A DICTIONARY ENGLISH AND SANSKRIT

A DICTIONARY ENGLISH AND SANSKRIT

BY

MONIER WILLIAMS, M.A.
PROFESSOR AT THE EAST-INDIA COLLEGE, HAILEYBURY,
FORMERLY BODEN SANSKRIT SCHOLAR IN THE UNIVERSITY OF OXFORD

GYAN

Published by

Gyan Publishing House
5, Ansari Road
Daryaganj, New Delhi-110002
Phone: 011-47034999, 9811692060
E-mail: books@gyanbooks.com

Distribution Network
gyanbooks.com
India, USA, Canada, UK, Australia, France

ISBN : 978-81-212-4343-8 (PB)
First Published, 1851

2nd Impression 2020

Printed at: Gyan Press, Delhi.

A
Dictionary English and Sanskrit
Author: Monier Williams

A

DICTIONARY, ENGLISH AND SANSKRIT,

BY

MONIER WILLIAMS, M.A.

PROFESSOR AT THE EAST-INDIA COLLEGE, HAILEYBURY,

FORMERLY BODEN SANSKRIT SCHOLAR IN THE UNIVERSITY OF OXFORD.

PUBLISHED UNDER THE PATRONAGE

OF THE

HONOURABLE EAST-INDIA COMPANY.

LONDON:

W^M. H. ALLEN AND CO.,

BOOKSELLERS TO THE HONOURABLE EAST-INDIA COMPANY,

7 LEADENHALL STREET.

1851.

TO

JOHN SHEPHERD, ESQ., CHAIRMAN,

SIR JAMES WEIR HOGG, BART., M.P., DEPUTY CHAIRMAN,

WILLIAM WIGRAM, ESQ.,
SIR ROBERT CAMPBELL, BART.,
JOHN LOCH, ESQ.,
CHARLES MILLS, ESQ.,
JOHN PETTY MUSPRATT, ESQ.,
HENRY ALEXANDER, ESQ.,
LIEUT.-GEN. SIR Js. L. LUSHINGTON, G. C. B.,
HENRY SHANK, ESQ.,
JOHN COTTON, ESQ.,
SIR HENRY WILLOCK, K. L. S.,
MARTIN TUCKER SMITH, ESQ., M.P.,
LIEUT.-COL. WILLIAM HENRY SYKES,
WILLIAM HENRY C. PLOWDEN, ESQ., M.P.,
ELLIOT MACNAGHTEN, ESQ.,
MAJOR JAMES OLIPHANT,
JOHN CLARMONT WHITEMAN, ESQ.,
THE HON. WILLIAM H. L. MELVILLE,
MAJOR-GEN. JAMES CAULFIELD, C. B.,
WILLIAM JOSEPH EASTWICK, ESQ.,
HENRY THOBY PRINSEP, ESQ.,
WILLIAM DENT, ESQ.,
JOHN H. ASTELL, ESQ.,

DIRECTORS

FOR MANAGING THE AFFAIRS

OF

THE HONOURABLE EAST-INDIA COMPANY,

THIS DICTIONARY

IS RESPECTFULLY DEDICATED,

BY THEIR OBLIGED AND OBEDIENT SERVANT,

MONIER WILLIAMS.

CONTRACTIONS.

s. for substantive
a. — adjective.
pron. — pronoun.
adv. — adverb.
prep. — preposition.
v. a. — verb active.
v. n. — verb neuter.
p. p. — passive participle.
part. — participle.
c. — conjugation or class.
caus. — causal form.
pass. — passive form.
des. — desiderative form.
freq. — frequentative form.

nom. for nominal verb.
impers. — impersonal.
irreg. — irregular.
def. — definite.
pres. — present.
pret. — preterite.
par. — parasmaipada.
átm. — átmanepada.
m. — masculine gender.
f. — feminine.
n. — neuter.
sing. — singular number.
du. — dual.
pl. — plural.

indec. for indeclinable.
in comp. — in composition.
nom. c. — nominative case.
acc. c. — accusative case.
inst., *instrum.* — instrumental case.
dat. c. — dative case.
abl. c. — ablative case.
gen. c. — genitive case.
loc. c. — locative case.
conj. — conjunction.
interj. — interjection.
exclam. — exclamation.

PREFACE.

Roger Ascham, in bearing testimony to the classical proficiency of his illustrious pupils, Edward and Elizabeth, said of them, that they not only understood, but composed in Latin, skilfully and with ease. Such an assertion, made three centuries since by the great preceptor of the age, leads to the inference, that, even in that early period, the value of composition as a criterion of scholarship was duly appreciated. It would be needless to quote the more express statements of scholars and linguists of modern times, in proof of the estimation in which this accomplishment is now held as a test of sound proficiency. It is sufficient to know, that in these days of intellectual progress and competition, no classical examination is considered effectual in which a prominent place is not assigned to composition. Indeed, an increasingly high standard of excellence in this branch of education is now demanded by all collegiate tribunals.

In unison with these opinions, the framers of the Statutes of the East-India College have provided, that no student shall be pronounced qualified for Indian service until he can make an intelligible translation from an English passage into the Oriental languages in which he has been instructed. And if this requirement has been wisely made, as a test of scholarship in the spoken dialects, much more has it so been made in regard to Sanskrit, the classical language of India, which bears a far closer relation to those dialects than Greek and Latin bear to the living languages of Europe. If at our Universities and Colleges, where are educated many who are destined to fill the highest offices in our home government, the composition of Latin prose is demanded of all candidates for degrees, with much more reason may Sanskrit composition be made an essential at this Institution, where are trained the whole body of civilians to whom the government of our Indian Empire is to be intrusted.

Nevertheless, it must be admitted that a student can hardly be expected to practice composition and translation in a difficult language, if the usual aids are not placed at his disposal. That such aids have not hitherto been made available in Sanskrit has been owing to the great difficulty of compiling a good English and Sanskrit Dictionary. Reverse Dictionaries are sufficiently within the reach of the student of Greek and Latin. In truth, the time that has been spent in investigating these languages, during many centuries, by a succession of learned men, each improving upon the results of his predecessor's labours, has led to the production of such a variety of dictionaries, phrase-books, and vocabularies, that the work of Greek and Latin lexicography, in the present day, has become a mere process of sifting and digesting the mass of existing materials. Yet, even in these languages, so great has been the difficulty of compiling a good Reverse Dictionary, that, after numerous incomplete attempts, it has only been within recent years that any really valuable English-Greek or English-Latin Dictionary has been published.

With reference to some of the spoken languages of the East, much has been done to facilitate translation and composition. In Hindustáni, it will scarcely be necessary to allude to the labours of that eminent scholar, Dr. Gilchrist, and in more recent times to the works of Mr. Shakespear and Dr. Duncan Forbes. In Bengálí, great assistance is afforded to the student by the copious English-Bengálí Dictionary of Rám Comul Sen: in Maráthí, still greater, by the admirable English and Maráthí Dictionary of Major Candy: in Telugu, by that of Mr. Morris: in Carnátaca, or Canarese, by that of Mr. Reeve. In Persian and Arabic, the dictionary of Professor Johnson, now passing through the press, will offer to the student a complete Persian, Arabic, and English Lexicon; but, although Reversed Dictionaries of English and Persian are procurable, a good lexicon in this form remains yet to be compiled. The English and Persian Dictionaries, or rather Vocabularies, of Meninski and Wilkins, are proofs of how little assistance is rendered to the student, in translating European ideas and phrases, by a mere supplementary vocabulary which is a reversed counterpart of the preceding lexicon. In most of the other spoken dialects of India such vocabularies exist, and are, without doubt, useful aids in the absence of more complete works. But in Sanskrit, nothing of this description, deserving of notice, has hitherto been effected. The Sanskrit and English Dictionary of Professor H. H. Wilson is, indeed, too well known as one of the best lexicons in any language to require comment in this place; and if the labours of that eminent Orientalist had been directed to the composition of an English and Sanskrit Dictionary, the student would long since have enjoyed the advantage of an aid to composition, far more effective than that which the present work can supply.

Such as it is, however, this Volume appears before the public as the result of the first attempt that has yet been made to meet a want, which the experience of every day renders increasingly felt. For it is not too much to allege, that the great development of the study of Sanskrit, during late years, has caused the absence of a Reverse Dictionary to be recognised as a want by many very different and very important members of the community, both at home and abroad; by students and civilians, by scholars and philologists, by chaplains and missionaries; by all those zealous men who have devoted themselves to the social, religious, and intellectual improvement of the natives of our Indian Empire.

With missionaries, and other philanthropists and scholars, whose aim has been to communicate scriptural and scientific truth to the learned natives, through the medium of their classical language, and to the uneducated, through their vernacular tongues, the absence of an aid to composition has doubtless enhanced the difficulties by which their labours have been retarded. It will be sufficient to mention the well-known names of Dr. Carey and Dr. Yates, whose translations of parts of the Bible are valued by all promoters of the cause of Christianity in the East; of Dr. Mill, formerly

Principal of Bishop's College at Calcutta, whose history of Christ in Sanskrit dialogue is still more acceptable to the natives of India, from its adaptation to their own system of teaching; of Mr. John Muir, whose zeal for the welfare of the Hindús has been displayed by carrying out and improving the system of Dr. Mill, in numerous excellent tracts; and lastly, of Dr. James Ballantyne, the energetic Principal of the College at Benares, whose Sanskrit lectures on the elements of general knowledge, and other scholarlike writings, prove him to be eminently fitted for the post to which he has been appointed.

The labours of these, and many other able and devoted men, are based upon the theory, that if the natives of India are to be effectively imbued with the principles of truth, whether religious or scientific, it must be through the medium of the only language through which they will be disposed to accept such information. Proficiency in English may be deemed indispensable to the liberal education of a native, but the attempt to make English the sole vehicle of instilling sound ideas respecting religion and philosophy, is not likely to be successful. The learned natives will be averse to receive any new truths which are not imparted by means of the language which they are accustomed to regard as the channel of all truth; and the more uneducated classes are found to be incapable of comprehending new ideas, excepting through their vernacular tongues. And since it is found that no vernacular tongue is adequate to express the ideas of religion and science, without borrowing its terms from the Sanskrit, the utility of an English and Sanskrit Dictionary will be recognised by all who have to compose in these dialects, whether in Hindí, Bengálí, Uriya, Telugu, Canarese, Tamil, Malayálam, or Maráthí.

Among philological scholars, whether in Europe or the East, the need of a complete compendium of synonymous words and vocables, in a language which is the key to the solution of every problem in comparative philology, is too obvious to require demonstration.

With respect to the civil servants of India, there can be no doubt that the want of a Reverse Sanskrit Dictionary has contributed to render unpopular the study of a language which must force itself, however distastefully, on their observation, by the influence which it exercises on the spoken dialects of India—an influence far greater than that of Latin on English, Italian, or French. But it is by the candidates for the civil service who are educated at the East-India College that this want has been chiefly acknowledged. Here it has seriously affected the popularity of a study which, above all others, ought to be cultivated, if on no other grounds, at least on the score of its adapting itself, more than any other, to the condition of students, who, being ignorant of their precise destination in India, are undergoing that course of general training which is best suited to fit them for the special requirements of particular localities.

Such is the want, then, which the Compiler of this dictionary has attempted to supply. But not even his firm persuasion of its magnitude could have emboldened him to address himself to a task of so much difficulty, had he not been liberally encouraged by the Honourable Directors of the East-India Company, whom he has the honour to serve. The public does not require to be informed, that it is the desire of those generous Rulers to win the attachment of their Indian subjects, by furthering every undertaking which aims at improving the knowledge of their languages and literature. A long enumeration might be made of dictionaries, vocabularies, and important publications, which have issued, and are now issuing, from the press, under the patronage of the Honourable Court. The present is but one out of numerous instances in which the authors of long and laborious works have had to record their gratitude for the countenance thus wisely extended.

It will not be necessary for the Compiler to dwell on the many difficulties he has had to encounter in pursuing his solitary labours, unassisted by the native Pandits and transcribers, who lighten the toil of the lexicographer in India. Those who understand what it is to be a pioneer in any work of lexicography, to be, as it were, the first to break and clear the ground over an untrodden field of inquiry, will doubtless, in their candour, appreciate at its full value the labour he has undergone in carrying this Volume to its completion. They will also be prepared to expect inequality in the execution, especially of the earlier pages, and many defects and inconsistencies throughout the whole body of the dictionary, agreeably to the inevitable law of expansion and improvement to which such a work must be subject in its progress through the press. No apology need, therefore, be made for these imperfections. But a brief account of the method in which, during nearly eight years, the Compiler has prosecuted his labours would seem to be expected of him, and is, in fact, rendered necessary by the entire novelty of his work.

He commenced by transcribing carefully, and then arranging in alphabetical order, all the English words, with their Sanskrit synonyms, contained in the Kosha of Amara Sinha, edited by the late Mr. Colebrooke. His next step was, to have copied, on nearly two thousand pages of large folio paper, with suitable intervals, all the English words in Riddle's English-Latin Dictionary, known to be very useful in Latin composition. Having thus prepared a kind of thesaurus, or repository for the collection of words and phrases, he proceeded to insert therein, in their proper places, all the words of the Amara Kosha, above referred to, as well as all those contained in the Hitopadeśa, the Selections from the Mahábhárata, edited by Professor Johnson, the Meghadúta, the Anthology of Professor Lassen, and all the roots, with some of the examples, comprised in that most learned and admirable compilation, the Radices Linguæ Sanskritæ of Professor Westergaard.

A sound and solid foundation of useful household words being thus laid, the Compiler commenced reversing the second edition of Professor Wilson's Sanskrit and English Dictionary, incorporating in his thesaurus all the new words as they occurred, and omitting only those which represented ideas or things having no approximate equivalent in English. This was a process of much time and labour, requiring a very attentive perusal of the dictionary, accompanied by much transcribing, collating, arranging, and inserting of words and phrases. It might be hastily inferred, that having accomplished thus much, considerable advance had been made towards the completion of the work; and if the object of the Compiler had been to compose a good vocabulary, reversing the senses of the words in the Sanskrit and English Dictionary, and nothing more, such would have been the case. But a complete dictionary, which was intended to offer an effectual help to the student in practising translation, was not merely to be compiled by collecting words and reversing meanings. It was to be continuously composed with a thoughtful consideration of the best Sanskrit equivalents for modern expressions and idioms, and a careful disposition, under each English word, of its several equivalents, in their proper order, and in their proper connection with its several shades of meaning. In fact, the real business of writing the Dictionary had now to be commenced. Having procured the latest edition of Webster's English Dictionary, in which are contained all the words of Tod's edition of Dr. Johnson, with many modern additions, as well as all the participles and adverbs, the Author proceeded to translate it systematically into Sanskrit, either gathering his materials from his own collection of classical words; or assisting his memory by suggestions from the Bengálí Lexicon of Rám Comul Sen, and omitting only those expressions which seemed obsolete or obsolescent, or of which no classical equivalent could be found or suggested.

Having thus progressed as far as the letter C, and the exigency of the case seeming to require the speedy appearance of the work, even at the risk of incompleteness, the printing of it was commenced, the Compiler feeling confident that, by great diligence, he might keep in advance of the press. It was not till some progress had been made that the inexpediency of this step was manifested by various omissions, which, though overlooked in the manuscript, became gradually apparent in the printed pages of the work. As soon as this discovery was made, one of two courses remained to be pursued, either to cancel the earlier pages of the work, or to supply their deficiencies by an Appendix. The latter of these courses was adopted, and the process of printing was first suspended, and then retarded, until, by a more extensive course of reading and research, the stock of classical materials was enlarged. To effect this, the Compiler undertook a second and more minute perusal of Professor Wilson's Sanskrit and English Dictionary, and noted numerous words and terms which had before escaped his observation. He also reversed the Sanskrit part of the excellent English and Maráthí Dictionary of Captain Molesworth, collecting from this source many valuable words, and much useful information. He then read through the Code of Manu, and the Commentary of Kullúka Bhaṭṭa, with the view of obtaining therefrom a store of choice phrases and idioms. And lastly, he studied attentively, with the same object, the plays of Kálidása, and parts of the Raghuvansa, Rámáyana, Mahábhárata, and Bhaṭṭi Kávya. He moreover extracted some good words from the Glossarium Sanskritum of Professor Bopp, and made extracts also from some modern Sanskrit writings and translations of the Scriptures. Without detracting from the acknowledged merit of these translations, he believes that little value is to be accorded to suggestions adopted from a source which is not classical.

But he avails himself of this opportunity of gratefully acknowledging his obligation to his friend and colleague, Professor Johnson, for furnishing him with a list of words, collected by him in the course of his reading, chiefly from the following standard classical works :—The Text of Manu, with the Commentary of Kullúka; the two law-treatises of Jímútaváhana, called Dáyabhága and Mitákshara; the Vikramorvaśí, Śakuntalá, Mṛichchhakati, Málatímádhava, Mudrárákshasa, Ratnávalí, Uttararámacharitra, and the Rájataranginí, published by Capt. Troyer.

Having enriched his store of materials with words and phrases from these approved sources, the composition and printing of his Dictionary was gradually advanced to the end of the letter H. At this point a copy of Major Candy's English and Maráthí Dictionary came first to hand. Had an impression of this work been received earlier, it would have saved the Compiler the time and labour consumed by him in reversing Captain Molesworth's Maráthí and English Dictionary, a task which he had not completed, until three hundred pages of his own work had been printed off, and excluded from any improvement derivable from this source.

It is, however, right to acknowledge, that the Dictionary of Major Candy, although it often furnished little more than a repetition of what the Compiler had himself collected, either from the Sanskrit or Maráthí Lexicons, provided him with numerous additional words, and much useful information, upon Hindú mythology and science, the value of which cannot be too highly estimated. Indeed, it would be difficult to make mention of Major Candy's work excepting in the highest terms of praise. By these aids, and with the addition of some happy renderings of scientific terms from Dr. Ballantyne's Lectures, and of some classical words from the Appendix to the late Dr. Yates' abridgment of Professor Wilson's Sanskrit Dictionary, the remainder of the present work, from the letter I to the end, was composed and printed in a comparatively short period.

The foregoing statement is the best apology for any want of uniformity discoverable in the plan of this Volume. A general uniformity, sufficient, it is hoped, for all the purposes of reference, has been sustained throughout. But perfect unity is hard to be maintained, at least in the first edition of a laborious work, compiled by gradual accretion from an increasing store of materials, and liable in its growth to occasional improvement and expansion.

If consistency has been sacrificed, it has only been in cases where improvements were admissible without endangering facility of reference, which should be the paramount consideration. For the convenience, therefore, of all consulters of the Dictionary, the use of too many symbols or abbreviations has been avoided. Whenever a substantive or adjective is followed by the parts of speech in connexion with it, or a verb by its participles and participial adjectives, and whenever, under each of these heads, separate gradations of meaning occur, the student will find the different meanings exhibited at full under the first word, and repeated at full under the others, the same relative order being generally preserved. For example, let him turn to the words Nobility, Noble, Nobly. Under the substantive Nobility, the first meaning given is, 'antiquity of family;' the second, 'greatness of mind;' the third, 'distinction;' the fourth, 'magnificence.' Under the adjective, instead of referring back to the substantive by symbols, as in some other dictionaries, the meanings have been repeated thus: 'of ancient family,' 'great in mind,' 'distinguished,' 'magnificent;' and similarly under the adverb, thus: 'with nobleness of birth,' 'with greatness of mind,' &c. The better to effect this clear exhibition of successive meanings, close printing has been employed, and no needless blanks admitted; so that the spaces occupied by the words Nobility, Noble, and Nobly, is not so large, in comparison to the number of equivalents given, as the spaces occupied by the same words in the Maráthí Dictionary. If the order of the meanings has not always been preserved, it is because the object has been, under each word, to dispose the gradations of senses according to what appeared to be the ratio of their commonness.

On the other hand, many meanings which appeared unusual or obsolete have been omitted; and under some words references have been made to preceding or succeeding parts of the Dictionary; but in all such cases a few of the commonest equivalents are generally given, of which the student can avail himself if indisposed to follow out the reference. Thus, under the word Vigilant, two meanings are given, viz. 'wakeful,' and 'wary.' In connexion with the first of these, a few of the commonest Sanskrit words are specified, but for a fuller enumeration the student must consult the word Wakeful itself. So also in connexion with the sense 'wary;' after mentioning the most useful equivalents, the student is referred back to the word Circumspect, for a more complete list. And in cases where no direct reference is made, as under the substantive, Vigilance, the student will infer that the word 'wakefulness,' in brackets, is intended not only to exhibit the variation of meaning, but also to direct his attention to the quarter of the Dictionary where additional synonyms may be found.

If objection be raised to the multiplication of Sanskrit equivalents under each English word, and the several meanings of which it is susceptible, the Compiler may state, in explanation, that in striving to render his work as complete as possible, he has been forced, at the risk of surplusage, into a copious enumeration of words and significant terms. Whenever it has been possible to give a complete list of synonymous Sanskrit words, it has been done. At the same time, the attempt has been made to dispose the words in the order of their usefulness. Indeed, for the simple purposes of prose composition or translation it will be advisable that the student should choose the Sanskrit word standing first in the list, or at least should make his selection from the first few equivalents enumerated; excepting in the case of such comprehensive terms as Sun, Moon, Earth, Fire, Water, &c., where the number of Sanskrit words is so great that the selection may be fairly made from the first few lines. The remaining equivalents given under such examples would, in any other language, be regarded as epithets rather than words, and would probably be restricted to poetical composition. And in fact, as regards their adaptation to plain Sanskrit prose, it will be better for the student so to treat them.

It should be observed, notwithstanding, that no distinction is rightly to be made, in an English and Sanskrit Dictionary, between strictly prose and strictly poetical terms. Sanskrit is peculiarly the language of poetry, Nearly the whole of its immense and wonderful literature is poetical; and the little prose that exists makes free use of poetical expressions. In fact, the commonest names for some of the most ordinary objects are proofs that a rich poetical vein runs throughout the language. Thus, one of the common words for 'earth' is, 'repository of wealth,' वसुधा; for the sea, 'receptacle of water,' जलनिधिः; for a cloud, 'water-giver,' जलदः, or 'water-holder,' जलधरः; for fire, 'purifier,' पावकः; for the moon, 'lord of the night,' निशापतिः; for the sun, 'generator,' सविता; for a good man, 'mine of merit,' गुणाकरः, or 'ocean of merit,' गुणसागरः. And if the remaining equivalents under each of these heads were examined, many of them would be found to possess a still more poetical character. In proof of which the reader is referred to the words Sun, Moon, Cloud, as they stand in the pages of the Dictionary.

Again, the English verb 'to kill,' may be rendered in Sanskrit either by the use of the simple root हन्, or by वधं कृ, 'to make killing,' or by प्राणहत्यां कृ, 'to make destruction of life,' or by पञ्चत्वं गम्, in the causal form, 'to cause to go the state of the five elements,' or by लोकान्तरं गम्, 'to cause to go to the other world.' All these expressions are legitimate, whatever be the form of composition; but the student, in writing prose, will do well to adopt those which come first in order.

Under the head of natural objects, and the terms of religion, literature, mythology, science, and social life, the copious enumeration of equivalent words and significant phrases will be valued, not only by the student of Sanskrit and its various cognate languages, but also by many of those learned and zealous men who are seeking to promote a sympathy between Hindús and Europeans, by diffusing amongst the latter a correct knowledge of Oriental customs, habits of thought, religious tenets, and ceremonial observances. It has been the desire of the Compiler to make this Volume not only a thesaurus of synonyms and phrases, but a repository of much useful information in connexion with such subjects. In illustration of this, the reader may turn to the words Water, Fire, Hand, Lotus, Vishnu, Śiva, Indra, Veda, Scripture, Rite, Sacrament, Manes, School, Marriage, Measure, Planet, &c.

The significant expressions collected under such words will, it is hoped, facilitate inquiry into the manners and customs of the Hindús, their mythological fictions, and the state of their scientific knowledge. Naturalists, also, may be expected to appreciate a collection of terms, the analysis of which must throw light on some particulars connected with botany and zoology. A comparison of the number of Sanskrit equivalents brought together under some of these heads might, at least, be a guide to the comparative value or utility of certain animals, plants, and minerals. In illustration, the reader may compare the words Elephant, Horse, Cow, Wolf, Frog, Camel, Lotus, Sandal, Mango, Musk, Myrobalan, Pyrites, Coal, Copper, Lead, Iron, Vitriol, &c.

It is not unlikely, however, that under some heads an exception may be taken to the number of Sanskrit equivalents enumerated: as, for example, under the various scarcely-distinguishable shades of meaning belonging to numerous common nouns, adjectives, and verbs: or again, under the head of many English words of which no precise Sanskrit representative could be offered. In the first of these cases the impossibility of observing the proper medium, at least in the first edition of a work like the present, has led the Compiler to prefer erring on the side of excess rather than on that of deficiency. In the other case, where the great disparity between Hindú and European habits of thought and condition prevented the exhibition of any classical equivalent, the Compiler has been forced, almost against his will, into occasional redundancy, by the pliancy and malleability, so to speak, of the Sanskrit, and its amazing power of expressing exotic ideas by the employment of an infinite variety of compound words. As examples, the reader may take Cannon, Canon, Camera-obscura, Certificate, Episcopacy, *To* Farm, Laymen, Lay, *To* Lease, Navy, Parliament, Penitentiary, Phrenology, Rubric, Sail, Sabbatarian, Steam-engine, Steam-boat, &c.

In rendering such words, respect has been paid to the learned Hindús in their study of English. The comprehension of European ideas by the educated natives is as necessary to reciprocal sympathy as the comprehension of Hindú ideas by ourselves.

In the rendering of the verbs some difficulty has been experienced. It is usual in an English Dictionary to prefix to the verb the infinitive sign 'to.' Consistently with this, in Greek and Latin, and some other Reversed Dictionaries, the infinitive of the equivalent verb is generally exhibited. But in Sanskrit the infinitive is a form of the verb very limited in its application, resembling, in some respects, the Latin supines in *um* and *u*. It has therefore been thought more proper to exhibit the root in the first place, specifying the infinitive, with the third person singular of the present tense, between brackets. The student will thus bear in mind, that the root is not to be regarded as representing the infinitive, or indeed any part of the verb, excepting the general idea expressed by it.

Another source of difficulty was, the limitation in regard to the number of roots properly available in Sanskrit for the formation of legitimate verbs, supported by classical authority. It is well known that in this language there are about 1900 roots, or elementary sounds, which are generally monosyllabic. These are the imaginary sources of both nouns and verbs, and are the representatives of the simple ideas contained in them. Thus the root गम् represents the idea of 'going;' अद्, of 'eating;' युज्, of 'joining;' कृ, of 'making.' As a matter of convenience, grammarians have connected these roots more directly with verbs than nouns; and their theory is, that every root may serve as the basis on which to construct five distinct forms of verbs: First, a Primitive verb; second, a Causal; third, a Passive; fourth, a Desiderative; and fifth, a Frequentative. So, also, from every noun certain verbs, called Nominals, may theoretically be derived, and, not unfrequently, are so derived. It might reasonably be imagined that, amongst a collection of 1900 roots, each capable of five-fold multiplication, besides innumerable nominals, there would be little difficulty in finding equivalents for any form of English verb that might present itself. But it will be found, on examination, that nearly two-thirds of these 1900 roots do not occur in this Dictionary in any form, excepting in that of the nouns to which they give origin. It will be observed, too, that of these, certain particular roots, such as कृ, भू, दा, गम्, इ, या, ज्ञा, स्था, वृत्, अस्, नी, हृ, युज्, वृ, recur perpetually, and, by the aid of prepositions and other affixes, are applied to the expression of the most varied and opposite ideas.

In explanation, the Compiler thinks it proper to state, that he has been careful to follow only classical usage in the admission of verbs into his Dictionary; and that no verb has been so admitted unless a good example of its use could be adduced, either from the pages of Westergaard or other authentic sources. Rather than violate this rule, he has constantly been obliged to employ a noun with the auxiliaries कृ, गम्, &c., or a participle with the auxiliaries भू and अस्, in place of a direct verb.

In every case it is allowable thus to employ the auxiliaries, in the absence of legitimate verbs; and even should such verbs be available, the student may, if he please, still take the noun, participle, or adjective, and combine them with the auxiliaries, in place of using the more direct form. Thus, under the verb 'to resent,' he may either directly employ the roots कुप्, क्रुध्, रुष्, in the conjugations specified, or he may combine the equivalents given under the substantive with the auxiliaries, thus मन्युं कृ, क्रोधं कृ, कोपं कृ, रोषं गम्; or under the adjective, thus, समन्युः -न्युः -न्यु भू, जातमन्युः -न्युः -न्यु भू or अस्. Again, under the verb 'to perish,' he may either directly make use of the roots मृ or नश् in the passive form, or he may substitute नाशं गम्, नष्टः -ष्टा -ष्टं भू, &c.

In the specification of roots, the third person singular of the present tense has been chosen for exhibition in brackets in conjunction with the infinitive, as being the best guide to the conjugational form of the verb; whilst the infinitive furnishes a mark for the formation of some of the most useful non-conjugational forms. At the same time the conjugation or class of the verb is indicated by a figure; and if the verb is to be conjugated in the causal, passive, desiderative, or frequentative form, or as a nominal, it is so specified. But as the causal form is identical with that of the tenth conjugation, it has sometimes been more convenient to designate causal verbs as belonging to that conjugation.

When a root is compounded with prepositions, these are not repeated in the bracket, that the student may more readily perceive the simple form of the root, but a small hyphen is used, to show that the preposition cannot be dispensed with in conjugating the verb.

If a root occur more than once under the same verb, it has not been thought necessary to repeat the present tense and infinitive in connexion with it. Indeed, under some verbs towards the end of the Dictionary, these forms are omitted altogether, as having been frequently notified under the synonymous expressions, to which a reference is indicated. Thus, under the verb '*To* Part,' *v. a.*, the student must refer to the synonymous terms, Disunite, Divide, Separate, for any particulars relating to these grammatical forms.

In regard to participles, this Dictionary will be found so copious that here also an exception may perhaps be taken to the number of equivalents enumerated. The explanation is to be sought in the genius of the Sanskrit language, which abounds in participles to an extent wholly unparalleled in any other language, living or dead. These participles are often idiomatically substituted for the tenses of the verb itself. They are constantly employed in place of the past and future tenses, especially of passive verbs; so that an example of a passive tense is of rare occurrence, excepting in the form of the third person singular or plural of the present and imperative.

If, therefore, the student desire to write idiomatic Sanskrit, he must make free use of the participles in this Dictionary, especially of the passive past participle. This latter is the most useful derivative in the language, and should be abundantly employed in translation and composition. It corresponds with the Latin participle in *tus*, and, like it, often supplies the place of the past tense. Thus, in translating the phrase, 'he reproved his own son,' the student might employ the simple root, thus, स स्वपुत्रम् अनिन्दत्, or he might idiomatically use the passive participle, thus, तेन स्वपुत्रो निन्दितः, the agent being placed in the instrumental case, and the participle agreeing with the object.

With respect to the rendering of nouns in this dictionary, it will be proper to state, that the system of Amara Sinha has been followed, in exhibiting substantives and adjectives in their nominative case rather than in their crude state. Whenever the crude form differs from the nominative more than in rejecting the final visarga or anuswára, it has been indicated by giving the final of the crude in brackets. Thus, under the word Fire, अग्निः being the nominative case, the final of the crude is ascertained by rejecting the visarga, thus अग्नि. Similarly अनलः becomes अनल in the crude form; तेजः becomes तेजस्; कृष्णवर्त्मा becomes कृष्णवर्त्मन्; हुतभुक् becomes हुतभुज्; तनूनपात् becomes तनूनपाद्; आश्रयध्वंसी becomes आश्रयध्वंसिन्; दमुनाः becomes दमुनस्; जुहुवान् becomes जुहुवत्; अर्चिष्मान् becomes अर्चिष्मत्.

It is necessary to be thus particular in exhibiting the crude form as distinct from the nominative case, both as a guide to the declension of the noun, which must always depend on the final of the crude, and because the crude state is that which is employed in the formation of compound words. In all such words, with but few exceptions, the last number of the compound alone admits of declension, and the preceding word or words require to be placed in the crude form, this form admitting of a plural as well as singular acceptation. For an explanation of compound words the Student must of course consult his grammar; but it will not be out of place to remark here, that in a language which, like Sanskrit, abounds in compounds more than any other language in the world, it will not be possible for him to compose idiomatically until he has made himself conversant with the principles of their formation.

Under adjectives the nominative case in three genders has generally been given, and the final of the crude state exhibited when necessary, as in substantives. The genders are not specified, as the student will himself take for granted that साधुः -धुः -ध्वी -धु, meaning 'good,' stands for the nominative case of the adjective in its three genders; साधुः being the nominative of the masculine form, साधुः being also the nominative of the feminine form, साध्वी of a second feminine form, and साधु of the neuter form; the crude state being साधु: Similarly भद्रः -द्रा -द्रं, stands for भद्रः the nominative of the masculine, भद्रा of the feminine, भद्रं of the neuter, the crude being भद्र; सारवान् -वती -वत् (त्) for सारवान् the nominative of the masculine, सारवती of the feminine, and सारवत् of the neuter, the last standing also for the crude form. Again, सुकृती -तिनी -ति (न्) is for सुकृती the nominative of the masculine, सुकृतिनी of the feminine, सुकृति of the neuter, the crude form being सुकृतिन्.

When, however, under one head a variety of similar adjectives are enumerated, it has not been deemed necessary in all cases to give the nominative case in more than the masculine form; but the addition of the sign, &c. indicates that the student must himself supply the other forms thus: दृष्टः &c., stands for दृष्टः -ष्टा -ष्टं. Similarly, धनवान् &c., for धनवान् -वती -वत् (त्), धनी &c., for धनी -निनी -नि (न्), and महात्मा &c., for महात्मा -त्मा -त्म (न्).

In the case of compound adjectives formed from neuter substantives, whose crude form ends in उस् or इस्, such as उत्पलचक्षुस्, 'lotus-eyed;' दीर्घायुस्, 'long-lived;' निराशिस्, 'unblessed;' शुचिरोचिस्: 'clear-shining;' the nominative case in the three genders has been exhibited thus, उत्पलचक्षूः -क्षूः -क्षुः, (स्), दीर्घायूः -यूः -युः (स्), निराशीः -शीः -शिः (स्), शुचिरोचीः &c.

In some cases, however, as in the case of दीर्घायुस्, where a masculine noun आयुः exists as well as a neuter आयुस्, the nominative case of the compound adjective is susceptible of two forms, दीर्घायूः and दीर्घायुः. Some notice of this point seems to be required, as it appears to have been overlooked, if not erroneously explained, by the generality of European scholars. That the Compiler's view is correct, may be shown by a reference to Professor Wilson's Dictionary, under the words सजुस् or सजुष्, आशिस्, उत्पलचक्षुस्, शुचिरोचिस्; by referring also to the declension of सजुष्, and आशिस्, in Professor Wilson's Grammar, p. 68; and by the analogy of compound adjectives, like महामनाः -नाः -नः, 'high-minded,' derived from a neuter substantive ending in अस्.

The exhibition, in all cases, of the nominative case of nouns, whether substantive or adjective, has prevented the necessity of specifying the gender of substantives ending in अः, like देवः, 'a god,' which are invariably masculine; or of substantives ending in अं, like दानं, 'a gift,' which are invariably neuter; or of those ending in आ and ई, like माला, 'a garland,' and देवी, 'a goddess,' which are always feminine. The gender of all such substantives will be taken for granted. The student might also have been left to infer for himself the gender of substantives ending in ति: in the nominative, like मति:, 'the mind,' which are feminine, and of substantives ending in धि:, derived from the root धा, like सन्धि:, 'peace,' which are masculine. But since, in these latter instances, some slight occasional variation might occur, it has been thought desirable to notify the gender of substantives in these cases, as well as in every other where any doubt could possibly arise.

The Compiler has now only the grateful duty to discharge of expressing his further obligation to Professor Johnson, for his invaluable assistance in correcting the greater number of the proof-sheets of this work. Nor does he think it just to conclude without some tribute of acknowledgment to the Printer, Mr. Watts, for the accuracy and clearness with which the typography has been executed.

East-India College, Haileybury,
November 5th, 1851.

ENGLISH AND SANSKRIT DICTIONARY.

A. As an indefinite article before nouns singular, for the most part not expressed in Sanskrit; as, 'a lion,' सिंहः; (One) एकः -का -कं.—(Some, a certain) कश्चित्; as, 'a certain man,' कश्चित् पुरुषः.—(Each, every) expressed by प्रति or अनु, before the acc. neut.; as, 'a day,' 'each day,' प्रतिदिनं or अनुदिनं. When 'a' comes before a participle, after a verb of motion, it is expressed by the dat. c.; as, 'he went a hunting,' मृगयायै गतः; or by अर्थं preceded by the crude form of a noun; as, मृगयार्थं गतः; or by the infinitive; as, मृगयां कर्तुं गतः.

Abaft, *adv.* (Towards the stern of the ship) नावः पश्चिमभागं प्रति.

To abandon, *v. a.* त्यज् (c. 1. त्यजति, त्यक्तुं), परित्यज्, सन्त्यज्; हा (c. 3. जहाति, हातुं), अपहा, विहा, प्रहा, अपाहा; उत्सृज् (c. 6. -सृजति, -स्रष्टुं), अतिसृज्, व्यपसृज्; उज्झ् (c. 6. उज्झति, उज्झितुं), प्रोज्झ्.

Abandoned, *p. p.* त्यक्तः -क्ता -क्तं, परित्यक्तः -क्ता -क्तं, उत्सृष्टः -क्ता -क्तं, हीनः -ना -नं, उत्सृष्टः -ष्टा -ष्टं, प्रोज्झितः -ता -तं, समुज्झितः -ता -तं, रहितः -ता -तं, विरहितः -ता -तं, विसर्ज्जितः -ता -तं, विनाकृतः -ता -तं.—(Reprobate) पापात्मा -त्मा -त्म (न्), पापमतिः -तिः -ति.

Abandonment, *s.* त्यागः, परित्यागः, उत्सर्गः, विरहः, प्रोज्झनं.—(Of worldly connexions) सन्न्यासः.

To abase *v. a.* स्वस्थानाद् अपकृष् (c. 1. -कर्षति, c. 6. -कृषति, -क्रष्टुं), स्वस्थानाद् भ्रंश् in caus. (भ्रंशयति, भ्रंशयितुं) or निपत् in caus. (-पातयति, -पातयितुं).

Abased, *p. p.* भग्नदर्पः -र्पा -र्पं, अपकृष्टः -ष्टा -ष्टं, पराभूतः -ता -तं, अभिभूतः -ता -तं.

Abasement, *s.* (The act of bringing low) अपकर्षः, -र्षणं, अभिभवः.—(A low state), अपकृष्टता, -त्वं, अपकीर्त्तिः *f.*

To abash, *v. a.* लज्ज् in caus. (लज्जयति, लज्जयितुं), ह्री in caus. (ह्रेपयति, ह्रेपयितुं), त्रप् in caus. (त्रपयति, त्रपयितुं).

Abashed, *p. p.* लज्जितः -ता -तं, त्रपितः -ता -तं, व्रीडितः -ता -तं, ह्रीपरिगतः -ता -तं.

To abate, *v. a.* (To diminish) ह्रस् in caus. (ह्रासयति, ह्रासयितुं), ऊन् (nom. ऊनयति, ऊनयितुं), लघ् (nom. लघयति, लघयितुं), शम् in caus. (शमयति, शमयितुं).—(To let down the price in selling) मूल्यं न्यूनीकृ.—(To depress) अवसद् in caus. (-सादयति, -यितुं).

To abate, *v. n.* (To grow less) क्षि in pass. (क्षीयते), ह्रस् (c. 1. ह्रसति, ह्रसितुं).—(To subside) शम् (c. 4. शाम्यति, शमितुं), उपशम्, प्रशम्.

Abated, *p. p.* (Subsided) उपशान्तः -न्ता -न्तं, प्रशान्तः -न्ता -न्तं.

Abbess, *s.* विहारस्य or मठस्य or आश्रमस्य प्रधाना स्त्री.

Abbey, *s.* विहारः, धर्म्मचारिणां मठः.

Abbot, *s.* विहारस्य प्रधानपुरुषः, मठाध्यक्षः, गुरुः.

To abbreviate, *v. a.* (To shorten by contraction) संह्र (c. 1. -हरति, -हर्तुं), संक्षिप् (c. 6. -क्षिपति, -क्षेप्तुं), ह्रस् in caus. (ह्रासयति, ह्रासयितुं).

Abbreviature, *s.* सङ्क्षेपः, -पणं, समसनं, सङ्ग्रहः.

To abdicate, *v. a.* (To resign an office) राज्यं or अधिकारं or पदं त्यज् (c. 1. त्यजति, त्यक्तुं).

Abdication, *s.* राज्यत्यागः, अधिकारत्यागः, पदत्यागः.

Abdomen, *s.* वस्तिः *m.*, उदरं, कुक्षिः *m.*

Abdominal, *a.* वास्तेयः -यी -यं, उदरकः -का -कं, कौक्षः -क्षी -क्षं.

Aberration, *s.* विभ्रमः, भ्रान्तिः, भ्रंशः, च्युतिः *f.*, पथभ्रष्टता, उन्मार्गगमनं.

To abet, *v. a.* (To encourage) प्रोत्सह् in caus. (-साहयति, -साहयितुं), प्रवृत् in caus. (-वर्त्तयति, -वर्त्तयितुं).—(To help) उपकृ (c. 8. -करोति, -कर्तुं), उपचर् (c. 1. -चरति, -चरितुं), उपकारं or साहाय्यं कृ.

Abettor, *s.* प्रोत्साहकः, प्रवर्त्तकः, उपकारकः.

Abeyance, *s.* अपेक्षा, विलम्बः.

To abhor, *v. a.* गर्ह् (c. 1. गर्हते, गर्हितुं), बाध् in des. (बीभत्सते, बीभत्सितुं), घृणां कृ, द्विष् (c. 2. द्वेष्टि, द्वेष्टुं), प्रद्विष्.

Abhorrence, *s.* बीभत्सः, -त्सं, गर्हणं, घृणा, अरुचिः *f.*

Abhorrent, *a.* (Struck with abhorrence) बीभत्सान्वितः -ता -तं.—(Inconsistent with) विरुद्धः -द्धा -द्धं, अयोग्यः -ग्या -ग्यं, असङ्गतः -ता -तं, असंस्थितः -ता -तं, विपरीतः -ता -तं.

To abide, *v. n.* (To dwell) वस् (c. 1. वसति, वस्तुं).—(To remain) स्था (c. 1. तिष्ठति -ते, स्थातुं), वृत् (c. 1. वर्त्तते, वर्त्तितुं).

To abide, *v. a.* (To wait for, expect) प्रतीक्ष् (c. 1. -ईक्षते, -ईक्षितुं), उद्दृश् (c. 1. -पश्यति, -द्रष्टुं), प्रतिपाल् (c. 10. -पालयति, -पालयितुं).—(To bear, support) सह् (c. 1. सहते, सोढुं), क्षम् (c. 1. क्षमते, क्षन्तुं), तिज् in des. (तितिक्षते, तितिक्षितुं).—(To abide by one's promise) प्रतिज्ञातं पाल्.

Abiding, *a.* स्थायी -यिनी -यि (न्), वर्त्ती -र्त्तिनी -र्त्ति (न्), वृत्तिमान् -मती -मत् (त्).

Ability, *s.* शक्तिः *f.*, शक्तता, बलं, सामर्थ्यं.—(Skill) कुशलता, प्रवीणता. 'To the utmost of one's ability,' यथाशक्ति *ind.*, यावच्छक्यं, सर्व्वयत्नैः, यथासामर्थ्यं.

Abject, *a.* कृपणः -णा -णं, अधमः -मा -मं, अपकृष्टः -ष्टा -ष्टं, निकृष्टः -ष्टा -ष्टं, नीचः -चा -चं, अवगर्हितः -ता -तं.—(Without hope) निराशः -शा -शं.

Abjectly, *ad.v* कृपणं, कार्पण्येन, निकृष्टं, नीचतया, अधमप्रकारेण.

Abjectness or abjection, *s.* कार्पण्यं, अधमत्वं, अपकृष्टता, निकृष्टता.

Abjuration, *s.* (Renouncing with oath) शपथेन त्यागः.

To abjure, *v. a.* (To renounce with oath) शपथेन त्यज् (c. 1. त्यजति, त्यक्तुं).—(To renounce) प्रत्याख्या (c. 2. -ख्याति -ख्यातुं), परित्यज्.

Ablative case, अपादानं, पञ्चमी विभक्तिः.

Able, *a.* (Of power sufficient) समर्थः -र्था -र्थं, क्षमः -मा -मं, शक्तः -क्ता -क्तं.—(Powerful) प्रबलः -ला -लं, बलवान् -वती -वत् (त्), शक्तिमान् -मती -मत् (त्).

To be able, *v. n.* शक् (c. 5. शक्नोति, c. 4. शक्यति -ते, शक्तुं), क्षम् (c. 1. क्षमते, क्षन्तुं), उत्सह् (c. 1. -सहते -सोढुं) with inf.; प्रभू (c. 1. -भवति -भवितुं) with dat.; as, 'they are able to destroy the world,' प्रभवन्ति क्षयाय जगतः.

ABLE-BODIED, *a.* प्रबलशरीरः -रा -रं, प्रबलकायः -या -यं, दृढाङ्गः -ङ्गा -ङ्गं.

ABLUTION, *s.* स्नानं, मज्जनं, धावनं.

ABNEGATION, *s.* निह्नवः, अपह्नवः, प्रत्याख्यानं.

ABODE, *s.* (Place of residence) गृहं, वेश्म *n.* (न्), आयतनं, निवासः, निलयः, -यनं, आलयः.—(Continuance in a place) वसतिः, अवस्थानं.

To ABOLISH, *v. a.* (To annul) लोपं कृ, निरर्थकं -कां -कं कृ.—(To destroy) नश् in caus. (नाशयति, नाशयितुं), विनश्; सद् in caus. (सादयति, सादयितुं), उत्सद्, प्रोत्सद्; उद्धृ (c. 1. -हरति -हर्त्तुं), उच्छिद् (c. 7. -छिनत्ति, -छेत्तुं).

ABOLISHED, *p. p.* लुप्तः -प्ता -प्तं.

ABOLITION, *s.* (Act of annulling) लोपः.—(Destruction) विनाशः, उद्धरणं, उच्छेदः.

ABOMINABLE, *a.* गर्हणीयः -या -यं, द्वेष्यः -ष्या -ष्यं, घृणार्हः -र्हा -र्हं.

ABOMINABLY, *adv.* गर्ह्यप्रकारेण, गर्हितं.

To ABOMINATE, *v. a.* गर्ह् (c. 1. गर्हते, गर्हितुं), बाध् in des. (बीभत्सते, बीभत्सितुं).

ABOMINATED, *p. p.* गर्हितः -ता -तं.

ABOMINATION, *s.* (Detestation) बीभत्सः, गर्हा, गर्हणं.—(An abominated thing, the object of detestation) गर्हितं, अशुद्धद्रव्यं.

ABORTION, *s.* गर्भस्रावः, अकालप्रसवः.

ABORTIVE, *a.* (Producing abortion) गर्भस्रावी -विणी -वि (न्).—(Brought forth prematurely) गर्भस्रस्तः -स्ता -स्तं, अपूर्णकालः -ला -लं.—(That does not succeed) निष्फलः -ला -लं, मोघः -घा -घं, व्यर्थः -र्था -र्थं.

To ABOUND, *v. n.* (Followed by with or in) सङ्कॄ in pass. (-कीर्य्यते) with inst. c.; पॄ in pass. (पूर्य्यते), आपॄ with inst. c.—(To be in great plenty) बहुलीभू (c. 1. -भवति, -भवितुं).

ABOUNDING IN, आढ्यः -ढ्या -ढ्यं, सङ्कीर्णः -र्णा -र्णं, चितः -ता -तं, निचयी -यिनी -यि (न्), संवलितः -ता -तं.

ABOUT, *prep.* (Encircling) परि prefixed.—(Near to, in time) प्रति.—(In number) देशीय affixed; as, 'about twelve years old,' द्वादशवर्षदेशीयः; न्यूनाधिकं.—(Concerning, relating to) प्रति, प्रतीक्ष्य, उद्दिश्य.—(On account of) हेतोः, हेतौ, अर्थं, अर्थे, कृते, निमित्ते, कारणात्, with the crude form, or sometimes the gen. c. of the preceding noun.—(Engaged in any thing) व्यापृतः, निष्ठितः, निरतः, with loc. c.—(Close to one's person) पार्श्वतस् *ind.*, निकटे, समीपं.

ABOUT, *adv.* (Circularly) परितस् *ind.*, अभितस् *ind.*—(Nearly) प्रायशस् or प्रायस् *ind.*—(Here and there) इतस्ततस् *ind.*, सर्व्वतस् *ind.*—(To be about to do any thing) expressed by उद्यतः, 'prepared,' with the infin.; as, 'about to kill,' हन्तुम् उद्यतः; or by the act. part. of the 2d fut.; as, गमिष्यन्, 'about to go,' एधिष्यमाणः, 'about to increase'; or, by the desid. adj.; as, जिगमिषुः, 'about to go,' मुमूर्षुः 'about to die.'

ABOVE, *prep.* or *adv.* (Higher in place) अधि or अभि prefixed; उपरि, उपरिष्टात्, ऊर्द्ध्वं.—(More in quantity) अधिकं, उत्तरं.—(Higher in rank) उत्तरः -रा -रं, विशिष्टः -ष्टा -ष्टं, श्रेष्ठः -ष्ठा -ष्ठं.—(Superior to, beyond) अति; as, 'above man's power,' अतिमानुषं.—(Above all, especially) विशेषतस् *ind.*, प्राधान्यतस् *ind.*

To be ABOVE, *v. n.* (To excel) अभिभू (c. 1. -भवति -भवितुं), प्रभू, अतिभू; विशिष् in pass. (-शिष्यते).—(To be higher) ऊर्द्ध्वं स्था (c. 1. तिष्ठति, स्थातुं).

ABOVE-GROUND, *a.* (Not in the grave, still existing) वर्त्तमानः -ना -नं, जीवन् -वन्ती -वत् (त्).

ABOVE-MENTIONED, *a.* पूर्व्वोक्तः -क्ता -क्तं, पूर्व्वोदितः -ता -तं, प्रागुक्तः -क्ता -क्तं.

ABREAST, *adv.* पार्श्वापार्श्वि.

To ABRIDGE, *v. a.* संहृ (c. 1. -हरति -ते -हर्त्तुं) उपसंहृ; संक्षिप् (c. 6. -क्षिपति -क्षेप्तुं).—(To shorten) ह्रस् in caus. (ह्रासयति, ह्रासयितुं).—(To deprive of, cut off) उच्छिद् (c. 7. -छिनत्ति -छेत्तुं), वियुज् in caus. (-योजयति -योजयितुं).

ABRIDGMENT, *s.* प्रत्याहारः, सङ्क्षेपः, -पणं, समसनं, सङ्ग्रहः, समाहारः, समाहृतिः *f.*

ABROAD, *adv.* (In another country) विदेशे loc. c.—(At large, unconfined) निर्विघ्नं.—(Out of the house) बहिस्.—(In all directions) सर्व्वत्र, इतस्ततस् *ind.*—(Sojourn abroad in a foreign country) प्रवसनं.—(A sojourner abroad) प्रवासी (न्), प्रोषितः.

To ABROGATE, *v. a.* लोपं कृ.

ABROGATED, *p. p.* लुप्तः -प्ता -प्तं.

ABROGATION, *s.* लोपः, लोपकरणं.

ABRUPT, *a.* (Broken, craggy) भग्नः -ग्ना -ग्नं, भिन्नः -न्ना -न्नं, रूक्षः -क्षा -क्षं.—(Sudden) आकस्मिकः -की -कं.—(Unconnected) असम्बन्धः -न्धा -न्धं.

ABRUPTLY, *adv.* (Hastily) सहसा, अकस्मात्, झटिति.

ABSCESS, *s.* विद्रधिः *m.*, पूयसम्पूर्णः स्फोटः.

To ABSCOND, *v. n.* (To hide one's self) आत्मानं गुह् (c. 1. गूहति -ते, गोढुं), निगुह्; गुप्तः -प्ता -प्तं or प्रच्छन्नः -न्ना -न्नं भू.—(To disappear) अन्तर्धा in pass. (-धीयते).—(To escape privately) पलाय् (c. 1. पलायते -यितुं), निष्पत् (c. 1. -पतति -पतितुं), व्यपसृप् (c. 1. -सर्पति -सर्पितुं).

ABSENCE, *s.* अभावः, परोक्षं, अनुपस्थितिः *f.*, अनुपस्थानं, अविषयः, असन्निधिः *m.*—(Absence from) विरहः, वियोगः.—(Of mind) अमनोयोगः, अन्यमानसत्वं, समाधिः *m.*—(In one's absence) परोक्षे.

ABSENT, *a.* (Not present) अवर्त्तमानः -ना -नं, अविद्यमानः -ना -नं, परोक्षः -क्षा -क्षं, स्थानान्तरङ्गतः -ता -तं, अनुपस्थितः -ता -तं, अनुपस्थायी -यिनी -यि (न्), असमक्षः -क्षा -क्षं, अप्रत्यक्षः -क्षा -क्षं.—(Abroad) प्रोषितः -ता -तं.—(Absorbed in meditation) समाहितः -ता -तं.—(Thinking of something else) अन्यमानसः -सी -सं or -मनाः -नाः -नः (स्), शून्यहृदयः -या -यं.

To be ABSENT, *v. n.* अन्यत्र, or स्थानान्तरे, or असाक्षात् वृत् (c. 1. वर्त्तते, वर्त्तितुं) or अस् (c. 2. अस्ति).

ABSENTEE, *s.* प्रोषितः, प्रवासी *m.* (न्), अदेशस्थः.

ABSOLUTE, *a.* (Complete) सम्पूर्णः -र्णा -र्णं, समाप्तः -प्ता -प्तं, समग्रः -ग्रा -ग्रं, पर्य्याप्तः -प्ता -प्तं.—(Not relative, simple) मात्रकः -का -कं, केवलः -ला -लं.—(Sovereign, paramount) परमः -मा -मं, उत्तमः -मा -मं.—(An absolute king) अधिराजः, सम्राट् (ज्).

ABSOLUTELY, *adv.* (Entirely) सर्व्वशस्, केवलं.

ABSOLUTION, *s.* पापमोचनं, पापक्षमा, निष्कृतिः *f.*, क्षमा, मुक्तिः *f.*

To ABSOLVE, *v. a.* (To acquit of a crime) पापात् मुच् (c. 6. मुञ्चति -ते, मोक्तुं), विमुच्, or in caus. (मोचयति -यितुं), पापं क्षम् (c. 1. क्षमते, क्षन्तुं), अपराधं क्षम्; 'he is absolved from crime,' दुष्कृतात् पूयते.

ABSOLVED, *p. p.* पापमुक्तः -क्ता -क्तं.

To ABSORB, *v. a.* निपा (c. 1. -पिबति, -पातुं), उत्पा; शुष् in caus. (शोषयति -यितुं), उच्छुष्, उपशुष्; ग्रस् (c. 1. ग्रसते, ग्रसितुं), उपग्रस्.

ABSORBED, *p. p.* (Absorbed in any occupation) निरतः -ता -तं, निविष्टः -ष्टा -ष्टं, परायणः -णा -णं, आसक्तः -क्ता -क्तं.—(In meditation) समाहितः -ता -तं, एकाग्रः -ग्रा -ग्रं; (Drunk in) निपीतः -ता -तं, ग्रस्तः -स्ता -स्तं.

ABSORPTION, निपानं, शोषणं, ग्रसनं.

To ABSTAIN, *v. n.* निवृत् (c. 1. -वर्त्तते -वर्त्तितुं) with abl.; as, 'he abstains from eating flesh,' निवर्त्तते मांसभक्षणात्; वृज् in caus. (वर्जयति -यितुं), परिवृज्, विवृज् with acc.

ABSTEMIOUS, *a.* अल्पाहारी -रिणी -रि (न्), अभोजी -जिनी -जि (न्), मिताशनः -ना -नं, मितभुक् *m. f. n.* (ज्), परिमिताहारः -रा -रं, नियताहारः -रा -रं, यताहारः -रा -रं, लघ्वाशी -शिनी -शि (न्), लघ्वाहारः -रा -रं.

ABSTEMIOUSNESS, *s.* आहारपरित्यागः, अल्पाहारित्वं.

ABSTINENCE, *s.* (Abstaining from food) उपवासः, अभोजनं.—(Restraint of the passions) जितेन्द्रियत्वं, संयमनं, संयामः.—(Forbearance from any thing) निवृत्तिः *f.*, क्षान्तिः, *f.*

ABSTINENT, *a.* (Temperate) जितेन्द्रियः -या -यं, निवृत्तरागः -गा -गं, संयमी -मिनी -मि (न्), संयतात्मा -त्मा -त्म (न्).—(Fasting) उपवासी -सिनी -सि (न्).

To ABSTRACT, *v. a.* अपहृ (c. 1. -हरति-ते -हर्त्तुं), व्यपहृ; अपकृष् (c. 1. -कर्षति, c. 6. -कृषति -क्रष्टुं), अपाकृष्, अवकृष्, व्यपकृष्; आदा (c. 3. -दत्ते -दातुं), उपादा, अभ्यादा.—(To reduce to an epitome) सङ्क्षिप् (c. 6. -क्षिपति -क्षेप्तुं), संहृ.

ABSTRACT, *a.* विभिन्नः -न्ना -न्नं, वियुक्तः -क्ता -क्तं, विविक्तः -क्ता -क्तं, पृथक्कृतः -ता -तं, केवलः -ला -लं.—(From material objects) विषयविविक्तः -क्ता -क्तं, विषयापकृष्टः -ष्टा -ष्टं—(Metaphysical) आन्वीक्षिकः -की -कं. —(Abstracted in mind) समाहितः -ता -तं, अनन्यमनाः -नाः -नः (स्).

ABSTRACT, *s.* (An epitome) सङ्ग्रहः, प्रत्याहारः, सङ्क्षेपः, सारः, वस्तु *n.* वस्तुमात्रं.—(An abstract noun) भाववाचकः.

ABSTRACTEDLY, ABSTRACTLY, *adv.* विविक्तं, विविक्तप्रकारेण.—(Simply) केवलं, मात्रं.

ABSTRACTION, *s.* (Taking away) प्रत्याहारः, उपादानं.—(Separation) विवेकः, विभेदः, पार्थक्यं, पृथक्करणं.—(From material objects) विषयविविक्तत्वं.—(Of the mind) समाधिः *m.*, एकाग्रता.

ABSTRUSE, *a.* (Hidden) गूढः -ढा -ढं, गुप्तः -प्ता -प्तं, प्रच्छन्नः -न्ना -न्नं.—(Remote from apprehension, obscure) निगूढः -ढा -ढं, निगूढार्थः -र्था -र्थं, दुर्ज्ञेयः -या -यं, बोधागम्यः -म्या -म्यं, कठिनः -ना -नं.

ABSURD, *a.* अनर्थकः -का -कं, न्यायविरुद्धः -द्धा -द्धं, विचारविरुद्धः -द्धा -द्धं, अन्यायी -यिनी -यि (न्).

ABSURDITY, *s.* (That which is absurd) मृषार्थकं, अनर्थकं, शशविषाणं, शशशृङ्गं, गगनकुसुमं, गगनपुष्पं.

ABSURDNESS, *s.* आनर्थक्यं, अन्याय्यत्वं, अयाथार्थ्यं.

ABSURDLY, *adv.* अन्यायतस् *ind.*, आनर्थक्येन, अविचारेण.

ABUNDANCE, *s.* बाहुल्यं, बहुत्वं, प्रचुरत्वं.

ABUNDANT, *a.* बहुः -हुः or -ह्वी -हु, बहुलः -ला -लं, प्रचुरः -रा -रं, भूरिः -रिः -रि, विपुलः -ला -लं, समधिकः -का -कं.

ABUNDANTLY, *adv.* बहुशस् *ind.*, भूरिशस् *ind.*, भूयस् *ind.*, अनेकशस् *ind.*

To ABUSE, *v. a.* (Make ill use of) वृथा or मृषा or अन्यायतः प्रयुज् (c. 7. -युंक्ते -योक्तुं), or in caus. (-योजयति -यितुं), कदर्थीकृ, व्यर्थीकृ, वृथाकृ.—(Revile) कुत्स् (c. 10. कुत्सयति -यितुं), अभिकुत्स्, आक्षिप् (c. 6. -क्षिपति -क्षेप्तुं), परिक्षिप्, आक्रुश् (c. 1. क्रोशति -क्रोष्टुं), समाक्रुश्, तिरस्कृ (c. 8. -करोति, -कुरुते -कर्त्तुं), अपवद् (c. 1. -वदते -वदितुं), अवगुर् (c. 6. गुरते, -गुरितुं), with dat. or loc.; शप् (c. 1. शपति, c. 4. शप्यति शप्तुं), अभिशप्, परिशप्; खर्, in caus. (-खारयति -यितुं), मुखरीकृ, अतिब्रू (c. 2. -ब्रवीति -वक्तुं)—(To abuse in return) प्रत्याक्रुश्.

ABUSE, *s.* पारुष्यं, अभिवादः, तिरस्कारः, परिभाषणं, आक्रोशः, विक्रोशनं, अपक्रोशः, निन्दा, मौखर्यं, उपालम्भः, जुगुप्सा, -प्सनं, वाक्पारुष्यं, वाग्दोषः, खलोक्तिः *f.*, निर्भर्त्सनं, दुरालापः, दुर्वचः *n.* (स्), परुषवचनं, परुषोक्तिः *f.*; (Ill use) कुप्रयोगः, कुव्यवहारः, दुर्व्यवहारः, कदर्थीकरणं.

ABUSED, *p.p.* (Badly employed) कुप्रयुक्तः -क्ता -क्तं.—(Reviled) आक्षिप्तः -प्ता -प्तं, आक्रुष्टः -ष्टा -ष्टं.

ABUSIVE, *a.* निन्दकः -का -कं, परुषः -षा -षं, मुखरः -रा -रं, आक्रोशकः -की -कं, दुर्वादः -दा -दं, कुत्सावादी -दिनी -दि (न्), वाग्दुष्टः -ष्टा -ष्टं.

ABYSS, *s.* अगाधदरी *f.*, अगाधरन्ध्रं, अतलस्पर्शखातं, गम्भीररन्ध्रं, नरकः.

ACADEMY, *s.* पाठशाला, विद्यालयः, विद्याभ्यासस्थानं.

To ACCEDE, *v. n.* (To be added to) मिल् (c. 1. मिलति, मेलितुं), समि (c. 2. -एति -एतुं), सङ्क्रम् (c. 1. -गच्छति -गन्तुं).—(To assent) अनुज्ञा (c. 9. -जानाति -नीते -ज्ञातुं), अनुमन् (c. 4. -मन्यते -मन्तुं), सम्मतिं कृ.

To ACCELERATE, *v. a.* त्वर् in caus. (त्वरयति -यितुं), सन्त्वर्, प्रवृत् in caus. (-वर्त्तयति -यितुं).

ACCENT, *s.* (The sound of a syllable) स्वरः.—(The manner of speaking) उच्चारणं.—(The mark of a syllable) उच्चारणचिह्नं, स्वरचिह्नं.—(Acute accent) उदात्तः.

To ACCENT, *v. a.* (To pronounce with a proper accent) सूत्रानुसारतः or सूत्रानुरूपम् उच्चर् in caus. (-चारयति -यितुं) or स्वरोच्चारणं कृ.

ACCENTED, *p. p.* स्वरितः -ता -तं, उदात्तः -त्ता -त्तं.

To ACCENTUATE, *v. a.* स्वरस्य उपरि उच्चारणचिह्नं दा (c. 3. ददाति, दातुं).

To ACCEPT, *v. a.* ग्रह् (c. 9. गृह्णाति, गृह्णीते, ग्रहीतुं), प्रतिग्रह् सङ्ग्रह्, उपसङ्ग्रह्; आदा (c. 3. -ददाति -दत्ते, -दातुं), प्रतीष् (c. 6. -इच्छति -एष्टुं), स्वीकृ (c. 8. -करोति -कर्त्तुं).

ACCEPTABLE, *a.* ग्राह्यः -ह्या -ह्यं, ग्रहणीयः -या -यं, आदेयः -या -यं, उपादेयः -या -यं, समादेयः -या -यं.—(Agreeable) रमणीयः -या -यं, मनोरमः -मा -मं, प्रियः -या -यं.

ACCEPTABLENESS, *s.* ग्राह्यत्वं, रमणीयत्वं, प्रियता.

ACCEPTANCE, *s.* प्रतिग्रहः, परिग्रहः, आदानं, स्वीकरणं.—(Acceptance of money) धनादानं.

ACCEPTATION, *s.* (Meaning) अर्थः, अभिप्रायः, आशयः.

ACCEPTED, *p. p.* गृहीतः -ता -तं, आदत्तः -त्ता -त्तं.

ACCESS, *s.* (The way by which any thing may be approached) आगमः, अभिगमः, उपगमः.—(Increase, addition) वृद्धिः *f.*, उपचयः.

ACCESSARY *or* -ORY, *a.* (Co-operator) सहकारी -रिणी -रि (न्).—(To a crime) पापसहायः.

ACCESSIBLE, *a.* अभिगम्यः -म्या -म्यं, गम्यः -म्या -म्यं, सुगमः -मा -मं, -लभ्यः -भ्या -भ्यं, सुलभः -भा -भं, सुखोपसर्प्यः -र्प्या -र्प्यं.

ACCESSION, *s.* (Increase by something added) आगमः, वृद्धिः *f.*, उपचयः.—(Accession of wealth) धनागमः.—(The act of joining one's self to) उपगमः, अभिगमनं, मिलनं, उपस्थितिः *f.*—(Accession to a throne) राज्यप्राप्तिः *f.*

ACCESSORY, *a.* (Additional) अधिकः -का -कं.—(Associated with) सहितः -ता -तं, or सम्मिलितः -ता -तं, or संयुक्तः -क्ता -क्तं.

ACCIDENCE, *s.* (Rudiments of grammar) व्याकरणारम्भः, व्याकरणस्य आदिप्रकरणग्रन्थः.

ACCIDENT, *s.* (A casualty, chance) सङ्गतिः *f.*, दैवयोगः, दैवगतिः *f.*, दैवात् or अकस्मात् सङ्गतं, दैवघटनं or -ना, अतिवर्त्तनं, अभ्युदयः.—(Unfortunate accident) आपद् *f.*, विपद् *f.*—(A non-essential quality) अप्रकृतिः *f.*, असहजो गुणः.—(By accident) अकस्मात्, दैवात्, दैवेन, दैवगत्या.

ACCIDENTAL, *a.* (Casual) दैवायत्तः -त्ता -त्तं, आपतिकः -की -कं, साङ्गतिकः -की -कं, आकस्मिकः -की -कं.—(Non-essential) अप्रकृतः -ता -तं, असमवायी -यिनी -यि (न्).

ACCIDENTALLY, *adv.* दैवात्, अकस्मात्, सङ्गत्या, दैवयोगेन.

ACCLAMATION or ACCLAIM, *s.* प्रवादः, धन्यवादः, जयशब्दः, प्रशंसाशब्दः, सम्मतिप्रवादः, सांराविणं.

ACCLIVITY, *s.* उत्सङ्गः, स्थानं क्रमश उन्नम्यं.

To ACCOMMODATE, *v. a.* (To adapt, adjust) युज् in caus. (योजयति -यितुं), सन्धा (c. 3. -दधाति -धातुं), समाधा.—(To settle a difference) सन्धा, समाप् in caus. (-आपयति -यितुं).—(To supply with conveniences) सोपकारद्रव्याणि उपक्लृप् (c. 10. -कल्पयति -यितुं), युज् in caus. समायुज्.

ACCOMMODATION, *s.* (Supplying of conveniences) सोपकारद्रव्योपकल्पनं.—(Convenience) उपकरणं.—(Mutual accommodation) प्रत्युपकारः.—(Adaptation) संयोजनं, सन्धानं.

ACCOMPANIED, *p. p.* सहितः -ता -तं, संवृतः -ता -तं, सहायवान् -वती -वत्, परिवारितः -ता -तं, समेतः -ता -तं. As applied to two persons द्वितीय or सहाय may be used; as, 'Nakula accompanied by Sahadeva,' नकुलः सहदेवद्वितीयः; 'accompanied by Umā,' उमासहायः, Sometimes स is prefixed with this sense; as, 'accompanied by his ministers,' ससचिवः.

To ACCOMPANY, *v. a.* (As a companion) अनुया (c. 2. -याति -यातुं), समनुया, अन्वि (c. 2. -एति -एतुं), परिवृ in caus. (-वारयति -यितुं), सहायीभू.—(To join with) युज् (c. 7. युनक्ति, योक्तुं, c. 10. योजयति -यितुं), संयुज्.

ACCOMPLICE, *s.* (In crime) पापसहायः, पापसम्मितः, कुसहायः.—(Coadjutor) सहकारी *m.* (न्).—(Adherent) अनुषङ्गी *m.* (न्).

To ACCOMPLISH, *v. a.* सिध् or साध् in caus. (साधयति -यितुं) संसाध्; समाप् in caus. (-आपयति -यितुं), सम्पद् in caus. (-पादयति -यितुं), समाचर् (c. 1. -चरति -चरितुं), निर्वृत् in caus. (-वर्त्तयति -यितुं), समास्था (c. 1. तिष्ठति -ते -स्थातुं), अनुष्ठा, आस्था, कृ (c. 8. करोति, कर्त्तुं) सङ्कृ.

ACCOMPLISHABLE, साध्यः -ध्या -ध्यं, साधनीयः -या -यं, सम्पादनीयः -या -यं.

ACCOMPLISHED, सिद्धः -द्धा -द्धं, निर्वृत्तः -त्ता -त्तं, निष्पन्नः -न्ना -न्नं, सम्पन्नः -न्ना -न्नं, कृतार्थीभूतः -ता -तं.—(Clever) गुणवान् -वती -वत् (त्), गुणी -णिनी -णि (न्), निपुणः -णा -णं.

ACCOMPLISHMENT, *s.* सिद्धिः *f.*, समाप्तिः *f.*, निष्पत्तिः *f.*, आसाधनं, निर्वाहः, राद्धिः *f.*, निर्वृत्तिः *f.*—(Of one's object) कृतकृत्यता, कृतार्थता, स्वार्थसिद्धिः *f.*—(The condition of an accomplished man) गुणिता, सम्पूर्णभावः, निपुणता.—(Embellishment) परिष्कारः.

To ACCORD, *v. n.* (To agree, suit) युज् in pass. (युज्यते), अनुरूपः -पा -पं, or सदृशः -शा -शं, or तुल्यः -ल्या -ल्यं अस्.—(To be of the same opinion) एकचित्तीभू, सम्मतः -ता -तं भू.

ACCORD, *s.* (Concurrence) सम्मतिः *f.*, ऐकमत्यं, एकचित्तता, समता, समवाक्यं, स्वीकरणं.—(In music) एकतालः.—(Of one's own accord) स्वयं, कामतस् *ind.*, कामहैतुकः -की -कं.—(With one accord) एकचित्तीभूय.

ACCORDANCE, *s.* (Conformity) अनुसारः, अनुरूपता, सादृश्यं.

ACCORDING, *prep.* (According to) यथा, अनुरूपं, अनुसारतस् *ind.* अनुरूपेण, अनुसारेण, अनु prefixed; 'according to seniority,' अनुज्येष्ठं; 'according to one's desire,' यथेष्टं, यथाभिमतं; 'according to one's power,' यथाशक्ति *ind.*

ACCORDINGLY, *adv.* तथैव, तदनुसारतस् *ind.*, तदनुरूपेण.

To ACCOST, *v. a.* अभिभाष् (c. 1. -भाषते -भाषितुं), आभाष्, समाभाष्, अभिधा (c. 3. -दधाति -धातुं), आमन्त्र् (c. 10. -मन्त्रयति -ते -यितुं), समामन्त्र्.

ACCOSTED, *p. p.* अभिहितः -ता -तं, अभिभाषितः -ता -तं.

ACCOUNT, *s.* (A computation) गणितं, विगणनं, गणना -नं, सङ्ख्यानं, लेखा.—(Value, estimation) मूल्यं, अर्घः, सम्मानं.—(Great value) बहुमतिः.—(Narrative, explanation) कथा, कथनं, उपाख्यानं, यथातथं, यथास्थितं; 'on this account,' अतस् *ind.*, अनेन हेतुना, इति हेतोः; 'on what account?' केन हेतुना or केन कार्य्येण; 'on account of,' हेतोः, हेतौ, अर्थं or अर्थे, कृते, निमित्ते, कारणात् with the crude form; or expressed by simply putting the noun in the abl. c.; as, 'on account of anger,' कोपात्; or by the indec. part. of उद्दिश्; as, 'on which account,' यदुद्दिश्य.

To ACCOUNT, *v. a.* (To esteem) मन् (c. 4. मन्यते, मन्तुं, or caus. मानयति -यितुं), सम्मन् in caus.; ज्ञा (c. 9. जानाति, जानीते, ज्ञातुं).—(To reckon, compute) गण् (c. 10. गणयति -यितुं), विगण्, सङ्ख्या (c. 2. -ख्याति -ख्यातुं).—(To give an account or relation) कथ् (c. 10. कथयति -यितुं), आख्या, निविद् in caus. (-वेदयति -यितुं).

ACCOUNTABLE, *a.* परानुयोगाधीनः -ना -नं, अनुसन्धेयः -या -यं, अनुसन्धानायत्तः -त्ता -त्तं, आह्वानाधीनः -ना -नं, यो निक्षेपं or न्यासं प्रतिपादयितुम् अर्हति.

ACCOUNTANT, *s.* गणकः, लेखकः, लिपिकारः, मसिपण्यः.

ACCOUNT-BOOK, *s.* गणनापुस्तकं.

To ACCOUTRE, *v. a.* नह् (c. 4. -नह्यति -ते -नद्धुं), सन्नह्, पिनह्, सज्जीकृ (c. 8. -करोति -कर्त्तुं).

ACCOUTRED, सन्नद्धः -द्धा -द्धं, पिनद्धः -द्धा -द्धं, सज्जः -ज्जा -ज्जं, सज्जितः -ता -तं.

ACCOUTREMENT, *s.* सन्नाहः, सज्जा, परिधानं, अलङ्कारः.

To ACCRUE, *v. n.* (To be added) प्रतिवृत् (c. 1. -वर्त्तते -वर्त्तितुं), मिल् (c. 1. मिलति, मेलितुं), प्राप् in pass. (-आप्यते).—(To arise as profit) उत्पद् (c. 4. -पद्यते -पत्तुं), जन् (c. 4. जायते, जनितुं), सञ्जन्.

To ACCUMULATE, *v. a.* चि (c. 5. चिनोति, चेतुं), सञ्चि, समाचि, प्रचि, राशीकृ, एकत्र कृ.

To ACCUMULATE, *v. n.* उपचि in pass. (-चीयते), वृध् (c. 1. वर्धते, वर्धितुं), राशीभू.

ACCUMULATED, *p. p.* उपचितः -ता -तं, सञ्चितः -ता -तं, समाचितः -ता -तं. राशीकृतः -ता -तं, वर्द्धितः -ता -तं.

ACCUMULATION, *s.* सञ्चयः, समुदायः, सम्पत्तिः *f.*, सङ्घातः, सञ्चयः, ओघः, राशीकरणं.

ACCURACY, *s.* याथार्थ्यं, तथ्यं, याथातथ्यं, सम्यक्त्वं, शुद्धत्वं, सत्यता.—(Nicety) सूक्ष्मत्वं.

ACCURATE, *a.* यथार्थः -र्था -र्थं, सत्यः -त्या -त्यं, तथ्यः -थ्या -थ्यं, ऋतः -ता -तं, समञ्जसः -सा -सं, याथार्थिकः -की -कं.

ACCURATELY, *adv.* यथार्थं, सम्यक्, ऋतं, सत्यं, अञ्जसा, सूक्ष्मत्वेन.

ACCURSED, *p. p.* अभिशप्तः -प्ता -प्तं, शापग्रस्तः -स्ता -स्तं, आक्रुष्टः -ष्टा -ष्टं, आक्रोशनीयः -या -यं, अवगर्हितः -ता -तं.

ACCUSATION, *s.* अभियोगः, दोषकल्पनं, अपवादः.—(False) अभिशंसनं, अभिशापः.

ACCUSATIVE, *a.* (Case) कर्म्म *n.* (न्), द्वितीया विभक्तिः.

To ACCUSE, *v. a.* अभियुज् (c. 7. -युनक्ति -योक्तुं), अभियोगं कृ, अधिक्षिप् (c. 6. -क्षिपति -क्षेप्तुं), अपवद् (c. 1. -वदति -वदितुं), दोषकल्पनं कृ, परिशप् (c. 1. -शपति -शप्तुं), अभिशप्.—(To be accused), अभियुज् in pass. (-युज्यते).

ACCUSED, अभियुक्तः -क्ता -क्तं, अभिशप्तः -प्ता -प्तं, अभिशस्तः -स्ता -स्तं.

ACCUSER, *s.* अभियोगी *m.* (न्), अभियोक्ता *m.* (क्तृ), अपवादकः, परिवादकः.

To ACCUSTOM, *v. a.* अभ्यस् (c. 4. -अस्यति -असितुं), अभ्यासं or व्यवहारं कृ, शिक्ष् in caus. (शिक्षयति -यितुं).—(To be accustomed) अभ्यस्तः -स्ता -स्तं भू.

ACCUSTOMARY, *a.* आचारिकः -की -कं, आचरितः -ता -तं, व्यावहारिकः -की -कं, व्यवहारानुरूपः -पा -पं, स्वाभाविकः -की -कं.

ACCUSTOMED, *p. p.* अभ्यस्तः -स्ता -स्तं, शिक्षितः -ता -तं.

ACE, *s.* (On cards or dice) मुद्राविशेषः.—(Within an ace, all but) प्रायस्, यत्किञ्चित् न्यूनं, ईषदूनं.—'All but dead,' मृतकल्पः.

ACERBITY, *s.* कटुता, अम्लता, शुक्तता.—(Sharpness of temper) स्वभावकटुता, अरुन्तुदत्वं.

ACHE, *s.* वेदनं -ना, पीडा, व्यथा.—(Headache) शिरोवेदना.—(Toothache) दन्तवेदना.

To ACHE, *v. n.* पीड् in pass. (पीड्यते), व्यथ् (c. 1. व्यथते, व्यथितुं).

To ACHIEVE, *v. a.* (To perform, finish) समाप् in caus. (-आपयति -यितुं), सम्पद् in caus. (-पादयति -यितुं), सिध् in caus. (साधयति -यितुं).—(To obtain) प्राप् (c. 5. -आप्नोति -आप्तुं), समाप्, सम्प्राप्.

ACHIEVEMENT, *s.* (A noble exploit) प्रशंसनीयकर्म्म *n.* (न्), चेष्टितं, चरित्रं.—(In heraldry) पदचिह्नं.

ACID, *a.* अम्लः -म्ला -म्लं, शुक्तः -क्ता -क्तं, शौक्तः -क्ती -क्तं, शौक्तिकः -की -कं.

ACID, *s.* अम्लः, शुक्तं.

ACIDITY, *s.* अम्लता -त्वं, अम्लभावः, शुक्तता.—(Of stomach) अम्लपित्तः.

To ACIDULATE, *v. a.* अम्लीकृ; अम्लय् (nom. अम्लयति -यितुं).

ACIDULATED, *p. p.* अम्लाक्तः -क्ता -क्तं, अम्लीकृतः -ता -तं.

To ACKNOWLEDGE, *v. a.* अभिज्ञा (c. 1. -जानाति -नीते -ज्ञातुं), प्रत्यभिज्ञा, समभिज्ञा, प्रतिज्ञा; स्वीकृ, अङ्गीकृ, अनुभाष् (c. 1. -भाषते -भाषितुं).

ACKNOWLEDGMENT, *s.* स्वीकारः, अङ्गीकारः, प्रत्यभिज्ञानं.—(Of a fault) स्वपापस्वीकारः.

ACORN, *s.* प्रसिद्धवृक्षस्य फलं.

To ACQUAINT, *v. a.* ज्ञा in caus. (ज्ञापयति -यितुं), विज्ञा; बुध् in caus. (बोधयति -यितुं), प्रबुध्, प्रतिबुध्, अवबुध्, निविद् in caus. (-वेदयति -यितुं).

ACQUAINTANCE, *s.* परिचयः.—(Knowledge) ज्ञानं, परिज्ञानं.—(An acquaintance, friend) मित्रं, संसर्गी *m.* (न्), विभावः.—(Familiarity) संसर्गः, संस्तवः.

ACQUAINTED, परिचितः -ता -तं, संस्तुतः -ता -तं.—(Known) ज्ञातः -ता -तं.

To ACQUIESCE, *v. n.* तुष् (c. 4. तुष्यति तोष्टुं), सन्तुष् with inst. or loc.—(In an opinion) सम्मतिं कृ.—(To assent) अनुमन् (c. 4. -मन्यते -मन्तुं), अनुज्ञा (c. 9. -जानाति -ज्ञातुं).

ACQUIESCENCE, *s.* तुष्टिः *f.*, परितोषः, सन्तोषः, सम्मतिः *f.*, अनुमतिः *f.*, क्षान्तिः *f.*—(Submission) क्षान्तिः *f.*

ACQUIRABLE, *a.* प्राप्यः -प्या -प्यं, लभ्यः -भ्या -भ्यं.

To ACQUIRE, *v. a.* अर्ज् (c. 1. अर्जति अर्जितुं), उपार्ज्, लभ् (c. 1. लभते लब्धुं), उपलभ्, प्राप् (c. 5. -आप्नोति -आप्तुं), अवाप्; प्रतिपद् (c. 4. -पद्यते -पत्तुं), अश् (c. 5. अश्नुते, अशितुं), उपाश्, समश्; आविश् (c. 6. -विशति -वेष्टुं), समाविश्.

ACQUIRED, *p. p.* प्राप्तः -प्ता -प्तं, लब्धः -ब्धा -ब्धं, आपन्नः -न्ना -न्नं, अर्ज्जितः -ता -तं, उपार्ज्जितः -ता -तं.

ACQUISITION OR ACQUIREMENT, *s.* लाभः, लब्धिः *f.*, अर्ज्जनं, प्राप्तिः *f.*, अवाप्तिः *f.*, सम्प्राप्तिः *f.*, प्रतिपत्तिः *f.*, ग्रहणं.—(The thing gained) आगमः.—(Acquirement of knowledge) विद्याप्राप्तिः *f.*, विद्यार्ज्जनं, विद्यागमः.—(Acquisition of property) धनार्ज्जनं.—(Various acquirement) विप्रतिपत्तिः *f.*

To ACQUIT, *v. a.* पापात् मुच् (c. 6. मुञ्चति, मोक्तुं), विमुच्, or in caus. (मोचयति -यितुं), शुध् in caus. (शोधयति -यितुं), निस्तॄ in caus. (-तारयति -यितुं).

ACQUITTAL, *s.* शुद्धिः *f.*, शोधनं, मुक्तिः *f.*, मोक्षः.

ACQUITTANCE, *s.* निस्तारः, आनृण्यं, निष्कृतिः *f.*

ACQUITTED, *p. p.* शुद्धः -द्धा -द्धं, मुक्तः -क्ता -क्तं.

ACRID, ACRIMONIOUS, *a.* कटुः -टुः or -ट्वी -टु, उग्रः -ग्रा -ग्रं, अरुन्तुदः -दा -दं, प्रखरः -रा -रं.

ACRIMONY, *s.* कटुता, उग्रत्वं, प्राखर्य्यं.—(Of temper) स्वभावकटुता.

ACROSS, *adv.* (To the other side) पारं, तीरान्तरं; as, 'across the sea,' समुद्रपारं.—(Transversely) व्यत्यस्तं.—(With hands across) व्यत्यस्तपाणिना.

ACROSTIC, *s.* श्लोकविशेषः.

To ACT, *v. n.* चेष्ट् (c. 1. चेष्टते, चेष्टितुं), विचेष्ट्, सञ्चेष्ट्, कृ (c. 8. करोति, कुरुते, कर्त्तुं), विधा (c. 3. -दधाति -धातुं).—(To conduct one's self) व्यवहृ (c. 1. -हरति -ते -हर्त्तुं), आचर् (c. 1. -चरति -चरितुं)—(As a stage-player) नट् (c. 1. नटति, नटितुं).

To ACT, *v. a.* (To feign by action) नट् (c. 10. नाटयति -यितुं); as, 'Acting the sentiment of love,' शृङ्गारभावं नाटयन्ती; रूप् (c. 10. रूपयति -यितुं), अभिनयं कृ. The sense of acting a part may be expressed by nominal verbs; as, 'he acts the king,' राजायते.—(To assume disguise) छद्मवेशं कृ.

ACT, *s.* (A deed) कर्म्म *n.* (न्), कार्य्यं, चेष्टितं, क्रिया, कृतं, कृत्यं, विचेष्टितं.—(Of a play) अङ्कः, अङ्कं.—(A decree) व्यवस्था.

ACTION, *s.* कर्म्म *n.* (न्), क्रिया, कृत्या, चेष्टा, विचेष्टितं, प्रवृत्तिः *f.*, विधानं.—(Agency, operation) कारणं.—(The action of the wind) वाताहतिः *f.*—(Gesticulation) इङ्गितं, अङ्गहारः, अङ्गविक्षेपः.—(An action in law) अभियोगः, अर्थः.—(Fight, battle) युद्धं, सङ्ग्रामः, समरः, संयुगः.

ACTIONABLE, *a.* (In law) अभियोज्यः -ज्या -ज्यं, व्यवहार्य्यः -र्य्या -र्य्यं, व्यवहर्त्तव्यः -व्या -व्यं.

ACTIVE, *a.* (Engaged in action) उद्योगी -गिनी -गि (न्), प्रयत्नवान् -वती -वत् (त्), उद्युक्तः -क्ता -क्तं, कर्म्मोद्युक्तः -क्ता -क्तं, अनलसः -सा -सं, सयत्नः -त्ना -त्नं, व्यवसायी -यिनी -यि (न्), कर्म्मी -र्म्मिणी -र्म्मि (न्), सोत्साहः -हा -हं, सोद्योगः -गा -गं, कर्म्मनिष्ठः -ष्ठा -ष्ठं.—(Nimble) तीक्ष्णकर्म्मा -र्म्मा -र्म्म (न्), आशुकारी -रिणी -रि (न्), लघु -घुः -घु, त्वरितः -ता -तं, सत्वरः -रा -रं, अतन्द्रः -न्द्रा -न्द्रं.—(Having motion) गत्वरः -रा -रं.—(Active voice) परस्मैपदं, कर्त्तृवाच्यः.—(A verb in the active voice) कर्त्तरि वाच्यं, सकर्म्मकक्रिया.—(Fond of manly exercise) व्यायामशीलः -ला -लं, व्यायामी -मिनी -मि (न्).

ACTIVITY, *s.* कर्म्मोद्योगः, सयत्नता, व्यवसायः, प्रवृत्तिः *f.*, प्रवर्त्तनं.—(Manly exercise) व्यायामः.—(Active life) प्रवृत्तिः *f.*—(With activity) प्रयत्नतस् *ind.*

ACTOR, *s.* (Stage-player) नटः, नर्त्तकः, कुशीलवः, चारणः, रङ्गजीवकः, रङ्गाजीवः, अभिनेता *m.* (तृ), शैलाली *m.* (न्), कृशाश्वी *m.* (न्).—(He that acts or does) कारी *m.* (न्), कारकः, कारः.

ACTRESS, *s.* नर्त्तकी, नटी, चारणदाराः *pl.*

ACTUAL, *a.* (True, real) तथ्यः -थ्या -थ्यं, वास्तवः -वी -वं, वास्तविकः -की -कं, सत्यः -त्या -त्यं, विद्यमानः -ना -नं.

ACTUALLY, *adv.* वस्तुतस् *ind.*, अर्थतस् *ind.*, कार्य्यतस् *ind.*, कार्य्यवत्.

ACTUARY, *s.* लेखकः, व्यवस्थारचकः.

ACUMEN, *s.* (Quickness of intellect) बुद्धिसूक्ष्मता, मतिप्रकर्षः, विदग्धता, कुशाग्रीयमतित्वं.

ACUMINATED, तीक्ष्णाग्रः -ग्रा -ग्रं, अंशुमान् -मती -मत् (त्).

ACUTE, *a.* (In intellect) सूक्ष्मबुद्धिः -द्धिः -द्धि, विदग्धः -ग्धा -ग्धं, कुशाग्रीयमतिः -तिः -ति.—(Not blunt) तीक्ष्णः -क्ष्णा -क्ष्णं, तीव्रः -व्रा -व्रं.—(Acute pain) तीव्रवेदना.

ACUTELY, *adv.* तीव्रं, तीक्ष्णं, सूक्ष्मतया.

ACUTENESS, *s.* (Of intellect) बुद्धिसूक्ष्मता, विदग्धता, वैदग्ध्यं.—(Sharpness) तैक्ष्ण्यं, तेजः *n.* (स्), तीव्रता.

ADAGE, *s.* सूत्रं, वचनं, प्राचीनपुरुषवचनं.

ADAGIO, *adv.* शनैः शनैः, मन्दं मन्दं.

ADAGIO, *s.* स्वरमान्द्यं.

ADAMANT, *s.* वज्रः or -ज्रं, अभेद्यप्रस्तरः.—(Diamond) हीरकः, हीरं, अशिरकं, वरारकं.

ADAMANTINE, *a.* वज्रमयः -यी -यं, वज्रः -ज्रा -ज्रं.

To **ADAPT**, *v. a.* युज् in caus. (योजयति -यितुं), सन्धा (c. 3. -धत्ते -धातुं).—(To be adapted) युज् in pass. (युज्यते).

ADAPTABLE, *a.* योग्यः -ग्या -ग्यं, योक्तव्यः -व्या -व्यं, संयोजनीयः -या -यं.

ADAPTED, *p. p.* युक्तः -क्ता -क्तं, योग्यः -ग्या -ग्यं, उपयुक्तः -क्ता -क्तं, पर्य्याप्तः -प्ता -प्तं, सम्भाव्यः -व्या -व्यं.

To **ADD**, *v. a.* (One thing to another) अन्यद् अन्येन संयुज् (c. 10. -योजयति -यितुं) or समायुज्; धा (c. 3. दधाति धातुं), समाक्षिप् (c. 6. -क्षिपति -क्षेप्तुं), उपर्य्युपरि धा, समाचि (c. 5. -चिनोति -चेतुं).—(To add together, cast up) परिसङ्ख्या (c. 2. -ख्याति -ख्यातुं), परिगण् (c. 10. -गणयति -यितुं).

ADDER, *s.* सर्पविशेषः.

To **ADDICT**, *v. a.* (One's self to any thing) आसञ्ज् in pass. (-सज्यते or -सज्जते -संक्तुं) with loc.; भज् (c. 1. भजति -ते, भक्तुं), आसेव् (c. 1. -सेवते, -सेवितुं), निविश् in caus. (-वेशयति -यितुं), निरतः -ता -तं or आसक्तः -क्ता -क्तं भू.

ADDICTED, *p. p.* सक्तः -क्ता -क्तं, आसक्तः -क्ता -क्तं, प्रसक्तः -क्ता -क्तं, निविष्टः -ष्टा -ष्टं, प्रजुष्टः -ष्टा -ष्टं, प्रवणः -णा -णं.

ADDICTION, सक्तिः *f.*, आसक्तिः *f.*, रक्तिः *f.*, उपसेवनं, निवेशः.

ADDITION, *s.* संयोजनं, समायोगः, समाक्षेपः.—(The state of being additional) आधिक्यं.—(In arithmetic) सङ्कलितं, परिसंख्या, परिगणनं.—(The thing added) अनुबन्धः.

ADDITIONAL, *a.* अधिकः -का -कं, अधिकतरः -रा -रं.

ADDLE, *a.* असम्पूर्णः -र्णा -र्णं, नष्टः -ष्टा -ष्टं, दुष्टः -ष्टा -ष्टं.

To **ADDRESS**, *v. a.* (By words) आमन्त्र् (c. 10. -मन्त्रयते -यितुं), समामन्त्र्, अभिभाष् (c. 1. -भाषते -भाषितुं), आभाष्, समाभाष्, प्रतिभाष्, अभिवद् (c. 1. -वदति -ते -वदितुं, c. 10. -वादयति -ते -यितुं), अभिवच् (c. 2. -वक्ति -वक्तुं), आलप् (c. 1. -लपति -लपितुं), निगद् (c. 1. -गदति -गदितुं).—(By name) सम्बोधनं कृ, नाम ग्रह् (c. 9. गृह्णाति, ग्रहीतुं).—(To address a letter, &c., to any one) पत्रसंज्ञां कृ.

ADDRESS, *s.* सम्बोधनं, अभिवादः, वाक्यं, वचनं, वाक्यारम्भः.—(By name) नामग्रहः.—(Courtship) भावकरणं.—(Dexterity) नैपुण्यं चतुरता.—(Direction of a letter) पत्रसंज्ञा, पत्रादेशः.

ADDRESSED, *p. p.* सम्बोधितः -ता -तं, अभिहितः -ता -तं, सम्भाषितः -ता -तं.

To **ADDUCE**, उपन्यस् (c. 4. -अस्यति -असितुं), उपनी (c. 1. -नयति -नेतुं), आनी, साक्षात् कृ.

ADDUCED, *p. p.* उपन्यस्तः -स्ता -स्तं, उपनीतः -ता -तं, आनीतः -ता -तं.

ADEPT, *s.* अभिज्ञः, पटुः, निपुणः, प्रवीणः.

ADEQUACY, *s.* सामर्थ्यं, पर्य्याप्तिः *f.*, क्षमता, योग्यत्वं.

ADEQUATE, *a.* पर्य्याप्तः -प्ता -प्तं, क्षमः -मा -मं, समर्थः -र्था -र्थं, प्रतिबलः -ला -लं, तुल्यः -ल्या -ल्यं, समानः -ना -नं, योग्यः -ग्या -ग्यं.

To **ADHERE**, *v. n.* संज् in pass. (सज्यते or सज्जते) अनुसंज्, आसंज्, प्रसंज्, संसंज् with loc.; संलग्नः -ग्ना -ग्नं, or अनुलग्नः -ग्ना -ग्नं, or संयुक्तः -क्ता -क्तं, or अवलम्बी -म्बिनी -म्बि, or दृढावलम्बी -म्बिनी -म्बि अस्; अनुबन्ध् (c. 9. -बध्नाति -बन्द्धुं) in pass. (-बध्यते), ली (c. 4. लीयते लेतुं), धृ in caus. (धारयति -यितुं).—'He adheres to his promise,' प्रतिज्ञातं पालयति.

ADHERENCE, *s.* आसङ्गः, अनुषङ्गः, आसक्तिः *f.*, प्रसक्तिः *f.*, निषेवनं.—(To a pursuit) परायणः, त्परायणं.

ADHERENT, *s.* अनुषङ्गी *m.* (न्), अनुगतः, अनुगामी *m.* (न्), सहायः, सहचरः.—(Follower of the same party) एकपक्षः, पक्षकः, सपक्षः, पार्श्विकः.

ADHESION, *s.* अनुलग्नता, संलग्नत्वं, संसक्तिः *f.*

ADHESIVE, *a.* अनुलग्नशीलः -ला -लं, संलग्नशीलः -ला -लं, अनुषङ्गिकः -की -कं.

ADIEU, *s.* आमन्त्रणं, आप्रच्छनं, प्रस्थानकाले आमन्त्रणं.—(To bid adieu) आप्रच्छ् (c. 6. -पृच्छते -प्रष्टुं), आमन्त्र् (c. 10. -मन्त्रयते -यितुं) अनुमन्त्र्.

ADJACENT, *a.* समीपः -पा -पं, आसन्नः -न्ना -न्नं, निकटः -टा -टं, सम्बद्धः -द्धा -द्धं, सन्निकृष्टः -ष्टा -ष्टं, संसक्तः -क्ता -क्तं, पार्श्वस्थः -स्था -स्थं.

ADJECTIVE, *s.* गुणवाचकः, शब्दविशेषणं.

To **ADJOIN**, *v. a.* आयुज् (c. 7. -युनक्ति -योक्तुं, c. 10. -योजयति -यितुं) समायुज् संयुज्.

To **ADJOIN**, *v. n.* समीपः -पा -पं स्था (c. 1. तिष्ठति स्थातुं), निकटे स्था, समीपवर्त्ती -र्त्तिनी -र्त्ति अस्.

ADJOINING. *See* ADJACENT.

To **ADJOURN**, *v. a.* निरूपितकालपर्य्यन्तं कार्य्यं त्यज् (c. 1. त्यजति त्यक्तुं).

ADJOURNMENT, *s.* निरूपितकालपर्य्यन्तं कार्य्यत्यागः.

ADIPOUS, *a.* मेदस्वी -स्विनी -स्वि (न्), वसायुक्तः -क्ता -क्तं.

To **ADJUDGE**, *v. a.* (To cause one of the parties to give up the thing controverted) दा in caus. (दापयति -यितुं).—(To decree judicially) तीर् (c. 10. तीरयति -यितुं), निर्णीतं -तां -तं कृ, निष्पन्नं -न्नां -न्नं कृ, विचारं कृ, पार् (c. 10. पारयति -यितुं).

ADJUDGED, *p. p.* दापितः -ता -तं, तीरितः -ता -तं, विचारितः -ता -तं.

ADJUDICATION, *s.* दापनं, तीरणं, विचारणं.

ADJUNCT, *a.* संयुक्तः -क्ता -क्तं, सहितः -ता -तं, सम्मिलितः -ता -तं.

ADJUNCT, *s.* (An indicatory affix to verbs) अनुबन्धः.

ADJUNCTION, (The act of adjoining) संयोजनं, सम्मिलनं.

ADJURATION, *s.* (The act of proffering an oath) शापनं.—(The form of oath proffered) शपथव्यवस्था.

To ADJURE, *v. a.* (To put upon oath) शप् in caus. (शापयति -यितुं).—(To charge earnestly) शपथेन समादिश् (c. 6. -दिशति -देष्टुं).

To ADJUST, *v. a.* समाधा (c. 3. -दधाति -धातुं), सन्धा, संविधा; आयुज् (c. 7. -युनक्ति -योक्तुं or in caus. -योजयति -यितुं), समायुज्; प्रतिसाध् in caus. (-साधयति -यितुं) तुल्यं -ल्यां -ल्यं कृ.

ADJUSTED, *p. p.* समाहितः -ता -तं, विहितः -ता -तं, आयोजितः -ता -तं.

ADJUSTMENT, *s.* समाधानं, सन्धानं, विधानं, समायोगः.

ADJUTANT, *s.* (A helper) सहायः, उपकारकः, सहकारी *m.* (न्), साहाय्यकारी *m.* (न्).—(In the army) सैन्यपदविशेषः.

ADMENSURATION, *s.* परिमाणं, मापनं, परिमाणविद्या.

To ADMINISTER, *v. a.* (Give, afford, supply) दा (c. 3. ददाति दातुं), उपपद् in caus. (-पादयति -यितुं), प्रयुज् in caus. (-योजयति -यितुं).—(To conduct) निर्वह् in caus. (-वाहयति -यितुं), निर्वृत् in caus. (-वर्त्तयति -यितुं), प्रवृत्; आवस् (c. 1. -वसति -वस्तुं).—(Justice, punishment, &c.) प्रणी (c. 1. -नयति -नेतुं), सम्प्रणी; प्रवृत् in caus. (-वर्त्तयति -यितुं).

ADMINISTERED, *p. p.* (As justice) प्रवर्त्तितः -ता -तं, प्रणीतः -ता -तं.

ADMINISTRATION, *s.* (The act of administering an office) प्रणयनं, कर्म्मनिर्वाहः, राज्यधुरा.—(Those to whom the care of public affairs is committed) सचिवाः *pl.*; 'ministers of action,' कर्म्मसचिवाः *pl.*; 'ministers of counsel,' धीसचिवाः *pl.*—(The ministerial office) साचिव्यं, मन्त्रित्वं.—(Act of administering medicine, &c.) भेषजप्रयोगः.

ADMINISTRATOR, *s.* (One entrusted with the care of the effects of a deceased man) मृतद्रव्यनिरूपणाधिकृतः, प्रेतजनद्रव्यरक्षकः.—(One that conducts any thing) प्रणेता *m.* (तृ), सम्प्रणेता *m.* (तृ), प्रवर्त्तयिता *m.* (तृ), प्रवर्त्तकः.

ADMIRABLE, *a.* श्लाघ्यः -घ्या -घ्यं, प्रशंसनीयः -या -यं, अद्भुतः -ता -तं, अनुपमः -मा -मं, सुन्दरः -रा -री -रं.

ADMIRABLY, *adv.* श्लाघ्यप्रकारेण, प्रशंसनीयप्रकारेण, अद्भुतं.

ADMIRAL, *s.* जलयोधाधिपतिः, वृहन्नौसमूहाधिपतिः, जलयोधाध्यक्षः.

ADMIRALSHIP, *s.* वृहन्नौसमूहाधिपत्यं, जलयोधाधिपतित्वं.

ADMIRALTY, *s.* (The officers appointed to administer naval affairs) सामुद्रकार्य्याधिकृतः सचिवसमाजः, जलयुद्धव्यवस्थानिरूपणे नियुक्तः समाजः.

ADMIRATION, *s.* प्रशंसा, श्लाघा.—(Wonder) विस्मयः, आश्चर्य्यं, चमत्कारः.

To ADMIRE, *v. n.* प्रशंस् (c. 1. -शंसति -शंसितुं), श्लाघ् (c. 1. श्लाघते श्लाघितुं).—(To regard with wonder) विस्मयेन दृश् (c. 1. पश्यति द्रष्टुं) or अपेक्ष् (c. 1. -ईक्षते -ईक्षितुं).—(To regard with love) स्नेहेन or अनुरागेण अवेक्ष्.

ADMIRER, *s.* (The person who admires) विस्मयी *m.* (न्), श्लाघकः, प्रशंसकः.—(A lover) कामी *m.* (न्), अनुरागवान् *m.* (त्), प्रणयी *m.* (न्), स्नेही *m.* (न्).

ADMISSIBLE, *a.* ग्राह्यः -ह्या -ह्यं, आदेयः -या -यं, उपादेयः -या -यं, प्रगृह्यः -ह्या -ह्यं, स्वीकरणीयः -या -यं.

ADMISSION, *s.* (The act of admitting) प्रवेशनं.—(Admittance, entry) प्रवेशः.—(Allowing an argument) वाक्यग्रहणं, स्वीकारः, अनुज्ञा, अङ्गीकरणं.

To ADMIT, *v. a.* प्रविश् in caus. (-वेशयति -यितुं), निविश्, आविश्.—(Allow, approve of) ग्रह् (c. 9. गृह्णाति -ह्णीते ग्रहीतुं), अनुग्रह्, स्वीकारं कृ, अङ्गीकृ.

ADMITTANCE, *s.* (Entry) प्रवेशः.—(Allowance) वाक्यस्वीकारः, ग्रहणं.

ADMITTED, *p. p.* प्रवेशितः -ता -तं, निवेशितः -ता -तं.

To ADMIX, *v. a.* मिश्र् (c. 10. मिश्रयति -यितुं), विमिश्र्, सम्मिश्रं -श्रां -श्रं कृ, मिश्रणं कृ, संयोगं कृ.

ADMIXED, *p. p.* मिश्रितः -ता -तं, सम्मिश्रितः -ता -तं.

ADMIXTION, *s.* मिश्रणं, सम्पर्कः, साङ्कर्य्यं.

To ADMONISH, *v. a.* प्रदिश् in caus. (-देशयति -यितुं), उपदिश् (c. 6. -दिशति -देष्टुं), प्रत्यादिश्, प्रबुध् or सम्बुध् in caus. (-बोधयति -यितुं), समाविद् in caus. (-वेदयति -यितुं), शिक्ष् in caus. (शिक्षयति -यितुं), विज्ञा in caus. (-ज्ञापयति -यितुं), मन्त्र् (c. 10. मन्त्रयति -यितुं), निदृश् in caus. (-दर्शयति -यितुं), अनुयोगं कृ.

ADMONISHED, *p. p.* प्रत्यादिष्टः -ष्टा -ष्टं, उपदिष्टः -ष्टा -ष्टं, बोधितः -ता -तं.

ADMONISHER, *s.* उपदेशकः, प्रत्यादेशकः, प्रबोधकः, अनुयोगकारी *m.* (न्), अनुयोजकः, शिक्षादाता *m.* (तृ), शिक्षकः.

ADMONITION, *s.* उपदेशः, प्रत्यादेशः, मन्त्रणं, प्रबोधनं, प्रबोधः, शिक्षा, अनुयोगः.

ADMONITORY, *a.* उपदेशकः -का -कं, शिक्षकः -का -कं, बोधकारः -री -रं, अनुज्ञापकः -का -कं.

ADO, *s.* (Trouble) दुःखं, कष्टं, श्रमः.—(Bustle, tumult) तुमुलं, कलहः, कोलाहलः.

ADOLESCENCE OR ADOLESCENCY, *s.* यौवनं, कौमारं, यौवनावस्था.

To ADOPT, *v. a.* (As a child) कृत्रिमपुत्रं कृ, पोष्यपुत्रं कृ.—(To assume) ग्रह् (c. 9. गृह्णाति -ह्णीते, ग्रहीतुं), आत्मसात्कृ.

ADOPTED, *p. p.* गृहीतः -ता -तं, आत्मसात्कृतः -ता -तं; 'an adopted son,' पोष्यपुत्रः, कृत्रिमपुत्रः, दत्तकपुत्रः, दत्त्रिमपुत्रः.—(Not natural) कृत्रिमः -मा -मं, कृतकः -का -कं.

ADOPTER, *s.* (Of a child) कृत्रिमपुत्रकारी, पोष्यपुत्रकारी (न्).

ADOPTION, *s.* (Of a child) कृत्रिमपुत्रकरणं, पोष्यपुत्रकरणं.—(Assumption) ग्रहणं, आत्मसात्करणं.

ADORABLE, *a.* पूज्यः -ज्या -ज्यं, अर्च्चनीयः -या -यं, भगवान् -वती -वत् (त्).

ADORATION, *s.* पूजा, अर्च्चा, अभ्यर्च्चनं, भजनं, नमस्कारः, नमस्या.

To ADORE, *v. a.* नमस्य् (nom. नमस्यति -स्यितुं), पूज् (c. 10. पूजयति -यितुं), अर्च् (c. 1. अर्चति, अर्चितुं), अभ्यर्च्, समर्च्, नमस्कृ (c. 8. -करोति -कुरुते -कर्त्तुं), सभाज् (c. 10. सभाजयति -यितुं), वरिवस्य् (nom. वरिवस्यति -स्यितुं).

ADORED, *p. p.* पूजितः -ता -तं, नमस्कृतः -ता -तं, अर्चितः -ता -तं.

ADORER, *s.* पूजकः, अर्च्चकः, भक्तः, नमस्कर्त्ता *m.* (र्तृ).

To ADORN, *v. a.* भूष् (c. 1. भूषति, भूषितुं, c. 10. भूषयति -यितुं), विभूष्, अलङ्कृ (c. 8. -करोति -कुरुते -कर्त्तुं), परिष्कृ, समलङ्कृ; शुभ् in caus. (शोभयति -यितुं), उपशुभ्; मण्ड् (c. 10. मण्डयति -यितुं).

ADORNED, *p. p.* अलङ्कृतः -ता -तं, भूषितः -ता -तं, उपशोभितः -ता -तं, मण्डितः -ता -तं.

ADORNING, *s.* अलङ्कारः, अलङ्क्रिया, भूषणं.

ADRIFT, *adv.* इतस्ततः प्लवमानः -ना -नं.

ADROIT, *a.* निपुणः -णा -णं, दक्षः -क्षा -क्षं, चतुरः -रा -रं, लघुः -घुः -घु.

ADROITLY, *adv.* सदाक्ष्यं, चतुरं, नैपुण्येन.

ADROITNESS, *s.* नैपुण्यं, दाक्ष्यं, चातुर्य्यं, लाघवं.

ADRY, *a.* शुष्कः -ष्का -ष्कं, तृषितः -ता -तं, तृषार्त्तः -र्त्ता -र्त्तं.

ADULATION, *s.* अतिप्रशंसा, मिथ्याप्रशंसा, चाटुकारः, चाटूक्तिः *f.*, श्लाघा, अनुनयः, स्तुतिः *f.*

Adulatory, *s.* अतिप्रशंसकः -का -कं, अतिप्रशंसायुक्तः -क्ता -क्तं, श्लाघान्वितः -ता -तं, अनुनयी -यिनी -यि (न्).

Adult, *s.* प्रौढः -ढा -ढं, प्रवृद्धः -द्धा -द्धं, उन्नतः -ता -तं, मानुष्यप्राप्तः -प्ता -प्तं, दृहितः -ता -तं.

To adulterate, *v. a.* दुष् in caus. (दूषयति -यितुं), मिश्र् (c. 10. मिश्रयति -यितुं), अशुद्धीकृ, अपवित्रीकृ.

Adulterate or adulterated, *p. p.* दूषितः -ता -तं, अशुद्धीकृतः -ता -तं, मिश्रः -श्रा -श्रं, संसृष्टरूपः -पी -पं.

Adulteration, *s.* दूषणं, अशुद्धीकरणं, मिश्रणं.

Adulterer, *s.* पारदारिकः, परदारगामी *m.* (न्), व्यभिचारी *m.* (न्), पारजायिकः.

Adulteress, *s.* बन्धकी *f.*, व्यभिचारिणी, अभिसारिका *f.*

Adulterine, *s.* जारजः.

Adulterous, *s.* व्यभिचारी -रिणी -रि (न्).—(Corrupt) दुष्टः -ष्टा -ष्टं, अशुद्धः -द्धा -द्धं.

Adultery, *s.* पारदार्य्यं, परदारगमनं, परकलत्राभिगमनं, भार्य्यातिक्रमः, व्यभिचारः.—(To commit adultery) व्युच्चर् (c. 1. -चरति -चरितुं), परस्त्रिया सह रम् (c. 1. रमते रन्तुं).

To adumbrate, *v. a.* पाण्डुलेख्यं कृ, पाण्डुलिपिं कृ, प्रतिच्छायां कृ, चित्रारम्भं कृ.

Adumbration, *s.* प्रतिच्छाया, प्रतिबिम्बं.—(The act of adumbrating) प्रतिच्छायाकरणं, पाण्डुलेख्यकरणं.—(Sketch) पाण्डुलेख्यं, पाण्डुलिपिः *f.*, चित्रारम्भः.

Aduncity, *s.* वक्रता, जैह्म्यं, विजिह्मता, अनृजुता.

To advance, *v. n.* प्रया (c. 2. -याति -यातुं), प्रगम् (c. 1. -गच्छति -गन्तुं), प्रस्था (c. 1. -तिष्ठति -ते -स्थातुं), चल् (c. 1. चलति चलितुं), प्रचल्, प्रसृ (c. 1. -सरति -सर्त्तुं), प्रसृप् (c. 1. -सर्पति -सर्प्तुं or -सर्पितुं), क्रम् (c. 1. क्रमते, क्रमितुं).—(To improve) वृध् (c. 1. वर्धते वर्धितुं).

To advance, *v. a.* आनी (c. 1. -नयति -नेतुं), प्रणी, अग्रे नी, पुरस्कृ; 'to advance an army,' बलं पुरस्कर्त्तुं.—(To aggrandize) वृध् in caus. (वर्धयति -यितुं).—(To accelerate) त्वर् in caus. (त्वरयति -यितुं).—(To pay beforehand) प्राग् विहितकालात् मूल्यं दा.

Advance, *s.* प्रगमनं, प्रयाणं, अग्रगमनं, अग्रसरणं.—(Improvement) आगमः, वर्द्धनं, क्रमशो वृद्धिः *f.*, उत्तरोत्तरवर्द्धनं.

Advanced, *p.p.* (Brought forward) आनीतः -ता -तं, वर्धितः -ता -तं.—(In knowledge) कृतागमः -मा -मं.—(In life) गतायूः -यूः -युः (स् or ष्), प्रवयाः -याः -यः (स्).

Advancement, *s.* प्रगमनं.—(Promotion) वर्द्धनं, समुन्नतिः *f.*, उन्नतिः *f.*, उच्चपदप्राप्तिः *f.*—(In knowledge) विद्यागमः.

Advantage, *s.* (Gain, profit) फलं, लाभः, अर्थः.—(Superiority over) प्राधान्यं, आधिक्यं.—(Opportunity) अवसरः, अवकाशः; 'for one's own advantage,' आत्मविवृद्धये dat. c.; 'dressed to advantage,' सुवेशी -शिनी -शि (न्).

To advantage *v. a.* उपकृ (c. 8. -करोति -कर्त्तुं), उपचर् (c. 1. -चरति -चरितुं), उपग्रह् (c. 9. -गृह्णाति -ग्रहीतुं), फलं or लाभं दा (c. 3. ददाति दातुं).

Advantageous, *a.* फली -लिनी -लि (न्), फलदः -दा -दं, सफलः -ला -लं, अर्थशीलः -ला -लं, अर्थयुक्तः -क्ता -क्तं, अर्थकरः -रा or -री -रं, लभनीयः -या -यं.

Advantageously, *adv.* (Profitably) लाभेन, सफलं, सलाभं, सार्थं.—(Conveniently) सावकाशं.

Advantageousness, *s.* सफलत्वं, लभ्यता, फलित्वं.

Advent, *s.* आगमनं.—(Of Christ) खृष्टागमनं.

Adventitious, *a.* आगन्तुकः -का or -की -कं, आहार्य्यः -र्य्या -र्य्यं; 'adventitious beauty,' आहार्य्यशोभा.

Adventure, *s.* चरित्रं, वृत्तान्तः, चेष्टितं, चरितं, घटनं, दैवघटनं.

To Adventure, *v. n.* (To try the chance) सन्दिग्धकर्म्म दैवायत्तं or दैवाधीनं कृ.—(To attempt with daring) साहसेन व्यवसो (c. 4. -स्यति -सातुं).

Adventurer, *s.* सन्दिग्धकर्म्मरतः, सन्दिग्धकार्य्यप्रवृत्तः, कठिनकर्म्मव्यवसायी *m.* (न्).

Adventurous, *a.* (Inclined to adventure) साहसिकः -की -कं, निर्भयः -या -यं, प्रगल्भः -ल्भा -ल्भं.—(Dangerous) भययुक्तः -क्ता -क्तं, भयावहः -हा -हं, सन्दिग्धः -ग्धा -ग्धं, अदृष्टः -ष्टा -ष्टं.

Adventurously, *adv.* साहसेन, धृष्टं, प्रगल्भं, निर्भयं.

Adverb, *s.* क्रियाविशेषणं, अव्ययशब्दः.

Adverbial, *a.* क्रियाविशेषकः -का -कं, अव्ययः -या -यं, क्रियाविशेषणसम्बन्धी -न्धिनी -न्धि (न्).

Adverbially, *adv.* क्रियाविशेषणवत्, अव्ययभावे.

Adversary, *s.* वैरी *m.* (न्), शत्रुः *m.*, अरिः *m.*, विपक्षः, सपत्नः.

Adverse, *a.* प्रतिकूलः -ला -लं, विरुद्धः -द्धा -द्धं, वैरी -रिणी -रि (न्), प्रतिघः -घा -घं, प्रतिघाती -तिनी -ति (न्), विपक्षः -क्षा -क्षं.

Adversity, *s.* विपत् *f.* (-द्), आपत् *f.* (-द्), विपत्तिः *f.*, विपत्कालः अपचयः.

To advert, *v. n.* (To attend to, regard) मनः समाधा (c. 3. -धत्ते -धातुं), मनो युज् (c. 7. युनक्ति योक्तुं. c. 10. योजयति -यितुं), आलक्ष् (c. 10. -लक्षयति -यितुं), समीक्ष् (c. 1. -ईक्षते -ईक्षितुं), अवेक्ष्; अनुदृश् (c. 1. -पश्यति -द्रष्टुं), अवधानं or मनोयोगं कृ.

Advertence, *s.* अवधानं, मनोयोगः, अवेक्षा.

To advertise, *v. a.* (To inform) ज्ञा in caus. (ज्ञापयति -यितुं), विज्ञा; निविद् in caus. (-वेदयति -यितुं), समाविद्; बुध् in caus. (बोधयति -यितुं); सूच् (c. 10. सूचयति -यितुं).—(Give notice, publish) प्रकाश् in caus. (-काशयति -यितुं), विकाश्; विबुध् in caus. (-बोधयति -यितुं); संवादपत्रेण प्रकाश्.

Advertisement, *s.* (Instruction) सूचनं, बोधनं, प्रबोधनं, उपदेशः.—(Intelligence) संवादः, समाचारः.—(By public paper) संवादपत्रं.

Advertiser, *s.* (He that gives intelligence) संवादकः, ज्ञापकः, प्रकाशकः.—(The paper in which advertisements are published) समाचारपत्रं.

Advice, *s.* उपदेशः or -शनं, मन्त्रः, आदेशः, मन्त्रणं -णा, आमर्शः, प्रत्यवमर्शः, बोधनं.—(Intelligence) संवादः, समाचारः.

Advice-boat, *s.* संवादवाहिनी नौः or नौका.

Advisable, *a.* (Prudent) उचितः -ता -तं, योग्यः -ग्या -ग्यं, युक्तः -क्ता -क्तं.—(Open to advice) उपदेश्यः -श्या -श्यं, उपदेशग्राही -हिणी -हि (न्).

To advise, *v. a.* (To give counsel) उपदिश् (c. 6. -दिशति -देष्टुं), शिक्ष् in caus. (शिक्षयति -यितुं), अनुशास् (c. 2. -शास्ति -शासितुं).—(To inform) ज्ञा in caus. (ज्ञापयति -यितुं), निविद् in caus. (-वेदयति -यितुं), बुध् in caus. (बोधयति -यितुं).

To advise, *v. n.* (To consult) मन्त्र् (c. 10. मन्त्रयते -यितुं).—(To deliberate) विचर् in caus. (-चारयति -यितुं).

Advised, उपदिष्टः -ष्टा -ष्टं.—(Informed) ज्ञापितः -ता -तं, निवेदितः -ता -तं.

Advisedly, *adv.* (Prudently) मन्त्रतस् *ind.*, अवधानतस् *ind.*, अवधानपुरःसरं, सावधानं.—(Purposely) ज्ञानतस् *ind.*, अभिप्रायेण.

Adviser, *s.* उपदेशकः, उपदेष्टा *m.* (ष्टृ), उपदेशी *m.* (न्), आदेशी *m.* (न्) मन्त्री *m.* (-न्).—(Counsellor) अमात्यः, सचिवः, मन्ता *m.* (न्तृ).

Advocate, *s.* (A pleader in law) उत्तरवादी *m.* (न्), परार्थं प्रतिवादी *m.* (न्), प्रतिनिधिः *m.*—(Any defender) प्रतिपालकः, रक्षकः, आश्रयः.

To advocate, *v. a.* परार्थं वद् (c. 1. वदति वदितुं); प्रतिनिधिः अस्; रक्ष् (c. 1. रक्षति रक्षितुं), परिरक्ष्, अभिरक्ष्; प्रतिपाल् (c. 10. -पालयति -यितुं).

Advowee, *s.* (He that has the right of advowson) धर्म्माध्यापने यो ऽन्यं नियोक्तुम् अर्हति.

Advowson, *s.* (A right to present to a benefice) धर्म्माध्यापने नियोजनाधिकारः.

Adze, *s.* तक्षणी, कुठारिका, वासिः *m.* -सी *f.*

Aerial, *a.* (Belonging to the air) आकाशीयः -या -यं, वायवः -वी -वं, वैहायसः -सी -सं.—(Produced in the air) आकाशजः -जा -जं, वायुजः -जा -जं.—(Inhabiting the air) वायुगः -गा -गं, आकाशस्थः -स्था -स्थं, खेचरः -रा -रं, नभःस्थः -स्था -स्थं.—(Lofty) उच्चः -च्चा -च्चं.

Aerie, *s.* (A hawk's nest) श्येननीडः, शकुनिनीडः.

Aerology, *s.* आकाशविद्या, वायुविद्या.

Aeronaut, *s.* आकाशगामी *m.* (न्), आकाशचरः.

Æther, *s.* आकाशः, वायुः *m.*, नभः *n.* (स्), विहायः *n.* (स्).

Afar, *adv.* (At a great distance) दूरं, दूरे, अतिदूरं, दूरतस् *ind.*—(To a great distance) दूरपर्य्यन्तं.—(From afar) दूरतस्, दूरात्.—(Afar off) दूरस्थः -स्था -स्थं.

Affability, *a.* मृदुशीलत्वं, सुशीलत्वं, अभिगम्यता, चाटूक्तिः *f*, कोमलत्वं, मृदुता.

Affable, *a.* मृदुशीलः -ला -लं, कोमलस्वभावः -वा -वं, सुशीलः -ला -लं, अभिगम्यः -म्या -म्यं, मृदुः -द्वी -दु, चाटुवादी -दिनी -दि (न्), प्रियवादी -दिनी -दि (न्).

Affably, *adv.* मृदु, मृदुवचनेन, चाटूक्त्या, मृदुतया, मृदुजनवत्.

Affair, *s.* कार्य्यं, कर्म्म *n.* (न्), व्यापारः, विषयः, अर्थः.

To affect, *v. a.* (Aim at) सेव् (c. 1. सेवते सेवितुं), उपसेव् निषेव्; समाचर् (c. 1. -चरति -चरितुं); भज् (c. 1. भजते, भक्तुं).—(Operate upon) विकृ (c. 8. -करोति -कर्त्तुं); उपहन् (c. 2. -हन्ति -हन्तुं); चल् in caus. (चालयति -यितुं).—(To move with grief, &c.) शोकोपहतं -तां -तं कृ; 'to affect with joy,' हर्षाकुलं -लां -लं कृ.—(To pretend) छद्म or छलं कृ; मिथ्या वद्; 'to affect to befriend a person,' मिथ्योपचारं कृ.—(To think one's self) मन् (c. 10. मानयते); 'one who affects learning,' पण्डितम्मन्यः.

Affectation, *s.* अहङ्कारः, वैलक्ष्यं, मानित्वं; महापण्डितो ऽहम् इति अतिसुन्दरी अहम् इति बुद्धिर् व्यवहारो वा; 'affectation of learning,' पण्डितम्मन्यत्वं.—(A branch of feminine action) अवहित्थं, -त्था, विलासः, हावः.—(False pretence) उपधा, छलं, छद्म *n.* (न्).

Affected, *part. a.* (Pretended) कृत्रिमः -मा -मं; मिथ्या prefixed, as, मिथ्योपचारः, 'affected kindness.'—(Full of affectation) सवैलक्ष्यः -क्ष्या -क्ष्यं, अहङ्कारी -रिणी -रि (न्), मानी -निनी -नि (न्), विलासवान् -वती -वत्.—(Affected by, disturbed by) उपहतः -ता -तं, आकुलः -ला -लं, ग्रस्तः -स्ता -स्तं, रञ्जितः -ता -तं.

Affectedly, *adv.* वैलक्ष्येण, साहङ्कारं, अहङ्कारेण.

Affecting, *a.* हृदयङ्गमः -मा -मं, मर्म्मभेदी -दिनी -दि (न्).

Affection, *s.* स्नेहः *m.*, प्रियता *f.*, अनुरक्तिः *f.*, अनुरागः, प्रणयः, प्रेमा *m.* or -म *n.* (-मन्), हार्द्दं, प्रश्रयः.—(Passion of any kind) रागः, भावः, रसः.—(Of the mind) मनसो भावः.—(Of the body) शरीरस्य भावः.—(Parental) वात्सल्यं; 'I have great affection for him' तेन सह मम महान् स्नेहः or तस्मिन् अनुरागवान् अस्मि.

Affectionate, *a.* स्नेही -हिनी -हि (न्), स्निग्धः -ग्धा -ग्धं, स्नेहशीलः -ला -लं, सुहृत्तमः -मा -मं, अनुरागी -गिणी -गि (न्), प्रीतिमान् -मती -मत् (त्), वत्सलः -ला -लं, हितः -ता -तं, प्रणयी -यिणी -यि (न्), सप्रणयः -या -यं, जातहार्द्दः -र्द्दा -र्द्दं.

Affectionately, *adv.* स्नेहेन, प्रीत्या, प्रीतिपूर्व्वं, स्नेहपुरःसरं, सानुरागं.

Affiance, *s.* (A marriage-contract) वाग्दानं, विवाहसम्बन्धः.—(Trust, confidence) विश्वासः, प्रत्ययः, श्रद्धा, आस्था.

To affiance, *v. a.* (To betroth) वाग्दानं कृ, विवाहनियमं कृ.—(To confide) विश्वस् (c 2. -श्वसिति -श्वसितुं).

Affianced, *p. p.* वाग्दत्तः -त्ता -त्तं.

Affidavit, *s.* शपथपत्रं.—(To make affidavit) तथेति or नेति शपथेन ब्रू (c. 2. ब्रवीति वक्तुं), शपथं शप् (c. 1. शपति शप्तुं).

Affiliation, *s.* कृत्रिमपुत्रकरणं, पोष्यपुत्रग्रहणं.

Affinity, *s.* सम्बन्धः, सम्पर्कः, योगः, ज्ञातित्वं, बन्धुता.

To affirm, *v. n.* (Opposed to deny) तथेति ब्रू (c. 2. ब्रवीति, ब्रूते वक्तुं).—(Maintain, declare positively) दार्ढ्येन वद् (c. 1. वदति वदितुं).—(Ratify) स्थिरीकृ, दृढीकृ, निश्चितं -तां -तं कृ, संस्तम्भ् (c. 5. -स्तभ्नोति, c. 9. -स्तभ्नाति -स्तम्भितुं), प्रमाणीकृ.

Affirmation, *s.* (Declaring positively) दृढोक्तिः *f.*, वचनं, दृढवचनं.—(Argumentative statement) पक्षः.—(Confirmation) प्रमाणीकरणं, निश्चयः, दृढीकरणं, स्थिरीकरणं.—(False) विप्रलापः.

Affirmative, *a.* (That which affirms) वादी -दिनी -दि (न्), निश्चायकः -का -कं.—(Favourable to the argument) पक्षानुकूलः -ला -लं.

To affix, *v. a.* अनुबन्ध् (c. 9. -बध्नाति -बन्द्धुं), निबन्ध्, सम्बन्ध्; संयुज् (c. 7. -युनक्ति, c. 10. -योजयति -यितुं), आयुज्, उपयुज्.

Affix, *s.* (Grammatical) अनुबन्धः, प्रयोगः, आमोक्तिः *f.*

To afflict, *v. a.* क्लिश् (c. 9. क्लिश्नाति क्लेशितुं or क्लेष्टुं), पीड् (c. 10. पीडयति -यितुं), अभिपीड्, उपपीड्, परिपीड्; व्यथ् in caus. (व्यथयति -यितुं), आयस् in caus. (-यासयति -यितुं).—(To be afflicted with disease) रोगेण पीड् in pass. (पीड्यते) or बाध् in pass.

Afflicted, *p. p.* व्यसनार्त्तः -र्त्ता -र्त्तं, दुर्गतः -ता -तं, आपद्ग्रस्तः -स्ता -स्तं, आपन्नः -न्ना -न्नं.—(Afflicted with) पीडितः -ता -तं, आतुरः -रा -रं, आर्त्तः in composition; 'afflicted with disease,' रोगपीडितः -ता -तं.

Affliction, *s.* क्लेशः, शोकः, दुःखं, कष्टं, व्यथा, पीडा, विडम्बना.

Afflictive, *a.* क्लेशकः -का -कं, क्लेशी -शिनी -शि (न्), दुःखकरः -री -रं, व्यथाकरः -री -रं.

Affluence or -ency, *s.* धनबाहुल्यं, धनसम्पत्तिः, धनित्वं, समृद्धिः *f.*, समृद्धता.—(The act of flowing to any one place) एकस्थानं प्रति प्रवाहः.

Affluent, *a.* महाधनः -ना -नं, बहुधनः -ना -नं, धनी -निनी -नि (न्), धनवान् -वती -वत् (त्), समृद्धः -द्धा -द्धं, वसुमान् -मती -मत् (त्), धनाढ्यः -ढ्या -ढ्यं.—(Flowing to any one place) एकस्थानं प्रति प्रवाहकः -का -कं.

Afflux or affluxion, *s.* एकस्थानं प्रति स्रोतसां प्रवाहः.

To afford *v. a.* (Give) दा (c. 3. ददाति, c. 1. यच्छति दातुं), प्रादा, अभिदा, प्रदा; उपपद् in caus. (-पादयति -यितुं).—(To be able to bear expenses) व्ययं कर्त्तुं समर्थः -र्था -र्थं अस् or शक् (c. 8. शक्नोति शक्तुं), or व्ययाय उपकॢप् (c. 1. -कल्पते -कल्पितुं or -कल्प्तुं).

To AFFRANCHISE, *v. a.* मुच् (c. 10. मोचयति -यितुं, c. 6. मुञ्चति मोक्तुं), विमुच्; मोक्ष् (c. 10. मोक्षयति -यितुं), विमुक्ष्.

AFFRAY, *s.* सङ्ग्रामः, समरः, संयुगः, युद्धं, कलहः, डिम्बः, डमरः, डामरः.

To AFFRIGHT, *v. a.* त्रस् in caus. (त्रासयति -यितुं), वित्रस्; भी in caus. (भाययति or भीषयति -ते -यितुं), उद्विज् in caus. (-वेजयति -यितुं).

AFFRIGHT, *s.* त्रासः, सन्त्रासः, साध्वसं, भयं.

AFFRIGHTEDLY, *adv.* सत्रासं, सभयं, सन्त्रासेन.

AFFRONT, *s.* अपमानं, विप्रियं, क्षेपः, अवज्ञानं, धर्षणं, तिरस्कारः.

To AFFRONT, *v. a.* (Offer open insult) साक्षात्, or सम्मुखं, or प्रतिमुखं, or मुखामुखि, or प्रत्यक्षं अवमन् (c. 4. -मन्यते -मन्तुं), अवज्ञा (c. 9. -जानाति -ज्ञातुं), तिरस्कृ (c. 8. -करोति -कर्त्तुं), आक्षर् in caus. (-क्षारयति -यितुं), अधिक्षिप् (c. 6. -क्षिपति -क्षेप्तुं), अवक्षिप्, परिक्षिप्.

AFFRONTED, *p. p.* अपमानितः -ता -तं, अवज्ञातः -ता -तं, तिरस्कृतः -ता -तं, अधिक्षिप्तः -प्ता -प्तं.

AFFRONTER, *s.* साक्षात् or प्रतिमुखम् अपमानकः, अवज्ञानकर्त्ता *m.* (र्त्तृ).

AFFRONTIVE, *a.* अपमानकः -का -कं, अपमानोपेतः -ता -तं, अवज्ञानयुक्तः -क्ता -क्तं.

AFFUSION, *s.* आसेकः, आसेचनं, अभिषेकः.

To AFFY, *v. a.* (Betroth) वाग्दानं कृ, प्रतिज्ञापत्रेण विवाहसम्बन्धं कृ, नियमपत्रेण विवाहप्रतिज्ञां कृ.

AFLOAT, *adv.* (Floating) प्लवमानः -ना -नं, प्लवः -वा -वं.

AFOOT, *adv.* (On foot) पादेन, पदेन.—(Going on foot) पादगः -गा -गं.—(In action, or use) प्रचलः -ला -लं, प्रचलितः -ता -तं, प्रचरितः -ता -तं.—(Set on foot) आरब्धः -ब्धा -ब्धं, उद्यतः -ता -तं.

AFORE, *prep.* (In front) प्रतिमुखं, अभिमुखं, सम्मुखं, अग्रे, पुरस्, पुरतस्, साक्षात्.—(In former time) पूर्व्वकाले, गतकाले, पूर्व्वं, पूर्व्वसमये, पुरा.

AFORESAID, *p. p.* पूर्व्वोक्तः -क्ता -क्तं, पूर्व्वोदितः -ता -तं, प्रागुक्तः -क्ता -क्तं.

AFORETIME, *adv.* पूर्व्वकाले, गतकाले, पुरा, पूर्व्वं.

AFRAID, *a.* भीतः -ता -तं, भयान्वितः -ता -तं, शङ्कान्वितः -ता -तं; 'to be afraid of,' भी (c. 3. बिभेति भेतुं), with abl. or gen.; as, 'he is afraid of the dog,' कुक्कुरात् or कुक्कुरस्य बिभेति. So also त्रस् (c. 4. त्रस्यति त्रसितुं), उद्विज् (c. 6. -विजते -विजितुं).

AFRESH, *adv.* पुनर्, पुनरपि, नूतनं, अभिनवं, प्रतिनवं.

AFT, *s.* (The part of a ship towards the stern) नावः पश्चिमभागः.

AFT, *adv.* (Towards the stern of a ship) नावः पश्चिमभागं प्रति, नावः पश्चाद्भागं प्रति.

AFTER, *prep.* अनु or पश्चात् prefixed; as, 'to go after,' अनुगन्तुं; 'to run after,' पश्चाद् धावितुं.—(Of time) पश्चात्, परं, अनन्तरं, ऊर्द्ध्वं, अर्व्वाक् with abl.—(According to) अनु, अनुरूपं, अनुसारतस्, अनुरूपेण, अनुसारेण; 'after that,' तदनन्तरे, or तदनन्तरं, or तस्मात् परं, or अत ऊर्द्ध्वं; 'after one another,' अनुपूर्व्वशस्; 'a century after,' वर्षशते गते; 'after eating,' भोजनानन्तरं or भोजनात् परं; 'after the rising of the sun,' सूर्य्योदयाद् ऊर्द्ध्वं; 'after a few days,' दिनेषु गच्छत्सु. Sometimes 'after' is expressed by the indec. part.; as, 'after ascending the tree the nests were destroyed,' वृक्षम् आरुह्य नीडा भग्नाः, or even by पूर्व्वकं; as, 'after laying down a stake,' पणस्थापनपूर्व्वकं; or by repeating the word in such phrases as, 'he waters tree after tree,' वृक्षं वृक्षं सिञ्चति.

AFTER, *adv.* (In after time) परं, परकाले, आगामिकाले, उत्तरकाले.—(Following after another) पश्चात्.—(Subsequently) परस्तात्, उत्तरत्र, उत्तरतस् *ind.*

AFTER-AGES, *s.* उत्तरकालः, परकालः, आगामिकालः, भाविकालः.—(Descendants) पुत्रपौत्राः *m. pl.*

AFTER ALL, अन्ततस् *ind.*, अन्ते, परं, शेषे, अवशेषे.

AFTER-BIRTH, *s.* गर्भपरिस्रवः.

AFTER-COMER, *s.* उत्तरागामी *m.* (न्), परम् उपतिष्ठति यः, उत्तरकाले जीवति यः.

AFTER-CROP, *s.* शस्यस्य द्वितीयसङ्ग्रहः or द्वितीयोत्पत्तिः *f.*, फलस्य द्वितीयसङ्ग्रहः.

AFTER-DINNER, *s.* भोजनानन्तरं, भोजनात् परं, भोजनोत्तरं.

AFTER-ENDEAVOUR, *s.* उत्तरोद्योगः, द्वितीययत्नः.

AFTER-GAME, *s.* उत्तरोपायः.

AFTER-GRASS or AFTER-MATH, *s.* द्वितीयतृणं, द्वितीयतृणोत्पत्तिः *f.*

AFTER-INQUIRY, *s.* उत्तरानुसन्धानं, उत्तरजिज्ञासा.

AFTER-LIFE, *s.* जीवनावशेषः.

AFTERNOON, *s.* अपराह्णः, पराह्णः, वैकालः, विकालः.—(Relating to the afternoon) आपराह्णिकः -की -कं, वैकालिकः -की -कं.

AFTER-PAINS, *s.* अनुतापः, उत्तरव्यथा.—(At childbirth) प्रसवानन्तरं वेदना.

AFTER-STATE, *s.* परावस्था, उत्तरावस्था, भाव्यवस्था.

AFTER-TASTE, *s.* उत्तरस्वादः, अनुस्वादः.

AFTER-THOUGHT, *s.* अनुबोधः, उत्तरचिन्ता, कार्य्यानन्तरं विचारणं.

AFTER-TIMES, *s.* उत्तरकालः, परकालः, आगामिकालः.—(Descendants) पुत्रपौत्राः *m. pl.*

AFTERWARDS, *s.* पश्चात् *ind.*, तत्पश्चात्, तदनन्तरं, अनन्तरं, ततः परं, परं *ind.*, अपरं, परस्तात्, उत्तरतस्, ततस्.

AGAIN, *adv.* पुनर्, पुनरपि, भूयस् *ind.*—(Moreover) अन्यच्च, किञ्च, इतरम् *indec.*—(On the other hand) अन्यपक्षे, पुनर्.—(Repeatedly) मुहुस्, पुनःपुनर्, असकृत्, भूयो भूयस्, वारंवारं.—(Further, in argument) अङ्ग.—(As much again) द्विगुणः -णा -णं.—(Back again, as *re* in English or Latin) प्रति.—(In return for) प्रति.

AGAINST, *prep.* प्रति, अभि.—(Opposed to) विरुद्धः -द्धा -द्धं, प्रतिकूलः -ला -लं, विपक्षः -क्षा -क्षं.—(Over against) अभिमुखं, प्रतिमुखं, सम्मुखं; 'against the wind,' प्रतिवातं, वाताभिमुखं; 'against the stream,' प्रतिस्रोतस् *ind.* 'Against' may be expressed by अर्थे or अर्थं, in such phrases as 'one should store up money against misfortune,' आपदर्थे धनं रक्षेत्.

AGAPE, *adv.* जृम्भमाणः -णा -णं, विस्मयोत्फुल्लनयनः -ना -नं, फुल्ललोचनः -ना -नं.

AGARIC, *s.* वृक्षरुहः छत्राकविशेषः, तरूरोही, औषधीयछत्राकविशेषः.

AGASTYA, *s.* (A celebrated Saint, son of Mitra and Varuna, and regent of the star Canopus) अगस्त्यः, मैत्रावारुणिः.

AGATE, *s.* रत्नविशेषः, नानावर्णः प्रस्तरविशेषः, नानाच्छायान्वितः प्रस्तरविशेषः.

AGE, *s.* (Period) युगं, कालः, समयः.—(Life) आयुः *n.* (स्), जीवितकालः, वयः *n.* (स्).—(Age of the world) कल्पः.—(Old age) वृद्धत्वं, वार्द्धक्यं, वृद्धभावः; 'a youth who has come of age,' व्यवहारप्राप्तः, व्यवहारज्ञः; 'a son twenty years of age,' विंशतिवर्षीयः पुत्रः; 'of the same age,' समानवयस्कः -स्का -स्कं.

AGED, *a.* वृद्धः -द्धा -द्धं, जीर्णः -र्णा -र्णं, प्राचीनः -ना -नं, वयोगतः -ता -तं, आयुषः -षी -षं.

Agency, *s.* (State of an agent) कर्त्तृत्वं, कर्त्तृकत्वं.—(Operation) कारयत्वं, हेतुता, कारणं; 'human agency,' पौरुषेयत्वं.—(Office of a deputy) नियोगिपदं, नियोगित्वं.

Agent, *s.* (Doer) कर्त्ता *m.* (र्त्तृ), कर्त्तृकः, कारः, कारकः, करः in comp.—(A deputy) नियोगी *m.* (न्), प्रतिपुरुषः, कार्य्याधीशः, प्रतिनिधिः *m.*—(That which has the power of operating) हेतुकः, हेतुः *m.*, कारणं, साधनं.

To agglomerate, *v. a.* सञ्चि (c. 5. -चिनोति -चेतुं), समाचि, उपचि; समाक्षिप् (c. 6. -क्षिपति -क्षेप्तुं); राशीकृ; पुञ्जं कृ, एकत्र कृ.

Agglomerated, *p. p.* सञ्चितः -ता -तं, उपचितः -ता -तं, राशीकृतः -ता -तं.

To agglutinate, *v. n.* संश्लिष् in caus. (-श्लेषयति -यितुं), संयुज् (c. 7. -युनक्ति -योक्तुं, c. 10. -योजयति -यितुं), संहन् (c. 2. -हन्ति -हन्तुं), संलग्नं -ग्नां -ग्नं कृ.

To aggrandise, *v. a.* वृध् in caus. (वर्धयति -यितुं), संवृध्, ऋध् in caus. (ऋधयति -यितुं), आप्यै (caus. -प्याययति -यितुं), स्फाय् in caus. स्फावयति -यितुं), प्रचुरीकृ, स्फीतीकृ, तन् (c. 8. तनोति तनितुं).

Aggrandisement, *s.* वृद्धिः *f.*, वर्द्धनं, विवृद्धिः *f.*, उन्नतिः *f.*, समुन्नतिः *f.* उपचयः, स्फातिः *f.*, अभ्युदयः; 'for one's own aggrandisement,' आत्मविवृद्धये *dat. c.* or आत्मोदयाय *dat. c.*

To aggravate, *v. a.* (To increase) वृध् in caus. (वर्धयति -यितुं), अधिकं -कां -कं कृ, अतिरिक्तं -क्तां -क्तं कृ, गरय् (nom. गरयति).—(To irritate, provoke) प्रकुप् in caus. (-कोपयति -यितुं), प्रपीड् (c. 10. -पीडयति -यितुं).

Aggravated, *p. p.* (Increased) वर्धितः -ता -तं. — (Provoked) प्रकोपितः -ता -तं.

Aggravation, *s.* (Act of irritating) प्रकोपणं, पीडनं, पीडाकरणं. (Act of increasing) संवर्द्धनं, वर्द्धनं, उद्दीपनं.—(Aggravating circumstance) अनुपशयः, आधिक्यं.

Aggregate, *s.* समूहः, सञ्चयः, सन्निपातः, समवायः, सङ्ग्रहः, राशिः *m.*, पुञ्जः.

To aggregate, *v. a.* समाक्षिप् (c. 6. -क्षिपति -क्षेप्तुं), सञ्चि (c. 5. -चिनोति -चेतुं), समाचि, उपचि; समूहं कृ, राशीकृ, एकत्र कृ.

Aggregated, *p. p.* सञ्चितः -ता -तं, उपचितः -ता -तं, राशीकृतः -ता -तं, समवायी -यिनी -यि (न्).

Aggregation, *s.* (The act of aggregating) समाहारः -हरणं, राशीकरणं, सञ्चयनं, सङ्ग्रहणं. — (A sum, collection) समूहः, सन्निपातः, सङ्ग्रहः.

To aggress, *v. a.* आक्रम् (c. 1. -क्रामति, c. 4. -क्राम्यति -क्रमितुं), अतिक्रम्; लङ्घ् (c. 10. लङ्घयति -यितुं). — (To be the first to injure) हिंसारम्भं or लङ्घनारम्भं कृ.

Aggression, *s.* आक्रमः -मणं, अतिक्रमः, लङ्घनं.—(The first act of injury) हिंसारम्भः, अपकारारम्भः, प्रथमापकारः, आक्रमारम्भः.

Aggressor, *s.* आक्रामकः, अतिक्रामकः, द्रोही *m.* (न्), प्रथमापकारकरः, प्रथमं हिंसां करोति यः.

Aggrievance, *s.* (Wrong endured) हिंसा, अपकारः, द्रोहः, क्लेशः, दुःखं, व्यथा.

To aggrieve, *v. a.* दुःख् (c. 10. दुःखयति -यितुं), शुच् in caus. (शोचयति -यितुं), क्लिश् (c. 9. क्लिश्नाति क्लेष्टुं), व्यथ् in caus. (व्यथयति -यितुं), अर्द् in caus. (अर्दयति -यितुं), समर्द्, हिंस् (c. 1. हिंसति, c. 7. हिनस्ति, हिंसितुं).

Aghast, *a. a.* विस्मयाकुलः -ला -लं, भयव्याकुलः -ला -लं, भयमोहितः -ता -तं, साध्वसोपहतः -ता -तं.

Agile, *a.* लघुः -घुः -घु, त्वरितः -ता -तं, चञ्चलः -ला -लं, द्रुतस्वभावः -वा -वं, लघुशरीरः -रा -रं.

Agility, *s.* लघुता, द्रुतत्वं, चञ्चलत्वं, लघुशरीरता.

Agillochum, *s.* (Aloe-wood) अगुरुः *m.*, -रु *n.*, अगुरुकाष्ठं.

Agistment, *s.* निरूपितमूल्येन सर्व्वसामान्यक्षेत्रे पश्वादिप्रतिपालनं.—(Embankment) सेतुः *m.*

Agitable, *a.* क्षोभणीयः -या -यं, मन्थनीयः -या -यं, चालनीयः -या -यं.

To agitate, *v. a.* क्षुभ् in caus. (क्षोभयति -यितुं), विक्षुभ्; धू (c. 5. धूनोति, c. 9. धुनाति धवितुं or धोतुं), आधू; मन्थ् (c. 1. मन्थति, c. 9. मथ्नाति मन्थितुं), प्रमन्थ्; चल् in caus. (चलयति or चालयति -यितुं); गाह् (c. 1. गाहते गाहितुं or गाढुं); लुड् (c. 1. लोडति लोडितुं or caus. लोडयति), आलुड्, समालुड्, परिलुड्, विलुड्, संलुड्.—(To be agitated) क्षुभ् (c. 4. क्षुभ्यति क्षोभितुं); विह्वल् (c. 1. -ह्वलति -ह्वलितुं).

Agitated, *p. p.* क्षुब्धः -ब्धा -ब्धं, धूतः -ता -तं, आकुलितः -ता -तं, प्रमथितः -ता -तं, उद्भ्रान्तः -न्ता -न्तं, सम्भ्रान्तः -न्ता -न्तं, विह्वलः -ला -लं, विधुरः -रा -रं, लुलितः -ता -तं, कातरः -रा -रं, पारिप्लवः -वा -वं, विप्लवः -वा -वं.

Agitation, *s.* क्षोभः, मन्थनं, उन्मन्थनं, आलोडनं, विधुवनं, दवथुः.—(Of mind, &c.) व्याकुलत्वं, उत्कम्पः.—(Discussion) वादानुवादः, विचारणं.

Agitator, *s.* (He who agitates) क्षोभकः, उन्मन्थकः, मथनकारी *m.* (न्).—(Manager of affairs) कार्य्याधीशः, कार्य्याधिष्ठाता *m.* (तृ), नायकः.

Agnail, *s.* नखरोगः, चिप्पं, नखम्पचः.

Agnate, *a.* (Allied to) सम्बन्धी -न्धिनी -न्धि (न्), सम्पर्कीयः -या -यं.

Agnation, *s.* (Relationship) ज्ञातित्वं, बन्धुत्वं, सम्बन्धः, सम्पर्कः.

Ago, agone, *adv.* पुरा, पूर्व्वं, पूर्व्वकाले, गतकाले, पुरस्तात्.

Agog, *adv.* कुतूहली -लिनी -लि (न्), कौतुकाकुलः -ला -लं, अन्यथावृत्तिः -त्तिः -त्ति.

Agoing, *part.* चलः -ला -लं, प्रचलः -ला -लं, प्रचलितः -ता -तं, प्रचरितः -ता -तं.

To agonise, *v. n.* व्यथ् (c. 1. व्यथते व्यथितुं), परितप् in pass. (-तप्यते), सन्तप्.

Agony, *s.* तीव्रवेदना, अतिव्यथा, व्यथा, अन्तस्तापः, विबाधा, दुःखदुःखं, यन्त्रं.

Agrarian, *a.* क्षेत्रविषयकः -का -कं, क्षैत्रिकः -की -कं, भूमिविषयकः -का -कं.

To agree, *v. n.* (Be in concord) सम्मन् (c. 4. -मन्यते -मन्तुं), सम्मतः -ता -तं भू.—(Assent to) स्वीकृ, अङ्गीकृ, अनुमन् (c. 4. -मन्यते -मन्तुं), अभिमन्; अनुज्ञा (c. 9. -जानाति -ज्ञातुं), अनुवद् (c. 1. -वदति -वदितुं), ग्रह् (c. 9. गृह्णाति ग्रहीतुं), उपगम् (c. 1. -गच्छति -गन्तुं).—(Settle by stipulation) सन्धा (c. 3. -धत्ते -धातुं), संविदा निष्पन्नं -न्नां -न्नं कृ.—(Be of the same mind) एकचित्तीभू, एकमतः -ता -तं भू.—(Be consistent or suitable) युज् in pass. (युज्यते).

To agree, *v. a.* सन्धा (c. 3. -दधाति -धत्ते -धातुं), सम्मतं -तां -तं or संविदितं -तां -तं कृ.

Agreeable, *a.* (Pleasant) रम्यः -म्या -म्यं, काम्यः -म्या -म्यं, सुभगः -गा -गं, अभिमतः -ता -तं, मनोज्ञः -ज्ञा -ज्ञं, सन्तोषकः -का -कं, तुष्टिकरः -री -रं. — (Suitable, comfortable) अनुरूपः -पा -पं, उपयुक्तः -क्ता -क्तं, योग्यः -ग्या -ग्यं, सदृशः -शी -शं, तुल्यः -ल्या -ल्यं.—(To be agreeable, please) रुच् (c. 1. रोचते, रोचितुं).

Agreeableness, *s.* (Consistency with) योग्यता, उपयुक्तता, अनुरूपता, सादृश्यं.—(The quality of pleasing) रम्यत्वं, काम्यत्वं, अभिमतता.—(Resemblance) तुल्यता, सदृशता.

Agreeably, *adv.* सुखं, अभिमतं, सुभगं, यथाभिमतं, यथासुखं.—(According to) अनुरूपं, अनुसारतस् *ind.*, योगतस् *ind.*—(Agreeably to one's nature) स्वभावानुरूपं.

AGREED, *p. p.* संविदितः -ता -तं, सम्मतः -ता -तं, उपगतः -ता -तं, अभ्युपेतः -ता -तं, अभ्युपगतः -ता -तं, स्वीकृतः -ता -तं, अनुज्ञातः -ता -तं; 'he has agreed to a separation,' भेदम् उपगतः.

AGREEMENT, *s.* (Compact) संविद् *f.*, प्रतिज्ञानं, नियमः, संस्कारः, अङ्गीकारः, उपगमः, समयः, अभ्युपगमः, सङ्केतः, संवादः, व्यवस्था.—(Making an agreement) समयकारः.—(Breaking an agreement) समयभेदः. — (Concord) सम्मतिः *f.*, एकचित्तता, अनुवादः, ऐक्यं.—(Resemblance) सदृशता, अनुरूपता, सादृश्यं, तुल्यत्वं.

AGRICULTURE, *s.* कृषिः *f.*, कर्षणं, हलभृतिः *f.*, वैश्यक्रिया, वैश्यवृत्तिः *f.* (The science) कृषिविद्या.

AGRICULTURIST, *s.* कर्षकः, क्षेत्राजीवः, कृषकः, क्षेत्रिकः, क्षेत्री *m.* (न्), कृषिविद्याज्ञः.—(A man of the third class) वैश्यः, विट् (श्).

AGROUND, *adv.* उच्चैरस् *ind.*, तटस्थः -स्था -स्थं, सैकतस्थः -स्था -स्थं, पुलिनस्थः -स्था -स्थं.

AGUE, *s.* कम्पज्वरः.—(A tertian ague) तृतीयकः, तृतीयकज्वरः.—(A quartan) चातुर्थकः.

AGUE-FIT, *s.* कम्पज्वराक्रमः.

AGUISH, *a.* कम्पज्वरशीलः -ला -लं, कम्पज्वरस्वभावः -वा -वं.

AH, *interj.* आ, आस्, हन्त, हा, अहो, अहह.

AHEAD, *adv.* अग्रे, अग्रतस् *ind.*, पुरस् *ind.*, पुरतस् *ind.*—(Headlong) अधोमुखं.

AJAR, *adv.* अर्द्धविवृतः -ता -तं, अर्द्धोद्घाटितः -ता -तं.

AID, *s.* साहाय्यं, उपकारः, उपकृतं, साहित्यं, शरणं, उपग्रहः. — (An assistant) सहायः, उपकारकः, उत्तरसाधकः.

To AID, *v. a.* उपकृ (c. 8. -करोति -कर्त्तुं), उपचर् (c. 1. -चरति -चरितुं), उपग्रह् (c. 9. -गृह्णाति -ग्रहीतुं), साहाय्यं कृ, अभिरक्ष् (c. 1. -रक्षति -रक्षितुं).

AIDED, *p. p.* उपकृतः -ता -तं, कृतोपकारः -रा -रं.

AIDE-DE-CAMP, *s.* परिधिस्थः, सेनापतिसहायः, सेनापत्याज्ञावहः.

AIDER, *s.* सहायः, साहाय्यकर्त्ता *m.* (र्तृ), उपकारकः.

AIDLESS, *a.* साहाय्यरहितः -ता -तं, उपकारहीनः -ना -नं, असहायः -या -यं.

To AIL, *v. a.* (To give pain) पीड् (c. 10. पीडयति -यितुं).—(To be ailing) ईषद्रोगेण or क्षुद्ररोगेण, पीड् in pass. (पीड्यते).

AIL OF AILMENT, *s.* ईषद्रोगः, ईषद्व्याधिः *m.*, क्षुद्ररोगः, क्षुद्रव्याधिः *m.*

AILING, *a.* रोगी -गिणी -गि (न्), क्षुद्ररोगपीडितः -ता -तं, व्याधितः -ता -तं.

To AIM, *v. a.* and *n.* (As at a mark) अभिसन्धा (c. 3. -दधाति -धातुं), उद्दिश् (c. 6. -दिशति -देष्टुं) with acc.; as, 'aiming at him,' तमुद्दिश्य; लक्षीकृ.—(Endeavour after) आप् in des. (ईप्सति ईप्सितुं), अभ्याप्; सेव् (c. 1. सेवते सेवितुं), उपसेव्, निषेव्; समाचर् (c. 1. -चरति -चरितुं); काङ्क्ष् (c. 1. काङ्क्षति काङ्क्षितुं), आकाङ्क्ष्, अनुकाङ्क्ष्.—(To direct the weapon) अभिसन्धा, लक्ष्यं प्रति अस्त्रं क्षिप् (c. 6. क्षिपति, क्षेप्तुं).

AIM, *s.* (The point to which a missive weapon is thrown) लक्षं, लक्ष्यं, बाणलक्ष्यं, शरव्यं.—(The direction of the weapon) सन्धानं.—(A purpose, design) अभिप्रायः, चिकीर्षितं, आशयः, काङ्क्षा, वाञ्छा.—(Conjecture) अनुमानं.

AIMLESS, *a.* असन्धानः -ना -नं, सन्धानरहितः -ता -तं, अलक्ष्यः -क्ष्या -क्ष्यं.

AIR, *s.* आकाशः, वायुः *m.*, नभः *n.* (स्), विहायः *n.* (स्), समीरणः, समिरः.—(Air in motion) वायुः, वातः, समीरणः.—(In music) तालः, मूर्च्छना, निशारुकं.—(Appearance) रूपं, आकारः, आकृतिः *f.*—(Gesture, mien) गतिः *f.*, वदनं, रीतिः *f.*—(Manner) विधिः *m.*, प्रकारः, रूपं.—(Scent, vapour) वासः, वाष्पः, गन्धः; 'aloft in air,' विहायसा *ind.*; 'to build castles in the air,' गगनकुसुमानि कृ.

To AIR, *v. a.* (To expose to the air) वायुव्याप्यं -प्यां -प्यं कृ.—(To dry) शुष् in caus. (शोषयति -यितुं), शुष्कीकृ, निर्जलं -लां -लं कृ.

AIR-BALLOON, *s.* आकाशयानं, व्योमयानं, आकाशवर्त्मना गमनार्थं विमानं.

AIR-BLADDER, *s.* (Any cuticle filled with air) वायुकोषः, अनिलपूरिता नाडिः

AIR-BORN, *a.* वायुजः -जा -जं, आकाशजः -जा -जं.

AIR-GUN, *s.* शरादिप्रासनार्थं वायुपूरितं यन्त्रं.

AIR-HOLE, *s.* वातायनं, गवाक्षः, जालं, वायुच्छिद्रं, वायुपथः.

AIRING, *s.* वायुसेवनं, विहारः, वायुहेतोः परिक्रमः.

AIR-PUMP, *s.* वायुप्रक्षेपको नालः.

AIR-SHAFT, *s.* आकरे वायुगमनार्थं पथः or छिद्रं.

AIRY, *a.* (Composed of air) वायुमयः -यी -यं, आकाशीयः -या -यं, वैहायसः -सी -सं.—(Open to the air) वायुव्याप्यः -प्या -प्यं.—(Wanting reality, vain, empty) शून्यः -न्या -न्यं, लघुः -घुः -घ्वी -घु, अवास्तवः -वी -वं, असारः -रा -रं, चपलः -ला -लं, वायुसमः -मा -मं.

AISLE, *s.* (A path in a church) पूजाशालाभ्यन्तरे पथः.

AKIN, *a.* (Allied by blood, used of persons) सगोत्रजः -जा -जं, सजातीयः -या -यं.—(Used of things) सम्बन्धी -न्धिनी -न्धि (न्), सम्पर्कीयः -या -यं.

ALABASTER, *s.* श्वेतप्रस्तरविशेषः.

ALACK, *interj.* (Alas!) कष्टं, आस्, हा, हन्त, अहह, हाहा, हाहो.

ALACRITY, *s.* लाघवं, चञ्चलत्वं, सोद्यमत्वं, शीघ्रत्वं, अविलम्बत्वं, क्षिप्रता.

ALAMODE, *adv.* व्यवहारानुरूपं, रीत्यनुसारेण.

ALARM, *s.* (Fright) त्रासः, भयं, साध्वसं, शङ्का, भयप्रस्तावः.—(A cry by which soldiers are summoned to arms) सान्नाहनिकं, युद्धाय योधाह्वानं.—(Alarm-cry in general) भयध्वनिः *m.*

To ALARM, *v. a.* भी in caus. (भाययति -यितुं or भीषयति -ते), त्रस् in caus. (त्रासयति -यितुं), वित्रस्, सन्त्रस् in caus.

ALARMED, *p. p.* भीतः -ता -तं, भयार्त्तः -र्त्ता -र्त्तं, चकितः -ता -तं, शङ्कितः -ता -तं, भीषितः -ता -तं.

ALARM-BELL, *s.* भयसूचका घण्टा, शत्रोर् आगमनसमये वाद्यते या घण्टा.

ALARMING, *a.* भयङ्करः -रा -रं, भयानकः -का -कं, त्रासजनकः -का -कं, भयदः -दा -दं.

ALARMIST, *s.* भयोत्पादकः, भयकारकः.

ALARM-POST, *s.* भयसमये सैन्यसमागमार्थं निरूपितस्थानं.

ALARUM, *s.* सान्नाहनिकं, भयध्वनिः *m.*, निरूपितसमये निद्रालसं प्रबोधयति या घटी.

ALAS, *interj.* कष्टं, आ, आस्, हा, हन्त, अहह, अहोवत्.

ALB, *s.* (A white garment worn by priests) धर्म्मोपाध्यायैर् भृतः श्वेतवस्त्रविशेषः.

ALBATROSS, समुद्रीयपक्षिविशेषः, दक्षिणसमुद्रसेवी पक्षी.

ALBEIT, *adv.* तथापि, यद्यपि.

ALBION, *s.* श्वेतद्वीपः.

ALBUGINEOUS, *a.* अण्डशुक्लांशोपमः -मा -मं.

ALBUGO, *s.* शुक्लं, चक्षूरोगः, शुक्लमण्डलरोगः.

ALBUM, *s.* विशिष्टश्लोकरक्षार्थं पुस्तकं.

ALCHYMICAL, *a.* रसायनविद्याविषयकः -का -कं, रसायनजः -जा -जं.

ALCHYMIST, *s.* रसज्ञः, रसायनविद्याज्ञः, रससिद्धः.

ALCHYMY, *s.* रसायनविद्या, रसायनं, रससिद्धिः *f.*

ALCOHOL, *s.* मद्यसारः.—(Impalpable powder) सूक्ष्मभस्म *n.* (न्).

ALCOVE, *s.* कुञ्जः, कुञ्जकुटीरः, पर्णशाला, पल्लवशाला, निभृतस्थानं.

ALDER, *s.* वृक्षविशेषः.

ALDERMAN, *s.* पुराध्यक्षः, नगरस्य प्रधानपुरुषः, मान्यपदस्थः, पौरजनः, वृद्धः, वृद्धजनः, गुरुजनः.

ALDERMANLY, *adv.* वृद्धजनवत् *ind.*, गुरुजनवत् *ind.*, गुरुजनप्रकारेण.

ALE, *s.* यवसुरं, यवनिर्म्मितो मद्यविशेषः.

ALE-HOUSE, *s.* यवसुरालयः, यवसुरस्थानं.

ALE-HOUSE-KEEPER, *s.* यवसुरविक्रयी *m.* (न्), शौण्डिकः.

ALEMBIC, *s.* वकः, वकयन्त्रं, काचवकयन्त्रं, मुषा, द्रवद्रव्यसारनिर्हारार्थं मुषा.

ALERT, *a.* त्वरितः -ता -तं, क्षिप्रः -प्रा -प्रं, उद्यमी -मिनी -मि (न्), उद्योगी -गिनी -गि (न्), सावहितः -ता -तं, अतन्द्रः -द्रा -द्रं.

ALERTNESS, *s.* क्षिप्रता, अतन्द्रता, सत्वरता, सोद्योगत्वं.

ALGEBRA, *s.* वीजगणितं, गणनाविद्या.

ALGEBRAICAL, *a.* वीजगणितविषयकः -का -कं, गणनाविद्यासम्बन्धी -न्धिनी -न्धि (न्).

ALGID, *a.* शीतः -ता -तं, शीतलः -ला -लं, शिशिरः -रा -रं, हिमवान् -वती -वत् (त्).

ALIEN, *s.* (A foreigner) विदेशी *m.* (न्), विदेशीयः, भिन्नजातीयः.

ALIEN, *a.* अन्यदेशीयः -या -यं, विदेशीयः -या -यं, पारक्यः -क्या -क्यं.—(Estranged from) विरक्तः -क्ता -क्तं.—(Adverse to) विरुद्धः -द्धा -द्धं, विपरीतः -ता -तं, भिन्नः -न्ना -न्नं.

ALIENABLE, *a.* विच्छेदनीयः -या -यं, विभेद्यः -द्या -द्यं.—(Alienable property) पराधीनं कर्त्तुं शक्यते यद् द्रव्यं.

To ALIENATE, *v. a.* (To withdraw the affections) विरञ्ज् in caus. (-रञ्जयति -यितुं).—(To transfer property) द्रव्याधिकारित्वं पराधीनं or परवशं कृ, or परस्वत्वे प्रतिपद् in caus. (-पादयति -यितुं).

ALIENATE, *a.* विभिन्नः -न्ना -न्नं, विरक्तः -क्ता -क्तं, विच्छिन्नः -न्ना -न्नं, पराधीनः -ना -नं.

ALIENATED, *p. p.* विरक्तः -क्ता -क्तं. *See* ALIENATE.

ALIENATION, *s.* (Coldness of affection) विरागः, विरक्तिः *f.*, वैरक्त्यं.—(Transferring of property) स्वस्वत्वत्यागानन्तरं परस्वत्वापादनं.

To ALIGHT, *v. n.* अवतॄ (c. 1. -तरति -तरितुं -तरीतुं), उपविश् (c. 6. -विशति -वेष्टुं), निपत् (c. 1. -पतति -पतितुं).

ALIGHTED, *p. p.* अवतीर्णः -र्णा -र्णं, उपविष्टः -ष्टा -ष्टं, निपतितः -ता -तं.

ALIKE, *a.* सदृशः -शी -शं, तुल्यः -ल्या -ल्यं, समानः -ना -नं, एकप्रकारः -रा -रं, तुल्यरूपः -पी -पं, तुल्याकृतिः -तिः ति.

ALIMENT, *s.* आहारः, भोजनं, भक्ष्यं, भोज्यं, अन्नं, खाद्यं, पौष्टिकं.

ALIMENTAL or ALIMENTARY, *a.* पौष्टिकः -की -कं, पोषकः -का -कं, पुष्टिदः -दा -दं, प्रतिपालकः -का -कं, भरणशीलः -ला -लं.

ALIMENTARINESS, *s.* पोषकत्वं, प्रतिपालकत्वं, भरिमा *m.* (न्), भरणशीलता.

ALIMENTATION, *s.* पोषणं, भरणं, प्रतिपालनं, पुष्टिः *f.*

ALIMONY, *s.* स्त्रीपुरुषविभेदसमये यो धनस्य न्यायांशो भार्य्यायै दीयते.

ALIVE, *a.* जीवन् -वन्ती -वत् (त्), वर्त्तमानः -ना -नं, सजीवः -वा -वं, सचेतनः -ना -नं, आयुष्मान् -ष्मती -ष्मत् (त्).—(Cheerful, sprightly) त्वरितः -ता -तं, अतन्द्रः -न्द्रा -न्द्रं, चपलः -ला -लं.

ALKALI, *s.* सर्ज्जिका, सर्ज्जिः *f.*, क्षारः, सर्ज्जिकाक्षारः, यवक्षारः, गोगवाही *m.* (न्).

ALKALINE, *a.* क्षारस्वभावः -वा -वं, क्षारविशिष्टः -ष्टा -ष्टं, सर्ज्जियुक्तः -क्ता -क्तं.

ALL, *a.* सर्व्वः -र्व्वा -र्व्वं, विश्वः -श्वा -श्वं, कृत्स्नः -त्स्ना -त्स्नं, निखिलः -ला -लं, अखिलः -ला -लं, समस्तः -स्ता -स्तं, सकलः -ला -लं.

ALL, *s.* (The whole) सर्व्वं, कार्त्स्न्यं, कात्स्न्यं, साकल्यं; 'In all, altogether,' सर्व्वशस्, साकल्येन, कृत्स्नशस्; 'not at all,' न कथञ्चन, न मनाक्; 'at all times,' सर्व्वदा; 'all but,' प्रायस् *ind.*, प्रायशस्, ईषदूनः -ना -नं; 'all of a sudden,' अकस्मात्; 'all I can,' यथाशक्ति *ind.*, यथाबलं, यथासामर्थ्यं; 'all around,' सर्व्वतस्, समन्ततस्, परितस्, चतुर्दिक्षु; 'by all means,' सर्व्वथा; 'all at once,' युगपत् *ind.*, 'most of all,' भूयिष्ठं, विशेषतस्; 'all hail,' नमस् *ind.*

ALL-ATONING, *a.* सर्व्वपापनाशकः -का -कं, सर्व्वपापशोधकः -का -कं.

ALL-BEARING, *a.* सर्व्वसहः -हा -हं.—(Omniparous) सर्व्वप्रसवी -विनी -वि (न्).

ALL-CONQUERING, *a.* सर्व्वजयी -यिनी -यि (न्), सर्व्वदमनः -ना -नं, सर्व्वन्दमः -मा -मं.

ALL-GLORIOUS, *a.* सर्व्वतेजोमयः -यी -यं, सर्व्वप्रतापवान् -वती -वत् (त्).

ALL-KNOWING, *a.* सर्व्वज्ञः -ज्ञा -ज्ञं, सर्व्ववेदी -दिनी -दि (न्).

ALL-LOVING, *a.* सर्व्वप्रियः -या -यं, सर्व्वहितैषी -षिणी -षि (न्).

ALL-MATURING, *a.* सर्व्वपाचकः -का -कं, सर्व्वपाचनशीलः -ला -लं.

ALL-PENETRATING, *a.* सर्व्वभेदकः -का -कं, सर्व्वप्रवेशकः -का -कं.

ALL-PERVADING, सर्व्वगतः -ता -तं, सर्व्वव्यापी -पिनी -पि (न्), सर्व्वगः -गा -गं.

ALL-SEEING, *a.* सर्व्वदर्शी -र्शिनी -र्शि (न्), सर्व्वद्रष्टा -ष्ट्री -ष्टृ (ष्टृ).

ALL-SUFFICIENCY, *n.* सर्व्वशक्तिता, सर्व्वसामर्थ्यं.

ALL-SUFFICIENT, सर्व्वसमर्थः -र्था -र्थं, सर्व्वशक्तिमान् -मती -मत् (त्).

ALL-WISE, *a.* सर्व्वज्ञः -ज्ञा -ज्ञं, सर्व्वविद् *m. f. n.*, सर्व्ववेदी -दिनी -दि (न्). सर्व्वज्ञानमयः -यी -यं.

To ALLAY, *v. a.* (To mitigate) शम् in caus. (शमयति -यितुं), प्रशम्, उपशम्; शान्त्व् or सान्त्व् (c. 10. शान्त्वयति -यितुं) अभिशान्त्व्, परिशान्त्व्; तुष् in caus. (तोषयति -यितुं).—(To mix one metal with another) धातुं धातुना मिश्र् (c. 10. मिश्रयति -यितुं); सुवर्णं रूप्यं वा कुप्येन मिश्र्.

ALLAY or ALLAYMENT, *s.* (Mitigation) शान्तिः *f.*, प्रशमनं, प्रशान्तिः *f.*, सान्त्वनं; 'allayment of fear,' भयोपशमः; 'allayment of hunger,' क्षुत्प्रतीकारः.—(Mixture of base metal) कुप्यसम्पर्कः.

ALLAYED, *p. p.* प्रशान्तः -न्ता -न्तं, उपशान्तः -न्ता -न्तं, प्रशमितः -ता -तं.

ALLAYER, *s.* शमकः, शान्तिकरः, शान्तिकर्त्ता *m.* (र्तृ), शान्तिदः.

ALLEGATION, *s.* (Affirmation) वचनं, अभियोगः, वाक्यं, अभिधानं.—(False allegation) मिथ्याभिशंसनं.—(Excuse, plea) छद्म *n.* (न्), उपदेशः, व्यपदेशः.

To ALLEGE, *v. a.* (To affirm, declare) वद् (c. 1. वदति, वदितुं), तथेति ब्रू (c. 2. ब्रवीति ब्रूते वक्तुं).—(To plead as an excuse) छद्म कृ, व्यपदिश् (c. 6. -दिशति -देष्टुं), मिथ्या वद्.

ALLEGEABLE, *a.* वचनीयः -या -यं, वदनीयः -या -यं, कथनीयः -या -यं.

ALLEGIANCE, *s.* भक्तिः *f.*, अनुरागः, वशीभूतत्वं, अधीनत्वं.

ALLEGIANT, *a.* भक्तिमान् -मती -मत् (त्), अनुरागी -गिणी -गि (न्).

ALLEGORICAL, *a.* रूपकमयः -यी -यं, दृष्टान्तरूपः -पी -पं, लाक्षणिकः -की -कं.

ALLEGORICALLY, *adv.* दृष्टान्ततस् *ind.*, लाक्षणिकप्रकारेण, रूपकक्रमेण.

To ALLEGORISE, *v. a.* दृष्टान्तीकृ, दृष्टान्तय् (*nom.* दृष्टान्तयति -यितुं), लाक्षणिकप्रकारेण वद् (c. 1. वदति, वदितुं).

ALLEGORY, *s.* रूपकं, दृष्टान्तः, उदाहरणं, लाक्षणिकवाक्यं, युक्तिः *f.*

ALLEGRO, *adv.* त्वरितं, क्षिप्रं, शीघ्रं.

To ALLEVIATE, *v. a.* शम् in caus. (शमयति -यितुं), प्रशम्, उपशम्; शान्त्व् or सान्त्व् (c. 10. सान्त्वयति -यितुं), अभिशान्त्व्, उपसान्त्व्, परिशान्त्व्; लघ् (*nom.* लघयति -यितुं), उद्धृ (c. 1. -हरति -ते -हर्त्तुं), लघूकृ.

ALLEVIATED, *p. p.* प्रशमितः -ता -तं, प्रशान्तः -न्ता -न्तं, उपशान्तः -न्ता -न्तं, लघूकृतः -ता -तं.

ALLEVIATION, *s.* शान्तिः *f.*, प्रशमनं, प्रशान्तिः, उपशमः, लघूकरणं, लाघवं.

ALLEVIATIVE, *a.* (Giving alleviation) शान्तिदः -दा -दं, शान्तिकरः -रा -रं, शमकः -का -कं.

ALLEY, *s.* (A narrow passage) सङ्कटपथः, सम्बाधपथः, सङ्कुचितवीथिः *f.* —(A walk in a garden) उद्यानपथः.

ALLIANCE, *s.* (League) सन्धिः *m.*, साहित्यं, संयोगः, साहाय्यं, सहायता, ऐक्यं.—(Relation by marriage, &c.) सम्बन्धः, ज्ञातिसम्पर्कः; 'offensive and defensive alliance,' परस्परोपकारः.

ALLIED, *p. p.* सन्धितः -ता -तं, सहितः -ता -तं, सम्बद्धः -द्धा -द्धं, संयुक्तः -क्ता -क्तं.

To ALLIGATE, *v. a.* सम्बन्ध् (c. 9. -बध्नाति -बन्द्धुं or caus. -बन्धयति -यितुं), अनुबन्ध्, आबन्ध्.

ALLIGATION, *s.* (Tying together) सन्धानं, सम्बन्धनं, संयोजनं.—(Rule in arithmetic) सम्मिश्रद्रव्याणां मूल्यं निरूपयति यो गणनाविधिः, अर्घसंस्थापनं.

ALLIGATOR, *s.* नक्रः, ग्राहः, कुम्भीरः.

ALLITERATION, *s.* अनुप्रासः.

ALLODIAL, *a.* अनधीनः -ना -नं, अनायत्तः -त्ता -त्तं, स्वाधीनः -ना -नं.

To ALLOO, *v. a.* (Set on by crying alloo) हे है इत्यादिशब्दैः कुक्कुरान् प्रबुद् (caus. -बोधयति -यितुं).

To ALLOT, *v. a.* (Distribute by lot) विभज् (c. 1. -भजति -ते -भक्तुं), प्रविभज्; चंस् (c. 10. -चंसयति -यितुं), अंश् (c. 10. अंशयति -यितुं), विन्यस् (c. 4. -अस्यति -असितुं), न्यस्; क्लृप् (c. 10. कल्पयति -यितुं), परिक्लृप्.—(To grant) प्रदा (c. 3. -ददाति -दातुं).

ALLOTMENT, *s.* (Distributing by lot) विभागः, अंशनं, विभागकल्पना. —(The portion granted) अंशः, भागः, विभागः.

To ALLOW, *v. a.* अनुज्ञा (c. 9. -जानाति -ज्ञातुं), अभ्यनुज्ञा; अनुमन् (c. 4. -मन्यते -मन्तुं), सह् (c. 1. सहते सोढुं), विषह्, अनुमुद् (c. 1. -मोदते -मोदितुं).—(To admit an argument) ग्रह् (c. 9. गृह्णाति ग्रहीतुं).—(To allow wages) वर्त्तनं दा or अनुदा (c. 3. -ददाति -दातुं).—(To abate) उद्धारं कृ, न्यूनीकृ.

ALLOWABLE, *a.* धर्म्यः -र्म्या -र्म्यं, अनुज्ञेयः -या -यं, अनुज्ञातव्यः -व्या -व्यं, स्वीकरणीयः -या -यं, अनुज्ञायोग्यः -ग्या -ग्यं, दातव्यः -व्या -व्यं.—(Admissible) ग्राह्यः -ह्या -ह्यं, गृह्यः -ह्या -ह्यं, प्रगृह्यः -ह्या -ह्यं.

ALLOWANCE, *s.* अनुज्ञा, अनुमतिः *f.*—(Stipulated pay) वर्त्तनं, वेतनं, निरूपितमूल्यं, परिमितमूल्यं.—(Abatement) उद्धारः, न्यूनीकरणं.

ALLOWED, *p. p.* अनुज्ञातः -ता -तं, अभ्यनुज्ञातः -ता -तं, अनुमतः -ता -तं.

ALLOY, *s.* अपद्रव्यं, कुप्यं, कूटस्वर्णं, अल्पमूल्यको धातुः, दूषणं, दोषः, मलं. —(Abatement, impairment) न्यूनता, क्षयः, विघ्नः.

ALLOYED, *p. p.* दूषितः -ता -तं, दुष्टः -ष्टा -ष्टं.

To ALLUDE, *v. n.* (Hint at) उद्दिश् (c. 6. -दिशति -देष्टुं), समुद्दिश्, सूच् (c. 10. सूचयति -यितुं), इङ्गं or इङ्गितं or सङ्केतं कृ, स्मृ in caus. (स्मारयति -यितुं), प्रबुध् in caus. (-बोधयति -यितुं).

ALLUDED, *p. p.* उद्दिष्टः -ष्टा -ष्टं, सूचितः -ता -तं, स्मृतः -ता -तं.

To ALLURE, *v. a.* आकृष् (c. 1. -कर्षति or c. 6. -कृषति -क्रष्टुं), समाकृष्; प्रलुभ् in caus. (-लोभयति -यितुं).

ALLURED, *p. p.* आकृष्टः -ष्टा -ष्टं or आकर्षितः -ता -तं, प्रलोभितः -ता -तं.

ALLUREMENT, *s.* प्रलोभनं, आकर्षणं, विलोभनं, वञ्चनं, भोगः.

ALLURING, *a.* आकर्षकः -का -कं, आकर्षी -र्षिणी -र्षि (न्), प्रलोभकः -का -कं, वञ्चकः -का -कं.

ALLURINGLY, *adv.* प्रलोभनपूर्व्वकं, प्रलोभनेन, आकर्षणप्रकारेण.

ALLUSION, *s.* (Hint) इङ्गं, इङ्गितं, सङ्केतः, आकारः.—(Allusion to) उद्देशः, सूचनं.—(In allusion to) उद्दिश्य, समुद्दिश्य.

ALLUSIVE, *a.* उद्देशकः -का -कं, सूचकः -का -कं.

ALLUVION, *s.* पुलिनं, नदीरयेण or जलप्रवाहेण समानीता मृत्तिका.

ALLUVIOUS, *a.* नदीरयेण समानीतः -ता -तं, पुलिनमयः -यी -यं.

ALLY, *s.* सहायः, सहकारी *m.* (न्), मित्रं, सुहृद् *m.*, परस्परोपकारी *m.* (न्), सम्बन्धी *m.* (न्).

To ALLY, *v. a.* सन्धा (c. 3. -दधाति -धत्ते -धातुं), सम्बन्ध् (caus. -बन्धयति -यितुं), संयुज् (c. 10. -योजयति -यितुं), संश्लिष् in caus. (-श्लेषयति -यितुं).

ALMANAC, *s.* पत्रिका, पञ्जिः *f.*

ALMANAC-MAKER, *s.* पञ्जीकारः, पत्रिकारचकः.

ALMIGHTINESS, *s.* सर्व्वशक्तिमत्त्वं, सर्व्वसामर्थ्यं.

ALMIGHTY, *a.* सर्व्वशक्तिमान् -मती -मत् (त्), सर्व्वसमर्थः -र्था -र्थं, सर्व्वशक्त *m. f. n.*, अमितौजाः -जाः -जः (स्).

ALMOND, *s.* पारसीकजनैर् बादामित्य् अभिधीयते यत् फलं.

ALMONER, *s.* दानधर्म्मे नियुक्तः, भिक्षावितरणे अधिकृतः, दरिद्रेषु यद् धनं दातव्यं तद्वितरणे अधिकृतः.

ALMONRY, *s.* दानधर्म्मे नियुक्तस्य गृहं, भिक्षावितरणशाला.

ALMOST, *adv.* प्रायस्, प्रायशस्, भूयिष्ठं, ईषदूनः -ना -नं, कल्पः affixed. —(Somewhat less) ईषदूनं, यत् किञ्चिन् न्यूनं; 'almost four,' उपचतुराः *m. pl.*; 'almost every person,' प्रायः सर्व्वजनः; 'almost dead,' मुमूर्षुः or मृतप्रायः or मृतकल्पः; 'almost finished,' समाप्तभूयिष्ठः; 'seven days being almost ended,' सप्तसु दिनेषु समाप्तकल्पेषु.

ALMS, *s.* भैक्षं, भैक्ष्यं, भिक्षा, भिक्षान्नं, दानं; 'to beg alms,' भिक्ष् (c. 1. भिक्षते भिक्षितुं), भैक्ष्यं चर् (c. 1. चरति, चरितुं), भिक्षाटनं कृ.

ALMS-BOX, *s.* भिक्षापात्रं, दानाधारः.

ALMS-GIVER, *s.* भिक्षादाता *m.* (तृ), दरिद्रपोषकः.

ALMS-GIVING, *s.* दानधर्म्मः, दानकार्य्यं, भिक्षादानं, दरिद्रपोषणं.

ALMS-HOUSE, *s.* दरिद्रपोषणशाला, भिक्षावितरणशाला.

ALMS-MAN, *s.* भिक्षाचरः, भिक्षुकः, भिक्षाशी *m.* (न्), भिक्षोपजीवी *m.* (न्).

ALOE, *s.* (The plant) कुमारी, सहा, स्थूलदला.—(A precious wood) अगुरुः, अगुरुकाष्ठं.

ALOFT, *adv.* ऊर्द्ध्वं, उपरि, उपरिष्टात्, उच्चं.—(In air) विहायसा.

ALONE, *a.* एकाकः -का -कं, एकः -का -कं, एकाकी -किनी -कि (न्), निभृतः -ता -तं, केवलः -ला -लं, केवली -लिनी -लि (न्), अद्वितीयः -या -यं.—(Only) केवलं, मात्रं.

ALONG, *prep.* (At length, all along the side of) अनु prefixed to the acc. c. neuter; as, 'along the Ganges,' अनुगङ्गं; 'along the bank,' अनुकूलं.—(Forward) अग्रे, पुरस् *ind.*, पुरस्तात्.—(Along with) सह, सार्द्धं, सहितः -ता -तं.—(All along, from first to last) प्रथमावधेः प्रभृति शेषपर्य्यन्तं, सर्व्वत्र.—(Along-side) पार्श्वतस् *ind.*

ALOOF, *adv.* दूरे, कियद्दूरे, ईषद्दूरे, अन्तरे, निभृतं, पृथक्.—(Standing aloof) दूरस्थः.

ALOUD, *adv.* प्रकाशं, उच्चैस् *ind.*, उच्चकैस्, प्रोच्चैस्, उच्चैःस्वरेण, महानादेन, उच्चैस्तमाम् *ind.*, मुक्तकण्ठं.

ALPHABET, *s.* वर्णमाला, वर्णक्रमः, अक्षरविन्यासः, वर्णसङ्घातः.

ALPHABETICAL, *a.* वर्णक्रमानुसारी -रिणी -रि (न्), वर्णमालाश्रेण्यनुरूपः -पा -पं.

ALPHABETICALLY, *adv.* वर्णक्रमानुसारतस् *ind.*, वर्णमालाश्रेण्यनुरूपं.

ALREADY, *adv.* (Some time ago) तत्पूर्व्वं, पूर्व्वं, पुरा, पूर्व्वकाले, प्राग् वर्त्तमानकालात्.—(At the present time) तत्क्षणे, सम्प्रति, तत्काले.

Also, *adv.* च, चैव, अपिच, एवं, अपरञ्च, पुनरपि, पुनश्च.—(In like manner) तद्वत् *ind.*, तद्विधे, तत्प्रकारे.

Altar, *s.* चैत्यं, आयतनं, वेदिः *m.* or -दी *f.*, चयनं, यज्ञवेदिः, स्थण्डिलं.

To alter, *v. a.* अन्यथा कृ, अन्यरूपं -पां -पं कृ, अन्यप्रकारं -रां -रं कृ, विपर्य्यस् (c. 4. -अस्यति -असितुं), परिवृत् in caus. (-वर्त्तयति -यितुं).—(To alter for the worse) विकृ (c. 8. -कुरुते -कर्त्तुं), विरूप् (c. 10. -रूपयति -यितुं).

To alter, *v. n.* अन्यथा or अन्यरूपः -पा -पं or अन्यप्रकारः -रा -रं भू.—(For the worse) विकृ (c. 8. -कुरुते).—(To alter in mind and feelings) विमनीभू.

Alterable, *a.* विकार्य्यः -र्य्या -र्य्यं, अन्यथा करणीयः -या -यं, विकारशीलः -ला -लं, परीवर्त्तनीयः -या -यं, परिणामयोग्यः -ग्या -ग्यं.

Alterage, *s.* (The fostering of a child) बालकपोषणं, पुत्रप्रतिपालनं.

Alteration, *s.* विकारः, विक्रिया, विकृतिः *f.*, परिणामः, परीवर्त्तनं, अन्यथाभावः, वैकृतं.

Alterative, *a.* विकारी -रिणी -रि (न्), परिवर्त्तकः -का -कं, परिणामकरः -रा -रं.

To altercate, *v. n.* विवद् (c. 1. -वदते -वदितुं), व्यवक्रुश् (c. 1. क्रोशति -क्रोष्टुं).

Altercation, *s.* विप्रलापः, व्यवक्रोशनं, व्यावभाषी *f.*, वादानुवादः, विवादः, उत्तरप्रत्युत्तरं, वाक्यविरोधः, वाग्युद्धं, वाक्यं.

Altered, *p. p.* विकृतः -ता -तं, वैकृतः -ता -तं, अन्यरूपः -पा -पं, अन्यथा कृतः -ता -तं, कृतविक्रियः -या -यं.—(In mind) विमनीकृतः -ता -तं.

Alternate, alternately, *adv.* विपर्य्ययेण, वारं वारं, अन्योन्यं, परस्परतस्, परस्परम्, परिवृत्य; 'alternate sleeping and waking,' पर्य्यायशयनं.

To alternate, *v. a.* परिवृत् in caus. (-वर्त्तयति -यितुं), विहृ (c. 1. -हरति -हर्त्तुं).

To alternate, *v. n.* परिवृत् (c. 1. -वर्त्तते -वर्त्तितुं).

Alternation, *s.* विपर्य्ययः, पर्य्यायः, परिवर्त्तनं, परिवृत्तिः *f.*—(Alternation of employment or duty) कर्म्मविपर्य्ययः.

Alternative, विकल्पः, अनुकल्पः, पाक्षिकः, पक्षः, वाग्यः.—(In grammar) विभाषा *f.*

Although, *conj.* यद्यपि. 'Although' is sometimes expressed by the potential mood of the verb; as, 'although it be not,' न भवेत्.—(Notwithstanding) तथापि, किन्तु.

Altiloquence, *s.* गर्व्वितवाक्यं, साटोपोक्तिः *f.*

Altisonant, *a.* उच्चैःस्वरकारी -रिणी -रि (न्), महास्वनः -ना -नं.

Altivolant, *a.* उच्चैर् उड्डीयमानः -ना -नं, उच्चैर् उड्डीनः -ना -नं.

Altitude, *s.* उच्चत्वं, उच्छ्रितिः *f.*, उच्छ्रायः, उत्तुङ्गता, उत्सेधः.—(Superiority) प्रधानत्वं.

Altogether, *adv.* सर्व्वथा, सर्व्वतस् *ind.*, सम्यक्. अशेषतस् *ind.*, अशेषेण, कृत्स्नशस् *ind.*, अखिलेन, साकल्येन, कार्त्स्न्येन.—(Conjunctly) समं, एकचित्तीभूय *ind.*, सहितः -ता -तं, संहतः -ता -तं.

Alum, *s.* स्फटी, लवणविशेषः.

Aluminous, *a.* स्फटीमयः -यी -यं, स्फटीसम्बन्धी -न्धिनी -न्धि (न्).

Always, *adv.* सर्व्वदा, सदा, सततम्, नित्यदा, अनिशं, अनवरतं, निरन्तरं, सर्व्वकाले.

Amain, *adv.* (Violently) प्रसभं, प्रसह्य, बलात्, बलवत् *ind.*—(With impetuosity) सवेगं, वेगतस् *ind.*, जवेन.

Amalgam, *s.* कांस्यं.

To amalgamate, *v. n.* पारेण धातून् मिश्र् (c. 10. मिश्रयति -यितुं).—(To unite together) संयुज् (c. 10. -योजयति -यितुं), संश्लिष् in caus. (-श्लेषयति -यितुं), संहन् (c. 2. -हन्ति -हन्तुं), एकीकृ.

Amalgamation, *s.* (Of metals) धातुमिश्रणं, योगः.—(Junction) संश्लेषः, संयोजनं.

Amanuensis, *s.* लेखकः, लिपिकारः, यद् अन्येन कथितं तल्लेखकः.

Amaranth, *s.* अम्लानः, अम्लानपुष्पं.

Amarantine, *a.* अम्लानी -निनी -नि (न्), अम्लानवान् -वती -वत् (त्), अम्लानपुष्पयुक्तः -क्ता -क्तं.

Amaritude, *s.* तिक्तता, -त्वं, कटुता.

To amass, *v. a.* सञ्चि (c. 5. -चिनोति -चेतुं), उपचि, सम्भृ (c. 1. -भरति -ते -भर्त्तुं), समाक्षिप् (c. 6. -क्षिपति -क्षेप्तुं), एकत्र कृ, राशीकृ.

Amassed, *p. p.* सञ्चितः -ता -तं, उपचितः -ता -तं, सम्भृतः -ता -तं, राशीकृतः -ता -तं.

Amassment, *s.* सञ्चयः, पुञ्जः, समुच्चयः, संहतिः *f.*, ओघः, समुदायः, राशीकरणं.

Amateur, *s.* काञ्चिद् विद्यां स्वेच्छातः or आत्मविनोदार्थं सेवते यः.—(In music) गन्धर्व्वविद्याप्रियः, गन्धर्व्वविद्याकामः.

Amatory, *a.* कामी -मिनी -मि (न्), स्नेही -हिनी -हि (न्), प्रीतिमान् -मती -मत् (त्), अनुरागी -गिणी -गि (न्), प्रेमशीलः -ला -लं, शृङ्गारी -रिणी -रि (न्), रसिकः -का -कं.

To amaze, *v. a.* विस्मि in caus. (-स्माययति -ते -यितुं), आकुलीकृ, व्याकुलीकृ, विस्मयाकुलं -लां -लं or साश्चर्य्यं -र्य्यां -र्य्यं or व्यस्तं -स्तां -स्तं कृ.

Amaze, *s.* विस्मयः, आश्चर्य्यः, चमत्कारः.—(Confusion) आकुलत्वं, व्याकुलता.

Amazed, *p. p.* विस्मितः -ता -तं, चमत्कृतः -ता -तं, मोहितः -ता -तं, व्याकुलितः -ता -तं, आकुलीकृतः -ता -तं, व्याकुलमनाः -नाः -नः (स्).

Amazedly, *adv.* सविस्मयं, साश्चर्य्यं, विस्मयेन, चमत्कारेण.

Amazement, *s.* विस्मयः, आश्चर्य्यत्वं, अद्भुतं, व्याकुलता, कातरता.

Amazing, *part. a.* (Astonishing) विस्मयकारी -रिणी -रि (न्), विचित्रः -त्रा -त्रं, अद्भुतः -ता -तं, चमत्कारी -रिणी -रि (न्).—(Excessive) अतिरिक्तः -क्ता -क्तं; 'amazing power,' अतिशक्तिः *f.*

Amazingly, *adv.* अद्भुतं, विचित्रं, विचित्रप्रकारेण.—(Excessively) निर्भरं, अतीव, अतिरिक्तं, अतिशयं; 'amazingly covetous,' अतिलुब्धः.

Amazon, *s.* स्वस्तनच्छेदनपूर्व्वकं रणे विक्रमं दर्शयित्वा या स्त्रीजातिः प्राङ्गलीनपुस्तकेषु प्रशस्यते.

Ambages, *s.* वक्रोक्तिः *f.*, वक्रभणितं.

Ambassador, *s.* दूतः, सन्देशहरः, राजदूतः, राजचारः, मन्त्री *m.* (न्).

Ambassage, *s.* दूत्यं, दौत्यं, दूतप्रेरणं.

Amber, *s.* तृणमणिः *m.*, तृणग्राही *m.* (न्), शूकापुट्ठः.

Amber, *a.* तृणमणिमयः -यी -यं, शूकापुट्ठरूपः -पी -पं.

Ambergris, *s.* औषधविशेषः.

Amber-tree, *s.* सुगन्धिवृक्षविशेषः.

Ambidexter or ambidextrous, *a.* (Having equally the use of both hands) सव्यसाची -चिनी -चि (न्), उभयहस्तकुशलः -ला -लं.—(Equally ready to act on both sides) द्विपक्षपाती *m.* (न्).

Ambient, *a.* वेष्टकः -का -कं, परिवेष्टकः -का -कं, व्यापकः -का -कं.

Ambiguity, ambiguousness, *s.* द्व्यर्थः, सन्दिग्धार्थः, सन्देहार्थः, अस्पष्टार्थः, अस्पष्टता, वक्रोक्तिः *f.*, वक्रता.

Ambiguous, *a.* द्व्यर्थः -र्था -र्थं, सन्दिग्धार्थः -र्था -र्थं, अस्पष्टार्थः -र्था -र्थं, अस्पष्टः -ष्टा -ष्टं, अव्यक्तः -क्ता -क्तं, वक्रः -क्रा -क्रं.

Ambiguously, *adv.* द्व्यर्थतस् *ind.*, अस्पष्टं, अव्यक्तं, वक्रोक्त्या, सन्दिग्धप्रकारेण.

Ambit, *s.* मण्डलं, वेष्टनं, चक्रवालं.

Ambition, *s.* कीर्त्तिस्पृहा, अभिरुचिः *f.*, ऐश्वर्य्याकाङ्क्षा, उत्कृष्टपदवाञ्छा, राज्यलोभः.

Ambitious, *s.* कीर्त्तिप्रेप्सुः -प्सुः -प्सु, यशस्कामः -मा -मं, यशस्काम्यन् -म्यती -म्यत् (त्), आजिगीषुः -षुः -षु, उत्कृष्टपदप्रेप्सुः -प्सुः -प्सु, अभिरुचिमान् -मती -मत् (त्), ऐश्वर्य्यप्रेप्सुः -प्सुः -प्सु, अभिप्रेतः -ता -तं.

Ambitiously, *adv.* कीर्त्तिस्पृहातस् *ind.*, ऐश्वर्य्याकाङ्क्षया, उत्कृष्टपदवाञ्छया, अभिरुच्या.

To amble, *v. n.* सुन्दरगत्या चल् (c. 1. चलति चलितुं), सुन्दरप्रकारेण प्रु (c. 1. प्रवते प्रोतुं) or धोर् (c. 1. धोरति धोरितुं).

Amble, *s.* अश्वस्य गतिविशेषः, प्लुतः, धोरितं, सुन्दरगतिः *f.*

Ambler, *s.* धोरितशीलः, सुन्दरगतियायी *m.* (न्).

Ambrosia, *s.* अमृतं, त्रिदशाहारः, पीयूषं, देवान्नं, परमान्नं.

To ambulate, *v. a.* विचर् (c. 1. -चरति -चरितुं). क्रम् in freq. (चंक्रम्यते), परिक्रम् (c. 4. -क्राम्यति क्रमितुं), इतस्ततश् चर्.

Ambulation *s.* परिक्रमः, इतस्ततो भ्रमणं.

Ambuscade, ambush, *s.* (A place where persons lie in wait) पराक्रमणार्थे निभृतस्थानं.—(The liers in wait) सैन्यं निभृते स्थापितं.

To ameliorate, *v. a.* भद्रतरं -रां -रं, or श्रेयांसं -यसीं -यः or श्रेष्ठतरं -रां -रं, or साधीयांसं -यसीं -यः कृ.

Amelioration, *s.* श्रेयस्त्वं, भद्रतरता, श्रेष्ठता, श्रैष्ठ्यं, वृद्धिः *f.*

Amen, *adv.* तथास्तु, एवमस्तु.

Amenable, *a.* अभियोक्तुराह्वानाधीनः -ना -नं, परानुयोगाधीनः -ना -नं, अनुसन्धेयः -या -यं.

To amend, *v. a.* (To correct) शुध् in caus. (शोधयति -यितुं), परिशुध् विशुध्, संशुध्; समाधा (c. 3. -दधाति -धत्ते -धातुं).—(To amend one's life, leave wickedness) पापात् निवृत् (c. 1. -वर्त्तते -वर्त्तितुं), पापं त्यक्त्वा धर्म्मम् आचर् (c. 1. -चरति -चरितुं), or साधून् आचारान् आस्था (c. 1. -तिष्ठति -स्थातुं), विप्रतीसारं कृ.

To amend, *v. n.* (As the life or manners) शुध् (c. 4. शुध्यति शोद्धुं), विशुध्, संशुध्, समाधा in pass. (-धीयते), भद्रतरः -रा -रं भू, साधुः -धुः or -ध्वी -धु भू.—(As a disease) शम् (c. 4. शाम्यति शमितुं) उपशम्.

Amended, *p. p.* शोधितः -ता -तं, संशुद्धः -द्धा -द्धं.—(Ceased from evil) निवृत्तपापः -पा -पं.

Amendment, *s.* शोधनं, संशुद्धिः *f.*, प्रतिसमाधानं, समाधानं, विप्रतीसारः, श्रेयस्त्वं, श्रेष्ठता, श्रैष्ठ्यं.—(Of life) आचारशोधनं, दोषशोधनं.—(Of a disease) उपशमः, स्वास्थ्यं.

Amends, *s.* निस्तारः, निष्कृतिः *f.*, पारितोषिकं, शोधनं, संशुद्धिः *f.*

Amenity, *s.* रम्यता, प्रियता, अभिरामत्वं, सुनन्दता.

To amerce, *v. a.* दण्ड् (c. 10. दण्डयति -यितुं) with two accusatives.

Amerced, *p. p.* दण्डितः -ता -तं, साधितः -ता -तं.

Amercement, *s.* दण्डः, धनदण्डः.—(Loss) हानिः *f.*, क्षयः, अपचयः.

Amethyst, *s.* मणिविशेषः, नीलवर्णः प्रस्तरप्रभेदः, मर्दौष्मणिः.

Amiable, *a.* सुशीलः -ला -लं, सुप्रियः -या -यं, सुशीलवान् -वती -वत् (त्), प्रीतिमान् -मती -मत् (त्), प्रियदर्शनः -ना -नं, स्नेहार्हः -र्हा -र्हं, प्रियङ्करः -रा -रं.—(Pleasant) रमणीयः -या -यं.

Amiableness, *s.* सुशीलत्वं, सद्भावः, प्रियता, प्रियम्भविष्णुता, प्रियम्भावुकता.

Amiably, *adv.* सुशीलजनवत्, सुप्रियं, प्रीतिपूर्व्वकं, प्रीत्या.

Amicable, *a.* मैत्रः -त्री -त्रं, हितः -ता -तं, साख्येयः -या -यं, स्नेहशीलः -ला -लं.

Amicableness, *s.* मित्रत्वं, साख्यं, सौहार्द्दं, सहायता, अनुकूलता.

Amid, amidst, *prep.* मध्ये, अन्तरेण, अन्तरे, अन्तरा, अभ्यन्तरे.

Amiss, *adj.* दोषी -षिणी -षि (न्), अपराधी -धिनी -धि (न्), अनुचितः -ता -तं, अयुक्तः -क्ता -क्तं. *adv.* दुष्टु, दोषेण, अपराधतस्, अनुचितं, अयुक्तं.

Amity, *s.* मैत्र्यं, साख्यं, बन्धुता, ऐक्यं.—(Between nations) सन्धिः *m.*

Ammoniac, *s.* (Gum ammoniac) निर्यासप्रकारः.—(Sal ammoniac) लवणप्रकारः.

Ammunition, *s.* युद्धोपकरणं, युद्धसज्जा.

Amnesty, *s.* राजक्षमा, दोषक्षमा, दोषविस्मरणव्यवस्था.

Among, amongst, *prep.* मध्ये, अभ्यन्तरे, अन्तरे, अन्तरेण, अन्तरा, अन्तर्.

Amorous, *a.* कामी -मिनी -मि (न्), प्रकामः -मा -मं, कामुकः -का -कं, मन्मथी -थिनी -थि (न्), शृङ्गारी -रिणी -रि (न्), रसिकः -का -कं, प्रेमशीलः -ला -लं, कामाक्रान्तः -न्ता -न्तं.

Amorously, *adv.* कामेन, कामतस् *ind.*, रसिकभावेन, प्रीतिपूर्व्वकं.

To amount, *v. n.* उपचि in pass. (-चीयते), सञ्चि, समुदि in pass. (-ईयते), सङ्ख्या in pass. (-ख्यायते); 'amounting to,' संख्यकः -का -कं.

Amount, *s.* परिमाणं, सङ्ख्या, समुदायः, उपचायः, सारः, सर्वः; 'money to the amount of a lac,' लक्षसंख्यानि धनानि.—(Value, price) मूल्यं.

Amphibious, *a.* भूजलचरः -रा -रं, स्थलजलचरः -रा -रं, जलवायुगः -गा -गं, द्विधागतिः -तिः -ति, स्थलेशयः.

Amphitheatre, *s.* अर्द्धचन्द्राकारो रङ्गः, अर्द्धमण्डलाकारो रङ्गः, रङ्गभूमिः *f.*, रङ्गाङ्गणं.

Ample, *a.* विशालः -ला -लं, विपुलः -ला -लं, विस्तृतः -ता -तं, बृहन् -हती -हत् (त्), प्रचुरः -रा -रं, बहुलः -ला -लं, यथेष्टः -ष्टा -ष्टं.

Ampleness, *s.* विशालता, विपुलता, विस्तीर्णता, बृहत्त्वं, प्राचुर्य्यं.

Amplification, *s.* विस्तारत्वं, विस्तरः, वृद्धिः *f.*, वर्द्धनं.—(In rhetoric) अत्युक्तिः *f.*

To amplify, amplificate, *v. a.* वृध् in caus. (वर्धयति -यितुं), संवृध्; विस्तृ (c. 5. -स्तृणोति, c. 9. -स्तृणाति -स्तरितुं, -स्तरीतुं, caus. -स्तारयति), आप्यै in caus. (-प्याययति -यितुं), समाप्यै; तन् (c. 8. तनोति तनितुं).

Amplitude, *s.* (Extent) विस्तीर्णता, विस्तारः, विपुलता.—(Greatness) बृहत्त्वं, महत्त्वं, महिमा *m.* (न्).—(Capacity) आधारशक्तिः, सामर्थ्यं.—(Abundance) प्रचुरत्वं, सम्पूर्णत्वं, बहुत्वं.

Amply, *adv.* विस्तरेण, विस्तरशस् *ind.*, विपुलं, यथेष्टं.

To amputate, *v. a.* अङ्गं छिद् (c. 7. छिनत्ति छेत्तुं), लू (c. 9. लुनाति -नीते लवितुं), निकृत् (c. 6. -कृन्तति -कर्त्तितुं), अङ्गच्छेदनं कृ.

Amputated, *p. p.* छिन्नः -न्ना -न्नं, लूनः -ना -नं, कृत्तः -त्ता -त्तं.

Amputation, *s.* छेदः, अङ्गच्छेदनं, कर्त्तनं, अङ्गकर्त्तनं.

Amulet, *s.* कवचः, रक्षा, रोगनिवारणार्थं किञ्चिद् द्रव्यं or औषधं.

To amuse, *v. a.* नन्द् in caus. (नन्दयति -यितुं), अभिनन्द्, प्रतिनन्द्; रम् in caus. (रमयति -यितुं), विनुद् in caus. (नोदयति -यितुं).—(To amuse one's self) विलस् (c. 1. -लसति -लसितुं).

Amused, *p. p.* विनोदितः -ता -तं, अभिनन्दितः -ता -तं.

Amusement, *s.* विनोदः, परीहासः, क्रीडा, केलिः *f.*, खेला, विलासः, आह्लादः, नर्म्म *n.* (न्), कौतुकं, कुतूहलं.

Amuser, *s.* विनोदयिता *m.* (तृ), नन्दकः.

An. *See* A.

Anabaptism, *s.* पुनर्जलसंस्कारः, पुनर्मज्जनं.

Anabaptist, *s.* पुनर्जलसंस्कारमतावलम्बी, पुनर्जलसंस्कारमतं धारयन्.

Anachronism, *s.* कालगणनाभ्रमः.

Anagram, नामाक्षरपरिवर्त्तनात् सार्थवाक्यरचनं यथा देवराजः, वेद जारः.

Analogical or analogous, सम्बन्धी -न्धिनी -न्धि (न्), सम्बन्धकः -का -कं, सदृशः -शी -शं, उपमः -मा -मं, अनुरूपः -पा -पं, समानः -ना -नं,

अनुगुणः -णा -णं, तुल्यः -ल्या -ल्यं, सम्पर्क्की -र्क्किणी -र्क्कि (न्), आनुषङ्गिकः -की -कं, तुल्यरूपः -पा -पी -पं.

Analogically, *adv.* सादृश्येन, औपम्येन, सामान्यतस् *ind.*, सादृश्यतस् *ind.*

Analogy, *s.* सम्बन्धः, सादृश्यं, औपम्यं, सम्पर्कः, सामान्यं, समानभावः, उपमितिः.

Analysis, *s.* उपोद्घातः, पृथक्करणं, विच्छेदः, व्यवच्छेदः, परिच्छेदः, विभेदः, विभागः, विवेचनं, विवेकः, द्रावणं, व्याकारः.—(The essence of any thing) सारः, वस्तु *n.*

To analyze, *v. a.* उपोद्घातं कृ, किञ्चित् समस्तद्रव्यं पृथक्कृ, or खण्डशस् कृ, or भागशस् कृ, विविक्तं -क्तां -क्तं or विभिन्नं -न्नां -न्नं कृ, व्याकृ, विभज् (c. 1. -भजति -ते -भक्तुं), विच्छिद् (c. 7. -छिनत्ति -छेत्तुं), द्रु in caus. (द्रावयति -यितुं), द्रवीकृ.

Anarchical, *a.* अराजकः -का -कं, अनीश्वरः -रा -रं, अशिष्टः -ष्टा -ष्टं, राजनीतिरहितः -ता -तं, अशासितः -ता -तं, अस्थिरः -रा -रं, अव्यवस्थितः -ता -तं.

Anarchy, *s.* अराज्यं, अशासनं, प्रभुत्वराहित्यं, शासनहीनत्वं, अनधीनता, अनीश्वरता.

Anathema, *s.* शापः, अभिशापः, परिशापः, आक्रोशनं, अवक्रोशः.

To anathematize, *v. a.* शप् (c. 1. शपति, c. 4. शप्यति, शप्तुं), अभिशप्; आक्रुश् (c. 1. -क्रोशति -क्रोष्टुं).

Anatomical, *a.* व्यवच्छेदविद्यासम्बन्धकः -का -कं, व्यवच्छेदविद्यानुरूपः -पा -पं.

Anatomically, *adv.* व्यवच्छेदविद्यानुरूपं, विशसनविद्याक्रमेण, व्यवच्छेदविद्यावत्.

To anatomise, *v. a.* शरीरं व्यवच्छिद् (c. 7. -छिनत्ति -छेत्तुं), विच्छिद्, सञ्छिद्; विशस् (c. 1. -शसति -शसितुं), खण्डशस् कृ, पृथक्कृ.—(To lay open distinctly) विवृ (c. 5. -वृणोति, -वरितुं or -वरीतुं), अपवृ; प्रकटीकृ, व्याख्या (c. 2. -ख्याति -ख्यातुं).

Anatomised, *p. p.* व्यवच्छिन्नः -न्ना -न्नं, विशसितः -ता -तं, पृथक्कृतः -ता -तं.

Anatomist, *s.* व्यवच्छेदविद्याज्ञः, व्यवच्छेदकः, विशसिता *m.* (तृ).

Anatomy, *s.* शरीरव्यवच्छेदविद्या, विशसनविद्या, विशसनं.—(Division of any thing) विच्छेदः, विभेदः, पृथक्करणं.

Ancestor, *s.* पूर्व्वपुरुषः.—(Ancestors) पूर्व्वजाः *m. pl.*, पितरः *m. pl.*, पितृलोकः.

Ancestral, *a.* पित्र्यः -त्र्या -त्र्यं, पितृकः -का -कं, कौलिकः -की -कं, पैत्रः -त्री -त्रं, पैत्रिकः -की -कं.

Ancestry, *s.* पितरः *m. pl.*, पूर्व्वजाः *m. pl.*, पितृसामान्यं, पितृश्रेणी *f.*, पितृपितामहादि *n.*—(Birth, the honour of descent) वंशः, अन्वयः, कुलमर्य्यादा.

Anchor, *s.* नौबन्धनकीलः, लोहमययन्त्रं येन नौका बध्यते or स्थिरीक्रियते.—(A post for mooring vessels) कूपकः.

To anchor, *v. a.* लौहयन्त्रेण नावं बन्ध् (c. 9. बध्नाति बन्द्धुं) or स्थिरीकृ.

Anchorage, *s.* स्थानं नौबन्धनयोग्यं.—(The duty paid for anchoring) नौकाबन्धनानन्तरं यत् शुल्कं नौकारूढैर् दीयते.

Anchorite, *s.* वनवासी *m.* (न्), यती *m.* (न्), यतिः *m.*, तपस्वी *m.* (न्), सन्न्यासी *m.* (न्), वनी *m.* (न्).—(Brahman of the 3d order) वानप्रस्थः, गृहस्थाश्रमत्यागी *m.* (न्).

Anchovy, *s.* क्षुद्रमत्स्यविशेषः.

Ancient, *a.* पुराणः -णा or -णी -णं, पुरातनः -नी -नं, प्राक्कालीनः -ना -नं, पौराणः -णी -णं, प्राक्तनः -नी -नं, वृद्धः -द्धा -द्धं, प्राचीनः -ना -नं, पूर्व्वकालीनः -ना -नं, चिरन्तनः -नी -नं.

Ancient, *s.* वृद्धः, प्राचीनपुरुषः, पूर्व्वकालीनलोकः.—(The flag of a ship) नावो ध्वजः or पताका.—(Flag-bearer) पताकी *m.* (न्).

Anciently, *adv.* पूर्व्वकाले, गतकाले, पुरा, पूर्व्वं.

Ancientness, *s.* प्राचीनता, पुरातनत्वं, प्राक्कालीनता, वृद्धत्वं.

Ancients, *s.* पूर्व्वजाः *m. pl.*, प्राचीनपुरुषाः *m. pl.*, पूर्व्वकालीनमनुष्याः *m. pl.*

And, *conj.* च placed after the word which it connects with another. In many cases 'and' may be omitted in Sanskrit, and the connection expressed by the use of the indeclinable participle; as, 'the beasts assembled *and* informed the lion,' पशुभिर्मिलित्वा सिंहो विज्ञप्तः.—(Moreover) अपिच, किञ्च, अपरं, अन्यच्च.—(And then) अथ.

Andante, *s.* घनं, तत्त्वं, विलम्बितं, स्पष्टं.

Andiron, *s.* लोहनिर्म्मितः शूलाधारः.

Androgynal or androgynous, *a.* द्विलिङ्गविशिष्टः -ष्टा -ष्टं.

Anecdote, *s.* उपकथा, उपाख्यानं.

Anent, *prep.* (Concerning) प्रति, उद्दिश्य *ind.*, प्रतीक्ष्य *ind.*, विषयकः -का -कं.

Aneurism, *s.* नाडिस्फातिः *f.*, नाडीनां रक्तप्रवाहकाणाम् अतिशयस्फातिः.

Anew, *adv.* (Over again) पुनर्, पुनःपुनर्, पुनरपि.—(Newly) नूतनं, प्रतिनवं.

Angel, *s.* ईश्वरदूतः, देवदूतः, ईश्वरप्रेष्यः, स्वर्गी *m.* (न्), परमेश्वरप्रेरितः, स्वर्गीयदूतः, स्वर्गदूतः, दिव्यदूतः.

Angelical, angelic, *a.* ईश्वरदूतोपमः -मा -मं, दिव्यः -व्या -व्यं, देवरूपी -पिणी -पि (न्), स्वर्गीयः -या -यं.

Angelically, *adv.* ईश्वरदूतवत्, स्वर्गीयजनवत्, दिव्यप्रकारेण.

Anger, *s.* क्रोधः, कोपः, अमर्षः, रोषः, चेतोविकारः; 'my anger is appeased,' मम क्रोधः शाम्यति; 'through anger,' कोपात्.—(Smart of a sore) व्रणवेदना.

To anger, *v. a.* कुप् in caus. (कोपयति -यितुं), प्रकुप्, सङ्कुप्; क्रुध् in caus. (क्रोधयति -यितुं).

Angle, *s.* अस्रः, कोणः, द्विभुजः.—(Apparatus to take fish) मत्स्यवेधनोपकरणं.

To angle, *v. a.* वडिशेन मत्स्यान् जलाद् उद्धृ (c. 1. -हरति -ते -हर्त्तुं), वडिश (nom. वडिशयति), मत्स्यवेधनेन मीनान् व्यध् (c. 4. विध्यति व्यद्धुं) or ग्रह् (c. 9. गृह्णाति ग्रहीतुं).

Angle-rod or angling-rod, *s.* मत्स्यग्रहणार्थं दण्डं.

Angler, *s.* मत्स्यवेधकः, मत्स्यबन्धी *m.* (न्), यो वडिशेन मत्स्यान् गृह्णाति.

Angling, *s.* वडिशेन मत्स्यवेधनं, मत्स्यबन्धनं.

Angling-line, *s.* मत्स्यग्रहणार्थं सूत्रं or रज्जुः *m.*

Angrily, *adv.* सकोपं, सरोषं, सामर्षं, कोपेण, क्रोधात्.

Angry, *a.* क्रुद्धः -द्धा -द्धं, क्रोधी -धिनी -धि (न्), कोपी -पिनी -पि (न्), जातामर्षः -र्षा -र्षं, रुष्टः -ष्टा -ष्टं, क्रोधाक्रान्तः -न्ता -न्तं, सामर्षः -र्षा -र्षं, कृतकोपः -पा -पं, कृतक्रुधः -धा -धं, आगतमन्युः -न्युः -न्यु, सरोषः -षा -षं, रोषणः -णा -णं, सकोपः -पा -पं, समन्युः -न्युः -न्यु.—(To be angry) क्रुध् (c. 4. क्रुध्यति क्रोद्धुं), अनुक्रुध्, समभिक्रुध्, संक्रुध्, अभिसंक्रुध्; रुष् (c. 4. रुष्यति रोषितुं), कुप् (c. 4. कुप्यति कोपितुं), प्रकुप्, सङ्कुप् with dative; असूय् (असूयति -ते, असूयितुं) with acc.

Anguish, *s.* परितापः, वेदना, तीव्रवेदना, क्लेशः, पीडा, दुःखं, आधिः *m.*, मनस्तापः, परिवेदनं, विबाधा, कृच्छ्रं, कष्टं, तोदः.

Angular or angulous, *a.* अस्रः -स्रा -स्रं, कोणविशिष्टः -ष्टा -ष्टं, अस्रवान् -वती -वत् (त्), अस्रोपेतः -ता -तं.

Anhelation, *s.* उच्छ्वसनं, निःश्वसनं.—(Palpitation) हृदयकम्पनं.

Animadversion, *s.* (Reproof) अनुयोगः, निन्दा, उपालम्भः, घृणा.—

(Infliction of punishment) दण्डयोगः.—(Observation) चर्चा, निरीक्षणं, अन्वेषणं.

To Animadvert, *v. n.* (To pass censure on) प्रतिनिन्द् (c. 1. -निन्दति -निन्दितुं), उपालभ् (c. 1. -लभते -लब्धुं).—(To punish) दण्डं प्रणी (c. 1. -नयति -नेतुं), दण्ड् (c. 10. दण्डयति -यितुं).—(To make observation) निरीक्ष् (c. 1. -ईक्षते -ईक्षितुं), चर्चां कृ.

Animadverted, *p.p.* प्रतिनिन्दितः -ता -तं.—(Punished) दण्डितः -ता -तं.

Animadverter, *s.* प्रतिनिन्दकः, दण्डप्रणेता *m.* (तृ), अनुयोगी *m.* (न्).

Animal, *s.* जन्तुः *m.*, प्राणी *m.* (न्), चेतनः, जीवी *m.* (न्), जन्तुः *m.*, जन्मी *m.* (न्), शरीरी *m.* (न्).—(Beast) पशुः *m.*, तिर्य्यङ् *m.* (-च्).

Animal, *a.* जीवी -विनी -वि (न्), प्राणी -णिनी -णि (न्), चेतनः -ना -नं, चेतनावान् -वती -वत् (त्).—(Animal food) मांसाहारः.

Animalcule, *s.* क्षुद्रजीवी *m.* (न्), क्षुद्रजन्तुः *m.*

To Animate, *v. a.* जीव् in caus. (जीवयति -यितुं), प्राण् in caus. (-आनयति -यितुं), आश्वस् in caus. (-श्वासयति -यितुं), समाश्वस्, विश्वस्, परिविश्वस् in caus.; उत्था in caus. (उत्थापयति -यितुं), उद्युज् in caus. (-योजयति -यितुं), प्रोत्सह् in caus. (-साहयति -यितुं), उत्तिज् (c. 10. -तेजयति -यितुं).

Animate, animated, *part. a.* (Inspirited) आश्वासितः -ता -तं, उद्युक्तः -क्ता -क्तं, उत्तेजितः -ता -तं.—(Living) चेतनः -ना -नं, प्राणी -णिनी -णि (न्).—(Vivacious) प्रफुल्लवदनः -ना -नं, हृष्टहृदयः -या -यं, रसिकः -का -कं, सारवान् -वती -वत् (त्).

Animation, *s.* (The act of enlivening) आश्वासनं, उत्तेजनं.—(The state of being enlivened, vivacity) प्रफुल्लता, हृष्टता.

Animator, *s.* आश्वासकः, जीवदः, प्राणदः, प्रोत्साहकः.

Animosity, *s.* वैरं, द्वेषः, विरोधः, मात्सर्य्यं.

Anise, *s.* छत्रा, सालेयः, शीतशिवः, मधुरिका, मिशी, मिश्रेया.

Anker, *s.* रसानां परिमाणविशेषः.

Ankle, *s.* गुल्फः -ल्फं, घुटिका or घटिका, घुटिः *f.*, चरणग्रन्थिः *f.*

Ankled, *a.* गुल्फयुक्तः -क्ता -क्तं, गुल्फसम्बन्धी -न्धिनी -न्धि (न्).

Anklet, *s.* नूपुरः, पादाङ्गदं, मञ्जीरं, पादकटकः.

Annalist, *s.* क्रमानुसारेण चरित्ररचकः, चरित्रलेखकः, पुरावृत्तरचकः, आख्यानरचकः, वृत्तान्तलेखकः, आख्यानसङ्ग्राहकः.

To Annalize, *v. a.* चरित्राणि or पुरावृत्तकथा रच् (c. 10. रचयति -यितुं).

Annals, *s.* क्रमानुसारेण सङ्गृहीत इतिहासः, पुरावृत्तं, पुरावृत्तकथा, चरित्राख्यानं, वृत्तान्तविवरणं.

Annates, *s.* प्रथमफलं, नवशस्यं.—(Sacrifice of first-fruits) आग्रायणं.

To Anneal, *v. n.* रङ्गस्थिरीकरणनिमित्ते काचं तप् (c. 1. तपति तप्तुं or caus. तापयति -यितुं).

Annealing, *s.* यत् काचस्य तपनं रङ्गस्थिरीकरणाय क्रियते.

To Annex, *v. a.* अनुबन्ध् (c. 9. -बध्नाति -बन्धुं), आबन्ध्; संयुज् in caus. (-योजयति -यितुं), उपाधा (c. 3. -दधाति -धत्ते -धातुं), आधा; उपस्था in caus. (-स्थापयति -यितुं).

Annexed, *p. p.* संयोजितः -ता -तं, उपाहितः -ता -तं, अनुबद्धः -द्धा -द्धं.

Annexation, *s.* अनुबन्धनं, उपस्थापनं, संयोगः, संयोजनं, उपधानं.

Annexment, *s.* (The act of annexing). *See the last.*—(The thing annexed) अनुबन्धः, उपाहितं, संयुक्तभागः.

To Annihilate, *v. a.* नश् in caus. (नाशयति -यितुं), विनश्; प्रली in caus. (-लापयति or -लाययति -यितुं), उद्धृ (c. 1. -हरति -ते -हर्त्तुं), उच्छिद् (c. 7. -छिनत्ति -छेत्तुं), लोपं कृ.

Annihilated, *p. p.* उच्छिन्नः -न्ना -न्नं, विनाशितः -ता -तं.

Annihilation, *s.* नाशः, क्षयः, प्रलयः, विनाशः, अभावः, समुच्छेदः, लोपः, निर्भावः, प्रलीनता.

Anniversary, *s.* दिवसः केनापि सविशेषेण कारणेन वत्सरे वत्सरे प्रसिद्धः, प्रतिवार्षिक उत्सवः, वत्सरे वत्सरे सेवितो महोत्सवः.

Anniversary, *a.* सांवत्सरिकः -की -कं, सांवत्सरः -री -रं, प्रतिवार्षिकः -का -कं.

To Annotate, *v. n.* टीकां or भाष्यं लिख् (c. 6. लिखति लेखितुं) or रच् (c. 10. रचयति -यितुं).

Annotation, *s.* टीका, भाष्यं, टिप्पनी *f.*

Annotator, *s.* टीकालेखकः, भाष्यकरः, भाष्यकृत्.

To Announce, *v. a.* आख्या (c. 2. -ख्याति -ते -ख्यातुं), समाख्या; ख्या in caus. (ख्यापयति -यितुं), आख्या in caus.; विघुष् (c. 1. -घोषति -घोषितुं or c. 10. घोषयति), विद् in caus. (वेदयति -यितुं), निविद्, आविद्, समाविद्, विनिविद्, सन्निविद्; ज्ञा in caus. (-ज्ञापयति -यितुं).

Announced, *p. p.* प्रकाशितः -ता -तं, निवेदितः -ता -तं, आवेदितः -ता -तं, अवघुष्टः -ष्टा -ष्टं, आख्यातः -ता -तं, परिकीर्त्तितः -ता -तं.

Announcement, *s.* ख्यापनं, विज्ञापनं, विज्ञप्तिः *f.*, निवेदनं, विघोषणं.—(News) सन्देशः, समाचारः, संवादः.

Announcer, *s.* आख्यायकः, विज्ञापकः, विघोषकः, सन्देशहरः.

To Annoy, *v. a.* पीड् (c. 10. पीडयति -यितुं), अभिपीड्, उपपीड्, प्रपीड्, प्रतिपीड्, सम्पीड्; तप् in caus. (तापयति -यितुं), सन्तप्, परितप्; क्लिश् (c. 9. क्लिश्नाति क्लेष्टुं), अर्द् in caus. (अर्दयति -यितुं), समर्द्, बाध् (c. 1. बाधते, बाधितुं).

Annoyance, *s.* व्यथा, क्लेशः, विडम्बना, दुःखं, पीडा, बाधा.—(The act of annoying) पीडनं.—(A source of annoyance) कण्टकः, -कं.

Annoyed, *p.p.* क्लिष्टः -ष्टा -ष्टं, परिक्लिष्टः -ष्टा -ष्टं, सव्यथः -था -थं, व्यथितः -ता -तं.

Annoyer, *s.* क्लेशकः, दुःखकरः, व्यथाकरः.

Annoying, *a.* क्लेशी -शिनी -शि (न्), क्लेशकः -का -कं, दुःखकरः -री -रं.

Annual, *a.* वार्षिकः -की -कं, आब्दिकः -की -कं, सांवत्सरः -री -रं, वर्षिकः -का -कं, समीनः -ना -नं.—(Lasting only for a year) एकवर्षपर्य्यन्तजीवी -विनी -वि (न्); 'an annual plant,' ओषधिः *f.*

Annually, *adv.* प्रतिवर्षं, प्रतिवत्सरं, वत्सरे वत्सरे, वत्सरक्रमेण.

Annuity, *s.* वार्षिकं or सांवत्सरिकं वेतनं or वर्त्तनं, यन् निरूपितमूल्यं वत्सरे वत्सरे कस्मैचिद् दीयते.

To Annul, *v. a.* लोपं कृ, निरर्थकं -कां -कं कृ, विनश् in caus. (-नाशयति -यितुं).

Annular, *a.* मण्डलाकारः -रा -रं, वलयाकारः -रा -रं, वलयाकृतिः -तिः -ति, अङ्गुरीयाकारः -रा -रं.

Annulet, *s.* क्षुद्रवलयः, क्षुद्राङ्गुरीयः, -यं.

Annulment, *s.* लोपः, नाशः, विनाशः.

To Annumerate, *v. a.* संख्यां संख्यया संयुज् (c. 7. -युनक्ति -युङ्क्ते -योक्तुं).

Annumeration, *s.* संख्या संख्यया संयोजनं.

Annunciation, *s.* प्रत्यादेशः, घोषणं, -णा, ख्यापनं, विज्ञापनं.

Anodyne, *a.* शूलघ्नः -घ्नी -घ्नं, वेदनाशान्तिकः -की -कं, पीडाशमकः -का -कं.

Anodyne, *s.* शूलघ्नं, वेदनाशान्तिकं.

To Anoint, *v. a.* लिप् (c. 6. लिम्पति -ते लेप्तुं), अनुलिप्, आलिप्, समालिप्, उपलिप्, विलिप्; अञ्ज् (c. 7. अनक्ति अंक्तुं) or caus. (अञ्जयति -यितुं), समालभ् (c. 1. -लभते -लब्धुं).—(To consecrate by unction) अभिषिच् (c. 6. -सिञ्चति -सेक्तुं).

Anointed, *p. p.* लिप्तः -प्ता -प्तं, अभिषिक्तः -क्ता -क्तं, दिग्धः -ग्धा -ग्धं, अनुलिप्तः -प्ता -प्तं, अभ्यक्तः -क्ता -क्तं, कृताभिषेकः -का -कं.

Anointer, *s.* अभिषेचकः, लेपकः, अञ्जनकर्त्ता *m.* (र्तृ).

ANOINTING, *s.* अभिषेकः, -चनं, विलेपनं, समालम्भः, अभ्यञ्जनं, अञ्जनं.

ANOMALOUS, *a.* विधिविरुद्धः -द्धा -द्धं, विधिहीनः -ना -नं, विधिघ्नः -घ्नी -घ्नं, नियमविरुद्धः -द्धा -द्धं, अविधिः -धिः -धि.

ANOMALOUSLY, *adv.* अविधानतस् *ind.*, अविधिवत् *ind.*, अनियमतस् *ind.*

ANOMALY, *s.* अविधिः *m.*, अविधानं, विधिविरुद्धता, अनियमः.

ANON, *adv.* (Quickly, soon) शीघ्रं, सपदि, झटिति.—(Now and then) कदापि, कदाचित्.

ANONYMOUS, *a.* अनामकः -का -कं, नामहीनः -ना -नं, सञ्ज्ञारहितः -ता -तं.

ANONYMOUSLY, *adv.* नामव्यतिरेकेण, संज्ञाव्यतिरेकेण, संज्ञां विना.

ANOTHER, *a.* अन्यः -न्या -न्यत्, इतरः -रा -रं, परः -रा -रं, अपरः -रा -रं, परकीयः -या -यं, अन्यदीयः -या -यं. Another is often expressed by अन्तर in composition; as, 'another place,' स्थानान्तरं; 'along with another king,' राजान्तरेण सह. 'In another place,' अन्यत्र; 'in another manner,' अन्यथा; 'at another time,' अन्यदा; 'one after another,' अनुपूर्व्वशस् *ind.*, प्रत्येकं एकैकशस्; 'a defect in another,' परच्छिद्रं; 'another's wife,' परदाराः; 'another man's goods,' परद्रव्यं, परस्वं; 'another's right,' परस्वत्वं; 'another day,' अन्यस्मिन् दिवसे, अन्येद्युः (स्).

To ANSWER, *v. n.* (To speak in reply) प्रतिवच् (c. 2. -वक्ति -वक्तुं), प्रतिभाष् (c. 1. -भाषते -भाषितुं), प्रतिवद् (c. 1. -वदति -ते -वदितुं), प्रतिब्रू (c. 2. -ब्रवीति -वक्तुं), व्याहृ (c. 1. -हरति -ते -हर्तुं), प्रतिभण् (c. 1. -भणति -भणितुं), प्रतिजल्प् (c. 1. -जल्पति -जल्पितुं).—(To correspond, to suit) युज् in pass. (युज्यते), अनुरूपः -पा -पं or तुल्यरूपः -पा -पं or सदृशः -शी -शं अस्.—(To succeed) सम्पद् (c. 4. -पद्यते -पत्तुं), संसिध् (c. 4. -सिध्यति -सेद्धुं).—(To be accountable for) प्रतिभूः or प्रतिनिधिः अस्, लग्नकं दा (c. 3. ददाति दातुं).

ANSWER, *s.* प्रतिवचनं, प्रतिवाक्यं, प्रतिवाक् *f.* (च्), उत्तरं, प्रत्युत्तरं, प्रत्युक्तिः *f.*, प्रतिवाणिः *f.*—(Refutation of a charge) वाक्यखण्डनं, वाक्याघातः.

ANSWERABLE, *a.* प्रतिवाच्यः -च्या -च्यं.—(Responsible) परानुयोगाधीनः -ना -नं, पराज्ञानाधीनः -ना -नं, अभियोक्तव्यः -व्या -व्यं, येन प्रत्युत्तरं दातव्यं सः, यो लग्नकं दातुम् अर्हति.—(Corresponding to) योग्यः -ग्या -ग्यं, अनुरूपः -पा -पं, अनुसारी -रिणी -रि (न्).

ANSWERED, *p. p.* प्रत्युक्तः -क्ता -क्तं, प्रतिभाषितः -ता -तं, प्रतिभणितः -ता -तं.

ANT, *s.* पिपीलिका, पुत्तिका.

ANT-BEAR, *s.* पिपीलिकाखादको जन्तुविशेषः.

ANT-HILL, *s.* वल्मीकः, -कं, कृमिशैलः, कूलकः, भूश्रवाः *m.* (स्), वम्रीकूटं, वामलूरः, स्यमीकः, मृत्तिकाकूटं.

ANTAGONIST, *s.* विरोधी *m.* (न्), विपक्षः, वैरी *m.* (न्), शत्रुः *m.*, अभियोक्ता *m.* (तृ), पर्य्यवस्थाता *m.* (तृ), प्रतिबन्धकः.

ANTAGONISTIC, *a.* विरोधी -धिनी -धि (न्), विपक्षः -क्षा -क्षं, विपरीतः -ता -तं.

ANTALGIC, *a.* वेदनाशमकः -का -कं, शूलघ्नः -घ्नी -घ्नं, शोकापनुदः -दा -दं.

ANTARCTIC, *adj.* दक्षिणकेन्द्रीयः -या -यं.—(The south pole) दक्षिणकेन्द्रं, कुमेरुः *m.*

ANTECEDENT, *a.* पूर्व्वगतः -ता -तं, अग्रगतः -ता -तं, अग्रगामी -मिनी -मि (न्).

ANTECEDENTLY, *adv.* पूर्व्वं, अग्रे, पूर्व्वतस्, अग्रतस्.

ANTEDILUVIAN, *a.* प्राग् भूतसम्प्लवाद् विद्यमानः -ना -नं, प्राग् जलाप्लावनाद् वर्त्तमानः -ना -नं.

ANTELOPE, *s.* मृगः, हरिणः, एणेयः, कुरङ्गः -ङ्गकः, -ङ्गमः.

ANTEMERIDIAN, *a.* पूर्व्वाह्णेतनः -नी -नं.

ANTEMUNDANE, *a.* प्राग् जगत्सृष्टेर् वर्त्तमानः -ना -नं.

ANTEPAST, *s.* पूर्व्वभुक्तिः *f.*, पूर्व्वभोजनं, पूर्व्वाशनं, अग्रग्रहणं.

ANTEPENULTIMATE, *s.* उपधायाः पूर्व्वं विद्यते यद् अक्षरं, पूर्व्वोपान्त्यः.

ANTERIOR, *a.* प्राक्तनः -नी -नं, पूर्व्वः -र्व्वा -र्व्वं, अग्र्यः -ग्र्या -ग्र्यं.

ANTHEM, *s.* ईश्वरस्तवात्मकं गीतं, ईश्वरस्तुतिरूपकं गानं.

ANTHONY'S FIRE, *s.* उदर्दः, रोगविशेषः.

ANTHROPOPHAGI, *s.* नृजग्धाः *m. pl.*, आममांसाशिनः *m. pl.*, क्रव्याशिनः *m. pl.*, असृक्पाः *m. pl.*, राक्षसाः *m. pl.*

ANTIBILIOUS, *a.* पित्तघ्नः -घ्नी -घ्नं.

ANTIC, *a.* (Buffoon-like) भण्डोपमः -मा -मं.—(Odd, unnatural) अपरूपः -पा -पं, विरूपः -पा -पं, असङ्गतः -ता -तं, अयोग्यः -ग्या -ग्यं.

ANTIC, *s.* (A buffoon) भण्डः, भाण्डकरः.—(An odd gesture) असङ्गतप्रकारेण हस्तादिविक्षेपः, विरूपो ऽङ्गविक्षेपः.

ANTI-CHAMBER, *s.* उपशाला.

To ANTICIPATE, *v. a.* (Before the time) पूर्व्वतस् ग्रह् (c. 9. गृह्णाति ग्रहीतुं), प्रवेक्ष् (c. 1. -ईक्षते -ईक्षितुं).—(To foretaste) पूर्व्वास्वादनं कृ, अग्रतस् अनुभू (c. 1. -भवति -भवितुं), पूर्व्वं ज्ञा (c. 9. जानाति ज्ञातुं) or भुज् (c. 7. भुनक्ति, भुंक्ते, भोक्तुं), उत्प्रुश् (c. 1. उत्पश्यति उद्द्रष्टुं), प्रदृश्.

ANTICIPATED, *p. p.* पूर्व्वभुक्तः -क्ता -क्तं, पूर्व्वतस् अनुभूतः -ता -तं, प्रदृष्टः -ष्टा -ष्टं, प्रवेक्षितः -ता -तं, सन्दृष्टः -ष्टा -ष्टं, चित्तकलितः -ता -तं, पुरस्कृतः -ता -तं.

ANTICIPATION, *s.* पूर्व्वभुक्तिः *f.*, पूर्व्वभोजनं, पूर्व्वाशनं, प्रवेक्षणं.

ANTIDOTAL, *a.* विषनाशी -शिनी -शि (न्), विषघाती -तिनी -ति (न्), विषघ्नः -घ्नी -घ्नं, गरघ्नः -घ्नी -घ्नं.

ANTIDOTE, *s.* विषनाशनं, प्रतिविषं.—(Dealer in) विषवैद्यः, जाङ्गुलिकः.

ANTIFEBRILE, *a.* ज्वरघ्नः -घ्नी -घ्नं, ज्वरनाशकः -का -कं, ज्वरान्तकः -का -कं.

ANTIMONY, *s.* स्रोतोञ्जनं, सौवीरं, कापोताञ्जनं, यामुनं.—(Made of antimony) स्रोतोञ्जनमयः -यी -यं.

ANTIPATHY, *s.* सहजो विरोधः, द्वन्द्वभावः, विरक्तिः *f.*, वैरिता, शत्रुता, विमतिः *f.*, अनिच्छा.

ANTIPHLEGMATIC, *a.* कफनाशनः -नी -नं, कफघ्नः -घ्नी -घ्नं, श्लेष्मघ्नः -घ्नी -घ्नं.

ANTIPHONY, *s.* प्रतिगानं, परस्परगीतिः *f.*, प्रतिध्वनिः *f.*

ANTIPODES, *s.* भूमण्डलस्य विपरीतभागे वर्त्तिनः; अन्यतरस्मिन् भूगोलभागे वर्त्तिनः परस्परम् अभिमुखपादतला जनाः.

ANTIQUARIAN, *a.* प्राक्कालीनः -ना -नं, पूर्व्वकालीनः -ना -नं, प्राक्तनः -नी -नं.

ANTIQUARY, ANTIQUARIAN. *s.* प्राक्कालीनविषयेषु पण्डितः, पुरातनद्रव्यानुसन्धायी *m.* (न्).

ANTIQUE, *a.* (Ancient) पुराणः -णा or -णी -णं, पुरातनः -नी -नं, प्राक्तनः -नी -नं, पूर्व्वकालीनः -ना -नं, चिरन्तनः -नी -नं.—(Old-fashioned) अप्रचलः -ला -लं, अपरूपः -पा -पं.

ANTIQUE, *s.* प्राचीनद्रव्यं, प्राक्कालीनविषयः.

ANTIQUITY, *s.* (Old-times) प्राक्कालं, पूर्व्वकालं, गतकालं.—(The ancients) प्राचीनपुरुषाः *m. pl.*—(Ancientness) पुरातनत्वं, प्राचीनत्वं.

ANTISEPTIC, *a.* पूतिघ्नः -घ्नी -घ्नं, पूतिनिवारकः -का -कं, पूतिनाशकः -का -कं.

ANTISTES, *s.* प्रधानपुरोहितः, धर्म्माध्यक्षः.

ANTITHESIS, *s.* अर्थान्तरन्यासः, अर्थवैपरीत्यं, विकल्पः, प्रतिपक्षता, विरोधः.

ANTITYPE, *s.* प्रतिमूर्त्त्या प्रदर्शिता मूर्त्तिः *f.*, मूलमूर्त्तिः *f.*, वस्तु *n.*, आदर्शः.

ANTLER, *s.* मृगशृङ्गं, मृगशृङ्गशाखा, मृगविषाणं.

ANTLERED, *a.* शृङ्गी -ङ्गिणी -ङ्गि (न्), विषाणी -णिनी -णि (न्).

ANUS, गुदं, पायुः *m.*, मेढ्रः, अपानं.

ANVIL, *s.* सूर्म्मी *f.*, शूर्म्मिः *m.*, स्थूणा, लोहप्रतिमा.

ANXIETY, *s.* चिन्ता, चित्तोद्वेगः, औत्सुक्यं, मनोदुःखं, मनस्तापः, चित्तवेदना, आधिः *m.*, व्यग्रता, उद्वेगः -जनं, उत्तापः, चिन्ताभारः, मानसी व्यथा.

Anxious, *a.* (Solicitous) उद्विग्नः -ग्ना -ग्नं, उद्विग्नमनाः -नाः -नः (स्), चिन्तापरः -रा -रं, व्यग्रः -ग्रा -ग्रं, उत्सुकः -का -कं, विधुरः -रा -रं, समन्युः -न्युः -न्यु.—(Eagerly endeavouring) सयत्नः -त्ना -त्नं.—(Desirous of) ईप्सुः -प्सुः -प्सु, इच्छुः -च्छुः -च्छु; 'anxious to see,' दर्शनेप्सुः; 'anxious to do,' कर्त्तुकामः -मा -मं.—(To be anxious) उत्सुकाय् (nom. उत्सुकायते).

Anxiously, *adv.* औत्सुक्येन, उद्वेगेन, मनोदुःखेन, चिन्तया, सोद्वेगं, सयत्नं.

Any, *a.* कश्चित् *m.* काचित् *f.* किञ्चित् *n.*, को ऽपि *m.* कापि *f.* किमपि *n.*, कश्चन *m.* काचन *f.* किञ्चन *n.*; 'any thing,' किञ्चित्, किमपि; 'any where,' क्वचित्, क्वापि, कुत्रचित्, कुत्रापि; 'any longer,' पुनर्; 'any how,' कथञ्चन, कथञ्चित्, यथातथा; 'at any time,' कदाचित्, कर्हिचित्; 'any further,' दूरतरं; 'any one soever,' यः कश्चित्.

Aorta, *s.* हृत्पिण्डवामकोषनिर्गता रक्तप्रवाहका वृहन्नाडी.

Apace, *adv.* सत्वरं, शीघ्रं, क्षिप्रं, सहसा, द्रुतं, सवेगं.

Apart, *adv.* Often expressed by the prep. वि; पृथक्, विरलं, प्रविरलं, प्रगतः -ता -तं, उज्ज्ञुभ्नः -भ्ना -भ्नं; 'having the knees apart,' प्रगतजानुः -नुः -नु.—(Privately) एकान्ते, एकान्ततस् *ind.*, निभृतं, रहसि, विविक्ते, विजने.—(At a distance) दूरे, कियद्दूरे.—(Aside, to one's self) स्वगतं, विजने, जनान्तिकं.

Apartment, *s.* शाला, कोष्ठः, आवासः, आगारं, गृहं.—(The inner apartments) अन्तःपुरं, अन्तर्गृहं.

Apathetic, *a.* वीतरागः -गा -गं, निःसङ्गः -ङ्गा -ङ्गं, निःस्पृहः -हा -हं, निरीहः -हा -हं, निरपेक्षः -क्षा -क्षं.

Apathy, *s.* विरागः, वैराग्यं, निरीहता, जाड्यं, मान्द्यं.

Ape, *s.* वानरः, अपुच्छः कपिः *m.*, प्लवङ्गः.—(Imitator) अनुकारी *m.* (न्).

To ape, *v. a.* वानरवत् or कपिवत् अनुकृ (c. 8. -करोति -कर्त्तुं).

Apepsy, *s.* अजीर्णं, आमयावित्वं, तीक्ष्णाग्निः *m.*

Aperient, *a.* रेचकः -की -कं.—(An aperient medicine) रेचकः.

Aperture, *s.* छिद्रं, रन्ध्रं, द्वारं, पथः.—(Act of opening) व्यादानं.

Apetalous, *a.* दलहीनः -ना -नं, पुष्पपत्ररहितः -ता -तं, निष्पत्रः -त्रा -त्रं.

Apex, *s.* शिखा, शिखरं, अग्रं, चूडा, शिरः *n.* (स्).

Aphorism, *s.* सूत्रं, वचनं, तत्त्वं, उपदेशवाक्यं, आदेशः.

Aphrodisiac, *a.* (Exciting passion) वाजीकरः -रा -रं, कामाग्निदीपनः -ना -नं.

Apiary, *s.* करण्डः, छत्रकः, मधुमक्षिकारक्षणस्थानं, मधुकरस्थानं.

Apiece, *adv.* प्रत्येकं, एकैकशस् *ind.*, एकशस् *ind.*, एकतस् *ind.*, एकैकं, पृथक् पृथक्, विभागशस् *ind.*

Apish, *a.* कापेयः -यी -यं, कपिस्वभावः -वा -वं, वानरोपमः -मा -मं.—(Imitative) अनुकारशीलः -ला -लं.

Apishness, *s.* कापेयं, वानरता, अनुकारशीलता.

Apitpat, *adv.* पटपटा *ind.*

Apocalypse, *s.* प्रकाशितं भविष्यद्वाक्यं, प्रकाशनं, विवृतिः *f.*, स्पष्टीकरणं.

Apocrypha, *s.* धर्म्मग्रन्थानां मध्ये गणितः सन्दिग्धप्रमाणो ग्रन्थः.

Apocryphal, *a.* (Of uncertain authority) सन्दिग्धप्रमाणः -णा -णं, असिद्धप्रमाणः -णा -णं.

Apologetic, apologetical, *a.* व्यपदेशकः -का -कं, पक्षपाती -तिनी -ति (न्), प्रतिवादकः -का -कं, क्षामिकः -की -कं.

Apologist, *s.* (For another) पक्षपातकर्त्ता *m.* (र्तृ), परस्वार्थं वादी *m.* (न्), प्रतिवादी *m.* (न्), उत्तरवादी *m.*—(For one's self) व्यपदेष्टा *m.* (-ष्टृ), छलकारी, स्वदोषस्वीकारी *m.* (न्), प्रत्यवस्कन्दकारी *m.* (न्).

Apologise, *v. n.* (To state some plea) व्यपदिश् (c. 6. -दिशति -देष्टुं), छल or व्यपदेशं or प्रत्यवस्कन्दं कृ.—(To acknowledge one's fault) स्वदोषस्य स्वीकारं कृ.—(To apologise for another) पक्षपातं कृ, परस्वार्थं प्रतिवद् (c. 1. -वदति -वदितुं).

Apologue, *s.* उपकथा, हितोपदेशकं उपाख्यानं, नीतिवाक्यं.

Apology, *s.* व्यपदेशः, अपदेशः, उपदेशः, प्रतिवादः, उत्तरं, छल *n.* (न्), प्रत्यवस्कन्दः, स्वदोषस्वीकारः, छलकरणं.—(For another) पक्षपातः, परस्वार्थं प्रतिवादः.

Apophlegmatic, *a.* कफनाशनः -नी -नं, कफघ्नः -घ्नी -घ्नं, श्लेष्मघ्नः -घ्नी -घ्नं.

Apophthegm, *s.* सूत्रं, नीतिवाक्यं, वचनं, आदेशः.

Apoplectical, apoplectic, *a.* (Relating to apoplexy) अङ्गविकृतिविषयः -या -यं.—(Inclined to apoplexy) अङ्गविकृतिशीलः -ला -लं.

Apoplexy, *s.* अङ्गविकृतिः *f.*

Apostacy, *s.* स्वधर्म्मत्यागः, स्वधर्म्मच्युतिः *f.*, अवहारः, स्वधर्म्मभ्रंशः, भ्रष्टत्वं, स्वजातीयधर्म्मत्यागानन्तरं परधर्म्माश्रयः.

Apostate, *s.* स्वधर्म्मत्यागी *m.* (न्), स्वजातीयव्यवहारभ्रष्टः, आत्मधर्म्मच्युतः, अन्यशाखः, स्वजातीयधर्म्मं त्यक्त्वा परधर्म्माश्रितः.

To apostatize, *v. n.* स्वधर्म्मात् or स्वजातीयव्यवहाराद् भ्रंश् (c. 4. भ्रश्यति, c. 1. भ्रंशते भ्रंशितुं) or च्यु (c. 1. च्यवते च्योतुं), विच्यु; स्वजातीयधर्म्मं त्यक्त्वा परधर्म्मं आश्रि (c. 1. -श्रयति -श्रयितुं).

Aposteme, aposthume, *s.* व्रणः, विद्रधिः *m.*, शोफः, स्फोटः, पूयसम्पूर्णः स्फोटः.

Apostle, *s.* ईश्वरप्रेरितः, ईश्वरदूतः, ईश्वराज्ञावहः, प्रेरितः.

Apostleship, *s.* ईश्वरप्रेरितत्वं, ईश्वरदौत्यं, प्रेरितत्वं.

Apostolical, apostolic, *a.* (Enjoined by an apostle) ईश्वरप्रेरितेनादिष्टः -ष्टा -ष्टं.—(Relating to the Apostles) ईश्वरप्रेरितसम्बन्धी -न्धिनी -न्धि (न्).

Apostrophe, *s.* सम्बोधनं, वाक्यालङ्कारविशेषः.

To apostrophise, *v. a.* सम्बोधनं कृ, सम्बोधनेन आमन्त्र् (c. 10. -मन्त्रयते -यितुं).

Apostume, *s.* पूयसम्पूर्णः स्फोटः, विद्रधिः *m.*

Apothecary, *s.* विक्रयार्थं औषधपेषकः, भेषजविक्रेता *m.* (तृ), औषधविक्रेता *m.* (तृ), अगदङ्कारः.

Apothegm, *s.* *See* Apophthegm.

Apotheosis, *s.* देवत्वं, ब्रह्मत्वं, ब्रह्मनिर्वाणं, देवगणितत्वं.

To appal, *v. a.* भी in caus. (भाययति or भीषयति -यितुं), त्रस् in caus. (त्रासयति -यितुं), वित्रस्, सन्त्रस्; उद्विज् in caus. (-वेजयति -यितुं), व्याकुलीकृ.

Appalled, *p. p.* भयविप्लुतः -ता -तं, भयसंहृष्टरोमा -मा -म (न्), शङ्कितः -ता -तं, सन्त्रस्तः -स्ता -स्तं, व्याकुलीकृतः -ता -तं.

Apparatus, *s.* उपकरणं, सज्जा, यन्त्रं, सामग्र्यं, सामग्री *f.*—(Military apparatus) शस्त्रोपकरणं.

Apparel, *s.* वेशः, वस्त्रं, परिधानं, परिच्छदः, अम्बरं, आभरणं, संव्यानं.

To apparel, *v. a.* वस्त्र (nom. वस्त्रयति -यितुं), आच्छद् (c. 10. -छादयति -यितुं); वेष्ट् (c. 1. वेष्टते, वेष्टितुं), वस् in caus. (वासयति -यितुं), प्रवस्; प्रवृ (c. 5. -वृणोति, -वरितुं or -वरीतुं), संव्ये (c. 1. -व्ययति -व्यातुं).—(To apparel one's self) वस् (c. 2. वस्ते, वसितुं).

Apparelled, *p. p.* आच्छादितः -ता -तं, प्रच्छादितः -ता -तं, परिच्छन्नः -न्ना -न्नं, वस्त्रवेष्टितः -ता -तं, संवीतः -ता -तं.

Apparent, *a.* व्यक्तः -क्ता -क्तं, अभिव्यक्तः -क्ता -क्तं, प्रव्यक्तः -क्ता -क्तं, स्पष्टः -ष्टा -ष्टं, स्फुटः -टा -टं, प्रेक्षणीयः -या -यं, प्रेक्ष्यः -क्ष्या -क्ष्यं, प्रत्यक्षः -क्षा -क्षं.—(Not real) अवास्तवः -वी -वं; 'apparent praise,' 'not real,' व्याजस्तुतिः *f.*, मिथ्याप्रशंसा; 'heir-apparent,' युवराजः.—(To make apparent) प्रादुष्कृ, आविष्कृ, प्रत्यक्षीकृ, स्पष्टीकृ, प्रकटीकृ.

APPARENTLY, *adv.* प्रादुस् *ind.*, साक्षात् *ind.*, आविस्, प्रत्यक्षतस्, स्पष्टं.

APPARITION, *s.* (Appearance, form) आभासः, आभा, छाया, आकारः, आकृतिः *f.*, रूपं.—(Spectre, walking spirit) रात्रिचरः, प्रेतनरः, प्रेतः, वेतालः.

APPARITOR, *s.* यष्टिधरः, प्रेष्यजनः, राजदूतः.

APPEACHMENT, *s.* अभियोगः, अपवादः.

To APPEAL, *v. n.* परावर्त्तं प्रार्थ् (c. 10. -अर्थयते -यितुं); यत् कार्य्यं अवरप्राड्विवाकेन तीरितं or निर्णीतं तस्यापि पुनर्विचारम् उत्तमप्राड्विवाकसकाशात् प्रार्थ्.—(To call another as witness) साक्षिणं कृ, आह्वे (c. 1. -ह्वयति -ते -ह्वातुं).

APPEAL, *s.* परावर्त्तव्यवहारः, पुनराह्वानं, पुनर्विचारप्रार्थना, उत्तमप्राड्विवाकसाक्षाद् आह्वानं.—(The calling upon any one as witness or judge) आह्वानं.

To APPEAR, *v. n.* (To become visible) दृश् in pass. (दृश्यते), अभिदृश्, प्रतिदृश्; प्रभू (c. 1. -भवति -भवितुं), सम्भू, प्रकाश् (c. 1. -काशते -काशितुं), सम्प्रकाश्, सङ्काश्, उदि (c. 1. उदयति -यितुं), अभ्युदि, उच्चर् (c. 1. -चरति -चरितुं).—(Show one's self) आत्मानं दृश् in caus. (दर्शयति -यितुं), दर्शनं दा.—(To seem) प्रतिभा (c. 2. -भाति -भातुं), सम्प्रभा, निभा, आभा; लक्ष् in pass. (लक्ष्यते).—(To be evident) प्रकाश्, प्रादुर्भू (c. 1. -भवति -भवितुं), आविर्भू; प्रादुरस् (c. 2. -अस्ति); 'you appear dismayed,' विस्मित इव प्रतिभासि.

APPEARANCE, *s.* (Coming into sight) दर्शनं, सन्दर्शनं.—(Entry into a place or company) उपस्थितिः *f.*, प्रवेशनं.—(The thing seen) रूपं, आकृतिः *f.*, मूर्त्तिः *f.*, आकारः.—(Semblance, not reality) छाया, आभासः, आभा, अवस्तुता.—(Presence, mien) रूपं, अवस्था, भावः, आकारः.—(Probability) अनुमेयत्वं, अनुभवनीयत्वं.

To APPEASE, *v. a.* शम् in caus. (शमयति -यितुं), उपशम्, प्रशम्; सान्त्व् or शान्त्व् (c. 10. सान्त्वयति -यितुं), अभिशान्त्व्, परिशान्त्व्, उपसान्त्व्; तुष् in caus. (तोषयति -यितुं), परितुष्, सन्तुष्; प्रसद् in caus. (-सादयति -यितुं), अभिप्रसद्, सम्प्रसद्; सुस्थिरं -रां -रं कृ; परिमृश् (c. 6. -मृशति -म्रष्टुं), परामृश्, अनुनी (c. 1. -नयति -ते -नेतुं).—(To be appeased) शम् (c. 4. शाम्यति, शमितुं), उपशम्; प्रसद् (c. 1. -सीदति -सत्तुं).

APPEASED, *p. p.* शान्तः -न्ता -न्तं, शमितः -ता -तं, प्रशान्तः -न्ता -न्तं, आराधितः -ता -तं, अनुनीतः -ता -तं, प्रसन्नः -न्ना -न्नं, प्रसादितः -ता -तं.

APPEASING, *s.* शान्तिः *f.*, उपशान्तिः *f.*, प्रशान्तिः *f.*, आराधनं, प्रसादनं.

APPELLANT, *s.* उत्तमप्राड्विवाकसकाशात् परावर्त्तप्रार्थकः, परावर्त्तप्रार्थयिता *m.* (तृ), पुनराह्वानकर्त्ता *m.* (र्त्तृ), आह्वानकर्त्ता *m.* (र्त्तृ), आवेदकः.

APPELLATE, *s.* पुनराहूतः, उत्तमप्राड्विवाकसाक्षाद् आहूतः, प्रत्यर्थी *m.* (न्).

APPELLATION, *s.* नामधेयं, नाम *n.* (न्), आख्या, संज्ञा, अभिधानं, अभिधा, अभिख्या, आह्वा.

APPELLATIVE, *a.* अभिधायिकः -का -कं, अभिधानीयकः -का -कं.—(Common) सामान्यः -न्या -न्यं, साधारणः -णा -णं.

APPELLEE, *s.* आहूतः, अभियुक्तः, प्रत्यर्थी *m.* (न्).

To APPEND, *v. a.* अनुबन्ध् (c. 9. -बध्नाति -बन्द्धुं or caus. -बन्धयति -यितुं), आबन्ध्; उपाधा (c. 3. -दधाति -धत्ते -धातुं), आधा; अवलम्ब् in caus. (-लम्बयति -यितुं).

APPENDAGE, *s.* अनुबन्धः, सम्बन्धः, उपाहितं, शेषांशः, उपाहितभागः.

APPENDANT, *adj.* अनुबन्धी -न्धिनी -न्धि (न्), सम्बन्धी -न्धिनी -न्धि (न्), अवलम्बी -म्बिनी -म्बि (न्).

APPENDIX, *s.* परिशिष्टं, उपग्रन्थः, शेषग्रन्थः.

To APPERTAIN, *v. n.* (To belong to one's self) आत्मसात् or आत्माधीनः -ना -नं, or स्वाधीनः -ना -नं, or स्वकीयः -या -यं अस्.—(To belong, in general) सम्बन्ध् in pass. (-बध्यते). The sense of 'appertaining' may often be expressed by the root अस् or विद् with the gen. case; as, 'money appertains to me,' मम धनं विद्यते.

APPERTAINING, *p.* सम्बन्धी -न्धिनी -न्धि (न्), अनुबन्धी -न्धिनी -न्धि (न्).

APPERTENANCE, *s.* अनुबन्धः, सम्बन्धः, उपकरणं, सामग्री.

APPETENCY, *s.* कामः, लोभः, अभिलाषः, वाञ्छा, इच्छा.

APPETITE, *s.* (Desire) कामः, लोभः, रागः, रुचिः *f.*, अभिरुचिः *f.*, अतिवाञ्छा, अतिशयलोभः, अभिलाषः, इच्छा.—(Hunger) बुभुक्षा, क्षुधा, आहारादिवाञ्छा, भक्तच्छन्दः.—(The digestive faculty causing appetite) अग्निः *m.*, वह्निः *m.*, अग्निवृद्धिः *f.*—(One who has no appetite for food) अग्निरहितः.

APPETITIVE, *a.* कामुकः -का -कं, अभिलाषुकः -का -कं, इच्छुकः -का -कं.

To APPLAUD, *v. a.* प्रशंस् (c. 1. -शंसति -शंसितुं), अभिप्रशंस्; प्रतिनन्द् (c. 1. -नन्दति -नन्दितुं), प्रवादेन प्रशंस्, प्रशंसां कृ, श्लाघां कृ.—(By clapping the hands) करतालेन प्रशंस्.

APPLAUDER, *s.* प्रशंसकः, स्तावकः, श्लाघाकर्त्ता *m.* (र्त्तृ).

APPLAUSE, *s.* (Loudly expressed) प्रवादः, जयशब्दः, धन्यवादः, प्रशंसाशब्दः, साराविणं, भुजनिःस्वनः, शब्दोऽनुरागजः.—(Praise) श्लाघा, प्रशंसा, स्तुतिः *f.*

APPLAUSIVE, *a.* प्रशंसकः -का -कं, स्तुतिमयः -यी -यं, श्लाघान्वितः -ता -तं.

APPLE, *s.* (A kind of fruit) फलप्रभेदः.—(Pupil of the eye) नयनतारा, कनीनिका, चक्षुर्गोलकः.

APPLIANCE, *s.* (The means applied) उपायः, अभ्युपायः, उपकरणं, सामग्री.—(The act of applying) योगः, अर्पणं.

APPLICABILITY, *s.* योग्यता, प्रयोज्यत्वं, सामञ्जस्यं, साङ्गत्यं.

APPLICABLE, *a.* योग्यः -ग्या -ग्यं, प्रयोक्तव्यः -व्या -व्यं, प्रयोज्यः -ज्या -ज्यं, उपयोग्यः -ग्या -ग्यं, व्यवहरणीयः -या -यं, अर्पणीयः -या -यं, अर्प्यः -र्प्या -र्प्यं, संयोजनीयः -या -यं, व्यापी -पिनी -पि (न्), समञ्जसः -सा -सं.

APPLICATION, *s.* (Of one thing to another) योगः, अर्पणं, न्यसनं.—(Attention to) आसक्तिः *f.*, अनुष्ठानं, योगः, प्रवेशः, व्यसनं.—(Use) उपयोगः, प्रयोगः, प्रयोजनं.—(Application of mind, study) मनःप्रवेशः, अभिनिवेशः, प्रवेशः, अभ्यसनं, अभ्यासः, विद्याभ्यासः, अध्यवसायः, अभियुक्तता, मनोयोगः.—(Petition) याच्ञा, प्रार्थना, निवेदनपत्रं.

APPLIED, *p. p.* प्रयुक्तः -क्ता -क्तं, अर्पितः -ता -तं, न्यस्तः -स्ता -स्तं, निहितः -ता -तं, निवेशितः -ता -तं.

APPLIER, *s.* उपेता *m.* (तृ), प्रयोजकः.

To APPLY, *v. a.* (One thing on another) संयुज् (c. 10. -योजयति -यितुं), न्यस् (c. 4. -अस्यति, -असितुं), विन्यस्; ऋ in caus. (अर्पयति -यितुं), सङ्क्रम् in caus. (-गमयति -यितुं), प्रविश् in caus. (-वेशयति -यितुं), निविश्, संलग्नीकृ.—(To make use of) प्रयुज् (c. 7. -युनक्ति -युङ्क्ते -योक्तुं), उपयुज्.—(To attend to) आस्था (c. 1. -तिष्ठति -ते -स्थातुं), समास्था, अनुष्ठा.—(To have recourse to, solicit) प्रयाच् (c. 1. -याचति -याचितुं), अभियाच्, आश्रि (c. 1. -श्रयति -ते -श्रयितुं), प्रार्थ् (c. 10. -अर्थयति -ते -यितुं).—(To make effort, study) अभ्यस् (c. 4. -अस्यति -असितुं), यत् (c. 1. यतते, यतितुं), प्रयत्.

To APPLY, *v. n.* (Suit, fit) युज् in pass. (युज्यते), संयुज्, उपपद्

(c. 4. -पद्यते -पत्तुं), सङ्गतः -ता -तं भू.—(Have recourse as a petitioner) कार्य्यसिद्धिनिमित्ते अन्यम् आश्रि (c. 1. -श्रयति -ते -श्रयितुं), अर्थ् (c. 10. अर्थयते -यितुं), प्रार्थ्.

To APPOINT, *v. a.* निधा (c. 3. -दधाति -धातुं), स्था in caus. (स्थापयति -यितुं), अवस्था, प्रस्था; युज् (c. 10. योजयति -यितुं).—(To appoint over any office) अधिकृ (c. 8. -करोति -कुरुते -कर्त्तुं), प्रकृ; नियुज् (c. 10. -योजयति -यितुं, c. 7. -युनक्ति -योक्तुं), with acc. of the pers. and loc. of the thing; अभिषिच् (c. 6. -सिञ्चति -सेक्तुं), with two acc. or with acc. and loc.; समादिश् (c. 6. -दिशति -देष्टुं), व्यादिश्.—(To make an appointment) समयं कृ, समयाकृ.

APPOINTED, *p. p.* स्थापितः -ता -तं, प्रस्थापितः -ता -तं, नियोजितः -ता -तं, नियतः -ता -तं, विहितः -ता -तं, नियुक्तः -क्ता -क्तं, व्यवस्थितः -ता -तं.—(To any office) अधिकृतः -ता -तं, व्यापृतः -ता -तं, वावृत्तः -त्ता -त्तं.—(An appointed duty) नियोगः.—(An appointed time) कालावधिः *m.*—(Agreed upon) कृतसङ्केतः -ता -तं.—(As to time) कृतकालः -ला -लं, कृतावधिः -धिः -धि.

APPOINTMENT, *s.* नियोगः, -जनं, नियुक्तिः *f.*, प्रस्थापनं, निरूपणं, कल्पनं.—(Engagement) समयः, प्रज्ञप्तिः *f.*—(Breaking an appointment) समयभेदः, समयव्यभिचारः.—(Stipulation) समयः, नियमः, सङ्केतः.—(Order) आज्ञा.—(Decree) नियमः, विधिः *m.*—(Office) अधिकारः, पदं.—(Equipment, furniture) सज्जा, उपकरणं, सामग्री.—(Allowance) वर्त्तनं, निरूपितमूल्यं.—(Assignation) अभिसारः.

To APPORTION, *v. n.* विभज् (c. 1. -भजति -ते -भक्तुं), प्रविभज्, संविभज्; अंश् (c. 10. अंशयति -यितुं), व्यंश्; विन्यस् (c. 4. -अस्यति -असितुं), परिकॢप् (c. 10. -कल्पयति -यितुं), विधा (c. 3. -दधाति -धातुं).

APPORTIONMENT, *s.* विभागः, संविभागः, अंशनं, परिकल्पनं, विन्यासः.

APPOSITE, *a.* योग्यः -ग्या -ग्यं, युक्तः -क्ता -क्तं, उपयुक्तः -क्ता -क्तं, सङ्गतः -ता -तं, हृदयङ्गमः -मा -मं, यथार्थः -र्था -र्थं, यथार्हः -र्हा -र्हं.

APPOSITELY, *adv.* स्थाने, यथार्हतस् *ind.*, यथार्थं, सङ्गतप्रकारेण.

To APPRAISE, *v. a.* (Set a price on) अर्घं संख्या in caus. (-ख्यापयति -यितुं), मूल्यं निरूप् (c. 10. -रूपयति -यितुं) or व्यवसो, (c. 4. -स्यति -सातुं), मूल्यनिर्णयं कृ, मूल्यं निश्चितं कृ.

APPRAISER, *s.* अर्घसंख्यापकः, मूल्यनिरूपकः, मूल्यविज्ञापकः.

APPRAISING, *s.* अर्घसंख्यापनं, मूल्यनिरूपणं, मूल्यविज्ञापनं.

To APPRECIATE, *v. a.* मूल्यं or अर्घं or गुणागुणं or भद्राभद्रतां or सारासारं विज्ञा (c. 9. -जानाति -नीते -ज्ञातुं), or निरूप् (c. 10. -रूपयति -यितुं), or निश्चितं कृ or विविच् (c. 7. -विनक्ति -वेक्तुं); 'one who knows how to appreciate,' गुणज्ञः, गुणागुणज्ञः, गुणग्राही *m.* (न्), मर्म्मज्ञः.

APPRECIATION, *s.* मूल्यविज्ञानं, गुणागुणज्ञानं, भद्राभद्रनिरूपणं, दोषादोषबोधः, विज्ञानं.

To APPREHEND, *v. a.* (Lay hold on) ग्रह् (c. 9. गृह्णाति -ह्णीते ग्रहीतुं), परिग्रह्, सङ्ग्रह्; परामृश् (c. 6. -मृशति -म्रष्टुं), धृ (c. 1. धरति धर्त्तुं).—(Seize in order for trial) आसिध् (c. 1. -सेधति -सेद्धुं); ग्रह्, धृ, आक्रम् (c. 1. -क्रामति -क्रमति -क्रमितुं).—(By the mind) उपलभ् (c. 1. -लभते -लब्धुं), ऊह् (c. 1. ऊहते ऊहितुं); अनुमा (c. 2. -माति -मातुं), अवगम् (c. 1. -गच्छति -गन्तुं), अवबुध् (c. 4. -बुध्यते -बोद्धुं).—(To fear) शङ्क् (c. 1. शङ्कते शङ्कितुं) आशङ्क्; भी (c. 3. बिभेति भेतुं).

APPREHENDED, *p. p.* (Understood) उपलब्धः -ब्धा -ब्धं, अवगतः -ता -तं.—(Arrested) आसिद्धः -द्धा -द्धं.

APPREHENSIBLE, ग्राह्यः -ह्या -ह्यं, धीगम्यः -म्या -म्यं, उपलभ्यः -भ्या -भ्यं.

APPREHENSION, *s.* (Fear) भयं, शङ्का, आशङ्का, सन्देहः.—(Opinion) मतिः *f.*, बुद्धिः *f.*, बोधः.—(Seizure) ग्रहणं, आक्रमणं, धरणं.—(Arrest) आसेधः.—(Conception) उपलब्धिः *f.*, मेधा, अनुभवः, अनुमानं, अवगमः, अनुबोधः, उपलम्भः.

APPREHENSIVE, *a.* शङ्कितः -ता -तं, शङ्की -ङ्किनी -ङ्कि (न्), शङ्कान्वितः -ता -तं, कृतभयः -या -यं.

APPRENTICE, *s.* शिल्पविद्याशिष्यः, शिष्यः, निरूपितकालपर्य्यन्तं शिल्पविद्याशिक्षार्थे नियमपत्रेण स्थापितः or धृतः सेवकः.

To APPRENTICE, *v. a.* आविहितकालात् शिल्पविद्याशिक्षार्थे नियमपत्रेण शिष्यं or सेवकं स्था in caus. (स्थापयति -यितुं).

APPRENTICESHIP, *s.* शिल्पविद्याशिक्षावधिः *m.*, शिल्पशिक्षासमयः, सेवाकालः, दास्यकालः.

To APPRIZE, *v. a.* ज्ञा in caus. (ज्ञापयति -यितुं), विज्ञा; विद् in caus. (वेदयति -यितुं), निविद्, समाविद्; बुध् in caus. (बोधयति -यितुं), सूच् (c. 10. सूचयति -यितुं).

APPRIZED, *p. p.* विज्ञापितः -ता -तं, अनुज्ञापितः -ता -तं, विज्ञप्तः -प्ता -प्तं, सन्दिष्टः -ष्टा -ष्टं, प्रत्यादिष्टः -ष्टा -ष्टं, बोधितः -ता -तं.

To APPROACH, *v. n.* (Draw near to) अधिगम् (c. 1. -गच्छति -गन्तुं), आगम्, अभिगम्, अभ्यागम्, उपागम्, उपगम्, समुपगम्; या (c. 2. याति यातुं), अभिया, आया, उपाया, प्रत्याया, समाया, उपया, समुपया; उपस्था (c. 1. -तिष्ठति -ते -स्थातुं), ऋ (c. 1. ऋच्छति अर्त्तुं), अभ्यृ; अभिवृत् (c. 1. -वर्त्तते -वर्त्तितुं), उपावृत्, प्रतिवृत्, उपवृत्; समभ्यागा used only in the 3d pret.; as, 'he approached,' समभ्यागात्. इ, *i. e.* इ with आ (c. 2. एति, एतुं), अभ्ये, उपे, अभी (अभ्येति); उपसृप् (c. 1. -सर्पति -सर्प्तुं), समुपसृप्; आक्रम् (c. 1. -क्रामति -क्रमितुं), उपक्रम्; आव्रज् (c. 1. -व्रजति -व्रजितुं), प्रतिव्रज्, अभिपद् (c. 4. -पद्यते -पत्तुं), समापद्, समुपपद्, प्रतिपद्; अंह् (c. 1. अंहते अंहितुं).

To APPROACH, *v. a.* उपस्था in caus. (-स्थापयति -यितुं), समीपं स्था in caus.; समीपं धा (c. 3. -दधाति -धत्ते -धातुं), निकटे धा; सङ्गम् in caus. (-गमयति -यितुं).

APPROACH, *s.* आगमः, अभिगमनं, आगमनं, उपगमः, उपस्थितिः *f.*, उपसन्नता.

APPROACHABLE, *a.* आगम्यः -म्या -म्यं, उपगम्यः -म्या -म्यं, उपसार्य्यः -र्य्या -र्य्यं.

APPROACHED, *p. p.* अभिगतः -ता -तं, उपगतः -ता -तं, उपस्थितः -ता -तं, अभ्यागतः -ता -तं, प्रत्युपस्थितः -ता -तं.

APPROACHING, *a.* (Near at hand) उपस्थितः -ता -तं, समुपस्थितः -ता -तं, आसन्नः -न्ना -न्नं.

APPROBATION, *s.* सम्मतिः *f.* or -तं, अनुमतिः *f.* or -तं, प्रशंसा, प्रसादः, मनःसन्तोषः, ग्रहणं.

To APPROPRIATE, *v. a.* (To consign to some particular use) प्रयुज् (c. 7. -युनक्ति -युंक्ते -योक्तुं, caus. -योजयति -यितुं), उपयुज्, विनियुज्.—(To claim to one's self by an exclusive right) स्वीकृ, स्वीयमिति or ममेति वद् (c. 1. वदति वदितुं), स्वकीयं -यां -यं or आत्मीयं -यां -यं or स्वाधीनं -नां -नं or आत्माधीनं -नां -नं or आत्मसात् कृ, स्वस्वत्वं बुध् in caus. (बोधयति -यितुं), or ज्ञा in caus. (ज्ञापयति -यितुं.)

APPROPRIATE, *a.* (Suited to the occasion) प्रस्तावसदृशः -शी -शं.—(Belonging peculiarly) आत्मनीनः -ना -नं, स्वकीयः -या -यं, सम्बन्धी -न्धिनी -न्धि (न्), सम्बन्धकः -का -कं, विशेषकः -का -कं, जनीनः -ना -नं.—(Suitable) युक्तः -क्ता -क्तं, योग्यः -ग्या -ग्यं, सङ्गतः -ता -तं, उपयोगी -गिनी -गि (न्).

APPROPRIATED, *p. p.* (Made one's own) आत्मसात्कृतः -ता -तं.

APPROPRIATELY, *adv.* युक्तं, यथायोग्यं, यथोचितं, यथातथा, स्थाने.

Appropriateness, *s.* (Fitness of application) युक्तता, योग्यत्वं, औचित्यं, उपयुक्तता, सामञ्जस्यं, सङ्गतता.

Appropriation, *s.* (The application of something to a particular purpose) उपयोगः, प्रयोगः, विनियोगः.—(Claiming any thing as peculiar) आत्मग्रहणं, स्वत्वबोधनं, आत्मसात्करणं.

Approval, *s.* अनुमतिः *f.*, सम्मतिः *f.*, अनुमतं, सम्मतं, प्रशंसा.

To approve, *v. a.* अनुमन् (c. 4. -मन्यते -मन्तुं), सम्मन्; प्रशंस् (c. 1. -शंसति -शंसितुं), रुच्, in caus. (रोचयति -यितुं), अनुरुच्; 'that is approved by me,' तन् मया प्रशस्यते or तन् मह्यं रोचते. प्रतिनन्द् (c. 1. -नन्दति -नन्दितुं), अनुरुध् (c. 4. -रुध्यते -रोद्धुं).—(To prove, show) प्रमाणीकृ, प्रमाण् (nom. प्रमाणयति -यितुं), विभू in caus. (-भावयति -यितुं).

Approved, *p. p.* सम्मतः -ता -तं, अभिमतः -ता -तं, मतः -ता -तं, यथाभिमतः -ता -तं, प्रशस्तः -स्ता -स्तं, शिष्टः -ष्टा -ष्टं.—(Tried) परीक्षितः -ता -तं.—(Of tried probity) उपधाशुचिः -चिः -चि.

To approximate, *v. n.* उपस्था (c. 1. -तिष्ठति -ते -स्थातुं), समीपं or निकटं वृत् (c. 1. वर्त्तते वर्त्तितुं), or स्था, उपागम् (c. 1. -गच्छति -गन्तुं), उपगम्, समुपगम्, अभिगम्.—(To be like) तुल्यः -ल्या -ल्यं or सदृशः -शी -शं अस्.

To approximate, *v. a.* नेद् (nom. नेदयति -यितुं), उपस्था in caus. (-स्थापयति -यितुं), समीपं स्था in caus., उपनी (c. 1. -नयति -नेतुं), सङ्क्रम् in caus. (-गमयति -यितुं).

Approximate, *a.* समीपः -पा -पं, आसन्नः -न्ना -न्नं, सन्निकृष्टः -ष्टा -ष्टं, उपस्थायी -यिनी -यि (न्).

Approximated, *p. p.* उपस्थापितः -ता -तं, उपनीतः -ता -तं, उपनतः -ता -तं, उपसन्नः -न्ना -न्नं, कृतसन्निधानः -ना -नं.

Approximation, *s.* (Approach) उपगमः, समुपगमः, समीपगमनं, संहतता -त्वं, उपस्थितिः *f.*, उपस्थानं, समुपस्था.—(Nearness) नैकट्यं, सामीप्यं, सान्निध्यं, सन्निधानं.

Appulse, *s.* आघातः, आघातनं, प्रतिहननं, प्रतिघातः.

Appurtenance, *s.* *See* Appertenance.

Apricot, *s.* फलविशेषः.

April, *s.* चैत्रः, चैत्रिकः, मधुः, वैशाखः, माधवः, राधः.

Apron, *s.* मलनिवारणार्थं स्त्रीभिर् भृतम् आच्छादनं.

Apropros, *adv.* स्थाने, यथायोग्यं, यथावसरं, यथावकाशं.

Apsis, *s.* (In astronomy) मन्दोच्चः.

Apt, *a.* (Fit) उपयुक्तः -क्ता -क्तं, योग्यः -ग्या -ग्यं, युक्तः -क्ता -क्तं, आप्तः प्ता -प्तं.—(Having a tendency to) expressed by शीलः in composition; as, 'disposed to piety,' धर्म्मशीलः -ला -लं, or by the affix आलु; as, 'apt to sleep,' शयालुः -लुः -लु, or by the desiderative adjective; as, 'apt to do,' चिकीर्षुः -र्षुः -र्षु; 'apt to fall,' पिपतिषुः -षुः -षु.—(Skilful) कुशलः -ला -लं, दक्षः -क्षा -क्षं, पटुः -टुः -ट्वी -टु, अभिज्ञः -ज्ञा -ज्ञं.—(Ready, quick) त्वरितः -ता -तं, उद्युक्तः -क्ता -क्तं.

Aptitude, *s.* (Fitness) योग्यता, पात्रता or -त्वं, उपयोगिता, आप्तिः *f.*—(Tendency) शीलत्वं, -ता, अभिप्रायः, आशयः.—(Disposition) शीलः, स्वभावः, भावः, रीतिः *f.*

Aptly, *adv.* यथायोग्यं, योगतस् *ind.*, स्थाने.—(Skilfully) दाक्ष्येण, चातुर्य्येण, सपाटवं.

Aptness. *s.* (Fitness) योग्यता.—(Skill) कुशलता, पाटवं, विदग्धता, चातुर्य्यं.—(Ability) शक्तिः *f.*, सामर्थ्यं.

Aquatic, *a.* (Inhabiting the water) जलेचरः -रा -रं, जलजः -जा -जं, वारिजः -जा -जं, वारिचरः -रा -रं, अम्बुचरः -रा -रं, अम्बुजः -जा -जं, आम्भसिकः -की -कं, जलोद्भवः -वा -वं, जलभूः -भूः -भु.—(Growing in the water) अम्भोरुहः, जलरुहः.—(Watery) औदकः -की -कं, आप्यः -प्या -प्यं; 'an aquatic animal,' जलजन्तुः *m.*

Aqueduct, *s.* जलमार्गः, जलपथः, जलनिर्गमः, जलप्रणाली.

Aqueous, *a.* अम्मयः -यी -यं, सजलः -ला -लं, जलसः -सा -सं, अनूपः -पा -पं.

Aqueousness, *s.* सजलता, औदकत्वं, अनूपता,

Aquiline, *a.* (Resembling an eagle) उत्क्रोशरूपः -पा -पं, गृध्राकारः -रा -रं.—(Hooked) वक्रः -क्रा -क्रं, कुञ्चितः -ता -तं, वृजिनः -ना -नं; 'having an aquiline nose,' प्रलम्बघोणः.

Arabia, *s.* यवनः, यवनदेशः.

Arabian, *a.* यवनसम्बन्धी -न्धिनी -न्धि (न्), यवनदेशीयः -या -यं; 'an Arabian,' यवनदेशजः.

Arable, *a.* कृषियोग्यः -ग्या -ग्यं, कर्षणीयः -या -यं, फालकृष्टः -ष्टा -ष्टं.

Aration, *s.* कृषिः *f.*, कार्षिः *f.*, कर्षणं, हलहतिः *f.*

Arbiter, *s.* प्रमाणपुरुषः, मध्यस्थः, निर्णेता *m.* (तृ), विचारकर्त्ता *m.* (र्त्तृ).

Arbitrable, *a.* निर्णेयः -या -यं, विचारणीयः -या -यं.

Arbitrarily, *adv.* स्वेच्छया, स्वेच्छातस् *ind.*, स्वकामतस् *ind.*

Arbitrary, *a.* (Following the will) कामकारी -रिणी -रि (न्), यथाकामी -मिनी -मि (न्), स्वतन्त्रः -न्त्रा -न्त्रं, स्वच्छन्दः -न्दा -न्दं, स्वाधीनः -ना -नं, अनायत्तः -त्ता -त्तं, स्वैरवृत्तः -त्ता -त्तं.—(Capricious) चपलः -ला -लं.—(Tyrannical) क्रूरचरितः -ता -तं.—(Depending on no rule) अविहितः -ता -तं.

To arbitrate, *v. n.*, *v. a.* विचर् in caus. (-चारयति -यितुं), निर्णी (c. 1. -नयति -ते -नेतुं), निश्चि (c. 5. -चिनोति -चेतुं), तीर् (c. 10. तीरयति -यितुं), निश्चयं or विचारं or निर्णयं or परिच्छेदं कृ.

Arbitrated, *p. p.* निर्णीतः -ता -तं, तीरितः -ता -तं, निश्चितः -ता -तं, कृतनिश्चयः -या -यं.

Arbitration, *s.* (Determination) निर्णयः, विचारः, -रणं, निश्चयः, परिच्छेदः.—(Mediation) माध्यस्थ्यं.

Arbitrator, *s.* प्रमाणपुरुषः, स्थेयः, मध्यस्थः, निर्णेता *m.* (तृ), निश्चायकः, विचारकः.

Arborous, *a.* वार्क्षः -र्क्षी -र्क्षं, वार्क्ष्यः -र्क्ष्यी -र्क्ष्यं, वृक्षसम्बन्धी -न्धिनी -न्धि (न्).

Arbour, *s.* लतागृहं, कुञ्जः, निकुञ्जः, पर्णशाला, मण्डपः -पं, कुडुङ्गकः, छत्वरः.

Arc, *s.* (Segment of a circle) खण्डमण्डलं, वृत्तखण्डं, गोलखण्डं.—(Arched gateway) तोरणः.

Arcade, *s.* (Garden-walk) वृक्षैर् आच्छादित उद्यानपथः.—(A street arched over) इष्टकानिर्म्मिततोरणाकारपटला वीथिः, or धनुराकारेण पटलेन आवृता वीथिः.

Arch, *s.* (Part of a circle) खण्डमण्डलं, वृत्तखण्डं, गोलखण्डं.—(Arched gateway) तोरणः -णं.—(The arched roof of a house) खोडकशीर्षं.—(Vault of heaven) खगोलः, नभोमण्डलं.

Arch, *a.* (Sly, waggish) क्रीडाशीलः -ला -लं, रसिकः -का -कं, लोलापाङ्गः -ङ्गा -ङ्गं, विदग्धः -ग्धा -ग्धं.—(Chief) प्रधानः -ना -नं, मुख्यः -ख्या -ख्यं, उत्तमः -मा -मं, श्रेष्ठः -ष्ठा -ष्ठं.

To arch, *v. a.* (To make in the form of an arch) मण्डलीकृ, गोलीकृ तोरणरूपेण निर्मा (c. 2. -माति, c. 4. -मायते -मातुं) or कृ in caus. (कारयति -यितुं), तोरणाकारपटलेन आच्छद् (c. 10. -छादयति -यितुं).—(To build an arch) तोरणं निर्मा.

Archangel, *s.* ईश्वरदूतानां मध्ये मुख्यदूतः or प्रधानदूतः, ईश्वरदूताधिष्ठाता *m.* (तृ).

ARCHBISHOP, *s.* धर्म्माध्यक्षाणां मध्ये प्रधानो or मुख्यो धर्म्माध्यक्षः.

ARCHDEACON, *s.* (The bishop's vicegerent) धर्म्माध्यक्षसहायः, धर्म्माध्यक्षोपकारकः.

ARCHAIOLOGY or ARCHÆOLOGY, *s.* प्राक्कालीनव्यवहारविषयं वाक्यं, पुरातनशास्त्रं.

ARCHED, *p. p.* मण्डलीकृतः -ता -तं, गोलीकृतः -ता -तं, तोरणाकारः -रा -रं, कुञ्चितः -ता -तं.

ARCHER, *s.* धनुर्धरः, धन्वी *m.* (न्), धन्वा *m.* (न्), धनुष्मान् *m.* (-त्), धानुष्कः, धनुर्धारी *m.* (न्), इष्वासः, इषुधरः, काण्डीरः, निषङ्गी *m.*, अस्त्री *m.*

ARCHERY, *s.* धनुर्विद्या, शराभ्यासः, उपासनं, शराघातः, बाणमोक्षणं.—(Skilled in) कृतहस्तः, सुप्रयोगविशिखः, कृतपुङ्खः.

ARCHETYPE, *s.* मूलं, मूलमूर्त्तिः *f.*, आदर्शः, सूक्ष्मशरीरं.

ARCHITECT, *s.* स्थपतिः *m.*, गृहादिनिर्म्माणविद्याज्ञः, गृहनिर्म्माणाध्यक्षः, निर्म्माता *m.* (तृ).

ARCHITECTURAL, *a.* निर्म्माणविद्यासम्बन्धी -न्धिनी -न्धि (न्).

ARCHITECTURE, *s.* निर्म्माणविद्या, निर्म्माणशिल्पं, गृहादिनिर्म्माणशिल्पं.

ARCHITRAVE, *s.* गृहस्य यो भागः स्तम्भाग्रे अवलम्बते or निवेश्यते.

ARCHIVES, *s.* प्राक्कालीनग्रन्थरक्षागारं.—(Ancient records) इतिहासः, पुरावृत्तं.

ARCHNESS, *s.* विदग्धता, वैदग्ध्यं, रसित्वं.

ARCHWISE, *adv.* तोरणरूपेण, अर्द्धमण्डलाकारेण, तोरणवत्; धनुराकारेण.

ARCTIC, *a.* उत्तरः -रा -रं, उदीचीनः -ना -नं, उत्तरकेन्द्रीयः -या -यं, चित्रशिखण्ड्यधःस्थितो भूगोलभागः.

ARDENCY, *s.* उत्तापः, उत्साहः, उग्रता, व्यग्रता, कौतूहलं, उत्सुकता.

ARDENT, *a.* (Hot) उत्तप्तः -प्ता -प्तं, प्रचण्डः -ण्डा -ण्डं.—(Eager) कुतूहली -लिनी -लि (न्), उत्सुकः -का -कं, अतीच्छः -च्छा -च्छं, व्यग्रः -ग्रा -ग्रं, उत्साही -हिनी -हि (न्).—(Affectionate) अनुरागी -गिणी -गि (न्).

ARDENTLY, *adv.* उत्तापेन, कौतूहलेन, औत्सुक्येन, सानुरागं.

ARDOUR, *s.* उत्तापः, आसक्तिः *f.*, उग्रता, व्यग्रता, कौतूहलं, औत्सुक्यं, उत्साहः.—(Of affection) अनुरागः.

ARDUOUS, *a.* (Lofty) उच्चः -च्चा -च्चं, प्रांशुः -शुः -शु, आरोहणदुर्गम्यः -म्या -म्यं.—(Difficult) दुष्करः -रा -रं, सुदुष्करः -रा -रं, अतिदुष्करः -रा -रं, कठिनः -ना -नं, दुर्गम्यः -म्या -म्यं, दुःसाध्यः -ध्या -ध्यं, दुस्तरः -रा -रं.

ARDUOUSNESS, *s.* उच्चता, उत्तुङ्गता.—(Difficulty) कठिनता, काठिन्यं.

AREA, *s.* अङ्गणं, प्राङ्गणं, अभ्यन्तरस्थानं.

ARENA, *s.* रङ्गः, रङ्गभूमिः *f.*, मल्लभूः, अक्षवाटः.

ARGENT, *a.* रूप्यः -प्या -प्यं, रौप्यः -प्यी -प्यं, राजतः -ती -तं.

ARGILLOUS, *a.* मृण्मयः -यी -यं, मार्त्तिकः -की -कं, चिक्कणमृत्तिकामयः -यी -यं.

To ARGUE, *v. n.* (To reason) विचर् in caus. (-चारयति -यितुं), तर्क् (c. 10. तर्कयति -यितुं), वितर्क्, विवेचनं कृ.—(To dispute) विवद् (c. 1. -वदते -वदितुं), वादानुवादं or उत्तरप्रत्युत्तरं कृ.

To ARGUE, *v. a.* (To prove by argument) प्रमाण्, (nom. प्रमाणयति -यितुं), प्रमाणीकृ, प्रमाणेन or तर्केण or विचारेण सिद्धीकृ; सूच् (c. 10. सूचयति -यितुं).—(To charge with, as a crime) दोषारोपं कृ, अपवद् (c. 1. -वदति -वदितुं), अधिक्षिप् (c. 6. -क्षिपति -क्षेप्तुं).

ARGUER, *s.* तर्की *m.* (न्), विवादी *m.* (न्), विचारकः, प्रतिवादी *m.* (न्), न्यायी *m.* (न्).

ARGUMENT, *s.* (A reason stated) पक्षः, प्रमाणं, हेतुः *m.*, कारणं, वितर्कः, न्यायः; 'a false argument,' पक्षाभासः; 'a different side of the argument,' पक्षान्तरं.—(Controversy) वादानुवादः, वादयुद्धं, वाक्कलहं, विचारः, वितर्कः, विवादः, वितण्डा.—(The subject of any work) विषयः.—(Table of contents) अनुक्रमणिका, निर्घण्टः.

ARGUMENTATION, *s.* वितर्कणं, विचारणं, न्यायः.

ARGUMENTATIVE, *a.* (Consisting of argument) तार्किकः -की -कं, वितर्की -र्किणी -र्कि (न्), विवादी -दिनी -दि (न्), न्यायी -यिनी -यि (न्), विचारी -रिणी -रि (न्).—(Disposed to controversy) विवादशीलः -ला -लं, विवादार्थी -र्थिनी -र्थि (न्), विवादप्रियः -या -यं.

ARGUMENTATIVELY, *adv.* सवितर्कं, वादानुवादपूर्व्वकं, वितर्कपूर्व्वकं, न्यायवत्.

ARID, *a.* शुष्कः -ष्का -ष्कं, शोषितः -ता -तं, परिशुष्कः -ष्का -ष्कं; 'arid soil,' मरुः *m.*, मरुस्थली, धन्वा *m.* (न्).

ARIDITY, *s.* शुष्कता, -त्वं, शोषः, शोषणं, परिशोषः.

ARIGHT, *adv.* युक्तं, ऋतं, यथातथं, यथोचितं, यथायोग्यं, सम्यक्, यथार्हं.

To ARISE, *v. n.* (To stand up) उत्था for उत्स्था (c. 1. -तिष्ठति -ते -थातुं).—(To have origin) उत्पद् (c. 4. -पद्यते -पत्तुं), समुत्पद्; उच्चर् (c. 1. -चरति -चरितुं), उदि (c. 1. -अयति -एतुं), अभ्युदि, समुदि; प्रभू (c. 1. -भवति -भवितुं), सम्भू, आविर्भू, प्रादुर्भू; प्रवृत् (c. 1. -वर्त्तते -वर्त्तितुं), प्रसृ (c. 1. -सरति -सर्त्तुं), उद्भा (c. 2. -भाति -भातुं), निर्भा; आत्मानं दृश् in caus. (दर्शयति -यितुं), जन् (c. 4. जायते जनितुं), अभिजन्, उपजन्, सञ्जन्.—(From death) प्रतिसञ्जन्, समुत्था.

ARISEN, *p. p.* उत्थितः -ता -तं, सञ्जातः -ता -तं, जातः -ता -तं, जनितः -ता -तं, उत्पन्नः -न्ना -न्नं, समुत्पन्नः -न्ना -न्नं, विनिःसृतः -ता -तं, जन्यः -न्या -न्यं.

ARISTOCRACY, *s.* (A form of government) कुलीनजनाधिष्ठितं राज्यं, कुलीनवर्गप्रमुखं राज्यं, कुलीनवर्गप्रभुत्वं.—(The persons of whom it is composed) कुलीनजनाः, कुलीनवर्गः.

ARISTOCRATICAL, *a.* कुलीनः -ना -नं, कुलीनकः -का -कं, कौलेयः -यी -यं, कुलीनवर्गयोग्यः -ग्या -ग्यं, उत्कृष्टः -ष्टा -ष्टं.

ARISTOCRATICALLY, *adv.* कुलीनजनवत्, राजन्यवत्, कुलीनकप्रकारेण.

ARITHMETIC, *s.* गणनाविद्या, गणितं, पाटीगणितं, अङ्कविद्या, परिपाटिः *f.* -टी, परिकर्म्म *n.* (न्); 'the eight rules of arithmetic,' परिकर्म्माष्टकं.

ARITHMETICAL, *a.* गणनाविद्यानुरूपः -पा -पं, अङ्कविद्यानुसारी -रिणी -रि (न्).

ARITHMETICIAN, *s.* गणनाविद्याज्ञः, गणनाशास्त्रपण्डितः, अङ्कविद्याज्ञः, गणकः.

ARK, *s.* (A vessel, ship) नौः, नौका, पोतः, तरणी, वृहन्नौका.—(A chest) आधारः, कोषः, पेटिका, पेटः -टा -टी.

ARM, *s.* (Of the body) बाहुः *m. f.*, भुजः or -जा *f.*, दोषा *f.*, दोः *m.* (-स्), प्रवेष्टः.—(Of a tree) शाखा, उपशाखा.—(Of the sea) समुद्रवङ्कः.—(Of a river) वक्रं, वङ्कः, नदीवङ्कः, नदीवक्रं, पुटभेदः.—(Power, might) बलं, शक्तिः *f.*; 'a dominion acquired by one's own arm,' स्वभुजोपार्ज्जितं राज्यं.—(The upper arm) प्रगण्डः.

To ARM, *v. a.* सन्नह् (c. 4. -नह्यति -नद्धुं), सज्जीकृ, अस्त्रैः or शस्त्रैः सज्जीकृ, or युज् in caus. (योजयति -यितुं), or समायुज्.—(To arm one's self, put on one's arms) नह् (c. 4. नह्यते नद्धुं), सन्नह्.—(To put on armour) वर्म्म् (nom. वर्म्मयति -यितुं or संवर्म्मयति).

ARMADA, *s.* वृहन्नौकासमूहः, समुद्रयुद्धाय सज्जीकृतो वृहन्नौकासमूहः.

ARMADILLO, *s.* घुणः, कवचाकारचर्म्मधारी विलवासी क्षुद्रजन्तुः.

ARMAMENT, *s.* सैनिकः, युद्धाय सज्जीकृतं बलं, योद्धृसज्जनं.

ARMED, *p. p.* सज्जः -ज्जा -ज्जं, वर्म्मितः -ता -तं, सन्नद्धः -द्धा -द्धं, अभिसन्नद्धः -द्धा -द्धं, सायुधः -धा -धं, कृतास्त्रः -स्त्रा -स्त्रं, शस्त्री -स्त्रिणी -स्त्रि (न्).—(Having a weapon in the hand) शस्त्रपाणिः -णिः -णि.

ARM-HOLE, *s.* कक्षः, बाहुमूलं, भुजकोटरः, कक्षस्थानं, दोर्मूलं.

ARMISTICE, *s.* किञ्चित्कालपर्य्यन्तं युद्धनिवर्त्तनं, सन्धिः *m.*, क्षमा.

ARMLESS, *a.* (Without an arm) अभुजः -जा -जं.—(Without weapons) अस्त्रहीनः -ना -नं, अशस्त्रः -स्त्रा -स्त्रं.

ARMLET. *s.* (Bracelet) वलयः or यं, केयूरं, अङ्गदं.—(A little arm) क्षुद्रबाहुः *m.*, उपशाखा.

ARMORIAL, *a.* कावचिकः -की -कं, आयुधिकः -का -कं, आयुधीयः -या -यं.—(Belonging to the escutcheon of a family) कुलचिह्नसम्बन्धी -न्धिनी -न्धि (न्).

ARMORY, *s.* आयुधागारं, शस्त्रागारं, अस्त्रागारः.—(A collection of arms) शस्त्रसंहतिः *f.*, शस्त्रसमूहं.

ARMOUR, *s.* वर्म्म *n.* (न्), लौहवर्म्म *n.* (न्), तनुत्रं, तनुत्राणं, कवचः or -चं, वारवाणः, कञ्चुकः, त्वक्त्रं, दंशनं, सन्नाहः, देहावरणं, युद्धास्त्रं, तनुवारं, सज्जा.—(Chain-armour) जालिका, जालप्राया; 'arrayed in armour,' वर्म्मितः -ता -तं, कवची -चिनी -चि (न्).

ARMOUR-BEARER, *s.* सान्नहानिकः, वर्म्मवाहकः.

ARMOURER, *s.* अस्त्रकारकः, शस्त्रकारः, शस्त्रमार्जः, अस्त्रनिर्म्माणशिल्पज्ञः, सज्जाकर्त्ता *m.* (र्तृ), असिधावकः.

ARM-PIT, *s.* कक्षः, बाहुमूलं, भुजकोटरः, दोर्मूलं.

ARMS, *s.* अस्त्रं, शस्त्रं, आयुधः, युद्धास्त्रं, शस्त्रास्त्रं.—(War in general) विग्रहः, समरः, रणः, युद्धं, सङ्ग्रामः.—(State of hostility) युद्धावस्था, रणसमयः; 'dexterity in arms,' अस्त्रलाघवं; 'the taking up of arms,' अस्त्रग्रहणं, युद्धे प्रवृत्तिः, अस्त्रधारणं; 'passage of arms,' अस्त्रशिक्षा, शस्त्राभ्यासः; 'a brother in arms,' सहयुध्वा *m.* (न्).—(The ensigns armorial of a family) कुलीनपदसूचकचिह्नं, कुलचिह्नं.

ARMY, *s.* सेना *f.*, सैन्यं, बलं, वाहिनी, चमूः *f.*, दण्डः or -ण्डं, अनीकं, चक्रं, ध्वजिनी, व्यूहः, योधसमूहः, पृतना, वरूथिनी.—(A complete army) अक्षौहिणी, चतुरङ्गः.—(In motion) प्रचक्रं.

AROMA, *s.* गन्धः, वासः, आमोदः, धूपः, परिमलः.

AROMATIC. *a.* सुगन्धीयः -या -यं, गन्धी -न्धिनी -न्धि (न्), तिक्तः -क्ता -क्तं, सुरभितः -ता -तं, सुवासितः -ता -तं, धूपितः -ता -तं.

AROMATICS, *s.* उपस्कराः *m. pl.*, सुगन्धिद्रव्याणि *n. pl.*, सुगन्धानि *n. pl.*

To AROMATISE, *v. a.* वास् (c. 10. वासयति -यितुं), धूप् (c. 1. धूपायति, धूपितुं).

AROUND, *adv.* (Circularly) परितस्, अभितस्.—(On every side) समन्ततस्, सर्व्वतस्, विश्वतस्, समन्तात्.

AROUND, *prep.* परि, अभि.

To AROUSE, *v. a.* (To excite) उत्सह् in caus. (-साहयति -यितुं), प्रोत्सह्, उत्था for उत्स्था in caus. (उत्थापयति -यितुं), उद्बुध् in caus. (-बोधयति -यितुं), प्रबुध्.—(To wake from sleep) जागृ in caus. (जागरयति -यितुं), प्रबुध् in caus., निद्रां भञ्ज् (c. 7. भनक्ति भंक्तुं).

AROUSED, *p. p.* प्रोत्साहितः -ता -तं.—(Awaked) प्रबोधितः -ता -तं, प्रबुद्धः -द्धा -द्धं, निद्राभङ्गः -ङ्गा -ङ्गं.

To ARRAIGN, *v. a.* (To set in order) विरच् (c. 10. -रचयति -यितुं), स्वस्थाने स्था in caus. (स्थापयति -यितुं).—(To accuse) अभियोगं कृ, आह्वे (c. 1. -ह्वयति -ह्वातुं), अपवद् (c. 1. -वदति -वदितुं), अभिशप् (c. 1. -शपति -शप्तुं).

ARRAIGNED, *p. p.* अभियुक्तः -क्ता -क्तं, आहूतः -ता -तं, अभिशप्तः -प्ता -प्तं.

ARRAIGNMENT, *s.* अभियोगः, आह्वानं, अपवादः.

To ARRANGE, *v. a.* रच् (c. 10. रचयति -यितुं), विरच्; विधा (c. 3. -दधाति -धातुं), संविधा; क्रमेण or यथाक्रमं स्था in caus. (स्थापयति -यितुं), ग्रन्थ् (c. 1. ग्रन्थति, c. 9. ग्रथ्नाति, ग्रन्थितुं).

ARRANGED, *p. p.* विरचितः -ता -तं, ग्रथितः -ता -तं, विन्यस्तः -स्ता -स्तं, विहितः -ता -तं, प्रतिविहितः -ता -तं, परिमितः -ता -तं, व्यूढः -ढा -ढं; 'well-arranged,' सुघटितः -ता -तं.

ARRANGEMENT, *s.* विन्यासः, पर्य्यायः, प्रतिविधानं, व्यूहनं, व्यूढिः *f.*, रचना, विरचनं, ग्रन्थनं, -ना, व्यवस्थापनं, अनुसन्धानं, क्रमेण स्थापनं, परिपाटिः *f.*—(The state of being in order) क्रमः.

ARRANGER, *s.* विरचकः, उपायज्ञः, उपेता *m.* (तृ), व्यासः.

ARRANT, *a.* (Bad in a high degree) अतिदुष्टः -ष्टा -ष्टं, अतिनिकृष्टः -ष्टा -ष्टं, अतिकुत्सितः -ता -तं.—(Excessive) अत्यन्तः -न्ता -न्तं.

ARRAS, *s.* नानावर्णानि चित्रितवस्त्राणि.

ARRAY, *s.* (Of battle) व्यूहः, or -हनं, व्यूढिः *f.*, बलविन्यासः; 'to draw up in battle array,' व्यूह् (c. 1. -ऊहते -ऊहितुं).—(Order) क्रमः, श्रेणी, पङ्क्तिः *f.*, रचना.—(Dress) आभरणं, भूषणं, परिच्छदः.

To ARRAY, *v. a.* (To put in order) क्रमेण or व्यूहेन रच् (c. 10. रचयति -यितुं), विरच् or स्था in caus. (स्थापयति -यितुं), or व्यवस्था; or विधा (c. 3. -दधाति -धातुं), or सज्जीकृ.—(To dress) वस्त्रम् आच्छद् (c. 10. -छादयति -यितुं), संव्ये (c. 1. -व्ययति -व्यातुं), भूष् (c. 10. भूषयति -यितुं); अलङ्कृ, परिष्कृ.

ARREAR, *s.* ऋणशेषं, ऋणशेषांशः, ऋणस्य अशोधितो भागः, ऋणस्य शोधनीयो भागः.

ARREST, *s.* आसेधः, धरणं, ग्रहणं, निरोधः, बन्धनं.—(Stop) निवारणं.

To ARREST, *v. a.* (As a bailiff) आसिध् (c. 1. -सेधति -सेद्धुं), निरुध् (c. 7. -रुणद्धि -रोद्धुं), ऋणहेतोः or दोषहेतोः राजलेखेन or राजाज्ञया बन्ध् (c. 9. बध्नाति -बन्द्धुं), or ग्रह् (c. 9. गृह्णाति, ग्रहीतुं) or धृ (c. 1. धरति, धर्त्तुं).—(Stop, bring to a stand) स्तम्भ् in caus. (स्तम्भयति -यितुं), विष्टम्भ् (c. 5. -स्तभ्नोति, c. 9. -स्तभ्नाति -स्तम्भितुं), निवृ in caus. (-वारयति -यितुं).

ARRESTED, *p. p.* आसिद्धः -द्धा -द्धं, धृतः -ता -तं, बद्धः -द्धा -द्धं, निरुद्धः -द्धा -द्धं.

ARRIVAL, *s.* आगमनं, अभिगमनं, उपस्थितिः *f.*, उपयातं, आयः.

To ARRIVE, *v. n.* आगम् (c. 1. -गच्छति -गन्तुं), अभिगम्, उपगम्; उपस्था (c. 1. -तिष्ठति -स्थातुं), प्राप् (c. 5. -आप्नोति -आप्तुं), सम्प्राप्, अवाप्, अनुसम्प्राप्, उपसम्प्राप्, आया (c. 2. -याति -यातुं), अभिया, उपाया, समाया.

ARRIVED, *p. p.* आगतः -ता -तं, समायातः -ता -तं, उपस्थितः -ता -तं, प्राप्तः -प्ता -प्तं.

ARROGANCE, *s.* गर्व्वः, धर्षः, दर्पः, मानः, अभिमानः, मदः, अवलेपः, अहङ्कारः, प्रागल्भ्यं, प्रगल्भता, आटोपः, चित्तसमुन्नतिः, औद्धत्यं, प्रतिभानं.

ARROGANTLY, *adv.* सगर्व्वं, सदर्पं, साटोपं, गर्व्वेण, धर्षेण, प्रगल्भं.

ARROGANT, *a.* प्रगल्भः -ल्भा -ल्भं, गर्व्वी -र्व्विणी -र्व्वि (न्), अतिगर्व्वितः -ता -तं, सगर्व्वः -र्व्वा -र्व्वं, मानी -निनी -नि (न्), मदोद्धतः -ता -तं, अहङ्कारी -रिणी -रि (न्), आत्मश्लाघी -घिनी -घि (न्), प्रधर्षितः -ता -तं, अवलिप्तः -प्ता -प्तं, उद्धतः -ता -तं, प्रतिभामुखः -खी -खं.—(To be arrogant) प्रगल्भ् (c. 1. -गल्भते -गल्भितुं), दृप् (c. 4. दृप्यति, दर्प्तुं द्रप्तुं).

To ARROGATE, *v. a.* (To claim proudly) गर्व्वपूर्व्वकं or सगर्व्वं or अनर्हतस् or अधर्म्मतस् or मिथ्या ग्रह् (c. 9. गृह्णाति ग्रहीतुं), अभिग्रह्, परिग्रह्; or लभ् (c. 1. लभते लब्धुं), or आदा (c. 3. -ददाति -दातुं), or अभ्यनुज्ञा (c. 9. -जानाति -ज्ञातुं), or आत्मीयं -यां -यं कृ or स्वीकृ; मृषा or मिथ्या ग्रह्; उपधां कृ, ध्वजीकृ.

ARROGATION, *s.* सगर्व्वग्रहणं, अनर्हग्रहणं, अभिग्रहणं, अन्याय्यग्रहणं, मिथ्याग्रहणं, ध्वजीकरणं, उपधा.

ARROW, *s.* शरः, बाणः, इषुः *m.*, शायकः, काण्डं, शल्यं, विपाठः, विशिखः, पृषत्कः, पत्री *m.* (न्), भल्लः, नाराचः, प्रक्ष्वेडनः, अजिह्मगः, खगः, आशुगः, मार्गणः, कलम्बः, रोपः; 'arrow-head,' बाणाग्रं; 'arrow-shaft,' शरकाण्डं; 'a shower of arrows,' शराक्षेपः, शरवर्षं.

ARROWY, *a.* (Consisting of arrows) बाणी -णिनी -णि (न्), बाणवान्

-वती -वत् (त्).—(Arrow-shaped) बाणाकारः -रा -रं.

ARSENAL, *s.* आयुधागारं, आयुधगृहं, शस्त्रागारं, अस्त्रागारं, युद्धभाण्डागारं. —(A collection of arms) शस्त्रसंहतिः, शस्त्रसमूहः.

ARSENIC, *s.* मनःशिला, शिला, मनोगुप्ता, नागजिह्विका, नैपाली, कुनटी.

ARSON, *s.* आगारदाहः, गृहदाहापराधः.

ART, *s.* शिल्पं, शिल्पविद्या, कला, व्यवसायः, कर्म्म *n.* (न्).—(Invention) कल्पनं, -ना.—(Science) विद्या.—(Skill) निपुणता, पाण्डित्यं, दक्षता, युक्तिः *f.*, शिक्षाशक्तिः *f.*—(Cunning) विदग्धता, वैदग्ध्यं, माया.

ARTERY, *s.* नाडी, नाडिः *f.*, कण्डरा, नाली, नालिः *f.*, सिरा, रक्तवाही *m.* (न्).

ARTERIAL, *a.* नाडीसम्बन्धी -न्धिनी -न्धि (न्), रक्तवाही -हिनी -हि (न्).

ARTFUL, *a.* (Performed with art) शिल्पेन or पाण्डित्येन कृतः -ता -तं. —(Skilful) शिक्षितः -ता -तं, निपुणः -णा -णं, पटुः -टुः -ट्वी -टु.—(Cunning) उपायज्ञः -ज्ञा -ज्ञं, विदग्धः -ग्धा -ग्धं, छलान्वितः -ता -तं, मायी -यिनी -यि (न्).

ARTFULLY, *adv.* पाण्डित्येन, नैपुण्येन, सपाटवं, वैदग्ध्येन, छलेन.

ARTFULNESS, *s.* (Skill) पाण्डित्यं, निपुणता, चातुर्य्यं, दक्षता, पटुता.—(Cunning) विदग्धता, वैदग्ध्यं, शठता.

ARTHRITIC, *a.* (Gouty) वातकी -किनी -कि (न्).—(Relating to the joints) ग्रन्थिलः -ला -लं.

ARTICHOKE, *s.* शाकविशेषः.

ARTICLE, *s.* (Part of speech) वाक्यार्थनिर्णायकोऽव्ययशब्दः.—(A particular part of any complex thing) अंशः, भागः, पदं, विषयः. —(Thing) द्रव्यं, वस्तु *n.*, विषयः.—(Apparatus) सामग्री *f.*—(Terms, stipulation) नियमपत्रं, समयः; 'articles of peace,' सन्धिसमयः. —(A point of time) क्षणः, समयः, वेला.

To ARTICLE, *v.n.* समयं कृ, नियमपत्रेण स्थिरीकृ, सङ्कट् (c. 1. -ङ्कटते -ङ्कटितुं).

ARTICULAR, *a.* ग्रन्थिलः -ला -लं, ग्रन्थिसम्बन्धकः -का -कं.

ARTICULATE, *a.* (Distinct) व्यक्तः -क्ता -क्तं, स्पष्टः -ष्टा -ष्टं.

To ARTICULATE, *v. a.* (To utter words distinctly) स्पष्टं or व्यक्तं उच्चर् in caus. (-चारयति -यितुं), or उदीर् (c. 10. -ईरयति -यितुं, c. 1. -ईरति -ईरितुं), or उदाहृ (c. 1. -हरति -हर्तुं).—(To joint) ग्रन्थ् (c. 1. ग्रन्थति, c. 9. ग्रथ्नाति ग्रन्थितुं).

ARTICULATED, *p.p.* (Uttered) उच्चारितः -ता -तं.—(Jointed) ग्रन्थितः -ता -तं, सन्धितः -ता -तं.

ARTICULATION, *s.* (Of words) उच्चारणं, उदाहरणं.—(The juncture of bones) ग्रन्थिः *m.*, अस्थिसन्धिस्थानं, सन्धिः *m.*

ARTIFICE, *s.* (Stratagem, contrivance) उपायः, छद्म *n.* (न्), छलं, व्यपदेशः, कपटः -टं, कौशलं.

ARTIFICER, *s.* (An artist) शिल्पकारः, शिल्पी *m.* (न्), कर्म्मकारः, कर्म्मारः, कारुः *m.*—(Maker) कर्त्ता *m.* (र्तृ), निर्म्माता *m.* (तृ).—(Contriver) उपेता *m.* (तृ), उपायज्ञः.

ARTIFICIAL, *a.* शिल्पिकः -की -कं, कृत्रिमः -मा -मं, कृतकः -का -कं, काल्पनिकः -की -कं, प्रतियत्नपूर्व्वः -र्व्वा -र्व्वं.—(Made by art) कल्पितः -ता -तं, शिल्पनिर्म्मितः -ता -तं; 'an artificial lake,' क्रीडासरः *n.* (स्).

ARTIFICIALLY, *adv.* शिल्पेन, कृत्रिमप्रकारेण, शिल्पिकप्रकारेण.

ARTILLERY, *s.* अग्न्यस्त्रं, युद्धास्त्रं, आग्नेयानि अस्त्राणि *n. pl.*

ARTISAN, *s.* शिल्पी *m.* (न्), शिल्पकारः, कर्म्मकारः, कारुकः.

ARTIST, *s.* शिल्पी *m.* (न्).—(A skilful man) पण्डितः, निपुणः, पटुः. —(Painter) चित्रकरः.

ARTLESS, *a.* (Without fraud) अमायः -या -यं, अमायिकः -की -कं, कपटहीनः -ना -नं, दक्षिणः -णा -णं, सरलः -ला -लं, शुद्धमतिः -तिः -ति, छलरहितः -ता -तं, निर्व्याजः -जा -जं.—(Void of art) अपटुः -टुः -टु, अदक्षः -क्षा -क्षं, अनभिज्ञः -ज्ञा -ज्ञं.

ARTLESSLY, *adv.* छलव्यतिरेकेण, मायां विना, कपटव्यतिरेकेण, अमायया, दाक्षिण्येन.

ARTLESSNESS, *s.* अमाया, सरलता, दाक्षिण्यं.

ARUNDINEOUS, *a.* वेत्रकः -की -कं, वेत्रकीयः -या -यं, नडकीयः -या -यं, वेतस्वान् -स्वती -स्वत् (त्), वेत्रवान् -वती -वत् (त्).

AS, *conj.* (In the same manner with something else) यथा.—(Like) इव; वत् affixed; 'to act as a fool,' मूर्खवत् कृ.—(In the manner that) यथा, यद्वत्, यत्प्रकारेण, रूपेण; 'they did as he commanded,' तस्य यथानिदेशं चक्रुः.—(According as) अनुरूपेण, अनुसारेण.—(So as) यथा तथा.—(While, at the same time) यावत्, यत्समये, यत्काले.—(Because that) यतस्.—(As many as, as much as) यावान् -वती -वत् (त्), यावत्संख्यकः -का -कं or यत्संख्यकः, यति *ind.*—(As long as, as far as) यावत्, आ prefixed with the abl. c.; as, 'as far as the ocean,' आसमुद्रात्; 'as long as the vow lasted,' आसमापनाद् व्रतस्य. —Sometimes पर्य्यन्तं or अन्त are affixed with the sense, 'as far as;' as, 'the land as far as the ocean,' सागरपर्य्यन्तं पृथिवी, or सागरान्ता पृथिवी.—(As soon as) यदा; मात्रात् affixed; 'as soon as he had spoken,' कथनमात्रात्.—(As well as) यथा.—(As yet) अद्य यावत्, अद्यपर्य्यन्तं, अद्यापि, एतत् कालं यावत्. —(As how) यथा.—(Equally with) तुल्यरूपेण, समं.—(As if, as though) इव, प्रायस्.—(As to, with reference to) प्रति, प्रतीक्ष्य, उद्दिश्य.—(As high as) दघ्नं, मात्रं; as, 'water as high as the knees,' जानुदघ्नं जलं.

To ASCEND, *v. n.* (Rise up) उदि (c. 1. -अयति -एतुं), अभ्युदि, समुदि, आक्रम् (c. 1. -क्रमते -क्रमितुं), ऊर्द्ध्वं गम् (c. 1. गच्छति, गन्तुं), उपरि गम्, ऊर्द्ध्वं व्रज् (c. 1. व्रजति, व्रजितुं).

To ASCEND, *v. a.* (Mount upon) आरुह् (c. 1. -रोहति -रोढुं), अधिरुह्, अभिरुह्, अध्यारुह्, उपरुह्, प्ररुह्, समारुह्; अधिक्रम् (c. 1. -क्रामति, c. 4. क्राम्यति -क्रमितुं).

ASCENDABLE, *a.* आरोहणीयः -या -यं, अधिरोहणीयः -या -यं, आक्रमणीयः -या -यं.

ASCENDANT, *a.* (Rising upwards) ऊर्द्ध्वगः -गा -गं, अधिरोही -हिणी -हि (न्).—(Superior) उत्तमः -मा -मं, प्रबलः -ला -लं, प्रधानः -ना -नं, प्रभविष्णुः -ष्णुः -ष्णु.

ASCENDANT, *s.* (Height, Elevation) ऊर्द्ध्वत्वं, उच्चता, उच्छ्रायः, उत्तुङ्गता. —(Superiority, influence) प्रधानता, प्रभुत्वं.—(In astronomy) लग्नं, नाक्षत्रिकी.

ASCENDANCY, *s.* (Influence, power) प्राधान्यं, प्रभुत्वं, प्राबल्यं, प्राभवं, प्रभुतता, गौरवं.

ASCENDED, *p. p.* आरूढः -ढा -ढं, अधिरूढः -ढा -ढं, ऊर्द्ध्वगतः -ता -तं, उपरिगतः -ता -तं.

ASCENSION, *s.* आरोहणं, ऊर्द्ध्वगतिः *f.*, ऊर्द्ध्वगमनं.—(To heaven) स्वर्गारोहणं.

ASCENSION-DAY, *s.* ख्रीष्टस्य स्वर्गारोहणदिवसः.

ASCENT, *s.* आरोहणं, ऊर्द्ध्वगतिः *f.*, उद्गमः, समुद्गमः, समुत्क्रमः, उदयः, समुदयः, उत्पातः, उद्वर्त्तनं, समुत्थानं.—(The way by which one rises) आरोहणपथः, सोपानं, अधिरोहणी; 'difficult of ascent,' दुरारोहः -हा -हं.

To ASCERTAIN, *v. a.* (Find out) ज्ञा (c. 9. जानाति -नीते, ज्ञातुं), विज्ञा;

ज्ञा in desid. (जिज्ञासते -सितुं), निरूप् (c. 10. -रूपयति -यितुं), विद् (c. 2. वेत्ति, वेदितुं).—(Determine) निश्चि (c. 5. -चिनोति -चेतुं), निर्णी (c. 1. -णयति -ते -णेतुं), व्यवसो (c. 4. -स्यति -सातुं), स्थिरीकृ; 'that is ascertained,' निर्णीयते तत्.

ASCERTAINABLE, *a.* निरूपणीयः -या -यं, निर्धारणीयः -या -यं, निर्णेयः -या -यं.

ASCERTAINED, *p. p.* निरूपितः -ता -तं, निश्चितः -ता -तं, निर्णीतः -ता -तं, निर्धारितः -ता -तं.

ASCERTAINMENT, *s.* निश्चयः, निर्णयः, अवगमः, निर्धारणं.

ASCETIC, *s.* वानप्रस्थः, तपस्वी *m.* (न्), योगी *m.* (न्), तापसः, यतिः *m.*, यती *m.* (न्), वैरागी *m.* (न्), वैरङ्गिकः, मुनिः, सन्न्यासी *m.*, पारिकाङ्क्षी *m.*

ASCETICISM, *s.* वैराग्यं, सन्न्यासः.

ASCITITIOUS, *a.* अप्रकृतः -ता -तं, असमवायी -यिनी -यि (न्), आरोपितः -ता -तं.

ASCLEPIAS, *s.* (Moon-plant) सोमः.—(A drinker of its juice) सोमपः, सोमपाः *m.*

ASCRIBABLE, *a.* आरोपणीयः -या -यं, अभिसम्बन्धनीयः -या -यं, दातव्यः -व्या -व्यं.

To ASCRIBE, (an action, cause, quality, &c., to anybody) कर्म्म कारणं गुणं वा इत्यादि कस्मिंश्चित् or कस्मैचिद् आरुह् in caus. (-रोपयति -यितुं), or अध्यारुह्, or अभिसम्बन्ध् (c. 9. -बध्नाति -बन्द्धुं), or सम्बन्ध्, or दा (c. 3. ददाति -दातुं).—(To ascribe a fault) दोषारोपणं, or दोषप्रसङ्गं, or दोषकल्पनं कृ.

ASCRIPTION, *s.* आरोपः -पणं, अध्यारोपः, अभिसम्बन्धनं, सम्बन्धनं, प्रसङ्गः.

ASH, *s.* वन्यपादपविशेषः.

ASHAMED, *a.* ह्रीणः -णा -णं, ह्रीतः -ता -तं, लज्जितः -ता -तं, व्रीडितः -ता -तं, लज्जमानः -ना -नं, लज्जावान् -वती -वत् (त्), त्रपितः -ता -तं, त्रपमाणः -णा -णं, त्रपान्वितः -ता -तं.—(To be ashamed) लज्ज् (c. 6. लज्जते, लज्जितुं), विलज्ज्, संलज्ज्; व्रीड् (c. 4. व्रीड्यति, व्रीडितुं); त्रप् (c. 1. त्रपते, त्रपितुं), अपत्रप्, व्यपत्रप्; ह्री (c. 3. जिह्रेति, ह्रेतुं), with abl. or gen. of the thing of which one is ashamed. To be ashamed of any thing, may be expressed by किञ्चिद् लज्जास्पदं ज्ञा.—(To make ashamed) ह्री in caus. ह्रेपयति -यितुं).

ASH-COLOURED, *a.* भस्मवर्णः -र्णा -र्णं, पांशुवर्णः -र्णा -र्णं, पाण्डुः -ण्डुः -ण्डु.

ASHEN, *a.* पूर्व्वोक्तपादपनिर्म्मितः -ता -तं or -मयः -मयी -मयं.

ASHES, *s.* भस्म *n.* (न्), भसितं, भूतिः *f.*, पांशुः *m.*, रक्षा ; 'to reduce to ashes,' भस्मसात् कृ; 'reducing to ashes,' भस्मीकरणं; 'reduced to ashes,' भस्मसात्कृतः -ता -तं, भस्मीभूतः -ता -तं.

ASH-WEDNESDAY, *s.* चत्वारिंशद्दिनपर्य्यन्तं महोपवासस्य प्रथमदिवसः.

ASHORE, *adv.* उत्तीरम् *ind.*, तीरे, तटे, वेलायां, तटस्थः -स्था -स्थं.

ASHY, *a.* भास्मनः -नी -नं, पांशुवर्णः -र्णा -र्णं.—(Turned into ashes) भस्मीकृतः -ता -तं, भस्मलिप्तः -प्ता -प्तं.

ASIDE, *adv.* (On one side) एकपार्श्वे.—(To another side) अन्यपार्श्वे.—(By the side) पार्श्वतस् *ind.*—(In private, in concealment) निभृते, एकान्ते.—(In stage language) स्वगतं, आत्मगतं, अपवार्य्य, विजने, जनान्तिके.

ASININE, *a.* गर्द्दभीयः -या -यं, खरसम्बन्धकः -का -कं.

To ASK, *v. a.* (To beg, request) याच् (c. 1. याचति -ते, याचितुं), अभियाच्, प्रयाच्, सम्प्रयाच्, संयाच्, अर्थ् (c. 10. अर्थयते -यितुं), अभ्यर्थ्, प्रार्थ्, सम्प्रार्थ्; भिक्ष् (c. 1. भिक्षते, भिक्षितुं).—(To ask a question, inquire) प्रच्छ् (c. 6. पृच्छति प्रष्टुं), अनुप्रच्छ्, समनुप्रच्छ्, परिप्रच्छ्; ज्ञा in des. (जिज्ञासते, जिज्ञासितुं), अनुयुज् (c. 7. -युनक्ति -युङ्क्ते -योक्तुं).

ASKED, *p. p.* अर्थितः -ता -तं, प्रार्थितः -ता -तं, अभ्यर्थितः -ता -तं, याचितः -ता -तं, प्रयाचितः -ता -तं.—(Questioned) पृष्टः -ष्टा -ष्टं, अनुयुक्तः -क्ता -क्तं.

ASKANCE, ASKAUNCE, ASKAUNTE, *adv.* साचि *ind.*, तिरस् *ind.*, तिर्य्यक् *ind.*, तिरश्चीनः -ना -नं.—(Looking askance) साचिविलोकी -किनी -कि (न्), लोलापाङ्गः -ङ्गा -ङ्गं, अपाङ्गदर्शी -र्शिनी -र्शि (न्).

ASKER, *s.* (Petitioner) प्रार्थकः, याचकः, अर्थी *m.* (न्).—(Inquirer) प्रष्टा *m.* (ृ).

ASKEW, *adv.* तिरस्, साचि, तिर्य्यक्, तिरश्चीनः -ना -नं, साचीकृतः -ता -तं.

ASKING, *s.* याञ्चा, याचना, अर्थना, प्रार्थनं -ना, अभ्यर्थना, अभिशस्तिः *f.* —(Questioning) प्रच्छना, जिज्ञासा.

ASLANT, *adv.* आवर्ज्यं *ind.*, तिर्य्यक् *ind.*, वक्रं, जिह्मं, अनृजु, कुटिलं.

ASLEEP, *a.* सुप्तः -प्ता -प्तं, निद्राणः -णा -णं, शयितः -ता -तं, प्रसुप्तः -प्ता -प्तं, निद्रितः -ता -तं, शयानः -ना -नं, निद्रालसः -सा -सं.—(Fast asleep) सुषुप्तः -प्ता -प्तं.—(To fall asleep) स्वप् (c. 2. स्वपिति, स्वपितुं), प्रस्वप्.

ASLOPE, *adv.* (Declivous) प्रवणः -णा -णं.—(With declivity) प्रवणं, प्रवणप्रकारेण.

ASÓCA, *s.* (Flower) अशोकः, वञ्जुलः.

ASP, ASPIC, *s.* अतिविषालुः क्षुद्रसर्पप्रभेदः.

ASPARAGUS, *s.* शतमूली, एकमूला, बहुसुता, अभीरुः *f.*, शतावरी, अहेरुः.

ASPECT, *s.* (Appearance, look) रूपं, आकारः, आकृतिः *f.*, आभा, मूर्त्तिः *f.*—(Countenance) वदनं.—(State) अवस्था, दशा.—(Act of beholding) आलोकनं, दर्शनं, निरीक्षणं.—(Relation) सम्पर्कः, सम्बन्धः.—(Situation) अवस्थानं.—(Disposition of a planet) दशा.

ASPEN, *s.* स्फुरितपत्रशीलो वृक्षविशेषः.

ASPEN, *a.* (Like the aspen-tree) पूर्व्वोक्तवृक्षोपमः -मा -मं.—(Made of the aspen) पूर्व्वोक्तवृक्षनिर्म्मितः -ता -तं.

ASPERITY, *s.* (Unevenness of surface) रूक्षता, असमानत्वं, वैषम्यं. (Of temper) कार्कशत्वं, अरुन्तुदत्वं, स्वभावकटुता.—(Sharpness) तैक्ष्ण्यं, तीव्रता.

To ASPERSE, *v. a.* (To sprinkle) सिच् (c. 6. सिञ्चति -ते, सेक्तुं), निषिच्, संसिच्, उक्ष् (c. 1. उक्षति, उक्षितुं), अभ्युक्ष्, प्रोक्ष्, समुक्ष्.—(To calumniate) अवक्षिप् (c. 6. -क्षिपति -क्षेप्तुं), अधिक्षिप्; कलङ्क (nom. कलङ्कयति -यितुं), कलङ्कं कृ, परिवद् (c. 1. -वदति -वदितुं), अपवद्; अभिशप् (c. 1. -शपति -ते -शप्तुं).

ASPERSED, *p. p.* (Sprinkled) सिक्तः -क्ता -क्तं, प्रोक्षितः -ता -तं.—(Calumniated) अवक्षिप्तः -प्ता -प्तं, कलङ्कितः -ता -तं.

ASPERSER, *s.* कलङ्ककारः, परिवादकः, अपवादकः, अवक्षेपकः.

ASPERSION, *s.* (Sprinkling) सेकः, सेचनं, निषेकः, प्रोक्षणं, उक्षोतः, प्रासारः.—(Calumny) अपवादः, कलङ्कः, अवक्षेपः, क्षेपः, गुणनिन्दा.

ASPIRANT, *s.* अर्थी *m.* (न्), प्रार्थयिता *m.* (तृ), आकाङ्क्षी *m.* (न्), कुतूहली *m.* (न्), अभिलाषुकः.

ASPIRATE, *s.* महाप्राणः, महाप्राणसूचकं चिह्नं.—(The soft aspirate) अभिनिष्ठानं, अल्पप्राणः.

To ASPIRATE, *v. n.* महाप्राणेन उच्चर् in caus. (-चारयति -यितुं).

ASPIRATED, *p. p.* महाप्राणेन उच्चारितः -ता -तं.

ASPIRATION, *s.* (An ardent wish) आकाङ्क्षा, लालसा, महाकाङ्क्षा, कौतूहलं, स्पृहा, अभिरुचिः *f.*, अभिलाषः.—(Pronunciation with a full breath) महाप्राणेन उच्चारणं, महाप्राणः.

To ASPIRE TO OR AFTER, *v. n.* अभिरुच् in caus. (-रोचयति -यितुं), अभिलष् (c. 1. -लषति -लषितुं), अभिकाङ्क्ष् (c. 1. -काङ्क्षति -काङ्क्षितुं), आकाङ्क्ष्; अभ्याप् in des. (-ईप्सति -ईप्सितुं), स्पृह् (c. 10. स्पृहयति -यितुं), उपजीव् (c. 1. -जीवति -जीवितुं).

Ass, *s.* गर्द्दभः *m.* -भी *f.*, खरः, रासभः *m.* -भी *f.*, चक्रीवान् *m.* (त्), वालेयः. —(A stupid fellow) मन्दबुद्धिः, दुर्मतिः.—(Skin of an ass) गर्द्दभाजिनं.

Assa-fœtida, *s.* सहस्रवेधि *n.* (न्), रामठं, जतुकं, वाह्लीकं, हिङ्गुः *m.*

To assail, *v. a.* आक्रम् (c. 1. -क्रामति, c. 4. -क्राम्यति -क्रमितुं), अभियुज् (c. 7. -युनक्ति -युंक्ते -योक्तुं), आसद् (c. 10. -सादयति -यितुं), समासद्, अभिद्रु (c. 1. -द्रवति -द्रोतुं), आविश् (c. 6. -विशति -वेष्टुं), अभिधाव् (c. 1. -धावति -ते -धावितुं), प्रतियुध् (c. 4. -युध्यते -योद्धुं), अभिशस् (c. 1. -शसति -शसितुं).—(To storm) आस्कन्द् (c. 1. -स्कन्दति -स्कन्तुं), अवस्कन्द्.

Assailable, आक्रमणीयः -या -यं, अभियोज्यः -ज्या -ज्यं, आसादनीयः -या -यं.

Assailant, *s.* आक्रमिता *m.* (तृ), आक्रामकः, आघातकः, अभियोक्ता *m.* (क्तृ), अभिघाती *m.* (न्).

Assailed, *p. p.* आक्रान्तः -न्ता -न्तं, अभियुक्तः -क्ता -क्तं, उपद्रुतः -ता -तं.

Assassin, *s.* घातकः, हन्ता *m.* (न्तृ), नृघातकः, वधकः, वधोद्यतः.

To assassinate, *v. a.* निभृतं or छलेन or गोपनेन हन् (c. 2. हन्ति हन्तुं), or in caus. (घातयति -यितुं), or मृ in caus. (मारयति -यितुं).

Assassination, *s.* छलेन or गोपनेन हननं, नृहत्या, घातनं, प्राणान्तिकं, वधः, मारणं.

Assassinator, *s.* निभृतं or छलेन हन्ति यो घातकः.

Assault, *s.* अभियोगः, आक्रमणं, अवगोरणं, अभ्याघातः, आघातः, उपघातः.—(Storm) अवस्कन्दः -न्दनं.—(Violence) प्रसभं, साहसं, प्रमाथः, बलात्कारः.

To assault, *v. a.* आक्रम् (c. 1. -क्रामति, c. 4. -क्राम्यति -क्रमितुं), आसद् (c. 10. -सादयति -यितुं), समासद्; अभिद्रु (c. 1. -द्रवति -द्रोतुं), समाद्रु, उपद्रु, समुपद्रु, अवगुर् (c. 6. -गुरते or -ति, -गुरितुं), अभिधाव् (c. 1. -धावति -ते -धावितुं).—(To storm) आस्कन्द् (c. 1. -स्कन्दति -स्कन्तुं), अवस्कन्द्, लङ्घ् (c. 10. लङ्घयति -यितुं).

Assaulted, *p. p.* अभियुक्तः -क्ता -क्तं, आक्रान्तः -न्ता -न्तं.—(By storm) अवस्कन्दितः -ता -तं.

Assay, *s.* परीक्षा, प्रमाणीकरणं, उपधा.—(Touchstone) निकषः.—(Of coin) नाणकपरीक्षा.—(First attempt) आरम्भः, प्रवृत्तिः *f.*

To assay, *v. a.* परीक्ष् (c. 1. -ईक्षते -ईक्षितुं), ज्ञा in des. (जिज्ञासते जिज्ञासितुं).—(Endeavour) यत् (c. 1. यतते, यतितुं), व्यवसो (c. 4. -स्यति -सातुं), चेष्ट् (c. 1. चेष्टते, चेष्टितुं).

Assayer, *s.* (An officer of the mint) नाणकपरीक्षी *m.* (न्), धातुवादी *m.* (न्), धातुपरीक्षकः, परीक्षकः.

Assemblage, *s.* समूहः, सङ्घातः, समाहारः, समुच्चयः, समवायः, वृन्दं, चयः, सञ्चयः, समुदयः, गणः, ओघः, संहतिः *f.*, संहारः, सन्निपातः, सङ्घः, अक्षौहिणी, साहित्यं, ग्रामः in composition; 'an assemblage of people,' पुरुषसमवायः, जनसमागमः, जननिवहः; 'of princes,' राजकं; 'the assemblage of the organs,' इन्द्रियग्रामः.

To assemble, *v. n.* सङ्गम् (c. 1. -गच्छति -गन्तुं), समागम्; समे (root इ with सम् and आ, c. 2. समैति समैतुं), समभ्ये; एकत्र मिल् (c. 6. मिलति -ते, मेलितुं), समावृत् (c. 1. -वर्त्तते -वर्त्तितुं), सन्निपत् (c. 1. -पतति -पतितुं), समूहीभू.

To assemble, *v. a.* सङ्गम् in caus. (-गमयति -यितुं), समाहृ (c. 1. -हरति -ते -हर्त्तुं), उपसंहृ; सन्निपत् in caus. (-पातयति -यितुं), एकत्र कृ, समूहीकृ.

Assembled, *p. p.* मिलितः -ता -तं, समेतः -ता -तं, समागतः -ता -तं, समुपागतः -ता -तं, संहतः -ता -तं, समूढः -ढा -ढं, समवेतः -ता -तं.

Assembling, *s.* मिलनं, सङ्गमः, समागमः, समागतिः *f.*

Assembly, *s.* सभा, सदः *n.* (स्), समज्या, समाजः, परिषद् *f.*, समागमः, संसद् *f.*, गोष्ठी *f.*, समूहः, मेलकः, मेलः, सन्निवेशः; 'an assembly of lords or nobles,' शिष्टसभा.—(A collection) समाहारः, समुच्चयः, सन्निपातः, समुदयः, समवायः, संहारः, समूहः.—(A party) पंक्तिः *f.*

Assembly-room, *s.* समागमस्थानं, सभाशाला, इन्द्रकं.

Assent, *s.* सम्मतिः *f.*, अनुमतिः *f.*, सम्मतं, अनुज्ञा, प्रतिग्रहः, परिग्रहः, स्वीकारः, अङ्गीकारः, प्रतिश्रवः, समनुज्ञानं, अनुवादः.

To assent, *v. n.* अनुज्ञा (c. 9. -जानाति -ज्ञातुं), अनुमन् (c. 4. -मन्यते -ते -मन्तुं), सम्मन्, प्रतिग्रह् (c. 9. -गृह्णाति -गृह्णीते -ग्रहीतुं), स्वीकृ, अङ्गीकृ, उरीकृ, सम्मतीष् (c. 6. -इच्छति -एष्टुं).

Assentation, *s.* स्वीकरणं, चाटुकारः, अनुरोधः, अनुवृत्तिः *f.*

Assented, *p. p.* अनुमतः -ता -तं, सम्मतः -ता -तं, अनुज्ञातः -ता -तं, प्रतिश्रुतः -ता -तं, समनुज्ञातः -ता -तं.

Assenter, *s.* अनुमन्ता *m.* (न्तृ), अनुवादकः, अनुज्ञाता *m.* (तृ), स्वीकर्त्ता *m.* (र्त्तृ).

To assert, *v. a.* (To maintain) दार्ढ्येन वद् (c. 1. वदति, वदितुं).—(To affirm) वद्, तथेति ब्रू (c. 2. ब्रवीति, ब्रूते, वक्तुं).—(To claim) ममेति वद्, स्वीकृ, स्वस्वत्वं ज्ञा in caus. (ज्ञापयति -यितुं).

Assertion, *s.* (The act of asserting) वचनं, उक्तिः *f.*—(The position advanced) वचनं, वाक्यं, उक्तवाक्यं.—(The first part of an argument) प्रतिज्ञा, पूर्व्वपक्षः, पक्षः.

To assess, *v. a.* राजस्वं or करं or शुल्कं दा in caus. (दापयति -यितुं), or ग्रह् (c. 9. गृह्णाति, ग्रहीतुं), or अवहृ in caus. (-हारयति -यितुं), or स्था in caus (स्थापयति -यितुं), or निरूप् (c. 10. -रूपयति -यितुं).

Assessment, *s.* करग्रहणं, शुल्कग्रहणं, राजस्वग्रहणं.—(The sum levied) करः, शुल्कः, शुल्कं, राजस्वं.

Assessor, *s.* (One who sits by) सभ्यः, सभासद् *m.*, उपासिता *m.* (तृ), उपासीनः.—(Tax-gatherer) करग्रहः, शुल्कग्राही *m.* (न्), राजस्वनिरूपकः.

Assets, *s.* मृतजनस्य ऋणशोधनार्थं अवशिष्टधनं.—(Goods) अर्थः, विभवः, सम्पत्तिः *f.*

To assever, asseverate, *v. a.* स्थैर्य्येण, or दार्ढ्येन, or शपथेन, or शपथपूर्व्वकं वद् (c. 1. वदति, वदितुं), or ब्रू (c. 2. ब्रवीति, ब्रूते, वक्तुं).

Asseveration, *s.* शपथपूर्व्वकं वचनं, स्थिरवचनं, दृढवचनं.

Assiduity, *s.* उद्योगः, उद्यमः, अभ्यसनं, व्यवसायः, प्रसक्तिः *f.*, मनोयोगः, चेष्टा, यत्नः, मनोनिवेशः, प्रवेशः, परायणः, प्रयासः.

Assiduous, *a.* उद्योगी -गिनी -गि (न्), सोद्योगः -गा -गं, व्यवसायी -यिनी -यि (न्), परायणः -णा -णं, प्रयत्नवान् -वती -वत् (त्), प्रसक्तः -क्ता -क्तं, प्रसितः -ता -तं.

Assiduously, *adv.* प्रयत्नतस्, यत्नतस्, व्यवसायेन, उद्योगेन, अविरतं, प्रसक्तं.

Assignable, *a.* प्रकल्पनीयः -या -यं, निर्देष्टव्यः -व्या -व्यं, आरोपणीयः -या -यं.

To assign, *v. a.* (Mark out) निरूप् (c. 10. -रूपयति -यितुं), विधा (c. 3. -दधाति -धातुं), निर्णी (c. 1 -नयति -नेतुं), प्रकॢप् (c. 10. -कल्पयति -यितुं), निर्दिश् (c. 6. -दिशति -देष्टुं), समादिश्.—(Appoint) नियुज् (c. 7. -युनक्ति -युंक्ते -योक्तुं), स्था in caus. (स्थापयति -यितुं), व्यवस्था.—(Make over property) द्रव्यं or धनं समृ in caus. (-अर्पयति -यितुं), or दा in caus. (दापयति -यितुं); निबन्धं कृ.—(Attribute) आरुह् in caus. (-रोपयति -यितुं).—(He assigns a reason) स हेतुम् आह.

Assignation, *s.* (An appointment to meet another) अभिसारः, सङ्केतः, प्रज्ञप्तिः *f.*, समागमनियमः.—(Going to an assignation) अभिसारी -रिणी -रि (न्).—(Place of assignation) सङ्केतस्थानं.—(A making over property to another) द्रव्यसमर्पणं, धनसमर्पणं, निबन्धदानं.

Assigned, *p. p.* निर्दिष्टः -ष्टा -ष्टं, आदिष्टः -ष्टा -ष्टं, नियमितः -ता -तं,

नियोजितः -ता -तं, समर्पितः -ता -तं, दापितः -ता -तं, व्यवस्थापितः -ता -तं, प्रकल्पितः -ता -तं, आरोपितः -ता -तं.

ASSIGNEE, *s.* नियोगी *m.* (न्), कार्य्येषु नियुक्तः, प्रतिनिधिः, प्रतिपुरुषः.

ASSIGNMENT, *s.* (Of goods) निबन्धनं, समर्पणं.—(Appointment) नियोजनं.

To ASSIMILATE, *v. a.* (To bring to a likeness) समीकृ, तुल्यीकृ.—(To perform the act of converting food to nourishment) जीर्णिपूर्व्वकं समीकृ, परिणामं कृ.

ASSIMILATION, *s.* (The act of) समीकरणं, तुल्यीकरणं.—(The state of) समता, समानता, तुल्यता, साम्यं.—(Of food) परिणामः, परिणतत्वं, विपाकः, परिपक्वता.—(Of fractions) भागजातिः *f.*

To ASSIMULATE, *v. a.* छल् (nom. छलयति -यितुं), छद्म or कपटं कृ.

ASSIMULATION, *s.* छलनं, कपटः -टं, छद्म *n.* (न्).

To ASSIST, *v. a.* उपकृ (c. 8. -करोति -कर्त्तुं), उपचर् (c. 1. -चरति -चरितुं), उपग्रह् (c. 9. -गृह्णाति -ग्रहीतुं), अभिरक्ष् (c. 1. -रक्षति -रक्षितुं), उपकारं कृ, साहाय्यं कृ, पक्षपातं कृ.

ASSISTANCE, *s.* उपकारः, उपकारिता, उपकृतं, साहाय्यं, साहित्यं, उपग्रहः, अनुग्रहः, पक्षपातः.

ASSISTANT, *s.* उपकारी *m.* (न्), उपकारकः, साहाय्यकर्त्ता *m.* (र्त्तृ), सहायः, उत्तरसाधकः.

ASSISTED, *p. p.* उपकृतः -ता -तं, कृतोपकारः -रा -रं, उपचरितः -ता -तं.

ASSIZE, *s.* (A court of justice) दोषादोषविचारसभा, दण्डयोगसभा, दण्डप्रणयनसभा.—(Market rate, measure) आपणिकः, अर्घबलाबलं, परिमाणं, मानं.

To ASSIZE, *v. a.* (To fix the rate of any thing) अर्घं संख्या in caus. (-स्थापयति -यितुं), अर्घबलाबलं or द्रव्यादिमूल्यं or परिमाणं निरूप् (c. 10. -रूपयति -यितुं), or स्था in caus. (स्थापयति -यितुं).

ASSIZER, *s.* अर्घसंस्थापकः, मूल्यनिरूपकः, विक्रेयद्रव्यादिपरिमाणनिरूपकः.

ASSOCIATE, *s.* (A partner, confederate) सहायः, सङ्गी *m.* (न्), अनुषङ्गी *m.* (न्), उत्सङ्गी *m.* (न्), सहकारी *m.* (न्), सजूः *m.* (-जुस्), सहवासी *m.* (न्).—(A companion, equal) वयस्यः.

To ASSOCIATE, *v. a.* संयुज् (c. 7. -युनक्ति -योक्तुं, c. 10. -योजयति -यितुं), सङ्क्रम् in caus. (-गमयति -यितुं), सम्बन्ध् in caus. (-बन्धयति -यितुं), संश्लिष् in caus. (-श्लेषयति -यितुं).

To ASSOCIATE WITH, *v. n.* संवस् (c. 1. -वसति -वस्तुं), सह वस्; सहितः -ता -तं भू, मिल् (c. 6. मिलति -ते, मेलितुं), सम्मिल्; सह गम् (c. 1. गच्छति, गन्तुं), सहवासं कृ.—(Not to be associated with) अपाङ्क्तेयः -या -यं.

ASSOCIATED, *p. p.* संयुक्तः -क्ता -क्तं, संश्लिष्टः -ष्टा -ष्टं, संहतः -ता -तं, सहितः, -ता -तं, सहगतः -ता -तं, सङ्घातवान् -वती -वत् (त्), उत्सङ्गितः -ता -तं.

ASSOCIATION, *s.* संयोगः, साहित्यं, साहाय्यं, सार्थं, सङ्क्रमः, सङ्गतिः *f.*, संसर्गः, सहायता or -त्वं, साहचर्य्यं, समागमः, सङ्घातः, आसङ्गः, सङ्गः, संश्लेषः.—(Evil association) असत्संसर्गः.—(Set, club) पङ्क्तिः *f.*—(Partnership) समांशिता.

To ASSORT, *v. a.* यथाक्रमं or क्रमेण स्था in caus. (स्थापयति -यितुं), विधा (c. 3. -दधाति -धातुं), संविधा; रच् (c. 10. रचयति -यितुं), विरच्; ग्रन्थ् (c. 1. ग्रन्थति, c. 9. ग्रथ्नाति, ग्रन्थितुं), पृथक् पृथक् स्था in caus. or कृ.

ASSORTED, *p. p.* विरचितः -ता -तं, व्यूढः -ढा -ढं, विन्यस्तः -स्ता -स्तं.

ASSORTMENT, *s.* विरचनं, पृथक्करणं, विन्यासः, प्रतिविधानं, ग्रन्थनं -ना, व्यूहनं, व्यूढिः *f.*, परिपाटिः *f.*—(A mass of things assorted) सञ्चयः, सङ्घातः, वृन्दं, ओघः.

To ASSUAGE, *v. a.* शम् in caus. (शमयति -यितुं), उपशम्, प्रशम्; सान्त्व् or शान्त्व् (c. 10. सान्त्वयति -यितुं), अभिशान्त्व्, परिशान्त्व्; तुष् in caus. (तोषयति -यितुं), परितुष्.

To ASSUAGE, *v. n.* शम् (c. 4. शाम्यति, शमितुं), उपशम्, प्रशम्; तुष् (c. 4. तुष्यति, तोष्टुं).

ASSUAGED, *p. p.* शान्तः -न्ता -न्तं, प्रशमितः -ता -तं, प्रशान्तः -न्ता -न्तं.

ASSUAGEMENT, *s.* प्रशमनं, शान्तिः *f.*, उपशान्तिः *f.*, सान्त्वनं.

ASSUASIVE, *a.* शान्तिकः -की -कं, शमकः -का -कं, शान्तिदः -दा -दं.

To ASSUME, *v. a.* (To take) ग्रह् (c. 9. गृह्णाति, ग्रहीतुं), परिग्रह्, प्रतिग्रह्; लभ् (c. 1. लभते, लब्धुं).—(To arrogate) अधर्म्मतस् or मिथ्या ग्रह् or आत्मसात्कृ, परधर्म्मं ग्रह्; 'he assumes the king,' राजायते.—(To suppose something granted) अप्रमाणीकृत्य or अप्रमाणतस् or निष्प्रमाणेन वद् (c. 1. वदति, वदितुं), अनुमतं -तां -तं ज्ञा (c. 9. जानाति, ज्ञातुं).

ASSUMED, *p. p.* गृहीतः -ता -तं, आदत्तः -त्ता -त्तं.—(Not natural) कृतकः -का -कं.

ASSUMPTION, *s.* (The act of taking) ग्रहणं, आदानं, प्रतिग्रहः, परिग्रहः, आत्मसात्करणं; 'false assumption,' मिथ्याग्रहणं.—(The supposition of any thing granted) निष्प्रमाणेन or अप्रमाणतस् ग्रहणं, प्रमाणव्यतिरेकेण कस्यचित् मतस्य धारणं; 'on the assumption,' न्यायात्.—(The thing supposed) प्रतिज्ञा, प्रमेयं, उपन्यासः.—(Of a disguise) वेशधारणं, विडम्बनं.

ASSURANCE, *s.* (Certain expectation) विश्वासः, प्रत्ययः, प्रत्याशा, निश्चयः, दृढः प्रत्ययः.—(Want of modesty) धार्ष्ट्यं, प्रगल्भता, साहसं, निर्लज्जता.—(Reason for confidence) विश्वासकारणं, प्रत्ययहेतुः.—(Insurance, assurance of safety) योगक्षेमः, अभयवाक् *f.* (च्), सहाय्यत्वं.

To ASSURE, *v. a.* स्थिरीकृ, दृढीकृ, संस्तम्भ् (c. 5. -स्तभ्नोति, c. 9. -स्तभ्नाति, -स्तम्भितुं, or caus. -स्तम्भयति -यितुं), विश्वासं दा, प्रमाणं दा, असन्दिग्धं -ग्धां -ग्धं कृ, सुनिश्चितं -तां -तं कृ.—(To affirm) दार्ढ्येन वद् (c. 1. वदति).

ASSURED, *p. p.* (Certain) स्थिरः -रा -रं, दृढः -ढा -ढं, सुनिश्चितः -ता -तं, असन्दिग्धः -ग्धा -ग्धं, असंशयः -या -यं.

ASSUREDLY, *adv.* निश्चितं, सुनिश्चितं, असंशयं, निःसन्देहेन, नूनं, एवं, खलु, किल, सुतरां.

ASTERISK, *s.* नक्षत्राकारश् चिह्नविशेषः.

ASTERISM, *s.* नक्षत्रं, ऋक्षः, तारा, तारकः, ज्योतिषी, दाक्षायिणी.

ASTERN, *adv.* नावः पश्चाद्भागे or पश्चिमभागं प्रति.

ASTHMA, *s.* दुःश्वासः, दुःश्वसनं, श्वासरोगः.

ASTHMATICAL, ASTHMATIC, *a.* दुःश्वासशीलः -ला -लं, श्वासरोगपीडितः -ता -तं.

To ASTONISH, *v. a.* विस्मि in caus. (-स्माययति -ते -यितुं), व्याकुलीकृ, आकुलीकृ, चमत्कारं or विस्मयं जन् in caus. (जनयति -यितुं), चमत्कृ.

ASTONISHED, *p. p.* विस्मितः -ता -तं, विस्मयान्वितः -ता -तं, विस्मयाकुलः -ला -लं, चमत्कृतः -ता -तं, विलक्षः -क्षा -क्षं.—(To be astonished) विस्मि (c. 1. -स्मयते -स्मेतुं), आश्चर्य्यं ज्ञा (c. 9. जानाति, ज्ञातुं) or मन् (c. 4. मन्यते, मन्तुं).

ASTONISHING, *a.* आश्चर्य्यः -र्य्या -र्य्यं, अद्भुतः -ता -तं, विचित्रः -त्रा -त्रं.

ASTONISHMENT, *s.* विस्मयः, आश्चर्य्यत्वं, चमत्कारः, व्याकुलता.—(With astonishment) साश्चर्य्यं, सविस्मयं.—(Matter of astonishment) विस्मयहेतुः *m.*, विस्मयकारणं, अद्भुतं.

To ASTOUND *v. a.* मुह् in caus. (मोहयति -यितुं), व्यामुह्, व्याकुलीकृ, विस्मयाकुलं -लां -लं कृ.

ASTOUNDED, *p. p.* विस्मयाकुलः -ला -लं, मोहितः -ता -तं, आकुलीकृतः -ता -तं.

Astral, *a.* आर्क्षः -र्क्षी -र्क्षं, तारकी -किनी -कि (न्), तारकितः -ता -तं.

Astray, *adv.* उत्पथं, पथभ्रष्टः -ष्टा -ष्टं, विमार्गगामी -मिनी -मि (न्), विपथगामी -मिनी -मि (न्), भ्रान्तः -न्ता -न्तं.—(To lead astray) उत्पथं नी (c. 1. नयति, नेतुं).

Astride, *adv.* (To stand with the legs apart) पादौ पृथक् कृत्वा or प्रगतजङ्घः -ङ्घा -ङ्घं स्था (c. 1. तिष्ठति, स्थातुं).

To astringe, *v. a.* सङ्कुच् (c. 1. -कोचति, c. 6. -कुचति -कोचितुं); कषाय् (nom. कषायति -यितुं).

Astringency, *s.* सङ्कोचनं, कषायः -यं, तुवरः -रं.

Astringent, *a.* कषायः -या -यं, सङ्कोचनशीलः -ला -लं, रूक्षः -क्षा -क्षं, तुवरः -रा -रं, ग्राही -हिणी -हि (न्), विरूक्षणः -णी -णं.

Astrologer, *s.* गणकः, ज्यौतिषिकः, दैवज्ञः, मौहूर्त्तः, मौहूर्त्तिकः, दैवलेखकः, कार्त्तान्तिकः, ज्योतिःशास्त्रानुरूपं भाविविषयकथकः or भाविकथकः or भाविव्यक्तीकर्त्ता *m.* (र्त्तृ), सांवत्सरः, ज्ञानी *m.* (न्).

Astrological, *a.* ज्योतिषः -षी -षं, ज्योतिर्विद्याविषयः -या -यं, नाक्षत्रः -त्री -त्रं.

Astrologically, *adv.* ज्योतिर्विद्यानुसारात्, ज्योतिःशास्त्रानुरूपं, ज्योतिःशास्त्रवत्.

Astrology, *s.* नक्षत्रविद्या, ज्योतिषं, दैवप्रश्नः, देवप्रश्नं, ज्योतिःशास्त्रमूला भाविव्यक्तीकरणविद्या; ज्योतिःशास्त्रज्ञानात् or -ज्ञानेन भाविकथनविद्या.

Astronomer, *s.* ज्योतिःशास्त्रज्ञः, ज्योतिर्विद्, ज्योतिषः, ज्यौतिषिकः, राशिग्रहनक्षत्रादिगतिज्ञः, ग्रहनक्षत्रादिविद्याज्ञः.

Astronomical, *a.* ज्योतिषः -षी -षं, ज्योतिःशास्त्रविषयः -या -यं, नाक्षत्रिकः -की -कं.

Astronomically, *adv.* ज्योतिःशास्त्रानुसारात्, ज्योतिःशास्त्रानुरूपं, ज्योतिःशास्त्रवत्.

Astronomy, *s.* ज्योतिःशास्त्रं, ज्योतिर्विद्या, राशिग्रहनक्षत्रादिविद्या, ज्योतिषं, खगोलविद्या.

Astute, *a.* विदग्धः -ग्धा -ग्धं, सव्याजः -जा -जं, चतुरः -रा -रं.

Asunder, *adv.* विरलं, पृथक्, प्रगतः -ता -तं, विगतः -ता -तं.—'Asunder' may often be expressed by the prep. वि; as, 'cut asunder,' विच्छिन्नः.

Aświns, (Nāsatya and Dasra, the twin sons of the Sun by the constellation Aświnī, physicians of heaven) अश्विनौ *du.*, स्वर्वैद्यौ *du.*, नासत्यौ *du.*, दस्रौ *du.*, अश्विनीसुतौ *du.*, आश्विनेयौ *du.*

Asyle, Asylum, *s.* आश्रयः, आशयः, शरणं, संश्रयः, गतिः *f.*, प्रतिश्रयः, विषयः.—(To seek asylum with) आश्रि (c. 1. -श्रयति -ते -श्रयितुं), उपाश्रि, समुपाश्रि, संश्रि.

At, *prep.* expressed by आ or अभि prefixed to roots, as, 'to arrive at,' आगम्, अभिगम्.—Before names of towns, expressed by the loc. c.; as, 'at Ayodhyā,' अयोध्यायां. At home,' स्वगृहे, स्वस्थाने; 'at night,' रात्रौ; 'at evening,' आसन्ध्यं; 'at this time,' तत्काले, तत्क्षणे; 'at the moment,' सपदि; 'at present,' वर्त्तमाने काले, अधुना, सम्प्रति; 'at first,' प्रथमतस्, पूर्व्वं; 'at last,' अनन्तरं, शेषे; 'at least,' तावत्; 'at all,' कथञ्चन, मनाक्; 'at the sight,' आदर्शनात्; 'at ease,' यथासुखं, सुखेन; 'at large,' निर्विघ्नं; 'at the price,' मूल्येन; 'at once,' युगपत्, एकदा, एककाले.—'At,' may often be expressed by the indec. part., as, 'at the sight of that,' तद् दृष्ट्वा; or by the loc. c., as, 'at their arrival,' तेषु आगतेषु; or by the abl. c., as. 'at his bidding,' तस्य निदेशात्; or by the instr. c., as, 'at the king's command,' राजाज्ञया.

At-hand, *adv.* उपस्थितः -ता -तं, आसन्नः -न्ना -न्नं; 'to be at hand,' उपस्था (c. 1. -तिष्ठति -ते -स्थातुं), प्रत्युपस्था.

Atheism, *s.* नास्तिकता, नास्तिक्यं, देवनिन्दा, परलोकाभावबुद्धिः.

Atheist, *s.* नास्तिकः, देवनिन्दकः, अनीश्वरवादी *m.* (न्), नास्तिकमते स्थितः.

Atheistical, *a.* (Given to atheism) नास्तिकवृत्तिः -त्तिः -त्ति, देवनिन्दकः -का -कं.

Athirst, *a.* तृषार्त्तः -र्त्ता -र्त्तं, तृषितः -ता -तं, पिपासुः -सुः -सु.

Athlete, *s.* मल्लयोद्धा *m.* (द्धृ), मल्लः, झल्लः.

Athletic, *a.* (Belonging to wrestling) मल्लयुद्धसम्बन्धकः -का -कं.—(Strong) बाहुवीरः -रा -रं, मल्लः -ल्ला -ल्लं, व्यायामी -मिनी -मि (न्), व्यायामशीलः -ला -लं, व्यूढोरस्कः -स्का -स्कं, पृथुशरीरः -रा -रं, बलवान् -वती -वत् (त्).—(Athletic exercise) व्यायामः.

Athwart, *prep.* कोणाकोणि, विपरीतं, विलोमं, व्यत्यस्तं, प्रतिकूलं; 'athwart the way,' प्रतिमार्गं; 'athwart the stream,' प्रतिस्रोतस्; 'athwart the river,' नदीपारं, नदीतीरान्तरं.

Atlantic, *a.* महासमुद्राणां मध्ये य एट्लण्टिकिति अभिधीयते महासमुद्रः.

Atlas, *s.* भूगोलस्य यत् किञ्चिद् देशसमुद्रनगरादि विद्यते तदाकारनामादिमुद्रितः पत्रसमूहः.

Atmosphere, *s.* आकाशः, नभः *n.* (स्), गगणं, अभ्रं, अन्तरीक्षं, वायुवर्त्म *n.*, (न्), विहायसः -सं, मण्डलं, शून्यं, शून्यत्वं, आड्डं.

Atmospherical, *a.* आकाशीयः -या -यं, आन्तरीक्षः -क्षी -क्षं, वायवः -वी -वं, वैहायसः -सी -सं, विहायसीयः -या -यं.

Atom, *s.* परमाणुः *m.*, अणुः *m.*, कणः, लवः, लेशः, कणिका, सूक्ष्मः.

Atomical, *a.* (Consisting of atoms) आणवकः -की -कं, अणुकः -का -कं, परमाणुमयः -यी -यं.—(Minute) सूक्ष्मः -क्ष्मा -क्ष्मं.—(Relating to atoms) अणुविषयः -या -यं, परमाणुसम्बन्धकः -का -कं.

At-once, एकदा, युगपत्, एकपदे, एककाले.

To atone, *v. a.* (To expiate, answer for) प्रायश्चित्तं कृ, निष्कृतिं कृ, प्रायश्चित्तेन पापं परिशुध् in caus. (-शोधयति -यितुं), or पापात् मुच् (c. 6. मुञ्चति मोक्तुं); पापक्षमां सिध् in caus. (साधयति -यितुं).—(To reconcile) सन्धा (c. 3. -दधाति -धातुं), अनुनी (c. 1. -नयति -नेतुं), प्रशम् in caus. (-शमयति -यितुं).

To atone, *v. n.* (To agree) सम्मन् (c. 4. -मन्यते -मन्तुं).—(To stand as an equivalent) प्रायश्चित्तः or प्रतिनिधिः or प्रतिभूः भू.

Atonement, *s.* प्रायश्चित्तः, निष्कृतिः *f.*, पापक्षमासाधनं, पापनाशः, अग्निष्टुत् *f.*—(One who atones) प्रायश्चित्तकारी *m.* (न्), निष्कृतिकर्त्ता *m.* (र्त्तृ), पापक्षमासाधकः.

Atonic, *a.* अग्निनाशकः -का -कं, अतेजस्वी -स्विनी -स्वि (न्).

Atrabilarious, *a.* कालपित्तसम्पूर्णः -र्णा -र्णं, दुर्मनाः -नाः -नः (स्).

Atramentous, *a* मसिवर्णः -र्णा -र्णं, कृष्णवर्णः -र्णा -र्णं.

Atrocious, *a.* अतिपापी -पिनी -पि (न्), अतिदोषी -षिणी -षि (न्), अतिपातकी -किनी -कि (न्), अतिपापिष्ठः -ष्ठा -ष्ठं, अत्यन्तदुराचारः -रा -रं, दुर्वृत्तः -त्ता -त्तं, दारुणः -णा -णं.

Atrocity, atrociousness, *s.* अतिपातकं, अतिपापं, अतिदोषः, अतिदुष्टता.

Atrophy, *s.* क्षयः, क्षयरोगः, शरीरशोषणं, अग्न्यभावः, अजीर्णता.

To attach, *v. a.* (To fix to one's interests, win over) सञ्ज् in caus. (सञ्जयति -यितुं), अनुरञ्ज् in caus. (-रञ्जयति -यितुं).—(To connect) सम्बन्ध् (c. 9. -बध्नाति -बन्द्धुं).—(To seize) आसेधं कृ; धृ (c. 1. धरति, धर्त्तुं), आक्रम् (c. 1. -क्रामति -क्रमितुं).—(To attribute) आरुह् in caus. (-रोपयति -यितुं).—(To be attached) आसञ्ज् in pass. (-सज्यते), अनुरञ्ज् in pass. (-रज्यते).—(To be connected)

संबन्ध् in pass. (-बध्यते).

ATTACHED, *p. p.* अनुरक्तः -क्ता -क्तं, आसक्तः -क्ता -क्तं, संसक्तः -क्ता -क्तं, प्रसक्तः -क्ता -क्तं, लग्नः -ग्ना -ग्नं, लगितः -ता -तं, भक्तः -क्ता -क्तं, भक्तिमान् -मती -मत् (त्), अविरक्तः -क्ता -क्तं, संहितः -ता -तं, अनुरागवान् -वती -वत् (त्), सानुरागः -गा -गं.

ATTACHMENT, *s.* आसक्तिः *f.*, प्रसक्तिः *f.*, अनुरागः, अनुरक्तिः *f.*, रक्तिः *f.* सङ्गः, आसङ्गः, प्रसङ्गः, भक्तिः *f.*, चित्तासङ्गः, सम्प्रीतिः *f.*, परायणः, तुरायणः.

To ATTACK, *v. a.* आक्रम् (c. 1. -क्रामति, c. 4. -क्राम्यति -क्रमितुं), उपक्रम्, उपाक्रम्, अभिक्रम्; आसद् (c. 10. -सादयति -यितुं), आस्कन्द् (c. 1. -स्कन्दति -स्कन्तुं); आयुध् (c. 4. -युध्यते -योद्धुं), प्रतियुध्, युध् in caus. (योधयति -यितुं), अभिद्रु (c. 1. -द्रवति -द्रोतुं), उपद्रु, समाद्रु, अभिधाव् (c. 1. -धावति -ते -धावितुं), अभिप्रया (c. 2. -याति -यातुं).

ATTACK, *s.* अभियोगः, अभिग्रहः, अभिक्रमः, आक्रमः, अवस्कन्दः, अभिमर्दः.

ATTACKED, *p. p.* अभियुक्तः -क्ता -क्तं, आक्रान्तः -न्ता -न्तं, आसादितः -ता -तं.

To ATTAIN, *v. a.* प्राप् (c. 5. -आप्नोति -आप्तुं), सम्प्राप्; लभ् (c. 1. लभते, लब्धुं), गम् (c. 1. गच्छति, गन्तुं), with acc., अधिगम्; या (c. 2. याति, यातुं), आया; इ (c. 2. एति, एतुं), अभी (अभ्येति); ऋ (c. 1. ऋच्छति, अर्त्तुं), अश् (c. 5. अश्नुते, अशितुं), उपाश्, समश्; स्पृश् (c. 6. स्पृशति, स्प्रष्टुं), आविश् (c. 6. -विशति -वेष्टुं).

ATTAINABLE, *a.* प्राप्यः -प्या -प्यं, प्रापणीयः -या -यं, गम्यः -म्या -म्यं, लभ्यः -भ्या -भ्यं, समासाद्यः -द्या -द्यं, सुलभः -भा -भं, साध्यः -ध्या -ध्यं.

ATTAINDER, *s.* (The conviction of a crime) आधर्षणं.—(Taint, sully of character) कलङ्कः, अपयशः *n.* (स्), अपकीर्त्तिः *f.*

ATTAINED, *p. p.* प्राप्तः -प्ता -प्तं, लब्धः -ब्धा -ब्धं, अधिगतः -ता -तं,

ATTAINMENT, *s.* लाभः, लब्धिः *f.*, प्राप्तिः *f.*, अवाप्तिः *f.*, उत्पत्तिः *f.*, अर्ज्जनं, उपार्ज्जनं; 'attainment of knowledge,' विद्यागमः.

To ATTAINT, *v. a.* (To corrupt, disgrace) दुष् in caus. (दूषयति -यितुं), कलङ्क (nom. कलङ्कयति -यितुं), कलङ्कं कृ.—(To convict) आधृष् (c. 10. -धर्षयति -यितुं), आधर्षणं कृ.

ATTAINTED, *p. p.* (Convicted) आधर्षितः -ता -तं.—(Corrupted) दूषितः -ता -तं.

To ATTEMPER, *v. a.* (To mingle in just proportions) यथांशतस् मिश्र् (c. 10. मिश्रयति -यितुं) or संयुज् in caus. (-योजयति -यितुं); द्रवीकृ.—(To soften, mollify) शम् in caus. (शमयति -यितुं), मृद् (nom. मृदयति -यितुं), स्निग्धीकृ.—(To regulate) नियम् (c. 1. -यच्छति -यन्तुं).

To ATTEMPT, *v. a.* (To try) यत् (c. 1. यतते, यतितुं), उपक्रम् (c. 1. -क्रमते -क्रमितुं), आरभ् (c. 1. -रभते -रब्धुं), समारभ्; उद्यम् (c. 1. -यच्छति -यन्तुं), प्रवृत् (c. 1. -वर्त्तते -वर्त्तितुं), घट् (c. 1. घटते, घटितुं), व्यवसो (c. 4. -स्यति -सातुं), चेष्ट् (c. 1. चेष्टते, चेष्टितुं), उद्योगं कृ.—(To attack) आक्रम् (c. 1. -क्रामति, c. 4. -क्राम्यति, -क्रमितुं).

ATTEMPT, *s.* समुद्यमः, उद्यमः, आरम्भः, उपक्रमः, उद्योगः, प्रवृत्तिः *f.*, चेष्टा, ग्रहः, साधनं, व्यापारः.—(Attack) आक्रमः.

ATTEMPTED, *p. p.* आरब्धः -ब्धा -ब्धं, अध्यवसायितः -ता -तं, समुद्यतः -ता -तं.

ATTEMPTER, *s.* आरम्भकः, प्रवर्त्तकः, उपक्रमिता *m.* (तृ), आक्रामकः.

To ATTEND, *v. a.* (To listen to) श्रु (c. 5. शृणोति, श्रोतुं), आश्रु, उपश्रु; आकर्ण् (c. 10. -कर्णयति -यितुं).—(To fix the attention upon) अवधा (c. 3. -धत्ते -धातुं), प्रणिधा, समाधा; मनो युज् (c. 7. युनक्ति, योक्तुं), सेव् (c. 1. सेवते, सेवितुं).—(To wait upon) श्रु in desid. (शुश्रूषते, शुश्रूषितुं), आश्रु, प्रतिश्रु; सेव्, उपसेव्; उपस्था (c. 1. -तिष्ठति -ते -स्थातुं), पर्युपस्था, उपचर् (c. 1. -चरति -चरितुं), परिचर्, उपाचर्; परिविश् (c. 6. -विशति -वेष्टुं), उपास् (c. 2. -आस्ते -आसितुं).—(To accompany) अनुया (c. 2. -याति -यातुं), परिवृ in caus. (-वारयति -यितुं).—(To stay for) प्रतीक्ष् (c. 1. -ईक्षते -ईक्षितुं).

To ATTEND, *v. n.* (To be attentive) अवधा in pass. (-धीयते); 'let attention be paid,' अवधीयतां.—(To delay) विलम्ब् (c. 1. -लम्बते -लम्बितुं).

ATTENDANCE, *s.* शुश्रूषा, परिचर्य्या, उपासनं, उपचारः, सेवा, उपसेवा, अनुगमनं.

ATTENDANT, *a.* सहगामी -मिनी -मि (न्), सहचारी -रिणी -रि (न्).

ATTENDANT, *s.* सेवकः, परिचरः, सहचारी *m.* (न्), अनुयायी *m.* (न्), अनुसारी *m.* (न्), अनुचरः, पारिषदः, परिधिस्थः.—(Train of attendants) परिवारः, परिवर्हः.—(Of Siva) प्रमथः.

ATTENDED, *p. p.* (Accompanied) सहितः -ता -तं, समेतः -ता -तं, परिवारितः -ता -तं, परिवृतः -ता -तं, वृतः -ता -तं, समन्वितः -ता -तं.—(Attended to) अनुष्ठितः -ता -तं. When only two persons are referred to, द्वितीय or सहाय may be used; as, 'attended by Indrasena,' इन्द्रसेनद्वितीयः -या -यं or इन्द्रसेनसहायः -या -यं; 'attended by servants,' सप्रेष्यः -ष्या -ष्यं.

ATTENT, *a.* निविष्टः -ष्टा -ष्टं, अवहितः -ता -तं, आहितः -ता -तं.

ATTENTION, *s.* अवधानं, अवधानता, अवेक्षा, अन्ववेक्षा, अपेक्षा, अभिनिवेशः, मनोनिवेशः, मनोनिधानं, मनःप्रवेशः, निविष्टचित्तता, मनोयोगः, आसक्तिः *f.*, अनुरागः, अप्रमादः.—(To a pursuit) परायणः, अनुष्ठानं, सेवनं, उपसेवा.—(To discourse) कथानुरागः.—(To one object) एकाग्रता.

ATTENTIVE, *a.* सावधानः -ना -नं, अवहितः -ता -तं, दत्तावधानः -ना -नं, कृतावधानः -ना -नं, अभिनिविष्टः -ष्टा -ष्टं, आसक्तः -क्ता -क्तं, आसक्तचित्तः -त्ता -त्तं, आश्रवः -वा -वं, समाहितः -ता -तं, प्रमादरहितः -ता -तं, यत्नवान् -वती -वत् (त्), प्रसितः -ता -तं, अप्रमत्तः -त्ता -त्तं.—(Closely attentive) अनन्यमनाः -नाः -नः (स्), एकाग्रः -ग्रा -ग्रं, अनन्यवृत्तिः -त्तिः -त्ति, एकतानः -ना -नं, एकायनः -ना -नं.

ATTENTIVELY, *adv.* सावधानं, अवधानात्, अवहितं, मनःप्रवेशेन, प्रमादव्यतिरेकेण.

To ATTENUATE, *v. a.* कृश् (nom. कृशयति -यितुं), तनूकृ, क्षि in caus. (क्षपयति -यितुं), श्लक्ष्ण (nom. श्लक्ष्णयति -यितुं), सूक्ष्मीकृ.

ATTENUATED, *p. p.* कृशः -शा -शं, प्रकृशितः -ता -तं, परिकृशः -शा -शं, तनुः -नुः -न्वी -नु, क्षीणः -णा -णं, शीर्णः -र्णा -र्णं, क्षामः -मा -मं.—(In body) कृशाङ्गः -ङ्गी -ङ्गं, शुष्काङ्गः -ङ्गी -ङ्गं.

ATTENUATION, *s.* कार्श्यं, क्षामता, क्षीणता.—(Of body) कृशाङ्गत्वं, शरीरशोषणं.

To ATTEST, *v. a.* (To bear witness of) साक्ष्यं or साक्षितां दा (c. 3. ददाति, दातुं), साक्ष्येण or साक्षिणा or प्रत्यक्षदर्शनेन प्रमाणं दा, or प्रमाणीकृ, or दिश् (c. 6. दिशति देष्टुं).—(To call to witness) आह्वे (c. 1. -ह्वयति -ते -ह्वातुं), साक्षिणं कृ.

ATTEST, ATTESTATION, *s.* साक्ष्यं, साक्षिता, प्रमाणं, दृष्टोक्तिः, प्रत्यक्षप्रमाणं.

ATTIC, *s.* (Upper room) अट्टः, क्षौमः, शिरोगृहं.

To ATTIRE, *v. a.* (To attire one's self) वस् (c. 2. वस्ते, वसितुं).—(To clothe) वेष्ट् (c. 1. वेष्टते, वेष्टितुं), वस्त्र (nom. वस्त्रयति -यितुं), आच्छद् (c. 10. -छादयति -यितुं), संव्ये (c. 1. -व्ययति -व्यातुं).—(To adorn) परिष्कृ (c. 8. -करोति -कर्त्तुं), अलङ्कृ, संस्कृ; भूष् (c. 10. भूषयति -यितुं).

ATTIRE, *s.* वस्त्रं, वेशः, परिधानं, परिच्छदः, आभरणं, भूषणं, अम्बरं.

संस्थानं, अलङ्कारः, परिष्कारः.

ATTIRED, *p.p.* आच्छादितः -ता -तं, प्रच्छादितः -ता -तं, परिच्छन्नः -न्ना -न्नं, संवीतः -ता -तं, प्रावृतः -ता -तं, अलङ्कृतः -ता -तं, परिष्कृतः -ता -तं.

ATTITUDE, *s.* स्थानं, भावः, अवस्था, स्थितिः *f.*, आकारः, रूपं, वृत्तिः *f.*, भूमिः *f.*

ATTORNEY, *s.* परकार्य्यसाधकः, परकार्य्यसम्पादकः, प्रतिपुरुषः, प्रतिहस्तः.

To ATTRACT, *v. a.* आकृष् (c. 1. -कर्षति, c. 6. -कृषति -क्रष्टुं), समाकृष्, प्रतिकृष्, समुपकृष्; अभिप्रणी (c. 1. -णयति -णेतुं).—(To beguile) मुह् in caus. (मोहयति -यितुं), विमुह्, सम्मुह्; प्रलुभ् in caus. (-लोभयति -यितुं), विलुभ्.

ATTRACTED, *p.p.* आकृष्टः -ष्टा -ष्टं, आकर्षितः -ता -तं, प्रलोभितः -ता -तं, विलोभितः -ता -तं, मोहितः -ता -तं.

ATTRACTION, *s.* आकर्षः -र्षणं, आकृष्टिः *f.*, सन्निकर्षणं.—(Allurement) प्रलोभनं, विलोभः, विलोभनं; 'desire to blend,' यियविषा.

ATTRACTIVE, *a.* आकर्षकः -की -कं, कर्षकः -का -कं, मनोहरः -रा -रं, आकर्षणशीलः -ला -लं, चित्तापहारी -रिणी -रि (न्).—(Beguiling) मोही -हिनी -हि (न्), प्रलोभकः -का -कं.—(Winning friends) मित्रयुः -युः -यु.

ATTRIBUTABLE, *a.* आरोपणीयः -या -यं, अध्यारोपणीयः -या -यं, अभिसम्बन्धनीयः -या -यं.

To ATTRIBUTE, *v. a.* (As an action, quality, &c., to any one) कर्म्म गुणं वा इत्यादि कस्मिंश्चित् or कस्मैचिद् आरुह् in caus. (-रोपयति -यितुं), अध्यारुह् or अभिसम्बन्ध् (c. 9. -बध्नाति -बन्द्धुं) or सम्बन्ध्, or दा (c. 3. ददाति, दातुं).—(To attribute a fault) दोषारोपणं or दोषकल्पनं or दोषप्रसङ्गं कृ.

ATTRIBUTE, *s.* गुणः, विशेषः, विशेषणं, संज्ञाविषयः.

ATTRIBUTIVE, *a.* वाच्यः -च्या -च्यं, विशेषकः -का -कं, विशेषणः -णा -णं.

ATTRITION, *s.* (The act of wearing things by rubbing one against another) घर्षणं, सम्मर्द्दः -र्द्दनं, पेषणं, क्षयः, क्षीणत्वं.—(Grief for sin) भयमूलः पश्चात्तापः, अनुतापः, सन्तापः.

To ATTUNE, *v. a.* (To make any thing musical) सुस्वरं -रां -रं कृ, तालोपेतं -तां -तं कृ.—(To tune one thing to another) गीतवादित्रादि तुल्यस्वरं कृ, गीतवादित्रादीनाम् एकतालं कृ, तौर्य्यत्रिकं कृ, नानाध्वनीनां तूर्य्यादीनाम् ऐक्यं कृ.

AUBURN, *a.* श्यावः -वा -वं, कपिशः -शा -शं, पाण्डुवर्णः -र्णा -र्णं.

AUCTION, *s.* वर्द्धमानमूल्येन नानाद्रव्यविक्रयः, घोषणपूर्व्वकं नानाद्रव्यविक्रयः.—(Auction-room) द्रव्यविक्रयगृहं.

AUCTIONEER, *s.* विक्रेता *m.* (तृ), विक्रयिकः, विक्रयी *m.* (न्), यो घोषणपूर्व्वकं विक्रेयाणि द्रव्याणि विक्रीणाति.

AUDACIOUS, *a.* प्रगल्भः -ल्भा -ल्भं, गल्भः -ल्भा -ल्भं, धृष्टः -ष्टा -ष्टं, साहसिकः -की -कं, निर्लज्जः -ज्जा -ज्जं, प्रतिभानवान् -वती -वत् (त्), निर्भयः -या -यं; 'to be audacious,' धृष् (c. 5. धृष्णोति, धर्षितुं).

AUDACIOUSLY, *adv.* प्रगल्भं, साहसेन, निर्भयं, धार्ष्ट्येन, लज्जां विना.

AUDACIOUSNESS, AUDACITY, *s.* प्रगल्भता, धार्ष्ट्यं, धृष्टता, साहसं, निर्लज्जत्वं, प्रतिभानं.

AUDIBLE, *a.* श्राव्यः -व्या -व्यं, श्रोतव्यः -व्या -व्यं, कर्णगोचरः -रा -रं, कर्णश्रवः -वा -वं, श्रवणार्हः -र्हा -र्हं, श्रवणयोग्यः -ग्या -ग्यं, श्रोत्रग्राह्यः -ह्या -ह्यं.

AUDIBLY, *adv.* श्राव्यप्रकारेण, कर्णगोचरं.

AUDIENCE, *s.* (The act of hearing) श्रवणं, आकर्णनं, निशमनं.—(Liberty of speaking to or seeing a superior) राजदर्शनं, दर्शनं; 'he is come begging an audience,' दर्शनार्थम् आगतोऽस्ति.—(An auditory, hearers) श्रोतारः *m. pl.* (तृ), सभा, सभासदः *m. pl.*, सदः *n.* (स्), परिषद् *f.*, प्रेक्षकाः *m. pl.*—(Audience-chamber) दर्शनशाला, दर्शनगृहं.

AUDIT, *s.* गणितशोधनं, गणितशुद्धीकरणं, गुणनी, विगणनं, अनुसन्धानं, अनुयोगः, परीक्षणं.

To AUDIT, *v. a.* गणितानि शुध् in caus. (शोधयति -यितुं), or शुद्धीकृ or अनुसन्धा (c. 3. -दधाति -धत्ते -धातुं), or अनुयुज् (c. 7. -युनक्ति -योक्तुं) or परीक्ष् (c. 1. -ईक्षते -ईक्षितुं); गुणनीं कृ, विगणनं कृ.

AUDITED, *p. p.* शुद्धीकृतः -ता -तं, शोधितः -ता -तं, विगणितः -ता -तं.

AUDITOR, *s.* श्रोता *m.* (तृ).—(One employed to take an account) गणितशोधकः, अनुसन्धायी *m.* (न्), गुणकः.

AUDITORY, *s.* (A collection of hearers) श्रोतारः *m. pl.*, सभासदः *m. pl.*, सभा, सदः *n.* (स्), परिषद् *f.*—(A lecture room) पाठशाला, श्रवणशाला.

AUGER, *s.* आस्फोटनी, वेधनिका, आविधः.

AUGHT, *s.* किञ्चित्, किमपि, किञ्चन.

To AUGMENT, *v. a.* वृध् in caus. (वर्धयति -यितुं), संवृध्, परिवृध्; ऋध् in caus. (ऋधयति -यितुं), समेध्; प्रचुरीकृ; आप्यै in caus. (-प्याययति -यितुं), समाप्यै.

To AUGMENT, *v. n.* वृध् (c. 1. वर्धते, वर्धितुं), अभिवृध्, प्रवृध्, विवृध्; ऋध् (c. 5. ऋध्नोति, c. 4. ऋध्यति, अर्धितुं), समृध्; उपचि in pass. (-चीयते), प्यै (c. 1. प्यायते, प्यातुं), वृंह् in caus. (वृंहयति -यितुं), उपवृंह्, समुपवृंह्.

AUGMENT, *s.* वृद्धिः *f.*—(In grammar) आगमोक्तिः *f.*

AUGMENTATION, *s.* (The act) वर्द्धनं.—(The state) वृद्धिः *f.*, विवृद्धिः *f.*, ऋद्धिः *f.*, उपचयः, उन्नतिः *f.*, समुन्नतिः *f.*

AUGMENTED, *p. p.* संवर्द्धितः -ता -तं, वृद्धः -द्धा -द्धं, प्रवृद्धः -द्धा -द्धं, उपचितः -ता -तं, प्रचुरीकृतः -ता -तं, समेधितः -ता -तं.

AUGUR, *s.* शकुनपरीक्षकः, अजन्यज्ञः, पूर्व्वचिह्ननिरीक्षकः, पूर्व्वलक्षणज्ञः, पक्षिगतिहस्तरेखादिलक्षणात् शुभाशुभदर्शकः, भूकम्पाद्युत्पातपक्षिगतिचक्षुःस्पन्दादिनिमित्तफलकथकः.

To AUGUR, *v. n.* भूकम्पाद्युत्पातपक्षिगतिचक्षुःस्पन्दादिनिमित्तफलकथनेन शुभाशुभं or मङ्गलामङ्गलं or लक्षणानि प्रदृश् in caus. (-दर्शयति -यितुं); शकुनानि or पूर्व्वलिङ्गानि परीक्ष् (c. 1. -ईक्षते -ईक्षितुं).—(To conjecture) अनुमा (c. 2. -माति -मातुं), शङ्क् (c. 1. शङ्कते, शङ्कितुं).

AUGURED, *p.p.* (Foreshewn) प्रदर्शितः -ता -तं.—(Inferred) अनुमितः -ता -तं.

AUGURY, *s.* (The act of prognosticating) पक्षिगतिहस्तरेखाचक्षुःस्पन्दादिलक्षणात् शुभाशुभदर्शनं or भविष्यदनुमानं, शकुनपरीक्षणं, पूर्व्वलक्षणज्ञानं.—(An omen) शकुनं, अजन्यं, पूर्व्वचिह्नं, पूर्व्वलक्षणं.

AUGUST, *a.* ऐश्वरः -री -रं, ऐशिकः -की -कं, प्रतापवान् -वती -वत् (त्), महामहिमा -मा -म (न्), अतुलकृष्टः -ष्टा -ष्टं, अतिमहान् -हती -हत् (त्), राजयोग्यः -ग्या -ग्यं.

AUGUST, *s.* श्रावणः, नभाः *m.* (स्), भाद्रः, नभस्यः, प्रोष्ठपदः.

AUGUSTNESS, *s.* महाप्रतापः, अतिमहत्त्वं, अतुल्कृष्टता, प्रतापः.

AUNT, *s.* (By the mother's side) मातुली, -ला, -लानी.—(Father's sister) पितृष्वसा *f.* (सृ).

AURICLE, *s.* (The external ear) कर्णशष्कुली *f.*, कर्णबहिर्भागः.—(Of the heart) हृद्रक्तधृत् कर्णाकारः कोषः.

AURICULAR, *a.* (Relating to the ear) कार्णः -र्णी -र्णं, कार्णिकः -की -कं, श्रावणः -णी -णं, श्रौतः -ती -तं.—(Told in the ear, secret) उपकर्ण

or कर्णे अर्पितः -ता -तं or अप्यः -प्या -प्यं, सुगुप्तः -प्ता -प्तं.—(Within the sense of hearing) कर्णगोचरः -रा -रं.

AURORA, *s.* (The dawn) अरुणः, दिवसमुखं, अहर्मुखं, उषः, पूर्व्वसन्ध्या.

AUSPICE, *s.* (An omen drawn from birds) शकुनं, निमित्तं, पक्षिगतिप्रयुक्तं पूर्व्वलक्षणं, पूर्व्वचिह्नं.—(Favour, protection) आश्रयः, अनुग्रहः.

AUSPICIOUS, *a.* शुभः -भा -भं, कल्याणः -णी -णं, शङ्करः -री -रं, शिवङ्करः -रा -रं, भद्रः -द्रा -द्रं, मङ्गल्यः -ल्या -ल्यं, माङ्गलिकः -की -कं, शर्म्मवान् -वती -वत् (त्), शुभङ्करः -रा -रं, क्षेमकरः -रा -रं, तिष्यः -ष्या -ष्यं.—(Prosperous) सौभाग्यवान् -वती -वत् (त्), श्रीयुक्तः -क्ता -क्तं, क्षेमवान् -वती -वत् (त्).—(Favourable) प्रसन्नः -न्ना -न्नं, अनुग्राही -हिणी -हि (न्); 'an auspicious moment,' शुभलग्नः, लग्नवेला.

AUSPICIOUSLY, *adv.* दिष्ट्या, शुभलग्ने, शुभक्षणे, सौभाग्येन, कौशल्येन, क्षेमेण.

AUSPICIOUSNESS, *s.* कल्याणं, मङ्गलं, माङ्गल्यं, कौशल्यं, क्षेमः.

AUSTERE, *a.* निष्ठुरः -रा -रं, कर्कशः -शा -शं, कठिनः -ना -नं, उग्रः -ग्रा -ग्रं, कटुमतिः -तिः -ति, कठोरः -रा -रं, निर्दयः -या -यं.—(In taste) शुक्तः -क्ता -क्तं.

AUSTERELY, *adv.* निष्ठुरं, काठिन्येन, कठोरं, नैष्ठुर्य्येण, उग्रं.

AUSTERENESS, AUSTERITY, *s.* (Severity) कार्कश्यं, काठिन्यं, कठिनता, उग्रता, निष्ठुरता, नैष्ठुर्य्यं, कठोरता, कटुता.—(Penance) तपः *n.* (स्), कृच्छ्रं; 'patient of austerities,' तपःक्लेशसहः; 'to practise austerities,' तप् in pass. (तप्यते), सन्तप्; तपस्य् (nom. तपस्यति).

AUSTRAL, *a.* (Southern) दक्षिणः -णा -णं, अपाचीनः -ना -नं.

AUTHENTICAL, AUTHENTIC, *a.* सिद्धप्रमाणः -णा -णं, अलब्धप्रमाणः -णा -णं, प्रामाणिकः -की -कं, प्रमाणयुक्तः -क्ता -क्तं, आप्तः -प्ता -प्तं.—(Real, genuine) वास्तवः -वी -वं, वास्तविकः की -कं, निर्व्यलीकः -का -कं, निर्व्याजः -जा -जं, अकृत्रिमः -मा -मं, अकल्पितः -ता -तं, मूलिकः -की -कं, सारः -रा -रं, तथ्यः -थ्या -थ्यं, सत्यः -त्या -त्यं.

AUTHENTICALLY, *adv.* प्रमाणतस् *ind.*, प्रमाणानुरूपेण, वस्तुतस्, तत्त्वतस्, निर्व्यलीकं, सारतस्.

To AUTHENTICATE, *v. a.* प्रमाणीकृ, प्रमाण (nom. प्रमाणयति -यितुं), सत्याकृ.

AUTHENTICITY, *s.* प्रामाण्यं, प्रमाणत्वं, वास्तवता, निर्व्यलीकता, अकृत्रिमता, मौलता, सारता, सत्यता.

AUTHOR, *s.* (The first beginner of any thing) प्रयोजकः, प्रवर्त्तकः, आरम्भकः, आदिकर्त्ता *m.* (र्तृ).—(The effector) साधकः, उत्पादकः, सम्पादकः, जनकः, कर्त्ता *m.* (र्तृ), कारकः, निर्व्वाहकः.—(A writer) निबन्धा *m.* (न्धृ), ग्रन्थकारः, ग्रन्थकर्त्ता *m.* (र्तृ), रचकः.

To AUTHORISE, *v. a.* (To establish by authority) प्रमाणीकृ, प्रमाणेन सिद्धीकृ or स्थिरीकृ or संस्था in caus. (-स्थापयति -यितुं), सप्रमाणं -णां -णं कृ, प्रमाणवन्तं -वतीं -वत् कृ.—(To give authority to any one) नियुज् (c. 7. -युनक्ति -युंक्ते -योक्तुं, c. 10. -योजयति -यितुं), अधिकारित्वं दा (c. 3. ददाति, दातुं).—(To permit) अनुज्ञा (c. 9. -जानाति -नीते -ज्ञातुं), अनुमन् (c. 4. -मन्यते -मन्तुं).

AUTHORISED, *p. p.* प्रमाणीकृतः -ता -तं, सप्रमाणः -णा -णं, नियुक्तः -क्ता -क्तं, अधिकृतः -ता -तं, नियोगी -गिनी -गि (न्), विधीयमानः -ना -नं.—(Permitted) अनुज्ञातः -ता -तं, अनुमतः -ता -तं.

AUTHORITATIVE, *a.* प्रामाणिकः -की -कं, प्रमाणधारी -रिणी -रि (न्), वैधिकः -की -कं, आचारिकः -की -कं, शासनानुरूपः -पा -पं.

AUTHORITATIVELY, *adv.* प्रमाणतस् *ind.*, प्रमाणानुसारेण, विधिवत्, आचारानुरूपं, शासनात्.

AUTHORITY, *s.* (Weight of testimony, credit) प्रमाणं, प्रामाण्यं.—(Power, influence, control) शक्तिः *f.*, प्रभावः, वशं.—(Dominion) ऐश्वर्य्यं, राज्यं, प्रभुत्वं.—(Weight) गुरुत्वं, गौरवं.—(Credibility) श्रद्धेयता.—(Legal power, title) अधिकारित्वं, अधिकारः, आधिपत्यं, नियोगः, कर्तृत्वं, प्रभुत्वं.—(A received text) आप्तवचनं, निदर्शनं.—(Testimony) साक्ष्यं.—(A person invested with legal powers) अधिकारी *m.* (न्), नियोगी *m.* (न्), प्रभुः *m.*—(An authority, a guide) निर्देष्टा *m.* (ष्टृ); 'of little authority,' अल्पप्रमाणः -णा -णं, अल्पप्रभावः -वा -वं; 'by his authority,' तस्य आज्ञया.

AUTHORSHIP, *s.* निबन्धृत्वं, ग्रन्थकर्तृत्वं, कर्तृत्वं.

AUTO-BIOGRAPHY, *s.* आत्मवृत्तान्तरचनं, आत्मचरित्ररचनं.

AUTOCRASY, *s.* साम्राज्यं, आधिराज्यं, राजाधिराज्यं, स्वाधिपत्यं, स्वाधीनता.

AUTOCRAT, *a.* सम्राट् *m.* (ज्), अधिराजः, राजाधिराजः.

AUTOCRATICAL, *a.* साम्राज्ययोग्यः -ग्या -ग्यं, स्वाधीनः -ना -नं.

AUTOGRAPH, *s.* स्वहस्तलिखितं, स्वहस्ताक्षरं, स्वहस्तलेखः, स्वहस्तलिपिः *f.*

AUTOMATON, *s.* स्वयं चलति यद् यन्त्रं, स्वयञ्चक्रमा मूर्त्तिः.

AUTUMN, *s.* शरद् *f.*, शरदा, शरत्कालं, श्रावणावधिः *m.*, वर्षावसानः.

AUTUMNAL, *a.* शरत्कालीनः -ना -नं, शारदीयः -या -यं, शारदः -दी -दं, शारदी -दिनी -दि (न्).—(Produced in autumn) शरदिजः -जा -जं. शरदुद्भवः -वा -वं.

AUXILIARY, *s.* सहायः, सहकारी *m.* (न्), उपकारकः, उपकारी *m.* (न्), उत्तरसाधकः.

AUXILIARY, *a.* उपकारकः -का -कं or -री -रिणी -रि (न्), सहकारी -रिणी -रि (न्), उत्तरसाधकः -का -कं.—(Auxiliary verb) गौणक्रिया.

To AVAIL, *v. a.* (To assist) उपकृ (c. 8. -करोति -कर्त्तुं), हितं कृ, साहाय्यं कृ, अनुग्रह् (c. 9. -गृह्णाति -ग्रहीतुं).—(To avail one's self of) प्रयुज् (c. 7. -युनक्ति -युंक्ते -योक्तुं), उपयुज्.

To AVAIL, *v. n.* (To be of use) सोपकारः -रा -रं or सफलः -ला -लं भू or अस्, हिताय or फलाय or लाभाय भू.

AVAIL, *s.* (Use) प्रयोजनं, उपयोगः.—(Profit) फलं, हितं, लाभः, साफल्यं, अर्थः.—(Aid) उपकारः.

AVAILABLE, *a.* (To be used) प्रयोज्यः -ज्या -ज्यं, उपयोजनीयः -या -यं, प्रयोगी -गिनी -गि (न्).—(Profitable) सफलः -ला -लं, अर्थकरः -री -रं.

AVANT-GUARD, *s.* सेनामुखं, ध्वजिनीमुखं, रणमूर्द्धा *m.* (न्), नासीरं, अग्रव्यूहः, प्रथमपङ्क्तिः *f.*

AVARICE, *s.* लोभः, अतिकाङ्क्षा, लालसा, जिघृक्षा.—(Desire of wealth) अर्थकामः, वित्तेहा, धनतृष्णा, धनलोभः.

AVARICIOUS, *a.* लोभी -भिनी -भि (न्), लुब्धः -ब्धा -ब्धं, लोभवान् -वती -वत् (त्), कृपणः -णा -णं, अर्थपरः -रा -रं, अर्थलुब्धः -ब्धा -ब्धं, धनलुब्धः -ब्धा -ब्धं, धनार्थी -र्थिनी -र्थि (न्), लिप्सुः -प्सुः -प्सु, मितम्पचः -चा -चं.

AVARICIOUSNESS, *s.* कृपणत्वं, कार्पण्यं, लुब्धता, धनलुब्धता, अतिलोभः.

AVARICIOUSLY, *adv.* लोभेन, लोभात्, सलोभं, कार्पण्येन, कृपणं, अतिकाङ्क्षया.

AVAUNT, *interj.* अपैहि, अपसर, दूरम् अपसर.

To AVENGE, *v. a.* प्रतिकृ (c. 8. -करोति -कुरुते -कर्त्तुं), परिष्कृ, प्रतिहिंस् (c. 1. -हिंसति, c. 7. हिनस्ति -हिंसितुं), प्रतीकारं or प्रतिहिंसां कृ.—(To punish) दण्ड् (c. 10. दण्डयति -यितुं).—(To wipe out a grudge) वैरं शुध् in caus. (शोधयति -यितुं).

AVENGED, *p. p.* प्रतिकृतः -ता -तं, प्रतिहिंसितः -ता -तं, प्रतिहतः -ता -तं, निर्यातितः -ता -तं.—(Wiped out as a grudge) शोधितः -ता -तं.—(Punished) दण्डितः -ता -तं.

AVENGEMENT, *s.* प्रतीकारः, प्रतिक्रिया, प्रतिहिंसा, निर्यातनं, वैरशुद्धिः *f.*

AVENGER, *s.* प्रतिहिंसकः, प्रतिहन्ता *m.* (न्तृ), प्रतीकारकर्त्ता *m.* (र्तृ), वैरशोधकः.

AVENUE, *s.* (An approach) पथः, आगमः, द्वारं.—(An alley of

trees) तरुपंक्तिः *f.*, मार्गे उभयतो रोपिता वृक्षश्रेणी.

To AVER, *v. a.* शपथेन or दिव्येन or दार्ढ्येन वद् (c. 1. वदति, वदितुं).

AVERAGE, *s.* (Mean proportion) मध्यस्थता, मध्यत्वं, मध्यं, मध्यमावस्था, समं.

AVERMENT, *s.* दृढवाक्यं, दृढवचनं, दृढोक्तिः *f.*, स्थिरवचनं.

AVERSE, *a.* विरक्तः -क्ता -क्तं, प्रतिकूलः -ला -लं, विपरीतः -ता -तं, विमतः -ता -तं, विमनीभूतः -ता -तं, द्वेषी -षिणी -षि (न्), वैरी -रिणी -रि (न्).—(To be averse) विरञ्ज् in pass. (-रज्यते), अपावृत् (c. 1. -वर्त्तते -वर्त्तितुं), प्रतीप (nom. प्रतीपायते).—(Averting the face) पराङ्मुखः -खी -खं, विमुखः -खी -खं.

AVERSELY, *adv.* निष्कामं, प्रतिकूलं, विपरीतं, विरक्तं, विरक्त्या.

AVERSENESS, AVERSION, *s.* वैरक्त्यं, विरक्तिः *f.*, निग्रहः, प्रतिकूलता, विमतिः *f.*, पराङ्मुखता, वैमुख्यं, वैपरीत्यं, अप्रियता, अप्रीतिः *f.*, द्वेष्यता: 'aversion to business,' कार्य्यप्रद्वेषः.

To AVERT, *v. a.* अपवृत् in caus. (-वर्त्तयति -यितुं), व्यावृत्, निवृत्, विनिवृत्, निवृ in caus. (-वारयति -यितुं), प्रतिवृ, अपानुद् (c. 6. -नुदति -नोत्तुं), व्यपानुद्, विमुखीकृ.

AVERTED, *p. p.* (Having the face averted) पराङ्मुखः -खी -खं, विमुखः -खी -खं, विमुखीकृतः -ता -तं, विमुखी -खिनी -खि (न्), पराचीनः -ना -नं.—(Kept off) निवारितः -ता -तं, व्यावृत्तः -त्ता -त्तं.

AVIARY, *s.* विटङ्कः, पञ्जरं, पिञ्जरं, वीतंसः, कपोतपालिका, पक्षिशाला, कुलायिका.

AVIDITY, *s.* अतिक्षुधा, गृध्नता, गर्द्धः, अतिस्पृहा, कौतूहलं, लालसा, अतिलोभः.

AVOCATION, *s.* (Calling aside, withdrawing) अपकर्षणं, आकर्षः, अपहरणं.—(Business that calls aside) कार्य्यं, कर्म्म *n.* (न्), विकर्म्म *n.* (न्), व्यापारः, व्यवसायः.

To AVOID, *v. a.* वृज् in caus. (वर्जयति -यितुं), परिवृज्, विवृज्; परिहृ (c. 1. -हरति -ते -हर्त्तुं); प्रोज्झ् (c. 6. -उज्झति -उज्झितुं); हा (c. 3. जहाति, हातुं); त्यज् (c. 1. त्यजति, त्यक्तुं).

AVOIDABLE, *a.* (To be avoided) परिहरणीयः -या -यं, परिहर्त्तव्यः -व्या -व्यं, परित्याज्यः -ज्या -ज्यं, हेयः -या -यं, हातव्यः -व्या -व्यं, त्याज्यः -ज्या -ज्यं.

AVOIDANCE, *s.* त्यागः, परित्यागः, परिहारः, परिहरणं, प्रतिहरणं, वर्जनं, प्रोज्झनं.

AVOIDED, *p. p.* परिहृतः -ता -तं, त्यक्तः -क्ता -क्तं, परित्यक्तः -क्ता -क्तं, विवर्जितः -ता -तं, प्रोज्झितः -ता -तं.

To AVOUCH, *v. a.* (To affirm) दार्ढ्येन or स्थैर्य्येण or शपथेन वद् (c. 1. वदति, वदितुं).—(To vindicate, assert any thing in favour of another) परार्थे प्रतिवद्.

To AVOW, *v. a.* (To confess) स्वीकृ, अङ्गीकृ, उरीकृ, अनुभाष् (c. 1. -भाषते -भाषितुं).—(To declare openly) प्रकाशं or व्यक्तं वद् (c. 1. वदति, वदितुं).

AVOWED, *p. p.* स्वीकृतः -ता -तं, अङ्गीकृतः -ता -तं, व्यक्तोदितः -ता -तं.

AVOWEDLY, *adv.* प्रकाशं, व्यक्तं, प्रकटं, अगूढं.

To AWAIT, *v. a.* अपेक्ष् (c. 1. -ईक्षते -ईक्षितुं), उदीक्ष्, प्रतीक्ष्; प्रतिपाल् (c. 10. -पालयति -यितुं), उद्दृश् (c. 1. -पश्यति -द्रष्टुं), अपेक्षां कृ.

To AWAKE, AWAKEN, *v. a.* जागृ in caus. (जागरयति -यितुं), बुध् in caus. (बोधयति -यितुं), प्रबुध्, प्रतिबुध्, विबुध्; निद्रां भञ्ज् (c. 7. भनक्ति, भंक्तुं), निद्राभङ्गं कृ.—(To incite) उत्था in caus. (-थापयति -यितुं), उत्सह् in caus. (-साहयति -यितुं), प्रोत्सह्; उत्तिज् (c. 10. -तेजयति -यितुं).

To AWAKE, *v. n.* जागृ (c. 2. जागर्त्ति, जागरितुं), प्रजागृ; बुध् (c. 4. बुध्यते, बोद्धुं), अनुबुध्, प्रबुध्, प्रतिबुध्, विबुध्, प्रतिसबुध्.

AWAKE, *a.* जागरः -रा -रं, प्रबुद्धः -द्धा -द्धं, प्रतिबुद्धः -द्धा -द्धं, विप्रबुद्धः -द्धा -द्धं, प्रजागरः -रा -रं, उन्निद्रः -द्रा -द्रं; 'that which keeps one awake at night,' रात्रिजागरदः.

AWAKENED, *p. p.* जागरितः -ता -तं, प्रबोधितः -ता -तं, निद्राभङ्गः -ङ्गा -ङ्गं.

AWAKENING, *s.* प्रबोधनं, प्रबोधः, निद्राभञ्जनं.

To AWARD, *v. a.* दा in caus. (दापयति -यितुं), तीर् (c. 10. तीरयति -यितुं).

AWARD, *s.* (Judgment, sentence) विचारः, निर्णयः, निष्पत्तिः *f.*, तीरणं, समाधानं, दण्डः, आज्ञा.

AWARDED, *p. p.* दापितः -ता -तं, तीरितः -ता -तं.

AWARDER, *s.* विचारकः, निर्णेता *m.* (तृ), दापकः.

AWARE, *a.* (Excited to consciousness) विज्ञापितः -ता -तं, बोधितः -ता -तं.—(Knowing) वेदी -दिनी -दि (न्), ज्ञः -ज्ञा -ज्ञं in comp.—(Vigilant, attentive) सावधानः -ना -नं, जागरः -रा -रं, -री -रिणी -रि (न्); 'he is aware,' वेत्ति, जानाति.

AWAY, *a.* and *adv.*, expressed by the preposition अव.—(Absent) परोक्षः -क्षा -क्षं, स्थानान्तरङ्गतः -ता -तं, अनुपस्थितः -ता -तं, अविद्यमानः -ना -नं.—(Far away) दूरस्थः -स्था -स्थं, दूरस्थायी -यिनी -यि (न्).—(Come along) यातु.—(Begone!) अपैहि, अपसर, हुम्; 'away with this fear,' अलम् अनया शङ्कया.

AWE, *s.* आदरः, सम्भ्रमः, विस्मयः, त्रासः, आतङ्कः, आदरप्रयुक्तं भयं.—(To stand in awe of) भी (c. 3. बिभेति, भेतुं), त्रस् (c. 4. त्रस्यति, त्रसितुं) with abl., आदृ (c. 6. -द्रियते) with acc.

To AWE, *v. a.* (To strike terror into) भी in caus. (भाययति or भीषयति -यितुं), त्रस् in caus. (त्रासयति -यितुं), व्याकुलीकृ, आकुलीकृ, सम्भ्रमेण उपहन् (c. 2. -हन्ति -हन्तुं).

AWE-STRUCK, *a.* सम्भ्रान्तः -न्ता -न्तं, विस्मयाकुलः -ला -लं, भयविप्लुतः -ता -तं.

AWFUL, *a.* घोरः -रा -रं, दारुणः -णा -णं, भैरवः -वा -वं, भीषणः -णा -णं, भयङ्करः -रा -रं, भयानकः -का -कं.—(Worshipful) आदरणीयः -या -यं, आदृत्यः -त्या -त्यं, पूज्यः -ज्या -ज्यं.

AWFULLY, *adv.* दारुणं, घोरं, यथा सम्भ्रम उत्पद्यते तथा.

AWFULNESS, *s.* घोरता, दारुणता, भीषणं, भैरवं, भीष्मं.

AWHILE, *adv.* कियत्कालं, किञ्चित्कालं, अल्पकालं, इयत्कालं, मुहूर्त्तं, क्षणं, यत्किञ्चित्समयं.

AWKWARD, *a.* (Clumsy, unskilful) अदक्षः -क्षा -क्षं, अनाप्तः -प्ता -प्तं, अपटुः -टुः -टु, अक्षिप्रः -प्रा -प्रं, अविज्ञः -ज्ञा -ज्ञं, अकृती -तिनी -ति (न्).—(Inelegant) विरूपः -पी -पं, स्थूलः -ला -लं.

AWKWARDLY, *adv.* अपटु, अदक्षं, अक्षिप्रं, अनाप्तं.

AWKWARDNESS, *s.* (Unskilfulness) अपाटवं, अपटुता, अदक्षत्वं, अक्षिप्रत्वं.—(Inelegance) स्थूलता, वैरूप्यं.

AWL, *s.* आरा, चर्म्मप्रभेदिका, आविधः, वेधनिका.

AWN, *s.* (A beard of corn) शूकः -कं, शस्यशूकं, किंशारुः *m.*

AWNING, *s.* वितानं, वितानकं, आच्छादनं, उल्लोचः.

AWRY, *adv.* तिरस्, साचि, तिर्य्यक्, कुटिलं, जिह्मं, अनृजु.—(Perversely) विपरीतं, प्रतिकूलं, विलोमं.

AXE, *s.* टङ्कः, कुठारः, परशुः *m.*, परश्वधः, छिदिः *f.*, वृक्षभिद् *f.*, वृक्षभेदी *m.* (न्), स्वधितिः *m.*

AXIOM, *s.* तत्त्वं, सूत्रं, सिद्धान्तः, आदेशः, वचनं.

AXIOMATIC, *a.* सौत्रः -त्री -त्रं, सिद्धान्ती -न्तिनी -न्ति (न्).

AXIS, *s.* अक्षः, ध्रुवः, मेरुः *m.*

AXLE, AXLE-TREE, *s.* अक्षाग्रं, अक्षदन्तः.

AY, *adv.* तथेति, एवं, हूम्, आम्.

AYE, *adv.* सर्व्वदा, सदा, नित्यं, नित्यदा, शाश्वतं, अजस्रं, शाश्वतीः समाः.

AZURE, *a.* नीलः -ला -लं, नीलवर्णः, -र्णा -र्णं, आकाशवर्णः -र्णा -र्णं.

B.

To BAA, *v. n.* उ (c. 1. अवते, ओतुं), मेषवत् or उरभ्रवत् शब्दं कृ.

To BABBLE, *v. n.* (To prattle like a child) बालवत् जल्प् (c. 1. जल्पति, जल्पितुं).—(To talk idly) जल्प्.—(To tell secrets) रहस्यं प्रकाश् in caus. (-काशयति -यितुं) or विख्या, in caus. (-ख्यापयति -यितुं), रहस्यभेदं कृ.

BABBLE or BABBLING, *s.* जल्पः, जल्पनं, वावदूकता, बालवचनं, आख्यायिका.

BABBLER, *s.* वाचालः, जल्पकः, उपजल्पी *m.* (न्), वाचाटः, जल्पाकः, वावदूकः.

BABE, BABY, *s.* बालः -ला, बालकः, शिशुः *m.*, शावकः.—(At the breast) स्तनन्धयः, स्तनपाः *m.* (पा), क्षीरपः.

BABEL, *s.* (Confusion) सङ्करः, साङ्कर्य्यं, तुमुलं, कोलाहलः, कालकीलः.

BABOON, *s.* वानरः, कपिः, मर्कटः, प्लवङ्गः, प्लवगः, शाखामृगः, वलीमुखः.

BABYHOOD, *s.* बाल्यं, बालकत्वं, बालभावः, शैशवं.

BABYISH, *a.* बालकीयः -या -यं, बालिशः -शा -शं, बालेयः -यी -यं.

BACCHANALIAN, *s.* पानरतः, पानप्रसक्तः, मद्यपीतः, मद्यप्रियः, सम्पीतिरतः.

BACHELOR, *s.* (A man unmarried) अविवाहितः, अकृतदारः, अकृतदारसङ्ग्रहः, अकृतविवाहः.—(One who takes his first degree) विद्यालये पूर्व्वपदप्राप्तः.

BACK, *s.* पृष्ठं, विग्रहावरं; 'to turn the back, avert the face,' पराङ्मुखः -खी -खं or पराचीनः -ना -नं भू; 'to turn back, away from,' अपवृत् (c. 1. -वर्त्तते -वर्त्तितुं), विनिवृत्, अपावृत्, निवृत्; 'turned back,' विपरिवर्त्तितः -ता -तं; 'at one's back, behind the back,' पृष्ठतस्; 'behind one's back, in one's absence,' परोक्षे.—(The hinder part) पृष्ठदेशः, पश्चाद्देशः, पश्चाद्भागः, पृष्ठं, नितम्बः; 'the back of the hand,' करपृष्ठं.

BACK, *adv.* (To the place whence one came) commonly expressed by प्रति prefixed; as, 'to go back,' प्रतिगम्; 'come back,' प्रत्यावृत्तः -त्ता -त्तं, पुनरागतः -ता -तं; 'brought back,' प्रत्यानीतः -ता -तं.—(Backward from the present station) expressed by परा, प्रति, or पश्चात् prefixed; as, 'to beat back,' पराहन्, प्रत्याहन्.—(Again) expressed by पुनर्, प्रति, or अनु prefixed; as, 'to give back,' प्रतिदा.—(Kept back) निगृहीतः -ता -तं, निवारितः -ता -तं; 'in the back-ground,' दूरस्थः -स्था -स्थं, निभृते.

To BACK, *v. a.* (To mount a horse) आरुह् (c. 1. -रोहति -रोढुं), अधिरुह्, समारुह्.—(To support, justify) रक्ष् (c. 1. रक्षति, रक्षितुं), अभिरक्ष्, संरक्ष्; पक्षपातं कृ, उपकृ, अनुग्रह् (c. 9. -गृह्णाति -ग्रहीतुं).—(To impel backwards) पराणुद् (c. 6. -णुदति -णोत्तुं), विपरीतं प्रणुद्.

To BACK, *v. n.* (To go backwards) अपक्रम् (c. 1. -क्रामति, c. 4. -क्राम्यति, -क्रमितुं), व्यपक्रम्, परावृत् (c. 1. -वर्त्तते -वर्त्तितुं).

To BACKBITE, *v. a.* पृष्ठमांसं खाद् (c. 1. खादति, खादितुं).—(To slander) परिवद् (c. 1. -वदति -ते -वदितुं), अपवद्.

BACKBITER, *s.* पृष्ठमांसादः, परोक्षे अपवादकः, परिवादकः, पिशुनः.

BACKBITING, *s.* परिवादः, अपवादः, पिशुनवाक्यं.

BACKBONE, *s.* कशेरुका, पृष्ठवंशः, पृष्ठास्थि *n.*, रीढकः.

BACKDOOR, *s.* पक्षद्वारं, अन्तर्द्वारं, उपद्वारं, प्रच्छन्नं, पक्षकः, खडक्किका.

BACKGAMMON, *s.* चर्म्मपट्टिकाक्रीडा.—(Backgammon-board) चर्म्मपट्टिका, अष्टापदं, अक्षः.

BACKROOM, *s.* अन्तर्गृहं, अन्तःशाला, उपरोधकं, उपशाला.

BACKSIDE, *s.* (The hinder part of any thing) पृष्ठदेशः, पश्चाद्देशः, पश्चाद्भागः, अधोदेशः.—(The hinder part of any animal) नितम्बः, पृष्ठं.

To BACKSLIDE, *v. n.* स्वधर्म्मात् परिभ्रंश् (c. 4. -भ्रश्यति -भ्रंशितुं) or च्यु (c. 1. च्यवते, च्योतुं), स्वधर्म्मं त्यज् (c. 1. त्यजति, त्यक्तुं).

BACKSLIDER, *s.* धर्म्मच्युतः, धर्म्मभ्रष्टः, स्वधर्म्मत्यागी *m.* (न्), उन्मार्गगामी *m.* (न्), अन्यशास्त्रकः.

BACKSTAIRS, *s.* उपसोपानं, अन्तःसोपानं, पक्षसोपानं, प्रच्छन्नसोपानं.

BACKWARD or BACKWARDS, *adv.* Expressed by परा or प्रति prefixed; पश्चात्, प्रतीपं, विपरीतं, अवकटं; 'to walk backwards and forwards,' गतागतानि or प्रतिगतागतं or गमनागमने or यातायातं कृ.

BACKWARD, *a.* (Unwilling) प्रतीपः -पा -पं, अनिच्छः -च्छा -च्छं, असम्मतः -ता -तं, अनिच्छुकः -का -कं.—(Sluggish) मन्दः -न्दा -न्दं, अलसः -सा -सं, विलम्बी -म्बिनी -म्बि (न्).—(Dull of apprehension) मन्दमतिः -तिः -ति.—(Late, after its time) अतीतकालः -ला -लं, अतिक्रान्तकालः -ला -लं, दीर्घकालीनः -ना -नं, दीर्घपक्वः -क्वा -क्वं, दीर्घपक्वशीलः -ला -लं.

BACKWARDNESS, *s.* (Unwillingness) अनिच्छा, अस्वीकारः, असम्मतिः *f.*—(Sluggishness) आलस्यं, मान्द्यं, विलम्बत्वं.—(Dulness) मन्दमतिता.—(Lateness) दीर्घकालीनता, अतीतकालत्वं, दीर्घता, दीर्घपक्वता.

BACON, *s.* वल्लूरं, शूकरस्य शुष्कमांसं.

BAD, *a.* (Vicious, corrupt) पापः -पा -पं, दुष्टः -ष्टा -ष्टं, अधमः -मा -मं, नीचः -चा -चं, खलः -ला -लं, कुत्सितः -ता -तं, कदर्य्यः -र्य्या -र्य्यं.—(Not good) अभद्रः -द्रा -द्रं, असाधुः -धुः -धु, अधार्म्मिकः -की -कं, असारः -रा -रं, असन् -सती -सत् (त्).—(Worthless) निर्गुणः -णा -णं.—(Hurtful, unwholesome) हिंस्रः -स्रा -स्रं, अहितः -ता -तं, अपथ्यः -थ्या -थ्यं, रुजाकरः -रा -रं.—(Sick) रोगी -गिणी -गि (न्), व्याधितः -ता -तं.—(Sick of) आतुरः -रा -रं, आर्त्तः -र्त्ता -र्त्तं in comp.—(Unfortunate) विपन्नः -न्ना -न्नं, दुर्गतः -ता -तं. 'Bad,' as a general word, is often expressed by दुर्, कु, कत्, or sometimes by वि or अप prefixed; as, 'a bad road,' दुरध्वः, कुपथं, कदध्वा *m.* (न्), विमार्गः; 'a bad man,' दुर्ज्जनः, दुराचारः; 'bad weather,' दुर्द्दिनं; 'bad food,' कदन्नं; 'bad thing,' अपद्रव्यं; 'bad conduct,' दुर्णयः, कुकर्म्म *n.* (न्), अपकर्म्म *n.* (न्); 'bad policy,' अनीतिः *f.*

BADGE, *s.* चिह्नं, लिङ्गं, व्यञ्जनं, लक्षणं.—(Badge of rank) पदचिह्नं, पदसूचकं चिह्नं.

BADGER, *s.* गर्त्तवासी जन्तुविशेषः.

BADINAGE, *s.* लघुवाक्यं, लघूक्तिः *f.*, हास्यवाक्यं, नर्म्म *n.* (न्), ठट्टरी.

BADLY, *adv.* दुष्टु, दुष्टं, अभद्रं. Often expressed by दुर्, कु, अप prefixed; as, 'badly managed,' दुर्णीतः -ता -तं; 'badly shaped,' कुरूपः -पी -पं; 'badly-behaved,' दुःशीलः, कुशीलः; 'badly done,' दुष्कृतः -ता -तं, अपकृतः -ता -तं.

BADNESS, *s.* दुष्टता, दौष्ट्यं, निर्गुणत्वं, नीचता, अभद्रता, कदर्य्यत्वं.—(Of character) दुरात्मता, दुराचारत्वं.

To BAFFLE, *v. a.* (To make ineffectual) मोघीकृ, निष्फलय् (nom. निष्फलयति -यितुं), खण्ड् (c. 10. खण्डयति -यितुं), व्यर्थीकृ, प्रतिहन् (c. 2. -हन्ति -हन्तुं), मुधा कृ, वृथा कृ.—(To defeat) पराभू (c. 1. -भवति -भवितुं), पराजि (c. 1. -जयति -ते -जेतुं).

BAFFLED, *p. p.* प्रतिहतः -ता -तं, मोघाशः -शा -शं, भग्नोहतः -ता -तं, प्रति-

बद्धः -द्धा -द्धं, भग्नोद्यमः -मा -मं, खण्डितः -ता -तं, खण्डिताशंसः -सा -सं, पराजितः -ता -तं.

BAG, *s.* शाणपुटः -टं, स्यूतः, स्योतः, कोषः, आधारः.

To BAG, *v. a.* (To put into a bag) शाणपुटे or स्यूते or कोषे निधा (c. 3. -दधाति -धातुं) or निविश् in caus. (-वेशयति -यितुं).—(To make tumid) श्वि in caus. (श्वाययति -यितुं).

To BAG, *v. n.* (To swell out like a bag) स्यूतवत् लम्ब् (c. 1. लम्बते, लम्बितुं), प्रलम्ब्, or पॄ in pass. (पूर्य्यते), or श्वि (c. 1. श्वयति, श्वयितुं).

BAGATELLE, *s.* स्वल्पविषयः, अल्पमूल्यद्रव्यं, क्षुद्रद्रव्यं, क्षुद्रविषयः.

BAGGAGE, *s.* (The furniture of an army) सामग्री -ग्र्यं, भारः, उपकरणं, परिच्छदः.—(A worthless woman) पुंश्चली *f.*, वेश्या, बन्धकी.

BAGNIO, *s.* (A house for bathing) स्नानागारं, गात्रमार्ज्जनशाला.—(A brothel) वेश्यालयः.

BAIL, *s.* (Security for one's appearance) दर्शनप्रतिभूः *m.*, दर्शनप्रातिभाव्यं, प्रतिनिधिः *m.*, प्रतिभूः *m.*, प्रातिभाव्यं, पारिभाव्यं, लग्नकः, न्यासः, अन्वाधिः *m.*, बन्धकः, तृणमत्कुणः.—(The person who gives the security) प्रतिनिधिः *m.*, प्रतिभूः *m.*, लग्नकदायी *m.* (न्).

To BAIL, *v. a.* (To give bail for another) प्रतिनिधिः or प्रतिभूः भू, लग्नकं दा (c. 3. ददाति, दातुं).

BAILABLE, *a.* यो लग्नकं दत्त्वा मोक्तुं शक्यते or शक्यः.

BAILIFF, *s.* (An officer who arrests) आसेद्धा *m.* (द्धृ), आसेधकर्त्ता *m.* (र्तृ), ग्राहकः, यष्टिधरः, दण्डनायकः.—(A steward) कार्य्याधीशः.

BAILMENT, *s.* आक्षेपः.

BAIRN, *s.* बालः, बालकः, शिशुः *m.*

To BAIT, *v. a.* (To put meat on a hook to tempt animals) मत्स्यादिग्रहणार्थं बडिशे आमिषादि निधा (c. 3. -दधाति -धातुं), or निविश् in caus. (-वेशयति -यितुं).—(To give food to horses on the road) मध्ययाने यवादिना वाहनानि भुज् in caus. (भोजयति -यितुं), यानश्रान्तानि वाहनानि विश्रम् in caus. (-श्रामयति -यितुं).—(To incite dogs to attack a bull) वृषभम् आक्रमितुं कुक्कुरान् प्रचुद् in caus. (-चोदयति -यितुं).

To BAIT, *v. n.* (To stop on the road for refreshment) मध्ययाने भोजनार्थं विश्रम् (c. 4. -श्राम्यति -श्रमितुं).

BAIT, *s.* मत्स्यग्रहणार्थं यद् आमिषं बडिशे निवेश्यते.—(Temptation) प्रलोभनं.

BAIZE, *s.* शाणं, कम्बलः, ऊर्णामयो वस्त्रविशेषः.

To BAKE, *v. a.* आपाके or कन्दौ or चुल्लौ पच् (c. 1. पचति, पक्तुं) or तप् (c. 1. तपति, तप्तुं, c. 10. तापयति -यितुं) or भ्रस्ज् (c. 6. भृज्जति, भ्रष्टुं), कान्दवीकृ.

To BAKE, *v. n.* (To be heated) तप् in pass. (तप्यते), पच् in pass. (पच्यते).

BAKED, *p. p.* कान्दवः -वा -वं, उख्यः -ख्या -ख्यं, कन्दुपक्वः -क्वा -क्वं.

BAKEHOUSE, *s.* आपाकः, कन्दुः *m. f.*, पूपागारं, पूपशाला.

BAKE-MEATS, *s.* कान्दवं, कान्दवान्नं, उख्यं, पक्वान्नं, आपूपिकं, शाष्कुलिकं.

BAKER, *s.* आपूपिकः, कान्दविकः, मोदककृत्, भक्ष्यकारः.

BAKING, *s.* कन्दुपचनं, चुल्लिपचनं, पचनं, तपनं, तापनं.

BALANCE, *s.* (Scales) तुला, मापनः, मापनदण्डं, तौलं, तौलदण्डं.—(The act of comparing two things in the mind) विवेचनं, विकल्पनं, विगणनं, उपमानं.—(That which is wanting to make two parts of an account even) अवशेषः, शेषं, शेषभागः, अधिकांशः, न्यूनांशः.—(Equipoise) तुल्यता, भारतुल्यता.

To BALANCE, *v. a.* (To weigh in a balance) तुल् (nom. तुलयति -यितुं), तूल् (c. 10. तूलयति).—(In the mind) विकॢप् in caus. (-कल्पयति -यितुं), विगण् (c. 10. -गणयति -यितुं).—(To equipoise) समीकृ, तुल्यभारं -रां -रं कृ.—(To regulate an account) शुध् in caus. (शोधयति -यितुं), समीकृ, अपनयनं कृ, विगणनं कृ.

To BALANCE, *v. n.* (To hesitate, fluctuate) दोल (nom. दोलायते यितुं), विकॢप् (c. 1. -कल्पते -कल्पितुं).—(To be equipollent) समीभू, तुल्यीभू.

BALANCED, *p. p.* तुलितः -ता -तं, समीकृतः -ता -तं, तुल्यभारः -रा -रं.—(As an account) शोधितः -ता -तं, अपनीतः -ता -तं, विगणितः -ता -तं.

BALARÁMA, *s.* (A celebrated demigod, half-brother to Kṛishńa, and the third of the Rámas; and considered to be the eighth avatár of Vishńu) बलरामः, बलदेवः, रामः.—As elder brother of Kṛishńa) अच्युताग्रजः.—(As armed with a plough-share) हलायुधः, हलभृत् *m.*, हली *m.* (न्), सीरपाणिः, सङ्कर्षणः.—(As carrying a pestle-like club) मुसली *m.* (न्).—(As having the palm for a banner) तालध्वजः, तालाङ्कः.—(As diverting the stream of the Yamuná) कालिन्दीभेदनः.—(As dressed in blue) नीलाम्बरः.—(As husband of Revatí) रेवतीरमणः.—(As killer of a certain demon) प्रलम्बघ्नः.—(As guardian of Káma) कामपालः.

BALCONY, *s.* वरण्डः, इन्द्रकोषः, प्रग्रीवः -वं, निष्काशः, वितर्द्धिः *f.* or -र्द्धी.

BALD, *a.* (Without hair) मुण्डः -ण्डा -ण्डं, मुण्डितः -ता -तं, अकेशः -शा -शं, विकेशः -शी -शं, केशहीनः -ना -नं.—(Without natural covering) अनावृतः -ता -तं, विवृतः -ता -तं, नग्नः -ग्ना -ग्नं.—(Unadorned, inelegant) असंस्कृतः -ता -तं, अपरिष्कृतः -ता -तं, असभ्यः -भ्या -भ्यं.—(As style) अलङ्कारहीनः -ना -नं, अव्यञ्जनः -ना -नं.

BALDERDASH, *s.* (Any thing jumbled together) प्रकीर्णकं.—(Nonsense) अनर्थकवाक्यं, आलस्यवचनं, वृथाकथा.

BALDNESS, *s.* मौण्ड्यं, मुण्डता, अकेशत्वं.—(Inelegance) असभ्यता.

BALD-PATED, *a.* मुण्डितशिराः -राः -रः (स्), मुण्डमस्तकः -का -कं. नग्नमस्तकः -का -कं.

BALDRICK, *s.* (A girdle) मेखला, काञ्ची.—(The zodiac) राशिचक्रं, राशिमण्डलं, लग्नमण्डलं, ज्योतिश्चक्रं.

BALE, *s.* भाण्डकं, भाण्डं, द्रव्यकूर्चं, पोटलिका, द्रव्यपोट्टली, भारः.

To BALE, *v. a.* (To make up into a bale) भाण्डं कृ, द्रव्याणि कूर्चीकृ. (To bale out water) अभ्रिणा or द्रोण्या जलम् उत्क्षिप् (c. 6. -क्षिपति -क्षेप्तुं) or उत्तुल् (c. 10. -तोलयति -यितुं).

BALEFUL, *a.* (Full of misery) क्लेशी -शिनी -शि (न्), दुःखी -खिनी -खि (न्), सशोकः -का -कं, शोकान्वितः -ता -तं.—(Destructive) नाशी -शिनी -शि (न्), आत्ययिकः -की -कं, प्राणहरः -रा -रं, क्लेशकः -की -कं, हिंस्रः -स्रा -स्रं.

BALEFULLY, *adv.* सशोकं, सक्लेशं, दुःखेन, यथा हिंसा जायते तथा.

BALING-VESSEL, *s.* सेकपात्रं, सेचनं, सेक्त्रं, अब्भ्रि *n.*, अभ्रिः *f.*, अम्बुसेचनी, द्रोणिः *f.*, -णी, अवगाहः, काष्ठकुद्दालः, काष्ठाम्बुवाहिनी *f.*

BALK, *s.* (A ridge of land left unploughed) सेतुः *m.*

To BALK *v. a.* (To frustrate, disappoint) खण्ड् (c. 10. खण्डयति -यितुं), प्रतिहन् (c. 2. -हन्ति -हन्तुं), वृथा कृ, मुधा कृ, भग्नाशं -शां -शं कृ, मोघाशं -शां -शं कृ, व्यर्थीकृ, मोघीकृ, वञ्च् in caus. (वञ्चयति -यितुं).

BALKED, *p. p.* प्रतिहतः -ता -तं, भग्नोद्यमः -मा -मं, खण्डितः -ता -तं, वञ्चितः -ता -तं, परिवञ्चितः -ता -तं, विप्रलब्धः -ब्धा -ब्धं.

BALKH, *s.* (The country) वाह्लीकः.

BALL, *s.* (Any thing round) गोलः -लं, मण्डलं, परिमण्डलं, गोलकः, वर्त्तुलः, निघः, पिण्डं.—(The ball of the earth) भूगोलः, भूमण्डलं.—(For playing) कन्दुकः, गुडः, गेन्दुः *m.*, गेन्दुकः, गिरिः *m.*—(A dancing party) सहनर्त्तनं, नृत्यक्रीडा.—(A ball of thread) सूत्रकोषं.—(Ball of the eye) अक्षिगोलः.—(Ball-room) नृत्यस्थानं, रङ्गशाला, वासकर्णी *f.*

To BALL, *v. a.* (To make into a ball) वर्त्तुलीकृ, गोलीकृ.

BALLAD, *s.* (A song) गीतं, गानं, गीतिः *f.*, सङ्गीतं.

BALLAD-SINGER, *s.* गायकः, गाथाकारः, गायकः, गाता *m.* (तृ).

BALLAST, *s.* नाव अधोभागे स्थापितो भारः, पोतस्थिरीकरणाय तदधोभागे यत् प्रस्तरवालुकादि द्रव्यं निवेश्यते, स्थैर्य्यद्रव्यं.

To BALLAST, *v. a.* नौकायाः स्थिरीकरणाय तदधोभागे भारं स्था in caus. (स्थापयति -यितुं), स्थिरीकृ.

BALLOON, *s.* आकाशयानं, व्योमयानं, आकाशवर्त्मना गमनार्थं विमानं.

BALLOT, *s.* (A ball or ticket used in voting) गुटिका, गुलिका, काकिनी *f.*, कपर्द्दकः, स्वीकृतास्वीकृतचिह्नं.—(The act of voting by ballot) गुटिकां निभृतं पातयित्वा स्वीकृतास्वीकृतज्ञापनं or मतामतसूचनं.

To BALLOT, *v. n.* स्वीकृतास्वीकृतज्ञापनाय गुटिकां निभृतं पत् in caus. (पातयति -यितुं).

BALM, *s.* (The juice of a shrub) गुग्गुलुः *m.*—(That which alleviates) प्रशमनं, शान्तिः *f.*, उपशान्तिः *f.*, वेदनाशान्तिः *f.*

BALMY, *a.* (Having the qualities of balm) पूर्व्वोक्तवृक्षरसोपेतः -ता -तं.—(Soothing) उपशमकः -का -कं, उपशायी -यिनी -यि (न्).—(Fragrant) सौगन्धिकः -की -कं, सुरभिः -भिः -भि.

BALSAM, *s.* (Ointment, unguent) विलेपः, विलेपनं, उपदेहः, अभ्यञ्जनं.

BALSAMIC, *a.* (Unctuous) स्निग्धः -ग्धा -ग्धं, मेदुरः -रा -रं, प्रमेदितः -ता -तं, पिच्छिलः -ला -लं, स्नेही -हिनी -हि (न्), मृदुः -द्वी -दु.

BALUSTRADE, *s.* पङ्क्तिक्रमेण रचितः क्षुद्रस्तम्भसमूहः, क्षुद्रस्तम्भश्रेणी.

BAMBOO, *s.* वेणुः, वंशः, वेतसः, त्वक्सारः, शतपर्व्वा *m.* (न्), मस्करः, तृणध्वजः, यवफलः, तेजनः, कर्म्मारः.—(When rattling) कीचकः.

To BAMBOOZLE, *v. a.* (To cheat) वञ्च् in caus. (वञ्चयते -यितुं), परिवञ्च्, प्रलभ् (c. 1. -लभते -लब्धुं), विप्रलभ्, छल् (c. 10. छलयति -यितुं).

BAMBOOZLED, *p. p.* वञ्चितः -ता -तं, प्रलब्धः -ब्धा -ब्धं, विप्रलब्धः -ब्धा -ब्धं.

BAMBOOZLER, *s.* वञ्चकः, छली *m.* (न्), धूर्त्तः, कूटकः, कितवः, प्रतारकः.

BAN, *s.* (Public notice of any thing) घोषणं -णा, घोषणापत्रं, उत्कीर्त्तनं, समाचारः.—(A curse) शापः, अभिशापः, आक्रोशः; 'under a ban,' शापग्रस्तः -स्ता -स्तं.—(Interdiction) निषेधः, प्रतिषेधः, वारणं, विरोधः.

To BAN, *v. a.* (To curse) शप् (c. 1. शपति -ते, c. 4. शप्यति, शप्तुं), अभिशप्, परिशप्.

BANANA, *s.* कदली, तृणसारा, गुच्छफला, वारणवुषा, रम्भा, मोचा, काष्ठीला.

BAND, *s.* (That which binds) बन्धनं or -नी or -नः.—(Bond) पाशः, शृङ्खलं.—(Union or connection) सम्बन्धः, संयोगः.—(A company of persons) पङ्क्तिः *f.*, समूहः, श्रेणी, समागमः.—(Of musical instruments) वाद्यभाण्डं, वादित्रगणः, तूर्य्यौघः.—(A company of soldiers) गुल्मः, सैनिकः.

To BAND, *v. a.* संयुज् (c. 10. -योजयति -यितुं), एकत्र कृ.

To BAND, *v. n.* एकत्र मिल् (c. 6. मिलति, मेलितुं), सम्मिल्.

BANDAGE, *s.* पट्टः, बन्धनं, पट्टकः, आवेष्टनं, कवलिका.—(Securing with bandages in surgery) अनुवेल्लितं.

BANDBOX, *s.* यत् किञ्चिल्लघुवस्त्रं स्त्रीलोकेन भृतं तदाधानयोग्यः सम्पुटकः or आधारः.

BANDIT, *s.* परिपन्थी *m.* (न्), दस्युः, प्रसह्यचौरः, चौरः, विप्रवकारी *m.* (न्), सारथिकघ्नः.

To BANDY, *v. a.* (To toss to and fro) इतस्ततः or इतश्चेतः क्षिप् (c. 6. क्षिपति, क्षेप्तुं).—(To give and take reciprocally) निमे (c. 1. -मयते -मातुं), विनिमे, परिवृत् in caus. (-वर्त्तयति -यितुं).

BANDY-LEGGED, *a.* प्रज्ञुः -ज्ञुः -ज्ञु, प्रगतजानुः -नुः -नु, विरलजानुः -नुः -नु.

BANE, *s.* (Poison) विषं, गरः -रं, हलाहलः.—(Ruin) नाशः, विनाशः, अत्ययः, दूषणं.—(Causing ruin) दूषकः.

BANEFUL, *a.* (Poisonous) विषधरः -रा -रं, गरली -लिनी -लि (न्). विषान्वितः -ता -तं, विषतुल्यः -ल्या -ल्यं.—(Destructive) नाशी -शिनी -शि (न्). विनाशकः -का -कं, आत्ययिकः -की -कं, दूषकः -का -कं, हिंस्रः -स्रा -स्रं.

BANEFULNESS, *s.* विषालुता, नाशित्वं, हिंस्रता, सगरता.

To BANG, *v. a.* (To beat, thump) तड् (c. 10. ताडयति -यितुं), प्रहृ (c. 1. -हरति -हर्त्तुं), तुद् (c. 6. तुदति -तोत्तुं), आतुद्.

BANG, *s.* आघातः, अभिघातः, प्रहारः, मुष्टिपातः, कराघातः.

To BANISH, *v. a.* (To another country) विवस् in caus. (-वासयति -यितुं), निर्वस्, प्रवस्, विप्रवस्, प्रव्रज् in caus. (-व्राजयति -यितुं), देशान्तरीकृ.—(To drive away) निराकृ (c. 8. -करोति -कर्त्तुं), वहिष्कृ or वहिः कृ, निःसृ, in caus. (-सारयति -यितुं), उत्सृ; अपानुद् (c. 6. -नुदति -नोत्तुं), निरस् (c. 4. -अस्यति -असितुं).

BANISHED, *p. p.* प्रवासितः -ता -तं, विवासितः -ता -तं, निःसारितः -ता -तं, वहिष्कृतः -ता -तं, निरस्तः -स्ता -स्तं, निराकृतः -ता -तं, निःकासितः -ता -तं, अवकृष्टः -ष्टा -ष्टं.

BANISHMENT, *s.* (The act) प्रवासनं, विवासनं, निर्वासनं, प्रव्राजनं, निःसारणं, निरसनं, अपनोदनं, निराकरणं.—(The state) प्रवासः, विवासः.

BANISTER, *s.* सोपाने उभयतः स्थापिता क्षुद्रस्तम्भपङ्क्तिः.

BANK, *s.* (Of a river) तीरं, तटं -टः, कूलं, प्रतीरं, कच्छः, रोधः *n.* (स्); 'the opposite bank,' पारं, तीरान्तरं; 'the near bank,' अवारं.—(Any heap) चयः, कूलं, पिण्डनः, वप्रः; 'sand-bank,' सैकतं.—(A place where money is laid up) धनागारं, मुद्रागारं, निक्षिप्तधनागारं, टङ्कागारं.

To BANK, *v. a.* (To inclose with a bank) कूलेन or वप्रेण परिवेष्ट् (c. 1. -वेष्टते -वेष्टितुं).—(To lay up money in a bank) धनागारे धनं निक्षिप् (c. 6. -क्षिपति -क्षेप्तुं) or न्यस् (c. 4. -अस्यति -असितुं), कुसीदिकं निकटे धनं स्था in caus. (स्थापयति -यितुं).

BANK-BILL, BANK-NOTE, *s.* आनृण्यप्रतिज्ञापत्रं or ऋणशोधनप्रतिज्ञापत्रं यद्दर्शनाद् मुद्रागारे निक्षिप्तधनं प्रतिदीयते, निक्षिप्तधनविनिमयेन यत् प्रतिज्ञापत्रं प्रचलीक्रियते.

BANKER, *s.* (Keeper of a bank) धनागारपतिः *m.*, मुद्रागारपतिः.—(Trader in money) कुसीदिकः, कलोपजीवी *m.* (न्).

BANKRUPT, *s.* परिक्षीणः, ऋणशोधनाय अक्षम ऋणी (न्) or अधमर्णः or ऋणवान् (त्), असमर्थर्णशोधनः, अशक्तानृण्यः, गतविभवः, सर्व्वस्वच्युतः, निर्धनः, हतसम्पदः.

BANKRUPTCY, *s.* परिक्षीणता, ऋणशोधनाशक्तिः *f.*, ऋणमोक्षासामर्थ्यं, निर्धनता.

BANNER, *s.* पताका, ध्वजः or -जं, केतनं, वैजयन्ती *f.*, ध्वजपटः.

BANNS, *s.* (Of marriage) विवाहघोषणा, विवाहघोषणापत्रं.

BANQUET, *s.* उत्सवः, सम्भोजनं, स्वाद्वन्नभोजनं.

To BANQUET, *v. a.* स्वाद्वन्नैः or मिष्टान्नैः or भोजनविशेषैः or सविशेषान्नैः भुज् in caus. (भोजयति -यितुं) or सन्तुष् in caus. (-तोषयति -यितुं)

or संवृध् in caus. (-वर्द्धयति -यितुं) or तृप् in caus. (तर्पयति -यितुं).

To BANQUET, *v. n.* उत्सवं कृ, विशिष्टान्नं or स्वाद्वन्नं or भोजनविशेषान् or सविशेषान्नं भुज् (c. 7. भुंक्ते, भोक्तुं), विशिष्टरूपेण आहारं कृ, आत्मम्भरिः -रिः -रि अस्.

BANQUETER, *s.* उत्सवकर्त्ता *m.* (र्त्तृ), विशिष्टान्नभोक्ता *m.* (क्तृ), स्वाद्वन्नसन्तोषितः, स्वाद्वन्नभक्षकः.

BANQUETING, *s.* उत्सवकरणं, विशिष्टान्नभोजनं, स्वाद्वन्नखादनं.

To BANTER, *v. a.* अवहस् (c. 1. -हसति -हसितुं), अपहस्, विहस् with acc.; अवक्षिप् (c. 6. -क्षिपति -क्षेप्तुं), भर्त्स् (c. 10. भर्त्सयते -ति -यितुं), निन्द् (c. 1. निन्दति, निन्दितुं).

BANTERER, *s.* अवक्षेपकः, क्षेपकः, निन्दकः, परिहासवेदी *m.* (न्).

BANTLING, *s.* बालः, -ला, बालकः, शिशुः *m.*

BANYAN-TREE, *s.* वटः, न्यग्रोधः, पर्कटी.

BAPTISM, *s.* मज्जनं, जलसंस्कारः, अवगाहनं.

BAPTISMAL, *a.* मज्जनसम्बन्धी -न्धिनी -न्धि (न्), जलसंस्कारविषयः -या -यं.

BAPTIST, *s.* मज्जयिता *m.* (तृ), अवगाहकः, जलसंस्कारकर्त्ता *m.* (र्त्तृ).

BAPTISTERY, *s.* मज्जनस्थानं, अवगाहनस्थानं, जलसंस्कारकरणस्थानं.

To BAPTIZE, *v. a.* मज्ज् in caus. (मज्जयति -यितुं), निमज्ज्, अवगाह् in caus. (-गाहयति -यितुं), जलसंस्कारं कृ.

BAR, *s.* (Of a door) अर्गलं.—(Of a cage) शलाका.—(Any obstacle) विघ्नः, अवरोधः -धकं, व्याघातः, प्रतिष्टम्भः, बाधकः, प्रतिबन्धः, प्रत्यूहः.—(A sand-bank) सैकतं.—(The place where criminals are tried) धर्म्मसभा, विचारस्थानं.—(A solid mass of metal) लोहपिण्डः -ण्डं, कुशी.—(In music) तालनियामका रेखा.—(In a tavern) शुण्डापाने मद्यक्रेतृविक्रेत्रोरभ्यन्तरे स्थापितम् अवरोधकं तत्र च तन्मध्ये विगणनं क्रियते.

To BAR, *v. a.* (To fasten with a bar) अर्गलेन बन्ध् (c. 9. बध्नाति, बद्धुं).—(To hinder) वृ in caus. (वारयति -यितुं), निवृ, प्रतिवृ; प्रतिरुध् (c. 7. -रुणद्धि -रोद्धुं), निरुध्, विरुध्, प्रतिबन्ध्.—(To shut out from) निराकृ, निरस् (c. 4. -अस्यति -असितुं).—(To exclude) बहिष्कृ, निराकृ.—(To prohibit) प्रतिषिध् (c. 1. -सेधति -सेद्धुं), निषिध्; अन्तःख्या (c. 2. -ख्याति -ख्यातुं).

BARB, *s.* (A species of horse brought from Barbary) विदेशजातीयः सुतनुकायविशिष्टस् तुरगप्रभेदः.—(A crooked point) फलं, कर्णः, शूलाग्रं, शरफलं.—(Armour for horses) प्रखरः, प्रक्षरः, अश्वतनुत्रं, अश्वसज्जा.

BARBACAN, *s.* प्राकारीयनगरोपान्ते निर्म्मितं दुर्गं.

BARBARIAN, *s.* म्लेच्छः, म्लेच्छजातिः *m.*, शबरः, किरातः, खुधुनः, पुलिन्दः.—(An uncivilized man) असभ्यलोकः, पुरुषपशुः.—(A foreigner) विदेशी *m.* (न्).—(A cruel tyrant) निर्दयः.—(The country of barbarians) प्रत्यन्तः.

BARBARIAN, BARBARIC, *a.* (Belonging to barbarians) म्लेच्छी -च्छिनी -च्छि (न्). विदेशी -शिनी -शि (न्), वैदेशिकः -की -कं.—(Uncivilized) असभ्यः -भ्या -भ्यं, असंस्कृतः -ता -तं, अशिष्टः -ष्टा -ष्टं.

BARBARISM, *s.* (In grammar) म्लेच्छितं.—(Savageness of manners) क्रूरता, क्रूराचारता, म्लेच्छत्वं, पशुता, दुराचारत्वं.

BARBARITY, *s.* (Cruelty) निष्ठुरता, निर्दयत्वं, क्रूरता.—(Of manners) असभ्यता, क्रूराचारता.

BARBAROUS, *a.* (Foreign) म्लेच्छीयः -या -यं, वैदेशिकः -की -कं.—(Savage in manners) क्रूराचारः -रा -रं, कुशीलः -ला -लं, दुराचारः -रा -रं, अशिष्टः -ष्टा -ष्टं, श्वापदः -दी -दं.—(Cruel) निष्ठुरः -रा -रं, निर्दयः -या -यं, क्रूरः -रा -रं.

BARBAROUSLY, *adv.* म्लेच्छवत्, असभ्यलोकवत्, पशुवत्, श्वापदवत्.—(Cruelly) निर्दयं, निष्ठुरं, अतिक्रूरतया.

BARBED, *a.* कर्णी -र्णिनी -र्णि (न्), फलयुक्तः -क्ता -क्तं, लौहाग्रयुक्तः -क्ता -क्तं.—(Mailed) वर्म्मितः -ता -तं, कवची -चिनी -चि (न्), परिदंशितः -ता -तं.

BARBEL, *s.* नादेयमत्स्यविशेषः.

BARBER, *s.* नापितः, क्षुरी *m.* (न्), मुण्डी *m.* (न्), क्षौरिकः, अन्तावसायी *m.* (न्), दिवाकीर्त्तिः *m.*; 'a barber's business,' नापित्यं.

BARBES, *s. pl.* (A disease of horses) अश्वीयरोगविशेषः.

BARD, *s.* मागधः, वन्दी *m.* (न्), मधुकः.—(Poet) कविः *m.*, काव्यशास्त्रज्ञः.

BARDICK, *a.* मागधसम्बन्धी -न्धिनी -न्धि (न्), काव्यशास्त्रसम्बन्धीयः -या -यं.

BARE, *a.* (Naked) नग्नः -ग्ना -ग्नं.—(Without ornament) अभूषितः -ता -तं, अनलङ्कृतः -ता -तं, असंस्कृतः -ता -तं.—(Unclothed) विवस्त्रः -स्त्रा -स्त्रं.—(Uncovered) अनावृतः -ता -तं, विवृतः -ता -तं, अपवृतः -ता -तं.—(Mere) केवलः -ला -लं, मात्रकः -का -कं, मात्रं.—(Threadbare, worn) जीर्णः -र्णा -र्णं; 'the bare ground,' केवला भूमिः, पृथिवीतलं, भूतलं.

To BARE, *v. a.* (To strip, uncover) नग्नीकृ; व्यक्तीकृ; उच्छद् (c. 10. -छादयति -यितुं), विवृ (c. 5. -वृणोति -वरितुं -वरीतुं).

BARED, *p. p.* नग्नीकृतः -ता -तं, व्यक्तीकृतः -ता -तं, विवृतः -ता -तं.

BAREFACED, *a.* (Shameless) निर्लज्जः -ज्जा -ज्जं, लज्जाहीनः -ना -नं, धृष्टः -ष्टा -ष्टं.

BAREFACEDNESS, *s.* निर्लज्जत्वं, धृष्टता, धार्ष्ट्यं, प्रगल्भता, प्रागल्भ्यं, वैयात्यं.

BAREFOOT, *a.* नग्नपादः -दा -दं, शून्यपादः -दा -दं, पादुकाहीनः -ना -नं.

BAREHEADED, *a.* नग्नशिराः -राः -रः (स्), शून्यमस्तकः -का -कं, अनावृतशिराः -राः -रः (स्).

BARELY, *adv.* (Merely) मात्रं, केवलं.—(Hardly) कष्टं, कष्टेन, कृच्छ्रेण.—(Nakedly)—नग्नं, शून्यं, आच्छादनव्यतिरेकेण.—(Without ornament) अलङ्कारव्यतिरेकेण, भूषणं विना.

BARENESS, *s.* (Nakedness) नग्नत्वं, शून्यता, रिक्तता.—(Leanness, poverty) क्षीणता, दरिद्रता, दैन्यं.

BARGAIN, *s.* (A contract, agreement) समयः, नियमः, संविद् *f.*, उपगमः, अभ्युपगमः, संश्रवः, आश्रवः, समाधिः *m.*, उद्देशः.—(Contract concerning the price of a thing sold) पणः, विपणः, क्रयनियमः, क्रयविक्रयनियमः, क्रयपत्रं.

To BARGAIN, *v. n.* पण् (c. 1. पणते, पणितुं or पणायति -यितुं), पणं कृ, सङ्घट्ट् (c. 1. -घट्टते -घट्टितुं), समयाकृ, नियमीकृ, क्रयविक्रयनियमं कृ.

BARGAINED, *p. p.* पणितः -ता -तं, पणायितः -ता -तं, सङ्घट्टितः -ता -तं.

BARGE, *s.* तरालुः *m.*, तरान्धुः *m.*, वहित्रं.—(Pleasure-boat) केलिनौका.

BARGEMAN, *s.* नाविकः, पोतवाहः, पूर्व्वोक्तनौकाकर्णधारः, तरिकः.

BARK, *s.* वल्कलः -लं, वल्कं, त्वक् *f.* (च्), त्वचं, छल्ली *f.*, शल्कं, शल्कलं; 'bark of a tree,' तरुत्वक् *f.* (च्).—(Made of bark) त्वङ्मयः -यी -यं, तरुत्वङ्निर्म्मितः -ता -तं, वाल्कलः -ली -लं.—(Garment of) वल्कलः.—(A small ship) पोतः, क्षुद्रनौका.

To BARK, *v. a.* (To strip trees of their bark) त्वच् (nom. त्वचयति -यितुं), वल्क् (nom. वल्कयति -यितुं), त्वक्ष् (c. 1. त्वक्षति, त्वक्षितुं), वल्कम् उत्कृष् (c. 1. -कर्षति -क्रष्टुं) or निष्कृष्.—(To enclose, as bark) वल्कलवत् परिवेष्ट् (c. 1. -वेष्टते -वेष्टितुं).

To BARK, *v. n.* भष् (c. 1. भषति, भषितुं), बुक्क् (c. 1. बुक्कति, बुक्कितुं, c. 10. बुक्कयति -यितुं), रै (c. 1. रायति, रातुं).—(To revile) आक्रुश् (c. 1. -क्रोशति -क्रोष्टुं), मुखरीकृ.

BARKER, *s.* भषकः.—(Reviler) आक्रोशकः.

BARKING, *s.* (Of dogs) भषणं, बुक्कनं, रायणं, रुतं.

BARKY, *a.* वाल्कः -ल्की -ल्कं, वाल्कलः -ली -लं, त्वङ्मयः -यी -यं.

BARLERIA, *s.* (A flower) वाणा, आर्त्तगलः, कुरवकः, सहचरी, क्षुरः.

BARLEY, *s.* यवः, यवकः, तीक्ष्णशूकः, प्रवेटः, शितशूकः; 'unripe barley,' तोक्मः, यावकः, कुल्माषं; 'barley-meal,' यवक्षोदः; 'barley-water,' उदमन्थः; 'made of barley,' यवमयः -यी -यं; 'sown with barley,' यव्यः -व्या -व्यं.

BARLEY-BROTH, *s.* यवसुरं, यवनिर्म्मितं पानीयं, यवरसः.

BARLEY-CORN, *s.* यवः, तिर्य्यग्यवोदरं.

BARLEY-MOW, *s.* लूनयवसङ्ग्रहस्थानं, यवे लूने सति तत्सञ्चयनस्थानं.

BARLEY-SUGAR, *s.* यवरससङ्क्वथित इक्षुसारः, माधिकशर्करा, शुक्लोपला.

BARM, *s.* सुरामण्डः, मद्यमण्डः, कारोत्तरः, कारोत्तमः, अभिषवः.

BARN, *s.* कुशूलः, शस्यभाण्डं, भाण्डागारः, धान्यागारः, धान्यकोष्ठकं, धान्यसङ्ग्रहस्थानं.

BARNACLE, *s.* (A kind of shell-fish) नौकाकाष्ठलग्नः शम्बूकविशेषः.—(An instrument to hold a horse by the nose) पाशविशेषो येन तुरङ्गो मुखदेशे नियम्यमाणोऽश्वचिकित्सकेन चिकित्सितुं शक्यते.—(A kind of bird) हंसजातीयः पक्षिप्रभेदः.

BAROMETER, *s.* आकाशतोलनयन्त्रं, आकाशपरिमाणार्थं पारदपूरिता काचनाली.

BARON, *s.* क्रमागतानां कुलीनपदानां मध्ये पदप्रभेदः, अधिपतिः *m.*, स्वामी *m.* (न्).—(Baron of beef) गोपृष्ठं, उभयपार्श्वीयपञ्जरयुक्तं गोमांसं.

BARONESS, *s.* वक्ष्यमाणकुलीनपदस्थितस्य पुरुषस्य पत्नी or भार्य्या.

BARONET, *s.* क्रमागतानां कुलीनपदानां मध्ये अवरपदं यस्य सः.

BARONIAL, *a.* पूर्व्वोक्तकुलीनपदसम्बन्धी -न्धिनी -न्धि (न्).

BARONY, *s.* पूर्व्वोक्तकुलीनपदसम्बन्धीयम् आधिपत्यं or स्वाम्यं.

BARRACK, *s.* सैन्यागारं, सैन्यालयः, अयुद्धसमये सैन्यनिवासस्थानं, सैन्यावासः.

To BARRACK, *v. a.* सैन्यान् सैन्यागारे पृथक् पृथक् स्था in caus. (स्थापयति -यितुं), or वस् in caus. (वासयति -यितुं).

BARRED, *p. p.* विरुद्धः -द्धा -द्धं, प्रतिबद्धः -द्धा -द्धं, निषिद्धः -द्धा -द्धं, बाधितः -ता -तं.

BARREL, *s.* (A small cask) दीर्घगोलाकारं काष्ठनिर्म्मितं पात्रं or भाण्डं.—(A cylinder, as of a gun) नाडिः -डी *f.*, नाली or -ला.

To BARREL, *v. a.* (To put in a barrel) पूर्व्वोक्तपात्रे निविश् in caus. (-वेशयति -यितुं).

BARREN, *a.* (Not prolific) वन्ध्यः -न्ध्या -न्ध्यं, असुती -तिनी -ति (न्), अप्रसवी -विनी -वि (न्), प्रजारहितः -ता -तं.—Unfruitful) निष्फलः -ला -लं, अफलः -ला -लं, अवकेशी -शिनी -शि (न्), शुष्कः -ष्का -ष्कं, —(Useless) व्यर्थः -र्था -र्थं, अनर्थकः -का -कं, मोघः -घा -घं.—(Empty) शून्यः -न्या -न्यं, रिक्तः -क्ता -क्तं; 'a barren woman,' वन्ध्या, अप्रसूता; 'a barren soil,' मरुस्थलं or -ली.

BARRENNESS, *s.* वन्ध्यता, निष्फलता, वैयर्थ्यं, शुष्कता, शून्यता.—(In a female) वन्ध्यात्वं.

BARRICADE OR BARRICADO, *s.* प्राचीरं, प्राकारः, वप्रः -प्रं, अवरोधकं, पथावरोधः.

To BARRICADE OR BARRICADO, *v. a.* and *n.* रुध् (c. 7. रुणद्धि, रोद्धुं), प्रतिरुध्, संरुध्; प्रतिबन्ध् (c. 9. -बध्नाति -बद्धुं); प्राचीरेण पथम् अवरुध्.

BARRIER, *s.* (A barricade) प्राकारः, प्राचीरं, परिकूटं, वप्रः.—(An obstacle) विघ्नः, प्रतिष्टम्भः, अवरोधकं, प्रतिरोधः, प्रतिबन्धः, सम्बाधनं. प्रत्यूहः.—(A boundary) सीमा, पर्य्यन्तं, परिसीमा.

BARRISTER, *s.* उत्तरवादी *m.* (न्), परार्थं वादी *m.* (न्), प्रतिवादी *m.* (न्), परार्थे वादानुवादकर्त्ता *m.* (र्तृ), मन्त्री *m.* (न्), मन्त्रकृत्, व्यवस्थानिरूपकः, व्यवहारपण्डितः, स्मृतिशास्त्रज्ञः, धीसचिवः.

BARROW, *s.* (A kind of vehicle) हस्तप्रचालितं वाहनं or यानं.—(A hog) शूकरः.—(A mound) मृत्तिकाराशिः *f.*, उन्नतभूभागः.

To BARTER, *v. n.* (To trade) भाण्डविनिमयेन वाणिज्यं कृ.

To BARTER, *v. a.* (To exchange one article for another) निमे (c. 1. -मयते -मातुं), विमे, विनिमे, भाण्डविनिमयं कृ, परिवृत् in caus. (-वर्त्तयति -यितुं), भाण्डं प्रति भाण्डं दा (c. 3. ददाति, दातुं); 'capable of being bartered,' परिवर्त्तनीयः -या -यं.

BARTER, *s.* भाण्डविनिमयः, निमेयः, नैमेयः, विमयः, विनिमयः, वैमेयः, प्रतिदानं, परिदानं, परिवृत्तिः *f.*, परीवर्त्तः, परिवर्त्तः, निमया, व्यतिहारः; 'any thing obtained by barter,' आपमित्यकं.—(Rule of barter in arithmetic) भाण्डप्रतिभाण्डकः.

BARTON, *s.* (A poultry-yard) ग्रामकुक्कुटादिरक्षणार्थं वृतिः.

BASALT, *s.* लोहसदृश अतिदृढः कृष्णवर्णः प्रस्तरविशेषः.

BASALTIC, पूर्व्वोक्तप्रस्तरसम्बन्धी -न्धिनी -न्धि (न्).

BASE, *a.* (Mean, vile) नीचः -चा -चं, अधमः -मा -मं, निकृष्टः -ष्टा -ष्टं, अपकृष्टः -ष्टा -ष्टं, खलः -ला -लं, अनार्य्यः -र्य्या -र्य्यं, निर्गुणः -णा -णं, दुष्टः -ष्टा -ष्टं, तुच्छः -च्छा -च्छं, जघन्यः -न्या -न्यं, कदर्य्यः -र्य्या -र्य्यं, हीनः -ना -नं, कुत्सितः -ता -तं; 'a base man,' कापुरुषः.—(Of mean parentage) अकुलः -ला -लं, अकुलीनः -ना -नं.—(Of mean spirit) कृपणः -णा -णं, दुष्टभावः -वा -वं; 'base metal,' कुप्यं.

BASE OR BASS, *a.* (As sound) गम्भीरः -रा -रं, धीरः -रा -रं.—(A base sound) मन्द्रः.

BASE, *s.* (The bottom of any thing) अधोभागः, मूलं, तलं, उपष्टम्भः, उपान्तं.—(In geometry) भूमिः *m.* (न्), भूमिः *f.*—(Base of a pillar) उपष्टम्भः, स्तम्भस्य अधोभागः.—(Base of a tree) तरुतलं. —(Foundation of a house) भित्तिमूलं, पोटः.

BASE-BORN, *a.* विहीनयोनः -निः -नि, विजातः -ता -तं, कलुषयोनिजः -जा -जं, हीनजातिः -तिः -ति.—(Bastard) जारजः, कुण्डः.

BASE-MINDED, *a.* दुष्टमतिः -तिः -ति, दुष्टचेताः -ताः -तः (स्).

BASED, *p. p.* (Founded) मूलः -ला -लं in comp.; 'based on knowledge,' ज्ञानमूलः -ला -लं.

BASELESS, *a.* निर्म्मूलः -ला -लं, अमूलः -ला -लं.

BASELY, *adv.* अपकृष्टं, निकृष्टं, नीचतया, सदैन्यं, दुष्टजनवत्, अधमप्रकारेण, कार्पण्येन.

BASEMENT, *s.* (Foundation of a house) गृहस्य भित्तिमूलं, वास्तु *n.*, पोटः.

BASENESS, *s.* (Meanness) नीचता, दुष्टता, निकृष्टता, दैन्यं, कदर्य्यत्वं, अनार्य्यता, खलता.—(Of birth) हीनजातिता, वैजात्यं.—(Of Sound) गाम्भीर्य्यं.—(Of metal) मलं, कुप्यत्वं.

BASHAW, *s.* तर्कीयदेशे ख्यातिविशेषः, सेनानीः *m.*, सेनापतिः *m.*, अधिपतिः *m.*

BASHFUL, *a.* ह्रीमान् -मती -मत् (त्), लज्जावान् -वती -वत् (त्), अपत्रपिष्णुः -ष्णुः -ष्णु, त्रपितः -ता -तं, त्रपायुक्तः -क्ता -क्तं, व्रीडितः -ता -तं, शालीनः -ना -नं.—(Timorous) भीरुः -रुः -रु.

BASHFULLY, *adv.* लज्जया, सत्रपं, सव्रीडनं.—(Timorously) सचकितं, सभयं.

BASHFULNESS, *s.* ह्रीः *f.*, लज्जा, त्रपः -पा, अपत्रपा, व्रीडा, व्रीडनं, शालीनत्वं, मन्दाक्षं.—(Timidity) भीरुता.

BASIL, *s.* (A plant) तुलसी, मरुवकः, समीरणः, प्रस्थपुष्पः, फणिज्झकः, पर्णासः, जम्भीरः, कठिञ्जरः, कुठेरकः, अर्ज्जकः.

BASILICA, *s.* (The middle vein of the arm) बाहुमध्यस्था वृहन्नाडिः *f.*

BASILICK, *s.* वृहत्पूजाशाला.

BASILISK, *s.* (A kind of serpent) चूडायुक्तः सर्पभेदः.

BASIN, *s.* तडागः, जलाशयः, जलाधारः, खातं. See Bason.

BASIS, *s.* (Foundation of any thing) मूलं, अधोभागः, उपष्टम्भः, तलं.—(Basis of a pillar) स्तम्भस्य अधोभागः.—(The groundwork of any thing) मूलं, वस्तु *n.*, योनिः *m.*; 'prosperity has virtue for its basis,' धर्म्ममूला सम्पत्तिः; 'the basis or material of cloth,' वस्त्रयोनिः.

To BASK, *v. n.* सूर्य्यातपं or सूर्य्यतेजः सेव् (c. 1. सेवते, सेवितुं), प्रतिसूर्य्यं शी (c. 2. शेते, शयितुं) or संविश् (c. 6. -विशति -वेष्टुं).

BASKET, *s.* पिटकः, पेटकः, पेटा, डलकं, डल्लकः, करण्डः, मञ्जूषा, कण्डोलः; 'basket-maker,' वैणवः, वैदलकारः; 'basket-work,' वैदलं.

BASON or BASIN, *s.* (Reservoir) तडागः, जलाशयः, वेशन्तः, पल्वलः -लं, अल्पसरः *n.* (स्), खातं, क्रीडासरः *n.* (स्).—(Round the foot of a tree) आलवालं, आवालं, आवापः.—(Vessel to hold water) द्रोणी, पात्रं, भाण्डं, जलाधारः, काष्ठाम्बुवाहिनी.—(Harbour) खातं, पोतबन्धनस्थानं.—(Scale of a balance) तुलापटः.

BASS, *a.* (In music.) See Base.

BASS, *s.* (Mat) कटः, तृणपूली, तलाची, पादपाशी.

BASSO-RELIEVO or BASS-RELIEF *s.* प्रतिच्छाया, प्रतिच्छन्दः, उच्चैःप्रकारेण तक्षिता चित्रलेखा.

BASSOON, *s.* शुषिरविशेषः, शुषिरवाद्यप्रभेदः.

BASTARD, *s.* जारजः, असतीसुतः, कुण्डः -ण्डी *m.* (न्), उपस्त्रीजातः, दासीपुत्रः, कौलटेरः, कौलटेयः, बन्धुलः, बान्धकिनेयः.—(Born after the death of a husband) गोलकः.

BASTARD, *a.* (Illegitimate) विजनितः -ता -तं, विजातः -ता -तं.—(Spurious) कृत्रिमः -मा -मं, कल्पितः -ता -तं.

BASTARDY, *s.* जारजातता, जारजत्वं, कुण्डावस्था, उपस्त्रीजातदशा.

To BASTE, *v. a.* (To beat with a stick) लगुडेन or गदया तड् (c. 10. ताडयति -यितुं), or प्रहृ (c. 1. -हरति -हर्त्तुं), or अभिहन् (c. 2. -हन्ति -हन्तुं), or तुद् (c. 6. तुदति, तोत्तुं).—(To sprinkle meat that is roasting) पच्यमानं or शूलाकृतं मांसं घृतेन सिच् (c. 6. सिञ्चति, सेक्तुं).—(To sew) सीव् (c. 4. सीव्यति, सेवितुं).

BASTILE, *s.* प्राकारयुक्तं कारागारं, दुर्गं, दुर्गपरिगतं परिखाप्राचीरादि.

BASTINADE or BASTINADO, *s.* लगुडेन ताडनं, दण्डाघातः, गदाप्रहारः.

BASTING, *s.* दण्डाघातनं, लगुडपातनं, गदाप्रहरणं, अभिघातः, ताडनं.

BASTION, *s.* वप्रः -प्रं, दुर्गबहिःपार्श्वे राशीकृता मृत्तिका or उपचितो वप्रः.

BAT, *s.* जतुका, जतूका, अजिनपत्रा, चर्म्मचटका, चर्म्मचटी, भङ्कारी.—(A club) गुलिकाक्रीडायां गुलिकाप्रणोदार्थं यष्टिः *m.* or गदा or लगुडः.

BAT-FOWLER, *s.* रात्रिकाले जतुकादिव्याधः or पक्षिग्राहकः.

BAT-FOWLING, *s.* प्रदोषकाले or रात्रिसमये पक्षिग्रहणं.

BATCH, *s.* (A number of things) गणः, सङ्घं, सङ्घातः.—(A single baking) आपूपिकं, पैष्टिकं, शाष्कुलिकं, यत्पिष्टकपूपादि एककाले पच्यते.

BATCHELOR, *s.* अविवाहितः, अकृतदारः, अकृतविवाहः.

To BATE, *v. a.* न्यूनीकृ, अल्पीकृ, ह्रस् in caus. (ह्रासयति -यितुं), कन् (nom. कनयति -यितुं), लघ् (nom. लघयति -यितुं), शम् in caus. (शमयति -यितुं), उद्धारं कृ.

To BATE, *v. n.* क्षि in pass. (क्षीयते), न्यूनीभू, अल्पीभू, ह्रस् (c. 1. ह्रसति, ह्रसितुं), शम् (c. 4. शाम्यति, शमितुं).

BATEFUL, *a.* कलहकारी -रिणी -रि (न्), विवादशीलः -ला -लं.

BATEMENT, *s.* न्यूनीकरणं, अल्पीकरणं, न्यूनता, उद्धारः, उद्धरणं.

BATH, *s.* स्नानकुण्डं, स्नानागारं, स्नानशाला, अवगाहः, अवगाहनस्थानं.

To BATHE, *v. a.* स्ना in caus. (स्नापयति -यितुं), धाव् (c. 1. धावति, धावितुं or caus. धावयति -यितुं), प्रधाव् in caus., क्षल् (c. 10. क्षालयति -यितुं), प्रक्षल्, निमज्ज् in caus. (-मज्जयति -यितुं), आप्लु in caus. (-प्लावयति -यितुं).

To BATHE, *v. n.* स्ना (c. 2. स्नाति, स्नातुं), निमज्ज् (c. 6. -मज्जति -मज्जितुं), अवगाह् (c. 1. -गाहते -गाहितुं -गाढुं), आप्लु (c. 1. -प्लवते -प्लोतुं), अभिषेकं कृ.—(With one's clothes on) सचेलः स्ना.

BATHED, *p. p.* स्नातः -ता -तं, कृतस्नानः -ना -नं, अवगाहितः -ता -तं, अवगाढः -ढा -ढं, आप्लुतः -ता -तं, निमग्नः -ग्ना -ग्नं, धौतः -ता -तं, जलशुचिः -चिः -चि.

BATHER, *s.* स्नायी *m.* (न्), कृतस्नानः, स्नाता *m.* (तृ), आप्लवकः, निमज्जनकृत्.

BATHING, *s.* (Act of) स्नानं, मज्जनं, निमज्जनं, आप्लवः, आप्लावः, अवगाहनं, अभिषेकः.—(Religious bathing) सवनं, अभिषवः, सूत्या.—(Relating to bathing) स्नानीयः -या -यं.—(Bathing-gown) स्नानवस्त्रं.

BATHOS, *s.* वाक्यालङ्कारविशेषः, गम्भीरता, गाम्भीर्य्यं, नीचता.

BATING, *prep.* वर्ज्जयित्वा, वर्ज्जं, ऋते, अपास्य, व्यतिरिक्तं, व्यतिरेकेण.

BATLET, *s.* वस्त्रधावने रजकैः प्रयुक्तश् चतुष्कोणः काष्ठमुद्गरः.

BATOON, *s.* दण्डः, गदा, लगुडः, यष्टिः *m.*, वेत्रं.

BATTALION, *s.* वाहिनी, सैन्यदलं, गुल्मः, व्यूहः, सेनामुखं.

BATTEL, *s.* यः कश्चिद् व्ययो राजविद्यालये अन्तेवासिना क्रियते तद्गणनापत्रं.

To BATTEN, *v. a.* (To make fat) प्यै in caus. (प्याययति -यितुं), स्फाय् in caus. (स्फावयति -यितुं), संवृध् in caus. (-वर्धयति -यितुं), तृप् in caus. (तर्पयति -यितुं), पीनं -नां -नं कृ.—(To fertilize) सफल (nom. सफलयति -यितुं).

To BATTEN, *v. n.* (To grow fat) प्यै (c. 1. प्यायते, प्यातुं), स्फाय् (c. 1. स्फायते, स्फायितुं), संवृध् (c. 1. -वर्धते -वर्धितुं), आत्मम्भरिः -रिः -रि or उदरम्भरिः -रिः -रि अस्.

To BATTER, *v. a.* (To shatter) मृद् (c. 9. मृद्गाति, मर्द्दितुं), अवमृद्, प्रमृद्; चूर्ण् (c. 10. चूर्णयति -यितुं), प्रचूर्ण्, मथ् (c. 9. मथ्नाति, मन्थितुं or मथितुं), विमथ्, पिष् (c. 7. पिनष्टि, पेष्टुं), निष्पिष्, प्रतिपिष्; चूर्णीकृ, भञ्ज् (c. 7. भनक्ति, भंक्तुं), प्रभञ्ज्; तड् (c. 10. ताडयति -यितुं), तुद् (c. 6. तुदति, तोत्तुं).

BATTERED, *p. p.* मृदितः -ता -तं, मर्द्दितः -ता -तं, विमथितः -ता -तं, चूर्णितः -ता -तं, भग्नः -ग्ना -ग्नं, ताडितः -ता -तं, निष्पिष्टः -ष्टा -ष्टं.

BATTERING-RAM, *s.* दुर्गभित्तिमर्द्दने or नगरप्राचीरभञ्जने पूर्व्वकालीनयोधैः प्रयुक्तो मेषमस्तकाकारायो वृहद्दण्डः.

BATTERY, *s.* (The act of battering) मर्द्दनं, पेषणं, भञ्जनं, आघातनं.—(In law) दण्डपारुष्यं.—(A line of cannon) युद्धयन्त्रश्रेणी.

BATTLE, *s.* युद्धं, रणः, रणं, सङ्ग्रामः, समरः -रं, विग्रहः, संयुगः, आहवः, आयोधनं, प्रयुद्धं, प्रधनं, संख्यं, सङ्गरः, कलहः, प्रघातः, प्राघातः, समाघातः, मृधं, सम्परायः -यकं, साम्परायिकं, युत् *f.* (ध्), कलिः *m.*, सम्प्रहारः, प्रविदारणं, समुदायः, समित् *f.*, समितिः, समीकं, जन्यं, संयत् *f.*, संस्फोटः, अभिसम्पातः, अभ्यामर्द्दः, अभ्यागमः, आजिः *f.*—(Close fight) नियुद्धं, बाहुयुद्धं.—(Mingled fight) तुमुलं, रणसङ्कुलं.—(Battle-cry) सिंहनादः, क्ष्वेडितं; 'field of battle,' रणभूमिः *f.*

To BATTLE, *v. n.* युध् (c. 4. युध्यते, योद्धुं), कलह् (nom. कलहायते); 'to desire battle,' युध् in des. (युयुत्सते) रणकाम्य् (nom. रणकाम्यति).

BATTLE-ARRAY, *s.* सैन्यव्यूहः, सैन्यविन्यासः, बलविन्यासः, व्यूढिः *f.*, योद्धृश्रेणी.

BATTLE-AXE, *s.* परश्वधः, परशुः *m.*—(Armed with) पारश्वधिकः.

BATTLEDOOR, *s.* गुलिकाक्रीडायां दण्डो येद्द्वारा गुलिका प्रणुद्यते or आहन्यते,

कन्दुकप्रहरणार्थं यष्टिः.

BATTLE-FIELD, *s.* रणभूमिः *f.*, आयोधनं, रणः, रणाङ्गणं, रणाजिरं, मल्लभूः *f.*, मल्लभूमिः *f.*, रङ्गः, रङ्गभूमिः *f.*

BATTLEMENT, *s.* भित्तिः *f.*, छिद्रयुक्तः प्राकारः, बाणादिप्रक्षेपार्थं प्राकारच्छिद्रं.

BATTOLOGIST, *s.* येन निरर्थिका पुनरुक्तिः क्रियते सः, निरर्थकवक्ता *m.* (क्तृ).

BATTOLOGY, *s.* निरर्थिका पुनरुक्तिः or मुहुर्भाषा, निरर्थकवाक्यं.

BAVIN, *s.* इन्धनयोग्यं शुष्ककाष्ठखण्डं, शुष्ककाष्ठं.

BAWBLE, *s.* अल्पमूल्यकम् आभरणं or कङ्कणं, बल्यार्थं क्रीडाद्रव्यं, कङ्कणं, किङ्किणी, कदर्थद्रव्यं.

BAWD, *s.* कुट्टनी, कुट्टिनी, दूती, चुन्दी, शम्भली, घटदासी, वेश्याचार्यः *m.*

BAWDILY, *adv.* अशुद्धं, लम्पटवत्, वैयात्येन, गर्हितं, गर्ह्यप्रकारेण.

BAWDINESS, *s.* अवाच्यता, गर्ह्यता, अनाचारं, वैयात्यं, लम्पटता.

BAWDRY, *s.* कुट्टनीकर्म्म *n.* (न्), वेश्याकर्म्म *n.* (न्), दूतीकार्य्यं.

BAWDY, *a.* अवाच्यः -च्या -च्यं, अवक्तव्यः -व्या -व्यं, अकथ्यः -थ्या -थ्यं, गर्हितः -ता -तं, गर्ह्यः -र्ह्या -र्ह्यं, नीचः -चा -चं, अधमः -मा -मं, अशुद्धः -द्धा -द्धं, अविनीतः -ता -तं.

BAWDY-HOUSE, *s.* वेश्याजनसमाश्रयः, वेश्यागृहं, वेश्याश्रयः, गणिकागृहं, वेशः.

To BAWL, *v. n.* उत्क्रुश् (c. 1. -क्रोशति -क्रोष्टुं), प्रक्रुश्, विक्रुश्, नद् (c. 1. नदति, नदितुं), प्रणद्, विनद्; उद्घुष् (c. 10. -घोषयति -यितुं), चीत्कारं कृ; चीत् शब्दं कृ, रस् (c. 1. रसति, रसितुं).

BAWLER, *s.* उत्क्रोष्टा *m.* (-ष्टृ), विक्रोष्टा *m.* (-ष्टृ), घोषकः, उद्घोषकः.

BAWLING, *s.* विक्रोशनं, उत्क्रोशनं, घोषणं, चीत्कारशब्दः, रासः.

BAY, *s.* (An opening of the sea into the land) खलातं, खातं, पुटभेदः, समुद्रवङ्कः, वङ्कः, वक्रिः.—(An honorary garland) श्यामवृक्षनिर्म्मिता मानसूचका माला.—(An opening in a wall) गृहाक्षः; 'to stand at bay,' शत्रुं प्रति or शत्रुप्रतिमुखं or अभिमुखं or मुखामुखि स्था (c. 1. तिष्ठति, स्थातुं).

BAY, *a.* (Colour) पिङ्गलः -ला -लं, पिङ्गः -ङ्गा -ङ्गं.—(A bay horse) उकनाहः, कियाहः.

To BAY, *v. n.* रै (c. 1. रायति, रातुं), भष् (c. 1. भषति, भषितुं).

BAY-SALT, *s.* समुद्रलवणं, सिन्धुलवणं, सामुद्रं, सैन्धवं, वसिरं, अक्षीवं.

BAY-TREE, *s.* श्यामवृक्षो यस्य पत्राणि मानसूचकहाररचने प्रयुज्यन्ते.

BAY-WINDOW, *s.* पुटाकारो गवाक्षः, भित्तिबहिर्लम्बो गृहाक्षः, पुटरूपवातायनं.

BAYONET, *s.* या लोहगुलिकाप्रक्षेपणे अधुनातनयोद्धृभिः प्रयुज्यते नाडिस् तदग्रे बद्धा कृपाणी or छुरिका.

BAZAR, *s.* पण्यवीथी, पण्यशाला, आपणः, हट्टः, क्रयारोहः.

BDELLIUM, *s.* गुग्गुलुः *m.*, कुम्भं, उलूखलकं, सर्व्वसहः, कौशिकः, पुरः, कङ्कोलः, कोलकं, कोशफलं.

To BE, *v. n.* (To be in some state) अस् (c. 2. अस्ति), आस् (c. 2. आस्ते).—(To enter into some state) भू (c. 1. भवति, भवितुं).—(To exist) अस्, वृत् (c. 1. वर्त्तते, वर्त्तितुं), विद् in pass. (विद्यते), जन् in pass. (जायते).—(To be in or at) वृत्, स्था (c. 1. तिष्ठति, स्थातुं); 'be it so,' एवम् अस्तु. The verb 'to be' is often expressed by the use of the passive form of the Sanskrit verb, and is not unfrequently omitted altogether.

BEACH, *s.* समुद्रतीरं, समुद्रकूलं, समुद्रतटं, वेला.

BEACHED, *a.* समुद्रतीरस्थः -स्था -स्थं, उत्तरङ्गः -ङ्गा -ङ्गं.

BEACHY, *a.* तीरविशिष्टः -ष्टा -ष्टं, तटयुक्तः -क्ता -क्तं, कूलमयः -यी -यं.

BEACON, *s.* आकाशदीपः, उन्नतभूभागे स्थापिता शत्रोर् आगमनसमये जाज्वल्यमाना महोल्का, समुद्रगामिनां पथदर्शनार्थम् उच्चीकृतं चिह्नं.

BEAD, *s.* (Little globular body) गुलिका, गुटिका, गुली, वर्त्तुलः.—(A string of beads) माला, हारः.—(A rosary of beads) जपमाला.

BEADLE, *s.* गड्डोटः, यष्टिधरः, राजदूतः, दण्डधरः, दण्डी *m.* (न्), दण्डहस्तः.

BEADROLL, *s.* ये लोका जपे कथयितव्यास् तत्परिसंख्या.

BEADSMAN, *s.* परार्थं or अन्यनिमित्ते जपकरणे नियुक्तो जनः.

BEAGLE, *s.* शशाखेटकः कुक्कुरप्रभेदः, शशाखेटे शिक्षितो मृगव्यश्वा *m.* (न्).

BEAK, *s.* (Of a bird) चञ्चुः *f.*, चञ्चूः *f.*, चोटी -टिः *f.*, मुखः, तुण्डिः *m.*, तुण्डः.—(Of a ship) पित्तलमयं चञ्चुरूपेण तक्षितं नौकाग्रं.

BEAKED, *a.* चञ्चुमान् -मती -मत् (त्), चञ्चुरूपः -पी -पं, चञ्चुविशिष्टः -ष्टा -ष्टं.

BEAM, *s.* (Piece of timber) स्थूणा, दीर्घकाष्ठं, काष्ठं, गृहकाष्ठं, नासा, यष्टिः *m.*—(Main support of a house) वेश्मस्थूणा.—(Ray of light) रश्मिः *m.*, मरीचिः *m. f.*, किरणः, अंशुः *m.*—(Part of a balance) तुलाधारः, तुलादण्डः.—(Pole of a carriage) धूः *f.* (धुर्), कूबरः.—(Part of a weaver's loom) वायदण्डः, वापदण्डः.

To BEAM, *v. n.* (To emit rays of light) स्फुर् (c. 6. स्फुरति, स्फुरितुं), अंशु (nom. अंशूयति -यितुं), किरण (nom. किरणायते -यितुं), दीप् (c. 4. दीप्यते, दीपितुं), वर्च्चस् (nom. वर्च्चायते -यितुं).

BEAMLESS, *a.* रश्मिहीनः -ना -नं, निस्तेजाः -जाः -जः (स्), निष्प्रभः -भा -भं.

BEAMY, *a.* (Radiant) अंशुमान् -मती -मत् (त्), अंशुलः -ला -लं, किरणमयः -यी -यं, मरीचिमाली -लिनी -लि (न्), प्रभावान् -वती -वत् (त्), देदीप्यमानः -ना -नं.

BEAN, *s.* शिम्बिकः, शिम्बा, मुद्गः, माषः.

BEAR, *s.* ऋक्षः, भल्लकः, भल्लुकः, भल्लः, भालुकः, अच्छः, अच्छभल्लः.—(The Great Bear, constellation) चित्रशिखण्डिनः *m. pl.*

To BEAR, *v. a.* (Carry) वह् (c. 1. वहति -ते, वोढुं), सह् (c. 1. सहते, सोढुं); 'he bore his mother on his back,' मातरं पृष्ठेन अवहत्; 'he is borne on a horse,' अश्वेन उह्यते or अश्वेन सञ्चरति.—(Support) भृ (c. 1. भरति -ते, c. 3. बिभर्त्ति, भर्त्तुं), धृ (c. 1. धरति -ते, धर्त्तुं or in caus. धारयति -यितुं), आलम्ब् (c. 1. -लम्बते -लम्बितुं).—(Suffer, endure) सह्, विषह्, क्षम् (c. 1. क्षमते, क्षन्तुं), सङ्क्षम्; तिज् in des. (तितिक्षते -क्षितुं), मृष् (c. 4. मृष्यति -ते, मर्षितुं, c. 10. मर्षयति -यितुं); 'that is not to be borne,' न सह्यं तत्.—(Permit) अनुज्ञा (c. 9. -जानाति -ज्ञातुं).—(Admit) ग्रह् (c. 9. गृह्णाति, ग्रहीतुं).—(Produce) उत्पद् in caus. (-पादयति -यितुं), जन् in caus. (जनयति -यितुं).—(Bring forth) सु (c. 1. सवति, c. 2. सौति, सोतुं), प्रसु; प्रजन् (c. 4. -जायते -जनितुं) or जन् in caus.—(Bear in mind) अनुस्मृ (c. 1. -स्मरति -स्मर्त्तुं), अनुचिन्त् (c. 10. -चिन्तयति -यितुं).—(Bear witness) साक्ष्यं दा (c. 3. ददाति, दातुं).—(Keep afloat) प्लु in caus. (प्लावयति -यितुं).—(Bear fruit) फल् (फलति, फलितुं).—(Possess) भृ, धा, धृ in caus.—(Bear up) उद्वह्.—(Bear away) अपवह्.—(Bear down) निपत् in caus. (-पातयति -यितुं).—(Be capable of) उत्सह् with inf.—(Bear on, incite) प्रोत्सह् in caus. (-साहयति -यितुं).—(Bear the blame) दोषं स्वीकृ; 'I will bear the blame,' दोषो मयि वर्त्तिष्यते.—(Bear one's self, behave) वृत् (c. 1. वर्त्तते, वर्त्तितुं), काचिद् वृत्तिम् अनुष्ठा (c. 1. -तिष्ठति -स्थातुं).—(Bear malice) द्रुह् (c. 4. द्रुह्यति, द्रोहितुं). When this verb occurs in phrases such as, 'to bear company,' 'to bear aid,' 'to bear resemblance,' *see* '*to* ACCOMPANY,' '*to* AID,' '*to* RESEMBLE.'

To BEAR, *v. n.* (To be patient) सह् (c. 1. सहते, सोढुं), सोढ (nom. सोढयते -यितुं).—(To wait patiently) विलम्ब् (c. 1. -लम्बते -लम्बितुं).—(To be fruitful) फल् (c. 1. फलति, फलितुं), फलं दा (c. 3. ददाति,

दातुं), सफलः -ला -लं भू.—(To be situated towards) प्रतिष्ठा (c. 1. -तिष्ठति -स्थातुं), दिश्यः -श्या -श्यं अस्; as, 'bearing towards the east,' पूर्व्वदिश्यः.—(To bear up) मनःस्थैर्य्यं कृ.

BEARD, *s.* श्मश्रु *n.*, मासुरी, मुखजं रोम *n.* (न्), मुखरोम *n.*—(Of corn) शस्यशूकं, शूकं, किंशारुः *m.*—(Barb of an arrow) फलं, कर्णः.

To BEARD, *v. a.* (To take by the beard) अवज्ञानात् परश्मश्रु सङ्ग्रह् (c. 9. -गृह्णाति -ग्रहीतुं).—(To insult to the face) मुखरीकृ, प्रतिमुखं or प्रत्यक्षे अवज्ञा (c. 9. -जानाति -ज्ञातुं), अवक्षिप् (c. 6. -क्षिपति -क्षेप्तुं).

BEARDED, *a.* (Having a beard) सश्मश्रुः -श्रुः -श्रु, श्मश्रुमान् -मती -मत् (त्), श्मश्रुलः -ला -लं.—(As corn) शूकवान् -वती -वत् (त्); 'bearded corn,' शूकधान्यं.—(As an arrow) कर्णी -र्णिनी -र्णि (न्).—(A bearded dart) प्रासः, कुन्तः.—(Insulted) अवज्ञातः -ता -तं.

BEARDLESS, *a.* श्मश्रुहीनः -ना -नं.—(A stripling) अप्राप्तव्यवहारः, वटुः, माणवकः.

BEARER, *s.* वाहकः, वाही *m.* (न्).—(Of burdens) भारवाहः -हनः, भारहारः, धुरन्धरः; 'one who carries out the dead,' प्रेतनिर्हारकः; 'letter-bearer,' पत्रवाहः; 'bearer of news,' सन्देशहरः.

BEARING, *s.* (The relative situation of a place) दिश्यं, दिक् *f.* (श्), अवस्थानं, अवस्थितिः *f.*, स्थानं.—(Behaviour) वृत्तिः *f.*, दर्शनं, रीतिः *f.*, गतिः *f.*, भावः, वर्त्तनं.

BEARISH, *a.* ऋक्षशीलः -ला -लं, भल्लूकस्वभावः -वा -वं, अशिष्टः -ष्टा -ष्टं.

BEAST, *s.* पशुः *m.*, जन्तुः *m.*, तिर्य्यङ् (च्).—(Four-footed beast) चतुष्पात् *m. f. n.* (द्).—(Beast of prey) श्वापदः.—(Of burden) धुरीणः, धुरीयः, धुर्य्यः, भारवाहनः.—(Applied to a man) पुरुषपशुः *m.*, दुराचारः.

BEASTLINESS, *s.* पशुता -त्वं, पाशवं, पशुशीलता, अमनुष्यता.

BEASTLY, *a.* पाशवः -वी -वं, पशुशीलः -ला -लं, पशुव्यवहारः -रा -रं, अमानुषः -षी -षं.

BEASTLY, *adv.* पशुवत्, पशुव्यवहारानुसारेण, मानुषाचारविरुद्धं.

BEAT, *s.* आघातः, घातः, प्रहारः, पातः.—(Of the pulse or heart) स्पन्दनं, स्फुरणं, विस्पन्दः; 'at the beat of the drum,' आहतेषु पटहेषु.

To BEAT, *v. a.* तड् (c. 10. ताडयति -यितुं), वितड्; हन् (c. 2. हन्ति, हन्तुं), निहन्, अभिहन्; प्रहृ (c. 1. -हरति -ते -हर्त्तुं), तुद् (c. 6. तुदति, तोत्तुं), आतुद्, वितुद्.—(With a stick) वेत्राघातं कृ.—(To conquer, excel) पराजि (c. 1. -जयति -ते -जेतुं), विजि; अभिभू (c. 1. -भवति -भवितुं), अती (c. 2. अत्येति, अत्येतुं).—(To mix by beating) आलुड् (c. 1. -लोडति -लोडितुं), मन्थ् (c. 1. मथति, मथितुं).—(To bruise) चूर्ण् (c. 10. चूर्णयति -यितुं), मृद् (c. 9. मृद्नाति, मर्द्दितुं).—(To beat off, beat back) प्रतिहन् (c. 2. -हन्ति -हन्तुं).—(To beat down) निपत् in caus. (-पातयति -यितुं).—(To beat down the price) मूल्यं न्यूनीकृ or ह्रस् in caus. (ह्रासयति -यितुं).—(To flap the wings) पक्षास्फालं कृ, पक्षौ चल् in caus. (चालयति -यितुं).—(To rouse game by striking the bushes) मृगयासमये यथा मृगाः स्वस्थानानि त्यजन्ति तथा कोलाहलेन गुल्मादिताडनं कृ, मृगान्वेषणे यथा मृगो निजाश्रयात् पलायते तथा गुल्मादीन् तड्.

To BEAT, *v. n.* (To palpitate) स्पन्द् (c. 1. स्पन्दते, स्पन्दितुं), परिस्पन्द्; कम्प् (c. 1. कम्पते, कम्पितुं), स्फुर् (c. 6. स्फुरति, स्फुरितुं).

BEATEN, *part. a.* आहतः -ता -तं, ताडितः -ता -तं.—(Conquered) पराजितः -ता -तं; 'beaten by the waves,' उत्तरङ्गः -ङ्गा -ङ्गं.—(One that deserves to be beaten) कश्यः -श्या -श्यं, कशार्हः -र्हा -र्हं.

BEATER, *s.* ताडयिता *m.* (तृ), ताडकः, घाती *m.* (न्).—(A gold-beater) मुद्गरादिना यः सुवर्णम् अतिशयेन सूक्ष्मीकरोति स्वर्णकारविशेषः; स्वर्णपत्रकृत्.—(An instrument for comminuting) मुद्गरः.

BEATIFIC OR BEATIFICAL, *a.* अपवर्गदः -दा -दं, परमसुखावहः -हा -हं, परमानन्दकरः -री -रं.

BEATIFICATION, *s.* अमुकसाधुजनः स्वर्गं or अपवर्गं or सिद्धिं प्राप्तवान् इति घोषणापत्रेण महाधर्म्माध्यक्षकाज्ञाद् विज्ञापनं, स्वर्गीयलोकमध्ये आरोपणं.

BEATIFIED, *p. p.* गृहीतापवर्गः -र्गा -र्गं, स्वर्गप्राप्तः -प्ता -प्तं, स्वर्गारोपितः -ता -तं.

To BEATIFY, *v. a.* (To make happy) सुख् (c. 10. सुखयति -यितुं), परमसुखं or परमानन्दं दा (c. 3. ददाति -दातुं).—(To proclaim publicly that a person is received into heaven) अमुकसाधुजनः स्वर्गं or सिद्धिं प्राप्तवान् इति महाधर्म्माध्यक्षाज्ञया घोषणापत्रं प्रचर् in caus. (-चारयति -यितुं); स्वर्गीयलोकमध्ये आरुह् in caus. (-रोपयति -यितुं).

BEATING, *s.* ताडनं, आघातः, घातः, दण्डः.—(With a stick) वेत्राघातः.—(Throbbing) स्पन्दनं, स्फुरणं.

BEATITUDE, *s.* मुक्तिः *f.*, मोक्षः, निर्वाणं, सिद्धिः *f.*, अपवर्गः, स्वर्गप्राप्तिः *f.*, परमागतिः *f.*, श्रेयः *n.* (स्) or निःश्रेयः, अमृतता, कैवल्यं.—(Felicity) परमसुखं, परमानन्दः, श्रेयस्त्वं, सुखं.—(Desirous of) मुमुक्षुः.

BEAU, *s.* सुवेशी *m.* (न्), सुवेशः, सुवस्त्रपरिच्छदः, दर्शनीयमानी *m.* (न्).

BEAU-MONDE, *s.* नृत्यगीतखाद्यभोजनमद्यपानसुवस्त्रपरिधानादिभोगतत्परो लोकः, भोगासक्तो लोकः.

BEAUTEOUS OR BEAUTIFUL, *a.* चारुः -र्व्वी -रु, सुन्दरः -रा -री -रं, रुचिरः -रा -रं, सुदृश्यः -श्या -श्यं, शोभनः -ना -नं, कान्तः -न्ता -न्तं, वामः -मा -मं, रूपवान् -वती -वत् (त्), रूपी -पिणी -पि (न्), सुरूपः -पी -पं, मनोरमः -मा -मं, मनोज्ञः -ज्ञा -ज्ञं, लावण्यवान् -वती -वत् (त्), साधुः -धुः -ध्वी -धु, सौम्यः -म्या -म्यं, श्रीयुक्तः -क्ता -क्तं, सुमुखः -खी -खं, अभिरामः -मा -मं, सुषमः -मा -मं, पेशलः -ला -लं, रूप्यः -प्या -प्यं, मञ्जुः -ञ्जुः -ञ्जु, मञ्जुलः -ला -लं, वृन्दारः -रा -रं. Often expressed by सु; as, 'a beautiful day,' सुदिनं. 'A beautiful woman,' रूपवती, प्रमदा; 'to be beautiful,' शुभ् (c. 1. शोभते, शोभितुं).

BEAUTEOUSLY OR BEAUTIFULLY, *adv.* साधु, सुन्दरं, रुचिरं, सुष्ठु, सुन्दरप्रकारेण, सु prefixed; as, 'beautifully dressed,' सुवेशी -शिनी -शि (न्).

BEAUTEOUSNESS, *s.* कान्तता, अभिरामता, वामता, रूपवत्त्वं, रमणीयता, मुग्धता.

BEAUTIFIED, *p. p.* शोभितः -ता -तं, उपशोभितः -ता -तं, कृतशोभः -भा -भं.

BEAUTIFIER, *s.* शोभकृत्, शोभकः, शोभयिता *m.* (तृ), भूषणः.

To BEAUTIFY, *v. a.* शुभ् in caus. (शोभयति -यितुं), उपशुभ्, अलङ्कृ, परिष्कृ, भूष् (c. 10. भूषयति -यितुं), विभूष्.

BEAUTY, *s.* सौन्दर्य्यं, चारुता, शोभा, कान्तिः *f.*, रूपं, लावण्यं, रूपलावण्यं, श्रीः, आभा, अभिख्या, द्युतिः *f.*, छविः *f.*, मञ्जिमा *m.* (न्), सुषमा.

BEAUTY-SPOT, *s.* तिलकः -कं, सौन्दर्य्यवर्द्धकं चिह्नं, कान्तिदायकम् अङ्कं.

BEAVER, *s.* (An animal) स्थलजलचरजन्तुप्रभेदो यल्लोमनिर्म्मितं शिरस्त्रम् अधुनातनजनैर् ध्रियते.—(A hat) पूर्व्वोक्तजन्तुलोमनिर्म्मितं शिरस्कं or शिरस्त्राणं.—(Part of a helmet) शिरस्त्राणस्य यो भागश् चिबुकदेशं or मुखस्य अधोभागं प्रच्छादयति.

BECAFICO, *s.* अञ्जीरद्राक्षादिखादको विदेशीयपक्षिभेदः, अञ्जीरप्रतुदः.

To BECALM, *v. a.* (To still the elements) निर्व्वातं -तां -तं कृ, वायुं निवृत् in caus. (-वर्त्तयति -यितुं), निस्तरङ्गं -ङ्गां -ङ्गं कृ.—(To quiet) शम् in caus. (शमयति -यितुं), उपशम्, प्रशम्.

BECALMED, *p. p.* निर्व्वातः -ता -तं, निर्वेगः -गा -गं, निस्तरङ्गः -ङ्गा -ङ्गं.

BECAME, the preterite of 'become;' which *see*. Sometimes expressed by जातः -ता -तं.

Because, *conj.* यतस्, यत्, येन, यस्मात्, इति हेतोः, यतोहेतोः, हि. 'Because' may be often expressed by the abl. or inst. c. of the abstract noun; as, 'because it had no deepness of earth,' मृदल्पत्वात्; 'because he was a just man,' सज्जनत्वात्; 'because he was a friend,' मित्रतया. It may even be expressed by इति; thus, 'I am come, because a servant ought to be present at the fitting occasion,' अनुजीविना प्राप्तकाले सान्निध्यं कर्त्तव्यम् इति आगतोऽस्मि.

Because of, *prep.* (By reason of) हेतोः, हेतौ, कारणात्.—(For the sake of) अर्थं, अर्थे, कृते, निमित्ते affixed to a crude noun; 'because of that,' अनेन हेतुना, इति हेतोः. 'Because of' is often expressed by the abl. c. of the noun; as, 'because of their unbelief,' तेषाम् अविश्वासात्.

Beck, *s.* सङ्केतः, इङ्गितं.—(With the hand) करसङ्केतः.

To beckon, *v. n.* शिरसा or हस्तेन सङ्केतं or इङ्गितं दा (c. 3. ददाति, दातुं) or कृ.—(To summon with a sign) इङ्गितेन समाह्वे (c. 1. -ह्वयति -ह्वातुं).

To become, *v. n.* भू (c. 1. भवति, भवितुं), सम्भू; सम्पद् (c. 4. -पद्यते -पत्तुं), प्रतिपद्, वृत् (c. 1. वर्त्तते, वर्त्तितुं), संवृत्, जन् (c. 4. जायते), सञ्जन्. The pass. part. of जन् (जात) is often used in the sense 'became.' आहृ in caus. (-हारयति -यितुं) with acc.

To become, *v. a.* (Suit) युज् in pass. (युज्यते), उपपद् (c. 4. -पद्यते -पत्तुं) with loc.

Becoming, *a.* युक्तः -क्ता -क्तं, योग्यः -ग्या -ग्यं, यथायोग्यः -ग्या -ग्यं, उचितः -ता -तं, यथोचितः -ता -तं, समुचितः -ता -तं, समञ्जसः -सा -सं.

Becomingly, *adv.* यथायोग्यं, यथोचितं, युक्तं, यथार्हं, यथातथं, यथायथं, योगतस्.

Becomingness, *s.* युक्तता, औचित्यं, योग्यता, उपयुक्तत्वं, सामञ्जस्यं, उपपत्तिः *f.*, याथातथ्यं.

Bed, *s.* शय्या, शयनं, पर्य्यङ्कः, तल्पः, खट्वा, संस्तरः, पल्यङ्कः, स्तरिमा *m.* (न्), शयनीयं, मञ्चः, मञ्चकः, प्रस्तरः, आस्तरणं.—(To go to bed) शी (c. 2. शेते, शयितुं); 'gone to bed,' शय्यागतः, खट्वारूढः -ढा -ढं.—(To make a bed) शय्यां प्रस्तुतीकृ or उपस्तृ (c. 5. -स्तृणोति -स्तरितुं -स्तरीतुं), आस्तृ.—(To lie down in bed) शय्याम् अधिशी.—(Channel of a river) गर्भः, नदीमध्यं, नदीवहनपथः, नदीरयपथः.—(Garden-bed) स्थलं, उद्याने पुष्पोत्पत्तियोग्य ईषदुन्नतो भूभागः.—(Marriage) विवाहः.—(A layer) फलकः.

To bed, *v. a.* (To place in a bed) खट्वाम् आरुह् in caus. (-रोपयति -यितुं).—(To cohabit with) उपगम् (c. 1. -गच्छति -गन्तुं).

To bedabble or bedash, *v. a.* सिच् (c. 6. सिञ्चति, सेक्तुं), अवसिच्, संसिच्, अवकॄ (c. 6. -किरति -करितुं -करीतुं), प्रोक्ष् (c. 1. -उक्षति -उक्षितुं).

To bedaggle or bedash, *v. a.* कर्द्दमेन or पङ्केन or मलेन लिप् (c. 6. लिम्पति, लेप्तुं) or दुष् in caus. (दूषयति -यितुं), मलिन (nom. मलिनयति -यितुं).

To bedaub, *v. v.* लिप् (c. 6. लिम्पति, लेप्तुं), आलिप्, उपलिप्, अञ्ज् (c. 7. अनक्ति, अङ्क्तुं) or in caus. (अञ्जयति -यितुं).

To bedazzle, *v. a.* अतिशयतेजसा दृष्टिम् उपहन् (c. 2. -हन्ति -हन्तुं).

Bedchamber, *s.* शयनागारः, शयनगृहं, स्वप्ननिकेतनं, निद्राशाला, विश्रामशाला, वासगृहं, वासागारं.

Bedclothes, *s. pl.* शय्यास्तरणं, शय्यावरणं, खट्वासम्बन्धि वस्त्रादिद्रव्यं, उत्तरच्छदः, मन्दुरा.

Bedding, *s.* शय्या, शय्योपकरणं, आस्तरणं, चोरपट्टी, खट्वासामग्री.

To bedeck, *v. a.* भूष् (c. 10. भूषयति -यितुं), विभूष्, मण्ड् (c. 10. मण्डयति -यितुं), अलङ्कृ, परिष्कृ, शुभ् in caus. (शोभयति -यितुं).

Bedecked, *p. p.* भूषितः -ता -तं, अलङ्कृतः -ता -तं, मण्डितः -ता -तं.

To bedew, *v. a.* शिशिरेण or नीहारेण क्लिद् in caus. (क्लेदयति -यितुं) or अवसिच् (c. 6. -सिञ्चति -सेक्तुं) or प्रोक्ष् (c. 1. -उक्षति -उक्षितुं) or आर्द्रीकृ.

Bedewed, *p. p.* क्लिन्नः -न्ना -न्नं, आर्द्रः -र्द्रा -र्द्रं, प्रोक्षितः -ता -तं, तिमितः -ता -तं.

Bedfellow, *s.* सहशायी *m.* -यिनी *f.* (न्), एकखट्वाशायी *m.* -यिनी *f.* (न्).

Bed-hangings, *s.* मशहरी, चतुष्की, शय्यातिरस्करिणी.

To bedim, *v. a.* तिमिर (nom. तिमिरयति -यितुं), तिमिरीकृ, मलिनीकृ.

To bedizen, *v. a.* भूष् (c. 10. भूषयति -यितुं), विभूष्, परिभूष्, अलङ्कृ, परिष्कृ.

Bedizened, *p. p.* भूषितः -ता -तं, अलङ्कृतः -ता -तं, शोभितः -ता -तं.

Bedlam, *s.* उन्मत्तानाम् आरोग्यशाला, वातुलागारं, वातुलालोकालयः.

Bedlam, *a.* उन्मत्तः -त्ता -त्तं, उन्मादः -दा -दं, वातुलः -ला -लं.

Bedlamite, *s.* उन्मत्तः, उन्मादी *m.* (न्), वातुलः, मत्तः.

Bed-maker, *s.* राजविद्यालये या स्त्री or यो जनो ऽन्तेवासिनां शय्यास्तरणं करोति; शयनकल्पिका, शय्यां कल्पयति या परिचारिका.

Bedpost, *s.* खट्वास्तम्भः, खट्वादण्डः, शयनस्थूणा.

Bedrid or bedridden, *a.* शयनाद् उत्थातुम् अक्षमः; अतिशीर्णः -र्णा -र्णं, अतिवृद्धः -द्धा -द्धं.

Bedroom, *s.* शयनगृहं, स्वप्ननिकेतनं, शयनागारः, निद्राशाला, विश्रामशाला.

Bedside, *s.* शय्यापार्श्वः, खट्वापार्श्वः, शयनोपान्तं, खट्वासमीपं.

Bedstead, *s.* पर्य्यङ्कः, खट्वा, मञ्चः, मञ्चकः, पल्यङ्कः, तल्पः.

Bedtime, *s.* शयनकालः, स्वप्नकालः, निद्राकालः, शय्यागमनसमयः, विश्रामकालः.

Bee, *s.* मधुकरः -कारी *m.* (न्), अलिः *m.*, मधुकृत् *m.*, मधुपायी *m.* (न्), मधुपः, मधुमक्षिका, मधुलिट् *m.* (ह्), भृङ्गः, पुष्पन्धयः, पुष्पलिट् *m.* (ह्), षट्पदः, द्विरेफः, भ्रमरः, मधुव्रतः, सरघा.

Beech, *s.* भूर्जजातीयो वन्यवृक्षप्रभेदः.

Beechen, *a.* पूर्वोक्तवृक्षकाष्ठमयः -यी -यं.

Bee-eater, *s.* मधुमक्षिकाखादकः पक्षिप्रभेदः.

Beef, *s.* गोमांसं; 'roast beef,' शूलिकगोमांसं; 'boiled beef,' शृतगोमांसं.

Beef-eater, *s.* राजपरिचरः -परिचारकः, राजोपासकः.

Bee-garden, *s.* मधुमक्षिकापालनस्थानं, मधुकरपालनोद्यानं.

Bee-hive, *s.* मधुकोषः, करण्डः, छत्रकः, मधुमक्षिकाधारः.

Bee-master, *s.* मधुमक्षिकापालकः, मधुकररक्षकः.

Beeswax, *s.* मधूच्छिष्टं, मधुजं, शिक्थं, सिक्थकं.

Beer, *s.* यवसुरं, यवमद्यं, यवरसः, यवनिर्म्मितं पानीयं.

Beer-house, *s.* यवसुराविक्रयस्थानं, यवसुरगृहं, आपानं, पानगोष्ठिका.

Beet, *s.* (A plant) पालङ्कः, पालङ्कशाकः.

Beetle, *s.* भ्रमरभेदः, भृङ्गप्रभेदः, परोष्णी, पिङ्गकपिशा.—(A mallet) मुद्गरः.

To beetle, *v. n.* बहिर् लम्ब् (c. 1. लम्बते, लम्बितुं), प्रलम्ब्.

Beetle-browed, *a.* ललाटाभोगविशिष्टः -ष्टा -ष्टं, प्रलम्बललाटः -टा -टं.

Beeves, *s.* (Oxen) गावः *m. pl.*, गोकुलं.

To befall, *v. n.* घट् (c. 1. घटते, घटितुं), निपत् (c. 1. -पतति -पतितुं), उपस्था (c. 1. -तिष्ठति -स्थातुं), सम्पद् (c. 4. -पद्यते -पत्तुं), उपपद्, सम्भू (c. 1. -भवति -भवितुं).

Befallen, *p. p.* आपतितः -ता -तं, उपस्थितः -ता -तं, समुपस्थितः -ता -तं, समापन्नः -न्ना -न्नं, उपपन्नः -न्ना -न्नं, घटितः -ता -तं, वृत्तः -त्ता -त्तं.

To befit, *v. a.* युज् in pass. (युज्यते), उपपद् (c. 4. -पद्यते -पत्तुं) with loc.

BEFITTING, *a.* योग्यः -ग्या -ग्यं, यथायोग्यः -ग्या -ग्यं, यथोचितः -ता -तं.

To BEFOOL, *v. a.* मुह् in caus. (-मोहयति -यितुं), व्यामुह्, विप्रमुह्, भ्रम् in caus. (भ्रमयति -यितुं), वञ्च् in caus. (वञ्चयति -ते -यितुं).

BEFORE, *prep.* and *adv.* प्र, अभि prefixed.—(In the front of, not behind) अग्रे, अग्रतस्, पुरस्, पुरतस्, पुरस्तात्, अभितस्, प्रतिमुखं, अभिमुखं; 'going before,' पुरोगः -गा -गं, अग्रेसरः -रा -रं; 'before the fire,' अभ्यग्नि.—(In the presence of) साक्षात्, प्रत्यक्षे, अग्रे, समक्षं, प्रतिमुखं; 'he took them before the king,' तान् राजसमीपम् आनीतवान्.—(In the sight of, before the face) समक्षं, प्रत्यक्षं, प्रत्यक्षतस्, साक्षात्, सम्मुखं; 'before many persons,' बहुजनसमक्षं.—(Earlier in time, sooner than) प्राक्, पूर्व्वं, with the abl. c.; अग्रे; 'before offering the cakes,' पिण्डदानात् पूर्व्वं; 'before the appointed time,' निरूपितसमयात् पूर्व्वं or प्राग् विहितकालात्; 'he knows your necessities before you ask,' यत् तव प्रयोजनं तद् याञ्चातः पूर्व्वं जानाति; 'before dinner,' भोजनात् पूर्व्वं; 'before the event,' प्राग् घटनात्; 'before me,' मदग्रे.—(In time past) पुरा, पूर्व्वं, पूर्व्वकाले.—(As yet, hitherto) अद्य यावत्, अद्यपर्य्यन्तं, एतत् कालं यावत्, अद्यापि.—(Already) तत्पूर्व्वं, प्राग् वर्त्तमानकालात्; 'before mentioned,' पूर्व्वोक्तः -क्ता -क्तं, प्रागुक्तः -क्ता -क्तं, पूर्व्वचोदितः -ता -तं; 'the day before yesterday,' अपरेद्युस्; 'before and after,' पूर्व्वोत्तरं.

BEFORE-HAND, *adv.* पूर्व्वे, अग्रे, पूर्व्वं, अग्रतस्, पूर्व्वतस्; 'determining beforehand,' अग्रनिरूपणं; 'to taste beforehand,' पूर्व्वस्वादनं कृ.

BEFORE-TIME, *adv.* पुरा, पूर्व्वं, पूर्व्वकाले, गतकाले.

To BEFOUL, *v. a.* मलिन (nom. मलिनयति -यितुं), दुष् in caus. (दूषयति -यितुं), कलुष (nom. कलुषयति -यितुं), आविल (nom. आविलयति -यितुं), समलं -लां -लं कृ.

To BEFRIEND, *v. a.* मित्र (nom. मित्रीयते -यितुं), उपकृ (c. 8. -करोति -कुरुते -कर्त्तुं), अनुग्रह् (c. 9. -गृह्णाति -ग्रहीतुं), साहाय्यं कृ.

BEFRIENDED, *p. p.* कृतोपकारः -रा -रं, उपकृतः -ता -तं, अनुगृहीतः -ता -तं.

To BEG, *v. a.* (To ask) अर्थ् (c. 10. अर्थयते -यितुं), अभ्यर्थ्, प्रार्थ्, सम्प्रार्थ्, याच् (c. 1. याचति -ते, याचितुं), अभियाच्, प्रयाच्, सम्प्रयाच्, संयाच्.—(To ask alms) भिक्ष् (c. 1. भिक्षते, भिक्षितुं).—(To beg as a favour) वृ (c. 9. वृणीते, वरितुं, वरीतुं) or in caus. (वारयति -यितुं) with 2 acc., प्रसद् in caus. (-सादयते -यितुं).—(To beg for pardon) क्षम् in caus. (क्षमयति -यितु) with acc. of the pers.

To BEG, *v. n.* भिक्ष् (c. 1. भिक्षते, भिक्षितुं), भैक्ष्यं चर् (c. 1. चरति, चरितुं), भिक्षाटनं कृ.

To BEGET, *v. a.* जन् in caus. (जनयति -यितुं), विजन्, सञ्जन्, प्रसु (c. 2. -सूते, c. 4. -सूयते -सोतुं).—(To produce, cause) उत्पद् in caus. (-पादयति -यितुं).—(To create) सृज् (c. 6. सृजति, स्रष्टुं).

BEGETTER, *s.* जनकः, जननः, जनयिता *m.* (तृ), जनिता *m.* (तृ), जन्मदः, सुती *m.* (न्), उत्पादकः.

BEGGAR, *s.* (One who lives on alms) भिक्षुः *m.*, भिक्षुकः -की *f.*, भिक्षोपजीवी *m.* (न्), भिक्षाचरः, दरिद्रः.—(A petitioner) प्रार्थकः, अर्थी *m.* (न्) -र्थिनी *f.*, प्रार्थयिता *m.* (तृ), याचकः, याचनकः, मार्गणः -णकः, वनीयकः.—(In ragged garments) कर्पटी *m.* (न्).

To BEGGAR, *v. a.* दरिद्रीकृ, सर्व्वस्वं हृ (c. 1. हरति, हर्त्तुं), धनाद् भ्रंश् in caus. (भ्रंशयति -यितुं).

BEGGARED, *a.* दरिद्रितः -ता -तं, धनच्युतः -ता -तं, हृतसर्व्वस्वः -स्वा -स्वं, परिक्षीणः -णा -णं, गतवित्तः -त्ता -त्तं, नष्टार्थः -र्था -र्थं, गतविभवः -वा -वं, गतलक्ष्मीकः -का -कं, गतश्रीकः -का -कं; 'he is beggared,' अभगायते.

BEGGARLY, *a.* (Indigent) दरिद्रः -द्रा -द्रं, निर्धनः -ना -नं, दुर्गतः -ता -तं, कृपणः -णा -णं, दीनः -ना -नं.—(Mean) तुच्छः -च्छा -च्छं, नीचः -चा -चं, अपकृष्टः -ष्टा -ष्टं.

BEGGARLY, *adv.* कृपणं, कार्पण्येन, दीनं, नीचप्रकारेण.

BEGGARY, *s.* (Indigence) दरिद्रता, दारिद्र्यं -द्र्यं, निर्धनता, परिक्षीणता, कार्पण्यं, अर्थिता, दीनता.

BEGGED, *p. p.* प्रार्थितः -ता -तं, याचितः -ता -तं, भिक्षितः -ता -तं.

BEGGING, (Act of) *s.* भिक्षा, भिक्षाटनं, भैक्षचर्य्या, अर्थना, अभ्यर्थना, याचना, याञ्चा, प्रार्थनं -ना, अर्हना, अभिशस्तिः *f.*

To BEGIN, *v. a.* and *n.* आरभ् (c. 1. -रभते -रब्धुं), अभ्यारभ्, प्रारभ्, समारभ्, प्रक्रम् (c. 1. -क्रमते -क्रमितुं), उपक्रम्, समुपक्रम्, प्रवृत् (c. 1. -वर्त्तते -वर्त्तितुं); प्रकृ, सम्प्रकृ; प्रस्तु (c. 2. -स्तौति -स्तोतुं); 'he began to cut,' छेत्तुं प्रवृत्तः.

BEGINNER, *s.* (One who begins) आरब्धा *m.* (ब्धृ), आरम्भकः, उपक्रन्ता *m.* (न्तृ), उपक्रमिता *m.* (तृ), उपक्रमकारी *m.* (न्).—(A novice) नवच्छात्रः, नूतनशिष्यः, प्राथमकल्पिकः.

BEGINNING, *s.* आरम्भः, प्रारम्भः, समारम्भः, प्रारब्धिः *f.*, आदिः *m.* उपक्रमः, प्रक्रमः, उद्घातः, उपोद्घातः, अभ्यादानं.—(Origin, source) मूलं, योनिः *m. f.*, उद्भवः, प्रभवः, गर्भः, जन्म *n.* (न्).—(Rudiments) आरम्भः.—(Elementary property) कारणगुणः; 'without beginning,' अनाद्यः -द्या -द्यं; 'from beginning to end,' आद्यन्तं, आप्रथमात् शेषं यावत्; 'beginning, middle, and end,' आदिमध्यावसानं; 'beginning with,' आदि, आद्य affixed.

To BEGIRD, *v. a.* परिवेष्ट् (c. 1. -वेष्टते -वेष्टितुं), अवरुध् (c. 7. -रुणद्धि -रोद्धुं).

BEGIRT, *p. p.* परिवेष्टितः -ता -तं, परिगतः -ता -तं, वलयितः -ता -तं, आवृतः -ता -तं; 'begirt with the sea,' समुद्रमेखलः -ला -लं.

BEGONE, *interj.* अपेहि, अपसर, दूरम् अपसर.

BEGOTTEN, *p. p.* जनितः -ता -तं, उत्पादितः -ता -तं, प्रसूतः -ता -तं.

To BEGREASE, *v. a.* वसया or स्नेहेन or तैलेन or घृतेन लिप् (c. 6. लिम्पति -लेप्तुं), स्निग्धीकृ.

To BEGRIME, *v. a.* मलेन दुष् in caus. (दूषयति -यितुं), मलिन (nom. मलिनयति -यितुं), कलुष (nom. कलुषयति -यितुं), कलङ्क (nom. कलङ्कयति -यितुं).

BEGRIMED, *p. p.* मलदूषितः -ता -तं, कलुषितः -ता -तं, कलङ्कितः -ता -तं.

To BEGRUDGE, *v. a.* स्पृह् (c. 10. स्पृहयति -यितुं), असूय (nom. असूयति -यितुं).

To BEGUILE, *v. a.* मुह् in caus. (मोहयति -यितुं), विप्रमुह्, व्यामुह्, वञ्च् in caus. (वञ्चयते -यितुं), परिवञ्च्, प्रवञ्च्, भ्रम् in caus. (भ्रमयति -यितुं), प्रलभ् (c. 1. -लभते -लब्धुं), विप्रलभ्, आकृष् (c. 1. -कर्षति -क्रष्टुं -कर्षितुं).—(To beguile the time) विनुद् in caus. (-नोदयति -यितुं).

BEGUILED, *p. p.* मोहितः -ता -तं, विमोहितः -ता -तं, वञ्चितः -ता -तं, विप्रलब्धः -ब्धा -ब्धं, विमूढः -ढा -ढं, प्रपञ्चितः -ता -तं, प्रलोभितः -ता -तं, विलोभितः -ता -तं, प्रतारितः -ता -तं.

BEGUN, *p. p.* आरब्धः -ब्धा -ब्धं, प्रारब्धः -ब्धा -ब्धं, उपक्रान्तः -न्ता -न्तं.

BEHALF, *s.* (In behalf of) अर्थं, अर्थे, हेतोः, हेतौ, कारणात्, निमित्ते, कृते, generally affixed to the crude of a noun; 'on my behalf,' मत्कृते or मदर्थे; 'on behalf of (his) son,' पुत्रहेतोः.—(Favour) अनुग्रहः, प्रसादः.

To BEHAVE, *v. n.* चर् (c. 1. चरति, चरितुं), आचर्, समाचर्, वृत् (c. 1.

वर्त्तते, वर्त्तितुं); sometimes वृत्तिं is added; as, 'in whatever way you behave towards them,' यां वृत्तिं तेषु वर्त्तसे. वृत्तिम् अनुष्ठा (c. 1. -तिष्ठति -स्थातुं), व्यवहृ (c. 1. -हरति -हर्त्तुं).—Well-behaved) सदाचारयुक्तः -क्ता -क्तं, सदाचारवान् -वती -वत् (त्).

Behaviour, *s.* वृत्तिः *f.*, वृत्तं, आचारः, रीतिः *f.*, व्यवहारः, चरित्रं, चरितं, आचरणं, गतिः *f.*, चेष्टितं, स्थितिः *f.*

To behead, *v. a.* शिरः or मस्तकं छिद् (c. 7. छिनत्ति, छेत्तुं), विमस्तक (nom. विमस्तकयति -यितुं).

Beheaded, *p. p.* विमस्तकितः -ता -तं, छिन्नमस्तः -स्ता -स्तं, -स्तकः -का -कं.

Beheading (act of) *s.* शीर्षच्छेदः.—(Worthy of) शीर्षच्छेद्यः -द्या -द्यं.

Beheld, *p. p.* आलोकितः -ता -तं, दृष्टः -ष्टा -ष्टं, आलोचितः -ता -तं, ईक्षितः -ता -तं. ईक्ष्यमाणः -णा -णं.

Behest, *s.* आज्ञा, आदेशः, निर्देशः, निदेशः, शासनं, वशः.

Behind, *prep.* or *adv.* पश्चात्, अनु prefixed.—(Behind the back, at the back of) पृष्ठतस्; 'following behind,' अनुगामी -मिनी -मि (न्).—(Below, inferior) अधस्तात्, अधरस्तात्.—(Posterior) अवरतस्, अवरस्तात्.—(At a distance) दूरतस्, दूरे.—(The hinder part) पृष्ठदेशः, पश्चाद्देशः, पृष्ठं, नितम्बः.

Behindhand, *adv.* अतीतकालः -ला -लं, विलम्बी -म्बिनी -म्बि (न्), दीर्घकालीनः -ना -नं.—(Surpassed by another) अतिक्रान्तः -न्ता -न्तं.

To behold, *v. a.* दृश् (c. 1. पश्यति, द्रष्टुं), अभिदृश्, विदृश्, सन्दृश्; ईक्ष् (c. 1. ईक्षते, ईक्षितुं), समीक्ष्, वीक्ष्, अभिवीक्ष्, प्रेक्ष्, अभिप्रेक्ष्, सम्प्रेक्ष्, उदीक्ष्, अवेक्ष्, अन्वीक्ष्, अवलोक् (c. 10. -लोकयति -यितुं, c. 1. -लोकते -लोकितुं), आलोक्, समालोक्, विलोक्, लक्ष् (c. 10. लक्षयति -ते -यितुं), आलक्ष्, समालक्ष्, उपलक्ष्, संलक्ष्; आलोच् (c. 10. -लोचयति -यितुं).

Behold, *interj.* पश्य, प्रेक्षस्व.

To be beholden, *v. n.* कृतोपकारस्मरणेन पराधीनः -ना -नं or परायत्तः -त्ता -त्तं भू, प्राप्तोपकारहेतोर् बद्धः -द्धा -द्धं or निबद्धः -द्धा -द्धं भू or अस्, कृतोपकारं ज्ञा (c. 9. जानाति, ज्ञातुं), प्रत्युपकारः करणीय इति ज्ञा, आप्राप्तोपकारमोक्षात् परवशं ज्ञा.

Beholder, *s.* प्रेक्षकः, द्रष्टा *m.* (ष्टृ), प्रेक्षमाणः, दर्शी *m.* (न्), पश्यन् *m.* (त्).

Behoof, *s.* अर्थः, फलं, लाभः, वृद्धिः *f.*, विवृद्धिः *f.*, फलोदयः.

Behoveful, *a.* यथोचितः -ता -तं, योग्यः -ग्या -ग्यं, अर्थकरः -री -रं.

It behoves, *v. imp.* Expressed by the future passive participle; as, 'it behoves you to marry the damsel,' त्वया कन्या वोढव्या; or by the potential mood, as, त्वं कन्यां वहेः; or by the use of the verb अर्ह् (c. 1. अर्हति), as त्वं कन्यां वोढुम् अर्हसि; 'to act as it behoves one,' यथोचितं कृ.

Being, *s.* (A being) भूतं, सत्त्वः.—(A sentient being) प्राणी *m.* (न्), प्राणभृत् *m. f. n.*, शरीरी *m.* (न्), देही *m.* (न्), जन्तुः *m.*, जन्युः *m.*, चेतनः, जन्मी *m.* (न्).—(Existence) प्राणधारणं, असुधारणं, निश्वसनप्रश्वसनं, सम्भवः, अस्ति *ind.*, वृत्तिः *f.*, सत्त्वं.—(Particular state) भावः, अवस्था, दशा, वृत्तिः *f.*—(Supreme Being) परमेश्वरः.—(Pres. part.) सन् सती सत् (त्), वर्त्तमानः -ना -नं.

Being that, *conj.* (Since) यतस्, यस्मात्, येन, इति हेतोः, यतोहेतोः. 'Being,' is often expressed by the loc. c. of सत्, as, 'the man being gone,' पुरुषे गते सति; 'it being so,' एवं सति, तथात्वे, एवम्भूत्वा. 'Being' may also be expressed by the abl. c. of the abstract noun in such phrases as 'he being a good man,' सज्जनत्वात्.

Be it so, एवमस्तु, तथास्तु, भवतु, अस्त्वेवं.

To belabour, *v. a.* तड् (c. 10. ताडयति -यितुं), हन् (c. 2. हन्ति, हन्तुं), अभिहन्, अभ्याहन्, समाहन्; प्रहृ (c. 1. -हरति -हर्त्तुं).—(With a stick) वेत्राघातं कृ.

To belay, *v. a.* (Block up) प्रतिरुध् (c. 7. -रुणद्धि -रोद्धुं), उपरुध्.

To belch, *v. a.* उद्वम् (c. 1. -वमति -वमितुं), उद्गॄ (c. 6. -गिरति -गरितुं -गरीतुं).

Belch, belching, *s.* उद्वमः, उद्वमनं, उद्गारः, उद्गिरणं.

Beldam, *s.* वृद्धा स्त्री, जरिणी, जरापरिणता स्त्री, कुट्टिनी, कुरूपी.

To beleaguer, *v. a.* (To besiege) रुध् (c. 7. रुणद्धि, रोद्धुं), अवरुध्, उपरुध्; परिवेष्ट् (c. 1. -वेष्टते -वेष्टितुं).

Beleaguered, *p. p.* परिवेष्टितः -ता -तं, उपरुद्धः -द्धा -द्धं, बाधितः -ता -तं.

Belfounder, *s.* घण्टाकारी *m.* (न्), घण्टानिर्म्माणकर्त्ता *m.* (र्त्तृ), कांस्यकारः.

Belfry, *s.* घण्टाताडनयोग्यं प्रासादशृङ्गं, घण्टास्थानं, घण्टाशाला.

To belie, *v. a.* (To counterfeit, imitate) छल् (c. 10. छलयति -यितुं), छद्म or छद्मवेशं कृ, अनुकृ (c. 8. -करोति -कर्त्तुं).—(To charge any one with falsehood, to argue) अनृतं or असत्यं or मिथ्यावादं कस्मैचिद् आरुह् in caus. (-रोपयति -यितुं), पिशुन (nom. पिशुनयति -यितुं).—(To calumniate) परिवद् (c. 1. -वदति -वदितुं), अपवद्, कलङ्कं कृ, मिथ्याभियोगं कृ.

Belief, *s.* (Credence) प्रत्ययः, विश्वासः, विश्रम्भः, प्रमाणं.—(Religious belief) श्रद्धं -द्धा, भक्तिः *f.*, विश्वासः.—(Opinion) मतिः *f.*, बुद्धिः *f.*, बोधः.—(The thing believed in, tenet) मतं; 'my belief is,' मन्ये.

Believable, *a.* विश्वास्यः -स्या -स्यं, श्रद्धेयः -या -यं, विश्वासयोग्यः -ग्या -ग्यं.

To believe, *v. a.* (To give credit to) प्रती (c. 2. प्रत्येति, प्रत्येतुं), प्रत्ययीकृ.—(To have religious belief in) विश्वस् (c. 2. -श्वसिति -श्वसितुं) with loc. c.

To believe, *v. n.* (To exercise religious faith) श्रद्धा (c. 3. -दधाति -धातुं), विश्वासं कृ, प्रत्ययं कृ.—(To believe in, hold as an object of faith) विश्वस् (c. 2. -श्वसिति -श्वसितुं) with loc. c.—(To think) मन् (c. 4. मन्यते, मन्तुं).

Believed, *p. p.* विश्वसितः -ता -तं, विश्वस्तः -स्ता -स्तं, प्रतीतः -ता -तं.

Believer, *s.* श्रद्धान्वितः, आस्तिकः, प्रत्ययी *m.* (न्), विश्वासी *m.* (न्).

Believing, *a.* श्रद्दधानः -ना -नं, श्रद्धालुः -लुः -लु, श्राद्धः -द्धा -द्धं, श्रद्धावान् -वती -वत् (त्), ज्ञातविश्वासः -सा -सं, विश्वासी -सिनी -सि (न्), प्रत्ययी -यिनी -यि (न्).

Belike, *adv.* अपिनाम, किंस्वित्, किल, स्यात्.

Bell, *s.* घण्टा, घण्टिका, घनं.—(Tinkling ornaments) किङ्किणी; 'to ring a bell,' घण्टां हन् (c. 2. हन्ति, हन्तुं) or तड् (c. 10. ताडयति -यितुं) or वद् in caus. (वादयति -यितुं); 'bell-shaped,' घण्टाकारः -रा -रं.

Bell-clapper, *s.* घण्टावादकः, घण्टाकोणः, घण्टाभ्यन्तरे लम्बमान इतस्ततो दोलायमानस् तद्वादनयोग्यो लवङ्गाकारः कोणः; घण्टाभ्यन्तरे लग्नः स्थूलशिरस्को मुसलाकार आयसकीलो येन इतस्ततो लोलमाना घण्टा वाद्यते.

Belle, *s.* सुन्दरी *f.*, सुरूपी *f.*, रूपवती *f.*, सुवेशिनी *f.*, प्रमदा.

Belles-lettres, *s.* अलङ्कारविद्या, रसविद्या, रसिका विद्या, वाङ्मयं.

Belligerent, *a.* युध्यमानः -ना -नं, रणशीलः -ला -लं, युयुत्सुः -त्सुः -त्सु.

Bellipotent, *a.* रणवीरः -रा -रं, विक्रमी -मिणी -मि (न्), महावीर्य्यः -र्य्या -र्य्यं.

Bell-metal, *s.* कांस्यं, घण्टाशब्दं, घोषः, ताम्रार्द्धं, घोरपुष्पः, पीतलोहं.

To bellow, *v. n.* गर्ज् (c. 1. गर्जति, गर्जितुं), नर्द् (c. 1. नर्दति, नर्दितुं), विनर्द्, रस् (c. 1. रसति, रसितुं), रु (c. 2. रौति, रवितुं), विरु, संरु; रट् (c. 1. रटति, रटितुं), गज् (c. 1. गजति, गजितुं), हम्भ (nom. हम्भायते -यितुं).

BELLOWED, *p. p.* गर्ज्जितः -ता -तं, नर्द्दितः -ता -तं, प्रणर्द्दितः -ता -तं.
BELLOWING, *s.* गर्ज्जनं, नादः, रुतं, नर्दनं, नर्द्दितं.
BELLOWS, *s.* भस्त्रा *f.*, भस्त्री, भस्त्रका, चर्म्मप्रसेवकः -विका, व्यजनं, दृतिः *f.*
BELL-RINGER, *s.* घण्टाताडः -डकः, घण्टावादकः, घण्टावादयिता *m.* (तृ).
BELLUINE, *a.* पाशवः -वी -वं, पशुशीलः -ला -लं, अमानुषः -षी -षं.
BELLY, *s.* उदरं, जठरं -रा, कुक्षिः *m.*, पिचिण्डः, पिचण्डः, तुन्दं, तुन्दि *n.*
To BELLY or BELLY-OUT, *v. n.* (To swell out, bulge out) उदरवत् or उदररूपेण लम्ब् (c. 1. लम्बते, लम्बितुं) or पॄ in pass. (पूर्य्यते).
BELLY-ACHE, *s.* उदरवेदना, उदरामयः.
BELLY-BAND, *s.* उदरत्राणं, उदरदाम *n.* (न्), अश्वसक्थिका.
BELLY-BOUND, *a.* आनद्धः -द्धा -द्धं, निबद्धः -द्धा -द्धं, बद्धोदरः -रा -रं.
BELLY-FULL, *s.* उदरपूरणं, पिचिण्डपूरणं, जठरपूरणं.
BELLY-GOD, *s.* उदरम्भरिः *m.*, कुक्षिम्भरिः *m.*, औदरिकः, उदरकामुकः, आत्मम्भरिः *m.*
BELLY-WORMS, *s. pl.* उदरावेष्टः, मीवा, कृमिः *m.*, क्रिमिः *m.*
BELMAN, *s.* घोषकः, घण्टाधरः, घण्टाताडनपूर्व्वकं घोषणाकर्त्ता *m.*, वैबोधिकः.
To BELONG, *v. n.* (To be one's own property) आत्मीयः -या -यं or स्वकीयः -या -यं or स्वाधीनः -ना -नं अस्. But the sense of 'belonging' is more usually expressed by the use of the roots अस् or भू or विद् with the gen. c.; as, 'money belongs to me,' मम धनं विद्यते or अस्ति.—(To have relation to) सम्बन्ध् in pass. (-बध्यते).—(To be fit, or becoming) युज् in pass. (युज्यते); 'this belongs to me,' *i.e.* 'this is my business,' मम अयं व्यापारः.
BELONGING, *part.* सम्बन्धी -न्धिनी -न्धि (न्), सम्बन्धकः -का -कं.
BELOVED, *a.* प्रियः -या -यं, सुप्रियः -या -यं, दयितः -ता -तं, इष्टः -ष्टा -ष्टं, अभीष्टः -ष्टा -ष्टं, इष्टतमः -मा -मं, प्रेष्ठः -ष्ठा -ष्ठं, प्रीतः -ता -तं, हृद्यः -द्या -द्यं, वल्लभः -भा -भं, अभीप्सितः -ता -तं.—(Dear as one's life) असुसमः -मा -मं, प्राणैर् गरीयान् -यसी -यः (स्).
BELOW, *prep.* (Under in place) अधस्, अधस्तात्, तले, नीचे, अधोऽधस्; 'below the bed,' खट्वातले or खट्वाऽधः.—(Inferior, beneath) अवरः -रा -रं, अधःस्थः -स्था -स्थं, अवरतस्, अवरस्तात्, अधरेण, अधरात्, अधरतस्, अधरस्तात्.—(Unworthy of) अयोग्यः -ग्या -ग्यं, अनर्हः -र्हा -र्हं.—(Subject to) अधीनः -ना -नं.—(Less than) ऊनः -ना -नं; 'below two years of age,' ऊनद्विवार्षिकः or अप्राप्तद्वितीयवर्षः.
BELOW, *adv.* अधस्, नीचे, नीचकैस्, अधःस्थाने, अधोभागे, अधःस्थः -स्था -स्थं.—(On earth, as opposed to heaven) इहलोके, इह.—(In hell) अधोलोके, अधोभुवने.
BELROPE, *s.* घण्टारज्जुः *m.*, घण्टासूत्रं, अधुनातनगृहेषु घण्टावादने प्रयुक्तं सूत्रं.
BELT, *s.* मेखला, काञ्ची, कटिसूत्रं, शृङ्खलं -ला, रसना.
To BELT, *v. a.* मेखलारूपेण परिवेष्ट् (c. 1. -वेष्टते -वेष्टितुं).
BELWETHER, *s.* यो मेषश् चरन् चरन् कण्ठलग्नां घण्टां वादयति शब्दकारेण च मेषयूथम् एकत्र करोति सः; मेषयूथाग्रगः, मेषयूथपः.
To BEMANGLE, *v. a.* व्रश्च् (c. 6. वृश्चति, व्रश्चितुं, व्रष्टुं), प्रव्रश्च्, खण्डशः कृ, खण्डं खण्डं कृ, शकलीकृ, व्यवछिद् (c. 7. -छिनत्ति -छेत्तुं).
To BEMIRE, *v. a.* मलिन (nom. मलिनयति -यितुं), कलुष (nom. कलुषयति -यितुं), पङ्केन or मलेन दुष् in caus. (दूषयति -यितुं).
BEMIRED, *p. p.* मलदूषितः -ता -तं, मलपङ्की -ङ्किनी -ङ्कि (न्).
To BEMOAN, *v. a.* विलप् (c. 1. -लपति -लपितुं), अनुशुच् (c. 1. -शोचति -शोचितुं), परिदेव् (c. 1. -देवते देवितुं), लप् in freq. (लालप्यते).
BEMOANING, *s.* विलपनं, विलापः, परिदेवनं, क्रन्दितं, अनुशोचनं, रोदनं.

BENCH, *s.* दीर्घासनं, दीर्घपीठं, आसनं, फलकः -कं; 'carpenter's bench,' उद्घनः.—(Seat of justice) धर्म्मासनं, विचारासनं.
BENCHER, *s.* विचारकर्त्तॄणां संसर्गे ज्येष्ठः or उत्तमपदप्राप्तः, सभ्यः, सभासद् *m.*—(Judge) प्राड्विवाकः.
To BEND, *v. a.* (To bow, inflect) नम् in caus. (नामयति -यितुं), अवनम्, आनम्; नम्रीकृ.—(To make crooked) वक्रीकृ, जिह्म (nom. जिह्मयति -यितुं), अञ्च् (c. 1. अञ्चति, अञ्चितुं).—(To direct towards) आवृज् in caus. (-वर्जयति -यितुं).—(To bend a bow) धनुर् विस्फुर् in caus. (-स्फारयति -यितुं) or आयम् (c. 1. -यच्छति -यन्तुं).—(To bend the brow) भ्रूभङ्गं कृ.—(To bend the mind) मनः प्रविश् in caus. (-वेशयति -यितुं).—(To subdue) वशीकृ.
To BEND, *v. n.* (To be incurvated) नम् (c. 1. नमति, नन्तुं), अवनम्, आनम्; नम्रीभू, वक्रीभू.—(To jut over) प्रणतः -ता -तं अस्; प्रलम्ब् (c. 1. -लम्बते -लम्बितुं).—(To be bent or resolved on) कृतनिश्चयः -या -यं or दृढनिश्चयः -या -यं or सुनिश्चितः -ता -तं अस्.—(To be submissive) आनतः -ता -तं or वश्यः -श्या -श्यं भू.
BEND, *s.* (Incurvation) नतिः *f.*, वक्रता, जिह्मता, वक्रिमा *m.* (न्), कुञ्चनं, अवकुञ्चनं, भङ्गी.—(Bend of a river) वङ्क्रः वङ्कः, पुटभेदः, भङ्गुरः.
BENEATH, *prep.* (Lower in place) अधस्, अधस्तात्, तले, नीचे, अधोऽधस्, अधरस्तात्, अधरतस्, अधरात्; 'beneath the tree,' वृक्षतले or वृक्षस्याधस्तात्; 'the water beneath the earth,' धरण्या अधःस्थं तोयं.—(Inferior) अवरः -रा -रं, अवरतस्, अवरस्तात्.—(Unbeseeming) अयोग्यः -ग्या -ग्यं, अनर्हः -र्हा -र्हं.
BENEATH, *adv.* अधस्, नीचे, अधःस्थाने, नीचस्थाने, अधःस्थः -स्था -स्थं; 'the earth beneath,' नीचस्था पृथिवी.
BENEDICTION, *s.* आशीः *f.* (स्), आशीर्वचनं, आशीर्वादः, स्वस्ति *ind.* धन्यवादः.—(Praise) स्तवः, स्तुतिः *f.*—(The advantage conferred) मङ्गलं, धन्यत्वं, वरः.
BENEDICTORY, *a.* सौवस्तिकः -की -कं, स्वस्तिमान् -मती -मत् (त्), माङ्गलिकः -की -कं.
BENEFACTION, *s.* उपकारः, उपकृतं, उपकारकत्वं, हितं, प्रसादः.
BENEFACTOR, *s.* हितकरः, उपकर्त्ता *m.* (र्त्तृ), उपकारकः, उपकारी *m.* (न्), उपकारकरः, कृतोपकारः, प्रियकृत्, प्रियकारः, परवाञ्छापूरकः.
BENEFACTRESS, *s.* हितकरी, उपकारिणी, उपकर्त्री, प्रियकारी.
BENEFICE, *s.* धर्म्माध्यापकवृत्तिः *f.*, धर्म्मशिक्षकवृत्तिः *f.*, धर्म्माध्यापकप्रतिपत्तिः *f.*
BENEFICENCE, *s.* परोपकारकत्वं, परोपकारः, उपकारशीलता, दानशीलता, दया, कृपा, स्थूललक्ष्यत्वं, त्यागशीलता, त्यागिता.
BENEFICENT, *a.* परोपकारकः -का -कं, परोपकारी -रिणी -रि (न्), उपकारशीलः -ला -लं, उपकारपरः -रा -रं, हितकरः -री -रं, दानशीलः -ला -लं, त्यागशीलः -ला -लं, स्थूललक्ष्यः -क्ष्या -क्ष्यं, प्रियकारः -री -रं, प्रियङ्करः -री -रं, दयाकरः -रा -रं.
BENEFICENTLY, *adv.* हितकरवत्, प्रियकरवत्, वदान्यवत्, स्थूललक्ष्यतया, दयापूर्व्वं.
BENEFICIAL, *a.* हितः -ता -तं, फलवान् -वती -वत् (त्), सफलः -ला -लं, सोपकारः -रा -रं, हितवान् -वती -वत् (त्), अर्थकरः -री -रं, उपकारकः -का -कं, उपकारी -रिणी -रि (न्), लाभवान् -वती -वत् (त्), लाभजनकः -का -कं, अर्थजनकः -का -कं.—(Medicinally wholesome) पथ्यः -थ्या -थ्यं, औषधीयः -या -यं.
BENEFICIALLY, *adv.* सोपकारं, सफलं, सलाभं, सार्थं, फलाय, लाभाय.
BENEFICIARY, *a.* पराधीनः -ना -नं, पराश्रितः -ता -तं, परतन्त्रः -न्त्रा -न्त्रं.—(One who holds a benefice) धर्म्माध्यापनवृत्तिभागी *m.* (न्).

BENEFIT, *s.* (Favour conferred) हितं, उपकारः, उपकृतं, उपकारकत्वं -ता, अनुग्रहः, प्रसादः, मङ्गलं.—(Advantage, profit) फलं, लाभः, अर्थः; 'for the public benefit,' प्रजार्थं.

To BENEFIT, *v. a.* उपकृ (c. 8. -करोति -कुरुते -कर्त्तुं) with loc. or acc. c., हितं कृ, अनुग्रह् (c. 9. -गृह्णाति -ग्रहीतुं), उपचर् (c. 1. -चरति -चरितुं), फलं or लाभं दा (c. 3. ददाति, दातुं).

To BENEFIT, *v. n.* उपकारं or फलं or लाभं or हितं प्राप् (c. 5. -आप्नोति -आप्तुं).

BENEFITTED, *p. p.* उपकृतः -ता -तं, कृतोपकारः -रा -रं, कृतलाभः -भा -भं.

BENEVOLENCE, *s.* परहितेच्छा, हितेच्छा, प्रेम *n.* (न्), दयालुत्वं, परोपकारशीलता, हितकाम्या, सौजन्यं, परवाञ्छापूरणं, दया, कृपा.

BENEVOLENT, *a.* हितकामः -मा -मं, परहितैषी -षिणी -षि (न्), परोपकारशीलः -ला -लं, हितप्रेप्सुः -प्सुः -प्सु, प्रियैषी -षिणी -षि (न्), परहितः -ता -तं, उपकारपरः -रा -रं, दयालुः -लुः -लु, सुशीलः -ला -लं, सुहृदयः -या -यं.

BENEVOLENTLY, *adv.* सुशीलवत्, प्रेम्णा, प्रियं, दयापूर्व्वं, सद्भावात्, कृपया.

BENGAL, *s.* (The country) वङ्गः.—(Belonging to it) वाङ्गः -ङ्गी -ङ्गं.

To BENIGHT, *v. a.* तिमिर (nom. तिमिरयति -यितुं), तमसा प्रच्छद् in caus. (-छादयति -यितुं).

BENIGHTED, *p. p.* निशाक्रान्तः -न्ता -न्तं, रात्रिग्रस्तः -स्ता -स्तं, तमोवृतः -ता -तं, तमोभूतः -ता -तं, सन्तमसः -सा -सं, तमसाछन्नः -न्ना -न्नं.

BENIGN, BENIGNANT, *a.* प्रियः -या -यं, हितः -ता -तं, प्रीतः -ता -तं, दयाशीलः -ला -लं, दयालुः -लुः -लु, सुशीलः -ला -लं, कृपालुः -लुः -लु. मृदुः -द्वी -दु, प्रेमपरः -रा -रं.

BENIGNITY, *s.* प्रियता, प्रेम *n.* (न्), प्रीतिः *f.*, स्नेहः, दया, कृपा, कृपालुत्वं, मृदुता, मार्द्दवं, दयालुत्वं, अनुग्रहः.—(Wholesomeness) पथ्यता.

BENIGNLY, *adv.* प्रियं, प्रीत्या, दयापूर्व्वं, कृपया, सद्भावात्, प्रसादात्.

BENISON, *s.* आशीः *f.* (स्), आशीर्वचनं, स्वस्ति *ind.*, धन्यवादः.

BENJAMIN, *s.* कालानुसार्य्यं, शैलनिर्य्यासः, शिलारसः, शिलाजं, वल्कली.

BENT, *s.* (Curvature) नतिः *f.*, वक्रता, नम्रत्वं, जिह्मता, वक्रिमा *m.* (न्), कुब्जत्वं.—(Declivity) प्रवणः, पातुकः.—(Inclination) शीलः, भावः, स्वभावः, प्रकृतिः *f.*, वाञ्छा, इच्छा.—(Determination) निश्चयः.—(Purpose) चिकीर्षितं, अभिप्रायः.—(Application of mind) मनःप्रवेशः.—(A kind of grass) दूर्व्वा, शकुलाक्षकः.

BENT, *p. p.* नतः -ता -तं, नामितः -ता -तं, आनतः -ता -तं, प्रणतः -ता -तं, नम्रः -म्रा -म्रं, परिणतः -ता -तं, भुग्नः -ग्ना -ग्नं, अवभुग्नः -ग्ना -ग्नं, विभुग्नः -ग्ना -ग्नं, रुग्नः -ग्ना -ग्नं, वक्रिमः -मा -मं, प्रवणः -णा -णं, प्रह्वः -ह्वा -ह्वं, कुचितः -ता -तं, आकुञ्चितः -ता -तं, अवाग्रः -ग्रा -ग्रं.

To BENUMB, *v. a.* जडीकृ, मुह् in caus. (मोहयति -यितुं), स्तम्भ् (c. 5. स्तभ्नोति, c. 9. स्तभ्नाति, स्तम्भितुं).

BENUMBED, *p. p.* शीताकुलः -ला -लं, जडीकृतः -ता -तं, जडीभूतः -ता -तं, स्तम्भितः -ता -तं, सुप्तत्वक् *m. f. n.* (च्).

BENZOIN, *s.* कालानुसार्य्यं, अश्मपुष्पं, शीतशिवं, वृद्धं, शैलं, वल्कली, शिलाजं, शिलाभवं, शैलनिर्य्यासः.

To BEPAINT, *v. a.* चित्र् (c. 10. चित्रयति -यितुं), रञ्ज् in caus. (रञ्जयति -यितुं).

To BEPISS, *v. a.* अवमूत्र् (c. 10. -मूत्रयति -यितुं).

To BEQUEATH, *v. a.* प्राग् मरणात् or मरणात् पूर्व्वं or आसन्ने मरणकाले नियमपत्त्रेण स्वरिक्थं दायादादिभ्यः प्रदा (c. 1. -यच्छति -दातुं) or प्रतिपद् in caus. (-पादयति -यितुं) or समृ in caus. (-अर्पयति -यितुं).

BEQUEATHED, *p. p.* रिक्थहारिणे प्रदत्तः -त्ता -त्तं or प्रत्तः -त्ता -त्तं or प्रतिपादितः -ता -तं.

BEQUEST, *s.* मुमूर्षुदानं, उत्तरदानं, आसन्ने मरणकाले दायादादिभ्यो रिक्थप्रदानं.

To BEREAVE, *v. a.* वियुज् in caus. (-योजयति -यितुं), विप्रयुज् with abl. or inst. c., अपहृ (c. 1. -हरति -हर्त्तुं), अपनी (c. 1. -नयति -नेतुं), भ्रंश् in caus. (भ्रंशयति -यितुं).—(To be bereaved) हा in pass. (हीयते), परिहा in pass. with inst. c., भ्रंश् (c. 4. भ्रश्यति, भ्रंशितुं) with abl. c., वियुज् in pass. (-युज्यते).

BEREAVED OR BEREFT, *a.* हीनः -ना -नं, रहितः -ता -तं, वर्जितः -ता -तं, हृतः -ता -तं, अपहृतः -ता -तं, परित्यक्तः -क्ता -क्तं, वियुक्तः -क्ता -क्तं; 'bereft of money,' धनहीनः -ना -नं; 'bereft of one's all,' हृतसर्व्वस्वः; 'bereft of life,' हतजीवितः -ता -तं. Often expressed by गत in the first member of a compound; as, 'bereft of feeling,' गतचेतनः -ना -नं.

BEREAVEMENT, *s.* हानिः *f.*, वियोगः, विप्रयोगः, अपहारः, अपचयः.

BERGAMOT, *s.* फलभेदः, सुगन्धविशिष्टो निर्य्यासविशेषः.

To BERHYME, *v. a.* उपगीतं -तां -तं कृ, कवि (nom. कव्यति).

BERRY, *s.* वीजपूर्णं गुटिकाकारं क्षुद्रफलं, गुटिका, गुली.

BERYL, *s.* गोमेदः, गोमेदकः -कं.

To BESCATTER, *v. a.* अवकॄ (c. 6. -किरति -करितुं, करीतुं), पर्य्यवकॄ.

To BESEECH, *v. a.* प्रार्थ् (c. 10. -अर्थयते -यितुं), अभ्यर्थ्, सम्प्रार्थ्; विनयेन प्रार्थ्, विनी (c. 1. -नयति -नेतुं), याच् (c. 1. याचति -ते, याचितुं), अभियाच्, प्रयाच्, सम्प्रयाच्; प्रसद् in caus. (-सादयते -यितुं).

BESEECHED, *p. p.* विनयेन प्रार्थितः -ता -तं, अभ्यर्थितः -ता -तं, याचितः -ता -तं.

BESEECHER, *s.* प्रार्थकः, प्रार्थयिता *m.* (तृ), अर्थी *m.* (न्), याचकः.

To BESEEM, *v. a.* युज् in pass. (युज्यते), उपपद् (c. 4. -पद्यते -पत्तुं) with loc. c.

BESEEMLY, *a.* युक्तः -क्ता -क्तं, योग्यः -ग्या -ग्यं, यथोचितः -ता -तं.

To BESET, *v. a.* (To besiege) रुध् (c. 7. रुणद्धि, रोद्धुं), उपरुध्, आक्रम् (c. 1. -क्रामति -क्रमितुं).—(To surround) परिवेष्ट् (c. 1. -वेष्टते -वेष्टितुं), उपवेष्ट्, संवेष्ट्; परिष्ठा (c. 1. -तिष्ठति -ते -स्थातुं), पर्य्युपस्था.—(To embarrass) आकुलीकृ, बाध् (c. 1. बाधते, बाधितुं), परिक्लिश् (c. 9. -क्लिश्नाति -क्लेष्टुं).

BESET, *p. p.* रुद्धः -द्धा -द्धं, उपरुद्धः -द्धा -द्धं, वेष्टितः -ता -तं, परिवेष्टितः -ता -तं, आक्रान्तः -न्ता -न्तं, परिगतः -ता -तं, अभिपरिप्लुतः -ता -तं, बाधितः -ता -तं, परीतः -ता -तं, अभिपरीतः -ता -तं.

To BESHREW, *v. a.* दुर्भाग्यं or अमङ्गलं प्रार्थ् (c. 10. -अर्थयते -यितुं), धिक्कृ.

BESIDE OR BESIDES, *prep.* (At the side of) पार्श्वे, पार्श्वतस्, निकटे, समीपे, सन्निधाने, अभितस्; 'beside the river,' नदीतीरे, नदीसमीपे.—(Over and above) अधिकं, व्यतिरिक्तं, अन्तरेण, मुक्त्वा.—(Except) ऋते with abl. or acc., विना with inst. or acc.—(Beside one's self) हतज्ञानः -ना -नं, उपहतबुद्धिः -द्धिः -द्धि, उन्मत्तः -त्ता -त्तं.

BESIDE OR BESIDES, *adv.* अपरञ्च, अपरं, अन्यच्च, अपिच, किञ्च, अधिकन्तु, अधिकं; 'are there any here besides?' किम् अत्र अपरे सन्ति.

To BESIEGE, *v. a.* रुध् (c. 7. रुणद्धि, रोद्धुं), अवरुध्, उपरुध्, परिवेष्ट् (c. 1. -वेष्टते -वेष्टितुं), आक्रम् (c. 1. -क्रामति -क्रमितुं), बाध् (c. 1. बाधते, बाधितुं).

BESIEGED, *part. a.* रुद्धः -द्धा -द्धं, परिवेष्टितः -ता -तं, बाधितः -ता -तं.

BESIEGER, *s.* अवरोधकः, रोधी *m.* (न्), अवरोधी *m.* (न्), वेष्टकः, बाधकः.

To BESLAVE, *v. a.* वशीकृ, दासीकृ, करदीकृ, दम् in caus. (दमयति -यितुं).

To BESMEAR, *v. a.* लिप् (c. 6. लिम्पति -ते -लेप्तुं), आलिप्, समालिप्, उपलिप्, अञ्ज् (c. 7. अनक्ति, अंक्तुं), or caus. (अञ्जयति -यितुं), दिह् (c. 2. देग्धि, देग्धुं), प्रदिह्.

BESMEARED, *p. p.* लिप्तः -प्ता -प्तं, विलिप्तः -प्ता -प्तं, उपलिप्तः -प्ता -प्तं, अभ्यक्तः -क्ता -क्तं, दिग्धः -ग्धा -ग्धं; 'besmeared with blood,' रक्ताक्तः -क्ता -क्तं, शोणिताक्तः -क्ता -क्तं, शोणितोक्षितः -ता -तं.

Besom, *s.* मार्ज्जनी, सम्मार्ज्जनी, शोधनी, विमार्गः, अहनी, समूहनी.

To besort, *v. a.* युज् in pass. (युज्यते), उपपद् (c. 4. -पद्यते -पत्तुं).

To besot, *v. a.* मुह् in caus. (मोहयति -यितुं), जडीकृ, मूढीकृ.

Besotted, *p. p.* मूढचेताः -ताः -तः (स्), मूढबुद्धिः -द्धिः -द्धि, मूढात्मा -त्मा -त्म (न्), प्रमूढसंज्ञः -ज्ञा -ज्ञं, मोहितः -ता -तं, जडीकृतः -ता -तं.

Besottedness, *s.* मोहः, सम्मोहः, मूढता, जडता, जडिमा *m.* (न्).

To bespangle, *v. a.* नक्षत्राकारैर् भूषणैर् अनुव्यध् (c. 4. -विध्यति -व्यद्धुं) or शुभ् in caus. (शोभयति -यितुं), उपशुभ्.

To bespatter, *v. a.* पङ्केन or मलेन सिच् (c. 6. सिञ्चति -ते, सेक्तुं), अवसिच् or अवकृ (c. 6. -किरति -करितुं -करीतुं), अभ्यवकृ or उक्ष् (c. 1. उक्षति उक्षितुं), प्रोक्ष्; मलिन (nom. मलिनयति -यितुं), कलुष (nom. कलुषयति -यितुं), कलङ्क (nom. कलङ्कयति -यितुं).

Bespattered, *p. p.* मलदूषितः -ता -तं, कलङ्कितः -ता -तं, कलुषितः -ता -तं.

To bespeak, *v. a.* (To order beforehand) प्रख्या (c. 2. -ख्याति -ख्यातुं), पूर्व्वादेशं कृ; अग्रनिवेदनं कृ; मम पूर्व्वभुक्तिः स्यादिति वद् (c. 1. वदति, वदितुं).—(To betoken, indicate) सूच् (c. 10. सूचयति -यितुं), प्रदिश् (c. 6. -दिशति -देष्टुं).—(To forebode) अग्रनिरूपणं कृ, प्रदृश् in caus. (-दर्शयति -यितुं).

To bespeckle, *v. a.* चित्र् (c. 10. चित्रयति -यितुं), शवलीकृ, कर्व्वुरीकृ.

To bespit, *v. a.* निष्ठीव् (c. 1. -ष्ठीवति -ष्ठेवितुं), अवनिष्ठीव्.

Bespoken, *p. p.* प्रख्यातः -ता -तं, पूर्व्वादिष्टः -ष्टा -ष्टं, अग्रनिवेदितः -ता -तं.—(Any commodity bespoken) प्रख्यातभाण्डं.

Bespread, *p. p.* आस्तीर्णः -र्णा -र्णं, आवृतः -ता -तं, परिच्छन्नः -न्ना -न्नं.

To besprinkle, *v. a.* सिच् (c. 6. सिञ्चति -ते, सेक्तुं), अवसिच्, निषिच्, संसिच्, अवकृ (c. 6. -किरति -करितुं -करीतुं), अभ्यवकृ, पर्य्यवकृ, समवकृ, उक्ष् (c. 1. उक्षति, उक्षितुं), अभ्युक्ष्, प्रोक्ष्; क्लिद् in caus. (क्लेदयति -यितुं).

Besprinkled, *p. p.* सिक्तः -क्ता -क्तं, उक्षितः -ता -तं, प्रोक्षितः -ता -तं.

Best (superl. of good), *a.* सर्व्वोत्तमः -मा -मं, उत्तमः -मा -मं, अनुत्तमः -मा -मं, सत्तमः -मा -मं, श्रेष्ठः -ष्ठा -ष्ठं, सर्व्वश्रेष्ठः -ष्ठा -ष्ठं, परमः -मा -मं, परः -रा -रं, भद्रतमः -मा -मं, अर्हत्तमः -मा -मं, प्रवरः -रा -रं, प्रशस्तः -स्ता -स्तं, अग्रिमः -मा -मं, परार्द्ध्यः -र्द्ध्या -र्द्ध्यं; 'which is the best of these?' एतेषां को भद्रतमः; 'best beloved,' इष्टतमः -मा -मं. Any thing the best of its kind may sometimes be expressed by रत्नं.

Best (superl. of well), *adv.* उत्तमं, श्रेष्ठं, सत्तमं, श्रेष्ठतस्.

Bestained, *p. p.* कलङ्कितः -ता -तं, दूषितः -ता -तं, परिमलितः -ता -तं.

To bestead, *v. a.* (To profit) फलाय or लाभाय भू or अस्.

Bestial, *a.* पाशवः -वी -वं, पशुशीलः -ला -लं, पशुव्यवहारः -रा -रं, पशुसदृशः -शी -शं, अमानुषः -षी -षं, क्रूराचारः -रा -रं.

Bestiality, *s.* पशुता -त्वं, पशुशीलता, अमनुष्यता, क्रूराचारत्वं, पशुगमनं.

To bestialize, *v. a.* पशूकृ, पशुसदृशं -शीं -शं कृ.

Bestially, *adv.* पशुवत्, पशुरूपेण, पशुव्यवहारानुसारात्, मानुषाचारविरुद्धं.

To bestir one's self, *v. r.* चेष्ट् (c. 1. चेष्टते, चेष्टितुं), विचेष्ट्, आत्मानं चेष्ट् in caus. (चेष्टयति -यितुं), यत् (c. 1. यतते, यतितुं), प्रयत्, घट् (c. 1. घटते, घटितुं), व्यवसो (c. 1. -स्यति -सातुं), उद्यमं or उत्साहं कृ.

To bestow, *v. a.* (To give) दा (c. 3. ददाति, c. 1. यच्छति, दातुं), प्रदा, अभिदा, अनुदा, वितृ (c. 1. -तरति -तरितुं -तरीतुं), प्रतिपद् in caus. (-पादयति -यितुं), उपपद्; निक्षिप् (c. 6. -क्षिपति -क्षेप्तुं); उपाकृ.—(To apply, lay out) प्रयुज् (c. 7. -युनक्ति -युंक्ते -योक्तुं), उपयुज्; निधा (c. 3. -दधाति -धातुं).—(To give in marriage) कन्यां प्रदा.

To bestow one's self, *v. r.* (Attend to) सेव् (c. 1. सेवते, सेवितुं). उपसेव्; आस्था (c. 1. -तिष्ठति -स्थातुं), मनो निविश् in caus. (-वेशयति -यितुं).

Bestowed, *p. p.* दत्तः -त्ता -त्तं, प्रदत्तः -त्ता -त्तं, प्रत्तः -त्ता -त्तं, निहितः -ता -तं, विश्राणितः -ता -तं, प्रतिपादितः -ता -तं, निक्षिप्तः -प्ता -प्तं, वितीर्णः -र्णा -र्णं.

Bestower, *s.* दाता *m.* (तृ), प्रदाता *m.* (तृ), प्रदः or दः in comp.

Bestraught, *p. p.* चिन्ताकुलः -ला -लं, व्यग्रः -ग्रा -ग्रं, उपहतबुद्धिः -द्धिः -द्धि.

To bestrew, *v. a.* आस्तृ (c. 5. -स्तृणोति -स्तरितुं -स्तरीतुं).

To bestride, *v. a.* (A horse) पादौ or जङ्घे पृथक्कृत्वा अश्वम् आरुह् (c. 1. -रोहति -रोढुं), अधिरुह्, अध्यारुह्; अधिक्रम् (c. 1. -क्रामति -क्रमितुं); 'bestriding a horse,' अश्वारूढः.

To bestud, *v. a.* गण्डादिभूषणैर् अनुव्यध् (c. 4. -विध्यति -व्यद्धुं) or खच् (c. 10. खचयति -यितुं).

Bestudded, *p. p.* अनुविद्धः -द्धा -द्धं, खचितः -ता -तं, प्रत्युप्तः -प्ता -प्तं.

Bet, *s.* (Wager) पणः, प्रतिज्ञा, आक्षिकपणः.

To bet, *v. n.* पण् (c. 1. पणते, पणितुं), विपण्; दिव् (c. 4. दीव्यति, देवितुं).

To betake one's self, *v. r.* आश्रि (c. 1. -श्रयति -ते -श्रयितुं), अभिश्रि, उपाश्रि, संश्रि, समुपाश्रि.

Betel, *s.* (Nut) ताम्बूलं, पूगं, उद्वेगं, पूगफलं.—(The plant) ताम्बूली, ताम्बूलवल्ली, नागवल्ली.—(A seller of it) ताम्बूलिकः.—(Relating to it) ताम्बूली -लिनी -लि (न्).—(Betel box) पूगपात्रं, ताम्बूलपेटिका.—(Betel-bearer) ताम्बूलवाहकः, ताम्बूलदः, वाग्गुलिः *m.*

To bethink one's self, *v. r.* अनुचिन्त् (c. 10. -चिन्तयति -यितुं), सञ्चिन्त्, अनुध्यै (c. 1. -ध्यायति -ध्यातुं), विमृश् (c. 6. -मृशति -मर्ष्टुं -म्रष्टुं), अनुबुध् (c. 4. -बुध्यते -बोद्धुं), अनुस्मृ (c. 1. -स्मरति -स्मर्त्तुं).

To bethump, *v. a.* तड् (c. 10. ताडयति -यितुं), प्रहृ (c. 1. -हरति -हर्त्तुं).

To betide, *v. n.* सम्भू (c. 1. -भवति -भवितुं), उपस्था (c. 1. -तिष्ठति -स्थातुं), निपत् (c. 1. -पतति -पतितुं), सम्पद् (c. 4. -पद्यते -पत्तुं), घट् (c. 1. घटते, घटितुं); 'may good betide you,' भद्रं ते भूयात्; 'woe betide you,' अवग्राहस्ते or अजीवनिस्ते or अकरणिस्ते भूयात्.

Betimes, *adv.* प्रभाते, सकालं, प्रातर्, व्युष्टे, प्रत्यूषे, समया, समये, उपयुक्तसमये, वेलायां.

To betoken, *v. a.* सूच् (c. 10. सूचयति -यितुं), प्रदिश् (c. 6. -दिशति -देष्टुं), सन्दिश्; अभिदृश् in caus. (-दर्शयति -यितुं).—(To foreshew) प्रदृश् in caus.; 'betokening,' सूचकः -का -कं, वाचकः -का -कं.

To betoss, *v. a.* क्षुभ् in caus. (क्षोभयति -यितुं), क्षिप् (c. 6. क्षिपति, क्षेप्तुं).

To betray, *v. a.* परहस्तेषु or शत्रुकरेषु or शत्रुपाणिषु or अन्येषां करेषु समृ in caus. (-अर्पयति -यितुं), परादा (c. 3. -ददाति -दातुं), प्रदा, वञ्च् (c. 10. वञ्चयते -यितुं), विश्वासघातं or विश्वासभङ्गं कृ, खण्ड् (c. 10. खण्डयति -यितुं), शत्रोरायत्तं -त्तां -त्तं कृ.—(To shew, discover) सूच् (c. 10. सूचयति -यितुं); दृश् in caus. (दर्शयति -यितुं), पिशुन (nom. पिशुनयति -यितुं), व्यक्तीकृ, प्रकटीकृ.—(To betray secrets) गोप्यानि प्रकाश् in caus. (-काशयति -यितुं), मन्त्रभेदं कृ.

Betrayed, *p. p.* शत्रुहस्तार्पितः -ता -तं, वञ्चितः -ता -तं, परादत्तः -त्ता -त्तं.

Betrayer, *s.* परहस्तार्पकः, वञ्चकः, विश्वासघातकः, प्रदाता *m.* (तृ).

To betrim, *v. a.* भूष् (c. 10. भूषयति -यितुं), अलङ्कृ, परिष्कृ.

To betroth, *v. a.* वाग्दानं कृ, नियमपत्रेण विवाहप्रतिज्ञां कृ, प्रतिज्ञापत्रेण विवाहसम्बन्धं कृ.

Betrothed, *p. p.* वाग्दत्तः -त्ता -त्तं, प्रदत्तः -त्ता -त्तं, प्रत्तः -त्ता -त्तं, प्रतिज्ञाविवाहितः -ता -तं.—(Woman) वाग्दत्ता, प्रत्ता.

Betrothment, *s.* वाग्दानं, कन्याप्रदानं.

To betrust, *v. a.* परिदा (c. 3. -ददाति -दातुं), नियुज् in caus. (-योजयति

-यितुं), समृ in caus. (-अर्पयति -यितुं).

Better, (compar. of good) *a.* भद्रतरः -रा -रं, श्रेयान् -यसी -यः (स्), श्रेष्ठः -ष्ठा -ष्ठं, गरीयान् -यसी -यः (स्), प्रशस्तः -स्ता -स्तं, अर्हत्तरः -रा -रं, साधीयान् -यसी -यः (स्), ज्यायान् -यसी -यः (स्).

Better (compar. of well) *adv.* वरं, प्रशस्तं, श्रेयस्, भद्रतरं, भद्रतरप्रकारेण, श्रेष्ठं.—(More) अधिकं, अधिकतरं, अतिरिक्तं.—(The better, the superiority) श्रेष्ठता, श्रेयस्त्वं, प्रधानता, प्रमुखत्वं.—(To get the better) अभिभू, अतिरिच् in pass. (-रिच्यते).

To better, *v. a.* भद्रतरं -रां -रं कृ, श्रेयांसं -यसीं -यः कृ.—(To advance) वृध् in caus. (वर्धयति -यितुं), संवृध्, परिवृध्, ऋध् in caus. (ऋधयति -यितुं), समेध्.—(To surpass) अतिरिच् in pass. (-रिच्यते), अभिभू.

Betters, *s. pl.* (Superiors) श्रेष्ठाः *m. pl.*, प्रधानपुरुषाः *m. pl.*, उत्तमपुरुषाः *m. pl.*

Betting, *s.* पणनं, पणकरणं, पणार्पणं, आक्षिकपणकरणं, प्रतिज्ञानं.

Bettor, *s.* पणकर्त्ता *m.* (र्त्तृ), पणकः, पणार्पकः.

Betty, *s.* द्वारकपाटादिभञ्जने सन्धिचौरैः प्रयुक्तं लोहयन्त्रं.

Between or betwixt, *prep.* मध्ये, अभ्यन्तरे, अन्तरेण, अन्तरे, अन्तर्, अन्तरा, मध्यतस्, मध्यस्थाने; 'the mediator between God and man,' ईश्वरस्य मानुषाणाञ्च मध्ये मध्यस्थः. Between is sometimes expressed by the gen. or inst. c.; as, 'there is a great difference between a master and a servant,' सेव्यसेवकयोर् महदन्तरं; 'great is the difference between thee and the ocean,' त्वया समुद्रेण च महदन्तरं; 'I will put enmity between thee and the woman,' त्वया नार्य्या च वैरितां जनिष्यामि; 'I am in a strait betwixt two,' उभाभ्यां सङ्कुचितोऽस्मि; 'they parted the paternal inheritance between them,' दायं पित्र्यं परस्परं व्यभजन्.

Bever, *s.* माध्यन्दिनभोजनानन्तरं प्रायाग्निभोजनात् तत्कालान्तरे लघ्वाहारः or अल्पाशनं.

Beverage, *s.* पानीयं, पेयं, पानं, पयः *n.* (स्).—(Of the gods) अमृतं.

Bevy, *s.* गणः, सङ्घः, समवायः, यूथं, कुलं; 'a bevy of young lasses,' तरुणीगणः.

To bewail, *v. a.* and *n.* विलप् (c. 1. -लपति -लपितुं), शुच् (c. 1. शोचति, शोचितुं), अनुशुच्, परिदेव् (c. 1. -देवति -ते -देवितुं); 'to grieve exceedingly,' शुच् in freq. (शोशुच्यते), परिशुच् in freq., लप् in freq. (लालप्यते).

Bewailable, *a.* शोच्यः -च्या -च्यं, शोचनीयः -या -यं, विलपनीयः -या -यं.

Bewailing, *s.* विलपनं, विलापः, परिदेवनं, अनुशोचनं, क्रन्दनं.

To beware, *v. n.* अवधा (c. 3. -धत्ते -धातुं), सावधानः -ना -नं भू, अवधानं कृ.—(Abstain from, avoid) परिहृ (c. 1. -हरति -हर्त्तुं), वृज् in caus. (वर्जयति -यितुं), विवृज्, परिवृज्; 'beware of men,' मानुषेभ्योऽवधत्त; 'beware of too great avarice,' अतिलोभात् सावधानो भव; 'beware lest any one deceive you,' सावधाना भवत कोऽपि युष्मान् न भ्रमयेत्.

To beweep, *v. a.* रुद् (c. 2. रोदिति, रोदितुं), अनुशुच् (c. 1. -शोचति, -शोचितुं).

To bewet, *v. a.* क्लिद् in caus. (क्लेदयति -यितुं), सिच् (c. 6. सिञ्चति, सेक्तुं).

To bewilder, *v. a.* मुह् in caus. (मोहयति -यितुं), व्यामुह्, परिमुह्, विप्रमुह्; आकुलीकृ, व्याकुलीकृ, विभ्रम् in caus. (-भ्रमयति -यितुं), सम्भ्रम्.

Bewildered, *p.p.* आकुलः -ला -लं, व्याकुलः -ला -लं, आकुलितः -ता -तं, आकुलीकृतः -ता -तं, सम्भ्रान्तः -न्ता -न्तं, कातरः -रा -रं, व्यग्रः -ग्रा -ग्रं, मोहितः -ता -तं, मुग्धः -ग्धा -ग्धं, विमूढः -ढा -ढं, विमुग्धः -ग्धा -ग्धं, भ्रान्तः -न्ता -न्तं, परिविह्वलः -ला -लं.

Bewilderment, *s.* व्याकुलता, आकुलत्वं, व्यग्रता, वैक्लव्यं, सम्भ्रमः, कातरता.

To bewitch, *v. a.* मन्त्रद्वारा वशीकृ or मुह् in caus. (मोहयति -यितुं), मोहं कृ, अभिमन्त्र् (c. 10. -मन्त्रयते -यितुं).—(To captivate) मनो हृ (c. 1. हरति, हर्त्तुं).

Bewitched, *p. p.* मोहितः -ता -तं, वशीकृतः -ता -तं, अभिमन्त्रितः -ता -तं.

Bewitcher, *s.* मोहकः, मोहनः, मायी *m.* (न्), वशीकर्त्ता *m.* (र्त्तृ), मायाकृत्.

Bewitchment, *s.* वशीक्रिया, वशिः *m.*, वशिता, वशीकरणं, मोहनं, परिमोहनं, विमोहनं, सम्मोहः, मोहः, माया, कार्म्मणत्वं.

Bewitching, *a.* मोही -हिनी -हि (न्), मोहनः -नी -नं, मनोहारी -रिणी -रि (न्), मनोहरः -रा -रं, प्रलोभकः -का -कं, आकर्षिकः -की -कं, मायी -यिनी -यि (न्).

Bewitchingly, *adv.* यथा मनो ह्रियते or वशीक्रियते तथा, मनोहरप्रकारेण, यथा मोहो जायते तथा, मायया, प्रलोभनाय.

To bewray, *v. a.* (To betray) परादा (c. 3. -ददाति -दातुं), प्रदा; शत्रुहस्तेषु समृ in caus. (-अर्पयति -यितुं).—(To indicate) सूच् (c. 10. (सूचयति -यितुं), पिशुन (nom. पिशुनयति -यितुं).

Beyond, *prep.* and *adv.* अति prefixed.—(On the farther side) पारं, पारे; 'beyond the sea,' समुद्रपारं; 'from beyond,' पारात्; 'to go beyond,' अतिक्रम् (c. 1. -क्रामति -क्रमितुं), अतिचर् (c. 1. -चरति -चरितुं).—(In front) अग्रे.—(Superior to) अतिरेकी -किणी -कि (न्), विशिष्टः -ष्टा -ष्टं.—(More than) अधिकं, or expressed by अति prefixed; as, 'beyond mortal strength,' अतिमानुषः -षा -षं; 'beyond's one's power,' अतिशक्ति; 'beyond measure,' अतिशयं, अतीव; 'passed beyond the range of sight,' चक्षुर्विषयम् अतिक्रान्तः.—(At a distance) दूरे.

Bezel or bezil, *s.* रत्नाधारयोग्योऽङ्गुरीयकभागः, अङ्गुरीयकस्य यत्स्थाने मणिः लग्यते or प्रणिधीयते तत्.

Bhavání, *s.* (The wife of the god Śiva, and the goddess of destruction; called Bhavání in her amiable form) भवानी, उमा, महादेवी, देवी.—(The pure one) गौरी.—(As terrible in form and irascible in temper) दुर्गा, काली, चण्डी, चण्डिका.—(As daughter of Himálá, the sovereign of the snowy mountains) पार्व्वती, हैमवती.—(As wife of Śiva) शिवा, ईश्वरी, रुद्राणी, शर्व्वाणी, मृडानी.—(The all-auspicious) सर्व्वमङ्गला.—(The mother) अम्बिका.—(As the performer of austerities) कात्यायनी, अपर्णा.

Biangulated, *a.* द्विकोणः -णा -णं, द्व्यस्रकः -का -कं, कोणद्वयविशिष्टः -ष्टा -ष्टं.

Bias, *s.* (Inclination) भावः, शीलः, शीलत्वं, वाञ्छा, स्वभावः, इच्छा, अभिलाषः, सङ्कल्पः, छन्दं, चिकीर्षा, स्पृहा, अभिप्रायः.—(Inclination to go on one side) पार्श्वे गमनेच्छा.—(Partiality) पक्षपातः, पक्षपातिता, साचीकृतं.—(That which biasses, or induces to act) प्रवर्त्तकः, प्रणोदः, प्रोत्साहः -हकः, प्रयोजकः.

To bias, *v. a.* प्रवृत् in caus. (-वर्त्तयति -यितुं), आवृज् in caus. (-वर्जयति -यितुं); साचीकृ; प्रणुद् (c. 6. -णुदति -णोत्तुं), आकृष् (c. 1. -कर्षति -क्रष्टुं), चेष्ट् in caus. (चेष्टयति -यितुं), प्रोत्सह् in caus. (-साहयति -यितुं), आकृ in caus. (-कारयति -यितुं), पक्षपातीकृ.

Biassed, *p. p.* प्रवर्त्तितः -ता -तं, प्रोत्साहितः -ता -तं, प्रणोदितः -ता -तं, साचीकृतः -ता -तं, आकृष्टः -ष्टा -ष्टं.—(In favour of a side) पक्षग्राही *m.* (न्).

Bib, *s.* बालकस्य वक्षस्थलछादनयोग्यं क्षौमीनिर्म्मितं उत्तरीयवस्त्रं.

Bibber, *s.* सुरापी *m.* (न्), सुरापः, मद्यपायी *m.* (न्), पानपरः, मद्यपः *m.*

Bible, *s.* धर्म्मपुस्तकं, ईश्वरवाक्यप्रकाशको ग्रन्थः.

Biblical, *a.* धर्म्मपुस्तकविषयः -या -यं, धर्म्मपुस्तकसम्बन्धकः -का -कं.

Bibliography, *s.* ग्रन्थविद्या, ग्रन्थविद्यानुसेवनं.

Bibliomania, *s.* प्राचीनपुस्तकप्राप्तौ व्यग्रता, दुर्लभग्रन्थान्वेषणे व्यग्रता.

Bibliotheke, *s.* पाठार्थं सुरक्षितो ग्रन्थसमूहः, विद्यानुसेवनार्थं ग्रन्थकुटी.

Bibulous, *a.* जलशोषकः -का -कं, जलनिपानशीलः -ला -लं.

Bicapsular, *a.* बीजकोशो द्वैधीकृतो यस्य, द्विधाभूतबीजकोशः -शा -शं.

Bicipital, *a.* द्विमुण्डः -ण्डा -ण्डं, द्विशीर्षकः -का -कं, द्विशिराः -राः -रः (स्).

To bicker, *v. n.* (To skirmish) डिम्बाहवं कृ; कलह (nom. कलहायते -यितुं), कलहं कृ.—(To wrangle) विवद् (c. 1. -वदते -वदितुं), वाग्युद्धं कृ.—(To quiver) स्फुर् (c. 6. स्फुरति, स्फुरितुं).

Bickering, *s.* कलहः, विप्रलापः, विवादः, द्वन्द्वं, वाग्युद्धं.—(Petty warfare) डिम्बः, डिम्बाहवः.

Bickern, *s.* सूच्याकाराग्रयुक्तः शूर्म्मिभागः, कर्म्मकारसेवितं लोहयन्त्रं.

Bicorne, *a.* द्विशृङ्गः -ङ्गा -ङ्गं, शृङ्गद्वयविशिष्टः -ष्टा -ष्टं.

To bid, *v. a.* (To invite) निमन्त्र् (c. 10. -मन्त्रयति -ते -यितुं), आह्वे (c. 1. -ह्वयति -ह्वातुं).—(To command) आज्ञा in caus. (-ज्ञापयति -यितुं), प्रेर् (c. 10. प्रेरयति -यितुं), आदिश् (c. 6. -दिशति -देष्टुं), समादिश्.—(To offer a price) अमुकमूल्यं दित्सामीति or दातुमिच्छामीति वद् (c. 1. वदति, वदितुं) or ख्या in caus. (ख्यापयति -यितुं) or घुष् (c. 10. घोषयति -यितुं) or अभिधा (c. 3. -दधाति -धातुं).—(To bid welcome) स्वागतमिति वद्.—(To bid adieu) आमन्त्र् (c. 10. -मन्त्रयते -यितुं), अनुमन्त्र्; आप्रच्छ् (c. 6. -पृच्छते -प्रष्टुं).—(To bid defiance) आह्वे, समाह्वे.

Bidden, *p. p.* (Commanded) आज्ञप्तः -प्ता -प्तं, प्रेरितः -ता -तं, चोदितः -ता -तं, देशितः -ता -तं, आदिष्टः -ष्टा -ष्टं.—(Invited) निमन्त्रितः -ता -तं, केतितः -ता -तं, आहूतः -ता -तं.

Bidder, *s.* क्रेता *m.* (तृ), क्रायकः, मूल्यदित्सुः *m.*, प्रकाशक्रयसमये अमुकमूल्यं दित्सामीति or दास्यामीति ख्यापयति यो जनः.

Bidding, *s.* (Command) आज्ञा, प्रेरणं, आदेशः, निर्देशः, शासनं.—(Offer of a price) मूल्यदित्साख्यापनं, अमुकमूल्यं दित्सामीति ख्यापनं, मूल्यदित्सा.

To bide, *v. a.* and *n.* (To remain) स्था (c. 1. तिष्ठति -ते, स्थातुं), वृत् (c. 1. वर्त्तते, वर्त्तितुं), वस् (c. 1. वसति, वस्तुं).—(To expect) प्रतीक्ष् (c. 1. -ईक्षते -ईक्षितुं), उद्दृश् (c. 1. -पश्यति -द्रष्टुं).—(To endure) सह् (c. 1. सहते, सोढुं), मृष् (c. 4. मृष्यति, मर्षितुं).

Bidental, *a.* द्विदन् -दती -दत् (त्), द्विदन्तः -न्ती -न्तं, द्विरदः -दा -दं.

Biennial, *a.* द्वैवर्षिकः -की -कं, द्विवर्षः -र्षा -र्षं, द्विवर्षीणः -णा -णं, द्विवर्षमात्रस्थायी -यिनी -यि (न्), वत्सरद्वयमात्रजीवी *m.* (न्).

Bier, *s.* शिविका, शववाहनं, शवयानं, कटः, खट्टिः *m.*, खाटः, खारुठः, प्रेतवाहनसाधनं खट्वादि.

Biesting, *s.* पेयूषः -षं, पीयूषः -षं, प्रसवानन्तरं प्रथमगोदुग्धं.

Bifid, bifidated, *a.* द्विखण्डीकृतः -ता -तं, द्वैधीकृतः -ता -तं.

Bifold, *a.* द्विगुणः -णा -णं, द्वैधः -धी -धं, द्विःप्रकारः -रा -रं.

Biformed, *a.* द्विरूपः -पा -पी -पं, द्विमूर्त्तिमान् -मती -मत् (त्).

Bifurcated, *s.* द्व्यग्रः -ग्रा -ग्रं, अग्रद्वयविशिष्टः -ष्टा -ष्टं.

Big, *a.* स्थूलः -ला -लं, बृहन् -हती -हत् (त्), विपुलः -ला -लं.—(Big-bodied) बृहत्कायः -या -यं, महाकायः -या -यं, महाङ्गः -ङ्गी -ङ्गं.—(A pregnant woman) गर्भिणी, गर्भवती.—(Bombastic) गर्व्वितः -ता -तं.—(Teeming with) सङ्कुलः -ला -लं, सङ्कीर्णः -र्णा -र्णं, आकीर्णः -र्णा -र्णं, पूर्णः -र्णा -र्णं.—(As big as) परिमाण or परिमित, or मात्र affixed; as, 'as big as an egg,' अण्डपरिमाणः -णा -णं; 'as big as a grain of mustard,' सर्षपपरिमितः -ता -तं; 'as big as a man,' पुरुषमात्रः -त्रा -त्रं.

Bigamist, *s.* द्विभार्य्यः, द्विपत्नीस्वामी *m.* (न्), एककाले विवाहद्वयकर्त्ता *m.* (तृ).

Bigamy, *s.* एककाले द्विविवाहकरणं, द्विपत्नीधारित्वं.

Big-bellied, *a.* पृथूदरः -रा -रं, स्थूलोदरः -रा -रं, लम्बोदरः -रा -रं, बृहत्कुक्षिः -क्षिः -क्षि, पिचण्डिलः -ला -लं, बृहन्नाभिः -भिः -भि, तुन्दवान् -वती -वत् (त्).

Big-boned, *a.* बृहदस्थिमान् -मती -मत् (त्), बृहदङ्गः -ङ्गी -ङ्गं.

Biggin, *s.* बालकयोग्यं शिरोवेष्टनं, बालशिरस्कं.—(A pot) पात्रं, आधारः.

Bigness, *s.* स्थूलता, स्थौल्यं, बृहत्त्वं, विपुलता.—(Size, comparative bulk) परिमाणं; 'of the bigness of an egg,' अण्डपरिमाणः -णा -णं.

Bignonia, *s.* पाटलिः *m. f.* -ला, अमोघा, काचस्थाली, फलेरुहा, कुबेराक्षी.

Bigot, *s.* स्वमतधारणे व्यग्रः, विचारणां विना or अविचार्य्य पक्षपाती *m.* (न्), निर्बन्धशीलः, व्यग्रचित्तः.

Bigoted, *a.* अविचार्य्य स्वमते स्थितः -ता -तं, स्वमतधारणे व्यग्रः -ग्रा -ग्रं, स्वमतेनिष्ठितः -ता -तं, साचीकृतः -ता -तं, स्वमतरक्षी -क्षिणी -क्षि (न्).

Bigotry, *s.* विचारणां विना स्वमते व्यवस्थितिः *f.* or अभिनिवेशः or अतिनिर्बन्धः, साचीकृतं.

Big-swoln, *a.* अतिस्फीतः -ता -तं, उच्छूनः -ना -नं, प्रवृद्धः -द्धा -द्धं.

Big-uddered, *a.* पीनोघ्नी *f.*, पीवरस्तनी *f.*, पीनस्तनधारिणी *f.*

Bilbo, *s.* कृपाणः, खड्गः, निस्त्रिंशः, असिः *m.*

Bile, *s.* पित्तं, मायुः *m.*, भ्राजकं, पलाग्निः *m.*

Bile, *s.* (A boil) स्फोटः, स्फोटकः, विस्फोटः.

To bilge, *v. n.* (To spring a leak) नौकातले or नौकापार्श्वे दारुस्फोटनप्रयुक्तं जलं गृहीत्वा मस्ज् (c. 6. मज्जति, मङ्क्तुं).

Biliary, *a.* पैत्तः -त्ती -त्तं, पित्तसम्बन्धी -न्धिनी -न्धि (न्).

Bilinguous, *a.* द्विजिह्वः -ह्वा -ह्वं, द्विभाषावादी -दिनी -दि (न्).

Bilious, *a.* पित्तलः -ला -लं, पैत्तः -त्ती -त्तं, पैत्तिकः -की -कं.

To bilk, *v. a.* वञ्च् in caus. (वञ्चयति -ते -यितुं), परिवञ्च्, प्रलभ् (c. 1. -लभते -लब्धुं), विप्रलभ्.

Bill, *s.* (Beak of a bird) चञ्चुः *f.*, तुण्डः, तुण्डिः *m.*, मुखः.—(A kind of hatchet) दात्रं, खनित्रः.—(An act of parliament) व्यवस्था.—(A written paper of any kind) पत्रं, लेखः -खा, लेख्यं.—(An account of money) विक्रयपत्रं.—(An advertisement) घोषणापत्रं.—(In law) भाषापादः, पूर्व्वपक्षपादः, अभियोगपत्रं.

To bill, *v. n.* (To kiss, embrace) चुम्ब् (c. 1. चुम्बति, चुम्बितुं), निंस् (c. 2. निंस्ते, निंसितुं), आलिङ्ग् (c. 1. -लिङ्गति -लिङ्गितुं), परिरिंसां कृ.

Billet, *s.* (A note) पत्रं, लेखः, लेख्यं.—(A ticket) निदर्शनपत्रं, चिह्नं.—(A log of wood) काष्ठखण्डं, काष्ठं.

To billet, *v. a.* निदर्शनपत्रेण सैन्यानाम् आवासस्थानं प्रक्लृप् (c. 10. -कल्पयति -यितुं); सैन्यान् वस् in caus. (वासयति -यितुं).

Billiards, *s. pl.* इदानीन्तनजनैः सेविता गुलिकाक्रीडा.

Billion, *s.* खर्व्वः.—(A million millions) नियुतनियुतानि, शङ्कुः.

Billow, *s.* ऊर्म्मिः *m. f.*, महोर्म्मिः *m. f.*, भङ्गः, तरङ्गः, उल्लोलः, पयोराशिः *f.*, वारिराशिः *f.*, कल्लोलः, अगेलः.

To billow, *v. n.* तरङ्ग (nom. तरङ्गायते), तरङ्गरूपेण प्रलुठ् (c. 1. -लोठति -लोठितुं), महावेलया प्रवृध् (c. 1. -वर्धते -वर्धितुं).

Billow-beaten, *a.* तरङ्गोद्धातः -ता -तं, तरङ्गक्षिप्तः -प्ता -प्तं, उत्तरङ्गः -ङ्गा -ङ्गं.

BILLOWY, *a.* ऊर्म्मिमान् -मती -मत् (त्), तरङ्गितः -ता -तं, महावेलः -ला -लं, महातरङ्गः -ङ्गा -ङ्गं, प्रलोठितः -ता -तं.

BILL-STICKER, *s.* घोषणापत्राणि राजमार्गादिषु जनसङ्कीर्णस्थानेषु स्थापयति यः.

BIN, *s.* धान्यकोष्ठकं, कुशूलः, पिटः.

BINARY, *a.* द्वैधः -धी -धं, द्विगुणः -णा -णं.

To BIND, *v. a.* (To tie) बन्ध् (c. 9. बध्नाति, बन्द्धुं), निबन्ध्, योक्त्र (nom. योक्त्रयति -यितुं), यन्त्र् (c. 10. यन्त्रयति -यितुं), संयम् (c. 1. -यच्छति -यन्तुं). —(To fasten to any thing, fasten on) आबन्ध्, अनुबन्ध्, आकच् (c. 1. -कचते -कचितुं), पिनद्धं -द्धां -द्धं कृ.—(To tie together) सम्बन्ध्, संश्लिष् in caus. (-श्लेषयति -यितुं), ग्रन्थ् (c. 9. ग्रथ्नाति, ग्रथितुं or caus. ग्रन्थयति -यितुं), संहृ (c. 1. -हरति -हर्त्तुं).—(To unite) संयुज् (c. 7. -युनक्ति -युंक्ते -योक्तुं or caus. -योजयति -यितुं).—(To connect closely) सम्बन्ध्, संश्लिष् in caus.; 'my life is bound up in his,' मम प्राणा अस्य प्राणैर् बद्धाः सन्ति.—(To constrain, compel) धृ (c. 1. धरति, धर्त्तुं).—(To bind one's self by a promise) प्रतिज्ञा (c. 9. -जानीते -ज्ञातुं), सम्प्रतिज्ञा; 'to bind one's self over to appear,' दर्शनप्रातिभाव्यं दा.—(To be bound, obliged) expressed by the fut. pass. part.; as, 'he is bound to marry the damsel,' तेन कन्या वोढव्या, or by the root अर्ह, as, कन्यां वोढुम् अर्हति.—(To bind books) ग्रन्थपत्राणि चर्म्मादिना छादयित्वा सम्बन्ध्.—(To make costive) आनद्धं -द्धां -द्धं कृ, निबद्धं -द्धां -द्धं कृ. —(To secure with bandages) अनुवेष्टितं कृ, क्षतानि बन्ध्.

BINDER, *s.* ग्रन्थपत्राणि चर्म्मादिना सम्बन्धा *m.* (न्धृ).

BINDING, *s.* (A bandage) बन्धनं, दाम *n.* (न्), उद्दानं, पट्टः.—(Of a book) ग्रन्थपत्राच्छादनं.

BINDWEED, *s.* क्षीरविदारी, महाश्वेता, विदारी, इक्षुगन्धा, क्रोष्ट्री, श्यामा.

BINOCULAR, *a.* द्विनयनः -नी -नं, द्विनेत्रः -त्रा -त्रं, चक्षुर्द्वयविशिष्टः -ष्टा -ष्टं.

BINOMIAL, *a.* (In algebra) द्विपदः -दा -दं.

BIOGRAPHER, *s.* शिष्टसमाचाररचकः, शिष्टजनचरित्ररचकः, मृतजनचरित्रनिबन्धा *m.* (न्धृ).

BIOGRAPHICAL, *a.* शिष्टसमाचारसम्बन्धकः -का -कं, शिष्टजनचरित्रविषयः -या -यं.

BIOGRAPHY, *s.* (The act of writing it) शिष्टजनचरित्ररचना, शिष्टसमाचाररचना.—(The book) शिष्टजनचरित्रग्रन्थः, शिष्टसमाचारः.

BIPARTITE, *a.* द्वैधः -धी -धं, द्वैधीकृतः -ता -तं.

BIPARTITION, *s.* द्वैधीकरणं, द्विधाकरणं, द्वैधीभावः.

BIPED, *a.* द्विपादः -दा -दं, द्विपदः -दा -दं, द्विपाद् -पदी -पत्.

BIPEDAL, *a.* द्विपादपरिमाणः -णा -णं, द्विपादवान् -वती -वत् (त्).

BIPENNATED, *a.* द्विपक्षः -क्षा -क्षं, पक्षद्वयविशिष्टः -ष्टा -ष्टं.

BIRCH or BIRCH-TREE, *s.* भूर्जः, भूर्जपत्रः, कवचपत्रं, चर्म्मी *m.* (न्), मृदुच्छदः, मृदुत्वचः, विश्वा, शृङ्गी, महौषधं, अरुणा, प्रतिविषा.

BIRCHEN, *a.* भूर्जमयः -यी -यं, भूर्जनिर्म्मितः -ता -तं.

BIRD, *s.* पक्षी *m.* (न्), पक्षिणी *f.*, खगः, विहगः, विहङ्गः -ङ्गमः, पतगः, पत्री *m.* (न्), पतत्री *m.* (न्), विहायाः *m.* (स्), गरुत्मान् *m.* (त्), नीडजः, नीडोद्भवः, द्विजः, अण्डजः, नगौकाः *m.* (स्), पक्षवाहनः, शकुनिः *m.* -नः, विकिरः, विष्किरः, वाजी *m.* (न्), पतन् *m.* (त्), शकुन्तः, नभसङ्गमः, पत्ररथः, विः *m.*, वी, पित्सन् *m.* (त्).

To BIRD, *v. n.* (To catch birds) पक्षिणो ग्रह् (c. 9. गृह्णाति, ग्रहीतुं) or धृ (c. 1. धरति, धर्त्तुं), or बन्ध् (c. 9. बध्नाति, बन्द्धुं), शकुन (nom. शकुनयति -यितुं).

BIRDCAGE, *s.* पञ्जरं, पिञ्जरं, वीतंसः, कुलायिका, पक्षिशाला, शालारं.

BIRDCALL, *s.* पक्षिप्रलोभनार्थं शाकुनिकैर् वादितं पक्षिरावानुकारिणी वंशी.

BIRD-CATCHER, *s.* शाकुनिकः, व्याधः, जालिकः, जीवान्तकः, वागुरिकः.

BIRD-FANCIER, *s.* पक्षिपोषकः, पक्षिपालकः, पक्षिप्रियः.

BIRDING, *s.* (Catching birds) पक्षिग्रहणं, पक्षिबन्धनं, श्यैनम्पाता.

BIRDLIKE, *a.* पक्षिसन्निभः -भा -भं, पक्षिसदृशः -शी -शं, पक्षिनिभः -भा -भं.

BIRDLIME, *s.* अतिश्यानम् उदपेषं येन लिप्तासु तरुशाखासु पक्षिणो बध्यन्ते.

BIRD'S-EYE-VIEW, *s.* यादृशं डीयमानेन पक्षिणा क्रियते तादृशं दर्शनं, उच्चैःस्थानाद् अवलोकनं.

BIRD'S-NEST, *s.* नीडः -डं, कुलायः, पक्षिशाला.

BIRTH, *s.* जन्म *n.* (न्), जातिः *f.*, जनिः *f.*, जननं, जनिमा *m.* (न्), उत्पत्तिः *f.*, उद्भवः, सम्भवः, भवः, जनुः *n.* (स्).—(The act of bringing forth) प्रसवनं, प्रसवः, उत्पादनं, प्रसूतिः *f.*—(Extraction, lineage) वंशः, कुलं, अन्वयः, जातिः *f.*—(Rise, origin) योनिः *m. f.*, मूलं, उद्भवः. —(Rank, high birth) कुलीनता, कौलीनं; 'of good birth,' कुलीनः -ना -नं, कुलजः -जा -जं, कौलेयः -यी -यं, सुजन्मा -न्मा -न्म (न्), महाकुलप्रसूतः -ता -तं, महाकुलः -ला -लं; 'pride of birth,' कुलाभिमानं; 'blind from birth,' जन्मान्धः -न्धा -न्धं, जात्यन्धः -न्धा -न्धं.—(To give birth to) सु (c. 1. सवति, c. 2. सौति, सोतुं), प्रसु, जन् in caus. (जनयति -यितुं), सञ्जन्.

BIRTHDAY, *s.* जन्मदिनोत्सवः, जन्मदिवसः, जन्मतिथिः *m.*, जन्मदिनं.

BIRTHPLACE, *s.* जन्मभूमिः *f.*, जन्मस्थानं, जन्मदेशः.

BIRTHRIGHT, *s.* ज्येष्ठत्वं, ज्यैष्ठ्यं, ज्येष्ठाधिकारः, ज्येष्ठभागः, पैतृकं.

BISCUIT, *s.* पिष्टकः, पूपः, अपूपः, सुकान्दवो गोधूमादिचूर्णमयः पिष्टकः.

To BISECT, *v. a.* द्वैधीकृ, द्विभागीकृ, द्विखण्डीकृ, द्विधा कृ or छिद् (c. 7. छिनत्ति, छेत्तुं) or कृत् (c. 6. कृन्तति, कर्त्तितुं).

BISECTED, *p. p.* द्वैधीकृतः -ता -तं, द्विखण्डीकृतः -ता -तं, द्विधा छिन्नः -न्ना -न्नं.

BISECTION, *s.* द्विधाकरणं, द्वैधीकरणं.

BISHOP, *s.* धर्म्माधिपतिः *m.*, धर्म्माध्यक्षः.

BISHOP, *s.* (A beverage) मद्यनागरङ्गरसादिनिर्म्मितं पानीयं.

BISHOPRIC, *s.* धर्म्माधिपतिपदं, धर्म्माध्यक्षाधिकारः.

BISMUTH, *s.* अतिदृढः शुक्लवर्णो विदेशीयधातुप्रभेदः.

BISON, *s.* अरण्यवृषभप्रभेदः.

BISSEXTILE, *s.* चतुर्थः संवत्सरो यस्मिन् अधिदिवसो निवेश्यते.

BIT, *s.* (Part of a bridle) खलीनः, कविका -कं, वल्गा, मुखयन्त्रणं, लङ्गनी.—(A piece) खण्डं, भागः, भित्तं, भित्रं, भित्तिः *f.*; 'in bits,' खण्डशस्, भागशस्, खण्डं खण्डं.—(A mouthful, morsel) पिण्डः -ण्डं, ग्रासः; 'a tit bit,' स्वाद्वन्नं, भोजनविशेषः; 'not a bit,' न मनागपि, न किञ्चिदपि, न सूक्ष्ममपि; 'a bit bigger,' किञ्चित्स्थूलतरं.

To BIT, *v. a.* खलीन (nom. खलीनयति -यितुं), अश्वमुखं खलीनेन यन्त्र् (c. 10. यन्त्रयति -यितुं).

BITCH, *s.* शुनी, कुक्कुरी, सरमा, कुलाक्षुता.—(A name of reproach) बन्धकी.

To BITE, *v. a.* दंश् (c. 1. दशति, दंष्टुं), विदंश्; 'to bite the lips,' दशनच्छदं or दन्तान् सन्दंश्.—(To gnaw) चर्व् (c. 1. चर्वति, चर्वितुं); 'to bite the nails,' नखान् खाद् (c. 1. खादति, खादितुं).—(To pain by cold) शीतार्त्तं -र्त्तां -र्त्तं कृ.—(To rail at) अवक्षिप् (c. 6. -क्षिपति -क्षेप्तुं).—(To vex) पीड् (c. 10. पीडयति -यितुं).—(To defraud) वञ्च् (c. 10. वञ्चयति -ते -यितुं).

BITE, *s.* दंशः, दंशनं, दन्ताघातः; 'the mark of the teeth,' दशनाङ्कः.

BITER, *s.* दंशकः, खादिता *m.* (तृ), दंष्टा *m.* (ष्टृ), वञ्चकः.

BITING, *a.* दंशकः -का -कं, दंशेरः -रा -रं, पीडाकरः -रा -रं.

BITTEN, *p. p.* दष्टः -ष्टा -ष्टं, सन्दष्टः -ष्टा -ष्टं, दंशितः -ता -तं.

BITTER, *a.* तिक्तः -क्ता -क्तं, तिक्तस्वादः -दा -दं, तिक्तरसः -सा -सं.—(Pungent) कटुः -टुः -ट्वी -टु, तीक्ष्णः -क्ष्णा -क्ष्णं, तिग्मः -ग्मा -ग्मं.—(Grievous) उग्रः -ग्रा -ग्रं, आत्ययिकः -की -कं.—(Cruel, severe) कठोरः -रा -रं, निष्ठुरः -रा -रं, पीडाकरः -रा -रं.—(Malicious) मत्सरः -रा -रं, पिशुनः -ना -नं.

BITTERGOURD, *s.* इन्द्रवारुणिका, अरुणा.

BITTERLY, *adv.* उग्रं, निष्ठुरं, उग्रतया; 'one who grieves bitterly,' उग्रशोकः -का -कं.

BITTERN, *s.* क्रौञ्चजातीयः पक्षिभेदः, क्रौञ्चः, कुडः, कलिकः.

BITTERNESS, *s.* तिक्तः, तिक्तत्वं, तिक्तरसः.—(Pungency) कटुता, तिग्मता, तीक्ष्णता.—(Malice) असूया, मात्सर्यं.—(Severity) उग्रत्वं -ता, निष्ठुरता, कठोरता.—(Sorrow) शोकः, उग्रशोकः, दुःखं.

BITUMEN, *s.* शिलाजतु *n.*, अश्मजतुकं, शिलादद्रुः *m.*, गिरिपुष्पकं, शैलं, शैलनिर्य्यासः.

BITUMINOUS, *a.* शिलाजतुमयः -यी -यं, शिलाजतुगुणविशिष्टः -ष्टा -ष्टं.

BIVALVE, *a.* द्विकपाटः -टा -टं, द्विकोषः -षा -षं.—(Bivalve shell) शम्बुः *m.*, शम्बुः *m.*, शम्बुकः -का, जलशुक्तिः *f.*, पङ्कमण्डुकः.

BIVOUAC, *s.* (A guard at night) वीरासनं.

To BLAB, *v. n.* and *a.* रहस्यं प्रकाश् in caus. (-काशयति -यितुं), रहस्यभेदं कृ.

BLAB, BLABBER, *s.* रहस्यभेदकः, रहस्यप्रकाशकः, वाचालः, वावदूकः, जल्पकः.

BLABBER-LIPPED, *a.* स्थूलोष्ठः -ष्ठा -ष्ठं, लम्बौष्ठः -ष्ठा -ष्ठं.

BLACK, *a.* कृष्णः -ष्णा -ष्णं, श्यामः -मा -मं, -मलः -ला -लं, कालः -ला -लं, कालकः -का -कं, कार्ष्णः -र्ष्णी -र्ष्णं, असितः -ता -तं, नीलः -ला -लं, मेचकः -का -कं, ध्यामः -मा -मं.—(Dark) तमस्वी -स्विनी -स्वि (न्), तिमिरः -रा -रं, अन्धकारयुक्तः -क्ता -क्तं, निष्प्रभः -भा -भं.—(Horrible) घोरः -रा -रं, दारुणः -णा -णं.—(Cloudy of countenance) म्लानवदनः -ना -नं.—(Black with crime) कृष्णकर्म्मा -र्म्मा -र्म्म (न्).—(White and black) सितासितः -ता -तं.

BLACK, *s.* (The colour) कृष्णः, कृष्णवर्णः.—(A blackamoor) कृष्णदेहः, श्यामाङ्गः; 'black clothes,' नीलवस्त्रं, नीलाम्बरं; 'clothed in black,' नीलवस्त्रः -स्त्रा -स्त्रं, नीलाम्बरः -रा -रं, श्यामवस्त्रः -स्त्रा -स्त्रं.—(Lamp-black) दीपकिट्टं, कज्जलं.

To BLACK, *v. a.* कृष्ण (nom. कृष्णायते -यितुं), कृष्णीकृ.

BLACKAMOOR, *s.* श्यामाङ्गः, श्यामदेहः, कृष्णदेहः, कृष्णाङ्गः.

BLACKBERRY, *s.* कृष्णवर्णं कण्टकगुल्मफलं, शृगालकण्टकफलं.

BLACKBEETLE, *s.* भ्रमरः, भृङ्गः, अलिः *m.*

BLACKBIRD, *s.* कृष्णवर्णो मधुररावविशिष्टः पक्षिभेदः.

To BLACKEN, *v. a.* कृष्णीकृ, कृष्ण (nom. कृष्णायते -यितुं), श्याम (nom. श्यामयति -यितुं), श्यामीकृ.—(To darken) तिमिर (nom. तिमिरयति -यितुं).

To BLACKEN, *v. n.* श्याम (nom. श्यामायते), नील (nom. नीलायते).

BLACKENED, *p. p.* कृष्णीकृतः -ता -तं, श्यामितः -ता -तं, कृष्णीभूतः -ता -तं, तमोवृतः -ता -तं, तमोभूतः -ता -तं, समामसः -सा -सं.

BLACKEYED, *a.* असितनयनः -नी -नं, कृष्णनयनः -नी -नं, नीलाक्षः -क्षी -क्षं.

BLACKGUARD, *s.* अधमाचारः, दुर्वृत्तः, दुराचारः, कृष्णकर्म्मा *m.* (न्), दुष्टः.

BLACKING, *s.* पादुकाञ्जनं, मसिः *f.* -सी, काली.

BLACKISH, *a.* ईषत्कृष्णः -ष्णा -ष्णं, ईषत्कालः -ला -लं. आकालः -ला -लं.

BLACKLEAD, *s.* सीसकप्रभेदो येन तूलिकायां निवेशितेन कृष्णरेखा क्रियते.

BLACKLY, *adv.* कृष्णवर्णेन, कृष्णं, दारुणं, अतिदुष्टतया.

BLACK-MOUTHED, *a.* दुर्मुखः -खी -खं, मुखरः -रा -रं, वाग्दुष्टः -ष्टा -ष्टं.

BLACKNESS, *s.* कृष्णता -त्वं, कृष्णिमा *m.* (न्), कालिमा *m.* (न्), श्यामत्वं, नीलिमा *m.* (न्).—(Darkness) तमः *n.* (स्), तमिस्रं, तिमिरं, अन्धकारः.—(Horribleness) घोरता, दारुणता.—(Atrocity) अतिदुष्टता.

BLACKPUDDING, *s.* अधुनातनजनखादितम् असृग्धान्यादिपूरितं शूकरपुरीतत्.

BLACKSMITH, *s.* लोहकारः, ध्माकारः, कर्म्मकारः, अयस्कारः, कर्म्मारः, व्योकारः.

BLADDER, *s.* वस्तिः *m. f.* मूत्राशयः, तिलकं, क्लोम *n.* (न्), क्लोमं.

BLADE, *s.* (The sharp part of a weapon) फलं, पत्रं, फलकः -कं, धारा, पत्त्रः, पुष्करं; 'the blade of a sword,' असिपत्रं.—(Spire of grass) काण्डं, दलः -लं, अङ्कुरः, तृणदलं, तृणकाण्डं, किसलः, कुशः.—(Of the shoulder) अंसः, स्कन्धास्थि *n.*, भुजशिरः *n.* (स्).

BLADED, *a.* काण्डवान् -वती -वत् (त्), मञ्जरितः -ता -तं, दलवान् -वती -वत् (त्).

BLAIN, *s.* विस्फोटः, स्फोटः, स्फोटकः, व्रणं, वटी, वरटी.

BLAMABLE, *a.* निन्दनीयः -या -यं, निन्द्यः -न्द्या -न्द्यं, निन्दार्हः -र्हा -र्हं, दोषी -षिणी -षि (न्), अपराधी -धिनी -धि (न्), अपराद्धः -द्धा -द्धं, सापराधः -धा -धं, गर्हितः -ता -तं, दूष्यः -ष्या -ष्यं, गर्ह्यः -र्ह्या -र्ह्यं, वाच्यः -च्या -च्यं.

BLAMABLENESS, *s.* निन्द्यता, निन्दार्हत्वं, अपराधिता -त्वं, दोषित्वं.

BLAMABLY, *adv.* सापराधं, अपराधेन, निन्द्यप्रकारेण, यथा दोषो जायते तथा.

To BLAME, *v. a.* (To lay the blame) दोषम् आरुह् in caus. (-रोपयति -यितुं), दोषीकृ.—(To censure) निन्द् (c. 1. निन्दति, निन्दितुं), प्रणिन्द्, प्रतिनिन्द्, विनिन्द्; तिरस्कृ; कुत्स् (c. 10. कुत्सयति -ते -यितुं), गुप् in des. (जुगुप्सते -प्सितुं), उपालभ् (c. 1. -लभते -लब्धुं), गर्ह् (c. 1. गर्हते, गर्हितुं, c. 10. गर्हयते -यितुं), विगर्ह्, परिगर्ह्; 'he casts the blame on him,' तस्मिन् दोषं क्षिपति.

BLAME, *s.* (Censure) निन्दा, परीवादः, अपवादः, आक्षेपः, घृणा, तिरस्कारः, गर्हा, परिभाषणं, जुगुप्सा, कलङ्कः, कुत्सा, निर्वादः, अवर्णः, उपालम्भः, उपक्रोशः.—(Fault) दोषः, अपराधः, वचनीयता, वाच्यता, —(Imputation of a fault) दोषारोपः; 'I am not to blame,' नाहम् अपराद्धः, or सापराधः, or निन्दार्हः.

BLAMED, *p. p.* निन्दितः -ता -तं, जुगुप्सितः -ता -तं, गर्हितः -ता -तं, तिरस्कृतः -ता -तं, धिक्कृतः -ता -तं, उपालब्धः -ब्धा -ब्धं, अवरीणः -णा -णं.

BLAMELESS, *a.* निर्दोषः -षा -षं, निरपराधः -धा -धं, अनिन्द्यः -न्द्या -न्द्यं, अनिन्दितः -ता -तं, अनेनाः -नाः -नः (स्), अविगर्हितः -ता -तं, अनघः -घा -घं.

BLAMELESSLY, *adv.* अपराधं विना, दोषव्यतिरेकेण, निरपराधं, अनघं, अनिन्द्यप्रकारेण.

BLAMELESSNESS, *s.* अनिन्द्यता, निर्दोषता, निरपराधता, शुद्धत्वं.

BLAMER, *s.* निन्दकः, दोषारोपकः, परिवादकः, निन्दाकर्त्ता *m.* (र्तृ), कलङ्ककरः.

BLAMEWORTHY, *a.* निन्दार्हः -र्हा -र्हं, निन्दनीयः -या -यं.

To BLANCH, *v. a.* (To whiten) शुक्लीकृ, धवलीकृ.—(To peel such things as have husks) निस्तुष (nom. -तुषयति -यितुं), तुषीकृ, त्वच् (nom. त्वचयति -यितुं), त्वचं निष्कृष् (c. 1. -कर्षति -क्रष्टुं), त्वक्परिपुटनं कृ.

BLAND, *a.* मृदुः -द्वी -दु, स्निग्धः -ग्धा -ग्धं, मसृणः -णा -णं, मेदुरः -रा -रं, श्लक्ष्णः -क्ष्णा -क्ष्णं, कोमलः -ला -लं, सोमालः -ला -लं.—(In speech) प्रियम्वदः -दा -दं.

BLANDATION, *s.* चाटूक्तिः *f.*, चाटुकारः, कोमलत्वं.

To BLANDISH, *v. a.* (To caress, flatter) शान्त्व् or सान्त्व् (c. 10. सान्त्वयति -यितुं), अभिशान्त्व्, परिशान्त्व्, प्रियं वद् (c. 1. वदति, वदितुं).

BLANDISHMENT, *s.* (Gesture of love) ललितं, हावः, विलासः, विभ्रमः. —(Soft words) प्रियवाक्यं, चाटूक्तिः *f.*, चाटुः *m.*

BLANK, *a.* (Empty, not written upon) शून्यः -न्या -न्यं, रिक्तः -क्ता -क्तं, लेखाशून्यः -न्या -न्यं, अलिखितः -ता -तं.—(White) शुक्लः -क्ला -क्लं.—(Pale, depressed) पाण्डुः -ण्डुः -ण्डु, विवर्णवदनः -ना -नं, म्लानवदनः -ना -नं, विषण्णः -ण्णा -ण्णं.—(Confused) विस्मितः -ता -तं, विलक्षः -क्षा -क्षं, आकुलः -ला -लं.—(Without rhyme) अनुप्रासहीनः -ना -नं, अमित्राक्षरः -रा -रं, यमकहीनः -ना -नं, छन्दोरहितः -ता -तं.

BLANK, *s.* (A void space) शून्यं, रिक्तं, शून्यत्वं -ता, रिक्तता, शून्यस्थानं.—(A paper without writing) लेखाशून्यं पत्रं,—(In a lottery) भाग्यस्परहिता or लाभरहिता गुटिका, दौर्भाग्यं.

To BLANK, *v. a.* शून्यीकृ, म्लानीकृ, आकुलीकृ, विस्मयाकुलं -लां -लं कृ.

BLANKET, *s.* कम्बलः, रल्लकः, ऊर्णायुः *m.*, सहस्ररोम *n.* (न्), मेषकम्बलः, लाशूकः, कुतपः.—(Covered with a blanket) काम्बलः -ली -लं, कम्बलाच्छादितः -ता -तं.

To BLANKET, *v. a.* कम्बलेन आच्छद् (c. 10. -च्छादयति -यितुं).

To BLASPHEME, *v. a.* परमेश्वरं निन्द् (c. 1. निन्दति, निन्दितुं) or अवमन् (c. 4. -मन्यते -मन्तुं) or अभिशप् (c. 1. -शपति -शप्तुं) or आक्रुश् (c. 1. -क्रोशति -क्रोष्टुं), ईश्वरनिन्दां कृ, पाषण्डीयकथां कथ् (c. 10. कथयति -यितुं).

BLASPHEMER, *s.* ईश्वरनिन्दकः, ईश्वराभिशापकः, ईश्वरावमानकृत्, पाषण्डः, गर्ह्यवादी *m.* (न्).

BLASPHEMOUS, *a.* ईश्वरनिन्दकः -का -कं, ईश्वरावमानकरः -री -रं, पाषण्डीयः -या -यं.

BLASPHEMOUSLY, *adv.* ईश्वरनिन्दापूर्वकं, ईश्वरनिन्दाक्रमेण, पाषण्डवत्.

BLASPHEMY, *s.* ईश्वरनिन्दा, ईश्वरावमानं, ईश्वराभिशापः, देवनिन्दा, पाषण्डता.

BLAST, *s.* (A gust of wind) वातः, वायुवेगः, वायुगुल्मः, वातरूषः, निर्घातः, प्रभञ्जनः, व्योममुद्गरः.—(Puff) श्वासः.—(Of a horn) शङ्खध्मानं.—(Blight) विनाशः, व्याघातः, क्षयः.

To BLAST, *v. a.* (To ruin, destroy) विनश् in caus. (-नाशयति -यितुं), क्षि in caus. (क्षययति -यितुं), विहन् (c. 2. -हन्ति -हन्तुं).—(To make to wither) मृ in caus. (मारयति -यितुं), म्लानीकृ, विशॄ in caus. (-शारयति -यितुं).

BLASTED, *p. p.* विनाशितः -ता -तं, मारितः -ता -तं, परिम्लानः -ना -नं, विशीर्णः -र्णा -र्णं.—(By lightning) विद्युद्धतः -ता -तं.

BLASTER, *s.* विनाशकः, मारकः, नाशयिता *m.* (तृ), विघाती *m.* (न्), विनाशकृत्.

BLAZE, *s.* ज्वालः -ला, ज्वलः, ज्वलका, ज्वालाग्निः *m.*, उल्का; 'a blaze of light,' रश्मिजालं, अंशुजालं.—(Publication) प्रकाशनं, प्रकटीकरणं, प्रचारणं.

To BLAZE, *v. n.* ज्वल् (c. 1. ज्वलति, ज्वलितुं), प्रज्वल्, सम्प्रज्वल्, or in freq. (जाज्वल्यते), दीप् (c. 4. दीप्यते, दीपितुं), आदीप्, प्रदीप् or in freq. (देदीप्यते).

To BLAZE ABROAD, *v. a.* प्रकाश् in caus. (-काशयति -यितुं), विकाश्, प्रचर् in caus. (-चारयति -यितुं), विघुष् (c. 10. -घोषयति -यितुं), विख्या in caus. (-ख्यापयति -यितुं), प्रकटीकृ.

BLAZING, *a.* ज्वाली -लिनी -लि (न्), ज्वालः -ली -लं, ज्वलन् -लन्ती -लत् (त्), उज्ज्वलः -ला -लं, जाज्वल्यमानः -ना -नं, ज्वलितः -ता -तं, प्रज्वलितः -ता -तं, उज्ज्वलः -ला -लं, प्रदीप्तः -प्ता -प्तं.

To BLAZON, *v. a.* (To draw coats of arms) कुलीनपदचिह्नानि लिख् (c. 6. लिखति, लेखितुं).—(To explain coats of arms) चित्रगतानि कुलीनपदचिह्नानि व्याख्या (c. 2. -ख्याति -ख्यातुं).—(To deck) भूष् (c. 10. भूषयति -यितुं), परिभूष्, परिष्कृ.—(To celebrate) प्रख्या, विख्या.—(To display, publish) प्रकाश् in caus. (-काशयति -यितुं), प्रचर् in caus. (-चारयति -यितुं).

To BLEACH, *v. a.* धाव् (c. 1. धावति, धावितुं, c. 10. धावयति -यितुं), वस्त्राणि वायुव्याप्यानि कृत्वा शुक्लीकृ or धवलीकृ or निर्णिज् (c. 3. -नेनेक्ति -नेक्तुं).

To BLEACH, *v. n.* वायुव्यापकत्वाद् धवलीभू or शुक्लीभू.

BLEACHED, *p. p.* धौतः -ता -तं, धवलितः -ता -तं, शुक्लीकृतः -ता -तं, धवलीकृतः -ता -तं, धवलीभूतः -ता -तं, वीतरागः -गा -गं; 'bleached silk,' धौतकौशेयं, पत्रोर्णं; 'a pair of bleached clothes,' उद्गमनीयं.

BLEACHER, *s.* धावकः, वस्त्रधावकः, वस्त्रनिर्णेजकः.

BLEAK, *a.* (Cold) शीतलः -ला -लं, शिशिरः -रा -रं, हिमः -मा -मं, हैमन्तः -न्ती -न्तं, -न्तिकः -की -कं, हिमशीतलः -ला -लं.—(Exposed to the weather) आभ्यवकाशिकः -की -कं, शीतावकाशिकः -की -कं.—(Cheerless) निरानन्दः -न्दा -न्दं.

BLEAKNESS, *s.* शीतता, शीतलता, शैत्यं, हिमता, शीतावकाशिकत्वं.

To BLEAR, *v. a.* चुल्लीकृ, तिमिर (nom. तिमिरयति -यितुं).

BLEAREDNESS, *s.* (Having blear eyes) चुल्लत्वं, पिल्लत्वं, क्लिन्नाक्षता.

BLEAR-EYED, *a.* क्लिन्नाक्षः -क्षा -क्षं, चुल्लः -ल्ली -ल्लं, चिल्लः -ल्ला -ल्लं, पिल्लः -ल्ली -ल्लं.

To BLEAT, *v. n.* उ (c. 1. अवते, ओतुं), मेषरुतं कृ, अविवत् शब्दं कृ.

BLEATING, *s.* मेषरुतं, मेषरावः, मेषशब्दः, उरभ्रनादः.

To BLEED, *v. n.* रक्तं or शोणितं स्रु (c. 1. स्रवति, स्रोतुं), प्रस्रु or मुष् (c. 6. मुञ्चति, मोक्तुं), प्रमुच्; 'the wound bleeds,' क्षतं शोणितं स्रवति.

To BLEED, *v. a.* रक्तं or शोणितं स्रु in caus. (स्रावयति -यितुं) or मुच् in caus. (मोचयति -यितुं) or मोक्ष् (c. 10. मोक्षयति -यितुं) or अवसिच् (c. 6. -सिञ्चति -सेक्तुं).

BLEEDER, *s.* रक्तस्रावकः, असृक्स्रावी *m.* (न्), रक्तमोचकः, सिराव्यधनकृत्, रक्तावसेचकः.

BLEEDING, *s.* (Venesection) रक्तस्रावः, असृक्स्रावः, रक्तमोक्षणं, असृग्विमोक्षणं, सिरामोक्षः, सिराव्यधः, रक्तावसेचनं.

To BLEMISH, *v. a.* मलिन (nom. मलिनयति -यितुं), कलङ्क (nom. कलङ्कयति -यितुं), दुष् in caus. (दूषयति -यितुं), अपयशः कृ, सदोषं -षां -षं कृ.

BLEMISH, *s.* दोषः, कलङ्कः, छिद्रं, कलुषं, अघं, आगः *n.* (स्).—(Loss of reputation) अपयशः *n.* (स्), अख्यातिः *f.*, अकीर्त्तिः *f.*, अपकीर्त्तिः *f.*, वाच्यता.—(Without blemish) अनघः -घा -घं, निश्छिद्रः -द्रा -द्रं.

BLEMISHED, *p. p.* कलङ्कितः -ता -तं, दूषितः -ता -तं, दोषवान् -वती -वत् (त्), सदोषः -षा -षं, कलुषितः -ता -तं.

To BLENCH, *v. n.* सहसा सङ्कोचं कृ, मील् (c. 1. मीलति, मीलितुं), निमील्.

To BLEND, *v. a.* मिश्र् (c. 10. मिश्रयति -यितुं), सम्मिश्र्, मिश्रीकृ, सम्पृच् (c. 7. -पृणक्ति -पर्चितुं), संयुज् (c. 7. -युनक्ति -योक्तुं), संश्लिष् in caus. -श्लेषयति -यितुं), एकीकृ, एकत्र कृ, व्यतिकरं कृ.—(To be mingled) सङ्कॄ in pass. (-कीर्य्यते), मिल् (c. 6. मिलति, मेलितुं), सम्मिल्.

BLENDED, *p. p.* मिश्रितः -ता -तं, मिश्रीकृतः -ता -तं, सम्मिश्रः -श्रा -श्रं, व्यामिश्रः -श्रा -श्रं, सम्पृक्तः -क्ता -क्तं, आश्लिष्टः -ष्टा -ष्टं, सङ्कीर्णः -र्णा -र्णं, मिलितः -ता -तं, एकीकृतः -ता -तं, करम्बितः -ता -तं, संसृष्टः -ष्टा -ष्टं, सन्निपतितः -ता -तं, संवलितः -ता -तं.

To BLESS, *v. a.* (To pronounce a blessing) आशिषं दा (c. 3. ददाति, दातुं), or वद् (c. 1. वदति, वदितुं), or गद् (c. 1. गदति, गदितुं), or आशंस् (c. 1. -शंसते -शंसितुं), धन्यवादं कृ, कुशलं वद्.—(To make happy) सुख् (c. 10. सुखयति -यितुं), सुखिनं -खिनीं -खि कृ, धन्यं -न्यां -न्यं कृ, मङ्गलं -लां -लं कृ, कुशलं -लां -लं कृ.—(To glorify, give thanks) कस्यचिद् धन्यं वद्, कस्यचिद् गुणान् वद् or कृत् (c. 10. कीर्त्तयति -यितुं), स्तु (c. 2. स्तौति, स्तोतुं); 'God bless you!' स्वस्ति,

मङ्गलं भूयात्, शुभं भूयात्.

Blessed, *a.* धन्यः -न्या -न्यं, मङ्गलः -ला -लं, कुशलः -ला -लं, प्राप्तमङ्गलः -ला -लं, कृतमङ्गलः -ला -लं, कल्याणः -णी -णं, क्षेमवान् -वती -वत् (त्), परमसुखभागी -गिनी -गि (न्), सुखी -खिनी -खि (न्).—(In the joys of heaven) प्राप्तस्वर्गः -र्गा -र्गं, सिद्धः -द्धा -द्धं.

Blessedness, *s.* धन्यत्वं, माङ्गल्यं, कौशल्यं, कल्याणं, परमसुखं, परमानन्दः, सद्गतिः *f.*—(In heaven) सिद्धिः *f.*, स्वर्गगतिः *f.*, परमपदं, परम्पदं, परमागतिः *f.*, अपवर्गः.

Blesser, *s.* आशीर्वादी *m.* (न्), आशंसिता *m.* (तृ), धन्यवादकृत् *m.*, कुशलवादी *m.* (न्).

Blessing, *s.* (Benediction) आशीः *f.* (स्), आशीर्वादः, धन्यवादः, आशीर्वचनं, कुशलवादः, कुशलं.—(A benefit received) वरः, हितं, कुशलं, उपकृतं, धन्यत्वं; 'wishing blessing,' आशंसुः -सुः -सु.

Blight, *s.* नाशः, क्षयः, विनाशः, व्याघातः, आघातः, दूषणं, कलङ्कः, विषं.

To blight, *v. a.* दुष् in caus. (दूषयति -यितुं), नश् in caus. (नाशयति -यितुं), विनश्, क्षि in caus. (क्षययति -यितुं) मृ in caus. (मारयति -यितुं), म्लानीकृ, विशीर्णी -र्णी -र्णी कृ, विफलीकृ.

Blighted, *p. p.* दूषितः -ता -तं, विनाशितः -ता -तं, मारितः -ता -तं.

Blind, *a.* अन्धः -न्धा -न्धं, अन्धकः -का -कं, अचक्षुः -क्षुः -क्षु (स्), विचक्षुः -क्षुः -क्षु (स्), गताक्षः -क्षा -क्षं, अनक्षः -क्षा -क्षं, नेत्रेन्द्रियविकलः -ला -लं, अदृक् *m.* (श्).—(Blind from birth) जात्यन्धः -न्धा न्धं, जन्मान्धः -न्धा -न्धं.—(Blind of one eye) काणः -णा -णं.—(Hard to find, private) अदृश्यः -श्या -श्यं, निभृतः -ता -तं; 'a blind well,' अन्धकूपः.—(Dark) तमस्वी -स्विनी -स्वि (न्).—(Ignorant) हतज्ञानः -ना -नं, अज्ञः -ज्ञा -ज्ञं, दुर्बुद्धिः -द्धिः -द्धि.

To blind, *v. a.* अन्धीकृ, तिमिरीकृ, तिमिर (nom. तिमिरयति -यितुं).

Blind, *s.* (Screen to hinder the sight) तिरस्करिणी, व्यवधा, -धानं.—(Something to mislead) छद्म *n.* (न्), कपटः, कपटवेशः, छद्मवेशः.

Blinded, *p. p.* अन्धीकृतः -ता -तं, अन्धीभूतः -ता -तं, तमोवृतः -ता -तं.—(By sin) पापतिमिरः -रा -रं.

To blindfold, *v. a.* वस्त्रेण नयने or दृशौ बन्ध् (c. 9. बध्नाति, बन्द्धुं), or अवरुध् (c. 7. -रुणद्धि -रोद्धुं), or विरुध्, or आवृ (c. 5. -वृणोति -वरितुं -वरीतुं), वस्त्रेण नयने आच्छद् (c. 10. -छादयति -यितुं).

Blindfold, *a.* वस्त्रावरुद्धनयनः -नी -नं, अवरुद्धदृष्टिः -ष्टिः -ष्टि, बद्धनेत्रः -त्री -त्रं.

Blindly, *adv.* अन्धवत्, अनालोचितं, अविचार्य्य, असमीक्ष्य, अविचिन्त्य, सहसा.

Blind-man's-buff, *s.* बालानाम् क्रीडाविशेषो यस्मिन् एकतमो वस्त्रावरुद्धनयनः or अवरुद्धदृष्टिर् इतरान् इतस्ततः पलायमानान् जिघृक्षयाऽनुधावति.

Blindness, *s.* अन्धता -त्वं, तिमिरं.—(Ignorance) अज्ञानं, आवरणं, दुर्बुद्धित्वं, मोहः.

To blink, *v. n.* मील् (c. 1. मीलति, मीलितुं), निमील् or in caus. (निमीलयति -यितुं), निमिष् (c. 6. -मिषति -मेषितुं).

Blink, *s.* निमेषः, निमिषः, मीलितं, दृष्टिनिपातः, अर्द्धवीक्षणं.

Blinking, *s.* मीलनं, निमीलनं, निमेषः, *part.* निमीलन् -लन्ती -लत् (त्).

Bliss, *s.* परमसुखं, परमाह्लादः, परमानन्दः, प्रहर्षः, सुखं, शर्म्म *n.* (न्), प्रह्लादः, अत्यन्तसुखं, धन्यता, कल्याणं.—(Celestial life) अपवर्गः, मोक्षः, सिद्धिः *f.*, मुक्तिः *f.*, स्वर्गगतिः *f.*, परमपदं, परम्पदं.

Blissful, *a.* परमसुखमयः -यी -यं, आनन्दमयः -यी -यं, परमाह्लादवान् -वती -वत् (त्), सुखी -खिनी -खि (न्), धन्यः -न्या -न्यं, सानन्दः -न्दा -न्दं, प्रमोदी -दिनी -दि (न्).

Blissfully, *adv.* परमसुखेन, परमाह्लादेन, परमानन्दपूर्व्वकं, सानन्दं.

Blissless, *a.* सुखहीनः -ना -नं, आह्लादरहितः -ता -तं, निरानन्दः -न्दा -न्दं.

Blister, *s.* त्वक्स्फोटः, स्फोटः, स्फोटकः, विस्फोटः, शोफः, व्रणं.—(On the foot) पादस्फोटः, स्फुटिः *f.*, विपादिका.—(A blistering plaster) त्वक्स्फोटोत्पादक उपनाहः.

To blister, *v. a.* त्वक्स्फोटम् उत्पद् in caus. (-पादयति -यितुं).

To blister, *v. n.* व्रणरूपेण श्वि (c. 1. श्वयति, श्वयितुं) or स्फुट् (c. 1. स्फोटते, स्फोटितुं).

Blistered, *p. p.* व्रणी -णिनी -णि (न्), शूनः -ना -नं, स्फातः -ता -तं.

Blithe, blithesome, *a.* हृष्टः -ष्टा -ष्टं, हृष्टमानसः -सी -सं, प्रहृष्टः -ष्टा -ष्टं, प्रफुल्लः -ल्ला -ल्लं, आनन्दी -न्दिनी -न्दि (न्), आह्लादी -दिनी -दि (न्), प्रमोदी -दिनी -दि (न्), पुलकितः -ता -तं, उल्लासितः -ता -तं, मुदान्वितः -ता -तं, प्रसन्नवदनः -नी -नं.

Blithely, *adv.* सहर्षं, हृष्टमनसा, प्रहृष्टं, प्रहर्षेण, प्रह्लादेन, सानन्दं.

Blitheness, blithesomeness, *s.* प्रहर्षः, हर्षः, प्रहृष्टता, प्रफुल्लता, आह्लादः, आनन्दः.

To bloat, *v. a.* मांसाद्याहारेण सन्तोष्य संशूनीकृ or पीनीकृ or स्थूलीकृ, स्फाय् in caus. (स्फावयति -यितुं), श्वि in caus. (श्वाययति -यितुं), आप्यै in caus. (-प्याययति -यितुं).

To bloat, *v. n.* मांसाद्युपभोगेन संशूनीभू or पीनीभू or स्थूलीभू, स्फाय् (c. 1. स्फायते, स्फायितुं), श्वि (c. 1. श्वयति, श्वयितुं), संश्वि, आप्यै (c. 1. (-प्यायते -प्यातुं).

Bloated, *p. p.* शूनः -ना -नं, मांसोपभोगसंशूनः -ना -नं, प्रोच्छूनः -ना -नं, पीनः -ना -नं, स्फीतः -ता -तं, स्फातः -ता -तं, प्रवृद्धः -द्धा -द्धं, स्थूलीभूतः -ता -तं.

Bloatedness, *s.* शूनता, स्थूलता, स्फातिः *f.*, स्फीतिः *f.*, पीनता.

Blobber-lipped, *a.* स्थूलोष्ठः -ष्ठा -ष्ठं, लम्बौष्ठः -ष्ठा -ष्ठं.

Block, *s.* (Of wood) स्थूलकाष्ठं, काष्ठं, काष्ठखण्डं.—(Any mass) पिण्डः -ण्डं.—(A massy body) स्थूलद्रव्यं, भारः, स्थूणा.—(Of stone) शिला.—(Obstruction) अवरोधः -धकं, विरोधः, प्रतिष्टम्भः, विष्टम्भः, प्रत्यूहः, विघ्नः.—(A washerman's block) फलकः.

To block up, *v. a.* प्रतिरुध् (c. 7. -रुणद्धि -रोद्धुं), उपरुध्, निरुध्, संरुध्, स्तम्भ् (c. 9. स्तभ्नाति, स्तम्भितुं or caus. स्तम्भयति -यितुं), अपिधा (c. 3. -दधाति -धातुं), पिधा, बाध् (c. 1. बाधते, बाधितुं), आवृ (c. 5. -वृणोति -वरितुं -वरीतुं), प्रतिबन्ध् (c. 9. -बध्नाति -बन्द्धुं).

Blockade, *s.* अवरोधः, रोधः, रोधनं, वेष्टनं, परिवेष्टनं, चिरारोधः.

To blockade, *v. a.* रुध् (c. 7. रुणद्धि, रोद्धुं), उपरुध्, संरुध्, निरुध्, प्रतिरुध्, विरुध्; परिवेष्ट् (c. 1. -वेष्टते -वेष्टितुं), बाध् (c. 1. बाधते, बाधितुं).

Blockaded, *p. p.* रुद्धः -द्धा -द्धं, परिवेष्टितः -ता -तं, बाधितः -ता -तं.

Blocked up, *p. p.* प्रतिरुद्धः -द्धा -द्धं, रुद्धः -द्धा -द्धं, प्रतिष्टब्धः -ब्धा -ब्धं, स्तब्धः -ब्धा -ब्धं, सबाधः -धा -धं, वारितः -ता -तं, विघ्नितः -ता -तं.

Blockhead, *s.* स्थूलबुद्धिः *m.*, स्थूलधीः *m.*, मन्दबुद्धिः *m.*, मूर्खः, मूढः, दुर्बुद्धिः *m.*, बर्ब्बरः.

Blood, *s.* असृक् *n.* (ज्), लोहितं, रक्तं, रुधिरं, शोणितं, क्षतजं, अस्रं; 'to lose blood,' रक्तं मुच् (c. 6. मुञ्चति, मोक्तुं); 'to flow with blood,' रक्तं स्रु (c. 1. स्रवति, स्रोतुं).—(Kindred, lineage) कुलं, वंशः, सन्तानः, गोत्रं, गोष्ठी; 'of whole blood,' सोदरः, सहोदरः, सोदर्य्यः, समानोदर्य्यः, सगर्भः, सनाभिः *m.*, एकशरीरः; 'of half blood,' भिन्नोदरः.—(Murder) वधः, नृहत्या, घातनं, मारणं.

To blood, *v. a.* (To stain with blood) असृजा or शोणितेन लिप् (c. 6. लिम्पति, लेप्तुं), अनुलिप् or अञ्ज् (c. 7. अनक्ति, अंक्तुं) or मलिन (nom. मलिनयति -यितुं).—(To let blood) रक्तं or शोणितं स्रु in caus. (स्रावयति -यितुं) or मुच् in caus. (मोचयति -यितुं).

BLOOD-BESPOTTED, *a.* रक्तमलिनः -ना -नं, शोणितोक्षितः -ता -तं.

BLOOD-DRINKING, *a.* रक्तपः -पा -पं, रक्तपायी -यिनी -यि (न्) or रुधिरपायी, शोणितपः -पा -पं, असृक्पः -क्पा.

BLOODHOUND, *s.* अतिक्रूरो मृगव्यकुक्कुरभेदः स च घ्राणबलेन मृगस्थानं नयति.

BLOODILY, *adv.* जिघांसया, क्रूरं, निष्ठुरं, नैष्ठुर्य्येण, निर्द्दयं.

BLOODINESS, *s.* रक्तपूर्णता.—(Disposition to kill) जिघांसा.

BLOODLESS, *a.* नीरक्तः -क्ता -क्तं, रक्तहीनः -ना -नं, निःशोणितः -ता -तं.

BLOODLETTER, *s.* रक्तस्रावकः, असृक्स्रावी *m.* (न्), रक्तमोक्षकः, सिरावेधकः.

BLOODSHED, *s.* रक्तपातः, असृक्पातः, वधः, नृहत्या, रिपुहत्या.

BLOODSHEDDER, *s.* रक्तपातकः, जिघांसुः *m.*, घातकः, हन्ता *m.* (न्तृ) or निहन्ता, वधोद्यतः.

BLOODSHOT, *a.* रक्तपूर्णः -र्णा -र्णं, शोणिताप्लुतः -ता -तं.—(Redness of the vessels of the eye) रक्ताभिष्यन्दः; 'having bloodshot eyes,' रक्तेक्षणः -णा -णं.

BLOOD-STAINED, *a.* असृग्लिप्तः -प्ता -प्तं, शोणिताक्तः -क्ता -क्तं, रक्ताक्तः -क्ता -क्तं, शोणितोक्षितः -ता -तं, रक्तमलिनः -ना -नं.

BLOODSUCKER, *s.* शोणितपः, रक्तपायी *m.* (न्) or रुधिरपायी, असृक्पः.—(A leech) जलौका, रक्तपा *f.*, जलौकाः *m.* (स्).

BLOODTHIRSTY, *a.* रक्तपिपासुः -सुः -सु, शोणितप्रियः -या -यं, जिघांसुः -सुः -सु, क्रूरः -रा -रं, वधोद्यतः -ता -तं.

BLOODVESSEL, *s.* असृग्वहा *f.*, नाडिः *f.*, रक्तप्रवाहकनाडिः *f.*, शिरा, रक्तवाही *m.* (न्).

BLOODY, *a.* रक्तमयः -यी -यं, शोणितमयः -यी -यं, रक्ताक्तः -क्ता -क्तं.—(Murderous) मारात्मकः -का -कं, क्रूरः -रा -रं.

BLOODY-FLUX, *s.* रक्तातीसारः, रक्तपित्तः, अधोगपित्तं, सारणः, प्रवाहिका.

BLOODY-MINDED, *a.* मारात्मकः-का-कं, जिघांसुः-सुः-सु, क्रूरचेताः-ताः-तः(स्).

BLOODY-RED, *a.* रक्तवर्णः -र्णा -र्णं, लोहितवर्णः -र्णा -र्णं.

BLOOM, *s.* (A blossom) पुष्पं, कुसुमं, पल्लवः, मुकुलः -लं.—(Fresh-colour) नववर्णः.—(In a state of bloom) अदृष्टपरिणामः.—(Bloom of youth) नवयौवनं, अक्षतयौवनं; 'in the bloom of youth,' प्रौढयौवनः -ना -नं.

To BLOOM, *v. n.* फुल्ल् (c. 1. फुल्लति, फुल्लितुं), पुष्प् (c. 4. पुष्प्यति, पुष्पितुं), कुसुम (nom. कुसुमयति -यितुं), विकस् (c. 1. -कसति -कसितुं).—(To flourish) ऋध् (c. 5. ऋध्नोति, अर्धितुं), समृध्; एध् (c. 1. एधते, एधितुं), वृध् (c. 1. वर्धते, वर्धितुं).

BLOOMING, *a.* फुल्लवान् -वती -वत् (त्), प्रफुल्लः -ल्ला -ल्लं, विकसन् -सन्ती -सत् (त्), स्फुटन् -टन्ती -टत् (त्), विकासी -सिनी -सि (न्).—(Flourishing) वर्द्धमानः-ना-नं, समृद्धः-द्धा-द्धं, उदयी-यिनी-यि (न्).

BLOSSOM, *s.* पुष्पं, कुसुमं, पल्लवः, मुकुलः -लं, क्षारकः, प्रसवः.

To BLOSSOM, *v. n.* फुल्ल् (c. 1. फुल्लति, फुल्लितुं), कुसुम (nom. कुसुमयति -यितुं), स्फुट् (c. 6. स्फुटति, स्फुटितुं, c. 1. स्फोटते, स्फोटितुं), पुष्प् (c. 4. पुष्प्यति, पुष्पितुं), विकस् (c. 1. -कसति -कसितुं).

BLOSSOMING, *a.* फुल्लवान् -वती -वत् (त्), पुष्पितः -ता -तं, पुष्पवान् -वती -वत् (त्), कुसुमितः -ता -तं, कुसुमवान् -वती -वत् (त्), स्फुटितपुष्पः -ष्पा -ष्पं.

To BLOT, *v. a.* मलिन (nom. मलिनयति -यितुं), मलिनीकृ, लिप् (c. 6. लिम्पति, लेप्तुं), दुष् in caus. (दूषयति -यितुं), कलङ्क (nom. कलङ्कयति -यितुं), कृष्णीकृ.—(To make indistinct) अस्पष्टीकृ.

To BLOT OUT, *v. a.* (To efface, destroy) विनश् in caus. (-नाशयति -यितुं), उच्छिद् (c. 7. -छिनत्ति -छेत्तुं), उद्धृ (c. 1. -हरति -हर्तुं), विलुप् in caus. (-लोपयति -यितुं).—(To erase) आमृष् (c. 1. -मर्षति -मर्षितुं), लोपं कृ.

BLOT, *s.* (Erasure) लोपः, आमर्षः.—(Spot, stain) कलङ्कः, अपकलङ्कः, कलुषं, मलं, दोषः.—(Disgrace) अपकीर्त्तिः *f.*, अपयशः *n.* (स्), अकीर्त्तिः *f.*

BLOTCH, *s.* किलासं, सिध्म *n.* (न्), स्फोटः, विस्फोटः, व्रणं, कक्षपिका.

To BLOTCH, *v. a.* किलासीकृ, मलिन (nom. मलिनयति -यितुं).

BLOTCHY, *a.* किलासी -सिनी -सि (न्), सिध्मलः -ला -लं, सिध्मवान् -वती -वत् (त्).

BLOTTED, *p. p.* मलिनितः -ता -तं, दूषितः -ता -तं, कलङ्कितः -ता -तं.

BLOTTING-PAPER, *s.* मसीशोषकः, मसीशोषणयोग्यं पत्रं.

BLOW, *s.* (A stroke) प्रहारः, आघातः, अभिघातः, घातः, पातः, पातनं, दण्डः, हतिः *f.*, आहतिः *f.*—(A blow with the fist) मुष्टिपातः; 'a blow which reduces to powder,' निष्पेषः.—(Blooming of flowers) फुल्लिः *f.*, फुल्लतिः *f.*, स्फुटनं, विकाशः.—(The act of a fly which infects meat by depositing eggs) मक्षिकया अण्डप्रसवेन खाद्यमांसदूषणं.

To BLOW, *v. n.* (As the wind) वा (c. 2. वाति, वातुं), प्रवा.—(To breathe) श्वस् (c. 2. श्वसिति, श्वसितुं), उच्छ्वस्, श्वासप्रश्वासं कृ.—(To pant) कृच्छ्रेण श्वस्, विनिश्वस्, दुःश्वासं कृ, यष्टिप्राणः -णा -णं भू.—(As a flower) फुल्ल् (c. 1. फुल्लति, फुल्लितुं), स्फुट् (c. 6. स्फुटति, स्फुटितुं), पुष्प् (c. 4. पुष्प्यति, पुष्पितुं).

To BLOW, *v. a.* ध्मा (c. 1. धमति, ध्मातुं), समाध्मा, प्रध्मा, उपध्मा; 'he blew his horn,' शङ्खं दध्मौ; 'fire blown by the wind,' वायुना ध्मायमानोऽग्निः.—(To blow away) अपध्मा, विध्मा.—(To blow out) निर्वा in caus. (-वापयति -यितुं).—(To blow upon) वीज् (c. 10. वीजयति -यितुं), अनुवीज्, उद्वीज्, उपवीज्; 'blown upon by sacred breezes,' पुण्यैर्वायुभिर् अनुवीजितः.—(To puff upon, to cool) फुत् कृ, फूत्कारं कृ.—(To blow the nose) नासिकां ध्मा.—(One who blows his nose) नासिकन्धमः.

BLOWING, *part.* (As a flower) स्फुटन् -टन्ती -टत् (त्), विकाशी -शिनी -शि (न्), फुल्लवान् -वती -वत् (त्).—(The act) फुल्लिः *f.*, स्फुटनं, प्रस्फोटनं, विकाशः.

BLOWN, *p. p.* (As a flower) फुल्लः -ल्ला -ल्लं, उत्फुल्लः -ल्ला -ल्लं, प्रफुल्लः -ल्ला -ल्लं, स्फुटः -टा -टं, व्याकोशः -शा -शं, विकसितः -ता -तं, विकचः -चा -चं, प्रस्फुटः -टा -टं.—(Inflated) आध्मातः -ता -तं.

BLOW-PIPE, *s.* नाडिः *f.*—(One who uses it) नाडिन्धमः.

BLOWZY, *a.* आतपदग्धवदनः -ना -नं, सूर्य्यतेजसा विकृतवर्णः -र्णा -र्णं.

BLUBBER, *s.* तिमिमेदः *n.* (स्), तिमिवसा, तिमितैलं, बृहन्मीनमेदः *n.* (स्).

To BLUBBER, *v. n.* यथा गण्डौ श्वयतस् तथा रुद् (c. 2. रोदिति, रोदितुं), अतिशयक्रन्दनाद् उच्छूनमुखो भू.

BLUDGEON, *s.* लगुडः, परिघः, परिघातनं, गदा.—(Armed with) लगुडहस्तः.

BLUE, *s.* (The colour) नीलः, नीलवर्णः.

BLUE, *a.* नीलः -ला -लं, नीलवर्णः -र्णा -र्णं, श्यामः -मा -मं.

To BLUE, *v. a.* नीलीकृ.—(To become blue) नील (nom. नीलायते).

BLUEBOTTLE, *s.* नीलशरीरः स्थूलमक्षिकाप्रभेदः, वर्वणा.

BLUE-EYED, *a.* नीलनयनः -नी -नं, नीलाक्षः -क्षी -क्षं.

BLUENESS, *s.* नैल्यं, नीलता -त्वं, श्यामता.

BLUFF, *a.* (Big) स्थूलः -ला -लं.—(Harsh) रूक्षः -क्षा -क्षं, परुषः -षा -षं, उग्रः -ग्रा -ग्रं, कर्कशः -शा -शं.—(Not pointed) घनाग्रः -ग्रा -ग्रं.—(Exposed to wind) वातावकाशिकः -की -कं.

BLUFFNESS, *s.* रूक्षता, कार्कश्यं, परुषत्वं, घनत्वं.

BLUISH, *a.* आनीलः -ला -लं, ईषन्नीलः -ला -लं. ईषत्श्यामः -मा -मं.

To BLUNDER, *v. n.* प्रमद् (c. 4. -माद्यति -मदितुं), स्खल् (c. 1. स्खलति, स्खलितुं), भ्रम् (c. 1. भ्रमति, c. 4. भ्राम्यति, भ्रमितुं), अनवधानं कृ.

BLUNDER, *s.* प्रमादः, स्खलितं, स्खलनं, दोषः, भ्रमः, कर्म्मदोषः, अनवधानं, अशुद्धं.

BLUNDERBUSS, *s.* अनेकशो लोहगुलिकाप्रक्षेपणी विशालमुखविशिष्टा नाडिः *f.*

BLUNDERER, *s.* प्रमादी *m.* (न्), प्रमादकर्त्ता *m.* (र्तृ), दोषकर्त्ता *m.* (र्तृ), स्खलनशीलः.

BLUNDERING, *a.* प्रमादी -दिनी -दि (न्), प्रमत्तः -त्ता -त्तं, स्खलन्मतिः -तिः -ति, अनवधानः -ना -नं, दोषी -षिणी -षि (न्).

BLUNDERINGLY, *adv.* प्रमादेन, प्रमादतस्, स्खलनपूर्व्वं, अनवधानेन, अवधानं विना.

BLUNT, *a.* (Not sharp) अतीक्ष्णः -क्ष्णा -क्ष्णं, अतीव्रः -व्रा -व्रं, अप्रखरः -रा -रं, धाराहीनः -ना -नं.—(Thick, obtuse) घनः -ना -नं, स्थूलः -ला -लं.—(Dull of understanding) मन्दमतिः -तिः -ति, अविदग्धः -ग्धा -ग्धं.—(Rough) रूक्षः -क्षा -क्षं, परुषः -षा -षं, कर्कशः -शा -शं, अमसृणः -णा -णं.

To BLUNT, *v. a.* घनीकृ, धाराम् अतीक्ष्णां कृ, विरुग्नधारं -रां -रं कृ, रुग्नीकृ, विरुग्नीकृ, स्थूलीकृ.—(To lessen) अल्पीकृ, न्यूनीकृ, शम् in caus. (शमयति -यितुं), ह्रस् in caus. (ह्रासयति -यितुं); 'one who blunts desire,' कामावसायिता *m.* (तृ).

BLUNTED, *p. p.* घनीकृतः -ता -तं, विरुग्नधारः -रा -रं, विरुग्नः -ग्ना -ग्नं.

BLUNTLY, *adv.* पारुष्येण, कार्कश्येन, कर्कशवाक्येन, परुषोक्त्या, सपारुष्यं.

BLUNTNESS, *s.* अतीक्ष्णता, धाराहीनता, घनत्वं, रूक्षता, स्थूलता.—(Of intellect) मन्दमतिता, अविदग्धता, बुद्धिमान्द्यं.—(Of manner) पारुष्यं, रूक्षता, कर्कशत्वं, कार्कश्यं.

BLUR, *s.* कलङ्कः, दोषः, कलुषं, मलं.

To BLUR, *v. a.* मलिन (nom. मलिनयति -यितुं), कलङ्क (nom. कलङ्कयति -यितुं), लिप् (c. 6. लिम्पति, लेप्तुं), दुष् in caus. (दूषयति -यितुं), कलुष (nom. कलुषयति -यितुं).

BLURRED, *p. p.* मलिनितः -ता -तं, परिमलितः -ता -तं, कलुषितः -ता -तं.

To BLURT, *v. a.* असमीक्ष्य or अविमृश्य or अविचार्य्य or प्रमादेन वद् (c. 1. वदति, वदितुं). जल्प् (c. 1. जल्पति, जल्पितुं).

To BLUSH, *v. n.* लज्ज् (c. 6. लज्जते, लज्जितुं), विलज्ज्, संलज्ज्, व्रीड् (c. 4. व्रीड्यति, व्रीडितुं), त्रप् (c. 1. त्रपते, त्रपितुं), ह्री (c. 3. जिह्रेति, ह्रेतुं); 'to blush at any thing,' ह्री with abl. or gen. c.—(To become red) अरुणीभू, ईषदरुणीभू, लोहित (nom. लोहितायते).—(In the face) लोहिताननः -नी -नं भू.

To BLUSH, *v. a.* (To make red) अरुणीकृ, अरुण (nom. अरुणयति -यितुं).

BLUSH, *s.* कपोलरागः.—(Colour in the face resulting from shame) लज्जाप्रयुक्तं वदनरक्तत्वं, व्रीडाजनितो मुखारुणिमा *m.* (न्).—(Bashfulness) लज्जा, ह्रीः *f.*, व्रीडा, त्रपा; 'full of blushes,' ह्रीपरिगतः -ता -तं.—(To put to the blush) ह्री in caus. (ह्रेपयति -यितुं); 'put to the blush,' ह्रेपितः -ता -तं.—(At the first blush or aspect) प्रथमदर्शने, आदावेव.

To BLUSTER, *v. n.* (To roar) गर्ज् (c. 1. गर्जति, गर्जितुं).—(To be tumultuous) तुमुलं कृ, मुखरीभू, शब्द (nom. शब्दायते).—(To brag) विकत्थ् (c. 1. -कत्थते -कत्थितुं).—(To be violent) भृश (nom. भृशायते).—(To bully) तर्ज् (c. 1. तर्जति, तर्जितुं), मुखरीकृ, भर्त्स् (c. 10. भर्त्सयते -यितुं).

BLUSTERER, *s.* शूरम्मन्यः, भर्त्सनकारः, कलहकारः, दाम्भिकः, विकत्थी *m.* (न्).

BLUSTERING, *s.* गर्ज्जनं, गर्ज्जितं, तुमुलं, कोलाहलः, भर्त्सनं, विकत्थनं.

BLUSTEROUS, *a.* गर्जनकारी -रिणी -रि (न्), महास्वनः -ना -नं, मुखरः -रा -रं.

BOA-CONSTRICTOR, *s.* (A snake) अजगरः, वाहसः, शयुः *m.*, वोड्रः.

BOAR, *s.* वराहः, शूकरः, दंष्ट्री *m.* (न्), स्थूलनासः, पृथुस्कन्धः, कोलः, किरः, दृढलोमा *m.* (न्), वक्रदंष्ट्रः; 'wild boar,' वनशूकरः.

BOARD, *s.* (A plank) फलकः -कं, दीर्घकाष्ठं.—(A table) भोजनाधारः, फलकः, भोजनासनं, मञ्चः.—(Food) भोजनं, आहारः, भृतिः *f.*, अन्नजलं. 'board and clothing,' ग्रासाच्छादनं; 'board and lodging,' ग्रासावासौ *du.*—(A council) सभा; 'the members of it,' सभासदः *m. pl.*—(The deck of a ship) नौकापृष्ठं, पोतपृष्ठं, नौकातलं, नौकाफलकं, पोतास्तरणं; 'on board,' नौकारूढः -ढा -ढं.—(A board for playing drafts, &c.) अष्टापदं, शारिफलं, नयपीठी.

To BOARD, *v. a.* (To enter a ship by force) नावं बलात् or बलेन or प्रसह्य आरुह् (c. 1. -रोहति -रोढुं) or अधिक्रम् (c. 1. -क्रामति -क्रमितुं) or आक्रम् or अवप्लु (c. 1. -प्लवते -प्लोतुं).—(To lay with boards) फलक (nom. फलकयति -यितुं), फलकैः or दीर्घकाष्ठैः or काष्ठफलकेन आस्तृ (c. 9. -स्तृणाति -स्तरितुं -स्तरीतुं).—(To diet another at a settled rate) निरूपितमूल्येन स्वगृहे अन्तेवासिनं भुज् in caus. (भोजयति -यितुं) or भृ (c. 3. बिभर्त्ति, भर्तुं).

To BOARD, *v. n.* (To diet with another at a settled rate) निरूपितवेतनं दत्त्वा or निरूपितमूल्येन परगृहे भोजनशयनादि कृ or अन्तेवासी भू.

BOARDER, *s.* (One who diets with another) निरूपितमूल्येन परगृहे भोजनशयनादिकर्त्ता *m.* (र्तृ), सहभोजी *m.* (न्), सहभोक्ता *m.* (क्तृ), पांक्तः.—(A pupil at a boarding-school) अन्तेवासी *m.* (न्).

BOARDING-SCHOOL, *s.* यस्मिन् विद्यालये अन्तेवासिनः शिक्षकगृहे भोजनशयनादि कुर्व्वन्ति सः.

BOARD-WAGES, *s.* भोजनशयनार्थं वेतनं, अन्नक्रयणार्थं वर्त्तनं, भोजनात् प्रति वेतनं.

BOARISH, *a.* वाराहः -ही -हं, सौकरः -री -रं, असभ्यः -भ्या -भ्यं.

To BOAST, *v. n.* आत्मानं श्लाघ् (c. 1. श्लाघते, श्लाघितुं), कत्थ् (c. 1. कत्थते, कत्थितुं), विकत्थ् with inst. of the thing of which boast is made, दम्भं कृ, परिकॄत् (c. 10. -कीर्त्तयति -यितुं), दृप् (c. 4. दृप्यति, द्रप्तुं), गर्व्व् (c. 1. गर्व्वति, गर्व्वितुं).

BOAST, BOASTING, *s.* आत्मश्लाघा, विकत्था, विकत्थनं, परिकीर्त्तनं, अहङ्कारोक्तिः *f.*, शूरमानं, दम्भः, दर्पकरणं, दर्पः, गर्व्वः, अभिमानं, आहोपुरुषिका, अहमहमिका.

BOASTED, *p. p.* श्लाघितः -ता -तं, परिकीर्त्तितः -ता -तं.

BOASTER, *s.* आत्मश्लाघी *m.* (न्), विकत्थी *m.* (न्), -त्थिनी *f.*, -त्थनः, उपजल्पी *m.* (न्), दम्भी *m.* (न्), शूरम्मन्यः, शूरमानी *m.* (न्).

BOASTFUL, *a.* दाम्भिकः -की -कं, दम्भी -म्भिनी -म्भि (न्), गर्व्वितः -ता -तं, गर्व्वपूर्णः -र्णा -र्णं, विकत्थनः -ना -नं, अवलिप्तः -प्ता -प्तं, वाचालः -ला -लं.

BOASTFULLY, *adv.* गर्व्वेण, दम्भेन, सदर्पं, सगर्व्वं, सदम्भं, विकत्थनपूर्व्वं.

BOASTLESS, *a.* दम्भहीनः -ना -नं, अगर्व्वः -र्व्वा -र्व्वं, अभिमानरहितः -ता -तं.

BOAT, *s.* नौः *f.*, नौका, पोतः, तरी, तरणी, तरण्डः, उडुपः.

BOATFUL, *s.* नौकापूरणं, पोतपूरणं.

BOATLOAD, *s.* नौकाभारः, पोतभारः.

BOATMAN, *s.* नाविकः, पोतवाहः, नियामः, नौकारूढः, औडुपिकः.

BOATSWAIN, *s.* मुख्यनाविकः, प्रधाननाविकः, नाविकः, कर्णधारः, नियामाधिष्ठाता *m.* (तृ).

To BOB, *v. a.* (To crop) ह्रस् in caus. (ह्रासयति -यितुं).—(To beat) तड् in caus. (ताडयति -यितुं).

To BOB, *v. n.* (To play backwards and forwards) इतस्ततो लुट्

(c. 6. लुठति, लुठितुं) or स्फुर् (c. 6. स्फुरति, स्फुरितुं) or प्रेङ्ख् (c. 1. प्रेङ्खति, प्रेङ्खितुं), दोल (nom. दोलायते -यितुं), चञ्च् (c. 1. चञ्चति, चञ्चितुं), चञ्चल (nom. चञ्चलायते).

Bob, *s.* (Ear-ring) कुण्डलं, कर्णिका.—(A blow) प्रहारः, आघातः.

Bobbin, *s.* कपालनालिका, सूत्रगण्डिका, तनुकीलः.

Bobtail, *s.* छिन्नबालधारी *m.* (न्), ह्रस्वपुच्छी *m.* (न्), कर्त्तितलाङ्गूली *m.* (न्).

Bobtailed, *a.* छिन्नवालः -ला -लं, ह्रस्वपुच्छः -च्छा -च्छं, ह्रसितलाङ्गूलः -ला -लं.

Bobwig, *s.* शिरोरुहहीनैर् भृतं परकीयकृत्रमकेशनिर्म्मितं शिरस्त्रं.

To bode, *v. a.* शुभाशुभं or मङ्गलामङ्गलं प्रदृश् in caus. (-दर्शयति -यितुं), इष्टानिष्टम् आविद् in caus. (-वेदयति -यितुं) or सूच् (c. 10. सूचयति -यितुं), पूर्व्वलिङ्गं or पूर्व्वचिह्नं or पूर्व्वलक्षणं दा (c. 3. ददाति, दातुं), निपातं or विनिपातं शंस् (c. 1. शंसति, शंसितुं).

Bodement, *s.* पूर्व्वलक्षणं, पूर्व्वचिह्नं, पूर्व्वलिङ्गं, चिह्नं, शुभाशुभलक्षणं, शुभाशुभचिह्नं, शकुनं, उत्पातः, अजन्यं, निमित्तं, उपसर्गः, उपलिङ्गं, भाविसूचकं चिह्नं.

Bodice, *s.* चोलः -ली, अङ्गिका, चेलिका, कञ्चुलिका, कूर्पासकः -कं.

Bodied, *a.* शरीरी -रिणी -रि (न्), देही -हिनी -हि (न्), अङ्गी -ङ्गिनी -ङ्गि (न्).

Bodiless, *a.* अशरीरः -रा -रं or -री -रिणी -रि (न्), अनङ्गः -ङ्गा -ङ्गं, अङ्गहीनः -ना -नं, निराकारः -रा -रं, अमूर्त्तः -र्त्ता -र्त्तं, व्यङ्गः -ङ्गी -ङ्गं.

Bodily, *a.* शारीरिकः -की -कं, दैहिकः -की -कं, शरीरजः -जा -जं, कायिकः -की -कं, आङ्गिकः -का -की -कं, आङ्गः -ङ्गी -ङ्गं.—(Bodily hardship) कायक्लेशः, देहक्लेशः, कृच्छ्रं.

Bodily, *adv.* शरीरतस्, सदेहं, सशरीरं, सकायं, साङ्गं.—(In a mass) साकल्येन.—(United with the body) शरीरसंयुक्तः -क्ता -क्तं, शरीरसम्पृक्तः -क्ता -क्तं.

Bodkin, *s.* सूचिविशेषः, सूचिः -ची, सूचिनी.—(A dagger) छुरिका, शङ्कुः *m.*—(Instrument for piercing) आविधः, वेधनिका.—(For the hair) केशरचनायोग्यः कीलविशेषः.

Body, *s.* (As opposed to the immaterial substance of an animal) शरीरं, देहः, कायः, गात्रं, मूर्त्तिः *f.*, अङ्गं, वपुः *n.* (स्), कलेवरं, वर्ष्म *n.* (न्), विग्रहः, संहननं, तनुः *f.* -नूः *f.*, करणं; 'a dead body,' मृतशरीरं, शवः, कुणपः; 'a little body,' शरीरकं.—(Substance) मूर्त्तिः *f.*; 'the body of cloth,' वस्त्रयोनिः *m.*—(A person) पुरुषः, जनः, मनुष्यः, लोकः.—(A collective mass) समूहः, समवायः, सङ्घातः, समुदायः, मण्डलं, सङ्घः, वृन्दं, निवहः, ओघः; 'a body of men,' जनसमूहः; 'a body of water,' पयोराशिः *m.*, वारिराशिः *m.*; 'in a body,' सङ्घशस्, सङ्गम्य, समूह्य.—(A society of men) संसर्गः, समागमः, पङ्क्तिः *f.*—(A corporate body) श्रेणी.—(A collegiate or religious body) आश्रमः.—(Strength) बलं.—(The main part) प्रधानभागः; 'body of a tree,' प्रकाण्डः, स्कन्धः; 'the body or interior of a building,' प्रासादाभ्यन्तरं, अन्तर्गृहं, अन्तर्भवनं, भवनोदरं, भवनगर्भः.—(A body of troops) गुल्मः, सैन्यदलं, सैनिकः; 'a body of reserve,' प्रतिग्रहः; 'body to body,' अङ्गाङ्गि.

Body-clothes, *s.* (Of horses) आस्तरः, पर्य्याणं, अश्वानां गात्रवस्त्रं.

To body-forth, *v. a.* कृप् (c. 10. कल्पयति -यितुं), निर्मा (c. 2. -माति -मातुं).

Body-guard, *s.* परिचरः, परिधिस्थः, अनुचरः, परिवारः.

Bog, *s.* अनूपः, अनूपभूः *f.*, कच्छः, कच्छभूः *f.*, पङ्कः, कर्द्दमः, पङ्कक्लेदः.

Bog-trotter, *s.* अनूपवासी *m.* (न्), कच्छभूमिवासी *m.* (न्), कच्छदेशस्थायी *m.* (न्).

To boggle, *v. n.* (To hesitate) शङ्क् (c. 1. शङ्कते, शङ्कितुं), विशङ्क्, अभिशङ्क्, आशङ्क्, सन्दिह् (c. 2. -देग्धि -देग्धुं), दोल (nom. दोलायते -यितुं), आन्दोल, विलम्ब् (c. 1. -लम्बते -लम्बितुं), विक्लृप् (c. 1. -कल्पते -कल्पितुं).

Boggler, *s.* सन्दिग्धमतिः, शङ्कितमतिः, संशयिता *m.* (तृ), संशयालुः, शङ्काशीलः.

Boggy, *a.* अनूपः -पा -पं, आनूपः -पी -पं, पङ्किलः -ला -लं, कार्द्दमः -मी -मं, कच्छः -च्छा -च्छं.

To boil, *v. n.* (To be effervescent) फेन् (nom. फेनायते -यितुं), मुत् कृ.—(To boil over) उत्सेचनं कृ.—(To be cooked by boiling) क्वथ् in pass. (क्वथ्यते), श्रा in pass. (श्रायते), पच् in pass. (पच्यते).—(To be hot) तप् in pass. (तप्यते).

To boil, *v. a.* क्वथ् (c. 1. क्वथति, क्वथितुं), स्थाल्यां पच्, श्रा (c. 2. श्राति, श्रातुं or caus. श्रपयति -यितुं), तप् in caus. (तापयति -यितुं).

Boil, *s.* व्रणं -णः, तनुव्रणः, विस्फोटः, स्फोटः, स्फोटकः, पिटकः -का, नालीव्रणः, गण्डः, पोटिकः; 'blind boil,' अन्धालजी.

Boiled, *p. p.* क्वथितः -ता -तं, श्राणः -णा -णं, शृतः -ता -तं, श्रपितः -ता -तं.—(In a caldron) पैठरः -री -रं, स्थालीपक्वः -क्वा -क्वं, उख्यः -ख्या -ख्यं; 'boiled rice,' भक्तं.

Boiler, *s.* स्थाली, ऋजीषं, पिष्टपचनं, पिठरः -रं, उखा, कन्दुः *m. f.*

Boisterous, *a.* (Stormy) वातवान् -वती -वत् (त्), वातलः -ला -लं, गर्जनकारी -रिणी -रि (न्); 'a boisterous wind,' प्रचण्डपवनः.—(Violent) प्रचण्डः -ण्डा -ण्डं, उच्चण्डः -ण्डा -ण्डं, रोषणः -णा -णं, साहसिकः -की -कं.—(Turbulent) कलहकारी -रिणी -रि (न्.—(Noisy) शब्दकारी -रिणी -रि (न्) or तुमुलकारी.—(Laughing violently) अट्टहासी -सिनी -सि (न्).

Boisterously, *adv.* प्रचण्डं, प्रचण्डतया, महारोषेण, महाशब्देन, कोलाहलेन.

Boisterousness, *s.* वातलत्वं, प्रचण्डता, साहसित्वं, सरोषता.

Bold, *a.* (Brave) शूरः -रा -रं, प्रवीरः -रा -रं, निर्भयः -या -यं, निर्विशङ्कः -ङ्का -ङ्कं.—(Daring, audacious) साहसी -सिनी -सि (न्), प्रगल्भः -ल्भा -ल्भं, प्रतिभान्वितः -ता -तं.—(Impudent) निर्लज्जः -ज्जा -ज्जं, धृष्टः -ष्टा -ष्टं, अनिभृतः -ता -तं, प्रतिभानवान् -वती -वत् (त्); 'to be bold,' धृष् (c. 5. धृष्णोति, धर्षितुं).

To bolden, *v. a.* निर्भयं -यां -यं कृ, अभयं दा (c. 3. ददाति, दातुं).

Bold-faced, *a.* प्रतिभामुखः -खी -खं, निर्लज्जमुखः -खी -खं, निर्लज्जः -ज्जा -ज्जं.

Boldly, *adv.* शूरवत्, साहसेन, प्रागल्भ्येन, निर्भयं, भयं विना; 'to speak boldly,' जल्प् (c. 1. जल्पति, जल्पितुं).

Boldness, *s.* (Courage) शौर्य्यं, शूरता, वीरता, निर्भयत्वं, अक्षोभः.—(Daringness) प्रागल्भ्यं, प्रगल्भता, साहसं, प्रतिभानं.—(Impudence) निर्लज्जत्वं, धार्ष्ट्यं, धृष्टता.

Bole, *s.* (Trunk of a tree) स्कन्धः, प्रकाण्डः, स्थाणुः *m.*

Boll, *s.* नाडिः -डी *f.*, नाली, काण्डः -ण्डं.

To boll, *v. n.* अतसीवत् स्फुट् (c. 6. स्फुटति, स्फुटितुं) or विकस् (c. 1. -कसति -कसितुं) or शस्ययुक्तः -क्ता -क्तं भू.

Bolster, *s.* उपधानं, उपधानीयं, उच्छीर्षकं, उपबर्हः, गभोलिकः.—(Bandage) पट्टः बन्धनं.—(A prop, support) उपस्तम्भः, उपघ्नः, आलम्बः.

To bolster up, *v. a.* (To support) संस्तम्भ् (c. 5. स्तभ्नोति, c. 9. स्तभ्नाति, स्तम्भितुं or caus. स्तम्भयति -यितुं), उपस्तम्भ्, विष्टम्भ्; धृ (c. 1. धरति, धर्तुं or caus. धारयति -यितुं), आलम्ब् (c. 1. -लम्बते -लम्बितुं), समवलम्ब्.

Bolt, *s.* (Of a door) अर्गलं, तालकं, कीलः, तालयन्त्रं, द्वारयन्त्रं, अपलं.—(A dart) बाणः, शूलः -लं, शल्यं, शङ्कुः *m.*, प्रासः, शरः.—(Thunder-bolt) वज्रं, कुलिशं, अशनिः *m. f.*

To BOLT, *v. a.* (To shut with a bolt) अर्गलेन or तालकेन द्वारं पिधा (c. 3. -दधाति -धातुं) or बन्ध् (c. 9. बध्नाति, बन्द्धुं).—(To sift) चालनेन पू (c. 9. पुनाति, पवितुं) or शुध् in caus. (शोधयति -यितुं), तितउना चल् in caus. (चालयति -यितुं).—(To blurt out) अविचार्य्य वद् (c. 1. वदति, वदितुं), जल्प् (c. 1. जल्पति, जल्पितुं).

To BOLT OUT, *v. n.* अकस्मात् or झटिति निर्गम् (c. 1. -गच्छति -गन्तुं) or निःसृ (c. 1. -सरति -सर्त्तुं), निष्पत् (c. 1. -पतति -पतितुं), विनिष्पत्, अभिनिष्पत्.

BOLTED, *p. p.* अर्गलेन बद्धः -द्धा -द्धं, कीलितः -ता -तं.

BOLTER, *s.* (A sieve) चालनं -नी, तितउः *m.* -तउ *n.*

BOLTHEAD, *s.* वकः, वकयन्त्रं, काचवकयन्त्रं.

BOLTING-HOUSE, *s.* शस्यचालनस्थानं, शस्यपवनस्थानं.

BOLTSPRIT or BOWSPRIT, *s.* नौकाग्रभागे स्थापितो महाकूपकावलम्बिताधरायो वहिर्प्रणतः क्षुद्रकूपकः, पोताग्रवहिःप्रलम्बो गुणवृक्षकः.

BOLUS, *s.* गुली, गुटिका, रोगिभिर् निगरणीय औषधीयगोलः.

BOMB, *s.* पुरमर्द्दने प्रयुक्तोऽग्न्यस्त्रविशेषः स च अन्तर्ज्वलनबलेन वज्रनिर्घोषतुल्यशब्देन विदीर्णो भूत्वा सहस्रखण्डशः पतति.

To BOMB or BOMBARD, *v. a.* पूर्व्वोक्तेन अग्न्यस्त्रेण पुरं मृद् (c. 9. मृद्नाति, मर्द्दितुं) or प्रमृद् or विमृद् or अवमृद्.

BOMBARDIER, *s.* पूर्व्वोक्तेन अग्न्यस्त्रेण पुरमर्द्दी *m.* (न्) or नगरविमर्द्दी *m.*

BOMBARDMENT, *s.* प्रागुक्तेन अग्न्यस्त्रेण पुरमर्द्दनं or नगरविमर्द्दनं.

BOMBASIN, *s.* दुकूलं, बन्धुमरणसमये शोकसूचकः सूक्ष्मकौशासरविशेषः.

BOMBAST, *s.* गर्व्वितवाक्यं, दर्पवाक्यं, असारवाक्यं, फल्गुवाक्यं, अतिशयोक्तिः *f.*

BOMBASTICAL, *a.* अतिगर्व्वितः -ता -तं, दर्पध्मातः -ता -तं, निरर्थकः -का -कं, फल्गुः -ल्गुः -ल्गु, असारः -रा -रं.

BOMBYX, *s.* तन्तुकीटः, कोषकारः, कोशकारकः.

BONA FIDE, *a.* अर्थतस्, तत्त्वतस्, वस्तुतस्, निर्व्याजं, निर्व्यलीकं.

BOND, *s.* बन्धनं, बन्धः, पाशः, आबन्धः.—(A written contract) प्रतिज्ञापत्रकं, पत्रं, लेख्यप्रसङ्गः, लेख्यं, करणं, काचनकी *m.* (न्).—(Union, tie) सन्धिः *m.*, श्लेषः, संहतिः *f.*, संसक्तिः *f.*—(Connection) संयोगः, सम्बन्धः.—(Captivity) बन्धनं.—(That which binds, obligation) नियमः, अवश्यकता.

BONDAGE, *s.* बन्दित्वं, दासत्वं, बन्धनं, प्रतिबन्धनं, परप्रेष्यत्वं.

BONDSMAID, *s.* दासी, दासिका, चेटी, किङ्करी.

BONDSMAN, *s.* दासः, क्रीतदासः, किङ्करः, चेटः.

BONE, *s.* अस्थि *n.*, अस्थिकं, कुल्यं, हड्डं, कीकसं; 'backbone,' पृष्ठास्थि *n.*

To BONE, *v. a.* निरस्थीकृ, अस्थीनि निष्कृष् (c. 1. -कर्षति -क्रष्टुं).

BONE-ACHE, *s.* अस्थिवेदना, अस्थिव्यथा.

BONED, *a.* (Bony) अस्थिमान् -मती -मत् (त्).—(Having the bones extracted) निरस्थिः -स्थिः स्थि.

BONELESS, *a.* अनस्थिः -स्थिः -स्थि, अस्थिहीनः -ना -नं, अस्थिरहितः -ता -तं.

To BONESET, *v. n.* त्रुटितास्थि or भिन्नास्थि स्वस्थं or सुस्थं कृ or स्वस्थाने पुनः संस्था in caus. (-स्थापयति -यितुं) or पुनः सन्धा (c. 3. -दधाति -धातुं), करपादादित्रोटनं or अस्थिभङ्गं समाधा or कित् in des. (चिकित्सति -त्सितुं).

BONESETTER, *s.* त्रुटितास्थि स्वस्थं करोति यो वैद्यः, त्रुटितास्थिसमाधाता *m.* (तृ), भग्नास्थिचिकित्सकः.

BONFIRE, *s.* उत्सवकाले or उद्धर्षसमये समिद्धो हर्षसूचनार्थं महाज्वालोऽग्निः, जयोग्निः *m.*

BON-MOT, *s.* रसवद्वाक्यं, परिहासवाक्यं, नर्म्म *n.* (न्), श्लेषवाक्यं, द्व्यर्थवाक्यं, टट्टरी.

BONNET, *s.* स्त्रीलोकभृतं शिरस्कं or शिरस्त्रं or शिरोवेष्टनं or मस्तकाभरणं.

BONNILASS, *s.* सुन्दरी, रूपवती, प्रमदा, सुमुखी, मुग्धा, सुरूपी.

BONNILY, *adv.* हृष्टवत्, हृष्टपुष्टवत्, सुष्ठु, सुन्दरं, रमणीयप्रकारेण, साधु.

BONNY, *a.* (Pretty) सुन्दरः -री -रं, रूपवान् -वती -वत् (त्), सुरूपः -पी -पं, सुदृश्यः -श्या -श्यं, चारुः -र्व्वी -रु.—(Cheerful) हृष्टः -ष्टा -ष्टं, हृष्टहृदयः -या -यं.—(Plump) हृष्टपुष्टः -ष्टा -ष्टं, सुललितः -ता -तं.

BONY, *a.* (Having bones) अस्थिमान् -मती -मत् (त्).—(Strong) दृढाङ्गः -ङ्गी -ङ्गं.—(Made of bone) अस्थिमयः -यी -यं.—(Full of bones) अस्थिपूर्णः -र्णा -र्णं.

BOOBY, *s.* मन्दबुद्धिः *m.*, दुर्मतिः *m.*, दुर्बुद्धिः *m.*, मूढः, मूर्खः, स्थूलधीः *m.*—(A kind of bird) वकः.

BOOK, *s.* पुस्तकं -की, ग्रन्थः, पत्रं, पत्रिका, पुस्तं -स्ती; 'a book of science,' शास्त्रं. This last may be used in connexion with some other word to limit its application; as, 'a book on law,' धर्म्मशास्त्रं; 'a poetical book,' काव्यशास्त्रं.—(A manuscript, written book) लेख्यं, लिखितं.

To BOOK, *v. a.* ग्रन्थे or पुस्तके or लेख्ये समारुह् in caus. (-रोपयति -यितुं) or अभिलिख् (c. 6. -लिखति -लेखितुं); 'booked, committed to writing,' लेख्यारूढः -ढा -ढं.

BOOKBINDER, *s.* चर्म्मादिना ग्रन्थपत्रसम्बन्धा *m.* (न्धृ), ग्रन्थाच्छादनकृत्.

BOOKCASE, *s.* ग्रन्थकुटी, ग्रन्थकोशः, ग्रन्थभाण्डं, ग्रन्थाधारः.

BOOKISH, *a.* ग्रन्थी -न्थिनी -न्थि (न्), पुस्तकी -किनी -कि (न्), शास्त्रज्ञः -ज्ञा -ज्ञं.

BOOKKEEPER, *s.* गणनाध्यक्षः, ग्रन्थसमारोपणकृत्, गणितलेखकः.

BOOKMATE, *s.* सहाध्यायी *m.* (न्).

BOOKSELLER, *s.* ग्रन्थविक्रेता *m.* (तृ), ग्रन्थविक्रयी *m.* (न्), पुस्तकविक्रेता *m.* (तृ).

BOOKWORM, *s.* ग्रन्थखादकः कीटः.—(Too closely given to books) ग्रन्थी *m.* (न्), ग्रन्थासक्तः, ग्रन्थपरः, शास्त्रगतः, ग्रन्थचुम्बकः.

BOOM, *s.* (A long pole) वातवसनप्रसारणार्थं दीर्घयष्टिः or दण्डः.—(A bar of wood laid across a harbour) पारक्यनौकाप्रवेशनिवारणार्थं पोतबन्धनखाते स्थापितम् अवरोधकं.

To BOOM, *v. n.* ऊर्म्मिवत् प्लुट् (c. 1. लोठति -लोठितुं) or उच्छल् (c. 1. -छलते -छलितुं) or पातोत्पातं कृ.

BOON, *s.* वरः, प्रसादः, दानं, प्रदानं, वरदानं, उपकृतं, हितं, अनुग्रहः; 'granting boons,' वरदः -दा -दं.

BOON, *a.* (Gay) हृष्टः -ष्टा -ष्टं, हृष्टहृदयः -या -यं, हासी -सिनी -सि (न्),—(Boon-companion) सहपायी *m.* (न्).

BOOR, *s.* ग्रामी *m.* (न्), ग्राम्यजनः, ग्रामवासी *m.* (न्), ग्रामिकः, क्षेत्रिकः, वृषलः.

BOORISH, *a.* ग्राम्यः -म्या -म्यं, ग्रामीयः -या -यं, ग्रामिकः -की -कं, क्षेत्रिकः -की -कं, असभ्यः -भ्या -भ्यं, अशिष्टः -ष्टा -ष्टं, प्राकृतः -ता -तं, असत्कृतः -ता -तं.

BOORISHLY, *adv.* ग्राम्यजनवत्, वृषलवत्, असभ्यजनवत्, असभ्यं, अशिष्टं, असत्कृतप्रकारेण.

BOORISHNESS, *s.* ग्राम्यत्वं -ता, असभ्यता, अशिष्टता, असत्कृतिः *f.*, वृषलत्वं.

BOOT, *s.* पादुका *f.*, पादूः *f.*, उपानत् *f.* (ह्), पत्रङ्गा *f.*, पत्रङ्गी, अनुपदीना, जङ्घात्राणं, पादत्रं, पादरक्षणं, पादरथः.—(Profit) फलं, लाभः, अर्थः.

To BOOT, *v. a.* (To profit) फलाय or लाभाय भू, फलं or लाभं दा (c. 3. ददाति, दातुं), उपकृ (c. 8. -करोति -कर्त्तुं).

To BOOT, *v. n.* (To put on boots) पादुके अधिरुह् (c. 1. -रोहति -रोढुं) or आरुह् or परिधा (c. 3. -दधाति -धत्ते -धातुं).

BOOT-TREE, *s.* पादुकानां चर्म्मशिथिलीकरणयोग्यं जङ्घाकृति काष्ठयन्त्रं.

BOOTED, *a.* सपादुकः -का -कं, उपानद्गूढपादः -दा -दं, पादुकारूढः -ढा -ढं.

BOOTH, *s.* मण्डपः -पं, पटमण्डपः, दूष्यं, औपकार्य्या.

BOOTLESS, *s.* निरर्थकः -का -कं, अनर्थकः -का -कं, व्यर्थः -र्था -र्थं, निष्फलः

-ला -लं, विफलः -ला -लं, निष्प्रयोजनः -ना -नं, अनामिषः -षा -षं.

BOOTMAKER, s. पादुकाकारः, पादुकाकृत्, पदत्राकृत्, पदत्राकारः, पादूकृत् m.

BOOTY, s. लोप्त्रं, लोत्रं or -तं, लुप्तं.—(In cattle) गोग्रहः.

BOPEEP, s. पितृपुत्रकयोः क्रीडाविशेषो यत्र पिता बालविनोदार्थं सन्त्रस्त इव स्वमुखगोपनं कृत्वा पश्चात् सन्त्रासनार्थम् अकस्मात् बालकमुखनिरीक्षणं करोति.

BORACHIO, s. सुराभाजनं, मद्यभाजनं, कुतूः f.—(Drunkard) पानरतः.

BORABLE, a. वेध्यः -ध्या -ध्यं, व्यध्यः -ध्या -ध्यं, छिद्रणीयः -या -यं.

BORAGE, s. खिलरुह ओषधिप्रभेदः.

BORAX, s. रसशोधनः, लोहद्रावी m. (न्), लोहश्लेषणः, चिडं, धातुमारिणी.

BORDEL, s. वेश्याजनसमाश्रयः, वेश्यागृहं, गणिकागृहं, वेश्याश्रयः.

BORDER, s. (Of a river, &c.) तीरं, कूलं, तटं, कच्छः, कच्छान्तः—(Edge of any thing) प्रान्तः, अन्तः -न्तं, उपान्तं, समन्तः, पर्य्यन्तं, सीमा, उत्सङ्गः, धारः.—(Frontier) सामन्तः, सामन्तं, पर्य्यन्तं, सीमा; 'dwelling on the border,' सामन्तवासी -सिनी -सि (न्), पर्य्यन्तस्थः -स्था -स्थं; 'the border of a wood,' वनान्तं; 'of a city,' नगरोपान्तं; 'along the border,' प्रान्ततस्.—(Of a garment) अञ्चलः, वस्त्राञ्चलं.—(A garden-bed) स्थलं.

To BORDER, v. a. (To surround with a border) प्रान्त (nom. प्रान्तयति -यितुं), समन्त (nom. समन्तयति -यितुं), पर्य्यन्तं कृ.

To BORDER UPON, v. n. प्रान्ततस् or पर्य्यन्ते or निकटे or समीपं स्था (c. 1. तिष्ठति, स्थातुं) or वृत् (c. 1. वर्त्तते, वर्त्तितुं) or वस् (c. 1. वसति, वस्तुं), स्पृश् (c. 6. स्पृशति, स्प्रष्टुं).—(To approach nearly to, resemble) कल्पः -ल्पा -ल्पं अस् in comp., सदृशः -शी -शं अस्.

BORDERED, p. p. प्रान्तितः -ता -तं, समर्य्यादः -दा -दं, वलयितः -ता -तं.

BORDERER, s. सामन्तवासी m. (न्), सीमावासी m. (न्), निकटवर्त्ती m. (न्), समीपवासी m. (न्), प्रतिवासी -सिनी -सि (न्).

BORDERING, a. प्रत्यन्तः -न्ता -न्तं, सामन्तः -न्ता -न्तं, पर्य्यन्तस्थः -स्था -स्थं.

BORE, s. (Hole made by boring) छिद्रं, रन्ध्रं.—(The instrument of boring) वेधनी, वेधनिका.—(Diameter of a hole) सुषिरं, शुषिरं, छिद्रं, व्यासं, छिद्रव्यासं.—(A swelling tide) वानं.

To BORE, v. a. व्यध् (c. 4. विध्यति, व्यद्धुं), छिद्र् (c. 10. छिद्रयति -यितुं), शुषिरीकृ.

BOREAL, a. उत्तरः -रा -रं, उदङ् -दीची -दक् (च्), उदीचीनः -ना -नं.

BOREAS, s. उत्तरवायुः m., उदीचीनवातः.

BORED, p. p. (Pierced) विद्धः -द्धा -द्धं, छिद्रितः -ता -तं, शुषिरः -रा -रं; 'having the ears bored,' छिद्रकर्णः -र्णा -र्णं.

BORER, s. वेधकः, छिद्रकर्त्ता.—(An instrument) वेधनी, वेधनिका.

To be BORN, v. pass. जन् (c. 4. जायते, जनितुं), अभिजन्, सञ्जन्, उत्पद् (c. 4. -पद्यते -पत्तुं), प्रसु in pass. (-सूयते), सम्भू (c. 1. -भवति -भवितुं).

BORN, p. p. जातः -ता -तं, जनितः -ता -तं, उपजातः -ता -तं, उत्पन्नः -न्ना -न्नं, उत्पादितः -ता -तं, सम्भूतः -ता -तं, प्रसूतः -ता -तं, प्रभवः -वा -वं, कृतजन्मा -न्मा -न्म (न्), उत्पतितः -ता -तं; 'born blind,' जात्यन्धः; 'a born slave,' गर्भदासः.

BORNE, p. p. सोढः -ढा -ढं, ऊढः -ढा -ढं, क्षान्तः -न्ता -न्तं; 'easy to be borne,' सुसहः -हा -हं, सुवहः -हा -हं; 'grass borne along by the wind,' वात्याप्रेरिततृणं; 'it is borne on the shoulder,' स्कन्धेन समुह्यते.

BOROUGH, s. नगरं -री, पुरं -री, प्रजाप्रतिनिधिसभायां सामाजिकजनप्रेरणाधिकारयुक्ता नगरी.

To BORROW, v. a. ऋणं ग्रह् (c. 9. गृह्णाति, ग्रहीतुं), ऋणं प्रार्थ् (c. 10. -अर्थयते -ति -यितुं), याच् (c. 1. याचति, याचितुं), ऋणं परियाच्, निरूपितकालपर्य्यन्तं परद्रव्यप्रयोगं प्रार्थ्.

BORROW, s. (The thing borrowed) याचितकं, प्रतिदेयं.

BORROWER, s. ऋणग्राही m. (न्), ऋणग्रहः, ऋणप्रार्थकः, ऋणप्रार्थयिता m. (तृ), याचकः, ऋणयाचकः.

BORROWING, s. ऋणग्रहः -हणं, ऋणयाचना, याचना, ऋणप्रार्थनं.

BOSKY, a. तरुगुल्मावृतः -ता -तं, वार्क्षः -र्क्षी -र्क्षं.

BOSOM, s. उरः n. (स्), क्रोडं -डा, अङ्कः, वत्सं, वक्षः n. (स्), वक्षस्स्थलं, भुजान्तरं.—(Female breast) स्तनः, स्तनौ m. du., कुचः, कुचतटं, वक्षोरुहः, वक्षोजं, उरसिजः, उरसिरुहः, स्तनकुड्मलं.—(The heart) हृदयं, अन्तःकरणं, चित्तं, मनः n. (स्), मर्म्म n. (न्).—(A secret receptacle) गर्भः.

BOSS, s. गण्डः, उच्चैःप्रकारेण खचित अलङ्कारः, पिण्डः.

BOSSED or BOSSY, a. गण्डखचितः -ता -तं, गण्डानुविद्धः -द्धा -द्धं.

BOTANIC, BOTANICAL, a. उद्भिद्विद्याविषयः -या -यं, वृक्षादिविद्यासम्बन्धकः -का -कं.

BOTANIST, s. उद्भिद्विद्याज्ञः, वृक्षादिविद्यातत्त्वज्ञः, वृक्षादिशास्त्रपण्डितः.

BOTANY, s. उद्भिद्विद्या, ओषधिविद्या, वृक्षलतातृणादिविद्या, वृक्षायुर्वेदः.

BOTCH, s. दद्रुः m., पाम n. -मा f. (न्), व्रणः, सिध्मं, कच्छूः f., त्वक्पुष्पं.—(Flaw) दोषः, छिद्रं.—(A patch) कन्था, कर्पटः.

To BOTCH, v. a. (To patch old clothes) जीर्णवस्त्राणि or चीरवस्त्राणि सिव् (c. 4. सीव्यति, सेवितुं) or सूच्या सन्धा (c. 3. -धत्ते -धातुं).—(To mark with stains) मलिन (nom. मलिनयति -यितुं).—(To spoil) दुष् in caus. (दूषयति -यितुं).

BOTCHER, s. जीर्णवस्त्रसूचिकः, चीरवस्त्रभेदकः, कर्पटवस्त्रभेदी m. (न्).

BOTCHY, a. पामनः -ना -नं, दद्रुणः -णा -णं, कच्छुरः -रा -रं, सिध्मलः -ला -लं. व्रणमयः -यी -यं, मली -लिनी -लि (न्), सदोषः -षा -षं.

BOTH, a. उभौ m. du., उभयः -या -यं, द्वयं; 'on both sides,' उभयतस्, उभयत्र; 'in both ways,' उभयथा; 'for both objects,' उभयार्थं; 'both hands,' हस्तद्वयं.

BOTH, *conj.* (And) च -च.—(As well as) तथा. 'Both' may be expressed by the use of the indeclinable participle; as, 'he both labours and suffers reproach,' परिश्रम्य निन्दां भुंक्ते.

To BOTHER, v. a. क्लिश् (c. 9. क्लिश्नाति, क्लेशुं), पीड् (c. 10. पीडयति -यितुं), अभिपीड्, प्रपीड्, बाध् (c. 1. बाधते, बाधितुं), व्यथ् (c. 10. व्यथयति -यितुं).

BOTHERED, p. p. क्लेशितः -ता -तं, पीडितः -ता -तं, व्यथितः -ता -तं.

BOTTLE, s. काचकूपी, कूपी, कुतूः f., काचपात्रं, काचभाजनं, सुराभाजनं, मद्यभाजनं, पुटग्रीवः.

To BOTTLE, v. a. काचकूप्यां or कुत्वां निविश् in caus. (-वेशयति -यितुं).—(To bottle wine, &c.) कूपीं or कुतूं मद्येन पृ in caus. (पूरयति -यितुं).

BOTTLED, a. (Big-bellied) लम्बोदरः -रा -रं.—(As wine) कूपीनिवेशितः -ता -तं.

BOTTLESCREW, s. कुतूमध्ये or काचकूपीमध्ये यत् छिद्रप्रतिबन्धकं तरुत्वक्निर्म्मितं द्रव्यं विद्यते तदाकर्षणयोग्यं परिवर्त्तकयन्त्रं or कुटिलयन्त्रं.

BOTTOM, s. (The lowest part of any thing) अधोभागः, तलं, अधःस्थानं, अधोदेशः; 'the bottom of a tree,' वृक्षतलं.—(Low ground) दरीभूः f., दरी, निम्नभूमिः f., प्रान्तरं, उपत्यका, शैलोपशल्यं.—(Dregs) मलं, खलः, किट्टं, शेषं, अवशेषं.—(Foundation) मूलं.

To BOTTOM, v. n. (To rest upon) अवलम्ब् (c. 1. -लम्बते -लम्बितुं),

समालम्ब. Sometimes expressed by मूल in comp.; as, 'all actions are bottomed upon money,' धनमूलाः क्रियाः सर्वाः.

Bottomless, *a.* अतलस्पर्शः -र्शा -र्शं, तलहीनः -ना -नं, अगाधः -धा -धं.

Bougie, *s.* (Wax taper) सिक्थकमयो दीपः, वर्त्ती.

Bough, *s.* शाखा, विटपः, तरुविटपः, लता.

Bought, *p. p.* क्रीतः -ता -तं, क्रयक्रीतः -ता -तं.

To bounce, *v. n.* (To make a sudden noise) स्वन् (c. 1. स्वनति, स्वनितुं), ध्वन् (c. 1. ध्वनति, ध्वनितुं), क्वण् (c. 1. क्वणति, क्वणितुं).—(To spring against with great force) प्रस्कन्द् (c. 1. -स्कन्दति -स्कन्तुं), प्रपत् (c. 1. -पतति -पतितुं), अभिप्लु (c. 1. -प्लवते -प्लोतुं).—(To spring, leap) प्लु, उत्प्लु.—(To boast, bully) विकत्थ् (c. 1. -कत्थते -कत्थितुं), तर्ज् (c. 1. तर्जति, तर्जितुं).

Bounce, *s.* (A sudden noise) ध्वनिः *m.*, क्वणः, क्वणितं.—(A sudden blow) एकपाताभिघातः, अकस्मादाघातः.—(A boast, threat) विकत्थनं -त्था, भर्त्सनं.

Bouncer, *s.* (A boaster, bully) विकत्थी *m.* (न्), शूरम्मन्यः, भर्त्सनकारः, दाम्भिकः.

Bound, *s.* (A limit) अन्तः -न्तं, समन्तः, पर्य्यन्तं, प्रान्तः, सीमा, परिसीमा, अवधिः *m.*, मर्य्यादा; 'without bounds,' अनन्तः -न्ता -न्तं, अत्यन्तः -न्ता -न्तं.—(A leap) प्लवः, प्लवनं, प्लुतं.—(Rebound) प्रतिघातः, प्रतिहतिः *f.*, उत्प्लवः, उत्पतनं.

To bound, *v. a.* (To limit) प्रान्त (nom. प्रान्तयति -यितुं), समन्त, समर्य्यादं -दां -दं कृ, पर्य्यन्तं कृ.—(To restrain) नियम् (c. 1. -यच्छति -यन्तुं), निग्रह् (c. 9. -गृह्णाति -ग्रहीतुं).

To bound, *v. n.* प्लु (c. 1. प्लवते, प्लोतुं), वल्ग् (c. 1. वल्गति, वल्गितुं), आवल्ग्.—(To rebound) उत्प्लु, उत्पत् (c. 1. -पतति -पतितुं).

Bound, *p. p.* बद्धः -द्धा -द्धं, निबद्धः -द्धा -द्धं, निबन्धितः -ता -तं, सन्धितः -ता -तं, सन्धानितः -ता -तं, सन्दितः -ता -तं, मृतः -ता -तं, मूर्णः -र्णा -र्णं, उद्दितः -ता -तं, सितः -ता -तं.—(In leather) चर्म्मावनद्धः -द्धा -द्धं, चर्म्माच्छादितः -ता -तं; 'dignity is bound up with (dependent on) riches,' गौरवं धननिबन्धितं or धनप्रतिष्ठितं or धनसम्बद्धं.

Bound for, *part. a.* जिगमिषुः -षुः -षु, प्रस्थितः -ता -तं, प्रयातः -ता -तं, प्रयास्यन् -स्यन्ती -स्यत् (त्).

Boundary, *s.* सीमा *f.* -मा *m.* (न्) or परिसीमा, पर्य्यन्तं, अन्तः -न्तं, समन्तः, प्रान्तः, वलयः, अवधिः *m.*, मर्य्यादा, परिसरः, उपकण्ठं.—(On the boundary) पर्य्यन्तस्थः -स्था -स्थं; 'boundary tree,' सीमावृक्षः; 'boundary mark,' सीमालिङ्गं, सीमाचिह्नं, स्थलसीमा *m.* (न्).

Bounded, *p. p.* प्रान्तितः -ता -तं, समर्य्यादः -दा -दं, वलयितः -ता -तं.

Bounden, *a.* बद्धः -द्धा -द्धं, निबद्धः -द्धा -द्धं; 'a bounden duty,' अवश्यकता, कर्त्तव्यता, नियमः.

Bounding-stone, *s.* बालानां क्रीडाप्रस्तरः.

Boundless, *a.* अनन्तः -न्ता -न्तं, अमितः -ता -तं, अपरिमितः -ता -तं, अप्रमेयः -या -यं, अमेयः -या -यं, अत्यन्तः -न्ता -न्तं; 'of boundless glory,' अमिततेजाः -जाः -जः (स्).

Boundlessness, *s.* अनन्तता, आनन्त्यं, अत्यन्तता, अप्रमेयता, अमेयत्वं.

Bounteous, bountiful, *a.* दानशीलः -ला -लं, वदान्यः -न्या -न्यं, बहुप्रदः -दा -दं, अतिदाता -त्री -तृ (तृ), त्यागशीलः -ला -लं, दायकः -का -कं, स्थूललक्ष्यः -क्ष्या -क्ष्यं, उदारः -रा -रं, दयालुः -लुः -लु, मुक्तहस्तः -स्ता -स्तं, अकृपणः -णा -णं.

Bounteously, bountifully, *adv.* वदान्यवत्, वदान्यतया, उदारवत्, स्थूललक्ष्यतया, अतिदानेन, अतित्यागेन, दयापूर्व्वकं, अकार्पण्येन.

Bounteousness, bountifulness, *s.* दानशीलत्वं, स्थूललक्ष्यत्वं, अतिदानं, त्यागशीलता, त्यागिता, अतिसर्ज्जनं, वदान्यता, मुक्तहस्तत्वं, अकार्पण्यं, दयालुत्वं.

Bounty, *s.* (Favour) अनुग्रहः, दया, कृपा, प्रसादः.—(Generosity) वदान्यता, त्यागशीलता, दयालुत्वं.—(Gift) दानं, प्रदानं, स्वेच्छया दानं; 'king's bounty,' राजवर्त्तनं.

Bouquet, *s.* कुसुमस्तवकः, स्तवकः, पुष्पगुच्छः, गुच्छः, समाली, गुलुञ्छः.

To bourgeon, *v. n.* स्फुट् (c. 6. स्फुटति, स्फुटितुं), अङ्कुर (nom. अङ्कुरयति -यितुं).

Bourn, *s.* अन्तः -न्तं, पर्य्यन्तं, समन्तः, अवधिः *m.*, मर्य्यादा, सीमा.

To bouse, *v. n.* अतिशयेन सुरापानं or मद्यपानं कृ.

Bousy, *a.* मद्यपीतः -ता -तं, पानप्रसक्तः -क्ता -क्तं, क्षीवः -वा -वं.

Bout, *s.* (A turn) वारः, वासरः; 'at one bout,' एकवारे.—(A drinking bout) सम्पीतिः *f.*

Bow, *s.* (Salutation) नमस् *ind.*, प्रणामः, प्रणतिः *f.*, नमस्कारः.—(A rainbow) इन्द्रायुधं, शक्रधनुः *n.* (स्), इन्द्रचापः.—(A knot) ग्रन्थिः *m.*, पाशः.—(Of a ship) पोताग्रं, नौकाग्रं, नावो ऽग्रभागः, मङ्गः.

Bow, *s.* (A weapon) धनुः *m.*, -नुः *n.* (स्), -नु *n.*, धन्वा *m.*, -न्व *n.* (न्), चापः, शरासनं, कार्म्मुकं, इष्वासः, कोदण्डः or -ण्डं, शरावापः; 'middle of the bow,' लस्तकः, धनुर्मध्यं.—(For playing stringed instruments) कोणः, शारिका, परिवादः.—(Bow of Arjuna) गाण्डीवः.—(Of Karńa) कालपृष्ठं.—(Of Siva) पिनाकः, अजगवं.

To bow, *v. a.* (To bend) नम् in caus. (नामयति or नमयति -यितुं) or नम् (c. 1. नमति, नन्तुं), प्रणम्, अभिनम्, विनम्, अवनम्, आनम्; कुञ्च् (c. 1. कुञ्चति, कुञ्चितुं), नम्रीकृ, प्रह्वीकृ, भुग्नीकृ.—(To bow the head) शिरसा प्रणम्.

To bow, *v. n.* नम् (c. 1. नमति, नन्तुं), प्रणम्, अभिनम्, विनम्, नम्रीभू; 'bowing the body,' प्रणम्य कायं; 'bowing the head,' प्रणम्य शिरसा, प्रह्वीभू.—(To submit, yield) क्षम् (c. 1. क्षमते, क्षमितुं, क्षन्तुं), अभ्युपे (-उपैति -उपैतुं).

Bow-bent, *a.* धनुराकृतिः -तिः -ति, कुटिलः -ला -लं, वक्रः -क्रा -क्रं.

Bowed, *p. p.* नतः -ता -तं, नामितः -ता -तं, आनतः -ता -तं, अवनतः -ता -तं, परिणतः -ता -तं, प्रणतः -ता -तं, अवनतः -ता -तं, नम्रः -म्रा -म्रं, नम्रमूर्त्तिः -र्त्तिः -र्त्ति, प्रह्वः -ह्वा -ह्वं, प्रह्वीकृतः -ता -तं.

Bowels, *s.* अन्त्रं *n. sing.*, अन्त्राणि *n. pl.*, नाड्यः *f. pl.*, कोष्ठः *m. sing.*—(Compassion) कृपा, दया.—(The inner part) अभ्यन्तरं, गर्भः, विलं, विवरं.

Bower, *s.* कुञ्जः, निकुञ्जः, मञ्जरीकुञ्जः, लतानिर्म्मितं मन्दिरं, कुञ्जकुटीरः, मण्डपः, क्लाटः, वल्लुरं, कुटङ्गकः.—(Cottage) कुटीरः. पर्णशाला.—(Anchor) नौकाया अग्रभागे स्थापितो ऽङ्कुशाकारो लोहबन्धः.

To bower, *v. a.* परिवेष्ट् (c. 1. -वेष्टते -वेष्टितुं), परिच्छद् (c. 10. -छादयति -यितुं).

Bowery, *a.* कुञ्जवान् -वती -वत् (त्), लतावृतः -ता -तं, लतापरिच्छन्नः -न्ना -न्नं.

Bowl, *s.* (A vessel for liquids) पात्रं, भाजनं, कंसः -सं, शरावः, पुटकः.—(A ball) गुलिका.—(The bowl, poison) विषं.

To bowl, *v. a.* गुलिकाम् आवृत् in caus. (-वर्त्तयति -यितुं).—(To play at bowls) गुलिकाभिः क्रीड् (c. 1. क्रीडति, क्रीडितुं).

Bowler, *s.* गुलिकावर्त्तनकृत्, गुलिकावर्त्तकः, गुलिकाक्रीडाकृत्.

Bow-legged, *a.* प्रज्ञुः -ज्ञुः -ज्ञु, प्रगतजानुः -नुः -नु, विरलजानुः -नुः -नु.

Bowling-green, *a.* गुलिकाक्रीडायोग्यं समस्थलं or समस्थलीकृतो भूभागः.

Bowman, *s.* धन्वी *m.* (न्), धनुष्मान् *m.* (त्), धानुष्कः, धनुर्धारी *m.* (न्), धनुर्धरः, धनुर्भृत् *m.*, इष्वासः, इषुधरः, काण्डीरः, काण्डवान् *m.* (त्),

निषङ्गी *m.* (न्), अस्त्री *m.* (न्), शार्ङ्गी *m.* (न्).

Bowshot, *s.* बाणगोचरं, शरगोचरं, धनुःक्षेपणं, शरक्षेपः.

Bowsprit, *s.* पोताग्रबहिःप्रलम्बो गुणवृक्षकः. *See* Boltsprit.

Bowstring, *s.* ज्या, गुणः, धनुर्गुणः, मौर्वी, भारवं, शिञ्जिनी, तावरं, पतञ्चिका.

Bow-window, *s.* धनुराकृति वातायनं, धनुराकारो गवाक्षः, प्रग्रीवः.

Bowyer, *s.* धनुर्धरः, धनुर्भृत् *m.*, धन्वी *m.* (न्), धनुष्मान् *m.* (त्).

Box, *s.* (A kind of tree) अतिदृढो वृक्षप्रभेदः.—(A case to hold any thing) भाण्डं, सम्पुटः, सम्पुटकः, मुद्राधारः, आधारः, पात्रं, भाजनं, समुद्गः, पेटिका, वासनं.—(For spectators) प्रेक्षागारं.—(A blow) मुष्ट्याघातः, मुष्टिप्रहारः, मुष्टिपातः, पाणिघातः, कराघातः, कीला, आघातः, प्रहारः, बाहुप्रहरणं.

To **box**, *v. n.* (To fight with the fist) मल्लयुद्धं कृ, मुष्ट्या युध् (c. 4. युध्यते, योद्धुं), मुष्टीमुष्टि or बाहूबाहवि युध्.

To **box**, *v. a.* (To strike with the fist) मुष्ट्या अभिहन् (c. 2. -हन्ति -हन्तुं), निहन्, or तड् (c. 10. ताडयति -यितुं) or प्रहृ (c. 1. -हरति -हर्त्तुं).—(To enclose in a box) सम्पुटके or भाण्डे निविश् in caus. (-वेशयति -यितुं) or निधा (c. 3. -दधाति -धातुं).

Boxen, *a.* पुष्टीलवृक्षकाष्ठनिर्म्मितः -ता -तं.

Boxer, *s.* मल्लयोधः, मल्लः, मल्लः, पाणिघातः, बाहुप्रहरणः, बाहुयोधी *m.* (न्), रङ्गावतारी *m.* (न्).

Boxing, *s.* मौष्टा, मल्लयुद्धं, मुष्टिपातः, पाणिघातः, बाहुयुद्धं, बाहुप्रहरणं.—(Boxing-match) मल्लयात्रा.

Boy, *s.* कुमारः -रकः, बालः, बालकः, पुत्रः, पुत्रकः, अप्राप्तव्यवहारः.—(A word of contempt for a young man) माणवः, माणवकः; 'multitude of boys,' माणव्यं.

Boyhood, *s.* बालकत्वं, बाल्यं, शैशवं, शिशुत्वं, कौमारं, कैशोरं, माणव्यं.

Boyish, *a.* बालिशः -शा -शं, बालेयः -या -यं, बालकीयः -या -यं, बालकशीलः -ला -लं, कौमारः -री -रं, शिशुयोग्यः -ग्या -ग्यं, माणवीनः -ना -नं.

Boyishly, *adv.* बालकरूपेण, बालकवत्, शिशुवत्, कुमारवत्, बालिशप्रकारेण.

Boyishness, *s.* बालिश्यं, बालेयत्वं, बालकत्वं, कुमारशीलत्वं, शिशुशीलता.

Brabble, *s.* कलहः, व्यवक्रोशनं, विवादः, वाग्युद्धं, विप्रलापः, द्वन्द्वं.

To **brabble**, *v. n.* कलह (nom. कलहायते -यितुं), व्यवक्रुश् (c. 1. -क्रोशति -क्रोष्टुं).

To **brace**, *v. a.* बन्ध् (c. 9. बध्नाति, बन्द्धुं), योक्त्र (nom. योक्त्रयति -यितुं).—(To strain up, tighten) सन्निबन्ध्, संस्तम्भ् (c. 9. -स्तभ्नाति -स्तम्भितुं), दृढ (nom. दृढयति -यितुं).

Brace, *s.* (A pair) युगं, युग्मं, युगलं, द्वयं, यमलं, यामलं.—(Bandage) बन्धनं, बन्धः.—(Strap) चर्म्मबन्धः -न्धनं.—(Of a coach) रथालम्बि चर्म्मबन्धादि.—(Of a ship) नौकासम्बन्धी रज्जुविशेषः.

Bracelet, *s.* वलयः -यं, कङ्कणं, करभूषणं, अङ्गदं, हस्तसूत्रं, वालकः, आवापकः, पारिहार्य्यः, कटकः.

Brachial, *a.* बाहुसम्बन्धी -न्धिनी -न्धि (न्).

Brachygraphy, *s.* सङ्क्षिप्तलिखनविद्या, सङ्क्षिप्ताक्षरलिखनं, सङ्केतलेखनविद्या.

Bracket, *s.* नागदन्तः -न्तकः, नागः, हस्तिदन्तः, गजदन्तः, नालेयः.

Brackish, *a.* क्षाररसयुक्तः -क्ता -क्तं, ईषल्लवणः -णा -णं, क्षारसंसृष्टः -ष्टा -ष्टं.

Brackishness, *s.* क्षारः, क्षारत्वं, क्षाररसः.

Brad, *s.* लोहमयः कीलविशेषः, क्षुद्रशङ्कुः *m.*

To **brag**, *v. n.* कत्थ् (c. 1. कत्थते, कत्थितुं), विकत्थ्, श्लाघ् (c. 1. श्लाघते, श्लाघितुं), with inst. of the thing, आत्मानं श्लाघ्.

Brag, *s.* अहङ्कारोक्तिः *f.*, विकत्था -त्थनं, दम्भः, आहोपुरुषिका, अहमहमिका, आत्मश्लाघा, गर्व्वितवाक्यं, शूरमानं, परिकीर्त्तनं.

Braggart, braggadocio, bragger, *s.* शूरम्मन्यः, शूरमानी *m.* (न्), पिण्डीशूरः, उपजल्पी *m.* (न्), विकत्थी *m.* (न्), अवलिप्तः, अहङ्कारी *m.* (न्), अहङ्कारपूर्णः, आत्मश्लाघी *m.* (न्).

Braggingly, *adv.* अहङ्कारेण, साहङ्कारं, विकत्थया, आत्मश्लाघापूर्व्वं, दम्भात्.

Brahmá, *s.* (The first deity of the Hindu triad, the Creator of the world, Providence) ब्रह्मा *m.* (न्), वेधाः *m.* (स्), विधिः *m.*, विरिञ्चिः *m.*, द्रुहिणः.—(As creator of the world) स्रष्टा *m.* (ष्टृ), विश्वसृक् -ड् (ज्).—(Born in the lotus which sprung from the navel of Vishńu) नाभिजः, नाभिभूः *m.*, अब्जजः, अब्जयोनिः, पद्मगर्भः, पद्मभूः *m.*, पद्मासनः, कमलासनः.—(The self-existent) स्वयम्भूः *m.*, आत्मभूः *m.*—(Born from the golden egg) हिरण्यगर्भः.—(As elder of the deities) सुरज्येष्ठः.—(The four-faced one) चतुर्म्मुखः, चतुराननः.—(The great father and lord of all) पितामहः, प्रजापतिः *m.*, लोकेशः.—(Supporter of all) धाता *m.* (तृ), विधाता *m.* (तृ).—(Exalted in heaven) परमेष्ठः -ष्ठी *m.* (न्).

Brahmin or bráhman, *s.* ब्राह्मणः, विप्रः, वाडवः.—(As the first-born among mortals) अग्रजन्मा *m.* (न्).—(As receiving second birth at his investiture with the sacred thread) द्विजः, द्विजातिः *m.*, द्विजन्मा *m.* (न्).—(As learned in the Vedas) श्रोत्रियः.—(As a deity upon earth) भूदेवः, भूमिदेवः.—(As born from the mouth of Brahmá) मुखजः.—(A Brahmin by birth but not by duties) ब्राह्मणब्रुवः.—(The wife of a Brahmin) ब्राह्मणी.—(The condition of a Brahmin) ब्राह्मण्यं, ब्राह्मणता.

Brahminical, *a.* ब्राह्मः -ह्मी -ह्मं, ब्राह्मणजातीयः -या -यं; 'the brahminical caste,' ब्राह्मणजातिः *f.*

Brahminicide, *s.* ब्रह्महत्या, ब्राह्मणवधः.—(One who kills a Brahmin) ब्रह्महा *m.* (न्).

To **braid**, *v. a.* वेणीकृ, वेणिरूपेण केशान् रच् (c. 10. रचयति -यितुं) or ग्रन्थ् (c. 9. ग्रथ्नाति, c. 1. ग्रन्थति, ग्रन्थितुं) or केशसंस्कारं कृ.—(Weave, interweave) वे (c. 1. वयति, वातुं), ग्रन्थ्, उत्खच् (c. 10. -खचयति -यितुं).

Braid, *s.* (Of hair) वेणिः -णी *f.*, प्रवेणिः, कबरः -री, धम्मिल्लः, केशवेशः, केशगर्भः.—(A knot) ग्रन्थिः *m.*, बन्धः.

Braided, *p. p.* वेणीभूतः -ता -तं, ग्रथितः -ता -तं, कबरः -री -रं.

Brain, *s.* मस्तिष्कं or -ष्कः, गोर्दं, मस्तकस्नेहः.—(Intellect) बुद्धिः *f.*, मतिः *f.*, धीः *f.*

To **brain**, *v. a.* मस्तकं निर्भिद्य मस्तिष्कं बहिःकृत्य हन् (c. 2. हन्ति, हन्तुं).

Brainish, *a.* मदोन्मत्तः -त्ता -त्तं, मदोत्कटः -टा -टं, उन्मत्तः -त्ता -त्तं.

Brainless, *a.* मस्तिष्कहीनः -ना -नं, निर्बुद्धिः -द्धिः -द्धि, दुर्म्मतिः -तिः -ति.

Brainpan, *s.* कपालः -लं, मस्तकः -कं, कर्प्परः, शिरोस्थि *n.*, मुण्डः, करोटः, शीर्षकं.

Brainsick, *a.* मूढबुद्धिः -द्धिः -द्धि, विभ्रान्तशीलः -ला -लं, चपलमतिः -तिः -ति.

Brainsickness, *s.* मूढता, चपलत्वं, चपलत्वं, प्रामादं, प्रमादित्वं.

Brake, *s.* (A thicket of brambles) कण्टकगहनं, गुल्मगहनं, कण्टः -टं.—(A snaffle) खलीनः -नं, मुखयन्त्रणं.—(That which moves a military engine) युद्धयन्त्रवाहनं, युद्धयन्त्रचालनसाधनं.

Bramble, *s.* कण्टकगुल्मः, कण्टकलता, शृगालकोलिः *m.*, शृगालकण्टकः, गोक्षुरः.

Brambly, *a.* शृगालकण्टकावृतः -ता -तं, कण्टकी -किनी -कि (न्).

Bramin, *s.* *See* Brahmin.

BRAN, *s.* तुषः -षा, धान्यकल्कं, धान्यत्वक् *f.* (च्), बुसं.

BRANCH, *s.* शाखा, लता, विटपः, तरुविटपः, तरुभुजः, काण्डः, विस्तारः; 'a large branch,' स्कन्धशाखा, शाला.—(Of a river) कुसरित् *f.*, उपनदी, उपसरित्, अल्पनदी, नदीवङ्कः, वङ्कुः *f.*, प्रणालः -ली.—(A section, subdivision) शाखा, अङ्कः, सर्गः, परिच्छेदः, विच्छेदः, अङ्गस्कन्धः; 'a branch of the Vedas,' वेदाङ्गः.—(Offspring) कुलसन्ततिः *f.*, कुलसन्तानः, अपत्यं, प्रवरं.

To BRANCH, *v. n.* शाखा (nom. शाखायते), लता (nom. लतायते), शाखारूपेण विस्तॄ in pass. (-स्तीर्य्यते) or भिन्नीभू or विभिद् in pass. (-भिद्यते) or विछिद् in pass. (-छिद्यते).—(To speak diffusely) विस्तरशस् or सुविस्तरं वद् (c. 1. वदति, वदितुं).

To BRANCH, *v. a.* शाखावत् पृथक्कृ or विभिद् (c. 7. -भिनत्ति -भेत्तुं).

BRANCHLESS, *a.* शाखाहीनः -ना -नं, विटपरहितः -ता -तं, अभिन्नः -न्ना -न्नं.

BRANCHY, *a.* शाखी -खिनी -खि (न्), शाखाढ्यः -ढ्या -ढ्यं, विस्तीर्णशाखः -खा -खं, काण्डीरः -रा -रं, विस्तीर्णः -र्णा -र्णं, विस्तारयुक्तः -क्ता -क्तं, विभिन्नः -न्ना -न्नं.

BRAND, *s.* (A burning stick) उल्का, दग्धकाष्ठं, तप्तकाष्ठं.—(A mark of infamy) अपकीर्त्तिचिह्नं, अभिशस्ताङ्कः, अङ्कः, अङ्कनं.

To BRAND, *v. a.* अपमानचिह्नेन अङ्क् (c. 10. अङ्कयति -यितुं), तप्तलोहेन चिह्न् (c. 10. चिह्नयति -यितुं), अभिशस्ताङ्कं कृ.

BRANDED, *p. p.* अपमानचिह्नाङ्कितः -ता -तं, अभिशस्ताङ्कचिह्नितः -ता -तं, कृताङ्कः -ङ्का -ङ्कं; 'branded with infamy,' दुर्नामग्रस्तः -स्ता -स्तं.

To BRANDISH, *v. a.* भ्रम् in caus. (भ्रमयति or भ्रामयति -यितुं); 'they brandished their pikes,' शूलानि भ्रमयाञ्चक्रुः; विधू (c. 5. -धूनोति -धवितुं), उज्ज्वल् in caus. (-ज्वालयति -यितुं), व्याव्यध् (c. 4. -विध्यति -व्यद्धुं).

BRANDISHED, *p. p.* उद्भ्रामितः -ता -तं, अवधूतः -ता -तं, उज्ज्वालितः -ता -तं.

BRANDLING, *s.* कृमिप्रभेदः स च मत्स्यप्रलोभार्थं कदाचिद् वडिशे निवेश्यते.

BRANDY, *s.* मद्यशुक्ता, मद्यासवं, सुरा, आसवं, शीधुः *m.*, वारुणी.

BRANGLE, *s.* (Squabble) व्यावक्रोशी, व्यवक्रोशनं, उच्चैर्भाषणं, कलहः, विप्रलापः.

BRANNY, *a.* तुषाकृतिः -तिः -ति, तुषमयः -यी -यं, धान्यत्वङ्मयः -यी -यं.

BRASIER or BRAZIER, *s.* (Worker in brass) ताम्रकारः, कांस्यकारः, कामन्धमी *m.* (न्).—(A pan to hold coals) अङ्गारशकटी, अङ्गारपात्रं.

BRASIERY, *s.* कुप्यशाला, सन्धानी.

BRASS, *s.* रीतिः *f.*, रैत्यं, आरः, ताम्रं, कांस्यं -स्यकं, पित्तलं, पीतलोहं, पीतलं -लकं, आरकूटः -टं.—(Impudence) निर्लज्जता, धार्ष्ट्यं, प्रगल्भता.

BRASSY, *a.* रैत्यः -त्यी -त्यं, कांस्यमयः -यी -यं, पित्तलगुणविशिष्टः -ष्टा -ष्टं.

BRAT, *s.* शिशुः *m.*, बालकः, बालः, पृथुकः, शावकः.

BRAVADO, *s.* विकत्था, अहङ्कारवाक्यं, आत्मश्लाघा, आहोपुरुषिका, अहमहमिका.

BRAVE, *a.* शूरः -रा -रं, वीरः -रा -रं, प्रवीरः -रा -रं, पराक्रान्तः -न्ता -न्तं, विक्रान्तः -न्ता -न्तं, निर्भयः -या -यं, धृष्टः -ष्टा -ष्टं, साहसिकः -की -कं, उद्धतः -ता -तं.—(Excellent) साधुः -धुः -धु, उत्तमः -मा -मं, प्रशस्तः -स्ता -स्तं.—(Noble) उदारः -रा -रं.

BRAVE, *s.* (A bully) शूरम्मन्यः, दम्भी *m.* (न्).—(Defiance) समाह्वानं, क्रन्दनं, आस्पर्द्धा.

To BRAVE, *v. a.* (To menace) भर्त्स् (c. 10. भर्त्सयते -यितुं), अभिभर्त्स्, अवभर्त्स्, परिभर्त्स्, तर्ज् (c. 1. तर्जति, तर्जितुं).—(To challenge) आह्वे (c. 1. -ह्वयते -ह्वातुं), समाह्वे, क्रन्दनं कृ, स्पर्ध् (c. 1. स्पर्धते, स्पर्धितुं).

To BRAVE, *v. n.* (To carry a boasting appearance) दाम्भिकवद् वृत् (c. 1. वर्त्तते, वर्त्तितुं) or चर् (c. 1. चरति, चरितुं), धृष् (c. 5. धृष्णोति, धर्षितुं), दृप् (c. 4. दृप्यति, द्रप्तुं).

BRAVED, *p. p.* (Challenged) आहूतः -ता -तं, समाहूतः -ता -तं.

BRAVELY, *adv.* (In a brave manner) सवीर्य्यं, शूरवत्, वीरवत्, अभीतवत्, सपराक्रमं, शौर्य्येण, निर्भयं, प्रसभं.—(Excellently) साधु, प्रशस्तं, सु prefixed.

BRAVERY, *s.* शूरता, शौर्य्यं, वीरता, वीर्य्यं, पराक्रमः, विक्रमः, कापेयराहित्यं; 'to show bravery in battle,' पराक्रम् (c. 1. -क्रमति -क्रमितुं), विक्रम्.—(Bravado, boast) विकत्था, आस्पर्द्धा.—(Magnificence) प्रतापः, तेजः *n.* (स्).

BRAVINGLY, *adv.* दाम्भिकवत्, सदम्भं, आह्वानपूर्व्वकं, समाह्वानक्रमेण.

BRAVO, *interj.* साधु.—(A murderer) घातकः, दस्युः *m.*, आततायी *m.* (न्).

To BRAWL, *v. n.* व्यवक्रुश् (c. 1. -क्रोशति -क्रोष्टुं), कलह (nom. कलहायते -यितुं), वैर (nom. वैरायते -यितुं), विवद् (c. 1. -वदति -वदितुं), विप्रलप् (c. 1. -लपति -लपितुं).

BRAWL, *s.* कलहः, व्यवक्रोशः, व्यावक्रोशी, आक्रोशः, उच्चैर्भाषणं, उच्चैर्घुष्टं, व्यावभाषी, विवादः, वाग्युद्धं, विप्रलापः, द्वन्द्वं, संरावः.

BRAWLER, *s.* कलहकारः -री *m.* (न्), कलहप्रियः, विरोधी *m.* (न्), कलिप्रियः, युयुत्सुः *m.*

BRAWN, *s.* (The flesh of a boar) शूकरमांसं.—(The musculous part of the body) स्नायुः *f.*, स्नसा.—(The arm) बाहुः *m.*—(A boar) शूकरः, वराहः.

BRAWNINESS, *s.* मांसलत्वं, दृढाङ्गता, शरीरदृढता, द्रढिमा *m.* (न्).

BRAWNY, *a.* मांसलः -ला -लं, स्नायुमान् -मती -मत् (त्), दृढाङ्गः -ङ्गी -ङ्गं.

To BRAY, *v. a.* (To pound) चूर्ण् (c. 10. चूर्णयति -यितुं), प्रचूर्ण्, विचूर्ण्, पिष् (c. 7. पिनष्टि, पेष्टुं), निष्पिष्, विनिष्पिष्, उत्पिष्.

To BRAY, *v. n.* (Like an ass) गर्दभवद् रु (c. 2. रौति, रवितुं) or चित्कारं कृ or नद् (c. 1. नदति, नदितुं).

BRAY, *s.* खरनादः, गर्दभनादः, गर्दभरावः, चित्कारः, खरशब्दः, नादः.

BRAYER, *s.* (One that brays like an ass) खरनादी *m.* (न्), नादी *m.* (न्), चित्कारकृत्.—(One that pounds) चूर्णकः, निष्पेष्टा *m.* (ष्टृ), पेषकः.

To BRAZEN, *v. n.* धृष् (c. 5. धृष्णोति, धर्षितुं), अभिभर्त्स् (c. 10. -भर्त्सयते -यितुं).

BRAZEN, *a.* रैत्यः -त्यी -त्यं, पित्तलमयः -यी -यं, ताम्रिकः -की -कं.—(Impudent) निर्लज्जः -ज्जा -ज्जं, धृष्टः -ष्टा -ष्टं.

BRAZEN-FACED, *a.* निर्लज्जमुखः -खी -खं, लज्जाहीनः -ना -नं, त्यक्तव्रीडः -डा -डं.

BRAZENNESS, *s.* रैत्यत्वं.—(Impudence) निर्लज्जता, धृष्टता, प्रगल्भता.

BRAZIER, *s.* ताम्रकारः, कांस्यकारः. *See* BRASIER.

BREACH, *s.* भङ्गः, भेदः, छेदः, खण्डं, रन्ध्रं, छिद्रं.—(The act of breaking) भञ्जनं, भेदनं, खण्डनं.—(A gap in a wall) सन्धिः *m.*, गृहरन्ध्रं, खानिकं, सुरङ्गा, कुड्यच्छेदः.—(Violation) अतिक्रमः, लङ्घनं, उल्लङ्घनं.—(Violation of a law) व्यवस्थातिक्रमः, व्यवस्थालङ्घनं.—(Breach of promise) प्रतिज्ञाभङ्गः.—(Breach of confidence) विश्वासभङ्गः.—(Separation of friendship) सुहृद्भेदः, विरोधः, विच्छेदः.

BREAD, *s.* अपूपः, पूपः, पिष्टकः, खाद्यं, अभ्यूषः.—(Food in general) अन्नं, आहारः, भोजनं.

BREAD-CORN, *s.* गोधूमः, सुमनाः *m.* (स्), सुमनः, शस्यं, धान्यं, आपूप्यं.

BREAD-FRUIT, *s.* पनसः, पनसनालिका, कण्टकिफलः, कण्टकफलः.

BREADTH, *s.* पृथुता, पार्थवं, प्रथिमा *m.* (न्), विशालता, विपुलता, विस्तारः, विस्तीर्णता, परिसरः, प्रस्थः, विततिः *f.*, आयामः, आयतनं, पाटः.

To BREAK, *v. a.* (Burst or part asunder by force) भञ्ज् (c. 7. भनक्ति, भंक्तुं), निभञ्ज्, विनिर्भञ्ज्, प्रभञ्ज्; भिद् (c. 7. भिनत्ति, भेत्तुं), खण्ड् (c. 10. खण्डयति -यितुं), परिखण्ड्, दॄ in caus. (-दारयति -यितुं), स्फुट् (c. 10. स्फोटयति -यितुं), रुज् (c. 6. रुजति, रोक्तुं), अवरुज्, आरुज्,

समारुज् ; क्षुद् (c. 7. क्षुणत्ति, क्षोत्तुं), प्रक्षुद् ; शकलीकृ, दल् in caus. (दालयति -यितुं), विदल्.—(Penetrate, break through) व्यध् (c. 4. विध्यति, व्यद्धुं), निर्भिद्, छिद्र् (c. 10. छिद्रयति -यितुं).—(Crush) मृद् (c. 9. मृद्नाति, मर्द्दितुं), पिष् (c. 7. पिनष्टि, पेष्टुं).—(Break or sink the spirit) मनो भञ्ज् or हन् (c. 2. हन्ति, हन्तुं) or प्रतिहन्, भग्नाशं -शां -शं कृ, आशाविभिन्नं -न्नां -न्नं कृ, खण्डिताशंसं -सां -सं कृ.—(Tame) दम् in caus. (दमयति -यितुं or c. 4. दाम्यति, दमितुं), प्रदम् ; विनी (c. 1. -नयति -नेतुं).—(Make bankrupt) परिक्षीणं -णां -णं कृ, निर्धनीकृ.—(Overcome) पराजि (c. 1. -जयति -ते -जेतुं).—(Break down, destroy) अवभञ्ज्, प्रभञ्ज्, विनश् in caus. (-नाशयति -यितुं), उच्छिद् (c. 7. -छिनत्ति -छेत्तुं).—(Violate a promise) संविदं व्यतिक्रम् (c. 1. -क्रामति -क्रमितुं), विसंवद् (c. 1. -वदति -वदितुं), विसंविद् (c. 2. -वेत्ति -वेदितुं).—(Infringe a law) व्यवस्थाम् अतिक्रम् or व्यतिक्रम् or लङ्घ् (c. 1. लङ्घते, लङ्घितुं, c. 10. लङ्घयति -यितुं), उल्लङ्घ्, विलङ्घ्, or अतिचर् (c. 1. -चरति -चरितुं) or लुप् in caus. (लोपयति -यितुं).—(Break a vow) व्रतं लुप् in caus.—(Interrupt) लुप्, विलुप्, विप्रलुप् in caus., उच्छिद्, विच्छिद्, प्रतिहन्, अभ्यर्द् (c. 2. -र्त्ति -र्त्तुं).—(Break intelligence) प्रथमसंवादं कृ, प्रथमाख्यानं कृ.—(Break the heart) दलद्धृदयं -यां -यं कृ, भग्नान्तःकरणं -णां -णं कृ.—(Break into a house) सन्धिं कृ, कुड्यं छिद्.—(Break a bone) अस्थि भञ्ज् or भिद्.—(Make to cease) निवृत् in caus. (-वर्त्तयति -यितुं).—(Separate) वियुज् (c. 7. -युनक्ति -युंक्ते -योक्तुं).—(Break off, relinquish) त्यज् (c. 1. त्यजति, त्यक्तुं).—(Reform a bad habit) दोषत्यजनं कृ.—(Dissolve friendship) सौहृदं भिद्.—(Break one's sleep) निद्रां भञ्ज्, निद्राभङ्गं कृ.—(Break one's fast) पारणं कृ, प्रातर्भोजनं कृ, उपवासानन्तरं प्रथमाहारं कृ.—(Break wind) पर्द् (c. 1. पर्दते, पर्दितुं), गुदरवं कृ.

To BREAK, *v. n.* (Part in two) भञ्ज् in pass. (भज्यते), भिद् in pass. (भिद्यते), विभिद्, विच्छिद् in pass. (-छिद्यते), त्रुट् (c. 4. त्रुट्यति, त्रुटितुं), विद् in pass. (-दीर्य्यते), स्फुट् (c. 6. स्फुटति, स्फुटितुं), शकलीभू.—(Dawn) प्रभा (c. 2. -भाति -भातुं), उष् (c. 1. ओषति, ओषितुं or उच्छति, उच्छितुं), व्युष्, समुष्.—(Open as a sore) पूय् (c. 1. पूयते, पूयितुं), पूयनं कृ, पक्कः -क्का -क्कं भू.—(Become bankrupt) परिक्षीणः -णा -णं भू.—(Decline, decay) जॄ (c. 4. जीर्य्यति, जरितुं, जरीतुं), क्षि in pass. (क्षीयते), क्षै (c. 1. क्षायति, क्षातुं), ध्वंस् (c. 1. ध्वंसते, ध्वंसितुं), सद् (c. 1. सीदति, सत्तुं), विनश् (c. 4. -नश्यति -नशितुं -नंष्टुं), विशॄ in pass. (-शीर्य्यते).—(Part friendship) विरञ्ज् in pass. (-रज्यते).—(Break in, force one's way in) बलात् or प्रसह्य प्रविश् (c. 6. -विशति -वेष्टुं), आपत्, (c. 1. -पतति -पतितुं), अभिपत्, अवलुप् (c. 6. -लुम्पति -लोप्तुं).—(Break forth) प्रपत् (c. 1. -पतति -पतितुं), निष्पत्.—(Break loose) प्रमुच् in pass. (-मुच्यते), विप्रमुच्.—(Break off, desist suddenly) अकस्मात् विरम् (c. 1. -रमति -रन्तुं) or निवृत् (c. 1. -वर्त्तते -वर्त्तितुं).—(Break out, arise suddenly) अकस्मात् उत्पद् (c. 4. -पद्यते -पत्तुं) or जन् (c. 4. जायते, जनितुं) or दृश् in pass. (दृश्यते) or प्रभू.—(Break up) विगम् (c. 1. -गच्छति -गन्तुं), निवृत्.—(Break forth, as fire) प्रज्वल् (c. 1. -ज्वलति -ते -ज्वलितुं).—(Break, as waves) भङ्गरूपेण प्रलुठ् (c. 1. -लोठति -लोठितुं).

BREAK, *s.* (Interruption) विच्छेदः, छेदः, अन्तरायः.—(Cessation) विरामः, विरतिः *f.*, निर्वृतिः *f.*, निवृत्तिः *f.*, उपशमः, क्षयः.—(Opening of the day) अरुणोदयः, प्रभातं, उदयः, दिवसमुखं, उषः ; 'at break of day,' प्रभाते, प्रातःकाले ; 'breaking a blood-vessel,' उरोक्षतं.

BREAKER, *s.* (One who breaks) भंक्ता *m.* (कृ), भञ्जकः, भङ्गकारः, भेदकः, भेदी *m.* (न्), विदारकः.—(Destroyer) नाशकः.—(A wave breaking over a sandbank) सैकतसूचको भङ्गः, भङ्गिः *f.*, -ङ्गी, तरलायितः, लहरिः *f.*, कल्लोलः, तरङ्गः.

BREAKFAST, *s.* प्रातर्भोजनं, प्रातराशः, कल्यवर्त्तः, कल्यजग्धिः *f.*, प्रथमाहारः.

To BREAKFAST, *v. n.* प्रातर्भोजनं or प्रातराशं कृ, प्रथमाहारं कृ.

BREAKFASTED, *p. p.* प्रातराशितः -ता -तं.

BREAKING, *s.* भङ्गः, भञ्जनं, भेदः, भेदनं, खण्डनं, शकलीकरणं, विदारणं.—(Breaking down) प्रभङ्गः.—(Breaking a vow) व्रतलोपनं.

BREAM, *s.* पृथुशरीरो मत्स्यभेदः.

BREAST, *s.* वक्षः *n.* (स्), उरः *n.* (स्), वक्षस्स्थलं or वक्षःस्थलं, क्रोडं -डा, अङ्कः, वत्सं, भुजान्तरं, हृदयस्थानं.—(Female breast) स्तनः, स्तनौ *m. du.*, स्तनकुट्मलं, कुचः, कुचतटं, वक्षोरुहः, वक्षोजं, उरसिजः, उरोजः.—(Heart) हृदयं, अन्तःकरणं, मनः *n.* (स्), चित्तं, मर्म्म *n.* (न्).

BREAST-BONE, *s.* वक्षोऽस्थि *n.*, उरोऽस्थि *n.*

BREAST-HIGH, *a.* वक्षोदघ्नः -घ्ना -घ्नं, वक्षोदेशपर्य्यन्तः -न्ता -न्तं.

BREAST-PLATE, *s.* कवचं, उरस्त्राणं, वक्षस्त्राणं, उरश्छदः, आयसी *f.*, नागोदरं, वारवाणः.

BREASTWORK, *s.* वक्षोदेशपर्य्यन्तं दुर्गप्राचीरं, वक्षःसमानः प्राकारः.

BREATH, *s.* प्राणः, श्वासः, श्वसितं, असुः *m.*—(Inspiration and expiration) श्वासप्रश्वासं, श्वासनिःश्वासं.—(Pause, respite) उच्छ्वासः, विरामः, उपशमः.—(Out of breath) उच्छ्वसन् -सन्ती -सती -सत् (त्), उच्छ्वसितः -ता -तं, यष्टिप्राणः -णा -णं.—(Holding one's breath) श्वासप्रश्वासधारणं.—(Breeze, moving air) समश्वासः, मृदुवातः, मन्दानिलः, अनिलः, समीरणः.

To BREATHE, *v. n.* श्वस् (c. 2. श्वसिति, श्वसितुं), आश्वस्, उच्छ्वस्, प्राण् (c. 2. प्राणिति, प्राणितुं).—(To inspire and expire) श्वासप्रश्वासं कृ, श्वासनिःश्वासं कृ.—(To live) जीव् (c. 1. जीवति, जीवितुं).—(To take breath, recover breath) प्रत्याश्वस्.

To BREATHE, *v. a.* (To inspire) श्वस् (c. 2. श्वसिति, श्वसितुं).—(To breathe forth, expire) निःश्वस्, प्रश्वस्.—(To exhale) प्रवा (c. 2. -वाति -वातुं).

BREATHING, *s.* श्वासः, श्वासप्रश्वासं, प्राणः, श्वसितं.—(Ardent wish) आकाङ्क्षा, स्पृहा, लालसा. *Part.* प्राणन् -णन्ती -णत् (त्), श्वसन् -सती -सन्ती -सत् (त्), असुमान् -मती -मत् (त्), प्राणभृत् *m. f. n.*—(Breathing through the nose) नासिकन्धमः.—(Accent) प्राणसूचकं चिह्नं ; 'the hard breathing,' महाप्राणः ; 'the soft breathing,' अभिनिष्ठानं.

BREATHING-HOLE, *s.* वातायनं, वायुच्छिद्रं, वायुपथः, गवाक्षः, जालं.

BREATHING-TIME, *s.* उच्छ्वासः, विश्रामः, विरामः, उपशमः, निर्वृतिः *f.*

BREATHLESS, *a.* (Without breath, lifeless) प्राणहीनः -ना -नं, अप्राणः -णा -णं, व्यसुः -सुः -सु, निरुच्छ्वासः -सा -सं, विचेतनः -ना -नं.—(Panting for breath) उच्छ्वसन् -सती -सत् (त्), उच्छ्वसितः -ता -तं, नष्टश्वासः -सा -सं, यष्टिप्राणः -णा -णं.—(Dead) मृतः -ता -तं.—(Half dead) मृतकल्पः -ल्पा -ल्पं.

BRED, *p. p.* (Born) जातः -ता -तं, उत्पन्नः -न्ना -न्नं.—(Produced) जनितः -ता -तं, उत्पादितः -ता -तं.—(Reared, educated) पुष्टः -ष्टा -ष्टं, शिक्षितः -ता -तं, गृहीतविद्यः -द्या -द्यं, विनीतः -ता -तं ; 'well-bred,' सुविनीतः -ता -तं ; 'ill-bred,' अनीतः -ता -तं, अविनीतः -ता -तं, अविनयः -या -यं, दुराचारः -रा -रं, दुःशीलः -ला -लं.

BREECH, *s.* (The back part of any thing) पश्चाद्भागः, पश्चिमो भागः, पश्चाद्देशः, अधोदेशः.—(Of an animal) नितम्बः. स्फिचौ *f. du.*, कटिदेशः, कटीरकं, कटिप्रोथः.—(Of a cannon) यस्माद् अन्तरग्निबलेन लोहगोलो निःसार्य्यते तस्य युद्धयन्त्रस्य पश्चाद्भागः.

BREECHES, *s.* कञ्चुकः, पुम्भिर् भृतं कटिवस्त्रं, पुरुषस्य कटिवस्त्रं, कटिजङ्घादिपरिधानं, कटीपटः, शाटकः.

To BREED, *v. a.* (To procreate, give birth to) सु (c. 1. सवति, c. 2. सौति, सोतुं), प्रसु, प्रजन् (c. 4. -जायते -जनितुं) or जन् in caus. (जनयति -यितुं), सञ्जन्; वृध् in caus. (वर्धयति -यितुं).—(To be pregnant) गर्भवती or गर्भिणी or सञ्जातगर्भा भू.—(To cause, produce) जन् in caus., उत्पद् in caus. (-पादयति -यितुं).—(To rear) पुष् (c. 9. पुष्णाति, c. 1. पोषति or in caus. पोषयति -यितुं), पाल् (c. 10. पालयति -यितुं), प्रतिपाल्.—(To educate) शिक्ष् (*i.e.* des. of शक्) in caus. (शिक्षयति -यितुं), विनी (c. 1. -नयति -नेतुं).—(To contrive, plot) घट् (c. 1. घटते, घटितुं).

To BREED, *v. n.* (To have birth) जन् (c. 4. जायते), उपजन्, अभिजन्; उत्पद् (c. 4. -पद्यते).—(To increase) वृध् (c. 1. वर्धते, वर्धितुं), पुष् (c. 4. पुष्यति, पोष्टुं).

BREED, *s.* (Race, family) वंशः, कुलं, जातिः *f.*, सन्तानः, सन्ततिः *f.*, अन्वयः.—(Offspring) अपत्यं, प्रजा; 'a horse of a good breed,' आजानेयः, भूमिपक्षः, भूमिरक्षकः.—(Number of animals born at once) शावकगणः, यः शावकगण एककाले डिम्बाद् उत्पद्यते or प्रसूयते.

BREEDBATE, *s.* कलहकारः, विवादार्थी *m.* (न्), कलिप्रियः, कलहप्रियः.

BREEDER, *s.* (A producer) जनकः, प्रजनिष्णुः, उत्पादकः, सुती *m.* (न्).—(A prolific female) सुतिनी, अवन्ध्या, प्रसविनी, प्रजायिनी, जननी.—(A rearer) पोषकः, पोष्टा *m.* (ष्टृ), पोषयिता *m.* (तृ), विनेता *m.* (तृ).

BREEDING, *s.* (Rearing) पोषः -षणं, पालनं.—(Education) शिक्षा, विनयः.—(Good manners) विनयः, सभ्यता, सुशीलता; 'a man of breeding,' सुविनीतः.

BREESE, *s.* दंशः, दंशकः, वनमक्षिका, गोमक्षिका.

BREEZE, *s.* मृदुवातः, मन्दानिलः, अनिलः, मारुतः, मरुत् *m.*, वायुः *m.*, सुवायुः *m.*, चारुवायुः *m.*, पवनः, श्वसनः, समीरणः, समीरः, मन्दसमीरणः; 'soft breezes,' सुखस्पर्शाः *m. pl.*

BREEZY, *a.* (Windy) वातलः -ला -लं, वातवान् -वती -वत् (त्), वायव्यः -व्यी -व्यं.—(Fanned by the breezes) वायुभिः or मन्दानिलैर् अनुवीजितः -ता -तं or उपवीजितः or उद्वीज्यमानः -ना -नं.

BRETHREN, *s.* (Plur. of brother) भ्रातरः *m. pl.*, समानोदर्य्याः.—(Of the same race) बान्धवाः *m. pl.*, सजातयः *m. pl.*, समानजातयः.—(Associates) संसर्गिणः *m. pl.*, सङ्गिनः *m. pl.*—(Spiritual brethren) एकगुरवः *m. pl.*, सतीर्थ्याः *m. pl.*

BREVET, *s.* अधिकवर्त्तनं विना श्रेष्ठपदमात्रप्रतिपत्तिः *f.*, अधिकवेतनव्यतिरेकेण ज्येष्ठख्यातिमात्रप्राप्तिः *f.*, पदमात्रवृद्धिः *f.*

BREVIARY, *s.* (A compendium) सङ्ग्रहः, संहिता.—(Of prayers) प्रार्थनासङ्ग्रहः, प्रार्थनासंहिता.

BREVIATE, *s.* सङ्ग्रहः, संहिता, संहारः, प्रत्याहारः.

BREVITY, *s.* सङ्क्षेपः -पणं, सङ्क्षिप्तिः *f.*, सङ्क्षिप्तत्वं, समस्तत्वं, उपसङ्क्षेपः, सङ्ग्रहः -हणं, समसनं, समासः, परिमितता, संहारः, समाहारः, अल्पत्वं.

To BREW, *v. a.* (To make beer) यवसुरं पच् (c. 1. पचति, पक्तुं) or क्वथ् (c. 1. क्वथति, क्वथितुं), यवमद्यं कृ.—(To mingle) मिश्र् (c. 10. मिश्रयति -यितुं).—(To contrive) घट् (c. 1. घटते, घटितुं), प्रचिन्त् (c. 10. -चिन्तयति -यितुं), परिचिन्त्.

BREWAGE, *s.* नानासम्मिश्रद्रव्यनिर्म्मितं पानीयं, मिश्रक्वाथः, सन्निपातः, प्रकीर्णकं.

BREWER, *s.* यवसुरक्वथिता *m.* (तृ), यवसुरपाचकः.

BREWERY or BREWHOUSE, *s.* यवसुरपचनस्थानं, यवसुरक्वथनस्थानं.

BREWING, *s.* यवसुरपचनं, यत्किञ्चिद् यवसुरम् एककाले पच्यते.

BREWIS, *s.* यूषक्वथितः पिष्टकः or अपूपः.

BRIBE, *s.* उत्कोचः -चा -चकः, उपप्रदानं, उपायनं, अभ्युपायनं, कौशलिकं, पारितोषिकं; 'the receiver of a bribe,' उत्कोचकः, उत्कोचादाता *m.* (तृ), उत्कोचग्राहकः.

To BRIBE, *v. a.* उत्कोचं दा (c. 3. ददाति, दातुं) or उपप्रदा, अन्याय्यकर्म्मसम्पादनार्थम् उपायनं दा.

BRIBER, *s.* उत्कोचदाता *m.* (तृ), उत्कोचदायी *m.* (न्), उपप्रदाता *m.* (तृ).

BRIBERY, *s.* उत्कोचस्य दानादानापराधः.—(Giving bribes) उत्कोचदानं, उत्कोचचर्य्या.—(Receiving bribes) उत्कोचग्रह -हणं.

BRICK, *s.* इष्टका, इष्टिका, सुधा; 'burnt brick,' पक्वेष्टका, न्यामकं; 'a brick-house,' इष्टकागृहं, सुधाभवनं; 'brick-built,' इष्टकानिर्म्मितः -ता -तं; 'a pile of bricks,' इष्टकाराशिः *f.*

To BRICK, *v. a.* इष्टकान्यासं कृ, इष्टकान्यासं कृत्वा निर्म्मा (c. 2. -माति -मातुं).

BRICK-BAT, *s.* इष्टकाशकलं, इष्टकाखण्डं, भिन्नेष्टका, भग्नेष्टकाशकलं.

BRICK-DUST, *s.* इष्टकाचूर्णं, इष्टकाक्षोदः, इष्टकाक्षोदितं.

BRICK-KILN, *s.* पाकपुटी, आपाकः, इष्टकापचनस्थानं, पचनं.

BRICKLAYER, *s.* लेपकः, लेपी *m.* (न्), लेप्यकृत् *m.*, प्रलेपकः, सुधाजीवी *m.* (न्), अट्टालिकाकारः, पलगण्डः.

BRICKMAKER, *s.* इष्टकाकारी *m.* (न्), इष्टकाकृत्, इष्टकाकारः, सुधाकृत्.

BRICKWORK, *s.* इष्टकान्यासः, सुधान्यासः, इष्टकानिर्म्माणं, इष्टकानिर्म्मितं यत्किञ्चिद् भवनादि.

BRIDAL, *s.* विवाहोत्सवः, विवाहपर्व्व *n.* (न्), विवाहः, विवाहकर्म्म *n.* (न्) or उद्वाहकर्म्म.

BRIDAL, *a.* वैवाहिकः -की -कं, औद्वाहिकः -की -कं, विवाहयोग्यः -ग्या -ग्यं, पाणिग्रहणिकः -की -कं; 'bridal clothes,' आनन्दपटं.

BRIDE, *s.* नवोढा, नववधूः, नववधूः *f.*, नवपत्नी, ऊढा, नवकारिका, नववरिका, पाणिगृहीता, सुवासिनी; 'one who chooses her own husband,' स्वयंवरा.

BRIDE-BED, *s.* विवाहशय्या, नवोढाशयनं, आनन्दशय्या, ऊढापोढ्रोः नवशयनं.

BRIDE-CAKE, *s.* विवाहोत्सवकाले गृहाभ्यागतैः खादनीयः पिष्टकः or अपूपः, आनन्दपिष्टकः.

BRIDEGROOM, *s.* वरः, वोढा *m.* (-ढृ), परिणेता *m.* (तृ), पाणिग्राहः, विवाहोत्सुकः.

BRIDEMAID, *s.* (Attendant on the bride) जन्या.

BRIDEMAN, *s.* (Attendant on the bridegroom) जन्यः.

BRIDEWELL, *s.* निग्रहगृहं, निग्रहागारं, दण्डप्रणयनगृहं, कारागारं, कारावेश्म *n.* (न्).

BRIDGE, *s.* सेतुः *m.*, पिण्डलः, पिच्छिलः, धरणः, संवरः, सञ्चरः.—(Foot-bridge) सङ्क्रमः.—(A bridge of boats) नौसेतुः *m.*—(Of the nose) नासावंशः.—(Of a musical instrument) तन्त्रालम्बः, तन्त्रधारणार्थं काष्ठखण्डं.

To BRIDGE, *v. a.* (Connect by a bridge) सेतुना बन्ध् (c. 9. बध्नाति, बन्धुं).

BRIDLE, *s.* वागा, रश्मिः *m.*, वल्गा, दन्तालिका.—(Restraint) संयमः, यमः, यन्त्रणं, निग्रहः.

To BRIDLE, *v. a.* रश्मिभिर् यम् (c. 1. यच्छति, यन्तुं).—(To restrain) यम्, नियम्, संयम्, निग्रह् (c. 9. -गृह्णाति -ग्रहीतुं), वशीकृ.

Bridlehand, *s.* अश्वारूढस्य यो हस्तो वल्गां सङ्गृह्णाति or धरति.

Brief, *a.* (Concise) सङ्क्षिप्तः -प्ता -प्तं, साङ्क्षेपिकः -की -कं, सामासिकः -की -कं, परिमितः -ता -तं, सङ्गृहीतः -ता -तं.—(Not long, as time, &c.) अचिरः -रा -रं, अल्पः -ल्पा -ल्पं, अल्पकालः -ला -लं.—(Contracted) सङ्कुचितः -ता -तं, संवृतः -ता -तं, ह्रस्वः -स्वा -स्वं; 'in a brief space of time,' अचिरेण, अचिरात्, न चिरेण; 'for a brief space,' अल्पमात्रं.

Brief, *s.* (Writing of any kind) पत्रं.—(An epitome) सङ्ग्रहः, सङ्क्षेपः, संहारः.—(A writ) आज्ञापत्रं.—(A writing explaining the case) निवेदनपत्रं, अर्थतत्त्वज्ञापकं पत्रं.

Briefly, *adv.* (Concisely) सङ्क्षेपेण, सङ्क्षेपात्, सङ्क्षेपतस्, समासतस्, अविस्तरशस्, न विस्तरेण, परिमितप्रकारेण.—(Quickly) अचिरेण, क्षिप्रं, आशु, अविलम्बितं.

Briefness, *s.* सङ्क्षिप्तिः *f.*, सङ्क्षिप्तत्वं, सङ्क्षेपः, उपसङ्क्षेपः, समस्तत्वं, समासः, समसनं, संहारः, परिमितता, अल्पत्वं -ता.—(Of life) आयुरल्पत्वं.

Brier or briar, *s.* गोक्षुरः, कण्टकगुल्मः, शृगालकण्टकः, शृगालकोलिः *m.*

Briery, *a.* कण्टकी -किनी -कि (न्), कण्टकितः -ता -तं, शृगालकण्टकावृतः -ता -तं.

Brig, *s.* कूपकद्वयविशिष्टः सामुद्रपोतप्रभेदः.

Brigade, *s.* व्यूहः, चमूः *f.*, गुल्मः, वाहिनी, सैन्यदलं, सेनामुखं.

To brigade, *v. a.* वाहिनीं व्यूह् (c. 1. -ऊहते -ऊहितुं), व्यूहीकृ.

Brigadier, *s.* वाहिनीपतिः *m.*, गुल्माधिपतिः *m.*, चमूपतिः *m.*, व्यूहाध्यक्षः, सैन्यव्यूहपतिः *m.*

Brigand, *s.* दस्युः *m.*, प्रसह्यचौरः, अपहारकः, साहसिकः, चौरः, लोप्त्रजीवी *m.* (न्).

Brigantine, *s.* सामुद्रदस्युभिः प्रयुक्तो लघुनौकाविशेषः.

Bright, *a.* दीप्तिमान् -मती -मत् (त्), दीप्तः -प्ता -प्तं, द्युतिमान् -मती -मत् (त्), प्रभावान् -वती -वत् (त्), सुप्रभः -भा -भं, वर्चस्वी -स्विनी -स्वि (न्), द्योती -तिनी -ति (न्), द्योतनः -ना -नं, शोभी -भिनी -भि (न्), शोभनः -ना -नं, रुचिरः -रा -रं, तेजोमयः -यी -यं, तैजसः -सी -सं, उज्ज्वलः -ला -लं, प्रतिभानवान् -वती -वत् (त्); 'having bright eyes,' दीप्ताक्षः -क्षी -क्षं, दीप्तलोचनः -ना -नं.—(Clear) विशदः -दा -दं, विमलः -ला -लं, निर्म्मलः -ला -लं, स्वच्छः -च्छा -च्छं, शुचिः -चिः -चि.—(Illustrious) कीर्त्तिमान् -मती -मत् (त्), विश्रुतः -ता -तं, महायशाः -शाः -शः (स्).—(Acute) सूक्ष्मबुद्धिः -द्धिः -द्धि, निपुणमतिः -तिः -ति.

To brighten, *v. a.* (To make to shine, &c.) द्युत् in caus. (द्योतयति -यितुं), भास् in caus. (भासयति -यितुं), प्रभास्, उद्भास्, भाज् in caus. (भाजयति -यितुं), विराज् in caus. (-राजयति -यितुं), प्रकाश् in caus. (-काशयति -यितुं), विमल (nom. विमलयति -यितुं).

To brighten, *v. n.* (To become bright) दीप्तीभू, विमलीभू.—(To be bright) शुभ् (c. 1. शोभते, शोभितुं), रुच् (c. 1. रोचते, रोचितुं), द्युत् (c. 1. द्योतते, द्योतितुं), भाज् (c. 1. भाजते, भाजितुं); भास् (c. 1. भासते, भासितुं), राज् (c. 1. राजति -ते, राजितुं), विराज्, काश् (c. 1. काशते, काशितुं), चकास् (c. 2. चकास्ति, चकासितुं), शुचि (nom. शुचीयते -यितुं).—(To become bright as the sky) गततोयदः -दा -दं भू.

Brightly, *adv.* तेजसा, दीप्त्या, द्युत्या, कान्त्या, दीप्तप्रकारेण, विमलं.

Brightness, *s.* द्युतिः *f.*, द्युतिमत्त्वं, दीप्तिः *f.*, दीप्तिमत्त्वं, दीप्तता, ज्योतिः *n.* (स्), रुचिः *f.*, प्रभा, उज्ज्वलता, छविः *f.*, कान्तिः *f.*, तेजः *n.* (स्), शोभा.—(Acuteness) बुद्धिसूक्ष्मत्वं, नैपुण्यं, मतिप्रकर्षः.—(Beauty) सौन्दर्य्यं.

Brilliancy, *s.* दीप्तिः *f.*, प्रभा, कान्तिमत्त्वं, द्युतिः *f.*, छविः *f.*, तेजः *n.* (स्), भ्राजिष्णुता.

Brilliant, *s.* अतिदीप्तिमान् बहुकक्षविशिष्टो वज्रभेदः, भिन्नच्छायो हीरविशेषः.

Brilliant, *a.* प्रभावान् -वती -वत् (त्), दीप्तिमान् -मती -मत् (त्), देदीप्यमानः -ना -नं, दीप्तः -प्ता -प्तं, कान्तिमान् -मती -मत् (त्), रोचिष्णुः -ष्णुः -ष्णु, तेजस्वी -स्विनी -स्वि (न्), तेजोमयः -यी -यं, द्योतमानः -ना -नं, प्रकाशमानः -ना -नं, उज्ज्वलः -ला -लं.

Brilliantly, *adv.* प्रभया, अतिकान्त्या, छव्या, तेजसा, दीप्तिपूर्व्वं.

Brim, *s.* (Edge of any thing) धारः -रा, प्रान्तः, अन्तः -न्तं, उपान्तं, पर्य्यन्तं, उत्सङ्गः.—(Edge of a vessel) कर्णः, धारः, मुखं.—(Margin of a river) तीरं, तटः, तटं, कच्छः.—(Border of a cloth, &c.) अञ्चलः; 'up to the brim,' आकर्णं, धारपर्य्यन्तं, आमुखात्.

To brim, *v. a.* आकर्णं पात्रं पॄ in caus. (पूरयति -यितुं), पात्रप्रान्तं कृ.

Brimful, *a.* आकर्णं or धारपर्य्यन्तं पूर्णः -र्णा -र्णं, एकान्तपूर्णः -र्णा -र्णं.

Brimmer, *s.* आकर्णं or धारपर्य्यन्तं or मुखपर्य्यन्तं पूरितं पात्रं, अतिपूर्णं भाजनं.

Brimstone, *s.* गन्धकः, गन्धाश्मा *m.* (न्), गन्धमोदनं, क्रूरगन्धः, शुल्वारिः *m.*

Brimstony, *a.* गन्धकमयः -यी -यं, गन्धकपूर्णः -र्णा -र्णं, गन्धकविशिष्टः -ष्टा -ष्टं.

Brinded or brindled, *a.* शबलः -ला -लं, चित्राङ्गः -ङ्गी -ङ्गं, चित्रः -त्रा -त्रं, चित्रितः -ता -तं, नानावर्णः -र्णा -र्णं, रेखाङ्कितः -ता -तं.

Brindle, *s.* शबलत्वं, शबलभावः, चित्राङ्गत्वं, चित्रता.

Brine, *s.* लवणोदं, लवणजलं.—(The briny deep) लवणाम्बुराशिः.—(Tears) बाष्पः, अश्रु *n.*, नयनसलिलं.

Brine-pit, *s.* लवणजलपूर्णं खातं or कुण्डं, लवणोदकूपः.

To bring, *v. a.* (Fetch from another place) आनी (c. 1. -नयति -ते -नेतुं), उपानी, आहृ (c. 1. -हरति -हर्त्तुं).—(Carry to a place) नी, आवह् (c. 1. -वहति -वोढुं), उपवह्, संवह्.—(Cause to come) आगम् in caus. (-गमयति -यितुं), प्राप् in caus. (-आपयति -यितुं), उपपद् in caus. (-पादयति -यितुं).—(Reduce to a particular state) गम् in caus., कृ; 'brought to misery,' कृच्छ्रगतः -ता -तं; 'brought low,' अल्पीकृतः -ता -तं, अस्तङ्गमितः -ता -तं.—(Induce) अनुनी, उपागम् in caus., प्रोत्सह् in caus. (-साहयति -यितुं), आकृष् (c. 1. -कर्षति -क्रष्टुं).—(Bring about) घट् (c. 1. घटते, घटितुं), सिध् in caus. (साधयति -यितुं), संसिध्, सम्पद् in caus. (-पादयति -यितुं), उपपद्.—(Bring back) प्रत्यानी, प्रतिपद् in caus., प्रत्यृ in caus. (-अर्पयति -यितुं).—(Bring down, humble) अपकृष्, अभिभू (c. 1. -भवति -भवितुं); 'having his pride brought down,' आप्तगर्व्वः, भग्नदर्पः.—(Bring forth, give birth to) सु (c. 1. सवति, c. 2. सौति, सोतुं), प्रसू; प्रजन् (c. 4. -जायते -जनितुं), जन् in caus. (जनयति -यितुं), उत्पद् in caus.; 'act of bringing forth,' प्रसवः.—(Bring forward) प्रणी, अभिप्रणी, आनी, उपनी, अग्रे नी, पुरस्कृ, प्रगम् in caus., सम्प्रस्था in caus. (-स्थापयति -यितुं), प्रसृ in caus. (-सारयति -यितुं); 'brought forward as an example,' उपन्यस्तः -स्ता -स्तं.—(Bring in) प्रविश् in caus. (-वेशयति -यितुं), निविश्, उपन्यस् (c. 4. -अस्यति, असितुं).—(Bring on) आवह्, उत्पद् in caus. (-पादयति -यितुं); 'that would bring on death,' तन्मृत्युम् आवहेत्; 'bringing happiness,' सुखावहः -हा -हं.—(Bring out) प्रकाश् in caus. (-काशयति -यितुं), प्रचर् in caus. (-चारयति -यितुं), प्रकटीकृ, दृश् in caus. (दर्शयति -यितुं). (Bring together) समानी, एकत्र नी or कृ, सम्भृ (c. 1. -भरति -भर्त्तुं).—(Bring under) अपकृष्, अभिभू, दम् in caus. (दमयति -यितुं), वशीकृ.—(Bring up) विनी, पुष् in caus. (पोषयति -यितुं), वृध् in caus. (वर्धयति -यितुं).—(Bring to an end) निर्वह् in caus. (-वाहयति -यितुं), निर्वृत् in caus. (-वर्त्तयति -यितुं), समाप् in caus. (-आपयति -यितुं), सिध् in caus.—(Bring to light) प्रकाश् in caus., स्पष्टीकृ.—(Bring to pass).

See Bring about.—(Bring word) निविद् in caus. (-वेदयति -यितुं), वार्त्ताम् or संवादम् आख्या (c. 2. -ख्याति -ख्यातुं), संवद् in caus. (-वादयति -यितुं).—(Bring an action against) अभियुज् (c. 7. -युनक्ति -योक्तुं), विवादास्पदीकृ.

BRINGER, *s.* आनेता *m.* (तृ), उपानेता *m.* (तृ), आवहः in comp.

BRINISH or BRINY, *a.* लवणः -णा -णं, लावणः -णी -णं, क्षाररसः -सा -सं.

BRINISHNESS, *s.* लावण्यं, लवणत्वं, क्षारता, क्षाररसः.

BRINK, *s.* (Of a river) तीरं, कूलं, तटं, कच्छः.—(Of any thing) प्रान्तः, अन्तः -न्तं, उपान्तं, पर्य्यन्तं, धारः -रा.—(Of a precipice) उत्सङ्गः, शैलकटकः.

BRISK, *a.* लघुः -घुः -घु, त्वरितः -ता -तं, अविलम्बः -म्बा -म्बं, क्षिप्रः -प्रा -प्रं, अतन्द्रः -न्द्रा -न्द्रं, प्रफुल्लः -ल्ला -ल्लं.—(Powerful, spirituous) प्रबलः -ला -लं, तीव्रः -व्रा -व्रं, तैजसः -सी -सं, सारवान् -वती -वत् (त्), सौरिकः -की -कं; 'a brisk shower,' धारासम्पातः.

BRISKET, *s.* पशोर् वक्षः *n.* (स्), or उरः *n.* (स्), or वक्षस्स्थलं.

BRISKLY, *adv.* त्वरितं, क्षिप्रं, सत्वरं, प्रयत्नतस्, सारतस्, अविलम्बितं, अतन्द्रितं, बलवत्.

BRISKNESS, *s.* लाघवं, क्षिप्रत्वं, शीघ्रता, अविलम्बता.—(Vigour) तेजः *n.* (स्), सारता, सत्त्वं, तीव्रता.

BRISTLE, *s.* शूकः -कं, दृढलोम *n.* (न्), स्तब्धरोम *n.* (न्), रोम *n.* (न्), सूचिः *f.*—(Of a hog) शूकरलोम *n.* (न्).

To BRISTLE, *v. n.* शूकवत् or शूकरलोमवद् हृष् (c. 4. हृष्यति, हर्षितुं) or पुलकितः -ता -तं or उन्नतः -ता -तं or उन्नतः -ता -तं भू or स्तब्धीभू; शूक (nom. शूकायते), पुलक (nom. पुलकायते); 'the hairs of his skin bristled up,' तस्य रोमाण्य् अहृषन्.

BRISTLING, *part.* हृषितः -ता -तं, हृष्टः -ष्टा -ष्टं, पुलकितः -ता -तं, पुलकी -किनी -कि (न्), दन्तुरः -रा -रं; 'bristling hairs,' हृषितानि रोमाणि.

BRISTLY, *a.* शूकी -किनी -कि (न्), शूकवान् -वती -वत् (त्), सूचीरोमा -मा -म (न्), दृढलोमा -मा -म (न्), स्तब्धरोमा -मा -म (न्).

BRITAIN, *s.* (The white island) श्वेतद्वीपः.

BRITISH, *a.* पूर्व्वोक्तदेशसम्बन्धी -न्धिनी -न्धि (न्).

BRITTLE, *a.* भङ्गुरः -रा -रं, भिदुरः -रा -रं, भिदेलिमः -मा -मं, सुखभेद्यः -द्या -द्यं, भेद्यः-द्या-द्यं, खण्डनीयः-या-यं, सुभङ्गः-ङ्गा-ङ्गं, कोमलः-ला-लं.

BRITTLENESS, *s.* भङ्गुरता-त्वं, सुभङ्गता, भिदुरत्वं, खण्डनीयता, भेद्यता, कोमलता.

BRIZE, *s.* दंशः, दंशकः, वनमक्षिका, गोमक्षिका.

BROACH, *s.* (A spit) शूलः, शलाका, शल्यं, शङ्कुः *m.*—(An ornament). *See* BROOCH.

To BROACH, *v. a.* (To spit) शूल् (c. 1. शूलति, शूलितुं), शूलाकृ.—(To tap a vessel) मद्यादिस्रावणार्थं सुराभाजने छिद्रं कृ, मद्यादिमोचनार्थं भाण्डं छिद्र् (c. 10. छिद्रयति -यितुं).—(To open) विवृ (c. 5. -वृणोति -वरितुं -वरीतुं), अपावृ, उद्घट् (c. 10. -घाटयति -यितुं).—(To give out, utter) उच्चर् in caus. (-चारयति -यितुं), प्रचर्, प्रकाश् in caus. (-काशयति -यितुं), निविद् in caus. (-वेदयति -यितुं), प्रचलीकृ.

BROAD, *a.* (Wide, large) पृथुः -थुः -थु, विशालः -ला -लं, विपुलः -ला -लं, प्रस्थः -स्था -स्थं.—(Spacious, expanded) विस्तीर्णः -र्णा -र्णं, विततः -ता -तं.—(Coarse) असभ्यः -भ्या -भ्यं, अपरिष्कृतः -ता -तं, अशुद्धः -द्धा -द्धं.—(Indelicate) अवाच्यः -च्या -च्यं, गर्हितः -ता -तं; 'to make broad,' प्रथ् (nom. प्रथयति -यितुं); 'broad-waisted,' पृथुमध्यः -ध्या -ध्यं.

BROAD-AWAKE, *a.* प्रजागरः -रा -रं, प्रबुद्धः -द्धा -द्धं, उन्निद्रः -द्रा -द्रं.

BROAD-BREASTED, *a.* व्यूढोरस्कः -स्का -स्कं, उरस्वान् -स्वती -स्वत् (त्), उरसिलः -ला -लं.

BROAD-BRIMMED, *a.* पृथुधारः -रा -रं, विशालाञ्चलः -ला -लं, विपुलधारः -रा -रं.

BROAD-CLOTH, *s.* अधुनातनजनैर् भृतं मेषलोमनिर्म्मितं सूक्ष्मवस्त्रं.

To BROADEN, *v. n.* प्रथ् (c. 1. प्रथते, प्रथितुं), विप्रथ्, विस्तॄ in pass. (-स्तीर्य्यते).

BROADNESS, *s.* पृथुता, पार्थवं, प्रथिमा *m.* (न्), विशालता, विस्तारः, विस्तीर्णता, विपुलता, प्रस्थता, परिसरः, पाटः.—(Coarseness) असभ्यता, अशुद्धता, अवाच्यत्वं, गर्ह्यता.

BROAD-SHOULDERED, *a.* पृथुस्कन्धः -न्धा -न्धं, अंसलः -ला -लं, पृथुबाहुः -हुः -हु.

BROADSIDE, *s.* नौपार्श्वः -र्श्वं, नौकापार्श्वः, पोतपार्श्वः.—(Volley of shot) सामुद्रयुद्धसमये ये लोहगोलका एककाले नौकापार्श्वात् प्रक्षिप्यन्ते.

BROADSWORD, *s.* पृथुपत्रः खड्गविशेषः, पृथुफलकविशिष्टः कृपाणः.

BROCADE, *s.* सुवर्णरूप्यतन्तुस्यूतं दुकूलं, कार्म्मिकवस्त्रं, नानावर्णकौशाम्बरं.

BROCADED, *a.* चित्रदुकूलाम्बरः -रा -रं, नानावर्णदुकूलालङ्कृतः -ता -तं.

BROCAGE, BROKAGE, or BROKERAGE, *s.* (The profit gotten by promoting bargains) शुल्कः -ल्कं, पारितोषिकं, क्रेतृविक्रेत्रोर्मध्ये पणसम्पादकेन गृहीतं शुल्कं or मूल्यं, परकार्य्यनिर्व्वाहणात् प्रति निरूपितप्रतिफलं, पणप्रयोजकपारितोषिकं.—(The trade of dealing in old things) जीर्णद्रव्याणां क्रयविक्रयः.—(The transaction of business for other men) परस्य कृते पणाया or पणसम्पादनं, परकार्य्यनिर्व्वाहः.

BROCOLI, *s.* शाकप्रभेदः, हरितकभेदः, शिग्रुः *m.*, पोतकी.

BROCKET, *s.* द्विवर्षीयस् तावतनुविशिष्टो हरिणप्रभेदः.

BROGUE, *s.* भ्रष्टभाषा, प्राकृतभाषा, अपशब्दः, अशुद्धोच्चारणं, असभ्यव्याहरणं, म्लेच्छभाषा.—(A kind of shoe) चर्म्मपादुकाविशेषः.

To BROIDER, *v. a.* सूच्या पुष्पाद्यलङ्कारान् सिव् (c. 4. सीव्यति, सेवितुं) or निषिव्, or चित्र् (c. 10. चित्रयति -यितुं) or लिख् (c. 6. लिखति, लेखितुं).

BROIDERY, *s.* सूचिकर्म्म *n.* (न्), सूचिता, सूच्या पुष्पाद्यलङ्कारसीवनं.

BROIL, *s.* (A quarrel) कलहः, द्वन्द्वं, विरोधः, व्यवक्रोशनं, कलिः *m.*, तुमुलं; 'to raise broils,' कलह (nom. कलहायते).

To BROIL, *v. a.* भ्रस्ज् (c. 6. भृज्जति, भ्रष्टुं), भृज् (c. 1. भर्जते, भर्जितुं), ऋञ्ज (c. 1. ऋञ्जते, ऋञ्जितुं).

To BROIL, *v. n.* (To be hot) तप् in pass. (तप्यते), पच् in pass. (पच्यते).

BROILED, *p. p.* भर्जितः -ता -तं, भृष्टः -ष्टा -ष्टं, तप्तः -प्ता -प्तं.

To BROKE, *v. n.* पणं or परकार्य्याणि सम्पद् in caus. (-पादयति -यितुं) or सिध् in caus. (साधयति -यितुं); परार्थं पण् (c. 1. पणते, पणितुं or पणायति -यितुं).

BROKEN, *p. p.* भग्नः -ग्ना -ग्नं, भिन्नः -न्ना -न्नं, खण्डितः -ता -तं, रुग्नः -ग्ना -ग्नं, विदीर्णः -र्णा -र्णं, शकलीकृतः -ता -तं, विघट्टितः -ता -तं, त्रुटितः -ता -तं.—(Trained) विनीतः -ता -तं, दमितः -ता -तं.

BROKEN-HEARTED, *a.* भग्नहृदयः -या -यं, दलद्धृदयः -या -यं, विदीर्णहृदयः -या -यं, भग्नान्तःकरणः -णा -णं, शोकाकुलः -ला -लं, भग्नाशः -शा -शं.

BROKEN-KNEED, *a.* भग्नजानुः -नुः -नु, भिन्नजानुः -नुः -नु.

BROKEN-WINDED, *a.* नष्टश्वासः -सा -सं, नष्टप्राणः -णा -णं, यष्टिप्राणः -णा -णं.

BROKER, *s.* निरूपितशुल्केन or निरूपितपारितोषिकेण परार्थे क्रेता विक्रेता वा or परार्थे व्यवसायी *m.* (न्) or क्रयविक्रयप्रयोजकः or परकार्य्यनिर्व्वाहकः or परकार्य्यसम्पादकः, घटकः.—(A dealer in old things) जीर्णद्रव्यक्रयविक्रयिकः, जीर्णपरिच्छदक्रयविक्रयी *m.* (न्).

BROKERAGE, *s.* *See* BROCAGE.

BRONCHIAL, *a.* कण्ठ्यः -ण्ठ्या -ण्ठ्यं, कण्ठसम्बन्धीयः -या -यं, ग्रैवेयः -यी -यं.

BRONZE, *s.* कांस्यं, पित्तलं, ताम्रं, रीतिः *f.*, रैत्यं, आरः.

To BRONZE, *v. a.* पित्तलीकृ, ताम्रसात्कृ, पित्तलरूपेण कठिनीकृ.

BRONZED, *p. p.* ताम्रसात्कृतः -ता -तं, रैत्यः -त्यी -त्यं, कांस्यतुल्यः -ल्या -ल्यं.

BROOCH, *s.* (A kind of ornament) वस्त्राञ्चलसङ्ग्रहणयोग्यो वक्षःस्थले भृतः सुवर्णकीलः, उरसि कीलितः सूक्ष्मसुवर्णशङ्कुयुक्तालङ्कारो यद्द्वारेण वस्त्राञ्चलद्वयं संलग्नीकृतं, उरोमणिः, वक्षोभूषणं.

To BROOD, *v. n.* (To sit on eggs) कुलायनिलायं or नीडनिलायं कृ, कुलायं निली (c. 4. -लीयते -लेतुं), अण्डप्रसवानन्तरम् आपक्षिशावको-त्पत्तेर् नीडं निली; अण्डानाम् उपरि उपविश् (c. 6. -विशति -वेष्टुं).

To BROOD-OVER, *v. a.* चिन्ताकुलीभू, चिन्ताव्यग्रः -ग्रा -ग्रं भू, अवसन्नेन मनसा चिन्त् (c.10. चिन्तयति -यितुं),यथा महद्दुःखं जायते तथा सुचिरं चिन्त्.

BROOD, *s.* (A hatch) शावकगणः, यः शावकगण एककाले डिम्बाद् उत्पद्यते. —(Offspring) प्रजा, अपत्यं, सन्तानः.

BROODING, *s.* (The act of sitting on eggs) कुलायनिलायः.

BROODY, *a.* कुलायनिलायी -यिनी -यि (न्).

BROOK, *s.* अल्पनदी,अल्पसरित् *f.*,कुसरित् *f.*,क्षुद्रसरित् *f.*,अल्पस्रोतः *n.* (स्).

To BROOK, *v. a.* and *v. n.* सह् (c. 1. सहते, सोढुं), विषह्, क्षम् (c. 1. क्षमते, क्षन्तुं), सङ्क्षम्; तिज् in des. (तितिक्षते -क्षितुं), मृष् (c. 4. मृष्यति -ते, मर्षितुं, c. 10. मर्षयति -यितुं).

BROOKLIME, *s.* नदीकूलप्रियः or कच्छरुहो नीलपुष्पविशिष्ट ओषधिभेदः.

BROOM, *s.* (For cleaning) मार्जनी, सम्मार्जनी, शोधनी *f.*, विमार्गः, ऊहनी, समूहनी.—(A shrub) क्षुपप्रभेदस् तस्य च क्षुद्रविटपा मार्ज-नीनिर्म्माणे कदापि प्रयुज्यन्ते.

BROOMSTAFF, *s.* मार्जनीदण्डः, शोधनीदण्डः, विमार्गयष्टिः *m.*

BROTH, *s.* जूषं, यूषं, सूपः, निष्क्वाथः.

BROTHEL, *s.* वेश्याजनसमाश्रयः,गणिकागृहं, वेश्याश्रयः, वेश्यागृहं, वेश्यालयः, वेश्यावेश्म *n.* (न्), केलिगृहं.

BROTHER, *s.* भ्राता *m.* (तृ).—(Of whole blood) सोदरः, सहोदरः, सोदर्य्यः, समानोदर्य्यः, सगर्भः, सगर्भ्यः, सनाभिः *m.*, स्वयोनिः *m.*, सहजः. —(Of half blood) भिन्नोदरः.—(Half-brother, step-mother's son) वैमात्रेयः,विमातृजः.—(Brother in law, husband's brother) देवा *m.* (वृ), देवरः.—(Wife's brother) श्यालः.—(Brother's wife) भ्रातृजाया, प्रजावती.—(Brother and sister) भ्रातृभगिन्यौ *m. du.*, भ्रातरौ *m. du.*—(Any one closely united) बन्धुः *m.*, बान्धवः, सजातिः *m.*, समानगोत्रः, सहायः, सहकारी *m.* (न्), संसर्गी *m.* (न्); 'a brother in arms,' सहयुध्वा *m.* (न्).

BROTHERHOOD, *s.* भ्रातृत्वं, सौभ्रात्रं.—(Association) संसर्गित्वं, समांशिता, सहकारिता, साहचर्य्यं, साहित्यं, बन्धुता, संसर्गः.

BROTHERLESS, *a.* अभ्रातृकः -का -कं, भ्रातृहीनः -ना -नं.

BROTHERLY, *a.* भ्रातृकः -का -कं, भ्रात्रीयः -या -यं, भ्रातृसन्निभः -भा -भं.

BROTHERLY, *adv.* भ्रातृवत्, सोदरवत्, भ्रातृरूपेण, भ्रातृकप्रकारेण.

BROUGHT, *p.p.* नीतः -ता -तं, आनीतः -ता -तं, उपानीतः -ता -तं, आहृतः -ता -तं.—(Brought forth) प्रसूतः -ता -तं, जातः -ता -तं, उत्पादितः -ता -तं, उत्पन्नः -न्ना -न्नं.—(Brought up) गृहीतविद्यः -द्या -द्यं, लब्धविद्यः -द्या -द्यं, विनीतः -ता -तं, वर्धितः -ता -तं.

BROW, *s.* (The forehead) ललाटं, मूर्द्धा *m.* (न्), गोधिः *m.*—(The countenance) वदनं, मुखं, आननं.—(The arch of hair over the eye) भ्रूः *f.*, भ्रूलता.—(The edge of any high place) शैलकटकः, गिरिमूर्द्धा *m.* (न्), उत्सङ्गः, नितम्बः, गिरिपृष्ठं.

To BROWBEAT, *v. a.* भ्रूभङ्गेन or सभ्रूभङ्गं or सभ्रुकुटीमुखं or कटाक्षेण or सदर्पं निरीक्ष् (c. 1.-ईक्षते -ईक्षितुं); 'brow-beaten,' कटाक्षितः -ता -तं.

BROWBOUND, *a.* किरीटी -टिनी -टि (न्), किरीटधारी -रिणी -रि (न्).

BROWN, *a.* श्यावः -वा -वं, कपिशः -शा -शं, कपिलः -ला -लं, पिङ्गलः -ला -लं, पिशङ्गः -ङ्गा -ङ्गं, ताम्रः -म्री -म्रं, ताम्रवर्णः -र्णा -र्णं.—(Browned, made brown) कपिशितः -ता -तं.

BROWNISH, *a.* ईषत्कपिशः -शा -शं, ईषत्पिङ्गलः -ला -लं, आताम्रः -म्री -म्रं.

BROWNNESS, *s.* कपिशः, कपिशवर्णः, पिङ्गलता, श्यावः, ताम्रवर्णः.

BROWNSTUDY, *s.* समाधानं, अन्तर्ध्यानं, अन्यमनस्कत्वं, चिन्ताव्यग्रभावः, चिन्ताकुलता.

BROWSE, *s.* किसलः -लं, किसलयं, नवपल्लवं, पल्लवं, गवादनं, छागादनं, छागादिभक्षणीयं नवशाखागुल्मादि.

To BROWSE, *v. n.* छागादिवत् किसलशाखादि भक्ष् (c. 1. भक्षति, भक्षितुं) or खाद् (c. 1. खादति, खादितुं), चर् (c. 1. चरति, चरितुं).

BROWSICK, *a.* विषण्णवदनः -नी -नं, अधोमुखः -खी -खं, नतमूर्द्धा -र्द्धा -र्द्ध (न्).

BROWSING, *s.* नवकिसलयं, नवपल्लवं, नवतृणं, यवसः, शाद्वलं, पत्त्रयौवनं, मृगभोजनीयं नवाङ्कुरलतादि.

BRUISE, *s.* क्षतं, परिक्षतं, अष्ठीला, प्रहारक्षतं, प्रहारार्त्तिः *f.*; प्रहारः, आघातः.

To BRUISE, *v. a.* (Hurt by a blow) प्रहारेण हिंस् (c. 7. हिनस्ति, हिंसितुं) or क्षतं कृ, or क्षण् (c. 8. क्षणोति, क्षणितुं), अष्ठीलां कृ.—(Reduce to powder, crush) चूर्ण् (c. 10. चूर्णयति -यितुं), मृद् (c. 9. मृद्नाति, मर्द्दितुं), अवमृद्, विमृद्, चूर्णीकृ.

BRUISED, *p. p.* प्रहारार्त्तः -र्त्ता -र्त्तं, क्षतः -ता -तं, परिक्षतः -ता -तं, विक्षतः -ता -तं, चूर्णितः -ता -तं, चूर्णीकृतः -ता -तं, मर्द्दितः -ता -तं.

BRUISER, *s.* (Boxer) मल्लः, मल्लयोधः, पाणिघातः, बाहुप्रहरणः, बाहुयोधी *m.* (न्).

BRUIT, *s.* (Noise) शब्दः, ध्वनिः *m.*—(Rumour) प्रवादः, जनप्रवादः, समाचारः, संवादः, किंवदन्ती, वार्त्ता.

To BRUIT, *v. a.* घुष् in caus. (घोषयति -यितुं), आघुष्, विघुष्, ख्या in caus. (ख्यापयति -यितुं), आख्या, प्रकाश् in caus. (-काशयति -यितुं).

BRUMAL, *a.* हैमनः -नी -नं, -मन्तिकः -की -कं, शीतकालीनः -ना -नं.

BRUNETTE, *s.* श्यामा, श्यामला, श्यावाङ्गी, ताम्रमुखी, कपिशमुखी.

BRUNT, *s.* (Attack) आक्रमः, अभिक्रमः, प्रथमाक्रमः, सङ्घट्टः, अभिमर्द्दः, बलात्कारः.—(Blow) आघातः, प्रहारः, समाघातः.

BRUSH, *s.* आघर्षणी, निघर्षणकः, मार्जनी, शूकरलोममयी मार्जनी, शोधनी, विमार्गः, कूर्चः, कूर्चकं.—(Painter's brush) ईषिका, तूलिका, वर्त्तिका, लेख्यचूर्णिका.—(Tail of a fox) लोमशवालः.—(A rude encounter) सङ्घट्टः, समाघातः, बलात्कारः.

To BRUSH, *v. a.* (To rub or clean with a brush) मृज् (c. 2. मार्ष्टि, मार्ष्टुं, c. 1. मार्जति, मार्जितुं), अपमृज्, प्रमृज्, परिमृज्, अवमृज्, सम्मृज्, आघृष् (c. 1. -घर्षति -घर्षितुं), आघर्षणीद्वारेण शुध् in caus. (शोधयति -यितुं), प्रक्षल् (c. 10. -क्षालयति -यितुं).—(To strike lightly) घृष्, लघु or लाघवेन तड् (c. 10. ताडयति -यितुं).

To BRUSH, *v. n.* (To brush by, pass hastily by) लघुगत्या अतिक्रम्य परवस्त्रं घृष् (c. 1. -घर्षति -घर्षितुं).—(To brush off, hasten off) अपधाव् (c. 1. -धावति -धावितुं).—(To skim lightly, glide) विसृप् (c. 1. सर्पति -सर्प्तुं -स्रप्तुं).

BRUSHED, *p. p.* आघर्षितः -ता -तं, मार्जितः -ता -तं, आघट्टितः -ता -तं.

BRUSHER, *s.* मार्जनकृत्, आघर्षणकृत्, प्रक्षालकः, मार्जनीद्वारा शोधनकृत्.

BRUSH-MAKER, *s.* मार्जनीकारः, आघर्षणीकारः.

BRUSHWOOD, *s.* जङ्गलः, गुल्मः, क्षाटः -टं, क्षुपः, प्रस्तारः, इन्धनं.

BRUSHY, *a.* लोमशः -शा -शं, दृढलोमा -मा -म (न्), खरलोमा -मा -म (न्).

BRUTAL, *a.* (Like a brute) शौवापदः -दी -दं, पशुशीलः -ला -लं, पशुव्यवहारः -रा -रं, पशुसदृशः -शी -शं, अमानुषः -षी -षं.—(Cruel) निर्दयः -या -यं, क्रूरः -रा -रं, क्रूराचारः -रा -रं, निष्ठुरः -रा -रं.

BRUTALITY, *s.* पशुत्वं -ता, तिर्य्यक्त्वं, पशुशीलता, अमनुष्यता, क्रूराचारता.

To BRUTALIZE, *v. a.* पशूकृ, पशुशीलं -लां -लं कृ, शौवापदीकृ.

BRUTALLY, *adv.* पशुवत्, पशुरूपेण, पशुव्यवहारानुसारेण, अतिक्रौर्य्येण, निर्द्दयं.

BRUTE, *s.* पशुः *m.*, जन्तुः *m.*, तिर्य्यङ् (ञ्च्), प्राणी *m.* (न्).—(A savage) पुरुषपशुः *m.*, दुराचारः, दुर्वृत्तः, क्रूराचारः, असभ्यजनः.

BRUTE, *a.* (Irrational) अज्ञानी -निनी -नि (न्), अप्राज्ञः -ज्ञा -ज्ञं.—(Savage) क्रूरकर्म्मशाली -लिनी -लि (न्), असभ्यः -भ्या -भ्यं.—(Senseless) विचेतनः -ना -नं, विमूढात्मा -त्मा -त्म (न्).—(Bestial) शौवापदः -दी -दं, पाशवः -वी -वं.

BRUTISH, *a.* पशुसदृशः -शी -शं, जडः -डा -डं, मूढः -ढा -ढं. *See* BRUTAL.

BRUTISHLY, *adv.* पशुवत्, जडवत्, मूढवत्. *See* BRUTALLY.

BRUTISHNESS, *s.* पशुत्वं, जडता, मूढता, क्रौर्य्यं, दुराचारता, नैष्ठुर्य्यं.

BRYONY, *s.* तुण्डिकेरी, रक्तफला, विम्बिका, पीलुपर्णी.

BUBBLE, *s.* बुद्बुदः, जलबुद्बुदः, डिम्बिका, स्फारः, गण्डः, फेनायं.—(Any thing unreal, a trifle) अवस्तु *n.*, असारवस्तु *n.*, स्वल्पविषयः.—(A cheat) वञ्चकः, कपटी *m.* (न्).

To BUBBLE, *v. n.* बुद्बुद (nom. बुद्बुदायते -यितुं), फेन (nom. फेनायते -यितुं), उत्सेचनं कृ.

To BUBBLE, *v. a.* (To cheat) वञ्च् in caus. (वञ्चयते -यितुं), प्रलभ् (c. 1. -लभते -लब्धुं), विप्रलभ्, छल् (c. 10. छलयति -यितुं).

BUBBY, *s.* स्तनः, स्तनकुट्मलं, कुचः, वक्षोजं, उरसिजः.

BUBO, *s.* व्रणः, उपदंशः, स्फोटः, विस्फोटः.

BUCCANIER OR BUCCANEER, *s.* आमेरिकादेशीयः समुद्रयायी दस्युविशेषः.

BUCK, *s.* (Male of the deer) पुम्मृगः; 'male of the rabbit,' पुंशशकः; 'male of the goat,' पुंच्छागः.—(Liquor in which clothes are washed) वस्त्रधावनार्थं जलं.—(Clothes washed in that liquor) पूर्व्वोक्तजलधावितं वस्त्रं.—(A fop) दर्शनीयमानी *m.* (न्), सुवेशी *m.* (न्), रूपगर्व्वितः.

To BUCK, *v. a.* (To wash clothes) वस्त्राणि धाव् (c. 1. धावति, धावितुं) or प्रक्षल् (c. 10. -क्षालयति -यितुं).

BUCK-BASKET, *s.* तरिः *f.*, पेटः, पेटकः, पेडा, पिटकः.

BUCKET, *s.* सेक्तं, पात्रं, द्रोणी, सेकपात्रं, सेचनं -नी.—(Bucket of a well) नीरोत्तोलनपात्रं, उद्घाटनं, घटीयन्त्रं.

BUCKLE, *s.* द्रव्यद्वयसंलग्नीकरणार्थं कीलयुक्तं धातुमयचक्रं, वस्त्राञ्चलपादुकाबन्धनादिसङ्ग्रहणार्थं मध्यस्थकीलविशिष्टः कुडुपविशेषः, उपानद्बन्धनकुडुपः, कुडुपः, निदर्शनमुद्रा.—(A curl, crisp) अलकः, कर्करालः.

To BUCKLE, *v. a.* पूर्व्वोक्तकुडुपद्वारेण बन्ध् (c. 9. बध्नाति, बन्द्धुं) or संलग्नीकृ.

To BUCKLE TO, *v. n.* (To a business) आस्था (c. 1. -तिष्ठति -स्थातुं), अनुष्ठा; सेव् (c. 1. सेवते, सेवितुं), परायणः -णा -णं or आसक्तः -क्ता -क्तं भू.—(To engage in close fight) नियुद्धं कृ, बाहुयुद्धं कृ.

BUCKLER, *s.* चर्म्म *n.* (न्), फलकः -कं.—(Armed with) फलकपाणिः, फलकी *m.* (न्).

BUCKRAM, *s.* दृढवस्त्रविशेषः, स्तब्धक्षौमपटविशेषः, स्तब्धीकृतवस्त्रं, स्थूलपट्टं, स्थूलशाटिः *m.*, पटी.—(Stiff, formal) कठिनः -ना -नं, दृढः -ढा -ढं.

BUCKSKIN, *a.* मृगाजिनमयः -यी -यं, मृगचर्म्मनिर्म्मितः -ता -तं.

BUCKTHORN, *s.* रेचकफलदायी वृक्षप्रभेदः.

BUCKWHEAT, *s.* शस्यक्षेत्ररुह ओषधिप्रभेदः.

BUCOLICS, *s. pl.* गोमेषादिविषयं गीतं, पशुपालनादिविषयकं काव्यं.

BUD, *s.* मुकुलः -लं, कुट्मलः -लं, कुड्मलः, जालकं, क्षारकः, कलिका, प्ररोहः, अङ्कुरः, पल्लवः -वं, कोषः, कोरकः -कं, मुकुलोद्गमः.

To BUD, *v. n.* स्फुट् (c. 6. स्फुटति, स्फुटितुं), फुल्ल् (c. 1. फुल्लति, फुल्लितुं), विकस् (c. 1. -कसति -कसितुं), अङ्कुर (nom. अङ्कुरयति -यितुं).

BUDDED, *p. p.* स्फुटितः -ता -तं, विकसितः -ता -तं, व्याकोशः -शा -शं, कुड्मलितः -ता -तं, अङ्कुरितः -ता -तं, प्रस्फुटः -टा -टं, पल्लववान् -वती -वत् (त्).

BUDDING, *a.* उद्भिज्जः -ज्जा -ज्जं, प्ररोही -हिणी -हि (न्), पल्लववान् -वती -वत् (त्).

BUDDHA, *s.* (The name applied to the ninth incarnation of Vishńu, and to the founder of the Buddhist religion) बुद्धः, शाक्यमुनिः *m.*, शाक्यसिंहः, गौतमः, मुनिः *m.*, मुनीन्द्रः, शास्ता *m.* (स्तृ), श्रीघनः, सर्व्वार्थसिद्धः, शौद्धोदनिः *m.*, अर्कबन्धुः *m.*, मायादेवीसुतः.

To BUDGE, *v. n.* चल् (c. 1. चलति, चलितुं), प्रचल्; अपसृ (c. 1. -सरति -सर्त्तुं).

BUDGET, *s.* (Bag) शाणपुटः, पुटः, कोषः, दृतिः *f.*, आधारः, स्यूतः.—(Stock, store) कोषः, सामग्र्यं, सङ्ग्रहः, सञ्चयः.—(The statement made by the chancellor of the exchequer) कोशाधीशेन प्रजाप्रतिनिधिसभायाम् आगामिसंवत्सरे प्रत्य आयव्यययोर् ज्ञापनपत्रं.

BUFF, *s.* (Leather made of the skin of the buffalo) महिषचर्म्म *n.* (न्), महिषाजिनं.—(A light yellow colour) ईषत्पीतः, पाण्डुवर्णः.

BUFFALO, *s.* महिषः -षी *f.*, कासरः, गवलः, लुलापः, वाहद्विषन् *m.* (त्), सैरिभः.

BUFFET, *s.* (A blow) मुष्ट्याघातः, मुष्टिघातः, कराघातः, पाणिघातः, बाहुप्रहरणं, चपेटाघातः, चपेटिका.—(A cupboard) कुशूलः, कोष्ठः.

To BUFFET, *v. a.* मुष्टिना or पाणिना or चपेटेन हन् (c. 2. हन्ति, हन्तुं) or प्रहृ (c. 1. -हरति -हर्त्तुं) or तड् (c. 10. ताडयति -यितुं).

BUFFETER, *s.* प्रहर्त्ता *m.* (र्त्तृ), पाणिघातः, बाहुप्रहरणः, कराघातकृत्.

BUFFOON, *s.* भण्डः, वैहासिकः, विदूषकः, परिहासवेदी *m.* (न्), नर्म्मसचिवः.

BUFFOONERY, *s.* भाण्डं, वैहासिककर्म्म *n.* (न्), विहासः, हास्यं, परिहासः, नर्म्म *n.* (न्).

BUG, *s.* मत्कुणः, उत्कुणः, उद्गुणः, ओकणः, उद्दंशः, किटिभः, तल्पकीटः.

BUGBEAR, *s.* भयानकं or सन्त्रासजनकं यत्किञ्चित्, भयहेतु *n.*, त्रासदायी -यिनी -यि (न्), त्रासकरः -री -रं.

BUGGY, *a.* (Full of bugs) मत्कुणपूर्णः -र्णा -र्णं, समत्कुणः -णा -णं.

BUGLE, *s.* शृङ्गः -ङ्गं, मृगव्यशृङ्गः, व्याधवादितं शृङ्गं or विषाणं.

BUGLOSS, *s.* खिलरुह ओषधिप्रभेदः, गोजिह्वा.

To BUILD, *v. a.* निर्म्मा (c. 2. -माति -मातुं or in caus. -मापयति -यितुं or c. 4. -मीयते), निचि (c. 5. -चिनोति -चेतुं), कृ in caus. (कारयति -यितुं); 'to build castles in the air,' गगणकुसुमानि कृ.

To BUILD UPON, *v. a.* (To rely upon) अवलम्ब् (c. 1. -लम्बते -लम्बितुं), समालम्ब्, संश्रि (c. 1. -श्रयति -ते -श्रयितुं), समाश्रि, उपाश्रि.

BUILDER, *s.* निर्म्माता *m.* (तृ), निर्म्माणकर्त्ता *m.* (र्त्तृ), कारकः, निचेता *m.* (तृ), विधायकः.—(Of houses) स्थपतिः *m.* गृहकारकः, गृहकारी *m.* (न्).

BUILDING, *s.* (The act of building) निर्म्माणं, निर्म्मापणं, निचयनं, गृहकरणं.—(The fabric built) प्रासादः, गृहं, भवनं, हर्म्म्यं.

BUILT, *p. p.* निर्म्मितः -ता -तं, कारितः -ता -तं, निचितः -ता -तं.

BULB, *s.* कन्दः -न्दं, गोलमूलं, स्थूलकन्दः, वृहत्कन्दः.

BULBOUS, *a.* कन्दी -न्दिनी -न्दि (न्), गोलमूलविशिष्टः -ष्टा -ष्टं, कन्दाकृतिः -तिः -ति.

To BULGE, *v. n.* (To founder) दारुस्फोटनात् पोतपार्श्वे जलं गृहीत्वा मज्ज् (c. 6. मज्जति, मज्जितुं).—(To bag down, jut out) पुटरूपेण लम्ब् (c. 1. लम्बते लम्बितुं), वहिर्लम्ब्.

BULK, *s.* (Bigness) स्थूलता, स्थौल्यं, वृहत्त्वं, परिमाणं, स्थूलाकारता.—(The greatest part of a thing) प्रधानभागः, अधिकभागः, बहुतरभागः.—(Part of a building jutting out) वहिर्लम्बो हर्म्म्यभागः.

BULKHEAD, *s.* नौकाभ्यन्तरे पार्श्वापार्श्वि स्थापिता काष्ठमयी भित्तिः.

BULKINESS, *s.* स्थूलता, वृहत्त्वं, स्थूलकायता. *See* BULK.

BULKY, *a.* स्थूलः -ला -लं, वृहन् -हती -हत् (त्), महाकायः -या -यं, महाङ्गः -ङ्गी -ङ्गं, स्थूलकायः -यी -यं, वृहदङ्गः -ङ्गी -ङ्गं, स्थूलाकारः -रा -रं.

BULL, *s.* वृषभः, वृषः, पुङ्गवः, ऋषभः, गौः *m.* (गो), बलीवर्द्दः, उक्षा *m.* (न्), सौरभेयः, गोनाथः, ककुद्मान् (त्), अनड्वान् *m.* (-डुह्), भद्रः; 'a cow which is fit for the bull,' काल्या, उपसर्य्या; 'one which has gone to the bull,' वृषभेण आक्रान्ता, सन्धिनी; 'one which is bulling,' सन्धिनी, वृषस्यन्ती.—(A letter published by the pope) महाधर्म्माध्यक्षेण प्रकाशितम् आज्ञापत्रं.—(A blunder) स्खलितं, प्रमादः, वाग्दोषः.

BULLACE, *s.* अम्लरसविशिष्टः फलप्रभेदः.

BULL-BAITING, *s.* कुक्कुरवृषभयोर् युद्धं यत्र मनुष्याः क्रीडार्थं वृषभम् आक्रमितुं कुक्कुरान् प्रचोदयन्ति.

BULL-DOG, *s.* वृषभाक्रमणाय शिक्षितो ऽतिशयक्रूरस्वभावो बृहन्मुखः कुक्कुरभेदः.

BULLET, *s.* अधुनातनयोद्धृभिः सेविता सीसकगुलिका या ऽग्निबलेन नाडिच्छिद्राद् अतिदूरे निःसार्य्यते, दूरवेधिनी गुलिका, सीसकगुलिका.

BULLETIN, *s.* राजाज्ञया प्रचारितं समाचारपत्रं, राजकीयचिकित्सकैः प्रकाशितं रोगार्त्तमहीपतेः शरीरस्थितिज्ञापनपत्रं.

BULL-FINCH, *s.* वागनुकरणशीलः क्षुद्रपक्षिभेदः.

BULL-HEAD, *s.* स्थूलबुद्धिः *m.*, स्थूलधीः *m.*, दुर्बुद्धिः *m.*, मूढः, मूर्खः, जडः.

BULLION, *s.* हिरण्यं, रूप्यं, अमुद्रितं सुवर्णं रूप्यं वा, कोशः.

BULLITION, *s.* (The act or state of boiling) क्वथनं, क्वाथः, उत्सेचनं.

BULLOCK, *s.* शातोक्षः, वृषभः, वृषः, पुङ्गवः, अभिनववयस्को वृषभः.

BULL'S EYE, *s.* (A kind of window) गवाक्षः.

BULLY, *s.* (A blustering coward) शूरम्मन्यः, दम्भी *m.* (न्), दाम्भिकः, कुम्भः, विटः, पिण्डीशूरः, भर्त्सनकारी *m.* (न्), तर्जनकृत्, कलहकारः.

To BULLY, *v. a.* भर्त्स् (c. 10. भर्त्सयति -ते -यितुं), तर्ज् (c. 1. तर्जति, तर्जितुं), तिरस्कृ, मुखरीकृ.

BULRUSH, *s.* पर्व्वहीनो दूर्व्वाप्रभेदः, नलः, शरः.

BULWARK, *s.* वप्रः, प्राकारः, प्राचीरं, दुर्गं, परिकूटं.—(Shelter, protection) आश्रयः, संश्रयः, शरणं, आलयः, उपस्तम्भः.

BUM, *s.* नितम्बः, स्फिचौ *f. du.*, कटिप्रोथः.

BUMBAILIFF, *s.* ग्राहकः, आसेद्धा *m.* (द्धृ), आसेधकर्त्ता *m.* (र्तृ), राजपुरुषः.

BUMBARD, *s.* *See* BOMB, BOMBARD.

BUMBLE-BEE, *s.* वनमोदी *m.* (न्).

BUMP, *s.* (A swelling) स्फोटः, विस्फोटः, श्वयथुः *m.*, शोफः, शोथः, गण्डः, गण्डका, आभोगः.

To BUMP, *v. a.* (To strike) तड् (c. 10. ताडयति -यितुं), तुद् (c. 6. तुदति, तोत्तुं), हन् (c. 2. हन्ति, हन्तुं), प्रहृ (c. 1. -हरति -हर्त्तुं).

To BUMP, *v. n.* (To swell) श्वि (c. 1. श्वयति, श्वयितुं).—(To make a noise) आस्फोटनं कृ.

BUMPER, *s.* आकर्णं or आरपर्य्यन्तं पूरितं पात्रं, अतिपूर्णं भाजनं.

BUMPKIN, *s.* ग्राम्यजनः, ग्रामिकः, ग्रामेवासी *m.* (न्), वृषलः, जानपदः, प्राकृतजनः.

BUNCH, *s.* (A hard lump) पिण्डः -ण्डं, गण्डः, गण्डका.—(A cluster) गुच्छः, गुच्छकः, स्तबकः; 'a bunch of grapes,' द्राक्षास्तबकः.—(A number of things tied together) कूर्चः, पोट्टली.—(A knot, a tuft) ग्रन्थिः *m.*, चूडा, शेखरः.

To BUNCH OUT, *v. n.* पिण्डीभू, पिण्डाकारः -रा -रं अस्, प्रलम्ब् (c. 1. -लम्बते -लम्बितुं).

BUNCHY, *a.* पिण्डाकारः -रा -रं, स्तबकमयः -यी -यं, गुच्छाकारः -रा -रं.

BUNDLE, *s.* कूर्चः, कूर्चं, भारः, कृतकूर्चः, गुच्छः, गुच्छकः, पोटलिका, पोट्टली, वीटिका; 'a bundle of goods,' भाण्डकं; 'bundle off,' दूरम् अपसर, अपैहि.

To BUNDLE UP, *v. a.* कूर्चं कृ, कूर्चीकृ, गुच्छीकृ, पोटलिकां कृ.

BUNDLED UP, *p. p.* कृतकूर्चकः -का -कं, कृतपोटलिकः -का -कं, कृतगुच्छः -च्छा -च्छं.

BUNG, *s.* पात्रमध्ये छिद्रप्रतिबन्धकं तरुत्वङ्निर्म्मितं द्रव्यं, यवसुराभाजने छिद्रावरोधनार्थं काष्ठखण्डं, भाण्डछिद्रस्तम्भनकाष्ठं, पात्रछिद्रपिधानं.

To BUNG, *v. n.* छिद्रं or रन्ध्रं or धारां पिधा (c. 3. -दधाति -धातुं) or प्रतिबन्ध् (c. 9. -बध्नाति -बन्धुं) or निरुध् (c. 7. -रुणद्धि -रोद्धुं) or स्तम्भ् in caus. (स्तम्भयति -यितुं).

BUNG-HOLE, *s.* पात्रछिद्रं, पात्ररन्ध्रं, पात्रधारा, भाण्डशुषिरं, यवसुराभाजनछिद्रं.

To BUNGLE, *v. n.* प्रमादतस् or अदक्षप्रकारेण or अनाप्तं किञ्चित् कार्य्यं निर्व्वह् in caus. (-वाहयति -यितुं), प्रमद् (c. 4. -माद्यति -मदितुं), स्खल् (c. 1. स्खलति, स्खलितुं), भ्रम् (c. 4. भ्राम्यति, भ्रमितुं), दोषं कृ.

BUNGLE, *s.* प्रमादः, दोषः, भ्रमः, दुर्णयः, छिद्रं, स्खलनं, स्खलितं.

BUNGLED, *p. p.* दुर्णीतः -ता -तं, दुर्घटितः -ता -तं, दूषितः -ता -तं.

BUNGLER, *s.* अकृती *m.* (न्), अनाप्तः, अनिपुणः, अदक्षः, अपटुः *m.*, प्रमादी *m.* (न्), स्खलन्मतिः *m.*

BUNGLINGLY, *adv.* प्रमादतस्, प्रमादेन, अनाप्तं, अदक्षतया, सदोषं, स्खलनेन.

BUNN, *s.* मिष्टापूपः, पिष्टकः, पिण्डः, गोधूमचूर्णमिष्टाद्विनिर्म्मितः पिष्टकः.

BUNT, *s.* पुटः, पुटकं, क्रमशो विस्तीर्य्यमाणं रन्ध्रं, क्रमशो विवारः.

BUNTER, *s.* कुत्सितकर्म्मजीविनी, वृषली, बन्धकी, दुष्टा.

BUNTING, *s.* पताकानिर्म्माणयोग्यो or ध्वजवसनकरणयोग्यो विरलपटविशेषः, ध्वजपटः, केतुवसनः.

BUOY, *s.* समुद्रगाणां पथदर्शनार्थं or प्रच्छन्नसैकतशिलादिभयस्थानसूचनार्थं जलोपरि प्लवमानं काष्ठखण्डं.—(For mooring vessels) कूपकः.

To BUOY UP, *v. a.* (To keep afloat) उन्मज्ज् in caus. (-मज्जयति -यितुं), प्लु in caus. (प्लावयति -यितुं), उत्पत् in caus. (-पातयति -यितुं).—(To bear up, support) भृ in caus. (धारयति -यितुं), सन्धृ, अभिधृ, स्तम्भ् in caus. (स्तम्भयति -यितुं), उत्तम्भ्, संस्तम्भ्, आलम्ब् (c. 1. -लम्बते -लम्बितुं).

BUOYANCY, *s.* प्लवनशीलता, उत्पतिष्णुता, लघुता, लाघवं, लघिमा *m.* (न्).

BUOYANT, *a.* प्लवनशीलः -ला -लं, तरणशीलः -ला -लं, लघुः -घुः -घु, उत्पतिष्णुः -ष्णुः -ष्णु.

BUR, *s.* अङ्कुशाकारलोमविशिष्टो वस्त्रानुबन्धनशीलो वक्ष्यमाणक्षुद्रगुल्मसम्बन्धी दलपिण्डः.

BURDEN, *s.* भारः, धुरा, धूः (धुर्) *f.*—(Something grievous) पीडाकरः -रा -रं; 'burden-bearing,' भारवाहनः -ना -नं, धुरन्धरः -रा -रं, भारसहः -हा -हं, धुर्व्वहः -हा -हं, भारहरः -रा -रं.—(Beast of burden) भारवाहनः, धुरीणः, धुरीयः, धुर्य्यः, धौरेयः -यी -यं.—(Of a song) ध्रुवका, कथितपदं, आवर्त्तनीयश्लोकः, परिवर्त्तकश्लोकः.

To BURDEN, *v. a.* भारं न्यस् (c. 4. -अस्यति -असितुं) with loc. c. or दा (c. 3. ददाति, दातुं); 'to lay a burden on the shoulder,' भारं स्कन्धे न्यस् or निविश् in caus. (-वेशयति -यितुं) or समृ in caus. (-अर्पयति -यितुं).

BURDENED, *p. p.* भारवान् -वती -वत् (त्), भारी -रिणी -रि (न्), धुरीणः -णा -णं, भाराक्रान्तः -न्ता -न्तं, भारग्रस्तः -स्ता -स्तं, भारयुक्तः -क्ता -क्तं.

BURDENSOME, *a.* (Troublesome to be borne) दुर्भरः -रा -रं, दुःसहः -हा -हं, दुर्व्वहः -हा -हं, दुरुद्वहः -हा -हं.—(Grievous, oppressive) पीडाकरः -रा -रं, कष्टकरः -रा -रं, दुःखी -खिनी -खि (न्).

BURDOCK, *s.* पूर्व्वोक्तदलपिण्डविशिष्टः क्षुद्रगुल्मप्रभेदः.

BUREAU, *s.* (A chest, receptacle) आगारं, आधारः, निधानं, गोपनस्थानं, भाण्डागारं.—(An office for writing, &c.) लेख्यस्थानं, ग्रन्थकुटी.

Burg or burgh, *s.* महासभायां प्रतिनिधिप्रेरणाधिकारयुक्ता नगरी, कर्वटः -टं, नगरं -री, पुरं -री.

Burgess, *s.* (A citizen) पौरजनः, नगरजनः, पौरः, नगरस्थः.—(A representative of a city) नगरप्रतिनिधिः *m.*, नगरप्रतिभूः *m.*, नगरजनप्रतिनिधिः *m.*, प्रजाप्रतिनिधिः *m.*

Burgher, *s.* नगरजनाधिकारभोगी *m.* (न्), प्रधाननगरजनः, मुख्यपौरजनः, नगरसभासद् *m.*

Burghership, *s.* नगरजनाधिकारः, नगरजनपदं, नगरसभासदधिकारः.

Burglar, *s.* भित्तिचौरः, कुड्यच्छेदी *m.* (न्), कपाटघ्नः, गृहभङ्गकृत्, गृहरन्ध्रकृत्, सन्धिचौरः, कारुचौरः, बन्दिचौरः, बन्दीकारः, बन्दिग्राहः, खानिलः, कुम्भिलः, सुरुङ्गाहिः *m.*, सुरुङ्गाकृत्.

Burglary, *s.* गृहभङ्गः, गृहभङ्गापराधः, कुड्यच्छेदः, भित्तिचौर्य्यं.

Burgomaster, *s.* नगराधिष्ठाता *m.* (तृ), नगराध्यक्षः, पुराध्यक्षः, प्रधाननगरजनः, मुख्यपौरजनः, नगरव्यवहारेषु नियुक्तः, नगराधिपतिः, पुराधिकारी *m.* (न्).

Burial, *s.* भूमिखननं, निखननं, भूमौ निखननं, श्मशाने स्थापनं, श्मशानयापनं, भूमिसमर्पणं, प्रेतनिर्हारः.—(Funeral rites) प्रेतकर्म्म *n.* (न्), प्रेतकार्य्यं, मृतकसत्कर्म्म *n.* (न्), सत्क्रिया.

Burial-ground, *s.* श्मशानं, प्रेतवनं, पितृवनं, प्रेतगृहं, मृतशरीरस्थानं.

Buried, *p. p.* निखातः -ता -तं, भूमिनिखातः -ता -तं, श्मशानशायी -यिनी -यि (न्), श्मशानस्थापितः -ता -तं, श्मशानसमर्पितः -ता -तं.

Burier, *s.* प्रेतनिर्हारकः, प्रेतहारः, मृतपाः *m.*, शववाहकः.

Burine, *s.* तक्षणयन्त्रं, तक्षणी, तङ्कः, टङ्कः, शैलभित्तिः *f.*

To burl, *v. a.* लोहसन्दंशद्वारा or तुरीद्वारा निष्प्रवाणपटं श्लक्ष्णीकृ.

Burlesque, *a.* परिहासकरः -रा -रं, हास्यः -स्या -स्यं, हास्यजनकः -का -कं, प्रहासी -सिनी -सि (न्), अवहास्यः -स्या -स्यं, हासोत्पादकः -का -कं, नर्म्मदः -दा -दं.

Burlesque, *s.* भाण्डं, परिहासः, परीहासः, प्रहासः, प्रहसितं, उपहासः, अपहासः, नर्म्म *n.* (न्), टट्ठरी, परिहासवाक्यं, उत्प्रासनं.

To burlesque, *v. a.* अपहस् (c. 1. -हसति -हसितुं), अवहस्, प्रहस्, उपहस्, उपहासास्पदं कृ.

Burliness, *s.* स्थूलता, स्थौल्यं, वृहत्त्वं, स्थूलशरीरता, वृहदङ्गत्वं.

Burly, *a.* स्थूलः -ला -लं, स्थूलशरीरः -रा -रं, वृहत्कायः -यी -यं, महाङ्गः -ङ्गी -ङ्गं, वृहदङ्गः -ङ्गी -ङ्गं.

Burn, *s.* अग्निकृतं क्षतं, अग्निक्षतं, सन्तापः, सञ्ज्वरः, दाहः, अग्निदाहः.

To burn, *v. a.* दह् (c. 1. दहति, दग्धुं), अनुदह्, आदह्, निदह्, निर्दह्, परिदह्, प्रदह्, सम्प्रदह्; तप् (c. 1. तपति, तप्तुं) or in caus. (तापयति -यितुं), सन्तप् in caus., उष् (c. 1. ओषति, ओषितुं), दीप् in caus. (दीपयति -यितुं), आदीप्, उद्दीप्, उपदीप्, प्रदीप्, सन्दीप्; सन्धुक्ष् in caus. (-धुक्षयति -यितुं); ज्वल् in caus. (ज्वालयति -यितुं), प्रज्वल्, प्लुष् (c. 1. प्लोषति, प्लोषितुं).

To burn, *v. n.* दह् (c. 4. दह्यति, दग्धुं or in pass. दह्यते), सम्परिदह्, दीप् (c. 4. दीप्यते, दीपितुं), आदीप्, प्रदीप्, सम्प्रदीप्, विदीप्, सन्दीप्, तप् in pass. (तप्यते or c. 1. तपति, तप्तुं), प्रतप्, ज्वल् (c. 1. ज्वलति, ज्वलितुं), प्रज्वल्, सन्धुक्ष् (c. 1. -धुक्षते -धुक्षितुं); 'to be inflamed with passion, &c.,' दह् in pass. (दह्यते); 'with anger,' कोपदीप्तः -प्ता -प्तं भू; 'to burn after,' उत्कण्ठ् (c. 1. -कण्ठते -कण्ठितुं), अभिकाङ्क्ष् (c. 1. -काङ्क्षति -काङ्क्षितुं).

Burnable, *a.* दहनीयः -या -यं, दाह्यः -ह्या -ह्यं, दग्धव्यः -व्या -व्यं, ज्वलनीयः -या -यं, दीपनीयः -या -यं, तपनीयः -या -यं.

Burner, *s.* दाहकः, दग्धा *m.* (ग्धृ), दाहनकृत्, अग्निदः, तापकः, दीपकः.

Burnet, *s.* अनूपप्रदेशरुहः क्षुद्रगुल्मप्रभेदः.

Burning, *s.* दाहः, दाहनं, ज्वलनं, दीपनं, तापः, प्लोषः, ओषः.

Burning, *a.* दाहकः -का -कं, तापकः -का -कं, दीपनः -ना -नं, नैदाघः -घी -घं, ज्वाली -लिनी -लि (न्).—(That is on fire) दह्यमानः -ना -नं, दहन् -हन्ती -हत् (त्), ज्वलन् -लन्ती -लत् (त्), दाहवान् -वती -वत् (त्).—(Vehement) तैजसः -सी -सं, चण्डः -ण्डा -ण्डं.

Burning-glass, *s.* सूर्य्यतेजःसंघट्टनार्थं तदंशुसङ्ग्रहणयोग्यं काचपत्रं, दीप्तोपलः, अर्काश्मा *m.* (न्).

To burnish, *v. a.* तिज् in caus. (तेजयति -यितुं), निघृष् in caus. (निघर्षयति -यितुं), कान्तिं दा (c. 3. ददाति, दातुं), परिष्कृ, निशो (c. 4. -श्यति -शातुं).

Burnished, *part.* तेजितः -ता -तं, तैजसः -सी -सं, सुनिघृष्टः -ष्टा -ष्टं, निर्धौतः -ता -तं, प्रमृष्टः -ष्टा -ष्टं, निशातः -ता -तं, निशितः -ता -तं, परिष्कृतः -ता -तं.

Burnisher, *s.* तेजकः, धावकः, मार्ज्जनकृत्, कान्तिदायकः.

Burnishing, *s.* तेजनं, मार्ज्जनं, परिष्कारः, धावनं.

Burnt, *a.* and *part.* दग्धः -ग्धा -ग्धं, अग्निदग्धः -ग्धा -ग्धं, प्लुष्टः -ष्टा -ष्टं, विप्लुष्टः -ष्टा -ष्टं, प्लुष्टः -ष्टा -ष्टं, ज्वलितः -ता -तं, तप्तः -प्ता -प्तं, सन्तप्तः -प्ता -प्तं, उषितः -ता -तं; 'burnt up,' उत्तप्तः -प्ता -प्तं; 'burnt as a sacrifice,' वषट्कृतः -ता -तं; 'burnt brick,' पक्वेष्टका.

Burnt-offering, *s.* होमः, वषट्कारः, वैतानिकं, वैतानं.

Burr, *s.* (Lobe of the ear) कर्णलतिका, पालिका, कर्णपालिका.

Burrow, *s.* (Hole) गर्त्तः, विवरं, बिलं, खातं, श्वभ्रं.

To burrow, *v. n.* गर्त्ते or विवरं कृ, गर्त्ते वस् (c. 1. वसति, वस्तुं).

Burrowing, *a.* बिलवासी -सिनी -सि (न्), गर्त्तवासी -सिनी -सि (न्).

Bursar, *s.* विद्यालये धनाधिकारी *m.* (न्), धनाध्यक्षः, कोषाध्यक्षः.

Bursarship, *s.* अर्थाधिकारः, धनाधिकारः, धनाध्यक्षाधिकारः, कोषाध्यक्षपदं.

Bursary, *s.* विद्यालये धनगृहं, धनागारः, कोषः, धनकोष्ठकं.

Burse, *s.* वणिक्समागमचत्वरं, श्रेष्ठिचत्वरं, पण्यशाला, निगमस्थानं.

To burst, *v. a.* भिद् (c. 7. भिनत्ति, भेत्तुं or caus. भेदयति -यितुं), विभिद्, निर्भिद्, भञ्ज् (c. 7. भनक्ति, भंक्तुं), प्रभञ्ज्, विभञ्ज्, खण्ड् (c. 10. खण्डयति -यितुं), स्फुट् (c. 10. स्फोटयति -यितुं), दॄ in caus. (दारयति -यितुं), विदॄ, अवदॄ, शकलीकृ, खण्डशः कृ, विदल् in caus. (-दलयति -यितुं), लुप् (c. 6. लुम्पति, लोप्तुं), अवलुप्.

To burst, *v. n.* भिद् in pass. (भिद्यते), विभिद्, निर्भिद्; भञ्ज् in pass. (भज्यते), प्रभञ्ज्, विभञ्ज्, स्फुट् (c. 6. स्फुटति, स्फुटितुं, c. 1. स्फोटते, स्फोटितुं), विदॄ in pass. (-दीर्य्यते), अवदॄ, विदल् (c. 1. -दलति -दलितुं), विशॄ in pass. (-शीर्य्यते), परिशॄ.—(To burst in pieces) शकलीभू, खण्डशो भिद् in pass. or भञ्ज् in pass.—(To burst forth, break out) प्रपत् (c. 1. -पतति -पतितुं).—(As seeds) प्रोद्भिद्.

Burst, *s.* (Sudden rending) स्फोटनं, स्फुटनं, अकस्माद् भञ्जनं, भङ्गः, विभङ्गः, भेदनं, भेदः.—(Of laughter) प्रहसनं, प्रहसितं, अतिहसितं, अट्टहासः.—(Of light) ज्वाला.

Burst, *p. p.* स्फुटः -टा -टं, स्फुटितः -ता -तं, विदीर्णः -र्णा -र्णं, विभग्नः -ग्ना -ग्नं, विघटितः -ता -तं, विदलितः -ता -तं, भिन्नः -न्ना -न्नं, विभिन्नः -न्ना -न्नं.—(Diseased with hernia) अन्त्रवृद्धिपीडितः -ता -तं.

Burthen, *s.* भारः, धुरा. *See* Burden.

To bury, *v. a.* श्मशाने or भूमौ स्था in caus. (स्थापयति -यितुं) or निधा (c. 3. -दधाति -धातुं) or निखन् (c. 1. -खनति -खनितुं or -खातुं), निर्हृ (c. 1. -हरति -ते -हर्त्तुं).

Burying, *s.* भूमिखननं, निखननं, श्मशाने स्थापनं, भूमिसमर्पणं, प्रेतनिर्हारः.

BURYING-GROUND, *s.* श्मशानं, प्रेतवनं, प्रेतगृहं, पितृवनं, मृतशरीरस्थानं.

BUSH, *s.* गुल्मः, स्तुपः, स्तम्बः, क्षुपः, कुरुटः, कटिः *m.*—(A bough of a tree fixed at the door of a tavern) अत्र सुरादि विक्रीयते इति घोषणार्थं द्वारोपरि स्थापिता तरुशाखा; सुराध्वजः.—(Tail of a fox) लोमशापुच्छं.

BUSHEL, *s.* (A measure) द्रोणः -णं, आढकः.

BUSHY, *a.* (Full of bushes) गुल्मी -ल्मिनी -ल्मि (न्), तरुगुल्मावृतः -ता -तं.—(Thick) घनः -ना -नं, निविडः -डा -डं, अविरलः -ला -लं.—(Formed like a bush) गुल्माकारः -रा -रं.

BUSILESS, *s.* कार्य्यरहितः -ता -तं, शून्यः -न्या -न्यं, निष्कर्म्मा -र्म्मा -र्म्म (न्).

BUSILY, *adv.* अनलसं, अतन्द्रितं, मनःप्रवेशेन, अभिनिवेशेन, औत्सुक्येन.—(Inquisitively) चर्चया.

BUSINESS, *s.* (Affair) कर्म्म *n.* (न्), कार्य्यं, अर्थः.—(Employment) व्यापारः, व्यवसायः, व्यवहारः, कार्य्योद्योगः, नियोगः, प्रवृत्तिः *f.*, प्रवर्त्तनं, चरितं, सम्बन्धः.—(Something to be done) कृत्यं, कर्त्तव्यं, कार्य्यं.—(Object) विषयः, अर्थः, प्रयोजनं.—(A point, case) अर्थः, पदं.—(Means of livelihood, profession) वृत्तिः *f.*, वर्त्तनं, जीविका, आजीवनार्थं.—(Point, matter of discussion) स्थलं; 'a man of business, one who knows the proper ways of acting,' क्रियाविधिज्ञः, कार्य्ये कुशलः, दृष्टकर्म्मा *m.* (न्); 'what business have I with that?' कोऽर्थो मे तेन.

BUSK, *s.* चेलिकास्तम्भीकरणे स्त्रीजनैः प्रयुक्तः शृङ्गलोहादिनिर्म्मितः फलकविशेषः.

BUSKIN, *s.* (A half-boot) अर्द्धजङ्घापरिमाणः पादुकाविशेषः, पत्रङ्गा, अनुपदीना, उपानत् *f.* (ह्).—(A high-heeled shoe worn by ancient actors) उच्चपार्ष्णियुक्तो गौरवसूचकः पूर्व्वकालीननटैर् भृतः पादुकाविशेषः.

BUSKINED, *p. p.* पूर्व्वोक्तपादुकारूढः -ढा -ढं, सपादुकः -का -कं.

BUSS, *s.* चुम्बनं, परिरिंसा, निम्बितकं.

To BUSS, *v. a.* चुम्ब् (c. 1. चुम्बति, चुम्बितुं), निंस् (c. 2. निंस्ते, निंसितुं).

BUST, *s.* मस्तकाद्यात्मभृति वक्षःस्थलपर्य्यन्तम् अर्द्धशरीरप्रतिमा, अर्द्धकायप्रतिमा.

BUSTARD, *s.* आरण्यपक्षिप्रभेदः.

To BUSTLE, *v. n.* चेष्ट् (c. 1. चेष्टते, चेष्टितुं), आत्मानं चेष्ट् in caus. (चेष्टयति -यितुं), व्यवसो (c. 4. -स्यति -सातुं), कार्य्यव्यग्रत्वाद् इतस्ततो धाव् (c. 1. धावति, धावितुं).

BUSTLE, *s.* (Hurry, confusion) सम्भ्रमः, वैक्लव्यं, विभ्रमः, त्वरा, व्यग्रता, आकुलत्वं, व्यस्तता.—(Tumult) तुमुलं, कोलाहलः.

BUSTLER, *s.* व्यवसायी *m.* (न्), चेष्टाशीलः, सचेष्टः, तीक्ष्णकर्म्मा *m.* (न्).

BUSY, *a.* व्यापारी -रिणी -रि (न्), व्यापृतः -ता -तं, व्यवसायी -यिनी -यि (न्), कर्म्मी -र्म्मिणी -र्म्मि (न्), कर्म्मोद्युक्तः -क्ता -क्तं, कार्य्योद्युक्तः -क्ता -क्तं, कार्य्यनिविष्टः -ष्टा -ष्टं, कर्म्मिष्ठः -ष्ठा -ष्ठं, कार्य्यी -र्य्यिणी -र्य्यि (न्), कार्य्यवान् -वती -वत् (त्), सचेष्टः -ष्टा -ष्टं, प्रयत्नवान् -वती -वत् (त्), सोत्साहः -हा -हं, सोद्योगः -गा -गं, प्रवृत्तः -त्ता -त्तं, अतन्द्रितः -ता -तं, अनलसः -सा -सं, कार्य्यनिमग्नः -ग्ना -ग्नं.—(Meddling) परकार्य्यचर्चाशीलः -ला -लं.

To BUSY, *v. a.* (To employ) व्यापृ in caus. (व्यापारयति -यितुं), कार्य्ये नियुज् in caus. (-योजयति -यितुं, c. 7. -युनक्ति -योक्तुं) or अधिकृ.

BUSYBODY, *s.* परकार्य्यचर्चकः, पराधिकारचर्चकः, छिद्रान्वेषी *m.* (न्).

BUT, *conj.* (As an adversative) किन्तु, तु, परन्तु, पुनर्, अथवा.—(Except) ऋते with abl., विना with acc. or inst., अन्यः with abl.; as, 'any one but the father,' पितुर् अन्यः.—(But for, without) व्यतिरेकेण, अन्तरेण, विना; as, 'but for sin every thing flourishes,' पापं विना सर्व्वं फलति.—(But yet, howbeit) तथापि.—(Only) केवलं, मात्रं.—(All but) अल्पोनः -ना -नं, ईषदूनः -ना -नं; 'next but one,' एकान्तरः -रा -रं.—(If it were not, unless) यदि न.—(Moreover) किञ्च, अपरञ्च, अधिकन्तु.—(On the other hand) पुनर्.—(Otherwise than) अन्यथा with abl. 'But' may often be omitted in Sanskrit, or expressed by another form of sentence; as, 'he will not gain his end but by doing that,' तद् अकृत्वा प्राप्तार्थो न भविष्यति; 'I do not doubt but I am to blame,' सापराधो ऽस्मि इति न संशयः; 'but a short time since,' न चिरात्; 'there is none but fears him,' सर्व्वे तस्माद् बिभ्यति; 'she does nothing but grieve,' सा निरन्तरं शोचति; "who but a child weeps," को रोदित्य् अबालिशः.

BUTCHER, *s.* (Seller of meat) मांसविक्रयी *m.* (न्), मांसिकः, शौनिकः, सौनिकः, शूनावान् *m.* (त्), सूनी *m.* (न्), पशुमारणपूर्व्वकं मांसविक्रयजीवी *m.* (न्), प्राणिहिंसापरः.—(Butcher's meat) सौनं, घातस्थानभवं मांसं.

To BUTCHER, *v. a.* हन् (c. 2. हन्ति, हन्तुं), निहन्, or in caus. (घातयति -यितुं), मृ in caus. (मारयति -यितुं), वध् (defective, usually found in the 3d pret. अवधीत् and fut. वधिष्यति -ते), विशस् (c. 1. -शसति -शसितुं), निसूद् in caus. (-सूदयति -यितुं), अभिसूद्, विनिसूद्.

BUTCHERY, *s.* वधः, हननं, निहननं, घातनं, निषूदनं, विशसनं.—(The place where animals are killed) शूना, सूना, वधस्थानं, वधस्थली, वध्यभूमिः *f.*, घातस्थानं, पशुमारणस्थानं.

BUTEA, *s.* (A plant) किंशुकः, पलाशः, वातपोथः, पर्णः.

BUT-END, *s.* घनाग्रं, स्थूलाग्रं, अतीक्ष्णाग्रं.—(Hilt) त्सरुः *m.*

BUTLER, *s.* पानपात्रवाहकः, मद्यरक्षकः, मद्यागाराधिकृतः.

BUTMENT, *s.* उभयतस् तोरणमूलोत्तम्भकः सेतुहर्म्यादिभागः.

BUTT, *s.* (For shooting at) लक्षं, लक्ष्यं, शरव्यं, वेध्यं, व्यध्यः, प्रतिकायः, दृष्टिगुणः.—(Aim, end) अभिप्रायः, आशयः, उद्देशः, चिकीर्षितं.—(Object of jest) उपहासस्थानं, परिहासास्पदं, हास्यभूमिः *f.*—(A cask) पात्रं, भाण्डं, सुराभाजनं.

To BUTT, *v. n.* (To strike with the head like horned animals) शृङ्गिणवत् or मेषादिवत् शिरसा आहन् (c. 2. हन्ति हन्तुं).

BUTTER, *s.* नवनीतं, क्षीरसारः, दधिजं, दधिसारः, किलाटः -टी, मन्थजं, नवोद्धृतं.—(Clarified butter or ghee) घृतं, हविः *n.* (स्), सर्पिः *n.* (स्), पुरोडाशः, आज्यं.—(Of yesterday's milk) हैयङ्गवीनं.

To BUTTER, *v. a.* नवनीतेन लिप् (c. 6. लिम्पति, लेप्तुं) or अञ्ज् (c. 7. अनक्ति, अंक्तुं).

BUTTER-BUMP, *s.* क्रौञ्चजातीयः पक्षिभेदः, क्रौञ्चः, बकप्रभेदः.

BUTTER-CUP, BUTTER-FLOWER, *s.* पीतपुष्पप्रभेदः स च वसन्तसमये यवसमध्ये प्ररोहति.

BUTTERED, *p. p.* नवनीताक्तः -क्ता -क्तं, घृताक्तः -क्ता -क्तं, घृताभ्यक्तः -क्ता -क्तं.

BUTTERFLY, *s.* चित्रपतङ्गः, चित्राङ्गः पतङ्गभेदः, आपक्षपक्षः कीटभेदः, कीटोद्भवपक्ष चित्रपतङ्गः, सपक्षः कीटः.

BUTTERIS, *s.* (An instrument for paring the hoof of a horse) अश्वखुरतक्षणयोग्या कर्त्तरिका, तुरगक्षुरकर्त्तनार्थं यन्त्रविशेषः.

BUTTER-KNIFE, *s.* कुन्तलिका, घृतकुन्तलिका, नवनीतकर्त्तरिका.

BUTTER-MAN, *s.* नवनीतविक्रयी *m.* (न्), नवनीतविक्रयजीवी *m.* (न्), घृतविक्रेता *m.* (तृ).

BUTTER-MILK, *s.* दण्डाहतं, तक्रं, प्रमथितं, अरिष्टं, कालशेयं, गोरसः, कट्वरं.

BUTTER-PRINT, *s.* नवनीताङ्कनयोग्या काष्ठमयी मुद्रा.

BUTTER-TEETH, *s.* मुखाग्रभागे बृहद्दन्तद्वयं, सम्मुखस्थौ छेदकदन्तौ.

BUTTERY, *a.* नवनीतगुणविशिष्टः -ष्टा -ष्टं, घृतमयः -यी -यं.

BUTTERY, *s.* (The room where provisions are laid up) खाद्यद्रव्यागारं, विद्यालये पूपनवनीतयवसुरादिकोष्ठकं, कुशूलः, अन्नकोष्ठकं.

BUTTOCK, *s.* स्फिचौ *f. du.* (स्फिच्), नितम्बः, कटिप्रोथः.

BUTTON, *s.* (Catch by which clothes are fastened) गण्डः, पुंसो वस्त्राञ्चलद्वयसङ्ग्रहणार्थं गुलिका.—(Bud) मुकुलं, कुड्मलं, पल्लवः.

To BUTTON, *v. a.* (To dress) संव्ये (c. 1. -व्ययति -व्यातुं), वेष्ट् (c. 1. वेष्टते, वेष्टितुं).—(To fasten with buttons) पूर्व्वोक्तगण्डेन सङ्ग्रह् (c. 9. -गृह्णाति -ग्रहीतुं) or संलग्नीकृ or बन्ध् (c. 9. बध्नाति, बन्द्धुं).

To BUTTON, *v. n.* (To bud) गण्डाकारमुकुलवत् स्फुट् (c. 6. स्फुटति, स्फुटितुं).

BUTTON-HOLE, *s.* गण्डाधारः, गण्डछिद्रं, गुलिकाग्रहणयोग्यं छिद्रं, छिद्रं.

BUTTON-MAKER, *s.* गण्डकृत्, गण्डकारी *m.* (न्), गुलिकाकारः.

BUTTRESS, *s.* वप्रः, भवनस्य वहिरालम्बः, भित्तिस्तम्भनार्थं वप्रः or प्राकारः.—(Prop, support) उपस्तम्भः, आलम्बः, उपघ्नः, आश्रयः, आधारः.

To BUTTRESS, *v. a.* (To prop) पूर्व्वोक्तवप्रेण उत्तम्भ् (c. 9. उत्तभ्नाति, उत्तम्भितुं).

BUXOM, *a.* (Gay, lively) हृष्टः -ष्टा -ष्टं, प्रहसितवदनः -ना -नं, प्रहासी -सिनी -सि (न्), प्रफुल्लवदनः -ना -नं, आनन्दी -न्दिनी -न्दि (न्), सरसः -सा -सं.—(Wanton) ललितः -ता -तं, विलासी -सिनी -सि (न्).

BUXOMLY, *adv.* सानन्दं, सहर्षं, सललितं, सविलासं, सरसं.

BUXOMNESS, *s.* (Wantonness) लालित्यं, सविलासता, सरसता, लीला.

To BUY, *v. a.* क्री (c. 9. क्रीणाति -णीते, क्रेतुं), उपक्री, सङ्क्री, मूल्यं दत्त्वा लभ् (c. 1. लभते, लब्धुं) or प्राप् (c. 5. -आप्नोति, -आप्तुं).

BUYER, *s.* क्रेता *m.* (तृ), क्रयी *m.* (न्), क्रायकः, क्रयिकः.—(Buyer and seller) क्रयविक्रयी *m.* (न्).

BUYING, *s.* क्रयः.—(Buying and selling) क्रयविक्रयः.

To BUZZ, *v. n.* रु (c. 2. रौति, रवितुं), गुञ्ज् (c. 1. गुञ्जति, गुञ्जितुं), रण् (c. 1. रणति, रणितुं), रणरणं कृ.

BUZZ, BUZZING, *s.* गुञ्जनं, गुञ्जितं, कलः, कलकलः, मर्म्मरः, रणत्कारः, कलरवः, कलस्वरः; *part.* गुञ्जन् -ञ्जन्ती -ञ्जत् (त्), रणन् -णन्ती -णत् (त्).

BUZZARD, *s.* अपकृष्टजातिः श्येनभेदः, श्येनकः.—(A blockhead) स्थूलधीः *m.*, मन्दमतिः *m.*, मूर्खः.

BY, *prep.* (By the side of) expressed by उप prefixed; as, 'he sits by me,' माम् उपास्ते; 'a tank by a well,' उपकूपजलाशयः.—(Beside, denoting passage) expressed by अति prefixed; as, 'he passes by me,' माम् अत्येति.—(Denoting the agent, instrument, cause, means or manner) expressed by the instr. case; as, 'by him,' 'by that,' 'on that account,' 'by that means,' 'in that manner,' may all be expressed by तेन. In modern Sanskrit the instrument and agent are often expressed by द्वारा or द्वारेण and कर्त्तृक; as, 'to hit with a stick,' काष्ठद्वारा or काष्ठद्वारेण तड्; 'sacrifices by sages,' ऋषिकर्त्तृकयज्ञाः. 'By,' in some of these senses, may often be expressed by the indec. part.; 'a man may be happy by doing penance,' तपस् तप्त्वा सुखी भवेत्.—(According to) अनुरूपं, अनुसारेण; 'by rule,' विधिवत्, विधितस्, यथाविधि.—(As soon as, not later than) मध्ये; as, 'by next year,' आगामिवत्सरमध्ये.—(The quantity at one time) expressed by the affix शस्; as, 'by thousands,' सहस्रशस्; 'by twos and threes,' द्विशस् त्रिशस्; 'by companies,' पंक्तिभिः.—(Successive action) expressed by प्रति or अनु, or by repeating the word; as, 'man by man,' प्रतिपुरुषं; 'day by day,' प्रतिदिवसं or अनुदिवसं or दिवसे दिवसे.—(By himself, alone) एकान्ततस्, निभृतं, रहसि, रहोभूतः -ता -तं.—(In swearing or adjuring) expressed by the instr. c.; as, 'swear not at all, neither by heaven, nor by earth,' शपथं मा कार्ष्ट स्वर्गेण न पृथिव्या न; 'by name,' नाम्ना, नामतस्, नामधेयतस्; 'by force,' बलात्, बलात्कारेण, प्रसह्य; 'by chance,' दैवात्; 'by day,' दिवा.

BY, *adv.* (Near) निकटे, समीपे, अन्तिके, अभितस्, आरात्.—(By the side) पार्श्वतस्, पार्श्वे.—(Passing by) expressed by the prep. अति; as, 'he passes by,' अतिक्रामति.—(In presence) सन्निधाने, साक्षात्, अग्रे, समक्षं, सम्मुखे.

BY, *s.* (Something not the direct object of regard) expressed, when in composition, by उप; as, 'a duty by the by,' *i. e.* 'a secondary duty,' उपधर्म्मः.

BY AND BY, *adv.* अनन्तरं, क्षणान्तरे, न चिरेण, अचिरेण, अचिरात्.

BY THE BY, OR BY THE WAY, *adv.* (Exclusively of the subject in hand) प्रस्तुतम् अन्तरेण, प्रस्तुतविषयव्यतिरेकेण.—(Besides, moreover) किञ्च, अपरञ्च, अन्यच्च.—(In reference to that) तदुद्दिश्य.

BY-DEGREES, *adv.* क्रमशस्, क्रमे क्रमे, पदे पदे, प्रतिपदं.

BY-CONCERNMENT, *s.* उपविषयः, अप्रधानकार्य्यं.

BY-END, *s.* स्वहितं, स्वार्थः, आत्मविवृद्धिः *f.*, आत्मोदयः.

BY-GONE, *a.* अतिक्रान्तः -न्ता -न्तं, अतीतः -ता -तं, गतः -ता -तं, पुरातीतः -ता -तं.

BY-LANE, BY-STREET, BY-ROAD, *s.* उपमार्गः, उपपथः, उपरथ्या, उपप्रतोली, गूढमार्गः.

BY-LAW, *s.* उपधर्म्मः, उपव्यवस्था, उपविधिः *m.*, अनुव्यवस्था.

BY-NAME, *s.* उपाधिः *m.*, उपनाम *n.* (न्).

BY-PATH, *s.* उपमार्गः, उपपथः, उत्पथः, गूढपथः.

BY-ROOM, *s.* उपरोधकं, उपशाला, उपकोष्ठः, अन्तर्गृहं, कक्षान्तरं.

BYSTANDER, *s.* पार्श्वस्थः, समीपस्थः, निकटस्थः, तटस्थः, समीपवर्त्ती *m.* (न्), उपस्थायी *m.* (न्).—(At a sacrifice) सदस्यः, विधिदर्शी *m.* (न्).

BY-WEST, *a.* (Westward, to the west of) पश्चिमदिश्यः -श्या -श्यं.

BY-WORD, *s.* उपकथा, उपवाक्यं.—(Subject of scorn) तिरस्कारविषयः, उपकथनविषयः, अपवादविषयः, उपहासस्थानं, उपहासास्पदं, अवहासभूमिः *f.*

C.

CABAL, *s.* (An union of a few persons in some secret design) गोपनीयकार्य्यसाधनार्थं कतिपयजनसंसर्गः or पंक्तिः *f.*—(Intrigue) कुमन्त्रणा, कुविचारणा, कुपरामर्शः, कुयुक्तिः *f.*, कुसंसर्गः.

To CABAL, *v. n.* गोपनीयकर्म्मसम्पादनार्थं सुनिभृतं सम्मिल् (c. 6. -मिलति -मेलितुं) or सह गम् (c. 1. गच्छति, गन्तुं) or संयुज् in pass. (-युज्यते) or सङ्घट्ट् (c. 1. -घट्टते -घट्टितुं) or संसर्गं कृ.

CABALA, *s.* (A secret science) निगूढविद्या, निगूढशास्त्रं, गूढशास्त्रं, गुह्यविद्या, परमगहनविद्या.

CABALIST, *s.* (One skilled in occult sciences) निगूढविद्याज्ञः, निगूढशास्त्रज्ञः.

CABALISTICAL, *a.* (Having an occult meaning) निगूढार्थः -र्था -र्थं, अतिगुप्तार्थः -र्था -र्थं, परमगहनः -ना -नं, गूढः -ढा -ढं, गुह्यः -ह्या -ह्यं, रहस्यः -स्या -स्यं.

CABALISTICALLY, *adv.* अतिगुप्तं, निगूढं, सरहस्यं, परमगहनप्रकारेण.

CABALLER, *s.* कुमन्त्रणाकृत्, कुमन्त्री *m.* (न्), भेत्ता *m.* (तृ), भेदकरः,

राजद्रोही *m.* (न्).

CABBAGE, *s.* (A pot-herb) शाकप्रभेदः, शाकं, हरितकं, शूरणं, शिग्रुः *m.* —(Any thing stolen) मूषितं, मुष्टं, अपहारः, लोप्त्रं, होढं.

To CABBAGE, *v. n.* (To steal in cutting clothes) सूचिकवत् पटखण्डम् अपछिद्य चुर् (c. 10. चोरयति -यितुं) or मुष् (c. 9. मुष्णाति, मोषितुं).

CABBAGE-TREE, *s.* (A species of palm) तालजातीयो वृक्षप्रभेदः, उच्चतरुः *m.*

CABIN, *s.* (A small room) कुटिः *f.*, कुटी, कोष्ठः, शालिका, शाला, स्थलं.—(A chamber in a ship) नौकाभ्यन्तरे कुटिः or कोष्ठः or कक्षः or वेश्म *n.* (न्).—(A cottage) कुटीरः, वेश्म *n.* (न्), कुट्टिमः, पर्णशाला.—(A tent) पटकुटिः *f.*, पटवेश्म *n.* (न्), मण्डपः.

To CABIN, *v. n.* (To live in a cabin) कुटीरे वस् (c. 1. वसति, वस्तुं).

CABIN-BOY, *s.* नौकारूढानां परिचारकः or सेवकः or प्रेष्यः.

CABINET, *s.* (Private room) कक्षः, उपरोधकं, कक्षान्तरं, अन्तःशाला. —(Private council of the state) प्रधानमन्त्रिणां गूढसभा, धीसचिवानां सभा, शिष्टसभा, गूढमन्त्रणं, गूढभाषितं; 'a cabinet-minister,' मुख्यमन्त्री *m.* (न्), प्रधानमन्त्री *m.*, गूढमन्त्री *m.*—(A place in which rare things are kept) विशिष्टाधारः, दुर्लभद्रव्याधारः, रत्नकोष्ठः, रत्नाधारः, रत्नपात्रं, रत्नभाण्डं.—(A kind of box) समुद्गः, समुद्गकः, सम्पुटः.

CABINET-MAKER, *s.* रत्नाधारकृत्, रत्नभाण्डकृत्, समुद्गकारः, सम्पुटकृत्.

CABLE, *s.* नौरज्जुः *m.*, नौबन्धनरज्जुः *m.*, शाखारज्जुः, नौबन्धनार्थं स्थूलरज्जुः or महारज्जुः, नौकाया महागुणः or बृहद्गुणः.

CABLED, *a.* रज्जुना or गुणेन बद्धः -द्धा -द्धं, रज्जुबद्धः -द्धा -द्धं.

CABRIOLET, *s.* चक्रद्वययुक्तः सपिधानो रथविशेषः, कर्णीरथः, ह्ययनं.

CACHECTICAL, *a.* दोषत्रयपीडितः -ता -तं, दुष्टशरीरः -रा -रं, अस्वस्थः -स्था -स्थं.

CACHEXY, *s.* शरीरदोषः, रक्तदूषणं, दोषत्रयं, शरीरस्य अस्वास्थ्यं.

CACHINNATION, *s.* अट्टहासः, आच्छुरितं, अपच्छुरितं, प्रहासः, प्रहसनं.

CACKLE or CACKLING, *s.* कूजनं, हंसनादः, हंसरुतं, कुक्कुटीशब्दः.—(Making a cackle) हंसनादी -दिनी -दि (न्).—(Idle talk) जल्पनं, आलस्यवचनं, वृथाकथा, असम्बद्धं.

To CACKLE, *v. n.* कूज् (c. 1. कूजति, कूजितुं), हंसनादं कृ, हंसवत् or कुक्कुटीवत् शब्दं कृ.

CACKLER, *s.* हंसरूपेण नादी *m.* (न्), कूजकः, कूजनकृत्.—(A tell-tale) जल्पकः, वाचालः, रहस्यभेदकः.

CACOCHYMY, *s.* शरीरविकारः, रक्तविकारः, शरीरदोषः, दोषत्रयं.

CACODŒMON, *s.* अपदेवता, पिशाचः, वेतालः, भूतः, दैत्यः.

CACOPHONY, *s.* विस्वरपदं, अपरवः, अपक्वणः, कष्टपदं, कटुश्रुतिः *f.*

CADAVEROUS, *a.* मृतशरीरोपमः -मा -मं, शवसवर्णः -र्णा -र्णं.

CADE, *s.* (A barrel) दीर्घगोलाकारः काष्ठमयो भाण्डविशेषः.

CADE, *a.* कोमलः -ला -लं, सुकुमारः -री -रं, गृह्यकः -का -कं.

To CADE, *v. a.* कोमलतया or कोमलप्रकारेण पुष् (c. 9. पुष्णाति, c. 1. पोषति, पोषितुं) or संवृध् in caus. (-वर्धयति -यितुं).

CADENCE, *s.* (Fall, state of sinking) पातः, पतनं, अवपातः, च्युतिः *f.* —(Modulation of the voice, tone) स्वरः, कलः, स्वनः, निःस्वनः, निह्रादः, विरावः, क्वणः, विरिब्धः, छन्दः *n.* (स्).

CADENT, *a.* (Falling down) पातुकः -का -कं, पतयालुः -लुः -लु.

CADET, *s.* अनुजः, अवरजः, जघन्यजः, कनिष्ठः.—(A young volunteer) युद्धकर्म्मशिक्षार्थं वेतनं विना क्षत्रियधर्म्मम् आचरति यो कुलीनयुवा.

CADGER, *s.* विपणी *m.* (न्), प्रापणिकः, आपणिकः, अण्डनवनीतादिविक्रयिकः.

CADI, *s.* तर्कीयदेशे प्राड्विवाकः, धर्म्माध्यक्षः, दण्डनायकः, न्यायाधिपतिः.

CADUCITY, *s.* पातुकता, पतयालुत्वं, पतनशीलता, सद्यःपातित्वं, अस्थिरता.

CÆSURA, *s.* विच्छित्तिः *f.*, विच्छेदः, यवच्छेदः, विरामः.

CAG, *s.* (A barrel) दीर्घगोलाकृतिः काष्ठनिर्म्मितः पात्रविशेषः.

CAGE, *s.* पञ्जरं, पिञ्जरं, वीतंसः, कुलायिका, पक्षिशाला, शालारं.—(A prison) कारा, कारागारं, कारावेश्म *n.* (न्), बन्धनगृहं.

To CAGE, *v. a.* पञ्जरे or कारागारे निरुध् (c. 7. -रुणद्धि -रोद्धुं) or अवरुध् or बन्ध् (c. 9. बध्नाति, बन्द्धुं).

To CAJOLE, *v. a.* (To flatter, wheedle) शान्त्व् or सान्त्व् (c. 10. शान्त्वयति, सान्त्वयति -यितुं), लल् in caus. (लालयति -यितुं).—(With intent to overreach) वञ्च् in caus. (वञ्चयते -यितुं), परिवञ्च्, प्रलभ् (c. 1. -लभते -लब्धुं), विप्रलभ्, छल् (c. 10. छलयति -यितुं).

CAJOLED, *p. p.* लालितः -ता -तं, मधुरैर्वचोभिः संलापितः -ता -तं, वञ्चितः -ता -तं, विप्रलब्धः -ब्धा -ब्धं, प्रतारितः -ता -तं.

CAJOLER, *s.* (Coaxer) लालनकृत् *m.*, चाटुकारः.—(Deceiver) वञ्चकः, प्रतारकः, कूटकः, कूटकारः, कपटिकः.

CAJOLERY, *s.* (Coaxing) लालनं, चाटूक्तिः *f.*—(Overreaching) छलं, वञ्चनं, प्रतारणं, कूटता, कपटः, व्याजः.

CAITIFF, *s.* दुर्वृत्तः, दुरात्मा *m.* (न्), नराधमः, खलः, धूर्त्तः, शठः.

CAITIFF, *a.* दुर्वृत्तः -त्ता -त्तं, खलः -ला -लं, शठः -ठा -ठं, अधमः -मा -मं.

CAIRN, *s.* प्रस्तरचितिः *f.*, पाषाणचितिः *f.*, शिलाराशिः *m.*, पाषाणोत्करः.

CAKE, *s.* पूपः, अपूपः, पिष्टकः, पोलिका, करम्भः.—(A mass of any thing) पिण्डः.

To CAKE, *v. n.* पिण्डीभू, पिण्ड (nom. पिण्डायते), पिष्टकरूपेण घनीभू.

CAKED, *p. p.* पिण्डितः -ता -तं, पिण्डीभूतः -ता -तं, घनीकृतः -ता -तं.

CALABASH, *s.* बृहदलाबूप्रभेदः, अलाबूः *f.*, चिचिका.

CALAMANCO, *s.* ऊर्णानिर्म्मितः पटविशेषः, ऊर्णामयवस्त्रं.

CALAMINE, *s.* शिलाजतुस्वभावो भूमिविशेषो यत्संसर्गेण ताम्रं पित्तलः सम्पद्यते.

CALAMITOUS, *a.* व्यसनी -निनी -नि (न्), आत्ययिकः -की -कं, विपन्नः -न्ना -न्नं, विपद्युक्तः -क्ता -क्तं, आपद्ग्रस्तः -स्ता -स्तं, दुर्गतः -ता -तं, विधुरः -रा -रं, दैवोपहतः -ता -तं, उपाकृतः -ता -तं, दुःखी -खिनी -खि (न्), क्लेशी -शिनी -शि (न्), औत्पातिकः -की -कं, शोकपूर्णः -र्णा -र्णं, व्यथाकरः -रा -रं.

CALAMITY, *s.* विपद् *f.*, आपद् *f.*, विपत्तिः *f.*, व्यसनं, व्यापद् *f.*, विप्लवः, उपप्लवः, दुर्घटना, दौर्गत्यं, दुर्दैवं, दौर्भाग्यं, दुःखं, क्लेशः.—(From heaven) विनिपातः, उत्पातः, विनिहतः.

CALAMUS, *s.* सुगन्धिवेतसप्रभेदः, वेत्रः, वेणुः *m.*, वंशः, नडः, नलः.

CALASH, *s.* (A pleasure-carriage) क्रीडारथः, पुष्परथः, केलिरथः.

CALCAREOUS, *a.* शार्करिकः -का -कं, शार्करीयः -यी -यं, शर्करावान् -वती -वत् (त्).

CALCEATED, *p. p.* सपादुकः -का -कं, पादुकारूढः -ढा -ढं, उपानद्युक्तः -क्ता -क्तं.

CALCEDONY, *s.* (A kind of opal) शिवधातुः *m.*, गोमेदसन्निभः.

To CALCINATE or CALCINE, *v. a.* भस्मीकृ, आतप्तनं कृ, प्रतीवापं कृ.

CALCINATION, *s.* भस्मीकरणं, आतप्तनं, प्रतीवापः.—(Apparatus for) पातालः.

CALCINED, *p. p.* भस्मीकृतः -ता -तं, भस्मीभूतः -ता -तं.

CALCULABLE, *a.* गणनीयः -या -यं, विगण्यः -ण्या -ण्यं, संख्येयः -या -यं.

To CALCULATE, *v. n.* गण् (c. 10. गणयति -यितुं), विगण्, प्रगण्, संख्या (c. 2. -ख्याति -ते -ख्यातुं), परिसंख्या, सम्परिख्या, कल् (c. 10. कलयति -यितुं), सङ्कल्.

CALCULATED, *p. p.* गणितः -ता -तं, विगणितः -ता -तं, परिगणितः -ता -तं, राशिगतः -ता -तं, चित्तकल्लितः -ता -तं.—(Adapted, suited) युक्तः -क्ता

-क्तं, उपयुक्तः -क्ता -क्तं, योग्यः -ग्या -ग्यं, उचितः -ता -तं, पर्य्याप्तः -प्ता -प्तं.

CALCULATION, *s.* (The act) गणनं *n.* -ना, विगणनं, सङ्ख्यानं, परिसङ्ख्यानं, गुणनं.—(The result) गणितं.

CALCULATOR, *s.* गणकः, विगणकः, गणनकृत्, गुणकः, गुणकारः, सङ्ख्याकृत्.

CALCULOUS, *a.* शार्करः -री -रं, आश्मिकः -की -कं, अश्मरः -रा -रं, आश्मनः -नी -नं, अश्ममयः -यी -यं, शिलामयः -यी -यं.

CALCULUS, *s.* (Stone in the bladder) अश्मरी, अश्मीरः, शर्करा, मूत्रकृच्छ्रं.

CALDRON, *s.* पिठरः, उखा, स्थाली, उदस्थाली, पिष्टपचनं, कन्दुः *m.*, कटाहः.

CALECHE, *s.* क्रीडारथः, पुष्परथः, केलिरथः.

CALEFACTION, *s.* तपनं, तापनं, प्रतापनं, दाहनं, सिद्धकरणं.

CALEFACTORY, *a.* तापकः -का -कं, तापनः -नी -नं, तापकरः -री -रं.

To CALEFY, *v. n.* (To be heated) तप् (c. 1. तपति, तप्तुं), प्रतप्.

CALENDAR, *s.* (Almanack) पञ्जिः *f.*, पत्री, पञ्जिका, तिथिपत्रपत्रं.

CALENDER, *s.* (A hot-press) वस्त्रस्निग्धीकरणार्थं or पटश्लक्ष्णीकरणार्थं or वस्त्रमार्जनार्थं चक्रयन्त्रं.

To CALENDER, *v. a.* (To dress cloth) पूर्व्वोक्तयन्त्रेण वस्त्रं or पटं स्निग्धीकृ or श्लक्ष्णीकृ or मृज् (c. 2. मार्ष्टि, मार्ष्टुं), प्रमृज्.

CALENDS, *s.* मासस्य प्रथमदिनं, शुक्लपक्षस्य प्रथमदिवसः, अशुक्लदिनं, प्रतिपद् *f.*, पक्षतिः *f.*

CALENTURE, *s.* समुद्रयायिनां व्याधिप्रभेदस् तद्रोगग्रस्तः पोतवाहः शस्यक्षेत्रम् इति बुद्ध्या समुद्रमध्ये आत्मानं प्रक्षिपति.

CALF, *s.* गोवत्सः, वत्सः, वष्कयः, शकृत्करिः *m.* -री *f.*, दोग्धकः.—(New-born) तर्णः, तर्णकः.—(A herd of calves) वात्सकं.—(The thick part of the leg) जङ्घायाः स्थूलभागः or मांसलभागः, जङ्घापिण्डः, जङ्घामध्यं, मांसपिण्डाङ्गं.—(A dolt) स्थूलबुद्धिः, जडः.

CALIBRE, *s.* (Bore of a gun, &c.) छिद्रं, यन्त्रछिद्रं, सुषिरं, शुषिरं, व्यासं, छिद्रव्यासं, विस्तारः, छिद्रविस्तृतिः *f.*—(Size, measure) परिमाणं, मात्रा.—(Sort, kind) प्रकारः.

CALICE, *s.* कंसः, पात्रं, भाजनं, पुटकं.

CALICO, *s.* कार्पासं, नानावर्णमूर्त्तिमुद्रितः कार्पासपटः, चित्रितकार्पासं.

CALID, *a.* उष्णः -ष्णा -ष्णं, तप्तः -प्ता -प्तं, नैदाघः -घी -घं.

CALIDITY, *s.* तापः, उष्णता, घर्म्मः, निदाघः, अशिशिरता.

CALIGATION, *s.* अन्धकारः, तिमिरं, तमः *n.* (स्), तमिस्रं, मेघतिमिरं.

CALIGINOUS, *a.* तमस्वी-स्विनी-स्वि (न्), अन्धकारयुक्तः-क्ता-क्तं, तमोवृतः-ता-तं.

CALIGRAPHY, *s.* चारुलेखनं, शुभलेखनं, सुलेखनं, चारुलेखनशिल्पं.

CALIX, *s.* पुष्पगर्भः, पुष्पकोषः, पुष्पाधारः, कुसुमपुटी, उपदलं, पुष्पसम्बन्धी दलमयो वहिःकोषः or पुटः, पुष्पधारको दलपुटः.

To CALK, *v. a.* नौकातले दारुस्फोटनप्रयुक्तानि छिद्राणि शणसूत्रादिना निरुध् (c. 7. -रुणद्धि -रोद्धुं) or पिधा (c. 3. -दधाति -धातुं).

CALKER, *s.* नौकातले शणसूत्रादिना छिद्रावरोधी *m.* (न्) or छिद्रप्रतिबन्धकः.

CALL, *s.* (Summon) आह्वानं, आहूतिः *f.*, आह्वयः, आकारणं.—(Invitation) निमन्त्रणं.—(Address by name) सम्बोधनं, नामग्रहः.—(Impulse) वेगः.—(Divine vocation) प्रत्यादेशः, आकाशवाणी, ईश्वराह्वानं.—(Requisition, obligation) प्रयोजनं, अवश्यकता.—(Claim, demand) अभियोगः.—(Authority) अधिकारः.—(A visit) अभिगमः, अभ्यागमः, समायः.—(Challenge) आहूतिः *f.*—(A calling over the names of the members of parliament) महासभायां प्रत्यक्षाप्रत्यक्षनिर्णयनार्थम् एकैकशः प्रतिनिधिनामव्याहरणं.

To CALL, *v. a.* (Name, denominate) अभिधा (c. 3. -दधाति -धातुं), आख्या (c. 2. -ख्याति -ख्यातुं), प्रचक्ष् (c. 2. -चष्टे), कृत् (c. 10. कीर्त्तयति -यितुं), प्रकृत्, नाम कृ; 'they called his name Rama,' तस्य नाम राम इति चक्रुः; 'to call upon by name,' सम्बोधनं कृ; 'to be called,' अभिधा in pass. (-धीयते), ख्या in pass. (ख्यायते).—(Summon) आह्वे (c. 1. -ह्वयति -ह्वातुं).—(Invite) निमन्त्र् (c. 10. -मन्त्रयति -यितुं), आमन्त्र्.—(Convoke) समाह्वे, आह्वे, सङ्घट्ट् (c. 10. -घट्टयति -यितुं).—(Appeal to, invoke) ह्वे, आह्वे, उपह्वे.—(Call forth, put in action, excite) प्रोत्सह् in caus. (-साहयति -यितुं), उद्युज् in caus. (-योजयति -यितुं), चेष्ट् in caus. (चेष्टयति -यितुं).—(Call back, revoke) निवृत् in caus. (-वर्त्तयति -यितुं), खण्ड् (c. 10. खण्डयति -यितुं), प्रत्यादिश् (c. 6. -दिशति -देष्टुं).—(Call for, require) अर्ह् (c. 1. अर्हति, अर्हितुं), प्रार्थ् (c. 10. -अर्थयते -यितुं), याच् (c. 1. याचति, याचितुं); 'this matter calls for deliberation,' अत्र विचारेण प्रयोजनं.—(Call in, as coin) मुद्राप्रचलनं निवृत्, मुद्राप्रचार्य्यं निवृ in caus. (-वारयति -यितुं).—(Call over names) प्रत्यक्षाप्रत्यक्षनिश्चयनार्थं नामानि एकैकश उदाहृ (c. 1. -हरति -हर्त्तुं) or परिसंख्या or वच् in caus. (वाचयति -यितुं).—(Call out, exclaim) उत्क्रुश् (c. 1. -क्रोशति -क्रोष्टुं), प्रक्रुश्, विक्रुश्, उच्चैःस्वरे घुष् (c. 10. घोषयति -यितुं), उद्घुष्, चित्कारं कृ, चीत्कृ.—(Call out, challenge) आह्वे, उपाह्वे.—(Call to witness) साक्षिणं कृ or आह्वे.—(Call to mind) स्मृ (c. 1. स्मरति, स्मर्त्तुं).—(Call to account) अनुयुज् (c. 7. -युंक्ते -योक्तुं), अभियुज्, अनुसन्धा (c. 3. -दधाति -धातुं), निबद्धं -द्धां -द्धं कृ.—(Call up, from sleep) जागृ in caus. (जागरयति -यितुं), प्रबुध् in caus. (-बोधयति -यितुं).—(Address) आमन्त्र्, आलप् (c. 1. -लपति -लपितुं); 'by name,' नाम ग्रह् (c. 9. गृह्णाति, ग्रहीतुं).—(Call upon, implore) प्रार्थ् (c. 10. -अर्थयते -यितुं), विनयेन प्रार्थ्.—(To visit) अभिगम् (c. 1. -गच्छति -गन्तुं), अभ्यागम्, अभिसृ in caus. (-सारयति -यितुं).

CALLED, *p. p.* (Named) प्रोक्तः -क्ता -क्तं, अभिहितः -ता -तं, उदाहृतः -ता -तं, परिकीर्त्तितः -ता -तं, स्मृतः -ता -तं, शब्दितः -ता -तं, संज्ञितः -ता -तं. The following are used in composition only: नामा -मा -म, अभिधानः -ना -नं, आख्यः -ख्या -ख्यं, आह्वः -ह्वा -ह्वं, आह्वयः -या -यं, नामधेयः -या -यं; thus, 'a lake called blue-lotus,' नीलोत्पलनाम or नीलोत्पलाभिधानं सरः.—(Summoned, invited) आहूतः -ता -तं, निमन्त्रितः -ता -तं.

CALLING, *s.* (Inviting) आह्वानं, हूतिः *f.*, हवः, निमन्त्रणं.—(Addressing by name) सम्बोधनं, नामग्रहः.—(Giving name) नामकरणं.—(Profession, employment) वृत्तिः *f.*, जीविका, उपजीविका, व्यापारः, व्यवसायः.—(Divine vocation) प्रत्यादेशः, आकाशवाणी.

CALLOSITY, *s.* (Induration of the skin) कदरः, किणः, त्वक्काठिन्यं, त्वग्घनता, त्वग्दृढता, तनुकूपघनता.

CALLOUS, *a.* कठिनः -ना -नं, दृढः -ढा -ढं, घनः -ना -नं, घनीकृतः -ता -तं.—(Hard-hearted) कठिनहृदयः -या -यं.—(Insensible, unfeeling) विचेतनः -ना -नं, कर्कशः -शा -शं, निर्दयः -या -यं, कृपाहीनः -ना -नं.—(Shameless) निर्लज्जः -ज्जा -ज्जं.

CALLOUSLY, *adv.* काठिन्येन, सकार्कश्यं, दार्ढ्येन, निर्दयं, लज्जां विना.

CALLOUSNESS, *s.* (Hardness) कठिनता, काठिन्यं, कार्कश्यं, दृढता, दार्ढ्यं, द्रढिमा *m.* (न्).—(Insensibility, want of feeling) अचैतन्यं, हृदयकाठिन्यं, निर्दयता, निर्लज्जता.

CALLOW, *a.* पक्षहीनः -ना -नं, अजातपक्षः -क्षा -क्षं, अजातपर्णः -र्णा -र्णं, अनुत्पन्नपक्षः -क्षा -क्षं, गरुद्रहितः -ता -तं, नग्नदेहः -हा -हं, अकृतडीनः -ना -नं.

CALM, *s.* (Freedom from wind and waves) निर्वातः, वायुनिवृत्तिः *f.*, निर्वेगता, निस्तरङ्गता.—(Quiet, repose) शान्तिः *f.*, शमः, प्रशान्तिः *f.*,

विश्रामः, विश्रान्तिः f., प्रसन्नता, प्रसादः.

CALM, a. (Free from wind and waves) निर्वातः -ता -तं, गतानिलः -ला -लं, निवृत्तवायुः -युः -यु, निर्वेगः -गा -गं, निस्तरङ्गः -ङ्गा -ङ्गं.—(Quiet, composed in mind) शान्तः -न्ता -न्तं, प्रशान्तः -न्ता -न्तं, विश्रान्तः -न्ता -न्तं, प्रसन्नः -न्ना -न्नं, अव्याकुलः -ला -लं, निराकुलः -ला -लं, समाहितः -ता -तं, प्रशान्तात्मा -त्मा -त्म (न्), स्थिरमतिः -तिः -ति, शान्तचेताः -ताः -तः (स्), अन्तर्वेगहीनः -ना -नं, असम्भ्रमः -मा -मं, अनुग्रः -ग्रा -ग्रं.—(In countenance) प्रसन्नमुखी -खिनी -खि (न्).

To CALM, v. a. शम् in caus. (शमयति -यितुं), प्रशम्, उपशम्, तुष् in caus. (तोषयति -यितुं), परितुष्, प्रसद् in caus. (-सादयति -यितुं), अभिप्रसद्, शान्त्व् or सान्त्व् (c. 10. सान्त्वयति -यितुं), अभिशान्त्व्, परिशान्त्व्; 'to be calm,' शम् (c. 4. शाम्यति, शमितुं), प्रसद् (c. 1. 6. -सीदति -सत्तुं), सम्प्रसद्; 'the sea became calm,' प्रससाद सागरः; 'my mind is calm,' अन्तरात्मा प्रसीदति.

CALMED, p. p. शमितः -ता -तं, प्रशमितः -ता -तं, प्रसादितः -ता -तं.

CALMER, s. शमकः, शान्तिकर्त्ता m. (र्त्तृ), शान्तिकरः, शान्तिदः, तुष्टिकरः.

CALMLY, adv. शान्त्या, शान्तं, मनःप्रसादेन, असम्भ्रमं, प्रशान्तचेतसा.

CALMNESS, s. शान्तता, प्रशान्तता, शान्तिः f., विश्रान्तता, प्रसादः, निराकुलता, अव्याकुलता, स्थिरता, असम्भ्रमः.—(Of the sea) निर्वातत्वं.

CALOMEL, s. षड्गुणः शोधितः or ऊर्द्ध्वपातितः पारदः स च चिकित्सकैर् नानाव्याधिप्रतिकाराय रोगार्त्तेषु प्रयुज्यते.

CALORIFIC, a. तापकरः -री -रं, तापजनकः -का -कं, निदाघकरः -री -रं.

CALOTTE, s. धर्म्मोपाध्यायैर् भृतं शरावाकृति मस्तकाभरणं or शिरोवेष्टनं.

CALTROP, s. विग्रहसमये शत्रोर् अश्वखुरवेधनार्थं रणभूमौ न्यस्तं शूलत्रययुक्तं लोहयन्त्रं.—(The plant) गोक्षुरः -रकः, गोखुरः -रकः.

To CALVE, v. n. वत्सं or तर्णं सु (c. 2. सूते, c. 4. सूयते, सोतुं) or प्रसु or जन् in caus. (जनयति -यितुं) or प्रजन् (c. 4. -जायते -जनितुं); 'a cow that calves often,' बहुसूतिः f., चिरसूता, बष्कयणी; 'cows calve every year,' प्रतिवर्षं प्रसूयन्ते गावः; 'a cow that has lately calved,' नवसूतिका; 'calving of a cow,' गोप्रसवः.

To CALUMNIATE, v. a. परिवद् (c. 1. -वदति -वदितुं), अपवद्, निन्द् (c. 1. निन्दति, निन्दितुं), मिथ्या अभियुज् (c. 7. -युनक्ति -युंक्ते -योक्तुं), अभिशप् (c. 1. -शपति -शप्तुं), अभिशंस् (c. 1. -शंसति -शंसितुं), अपक्षिप् (c. 6. -क्षिपति -क्षेप्तुं), आक्षर् in caus. (-क्षारयति -यितुं), कलङ्क (nom. कलङ्कयति -यितुं), परगुणान् अपवद्.

CALUMNIATED, p. p. अभिशस्तः -स्ता -स्तं, मिथ्याभिशस्तः -स्ता -स्तं, मिथ्याभियुक्तः -क्ता -क्तं, आक्षारितः -ता -तं, क्षारितः -ता -तं, कलङ्कितः -ता -तं.

CALUMNIATOR, s. परिवादी m. (न्) -दकः, पिशुनः, अभिशंसकः, अभिशापकः, मिथ्याभियोगी m. (न्), अभ्यसूयकः, निन्दकः, गुणघाती m. (न्), गुणापवादकः, कलङ्ककरः, कुवादः.

CALUMNIOUS, a. पिशुनः -ना -नं, असूकः -का -कं, अभ्यसूयकः -का -कं, वाग्दुष्टः -ष्टा -ष्टं, कलङ्ककरः -री -रं, कलङ्कमयः -यी -यं, कलङ्की -ङ्किनी -ङ्कि (न्).

CALUMNIOUSLY, adv. परिवादेन, सापवादं, गुणापवादेन, असूयया, सकलङ्कं, पैशुन्येन, पिशुनवचनेन, निन्दापूर्व्वकं, सासूयं.

CALUMNY, s. परिवादः, अपवादः, असूया f. -यनं, असूयुः m., अभ्यसूया, पिशुनवचनं, पिशुनवाक्यं, पैशुन्यं, अभिशंसनं, मिथ्याभिशंसनं, अभिशपनं, अभिशापः, आक्षारः -रणं, कलङ्कः, गुणापवादः, वाग्दोषः, मिथ्याभियोगः, निन्दा, परदोषवादः, अलीकप्रवादः.

CALX, s. चूर्णं, भस्म n. (न्).—(Of brass) रीतिपुष्पं, रीतिका, पुष्पकेतु n., पौष्पकं, कुसुमाञ्जनं.

CALYCLE, s. क्षुद्रमुकुलं, क्षुद्रकुड्मलं, नवजालकं.

CÁMADEVA, s. See KÁMADEVA.

CAMBIST, s. हुण्डिकापत्रक्रयविक्रयजीवी m. (न्).

CAMBRIC, s. अंशुकं, दुकूलं, कुलीनस्त्रीलोकेन भृतः सूक्ष्मक्षौमपटविशेषः.

CAMEL, s. उष्ट्रः, क्रमेलः, क्रमेलकः, महाङ्गः, मयः, वणिग्वहः, शरभः, द्विककुद् m., दीर्घग्रीवः; 'a young camel,' करभः; 'a flock of camels,' औष्ट्रकं.

CAMELEON, s. सरटः, सरटुः m., प्रतिसूर्य्यः, कृकलासः, कृकवाकुः m.

CAMELOPARD, s. तरक्षुरूपेण चित्रित उष्ट्रजातीयो दीर्घग्रीवो जन्तुप्रभेदः.

CAMELOT, s. (A stuff made of camel's hair, &c.) उष्ट्रलोमादिनिर्म्मितं वस्त्रं.

CAMEO, s. तक्षितुं शक्यो द्विवर्णप्रस्तरविशेषः, तक्षणीयत्वक्षमः वस्तुविशेषः.

CAMERA-OBSCURA, s. सान्धकारकुटीपटलनिवेशितश् चाक्षुषयन्त्रविशेषो यद्द्वारेण अन्तरस्थश्वेतफलके प्रतिबिम्बिता बहिःस्था विषया दृश्या भवन्ति.

CAMERATED, a. (Arched) तोरणाकारपटलयुक्तः -क्ता -क्तं, तोरणीकृतः -ता -तं.

CAMISADO, s. सौप्तिकं, सौप्तिकवधः, नैशाक्रमः, नैशाभिक्रमः, रात्रियुद्धं, रात्रौ or अन्धकारे अभियोगः or अवस्कन्दः.

CAMOYS or CAMOUS, a. (Flat, said of the nose) चिपिटः -टा -टं, चिक्किनः -ना -नं, अवभटः -टा -टं.

CAMP, s. वाहिनीनिवेशः, निवेशः, शिबिरं, कटकः, मन्दिरं, स्कन्धावारः, बलस्थितिः f., पटकः; 'camp-follower,' सेनाचरः.

To CAMP, v. n. (To pitch a camp, to lodge in a camp) निविश् (c. 6. -विशते -वेष्टुं), सैन्यं निविश् in caus. (-वेशयति -यितुं), शिबिरे वस् (c. 1. वसति, वस्तुं).

CAMPAIGN, s. (A level open tract of ground) समभूमिः f., समस्थलं, तरुगुल्मरहितः समो भूभागः, निर्वनभूमिः.—(The time for which any army keeps the field) अभियोगनकालः, युद्धकालः, रणक्षेत्रे वर्त्तनकालः, वत्सरमध्ये यत्कालपर्य्यन्तं सैन्या रणक्षेत्रे युयुत्सवो विचरन्ति.

CAMPANIFORM, a. (As a flower) घण्टाकारः -रा -रं, घण्टाकृतिः -तिः -ति.

CAMPESTRAL, a. क्षेत्रिकः -की -कं, कैदारः -री -रं, जाङ्गलः -ली -लं.

CAMPHOR or CAMPHIRE, s. कर्पूरः -रं, चन्द्रः, सोमः, सोमसंज्ञं, सिताभः, ताराभः, सुधांशुः m., घनसारः, हिमवालुका.

CAMPHORATED, a. कर्पूरसंसृष्टः -ष्टा -ष्टं, कर्पूरीयः -या -यं.

CAN, s. कंसः, कांस्यः, त्रापुषकुम्भः, लौहकुण्डः, धातुमयपात्रं, भाजनं.

To CAN, v. n. (To be able) शक् (c. 5. शक्नोति, c. 4. शक्यति, शक्तुं), समर्थः -र्था -र्थं अस्, क्षम् (c. 1. क्षमते, क्षन्तुं), प्रभू (c. 1. -भवति -भवितुं).

CANAILLE, s. अन्त्याः m. pl., अन्त्यजातीयाः m. pl., अन्त्यजाः m. pl., प्राकृतमनुष्याः m. pl., अधमजातीयाः m. pl., खलाः m. pl., हीनवर्णाः m. pl., पृथग्जनाः m. pl., इतरजनाः m. pl.

CANAL, s. कुल्या, उपकुल्या, खातं, प्रणालः -ली, खल्लः, जलनिर्गमः, सारणिः f., कृत्रिमा सरित्.

CANARY-BIRD, s. उत्तालरुतविशिष्टः पीतवर्णो विजातीयः क्षुद्रपक्षी.

To CANCEL, v. a. (To annul, obliterate) लुप् (c. 6. लुम्पति, लोप्तुं), लोपं कृ, उच्छिद् (c. 7. -छिनत्ति -छेत्तुं), अपमृज् (c. 2. -मार्ष्टि -मार्ष्टुं), निर्मृज्, व्यामृज्, परिमृज्, उद्धृ (c. 1. -हरति -हर्त्तुं).—(To mark a writing with cross lines) लिखितलोपसूचनार्थं व्यत्यस्तरेखाङ्कयेन पत्रं चिह्न् (c. 10. चिह्नयति -यितुं).

CANCELLATED, p. p. व्यत्यस्तरेखाचिह्नितः -ता -तं.

CANCELLED, p. p. लुप्तः -प्ता -प्तं, उच्छिन्नः -न्ना -न्नं, व्यामृष्टः -ष्टा -ष्टं.

CANCER, s. (A sore) विद्रधिः m., व्रणः, गलितक्षतं, नालीव्रणः, तनुव्रणः, उपदंशः, विस्फोटः, नाडी.—(The sign of the summer solstice) कर्कटः, कर्कः, कर्कटराशिः *m.*; 'stars in cancer,' पुष्यः, सिध्यः, तिष्यः.—(A crab-fish) कुलीरः, कर्कटः.

To CANCERATE, *v. n.* (To become a cancer) व्रणीभू, विद्रधीभू, व्रण (nom. व्रणायते).

CANCEROUS, *a.* विद्रधिगुणविशिष्टः -ष्टा -ष्टं, विद्रधीयः -या -यं.

CANCRINE, *a.* कर्कटीयः -या -यं, कुलीरसम्बन्धी -न्धिनी -न्धि (न्).

CANDENT, *a.* प्रचण्डः -ण्डा -ण्डं, अत्युष्णः -ष्णा -ष्णं, अत्यन्ततप्तः -प्ता -प्तं.

CANDID, *a.* (Fair, upright) सरलः -ला -लं, दक्षिणः -णा -णं, उदारः -रा -रं, अवक्रः -क्रा -क्रं, अजिह्मः -ह्मा -ह्मं, शुद्धमतिः -तिः -ति, ऋजुः -जुः -जु, अगूढभावः -वा -वं, विमलात्मा -त्मा -त्म (न्), निर्व्यलीकः -का -कं.—(Pure) शुचिः -चिः -चि, विमलः -ला -लं, निर्म्मलः -ला -लं.—(White) शुक्लः -क्ला -क्लं.

CANDIDATE, *s.* अर्थी *m.* (न्), प्रार्थकः, याचकः, प्रत्याशी *m.* (न्), पदान्वेषी *m.* (न्), अभियोक्ता *m.* (क्तृ).

CANDIDLY, *adv.* सरलं, दाक्षिण्येन, अजिह्मं, धर्म्मतस्, अमायया, निर्व्यलीकं, निर्व्याजं, कपटं विना, मायाव्यतिरेकेण.

CANDIDNESS, *s.* सरलता, सारल्यं, दाक्षिण्यं, शुचिता, ऋजुता, आर्जवं, अजिह्मता, निर्व्यलीकता, अमाया.

CANDIED, *a.* घनीभूतः -ता -तं.—(Sugar) खण्डमोदकः, माक्षिकशर्करा, उपला, दृढगात्रिका.

To CANDIFY, *v. a.* शुक्लीकृ, धवलीकृ, धवल (nom. धवलयति -यितुं).

CANDLE, *s.* दीपः -पकः, दीपिका, प्रदीपः, वर्त्ती, वर्त्तिः *f.*, दशाकर्षः, शिखी *m.* (न्), कज्जलध्वजः.

CANDLEHOLDER, *s.* दीपधारी *m.* (न्), दीपवाहः, प्रदीपभृत्, दीपहस्तः.

CANDLELIGHT, *s.* दीपद्युतिः *f.*, प्रदीपद्युतिः, दीपप्रभा, वर्त्तिदीप्तिः *f.*

CANDLEMAS, *s.* मरियम्नामिकायाः कन्यायाः शुचित्वम् उद्दिश्य महोत्सवो यस्य सेवनकाले भूरिप्रदीपाः समिद्धा भवन्ति.

CANDLESTICK, *s.* दीपाधारः, दीपपादपः, प्रदीपपादपः, दीपवृक्षः, वर्त्त्याधारः, शिखातरुः *m.*, शिखावृक्षः, कौमुदीवृक्षः, कज्जलरोचकः.

CANDLESTUFF, *s.* दीपिकानिर्म्माणार्थं तैलवसादि द्रव्यं, वसा, तैलं, स्नेहः.

CANDOUR, *s.* सरलता, दाक्षिण्यं, शुचिता, अमाया, ऋजुता, सत्यता, सत्यवादित्वं, विमलात्मता, मनोनिर्म्मलत्वं, निर्व्यलीकता, औदार्य्यं, सुशीलता.

To CANDY, *v. a.* (To form into congelations) खण्डीकृ, खण्डमोदकाकारं -रां -रं or उपलाकारं कृ, घनीकृ or सान्द्रीकृ or संहतीकृ, श्यै in caus. (श्यापयति -यितुं).

To CANDY, *v. n.* (To grow congealed) खण्डीभू, खण्डमोदकवद् घनीभू or सान्द्रीभू, उपलाकारः -रा -रं भू, श्यै (c. 1. श्यायते, श्यातुं).

CANDY, *s.* (Sugar) खण्डमोदकः, खण्डः, उपला, शुक्लोपला, माक्षिकशर्करा, शर्करा, दृढगात्रिका.

CANE, *s.* वेतसः, वेणुः *m.*, वेत्रः, वेत्रं, वंशः, कीचकः, वानीरः; 'made of cane,' वैणवः -वी -वं, वैत्रकः -की -कं, वैदलः -ली -लं; 'a worker in cane,' वेणुच्छेदनजीवी *m.* (न्), वैदलकारः; 'a blow with a cane,' वेत्राघातः, वेत्रेण आघातः.—(A stick) यष्टिः *m. f.*, दण्डः; 'a cane stick,' वैणवी यष्टिः.—(Sugar-cane) इक्षुः *m.*, इक्षुयष्टिः *m.*, इक्षुदण्डः.—(Cane-chair) वेत्रासनं.

To CANE, *v. a.* (To beat with a cane) दण्डेन or वेत्रेण or यष्टिना हन् (c. 2. हन्ति, हन्तुं) or तड् (c. 1. ताडयति -यितुं), वेत्राघातं कृ.

CANICULAR, *a.* (Belonging to the dog-star) कुक्कुराख्यनक्षत्रसम्बन्धी -न्धिनी -न्धि (न्).

CANINE, *a.* कुक्कुरसम्बन्धकः -का -कं, कुक्कुरीयः -या -यं, शौवः -वी -वं.

CANISTER, *s.* (A basket) डल्लकः, करण्डः.—(A tin-box) त्रापुषपात्रं.

CANKER, *s.* (A corroding sore) गलितक्षतं, विद्रधिः *m.*, नालीव्रणः.—(A worm that destroys fruits) फलनाशकः कीटः.—(Any thing that corrupts or corrodes) कलङ्कः, विषं, दूषकः, गरः.—(Corrosion, consuming) दूषणं, विलयः, विलयनं, क्षयः, नाशः, विनाशः.—(Virulence) विषालुता, सगरता.

To CANKER, *v. a.* (To corrupt, corrode) दुष् in caus. (दूषयति -यितुं), कलङ्क (nom. कलङ्कयति -यितुं), विली in caus. (-लाययति -यितुं), विनश् in caus. (-नाशयति -यितुं), क्षि in caus. (क्षययति -यितुं), मृ in caus. (मारयति -यितुं).

To CANKER, *v. n.* (To grow corrupt) दुष् (c. 4. दुष्यति, दोष्टुं), प्रदुष्, विली (c. 4. -लीयते -लेतुं), विषसम्पर्कात् or विषसंसर्गात् क्षी in pass. (क्षीयते), गल् (c. 1. गलति, गलितुं), विगल्.

CANKER-BIT, *a.* विषाक्तदन्तेन दष्टः -ष्टा -ष्टं or दंशितः -ता -तं.

CANKERED, *p. p.* कलङ्कितः -ता -तं, दूषितः -ता -तं, विषाक्तः -क्ता -क्तं, गरली -लिनी -लि (न्).—(In disposition) प्रतीपः -पा -पं, दुःशीलः -ला -लं, विषहृदयः -या -यं.

CANNABINE, *a.* शाणः -णी -णं, भाङ्गीनः -ना -नं, शणसूत्रमयः -यी -यं.

CANNIBAL, *s.* पुरुषादः, नृजग्धः, नरभुक् *m.* (ज्), मनुष्यभोजी *m.* (न्), असृपः, पिशिताशः, क्रव्याशी *m.* (न्), आममांसाशी *m.* (न्), राक्षसः.

CANNIBALISM, *s.* नृजग्धत्वं, क्रव्याशिता, मनुष्यभोजित्वं.

CANNON, *s.* अन्तरग्निबलेन लोहगुलिकाप्रक्षेपणं युद्धयन्त्रं, वृहन्नोलप्रक्षेपार्थं सुषिरयन्त्रं, गोलासनं, गुलिप्रक्षेपणी वृहल्लोहनाडिः *f.*

To CANNONADE, *v. a.* पूर्व्वोक्तेन यन्त्रेण मृद् (c. 9. मृद्नाति, मर्द्दितुं) or प्रमृद्.

CANNON-BALL, *s.* रणगुलिः *f.*, रणगोलः, गुलिः *f.* -ली, अयोगुडः, पूर्व्वोक्तवृहन्नाडेः प्रक्षेपणीयो लोहगोलकः, दूरवेधिनी गुलिका, आग्नेयास्त्रं.

CANNONEER, *s.* पूर्व्वोक्तयन्त्रेण मर्द्दी *m.* (न्) or विमर्द्दी, रणगुलिप्रक्षेपकः, रणगोलासः, आग्नेयास्त्रप्रक्षेपकः.

CANOE, *s.* वृक्षस्य खातस्कन्धनिर्म्मिता क्षुद्रनौका, लघुनौका.

CANON, *s.* (A rule, a law) विधिः *m.*, नियमः, सूत्रं, व्यवस्था, शास्त्रं, रीतिः *f.*—(Ecclesiastical law) पौरोहितधर्म्मशास्त्रं, धर्म्माध्यक्षसमाजेन व्यवस्थापिता धर्म्मसंहिता, पौरोहित्यसम्बन्धि स्मृतिशास्त्रं, याजकीयधर्म्मशास्त्रं.—(The received books of Holy Scripture) धर्म्ममूलं, धर्म्मपुस्तकसंहिता, धर्म्मनिदर्शनं.—(A dignitary of a Cathedral) महापूजाशालासम्बन्धीयमठे गुरुः or सभासद्, महाभजनप्रासादे प्रधानपुरोहितः, महापूजाशालायां मुख्यधर्म्माध्यापकः.

CANONESS, *s.* पूर्व्वोक्तपुरोहितव्यवहारानुसारिणी स्त्री or नारी.

CANONICAL, *a.* वैधिकः -की -कं, नैयमिकः -की -कं, शास्त्रीयः -या -यं, धर्म्मशास्त्रीयः -या -यं, रीत्यनुसारी -रिणी -रि (न्), व्यावहारिकः -की -कं, पौरोहितधर्म्मानुरूपः -पा -पं.

CANONICALLY, *adv.* विधिवत्, शास्त्रवत्, विधितस्, शास्त्रतस्, विधिपूर्व्वकं, रीतिपूर्व्वकं, नियमपूर्व्वकं, यथाविधि, यथाशास्त्रं, पौरोहितधर्म्मानुसारेण, याजकीयस्मृतिशास्त्रक्रमेण.

CANONICALS, *s. pl.* धर्म्माध्यापकलाक्षणिकं वस्त्रादि, पुरोहितवेशः, याजकवेशः.

CANONIST, *s.* पौरोहितधर्म्मशास्त्रज्ञः, पुरोहितव्यवहारपण्डितः, याजकीयधर्म्मशास्त्रज्ञः.

CANONIZATION, *s.* सिद्धानाम् मध्ये आरोपणं, अमुकसाधुजनः सिद्धिं प्राप्तवान् इति घोषणापत्रेण विज्ञापनं.

To CANONIZE, *v. a.* सिद्धलोकमध्ये आरुह् in caus. (-रोपयति -यितुं), अमुकसाधुजनः सिद्धानां मध्ये विगणनीय इति घोषणापत्रेण विज्ञा in caus. (-ज्ञापयति -यितुं).

CANONIZED, *p. p.* सिद्धलोकारोपितः -ता -तं, सिद्धानां मध्ये संख्यातः -ता -तं.

Canonry or canonship, *s.* पूर्व्वोक्तपुरोहितसम्बन्धि पदं or वर्त्तनं.

Canopied, *p. p.* वितानीकृतः -ता -तं, वितानाच्छादितः -ता -तं.

Canopy, *s.* वितानं -नकं, चन्द्रातपः, उल्लोचः, आच्छादनं, पिधानं, व्यवधा.

To canopy, *v. a.* वितानीकृ, चन्द्रातपेन आच्छद् (c. 10. -च्छादयति -यितुं).

Canorous, *a.* सुस्वरः -रा -रं, सुधारुस्वनः -ना -नं, स्वरयुक्तः -क्ता -क्तं.

Cant, *s.* (A technical form of speaking) परिभाषा, लाक्षणिकवाक्यं, कल्पितवाक्यं, कल्पितसंज्ञा, रचितवाक्यं.—(A corrupt dialect) भ्रष्टभाषा, अपभाषा, कुभाषा, अपशब्दः.—(A whining pretension to goodness) अन्तर्दुष्टस्य धर्म्मध्वजीकरणार्थं सद्भावकमात्रं, साधुवाङ्मात्रं, दम्भोक्तिः *f.*, दाम्भिकवचनं, धर्म्मोपदेशकवाक्यं, निःसत्यवाक्यं, वैलक्ष्यवचनं, वाक्छलं, छाद्मिकवचनं.

To cant, *v. n.* (To talk in technical language) परिभाष् (c. 1. -भाषते -भाषितुं), लाक्षणिकवाक्यं or रचितवाक्यं वद् (c. 1. वदति, वदितुं).—(To speak hypocritically) धर्म्मध्वजीकरणार्थं or धर्म्मोपदेशमात्रात् सज्जन इव वद्, दम्भार्थं स्वव्यवहारविरुद्धं सद्भावकमात्रं वद्.

Cantation, *s.* (The act of singing) गानं, गीतिः *f.*, गीतं, गानकरणं.

Canteen, *s.* सैन्यानां प्रस्थानकाले मद्यशुण्डादिधारणयोग्यं त्रापुषभाण्डं.

Canter, *s.* (Pace of a horse) अर्द्धपुलायितं, अर्द्धवल्गितं, विक्रान्तिः *f.*—(A canting hypocrite) दम्भार्थं वादी *m.* (न्), वाङ्मात्रेण धार्म्मिकः, दाम्भिकः, छद्मतापसः, धर्म्मध्वजी *m.* (न्), सार्थ्यलिङ्गी *m.* (न्), साधुम्मन्यः.

To canter, *v. n.* अर्द्धपुलायितेन or अर्द्धवल्गितेन चल् (c. 1. चलति, चलितुं).

Cantharides, *s. pl.* त्वक्स्फोटोत्पादका विदेशीयमक्षिकाप्रभेदाः.

Canthus, *s.* (Corner of the eye) अपाङ्गं -ङ्गकं, नयनोपान्तः, नेत्रपर्य्यन्तः.

Canticle, *s.* उपगीतं, उपगानं, ईषद्गीतं, काव्यबन्धः.—(Book of the Bible) सुलेमान्नाम्ना राज्ञा रचितं धर्म्मग्रन्थानां मध्ये गणितं गीतं.

Cantle or cantlet, *s.* (A piece) खण्डं, भिन्नं, भागः, विभागः, शकलं.

Canto, *s.* अध्यायः, सर्गः, पर्व्व *n.* (न्), परिच्छेदः, विच्छेदः, स्कन्धः, खण्डः -ण्डं, उच्छ्वासः, काण्डः, परिवर्त्तः.

Canton, *s.* मण्डलं, उपमण्डलं, चक्रं, भूप्रदेशः, भूमिभागः, भूभागः, देशः.

To canton, *v. n.* (To divide into parts) खण्डशस् or भागशस् or खण्डं खण्डं विभज् (c. 1. -भजति -भक्तुं) or परिकॢप् (c. 10. -कल्पयति -यितुं) or अंश् (c. 10. -अंशयति -यितुं).—(To canton a town for soldiers) नगरे स्वं स्वम् आवासं सैन्यानां कॢप् (c. 10. कल्पयति -यितुं).

Cantonment, *s.* सैन्यावासः, नगरे पृथक् पृथक् परिकल्पितं सैन्यनिवासस्थानं.—(Camp) कटकः, शिविरं.

Canvass, *s.* (A coarse cloth) शाणं, शणवस्त्रं, पटः, पटी, स्थूलपट्टं, स्थूलशाटिः *m.*—(Sails of a ship) वातवसनं.—(Solicitation upon an election) अमुकपदप्रेप्सया परसम्मतप्रार्थनं.

To canvass, *v. a.* (To sift, examine) परीक्ष् (c. 1. -ईक्षते -ईक्षितुं), निरूप् (c. 10. -रूपयति -यितुं), अनुसन्धा (c. 3. -दधाति -धातुं).—(To debate) विचर् in caus. (-चारयति -यितुं), तर्क् (c. 10. तर्कयति -यितुं), वितर्क्.

To canvass, *v. n.* (To solicit votes) अमुकपदप्रेप्सया परेषां सम्मतं or आश्रयं or आग्रहं or अनुपालनं or संवर्द्धनं प्रार्थ् (c. 10. -अर्थयते -यितुं).

Canvasser, *s.* प्रार्थकः, अर्थी *m.* (न्), अमुकपदप्रेप्सुः *m.*, पराश्रयप्रार्थकः.

Cany, *a.* वेतस्वान् -स्वती -स्वत् (त्), वैत्रकः -की -कं, वैदलः -ली -लं, वैणवः -वी -वं.

Canzonet, *s.* (A little song) उपगीतं, उपगानं, गीतकः, ईषद्गीतं.

Cap, *s.* शिरोवेष्टः -ष्टनं, शिरस्कं, शिरस्त्रं, शिरस्त्राणं, शिरोवस्त्रं, मस्तकाभरणं.

To cap, *v. n.* (To take off the cap in salutation) मस्तकम् उच्छाद्य or शिरस्कम् उन्नम्य अभिवद् (c. 10. -वादयति -ते -यितुं); अभिवादनार्थं

शिरस्त्रम् अवतॄ in caus. (-तारयति -यितुं), or अवमुच् (c. 6. -मुञ्चति -मोक्तुं).

To cap, *v. a.* (To cover) पिधा (c. 3. -दधाति -धातुं), सपिधानं -ना -नं कृ; 'to cap verses,' प्रतिमालां कृ.

Capability, *s.* शक्यत्वं, शक्तिः *f.*, शक्तता, सामर्थ्यं, समर्थता, क्षमता, उपयोगिता, योग्यता, युक्तिः *f.*, पात्रता, सामञ्जस्यं; 'of acting,' क्रियाशक्तिः *f.*

Capable, *a.* (Having powers equal to any thing) क्षमः -मा -मं, समर्थः -र्था -र्थं, शक्तः -क्ता -क्तं, योग्यः -ग्या -ग्यं, उचितः -ता -तं; 'capable of building a house,' गृहकरणे शक्तः; 'capable of a journey,' अध्वनि क्षमः; 'capable of toils,' क्लेशानाम् उचितः; 'capable of being done,' शक्यः -क्या -क्यं; 'to be capable of,' शक् (c. 5. शक्नोति or pass. शक्यते), क्षम् (c. 1. क्षमते), उत्सह् (c. 1. -सहते) with inf.; कॢप् (c. 1. कल्पते), उपकॢप्; 'I am not capable of leaving thee,' त्वाम् उत्स्रष्टुं नोत्सहे; 'he is rendered capable of immortality,' अमृतत्वाय कल्पते.—(Qualified, competent) उपयुक्तः -क्ता -क्तं, पात्रिकः -का -कं.—(A competent person) पात्रं, सत्पात्रं.—(One endowed with good qualities, intelligent) गुणवान् -वती -वत् (त्), बुद्धिमान् -मती -मत् (त्), कृती -तिनी -ति (न्).—(Capable of holding) धारणक्षमः -मा -मं, आदानयोग्यः -ग्या -ग्यं.

Capacious, *a.* विशालः -ला -लं, विस्तीर्णः -र्णा -र्णं, विस्तृतः -ता -तं, पृथुः -थुः -थु, विवृतः -ता -तं, विपुलः -ला -लं, उरुः -रुः -रु, प्रसृतः -ता -तं, प्रस्थः -स्था -स्थं.

Capaciousness, *s.* विशालता, विस्तीर्णता, पृथुता, परिसरः, उरुत्वं.

To capacitate, *v. a.* क्षमीकृ, उपयुक्तं -क्तां -क्तं कृ, उपयोगित्वं दा (c. 3. ददाति, दातुं).

Capacity, *s.* (Size) परिमाणं.—(Power of holding) धारणशक्तिः *f.*, कोषः.—(Room) प्रसरः, विस्तृतिः *f.*, विस्तारः.—(Power of the mind) धीशक्तिः *f.*, बुद्धिपात्रता.—(Power, ability, fitness) शक्तिः *f.*, सामर्थ्यं, बलं, योग्यता, उपयुक्तता, उपयोगित्वं, पात्रता; 'according to one's capacity,' यथाशक्ति, यथासामर्थ्यं, यथाबलं; 'beyond one's capacity,' अतिशक्ति.—(State, profession) भावः, दशा, अवस्था, वृत्तिः *f.*

Cap-à-peé or cap-à-pié, अङ्गप्रत्यङ्गं, मस्तकात्प्रभृति पादपर्य्यन्तं, सर्व्वाङ्गं.—(Completely armed) संवर्म्मितः -ता -तं.

Caparison, *s.* (Of a horse or elephant) आस्तरः -रणं, परिस्तोमः, वर्णः, जयनं, सज्जा, अश्वसज्जा, अश्वपरिधानं, प्रखरः.

To caparison, *v. a.* परिस्तोमं or आस्तरं परिधा (c. 3. -दधाति -धातुं), सज्जीकृ.

Caparisoned, *p. p.* परिस्तोमभूषितः -ता -तं, सज्जितः -ता -तं, जयनयुक् *m. f. n.* (ज्).

Capcase, *s.* लघुवस्त्राधारः, भाण्डं, समुद्गः -द्गकः, सम्पुटः.

Cape, *s.* (Promontory) अन्तरीपः -पं, नासारूपेण समुद्रमध्ये प्रलम्बो भूमिभागः, समुद्रमध्ये उदग्रा गिरिनासिका, स्थलाभोगः.—(Neck-piece of a cloak) ग्रीवाप्रच्छदः, स्कन्धप्रच्छदः, स्कन्धप्रावरणं, उत्तरप्रच्छदः.—(A small cloak) अरत्निपर्य्यन्तं लम्बमानः क्षुद्रप्रावारः.

Caper, *s.* (A jump) प्लुतं, प्लवः, झम्पः, वल्गितं, उत्फालः, लङ्घनं, नर्त्तनं.—(A kind of pickle) सन्धितविशेषः.

To caper, *v. n.* प्लु (c. 1. प्लवते, प्लोतुं), नृत् (c. 4. नृत्यति, नर्त्तितुं), वल्ग् (c. 1. वल्गति, वल्गितुं), उत्पत् (c. 1. -पतति -पतितुं).

Capillament, *s.* केशरः, केसरः, पक्ष्म *n.* (न्), किञ्जलः, किञ्जल्कः.

Capillary, *a.* (Resembling hair) केशोपमः -मा -मं, केशिकः -की -कं, केशरी -रिणी -रि (न्).—(Minute) सूक्ष्मः -क्ष्मा -क्ष्मं, कणीकः -का -कं.

Capillary, *s.* सूक्ष्मतृणाकारदलविशिष्ट ओषधिभेदः.—(Vein) सूक्ष्मनाडिः *f.*

CAPITAL, *a.* (Relating to the head) मस्तकसम्बन्धी -न्धिनी -न्धि (न्). —(Chief, principal) परमः -मा -मं, मुख्यः -ख्या -ख्यं, उत्तमः -मा -मं, अग्र्यः -ग्र्या -ग्र्यं, विशिष्टः -ष्टा -ष्टं, श्रेष्ठः -ष्ठा -ष्ठं, प्रधानः in comp. —(Criminal in the highest degree, worthy of death) महापातकी -किनी -कि (न्), वधार्हः -र्हा -र्हं, वधदण्डार्हः -र्हा -र्हं; 'a capital crime,' महापातकं, महापापं.—(A capital city) पुरोत्तमः, *see* the next.—(Capital punishment) वधदण्डः, उत्तमसाहसं, प्राणहननं, प्राणदण्डः.—(Capital stock) मूलद्रव्यं.

CAPITAL, *s.* (In money, &c.) मूलं, मूलधनं, मूलद्रव्यं, नीवी -विः *f.*, परिपणं.—(A capital city) राजधानं -नी, स्कन्धावारः, कर्व्वटः -टं, खर्व्वटः -टं.—(A large letter) वृहदक्षरं, महाक्षरं.—(Top of a pillar) स्तम्भशीर्षं, स्तम्भाग्रं, स्तम्भशृङ्गं.

CAPITALIST, *s.* कोटीश्वरः, मूलधनाढ्यः, धनाढ्यः, धनवान् *m.* (त्), कोषवान् *m.* (त्), सधनः, विभवान् *m.* (त्).

CAPITALLY, *adv.* उत्तमसाहसेन, प्राणदण्डेन, परमं, उत्तमप्रकारेण.

CAPITATION, *s.* मस्तकसंख्या, शरीरगणना, व्यक्तितः परिसंख्या, प्रत्येकं or एकशस् or एकतस् or एकैकशस् or पृथक् पृथक् संख्यानं or परिगणना.

CAPITOL, *s.* रोमनगरे पूजितस्य युपितराख्यस्य आदिदेवस्य प्रासादः.

CAPITULAR, *s.* (The statutes of the chapter of a cathedral) महाभजनप्रासादे सर्व्वसभासद्भिर् विहिता व्यवस्थासंहिता.—(A member of the chapter) महाभजनप्रासादे सभासद् *m.*, महापूजाशालासम्बन्धी-मठे सभासद्.

CAPITULAR, *a.* पूर्व्वोक्तमठव्यवस्थासम्बन्धी -न्धिनी -न्धि (न्).

To CAPITULATE, *v. n.* (To surrender on certain stipulations) समयं or नियमं कृत्वा शत्रुवशे or शत्रुस्वत्वे or शत्रोरधिकारे परादा (c. 3. -ददाति -दातुं) or प्रदा, or सम्प्रदा or समृ in caus. (-अर्पयति -पितुं) or शत्रोरधीनः -ना -नं भू or शत्रोर् वशीभू.—(To draw up any thing in heads) मार्गेषु निबन्ध् (c. 9. -बध्नाति -बन्द्धुं) or रच् (c. 10. रचयति -यितुं), सम्प्रवच् (c. 2. -वक्ति -वक्तुं), समासतस् or सङ्क्षेपतस् लिख् (c. 6. लिखति, लेखितुं).

CAPITULATION, *s.* (Surrendering on certain stipulations) नियमपूर्व्वकं परादानं or सम्प्रदानं or प्रदानं or समर्पणं.—(Reduction to heads) मार्गेषु निबन्धनं or रचना, समासतो लिखनं.

CAPITULATOR, *s.* नियमपूर्व्वकं परादाता *m.* (तृ) or सम्प्रदाता *m.* (तृ), समयकर्त्ता *m.* (र्तृ).

CAP-MAKER, *s.* शिरस्त्रकारी *m.* (न्), शिरोवेष्टनकृत्, मस्तकाभरणविक्रेता *m.* (तृ).

CAPON, *s.* छिन्नवृषणः कुक्कुटः, वृषणहीनः कृकवाकुः *m.*

CAPOT, *s.* पिकेटाख्यायां क्रीडायां सर्व्वद्यूतपत्राणां निर्जयः or स्वीकरणं.

To CAPOT, *v. a.* पूर्व्वोक्तक्रीडायां सर्व्वद्यूतपत्राणि निर्जि (c. 1. -जयति -जेतुं) or स्वीकृ.

CAPOUCH, *s.* (A monk's hood) सन्न्यासिभिर् भृतं शिरःपिधानं.

CAPRICE, *s.* मनोलौल्यं, लौल्यं, चापलं, निर्बन्धः, असद्ग्रहः *m.*, असद्ग्रहः, स्फातिः *f.*

CAPRICIOUS, *a.* चपलः -ला -लं, चञ्चलः -ला -लं, लोलः -ला -लं, अस्थिरः -रा -रं, सङ्कसुकः -का -कं, चञ्चलहृदयः -या -यं, लोलचेताः -ताः -तः (स्), चलचित्तः -त्ता -त्तं, चपलात्मकः -का -कं, प्रकृतितरलः -ला -लं, नैकभावाश्रयः -या -यं, असदाग्रः -ग्रा -ग्रं.

CAPRICIOUSLY, *adv.* मनोलौल्येन, चापल्येन, चाञ्चल्येन, लोलचेतसा.

CAPRICIOUSNESS, *s.* चापल्यं, चपलता, चाञ्चल्यं, चञ्चलता, अस्थिरता, चलता, हृदयचाञ्चल्यं, चलचित्तता, चित्ततरलता.

CAPRICORN, *s.* (Sign of the zodiac) मकरराशिः *m.*, मकरः.

CAPRIOLE, *s.* अश्वप्लुतं, तुरङ्गवल्गितं, अश्वस्य गतिविशेषः.

CAPSTAN, *s.* गुरुभाराकर्षणार्थं यष्टिभिः सञ्चारितं चक्रयन्त्रं.

CAPSULAR, CAPSULARY, *a.* बीजकोशाकारः -रा -रं, पुटाकारः -रा -रं.

CAPSULATED, *a.* कोशस्थः -स्था -स्थं, कोशपरिगतः -ता -तं.

CAPSULE, *s.* बीजकोशः, बीजगुप्तिः *f.*, कोषः, पुटः, सिम्बा.

CAPTAIN, *s.* (In the army) सैन्याधिपतिः *m.*, सैन्याध्यक्षः, व्यूहपतिः *m.*, गुल्मपतिः, योधमुख्यः, दण्डनायकः, सेनानीः *m.*—(Of a ship) नौकाधिपतिः *m.*, नौकाधिष्ठाता *m.* (तृ), पोताध्यक्षः, नौपतिः.—(Any chief) मुख्यरः, नायकः, नेता *m.* (तृ), पुरोगः -गमः, अग्रगः.

CAPTAINSHIP, *s.* सैन्याधिपतिपदं, नौकाध्यक्षाधिकारः, नेतृत्वं, मुख्यत्वं.

CAPTATION, *s.* (Courting favour) लोकरञ्जनं, लोकानुरञ्जनं, लोकसेवनं, लोकप्रशंसासेवनं, जनप्रसादलिप्सा.

CAPTION, *s.* (Seizure of person) आसेधः.—(Overreaching) प्रलम्भः, प्रतारणं, छलं.

CAPTIOUS, *a.* (Censorious) छिद्रान्वेषी -षिणी -षि (न्), छिद्रानुसारी -रिणी -रि (न्), घृणी -णिनी -णि (न्), दोषग्राही -हिणी -हि (न्), विवादशीलः -ला -लं, उद्ग्राहशीलः -ला -लं.—(Fallacious, insidious) मोही -हिनी -हि (न्), भाक्तिकरः -री -रं.

CAPTIOUSLY, *adv.* विवादार्थं, विवादमात्रवाञ्छया, छिद्रान्वेषिवत्, उद्ग्राहशीलत्वात्, घृणया.

CAPTIOUSNESS, *s.* छिद्रान्वेषिता, विवादशीलता, घृणा, दोषग्राहित्वं, उद्ग्राहशीलता.

To CAPTIVATE, *v. a.* (To bring into bondage) वशीकृ, वन्दीकृ, दासीकृ, करदीकृ, दम् in caus. (दमयति -यितुं).—(To charm) वशीकृ, चित्तं or मनो हृ (c. 1. हरति, हर्त्तुं) or अपहृ, हृदयं ग्रह् (c. 9. गृह्णाति, ग्रहीतुं), मुह् in caus. (मोहयति -यितुं).

CAPTIVATED, *p. p.* वशीकृतः -ता -तं, वशीभूतः -ता -तं, वशतापन्नः -न्ना -न्नं.

CAPTIVATING, *a.* मनोहरः -रा -रं, चित्तहारी -रिणी -रि (न्), चित्तापहारी -रिणी -रि (न्), हृदयग्राही -हिणी -हि (न्), मोहनः -ना -नी -नं, मोही -हिनी -हि (न्).

CAPTIVATION, *s.* वशीकरणं, ग्रहणं, बन्धनं, दासीकरणं, वन्दीकरणं.

CAPTIVE, *a.* वन्दीकृतः -ता -तं, दासीभूतः -ता -तं, शत्रुधृतः -ता -तं, शत्रुवशः -शा -शं, शत्रुग्रस्तः -स्ता -स्तं, कारास्थितः -ता -तं, कारागुप्तः -प्ता -प्तं, ग्रहणः -णा -णं.

CAPTIVE, *s.* वन्दिः *f.*, वन्दी, शत्रुधृतः, कारास्थः, कारागुप्तः, ग्रहणः, उपग्रहः, प्रग्रहः, करदः, कयरकी; 'taken alive,' जीवग्राहः.—(Slave) दासः; 'to take captive,' वन्दीकृ, दासीकृ.—(One charmed by beauty, &c.) वशीभूतः, मोहितः.

CAPTIVITY, *s.* बन्धनं, वन्दिभावः, कारागोपनं, वशित्वं, वश्यता, शत्रुवशिता. —(Servitude) दासत्वं, दास्यं, दासभावः.

CAPTOR, *s.* वन्दीकर्त्ता *m.* (र्तृ), ग्राहकः, जेता *m.* (तृ), लोप्त्रकृत्.

CAPTURE, *s.* (The act of taking) ग्रहणं; 'capture of a fort,' दुर्गलङ्घनं, दुर्गभङ्गः.—(The prize taken) लोप्त्रं, लोत्रं; 'capture of cattle,' गोग्रहः.

To CAPTURE, *v. a.* ग्रह् (c. 9. गृह्णाति, ग्रहीतुं), वन्दीकृ, दासीकृ, करदीकृ; 'to capture a fort,' दुर्गं भञ्ज् (c. 7. भनक्ति, भंक्तुं) or लङ्घ् (c. 10. लङ्घयति -यितुं).

CAPUCHIN, *s.* रोमीयमतस्थः सन्न्यासिविशेषः.

CAPUT MORTUUM, *s.* मलं, खलं, किट्टं, कल्कं, विनीयः, शेषं.

CAR, *s.* रथः, चक्रयानं, गन्त्री, गन्त्रीरथः, शकटः; 'of the gods,' विमानः -नं; 'war-car,' स्यन्दनः, शताङ्गः; 'pleasure-car,' क्रीडारथः,

पुष्यरथः; 'a covered car,' कर्णीरथः, ह्यनं, प्रवहणं; 'multitude of cars,' रथ्या, रथकट्या; 'car-maker,' रथकारः.

Carabine or carbine, *s.* (A short gun used by the light horse) सङ्ग्रामसमये अश्वारूढैर् भृता सीसकगोलकप्रक्षेपणी बाहुपरिमाणा लोहनाडिः.

Carabineer, *s.* पूर्व्वोक्तशस्त्रधारी हयारूढः, पूर्व्वोक्तशस्त्रभृत्.

Carack, *s.* (A large ship of burthen) भारवाहिनी बृहन्नौका.

Caracole, *s.* तिर्य्यक्प्लुतं, तिर्य्यग्वल्गितं, वक्रगतिः *f.*, कुटिलगतिः, अर्द्धचन्द्राकारा तुरङ्गगतिः.

To caracole, *v. a.* तिर्य्यक् प्लु (c. 1. प्लवते, प्लोतुं) or वल्ग् (c. 1. वल्गति, वल्गितुं), अश्ववद् वक्रगत्या or अर्द्धचन्द्राकारगत्या चल् (c. 1. चलति, चलितुं).

Carat, caract, *s.* (A weight of four grains) रक्तिकाद्वयसम उन्मानविशेषः.—(Manner of expressing the fineness of gold) स्वर्णकारभाषायां सुवर्णनिर्म्मोल्यवाचिकः शब्दः.

Caravan, *s.* सार्थः, पथिकसन्ततिः *f.*, यात्रा, यात्रिकसङ्घः, सार्थवाहसमूहः, समङ्गगनिवहः.

Caravansary, *s.* पथिकाश्रयः, पथिकावासस्थानं, सार्थवाहानाम् उत्तरणस्थानं, उपकारी.

Caraway or carway, *s.* अजमोदा, क्षुद्रबीजप्रभेदः स च पिष्टकापूपादिना कदापि संसृज्यते.

Carbonado, *s.* भक्षणार्थं छिन्नमांसं or व्यवच्छिन्नमांसं, भक्षणयोग्यं विनिकृत्तमांसं.

To carbonado, *v. a.* भक्षणार्थं मांसं व्यवच्छिद् (c. 7. -छिनत्ति -छेत्तुं) or विनिकृत् (c. 6. -कृन्तति -कर्त्तितुं) or विशस् (c. 1. -शसति -शसितुं).

Carbuncle, *s.* (Swelling) व्रणः -णं, विस्फोटः, स्फोटः, गण्डः.—(Jewel) पद्मरागः, सर्पमणिः.

Carbuncled, *a.* (Having swellings) व्रणी -णिनी -णि (न्).—(Set with the jewel) पद्मरागमयः -यी -यं, सर्पमणिखचितः -ता -तं.

Carcanet, *s.* (A chain or necklace of jewels) रत्नावलिः *f.*, मणिमाला, मुक्तावली.

Carcass, *s.* (A dead body) शवः -वं, मृतशरीरं, मृताङ्गं, मृतकं, कुणपः -पं.—(The remains, ruins) शेषभागः, जीर्णभागः.

Carcelage, *s.* (Prison fees) काराध्यक्षशुल्कं, कारारक्षकेण गृहीतं शुल्कं.

Carceral, *a.* कारासम्बन्धी -न्धिनी -न्धि (न्), बन्धनालयसम्बन्धकः -का -कं.

Card, *s.* (A painted paper used in games of chance) क्रीडापत्रं, द्यूतपत्रं, चित्रितद्यूतपत्रं.—(The paper on which the points of the compass are marked under the needle) दिग्विदिगङ्कितं पत्रं.—(The instrument for combing wool, flax, &c.) ऊर्णाशणादिमार्जनार्थं लोहदन्तयुक्तं यन्त्रं, ऊर्णामार्जनी, ऊर्णानिर्घर्षणयन्त्रं.

To card, *v. a.* (To comb wool) पूर्व्वोक्तयन्त्रेण ऊर्णां सम्मृज् (c. 2. -मार्ष्टि -मार्ष्टुं) or निर्घृष् (c. 1. -घर्षति -घर्षितुं).

Cardamom, *s.* (Large) एला, एलीका, पृथ्वीका, चन्द्रवाला, निष्कुटिः *f.*, बहुला.—(Small) तुत्था, त्रिपुटा, त्रुटिः *f.*, कोरङ्गी, कुञ्चिका.

Carder, *s.* (One that cards wool) ऊर्णामार्जकः, ऊर्णानिर्घर्षकः.—(One that plays much at cards) द्यूतपत्रक्रीडासक्तः.

Cardiacal, cardiac, *a.* तेजस्करः -री -रं, दीपनः -ना -नं, अग्निदः -दा -दं.

Cardinal, *a.* (Chief) परमः -मा -मं, मुख्यः -ख्या -ख्यं, उत्तमः -मा -मं, श्रेष्ठः -ष्ठा -ष्ठं, विशिष्टः -ष्टा -ष्टं, अग्र्यः -ग्र्या -ग्र्यं, प्रधानः in comp.

Cardinal, *s.* रोमनगरे महाधर्म्माध्यक्षसमाजे सभासद्, रोमीयमतधारिणां मध्ये धर्म्माधिपतिः *m.*

Cardinalate or cardinalship, *s.* पूर्व्वोक्तधर्म्माधिपतेः पदं or अधिकारः.

Cardinal-point, *s.* उत्तरदिक्, पूर्व्वदिक्, पश्चिमदिक्, दक्षिणदिक् *f.* (श्).

Cardmatch, *s.* (Game at cards) द्यूतपत्रक्रीडा, चित्रितपत्रद्यूतं.

Care, *s.* (Anxiety) चिन्ता, चित्तोद्वेगः, चित्तवेदना, मनोदुःखं, मनस्तापः, आधिः *m.*, चर्चा, औत्सुक्यं, उद्वेगः -जनं, चिन्ताभारः, मानसी व्यथा; 'cares of this world,' सांसारिकी चिन्ता.—(Diligence, pains) प्रयत्नः, यत्नः, व्यवसायः, आस्था; 'with care,' प्रयत्नतस्.—(Regard, attention) अपेक्षा, अपेक्षा, मनःप्रवेशः, मनोयोगः. —(Caution, heed) अवधानं, अप्रमादः; 'to take care,' अवधा (c. 3. -दधाति -धातुं), सावधानः -ना -नं भू.—(Heed, in order to protection) गुप्तिः *f.*, रक्षणं, रक्षा, पालनं; 'to take care of, protect,' रक्ष् (c. 1. रक्षति, रक्षितुं), पाल् (c. 10. पालयति -यितुं), गुप् (c. 1. गोपायति, गोप्तुं).—(The object of care) रक्षणीयः -या -यं, अपेक्षाभूमिः *f.*—(Care and management) योगक्षेमः.

To care, *v. n.* (To care for, concern one's self about) अपेक्ष् (c. 1. -ईक्षते -ईक्षितुं), अवेक्ष्, चिन्त् (c. 10. चिन्तयति -यितुं), अनुचिन्त्, सेव् (c. 1. सेवते, सेवितुं), भज् (c. 1. भजति -ते, भक्तुं), मनो धा (c. 3. दधाति, धातुं) with loc.

Care-crazed, *a.* चिन्ताव्याकुलः -ला -लं, चिन्ताकुलः -ला -लं, चिन्ताव्यग्रः -ग्रा -ग्रं.

To careen, *v. a.* (To calk) दारुजीर्णत्वाद् दारुस्फोटनाद् वा नौकां पार्श्वे पर्य्यस्य छिद्राणि पिधा (c. 3. -दधाति -धातुं).

Career, *s.* (A race-ground) धावनस्थानं, चर्य्यास्थानं.—(A race) चर्य्या, मार्गः, पणलाभार्थं धावनं.—(Course of action, &c.) गतिः *f.*, मार्गः, क्रियाप्रसङ्गः, प्रसरः, पर्य्यायः, क्रमः, रीतिः *f.*, गमनं, चलनं; 'in full career, at full speed,' परमवेगेन, सरभसं, सर्व्ववेगेन.

To career, *v. n.* परमवेगेन धाव् (c. 1. धावति -वितुं), त्वर् (c. 1. त्वरते -रितुं).

Careful, *a.* (Heedful, attentive) सावधानः -ना -नं, अवहितः -ता -तं, कृतावधानः -ना -नं, अप्रमत्तः -त्ता -त्तं, अप्रमादी -दिनी -दि (न्), सयत्नः -त्ना -त्नं, यत्नवान् -वती -वत् (त्), प्रयत्नवान् -वती -वत्.—(Anxious, full of care) चिन्तावान् -वती -वत् (त्), सचिन्तः -न्ता -न्तं, उत्सुकः -का -कं, व्यग्रः -ग्रा -ग्रं.

Carefully, *adv.* सावधानं, सयत्नं, प्रयत्नतस्, यत्नतस्, प्रयत्नेन, प्रयत्नात्, यत्नात्, प्रमादं विना, अप्रमत्तं, प्रमादव्यतिरेकेण.

Carefulness, *s.* अवधानता, सावधानता, सयत्नता, अप्रमादः, अप्रमादित्वं.

Careless, *a.* प्रमत्तः -त्ता -त्तं, प्रमादी -दिनी -दि (न्), प्रमादवान् -वती -वत् (त्), अनवहितः -ता -तं, अनवधानः -ना -नं, निरपेक्षः -क्षा -क्षं, असावधानः -ना -नं, असमीक्ष्यकारी -रिणी -रि (न्).—(To be careless of) प्रमद् (c. 4. -माद्यति -मदितुं) with abl.; 'he is careless of his own interest,' स्वहितात् प्रमाद्यति.

Carelessly, *adv.* प्रमादेन, प्रमादतस्, सप्रमादं, निरपेक्षं, अनपेक्षया, अवधानं विना, अनवधानेन.—(Implying absence of restraint) निर्यन्त्रणं.

Carelessness, *s.* अनवधानं -नता, असावधानता, प्रमत्तता, प्रमादः, अनपेक्षा.

To caress, *v. a.* आलिङ्ग् (c. 1. -लिङ्गति -लिङ्गितुं), समालिङ्ग्, भज् (c. 1. भजते, भक्तुं), स्वञ्ज् (c. 1. स्वजते, स्वंक्तुं), परिष्वञ्ज्; क्रोडीकृ; परिमृश् (c. 6. -मृशति -मर्ष्टुं), परिरभ् (c. 1. -रभते -रब्धुं), प्रेम कृ.

Caress, *s.* आलिङ्गितं -ङ्गनं, परिष्वङ्गः, ललितं, क्रोडीकृतिः *f.*, अङ्कपाली, अङ्कपालिः *m.*, परिरम्भः.

Caressed, *p. p.* आलिङ्गितः -ता -तं, क्रोडीकृतः -ता -तं, परिमृष्टः -ष्टा -ष्टं, परिरब्धः -ब्धा -ब्धं, परिष्वक्तः -क्ता -क्तं, उपगूढः -ढा -ढं.

Caret, *s.* इह किञ्चिद् अधिकं विस्मृतं वा निवेशयितव्यम् इति सूचनार्थं हंसपादाकृति चिह्नं.

CARGO, *s.* नौकाभारः, पोतभारः, पौतिकं, पोतस्थद्रव्यं, पोतस्थं भाण्डं.

CARICATURE, *s.* विकृताकारत्वाद् हास्यजनकं प्रतिमानं or उपमानं, हास्यप्रतिमानं, हास्योपमानं, हास्यचित्रं, विकृतचित्रं, हास्यप्रकारेण or अतिशयेन चित्रितम् आलेख्यं.

To CARICATURE, *v. a.* आकारं or मूर्त्तिं विकृत्य or साचीकृत्य हास्यप्रकारेण चित्र् (c. 10. चित्रयति -यितुं) or आलिख् (c. 6. -लिखति -लेखितुं), हास्यप्रतिमानं कृ, मूर्त्तिविकारपूर्व्वकं प्रतिमूर्त्तिं चित्रे लिखित्वा हास्यभूमिं कृ.

CARICATURED, *p. p.* हास्यप्रकारेण चित्रलिखितः -ता -तं, अङ्गविकारपूर्व्वकम् आलिखितः -ता -तं.

CARICATURIST, *s.* हास्यप्रकारेण उपमाता *m.* (तृ), हास्यप्रतिमानकृत्, हास्यचित्रकर्त्ता *m.* (र्त्तृ), विकृतप्रतिमानकृत्, यो मूर्त्तिम् चित्रे विकृत्य प्रतिमूर्त्तिं हास्यास्पदं करोति.

CARIES or CARIOSITY, *s.* अस्थिगलितत्वं, अस्थिपूयनं, अस्थिव्यसनं, अस्थिपाकः, अस्थिक्षयः, अस्थिशोषः.—(Of the teeth) दन्तव्यसनं.

CARIOUS, *a.* गलितः -ता -तं, पूयपूर्णः -र्णा -र्णं, क्षीणः -णा -णं, पूतिगन्धः -न्धा -न्धं.

To CARK, *v. n.* (To be anxious) चिन्ताव्याकुलः -ला -लं or चिन्ताव्यग्रः -ग्रा -ग्रं अस्, उत्सुक (nom. उत्सुकायते).

CARLE, *s.* दुर्वृत्तः, दुराचारः, अधमाचारः, कुशीलः, असभ्यः, निकृष्टः.

CARMAN, *s.* रथिकः, रथी *m.* (न्), रथवाहकः, चातुरिकः, सारथिः *m.*

CARMELITE, *s.* (Belonging to the order of Carmelites) रोमीयमतधारी सन्न्यासिविशेषः.

CARMINATIVE, *a.* वातघ्नः -घ्ना -घ्नं, वायुघ्नः -घ्ना -घ्नं, वायुनाशी -शिनी -शि (न्), रोचकः -का -कं, रूचकः -का -कं, अग्निदः -दा -दं, स्वेदजनकः -का -कं.

CARMINE, *s.* जतुसवर्णो रक्तरङ्गः, सिन्दूरोपमः or ओड्रपुष्पसवर्णो रङ्गः, जतुजरङ्गः, रक्तरेणुः *m.*

CARNAGE, *s.* संहारः, विशसनं, वधः, हत्या, यातनं, निहननं, निषूदनं.

CARNAL, *a.* (Fleshly, bodily) शारीरिकः -की -कं, शरीरजः -जा -जं, दैहिकः -की -कं, कायिकः -की -कं, वापुषिकः -की -कं.—(Worldly) सांसारिकः -की -कं, लौकिकः -की -कं, ऐहिकः -की -कं, ऐहलौकिकः -की -कं.—(Sensual) विषयी -यिणी -यि (न्), विषयासक्तः -क्ता -क्तं, विषयसङ्गी -ङ्गिनी -ङ्गि (न्), विषयानुरागी -गिणी -गि (न्), विषयोपसेवी -विनी -वि (न्), कामासक्तः -क्ता -क्तं, भोगासक्तः -क्ता -क्तं, कामुकः -का -कं; 'carnal desire,' कामः; 'carnal connexion,' अङ्गसङ्गः, सङ्गमणं.

CARNALITY, *s.* विषयासक्तिः *f.*, विषयोपसेवा, विषयकामः, कामासक्तिः, विषयसङ्गः, शारीरिकविषयेषु अनुरागः, सङ्गः, कामिता.

CARNALLY, *adv.* शारीरिकरीतिक्रमेण, सांसारिकरीत्यनुसारात्, विषयसङ्गात्, कामुकवत्; 'to know carnally,' भज् (c. 1. भजते, भक्तुं).

CARNATION, *s.* (Flesh colour) मांसवर्णः.—(The flower) मांसवर्णविशिष्टः पुष्पप्रभेदः.

CARNELIAN or CORNELIAN, *s.* मांसवर्णः प्रस्तरविशेषः.

CARNEOUS, *a.* मांसलः -ला -लं, मांसशीलः -ला -लं, मांसगुणविशिष्टः -ष्टा -ष्टं.

To CARNIFY, *v. n.* and *a.* मांसीभू, मांससाद्भू, मांससात्कृ.

CARNIVAL, *s.* (The feast held before Lent) वसन्तसमये प्राग्महोपवासाद् रोमीयमतधारिभिः सेवितो महोत्सवः, दोलोत्सवः, होलाका.

CARNIVOROUS, *a.* क्रव्यादः -दा -दं, क्रव्यभुक् *m. f. n.* (ज्), क्रव्यभोजनः -ना -नं, मांसाशी -शिनी -शि (न्), मांसभक्षः -क्षा -क्षं, आमिषाशी -शिनी -शि (न्) or पिशिताशी, आममांसभक्षी -क्षिणी -क्षि (न्).

CARNOSITY, *s.* अर्बुदः, गण्डः, मेदोग्रन्थिः *m.*, अर्शः *n.* (स्), दुष्टमांसं, मांसवृद्धिः *f.*

CAROB-BEAN, *s.* सिम्बाप्रभेदः, सिम्बिका, शिम्बा.

CAROCHE, *s.* क्रीडारथः, पुष्परथः, रथः, प्रवहणं, चातुरं.

CAROL, *s.* (A song of joy) हर्षगीतं, हर्षगानं, आनन्दगीतं, जयगीतं जयशब्दः, आह्लादसूचकं गीतं.—(A song of devotion) स्तवगीतं, भक्तिगीतं, गीतं, स्तुतिः *f.*, स्तोत्रं, गाथा, खेलिः *f.*, सङ्कीर्तं.

To CAROL, *v. n.* गै (c. 1. गायति, गातुं), सुख (nom. सुखायते); 'to celebrate in song, &c.' उपगै, स्तु (c. 2. स्तौति, स्तोतुं), उपवीण (nom. उपवीणयति -यितुं).

CAROTID, *s.* (Two arteries) हृत्पिण्डाद् रक्तप्रवाहकं बृहन्नाडिद्वयं, कण्डराद्वयं.

To CAROUSE, *v. n.* (To drink largely) अतिशयेन पा (c. 1. पिबति, पातुं) or सम्पा, अतिशयसम्पीत्या क्षीबः -बा -बं भू, उत्सवं कृ.

CAROUSE or CAROUSAL, *s.* सम्पीतिः *f.*, अतिपानं, अतिशयसम्पीतिः *f.*, उत्सवः.

CAROUSER, *s.* पानप्रसक्तः, पानरतः, सम्पीतिरतः, मद्यपीतः, अतिपायी *m.* (न्).

CARP, *s.* (A fish) शफरी, सफरी, प्रोष्ठी, प्रोष्ठः, रोहितः.

To CARP AT, *v. n.* निन्द् (c. 1. निन्दति -न्दितुं), प्रतिनिन्द्, गर्ह् (c. 1. गर्हते, गर्हितुं, c. 10. गर्हयति -ते -यितुं), अधिक्षिप् (c. 6. -क्षिपति -क्षेप्तुं), अवक्षिप्, दोषीकृ, दोषं or छिद्रम् अन्विष् (c. 6. -इच्छति -एषितुं), असूय (nom. असूयति -यितुं).

CARPENTER, *s.* तक्षकः, तक्षा *m.* (न्), सूत्रधारः, त्वष्टा *m.* (ष्टृ), काष्ठतक्षकः, काष्ठतट् (क्ष्), तष्टा *m.* (ष्टृ), स्थपतिः *m.*, वर्द्धकिः *m.*, रथकारः; 'carpenter's bench,' उद्घनः.

CARPENTRY, *s.* त्वष्टिः *f.*, तक्षणं, काष्ठतक्षणं, सूत्रधारकर्म्म *n.* (न्), तक्षकक्रिया.

CARPER, *s.* दोषग्राही *m.* (न्), दोषकथकः, छिद्रान्वेषी *m.* (न्), दोषैकदृक् *m.* (श्), घृणी *m.* (न्), पापदर्शी *m.* (न्), गुणघाती *m.* (न्), निन्दकः, विवादशीलः, विवादप्रियः.

CARPET, *s.* आस्तरणं, पादपाशी, कुथः, कुथा, चित्रितवस्त्रं, पुष्पालङ्कृतवस्त्रं, आसनवस्त्रं; 'a carpet of grass,' दर्भास्तरणं; 'brought on the carpet,' प्रस्तुतः -ता -तं, उपन्यस्तः -स्ता -स्तं, प्रतिज्ञातः -ता -तं.

To CARPET, *v. a.* चित्रितवस्त्रादिना आस्तृ or आस्तॄ (c. 5. -स्तृणोति, c. 9. -स्तृणाति -स्तरितुं -स्तरीतुं).

CARPING, *a.* दोषग्राही -हिणी -हि (न्), घृणी -णिनी -णि (न्), निन्दकः -का -कं.

CARPING, *s.* (Cavil) निन्दा, गर्हा -र्हणं, घृणा, अपवादः, दोषकल्पनं, दोषप्रसङ्गः, दोषीकरणं, छिद्रान्वेषः, असूया, जुगुप्सा, ऋतीया, आक्षेपः, उद्ग्राहः.

CARPINGLY, *adv.* निन्दया, घृणया, असूयया, विवादशीलत्वात्, जुगुप्सया, सापवादं.

CARRIAGE, *s.* वाहनं, यानं, रथः, गन्त्री, चातुरं, वाहः, प्रवहणं, चङ्कुरः; 'travelling-carriage,' अध्वरथः, पुष्परथः; 'bullock-carriage,' वृषभयानं; 'one who has a carriage,' रथी *m.* (न्), रथिकः; 'riding in a carriage,' रथारूढः -ढा -ढं; 'alighting from a carriage,' रथावरोही -हिणी -हि (न्); 'carriage-road,' रथ्या; 'carriage-horse,' रथ्यः, प्रवहणवाजी *m.* (न्); 'bottom of a carriage,' अनुकर्षः.—(Framework of a gun) युद्धयन्त्रवाहनं.—(Behaviour) गतिः *f.*, चरितं, आचारः, चलनं, व्यवहारः.—(Management) नयः, प्रणयनं.

CARRIED, *p. p.* ऊढः -ढा -ढं, भृतः -ता -तं, धृतः -ता -तं, आहृतः -ता -तं, सञ्चारितः -ता -तं; 'grass carried along by the wind,' वातप्रेरितं तृणं.

CARRIER, *s.* वाहकः, वाही *m.* (न्).—(One who lives by carrying goods) भाण्डवाहनजीवी *m.* (न्).—(Carrier of news) सन्देशहरः.—(Pigeon) पत्रवाहकः कपोतः.

CARRION, *s.* पूतिमांसं, मृतं, मृतकं, अखाद्यमांसं, अखाद्यं, अमेध्यकुणपः.

CARROT, *s.* गर्जरं, पीतकन्दं, शिखामूलं, स्वादुमूलं, पिण्डमूलं.

CARROTINESS, *s.* रक्तत्वं, पिङ्गलत्वं.—(Of hair) केशरक्तत्वं, केशपिङ्गलता.

CARROTY, *a.* रक्तः -क्ता -क्तं, पिङ्गलः -ला -लं, गर्जरवर्णः -र्णा -र्णं.—(Carroty haired) पिङ्गलकेशी -शिनी -शि(न्) or रक्तकेशी, यूषिकाकेशः -शी -शं.

To CARRY, *v. a.* (Convey, transport) वह् (c. 1. वहति -ते, वोढुं), आवह्, उपवह्, संवह्, आनी (c. 1. -नयति -नेतुं), तॄ in caus. (तारयति -यितुं) गम् in caus. (गमयति -यितुं); 'he is carried on horse-back,' अश्वेन उह्यते or अश्वेन सञ्चरति.—(Bear as a burden) वह्, प्रवह्, उद्वह्; भृ (c. 3. बिभर्त्ति, भर्तुं), हृ (c. 1. हरति, हर्तुं); 'he carried his son on his back,' पुत्रम् अवहत् पृष्ठेन.—(Gain, carry a cause) साध् in caus. (साधयति -यितुं); 'to carry a fortress,' दुर्गं लङ्घ् (c. 10. लङ्घयति -यितुं) or भञ्ज् (c. 7. भनक्ति, भंक्तुं); 'to carry one's point,' अभिप्रेतसिद्धिं कृ, प्रतिज्ञापूरणं कृ.—(Carry about) परिवह्, पर्य्यानी.—(Carry away) अपवह्, अपनी (c. 1. -नयति -नेतुं), व्यपनी, अपोह् (c. 1. -ऊहते -ऊहितुं), व्यपोह्; 'to carry away with one,' समुपादा (c. 3. -ददाति -दातुं).—(Carry back) प्रत्यानी, प्रतिनी.—(Carry forth) निर्हृ.—(Carry off) अपवह्, अपनी, हृ, अपहृ, व्यपहृ, अपकृ (c. 8. -करोति -कुरुते -कर्तुं), कल् (c. 10. कालयति -यितुं).—(Carry on) कृ, प्रणी, सम्प्रणी, विधा (c. 3. -दधाति -धातुं).—(To carry on war) विग्रह् (c. 9. -गृह्णाति -ग्रहीतुं), सङ्ग्रामं कृ, युद्धं कृ.—(Carry out, effect) निर्वह् in caus. (-वाहयति -यितुं), सम्पद् in caus. (-पादयति -यितुं), निष्पद्.—(Carry letters) पत्राणि वह् or हृ.—(Carry arms) शस्त्राणि ग्रह् (c. 9. गृह्णाति, ग्रहीतुं), भृ or धृ, सैनिकवृत्तिम् आस्था (c. 1. -तिष्ठति -स्थातुं).

To CARRY ONE'S SELF, *v. n.* (Behave) चर् (c. 1. चरति, चरितुं), आचर्, वृत् (c. 1. वर्त्तते, वर्त्तितुं), व्यवहृ (c. 1. -हरति -हर्तुं).

CART, *s.* शकटः, गन्त्री, गन्त्रीरथः, चक्रयानं, वाहनं, अनः *n.* (स्), चातुरः.

To CART, *v. a.* (To carry in a cart) शकटेन वह् (c. 1. वहति, वोढुं).—(To place in a cart) शकटे आरुह् in caus. (-रोपयति -यितुं) or निविश् in caus. (-वेशयति -यितुं).

CARTE-BLANCHE, *s.* अलिखितपत्रं, लिखनशून्यं पत्रं.—(Permission to act as one pleases) स्वेच्छातः or स्वेच्छया कर्तुम् अनुमतिः or अनुज्ञा.

CARTED, *a.* शकटारूढः -ढा -ढं, शकटारोपितः -ता -तं, शकटनिवेशितः -ता -तं.

CARTEL, *s.* (A paper containing a challenge) द्वन्द्वयुद्धार्थं or नियुद्धार्थम् आह्वानपत्रं.—(Compact for exchange of prisoners) सङ्ग्रामसमये परस्परं बन्दीकृतानां योधानां परिवर्त्तनार्थं नियमपत्रं.

CARTER, *s.* शाकटिकः, शकटवाहकः, गन्त्रीवाहकः, चातुरिकः.

CART-HORSE, *s.* शाकटः, शकटवाजी *m.* (न्), शकटवाहनः, धुर्य्यः, धुरीणः.

CARTHUSIAN, *s.* रोमीयमतधारी सन्न्यासिविशेषः.

CARTICEYA. *See* KARTIKEYA.

CARTILAGE, *s.* तरुणास्थि *n.*, सन्धिबन्धनं, उपास्थि *n.*, कोमलास्थि *n.*

CARTILAGINOUS, *a.* तरुणास्थिमयः -यी -यं, तरुणास्थिविशिष्टः -ष्टा -ष्टं.

CART-LOAD, *s.* शाकटं, शाकटीनः, शाकटो भारः, आचितः -तं, शलाटः.

CARTOON, *s.* पटे लिखितश् चित्रारम्भः, कार्पासगतश् चित्रारम्भः, चित्रितपटं.

CARTOUCH, *s.* (A box for charges) वक्ष्यमाणचूर्णकोषधारणयोग्यः सम्पुटकः.—(A case filled with balls fired from a mortar) अनेकगुलिकागर्भो युद्धयन्त्रात् प्रक्षेपणीयः काष्ठादिमयः सम्पुटः.

CARTRIDGE, *s.* आग्नेयचूर्णकोषः, चूर्णगुलिकाकोशः; यौ चूर्णगोलकौ एकधारे युद्धनाडी निवेशयितव्यौ तयोः पूर्णम् आवेष्टनं.

CART-RUT, *s.* शकटचक्रचिह्नं, चक्राङ्कं, चक्रचिह्नं, चक्रपदवी, चक्रपद्धतिः *f.*

CARTULARY, *s.* आगमपत्रं, पांशुपत्रं, पट्टोलिका, पञ्जिका.

CART-WAY, *s.* रथ्या, रथमार्गः, शकटमार्गः, शकटपथः, गन्त्रीमार्गः.

CART-WRIGHT, *s.* रथकारः, शकटकारः, गन्त्रीकारकः, चक्रकारः.

To CARVE, *v. a.* (To cut) कृत् (c. 6. कृन्तति, कर्त्तितुं), विकृत्, छिद् (c. 7. छिनत्ति छेत्तुं).—(To cut meat) भोजनकाले परपरिवेषणार्थं खाद्यमांसादि निकृत् or व्यवछिद्, मांसादि परिविष् or परिविश् in caus. (-वेषयति -यितुं).—(To engrave) तक्ष् (c. 1. तक्षति, c. 5. तक्ष्णोति, तक्षितुं), त्वक्ष् (c. 1. त्वक्षति, त्वक्षितुं), रेखादिना अलङ्कृ or मुद्रीकृ, मुद्र (nom. मुद्रयति -यितुं).—(To apportion) कॢप् (c. 10. कल्पयति -यितुं), परिकॢप्, विभज् (c. 1. -भजति -भक्तुं).

CARVED, *p. p.* निकृत्तः -त्ता -त्तं, व्यवछिन्नः -न्ना -न्नं, तष्टः -ष्टा -ष्टं, परिकल्पितः -ता -तं.

CARVER, *s.* (A sculptor) तक्षकः, तष्टा *m.* (ष्टृ), त्वष्टा *m.* (ष्टृ), मुद्राकारः.—(One who cuts meat at a table) भोजनकाले परपरिवेषणार्थं खाद्यमांसव्यवच्छेदकः, परिवेषकः, परिवेशकः.—(One that apportions) परिकल्पकः, विभागकल्पयिता *m.* (तृ).

CARVING, *s.* (Sculpture, engraving) तक्षणं, तक्षणकर्म्म *n.* (न्).—(Cutting up meat) खाद्यमांसादिव्यवच्छेदः.—(Distributing) परिकल्पनं, विभागकल्पना.—(Carved wood, &c.) तष्टकाष्ठं, नानारेखालङ्कृतं काष्ठादि.

CARUNCLE, *s.* (A fleshy protuberance) अधिमांसः, मांसपिण्डः, गण्डः, त्वक्पुष्पं, मांसवृद्धिः *f.*

CASCADE, *s.* निर्झरः -री, झरः, वारिप्रवाहः, प्रपातः, सरः -री, प्रस्रवणं, झा.

CASE, *s.* (A covering, sheath) आच्छादनं, कोशः, कोषः, पुटः, पटलं, आवेष्टनं, आवरणं, पिधानं, व्यवधानं, तिरोधानं.—(A box) भाण्डं, आधारः, सम्पुटः, समुद्गः, पिधानं; 'a case for books,' ग्रन्थभाण्डं, ग्रन्थाधारः; 'a case for razors,' क्षुरभाण्डं.—(State of the case, matter) अर्थः, वृत्तान्तः, विषयः.—(Point, question) स्थलं, पदं, अधिकरणं.—(A position advanced) पक्षः, प्रतिज्ञा.—(Condition) अवस्था, दशा, भावः, स्थितिः *f.*, वृत्तिः *f.*—(State of the body) शरीरस्थितिः *f.*—(Contingence, occurrence) सङ्गतिः *f.*, सङ्गतं, वृत्तं.—(Inflection of nouns) विभक्तिः *f.*, व्यक्तिः *f.*; 'the true state of the case,' अर्थतत्त्वं; 'case in point,' दृष्टान्तः; 'in both cases,' उभयथा, पक्षद्वये; 'in certain cases,' क्वचित्; 'this being the case,' एवं सति, तथा सति; 'in case, if it should happen,' यदि, चेत्, यदि सम्भवेत्, एवं सति; 'upon the supposition,' पक्षे.

To CASE, *v. a.* (To put in a case) भाण्डे or आधारे निविश् in caus. (-वेशयति -यितुं).—(To cover) पिधा (c. 3. -दधाति -धातुं), आच्छद् (c. 10. -छादयति -यितुं).

To CASEHARDEN, *v. a.* बाह्यतस् or बहिर्भागे दृढीकृ or कठिनीकृ.

CASEMATE, *s.* वप्रस्य पार्श्वभागाभ्यन्तरे तोरणाकारा प्रस्तरनिर्म्मिता गुप्तिः.

CASEMENT, *s.* जालं -लिका, गवाक्षः, वातायनं, गवाक्षजालं, आकाशजननी *m.* (न्).

CASEWORM, *s.* कोषकारः, कोशकारः -रकः, कोशस्थः.

CASH, *s.* टङ्कः, टङ्ककः, मुद्रा, नाणकं, धनं.

CASH-KEEPER OR CASHIER, *s.* टङ्करक्षकः, टङ्काधीशः, टङ्काधिकृतः.

To CASHIER, *v. a.* पदात् or अधिकारात् भ्रंश् in caus. (भ्रंशयति -यितुं), प्रभ्रंश्, or निपत् in caus. (-पातयति -यितुं) or अवरुह् in caus. (-रोपयति -यितुं) or अपसृ in caus. (-सारयति -यितुं) or विसृज् in caus. (-सर्जयति -यितुं), or च्यु in caus. (च्यावयति -यितुं).

CASHIERED, *p. p.* च्युताधिकारः -रा -रं, भ्रष्टाधिकारः -रा -रं, पदात्प्रभ्रंशितः -ता -तं, अधिकारात्प्रभ्रंशितः -ता -तं or निराकृतः -ता -तं or अवरोपितः -ता -तं, अपसृष्टः -ष्टा -ष्टं.

Casing, *s.* छादनं, आच्छादनं, पटलं, पुटः, कोषः, कोशः, आवेष्टनं.

Cask, *s.* भाण्डं, भाजनं, दीर्घगोलाकृति काष्ठमयभाण्डं.

Casket, *s.* सम्पुटः -टकः, समुद्गः, स्थलिका, पेटिका, पेटकः, करण्डः; 'of jewels,' रत्नभाण्डं.

Casque, *s.* शिरस्त्राणं, शिरस्त्रं, शिरस्कं, शीर्षरक्षं, शीर्षण्यं.

To **cassate**, *v.a.* (Invalidate) खण्ड् (c.10. खण्डयति -यितुं), मोघीकृ, अधरीकृ.

Cassia, *s.* (A plant) प्रपुन्नाडः, एडगजः, दद्रुघ्नः, चक्रमर्द्दकः, शिग्रुः.—(Woody cassia) त्वक्पत्रं, उत्कटं, भृङ्गं.—(Bark) गन्धवल्कलं, गुडत्वक्, सुरसं.

Cassiowary, *s.* बृहत्कायः प्लवभेदः, अतिमहान् पक्षिप्रभेदः.

Cassock, *s.* (Part of a priest's dress) अधुनातनपुरोहितैर् भृतं परिधानं or अन्तरीयं or उपसंव्यानं.

To **cast**, *v. a.* (Throw) क्षिप् (c. 6. क्षिपति, क्षेप्तुं), प्रक्षिप्, अस् (c. 4. अस्यति, असितुं), प्रास्, मुच् (c. 6. मुञ्चति, मोक्तुं), प्रमुच्, सृज् (c. 6. सृजति, स्रष्टुं), ईर् (c. 10. ईरयति -यितुं), उदीर्, पत् in caus. (पातयति -यितुं); 'to cast one's self at another's feet,' परस्य पादयोः पत् (c. 1. पतति, पतितुं); 'into prison,' कारायां प्रविश् in caus. (-वेशयति -यितुं) or बन्ध् (c. 9. बध्नाति, बन्द्धुं).—(Compute) विगण् (c.10. -गणयति -यितुं), संख्या (c. 2. -ख्याति -ख्यातुं), कल् (c. 10. कलयति -यितुं).—(Cast in a law-suit) साध् in caus. (साधयति -यितुं), दा in caus. (दापयति -यितुं).—(Condemn) दोषीकृ, दोषिणं -णीं -षि कृ.—(Found as metals) लोहादि द्रावयित्वा or विलाप्य सन्धा (c. 3. -दधाति -धातुं).—(Consider, weigh) विचिन्त् (c. 10. -चिन्तयति -यितुं), विचर् in caus. (-चारयति -यितुं), विगण्.—(Shed, moult) निर्मुच् (c. 6. -मुञ्चति -मोक्तुं), पत् in caus. (-पातयति -यितुं).—(Cast away) अपास्, व्युदस्, प्रास्, प्रक्षिप्, अपव्यध् (c. 4. -विध्यति -ते -व्यद्धुं), परित्यज् (c. 1. -त्यजति -त्यक्तुं).—(Cast down) पत् in caus. निपत्, विनिपत्, अधःपत्, अवक्षिप्, पर्य्यस्, अधःक्षिप्, निक्षिप्.—(Cast forth, emit) उदीर्, मुच्, प्रमुच्, निरस्, उत्सृज्, उद्गृ (c. 6. -गिरति -गरितुं -गरीतुं), उद्वम् (c. 1. -वमति -वमितुं).—(Cast off) अवमुच्, अपास्, प्रतिक्षिप्, विक्षिप्, पराकृ (c. 8. -करोति -कर्त्तुं), अपाहा (c. 3. -जहाति -हातुं), निर्णुद् (c. 6. -णुदति -णोत्तुं).—(Cast out, expel) निरस्, बहिःक्षिप्, बहिर्निक्षिप्, बहिष्कृ, निराकृ, निर्या in caus. (-यापयति -यितुं), निःसृ in caus. (-सारयति -यितुं), भ्रंश् in caus. (भ्रंशयति -यितुं), अपानुद्, निष्कस् in caus. (-कासयति -यितुं).—(Cast the eye, glance) दृष्टिं पत् in caus., ईषद्दर्शनं कृ.—(Cast lots) गुटिकां पत् in caus.

Cast, *p. p.* क्षिप्तः -प्ता -प्तं, अस्तः -स्ता -स्तं, प्रास्तः -स्ता -स्तं, ईरितः -ता -तं, पातितः -ता -तं, मुक्तः -क्ता -क्तं, नुन्नः -न्ना -न्नं.—(Cast off) अपास्तः -स्ता -स्तं, समाक्षिप्तः -प्ता -प्तं.—(Cast in a law-suit) साधितः -ता -तं, दापितः -ता -तं.

Cast, *s.* (A throw) क्षेपः, क्षेपणं, असनं, पातनं; 'cast of a stick,' यष्टिपातः.—(Oblique direction of the eye) दृष्टितिर्य्यक्त्वं, दृष्टिविक्षेपः; 'having a cast in the eye,' तिर्य्यग्दृष्टिः *m.*, दूरेरितेक्षणः, केकराक्षः.—(Mould) संस्कारः, संयानः, कल्पः, आकारः, संस्थानं, मूर्त्तिः *f.*

Castanets, *s.* करर्द्धिः *m.*, एकताली, एकपर्णी, करताली.

Castaway, *s.* त्याज्यः, अग्राह्यः, अग्रहणीयः, उत्सन्नः, महापातकी *m.* (न्), अपांक्तेयः.

Caste, *s.* वर्णः, वर्गः, कुलं, जातिः *f.*; 'of low caste,' विवर्णः, नीचः, प्राकृतः, हीनजातिः *m. f.*, निकृष्टजातिः *m. f.*; 'of good caste,' सुवर्णः, वर्णश्रेष्ठः, उत्कृष्टजातिः; 'of mixed caste,' सङ्कीर्णः; 'loss of caste,' जातिभ्रंशः.—(Outcaste) जातिहीनः -ना -नं, वर्णहीनः, अपसदः, चाण्डालः.

Castellan, *s.* दुर्गाधिपतिः *m.*, दुर्गाधिकारी *m.* (न्), दुर्गाध्यक्षः, कोटिपालः.

Castellated, *s.* (Formed like a castle) दुर्गाकारः -रा -रं, कुटाकृतिः -तिः -ति.

Caster, *s.* (A thrower) क्षेपकः, क्षेप्ता *m.* (प्तृ), असिता *m.* (तृ), प्रासकः.—(A calculator) गणकः, गणयिता *m.* (तृ).

To **castigate**, *v. a.* दण्ड् (c. 10. दण्डयति -यितुं), तड् (c. 10. ताडयति -यितुं), शास् (c. 2. शास्ति, शासितुं or caus. शासयति -यितुं), अनुशास्.

Castigation, *s.* दण्डः, साहसं, शिष्टिः *f.*, अनुशासनं, ताडः, ताडनं, निग्रहः.

Castigatory, *a.* दाण्डः -ण्डी -ण्डं, साहसिकः -की -कं, प्रायश्चित्तिकः -की -कं.

Casting-house, *s.* सन्धानी, लोहादिद्रावणस्थानं, धातुविलयनशाला, कुप्यशाला.

Casting-net, *s.* क्षेपणिः *f.* -णी, हस्तेन प्रक्षेपणीयं सन्नद्धोत्तोलनीयं लघुजालं.

Castle, *s.* दुर्गं, कुटः, कूटः, कोटः, कोटिः *f.*—(Castle in the air) गगनकुसुमं, अनर्थकवासना, अनर्थकभावना, मनोरथसृष्टिः *f.*

Castling, *s.* गर्भपतितः, गर्भच्युतः, गर्भभ्रष्टः.

Castor, *s.* (A beaver) जलजन्तुविशेषः, जलमार्जारविशेषः.—(A hat) पूर्व्वोक्तजलजन्तुलोमनिर्म्मितम् अधुनातनपुम्भिर् भृतं शिरस्कं, शिरस्त्रं.

Castor-oil, *s.* एरण्डतैलं, एरण्डरसः, रुबुतैलं, अमण्डतैलं.

Castrametation, *s.* शिबिरनिवेशनविद्या, कटकनिवेशनं, कटकसमावासः, रचना.

To **castrate**, *v. a.* वृषणौ उत्कृत् (c. 6. -कृन्तति -कर्त्तितुं) or छिद् (c. 7. छिनत्ति, छेत्तुं), वृषणद्वयं उत्पट् in caus. (-पाटयति -यितुं).

Castrated, *p.p.* छिन्नवृषणः -णा -णं, छिन्नमुष्कः -ष्का -ष्कं, मुष्कशून्यः -न्या -न्यं.

Castration, *s.* वृषणच्छेदः, वृषणोत्कर्त्तनं, मुष्कच्छेदनं, वृषणोत्पाटनं.

Castrel, *s.* श्येनः, कपोतारिः *m.*, श्येनजातीयः पक्षिभेदः.

Castrensian, *a.* शिबिरसम्बन्धी -न्धिनी -न्धि (न्), सैनिकः -की -कं.

Casual, *a.* आगन्तुकः -का -कं, आकस्मिकः -की -कं, आपातिकः -की -कं, दैवायत्तः -त्ता -त्तं, दैविकः -की -कं, अकाण्डः -ण्डा -ण्डं, अदृष्टः -ष्टा -ष्टं, अचिन्तितः -ता -तं, अतर्कितः -ता -तं, नैमित्तिकः -की -कं.

Casually, *adv.* अकस्मात्, दैवात्, आगन्तुकप्रकारेण, अचिन्तितं, अतर्कितं.

Casualness, *s.* आकस्मिकत्वं, आगन्तुकत्वं, दैवायत्तता, दैवाधीनता.

Casualty, *s.* सङ्गतिः -तं, अकस्मात्सङ्गतं, दैवगतिः *f.*, दैवयोगः, दैवघटनं, आगन्तुः *m.*, अतिवर्त्तनं.—(Unseen danger) अदृष्टं.

Casuist, *s.* धर्म्माधर्म्मविचारकः, धर्म्माधर्म्मविषये विवादी *m.* (न्) or वादानुवादविज्ञः, धर्म्माधर्म्मोपदेशकः, कार्य्याकार्य्यनिर्णयविदग्धः.

Casuistical, *a.* धर्म्माधर्म्मविचारणविषयः -या -यं, धर्म्माधर्म्मोपदेशसम्बन्धी -न्धिनी -न्धि (न्).

Casuistry, *s.* धर्म्माधर्म्मविचारणविद्या, धर्म्माधर्म्मविषये वादानुवादविद्या, कार्य्याकार्य्यनिर्णयः, धर्म्माधर्म्मोपदेशः, इदं कर्त्तव्यं इदम् अकर्त्तव्यं इति विवेचनविद्या.

Cat, *s.* मार्जारः, बिडालः, ओतुः *m.*, वृन्दमः, मूषकारातिः *m.*, आखुभुक् *m.* (ज्), वृषदंशकः, पयस्यः, व्याघ्रास्यः, दीप्ताक्षः.

Cat-o'-nine-tails, *s.* नवबलिसज्जयुक्ता कशा, नवरज्जुयुक्ता ताडनी, नवग्रन्थिष्कशयुक्ता चर्म्मयष्टिः.

Catachresis, *s.* कुव्यञ्जकविशेषः यथा कर्णाभ्यां पीयते सुरूपी शब्द इति.

Cataclysm, *s.* भूतसम्प्लवः, आप्लावः, जलाप्लावनं, पृथिवीप्लावः.

Catacombs, *s.* भूमौ खाताः शवगोपनयोग्या गूढमार्गाः, अन्तर्भौमश्मशानं.

Catalectick, *a.* न्यूनैकाक्षरः -रा -रं, छन्दोविशेषः.

Catalepsis, *s.* महामयः, अपस्मारः, भ्रामरं, भूतविक्रिया, अङ्गविकृतिः *f.*

Catalogue, *s.* परिसंख्या, अनुक्रमणिका, परिगणना, एकैकशः परिसंख्या, सङ्ग्रहः, सूचिः *f.*; 'of names,' नामावलिः *f.*

CATAMENIA, *s.* ऋतुः *m.*, आर्त्तवं, रजः *n.* (स्), पुष्पं, योनिरञ्जनं.

CATAPHRACT, *s.* संवर्म्मितः or सर्व्वसन्नाहयुक्त अश्वारूढः सैनिकः.

CATAPLASM, *s.* उत्कारिका, लेपः, प्रलेपः, उपनाहः.

CATAPULT, *s.* पूर्व्वकालीनयोद्धृभिः प्रस्तरप्रक्षेपणे प्रयुक्तो युद्धयन्त्रविशेषः.

CATARACT, *s.* निर्झरः -री, झरः, वारिप्रवाहः, प्रपातः, सरः -री, प्रस्रवणं, उच्चदेशात् तोयपतनं.—(Disease of the eye) मन्थः, लिङ्गनाशः, शुक्रः, नेत्रपटलं.

CATARRH, *s.* पीनसः, प्रतिश्यायः, काशः -सः, श्लेष्मा *m.* (न्), कफः.—(Having one) पीनसी *m.* (न्), काशी *m.* (न्).

CATARRHAL, *a.* पीनसी -सिनी -सि (न्), काशी -शिनी -शि (न्), कफी -फिनी -फि (न्), श्लेष्मलः -ला -लं, पीनससम्बन्धी -न्धिनी -न्धि (न्).

CATASTROPHE, *s.* (Of a drama) निष्ठा, निर्व्वहणं.—(Conclusion) परिणामः, निर्व्वाहः, निर्वृत्तिः *f.*—(Event) सङ्गतिः *f.*—(Misfortune) आपद् *f.*, विपद् *f.* दुर्गतिः *f.*

CAT-CALL, *s.* रङ्गे प्रेक्षकाणाम् अप्रसादवाचको विस्वरवाद्यविशेषः.

To CATCH, *v. a.* ग्रह् (c. 9. गृह्णाति, ग्रहीतुं), धृ (c. 1. धरति, धर्त्तुं), लभ् (c. 1. लभते, लब्धुं), प्राप् (c. 5. -आप्नोति -आप्तुं).—(Lay hold with the hand) सङ्ग्रह्, परिग्रह्, परामृश् (c. 6. -मृशति -म्रष्टुं), अवलम्ब् (c. 1. -लम्बते -लम्बितुं).—(Receive suddenly) अकस्माद् ग्रह् or लभ् or प्राप्; 'to catch cold,' पीनसग्रस्तः -स्ता -स्तं भू, पीनसोपहतः -ता -तं भू; 'to catch a distemper,' सम्पर्कात् or संसर्गाद् रोगग्रस्तः -स्ता -स्तं भू; 'to catch fire,' अकस्माद् दह् in pass. (दह्यते) or दीप् (c. 4. दीप्यते, दीपितुं), लब्धदाहः -हा -हं भू, अग्निदीप्तः -प्ता -प्तं भू, अग्निं ग्रह्.—(Ensnare, entrap) ग्रह्, धृ, बन्ध् (c. 9. बध्नाति, बन्द्धुं), प्रलुभ् in caus. (लोभयति -यितुं), वञ्च् in caus. (वञ्चयते -यितुं); 'to catch fish,' मत्स्यान् धर्त्तुं or ग्रहीतुं.—(Come upon unexpectedly) अकस्माद् आसद् (c. 10. -सादयति -यितुं) or समासद् or प्राप्; 'caught out in a fault,' दृष्टदोषः -षा -षं, 'I caught him in the act of stealing,' चोरयन्तमेव तम् आसादयं or उपातिष्ठं.—(Allure) प्रलुभ् in caus., आकृष् (c. 1. -कर्षति -क्रष्टुं).—(Catch up, snatch, seize) हृ (c. 1. हरति, हर्त्तुं), अपहृ, हृत्वा अपनी.—(To spread as contagion) सञ्चर् (c. 1. -चरति -चरितुं).

CATCH, *s.* (Seizure) ग्रहणं, ग्रहः, सङ्ग्रहणं, सङ्ग्राहः, धरणं, हरणं.—(Any thing that catches) ग्राहकः -कं, ग्रहः, धरः; 'a latch,' तालकं; 'a clasp,' कुडुपः.—(Prize, advantage) लाभः, प्राप्तिः *f.*, लोप्त्रं, फलं.—(A song sung in succession) पर्य्यायगीतं, परस्परगीतं, परिवर्त्तकगीतं.

CATCHER, *s.* ग्राहकः, वागुरिकः, जालिकः, लुब्धकः.—(That in which fish, &c. are caught, a snare for animals) मत्स्यधानी, मृगबन्धिनी, वागुरा, जालं.

CATCHING, *a.* (Contagious) सञ्चारकः -का -कं, सञ्चारी -रिणी -रि (न्), सम्पर्कीयः -या -यं, त्वाचः -ची -चं.

CATCHPOLE, *s.* आसेद्धा *m.* (द्धृ), आसेधकर्त्ता *m.* (र्त्तृ), ग्राहकः, यष्टिधरः.

CATCHWORD, *s.* मुद्राकरभाषायां परपत्रगः शब्दः.

CATECHETICAL, *a.* प्राश्नोत्तरिकः -की -कं, प्रश्नोत्तरमयः -यी -यं, प्रश्नोत्तरविशिष्टः -ष्टा -ष्टं, सप्रश्नोत्तरः -रा -रं.

CATECHETICALLY, *adv.* प्रश्नोत्तरक्रमेण, सप्रश्नोत्तरं, प्रश्नोत्तरद्वारेण.

To CATECHISE, *v. a.* प्रश्नोत्तरद्वारेण or प्रश्नोत्तरक्रमेण उपदिश् (c. 6. -दिशति -देष्टुं) or शिक्ष् in caus. (शिक्षयति -यितुं) or अधी in caus. (अध्यापयति -यितुं).—(To interrogate) प्रच्छ् (c. 6. पृच्छति, प्रष्टुं), परीक्ष् (c. 1. -ईक्षते -ईक्षितुं).

CATECHISING, *s.* प्रश्नोत्तरद्वारेण शिक्षा or उपदेशः or अध्यापनं, परीक्षा.

CATECHISM, *s.* (Form of question and answer) प्रश्नोत्तरं, कथोपकथनं, उत्तरप्रत्युत्तरं, प्रश्नोत्तरविधिः *m.*, प्रश्नोत्तररीतिः *f.*, सप्रश्नोत्तरः पाठः.

CATECHIST OF CATECHISER, *s.* प्रश्नोत्तरद्वारेण or प्रश्नोत्तरक्रमेण or प्रश्नोत्तरविधिना उपदेशकः or शिक्षकः or अध्यापकः or पाठकः.

CATECHUMEN, *s.* नवछात्रः, नवशिष्यः, नवाधीयानः, प्राथमकल्पिकः.

CATEGORICAL, *a.* एकार्थः -र्था -र्थं, व्यक्तः -क्ता -क्तं, सुव्यक्तः -क्ता -क्तं, अवक्रः -क्रा -क्रं, स्पष्टः -ष्टा -ष्टं, स्पष्टार्थः -र्था -र्थं, वाचकः -का -कं, नियतः -ता -तं, पर्य्याप्तः -प्ता -प्तं, अव्यञ्जनः -ना -नं.

CATEGORICALLY, *adv.* एकार्थं, सुव्यक्तं, स्पष्टं, स्पष्टार्थं, अवक्रं, वाचकतया.

CATEGORY, *s.* पदार्थः, समानाधिकरणं, समानपदं, समानवर्गः, पदं.—(Of individual application) अव्याप्यवृत्तिः *f.*

CATENARIAN, *a.* शृङ्खलाकारः -रा -रं, शृङ्खलसम्बन्धी -न्धिनी -न्धि (न्).

CATENATION, *s.* शृङ्खलता, शृङ्खलत्वं, पर्य्यायः, सम्बन्धः.

To CATER, *v. a.* भोजनादि परिकॢप् (c. 10. -कल्पयति -यितुं) or उपकॢप् or सम्भृ (c. 1. -भरति, c. 3. -बिभर्त्ति -भर्त्तुं) or युज् in caus. (योजयति -यितुं).

CATERER, *s.* भोजनाधिकारी *m.* (न्), भोजनाधिकृतः, भोजनाधिष्ठाता *m.* (तृ), अन्नादिपरिकल्पकः.

CATERPILLAR, *s.* वृश्चिकः, शूककीटः, कोशवासी *m.* (न्), कोषकारी *m.* (न्).

To CATERWAUL, *v. n.* मत्तविडालवद् रु (c. 2. रौति, रवितुं), मेनादं कृ.

CATERWAULING, *s.* मत्तविडालरुतं, मत्तमार्ज्जारचित्कारः, कर्कशरावः, मेनादः.

CATES, *s. pl.* स्वाद्वन्नं, विशिष्टान्नं, भोजनविशेषाः *m. pl.*, मिष्टान्नं.

CAT-GUT, *s.* विडालादिपुरीतन्निर्म्मिता तन्त्रीः, जन्तुनाडिमयं सूत्रं, तन्तुः *m.*

CATHARTIC, *s.* रेचकः, रेचनं, विरेकः, विरेचनं, उदरशोधनं.

CATHARTICAL, *a.* रेचकः -की -कं, विरेचकः -की -कं, अधोभागहरः -रा -रं, अतिसारी -रिणी -रि (न्), शोधकः -का -कं.

CATHEDRAL, *s.* महापूजाशाला, महाभजनभवनं, महामण्डपः, महामन्दिरं, महाधर्म्माध्यक्षाधिष्ठिता पूजाशाला.

CATHEDRAL, *a.* महाधर्म्माध्यक्षमठसम्बन्धी -न्धिनी -न्धि (न्), महापूजाशालासम्बन्धीयः -या -यं.

CATHETER, *s.* मूत्रकृच्छ्रपीडितानां मेहमोचनार्थं मूत्रमार्गे निवेशयितव्या चक्रनाडिः.

CATHOLIC, *a.* सामान्यः -न्या -न्यं, सर्व्वसामान्यः -न्या -न्यं, साधारणः -णा -णं, सर्व्वसाधारणः -णा -णं, सार्व्वः -र्व्वी -र्व्वं, सार्व्वत्रिकः -की -कं, सर्व्वीयः -या -यं, सार्व्वलौकिकः -की -कं, सार्व्वजनिकः -की -कं, सर्व्वजनीनः -ना -नं.

CATHOLIC, *s.* सर्व्वसाधारणमतस्थः, सर्व्वसामान्यमतधारी *m.* (न्).—(Roman Catholic) रोमीयमतधारी *m.* (न्).

CATHOLICISM, *s.* साधारण्यं, सामान्यं, सर्व्वसाधारण्यं, सर्व्वसामान्यं.

CATHOLICON, *s.* सर्व्वसाधारणभेषजं, सर्व्वसम्मतभेषजं.

CATKINS, *s.* तरुशाखातो लम्बमाना विडालपुच्छाकारा हरितपुष्पश्रेणी.

CATLING, *s.* शस्त्रचिकित्सकैर् अङ्गच्छेदने प्रयुक्तः कर्त्तरिकाविशेषः.

CATOPTRICAL, *a.* वक्ष्यमाणचाक्षुषविद्याङ्गसम्बन्धी -न्धिनी -न्धि (न्).

CATOPTRICS, *s.* चाक्षुषविद्यायाः प्रतिबिम्बविषयकम् अङ्गं.

CATTLE, *s.* गावः *m. pl.*, गोधनं, गोकुलं; 'cattle for draught,' धुरीणः, धुर्य्यः; 'fit for any draught,' सर्व्वधुरीणः, सर्व्वधुरावहः; 'rich in cattle,' गोमान् -मती -मत् (त्), गोमी -मिनी -मि (न्); 'capture of cattle,' गोग्रहः; 'cattle-keeper,' गोपालः, पशुपालः; 'the keeping of cattle,' पाशुपाल्यं.

CAVALCADE, *s.* आश्विकयात्रा, सादिनां or अश्वारोहिणां यात्रा or श्रेणी.

CAVALIER, *s.* सादी *m.* (न्), अश्ववारः, आश्विकः, अश्वारूढः, अश्वारोही *m.* (न्), अश्ववहः, हयारूढः, तुरगी *m.* (न्), तुरङ्गी *m.* (न्).

CAVALIERLY, *adv.* (Disdainfully) सावमानं, अवमानेन, सदर्पं, सगर्व्वं,

सावलेपं, सावहेलं.—(To treat cavalierly) अवमन् (c. 4. -मन्यते -मन्तुं), अवज्ञा (c. 9. -जानाति -ज्ञातुं), कदर्थीकृ, लघूकृ.

CAVALRY, *s.* आश्वं, आश्विकं, अश्वीयं, अश्वाः *m. pl.*, अश्वारोहाः *m. pl.*, अश्वारोहं सेनाङ्गं, अश्वारूढाः *m. pl.*, अश्वारोहिणः *m. pl.*, हयारूढाः *m. pl.*, अश्ववहाः *m. pl.*, सादिनः *m. pl.*, तुरङ्गिणः *m. pl.*, तुरङ्गयायिनः *m. pl.*

To CAVATE, *v. a.* (To hollow) खन् (c. 1. खनति, खनितुं, खातुं), शुषिरीकृ.

CAVATION, *s.* गृहतले खातं, गृहस्याधस्तात् खाता गुप्तिः.

CAUDATED, *a.* पुच्छी -च्छिनी -च्छि (न्), लाङ्गूली -लिनी -लि (न्).

CAUDLE, *s.* प्रसूताभिर् आहार्य्यं मद्यादिसम्मिश्रितं पानीयं.

CAVE OR CAVERN, *s.* विलं, विवरं, कन्दरः -रा, गर्त्तः, गह्वरं -री, रन्ध्रं, गुहा, गुहागृहं, निर्झरिः *m.*, दरी *f.*, शैलरन्ध्रं.—(Excavation) खातं, देवखातं, देवखातविलं.

CAVEAT, *s.* सावधानो भव इति विज्ञापनं, निषेधः, निषेधपत्रं.

CAVERNED, *a.* (Full of caverns) गह्वरी -रिणी -रि (न्).—(Excavated) खातः -ता -तं.—(Inhabiting caverns) गह्वरवासी -सिनी -सि (न्) or -भाक् (ज्), विलवासी -सिनी -सि (न्).

CAVESSON, *s.* अश्वदमने प्रयुक्तं नासायन्त्रणं.

CAUGHT, *p. p.* गृहीतः -ता -तं, धृतः -ता -तं, प्राप्तः -प्ता -प्तं, लब्धः -ब्धा -ब्धं, बद्धः -द्धा -द्धं; 'caught in a net,' जालबद्धः -द्धा -द्धं; 'caught hold of,' सङ्गृहीतः -ता -तं, अवलम्बितः -ता -तं; 'caught out in a crime,' दृष्टदोषः -षा -षं; 'caught by a glance,' कटाक्षमुष्टः -ष्टा -ष्टं.

CAVIAR, *s.* लवणादिसम्मिश्रितं वृहन्मत्स्याण्डं, लवणाक्तं मीनाण्डं.

To CAVIL, *v. a.* मिथ्या विवद् (c. 1. -वदते-वदितुं) or निन्द् (c. 1. निन्दति -न्दितुं), वाक्यं खण्ड् (c. 10. खण्डयति -यितुं), दोषं or छिद्रम् अन्विष् (c. 6. -इच्छति -एषितुं) or ग्रह् (c. 9. गृह्णाति, ग्रहीतुं), विप्रलप् (c. 1. -लपति -लपितुं), दोषीकृ.

CAVIL, *s.* मिथ्याविवादः, विवादः, उद्ग्राहः, मिथ्योद्ग्राहः, दोषग्राहः, दोषकल्पनं, दोषप्रसङ्गः, छिद्रान्वेषः, मिथ्यापत्तिः *f.*, मिथ्यावितर्कः, विप्रलापः, वाक्यखण्डनं, वाक्यविरोधः, अपवादः, वाग्युद्धं, वितण्डा, विप्रतिपत्तिः *f.*

CAVILLER, *s.* विवादशीलः, उद्ग्राहशीलः, मिथ्याविवादी *m.* (न्), उद्ग्राहमल्लः.

CAVILLING, *a.* दोषग्राही -हिणी -हि (न्), विवादी -दिनी -दि (न्), छिद्रान्वेषी -षिणी -षि (न्), छिद्रानुसारी -रिणी -रि (न्), घृणी -णिनी -णि (न्), निन्दकः -का -कं, अपवादकः -का -कं, विसंवादी -दिनी -दि (न्).

CAVILLINGLY, *adv.* मिथ्याविवादपूर्व्वकं, विवादशीलत्वात्, छिद्रान्वेषिवत्.

CAVITY, *s.* गर्त्तः, छिद्रं, विवरं, खातं, विलं, रन्ध्रं, कोटरः, कुहरं, अवटः, अवटिः *m.*

CAUL, *s.* (Covering for the head) शिरोवेष्टनं.—(Integument of the bowels) अन्त्रावेष्टनं, पुरीतदावेष्टनं.—(Membrane encompassing the head of a new-born child) सद्यो योनिजातस्य बालकस्य मस्तकावेष्टकः कोशविशेषः, गर्भवेष्टनं, गर्भाशयः.

CAULIFEROUS, *a.* प्रकाण्डविशिष्टः -ष्टा -ष्टं, काण्डवान् -वती -वत् (त्), मञ्जरितः -ता -तं.

CAULIFLOWER, *s.* शाकप्रभेदः, हरितकः, शिग्रुः *m.*

CAUSABLE, *a.* उत्पादनीयः -या -यं, उत्पादयितुं शक्यः -क्या -क्यं.

CAUSAL, *a.* कारणिकः -की -कं, हेतुकः -का -कं, हैतुकः -की -कं.—(Causal verb) प्रेरणं.

CAUSALITY OR CAUSATION, *s.* कारणत्वं -ता, हेतुता -त्वं, निमित्तत्वं, प्रयोजककर्तृत्वं.

CAUSATIVE, *a.* उत्पादकः -का -कं, जनिकः -का -कं, जनयिता -त्री -तृ (तृ).

CAUSE, *s.* (That which effects, motive, reason) कारणं, हेतुः *m.*, निमित्तं -त्तकं, निदानं, प्रयोजनं, निबन्धनं, करणं, उपाधिः *m.*—(Origin) प्रभवः, उद्भवः, सम्भवः, योनिः *f.*, बीजं, वैजिकं, मूलं; 'without cause,' अकस्मात्; 'for this cause,' अनेन हेतुना, तदर्थं, तस्य हेतोः; 'primary cause,' आद्यबीजं, आदिकारणं; 'a good cause,' सन्निमित्तं; 'cause and effect,' कार्य्यकारणं.—(The person who effects) उत्पादकः, कारकः, कर्त्ता *m.* (र्तृ), प्रयोजकः, प्रवर्त्तकः.—(Subject of litigation) अर्थः; 'one who has lost his cause,' साधितः.—(Occasion) प्रयोजनं, कारणं, स्थानं, अवसरः.—(Side, party) पक्षः; 'one's own cause,' आत्मपक्षः.

To CAUSE, *v. a.* जन् in caus. (जनयति -यितुं), उत्पद् in caus. (-पादयति -यितुं), कृ (c. 8. करोति, कर्तुं), साध् in caus. (साधयति -यितुं), निमित्त (nom. निमित्तायते). Sometimes भू is used with the dat. c.; as, 'that will cause my destruction,' तन्मम विनाशाय भविष्यति: or even the dative alone may be used; as, तन्मम विनाशाय. Sometimes a phrase like the following may be found; 'I was not the cause of this deed,' इदं कर्म्म न मत्स्वामिकं or मत्कर्तृकं.

CAUSED, *p. p.* कारितः -ता -तं, कृतः -ता -तं, जनितः -ता -तं, उत्पादितः -ता -तं, कारणभूतः -ता -तं, उद्भवः -वा -वं or प्रभवः -वा -वं in comp.; as, 'caused by the wind,' अनिलोद्भवः -वा -वं.

CAUSELESS, *a.* निष्कारणः -णा -णं, निर्निमित्तः -त्ता -त्तं, अनिमित्तः -त्ता -त्तं, निष्प्रयोजनः -ना -नं, अहेतुकः -का -कं, अनिदानः -ना -नं, हेतुशून्यः -न्या -न्यं; 'causeless state,' विलक्षणं.

CAUSELESSLY, *adv.* निष्प्रयोजनं, अकारणं, अकारणात्, निष्कारणं, अनिमित्ततस्, निर्निमित्तं, असति प्रयोजने, हेतुना विना, हेतुं विना.

CAUSER, *s.* कारकः, कर्त्ता *m.* (र्तृ), करः, कारः, उत्पादकः, जनकः, जनयिता *m.* (तृ), प्रयोजकः, प्रवर्त्तकः.

CAUSEWAY, *s.* सेतुः *m.*, सेतुबन्धः, पाली, पिच्छलः, पिच्छिलः, भरणः, संवरं.

CAUSTIC, *a.* (Burning, corrosive) दाहकः -का -कं, अरुन्तुदः -दा -दं, अरुष्करः -रा -रं, क्षयकरः -री -रं, तिग्मः -ग्मा -ग्मं.—(Biting, satirical) अरुन्तुदः -दा -दं, दंशेरः -रा -रं, मर्म्मभेदी -दिनी -दि (न्), मर्म्मस्पृक् *m. f. n.* (श्).

CAUSTICITY, *s.* अरुन्तुदत्वं -ता, अरुष्करत्वं -ता.

CAUTELOUS, *a.* (Cunning, wily) विदग्धः -ग्धा -ग्धं, विचक्षणः -णा -णं.

CAUTERIZATION, *s.* दाहः, दाहनं, उपयन्त्रेण or तप्तलोहेन or तिग्मौषधप्रयोगेण मांसदाहनं, क्षारकर्म्म *n.* (न्), कृष्णकर्म्म, क्षारार्पणं.

To CAUTERIZE, *v. a.* दह् in caus. (दाहयति-यितुं), तप्तलोहेन or उपयन्त्रेण or तिग्मौषधप्रयोगेण मांसं दह्, क्षारम् ऋ in caus. (अर्पयति -यितुं).

CAUTERY, *s.* (Actual) दाहः, उपयन्त्रं, तप्तलोहेन मांसदाहः, क्षारः.—(Potential) दाहः, औषधीयारुन्तुदद्रव्यप्रयोगेण मांसदाहः.

CAUTION, *s.* (Prudent care) अवधानं -नता, सावधानता, समीक्षा -क्षणं, प्रसमीक्षा, अवेक्षा, अन्ववेक्षा, अपेक्षा, अप्रमादः, चिन्ता, कार्य्यचिन्ता, विवेचनं, चेतना, आशङ्का, आशङ्काशीलता.—(Warning) प्रत्यादेशः, अवधेहि or सावधानो भव इति विज्ञापनं, सन्देशः.—(Security) प्रातिभाव्यं, पारिभाव्यं, बन्धकः, आधिः *m.*

To CAUTION AGAINST, *v. a.* प्रत्यादिश् (c. 6. -दिशति -देष्टुं), सन्दिश्; अवधेहि or अवधत्स्व or सावधानो भव इति विज्ञा in caus. (-ज्ञापयति -यितुं); 'he cautioned his sons against evil company,' असत्संसर्गात् सावधाना भवत or अवधत्त इति पुत्रान् प्रत्यादिशत्.

CAUTIONARY, *a.* (Containing a security) सबन्धकः -का -कं, सपारिभाव्यः -व्या -व्यं.—(Containing a warning) प्रत्यादेशकः -का -कं.

CAUTIONED, *p. p.* प्रत्यादिष्टः -ष्टा -ष्टं, सन्दिष्टः -ष्टा -ष्टं.

CAUTIOUS, *a.* सावधानः -ना -नं, कृतावधानः -ना -नं, अवहितः -ता -तं,

स्ववहितः -ता -तं, अप्रमत्तः -त्ता -त्तं, अप्रमादी -दिनी -दि (न्), समीक्ष्यकारी -रिणी -रि (न्), विमृश्यकारी -रिणी -रि (न्), आशङ्काशीलः -ला -लं, कार्य्यचिन्तकः -का -कं, बुधः -धा -धं.

CAUTIOUSLY, *adv.* सावधानं, अवधानेन, अवहितं, अप्रमादेन, अवेक्षया, साशङ्कं.

CAUTIOUSNESS, *s.* अवधानता, सावधानता, अप्रमत्तता, अप्रमादित्वं.

To CAW, *v. n.* काकवद् रु (c. 2. रौति, रवितुं), कै (c. 1. कायति, कातुं), ध्रांक्ष् (c. 1. ध्रांक्षति, ध्रांक्षितुं), ध्वांक्ष् (c. 1. ध्वांक्षति -क्षितुं).

CAYENNE, *s.* मरीचगुणोपेतः सुतिग्मो रक्तवर्णो उपस्करविशेषः.

To CEASE, *v. n.* (To be at an end) विरम् (c. 1. -रमति -रन्तुं), उपरम्, निवृत् (c. 1. -वर्त्तते -वर्त्तितुं), निर्वृत्, विनिवृत्, शम् (c. 4. शाम्यति, शमितुं), अपया (c. 2. -याति -यातुं), विगम् (c. 1. -गच्छति -गन्तुं), विच्छिद् in pass. (-छिद्यते), विश्रम् (c. 4. -श्राम्यति -श्रमितुं).—(To desist from) विरम् or निवृत् with abl. c.; 'he ceases from wickedness,' पापाद् विरमति.

To CEASE, *v. a.* (To put a stop to) निवृत् in caus. (-वर्त्तयति -यितुं), निर्वृत्, विरम् in caus. (-रमयति -यितुं), उपरम्, शम् in caus. (शमयति -यितुं).

CEASED, *p. p.* विरतः -ता -तं, उपरतः -ता -तं, अवरतः -ता -तं, व्युपरतः -ता -तं, निवृत्तः -त्ता -त्तं, प्रशान्तः -न्ता -न्तं, शान्तः -न्ता -न्तं, विगतः -ता -तं, विश्रान्तः -न्ता -न्तं, विच्छिन्नः -न्ना -न्नं, निरस्तः -स्ता -स्तं; 'one whose fever has ceased,' विगतज्वरः or गतज्वरः or वीतज्वरः or शान्तज्वरः; 'one who has ceased from desire after worldly objects,' उपरतविषयाभिलाषः -षा -षं.

CEASELESS, *a.* अविरतः -ता -तं, अनवरतः -ता -तं, निरन्तरः -रा -रं, अनिवृत्तः -त्ता -त्तं, अविश्रान्तः -न्ता -न्तं, नित्यः -त्या -त्यं.

CEASELESSLY, *adv.* अविरतं, अनवरतं, निरन्तरं, नित्यं.

CEASING, *s.* विरतिः *f.*, निवृत्तिः *f.*, अवरतिः *f.*, उपरामः -रमः -रतिः *f.*, आरतिः *f.*

CECITY, *s.* अन्धता -त्वं, तिमिरं, अदृष्टिः *f.*, दृष्टिहीनता.

CECUTIENSY, *s.* दृष्टिवैकल्यं, नेत्रेन्द्रियवैकल्यं, नाकुलान्ध्यं, कुदृष्टिः *f.*

CEDAR, *s.* देवदारुः *m.* -रु *n.*, दारः *n.* (स्), दारुस्तरुः *m.*

To CEDE, *v. a.* (To give up) उत्सृज् (c. 6. -सृजति -स्रष्टुं), विसृज्, वितॄ (c. 1. -तरति -तरितुं -तरीतुं), त्यज् (c. 1. त्यजति, त्यक्तुं), परित्यज्, अनुदा (c. 3. -ददाति -दातुं), अनुज्ञा (c. 9. -जानाति -ज्ञातुं), प्रोत्सृ in caus. (-सारयति -यितुं).—(To go over) अभ्युपे (c. 2. अभ्युपैति, अभ्युपैतुं), वशीभू.

CEDED, *p. p.* उत्सृष्टः -ष्टा -ष्टं, विसर्ज्जितः -ता -तं, प्रोत्सारितः -ता -तं, वितीर्णः -र्णा -र्णं, त्यक्तः -क्ता -क्तं.

CEDRINE OR CEDARN, *a.* देवदारुमयः -यी -यं, देवदारुसम्बन्धीयः -या -यं.

To CEIL, *v. a.* अन्तःपटलेन छद् (c. 10. छादयति -यितुं), आच्छद्.

CEILING, *s.* अन्तःपटलः, अन्तश्छादं -दनं, अन्तराच्छादनं, पटलः, चालः.

CELANDINE, *s.* अरुष्करनिर्य्यासविशिष्टः पीतपुष्प ओषधिभेदः, बहुदुग्धिका.

CELATURE, *s.* तक्षणं, तक्षणकर्म्म *n.* (न्), नानारेखादिना अलङ्करणविद्या.

To CELEBRATE, *v. a.* प्रशंस् (c. 1. -शंसति -शंसितुं), स्तु (c. 2. स्तौति, स्तोतुं), विख्या (c. 2. -ख्याति -ख्यातुं), कृत् (c. 10. कीर्त्तयति -यितुं), श्लाघ् (c. 1. श्लाघते, श्लाघितुं), वन्द् (c. 1. वन्दते -न्दितुं), पूज् (c. 10. पूजयति -यितुं), आश्रु in caus. (-श्रावयति -यितुं), प्रथ् in caus. (प्रथयति -यितुं), प्रकाश् in caus. (-काशयति -यितुं), अनुवर्ण् (c. 10. -वर्णयति -यितुं).—(To perform solemnly) सेव् (c. 1. सेवते, सेवितुं), विधिवत् कृ, यथाविधि अनुष्ठा (c. 1. -तिष्ठति -ष्ठातुं) or सम्पद् in caus. (-पादयति -यितुं) or निर्वह् in caus. (-वाहयति -यितुं) or पाल् (c. 10. पालयति -यितुं) or आचर् (c. 1. -चरति -चरितुं) or पॄ (c. 10. पारयति -यितुं).—(To celebrate on the lyre) उपवीण् (nom. -वीणयति -यितुं).

CELEBRATED, *a.* विश्रुतः -ता -तं, ख्यातः -ता -तं, विख्यातः -ता -तं, प्रथितः -ता -तं, प्रसिद्धः -द्धा -द्धं, कीर्त्तिमान् -मती -मत् (त्), कीर्त्तितः -ता -तं, स्तुत्यः -त्या -त्यं, अनुवर्णितः -ता -तं, लब्धशब्दः -ब्दा -ब्दं, यशस्वी -स्विनी -स्वि (न्), यशस्वान् -स्वती -स्वत् (त्), प्रतीतः -ता -तं, विज्ञातः -ता -तं, विज्ञः -ज्ञा -ज्ञं.—(In song) उपगीतः -ता -तं, उपगीयमानः -ना -नं; 'to be celebrated,' प्रशंस् in pass. (-शस्यते), विश्रु in pass. (-श्रूयते), प्रथ् (c. 1. प्रथते, प्रथितुं); 'by mention,' अतिपद् in pass. (पद्यते), परिपठ्.—(As a festival) अभ्युदितः -ता -तं.

CELEBRATION, *s.* (Solemn performance) सेवनं, निषेवनं, विधिवत् पालनं or अनुष्ठानं or आचरणं, अभ्युदयः.—(Praise) स्तुतिः *f.*, स्तवः, वर्णना, प्रशंसा, पूजा, कीर्त्तनं, उत्कीर्त्तनं, श्लाघा.

CELEBRITY, *s.* (Fame) कीर्त्तिः *f.*, यशः *n.* (स्), ख्यातिः *f.*, सुख्यातिः *f.*, विश्रुतिः *f.*, प्रसिद्धिः *f.*, प्रकीर्त्तिः *f.*, विख्यातिः *f.*, प्रविख्यातिः *f.*, प्रतिख्यातिः *f.*, प्रतिपत्तिः *f.*, विश्रावः, प्रथा, सम्प्रथा, प्रथितिः *f.*, प्रतिष्ठा; 'conferring celebrity,' यशस्करः -री -रं, कीर्त्तिकरः -री -रं.

CELERITY, *s.* शीघ्रता, वेगः, जवः, त्वरा, रभसः, तूर्णिः *m.*, आशुगमनं.

CELERY, *s.* अजमोदाजातीयः शाकप्रभेदः.

CELESTIAL, *a.* (Relating to heaven, or the sky, divine) स्वर्गीयः -या -यं, दिव्यः -व्या -व्यं, दिविजः -जा -जं, दिविष्ठः -ष्ठा -ष्ठं, दैवः -वी -वं, देवकीयः -या -यं, देवार्हः -र्हा -र्हं, सौरः -री -रं, आन्तरीक्षः -क्षी -क्षं, वैहायसः -सी -सं, विहायसीयः -या -यं, नभःस्थः -स्था -स्थं; 'clothed in celestial raiment,' दिव्यवस्त्रः -स्त्रा -स्त्रं; 'celestial nymph,' स्वर्वेश्या.—(Excellent) परमः -मा -मं, उत्तमः -मा -मं.

CELIBACY OR CELIBATE, *s.* अविवाहः, अनुद्वाहः, अपरिणयनं, अपाणिग्रहणं, अविवाहावस्था, अकृतविवाहत्वं; 'living in celibacy,' अविवाहितः.

CELL, *s.* (A small cavity) बिलं, छिद्रं, रन्ध्रं, कूपः, कुहरं.—(A small apartment) कुटी, कक्षः.—(In a prison) कारागारे कुटी or कक्षः or उपरोधकं, अवरोधनशालिका, गुप्तिः *f.*—(A cottage) कुटीरः.—(The habitation of a religious person) मठः, आश्रमः.

CELLAR, *s.* गुप्तिः *f.*, भूतिकीलः, अवटः -टिः *m.*, गृहतले or गृहस्याधस्ताद् भूमौ खातो मद्यादिकोष्ठः.

CELLARIST, *s.* धर्म्मचारिणां मठे मद्यादिरक्षकः or भोजनाधिकारी *m.* (न्).

CELLULAR, *a.* सूक्ष्मकूपविशिष्टः -ष्टा -ष्टं, सूक्ष्मरन्ध्रपूर्णः -र्णा -र्णं, मधुकोषाकारः -रा -रं.

CELSITUDE, *s.* उच्चता, ऊर्द्धत्वं, उच्छ्रयः, उत्सेधः, समुन्नतिः *f.*, उत्कर्षः.

CEMENT, *s.* (The matter with which two bodies are made to cohere, as mortar) सुधा, लेपः, विलेपः, संलग्नीकरणार्थम् अतिश्यानद्रव्यं.—(Bond of union) बन्धनं, सम्बन्धः, आबन्धः, सन्धिः *m.*

To CEMENT, *v. a.* संलग्नीकृ, संयुज् (c. 7. -युनक्ति -योक्तुं, c. 10. -योजयति -यितुं), संश्लिष् in caus. (-श्लेषयति -यितुं), सम्बन्ध् (c. 9. -बध्नाति -बन्द्धुं), सन्धा (c. 3. -दधाति -धातुं).

CEMENTATION, *s.* संलग्नीकरणं, संयोजनं, संयोगः, सन्धानं, संश्लेषः.

CEMENTED, *p. p.* संलग्नीकृतः -ता -तं, संयुक्तः -क्ता -क्तं, संश्लिष्टः -ष्टा -ष्टं, सम्बद्धः -द्धा -द्धं, सन्धितः -ता -तं.

CEMETERY, *s.* श्मशानं, प्रेतवनं, पितृवनं, पितृकाननं, पितृवसतिः *f.*, शवस्थानं, शतानकं, रुद्राक्रीडः.

CENATORY, *a.* रात्रिभोजनसम्बन्धी -न्धिनी -न्धि (न्), नक्तभोजनविषयकः -का -कं.

CENOTAPH, *s.* शून्यचैत्यं, चैत्यं, चित्यं, स्थानान्तरे निखाते मृतजनमुद्दिश्य स्मरणचैत्यं.

CENSE, *s.* करः, राजकरं, राजस्वं, शुल्कः.—(Rank) पदं.

CENSER, *s.* धूपाधारः, धूपपात्रं.—(Fire-pan) अङ्गारधानिका.

CENSOR, *s.* नीतिशास्ता *m.* (स्तृ), धर्म्माध्यक्षः, धर्म्माधिकारी *m.* (न्), व्यवहारद्रष्टा *m.* (ष्टृ), आचारोपद्रष्टा *m.* (ष्टृ), कण्टकोद्धर्त्ता *m.* (र्त्तृ), दण्डप्रणेता *m.* (तृ), दोषनिग्रहीता *m.* (तृ), पापनिग्रहकृत्.

CENSORIAN, *a.* नीतिशिष्टिसम्बन्धी -न्धिनी -न्धि (न्) or आचारदर्शनसम्बन्धी.

CENSORIOUS, *a.* निन्दकः -का -कं, घृणी -णिनी -णि (न्), दोषग्राही -हिणी -हि (न्), गुणघाती -तिनी -ति (न्), अपवादकः -का -कं, -दी -दिनी -दि (न्), सापवादः -दा -दं, कुवादः -दा -दं, कुवदः -दा -दं, पापदर्शी -र्शिनी -र्शि (न्), निन्दाशीलः -ला -लं, छिद्रान्वेषी -षिणी -षि (न्), छिद्रानुसारी -रिणी -रि (न्), कुत्सावादी -दिनी -दि (न्) or अगुणवादी, कुचरः -रा -रं, दोषैकदृक् *m.f.n.*, पुरोभागी -गिनी -गि (न्).

CENSORIOUSLY, *adv.* घृणया, सापवादं, निन्दापूर्व्वकं, जुगुप्सया, अपवादशीलत्वात्, छिद्रान्वेषिवत्.

CENSORIOUSNESS, *s.* निन्दकता, अपवादशीलत्वं, छिद्रान्वेषः, परदोषकीर्त्तनं.

CENSORSHIP, *s.* नीतिशास्तृपदं, आचारद्रष्टृपदं, धर्म्माधिकारः, -करणं.

CENSURABLE, *a.* निन्द्यः -न्द्या -न्द्यं, निन्दनीयः -या -यं, निन्दार्हः -र्हा -र्हं, वचनीयः -या -यं, वाच्यः -च्या -च्यं, गर्ह्यः -र्ह्या -र्ह्यं, गर्हणीयः -या -यं, विगर्ह्यः -र्ह्या -र्ह्यं, दोषी -षिणी -षि (न्), अपराधी -धिनी -धि (न्).

CENSURABLENESS, *s.* निन्द्यता, वाच्यता, वचनीयता, सापराधता.

CENSURE, *s.* निन्दा, अपवादः, परीवादः, जुगुप्सा -प्सनं, उपक्रोशः, परिभाषणं, तिरस्कारः, घृणा, उपालम्भः, आक्षेपः, गर्हा, गर्हणं, कुत्सा, निर्वादः, अवर्णः, अर्हणं, ऋतीया.

To CENSURE, *v. a.* निन्द् (c. 1. निन्दति, निन्दितुं), प्रणिन्द्, प्रतिनिन्द्, विनिन्द्; प्रत्यादिश् (c. 6. -दिशति -देष्टुं), परिवद् (c. 1. -वदति -वदितुं), अपवद्, गर्ह् (c. 1. गर्हते, गर्हितुं, c. 10. गर्हयति -ते -यितुं), विगर्ह्, परिगर्ह्; तिरस्कृ; कुत्स् (c. 10. कुत्सयति -यितुं), अभिकुत्स्, गुप् in des. (जुगुप्सते -प्सितुं), असूय (nom. असूयति -यितुं), उपालभ् (c. 1. -लभते -लब्धुं), दोषीकृ, धिक्कृ.

CENSURED, *p. p.* निन्दितः -ता -तं, जुगुप्सितः -ता -तं, तिरस्कृतः -ता -तं, विगर्हितः -ता -तं, निर्भर्त्सितः -ता -तं, धिक्कृतः -ता -तं, अवरीणः -णा -णं, उपालब्धः -ब्धा -ब्धं.

CENSURER, *s.* निन्दकः, अपवादकः, अपवादी *m.* (न्), परिवादी *m.* (न्), निन्दाकृत्.

CENT, *s.* शतं; 'five per cent.,' शते विंशभागः, पञ्चकं शतं, पञ्चोत्तरं; 'two per cent.,' द्विकं शतं.

CENTAUR, *s.* जन्तुविशेषो यस्य पूर्व्वभागः पुरुषाकारः पश्चिमभागश्च अश्वाकृतिः, पूर्व्वकालीनकविभिः कल्पितो नरोर्द्धकायो वाज्यधःकायो जन्तुविशेषः, अर्द्धेन अश्वो ऽर्द्धेन पुरुषो जन्तुः, राक्षसः, दैत्यः.

CENTAURY, *s.* तिक्तस्वाद ओड्रपुष्पसवर्णो ओषधिप्रभेदः.

CENTENARIAN, *s.* (One a hundred years of age) शतायुः *m.* (स्), शतवर्षः.

CENTENARY, *a.* शतकः -का -कं, शतिकः -की -कं, शत्यः -त्या -त्यं.

CENTENARY, *s.* शतकः, शतं; 'a centenary of years,' वर्षशतं, अब्दशतं, शतवर्षं.

CENTENNIAL, *a.* शतवर्षः -र्षा -र्षं, शताब्दः -ब्दा -ब्दं, शतवत्सरः -रा -रं.

CENTESIMAL, *a.* शततमः -मी -मं.—(Hundredth part) शतभागमध्ये एकभागः.

CENTIFOLIOUS, *a.* शतपत्रः -त्री -त्रं, शतपर्णः -र्णी -र्णं, शतच्छदः -दा -दं.

CENTIPEDE, *s.* शतपदी *f.*, शतपाद् *f.*, शतपादिका, पृषिका, वृश्चिकः, कर्णजलौका -काः (स्).

CENTO, *s.* (A poem formed by scraps) प्रकीर्णकाव्यं, खण्डकाव्यं, नानाग्रन्थसङ्गृहीतं काव्यं.—(A collection of a hundred stanzas) शतकः.

CENTRAL or CENTRICAL, *a.* मध्यः -ध्या -ध्यं, मध्यमः -मा -मं, मध्यमीयः -या -यं, मध्यस्थः -स्था -स्थं, मध्यस्थायी -यिनी -यि (न्), गर्भस्थः -स्था -स्थं, मध्यवर्त्ती -र्त्तिनी -र्त्ति (न्).

CENTRALITY, *s.* मध्यत्वं, मध्यस्थता -त्वं, मध्यमत्वं.

CENTRE, *s.* (The middle, interior) मध्यं, मध्यः, मध्यस्थानं, मध्यस्थलं, गर्भः, उदरं, अभ्यन्तरं, हृदयं; 'in the centre,' मध्ये, अभ्यन्तरे.—(Of a circle) केन्द्रं, चतुष्टयं.

To CENTRE, *v. n.* (To rest on) अवलम्ब् (c. 1. -लम्बते -लम्बितुं), समालम्ब्, संश्रि (c. 1. -श्रयति -श्रयितुं).—(To meet together in one point) मध्यस्थानं or एकस्थानं प्रति समि (c. 2. समेति, समेतुं), एकत्र समागम् (c. 1. -गच्छति -गन्तुं) or सम्मिल् (c. 6. -मिलति -मेलितुं).

CENTRICALLY, *adv.* मध्यतस्, मध्यं प्रति, मध्ये, मध्यस्थाने, मध्यमुद्दिश्य.

CENTRIFUGAL, *a.* केन्द्रापजिगमिषुः -षुः -षु, मध्यापजिगमिषुः -षुः -षु.

CENTRIPETAL, *a.* केन्द्रजिगमिषुः -षुः -षु, केन्द्राभिपिपतिषुः -षुः -षु, मध्यं प्रति पतयालुः -लुः -लु or पातुकः -का -कं.

CENTUPLE, *s.* शतगुणः -णा -णं, शतधा *ind.*

To CENTUPLICATE, *v. a.* शतगुणं -णां -णं कृ, शतगुणीकृ, शतधा कृ.

To CENTURIATE, *v. a.* शतभागशः कृ, शतखण्डशः कृ, शतधा कृ, शतखण्डीकृ.

CENTURION, *s.* शतसेनापतिः *m.*, शतयोधमुख्यः, शतसैन्याधिपतिः *m.*

CENTURY, *s.* (Space of a hundred years) वर्षशतं, शतवर्षं, वत्सरशतं, अब्दशतं.—(A hundred) शतं, शतकः.

CEPHALALGY, *s.* शिरोवेदना, शीर्षवेदना, शिरःपीडा, शिरोऽर्त्तिः *f.*, शिरोरोगः.

CEPHALIC, *a.* मस्तकपथ्यः -थ्या -थ्यं, मस्तिष्करोगघ्नः -घ्नी -घ्नं.

CERASTES, *s.* शृङ्गविशिष्टः सर्पप्रभेदः, विषाणी व्यालः, शृङ्गी.

CERATE, *s.* सिक्थादिनिर्म्मितः or सिक्थतैलादिमयः क्षतशमक उपनाहः.

CERATED, *a.* सिक्थाक्तः -क्ता -क्तं, सिक्थमयः -यी -यं, सिक्थानुलिप्तः -प्ता -प्तं.

To CERE, *v. a.* सिक्थेन लिप् (c. 6. लिम्पति, लेप्तुं) or अञ्ज् (c. 7. अनक्ति, अंक्तुं).

CEREBRAL, *a.* मस्तिष्कसम्बन्धकः -का -कं; 'a cerebral letter,' मूर्द्धन्यं.

CEREBRUM, *s.* मस्तिष्कं, मस्तिस्कः, गोर्दं, मस्तकस्नेहः.

CERECLOTH or CEREMENT, *s.* सिक्थाक्तं वस्त्रं, शववस्त्रं.

CEREMONIAL, *s.* व्यवहारः, आचारः, रीतिः *f.*, विधिः *m.*, विधानं, नियमः, कृत्यं, नित्यकृत्यं, आह्निकाचारः, संस्कारः, क्रियाविधिः *m.*, शास्त्रविधानं.—(Sacrificial) यज्ञकर्म्म *n.* (न्), विधियज्ञः, इष्टिः *f.*

CEREMONIAL, *a.* वैधिकः -की -कं, वैधः -धी -धं, नैयमिकः -की -कं, आचारिकः -की -कं, व्यावहारिकः -की -कं, ऐष्टिकः -की -कं, पौर्त्तिकः -की -कं.

CEREMONIOUS, *a.* अतिशयेन आदरकृत्, अतिशयेन आदृतः -ता -तं or सभ्याचारसेवी -विनी -वि (न्), अतिसभ्यः -भ्या -भ्यं or अत्यञ्जलिकृत्, एकान्तसभ्यः -भ्या -भ्यं, सभ्यम्मन्यः -न्या -न्यं, एकान्तप्रश्रितः -ता -तं, एकान्तप्रणयी -यिनी -यि (न्), अतिसमादरकृत्, अत्यादृतः -ता -तं, अतिसभाजनकृत्, अत्यानन्दनकृत्, अत्यनुनयी -यिनी -यि (न्).

CEREMONIOUSNESS, *s.* (The use of too much ceremony) अत्यादरः, अतिशयेन शिष्टाचारानुष्ठानं, or सभ्याचारसेवनं, अतिसौजन्यं, अतिप्रश्रयः, अत्यनुनयः, अतिसभाजनं, अतिसमादरः, अत्यानन्दनं.

CEREMONIOUSLY, *adv.* एकान्तादरपूर्व्वं, अतिसमादरेण, अतिप्रश्रयेण, सातिशयसभाजनं.

CEREMONY, *s.* (Rite) विधिः *m.*, नियमः, संस्कारः, विधानं, कृत्यं, नित्यकृत्यं, कर्म्म *n.* (न्), नित्यकर्म्म *n.* (न्), क्रिया, आह्निकाचारः, दीक्षा; 'engaged in ceremonies,' दीक्षितः; 'occasional ceremony,' नैमित्तिककर्म्म *n.* (न्); 'marriage ceremony,' विवाहविधिः *m.*—(Form of civility) शिष्टाचारविधिः *m.*, सभ्याचारविधिः *m.*, सौजन्यरीतिः *f.*

CERTAIN, *a.* (Sure) ध्रुवः -वा -वं, अवश्यकः -का -कं, सुनिश्चितः -ता -तं. —(Not admitting doubt) असन्दिग्धः -ग्धा -ग्धं, असंशयः -या -यं, निःसन्दिग्धः -ग्धा -ग्धं, निःसन्देहः -हा -हं, निःसंशयः -या -यं; 'it is certain,' अत्र न संशयः.—(Settled, determined, resolved) निश्चितः -ता -तं, कृतनिश्चयः -या -यं, निष्पन्नः -न्ना -न्नं, नियतः -ता -तं; 'as to time,' कृतकालः -ला -लं.—(Regular) नित्यः -त्या -त्यं.—(Infallible) अमोघः -घा -घं.—(Particular) सविशेषः -षा -षं.—(Some) कश्चित् काचित् किञ्चित्, कोऽपि कापि किमपि, कश्चन काचन किञ्चन; 'some few,' कतिचित् *ind.*, कतिपयः -या -यं, कियान् -यती -यत् (त्); 'a certain person,' कश्चित्; 'a certain lion,' कश्चित् सिंहः, or in more modern Sanscrit एकः सिंहः; 'certain people,' कतिपयलोकाः; 'certain teachers,' कियन्तोऽध्यापकाः; 'on a certain time,' एकदा, कदाचित्, विशेषकाले.

CERTAINLY, *adv.* अवश्यं, निश्चितं, सुनिश्चितं, असंशयं, ध्रुवं, नूनं, खलु, किल, नाम, तत्त्वतस्, संशयं विना, अत्र न संशयः, कः सन्देहः, कोऽत्र सन्देहः.

CERTAINNESS, or CERTAINTY, or CERTITUDE, *s.* निश्चयः, निर्णयः, नैश्चित्यं, अवश्यकता, दृढप्रमाणं, ध्रुवत्वं, असन्दिग्धता; 'certainties,' ध्रुवाणि.

CERTIFICATE, *s.* प्रमाणपत्रं, अभिज्ञानपत्रं, निर्णयपत्रं, निश्चयपत्रं, सत्यापनपत्रं, निदर्शनपत्रं, आगमपत्रं, निर्णेता *m.* (तृ).

To CERTIFY, *v. a.* (To inform) ज्ञा in caus. (ज्ञापयति -यितुं), विज्ञा.—(To bear testimony, give proof) प्रमाणीकृ, सप्रमाणं -णां -णं कृ, दृढीकृ, स्थिरीकृ, सत्याकृ, प्रमाणपत्रेण or अभिज्ञानपत्रेण निर्णयं कृ.

CERVICAL, *a.* ग्रैवः -वी -वं, ग्रैवेयः -यी -यं, कण्ठ्यः -ण्ठ्या -ण्ठ्यं.

CERULEAN, *a.* नीलः -ला -लं, नीलवर्णः -र्णा -र्णं, आकाशवर्णः -र्णा -र्णं.

CERUMEN, *s.* (Ear-wax) कर्णमलः -लं, तोक्मं, कर्णगूथः, कर्णविट् (ष्).

CERUSE, *s.* (White lead) श्वेताञ्जनं, शुक्लवर्णः सीसकविशेषः.

CESARIAN, *a.* (Operation) गर्भोच्छेदनं, भ्रूणोत्कर्त्तनं.

CESS, *s.* (A sum levied) करः, शुल्कः -ल्कं, राजस्वं.—(The act of assessing) करग्रहणं, शुल्कग्रहणं.

To CESS, *v. a.* (To assess) करं or शुल्कं or राजस्वं ग्रह् (c. 9. गृह्णाति, ग्रहीतुं) or दा in caus. (दापयति -यितुं).

CESSATION, *s.* विरतिः *f.*, विरामः, अवरतिः *f.*, उपरतिः *f.*, निवृत्तिः *f.*, विनिवृत्तिः *f.*, निर्वृतिः *f.*, निवर्त्तनं, निर्वर्त्तनं, विच्छेदः, उपशमः, अपशमः, क्षयः; 'cessation of arms,' अवहारः.—(Without cessation) अविरतं, अनवरतं, निरन्तरं; 'cessation of affection,' स्नेहच्छेदः.

CESSAVIT, *s.* अमुकजनो वर्षद्वयप्रभृति अद्य यावत् करं न दत्तवान् इति ज्ञापनार्थं लेख्यं.

CESSIBLE, *a.* त्याज्यः -ज्या -ज्यं, प्रदेयः -या -यं, विसर्ज्जनीयः -या -यं.

CESSION, *s.* त्यागः, परित्यागः, प्रदानं, वितरणं, विसर्ज्जनं, समर्पणं.

CESSMENT, *s.* करग्रहणं, शुल्कग्रहणं, राजस्वग्रहणं, करदापनं.

CESSOR, *s.* नियतधर्म्मनिरपेक्षत्वात् or करदानमन्दादरत्वात् पूर्व्वोक्तलेख्यद्वारेण अभियोक्तव्यः.

CESTUS, *s.* रतिमेखला, रतिरसना, रतिकलापः.

CETACEOUS, *a.* तिमिजातीयः -या -यं, मीनरजातीयः -या -यं.

CEYLON, *s.* (The island) सिंहलद्वीपः, सिंहलं, लङ्का.

CHAD, *s.* पाठीनः, मद्गुरः, शृङ्गी *f.*

To CHAFE, *v. a.* (To rub, make hot by rubbing) घृष् (c. 1. घर्षति, घर्षितुं), आघृष्, निर्घृष्, संवाहं कृ, घर्षणेन तप् in caus. (तापयति -यितुं).—(To irritate) तप् in caus., परितप्, बाध् (c. 1. बाधते, बाधितुं).—(To make angry) कुप् in caus. (कोपयति -यितुं), प्रकुप्, रुष् in caus. (रोषयति -यितुं).

To CHAFE, *v. n.* तप् in pass. (तप्यते), परितप्, सन्तप्, दुर्मनस् (nom. दुर्मनायते), क्लिश् (c. 4. क्लिश्यते, क्लेशितुं), कुप् (c. 4. कुप्यति -ते, कोपितुं), प्रकुप्, रुष् (c. 4. रुष्यति, रोषितुं), क्रुध् (c. 4. क्रुध्यति, क्रोद्धुं), मन्तु (nom. मन्तूयति); 'chafing,' आतप्यमानः -ना -नं.

CHAFE, *s.* प्रकोपः, उत्तापः, परितापः, मनस्तापः, क्लेशः, रोषः, मन्युः *m.*, अमर्षः.

CHAFER, *s.* पिङ्गशरीरो वनमोदी भ्रमरप्रभेदः.

CHAFF, *s.* बुसं, बुषं, तुषः -षा, तुच्छं, तुच्छधान्यकं, धान्यकल्कं, कडङ्गरः, निष्पावः.—(Freed from the chaff) निस्तुषः -षा -षं.

To CHAFFER, *v. a.* पण् (c. 1. पणते, पणितुं or पणायति -यितुं), पणं कृ, पणीकृ, विपणीकृ, कुत्सितप्रकारेण पणायां कृ or क्रयविक्रयं कृ.

CHAFFERN, *s.* उदस्थाली, स्थाली, पिठरः, उखा.

CHAFFINCH, *s.* बुसप्रियः क्षुद्रपक्षिप्रभेदः.

CHAFFLESS, *a.* निस्तुषः -षा -षं, बुसहीनः -ना -नं, तुषरहितः -ता -तं.

CHAFFY, *a.* तुषमयः -यी -यं, तुषोपमः -मा -मं, लघुः -घुः -घु.

CHAFING-DISH, *s.* अङ्गारधानिका, अङ्गारशकटी *f.*, अङ्गारिः *f.* -रिणी, कटाहः.

CHAGRIN, *s.* क्लेशः, मन्युः *m.*, शोकः, विडम्बना, व्यथा, असन्तोषः.

To CHAGRIN, *v. a.* दुःख् (c. 10. दुःखयति -यितुं), क्लिश् (c. 9. क्लिश्नाति, क्लेशितुं), व्यथ् in caus. (व्यथयति -यितुं), तप् in caus. (तापयति -यितुं), सन्तप्, परितप्, शुच् in caus. (शोचयति -यितुं).

CHAGRINED, *p. p.* आगतमन्युः -न्युः -न्यु, सव्यथः -था -थं, दुःखितः -ता -तं, उद्विग्नः -ग्ना -ग्नं.

CHAIN, *s.* शृङ्खलः -ला -लं, दामः.—(Fetter) लोहबन्धनं, लौहबन्धं, निगडः -डं, बन्धनं, पाशः; 'a gold chain,' कनकसूत्रं.—(A series) श्रेणी, पर्य्यायः, पंक्तिः *f.*, अनुक्रमः, माला; 'a chain of causes,' कारणमाला.

To CHAIN, *v. a.* शृङ्खलया or निगडेन बन्ध् (c. 9. बध्नाति, बन्द्धुं), शृङ्खल (nom. शृङ्खलयति -यितुं), निगड (nom. निगडयति -यितुं).

CHAINED, *p. p.* शृङ्खलितः -ता -तं, निगडितः -ता -तं, शृङ्खलाबद्धः -द्धा -द्धं.

CHAIN-PUMP, *s.* शृङ्खलासञ्चारितं जलोत्तोलनयन्त्रं or घटीयन्त्रं.

CHAIN-SHOT, *s.* शृङ्खलाबद्धं युद्धयन्त्रात् प्रक्षेपणीयं लोहगोलद्वयं.

CHAIN-WORK, *s.* शृङ्खलकर्म्म *n.* (न्), शृङ्खलारूपेण निर्म्मितं यत् किञ्चिद् विरलकर्म्म.

CHAIR, *s.* पीठं, आसनं, विष्टरः, विस्तरः, संवेशः.—(Wheel-chair) पर्यं.

CHAIRMAN, *s.* सभापतिः *m.*, सभाधिकृतः, गोष्ठीपतिः, श्रेष्ठी *m.* (न्), प्रामाणिकः.—(One whose profession it is to carry a chair) प्रवहणिकः.

CHAISE, *s.* यानविशेषः, रथः, क्रीडारथः, पुष्परथः, वाहनं.

CHALCOGRAPHY, *s.* ताम्रफलके or पित्तलफलके लिखनविद्या.

CHALDRON, *s.* पिठरः, उखा, स्थाली, उदस्थाली, पिष्टपचनं.

CHALICE, *s.* कंसः, पात्रं, भाजनं, शरावः, यज्ञपात्रं, यज्ञभाजनं.

CHALK, *s.* कठिनी, खटिनी, कठिका, खटिका, खडिका, चूर्णः -र्णं, श्वेतधातुः *m.*, शुक्लधातुः, वर्णलेखा, पाण्डुमृत् *f.*, शिलाधातुः, सितोपलः, पाकशुक्ला, धवलमृत्तिका.—(Red chalk) गैरेयं, अर्घ्यं, गिरिजं, अश्मजं, शिलाजतु *n.*

To CHALK, *v. a.* (To mark with chalk) कठिन्या चिह्न् (c. 10. चिह्नयति -यितुं) or लिख् (c. 6. लिखति, लेखितुं).

CHALK-CUTTER, *s.* कठिनीखनकः, कठिनीखनिता *m.* (तृ), शुक्लधातुखनकः.

CHALKY, *a.* कठिनीमयः -यी -यं, श्वेतधातुपूर्णः -र्णा -र्णं, कठिनीसंसृष्टः -ष्टा -ष्टं.

To CHALLENGE, *v. a.* आह्वे (c. 1. -ह्वयति -ते -ह्वातुं), उपाह्वे, समाह्वे; द्वन्द्वयुद्धार्थं or नियुद्धार्थम् आह्वे; स्पर्द्ध् (c. 1. स्पर्द्धते, स्पर्द्धितुं), आक्रन्द् (c. 1. -क्रन्दति -क्रन्दितुं), प्रत्यर्प् (c. 10. -अर्पयति -यितुं).—(To accuse) अभियुज् (c. 7. -युनक्ति -योक्तुं).—(To claim as one's own due)

आत्मसात्कृ, स्वीकृ, मम देयं or मह्यं दातव्यमिति ज्ञापयित्वा ग्रह् (c. 9. गृह्णाति, ग्रहीतुं) or in des. (जिघृक्षति -क्षितुं).

CHALLENGE, s. आह्वानं, समाह्वयः -ह्वानं, योधसंरावः, क्रन्दितं, अभिग्रहः.—(A writing containing a challenge) युद्धाह्वानपत्रं, द्वन्द्वयुद्धार्थम् आह्वानपत्रं.

CHALLENGED, p. p. आहूतः -ता -तं, समाहूतः -ता -तं, कृताह्वानः -ना -नं.

CHALLENGER, s. आह्वानकर्त्ता m. (र्त्तृ), समाह्वानकृत्, समाह्वाता m. (तृ), अभियोक्ता m. (क्तृ).

CHALLENGING, s. (Act of) आह्वानं, हूतिः f., हवः, क्रन्दनं, स्पर्द्धा.

CHALYBEATE, a. अयःसंसृष्टः -ष्टा -ष्टं, लोहव्याप्तः -प्ता -प्तं, लोहगुणविशिष्टः -ष्टा -ष्टं, लोहघटितः -ता -तं ; 'a chalybeate pill,' अयोगुडः.

CHAMADE, s. युद्धे पराजयसूचकं or सम्प्रदानसूचकं पटहताडनं.

CHAMBER, s. कोष्ठः, प्रकोष्ठः, शाला, शालिका, आगारः -रं, गृहं, स्थलं, आवासः, वासभवनं, कक्षः, कुटी, कुटिः f.; 'bed-chamber,' शयनागारः, स्वप्ननिकेतनं, शयनशाला, शय्यावेश्म n. (न्); 'an inner chamber,' उपरोधकं, कक्षान्तरं ; 'an upper chamber,' उपरिस्थः प्रकोष्ठः ; चन्द्रशालिका, शिरोगृहं.—(A cavity) कोष्ठः, गर्त्तः, बिलं, कुहरं.

To CHAMBER, v. n. लम्पटवत् स्त्रियो गम् (c. 1. गच्छति, गन्तुं) or अभिगम्, लम्पटाचारः -रा -रं अस्.

CHAMBERING, s. स्त्रीगमनं, नार्य्यभिगमनं, स्त्रीसेवा, नारीप्रसङ्गः, लम्पटता.

CHAMBERLAIN, s. शयनाधिकृतः, अन्तःपुरवर्त्ती m. (न्), अन्तर्वंशिकः, कञ्चुकी m. (न्), स्थापत्यः, वस्त्रगृहाधीशः, द्वाःस्थितदर्शकः, वन्धुलः.

CHAMBERMAID, s. शयनशालायां शय्यादिपरिकल्पिका परिचारिका or दासी.

CHAMELEON, s. सरटः, सरटुः, प्रतिसूर्य्यः, कुलाहकः. See CAMELEON.

To CHAMFER, v. a. स्तम्भस्य परितः सीताकारा रेखा लिख् (c. 6. लिखति, लेखितुं).

CHAMFER or CHAMFRET, s. स्तम्भस्य परितो लिखिता सीताकारा रेखाः, स्तम्भरेखा, स्तम्भसीता.

CHAMOIS, s. वातप्रमीयः, वनछागजातीयो गिरिप्रियो महावेगो जन्तुभेदः.

CHAMOMILE, s. अतितिक्तरसविशिष्टः सुगन्ध ओषधिभेदः.

To CHAMP, v. a. चर्व् (c. 1. चर्वति, चर्वितुं), दंश् (c. 1. दशति, दंष्टुं), परिदंश्, दन्तचर्वं कृ ; 'to champ the bit,' खलीनं परिदंश्.

CHAMPAIGN, s. समभूमिः f., समभूभागः, समस्थलं -ली, समप्रदेशः, निम्नभूमिः f.

CHAMPAKA, s. (A plant) चम्पकः, चाम्पेयः, हेमपुष्पकः, स्थिरगन्धः, स्थिरपुष्पः.—(Its flower) गन्धफली.

CHAMPIGNON, s. छत्राप्रभेदः, छत्राकं, उच्छिलीन्ध्रं, शिलीन्ध्रं.

CHAMPION, s. (A warrior) भटः, सुभटः, वीरः, प्रवीरः, योद्धा m. (द्धृ), प्रयुयुत्सुः m., विक्रान्तः, गण्डीरः, नासीरः.—(A defender) रक्षकः, रक्षिता m. (तृ), परिरक्षी m. (न्).

CHANCE, s. दैवं, दैवयोगः, दैवगतिः f., घटना, दैवघटना, सङ्गतिः f., अकस्मात्सङ्गतं, आगन्तुः m., अतिवर्त्तनं.—(Unfortunate chance) विपद्, आपद् ; 'a game of chance,' अक्षादिक्रीडा, द्यूतं ; 'trusting too much to chance,' दैवपरः, दैवायत्तः, दैवचिन्तकः ; 'by chance,' अकस्मात्, दैवात्, दैववशात्, घटनया, अनपेक्षं, प्रमादेन.—(State of doubt) संशयः ; 'committed to chance,' संशयस्थः -स्था -स्थं.

To CHANCE, v. n. अकस्मात् सम्भू (c. 1. -भवति -भवितुं) or सम्पद् (c. 4. -पद्यते -पत्तुं) or समापद् or उपस्था (c. 1. -तिष्ठति -स्थातुं) or समुपस्था, or आपत् (c. 1. -पतति -पतितुं).

CHANCEL, s. पूजाशालायाः पूर्व्वदिश्यो महापवित्रत्वाद् व्यवधानेन अवरुद्धो भागः, मन्दिरस्य प्राचीनभागः.

CHANCELLOR, s. महाप्राड्विवाकः, प्रधानधर्म्माध्यक्षः, महाविचारकः, महाशासनकर्त्ता m. (र्त्तृ).—(Chancellor of the Exchequer) कोशाधीशः.—(Of the University) राजविद्यालयाधिपतिः m.

CHANCELLORSHIP, s. महाप्राड्विवाकत्वं, प्रधानधर्म्माध्यक्षस्य पदं or अधिकारः.

CHANCE-MEDLEY, s. विवादे अनिच्छातो नृहत्या or मनुष्यमारणं.

CHANCER, s. विद्रधिः m., उपदंशः, गलितक्षतं. See CANCER.

CHANCERY, s. दण्डनैष्ठुर्य्यशमका महाविचारसभा, महाविचारस्थानं, धर्म्मोग्रतानियामका सभाविशेषः.

CHÁNDÁLA, s. (An outcaste or man of a degraded tribe) चाण्डालः, चण्डालः, मातङ्गः, निषादः, दिवाकीर्त्तिः, श्वपचः, जनङ्गमः, अन्तेवासी, पुक्कसः, प्लवः.

CHANDELIER, s. दीपवृक्षः, दीपपादपः, शिखातरुः, शिखावृक्षः, दीपाधारः.

CHANDLER, s. (A huckster) वार्त्तावहः, वैवधिकः, विवधिकः ; 'a corn-chandler,' धान्यमायः.—(One who makes or sells candles) दीपिकाकृत्, दीपविक्रेता m. (तृ).

To CHANGE, v. a. विकृ (c. 8. -करोति -कर्त्तुं), अन्यरूपं -पीं -पं कृ, भिन्नरूपं -पीं -पं कृ, विपर्यस् (c. 4. -अस्यति, असितुं).—(To barter) निमे (c. 1. -मयते -मातुं), विमे, विनिमे, परिवृत् in caus. (-वर्त्तयति -यितुं) ; 'he changes beans for sesamum-seed,' तिलेभ्यः प्रति माषान् ददाति.—(To change the mind) अन्यमानसीभू, विपरीतं विज्ञा (c. 9. -जानाति -ज्ञातुं).—(To change a note) हुण्डिकापत्रं सुवर्णरूप्यादिभिः परिवृत्.—(To change gold for coin of less value) सुवर्णरूप्यादिकं कुप्यनाणकपणकपर्दादिभिः परिवृत्.—(To change one's clothes) वासांसि अवतार्य्य or विहाय or अवमुच्य अपराणि परिधा (c. 3. -दधाति -धातुं).

To CHANGE, v. n. विकृ (c. 8. -कुरुते), विकृतीभू, अन्यथा भू, अन्यरूपः -पा -पं भू, भिन्नरूपः -पा -पं भू, विकृताकारः -रा -रं भू ; 'the mouse was changed into a cat,' मूषिको विडालः कृतः.—(To change in mind) विमनीभू.—(To change one's evil course) पापाद् विनिवृत् (c. 1. -वर्त्तते -वर्त्तितुं) or निवृत्.

CHANGE, s. विकारः, विकृतिः f., विक्रिया, वैकृतं, परिणामः, विपरिणामः, विपर्य्ययः, परिवर्त्तः, अन्यथाभावः.—(Vicissitude) आवृत्तिः f., परिवृत्तिः f. ; 'of the seasons,' ऋतुपर्य्यायः.—(Variety) वैचित्र्यं, विभेदः.—(Reformation) निवर्त्तनं.—(Small money) अल्पसारं धनं यथा कुप्यनाणकपणकपर्दकादि, अल्पार्घमुद्रा, क्षुद्रमुद्रा.—(Place where merchants meet) वणिक्समागमचत्वरं, श्रेष्ठिचत्वरं.—(Of the moon) अमावसी, प्रतिपत्, चन्द्रपरिवर्त्तः, पर्व्वसन्धिः m. ; 'of mind,' बुद्धिभेदः.

CHANGEABLE, a. (Possible to be changed) विकार्य्यः -र्य्या -र्य्यं.—(Fickle) अस्थायी -यिनी -यि (न्), अस्थिरः -रा -रं, अधीरः -रा -रं, चलः -ला -लं, चलचित्तः -त्ता -त्तं, चपलः -ला -लं, सङ्कुसुकः -का -कं, नैकभावाश्रयः -या -यं, प्रकृतितरलः -ला -लं, अन्यमनाः -नाः -नः (स्), अन्यमानसः -सी -सं.—(Inconstant) अनित्यः -त्या -त्यं.

CHANGEABLENESS, s. अस्थिरता, अस्थैर्य्यं, चलचित्तता, चञ्चलत्वं, चापल्यं.

CHANGED, p. p. विकारितः -ता -तं, विकृतः -ता -तं, वैकृतः -ता -तं, कृतविक्रियः -या -यं, अन्यरूपः -पी -पं, परिणतरूपः -पी -पं, विपर्यस्तः -स्ता -स्तं, विकृताकारः -रा -रं.—(In feelings) विमनीकृतः -ता -तं, विमनीभूतः -ता -तं.

CHANGELING, s. कुलीनपुत्रेण परिवर्त्तितो धात्रीपुत्रः ; वेतालेन सुरूपबालकम् अपहृत्य तस्य स्थाने उपसर्ज्जितः कुरूपबालक इति केचिन् मन्यन्ते ; उपसर्ज्जितपुत्रः, उपकल्पितपुत्रः, कृत्रिमपुत्रः, पुत्रप्रतिनिधिः m.

CHANGER, s. हुण्डिकापत्रसुवर्णरूप्यादिपरिवर्त्तकः.

CHANNEL, *s.* (A strait) सङ्कटं.—(The bed of a river) नदीभाण्डं, नदीपात्रं, गर्भः, नदीगर्भः.—(A long excavation, a canal) कुल्या, उपकुल्या, खातं, नालः, प्रणालः.—(A narrow passage) सङ्कीर्णपथः.—(Furrow of a pillar) स्तम्भरेखा, स्तम्भसीता.—(A stream) स्रोतः *n.* (स्).

To CHANNEL, *v. a.* खन् (c. 1. खनति, खनितुं, खातुं), उत्खन्, कुल्याः कृ, सीताः कृ.

To CHANT, *v. n.* गै (c. 1. गायति, गातुं), प्रगै, उद्गै, सुख (nom. सुखायते), पठ् (c. 1. पठति, पठितुं).

CHANT, *s.* गीतं, गेयं, गानं, गाथा, खेलिः *f.*, स्तोत्रं.

CHANTED, *p. p.* गीतः -ता -तं, परिगीतः -ता -तं, पठितः -ता -तं.

CHANTER, *s.* उद्गाता *m.* (तृ), गायकः, गेष्णुः, गाथिकः, सुखयुः *m.*

CHANTICLEER, *s.* उषाकलः, कुक्कुटः, कृकवाकुः, यामघोषः.

CHAOS, *s.* महाभूतादिसाङ्कर्य्यं, प्राग्जगत्सृष्टेर् जलादिभूतानाम् अत्यस्तता, एकार्णवः.—(Confusion) सङ्करः, साङ्कर्य्यं, संक्षोभः, व्यस्तता, अव्यक्तता.

CHAOTIC, *a.* सङ्करीकृतः -ता -तं, व्यस्तव्यस्तः -स्ता -स्तं, अधरोत्तरः -रा -रं, सङ्कीर्णः -र्णा -र्णं, सङ्कुलः -ला -लं, एकार्णवीभूतः -ता -तं, अव्यक्तः -क्ता -क्तं, अलक्षणः -णा -णं.

To CHAP, *v. n.* (To break into gapings from the effect of cold) शीतोपहतत्वात् त्रुट् (c. 4. त्रुट्यति, त्रुटितुं) or विदल् (c. 1. -दलति -दलितुं) or विभिद् in pass. (-भिद्यते) or विदॄ in pass. (-दीर्य्यते) or छिद् in pass. (छिद्यते) or स्फुट् (c. 6. स्फुटति, स्फुटितुं).

CHAP, *s.* (Cleft, chink) त्रुटितं, त्रुटिः *f.* -टी, छिद्रं, रन्ध्रं, गर्त्तः, भित्तिः *f.*; 'in the feet,' पाददारी, अलसः.—(A person, a fellow, contemptuously) माणवः -वकः, मनुष्यकः, नागरः.

CHAPE, *s.* (The catch of any thing by which it is held) बन्धनी, बन्धनकीलकः, सङ्ग्रहणार्थं दमकः, ग्रहणी, रक्षणी, आलानं.

CHAPEL, *s.* (Shrine) देवागारः, देवतागारः, देवायतनं, देवालयं.—(A small place of worship subject to a church) महामन्दिराधीना क्षुद्रपूजाशाला, अप्रधानमन्दिरं.—(Of ease) दूरस्थैः सेवितं क्षुद्रभजनभवनं.

CHAPELRY, *s.* क्षुद्रमन्दिराधिकारः, पूर्व्वोक्तपूजाशालाधीनो भूमिभागः.

CHAPERON, *s.* नृत्यगीतादिसमाजे अनूढाम् तरुणीम् उपास्ते या मध्यमवयस्का भाविनी or कुलीना स्त्री.

To CHAPERON, *v. a.* नृत्यगीतादिसमाजे अनूढां तरुणीं युवतिगणं वा उपास् (c. 2. -आस्ते -आसितुं) or उपस्था (c. 1. -तिष्ठति -स्थातुं), or उपचर् (c. 1. -चरति -चरितुं).

CHAPFALLEN, *a.* म्लानवदनः -नी -नं, मलिनमुखः -खी -खं, हताशः -शा -शं.

CHAPITER, *s.* स्तम्भशीर्षं, स्तम्भमस्तकः, स्तम्भशृङ्गं, अर्द्धस्तम्भः, स्तम्भस्य अर्द्धभागः.

CHAPLAIN, *s.* पुरोहितः, कुलाचार्य्यः, ऋत्विक् *m.* (ज्), कुलगुरुः *m.*, कुलविप्रः.

CHAPLAINSHIP, *s.* पौरोहित्यं, पुरोहितपदं, कुलाचार्य्यपदं, आर्त्विज्यं.

CHAPLET, *s.* माला, माल्यं, स्रक् *f.* (ज्), दाम *n.* (न्), कुसुमावतंसकं, निर्य्यूहः, आपीडः, पीडा; 'chaplet-maker,' मालाकारः, मालिकः; 'chaplets worn in different positions,' गर्भकः, प्रभ्रष्टकं, ललामकं, प्रालम्बं, वैकक्षकं, आपीडः, शेखरः.

CHAPMAN, *s.* आपणिकः, विपणी *m.* (न्), क्रयिकः, विक्रयिकः.

CHAPPED, *p. p.* त्रुटितः -ता -तं, त्रुटितवान् -वती -वत् (त्), विदलितः -ता -तं, विभिन्नः -न्ना -न्नं, विदीर्णः -र्णा -र्णं, छिन्नः -न्ना -न्नं.

CHAPS, *s. pl.* (The mouth of a beast of prey) आस्यं, मुखं, वदनं, हनुः *m.*—(Entrance of a channel) सङ्कटमुखं, सङ्कटप्रवेशः.

CHAPTER, *s.* (Division) अध्यायः, अध्ययः, सर्गः, पर्व्व *n.* (न्), परिच्छेदः, विच्छेदः, काण्डः -ण्डं, खण्डः -ण्डं, स्कन्धः, उच्छ्वासः, आश्वासः, प्रकरणं, लम्बकः.—(An assembly of canons) महामन्दिरे प्रधानपुरोहितानां सभा.

To CHAR, *v. a.* (To burn wood to a cinder) अङ्गारसात्कृ, अङ्गारीकृ, अङ्गार (nom. अङ्गारयति -यितुं); ईषद्दह् (c. 1. -दहति -दग्धुं).

To CHAR, *v. n.* (To work at other's houses by the day) गृहसम्मार्ज्जने उदकवाहने इत्यादिकुत्सितकर्म्मणि एकदिनमात्रं यावद् व्यापृता भू or नियुज् in pass. (-युज्यते).

CHAR-WOMAN, *s.* गृहसम्मार्ज्जने उदकवाहने इत्यादिकुत्सितकर्म्मणि एकदिनमात्रं नियुक्ता or व्यापृता चेटी, प्रत्यहं भृतिं गृह्णाति या कर्म्मकरी, दिनिकाचेटी, दिनिकाप्रेष्या, प्रेष्या, सैरिन्ध्री.

CHARACTER, *s.* (Disposition) शीलः -लं, शीलत्वं -ता, स्वभावः, वृत्तिः *f.*, स्वरूपं, स्वाभिप्रायः, चारित्रं.—(Property, peculiarity) भावः, गुणः, विशेषः.—(Natural character) स्वभावः, निसर्गः, प्रकृतिः *f.*—(Mark) लक्षणं, चिह्नं, अभिज्ञानं.—(Letter) अक्षरं, वर्णः -र्णं.—(Handwriting) स्वहस्ताक्षरं.—(Personage in a drama) भूमिका.—(Reputation, honour) मर्य्यादा, कीर्त्तिः *f.*, यशः *n.* (स्).—(Dignity) गौरवं

CHARACTERISTIC, *a.* लाक्षणिकः -की -कं, लाक्षण्यः -ण्या -ण्यं, विशेषकः -का -कं, विशेषणः -णा -णं, स्वाभाविकः -की -कं, गुणवाचकः -का -कं.

CHARACTERISTIC, *s.* लक्षणं, विशेषलक्षणं, संलक्षणं, लिङ्गं, चिह्नं, विशेषः -षणं, अभिज्ञानं, संज्ञा, गुणः, उपाधिः *m.*, स्वधर्म्मः, स्वभावः; 'generic property,' समानाधिकरणं; 'specific property,' जातित्वं.

CHARACTERISTICALLY, *adv.* विशेषतस्, सविशेषं, लक्षणतस्.

To CHARACTERIZE, *v. a.* लक्ष् (c. 10. लक्षयति -यितुं), संलक्ष्, उपलक्ष्; विशिष् in caus. (-शेषयति -यितुं), चिह्न् (c. 10. चिह्नयति -यितुं).—(To give an account of the personal qualities) गुणदोषान् व्याख्या (c. 2. -ख्याति -ख्यातुं).

CHARACTERIZED, *p. p.* विशिष्टः -ष्टा -ष्टं, विशेषितः -ता -तं, सविशेषः -षा -षं -षणः -णा -णं, लक्षितः -ता -तं, संलक्षितः -ता -तं, उपलक्षितः -ता -तं, कृतलक्षणः -णा -णं, लिङ्गी -ङ्गिनी -ङ्गि (न्).

CHARADE, *s.* सर्व्वतोभद्रः, वर्द्धमानः, प्रवह्लिका, पद्यविरचिता प्रश्नदूती यथा किंस्वित् शीघ्रतरं वायोः किंस्विद्बहुतरं तृणात् मनः शीघ्रतरं वाताच्चिन्ता बहुतरा तृणादिति.

CHARCOAL, *s.* अङ्गारः -रं, निधापकः, दग्धकाष्ठं, दग्धेध्मं.

To CHARGE, *v. a.* (Accuse) अभियुज् (c. 7. -युनक्ति -योक्तुं), अभिशप् (c. 1. -शपति -शप्तुं), अभिशंस् (c. 1. -शंसति -शंसितुं), अधिक्षिप् (c. 6. -क्षिपति -क्षेप्तुं).—(Impute a crime to any one) दोषं कस्मिंश्चिद् आरुह् in caus. (-रोपयति -यितुं).—(Enjoin, exhort) आदिश् (c. 6. -दिशति -देष्टुं), समादिश्, प्रत्यादिश्, निर्दिश्, उपदिश्; आज्ञा in caus. -ज्ञापयति -यितुं).—(Intrust) निक्षिप्, न्यस् (c. 4. -अस्यति -असितुं), सम् in caus. (-अर्पयति -यितुं).—(Impose as a task) नियुज् (c. 7. -युनक्ति -युंक्ते -योक्तुं, c. 10. -योजयति -यितुं).—(Attack) अभिद्रु (c. 1. -द्रवति -द्रोतुं); आस्कन्द् (c. 1. -स्कन्दति -स्कन्तुं), आक्रम् (c. 1. -क्रामति -क्रमितुं), अभिधाव् (c. 1. -धावति -ते -धावितुं).—(Burden, load) भारं न्यस्, or निविश् in caus. (-वेशयति -यितुं) or आरुह् in caus. (-रोपयति -यितुं), पृ (c. 10. पूरयति -यितुं) with inst. c.—(Ask a price) मूल्यं प्रार्थ् (c. 10. -अर्थयते -ति -यितुं).

CHARGE, *s.* (Care, custody) गुप्तिः *f.*, रक्षा, रक्षणं; 'to take charge of,' रक्ष् (c. 1. रक्षति, रक्षितुं), अधिष्ठा (c. 1. -तिष्ठति -ष्ठातुं).—(Trust) निक्षेपः, उपनिक्षेपः, न्यासः, उपन्यासः, उपनिधिः *m.*; 'to give in charge,' निक्षिप् (c. 6. -क्षिपति -क्षेप्तुं), न्यस् (c. 4. -अस्यति -असितुं), नियुज् (c. 7. -युनक्ति -युंक्ते -योक्तुं).—(Commission, office, task, duty) नियोगः, अधिकारः, भारः, व्रतं, धर्म्मः.—(Mandate, command) आदेशः, आज्ञा, शासनं.—(Exhortation) प्रत्यादेशः, उपदेशः.—(Accusation) अभियोगः, अभिशापः, अभिशंसनं, अपवादः.—(Imputation) दोषारोपः, दोषकल्पनं; 'to lay a crime to any one's charge,' दोषं कस्मिंश्चिद् आरुह् in caus. (-रोपयति -यितुं).—(Onset, attack) संशरणं, आस्कन्दः, अभ्यवस्कन्दः, उपघातः, अभिक्रमः, आक्रमः; 'charge sounded by musical instruments,' आडम्बरः.—(Burden) भारः, धुरा.—(Charge of a gun) यद्चूर्णगुलिकादिकम् एकवारे युद्धनाडी निवेशयितव्यं.—(Expense) व्ययः.—(Price) मूल्यं, अर्घः.

CHARGEABLE, *a.* (Liable to be accused) अभियोक्तव्यः -व्या -व्यं, अभियोज्यः -ज्या -ज्यं.—(Imputable) आरोपणीयः -या -यं.—(Causing expense) व्ययकारी -रिणी -रि (न्).

CHARGED, *p. p.* (Loaded) धुर्वहः -हा -हं, धुरीणः -णा -णं, धुरीयः -या -यं, भारवान् -वती -वत् (त्), भाराक्रान्तः -न्ता -न्तं, अभिपूर्णः -र्णा -र्णं, गर्भः -र्भा -र्भं in comp.; as, 'a cloud charged with water,' अम्भोगर्भो जलदः.—(Accused) अभियुक्तः -क्ता -क्तं, अभिशस्तः -स्ता -स्तं.—(Injoined) समादिष्टः -ष्टा -ष्टं, प्रत्यादिष्टः -ष्टा -ष्टं.—(Made to pay) दापितः -ता -तं.—(Imputed) आरोपितः -ता -तं.

CHARGER, *s.* (Large dish) बृहत्पात्रं, पात्रं, भाजनं.—(War-horse) वारकीरः, योधहरः, युद्धाश्वः, युद्धवाजी *m.* (न्).

CHARILY, *adv.* परिमितप्रकारेण, मितप्रकारेण, परिमितं, अमुक्तहस्तेन, अल्पशस्.

CHARIOT, *s.* रथः, चक्रयानं, गन्त्री, गन्त्रीरथः; 'of war,' स्यन्दनः, शताङ्गः; 'of the gods,' विमानः -नं; 'covered chariot,' कर्णीरथः, ह्रयनं; 'pleasure-chariot,' क्रीडारथः; 'chariot-race,' रथचर्य्या; 'chariot-horse,' रथ्यः; 'warrior mounted on a chariot,' स्यन्दनारोहः, रथारूढः, रथी *m.* (न्).

CHARIOTEER, *s.* सूतः, यन्ता *m.* (न्तृ), नियन्ता (न्तृ), अधिरथः, रथवाहकः, सादिः *m.*, सारथिः *m.*, चातुरिकः, प्राजिता *m.* (तृ), क्षत्ता *m.* (तृ), सव्येष्टा *m.* (ष्टृ), दक्षिणस्थः, प्रवेता *m.* (तृ).

CHARITABLE, *a.* (Kind in giving alms and assisting the poor) कृपणवत्सलः -ला -लं, दरिद्रवत्सलः -ला -लं, दीनवत्सलः -ला -लं, कल्याणकः -का -कं, दानशीलः -ला -लं, दरिद्रोपकारी -रिणी -रि (न्) or परोपकारी, अन्नदाता -त्री -तृ (तृ) or भिक्षादाता, दयालुः -लुः -लु, दरिद्रपोष्टा -ष्ट्री -ष्टृ (ष्टृ), दरिद्रपालकः -का -कं, सर्व्वभूतानुकम्पकः -का -कं, धर्म्मात्मा -त्मा -त्म (न्).—(Kind in judging of others) परदोषसहनः -ना -नं, अनसूयकः -का -कं, अमत्सरः -रा -रं.

CHARITABLY, *adv.* दरिद्रोपकारशीलत्वात्, दयया, सदयं, दयालुवत्, दीनवत्सलवत्, दरिद्रपोष्टृवत्, सानुकम्पं.—(Without malignity) अनसूयया, अमत्सरं, परदोषसहनवत्.

CHARITY, *s.* (Kindness to the poor, liberality) दरिद्रोपकारः, दरिद्रपालनं, दरिद्रपोषणं, दया, कारुण्यं, दयालुत्वं, दानशीलता, कृपा, सुकरं, पूर्त्तं.—(Almsgiving) भिक्षादानं, दानं, दानधर्म्मः.—(Alms) भिक्षा, भैक्षं, भिक्षान्नं, पुण्यं, पुण्यकं; 'for charity,' पुण्यार्थे.—(Christian charity, love) प्रेम *n.* (न्), सर्व्वभूतानुकम्पा, सर्व्वप्राणिनः प्रति प्रेम.

CHARLATAN, *s.* मिथ्याचिकित्सकः, दुश्चिकित्सकः, कुवैद्यः, आयुर्वेदानभिज्ञः.—(Deceiver) छली *m.* (न्), मायी *m.* (न्), कपटी *m.* (न्).

CHARLATANICAL, *a.* आयुर्वेदविरुद्धः -द्धा -द्धं, मिथ्याचिकित्सासम्बन्धीयः -या -यं, कापटिकः -की -कं, छाद्मिकः -की -कं, दाम्भिकः -की -कं.

CHARLATANRY, *s.* मिथ्याचिकित्सा, दुश्चिकित्सा, आयुर्वेदानभिज्ञता, छलं, कपटः -टं, छद्म *n.* (न्), दम्भः, प्रतारणं, वञ्चनं, वाक्छलं.

CHARLES'S WAIN, *s.* सप्तर्षयः *m. pl.*, चित्रशिखण्डिनः *m. pl.*, शकटाकृति नक्षत्रं.

CHARLOCK, *s.* शस्यक्षेत्रप्ररोही पीतपुष्पविशिष्ट ओषधिभेदः.

CHARM, *s.* (Words having mystic power) मन्त्रः, अभिचारमन्त्रः.—(Charm, amulet) कवचः -चं, संवदनं -ना, गारुडः; 'subduing by charms, &c.' वशक्रिया, अभिचारः, संवदनं -ना; 'under the influence of a charm,' अनुमन्त्रितः -ता -तं, अभिमन्त्रितः -ता -तं.—(Something of power to charm or allure) प्रलोभनं, विलोभनं.—(Beauty) मुग्धता, शोभा, कान्तिः *f.*, श्रीः, सौन्दर्य्यं.

To CHARM, *v. a.* (To enchant) मन्त्रद्वारेण वशीकृ or मुह् in caus. (मोहयति -यितुं), अभिमन्त्र् (c. 10. -मन्त्रयते -यितुं), अनुमन्त्र्, अभिचर् (c. 10. -चारयति -यितुं).—(To rejoice the mind) मनो हृ (c. 1. हरति, हर्त्तुं) or रम् in caus. (रमयति -यितुं), हृष् in caus. (हर्षयति -यितुं).—(To allure) प्रलुभ् in caus. (-लोभयति -यितुं).

CHARMED, *p. p.* (With joy) हृतमानसः -सा -सं, हृष्टमानसः -सा -सं, प्रह्लादितः -ता -तं. उल्लासितः -ता -तं.—(By incantations, &c.) अभिमन्त्रितः -ता -तं, अनुमन्त्रितः -ता -तं, अभिचारितः -ता -तं, वशः -शा -शं, वशीभूतः -ता -तं, वशीकृतः -ता -तं, वशतापन्नः -न्ना -न्नं, मोहितः -ता -तं, आकृष्टः -ष्टा -ष्टं.

CHARMER, *s.* (A dealer in charms) गारुडिकः, जाङ्गुलिकः.—(An enchanter) अभिचारी *m.* (न्), -रिणी *f.*, मायी *m.* (न्), -यिनी *f.*, मायाकारः, मोही *m.* (न्), -हिनी *f.*—(Word of endearment applied to a woman) प्रिया, वत्सा, मुग्धा.

CHARMING, *a.* मनोहरः -रा -रं, मनोरमः -मा -मं, रम्यः -म्या -म्यं, रमणीयः -या -यं, कमनीयः -या -यं, सुभगः -गा -गं, कान्तः -न्ता -न्तं, मोदकः -का -कं, हर्षकरः -री -रं, चित्रचित्रः -त्रा -त्रं, सत्रीकः -का -कं, आकर्षकः -का -कं, आकृष्टवान् -वती -वत् (त्), आसेचनकः -का -कं; 'a charming woman,' मुग्धा, प्रमदा.

CHARMINGLY, *adv.* मनोरमं, रमणीयप्रकारेण, रम्यं, रमणीयतया, चित्रचित्रं, सुभगं, यथा मनो ह्रियते तथा, मनोहरप्रकारेण.

CHARMINGNESS, *s.* रम्यत्वं, रमणीयता, कमनीयता, मनोहरत्वं, सश्रीकता.

CHARNEL-HOUSE, *s.* शवास्थिस्थानं, अस्थिसञ्चयस्थानं, श्मशानं, शवास्थिगृहं.

CHARRED, *p. p.* अङ्गारितः -ता -तं, अङ्गारसात्कृतः -ता -तं, अर्द्धदग्धः -ग्धा -ग्धं.

CHART, *s.* वेलालेख्यं, वेलापटः, समुद्रयायिनां पथदर्शनार्थं नदीसमुद्रवेलासैकतादिभिर् अङ्कितं पत्रं, समुद्रद्वीपादीनाम् आलेख्यं, नौकारूढानां पथदर्शकं पत्रं.

CHARTER, *s.* शासनं, शासनपत्रं, राजाज्ञापत्रं, प्रामाणिकपत्रं, धर्म्मकीलः, पट्टः.—(Privilege) अधिकारः.

CHARTERED, *p. p.* राजादिसकाशात् शासनपत्रेण अधिकारयुक्तः -क्ता -क्तं.

CHARY, *a.* परिमितः -ता -तं, मितः -ता -तं, अमुक्तहस्तः -स्ता -स्तं, सावधानः -ना -नं, अवहितः -ता -तं, विचक्षणः -णा -णं.

To CHASE, *v. a.* (To hunt) मृग् (c. 10. मृगयते -यितुं), मृगयां कृ, आखिद् (c. 1. -खेटति -खेटितुं), परिकल् (c. 10. -कालयति -यितुं).—(To pursue) अनुधाव् (c. 1. -धावति -धावितुं), पश्चाद्धाव्, अभिधाव्, अनुसृ (c. 1. -सरति -सर्त्तुं), अन्विष् (c. 4. -इष्यति -एषितुं), अनुष्ठा (c. 1. -तिष्ठति -ष्ठातुं), अनुवृत् (c. 1. -वर्त्तते -र्त्तितुं), पश्चाद्वृत्.—(To drive away) निरस् (c. 4. -अस्यति -असितुं), अपास्; निराकृ; अपानुद् (c. 6. -नुदति -नोत्तुं), द्रु in caus. (द्रावयति -यितुं).—(To chase gold and silver vessels) राजतानि भाजनानि रेखादिना अलङ्कृ or उपस्कृ.

CHASE, *s.* (Hunting) मृगव्यं, मृगया *f.*, खेटः -टं, आखेटः, आच्छोदनं, पापर्द्धिः *f.*, आच्छोदनं, पराधिः *f.*; 'he went to the chase,' मृगयायै गतः or मृगयां कर्त्तुं गतः.—(The game hunted) आक्रन्दं.—(Pursuit, running after) अनुधावनं, अभिधावनं, पश्चाद्धावनं, अनुसरणं, अन्वेषणं, मृगया.—(Open ground fit for hunting) मृगव्यायोग्यो निर्विघ्नभूमिभागः, जाङ्गलभूमिः.

CHASED, *p. p.* अनुधावितः -ता -तं, मृगितः -ता -तं, द्रावितः -ता -तं.

CHASER, *s.* मृगयुः *m.*, आखेटकः, अनुधावकः, अनुसारी *m.* (न्), द्रावकः, पश्चाद्धावकः.

CHASM, *s.* छिद्रं, अवटः -टिः *m.*, विवरं, बिलं, रन्ध्रं, दरी, गर्त्तः, कुहरं, शुषिरं, रोकं, विरोकं, विद्रं, टङ्कः, भङ्गः, भर्करा, रोपं, रुहकं.

CHASTE, *a.* अलम्पटः -टा -टं, यतमैथुनः -ना -नं, सद्वृत्तः -त्ता -त्तं, अकामः -मा -मं, अपांशुलः -ला -लं, यतेन्द्रियः -या -यं, जितेन्द्रियः -या -यं, निष्कामः -मा -मं, ऊर्द्ध्वरेताः -ताः -तः (स्), अव्यसनी -निनी -नि (न्), धर्म्मचारी -रिणी -रि (न्), संयतोपस्थः -स्था -स्थं, अव्यभिचारी -रिणी -रि (न्); 'a chaste wife,' पतिव्रता, साध्वी, सती *f.*, अव्यभिचारिणी, कुलवधूः; 'most chaste,' महासती; 'a chaste woman,' कुलस्त्री, कुलपालिका.—(Pure, correct, as language, &c.) शुद्धः -द्धा -द्धं, विशुद्धः -द्धा -द्धं, शुचिः -चिः -चि, निर्म्मलः -ला -लं.

CHASTELY, *adv.* निष्कामं, उपस्थनिग्रहेण, इन्द्रियसंयमेन, शुद्धं, शुचि.

To CHASTEN or CHASTISE, *v. a.* शास् (c. 2. शास्ति, शासितुं), अनुशास्, दण्ड् (c. 10. दण्डयति -यितुं), वियत् (c. 10. -यातयति -यितुं), दण्डं प्रणी (c. 1. -णयति -णेतुं).

CHASTISED, *p. p.* शिष्टः -ष्टा -ष्टं, शासितः -ता -तं, दण्डितः -ता -तं, ताडितः -ता -तं, दुःखितः -ता -तं.

CHASTISEMENT, *s.* शिष्टिः *f.*, शास्तिः *f.*, दण्डः, साहसं, अनुशासनं, निग्रहः.—(Of a pupil) शिष्यशिष्टिः *f.*

CHASTISER, *s.* शासिता *m.* (तृ), शास्ता *m.* (स्तृ), दण्डप्रणेता *m.* (तृ), साहसकृत्.

CHASTITY, *s.* उपस्थनिग्रहः, उपस्थसंयमः, इन्द्रियनिग्रहः, जितेन्द्रियत्वं, यतेन्द्रियत्वं, निष्कामता, ब्रह्मचर्य्यं.—(In a woman) सतीत्वं, साध्वीत्वं, पातिव्रत्यं, कुलवधूत्वं; 'a sage of perfect chastity,' ऊर्द्ध्वमन्थी *m.* (न्).

To CHAT, *v. n.* संलप् (c. 1. -लपति -लपितुं), कथोपकथनं कृ, वृथाकथां कृ, आलस्यवचनं कृ, सम्भाष् (c. 1. -भाषते -भाषितुं).

CHAT, *s.* कथोपकथनं, संलापः, वृथाकथा, अनर्थककथा, सम्भाषः, सङ्कथा, कथायोगः, सम्प्रवदनं, आलस्यवचनं.

CHATELLANY, *s.* दुर्गाधिकाराधीनं भूमिमण्डलं, दुर्गाधीनो भूमिप्रदेशः.

CHATTELS, *s. pl.* अस्थावरधनं, द्रव्यं, विभवः, सामग्री -ग्र्यं.

To CHATTER, *v. n.* (To talk idly) जल्प् (c. 1. जल्पति, जल्पितुं), प्रलप् (c. 1. -लपति -लपितुं, c. 10. -लापयति -यितुं), विलप्, कथोपकथनं कृ, वृथाकथां कृ.—(To make a noise as a jay, &c.) किकि or चटचट or चित् शब्दं कृ, चटचट (nom. चटचटायते), कै c. 1. (कायति, कातुं), कूज् (c. 1. कूजति, कूजितुं).—(To make a noise by colliding the teeth) कटकट (nom. कटकटापयति -यितुं), दन्तैर् दन्तान् निष्पिष् (c. 7. -पिनष्टि -पेष्टुं).

CHATTER or CHATTERING, *s.* (Idle prate) वृथाकथा, प्रलापः, विप्रलापः, विलपनं, जल्पनं, प्रजल्पः, वाक्चापल्यं, अतिकथा, इतिकथा, निरर्थककथा, कलना.—(Noise of a jay, &c.) चटचट *ind.*, रुत *f.* (त्), किकि शब्दः, चित् शब्दः.

CHATTERER, *s.* जल्पकः, जल्पाकः, उपजल्पी *m.* (न्), वाचालः, गायनः, वावदूकः.

CHATTY, *a.* संलापी -पिनी -पि (न्) or प्रलापी, कथोपकथनकृत् *m. f. n.*

CHAUNT, *s.* *See* CHANT.

To CHAW, *v. a.* चर्व् (c. 1. चर्वति, चर्वितुं, c. 10. चर्वयति -यितुं).

CHAWDRON, *s.* अन्त्रं, पुरीतत् *m. n.*, नाडिः *f.*, -डी, धमनी.

CHEAP, *a.* अल्पमूल्यः -ल्या -ल्यं, अल्पार्घः -र्घा -र्घं, सुमूल्यः -ल्या -ल्यं, सुलभः -भा -भं, अल्पमूल्येन क्रेयः -या -यं or लभ्यः -भ्या -भ्यं, न्यूनः -ना -नं.

To CHEAPEN, *v. a.* (To bid for, attempt to purchase) अमुकमूल्यं दित्सामीति वद् (c. 1. वदति -दितुं); न्यूनमूल्यं दा in des. (दित्सति -त्सितुं).—(To lessen value) मूल्यं न्यूनीकृ or अल्पीकृ.

CHEAPLY, *adv.* अल्पमूल्येन, अल्पार्घेण, सुमूल्येन, सुलभं.

CHEAPNESS, *s.* सुमूल्यं, अल्पमूल्यता, अल्पार्घत्वं, मूल्यन्यूनता, सुलभता.

To CHEAT, *v. a.* वञ्च् in caus. (वञ्चयते -ति -यितुं), परिवञ्च्, प्रलभ् (c. 1. -लभते -लब्धुं), विप्रलभ्, छल् (c. 10. छलयति -यितुं).

CHEAT, *s.* (Fraud) छलं, वञ्चनं, कपटः.—(Cheater) वञ्चकः, छली *m.* (न्), धूर्त्तः, प्रतारकः, कूटकः, कपटिकः, कपटी *m.* (न्), कितवः, कूटकारः, दाम्भिकः, कुहकः, उपधिकः.

CHEATED, *p. p.* वञ्चितः -ता -तं, परिवञ्चितः -ता -तं, प्रलब्धः -ब्धा -ब्धं, विप्रलब्धः -ब्धा -ब्धं, मुषितः -ता -तं, अतिसंहितः -ता -तं.

CHEATING, *s.* वञ्चनं, छलनं, प्रतारणं -णा, कपटः -टं, व्याजः, कैतवं, अतिसन्धिः *m.*, अतिसन्धानं, कूटः -टं.

To CHECK, *v. a.* यम् (c. 1. यच्छति, यन्तुं), संयम्, नियम्, विनियम्, निग्रह् (c. 9. -गृह्णाति -गृह्णीते -ग्रहीतुं), विनिग्रह्, सन्निग्रह्, वृ in caus. (-वारयति -यितुं), निवृ, निरुध् (c. 9. -रुणद्धि -रोद्धुं), अवरुध्, सन्निरुध्, प्रतिषिध् (c. 1. -षेधति -षेद्धुं), विधृ in caus. (-धारयति -यितुं), स्तम्भ् in caus. (स्तम्भयति -यितुं), विष्टम्भ्.

CHECK, *s.* संयमः, निग्रहः, निवारः -रणं, यन्त्रणं, निरोधः, विरोधः, संरोधः, प्रतिषेधः, यन्ता -न्त्री -न्तृ (न्तृ).—(As of the perspiration) विष्टम्भः.

CHECKED, *p. p.* संयमितः -ता -तं, संयतः -ता -तं, नियमितः -ता -तं, रुद्धः -द्धा -द्धं, निरुद्धः -द्धा -द्धं, संरुद्धः -द्धा -द्धं, निवारितः -ता -तं, नियन्त्रितः -ता -तं.

To CHECKER or CHEQUER, *v. a.* अष्टापदप्रकारेण व्यत्यस्तरेखा लिखित्वा चित्रविचित्रीकृ or चित्र् (c. 10. चित्रयति -यितुं) or चित्रङ्गीकृ or नानारङ्गीकृ or कर्बुरीकृ.

CHECKERED, *p. p.* चित्रविचित्रः -त्रा -त्रं, अष्टापदप्रकारेण चित्रितः -ता -तं, कर्बुरितः -ता -तं, चित्रङ्गीकृतः -ता -तं, नानावर्णः -र्णा -र्णं.

CHECKERWORK, *s.* अष्टापदप्रकारेण चित्रविचित्रकर्म्म *n.* (न्), चित्रविचित्रकार्य्यं.

CHECKMATE, *s.* जयकारी शारिपरीणायः, शारिपरीणायो येन परः स्वशारीन् परिणेतुम् अक्षमः सन् पराजितो भवति.

CHEEK, *s.* गण्डः -ण्डं, कपोलः, कन्दलः, गण्डस्थलः -ली, गल्लः; 'the two cheeks,' गण्डौ; 'colour in the cheek,' कपोलरागः.

CHEEKBONE, *s.* कपोलफलकः, गण्डफलकः -कं.

CHEER, *s.* (Provisions, entertainment) आहारः, भोजनं, भोज्यं, सत्कारः.—(Heart, courage) वीर्य्यं, धैर्य्यं, स्थैर्य्यं, स्थिरता, तेजः *n.* (स्); 'be of good cheer,' समाश्वसिहि.—(Air of countenance) वदनं, मुखं, आकारः.—(Shout of joy) प्रणादः, जयशब्दः, जयध्वनिः *m.*, जयकोलाहलः, धन्यवादः.

To CHEER, *v. a.* (Incite) प्रोत्सह् in caus. (-साहयति -यितुं), प्रचुद् (c. 10. -चोदयति -यितुं).—(Gladden) हृष् in caus. (हर्षयति -यितुं), परिहृष्, प्रहृष्, ह्लाद् in caus. (ह्लादयति -यितुं), आह्लाद्, प्रह्लाद्, नन्द् in caus. (नन्दयति -यितुं), उल्लस् in caus. (-लासयति -यितुं).—(Comfort) आश्वस् in caus. (-श्वासयति -यितुं), समाश्वस्, विश्वस्, सान्त्व् (c. 10. सान्त्वयति -यितुं).

To CHEER-UP, *v. n.* प्रत्याश्वस् (c. 2. -श्वसिति -श्वसितुं), आश्वस्, समुत्था (c. 1. -तिष्ठति -थातुं), हृष् (c. 4. हृष्यति, हर्षितुं), प्रतिसंहृष्, आनन्द् (c. 1. -नन्दति -नन्दितुं), ह्लाद् (c. 1. ह्लादते, ह्लादितुं); 'cheer up!' समाश्वसिहि, साहसं कुरु, सुस्थिरो भव.

CHEERED, *p. p.* प्रहर्षितः -ता -तं, समाश्वासितः -ता -तं, आश्वासितः -ता -तं.

CHEERER, *s.* आश्वासकः, हर्षकरः, आनन्ददः, प्रह्लादकः, प्रहर्षकः.

CHEERFUL, *a.* आनन्दी -न्दिनी -न्दि (न्), सानन्दः -न्दा -न्दं, हृष्टः -ष्टा -ष्टं, प्रहृष्टः -ष्टा -ष्टं, हर्षयुक्तः -क्ता -क्तं, हृष्टहृदयः -या -यं, हृष्टमानसः -सी -सं, हर्षमाणः -णा -णं, प्रफुल्लः -ल्ला -ल्लं, प्रमनाः -नाः -नः (स्), उल्लसः -सा -सं -सितः -ता -तं, उल्लासितः -ता -तं, विकुर्वाणः -णा -णं.—(Having a cheerful countenance) प्रफुल्लवदनः -ना -नं or फुल्लवदनः, सुहसाननः -ना -नं, प्रसन्नवदनः -ना -नं, सदैव प्रहसितवदनः -ना -नं.

CHEERFULLY, *adv.* सहर्षं, सानन्दं, हृष्टमनसा, हृष्टवत्, प्रसन्नचेतसा.

CHEERFULNESS, *s.* हर्षः, हृष्टिः *f.*, आनन्दः, आह्लादः, प्रफुल्लता, चित्तप्रसन्नता, उल्लासः.

CHEERLESS, *a.* निरानन्दः -न्दा -न्दं, अहर्षः -र्षा -र्षं, हर्षरहितः -ता -तं.

CHEERLESSLY, *adv.* अहर्षं -र्षितं, निरानन्दं, आनन्दं विना.

CHEESE, *s.* किलाटः -टी, दधिजं, मन्थजं, क्षीरविकृतिः *f.*

CHEESECAKE, *s.* किलाटपिष्टकः, दधिनवनीतादिमयो मोदकविशेषः.

CHEESE-CURDS, *s.* दधि *n.*, किलाटः, पयस्यं, क्षीरजं, आमिक्षा.

CHEESE-MONGER, *s.* किलाटविक्रेता *m.* (तृ), दधिविक्रयी *m.* (न्), किलाटविक्रयोपजीवी *m.* (न्).

CHEESE-PRESS, *s.* दधिसम्पीडनयन्त्रं येन किलाटः सम्पद्यते.

CHEESY, *adv.* किलाटमयः -यी -यं, किलाटगुणोपेतः -ता -तं.

CHELY, *s.* कर्कटनखः, कुलीरादिनखः, कुलीराङ्घ्रिः *m.*, कर्कटपाणिः *m.*

CHEMISE, *s.* स्त्रीलोकभृतम् अन्तरीयं or अधोवसनं.

CHEMISTRY, *s.* रसायनं. *See* CHYMISTRY.

To CHERISH, *v. a.* पुष् (c. 1. पोषति, c. 9. पुष्णाति, पोषितुं, c. 10. पोषयति -यितुं), परिपुष्, पाल् (c. 10. पालयति -यितुं), संवृध् in caus. (-वर्धयति -यितुं), भृ (c. 1. भरति -ते, भर्तुं), भज् (c. 1. भजति -ते, भक्तुं), उपास् (c. 2. -आस्ते -आसितुं), दय् (c. 1. दयते, दयितुं), लल् (c. 10. लालयति -यितुं).

CHERISHED, *p. p.* पालितः -ता -तं, पोषितः -ता -तं, पुष्टः -ष्टा -ष्टं, संवर्द्धितः -ता -तं, भर्त्रिमः -मा -मं, अभीष्टः -ष्टा -ष्टं, हृद्यः -द्या -द्यं, हृन्नतः -ता -तं, दयितः -ता -तं, हृदिस्पृक् (श्), लालितः -ता -तं.

CHERISHER, *s.* पोष्टा *m.* (ष्टृ), पोषकः, पालकः, पालयिता *m.* (तृ), भर्त्ता *m.* (र्त्तृ).

CHERISHING, *s.* पोषः -षणं, पालनं, भरणं, भरिमा *m.* (न्).

CHERRY, *s.* अष्ठिगर्भः क्षुद्रफलविशेषः.

CHERRY-ORCHARD, *s.* वक्ष्यमाणवृक्षवाटिका or -वाटी.

CHERRY-TREE, *s.* पूर्व्वोक्तफलविशिष्टो वृक्षभेदः.

CHERSONESE, *s.* द्वीपः, अन्तरीपः -पं.

CHERUB, *s.* स्वर्गी *m.* (न्), स्वर्गदूतः, स्वर्गीयजनः, दिव्यदूतः, देवदूतः. Modern scholars coin the word किरूबः.

CHERUBIC, *a.* स्वर्गीयः -या -यं, दिव्यः -व्या -व्यं, स्वर्ग्यः -र्ग्या -र्ग्यं.

To CHERUP, *v. n.* क्विण् or चिक्क् शब्दं कृ. *See To* CHIRP.

CHERVIL, *s.* ओषधिभेदो यस्मिन् एककाण्डाग्राद् अनेकमञ्जर्य्य आतपत्ररूपेण प्ररोहन्ति.

CHESS, *s.* चतुरङ्गं; 'moving a piece at chess,' परीणायः.

CHESS-BOARD, *s.* अष्टापदं, शारिफलकं, पञ्चनी, पञ्चली, पञ्चारी, नयपीठी.

CHESSMAN, *s.* जतुपुत्रकः, सारः, शारः, शारिः *m.*, सारिः *m* -री *f.*, सारिका, खेलिनी, खेलनी.

CHEST, *s.* (The breast) उरः *n.* (स्), वक्षः *n.* (स्), भुजान्तरं, क्रोडं -डा; 'broad-chested,' उरस्वान् -स्वती -स्वत् (त्), उरस्कः -स्का -स्कं, उरसिलः.—(A box) भाण्डं, सम्पुटः -टकः, समुद्गः, भाजनं.

CHESTNUT or CHESNUT, *s.* श्यावफलविशेषः; 'a chestnut horse,' शोणः, उकनाहः.

CHEVALIER, *s.* सादी *m.* (न्), अश्वारोही *m.* (न्), रथी *m.* (न्), महारथः, महावीरः, राजर्षिः *m.*, मानसूचका ख्यातिः.

CHEVAUX DE FRISE, *s.* नागदन्तयुक्तं प्राचीरं, युद्धसमये पारकाश्वावेधनार्थं शितशल्ययुक्तम् अवरोधकं.

CHEVERIL, *s.* (A kid) छागशावकः, अजशावकः.—(Kid leather) अजचर्म्म *n.* (न्).

To CHEW, *v. a.* चर्व् (c. 1. चर्वति, चर्वितुं, c. 10. चर्वयति -यितुं), दन्तैः पिष् (c. 7. पिनष्टि, पेष्टुं), विदंश् (c. 1. -दशति -दंष्टुं); 'to chew the cud,' रोमन्थ (nom. रोमन्थायते).

CHEWED, *p. p.* चर्वितः -ता -तं, अवलीढः -ढा -ढं, दन्तैः पिष्टः -ष्टा -ष्टं.

CHEWING, *s.* चर्वणं, दन्तपेषणं, रोमन्थः.

CHICANE, *s.* (Prolonging a judicial contest) विवादिभिर् मिथ्योत्तरद्वारा or असद्ग्रहोद्ग्राहद्वारेण अर्थनिर्णयविलम्बनं, मिथ्याप्रौढिः *f.*, मिथ्यापत्तिः *f.*—(Artifice in general) छद्म *n.* (न्), छलं, व्यपदेशः, अपदेशः, कपटः.

To CHICANE, *v. n.* विवादसमये मिथ्योत्तरद्वारा or असद्ग्रहोद्ग्राहद्वारेण अर्थनिर्णयविलम्बनं कृ.

CHICANER, *s.* मिथ्याविवादी *m.* (न्), मिथ्यातार्किकः, वाग्जीवकः, मिथ्योत्तरवादी *m.* (न्), असद्ग्रहोद्ग्राहकृत्, जल्पकः.

CHICANERY, *s.* मिथ्याविवादः, हेत्वाभासः, पक्षाभासः, मिथ्यावादः, मिथ्यातर्कः, मिथ्याहेतुः, वाक्छलं, मिथ्याप्रौढिः *f.*, जल्पः, कपटः.

CHICK or CHICKEN, *s.* कुक्कुटशावकः, पक्षिशावकः.

CHICKEN-HEARTED, *a.* भीरुहृदयः -या -यं, हरिणहृदयः -या -यं.

CHICKEN-POX, *s.* रक्तवटीविशिष्टो बालानां रोगः.

CHICK-PEAS, *s.* चणकः, हरिमन्थः -न्थकः.

CHICK-WEED, *s.* पक्षिभक्ष्यः क्षुद्रौषधिभेदः.

CHIDDEN, *p. p.* निन्दितः -ता -तं, निर्भर्त्सितः -ता -तं, धिक्कृतः -ता -तं.

To CHIDE, *v. a* निन्द् (c. 1. निन्दति, निन्दितुं), प्रतिनिन्द्, विनिन्द्, भर्त्स् (c. 10. भर्त्सयते -ति -यितुं), गुप् in des. (जुगुप्सते -प्सितुं), गर्ह् (c. 1. गर्हते, गर्हितुं), धिक्कृ, आक्रुश् (c. 1. -क्रोशति -क्रोष्टुं).

To CHIDE, *v. n.* (Clamour) उत्क्रुश् (c. 1. -क्रोशति -क्रोष्टुं), प्रक्रुश्, विक्रुश्.—(Quarrel) विवद् (c. 1. -वदते -वदितुं), विप्रवद्, वाक्कलहं कृ.

CHIDER, *s.* निन्दकः, धिक्कर्त्ता *m.* (र्त्तृ), परिवादकः, आक्रोशकः.

CHIDING, *s.* निन्दा, परिभाषणं, परीवादः, जुगुप्सा, उपक्रोशः, तिरस्कारः, उपालम्भः, निर्भर्त्सनं, धिक्कारः, धिक्क्रिया, विप्रलापः, वाग्युद्धं.

CHIEF, *a.* परमः -मा -मं, परः -रा -रं, उत्तमः -मा -मं, मुख्यः -ख्या -ख्यं, प्रमुखः -खा -खं, अग्रः -ग्रा -ग्रं, अग्र्यः -ग्र्या -ग्र्यं, प्राग्र्यः -ग्र्या -ग्र्यं, अग्रीयः -या -यं, अग्रियः -या -यं, प्रधानः -ना -नं, शिष्टः -ष्टा -ष्टं, विशिष्टः -ष्टा -ष्टं, उत्कृष्टः -ष्टा -ष्टं, अनुत्तमः -मा -मं, पारमिकः -की -कं, वर्य्यः -र्य्या -र्य्यं, प्रवरः -रा -रं, वरेण्यः -ण्या -ण्यं, पुरोगमः -मा -मं, प्रवर्हः -र्हा -र्हं, परार्द्ध्यः -र्द्ध्या -र्द्ध्यं, अनवरार्द्ध्यः -र्द्ध्या -र्द्ध्यं, वृन्दारकः -का -कं, प्रष्ठः -ष्ठा -ष्ठं, इन्द्रः -न्द्रा -न्द्रं in comp., पुङ्गवः -वा -वं in comp., ऋषभः -भा -भं in comp.; 'chief minister,' प्रधानमन्त्री *m.* (न्); 'chief priest,' प्रधानयाजकः; 'chief justice,' धर्म्माधिकारी *m.* (न्), धर्म्माध्यक्षः; 'chief seat,' अग्रासनं; 'chief of sages,' देवर्षिः *m.*; 'chief person,' आदिपुरुषः.

CHIEF, *s.* पतिः *m.*, ईश्वरः, ईशः, नायकः, मुख्यः, पुरोगः, अग्रगः, अधिपः, अधिपतिः *m.*, अधिष्ठाता *m.* (तृ), अध्यक्षः, श्रेष्ठी *m.* (न्), शिष्टः, गणपतिः, प्रष्ठः, उड्डहः, शिरोवर्त्ती *m.* (न्), वृन्दारकः.—(Military chief) सेनापतिः, सेनाग्रगः, सेनानीः *m.*

CHIEFLESS, *a.* अनायकः -का -कं, अनीश्वरः -रा -रं, अराजकः -का -कं.

CHIEFLY, *adv.* प्रधानतस्, प्राधान्यतस्, मुख्यशस्, विशेषतस्, परमं.

CHIEFTAIN, *s.* (Leader) मुखरः, पुरोगः, अग्रगः, नायकः, पतिः *m.*, ईश्वरः.—(Commander) सेनापतिः, सेनानीः *m.*—(Head of a clan) गणपतिः, सामन्तः.

CHIEFTAINSHIP, *s.* मुख्यता, गाणपत्यं, सैनापत्यं, ऐश्वर्य्यं.

CHILBLAIN, *s.* पादस्फोटः, पाददारी *f.*, शिशिरजातं क्षतं.

CHILD, *s.* बालः -ला, बालकः, शिशुः *m.*, वत्सः -त्सा -त्सकः, सुतः, पुत्रः, शावकः, सन्तानः, सन्ततिः *f.*, अपत्यं, बालापत्यं, दारकः, तोकं, अर्भः, अर्भकः, माणवकः.—(The compellation of an old to a young man) वत्स.—(To be with child) गर्भवती or सञ्जातगर्भा भू.

CHILDBEARING, *s.* प्रसवः, सवनं, सूः *f.*; 'past childbearing,' विगतार्त्तवा, निष्फला; 'capable of childbearing,' सरजस्का.

CHILDBED, *s.* प्रसवावस्था, प्रसवकालः, प्रसववेदना, गर्भवेदनावस्था.

CHILDBIRTH, *s.* प्रसवः, प्रसूतिः *f.*, सूतिः *f.*, जननं; 'the pains of childbirth,' प्रसववेदना, गर्भवेदना; 'to suffer the pains of childbirth,' प्राप्तप्रसववेदना भू.

CHILDERMAS-DAY, *s.* हेरोद्नाम्नो यिहुदीयराज्ञ आज्ञया अपापशिशूनां वधमुद्दिश्य पर्व्व *n.* (न्).

CHILDHOOD, *s.* बाल्यं, शैशवं, शिशुत्वं, बालकत्वं, बालभावः, कौमारं, शैशवकालः, बाल्यकालः, बाल्यावस्था, अपत्यता, अर्भत्वं.

CHILDISH, *a.* बालिशः -शा -शं, बालेयः -या -यं, बालकीयः -या -यं, बालयोग्यः -ग्या -ग्यं; 'childish prattle,' बालवचनं; 'childish understanding,' बालबुद्धिः.

CHILDISHLY, *adv.* बालवत्, शिशुवत्, बालकवत्, बालरूपेण.

CHILDISHNESS, *s.* बालिश्यं, बालेयत्वं, बालकीयता, बालरूपत्वं.

CHILDLESS, *a.* अपुत्रः -त्रा -त्रं -त्रकः -का -कं, निष्पुत्रः -त्रा -त्रं, असुतः -ता -तं, अप्रसुतः -ता -तं, पुत्ररहितः -ता -तं, पुत्रशून्यः -न्या -न्यं, अनपत्यः -त्या -त्यं, असन्तानः -ना -नं, निःसन्तानः -ना -नं, अप्रजः -जा -जं, निरन्वयः -या -यं, निर्वंशः -शा -शं; 'a childless woman,' वन्ध्या, अशिश्वी; 'the state of being childless,' आनपत्यं.

CHILDLIKE, *a.* बालोपमः -मा -मं, बालसदृशः -शी -शं, बालेयः -या -यं.

CHILIAEDRON, *s.* सहस्रभुजः, सहस्रकोणः, सहस्रास्रं.

CHILIFACTORY, *a.* रसजनकः -का -कं. *See* CHYLIFACTORY.

To CHILL, *v. a.* शीतीकृ, शीतलीकृ.—(Check the perspiration) स्वेदं विष्टम्भ् in caus. (-स्तम्भयति -यितुं).—(Discourage) निर्विण्णं -ण्णां -ण्णं कृ, तेजोहीनं -नां -नं कृ.

CHILL, *a.* शीतलः -ला -लं, शिशिरः -रा -रं, शीतः -ता -तं.

CHILL, *s.* शीतं, शीतता, हिमं; 'a check to the perspiration,' स्वेदविष्टम्भः.

CHILLED, *p. p.* शीतीकृतः -ता -तं, हिमार्त्तः -र्त्ता -र्त्तं, हततापः -पा -पं.

CHILLINESS, *s.* शीतता, शीतलता, शैत्यं, शीतभावः, शिशिरत्वं.

CHILLY, *a.* शिशिरः -रा -रं, ईषच्छीतः -ता -तं, आशीतलः -ला -लं.

CHIME, *s.* नानावादित्राणाम् एकतालः or एकतानः or तालैक्यं, अनेकवाद्यानाम् तानैक्यं or तौर्य्यैक्यं, शब्दैक्यं.—(Of bells) अनेकघण्टानां तालैक्यं, ताड्यमानानाम् अनेकघण्टानां सुस्वरशब्दः, घण्टाशिञ्जितं.

To CHIME, *v. a.* यथा स्वरैक्यं or तालैक्यं जायते तथा नानावादित्राणि वद् in caus. (वादयति -यितुं) or तड् (c. 10. ताडयति -यितुं); घण्टां तड्.

To CHIME, *v. n.* (To agree) संवद् (c. 1. -वदति -वदितुं), अनुवद्, एकीभू, अनुगुणः -णा -णं भू, अनुरूपः -पा -पं भू.

CHIMERA, *s.* वृथावासना, असम्भवकल्पना, अनर्थकवासना, मिथ्यावासना, दुर्वासना, अनर्थकचिन्ता, अनर्थकभावना, मनोरथसृष्टिः *f.*, आभासः, मृषार्थकं, शशविषाणं, कूर्म्मलोमतन्तुवाणं.

CHIMERICAL, *a.* काल्पनिकः -की -कं, मानसिकः -की -कं, मनोरथसृष्टः -ष्टा -ष्टं, वासनाकल्पितः -ता -तं, अमूलकः -का -कं.

CHIMNEY, *s.* धूमरन्ध्रं, धूमपथः, धूमनिर्गमः.—(Fire-place) चुल्लिः *f.*, -ल्ली, जातिः *f.*, तेमनी, अग्निकुण्डं.

CHIMNEY-CORNER, *s.* चुल्लिपार्श्वः, चुल्लेरुपान्तं, चुल्लिपार्श्वे आसनं.

CHIMNEY-PIECE, *s.* चुल्लिशीर्षं, चुल्लिशिला, चुल्लेरुपरि प्रस्तरः.

CHIMNEY-SWEEPER, *s.* धूमरन्ध्रसम्मार्ज्जकः, चुल्लिसम्मार्ज्जकः.

CHIN, *s.* चिबुकं, चिबुः *m.*, हनुः *m. f.*, चिविः *m.*, पोथं, जम्भः.

CHIN-COUGH, *s.* बालानाम् आक्षेपकः कासः, महाकासः.

CHINA, *s.* (Porcelain) कौलालकं, मृन्मयं भाण्डं, मार्त्तिकं भाण्डं.—(The country) चीनः; 'China-cloth,' चीनांशुकं; 'China-rose,' ओड्रपुष्पं, जवा.

CHINE, *s.* सपृष्ठास्थि पृष्ठमांसं, सवंशः पृष्ठभागः, पृष्ठं, कशेरुका.

To CHINE, *v. a.* पृष्ठास्थिरूपेण छिद् (c. 7. छिनत्ति, छेत्तुं), पृष्ठवंशानुलोमं छिद्.

CHINK, *s.* (Aperture) छिद्रं, रन्ध्रं, सन्धिः *m.*—(Sound) शिञ्जितं, क्वणितं.

To CHINK, *v. n.* (To open in gaps) स्फुट् (c. 6. स्फुटति, स्फुटितुं), विदॄ in pass. (-दीर्य्यते), फल् (c. 1. फलति, फलितुं).—(To ring as metal) क्वण् (c. 1. क्वणति, क्वणितुं), शिञ्ज् (c. 2. शिंक्ते, शिञ्जितुं).

CHINKY, *a.* छिद्रपूर्णः -र्णा -र्णं, छिद्रितः -ता -तं, बहुरन्ध्रवान् -वती -वत् (त्).

CHINTZ, *s.* चित्रितपटं, चित्रकार्पासं, पटी, पटोलं, चीनांशुकं.

CHIP, *s.* विदलं, तष्टं, भिन्नं, भित्तिः *f.*, भित्तं, खण्डं, शकलं; 'a chip of wood,' काष्ठखण्डं.

To CHIP, *v. a.* तक्ष् (c. 1. तक्षति, तक्षितुं), विदलीकृ, खण्डीकृ.

CHIP-AXE, *s.* तक्षणी, छिदिः *f.*, टङ्कः, वृक्षभिद्.

CHIPPINGS, *s. pl.* विदलानि, भित्तानि, खण्डानि, तष्टानि.

CHIRAGRA, *s.* वातरोगविशेषो यत्र करमात्रम् उपहतं, हस्तशोथः.

CHIROGRAPHER, *s.* हस्तलेखकः, लिपिकरः, कायस्थः, अक्षरजीवकः.

CHIROGRAPHY, *s.* हस्तलेखनं, लेखनविद्या, लिपिः *f.*, लिखनं.

CHIROMANCER, *s.* हस्तरेखालक्षणात् शुभाशुभदर्शकः, हस्तरेखाविद्याज्ञः.

CHIROMANCY, *s.* हस्तरेखालक्षणात् शुभाशुभदर्शनं, हस्तरेखाविद्या, अङ्गविद्या.

To CHIRP, *v. n.* पक्षिवत् कूज् (c. 1. कूजति, कूजितुं), अनुकूज्, विकूज्, क्विण् or च्विण् शब्दं कृ, सुरारिं कृ.

CHIRPING, *s.* कूजितं, रावः, सुरारिः *m.*, वाशितं, रुतं, काकली -लिः.

CHIRURGEON, *s.* कायशल्यादिभिषक् *m.* (ज्). *See* SURGEON.

CHISEL, *s.* व्रश्चनः, तक्षणी, टङ्कः, वृक्षभेदी *m.* (न्), वृक्षादनः, शिलाभेदः, शिलाकुट्टकः, शैलभित्तिः *f.*

To CHISEL, *v. a.* तक्ष् (c. 1. तक्षति, तक्षितुं), व्रश्च् (c. 6. वृश्चति, व्रश्चितुं).

CHIT, *s.* (A child) बालः -ला, बालकः, शिशुः *m.*, शावकः.—(A freckle) तिलः -लकः, जडुलः.

CHIT-CHAT, *s.* विस्रम्भालापः, विस्रम्भकथितं, वृथाकथा, सङ्कथा, जल्पः.

CHITTERLINGS, *s. pl.* पश्वन्त्राणि *n. pl.*, पशुनाड्यः *f. pl.*, पुरीतत् *m. n.*

CHITTY, *a.* बालकीयः -या -यं, बालेयः -यी -यं, बालिशः -शा -शं.

CHIVALROUS, *a.* सुविक्रान्तः -न्ता -न्तं, महावीर्य्यः -र्य्या -र्य्यं, धामवान् -वती -वत् (त्).

CHIVALRY, *s.* (Knighthood) सादिपदं, रथिपदं, महारथत्वं.—(Prowess) सुविक्रमः, सुवीर्य्यं, धाम *n.* (न्), पौरुषं, कर्म्मोदारं, रणोत्साहः.

CHIVES, *s.* पुष्पकेशराग्रं, पुष्पपक्ष्माग्राणि *n. pl.*

CHOCOLATE, *s.* आमेरिकादेशीयवृक्षफलं, तत्फलनिर्द्धृतं पानीयं.

CHOICE, *s.* (The act) वरणं, वृतिः *f.*, वरः.—(The power of choice between two things) विकल्पः -ल्पकः; 'choice of a husband by a bride,' स्वयंवरः; 'the best of any thing,' उत्तमभागः, परभागः, उत्तमांशः, रत्नं in comp.; 'of one's own choice,' कामतस्, इच्छातस्, यथेप्सितं, यथेष्टं, यथाकामं.

CHOICE, *a.* उत्तमः -मा -मं, सर्व्वोत्तमः -मा -मं, विशिष्टः -ष्टा -ष्टं, शिष्टः -ष्टा -ष्टं, अनुत्तमः -मा -मं, मनोनीतः -ता -तं, विशेषः -षा -षं, सारः -रा -रं, सारवान् -वती -वत् (त्), उत्कृष्टः -ष्टा -ष्टं, अभीष्टः -ष्टा -ष्टं, प्रशस्तः -स्ता -स्तं, भद्रतमः -मा -मं, सर्व्वश्रेष्ठः -ष्ठा -ष्ठं; 'choice food,' भोजनविशेषः, विशिष्टान्नं.

CHOICELESS, *a.* अविकल्पः -ल्पा -ल्पं, अवैकल्पिकः -की -कं.

CHOICELY, *adv.* विशिष्टप्रकारेण, सविशेषं, उत्तमप्रकारेण, प्रशस्तं.

CHOICENESS, *s.* उत्कृष्टता, प्रकृष्टत्वं, वैशिष्ट्यं, विशिष्टता, श्रेष्ठता, प्राशस्त्यं, श्रौत्तम्यं.

CHOIR, *s.* गायकचक्रं, गाथकचक्रं, गायकसमूहः, चाक्रिकगणः.—(Part of a church) पूजाशालायाः सङ्कीर्त्तनयोग्यं मध्यमस्थलं.

To CHOKE, *v. a.* (To suffocate) कण्ठं सम्पीड् (c. 10. -पीडयति -यितुं) or ग्रस् (c. 1. ग्रसति, ग्रसितुं), गलहस्त (nom. गलहस्तयति -यितुं), गलग्रहं कृ, श्वासावरोधं कृ, श्वासधारणं कृ.—(To obstruct) रुध् (c. 7. रुणद्धि, रोद्धुं), निरुध्, अवरुध्, संरुध्; प्रतिबन्ध् (c. 9. -बध्नाति -बन्धुं).

CHOKED, *p. p.* अवरुद्धश्वासः -सा -सं, रुद्धकण्ठः -ण्ठा -ण्ठं, निरुद्धः -द्धा -द्धं.

CHOKER, *s.* (Argument that stops the mouth) गलहस्तः.

CHOLAGOGUES, *s.* पित्तद्रावनं, पित्तद्रावकः, पित्तघ्नं, पित्तनाशनं.

CHOLER, *s.* (Bile) पित्तं.—(Rage) क्रोधः, कोपः, रोषः, अमर्षः.

CHOLERA, *s.* विसूचिका, विषूचिका, महामारी.

CHOLERIC, *a.* पित्तवेगी -गिनी -गि (न्), क्रोधी -धिनी -धि (न्), कोपी -पिनी -पि (न्), चण्डः -ण्डा -ण्डं; 'choleric constitution,' पित्तप्रकृतिः.

CHOLIC, *s.* शूलः -लं, पक्तिशूलं. *See* COLIC.

To CHOOSE, *v. a.* (Select) वृ (c. 5. वृणोति -णुते, c. 9. वृणाति -णीते, c. 1. वरति, वरितुं, वरीतुं), आवृ, प्रवृ; or in caus. (वरयति -यितुं), अनुरुच् in caus. (-रोचयति -यितुं), वावृत् (c. 4. वावृत्यते).—(Take) ग्रह् (c. 9. गृह्णाति, ग्रहीतुं).—(Appoint) नियुज् (c. 10. -योजयति -यितुं), निरूप् (c. 10. -रूपयति -यितुं).

To CHOOSE, *v. n.* (To be willing) इष् (c. 6. इच्छति, एषितुं), रुच् (c. 1. रोचते) used impersonally. न प्रत्याख्या (c. 2. -ख्याति -ख्यातुं), अभिरुच् in caus. (-रोचयते -यितुं).

To CHOP, *v. a.* (To cut into pieces) खण्डं खण्डं कृ or खण्डशः कृ or छिद् (c. 7. छिनत्ति, छेत्तुं), शकलीकृ, विदलीकृ.

CHOP, *s.* खण्डं, शकलं, भिन्नं, भित्तिः, विदलं.—(Of meat) मांसखण्डं.—(A mutton chop) औरभ्रखण्डं.

CHOP-HOUSE, *s.* पक्वमांसविक्रयस्थानं, पाकशाला.

CHOPPING, *a.* हृष्टपुष्टः -ष्टा -ष्टं, मांसलः -ला -लं, स्थूलः -ला -लं.

CHOPPING-KNIFE, *s.* मांसच्छेदनार्थं छुरिका, मांसखण्डनी छुरिका.

CHOPS, *s.* (Mouth) मुखं, आननं, आस्यं.—(Of a river) सम्भेदः.

CHORAL, *a.* साङ्गीतिकः -की -कं, गानीयः -या -यं, चाक्रिकः -की -कं.

CHORD, *s.* (A string) गुणः. *See* CORD.—(Of an instrument) तन्त्री *f.*—(Of arc) त्रिज्या, ज्या, ज्यका, जीवा.

CHORDED, *p. p.* तन्त्री -न्त्रिणी -न्त्रि (न्).

CHORIAMBUS, *s.* (In prosody) विप्रः.

CHORION, *s.* गर्भकोशः, गर्भवेष्टनं, गर्भाशयः, गर्भावरणं चर्म्म.

CHORISTER, *s.* प्रधानमन्दिरस्य गायकः or गायकः, चाक्रिकः, तालावचरः, किन्नरः, किन्नरपुरुषः.

CHOROGRAPHER, *s.* देशविवरणकृत्, देशवर्णनकृत्, देशपर्य्यन्तलेखकः.

CHORUS, *s.* (Number of singers) गायकगणः, गायकसमूहः.—(Dramatic) पार्श्वस्थः, पारिपार्श्विकः.—(Of a song) ध्रुवकः, ध्रुवः, अनुपदं.

CHOSEN, *p. p.* मनोनीतः -ता -तं, वृतः -ता -तं, वृतः -ता -तं, वावृतः -ता -तं.

CHOUGH, *s.* काकजातीयः समुद्रवेलासेवी पक्षिभेदः.

To CHOUSE, *v. a.* वञ्च् (c. 10. वञ्चयते -ति -यितुं), प्रलभ् (c. 1. -लभते -लब्धुं), छल् (c. 10. छलयति -यितुं).

CHOUSE, *s.* (Trick) छलं, कूटः -टं, व्याजः.—(A cheater) वञ्चकः.

CHOWRIE, *s.* (Tail used to drive away flies) चामरं, बालचूलकं, रोमगुच्छः, रोमकेशरं.

CHRISM, *s.* अभ्यञ्जनं, अञ्जनं, अभिषेकः -षेचनं.

CHRIST, *s.* (The anointed) अभिषिक्तः.—(The anointed Saviour) अभिषिक्तत्राता *m.* (तृ). Modern scholars coin the word ख्रीष्टः.

To CHRISTEN, *v. a.* (To baptize) जलसंस्कारेण ख्रीष्टीयं -यां -यं कृ, जलसंस्कारेण ख्रीष्टीयमतधारिणां or ख्रीष्टीयानां मध्ये प्रविश् in caus. (-वेशयति -यितुं).—(To name) नाम कृ, नाम दा (c. 3. ददाति, दातुं).

CHRISTENDOM, *s.* ख्रीष्टीयमतधारिणां कृत्स्नसमूहः, ख्रीष्टीयदेशसामग्र्यं, ये केचिद् देशाः ख्रीष्टीयमतं धारयन्ति तत्साकल्यं.

CHRISTENING, *s.* जलसंस्कारः, जलसंस्कारेण ख्रीष्टीयानां मध्ये प्रवेशनं.—(Naming) नामकरणं.

CHRISTIAN, *s.* ख्रीष्टीयः, ख्रीष्टीयमतधारी *m.* (न्), ख्रीष्टीयमतावलम्बी *m.* (न्).

CHRISTIAN-NAME, *s.* जलसंस्कारकाले दत्तं नाम *n.* (न्), नाम, गुप्तनाम, राशिनाम.

CHRISTIANITY, *s.* ख्रीष्टीयमतं, ख्रीष्टीयानां मतं, ख्रीष्टीयधर्म्मः.

CHRISTIANLY, *adv.* ख्रीष्टीयवत्, ख्रीष्टीयधर्म्मानुसारेण.

CHRISTMAS-BOX, *s.* ख्रीष्टजन्मोत्सवकाले दत्तं (or देयं) पारितोषिकं.

CHRISTMAS-DAY, *s.* ख्रीष्टजन्मदिवसमुद्दिश्य महोत्सवः, ख्रीष्टजन्मपर्व्व *n.* (न्).

CHROMATIC, *a.* (Relating to colour) वर्णसम्बन्धी -न्धिनी -न्धि (न्), रङ्गी -ङ्गिणी -ङ्गि (न्).—(In music) ग्रामीणः -णा -णं, ग्रामिकः -की -कं.

CHRONIC or CHRONICAL, *a.* कालिकः -की -कं, दीर्घकालीनः -ना -नं, अनिसर्गी -र्गिणी -र्गि (न्); 'chronical distemper,' दीर्घरोगः, दीर्घव्याधिः *m.*

CHRONICLE, *s.* इतिहासः, पुरावृत्तविवरणं, वृत्तविवरणं or -रणपुस्तकं, पुरावृत्ताख्यानं, पुरावृत्तग्रन्थः, समाचारग्रन्थः, शिष्टसमाचारः.

To CHRONICLE, *v. a.* इतिहासपुस्तकेषु समारुह् in caus. (-रोपयति -यितुं) or अभिलिख् (c. 6. -लिखति -लेखितुं), यथाक्रमं वृत्तविवरणं कृ or वृत्तानि रच् (c. 10. रचयति -यितुं).

CHRONICLER, *s.* ऐतिहासिकः, इतिहासलेखकः, पुरावृत्तरचकः, वृत्तविवरणकृत्, शिष्टसमाचाररचकः.

CHRONOGRAM, *s.* यथा अक्षरविन्यासात् संवत्सरादिकालो निर्णेतुं शक्यते तथा प्रस्तरादौ लिखितम् अमुकप्रसिद्धवृत्तविवरणं.

CHRONOLOGIST, *s.* कालगणकः, कालगणनाविज्ञः, कालज्ञः, यथाकालं or कालक्रमेण पुरावृत्तरचकः, वृत्तकालनिरूपकः, गतकालनिर्णेता *m.* (तृ).

CHRONOLOGICAL, *a.* कालगणनाविषयकः -का -कं, कालिकः -की -कं.

CHRONOLOGICALLY, *adv.* यथाकालं, कालक्रमेण, कालक्रमानुसारेण.

CHRONOLOGY, *s.* कालगणनाविद्या, कालनिरूपणविद्या, कालनिर्णयविद्या, कालक्रमेण पुरावृत्तरचना.

CHRONOMETER, *s.* कालपरिमाणार्थं यन्त्रं, घटी, यामनाली.

CHRYSALIS, *s.* कोशस्थः, कोशवासी *m.* (न्), कोषकारः, डिम्भः, गुटिका.

CHRYSOLITE, *s.* चन्द्रकान्तः, हरिताश्म *n.* (न्), पीतमणिः *m.*

CHUB, *s.* स्थूलशिरस्को नादेयमत्स्यभेदः.

CHUBBED, *a.* स्थूलशिरस्कः -स्का -स्कं, स्थूलमस्तकः -का -कं.

CHUBBY-FACED, *a.* स्थूलास्यः -स्या -स्यं, स्थूलाननः -नी -नं.

CHUCK, *s.* (The cry of a hen) कुक्कुटीरावः, कुक्कुटीनादः.—(A term of endearment) प्रिये voc. c. *f.*, वत्स voc. c. *m.*, वत्से voc. c. *f.*

To CHUCK, *v. n.* (To call as a hen) कुक्कुटीवद् रु (c. 2. रौति, रवितुं). —(To give a gentle blow under the chin) बालस्यात् परचिबुकम् ईषत्प्रहारेण उन्नम् in caus. (-नमयति -यितुं).

CHUFF, *s.* (A loutish clown) ग्राम्यजनः, ग्रामिकः, ग्रामबुद्धिः, स्थूलबुद्धिः, असभ्यः, जडः.

CHUFFY, *a.* ग्राम्यः -म्या -म्यं, मन्दमतिः -तिः -ति, स्थूलः -ला -लं.

CHUM, *s.* वयस्यः, सहवासी *m.* (न्), सङ्गी *m.* (न्), प्रियमित्रं, संसर्गी *m.* (न्).

CHUMP, *s.* स्थूलकाष्ठं, स्थूलदारु *m.*, बृहत्काष्ठखण्डं.

CHURCH, *s.* (Place of worship) मन्दिरं, पूजाशाला, भजनभवनं, भजनगृहं, प्रासादः, मण्डपः.—(The body of Christians) ख्रीष्टमतधारिणां कृत्स्नसमूहः, मण्डली -लं, समाजः.

To CHURCH, *v. a.* प्रसवसमुत्थितां स्त्रीं परमेश्वरस्य धन्यवादं कृ in caus. (कारयति -यितुं).

CHURCHMAN, *s.* पुरोहितः, याजकः, धर्म्माध्यापकः.

CHURCHWARDEN, *s.* मन्दिररक्षकः, भजनगृहपालकः, पूजाशालाध्यक्षः.

CHURCHYARD, *s.* श्मशानं, प्रेतवनं, पितृवनं, शवनिखननस्थानं; 'churchyard flowers,' पितृवनसुमनः *n.* (स्).

CHURL, *s.* (A rustic) ग्राम्यजनः, ग्रामजः, ग्रामी *m.* (न्), असभ्यः.—(A rude man) कुशीलः, दुःशीलः, वामशीलः.—(A miser) कृपणः, कदर्य्यः, मुष्टेरुकः.

CHURLISH, *a.* दुराचारः -रा -रं, दुष्प्रकृतिः -तिः -ति, अविनयः -या -यं, अशिष्टः -ष्टा -ष्टं, अश्लीलः -ला -लं, क्रूराचारः -रा -रं, खलः -ला -लं, कदर्य्यः -र्य्या -र्य्यं.

CHURLISHLY, *adv.* असभ्यवत्, कदर्य्यवत्, कृपणं, अश्लीलं.

CHURLISHNESS, *s.* कुशीलता, अश्लीलता, अशिष्टता, अविनयः, असभ्यता.

CHURN, *s.* मन्थनी, मन्थिनी, गर्गरी, मन्थनघटी, आलगर्गणिका.

To CHURN, *v. a.* मथ् (c. 1. मथति, मथितुं) or मन्थ् (c. 1. मन्थति, c. 9. मथ्नाति, मन्थितुं), उन्मन्थ्, निर्मन्थ्, खज् (c. 1. खजति, खजितुं), समालुड् (c. 1. -लोडति -लोडितुं, c. 10. -लोडयति -यितुं).

CHURNED, *p. p.* मथितः -ता -तं, प्रमथितः -ता -तं, आलोडितः -ता -तं, दण्डाहतः -ता -तं, व्याघट्टितः -ता -तं, क्षोभः -भा -भं.

CHURNING, *s.* मन्थः, मन्थनं, मथनं, आलोडनं, समालोडा, खजा, क्षोभः.

CHURN-STAFF, *s.* मन्थः, मन्था *m.* (मथिन्), मन्थदण्डकः, मन्थानः, दधिचारः, वैशाखः, खजकः.

CHYLE, *s.* अन्नरसः, धातुपः, रसः, भोज्यसम्भवः, असमातृका, अन्नसारः.

CHYLIFACTORY, *a.* धातुपकारी -रिणी -रि (न्), अन्नरसोत्पादकः -का -कं.

CHYLOUS, *a.* अन्नरसमयः -यी -यं, धातुपरूपः -पा -पं.

CHYMIC OR CHYMICAL, *a.* रसायनविद्यासम्बन्धी -न्धिनी -न्धि (न्), रसायनज्ञः -ज्ञा -ज्ञं.

CHYMICALLY, *adv.* रसायनविद्यानुसारात्, रसायनविद्यानुरूपेण.

CHYMIST, *s.* रसायनविद्याज्ञः, रसज्ञः, रसायनः.

CHYMISTRY, *s.* रसायनं, रसायनविद्या, रसविद्या, रसज्ञता.

CIBARIOUS, *a.* अन्नमयः -यी -यं, भोज्यः -ज्या -ज्यं, खाद्यः -द्या -द्यं.

CICATRICE, *s.* किण *n.* (न्), किणं, शुष्कव्रणः, रूढक्षतचिह्नं, रूढक्षतं.

CICATRIZATION, *s.* व्रणविशोषणं, व्रणशोधनं, रोपणं, व्रणरोपणं, समुत्थानं, प्रतिसारणं, प्रतिसरः.

To CICATRIZE, *v. a.* क्षतं रुह् in caus. (रोपयति -यितुं) or शुष् in caus. (शोषयति -यितुं) or शुष्कीकृ, प्रतिसृ in caus. (सारयति -यितुं).

CICATRIZED, *p. p.* रूढः -ढा -ढं, रोपितः -ता -तं, शुष्कः -ष्का -ष्कं, समुत्थितः -ता -तं, प्रतिसारितः -ता -तं.

To CICURATE, *v. a.* दम् in caus. (दमयति -यितुं), वशीकृ, निग्रह् (c. 9. -गृह्णाति -ग्रहीतुं).

CIDER, *s.* अम्लरसः पानीयविशेषः, अम्लफलनिर्म्मितो मद्यविशेषः.

CILIARY, *a.* नेत्रच्छदसम्बन्धी -न्धिनी -न्धि (न्), पक्ष्मसम्बन्धी &c.

CILICIOUS, *a.* लोममयः -यी -यं, लोमजः -जा -जं.

CIMETER, *s.* वक्रखड्गः, चन्द्रहासः, मण्डलाग्रः, खड्गः, निस्त्रिंशः, कृपाणः -णकः, असिरिष्टिः *m.*

CINCTURE, *s.* मेखला, कटिसूत्रं, रसना, काञ्ची, बन्धनं.

CINDER, *s.* अग्नेरुच्छिष्टं, दग्धाङ्गारोच्छिष्टं, अङ्गारः -रं, भस्म *n.* (न्).

CINERATION, *s.* भस्मीकरणं, भस्मसात्करणं.

CINERITIOUS, *a.* भास्मनः -नी -नं, भस्मरूपः -पा -पं.

CINNABAR, *s.* रससिन्दूरं, रसस्थानं, रक्तपारदं.

CINNAMON, *s.* दारुगन्धः, तिक्तवल्कलं, सुगन्धत्वक् *f.* (च्), गन्धवल्कलं.

CINNAMON-TREE, *s.* पूर्व्वोक्तितिक्तवल्कलविशिष्टः सिंहलद्वीपरोही क्षुद्रवृक्षः.

CINQUE, *s.* (A five) पञ्चकः, पञ्चतं.

CINQUEFOIL, *s.* पञ्चपर्णी, पञ्चपत्री, पञ्चदली.

CINQUE-SPOTTED, *a.* पञ्चबिन्दुविशिष्टः -ष्टा -ष्टं, पञ्चतिलवान् -वती -वत् (त्).

CION, *s.* पल्लवं, नवपल्लवं, किसलः -लं, किसलयः -यं.

CIPHER, *s.* (An arithmetical character) अङ्कः, गुणनिका.—(Character in general) अक्षरं, वर्णः.—(Mark standing for nothing) शून्यं, बिन्दुः *m.*, वटः, हः, ठः, खं.—(Occult character in writing) बीजाक्षरं, बीजं.

To CIPHER, *v. a.* (To practise arithmetic) अङ्कविद्याम् अभ्यस् (c. 4. -अस्यति -असितुं) or शिक्ष् (c. 1. शिक्षते, शिक्षितुं).—(To write in occult characters) बीजाक्षरैर् अङ्क् (c. 10. अङ्कयति -यितुं) or लिख् (c. 6. लिखति, लेखितुं).

CIPHERING, *s.* अङ्कनं, गणितं, अङ्कविद्या, गणनविद्या, पाटीगणितं.

CIRCLE, *s.* (A round line) मण्डलं, परिमण्डलं, चक्रं, चक्रवालं, वृत्तं, गोलः -लं, निवः, चन्द्रकः, वटः, पर्य्येकः, वलयः -यं.—(Circuit, circumference) परिणाहः, परिधिः *m.*, परिवेष्टनं, वृत्तिः *f.*, परिवेशः; 'the circle of the earth,' भूपरिधिः *m.*, भूमण्डलं.—(A circle of people, assembly) मण्डलं, परिषद् *f.*, पंक्तिः *f.*—(Circle on the forehead) तिलकः -कं, तमालपत्रं, चित्रकं, विशेषकं; 'segment of a circle,' वृत्तखण्डं, खण्डमण्डलं; 'area of a circle,' फलं.

To CIRCLE, *v. a.* (To surround) परिवेष्ट् (c. 1. -वेष्टते -वेष्टितुं), परिवृ (c. 5. -वृणोति -वरितुं -वरीतुं), परिष्ठा (c. 1. -तिष्ठति, -ष्ठातुं), मण्डल (nom. मण्डलयति -यितुं).

To CIRCLE, *v. n.* (To move circularly) चक्रवत् परिवृत् (c. 1. -वर्त्तते -वर्त्तितुं), or आवृत् or परिभ्रम् (c. 1. -भ्रमति, c. 4. -भ्राम्यति -भ्रमितुं), मण्डल (nom. मण्डलायते).

CIRCLED, *p. p.* मण्डलितः -ता -तं, परिमण्डलितः -ता -तं, वलयितः -ता -तं. —(Having the form of a circle) मण्डली -लिनी -लि (न्), मण्डलाकारः -रा -रं, चक्राकारः -रा -रं.

CIRCUIT, *s.* (Compass, circumference) मण्डलं, परिमण्डलं, परिधिः *m.*, परिणामः, परिणाहः, परीणाहः, परिवेष्टनं.—(Act of moving round) परिवर्त्तनं, आवर्त्तः, आवृत्तिः *f.*, आवर्त्तनं, विवर्त्तः, भ्रमणं, परिभ्रमः, घूर्णिः *f.*—(Visitation of a judge) धर्म्माध्यक्षाभ्यागमनं, प्राड्विवाकभ्रमणं.

To CIRCUIT, *v. n.* परिभ्रम् (c. 4. -भ्राम्यति -भ्रमितुं), परिवृत् (c. 1. -वर्त्तते -वर्त्तितुं).

Circuitous, *a.* वक्रः -क्रा -क्रं, कुटिलगामी -मिनी -मि (न्), सुदीर्घः -र्घा -र्घं.

Circular, *a.* वर्त्तुलः -ला -लं, मण्डली -लिनी -लि (न्), चाक्रिकः -की -कं, चक्राकारः -रा -रं, चक्राकृतिः -तिः -ति, चक्री -क्रिणी -क्रि (न्), चक्रवान् -वती -वत् (त्), चाक्रेयः -यी -यं, वटी -टिनी -टि (न्), निघः -घा -घं, विष्वक्समः -मा -मं.

Circularity, *s.* मण्डलता, परिमण्डलता, वर्त्तुलत्वं, चक्राकारता, गोलाकारत्वं.

Circularly, *adv.* चक्रवत्, चक्ररूपेण, गोलवत्, मण्डलवत्, मण्डलतस्.

To circulate, *v. n.* प्रचल् (c. 1. -चलति -चलितुं), प्रचर् (c. 1. -चरति -चरितुं), परिवृत् (c. 1. -वर्त्तते -वर्त्तितुं), सम्परिवृत्, विपरिवृत्, विवृत्.

To circulate, *v. a.* परिवृत् in caus. (-वर्त्तयति -यितुं), प्रचल् in caus. (-चालयति -यितुं).

Circulated, *p. p.* प्रचलितः -ता -तं, परिवर्त्तितः -ता -तं, प्रचारितः -ता -तं, व्यावर्त्तकः -का -कं.

Circulating, *a.* प्रचलः -ला -लं, परिवर्त्ती -र्त्तिनी -र्त्ति (न्), व्यावर्त्तकः -का -कं.

Circulation, *s.* परिवर्त्तः -र्त्तनं, व्यावर्त्तः, प्रचारः, प्रचलनं, प्रचरः, भ्रमणं, परिभ्रमणं, चलनं, प्राचुर्य्यं.—(Of the blood) रक्तचलनं, रक्तवहनं.

Circulatory, *a.* वर्त्तुलः -ला -लं, चाक्रिकः -की -कं, मण्डली -लिनी -लि (न्).

Circumambiency, *s.* परिवेष्टनं, व्याप्तिः *f.*, व्यापनं, व्यापकत्वं, परिगमनं.

Circumambient, *a.* परिवेष्टकः -का -कं, व्यापकः -का -कं, परिगतः -ता -तं.

To circumambulate, *v. n.* परिक्रम् (c. 1. -क्रामति -क्रमितुं), परिभ्रम् (c. 4. -भ्राम्यति -भ्रमितुं).

Circumambulation, *s.* परिक्रमः, परिभ्रमणं, परिसर्य्या, परीसारः, पर्य्यटनं.—(Reverential) प्रदक्षिणः -णा -णं.

To circumcise, *v. a.* त्वचं छिद् (c. 7. छिनत्ति, छेत्तुं), लिङ्गाग्रचर्म्म छिद्, परिच्छिद्, परिकृत् (c. 6. -कृन्तति -कर्त्तितुं).—(A circumcised man) दुश्चर्म्मा *m.* (न्), वण्डः, वण्ठः, दुर्बलः, छिन्नगन्नकः.

Circumcision, *s.* त्वक्छेदनं, लिङ्गाग्रचर्म्मछेदनं, दौश्चर्म्म्यं, परिकर्त्तनं.

To circumduct, *v. a.* लुप् (c. 6. लुम्पति, लोप्तुं), व्यर्थीकृ, मोघीकृ, निष्फलीकृ.

Circumduction, *s.* लोपः, अनिष्पादनं, मोघीकरणं, व्यर्थीकरणं.

Circumference, *s.* परिधिः *m.*, मण्डलं, परीणाहः, परिणाहः, परिमाणं, वृत्तिः *f.*, चक्रवालं, पालिः *f.*, परिवेशः -षः, परिवेष्टनं.—(Of a wheel) चक्रपरिधिः *m.*, नेमिः *f.*, प्रधिः *m.*, प्रधिमण्डलं, नीध्रं, नीव्रः.—(Of the earth) भूपरिधिः *m.*

Circumflex, *s.* (Accent) स्वरितः, तृतीयम् उच्चारणचिह्नं.

Circumfluence, *s.* परिस्रवः, परिप्लवः, परिवाहः, परिस्यन्दनं, परिगलनं.

Circumfluent or circumfluous, *a.* परिस्रुतः -ता -तं, परिसारी -रिणी -रि (न्), परिस्यन्दी -न्दिनी -न्दि (न्), परिस्यन्नः -न्ना -न्नं, परिगलितः -ता -तं.

Circumforaneous, *a.* गृहाद्गृहम् अटमानः -ना -नं, अटाट्यमानः -ना -नं.

To circumfuse, *v. a.* परिप्लु in caus. (-प्लावयति -यितुं), समाप्लु.

Circumfused, *p. p.* परिप्लुतः -ता -तं, समाप्लुतः -ता -तं, परिगलितः -ता -तं, परिगतः -ता -तं, व्याप्तः -प्ता -प्तं, समाक्रान्तः -न्ता -न्तं.

Circumfusile, *a.* परिस्रावी -विनी -वि (न्), व्यापकः -का -कं, व्यप्लुवानः -ना -नं.

Circumfusion, *s.* परिस्रावः, परिप्लवः, व्याप्तिः *f.*, व्यापकत्वं, परिगलनं.

To circumgyrate, *v. n.* परिवृत् (c. 1. -वर्त्तते -वर्त्तितुं), व्यावृत्, घूर्ण् (c. 1. घूर्णते, घूर्णितुं), परिघूर्ण्, व्याघूर्ण्.

Circumgyration, *s.* चक्रावर्त्तः, आवर्त्तः, परिवर्त्तः, आवृत्तिः *f.*, घूर्णिः *f.*

Circumjacent, *a.* पर्य्यन्तस्थः -स्था -स्थं, सामन्तस्थः -स्था -स्थं, उपान्तिकः -की -कं.

Circumition, *s.* परिगमः, परिक्रमः, परिसर्य्या, परिभ्रमः.

Circumlocution, *s.* वाग्विस्तारः, वाक्यविस्तरः, वक्रोक्तिः *f.*, वक्रभणितं, व्याजोक्तिः *f.*, अत्युक्तिः, अतिशयोक्तिः, बहुवाक्यं, बहूक्तिः, वाक्यबाहुल्यं.

Circumlocutory, *a.* बहुवाक्यः -क्या -क्यं, विस्तीर्णवाक्यः -क्या -क्यं, वक्रः -क्रा -क्रं.

Circumnavigable, *a.* समन्तात् or परितो नावा तार्य्यः -र्य्या -र्य्यं.

To circumnavigate, *v. a.* समन्तात् नावा तॄ (c. 1. तरति, तरितुं, तरीतुं) or प्लु (c. 1. प्लवते, प्लोतुं).

Circumnavigation, *s.* नौकया समन्तात् तरणं.

Circumrotation, *s.* चक्रावर्त्तः, परिवर्त्तः, आवर्त्तः, आवृत्तिः *f.*, घूर्णिः *f.*

Circumrotatory, *a.* चक्रवत् परिवर्त्ती -र्त्तिनी -र्त्ति (न्), आवर्त्तमानः -ना -नं, घूर्णायमानः -ना -नं.

To circumscribe, *v. a.* परिमा (c. 2. -माति, c. 3. मिमीते -मातुं), संहृ (c. 1. -हरति -हर्त्तुं), संयम् (c. 1. -यच्छति -यन्तुं), नियम्, समन्त (nom. समन्तयति -यितुं).

Circumscribed, *p. p.* परिमितः -ता -तं, संहृतः -ता -तं, संयतः -ता -तं, सबाधः -धा -धं, सङ्कुचितः -ता -तं, संवृतः -ता -तं, समर्य्यादः -दा -दं, सावधिकः -की -कं, सुसंस्थितः -ता -तं, सुसङ्गृहीतः -ता -तं.

Circumscription, *s.* परिमाणं, संयमनं, संहरणं, सङ्कोचः, संवारः, संवृतिः *f.*

Circumspect, *a.* अवहितः -ता -तं, सुवहितः -ता -तं, सावधानः -ना -नं, समीक्ष्यकारी -रिणी -रि (न्) or विमृश्यकारी, अप्रमत्तः -त्ता -त्तं, परिणामदर्शी -र्शिनी -र्शि (न्).

Circumspection, *s.* अवधानं -नता, सावधानता, अप्रमादः, समीक्ष्यकारित्वं.

Circumspectly, *adv.* अवेक्षया, सावधानं, सुसमीक्ष्य, सुविमृश्य.

Circumstance, *s.* (Something adjunct to a fact) सम्बन्धः, अनुबन्धः.—(A thing, fact) विषयः, वस्तु *n.*, भूतं, विषयकत्वं.—(Incident, event) वृत्तं, वृत्तान्तः, सम्भवः.—(Condition, state) अवस्था, दशा, स्थितिः *f.*, संस्थितिः *f.*, भावः, वृत्तिः *f.*, गतिः *f.*; 'he related all the circumstances as they occurred,' सकलवृत्तान्तं यथावृत्तं न्यवेदयत्; 'according to circumstances,' यथासम्भवं, यथास्थितं; 'in good circumstances,' सुस्थितः -ता -तं, सुस्थः -स्था -स्थं; 'in bad circumstances,' दुःस्थः -स्था -स्थं, दुर्गतः -ता -तं.

Circumstanced, *p. p.* स्थितः -ता -तं, अवस्थितः -ता -तं, स्थः -स्था -स्थं in comp., भूतः -ता -तं, वर्त्ती -र्त्तिनी -र्त्ति (न्); 'so circumstanced,' एवम्भूतः -ता -तं, इत्थम्भूतः -ता -तं, एवंविधः -धा -धं, तथाविधः -धा -धं.

Circumstant, *a.* समन्तात् स्थायी -यिनी -यि (न्) or वर्त्ती -र्त्तिनी -र्त्ति (न्).

Circumstantial, *a.* (In detail) सविस्तरः -रा -रं, विस्तीर्णः -र्णा -र्णं, सविशेषः -षा -षं, सोपवर्णः -र्णा -र्णं, सविवरणः -णा -णं.—(Not essential) अप्रकृतः -ता -तं.—(Incidental) आगन्तुकः -का -कं.

Circumstantially, *adv.* यथावृत्तं, यथास्थितं, सुविस्तरं, विस्तरेण, उपवर्णेन, सुविवरणपूर्व्वकं, निरवशेषतस्.

Circumstantiated, *p. p.* विशेषभाववर्त्ती -र्त्तिनी -र्त्ति (न्). *See* Circumstanced.

To circumvallate, *v. a.* परिखाप्राचीरादिना परिवेष्ट् (c. 1. -वेष्टते -वेष्टितुं), समन्तात् उपरुध् (c. 7. -रुणद्धि -रोद्धुं).

Circumvallation, *s.* (The act) परिखाप्राचीरादिना नगरपरिवेष्टनं, समन्तादुपरोधनं.—(The trenches, &c., round a besieged town) रुद्धनगरपरिगतं परिखाप्राचीरादि.

To circumvent, *v. a.* वञ्च् in caus. (वञ्चयते -ति -यितुं), परिवञ्च्, प्रलभ् (c. 1. -लभते -लब्धुं), विप्रलभ्, छल् (c. 10. छलयति -यितुं).

Circumvented, *p. p.* वञ्चितः -ता -तं, परिवञ्चितः -ता -तं, विप्रलब्धः -ब्धा -ब्धं.

Circumvention, *s.* प्रवञ्चना, वञ्चनं, छलं -लना, अतिसन्धानं, कपटः, कापट्यं, स्खलितं, प्रपञ्चः, प्रलम्भः.

To circumvest, *v. a.* परिव्ये (c. 1. -व्ययति -व्यातुं), परिधा (c. 3. -दधाति -धातुं), परिवेष्ट् (c. 1. -वेष्टते -वेष्टितुं).

Circumvolation, *s.* (Flying round) परिडीनं -नकं.

To CIRCUMVOLVE, *v. a.* परिवृत् in caus. (-वर्त्तयति -यितुं), लुट् in caus. (लोठयति -यितुं), संसृ in caus. (-सारयति -यितुं).

To CIRCUMVOLVE, *v. n.* चक्रवत् परिवृत् (c. 1. -वर्त्तते -वर्त्तितुं), लुट् (c. 1. -लोठति -ते -लोठितुं), प्रलुट्, परिघूर्ण् (c. 6. घूर्णति -ते -र्णितुं).

CIRCUMVOLUTION, *s.* परिवर्त्तनं, परिवृत्तिः *f.*, आवर्त्तनं, आवृत्तिः *f.*, विवर्त्तः, व्यावर्त्तनं, प्रलोठनं, घूर्णिः *f.*; 'of a wheel,' चक्रावर्त्तः.

CIRCUS or CIRQUE, *s.* दीर्घमण्डलाकारो रथचर्य्यादिक्रीडायोग्यो भूमिभागः, क्रीडारङ्गः, क्रीडाङ्गनं, केलिरङ्गः.

CISSUS, *s.* (Plant) गोधापदी -दिका, सुवहा.

CIST, *s.* कोशः, पुटः, पटलं, आवेष्टनं.—(Excavation) खातं.

CISTERN, *s.* उदकाधारः, जलाशयः, जलकुण्डं, कुण्डं, पानीयस्थानं, वरासनं, वारासनं, जलदानगृहं.

CIT, *s.* नागरजनः, नागरकः, पौरजनः, पृथग्जनः, अवरवर्णः.

CITADEL, *s.* दुर्गं, कोटिः *f.*, कलत्रं.—(Commander of) कोटिपालः.

CITAL, *s.* (Impeachment, summons) अभियोगः, आह्वानं, अपवादः.

CITATION, *s.* (Summons) आह्वानं, अभियोगः.—(Quotation) उद्धारः, अवतरणं, -तारणं; 'of the Vedas,' श्रुतादानं.—(Passage quoted) उपनीतवचनं, उद्धृतवाक्यं, अवतारितवाक्यं.

CITATORY, *a.* आह्वायकः -का -कं, अपवादकः -का -कं.

To CITE, *v. a.* (To summon before a judge) प्राड्विवाकसाक्षाद् आह्वे (c. 1. -ह्वयति -ह्वातुं), अभियुज् (c. 7. -युनक्ति -योक्तुं).—(To adduce, quote) उपनी (c. 1. -नयति -नेतुं), उद्धृ (c. 1. -हरति -हर्त्तुं), अवतॄ in caus. (-तारयति -यितुं); 'to cite the Vedas,' श्रुतादानं कृ.

CITED, *p. p.* (Quoted) उपनीतः -ता -तं, उद्धृतः -ता -तं, अवतारितः -ता -तं, उपन्यस्तः -स्ता -स्तं.—(Before a court of justice) निबद्धः -द्धा -द्धं, आहूतः -ता -तं, अभियुक्तः -क्ता -क्तं, व्यवहाराभिशस्तः -स्ता -स्तं.

CITER, *s.* (Impeacher) अभियोगी *m.* (न्), अभियोक्ता *m.* (क्तृ).—(Quoter) उपनेता *m.* (तृ).

CITHERN, *s.* (A harp) वीणाविशेषः, वल्लकी, विपञ्ची, तन्त्रीः.

CITIZEN, *s.* पौरः, पौरजनः, नगरजनः, नागरजनः, नगरस्थः, पुरवासी *m.* (न्), नगरौकाः *m.* (स्), पौरलोकः; 'a fellow-citizen,' एकपौरः.

CITIZENLIKE, *adv.* नगरजनवत्, पौरवत्, सभ्यरूपेण, आर्य्यवत्.

CITIZENSHIP, *s.* नगरजनाधिकारः, पौराधिकारः, पौरत्वं; 'fellow-citizenship,' पौरसख्यं.

CITRINE, *s.* जम्बीरवर्णः -र्णा -र्णं, घनपीतः -ता -तं.

CITRON, *s.* (The tree) जम्बीरः, जम्भः -म्भकः -म्भलः -म्भरः, अम्लकेशरः, केशराम्लः, फलपूरः -रकः, बीजपूरः, गिलः, दन्तशठः, रुचकः, इक्षकः, वृहच्चित्रः, मातुलुङ्गकः, पूर्णबीजः, छोलङ्गः, बीजकः -जपूर्णः.—(The fruit) जम्बीरफलं.

CITY, *s.* पुरं -री, नगरं -री, पूः *f.* (पुर्), पत्तनं, पृथुपत्तनं, पट्टनं, पट्टं, पुरिः *f.*, कर्व्वटं, ढक्कः, पल्ली, पुटभेदनं, स्थानीयं, निगमः; 'city-gate,' नगरद्वारं, पुरद्वारं; 'city-police,' नगररक्षिपुरुषः.

CITY, *a.* पौरः -री -रं, नागरः -री -रं, -रेयकः -की -कं, नगरस्थः -स्था -स्थं.

CIVET, CIVET-CAT, *s.* गन्धमार्जारः, गन्धोतुः *m.*, खट्टाशः -शी, पूतिशारिजा, कस्तूरीमृगः.

CIVIC, *a.* पौराचारसम्बन्धी -न्धिनी -न्धि (न्) पौरः -री -रं.

CIVIL, *a.* (Relating to the usages of citizens) पुरव्यवहारसम्बन्धी -न्धिनी -न्धि (न्), नगराचारसम्बन्धीयः -या -यं, नीतिसम्बन्धीयः -या -यं, पौरः -री -रं; 'civil war, popular disturbance,' प्रकृतिक्षोभः, विप्लवः.—(Complaisant, gentle) अनुग्राही -हिणी -हि (न्), अनुनयी -यिनी -यि (न्), सानुनयः -या -यं, अनुकूलः -ला -लं, अनुरोधी -धिनी -धि (न्), चाटुकारः -रा, -रं, सुप्रसादः -दा -दं, दक्षिणः -णा -णं.—(Civil in speech) प्रियंवदः -दा -दं, अभिवादकः -का -कं, वन्दारुः -रुः -रु, शक्कुः -क्कुः -क्कु.—(Civilized) सभ्यः -भ्या -भ्यं.

CIVILIAN, *s.* स्मार्त्तः, स्मृतिज्ञः, धर्म्मशास्त्रज्ञः, व्यवहारविधिज्ञः, नीतिज्ञः, नयविद्, व्यवस्थाकुशलः, राजकर्म्मव्यवसायी *m.* (न्), राजव्यापारी *m.* (न्).

CIVILISATION, *s.* सभ्यता, शिष्टता, शिष्टाचारत्वं, आर्य्यवृत्तभावः, सुशीलत्वं.

CIVILITY, *s.* (Politeness) आनन्दनं, अनुग्रहः, अनुरोधः, अनुनयः, अभिनीतिः *f.*, अनुकूलता, अनुवृत्तिः *f.* -वर्त्तनं, सभाजनं, सौजन्यं, प्रश्रयः, सभ्यता, सुशीलता, शिष्टता.

To CIVILIZE, *v. a.* शिष्टाचारान् or आर्य्यव्यवहारान् शिक्ष् in caus. (शिक्षयति -यितुं) or शास् (c. 2. शास्ति, शासितुं).

CIVILIZED, *p. p.* शिष्टः -ष्टा -ष्टं, सभ्यः -भ्या -भ्यं, विनीतः -ता -तं, शिष्टाचारसेवी -विनी -वि (न्), अग्राम्यः -म्या -म्यं, आर्य्यवृत्तः -त्ता -त्तं; 'civilized and rude,' आर्य्या म्लेच्छाश्च.

CIVILLY, *adv.* (Politely) अनुनयेन, आनन्दनपूर्व्वकं, सानुनयं, सुशीलवत्, सानुरोधं.—(In a manner relating to civil government) नीतिविद्यानुसारात्, पौरव्यवहारानुसारेण.

CLACK, *s.* (Incessant chattering) जल्पः -ल्पनं, वावदूकता, अतिशयजल्पः, वाक्चापल्यं, चटचटशब्दः, झम्झनं.—(Bell of a mill) पेषणीघण्टा.

To CLACK, *v. n.* अतिशयेन जल्प् (c. 1. जल्पति -ल्पितुं), पेषणीघण्टारूपेण शब्दं कृ, चटचटशब्दं कृ.

CLAD, *a.* आच्छादितः -ता -तं, प्रच्छादितः -ता -तं, वस्त्रवेष्टितः -ता -तं, वस्त्रान्वितः -ता -तं, परिहितः -ता -तं, प्रावृतः -ता -तं, आवृतः -ता -तं, परिच्छन्नः -न्ना -न्नं, पिनद्धः -द्धा -द्धं, संवीतः -ता -तं, अनग्नः -ग्ना -ग्नं, सवासाः -साः -सः (स्), सचेलः -ला -लं; 'lightly clad,' लघुवासाः -साः -सः (स्).

To CLAIM, *v. a.* स्वीकृ, अङ्गीकृ; याच् (c. 1. याचति -चितुं), प्रार्थ् (c. 10. प्रार्थयति -ते -यितुं), ममेति उक्त्वा ग्रह् (c. 9. गृह्णाति, ग्रहीतुं), मह्यं दातव्यमिति ज्ञापयित्वा ग्रह्; अभिमानं कृ; as, 'to claim money,' धनाभिमानं कृ; ममेति वद् (c. 1. वदति -दितुं), मदीयमिति or स्वीयमिति वद्, स्वाधिकारं or स्वस्वत्वं ज्ञा in caus. (ज्ञापयति -यितुं).—(To set up a claim) अङ्गीकृ.—(To have a claim to) अर्ह् (c. 1. अर्हति -ते -र्हितुं).

CLAIM, *s.* अधिकारः, अभियोगः, अभिमानं, याञ्चा, अभ्यर्थना, प्रार्थना; 'false claim,' मिथ्याभियोगः; 'claim laid to learning,' विद्याभिमानं.

CLAIMABLE, *a.* अभियोक्तव्यः -व्या -व्यं, याचनीयः -या -यं, प्रार्थनीयः -या -यं.

CLAIMANT, *s.* अभियोक्ता *m.* (क्तृ), अर्थी *m.* (न्), अधिकारी *m.* (न्), याचिता *m.* (तृ), प्रार्थयिता *m.* (तृ).

CLAIMED, *p. p.* अधिकृतः -ता -तं, याचितः -ता -तं, प्रार्थितः -ता -तं, अभियुक्तः -क्ता -क्तं, प्रख्यातः -ता -तं, मार्गितः -ता -तं.

CLAIR-OBSCURE, *s.* चित्रकर्म्मणि नानाछायाविन्यासविद्या.

To CLAM, *v. a.* (To clog with glutinous matter) श्यै in caus. (श्यापयति -यितुं), श्यानीकृ, सान्द्रीकृ.

To CLAMBER, *v. a.* पाणिपादेन or करचरणाभ्यां दुरारोहस्थानम् आयासेन आरुह् (c. 1. -रोहति -रोढुं) or अध्यारुह्.

CLAMBERING, *s.* पाणिपादेन विषमस्थानारोहणं, आयासेनारोहणं.

CLAMMINESS, *s.* श्यानता, शीनता, सान्द्रता, घनत्वं, अनुलग्नशीलत्वं.

CLAMMY, *a.* श्यानः -ना -नं, शीनः -ना -नं, सान्द्रः -न्द्रा -न्द्रं, घनः -ना -नं. अनुलग्नशीलः -ला -लं, संलग्नशीलः -ला -लं, आर्द्रः -र्द्रा -र्द्रं.

CLAMOUR, *s.* घोषणं -णा, उत्क्रोशः, कलकलः, संहूतिः *f.*, जनरवः, उच्चैर्घुष्टं,

उच्चैःस्वरः, रासः, बहुभिः कृता संहूतिः, प्रक्ष्वेडनं.

To CLAMOUR, *v. n.* उच्चैर् घुष् (c. 10. घोषयति -यितुं), उद्घुष्, उत्क्रुश् (c. 1. -क्रोशति -क्रोष्टुं), प्रक्ष्विड् (c. 1. -क्ष्वेडति -डितुं).

CLAMOUROUS, *a.* घोषकरः -री -रं, घोषणः -णा -णं, उच्चैःस्वरकारी -रिणी -रि (न्), तुमुलकारी &c., मुखरः -रा -रं, महास्वनः -ना -नं, बहुघोषः -षा -षं, अनल्पघोषः -षा -षं, प्रक्ष्वेडितः -ता -तं, प्रक्ष्वेडितवान् -वती -वत् (त्).

CLAMP, *s.* (A piece of iron for joining stones) शिलाद्वयसम्बन्धनार्थं कीलः.—(A quantity of brick) इष्टकाराशिः *f.*

To CLAMP, *v. a.* पाषाणद्वयं or काष्ठद्वयं कीलेन सम्बन्ध् (c. 9. -बध्नाति -बन्द्धुं).

CLAN, *s.* कुलं, वंशः, गोत्रं, सन्तानः, वर्णः, वर्गः, जातिः *f.*, कुटुम्बः, पंक्तिः *f.*, मण्डलं, सङ्घः, संसर्गः, शाखा.

CLANDESTINE, *a.* निभृतः -ता -तं, गुप्तः -प्ता -प्तं, गूढः -ढा -ढं, रहस्यः -स्या -स्यं, छन्नः -न्ना -न्नं, प्रच्छन्नः -न्ना -न्नं, निह्नुतः -ता -तं, अप्रकाशः -शा -शं, छलेन कृतः -ता -तं; 'a clandestine marriage,' चौरिकाविवाहः.

CLANDESTINELY, *adv.* निभृतं, रहः (स्), रहसि, रहस्यं, गुप्तं, छलेन, प्रच्छन्नं, निह्नवेन, अप्रकाशं.

CLANG or CLANGOUR, *s.* घुष्टं, तुमुलं, झम्झा, कः.—(Of arms) शस्त्रघोषः.

To CLANG, *v. n.* शिञ्ज् (c. 2. शिंक्ते, c. 1. शिञ्जते -ञ्जितुं), विशिञ्ज्, क्वण् (c. 1. क्वणति -णितुं), ध्वन् (c. 1. ध्वनति -नितुं), प्रक्ष्वेड् (c. 1. -क्ष्वेडति -डितुं), झम्झा (nom. झम्झायते).

CLANGOUS, *a.* घोषणः -णा -णं, तुमुलकरः -री -रं, शस्त्रघुष्टकरः -री -रं.

CLANK, *s.* शिञ्जितं, क्वणितं, घुष्टं, झम्झनं, झम्झा, प्रक्ष्वेडनं.

To CLAP, *v. a.* (Strike together suddenly) अकस्मात् संहन् (c. 2. -हन्ति -हन्तुं) or सङ्घट्ट् (c. 10. -घट्टयति -यितुं), आस्फल् in caus. (-स्फालयति -यितुं).—(The hands, arms) तालं कृ, करतालं कृ, आस्फुट् (c. 10. -स्फोटयति -यितुं).—(The wings) पक्षौ उत्क्षिप् (c. 6. -क्षिपति -क्षेप्तुं).—(To applaud) करतालेन प्रशंस् (c. 1. -शंसति -शंसितुं).—(To apply suddenly) अकस्मात् प्रविश् in caus. (-वेशयति -यितुं) or ऋ in caus. (अर्पयति -यितुं) or न्यस् (c. 4. -अस्यति -असितुं).

CLAP, *s.* स्तनितं, आस्फोटनं, ध्वनितं, क्वणितं, सङ्घट्टशब्दः.—(Of thunder) मेघनादः, मेघस्तनितं, वज्रनिर्घोषः, वज्रनिष्पेषः, स्फूर्जथुः *m.*—(Of the hand) तालः.—(Applause) करतालेन प्रशंसा, प्रशंसाशब्दः, अनुरागजः शब्दः.

CLAPPER, *s.* (Of a bell) घण्टालोला, घण्टावादकः, नादनः.—(Applauder) करतालेन प्रसादकारी *m.* (न्).

CLARET, *s.* प्रसन्नमद्यं, प्रसन्नेरा, रक्तवर्णः स्वच्छमद्यविशेषः.

CLARIFICATION, *s.* प्रसादनं, विशोधनं, पावनं, पवित्रीकरणं, मलापकर्षणं.

To CLARIFY, *v. a.* शुध् in caus. (शोधयति -यितुं), परिशुध्, विशुध्, संशुध्, पू (c. 9. पुनाति -नीते, पवितुं), परिपू, विपू; पवित्रीकृ, विमल (nom. विमलयति -यितुं).

To CLARIFY, *v. n.* प्रसद् (c. 6. -सीदति -सत्तुं), पवित्रीभू, विमलीभू.

CLARINET, *s.* वेणुः *m.*, वंशः, विवरनालिका, उदात्तस्वरो वेणुभेदः.

CLARION, *s.* शुषिरवाद्यविशेषः, तूर्य्यं, शङ्खः.

CLARITY, *s.* प्रसन्नता, स्वच्छता, कान्तिः *f.*, द्युतिः *f.*, दीप्तिः *f.*

To CLASH, *v. n.* सङ्घट्ट् (c. 1. -घट्टते -ट्टितुं), परस्परसमाघातं कृ, परस्परसङ्घट्टप्रयुक्तं झम्झाशब्दं कृ or झम्झा (nom. झम्झायते).—(To contradict, disagree) विवद् (c. 1. -वदते -दितुं), विप्रवद्, विसंवद्, परस्परम् विरुध् (c. 7. -रुणद्धि -रोद्धुं).

CLASH, *s.* समाघातः, सङ्घट्टः -ट्टनं, सङ्कुष्टः, कः, झम्झनं, क्वणितं, घर्घरः.—(Contradiction) वचनविरोधः, प्रतीपवचनं, विसंवादः.

CLASHING, *a.* (Contradictory) परस्परपराहतः -ता -तं, परस्परविरोधी -धिनी -धि (न्), विवदमानः -ना -नं, विरुद्धार्थः -र्था -र्थं.

CLASP, *s.* (Embrace) आलिङ्गनं -ङ्गितं, परिष्वङ्गः, आश्लेषः, संश्लेषः, परिरम्भः, उपगूढं, अङ्कः, अङ्कपाली.—(Hook, buckle) कुडुपः.

To CLASP, *v. a.* (Shut with a clasp) कुडुपेन बन्ध् (c. 9. बध्नाति, बन्द्धुं) or पिनह् (c. 4. -नह्यति -नद्धुं).—(Embrace) आलिङ्ग् (c. 1. -लिङ्गति -ङ्गितुं), समालिङ्ग्; आश्लिष् (c. 4. -श्लिष्यति -श्लेष्टुं), संश्लिष्, पीड् (c. 10. पीडयति -यितुं), स्वञ्ज् (c. 1. स्वजते, स्वंक्तुं), परिष्वञ्ज्, सम्परिष्वञ्ज्, उपगुह् (c. 1. -गूहति -गूहितुं), परिरभ् (c. 1. -रभते -रब्धुं), क्रोडीकृ.—(Enclose round) परिवेष्ट् (c. 1. -वेष्टते -ष्टितुं).—(Clasp the hands) हस्तौ बन्ध् or संहन् (c. 2. -हन्ति -हन्तुं), अञ्जलिं बन्ध् or संश्लिष्.

CLASPED, *p. p.* आलिङ्गितः -ता -तं, श्लिष्टः -ष्टा -ष्टं, आश्लिष्टः -ष्टा -ष्टं, संश्लिष्टः -ष्टा -ष्टं, परिरब्धः -ब्धा -ब्धं, परिष्वक्तः -क्ता -क्तं, परिमृष्टः -ष्टा -ष्टं, उपगूढः -ढा -ढं, पीडितः -ता -तं, पिष्टः -ष्टा -ष्टं, क्रोडीकृतः -ता -तं; 'with hands clasped,' बद्धाञ्जलिः -लिः -लि, कृताञ्जलिः -लिः -लि.—(Clasped in the arms) भुजापीडितः -ता -तं.

CLASPER, *s.* लताभूजः, वृक्षादिपरिवेष्टनशीलः लताविटपः.

CLASP-KNIFE, *s.* वारङ्गमध्ये निवेशयितुं शक्या छुरिका.

CLASS, *s.* (A rank or order of persons) वर्णः, वर्गः, पदं, आश्रमः, जातिः *f.*—(A set of things or beings) गणः, पंक्तिः *f.*, श्रेणी, संसर्गः, समूहः, गोत्रं; 'class of verbs,' गणः.—(A number of scholars) सहाध्यायिनां पंक्तिः, छात्रसमूहः; 'the lower classes,' अवरवर्णाः *m. pl.*, अन्त्यजातीयाः *m. pl.*

To CLASS or CLASSIFY, *v. a.* वर्णक्रमेण or यथावर्गं विरच् (c. 10. -रचयति -यितुं), or व्यस् (c. 4. -अस्यति -असितुं) or ग्रन्थ् (c. 1. ग्रन्थति, ग्रन्थितुं), गणीकृ, वर्गीकृ.

CLASSED or CLASSIFIED, *p. p.* गणीभूतः -ता -तं, वर्गीभूतः -ता -तं, वर्गीयः -या -यं, ग्रथितः -ता -तं, वर्गक्रमेण विन्यस्तः -स्ता -स्तं or व्यूढः -ढा -ढं.

CLASSICAL, *a.* (Refined) संस्कृतः -ता -तं, साधुः -धुः -ध्वी -धु.—(Of the first rank) प्रथमवर्गीयः -या -यं, श्रेष्ठः -ष्ठा -ष्ठं, प्रथमपदस्थः -स्था -स्थं. (Relating to ancient books) पूर्व्वकालीनग्रन्थसम्बन्धी -न्धिनी -न्धि (न्).

CLASSIFICATION, *s.* गणीकरणं, गणना, वर्गक्रमेण विन्यासः, प्रतिविधानं.

CLASSIFIER, *s.* गणकारः, व्यासः; 'of words,' पदसङ्घातः.

CLASSICK, *s.* ग्रन्थकर्त्तॄणां मध्ये श्रेष्ठः, पूर्व्वकालीनग्रन्थकारः.

To CLATTER, *v. n.* क्वण् (c. 1. क्वणति -णितुं), ध्वन् (c. 1. ध्वनति -नितुं), झम्झनं कृ, झम्झा (nom. झम्झायते), चटचट (nom. चटचटायते).—(To talk idly) जल्प् (c. 1. जल्पति -ल्पितुं).

CLATTER, *s.* क्वणितं, स्तनितं, ध्वनितं, तुमुलं, कः, झम्झनं, चटचट *ind.*

CLAVATED, *a.* ग्रन्थिलः -ला -लं, पिण्डी -ण्डिनी -ण्डि (न्), गण्डवान् -वती -वत् (त्).

CLAUDICATION, *s.* (Lameness) पङ्गुता, खञ्जत्वं, गतिवैकल्यं.

CLAVICLE, *s.* जत्रु *n.*, ग्रीवास्थि *n.*, कण्ठास्थि *n.*

CLAUSE, *s.* (Division of a subject) पदं, स्थानं, मार्गः, अधिकरणं, अङ्गं, शाखा.—(Sentence) वाक्यं.—(Particular stipulation) नियमपत्राङ्गं, नियमः.

CLAUSTRAL, *a.* मठसम्बन्धी -न्धिनी -न्धि (न्), विहारसम्बन्धी &c.

CLAW, *s.* नखः, नखरः, करजः, कररुहः, पाणिः *m.*, अर्द्धचन्द्रः, अर्द्धेन्दुः.

To CLAW, *v. a.* नखेन दॄ (c. 10. दारयति -यितुं) or आहन् (c. 2. -हन्ति -हन्तुं) or लिख् (c. 6. लिखति, लेखितुं), नखाघातं कृ.

CLAWED, *a.* नखी -खिनी -खि (न्), नखवान् -वती -वत् (त्).

CLAY, *s.* पङ्कः, कर्द्दमः, कर्दः, मृत् *f.* (द्), मृत्तिका, जम्बालः, शादः,

निपट्टरः, शिलोञ्छी.

To CLAY, *v. a.* पङ्केन लिप् (c. 6. लिम्पति, लेप्तुं); 'clayed sugar,' शार्करः -र्करः, शुक्ला, सितासखण्डः, सिता, श्वेता.

CLAYEY, CLAYISH, *a.* पङ्की -ङ्किनी -ङ्कि (न्), पङ्किलः -ला -लं, सजम्बालः -ला -लं, मार्त्तिकः -की -कं, कार्द्दमः -मी -मं, मृन्मयः -यी -यं.

CLEAN, *a.* (Free from dirt) विमलः -ला -लं, निर्म्मलः -ला -लं, अमलिनः -ना -नं, पवित्रः -त्रा -त्रं, शुद्धः -द्धा -द्धं, शुचिः -चिः -चि, परिष्कृतः -ता -तं, अकल्कः -ल्का -ल्कं, अकल्मषः -षा -षं, वीध्रः -ध्रा -ध्रं; 'having a clean face,' शुचिमुखः -खी -खं; 'having clean clothes,' शुद्धवासाः -साः -सः (स्); 'ceremonially clean,' स्पृश्यः -श्या -श्यं.—(Guiltless, innocent) शुचिः -चिः -चि, शुद्धमतिः -तिः -ति, अनघः -घा -घं, विमलात्मा -त्मा -त्म (न्).—(Neat, smooth) श्लक्ष्णः -क्ष्णा -क्ष्णं; 'having a clean figure,' तनुमध्यमः -मा -मं.

CLEAN, *adv.* अशेषतस्, अखिलेन, साकल्येन, सम्यक्, आमूलं.

To CLEAN, *v. a.* शुध् in caus. (शोधयति -यितुं), परिशुध्, पू (c. 9. पुनाति, पवितुं), पवित्रीकृ, धाव् (c. 10. धावयति -यितुं), प्रक्षल् (c. 10. -क्षालयति -यितुं), मृज् (c. 2. मार्ष्टि, मार्ष्टुं), शुचीकृ, परिष्कृ; 'to clean the teeth,' दन्तान् धाव् or शुध्.

CLEANED, *p. p.* शोधितः -ता -तं, पवित्रीकृतः -ता -तं, पूतः -ता -तं, क्षालितः -ता -तं, प्रक्षालितः -ता -तं, विगतकल्मषः -षा -षं.

CLEANING, *s.* शोधनं, प्रक्षालनं, मार्ज्जनं, पवः, निष्पावः, पावनं, विशोधित्वं, मार्ष्टिः *f.*, मृजा, मार्ज्जना *f.*—(Cleaning the teeth) दन्तशुद्धिः *f.*, दन्तधावनं.

CLEANLINESS, *s.* शुद्धता, शुद्धिः *f.*, पवित्रत्वं, शुचिता, शौचं, परिष्कृतिः *f.*, मार्ष्टिः *f.*; 'neatness,' विनीतता.

CLEANLY, *a.* पवित्रशरीरः -रा -रं or शुचिशरीरः, शुद्धदेहः -हा -हं, मृष्टकायः -या -यं, निर्म्मलः -ला -लं, विनीतः -ता -तं; 'in dress,' शुद्धवासाः -साः -सः (स्).

CLEANLY, *adv.* शुचि, पवित्रं, निर्म्मलं, विनीतं, शुद्धप्रकारेण.

CLEANNESS, *s.* शुचिता, शौचं, निर्म्मलत्वं, वैमल्यं, शुद्धत्वं, शुद्धिः *f.*, विशुद्धिः *f.*, परिष्कारः, वैशद्यं, अकल्कता.—(Innocence) शुद्धिः *f.*

To CLEANSE, *v. a.* शुध् in caus. (शोधयति -यितुं), परिशुध्, विशुध्, संशुध्, पू (c. 9. पुनाति -नीते, पवितुं), परिपू, विपू, प्रक्षल् (c. 10. -क्षालयति -यितुं), धाव् in caus. (धावयति -यितुं), प्रधाव्, निर्णिज् (c. 3. -नेनेक्ति -नेक्तुं), मृज् (c. 1. मार्ज्जति, c. 2. मार्ष्टि, मार्ष्टुं), सम्मृज्, पवित्रीकृ, शुचीकृ, परिष्कृ.—(From dust) नीरजीकृ.

CLEANSED, *p. p.* पूतः -ता -तं, पवित्रः -त्रा -त्रं, पवित्रितः -ता -तं, शोधितः -ता -तं, मार्ज्जितः -ता -तं, प्रक्षालितः -ता -तं, निर्णिक्तः -क्ता -क्तं, मृष्टः -ष्टा -ष्टं, परिष्कृतः -ता -तं, अनवस्करः -रा -रं, धौतः -ता -तं, निर्धौतः -ता -तं, शुचीकृतः -ता -तं, पवित्रीकृतः -ता -तं, निःशोध्यः -ध्या -ध्यं.

CLEANSER, *s.* प्रक्षालकः, निर्णेजकः, शोधकः, सम्मार्ज्जकः, पावकः.

CLEANSING, *s.* शोधनं, शुद्धिः *f.*, पावनं, मार्ष्टिः *f.*, मार्ज्जनं, प्रक्षालनं, निर्णेकः, मलापकर्षणं.

CLEAR, *a.* (Bright, transparent) प्रसन्नः -न्ना -न्नं, विशदः -दा -दं, विमलः -ला -लं, निर्म्मलः -ला -लं, अमलः -ला -लं -लिनः -ना -नं, अच्छः -च्छा -च्छं, स्वच्छः -च्छा -च्छं, शुद्धः -द्धा -द्धं or विशुद्धः, स्फटिकप्रभः -भा -भं, दीप्रः -प्रा -प्रं.—(Serene, as the sky) वितिमिरः -रा -रं, अनभः -भा -भं, निरभ्रः -भ्रा -भ्रं, व्यभ्रः -भ्रा -भ्रं, गततोयदः -दा -दं; 'as the mind,' प्रसन्नः -न्ना -न्नं.—(Indubitable) निःसन्देहः -हा -हं.—(Evident) व्यक्तः -क्ता -क्तं or प्रव्यक्तः or अभिव्यक्तः, स्पष्टः -ष्टा -ष्टं, स्फुटः -टा -टं, प्रत्यक्षः -क्षा -क्षं, सुप्रकाशः -शा -शं.—(Intelligible, perspicuous) स्पष्टार्थः -र्था -र्थं, भिन्नार्थः -र्था -र्थं, सुगम्यः -म्या -म्यं, सुग्राह्यः -ह्या -ह्यं.—(A clear understanding) विशुद्धबुद्धिः, शुद्धधीः.—(Innocent) शुद्धः -द्धा -द्धं, शुचिः -चिः -चि, अदृष्टदोषः -षा -षं.—(Out of debt) अनृणः -णा -णं.—(Sounding distinctly) पटुस्वरः -रा -रं, उच्चैःस्वरः -रा -रं.—(Open, free from trees, &c.) तरुगुल्मविविक्तः -क्ता -क्तं, निष्कण्टकः -का -कं, निर्वनः -ना -नं; 'a clear space,' विविक्तता.—(Entire, free from deductions) अशेषः -षा -षं, निरवशेषः -षा -षं, अभग्नः -ग्ना -ग्नं, निरुद्धारः -रा -रं.—(Unobstructed) असम्बाधः -धा -धं, निर्विघ्नः -घ्ना -घ्नं.

To CLEAR, *v. a.* (Make bright or clean) शुध् in caus. (शोधयति -यितुं), प्रसद् in caus. (-सादयति -यितुं), प्रसन्नीकृ, निर्म्मलीकृ, विमल (nom. विमलयति -यितुं), मृज् (c. 2. मार्ष्टि, मार्ष्टुं).—(Explain) व्याख्या (c. 2. -ख्याति -ख्यातुं), स्पष्टीकृ, व्यक्तीकृ, प्रत्यक्षीकृ, सम्बुध् in caus. (-बोधयति -यितुं), परिशुध् in caus.—(Liquidate) शुध् in caus., संशुध्, अपाकृ, विनी (c. 1. -नयते -ति -नेतुं).—(Clear a doubt) संशयम् अपनी.—(Free from incumbrances, &c.) विशुध् in caus., मुच् (c. 6. मुञ्चति, मोक्तुं), विघ्नान् विनी or हृ (c. 1. हरति, हर्तुं) or नश् in caus. (नाशयति -यितुं), निर्विघ्नं -घ्नां -घ्नं कृ, निष्कण्टकं -कां -कं कृ.—(Gain) निरवशेषं लभ् (c. 1. लभते, लब्धुं) or आप् (c. 5. -आप्नोति -आप्तुं).—(Justify) परिशुध् in caus., विशुध् in caus.; 'he clears himself,' आत्मानं निर्दोषं करोति.—(Clear the throat) उत्कासनं कृ.—(Purge) रिच् (c. 7. रिणक्ति, रेक्तुं), विरिच्.

To CLEAR, *v. n.* (Grow bright) विमलीभू, शुचि (nom. शुचीयते); 'as the weather,' निरभ्रीभू, गततोयदीभू.

CLEARANCE or CLEARING, *s.* शुद्धिः *f.*, विशुद्धिः *f.*, शोधनं, विशोधित्वं; 'clearance of a debt,' ऋणशोधनं, ऋणापाकरणं; 'of a grudge,' वैरशोधनं.—(Certificate from the custom-house) शुल्काध्यक्ष-सकाशात् शोधनपत्रं.

CLEARED, *p. p.* शोधितः -ता -तं, प्रसादितः -ता -तं, निर्म्मलीकृतः -ता -तं, रेचितः -ता -तं; 'as the weather,' गततोयदः -दा -दं.

CLEARER, *s.* शोधकः, प्रसादनः; 'of obstacles,' विघ्ननाशकः, विघ्नविनायकः.

CLEARLY, *adv.* (Plainly, evidently) व्यक्तं, सुव्यक्तं, स्पष्टं, प्रत्यक्षतस्, प्रत्यक्षेण, स्फुटं, स्पष्टरूपेण.—(Intelligibly) स्पष्टार्थं, भिन्नार्थं.—(Brightly) विमलं, प्रसन्नं, विशदं.—(Candidly) सरलं, दाक्षिण्येन.

CLEARNESS, *s.* (Brightness, transparency) प्रसादः, प्रसन्नता, निर्म्मल्यं, निर्म्मलत्वं, वैमल्यं, नैर्म्मल्यं, शुद्धत्वं, शुद्धिः *f.*, स्वच्छता, वैशद्यं, दीप्तिः *f.*, प्रभा.—(Distinctness, plainness) स्पष्टता, व्यक्तत्वं, प्रत्यक्षत्वं, स्फुटता, भिन्नार्थत्वं.

CLEAR-SIGHTED, *a.* विवेकदृश्वा -श्वा -श्व (न्), शुद्धदृष्टिः -ष्टिः -ष्टि, शुद्धधीः -धीः -धि, तीक्ष्णदृष्टिः -ष्टिः -ष्टि, दूरदर्शी -र्शिनी -र्शि (न्), मर्म्मज्ञः -ज्ञा -ज्ञं.

CLEAR-SIGHTEDNESS, *s.* शुद्धदृष्टिः *f.*, विवेकदृश्वत्वं, तीक्ष्णदृष्टिः *f.*, दूरदृष्टिः.

To CLEAR-STARCH, *v. a.* गोधूमसम्भवादिसान्द्रद्रव्यप्रक्षेपेण वस्त्रादि धावयित्वा स्तब्धीकृ or दृढीकृ.

CLEAR-STARCHER, *s.* गोधूमसम्भवादिसान्द्रद्रव्यप्रक्षेपेण वस्त्रधावकः.

CLEAR-STARCHING, *s.* पूर्व्वोक्तसान्द्रद्रव्यप्रक्षेपेण वस्त्रधावनं.

To CLEAVE, *v. n.* (To adhere) सञ्ज् in pass. (सज्यते or सज्जते), अनुषञ्ज्, आसञ्ज्, संसञ्ज्, अनुबन्ध् (c. 9. -बध्नाति -बन्द्धुं), संयुज् in pass. (-युज्यते), संलग्नीभू, अनुलग्नीभू.—(Divide in two parts) स्फुट् (c. 1. स्फोटति, c. 6. स्फुटति -टितुं), दल् (c. 1. दलति -लितुं), विदल्; विद्ृ in pass. (-दीर्य्यते), भिद् in pass. (भिद्यते), फल् (c. 1. फलति -लितुं).

To CLEAVE, *v. a.* (To divide with violence) भिद् (c. 7. भिनत्ति,

भिन्ने, भेत्तुं), विभिद्, निर्भिद्, or in caus. (भेदयति -यितुं), पट् (c. 10. पाटयति -यितुं), विपट्, दृ (c. 9. दृणाति, दरितुं -रीतुं or in caus. दारयति -यितुं), विदृ, अवदृ, दल् in caus. (दालयति, दलयति -यितुं), विदल्, विदलीकृ.

Cleaver, s. (One who cleaves) भेत्ता m. (त्तृ), भेदकः, दारकः.—(A chopping-knife) मांसच्छेदनार्थं छुरिका, मांसभेदी m. (न्), मांसभिद् f., छिदिः f.

Clef, s. (In music) गन्धर्व्वविद्यायां वाद्यसूचनार्थं चिह्नं.

Cleft, s. दरी -रा, टङ्कः, सन्धिः m., भेदः, विदीर्णं.

Cleft or cloven, a. भिन्नः -न्ना -न्नं, विभिन्नः -न्ना -न्नं, विदारितः -ता -तं, विदीर्णः -र्णा -र्णं, विदलितः -ता -तं, विदलः -ला -लं -लीकृतः -ता -तं, दलितः -ता -तं.

Clemency, s. कृपा, दया, क्षमा, कारुण्यं, अनुकम्पा, अनुक्रोशः, घृणा, प्रसादः, दयालुता.

Clement, a दयालुः -लुः -लु, कृपालुः -लुः -लु, दयाशीलः -ला -लं, वत्सलः -ला -लं, मृदुः -द्वी -दु, कारुणिकः -की -कं, सानुकम्पः -म्पा -म्पं, करुणार्द्रः -र्द्रा -र्द्रं, हृदयालुः -लुः -लु.

Clench. See Clinch.

Clergy, s. पौरोहित्यं, पुरोहितवर्गः, पुरोहितसमूहः, धर्म्माध्यापकानां समवायः.

Clergyman, s. पुरोहितः, धर्म्माध्यापकः, धर्म्मोपदेशकः, धर्म्मप्रचारकः, धर्म्मप्रदर्शकः, धर्म्मप्रवक्ता m. (क्तृ), याजकः.

Clerical, a. पौरोहितः -ती -तं, याजकीयः -या -यं, धर्म्मोपदेशविषयः -या -यं, पौरोहित्यसम्बन्धी -न्धिनी -न्धि (न्).

Clerk, s. (Man employed as a writer) कायस्थः, लेखकः, लिपिकरः, मसिपण्यः.—(Accountant) गणनाध्यक्षः.—(Scholar) विद्वान् m. (स्), पण्डितः, कृतविद्यः, ज्ञानी m. (न्).—(Clergyman) पुरोहितः, धर्म्माध्यापकः.—(Assistant of a clergyman) उपपुरोहितः, पुरोहितसहायः.

Clerkship, s. कायस्थता, कायस्थ्यं, कायस्थकर्म्म n. (न्).—(Scholarship) पाण्डित्यं.

Clever, a. चतुरः -रा -रं, पटुः -टुः -ट्वी -टु, दक्षः -क्षा -क्षं, अभिज्ञः -ज्ञा -ज्ञं, विचक्षणः -णा -णं, निपुणः -णा -णं, निपुणमतिः -तिः -ति, कुशलः -ला -लं, वैज्ञानिकः -की -कं, सुप्रयोगवान् -वती -वत् (त्), योग्यः -ग्या -ग्यं, दक्षः -क्षा -क्षं, विशारदः -दा -दं, पेशलः -ला -लं, विपश्चित् m. f. n., पण्डितः -ता -तं, कृती -तिनी -ति (न्), विदग्धः -ग्धा -ग्धं, प्रवीणः -णा -णं, कल्याणबुद्धिः -द्धिः -द्धि.

Cleverly, adv. चतुरं, चातुर्य्येण, सपाटवं, निपुणं, दाक्ष्येण.

Cleverness, s. चातुर्य्यं, चतुरता, नैपुण्यं, कुशलता, कौशल्यं, पटुत्वं, पाटवं, दाक्ष्यं, दाक्षिण्यं, प्रवीणता, प्रावीण्यं, सुप्रयोगता, वैचक्षण्यं, विदग्धता, वैदग्ध्यं, योग्यता, मतिप्रकर्षः, निर्देष्टा m. (ष्टृ), उद्देशकः.

Clew or clue, s. (A ball of thread) सूत्रकोषः -षं.—(A guide) सूत्रं, गहनमार्गनिर्गमोपायः, दर्शकः.

To clew, v. a. रज्जुद्वारेण नौकावसनम् उन्नम् (c. 1. -नमति -नन्तुं, c. 10. -नामयति -यितुं) यदनन्तरं वसनसंवरणं कर्त्तुं शक्यते.

To click, v. n. टँ टँ पट् पट् कट् कट् चित् चित् इत्यादिशब्दान् कृ, पटपट (nom. पटपटायते).

Client, s. (Dependent) आश्रितः, संश्रितः, अधीनः, आयत्तः, उपजीवी m. (न्), भाक्तिकः, अनुगतः, प्रत्याशी m. (न्).—(One who applies to an advocate for counsel) स्वार्थनिर्व्वाहणहेतोर् व्यवहारसचिवसंश्रितः.

Clientship, s. अधीनता, आयत्तत्वं, व्यवहारसचिवसंश्रितस्य दशा.

Cliff, s. प्रपातः, दरद् f., पातुकः, विषमं, अतटः, भृगुः m., समुद्रवेलायां पातुकभूमिः.

Climacter or climacteric, s. शरीरविकारपरिणामो विशेषवत्सरपर्य्यायः, शरीरविकाराणां वर्षचक्रं.

Climate or clime, s. (A region) देशः, प्रदेशः, दिक् f. (श्), राष्ट्रं, आशा.—(Temperature) जलवायुः, जलाकाशः, व्योम n. (न्), आकाशः, वायुगुणः.

Climax, s. सारं, क्रमशो वृद्धिः f., ऊर्द्ध्वगमनं, उत्तरोत्तरवृद्धिः f.

To climb, v. a. आयासेन आरुह् (c. 1. -रोहति -रोढुं), अध्यारुह्, अभिरुह्; अधिक्रम् (c. 1. -क्रामति -क्रमितुं) or अवस्कन्द् (c. 1. -स्कन्दति -स्कन्तुं).

To climb, v. n. ऊर्द्ध्वं or उच्चैः or उपरि गम् (c. 1. -गच्छति -गन्तुं).

Climber, s. आरोही m. (न्), अधिरोही m. (न्), आरोढा m. (ढृ).—(Plant) वल्लिः f.

Clime, s. (Region) देशः, प्रदेशः.—(Temperature) जलवायुः m., जलाकाशः.

To clinch or clench, v. a. (Grasp) दृढमुष्टिना सङ्ग्रह् (c. 9. -गृह्णाति -ग्रहीतुं) or धृ (c. 1. धरति, धर्त्तुं), मुष्टिसङ्ग्राहेण पीड् (c. 10. पीडयति -यितुं); 'to clinch the fist,' मुष्टिं बन्ध् (c. 9. बध्नाति, बन्द्धुं), मुष्टिबन्धं or -सङ्ग्राहं कृ.—(Confirm) दृढीकृ, स्थिरीकृ, दृढप्रमाणं दा (c. 3. ददाति, दातुं).—(Fix the point of a nail on the other side) कीलाग्रं पराग् आवर्त्य विपरीतभागे निखन् (c. 1. -खनति -निखनितुं).

Clinch, s. (A pun) द्व्यर्थवाक्यं, श्लेषवाक्यं, श्लेषः.

Clincher, s. (A hold-fast) बन्धनकीलः, कीलकः, बन्धनी -ना.

To cling, v. n. अवलम्ब् (c. 1. -लम्बते -म्बितुं), समालम्ब्, संलग्नीभू, अनुलग्नीभू, अनुबन्ध् (c. 9. -बध्नाति -बन्द्धुं or in pass. -बध्यते), सञ्ज् in pass. (सज्यते or सज्जते), अनुषञ्ज्, आसञ्ज्, प्रसञ्ज्, संसञ्ज्, ली (c. 4. लीयते, लेतुं); 'clinging to the neck,' कण्ठलग्नः -ग्ना -ग्नं.

Clingy, a. अनुलग्नशीलः -ला -लं, संलग्नशीलः -ला -लं, अनुषक्तिकः -की -कं.

Clinic or clinical, a. अचिकित्स्यरोगोपहतत्वात् शयनात् समुत्थातुम् अक्षमः, शय्यागतः; 'clinical lecture,' दुश्चिकित्स्यव्याधिग्रस्तस्य शयनोपान्ते चिकित्साविद्यार्थिनां रोगोपचारोपदेशः.

To clink, v. n. शिञ्ज् (c. 2. शिङ्क्ते, c. 1. शिञ्जते -ञ्जितुं), विशिञ्ज्, क्वण् (c. 1. क्वणति -णितुं), किङ्किण (nom. किङ्किणायते), विरु (c. 2. -रौति -रवितुं).

Clink, s. शिञ्जितं, आशिञ्जितं, क्वणितं, किङ्किणीशब्दः, घर्घरारवः.

Clinquant, a. हेमरत्नभूषितः -ता -तं, अलङ्कारिष्णुः -ष्णुः -ष्णु.

To clip, v. a. (Embrace, hug) गाढम् आलिङ्ग् (c. 1. -लिङ्गति -ङ्गितुं), बाहुभ्यां परिष्वञ्ज् (c. 1. -ष्वजते -ष्वंक्तुं) or उपगुह् (c. 1. -गूहति -गूहितुं).—(Shear) आवप् in caus. (-वापयति -यितुं), परिवप्, मुण्ड् (c. 1. मुण्डति -ण्डितुं).—(Cut off) छिद् (c. 7. छिनत्ति, छेत्तुं), लू (c. 9. लुनाति, लवितुं), निकृत् (c. 6. -कृन्तति -कर्त्तितुं).—(Shorten) ह्रस् in caus. (ह्रासयति -यितुं), संहृ (c. 1. -हरति -हर्त्तुं).

Clipped, p. p. छिन्नः -न्ना -न्नं, लूनः -ना -नं, क्लृप्तः -प्ता -प्तं, तष्टः -ष्टा -ष्टं, परिवापितः -ता -तं, कृतवापः -पा -पं, यमितः -ता -तं.

Clipper, s. (Debaser of coin) वञ्चकः.—(Barber) मुण्डी m. (न्).

Clipping, s. विदलं, छिन्नं, भिन्नं, लूनं, खण्डं.

Clitoris, s. योनिलिङ्गं, भगाङ्कुरः, स्मरछत्रं.

Cloak, s. प्रावारः -रकः, आवारः, पिधानं, प्रच्छदपटः, नीशारः. See Cloke.

To cloak, v. a. प्रावृ (c. 5. -वृणोति -वरितुं -रीतुं), छद् (c. 10. छादयति -यितुं).

Cloak-bag, s. प्रावारादिगात्रीयवस्त्रवाहनार्थं कोषः, वस्त्रकोषः.

Clock, s. घटी, घण्टा, यामघोषा, यामनाली.—(Of a stocking) पादाच्छादनपार्श्वयोः सूचिकर्म्म n. (न्).

Clockmaker, s. घटीकर्त्ता m. (र्त्तृ), घटीकारः, घण्टाकृत्, घण्टाविक्रेता m. (तृ).

Clockmaking, *s.* घटीनिर्म्माणं, यन्त्रकरणं, घटीनिर्म्माणशिल्पं.

Clockwork, *s.* घटीकर्म्म *n.* (न्), घटीक्रिया, सम्बहितकर्म्म, ससञ्चारितकर्म्म.

Clod, *s.* (A lump of earth) लोष्टं -ष्टः -ष्टुः *m.*, मृल्लोष्टं, लेष्टुः *m.*, क्षितिखण्डः, दलनी, दलिः *m.* -ली ; 'clod-crusher,' लोष्टमर्द्दी *m.* (न्).—(A lump of any thing) पिण्डः -ण्डं.

Cloddy, *a.* लोष्टमयः -यी -यं, लोष्टपूर्णः -र्णा -र्णं, मार्त्तिकः -की -कं.

Clodpate, or clodpoll, or clodhopper, *s.* जडः, स्थूलबुद्धिः *m.*, मूढः.

To clog, *v. a.* (To shackle) शृङ्खलया or निगडेन बन्ध् (c. 9. बध्नाति बन्द्धुं), शृङ्खल (nom. शृङ्खलयति -यितुं), पाश (nom. पाशयति -यितुं), पाशीकृ, योक्त्र (nom. योक्त्रयति -यितुं).—(To hinder) संयम् (c. 1. -यच्छति -यन्तुं), यन्त्र् (c. 10. यन्त्रयति -यितुं), विघ्न (nom. विघ्नयति -यितुं), रुध् (c. 7. रुणद्धि, रोद्धुं), प्रतिरुध्, अवरुध् ; प्रतिबन्ध्.

Clog, *s.* (A shackle) शृङ्खला, पादपाशी, पाशः, निगडः, बन्धनं, अनुबन्धः.—(Any hindrance) विघ्नः, अन्तरायः, व्याघातः, प्रतिबन्धः, विष्टम्भः, बाधा, प्रतिरोधः.—(A wooden shoe) काष्ठपादुका, उत्तरपादुका.

Clogged, *p. p.* संयमितचरणः -णा -णं, शृङ्खलितः -ता -तं, सशृङ्खलः -ला -लं, निगडितः -ता -तं, शृङ्खलाबद्धः -द्धा -द्धं, प्रतिरुद्धः -द्धा -द्धं, विघ्नितः -ता -तं.

Cloggy, *a.* प्रतिबन्धकः -का -कं, प्रतिरोधी -धिनी -धि (न्), विघ्नकरः -री -रं.

Cloister, *s.* मठः, विहारः, सन्न्यासिनां मठः, मुनिस्थानं, मुनिशाला, मौनिगृहं.—(Piazza) एकपार्श्वे वायुव्याप्यो विहारयोग्यश् छन्नपथः.

To cloister, *v. a.* सन्न्यासिनां मठे or मुनिशालायां प्रविश् in caus. (-वेशयति -यितुं).

Cloisteral, *a.* मठसम्बन्धी -न्धिनी -न्धि (न्), विविक्तसेवी -विनी -वि (न्).

Cloistered, *a.* मठप्रवेशितः -ता -तं, पूर्व्वोक्तछन्नपथधारी -रिणी -रि (न्).

Cloisterer, *s.* सन्न्यासी *m.* (न्), वानप्रस्थः, मठवासी *m.* (न्), मुनिः *m.* मौनी *m.* (न्).

Cloisteress, *s.* धर्म्मभगिनी, सन्न्यासिनी, धर्म्मचारिणी, मठवासिनी.

Cloke, *s.* प्रावारः, उत्तरीयं, गात्रीयवस्त्रं, आच्छादनवस्त्रं. *See* Cloak.

To close, *v. a.* (Shut) पिधा (c. 3. -दधाति -धातुं), अपिधा, तिरोधा ; संहृ (c. 1. -हरति -हर्त्तुं) ; 'they closed the doors,' द्वाराणि पिदधुः.—(Shut up) निरुध् (c. 7. -रुणद्धि -रोद्धुं).—(Finish) समाप् in caus. (-आपयति -यितुं), अवसो (c. 4. -स्यति -सातुं), निर्वृत् in caus. (-वर्त्तयति -यितुं), साध् (c. 10. साधयति -यितुं), निष्पद् in caus. (-पादयति -यितुं), सम्पद्.—(Close in) परिवेष्ट् (c. 1. -वेष्टते -ष्टितुं).—(Close the eyes) मील् (c. 1. मीलति -लितुं), निमील्, or in caus. (मीलयति -यितुं), निमिष् (c. 6. -मिषति -मेषितुं).—(Close the mouth) मुखं पिधा.—(Close the hands) हस्तौ बन्ध् (c. 9. बध्नाति, बन्द्धुं) or संहन् (c. 2. -हन्ति -हन्तुं), हस्तपुटितं कृ.—(Close a book) पुस्तकं बन्ध्.

To close, *v. n.* (Coalesce) मिल् (c. 6. मिलति, मेलितुं), सम्मिल्, संयुज् in pass. (-युज्यते), संश्लिष् in pass. (-श्लिष्यते), सङ्क्रम् (c. 1. -गच्छति -गन्तुं).—(Close with in fight) बाहूबाहवि or हस्ताहस्ति युध् (c. 4. युध्यते, योद्धुं), बाहुयुद्धे सङ्क्रम्.—(Close with, come to an agreement) सङ्घट्ट् (c. 1. -घट्टते -ट्टितुं), संविदम् उपगम्, संविदा निष्पन्नं कृ, सन्धा (c. 3. -धत्ते -धातुं).—(Come to an end) समाप् in pass. (-आप्यते), निवृत् (c. 1. -वर्त्तते -र्त्तितुं), विरम् (c. 1. -रमते -रन्तुं), निष्पद् in pass. (-पद्यते), विगम् (c. 1. -गच्छति -गन्तुं).

Close, *s.* (Place enclosed) वाटः -टिका, वृतिः *f.*—(Conclusion) अवसानं, अवसायः, सायः, क्षयः, अन्तं, पर्य्यन्तं, शेषः, निर्वृत्तिः *f.*, समाप्तिः *f.*, पर्य्यवसानं, निष्पत्तिः *f.*, अत्ययः, निधनं, सातिः *f.*, विरामः, उपरमः, उपसंहारः ; 'close of day,' दिवसात्ययः, दिवावसानं, सन्ध्याकालः, दिनान्तसमयः, सूर्य्यास्तकालः, सायाह्नः.

Close, *a.* (Shut fast) संवृतः -ता -तं, बद्धः -द्धा -द्धं, दृढबद्धः -द्धा -द्धं.—(Confined, contracted) सङ्कटः -टा -टं, सबाधः -धा -धं, सङ्कुचितः -ता -तं, अविस्तृतः -ता -तं, श्लिष्टः -ष्टा -ष्टं.—(Firm) गाढः -ढा -ढं, दृढः -ढा -ढं.—(Solid, dense, without interstices) घनः -ना -नं, सान्द्रः -न्द्रा -न्द्रं, अविरलः -ला -लं, निरन्तरः -रा -रं -रालः -ला -लं, अनन्तरः -रा -रं, निविडः -डा -डं, दृढसन्धिः -न्धिः -न्धि, निर्विवरः -रा -रं.—(Concise) संक्षिप्तः -प्ता -प्तं, साङ्क्षेपिकः -की -कं.—(Contiguous) समीपः -पा -पं, निकटः -टा -टं, सन्निकृष्टः -ष्टा -ष्टं, आसन्नः -न्ना -न्नं, पार्श्वगतः -ता -तं, पार्श्वस्थः -स्था -स्थं, उपस्थः -स्था -स्थं, उपान्तः -न्ता -न्तं ; 'close to the ear,' कर्णान्तिकः -का -कं, उपकर्णं.—(Intimate, on terms of close friendship) दृढसौहृदः -दी -दं, परिचितः -ता -तं.—(Reserved) वाग्यतः -ता -तं.—(Retired) विविक्तः -क्ता -क्तं.—(Attentive) निविष्टः -ष्टा -ष्टं or अभिनिविष्टः, आसक्तः -क्ता -क्तं, एकाग्रः -ग्रा -ग्रं.—(Without air) निर्वातः -ता -तं.—(Secret) गुप्तः -प्ता -प्तं.—(Niggardly) स्वल्पव्ययी -यिनी -यि (न्), कृपणः -णा -णं ; 'close attendance,' सान्निध्यं ; 'close proximity,' अनन्तरं ; 'close fight,' नियुद्धं, बाहुयुद्धं, रणसङ्कुलं, तुमुलं ; 'close study,' निरन्तराभ्यासः, अभिनिवेशः.

Closed, *p. p.* (Shut) बद्धः -द्धा -द्धं, संवृतः -ता -तं, पिहितः -ता -तं, पिधानवान् -वती -वत् (त्), सपिधानः -ना -नं, मुद्रितः -ता -तं.—(As a bud) मुकुलीकृतः -ता -तं, अविकचः -चा -चं.—(As the eye) निमीलितः -ता -तं ; 'with closed eye,' निमीलितनयनः.—(Settled, finished) निष्पन्नः -न्ना -न्नं, समाप्तः -प्ता -प्तं ; 'with closed hands,' बद्धाञ्जलिः, संश्लिष्टाभ्यां पाणिभ्यां.

Close-fisted or close-handed, *a.* दृढमुष्टिः -ष्टिः -ष्टि, गाढमुष्टिः -ष्टिः -ष्टि, बद्धमुष्टिः -ष्टिः -ष्टि, अमुक्तहस्तः -स्ता -स्तं.

Closely, *adv.* (Secretly) निभृतं, गुप्तं, सुनिभृतं, सुगुप्तं, रहसि.—(Nearly) निरन्तरं, अनन्तरं, सन्निकृष्टं, उपान्ते.—(Attentively) मनःप्रवेशेन, प्रयत्नात्.—(Firmly) गाढं, दृढं ; 'closely attentive,' निविष्टः -ष्टा -ष्टं, आसक्तः -क्ता -क्तं, एकाग्रः -ग्रा -ग्रं, एकायनः -ना -नं, अनन्यवृत्तिः -त्तिः -त्ति, एकतानः -ना -नं.

Closeness, *s.* (Nearness) समीपता, आनन्तर्य्यं, सान्निध्यं, उपस्थानं, नैकट्यं, सन्निकर्षः, अभ्यासत्वं.—(Secrecy) रहः *n.* (स्), गुप्तिः *f.*, सुगुप्तिः *f.*, गुप्तता, गूढत्वं.—(Compactness) घनता, सान्द्रता, नैबिड्यं, नैरन्तर्य्यं.—(Parsimony) स्वल्पव्ययः, कार्पण्यं.—(Want of air) निर्वातता.

Close-stool, *s.* शयनोपान्ते विण्मूत्राधारः, शयनपार्श्वस्थं मूत्रपुरीषभाजनं.

Closet, *s.* कुटिः, कुटी, आगारं, कोष्ठः, निभृतागारं, गोपनागारं.

To closet, *v. a.* कुट्यां निविश् in caus. (-वेशयति -यितुं) or गुप् (c. 1. गोपायति, गोप्तुं).

Closure, *s.* पिधानं, वेष्टनं, आवेष्टनं, प्रावरणं, प्रावृतिः *f.*

Clot, *s.* गुल्मः, पिण्डः -ण्डं, घनता ; 'clot of blood,' रक्तगुल्मः, घनलोहितं ; 'of hair,' जटा.

To clot, *v. n.* सान्द्रीभू, घनीभू.—(As hair) जट् (c. 1. जटति -टितुं), श्यै (c. 1. श्यायते, श्यातुं), पिण्डीभू.

Cloth, *s.* पटः, वस्त्रं, वासः, वासः *n.* (स्), वसनं, चेलः -लं, चैलं, अंशुकं, मृगरोमजम् आच्छादनं, प्रोतं ; 'fine cloth,' सुचेलकः, अंशुकं ; 'coarse cloth,' स्थूलशाटकः, वराशिः *m.* ; 'tattered cloth,' कर्पटः.—(Made of cloth) वास्त्रः -स्त्री -स्त्रं, वस्त्रमयः -यी -यं.—(Table-cloth) भोजनाधारपटः, फलकाच्छादनं.

To clothe, *v. a.* वेष्ट् (c. 1. वेष्टते -ष्टितुं), परिवेष्ट्, प्रवेष्ट् ; आच्छद् (c. 10.

-छादयति -यितुं), वस् in caus. (वासयति), विवस्, प्रतिवस्, परिधा in caus. (-धापयति -यितुं), प्रवृ (c. 5. -वृणोति -वरितुं -रीतुं), संव्ये (c. 1. -व्ययति -व्यातुं), वस्त्र (nom. वस्त्रयति -यितुं); 'to clothe one's self,' वस् (c. 2. वस्ते वसितुं), प्रवस्, विवस्; परिधा (c. 2. -धत्ते -धातुं); 'in armour,' सन्नह् (c. 4. -नह्यते -नद्धुं).

Clothed, *p. p.* आच्छादितः -ता -तं, प्रच्छादितः -ता -तं, परिच्छन्नः -न्ना -न्नं, प्रावृतः -ता -तं, संवीतः -ता -तं, परिहितः -ता -तं, वेष्टितः -ता -तं, पिनद्धः -द्धा -द्धं, आमुक्तः -क्ता -क्तं, प्रतिमुक्तः -क्ता -क्तं, वासी -सिनी -सि (न्), वेशी -शिनी -शि (न्), वस्त्रान्वितः -ता -तं, सवासाः -साः -सः (स्), सचेलः -ला -लं, अनग्नः -ग्ना -ग्नं.

Clothes, *s. pl.* वस्त्रं, वासः *n.* (स्), वेशः, वसनं, प्रसाधनं, परिधानं, अम्बरं, संव्यानं, आच्छादः -दनं, सिचयः; 'a suit of clothes,' वस्त्रयुग्मं; 'old clothes,' जीर्णवस्त्रं, चीरं, प्रोथः; 'relating to clothes,' वास्त्रिकः -की -कं; 'clothes basket,' तरिः *f.*; 'bed-clothes,' शय्यास्तरणं; 'to put on one's clothes,' वस्त्राणि आच्छद् (c. 10. -छादयति -यितुं) or प्रवृ (c. 5. -वृणोति -वरितुं -रीतुं) or परिधा (c. 3. -धत्ते -धातुं) or प्रसाध् (c. 10. -साधयति -यितुं) or आमुच् (c. 6. -मुञ्चति -मोक्तुं); 'to take off one's clothes,' वस्त्राणि अवतॄ in caus. (-तारयति -यितुं) or अवमुच् or उच्छद् or विहा (c. 3. -जहाति -हातुं); 'to change one's clothes,' अन्यवस्त्रं परिधा, निवस् (c.2.-वस्ते-वसितुं).

Clothier, *s.* पटकारः, वस्त्रकृत्, पटनिर्म्माणकृत्, पटनिर्म्माणोपजीवी *m.* (न्).

Clothing, *s.* परिधानं, प्रवारः, प्रच्छादनं, आच्छादनं, परिच्छदः; 'under-clothing,' अधोवसनं, अन्तर्वासः *n.* (स्), अन्तरीयं.

Clotpoll, *s.* जडः, मूढः, स्थूलबुद्धिः *m.*, मूर्खः, बर्ब्बरः.

Clotted or clotty, *a.* पिण्डीभूतः -ता -तं, पिण्डितः -ता -तं, गुल्मी -ल्मिनी -ल्मि (न्), घनीभूतः -ता -तं, श्यानः -ना -नं; 'blood,' घनलोहितं, रक्तगुल्मः; 'clotted hair,' जटिः, जुटकं, जूटः.

Cloud, *s.* अभ्रं, मेघः, घनः, पर्ज्जन्यः, वलाहकः, जीमूतः, वृष्टिमान् *m.* (त्), जलधरः, तोयधरः, पयोधरः, धाराधरः, नीरधरः, जलदः, पयोदः, वारिदः, नीरदः, पाथोदः, अर्णोदः, जलवाहः, वारिवाहः -हनः, तोयवाहः, अम्बुवाहः, अम्बुभृत्, शक्रवाहनः, वारितस्करः, पयोजन्मा *m.* (न्), जलमुक् *m.* (च्), वारिमुक् *m.* (च्) or वार्म्मुक्, पयोमुक् *m.* (च्), वारिरः, पर्व्वताश्रयः, तडित्वान् *m.* (त्), स्तनयित्नुः *m.*, धूमयोनिः *m.*, व्योमधूमः, नभोधूमः, जलमसिः *m.*, वारिमसिः *m.*, नीलाभ्रः, खचरः, नभश्चरः, गगणध्वजः, नभोदुहः, नभोगजः, देवः, पारणः, वासवः, मुदिरः, दर्दुरः, उरणकः, नभाट् *m.* (ज्); 'a black cloud,' नीलाभ्रः *m.*, असिताभ्रं, कालिका; 'a gathering of clouds,' घनजालं, जलदसंहतिः *f.*, घनौघः; 'a succession of clouds,' मेघमाला, कादम्बिनी; 'a cloud of dust,' रजोमेघः, धूलीपटलः.

To cloud, *v. a.* अभ्रं कृ, मेघं कृ, तिमिर (nom. तिमिरयति -यितुं), प्रच्छद् (c. 10. -छादयति -यितुं), तिमिरीकृ, मलिनीकृ.

To cloud, *v. n.* मेघावृतः -ता -तं भू, मेघाच्छन्नः -न्ना -न्नं भू, अभ्र (nom. अभ्रायते), मेघ (nom. मेघायते).

Clouded, *p. p.* मेघच्छन्नः -न्ना -न्नं, घनोपरुद्धः -द्धा -द्धं, दुर्द्दिनग्रस्तः -स्ता -स्तं, सतमस्कः -स्का -स्कं, तमोवृतः -ता -तं, मलिनः -ना -नं, मलिनप्रभः -भा -भं.

Cloud-capt, *a.* अभ्रशेखरः -रा -रं, असिताभ्रशेखरः -रा -रं, अभ्रंलिहः -हा -हं, नभोलिट् (ह्).

Cloudily, *adv.* साभ्रं, समेघं, तिमिरं, सान्धकारं, निगूढार्थं.

Cloudiness, *s.* साभ्रता, मेघाकीर्णता, मेघतिमिरं, जलदसंहतिः *f.*, दुर्द्दिनं.

Cloudless, *a.* अनभ्रः -भ्रा -भ्रं, व्यभ्रः -भ्रा -भ्रं, निरभ्रः -भ्रा -भ्रं, अमेघः -घा -घं, गततोयदः -दा -दं, वितिमिरः -रा -रं.

Cloudy, *a.* साभ्रः -भ्रा -भ्रं, अभ्रियः -या -यं, मेघाकीर्णः -र्णा -र्णं, नीरदी -दिनी -दि (न्), समेघः -घा -घं, सघनः -ना -नं, दार्दुरः -री -रं; 'cloudy weather,' दुर्द्दिनं.—(Dark, obscure) तिमिरः -रा -रं, तमस्वी -स्विनी -स्वि (न्), तमोवृतः -ता -तं, तामसः -सी -सं, अन्धकारयुक्तः -क्ता -क्तं.

Clough, *s.* (Cleft of a hill) दरी -रिः *f.*, दरद्, कन्दरः -री -रं.—(An allowance of two in every hundred) शते शते पञ्चाशत्तमभागदानं.

Clove, *s.* (The spice) लवङ्गं, तीक्ष्णपुष्पं, मादनं, देवकुसुमं, दिव्यगन्धं, वारिपुष्पं, श्रीः, श्रीसंज्ञं, सुपुष्पं, भृङ्गारं, वश्यं, शृङ्गारं, चन्दनपुष्पं.—(The clove tree) लवङ्गः, तोयधिप्रियः.—(Of garlic) रसुनमूलं.

Cloven, *a.* भिन्नः -न्ना -न्नं, भेदितः -ता -तं, विभिन्नः -न्ना -न्नं, छिन्नः -न्ना -न्नं, दलितः -ता -तं, विदलितः -ता -तं -लीकृतः -ता -तं, पृथक्कृतः -ता -तं; 'cloven tongued,' द्विखण्डजिह्वः -ह्वा -ह्वं, द्विजिह्वः -ह्वा -ह्वं.

Cloven-footed or cloven-hoofed, *a.* द्विशफः -फा -फं, द्विखण्डशफः -फा -फं.

Clover, *s.* (Trefoil) त्रिपर्णः -र्णी -र्णं, त्रिपत्रः -त्रा -त्रं; 'to live in clover,' महता विलासेन जीव् (c. 1. जीवति -वितुं), महासुखेन जीव्.

Clovered, *a.* त्रिपर्णाचितः -ता -तं, त्रिपत्राकीर्णः -र्णा -र्णं, सत्रिपत्रः -त्रा -त्रं.

Clout, *s.* (A cloth for any mean use) चीरं, कर्पटः, वस्त्रखण्डं.—(A patch) कन्था.—(An iron plate over an axle-tree) अक्षाग्रफलकं.

To clout, *v. a.* (To patch) कन्था (nom. कन्थायति -यितुं), जीर्णवस्त्राणि समाधा (c. 3. -दधाति -धत्ते -धातुं) चीरं चीरेण सन्धा.

Clouted, *a.* श्यानः -ना -नं, संश्यानः -ना -नं, घनीभूतः -ता -तं.

Clouterly, *a,* (Clumsy) अदक्षः -क्षा -क्षं, अकृती -तिनी -ति (न्).

Clown, *s.* ग्राम्यजनः, ग्रामिकः, ग्रामी *m.* (न्), ग्रामवासः, ग्रामेवासी *m.* (न्), वृषलः, जानपदः, प्राकृतजनः, असभ्यजनः, पृथग्जनः, मूढः.

Clownish, *a.* ग्राम्यः -म्या -म्यं -मीयः -या -यं -मीणः -णा -णं -मेयः -यी -यं -मिकः -की -कं, असभ्यः -भ्या -भ्यं, अशिष्टः -ष्टा -ष्टं, असंस्कृतः -ता -तं, ग्राम्यबुद्धिः -द्धिः -द्धि.

Clownishly, *adv.* ग्राम्यजनवत्, वृषलवत्, ग्रामीयप्रकारेण, असभ्यं.

Clownishness, *s.* ग्राम्यता, ग्रामीयत्वं, असभ्यता, अशिष्टता, ग्राम्यबुद्धित्वं.

To cloy, *v. a.* अतिसौहित्यं or अतितृप्तिं जन् in caus. (जनयति -यितुं) or कृ, अतिशयेन or एकान्ततस् or अतिरिक्तं तृप् in caus. (तर्पयति -यितुं), or सन्तुष् in caus. (-तोषयति -यितुं).

Cloyed, *p. p.* अतितृप्तः -प्ता -प्तं, अतिसुहितः -ता -तं, अतिसन्तोषितः -ता -तं.

Club, *s.* यष्टिः *m.*, लगुडः, गदा, परिघः, उद्घातः, तोमरः -रा -रं, घनः, द्रुघणः; 'armed with a club,' याष्टीकः, लगुडहस्तः, यष्टिग्रहः, याष्टिहेतिकः.—(An assembly of companions) पंक्तिः *f.*, गणः, संसर्गः, सहभोजिनां संसर्गः, समांशिता; 'club-dinner,' गणचक्रकं, गणान्नं.—(Share of a reckoning) भागः, अंशः, उद्धारः, समांशः.

To club, *v. n.* (Contribute to a common expense) सर्व्वसाधारणधनव्यये, स्वं स्वम् अंशं दा (c. 3. ददाति दातुं), or किञ्चित् किञ्चिद् दा.

Club-foot, *s.* श्लीपदं, स्थूलचरणं, कुब्जचरणं, गडुपादः, वक्रपादः.

Club-footed, *a.* श्लीपदी -दिनी -दि (न्), बृहत्पादः -दी -दं, स्थूलचरणः -णा -णं.

Clubheaded, *a.* स्थूलशिरस्कः -स्का -स्कं, बृहन्मस्तकः -का -कं.

Clubroom, *s.* एकपंक्तिसामान्यशाला, साधारणशाला, इन्द्रकं.

To cluck, *v. n.* कुक्कुटीवत् शावकाह्वानार्थकं शब्दं कृ, कट् कट् शब्दं कृ.

Clucking, *s.* शावकाह्वानसमये कुक्कुटीरावः, कट् कट् शब्दः

Clue, *s.* सूत्रकोषं, सूत्रं. *See* Clew.

Clump, *s.* (Of grass) गुल्मः, स्तम्बः, गुच्छः, गुत्सः, काण्डः, विततिः *f.*, पिण्डः -ण्डं; 'a clump of reeds,' शरस्तम्बः, वंशविततिः *f.*—(A shapeless mass of wood) स्थूलकाष्ठं.

Clumsily, *adv.* अदक्षं, अनार्जं, अकृतिवत्, दाक्ष्यं विना, अपटु, आदाक्ष्येण.

Clumsiness, *s.* आचतुर्य्यं, आदाक्ष्यं, अनैपुणं, अपाटवं, अकृतित्वं.

Clumsy, *a.* स्थूलः -ला -लं, अदक्षः -क्षा -क्षं, अनिपुणः -णा -णं, अकुशलः -ला -लं, अकृती -तिनी -ति (न्), अनार्जः -र्जा -र्जं, अविज्ञः -ज्ञा -ज्ञं, अपटुः, टुः -टु.

Cluster, *s.* (A bunch) गुल्मः, गुच्छः -च्छकः, स्तवकः, स्तवः, सान्द्रं, गुत्सः -त्सकः, गुलुच्छः, वितितिः *f.*, 'a number of beings,' सङ्घः, ओघः, समूहः, गणः, सङ्घातः, वृन्दं, निवहः; 'cluster of four houses,' चतुःशालं, सञ्जवनं; 'of reeds,' शरस्तम्बः, वंशवितितिः *f.*; 'of people,' जनौघं, जनसमूहः; 'of grapes,' द्राक्षास्तवकः; 'in clusters,' सङ्घशस्, गुल्मशस्.

To **cluster**, *v. a.* गुल्मीकृ, पिण्डीकृ, एकीकृ, सञ्चि (c. 5. -चिनोति -चेतुं).

To **cluster**, *v. n.* गुल्मीभू, पिण्डीभू, एकीभू, वृन्दीभू, स्तवकरूपेण रुह् (c. 1. रोहति, रोढुं)

Clustering, *a.* गुल्मी -ल्मिनी -ल्मि (न्), आलीनः -ना -नं, सस्तवकः -का -कं, स्तवकाचितः -ता -तं, प्रलीनः -ना -नं, प्रलीनः -ना -नं, गुच्छाकारः -रा -रं.

To **clutch**, *v. a.* (To grasp) ग्रह् (c. 9. गृह्णाति, ग्रहीतुं), सङ्ग्रह्, धृ (c. 1. धरति धर्तुं).—(To double the hand) मुष्टिं बन्ध् (c. 9. बध्नाति बन्धुं) or सङ्ग्रह्.

Clutch, *s.* सङ्ग्राहः, मुष्टिसङ्ग्राहः, ग्रहणं, मुष्टिबन्धः.—(Claw, hand) नखः -खं, पाणिः *m.*, हस्तः; 'to rescue from the clutches of the enemy,' शत्रुवशात् परित्रातुं.

Clutched, *p. p.* गृहीतः -ता -तं, धृतः -ता -तं, मुष्टिसङ्ग्राहपीडितः -ता -तं.

Clutter, *s.* कोलाहलः, हलहलाशब्दः, तुमुलं, कालकीलः.

To **clutter**, *v. n.* कोलाहलं कृ, हलहलाशब्दं कृ.

Clyster, *s.* वस्तिः *m. f.*, वस्तिकर्म्म *n.* (न्), वस्तिद्वारेण अन्त्रनिवेशितम् औषधीयद्रव्यं.

Clyster-pipe, *s.* नेत्रं, वस्तिशिरः *n.* (स्), वस्तिनाली.

To **coacervate**, *v. a.* सञ्चि (c. 5. -चिनोति -चेतुं), समाचि, समुपचि, राशीकृ, पिण्डीकृ, एकौघीकृ, पुञ्जीकृ, पूगीकृ.

Coacervated, *p. p.* राशिगतः -ता -तं, एकौघभूतः -ता -तं, पुञ्जितः -ता -तं.

Coacervation, *s.* राशीकरणं, एकौघीकरणं, सञ्चयनं, एकौघभावः.

Coach, *s.* रथः, चातुरं, चक्रयानं, यानं, गन्त्री, गन्त्रीरथः, शकटः, प्रवहणं, वाहनं; 'coach and four,' चतुरश्वो रथः; 'riding in a coach,' रथारोही *m.* (न्), रथारूढः, यानारूढः; 'he travels by coach,' रथेन सञ्चरति.

Coach-box, *s.* रथोपस्थः, सूतासनं, सारथिस्थानं.

Coach-driving, *s.* रथसारथ्यं, रथवाहनं.

Coachful, *s.* पूर्णरथः, चातुरकं, शाकटं, रथपूरणं.

Coach-horse, *s.* रथ्यः, प्रवहणवाही *m.* (न्), रथाश्वः.

Coach-house, *s.* रथस्थानं, रथशाला, रथागारं, रथाधारः.

Coachmaker, *s.* रथकारः, रथकरः, रथनिर्म्माणकृत्, रथविक्रेता *m.* (तृ).

Coachman, *s.* सूतः, सारथिः *m.*, यन्ता *m.* (न्तृ), नियन्ता *m.* (न्तृ), चातुरिकः, वाहकः, रथवाहकः, प्रवहणवाहकः, प्राजकः, प्राजिता *m.* (तृ), क्षत्ता *m.* (तृ), हयङ्कषः, सादिः *m.*, दक्षिणस्थः, चाक्रिकः, प्रचेता *m* (तृ).

Coaction, *s.* बलात्कारः, बलात्कारप्रयोगः, प्रमाथः, नियमनं, निग्रहः.

Coactive, *a.* बलात्कारी -रिणी -रि (न्), बलान्वितः -ता -तं, बली -लिनी -लि (न्), सबलः -ला -लं, प्रमाथी -थिनी -थि (न्), नैयमिकः -की -कं, नियामकः -का -कं, अवश्यकः -का -कं.

Coadjutor, *s.* सहकारी *m.* (न्), सहकृत्, सहकृत्वा *m.* (न्), सहायः, सम्भूयकारी *m.* (न्), प्रतियोगी *m.* (न्).

Coadjuvancy, *s.* सहकारः -रिता, साहाय्यं, सम्प्रतिपत्तिः *f.*, प्रतियोगिता.

Coagmentation, *s.* राशीकरणं, एकीकरणं, सञ्चयनं, पिण्डीकरणं, सन्निपातः.

Coagulable, *a.* श्यानीयः -या -यं, श्येयः -या -यं, घनीकर्तुं शक्यः -क्या -क्यं.

To **coagulate**, *v. a.* श्यै in caus. (श्यापयति -यितुं), श्यानीकृ, घनीकृ.

To **coagulate**, *v. n.* श्यै (c. 1. श्यायते, श्यातुं), घनीभू, श्यानीभू.

Coagulated, *p. p.* शीनः -ना -नं, श्यानः -ना -नं, आश्यानः -ना -नं, घनीभूतः -ता -तं, संहतः -ता -तं.

Coagulation, *s.* शीनता, घनता -त्वं, संहतत्वं, घनीभावः.

Coal, *s.* अङ्गारः -रं, आलातं, निधापकः, कृष्णमृत् *f.*-मृत्तिका, कृष्णभूमिः *f.*; 'burning coal,' तप्ताङ्गारः.

To **coal**, *v. a.* अङ्गार (nom. अङ्गारयति -यितुं), अङ्गारीकृ.

Coal-black, *a.* अङ्गारसवर्णः -र्णा -र्णं, घनकृष्णः -ष्णा -ष्णं, अत्यन्तकालः -ला -लं.

Coal-hole or **coal-house**, *s.* अङ्गारागारं, अङ्गारगुप्तिः *f.*, कृष्णमृत्तिकाधारः.

Coal-man, **coal-merchant**, *s.* अङ्गारविक्रेता *m.* (तृ), कृष्णभूमिविक्रयी *m.* (न्), अङ्गारविक्रयोपजीवी *m.* (न्).

Coal-mine, **coal-pit**, *s.* अङ्गाराकरः, अङ्गारखनिः *m.*, अङ्गारोत्पत्तिस्थानं.

To **coalesce**, *v. n.* संयुज् in pass. (-युज्यते), सम्मिल् (c. 6. -मिलति -मेलितुं), सङ्गम् (c. 1. -गच्छति -गन्तुं), संसृज् in pass. (-सृज्यते), एकीभू, एकत्र भू or गम्, संश्लिष् in pass. (-श्लिष्यते), संलग्नीभू.

Coalition, *s.* संयोगः, संसृष्टिः *f.*, संसर्गः, सङ्गः -ङ्गमः -ङ्गतिः *f.*, मेलनं, संश्लेषः, संसक्तिः, अनुषङ्गः, संहतिः *f.*, सङ्घातः.

Coaly, *a.* अङ्गारमयः -यी -यं, आङ्गारिकः -की -कं, अङ्गारपूर्णः -र्णा -र्णं.

Coaptation, *s.* समायोगः, संयोजनं, समाधानं, सन्धानं.

To **coarct**, *v. a.* सङ्कुच् (c. 1. -कोचति -कोचितुं), संहृ (c. 1. -हरति -हर्तुं).

Coarctation, *s.* सङ्कोचः -चनं, संवारः, संवृतिः, ह्रासः, संक्षेपः, संयमः.

Coarse, *a.* (Not fine) घनः -ना -नं, सान्द्रः -न्द्रा -न्द्रं, निबिडः -डा -डं, स्थूलः -ला -लं, निरन्तरः -रा -रं, नीरन्ध्रः -न्ध्रा -न्ध्रं.—(Unpolished) अपरिष्कृतः -ता -तं, असंस्कृतः -ता -तं, अशिष्टः -ष्टा -ष्टं.—(Indelicate, indecent) अवाच्यः -च्या -च्यं, अशुद्धः -द्धा -द्धं.—(Vulgar) असभ्यः -भ्या -भ्यं, प्राकृतः -ता -तं, ग्राम्यः -म्या -म्यं, श्लीलः -ला -लं, अश्लीलः -ला -लं.—(Vile) नीचः -चा -चं, निकृष्टः -ष्टा -ष्टं, कदर्य्यः -र्य्या -र्य्यं, कुत्सितः -ता -तं; 'coarse cloth,' स्थूलपट्टं, स्थूलशाटकः, वराशिः *m.*; 'coarse-minded,' प्राकृतचेताः -ताः -तः (स्); 'coarse fare,' मन्दाहारः; 'coarse abuse,' अश्लीलाक्षेपः; 'coarse language,' अश्लीलं, अलोक्तिः *f.*

Coarsely, *adv.* अशिष्टं, अशुद्धं, निकृष्टं, मन्दं, अश्लीलं, अपरिष्कृतं.

Coarseness, *s.* (Of substance) घनता, स्थूलता, सान्द्रता, स्थौल्यं, नैबिड्यं, नैरन्तर्य्यं.—(Want of polish, vulgarity) अपरिष्कारः, अशिष्टता, असभ्यता, अशुद्धिः *f.*, नीचता, अश्लीलत्वं.

Coast, *s.* (Sea-coast) समुद्रतीरं, समुद्रतटं, वेला, वेलामूलं, समुद्रान्तं, अब्धितीरं.—(Border, limit) सीमा, समन्तः, सामन्तं.—(Quarter) दिक् *f.*, (श्), देशः, प्रदेशः; 'the coast is clear,' गतं भयं, निर्विघ्नः पथः.

To **coast**, *v. n.* उपतीरं or उपतटं or वेलानिकटे नावं or पोतं वह् in caus. (वाहयति -यितुं), or नौकया वह् in pass. (उह्यते).

Coaster, *s.* उपतीरं पोतवाहकः, समुद्रवेलावर्त्ती *m.* (न्).

Coasting, *s.* उपतीरं नौकावाहनं, वेलानिकटे वर्त्तनं.

Coat, *s.* (An upper garment) प्रावारः, उत्तरीयं, परिधेयं, निचोलः, वस्त्रं; 'a covering,' पटलं, छादनं, छदनं, आच्छादनं, प्रावरणं, पुटः -टं, आवेष्टनं; 'coat of the eye,' अक्षिपटलं.—(Hair of a beast) रोम *n.* (न्), लोम *n.* (न्); 'coat of a horse,' अश्वरोम *n.* (न्).—(Coat of arms) कुलचिह्नपत्रं.

To COAT, *v. a.* छद् (c. 10. छादयति -यितुं), वेष्ट् in caus. (वेष्टयति -यितुं). —(Inlay) अनुव्यध् (c. 4. -विध्यति -व्यद्धुं).—(Coat with paint) लिप् (c. 6. लिम्पति, लेप्तुं).

COATED, *p. p.* छन्नः -न्ना -न्नं, आछन्नः -न्ना -न्नं, वेष्टितः -ता -तं, अनुविद्धः -द्धा -द्धं, रूषितः -ता -तं, छुरितः -ता -तं, लिप्तः -प्ता -प्तं.

COATING, *s.* पटलं, पुटः -टी -टं, छादनं.—(Of paint) लेपः.

To COAX, *v. n.* लल् (c. 10. लालयति -यितुं), सान्त्व् (c. 10. सान्त्वयति -यितुं), मधुरैर्वाक्यैः or चाटूक्त्या सान्त्व् or प्रलुभ् in caus. (-लोभयति -यितुं).

COAXED, *p. p.* लालितः -ता -तं, चाटुकारापन्नः -न्ना -न्नं.

COAXER, *s.* लाली *m.* (न्), चाटुवादी *m.* (न्), चाटुकारः, सान्त्ववादः, आश्वासकः.

COAXING, *s.* लालनं, चाटुः *m.* -टु *n.*, चाटूक्तिः *f.*, मधुरवचः *n.* (स्), मधुरवाक्यं, आश्वासनं; 'repeated coaxing,' चाटुशतं.

COB, *s.* (Sea-fowl) समुद्रीयपक्षिभेदः.—(Entire horse) वीताश्वः, सवृषणोऽश्वः.—(A small compact horse) दृढदेहः क्षुद्रवाजी *m.* (न्).

COBALT, *s.* (Mineral substance) चावर्त्तः, मधुधातुः *m.*, मनःशिलाधातुः.

To COBBLE, *v. a.* (To mend shoes) जीर्णपादुकाः सूच्या समाधा (c. 3. -दधाति -धातुं) or सन्धा.—(To make any thing clumsily) अादाक्ष्येण किञ्चित् कृ or निर्म्मा (c. 2. -माति -मातुं).

COBBLER, *s.* (A mender of old shoes) जीर्णपादुकासन्धाता *m.* (तृ). —(A clumsy workman) अदक्षः शिल्पी *m.* (न्), अनिपुणः, अनभिज्ञः.

COBIRON, *s.* मांससंस्कारे प्रयुक्तः स्थूलाग्रो लोहशूलः.

COBISHOP, *s.* धर्म्माध्यक्षसहायः, धर्म्माधिपतेः सहकारी *m.* (न्).

COBRA CAPELLO, *s.* (Snake) फणाकरः, फणी *m.* (न्). फणावान् *m.* (त्), नागः.

COBWEB, *s.* ऊर्णनाभजालः, जालः -लं, मर्कटवासः, मर्कटजालः, आशाबन्धः, समानिका, लूतातन्तुवितानं.

COCCIFEROUS, *a.* गुटिकाकारफलविशिष्टः -ष्टा -ष्टं.

COCHINEAL, *s.* (Insect) लाक्षा, जतु *n.* -तुकं, तितिभः, क्रिमिः *m.*

COCHLEARY or COCHLEATED, *a.* आवर्त्ती -र्त्तिनी -र्त्ति (न्), परिवर्त्तकः -का -कं.

COCK, *s.* (The male to the hen) कुक्कुटः, चरणायुधः, नखायुधः, स्वर्णचूडः, ताम्रचूडः, ताम्रशिखी *m.* (न्), शिखी *m.* (न्), शिखण्डी *m.* (न्) -ण्डिकः, कृकवाकुः *m.*, कलविकः, कालज्ञः, उषाकलः, निशावेदी *m.* (न्), रात्रिवेदी *m.* (न्), यामघोषः, रसाञ्जनः, सुपर्णः, पूर्णकः; 'relating to a cock,' कार्क्कवाकवः -वी -वं; 'cock's comb,' चूडा, शिखा; 'a cock-sparrow,' चटकः.—(Weathercock) प्रासादशृङ्गाग्रे स्थापितं कुक्कुटाकारं वातस्कन्धलक्षणं, वायुलक्षणं, वायुध्वजः, वायुस्कन्धलक्ष्म.—(Spout to let out water at will) सपिधानं जलनिर्गमरन्ध्रं, प्रणाली, जलनिर्गमः, जलस्रावणयन्त्रं.—(Notch of an arrow) बाणाग्रभागे अवच्छेदः.—(Cock of a gun) आग्नेयनाडिसम्बन्धी सूक्ष्ममुद्गरविशेषो यद्द्वारेण अन्तःस्थचूर्णं संज्वाल्यते.—(A leader) मुख्यः, मुखरः, पुरोगः. —(Heap of hay) शुष्कतृणचितिः *f.*, तृणोत्करः.—(Form of a hat) शिरस्कसंस्कारः, शिरस्त्राकारः; 'cock a hoop,' जयी *m.* (न्), दृप्तः, दर्पध्मातः, गर्व्वोद्धतः; 'cock and a bull story,' वृथाकथा, शशविषाणधनुर् अस्य इति मृषार्थकम् आख्यानं.

To COCK, *v. a.* (To set erect) उन्नम् in caus. (-नामयति -नमयति -यितुं), उच्छ्रि (c. 1. -श्रयति -यितुं), उत्क्षिप् (c. 6. -क्षिपति -क्षेप्तुं), उद्धन् (c. 2. -हन्ति -हन्तुं); 'to cock the ears,' कर्णौ स्तब्धीकृ; 'the tail,' उत्पुच्छ (nom. उत्पुच्छयते -यितुं).—(To put hay into cocks) शुष्कतृणम् उत्करीकृ.—(To cock a gun) आग्नेयनाडिसम्बन्धिनं पूर्व्वोक्तसूक्ष्ममुद्गरम् उन्नम् in caus. (-नमयति -यितुं).

To COCK, *v. n.* कुक्कुटवत् खेलगत्या चल् (c. 1. चलति -लितुं), दृप् (c. 4. दृप्यति).

COCKED, *p. p.* उन्नतः -ता -तं, समुन्नतः -ता -तं, उच्छ्रितः -ता -तं, उत्क्षिप्तः -प्ता -प्तं; 'with tail cocked,' समुन्नतलाङ्गूलः -ला -लं.

COCKADE, *s.* राजव्यापृतस्य सेवकेन शिरस्कोपरि भृता चूडा, कुक्कुटचूडाकारो मस्तकालङ्कारः.

COCKATRICE, *s.* अजगरः, वाहसः, कुक्कुटाण्डजः सर्पः or व्यालः.

COCKBOAT, *s.* उपनौका, क्षुद्रनौका, क्षुद्रपोतः, उपतरिः *f.*

COCKCHAFER, *s.* पिङ्गशरीरो ध्वनमोदी भ्रमरभेदः.

COCKCROWING, *s.* कुक्कुटरवः -वणं, चरणायुधशब्दः.—(Morning) प्रभातकालः, प्रातःकालः.

To COCKER, *v. a.* (To fondle) कोमलं or कोमलप्रकारेण पुष् (c. 9. पुष्णाति, c. 1. पोषति -षितुं), or संवृध् in caus. (-वर्धयति -यितुं), अनुरुध् (c. 4. -रुध्यते -रोद्धुं), क्रोडीकृ.

COCKEREL, *s.* (Young cock) कुक्कुटशावकः, चरणायुधशावकः.

COCKERING, *s.* पोषणं, संवर्धनं, अनुरोधः, छन्दोनुवृत्तं, कोमलता.

COCKET, *s.* शौल्किकमुद्रा, शुल्कस्थाने द्रव्यनिक्षेपानन्तरं शौल्किकसकाशात् प्रत्ययपत्रं.

COCKFIGHT, *s.* प्राणिद्यूतं, समाह्वयः, साह्वयः, कौलीनं.

COCKHORSE, *a.* अश्वारूढः -ढा -ढं, जयी -यिनी -यि (न्), दर्पध्मातः -ता -तं.

COCKLE, *s.* (Shell-fish) दुर्नामा *m.* -म्नी *f.* (न्) दीर्घकोषिका, सितालिका, शुक्तिः *f.*—(Weed growing in corn) कणः, शस्यक्षेत्ररुह ओषधिभेदः.

COCKLED, *a.* दुर्नामाकारः -रा -रं, शौक्तिकः -की -कं, आवर्त्ती -र्त्तिनी -र्त्ति (न्).

COCKLOFT, *s.* कूटागारं, क्षौमः -मं, चूला, चन्द्रशालिका, गृहस्य उपरिस्थः प्रकोष्ठः.

COCKMASTER, *s.* चरणायुधपालकः, युद्धकुक्कुटपोषकः.

COCKMATCH, *s.* कुक्कुटयुद्धं, चरणायुधसमाह्वयः, कौलीनं.

COCKNEY, *s.* नागरजनः, पुरवासी *m.* (न्), नगरवासी *m.*, प्राकृतजनः, पृथग्जनः.

COCKPIT, *s.* (Area where cocks fight) कुक्कुटयुद्धभूमिः.—(In a man of war) वृहद्युद्धनौकाया अधोभागे कायशल्यादिचिकित्सायोग्या कुटी.

COCKROACH, *s.* परोष्णी, तैलाधारा, तैलपा *f.* -पायिका, धारिका, पिङ्गकपिशा.

COCK'S-COMB, *s.* *See* COXCOMB.

COCKSURE, *a.* सुनिश्चितः -ता -तं, निःसन्देहः -हा -हं, असन्दिग्धः -ग्धा -ग्धं.

COCKSWAIN, *s.* उपनौकाकर्णधारः, क्षुद्रनौकापतिः *m.*

COCOA-NUT, *s.* नारिकेलः, नालिकेरः, नारिकेरः, नाडिकेलः, नारिकेली, पयोधरः, कौशिकफलं, जलोदकः, पुटोरकः, दाक्षिणात्यः.—(The tree) तृणद्रुमः, फलकेशरः, दृढफलः, मुखफलः, सदाफलः, शिरःफलः, सदापुष्पः, दृढमूलः, सुतुङ्गः, सुभङ्गः, लाङ्गली.—(The juice) नारिकेलरसः.

COCOON, *s.* (Of the silk worm) कृमिकोषः, कीटकोषः, गुटिका.

COCTION, *s.* निष्क्वाथः, क्वाथः, क्वथनं, पाचनं.

COD or COD-FISH, *s.* स्थूलशिरस्कः समुद्रीयमत्स्यभेदः.

COD, *s.* (Seed-vessel, pod) बीजकोशः, बीजगुप्तिः *f.*, शमी, पुटः.

CODDED, *p. p.* कोशस्थः -स्था -स्थं, कोषगुप्तः -प्ता -प्तं.

To CODDLE, *v. a.* (Parboil) ईषत्क्वथ् (c. 1. -क्वथति -थितुं), शनैः स्थाल्यां पच् (c. 1. पचति, पक्तुं) or तप् in caus. (तापयति -यितुं), कोष्णजलेन कोमलीकृ.—(Breed up tenderly) कोमलतया or सौकुमार्य्येण पुष् (c. 1. पोषति -षितुं).

CODE, *s.* (Of laws) धर्म्मसंहिता, स्मृतिशास्त्रं, धर्म्मशास्त्रं, स्मृतिः *f.*, व्यवहारविधिः *m.*

CODICIL, *s.* मुमूर्षुजनपत्रस्य अनुबन्धः or उपलेख्यं or उपाङ्गं or उत्तरलेख्यं.

CODLING, *s.* भोजनात्पूर्व्वम् ईषत्क्वथनीय आपक्वः काम्रफलभेदः.

COEFFICACY or COEFFICIENCY, *s.* सहकारिणाम् अनेकहेतुकानां प्रभावः, सहकारिता, संयोगिता, सम्प्रयोगिता, सम्प्रतिपत्तिः *f.*, सम्भूतिः *f.*

Coefficient, *s.* (In arithmetic) वर्णः, प्रकृतिः *f.*, गुणः.

Coemption, *s.* पूर्व्वक्रयः, प्रख्यातभाण्डक्रयः, अवच्छेदावच्छेदक्रयः, समुदयक्रयः.

Cœnobite, *s.* सर्व्वसामान्यो विभवो यस्य सौभ्रात्रमध्याद् एकभ्राता *m.* (तृ).

Coequal, *a.* अन्येन समः -मा -मं or समानः -ना -नं or तुल्यः -ल्या -ल्यं, समानपदस्थः -स्था -स्थं, समानजातीयः -या -यं, समभावः -वी -वं, सहधर्म्मी -र्म्मिणी -र्म्मि (न्), सधर्म्मा -र्म्मा -र्म्म (न्).

Coequality, *s.* अन्येन समता or समानता or तुल्यता, समानावस्था.

To coerce, *v. a.* बलात्कारेण यम् (c. 1. यच्छति, यन्तुं), नियम्, संयम्, विनियम्; or निग्रह् (c. 9. -गृह्णाति -ह्णीते -ग्रहीतुं) or शास् (c. 2. शास्ति, शासितुं), अनुशास्; यन्त्र् (c. 10. यन्त्रयति -यितुं), निरुध् (c. 7. -रुणद्धि -रोद्धुं), निषिध् (c. 1. -षेधति -धितुं).

Coerced, *p. p.* बलात्कारेण निगृहीतः -ता -तं, संयतः -ता -तं, निरुद्धः -द्धा -द्धं, संरुद्धः -द्धा -द्धं, यन्त्रितः -ता -तं, प्रत्याहृतः -ता -तं.

Coercible, *a.* निग्रहीतव्यः -व्या -व्यं, नियन्तव्यः -व्या -व्यं, यन्त्रणीयः -या -यं.

Coercion, *s.* संयमः -मनं, नियमनं, निग्रहः -हणं, निगृहीतिः *f.*, यन्त्रणं, प्रत्याहरणं.

Coercive, *a.* बलात्कारी -रिणी -रि (न्), प्रतिरोधी -धिनी -धि (न्), नियामकः -का -कं.

Coessential, *a.* समभावः -वी -वं, सहभावी -विनी -वि (न्).

Coessentiality, *s.* समभावः or भावसमानता, सहभावित्वं.

Coetaneous, *a.* समानवयस्कः -स्का -स्कं. See Coeval.

Coeternal, *a.* अन्येन सह नित्यकालस्थायी -यिनी -यि (न्) or अनन्तकालस्थायी or आद्यन्तहीनः -ना -नं or सनातनः -ना -नं.

Coeternity, *s.* समनित्यता, समानानन्तता, समाननित्यता.

Coeval, *a.* समानवयस्कः -स्का -स्कं, समवयस्कः -स्का -स्कं, समानवयाः -याः -यः (स्) or तुल्यवयाः or सवयाः, समानकालीनः -ना -नं, एककालीनः -ना -नं, समानजन्मा -न्मा -न्म (न्).

Coeval, *s.* वयस्यः, सहभावी *m.* (न्), सवयाः *m.* (स्), तुल्यवयाः.

To coexist, *v. n.* सम्भू (c. 1. -भवति -वितुं), सह or एककाले वृत् (c. 1. वर्त्तते -र्त्तितुं) or स्था (c. 1. तिष्ठति, स्थातुं) or जीव् (c. 1. जीवति -वितुं).

Coexistence, *s.* एककाले वर्त्तनं or जीवनं, सहवर्त्तनं, सहजीवनं.

Coexistent, *a.* सहवर्त्ती -र्त्तिनी -र्त्ति (न्) or एककाले वर्त्ती, सहजीवी -विनी -वि (न्) or एककाले जीवी, सहजः -जा -जं.

To co-extend, *v. n.* अन्येन समं व्याप् (c. 5. -आप्नोति -आप्तुं) or विस्तॄ in pass. (-स्तीर्य्यते).

Co-extension, *s.* समव्याप्तिः *f.*, अभिव्याप्तिः *f.*, समविस्तारः, सम्मूर्च्छनं.

Coffee, *s.* यवनदेशीयक्षुद्रफलनिर्म्मितः कृष्णवर्णः पानीयविशेषः, यावनपानं.

Coffee-house, *s.* पूर्व्वोक्तपानीयविक्रयस्थानं, यावनपानशाला.

Coffee-pot, *s.* पूर्व्वोक्तपानीयाधारः, यावनपानभाजनं, यावनपानपात्रं.

Coffer, *s.* मुद्राधारः, मुद्राकोषः, धनाधारः, धनभाण्डं, दीनारभाण्डं.

To coffer, *v. a.* मुद्राधारे or धनभाण्डे निधा (c. 3. -दधाति -धातुं).

Coffin, *s.* शवाधारः, मृतशरीराधारः, शवभाजनं.

To coffin, *v. a.* शवाधारे or शवभाजने निधा (c. 3. -दधाति -धातुं) or निविश् in caus. (-वेशयति -यितुं).

To cog, *v. a.* and *n.* (Flatter, wheedle) लल् (c. 10. लालयति -यितुं), चाटूक्त्या सान्त्व् (c. 10. सान्त्वयति -यितुं).—(Cog a die) कूटाक्षं or दुरक्षं कृ.—(Fix cogs to a wheel) चक्रनेमिं सदन्तां कृ.

Cog, *s.* (Tooth of a wheel) चक्रदन्तः, नेमिदन्तकः, प्रधिदन्तः.

Cogency, *s.* बलं, सामर्थ्यं, समर्थता, प्रभावः, शक्तिः *f.*, अवश्यकता.

Cogent, *a.* बली -लिनी -लि (न्), बलवान् -वती -वत् (त्) प्रबलः -ला -लं, शक्तिमान् -मती -मत् (त्), अवश्यकः -का -कं, अवश्यकर्त्तव्यः -व्या -व्यं, निरुत्तरः -रा -रं; 'a cogent reason,' बलवद्धेतुः *m.*, विशिष्टहेतुः.

Cogently, *adv.* बलात्, बलेन, बलवत्, अवश्यकं, निरुत्तरं.

Cogger, *s.* लाली *m.* (न्), चाटुकारः, सान्त्वनकृत् सान्त्ववादः.

Cogglestone, *s.* क्षुद्रशर्करा, चूर्णखण्डः, अष्ठीला.

Cogitable, *a.* ध्यानीयः -या -यं, ध्येयः -या -यं, चिन्तनीयः -या -यं.

Cogitate, *v. n.* ध्यै (c. 1. ध्यायति, ध्यातुं), अनुध्यै, अभिध्यै, प्रध्यै, सन्ध्यै, चिन्त् (c. 10. चिन्तयति -यितुं), विचिन्त्, सञ्चिन्त्, विचर् in caus. (-चारयति -यितुं), आलोच् (c. 10. -लोचयति -चितुं), भू in caus. (भावयति -यितुं), सम्भू, वितर्क् (c. 10. -तर्कयति -यितुं), अनुतर्क्, विमृश् (c. 6. -मृशति -म्रष्टुं), अनुमृश्, प्रविमृश्.

Cogitated, *p. p.* चिन्तितः -ता -तं, ध्यातः -ता -तं, आलोचितः -ता -तं.

Cogitation, *s.* चिन्ता, ध्यानं, विचारः -रणं, आलोचनं, चर्चा, भावना, मनःकल्पना, सङ्कल्पः, मनोगतं.

Cogitative, *a.* चिन्तापरः -रा -रं, ध्यानपरः -रा -रं, मानसिकः -की -कं.

Cognate, *a.* सहजः -जा -जं, सम्बन्धी -न्धिनी -न्धि (न्), समानजातीयः -या -यं, सजातिः -तिः -ति, सगोत्रः -त्रा -त्रं.

Cognation, *s.* (Relationship) बन्धुता, बान्धवत्वं, ज्ञातित्वं, ज्ञातिभावः, सजातित्वं, सम्बन्धः, सम्बन्धित्वं, सम्पर्कः, अनुषङ्गः.

Cognition, *s.* ज्ञानं, विज्ञानं, परिज्ञानं, प्रज्ञानं, स्वीकारः.

Cognitive, *a.* ज्ञानी -निनी -नि (न्), ज्ञानवान् -वती -वत् (त्), or प्रज्ञावान्.

Cognizable, *a.* ज्ञेयः -या -यं, विज्ञेयः -या -यं, बोध्यः -ध्या -ध्यं, ग्राह्यः -ह्या -ह्यं.—(By law) अभियोक्तव्यः -व्या -व्यं, विचार्य्यः -र्य्या -र्य्यं, विचारार्हः -र्हा -र्हं.

Cognizance, *s.* (Judicial notice) विचारः -रणा, अनुसन्धानं, जिज्ञासा, चर्चा, परीक्षा, अनुयोगः, निर्णयः, निरूपणं.—(Badge) संज्ञा, लिङ्गं, चिह्नं, लक्षणं, अभिज्ञानं.—(To take cognizance) ज्ञा (c. 9. जानाति, ज्ञातुं), ज्ञा in des. (जिज्ञासते -सितुं), विचर् (c. 10. -चारयति -यितुं), अनुसन्धा (c. 3. -दधाति -धातुं), अनुयुज् (c. 7. -युनक्ति -योक्तुं), निरूप् (c. 10. -रूपयति -यितुं).

Cognominal, *a.* एकनामकः -का -कं, एकसंज्ञकः -का -कं, समसंज्ञावान् -वती -वत् (त्).

Cognomination, *s.* पद्धतिः *f.* -ती, उपपदं, उपाधिः *m.*, कौलिकोपाधिः *m.*

Cognoscible, *a.* ज्ञातव्यः -व्या -व्यं, ज्ञेयः -या -यं, बोध्यः -ध्या -ध्यं.

To cohabit, *v. n.* (Dwell with another) सह वस् (c. 1. वसति वस्तुं), एकत्र वस्, सङ्गम् (c. 1. -गच्छति गन्तुं), संसर्गं कृ.—(As the sexes) स्त्रीपुरुषवत् सम्भोगं कृ.

Cohabitant, *s.* सहवासी *m.* (न्), एकपुरनिवासी *m.*, एकस्थानवासी *m.*

Cohabitation, *s.* सहवासः, एकत्र वासः, संसर्गः, सङ्गमः.—(Sexual) सम्भोगः, स्त्रीपुरुषसङ्गमः, औपस्थ्यं, उपभोगः.—(Cohabitation with men) पुंयोगः.—(With women) स्त्रीसङ्गः.

Coheir, *s.* समांशी *m.* (न्), समांशहारी *m.* (न्), अंशहारी *m.*, अंशभाक् *m.* (ज्), अंशी *m.* (न्), अंशकः, समाधिकारी *m.* (न्), दायादः, ऋक्थभागी *m.* (न्), विभागकर्त्ता *m.* (र्तृ), वन्त्रः.

Coheiress, *s.* समांशिनी, समांशहारिणी, समाधिकारिणी.

To cohere, *v. n.* (Stick together) संसञ्ज् in pass. (-सज्यते or -सज्जते), संश्लिष् in pass. (-श्लिष्यते), संलग्नीभू or संलग्नः -ग्ना -ग्नम् अस्, संयुज् in pass. (-युज्यते), संहन् in pass. (-हन्यते).—(Agree, suit) युज् in pass. (युज्यते), सम्बन्ध् in pass. (-बध्यते), योग्यः -ग्या -ग्यम् अस्.

Coherence, *s.* संसक्तिः *f.*, संश्लेषः, संलग्नत्वं, संहतिः *f.*, संयोगः, समासञ्जनं, सम्पर्कः.—(Connexion) सम्बन्धः, प्रबन्धः, अन्वयः, समन्वयः, अनुषङ्गः, सन्दर्भः.—(Consistency) अविरोधः, अनुसारित्वं.

COHERENT, *a.* संसक्तः -क्ता -क्तं, संश्लिष्टः -ष्टा -ष्टं, सुश्लिष्टः -ष्टा -ष्टं, संलग्नः -ग्ना -ग्नं, दृढसन्धिः -न्धिः -न्धि, संहतः -ता -तं, सुसंहतः -ता -तं.—(Consistent, adapted) अविरुद्धः -द्धा -द्धं, उपयुक्तः -क्ता -क्तं, अनुरूपः -पा -पं, अनुसारी -रिणी -रि (न्).—(Connected) सम्बद्धः -द्धा -द्धं, अनुसम्बद्धः -द्धा -द्धं, सान्वयः -या -यं, अन्वितः -ता -तं.

COHESION, *s.* संलग्नत्वं, संश्लेषः, संसक्तिः, संयोगः, समासञ्जनं, सङ्घट्टनं.

COHESIVE, *a.* संलग्नशीलः -ला -लं, सान्द्रः -न्द्रा -न्द्रं, श्यानः -ना -नं, स्निग्धः -ग्धा -ग्धं.

COHESIVENESS, *s.* संलग्नशीलत्वं, सान्द्रता, श्यानता, स्निग्धता, स्रैग्ध्यं.

To COHIBIT, *v. a.* यम् (c. 1. यच्छति, यन्तुं), निग्रह् (c. 9. -गृह्णाति -ग्रहीतुं).

To COHOBATE, *v. n.* पुनः सन्धा (c. 3. -दधाति -धातुं), द्विःसन्धानं कृ.

COHORT, *s.* सैन्यगुल्मः, सैन्यव्यूहः, सैन्यदलं, पञ्चशतसैन्यदलं, गणः.

COHORTATION, *s.* सुस्थिरो भवेति समाश्वासनं, प्रचोदनं, प्रोत्साहः.

COIF or COIFFURE, *s.* मस्तकाभरणं, शिरोवेष्टः -ष्टनं, शिरस्त्रं, मुकुटं.

COIFED, *a.* मुकुटी -टिनी -टि (न्), मुकुटधारी -रिणी -रि (न्), कृतमस्तकाभरणः -णा -णं.

To COIL, *v. a.* मण्डलीकृ, वर्त्तुलीकृ, मण्डलाकारेण पुटीकृ.

COIL, *s.* मण्डलं, मण्डलायितं, वृत्तं, आवर्त्तः -र्त्तनं.—(Tumult) तुमुलं, वैक्लव्यं, व्यस्तता, व्यग्रत्वं.

COILED, *p. p.* मण्डली -लिनी -लि (न्), मण्डलीकृतः -ता -तं, वर्त्तुलीकृतः -ता -तं.

COIN, *s.* (Stamped money) मुद्रा, टङ्कः, टङ्ककः, नाणकं, निष्कः -ष्कं; 'gold coin,' सुवर्णमुद्रा, सुवर्णः; 'silver coin,' रूप्यमुद्रा; 'copper coin,' ताम्रमुद्रा, पणः; 'base coin,' कूटनाणकं.—(Corner) कोणः.

To COIN, *v. a.* (To stamp metals for money) सुवर्णरूप्यादि मुद्रीकृ or मुद्र् (nom. मुद्रयति -यितुं) or मुद्रया अङ्क् (c. 1. अङ्कयति -यितुं) or आहन् (c. 2. -हन्ति -हन्तुं).—(Forge, invent) क्लृप् (c. 10. कल्पयति -यितुं), घट् (c. 1. घटते -टितुं), सृज् (c. 6. सृजति, स्रष्टुं).

COINAGE, *s.* मुद्राङ्कनं.—(Money coined) मुद्रा.—(Invention) कल्पना, वासना, सृष्टिः.

COINED, *p. p.* मुद्राङ्कितः -ता -तं, मुद्रितः -ता -तं, आहतः -ता -तं.—(Invented) कल्पितः -ता -तं, काल्पनिकः -की -कं, कृत्रिमः -मा -मं, सृष्टः -ष्टा -ष्टं.

To COINCIDE, *v. n.* (Agree in opinion) सम्मन् (c. 4. -मन्यते -मन्तुं), अनुमन्, स्वीकृ, एकचित्तीभू, एकमतीभू, अनुवद् (c. 1. -वदति -दितुं).—(Fall or meet together) सम्पत् (c. 1. -पतति -तितुं), सन्निपत्, सङ्गम् (c. 1. -गच्छति -गन्तुं).—(Be consistent, fitting) युज् in pass. (युज्यते), अनुरूपः -पा -पं or सदृशः -शी -शम् अस्, अनुसृ (c. 1. -सरति -सर्त्तुं), अनुवृत् (c. 1. -वर्त्तते -र्त्तितुं), न विरुध् in pass. (-रुध्यते).

COINCIDENCE, *s.* (Falling or meeting together) सन्निपातः, सम्पातः, सङ्गमः, सङ्गतिः *f.*, समागतिः *f.*—(Coincidence of opinion) ऐकमत्यं, एकचित्तता, सम्मतिः *f.*—(Accident) दैवयोगः, अकस्मात्, घटनं -ना, दैवघटनं; 'by an unlucky coincidence,' दुर्दैवात्, दैवदुर्घटनात्.

COINCIDENT, *a.* सन्निपतितः -ता -तं, सम्पाती -तिनी -ति (न्), सङ्गामी -मिनी -मि (न्).—(In time) समानकालीनः -ना -नं.—(Consistent) अविरुद्धः -द्धा -द्धं, अनुसारी -रिणी -रि (न्), सदृशः -शी -शं.

COINDICATION, *s.* एककारणमुद्दिश्य लक्षणबाहुल्यं.

COINER, *s.* (A minter) मुद्राङ्ककः, टङ्काङ्कयिता *m.* (तृ), मुद्राकारः, नाणककृत्, नैष्किकः.—(Inventor) कल्पकः, स्रष्टा *m.* (ष्टृ), कारकः.

COISTREL, *s.* कापुरुषः, हतकः, भीरुः *m.*, युद्धपराङ्मुखः.

COITION, *s.* मैथुनं, रतं, सुरतं, अङ्गसङ्गः, औपस्थ्यं, सम्भोगः, संयोजनं, रतिक्रिया, रतिकर्म्म *n.* (न्).

COKE, *s.* अर्द्धदग्धाङ्गारोच्छिष्टं, तप्तकृष्णमृत्तिकोच्छिष्टं.

COLANDER, *s.* चालनं -नी, सम्मार्ज्जनयन्त्रं, शोधनी, शोधनयन्त्रं.

COLATION, *s.* (The act of straining) शोधनं, सम्मार्ज्जनं, चालनं.

COLD, *a.* शीतः -ता -तं, शीतलः -ला -लं, शिशिरः -रा -रं, हिमः -मा -मं, हिमवान् -वती -वत् (त्), अनुष्णः -ष्णा -ष्णं, अतप्तः -प्ता -प्तं; 'suffering from cold,' शीतार्त्तः -र्त्ता -र्त्तं, हिमार्त्तः -र्त्ता -र्त्तं; 'a cold wind,' शीतलवातः; 'cold weather,' शीतकालः -लं.—(Indifferent, cold in disposition) विरक्तः -क्ता -क्तं, उदासीनः -ना -नं, जलाशयः -या -यं, निरीहः -हा -हं.—(Wanting in affection) निःस्नेहः -हा -हं.—(Cold-blooded) रक्तहीनः -ना -नं.

COLD, *s.* शीतं, शीतता, शैत्यं, शीतलं -लता, शिशिरः, हिमं; 'cold weather,' शीतकालः -लं, शिशिरकालः -लं; 'cold season,' हिमागमः, शिशिरं, शीतकः.—(Disease caused by cold) पीनसः, प्रतिश्यायः, काशः, कफः, श्लेष्म *n.* (न्); 'having a cold,' काशी -शिनी -शि (न्), पीनसी -सिनी -सि (न्), कफी -फिनी -फि (न्).

COLDISH, *a.* शीतलः -ला -लं, ईषच्छीतः -ता -तं, आशीतः -ता -तं.

COLDLY, *adv.* शीतं, शीतलं, शैत्येन, शिशिरं.—(Indifferently) विरक्तं, विरक्त्या, निःस्नेहं, स्नेहं विना, स्नेहव्यतिरेकेण.

COLDNESS, *s.* शीतता, शैत्यं, शीतं, शीतलता, हिमं, हैमं, शीतीभावः.—(Want of affection) नैःस्नेह्यं, निःस्नेहता.—(Indifference) विरक्तिः *f.*, वैराग्यं, औदास्यं, निरीहता.

COLE or COLEWORT, *s.* शाकः, हरितकं, शूरणं, शिग्रुः *m.*

COLIC, *s.* शूलं, वातशूलं, पक्तिशूलं, आमशूलं, जठरव्यथा, जठरज्वाला, उदरवेदना, वातगुल्मान्त्रं.—(Having the colic) शूली -लिनी -लि (न्).

COLIC, *a.* उदरवेदनाजनकः -का -कं, जठरव्यथाकारः -रा -रं.

To COLLAPSE, *v. n.* (Fall together) सम्पत् (c. 1. -पतति -तितुं), सन्निपत्.—(Shrink) सङ्कुच् in pass. (-कुच्यते), शॄ in pass. (शीर्य्यते), सङ्कोचम् इ (c. 2. एति, एतुं), संक्षिप् in pass. (-क्षिप्यते), संहृ in pass. (-ह्रियते), संहन् in pass. (-हन्यते), संश्यानीभू.

COLLAPSED, *p. p.* सङ्कुचितः -ता -तं, शीर्णः -र्णा -र्णं, संहतः -ता -तं, संहृतः -ता -तं, संक्षिप्तः -प्ता -प्तं, संवृतः -ता -तं, संश्यानः -ना -नं, सन्नः -न्ना -न्नं.

COLLAR, *s.* ग्रैवं -वेयं -वेयकं, गलमेखला, कण्ठभूषा, कण्ठलता, माला, ग्रीवाभरणं, माला.—(Halter for the neck) कण्ठपाशकः, कण्ठतलासिका.

To COLLAR, *v. a.* ग्रैवेयके धृ (c. 1. धरति, धर्त्तुं) or हस्तं दा (c. 3. ददाति, दातुं).

COLLAR-BONE, *s.* जत्रु *n.*, ग्रीवास्थि *n.*, कण्ठास्थि *n.*; 'the collar bones,' जत्रुणी *n. du.*

COLLARED, *p. p.* ग्रैवेयके or ग्रीवायां धृतः -ता -तं.

To COLLATE, *v. a.* (Compare one thing with another) उपमा (c. 2. -माति, c. 3. -मिमीते -मातुं), सम्प्रधृ in caus. (-धारयति -यितुं), with 2 acc.; साधारणीकृ.—(Collate books) गुणनीं कृ, शुध् in caus. (शोधयति -यितुं).—(Place in a benefice, confer) धर्म्माध्यापकाय वृत्तिं प्रतिपद् in caus. (-पादयति -यितुं) or प्रदा (c. 3. -ददाति -दातुं).

COLLATED, *p. p.* उपमितः -ता -तं, शोधितः -ता -तं, प्रदत्तः -त्ता -त्तं.

COLLATERAL, *a.* (Parallel, side to side) पार्श्वापार्श्विभूतः -ता -तं, पार्श्वापार्श्विगतः -ता -तं.—(Not direct) प्रासङ्गिकः -की -कं, आनुषङ्गिकः -की -कं, वक्रः -क्रा -क्रं, विलोमः -मा -मं, असरलः -ला -लं.—(Concurrent) अनुवादकः -का -कं.—(Sprung from a common ancestor) सगोत्रः -त्रा -त्रं, सपिण्डः, समानोदकः.

COLLATERALLY, *adv.* पार्श्वापार्श्वि.—(Indirectly) प्रसङ्गक्रमेण, वक्रं, असरलं.

COLLATION, *s.* (Comparison of one thing with another) उपमानं, उपमितिः *f.*—(Of books) गुणनी, शोधनं.—(Act of bestowing) प्रदानं, प्रतिपादनं.—(To a benefice) धर्म्माध्यापकाय वृत्तिप्रतिपादनं.

or वृत्तिप्रदानं.—(A cold repast) पूर्व्वेद्युःसिद्धानां मांसादिखाद्यानां सम्भारः.

COLLATOR, *s.* (One that compares books) ग्रन्थसंशोधनकर्त्ता *m.* (र्त्तृ), ग्रन्थशोधनकृत्.—(One that confers a benefice) धर्म्माध्यापकवृत्तिप्रदाता *m.* (तृ).

COLLEAGUE, *s.* सहकारी *m.* (न्), सम्भूयकारी *m.* (न्), तुल्यवृत्तिः *m.*, तुल्यव्यापारी *m.* (न्), एकविषयी *m.* (न्), सहायः, सङ्गी *m.* (न्).

To COLLECT, *v. a.* (Gather together) चि (c 5. चिनोति, चेतुं), अवचि, समाचि, आचि, प्रचि, सञ्चि, समानी (c. 1. -नयति -नेतुं), समुपानी, सम्भृ (c. 1. -भरति, c. 3. -बिभर्त्ति -भर्त्तुं), समादा (c. 3. -ददाति -दातुं), समाक्षिप् (c. 6. -क्षिपति -क्षेप्तुं), संहन् (c. 2. -हन्ति -हन्तुं), समाहृ (c. 1. -हरति -हर्त्तुं), उपसंहृ, समूह् (c. 1. -ऊहते -हितुं), सङ्ग्रह् (c. 9. -गृह्णाति -ग्रहीतुं), एकीकृ, एकत्र कृ.—(Collect into a heap) राशीकृ, पिण्ड् (c. 10. पिण्डयति -यितुं), पिण्डीकृ, पूगीकृ, एकौघीकृ.—(Collect themselves, assemble) समे (*i.e.* सम् and आ with rt. इ, समैति, समैतुं), सङ्गम् (c. 1. -गच्छति -गन्तुं), समागम्, एकत्र मिल् (c. 6. मिलति, मेलितुं).—(Collect taxes) करान् or शुल्कान् ग्रह्.—(Infer) अनुमा (c. 2. -माति c. 3. -मिमीते -मातुं), ऊह्, अवगम् (c. 1. -गच्छति -गन्तुं). (Collect one's self, recover one's self) मनः or चेतः समाधा (c. 3. -दधाति -धत्ते -धातुं), संज्ञां लभ् (c. 1. लभते, लब्धुं), स्वप्रकृतिम् आपद् (c. 4. -पद्यते -पत्तुं), or प्रतिपद्.

COLLECT, *s.* ख्रीष्टीयानां रविवारादिविशिष्टपर्व्वोद्देशमुद्दिश्य प्रार्थना, संक्षेपिकप्रार्थना, स्तुत् *f.* (त्).

COLLECTED, *p. p.* सञ्चितः -ता -तं, उपचितः -ता -तं, समुपचितः -ता -तं, समूढः -ढा -ढं, सङ्गूढः -ढा -ढं, सम्भृतः -ता -तं, सम्भूतः -ता -तं, एकीकृतः -ता -तं, एकस्थः -स्था -स्थं, सन्निपतितः -ता -तं, संहतः -ता -तं, समवेतः -ता -तं, सङ्कलितः -ता -तं.—(Heaped) राशीभूतः -ता -तं, पूगीकृतः -ता -तं, पुञ्जितः -ता -तं, एकौघभूतः -ता -तं, एकराशिभूतः -ता -तं.—(In mind) समाहितः -ता -तं, लब्धचेताः -ताः -तः (स्), लब्धसंज्ञः -ज्ञा -ज्ञं, निराकुलः -ला -लं, प्रकृतिमापन्नः -न्ना -न्नं, अव्यस्तः -स्ता -स्तं, अव्यग्रः -ग्रा -ग्रं.

COLLECTIBLE, *a.* चयनीयः -या -यं, चेयः -या -यं, चेतव्यः -व्या -व्यं, सञ्चेयः -या -यं, उपचेयः -या -यं, समूह्यः -ह्या -ह्यं.

COLLECTION, *s.* सञ्चयः, चयः, समुच्चयः, निचयः, प्रचयः, समूहः, सङ्ग्रहः -हणं, सन्निपातः, सङ्घातः, सङ्घः, संहतिः *f.*, ओघः समुदायः, वृन्दं, समवायः, संहारः, समाहारः, सञ्चयः, चायः, सङ्घः, अक्षौहिणी, राशिः *m. f.*, पुञ्जः, पिण्डः, पूगः, विन्यासः, सङ्कुलः, ग्रामः in comp.; 'collection of people,' जनसमूहः, जननिवहः, जनौघं, जनसमागमः; 'of clouds,' घनचयः, घनौघः, जलदसंहतिः *f.*—(Raising money) एकैकस्मात् किञ्चित्किञ्चिद्धनग्रहणं, धनोत्तोलनं.

COLLECTIVE, *a.* समवायी -यिनी -यि (न्), सञ्चयी -यिनी -यि (न्), सङ्कुलः -ली -लं, उपचितः -ता -तं, गणीभूतः -ता -तं, सामान्यः -न्या -न्यं, साधारणः -णी -णं.

COLLECTIVELY, *adv.* (Generally) साधारण्येन, साकल्येन.—(In a mass) सङ्घशस्, अपृथक्, समूहं, ओघशस्.

COLLECTOR, *s.* सञ्चेता *m.* (तृ), सञ्चयी *m.* (न्), सङ्ग्रहीता *m.* (तृ), सङ्ग्राहकः.—(A tax-gatherer) करग्रहः, शुल्कग्राही *m.* (न्).

COLLEGE, *s.* (For learning) विद्यालयः, विद्यावेश्म *n.* (न्), चतुष्पाठी, पाठशाला, छात्रादिनिलयः, अवसथः -थ्यः.—(For religion) मठः, आश्रमः, विहारः, वीहारः.—(A community of persons) श्रेणिः *m. f.*, जनसमूहः, पंक्तिः *f.*, गणः.

COLLEGIAN, *s.* छात्रः, विद्यार्थी *m.* (न्), विद्यालयस्थः, अन्तेवासी *m.* (न्).

COLLEGIATE, *a.* विद्यालयसम्बन्धी -न्धिनी -न्धि (न्), आश्रमिकः -की -कं, आश्रमी -मिणी -मि (न्), मठसम्बन्धीयः -या -यं.

COLLET, *s.* (Collar) ग्रैवेयकं, ग्रीवाभरणं.—(Of a ring) अङ्गुरीयकभागो यत्र मणिः प्रणिधीयते.

To COLLIDE, *v. a.* संहन् (c. 2. -हन्ति -हन्तुं), समाहन्, सङ्घट्ट (c. 10. -घट्टयति -यितुं), मृद् (c. 9. मृद्नाति, मर्द्दितुं), निष्पिष् (c. 7. -पिनष्टि -पेष्टुं), घृष् (c. 1. घर्षति -र्षितुं).

COLLIED, *p. p.* अङ्गारमलिनितः -ता -तं, मलीमसः -सा -सं, अङ्गारितः -ता -तं.

COLLIER, *s.* अङ्गारखनकः, कृष्णभूमिखनकः, अङ्गाराखनिकः, अङ्गारविक्रेता *m.* (तृ).

COLLIERY, *s.* अङ्गारखानिः *f.*, अङ्गारोत्पत्तिस्थानं, कृष्णभूमिखननस्थानं.

COLLIFLOWER, *s.* शाकः, हरितकं, शूरणं, पोतकी.

COLLIGATION, *s.* सम्बन्धनं, एकत्र बन्धनं, संश्लेषणं, संयोजनं.

COLLIMATION or COLLINEATION, *s.* सन्धानं, अभिसन्धानं, लक्ष्यीकरणं.

COLLIQUABLE, *a.* द्राव्यः -व्या -व्यं, गलनीयः -या -यं.

To COLLIQUATE, *v. a.* विली in caus. (-लापयति -लाययति -यितुं), द्रवीकृ.

COLLIQUATION, *s.* विलयनं, गलनं, द्रवीकरणं, विद्रावणं.

COLLIQUATIVE, *a.* विद्रावकः -का -कं, विलयनकारी -रिणी -रि (न्), गलनकृत्.

COLLISION, *s.* सङ्घट्टः -ट्टनं, परस्परसमाघातः, समाघातः, प्रतिघातः, सम्मर्द्दः, घर्षणं, घनाघनः, स्खलनं.

To COLLOCATE, *v. a.* स्था in caus. (स्थापयति -यितुं), अवस्था, प्रतिष्ठा, धा (c. 3. दधाति, धातुं), आधा, न्यस् (c. 4. -अस्यति -असितुं), विन्यस्, ऋ in caus. (अर्पयति -यितुं), नियुज् (c. 7. -युनक्ति -योक्तुं), निविश् in caus. (-वेशयति -यितुं).

COLLOCATED, *p. p.* स्थापितः -ता -तं, प्रतिष्ठापितः -ता -तं, आहितः -ता -तं, विनिवेशितः -ता -तं, न्यस्तः -स्ता -स्तं, अर्पितः -ता -तं, रोपितः -ता -तं.

COLLOCATION, *s.* स्थापनं, प्रतिष्ठापनं, न्यसनं, निवेशनं, अर्पणं, प्रयोगः.

COLLOCUTION, *s.* सम्भाषणं, आभाषणं, सम्प्रवदनं, कथायोगः, कथाप्रसङ्गः.

To COLLOGUE, *v. n.* लल् in caus. (लालयति -यितुं), चाटूक्त्या सान्त्व् (c. 10. सान्त्वयति -यितुं).

COLLOP, *s.* (Of meat) मांसखण्डं, आमिषखण्डं, मांसलवः.

COLLOQUIAL, *a.* संलापी -पिनी -पि (न्); 'colloquial style,' कथोपकथनयोग्यो वाग्व्यापारः.

COLLOQUY, *s.* सम्भाषा, संलापः, सङ्कथा, संवादः, कथोपकथनं.

To COLLUDE, *v. a.* पक्षपातं कृ, गणतां कृ, कूटसंविदं कृ, अङ्गाङ्गिभू.

COLLUSION, *s.* पक्षपातः -तिता, गणता, कूटगणता, अङ्गाङ्गिभावः, कूटसंविद्, प्रतारणा, कूटता, चापल्यं, शठता.

COLLUSIVE, *a.* पक्षपाती -तिनी -ति (न्), पक्षपातघटितः -ता -तं, कौटिकः -की -कं.

COLLUSIVELY, *adv.* पक्षपातेन, कूटगणतापूर्व्वकं, अङ्गाङ्गि.

COLLY, *s.* अङ्गारमलं, अङ्गारकिट्टं, अङ्गारकल्कं.

To COLLY, *v. a.* अङ्गारेण कृष्णीकृ or कृष्ण (nom. कृष्णायते) or मलीमसीकृ.

COLLYRIUM, *s.* अञ्जनं, रसाञ्जनं, नेत्राञ्जनं, दार्व्विका, कज्जलं, कर्परी, खर्परी, तुत्थं, रसगर्भं, तार्क्ष्यशैलं.

COLOCYNTH, *s.* चरुका, इन्द्रवारुणिका, दाला, गलङ्कः, काकमर्द्दः, पिठङ्काकी, सुमला, विषघ्नी.

COLON, *s.* (A point used to mark a pause) वाक्यपरिमापकं द्विबिन्दुचिह्नं, द्विबिन्दुः *m.*—(The great intestine) महापुरीतत् *m.*, महदन्त्रं, महानाली.

COLONEL, *s.* व्यूहपतिः *m.*, गुल्मपतिः, सैन्यदलाध्यक्षः, सैन्याधिपतिः *m.*

COLONELSHIP, *s.* व्यूहपतित्वं, गुल्मपतिपदं, सैन्यदलाध्यक्षत्वं.

COLONIAL, *a.* नवीनवसतिस्थानसम्बन्धी -न्धिनी -न्धि (न्), प्रादेशिकः -की -कं.

COLONIST, *s.* स्वदेशत्यागानन्तरं देशान्तरवासी *m.* (न्), अधिवासी *m.* (न्),

प्रदेशवासी, दूरवासी, प्रदेशस्थः.

COLONIZATION, *s.* स्वदेशं त्यक्तुकामानां दूरदेशाधिवासनं, देशान्तराधिवासनं, प्रदेशवासनं.

To COLONIZE, *v. a.* स्वदेशं त्यक्तुकामान् प्रदेशे वस् in caus. (वासयति -यितुं) or अधिवस्, अध्यास् in caus. (-आसयति -यितुं).

COLONIZED, *p. p.* अधिवासितः -ता -तं, अध्युषितः -ता -तं, वासितः -ता -तं, अध्यासितः -ता -तं.

COLONNADE, *s.* मण्डलरूपेण विन्यस्ता स्तम्भश्रेणी, स्तम्भपंक्तिपरिवेष्टितश् छन्नपथः, स्तम्भपंक्तिः *f.*

COLONY, *s.* (The country planted) स्वदेशत्यागिभिर् वासितः प्रदेशः, नवीनवसतिस्थानं, प्रदेशः.—(The people) प्रदेशवासिनः *m. pl.*, अधिवासिनः *m. pl.*, नवीनवासिनः.

COLOPHONY, *s.* अरालः, रालः, धूपनः, सर्ज्जरसः, अग्निवल्लभः. *See* RESIN.

COLOQUINTIDA, *s.* अरुणा, दाला, जलकुः, काकमर्द्दकः. *See* COLOCYNTH.

COLORATE, *a.* रागी -गिणी -गि (न्), सरागः -गा -गं, रङ्गी -ङ्गिनी -ङ्गि (न्).

COLORATION, *s.* रञ्जनं, वर्णनं.—(The state) रागः.

COLORIFIC, *a.* रङ्गी -ङ्गिनी -ङ्गि (न्), रागदः -दा -दं, वर्णदः -दा -दं.

COLOSSAL OF COLOSSEAN, *a.* बृहत्कायः -या -यं, बृहच्छरीरः -रा -रं, अतिमानुषाकारः -रा -रं, भीमविग्रहः -हा -हं, दानवाकारः -रा -रं, असम्भवमूर्त्तिः -र्त्तिः -र्त्ति.

COLOSSUS, *s.* बृहत्प्रतिमा -प्रतिमानं, बृहत्प्रतिच्छन्दकं, बृहत्सूर्म्मी, अतिमानुषपरिमाणा मूर्त्तिः.

COLOUR, *s.* (Hue, dye, tint) रागः, रङ्गः, वर्णः; 'of one colour,' एकवर्णः -र्णा -र्णं; 'of the same colour,' सवर्णः -र्णा -र्णं, समवर्णः -र्णा -र्णं; 'of various colours,' नानावर्णः -र्णा -र्णं; 'of lasting colour,' स्थिररङ्गः -ङ्गा -ङ्गं; 'to change colour,' विवर्णीभू; 'that has lost its colour,' वीतरागः -गा -गं.—(Paint) रङ्गः, वर्णकः -का, लेपः; 'a picture in colours,' चित्रलेखा, चित्रलिखितं, चित्रं.—(Complexion, colour in the cheek) कपोलरागः; 'of a ruddy colour,' अरुणवदनः -ना -नं, लोहिताननः -नी -नं; 'without colour,' विवर्णवदनः -ना -नं.—(Colours of a regiment) पताका, ध्वजः, वैजयन्ती.—(Pretext) अपदेशः, व्यपदेशः, छद्म *n.* (न्); 'under colour of a vow,' व्रतव्यपदेशेन.

To COLOUR, *v. a.* रञ्ज् in caus. (रञ्जयति -यितुं), वर्ण् (c. 10. वर्णयति -यितुं), चित्र् (c. 10. चित्रयति -यितुं), सरागं -गां -गं कृ.—(Excuse, palliate) व्यपदिश् (c. 6. -दिशति -देष्टुं), अपदिश्, शम् in caus. (शमयति -यितुं), छद् (c. 10. छादयति -यितुं).—(Make plausible) सत्यसङ्काशं -शां -शं कृ, सुदृश्यं -श्यां -श्यं कृ.

To COLOUR, *v. n.* (Take a colour) रञ्ज् in pass. (रज्यते), संरञ्ज्.—(Blush) सलज्जत्वाद् रक्तवदनः -नी -नं भू, लज्ज् (c. 1. लज्जते -ज्जितुं), व्रीड् (c. 4. व्रीड्यति, व्रीडितुं).

COLOURABLE, *a.* सत्यसङ्काशः -शा -शं, सुदृश्यः -श्या -श्यं, सम्भावनीयः -या -यं.

COLOURABLY, *adv.* सत्यसङ्काशं, सत्यसन्निभं, सत्यसदृशं, सुदृश्यतया.

COLOURED, *p. p.* रञ्जितः -ता -तं, रक्तः -क्ता -क्तं, रागी -गिणी -गि (न्), सरागः -गा -गं, रागान्वितः -ता -तं, वर्णितः -ता -तं, वर्णगतः -ता -तं; 'many-coloured,' नानावर्णः -र्णा -र्णं.

COLOURING, *s.* वर्णनं, रञ्जनं, चित्रकरणं.—(The art of colouring or painting) चित्रविद्या, चित्रकर्म्म *n.* (न्), आलेख्यकरणं.—(Rhetorical ornament) अलङ्कारः, वर्णनं.

COLOURIST, *s.* रञ्जकः, रङ्गाजीवः, चित्रकरः, वर्णी *m.* (न्), वर्णधारकः, तौलिकः.

COLOURLESS, *a.* अवर्णः -र्णा -र्णं, विवर्णः -र्णा -र्णं, वर्णहीनः -ना -नं, नीरक्तः -क्ता -क्तं, वीतरागः -गा -गं, रागहीनः -ना -नं.

COLT, *s.* किशोरः, अश्वशावः -वकः, वालः, अश्वपोतः, घोटकवत्सः.—(A young foolish fellow) किशोरः, चपलः, प्रमादी *m.* (न्).

COLTSFOOT, *s.* कासनाशिनी, कासघ्नी, कासमर्द्दः.

COLT'S-TOOTH, *s.* किशोरदन्तः, अश्वशावकदन्तः.

COLTER, *s.* लाङ्गलदन्तः, हलदन्तः, फालः, कृन्तत्रं, हलकीलः.

COLTISH, *a.* चपलः -ला -लं, प्रकृतितरलः -ला -लं, चञ्चलः -ला -लं.

COLUMBARY, *s.* (Dove-cot) कपोतपालिका, कपोतागारं, विटङ्कः.

COLUMBINE, *s.* (A plant) वनौषधिभेदः.—(Female character in a pantomime) रङ्गावतारिणी.

COLUMN, *s.* (A pillar) स्तम्भः, स्थूणा, यूपः -पं, यष्टिः *f.*—(An array of troops in column) भोगव्यूहः, सूचिव्यूहः.—(Half a page) अर्द्धपृष्ठं, अर्द्धपत्रं, अर्द्धफलकः.

COLUMNAR, *a.* स्तम्भाकारः -रा -रं, स्तम्भाकृतिः -तिः -ति.

COMA, *s.* अतिशयनिद्रालक्षितो रोगविशेषः.

COMATE, *s.* सहायः, सङ्गी *m.* (न्), सहवासी *m.* (न्), सहवर्त्ती *m.* (न्).

COMATOSE, *s.* अतिशयनिद्राग्रस्तः -स्ता -स्तं, अतिनिद्रातुरः -रा -रं.

COMB, *s.* कङ्कतः -ती -तं -तिका, केशमार्जकः -र्जनं -र्जनी, प्रसाधनी -नं, मार्जनी, दन्ती *m.* (न्).—(Crest of a cock) कुक्कुटचूडा, कुक्कुटशिखा.—(A valley) दरी, कन्दरी.—(Instrument for carding wool) ऊर्णामार्जनी.—(Honey-comb) मधुकोषः, करण्डः.

To COMB, *v. a.* केशान् मृज् (c. 2. मार्ष्टि, मार्ष्टुं) or सम्मृज् or विजटीकृ or निर्घृष् (c. 1. -घर्षति -र्षितुं), वितूस्त (nom. वितूस्तयति -यितुं).

COMB-MAKER, *s.* केशमार्जनकारः, कङ्कतकृत्, कङ्कतिकाविक्रयी *m.* (न्).

To COMBAT, *v. n.* युध् (c. 4. युध्यते, योद्धुं), विग्रह् (c. 9. -गृह्णाति -ग्रहीतुं), सङ्ग्राम् (c. 10. सङ्ग्रामयति -यितुं), सङ्ग्रामं कृ.

To COMBAT, *v. a.* (Oppose in fight) प्रतियुध् (c. 4. -युध्यते -योद्धुं or in caus. -योधयति -यितुं) with acc., प्रतिरुध् (c. 7. -रुणद्धि -रोद्धुं), प्रतिकूल (nom. प्रतिकूलयति -यितुं).—(In argument) विवद् (c. 1. -वदते -दितुं) with instr.; 'to combat one's passions,' इन्द्रियाणि निग्रह् (c. 9. -गृह्णाति -ग्रहीतुं).

COMBAT, *s.* युद्धं, युत् *f.* (ध्), रणः -णं, सङ्ग्रामः, समरः -रं, विग्रहः, कलहः, संयुगः, संख्यं, आहवः, आयोधनं, सङ्गरः, समाघातः, सम्परायः, जन्यं, मृधं, सम्प्रहारः, अभिसम्पातः, अभ्यागमः; 'hand to hand, combat,' बाहुयुद्धं; 'single combat,' द्वन्द्वयुद्धं; 'mingled combat,' तुमुलं, रणसङ्कुलं.

COMBATANT, *s.* योद्धा *m.* (द्धृ), योधः, युध्वा *m.* (न्), युयुत्सुः *m.*, प्रयुयुत्सुः, युधानः, प्रहर्त्ता *m.* (र्तृ).—(Duellist) द्वन्द्वयुद्धकृत्.—(Warrior) वीरः, सुभटः, भटः.

COMBER, *s.* ऊर्णामार्जकः, ऊर्णासम्मार्जनकृत्, ऊर्णानिर्घर्षणकः.

COMBINABLE, *a.* सन्धेयः -या -यं, सम्भाव्यः -व्या -व्यं, अविरुद्धः -द्धा -द्धं.

COMBINATION, *s.* योगः, संयोगः, सन्धिः *m.*, सन्धानं, संसर्गः, संश्लेषः, श्लेषः, सङ्गः -ङ्गमः, साहित्यं, संहतिः *f.*, सङ्घातः, संहतत्वं, सहायता, साहाय्यं, सार्थं, मेलकः, सम्भूतिः *f.*, संव्यूहः, समासक्तिः *f.*, आसक्तिः *f.*, समासञ्जनं, प्रसक्तिः.—(Commixture) सम्मिश्रणं, प्रक्षेपः; 'combination of letters,' सन्धिः *m.*—(Joint execution of work) सम्भूयकारित्वं, सम्भूयसमुत्थानं; 'in combination with his brethren,' भ्रातृसङ्घातवान् *m.* (त्).

To COMBINE, *v. a.* संयुज् (c. 7. -युनक्ति -योक्तुं or caus. -योजयति -यितुं), सन्धा (c. 3. -दधाति -धातुं), उपसन्धा, संहन् (c. 2. -हन्ति -हन्तुं), संश्लिष् in caus. (-श्लेषयति -यितुं), सङ्गम् in caus. (गमयति -यितुं), सम्मिश्

(c. 10. -मिश्रयति -यितुं), संलग्नीकृ, एकीकृ, एकत्र कृ.

To COMBINE, *v. n.* संयुज् in pass. (-युज्यते), सन्धा in pass. (-धीयते), संश्लिष् in pass. (-श्लिष्यते), सम्मिल् (c. 6. -मिलति -मेलितुं), संसृज् in pass. (-सृज्यते), सम्भू (c. 1. -भवति -वितुं), सङ्गम् (c. 1. -गच्छति -गन्तुं), संहन् in pass. (-हन्यते), संसञ्ज् in pass. (-सज्यते or -सज्जते), सम्मिश्रीभू, एकीभू, एकत्र मिल्.

COMBINED, *p. p.* संयुक्तः -क्ता -क्तं, संयोजितः -ता -तं, समायुक्तः -क्ता -क्तं, संश्लिष्टः -ष्टा -ष्टं, संहतः -ता -तं, सङ्घातवान् -वती -वत् (त्), सन्धितः -ता -तं, संहितः -ता -तं, सन्धानितः -ता -तं, सहितः -ता -तं, सहगतः -ता -तं, संसृष्टः -ष्टा -ष्टं, कृतसंसर्गः -र्गा -र्गं, सम्मिश्रः -श्रा -श्रं, मिश्रितः -ता -तं, सम्पृक्तः -क्ता -क्तं, मिलितः -ता -तं, संसक्तः -क्ता -क्तं, समासक्तः -क्ता -क्तं, समस्तः -स्ता -स्तं; 'having combined,' सम्भूय, मिलित्वा.

COMBLESS, *a.* चूडाहीनः -ना -नं, शिखाहीनः -ना -नं, चूडारहितः -ता -तं.

COMBUST, *a.* सूर्य्यस्य समीपवर्त्तिनी तारा.

COMBUSTIBLE, *a.* दहनीयः -या -यं, दाह्यः -ह्या -ह्यं, ज्वलनीयः -या -यं, दीपनीयः -या -यं, दीप्यः -प्या -प्यं, ज्वलनशीलः -ला -लं, ज्वलनार्हः -र्हा -र्हं.

COMBUSTIBLE, *s.* (A combustible) अग्निवल्लभः, शीघ्रं ज्वलनीयं किञ्चिद्वस्तु.

COMBUSTIBLENESS, *s.* दहनीयता, दाह्यत्वं, ज्वलनशीलत्वं.

COMBUSTION, *s.* (Burning) दाहः -हनं, ज्वलनं, दीपनं, तापः, ओषः, प्लोषः, प्रोषः.—(Tumult) तुमुलं, व्यस्तता, विप्लवः, वैक्लव्यं, कोलाहलः, आहवः.

To COME, *v. n.* आगम् (c. 1. -गच्छति -गन्तुं), अभ्यागम्, उपागम्, समुपागम्, अभिगम्, उपगम्; आया (c. 2. -याति -यातुं), समाया, उपाया, अभिया; उपस्था (c. 1. -तिष्ठति -स्थातुं), समुपस्था; ए (*i.e.* आ with rt. इ, c. 2. एति, एतुं), आव्रज् (c. 1. -व्रजति -जितुं), अभिपद् (c. 4. -पद्यते -पत्तुं), अभ्यृ (c. 1. -ऋच्छति -अर्त्तुं), उपक्रम् (c. 1. -क्रामति -क्रमितुं), अभिवृत् (c. 1. -वर्त्तते -र्त्तितुं), अभ्यावृत्; 'whence have you come,' कुतः समागतोऽसि.—(Come to, arrive at) प्राप् (c. 5. -आप्नोति -आप्तुं).—(Come and go) गमनागमनं कृ, गतागतं कृ, यातायातं कृ.—(Come about, come to pass) सम्पद्, संवृत्, सम्भू, उपस्था, निपत् (c. 1. -पतति -तितुं), आपत्.—(Come after) पश्चाद् आया, अन्वागम्, अन्वास्था.—(Come away) अपगम्, व्यपगम्, अपया, व्यपया.—(Come again) पुनर् आगम्, प्रत्यागम्, प्रत्यावृत्.—(Come behind) पृष्ठतः or पृष्ठेन आगम्.—(Come between) अन्तरागम्, अन्तर्वृत्, अन्तःस्था.—(Come back) प्रत्यागम्, प्रत्याया.—(Come down) अवरुह् (c. 1. -रोहति -रोढुं), अवतृ (c. 1. -तरति -रितुं -रीतुं).—(Come forth, come out) वहिर् आगम्, निर्गम्, निःसृ (c. 1. -सरति -सर्त्तुं). *See To* APPEAR.—(Come forward) अग्रतः स्था, सम्प्रस्था; 'in learning,' विद्यागमं कृ. *See To* ADVANCE.—(Come hither) अत्र आगम्.—(Come in). *See To* ENTER, ARRIVE, COMPLY.—(Come into) प्रविश् (c. 6. -विशति -वेष्टुं); 'be involved,' सम्बन्ध् in pass. (-बध्यते); 'come into trouble,' विपद्ग्रस्तः -स्ता -स्तं भू.—(Come near). *See To* APPROACH.—(Come out). *See To* APPEAR.—(Come to). *See To* AMOUNT, COST; 'that will come to a large sum of money,' तद् बहुधनव्ययसाध्यं.—(Come to one's self) संज्ञां or चेतनां लभ् (c. 1. लभते, लब्धुं) or प्राप् (c. 5. -आप्नोति, आप्तुं), सम्प्रकृतिम् आपद्.—(Come to an end) निवृत्, विनिवृत्. *See To* END.—(Come to life) उज्जीव् (c. 1. -जीवति -वितुं).—(Come to an agreement) संविदम् उपगम्.—(Come short) न्यूनीभू.—(Come together) समागम्, समे.—(Come upon) आक्रम्.

To COME, *adv.* (The time to come) भविष्यत्कालः, भविष्यत् *n.*, आगामिकालः, उत्तरकालः; 'generations to come,' पुत्रपौत्राः *m. pl.*

COME, *interj.* आगच्छ, एहि, आयाहि, यातु.—(Be quick) त्वरतां.—(Come up, said to horses) वहत वहत.

COME, *p. p.* आगतः -ता -तं, आयातः -ता -तं, उपस्थितः -ता -तं.—(Come to pass) सम्भूतः -ता -तं, समापन्नः -न्ना -न्नं, जातः -ता -तं, वृत्तः -त्ता -त्तं, संवृत्तः -त्ता -त्तं, उपावृत्तः -त्ता -त्तं.—(Come back) प्रत्यागतः -ता -तं.

COMEDIAN, *s.* (A comic actor) वैहासिकः.—(Stage-player) नटः, नाटकः, कुशीलवः, चारणः, रङ्गाजीवः, रङ्गावतारी *m.* (न्), अभिनेता *m.* (तृ), शैलाली *m.* (न्), नर्त्तकः.

COMEDY, *s.* नाटकः, नाटिका, भाणिका, प्रहसनं, दुर्मल्लिका.

COMELINESS, *s.* सुदृश्यता, सौन्दर्य्यं, सुन्दरत्वं, लावण्यं, सुरूपता, रूपं.

COMELY, *a.* सुदृश्यः -श्या -श्यं, सुन्दरः -रा -री -रं, चारुः -र्व्वी -रु, रूपवान् -वती -वत् (त्), सुरूपः -पी -पं, अभिरूपः -पी -पं, सौम्यः -म्यी -म्यं, अभिरामः -मा -मं.

COMER, *s.* आगन्ता *m.* (न्तृ), आगामी *m.* (न्), आयायी *m.* (न्); 'a new-comer,' आगन्तुः *m.* -न्तुकः, अभ्यागतः, आवेशिकः.

COMET, *s.* केतुतारा, धूमकेतुः *m.*, केतुः *m.*, अग्न्युत्पातः, शिखावज् ज्योतिः *n.* (स्), उत्पातः, उपग्रहः, उल्का.

COMETARY, *a.* धूमकेतुसम्बन्धी -न्धिनी -न्धि (न्), औत्पातिकः -की -कं.

To COMFIT, *v. a.* मोदकं कृ, मिष्टीकृ, मधुशर्करादिना उपस्कृ.

COMFIT or COMFITURES, *s. pl.* मोदकं -कः, मिष्टं, मिष्टान्नं, खण्डमोदकः, मधुमस्तकं, गुडकः, लड्डुकं, उपस्कराः.

To COMFORT, *v. a.* आश्वस् in caus. (-श्वासयति -यितुं), सान्त्व् or शान्त्व् (c. 10. सान्त्वयति -यितुं), अभिशान्त्व्, उपसान्त्व्, परिशान्त्व्, सन्तुष् in caus. (-तोषयति -यितुं), आप्यै in caus. (-प्याययति -यितुं).—(Gladden) नन्द् in caus. (नन्दयति -यितुं), हृष् in caus. (हर्षयति -यितुं).

COMFORT, *s.* (Ease) सुखं, सन्तोषः, सुस्थता, सौख्यं, सम्पत्तिः *f.*—(Consolation) आश्वासनं, सान्त्वनं -ना, शान्त्वं, उपशान्तिः *f.*, सन्तोषणं, शोकापनोदः, विनोदः, प्रबोधः.—(Of mind) मनःसन्तोषः.

COMFORTABLE, *a.* सुखमयः -यी -यं, सुखदः -दा -दं, स्वस्थः -स्था -स्थं, सुस्थः -स्था -स्थं, सन्तोषकः -का -कं, स्वास्थ्यजनकः -का -कं.—(Consolatory) आश्वासकः -सिका -कं, शान्तिदः -दा -दं, क्लेशापहः -हा -हं, शोकापहारकः -का -कं.

COMFORTABLENESS, *s.* स्वास्थ्यं, सुस्थता, सौख्यं, हृष्टपुष्टता.

COMFORTABLY, *adv.* सुखेन, सुखं, यथासुखं, मनःसन्तोषेण, अनायासेन, आनन्दं.

COMFORTED, *p. p.* आश्वासितः -ता -तं, सन्तोषितः -ता -तं, आप्यायितः -ता -तं, सन्तुष्टमनाः -नाः -नः (स्), गतोद्वेगः -गा -गं, प्रबोधितः -ता -तं, आनन्दितः -ता -तं.

COMFORTER, *s.* आश्वासकः, सन्तोषदः, सान्त्ववादः, शोकापनुदः, आश्वासशीलः, शोकापहर्त्ता *m.* (र्त्तृ), प्रबोधयिता *m.* (तृ).

COMFORTLESS, *a.* निरानन्दः -न्दा -न्दं, सन्तोषहीनः -ना -नं, अनाश्वासनीयः -या -यं.

COMIC or COMICAL, *a.* हासकरः -री -रं, हास्यः -स्या -स्यं, उपहास्यः -स्या -स्यं, हास्योत्पादकः -का -कं, कौतुकी -किनी -कि (न्).—(Odd, uncouth) अपरूपः -पा -पं, असङ्गतः -ता -तं.—(Relating to a comedy) प्रहसननाटकसम्बन्धी -न्धिनी -न्धि (न्).

COMICALLY, *adv.* यथा हास उत्पाद्यते तथा, हास्यप्रकारेण, असङ्गतं.

COMICALNESS, *s.* हास्यत्वं, उपहास्यता, कौतुकं, अपरूपता.

COMING, *s.* आगमः -मनं, अभिगमः -मनं, उपगमः, उपस्थितिः *f.*, उपस्थानं, उपसन्नता; 'coming and going,' गतागतं, गमनागमनं; 'coming on of night,' रात्रियोगः.

COMING, *a.* (Ready) उद्यतः -ता -तं, सुप्रस्तुतः -ता -तं.—(Future, to come) आगामी -मिनी -मि (न्), अनागतः -ता -तं, भावी -विनी -वि (न्), भविष्यन् -ष्यन्ती -ष्यत् (त्), उत्तरकालीनः -ना -नं.

COMING-IN, *s.* (Income) आयः, आगमः, धनागमः.—(Submission) परवशगमनं.

COMITY, *s.* अनुनयः, अनुकूलता, प्रश्रयः, अनुरोधः, सौजन्यं.

COMMA, *s.* पदविच्छेदचिह्नं, पदावच्छेदचिह्नं, वाक्यविच्छेदचिह्नं.

To COMMAND, *v. a.* (Give orders, enjoin) आज्ञा in caus. (-ज्ञापयति -यितुं), समाज्ञा, आदिश् (c. 6. -दिशति -देष्टुं), समादिश्, सन्दिश्, व्यादिश्, प्रतिसन्दिश्, चुद् (c. 10. चोदयति -यितुं), अभिचुद्, प्रक्लृप् (c. 10. -कल्पयति -यितुं).—(Govern, hold in subjection) शास् (c. 2. शास्ति, शासितुं), ईश् (c. 2. ईष्टे, ईशितुं), वशीकृ, अभिभू, निग्रह् (c. 9. -गृह्णाति -ग्रहीतुं); 'to command one's passions,' इन्द्रियाणि संयम् (c. 1. -यच्छति -यन्तुं).—(Have authority over any thing) अधिष्ठा (c. 1. -तिष्ठति -ष्ठातुं).—(Overlook) अवलोक् (c. 10. -लोकयति -यितुं), निरीक्ष् (c. 1. -ईक्षते -क्षितुं).

COMMAND, *s.* (Order) आज्ञा, आदेशः, आज्ञप्तिः, निदेशः, निर्देशः, नियोगः, शासनं, शास्तिः *f.*, शिष्टिः *f.*, चोदनं, वचनं, प्रयुक्तिः *f.*, नियमः, प्रेरणं -णा, मतं, अववादः; 'obedient to commands,' आज्ञाकरः -री -रं; 'word of command,' निदेशः.—(Authority, power, right of commanding) अधिकारः, अधिकारित्वं, प्रभावः, प्रभुत्वं, आधिपत्यं, अध्यक्षता, अधिष्ठातृत्वं.—(Subjection) वशं, अधीनता.—(Command of an army) सैनापत्यं; 'under one's command,' वशीकृतः -ता -तं, वशीभूतः -ता -तं, वशङ्गतः -ता -तं, स्वाधीनः -ना -नं; 'to bring any thing under one's command,' आत्मवशं नेतुं; 'self-command,' आत्मसंयमः, अन्तर्यमनं. Particles of command, परं, परमं.

COMMANDANT, *s.* अधिकारी *m.* (न्), अधिकृतः, अधिष्ठाता *m.* (तृ), अध्यक्षः.

COMMANDED, *p. p.* आज्ञापितः -ता -तं, आज्ञप्तः -प्ता -प्तं, आज्ञातः -ता -तं, आदिष्टः -ष्टा -ष्टं, समादिष्टः -ष्टा -ष्टं, दत्ताज्ञः -ज्ञा -ज्ञं, चोदितः -ता -तं, प्रचोदितः -ता -तं, प्रेरितः -ता -तं, विहितः -ता -तं.

COMMANDER, *s.* (One who orders) आज्ञापकः, आदेशी *m.* (न्), आदेष्टा *m.* (ष्टृ).—(Chief) अधिपतिः *m.*, पतिः *m.*, अधिष्ठाता *m.* (तृ), अधिकारी *m.* (न्), अधिकृतः, अध्यक्षः.—(Of an army) सेनानीः, सेनापतिः, सेनाग्रगः, सेनाध्यक्षः, योधमुख्यः.

COMMANDMENT, *s.* आज्ञा, आदेशः, विधिः *m.*, सूत्रं.—(Of God) ईश्वराज्ञा.

COMMANDRESS, *s.* अधिकारिणी, अधिष्ठात्री, आधिपत्यकारिणी.

COMMATERIAL, *a.* एकमूर्त्तिः -र्त्तिः -र्त्ति, एकवस्तुः -स्तुः -स्तु, एकभावः -वा -वं.

To COMMEMORATE, *v. a.* किञ्चित्स्मरणीयकर्म्मोद्दिश्य उत्सवं कृ or सेव् (c. 1. सेवते -वितुं) or आचर् (c. 1. -चरति -रितुं) or समाचर्, किञ्चित्कर्म्मस्मरणार्थं पर्व्व पाल् (c. 10. पालयति -यितुं), or विधिवत् कृ.—(Cause to remember) स्मृ in caus. (स्मारयति -यितुं).—(Celebrate in words) अनुवर्ण् (c. 10. -वर्णयति -यितुं), संवर्ण्, कृत् (c. 10. कीर्त्तयति -यितुं).

COMMEMORATED, *p. p.* स्मारितः -ता -तं, पालितः -ता -तं, अभ्युदितः -ता -तं.

COMMEMORATION, *s.* (Causing to remember) स्मारणं.—(Of a festival) किञ्चित्स्मरणीयकर्म्मोद्दिश्य उत्सवकरणं, उत्सवपालनं, उत्सवसेवनं, उत्सवाचरणं, अभ्युदयपालनं; 'in commemoration of,' उद्दिश्य, समुद्दिश्य.

COMMEMORATIVE, *a.* स्मारणः -णा -णं, स्मरणकृत्, उद्देशकः -का -कं.

To COMMENCE, *v. a.* and *n.* आरभ् (c. 1. -रभते -रब्धुं), समारभ्, अभ्यारभ्, प्रारभ्; प्रक्रम् (c. 1. -क्रमते -क्रमितुं), उपक्रम्, समुपक्रम्; प्रवृत् (c. 1. -वर्त्तते -र्त्तितुं); प्रस्तु (c. 2. -स्तौति -स्तुते -स्तोतुं); प्रकृ, सम्प्रकृ.—(Set about) अनुष्ठा (c. 1. -तिष्ठति -ष्ठातुं) व्यवसो (c. 4. -स्यति -सातुं); 'she commenced weeping,' रोदितुं प्रवृत्ता.

COMMENCED, *p. p.* आरब्धः -ब्धा -ब्धं, प्रारब्धः -ब्धा -ब्धं, समारब्धः -ब्धा -ब्धं, प्रक्रान्तः -न्ता -न्तं, उपक्रान्तः -न्ता -न्तं, प्रवृत्तः -त्ता -त्तं, प्रस्तुतः -ता -तं, अनुष्ठितः -ता -तं.

COMMENCEMENT, *s.* आरम्भः, प्रारम्भः, समारम्भः, प्रारब्धिः *f.*, उपक्रमः, प्रक्रमः, अभ्यादानं, समुद्यमः, आदरः, आमुखं.—(Prelude) प्रस्तावना, प्रकरणं.—(Setting about) अनुष्ठानं; 'from the commencement,' आदितस्.

COMMENCER, *s.* प्रक्रन्ता *m.* (न्तृ), उपक्रन्ता *m.* (न्तृ), आरम्भकः, आरब्धा *m.* (ब्धृ).

To COMMEND, *v. a.* प्रशंस् (c. 1. -शंसति -सितुं), स्तु (c. 2. स्तौति, स्तोतुं), अभिष्टु, संस्तु, श्लाघ् (c. 1. श्लाघते -घितुं, or in caus. श्लाघयति -यितुं), कृत् (c. 10. कीर्त्तयति -यितुं), अनुरागं कृ, रुच् in caus. (रोचयति -यितुं), अनुरुच्.—(Entrust) समृ in caus. (-अर्पयति -यितुं).—(Set off) प्रकाश् in caus. (-काशयति -यितुं).

COMMENDABLE, *a.* प्रशंसनीयः -या -यं, प्रशस्यः -स्या -स्यं, श्लाघ्यः -घ्या -घ्यं, स्तुत्यः -त्या -त्यं, वन्द्यः -न्द्या -न्द्यं, ईड्यः -ड्या -ड्यं, विकत्थनीयः -या -यं, कीर्त्तनीयः -या -यं.

COMMENDABLY, *adv.* प्रशस्तं, प्रशस्यं, प्रशंसनीयप्रकारेण, श्लाघ्यवत्.

COMMENDATION, *s.* प्रशंसा -सनं, श्लाघा, गुणश्लाघा, स्तुतिः *f.*, गुणस्तुतिः, स्तुतिवादः, ईडा.

COMMENDATORY, *a.* प्रशंसाकरः -री -रं, स्तुतिमयः -यी -यं, गुणप्रकाशकः -का -कं.

COMMENDED, *p. p.* प्रशंसितः -ता -तं, प्रशस्तः -स्ता -स्तं, श्लाघितः -ता -तं.

COMMENDER, *s.* प्रशंसकः, प्रशंसाकृत्, स्तावकः, स्तोता *m.* (तृ).

COMMENSALITY, *s.* सहभोजित्वं, गणान्नभोजित्वं.

COMMENSURABLE or COMMENSURATE, *a.* (Reducible to a common measure) सापवर्त्तः -र्त्ता -र्त्तं.—(Proportionate) अनुसारी -रिणी -रि (न्), अनुरूपः -पा -पं, अनुगुणः -णा -णं, सदृशः -शी -शं, समः -मा -मं; 'commensurable with one's strength,' आत्मशक्तिसमः -मा -मं.

COMMENSURABLENESS, *s.* अनुरूपता, अनुसारित्वं, सादृश्यं, समता.

COMMENSURABLY or COMMENSURATELY, *adv.* अनुरूपं -पेण, अनुसारेण -सारतस्.

To COMMENSURATE, *v. a.* (Reduce to a common measure) अपवृत् in caus. (-वर्त्तयति -यितुं).—(Make proportionable) अनुरूपं -पां -पं कृ, अनुगुणं -णां -णं कृ.

To COMMENT, *v. n.* (Expound) टीकां लिख् (c. 6. लिखति, लेखितुं), टीकाद्वारेण व्याख्या (c. 2. -ख्याति -ख्यातुं) or व्याकृ or व्याचक्ष् (c. 2. -चष्टे) or व्याहृ (c. 1. -हरति -हर्त्तुं) or प्रकाश् (c. 10. -काशयति -यितुं) or स्पष्टीकृ.—(Make remarks) प्रवद् (c. 1. -वदति -दितुं), चर्चां कृ, निरूप् (c. 10. -रूपयति -यितुं), अनुयुज् (c. 7. -युनक्ति -योक्तुं).

COMMENT or COMMENTARY, *s.* (Exposition, annotation) टीका, भास्यं, भाष्यं, टिप्पनी, व्याख्या, व्याकरणं, निबन्धः, वार्त्तिकं, सूत्रव्याख्या; 'having a commentary,' सटीकः -का -कं.—(Remarks, observations) प्रवादः, चर्चा, निरूपणं, अनुयोगः.

COMMENTATOR or COMMENTER, *s.* टीकालेखकः, भाष्यकृत्, भास्यकरः, निबन्धा *m.* (न्धृ), प्रवक्ता *m.* (क्तृ), प्रकाशकः, व्याख्याता *m.* (तृ), वाचकः, चूर्णिकृत् *m.*

COMMENTED, *p. p.* व्याकृतः -ता -तं, व्याख्यातः -ता -तं, निरूपितः -ता -तं.

COMMENTITIOUS, *a.* कल्पितः -ता -तं, काल्पनिकः -की -कं, कृत्रिमः -मा -मं.

COMMERCE, *s.* (Traffic) वाणिज्यं -ज्या, वणिक्पथं, वणिग्भावः, क्रयविक्रयः, सत्यानृतं, निगमः, पणाया, पाणः, महाजनकर्म्म *n.* (न्).—(Intercourse of society) लोकव्यवहारः, लोकसंसर्गः, लोकयात्रा, गमनागमनं, आनुगत्यं ; 'of sexes,' मिथुनीभावः, स्त्रीपुरुषसङ्गः.

To COMMERCE, *v. n.* वाणिज्यं कृ, पण् (c. 1. पणायति -यितुं), उपक्रीय विक्री (c. 9. -क्रीणाति -क्रेतुं).

COMMERCIAL, *a.* वाणिजः -जी -जं -जिकः -की -कं, वाणिज्यसम्बन्धी -न्धिनी -न्धि (न्), महाजनसम्बन्धी &c.

To COMMIGRATE, *v. n.* बहुजनैः सह देशं त्यक्त्वा देशान्तरं गम् (c.1. गच्छति, गन्तुं).

COMMIGRATION, *s.* बहुजनैर् देशं त्यक्त्वा देशान्तरगमनं, सहोत्क्रमणं.

COMMINATION, *s.* (Curse, threat) शापः, अभिशापः, अवक्रोशः, भर्त्सनं, तर्जनं.—(Recital of God's threatenings on stated days) निरूपितदिवसे परमेश्वरशापख्यापनं.

COMMINATORY, *a.* शापकः -का -कं, आभिशापिकः -की -कं, सशापः -पा -पं, आक्रोशकः -की -कं, सभर्त्सनः -ना -नं, सतर्जनः -ना -नं.

To COMMINGLE, *v. a.* मिश्र् (c. 10. मिश्रयति -यितुं), सम्मिश्र्, विमिश्र्, मिश्रीकृ ; सम्पृच् (c. 7. -पृणक्ति -पर्चितुं), संयुज् (c. 7. -युनक्ति -योक्तुं), एकीकृ, एकत्र कृ.

COMMINGLED, *p. p.* सम्मिश्रः -श्रा -श्रं -श्रितः -ता -तं, संसृष्टः -ष्टा -ष्टं, कृतसंसर्गः -र्गा -र्गं, सम्पृक्तः -क्ता -क्तं, संश्लिष्टः -ष्टा -ष्टं, संयुक्तः -क्ता -क्तं, सन्निपतितः -ता -तं.

COMMINUIBLE, *a.* चूर्णनीयः -या -यं, मर्द्दनीयः -या -यं, खण्डनीयः -या -यं, चूर्णयितुं शक्यः -क्या -क्यं, छेद्यः -द्या -द्यं, पेषणीयः -या -यं.

To COMMINUTE, *v. a.* चूर्ण् (c. 10. चूर्णयति -यितुं), प्रचूर्ण्, विचूर्ण्, चूर्णीकृ, मृद् (c. 9. मृद्नाति, मर्द्दितुं), अवमृद्, विमृद्, प्रमृद्, अभिमृद् or in caus. (मर्दयति -यितुं), पिष् (c. 7. पिनष्टि, पेष्टुं), निष्पिष्, विनिष्पिष्, प्रतिपिष्, उत्पिष्, खण्ड् (c.10. खण्डयति -यितुं), छिद् (c.7. छिनत्ति, छेत्तुं), खण्डशः कृ.

COMMINUTED, *p. p.* चूर्णितः -ता -तं, चूर्णीकृतः -ता -तं, सञ्चूर्णितः -ता -तं, खण्डितः -ता -तं, मर्द्दितः -ता -तं, पिष्टः -ष्टा -ष्टं, निष्पिष्टः -ष्टा -ष्टं.

COMMINUTION, *s.* चूर्णनं, सञ्चूर्णनं, चूर्णीकरणं, चूर्णता, पेषणं, मर्द्दनं, खण्डनं.

COMMISERABLE, *a.* अनुकम्प्यः -म्प्या -म्प्यं, दयार्हः -र्हा -र्हं, कृपार्हः -र्हा -र्हं.

To COMMISERATE, *v. a.* अनुकम्प् (c. 1. -कम्पते -म्पितुं) समनुकम्प्, दय् (c. 1. दयते -यितुं) with gen., करुण (nom. करुणायते), कृपा (nom. कृपायते), अनुकृपा ; दयां कृ.

COMMISERATED, *p. p.* अनुकम्पितः -ता -तं, दयितः -ता -तं, कृतानुकम्पः -म्पा -म्पं.

COMMISERATION, *s.* कारुण्यं, करुणः -णा, कृपा, दया, अनुकम्पा.

COMMISERATIVE, *a.* अनुकम्पकः -का -कं, दयाकरः -री -रं, दयालुः -लुः -लु, दयाशीलः -ला -लं, कृपामयः -यी -यं, करुणार्द्रः -र्द्रा -र्द्रं, करुणात्मकः -का -कं.

COMMISSARIAT, *s.* (The office) भोजनाधिकारः -रित्वं.—(The officers) भोजनाधिकृताः *m. pl.*

COMMISSARY, *s.* (A delegate) नियोगी *m.* (न्), नियुक्तः.—(Of provisions) भोजनाधिकारी *m.* (न्), सैन्यानां भोजनादिपरिकल्पकः.

COMMISSION, *s.* (Employment, charge, appointment) नियोगः, नियोजनं, नियुक्तिः *f.*, अधिकारः, प्रस्थापनं, प्रयोगः.—(Trust) निक्षेपः, न्यासः.—(A warrant, order) प्रत्ययपत्रं, आज्ञापत्रं, आदेशः, समादेशः, शासनं, शासनपत्रं, सङ्क्रामिताक्षरं.—(Employment) व्यापारः.—(Power of buying or selling for another) परस्य कृते क्रयशक्तिः or विक्रयशक्तिः *f.*—(Allowance made to the buyer or seller) शुल्कः -ल्कं.—(Act of committing or perpetrating) करणं, आचरणं, समाचरणं.—(Number of persons appointed to any office) कस्मिंश्चित् कार्य्ये नियुक्तो जनसमूहः.—(Commission in the army) सेनायाम् अधिकारः or पदं.

To COMMISSION, *v. a.* नियुज् (c. 7. -युनक्ति -योक्तुं or caus. -योजयति -यितुं), विनियुज्, सन्नियुज् ; प्रस्था in caus. (-स्थापयति -यितुं), समादिश् (c. 6. -दिशति -देष्टुं), व्यादिश्, अधिकृ, प्रकृ.

COMMISSIONED, *p. p.* नियुक्तः -क्ता -क्तं, नियोजितः -ता -तं, प्रस्थापितः -ता -तं, प्रहितः -ता -तं, अधिकृतः -ता -तं, अधिकारवान् -वती -वत् (त्).

COMMISSIONER, *s.* नियोगी *m.* (न्), नियुक्तः, अधिकारी *m.* (न्), अधिकारवान् *m.* (त्), राजकर्म्मनिर्वाहणे नियुक्तो जनः.

COMMISSURE, *s.* (Joint) सन्धिः *m.*, सन्धिस्थानं, सेवनं, ग्रन्थिः *m.*

To COMMIT, *v. a.* (Give in trust) ऋ in caus. (अर्पयति -यितुं), समृ, निक्षिप् (c. 6. -क्षिपति -क्षेप्तुं), न्यस् (c. 4. -अस्यति -असितुं), उपन्यस्, नियुज् (c. 7. -युनक्ति -योक्तुं or caus. -योजयति -यितुं), प्रतिपद् in caus. (-पादयति -यितुं), परिदा (c. 3. -ददाति -दातुं), समादिश् (c. 6. -दिशति -देष्टुं), प्रतिसन्दिश्, न्यासीकृ.—(Perpetrate) कृ, आचर् (c. 1. -चरति -रितुं), विधा (c. 3. -दधाति -धातुं).—(Imprison) कारागारे प्रविश् in caus. (-वेशयति -यितुं), आसिध् (c. 1. -सेधति -सेद्धुं).—(Expose to hazard) संशयस्थं -स्थां -स्थं कृ.—(Commit to writing) लेख्ये आरुह् in caus. (c. 1. -रोपयति -यितुं).—(To memory) अभ्यस् (c. 4. -अस्यति -असितुं), कण्ठस्थं -स्थां -स्थं कृ.

COMMITMENT, *s.* आसेधः, स्थानासेधः, कारागारप्रवेशनं, कारागृहप्रवेशः, निरोधनं, रोधः, प्रतिबन्धनं.

COMMITTED, *p. p.* अर्पितः -ता -तं, समर्पितः -ता -तं, निक्षिप्तः -प्ता -प्तं, न्यस्तः -स्ता -स्तं, न्यासीकृतः -ता -तं, प्रतिपादितः -ता -तं.—(Perpetrated, done) कृतः -ता -तं.—(Imprisoned) कारागुप्तः -प्ता -प्तं, कारागारप्रवेशितः -ता -तं, आसिद्धः -द्धा -द्धं.—(Committed to writing) लेख्यारूढः -ढा -ढं, पत्रे निवेशितः -ता -तं.—(To memory) अभ्यस्तः -स्ता -स्तं.

COMMITTEE, *s.* कस्मिंश्चित् कार्य्ये नियुक्ताः जनाः *m. pl.*, कार्य्यसम्पादने नियुक्तो जनसमूहः, कर्म्मसम्पादिका सभा.

COMMITTER, *s.* कर्त्ता *m.* (र्तृ), कृत् or करः in comp., कारः, विधायी *m.* (न्).

To COMMIX, *v. a.* सम्मिश्र् (c. 10. -मिश्रयति -यितुं), मिश्रीकृ, सम्मिश्रीकृ, एकीकृ.

COMMIXTURE, *s.* सम्मिश्रणं, मिश्रणं, सम्पर्कः, सन्निपातः, संयोजनं, संयोगः, संसर्गः, प्रक्षेपः, अनुषङ्गः.

COMMODE, *s.* स्त्रीजनभृतं मस्तकाभरणं or मुकुटं or उष्णीषं.

COMMODIOUS, *a.* योग्यः -ग्या -ग्यं, युक्तः -क्ता -क्तं, उपयुक्तः -क्ता -क्तं, उपयोगी -गिनी -गि (न्), उचितः -ता -तं, समुचितः -ता -तं, यथायोग्यः -ग्या -ग्यं, क्षमः -मा -मं, हितः -ता -तं, सोपकारः -रा -रं, उपपन्नः -न्ना -न्नं.

COMMODIOUSLY, *adv.* योग्यं, उपयुक्तं, यथायोग्यं, यथोचितं, युक्तं.

COMMODIOUSNESS, *s.* योग्यत्वं, युक्तता, उपयोगिता, उपयोगः, सोपकारत्वं.

COMMODITY, *s.* (Ware, merchandise) पण्यं, पणः, पणसः, द्रव्यं, भाण्डं ; 'price of a commodity,' पण्यमूल्यं.—(Profit, advantage) वृद्धिः *f.*, विवृद्धिः *f.*, अर्थः, लाभः, फलं, फलोदयः, प्राप्तिः *f.*, योगक्षेमः.

COMMODORE, *s.* युद्धनौकाधिपतिः, बृहन्नौकासमूहपतिः, जलयोधाध्यक्षः.

COMMON, *a.* (Belonging to more than one, general) सामान्यः -न्या -न्यं, साधारणः -णा -णी -णं, सार्व्वः -र्व्वी -र्व्वं, सर्व्वीयः -या -यं, सार्व्वलौकिकः -की -कं, सार्व्वजनिकः -की -कं, सर्व्वजनीयः -या -यं, सर्व्वमयः -यी -यं, समानः -ना -नं, व्यापकः -का -कं, अविविक्तः -क्ता -क्तं.—(Vulgar) प्राकृतः -ती -तं, ग्राम्यः -म्या -म्यं, लौकिकः -की -कं, अश्लीलः -ला -लं, वार्षलः -ली -लं, अधमः -मा -मं.—(Usual) प्रायिकः -की -कं, लोकसिद्धः -द्धा -द्धं, प्रसिद्धः -द्धा -द्धं, व्यावहारिकः -की -कं, आचारिकः -की -कं.—(Frequent) अभीक्ष्णः -क्ष्णा -क्ष्णं, असकृद्दृष्टपूर्व्वः -र्व्वा -र्व्वं.—(Having no owner) अस्वामिकः -का -कं.—(Having many owners) बहुस्वामिकः -का -कं.—(Easily attainable) अनायासेन

लभ्यः -भ्या -भ्यं, सुलभः -भा -भं ; 'common to all,' सर्व्वसामान्यः -न्या -न्यं ; 'common to others,' अन्यसाधारणः -णी -णं ; 'this affection is common to both,' अयं प्रणय उभयोः साधारणः ; 'common to the lower orders,' आपामरसाधारणः -णी -णं ; 'common to the beasts,' पश्वादिसाधारणः -णी -णं ; 'a common duty,' साधारणधर्म्मः ; 'a common, vulgar person,' पृथग्जनः, प्राकृतजनः, वृषलः ; 'the common people,' प्रजा, अवरवर्णाः *m. pl.*, अन्त्यजातीयाः *m. pl.* ; 'common-report,' जनप्रवादः, जनवार्त्ता ; 'common stock,' गणद्रव्यं ; 'common food,' गणान्नं ; 'common woman,' साधारणस्त्री, सामान्या ; 'common road,' प्रचारः ; 'in common,' साधारण्येन, सामान्येन.

COMMON, *s.* (Land) सर्व्वसामान्यभूमिः *f.*, सर्व्वसाधारणक्षेत्रं.—(Pasture ground) प्रचारः, सर्व्वसाधारणप्रचारः.

COMMON-LAW, *s.* देशाचारः, देशव्यवहारः, व्यवहारविधिः *m.*, देशाचारात्मिका स्मृतिः *f.*

COMMONAGE, *s.* सर्व्वसामान्यप्रचारे पश्वादिपालनाधिकारः, सर्व्वसाधारणक्षेत्रे पशुचारणाधिकारः,

COMMONALTY, *s.* प्रजा, लोकः, अवरवर्णाः *m. pl.*, अन्त्यवर्णाः, अन्त्यजातीयाः *m. pl.*

COMMONER, *s.* (One of the common people) अवरवर्णः -र्णकः, अन्त्यजातीयः, प्राकृतजनः, पृथग्जनः, अकुलीनः.—(A member of the House of Commons) प्रजाप्रतिनिधिः *m.*—(At the University) राजविद्यालये द्वितीयपदस्थः or गणान्नभोजी *m.* (न्).

COMMONITION, *s.* प्रत्यादेशः, उपदेशः, प्रबोधः -धनं, मन्त्रणं.

COMMONLY, *adv.* (Frequently, usually) बहुशस्, बाहुल्येन, प्रायस्, प्रायशस्, प्रायेण.—(Jointly, in common) साधारण्येन, सामान्यतस्.

COMMONNESS, *s.* साधारणत्वं -ता, सामान्यत्वं -ता, समानता, प्रसिद्धत्वं, बाहुल्यं.

COMMON-PLACE, *a.* (Ordinary) प्राकृतः -ती -तं, प्रसिद्धः -द्धा -द्धं, ग्राम्यः -म्या -म्यं.

COMMON-PLACE-BOOK, *s.* स्मरणार्थकं पुस्तकं, स्मरणीयवाक्यसंग्रहार्थं पुस्तकं, उद्धृतवाक्यसंग्रहणपुस्तकं.

COMMONS, *s. pl.* (The lower orders) अवरवर्णाः *m. pl.*, अन्त्यवर्णाः.—(House of Commons) अवरसभा, प्रजाप्रतिनिधिसभा, महासभा.—(Food eaten in common) गणान्नं.

COMMONWEAL or COMMONWEALTH, *s.* प्रजाधिपत्यं, प्रजाप्रभुत्वं, प्रजापालितं राज्यं, राज्यं यत्र प्रजायां न्यस्तो राज्यव्यवहारः ; 'for the commonweal,' प्रजार्थं.

COMMORANCY, *s.* वासः, निवासः, वसतिः *f.*, अवस्थानं, अधिष्ठानं.

COMMORANT, *a.* वासी -सिनी -सि (न्) or निवासी, स्थः स्था स्थं in comp.

COMMOTION, *s.* क्षोभः, व्याक्षोभः, विप्लवः, उपप्लवः, वैक्लव्यं, तुमुलं, आहवः, प्रकोपः, कलहः ; 'popular commotion,' प्रकृतिक्षोभः.

COMMOTIONER, *s.* विप्लवकृत्, विप्लावी *m.* (न्), कलहकारी *m.* (न्).

To COMMUNE, *v. n.* सम्भाष् (c. 1. -भाषते -षितुं), संवद् (c. 1. -वदति -दितुं), संलप् (c. 1. -लपति -पितुं), कथोपकथनं कृ, मन्त्र् (c. 10. मन्त्रयते -ति -यितुं), सम्मन्त्र्.

COMMUNICABLE, *a.* प्रतिपादनीयः -या -यं, प्रदेयः -या -यं, संवदनीयः -या -यं.

COMMUNICANT, *s.* ख्रीष्टमृत्युस्मरणार्थकस्य भोजनस्य सहभोजी *m.* (न्), ईश्वरवपुषः सहभागी *m.* (न्), प्रभुनिरूपितखाद्यस्य भोक्ता *m.* (क्तृ), महायज्ञकृत्.

To COMMUNICATE, *v. a.* (Reveal) प्रकाश् in caus. (-काशयति -यितुं), विवृ (c. 5. -वृणोति -वरितुं -रीतुं) ; 'to communicate one's designs to another,' अर्थानर्थं परस्य प्रकाशयितुं.—(Impart intelligence, knowledge) संवद् (c. 1. -वदति -दितुं), वद्, ब्रू (c. 2. ब्रवीति, वक्तुं), प्रब्रू, अनुब्रू, विज्ञा in caus. (-ज्ञापयति -यितुं), निविद् in caus. (-वेदयति -यितुं), समाविद्, प्रवच् (c. 2. -वक्ति -वक्तुं), सन्दिश् (c. 6. -दिशति -देष्टुं), ग्रह् in caus. (ग्राहयति -यितुं), समाचारं दा.—(Confer, bestow) प्रदा (c. 3. -ददाति, c. 1. -यच्छति -दातुं), अभिदा, प्रतिपद् in caus. (-पादयति -यितुं), उपपद्.

To COMMUNICATE, *v. n.* (Partake of the Lord's Supper) ख्रीष्टमृत्युस्मरणार्थं भोजनं कृ or खाद्यं भुज् (c. 7. भुंक्ते, भोक्तुं), ख्रीष्टनिरूपितभोजनं खाद् (c. 1. खादति -दितुं).—(Have intercourse) सङ्क्रम् (c. 1. -गच्छति -गन्तुं), समागम्, संसर्गं कृ.—(As houses) सद्मवनरूपेण सामान्यद्वारेण संयुज् in pass. (-युज्यते).

COMMUNICATED, *p. p.* प्रतिपादितः -ता -तं, प्रदत्तः -त्ता -त्तं, सन्दिष्टः -ष्टा -ष्टं, निवेदितः -ता -तं, प्रकाशितः -ता -तं.—(As disease) सञ्चारितः -ता -तं.

COMMUNICATION, *s.* (Of knowledge, intelligence) विज्ञापनं, विज्ञप्तिः *f.*, निवेदनं, संवदनं, संवादः, वादः, सन्देशवादः.—(Bestowing) सम्प्रदानं, प्रदानं.—(Intercourse) गमनागमनं, यातायातं, संसर्गः -र्गिता, सङ्क्रमः, सङ्गः, सङ्गतिः *f.*, समागमः.—(Conversation) संलापः, आलापः, सम्भाषः, सङ्कथा, सम्प्रवदनं.—(Common passage) सामान्यद्वारं, सामान्यपथः.—(Of disease) सञ्चारः.

COMMUNICATIVE, *a.* सम्प्रदानशीलः -ला -लं, संवदनशीलः -ला -लं, विज्ञापकः -का -कं ; 'not communicative,' वाग्यतः -ता -तं, परिमितकथः -था -थं.

COMMUNICATIVENESS, *s.* सम्प्रदानशीलता, संवादशीलत्वं, विज्ञापकत्वं.

COMMUNION, *s.* (Intercourse) सङ्गः, सङ्गमः, सङ्गतिः *f.*, संसर्गः, संसर्गिता, साहित्यं.—(Participation of the Lord's Supper) ख्रीष्टमृत्युस्मरणार्थकं भोजनं, ख्रीष्टभोजनं, ख्रीष्टनिरूपितभोजनं.

COMMUNITY, *s.* (Body of the people) प्रजा, प्रजालोकः.—(A body of people) जनसमूहः, जनता, गोष्ठी, श्रेणी.—(Commonness of possession) सामान्यं, समानता, साधारण्यं ; 'community of goods,' गणद्रव्यता.

COMMUTABLE, *a.* परिवर्त्तनीयः -या -यं, प्रतिदेयः -या -यं, विनिमातव्यः -व्या -व्यं ; 'not commutable,' अप्रतिपण्यः -ण्या -ण्यं.

COMMUTATION, *s.* (Change) विकारः, विक्रिया, परिणामः, विपर्य्ययः ; 'of a curse,' उच्छापः.—(Exchange) परिवर्त्तः -र्त्तनं, प्रतिदानं, परिदानं, निमयः, विनिमयः.

To COMMUTE, *v. a.* परिवृत् in caus. (-वर्त्तयति -यितुं), निमे (c. 1. -मयते -मातुं), विमे, विनिमे ; प्रतिनिधिं कृ, विपर्यस् (c. 4. -अस्यति -असितुं).

COMMUTED, *p. p.* परिवर्त्तितः -ता -तं, परिदत्तः -त्ता -त्तं, प्रतिदत्तः -त्ता -त्तं.

COMPACT, *s.* नियमः, संविद् *f.*, समयः, अङ्गीकारः, समाधिः *m.*, सङ्घट्टनं, अभ्युपगमः, उपगमः, संश्रवः, प्रतिश्रवः, आश्रवः, प्रतिज्ञानं, आगूः *f.* ; 'a written compact,' नियमपत्रं ; 'in compact,' प्रयुक्तः -क्ता -क्तं, संविदितः -ता -तं ; 'to make a compact,' सङ्घट्ट् (c. 1. -घट्टते -ट्टितुं), संविदम् उपगम् (c. 1. -गच्छति -गन्तुं).

COMPACT, *a.* घनः -ना -नं, दृढः -ढा -ढं, सान्द्रः -न्द्रा -न्द्रं, संहतः -ता -तं, सुसंहतः -ता -तं, दृढसन्धिः -न्धिः -न्धि, निःसन्धिः -न्धिः -न्धि, अविरलः -ला -लं, अनन्तरः -रा -रं, निरन्तरः -रा -रं, निविडः -डा -डं, व्यूढः -ढा -ढं.

To COMPACT, *v. a.* संहन् (c. 2. -हन्ति -हन्तुं), सन्धा (c. 3. -दधाति -धातुं), घनीकृ.

COMPACTED, *p. p.* संहतः -ता -तं, सन्धितः -ता -तं, संश्लिष्टः -ष्टा -ष्टं, सुश्लिष्टः -ष्टा -ष्टं, घनीभूतः -ता -तं, घनीकृतः -ता -तं.

COMPACTLY, *adv.* दृढं, निविडं, सुसंहतं, सान्द्रं, प्रगाढं, निरन्तरं.

COMPACTNESS, *s.* घनत्वं -ता, संहतिः *f.*, संहतत्वं, सान्द्रता, सन्धिः *m.*, दृढता, दार्ढ्यं, नैरन्तर्य्यं, नैबिड्यं.

COMPAGES, *s.* समासः, समाहारः, संहतिः *f.*, सङ्घातः, सन्निपातः संयोगः.

COMPANION, *s.* सहायः, सहचरः, सङ्गी *m.* (न्), मित्रं, सखा *m.* (खि), बन्धुः *m.*, सजूः *m.* (स्), सहवर्त्ती *m.* (न्), सहभावी *m.* (न्), अनुचरः, अभिसरः, अनुप्लवः, स्वकीयः; 'of the king,' नर्म्मसचिवः, महामात्रः, प्रधानं -नः; 'in arms,' सहयुध्वा *m.* (न्); 'at school,' सहाध्यायी *m.* (न्); 'in sorrow and joy,' समदुःखसुखः; 'at table,' सहभोजी *m.* (न्); 'boon companion,' सहपायी *m.* (न्); नर्म्मसुहृद्; 'a woman's female companion,' सखी.

COMPANIONABLE, *a.* साङ्गतिकः -की -कं, मैत्रेयः -यी -यं, प्रतिभावान् -वती -वत् (त्).

COMPANIONABLY, *adv.* ससहायवत्, सन्मित्रवत्, साङ्गतिकप्रकारेण.

COMPANIONSHIP, *s.* सहायता -त्वं, साहाय्यं, साहित्यं, साह्यं, संसर्गिता, सङ्गः -ङ्गतिः *f.*, साहचर्य्यं.

COMPANY, *s.* (Assembly of people, party) सभा, समाजः, पंक्तिः *f.*, परिषद् *f.*, रासेरसः; 'inadmissible into company,' अपांक्तेयः -या -यं; 'politeness to company,' सभाचातुर्य्यं, सभाजनं.—(Body of men) जनसमूहः, गणः.—(Band of soldiers) गुल्मः, सैन्यदलं; 'by companies,' पंक्तिभिः.—(Fellowship, society) सहायता, साहचर्य्यं, साहित्यं, संसर्गः, संवासः, समागमः; 'evil company,' असत्संसर्गः, कुसंसर्गः, कुसङ्गतिः *f.*—(Company of actors) पात्रवर्गः.—(Company of traders, corporate body) श्रेणी -णिः *m.f.*; 'to bear or keep company with,' सह चर् (c. 1. चरति -रितुं), अनुचर्, सह वस् (c. 1. वसति, वस्तुं), सह गम् (c. 1. गच्छति, गन्तुं).

COMPARABLE, *a.* उपमेयः -या -यं, तुलनीयः -या -यं, तुल्यः -ल्या -ल्यं.

COMPARATIVE, *a.* (Relative, not absolute) आनुषङ्गिकः -की -कं, प्रासङ्गिकः -की -कं, उपमानेन निर्णीतः -ता -तं.—(Having the faculty of comparing) तोलनः -ना -नं.

COMPARATIVELY, *adv.* उपमानेन, औपम्येन, सादृश्येन, उपमानपूर्व्वं.

To COMPARE, *v. a.* उपमा (c. 2. -माति, c. 3. -मिमीते -मातुं), तुल् (c. 10. तुलयति -यितुं), साधारणीकृ, सम्प्रधृ in caus. (-धारयति -यितुं) with two acc., उपदिश् (c. 6. -दिशति -देष्टुं).—(Liken, equal) समीकृ, तुल्यीकृ, सदृशीकृ, समान (nom. समानयति -यितुं).

COMPARED, *p. p.* उपमितः -ता -तं, उपमेतः -ता -तं, साधारणीकृतः -ता -तं, तुलितः -ता -तं, उत्प्रेक्षितः -ता -तं, समीकृतः -ता -तं.

COMPARISON, *s.* उपमा, उपमितिः *f.*, उपमानं, तोलनं, उत्प्रेक्षा, साधारणं, सादृश्यं, औपम्यं; 'by comparison with one's self,' आत्मौपम्येन; 'without comparison,' अतुलनीयः -या -यं, अतुल्यः -ल्या -ल्यं, असाधारणः -णा -णं.—(Simile) दृष्टान्तः, उपमा.

COMPARTMENT, *s.* (Division) छेदः, भागः, विभागः, परिच्छेदः, अंशः, खण्डः -ण्डं.—(Of an edifice) कक्षः.

COMPASS, *s.* (Circuit) परिवेष्टनं, मण्डलं, परिमण्डलं, परिधिः *m.*, परिणाहः.—(Extent, limits) परिमाणं, पर्य्यन्तं, विस्तारः, सीमा.—(Range, reach) विषयः, परिमाणं; 'within compass of the understanding,' बुद्धिगम्यः -म्या -म्यं; 'of the ear,' कर्णगोचरः -रा -रं.—(Due limits, moderation) परिमितत्वं, अनतिक्रमः, अप्रशक्तिः *f.*—(Instrument to find the quarter) दिक्सूचकयन्त्रं, उत्तरदिक्प्रदेशिनी सूचिः, दिक्सूचियन्त्रं, दिग्लक्षणं, समुद्रपथलक्षणं.

To COMPASS, *v. a.* (Surround) वेष्ट् (c. 1. वेष्टते -ष्टितुं), परिवेष्ट्, परिवृ (c. 5. -वृणोति -वरितुं -रीतुं), परिष्ठा (c. 1. -तिष्ठति -ष्ठातुं).—(Go round) परिगम् (c. 1. -गच्छति -गन्तुं), परिचर् (c. 1. -चरति -रितुं); 'reverentially,' प्रदक्षिणीकृ.—(Attain) अधिगम् (c. 1. -गच्छति -गन्तुं), गम्, प्रतिपद् (c. 4. -पद्यते -पत्तुं), अभिपद्; आपद्; आसद् in caus. (-सादयति -यितुं), लभ् (c. 1. लभते, लब्धुं), साध् in caus. (साधयति -यितुं).—(Contrive) घट् (c. 1. घटते -टितुं).

COMPASS OR COMPASSES, *s.* कर्कटः, कर्कटकः.

COMPASSION, *s.* कारुण्यं, करुणः -णा, दया, कृपा, अनुकम्पा, घृणा, अनुक्रोशः, अनुग्रहः, दयालुता -त्वं, करुणार्द्रता, हृल्लेखः *f.*, आपन्नरक्षणं.

To COMPASSIONATE, *v. a.* अनुकम्प् (c. 1. -कम्पते -म्पितुं), समनुकम्प् with acc.; दय् (c. 1. दयते -यितुं) with gen.; करुण (nom. करुणायते), कृपा (nom. कृपायते), अनुकृपा, दयां कृ, कृपां कृ, करुणां कृ.

COMPASSIONATE, *a.* दयालुः -लुः -लु, कृपालुः -लुः -लु, सदयः -या -यं, कारुणिकः -की -कं, सकरुणः -णा -णं, कारुण्यवेदी -दिनी -दि (न्), घृणी -णिनी -णि (न्), करुणामयः -यी -यं, करुणार्द्रः -र्द्रा -र्द्रं, अनुकम्पी -म्पिनी -म्पि (न्), सानुकम्पः -म्पा -म्पं, सानुक्रोशः -शा -शं, कृपावान् -वती -वत् (त्), कृपामयः -यी -यं, हृदयालुः -लुः -लु, दयायुक्तः -क्ता -क्तं, दयामयः -यी -यं, दयाशीलः -ला -लं, दयाकरः -रा -रं, दयान्वितः -ता -तं, सुरतः -ता -तं, आपन्नरक्षणशीलः -ला -लं, क्षमावान् -वती -वत् (त्).

COMPASSIONATELY, *adv.* सानुकम्पं, सदयं, सकारुण्यं, कारुण्येन, कृपया.

COMPATERNITY, *s.* धर्म्मपितृत्वं, धर्म्मपितुर् अवस्था or दशा or भावः.

COMPATIBILITY, *s.* योग्यता, उपयुक्तता, सम्भवः, सम्भाव्यता, अविरोधः, अविरुद्धता, अविगुणता, अनुसारित्वं.

COMPATIBLE, *a.* अविरुद्धः -द्धा -द्धं, योग्यः -ग्या -ग्यं, सम्भाव्यः -व्या -व्यं, अविगुणः -णा -णं, अनुसारी -रिणी -रि (न्), अनुगुणः -णा -णं, उपयुक्तः -क्ता -क्तं.

COMPATIBLY, *adv.* अविरुद्धं, अविगुणं, उपयुक्तं, अनुसारात् -रेण -रतस्.

COMPATRIOT, *s.* स्वदेशजः, स्वदेशीयः, एकदेशीयः, एकदेशवासी *m.* (न्), सांस्थानिकः.

COMPEER, *s.* वयस्यः, तुल्यपदभाक् *m.* (ज्), समानपदस्थः, समानवयस्कः, सवयाः *m.* (स्), तुल्यवृत्तिः, प्रतियोगी *m.* (न्), सङ्गी *m.* (न्).

To COMPEL, *v. a.*, Expressed by the causal form, usually in conjunction with the adverb बलात् or बलेन; as, 'the king should compel him to pay,' तं राजा बलाद् दापयेत्; 'he compels the Brahmans to perform the sacrifice,' ब्राह्मणान् यज्ञं कारयति. The root अर्ह् (c. 1. अर्हति -र्हितुं) has sometimes the sense of 'being compelled'; as, 'he is compelled to pay,' दातुम् अर्हति. In modern Sanskrit such expressions as the following are found; 'They compelled him to bear a burden,' भारं वोढुं तं बलाद् दधुः (root धा); 'Compel the people to come,' लोकान् आगन्तुं प्रवर्त्तय. *See* CONSTRAIN.

COMPELLABLE, *a.* Expressed by the fut. pass. part. of the causal form; as, 'compellable to pay,' दापनीयः -या -यं, दाप्यः -प्या -प्यं.

COMPELLATION, *s.* आभाषणं, आमन्त्रणं, अभिवादः, सम्बोधनं.

COMPELLED, *p. p.*, Expressed by the pass. part. of the causal form; as 'compelled to pay,' दापितः -ता -तं. The adverb बलात्, or बलेन may be joined with it.

COMPELLER, *s.* कारयिता *m.* (तृ), प्रवर्त्तकः, प्रयोजकः, प्रेरकः.

COMPENDIOUS, *a.* साङ्क्षेपिकः -की -कं, सामासिकः -की -कं, संक्षिप्तः -प्ता -प्तं, समस्तः -स्ता -स्तं, सङ्गृहीतः -ता -तं, परिमितः -ता -तं, अविस्तीर्णः -र्णा -र्णं.

COMPENDIOUSLY, *adv.* संक्षेपेण, संक्षेपात्, संक्षेपतस्, समासतस्, अविस्तरेण, अविस्तरशस्, संक्षिप्तप्रकारेण.

COMPENDIOUSNESS, *s.* संक्षिप्तता, संक्षिप्तिः *f.*, संक्षेपः, उपसंक्षेपः, समस्तत्वं, समासः, संहारः, लघुकत्वं.

COMPEND OR COMPENDIUM, *s.* संक्षेपः, सङ्ग्रहः, प्रत्याहारः, संहारः,

उपसंहारः, उपसंक्षेपः, संहिता, सारः.

COMPENSABLE, *a.* परितोषणीयः -या -यं, प्रतिफलार्हः -र्हा -र्हं.

To COMPENSATE, *v. a.* परितुष् in caus. (-तोषयति -यितुं), पारितोषिकं or प्रतिफलं or निष्कृतिं दा (c. 3. ददाति, दातुं), निष्कृ, अपाकृ, प्रतिकृ, शुध् in caus. (शोधयति -यितुं), परिशुध्, निस्तारं कृ.—(Be equivalent) तुल्यीभू, तुल्यबलः -ला -लम् अस्.

COMPENSATED, *p. p.* प्रतिफलितः -ता -तं, प्रत्युपकृतः -ता -तं, परितोषितः -ता -तं.

COMPENSATION, *s.* पारितोषिकं, निष्कृतिः *f.*, निस्तारः, प्रतिफलं, प्रत्युपकारः, क्षतिपूरणं, दण्डः.

COMPENSATIVE, *a.* पारितोषिकः -की -कं, प्रत्युपकारी -रिणी -रि (न्), क्षतिपूरकः -का -कं.

COMPETENCE or COMPETENCY, *s.* (Adequacy, sufficiency) सामर्थ्यं, योग्यत्वं, उपयुक्तत्वं, युक्तता, औचित्यं, सम्भावना, सामयिकसम्भावना, निर्वाहः.—(Fortune sufficient for subsistence) वृत्त्युचितं धनं, जीवननिर्वाहसमर्थं धनं.—(Bare subsistence, food and clothing) ग्रासाच्छादनं, अशनाच्छादनं (or -ने).—(Enough) अलं.

COMPETENT, *a.* (Adequate) शक्तः -क्ता -क्तं, क्षमः -मा -मं, योग्यः -ग्या -ग्यं, उपयुक्तः -क्ता -क्तं, उचितः -ता -तं, समर्थः -र्था -र्थं, पर्य्याप्तः -प्ता -प्तं.—(Adequate to any work) कार्य्यक्षमः -मा -मं, कर्म्मक्षमः -मा -मं, अलङ्कर्म्मीणः -णा -णं, कृती -तिनी -ति (न्).—(Reasonable, moderate) मितः -ता -तं, परिमितः -ता -तं, समः -मा -मं.

COMPETENTLY, *adv.* पर्य्याप्तं, युक्तं, उपयुक्तं, उचितं, सामर्थ्येन, योग्यप्रकारेण.—(Sufficiently) अलं, यथावत्.—(Moderately) परिमितं.

COMPETIBLE, *a.* योग्यः -ग्या -ग्यं, अविरुद्धः -द्धा -द्धं. *See* COMPATIBLE.

COMPETITION, *s.* जिगीषा, विजिगीषा, स्पर्द्धा, प्रतिस्पर्द्धा, आस्पर्द्धा, सङ्घर्षः, अहम्पूर्व्विका, परस्पराभिभवेच्छा, उपप्लवः, समवायः; 'of buyers,' प्रयामः.

COMPETITOR, *s.* जिगीषुः *m.*, विजिगीषुः *m.*, स्पर्द्धी *m.* (न्), प्रतिस्पर्द्धी *m.* (न्), अभियोक्ता *m.* (तृ), अर्थी *m.* (न्), दायादः, प्रतिपक्षः, एकार्थाभिलाषी *m.* (न्), एकचेष्टः, प्रतियोगी *m.* (न्).

COMPILATION, *s.* सङ्ग्रहः -हणं, सङ्क्षेपः, संहारः, समाहारः, समाहृतिः *f.*, संहिता, खिलः -लं.

To COMPILE, *v. a.* समाहृ (c. 1. -हरति -हर्त्तुं), संहृ, उद्धृ; सङ्ग्रह् (c. 9. -गृह्णाति -ग्रहीतुं), संक्षिप् (c. 6. -क्षिपति -क्षेप्तुं).

COMPILED, *p. p.* समाहृतः -ता -तं, संहृतः -ता -तं, सङ्गृहीतः -ता -तं, संक्षिप्तः -प्ता -प्तं, प्रणीतः -ता -तं.

COMPILER, *s.* व्यासः, समाहर्त्ता *m.* (र्त्तृ), उद्धर्त्ता *m.* (र्त्तृ), निबन्धा *m.* (न्धृ).

COMPLACENCE, COMPLACENCY, *s.* (Satisfaction, pleasure) प्रसन्नता, प्रसादः, तुष्टिः *f.*, सन्तोषः, परितोषः, सौमनस्यं, शान्तिः *f.*, प्रीतिः *f.*—(Civility, complaisance) अनुग्रहः, अनुकूलता, अनुवृत्तिः *f.*, अनुनयः.

COMPLACENT, *a.* प्रसन्नः -न्ना -न्नं, सन्तुष्टः -ष्टा -ष्टं, सुशीलः -ला -लं, अनुरोधी -धिनी -धि (न्), अनुनयी -यिनी -यि (न्), सुप्रसादः -दा -दं.

COMPLACENTLY, *adv.* प्रसादेन, प्रसन्नमनसा, सन्तोषेण, तुष्टमनसा.

To COMPLAIN, *v. n.* (Represent sorrowfully) सशोकं or विलापपूर्व्वकं or सविलापं स्वार्थं निविद् in caus. (-वेदयति -यितुं) or विज्ञा in caus. (-ज्ञापयति -यितुं), क्लेशं or दुःखम् आख्या (c. 2. -ख्याति -ख्यातुं) or कथ् (c. 10. कथयति -यितुं).—(Lament) विलप् (c. 1. -लपति -पितुं), परिदेव् (c. 1. -देवते -वितुं), क्रुश् (c. 1. क्रोशति, क्रोष्टुं), विक्रुश्, अनुशुच् (c. 1. -शोचति -चितुं), रुद् (c. 2. रोदिति -दितुं), क्रन्द् (c. 1. क्रन्दति -न्दितुं).—(Inform against) अभियुज् (c. 7. -युनक्ति -योक्तुं), पिशुन (nom. पिशुनयति -यितुं), परिवद् (c. 1. -वदति -दितुं).

COMPLAINANT, *s.* अभियोक्ता *m.* (क्तृ), अभियोगी *m.* (न्), विवादार्थी *m.* (न्), अर्थी *m.* (न्), पूर्व्वपक्षवादी *m.* (न्) or कारणवादी or क्रियावादी or परिवादी, पूर्व्वावेदकः.—(Informer) पिशुनः.

COMPLAINER, *s.* विलापी *m.* (न्), परिदेवी *m.* (न्), परिदेवकः, विलपनकृत्.

COMPLAINT, *s.* (Sorrowful representation) विलापेन or शोकेन स्वार्थनिवेदनं or स्वार्थविज्ञापनं or दुःखकथनं, क्लेशख्यापनं.—(Lamentation) विलापः, विलपनं, परिदेवनं.—(In law) अभियोगः, भाषापादः, पूर्व्वपक्षपादः, विवादः.—(Informing against) पैशुन्यं.—(Disease) रोगः, व्याधिः *m.*, आमयः, आर्त्तिः *f.*, पीडा.

COMPLAISANCE, *s.* अनुकूलता, अनुग्रहः, अनुवर्त्तनं, अनुवृत्तिः *f.*, अनुनयः, अनुरोधः -धनं, आनन्दनं, प्रश्रयः, अभिनीतिः *f.*, सभाजनं, सुशीलता, दाक्षिण्यं.

COMPLAISANT, *a.* अनुकूलः -ला -लं, अनुग्राही -हिणी -हि (न्), अनुनयी -यिनी -यि (न्), अनुरोधी -धिनी -धि (न्), सानुनयः -या -यं, चाटुकारः -रा -रं, दक्षिणः -णा -णं, वल्गुवाक्यः... वदान्यः; बद्धाह्रूः -रूः -रु, सुप्रसादः -दा -दं, प्रियंवदः -दा -दं.

COMPLAISANTLY, *adv.* अनुकूलं, सानुग्रहं, सानुरोधं, सानुनयं, आनन्दनपुरःसरं.

To COMPLANE, *v. a.* समीकृ, समान (nom. समानयति -यितुं), समस्थलीकृ.

COMPLEMENT, *s.* (Perfection, fulness) सम्पूर्णता, पूर्त्तिः *f.*—(The full quantity, complete set) सामग्र्यं, पूरणं, परिपूरकं, परिसंख्या, साकल्यं, समुदायः.—(Of an arc) कोटिः *f.*—(Of a segment) पीठः.

COMPLETE, *a.* (Perfect, full) सम्पूर्णः -र्णा -र्णं, पूर्णः -र्णा -र्णं, समाप्तः -प्ता -प्तं, सम्पन्नः -न्ना -न्नं, सिद्धः -द्धा -द्धं, संसिद्धः -द्धा -द्धं, पर्य्याप्तः -प्ता -प्तं, समस्तः -स्ता -स्तं, सकलः -ला -लं, निखिलः -ला -लं, अखिलः -ला -लं, समग्रः -ग्रा -ग्रं, कृत्स्नः -त्स्ना -त्स्नं, राद्धः -द्धा -द्धं, साधनः -ना -नं.—(Having no deficiencies) अशेषः -षा -षं, निःशेषः -षा -षं, अविकलः -ला -लं, अन्यूनः -ना -नं.—(Mature) पक्वः -क्वा -क्वं, परिपक्वः -क्वा -क्वं, परिणतः -ता -तं; 'complete army,' अक्षौहिणी, चतुरङ्गः.

To COMPLETE, *v. a.* समाप् in caus. (-आपयति -यितुं), सम्पॄ in caus. (-पूरयति -यितुं), समभिपॄ, सम्पद् in caus. (-पादयति -यितुं), निष्पद्; साध् in caus. (साधयति -यितुं), संसाध्, निर्वृत् in caus. (-वर्त्तयति -यितुं), निवृत्, संवृत्.

COMPLETED, *p. p.* समाप्तः -प्ता -प्तं, सम्पन्नः -न्ना -न्नं, निष्पन्नः -न्ना -न्नं, सम्पूर्णः -र्णा -र्णं, सिद्धः -द्धा -द्धं, साधितः -ता -तं, विपर्य्यस्तः -स्ता -स्तं, समापन्नः -न्ना -न्नं, अवसितः -ता -तं, निर्वृत्तः -त्ता -त्तं.

COMPLETELY, *adv.* अशेषतस्, अशेषेण, निःशेषेण, पर्य्याप्तं, सम्पूर्णं, साकल्येन, अखिलेन, निखिलेन, कृत्स्नशस्, कार्त्स्न्येन, सम्यक्, सर्व्वतस्, आमूलं, निरवशेषं, तत्त्वतस्.

COMPLETENESS, *s.* सम्पूर्णता, परिपूर्णता -त्वं, पूर्त्तिः *f.*, संसिद्धिः *f.*

COMPLETION, *s.* (The act) समापनं, साधनं, निष्पादनं, सम्पादनं, निर्वर्त्तनं, निर्व्वहणं, निर्व्वाहः.—(The state) सिद्धिः *f.*, संसिद्धिः *f.*, सम्पूर्णता, परिपूर्णता, समाप्तिः *f.*, निष्पत्तिः *f.*, निर्वृत्तिः *f.*, आभोगः.—(Maturity) परिणामः, परिणतिः *f.*, परिपाकः.

COMPLETIVE, *a.* पूरकः -का -कं, परिपूरकः -का -कं, समापकः -का -कं.

COMPLEX, *a.* सङ्कीर्णः -र्णा -र्णं, प्रकीर्णः -र्णा -र्णं, मिश्रितः -ता -तं, समस्तः -स्ता -स्तं, सामासिकः -की -कं, अनेकार्थः -र्था -र्थं, नानार्थकः -का -कं, बह्वर्थः -र्था -र्थं, नानाप्रकारः -रा -रं, असरलः -ला -लं.

COMPLEXION, *s.* (Colour of the face) मुखरागः, कपोलरागः, वदनवर्णः; 'having a pale complexion,' विवर्णवदनः -ना -नं, पाण्डुवर्णः -र्णा -र्णं.—(Temperament) भावः, प्रकृतिः *f.*, देहस्वभावः, शरीरभावः, शरीरस्थितिः *f.*

COMPLEXIONAL, *a.* प्राकृतः -ती -तं, देहस्वभावसम्बन्धी -न्धिनी -न्धि (न्).

COMPLEXITY, *s.* सङ्करः, साङ्कर्य्यं, सङ्कीर्णता, समस्तता, मिश्रता, नानार्थकत्वं.

COMPLIANCE, *s.* अनुकूलता, अनुरोधः -धनं, अनुरोधित्वं, अनुवृत्तिः *f.*,

अनुवर्त्तनं, अनुग्रहः, परिग्रहः, अनुनयः, स्वीकारः, सम्मतिः *f.*, अनुमतिः.

COMPLIANT, *a.* अनुरोधी -धिनी -धि (न्), अनुकूलः -ला -लं, अनुग्रही -हिणी -हि (न्), अनुनयी -यिनी -यि (न्), विनयग्राही -हिणी -हि (न्), विनेयः -या -यं, प्रणेयः -या -यं, विधेयः -या -यं, अनुविधायी -यिनी -यि (न्), वचनेस्थितः -ता -तं, नम्रः -म्रा -म्रं, कृतानुकूल्यः -ल्या -ल्यं, आश्रवः -वा -वं.

To COMPLICATE, *v. a.* सङ्करीकृ, मिश्रीकृ, सङ्कीर्णीकृ, सङ्कुलीकृ, व्यस्तव्यस्तीकृ, परस्परं सम्मिश्र् (c. 10. -मिश्रयति -यितुं) or सम्बन्ध् (c. 9. -बध्नाति, -बन्द्धुं) or संयुज् (c. 7. -युनक्ति -योक्तुं) or समस् (c. 4. -अस्यति -असितुं).

COMPLICATED, *p. p.* सङ्करीकृतः -ता -तं, सान्निपातिकः -की -कं, प्रकीर्णः -र्णा -र्णं, समस्तः -स्ता -स्तं, मिश्रितः -ता -तं, सम्बद्धः -द्धा -द्धं.

COMPLICATION, *s.* (The act) सङ्करीकरणं, सङ्कुलीकरणं, समसनं.—(The state) सन्निपातः, प्रकीर्णता, समस्तता, व्यस्तव्यस्तता.

COMPLICE, *s.* पापसहायः, पापसम्मितः, सहकारी *m.* (न्), सङ्गी *m.* (न्).

COMPLIER, *s.* अनुरोधी *m.* (न्), अनुग्रही *m.* (न्), अनुविधायी *m.* (न्), प्रणयी *m.* (न्).

COMPLIMENT, *s.* चाटूक्तिः *f.*, चाटुः *m.* -टु *n.*, सान्त्वं, सान्त्वोक्तिः *f.*, आलोकः, आलोकशब्दः, कोमलवाक् *f.* (च्), मधुरवाक्यं, प्रश्रयवाक्, मानोक्तिः *f.*, जयूलः; 'a complimentary present,' उपायनं.

To COMPLIMENT, *v. a.* चाटूक्त्या or आलोकेन or कोमलवाचा or मधुरवाक्यैः सान्त्व् (c. 10. सान्त्वयति -यितुं).

COMPLIMENTAL, COMPLIMENTARY, *a.* चाटुकारः -री -रं, सान्त्ववादः -दा -दं, सान्त्वकरः -री -रं, स्तुतिमयः -यी -यं, वन्दारुः -रुः -रु, प्रियवादी -दिनी -दि (न्), औपचारिकः -की -कं.

COMPLIMENTER, *s.* सान्त्ववादः, चाटुवादी *m.* (न्), प्रियवादी, आभाषनशीलः, आदरकृत्.

COMPLOT, *s.* गोपनीयकर्म्मसम्पादनार्थं पापसाहित्यं, कुसाहित्यं, कूटसाहित्यं, कूटसंविद् *f.*, कुमन्त्रणा, कुपरामर्शः, कूटसंसर्गः,

To COMPLOT, *v. n.* गोपनीयकर्म्मसम्पादनार्थं कुसाहित्यं कृ, कूटसाहित्यं कृ, कूटसंसर्गं कृ.

COMPLOTTER, *s.* पापसहितः, कूटसहितः, कूटसम्पादनार्थं अन्यसहितः or अन्यसङ्गातवान् *m.* (त्) or संशप्तकः.

To COMPLY, *v. n.* (Yield to, assent to) अनुमन् (c. 4. -मन्यते -ते -मन्तुं), अनुज्ञा (c. 9. -जानाति -ज्ञातुं), स्वीकृ, स्वीकारं कृ, प्रतिग्रह् (c. 9. -गृह्णाति -ग्रहीतुं), प्रतीष् (c. 6. -इच्छति -एषितुं), सम्प्रतीष्, अनुरुध् in pass. (-रुध्यते), अनुविधा in pass. (-धीयते), अनुकूल (nom. अनुकूलयति -यितुं).—(Suit with, accord with) युज् in pass. (युज्यते).—(Submit to) उपगम् (c. 1. -गच्छति -गन्तुं), अभ्युपे (c. 2. अभ्युपैति -पैतुं).

COMPONENT, *a.* साधकः -का -कं, रचकः -का -कं, विरचकः -का -कं, कल्पकः -का -कं.—(Component part) साधनं, अङ्गं, भागः; 'component part of an army,' सेनाङ्गं.

To COMPORT, *v. n.* (Agree, suit) युज् in pass. (युज्यते), उपपद् in pass. (-पद्यते); 'comport one's self,' आचर् (c. 1. -चरति -रितुं), वृत् (c. 1. वर्त्तते -र्त्तितुं), व्यवहृ (c. 1. -हरति -हर्त्तुं).

COMPORTABLE, *a.* योग्यः -ग्या -ग्यं, उपयुक्तः -क्ता -क्तं, अविरुद्धः -द्धा -द्धं.

COMPORTMENT, *s.* वृत्तिः *f.*, आचारः, व्यवहारः, स्थितिः *f.*, रीतिः *f.*, गतिः *f.*, चरित्रं, चरितं, चेष्टितं.

To COMPOSE, *v. a.* (Form by joining different things together) सन्धा (c. 3. -दधाति -धातुं), समाधा, संस्था in caus. (-स्थापयति -यितुं), कॢप् (c. 10. कल्पयति -यितुं), सङ्कॢप्, निर्म्मा (c. 2. -माति -मातुं), एकत्र कृ, सम्मिश्रीकृ.—(Arrange, adjust) रच् (c. 10. रचयति -यितुं), विरच्, विधा, संविधा, समाधा, विन्यस् (c. 4. -अस्यति -असितुं), ग्रन्थ् (c. 1. ग्रन्थति or ग्रथति -न्थितुं).—(Settle a difference) सन्धा, प्रशम् in caus. (-शमयति -यितुं).—(Compose a book) रच्, विरच्, निबन्ध् (c. 9. -बध्नाति -बन्द्धुं), ग्रन्थं कृ, कॢप्.—(Compile) सङ्ग्रह् (c. 9. -गृह्णाति -ग्रहीतुं), समस् (c. 4. -अस्यति -असितुं).—(Constitute) संस्था, कॢप्, निर्म्मा. *See* COMPOSED; 'the body is composed of five elements,' पञ्चभिर् निर्म्मितो देहः; 'whatever wealth composes the treasury,' यद् धनं कोषभूतं.—(Calm) शम् in caus. (शमयति -यितुं), प्रशम्, उपशम्; प्रसद् in caus. (-सादयति -यितुं), अभिप्रसद्, सान्त्व् (c. 10. सान्त्वयति -यितुं).—(Arrange the type) अक्षराणि or मुद्राक्षराणि विन्यस् or सन्धा or विधा.

COMPOSED, *p. p.* (Calm) शान्तः -न्ता -न्तं, उपशान्तः -न्ता -न्तं, प्रशान्तः -न्ता -न्तं, समाहितः -ता -तं, प्रसन्नः -न्ना -न्नं, अव्याकुलः -ला -लं, स्थिरः -रा -रं, अविक्षिप्तः -प्ता -प्तं.—(In mind) शान्तचेताः -ताः -तः (स्), प्रशान्तात्मा -त्मा -त्म (न्), स्थिरमतिः -तिः -ति, स्थितधीः -धीः -धि, अविक्षिप्तचित्तः -त्ता -त्तं, आवेगरहितः -ता -तं, असम्भ्रमः -मा -मं, निरुद्विग्नः -ग्ना -ग्नं.—(In countenance) प्रसन्नमुखः -खी -खं.—(Constituted, consisting of) आत्मकः -का or -त्मिका -कं in comp., रूपः -पा -पं in comp.; 'an army composed of elephants, horses, and infantry,' हस्त्यश्वपादातात्मकं बलं; 'composed of two,' द्व्यात्मकः -का -कं.—(Made of) निर्म्मितः -ता -तं, मयः -यी -यं in comp., सम्भृतः -ता -तं.—(Written, arranged, compiled) रचितः -ता -तं, विरचितः -ता -तं, कल्पितः -ता -तं, बद्धः -द्धा -द्धं, निबद्धः -द्धा -द्धं, ग्रथितः -ता -तं, प्रणीतः -ता -तं, सङ्गृहीतः -ता -तं; 'a story composed in verse,' श्लोकबद्धा कथा.—(As music) स्वरबद्धः -द्धा -द्धं.

COMPOSEDLY, *adv.* प्रशान्तं, निरुद्विग्नं, असम्भ्रमं, सम्भ्रमेण विना.

COMPOSEDNESS, *s.* शान्तता, शान्तिः *f.*, प्रसन्नता, निराकुलता, असम्भ्रमः, अभ्रमः.

COMPOSER, *s.* रचकः, विरचकः, ग्रन्थकारः, ग्रन्थकृत्, निबन्धा *m.* (न्धृ).—(Of music) स्वरबन्धा *m.* (न्धृ).

COMPOSING, *a.* (Causing sleep) उपशायी -यिनी -यि (न्), स्वप्नकृत् *m. f. n.*

COMPOSITION, *s.* (Conjunction, combination, union) सन्धिः *m.*, संयोगः, मिश्रणं, सङ्घातः, संश्लेषः, समासञ्जनं, संव्यूहः, संस्थापनं.—(Adjustment) समाधानं, सन्धानं, निष्पत्तिः *f.*—(Of differences) सन्धिः *m.*, सन्धानकरणं, समासः.—(Literary composition) रचना, विरचना, ग्रन्थकरणं.—(Poetical) काव्यरचना, कवनं.—(A poetical composition) काव्यं, काव्यबन्धः.—(A written work) ग्रन्थः.—(Compilation) संहिता, संहारः, समाहारः, सङ्ग्रहः, सन्निपातः.—(Art of rhetorical composition) अलङ्कारविद्या.—(Of words) समसनं, समासः, सङ्घातः.—(Agreement, compact) नियमः, संविद्, समयः.

COMPOSITIVE, *a.* सन्धानकरणः -णी -णं, सामासिकः -की -कं, मिश्रितः -ता -तं.

COMPOSITOR, *s.* मुद्रायन्त्रालये मुद्राक्षरविन्यासकृत्, यो जनो मुद्रायन्त्रे मुद्राक्षराणि विन्यस्यति.

COMPOST, *s.* (Manure) पांशुः *m.*, पांसुः, सारः, उर्व्वराकरणार्थं गोमयादिसम्मिश्रद्रव्यं.

To COMPOST, *v. a.* उर्व्वराकरणार्थं पांशुं or गोमयादिसम्मिश्रद्रव्यं भूमौ प्रक्षिप् (c. 6. -क्षिपति -क्षेप्तुं) or धा (c. 3. दधाति, धातुं).

COMPOSURE, *s.* (Act of composing) रचना, विरचनं -ना, निर्म्माणं.—(Combination, arrangement) सन्धिः *m.*, संयोगः, मिश्रणं, सङ्घातः, विन्यासः.—(Of mind) शान्तिः *f.*, शमः, समाधिः *m.*, प्रसादः, विश्रामः, अभ्रमः, असम्भ्रमः, निराकुलता, अक्षोभः, स्थिरता, स्थैर्य्यं.—(Settlement of differences) सन्धानं, सन्धिः *m.*, सन्धानकरणं, समासः.

Compotation, *s.* सपीतिः, सम्पीतिः *f.*, सहपानं, तुल्यपानं, एकत्र पानं.

Compotator, *s.* सहपायी *m.* (न्), अन्येन सह पायी *m.* (न्).

To compound, *v. a.* समस् (c. 4. -अस्यति -असितुं), मिश्र् (c. 10. मिश्रयति -यितुं), सम्मिश्र्, मिश्रीकृ, संश्लिष् in caus. (-श्लेषयति -यितुं), संयुज् (c. 7. -युनक्ति -योक्तुं), सन्धा (c. 3. -दधाति -धातुं), संहन् (c. 2. -हन्ति -हन्तुं), संलग्नीकृ, एकीकृ, एकत्र कृ, सङ्करीकृ; 'to compound ingredients,' प्रक्षेपं कृ; 'medicines,' संस्कारं कृ, योगं कृ.—(Settle differences) सन्धा (c. 3. -दधाति -धातुं), समाधा, समासं कृ.

To compound, *v. n.* (Settle a debt by agreement to abate something) समयपूर्व्वकम् ऋणभागम् अपास्य ऋणं शुध् in caus. (शोधयति -यितुं), समयपूर्व्वम् ऋणांशं शोधयित्वा आनृण्यं गम् (c. 1. गच्छति, गन्तुं), ऋणांशं वितीर्य्य आनृण्यं दा (c. 3. ददाति, दातुं).

Compound, *s.* मिश्रणं, समसनं, समासः, सङ्करः.—(The mass compounded) मिश्रितद्रव्यसमूहः.—(A compound substance) योगः, मिश्रितद्रव्यं; 'a compound word,' समस्तपदं, समासः; 'separating compound words,' पदभञ्जनं.

Compound, compounded, *a.* समस्तः -स्ता -स्तं, सामासिकः -की -कं, मिश्रितः -ता -तं, मिश्रः -श्रा -श्रं, सम्मिश्रः -श्रा -श्रं, संयुक्तः -क्ता -क्तं, संसृष्टः -ष्टा -ष्टं, एकत्रीकृतः -ता -तं, सङ्करीकृतः -ता -तं; 'a compound perfume,' कृत्रिमधूपः.

Compounder, *s.* मिश्रणकृत्, सङ्करकृत्, सन्धानकरणः -कर्त्ता *m.* (र्त्तृ), समाधाता *m.* (तृ); 'of medicines,' योगविद् *m.*

To comprehend, *v. a.* (Understand in the mind) ग्रह् (c. 9. गृह्णाति, ग्रहीतुं), उपलभ् (c. 1. -लभते -लब्धुं), अवगम् (c. 1. -गच्छति -गन्तुं), अवे (*i.e.* root इ with अव, अवैति -तुं), ऊह् (c. 1. ऊहते -हितुं), बुध् (c. 1. बोधति -धितुं), विद् (c. 2. वेत्ति, वेदितुं), अनुभू (c. 1. -भवति -भवितुं), भू in caus. (भावयति -यितुं).—(Include) परिग्रह्, अन्तर्गण् (c. 10. -गणयति -यितुं), परिसमाप् (c. 5. -आप्नोति -आप्तुं), व्याप्, प्रतिसंहृ (c. 1. -हरति -हर्त्तुं). 'Comprehending' is expressed by आत्मकः -का -कं or रूपः -पा -पं affixed; as, 'comprehending two,' द्व्यात्मकः -का -कं.

Comprehended, *p. p.* (Understood) गृहीतः -ता -तं, उपलब्धः -ब्धा -ब्धं, अवगतः -ता -तं.—(Included) अन्तर्गतः -ता -तं, परिसमाप्तः -प्ता -प्तं, आन्तर्गणिकः -की -कं, प्रतिसंहृतः -ता -तं, आकलितः -ता -तं, समाविष्टः -ष्टा -ष्टं, गर्भः -र्भा -र्भं in comp.

Comprehensible, *a.* ग्रहणीयः -या -यं, ग्राह्यः -ह्या -ह्यं, उपलभ्यः -भ्या -भ्यं, धीगम्यः -म्या -म्यं, मनोगम्यः -म्या -म्यं, विभाव्यः -व्या -व्यं, भावनीयः -या -यं, बोधनीयः -या -यं, अवधारणीयः -या -यं, व्यापनीयः -या -यं.

Comprehension, *s.* (Understanding) मेधा, उपलब्धिः *f.*, उपलम्भः, भावना, बुद्धिः *f.*, मतिः *f.*, बोधः, अवधारणं, अनुभवः, विवेचना.—(Act of comprising) ग्रहणं, परिग्रहः, परिवेष्टनं.—(Inclusion) प्रतिसंहारः, परिसमाप्तिः *f.*, व्याप्तिः *f.*, समासक्तिः *f.*, समावेशः, संवरः.

Comprehensive, *a.* (Comprising much) बहुग्रहः -हा -हं.—(Extending far and wide) व्यापी -पिनी -पि (न्), व्यापकः -का -कं, सुपर्य्याप्तः -प्ता -प्तं, सर्व्वमयः -यी -यं, बहुविस्तीर्णः -र्णा -र्णं.—(Compendious) साङ्क्षेपिकः -की -कं, सामासिकः -की -कं; 'a comprehensive speech,' बहुमर्म्मवाक्यं.

Comprehensively, *adv.* संक्षेपतस्, संक्षेपात्, समासतस्, कार्त्स्न्येन, निःशेषं.

Comprehensiveness, *s.* (Conciseness) संक्षेपः, संक्षिप्तता, सांक्षेपिकत्वं, समस्तता, उपसंहारः.—(Extensive diffusion) व्यापकत्वं, बहुविस्तीर्णता, सर्व्वगत्वं.

Compress, *s.* पट्टः, पट्टकः, आवेष्टनं, कवलिका, अनुवेल्लितं.

To compress, *v. a.* सङ्कुच् (c. 1. -कोचति -चितुं), संहृ (c. 1. -हरति -हर्त्तुं), प्रतिसंहृ, संवृ (c. 5. -वृणोति, c. 1. -वरति -वरितुं -रीतुं), संहन् (c. 2. -हन्ति -हन्तुं), सम्पीड् (c. 10. -पीडयति -यितुं).

Compressed, *p. p.* संहृतः -ता -तं, प्रतिसंहृतः -ता -तं, संहतः -ता -तं, सङ्कुचितः -ता -तं, आकुञ्चितः -ता -तं, सम्पीडितः -ता -तं, संवृतः -ता -तं, सङ्कलितः -ता -तं, पुटितः -ता -तं.

Compressibility, *s.* संहरणीयता, सङ्कोचक्षमत्वं, सम्पीडनीयत्वं, संवरितुं शक्यता.

Compressible, *a.* संहरणीयः -या -यं, प्रतिसंहरणीयः -या -यं, सङ्कोचनीयः -या -यं, सम्पीडनीयः -या -यं, संवारणीयः -या -यं, सङ्कोचक्षमः -मा -मं.

Compression, *s.* संहृतिः *f.*, संहारः, प्रतिसंहारः, समाहारः, संवृतिः *f.*, संवरः, पीडनं, सम्पीडनं, सङ्कोचः -चनं, आकुञ्चनं, समसनं, ह्रासः.—(Of the lips, &c.) संवारः.

To comprise, *v. a.* परिग्रह् (c. 9. -गृह्णाति -ग्रहीतुं), अन्तर्गण् (c. 10. -गणयति -यितुं), परिसमाप् (c. 5. -आप्नोति -आप्तुं), प्रतिसंहृ (c. 1. -हरति -हर्त्तुं); 'Karpúradwípa is comprised in Jambudwípa,' कर्पूरद्वीपो जम्बुद्वीपान्तर्गतः. 'Comprising' is expressed by आत्मकः -का -त्मिका -कं or रूपः -पा -पं; as, 'comprising two,' द्व्यात्मकः -का -कं.

Comprised, *p. p.* अन्तर्गतः -ता -तं, अन्तर्गणितः -ता -तं, आन्तर्गणिकः -की -कं, प्रतिसंहृतः -ता -तं, आकलितः -ता -तं, समाविष्टः -ष्टा -ष्टं, गर्भः -र्भा -र्भं in comp., गर्भितः -ता -तं.

Comprobation, *s.* प्रमाणं, प्रमाणीकरणं, साक्ष्यं, साक्षिता, सम्मतिः *f.*

Compromise, *s.* समयं कृत्वा परस्परेण स्वस्वत्वाद् अंशापासनं or अंशवितरणं or स्वाधिकारात् किञ्चिन्निवर्त्तनं or स्वस्वत्वात् किञ्चिन्निवृत्तिः *f.* or स्वाभियोगात् किञ्चिदपासनं.—(A mutual promise to refer a controversy to arbitrement) प्रमाणपुरुषः पृच्छ्यताम् इति परस्परविवादिनोः समयः.

To compromise, *v. a.* समयं कृत्वा परस्परं स्वाधिकारात् or स्वस्वत्वात् किञ्चिन् निवृत् (c. 1. -वर्त्तते -र्त्तितुं) or किञ्चिद् अपास् (c. 4. -अस्यति -असितुं) or अंशम् अपास् or वितॄ (c. 1. -तरति -रितुं -रीतुं).—(Bring into hazard) संशयस्थं -स्थां -स्थं कृ, सन्देहस्थं -स्थां -स्थं कृ.

Comprovincial, *s.* एकदेशीयः, एकदेशजः, सदेशः, सदेशीयः, एकप्रदेशस्थः.

To comptrol, *v. a.* अधिष्ठा (c. 1. -तिष्ठति -ष्ठातुं), कार्य्याण्य् अवेक्ष् (c. 1. -ईक्षते -क्षितुं).

Comptroller, *s.* अध्यक्षः, उपद्रष्टा *m.* (ष्टृ), कार्य्याधीशः, कार्य्यद्रष्टा *m.* (ष्टृ), अवेक्षिता *m.* (तृ), अधिकारी *m.* (न्), कार्य्याधिकृतः, अधिकर्म्मिकः.

Comptrollership, *s.* अध्यक्षता -त्वं, कार्य्येक्षणं, कार्य्यदर्शनं, कार्य्याधीशता.

Compulsion, *s.* बलात्कारः, बलं, साहसं, प्रमाथः, प्रसभं; 'by compulsion,' बलात्, बलेन, बलात्कारेण.

Compulsory, compulsive, *a.* बलात्कारी -रिणी -रि (न्), बलवान् -वती -वत् (त्), बली -लिनी -लि (न्), प्रबलः -ला -लं.—(Obligatory) आवश्यकः -का -कं.

Compulsorily, compulsively, *adv.* बलात्कारेण, बलेन, बलात्, प्रसह्य, प्रसभं.

Compunction, *s.* सन्तापः, अनुतापः, पश्चात्तापः, मनस्तापः, अनुशोकः, अनुशयः.

Compunctious, *a.* अनुतापी -पिनी -पि (न्), अनुशोचकः -का -कं, अनुशयी -यिनी -यि (न्).

Computable, *a.* गणनीयः -या -यं, विगण्यः -ण्या -ण्यं, संख्येयः -या -यं.

Computation, *s.* गणनं -ना, विगणनं, सङ्ख्यानं, परिसङ्ख्यानं, गुणनं.—(The sum computed) गणितं.

To COMPUTE, *v. a.* गण् (c. 10. गणयति -यितुं), विगण्, प्रगण्; संख्या (c. 2. -ख्याति -ते -तुं), परिसंख्या, सम्परिख्या; कल् (c. 10. कलयति -यितुं), सङ्कल्.

COMPUTED, *p. p.* गणितः -ता -तं, परिगणितः, संख्यातः -ता -तं, परिसंख्यातः -ता -तं, गुणितः -ता -तं, कलितः -ता -तं.

COMPUTER, *s.* गणकः, विगणकः, गुणकः, गुणकारः, संख्याता *m.* (तृ).

COMRADE, *s.* सङ्गी *m.* (न्), सहायः, सहचरः, सहवासी *m.* (न्), बन्धुः *m.*, सुहृद् *m.*, मित्रं, उपसङ्गी *m.* (न्), पक्षकः, भागी *m.* (न्).—(In arms) सहयुध्वा *m.* (न्).

To CON, *v. n.* (Study) अभ्यस् (c. 4. -अस्यति -असितुं), अधी (c. 2. अधीते, अध्येतुं).

To CONCATENATE, *v. a.* शृङ्खलारूपेण अन्यद् अन्येन सन्धा (c. 3. -दधाति -धातुं), अविच्छिन्नक्रमेण or अविच्छिन्नं or निरन्तरम् अन्यद् अन्येन संयुज् (c. 7. -युनक्ति -योक्तुं).

CONCATENATION, *s.* शृङ्खलता -त्वं, शृङ्खलारूपेण अन्यस्य अन्येन सन्धानं or संयोजनं.—(A series) श्रेणी, पंक्तिः *f.*, माला, प्रबन्धः, प्रसङ्गः; 'a concatenation of causes,' कारणमाला.

CONCAVE, *a.* उत्तानः -ना -नं, पुटाकारः -रा -रं, गर्भाकारः -रा -रं, उदराकृतिः -तिः -ति, अब्जाकारः -रा -रं, कूर्म्मपृष्ठाकारः -रा -रं.

CONCAVITY, *s.* उत्तानता, पुटः, पुटकं, गर्भः, उदरं.

To CONCEAL, *v. a.* गुह् (c. 1. गूहति -ते, गूहितुं, गोढुं), निगुह्, विनिगुह्; छद् (c. 10. छादयति -यितुं), आच्छद्, समाच्छद्, प्रच्छद्, प्रतिच्छद्, सञ्छद्; गुप् in des. (जुगुप्सते -प्सितुं), स्थग् (c. 10. स्थगयति -यितुं); निह्नु (c. 2. -ह्नुते -ह्नोतुं), अन्तर्धा (c. 3. -दधाति -धातुं), तिरोधा, उपनिधा, अपिधा, पिधा; अपवृ in caus. (-वारयति -यितुं), संवृ; गोपनं कृ; 'to be concealed,' तिरस्कृ in pass. (-क्रियते), रहस् (nom. रहायते).

CONCEALABLE, *a.* गुह्यः -ह्या -ह्यं, गोप्यः -प्या -प्यं, गोपनीयः -या -यं, प्रच्छादनीयः -या -यं, गोपनार्हः -र्हा -र्हं.

CONCEALED, *p. p.* गूढः -ढा -ढं, गुप्तः -प्ता -प्तं, सङ्गुप्तः -प्ता -प्तं, छन्नः -न्ना -न्नं, प्रच्छन्नः -न्ना -न्नं, उपच्छन्नः -न्ना -न्नं, छादितः -ता -तं, प्रच्छादितः -ता -तं, स्थगितः -ता -तं, अपवारितः -ता -तं, निवारितः -ता -तं, संवृतः -ता -तं, आवृतः -ता -तं, अन्तर्हितः -ता -तं, तिरोहितः -ता -तं, पिहितः -ता -तं, अन्तरितः -ता -तं, निभृतः -ता -तं, निह्नुतः -ता -तं, तिरस्कृतः -ता -तं, अपह्नुतः -ता -तं.

CONCEALER, *s.* प्रच्छादयिता *m.* (तृ), गोपनकृत्, गोप्ता *m.* (प्तृ), अपहर्त्ता *m.* (र्त्तृ).

CONCEALMENT, *s.* गोपनं, सङ्गोपनं, छादनं, प्रच्छादनं, गुप्तिः *f.*, अन्तर्धानं, तिरोधानं, अपिधानं, पिधानं, स्थगनं, अपवारणं, अपह्नुत्वं, अपहारः, निह्नवः, आवरणं; 'in concealment,' निभृते, रहसि, गोपने, प्रच्छन्नं, गुप्तं.

To CONCEDE, *v. a.* वितॄ (c. 1. -तरति -रितुं -रीतुं), त्यज् (c. 1. त्यजति, त्यक्तुं), अनुज्ञा (c. 9. -जानाति -नीते -ज्ञातुं), अनुमन् (c. 4. -मन्यते -मन्तुं), अनुदा (c. 3. -ददाति -दातुं), प्रयम् (c. 1. -यच्छति -दातुं), अनुग्रह् (c. 9. -गृह्णाति -ग्रहीतुं), प्रोत्सृ in caus. (-सारयति -यितुं), अनुमुद् (c. 1. -मोदते -दितुं), क्षम् (c. 1. क्षमते, क्षन्तुं).

CONCEDED, *p. p.* अनुज्ञातः -ता -तं, प्रोत्सारितः -ता -तं, प्रदत्तः -त्ता -त्तं, वितीर्णः -र्णा -र्णं, त्यक्तः -क्ता -क्तं, अङ्गीकृतः -ता -तं.

CONCEIT, *s.* (Self-conceit) गर्व्वः, अहङ्कारः, अहम्मतिः *f.*, मानः, मानिता, अभिमानः -नता, दर्पः, दर्पारम्भः, आटोपः, स्मयः.—(Conception, thought) मेधा, बोधः, बुद्धिः *f.*, चिन्ता, कल्पना, ध्यानं, सङ्कल्पः.—(Fancy) कल्पना, मनःकल्पना, भावना, वासना.—(Opinion) मतिः *f.*, मतं, बुद्धिः *f.*; 'idle-conceit,' मृषार्थकं; 'affectation of knowledge,' ज्ञानाभिमानं.

To CONCEIT, *v. a.* (Fancy, imagine) मन् (c. 4. मन्यते, मन्तुं), चिन्त् (c. 10. चिन्तयति -यितुं), बुध् (c. 1. बोधति -धितुं), मनसा क्लृप् (c. 10. कल्पयति -यितुं), भू in caus. (भावयति -यितुं).

CONCEITED, *a.* मानी -निनी -नि (न्), मानवान् -वती -वत् (त्) or अभिमानवान्, अहङ्कारी -रिणी -रि (न्), अहंयुः -युः -यु, आत्माभिमानी -निनी -नि (न्), गर्व्वितः -ता -तं, दृप्तः -प्ता -प्तं, उद्धतः -ता -तं, समुन्नद्धः -द्धा -द्धं, जातस्मयः -या -यं, साटोपः -पा -पं, अवलिप्तः -प्ता -प्तं, मत्तः -त्ता -त्तं, भावितः -ता -तं; 'one conceited of his appearance,' दर्शनीयमानी *m.* (न्); 'conceited of her beauty,' रूपगर्व्विता; 'one conceited of his learning,' पण्डितम्मन्यः, ज्ञम्मन्यः, असन्नद्धः.

CONCEITEDLY, *adv.* साभिमानं, सगर्व्वं, सदर्पं, अहङ्कारेण, साटोपं.

CONCEITEDNESS, *s.* अहङ्कारित्वं, अहङ्कृतिः *f.*, मानिता, अभिमानता, चित्तसमुन्नतिः *f.*

CONCEIVABLE, *a.* मनोगम्यः -म्या -म्यं, धीगम्यः -म्या -म्यं, बोधगम्यः -म्या -म्यं, विभाव्यः -व्या -व्यं, भावनीयः -या -यं, विभावनीयः -या -यं, बोध्यः -ध्या -ध्यं, मन्तव्यः -व्या -व्यं.

CONCEIVABLENESS, *s.* मनोगम्यता, धीगम्यत्वं, विभाव्यत्वं, बोध्यता.

To CONCEIVE, *v. a.* and *n.* (Imagine, think) चिन्त् (c. 10. चिन्तयति -यितुं), मन् (c. 4. मन्यते, मन्तुं), ध्यै (c. 1. ध्यायति, ध्यातुं).—(Comprehend, understand) उपलभ् (c. 1. -लभते -लब्धुं), ग्रह् (c. 9. गृह्णाति, ग्रहीतुं), अवगम् (c. 1. -गच्छति -गन्तुं), बुध् (c. 1. बोधति -धितुं), अवधृ in caus. (-धारयति -यितुं), अवबुध् (c. 4. -बुध्यते -बोद्धुं), भू in caus. (भावयति -यितुं), सम्भू, ऊह् (c. 1. ऊहते -हितुं), अवे (c. 2. अवैति -तुं).—(In the womb) गर्भं लभ् or उपलभ् or ग्रह् or धृ (c. 1. धरति, धर्त्तुं).

CONCEIVED, *p. p.* (Imagined, understood) चिन्तितः -ता -तं, भावितः -ता -तं, विभावितः -ता -तं, मतः -ता -तं, बुद्धः -द्धा -द्धं, उपलब्धः -ब्धा -ब्धं, गृहीतः -ता -तं, अवगतः -ता -तं, ऊहितः -ता -तं, प्रतिपन्नः -न्ना -न्नं, अनुभूतः -ता -तं.—(Contained in the womb) गर्भधारितः -ता -तं; 'a female who has conceived,' गृहीतगर्भा, धृतगर्भा, पूर्णगर्भा, सञ्जातगर्भा, प्ररूढगर्भा, ससत्वा.

To CONCENTRATE, *v. a.* (Drive towards the centre) केन्द्रं or मध्यस्थलं प्रति गम् in caus. (गमयति -यितुं).—(Contract into a narrow compass) अल्पस्थानं प्रति गम् in caus. or समाक्षिप् (c. 6. -क्षिपति -क्षेप्तुं), संक्षिप्; संहृ (c. 1. -हरति -हर्त्तुं).—(Collect into one spot) एकत्र समाचि (c. 5. -चिनोति -चेतुं) or उपचि or समुपचि, एकीकृ, राशीकृ.—(Concentrate one's thoughts) एकाग्रः -ग्रा -ग्रं or एकायनः -ना -नं or अनन्यमनाः -नाः -नः भू.

To CONCENTRATE, *v. n.* केन्द्रं or मध्यस्थलं प्रति समागम् (c. 1. -गच्छति -गन्तुं), एकत्र मिल् (c. 6. मिलति, मेलितुं) or सम्मिल्; 'his affections concentrate in her,' अस्यां बद्धभावोऽस्ति.

CONCENTRATED, *p. p.* केन्द्रं or मध्यस्थलं प्रति गमितः -ता -तं, एकत्र समाक्षिप्तः -प्ता -प्तं or समुपचितः -ता -तं, राशिगतः -ता -तं, एकीकृतः -ता -तं.

CONCENTRATION, *s.* एकत्र समाक्षेपणं, एकीकरणं.—(Of the thoughts) एकाग्रता.—(Essence) सारः.

CONCENTRIC or CONCENTRICAL, *a.* एककेन्द्रः -न्द्रा -न्द्रं, समानकेन्द्रः -न्द्रा -न्द्रं, साधारणकेन्द्रः -न्द्रा -न्द्रं.

CONCEPTION, *s.* (Comprehension) उपलब्धिः *f.*, उपलम्भः, मेधा, ग्रहणं, अनुभवः.—(Imagination) भावना, कल्पना, मनःकल्पना, वासना.—(Idea, thought) बुद्धिः *f.*, मतिः *f.*, चिन्ता, सङ्कल्पः, मनोगतं.—

2 H

(Becoming pregnant) गर्भग्रहणं, गर्भाधानं, गर्भधरणं.

To CONCERN, *v. a.* (Belong to) सम्बन्ध् in pass. (-बध्यते).—(Regard) प्रतीक्ष् (c. 1. -ईक्षते -क्षितुं), अवेक्ष्, उद्दिश् (c. 6. -दिशति -देष्टुं), समुद्दिश्.—(Disturb, trouble) क्लिश् (c. 9. क्लिश्नाति, क्लेशुं), तप् in caus. (तापयति -यितुं), बाध् (c. 1. बाधते -धितुं).—(Intermeddle, be busy about other's affairs) परकार्य्येषु व्यापृ in pass. (-व्रियते) or व्यापृतः -ता -तम् अस् or चर्चां कृ or चिन्त् (c. 10. चिन्तयति -यितुं) with acc. c.

CONCERN, CONCERNMENT, *s.* (Affair, business) विषयः, अर्थः, व्यापारः, कार्य्यं, प्रयोजनं, सम्बन्धः.—(Interest) अर्थः, स्पृहणीयत्वं, सम्बन्धः, अभिसन्धानं; 'one's own concern,' स्वार्थः.—(Importance) गौरवं, गुरुत्वं -ता.—(Regard for, affection) अवेक्षा, प्रतीक्षा, अपेक्षा, अनुरागः, प्रणयः, स्नेहः.—(Thought, attention) चिन्ता, विचारः, मनोनिवेशः, मनोयोगः.—(Meddling) चर्चा, व्यापारः.—(Anxiety) चित्तोद्वेगः, उद्वेगः, औत्सुक्यं, मनोदुःखं, मनस्तापः.

CONCERNED, *p. p.* (Anxious) उद्विग्नः -ग्ना -ग्नं, उत्सुकः -का -कं, व्यग्रः -ग्रा -ग्रं.—(Interested) सम्बन्धी -न्धिनी -न्धि (न्).

CONCERNING, *prep.* प्रति, प्रतीक्ष्य, उद्दिश्य, समुद्दिश्य, उद्देशेन, अधि. 'Concerning' may be expressed by the acc. or loc. case. (Relating to) सम्बन्धी -न्धिनी -न्धि (न्), विषयकः -का -कं.

CONCERT, *s.* (Symphony) सङ्गीतं, एकतालः, एकतानः, एकलयः, तौर्य्यत्रिकं, गान्धर्व्वं; 'concert-room,' सङ्गीतशाला.—(Common deliberation on measures) सम्प्रधारणा, अन्यैः सह कार्य्यचिन्ता or विमर्शः or परामर्शः or सञ्चिन्तनं.—(Mutual communication) संवादः, सम्प्रवदनं.—(Co-operation) सहकारिता, सम्प्रतिपत्तिः *f.*, प्रतियोगः, अङ्गाङ्गिभावः.—(Union of purpose) चित्तैक्यं; 'one who acts in concert,' सहकारी *m.* (न्), सम्भूयकारी.

To CONCERT, *v. n.* and *a.* (Communicate mutually) संवद् (c. 1. -वदति -दितुं), सम्प्रवद्.—(Deliberate together on measures) अन्यैः सह कार्य्याणि चिन्त् (c. 10. चिन्तयति -यितुं) or प्रचिन्त् or सञ्चिन्त्.—(Co-operate) सह कृ, सम्भूय कृ.—(Contrive) घट् (c. 1. घटते -टितुं).

CONCERTED, *p. p.* सञ्चिन्तितः -ता -तं; 'well concerted,' सुघटितः -ता -तं, पक्वः -क्वा -क्वं.

CONCESSION, *s.* प्रदानं, सम्प्रदानं, वितरणं, विसर्ज्जनं, त्यजनं, त्यागः, स्वीकारः, अङ्गीकारः, क्षमा.

CONCESSIONARY, CONCESSIVE, *a.* क्षमया प्रदत्तः -त्ता -त्तं, क्षमी -मिणी -मि (न्).

CONCH, *s.* (Shell) शङ्खः, कम्बुः *m.*, दरं, जलजं, रेचटः.—(Of Vishnu) दरेन्द्रः.

To CONCILIATE, *v. a.* (Procure good will) आराध् in caus. (-राधयति -यितुं), अभिराध्, प्रसद् in caus. (-सादयति -यितुं), अनुरञ्ज् in caus. (-रञ्जयति -यितुं), सान्त्व् (c. 10. सान्त्वयति -यितुं), प्रसाध् in caus. (-साधयति -यितुं), लल् in caus. (लालयति -यितुं).—(Reconcile) सन्धा (c. 3. -दधाति -धातुं), समाधा, अनुनी (c. 1. -नयति -नेतुं).

CONCILIATED, *p. p.* आराधितः -ता -तं, अनुरञ्जितः -ता -तं, प्रसादितः -ता -तं, लालितः -ता -तं.

CONCILIATION, *s.* सान्त्वः -न्त्वं, सान्त्वनं, साम *n.* (न्), आराधनं, प्रसादनं, अनुरञ्जनं, सन्धानं, प्रीतिः *f.*, शाम *n.* (न्).

CONCILIATOR, *s.* अनुरञ्जकः, आराधकः, सन्धानकरणः -कर्त्ता *m.* (र्त्तृ).

CONCILIATORY, *a.* अनुरञ्जकः -का -कं, आराधकः -का -कं, सान्त्वयन् -यन्ती -यत् (त्), प्रसादयन् -यन्ती -यत् (त्), हृदयग्राही -हिणी -हि (न्), हृदयङ्गमः -मा -मं.

CONCINNITY, *s.* विनीतत्वं -ता, विनयः, उपयुक्तता, योग्यः -ग्या -ग्यं.

CONCINNOUS, *a.* विनीतः -ता -तं, उपयुक्तः -क्ता -क्तं, योग्यः -ग्या -ग्यं.

CONCISE, *a.* सङ्क्षिप्तः -प्ता -प्तं, साङ्क्षेपिकः -की -कं, सामासिकः -की -कं, अविस्तीर्णः -र्णा -र्णं, सूचकः -का -कं, संहृतः -ता -तं.

CONCISELY, *adv.* सङ्क्षेपतस्, सङ्क्षेपात्, सङ्क्षेपेण, समासतस्, अविस्तरशस्, अविस्तरेण.

CONCISENESS, *s.* सङ्क्षिप्तता, सङ्क्षेपः, सामासिकत्वं, समस्तता, संहृतिः *f.*, संहारः, उपसंहारः, अविस्तरः, अविस्तीर्णता.

CONCISION, *s.* कर्त्तनं, उत्कर्त्तनं, छेदनं, उच्छेदः, उच्छित्तिः *f.*

CONCITATION, *s.* उत्थापनं, उत्तेजनं, समुत्तेजनं, प्रोत्साहनं, उत्तापः.

CONCLAMATION, *s.* संहूतिः *f.*, संरावः, सांराविणं, बहुभिः कृता संहूतिः.

CONCLAVE, *s.* (Assembly of cardinals) रोमनगरे धर्म्माधिपतिसभा.—(Secret assembly) गूढसभा, गूढसमाजः.—(Private apartment) अवरोधनं, कक्षान्तरं, अन्तःशाला.

To CONCLUDE, *v. a.* (End, finish) समाप् in caus. (-आपयति -यितुं), सम्पॄ in caus. (-पूरयति -यितुं), साध् in caus. (साधयति -यितुं), निवृत् in caus. (-वर्त्तयति -यितुं), निवृत्, अवसो (c. 4. -स्यति -सातुं), निष्पद् in caus. (-पादयति -यितुं).—(Infer by ratiocination) अनुमा (c. 2. -माति, c. 3. -मिमीते -मातुं), ऊह् (c. 1. ऊहते -हितुं), तर्क् (c. 10. तर्कयति -यितुं), अवगम् (c. 1. -गच्छति -गन्तुं).—(Determine, decide) निश्चि (c. 5. -चिनोति -चेतुं), निर्णी (c. 1. -णयति -णेतुं), व्यवसो, निर्दिश् (c. 6. -दिशति -देष्टुं).

To CONCLUDE, *v. n.* (End) विरम् (c. 1. -रमते -रन्तुं), उपरम्, निवृत् (c. 1. -वर्त्तते -र्त्तितुं), विगम् (c. 1. -गच्छति -गन्तुं).—(Determine) अनुमानं कृ, निश्चयं कृ.

CONCLUDED, *p. p.* (Completed) समाप्तः -प्ता -प्तं, समापितः -ता -तं, सम्पूर्णः -र्णा -र्णं, सिद्धः -द्धा -द्धं, साधितः -ता -तं, निर्वृत्तः -त्ता -त्तं, वृत्तः -त्ता -त्तं, निष्पन्नः -न्ना -न्नं, समापन्नः -न्ना -न्नं.—(Ended) अवसितः -ता -तं, अवसन्नः -न्ना -न्नं, पर्य्यवसितः -ता -तं, सितः -ता -तं, सन्नः -न्ना -न्नं, परिणतः -ता -तं, गतः -ता -तं, विपर्य्यस्तः -स्ता -स्तं.—(Inferred) अनुमितः -ता -तं, अवगतः -ता -तं.—(Determined) निश्चितः -ता -तं, निर्णीतः -ता -तं, निर्दिष्टः -ष्टा -ष्टं.

CONCLUSION, *s.* (Completion) समाप्तिः *f.*, समापनं, सिद्धिः *f.*, साधनं, निष्पादनं, निष्पत्तिः *f.*, निर्वर्त्तनं, निर्वृत्तिः *f.*—(Close, end) अवसानं, पर्य्यवसानं, अवसायः, सातिः *f.*, सायः, क्षयः, अन्तः -न्तं, पर्य्यन्तं, शेषः, परिणामः, गतिः *f.*, उपसंहारः; 'conclusion of a play or tale,' निष्ठा, निर्वहणं.—(Inference) अनुमानं, अनुमितिः *f.*, अनुमा, अनुभवः, ऊहनं, अवगमः.—(Consequence) फलं, फलमुत्तरं, उत्तरं, परिणामः, अनुवर्त्तनं.—(Decision, determination) निश्चयः, निर्णयः, निश्चितं, निर्णयनं.—(Demonstrated conclusion) सिद्धान्तः, राद्धान्तः, कृतान्तः.—(Last result of argument) उत्तरपक्षः.

CONCLUSIVE, *a.* निश्चायकः -का -कं, निर्णायकः -का -कं, निर्णयनः -ना -नं, प्रामाणिकः -की -कं, निर्देष्टा -ष्ट्री -ष्टृ (ष्टृ), सिद्धान्तकरणः -णा -णं, एकान्तिकः -की -कं.

CONCLUSIVELY, *adv.* निश्चितं, निर्णीतं, सनिश्चयं, निर्णयेन, सिद्धान्तपूर्व्वकं.

CONCLUSIVENESS, *s.* निश्चायकत्वं, निर्णायकत्वं, निर्णेतृत्वं, निर्देष्टृत्वं, प्रामाण्यं.

To CONCOCT, *v. a.* (Digest, mature by heat) जॄ in caus. (जरयति -यितुं), पच् (c. 1. पचति, पक्तुं), परिपच्, क्वथ् (c. 1. क्वथति -थितुं), निष्क्वथ्.—(Plot) घट् (c. 1. घटते -टितुं), सञ्चिन्त् (c. 10. -चिन्तयति -यितुं).

CONCOCTED, *p. p.* क्वथितः -ता -तं, परिपक्वः -क्वा -क्वं, घटितः -ता -तं.

CONCOCTION, *s.* (Digestion) पाकः, पाचनं, परिपाकः, पक्तिः *f.*, भुक्तस्य अन्नस्य पचनं, जीर्णिः *f.*—(A decoction) निष्क्वाथः, क्वाथः.

CONCOCTIVE, *a.* पाचकः -का -कं, पाचनः -ना -नं, परिपाकी -किणी -कि (न्).

CONCOLOUR, *a.* सवर्णः -र्णा -र्णं, समवर्णः -र्णा -र्णं, एकवर्णः -र्णा -र्णं.

CONCOMITANCE, *s.* सङ्गः, अनुषङ्गः, संयोगः, सहवर्त्तनं, अनुवर्त्तनं, समवायः, अन्वयः, समन्वयः.

CONCOMITANT, *a.* सङ्गी -ङ्गिनी -ङ्गि (न्), आनुषङ्गिकः -का -कं or आनुषङ्गिकः, संयुक्तः -क्ता -क्तं, सहवर्त्ती -र्त्तिनी -र्त्ति (न्), समवेतः -ता -तं, समेतः -ता -तं, समवायी -यिनी -यि (न्), सहितः -ता -तं, समितः -ता -तं, अन्वितः -ता -तं, समन्वितः -ता -तं.

CONCOMITANT, *s.* सङ्गी *m.* (न्), अनुषङ्गी *m.* (न्), सहचारी *m.* (न्), सहवर्त्ती *m.* (न्), सहभावी *m.* (न्).

CONCOMITANTLY, *adv.* अन्यैः सह or सहितं or संयुक्तं or समवेतं.

To CONCOMITATE, *v. n.* संयुज् in pass. (-युज्यते), अन्वि (c. 2. -एति -एतुं).

CONCORD, *s.* (Agreement of opinion, union) सम्मतिः *f.*, एकचित्तता, चित्तैक्यं, ऐक्यं, एकता, परस्परानुमतिः *f.*, संवादः, दाक्षिण्यं, संयोगः, सन्धिः *m.*, सङ्गः.—(Love) प्रीतिः *f.*, प्रणयः.—(Compact) समयः, संविद् *f.*, नियमः.—(Grammatical relation) अनुषञ्जनं, अनुषङ्गः, शब्दानां परस्परसंयोगः, अन्वयः.—(Harmony) तालैक्यं, स्वरैक्यं.

CONCORDANCE, (Agreement) ऐक्यं, एकता, सादृश्यं, अनुरूपता, आनुगुण्यं.—(To the Bible) धर्म्मपुस्तकसूची, धर्म्मपुस्तकनिर्घण्टं.

CONCORDANT, *a.* अनुरूपः -पा -पं, अनुगुणः -णा -णं, सदृशः -शी -शं.

CONCORDAT, *s.* नियमः, समयः, संविद् *f.*, संश्रवः, संवादः, उपगमः.

CONCORPORAL, *a.* एकशरीरः -रा -रं, समशरीरः -रा -रं, एकदेहः -हा -हं.

To CONCORPORATE, *v. a.* एकशरीरीकृ, एकौघीकृ, एकत्र कृ, एकीकृ, पिण्डीकृ.

CONCOURSE, *s.* (Of people) जनसमूहः, लोकसङ्घः, बहुजनमेलकः, लोकनिवहः, जनसम्मर्द्दः, जनौघः, जनसमागमः, जनता.—(Point of junction) सन्धिः *m.*, सङ्गमः.

CONCREMATION, *s.* (Of a widow with her dead husband) सहमरणं, अनुमरणं.

CONCREMENT, *s.* पिण्डः -ण्डं, घनता, संहतिः *f.*, लोष्टः -ष्टं, ओघः, राशिः *m. f.*, एकौघः, सान्द्रता, श्यानता.

To CONCRETE, *v. n.* पिण्डीभू, एकौघीभू, राशीभू, घनीभू, लोष्टीभू, संहन् in pass. (-हन्यते), श्यै (c. 1. श्यायते, श्यातुं).

To CONCRETE, *v. a.* पिण्डीकृ, एकौघीकृ, राशीकृ, घनीकृ, लोष्टीकृ, एकीकृ, सान्द्रीकृ, संहन् (c. 2. -हन्ति -हन्तुं), श्यै in caus. (श्यापयति -यितुं).

CONCRETE, *s.* पिण्डः -ण्डं, ओघः, लोष्टः -ष्टं, घनद्रव्यं, श्यानद्रव्यं, घनचयः.

CONCRETE, *a.* पिण्डीभूतः -ता -तं, एकौघभूतः -ता -तं, राशीभूतः -ता -तं, घनः -ना -नं, शीनः -ना -नं, श्यानः -ना -नं, संहतः -ता -तं, सान्द्रः -न्द्रा -न्द्रं.—(Not abstract) समवेतः -ता -तं, अन्वितः -ता -तं, अविविक्तः -क्ता -क्तं, संयुक्तः -क्ता -क्तं.

CONCRETION, *s.* (The act of concreting) पिण्डीकरणं, एकौघीकरणं, घनीकरणं.—(Coalition) संसक्तिः, संहतिः *f.*, सङ्घातः.—(Mass formed) पिण्डः -ण्डं, ओघः, लोष्टः -ष्टं.

CONCUBINAGE, *s.* उपस्त्रीसेवा, उपस्त्रीगमनं, उपपत्नीसम्भोगः, वेश्यासेवा.

CONCUBINE, *s.* उपस्त्री, उपपत्नी, वारस्त्री, भोग्या स्त्री, स्वैरिणी.—(As shut up in the haram) अवरुद्धा, अवरोधवधूः.

To CONCULCATE, *v. a.* पादेन सम्मृद् (c. 9. -मृद्नाति -मर्द्दितुं) or अवमृद् or प्रमृद् or प्रमन्थ् (c. 9. -मथ्नाति -मन्थितुं).

CONCUPISCENCE, *s.* कामः, कामिता, कामुकत्वं, कामाग्निः *m.*, रतार्थित्वं, अभिलाषः.

CONCUPISCENT, *a.* कामी -मिनी -मि (न्), कामुकः -का -कं, रतार्थी -र्थिनी -र्थि (न्), व्यवायी -यिनी -यि (न्), अभिलाषुकः -का -कं, लम्पटः -टा -टं, अनुकः -का -कं.

To CONCUR, *v. n.* (Meet in one point) एकत्र सङ्गम् (c. 1. -गच्छति -गन्तुं) or समागम् or मिल् (c. 6. मिलति, मेलितुं).—(Join in one action) अन्येन सह कृ or सम्भूय कृ.—(Agree, concur with) सम्मन् (c. 4. -मन्यते -मन्तुं), अनुमन्, अनुवद् (c. 1. -वदति -दितुं), उपगम् (c. 1. -गच्छति -गन्तुं), एकचित्तीभू, स्वीकृ.

CONCURRED, *p. p.* सम्मतः -ता -तं, अनुमतः -ता -तं, सम्प्रतिपन्नः -न्ना -न्नं.

CONCURRENCE, *s.* सम्मतिः *f.*, सम्मतं, अनुमतिः *f.*, अनुवादः -दनं, अनुवचनं, सम्प्रतिपत्तिः *f.*, समनुज्ञानं, स्वीकारः, परिग्रहः, इच्छा.—(Sameness of opinion) ऐकमत्यं, मतैक्यं; 'mutual concurrence,' परस्परानुमतिः *f.*; 'without the concurrence,' अनिच्छया, असम्मत्या, अगोचरेण; 'with his concurrence,' तस्य सम्मत्या or इच्छया or इच्छातस्; 'without his concurrence,' तस्य सम्मतिव्यतिरेकेण.

CONCURRENT, *a.* अनुवादकः -का -कं, अनुवादी -दिनी -दि (न्), आनुमतिकः -की -कं, सम्प्रतिपन्नः -न्ना -न्नं, एकचित्तः -त्ता -त्तं.—(Acting in conjunction) सहकारी -रिणी -रि (न्), सम्भूयकारी -रिणी -रि (न्).—(Concomitant) अनुषङ्गी -ङ्गिणी -ङ्गि (न्), सङ्गी -ङ्गिनी -ङ्गि (न्).

CONCURRENTLY, *adv.* सम्मतिपूर्व्वं, अनुमतिपूर्व्वं, सम्मत्या, अनुमत्या, सम्प्रतिपन्नं.

CONCUSSION, *s.* संक्षोभः, सङ्घट्टः, क्षोभः, विक्षोभः, विकम्पः, मन्थनं, विधुवनं.

To CONDEMN, *v. a.* (Find guilty) दोषीकृ, दोषिणं -षिणीं -षि कृ, सदोषं -षां -षं कृ, अपराधिनं -धिनीं -धि कृ, अपराध (nom. अपराधयति -यितुं), अपराधनिश्चयं कृ, अपराधनिर्णयं कृ.—(Doom to punishment) दण्ड् (c. 10. दण्डयति -यितुं).—(Condemn to death) वधदण्डार्हं -र्हां -र्हं ज्ञा (c. 1. जानाति, ज्ञातुं), हन्तुम् आदिश् (c. 6. -दिशति -देष्टुं), वधदण्डाज्ञां कृ.—(Censure) निन्द् (c. 1. निन्दति -न्दितुं), प्रणिन्द्, प्रत्यादिश् (c. 6. -दिशति -देष्टुं).—(Condemn to pay) दा in caus. (दापयति -यितुं); 'to be condemned,' दण्डं प्राप्.

CONDEMNED, *p. p.* (Found guilty) दोषीकृतः -ता -तं, अपराधितः -ता -तं, निर्णीतापराधः -धा -धं, निर्णीतदोषः -षा -षं.—(Doomed to punishment) दण्डितः -ता -तं, प्राप्तदण्डः -ण्डा -ण्डं, दण्डार्हः -र्हा -र्हं; 'condemned to death,' वध्यः -ध्या -ध्यं; 'condemned to pay,' दापितः -ता -तं; 'cast in a suit,' साधितः -ता -तं.

CONDEMNABLE, *a.* दण्डनीयः -या -यं, दण्ड्यः -ण्ड्या -ण्ड्यं, निन्दनीयः -या -यं, निन्दार्हः -र्हा -र्हं, अपराधी -धिनी -धि (न्), गर्हणीयः -या -यं, दूष्यः -ष्या -ष्यं.

CONDEMNATION, *s.* दण्डः, दण्डनं, दण्डकरणं, दण्डयोगः, दण्डाज्ञा, दोषीकरणं, अपराधनिर्णयः, अपराधनिश्चयः.

CONDEMNATORY, *a.* दण्डवादी -दिनी -दि (न्), निन्दकः -का -कं, अपवादकः -का -कं.

CONDEMNER, *s.* दण्डप्रणेता *m.* (तृ), दोषग्राही *m.* (न्), अपराधनिर्णेता *m.* (तृ), निन्दकः.

CONDENSABLE, *a.* घनीकरणीयः -या -यं, स्थूलीकर्त्तुं शक्यः -क्या -क्यं.

CONDENSATION, *s.* घनीकरणं, स्थूलीकरणं, सान्द्रीकरणं, निविडीकरणं.

To CONDENSE, *v. a.* घनीकृ, स्थूलीकृ, सान्द्रीकृ, निविडं -डां -डं कृ.

To CONDENSE, *v. n.* घनीभू, स्थूलीभू, सान्द्रीभू, पीवरः -रा -रं भू.

CONDENSE, *a.* घनः -ना -नं, स्थूलः -ला -लं, सान्द्रः -न्द्रा -न्द्रं, निविडः -डा -डं, निरन्तरः -रा -रं, दृढसन्धिः -न्धिः -न्धि, नीरन्ध्रः -न्ध्रा -न्ध्रं, अविरलः -ला -लं.

CONDENSED, *p. p.* घनीकृतः -ता -तं, घनीभूतः -ता -तं, स्थूलीभूतः -ता -तं.

CONDENSITY, *s.* घनता -त्वं, स्थूलता, सान्द्रता, नैबिड्यं, पीवरत्वं.

To CONDESCEND, *v. n.* (Lay aside dignity, yield, stoop) गर्व्वं or गौरवं or दर्पम् अपास् (c. 4. -अस्यति -असितुं), मानं or अभिमानं त्यज् (c. 1. त्यजति, त्यक्तुं), or उत्सृज् (c. 1. -सृजति -स्रष्टुं), नम्रीभू, आनतगर्व्वः

-र्व्वा -र्व्वं भू, त्यक्तगौरवः -वा -वं भू.—(Submit) वशीभू.—(Consent, concur with) अनुमन् (c. 4. -मन्यते -मन्तुं), उपगम् (c. 1. -गच्छति -गन्तुं), अनुज्ञा (c. 9. -जानाति -ज्ञातुं), अनुवृत् (c. 1. -वर्त्तते -र्त्तितुं). The 2d or 3d pers. pres. of the rt. अर्ह् is used in such phrases as, 'condescend to speak to me,' मां वक्तुम् अर्हसि or अर्हति भवान्.

CONDESCENDING, *a.* त्यक्तगर्व्वः -र्व्वा -र्व्वं, त्यक्तदर्पः -र्पा -र्पं, न्यस्तगौरवः -वा -वं, नम्रः -म्रा -म्रं, आनतः -ता -तं, अनुरोधी -धिनी -धि (न्), वशानुगः -गा -गं, वशवर्त्ती -र्त्तिनी -र्त्ति (न्), अनुविधायी -यिनी -यि (न्).

CONDESCENDINGLY, *adv.* अगर्व्वं, गर्व्वं विना, गौरवं विना, त्यक्तगर्व्वं, नम्रतया.

CONDESCENSION, *s.* गर्व्वापासनं, दर्पापासनं, अभिमानोत्सर्जनं, गौरवत्यागः, नम्रता, आनतिः *f.*, अनुरोधः, अनुवर्त्तनं.

CONDIGN, *a.* यथार्हः -र्हा -र्हं, योग्यः -ग्या -ग्यं, उपयुक्तः -क्ता -क्तं, अनुगुणः -णा -णं, समुचितः -ता -तं, 'condign punishment,' यथायोग्यदण्डः, यथोपयुक्तशिष्टिः *f.*

CONDIGNLY, *adv.* यथार्हं -र्हतस्, यथायोग्यं, यथोचितं, अनुगुणं.

CONDIGNNESS, *s.* यथार्हत्वं, योग्यता, उपयुक्तता, याथातथ्यं, उपपत्तिः *f.*

CONDIMENT, *s.* उपस्करः, उपकरणं, व्यञ्जनं, वेसवारः, वेशवारः, प्रहितं, तेमनं, निष्ठानं, सन्धितं, अग्निवर्द्धनः, मिष्टान्नं, मोदकं.

CONDISCIPLE, *s.* सहाध्यायी *m.* (न्), एकगुरुः *m.*, सतीर्थः, सब्रह्मचारी *m.* (न्).

To CONDITE, *v. a.* उपस्कृ, सन्धा (c. 3. -दधाति -धातुं), मिष्टीकृ.

CONDITE, *a.* सन्धितः -ता -तं, मिष्टः -ष्टा -ष्टं, सुस्वादुः -द्वी -दु.

CONDITION, *s.* (State) अवस्था, भावः, दशा, स्थितिः *f.*, वृत्तिः *f.*, संस्थितिः *f.*, दशास्थितिः *f.*, गतिः *f.*, रूपं; 'natural condition,' स्वभावः, स्वरूपं; 'calamitous condition,' विपद्दशा; 'ill condition,' दुःस्थितिः *f.*; 'good condition,' सुस्थितिः *f.*; 'in good condition,' सुस्थितः -ता -तं; 'in bad condition,' दुःस्थः -स्था -स्थं; 'in such a condition,' तथाविधः -धा -धं, एवंविधः -धा -धं, एवम्भूतः -ता -तं, इत्थम्भूतः -ता -तं. OBS. The condition or state of any thing is often expressed by the affixes त्व and ता, as, 'the condition of a worm,' कृमित्वं; 'of a Śúdra,' शूद्रता; 'of a wife,' पत्नीत्वं.—(Circumstances) वृत्तिः *f.*, अर्थः, स्थितिः *f.*—(Rank) पदं, आस्पदं, अधिकारः, वृत्तिः *f.*—(Stipulation) नियमः, समयः, नियमवाक्यं, प्रतिज्ञा, पणः, उद्देशः.—(State of body) शरीरस्थितिः *f.*; 'in good condition of body,' हृष्टपुष्टाङ्गः -ङ्गा -ङ्गं.—(Temperament) प्रकृतिः *f.*, भावः.—(Quality) गुणः.—(Attribute) उपाधिः *m.* विशेषणं.

To CONDITION, *v. n.* (Stipulate) समयम् उपगम् (c. 1. -गच्छति -गन्तुं), नियमं कृ.

CONDITIONAL, *a.* सामयिकः -की -कं, नैयमिकः -की -कं, सनियमवाक्यः -क्या -क्यं, नियमितः -ता -तं, नियतः -ता -तं, समयनिश्चितः -ता -तं, निबद्धः -द्धा -द्धं. सोपाधिकः -की -कं, सनियमः -मा -मं.—(In grammar) संशयवाचकं क्रियापदविशेषणं.

CONDITIONALLY, *adv.* नियमवाक्यपूर्व्वं, समयतस्, नियमतस्, समयपुरःसरं.

CONDITIONED, *p. p.* (Circumstanced) स्थितः -ता -तं, स्थः स्था स्थं in comp., भूतः -ता -तं, वर्त्ती -र्त्तिनी -र्त्ति (न्); 'ill-conditioned,' दुःस्थः -स्था -स्थं; 'well-conditioned,' सुस्थितः -ता -तं, सुस्थः -स्था -स्थं.

To CONDOLE, *v. n.* अन्येन सह शुच् (c. 1. शोचति -चितुं) or अनुशुच्, परदुःखं दृष्ट्वा or ज्ञात्वा विलप् (c. 1. -लपति -पितुं) or परिदेव् (c. 1. -देवते -वितुं) or परिखिद् in pass. (-खिद्यते) or परितप् in pass. (-तप्यते), शोकार्त्तं समशोकेन परिशान्त्व् (c. 10. -शान्त्वयति -यितुं), परदुःखभागित्वात् शोकम् अपनुद् (c. 6. -नुदति -नोत्तुं), अन्येन समं शोकं कृ, कुल्यं कृ, परस्य समदुःखः -खा -खम् अस्.

CONDOLENCE, *s.* अन्येन सह शोचनं or अनुशोचनं or शोककरणं, परदुःखार्थं विलपनं or परिदेवनं, समशोककरणं, कुल्यं, कुल्यकरणं.

CONDOLER, *s.* समदुःखः, परशोकसंविभागी *m.* (न्), परदुःखभागी *m.* (न्), समशोककारी *m.* (न्).

CONDONATION, *s.* क्षमा, क्षान्तिः *f.*, मार्ज्जना, अपराधक्षमा, अपराधमार्ज्जना.

To CONDUCE, *v. n.* (Lead to) नी (c. 1. नयति, नेतुं), आनी, गम् in caus. (गमयति -यितुं).—(Bring about) आवह् (c. 1. -वहति -वोढुं).—(Promote) प्रवृत् in caus. (-वर्त्तयति -यितुं), प्रयुज् in caus. (-योजयति -यितुं), सम्पद् in caus. (-पादयति -यितुं), सञ्जन् in caus. (-जनयति -यितुं).

CONDUCIVE, *a.* आवहः -हा -हं, प्रवर्त्तकः -का -कं, सम्पादकः -का -कं, प्रतिपादकः -का -कं, प्रयोजकः -का -कं, जनकः -का -कं, उपायिकः -का -कं; 'conducive to wealth,' अर्थावहः -हा -हं or अर्थोत्पादकः -का -कं; 'to satisfaction,' तृप्तिजनकः -का -कं; 'to virtue,' धर्म्मनिबन्धी -न्धिनी -न्धि (न्); 'to longevity,' आयुष्यः -ष्या -ष्यं; 'to beatitude,' आपवर्ग्यः -र्ग्या -र्ग्यं.

CONDUCT, *s.* (Management) नयः, प्रणयनं, निर्व्वाहः -हणं, नायः, प्रयोगः; 'conduct of affairs,' कर्म्मनिर्व्वाहः, क्रियाविधिः *m.*—(Behaviour) चरितं, चरित्रं, चारित्र्यं, व्यवहारः, चेष्टितं, आचारः, आचरणं, कर्म्म *n.* (न्), क्रिया, वृत्तिः *f.*, प्रवृत्तिः *f.*, वृत्तं, रीतिः *f.*, गतिः *f.*, स्थितिः *f.*, चर्य्या; 'good conduct,' सुचरितं, सुकृतं, सुकर्म्म *n.* (न्), शीलः -लं; 'bad conduct,' दुश्चरितं, दुष्कृतं, कुचर्य्या, कुकर्म्म *n.* (न्), दुश्चेष्टितं; 'improper course of conduct,' उन्मार्गः, विमार्गः; 'proper course,' सुमार्गः, सन्मार्गः.—(Act of leading) समानयनं.—(Convoy, guard) परिचरः.

To CONDUCT, *v. a.* (Lead) नी (c. 1. नयति, नेतुं), आनी, उपानी, समानी, गम् in caus. (गमयति -यितुं), प्राप् in caus. (-आपयति -यितुं).—(Manage) निर्वह् in caus. (-वाहयति -यितुं), प्रवृत् in caus. (-वर्त्तयति -यितुं), प्रणी, सम्प्रणी, विधा (c. 3. -दधाति -धातुं), घट् (c. 1. घटते -टितुं).—(Accompany, attend) अनुया (c. 2. -याति -यातुं), अनुव्रज् (c. 1. -व्रजति -जितुं); परिचर् (c. 1. -चरति -रितुं).—(Shew the way) पथं दृश् in caus. (दर्शयति -यितुं).—(Conduct one's self) व्यवहृ (c. 1. -हरति -हर्त्तुं), चर्, आचर्, समाचर्, वृत् (c. 1. वर्त्तते -र्त्तितुं); 'road conducting to the city,' नगरगामी मार्गः.

CONDUCTED, *p. p.* (Led) नीतः -ता -तं, आनीतः -ता -तं, समानीतः -ता -तं, उपानीतः -ता -तं, गमितः -ता -तं; 'conducted here,' सन्निधापितः -ता -तं; 'being conducted,' नीयमानः -ना -नं.—(Managed) निर्व्वाहितः -ता -तं, प्रणीतः -ता -तं, घटितः -ता -तं, प्रवर्त्तितः -ता -तं, वर्त्तितः -ता -तं; 'well-conducted,' सुघटितः -ता -तं; 'difficult to be conducted,' दुर्निर्व्वाहः -हा -हं.

CONDUCTOR, *s.* (Leader) नायकः, नेता *m.* (तृ), वाहकः, पुरोगः, अग्रगः, पथदर्शकः, सञ्चारकः.—(Manager) प्रणेता *m.* (तृ), सम्प्रणेता, घटकः, निर्व्वाहकः, प्रवर्त्तकः.

CONDUCTRESS, *s.* नायिका, नेत्री, सम्प्रणेत्री, निर्व्वाहिका, अग्रगामिनी.

CONDUIT, *s.* प्रणालः -ली, जलनिर्गमः, कुल्या, खातं, सारणिः *f.*, कृत्रिमासरित्.

CONE, *s.* (Pyramidal figure) सूचिः *f.* -ची, शिखा.—(Solid body, round at the base and pointed at the top) अधोभागे मण्डलाकारो ऽग्रभागे सूच्याकारो घनः.—(Fruit) देवदारुफलं.

To CONFABULATE, *v. n.* संलप् (c. 1. -लपति -पितुं), सञ्जल्प् (c. 1. -जल्पति -ल्पितुं), सम्भाष् (c. 1. -भाषते -षितुं), कथोपकथनं कृ, संवद् (c. 1.

-वदति -दितुं).

CONFABULATION, *s.* संलापः, आलापः, कथोपकथनं, सम्भाषा, विश्रम्भकथा, सम्प्रवदनं, वादः, द्वयोः संवादः.

CONFABULATORY, *a.* आलापी -पिनी -पि (न्), कथोपकथनयोग्यः -ग्या -ग्यं.

To CONFECT, *v. a.* उपस्कृ, सन्धा (c. 3. -दधाति -धातुं), मिष्टीकृ.

CONFECTION, *s.* (A preparation of sugar, &c.) उपस्करः, मोदकः -कं, मिष्टान्नं, मिष्टं, सन्धितं, खण्डमोदकः.—(A mixture) सन्निपातः.—(Electuary) अवलेहः.

CONFECTIONARY, *s.* (Where sweetmeats are sold) मिष्टान्नविक्रयस्थानं, मोदकवीथिः *f.*, मोदकशाला.

CONFECTIONER, *s.* मोदककृत्, मिष्टकर्त्ता *m.* (र्तृ), मिष्टान्नकृत्, आपूपिकः, खाण्डिकः, खण्डपालः.

CONFEDERACY, *s.* सन्धिः *m.*, सन्धानं, साहित्यं, सहायता, सङ्घातः, प्रतीहारः, सङ्घट्टनं, संयोगः, साम्यं, ऐक्यं, ऐकमत्यं, एकवाक्यता.

To CONFEDERATE, *v. n.* सन्धा (c. 3. -धत्ते -धातुं), सन्धिं कृ or विधा (c. 3. -दधाति -धातुं), संयुज् in pass. (-युज्यते), सङ्घट्ट् (c. 1. -घट्टते -ट्टितुं).

To CONFEDERATE, *v. a.* सन्धा (c. 3. -दधाति -धातुं), सन्धिं कृ in caus. (कारयति -यितुं)

CONFEDERATE, *a.* सन्धितः -ता -तं, कृतसन्धिः -न्धिः -न्धि, कृतसम्बन्धः -न्धा -न्धं, सङ्घातवान् -वती -वत् (त्), सहितः -ता -तं, संयुक्तः -क्ता -क्तं.

CONFEDERATE, *s.* सहायः, सहकारी *m.* (न्), सङ्गी *m.* (न्), सम्बन्धी *m.* (न्), परस्परोपकारी *m.* (न्).

CONFEDERATION, *s.* सन्धानं, परस्परोपकारार्थकः सन्धिः, सङ्घातः, सङ्गः.

To CONFER, *v. n.* (Hold conversation) सम्भाष् (c. 1. -भाषते -षितुं), संवद् (c. 1. -वदति -दितुं), संलप् (c. 1. -लपति -पितुं), कथोपकथनं कृ.—(Deliberate with another) अन्येन सह मन्त्र् (c. 10. मन्त्रयते -ति -यितुं) or सम्मन्त्र् or विचर् in caus. (-चारयति -यितुं), सम्भिन् (c. 10. -भिन्नयति -यितुं).

To CONFER, *v. a.* (Compare) उपमा (c. 2. -माति c. 3. -मिमीते -मातुं), सम्प्रधृ in caus. (-धारयति -यितुं).—(Bestow) दा (c. 3. ददाति, c. 1. यच्छति, दातुं), प्रदा, वितृ (c. 1. -तरति -रितुं -रीतुं), प्रतिपद् in caus. (-पादयति -यितुं), उपाकृ, उपकृ; 'confer a favour,' अनुग्रह् (c. 9. -गृह्णाति -ग्रहीतुं), अनुग्रहं कृ, प्रसादं कृ, अभ्युपपत्तिं कृ; 'conferring pleasure,' सुखदः -दा -दं, सुखावहः -हा -हं; 'conferring bliss,' अपवर्गदः -दा -दं, आपवर्ग्यः -र्ग्या -र्ग्यं.

CONFERENCE, *s.* (Conversation) संलापः, सम्भाषा -षणं, सम्प्रवदनं, सङ्कथा, वादः, द्वयोः संवादः.—(Deliberation) मन्त्रणं -णा, सम्मन्त्रणं, सम्प्रधारणा.—(Comparison) उपमितिः *f.*, उपमानं.

CONFERRED, *p. p.* दत्तः -त्ता -त्तं, प्रदत्तः -त्ता -त्तं, प्रत्तः -त्ता -त्तं, प्रतिपादितः -ता -तं, वितीर्णः -र्णा -र्णं, विश्राणितः -ता -तं, निहितः -ता -तं.

CONFERRER, *s.* दाता *m.* (तृ), प्रदाता *m.* (तृ), प्रदः or दः in comp.

To CONFESS, *v. a.* and *n.* (Own, acknowledge) स्वीकृ, अङ्गीकृ, उरीकृ, उररीकृ, अनुभाष् (c. 1. -भाषते -षितुं), प्रतिपद् (c. 4. -पद्यते -पत्तुं), सम्प्रतिपद्.—(Make a public avowal) ख्या in caus. (ख्यापयति -यितुं), विवृ (c. 5. -वृणोति -वरितुं -रीतुं), प्रकाश् in caus. (-काशयति -यितुं), प्रकाशं or व्यक्तं वद् (c. 1. वदति -दितुं).—(Disclose the state of the conscience to a priest) सर्व्वं मनोगतं गुरोर् कर्णे ख्या in caus. or प्रकाश् in caus., आचार्य्यनिकटे पापविवरणं कृ.—(Hear the confession of a penitent) अनुतापिना कर्णे अर्पितं पापस्वीकारं श्रु (c. 5. शृणोति श्रोतुं).—(Prove, show) सूच् in caus. (सूचयति -यितुं).

CONFESSEDLY, *adv.* निर्विवादं, असंशयं, सुनिश्चितं, प्रकाशं, व्यक्तं.

CONFESSION, *s.* स्वीकारः, अङ्गीकारः, उरीकारः.—(Of sins) पापस्वीकारः, स्वपापविवरणं, आत्मापराधस्वीकारः, पापानाम् अङ्गीकारः, काम्यकारः.—(Avowal, open declaration) ख्यापनं, प्रकाशनं, प्रतिपत्तिः *f.*, सम्प्रतिपत्तिः *f.*—(To a priest) आचार्य्यनिकटे मनोगतप्रकाशनं.

CONFESSIONAL, *s.* अपराधस्वीकारश्रोतुर् आसनं, पापविवरणश्रोतुर् आचार्य्यस्य कुटी.

CONFESSOR, *s.* (One who makes confession) ख्यापकः, काम्यकारः, स्वीकारकृत्, स्वीकर्त्ता *m.* (र्तृ), अङ्गीकर्त्ता.—(One who suffers for his faith) स्वधर्म्मार्थे दुःखभागी *m.* (न्).—(A priest who hears confession) पापस्वीकारश्रोता *m.* (तृ), कर्णे अर्पितं परपापविवरणं शृणोति य आचार्य्यः.

CONFIDANT, *s.* (A woman's female friend) सखी, वयस्या, दूती, दूतिका, आलिः *f.*, -ली.—(A man's intimate friend) सखा *m.* (खि), वयस्यः, समदुःखसुखः.

To CONFIDE, *v. n.* विश्वस् (c. 2. -श्वसिति -सितुं), परिविश्वस् with loc. or gen.; विश्रम्भ् (c. 1. -श्रम्भते -म्भितुं), प्रती (rt. इ with प्रति, प्रत्येति, प्रत्येतुं), श्रद्धा (c. 3. -दधाति -धातुं), विश्वासं कृ, प्रत्ययं कृ.

To CONFIDE, *v. a.* (Intrust) न्यस् (c. 4. -अस्यति -असितुं), न्यासीकृ, निक्षिप् (c. 6. -क्षिपति -क्षेप्तुं), सम्ॠ in caus. (-अर्पयति -यितुं).

CONFIDED, *p. p.* (Trusted in) विश्वस्तः -स्ता -स्तं, विश्रब्धः -ब्धा -ब्धं, प्रतीतः -ता -तं, प्रत्ययितः -ता -तं, समाश्वस्तः -स्ता -स्तं, न्यासीकृतः -ता -तं.—(Intrusted) निक्षिप्तः -प्ता -प्तं, न्यस्तः -स्ता -स्तं, न्यासीकृतः -ता -तं.

CONFIDENCE, *s.* (Trust, firm belief) विश्वासः, प्रत्ययः, विश्रम्भः -म्भणं, समाश्वासः, दृढप्रत्ययः, असंशयः, असन्देहः, असन्दिग्धता, श्रद्धा -द्धा, आशाबन्धः; 'breach of confidence,' विश्वासभङ्गः; 'an object of confidence,' विश्वासभूमिः *f.*, विश्वासपात्रं; 'worthy of confidence,' विश्वास्यः -स्या -स्यं; 'one whose confidence has been gained,' विश्वासप्रतिपन्नः -न्ना -न्नं; 'to inspire with confidence,' आश्वस् in caus. (-श्वासयति -यितुं) or विश्वस्; 'inspired with confidence,' विश्वासितः -ता -तं.—(Conviction, certainty) निश्चयः, दृढज्ञानं, दृढप्रमाणं.—(Boldness, want of modesty) प्रगल्भता, प्रतिभा -भानं, अविशङ्का, धार्ष्ट्यं, निर्लज्जता.

CONFIDENT, *a.* (Assured beyond doubt, certain) निश्चितः -ता -तं, कृतनिश्चयः -या -यं, असन्दिग्धः -ग्धा -ग्धं, निःसन्देहः -हा -हं, छिन्नसंशयः -या -यं; 'I am confident of that,' तन् मया निश्चितं.—(Trusting) विश्वासी -सिनी -सि (न्), प्रत्ययी -यिनी -यि (न्), विश्वस्तः -स्ता -स्तं.—(Bold) प्रगल्भः -ल्भा -ल्भं, प्रतिभानवान् -वती -वत् (त्) or प्रतिभावान्, अशङ्कितः -ता -तं, अविशङ्कितः -ता -तं, निर्विशङ्कः -ङ्का -ङ्कं.

CONFIDENTIAL, *a.* विश्वस्तः -स्ता -स्तं, विश्रब्धः -ब्धा -ब्धं, आप्तः -प्ता -प्तं, प्रत्ययितः -ता -तं, प्रात्ययिकः -की -कं; 'confidential conversation,' विश्रम्भालापः, विश्वासकथाप्रसङ्गः; 'confidential matters,' विश्वासकार्य्यं.

CONFIDENTIALLY, *adv.* विश्वासेन, विश्रम्भात्, विश्वस्तं, विश्रम्भपूर्व्वकं.

CONFIDENTLY, *adv.* सविश्वासं, असंशयं, निःशङ्कं, निर्विशङ्कं, असंशयं, निःसन्देहं.

CONFIDING, *a.* विश्वस्तः -स्ता -स्तं, विश्वासी -सिनी -सि (न्), सञ्जातविश्वासः -सा -सं, विश्रब्धः -ब्धा -ब्धं, विश्रम्भप्रवणः -णा -णं, प्रत्ययी -यिनी -यि (न्), जातप्रत्ययः -या -यं, समाश्वस्तः -स्ता -स्तं, श्रद्धत् -धती -धत् (त्), श्रद्दधानः -ना -नं, अविशङ्कमानः -ना -नं.

CONFIGURATION, *s.* संस्कारः, आकारः, आकृतिः *f.*, रूपं, मूर्त्तिः *f.*, विग्रहः, विधानं, संस्थानं, धरिमा *m.* (न्), संयानः.

CONFINE, *s.* (Border) सीमा, समन्तः, पर्य्यन्तं, अन्तः -न्तं, प्रान्तः, उपान्तं;

'dwelling on the confines,' सामन्तवासी -सिनी -सि (न्).

To CONFINE, *v. n.* समन्ते or पर्य्यन्ते or निकटे स्था (c. 1. तिष्ठति, स्थातुं), or वृत् (c. 1. वर्त्तते -र्त्तितुं) or वस् (c. 1. वसति, वस्तुं); स्पृश् (c. 6. स्पृशति, स्प्रष्टुं), समन्त (nom. समन्तयति -यितुं).

To CONFINE, *v. a.* (Circumscribe) परिमा (c. 2. -माति -मातुं), संहृ (c. 1. -हरति -हर्त्तुं), नियम् (c. 1. -यच्छति -यन्तुं), निबन्ध् (c. 9. -बध्नाति -बन्द्धुं).—(Imprison) कारायां or कारागारे बन्ध् or निरुध् (c. 7. -रुणद्धि -रोद्धुं) or आसिध् (c. 1. -सेधति -सेद्धुं).—(Restrain) यम्, संयम्, नियम्, परियम्, विनियम्; निग्रह् (c. 9. -गृह्णाति -ग्रहीतुं); निरुध्, अवरुध्; संहृ, निषिध्; 'to be confined in childbed,' प्राप्तप्रसवकाला भू.

CONFINED, *p. p.* (Circumscribed) मितः -ता -तं, परिमितः -ता -तं, नियतः -ता -तं, निबद्धः -द्धा -द्धं.—(Contracted) सम्बाधः -धा -धं, संहृतः -ता -तं, सङ्कुटः -टा -टं, सङ्कुचितः -ता -तं, संवृतः -ता -तं.—(Imprisoned) कारागुप्तः -प्ता -प्तं, कारायां बद्धः -द्धा -द्धं or निरुद्धः -द्धा -द्धं.—(Bound) बद्धः -द्धा -द्धं, कीलितः -ता -तं, अमोचितः -ता -तं.—(Restrained) यतः -ता -तं, संयतः -ता -तं, निगृहीतः -ता -तं, बाधितः -ता -तं, निरुद्धः -द्धा -द्धं, यन्त्रितः -ता -तं, प्रत्याहृतः -ता -तं.—(Confined in the bowels) आनद्धः -द्धा -द्धं, बद्धकोष्ठः -ष्ठा -ष्ठं, अवरुद्धमलः -ला -लं.—(In childbed) प्राप्तप्रसवकाला.

CONFINEMENT, *s.* (Restraint) रोधः, निरोधः, संरोधः, यमः, संयमः -मनं, निग्रहः, बन्धनं, अमुक्तिः *f.*, अमोक्षः—(Imprisonment, durance) रोधः, निरोधनं, बन्धनं, प्रतिबन्धनं, स्थानासेधः, सम्प्रतिरोधकः.—(Of the bowels) नाहः, आनाहः, निबन्धः, मलावरोधः, मलावष्टम्भः, गुदग्रहः.—(Childbed) प्रसवकालः, प्रसवावस्था.

To CONFIRM, *v. a.* (Strengthen) दृढीकृ, स्थिरीकृ, दृढ (nom. दृढयति -यितुं), सबलं -लां -लं कृ, संस्तम्भ् (c. 5. -स्तभ्नोति -स्तम्भितुं or caus. -स्तम्भयति -यितुं).—(Corroborate another's opinion by new evidence) प्रमाणं or दृढप्रमाणं दा (c. 3. ददाति, दातुं), सप्रमाणं -णां -णं कृ, प्रमाणीकृ, अनुवद् (c.1. -वदति -दितुं), अनुकरणवाक्यं वद्, परवाक्यं दृढीकृ.—(Strengthen in resolution) मनःस्थैर्य्यं कृ, सुस्थिरं -रां -रं कृ, सुस्थ (nom. सुस्थयति -यितुं).—(Ratify, settle) सत्याकृ, सत्यं कृ, स्थिरीकृ, दृढनिश्चयं दा.—(Confirm in the Christian faith by imposition of hands) हस्तार्पणेन ख्रीष्टीयधर्म्मे प्रवृत्तं -त्तां -त्तं कृ.

CONFIRMABLE, *a.* संस्तम्भनीयः -या -यं, दृढीकरणीयः -या -यं, स्थिरीकरणीयः -या -यं.

CONFIRMATION, *s.* दृढीकरणं, स्थिरीकरणं, संस्तम्भः, सत्याकृतिः *f.*, प्रमाणीकरणं, दृढप्रमाणदानं, अनुवादः, दृढोक्तिः *f.*—(Confirming in the Christian faith by imposition of hands) हस्तार्पणेन ख्रीष्टीयधर्म्मे प्रवर्त्तनं.

CONFIRMATORY, *a.* अनुवादकः -का -कं, प्रमाणीकरणः -णा -णं, संस्तम्भकृत्.

CONFIRMED, *p. p.* दृढीकृतः -ता -तं, स्थिरीकृतः -ता -तं, संस्तब्धः -ब्धा -ब्धं, सत्याकृतः -ता -तं, प्रमाणीकृतः -ता -तं, दृढनिश्चयः -या -यं, दृढः -ढा -ढं.—(Radicated) प्ररूढः -ढा -ढं, रूढः -ढा -ढं, संरूढः -ढा -ढं; 'a confirmed fool,' प्रतिनिविष्टमूर्खः; 'confirmed friendship,' रूढसौहृदं.

CONFIRMER, *s.* प्रमाणीकर्त्ता *m.* (र्त्तृ), दृढीकर्त्ता, स्थिरीकर्त्ता, दृढप्रमाणदाता *m.* (तृ), अनुवादी *m.* (न्).

To CONFISCATE, *v. a.* सर्व्वस्वं दण्ड् (c. 10. दण्डयति -यितुं) or हृ (c. 1. हरति, हर्त्तुं) or अपहृ or छिद् (c. 7. छिनत्ति, छेत्तुं) or आच्छिद्, सर्व्ववित्तं दण्डयित्वा राजाधीनं कृ.

CONFISCATED, *p. p.* राजहृतः -ता -तं, राजापहृतः -ता -तं.—(In all one's property) सर्व्वस्वदण्डः -ण्डा -ण्डं, हृतसर्व्वस्वः -स्वा -स्वं, छिन्नवृत्तिः -त्तिः -त्ति.

CONFISCATION, *s.* सर्व्वस्वदण्डं, सर्व्वस्वहरणं, सर्व्वहारः, सर्व्वस्वापहारः, वृत्तिच्छेदः, अर्थदूषणं.

CONFIT, *s.* मोदकः -कं, मिष्टं, मिष्टान्नं, मधुमस्तकं. *See* COMFIT.

CONFLAGRATION, *s.* (Burning) दाहः -हनं, ज्वलनं, ज्वालः, प्लोषः, ओषः, दीपनं.—(Great fire) महाग्निः *m.*; 'in a forest,' दवाग्निः, दावानलः.—(Fire that will consume the world) प्रलयाग्निः *m.*

CONFLATION, *s.* एककाले बहूनां शुषिरवाद्यानां ध्मानं.—(Casting of metals) सन्धानं.

To CONFLICT, *v. n.* युध् (c. 4. युध्यते, योद्धुं), कलह (nom. कलहायते), विग्रह् (c. 9. -गृह्णाति -ग्रहीतुं).—(Clash) सङ्घट्ट् (c. 1. -घट्टते -ट्टितुं), परस्परं विरुध् (c. 7. -रुणद्धि -रोद्धुं).

CONFLICT, *s.* युद्धं, सङ्ग्रामः, संयुगः, समरः -रं, रणः -णं, विग्रहः, सङ्गरः, संख्यं, सम्परायः, कलहः, कलिः *m.*, समित् *f.*, सम्प्रहारः.—(Clash) समाघातः, सङ्घट्टः -ट्टनं.

CONFLICTING, *a.* (Clashing) परस्परपराहतः -ता -तं, विप्रतिपन्नः -न्ना -न्नं, परस्परविरोधी -धिनी -धि (न्), विरुद्धः -द्धा -द्धं.

CONFLUENCE, *s.* (Of two rivers) सम्भेदः, सङ्गः, सङ्गमः, सम्पातः, वेणिः *f.*, निर्व्वाणं.—(Junction) संयोगः, समागमः.—(Concourse of people) जनसमागमः, जनसमूहः, जनसम्मर्द्दः, लोकसङ्घः.

CONFLUENT, *a.* एकस्थानं प्रति प्रवाहकः -का -कं, सम्मेलकः -का -कं.

CONFLUX, *s.* सङ्गमः, समागमः, सम्भेदः, वेणिः *f.*—(Crowd) बहुजनमेलकः.

To CONFORM, *v. a.* अनुरूपीकृ, सदृशीकृ, अनुरूपं -पां -पं कृ, सदृशं -शीं -शं कृ, तुल्यीकृ, समीकृ, योग्यं -ग्यां -ग्यं कृ, समान (nom. समानयति -यितुं).

To CONFORM, *v. n.* सादृश्यं or आनुरूप्यं गम् (c. 1. गच्छति, गन्तुं), सदृशः -शी -शं भू.—(Comply with) अनुवृत् (c. 1. -वर्त्तते -र्त्तितुं), अनुरुध् (c. 4. -रुध्यते -रोद्धुं), अनुविधा (c. 3. -दधाति -धातुं), अनुसृ (c. 1. -सरति -सर्त्तुं), अनुकृ, अनुमन् (c. 4. -मन्यते -मन्तुं), स्वीकृ.—(Be suitable) युज् in pass. (युज्यते).

CONFORMABLE, *a.* अनुरूपः -पा -पं, सदृशः -शी -शं, अनुसारी -रिणी -रि (न्), अनुगुणः -णा -णं, सरूपः -पी -पं, तुल्यरूपः -पा -पी -पं, समानः -ना -नं, तुल्यः -ल्या -ल्यं, समानाकारः -रा -रं, एकाकारः -रा -रं.—(Compliant) अनुवर्त्ती -र्त्तिनी -र्त्ति (न्), अनुविधायी -यिनी -यि (न्), अनुकूलः -ला -लं, अनुनयी -यिनी -यि (न्), अनुरोधी -धिनी -धि (न्).—(To what has been said) अनुवादकः -का -कं -दी -दिनी -दि (न्).—(Suitable) योग्यः -ग्या -ग्यं, युञ्जानः -ना -नं, युक्तः -क्ता -क्तं, उपयुक्तः -क्ता -क्तं.

CONFORMABLY, *adv.* अनुरूपं, अनुरूपेण, अनुसारतस्, अनुसारेण, अनुसारात्, युक्तं, योगतस्, योग्यं, यथावत्. Often expressed by यथा prefixed; as, 'conformably to rule,' यथाविधि.

CONFORMATION, *s.* संस्कारः, संयानः, आकारः, आकृतिः *f.*, संस्थानं, रूपं.

CONFORMIST, *s.* धर्म्मानुसारी *m.* (न्), वृत्तानुसारी, वृत्तानुवर्त्ती *m.* (न्), गतानुगतिकः.

CONFORMITY, *s.* अनुरूपं -पता, आनुरूप्यं, सादृश्यं, सदृशता, अनुसारः -रित्वं, समानता, समता, तुल्यत्वं, सरूपता, आनुगुण्यं.—(Compliance) अनुवृत्तिः *f.*, अनुरोधः, अनुकूलता.—(To what has been said) अनुवादत्वं.—(Suitableness) योग्यता, युक्तता, उपयुक्तत्वं; 'conformity to established practice,' वृत्तानुसारः, धर्म्मानुसारः.

To CONFOUND, *v. a.* (Perplex) मुह् in caus. (मोहयति -यितुं), विमुह्, व्यामुह्, आकुलीकृ, व्याकुलीकृ, व्याकुल (nom. व्याकुलयति -यितुं),

विस्मि in caus. (-स्माययति -यितुं).—(Agitate, disturb) क्षुभ् in caus. (क्षोभयति -यितुं), विक्षुभ्, संक्षुभ्, विलुप् (c. 6. -लुम्पति -लोप्तुं). —(Mingle, huddle together) सम्मिश्रीकृ, सङ्कीर्णीकृ, सम्मिश्र् (c. 10. -मिश्रयति -यितुं), विक्षिप् (c. 6. -क्षिपति -क्षेप्तुं), अस्तव्यस्तीकृ, सङ्कुलीकृ, भेदं जन् in caus. (जनयति -यितुं).—(Destroy) विनश् in caus. (-नाशयति -यितुं).—(Confound by argument) निरुत्तरं -रां -रं कृ; 'to be confounded,' मुह् (c. 4. मुह्यति), विमुह्, सम्मुह्; आकुलीभू, व्याकुलीभू.

Confounded, *a.* (Perplexed) मोहितः -ता -तं, विमोहितः -ता -तं, आकुलितः -ता -तं, व्याकुलितः -ता -तं, आकुलः -ला -लं, व्याकुलः -ला -लं, व्याकुलीकृतः -ता -तं, व्यग्रः -ग्रा -ग्रं, सङ्कीर्णः -र्णा -र्णं, व्यस्तः -स्ता -स्तं, विहस्तः -स्ता -स्तं, सम्भ्रान्तः -न्ता -न्तं, पिच्छलः -ला -लं, पिच्छः -च्छा -च्छं, विक्षिप्तचित्तः -त्ता -त्तं.—(Agitated) क्षोभितः -ता -तं, विक्षिप्तः -प्ता -प्तं. —(Huddled together) सङ्कुरीकृतः -ता -तं, सङ्कीर्णः -र्णा -र्णं, सङ्कुलः -ला -लं, अस्तव्यस्तः -स्ता -स्तं.—(Unfortunate) दैवोपहतः -ता -तं.—(Detestable) गर्ह्यः -र्ह्या -र्ह्यं, कुत्सितः -ता -तं.

Confoundedly, *adv.* अत्यन्तं, कुत्सितं, अत्यर्थं, गर्हितं, गर्ह्यप्रकारेण.

Confounder, *s.* मोहकः, विमोहनः, मोहनकृत्, विक्षेपकः, विक्षोभकर्त्ता *m.* (र्त्तृ).

Confraternity, *s.* सौभ्रात्रं, भ्रातृत्वं, सभ्यासिनां साहित्यं, सगोत्रं.

To confront, *v. a.* (Stand face to face) अभिमुखे or सम्मुखे or सम्मुखासम्मुखि or प्रत्यक्षतः स्था (c. 1. तिष्ठति, स्थातुं) or वृत् (c. 1. वर्त्तते -र्त्तितुं), सम्मुखीभू, अभिमुखं गम् (c. 1. गच्छति, गन्तुं), अभिवृत्. —(Compare) उपमा (c. 2. -माति -मातुं), सम्धृ in caus. (-धारयति -यितुं).—(Oppose plaintiff and defendant in court) अर्थिप्रत्यर्थिनौ प्राड्विवाकसाक्षाद् एककाले आनी (c. 1. -नयति -नेतुं).—(Oppose a witness to an accused party) अभियुक्तजनप्रतिमुखे साक्षिणं स्था in caus. (स्थापयति -यितुं).

Confrontation, *s.* (Of witnesses with an accused party) धर्म्मसभायाम् अभियुक्तजनप्रतिमुखे साक्षिस्थापनं.—(In battle) धाटी.

To confuse, *v. a.* विक्षिप् (c. 6. -क्षिपति -क्षेप्तुं), संक्षुभ् in caus. (-क्षोभयति -यितुं), विक्षुभ्, सङ्कुरीकृ, सङ्कॄ (c. 6. -किरति -करितुं -रीतुं), सम्मिश्र् (c. 10. -मिश्रयति -यितुं), अस्तव्यस्तीकृ; 'to be confused,' सङ्कॄ in pass. (-कीर्य्यते). *See To* confound.

Confused, *p. p.* (Crowded irregularly, disordered) सङ्कुलः -ला -लं, सङ्कीर्णः -र्णा -र्णं, आकीर्णः -र्णा -र्णं, विक्षिप्तः -प्ता -प्तं, सङ्कुरीकृतः -ता -तं, अस्तव्यस्तः -स्ता -स्तं.—(Disturbed in mind) व्यस्तः -स्ता -स्तं, आकुलः -ला -लं, व्याकुलः -ला -लं, विह्वलः -ला -लं, कातरः -रा -रं, पारिप्लवः -वा -वं, व्यग्रः -ग्रा -ग्रं, सम्भ्रान्तः -न्ता -न्तं, विस्मयाकुलः -ला -लं, आकुलचित्तः -त्ता -त्तं, पिच्छः -च्छा -च्छं, अधीरः -रा -रं, विपन्नः -न्ना -न्नं. *See* Confounded.—(Without order) क्रमहीनः -ना -नं. —(Abashed) ह्रीपरिगतः -ता -तं.—(Not clear) अस्पष्टः -ष्टा -ष्टं.

Confusedly, *adv.* (In a mixed manner) सङ्कुलं, सङ्कीर्णं, साङ्कर्य्येण. —(Without order) क्रमं विना, अक्रमेण.—(Not clearly) अस्पष्टं. —(With bewilderment) ससम्भ्रमं, व्यस्तचेतसा, व्याकुलमनसा.

Confusion, *s.* (The act) सङ्कुरीकरणं.—(Irregular mixture) सङ्करः, साङ्कर्य्यं, सङ्कीर्णत्वं, सङ्क्षोभः, व्यस्तता, व्यतिकरः.—(Bewilderment) आकुलत्वं, व्याकुलत्वं, वैक्लव्यं, कातरता, व्यस्तता, व्यग्रता, सम्भ्रमः, विस्मयः.—(Confusion of an army) समुत्पिञ्जः, पिञ्जलः.—(Want of order) अक्रमः, विसूत्रता, क्रमहीनता.—(Want of clearness) अस्पष्टता.—(Shame) ह्रीः, लज्जा, व्रीडा.—(Destruction) विनाशः; 'Confusion seize thee!' निग्राहस् ते भूयात्; 'confusion of ideas,' रोपः, रोपणं.

Confutable, *a.* खण्डनीयः -या -यं, प्रत्याख्येयः -या -यं, निराकरणीयः -या -यं.

Confutation, *s.* खण्डनं, वाक्यखण्डनं, पक्षाघातः, निराकरणं, प्रत्याख्यानं, निरासः, अधरीकरणं, बाधः, बाधा, उपमर्द्दः, अनिश्चयः.

To confute, *v. a.* खण्ड् (c. 10. खण्डयति -यितुं), निरस् (c. 4. -अस्यति -असितुं), परास्; प्रत्याख्या (c. 2. -ख्याति -तुं), संमूष् (c. 10. -मूषयति -यितुं), अधरीकृ, निराकृ, निरुत्तरीकृ.

Confuted, *p. p.* खण्डितः -ता -तं, निरस्तः -स्ता -स्तं, परास्तः -स्ता -स्तं, निराकृतः -ता -तं, अधरीकृतः -ता -तं, प्रत्याख्यातः -ता -तं, बाधितः -ता -तं.

Congé, *s.* (Bow, salutation) प्रणामः, प्रणतिः *f.*, नमस्कारः, अभिवादः -दनं, प्रणिपातः.—(Leave, farewell) अनुज्ञा, अनुमतिः *f.*, आमन्त्रणं.

To congeal, *v. a.* घनीकृ, श्यै in caus. (श्यापयति -यितुं), शीतीकृ, श्यानीकृ, पिण्डीकृ, संहन् (c. 2. -हन्ति -हन्तुं).

To congeal, *v. n.* घनीभू, संहन् in pass. (-हन्यते), श्यै (c. 1. श्यायते, श्यातुं), शीतीभू, शीनीभू, पिण्डीभू.

Congealable, *a.* श्यानीयः -या -यं, श्येयः -या -यं, घनीकरणीयः -या -यं.

Congealed, *p. p.* घनीकृतः -ता -तं, घनीभूतः -ता -तं, शीतः -ता -तं, शीनः -ना -नं, श्यानः -ना -नं, द्रवेतरः -रा -रं.

Congelation, *s.* (The state) शीतीभावः, शीतता, घनत्वं -ता, घनीभावः, संहतत्वं -ता, संहतिः *f.*—(The act) घनीकरणं, शीतीकरणं.

Congenial, *a.* (Of the same disposition) समानशीलः -ला -लं, समानभावः -वा -वं, एकस्वभावः -वा -वं, एकभावः -वा -वं, तुल्यशीलः -ला -लं, स्वाभाविकः -की -कं, सधर्म्मा -र्म्मा -र्म्म (न्).—(Kindred) समानजातीयः -या -यं, सजातिः -तिः -ति.—(Agreeable, suitable) अनुसारी -रिणी -रि (न्), अनुरूपः -पा -पं, अनुगुणः -णा -णं, प्रियकारः -री -रं.

Congeniality, *s.* समानशीलता, तुल्यशीलता, सजातित्वं, एकजातित्वं, सधर्म्मकत्वं, अनुसारित्वं, आनुगुण्यं, आनुरूप्यं.

Congenite, *a.* सहजः -जा -जं, सहजातः -ता -तं, समकालजः -जा -जं, एककाले जातः -ता -तं, एककालोत्पन्नः -न्ना -न्नं.

Conger, *s.* समुद्रव्यालः, जलव्यालः, समुद्रजः कुक्षिकाभेदः or अभ्याहिः *m.*

Congeries, *s.* राशिः *m. f.*, स्तूपः, पिण्डः, सञ्चयः, ओघः, पुञ्जः, पूगः, स्तोमः.

To congest, *v. a.* राशीकृ, पिण्डीकृ, एकौघीकृ, सञ्चि (c. 5. -चिनोति -चेतुं), समाचि, समुपचि, एकपूगीकृ, एकपुञ्जीकृ.

Congestible, *a.* सञ्चयनीयः -या -यं, एकराशीकरणीयः -या -यं.

Congestion, *s.* (Of blood) रक्तावरोधः, रक्तावष्टम्भः.

To conglobate, *v. a.* गोलीकृ, एकमण्डलीकृ, एकपिण्डीकृ, एकौघीकृ, वर्त्तुलीकृ.

Conglobate, *a.* एकपिण्डीभूतः -ता -तं, मण्डलीभूतः -ता -तं, एकमण्डलाकारः -रा -रं.

Conglobation, *s.* (The act) एकमण्डलीकरणं, एकौघीकरणं.—(A mass) एकपिण्डः, एकौघः, एकमण्डलं.

To conglomerate, *v. a.* एकराशीकृ, एकपिण्डीकृ, एकगोलीकृ, एकौघीकृ, एकवृन्दीकृ, सञ्चि (c. 5. -चिनोति -चेतुं), समुपचि, समाचि, सम्भृ (c. 1. -भरति -भर्त्तुं), समाक्षिप् (c. 6. -क्षिपति -क्षेप्तुं), एकत्र कृ, वर्त्तुलीकृ.

Conglomerated, *p. p.* एकराशिभूतः -ता -तं, एकौघभूतः -ता -तं, एकपिण्डीभूतः -ता -तं, एकत्रीभूतः -ता -तं.

Conglomeration, *s.* (The act) एकपिण्डीकरणं, एकराशीकरणं, समुपचयनं.—(A collection, heap) एकराशिः *m. f.*, एकौघः, एकपिण्डः, एकवृन्दं.

To conglutinate, *v. a.* संलग्नीकृ, संश्लिष् in caus. (-श्लेषयति -यितुं), सन्धा (c. 3. -दधाति -धातुं), संयुज् (c. 7. -युनक्ति -योक्तुं).—(Heal wounds) संरुह् in caus. (-रोपयति -यितुं).

To conglutinate, *v. n.* संसञ्ज् in pass. (-सज्यते), संलग्नीभू, संश्लिष् in pass. (-श्लिष्यते), सन्धा in pass. (-धीयते), संयुज् in pass. (-युज्यते). —(Be healed) संरुह् in caus. pass. (-रोप्यते).

Conglutination, *s.* (Junction) संसक्तिः *f.*, समासक्तिः, संश्लेषः, संयोगः, सन्धिः *m.*—(The act) संलग्नीकरणं.—(Healing) रोपणं, संरोपणं.

To congratulate, *v. a.* मङ्गलवचनं or कल्याणवचनं ब्रू (c. 2. ब्रवीति, वक्तुं) or वद् (c. 1. वदति -दितुं), काल्यं वद्, परमकुशलं ज्ञात्वा तेन सह धन्यवादं कृ, or कुशलवादं कृ or उत्सवं कृ; मङ्गलं or कुशलं भूयाद् इति वद्, आमन्त्र् (c. 10. -मन्त्रयति -ते -यितुं).

Congratulation, *s.* कल्याणवचनं, कल्यवादः, कल्यं, कल्या, मङ्गलवचनं, कल्याणोक्तिः *f.*, माङ्गल्यवाक्यं, कुल्यं, धन्यवादः, कुशलवादः, आमन्त्रणं, आशीः *f.* (स्), आशीर्वादः.

Congratulatory, *a.* कल्यवादः -दा -दं, मङ्गलवादी -दिनी -दि (न्), कल्योक्तिमयः -यी -यं, मङ्गलसूचकः -का -कं, माङ्गलिकः -की -कं, कल्याणकरः -री -रं, उत्सवकरः -री -रं.

To congregate, *v. a.* समाचि (c. 5. -चिनोति -चेतुं), समानी (c. 1. -नयति -नेतुं), समाहृ (c. 1. -हरति -हर्त्तुं), समूह् (c. 1. -ऊहते -हितुं), सङ्क्रम् in caus. (-गमयति -यितुं), सन्निपत् in caus. (-पातयति -यितुं), एकीकृ, एकत्रकृ, राशीकृ, समूहीकृ, यूथशः कृ, एकयूथीकृ.

To congregate, *v. n.* समे (सम् and आ with root इ, समैति -तुं), समभ्ये, सङ्गम् (c. 1. -गच्छति -गन्तुं), समागम्; सम्मिल् (c. 6. -मिलति -मेलितुं), एकत्र मिल्, एकत्र आगम्, यूथशः सम्मिल्; समावृत् (c. 1. -वर्त्तते -र्त्तितुं), सन्निपत् (c. 1. -पतति -तितुं).

Congregated, *a.* समेतः -ता -तं, समागतः -ता -तं, मिलितः -ता -तं, समूढः -ढा -ढं, समूहभूतः -ता -तं, एकस्थः -स्था -स्थं, सन्निपतितः -ता -तं.

Congregation, *s.* (Assembly) सभा, परिषद् *f.*, समाजः, समज्या, समूहः, समागमः, मेलकः, मेलः -ला, संसद् *f.*, मण्डलं, समवायः, निवहः, निकायः. (Collection) सञ्चयः -यनं, समाहारः, सन्निपातः, समुदयः.—(Assembly met to worship God) ईश्वरपूजार्थं समागतो जनसमूहः, ईश्वरपूजकानां परिषद्.

Congregational, *a.* सभ्यः -भ्या -भ्यं, सामाजिकः -की -कं, पारिषदः -दी -दं,

Congress, *s.* सभा, संसद् *f.*, सदः *n.* (स्), समाजः, मेलकः.—(Shock, collision) सङ्घट्टः -ट्टनं -ट्टना, समाघातः.—(Sexual) स्त्रीपुरुषसङ्गः,

Congressive, *a.* साङ्गतिकः -की -कं, सम्मेलकः -का -कं, सङ्घट्टनशीलः -ला -लं.

Congruence, *s.* आनुरूप्यं, अनुरूपता, सादृश्यं, अनुसारः -रित्वं, आनुगुण्यं, योग्यता, युक्तता, उपयुक्तता, सङ्गतत्वं, साङ्गत्यं.

Congruity, *s.* योग्यता, युक्तता, युक्तिः *f.*, सामञ्जस्यं, अनुसारिता, याथातथ्यं, औचित्यं, उचितता, उपपत्तिः *f.*, सदृशता. *See* Congruence.

Congruous, *a.* योग्यः -ग्या -ग्यं, युक्तः -क्ता -क्तं, सङ्गतः -ता -तं, अविरुद्धः -द्धा -द्धं, समञ्जसः -सा -सं, अनुसारी -रिणी -रि (न्), अनुगुणः -णा -णं, सदृशः -शी -शं, सम्भाव्यः -व्या -व्यं.

Congruously, *adv.* योग्यं, युक्तं, अनुसारेण -रात् -रतस्, अनुरूपं -पेण, अविरुद्धं, समञ्जसं, सङ्गतं, सङ्गतप्रकारेण.

Conic, conical, *a.* सूच्याकारः -रा -रं, शिखाकृतिः -तिः -ति, शुण्डाकारः -रा -रं.

Conically, *adv.* सूच्याकारेण, शुण्डाकारेण, सूचिरूपेण.

Conicks, *s.* सूचिच्छेदविषयका रेखागणितविद्यायाः शाखा or अङ्गं.

Coniferous, *a.* सूच्याकारफलप्रदः -दा -दं, शिखाकृतिफलवान् -वती -वत् (त्).

Conjecturable, *a.* वितर्क्यः -र्क्या -र्क्यं, अनुमेयः -या -यं, ऊहनीयः -या -यं.

Conjectural, *a.* आनुमानिकः -की -कं, वैतर्किकः -की -कं, ऊही -हिनी -हि (न्).

Conjecturally, *adv.* अनुमानेन, वितर्केण, सानुमानं, सवितर्कं, अनुमानपूर्व्वं.

To conjecture, *v. a.* अनुमा (c. 2. -माति, c. 4. -मायते, c. 3. -मिमीते -मातुं), शङ्क् (c. 1. शङ्कते -ङ्कितुं), तर्क् (c. 10. तर्कयति -यितुं), वितर्क्, ऊह् (c. 1. ऊहते -हितुं), अनुभू (c. 1. -भवति -वितुं).

Conjecture, *s.* वितर्कः -र्कणं, अनुमानं, अनुमानोक्तिः, ऊहा -हनं, अनुभवः, शङ्का.

Conjectured, *p. p.* अनुमितः -ता -तं, वितर्कितः -ता -तं, शङ्कितः -ता -तं.

Conjecturer, *s.* अनुमाता *m.* (तृ), अनुमानकर्त्ता *m.* (र्त्तृ), वितर्ककः, वितर्कणकृत्.

To conjoin, *v. a.* संयुज् (c. 7. -युनक्ति -योक्तुं, c. 10. -योजयति -यितुं), समायुज्; सन्धा (c. 3. -दधाति -धातुं), संश्लिष् in caus. (-श्लेषयति -यितुं).

To conjoin, *v. n.* संयुज् in pass. (-युज्यते), समायुज्; सन्धा (c. 3. -धत्ते -धातुं or pass. -धीयते), संश्लिष् in pass. (-श्लिष्यते).

Conjoined, *p. p.* संयुक्तः -क्ता -क्तं, समायुक्तः -क्ता -क्तं, संश्लिष्टः -ष्टा -ष्टं.

Conjoint, *a.* संयुक्तः -क्ता -क्तं, सहितः -ता -तं, सम्बद्धः -द्धा -द्धं, कृतसम्बन्धः -न्धा -न्धं, संहतः -ता -तं, सन्धितः -ता -तं, सङ्गतवान् -वती -वत् (त्).

Conjointly, *adv.* सहितं, सह, सार्द्धं, योगतस्, समं, साकं, अपृथक्.

Conjugal, *a.* वैवाहिकः -की -कं, उद्वाहिकः -का -कं, औद्वाहिकः -की -कं; 'the conjugal state,' पतित्वं, भर्तृत्वं; 'conjugal affection,' दम्पत्योः or भार्य्यापत्योः स्नेहः; 'conjugal fidelity in a woman,' सतीत्वं, पातिव्रत्यं; 'in a man,' एकपत्नीसेवा.

Conjugally, *adv.* दम्पतिवत्, यथा भार्य्यापती तथा महास्नेहेन, वैवाहिकप्रकारेण.

To conjugate, *v. a.* (In grammar) आख्या (c. 2. -ख्याति -ख्यातुं), रूपम् आख्या.

Conjugated, *p. p.* आख्यातः -ता -तं.—(Joined) संयुक्तः -क्ता -क्तं.

Conjugation, *s.* (In grammar) रूपं, वाच्यता, गणः, रूपकरणं.—(Union, compilation) संयोगः, समाहारः.

Conjunct, *a.* संयुक्तः -क्ता -क्तं, समायुक्तः -क्ता -क्तं, संश्लिष्टः -ष्टा -ष्टं, सङ्गतः -ता -तं; 'a conjunct consonant,' संयोगः.

Conjunction, *s.* (Union) संयोगः, सम्प्रयोगः, योगः, सन्धिः *m.*, सन्धानं, श्लेषः, संश्लेषः, सङ्गमः, समागमः, सङ्गः, अनुषङ्गः, समासञ्जनं, समासक्तिः *f.*, सम्पर्कः, संसर्गः, मेलः.—(In grammar) समुच्चयः, समुच्चयबोधकः शब्दः.—(Planetary) सङ्गमः; 'of sun and moon,' अर्केन्दुसङ्गमः, उपसर्गः; 'day of lunar conjunction,' अमावास्या; 'in conjunction,' सङ्गतः -ता -तं.

Conjunctive, *a.* साङ्गतिकः -की -कं, यौक्तिकः -की -कं, यौगिकः -की -कं, अनुषङ्गी -ङ्गिणी -ङ्गि (न्), आनुषङ्गिकः -की -कं.—(United) संयुक्तः -क्ता -क्तं, संश्लिष्टः -ष्टा -ष्टं.

Conjunctly, *adv.* योगतस्, सहितं, सह, सार्द्धं, संयुक्तं.

Conjuncture, *s.* योगः, संयोगः, सन्धिः *m.*—(Occasion) समयः, प्रस्तावः, अवकाशः, अवसरः.

Conjuration, *s.* (Magic) योगः, सम्प्रयोगः, माया, कुहकः, इन्द्रजालं, कुसृतिः *f.*—(Incantation, enchantment) मन्त्रं, अभिचारः, माया.—(Conspiracy) संशपः, संशपनं, सङ्कल्पः, दुष्कर्म्मसाधनार्थं बहुजनानां संसर्गः, ऐकमत्यं, एकवाक्यता.—(Charging earnestly by oath) शपनपूर्व्वकं सम्बोधनं, शपथपुरःसरं प्रत्यादेशः, शापनं.

To conjure, *v. a.* (Charge earnestly) शपनपूर्व्वकं or सशपनं समादिश् (c. 6. -दिशति -देष्टुं) or प्रत्यादिश् or सम्बुध् in caus. (-बोधयति -यितुं), शप् in caus. (शापयति -यितुं).

To conjure, *v. n.* (Use enchantment) मायां कृ, कुहकं कृ, इन्द्रजालं कृ, अभिचर् (c. 1. -चरति -रितुं).—(Conspire) शपथपुरःसरं अन्यैः सह सहायत्वम् कृ, दुष्कर्म्मसम्पादनार्थम् अन्यैः सह शप् (c. 4. शप्यति,

शप्तुं) or शपथपत्रः -त्रा -त्रम् अस्.

Conjurer, *s.* मायी *m.* (न्), मायाकारः -कृत्, मायाजीवी *m.* (न्), कुहककारः, कुहकजीवी *m.* (न्), इन्द्रजालिकः, ऐन्द्रजालिकः, योगी *m.* (न्), सम्प्रयोगी *m.* (न्), कौसृतिकः, अभिचारविद्.

Connascence, *s.* सहजत्वं, एककाले जन्म *n.* (न्) or उत्पत्तिः *f.*, समकालोत्पत्तिः.

Connate, *a.* सहजः -जा -जं, सहजातः -ता -तं, समकालजः -जा -जं, एककाले जातः -ता -तं, एककालोत्पन्नः -न्ना -न्नं, यमजः -जा -जं.

Connatural, *a.* सहजः -जा -जं, स्वाभाविकः -की -कं, स्वभावजः -जा -जं, अन्तर्जातः -ता -तं, एकभावः -वा -वं, एकस्वभावः -वा -वं.

To connect, *v. a.* संयुज् (c. 7. -युनक्ति -योक्तुं, c. 10. -योजयति -यितुं), सम्बन्ध् (c. 9. -बध्नाति -बन्धुं), अनुबन्ध्, सन्धा (c. 3. -दधाति -धातुं), उपसन्धा, संश्लिष् in caus. (-श्लेषयति -यितुं), संलग्नीकृ, योक्त्र (nom. योक्त्रयति -यितुं), ग्रन्थ् (c. 9. ग्रथ्नाति, ग्रन्थितुं), पिनह् (c. 4. -नह्यति -नद्धुं), व्यतिषञ्ज् (c. 1. -षजति -षंक्तुं); 'to be connected,' सम्बन्ध् in pass. (-बध्यते).

Connected, *p. p.* (Joined, related) संयुक्तः -क्ता -क्तं, समायुक्तः -क्ता -क्तं, संयुतः -ता -तं, प्रयुक्तः -क्ता -क्तं, यौक्तिकः -की -कं, सम्बद्धः -द्धा -द्धं, सम्बन्धी -न्धिनी -न्धि (न्), कृतसम्बन्धः -न्धा -न्धं, अनुषक्तः -क्ता -क्तं, अनुसम्बद्धः -द्धा -द्धं, प्रतिबद्धः -द्धा -द्धं, अन्वितः -ता -तं, समन्वितः -ता -तं, सान्वयः -या -यं, समितः -ता -तं; 'mutually connected,' व्यतिषक्तः -क्ता -क्तं.—(Continuous) अविच्छिन्नः -न्ना -न्नं, अपरिच्छिन्नः -न्ना -न्नं; 'a connected story,' प्रबन्धः.

Connectedly, *adv.* प्रबन्धेन, अविच्छेदेन, अविच्छिन्नं, योगतस्, सम्बद्धं.

Connexion, *s.* (Union) संयोगः, सम्प्रयोगः, योगः, सङ्गः, सङ्गमः, सङ्गतं, समासक्तिः *f.*, प्रसक्तिः *f.*, समासञ्जनं, अनुषङ्गः, संसर्गः, सन्धिः *m.*; 'mutual connexion,' व्यतिषङ्गः.—(Relation) सम्बन्धः -न्धित्वं, अभिसम्बन्धः, सम्बन्धी *m.* (न्), अन्वयः, समन्वयः, सम्पर्कः, सन्दर्भः.—(Family connexion) बान्धवः, बन्धुः *m.*, सम्बन्धी *m.* (न्).—(Connexion of a discourse) प्रबन्धः; 'to have connexion with,' सङ्गम् (c. 1. -गच्छति -गन्तुं).

Connexive, *a.* यौक्तिकः -की -कं, सम्बन्धकः -का -कं, आनुषङ्गिकः -की -कं.

Connivance, *s.* उपेक्षा, उपेक्षणं, अपह्नवः, ज्ञातापह्नवः, निह्नवः, निह्नुतिः *f.*, आकारगुप्तिः *f.*, ज्ञात्वा ज्ञातापह्नवः, दृष्ट्वा दृष्टोपेक्षणं, क्षमा.—(Winking) अक्षिनिकोचनं, अक्षिसङ्कोचनं.

To connive at, *v. n.* (Intentionally overlook) ज्ञानपूर्वकम् उपेक्ष् (c. 1. -ईक्षते -क्षितुं).—(Conceal knowledge) ज्ञात्वा ज्ञातं निह्नु (c. 2. -ह्नुते -ह्नोतुं) or अपह्नु.—(Bear with) क्षम् (c. 1. क्षमते, क्षन्तुं).—(Wink) अक्षि सङ्कुच् (c. 1. -कोचति -चितुं).

Connoisseur, *s.* विज्ञः, अभिज्ञः, गुणज्ञः, ज्ञानी *m.* (न्), बोद्धा *m.* (द्धृ), तद्विद् *m.*, परीक्षकः.

Connubial, *a.* वैवाहिकः -की -कं, उद्वाहिकः -का -कं, औद्वाहिकः -की -कं.

To conquer, *v. a.* जि (c. 1. जयति -ते, जेतुं), पराजि, विजि, सञ्जि, अभिभू (c. 1. -भवति -वितुं), पराभू, दम् in caus. (दमयति -यितुं), वशीकृ, धृष् in caus. (धर्षयति -यितुं), प्रधृष्, पर्यामृश् (c. 6. -मृशति -म्रष्टुं); 'one who has conquered his passions,' जितेन्द्रियः.

Conquerable, *a.* जेयः -या -यं, जयनीयः -या -यं, जय्यः -य्या -य्यं, जेतव्यः -व्या -व्यं, दमनीयः -या -यं, अभिभवनीयः -या -यं, पराभवनीयः -या -यं.

Conquered, *p. p.* जितः -ता -तं, पराजितः -ता -तं, विजितः -ता -तं, दान्तः -न्ता -न्तं, दमितः -ता -तं, अभिभूतः -ता -तं, पराभूतः -ता -तं, वशीकृतः -ता -तं.

Conquerer, *s.* जेता *m.* (तृ), विजेता *m.* (तृ), विजयी *m.* (न्), जयी *m.*, परन्तपः.

Conquest, *s.* जयः, विजयः, विजयसिद्धिः *f.*, अभिभवः, निग्रहः.—(The act of conquering) जयनं, विजयनं, वशीकरणं; 'foreign conquests,' दिग्विजयः.

Consanguineous, *a.* एकशरीरः -रा -रं, सहोदरः -रा -रं, समानोदर्य्यः -र्य्या -र्य्यं, सगर्भः -र्भा -र्भं, एकपिण्डः -ण्डा -ण्डं, सपिण्डः -ण्डा -ण्डं, सगोत्रः -त्रा -त्रं, एकवंशजातः -ता -तं, अन्तरङ्गः -ङ्गा -ङ्गं; 'consanguineous descent,' एकशरीरान्वयः.

Consanguinity, *s.* एकशरीरता, एकशरीरान्वयः, एकशरीरावयवत्वं, सपिण्डता, एकपिण्डता, समानोदर्य्यता, सगोत्रता, सगर्भत्वं, सम्बन्धित्वं.

Conscience, *s.* अन्तःकरणं, अन्तर्यामी *m.* (न्), अभिमन्ता *m.* (न्तृ), अन्तःसंज्ञा, मनः *n.* (स्), अन्तःशरीरं; 'remorse of conscience,' मनस्तापः, मनःसन्तापः, पश्चात्तापः.—(Consciousness) चेतना, वेदनं, अनुभवः.

Conscientious, *a.* शुद्धान्तःकरणः -णा -णं, शुद्धमतिः -तिः -ति, शुद्धात्मा -त्मा -त्म (न्), पुण्यशीलः -ला -लं, पुण्यात्मा -त्मा -त्म (न्), न्यायाचारः -रा -रं, शुचिः -चिः -चि, धर्म्मशीलः -ला -लं.

Conscientiously, *adv.* शुद्धमत्या, शुद्धमनसा, न्यायेन, पुण्यशीलत्वात्, निर्विशङ्कं.

Conscientiousness, *s.* मतिशुद्धत्वं, अन्तःकरणशुद्धिः *f.*, पुण्यशीलता, शुचिता.

Conscionable, *a.* न्याय्यः -य्या -य्यं, यथान्याय्यः -य्या -य्यं, यथार्थः -र्था -र्थं.

Conscionably, *adv.* यथान्याय्यं, यथार्थं, धर्म्मतस्, धर्म्मानुसारात्, यथोचितं.

Conscious, *a.* चेतनः -ना -नं, सचेतनः -ना -नं, प्रतिपन्नचेतनः -ना -नं, वेदी -दिनी -दि (न्), ज्ञानी -निनी -नि (न्), अनुभावी -विनी -वि (न्), सतर्कः -र्का -र्कं; 'internally conscious,' अन्तश्चैतन्यः -न्या -न्यं.

Consciously, *adv.* ज्ञानतस्, ज्ञानात्, ज्ञानपूर्वं, बुद्धिपूर्वं, मत्या.

Consciousness, *s.* चेतना, चैतन्यं, वेदनं, अनुभवः, अन्तःसंज्ञा, बोधः, अन्तर्बोधः, ज्ञानं, चित्ताभोगः, मनस्कारः, अहङ्कारः, चिदात्मकं, प्रमा; 'internal consciousness,' अन्तश्चैतन्यं; 'consciousness of pleasure,' सुखानुभवः, सुखवेदनं.

Conscript, *s.* नवयोद्धा *m.* (द्धृ), नवसैन्यः, सैन्यानां मध्ये अभिलिखितनामा *m.* (न्).

Conscription, *s.* सैन्यानां मध्ये नामाभिलेखनं or नामसमारोपणं.

To consecrate, *v. a.* संस्कृ, अभिसंस्कृ, प्रतिष्ठा in caus. (-ष्ठापयति -यितुं), अभिमन्त्र् (c. 10. -मन्त्रयति -ते -यितुं), उपनिमन्त्र्.—(By sprinkling) अभिषिच् (c. 6. -षिञ्चति -षेक्तुं), प्रोक्ष् (c. 1. -उक्षति -क्षितुं).—(Devote to any use) विनियुज् (c. 7. -युनक्ति -योक्तुं), प्रयुज्; समृ in caus. (-अर्पयति -यितुं).—(Present) उत्सृज् (c. 6. -सृजति -स्रष्टुं), निविद् in caus. (-वेदयति -यितुं).

Consecrate or consecrated, *a.* संस्कृतः -ता -तं, अभिसंस्कृतः -ता -तं, कृतसंस्कारः -रा -रं, अभिमन्त्रितः -ता -तं, प्रतिष्ठितः -ता -तं, सुप्रतिष्ठितः -ता -तं, प्रोक्षितः -ता -तं, सम्प्रोक्षितः -ता -तं, कृताभिषेकः -का -कं, अभिषिक्तः -क्ता -क्तं, प्रणीतः -ता -तं, विनियोजितः -ता -तं, उपकॢप्तः -प्ता -प्तं, समर्पितः -ता -तं, आहितः -ता -तं.

Consecrater, *s.* संस्कर्त्ता *m.* (र्तृ), प्रतिष्ठापकः, अभिमन्त्रणकृत्, अभिषेचकः, सङ्कल्पकृत्.

Consecration, *s.* संस्कारः, प्रतिष्ठा, सुप्रतिष्ठा, अभिमन्त्रणं, अभिषेकः -षेचनं, सम्प्रोक्षणं, प्रोक्षणं, उत्सर्गः, सङ्कल्पः; 'of a temple,' प्रासादप्रतिष्ठा; 'of one's self to God,' आत्मनिवेदनं; 'of one's person,' देहविनियोगः.

Consecution, *s.* प्रबन्धः, पर्य्यायः, क्रमः, अनुक्रमः, विपर्य्ययः, वीप्सा, सन्ततिः *f.*, समन्वयः, परम्परा, श्रेणी, माला.

Consecutive, *a.* निरन्तरः -रा -रं, अविरतः -ता -तं, आनुपूर्व्वः -र्व्वा -र्व्वं, क्रमकः -का -कं, क्रमागतः -ता -तं, अपरिच्छिन्नः -न्ना -न्नं, सम्प्रबन्धः -न्धा -न्धं, सन्ततः -ता -तं.

Consecutively, *adv.* निरन्तरं, प्रबन्धेन, अनुपूर्व्वशस्, अनुक्रमशस्, क्रमतस्, क्रमानुसारेण, यथाक्रमं, यथापूर्व्वं, अविरतं, अविच्छिन्नं.

Consecutiveness, *s.* आनन्तर्य्यं, नैरन्तर्य्यं, आनुपूर्व्यं, अविच्छेदः, अविरामः, अनुयायित्वं, अपरिच्छिन्नता, अविच्छिन्नत्वं, सम्बन्धत्वं.

Consent, *s.* सम्मतिः *f.*, सम्मतं, अनुमतिः *f.* -तं, अनुज्ञा, स्वीकारः, अनुकूलता, ग्रहणं, प्रतिग्रहः, अनुग्रहः, परिग्रहः, इच्छा.—(Unity of opinion) ऐकमत्यं, ऐक्यं, मतैक्यं, एकचित्तता, अनुवादः; 'mutual consent,' परस्परानुमतिः *f.*; 'with his consent,' तस्य सम्मत्या; 'without his consent,' तस्य अनुमतिव्यतिरेकेण; 'with the consent,' इच्छातस्, इच्छया; 'against consent,' अनिच्छया; 'a writing testifying consent,' सम्मतिपत्रं.

To consent, *v. n.* सम्मन् (c. 4. -मन्यते -ते -मन्तुं), अनुमन्; अनुज्ञा (c. 9. -जानाति -ज्ञातुं), समनुज्ञा, अभ्यनुज्ञा, स्वीकृ, ग्रह् (c. 9. गृह्णाति, ग्रहीतुं), प्रतिग्रह्, परिग्रह्, अनुग्रह्, प्रतीष् (c. 6. -इच्छति -एषितुं), सम्प्रतीष्, अनुमुद् (c. 1. -मोदते -दितुं), उपगम् (c. 1. -गच्छति -गन्तुं), एकचित्तीभू, एकमतीभू.

Consented, *p. p.* सम्मतः -ता -तं, अनुमतः -ता -तं, अनुज्ञातः -ता -तं.

Consentaneous, *a.* अनुसारी -रिणी -रि (न्), योग्यः -ग्या -ग्यं, युक्तः -क्ता -क्तं, अनुरूपः -पा -पं, सदृशः -शी -शं, अविरुद्धः -द्धा -द्धं, अनुगुणः -णा -णं.

Consentaneously, *adv.* अनुसारतस् -रेण -रात्, अनुरूपं -पेण, योग्यं, अविरुद्धं.

Consentient, *a.* एकमतः -ता -तं, सम्मतः -ता -तं, एकचित्तः -त्ता -त्तं, एकवाक्यः -क्या -क्यं.

Consentingly, *adv.* सम्मत्या, अनुमत्या, सम्मतिपूर्व्वं, कामतस्, बुद्धिपूर्व्वं.

Consequence, *s.* प्रयोगः, प्रयुक्तिः *f.*, फलं, फलमुत्तरं, उत्तरं, अनुसारः, अनुषङ्गः, परिणामः, शेषः, अन्वयः, समन्वयः, योगः, उदर्कः, व्युष्टिः *f.* -ष्टं, अर्थः, कार्य्यं, उत्पन्नं, उद्भूतं, सिद्धिः *f.*, प्रतिफलं, अनुभवः, अनुवृत्तं, अनुवर्त्तनं, प्रयोजनं, निमित्तं, प्रत्ययः; 'necessary consequence,' कार्य्यवशः; 'in consequence,' प्रयोगतस्, कार्य्यतस्; 'evil consequences,' मन्दफलं; 'visible consequence,' दृष्टार्थः; 'invisible consequence,' अदृष्टार्थः; 'immediate consequence,' सान्दृष्टिकं; 'happy consequence,' शुभफलं.—(Deduction, inference) अनुमानं, युक्तिः *f.*, ऊहा, अभ्यूहः, अपवाहः.—(Importance) गौरवं, गुरुता, प्रभावः; 'of little consequence,' अल्पप्रभावः; 'consequence or importance of an act,' कार्य्यगुरुता; 'a matter of some consequence,' गुरुकार्य्यं.

Consequent, *a.* प्रयुक्तः -क्ता -क्तं, प्रयोगी -गिणी -गि (न्), यौक्तिकः -की -कं, अनुषङ्गिकः -की -कं or आनुषङ्गिकः, अनुसारी -रिणी -रि (न्), अनुवर्त्ती -र्त्तिनी -र्त्ति (न्), अनुयायी -यिनी -यि (न्), जनितः -ता -तं; 'consequent upon that,' तत्फलः -ला -लं.

Consequent, *s.* प्रयोगः, अनुषङ्गः, अनुवृत्तं, फलं, अन्वयः, परिणामः.

Consequential, *a.* (Full of conceit) गर्व्वी -र्व्विणी -र्व्वि (न्), साटोपः -पा -पं, मानी -निनी -नि (न्).—(Following as effect and cause) प्रयुक्तः -क्ता -क्तं, आनुषङ्गिकः -की -कं.

Consequentially, *adv.* प्रयोगतस्, प्रयुक्तं.—(Arrogantly) साटोपं, सगर्व्वं.

Consequently, *adv.* प्रयोगतस्, प्रयुक्तं, कार्य्यतस्, कार्य्यवशात्, अनुसारेण, तदनुसारतस्, इति हेतोः, अतस्, अर्थात्, तदर्थं, तस्य हेतोः, तन्निमित्ते, अवश्यं, इति.

Consequentness, *s.* प्रयुक्तत्वं, अनुसारिता, प्रबन्धः, पूर्व्वापरसम्बन्धः.

Conservable, *a.* संरक्ष्यः -क्ष्या -क्ष्यं, संरक्षणीयः -या -यं, सन्धारणीयः -या -यं.

Conservation, *s.* संरक्षः -क्षणं, रक्षा, रक्षणं, परित्राणं, त्राणं, सन्धारणं, धरणं, गुप्तिः *f.*, पालनं, क्षेमः, क्षयनिवारणं.

Conservative, *a.* संरक्षकः -का -कं, पालकः -का -कं, सन्धारकः -का -कं.

Conservator, *s.* रक्षकः, संरक्षणशीलः, पालकः, परित्राता *m.* (तृ), गोप्ता *m.* (प्तृ).

Conservatory, *s.* रक्षास्थानं, गुप्तिः *f.*, धारकः, आधारः.—(For plants, &c.) विदेशीयतृणौषधिवृक्षादीनां रक्षणशाला or रक्षणगृहं.

To conserve, *v. a.* (Preserve) संरक्ष् (c. 1. -रक्षति -क्षितुं), परिरक्ष्; सन्त्रै (c. 1. -त्रायते -त्रातुं), सम्पाल् (c. 10. -पालयति -यितुं), परिपाल्; गुप् (c. 1. गोपायति, गोप्तुं), अभिसङ्गुप्, सन्धृ in caus. (-धारयति -यितुं).—(Preserve or pickle) सन्धा (c. 3. -दधाति -धातुं), उपस्कृ, मिष्टीकृ.

Conserve, *s.* मिष्टं, मोदकः -कं, खण्डमोदकः, खण्डः, सन्धितं, सन्धानं, गुडकः.

Consession, *s.* सहासनं, उपासनं, अन्येन सह उपवेशः.

Consessor, *s.* सभासद्, सहासीनः, उपासीनः, उपासिता *m.* (तृ), अन्येन सह आसीनः.

To consider, *v. a.* (Think upon) चिन्त् (c. 10. चिन्तयति -यितुं), विचिन्त्, सञ्चिन्त्, प्रविचिन्त्; बुध् (c. 1. बोधति -धितुं, c. 4. बुध्यते, बोद्धुं), विमृश् (c. 6. -मृशति -म्रष्टुं), परिमृश्, अनुमृश्; सम्भू in caus. (-भावयति -यितुं), ध्यै (c. 1. ध्यायति, ध्यातुं), सन्ध्यै, अनुध्यै, अवधृ in caus. (-धारयति -यितुं), सम्प्रधृ, उपधृ, समाधा (c. 3. -धत्ते -धातुं).—(Look at attentively) अवेक्ष् (c. 1. -ईक्षते -क्षितुं), समीक्ष्; आलोक् (c. 10. -लोकयति -यितुं), आलोच् (c. 10. -लोचयति -यितुं), दृश् (c. 1. पश्यति, द्रष्टुं), सन्दृश्, परिदृश्, आलक्ष् (c. 10. -लक्षयति -यितुं), उपलक्ष्, अवधा.—(Examine) निरूप् (c. 10. -रूपयति -यितुं), परीक्ष्, विचर् in caus. (-चारयति -यितुं).—(Weigh) विगण् (c. 10. -गणयति -यितुं), विकॢप् (c. 10. -कल्पयति -यितुं), विचर्, वितर्क् (c. 10. -तर्कयति -यितुं).—(Have regard to) अपेक्ष्, प्रतीक्ष्, अवेक्ष्, निरीक्ष्, अनुदृश्, उद्दिश् (c. 6. -दिशति -देष्टुं).—(Imagine, think) मन् (c. 4. मन्यते, मन्तुं), तर्क् (c. 10. तर्कयति -यितुं).—(Reverence) पूज् (c. 10. पूजयति -यितुं), अर्च् (c. 10. अर्चयति -यितुं), मन् (c. 10. मानयति -यितुं).—(Recompense) प्रत्युपकृ, सन्तुष् in caus. (-तोषयति -यितुं), परितुष्, सम्भू in caus.

To consider, *v. n.* चिन्त् (c. 10. चिन्तयति -यितुं), बुध् (c. 4. बुध्यते, बोद्धुं), ध्यै (c. 1. ध्यायति, ध्यातुं), समीक्षां कृ, विचारं कृ, परामर्शं कृ, विवेचनं कृ.

Considerable, *a.* (Respectable) प्रतीक्ष्यः -क्ष्या -क्ष्यं, मान्यः -न्या -न्यं, आर्य्यः -र्य्या -र्य्यं, आदरणीयः -या -यं.—(Important) गुरुः -र्व्वी -रु, बह्वर्थः -र्था -र्थं.—(Not little) अनल्पः -ल्पा -ल्पं, बहुः -ह्वी -हु, प्रचुरः -रा -रं, महान् -हती -हत् (त्), भूरिः -रिः -रि, महामूल्यः -ल्या -ल्यं, अर्घ्यः -र्घ्या -र्घ्यं.

Considerableness, *s.* गौरवं, गुरुता, मान्यता, आर्य्यत्वं, अर्घ्यता, अनल्पत्वं, प्राचुर्य्यं.

Considerably, *adv.* अनल्पं, बहु, गुरु, सु or अति prefixed, भूरि, भृशं, अतिशयं.

Considerate, *a.* (Prudent) समीक्ष्यकारी -रिणी -रि (न्), विमृश्यकारी -रिणी -रि (न्), कार्य्यचिन्तकः -का -कं, चिन्ताशीलः -ला -लं, परिणामदर्शी -र्शिनी -र्शि (न्), कृतावधानः -ना -नं, मतिमान् -मती -मत् (त्).—(Regardful) आदृतः -ता -तं, दत्तादरः -रा -रं, प्रतीतः -ता -तं.

Considerately, *adv.* समीक्ष्य, विमृश्य, अवधानतस्, मन्त्रतस्, अवेक्षया, असहसा, अप्रमत्तं, प्रमादं विना.

Considerateness, *s.* चिन्ता, कार्य्यचिन्ता, प्रसमीक्षा, चर्चा, सुविचारः.

Consideration, *s.* (Reflection, examination) चिन्ता, सुचिन्ता, सञ्चिन्तनं, विचारः -रणं -रणा, सुविचारः, समीक्षा -क्षणं, प्रसमीक्षा, चर्चा, वितर्कः, विवेचनं, विमर्शः, परामर्शः, भावना, सम्प्रधारणा, आध्यानं,

संप्रधानं, प्रणिधानं, विगणनं, परीक्षा, आस्था, संख्या.—(Regard for) प्रतीक्षा, अपेक्षा, अवेक्षा, उद्देशः, प्रतीतिः *f.*; 'in consideration of,' अपेक्षया.—(Motive, reason) हेतुः *m.*, निमित्तं, प्रयोजनं, कारणं, प्रयोगः —(Importance) गौरवं, गुरुता, प्रभावः.—(Estimation, honour) मानं, मान्यत्वं, आदरः, पूजा, पूज्यता, सम्भावना.—(Compensation) पारितोषिकं, परिवर्त्तः, परीवर्त्तः.

CONSIDERED, *p. p.* चिन्तितः -ता -तं, सुचिन्तितः -ता -तं, सञ्चिन्तितः -ता -तं, परामृष्टः -ष्टा -ष्टं, समीक्षितः -ता -तं, आलोचितः -ता -तं, निरूपितः -ता -तं, सुनिरूपितः -ता -तं, प्रतीक्षितः -ता -तं, निरीक्षितः -ता -तं, विचारितः -ता -तं, विगणितः -ता -तं, मतः -ता -तं, स्मृतः -ता -तं.

CONSIDERER, *s.* चिन्तकः, चिन्तापरः, ध्यानपरः, विचारकः, विवेचकः.

CONSIDERING, *part.* अपेक्षया, प्रतीक्ष्य, अवेक्ष्य, उद्दिश्य, प्रतीक्षकः -का -कं.

To CONSIGN, *v. a.* (Intrust) ऋ in caus. (अर्पयति -यितुं), समृ, प्रतिपद् in caus. (-पादयति -यितुं), निक्षिप् (c. 6. -क्षिपति -क्षेप्तुं), न्यस् (c. 4. -अस्यति -असितुं), न्यासीकृ, परिदा (c. 3. -ददाति -दातुं), आरुह् in caus. (-रोपयति -यितुं), नियुज् (c. 7. -युनक्ति -योक्तुं), प्रतिष्ठा in caus. (-ष्ठापयति -यितुं), प्रणिधा (c. 3. -दधाति -धातुं), विधा.—(Appropriate) प्रयुज्, उपयुज्, विनियुज्.

CONSIGNABLE, *p. p.* अर्पणीयः -या -यं, अर्प्यः -र्प्या -र्प्यं, समर्पणीयः -या -यं, प्रतिपादनीयः -या -यं, आरोपणीयः -या -यं.

CONSIGNED, *p. p.* अर्पितः -ता -तं, समर्पितः -ता -तं, प्रतिपादितः -ता -तं, निक्षिप्तः -प्ता -प्तं, न्यस्तः -स्ता -स्तं, न्यासीकृतः -ता -तं, प्रणिहितः -ता -तं.

CONSIGNMENT, *s.* समर्पणं, अर्पणं, न्यसनं, प्रतिपादनं, आरोपणं, परिदानं, विधायकत्वं.—(In writing) समर्पणपत्रं, चालनपत्रं.

To CONSIST, *v. n.* संस्था (c. 1. -तिष्ठति -स्थातुं), परिसंस्था, अवस्था, विष्ठा, सम्भू, वृत् (c. 1. वर्त्तते -र्त्तितुं), संवृत्.—(Be comprised, be composed) अन्तर्गतः -ता -तं भू. But in this sense आत्मकः -का -त्मिका -कं or रूपः -पा -पं are used; as, 'the army consists of elephants, horses, and infantry,' हस्त्यश्वपादातात्मकं बलं; 'the country consists of valleys and mountains,' दरीपर्व्वतरूपो विषयः.

CONSISTENCE, *s.* अचापल्यं.—(Thickness) घनता, सान्द्रता, श्यानता, पीवरत्वं.—(Firmness) दृढता, स्थिरता, अचापल्यं.—(Suitableness) योग्यता, अविरोधः.

CONSISTENCY, *s.* (Stability) स्थैर्य्यं, धीरत्वं, धृतिः *f.*, अचापल्यं, अव्यभिचारः.—(Congruity) अनुसारित्वं, अविरोधः, सादृश्यं, आनुरूप्यं.

CONSISTENT, *a.* (Stable) स्थिरः -रा -रं, धीरः -रा -रं, अचपलः -ला -लं, अव्यभिचारी -रिणी -रि (न्), अविगुणः -णा -णं, अविकलः -ला -लं.—(Not opposed, not contradictory) अविरुद्धः -द्धा -द्धं, अविपरीतः -ता -तं, अनुसारी -रिणी -रि (न्), योग्यः -ग्या -ग्यं, सङ्गतः -ता -तं, सदृशः -शी -शं.—(Solid, not fluid) घनः -ना -नं, दृढः -ढा -ढं, द्रवेतरः -रा -रं.

CONSISTENTLY, *adv.* अविरुद्धं, अविपरीतं, योग्यं, अनुसारतस्, -रेण, सङ्गतं.

CONSISTING OF, *p.* Expressed by आत्मकः -का -त्मिका -कं or रूपः -पा -पं; as, 'an army consisting of elephants, horses, chariots, and infantry,' हस्त्यश्वरथपादातात्मकं or -रूपं दण्डं; 'consisting of two,' द्व्यात्मकः -का -कं; 'consisting of troubles,' दुःखरूपः -पा -पं.—(Made of) मयः -यी -यं affixed.

CONSISTORIAL, *a.* धर्म्माध्यक्षसभासम्बन्धी -न्धिनी -न्धि (न्), पुरोहितसभासम्बन्धी.

CONSISTORY, *s.* धर्म्माध्यक्षसभा, पुरोहितसभा, रोमनगरे महाधर्म्माध्यक्षसमाजः.

CONSOCIATE, *s.* सङ्गी *m.* (न्), अनुषङ्गी *m.* (न्), सहायः, सहकारी *m.* (न्), सहवासी *m.* (न्), बन्धुः *m.*

To CONSOCIATE, *v. a.* संयुज् (c. 7. -युनक्ति -योक्तुं, c. 10. -योजयति -यितुं), संश्लिष् in caus. (-श्लेषयति -यितुं), सम्बन्ध् (c. 9. -बध्नाति -बन्द्धुं).

To CONSOCIATE, *v. n.* सङ्क्रम् (c. 1. -गच्छति -गन्तुं), सह गम्, संवस् (c. 1. -वसति -वस्तुं), सह वस्, मिल् (c. 6. मिलति, मेलितुं), सम्मिल्, संयुज् in pass. (-युज्यते).

CONSOCIATED, *p. p.* संयुक्तः -क्ता -क्तं, सहयुक्तः -क्ता -क्तं, समायुक्तः -क्ता -क्तं, संश्लिष्टः -ष्टा -ष्टं, सहितः -ता -तं, सङ्गतवान् -वती -वत् (त्), मिलितः -ता -तं, संसृष्टः -ष्टा -ष्टं, कृतसंसर्गः -र्गा -र्गं, सम्पृक्तः -क्ता -क्तं.

CONSOCIATION, *s.* साहाय्यं, सहायता, साहचर्य्यं, साहित्यं, संयोगः, सङ्क्रमः, सङ्गतिः *f.*, संसर्गः, सङ्गः, संश्लेषः, सङ्घातः.

CONSOLABLE, *a.* सान्त्वनीयः -या -यं, सन्तोषणीयः -या -यं, सन्तोष्टव्यः -व्या -व्यं, आश्वासनीयः -या -यं, प्रबोधनीयः -या -यं, विनोदनीयः -या -यं.

CONSOLATION, *s.* सान्त्वः -न्त्वं, सान्त्वनं -ना, शान्त्वं, आश्वासनं, समाश्वासनं, उपशान्तिः *f.*, शान्तिः *f.*, सन्तोषणं, शोकापनोदः, शोकापहारः, विनोदः, प्रबोधः.

CONSOLATORY, *a.* सान्त्वदः -दा -दं, सान्त्वनः -ना -नं, शान्तिकः -की -कं, शान्तिदः -दा -दं, शमकः -का -कं, सन्तोषकः -का -कं, आश्वासकः -सिका -कं, शोकापनुदः -दा -दं, क्लेशापहः -हा -हं, शोकापहारकः -का -कं, शोकच्छिद् *m. f. n.*

To CONSOLE, *v. a.* सान्त्व् or शान्त्व् (c. 10. सान्त्वयति -यितुं), अभिशान्त्व्, परिशान्त्व्, उपसान्त्व्, आश्वस् in caus. (-श्वासयति -यितुं), समाश्वस्, विश्वस्, परिविश्वस्, प्रबुध् in caus. (-बोधयति -यितुं), शम् in caus. (शमयति -यितुं), प्रशम्, उपशम्, शोकम् अपनुद् (c. 6. -नुदति -नोत्तुं) or विनुद् in caus. (-नोदयति -यितुं) or प्रतिकृ; सुस्थ (nom. सुस्थयति -यितुं), सुस्थिरं -रां -रं कृ.

CONSOLE, *s.* (In architecture) नागः, नागदन्तकः, सालारं, निर्य्यूहः.

CONSOLED, *p. p.* आश्वासितः -ता -तं, सन्तोषितः -ता -तं, विनोदितः -ता -तं.

CONSOLER, *s.* सान्त्ववादः, आश्वासकः, विनोदकर्त्ता *m.* (र्त्तृ), शोकापनुदः.

To CONSOLIDATE, *v. a.* संस्था in caus. (-स्थापयति -यितुं), प्रतिष्ठा, स्थिरीकृ, सुस्थिरं -रां -रं कृ, संस्तम्भ् (c. 5. -स्तभ्नोति -स्तम्भितुं, c. 10. -स्तम्भयति -यितुं), दृढीकृ, घनीकृ, संहन् (c. 2. -हन्ति -हन्तुं).

To CONSOLIDATE, *v. n.* संस्था in caus. pass. (-स्थाप्यते), स्थिरीभू, सुस्थिरीभू, दृढीभू, घनीभू, संहन् in pass. (-हन्यते).

CONSOLIDATED, *p. p.* संस्थापितः -ता -तं, संस्तम्भितः -ता -तं, संहतः -ता -तं, स्थिरीकृतः -ता -तं, दृढीभूतः -ता -तं, एकत्रीकृतः -ता -तं.

CONSOLIDATION, *s.* स्थिरीकरणं, दृढीकरणं, संस्तम्भः, संस्थापनं, घनीकरणं, एकीकरणं.

CONSONANCE, *s.* अनुसारः -रिता, आनुरूप्यं, योग्यता, अविरोधः, सादृश्यं.

CONSONANT, *a.* अनुसारी -रिणी -रि (न्), योग्यः -ग्या -ग्यं, उपयुक्तः -क्ता -क्तं, सदृशः -शी -शं, अनुगुणः -णा -णं, अविरुद्धः -द्धा -द्धं, तुल्यः -ल्या -ल्यं.

CONSONANT, *s.* (Letter) व्यञ्जनं; 'conjunct consonant,' संयोगः.

CONSONANTLY, *adv.* अनुसारतस् -रेण, अनुरूपेण, अविरुद्धं, योग्यं, यथा.

CONSONOUS, *a.* एकतालः -ला -लं, स्वरैक्यकारी -रिणी -रि (न्).

CONSORT, *s.* (Wife) पत्नी, भार्य्या, वधूः.—(Husband) पतिः *m.*, भर्त्ता *m.* (र्त्तृ).—(Royal consort, queen) राजपत्नी, राजमहिषी.—(Partner) सहवासी *m.* -सिनी *f.* (न्), सहवर्त्ती *m.* (न्), सहभावी *m.* (न्), सङ्गी *m.* (न्).

To CONSORT, *v. n.* (Keep company with) सह वस् (c. 1. वसति, वस्तुं), संवस्; सङ्क्रम् (c. 1. -गच्छति -गन्तुं), सह गम्, सह चर् (c. 1. चरति -रितुं).

CONSORTED, *p. p.* सङ्गतः -ता -तं, सहगतः -ता -तं, सङ्गतवान् -वती -वत् (त्).

CONSORTION, *s.* साहित्यं, सहायत्वं, साहाय्यं, सङ्गमः, साहचर्य्यं, संसर्गः.

CONSPERSION, *s.* सम्प्रोक्षणं, प्रोक्षणं, निषेकः, सेकः, सेचनं, प्रक्षेपः.

CONSPICUOUS, *a.* (Obvious to the sight) प्रकाशः -शा -शं, सुप्रकाशः -शा -शं, प्रत्यक्षः -क्षा -क्षं, स्पष्टः -ष्टा -ष्टं, सुस्पष्टः -ष्टा -ष्टं, स्फुटः -टा -टं, व्यक्तः -क्ता -क्तं, प्रव्यक्तः -क्ता -क्तं, प्रकाशमानः -ना -नं, प्रकाशितः -ता -तं, दीप्यमानः -ना -नं, देदीप्यमानः -ना -नं, पुरःस्फुरन् -रन्ती -रत् (त्).—(Eminent) प्रमुखः -खा -खं, उत्कृष्टः -ष्टा -ष्टं, प्रकृष्टः -ष्टा -ष्टं, विशिष्टः -ष्टा -ष्टं, सुख्यातः -ता -तं.

CONSPICUOUSLY, *adv.* प्रत्यक्षतस्, प्रकाशं, स्पष्टं, स्फुटं, व्यक्तं.

CONSPICUOUSNESS, *s.* प्रकाशता, सुप्रकाशत्वं, प्रत्यक्षत्वं, व्यक्तत्वं, स्फुटता, स्पष्टता, सुस्पष्टत्वं, प्रादुर्भावः.—(Eminence) प्रकृष्टत्वं, प्रमुखत्वं, विशिष्टता, विख्यातिः *f.*

CONSPIRACY, *s.* दुष्टकर्म्मसम्पादनार्थं बहुजनानां संसर्गः, बहूनां कुसाहित्यं, असत्साहित्यं, कुसंसर्गः, कुसाहाय्यं, कुमन्त्रणा, कपटप्रबन्धः, कुसङ्कल्पः, पणः, ऐकमत्यं, एकवाक्यता.—(Conjunction) संशापः, संशपनं.—(Against the king) द्रोहः, राजद्रोहः.

CONSPIRATOR, *s.* दुष्टकर्म्मसाधनार्थं बहुजनैः सह संसर्गी *m.* (न्) or सङ्गी *m.* (न्) or अनुषङ्गी *m.* (न्).—(Persons bound together by oath) संशप्तकाः *m.pl.*, दिव्यबद्धाः *m.pl.*, शपथबद्धाः *m.pl.*—(Against life) प्राणच्छेदकरः.—(Against the king) राजद्रोही *m.* (न्).—(Traitor) विश्वासघातकः.

To CONSPIRE, *v. n.* दुष्टकर्म्मसाधनार्थं संसर्गं कृ or कुसाहित्यं कृ or कुसाहाय्यं कृ or पणं कृ, द्रोहं कृ.—(Against the life of the king) राजा हन्तव्य इति परस्परं शपथेन बद्धा भूत्वा समयं कृ.—(Agree together, lead to one point) सम्मिल् (c. 6. -मिलति -मेलितुं), एकत्र नी (c. 1. नयति, नेतुं), समानी, अनुकूल (nom. अनुकूलयति -यितुं); 'all things conspire to make him happy,' तस्य सुखार्थं सर्व्वं सम्मिलति.

CONSTABLE, *s.* दण्डपाशिः *m.*, दण्डधरः, गड्डाटः, दण्डैटः, यष्टिधरः, राजपुरुषः, कोष्ठपालः, ग्राहकः.—(Chief constable) दण्डनायकः.

CONSTANCY, *s.* (Perpetuity) नित्यता -त्वं, अविरामः, नैरन्तर्य्यं, संस्थितिः *f.*, प्रत्यवस्थानं.—(Firmness) स्थिरता, स्थैर्य्यं, धीरत्वं, दार्ढ्यं, दृढता, द्रढिमा *m.* (न्), धृतिः *f.*, स्थेमा *m.* (न्).—(Perseverance) अभिनिवेशः, निर्बन्धः, अतिनिर्बन्धः, व्यवस्थितिः *f.*, ग्रहः.—(Faithfulness, lasting affection) दृढा भक्तिः, दृढं सौहृदं, दृढभक्तित्वं, अनुकूलता.

CONSTANT, *a.* (Perpetual) नित्यः -त्या -त्यं, नैत्यिकः -की -कं, अभीक्ष्णः -क्ष्णा -क्ष्णं, शाश्वतः -ती -तं, अविरतः -ता -तं, निरन्तरः -रा -रं, सनातनः -नी -नं, सर्व्वकालीनः -ना -नं, सार्व्वकालिकः -की -कं, चिरस्थायी -यिनी -यि (न्).—(Firm, steadfast) स्थिरः -रा -रं, दृढः -ढा -ढं, धीरः -रा -रं, व्यवस्थितः -ता -तं, धृतिमान् -मती -मत् (त्), प्रसक्तः -क्ता -क्तं, नियतः -ता -तं.—(Resolute) स्थिरमतिः -तिः -ति, स्थिरचेताः -ताः -तः (स्), स्थितधीः -धीः -धि.—(Constant in friendship) दृढसौहृदः -दी -दं, दृढभक्तिः -क्तिः -क्ति; 'a constant wife,' पतिव्रता, स्वीया, दृढाभक्तिः *f.*; 'a constant lover,' अनुकूलः.

CONSTANTLY, *adv.* नित्यं, नित्यशस्, नित्यदा, सततं, अजस्रं, नियतं, निरन्तरं, अविरतं, अनवरतं, अभीक्ष्णं, सर्व्वकालं, शश्वत्, अनिशं, सन्ततं, प्रतिक्षणं, अनुक्षणं, सना, वारं वारं, अश्रान्तं.—(With firmness) स्थिरमत्या, मनःस्थैर्य्येण.

CONSTELLATION, *s.* राशिः *m.*, नक्षत्रं, राशिनक्षत्रं, ऋक्षं, ताराराशिः *m.*, तारासमूहः.

CONSTERNATION, *s.* विस्मयः, सन्त्रासः, साध्वसं, त्रासः, सम्भ्रमः, आकुलत्वं, व्याकुलता, कातरता, भयं, चमत्कारः, अतिशङ्का.

To CONSTIPATE, *v. a.* अवरुध् (c. 7. -रुणद्धि -रोद्धुं), बन्ध् (c. 9. -बध्नाति -बन्द्धुं), निबन्ध्, स्तम्भ् (c. 9. स्तभ्नाति, स्तम्भितुं), विष्टम्भ्, अवष्टम्भ्; नह् (c. 4. नह्यति, नद्धुं).—(Crowd) सम्बाध् (c. 1. -बाधते -धितुं).—(Condense) घनीकृ, निबिडीकृ.

CONSTIPATED, *p. p.* अवरुद्धः -द्धा -द्धं, निरुद्धः -द्धा -द्धं, आनद्धः -द्धा -द्धं, बद्धकोष्ठः -ष्ठा -ष्ठं, निबद्धः -द्धा -द्धं, विष्टब्धः -ब्धा -ब्धं, अवष्टब्धः -ब्धा -ब्धं.

CONSTIPATION, *s.* मलावरोधः, मलावष्टम्भः, विष्टम्भः, नाहः, आनाहः, विड्ग्रहः, गुदग्रहः, विट्सङ्गः, निबन्धः, विबन्धः, कोष्ठनिबन्धः, बद्धकोष्ठं, आमवातः, वेगरोधः, वेगविधारणं; 'producing constipation,' ग्राही -हिणी -हि (न्), विष्टम्भी -म्भिनी -म्भि (न्).

CONSTITUENT, *a.* (Component, making) साधकः -का -कं, विधायी -यिनी -यि (न्), कल्पकः -का -कं, संस्थापकः -का -कं, निर्म्मायकः -का -कं, रचकः -का -कं.—(Essential) वास्तवः -वी -वं, सारभूतः -ता -तं, स्वाभाविकः -की -कं.

CONSTITUENT, *s.* साधनं, वस्तु *n.*, सारः, भूतं, मूलं, योनिः *m. f.*; 'a constituent part,' अङ्गं; 'of an army,' सेनाङ्गं.—(He who deputes) नियोजकः, प्रेरकः.

To CONSTITUTE, *v. a.* (Form, compose) निर्म्मा (c. 2. -माति, c. 3. -मिमीते -मातुं), विधा (c. 3. -दधाति -धातुं), कॢप् (c. 10. कल्पयति -यितुं), कृ (c. 8. कुरुते, कर्त्तुं), रच् (c. 10. रचयति -यितुं), साध् in caus. (साधयति -यितुं); संस्था in caus. (-स्थापयति -यितुं).—(Establish) स्था in caus., प्रस्था, संस्था, प्रतिष्ठा.—(Depute) नियुज् (c. 7. -युनक्ति -योक्तुं), प्रतिपद् in caus. (-पादयति -यितुं), समादिश् (c. 6. -दिशति -देष्टुं); 'whatever wealth constitutes the treasury,' यद् धनं कोषभूतं.

CONSTITUTED, *p. p.* (Composed, consisting of) निर्म्मितः -ता -तं, आत्मकः -का -त्मिका -कं in comp., रूपः -पा -पं in comp., मयः -यी -यं in comp.

CONSTITUTION, *s.* (State) भावः, स्वभावः, अवस्था, दशा, स्थितिः *f.*, वृत्तिः *f.*—(Form) रूपं, स्वरूपं.—(Structure) निर्म्मितिः *f.*, निर्म्माणं, संस्थितिः, व्यूहनं, विधानं, रचना, साधनं.—(Temperament) प्रकृतिः *f.*, भावः, स्वभावः, प्रकृतिस्वभावः, देहस्वभावः, शरीरस्थितिः *f.*, जन्मस्वभावः, जातिस्वभावः; 'of a sickly constitution,' जन्मरोगी -गिणी -गि (न्).—(Ordinance) व्यवस्था, विधिः *m.*—(System of government) राज्यरीतिः *f.*, राज्यस्थितिः *f.*, राज्यनीतिः *f.*, राज्यविधिः *m.*, राज्यप्रवृत्तिः *f.*, देशाचारः.—(Act of establishing) नियोजनं, प्रतिष्ठापनं, व्यवस्थापनं.

CONSTITUTIONAL, *a.* (Relating to the constitution of body) प्राकृतिकः -की -कं, स्वाभाविकः -की -कं.—(To the constitution of the state) राज्यव्यवस्थानुसारी -रिणी -रि (न्).—(Radical) मौलः -ली -लं.

To CONSTRAIN, *v. a.* (Compel an unwilling person to do any thing) बलेन or बलात्कारेण or यत्नेन अनिच्छन्तं जनं किञ्चित् कृ in caus. (कारयति -यितुं) or प्रवृत् in caus. (-वर्त्तयति -यितुं), or नियुज् in caus. (-योजयति -यितुं) with loc. c., बलात्कारं कृ, समाकृष् (c. 1. -कर्षति -क्रष्टुं). The causal form of any verb may be used to express 'constrain'; as, 'to constrain to give,' दा in caus. (दापयति -यितुं).—(Restrain) अवरुध् (c. 7. -रुणद्धि -रोद्धुं).

CONSTRAINABLE, *a.* बलात्काराधीनः -ना -नं, अवरोधनीयः -या -यं. Expressed by the fut. pass. part. of the caus. form.

CONSTRAINED, *p.p.* (Constrained to do) बलात्कारेण कारितः -ता -तं.

—(Constrained to give) दापितः -ता -तं.—(Constrained to be silent) यन्त्रितकथः -था -थं. The pass. part. of the caus. form of any verb may be used in this sense.

CONSTRAINT, *s.* (Compulsion) बलात्कारः, बलं.—(Necessity) अवश्यकत्वं -ता.—(Restraint) अवरोधः; 'by constraint,' बलात्, बलात्कारेण, अवश्यकत्वात्, बलापकर्षं.

To CONSTRICT or CONSTRINGE, *v. a.* सङ्कुच् (c. 1. -कोचति -चितुं), आकुच् (c. 1. -कुचति -चितुं), संहृ (c. 1. -हरति -हर्तुं), संवृ (c. 1. -वरति -रितुं -रीतुं), सन्निकृष् (c. 1. -कर्षति -क्रष्टुं).

CONSTRICTION, *s.* सङ्कोचः -चनं, संवारः, संवृतिः *f.*, आकुञ्चनं.

To CONSTRUCT, *v. a.* निर्म्मा (c. 2. -माति, c. 3. -मिमीते, c. 4. -मीयते -मातुं or caus. -मापयति -यितुं), कृ (c. 8. करोति, कर्तुं or caus. कारयति -यितुं), कॢप् (c. 10. कल्पयति -यितुं), विरच् (c. 10. -रचयति -यितुं), सञ्जन् in caus. (-जनयति -यितुं), घट् (c. 1. घटते -टितुं), विधा (c. 3. -दधाति -धातुं), निचि (c. 5. -चिनोति -चेतुं).

CONSTRUCTED, *p. p.* निर्म्मितः -ता -तं, कल्पितः -ता -तं, विरचितः -ता -तं, कारितः -ता -तं, घटितः -ता -तं, मयः -यी -यं in comp.

CONSTRUCTION, *s.* निर्म्माणं, निर्म्मितिः *f.*, रचना, विरचना, कल्पनं -ना, विधानं, घटनं, सन्धिः *m.*, सन्धानं.—(Of words) समर्थः -र्थता, अन्वयः. (Meaning) अर्थः, अभिप्रायः, आशयः, विवक्षा.

To CONSTRUE, *v. a.* (Interpret the meaning) अर्थं व्याख्या (c. 2. -ख्याति -तुं); व्याकृ; व्याहृ (c. 1. -हरति -हर्तुं); विब्रू (c. 2. -ब्रवीति -वक्तुं), परिशुध् in caus. (-शोधयति -यितुं), श्लिष्टिं कृ.—(Range words in order) शब्दविन्यासं कृ; 'to construe a sloke,' श्लोकलापनं कृ.

CONSTUPRATION, *s.* धर्षणं, दूषणं, साहसं, बलात्कारेणाभिगमः, राक्षसं, कन्याहरणं, स्त्रीहरणं, कन्यादूषणं.

CONSUBSTANTIAL, *a.* एकमूर्त्तिः -र्त्तिः -र्त्ति, समभावः -वा -वं, एकभावः -वा -वं, एकशरीरः -रा -रं, एकयोनिः -निः -नि, सजातीयः -या -यं.

CONSUL, *s.* पूर्व्वकाले रोमनगरे प्रजाभिर् नियुक्तो दण्डनायकः.—(An officer commissioned in foreign parts to superintend the commercial transactions of his own nation) विदेशे स्वदेशीयवाणिज्यव्यापारनिर्वाहणे नियुक्तो जनः.

CONSULATE, CONSULSHIP, *s.* पूर्व्वोक्तदण्डनायकस्य पदं or अधिकारः.

To CONSULT, *v. a.* and *n.* मन्त्र् (c. 10. मन्त्रयते -ति -यितुं), सम्मन्त्र्, विचर् in caus. (-चारयति -यितुं), सम्भाष् (c. 1. -भाषते -षितुं), संवद् (c. 1. -वदति -दितुं or c. 10. -वादयति -यितुं), विमृश् (c. 6. -मृशति -मर्ष्टुं), परामृश्, विनिश्चि (c. 5. -चिनोति -चेतुं), सञ्चिन्त् (c. 10. -चिन्तयति -यितुं), एकत्र परामर्शं कृ.—(Inquire of) निरूप् (c. 10. -रूपयति -यितुं).—(Regard) अवेक्ष् (c. 1. -ईक्षते -क्षितुं), प्रतीक्ष्, समीक्ष्; 'to consult with one's self,' मनसा विचर्.

CONSULTATION, *s.* मन्त्रः -न्त्रणं -णा, सम्मन्त्रणं, विचारः -रणं, सम्प्रधारणा, सम्भाषा -षणं, मर्शः, आमर्शः, प्रत्यवमर्शः, विमर्शः, परामर्शः, विवेचनं, संवादः, सम्प्रवदनं; 'private consultation,' गूढभाषितं.

To CONSUME, *v. a.* (Destroy) नश् in caus. (नाशयति -यितुं), विनश्, सद् in caus. (सादयति -यितुं), अवसद्, विध्वंस् in caus. (-ध्वंसयति -यितुं); 'by fire,' दह् (c. 1. दहति, दग्धुं), निर्दह्.—(Spend) उपयुज् (c. 7. -युनक्ति -योक्तुं), व्ययीकृ.—(Exhaust) निःशेषं -षां -षं कृ, निरवशेषीकृ.—(Waste) क्षि (c. 1. क्षयति c. 5. क्षिणोति or caus. क्षपयति -यितुं); 'to consume away,' नश् (c. 4. नश्यति, नशितुं), क्षि in pass. (क्षीयते), सद् (c. 6. सीदति, सत्तुं), अवसद्, परिहा in pass. (-हीयते).

CONSUMED, *p. p.* नष्टः -ष्टा -ष्टं, नाशितः -ता -तं, विनाशितः -ता -तं, दग्धः -ग्धा -ग्धं, भुक्तः -क्ता -क्तं, व्ययीभूतः -ता -तं, व्ययितः -ता -तं, क्षीणः -णा -णं, परिक्षीणः -णा -णं, क्षयितः -ता -तं, आलीढः -ढा -ढं.

CONSUMER, *s.* नाशकः, विनाशकः, क्षयकरः, क्षयी *m.* (न्), ध्वंसकारी *m.* (न्).

To CONSUMMATE, *v. a.* समाप् in caus. (-आपयति -यितुं), सम्पद् in caus. (-पादयति -यितुं), निष्पद्, साध् in caus. (साधयति -यितुं), संसाध्, सम्पॄ in caus. (-पूरयति -यितुं), निर्वृत् in caus. (-वर्त्तयति -यितुं).

CONSUMMATE, *a.* सम्पूर्णः -र्णा -र्णं, परिपूर्णः -र्णा -र्णं, सिद्धः -द्धा -द्धं, सम्पन्नः -न्ना -न्नं, समाप्तः -प्ता -प्तं, उत्कृष्टः -ष्टा -ष्टं, परमः -मा -मं.

CONSUMMATION. *s.* (The state) सिद्धिः *f.*, संसिद्धिः *f.*, निष्पत्तिः *f.*, समाप्तिः *f.*, सम्पूर्णता, परिपूर्णता.—(The act) समापनं, सम्पादनं, निष्पादनं, साधनं, निर्वर्त्तनं.

CONSUMPTION, *s.* (Pulmonary) क्षयः, शोषः, क्षयरोगः, क्षयथुः *m.*, क्षयकासः, यक्ष्मा *m.* (क्ष्मन्), यक्ष्मा *m.* (न्), कफक्षयः, नृपामयः, शरीरपाकः.—(Destruction, waste) क्षयः, परिक्षयः, उपक्षयः, नाशः, विनाशः, व्ययः -यनं, ध्वंसः -सनं, अपचयः.—(Use) उपयोगः, उपभोगः.

CONSUMPTIVE, *a.* क्षयी -यिणी -यि (न्), नाशी -शिनी -शि (न्), व्ययी -यिनी -यि (न्).—(Diseased with consumption) क्षयरोगी -गिणी -गि (न्), यक्ष्मी -क्ष्मिणी -क्ष्मि (न्).

CONTACT, *s.* स्पर्शः, संस्पर्शः, स्पृष्टिः *f.*, सम्पर्कः, पृक्तिः *f.*, समासञ्जनं, संसर्गः, आसङ्गः, सङ्गः, व्यतिकरः, उपघातः, संयोगः, परिमर्शः, उपयोगः; 'ascertainment by contact,' त्वाचप्रत्यक्षं; 'bodily contact,' अङ्गाङ्गि.

CONTAGION, *s.* (Communication of disease) सञ्चारः, स्पर्शसञ्चारः, संस्रवः, रोगाकर्षणं.—(Contagious disease) मारी, मारकः.

CONTAGIOUS, *a.* स्पर्शसञ्चारी -रिणी -रि (न्), सञ्चारकः -का -कं, सञ्चारी -रिणी -रि (न्), सम्पर्कीयः -या -यं, त्वाचः -ची -चं, संस्पर्शजः -जा -जं.

To CONTAIN, *v. a.* (Hold) धा (c. 3. दधाति, धत्ते, धातुं), आधा; आदा (c. 3. -ददाति -दत्ते -दातुं), धृ (c. 1. धरति, धर्तुं or caus., धारयति -यितुं), भृ (c. 3. बिभर्त्ति, भर्तुं).—(Comprise) परिग्रह् (c. 9. -गृह्णाति -ग्रहीतुं).—(Restrain) यम् (c. 1. यच्छति, यन्तुं), संयम्; निग्रह्; संहृ (c. 1. -हरति -हर्तुं), प्रतिसंहृ.

CONTAINABLE, *a.* आदेयः -या -यं, धारणीयः -या -यं, परिग्रहणीयः -या -यं.

CONTAINED, *p. p.* धृतः -ता -तं, धारितः -ता -तं, अन्तर्गतः -ता -तं, अन्तर्गणितः -ता -तं, समाविष्टः -ष्टा -ष्टं, परिगृहीतः -ता -तं, आकलितः -ता -तं, गर्भः -र्भा -र्भं in comp., वर्त्ती -र्त्तिनी -र्त्ति (न्); 'contained in the sentence,' वाक्यस्थः -स्था -स्थं.

CONTAINING, *p. p.* (Holding) आददानः -ना -नं, दधानः -ना -नं, धारकः -का -कं, गर्भः -र्भा -र्भं in comp. आत्मकः -का -कं; 'a box containing powder,' चूर्णगर्भं पात्रं.

To CONTAMINATE, *v. a.* दुष् in caus. (दूषयति -यितुं), प्रतिदुष्, लिप् (c. 6. लिम्पति, लेप्तुं), अनुलिप्, कलुष (nom. कलुषयति -यितुं), मलिन (nom. मलिनयति -यितुं), मलिनीकृ, कलङ्क (nom. कलङ्कयति -यितुं), दिह् (c. 2. देग्धि -ग्धुं), भ्रष्टीकृ; 'to be contaminated,' दुष् (c. 4. दुष्यति).

CONTAMINATED, *p. p.* दुष्टः -ष्टा -ष्टं, दूषितः -ता -तं, कलुषितः -ता -तं, मलिनितः -ता -तं, कलङ्कितः -ता -तं, लिप्तः -प्ता -प्तं, भ्रष्टः -ष्टा -ष्टं, अपवित्रः -त्रा -त्रं.

CONTAMINATION, *s.* दूषणं, कलुषं, मालिन्यं, अशौचं, अशौचत्वं, कलङ्कः, मलं.

To CONTEMN, *v. a.* अवज्ञा (c. 9. -जानाति -ज्ञातुं), अवमन् (c. 4. -मन्यते -मन्तुं), तृणाय मन्, अवधीर् (c. 10. -धीरयति -यितुं), परिभू; गर्ह् (c. 1. गर्हते -र्हितुं), निन्द् (c. 1. निन्दति -न्दितुं), गुप् in des. (जुगुप्सते -प्सितुं), कदर्थ (c. 10. -अर्थयते -यितुं), उपेक्ष् (c. 1. -ईक्षते -क्षितुं), कुत्स् (c. 10. कुत्सयति -यितुं), लघूकृ, तुच्छीकृ.

CONTEMNED, *p. p.* अवमतः -ता -तं, अपमानितः -ता -तं, अवज्ञातः -ता -तं,

अवधीरितः -ता -तं, परिभूतः -ता -तं, गर्हितः -ता -तं, निन्दितः -ता -तं, विमानितः -ता -तं, कदर्थितः -ता -तं, अवध्यातः -ता -तं, उपेक्षितः -ता -तं, कुत्सितः -ता -तं.

CONTEMNER, *s.* अवमन्ता *m.* (न्तृ), अवज्ञानकृत्, निन्दकः, निन्दाकरः, घृणाकरः.

To CONTEMPLATE, *v. a.* (Examine attentively) निरूप् (c. 10. -रूपयति -यितुं), अवेक्ष् (c. 1. -ईक्षते -क्षितुं), सम्प्रेक्ष्, अन्ववेक्ष्, समवेक्ष्; सन्दृश् (c. 1. -पश्यति -द्रष्टुं), अनुदृश्, परिदृश्; आलोक् (c. 10. -लोकयति -यितुं), आलोच् (c. 10. -लोचयति -यितुं), निर्वर्ण् (c. 10. -वर्णयति -यितुं).

To CONTEMPLATE, *v. n.* ध्यै (c. 1. ध्यायति, ध्यातुं), अनुध्यै, अभिध्यै, सन्ध्यै, प्रध्यै; चिन्त् (c. 10. चिन्तयति -यितुं), विचिन्त्, सञ्चिन्त्, भू in caus. (भावयति -यितुं), सम्भू, मनसा विचर् in caus. (-चारयति -यितुं), विमृश् (c. 6. -मृशति -म्रष्टुं), समाधा (c. 3. -धत्ते -धातुं).

CONTEMPLATED, *p. p.* ध्यातः -ता -तं, चिन्तितः -ता -तं, भावितः -ता -तं, सम्भावितः -ता -तं, विचारितः -ता -तं, मनोगुप्तः -प्ता -प्तं.

CONTEMPLATION, *s.* ध्यानं, अभिध्यानं, आध्यानं, अन्तर्ध्यानं, समाधिः *m.*, समाधानं, चिन्ता, भावना, सम्भावनं -ना, विचारणा, विमर्शः, ध्यानपरता, ध्याम *n.* (न्).

CONTEMPLATIVE, *a.* ध्यानपरः -रा -रं, चिन्तापरः -रा -रं, ध्यानशीलः -ला -लं, चिन्ताशीलः -ला -लं, समाधिमान् -मती -मत् (त्), चिन्तावान् -वती -वत् (त्), भावितात्मा -त्मा -त्म (न्), समाधिस्थः -स्था -स्थं, ध्याननिष्ठः -ष्ठा -ष्ठं, सचिन्तः -न्ता -न्तं.

CONTEMPLATOR, *s.* ध्यानकर्त्ता *m.* (र्त्तृ), ध्याता *m.* (तृ), समाधिकृत्, चिन्तकः विचारी *m.* (न्).

CONTEMPORARY, *a.* समकालीनः -ना -नं, एककालीनः -ना -नं, समानकालीनः -ना -नं, समानकालवर्त्ती -र्त्तिनी -र्त्ति (न्), समकालजः -जा -जं, समानवयस्कः -स्का -स्कं, सवयाः -याः -यः (स्); 'a contemporary associate,' वयस्यः.

CONTEMPT, *s.* अवमानं -नता, अवमतिः *f.*, अवज्ञा -ज्ञानं, परिभवः, परिभूतिः *f.*, परिभावः, गर्हा -र्हणं, अवधीरणं, कुत्सा -त्सनं, उपेक्षा -क्षणं, हेलनं, अवहेला -लं -लनं, घृणा, परीवादः, अपवादः, तिरस्कारः, न्यक्कारः, न्यग्भावनं, निन्दा; 'object of contempt,' तिरस्कारविषयः, परिभवपदं, परिभवास्पदं.

CONTEMPTIBLE, *a.* अवमान्यः -न्या -न्यं, अवमाननीयः -या -यं, अवमन्तव्यः -व्या -व्यं, अवक्षेयः -या -यं, अवज्ञातव्यः -व्या -व्यं, गर्ह्यः -र्ह्या -र्ह्यं, गर्हणीयः -या -यं, तुच्छः -च्छा -च्छं, कुत्सितः -ता -तं, निन्दार्हः -र्हा -र्हं, दूष्यः -ष्या -ष्यं, गर्हितः -ता -तं, अवगर्हितः -ता -तं, अवद्यः -द्या -द्यं, नीचः -चा -चं, क्षुद्रः -द्रा -द्रं, अपकृष्टः -ष्टा -ष्टं, निकृष्टः -ष्टा -ष्टं.

CONTEMPTIBLENESS, *s.* अवमान्यत्वं, गर्ह्यता, तुच्छत्वं, निन्दार्हत्वं, कौत्सित्यं, नीचत्वं.

CONTEMPTIBLY, *adv.* कुत्सितं, तुच्छं, अपकृष्टं, नीचतया, अवमान्यप्रकारेण.

CONTEMPTUOUS, *a.* अवमानी -निनी -नि (न्), अवमन्ता -न्त्री -न्तृ (न्तृ), परिभवी -विणी -वि (न्), परिभावी -विणी -वि (न्), परिभावुकः -का -कं, कुत्सावादी -दिनी -दि (न्), उपेक्षकः -का -कं, घृणी -णिनी -णि (न्).

CONTEMPTUOUSLY, *adv.* अवमानेन, अवज्ञानेन, सावमानं, परिभवेण, उपेक्षया; 'he treats contemptuously,' अवमन्यते or अवजानाति or उपेक्षते.

CONTEMPTUOUSNESS, *s.* अवमानिता, अवमानशीलता, परिभावुकत्वं.

To CONTEND, *v. n.* (Fight) युध् (c. 4. युध्यते, योद्धुं), प्रतियुध्, विग्रह् (c. 9. -गृह्णाति -ग्रहीतुं or in caus. -ग्राहयति -यितुं), कलह (nom. कलहायते), वैर (nom. वैरायते).—(Strive) यत् (c. 1. यतते -तितुं), प्रयत्; चेष्ट् (c. 1. चेष्टते -ष्टितुं), विचेष्ट्, व्यायम् (c. 1. -यच्छति -यन्तुं), व्यवसो (c. 4. -स्यति -सातुं), घट् (c. 1. घटते -टितुं).—(Oppose) विरुध् (c. 7. -रुणद्धि -रोद्धुं), प्रतिरुध्, संरुध्; प्रतिकृ; प्रतीप (nom. प्रतीपायते), प्रतिकूल (nom. प्रतिकूलयति -यितुं).—(Vie) स्पर्द्ध् (c. 1. स्पर्द्धते -र्द्धितुं), विस्पर्द्ध्, सङ्घृष् (c. 1. -घर्षति -र्षितुं).—(In argument) विवद् (c. 1. -वदते -दितुं), वाग्युद्धं कृ, वाक्कलहं कृ.

CONTENDENT, *a.* प्रतियोद्धा -द्ध्री -द्धृ (द्धृ), विरोधी -धिनी -धि (न्) or प्रतिरोधी, विरुद्धः -द्धा -द्धं, विवदमानः -ना -नं, विपक्षः -क्षा -क्षं, प्रतियोगी -गिनी -गि (न्), विपरीतः -ता -तं, प्रतीपः -पा -पं.

CONTENDER, *s.* विपक्षः, प्रतिपक्षः, योद्धा *m.* (द्धृ) or प्रतियोद्धा, वैरी *m.* (न्), प्रतिरोद्धा *m.* (द्धृ), विवादी *m.* (न्).

CONTENT, *a.* सन्तुष्टः -ष्टा -ष्टं, तृप्तः -प्ता -प्तं, अलुब्धः -ब्धा -ब्धं, अलिप्सुः -प्सुः -प्सु, तुष्टः -ष्टा -ष्टं, परितुष्टः -ष्टा -ष्टं, परितुष्टात्मा -त्मा -त्म (न्), निःस्पृहः -हा -हं, निस्पृहः -हा -हं, निष्पृहः -हा -हं, अस्पृहः -हा -हं, वितृष्णः -ष्णा -ष्णं, तृष्णाहीनः -ना -नं, अल्पाकांक्षी -क्षिणी -क्षि (न्) or निराकांक्षी, सुखी -खिनी -खि (न्), प्रीतः -ता -तं, हृष्टः -ष्टा -ष्टं, प्रशान्तः -न्ता -न्तं, शान्तः -न्ता -न्तं, प्रशान्तकामः -मा -मं, सुहितः -ता -तं, चरितार्थः -र्था -र्थं.

CONTENT, *s.* (Contentment) सन्तोषः, तृप्तिः *f.*, तुष्टिः *f.*, तोषः, परितोषः, शान्तिः *f.*, कामप्रशान्तिः *f.*, कामनिवृत्तिः *f.*, चित्तप्रशमः, अलोभः, अलुब्धत्वं, अलिप्सा, अस्पृहा, वितृष्णता, वैतृष्ण्यं, धृतिः *f.*, सौहित्यं; 'to the heart's content,' यथातृप्तं -तृप्ति; 'fruit to the heart's content,' प्रकामफलं.—(Contents, that which fills) पूरकः -कं, भरकः -कं; 'that which is contained,' अन्तर्गतं, अन्तर्भूतं, अन्तर्वर्त्ती -र्त्तिनी -र्त्ति (न्); 'the contents of a vessel,' भाण्डभरकः; 'contents of a writing,' अर्थः; 'contents of a solid in geometry,' घनफलं.—(Table of contents) अनुक्रमणिका, पत्रपञ्जी.

To CONTENT, *v. a.* तृप् in caus. (तर्पयति -यितुं), सन्तृप्, तुष् in caus. (तोषयति -यितुं), सन्तुष्, परितुष्; 'to be content,' तृप् (c. 4. तृप्यति -ते), तुष् (c. 4. तुष्यति), सन्तुष्.

CONTENTED, *p. p.* सन्तुष्टः -ष्टा -ष्टं, सन्तोषितः -ता -तं, तृप्तः -प्ता -प्तं, धृतिमान् -मती -मत् (त्), पूर्णाभिलाषः -षा -षं. *See* CONTENT.

CONTENTEDLY, *adv.* सन्तोषेण, तृप्त्या, तुष्ट्या, सन्तुष्टं, अलुब्धं, लोभं विना.

CONTENTION, *s.* (Strife) कलहः -हं, कलिः *m.*, विग्रहः, विरोधः, द्वन्द्वं, युद्धं, विपक्षता, विप्रतिपत्तिः *f.*—(Dispute, debate) वाक्कलहः -हं, वाग्युद्धं, विवादः, वादानुवादः, वादप्रतिवादः, विप्रलापः, विरोधोक्तिः *f.*, वाक्यविरोधः.—(Emulation) स्पर्द्धा, सङ्घर्षः, विजिगीषा.—(Application of mind) मनःप्रवेशः, अभ्यासः.

CONTENTIOUS, *a.* कलहकारी -रिणी -रि (न्) -कारः -री -रं, कलहप्रियः -या -यं, कलिप्रियः -या -यं, विवादी -दिनी -दि (न्), विरोधी -धिनी -धि (न्), विवादार्थी -र्थिनी -र्थि (न्), विवादशीलः -ला -लं, युयुत्सुः -त्सुः -त्सु.

CONTENTIOUSLY, *adv.* कलहकारिवत्, विवादार्थिवत्, विवादपूर्व्वकं, विवादशीलत्वात्.

CONTENTIOUSNESS, *s.* कलहकारित्वं, विवादार्थित्वं, कलहशीलता, कलहेच्छा, कलहप्रवृत्तिः *f.*

CONTENTLESS, *a.* असन्तुष्टः -ष्टा -ष्टं, अतृप्तः -प्ता -प्तं, तुष्टिहीनः -ना -नं.

CONTENTMENT, *s.* सन्तोषः, सन्तुष्टिः *f.*, तुष्टिः *f.*, तृप्तिः *f.*, तृप्तता, सन्तुष्टता, तोषः, परितोषः, अस्पृहा, अलिप्सा, अलोभः, निराकांक्षा, प्रीतिः *f.* *See* CONTENT.

CONTERMINOUS, *a.* सीमावासी -सिनी -सि (न्), सीमावर्त्ती -र्त्तिनी -र्त्ति (न्) or सामन्तवासी or समीपवासी or निकटवर्त्ती, प्रत्यन्तः -न्ता -न्तं, पर्य्यन्तस्थः -स्था -स्थं.

CONTERRANEOUS, *a.* एकदेशीयः -या -यं, एकदेशजः -जा -जं, सदेशः -शा -शं.

To contest, *v. a.* (Contend) युध् (c. 4. युध्यते, योद्धुं), प्रतियुध्, कलह (nom. कलहायते).—(Oppose) विरुध् (c. 7. -रुणद्धि -रोद्धुं), प्रतिरुध्.—(Dispute, litigate) विवद् (c. 1. -वदते -दितुं), विसंवद्, विवादास्पदीकृ.

Contest, *s.* (Contention) कलहः -हं, कलिः *m.*, युद्धं, विरोधः, विग्रहः.—(Dispute) विवादः, विप्रलापः, वाग्युद्धं, वाक्कलहं.—(Legal contest) विवादः, व्यवहारः; 'subject of contest,' विवादास्पदं.

Contestable, *a.* विवदनीयः -या -यं, विवादास्पदीकरणीयः -या -यं.

Contested, *p. p.* वादग्रस्तः -स्ता -स्तं, विवादास्पदीभूतः -ता -तं, विवादानुगतः -ता -तं.

Context, *s.* अन्वयः, प्रबन्धः, वाक्यप्रबन्धः, प्रसङ्गः, वाक्यप्रसङ्गः.

Context, *a.* संश्लिष्टः -ष्टा -ष्टं, सन्धितः -ता -तं, दृढसन्धिः -न्धिः -न्धि.

Contexture, *s.* समूतिः *f.*, विन्यासः, संस्थितिः *f.*, स्थितिः *f.*, रीतिः *f.*

Contiguity, *s.* समीपता, अन्तिक -कता, आसन्नता, सन्निधिः *m.*, सान्निध्यं, सन्निधानं, सन्निकर्षः, नैकट्यं, संसर्गः, उपस्थानं, संस्थितिः *f.*, आनन्तर्य्यं.

Contiguous, *a.* समीपः -पा -पं, आसन्नः -न्ना -न्नं, प्रत्यासन्नः -न्ना -न्नं, निकटः -टा -टं, उपान्तः -न्ता -न्तं, अन्तिकः -का -कं, उपस्थः -स्था -स्थं, उपस्थायी -यिनी -यि (न्), अव्यवधानः -ना -नं, अव्यवहितः -ता -तं, सन्निकृष्टः -ष्टा -ष्टं, सन्निहितः -ता -तं, अविदूरः -रा -रं, अदूरः -रा -रं, प्रत्यन्तः -न्ता -न्तं, संसक्तः -क्ता -क्तं, अविरलः -ला -लं, व्यतिकरः -रा -रं, अपटान्तरः -रा -रं; 'contiguous ground,' पर्य्यन्तभूः, परिसरः.

Contiguously, *adv.* समीपं, सन्निकृष्टं, निकटे, अविरलं, अन्तिकं, अविदूरं, पार्श्वे.

Continence, *s.* (Self-restraint) संयमः, आत्मसंयमः, आत्मवशः, दमः, धैर्य्यं.—(Chastity) उपस्थनिग्रहः, उपस्थसंयमः, संयतेन्द्रियता, जितेन्द्रियत्वं, इन्द्रियनिग्रहः, यतेन्द्रियत्वं, नियतविषयवृत्तिता, ब्रह्मचर्य्यं, अप्रतिषिद्धेष्वपि विषयेष्वनतिप्रसङ्गः.

Continent, *s.* महाद्वीपः, द्वीपः, स्थलं -ली, वर्षः, अविच्छिन्नभूमिः *f.*

Continent, *a.* (Restraining the passions) संयतः -ता -तं, संयतेन्द्रियः -या -यं, जितेन्द्रियः -या -यं, यतेन्द्रियः -या -यं, धैर्य्यशाली -लिनी -लि (न्).—(Chaste) यतमैथुनः -ना -नं, संयतोपस्थः -स्था -स्थं, अलम्पटः -टा -टं, अव्यभिचारी -रिणी -रि (न्), अव्यसनी -निनी -नि (न्), ऊर्द्ध्वरेताः -ताः -तः (स्).—(Moderate) मितः -ता -तं, परिमितः -ता -तं, असंसक्तः -क्ता -क्तं.

Continental, *a.* महाद्वीपीयः -या -यं, स्थलीयः -या -यं, वर्षीयः -या -यं.

Contingency, *s.* दैवं, दैवयोगः, दैवगतिः *f.*, दैवघटना, सङ्गतिः *f.*, आगन्तुः *m.*, अनिश्चयः, यदृच्छा.

Contingent, *a.* आगन्तुकः -का -कं, दैवायत्तः -त्ता -त्तं, दैववशः -शा -शं, आकस्मिकः -की -कं, आपतिकः -की -कं, अनिश्चितः -ता -तं; 'contingent upon,' आयत्तः -त्ता -त्तं, अधीनः -ना -नं.

Contingent, *s.* (Share to be supplied) अंशः, भागः, विभागः, उद्धारः.

Contingently, *adv.* दैवात्, दैवयोगेन, दैववशात्, अकस्मात्, अनिश्चितं, यदृच्छया.

Continual, *a.* (Without interruption of space) निरन्तरः -रा -रं.—(Of time) नित्यः -त्या -त्यं, नैत्यिकः -की -कं, शाश्वतः -ती -तं, सनातनः -नी -नं, सर्व्वकालीनः -ना -नं, अविरतः -ता -तं, अनवरतः -ता -तं, नियतः -ता -तं, अभीक्ष्णः -क्ष्णा -क्ष्णं, अविसर्गी -र्गिणी -र्गि (न्), अश्रान्तः -न्ता -न्तं, प्रसक्तः -क्ता -क्तं.—(Lasting) चिरस्थायी -यिनी -यि (न्), ध्रुवः -वा -वं.

Continually, *adv.* नित्यं, नित्यदा, नित्यशस्, सदा, सर्व्वदा, सततं, सन्ततं, अजस्रं, अनिशं, अनवरतं, अविरतं, अनारतं, निरन्तरं, शश्वत्, शाश्वतं, अभीक्ष्णं, अश्रान्तं, अविश्रान्तं, प्रतिक्षणं, अनुक्षणं, सना, नियतं, वारं वारं, पदे पदे, सर्व्वकालं.

Continuance, *s.* (Duration, lastingness) स्थायित्वं, चिरस्थायित्वं, स्थिरता, संस्थितिः *f.*, ध्रौव्यं, अविश्रान्तिः *f.*, नित्यता, अविरामः, अविरतिः *f.*—(Abode, continuance in a place) स्थितिः *f.*, अवस्थानं, प्रत्यवस्थानं, वसतिः *f.*—(Uninterrupted succession) प्रबन्धः, प्रसङ्गः, अन्वयः, अविच्छेदः, अविच्छिन्नत्वं, सन्ततिः *f.*—(Perseverance) अभिनिवेशः, व्यवस्थितिः *f.*, प्रवृत्तिः *f.*, निर्बन्धः.

Continuation, *s.* (The state) स्थायित्वं, स्थितिः *f.*, नित्यता, अविरतिः *f.*—(The act) प्रवर्त्तनं.—(The remaining part of a thing already begun) उत्तरभागः, उत्तरखण्डः -ण्डं, परिशेषः, परिशिष्टं, परिबृंहणं.—(Series) श्रेणी, पंक्तिः *f.*, अनुक्रमः, पर्य्यायः.

Continuator, *s.* प्रवर्त्तकः, निर्वाहकः, परिशेषकर्त्ता *m.* (र्त्तृ), सम्पादकः, उत्तरसाधकः.

To continue, *v. n.* (Proceed on in an undertaking) प्रवृत् (c. 1. -वर्त्तते -र्त्तितुं), प्रारब्धं सम्पद् in caus. (-पादयति -यितुं).—(Last) स्था (c. 1. तिष्ठति -ते, स्थातुं), चिरस्थायी -यिनी -यि भू.—(Persevere) पर्य्यवस्था, निर्बन्धं कृ, आस्थां कृ.—(Remain in the same state) expressed by आस् (c. 2. आस्ते) with the present or indeclinable part. of another verb; as, 'he continues eating the animals,' पशून् भक्षयन् आस्ते; 'he continues following me,' मम पश्चाद् आगच्छन् आस्ते; 'let him continue besieging the foe,' उपरुध्य अरिम् आसीत.

To continue, *v. a.* (Carry on) प्रवृत् in caus. (-वर्त्तयति -यितुं), निर्वह् in caus. (-वाहयति -यितुं), सम्पद् in caus. (-पादयति -यितुं).—(Prolong) दीर्घीकृ.—(Extend) तन् (c. 8. तनोति -नितुं), प्रतन्; 'he continued speaking,' पुनराह.

Continuing, *a.* स्थायी -यिनी -यि (न्) or चिरस्थायी or दीर्घकालस्थायी, संस्थः -स्था -स्थं, अविसर्गी -र्गिणी -र्गि (न्).

Continuity, *s.* नैरन्तर्य्यं, आनन्तर्य्यं, प्रबन्धः, सन्ततिः *f.*, अविरामः, अविरतिः *f.*, अविच्छेदः, अपरिच्छेदः, अविच्छिन्नत्वं, अन्वयः, समन्वयः.

Continuous, *a.* निरन्तरः -रा -रं, अनन्तरः -रा -रं, अविरतः -ता -तं, अनवरतः -ता -तं, सन्ततः -ता -तं, अविच्छिन्नः -न्ना -न्नं, अपरिच्छिन्नः -न्ना -न्नं, अन्वितः -ता -तं; 'a continuous story,' प्रबन्धः.

Continuously, *adv.* निरन्तरं, अविरतं, अनवरतं, अविच्छिन्नं, प्रबन्धेन.

To contort, *v. a.* आकुञ्च् (c. 1. -कुञ्चति -ञ्चितुं or caus. -कुञ्चयति -यितुं), आकृष् (c. 1. -कर्षति -क्रष्टुं), विकृ, विरूपीकृ, वक्रीकृ, साचीकृ, कुटिलीकृ.

Contorted, *p. p.* आकुञ्चितः -ता -तं, आकर्षितः -ता -तं, विरूपीकृतः -ता -तं, विकृताकारः -रा -रं; 'having the features contorted,' विकृतवदनः -ना -नं.

Contortion, *s.* आकुञ्चनं, विकारः, वक्रता, तिर्य्यक्त्वं, वैरूप्यं, आवर्त्तः, आकर्षः.

Contour, *s.* (Form) आकारः, आकृतिः *f.*, संस्कारः, रूपं.—(Circumference) परिमाणं, परिधिः *m.*, परीणाहः.—(Outline) वस्तुमात्रं, आरम्भः.

Contraband, *a.* निषिद्धः -द्धा -द्धं, प्रतिषिद्धः -द्धा -द्धं, व्यासिद्धः -द्धा -द्धं, विप्रतिसिद्धः -द्धा -द्धं, वर्ज्जितः -ता -तं, धर्म्मविरुद्धः -द्धा -द्धं.

Contract, *s.* नियमः, संविद् *f.*, समयः, प्रतिज्ञानं, संस्कारः, पणः, विपणः, उपगमः, अभ्युपगमः, व्यवस्था, अङ्गीकारः, समाधिः *m.*, संश्रवः, आगूः *f.*, उभयसम्मतिः *f.*; 'written contract,' नियमपत्रं, शासनपत्रं, प्रतिज्ञापत्रकं; 'contract of sale,' क्रयविक्रयनियमः, क्रयपत्रं, क्रयलेख्यं, पणापणं, विपणपत्रं; 'breaking a contract,' व्यवस्थातिक्रमः, संविद्व्यतिक्रमः, समयव्यभिचारः; 'marriage contract,' वाग्निश्चयः, विवाहसम्बन्धः, वाग्दानं.

To contract, *v. a.* (Cause to shrink, draw together) सङ्कुच्

(c. 1. -कोचति -चितुं), कुच् (c. 1. कुचति -चितुं or caus कुचयति -यितुं), आकुच्, संवृ (c. 1. -वरति, c. 5. -वृणोति -वरितुं -रीतुं), सन्निकृष् (c. 1. -कर्षति -क्रष्टुं), आकृष्; संहृ (c. 1. -हरति -हर्तुं), सम्बाध् (c. 1. -बाधते -धितुं), सङ्कुटीकृ; 'contracting the eye,' सङ्कुटाक्षः; 'contracting the brow,' संहतभ्रूः.—(Shorten) संक्षिप् (c. 6. -क्षिपति -क्षेप्तुं), संहृ, ह्रस् in caus. (ह्रासयति -यितुं).—(Make a contract) नियमं कृ, समयाकृ, पणं कृ, पण् (c. 1. पणते -णितुं, पणायति -यितुं), सङ्घट्ट् (c. 1. -घट्टते -ट्टितुं), संविदं कृ, संविद् (c. 2. -वेत्ति -वेदितुं).—(Betroth) वाग्दानं कृ; 'to contract a marriage,' विवाहं कृ, विवाहसम्बन्धं कृ, दारपरिग्रहं कृ.—(Contract friendship) सख्यं बन्ध् (c. 9. बध्नाति, बन्धुं) or उपगम् (c. 1. -गच्छति -गन्तुं); 'I contracted a friendship with him,' अहं तस्य मित्रत्वम् उपगतः.—(Contract a debt) ऋणं कृ, ऋणग्रस्तः -स्ता -स्तं भू.

To CONTRACT, *v. n.* (Shrink up) सङ्कुच् in pass. (-कुच्यते), सङ्कोचं or कुचनम् इ (c. 2. एति, एतुं) or गम् (c. 1. गच्छति, गन्तुं), संक्षिप् in pass. (-क्षिप्यते), संहृ in pass. (-ह्रियते), कुच् in pass. (कुच्यते), संहन् in pass. (-हन्यते).

CONTRACTED, *p. p.* (Drawn together) सङ्कुचितः -ता -तं, कुचितः -ता -तं, आकुञ्चितः -ता -तं, निकुञ्चितः -ता -तं, संवृतः -ता -तं, निरुद्धः -द्धा -द्धं, पुटितः -ता -तं, संहतः -ता -तं, संश्यानः -ना -नं.—(Abridged) संहृतः -ता -तं, संक्षिप्तः -प्ता -प्तं, समस्तः -स्ता -स्तं.—(Narrow) सम्बाधः -धा -धं, सङ्कटः -टा -टं, निरन्तरालः -ला -लं, निरायतः -ता -तं.—(Agreed) संविदितः -ता -तं.

CONTRACTIBLE, *a.* संक्षेपणीयः -या -यं, सङ्कोचनीयः -या -यं, कुचनशीलः -ला -लं.

CONTRACTIBILITY, *s.* संक्षेपणीयत्वं, सङ्कोचनीयत्वं, संहरणीयत्वं, कुचनशीलता.

CONTRACTION, *s.* सङ्कोचः -चनं, आकुञ्चनं, कुचनं, अवकुञ्चनं, समसनं, संक्षेपः -पणं, संवारः, संवृतिः *f.*, ह्रासः, सङ्ग्रहः, निरोधः, न्यूनता; 'contraction of the vulva,' योनिसंवृतिः *f.*; 'of the urethra,' मूत्रमार्गनिरोधः; 'contraction of the skin by astringents,' सन्धानं; 'union of letters,' सन्धिः *m.*; 'a contracted letter,' संक्षिप्तवर्णः.

CONTRACTOR, *s.* नियमकृत्, समयकर्त्ता *m.* (र्त्तृ), पणकर्त्ता, पणायकः.

To CONTRADICT, *v. a.* विपरीतं वद् (c. 1. वदति -ते -दितुं), विवद्, अपवद्, अपवच् (c. 2. -वक्ति -वक्तुं), प्रत्याख्या (c. 2. -ख्याति -तुं), अधरीकृ.—(Oppose) विरुध् (c. 7. -रुणद्धि -रोद्धुं), प्रतिरुध्, प्रतिकूल (nom. -कूलयति -यितुं), प्रतिकृ, प्रतीप (nom. प्रतीपायते); 'to contradict one's self,' विप्रवद्.

CONTRADICTED, *p. p.* अपवादितः -ता -तं, प्रत्याख्यातः -ता -तं, पराहतः -ता -तं, अधरीकृतः -ता -तं, विरुद्धः -द्धा -द्धं, बाधितः -ता -तं, विप्रतिपन्नः -न्ना -न्नं, विप्रतिकृतः -ता -तं.

CONTRADICTER, *s.* विपरीतवादी *m.* (न्), प्रत्याख्याता *m.* (तृ), अपवादकः, विवादी *m.* (न्), प्रतिवादी.

CONTRADICTION, *s.* (Verbal opposition) वचनविरोधः, प्रतीपवचनं, विपरीतवचनं, विरोधोक्तिः *f.*, विपरीतार्थं वचनं, प्रत्याख्यानं, विगीतिः *f.*—(Disagreement, incongruity) विसंवादः, असङ्गतिः *f.*, विरुद्धता, असंस्थितिः *f.*—(Controversial assertion) वितण्डा, प्रतिवादः, विप्रलापः.—(Opposition) विरोधः -धनं, विपरीतता, विप्रतिपत्तिः *f.*, विपक्षता, प्रतिपक्षता, विप्रतिकारः, पर्यवस्थानं, प्रातिकूल्यं, प्रतिकूलता, प्रतिबन्धिः *m.* -न्धकता, बाधः.

CONTRADICTORILY, *adv.* विरुद्धं, विपरीतं, प्रतीपं, विरोधेन, असङ्गतं.

CONTRADICTORY, *a.* विपरीतः -ता -तं, विरुद्धः -द्धा -द्धं, विरुद्धार्थः -र्था -र्थं, प्रतीपः -पा -पं, विपक्षः -क्षा -क्षं, विपरीतार्थः -र्था -र्थं, विभिन्नः -न्ना -न्नं, प्रतिकूलः -ला -लं, विगीतः -ता -तं, प्रतिषेधकः -का -कं, द्विष्टः -ष्टा -ष्टं, बाधितः -ता -तं.—(Inconsistent) परस्परविरोधी -धिनी -धि (न्), परस्परपराहतः -ता -तं, विवदमानः -ना -नं.

CONTRADISTINCTION, *s.* व्यतिरेकः, प्रतिपक्षता, विपक्षता, विरुद्धता, विपरीतता, वैपरीत्यं, प्रातिकूल्यं, वैलक्षण्यं, विपरीतगुणविशिष्टता.

To CONTRADISTINGUISH, *v. a.* विपरीतगुणैः or विरुद्धगुणैर् विशिष् (c. 7. -शिनष्टि -शेष्टुं) or caus. -शेषयति -यितुं).

CONTRADISTINGUISHED, *p. p.* विपरीतगुणविशिष्टः -ष्टा -ष्टं, व्यतिरिक्तः -क्ता -क्तं.

CONTRAINDICATED, *p. p.* विलक्षः -क्षा -क्षं, अपथ्यः -थ्या -थ्यं, विहितः -ता -तं.

CONTRAINDICATION, *s.* अपथ्यलक्षणं, अपथ्यौषधलक्षणं, अपथ्यता.

CONTRAPOSITION, *s.* सम्मुखे or प्रतिमुखे स्थापनं or प्रतिष्ठापनं.

CONTRARIETY, *s.* विपर्य्ययः -र्य्यायः, पर्य्ययः, विपरीतता, वैपरीत्यं, विपर्य्यासः, वैलक्षण्यं -लक्षण्यं, प्रतिकूलता, प्रातिकूल्यं, विरोधः, प्रतिरोधः, विरुद्धता, प्रतिपक्षता, पर्य्यवस्था, विप्रतिकारः, प्रतिबन्धिता, व्यतिक्रमः, व्यत्ययः, व्यत्यासः, अवकुटारं.

CONTRARILY, *adv.* विपरीतं, विरुद्धं, प्रातिकूल्येन, विपर्य्ययेण, अभिमुखं.

CONTRARIWISE, *adv.* पुनर्, परन्तु, वरं, विपरीतं, वैपरीत्येन.

CONTRARY, *a.* प्रतिकूलः -ला -लं, विरोधी -धिनी -धि (न्), विरुद्धः -द्धा -द्धं, विपरीतः -ता -तं, प्रतीपः -पा -पं, विप्रतीपः -पा -पं, प्रातीपिकः -की -कं, विलोमः -मी -मं, प्रतिलोमः -मा -मं, विपर्य्यस्तः -स्ता -स्तं, विपर्य्यासितः -ता -तं, विभिन्नः -न्ना -न्नं, अपसव्यः -व्या -व्यं, प्रसव्यः -व्या -व्यं, विपक्षः -क्षा -क्षं, प्रतिपक्षः -क्षी -क्षं, द्वन्द्वः -द्वा -द्वं, अवकटः -टा -टं, अवकुटारः -रा -रं, अभिमुखः -खा -खं, अभिमुखगतः -ता -तं, प्रतिपः -पा -पं.—(Hostile) वैरी -रिणी -रि (न्).—(Acting contrary) विपरीतकारी -रिणी -रि (न्); 'a contrary wind,' सम्मुखागतो वातः. 'Contrary' is sometimes expressed by इतर; as, 'the contrary of moveable,' *i. e.* 'stationary,' जङ्गमेतरः -रा -रं.

CONTRARY, *s.* विपर्य्ययः -र्य्यायः, पर्य्ययः, विपर्य्यासः, व्यत्ययः, विपरीतं, व्यतिक्रमः.—(Contrary proposition) प्रतिपक्षः, उत्तरपक्षः; 'to the contrary,' विपरीताभिप्रायेण; 'on the contrary,' पुनर्, परन्तु, वरं.

CONTRARY, CONTRARILY, *adv.* पुनर्, वरं, परन्तु, विपरीततस्, अन्यथा, प्रतिकूलं; 'contrary to that,' तद्विपरीतं; 'contrary to custom,' रीतिव्यत्ययेन; 'contrary to promise,' प्रतिज्ञाविरोधेन.

CONTRAST, *s.* प्रतिपक्षः, प्रतिपक्षता, व्यतिरेकः, विरोधः, विपर्य्ययः, वैपरीत्यं, व्यत्ययः, वैलक्ष्यं, पृथक्त्वं, भिन्नाभिप्रायः, विभिन्नभावः; 'illustration by contrast,' व्यतिरेकदाहरणं.

To CONTRAST, *v. a.* विपर्यस् (c. 4. -अस्यति -असितुं), परस्परविपर्य्ययेण उपमा (c. 2. -माति -मातुं), परस्परविरुद्धं -द्धां -द्धं कृ, व्यतिरेकं कृ, विपर्य्ययं कृ, पृथक्त्वेन अभिधा (c. 3. -दधाति -धातुं), परस्परवैपरीत्यं कृ.

To CONTRAST, *v. n.* (Be in contrast) विपर्यस् in pass. (-अस्यते), विरुध् in pass. (-रुध्यते), व्यतिरिच् in pass. (-रिच्यते).

CONTRASTED, *p. p.* विपर्य्यस्तः -स्ता -स्तं, व्यतिरिक्तः -क्ता -क्तं, विरुद्धः -द्धा -द्धं.

CONTRAVALLATION, *s.* परिखा, परिकूटं, प्रतिकूपः, नगरप्राचीराभिमुखं परिखाप्राचीरादि.

To CONTRAVENE, *v. a.* प्रतिरुध् (c. 7. -रुणद्धि -रोद्धुं), संरुध्, विरुध्; प्रतिकृ; प्रतिबन्ध् (c. 9. -बध्नाति -बन्धुं), प्रतिकूल (nom. प्रतिकूलयति -यितुं), विहन् (c. 2. -हन्ति -हन्तुं), व्याहन्, निषिध् (c. 1. -षेधति -षेद्धुं), प्रतीप (nom. प्रतीपायते), विघ्न (nom. विघ्नयति -यितुं).

CONTRAVENTION, *s.* प्रतिरोधः, विरोधः, प्रतिकारः, विप्रतिकारः, प्रतियत्नः,

प्रतियोगः, निषेधः, व्याघातः, बाधः, प्रतिबन्धः, प्रतिबन्धकता.

CONTRECTATION, *s.* संस्पर्शः, स्पर्शः, परिमर्शः, स्पृष्टिः *f.*, सम्पर्कः, परिष्वङ्गः.

CONTRIBUTARY, *a.* एकराज्ञे करदः -दा -दं, एकराजाधीनः -ना -नं.

To CONTRIBUTE, *v. a.* किञ्चित् किञ्चिद् दा (c. 3. ददाति, दातुं) or स्था in caus. (स्थापयति -यितुं), स्वं स्वम् अंशं or भागं or उद्धारं दा.—(Assist, promote) साहाय्यं कृ, उपकृ, प्रवृध् in caus. (-वर्धयति -यितुं), प्रवृत् in caus. (-वर्त्तयति -यितुं).

CONTRIBUTION, *s.* (The act) अंशदानं, उद्धारदानं, करदानं.—(The share contributed) अंशः, भागः, विभागः, उद्धारः, दत्तांशः, करः.

CONTRIBUTOR, *s.* अंशदाता *m.* (तृ), उद्धारदाता, अंशदायी *m.* (न्).—(Assister, promoter) उपकारी *m.* (न्), साहाय्यकर्त्ता *m.* (र्त्तृ), प्रवर्त्तकः, प्रयोजकः, प्रवर्त्तकः, उत्तरसाधकः.

CONTRIBUTORY, *a.* साहाय्यकारी -रिणी -रि (न्), सम्पादकः -का -कं.

CONTRITE, *a.* अनुतापी -पिनी -पि (न्), जातानुतापः -पा -पं, कृतपश्चात्तापः -पा -पं, सञ्जातपश्चात्तापः -पा -पं, अनुशोचकः -का -कं, अनुशोकसन्तप्तः -प्ता -प्तं, क्षुण्णमनाः -नाः -नः (स्), शोकाग्निसन्तप्तः -प्ता -प्तं.

CONTRITELY, *adv.* सानुतापं, सन्तापेन, सखेदं, सन्तापपूर्व्वकं, अनुशोकात्.

CONTRITION, *s.* पश्चात्तापः, अनुतापः, सन्तापः, अनुशोकः, अनुशोचनं, अनुशयः, खेदः, विसूरितं, काप्यकारः, विप्रतीसारः.

CONTRIVABLE, *a.* प्रचिन्तनीयः -या -यं, विधेयः -या -यं, कल्पनीयः -या -यं.

CONTRIVANCE, *s.* (Act of contriving) उपायचिन्तनं, घटनं, विधानं, कल्पनं -ना, परिकल्पनं, कृतिः *f.*, मन्त्रणा, युक्तिप्रयुक्तिः *f.*—(Scheme, plan) उपायः, अपदेशः, व्यपदेशः, साधनं, चेष्टा, व्यवसायः, विधः, छलं.

To CONTRIVE, *v. a.* प्रचिन्त् (c. 10. -चिन्तयति -यितुं), परिचिन्त् or उपायं प्रचिन्त् or निश्चि (c. 5. -चिनोति -चेतुं), घट् (c. 1. घटते -टितुं), विधा (c. 3. -दधाति -धातुं), अनुसन्धा, कॢप् (c. 10. कल्पयति -यितुं), परिकॢप्, मन्त्र् (c. 10. मन्त्रयति -यितुं), सम्प्रधृ in caus. (-धारयति -यितुं).

To CONTRIVE, *v. n.* उपायं कृ, उपायचिन्तां कृ, चेष्ट् (c. 1. चेष्टते -ष्टितुं), व्यवसो (c. 4. -स्यति -सातुं).

CONTRIVED, *p. p.* प्रचिन्तितः -ता -तं, विहितः -ता -तं, घटितः -ता -तं, कल्पितः -ता -तं, परिकल्पितः -ता -तं, चेष्टितः -ता -तं; 'well contrived,' सुघटितः; 'badly contrived,' दुर्णीतः -ता -तं.

CONTRIVER, *s.* उपेता *m.* (तृ), उपायज्ञः, उपायचिन्तकः, परिकल्पकः, व्यवसायी *m.* (न्).

CONTROL, *s.* (Restraint, check) संयमः, विनियमः, यमः, निग्रहः, निरोधः, संरोधः, दमः, दमनं, दमथः -थं, यन्त्रणं, निवारः -रणं.—(Power, authority) वशं, प्रभुत्वं, अधिकारः, अधीनता; 'under your control,' त्वदधीनः -ना -नं; 'mental control,' मनःसंयमनं, मनोदण्डः.—(Counter-reckoning) प्रतिगणितं, प्रतिगणना.

To CONTROL, *v. a.* वशीकृ or वशे कृ, यम् (c. 1. यच्छति, यन्तुं), नियम्, संयम्, सन्नियम्, विनियम्; निग्रह् (c. 9. -गृह्णाति -ग्रहीतुं), विनिग्रह्, सन्निग्रह्; संहृ (c. 1. -हरति -हर्त्तुं), दम् in caus. (दमयति -यितुं), शास् (c. 2. शास्ति, शासितुं), निरुध् (c. 7. -रुणद्धि -रोद्धुं), अवरुध्, निषिध् (c. 1. -षेधति -षेद्धुं), यन्त्र् (c. 10. यन्त्रयति -यितुं), नियन्त्र्.—(By a counter-reckoning) प्रतिगणनां कृ.

CONTROLLABLE, *a.* संयमनीयः -या -यं, दमनीयः -या -यं, वश्यः -श्या -श्यं, निग्रहणीयः -या -यं, शासनीयः -या -यं, प्रत्याहरणीयः -या -यं.

CONTROLLED, *p. p.* यतः -ता -तं, संयतः -ता -तं, संयमितः -ता -तं, नियमितः -ता -तं, विनियतः -ता -तं, वशीकृतः -ता -तं, शासितः -ता -तं, निरुद्धः -द्धा -द्धं, निगृहीतः -ता -तं, प्रत्याहृतः -ता -तं, अधीनः -ना -नं.

CONTROLLER, *s.* शास्ता *m.* (स्तृ), अनुशासिता *m.* (तृ), अध्यक्षः, अभिरक्षिता *m.* (तृ), अधिकारी *m.* (न्).

CONTROLLERSHIP, *s.* अध्यक्षता -त्वं, अभिरक्षितृत्वं, अनुशास्तृत्वं.

CONTROVERSIAL, *a.* विवादी -दिनी -दि (न्), वादानुवादी -दिनी -दि (न्), वितर्की -र्किणी -र्कि (न्), सांवादिकः -की -कं, विसंवादी -दिनी -दि (न्).

CONTROVERSIALIST, *s.* विवादार्थी *m.* (न्), विवादी *m.* (न्), वादी *m.* (न्), तर्की *m.* (न्), सांवादिकः.

CONTROVERSY, *s.* वादानुवादः, वादप्रतिवादः, वितण्डा, वादयुद्धं, विवादः, संवादः, विसंवादः, वादः, वितर्कः, तर्कः, वाक्कलहः, विरोधोक्तिः *f.*, शास्त्रार्थकलहः, विपक्षता, विप्रतिपत्तिः *f.*, विचारः.

To CONTROVERT, *v. a.* विवद् (c. 1. -वदति -ते -दितुं), विसंवद्; विपरीतं वद्; विचर् in caus. (-चारयति -यितुं), विवादास्पदीकृ, प्रत्याख्या (c. 2. -ख्याति -तुं), अधरीकृ, वादानुवादं कृ, वितण्ड् (c. 1. -तण्डते -ण्डितुं).

CONTROVERTED, *p. p.* वादग्रस्तः -स्ता -स्तं, विवादास्पदीकृतः -ता -तं, विचारितः -ता -तं, प्रत्याख्यातः -ता -तं.

CONTROVERTIBLE, *a.* प्रत्याख्येयः -या -यं, विवदनीयः -या -यं, विचारणीयः -या -यं.

CONTROVERTIST, *s.* शास्त्रविरोधदर्शी *m.* (न्), विवादी *m.* (न्), वादप्रतिवादकृत्, नैयायिकः.

CONTUMACIOUS, *a.* विपरीतकारी -रिणी -रि (न्), प्रतीपः -पा -पं, विप्रतीपः -पा -पं, प्रतिकूलः -ला -लं, धृष्टः -ष्टा -ष्टं, दुर्विनीतः -ता -तं, दुःशीलः -ला -लं, विलोमः -मा -मं.

CONTUMACIOUSLY, *adv.* प्रतीपं, प्रतिकूलं, सदर्पं, सधर्षं, सधार्ष्ट्यं, धार्ष्ट्येन, दुर्विनीतं.

CONTUMACY, *s.* प्रतीपता, धार्ष्ट्यं, दर्पः, धर्षः, प्रतिकूलता, दुःशीलता, दुर्विनीतता, विपरीतकारिता, व्यलीकता.

CONTUMELIOUS, *a.* परुषः -षा -षं, निष्ठुरः -रा -रं, धर्षकः -का -कं, अवमानी -निनी -नि (न्), निन्दकः -का -कं, घृणाकरः -री -रं.

CONTUMELIOUSLY, *adv.* पारुष्येण, सधर्षणं, सपारुष्यं, सनैष्ठुर्य्यं, सनिकारं, सावमानं.

CONTUMELY, *s.* पारुष्यं, परुषवचनं, निष्ठुरवचनं, परिभाषणं, परीवादः, अपवादः, धर्षः -र्षणं, अवज्ञा, अवमानं, निष्ठुरता, नैष्ठुर्य्यं, निन्दा, तिरस्कारः, वाच्यता, वचनीयता, धिक्क्रिया, दुर्वाक्यं, जुगुप्सा, घृणा, गर्हा, उपक्रोशः, निकारः, उपालम्भः.

To CONTUSE, *v. a.* चूर्ण् (c. 10. चूर्णयति -यितुं), चूर्णीकृ, मृद् (c. 9. मृद्नाति, मर्द्दितुं), अवमृद्, विमृद्, क्षुद् (c. 7. क्षुणत्ति, क्षोत्तुं), क्षण् (c. 8. क्षणोति -णितुं), पिष् (c. 7. पिनष्टि, पेष्टुं), निष्पिष्, सम्पिष्, तुद् (c. 6. तुदति, तोत्तुं).

CONTUSED, *p. p.* क्षुण्णः -ण्णा -ण्णं, क्षतः -ता -तं, चूर्णितः -ता -तं, मर्द्दितः -ता -तं.

CONTUSION, *s.* अष्ठीला, नीलिका, क्षतं, मर्द्दनं, सम्मर्द्दः, निष्पेषः.

CONUNDRUM, *s.* प्रवह्लिः *f.* -ह्लिका, प्रश्नदूती, प्रहेलिका, श्लेषः, श्लेषोक्तिः *f.*

CONVALESCENCE, *s.* समुत्थानं, निरामयं, कल्यत्वं, शमः, उपशमः, रोगोपशमः, स्वास्थ्यं.

CONVALESCENT, *a.* समुत्थितः -ता -तं, वीतरोगः -गा -गं, निरामयः -या -यं, नीरुजः -जा -जं, व्याधिरहितः -ता -तं, कल्यः -ल्या -ल्यं, अपगतव्याधिः -धिः -धि, उल्लाघः -घा -घं, प्रोल्लाघितः -ता -तं.

To CONVENE, *v. a.* आह्वे (c. 1. -ह्वयति -ह्वातुं), समाह्वे, सङ्घुष् (c. 10. -घोषयति -यितुं), आह्वानपूर्व्वकं समानी (c. 1. -नयति -नेतुं), एकत्र कृ.

To CONVENE, *v. n.* सङ्गम् (c. 1. -गच्छति -गन्तुं), समागम्; समे (rt. इ with सम्, आ, c. 2. समैति -तुं); सम्मिल् (c. 6. -मिलति -मेलितुं), एकत्र मिल्.

CONVENIENCE, *s.* (Fitness) युक्तिः *f.*, उपयोगः, उपयोगिता, योग्यता, पात्रत्वं -ता, उपपत्तिः *f.*, याथातथ्यं.—(Commodiousness, comfort) सुस्थता, सुखं, सौख्यं, सोपकारत्वं.—(Fitness of time) अवकाशः, अवसरः; 'when it suits your convenience,' अवकाशं प्राप्य or अवसरं प्राप्य or यथावकाशं.

CONVENIENT, *a.* योग्यः -ग्या -ग्यं, उपयुक्तः -क्ता -क्तं, युक्तः -क्ता -क्तं, उचितः

-ता -तं, यथायोग्यः -ग्या -ग्यं, उपपन्नः -न्ना -न्नं, समुचितः -ता -तं, यथोचितः -ता -तं, समञ्जसः -सा -सं, सोपकारः -रा -रं.

CONVENIENTLY, *adv.* युक्तं, यथायोग्यं, योग्यं, यथोचितं, उपयुक्तं, साम्प्रतं, स्थाने, यथातथा, अनायासेन, यथावसरं, यथावकाशं.

CONVENT, *s.* मठः, अवसथः, आश्रमः, वीहारः, विहारः, धर्म्मशाला, धर्म्मचारिणां मठः.

CONVENTICLE, *s.* सभा, समाजः, मेलकः, ईश्वरपूजकानां गूढसभा, व्यवहारविरुद्धः समाजः.

CONVENTICLER, *s.* सभासद्, गूढसभासेवी *m.* (न्), व्यवहारविरुद्धसमाजसेवी.

CONVENTION, *s.* (Agreement) समयः, नियमः, संविद् *f.*, उपगमः, संवादः, सङ्केतः.—(Assembly) सभा, समाजः, संसद् *f.*, मेलकः.

CONVENTIONAL, *a.* सामयिकः -की -कं, नैयमिकः -की -कं, नियमितः -ता -तं, सर्व्वसम्मतः -ता -तं, निरूढः -ढा -ढं, रूढः -ढा -ढं.

CONVENTUAL, *a.* मठसम्बन्धी -न्धिनी -न्धि (न्), आश्रमी -मिणी -मि (न्).

To CONVERGE, *v. n.* नानादिग्देशाद् एकस्थानं प्रति गम् (c. 1. गच्छति, गन्तुं) or समागम्; एककेन्द्राभिमुखम् इ (c. 2. एति, एतुं).

CONVERGENCE, *s.* एकस्थानं प्रति गमनशीलता, एककेन्द्राभिमुखता.

CONVERGENT, *a.* एकस्थानं प्रति or एककेन्द्रं प्रति गमनशीलः -ला -लं, एककेन्द्राभिमुखः -खा -खं, केन्द्राभिपिपतिषुः -षुः -षु.

CONVERSABLE, *a.* कथोपकथनयोग्यः -ग्या -ग्यं, आलापी -पिनी -पि (न्), आलापकरणपटुः -टुः -टु.

CONVERSABLENESS, *s.* सभाचातुर्य्यं, आलापकरणे पाटवं.

CONVERSANCE or CONVERSANCY, *s.* पाटवं, परिज्ञानं, परिचयः, नैपुण्यं, व्युत्पत्तिः *f.*, चातुर्य्यं, कुशलता, पाण्डित्यं, विदग्धता, विज्ञता, अभिज्ञता.

CONVERSANT, *a.* विज्ञः -ज्ञा -ज्ञं, अभिज्ञः -ज्ञा -ज्ञं, निपुणः -णा -णं, शिक्षितः -ता -तं, सम्पन्नः -न्ना -न्नं, व्युत्पन्नः -न्ना -न्नं, विप्रतिपन्नः -न्ना -न्नं, चतुरः -रा -रं, पटुः -टुः -टु, कुशलः -ला -लं, अभिनिविष्टः -ष्टा -ष्टं, विचक्षणः -णा -णं, विशारदः -दा -दं, वेत्ता -त्री -तृ (तृ), पण्डितः -ता -तं, कृती -तिनी -ति (न्), व्यवहर्त्ता -र्त्री -र्तृ (र्तृ), चञ्चुरः -रा -रं, शीलितः -ता -तं, ज्ञः ज्ञा ज्ञं in comp.; 'well read,' स्वधीतः -ता -तं; 'conversant with law,' स्मृतिज्ञः; 'with the Scriptures,' शास्त्रविद्.

CONVERSATION, *s.* सम्भाषा -षणं, संलापः, आलापः, आभाषणं, सङ्कथा, कथायोगः, सम्प्रवदनं, कथोपकथनं, वादः, विस्रम्भकथा, संवादः, कथावार्त्ता, द्वयोः संवादः, आपृच्छा.—(Criminal) स्त्रीपुरुषसङ्गः.—(Behaviour) वृत्तिः *f.*, रीतिः *f.*, आचारः, व्यवहारः, व्यापारः.

CONVERSE, *s.* आलापः, सम्भाषा, संसर्गः, सङ्गमः, सङ्गः, सङ्गतिः *f.*, सम्पर्कः.—(The contrary) विपर्य्ययः.

To CONVERSE, *v. n.* (Hold conversation) सम्भाष् (c. 1. -भाषते -षितुं), संवद् (c. 1. -वदति -ते -दितुं), सम्प्रवद्, संलप् (c. 1. -लपति -पितुं), आलप्, संवच् (c. 2. -वक्ति -वक्तुं), सञ्जल्प् (c. 1. -जल्पति -ल्पितुं).—(Have intercourse) संसर्गं कृ, सङ्गम् (c. 1. -गच्छति -गन्तुं).—(As the sexes) स्त्रीपुरुषवत् सम्भोगं कृ or सङ्गम्.

CONVERSELY, *adv.* विपर्य्ययेण, विपर्य्ययतस्, व्यतिक्रमेण, विपरीततस्.

CONVERSION, *s.* (Change from one state to another) विकारः, विकृतिः *f.*, विक्रिया, परिवर्त्तः, परिणामः, अन्यथाकरणं, अन्यथाभावः, विपर्य्ययः, भावान्तरप्राप्तिः *f.* OBS. Change from one substance to another is often expressed by the affix सात्; as, 'conversion to water,' जलसात्करणं; 'to ashes,' भस्मसात्करणं.—(Moral change) निवर्त्तनं, पापनिवर्त्तनं, विप्रतीसारः.—(To another religion or opinion) परमतग्रहणं, परधर्म्माश्रयः, धर्म्मपरिवर्त्तः, मतिभेदः, स्वस्वधर्म्मत्यागात् सत्यधर्म्मग्रहणं.

CONVERT, *s.* परधर्म्माश्रितः, परमतग्रहीता *m.* (तृ), स्वधर्म्मत्यागी *m.* (न्), धर्म्मपरिवर्त्तकः.

To CONVERT, *v. a.* (Change) विकृ, अन्यभावं -वां -वं कृ, भिन्नभावं -वां -वं कृ, भावान्तरीकृ, अन्यथा कृ, विकृताकारं -रां -रं कृ, परिवृत् in caus. (-वर्त्तयति -यितुं), परावृत्. OBS. To convert from one substance to another is often expressed by सात्; as, 'to convert to ashes,' भस्मसात् कृ; 'to water,' जलसात् कृ; 'to one's own substance,' आत्मसात् कृ.—(Cause to reform) पापाद् विरम् in caus. (-रमयति -यितुं) or निवृत् in caus. (-वर्त्तयति -यितुं).—(Cause to change from one religion or opinion to another) स्वधर्म्मत्यागानन्तरं परधर्म्मग्रहणे प्रवृत् in caus. (-वर्त्तयति -यितुं) or परधर्म्मं ग्रह् in caus. (ग्राहयति -यितुं).—(Apply to some use) प्रयुज् (c. 7. -युनक्ति -योक्तुं), उपयुज्, विनियुज्.

To CONVERT, *v. n.* (Be converted) विकृ (c. 8. -कुरुते), विकृतीभू, अन्यथाभू, विकृताकारः -रा -रं भू, भावान्तरम् इ (c. 2. एति, एतुं) or प्राप् (c. 5. -आप्नोति -आप्तुं), भावान्तरीभू.—(From sin) पापाद् विरम् (c. 1. -रमति -रन्तुं) or निवृत् (c. 1. -वर्त्तते -र्त्तितुं).—(Change one's religion) धर्म्मं परिवृत् in caus. (-वर्त्तयति -यितुं), स्वधर्म्मं त्यज् or अपास्य परधर्म्मं ग्रह् (c. 9. गृह्णाति, ग्रहीतुं) or आश्रि (c. 1. -श्रयति -यितुं).—(Change in mind) अन्यमानसीभू, विमनीभू.

CONVERTIBILITY, *s.* परिवर्त्तनीयता, विकार्य्यता, परिवर्त्तनक्षमता.

CONVERTIBLE, *s.* परिवर्त्तनीयः -या -यं, विकार्य्यः -र्य्या -र्य्यं, परिवर्त्तनयोग्यः -ग्या -ग्यं.

CONVEX, *a.* न्युब्जः -ब्जा -ब्जं, विम्बाकारः -रा -रं, कूर्म्मपृष्ठाकारः -रा -रं, आभोगवान् -वती -वत् (त्), गोलपृष्ठाकृतिः -तिः -ति, गण्डाकारः -रा -रं.

CONVEXITY, *s.* न्युब्जत्वं -ता, विम्बाकारता, गण्डाकारभावः, आभोगः.

CONVEXLY, *adv.* कूर्म्मपृष्ठाकारेण, आभोगरूपेण, न्युब्जतस्.

CONVEXO-CONCAVE, *a.* अर्द्धचन्द्राकृतिः -तिः -ति, अर्द्धचन्द्ररूपः -पा -पं.

To CONVEY, *v. a.* (Carry) वह् (c. 1. वहति -ते, वोढुं), आवह्, उपवह्, संवह्; आनी (c. 1. -नयति -नेतुं), तॄ in caus. (तारयति -यितुं), गम् in caus. (गमयति -यितुं), प्राप् in caus. (प्रापयति -यितुं), स्थानान्तरीकृ.—(Transmit) सञ्चर् in caus. (-चारयति -यितुं), चल् in caus. (चालयति -यितुं), अभिवह्.—(Make over to another) परस्मै or परस्मिन् समृ in caus (-अर्पयति -यितुं).

CONVEYANCE, *s.* (Vehicle) वाहनं, यानं, प्रवहणं, वाहः, रथः, चातुरं.—(Act of making over to another) परस्मै समर्पणं.—(Act of conveying) वाहनं, तारणं, आनयनं, अभिवाहः, सञ्चारणं, चालनं.—(Deed of sale or transfer) क्रयलेख्यं, समर्पणपत्रं.

CONVEYANCER, *s.* क्षेत्रद्रव्यादीनां दानपत्रलेखकः, स्थावरास्थावराणां समर्पणपत्रलेखकः or क्रयपत्रलेखकः.

CONVEYED, *p. p.* ऊढः -ढा -ढं, भृतः -ता -तं, सञ्चारितः -ता -तं, चालितः -ता -तं, तारितः -ता -तं; 'being borne along,' उह्यमानः -ना -नं, नीयमानः -ना -नं.

CONVEYER, *s.* वाहकः, वाही *m.* (न्), तारकः, तारी *m.* (न्), सञ्चारकः.

To CONVICT, *v. a.* आधृष् (c. 10. -धर्षयति -यितुं, c. 1. -धर्षति -र्षितुं), संसूच् (c. 10. -सूचयति -यितुं), अपराधनिश्चयं कृ, अपराधनिर्णयं कृ, निर्णीतापराधं -धां -धं कृ, दोषप्रमाणं कृ, सदोषं or सापराधं or अपराधिनं -धिनीं -धि ज्ञा (c. 9. जानाति, ज्ञातुं), अभियुक्तजनं निरुत्तरं कृ, असौ सापराध इति निश्चि (c. 5. -चिनोति -चेतुं), दृष्टदोषम् आख्या (c. 2. -ख्याति -तुं).

CONVICT or CONVICTED, *p. p.* आधर्षितः -ता -तं, दृष्टदोषः -षा -षं,

दृष्टापराधः -धा -धं, निश्चितदोषः -षा -षं, निर्णीतदोषः -षा -षं, उपपादितदोषः -षा -षं; 'of falsehood,' दृष्टवितथवचनः -ना -नं.

CONVICT, s. साधर्षितः, दृष्टदोषः, दृष्टापराधः, दोषनिश्चयात् प्रवासितः or कायक्लेशे बलेन नियोजितः.

CONVICTION, s. (Of crime) साधर्षणं, दोषनिश्चयः, दोषनिर्णयः, अपराधनिर्णयः.—(Full persuasion) निश्चयः, निर्णयः, सुनिश्चयः, विश्वासः, प्रत्ययः, ग्रहणं, धारणं, परिज्ञानं.

To CONVINCE, *v. a.* (Make to acknowledge) स्वीकारं कृ in caus. (कारयति -यितुं), उरीकारं or अङ्गीकारं कृ in caus., अभिज्ञातुं or उरीकर्त्तुम् आनी (c. 1. -नयति -नेतुं) or अनुनी, निरुत्तरं -रां -रं कृ, निरुत्तरीकृ, अभिज्ञा in caus. (-ज्ञापयति -यितुं), परिज्ञा in caus., ग्रह in caus. (ग्राहयति -यितुं).—(Make to believe, persuade) प्रत्ययं or विश्वासं or निश्चयं कृ in caus. or जन् in caus. (जनयति -यितुं), प्रत्येतुं or विश्वसितुम् आनी or अनुनी.—(Destroy doubt) संशयं or सन्देहं छिद (c. 7. छिनत्ति, छेत्तुं) or खण्ड् (c. 10. खण्डयति -यितुं).

CONVINCED, *p. p.* कृतनिश्चयः -या -यं, कृतनिर्णयः -या -यं, जातनिश्चयः -या -यं, जातविश्वासः -सा -सं, जातप्रत्ययः -या -यं, निरुत्तरीकृतः -ता -तं, छिन्नसंशयः -या -यं.

CONVINCING *a.* निश्चायकः -का -कं, निर्णायकः -का -कं, निश्चयजनकः -का -कं, विश्वासकारी -रिणी -रि (न्), परिज्ञानकृत्, प्रत्ययजनकः -का -कं.

CONVINCINGLY, *adv.* यथा निश्चयो जायते तथा, निःसन्दिग्धं, अत्र न संशय इति प्रकारेण.

CONVIVIAL, *a.* औत्सविकः -की -कं, सम्भोजनः -नी -नं, उत्सवसम्बन्धी -न्धिनी -न्धि (न्); 'a convivial party,' सम्भोजनं, सहभोजनं, सम्प्रीतिः *f.*

CONVOCATION, *s.* (The act of calling together) समाह्वानं, आह्वानं.—(Assembly) सभा, समाजः, सदः *n.* (स्).—(Assembly of the clergy) पुरोहितसभा, धर्म्माध्यक्षसमाजः.

To CONVOKE, *v. a.* समाह्वे (c. 1. -ह्वयति -ह्वातुं), आह्वे, सङ्घट् (c. 10. -घट्टयति -यितुं).

To CONVOLVE, *v. a.* समावृत् in caus. (-वर्त्तयति -यितुं), आवृत्, व्यावृत्; संसृ in caus. (-सारयति -यितुं).

CONVOLVOLUS, *s.* क्षीरविदारी, विदारी, महाश्वेता, इक्षुगन्धा, क्षुद्रगन्धिका, क्रोष्ट्री, श्यामा, भूमिकुष्माण्डकः.

To CONVOY, *v. a.* (Attend by way of defence) रक्षार्थम् अनुव्रज् (c. 1. -व्रजति -जितुं) or अनुया (c. 2. -याति -यातुं).—(Guide) सञ्चर् in caus. (-चारयति -यितुं).—(Convey) आवह् (c. 1. -वाहयति -यितुं).—(Guard on a journey) अध्वनि रक्ष् (c. 1. रक्षति -क्षितुं).

CONVOY, *s.* (Attendance by way of defence) रक्षार्थम् अनुव्रजनं, अनुव्रज्या.—(Guide) सञ्चारकः.—(Guard) रक्षकः.—(A ship for convoy) वाणिज्यपोतरक्षका वृहद्युद्धनौका.

CONVOYED, *p. p.* अनुयातः -ता -तं, सञ्चारितः -ता -तं, अध्वनि रक्षितः -ता -तं.

To CONVULSE, *v. a.* (Agitate greatly) क्षुभ् in caus. (क्षोभयति -यितुं), आक्षुभ्, सङ्क्षुभ्, विक्षुभ्; कम्प् in caus. (कम्पयति -यितुं), प्रकम्प्.—(Contract convulsively) आकृष्, (c. 1. -कर्षति, c. 6. -कृषति -क्रष्टुं), आक्षिप् (c. 6. -क्षिपति -क्षेप्तुं), अपतन् in caus. (-तानयति -यितुं); 'to be convulsed,' क्षुभ् (c. 4. क्षुभ्यति, क्षोभितुं), सङ्क्षुभ्, सम्प्रक्षुभ्.

CONVULSION, *s.* (Spasm) आक्षेपकः, अपतानकः, अपतन्त्रकः, आकर्षः, अङ्गामयः, शूलं.—(Commotion) क्षोभः, व्याक्षोभः, कम्पः, कम्पनं, कम्पितं.

CONVULSIVE, *a.* आकर्षकः -का -कं, आक्षेपकः -का -कं, कम्पकः -का -कं, कम्पकरः -री -रं; 'a convulsive contraction,' आकर्षः, अपतानकः; 'convulsive utterance,' गद्गदः, गद्गदवाक् *f.* (च्).

CONY, *s.* शशः, शशकः, बिलवासी *m.* (न्), गर्त्तवासी *m.* (न्).

To coo, *v. n.* (As a bird) कु (c. 1. कवते, c. 6. कुवते, c. 2. कौति, कवितुं, कोतुं), कूज् (c. 1. कूजति -जितुं), अनुकूज्, कुकु शब्दं कृ.

COOING, *s.* कूजनं, कूजितं, अनुकूजनं, कुकु शब्दः.

COOK, *s.* सूपकारः, पाचकस्त्री *f.*, पचकः, पाचकः, पचः, पचेलुकः, सदः, सूदाध्यक्षः, भक्ष्यकारः, अन्नसंस्कर्त्ता *m.* (र्तृ), भक्तकारः, औदनिकः, आन्धसिकः.

To COOK, *v. a.* पच् (c. 1. पचति -ते, पक्तुं), श्रा in caus. (श्रपयति -ते -यितुं), अग्नावि संस्कृ or सन्धा (c. 3. -दधाति -धातुं) or सिद्धीकृ.

COOKED, *p. p.* पक्कः -क्का -क्कं, श्राणः -णा -णं, शृतः -ता -तं, श्रपितः -ता -तं, सिद्धः -द्धा -द्धं, संस्कृतः -ता -तं, प्रणीतः -ता -तं, उपसम्पन्नः -न्ना -न्नं, राद्धः -द्धा -द्धं.

COOKERY, *s.* (Art of) पाकविद्या.—(Act of cooking) पचनं, पाकः, पचा, पाचा, पाचिका, पाकनिष्पत्तिः *f.*

COOK-MAID, *s.* पाचकस्त्री, पाचिका, अन्नसंस्कर्त्री, भक्ष्यकारी, सूपकारी.

COOK-ROOM, *s.* पाकशाला, पाकस्थानं, पाकागारं, सूदशाला, महानसः -सं.

COOL, *a.* शीतलः -ला -लं, शीतः -ता -तं, शिशिरः -रा -रं, अतप्तः -प्ता -प्तं, अतपः -पा -पं, अघर्म्मः -र्म्मा -र्म्मं, अनुष्णः -ष्णा -ष्णं, शीतलस्पर्शः -र्शा -र्शं, जडः -डा -डं.—(Calm, composed) असम्भ्रमः -मा -मं, अव्यग्रः -ग्रा -ग्रं, शान्तः -न्ता -न्तं, धीरः -रा -रं.—(Without passion) वीतरागः -गा -गं.—(Cool in affection) विरक्तः -क्ता -क्तं; 'it grows cool,' शीतलायते.

COOL, *s.* शीतलं, शीतं, शीतलता, शीतता, शिशिरः, शैत्यं, अनुष्णता, अघर्म्मः.

To COOL, *v. a.* शीतलीकृ, शीतीकृ, शिशिरीकृ, शीतल (nom. शीतलयति -यितुं).—(Cause an abatement, extinguish) शम् in caus. (शमयति -यितुं), उपशम्, प्रशम्.

To COOL, *v. n.* शीतल (nom. शीतलायते), शीतलीभू, शिशिरीभू, शीतीभू.—(Abate, subside) शम् (c. 4. शाम्यति, शमितुं), उपशम्, प्रशम्.

COOLED, *p. p.* शीतीकृतः -ता -तं, शीतलीकृतः -ता -तं, हततापः -पा -पं.

COOLER, *s.* शीतलकारकः.—(For wine, &c.) मद्यादिशीतलीकरणार्थं मृन्मयभाजनं.

COOLING, *a.* शीतलकारी -रिणी -रि (न्), तापहरः -री -रं, सन्तापहरः -रा -रं, घर्म्मनाशकः -का -कं.—(Causing abatement) शमकः -का -कं, शान्तिदः -दा -दं; 'cooling breeze,' शीतलवातः, स्वेदचूषको वायुः.

COOLLY, *adv.* शीतलं, शिशिरं, सशैत्यं.—(Without discomposure) असम्भ्रमं, सम्भ्रमं विना, अव्यग्रं, शान्तं, प्रशान्तं, असहसा.

COOLNESS, *s.* शीतलता, शैत्यं, शीतता, शीतीभावः, शिशिरत्वं, अनुष्णता.—(Of affection) विरागः, विरक्तिः *f.*, निःस्नेहता.

COOM, *s.* (Soot that gathers over an oven's mouth) कन्दुमुखलग्नम् अङ्गारमलं.—(Grease which works out of the nave of a wheel) चक्रनाभिमध्याद् निर्गतः स्नेहः.

COOP, *s.* (Barrel) भाण्डं, भाजनं, काष्ठभाण्डं, काष्ठपात्रं.—(Cage for poultry) ग्राम्यकुक्कुटादिरक्षणार्थं पिञ्जरं or वीतंसः, कुक्कुटपालिका.

To COOP-UP, *v. a.* पिञ्जरे or वीतंसे प्रविश् in caus. (-वेशयति -यितुं).—(Confine in a narrow place) सङ्कटस्थाने निरुध् (c. 7. -रुणद्धि -रोद्धुं).

COOPER, *s.* काष्ठभाण्डकृत्, काष्ठभाजनकारः, काष्ठपात्रदोहनादीनां तक्षकः.

COOPERAGE, *s.* (Price paid for cooper's work) काष्ठपात्रादितक्षकस्य मूल्यं or भृतिः *f.*—(Cooper's work) काष्ठपात्रादितक्षकस्य कर्म्म *n.* (न्) or व्यापारः.

To CO-OPERATE, *v. n.* अन्येन सह व्यवसो (c. 4. -स्यति -सातुं) or आचर् (c. 1. -चरति -रितुं) or चेष्ट् (c. 1. चेष्टते -ष्टितुं); प्रतियोगं कृ, साहाय्यं

कृ; सहकारी -रिणी -रि भू.

Co-operation, *s.* सहकारः -रिता, साहाय्यं, सहायता, प्रतियोगः, प्रतियोगिता, सम्प्रतिपत्तिः *f.*, अङ्गाङ्गिभावः.

Co-operative, *a.* सहकारी -रिणी -रि (न्), सहोद्योगी -गिनी -गि (न्).

Co-operator, *s.* सहकारी *m.* (न्), सहकृत्वा *m.* (न्), प्रतियोगी *m.* (न्), साहाय्यकृत्, सम्भूयकारी *m.* (न्).

Coot, *s.* जलचरः कृष्णवर्णः क्षुद्रपक्षिभेदः.

Coparcenary, *s.* संसृष्टता -त्वं, संसृष्टिता, समांशिता.

Coparcener, *s.* समांशी *m.* (न्), समांशहारी *m.* (न्), अंशहरः, संसृष्टी *m.* (न्), संसृष्टः, रिक्थसंविभागी *m.* (न्), सहाधिकारी *m.* (न्).

Copartner, *s.* समांशी *m.* (न्), समांशहारी *m.* (न्), अंशी *m.* (न्), अंशभागी *m.* (न्), अंशहारी *m.* (न्), सम्भूयकारी *m.* (न्).

Copartnership, *s.* समांशिता, सम्भूयसमुत्थानं, अंशभागिता, अविभक्तत्वं.

Cope, *s.* (Covering for the head) मस्तकाभरणं, मस्तकाच्छादनं, शिरस्त्राणं, शिरस्त्रं.—(Sacerdotal cloak) पुरोहितप्रावारः, पुरोहितपरिधेयं.

To cope with, *v. n.* प्रतियुध् (c. 4. -युध्यते -योद्धुं), स्पर्ध् (c. 1. स्पर्धते -र्धितुं), सङ्घृष् (c. 1. -घर्षति -र्षितुं), प्रतिकूल (nom. प्रतिकूलयति -यितुं), विरुध् (c. 7. -रुणद्धि -रोद्धुं), प्रतियोगं कृ.

Copier or copyist, *s.* लेखकः, लिपिकरः -कारः, प्रतिलिपिकरः.—(Imitator) अनुकारी *m.* (न्), गतानुगतिकः.—(Plagiary) वागपहारकः, शब्दचोरः.

Coping, *s.* प्राकारशृङ्गं, कपिशीर्षं, क्रयशीर्षं, लोडकशीर्षं, सालशृङ्गं.

Copious, *a.* बहुः -हुः -ह्वी -हु, बहुलः -ला -लं, प्रचुरः -रा -रं, भूरिः -रिः -रि, पुष्कलः -ला -लं, सम्पूर्णः -र्णा -र्णं, परिपूर्णः -र्णा -र्णं, अनेकः -का -कं, विपुलः -ला -लं.

Copiously, *adv.* बाहुल्येन, बहुशस्, बहु, प्राचुर्य्येण, प्रचुरं, भूरि, भूरिशस्, विस्तारेण, विस्तरशस्, अनेकशस्.

Copiousness, *s.* बाहुल्यं, प्राचुर्य्यं, बहुत्वं, प्रचुरत्वं, प्रपञ्चनं, सम्पूर्णता, पुष्कलत्वं, विपुलता.

Copper, *s.* ताम्रं, ताम्रकं, शुल्वं, म्लेच्छं, द्विष्टं, नैपालिकं, तपनेष्टं, लोहितायः *n.* (स्), उदुम्बरं, ब्रह्मवर्द्धनं, अम्बकं, अरविन्दं, रविलोहं; 'copper vessel,' ताम्रपात्रं, ताम्रकटाहः, ताम्रस्थाली, ताम्रपिठरः; 'copper coin,' पणः.

Copper-coloured, *a.* ताम्रवर्णः -र्णा -र्णं, ताम्रमुखः -खी -खं, ताम्रतनुः -नुः -नु.

Copperas, *s.* तुत्थं -त्थकं, मूषातुत्थं, मलीमसः.

Copperplate, *s.* ताम्रफलकं, ताम्रपट्टं, ताम्रपत्रं, पट्टं.

Coppersmith, *s.* ताम्रकारः, ताम्रिकः, ताम्रकुट्टकः -कुटः, शौल्बिकः, कांस्यकारः.

Coppery, *a.* ताम्रः -म्री -म्रं, ताम्रिकः -की -कं, ताम्रमयः -यी -यं, औदुम्बरः -री -रं, कुङ्कुमताम्रः -म्रा -म्रं.

Coppice or copse, *s.* गुल्मावृतं स्थानं, इन्धनावृतं स्थानं, जङ्गलः, उपवनं, कृत्रिमवनं.

Copula, *s.* विशेष्यविशेषणसंज्ञा.

To copulate, *v. a.* संयुज् (c. 7. -युनक्ति -योक्तुं), सन्धा (c. 3. -दधाति -धातुं).

To copulate, *v. n.* स्त्रीपुरुषवत् सङ्गम् (c. 1. -गच्छति -गन्तुं), अभिगम्; मैथुनं कृ, सम्भोगं कृ, संसर्गं कृ.

Copulation, *s.* मैथुनं, रतं, सुरतं, रतिकर्म्म *n.* (न्), रतिक्रिया, शृङ्गारः, अङ्गसङ्गः, औपस्थ्यं, सम्भोगः, संसर्गः, सम्पर्कः, संयोजनं, व्यवायः, गमनं, अभिगमनं, महासुखं, रहः *n.* (स्), उपसृष्टं, अभिमानितं, वर्षितं, कामकेलिः, मोहनं.

Copulative, *a.* संयोगकारी -रिणी -रि (न्) or संसर्गकारी; 'copulative conjunction,' संयोगकारिणी अव्ययसंज्ञा.

Copy, *s.* (Transcript from an original) प्रतिलिपिः *f.*, प्रतिरूपं.—(An individual book) एकपुस्तकं, एकग्रन्थः.—(An original from which any thing is copied) आदर्शः, मूलं.—(Autograph) स्वहस्तलिखितं, हस्ताक्षरं, हस्तलिपिः *f.*

To copy, *v. a.* and *n.* (Transcribe) उद्धृ (c. 1. -हरति -र्तुं -रीतुं), लिपिं दृष्ट्वा प्रतिलिपिं कृ, रूपं दृष्ट्वा प्रतिरूपं कृ, मूलदर्शनाद् लिख् (c. 6. लिखति, लेखितुं).—(Imitate) अनुकृ, अनुगम् (c. 1. -गच्छति -गन्तुं).

Copy-book, *s.* प्रतिलिपिपुस्तकं, प्रतिलिखनपुस्तकं.—(The writing by looking at which boys learn to write) आदर्शः, पुस्तकं यस्य पत्त्रेषु वर्णविन्यासश्च चारुरूपेण लिख्यते यद्दर्शनाद् बालका लिखनशिक्षां कुर्व्वन्ति, बालानां लिखनशिक्षार्थम् पुस्तकारोपितानि अक्षराणि वाक्यानि वा.

Copyhold, *s.* (Land, &c.) ग्रामेश्वराधीनं क्षेत्रादि.

Copyholder, *s.* आहर्ता *m.* (र्तृ), ग्रामेश्वराधीनक्षेत्रधारी *m.* (न्).

Copyright, *s.* स्वकीयमुद्रितग्रन्थे निबन्धुर् अधिकारः, मुद्राङ्कितपुस्तके स्वत्वं.

To coquet, *v. n.* विलस् (c. 1. -लसति -सितुं), विलासं कृ, हावं कृ, लल् (c. 1. ललति -लितुं), खेला (nom. खेलायति -यितुं), प्रेमललितं कृ.

Coquetry, *s.* विलासः, हावः, ललितं, विभ्रमः, खेला, रसिकता, मोहनेच्छा, लालसा, रमस्यं.

Coquette, *s.* रसिका स्त्री, रसिनी, विलासिनी, विलासवती, दामिनी, मोहनकारिणी, लालिनी, कामिनी, लीलावती.

Coral, *s.* विद्रुमः, प्रवालः -लं, रत्नवृक्षः, मन्दटः, मन्दारः, रक्तकन्दः -न्दलः, हेमकन्दलः, रत्नकन्दलः, रत्नवृक्षः, लतामणिः *m.*, अङ्गारकमणिः, माहेयः, पारिजातः, पारिभद्रः, क्रिमिशत्रुः *m.*, भौमरत्नं, भोमीरा, सुपुष्पः, रक्तपुष्पकः.

Coralline, *a.* प्रवालमयः -यी -यं, विद्रुममयः -यी -यं, सप्रवालः -ला -लं.

Coralloid, *a.* प्रवालोपमः -मा -मं, विद्रुमसदृशः -शी -शं.

Cord, *s.* रज्जुः *m. f.*, पाशः, दाम *n.* (न्), दामनी, दामा, गुणः, सूत्रं, शणतन्तुः *m.*, शणसूत्रं, सन्दानं, रसना, शुल्बं, शुल्बः, योक्त्रं, वटः, वराटः -टकः, दोरकः; 'Brahminical cord,' उपवीतं, यज्ञोपवीतं, निवीतं, पञ्चवटः, मौञ्जी.—(A load of wood measured by a cord) रज्जुपरिमितः काष्ठभारः, इन्धनराशिः *m. f.*

To cord, *v. a.* रज्ज्वा बन्ध् (c. 9. बध्नाति, बन्द्धुं), पाश (nom. पाशयति -यितुं), योक्त्र (nom. योक्त्रयति -यितुं), यन्त्र् (c. 10. यन्त्रयति -यितुं).

Cordage, *s.* शणसूत्रं.—(Of a ship) नावो रज्ज्वादिसामग्र्यं.

Corded, *a.* (Fastened with a cord) रज्जुबद्धः -द्धा -द्धं, पाशितः -ता -तं.—(Made of ropes) रज्जुमयः -यी -यं.

Cordial, *s.* अग्निवर्द्धनं, रुचकं, रोचकः, रोचनः, बलवर्द्धकं or तेजोवर्द्धनम् औषधं.

Cordial, *a.* (Invigorating tonic) अग्निवर्द्धकः -का -कं, अग्निदः -दा -दं, तेजस्करः -रा -रं, दीपकः -का -कं, रुचकः -का -कं, रुचिरः -रा -रं, पौष्टिकः -की -कं, धातुपोषकः -का -कं.—(Sincere, friendly) सरलः -ला -लं, सौहार्द्दवान् -वती -वत् (त्), सुहृत्तमः -मा -मं.

Cordiality, *s.* सौहार्द्दं, सौहृद्यं, सुहृत्ता, सारल्यं, सरलता, सुशीलता.

Cordially, *adv.* सौहार्द्देन, सुहृत्तया, ससौहार्द्दं, ससारल्यं, सुशीलवत्.

Cordmaker, *s.* रज्जुकारः, शणसूत्रकारी *m.* (न्), शणतन्तुकृत्.

Cordon, *s.* (Of a rampart) प्राकारशीर्षं.—(Band) दाम *n.* (न्).

Cordwainer, *s.* पादुकाकारः, चर्म्मकारः, चर्म्मकृत्, चर्म्मपादुकाकृत्, पादूकृत्.

Core, *s.* (Heart, inner part) हृदयं, गर्भः, अन्तरं, मध्यभागः, बीजं, सारः.

Coriaceous, *a.* चर्म्ममयः -यी -यं, चार्म्मिकः -की -कं, चर्मिनीयः -या -यं.

Coriander, *s.* (Plant) धानी, धानः, धानेयः, सूक्ष्मपत्रः, तीक्ष्णपत्रः,

तीक्ष्णफलः, कुमटी.—(Seed) छत्रा, अवारिका, सुगन्धि n., धान्यकं, धान्यबीजं, तुम्बुरु n. -री, कुस्तुम्बुरुः f. -म्बुरी.

Cork, s. (Bark of a tree) विदेशीयतरुत्वक् f. (च्).—(Stopple of a bottle, &c.) पिधानं, कूपीछिद्रपिधानं, कूपीछिद्रनिरोधनार्थं तरुत्वङ्मयं पिधानं.

To cork, v. a. (Stop with a cork) पूर्व्वोक्तपिधानेन निरुध् (c. 7. -रुणद्धि -रोद्धुं), पिधा (c. 3. -दधाति -धातुं).

Corked, p. p. सपिधानः -ना -नं, पूर्व्वोक्तपिधाननिरुद्धः -द्धा -द्धं.

Cormorant, s. मत्स्यखादकः पक्षिभेदः.—(A glutton) अत्याहारी m. (न्), गृध्नः, घस्मरः, कुक्षिम्भरिः m.

Corn, s. (Grain) धान्यं.—(Growing corn) शस्यं, स्तम्बकरिः m., सीत्यं. (Food) अन्नं, खाद्यं, भक्ष्यं, आहारः, जीवसाधनं.—(Callosity on the foot) किणः, कदरः.

To corn, v. a. लवणीकृ, लवण (nom. लवणयति -यितुं), लवणाक्तं -क्तां -क्तं कृ.

Cornchandler, s. धान्यमायः, धान्यादिविक्रेता m. (तृ), वैवधिकः -की m. (न्).

Corncutter, s. किणच्छेदकः, कदरकृत्, कदरोच्छेदकः, किणोन्मूलकः.

Cornea, s. (Of the eye) शुक्लमण्डलं.

Cornel, s. (A tree) वक्ष्यमाणप्रस्तरसवर्णफलो वृक्षः.

Cornelian, s. (A precious stone) स्वच्छप्रस्तरभेदः.

Corneous, a. शार्ङ्गः -र्ङ्गी -र्ङ्गं, शृङ्गमयः -यी -यं, शृङ्गोपमः -मा -मं.

Corner, s. (Angle) कोणः, अस्रः, आरं.—(Of the mouth) सृक्क n. (न्), सृक्किणी.—(Of the eye) अपाङ्गं, नयनोपान्तः, नेत्रपर्य्यन्तः.—(Secret place, retreat) निर्जनदेशः, विविक्तदेशः, आश्रमः.

Cornered, p. p. सास्रः -स्रा -स्रं, सकोणः -णा -णं, कोणविशिष्टः -ष्टा -ष्टं.

Corner-stone, s. कोणप्रस्तरः, आरप्रस्तरः, प्रस्तरो येन प्राचीरद्वयं सम्बद्धं, प्रधानप्रस्तरः.

Corner-wise, adv. कोणाकोणि, आरारि, अस्रास्रि.

Cornet, s. (A musical instrument) शुषिरवाद्यभेदः.—(Officer of horse) आश्विकसैन्यदलनायकः, अश्वारूढसैन्यपताकाधारी कुलीनकुमारः, सादी m. (न्).—(Envelope of paper) कोशः, आवेष्टनं, प्रच्छदपटः.

Cornetcy, s. पूर्व्वोक्तस्य सैन्यदलनायकस्य पदं or अधिकारः.

Cornfield, s. शस्यक्षेत्रं, धान्यक्षेत्रं, सीत्यक्षेत्रं, सीत्यभूमिः f.

Cornflower, s. कक्षः, शस्यक्षेत्ररुह ओषधिभेदः.

Cornice, s. प्राकारशीर्षं, खोडकशीर्षं, कपिशीर्षं, क्रमशीर्षं, प्राकारशेखरः.

Cornigerous, a. शृङ्गी -ङ्गिणी -ङ्गि (न्), शृङ्गिणः -णा -णं.

Corn-mill, s. धान्यपेषणी, धान्यपेषणयन्त्रं, पेषणं -णिः f.

Corn-rose, s. खसखसजातीय ओषधिप्रभेदः,

Cornucopia, s. चित्रीभूतं सम्पत्तिसूचकं पुष्पफलादिसम्पूर्णं विषाणं, ओघमः.

Cornuted, a. व्यभिचारिणीभार्य्यावान् m. (त्), पुंश्चली स्त्री यस्य सः, बन्धकीभार्य्यः.

Corny, a. (Horny) शार्ङ्गः -र्ङ्गी -र्ङ्गं.—(Producing grain) धान्यवान् -वती -वत् (त्).

Corollary, s. अनुमानं, अपवाहः, सिद्धान्तः, उपलक्ष्यः, अभ्यूहः, ऊहा, युक्तिः f.

Coromandel, s. (Coast of) द्राविडः.

Coronal, s. मुकुटं, किरीटः, मौलिः m. f., शेखरः, माला.

Coronal, a. मस्तकाग्रसम्बन्धीयः -या -यं, मस्तकोपरिस्थः -स्था -स्थं.

Coronary, a. किरीटी -टिनी -टि (न्), मुकुटसम्बन्धीयः -या -यं.

Coronation, s. राजाभिषेकः, अभिषेकः, मुकुटधारणसंस्कारः.—(The hall of coronation) अभिषेकशाला.

Coroner, s. अपमृत्युविचारकः, अपमृत्युकारणपरीक्षकः, अपमृत्युवृत्तान्तविचारको राजप्रतिनिधिः.

Coronet, s. कुलीनवर्गेलाञ्छणिकः क्षुद्रकिरीटः, मौलिः m. f., मुकुटं.

Corporal, s. सेनायां पदभाजां मध्ये अवरपदभाक्, सेनारक्षाध्यक्षः.

Corporal, a. शारीरः -री -रं -रिकः -की -कं, शरीरी -रिणी -रि (न्), दैहिकः -की -कं, देही -हिनी -हि (न्), आङ्गः -ङ्गी -ङ्गं, अङ्गी -ङ्गिनी -ङ्गि (न्), आङ्गिकः -की -कं, अङ्गकः -का -कं, कायिकः -की -कं, कायकः -का -कं. *See* Corporeal.

Corporality, s. मूर्त्तिमत्त्वं, शरीरवत्ता, देहवत्त्वं, शारीरिकत्वं.

Corporally, adv. शरीरतस्, देहतस्, शारीरं, सशरीरं.

Corporate, a. सङ्घातवान् -वती -वत् (त्), कृतसंसर्गः -र्गा -र्गं, सामाजिकः -की -कं, समूहीभूतः -ता -तं.

Corporation, s. (Corporate body) श्रेणी -णिः m. f., ग्रामसङ्घः.

Corporeal, a. शरीरवान् -वती -वत् (त्), मूर्त्तिमान् -मती -मत् (त्), देहवान् -वती -वत् (त्), वपुष्मान् -ष्मती -ष्मत् (त्), सशरीरः -रा -रं, सदेहः -हा -हं, तनुमान् -मती -मत् (त्), विग्रहवान् -वती -वत् (त्), देहभाक् m. f. n. (ज्). *See* Corporal.

Corps, s. (Body of soldiers) सैन्यदलं, सैन्यगुल्मः, दण्डः, अनीकं.

Corpse, s. शवः -वं, कुणपः -पं, मृतकं, मृतशरीरं, मृतदेहः, पञ्चावस्थः, प्रेतं, शपः.

Corpulence or corpulency, s. मेदस्विता, मेदोवृद्धिः f., स्थूलता, शरीरस्थूलता, स्थूलकायत्वं, उन्मेदा, आप्यायनं.

Corpulent, a. स्थूलः -ला -लं, स्थूलकायः -या -यं, पृथूदरः -रा -रं, उदरी -रिणी -रि (न्), मेदस्वी -स्विनी -स्वि (न्), मांसलः -ला -लं, आप्यानः -ना -नं, पीनः -ना -नं, पीवरः -रा -रं, बृहत्कुक्षिः -क्षिः -क्षि, तुन्दवान् -वती -वत् (त्), तुन्दिकः -का -कं, वृद्धनाभिः -भिः -भि, स्थविष्ठः -ष्ठा -ष्ठं.

Corpuscle, s. अणुः m., परमाणुः, कणः, लवः, लेशः, कणिका, कणिकणिका, रेणुः m. f., अणुरेणुः f., सूक्ष्ममूर्त्तिः f.

Corpuscular, a. अणुविषयकः -का -कं, सूक्ष्ममूर्त्तिविषयकः -का -कं.

To correct, v. a. (Amend) शुध् in caus. (शोधयति -यितुं), परिशुध्, विशुध्, संशुध्; समाधा (c. 3. -दधाति -धत्ते -धातुं), निर्दोषं -षां -षं कृ.—(Chastise) शास् (c. 2. शास्ति, शासितुं), अनुशास्, दण्ड् (c. 10. दण्डयति -यितुं).—(Destroy or modify by the addition of opposite qualities) विपरीतगुणप्रक्षेपेण नश् in caus. (नाशयति -यितुं) or शम् in caus. (शमयति -यितुं) or प्रतिकृ.

Correct, a. शुद्धः -द्धा -द्धं, विशुद्धः -द्धा -द्धं, निर्दोषः -षा -षं, दोषरहितः -ता -तं, सत्यः -त्या -त्यं, यथार्थः -र्था -र्थं, ऋतः -ता -तं, तथ्यः -थ्या -थ्यं, अवितथः -था -थं, समञ्जसः -सा -सं, शुचिः -चिः -चि, यथातथः -था -थं, याथार्थिकः -की -कं, यथामार्गः -र्गा -र्गं, स्पष्टः -ष्टा -ष्टं, प्रकृतः -ता -तं.—(Correct in conduct) साधुवृत्तिः -त्तिः -त्ति.

Corrected, p. p. (Amended) शोधितः -ता -तं, विशोधितः -ता -तं.—(Counteracted) प्रतिकृतः -ता -तं.—(Chastised) शासितः -ता -तं, अनुशासितः -ता -तं.

Correction, s. (Chastisement) शास्तिः f., शिष्टिः f., शासनं, अनुशासनं, दण्डः -ण्डनं, साहसं, निग्रहः, प्रतिफलं.—(Amendment) शोधनं, विशोधनं, शुद्धिः f., संशुद्धिः f., प्रतिसमाधानं, समाधानं.

Corrective, a. (Destroying noxious qualities) नाशकः -का -कं -घ्नः -घ्ना -घ्नं in comp., अपनुदः -दा -दं, हरः -रा -रं, अपहः -हा -हं or -हः -हा -हं in comp.—(Counteracting) प्रतीकारकः -का -कं.—(Amending) शोधकः -का -कं.

Corrective, s. प्रतीकारः, प्रतिकारः, प्रतिसमाधानं, अपनोदनं, अभिघातः.

Correctly, adv. शुद्धं, यथार्थं, निर्दोषं, तथ्यं, ऋतं, सत्यं, अञ्जसा, अवितथं, समञ्जसं, शुचि, यथातथं, यथावत्, यथामार्गं, साधु.

Correctness, s. शुद्धत्वं, शुद्धिः f., विशुद्धिः f., निर्दोषता, यथार्थता,

सत्यता, याथातथ्यं, याथार्थ्यं, तथ्यता, सामञ्जस्यं, शुचिता, साधुत्वं.

CORRECTOR, *s.* (Chastiser) शास्ता *m.* (स्तृ), शासिता *m.* (तृ), दण्डप्रणेता *m.* (तृ).—(Amender) शोधकः, शोधनकृत्, समाधाता *m.* (तृ), प्रतिसमाधाता, प्रतिकारकः.

CORRELATIVE, *a.* परस्परसम्बन्धी -न्धिनी -न्धि (न्), अन्योन्यसम्बद्धः -द्धा -द्धं, इतरेतरसम्बद्धः -द्धा -द्धं, व्यतिकरः -रा -रं.

CORRELATIVENESS, *s.* परस्परसम्बन्धित्वं, अन्योन्यसम्बद्धभावः, व्यतिकरः.

To CORRESPOND, *v. n.* (Suit) युज् in pass. (युज्यते), उपयुज्, उपपद् in pass. (-पद्यते), अनुरूपः -पा -पं or सदृशः -शी -शम् अस्, अनुसृ (c. 1. -सरति -सर्तुं).—(Keep up intercourse by alternate letters) परस्परं पत्रलिखनेन संवद् (c. 1. -वदति -दितुं), लेखालेखि कृ, पत्रद्वारेण उत्तरप्रत्युत्तरं कृ.—(Assent) संवद्, अनुवद्.

CORRESPONDENCE, *s.* (Adaptation) योग्यता, युक्तिः *f.*, सादृश्यं, अनुरूपता, आनुरूप्यं, आनुगुण्यं, तुल्यता, समानता, अनुसारः, पर्य्याप्तिः *f.*, उपपत्तिः *f.* —(By letter) परस्परं पत्रलिखनेन संवादः, पत्रविनिमयः, लेखालेखिकरणं.—(Connexion, intercourse) सम्बन्धः, सम्पर्कः, सङ्गः, संसर्गः; 'correspondence of character,' प्रतिभावः.

CORRESPONDENT, *a.* योग्यः -ग्या -ग्यं, सदृशः -शी -शं, अनुरूपः -पा -पं, अनुगुणः -णा -णं, अनुसारी -रिणी -रि (न्), तुल्यः -ल्या -ल्यं, समानः -ना -नं, उपयुक्तः -क्ता -क्तं, पर्य्याप्तः -प्ता -प्तं, सङ्गतः -ता -तं, अविरुद्धः -द्धा -द्धं.

CORRESPONDENT, *s.* (One who interchanges letters) अन्येन सह पत्रलिखनेन संवादी *m.* (न्).—(An agent, a connexion) नियोगी *m.* (न्), प्रतिपुरुषः, सम्पर्की *m.* (न्), सम्बन्धी *m.* (न्).

CORRIDOR, *s.* दुर्गपरिगतश् छन्नपथः, गृहपरितश् छन्नपथः.

CORRIGIBLE, *a.* (Punishable) शासनीयः -या -यं, शास्यः -स्या -स्यं, अनुशासनीयः -या -यं, दण्डनीयः -या -यं.—(Capable of amendment) शोधनीयः -या -यं, साध्यः -ध्या -ध्यं, समाधातुं शक्यः -क्या -क्यं.

CORRIVAL, *s.* सपत्नः, प्रतिस्पर्द्धी *m.* (न्), प्रतियोगी *m.* (न्), प्रतिपक्षः.

CORRIVALRY, *s.* प्रतिस्पर्द्धा, सङ्घर्षः, विजिगीषा, परस्पराभिभवेच्छा.

To CORROBORATE, *v. a.* दृढीकृ, स्थिरीकृ, दृढ (nom. दृढयति -यितुं), संस्तम्भ् (c. 5. -स्तभ्नोति, c. 9. -स्तभ्नाति -स्तम्भितुं or caus. -स्तम्भयति -यितुं), सबलं -लां -लं कृ, सत्याकृ.—(Confirm another's opinion by new evidence) प्रमाणीकृ, प्रमाणं दा, दृढप्रमाणं दा, अनुवद् (c. 1. -वदति -दितुं), परवाक्यं दृढीकृ.

CORROBORATED, *p. p.* दृढीकृतः -ता -तं, स्थिरीकृतः -ता -तं, संस्तब्धः -ब्धा -ब्धं, प्रमाणीकृतः -ता -तं, सत्याकृतः -ता -तं, दृढनिश्चयः -या -यं, सप्रमाणः -णा -णं.

CORROBORATION, *s.* दृढीकरणं, स्थिरीकरणं, दार्ढ्यं, दृढोक्तिः *f.*, संस्तम्भः, सत्याकृतिः *f.*, प्रमाणीकरणं, दृढप्रमाणदानं, अनुवादः.

CORROBORATIVE, *a.* अनुवादकः -का -कं, दृढीकरणः -णा -णं, स्थिरीकरणः -णा -णं.

To CORRODE, *v. a.* क्रमशः क्षि in caus. (क्षययति, क्षपयति -यितुं) or नश् in caus. (नाशयति -यितुं) or भक्ष् (c. 10. भक्षयति -यितुं) or खाद् (c. 1. खादति -दितुं), विली in caus. (-लाययति -यितुं), विलयनं कृ.

CORRODED, *p. p.* क्षीणः -णा -णं, विलीनः -ना -नं, गलितः -ता -तं.

CORRODENT, *a.* क्षयकरः -री -रं, अरुन्तुदः -दा -दं, नाशकः -का -कं.

CORRODIBLE OR CORROSIBLE, *a.* गलनीयः -या -यं, क्षयणीयः -या -यं, विलयनीयः -या -यं, नाश्यः -श्या -श्यं.

CORRODY, *s.* (Assignment of money) निबन्धः, निबन्धदानं.

CORROSION, *s.* क्रमशः क्षयकरणं or नाशनं, विलयनं, गलनं, क्षारणं.

CORROSIVE, *a.* अरुन्तुदः -दा -दं, अरुष्करः -री -रं, तिग्मः -ग्मा -ग्मं, तीव्रः -व्रा -व्रं, विलयनः -ना -नं, मर्म्मस्पृक् *m. f. n.* (श्), मर्म्मभेदी -दिनी -दि (न्), खादकः -का -कं, व्रणकृत् *m. f. n.*, प्रखरः -रा -रं, कटुः -टुः -टु.

CORROSIVENESS, *s.* अरुन्तुदत्वं, अरुष्करत्वं, तैग्म्यं, खादकत्वं, तीव्रता.

To CORRUGATE, *v. a.* (The skin) त्वचं or चर्म्म कुच् (c. 1. कुचति -चितुं) or आकुच् or सङ्कुच् (c. 1. -कोचति -चितुं); त्वक्सङ्कोचं कृ, चर्म्मतरङ्गान् कृ.

CORRUGATION, *s.* कुचनं, आकुचनं, सङ्कोचनं, चर्म्मसङ्कोचः, त्वगाकुचनं.

To CORRUPT, *v. a.* (Vitiate) दुष् in caus. (दूषयति -यितुं), सन्दुष्, प्रतिदुष्; नश् in caus. (नाशयति -यितुं), भ्रष्टीकृ, क्षि in caus. (क्षपयति -यितुं).—(Change to a bad state) विकृ.—(Infect) पूतीकृ, पूतिगन्धं -न्धां -न्धं कृ.—(Bribe) उत्कोचं दा.

To CORRUPT, *v. n.* दुष् (c. 4. दुष्यति, दोष्टुं), विप्रदुष्, सम्प्रदुष्, पूतीभू, पूतिगन्धः -न्धा -न्धं भू, दुर्गन्धः -न्धा -न्धं भू.

CORRUPT, *a.* दुष्टः -ष्टा -ष्टं.—(In morals) दुष्टभावः -वा -वं or विप्रदुष्टभावः, दुष्टमतिः -तिः -ति, असद्दृष्टः -ष्टा -ष्टं, नष्टधीः -धीः -धि, दुराचारः -रा -रं, दुरात्मा -त्मा -त्म (न्), पापचेताः -ताः -तः (स्), शठः -ठा -ठं, मन्दचरित्रः -त्रा -त्रं.—(Stinking) पूतः -ता -तं, पूतिगन्धः -न्धा -न्धं -न्धिः -न्धिः -न्धि, दुर्गन्धः -न्धा -न्धं.

CORRUPTED, *p. p.* दूषितः -ता -तं, नष्टः -ष्टा -ष्टं, नाशितः -ता -तं, भ्रष्टः -ष्टा -ष्टं, विकारितः -ता -तं, विप्लुतः -ता -तं, विशीर्णः -र्णा -र्णं.

CORRUPTER, *s.* दूषकः, दूषणः, दूषणकृत्, नाशकः, भ्रंशकारी *m.* (न्).

CORRUPTIBILITY, *s.* दूषणीयता, दूषयितव्यत्वं, दूषणशीलत्वं, नश्वरता.

CORRUPTIBLE, *a.* दूष्यः -ष्या -ष्यं, दूषणीयः -या -यं, दूषणक्षमः -मा -मं, क्षयी -यिणी -यि (न्), क्षयिष्णुः -ष्णुः -ष्णु, नश्वरः -रा -रं.

CORRUPTION, *s.* (Act of corrupting) दूषणं.—(Putrescence) पूतिः *f.*, पूतता, दुर्गन्धत्वं, पूयं, दूष्यं, गलितत्वं.—(Depravation of morals) दुष्टता, दुष्टभावता, मतिदुष्टता, असद्दुष्टता, दौरात्म्यं, भ्रष्टता, शाठ्यं, दौर्जन्यं.—(In language) अपभ्रंशः, अपशब्दः.

CORRUPTIVE, *a.* दूषकः -का -कं, दूषणः -णा -णं, दूषयिष्णुः -ष्णुः -ष्णु.

CORRUPTLESS, *a.* अदुष्टः -ष्टा -ष्टं, अक्षयः -या -यं, निर्जरः -रा -रं.

CORRUPTLY, *adv.* दुष्टं, सदूषणं, सदोषं, भावदुष्टत्वात्, दुरात्मत्वात्.

CORRUPTNESS, *s.* दुष्टत्वं, दुष्टभावता, भ्रष्टता, कुसृतिः *f.* *See* CORRUPTION.

CORSAIR, *s.* समुद्रयायी दस्युः *m.*, समुद्रीयदस्युः *m.*

CORSE, *s.* शवः, कुणपः -पं, मृतकं, मृतशरीरं. *See* CORPSE.

CORSET, *s.* चेलिका, चोलः -ली, अङ्गिका, कञ्चुलिका, कूर्पासकः -कं.

CORSLET, *s.* कवचः -चं, उरस्त्राणं, वक्षस्त्राणं, उरश्छदः, शरीररक्षणी.

CORTICAL, *a.* वाल्कलः -ली -लं, त्वङ्मयः -यी -यं, त्वाचः -ची -चं.

CORTICATED, *a.* वृक्षवल्कलोपमः -मा -मं, तरुत्वग्रूपः -पी -पं.

CORUSCANT, *a.* स्फुरन् -रन्ती -रत् (त्), विद्योतमानः -ना -नं, उज्ज्वलः -ला -लं.

To CORUSCATE, *v. n.* स्फुर् (c. 6. स्फुरति -रितुं), विद्युत् (c. 1. -द्योतते -तितुं).

CORUSCATION, *s.* स्फुरणं, स्फुरितं, विद्युद्दाम *n.* (न्), छटा, विद्युदाभा.

CORYMBIFEROUS, *a.* गुच्छाकारफलविशिष्टः -ष्टा -ष्टं.

COSINE, *s.* ज्या, ज्यका.—(Of a right-angled triangle) कोटिज्या.

COSMETIC, *a.* त्वक्कान्तिकरः -री -रं, कान्तिवर्द्धकः -का -कं, अङ्गरागकारी -रिणी -रि (न्), शोभकृत्; 'a cosmetic,' गात्रमार्जनद्रव्यं.

COSMICAL, *a.* जगत्सम्बन्धीयः -या -यं, पार्थिवः -वी -वं.

COSMOGONY, *s.* जगदुत्पत्तिः *f.*, जगत्सृष्टिः *f.*, पृथिवीसृष्टिः *f.*, पृथिव्युत्पत्तिः.

COSMOGRAPHER, *s.* जगद्विवरणकृत्, जगद्वर्णनकर्त्ता *m.* (र्तृ), पृथिवीविवरणरचकः.

COSMOGRAPHICAL, *a.* जगद्विवरणविषयः -या -यं, जगद्वर्णनसम्बन्धीयः -या -यं.

COSMOGRAPHY, *s.* जगद्विवरणं, जगद्वर्णनं, पृथिवीविवरणविद्या.

Cosmopolite, *s.* जगद्वासी *m.* (न्), पृथिवीवासी, सर्व्वत्रवासी, सर्व्वत्रस्थायी *m.* (न्), सर्व्वदेशवासी *m.* (न्), निर्व्विशेषेण सर्व्वलोकाभिज्ञं.

Cost, *s.* (Price) मूल्यं, अर्घः.—(Expense) व्ययः; 'high cost,' दुर्मूल्यं, बहुमूल्यं, माहार्घ्यं; 'little cost,' अल्पमूल्यं, अल्पव्ययः; 'at the cost of life,' प्राणव्ययेन; 'at the cost of a large sum,' बहुधनव्ययेन.

To cost, *v. n.* अर्घ् (c. 10. अर्घयति -यितुं). Usually expressed by the inst. c. of मूल्यं or व्ययः in conjunction with some other verb; as, 'what does it cost?' कियता मूल्येन विक्रीयते; 'the building of the house cost a large sum of money,' बहुधनव्ययेन गृहं निर्म्मितं.

Costal, *a.* पञ्जरसम्बन्धी -न्धिनी -न्धि (न्), पार्श्वीयः -या -यं.

Costive, *a.* आनद्धः -द्धा -द्धं, निबद्धः -द्धा -द्धं, बद्धकोष्ठः -ष्ठा -ष्ठं, अवरुद्धमलः -ला -लं, बद्धमलः -ला -लं. *See* Constipated.

Costiveness, *s.* मलावरोधः, मलावष्टम्भः, आनाहः, नाहः, निबन्धः, बद्धकोष्ठं.

Costliness, *s.* बहुमूल्यता, महार्घता, माहार्घ्यं, महार्हता, दुर्मूल्यता.

Costly, *a.* बहुमूल्यः -ल्या -ल्यं, महार्घः -र्घा -र्घं, महाधनः -ना -नं, महार्हः -र्हा -र्हं, दुर्मूल्यः -ल्या -ल्यं, उत्कृष्टः -ष्टा -ष्टं, अर्घार्हः -र्हा -र्हं, अर्घ्यः -र्घ्या -र्घ्यं.

Costume, *s.* (Dress) वेशः -षः, नेपथ्यं.—(Conformity of dress), वेषसारूप्यं.

Cot, *s.* कुटीरः, कुटेरः, कुटिरं, उटजः, कुट्टिमः -मं, वेश्म *n.* (न्), पर्णशाला, तृणकुटी, तृणौकः *n.* (स्), कायमानं.—(A small bed) खट्वा, दोला, प्रेङ्खा, प्रेङ्खोलनं.

Cotemporary, *a.* समानकालीनः -ना -नं, एककालीनः -ना -नं, समकालवर्त्ती -र्त्तिनी -र्त्ति (न्), सवयाः -याः -यः (स्), समानवयस्कः -स्का -स्कं. *See* Contemporary.

Coterie, *s.* भोगासक्तजनानां संसर्गः or पंक्तिः *f.* or गणः.

Cotquean, *s.* गेहशूरः, गेहनर्द्दी *m.* (न्), गेहमेही *m.* (न्), स्त्रीकार्य्यचर्चकः.

Cottage, *s.* कुटीरः, उटजः, वेश्म *n.* (न्), पर्णशाला. *See* Cot.

Cottager or cotter, *s.* कुटीरवासी *m.* (न्), ग्रामवासी *m.*, ग्रामीयः.

Cottier, *s.* कुटीरस्थः, उटजवासी *m.* (न्), ग्रामीणः.

Cotton, *s.* पिचुलः, पिचुः, पिचुतूलं, तूलः -लं, तूलकं, तूलपिचुः *m.*, बदरा -री.—(The plant) कर्पासी, कार्पासी, पिचव्यः; 'roll of cotton,' तूलनाली.—(Cotton cloth) कार्पासं, कार्पासाम्बरं, तूलावस्त्रं, अम्बरं, फालवस्त्रं.

Cottony, *a.* कार्पासः -सी -सं -सिकः -की -कं, फालः -ली -लं, बादरः -री -रं.

Couch, *s.* केलिशयनं, शय्या, शयनीयं, शयः -यनं, पर्य्यङ्कः, मञ्चः, प्रस्तरः, प्रस्तारः, तल्पः, पालङ्कः, विश्रामस्थानं.

To couch, *v. n.* शी (c. 2. शेते, शयितुं), शयनं कृ, संविश् (c. 6. -विशति -वेष्टुं).

To couch, *v. a.* (Cause to lie, lay down) शी in caus. (शाययति -यितुं), निधा (c. 3. -दधाति -धातुं), निविश् in caus. (-वेशयति -यितुं).—(Comprise) परिग्रह् (c. 9. -गृह्णाति -ग्रहीतुं).—(Hide) छद् (c. 10. छादयति -यितुं).—(Cut out cataract of the eye) नेत्रमन्यम् उच्छिद् (c. 7. -छिनत्ति -छेत्तुं).

Couchant, *a.* शायी -यिनी -यि (न्), शयितः -ता -तं, शयः -या -यं.

Couched, *p. p.* (Hidden, involved, comprised) समाच्छन्नः -न्ना -न्नं, छादितः -ता -तं, समाविष्टः -ष्टा -ष्टं, उपलक्षितः -ता -तं, सन्नद्धः -द्धा -द्धं, संसृष्टः -ष्टा -ष्टं, अन्तर्गतः -ता -तं.

Couchfellow, *s.* सहशायी *m.* -यिनी *f.* (न्), एकपर्य्यङ्कशायी, सहशयनः.

Couchgrass, *s.* तृणविशेषः, तृणं, कक्षः.

Cough, *s.* काशः, कासः, उत्कासः -सनं, क्षिवायः, क्षवः, क्षवथुः *m.*, क्षुत् *f.*, क्षुतः -ता; 'having a cough,' काशी -शिनी -शि (न्), क्षुतवान् -वती -वत् (त्).

To cough, *v. n.* कास् (c. 1. कासते -सितुं), क्षु (c. 2. क्षौति, क्षवितुं).—(Coughing up of phlegm) उत्कासनं.

Cougher, *s.* काशी *m.* (न्), उत्कासी *m.* (न्), खुत्कारी *m.* (न्), क्षवकृत्.

Coulter, *s.* लाङ्गलदण्डः, फालदण्डः, लाङ्गलकीलः, कृन्तत्रं, गोदारणं.

Council, *s.* सभा, समाजः, सदः *n.* (स्), संसद् *f.*; 'council of state,' शिष्टसभा, महासभा; 'privy council,' मन्त्रिसभा, गूढसभा; 'council-room,' चिन्तावेश्म *n.* (न्), मन्त्रशाला, दार्व्वटं.

Counsel, *s.* (Advice) मन्त्रः -न्त्रणं -णा, उपदेशः, उपदिष्टं, मन्त्रितं, मन्त्रोपष्टम्भः.—(Deliberation) विचारः -रणं, चिन्ता, सुचिन्ता, संचिन्तनं, विवेचनं, मर्शः, आमर्शः, परामर्शः, प्रत्यवमर्शः; 'good counsel,' सुमन्त्रितं; 'betraying of counsel,' मन्त्रभेदः.—(Plan, scheme, design) उपायः, व्यवसायः, चिन्ता, अभिप्रायः.—(Advocate, pleader) प्रतिवादी *m.* (न्), प्रतिनिधिः *m.*

To counsel, *v. a.* मन्त्र् (c. 10. मन्त्रयते -ति -यितुं), सम्मन्त्र्, मन्त्रणां कृ, मन्त्रं दा, उपदिश् (c. 6. -दिशति -देष्टुं), आदिश्, प्रत्यादिश्, परामर्शं कृ.

Counselled, *p. p.* मन्त्रितः -ता -तं, उपदिष्टः -ष्टा -ष्टं, आदिष्टः -ष्टा -ष्टं.

Counsellor, *s.* (On public affairs) मन्त्री *m.* (न्), अमात्यः, सचिवः.—(Adviser in general) मन्ता *m.* (न्तृ), अभिमन्ता *m.* (न्तृ), मन्त्रकृत्, मन्त्रवित्, मन्त्रदः, मन्त्रज्ञः, उपदेशकः, उपदेष्टा *m.* (ष्टृ), आदेष्टा *m.*, बुद्धिसहायः, भाक्तिहरः, कुल्यः.—(Courtier) शिष्टः.

Counsellorship, *s.* मन्त्रित्वं, साचिव्यं, प्रधानमन्त्रिपदं, अमात्यत्वं.

Count, *s.* (Reckoning) गणना -नं, गणितं, संख्या, गणितसंख्या.—(A title of foreign nobility) विदेशीयख्यातिविशेषः.—(Charge in an indictment) पूर्व्वपक्षपादः, भाषापादं, अभियोगः.

To count, *v. a.* (Number) सङ्ख्या (c. 2. -ख्याति -तुं), सम्परिख्या, परिसङ्ख्या, कल् (c. 10. कलयति -यितुं), अङ्क् (c. 10. अङ्कयति -यितुं).—(Calculate) गण् (c. 10. गणयति -यितुं), विगण्, प्रगण्.—(Esteem) मन् (c. 4. मन्यते, मन्तुं or caus. मानयति -यितुं), सम्मन्, प्रतिमन्.

To count-upon, *v. a.* अवलम्ब् (c. 1. -लम्बते -म्बितुं), समालम्ब्, संश्रि (c. 1. -श्रयति -ते -यितुं), समाश्रि, उपाश्रि; विश्वस् (c. 2. -श्वसिति -तुं); 'counting upon,' अवलम्बः.

Counted, *p. p.* संख्यातः -ता -तं, गणितः -ता -तं, अङ्कितः -ता -तं, मतः -ता -तं.

Countenance, *s.* (Face) मुखं, आननं, वदनं, आस्यं, वक्त्रं.—(Air, look) वदनं, रूपं, आकारः, आभा.—(Sanction, patronage) दृष्टिः *f.*, अनुग्रहः, आग्रहः, सङ्ग्रहः, आश्रयः, आधारः, अनुपालनं, संवर्द्धनं, प्रसादः, आनुकूल्यं, साहाय्यं, उपकारः; 'one who preserves a composed countenance,' प्रसन्नमुखी *m.* (न्).

To countenance, *v. a.* अनुग्रह् (c. 9. -गृह्णाति -ग्रहीतुं), अनुपाल् (c. 10. -पालयति -यितुं), प्रतिपाल्, अनुकूल् (nom. अनुकूलयति -यितुं), संवृध् in caus. (-वर्धयति -यितुं), उपकृ, साहाय्यं कृ.

Countenancer, *s.* अनुग्राही *m.* (न्), अनुपालकः, उपकारकः, संवर्धकः, सहायः.

Counter, *s.* (Table to count money on) गणनफलकं, वणिक्फलकं, वणिजां मुद्रासनं.—(Round piece to count with) गणनार्थं मुद्रा or काकिणी or कपर्द्दकः or वटः or वराटकः or वटीला or अक्षः.

Counter, *adv.* प्रति, अभि, प्रतिकूलं, विरुद्धं, विपरीतं, प्रातिकूल्येन, विरोधेन, प्रतिमुखं, प्रतिलोमं, विलोमं; 'a counter-charge,' प्रत्यभियोगः; 'a counter-pledge,' प्रतिपणः.

To counteract, *v. a.* प्रतिकृ, विप्रतिकृ, विप्रकृ, प्रतिहन् (c. 2. -हन्ति, -हन्तुं), प्रतीकारेण or प्रतियत्नेन विरुध् (c. 7. -रुणद्धि -रोद्धुं) or प्रतिरुध् or निवृ in caus. (-वारयति -यितुं), प्रतिकूल (nom. प्रतिकूलयति -यितुं).

Counteracted, *p. p.* प्रतिकृतः -ता -तं, विप्रतिकृतः -ता -तं, विप्रकृतः -ता -तं.

Counteraction, *s.* प्रतीकारः, प्रतिकारः, विप्रतिकारः, प्रतिक्रिया, विप्रकारः, विप्रकृतिः *f.*, प्रतिघातः, प्रतियत्नः, प्रतियोगः, विपरीतक्रिया, विरुद्धक्रिया, व्याघातः, अभिघातः.

To counterbalance, *v. a.* प्रतितुल् (c. 10. -तुलयति -यितुं), समीकृ, समतोलीकृ, तुल्यीकृ, तुल्यबलं -लां -लं कृ, तुल्यभारं -रां -रं कृ, समानीकृ.

To counterbuff, *v. a.* प्रतिहन् (c. 2. -हन्ति -हन्तुं), अभिहन्, प्रतिघातं कृ.

Counterbuff, *s.* प्रतिघातः, प्रतिहतिः *f.*, प्रतीघातः, अभिघातः.

Counterchange, *s.* परिवर्त्तः -र्त्तनं, विनिमयः, विपर्य्ययः, परस्परपरिवर्त्तनं, आदानप्रतिदानं, व्यतिकरः, इतरेतरयोगः.

To counterchange, *v. a.* परस्परं परिवृत् in caus. (-वर्त्तयति -यितुं) or विनिमे (c. 1. -मयते -मातुं) or आदानप्रतिदानं कृ.

To countercharm, *v. a.* मन्त्रं or अभिचारं or वशक्रियां प्रतिकृ, मन्त्रच्छेदं कृ.

Countercheck, *s.* प्रतिरोधः, प्रतिष्टम्भः, प्रतिबन्धः, प्रतिषेधः, प्रतिघातः.

Counterevidence, *s.* प्रतिकूलसाक्षी *m.* (न्), विरुद्धसाक्ष्यं, विपरीतसाक्ष्यं, प्रतिपक्षप्रमाणं.

To counterfeit, *v. a.* (Feign) छल (nom. छलयति -यितुं), छद्म कृ, कपटं कृ, कूटं कृ; 'to counterfeit a writing,' कपटलेख्यं or कूटलेखं कृ.—(Imitate) अनुकृ.—(Impose upon) प्रलभ् (c. 1. -लभते -लब्धुं), प्रतॄ in caus. (-तारयति -यितुं); 'to counterfeit sleep,' मिथ्याप्रसुप्तः -प्ता -प्तं भू; 'he counterfeits sleep,' आत्मानं प्रसुप्तमिव दर्शयति.

Counterfeit, *s.* कूटं, कपटः -टं, छद्म *n.* (न्), व्याजः.—(Forgery) कपटलेखः -ख्यं.

Counterfeit, *a.* कृत्रिमः -मा -मं, कल्पितः -ता -तं, छाद्मिकः -की -कं, लक्ष्यः -क्ष्या -क्ष्यं, सव्याजः -जा -जं, कपटी -टिनी -टि (न्); 'a counterfeit dress,' कपटवेशः, छद्मवेशः; 'counterfeit gold,' कूटस्वर्णं; 'counterfeit writing,' कपटलेख्यं; 'counterfeit order,' कूटशासनं.

Counterfeiter, *s.* (Forger) कूटकः, कूटकृत्, कपटलेख्यकारी *m.* (न्).—(Imposter) कापटिकः, छली *m.* (न्), प्रतारकः, वञ्चकः.

Counterfeitly, *adv.* मिथ्या, सकूटं, सकपटं, सव्याजं, छद्मना, कृत्रिमप्रकारेण.

To countermand, *v. a.* प्रत्यादिश् (c. 6. -दिशति -देष्टुं), प्रत्याज्ञा in caus. (-ज्ञापयति -यितुं), विपरीताज्ञां दा, अन्यथा आज्ञा in caus.

Countermand, *s.* विपरीताज्ञा, प्रत्यादेशः, विपरीतादेशः.

To countermarch, *v. n.* प्रतिक्रम् (c. 1. -क्रामति -क्रमितुं), व्यतिक्रम्, विपरीतयात्रां कृ, प्रतिया (c. 2. -याति -तुं), विपरीतं या.

Countermarch, *s.* विपरीतयात्रा, प्रतियानं, प्रतिगमनं, विपरीतगतिः *f.*, व्यतिक्रमः, प्रतियात्रा.

Countermark, *s.* प्रतिचिह्नं, प्रतिलक्षणं, चिह्नं चिह्नेन सहितं.

To countermark, *v. a.* प्रतिचिह्न (nom. -चिह्नयति -यितुं), चिह्नं चिह्नेन दृढीकृ.

Countermine, *s.* प्रतिसुरुङ्गा, प्रतिसन्धिः *m.*, प्रतिखानिकं, शत्रुसुरुङ्गाभिमुखगता सुरुङ्गा.

To countermine, *v. a.* प्रतिसुरुङ्गां कृ, शत्रुसन्धिप्रतिमुखम् अन्यसन्धिं खन् (c. 1. खनति -नितुं).

Countermure, *s.* प्राचीरपश्चात् प्राचीरं, प्राकारस्य पश्चाद् उपप्राकारः.

Counterpane or counterpoint, *s.* शय्याप्रच्छदः. शयनीयप्रच्छदपटः, शय्याच्छादनं, शयनास्तरणं.

Counterpart, *s.* प्रतिरूपं, प्रतियोगः, प्रतियोगी *m.* (न्), प्रतिमूर्त्तिः *f.*, प्रतिमा, प्रतिमानं, प्रतिबिम्बं, अनुरूपं.

Counterplea, *s.* प्रत्यर्थं, प्रत्यभियोगः, प्रत्युत्तरं, उद्ग्राहः.

Counterplot, *s.* प्रतियत्नः, प्रतियोगः, प्रतिचेष्टा, प्रतीकारः, प्रत्युपायः.

To counterplot, *v. a.* उपायं प्रत्यु अन्योपायं प्रयुज् (c. 7. -युनक्ति -योक्तुं).

To counterpoise, *v. a.* प्रतितुल् (c. 10. -तुलयति -यितुं), तुल्यभारं -रां -रं कृ, तुल्यबलं -लां -लं कृ, तुल्यीकृ, समतोलीकृ, समीकृ.

Counterpoise, *s.* तुल्यभारत्वं, तुल्यबलत्वं -ता, समतोलत्वं.

Counter-poison, *s.* प्रतिविषं, विषनाशनं, विषघ्नं, गरघ्नं,

Counterscarp, *s.* कटकनिकटवर्त्ती परिखापार्श्वः.

To countersign, *v. a.* परहस्ताक्षरं स्वहस्ताक्षरेण दृढीकृ.

Countersign, *s.* प्रत्याभिज्ञानं.—(Watchword) सम्भाषा, संविद्.

Counter-tenor, *s.* उदात्तविपरीतः स्वरमार्गः.

Counter-tide, *s.* प्रतिवेला, विपरीतवेला, प्रतिरयः, विपरीतप्रवाहः.

To countervail, *v. a.* तुल्यबलः -ला -लम् अस्, तुल्यीभू, समानबलीभू.

Countess, *s.* विशिष्टपदस्थितस्य कुलीनपुरुषस्य पत्नी.

Counting, *s.* गणनं -ना.—(Counting-house) लेख्यस्थानं.

Countless, *a.* असंख्येयः -या -यं, असंख्यः -ख्या -ख्यं, असंख्यकः -का -कं, अगण्यः -ण्या -ण्यं, अगणनीयः -या -यं, लक्षगुणः -णा -णं, अस्तसंख्यः -ख्या -ख्यं.

Country, *s.* (A region) देशः, प्रदेशः, विषयः, राष्ट्रं, दिश् *f.* (श्), आशा, तायिकः, भिष्ण्यं; 'inhabitated country,' जनपदः, नीवृत्; 'barbarous country,' म्लेच्छदेशः.—(As opposed to the town) ग्रामः, जनपदः.—(Native country) जन्मभूमिः *f.*, स्वदेशः, स्वराष्ट्रं, स्वविषयः.—(Country-road) दिङ्मार्गः.

Country, *a.* जानपदः -दी -दं, ग्राम्यः -म्या -म्यं, ग्रामीयः -या -यं.

Country-dance, *s.* पंक्तिक्रमेण सम्मुखस्थानां स्त्रीपुरुषाणां नृत्यं.

Country-house, *s.* जाङ्गलप्रदेशे गृहं, पौरजनस्य नगरोपान्ते खेलिगृहं.

Country-life, *s.* जानपदानां व्यवहारः or व्यापारः, जनपदे or जङ्गलदेशे वर्त्तनं, वनवर्त्तिभिः प्रवृत्तं जीवनं.

Countryman, *s.* (Rustic) जानपदः, ग्राम्यजनः, ग्रामवासी *m.* (न्), ग्रामी *m.* (न्), ग्रामीयः.—(Fellow-countryman) स्वदेशीयः, स्वदेशजः, एकदेशस्थः, संस्थः, सांस्थानिकः, एकग्रामीणः, एकपौरः.

Country-parson, *s.* ग्राम्यगुरुः *m.*, ग्रामवासिनाम् आचार्य्यः, जानपदानां पुरोहितः.

County, *s.* मण्डलं, चक्रं, देशः, प्रदेशः, राष्ट्रं.

Couple, *s.* (A brace) मिथुनं, द्वन्द्वं, युगं, युग्मं, युगलं, यमलं, यामलं, यमः, यमकं, द्वयं in comp.; as, 'a couple of men,' पुरुषद्वयं; 'a couple of oxen,' गोयुगं, गोमिथुनं; 'a married couple,' दम्पती *m. du.* भार्य्यापती *m. du.*—(A tie for fastening two dogs together) कुक्कुरद्वयसम्बन्धनार्थं रज्जुः or शृङ्खला.

To couple, *v. a.* संयुज् (c. 7. -युनक्ति -योक्तुं), सन्धा (c. 3. -दधाति -धातुं), संश्लिष् in caus. (-श्लेषयति -यितुं), सम्बन्ध् (c. 9. -बध्नाति -बन्द्धुं), एकत्र कृ.

To couple, *v. n.* भार्य्यापतिभावेन सङ्गम् (c. 1. -गच्छति -गन्तुं) or सम्मिल् (c. 6. -मिलति -मेलितुं), मैथुनं कृ, विवाहं कृ.

Couplet, *s.* (Two lines in verse) श्लोकः.

Courage or courageousness, *s.* वीर्य्यं, वीरता, शौर्य्यं, शूरता, धीरत्वं, धैर्य्यं, विक्रमः, पराक्रमः, निर्भयता, साहसं, पौरुषं, धार्ष्ट्यं, तेजः *n.* (स्), प्रतापः; 'to take courage,' आश्वस् (c. 2. -श्वसिति -सितुं), प्रत्याश्वस्, समाश्वस्; 'to inspire with courage,' आश्वस् in caus. (-श्वासयति -यितुं), समाश्वस् in caus.

Courageous, *a.* वीरः -रा -रं, प्रवीरः -रा -रं, शूरः -रा -रं, धीरः -रा -रं, निर्भयः -या -यं, अभीतः -ता -तं, अभीरुः -रुः -रु, विक्रान्तः -न्ता -न्तं, पराक्रान्तः -न्ता -न्तं, साहसिकः -की -कं, धृष्टः -ष्टा -ष्टं,

Courageously, *adv.* सवीर्य्यं, सशौर्य्यं, वीर्य्येण, सधैर्य्यं, सविक्रमं, निर्भयं,

अभीतवत्, वीरवत्, शूरवत्, साहसपूर्व्वकं.

COURIER, *s.* वार्त्ताहरः, जङ्घालः, उड्डेगः, वेगी *m.* (न्), प्रजवी *m.* (न्), तरस्वी *m.* (न्), जङ्घाकारिकः, जङ्घालः, जाङ्घिकः, तूः *m.* (तुर्).—(Bearing letters) लेखहारी *m.* (न्).

COURSE, *s.* (Career) गतिः *f.*, चर्य्या, मार्गः, चलनं, गमनं.—(Progress) क्रमः, प्रक्रमः, प्रगमनं.—(Room, scope) प्रसरः.—(Track) पथः, मार्गः, पदवी, अयनं.—(Ship's course) नौमार्गः, नौपथः.—(Course of an arrow) बाणगोचरं, शरायणं, बाणायणं.—(Line of study) अध्ययनमार्गः, अध्ययनक्रमः; 'course of mathematics,' गणितमार्गः.—(Order of succession) क्रमः, अनुक्रमः, पर्य्यायः, आनुपूर्व्यं, परम्परा, श्रेणी, आवलिः *f.*—(Course of proceeding) क्रियाप्रसङ्गः, क्रियाविधिः *m.*, अनुष्ठानं.—(Manner) रीतिः *f.*, विधः, विधिः *m.*, प्रकारः, मार्गः.—(Manner of life or conduct) व्यवहारः, वृत्तिः *f.*, रीतिः *f.*, आचारः, चरित्रं, सृतिः *f.*; 'correct course of conduct,' सुमार्गः, सुपथः; 'incorrect course,' उन्मार्गः, विमार्गः, उत्पथः, विपथः, कुपथः, कुसृतिः *f.*—(Course or flow of a river) नदीपद्धतिः *f.*, नदीप्रवाहः, नदीरयः.—(Race-ground) चर्य्याभूमिः *f.*, वाजिधावनस्थानं.—(Number of dishes set on the table at once) यावन्ति भोजनपात्राणि युगपत् परिवेष्यन्ते.—(Catamenia) ऋतुः *m.*, रजः *n.* (स्), आर्त्तवं, पुष्पं; 'of course,' अवश्यं, निःसन्देहं, नूनं, सुनिश्चितं, असंशयं; 'in the course,' मध्ये; 'in the course of three years,' वर्षत्रयमध्ये; 'being in the course of proof,' साध्यमानः -ना -नं; 'course of nature,' सृष्टेरीतिः *f.*

To COURSE, *v. a.* and *n.* कुक्कुरैः शशकम् अनुसृ (c. 1. -सरति -सर्त्तुं), दृष्टिगोचरशशकानुसरणे शिक्षितैः कुक्कुरैर् मृगयां कृ.

COURSER, *s.* (Fleet horse) जवनः, जवाधिकः, जवी *m.* (न्).—(War-horse) वारकीरः.

COURT, *s.* (An inclosed place, a square) चत्वरं, अङ्गनं, प्राङ्गणं, चतुःशालं -ला, चतुश्शाला, निवसथः, प्रकोष्ठः, कक्ष्या; 'court of a house,' गृहाङ्गणं.—(Prince's residence) राजशाला, राजसभा, शाला, सभा, राजगृहं, राजमन्दिरं, राजधानी, राजधाम *n.* (न्), नृपवेश्म *n.* (न्), राजद्वारं.—(Court of justice) धर्म्मसभा, राजद्वारं, व्यवहारमण्डपः, विचारस्थानं, धर्म्माधिकरणं, सदः *n.* (स्); 'court-house,' दाण्डिकं.—(The judges) धर्म्माधिकारिणः *m. pl.*, प्राड्विवाकाः *m. pl.*, धर्म्माध्यक्षाः *m. pl.*—(The retinue of the prince) तन्त्रं, राजपरिवारः, राजपरिजनः, परिबर्हः.—(Endeavour to please, civility) अनुनयः, सभाजनं, आराधनं, आनन्दनं, अनुवृत्तिः *f.*, अनुकूलता, भजनं, भक्तिः *f.*

To COURT, *v. a.* (Endeavour to please, conciliate) अनुनी (c. 1. -नयति -नेतुं), आराध् in caus. (-राधयति -यितुं), अनुरञ्ज् in caus. (-रञ्जयति -यितुं), सेव् (c. 1. सेवते -वितुं), आश्रि (c. 1. -श्रयते -यितुं), भज् (c. 1. भजते, भक्तुं), सभाज् (c. 10. सभाजयति -यितुं).—(Solicit) प्रार्थ् (c. 10. -अर्थयते -ति -यितुं), याच् (c. 1. याचति -चितुं),—(Solicit to marriage) विवाहार्थं स्त्रियं प्रार्थ् or उपास् (c. 1. आस्ते -आसितुं).

COURT-CHAPLAIN, *s.* राजपुरोहितः, राजाचार्य्यः, राजगुरुः *m.*, राजविप्रः.

COURTED, *p. p.* अनुनीतः -ता -तं, आराधितः -ता -तं, अनुरञ्जितः -ता -तं, सभाजितः -ता -तं, सेवितः -ता -तं, अनुरुद्धः -द्धा -द्धं, प्रार्थितः -ता -तं.

COURT-DAY, *s.* विचारदिनं, विचारदिवसः, धर्म्मप्रणयनदिवसः.

COURT-FAVOUR, *s.* वाल्लभ्यं, राजानुग्रहः, राजप्रसादः.

COURTEOUS, *a.* अनुनयी -यिनी -यि (न्), अनुरोधी -धिनी -धि (न्), अनुकूलः -ला -लं, अनुग्राही -हिणी -हि (न्), सविनयः -या -यं, सानुनयः -या -यं, प्रश्रितः -ता -तं, सभ्यः -भ्या -भ्यं, प्रियंवदः -दा -दं, वल्गुवाक्यः -क्या -क्यं, सान्त्ववादः -दा -दं; 'courteous language,' सूनृतं; as in the phrase 'we are happy that you are come,' धन्या वयं भवदागमनात्.

COURTEOUSLY, *adv.* सानुनयं, सविनयं, सानन्दनं, सानुरोधं, सभाजनपूर्व्वं.

COURTEOUSNESS, *s.* सभ्यता, अनुकूलता, सुशीलता, शिष्टता, अभिनीतिः *f.*

COURTESY, *s.* अनुनयः, विनयः, अनुकूलता, अनुरोधः, अनुग्रहः, आनन्दनं, सभाजनं, सभाजनं, प्रणयः, प्रश्रयः, अनुवृत्तिः *f.* -वर्त्तनं, सौजन्यं, दाक्षिण्यं; 'in receiving or taking leave of a friend,' आमन्त्रणं, आप्रच्छनं; 'treated with courtesy,' सभाजितः -ता -तं.

COURTEZAN, *s.* वेश्या, गणिका, पण्यस्त्री, पण्याङ्गना, वारविलासिनी, वारस्त्री, बन्धकी, साधारणस्त्री, पुंश्चली, चर्षणी, रूपाजीवा.

COURTIER, *s.* राजवल्लभः, नृपवल्लभः, सभास्थो जनः, राजसेवकः, राजभृत्यः, सभ्यः, सभ्यलोकः, शिष्टः, राजसभासद्.

COURT-LIKE, *a.* सभ्यः -भ्या -भ्यं, शिष्टाचारः -रा -रं, सभ्याचारः -रा -रं.

COURTLINESS, *s.* सभ्यता, शिष्टता, सौजन्यं, सुजनता, सुशीलता.

COURTLY, *a.* सभ्यशीलः -ला -लं, सुजनः -ना -नं, सुन्दरः -री -रं.

COURT-MINION, *s.* राजवल्लभः, नृपवल्लभः, राजप्रियः.

COURTSHIP, *s.* (Of a woman) विवाहार्थं प्रार्थनं -ना or याञ्चा, स्त्र्युपासनं.—(Soliciting favour) आराधनं, अनुरञ्जनं, भजनं, आनन्दनं.

COURT-YARD, *s.* अङ्गनं, प्राङ्गणं, चत्वरं, चतुःशालं -ला, अभ्यन्तरचतुःशालकः, अजिरं, गृहाङ्गणं, गृहप्राङ्गणं, प्रकोष्ठः.

COUSIN, *s.* (Male, by father's brother) पितृव्यपुत्रः, पितृभ्रात्रीयः.—(Female) पितृव्यपुत्री, पितृभ्रात्रीया.—(Male, by father's sister) पितृष्वस्रीयः, पितृष्वसेयः.—(Female) पितृष्वस्रीया, पितृष्वसेयी.—(Male, by mother's brother) मातुलपुत्रः, मातृभ्रात्रीयः.—(Female) मातुलपुत्री, मातृभ्रात्रीया.—(Male, by mother's sister) मातृष्वस्रीयः, मातृष्वसेयः.—(Female) मातृष्वस्रीया, मातृष्वसेयी.—(A kinsman) ज्ञातिः *m.*, बान्धवः, सहजमित्रं.

COVE, *s.* वङ्कुः, खञ्जः, खातं, अखातं, पोतबन्धनस्थानं.

COVENANT, *s.* नियमः, संविद् *f.*, समयः, पणः, सङ्कट्टनं, समाधिः *m.*, उपगमः, संश्रवः; 'written covenant,' नियमपत्रं; 'covenant-breaker,' समयभेदी *m.* (न्), नियमलङ्घी *m.* (न्).

To COVENANT, *v. n.* नियमं कृ, नियमीकृ, समयं कृ, समयाकृ, सङ्कट्ट् (c. 1. -सङ्कट्टते -ट्टितुं), संविदम् उपगम् (c. 1. -गच्छति -गन्तुं), पणं कृ, पण् (c. 1. पणते -णितुं, पणायति -यितुं).

COVENANTED, *p. p.* नियमितः -ता -तं, संविदितः -ता -तं, पणितः -ता -तं.

COVENANTER, *s.* सामयिकः, नियमबद्धः, नैयमिकः, नियमकारी *m.* (न्).

COVER, *s.* (Any thing put over another) छादनं, आच्छादनं, आवरणं, पिधानं, पटलं, पुटः -टी -टं.—(Screen) व्यवधा -धानं, पटः -टं, अवगुण्ठनं.—(Wrapper) प्रावारः, प्रवारः, आच्छादनवस्त्रं, प्रच्छदपटः, उत्तरच्छदः, उत्तरीयं, निचोलः.—(Lid) मुद्गः, पिधानं, शरावः, वर्द्धमानकः.—(Of a dish) कूर्म्मपृष्ठकं.—(Of a book) पुस्तकवस्त्रं, पुस्तकाच्छादनं.—(Of a well) विनाहः, वीनाहः, नान्दीपटः, नान्दीमुखः.—(Of a carriage) रथगुप्तिः *f.*, रथगोपनं.—(Pretext) छद्म *n.* (न्), व्यपदेशः, अपदेशः.—(Shelter) संश्रयः, समाश्रयः.

To COVER, *v. a.* (Put one thing over another) छद् (c. 10. छादयति -ते -यितुं), आच्छद्, समाच्छद्, प्रच्छद्, परिच्छद्, प्रतिच्छद्, संछद्, अवच्छद्, वृ (c. 5. वृणोति, c. 9. वृणाति, वरितुं -रीतुं), आवृ, समावृ, निवृ, संवृ; पिधा (c. 3. -दधाति -धातुं), अपिधा, अवतन् (c. 8. -तनोति -तनितुं).—(Put on in quantities) आचि (c. 5. -चिनोति -चेतुं), समाचि,

वृ (c. 5. वृणोति -णाति, वरितुं -रीतुं), आवृ.—(Conceal, veil) छद्, गुह्, (c. 1. गूहति -हितुं), निगुह्, अन्तर्धा, व्यवधा, तिरस्कृ, स्थग् (c. 10. स्थगयति -यितुं), गुण्ठ् (c. 10. गुण्ठयति -यितुं), अवगुण्ठ्, ऊर्णु (c. 2. ऊर्णोति, ऊर्णौति, ऊर्णवितुं), प्रोर्णु.—(Cover with a garment) वस्त्रेण आच्छद् or प्रावृ or परिधा or व्ये (c. 1. व्ययति, व्यातुं) or वेष्ट् (c. 1. वेष्टते -ष्टितुं).—(As a horse) स्कु (c. 5. स्कुनोति, c. 9. स्कुनाति, स्कोतुं).

Covered. *p. p.* छन्नः -न्ना -न्नं, छादितः -ता -तं, आच्छन्नः -न्ना -न्नं, आच्छादितः -ता -तं, प्रच्छन्नः -न्ना -न्नं, प्रच्छादितः -ता -तं, परिच्छन्नः -न्ना -न्नं, समवच्छन्नः -न्ना -न्नं, समाच्छन्नः -न्ना -न्नं, आवृतः -ता -तं, प्रावृतः -ता -तं, संवृतः -ता -तं, वृतः -ता -तं, पिहितः -ता -तं, अवततः -ता -तं, आचितः -ता -तं, निचितः -ता -तं, आस्तीर्णः -र्णा -र्णं, आस्तृतः -ता -तं, गूढः -ढा -ढं, निगूढः -ढा -ढं, अन्तर्हितः -ता -तं, व्यवहितः -ता -तं, स्थगितः -ता -तं, गुण्ठितः -ता -तं, ऊर्णुतः -ता -तं, संवीतः -ता -तं, वेष्टितः -ता -तं, पिनद्धः -द्धा -द्धं, रूषितः -ता -तं, अपवारितः -ता -तं; 'a covered way,' छन्नपथः; 'covered with blossoms,' स्तवकाचितः -ता -तं.

Covering, *s.* छादनं, आच्छादनं, प्रच्छादनं, पिधानं, अपिधानं, पटलं, प्रावरणं, आवरणं, वरणं, छदनं, पुटः, अपवारणं, वेष्टनं.—(Screen) व्यवधा -धानं, तिरस्करिणी, तिरोधानं, अन्तर्द्धानं, प्रावृतं.—(Dress) आच्छादनं, परिधानं, प्रवारः, प्रावारः, परिच्छदः.

Coverlet, *s.* शय्याच्छादनं, शयनीयप्रच्छदपटः, उत्तरप्रच्छदः, उत्तरच्छदः.

Covert, *s.* (Shelter) संश्रयः, समाश्रयः, आश्रयणं.—(Thicket in which beasts hide themselves) गहनं, गह्वरं, गुहिनं, न्यटः, कुञ्जः.

Covert, *a.* (Sheltered from the wind) निर्वातः -ता -तं.—(Hidden, secret) गूढः -ढा -ढं, निगूढः -ढा -ढं, छन्नः -न्ना -न्नं, निभृतः -ता -तं, गुप्तः -प्ता -प्तं, रहस्यः -स्या -स्यं; 'covert expression,' व्याजोक्तिः *f.*, व्यङ्ग्योक्तिः *f.*; 'covert meaning,' निगूढार्थः.

Covertly, *adv.* निभृतं, तिरस्, रहस्, रहसि, छलेन, गुप्तं.

To covet, *v. a.* लुभ् (c. 4. लुभ्यति, लोभितुं, लोब्धुं), अभिलष् (c. 1. -लषति -षितुं), वाञ्छ् (c. 1. वाञ्छति -ञ्छितुं), अभिवाञ्छ्, कांक्ष् (c. 1. कांक्षति -क्षितुं), आकांक्ष्, अतिशयेन लभ् in des. (लिप्सते -प्सितुं), गृध् (c. 4. गृध्यति, गर्धितुं), कम् (c. 10. कामयते -यितुं), स्पृह् (c. 10. स्पृहयति -यितुं), अभिध्यै (c. 1. -ध्यायति -ध्यातुं).

Covetable, *a.* लोभनीयः -या -यं, लोभ्यः -भ्या -भ्यं, स्पृहणीयः -या -यं, स्पृह्यः -ह्या -ह्यं, अभिलषणीयः -या -यं, आकांक्षणीयः -या -यं, वाञ्छनीयः -या -यं.

Coveted, *p. p.* अभिलषितः -ता -तं, आकांक्षितः -ता -तं, लिप्सितः -ता -तं, वाञ्छितः -ता -तं, अभीप्सितः -ता -तं, अभीष्टः -ष्टा -ष्टं.

Covetous, *a.* लोभी -भिनी -भि (न्), लुब्धः -ब्धा -ब्धं, लोभयुक्तः -क्ता -क्तं, लोलुभः -भा -भं, लोभवान् -वती -वत् (त्), अभिलाषी -षिणी -षि (न्) -षुकः -का -कं, आकांक्षी -क्षिणी -क्षि (न्), गृध्नः -ध्ना -ध्नं, गर्द्धनः -ना -नं, गृध्नुः -ध्नुः -ध्नु, ईप्सुः -प्सुः -प्सु, अभीप्सुः -प्सुः -प्सु, इच्छुः -च्छुः -च्छु, जिघृक्षुः -क्षुः -क्षु, लिप्सुः -प्सुः -प्सु, कामवान् -वती -वत् (त्), स्पृहयालुः -लुः -लु, आशायुक्तः -क्ता -क्तं, लालसी -सिनी -सि (न्), तृष्णकः -का -कं.—(Of riches, gain) धनलुब्धः -ब्धा -ब्धं, धनाभिलाषुकः -का -कं, अर्थलुब्धः -ब्धा -ब्धं, धनार्थी -र्थिनी -र्थि (न्), अर्थपरः -रा -रं, लाभलिप्सुः -प्सुः -प्सु.

Covetously, *adv.* लोभेन, सलोभं, अतिलिप्सया, लुब्धत्वात्, लुब्धं.

Covetousness, *s.* लोभः, लुब्धता, लिप्सा, तृष्णा, लालसा, अभिलाषः, अतिशयेच्छा, जिघृक्षा, अतिशयलिप्सा, लिप्सातिशयः, अतिस्पृहा, अतिकांक्षा, आकांक्षा, अतिवाञ्छा, अभिध्या -ध्यानं, लौल्यं.—(Of wealth) धनलिप्सा, धनलोभः, धनाभिलाषः, धनतृष्णा, वित्तेहा, वित्तैषणा, अर्थकामः.

Covey, *s.* (Hatch of young birds) पक्षिशावकगणः.—(A number of birds) पक्षिगणः, पाक्षिकं, कापोतं; 'covey of partridges,' चकोरमाला, टिट्टिभगणः.

Covin, *s.* कूटसंविद्, कूटपणः, कूटसमयः, कपटसंविद्.

Cow, *s.* गौः *f.* (गो), शृङ्गिणी, तम्पा, तम्बा, माहा -हेयी, निलिम्पा, पीवरी, सुरभी, सौरभेयी, उस्रा, अर्जुनी, अघ्न्या, रोहिणी.—(Milch-cow) धेनुः *f.*, धेनुका, गोधेनुः, स्त्रीगवी, दोग्ध्री, पीतदुग्धा, पीनोघ्नी, पीवरस्तनी, धेनुष्या; 'excellent cow,' गोवृन्दारकः, गवोद्घः, गोप्रकाण्डं, गोमतल्लिका, नैचिकी; 'a herd of cows,' गोकुलं, गोवृन्दं, धैनुकं; 'cow anxious for her calf,' वत्सकामा, वत्सला; 'sacrifice of a cow,' गोमेधः; 'cow's milk,' गोदुग्धं, धेनुकादुग्धं; 'killing a cow,' गोहत्या, गोवधः; 'cow-killer,' गोघ्नः; 'cow's hoof,' गोखुरः, गोक्षुरः; 'cow's hide,' गोचर्म्म *n.* (न्); 'cow-tail,' चामरं, गोपुच्छः; 'owner of cows,' गवीश्वरः; 'belonging to a cow,' गव्यः -व्या -व्यं; 'cow-shaped,' गवाकृतिः -तिः -ति; 'cow-dung,' गोमयः -यं, गोकृतं, गोशकृत्, भूमिलेपनं, गोपुरीषं, गोहन्नं, गोविद् *f.* (ष्).

To cow, *v. a.* भी in caus. (भाययति -यितुं or भीषयति -यितुं), त्रस् in caus. (त्रासयति -यितुं), वित्रस्, सन्त्रस्.

Cowach, *s.* (A plant) कच्छुरा, कण्डूरा, महाहृस्वा, स्वगुप्ता, स्वयङ्गुप्ता, अव्यण्डा, अजलोमा *m.* (न्), अजहा, जडा, प्रावृषायणी, मर्कटी.

Coward, *s.* कातरः, कापुरुषः, कुपुरुषः, भीरुः, भीतः, अधीरः, वीर्य्यहीनः, हतकः, क्लीवः, शौर्य्यहीनः, युद्धपराङ्मुखः, युयुत्सारहितः, कृपणः.

Cowardice, *s.* कातर्य्यं, कापुरुषत्वं, निर्वीर्य्यं, अवीर्य्यं, अपौरुषं, भीरुता, कातरता, अविक्रमः, शौर्य्यहीनता, क्लैव्यं, कार्पण्यं.

Cowardly, *a.* निर्वीरः -रा -रं, वीर्य्यहीनः -ना -नं, वीर्य्यरहितः -ता -तं, कातरः -रा -रं, भीरुः -रुः -रु, भीरुहृदयः -या -यं, बभ्रुः -भ्रुः -भ्रु, क्लीवः -वा -वं, पौरुषहीनः -ना -नं, शौर्य्यरहितः -ता -तं, अविक्रान्तः -न्ता -न्तं.

Cowardly, *adv.* कापुरुषवत्, भीतवत्, क्लीववत्, सकातर्य्यं, सशङ्कितं.

Cowed, *p. p.* भीतः -ता -तं, त्रासितः -ता -तं, सन्त्रस्तः -स्ता -स्तं.

To cower, *v. n.* अवनतकायः -या -यं भू, प्रणतशरीरः -रा -रं भू, नताङ्गः -ङ्गी -ङ्गं भू, प्रह्वीभू, उत्कटुकासनं कृ.

Cow-herd, *s.* गोपः, गोपालः -लकः, गोरक्षकः, गोचारकः, अनुगवीनः, आभीरः, वत्सीयः.

Cow-house, *s.* गोष्ठं, गोगोष्ठं, गोस्थानकं, गोशाला -लः -लं, व्रजः, गोव्रजः, गोगृहं, सन्धानिनी, गोकुलं.

Cow-keeper, *s.* गोरक्षकः, गोपः, गोपालः -लकः, गवीश्वरः.

Cowl, *s.* सन्न्यासिभिर् भृतं फणाकृति मस्तकाभरणं.

Cow-pen, *s.* व्रजः, गोव्रजः, गोष्ठं, गोस्थानं. *See* Cow-house.

Cowrie, *s.* (Shell) काकिनी *f.*, कपर्द्दकः, वटः, वराटकः, हिरणं, हिरण्यं.

Cowslip, *s.* वसन्तसमये यवसादिमध्ये प्ररोही ओषधिभेदः.

Cow's-tongue, *s.* (A plant) गोजिह्विका, गोजिह्वा.

Coxcomb, *s.* दाम्भिकः, दम्भी *m.* (न्), गर्व्वी *m.* (न्), दृप्तः, आत्माभिमानी *m.* (न्), दर्शनीयमानी *m.* (न्), आत्मश्लाघी *m.* (न्).—(The plant) मयूरशिखा, मयूरचूडा, मयूरः, मयूरकः, वह्निशिखरः.

Coxcombry, *s.* दम्भः, गर्व्वः, दर्पः, दाम्भिकत्वं, दम्भिता.

Coxcomical, *a.* दम्भी -म्भिनी -म्भि (न्), दाम्भिकः -की -कं, गर्व्वितः -ता -तं.

Coy, *a.* (Modest) अप्रगल्भः -ल्भा -ल्भं, लज्जान्वितः -ता -तं, सलज्जः -ज्जा -ज्जं, व्रीडितः -ता -तं, विनीतः -ता -तं, सत्रपः -पा -पं, मन्दाक्षः -क्षी -क्षं, मन्दास्यः -स्यी -स्यं.—(Reserved, not accessible) अल्पभाषी -षिणी -षि (न्), परिमितकथः -था -थं, दुर्धर्षः -र्षा -र्षं.

To coy, *v. n.* लज्ज् (c. 6. लज्जते -ज्जितुं), व्रीड् (c. 4. व्रीड्यति, व्रीडितुं).

Coyly, *adv.* लज्जया, सलज्जं, सव्रीडं, सत्रपं, विनीतं.

Coyness, *s.* लज्जा, व्रीडा, त्रपा, सलज्जता, सव्रीडत्वं, लज्जावत्त्वं, अप्रागल्भ्यं, विनीतता, मन्दाक्षं, मन्दास्यं, दुर्धैर्यं.

To cozen, *v. a.* वञ्च् in caus. (वञ्चयते -ति -यितुं), परिवञ्च्, प्रलभ् (c. 1. -लभते -लब्धुं), विप्रलभ्, छल् (c. 10. छलयति -यितुं).

Cozenage, *s.* वञ्चनं, प्रतारणा, छलं -लनं, कपटः -टं, कूटः -टं.

Cozener, *s.* वञ्चकः, प्रतारकः, कितवः, कूटकः, कूटकारः.

Crab, *s.* कुलीरः, कर्कटः -टकः, तिर्य्यग्यानः, बहिश्चरः, पार्श्वोदरप्रियः, बहिःकुटीचरः, जलबिल्वः, अपत्यशत्रुः *m.*, बहुकः, षोडशाङ्घ्रिः *m.*, मृतसूतिः *f.*, पङ्कवासः, कुरचिल्लः.

Crabbed, *a.* (Harsh, unpleasing) शुष्कः -ष्का -ष्कं, कर्कशः -शा -शं, परुषः -षा -षं, उग्रः -ग्रा -ग्रं, निष्ठुरः -रा -रं, कष्टः -ष्टा -ष्टं, व्यलीकः -का -कं, विरुद्धः -द्धा -द्धं.—(Peevish, morose) दुःशीलः -ला -लं, वामशीलः -ला -लं, नैकृतिकः -की -कं, प्रतीपः -पा -पं.—(Difficult, perplexing) विषमः -मा -मं, दुर्ज्ञेयः -या -यं, निगूढार्थः -र्था -र्थं, अव्याख्येयः -या -यं, सशल्यः -ल्या -ल्यं; 'crabbed or harsh speech,' कर्कशवाक्यं, परुषवचनं, शुष्कं; 'a crabbed case,' सशल्योऽर्थः.

Crabbedly, *adv.* कर्कशं, सकार्कश्यं, निष्ठुरं, वामशीलत्वात्, विषमं.

Crabbedness, *s.* (Harshness) कार्कश्यं, शुष्कता, पारुष्यं, नैष्ठुर्य्यं, उग्रत्वं, व्यलीकता.—(Moroseness) दौःशील्यं, निकृतिः *f.*—(Difficulty) वैषम्यं, दुर्ज्ञेयत्वं, सशल्यत्वं.

Crack, *s.* (Chink, breach) छिद्रं, रन्ध्रं, बिलं, सन्धिः *m.*, भित्तिः *f.*, भङ्गः.—(A sudden disruption) स्फोटनं, स्फुटनं, भञ्जनं, भेदनं, विदारणं, खण्डनं.—(Sudden sound of any thing bursting) क्वणितं, स्फुत्कारः, ध्वनितं, आकस्मिकशब्दः; 'cracking the finger-joints,' अङ्गुलिस्फोटनं.

To crack, *v. a.* स्फुट् in caus. (-स्फोटयति -यितुं), विदृ in caus. (-दारयति -यितुं), भञ्ज् (c. 7. भनक्ति, भंक्तुं), भिद् (c. 7. भिनत्ति, भेत्तुं), खण्ड् (c. 10. खण्डयति -यितुं), छिद्र् (c. 10. छिद्रयति -यितुं); 'to crack the finger-joints,' अङ्गुलिभङ्गं कृ.

To crack, *v. n.* (Open in chinks) स्फुट् (c. 6. स्फुटति -टितुं, c. 1. स्फोटति -टितुं), भिद् in pass. (भिद्यते), भञ्ज् in pass. (भज्यते), विदृ in pass. (-दीर्य्यते), विदल् (c. 1. -दलति -लितुं).—(Utter a sudden sound) अकस्मात् क्वण् (c. 1. क्वणति -णितुं), स्तन् (c. 1. स्तनति -नितुं), ध्वन् (c. 1. ध्वनति -नितुं).—(Boast) विकत्थ् (c. 1. -कत्थते -त्थितुं).

Crack-brained, *a.* वातूलः -ला -लं, उन्मत्तः -त्ता -त्तं, हतज्ञानः -ना -नं.

Cracked, *p. p.* स्फोटितः -ता -तं, स्फुटितः -ता -तं, भिन्नः -न्ना -न्नं, भग्नः -ग्ना -ग्नं, विदीर्णः -र्णा -र्णं, विदलितः -ता -तं, विदलीकृतः -ता -तं, विघट्टितः -ता -तं, छिद्रितः -ता -तं, दरितः -ता -तं, दर्दरः -रा -रं.—(As sound) स्वरभग्नः -ग्ना -ग्नं; 'a cracked note,' अपस्वरः, विस्वरः; 'a cracked voice,' काकस्वरं.—(Crazy) वातुलः -ला -लं, बुद्धिविकलः -ला -लं.

Cracker, *s.* (Boaster) दाम्भिकः, विकत्थी *m.* (न्).—(A small packet filled with gunpowder, which, being ignited, explodes with a loud noise) आग्नेयचूर्णगर्भः क्षुद्रपुटो यो वह्निस्पर्शात् महाशब्देन स्फुटति.

Crack-hemp or crack-rope, *s.* पाशदण्डार्हः, रज्जुपाशदण्ड्यः, उद्बन्धनार्हः.

To crackle, *v. n.* स्फुट् (c. 6. स्फुटति -टितुं), स्फुत्कृ, पटपट (nom. पटपटायति), शकशक (nom. शकशकायति), स्वन् (c. 1. स्वनति -नितुं), रट् (c. 1. रटति -टितुं).

Crackling, *s.* स्फुत्कारः, स्फुत्कृतं, स्वनितं, पटपट शकशक इत्यादिशब्दाः.—(Of flame) रटितं, रिटिः *f.*, सङ्करः, सङ्कारः.

Cracknel, *s.* अतिभङ्गुरो दृढपिष्टकभेदः.

Cradle, *s.* शिशुखट्वा, शिशुदोला, दोलिका, प्रेङ्खा, प्रेङ्खोलनं.

To cradle, *v. a.* दोलायां शी in caus. (शाययति -यितुं).—(Rock in cradle) प्रेङ्खायाम् आरोप्य चल् in caus. (चालयति -यितुं).

Craft, *s.* (Manual art) शिल्पं, शिल्पकर्म्म *n.* (न्), शिल्पिकं, शिल्पविद्या.—(Trade) व्यापारः, वृत्तिः *f.*, व्यवसायः.—(Cunning) शाठ्यं, वैदग्ध्यं, धूर्त्तता, कपटः -टं, छलं, कौटिल्यं.—(Skill) चातुर्य्यं, नैपुण्यं, कुशलता, दक्षता, हस्तकौशल्यं, सूक्ष्मता.—(A small vessel) क्षुद्रनौका.

Craftily, *adv.* (Cunningly) सशाठ्यं, सवैदग्ध्यं, विदग्धं, छलेन, सकौटिल्यं, धूर्त्तवत्, कितववत्.—(Skilfully) चतुरं, सकौशल्यं, सदाक्ष्यं.

Craftiness, *s.* शठता, विदग्धता, वैदग्ध्यं, वक्रता, विचिक्षता, कैतवं, कूटता.

Craftsman, *s.* शिल्पी *m.* (न्), शिल्पकारः, कर्म्मकारः, व्यापारी *m.* (न्).

Crafty, *a.* विदग्धः -ग्धा -ग्धं, धूर्त्तः -र्त्ता -र्त्तं, वञ्चकः -का -कं, विचिक्षः -क्षा -क्षं, कुटिलः -ला -लं, शठः -ठा -ठं, छलनापरः -रा -रं, सव्याजः -जा -जं, विपश्चित्पुः -पुः -पु, चतुरः -रा -रं, फेरवः -वा -वं, विसंवादी -दिनी -दि (न्).

Crag, *s.* विषमं, शृङ्गं, कूटः -टं, शैलशिखरं, पर्व्वतशृङ्गं, ग्रावा *m.* (न्).

Cragged or craggy, *a.* विषमः -मा -मं, असमः -मा मं, अत्यसमः -मा -मं, शृङ्गी -ङ्गिणी -ङ्गि (न्), शिखरी -रिणी -रि (न्), कूटवान् -वती -वत् (त्), शिलेयः -यी -यं.

Craggedness or cragginess, *a.* वैषम्यं, विषमता, शिलेयत्वं, कूटवत्त्वं.

To cram, *v. a.* (Fill to excess) अत्यन्तं पॄ in caus. (पूरयति -यितुं), आकीर्णीकृ, सम्बाध् (c. 1. -बाधते -धितुं).—(Satiate) अतिशयेन तृप् in caus. (तर्पयति -यितुं), अतितृप्ति भोजनेन सन्तुष् in caus. (-तोषयति -यितुं), or अन्नं भुज् in caus. (भोजयति -यितुं), सौहित्यं जन् in caus. (जनयति -यितुं).—(Thrust in by force) बलात् or प्रसभं निविश् in caus. (-वेशयति -यितुं).

To cram, *v. n.* (Eat beyond satiety) अतितृप्ति भुज् (c. 7. भुङ्क्ते, भोक्तुं) or भोजनेन आत्मानं पॄ in caus. (पूरयति -यितुं).

Crammed, *p. p.* सङ्कीर्णः -र्णा -र्णं, आकीर्णः -र्णा -र्णं, सङ्कुलः -ला -लं; 'with food,' अतितृप्तः -प्ता -प्तं, सुहितः -ता -तं; 'with people,' बहुजनाकीर्णः -र्णा -र्णं.

Cramp, *s.* (Spasm, numbness) आकर्षः, अङ्गाकर्षः, आक्षेपकः, शूलं, अङ्गग्रहः, अपतन्त्रकः, अपतानकः, स्तम्भः, विष्टम्भः, त्वक्सुप्तिः *f.*—(Obstruction, contraction) स्तम्भनं, प्रतिरोधः, अवरोधः, संरोधः, प्रतिबन्धः, संवृतिः *f.*, संक्षेपः, सङ्कोचः.—(Piece of iron to join two bodies) द्रव्यद्वयसम्बन्धनार्थं कीलः, लौहबन्धनी.

To cramp, *v. a.* (Pain with cramps) अङ्गम् आकृष् (c. 1. -कर्षति -क्रष्टुं), अङ्गग्रहं कृ, अङ्गशूलं कृ, अङ्गस्तम्भं कृ, त्वक्सुप्तिं जन् in caus. (जनयति -यितुं).—(Contract, obstruct) सङ्कुच् (c. 1. -कोचति -चितुं), सम्बाध् (c. 1. -बाधते -धितुं), स्तम्भ् (c. 9. स्तभ्नाति, स्तम्भितुं or caus. स्तम्भयति -यितुं), प्रतिरुध् (c. 7. -रुणद्धि -रोद्धुं), निरुध्, संरुध्; प्रतिबन्ध् (c. 9. -बध्नाति -बन्द्धुं).—(Fasten with a cramp) कील् (c. 10. कीलयति -यितुं), लौहकीलेन सम्बन्ध्.

Cramped, *p. p.* सम्बाधः -धा -धं, निरुद्धः -द्धा -द्धं, सङ्कटः -टा -टं, संवृतः -ता -तं, क्लिष्टः -ष्टा -ष्टं, कष्टः -ष्टा -ष्टं, बाधितः -ता -तं; 'we are much cramped in this house,' अस्मिन् गृहे महत् कष्टम् अस्माकं जायते.

Cramp-fish, *s.* विदेशीयमत्स्यभेदो यस्य स्पर्शात् करसुप्तिः सम्भवति.

Cramp-iron, *s.* लौहबन्धनी, लौहग्रहणी, लौहकीलः, कीलः, बन्धनकीलः.

CRANE, *s.* बकः, सारसः, मल्लरङ्गः, दीर्घजङ्घः, कुरङ्करः, कलाङ्कुरः, निशैतः, कङ्कः, शुक्लवायसः; 'Numidian crane,' करटुः *m.*, कर्कटुः *m.*, करेटुः, कर्कटेटुः.—(Machine for lifting weights) भारोद्धरणयन्त्रं, भारोत्तोलनयन्त्रं, भारोद्वहनयन्त्रं.—(A crooked pipe) बकः, वक्रनाडिः *f.*

CRANIAL, *a.* कापालः -ली -लं, कापालिकः -की -कं.

CRANIUM, *s.* कपालः -लं, कर्परः, शिरोस्थि *n.*, करोटः -टी, मस्तकः -कं, शीर्षकं, मुण्डः -ण्डं.

CRANK, *s.* (The end of an iron axle bent in the form of an elbow) चक्रोत्तोलनादिहेतोर् भुजाकृतिरूपेण भग्नं लोहदण्डाग्रं.—(A winding passage) वक्रमार्गः.—(Ambiguous expression) वक्रोक्तिः *f.*, वक्रभणितं.

CRANK, *a.* (As a ship) सङ्कटाकारः -रा -रं, परिवर्त्तनशीलः -ला -लं.

CRANKNESS, *s.* नाविकभाषायां सङ्कटाकारत्वात् परिवर्त्तनशीलता.

CRANNIED *a.* छिद्रितः -ता -तं, छिद्रपूर्णः -र्णा -र्णं, रन्ध्रवान् -वती -वत् (त्).

CRANNY, *s.* छिद्रं, रन्ध्रं, भित्तिः *f.*, भङ्गः, सन्धिः *m.*, भेदः, दरी, टङ्कः.

CRAPE, *s.* बन्धुजनमरणकाले शोकसूचकं नीलवासः *n.* (स्), नीलवर्णो विरलपटः, कृष्णवस्त्रं, कालाशौचे भृतं नीलाम्बरं.

CRAPULENCE, *s.* मदात्ययः, मदातङ्कः, अतिशयमद्यपानजा शिरोवेदना or विवमिषा or वमनेच्छा.

CRAPULOUS, *a.* मदात्ययग्रस्तः -स्ता -स्तं, मदातङ्कपीडितः -ता -तं.

To CRASH, *v. n.* झञ्झा (nom. झञ्झायते), झङ् झञ्झा झनत् इत्यादिशब्दान् कृ, स्तन् (c. 1. स्तनति -नितुं), ध्वन् (c. 1. ध्वनति -नितुं), कोलाहलं कृ.

To CRASH, *v. a.* भञ्ज् (c. 7. भनक्ति, भंक्तुं), निभञ्ज्, अवभञ्ज्, प्रभञ्ज्, भिद् (c. 7. भिनत्ति, भेत्तुं), निर्भिद्; मृद् (c. 9. मृद्नाति, मर्द्दितुं), पिष् (c. 7. पिनष्टि, पेष्टुं).

CRASH, *s.* झञ्झा, झनत्कारः, स्तनितं, ध्वनितं, कोलाहलः, कालकीलः, मडः.

CRASS, *a.* स्थूलः -ला -लं, घनः -ना -नं, असूक्ष्मः -क्ष्मा -क्ष्मं.

CRASSITUDE, *s.* स्थूलता, स्थौल्यं, घनता, सान्द्रता, असूक्ष्मत्वं.

CRASTINATION, *s.* कालयापनं, कालक्षेपः, विलम्बः,

CRASTINE, *a.* श्वस्तनः -नी -नं, श्वस्त्यः -स्त्या -स्त्यं, शौवस्तिकः -की -कं.

CRATCH, *s.* गवादनी, द्रोणिः *f.* -णी, गवादनाधारः, तृणाधारः.

CRAVAT, *s.* ग्रीवावेष्टनं, गलावेष्टनं, गलवस्त्रं, ग्रीवाच्छादनं, ग्रैवेयकं, ग्रीवाभरणं.

To CRAVE, *v. a.* (Entreat) प्रार्थ् (c. 10. -अर्थयते -ति -यितुं), अभ्यर्थ्, सम्प्रार्थ्; याच् (c. 1. याचति -चितुं), अभियाच्, प्रयाच्, सम्प्रयाच्; विनयेन प्रार्थ्; 'to crave indulgence,' प्रसद् in caus. (-सादयते -यितुं).—(Long for) अत्यन्तम् अभिलष् (c. 1. -लषति -षितुं) or अभिवाञ्छ् (c. 1. -वाञ्छति -ञ्छितुं) or लभ् in des. (लिप्सते -प्सितुं), भुज् in des. (बुभुक्षति -ते -क्षितुं), तृष् (c. 4. तृष्यति, तर्षितुं).

CRAVEN, *s.* कापुरुषः, कातरः, हतकः, क्लीवः, भीरुः, निर्वीरः.

CRAVING, *s.* अतिस्पृहा, अतिशयवाञ्छा, अतिकांक्षा, अभिलाषः, अभिकांक्षा, लालसा, उत्कण्ठा, कौतूहलं, औत्सुक्यं, तृष्णा, तृषा; 'for food,' अन्नलिप्सा, बुभुक्षा, अतिक्षुधा, गृध्नता; 'for drink,' पिपासा.

To CRAUNCH, *v. a.* चर्व् (c. 1. चर्वति -र्वितुं c. 10. चर्वयति -यितुं), दन्तैः पिष् (c. 7. पिनष्टि, पेष्टुं).

CRAW, *s.* पक्षिणां जठरः or उदरं or उपजठरः or पूर्व्वजठरः, पक्वाशयः.

CRAWFISH OR CRAYFISH, *s.* नादेयकर्कटः, नादेयकुलीरः, कर्कटजातीयो नादेयमत्स्यः,

CRAWL, *s.* गुप्तिः *f.*, पोतोदरं, नौकागुप्तिः, नौकोदरं, नौकूपः,

To CRAWL, *v. n.* सृप् (c. 1. सर्पति, सप्तुं), विसृप्, उपसृप्, प्रसृप्, चुप् (c. 1. चोपति -पितुं), उरसा गम् (c. 1. गच्छति, गन्तुं), उरोगमनं कृ, कीटवद् गम्, मन्दं प्रसृ (c. 1. -सरति -सर्तुं), मन्दगत्या चल् (c. 1. चलति -लितुं), रिङ्ग् (c. 1. रिङ्गति -ङ्गितुं).

CRAWLER, *s.* सर्पी *m.* -र्पिणी *f.* (न्), विसर्पी *m.* (न्), उरोगामी *m.* (न्).

CRAYON, *s.* वर्त्तिका, चित्रवर्त्तिका, ईषिका, तूलिका, लेख्यचूर्त्तिका; 'crayon-box,' वर्त्तिकाकरण्डकः.

To CRAZE, *v. a.* (Break) खण्ड् (c. 10. खण्डयति -यितुं), भञ्ज् (c. 7. भनक्ति, भंक्तुं), जर्ज्जरीकृ.—(Pulverise) चूर्ण् (c. 10. चूर्णयति -यितुं), क्षोदीकृ.—(Impair the intellect) वातुलीकृ, मुह् in caus. (मोहयति -यितुं).

CRAZINESS OR CRAZEDNESS, *s.* (Of intellect) बुद्धिवैकल्यं, वातुलता.—(Weakness) दौर्बल्यं, जीर्णिः *f.*, जीर्णता; 'as of a house,' जर्ज्जरत्वं.

CRAZY, *a.* (Shattered in mind, mad) वातुलः -ला -लं, वातूलः -ला -लं, न्यूनधीः -धीः -धि, बुद्धिविकलः -ला -लं, विकलान्तःकरणः -णा -णं, भ्रष्टबुद्धिः -द्धिः -द्धि, हतज्ञानः -ना -नं, उन्मादवान् -वती -वत् (त्), उन्मत्तः -त्ता -त्तं, सोन्मादः -दा -दं, अपध्वस्तः -स्ता -स्तं, विमनाः -नाः -नः (स्), उत्सिक्तमनाः -नाः -नः (स्).—(Broken, shattered) जर्ज्जरः -रा -रं, जर्ज्जरीकः -का -कं, जीर्णः -र्णा -र्णं; 'a crazy house,' जर्ज्जरगृहं, जीर्णगृहं.

To CREAK, *v. n.* विरु (c. 2. -रौति -रवितुं), कर्कशं शब्द् (nom. शब्दायते).

CREAKING, *s.* (Of a door) कपाटोद्घाटनात् कर्कशशब्दः, द्वारसन्धिचीत्कृतं.

CREAM, *s.* शरः, क्षीरशरः, दुग्धफेनं, दुग्धतालीयं, क्षीरजं, किलाटः -टी, शार्करः, शार्करः, कूर्चिका, सारः, सरः, सन्तानिका.—(The best part or essence of any thing) सारः, तात्त्विकं, उत्तमांशः.

To CREAM, *v. n.* शरं बन्ध् (c. 9. बध्नाति, बन्द्धुं).—(Froth) फेन (nom. फेनायते).

To CREAM, *v. a.* (Skim milk) दुग्धफेनम् उद्धृ (c. 1. -हरति -हर्तुं), क्षीरशरम् अपनी (c. 1. -नयति -नेतुं).—(Take the best part) सारम् उद्धृ.

CREAMY, *a.* शरमयः -यी -यं, क्षीरफेणयुक्तः -क्ता -क्तं, शरोपमः -मा -मं.

CREASE, *s.* ऊर्म्मी, ऊर्म्मिका, ऊर्म्मिचिह्नं, पुटचिह्नं, वस्त्रभङ्गः, वलिः *f.*, व्यावर्त्तनं.

To CREASE, *v. a.* पुटीकरणेन चिह्न् (c. 10. चिह्नयति -यितुं), चूर्ण् (c. 10. चूर्णयति -यितुं).

To CREASE, *v. n.* ऊर्म्मिकां बन्ध् (c. 9. बध्नाति, बन्द्धुं), कूण् (c. 10. कूणयते -यितुं).

CREASED, *p. p.* ऊर्म्मिचिह्नितः -ता -तं, कूणितः -ता -तं.

To CREATE, *v. a.* (Call into being) सृज् (c. 6. सृजति, स्रष्टुं), विसृज्; जन् (c. 10. जनयति -यितुं), विजन्, सञ्जन्; उत्पद् in caus. (-पादयति -यितुं), उपपद्, सम्पद्; निर्मा (c. 2. -माति, c. 3. -मिमीते, c. 4. -मायते -मातुं), साध् (c. 10. साधयति -यितुं), तन् (c. 8. तनोति -नितुं) कृ, सङ्कृ, विधा (c. 3. -दधाति -धातुं).—(Produce by invention) क्लृप् (c. 10. कल्पयति -यितुं), सङ्क्लृप्, सम्प्रक्लृप्, परिक्लृप्, रच् (c. 10. रचयति -यितुं).—(Invest with new rank) नवपदे नियुज् (c. 7. -युनक्ति -योक्तुं) or अभिषिच् (c. 6. -षिञ्चति -षेक्तुं).

CREATED, *p. p.* सृष्टः -ष्टा -ष्टं, जनितः -ता -तं, उत्पादितः -ता -तं, उत्पन्नः -न्ना -न्नं, निर्म्मितः -ता -तं, साधितः -ता -तं, कारितः -ता -तं, कल्पितः -ता -तं, सम्प्रकल्पितः -ता -तं, विहितः -ता -तं; 'a created thing,' भूतं; 'all created things,' सर्व्वभूतानि *m. pl.*, चेतनाचेतनं.

CREATION. *s.* सर्ज्जनं, सृष्टिः *f.*, उत्पादनं, जननं, निर्म्माणं, उत्पत्तिः *f.*, सर्गः, निसर्गः, भावनं; 'creation of the world,' जगत्सृष्टिः *f.*—(Invention) कल्पना -नं, क्लृप्तिः *f.*, परिकल्पनं, कल्पनासृष्टिः *f.*, भावना; 'creation of the mind,' मनःकल्पितं, मनःसृष्टिः *f.*; 'creation of one's own brain,' स्वकपालकल्पितं.—(Any thing produced) उत्पन्नं, भूतं.—(The things created, the universe) सर्गः, जगत्सृष्टिः, जगत्समग्रं, विश्वजगत् *n.*, चराचरं, विश्वं, सर्वभूतानि *n. pl.*, कल्पः.—(Investing with new rank) नवपदे नियोजनं or अभिषेचनं.

CREATIVE, *a.* उत्पादकः -का -कं, सृष्टिकरणः -णा -णं, जनकः -निका -कं, कारकः-रिका-कं,निर्म्माणशाली-लिनी-लि(न्),विधायी-यिनी-यि(न्).

CREATOR, *s.* स्रष्टा *m.* (सृ), जनकः, उत्पादकः, धाता *m.* (तृ), विधाता *m.* (तृ), सृक् *m.* (ज्), सृष्टिकर्त्ता *m.* (र्तृ), भावनः.—(Of the world) जगत्कर्त्ता *m.* (र्तृ), जगत्स्रष्टा *m.* (सृ), विश्वसृक् *m.* (ज्), विश्वविधायी *m.* (न्), विश्वकृत्, विश्वस्रष्टा *m.* (सृ), लोककृत् *m.*

CREATURE, *s.* (Being created) भूतं, सृष्टं, सृष्टिः *f.*, उत्पन्नं.—(Animal) जन्तुः *m.*, प्राणी *m.* (न्), जीवी *m.* (न्), शरीरी *m.* (न्), देही *m.* (न्), चेतनः, जन्मी *m.* (न्); 'living creatures,' प्राणिनः *m. pl.*, जीवन्तः *m. pl.*, जन्तवः *m. pl.*, प्रजाः *f. pl.*—(A word of contempt for a human being) तपस्वी *m.* (न्), जाल्मः, कृपणः.—(A word of tenderness) वत्सः -त्सा, प्रियः -या.—(A person who owes his fortune to another) आश्रितः, उपजीवी *m.* (न्), कार्पटः, भाक्तिकः.

CREDENCE, *s.* प्रत्ययः, विश्वासः, श्रद्धा, विस्रम्भः, भक्तिः *f.*—(That which gives a claim to credit) प्रमाणं; 'author worthy of credence,' प्रामाणिकः, प्रमाणं; 'to give credence,' प्रती (c. 2. प्रत्येति -तुं).

CREDENDA, *s.* धर्म्मविषये वस्तूनाम् अवश्यश्रद्धेयानां विधानं.

CREDENT, *a.* श्रद्दधानः -ना -नं, विश्वासी -सिनी -सि (न्), प्रत्ययी -यिनी -यि (न्).

CREDENTIALS, *s.* विश्वासपत्रं, अभिज्ञानपत्रं, प्रत्ययपत्रं, प्रत्ययकारिणी.

CREDIBILITY, *s.* श्रद्धेयता, विश्वास्यत्वं, विश्वासपात्रता, प्रामाणिकत्वं.

CREDIBLE, *a.* विश्वास्यः -स्या -स्यं, श्रद्धेयः -या -यं, प्रामाणिकः -की -कं.

CREDIBLY, *adv.* यथा विश्वासः क्रियते तथा, सप्रामाण्यं, प्रामाणिकवत्.

CREDIT, *s.* (Belief) प्रत्ययः, विश्वासः, विस्रम्भः, श्रद्धा, भक्तिः *f.*; 'worthy of credit,' विश्वासपात्रं, विश्वासभूमिः.—(Reputation) मानं, सम्मानं, मान्यत्वं, आदरः, पूजा, यशः *n.* (स्), कीर्त्तिः *f.*, ख्यातिः *f.*—(Trust between buyer and seller) कालिका, क्रेतृविक्रेत्रोर् मध्ये क्रेता द्रव्यग्रहणात् प्रभृति मूल्यदानं यावद् विश्वासः, मूल्यदाने विलम्बः or अपेक्षा; 'buying on credit,' उद्धारः.—(Authority) प्रमाणं, प्रामाण्यं, श्रद्धेयता, प्रभावः, गौरवं.

To CREDIT, *v. a.* प्रती (c. 2. प्रत्येति -तुं), विश्वस् (c. 2. -श्वसिति -तुं), सत्यमिति मन् (c. 4. मन्यते, मन्तुं), श्रद्धा (c. 3. -दधाति -धातुं), प्रत्ययीकृ, विश्वासं कृ.—(Admit as proof) प्रमाणीकृ.

CREDITABLE, *a.* मान्यः -न्या -न्यं, सम्मान्यः -न्या -न्यं, श्लाघ्यः -घ्या -घ्यं, प्रशंसनीयः -या -यं, पूज्यः -ज्या -ज्यं, प्रशस्तः -स्ता -स्तं, कीर्त्तिकरः -री -रं.

CREDITABLENESS, *s.* मान्यता, सम्मान्यता, पूज्यत्वं, श्लाघ्यत्वं, ख्यातिः *f.*

CREDITABLY, *adv.* श्लाघ्यप्रकारेण, प्रशस्तं, पूज्यवत्, समानं.

CREDITED, *p. p.* प्रमाणीकृतः -ता -तं, विश्वस्तः -स्ता -स्तं, प्रतीतः -ता -तं.

CREDITOR, *s.* उत्तमर्णः -र्णिकः -र्णी *m.* (न्), धनार्थी *m.* (न्), धनी *m.* (न्), धनिकः, धनैषी *m.* (न्).

CREDULITY, *s.* प्रत्ययशीलता, विश्वासशीलता, श्रद्धालुता, अवितर्कः, अशङ्का.

CREDULOUS, *a.* प्रत्ययी -यिनी -यि (न्), प्रत्ययशीलः -ला -लं, विश्वासी -सिनी -सि (न्), विश्वासशीलः -ला -लं, विस्रम्भप्रवणः -णा -णं, श्रद्धालुः -लुः -लु, श्रद्धामयः -यी -यं, अवितर्की -र्किणी -र्कि (न्), अशङ्काशीलः -ला -लं, उदारः -रा -रं.

CREED, *s.* (Form of articles of religious belief) धर्म्मविषये वस्तूनाम् अवश्यश्रद्धेयानां विधानं.—(Tenet) मतं.

CREEK, *s.* वङ्कः, समुद्रवङ्कः, खातः, पुटभेदः, वक्रं, भङ्गः, भङ्गुरः, खातं.

CREEKY, *a.* वाङ्कः -ङ्की -ङ्कं, वङ्कवान् -वती -वत् (त्), वंक्यः -क्या -क्यं, वक्रः -क्रा -क्रं, भङ्गुरः -रा -रं.

To CREEP, *v. n.* सृप् (c. 1. सर्पति, सर्प्तुं), उपसृप्, विसृप्, संसृप्, प्रसृप्; चुप् (c. 1. चोपति -पितुं), उरसा चल् (c. 1. चलति -लितुं), उरोगमनं कृ, कीटवद् गम् (c. 1. गच्छति, गन्तुं), मन्दगत्या चल्, मन्दं मन्दं सृ (c. 1. सरति, सर्त्तुं) or प्रसृ or विसृ, रिङ्ख् (c. 1. रिङ्खति -ङ्खितुं); 'the work creeps on,' कर्म्म प्रसर्पति.

CREEPER, *s.* (Plant) लता, वल्ली *f.*, गुल्मिनी *f.*, लताप्रतानिनी, वृक्षा-दिरुहः, व्रततिः *f.*, वीरुद् (ध्), उलपः, खेदिनी, प्रतानी, प्रतानः, अतिरसा.—(Insect) उरोगामी *m.* (न्), सर्पी *m.* (न्), विसर्पी *m.*

CREEPING, *s.* सर्पः -र्पणं, संसर्पः, विसर्पः, रिङ्खणं. *Part. a.* सर्पी -र्पिणी -र्पि (न्), or विसर्पी, प्रसारी -रिणी -रि (न्) or विसारी, विसृत्वरः -रा -रं.

CREEPINGLY, *adv.* मन्दगत्या, मन्दं मन्दं, सर्पवत्, कीटवत्.

CREMATION, *s.* दाहः -हनं, दहनं, प्लोषः, अग्निसात्करणं, चितारोपणं.

CREOLE OR CREOLIAN, *s.* प्रदेशवासिनः सुतः or प्रसूतः.

To CREPITATE, *v. n.* स्फुटकृ, पटपट (nom. पटपटायति), रट् (c. 1. रटति -टितुं), स्वन् (c. 1. स्वनति -नितुं), पर्द् (c. 1. पर्दते -र्दितुं), शृध् (c. 10. शर्धयति -यितुं).

CREPITATION, *s.* स्फुटकारः, स्फुटकृतं, स्वनितं, रटितं, रिटिः *f.*, पर्दः, गुदरवः.

CREPUSCULE, *s.* सन्ध्या, सन्ध्याकालः -लं, सन्ध्यासमयः, विकालः -लकः, अरुणोदयकालः; 'morning crepuscule,' पूर्व्वसन्ध्या, प्राक्सन्ध्या, दिवसमुखं; 'evening crepuscule,' परसन्ध्या, पश्चिमसन्ध्या, रजनीमुखं, दिनावसानं.

CREPUSCULOUS, *a.* सान्ध्यः -न्ध्यी -न्ध्यं, वैकालिकः -की -कं, प्रादोषिकः -की -कं.

CRESCENT, *s.* अर्द्धचन्द्रः, चन्द्रार्द्धं, अर्द्धेन्दुः *m.*, इन्दुदलः, अपूर्णचन्द्रः.

CRESCENT, *a.* अर्द्धचन्द्रः -न्द्रा -न्द्रं, चन्द्रार्द्धाकृतिः -तिः -ति, चन्द्रार्द्धः -र्द्धा -र्द्धं.—(Increasing) वर्द्धमानः -ना -नं, वर्द्धी -र्द्धिनी -र्द्धि (न्).

CRESS, *s.* (An herb) जलभूमिरुहः शाकप्रभेदः.

CRESSET, *s.* आकाशदीपः, उन्नतभूभागे स्थापिता दीप्तिः or उल्का.

CREST, *s.* (On the head) चूडा, शिखा, मुकुटं, किरीटः, शिखरः -रं, शेखरः, मौलिः *m. f.*, अवतंसः, कोटीरः.—(Of a cock, &c.) चूडा, शिखा.—(Of a mountain) नगमूर्द्धा *m.* (न्); 'crest-gem,' चूडामणिः *m.*, शिरोरत्नं.

CRESTED, *a.* शिखी -खिनी -खि (न्), शिखरी -रिणी -रि (न्), शिखाधरः -रा -रं, किरीटी -टिनी -टि (न्), किरीटधारी -रिणी -रि (न्), चूडावान् -वती -वत् (त्), चूडालः -ला -लं, चौडः -डी -डं, शेखरितः -ता -तं, अवतंसितः -ता -तं.

CREST-FALLEN, *a.* भग्नदर्पः -र्पा -र्पं, खातगर्व्वः -र्व्वा -र्व्वं, भग्नमानः -ना -नं, विषण्णः -ण्णा -ण्णं, हतौजाः -जाः -जः (स्), दीनमनस्कः -स्का -स्कं, खिन्नः -न्ना -न्नं.

CRETACEOUS, *a.* कठिनीमयः -यी -यं, कठिनीसंसृष्टः -ष्टा -ष्टं, श्वेतधातुपूर्णः -र्णा -र्णं.

CREVICE, *s.* छिद्रं, रन्ध्रं, विवरं, बिलं, सन्धिः *m.*, भित्तिः *f.*, भङ्गः, दरी, गर्त्तः.

CREW, *s.* (Of a ship) पोतवाहाः *m. pl.*, नौकारूढाः *m. pl.*, नाविकाः *m. pl.*, पोतीयलोकाः *m. pl.*, नौस्थाः *m. pl.*, नियामकाः *m. pl.*—(A company of people) जनसमूहः, जनसंसर्गः, गणः, सङ्घः, मण्डलं.

CREWEL, *s.* कौशेयसूत्रकोषः, कोमलम् ऊर्णासूत्रं.

CRIB, *s.* (Rack of a stable) गवादनी, तृणाधारः, द्रोणिः *f.* -णी.—(Stall of an ox) गोष्ठं, गोस्थानं, व्रजः, गोगृहं.—(Infant's bed) शिशुखट्वा.—(Cottage) कुटिः -टी -टीरः.

CRIBBAGE, *s.* क्रिबिज्नामिका द्यूतपत्रक्रीडा.

CRIBBLE, *s.* चालनी -नं, धान्यचालनी, तितउः *m.* -उ *n.*, शोधनी.

CRIBRATION, *s.* चालनं, शोधनं, तितउचालनं.

Crick, *s.* (Noise of a door) कपाटोद्घाटनात् कर्कशशब्दः, द्वारसन्धिचीत्कारः.—(In the neck) मन्यास्तम्भः.

Cricket, *s.* (Insect) झिल्लिका, चीरी, चीरिका, झीरुका, झिरी, वर्षकरी, भिल्लिका, भृङ्गारी -रिका.—(Game with bat and ball) गुलिकाक्रीडा.

Crier, *s.* घोषकः, ख्यापकः, प्रकाशकः, घोषणाकृत्, अर्थिकः.

Crim. con., *s.* प्रतिषिद्धस्त्रीपुरुषालापः.

Crime, *s.* अपराधः, पापं, दोषः, पातकं, दुष्कृतं, दुष्कर्म्म *n.* (न्), पापकर्म्म, कल्मषं, कलुषं, दुरितं, दुरिष्टं, एनः *n.* (स्), आगः *n.* (स्), अघं, अन्यायः, मन्तुः *m.*, कल्कः; 'a heinous crime,' महापातकं.

Criminal, *a.* अपराधी -धिनी -धि (न्), अपराद्धः -द्धा -द्धं, सापराधः -धा -धं, कृतापराधः -धा -धं, पातकी -किनी -कि (न्), पापी -पिनी -पि (न्), पापवान् -वती -वत् (त्), पापकर्म्मा -र्म्मा -र्म्म (न्), दोषी -षिणी -षि (न्), सदोषः -षा -षं, दोषवान् -वती -वत् (त्), दुष्कृती -तिनी -ति (न्), कृतागाः -गाः -गः (स्), अन्यायी -यिनी -यि (न्), एनस्वी -स्विनी -स्वि (न्), अभिपन्नः -न्ना -न्नं; 'criminal law,' दण्डविधिः *m.*

Criminal, *s.* पापी *m.* (न्), पातकी *m.* (न्), अपराधी *m.* (न्), अपराद्धा *m.* (धृ), महापातकी *m.* (न्), दण्ड्यः, वध्यः, दोषग्रस्तः, प्राप्तदोषः.

Criminally, *adv.* सापराधं, सपापं, सदोषं, सपातकं, अन्यायं, दुर्जनवत्; 'according to criminal law,' दण्डविधिवत्.

Criminality, *s.* अपराधिता -त्वं, सापराधता, पापित्वं, सपापता, सदोषत्वं, प्रत्यवायः.

Criminated, *p.p.* अपराधितः -ता -तं, अभियुक्तः -क्ता -क्तं, अभिशस्तः -स्ता -स्तं.

Crimination, *s.* अभियोगः, दोषारोपः -पणं, दोषकल्पनं, दोषप्रसङ्गः, अभिशंसनं, अपवादः.

Criminatory, *a.* अपवादकः -का -कं, अभिशंसकः -का -कं, कलङ्ककरः -री -रं.

Crimp, *a.* (Brittle, crisp) भङ्गुरः -रा -रं, भिदुरः -रा -रं, भिदेलिमः -मा -मं, अशिथिलः -ला -लं, शिथिलेतरः -रा -रं.—(Inconsistent) असङ्गतः -ता -तं, विरुद्धः -द्धा -द्धं.

To crimp, *v. a.* (As fish) मत्स्यान् सद्यो मृतीकृतान् नानाछेदैर् अङ्क् (c. 10. अङ्कयति -यितुं) येन मांसं शिथिलं न भवति.

To crimple, *v. a.* सङ्कुच् (c. 1. -कोचति -चितुं), कुच् (c. 1. कुचति -चितुं), चूर्ण् (c. 10. चूर्णयति -यितुं), पुट् (c. 10. पुटयति -यितुं), पुटीकृ, सङ्कुठीकृ, सतरङ्ग -ङ्गा -ङ्गं कृ.

To crimson, *v. a.* शोण (nom. शोणयति -यितुं), लोहित (nom. लोहितायति -यितुं), अरुण (nom. अरुणयति -यितुं), शोणीकृ, अरुणीकृ.

Crimson, *s.* शोणः, शोणिमा *m.* (न्), लोहितः, रक्तः, रक्तिमा *m.* (न्), अरुणिमा *m.* (न्), कोकनदच्छविः *m.*

Crimson, *a.* शोणः -णा -णं, शोणितः -ता -तं, रक्तः -क्ता -क्तं, रक्तवर्णः -र्णा -र्णं, सुरक्तः -क्ता -क्तं, अरुणः -णा -णं, घनारुणः -णा -णं, लोहितः -ता -तं, रोहितः -ता -तं.

Crimsoned, *p.p.* अरुणितः -ता -तं, पाटलितः -ता -तं, सिन्दूरितः -ता -तं.

Crincum, *s.* सङ्कोचः, वलिः *f.*, लहरी, अस्तद्रिः *m.*, मनोलौल्यं.

Cringe, cringing, *s.* प्रणामः, अष्टाङ्गपातः, अष्टाङ्गप्रणामः, अञ्जलिकर्म्म *n.* (न्), अत्यादरः, लालनं, चाटुः *m.*, एकान्तनमस्कारः.

To cringe, *v. n.* साष्टाङ्गपातं प्रणम् (c. 1. -णमति -णन्तुं), अञ्जलिं कृ, एकान्ततो नमस्कृ, एकान्तादरं कृ, लल् (c. 10. लालयति -यितुं), सान्त्व् (c. 10. सान्त्वयति -यितुं).

Crinigerous, *a.* रोमवान् -वती -वत् (त्), प्रचुरलोमा -मा -म (न्).

To crinkle, *v. a.* ऊर्म्मिरूपेण व्यावृत् (c. 1. -वर्त्तते -र्त्तितुं), पुटीभू, भङ्गुरीभू.

Crinkle, *s.* वलिः *f.*, पुटः, भङ्गः, ऊर्म्मिका, व्यावर्त्तनं, आवर्त्तः.

Cripple, *s.* or *a.* खञ्जः -ञ्जा -ञ्जं, पङ्गुः -ङ्गुः -ङ्गु, विकलाङ्गः -ङ्गी -ङ्गं, पादविकलः -ला -लं, अङ्गहीनः -ना -नं, अपाङ्गः -ङ्गी -ङ्गं, व्यङ्गः -ङ्गी -ङ्गं, गतिविकलः -ला -लं, विकलगतिः -तिः -ति, गतिहीनः -ना -नं, पक्षः पांशुषः, कुणिः *m.*, श्रोणः.—(One who moves about in a chair) पीठसर्पी *m.* (न्).

To cripple, *v. a.* विकल (nom. विकलयति -यितुं), विकलीकृ, व्यङ्गीकृ, अपाङ्गीकृ.

Crippled, *p.p.* विकलीकृतः -ता -तं, न्यूनाङ्गः -ङ्गी -ङ्गं, हीनाङ्गः -ङ्गी -ङ्गं, गतिशक्तिरहितः -ता -तं, हस्तपादादिशक्तिवर्ज्जितः -ता -तं.

Crippleness, *s.* खञ्जत्वं, पङ्गुता, गतिवैकल्यं, अङ्गवैकल्यं, व्यङ्गता.

Crisis, *s.* (Of a disease) रोगावधिर् यत्प्रभृति रोगार्त्तो मरणं वा स्वास्थ्यं वा याति, व्याधिसीमा.—(Of any affair) लग्नं, शुभाशुभलग्नं, निर्व्वहणं, कार्य्यनिर्व्वहणक्षणः, परिवर्त्तनक्षणः, विकल्पक्षणः, सन्देहसमयः, शेषावस्था, समयः, तात्कालः.

Crisp, *a.* (Curled, indented) कुञ्चितः -ता -तं, भङ्गुरः -रा -रं, वन्धुरः -रा -रं.—(Brittle) भङ्गुरः -रा -रं, भिदुरः -रा -रं, भिदेलिमः -मा -मं.

To crisp, *v. a.* केशान् कुञ्च् (c. 1. कुञ्चति -ञ्चितुं) or आकुञ्च्, अलकान् रच् (c. 10. रचयति -यितुं), भङ्गुरीकृ, वन्धुरीकृ.

Crispation, *s.* कुञ्चनं, आकुञ्चनं, केशाकुञ्चनं, अलकाकुञ्चनं, अलकरचना.

Crisping-iron or crisping-pin, *s.* केशाकुञ्चनयन्त्रं, अलकरचनार्थं लोहकीलः.

Crispness, *s.* (Curledness) आकुञ्चितत्वं.—(Brittleness) भङ्गुरता, भिदुरत्वं.

Criss-cross-row, *s.* वर्णमाला, व्याकरणारम्भः, आरम्भः, प्रारम्भः.

Criterion, *s.* लक्षणं, चिह्नं, लिङ्गं, व्यञ्जनं, आकषः, निकषः, कषः, अभिज्ञानं, संज्ञा, अवगतिः *f.*, लाञ्छनं.

Critic, *s.* (Judge of writings, &c.) गुणज्ञः, गुणागुणज्ञः, गुणग्राही *m.* (न्), गुणदोषपरीक्षकः, गुणदोषनिरूपकः, विज्ञः, अभिज्ञः, तज्ज्ञः, तद्विद् *m.*—(A censor) दोषग्राही *m.* (न्), छिद्रान्वेषी *m.* (न्), वाक्यखण्डकः, वितण्डकः.

Critical, *a.* (Of judicious taste) गुणदोषज्ञः -ज्ञा -ज्ञं, गुणदोषग्राही -हिणी -हि (न्).—(Relating to criticism) गुणपरीक्षकः -का -कं, वितण्डी -ण्डिनी -ण्डि (न्).—(Censorious) दोषदर्शी -र्शिनी -र्शि (न्), छिद्रानुसारी -रिणी -रि (न्).—(Relating to a crisis, decisive) तात्कालिकः -की -कं, निर्व्वहणः -णा -णं; 'the critical time,' निर्व्वहणकालः.—(Dangerous, dubious) सन्दिग्धः -ग्धा -ग्धं, सांशयिकः -की -कं, वैकल्पिकः -की -कं.

Critically, *adv.* (In a critical or censorious manner) गुणज्ञवत्, गुणदोषपरीक्षया, सवितण्डं.—(At the exact point of time) तत्काले, तदानीमेव, तत्क्षणादेव.

To criticise, *v. a.* गुणदोषान् परीक्ष् (c. 1. -ईक्षते -क्षितुं), or निरूप् (c. 10. -रूपयति -यितुं), वितण्ड् (c. 1. -तण्डते -ण्डितुं), वाक्यं खण्ड् (c. 10. खण्डयति -यितुं), छिद्राणि or दोषान् अन्विष् (c. 4. -इष्यति -एषितुं).

Criticism, critique, *s.* गुणदोषपरीक्षा, गुणविज्ञानं, गुणागुणज्ञानं, गुणदोषनिरूपणविद्या, वाक्यखण्डनं, दोषानुसन्धानं, छिद्रान्वेषः, वितण्डा, वितण्डावादः,

To croak, *v. n.* (As a crow) कै (c. 1. कायति, कातुं), ध्राङ्क्ष् (c. 1. ध्राङ्क्षति -ङ्क्षितुं), ध्वाङ्क्ष् (c. 1. ध्वाङ्क्षति -ङ्क्षितुं), or वाङ्क्ष् or ध्वाङ्क्ष्; का शब्दं कृ.—(As a frog) भेकनादं कृ, भेकवद् रु (c. 2. रौति, रवितुं).—(Make a harsh sound) विरु, रट् (c. 1. रटति -टितुं), कर्कशशब्दं कृ.

Croaking or croak, *s.* भेकनादः, काकरावः, ध्वाङ्क्षरावः, का शब्द, कर्कशनादः.

Croceous, *a.* कौङ्कुमः -मी -मं, कुङ्कुमाक्तः -क्ता -क्तं, गौरः -रा -री -रं.

CROCK, *s.* मृद्भाण्डं, मृत्पात्रं, मृद्भाजनं, मृत्तिकापात्रं, मृण्मयभाण्डं.

CROCKERY, *s.* कौलालकं, मृद्भाण्डानि *n. pl.*, मृण्मयभाण्डानि, मार्त्तिकं.

CROCODILE, *s.* नक्रः, कुम्भीरः, आलास्यः, महामुखः, द्विधागतिः *m.*, असिदन्तः, जलशूकरः, जलहस्ती *m.* (न्).

CROCUS, *s.* वसन्तोद्भवः पीतपुष्प ओषधिभेदः.

CROFT, *s.* वाटः, वाटिका, वृतिः *f.*, प्रावृतिः *f.*

CROISADE or CRUSADE, *s.* पुण्यनगरप्रत्युद्धरणार्थं ख्रीष्टीयानां यावनैः सह युद्धं, ख्रीष्टधर्म्मविषये आस्तिकानां यावनैः सह युद्धं.

CROISES, *s. pl.* क्रूशध्वजा योधाः *m. pl.*, ख्रीष्टीयधर्म्मार्थं योद्धारः *m. pl.*, क्रूशलाञ्छनाः कार्पटिकाः, क्रूशलिङ्गाः तीर्थसेविनः *m. pl.*

CRONE, *s.* वृद्धा स्त्री, जरिणी, जरती, जरापरिणता, पलिक्नी.

CRONY, *s.* चिरमित्रं, चिरपरिचितः, प्रियसुहृत्, प्रियवयस्यः, सुहृत्तमः.

CROOK, *s.* आकर्षणी -र्षिणी, न्युब्जदण्डः, वक्राग्रो दण्डः, अङ्कुशाकाराग्रो दण्डः, कुञ्चिताग्रो यष्टिः; 'shepherd's crook,' मेषपालकदण्डः.

To CROOK, *v. a.* नम् in caus. (नामयति -यितुं), अञ्च् (c. 1. अञ्चति -ते -ञ्चितुं), कुञ्च् (c. 1. कुञ्चति -ञ्चितुं), आकुञ्च्, वक्रीकृ, कुटिलीकृ, साचीकृ.

CROOK-BACK, *s.* न्युब्जः -ब्जा -ब्जं, कुब्जः -ब्जा -ब्जं, गडुरः -रा -रं.

CROOKED, *a.* (Not straight) वक्रः -क्रा -क्रं, वक्रिमः -मा -मं, कुटिलः -ला -लं, जिह्मः -ह्मा -ह्मं, विजिह्मः -ह्मा -ह्मं, अनृजुः -जुः -जु, भङ्गुरः -रा -रं, अरालः -ला -लं, नतः -ता -तं, नामितः -ता -तं, कुञ्चितः -ता -तं, आकुञ्चितः -ता -तं, भुग्नः -ग्ना -ग्नं, अवभुग्नः -ग्ना -ग्नं, विभुग्नः -ग्ना -ग्नं, सम्भुग्नः -ग्ना -ग्नं, वृजिनः -ना -नं, वृजनः -ना -नं, न्युब्जः -ब्जा -ब्जं, ह्वेडः -डा -डं, ह्लोमः -मा -मं, साचिस्थितः -ता -तं, विषमः -मा -मं.—(Distorted, made crooked) वक्रीकृतः -ता -तं, साचीकृतः -ता -तं, विकृताकारः -रा -रं.—(Winding) वक्रः -क्रा -क्रं, कुटिलः -ला -लं, विसर्पी -र्पिणी -र्पि (न्).—(Perverse, depraved) प्रतीपः -पा -पं, निकृतः -ता -तं, वक्री -क्रिणी -क्रि (न्), अनृजुप्रकृतिः -तिः -ति, भ्रष्टभावः -वा -वं; 'crooked-armed,' बाहुकुब्जः -ब्जा -ब्जं, दोर्गडुः, कुण्यः, कूणिः *m.*, कुकरः; 'crooked-nosed,' वक्रनासः -सा -सं, निविडः -डीषः; 'crooked-legged,' वक्रपादः -दा -दं; 'crooked with age,' जरापरिणतः -ता -तं.

CROOKEDLY, *adv.* कुटिलं, वक्रं, जिह्मं, विजिह्मं, अनृजु, तिरस्, साचि, तिर्य्यक्, पराक्; 'moving crookedly,' तिर्य्यग्यानः, वक्रगामी *m.* (न्) कुटिलगामी *m.*, जिह्मगः -गा -गं.

CROOKEDNESS, *s.* वक्रता, वक्रिमा *m.* (न्), जिह्मता, जैह्म्यं, विजिह्मता, कुटिलता, कौटिल्यं, अनृजुता, अनार्जवं, वक्रीभावः, नतिः *f.*—(Of body) वैरूप्यं, न्युब्जता.

CROP, *s.* (Craw of a bird) पक्षिजठरः.—(Highest part of any thing) अग्रं, शिखा; 'ear of corn,' धान्यशीर्षकं.—(The harvest, product) शस्यसङ्ग्रहः, फलं, क्षेत्रफलं, कृषिफलं, उत्पन्नं.

To CROP, *v. a.* (Cut short) छिद् (c. 7. छिनत्ति, छेत्तुं), लू (c. 9. लुनाति, लवितुं), निकृत् (c. 6. -कृन्तति -कर्त्तितुं).—(Reap, gather corn, &c.) शस्यं लू or सङ्ग्रह् (c. 9. -गृह्णाति -ग्रहीतुं).—(As cattle) चर् (c. 1. चरति -रितुं), शस्यम् अद् (c. 2. अत्ति -त्तुं).

CROP-EARED, *a.* छिन्नकर्णः -र्णा -र्णं, लूनकर्णः -र्णा -र्णं.

CROP-FULL, *a.* परिपूर्णोदरः -रा -रं, पूर्णजठरः -रा -रं, अतितृप्तः -प्ता -प्तं.

CROP-SICK, *a.* अतिसौहित्यात् or अतितृप्तोदरत्वाद् वमथुपीडितः -ता -तं.

CRORE, *s.* (Ten millions) कोटिः *f.* -टी.

CROSIER, *s.* धर्म्माधिपतेः क्रूशाग्रो दण्डः, क्रूशलक्षितो धर्म्माध्यक्षदण्डः.

CROSS, *s.* (Two transverse pieces of wood) व्यत्यस्तकाष्ठद्वयं.—(The instrument by which Christ suffered death) क्रूशाभिधानं ख्रीष्टवधसाधनं. In modern Sanskrit क्रूशः or क्रुशः are used in this sense.—(An instrument for impaling criminals) शूला -लः -लं, कीलः.—(Any thing that thwarts, hindrance, vexation) व्याघातः, प्रतिरोधः, विघ्नः, प्रत्यूहः, बाधः, क्लेशः, दुःखं, कष्टं, शल्यं.—(Cross lines) व्यत्यस्तरेखाद्वयं, स्वस्तिकः.

CROSS, *a.* (Transverse) व्यत्यस्तः -स्ता -स्तं, तिर्य्यङ् तिरश्ची तिर्य्यक्, वक्रः -क्रा -क्रं.—(Adverse, contrary) विरोधी -धिनी -धि (न्), प्रतिकूलः -ला -लं, विपरीतः -ता -तं, विलोमः -मी -मं, प्रतिलोमः -मा -मं, विपर्य्यस्तः -स्ता -स्तं, प्रतिपक्षः -क्षा -क्षं, विपक्षः -क्षा -क्षं.—(Perverse, peevish) प्रतीपः -पा -पं, कर्कशः -शा -शं, वक्रभावः -वा -वं, सदावक्रः -क्रा -क्रं, नैकृतिकः -की -कं, विपरीतकारी -रिणी -रि (न्); 'a cross woman,' अधीरा; 'cross multiplication,' वज्राभ्यासः; 'cross threads,' पूरणं -णी; 'to be cross,' प्रतीप (nom. प्रतीपायते).

CROSS, *prep.* and *adv.* (Athwart) व्यत्यस्तं, कोणाकोणि, तिर्य्यक्.—(Over, to the other side) पारं, तीरान्तरं.

To CROSS, *v. a.* (Lay one body across another) व्यत्यस् (c. 4. -अस्यति -असितुं), व्यत्यासीकृ, अन्यद् अन्यस्योपरि व्यत्यस्तरूपेण धा (c. 3. दधाति, धातुं); 'to cross the legs,' व्यत्यस्तपादेन आस् (c. 2. आस्ते, आसितुं); 'to cross the arms,' बाहुव्यत्यासं कृ, स्वस्तिकं कृ.—(Go across) तॄ (c. 1. तरति -रितुं -रीतुं), अतितॄ, सन्तॄ, निस्तॄ, उत्तॄ, समुत्तॄ, अती (c. 2. -एति -एतुं), व्यती, अतिक्रम् (c. 1. -क्रामति -क्रमितुं), व्यतिक्रम्; 'if he crosses your sight,' यदि दर्शनपथम् अवतरति.—(Cross to the other side) पारं गम् (c. 1. गच्छति, गन्तुं); 'to cross the sea,' समुद्रपारं गम्; 'one who crosses a river,' अवारपारीणः, अवारीणः.—(Thwart) प्रतिरुध् (c. 7. -रुणद्धि -रोद्धुं), निरुध्, विरुध्, विघ्न (nom. विघ्नयति -यितुं), व्याहन् (c. 2. -हन्ति -हन्तुं), प्रतिकूल (nom. प्रतिकूलयति -यितुं).—(Cross out writing) लिखितलोपसूचनार्थं व्यत्यस्तरेखाद्वयेन चिह्न् (c. 10. चिह्नयति -यितुं).

CROSS-BOW, *s.* सृगप्रक्षेपणो धनुर्विशेषः, सृगासनं, गोलासनं.

CROSS-BOWMAN, *s.* पूर्व्वोक्तधनुर्धारी, सृगासनभृत्, सृगासः, गोलासः.

CROSSED, *p. p.* (Laid transversely) व्यत्यस्तः -स्ता -स्तं; 'with hands crossed,' व्यत्यस्तपाणिना.—(Gone across) तीर्णः -र्णा -र्णं, उत्तीर्णः -र्णा -र्णं, अतिक्रान्तः -न्ता -न्तं, व्यतिक्रान्तः -न्ता -न्तं, पारगतः -ता -तं.—(Thwarted) विरुद्धः -द्धा -द्धं, बाधितः -ता -तं.

To CROSS-EXAMINE, *v. a.* विपक्षसाक्षिणं नानाविधैः प्रश्नैर् मुह् in caus. (मोहयति -यितुं).

CROSS-GRAINED, *a.* विलोमः -मी -मं, प्रतिलोमः -मा -मं, प्रतीपः -पा -पं.

CROSSLY, *adv.* (Transversely) व्यत्यस्तं, तिर्य्यक्.—(Adversely) प्रतीपं, प्रतिलोमं, प्रतिकूलं, विपरीतं.—(Unsuitably) अयुक्तं, अस्थाने.—(Peevishly) कर्कशं.

CROSSNESS, *s.* प्रतीपता, कार्कश्यं, कर्कशत्वं, निकृतिः *f.*, भाववक्रता, अनार्जवं.

CROSS-ROAD, *s.* चतुष्पथं, त्रिपथं, त्रिकं, शृङ्गाटं -टकं, चारपथः, संस्थानं, प्रवणः.—(Not the direct high road) उपपथः.

CROTCH, *s.* आकर्षणी -र्षिणी, अङ्कुशः, वडिशी.

CROTCHET, *s.* (In music) गान्धर्व्वविद्यायां मध्यमतालसूचकं चिह्नं.—(A whim) मनोलौल्यं, मनश्चापलं, मनःकल्पना, अवद्धिः *m.*, लहरी.

To CROUCH, *v. n.* (Stoop down) कायं प्रणम् (c. 1. -णमति -णन्तुं or -णामयति -यितुं), नताङ्गः -ङ्गी -ङ्गं or नम्राङ्गः -ङ्गी -ङ्गं भू, प्रह्वीभू, नम्रीभू, कुटिलिकां कृ; 'to crouch servilely at another's feet,' साष्टाङ्गपातं परपादयोः प्रणिपत् (c. 1. -पतति -तितुं).—(Fawn) चाटुकारेण सान्त्व् (c. 10. सान्त्वयति -यितुं).

CROUCHING, *p. p.* अवनतकायः -या -यं, नम्रमूर्त्तिः -र्त्तिः -र्त्ति, आनतशरीरः -रा -रं, प्रह्वः -ह्वा -ह्वं, अवाग्रः -ग्रा -ग्रं.

CROUP, *s.* (Of a fowl) कुक्कुटस्य पश्चाद्भागः.—(Of a horse) अश्वनितम्बः.—(Disease of children) शिशूनां काशपीनसादिलक्षितो रोगः.

CROW, *s.* (The bird) काकः, वायसः, ध्वाङ्क्षः, ध्वांक्षः, ध्वांक्षरावी *m.* (न्), करटः, बलिभुक् *m.* (ज्), गृहबलिभुक्, बलिपुष्टः -ष्टा -ष्टं, चिरञ्जीवी *m.* (न्), काणः, काणूकः, मौकुलिः *m.*, दिवाटनः, शक्रजः, सकृत्प्रजः, मलभुक् *m.* (ज्), प्रातर्भोक्ता *m.* (क्तृ), कारवः, अन्यभृत् *m.*, धूङ्क्षाटिः *m.*; अरिष्टः, आत्मघोषः; 'carrion crow,' द्रोणः, दग्धकाकः, शवभुक् *m.* (ज्), कुणपभुक्, नालिजङ्घः; 'crow's nest,' वर्त्तूलकः.—(Crow-bar) लोहदण्डः, अर्गला, शर्गला, तोमरः, तङ्कः.—(Cry of the cock, cry of joy) कुक्कुटरवः, हर्षनादः.

To CROW, *v. n.* (As a cock) कुक्कुटवद् रु (c. 2. रौति, रवितुं) or नद् (c. 1. नदति -दितुं).—(Boast, bluster) विकत्थ् (c. 1. -कत्थते -त्थितुं), दृप् (c. 4. दृप्यति, द्रप्तुं), भर्त्स् (c. 10. भर्त्सयते -यितुं), दम्भं कृ.

CROWD, *s.* (A multitude) समूहः, सङ्घः, सङ्घातः, मेलः -लकः, समाजः, सञ्चयः, समयः, वृन्दं.—(Confused mass) सङ्कुलं.—(Crowd of people) बहुजनसमूहः, बहुजनमेलकः, जनसम्मर्दः, लोकसङ्घः, लोकनिवहः, जनसङ्कुलं, जनसमागमः, जनता, जनौघः.

To CROWD, *v. a.* (Fill to excess) अतिशयेन पॄ in caus. (पूरयति -यितुं), or परिपॄ, सङ्कुलीकृ, सङ्कीर्णीकृ, आकीर्णीकृ.—(Press close together) सम्मृद् (c. 9. -मृद्नाति -मर्द्दितुं), सम्बाध् (c. 1. -बाधते -धितुं), सङ्कटीकृ.

To CROWD, *v. n.* सङ्कॄ in pass. (-कीर्य्यते), पॄ in pass. (पूर्य्यते) or आपॄ, व्याप् in pass. (-आप्यते), सङ्कुलीभू, बहुलीभू.

CROWDED, *p. p.* सङ्कीर्णः -र्णा -र्णं, आकीर्णः -र्णा -र्णं, अनुकीर्णः -र्णा -र्णं, सङ्कुलः -ला -लं, समाकुलः -ला -लं, व्याप्तः -प्ता -प्तं, सम्बाधः -धा -धं, सङ्कटः -टा -टं, गुप्तः -प्ता -प्तं, प्रस्तीमः -मा -मं, प्रस्तीतः -ता -तं, अनवकाशः -शा -शं, निरुच्छ्वासः -सा -सं; 'with people,' बहुजनाकीर्णः -र्णा -र्णं.

CROWDER, *s.* (Player on the violin) शारङ्गीवादकः, पिनाकीवादः.

CROWFOOT, *s.* (Caltrop). *See* the word.—(Plant) गोक्षुरः, गोक्षुरः.

CROWING, *s.* (Of a cock) कुक्कुटरवः, कुक्कुटध्वनिः *m.*, चरणायुधशब्दः.

CROWN, *s.* (Ornament for the head denoting royalty) मुकुटं, किरीटः, राजमुकुटं, मौलिः *m. f.*, राजमौलिः, राजपट्टः, राजाभरणं.—(Garland) स्रक् *f.* (ज्), माला.—(Regal power, royalty) राज्यं, राजत्वं.—(Top of the head) मस्तकाग्रं.—(Top of any thing) अग्रं, शिखा, मस्तकं, शिरः *n.* (स्), शीर्षकं; 'of a mountain,' गिरिशृङ्गं, गिरिपृष्ठं.—(Crown of a hat) शिरस्काग्रं, शिरस्त्रस्य अग्रभागः. (Piece of silver) रूप्यमुद्रा.

To CROWN, *v. a.* मुकुटेन अलङ्कृ, मुकुटं शिरसि धा (c. 3. -दधाति -धातुं), किरीट (nom. किरीटयति -यितुं), मुकुट (nom. मुकुटयति -यितुं), किरीटं शिरसि धा or ऋ in caus. (अर्पयति -यितुं), किरीटार्पणसंस्कारं कृ; 'with a garland,' स्रज् (nom. स्रजयति -यितुं).—(Complete, perfect) सम्पद् in caus. (-पादयति -यितुं), निष्पद्, समाप् in caus. (-आपयति -यितुं), संस्कृ, पुरस्कृ.

CROWNED, *p. p.* किरीटी -टिनी -टि (न्), मुकुटधारी -रिणी -रि (न्).

CROWN-SCAB, *s.* अश्वखुरस्य अग्रभागे व्रणः or क्षतं or पाम *n.* (न्).

To CRUCIATE, *v. a.* क्लिश् (c. 9. क्लिश्नाति, क्लेशुं), व्यथ् in caus. (व्यथयति -यितुं), तप् in caus. (तापयति -यितुं), प्रमथ् (c. 1. -मथति -थितुं), यत् in caus. (यातयति -यितुं).

CRUCIBLE OR CRUSET, *s.* मूषः -षी -षा -षिका, अन्धमूषा, वकः, वकयन्त्रं, आवर्त्तनी, तैजसावर्त्तिनी, शिलाञ्जिका.

CRUCIFEROUS, *a.* क्रूशचिह्नधारी -रिणी -रि (न्).

CRUCIFIX, *s.* क्रूशारोपितस्य ख्रीष्टस्य प्रतिमा or मूर्त्तिः *f.*

CRUCIFIXION, *s.* ख्रीष्टस्य क्रूशारोपणं or क्रूशनिवेशनं or क्रूशे बन्धनं.

CRUCIFORM, *a.* क्रूशाकारः -रा -रं, क्रूशाकृतिः -तिः -ति.

To CRUCIFY, *v. a.* क्रूशे आरुह् in caus. (-रोपयति -यितुं) or समारुह् or निविश् in caus. (-वेशयति -यितुं) or बन्ध् (c. 9. बध्नाति, बन्द्धुं) or व्यध् (c. 4. विध्यति, व्यद्धुं).

CRUDE, *a.* (Raw) आमः -मा -मं, बलः -ला -लं.—(Unripe, uncooked) अपक्वः -क्वा -क्वं, अपरिपक्वः -क्वा -क्वं, अपरिणतः -ता -तं, आपक्वः -क्वा -क्वं, असंस्कृतः -ता -तं, अनुपस्कृतः -ता -तं, असिद्धः -द्धा -द्धं, यातयामः -मा -मं.—(Undigested) अजीर्णः -र्णा -र्णं, विदग्धः -ग्धा -ग्धं.—(Not brought to perfection) असम्पूर्णः -र्णा -र्णं, अपूर्णकालः -ला -लं, असमाप्तः -प्ता -प्तं, अपरिष्कृतः -ता -तं, अयत्नकृतः -ता -तं; 'crude form of a noun,' प्रातिपदिकं, पदं.

CRUDELY, *adv.* अपूर्णकाले, अपरिष्कृतं, असिद्धं, अयत्नपूर्व्वं.

CRUDENESS, CRUDITY, *s.* आमता, अपक्वता, अपरिपक्वत्वं, अपाकः, अपक्तिः *f.*, असिद्धत्वं, अजीर्णिः *f.*, अजीर्णता, असम्पूर्णत्वं, असमाप्तिः *f.*, अपरिष्कारः.

CRUEL, *a.* निठुरः -रा -रं, क्रूरः -रा -रं, क्रूरकर्म्मा -र्म्मा -र्म्म (न्), क्रूरकृत् *m. f. n.*, क्रूरकर्म्मशाली -लिनी -लि (न्), हिंस्रः -स्रा -स्रं, नृशंसः -सा -सं, प्राणिपीडाकरः -री -रं, क्लेशकः -का -कं, निर्दयः -या -यं, दयाहीनः -ना -नं, निष्कृपः -पा -पं, कठिनहृदयः -या -यं, अकरुणः -णा -णं, निष्करुणः -णा -णं, निर्घृणः -णा -णं, वीतघृणः -णा -णं, दुःखकरः -री -रं, पिशुनः -ना -नं, व्यालः -ला -लं, द्रोही -हिणी -हि (न्).

CRUELLY, *adv.* निठुरं, निर्दयं, क्रूरं, निष्करुणं, निर्घृणं, नैठुर्य्येण, क्रौर्य्येण.

CRUELNESS, CRUELTY, *s.* नैठुर्य्यं, निठुरता, क्रूरता, क्रौर्य्यं, हिंस्रत्वं, नृशंसता, निर्दयत्वं, निष्करुणता, वीतघृणता, पैशुन्यं, दौरात्म्यं, द्रोहः, अभिद्रोहः, उत्पातः; 'cruelty to animals,' प्राणिपीडा, प्राणिहिंसा.

CRUENTATE, *a.* रक्ताक्तः -क्ता -क्तं, रक्तलिप्तः -प्ता -प्तं, असृग्लिप्तः -प्ता -प्तं, शोणिताक्तः -क्ता -क्तं, शोणितोक्षितः -ता -तं, रक्तमलिनः -ना -नं.

CRUET, *s.* शुक्ततैलादिधारणार्थं क्षुद्रकाचकूपी, शुक्ततैलाद्याधारः.

CRUISE, *s.* (A small cup) क्षुद्रपात्रं, क्षुद्रभाजनं, क्षुद्रकूपी, क्षुद्रकंसः.—(A voyage in search of plunder) लोप्त्रहरणार्थम् इतस्ततः समुद्रभ्रमणं or समुद्रयानं.

To CRUISE, *v. n.* लोप्त्रहरणार्थम् इतस्ततः समुद्रं परिभ्रम् (c. 4. -भ्राम्यति -भ्रमितुं).

CRUISER, *s.* पारक्यनौकानुसरणे वा न वा नियुक्ता यत्र कुत्रचित् समुद्रयायिनी युद्धनौका.

CRUM, CRUMB, *s.* (Fragment of bread, leavings of a meal) गुडं, फेलकः, फेला -लिः *f.*, पिण्डोलिः *f.*, अतिरिक्तपूपः, अपूपलवः, अपूपखण्डः, अपूपशकलं, भुक्तसमुज्झितं, शेषान्नं, अन्नशेषः, भोजनपात्राद् उज्झितं.—(Soft part of bread) अपूपस्य कोमलभागः or कोमलांशः.

To CRUM OR CRUMBLE, *v. a.* चूर्ण् (c. 10. चूर्णयति -यितुं), विचूर्ण्, चूर्णीकृ; क्षुद् (c. 7. क्षुणत्ति, क्षोत्तुं), प्रक्षुद्, संक्षुद्; पिष् (c. 7. पिनष्टि, पेष्टुं), निष्पिष्; मृद् (c. 9. मृद्नाति, मर्द्दितुं), विमृद्; खण्ड् (c. 10. खण्डयति, -यितुं), खण्डशः कृ, खण्डं खण्डं कृ, शकलीकृ.

To CRUMBLE, *v. n.* चूर्णीभू, शकलीभू, खण्डशो भू, क्षुण्णीभू, विशीर्णीभू, विशॄ in pass. (-शीर्य्यते).

CRUMMY, *a.* कोमलः -ला -लं, मृदुलः -ला -लं, मसृणः -णा -णं.

CRUMP, *a.* कुब्जः -ब्जा -ब्जं, न्युब्जः -ब्जा -ब्जं, गडुरः -रा -रं.

CRUMPET, *s.* शिथिलपिष्टकविशेषः यो नवनीताक्तो भूत्वा खाद्यते.

To CRUMPLE, *v. a.* कुच् (c. 1. कुचति -चितुं), सङ्कुच् (c. 1. -कोचति -चितुं), पुट् (c. 10. पुटयति -यितुं), सम्पुट्, सम्मृद् (c. 9. -मृद्नाति -मर्द्दितुं),

चूर्ण् (c. 10. चूर्णयति -यितुं), रूक्षीकृ.

CRUMPLING, s. (The act of crumpling) कुञ्चनं, सङ्कोचनं, सम्मर्द्दः, अवमर्द्दः.—(Fruit) शिथिलत्वग्विशिष्टं क्षुद्रफलं.

CRUPPER, s. चर्म्मबन्धो येन पर्य्याणम् अश्वलाङ्गूलेन संयुज्यते, पुच्छबन्धः.

CRURAL, a. जाङ्घिकः -की -कं, जङ्घासम्बन्धी -न्धिनी -न्धि (न्).

CRUSADE, CRUSADER. *See* CROISADE, CROISES, s.

CRUSH, s. (Act of crushing) मर्द्दनं, सम्मर्द्दः, अवमर्द्दः, सम्पेषः, निष्पेषः, सङ्घट्टः -ट्टनं, घर्षणं, समाघातः.—(A crowd) जनसम्मर्द्दः, जनौघः.

To CRUSH, *v. a.* (Squeeze) पीड् (c. 10. पीडयति -यितुं), सम्पीड्.—(Collide) मृद् (c. 9. मृद्नाति, मर्द्दितुं), सम्मृद्, प्रमृद्, विमृद्, आमृद्; पिष् (c. 7. पिनष्टि, पेष्टुं), सम्पिष्, निष्पिष्, विनिष्पिष्; चूर्ण् (c. 10. चूर्णयति -यितुं), प्रचूर्ण्, अवचूर्ण्, विचूर्ण्; घृष् (c. 1. घर्षति -र्षितुं); प्रभञ्ज् (c. 7. -भनक्ति -भंक्तुं); खण्ड् (c. 10. खण्डयति -यितुं); मन्थ् (c. 9. मथ्नाति, मन्थितुं, c. 1. मथति -थितुं); क्षुद् (c. 7. क्षुणत्ति, क्षोत्तुं), पुष् in caus. (पोषयति -यितुं).—(Beat down) निपत् in caus. (-पातयति -यितुं), अवमृद्.—(Demolish, subdue) नश् in caus. (नाशयति -यितुं), विनश्, दम् in caus. (दमयति -यितुं).

CRUSHED, *p. p.* मर्द्दितः -ता -तं, सम्मर्द्दितः -ता -तं, परिमृदितः -ता -तं, सम्पिष्टः -ष्टा -ष्टं, निष्पिष्टः -ष्टा -ष्टं, चूर्णितः -ता -तं, घर्षितः -ता -तं.

CRUST, s. (An external coat or skin by which a body is enveloped) त्वक् *f.* (च्), बाह्यभागः, पटलं, बाह्यपटलं, बाह्यकोशः, बहिःकोशः, छल्लिः *f.* -ल्ली, चोचं, चोलकं, वल्कं, शल्कं, बहिरावेष्टनं, पेशी.—(Hard incrustation) घनपटलं, घनीभूतं बाह्यपटलं, शीनीभूतो बाह्यभागः.—(Crust of bread) अपूपस्य बाह्यभागः or घनभागः.—(Pie-crust) शष्कुलस्य वहिर्भागः or उपरिभागः.

To CRUST, *v. a.* बाह्यतस् or वहिर्भागे घनीकृ, घनपटलेन वेष्ट् in caus. (वेष्टयति -यितुं) or आच्छद् (c. 10. -छादयति -यितुं) or शीनीकृ or संहतीकृ.

To CRUST, *v. n.* बाह्यतस् or बाह्यभागे घनीभू, घनपटलं बन्ध् (c. 9. बध्नाति, बन्द्धुं), वहिर्भागे संहतीभू or श्यानीभू.

CRUSTACEOUS, *a.* कवची -चिनी -चि (न्), काशवः -वी -वं, वल्कवान् -वती -वत् (त्).

CRUSTILY, *adv.* (Peevishly) कर्कशं, प्रतीपं, परुषं, कटुभावेन.

CRUSTINESS, s. कर्कशत्वं, प्रतीपता, निकृतिः *f.*, भावरूक्षता, भावकटुता.

CRUSTY, *a.* (Covered with a crust) त्वाचः -ची -चं, घनपटलोपेतः -ता -तं.—(Peevish) कर्कशः -शा -शं, प्रतीपः -पा -पं, नैकृतिकः -की -कं.

CRUTCH, s. वृद्धभृतो दण्डः, पङ्गुना कक्षेणावलम्बितो दण्डः, अरिणोपाश्रितो यष्टिः, खञ्जालम्बनार्थं दण्डः.

To CRUTCH, *v. a.* दण्डेन आलम्ब् (c. 1. -लम्बते -म्बितुं) or उत्तम्भ् in caus. (-तम्भयति for -स्तम्भयति -यितुं).

To CRY, *v. n.* (Weep, utter lamentations) क्रन्द् (c. 1. क्रन्दति -न्दितुं), आक्रन्द्; रुद् (c. 2. रोदिति -तुं), प्ररुद्; परिदेव् (c. 1. -देवते -वितुं); विलप् (c. 1. -लपति -पितुं), क्रुश् (c. 1. क्रोशति, क्रोष्टुं), विक्रुश्, परिक्रुश्.—(Shed tears) अश्रूणि or वाष्पं पत् in caus. (पातयति -यितुं) or मुच् (c. 6. मुञ्चति, मोक्तुं) or सृज् (c. 6. सृजति, स्रष्टुं), वाष्प (nom. वाष्पायते).—(Utter inarticulate sounds, scream) रु (c. 2. रौति, रवितुं), विरु; नद् (c. 1. नदति -दितुं), रस् (c. 1. रसति -सितुं), क्रुश्, विक्रुश्, वाश् (c. 4. वाश्यते, c. 1. वाशते -शितुं), कु (c. 1. कवते -वितुं), स्वरं कृ, चीत् शब्दं कृ, चित्कारं कृ, चीत्कृ.—(Cry out, exclaim) उत्क्रुश्, प्रकाशं or उच्चैःस्वरेण घुष् in caus. (घोषयति -यितुं), उद्घुष्; प्रक्ष्विड् (c. 1. -क्ष्वेडति -डितुं).—(Proclaim) घुष् in caus., विघुष् in caus.; प्रख्या in caus. (-ख्यापयति -यितुं), प्रकाश् in caus. (-काशयति -यितुं), उच्चर् in caus. (-चारयति -यितुं), उत्कृत् (c. 10. -कीर्त्तयति -यितुं).

To CRY DOWN, *v. a.* (Depreciate) अपवद् (c. 1. -वदति -दितुं), परिवद्; अपकृष् (c. 1. -कर्षति -क्रष्टुं), कन (nom. कनयति -यितुं).—(Prohibit) निषिध् (c. 1. -षेधति -षेद्धुं), प्रतिषिध्.

To CRY UNTO, *v. a.* आह्वे (c. 1. -ह्वयति -ह्वातुं), प्रार्थ् (c. 10. प्रार्थयति -यितुं).

To CRY UP, *v. a.* प्रशंस् (c. 1. -शंसति -सितुं), कृत् (c. 10. कीर्त्तयति -यितुं).

CRY s. (Lamentation, weeping) क्रन्दनं, क्रन्दितं, रोदनं, रुदितं, विलपनं, विलापः, परिदेवनं -ना, क्रुष्टं.—(Clamour) उत्क्रोशः, उत्क्रुष्टं, घोषणं -णा, उच्चैर्घुष्टं, उच्चैःस्वरः, जनरवः, संहूतिः.—(Confused noise, scream) कोलाहलः, शब्दः, रुतं, रावः, चित्कारः, चीत्कारः, नादः, विक्रुष्टं, रासः, स्वरः; 'cry of joy,' हर्षनादः, हर्षस्वनः; 'cry of pain,' आर्त्तनादः.

CRYER, s. घोषकः, प्रकाशकः, घोषणाकृत्, उच्चैःस्वरेण ख्यापकः.

CRYPT, s. पूजाशालाया अधोभागे खातं शवनिखननस्थानं, गुहा, गुहागृहं.

CRYSTAL, s. स्फटिकः, स्फटिकाश्मा *m.* (न्), स्फटिकोपलं, काचमणिः *m.*, सितमणिः *m.*, विमलमणिः, शुचिमणिः, अच्छः, सितोपलः, कुवक्रकं, केलासः, सिध्मं, धौतशिलं, निस्तुषरत्नं, शालिपिष्टं, रागदः.

CRYSTAL, CRYSTALLINE, *a.* स्फाटिकः -की -कं, स्फटिकमयः -यी -यं.—(Transparent) स्फटिकप्रभः -भा -भं, स्वच्छः -च्छा -च्छं, विमलः -ला -लं.

To CRYSTALLIZE, *v. a.* स्फटिकाकारेण घनीकृ or श्यानीकृ, स्फटिकसात्कृ.

To CRYSTALLIZE, *v. n.* स्फटिकाकारेण घनीभू or श्यै (c. 1. श्यायते, श्यातुं), स्फटिकाकृतिः -तिः -ति भू, स्फटिकं बन्ध् (c. 9. बध्नाति, बन्द्धुं).

CUB, s. (Young of a beast) शावः -वकः, वत्सः, शिशुः *m.*, पोतः; 'bear's cub,' ऋक्षशावकः; 'fox's cub,' लोमशावत्सः; 'jackal's cub,' शृगालवत्सः; 'lion's cub,' सिंहशावः, बालमृगेन्द्रः; 'tiger's cub,' शार्दूलपोतः; 'elephant's cub,' हस्तिशावकः, इभयुवतिः *f.*, इभपोटा.

CUBE, s. घनः; 'cube-root,' घनमूलं, घनपदं.

CUBIC, CUBICAL, *a.* घनाकारः -रा -रं, घनाकृतिः -तिः -ति; 'cubical contents,' घनफलं.

CUBIT, s. अरत्निः *m.*, रत्निः *m.*, हस्तः, काकिणी *f.*, किष्कुः *m. f.*, चिपुटः.

CUBITAL, s. अरत्निपरिमाणः -णा -णं, हस्तपरिमाणः -णा -णं.

CUCKOLD, s. कुलटापतिः *m.*, असतीपतिः *m.*, बन्धकीभार्य्यः, पुंश्चलीभार्य्यः, व्यभिचारिणीपतिः *m.*, अभिसारिकाभार्य्यः.

To CUCKOLD, *v. a.* भार्य्याभिगमनेन परं तिरस्कारास्पदं कृ.

CUCKOLD-MAKER, s. परदारगामी *m.* (न्), परकलत्राभिगामी *m.*, पारदारिकः.

CUCKOO, s. कोकिलः, परभृतः, परपुष्टः, परैधितः, पिकः, वसन्तदूतः, चातकः, मदालापी *m.* (न्), शारङ्गः, वनप्रियः; 'its note,' कोकिलाभिरुतं.

CUCUMBER, s. कर्कटी, पटोलः -लिका, बालुी, कापालः, चेलाल, इर्वारुः *m. f.*, सुधाशः, त्रिसं, त्रपुषं, मानधानिका, राजफलं, वृषभोजनं, ज्योत्स्नी, चिर्भा, गवाक्षी, गोडुम्बा.

CUCURBITACEOUS, *a.* अलाबूजातीयः -या -यं, तुम्बाकारः -रा -रं.

CUCURBITE, s. अलाबूस्वरूपं सन्धानयन्त्रं.

CUD, s. (Food swallowed to be chewed again) पुनश्चर्व्य आहारः, पुनश्चर्वणीयं तृणादिभोजनं; 'chewing the cud,' रोमन्थः -न्थनं; 'to chew the cud,' रोमन्थ (nom. रोमन्थायते).

To CUDDLE, *v. n.* निकटे or अङ्के or पार्श्वतः शी (c. 2. शेते, शयितुं), उत्कटुकासनं कृ.

CUDGEL, s. यष्टिः *m. f.*, गदा, लगुडः, वेत्रं, दण्डः, काष्ठं, मुद्गरः, इली, ईली, करपालिका, करवालिका.

To CUDGEL, *v. a.* वेत्रेण or गदया or लगुडेन तड् (c. 10. ताडयति -यितुं) or आहन् (c. 2. -हन्ति -हन्तुं) or प्रहृ (c. 1. -हरति -हर्तुं).

CUDGELING, *s.* वेत्राघातः, यष्ट्याघातः, दण्डपारुष्यं.

CUDGEL-PLAY, *s.* गदायुद्धं, दण्डादण्डि, वेत्रयुद्धं.

CUDGEL-PLAYER, *s.* गदायोधी *m.* (न्), यष्टिप्रहरणः, याष्टीकः, मल्लः.

CUE, *s.* (Tail or end of any thing) वालः, पुच्छः -च्छं, अञ्चलः.—(Hint) सङ्केतः, इङ्गितं, आकूतं.—(Humour) छन्दः *n.* (स्), छन्दं, मनोभावः.

CUFF, *s.* (Blow with the fist) मुष्ट्याघातः, मुष्टिप्रहारः, कराघातः, पाण्याघातः, आघातः, प्रहारः.—(End of a sleeve) पिप्पलस्य अग्रभागः, पिप्पलाञ्चलः ; 'fisticuffs,' मुष्टीमुष्टि.

To CUFF, *v. a.* मुष्टिना or करेण or पाणिना तड् (c. 10. ताडयति -यितुं) or आहन् (c. 2. -हन्ति -हन्तुं) or प्रहृ (c. 1. -हरति -हर्तुं).

To CUFF, *v. n.* मुष्टियुद्धं कृ, मुष्टीमुष्टि युध् (c. 4. युध्यते, योद्धुं).

CUIRASS, *s.* कवचः -चं, उरस्त्राणं, वक्षस्त्राणं, उरश्छदः, उदरत्राणं, कूर्पासः, तनुत्रं, वाणवारः, वारवाणः, नागोदरं, आयसी, निचुलकं, निचोलकः.

CUIRASSIER, *s.* कवची *m.* (न्), वर्म्मवान् *m.* (त्), तनुत्रवान् *m.* (त्), वर्म्मितः.

CUISH, *s.* जङ्घात्राणं, मेखला, मंजुषा, ऊरुत्राणं, ऊरुवर्म्म *n.* (न्).

CULINARY, *a.* पाकसम्बन्धी -न्धिनी -न्धि (न्), पाचकः -का -कं ; 'culinary utensil,' पाकपात्रं, पाकभाण्डं ; 'culinary skill,' पाकनिष्पत्तिः *f.*

To CULL, *v. a.* उद्धृ (c. 1. -हरति -हर्तुं), समुद्धृ, वृ (c. 5. वृणोति, वरितुं -रीतुं), उद्वृ ; 'to cull passages from a book,' चूर्णिं कृ.

CULLER, *s.* उद्धर्त्ता *m.* (र्तृ), समुद्धर्त्ता, चूर्णिकृत् *m.*

CULLION, *s.* धूर्त्तः, दुरात्मा *m.* (न्), नराधमः, शाल्मः, कृपणः.

CULLY, *s.* कामकूटः, वेश्याश्रितः, वेश्यावशवर्त्ती *m.* (न्), धूर्त्तवञ्चितः.

CULM, *s.* (Stalk) नालं -ली, नाडिः *f.* -डी, काण्डः, स्तम्भः, मञ्जरिः *f.*

To CULMINATE, *v. n.* ऊर्द्ध्वदेशं or उच्चस्थानं or मस्तकोपरिस्थानं or अग्रस्थानं प्राप् (c. 5. -आप्नोति -आप्तुं) or संक्रम् (c. 1. -क्रामति -क्रमितुं).

CULPABLE, *a.* दोषी -षिणी -षि (न्), अपराधी -धिनी -धि (न्), अपराद्धः -द्धा -द्धं, सापराधः -धा -धं, सदोषः -षा -षं, कृतापराधः -धा -धं, निन्दनीयः -या -यं, निन्द्यः -न्द्या -न्द्यं, निन्दार्हः -र्हा -र्हं, गर्ह्यः -र्ह्या -र्ह्यं, दूष्यः -ष्या -ष्यं, सागाः -गाः -गः (स्), वाच्यः -च्या -च्यं ; 'to be culpable,' अपराध् (nom. अपराध्यति).

CULPABLENESS, CULPABILITY, *s.* अपराधिता -त्वं, सापराधता, सदोषता, दोषित्वं, निन्दनीयत्वं, निन्द्यता, निन्दार्हत्वं, गर्ह्यता.

CULPABLY, *adv.* सापराधं, सदोषं, अपराधिवत्, निन्दनीयं.

CULPRIT, *s.* दोषी *m.* (न्), अपराधी *m.* (न्), अपराद्धा *m.* (द्धृ), पापी *m.* (न्), दोषग्रस्तः, दुष्टदोषः, निश्चितदोषः, वध्यः.

To CULTIVATE, *v. a.* (Till the land) कृष् (c. 6. कृषति, क्रष्टुं).—(Labour at, promote) सेव् (c. 1. सेवते -वितुं), आसेव्, अनुसेव्, उपसेव्, निषेव् ; भज् (c. 1. भजति -ते -भक्तुं) ; अनुष्ठा (c. 1. -तिष्ठति -ष्ठातुं) ; अनुपाल् (c. 10. -पालयति -यितुं), प्रतिपाल् ; संवृध् in caus. (-वर्धयति -यितुं).

CULTIVATED, *p. p.* कर्षितः -ता -तं, कृष्टः -ष्टा -ष्टं, फालकृष्टः -ष्टा -ष्टं, सीत्यः -त्या -त्यं, सेवितः -ता -तं ; 'cultivated land,' क्षेत्रभूमिः *f.*, कर्म्मभूः *f.*, कर्म्मान्तः, सीतं.

CULTIVATION, CULTURE, *s.* (Of land) कर्षणं, कृषिः *f.*, कृषिकर्म्म *n.* (न्), कृष्टिः *f.*. कार्षिः *f.*—(Labouring at, promoting) सेवनं, अनुसेवनं, परिष्कारः, अनुष्ठानं, अनुपालनं, प्रतिपालनं, संवर्धनं ; 'of learning,' विद्यानुसेवनं.

CULTIVATOR, *s.* (Of land) कृषकः, कर्षकः, कार्षिकः, क्षेत्रिकः, क्षेत्री *m.* (न्), क्षेत्राजीवः, हालिकः.—(One who labours at or promotes) सेवी *m.* (न्), अनुसेवी, अनुष्ठायी *m.* (न्), अनुपाली *m.* (न्), प्रतिपाली *m.* (न्), संवर्धकः ; 'cultivator of learning,' विद्यानुसेवी, विद्यानुपाली.

CULVER, *s.* (Pigeon) कपोतः, पारवतः, पारावतः, कलरवः.

CULVER-HOUSE, *s.* कपोतपालिका, कपोतागारं, विटङ्कः.

To CUMBER, *v. a.* बाध् (c. 1. बाधते -धितुं), क्लिश् (c. 9. क्लिश्नाति, क्लेष्टुं), अवरुध् (c. 7. -रुणद्धि -रोद्धुं), अतिभारं भू, विघ्न (nom. विघ्नयति -यितुं), कष्टं जन् (c. 10. जनयति -यितुं).

CUMBER, *s.* अतिभारः, बाधः -धनं, क्लेशः, कण्टकः, शल्यं, कष्टं, विघ्नः.

CUMBERSOME, CUMBROUS, *a.* भारी -रिणी -रि (न्) or अतिभारी, क्लेशकः -की -कं, कष्टकरः -री -रं, दुःखकरः -री -रं, दुर्भरः -रा -रं, बाधकः -का -कं.

CUMBERSOMELY, *adv.* अतिभारेण, यथा क्लेशः or कष्टं or बाधा जायते तथा.

CUMBERSOMENESS, CUMBRANCE, *s.* भारः, अतिभारः, क्लेशः, कष्टं, विघ्नः, अवरोधः.

CUMIN, *s.* जीरकः, जीरः, जीर्णः, अजाजी, सुगन्धं, सूक्ष्मपत्रः, कृष्णजीरी, दूता, सुषवी, कणाजी, श्वेतः, कणा.

To CUMULATE, *v. a.* सञ्चि (c. 5. -चिनोति -चेतुं), समाचि, समुपचि ; राशीकृ, पूगीकृ, पिण्डीकृ, ओघीकृ, एकत्र कृ.

CUMULATION, *s.* सञ्चयः -यनं, निचयः, प्रचयः, राशीकरणं, पूगीकरणं.

CUNCTATION, *s.* विलम्बः, कालक्षेपः, कालयापः -पनं, दीर्घसूत्रता.

CUNEIFORM, *a.* कीलाकारः -रा -रं, कीलाकृतिः -तिः -ति, कीलसरूपः -पा -पं.

CUNNING, *a.* (Sly) विदग्धः -ग्धा -ग्धं, छली -लिनी -लि (न्), छलनापरः -रा -रं, सव्याजः -जा -जं, मायी -यिनी -यि (न्), मायान्वितः -ता -तं, कापटिकः -की -कं, कूटकृत् *m. f. n.*, विप्रलम्भकः -का -कं, धूर्त्तः -र्त्ता -र्त्तं, वञ्चनशीलः -ला -लं, प्रतारणशीलः -ला -लं.—(Skilful) निपुणः -णा -णं, चतुरः -रा -रं, पटुः -टुः -ट्वी -टु.

CUNNING, *s.* (Deceit, slyness) विदग्धता, वैदग्ध्यं, छलं -लना, व्याजः, माया, कपटः, कापट्यं, कूटः -टं, धूर्त्तता, वञ्चनं, प्रवञ्चना, शठता, वक्रता, कैतवं.—(Skill) पाटवं, नैपुण्यं, चातुर्य्यं, युक्तिः *f.*

CUNNINGLY, *adv.* विदग्धं, छलेन, सव्याजं, समायं, वैदग्ध्येन, सपाटवं.

CUP, *s* पात्रं, पानपात्रं, भाण्डं, भाजनं, कंसः -सं, कांस्यः -स्यं, चषकः, शरावः, कुतलः, कुशयः, शालाजिरः -रं, पानीयाधारः.—(Any thing hollow like a cup) पुटः -टकं ; 'the cup of a flower,' पुटं, पुष्पगर्भः, पुष्पकोषः ; 'cup of a balance,' शरावं.—(Drinking bout) सम्पीतिः *f.* ; 'one who loves a cup,' पानासक्तः.

To CUP, *v. a.* (Draw blood by applying cupping-glasses) आचूषणं कृ, आचूषणयन्त्रेण रक्तं सु in caus. (स्रावयति -यितुं) or मुच् in caus. (मोचयति -यितुं) or मोक्ष् (c. 10. मोक्षयति -यितुं).

CUPBEARER, *s.* पात्रवाहकः, पानपात्रवाही *m.* (न्), पात्रभृत्, मद्यरक्षकः.

CUPBOARD, *s.* भाण्डकोष्ठः, कुशूलः, कक्षोलः -लकः, भाण्डद्रव्याधारः.

To CUPBOARD, *v. a.* भाण्डकोष्ठे निधा (c. 3. -दधाति -धातुं) or निविश् in caus. (-वेशयति -यितुं).

CUPEL, *s.* स्वर्णकारैर् व्यवहारिता सुवर्णशोधनार्थं मूषा.

CUPID, *s.* कामः, कामदेवः, अनङ्गः, मदनः, कन्दर्पः. *See* KÁMADEVA.

CUPIDINOUS, *a.* कामी -मिनी -मि (न्), कामुकः -का -कं, लोभी -भिनी -भि (न्), लोलुभः -भा -भं, लोभाविष्टः -ष्टा -ष्टं, लाभलिप्सुः -प्सुः -प्सु, लिप्सुः -प्सुः -प्सु.

CUPIDITY, *s.* कामः -मिता, कामुकत्वं, अभिलाषः, लोभः, लुब्धता -त्वं, लाभलिप्सा, लिप्सा, कामना, तृष्णा, अभिकाङ्क्षा, अतिस्पृहा.

CUPOLA, *s.* अर्द्धगोलाकारं प्रासादशृङ्गं or हर्म्यशिखरं.

CUPPER, *s.* आचूषणयन्त्रेण रक्तमोचकः or असृक्स्रावी *m.* (न्).

Cupping-glass, *s.* रक्ताचूषणयन्त्रं, रक्तचूषणार्थं काचपात्रं.

Cur, *s.* श्वा *m.* (न्), शुनकः, कुक्कुरः, दुष्टकुक्कुरः; 'cur-like,' श्ववत्.

Curable, *a.* चिकित्स्यः -त्स्या -त्स्यं, साध्यः -ध्या -ध्यं, प्रतीकार्य्यः -र्य्या -र्य्यं, शमनीयः -या -यं, चिकित्सितुं शक्यः -क्या -क्यं, स्वास्थ्यक्षमः -मा -मं.

Curableness, *s.* चिकित्स्यत्वं, साध्यता, प्रतीकार्य्यत्वं, उपशमनीयता.

Curacy, *s.* उपपुरोहितस्य वृत्तिः *f.* or व्यापारः or अधिकारः.

Curate, *s.* उपपुरोहितः, उपयाजकः, पुरोहितप्रतिनिधिः *m.*, उपगुरुः.

Curative, *a.* रोगघ्नः -घ्नी -घ्नं, रोगहरः -रा -रं, रोगान्तकः -की -कं, व्याधिशमकः -का -कं, शान्तिकरः -री -रं, शान्तिदः -दा -दं.

Curator, *s.* अध्यक्षः, अधिकारी *m.* (न्), अधिकृतः, रक्षकः, अधीशः, अवेक्षिता *m.* (तृ), अधिकर्म्मिकः, द्रष्टा *m.* (ष्टृ).

Curb, *s.* (Of a bridle) मुखयन्त्रणं, वल्गाशृङ्खलः, वागासम्बन्धिनी शृङ्खला, अश्वमुखशृङ्खला.—(Restraint) यन्त्रणा, शृङ्खलता, संयमः, यमः, निग्रहः, अवरोधः, निषेधः.

To curb, *v. a.* (Hold a horse in with a curb) अश्वं मुखयन्त्रणेन or मुखशृङ्खलया यम् (c. 1. यच्छति, यन्तुं).—(Restrain) यम्, संयम्; यन्त्र् (c. 10. यन्त्रयति -यितुं), निग्रह् (c. 9. -गृह्णाति -ग्रहीतुं), अवरुध् (c. 7. -रुणद्धि -रोद्धुं), निरुध्.

Curbed, *p. p.* शृङ्खलितः -ता -तं, यन्त्रितः -ता -तं, संयतः -ता -तं.

Curb-stone, *s.* परिखस्तरोपान्ते सुदृढप्रस्तरः.

To curd or curdle, *v. n.* दधिरूपेण श्यै (c. 1. श्यायते, श्यातुं) or घनीभू.

To curd or curdle, *v. a.* दधिसात्कृ, श्यै in caus. (श्यापयति -यितुं), घनीकृ.

Curds, *s.* दधि *n.*, पयस्यं, क्षीरजं, गव्यं, किलाटः, गोरसजं, जप्यं, द्रप्सा, रसाला, मार्जिता.

Curdy or curdled, *a.* दधिमयः -यी -यं, श्यानः -ना -नं, शीनः -ना -नं, आश्यानः -ना -नं, घनीभूतः -ता -तं, दधिवत् संहतः -ता -तं.

Cure, *s.* (Act of healing) चिकित्सा -त्सनं -त्सितं, शमः, शान्तिः *f.*, उपशमः, रोगशान्तिः *f.*, रोगशमः, रोगोपशमः, समाधानं, प्रतिसमाधानं, रुक्प्रतिक्रिया, प्रतीकारः, रोगोपचारः.—(State of being healed) समुत्थानं, स्वास्थ्यं, सुस्थता.—(The remedy itself) भेषजं, भैषज्यं, औषधं, रोगघ्नं.—(Benefice of clergyman) पुरोहितवृत्तिः *f.*, धर्म्माध्यापकस्य व्यापारः or अधिकारः.

To cure, *v. a.* कित् in des. (चिकित्सति -त्सितुं), शम् in caus. (शमयति -यितुं), प्रशम्, उपशम्; स्वस्थं -स्थां -स्थं कृ, सुस्थं -स्थां -स्थं कृ, प्रतिकृ, समाधा (c. 3. -दधाति -धातुं), प्रतिसमाधा, समुत्था in caus. (-थापयति for -स्थापयति -यितुं), भिषज् (nom. भिषज्यति), साध् in caus. (साधयति -यितुं).—(Cure fish or meat) लवण (nom. लवणयति -यितुं), लवणीकृ.

Cured, *p. p.* चिकित्सितः -ता -तं, शमितः -ता -तं, शान्तः -न्ता -न्तं, उपशान्तः -न्ता -न्तं, प्रशान्तः -न्ता -न्तं, स्वस्थः -स्था -स्थं, सुस्थः -स्था -स्थं, प्रतिकृतः -ता -तं, समुत्थितः -ता -तं, रोगमुक्तः -क्ता -क्तं; 'cured of fever,' विगतज्वरः -रा -रं.

Cureless, *a.* अचिकित्स्यः -त्स्या -त्स्यं, असाध्यः -ध्या -ध्यं, दुरुपचारः -रा -रं.

Curer, *s.* चिकित्सकः, रोगशामकः, रोगहारी *m.* (न्), रोगहा *m.* (न्), औषदः.

Curfew, *s.* अग्निप्रदीपा निर्व्वापयितव्या इति पुरा निर्देशार्थं प्रदोषकाले वादिता घण्टा, प्रदोषकाले घण्टाशब्दः.

Curiosity, *s.* (Inquisitiveness) कौतूहलं, कुतूहलं, कौतुकं, कुतुकं, जिज्ञासा, जिज्ञासाकुतूहलं, पिपृच्छिषा, अनुसन्धानेच्छा, असति प्रयोजने किमेतदिति जिज्ञासा; 'one whose curiosity is excited,' उपजातकौतुकः.—(A rarity) दुर्लभद्रव्यं, दुष्प्राप्यद्रव्यं, बहुमतद्रव्यं, विशिष्टद्रव्यं, उत्कृष्टद्रव्यं.

Curious, *a.* (Inquisitive) कुतूहली -लिनी -लि (न्), कौतूहलान्वितः -ता -तं, कौतूहलपरः -रा -रं, कौतुकाविष्टः -ष्टा -ष्टं, जिज्ञासुः -सुः -सु, पिपृच्छिषुः -षुः -षु, अनुसन्धानेच्छुः -च्छुः -च्छु.—(Skilled in) अभिज्ञः -ज्ञा -ज्ञं, विचक्षणः -णा -णं.—(Exact, nice) सूक्ष्मः -क्ष्मा -क्ष्मं, सूक्ष्मदर्शी -र्शिनी -र्शि (न्).—(Worthy of being seen, rare) दर्शनार्हः -र्हा -र्हं, दर्शनीयः -या -यं, दुर्लभः -भा -भं, दुष्प्राप्यः -प्या -प्यं, बहुमतः -ता -तं.—(Strange, wonderful) अद्भुतः -ता -तं, चित्रः -त्रा -त्रं, विचित्रः -त्रा -त्रं, आश्चर्य्यः -र्य्या -र्य्यं, अपूर्व्वः -र्व्वा -र्व्वं.

Curiously, *adv.* (Inquisitively) कौतूहलात्, कुतूहलेन, कौतुकेन, जिज्ञासया.—(Skilfully, nicely, strangely) निपुणं, सूक्ष्मं, अद्भुतं.

To curl, *v. a.* (Turn the hair in curls) अलकरूपेण केशान् कुच् (c. 1. कुचति -चितुं or c. 10. कुचयति -यितुं), अलकान् कृ or रच् (c. 10. रचयति -यितुं).—(Twist) कुच्, आकुच्, व्यावृत् in caus. (-वर्त्तयति -यितुं).—(Raise in waves) तरङ्ग (nom. तरङ्गयति -यितुं), वन्धुरीकृ, उन्नतानतीकृ.

To curl, *v. n.* अलकरूपेण कुच् in pass. (कुच्यते) or आकुच् in pass., व्यावृत् (c. 1. -वर्त्तते -र्त्तितुं).—(Rise in waves) तरङ्ग (nom. तरङ्गायते), तरल (nom. तरलायते), वन्धुरीभू, उन्नतानतीभू.

Curl, *s.* अलकः, आवर्त्तः -र्त्तका, कुरलः, कर्केरालः -लं, चक्रुरः, काकपक्षः, चर्च्चरीकः, चूर्णकुन्तलः, झल्लरी, भ्रमरकः; 'row of curls,' अलकसंहतिः *f.*—(Undulation) ऊर्म्मिः *f.*, तरङ्गः.

Curlew, *s.* क्रौञ्चः, क्रुङ्, कलिकः, कालिकः, कालीकः, अतिजागरः.

Curmudgeon, *s.* कृपणः, कदर्य्यः, स्वल्पव्ययी *m.* (न्), मत्सरः, गाढमुष्टिः.

Currant, *s.* (The tree) अम्लफलविशिष्टः क्षुद्रवृक्षः.—(A small dried grape) शोषितरसा क्षुद्रद्राक्षा.

Currency, *s.* (Circulation, general reception) प्रचारः, प्रचरः, प्रचलनं, चलनं, हस्ताद्धस्तं चलनं, व्यवहारः, सर्व्वसाधारणव्यवहारः, सर्व्वग्रहणं, सर्व्वसम्मानं.—(Continuous flow or course) प्रवाहः, प्रसरः.—(Easiness of utterance) सुखोच्चारणं, सुखोच्चार्य्यता.—(Current coin) प्रचलमुद्रा, प्रचारितमुद्रा.

Current, *a.* (Circulatory, generally received) प्रचलः -ला -लं, प्रचलितः -ता -तं, प्रचलन् -लन्ती -लत् (त्), प्रचरितः -ता -तं, प्रचरन् -रन्ती -रत् (त्), चलमानः -ना -नं, परिचालितः -ता -तं, सञ्चारितः -ता -तं, सर्व्वसम्मतः -ता -तं, सर्व्वगृहीतः -ता -तं.—(Common, general, popular) सर्व्वसाधारणः -णी -णं, सर्व्वसामान्यः -न्या -न्यं, लोकप्रसिद्धः -द्धा -द्धं, लोकविश्रुतः -ता -तं, व्यावहारिकः -की -कं, आचारिकः -की -कं, लौकिकः -की -कं.—(Received as authority, allowable) प्रचलितः -ता -तं, प्रामाणिकः -की -कं, ग्राह्यः -ह्या -ह्यं.—(What is now passing) वर्त्तमानः -ना -नं, विद्यमानः -ना -नं; 'the current year,' वर्त्तमानवत्सरः; 'current moment,' आपातः; 'current report,' लोकप्रवादः, जनवादः.

Current, *s.* (A running stream) स्रोतः *n.* (स्), स्रवन्ती, स्रोतस्वती, स्रोतस्विनी.—(The flow or course of water) वेला, वेगः, रयः, प्रवाहः, उदकप्रवाहः, धारः -रा, स्रोतः *n.* (स्), ओघः, प्रस्रवः -वणं, संसृतिः *f.*, प्रवृत्तिः *f.*, पाथःसंस्कारः, अम्बुपद्धतिः *f.*, पाथःप्रकारः, रयभाटी, ऊर्म्मी, कूलङ्कषः, पुरोटिः *m.*; 'current of the Ganges,' गाङ्गौघं; 'against the current,' प्रतिस्रोतस्.

Currently, *adv.* (Generally, popularly) सामान्यतस्, साधारणतस्, लोकतस्, प्रसिद्धं; 'it is currently reported,' इति लोकप्रवादः श्रूयते; 'it is currently known,' लोकप्रसिद्धम् अस्ति.

Curricle, *s.* रथः, क्रीडारथः, केलिरथः, अश्वद्वयसञ्चारितो रथः

CURRIER, *s.* चर्म्मकारः -री *m.* (न्), चर्म्मछेदनकारी *m.*, चर्म्मोपजीवी *m.* (न्), कुरटः.

CURRISH, *a.* कुक्कुराचारः -रा -रं, खशीलः -ला -लं, शौवः -वी -वं, दुःशीलः -ला -लं, शौवापदः -दी -दं ; 'a currish man,' श्वनरः.

To CURRY, *v. a.* (Dress leather) चर्म्म परिष्कृ.—(Beat) तड् (c. 10. ताडयति -यितुं), प्रहृ (c. 1. -हरति -हर्त्तुं).—(Rub a horse with a curry-comb) अश्वलोम लोहकङ्कतेन मृज् (c. 2. मार्ष्टि, मार्ष्टुं).—(Curry favour) आराध् in caus. (-राधयति -यितुं), सान्त्व् (c. 10. सान्त्वयति -यितुं), लल् in caus. (लालयति -यितुं).

CURRY, *s.* (The dish) अन्नमिश्रणीयो or भक्तेन सह खाद्यो व्यञ्जनविशेषः.

CURRY-COMB, *s.* अश्वलोममार्जनार्थं लोहकङ्कतः, अश्वमार्जनी.

To CURSE, *v. a.* शप् (c. 1. शपति -ते, c. 4. शप्यति, शप्तुं), अभिशप्, परिशप्, शापं or अभिशापं दा or कृ ; अमङ्गलं or अनिष्टम् आशंस् (c. 1. -शंसते -सितुं); आक्रुश् (c. 1. -क्रोशति -क्रोष्टुं), गर्ह् (c. 1. गर्हते -र्हितुं), धिक्कृ, भर्त्स् (c. 10. भर्त्सयति -यितुं).

To CURSE, *v. n.* शप् (c. 1. शपते, शप्तुं), शपथं or शापं वद् (c. 1. वदति -दितुं) or ब्रू (c. 2. ब्रवीति, वक्तुं); 'to curse and swear,' शपथाभिशापौ कृ.

CURSE, *s.* (Malediction) शापः, अभिशापः, शपथः, शपः -पनं, परिशापः, आक्रोशनं, अवक्रोशः, भर्त्सनं, अभिषङ्गः, अभीषङ्गः, गालिः *m.*, मन्दवाञ्छा ; 'under a curse,' शापग्रस्तः -स्ता -स्तं.—(A pest) कण्टकः, दूषकः, अपकारकः. The following are forms of curses answering to 'confusion seize you,' &c., अजीवनिस्ते भूयात्, अकरणिस्ते ऽस्तु, निग्राहस्ते भूयात्, अवग्राहस्ते स्यात्, अजननिर् अस्तु तव.

CURSED, *p. p.* शप्तः -प्ता -प्तं, अभिशप्तः -प्ता -प्तं, शापार्हः -र्हा -र्हं, गर्हितः -ता -तं, गर्हणीयः -या -यं, घृणार्हः -र्हा -र्हं, धिक्कृतः -ता -तं, अपध्वस्तः -स्ता -स्तं.

CURSEDLY, *adv.* गर्हितं, गर्हणीयप्रकारेण, दुष्टं, दुष्टु.

CURSHIP, *s.* कुक्कुरत्वं, खशीलता, दुःशीलता, अधमाचारत्वं.

CURSITOR, *s.* महाविचारणसभासम्बन्धी लेखकविशेषः.

CURSORILY, *adv.* ईषदपेक्षया, ईषन्मनोयोगेन, चुम्बकवत्, ईषद्दर्शनेन, सत्वरं, अनवधानेन, अनपेक्षया.

CURSORY, *a.* त्वरितः -ता -तं, असावधानः -ना -नं, अनवहितः -ता -तं, अयत्नपूर्व्वः -र्व्वा -र्व्वं, शीघ्रः -घ्रा -घ्रं ; 'cursory view,' ईषद्दर्शनं, अर्द्धवीक्षणं.

CURST, *a.* कर्कशः -शा -शं, नृशंसः -सा -सं, दुष्टचेताः -ताः -तः (स्).

CURT, *a.* ह्रस्वः -स्वा -स्वं, खर्व्वः -र्व्वा -र्व्वं, संक्षिप्तः -प्ता -प्तं.

To CURTAIL, *v. a.* ह्रस् in caus. (ह्रासयति -यितुं), छिद् (c. 7. छिनत्ति, छेत्तुं), अवछिद्, संक्षिप् (c. 6. -क्षिपति -क्षेप्तुं), संहृ (c. 1. -हरति -हर्त्तुं).

CURTAILED, *p. p.* ह्रसितः -ता -तं, छिन्नः -न्ना -न्नं, संक्षिप्तः -प्ता -प्तं, क्षीणः -णा -णं, अवरोपितः -ता -तं, अल्पीकृतः -ता -तं.

CURTAIN, *s.* तिरस्करिणी, व्यवधानं, आवरणं, तिरोधानं, आवरणपटः, प्रच्छदपटः, जवनी, यवनिका, नीशारः ; 'bed-curtain,' चतुष्की, मशहरी.

To CURTAIN, *v. a.* आवरणपटेन परिवेष्ट् (c. 1. -वेष्टते -ष्टितुं) or परिवृ (c. 5. -वृणोति -वरितुं -रीतुं) or प्रच्छद् (c. 10. -छादयति -यितुं).

CURTAIN-LECTURE, *s.* रात्रिकाले शय्यागतपतिमुद्दिश्य भार्य्योक्तं निन्दावाक्यं or भर्त्सनवाक्यं or तर्ज्जनं.

CURTSY, *s.* स्त्रीलोकेन कृतः प्रणामः or जानुप्रणामः or नमस्कारः.

CURVATED, *a.* नतः -ता -तं, आनतः -ता -तं, प्रणतः -ता -तं, परिणतः -ता -तं, भुग्नः -ग्ना -ग्नं, अवभुग्नः -ग्ना -ग्नं, विभुग्नः -ग्ना -ग्नं, कुञ्चितः -ता -तं, आकुञ्चितः -ता -तं.

CURVATION, *s.* वक्रीकरणं, नम्रीकरणं, कुञ्चनं, आकुञ्चनं, अवकुञ्चनं.

CURVATURE, *s.* नतिः *f.*, आनतिः *f.*, वक्रता, वक्रिमा *m.* (न्), वक्रीभावः, जिह्मता, कुटिलता, कौटिल्यं, नतत्वं, रुग्नता ; 'of the spine,' अन्ध्यमतरायामः.

CURVE, *a.* वक्रः -क्रा -क्रं, वक्रिमः -मा -मं, नतः -ता -तं, कुटिलः -ला -लं, नम्रः -म्रा -म्रं, जिह्मः -ह्मा -ह्मं, भुग्नः -ग्ना -ग्नं, कुञ्चितः -ता -तं.

CURVE, *s.* नतिः *f.*, नतं, भुजः, कुटिः *m.*, वक्रता, वक्रिमा *m.* (न्), कुञ्चनं, अवकुञ्चनं ; 'a curve line,' धनुर्मार्गं, वक्ररेखा.

To CURVE, *v. a.* नम् in caus. (नामयति -यितुं), आनम्, अवनम् ; नम्रीकृ ; वक्रीकृ ; आवृज् in caus. (-वर्जयति -यितुं), कुच् (c. 1. कुचति -चितुं), कुटिलीकृ, अञ्च् (c. 1. अञ्चति -ञ्चितुं), जिह्म (nom. जिह्मयति -यितुं).

CURVED, *p. p.* नतः -ता -तं, नामितः -ता -तं, वक्रीभूतः -ता -तं, कुटिलीकृतः -ता -तं, जिह्मितः -ता -तं, विभुग्नः -ग्ना -ग्नं, अवभुग्नः -ग्ना -ग्नं, सम्भुग्नः -ग्ना -ग्नं, रुग्नः -ग्ना -ग्नं, कुञ्चितः -ता -तं, वृजिनः -ना -नं, प्रवणः -णा -णं.

To CURVET, *v. n.* प्लु (c. 1. प्लवते, प्लोतुं), वल्ग् (c. 1. वल्गति -ल्गितुं), आवल्ग्.

CURVET, *s.* प्लुतं, प्लवः, वल्गितं, लङ्घनं, उत्फालः, कम्पः.

CURVILINEAR, *a.* वक्ररेखः -खा -खं, धनुर्मार्गाकारः -रा -रं, वक्रः -क्रा -क्रं.

CURULE, *a.* (Chair) पूर्व्वं रोमनगरे विचारकर्तृणाम् आसनं.

CUSHION, *s.* उपधानं -नीयं, पीठोपधानं, बालिशं, विष्टरः, विस्तरः, आस्तरणं, पीठास्तरणं, पीठगण्डुः *m. f.*, उपबर्हः, पीठाजिनं, अजिनं, चर्म्म *n.* (न्).

CUSHIONED, *a.* उपधानसंविष्टः -ष्टा -ष्टं, अजिनशयानः -ना -नं, बालिशनिषण्णः -ण्णा -ण्णं.

CUSP, *s.* अर्द्धचन्द्रकोणः, अर्द्धेन्दुशिखा, अर्द्धचन्द्राग्रं, कलाग्रं, कलाकोणः.

CUSPATED, CUSPIDATED, *a.* सूक्ष्माग्रः -ग्रा -ग्रं, सूच्यग्रः -ग्रा -ग्रं.

CUSTARD, *s.* अण्डक्षीरादिमयं मिष्टलेह्यं.

CUSTODY, *s.* (Imprisonment) रोधः, निरोधनं, बन्धनं, स्थानासेधः, आसेधः, कारागारे निरोधः.—(Care, charge) गुप्तिः *f.*, रक्षा, रक्षणं.—(Defence) रक्षणं, पालनं, त्राणं.

CUSTOM, *s.* (Habit, established manner, fashion) आचारः, व्यवहारः, व्यवहृतिः *f.*, प्रचारः, समाचारः, रीतिः *f.*, नियमः, अभ्यासः, नित्यकृत्यं, धारा, मार्गः, स्थितिः *f.*, अनुसारः, आवृत्तिः *f.*, चर्य्या, चरितं, क्रमः, सम्प्रदायः, व्यापारः, शीलः ; 'according to custom,' यथाव्यवहारं.—(Practice of buying of one person) एकपण्यविक्रेतुः सदाक्रयः or नित्यक्रयः.—(Tribute, toll) शुल्कः -ल्कं, करः, राजस्वं, राजग्राह्यभागः, शौल्किकः.

CUSTOMABLE, *a.* व्यावहारिकः -की -कं, आचारिकः -की -कं, लोकसिद्धः -द्धा -द्धं.

CUSTOMABLY, *adv.* व्यवहारानुसारेण, व्यवहारतस्, आचारानुरूपं.

CUSTOMARILY, *adv.* यथाव्यवहारं, यथारीति, रीत्यनुसारात्, प्रायशस्.

CUSTOMARY, *a.* आचारिकः -की -कं, व्यावहारिकः -की -कं or व्यवहारिकः, व्यवहारानुसारी -रिणी -रि (न्), आचारानुयायी -यिनी -यि (न्), आचरितः -ता -तं, प्रचरितः -ता -तं, प्रचलः -ला -लं, प्रचलितः -ता -तं, नैयमिकः -की -कं, रीत्यनुसारी &c., यौगिकः -की -कं.—(Habitual) आभ्यासिकः -की -कं, नित्यः -त्या -त्यं.—(Usual) प्रायिकः -की -कं, लोकसिद्धः -द्धा -द्धं, लौकिकः -की -कं, प्रसिद्धः -द्धा -द्धं.

CUSTOMER, *s.* क्रेता *m.* (तृ), क्रयी *m.* (न्), नित्यक्रेता *m.*, सदाक्रयी.

CUSTOM-HOUSE, *s.* शुल्कग्रहणशाला, शुल्कस्थानं, करसञ्चयगृहं.

CUSTOM-HOUSE-OFFICER, *s.* शौल्कः, शौल्किकः, करग्राही *m.* (न्).

To CUT, *v. a.* कृत् (c. 6. कृन्तति, कर्त्तितुं), छिद् (c. 7. छिनत्ति, छेत्तुं), संछिद्, लू (c. 9. लुनाति, लवितुं), व्रश्च् (c. 6. वृश्चति, व्रश्चितुं), छो (c. 4. छ्यति, छातुं), दो or दा (c. 4. द्यति, c. 2. दाति -तुं).—(Cut in two) द्विधा छिद् or कृ, द्विखण्डीकृ.—(Divide) भिद् (c. 7. भिनत्ति, भेत्तुं), खण्ड् (c. 10. खण्डयति -यितुं).—(Pierce) व्यध् (c. 4. विध्यति,

व्यद्धुं), छिद् (c. 10. छिद्रयति -यितुं), निर्भिद्, खन् (c. 1. खनति -नितुं), छिद्.—(Carve, make by sculpture) तक्ष् (c. 1. तक्षति -क्षितुं).—(Hew) छिद्, विशस् (c. 1. -शसति -सितुं).—(Intersect) परिच्छिद्.—(Scratch) खुर् (c. 6. खुरति, खोरितुं).—(Cut away) अवकृत्, निकृत्, उच्छिद्.—(Cut down) अवकृत्, प्रकृत्, अवच्छिद्, अवभञ्ज् (c. 7. -भनक्ति -भंक्तुं), निभञ्ज्, प्रभञ्ज्; अवपत् in caus. (-पातयति -यितुं).—(Cut off) छिद्, अवच्छिद्, निकृत्, अवकृत्, लू; 'destroy,' उच्छिद्, उद्धृ (c. 1. -हरति -हर्त्तुं), उन्मूल् (c. 10. -मूलयति -यितुं); 'rescind,' लुप् (c. 6. लुम्पति, लोप्तुं); 'take away,' अपनी (c. 1. -नयति -नेतुं), अपहृ; 'intercept,' विच्छिद्, उच्छिद्, अवरुध् (c. 7. -रुणद्धि -रोद्धुं); 'interrupt,' विच्छिद्, खण्ड् (c. 10. खण्डयति -यितुं); 'preclude,' निवृ in caus. (-वारयति -यितुं), निरुध्; 'obviate,' परिच्छिद्; 'cut off a limb,' अङ्गं छिद्.—(Cut out) उत्कृत्, निष्कृत्; 'shape,' कृप् (c. 10. कल्पयति -यितुं), परिकृप्; 'contrive,' मनसा चिन्त् (c. 10. चिन्तयति -यितुं), परिकृप्; 'adapt,' युज् in caus. (योजयति -यितुं); 'outdo,' अतिभू, विशिष् in pass. (-शिष्यते); 'cut off a letter,' लुप्.—(Cut short, abridge) संहृ, संक्षिप् (c. 6. -क्षिपति -क्षेप्तुं), उच्छिद्, लुप्; 'interrupt abruptly,' सहसा विच्छिद्.—(Cut up) व्यवच्छिद्, विनिकृत्, निकृत्; 'eradicate,' उच्छिद्.—(Cut the hair) केशान् छिद् or वप् in caus. (-वापयति -यितुं) or परिवप्.—(Cut to the heart) मर्म्म भिद् or छिद् or व्यध्.

To cut, *v. n.* (Make way by dividing) उद्भिद् in pass. (-भिद्यते), प्रोद्भिद्, स्फुट् (c. 6. स्फुटति -टितुं), उत्पद् in pass. (-पद्यते), प्रभू.

Cut, *p. p.* छिन्नः -न्ना -न्नं, कृत्तः -त्ता -त्तं, कर्त्तितः -ता -तं, लूनः -ना -नं, खातः -ता -तं, दातः -ता -तं, छितः -ता -तं, दितः -ता -तं, वृक्णः -क्णा -क्णं, खण्डितः -ता -तं, त्रुटितः -ता -तं, क्लृप्तः -प्ता -प्तं, तष्टः -ष्टा -ष्टं, परिवापितः -ता -तं; 'cut up,' व्यवच्छिन्नः -न्ना -न्नं, छिन्नभिन्नः -न्ना -न्नं, निकृत्तः -त्ता -त्तं; 'cut off,' in grammar, लुप्तः -प्ता -प्तं.

Cut, *s.* (The blow of a sharp instrument) प्रहारः, आघातः; 'a sword-cut,' खड्गप्रहारः, खड्गाघातः; 'cut with a whip,' कशाघातः.—(Impression made by an edge) छेदः, लूनकः, व्रश्चनचिह्नं.—(Channel or canal) खातं, कुल्या, कृत्रिमा सरित्.—(Part cut off from the rest) खण्डः -ण्डं, छेदः, भिन्नं, भित्तिः *f.*, दलं.—(Small particle) लवः, कणः, लेशः.—(A direct road) ऋजुमार्गः, अविमार्गः, अदीर्घपथः.—(Print) मुद्रा, पत्रे मुद्रिता प्रतिमा or प्रतिमूर्त्तिः *f.*—(Fashion, form) रीतिः *f.*, रूपं, आकारः, विधानं, संस्कारः, संस्थानं.

Cutaneous, *a.* त्वाचः -ची -चं, चार्म्मिकः -की -कं, चर्म्मी -र्म्मिणी -र्म्मि (न्), त्वक्सम्बन्धी -न्धिनी -न्धि (न्); 'cutaneous disease,' त्वग्रोगः, चर्म्मदूषिका; 'cutaneous eruption,' दद्रुः *m.*, दद्रूः *m.*

Cuticle, *s.* अवभासिनी, बाह्यत्वक् *f.* (च्), बाह्यचर्म्म *n.* (न्).

Cuticular, *a.* त्वाचः -ची -चं, बाह्यत्वक्सम्बन्धी -न्धिनी -न्धि (न्).

Cutis, *s.* (The true skin) वेदनी.

Cutlass, *s.* कर्त्तरिका, खड्गः, कृपाणः, पृथुपत्रः खड्गः.

Cutler, *s.* छुरिकाकारः, शस्त्रकारः, छुरिकाविक्रेता *m.* (तृ), शस्त्रमार्जः.

Cutlet, *s.* खण्डः -ण्डं, पर्शुका, पार्श्वास्थि *n.*; 'of mutton,' औरभ्रमांसखण्डः.

Cutpurse, *s.* ग्रन्थिभेदः -दकः, चौरः, अपहारकः, तस्करः.

Cutter, *s.* (One who cuts) छेत्ता *m.* (त्तृ), छेदकरः, छिद् in comp.; 'wood-cutter,' वनच्छिद्.—(Cutting instrument) कर्त्तरिका, कृन्तत्रं, छित्वरः.—(A nimble boat) लघुनौका.—(Front-teeth) छेदकदन्ताः *m. pl.*, राजदन्ताः *m. pl.*

Cut-throat, *s.* घातकः, सुप्तघातकः, प्राणघातकः, आततायी *m.* (न्).

Cut-throat, *a.* वधोद्यतः -ता -तं, मारात्मकः -का -कं, क्रूरः -रा -रं.

Cutting, *s.* (Piece cut off) विदलं, खण्डः -ण्डं, तष्टं, भित्तिः *f.* शकलं, भिन्नं.—(Act of cutting) छेदनं, कर्त्तनं, व्रश्चनं, खण्डनं, छिदा, छित्तिः *f.*, लूनिः *f.*, लावः, दातिः *f.*, दानं.

Cutting, *a.* छित्वरः -रा -रं, छिदुरः -रा -रं.—(Caustic) खरः -रा -रं, अरुन्तुदः -दा -दं, मार्म्मिकः -की -कं, मर्म्मभेदी -दिनी -दि (न्).

Cuttle, *s.* (A fish, or its bone) फेनः -नकः, समुद्रफेनः, सिन्धुकफः, अब्धिकफः, हिण्डीरः, हिण्डिरः, पिण्डीरः, श्वेतधामा *m.* (न्), मुफेनं, मलं.—(A foul-mouthed fellow) मुखरः, वाग्दुष्टः, दुर्मुखः.

Cuvera, *s.* *See* Kuvera.

Cycle, *s.* चक्रं, कालचक्रं, आवृत्तिः *f.*, कालावृत्तिः *f.*, कालावर्त्तः, परिवृत्तिः *f.*, परिवर्त्तः, पर्य्यायः, आवलिः *f.*; 'of the seasons,' ऋतुपर्य्यायः.

Cyclopædia, *s.* ज्ञानचक्रं, विद्याचक्रं, विद्यापर्य्यायः, विद्याहारावलिः *f.*

Cycloptic, cyclopean, *a.* क्रूराचारः -रा -रं, दारुणः -णा -णं, पशुव्यवहारः -रा -रं, अतिमहान् -हती -हत् (त्).

Cygnet, *s.* हंसशावकः, बालहंसः, युवहंसः, हंसापत्यं.

Cylinder, *s.* गोलः, नलः, स्तम्भः, शलाका, निघः.

Cylindrical, *a.* वर्त्तुलः -ला -लं, गोलाकारः -रा -रं, स्तम्भाकारः -रा -रं.

Cymbal, *s.* घनं, झल्लरी, झल्लकं, झिञ्झिः *f.*, झर्झरी, भेरी, करतालं.

Cynegetics, *s.* मृगव्यं, मृगया, मृगव्यविद्या, आखेटविद्या.

Cynic, *s.* (A misanthrope) सर्व्वाभिसन्धकः -सन्धी *m.* (न्), पुरुषद्वेषी *m.* (न्).

Cynical, *a.* सदावक्रः -क्रा -क्रं, अपरिचयी -यिनी -यि (न्), निरानन्दः -न्दा -न्दं, कुटिलभावः -वा -वं, निन्दाशीलः -ला -लं, चिरदुःखी -खिनी -खि (न्), अनालाप्यः -प्या -प्यं, परश्रीकातरः -रा -रं.

Cynosure, *s.* ध्रुवः, नक्षत्रनेमिः *m.*, द्युतिकरः, ज्योतीरथः.

Cypher, *s.* अङ्कः, शून्यं, गुणनिका. *See* Cipher.

Cyphering, *s.* अङ्कनं, अङ्कविद्या, गणनविद्या. *See* Ciphering.

Cypress-tree, *s.* श्मशानरोपितः शोकलाक्षणिकस् तिक्तपत्रो दीर्घवृक्षः.

D.

To dab, *v. a.* आर्द्रद्रव्यलघ्वाघातेन सिच् (c. 6. सिञ्चति, सेक्तुं) or प्रोक्ष् (c. 1. -उक्षति -क्षितुं), सिक्तद्रव्येण लघु आहन् (c. 2. -हन्ति -हन्तुं).

Dab, *s.* (Small lump) क्षुद्रपिण्डः, पिण्डः, क्षुद्रखण्डः.—(Blow with something moist) सिक्तद्रव्येण लघुप्रहारः or लघ्वाघातः, सेचनं, निषेकः.—(Something muddy thrown upon one) मलसेचनं, क्षिप्तपङ्कः.—(A man expert at something) निपुणः, पटुः, कुशलः, दक्षः.

To dabble, *v. a.* सिच् (c. 6. सिञ्चति, सेक्तुं), अवसिच्, निषिच्, लिप् (c. 6. लिम्पति, लेप्तुं), उक्ष् (c. 1. उक्षति -क्षितुं), प्रोक्ष्, क्लिद् in caus. (क्लेदयति -यितुं).

To dabble, *v. n.* (Play in water) जले or पङ्के क्रीड् (c. 1. क्रीडति -डितुं).—(Dabble in books, read superficially) शास्त्राणि चुष् (c. 1. चुषति -षितुं).

Dabbler, *s.* (One that plays in water or mud) जलक्रीडः, पङ्कक्रीडः.—(Superficial reader) शास्त्रचुषकः, शास्त्रगण्डः, किञ्चिज्ज्ञः, अल्पमात्रविद्.

Dace, *s.* नदीचरः क्षुद्रमत्स्यभेदः.

Dactyl, *s.* चरणः -णं, भगणः, छन्दःशास्त्रेषु असमानपदं.

Dad, daddy, *s.* बालकभाषायां पितृसमानार्थः शब्दः, बाबा, तातः.

Dædal, *a.* चित्रविचित्रः -त्रा -त्रं, नानाप्रकारः -रा -रं, बहुविधः -धा -धं.

DAFFODIL, DAFFODOWNDILLY, *s.* उत्पलजातीयः पुष्पप्रभेदः.

DAGGER, *s.* कट्टारः, कृपाणी, छुरिका, शङ्कुः *m.*, असिपुत्रिका, कर्त्तरी.

To DAGGLE, *v. a.* मलेन or पङ्केन लिप् (c. 6. लिम्पति, लेप्तुं).

To DAGGLE, *v. n.* पङ्के or कर्द्दमे लुट् (c. 6. लुठति -ठितुं).

DAGGLETAIL, *a.* मलपङ्की -ङ्किनी -ङ्कि (न्), मलदूषितः -ता -तं.

DAILY, *a.* आह्निकः -की -कं, दैनिकः -की -कं, दैनः -नी -नं, दैवसिकः -की -कं, प्रात्यहिकः -की -कं, दिवातनः -नी -नं, अन्वाहिकः -की -कं, नैत्यिकः -की -कं, अवश्यकः -का -कं; 'daily occupation,' आह्निकं, नित्यकृत्यं.

DAILY, *adv.* प्रतिदिनं, प्रतिदिवसं, प्रत्यहं, प्रतिवासरं, अनुदिनं, अन्वहं, दिवसे दिवसे, दिने दिने, अहनि अहनि, अहरहः.

DAINTILY, *adv.* ललितं, सलालित्यं, सलौल्यं, सुकुमारं, कोमलं, विलासेन.

DAINTINESS, *s.* (Delicacy, softness) सौकुमार्य्यं, कोमलता, मृदुता.—(Elegance, nicety) लालित्यं, लौल्यं, लावण्यं, विलासः, सूक्ष्मता, विनीतता.—(Deliciousness) सुस्वादुता, सुरसत्वं, सौरस्यं.

DAINTY, *a.* (Delicious) स्वादुः -दुः -द्वी -दु or सुस्वादुः, सुरसः -सा -सं, रसिकः -का -कं, सरसः -सा -सं, मिष्टः -ष्टा -ष्टं, स्वादुकारः -रा -रं, सुखाद्यः -द्या -द्यं.—(Delicate, nice) सुकुमारः -रा -रं, कोमलः -ला -लं, मृदुः -द्वी -दु, विनीतः -ता -तं, सूक्ष्मः -क्ष्मा -क्ष्मं.—(Over-nice, ceremonious) अतिविनीतः -ता -तं, अतिसभ्यः -भ्या -भ्यं.

DAINTY, *s.* सुग्रासः, स्वाद्वन्नं, स्वादुभोजनं, विशिष्टान्नं, भोजनविशेषः, सुखाद्यं.

DAIRY, *s.* क्षीरमन्थनशाला, दधिमन्थनगृहं, गोदुग्धागारं, पयोरक्षणस्थानं.

DAIRY-MAID, *s.* गोदोहिनी, क्षीरमन्थिनी, गोदुग्धरक्षिका, गोपी, आभीरी.

DAISY, *s.* वसन्तसमये यवसप्ररोही शुक्लदलः क्षुद्रपुष्पभेदः.

DALE, *s.* दरी -रा, दरीभृः *f.*, कन्दरः -री, अद्रिद्रोणी, उपत्यका, प्रान्तरं.

DALLIANCE, *s.* (Act of fondness) कामचेष्टा, हावः, ललितं, लालसा, रमणं, रमण्यं, विलासः, विलसितं.—(Delay) विलम्बः, कालयापः.

To DALLY, *v. n.* (Sport, play, trifle) क्रीड् (c. 1. क्रीडति -डितुं), प्रक्रीड्; रम् (c. 1. रमते, रन्तुं), लल् (c. 1. ललति -लितुं), विलस् (c. 1. -लसति -सितुं), कुड् (c. 6. कुडति -डितुं).—(Caress a woman) स्त्रिया सह रम् or विलस्, कामचेष्टां कृ.—(Delay) विलम्ब् (c. 1. -लम्बते -म्बितुं).

DAM, *s.* (Mother, said of animals) जननी, जनिका, प्रजनिका, प्रजायिनी, प्रसूः *f.*, जनयित्री, अम्बा, माता *f.* (तृ).—(Bank to confine water) सेतुः *m.*, सेतुबन्धः, जलबन्धकः, धरणं, पिण्डनः, आलिः *f.*

To DAM UP, *v. a.* सेतुना जलं बन्ध् (c. 9. बध्नाति, बन्धुं) or संस्तम्भ् (c. 9. -स्तभ्नाति -स्तम्भितुं) or निरुध् (c. 7. -रुणद्धि -रोद्धुं).

DAMAGE, *s.* क्षतिः *f.*, क्षतं, अपचयः, अपायः, हानिः *f.*, नाशः, दोषः, दूषणं, क्षयः, उपक्षयः, अपकारः, अपकृतं, हिंसा, द्रोहः, ध्वंसः, प्रध्वंसः, भ्रंशः, अनिष्टं.—(Damages in law) क्षतिपूरणं, दण्डः, पारितोषिकं, प्रतिफलं, निष्कृतिः *f.*, प्रायश्चित्तं.

To DAMAGE, *v. a.* हिंस् (c. 7. हिनस्ति c. 1. हिंसति -सितुं), उपहिंस्, विहिंस्; दुष् in caus. (दूषयति -यितुं); अपकृ; अर्द् in caus. (अर्दयति -यितुं); क्षण् (c. 8. क्षणोति -णितुं), परिक्षण्; नश् in caus. (नाशयति -यितुं), द्रुह् (c. 4. द्रुह्यति, द्रोग्धुं).

DAMAGEABLE, *a.* हिंसनीयः -या -यं, दूष्यः -ष्या -ष्यं, अपचयक्षमः मा -मं.—(Mischievous) हिंस्रः -स्रा -स्रं, दूषकः -का -कं, अपकारकः -का -कं.

DAMAGED, *p. p.* क्षतः -ता -तं, परिक्षतः -ता -तं, विक्षतः -ता -तं, दूषितः -ता -तं, सदोषः -षा -षं, अर्दितः -ता -तं, कृतापकारः -रा -रं, अपकृतः -ता -तं.

DAMASK, *s.* पुष्पादिसूचिकर्म्मोत्कृतं दमस्कनाम चित्रदुकूलं.

To DAMASK, *v. a.* (Adorn stuffs with flowers) दुकूलं सूचिकर्म्मद्वारा पुष्पादिना अलङ्कृ.—(Variegate) चित्र् (c. 10. चित्रयति -यितुं), कर्बुरीकृ.

DAMASK-ROSE, *s.* हेमपुष्पं, रक्तपुष्पो जवाप्रभेदः.

DAME, *s.* (Lady) आर्य्या, भाविनी.—(Woman) स्त्री, वधूः, गृहिणी.

To DAMN, *v. a.* (Doom to hell or eternal torments) नरकं गम्यता इति शापं वद् (c. 1. वदति -दितुं); अनन्तदण्डं or नरकदण्डं प्राप्नुया इति ब्रू (c. 2. ब्रवीति, वक्तुं), अनन्तदुःखं or अनन्तयातना ते भूयाद् इति धिक्कृ, स नरकं व्रजतु or अधो ऽधो निरये पततु इति शापं कृ, नरकदण्डार्हं ज्ञा (c. 9. जानाति, ज्ञातुं), नरके निपत् in caus. (-पातयति -यितुं).—(Condemn) दण्ड् (c. 10. दण्डयति -यितुं), दण्डार्हं ज्ञा.—(Hiss any public performance) रङ्गे नाटकं प्रेक्ष्य कर्कशशब्दैर् अप्रसादं सूच् (c. 10. सूचयति -यितुं).

DAMNABLE, *a.* अनन्तदण्डार्हः -र्हा -र्हं, नरकदण्डार्हः -र्हा -र्हं, नरके पतनार्हः -र्हा -र्हं.—(Odious) गर्हितः -ता -तं, गर्हणीयः -या -यं.

DAMNABLY, *adv.* यथा नरकदण्डार्हो भवति तथा, गर्हितं.

DAMNATION, *s.* अनन्तदण्डः, नरकदण्डः, अनन्तयातना, नरकयातना, नरके पतनं, नरकगमनं, अधोगमनं, अभिसम्पातः, ईश्वरकृपावहिष्करणं.

DAMNED, *p. p.* नरकगतः -ता -तं, नरकपतितः -ता -तं, नरकस्थः -स्था -स्थं, नारकी -किणी -कि (न्), नैरयः -यी -यं, नरकप्राप्तः -प्ता -प्तं, अभिशप्तः -प्ता -प्तं, गर्हितः -ता -तं, गर्हणीयः -या -यं, घृणार्हः -र्हा -र्हं.

DAMNIFIC, *a.* क्षतिकारकः -का -कं, अपकारी -रिणी -रि (न्), दूषकः -का -कं.

To DAMNIFY, *v. a.* दुष् in caus. (दूषयति -यितुं), अपकृ, क्षतं -तां -तं कृ.

DAMP, DANK, *a.* (Moist) आर्द्रः -र्द्रा -र्द्रं, सार्द्रः -र्द्रा -र्द्रं, जलार्द्रः -र्द्रा -र्द्रं, क्लिन्नः -न्ना -न्नं, तिमितः -ता -तं, स्तिमितः -ता -तं, उन्नः -न्ना -न्नं, समुन्नः -न्ना -न्नं, सरसः -सा -सं, जलसिक्तः -क्ता -क्तं, अनूपः -पा -पं, समुक्षितः -ता -तं, थोदः -दा -दं, उत्तः -त्ता -त्तं.—(Dejected) म्लानः -ना -नं, म्लानः -ना -नं, विषण्णः -ण्णा -ण्णं.

DAMP, *s.* (Moisture) क्लेदः, सङ्क्लेदः, स्तेमः, तेमः -मनं, समुन्दनं, जलावसेकः, चिक्लिदं.—(Fog, vapour) बाष्पः, सबाष्पः, धूमः -मिका, स्वेदः.—(Dejection) विषादः, ग्लानिः *f.*; 'to be damp,' क्लिद् (c. 4. क्लिद्यति) तिम् (c. 4. तिम्यति or तीम्यति).

To DAMP, *v. a.* (Moisten) क्लिद् in caus. (क्लेदयति -यितुं), परिक्लिद्; सिच् (c. 6. सिञ्चति, सेक्तुं), अवसिच्; उक्ष् (c. 1. उक्षति -क्षितुं), समुक्ष्; उन्द् (c. 7. उनत्ति, उन्दितुं), आर्द्रीकृ.—(Dispirit) मनो दण्ड् (c. 10. दण्डयति -यितुं), खण्डिताशंसं -सां -सं कृ, भग्नाशं -शां -शं कृ, म्लानाशं -शां -शं, कृ.

DAMPISH, *a.* ईषदार्द्रः -र्द्रा -र्द्रं, ईषत्स्तिमितः -ता -तं, आक्लिन्नः -न्ना -न्नं.

DAMPNESS, *s.* आर्द्रता, सार्द्रता, जलार्द्रत्वं, क्लिन्नता, जलसिक्तत्वं, अनूपता.

DAMPY, *a.* विषादी -दिनी -दि (न्), अवसन्नः -न्ना -न्नं, उद्विग्नः -ग्ना -ग्नं.

DAMSEL, *s.* कन्या, कुमारी -रिका, कन्यका, युवतिः *f.* -ती, यूनी, बाला -लिका, अविवाहिता स्त्री; 'damsel's child,' कानीनः -नी.

DAMSON, *s.* दाम्सन्नामकः कृष्णवर्णः शुक्लफलप्रभेदः.

To DANCE, *v. n.* नृत् (c. 4. नृत्यति, नर्त्तितुं), प्रनृत्, उपनृत्, सम्प्रनृत्, नट् (c. 1. नटति -टितुं), नृत्यं कृ, नर्त्तकवद् हस्तपादादि सञ्चल् in caus. (-चालयति -यितुं); 'to dance attendance,' उपास् (c. 2. -आस्ते -आसितुं).

To DANCE, *v. a.* नृत् in caus. (नर्त्तयति -यितुं), चल् in caus. (चालयति -यितुं).

DANCE, *s.* नृत्यं, नाट्यं, ताण्डवं, लास्यं, चारणत्वं, पादन्यासः, गुणनिका.

DANCER, *s.* नर्त्तकः -की *f.*, नटः -टी *f.*, कुशीलवः, लासकः -की *f.*, लासिका *f.*, चारणः, चारणदाराः *f. pl.*, शैलाली *m.* (न्), शैलूषः, नाटकः -की *f.*, कृशाश्वी *m.* (न्), नर्त्तनवृत्तिः *m. f.*, नृत्यकुशलः, भरतः, भारतः, जायाजीवः, तालावचरः.

DANCING, *s.* नृत्यं, नर्त्तनं, नाट्यं, नटनं, प्रनर्त्तनं, लास्यं, लासः, ताण्डवं,

कौशीलव्यं, चारणत्वं, गुणनिका, हस्तपादादिसञ्चालनं.

DANCING-MASTER, *s.* नृत्याचार्य्यः, नृत्यशिक्षकः, नृत्यगुरुः *m.*

DANCING-SCHOOL, *s.* नृत्यशिक्षणशाला, नृत्यशाला, नृत्यशिक्षावेश्म *n.* (न्).

DANDELION, *s.* सिंहपर्णी, सिंहदन्तसरूपपत्रः क्षुद्रौषधिभेदः.

DANDIPRAT or DAPPERLING, *s.* बालकः, पुत्रकः, माणवकः, वामनः.

To DANDLE, *v. a.* ऊरुदेशे बालकं धृत्वा लल् in caus. (लालयति -यितुं).

DANDLED, *p. p.* लालितः -ता -तं, सान्त्वकरणार्थं जानुदेशे धृतः -ता -तं.

DANDRIFF, DANDRUFF, *s.* मञ्जा, शिरोमध्ये पिच्छितस्नेहः, शिरोमलं.

DANDY, *s.* सुवेशी *m.* (न्), सुवसनः, दर्शनीयमानी *m.* (न्), छेकः.

DANGER, *s.* भयं, भयहेतुः *m.*, संशयः, शङ्का, सन्देहः, विकल्पः, आतङ्कः, आपद् *f.*, विपद् *f.*, अपायः, विपत्तिः *f.*, उत्पातः, बाधा, व्याघातः; 'any thing exposed to danger,' भयस्थानं, संशयस्थानं, शङ्कास्पदं; 'danger of life,' जीवितसंशयः, प्राणनाशसंशयः, प्राणबाधः; 'we are in danger of being led to justice,' अस्माकं विचारस्थाने आनयनशङ्का विद्यते; 'in danger of punishment,' दण्डयोग्यः -ग्या -ग्यं; 'brought into danger,' संशयितः -ता -तं; 'an act attended with danger,' सन्दिग्धकर्म्म *n.* (न्).

To DANGER, *v. a.* संशयस्थं -स्थां -स्थं कृ, शङ्कास्पदं कृ, सन्देहस्थं -स्थां -स्थं कृ; 'one who dangers his life,' संशयितजीवितः.

DANGEROUS, *a.* भयङ्करः -रा -रं, भयानकः -की -कं, भयहेतुकः -का -कं, सन्दिग्धः -ग्धा -ग्धं, सांशयिकः -की -कं, संशयस्थः -स्था -स्थं, संशयापन्नः -न्ना -न्नं, शङ्काक्रान्तः -न्ता -न्तं, भयाक्रान्तः -न्ता -न्तं, भयजनकः -का -कं, भैरवः -वी -वं, विपत्तिजनकः -का -कं; 'a dangerous illness,' सन्निपातकः.

DANGEROUSLY, *adv.* यथा संशयः or भयहेतुर् उत्पद्यते तथा, भैरवं, शङ्कापूर्व्वकं, भयानकं, सन्दिग्धं; 'dangerously ill,' सन्निपातकरोगग्रस्तः.

DANGEROUSNESS, *s.* भयानकत्वं, सन्दिग्धता, सांशयिकत्वं, शङ्काक्रान्तत्वं.

To DANGLE, *v. n.* लुठ् (c. 6. लुठति -ठितुं), चञ्च् (c. 1. चञ्चति -ञ्चितुं), लम्ब् (c. 1. लम्बते -म्बितुं), अवलम्ब्, लुल् (c. 1. लोलति -ते -लितुं).

DANGLER, *s.* स्त्रीणाम् उपासने or स्त्रीभिः सह विलासकरणे कालक्षेपकः.

DANGLING, *a.* चञ्चन् -ञ्चन्ती -ञ्चत् (त्), लोलः -ला -लं, लोलमानः -ना -नं, लुठन् -ठन्ती -ठत् (त्), लम्बमानः -ना -नं, अवलम्बितः -ता -तं, लुलितः -ता -तं.

DAPPER, *a.* विनीतः -ता -तं, क्षुद्राकारः -रा -रं, ललितरूपः -पा -पं.

To DAPPLE, *v. a.* चित्र् (c. 10. चित्रयति -यितुं), चित्रविचित्रीकृ, कर्बुरीकृ.

DAPPLED, *a.* चित्रितः -ता -तं, कर्बुरितः -ता -तं, नानावर्णः -र्णा -र्णं.

To DARE, *v. n.* धृष् (c. 5. धृष्णोति, धर्षितुं), साहसं कृ, साहसेन व्यवसो (c. 4. -स्यति -सातुं); 'I dare not ask him,' न तं प्रष्टुं धृष्णोमि.

To DARE, *v. a.* (Challenge) आह्वे (c. 1. -ह्वयति -ह्वातुं), समाह्वे, नियुद्धार्थम् आह्वे, स्पर्ध् (c. 1. स्पर्धते -र्धितुं), आक्रन्द् (c. 1. -क्रन्दति -न्दितुं).

DARE, *s.* आह्वानं, समाह्वानं, योधसंरावः, क्रन्दितं, अभिग्रहः.

DARED, *p. p.* (Challenged) आहूतः -ता -तं, समाहूतः -ता -तं.

DARING, *s.* साहसं, प्रतिभा, धार्ष्ट्यं; 'act of daring,' अत्याहितं.

DARING, *a.* साहसी -सिनी -सि (न्), साहसिकः -की -कं, धृष्टः -ष्टा -ष्टं, धृष्णुः -ष्णुः -ष्णु, प्रगल्भः -ल्भा -ल्भं, वीरः -रा -रं, प्रवीरः -रा -रं, शूरः -रा -रं, निर्भयः -या -यं, अभीतः -ता -तं, निर्विशङ्कः -ङ्का -ङ्कं, अकुतोभयः -या -यं, विक्रान्तः -न्ता -न्तं, पराक्रमी -मिणी -मि (न्), प्रतिभानवान् -वती -वत् (त्), प्रतिभान्वितः -ता -तं.

DARINGLY, *adv.* साहसेन -सात्, साहसपूर्व्वकं, धृष्टं, धृष्टत्वात्, सशौर्य्यं, प्रगल्भं, निर्भयं, निर्विशङ्कं, सविक्रमं, सप्रतिभानं, वीरवत्.

DARINGNESS, *s.* साहसं, साहसिकत्वं, धृष्टता, धृष्णुता, धार्ष्ट्यं, प्रगल्भता, प्रागल्भ्यं, प्रतिभा -भानं, निर्भयत्वं, वीरता, शौर्य्यं, धैर्य्यं, विक्रमः.

DARK, *a.* तामसः -सी -सं -सिकः -की -कं, तमस्वी -स्विनी -स्वि (न्), सान्धकारः -रा -रं, अन्धकारयुक्तः -क्ता -क्तं, सतिमिरः -रा -रं, तिमिरयुक्तः -क्ता -क्तं, तमोवृतः -ता -तं, तमोमयः -यी -यं, तमोभूतः -ता -तं, निरालोकः -का -कं, निष्प्रभः -भा -भं, अप्रकाशः -शा -शं, हतज्योतीः -तीः -तिः (स्).—(Obscure) गूढः -ढा -ढं, निगूढः -ढा -ढं, दुर्ज्ञेयः -या -यं, अस्पष्टः -ष्टा -ष्टं, दुर्दर्शः -र्शा -र्शं.—(Dark-coloured) कृष्णः -ष्णा -ष्णं, श्यामः -मा -मं, कालेयः -यी -यं, मेचकः -का -कं, नीलः -ला -लं, सितेतरः -रा -रं,—(Opaque) अस्वच्छः -च्छा -च्छं; 'a dark night,' तामसी, तमिस्रा, नष्टचन्द्रा रात्रिः.

DARK, *s.* तमः *n.* (स्), अन्धकारः, तिमिरं, तमिस्रं, अन्धं.

To DARKEN, *v. a.* तिमिर (nom. तिमिरयति -यितुं), तिमिरीकृ, अन्धीकृ.

To DARKEN, *v. n.* तमस्वी -स्विनी -स्वि भू, तिमिरीभू, अन्धीभू.

DARKENED, *p. p.* तमोवृतः -ता -तं, तिमिरीकृतः -ता -तं, सन्तमसः -सा -सं.

DARKISH, *a.* तमस्कल्पः -ल्पा -ल्पं, ईषत्तामसः -सी -सं.—(In colour) ईषत्कृष्णः -ष्णा -ष्णं, आकालः -ला -लं, आनीलः -ला -लं.

DARKLING, *a.* तमोवर्त्ती -र्त्तिनी -र्त्ति (न्) or अन्धकारवर्त्ती.

DARKLY, *adv.* अस्पष्टं, अप्रकाशं, अव्यक्तं, सान्धकारं, अन्धवत्, अन्धं.

DARKNESS, *s.* अन्धकारः, तमः *n.* (स्), तिमिरं, तमिस्रं, तमसं, ध्वान्तं, निरालोकता, सान्धकारत्वं, निष्प्रभता, अन्धं, शार्वरं, रात्रिवासः *n.* (स्), निशाचर्म्म *n.* (न्), भूच्छाया, खलुक् *m.* (च्); 'slight darkness,' अवतमसं; 'great darkness,' अन्धतमसं, तमस्ततिः *f.*; 'universal darkness,' सन्तमसं,

DARKSOME, *s.* तमस्वी -स्विनी -स्वि (न्), तमस्कल्पः -ल्पा -ल्पं, निष्प्रभः -भा -भं,

DARLING, *s.* प्रियः -या, हृदयप्रियः -या, दयितः -ता, स्नेहपात्रं.

DARLING, *a.* हृदयप्रियः -या -यं, सुप्रियः -या -यं, प्रियतमः -मा -मं, हृद्यः -द्या -द्यं, वल्लभः -भा -भं, इष्टः -ष्टा -ष्टं, इष्टतमः -मा -मं.

DARN, *s.* वस्त्रयोन्यनुकृतं जीर्णवस्त्रसीवनं, वस्त्रसन्धिः *m.*

To DARN, *v. a.* जीर्णवस्त्राणि सिव् (c. 4. सीव्यति, सेवितुं) or सूक्ष्मसूचिकर्म्मद्वारा सन्धा (c. 3. -दधाति -धातुं).

DARNEL, *s.* कक्षः, शस्यक्षेत्ररुहः कक्षप्रभेदः.

DART, *s.* शूलः -लं, प्रासः, शल्यं, शङ्कुः *m.*, क्षिपणिः *m.*, पाणिमुक्तं, करमुक्तं, मुक्तकं, बाणः, अस्त्रं, समिकं, दूरवेधी *m.* (न्).

To DART, *v. a.* अस् (c. 4. अस्यति, असितुं), प्रास्, क्षिप् (c. 6. क्षिपति, क्षेप्तुं), मुच् (c. 6. मुञ्चति, मोक्तुं), प्रमुच्, सृज् (c. 6. सृजति, स्रष्टुं), ईर् (c.10. ईरयति -यितुं), पत् in caus. (पातयति -यितुं), प्रहृ (c. 1. -हरति -हर्त्तुं).

To DART, *v. n.* (As lightning) स्फुर् (c. 6. स्फुरति -रितुं).—(Dart upon one) आपत् (c. 1. -पतति -तितुं), अभिद्रु (c. 1. -द्रवति -द्रोतुं).

To DASH, *v. a.* (Throw or strike any thing suddenly or forcibly against another) सहसा or प्रसभं क्षिप् (c. 6. क्षिपति, क्षेप्तुं) or प्रक्षिप् or अस् (c. 4. अस्यति, असितुं) or प्रास् or पत् in caus. (पातयति -यितुं), or अभिहन् (c. 2. -हन्ति -न्तुं), or अभ्याहन् or प्रतिहन् or प्रहृ (c. 1. -हरति -हर्त्तुं).—(Break by collision, dash in pieces) मृद् (c. 9. मृद्नाति, मर्द्दितुं), निष्पिष् (c. 7. -पिनष्टि -पेष्टुं), प्रभञ्ज् (c. 7. -भनक्ति, भंक्तुं), विघट्ट् (c. 10. -घट्टयति -यितुं), भूमौ प्रक्षिप्य खण्डं खण्डं कृ or खण्डशः कृ or लवशः कृ or चूर्ण् (c. 10. चूर्णयति -यितुं),—(Bespatter, besprinkle) अवकॄ (c. 6. -किरति -करितुं -रीतुं), अभ्यवकॄ, समवकॄ; उक्ष् (c. 1. उक्षति -क्षितुं), अभ्युक्ष्, प्रोक्ष्; अवसिच् (c. 6. -सिञ्चति -सेक्तुं),—(Mingle, adulterate) मिश्र् (c. 10. मिश्रयति -यितुं), सम्मिश्र्, संसृज् (c. 6. -सृजति -स्रष्टुं).—(Confound) मुह् in caus. (मोहयति -यितुं), विनश् in caus. (-नाशयति -यितुं).—(Obliterate) व्यामृज् (c. 2. -मार्ष्टि -मार्ष्टुं), उच्छिद् (c. 7. -छिनत्ति -छेत्तुं), विलुप्

in caus. (-लोपयति -यितुं); 'dash one's hopes,' आशा भञ्ज् or खराट् (c. 10. खराट्यति -यितुं); 'dash out the brains,' मस्तकं निष्पिष्.

To DASH, *v. n.* (Rush against with a violent motion) प्रपत् (c. 1. -पतति -तितुं), प्रोत्पत्, आपत्, प्रस्कन्द् (c. 1. -स्कन्दति -स्कन्तुं), उत्प्लु (c. 1. -प्लवते -प्लोतुं), अभिद्रु (c. 1. -द्रवति -द्रोतुं).—(Be dashed in pieces), प्रभञ्ज् in pass. (-भज्यते).

DASH, *s.* (Collision) सङ्घट्टः -ट्टनं, समाघातः, प्रतिघातः, अभिघातः, परस्पराघातः, प्रभङ्गः, सम्मर्द्दः, मर्द्दनं, निष्पेषः.—(Infusion, admixture) प्रक्षेपः, मिश्रणं, सम्पर्कः, संसर्गः; 'a dash, a slight quantity,' किञ्चित्, ईषत्.—(A line in writing to denote a pause or omission) लिखने विरामसूचनार्थं or त्यागसूचनार्थं क्षुद्ररेखा.—(Blow) प्रहारः, आघातः, आहतिः *f.*

DASTARD, *s.* कापुरुषः, कुपुरुषः, हतकः, क्लीवः, कातरः, कृपणः, भीरुः.

To DASTARD or DASTARDISE, *v. a.* त्रस् in caus. (त्रासयति -यितुं), सन्त्रस्; भी in caus. (भाययति or भीषयति -यितुं), दीनचेतसं -सां -सं कृ.

DASTARDLY, *a.* अमनुष्यः -ष्या -ष्यं, कातरः -रा -रं, निर्वीरः -रा -रं, क्लीवः -वा -वं, अपौरुषेयः -यी -यं, दीनमनस्कः -स्का -स्कं.

DASTARDY, *s.* कापुरुषत्वं, अमनुष्यता, अपौरुषं, कातर्य्यं, क्लैव्यं, दीनता.

DATA, DATUM, *s.* तत्त्वानि *n. pl.*, सत्यानि *n. pl.*, सर्व्वानुमतं तत्त्वं, उपन्यासः.

DATE, *s.* (Time at which a letter, &c. is written) लिखनकालः, लिखनदिवसः, दिवसः, दिनं, तिथिः *m. f.*—(Time at which a thing was done) कालः, कालिकता, तत्कालः.—(Period, term) अवधिः *m.*, कालावधिः *m.*, परिमाणं.—(Fruit) खर्ज्जूरः, काठिनः; 'out of date,' अव्यवहारितः -ता -तं, निरूढः -ढा -ढं.

To DATE, *v. a.* कालं or दिवसं or दिनं or तिथिं लिख् (c. 6. लिखति, लेखितुं).

DATED, *p. p.* कालसम्पन्नः -न्ना -न्नं, सकालः -ला -लं, कृतकालः -ला -लं.

DATE-TREE, *s.* खर्ज्जूरः, तृणद्रुमः, यवनामयः; 'marshy date-tree,' हिन्तालः, हीन्तालः, हिमहासकः.

DATIVE, *a.* (Case) सम्प्रदानं, सम्प्रदानकारकः, चतुर्थी विभक्तिः.

To DAUB, *v. a.* लिप् (c. 6. लिम्पति, लेप्तुं), आलिप्, उपलिप्, समालिप्; अञ्ज् (c. 7. अनक्ति, अंक्तुं or caus. अञ्जयति -यितुं), दिह् (c. 2. देग्धि -ग्धुं), प्रदिह्.—(Cover over) छद् (c. 10. छादयति -यितुं), प्रच्छद्.

DAUB, *s.* लेपः, विलेपः.—(Bad painting) कुचित्रं, कुचित्रलेखा, मन्दचित्रं.

DAUBED, *p. p.* लिप्तः -प्ता -प्तं, उपलिप्तः -प्ता -प्तं, विलिप्तः -प्ता -प्तं, अक्तः -क्ता -क्तं, अभ्यक्तः -क्ता -क्तं, दिग्धः -ग्धा -ग्धं, निदिग्धः -ग्धा -ग्धं.

DAUBER, *s.* लेपकः, लेपकरः, प्रलेपकः.—(Coarse painter) अनभिज्ञचित्रकरः, कुचित्रलिक् *m.* (ख्), चित्रकरदेशीयः, चित्रकरपाशः.

DAUBY, *a.* श्यानः -ना -नं, शीनः -ना -नं, सान्द्रः -न्द्रा -न्द्रं, लेप्यः -प्या -प्यं.

DAUGHTER, *s.* दुहिता *f.* (तृ), पुत्री, पुत्रिका, पुत्रका, सुता, सूनुः -नूः *f.*, आत्मजा, स्वजा, अङ्गजा, कन्या, तनया, कन्यकाजनः, जाता, दारिका, प्रसूतिः *f.*, विट् *f.* (श्); 'legitimate daughter,' औरसी, धर्म्मजा; 'daughter in law,' स्नुषा, जनी, पुत्रवधूः *f.*, वधूः *f.*, वधूटी, सुतस्त्री; 'adopted daughter,' करणीसुता, पुत्रिका, पोष्यपुत्री, क्रीतपुत्री; 'daughter's husband,' जामाता *m.* (तृ), दुहितुःपतिः *m.*

To DAUNT, *v. a.* त्रस् in caus. (-त्रासयति -यितुं), सन्त्रस्, भी in caus. (भाययति or भीषयति -यितुं), भयं जन् in caus. (जनयति -यितुं), मनो भञ्ज् (c. 7. भनक्ति, भंक्तुं), मनोहतं -तां -तं कृ.

DAUNTLESS, *a.* निर्भयः -या -यं, अशङ्कः -ङ्का -ङ्कं, विशङ्कः -ङ्का -ङ्कं, अभीतः -ता -तं, अकुतोभयः -या -यं, अपभीः -भीः -भि, निःसाध्वसः -सा -सं.

DAUNTLESSNESS, *s.* निर्भयत्वं, अभीतिः *f.*, अभयं, अभीरुता, विशङ्कता.

DAUPHIN, *s.* युवराजः, ज्येष्ठो राजपुत्रः, राज्ञः पूर्व्वजपुत्रः.

To DAWDLE, *v. n.* विलस् (c. 1. -लसते -सितुं), कालं क्षिप् (c. 6. क्षिपति, क्षेप्तुं).

DAWDLER, *s.* विलासी *m.* (न्), कालक्षेपकः, दीर्घसूत्री *m.* (न्).

To DAWN, *v. n.* प्रभा (c. 2. -भाति -तुं), उषस् (nom. उषस्यति), उष् (c. 1. उच्छति, ओषितुं), व्युष्, समुष्, प्रभातीभू.

DAWN, *s.* अरुणः, प्रभातं, उषः -षः *n.* (स्), प्रत्युषः -षः *n.* (स्), प्रत्यूषः -षः *n.* (स्), अरुणोदयः, व्युष्टं, विभातं, भातः, उदयः, प्रातःकालः, कल्यं, काल्यं, पूर्व्वसन्ध्या, प्राक्सन्ध्या, सन्ध्या, दिवसमुखं, अहर्मुखं, दिनारम्भः, दिनादिः *m.*, निशावसानं, निशान्तं, क्षपान्तः, रात्रिविगमः, गोसर्गः, प्राबोधिकः; 'at dawn,' प्रभाते, उषा, प्रातःकाले, प्रातर्; 'belonging to the dawn,' उषस्यः -स्या -स्यं, प्रभातीयः -या -यं, प्रातःकालीनः -ना -नं.

DAY, *s.* दिवसः -सं, दिनं, अहः *m.* (न्), वासरः, वारः, द्यु *n.*, घस्रः, वास्रः; 'a lunar day,' तिथिः *m. f.* -थी; 'to day,' अद्य; 'by day,' दिवा, अह्नाय; 'day by day,' प्रतिदिनं, प्रतिदिवसं, प्रतिवासरं, प्रत्यहं, दिवसे दिवसे, अहन्यहनि, अहरहः, दिने दिने; 'day and night,' अहोरात्रं, अहर्निशं, दिवानिशं, दिवारात्रं, क्षपाहं, द्युनिशं, द्युनिशौ; 'from day to day,' दिनाद्दिनं, वारं वारं; 'one day,' एकदा; 'a former day,' पूर्व्वेद्युस्; 'a future day,' उत्तरेद्युस्; 'another day,' अन्येद्युस्; 'next day,' परेद्युस्, परेद्यवि; 'the day before yesterday,' अपरेद्युस्; 'the day after to-morrow,' परश्वस्, अधरेद्युस्; 'a night and two days or a day and two nights,' पक्षिणी; 'a day of Brahma,' ब्राह्मः; 'a day of the gods,' दैवतः; 'a rainy day,' दुर्द्दिनं, वार्द्दलं; 'day's hire,' दिनिका, दैनिकी.

DAY-BOOK, *s.* महाजनस्य दैनिकपुस्तकं, वाणिजपुस्तकं यस्मिन् दिवसे दिवसे पण्यायावृत्तान्तो लिख्यते or आरोप्यते.

DAY-BREAK, *s.* अरुणोदयः, उदयकालः, उषः, प्रत्युषः, प्रभातं, प्रभातकालः, दिवसमुखं, अहर्मुखं, दिनारम्भः, दिनादिः *m.*, रात्र्यवसानं, निशान्तं.

DAY-LABOUR, *s.* व्रातं, दैनिककर्म्म *n.* (न्), आह्निकक्रिया, दिवाकर्म्म *n.*

DAY-LABOURER, *s.* व्रातीनः, व्रातकरः, व्रातव्यापृतः, दैनिककर्म्मकरः.

DAY-LIGHT, *s.* दिनज्योतिः *n.* (स्), सूर्य्यकालः, सूर्य्यरश्मिः *m.*, दिनालोकः, दीप्तिः *f.*

DAY-SPRING, *s.* अरुणोदयः, उदयः, सूर्य्योदयः, दिवसमुखं, दिनारम्भः.

DAY-STAR, *s.* प्रभातनक्षत्रं, प्रभातीयतारा, प्रातरुदयिनी तारा, शुक्रतारा.

DAY-TIME, *s.* दिवसकालः, सूर्य्यकालः, सूर्य्यसमयः, दिनकालः, रविकालः.

DAY-WORK, *s.* दिवसकर्म्म *n.* (न्), दिवाकर्म्म, आह्निकक्रिया, व्रातं.

To DAZZLE, *v. a.* अतिशयतेजसा दृष्टिं सन्तप् in caus. (-तापयति -यितुं) or उपहन् (c. 2. -हन्ति -न्तुं) or अवरुध् (c. 7. -रुणद्धि -रोद्धुं).

To DAZZLE, *v. n.* अतिदीप्त्युपहतत्वात् सन्तापितदृष्टिः -ष्टिः -ष्टि भू.

DAZZLED, *p. p.* उपहतदृष्टिः -ष्टिः -ष्टि or अवरुद्धदृष्टिः, उपहतनयनः -ना -नं.

DAZZLING, *a.* अतितैजसः -सी -सं, उज्ज्वलः -ला -लं, दृष्टिसन्तापकः -का -कं, दुरालोकः -का -कं, दुर्निरीक्ष्यः -क्ष्या -क्ष्यं, दुर्दर्शः -र्शा -र्शं, नयनोपघाती -तिनी -ति (न्).

DEACON, *s.* उपपुरोहितः, उपधर्म्माध्यापकः, पुरोहितसहायः -सहकारी *m.* (न्).

DEACONESS, *s.* पूर्व्वकाले ख्रीष्टीयसमाजे पुरोहितसहकारिणी स्त्री.

DEACONRY, DEACONSHIP, *s.* उपपुरोहितस्य पदं or व्यापारः or कर्म्म *n.* (न्).

DEAD, *a.* and *p.* मृतः -ता -तं, प्रेतः -ता -तं, परेतः -ता -तं, सम्मृतः -ता -तं, प्रेतीभूतः -ता -तं, अतीतः -ता -तं, व्यतीतः -ता -तं, अपगतः -ता -तं,

विगतः -ता -तं, अजीवः -वा -वं, निर्जीवः -वा -वं, व्यापन्नः -न्ना -न्नं, विपन्नः -न्ना -न्नं, संस्थितः -ता -तं, मृतः -ता -तं, प्रमीतः -ता -तं, नष्टः -ष्टा -ष्टं, उपरतः -ता -तं, अवसन्नः -न्ना -न्नं, त्यक्तजीवनः -ना -नं, प्रहीणजीवितः -ता -तं, न्यस्तदेहः -हा -हं, गतप्राणः -णा -णं, गतासुः -सुः -सु or उद्गतासुः, परासुः -सुः -सु, प्राप्तपञ्चत्वः -त्वा -त्वं, अभ्रियमाणः -णा -णं, नामशेषः -षा -षं, कीर्त्तिशेषः -षा -षं, कथाशेषः -षा -षं, दिष्टङ्गतः -ता -तं, प्रशान्तः -न्ता -न्तं; 'gone to heaven,' स्वर्यातः -ता -तं, ऊर्द्ध्वगतः -ता -तं; 'half-dead,' मृतकल्पः -ल्पा -ल्पं, मृतप्रायः -या -यं, मुमूर्षुः -र्षुः -र्षु.—(Inanimate) अप्राणी -णिनी -णि (न्), विचेतनः -ना -नं, व्यसुः -सुः -सु, प्राणहीनः -ना -नं.—(Motionless) निष्पन्दः -न्दा -न्दं, निश्चेष्टः -ष्टा -ष्टं, निश्चलः -ला -लं.—(Empty) शून्यः -न्या -न्यं.—(Dull) मन्दः -न्दा -न्दं, निस्तेजाः -जाः -जः (स्).—(Obtuse) जडः -डा -डं, अतीक्ष्णः -क्ष्णा -क्ष्णं.—(Vapid) विरसः -सा -सं, निस्सत्त्वः -त्त्वा -त्त्वं, निस्सारः -रा -रं, क्लीवः -वा -वं.—(Useless) विफलः -ला -लं.—(Numbed) स्तब्धः -ब्धा -ब्धं, सुप्तः -प्ता -प्तं.—(Dead body) मृतशरीरं, मृतकं, शवः -वं, कुणपः -पं.

Dead, *s.* (Of night) मध्यरात्रः, महारात्रः, महानिशा, अर्द्धरात्रः, अर्द्धनिशा, निशीथः; 'in the dead of night,' रात्रिमध्ये; 'of winter,' शीतकालमध्ये.

To **deaden**, *v. a.* दुर्बलीकृ, निर्बलीकृ, ग्लानीकृ, शिथिलीकृ, विरसीकृ, तेजो हृ (c. 1. हरति, हर्त्तुं) or उपहन् (c. 2. -हन्ति -न्तुं), शम् in caus. (शमयति -यितुं).

To **deaden**, *v. n.* ग्लै (c. 1. ग्लायति, ग्लातुं), क्षि in pass. (क्षीयते), शिथिलीभू.

Deadened, *p. p.* हृततेजाः -जाः -जः (स्) or ग्लानतेजाः or नष्टतेजाः, क्षीणशक्तिः -क्तिः -क्ति, शिथिलबलः -ला -लं, उपहतशक्तिः -क्तिः -क्ति.

Deadly, *a.* मारात्मकः -का -कं, व्यापादकः -का -कं, आत्ययिकः -की -कं, प्राणान्तिकः -की -कं or प्राणान्तकः or जीवान्तकः, प्राणहारी -रिणी -रि (न्) or प्राणापहारी, प्राणघातकः -का -कं, मृत्युजनकः -का -कं, निधनकारी -रिणी -रि (न्), विषतुल्यः -ल्या -ल्यं, सविषः -षा -षं, कालकल्पः -ल्पा -ल्पं, प्राणनाशकः -का -कं, मर्म्मान्तिकः -की -कं.—(Implacable) अशाम्यः -म्या -म्यं; 'deadly hatred,' बद्धवैरं; 'deadly poison,' मृत्युजनकगरलं.

Deadly, *adv.* (In a manner like the dead) मृतवत्, प्रेतवत्, शववत्.—(Mortally) मारात्मकं, प्राणान्तिकं; 'deadly wounded,' भिन्नमर्म्मा *m.* (न्); 'deadly pale,' शवसवर्णः -र्णा -र्णं.

Deadness, *s.* (Coldness, want of affection) निःस्नेहता, विरक्तिः *f.*, वैराग्यं.—(Languor, weakness) ग्लानिः *f.*, म्लानिः *f.*, अवसादः, मान्द्यं, निर्बलता, दौर्बल्यं, अशक्तिः *f.*, बलशैथिल्यं, शिथिलता.—(Want of motion) निष्पन्दता, निश्चलता.—(Want of spirit) तेजोहीनता, निस्सत्त्वता, वैरस्यं, जडत्वं.—(Numbness) सुप्तिः *f.*, स्तब्धता.—(Barrenness) वन्ध्यता, वैफल्यं.

Dead-reckoning, *s.* कुत्र समुद्रे नौका वर्त्तते इति जिज्ञासया सूर्य्यतारा-द्यभावे नाविकैः कृता गणना.

Deaf, *a.* बधिरः -रा -रं, एडः -डा -डं, अकर्णः -र्णा -र्णं, बन्धुरः -रा -रं, कल्लः -ल्ला -ल्लं, श्रोत्रविकलः -ला -लं, श्रवणेन्द्रियविकलः -ला -लं, श्रवणशक्तिरहितः -ता -तं, श्रुतिवर्ज्जितः -ता -तं; 'deaf and dumb,' एडमूकः -का -कं, कल्यः -ल्या -ल्यं.

To **deafen**, *v. a.* बधिरीकृ, बधिर (nom. बधिरयति -यितुं), कर्णौ उपहन् (c. 2. -हन्ति -न्तुं), श्रवणशक्तिं हृ (c. 1. हरति, हर्त्तुं).

Deafened, *p. p.* उपहतकर्णः -र्णा -र्णं, बधिरीकृतः -ता -तं.

Deafening, *a.* कर्णोपघाती -तिनी -ति (न्), श्रवणशक्तिहारी -रिणी -रि (न्).

Deafish, *a.* ईषद्बधिरः -रा -रं, ईषदेडः -डा -डं, अस्पष्टश्रवणः -णा -णं.

Deafly, *adv.* बधिरवत्, एडवत्, अश्रवणपूर्व्वं, अस्पष्टं.

Deafness, *s.* बधिरत्वं -ता, एडता, कल्लत्वं, अश्रवणं, श्रवणहीनता, श्रवणेन्द्रियवैकल्यं, श्रवणाक्षमता.

Deal, *s.* (Quantity) बाहुल्यं, बहुत्वं, प्राचुर्य्यं, प्रायः; 'a deal of, much,' बहुः -हुः -ह्वी -हु, भूरिः -रिः -रि, प्रचुरः -रा -रं, अनल्पः -ल्पा -ल्पं, अनेकः -का -कं; 'a deal of money,' बहुधनं; 'a good deal,' बहु, भृशं, अतिशयं, निर्भरं, गाढं, अत्यन्तं, अनल्पं, अति or सु prefixed; 'a good deal vexed,' सुदुःखितः.—(Fir wood) दारु *n.*, देवदारु, देवकाष्ठं, इन्द्रदारुः *m.*, किलिमं.

To **deal**, *v. a.* (Distribute) कॢप् (c. 10. कल्पयति -यितुं), परिकॢप्; पृथक् पृथग् विभज् (c. 1. -भजति -ते -भक्तुं) or विन्यस् (c. 4. -अस्यति -असितुं) or व्यंस् (c. 10. -अंसयति -यितुं) or विधा (c. 3. -दधाति -धातुं), वण्ट् (c. 10. वण्टयति -यितुं).—(Scatter) विकॄ (c. 6. -किरति -करितुं -रीतुं), विक्षिप् (c. 6. -क्षिपति -क्षेप्तुं), व्यस्; 'to deal blows,' मुष्टिं or दण्डं पत् in caus. (पातयति -यितुं).

To **deal**, *v. n.* (Transact business, trade) पण् (c. 1. पणते -णितुं or पणायति -यितुं), पणायां कृ, व्यवहृ (c. 1. -हरति -हर्त्तुं), व्यापृ (c. 6. -प्रियते), क्रयविक्रयं कृ.—(Behave, act) चर् (c. 1. चरति -रितुं), आचर्, समाचर्; वृत् (c. 1. वर्त्तते -र्त्तितुं), चेष्ट् (c. 1. चेष्टते -ष्टितुं), विधा (c. 3. -दधाति -धातुं).

To **deal with**, *v. a.* (Treat in any manner) विधा (c. 3. -दधाति -धातुं), आचर् (c. 1. -चरति -रितुं), समाचर्; व्यवहृ (c. 1. -हरति -हर्त्तुं); 'he deals honourably with me,' मयि यथान्यायं वृत्तिं वर्त्तते.—(Contend with) प्रतिकृ, विरुध् (c. 7. -रुणद्धि -रोद्धुं), प्रतिरुध्, प्रतिकूल (nom. प्रतिकूलयति -यितुं); 'how can one deal with such a monarch?' एवंविधे नृपे कुतो वशित्वं.—(Manage) प्रणी (c. 1. -णयति -णेतुं), विधा, घट् (c. 1. घटते -टितुं); 'an easy man to deal with,' विधेयः, प्रणेयः, वश्यः, गृह्यकः, अभिगम्यः, विनेयः; 'a hard man to deal with,' दुर्द्धर्षः.

Dealer, *s.* (One who has to do with any thing) व्यापारी *m.* (न्), व्यवसायी *m.* (न्), व्यवहर्त्ता *m.* (र्त्तृ), व्यवहारी *m.* (न्), कर्म्मकारी *m.* (न्).—(Trader) क्रयविक्रयिकः, विपणी *m.* (न्), आपणिकः, प्रापणिकः, पणिकः, वणिक् *m.* (ज्), वाणिजः, विक्रयिकः, विक्रेता *m.* (तृ).

Dealing, *s.* (Practice, mode of treatment) व्यापारः, व्यवहारः, व्यवसायः, कर्म्म *n.* (न्), क्रिया, कार्य्यं, चेष्टा, विचेष्टितं, प्रवृत्तिः *f.*, विधानं, आचारः, आचरणं, चरितं, वृत्तं, कर्म्मविधिः *m.*—(Intercourse) व्यवहारः, सङ्गतिः *f.*, सङ्गः, संसर्गः.—(Traffic) क्रयविक्रयः, विपणः, पणाया, पणः, पाणः, वाणिज्यं -ज्या, वणिक्पथः, महाजनकर्म्म *n.* (न्), निगमः, सत्यानृतं.

Dealt with, *p. p.* व्यवहारितः -ता -तं, आचरितः -ता -तं, पणायितः -ता -तं.

Deambulation, *s.* बहिर्गमनं, बहिर्भ्रमणं, परिक्रमः, पर्य्यटनं, भ्रमणं, विहारः.

Dean, *s.* प्रधानधर्म्माध्यक्षाधिकारे द्वितीयपदस्थः, महापूजाशालासम्बन्धीयमठे प्रधानसभासद्, दशपुरोहिताधिपतिः *m.*—(In a college) विद्यालये विनयाध्यक्षः.

Deanery, *s.* (House of a dean) पुरोहिताधिपतेर् गृहं or वेश्म *n.* (न्) or निवासः.

Deanship, *s.* पुरोहिताधिपतेः पदं or अधिकारः or व्यापारः.

Dear, *a.* (Beloved) प्रियः -या -यं, सुप्रियः -या -यं, हृदयप्रियः -या -यं, दयितः -ता -तं, इष्टः -ष्टा -ष्टं, अभीष्टः -ष्टा -ष्टं, प्रीतः -ता -तं, प्रेष्ठः -ष्ठा -ष्ठं, हृद्यः -द्या -द्यं, वल्लभः -भा -भं, अभीप्सितः -ता -तं, सुभगः -गा -गं,

कान्तः -न्ता -न्तं, प्रियतमः -मा -मं, इष्टतमः -मा -मं; 'a dear friend,' प्रियसुहृद् *m.*; 'dear as one's life,' असुसमः -मा -मं, प्राणाधिकः -का -कं, प्राणैर् गरीयान् -यसी -यः (स्).—(Of high price, costly) दुर्मूल्यः -ल्या -ल्यं, बहुमूल्यः -ल्या -ल्यं, महामूल्यः -ल्या -ल्यं, महार्घः -र्घा -र्घं, दुष्क्रेयः -या -यं, बहुधनव्ययेन क्रेयः -या -यं, गुरुः -र्वी -रु, महार्हः -र्हा -र्हं, अर्घ्यः -र्घ्या -र्घ्यं, उत्कृष्टः -ष्टा -ष्टं.

DEAR, *s.* (Word of endearment) प्रियः -या, दयितः -ता, कान्तः -न्ता, दयितः -ता, वत्सः -त्सा; 'my dear,' प्रिय voc. c. *m.*, प्रिये voc. c. *f.*

DEAR, *adv.* (Oh dear!) अहो, अहोबत्, कष्टं, आ, हा, हन्त, अहह.

DEAR-BOUGHT, *a.* दुष्क्रीतः -ता -तं, बहुमूल्येन क्रीतः -ता -तं.

DEARLY, *adv.* (With great fondness) प्रियं, सुप्रियं, प्रीत्या, सुप्रीत्या; 'dearly beloved,' अतिप्रियः -या -यं, प्रियतमः -मा -मं.—(At a high price) बहुमूल्येन, दुर्मूल्येन, महार्घेण, गुरु, गुरुमूल्येन.

DEARNESS, *s.* (Fondness) प्रियता, इष्टता, अभीष्टता, प्रीतिः *f.*—(High price) दुर्मूल्यं, बहुमूल्यं, माहार्घ्यं, महार्घता, महार्घः, मूल्यगुरुता, गुरुत्वं.

DEARTH, *s.* (Famine) दुर्भिक्षं, दुष्कालः, अनाकालं, दुर्भिक्ष्यं, नीवाकः, प्रयामः, उपद्रवः; 'dearth of provisions,' आहारविरहः.—(Want, need) अभावः, अप्राप्तिः *f.*, विरहः, असम्भवः, दौर्लभ्यं, वैरल्यं; 'dearth of money,' धनाभावः.

To DEARTICULATE, *v. a.* विसन्धीकृ, सन्धिस्फोटनं कृ, व्यङ्गीकृ.

DEARTICULATED, *p. p.* विसन्धितः -ता -तं, त्रुटितसन्धिः -न्धिः -न्धि.

DEATH, *s.* मृत्युः *m.*, मरणं, निधनं, पञ्चत्वं -ता, अत्ययः, अन्तः, अन्तकालः, अन्तकः, अपगमः, नाशः, विनाशः, प्रलयः, संस्थानं, संस्थितिः *f.*, अवसानं, निःसरणं, उपरतिः *f.*, अपायः, प्रयाणं, जीवनत्यागः, तनुत्यागः, जीवोत्सर्गः, देहक्षयः, प्राणवियोगः, मृतं, मृतिः *f.*, मरिमा *m.* (न्), महानिद्रा, दीर्घनिद्रा, कालः, कालधर्म्मः, कालदण्डः, कालान्तकः, नरान्तकः, दिष्टान्तः, व्यापद् *f.*, हान्द्रं, कथाशेषता, कीर्त्तिशेषः, लोकान्तरप्राप्तिः *f.*—(Murder) वधः, घातः, मारणं.—(Death personified) यमः, कालः, कृतान्तः; 'a violent death,' अपघातः, अपमृत्युः *m.*; 'death by lightning,' वज्रवधः; 'deserving of death,' वध्यः -ध्या -ध्यं, वधार्हः -र्हा -र्हं or प्रयाणार्हः; 'desire for death,' मुमूर्षा; 'desirous of death,' मुमूर्षुः -र्षुः -र्षु; 'at the point of death,' आसन्नमृत्युः, मुमूर्षुः, मृतप्रायः, मृतकल्पः; 'fearing death,' विवशः -शा -शं, अरिष्टदुष्टधीः -धीः -धि; 'put to death,' हतः -ता -तं, व्यापादितः -ता -तं, मारितः -ता -तं; 'to put to death,' हन् (c. 2. हन्ति -न्तुं), प्राणदण्डं कृ; 'angel of death,' यमदूतः; 'death-drum,' वध्यडिण्डिमः; 'hour of death,' मृत्युकालः, प्रयाणकालः; 'voluntary death by fasting,' प्रायः -यणं; 'after death,' प्रेत्य.

DEATH-BED, *s.* मृत्युशय्या, मरणशय्या, मृत्युशयनं, मुमूर्षुशयनं.

DEATHFUL, *a.* मारात्मकः -का -कं, आत्ययिकः -की -कं, मृत्युमयः -यी -यं, मृत्युजनकः -का -कं, प्राणान्तकः -का -कं, अन्तकरः -री -रं, घातुकः -का -कं.

DEATHLESS, *a.* अमरः -री -रं, मृत्युवर्ज्जितः -ता -तं, अमरणीयः -या -यं, अमर्त्यः -र्त्या -र्त्यं, अनन्तः -न्ता -न्तं, निरपायः -या -यं, अनश्वरः -रा -रं.

DEATH-LIKE, *a.* मृत्युसदृशः -शी -शं or कालसदृशः, कालकल्पः -ल्पा -ल्पं.

DEATH'S-DOOR, *s.* मृत्युद्वारं, यमद्वारं, यमालयद्वारं, यमपुरद्वारं.

DEATH'S-HEAD, *s.* शवशिरः *n.* (स्), मृतशरीरमस्तकः, कुणपमस्तकः, कपालः, नृकपालः.

DEATH'S MAN, *s.* वध्यपुरुषः, घातुकपुरुषः, वधकर्म्माधिकारी *m.* (न्), दण्डपाशिकः, मृतपाः *m.* (पा), घातकजनः.

DEATH-WATCH, *s.* मरणसूचकशब्दकारी कीटविशेषः.

To DEAURATE, *v. a.* रस् (c. 10. रसयति -यितुं), सुवर्ण (nom. सुवर्णयति -यितुं).

DEAURATE, *a.* रसितः -ता -तं, सुवर्णान्वितः -ता -तं, सुवर्णपङ्कः -ङ्का -ङ्कं.

To DEBAR, *v. a.* बाध् (c. 1. बाधते -धितुं), निरस् (c. 4. -अस्यति -असितुं), निराकृ, अपाकृ, बहिष्कृ, वृज् in caus. (वर्ज्जयति -यितुं), निषिध् (c. 1. -षेधति -षेद्धुं), वृ in caus. (वारयति -यितुं), निरुध् (c. 7. -रुणद्धि -रोद्धुं); 'is debarred,' परिह्रीयते.

DEBARRED, *p. p.* निषिद्धः -द्धा -द्धं, प्रतिषिद्धः -द्धा -द्धं, बाधितः -ता -तं, निवारितः -ता -तं, विघ्नितः -ता -तं, रुद्धः -द्धा -द्धं.

To DEBARK, *v. a.* उत्तॄ (c. 1. -तरति -रितुं -रीतुं), प्रत्युत्तॄ; नौकाया अवरुह् (c. 1. -रोहति -रोढुं) or अवतॄ.

DEBARKATION, *s.* उत्तरणं, प्रत्युत्तरणं, नौकाया अवतरणं or अवरोहणं.

To DEBASE, *v. a.* अपकृष् (c. 1. -कर्षति -क्रष्टुं), स्वपदात् पत् in caus. (पातयति -यितुं) or भ्रंश् in caus. (भ्रंशयति -यितुं) or अपध्वंस् in caus. (-ध्वंसयति -यितुं) or च्यु in caus. (-च्यावयति -यितुं), अवसद् in caus. (-सादयति -यितुं), न्यूनीकृ, अधःकृ, कन (nom. कनयति -यितुं).—(Make despicable) अपमानास्पदं कृ, खलीकृ, लघूकृ, तुच्छीकृ.

DEBASED, *p. p.* अपकृष्टः -ष्टा -ष्टं, स्थानभ्रष्टः -ष्टा -ष्टं, पातितः -ता -तं, अधःपातितः -ता -तं, पदच्युतः -ता -तं, अपध्वस्तः -स्ता -स्तं, अवज्ञोपहतः -ता -तं, भग्नदर्पः -र्पा -र्पं.

DEBASEMENT, *s.* (Act of) अपकर्षः -र्षणं, पातनं, पदभ्रंशनं, अपध्वंसः, अभिभवः, अपमानना, लघूकरणं, खलीकरणं.—(State of) अपकृष्टता, निकृष्टता, पतितत्वं, पातित्यं, अपमानभावः, न्यूनीभावः, अधोगतिः *f.*, अधोभावः, भ्रष्टता, वृषलत्वं.

DEBATABLE, *s.* विवदनीयः -या -यं, विचार्य्यः -र्य्या -र्य्यं, वितर्क्यः -र्क्या -र्क्यं, विचारणीयः -या -यं, सन्दिग्धः -ग्धा -ग्धं.

DEBATE, *s.* विवादः, वादानुवादः, वादप्रतिवादः, संवादः, विसंवादः, वादः, हेतुवादः, वादयुद्धं, विचारः, विरोधोक्तिः *f.*, वाग्युद्धं, वाक्कलहः, विप्रलापः, विप्रतिपत्तिः *f.*, वितण्डा, वितर्कः, तर्कः, वाक्यविरोधः, वाक्यं, सन्देहः, वाक्कलिः *m.*—(Contest) कलहः, विग्रहः, विरोधः, कलिः *m.*; 'matter of debate,' विवादास्पदं.

To DEBATE, *v. a.* and *n.* विवद् (c. 1. -वदति -ते -दितुं), विसंवद्; विचर् in caus. (-चारयति -यितुं), विवादास्पदीकृ, वादानुवादं कृ, वितर्क् (c. 10. -तर्कयति -यितुं), विप्रलप् (c. 1. -लपति -पितुं), वितण्ड् (c. 1. -तण्डते -ण्डितुं), कलह (nom. कलहायते), वैर (nom. वैरायते), वाक्कलहं कृ, मथ् (c. 1. मथति -थितुं).

DEBATED, *p. p.* विचारितः -ता -तं, वादग्रस्तः -स्ता -स्तं, मथितः -ता -तं.

DEBATEFUL, *a.* विवादी -दिनी -दि (न्), विवादशीलः -ला -लं, विवादार्थी -र्थिनी -र्थि (न्), कलहकारी -रिणी -रि (न्), वाक्कलहप्रियः -या -यं, वाग्युद्धप्रियः -या -यं, वाक्कलिप्रियः -या -यं, सन्नद्धः -द्धा -द्धं, विरोधी -धिनी -धि (न्).

DEBATER, *s.* विवादी *m.* (न्), विचारकः, विवादकृत्, तर्की *m.* (न्), वादी *m.* (न्), हेतुवादी, वितण्डाकारी *m.* (न्), न्यायी *m.* (न्), सांवादिकः.

To DEBAUCH, *v. a.* दुष् in caus. (दूषयति -यितुं), सन्दुष्, प्रतिदुष्, दुष्टीकृ; भ्रष्टीकृ, क्षतीकृ; नश् in caus. (नाशयति -यितुं); सव्यसनं -नां -नं कृ; धर्म्मभ्रष्टं -ष्टां -ष्टं कृ, धर्म्मविप्लुतं -तां -तं कृ, विकृ; 'to debauch a maiden,' कन्यां दुष् or धृष् in caus. (धर्षयति -यितुं), सतीत्वभ्रष्टां कृ.

DEBAUCH, *s.* मदावेशः, कामावेशः, व्यसनावेशः, आपीतिः *f.*, सम्पीतिः *f.*, सम्भोजनं, केलिः *m. f.*, स्त्रीमद्यादिसम्भोगार्थम् उत्सवः.

DEBAUCHED, *p. p.* दूषितः -ता -तं, दुष्टः -ष्टा -ष्टं; 'woman,' दूषिता, क्षतयोनिः.

DEBAUCHEE, *s.* व्यसनी *m.* (न्), व्यसनीयः, लम्पटः, विषयी *m.* (न्), सम्भोगी *m.* (न्), विषयासक्तः, विषयानुरागी *m.* (न्), कामासक्तः,

भोगासक्तः, दुराचारः, सम्प्रीतिरतः, पानरतः, नागरः, विटः.

DEBAUCHER, *s.* दूषकः, दूषणः, दूषयिता *m.* (तृ), भ्रंशकारी *m.* (न्), नाशकः.

DEBAUCHERY, *s.* लम्पटता, लाम्पट्यं, व्यसनं -निता, इन्द्रियासंयमः, विषयित्वं, विषयासक्तत्वं, अनवस्थितिः *f.*, धर्म्मापेतत्वं, कामासक्तिः *f.*, भोगासक्तिः *f.*, दुष्कर्म्म *n.* (न्).

DEBAUCHMENT, *s.* दूषणं, प्रतिदूषणं, भ्रष्टीकरणं, नाशनं.

To DEBELLATE, *v. a.* युद्धे पराजि (c. 1. -जयति -जेतुं), दम् (c. 10. दमयति -यितुं).

DEBENTURE, *s.* प्रतिज्ञापत्रकं, लेख्यप्रसङ्गः, लेख्यपत्रं, पत्रलेख्यं, ऋणशोधनप्रतिज्ञापत्रं, ऋणमार्गणपत्रं.

DEBILE, *a.* दुर्बलः -ला -लं, अल्पबलः -ला -लं, अल्पशक्तिः -क्तिः -क्ति, शिथिलबलः -ला -लं, शिथिलशक्तिः -क्तिः -क्ति, शिथिलः -ला -लं, अल्पवीर्य्यः -र्य्या -र्य्यं, अल्पतेजाः -जाः -जः (स्), अल्पसत्त्वः -त्त्वा -त्त्वं, फल्गुः -ल्गुः -ल्गु, ह्रासशक्तिः -क्तिः -क्ति, ग्लानः -ना -नं, कृशः -शा -शं, विगलिततेजाः -जाः -जः (स्), अवसन्नः -न्ना -न्नं, क्षामः -मा -मं, क्लीवः -वा -वं, क्षीणशक्तिः -क्तिः -क्ति.

To DEBILITATE, *v. a.* दुर्बलीकृ, शिथिलीकृ, अल्पबलीकृ, ग्लानीकृ, क्षामीकृ, क्षीणीकृ, तेजो हृ (c. 1. हरति, हर्त्तुं), क्लीव् in caus. (क्लीवयति -यितुं), कृश (nom. कृशयति -यितुं), क्षीणं -णां -णं कृ.

DEBILITATION, *s.* दुर्बलीकरणं, शिथिलीकरणं, क्षीणीकरणं, तेजोहरणं, ग्लानीकरणं.

DEBILITY, *s.* दौर्बल्यं, बलशैथिल्यं, शिथिलता, शक्तिशैथिल्यं, क्षीणशक्तित्वं, ग्लानिः *f.*, म्लानिः *f.*, अवसादः, अवसन्नता, विस्रंसः -सा, तेजोहीनता, अतेजः *n.* (स्), वीर्य्यहानिः *f.*, क्षामता, क्लैब्यं, कार्श्यं, सत्त्वहानिः *f.*, मान्द्यं.

To DEBIT, *v. a.* ऋणकर्त्तुः or क्रेतुः or द्रव्यग्रहीतुर् नाम पुस्तके समारुह् in caus. (-रोपयति -यितुं).

DEBONAIR, *a.* सभ्यः -भ्या -भ्यं, सुशीलः -ला -लं, मृदुशीलः -ला -लं, शिष्टः -ष्टा -ष्टं, कोमलस्वभावः -वा -वं, प्रियवादी -दिनी -दि (न्), अग्राम्यः -म्या -म्यं.

DEBONAIRLY, *adv.* सुशीलवत्, सभ्यवत्, मृदु, सुविनीतं, साधुजनवत्.

DEBT, *s.* ऋणं, धारः -रणा, उद्धारः, प्रामीत्यं, प्रामित्यं, अपमित्यकं, पर्य्युदञ्चनं; 'in debt,' ऋणी -णिनी -णि (न्), ऋणवान् -वती -वत् (त्), ऋणग्रस्तः -स्ता -स्तं; 'out of debt, free from debt,' अनृणः -णा -णं, अनृणी -णिनी -णि (न्) or अऋणी; 'to run into debt,' ऋणं कृ or ग्रह् (c. 9. गृह्णाति, ग्रहीतुं); 'to pay a debt,' ऋणं दा or शुध् in caus. (शोधयति -यितुं), आनृण्यं गम् (c. 1. गच्छति, गन्तुं); 'payment or discharge of a debt,' ऋणदानं, ऋणमुक्तिः *f.*, ऋणमोक्षः, ऋणशोधनं, ऋणापनयनं, ऋणापाकरणं, ऋणापनोदनं, आनृण्यं; 'recovery of a debt,' ऋणादानं, ऋणोद्धरणं; 'a debt at gambling,' आक्षिकं

DEBTOR, *s.* अधमर्णः -र्णी *m.* (न्) -र्णिकः, ऋणी *m.* (न्), ऋणिकः, ऋणवान् *m.* (त्), ऋणकर्त्ता *m.* (र्तृ), धारणकः, धारकः, ऋणग्रस्तः.

DECACUMINATED, *a.* छिन्नाग्रभागः -गा -गं, छिन्नमस्तकः -का -कं, कबन्धः.

DECADE, *s.* दशकः -कं, दशत्वं, दशता; 'decade of years,' दशवर्षी.

DECADENCY, *s.* अवपातः, अवसादः, सादः, विस्रंसा, क्षयः, ध्वंसः, भ्रंशः.

DECAGON, *s.* दशकोणः -णं, दशभुजः, दशास्रं -स्री, दशकोणा मूर्त्तिः *f.*

DECALOGUE, *s.* ईश्वरप्रोक्ता दशाज्ञाः *m. pl.* or दशनिदेशाः *m. pl.*, दशविधानं.

To DECAMP, *v. n.* कटकनिवेशनात् प्रया (c. 2. -याति -तुं) or प्रस्था (c. 1. -तिष्ठति -स्थातुं) or यात्रां कृ, कटकं त्यक्त्वा स्थानान्तरे निविश् (c. 6. -विशति -वेष्टुं), शिबिरं or मन्दिरं त्यज् (c. 1. त्यजति, त्यक्तुं).—(Move off) अपसृ (c. 1. -सरति -सर्तुं), अपसृप् (c. 1. -सर्पति -सर्प्तुं), पलाय् (c. 1. पलायते -यितुं), निष्पत् (c. 1. -पतति -तितुं), चल् (c. 1. चलति -लितुं).

DECAMPMENT, *s.* कटकनिवेशनात् प्रयाणं or प्रस्थानं or प्रगमनं or प्रस्थितिः *f.* or यात्राकरणं, कटकत्यागः, अपसरणं, अपसर्पणं, पलायनं, अपगमः, व्यपगमः.

To DECANT, *v. a.* मद्यभाजनम् ईषद्वनाम्य मद्यं विमलपात्रे शनैः शनैः प्रसु in caus. (-स्रावयति -यितुं) or निक्षिप् (c. 6. -क्षिपति -क्षेप्तुं) or निविश् in caus. (-वेशयति -यितुं) यथा भाजनाधःस्थं मलं नोर्द्ध्वगच्छति.

DECANTATION, *s.* यथोक्तं काचपात्रे or काचकूप्यां मद्यस्रावणं.

DECANTER, *s.* काचकूपी, काचपात्रं, कूपी, कुतूः *f.*, काचभाजनं, पुटग्रीवः.

To DECAPITATE, *v. a.* विमस्तक (nom. विमस्तकयति -यितुं), शिरः or मस्तकं छिद् (c. 7. छिनत्ति, छेत्तुं) or कृत् (c. 6. कृन्तति, कर्त्तितुं).

DECAPITATED, *p. p.* छिन्नमस्तकः -का -कं, छिन्नशिराः -राः -रः (स्) or कर्त्तितशिराः, विमस्तकितः -ता -तं, कबन्धः.

DECAPITATION, *s.* मस्तकच्छेदनं, शिरश्छेदः, शीर्षच्छेदः, शिरःकर्त्तनं, कबन्धता; 'meriting it,' शीर्षच्छेद्यः -द्या -द्यं, वध्यः -ध्या -ध्यं.

To DECAY, *v. n.* क्षि in pass. (क्षीयते), सद् (c. 1. सीदति, सत्तुं), अवसद्, व्यवसद्; ग्लै (c. 1. ग्लायति, ग्लातुं), जॄ (c. 4. जीर्य्यति, जरितुं -रीतुं), विशॄ in pass. (-शीर्य्यते), नश् (c. 4. नश्यति, नशितुं), विनश्, प्रणश्; ध्वंस् (c. 1. ध्वंसते -सितुं), विध्वंस्, प्रली (c. 4. -लीयते -लेतुं -लातुं), शद् (c. 6. शीयते, शत्तुं), क्षै (c. 1. क्षायति, क्षातुं), ह्रस् (c. 1. ह्रसति -सितुं), स्रंस् (c. 1. स्रंसते -सितुं), विस्रंस्, गल् (c. 1. गलति -लितुं), म्लै (c. 1. म्लायति, म्लातुं).

To DECAY, *v. a.* क्षि in caus. (क्षययति, क्षपयति -यितुं), अवसद् in caus. (-सादयति -यितुं), नश् in caus. (नाशयति -यितुं), ध्वंस् in caus. (ध्वंसयति -यितुं), ह्रस् in caus. (ह्रासयति -यितुं), विशीर्णीकृ, ग्लानीकृ.

DECAY, *s.* क्षयः, क्षिया, क्षीणता, परिक्षयः, संक्षयः, सादः, अवसादः, अवसन्नता, जीर्णिः *f.*, जीर्णता -त्वं, जरठः, शीर्णता, विशीर्णता, ग्लानिः *f.*, प्रलयः, नाशः, विनाशः, प्रणाशः, ध्वंसः, विध्वंसः, विस्रंसा, म्लानिः *f.*, हानिः *f.*, ह्रासः, अपचयः, व्ययः, क्षामता, गलनं; 'of the teeth,' दन्तव्यसनं, कृमिदन्तकः.

DECAYED, *p. p.* क्षीणः -णा -णं, जीर्णः -र्णा -र्णं, जीर्णवान् -वती -वत् (त्), शीर्णः -र्णा -र्णं, विशीर्णः -र्णा -र्णं, ग्लानः -ना -नं, नष्टः -ष्टा -ष्टं, गलितः -ता -तं, विगलितः -ता -तं, प्रलीनः -ना -नं, ध्वस्तः -स्ता -स्तं, क्षामः -मा -मं, विस्रस्तः -स्ता -स्तं, सन्नः -न्ना -न्नं, अवसन्नः -न्ना -न्नं, दीनः -ना -नं, हीनः -ना -नं.

DECAYING, *a.* क्षयी -यिणी -यि (न्), क्षयिष्णुः -ष्णुः -ष्णु, क्षीयमाणः -णा -णं, विशीर्य्यमाणः -णा -णं, परिजीर्णेन् -र्णमती -र्णत् (त्).

DECEASE, *s.* मरणं, अपगमः, संस्थानं, अत्ययः, प्रयाणं, निःसरणं, अपायः, जीवनत्यागः, तनुत्यागः, जीवोत्सर्गः.

To DECEASE, *v. n.* मृ (c. 6. म्रियते, मर्त्तुं), प्रे (c. 2. प्रैति -तुं, with प्र, प्रैति), देहं or जीवनं त्यज् (c. 1. त्यजति, त्यक्तुं) or उत्सृज् (c. 6. -सृजति -स्रष्टुं).

DECEASED, *p. p.* मृतः -ता -तं, प्रेतः -ता -तं, प्रेतीभूतः -ता -तं, अतीतः -ता -तं, व्यतीतः -ता -तं, संस्थितः -ता -तं, विपन्नः -न्ना -न्नं, प्रमीतः -ता -तं.

DECEIT, *s.* कपटः -टं, छलं -लना, वञ्चनं -ना, प्रवञ्चना, व्याजः, कैतवं, माया, कूटः -टं, कौटं, छद्म *n.* (न्), दम्भः, प्रलम्भः, विप्रलम्भः, अतिसन्धानं, अभिसन्धिः *m.* -न्धानं, प्रपञ्चः, प्रतारणं -णा, कुहकः, उपधिः *m.*, व्याकृतिः *f.*, दण्डाजिनं, संभत् *n.*, संख्य *n.*, निमीलिका.

DECEITFUL, *a.* कपटी -टिनी -टि (न्), कापटिकः -की -कं, छली -लिनी -लि (न्), छलनापरः -रा -रं, वञ्चकः -का -कं, वञ्चनः -ना -नं, प्रवञ्चकः -का -कं, मायी -यिनी -यि (न्), मोही -हिनी -हि (न्), मायान्वितः -ता -तं, कौटिकः -की -कं, प्रतारकः -का -कं, छाद्मिकः -की -कं, दाम्भिकः

-की -कं, प्रलम्भकः -का -कं, विप्रलम्भकः -का -कं, कृतकपटः -टा -टं, सव्याजः -जा -जं, विवञ्चिषुः -षुः -षु, विजिह्मः -ह्मा -ह्मं, उपधिकः -का -कं, दाम्भाजिनिकः -की -कं, तकिलः -ला -लं, वञ्चनशीलः -ला -लं, शठः -ठा -ठं, भ्रान्तिजनकः -का -कं.

DECEITFULLY, *adv.* सकपटं, सव्याजं, सकैतवं, छलेन, समायं, मायया, प्रलम्भात्, विप्रलम्भेन, दम्भात्, वञ्चनार्थं, धूर्त्तवत्, कितववत्, सकूटं.

DECEITFULNESS, *s.* कपटता, कापट्यं, कूटता, वञ्चकत्वं, शठता, सव्याजता.

DECEIVABLE, *a.* वञ्चनीयः -या -यं, प्रतारणीयः -या -यं, मोहनीयः -या -यं.

To DECEIVE, *v. a.* वञ्च् in caus. (वञ्चयते -ति -यितुं), परिवञ्च्, प्रवञ्च्; प्रलभ् (c. 1. -लभते -लब्धुं), विप्रलभ्; छल् (c. 10. छलयति -यितुं), प्रतॄ in caus. (-तारयति -यितुं), मुह् in caus. (मोहयति -यितुं), भ्रम् in caus. (भ्रमयति -यितुं), भ्रान्तिं जन् in caus. (जनयति -यितुं), प्रलुभ् in caus. (-लोभयति -यितुं), अतिसन्धा (c. 3. -दधाति -धातुं), अभिसन्धा, विनिकृ, व्यच् (c. 6. विचति, व्यचितुं), दम्भ् (c. 5. दभ्नोति, दम्भितुं).

DECEIVED, *p. p.* वञ्चितः -ता -तं, परिवञ्चितः -ता -तं, प्रलब्धः -ब्धा -ब्धं, विप्रलब्धः -ब्धा -ब्धं, प्रतारितः -ता -तं, प्रवञ्चितः -ता -तं, मोहितः -ता -तं, विमोहितः -ता -तं, अतिसंहितः -ता -तं, प्रलोभितः -ता -तं, विलोभितः -ता -तं.

DECEIVER, *s.* वञ्चकः, प्रतारकः, प्रवञ्चकः, विप्रलम्भकः, कपटी *m.* (न्), मायी *m.* (न्), दम्भी *m.* (न्), दम्भकः, कितवः, कूटकारः, कुहकः, नारकीटः, दाम्भिकः.

DECEMBER, *s.* आग्रहायणः -णिकः, अग्रहायणः, मार्गशीर्षः, मार्गशिरः, मार्गः -र्गकः, मृगः, सहाः *m.* (स्), शोभनमासः, पौषः, सहस्यः, तैषः, वत्सरस्य द्वादशमासः or शेषमासः.

DECEMPEDAL, *a.* दशपादपरिमाणः -णा -णं.

DECEMVIRATE, *s.* वक्ष्यमाणदशजनानाम् अधिकारः or आधिपत्यं.

DECEMVIRI, *s.* पूर्व्वकाले रोमीयदेशाधिष्ठातारो दशजनाः *m. pl.*, राज्यधुर्व्वहा दशशासितारः *m. pl.*

DECENCE, DECENCY, *s.* विनयः, विनीतत्वं -ता, मर्य्यादा, लज्जा, अनतिक्रमः, इतिकर्त्तव्यता, युक्तिः *f.*, उपपत्तिः *f.*, सामञ्जस्यं, याथातथ्यं, उपयुक्तता, याथार्थ्यं, औचित्यं, शिष्टता, संस्था, स्थितिः *f.*, अभेदः, धर्मांशः, शालीनत्वं, शिष्टाचारानुसारः.

DECENNIAL, *a.* दशवर्षीयः -या -यं, दशवर्षीणः -णा -णं, दशवत्सरी -रिणी -रि (न्), दशवार्षिकः -की -कं, दशाब्दिकः -की -कं, दशवर्षस्थायी -यिनी -यि (न्), दशवत्सरवर्त्ती -र्त्तिनी -र्त्ति (न्).

DECENT, *a.* विनीतः -ता -तं, विनयवान् -वती -वत् (त्), विनयोपेतः -ता -तं, अनतिक्रान्तमर्य्यादः -दा -दं, इतिकर्त्तव्यः -व्या -व्यं, सविनयः -या -यं, समर्य्यादः -दा -दं, सलज्जः -ज्जा -ज्जं, लज्जान्वितः -ता -तं, युक्तः -क्ता -क्तं, उपयुक्तः -क्ता -क्तं, योग्यः -ग्या -ग्यं, उचितः -ता -तं, समुचितः -ता -तं, सम्भाव्यः -व्या -व्यं, उपपन्नः -न्ना -न्नं, शिष्टाचारानुसारी -रिणी -रि (न्), शिष्टः -ष्टा -ष्टं.

DECENTLY, *adv.* सविनयं, विनीतवत्, विनयतस्, विनयात्, समर्य्यादं, युक्तं, उपयुक्तं, यथोचितं, समुचितं, सलज्जं, शिष्टाचारानुसारात्, लज्जापूर्व्वं.

DECEPTIBLE, *a.* वञ्चनीयः -या -यं, प्रतारणीयः -या -यं, प्रलभ्यः -भ्या -भ्यं.

DECEPTION, *s.* वञ्चनं -ना, प्रवञ्चना, छलना, प्रतारणं -णा, प्रलम्भः, विप्रलम्भः, कपटः -टं, छलं, व्याजः, माया, छद्म *n.* (न्), दम्भः, कूटः -टं.

DECEPTIOUS, DECEPTIVE, *a.* मायी -यिनी -यि (न्), मोही -हिनी -हि (न्), वञ्चकः -का -कं, भ्रान्तिजनकः -का -कं, ऐन्द्रजालिकः -की -कं, धिप्सुः -प्सुः -प्सु. *See* DECEITFUL.

DECERPT, *a.* अपच्छिन्नः -न्ना -न्नं, अवकर्त्तितः -ता -तं, अवलूनः -ना -नं.

DECERPTIBLE, *a.* अवच्छेद्यः -द्या -द्यं, अवकर्त्तनीयः -या -यं, लाव्यः -व्या -व्यं.

DECERPTION, *s.* अवच्छेदः -दनं, अवकर्त्तनं, अवचयः, अवलूनिः *f.*, लावः.

DECESSION, *s.* अपगमः, व्यपगमः, गमनं, अपासरणं, विगमः, अपायः.

To DECHARM, *v. a.* मन्त्रं or अभिचारं प्रतिकृ, विमन्त्र् (c. 10. विमन्त्रयति -यितुं).

To DECIDE, *v. a.* and *n.* निश्चि (c. 5. -चिनोति -चेतुं), निर्णी (c. 1. -णयति -णेतुं), व्यवसो (c. 4. -स्यति -सातुं), व्यवस्था in caus. (-स्थापयति -यितुं), साध् in caus. (साधयति -यितुं), सिद्धीकृ, निष्पद् in caus. (-पादयति -यितुं), निष्पत्तिं कृ, निश्चयं कृ, निर्णयं कृ, तीर् (c. 10. तीरयति -यितुं), विचर् in caus. (-चारयति -यितुं).

DECIDED, *p. p.* निश्चितः -ता -तं, निर्णीतः -ता -तं, सिद्धः -द्धा -द्धं, निष्पन्नः -न्ना -न्नं, व्यवसितः -ता -तं, नियतः -ता -तं, व्यवस्थापितः -ता -तं, व्यवस्थितः -ता -तं, तीरितः -ता -तं, विचारितः -ता -तं.

DECIDENCE, *s.* पतनशीलत्वं, पातः, अवपातः, निपातः, पतनं, विध्वंसः.

DECIDER, *s.* निर्णेता *m.* (तृ), निश्चायकः, निश्चयकारी *m.* (न्), निर्णयकृत्, विचारकर्त्ता *m.* (र्त्तृ), प्रमाणपुरुषः, मध्यस्थः, निष्पत्तिकारकः.

DECIDUOUS, *a.* पतयालुः -लुः -लु, पातुकः -का -कं, पतनशीलः -ला -लं, क्षयी -यिणी -यि (न्), एकवर्षस्थायी -यिनी -यि (न्) or अचिरस्थायी or अस्थायी, विध्वंसी -सिनी -सि (न्); 'an annual plant,' ओषधिः *f.* -धी.

DECIMAL, *a.* दशकः -का -कं, दशगुणितः -ता -तं, दशसंख्यकः -का -कं.

To DECIMATE, *v. a.* (Take the tenth) दशभागं or दशमभागं or दशमांशं ग्रह् (c. 9. गृह्णाति, ग्रहीतुं) or हृ (c. 1. हरति, हर्तुं).—(Select by lot every tenth soldier for punishment) गुटिकापातपूर्व्वं सर्व्वसैन्यमध्याद् दशमं दशमं सैनिकं वधार्थम् उद्धृ (c. 1. -हरति -हर्तुं).

DECIMATION, *s.* दशमभागग्रहणं, दशमांशहरणं, यथोक्तं सर्व्वसैन्यमध्याद् दशके दशके एकसैनिकोद्धारः.

To DECIPHER, *v. a.* (Explain occult characters) गूढाक्षराणि or घोभाक्षराणि व्याख्या (c. 2. -ख्याति -तुं) or व्याकृ or व्याहृ (c. 1. -हरति -हर्तुं) or व्याचक्ष् (c. 2. -चष्टे) or प्रकाश् in caus. (-काशयति -यितुं) or स्पष्टीकृ or परिशुध् in caus. (-शोधयति -यितुं), स्पष्ट (nom. स्पष्टयति -यितुं), निरूप् (c. 10. -रूपयति -यितुं).

DECIPHERER, *s.* व्याख्याता *m.* (तृ), स्पष्टीकर्त्ता *m.* (र्त्तृ), विवरणकृत्, निरूपकः.

DECIPHERING, *s.* व्याख्यानं, व्याकरणं, विवृतिः *f.*, स्पष्टीकरणं, निरूपणं.

DECISION, *s.* निश्चयः, निर्णयः -यणं, निश्चितं, निष्पत्तिः *f.*, सिद्धिः *f.*, व्यवसायः, व्यवस्थितिः *f.*, व्यवस्थापनं, सम्प्रधारणा, तीरणं, तीरितं.

DECISIVE, DECISORY, *a.* निश्चायकः -का -कं, निर्णायकः -का -कं, निर्णयनः -ना -नं, निष्पत्तिकारकः -का -कं, साधकः -का -कं, सिद्धीकरणः -णा -णं, प्रमाणीकारकः -का -कं, विचारकः -का -कं, निर्देशकः -का -कं, निष्पादकः -का -कं.

DECISIVELY, *adv.* निश्चितं, सुनिश्चितं, सनिश्चयं, निर्णयपूर्व्वं, सनिर्णयं.

DECISIVENESS, *s.* निश्चायकत्वं, निर्णायकत्वं, साधकत्वं, विचारकता, निष्पादकता.

To DECK, *v. a.* (Cover) छद् (c. 10. छादयति -ते -यितुं), आच्छद्, आस्तॄ (c. 9. -स्तृणाति -स्तरितुं -रीतुं); 'to deck a ship,' नौकां काष्ठफलकैर् आस्तॄ.—(Adorn) भूष् (c. 1. भूषति -षितुं, c. 10. भूषयति -यितुं), विभूष्, परिभूष्; शुभ् in caus. (शोभयति -यितुं), अलङ्कृ, समलङ्कृ, परिष्कृ, मण्ड् (c. 10. मण्डयति -यितुं).

DECK, *s.* (Of a ship) नौकापृष्ठं, नौपृष्ठं, नौकास्तरणं, नौकातलं, नौतलं, नौफलकं.—(Pack of cards) द्यूतपत्रराशिः *m. f.*

DECKED, *p. p.* भूषितः -ता -तं, अलङ्कृतः -ता -तं, शोभितः -ता -तं.

To DECLAIM, *v. n.* विस्मयोत्पादनार्थं or इन्द्रियमोहकरणार्थम् अलङ्कारमयं वाक्यं वद् (c. 1. वदति -दितुं), रसिकवाक्यं or शब्दालङ्कारपूर्व्वं वाक्यं ब्रू (c. 2. ब्रवीति, वक्तुं), वर्ण् (c. 10. वर्णयति -यितुं); 'to declaim against,' सवाक्यालङ्कारम् अवक्षिप् (c. 6. -क्षिपति -क्षेप्तुं).

Declamation, *s.* विस्मयोत्पादनार्थं वाक्यं, इन्द्रियमोहनार्थं वाक्यं, अलङ्कारमयं वाक्यं, रसिकवाक्यं, वर्णनवाक्यं, भारती, करुणावाक्यं, वक्तृत्वं, शब्दचातुर्य्यं, सुप्रलापः, सारस्वतवाक्यं.

Declamator, declaimer, *s.* वक्ता *m.* (क्तृ), वाक्पटुः *m.*, वागीशः, वाग्विदग्धः, प्रवचनपटुः *m.*, वर्णनकृत्, वाक्यद्वारेण विस्मयोत्पादकः or इन्द्रियमोहकः.

Declamatory, *a.* वागलङ्कारमयः -यी -यं, वाङ्मयः -यी -यं.—(Appealing to the passions) विस्मयोत्पादकः -का -कं, इन्द्रियमोहकः -का -कं.

Declarable, *a.* आख्येयः -या -यं, अभिधेयः -या -यं.—(Capable of proof) साध्यः -ध्या -ध्यं, सूच्यः -च्या -च्यं, प्रमेयः -या -यं.

Declaration, *s.* आख्यानं, ख्यापनं, निवेदनं, आवेदनं, ज्ञापनं, विज्ञापनं, विज्ञप्तिः *f.*, बोधनं, अभिधानं, अभिहितत्वं, प्रवचनं, वचनं, वादः, कथनं, कीर्त्तनं, अनुकीर्त्तनं, प्रकीर्त्तनं, प्रकाशनं, घोषणा, प्रतिज्ञा; 'repeated declaration,' वचनशतं; 'declaration of war,' प्रत्युत्क्रमः -मणं, प्रत्युत्क्रान्तिः *f.*

Declarative, declaratory, *a.* ख्यापकः -का -कं, ज्ञापकः -का -कं, विज्ञापकः -का -कं, बोधकः -का -कं, आवेदकः -का -कं, निवेदकः -का -कं, वाचकः -का -कं, अभिधायिकः -का -कं, प्रकाशकः -का -कं, कथकः -का -कं.

Declaratorily, *adv.* प्रवचनपूर्व्वं, निवेदनपूर्व्वं, व्यक्तं, सुव्यक्तं.

To declare, *v. a.* (Tell, make known) आख्या (c. 2. -ख्याति -तुं), समाख्या; ख्या in caus. (ख्यापयति -यितुं), ज्ञा in caus. (ज्ञापयति -यितुं), विज्ञा, विद् in caus. (वेदयति -यितुं), निविद्, आविद्, समाविद्, विनिविद्; कथ् (c. 10. कथयति -यितुं), वद् (c. 1. वदति -दितुं), प्रवच् (c. 2. -वक्ति -क्तुं), अभिधा (c. 3. -दधाति -धातुं), सूच् (c. 10. सूचयति -यितुं).—(Proclaim) प्रख्या in caus., कृत् (c. 10. कीर्त्तयति -यितुं), प्रकृत्, परिकृत्, अनुकृत्, घुष् in caus. (घोषयति -यितुं), विघुष्, आघुष्, उच्चर् in caus. (-चारयति -यितुं), प्रकाश् in caus. (-काशयति -यितुं), प्रकटीकृ, व्यक्तीकृ.

To declare, *v. n.* निवेदनं कृ, मतं or अभिप्रायं or सङ्कल्पं ज्ञा in caus. (ज्ञापयति -यितुं), साक्ष्यं or प्रमाणं दा, स्वीकृ.

Declared, *p.p* ख्यातः -ता -तं, आख्यातः -ता -तं, प्रोक्तः -क्ता -क्तं, उक्तः -क्ता -क्तं, आवेदितः -ता -तं, निवेदितः -ता -तं, कथितः -ता -तं, सूचितः -ता -तं, ज्ञापितः -ता -तं, विज्ञप्तः -प्ता -प्तं, अभिहितः -ता -तं, कीर्त्तितः -ता -तं, प्रकीर्त्तितः -ता -तं, परिकीर्त्तितः -ता -तं, विघुष्टः -ष्टा -ष्टं, आघोषितः -ता -तं, उच्चारितः -ता -तं, उदितः -ता -तं, प्रकाशितः -ता -तं, निरूपितः -ता -तं, व्यवस्थितः -ता -तं.

Declension, *s.* (Falling off) भ्रंशः, ध्वंसः, विध्वंसः, सादः, क्षयः, च्युतिः *f.*—(Inflexion of nouns) विभक्तिः *f.*, रूपं, रूपकरणं, शब्दविकारः, पदसाधनं, शब्दाख्यानं.

Declinable, *a.* वाच्यः -च्या -च्यं, विकार्य्यः -र्य्या -र्य्यं, आख्येयः -या -यं.

Declination, *s.* (Falling off, decay, descent) च्युतिः *f.*, भ्रंशः, क्षयः, अवसादः, विस्रंसा, अवपातः, अवतारः, अधोगतिः *f.*, अवनतिः *f.*—(Obliquity) वक्रता.—(Deviation) उत्क्रमः, भेदः, विक्रिया.—(In astronomy) क्रान्तिः *f.*, क्रान्तः, अपमः.

Decline, *s.* क्षयः, परिक्षयः, उपक्षयः, अवक्षयः, क्षिया, भ्रंशः, सादः, अवसादः, ध्वंसः, विध्वंसः, अपचयः, ह्रासः, विस्रंसा, व्ययः, अधःपतनं, अवपातः, च्युतिः *f.*, न्यूनता, अत्ययः, व्यसनं, ग्लानिः *f.*, ग्लानिः *f.*—(Consumption) देहक्षयः, क्षयरोगः, क्षयथुः *m.*, क्षयकासः, क्रमक्षयः, शरीरपाकः, शरीरशोषः.—(Decline of the sun, or of good fortune, &c.) अस्तः; 'decline of life,' जीवितक्षयः.

To decline, *v. a.* (Bend downwards) नम् in caus. (नामयति -यितुं), अवनम्; अवपीड् (c. 10. -पीडयति -यितुं), अपकृष् (c. 1. -कर्षति -क्रष्टुं), पत् in caus. (पातयति -यितुं).—(Refuse, shun) प्रत्याख्या (c. 2. -ख्याति -तुं), अन्तःख्या, अतिख्या, अपलप् (c. 1. -लपति -पितुं), प्रत्यादिश् (c. 6. -दिशति -देष्टुं), अपह्नु (c. 2. -ह्नुते -ह्नोतुं), निह्नु, अस्वीकृ; निरस् (c. 4. -अस्यति -असितुं), अपास्; वृज् in caus. (वर्ज्जयति -यितुं), परिहृ (c. 1. -हरति -हर्त्तुं).—(In grammar) आख्या (c. 2. -ख्याति -तुं), रूप् (c. 10. रूपयति -यितुं), शब्दरूपं कृ.

To decline, *v. n.* (Lean downwards) नम् (c. 1. नमति, नन्तुं), अवनम्, आनम्, नम्रीभू; 'as the sun,' अस्तं गम् (c. 1. गच्छति, गन्तुं), लघ् (c. 1. लघते -घितुं); 'declining towards the south,' दक्षिणाप्रवणः -णा -णं, दक्षिणादिगवनतः -ता -तं.—(Deviate) भ्रंश् (c. 4. भ्रश्यति, भ्रंशितुं), च्यु (c. 1. च्यवते, च्योतुं), विच्यु, विचल् (c. 1. -चलति -लितुं), पत् (c. 1. पतति -तितुं).—(Avoid) त्यज् (c. 1. त्यजति, त्यक्तुं), परित्यज्, हा (c. 3. जहाति, हातुं).—(Desist from) निवृत् (c. 1. -वर्त्तते -र्त्तितुं).—(Decay) क्षि in pass. (क्षीयते), परिक्षि, सद् (c. 6. सीदति, सत्तुं), अवसद्; भ्रंश्; ध्वंस् (c. 1. ध्वंसते -सितुं), विध्वंस्, विस्रंस् (c. 1. -स्रंसते -सितुं), अपचि in pass. (-चीयते), ग्लै (c. 1. ग्लायति, ग्लातुं), ह्रस् (c. 1. ह्रसति -सितुं), व्ययीभू, न्यूनीभू, विशॄ in pass. (-शीर्य्यते).

Declined, *p. p.* (Refused) प्रत्याख्यातः -ता -तं, प्रत्यादिष्टः -ष्टा -ष्टं, अस्वीकृतः -ता -तं.—(Deviated) भ्रष्टः -ष्टा -ष्टं, च्युतः -ता -तं, पतितः -ता -तं.—(Decayed) क्षीणः -णा -णं, सन्नः -न्ना -न्नं, अवसन्नः -न्ना -न्नं, ग्लानः -ना -नं, अस्तगतः -ता -तं, अपचितः -ता -तं, विशीर्णः -र्णा -र्णं.—(Inflected) आख्यातः -ता -तं.

Declivity, *s.* पातुकः, पातुकभूमिः *f.*, प्रवणभूमिः, प्रवः, उत्सङ्गः, निम्नता.

Declivous, *a.* क्रमशः पातुकः -की -कं or प्रवणः -णा -णं.

To decoct, *v. a.* क्वथ् (c. 1. क्वथति -थितुं), निष्क्वथ्; पच् (c. 1. पचति, पक्तुं), निष्पच्.

Decocted, *p. p.* निष्पक्वः -क्वा -क्वं, क्वथितः -ता -तं, निष्क्वथितः -ता -तं.

Decoction, *s.* (Act of) क्वाथः, क्वथनं, निष्क्वाथः, पाचनं.—(Preparation made by decocting) निर्य्यासः, निर्य्यूहः, कषायः -यं, घनरसः, क्वाथं.

Decollation, *s.* शिरश्छेदनं, शीर्षच्छेदः, मस्तकच्छेदः, शीर्षघातः.

To decompose, *v. a.* (Analyze a compound body) समस्तद्रव्यं पृथक्कृ or व्याकृ, विली in caus. (-लाययति -लापयति -यितुं), विद्रु in caus. (-द्रावयति -यितुं), पिश् in caus. (पेशयति -यितुं), उपोद्घातं कृ.

Decomposed, *p.p.* व्याकृतः -ता -तं, विद्रावितः -ता -तं, विलीनः -ना -नं.

Decomposite, *a.* (Twice compounded) द्विमिश्रितः -ता -तं, पुनर्मिश्रितः.

Decomposition, *s.* (Compounding twice) द्विमिश्रणं, पुनर्मिश्रणं.—(Resolution of parts, dissolution) उपोद्घातः, पृथक्करणं, विद्रावणं, विलयः, प्रलयः, परिक्षयः.

To decompound, *v. a.* (Compound a second time) पुनर् or द्विवारं मिश्र् (c. 10. मिश्रयति -यितुं) or सम्मिश्र्.—(Resolve into parts). *See* Decompose.

To decorate, *v. a.* भूष् (c. 10. भूषयति -यितुं), विभूष्; अलङ्कृ, परिष्कृ, समलङ्कृ, संस्कृ; मण्ड् (c. 10. मण्डयति -यितुं); शुभ् in caus. (शोभयति -यितुं), उपशुभ्, परिकर्म्म (nom. परिकर्म्मयति -यितुं).

Decorated, *p. p.* भूषितः -ता -तं, विभूषितः -ता -तं, अलङ्कृतः -ता -तं, परिष्कृतः -ता -तं, संस्कृतः -ता -तं, मण्डितः -ता -तं, शोभितः -ता -तं, सालङ्कारः -रा -रं, कृतालङ्कारः -रा -रं, कृताभरणः -णा -णं, कृतशोभः

-आ -अं, सवेशः -शा -शं, रञ्जितः -ता -तं, प्रसाधितः -ता -तं.

DECORATION, *s.* अलङ्कारः, अलङ्क्रिया, भूषणं, विभूषणं, भरणं, आभरणं, प्रसाधनं, परिष्कारः, परिष्कृतिः *f.*, परिकर्म्म *n.* (न्), प्रतिकर्म्म, संस्कारः, मण्डनं, शोभा -भनं, रञ्जनं, कल्पना, तल्पं, सज्जा, वेशः; 'stage decorations,' नेपथ्यं, आहार्य्यः.

DECORATOR, *s.* प्रसाधकः, भूषकः, शोभाकारी *m.* (न्), अलङ्कारकल्पकः.

DECOROUS, *a.* विनीतः -ता -तं, विनयी -यिनी -यि (न्), सविनयः -या -यं, अनतिक्रान्तः -न्ता -न्तं, अनतिक्रान्तमर्य्यादः -दा -दं, समर्य्यादः -दा -दं, शिष्टाचारानुसारी -रिणी -रि (न्), सुशीलः -ला -लं, युक्तः -क्ता -क्तं, उपयुक्तः -क्ता -क्तं, योग्यः -ग्या -ग्यं, यथायोग्यः -ग्या -ग्यं, उचितः -ता -तं, यथोचितः -ता -तं, समञ्जसः -सा -सं.

DECOROUSLY, *adv.* सविनयं, समर्य्यादं, अनतिक्रान्तं, युक्तं, यथोचितं.

To DECORTICATE, *v. a.* त्वच (nom. त्वचयति -यितुं), निस्त्वच; निस्त्वचीकृ; निर्वल्क (nom. निर्वल्कयति -यितुं); निस्तुष (nom. निस्तुषयति -यितुं), तुषीकृ, निस्तुषीकृ; त्वक्ष् (c. 1. त्वक्षति -क्षितुं), वल्कलं or त्वचम् उत्कृष् (c. 1. -कर्षति -क्रष्टुं) or निष्कृष्.

DECORTICATION, *s.* निस्त्वचीकरणं, निस्तुषीकरणं, त्वक्परिपुटनं, निर्वल्कलीकरणं.

DECORUM, *s.* विनयः, विनीतता -त्वं, मर्य्यादा, अनतिक्रमः, शिष्टाचारानुसारः, सदाचारता, सुशीलता, सभ्यता, शिष्टता, सुरीतिः *f.*, सुनीतिः *f.*, सुचरित्रं, सच्चरित्रं, युक्तता, उपयुक्तत्वं, औचित्यं, न्यायः -यता.

To DECOY, *v. a.* छलेन or कौटेन प्रलुभ् in caus. (-लोभयति -यितुं) or आकृष् (c. 1. -कर्षति -क्रष्टुं) or प्रवञ्च् in caus. (-वञ्चयते -यितुं) or प्रतॄ in caus. (-तारयति -यितुं).—(Entrap) जाले बन्ध् (c. 9. बध्नाति, बन्धुं).

DECOYED, *p. p.* प्रलोभितः -ता -तं, जालबद्धः -द्धा -द्धं, पाशबद्धः -द्धा -द्धं.

DECOY-BIRD, *s.* आकर्षकपक्षी *m.* (न्), शाकुनिकैर् अन्यपक्षिप्रलोभने शिक्षितः पक्षी.

To DECREASE, *v. n.* क्षि in pass. (क्षीयते), परिक्षि, परिहा in pass. (-हीयते), ह्रस् (c. 1. ह्रसते -सितुं), अल्पीभू, न्यूनीभू, ऊनीभू, अवसद् (c. 6. -सीदति -सत्तुं).

To DECREASE *v. a.* अल्पीकृ, ह्रस् in caus. (ह्रासयति -यितुं), ऊन् (c. 10. ऊनयति -यितुं), न्यूनीकृ, ऊन (nom. ऊनयति -यितुं), लघ (nom. लघयति -यितुं), क्षि in caus. (क्षपयति -यितुं).

DECREASE, DECREMENT, *s.* क्षयः, क्षिया, क्षितिः *f.*, ह्रासः, न्यूनत्वं -ता, न्यूनीभावः, अवसादः, अपचयः, हानिः *f.*; 'of the moon,' इन्दुक्षयः.

To DECREE, *v. n.* व्यवस्थाद्वारेण or आज्ञापत्रद्वारेण निश्चयं or सिद्धं or निर्णीतं कृ, व्यवस्थां कृ, आज्ञां कृ or दा, शासनं कृ, निष्पत्तिं कृ, निश्चयं कृ.

To DECREE, *v. a.* व्यवस्था in caus. (-स्थापयति -यितुं), प्रणी (c. 1. -णयति -णेतुं), आज्ञा in caus. (-ज्ञापयति -यितुं), आदिश् (c. 6. -दिशति -देष्टुं), समादिश्, निर्दिश्, विधा (c. 3. -दधाति -धातुं), प्रक्लृप् (c. 10. -कल्पयति -यितुं).

DECREE, *s.* व्यवस्था, व्यवस्थापत्रं, शासनं, शासनपत्रं, आज्ञापत्रं, राजाज्ञा, आज्ञा, विधानं, नियमः, नियोगः, निदेशः, आदेशः.

DECREED, *p. p.* व्यवस्थितः -ता -तं, व्यवस्थापितः -ता -तं, प्रणीतः -ता -तं, विहितः -ता -तं, निर्दिष्टः -ष्टा -ष्टं, प्रकल्पितः -ता -तं, आज्ञप्तः -प्ता -प्तं.

DECREPIT, *a.* जरी -रिणी -रि (न्), जीर्णः -र्णा -र्णं, जरातुरः -रा -रं, जराग्रस्तः -स्ता -स्तं, जरापरिणतः -ता -तं, जरठः -ठा -ठं, अतिवृद्धः -द्धा -द्धं.

DECREPITATION, *s.* मूषानिवेशितलवणस्य वह्निसम्पर्कात् स्फुटत्कारशब्दः.

DECREPITUDE, *s.* जरा, जीर्णिः *f.*, जीर्णता, जरावस्था, जरठः, जीर्णावस्था, अतिवृद्धभावः, अतिवार्धक्यं, विस्रसा, ज्यानिः *f.*, प्रातिका.

DECRESCENT, *a.* क्षयी -यिणी -यि (न्), क्षीयमाणः -णा -णं, अपचीयमानः -ना -नं,

DECRETAL, *a.* व्यवस्थाविषयः -या -यं, व्यवस्थापकः -का -कं, नैयमिकः -की -कं.

DECRETAL, *s.* (Body of laws or edicts) धर्म्मसंहिता, व्यवस्थासङ्ग्रहः.—(Collection of the pope's decrees) रोमनगरे महाधर्म्माध्यक्षप्रकाशितानां शासनपत्राणां संहिता.

DECRETORY, *a.* विचारकः -का -कं, प्रणयनः -ना -नं, निश्चायकः -का -कं.

DECRIAL, *s.* अपवादः, परीवादः, उपक्रोशः, उच्चैःस्वरेण कृता निन्दा.

To DECRY, *v. a.* अपवद् (c. 1. -वदति -दितुं), परिवद्, उच्चैःस्वरेण निन्द् (c. 1. निन्दति -न्दितुं) or अवक्षिप् (c. 6. -क्षिपति -क्षेप्तुं) or तिरस्कृ or दोषीकृ.

DECUMBENCE, *s.* शयनं, शय्यागमनं, पतनं, संवेशः, उपवेशनं.

DECUMBENT, *a.* शयानः -ना -नं, शयने संविष्टः -ष्टा -ष्टं, शयितः -ता -तं, निषण्णः -ण्णा -ण्णं, निलीनः -ना -नं, उपविष्टः -ष्टा -ष्टं.

DECUMBITURE, *s.* रोगार्त्तस्य शय्यावर्त्तनकालः, रोगावधिर् यत्पर्य्यन्तं शयने वर्त्तते रोगी.

DECUPLE, *a.* दशगुणः -णा -णं, दशगुणीकृतः -ता -तं, दशविधः -धा -धं.

DECURION, *s.* दशाध्यक्षः, दशसैन्याधिपतिः *m.*, दशयोधनायकः.

DECURSION, *s.* अधःपतनं, अधोगमनं, अवतरणं, अवधावनं, अधोद्रावः.

DECURTATION, *s.* उच्छेदः -दनं, विच्छेदः, ह्रस्वीकरणं, संक्षेपः -पणं.

DECUSSATION, *s.* अन्तर्लेखकरेखाव्यत्यासः, कोणाकोणि छेदनं.

To DEDECORATE, *v. a.* अकीर्त्तिं or अपयशः कृ, सापमानं -नां -नं कृ, कुख्यातिं जन् (c. 10. जनयति -यितुं), कलङ्क (nom. कलङ्कयति -यितुं).

DEDECORATION, *s.* अकीर्त्तिकरणं, अपयशस्करणं, कलङ्ककरणं, अपमानं.

DEDECOROUS, *a.* अकीर्त्तिकरः -री -रं, अयशस्यः -स्या -स्यं, कलङ्ककरः -री -रं, लज्जाकरः -री -रं, अपमानजनकः -का -कं, वाच्यः -च्या -च्यं.

To DEDICATE, *v. a.* (Appropriate to a sacred use) धर्म्मार्थं प्रयुज् (c. 7. -युनक्ति -योक्तुं) or विनियुज् or निर्दिश् (c. 6. -दिशति -देष्टुं), धर्म्ममुद्दिश्य दा or उत्सर्गं कृ.—(Consecrate) प्रतिष्ठा in caus. (-ष्ठापयति -यितुं), संस्कृ, अभिसंस्कृ, प्रणी (c. 1. -णयति -णेतुं), उपकॢप् in caus. (-कल्पयति -यितुं), उत्सृज् (c. 6. -सृजति -स्रष्टुं), निविद् in caus. (-वेदयति -यितुं), समृ in caus. (-अर्पयति -यितुं), अभिमन्त्र् (c. 10. -मन्त्रयति -यितुं), सङ्कल्पं कृत्वा दा.—(Dedicate a book) उपकारकजनस्य प्रथमपत्रे नामलिखनात् सचाटुवादं ग्रन्थं समृ in caus., or निविद् in caus. or सनाथीकृ.

DEDICATED, *p. p.* प्रतिष्ठितः -ता -तं, सुप्रतिष्ठितः -ता -तं, विनियोजितः -ता -तं, प्रणीतः -ता -तं, उत्सृष्टः -ष्टा -ष्टं, निर्दिष्टः -ष्टा -ष्टं, उपकॢप्तः -प्ता -प्तं, संस्कृतः -ता -तं, अभिसंस्कृतः -ता -तं, कृतसङ्कल्पः -ल्पा -ल्पं, निवेदितः -ता -तं, समर्पितः -ता -तं.—(As a book) उपकारकजनस्य प्रथमपत्रे नामलिखनात् समर्पितः -ता -तं or निवेदितः -ता -तं, उपकारकजननामसंज्ञितः -ता -तं, सनाथीकृतः -ता -तं.

DEDICATION, *s.* प्रतिष्ठा, सुप्रतिष्ठा, प्रतिष्ठाकरणं, निवेदनं, समर्पणं, विनियोगः, उत्सर्गः, सङ्कल्पकरणं, संस्कारः; 'of a book,' उपकारकजनस्य प्रथमपत्रे नामलिखनाद् ग्रन्थनिवेदनं, ग्रन्थस्य निवेदनपत्रं; 'of a temple,' प्रासादप्रतिष्ठा; 'of one's person,' आत्मनिवेदनं, देहविनियोगः.

DEDICATOR, *s.* उपकारकजनस्य प्रथमपत्रे नाम लिखित्वा ग्रन्थनिवेदकः or ग्रन्थसमर्पकः, अनुग्राहकजनद्वारा ग्रन्थप्रकाशकः, प्रतिष्ठाकारी *m.* (न्).

DEDICATORY, *a.* निवेदनपत्रलिखनविषयः -या -यं, ग्रन्थानुग्राहकगुणप्रकाशकः -का -कं, ग्रन्थोपकारकप्रशंसाकरः -री -रं, स्तुतिमयः -यी -यं.

DEDITION, *s.* समर्पणं, उत्सर्जनं, प्रदानं, प्रोत्सारणं, वितरणं, त्यागः.

To DEDUCE, *v. a.* अनुमा (c. 2. -माति -तुं, c. 3. -मिमीते), ऊह् (c. 1. ऊहते -हितुं), अपोह्; निर्णी (c. 1. -णयति -णेतुं), अवगम् (c. 1. -गच्छति -गन्तुं) समधिगम्, अपवह् (c. 1. -वहति -वोढुं).

DEDUCED, *p. p.* अनुमितः -ता -तं, निर्णीतः -ता -तं, अवगतः -ता -तं, समधिगतः -ता -तं, अपोढः -ढा -ढं, अपोहितः -ता -तं.

DEDUCEMENT, *s.* अनुमानं, अनुमितिः *f.*, ऊहनं, निर्णयः, अपवाहः, अपोहः -हनं.

DEDUCIBLE, *a.* अनुमेयः -या -यं, ऊहनीयः -या -यं, आनुमानिकः -की -कं, उपलक्ष्यः -क्ष्या -क्ष्यं, अवगम्यः -म्या -म्यं, समधिगम्यः -म्या -म्यं, यौक्तिकः -की -कं.

To DEDUCT, *v. a.* उद्धृ (c. 1. -हरति -हर्त्तुं), व्यवकल् (c. 10. -कलयति -यितुं), ऊन् (c. 10. ऊनयति -यितुं), अवछिद् (c. 7. -छिनत्ति -छेत्तुं), पृथक्कृ.

DEDUCTED, *p. p.* उद्धृतः -ता -तं, व्यवकलितः -ता -तं, अवछिन्नः -न्ना -न्नं; 'having a part deducted,' उद्धृतोद्धारः -रा -रं.

DEDUCTION, *s.* (Inference, consequence) अनुमा -मानं -मितिः *f.*, ऊहनं, ऊहा, अपवाहः, अपोहः -हनं, अभ्यूहः, उपलक्ष्यः, युक्तिः *f.*, प्रयुक्तिः *f.*, अन्वयः, अनुषङ्गः, अनुभवः, निर्णयः, परामर्शः.—(Part deducted) उद्धारः, उद्धृतभागः.

DEDUCTIVE, *a.* आनुमानिकः -की -कं, आनुषङ्गिकः -की -कं, यौक्तिकः -की -कं.

DEDUCTIVELY, *adv.* प्रयोगतस्, प्रयुक्त्या, अनुमानतस्, अनुषङ्गेण.

DEED, *s.* (Action) कर्म्म *n.* (न्), क्रिया, कार्य्यं, कृतं, कृत्यं, कृत्या, चेष्टा, प्रवृत्तिः *f.*, विधानं.—(Exploit) चेष्टितं, विचेष्टितं, चरित्रं, अद्भुतकर्म्म *n.* (न्), आश्चर्य्यकर्म्म *n.*—(Written evidence of any legal act) लेखपत्रं, लेखप्रमाणं, लिखितं, साधनपत्रं; 'deed of conveyance,' दानपत्रं; 'deed of sale,' विक्रयपत्रं, क्रयलेख्यं; 'title-deed,' आगमः, पट्टोलिका, पांशुकूलं, कूमकीला.—(Fact) वस्तु *n.*, भूतं, अर्थः, तत्त्वं; 'indeed,' तत्त्वतस्, सत्यं, वस्तुतस्, अवश्यं, अर्थतस्, परमार्थतस्; 'in very deed,' सत्यमेव.

To DEEM, *v. a.* and *n.* मन् (c. 4. मन्यते, मन्तुं), विचर् in caus. (-चारयति -यितुं), सम्भू in caus. (-भावयति -यितुं), वितर्क् (c. 10. -तर्कयति -यितुं), अनुमा (c. 2. -माति -तुं), अवगम् (c. 1. -गच्छति -गन्तुं), निर्णी (c. 1. -णयति -णेतुं).

DEEMED, *p. p.* मतः -ता -तं, स्मृतः -ता -तं, अवगतः -ता -तं, अनुमितः -ता -तं.

DEEP, *a.* (Having length downwards, profound) गम्भीरः -रा -रं, गभीरः -रा -रं, अगाधः -धा -धं, दीर्घः -र्घा -र्घं, गहनः -ना -नं, गाढः -ढा -ढं, अवगाढः -ढा -ढं, अधोगतः -ता -तं.—(Low) निम्नः -म्ना -म्नं, नीचः -चा -चं.—(Excessive) गाढः -ढा -ढं; 'deep grief,' गाढशोकः.—(Entering deep) मर्म्मभेदी -दिनी -दि (न्).—(Not obvious) गम्भीरार्थः -र्था -र्थं or निगूढार्थः, परमगहनः -ना -नं, अगम्यः -म्या -म्यं, दुर्ज्ञेयः -या -यं, रहस्यः -स्या -स्यं.—(Sagacious) गम्भीरबुद्धिः -द्धिः -द्धि, विदग्धः -ग्धा -ग्धं, दीर्घदृष्टिः -ष्टिः -ष्टि, अर्थज्ञः -ज्ञा -ज्ञं.—(Full of contrivance) उपायज्ञः -ज्ञा -ज्ञं.—(Grave in sound) गम्भीरः -रा -रं, मन्द्रः -न्द्रा -न्द्रं or आमन्द्रः, घनः -ना -नं, धीरः -रा -रं; 'a deep sound,' गभीरध्वनिः *m.*, गम्भीरशब्दः, घनध्वनिः.—(Dark coloured) घनः -ना -नं; 'deep red,' घनारुणः -णा -णं, सुरक्तः -क्ता -क्तं; 'deep blue,' घननीलः -ला -लं.—(Very deep) अतलस्पर्शः -र्शा -र्शं, अस्थागः -गा -गं, अस्थाघः -घा -घं, अस्थानः -ना -नं, अस्तारः -रा -रं; 'deep sleep,' सुषुप्तिः *f.*, सुनिद्रा, सुषुप्त्यवस्था, अघोरनिद्रा, साधिका; 'deep darkness,' घनान्धकारः, अन्धतमसं; 'deep sigh,' दीर्घनिश्वासः; 'knee-deep,' जानुदघ्नः -घ्ना -घ्नं, जानुद्वयसः -सा -सं, जानुमात्रः -त्रा -त्रं.

DEEP, *s.* (The sea) समुद्रः, सागरः, महोदधिः *m.*, महार्णवः, जलधिः *m.*, पयोनिधिः *m.*, अम्बुराशिः *m. f.*, वारिराशिः; 'deep of night,' निशीथः, महारात्रः, गभीररात्रः, घोररात्रः.

To DEEPEN, *v. a.* गम्भीरीकृ, अधिकगभीरं -रां -रं कृ, अगाधीकृ, घनतरं -रां -रं कृ, निम्नीकृ.—(Darken) तिमिर (nom. तिमिरयति -यितुं).

DEEPLY, *adv.* गम्भीरं, गभीरं, गाढं, प्रगाढं, निर्भरं, अत्यन्तं, नितान्तं, भृशं, दीर्घं; 'deeply grieving,' शोकमग्नः -ग्ना -ग्नं, शोकसागरमग्नः -ग्ना -ग्नं, शोकावगाढः -ढा -ढं; 'deeply sighing,' दीर्घनिश्वस्य; 'deeply rooted,' बद्धमूलः -ला -लं or दीर्घमूलः.

DEEP-MOUTHED, *a.* गभीरनादी -दिनी -दि (न्), घनध्वनिः -निः -नि.

DEEP-MUSING, *a.* चिन्तापरः -रा -रं, ध्यानमग्नः -ग्ना -ग्नं, चिन्ताकुलः -ला -लं.

DEEP-READ, *a.* सर्व्वशास्त्रपारगः -गा -गं, स्वधीतः -ता -तं, सर्व्वविषयज्ञः -ज्ञा -ज्ञं, सर्व्वशास्त्रनिष्ठितः -ता -तं.

DEEPNESS, *s.* (Profundity) गम्भीरता, गाम्भीर्य्यं, अगाधता, निम्नता, अधोगतत्वं, घनता, गाढता, नीचत्वं.—(Craft) विदग्धता, वैदग्ध्यं.

DEER, *s.* मृगः, हरिणः, कृष्णसारः, एणः, कुरङ्गः -ङ्गकः -ङ्गमः, रुरुः *m.*, रोहितः, रोहित् *m.*, पृषतः, पृषत् *m.* (त्), समूरुः *m.*, चमूरुः *m.*, चमरः, ऋश्यः, रिश्यः, रिष्यः, रङ्कुः *m.*, न्यङ्कुः *m.*, रौहिषः, सम्बरः, शम्बरः, समीचो, चीनः, कदली, कन्दली, प्रियकः, मृडीकः, गोकर्णः, भीतहृदयः, व्याधभीतः, पल्लवादः, वातायुः *m.*—(Deer-skin) मृगाजिनं, मृगचर्म्म *n.* (न्).—(Deer-killer) मृगवधाजीवः, मृगयुः *m.*

To DEFACE, *v. a.* नश् in caus. (नाशयति -यितुं), विनश्; उद्धृ (c. 1. -हरति -हर्त्तुं), उच्छिद् (c. 7. -छिनत्ति -छेत्तुं), विलुप् in caus. (-लोपयति -यितुं), लुप् (c. 6. लुम्पति, लोप्तुं), अपमृज् (c. 2. -मार्ष्टि -मार्ष्टुं), प्रमृज्, दुष् in caus. (दूषयति -यितुं), विरूपीकृ, विकृ.

DEFACED, *p. p.* विनाशितः -ता -तं, उच्छिन्नः -न्ना -न्नं, लुप्तः -प्ता -प्तं.

DEFACEMENT, *s.* लोपः, विलोपनं, उच्छेदः, दूषणं, विनाशः, व्यामर्दः.

DEFACER, *s.* दूषकः, विनाशकः, उद्धर्त्ता *m.* (र्तृ), उन्मूलकः, उत्पाटकः.

To DEFALCATE, *v. a.* उद्धृ (c. 1. -हरति -हर्त्तुं), ऊन् (c. 10. ऊनयति -यितुं), न्यूनीकृ, ह्रस् in caus. (ह्रासयति -यितुं), अल्पीकृ, लोपं कृ.

DEFALCATION, *s.* न्यूनता, हीनता, हानिः *f.*, उद्धारः, लोपः, ह्रासः, क्षीणता, अल्पत्वं, अपचयः, विच्छित्तिः *f.*, अवच्छेदः, उत्कर्त्तनं.

DEFAMATION, *s.* अपवादः, परिवादः, अभिशंसनं, अभिशापः, आक्षेपः, पिशुनवाक्यं, कलङ्कः, कलङ्ककरणं, असूया, निन्दा, परिभाषणं, वाग्दोषः, मौखर्य्यं, अकीर्त्तिकरणं, अयशस्करणं.

DEFAMATORY, *a.* अपवादकः -का -कं, अभिशंसकः -का -कं, कुवादः -दा -दं, कलङ्ककरः -री -रं, अकीर्त्तिकरः -री -रं, अपयशस्करः -री -रं, वाग्दुष्टः -ष्टा -ष्टं, पिशुनः -ना -नं, अभ्यसूयकः -का -कं, गुणापवादकः -का -कं, मुखरः -रा -रं.

To DEFAME, *v. a.* अपवद् (c. 1. -वदति -दितुं), परिवद्, परगुणान् अपवद्, अभिशंस् (c. 1. -शंसति -सितुं), कलङ्क (nom. कलङ्कयति -यितुं), असूय (nom. असूयति -यितुं), निन्द् (c. 1. निन्दति -न्दितुं), अपयशः कृ, अकीर्त्तिं कृ.

DEFAMER, *s.* अपवादी *m.* (न्), परिवादी *m.*, गुणापवादकः, असूयकः, अभ्यसूयकः, गुणघाती *m.* (न्), कलङ्ककरः, कुवादः, अभिशंसकः, परुषवादी *m.* (न्), पिशुनः, सूचकः, आक्षेपकः.

To DEFATIGATE, *v. a.* खिद् in caus. (खेदयति -यितुं), श्रम् in caus. (श्रामयति -यितुं), श्रान्तीकृ, श्रमार्त्तं -र्त्तां -र्त्तं कृ, क्लान्तं -न्तां -न्तं कृ.

DEFATIGATION, *s.* श्रान्तिः *f.*, क्लान्तिः *f.*, श्रमः, परिश्रमः, ग्लानिः *f.*, खेदः.

DEFAULT, *s.* (Omission) परित्यागः, अननुष्ठानं, परिलोपः, भंशः.—(Want, failure) अभावः, असम्भवः, अविद्यमानत्वं, विरहः, अप्राप्तिः *f.*, न्यूनता.—(Defect) दोषः, अगुणः, वैकल्यं, व्यतिक्रमः.—(Non-appearance) अदर्शनं, अनुपस्थानं; 'in default of evidence,' साक्ष्याभावे.

Defaulter, *s.* नियमव्यभिचारी *m.* (न्), नियमलङ्घी *m.* (न्), रुद्धः, ऋणशोधनार्थे निरूपितदिवसे विचारसभायाम् अनुपस्थायी *m.* (न्).

Defeasance, *s.* अनुशयः, विप्रतिपत्तिः *f.*, लोपः, नियमभङ्गः, नियमलोपः.

Defeasible, *a.* अनुशयितव्यः -व्या -व्यं, लोप्यः -प्या -प्यं, लोपनीयः -या -यं.

Defeat, *s.* पराजयः, पराभवः, परिभवः, अभिभवः, अभिभूतिः *f.*, अपजयः, व्यसनं, बलव्यसनं, भङ्गः, भेदः, नाशः, विनाशः, ध्वंसः.

To **defeat**, *v. a.* (Overthrow) जि (c. 1. जयति, जेतुं), पराजि, विजि; अभिभू (c. 1. -भवति -वितुं), पराहन् (c. 2. -हन्ति -न्तुं), परास् (c. 4. -अस्यति -असितुं), विद्रु in caus. (-द्रावयति -यितुं), धृष् (c. 10. धर्षयति -यितुं), प्रधृष्; पर्य्यामृश् (c. 6. -मृशति -म्रष्टुं), वशीकृ.—(Frustrate) व्याहन्, खण्ड् (c. 10. खण्डयति -यितुं), वृथाकृ, विफलीकृ.

Defeated, *p. p.* जितः -ता -तं, पराजितः -ता -तं, पराभूतः -ता -तं, अभिभूतः -ता -तं, पराहतः -ता -तं, परास्तः -स्ता -स्तं, कृतध्वंसः -सा -सं.

Defecate, *a.* अपकर्षितमलः -ला -लं, शोधितः -ता -तं, हृतमलः -ला -लं, निर्म्मलीकृतः -ता -तं, पवित्रीकृतः -ता -तं, परिष्कृतः -ता -तं.

To **defecate**, *v. a.* मलं हृ (c. 1. हरति, हर्तुं) or अपकृष् (c. 1. -कर्षति -क्रष्टुं), निर्म्मलीकृ, विमलीकृ, शुध् in caus. (शोधयति -यितुं), पवित्रीकृ, परिष्कृ.

Defecation, *s.* मलापकर्षणं, निर्म्मलीकरणं, विमलीकरणं, शोधनं.

Defect, *s.* (Fault) दोषः, अपराधः, छिद्रं, अगुणः, कलङ्कः, दूषणं, वैकल्यं, मन्तुः *m.*—(Want) अभावः, विरहः, न्यूनता.

Defectibility, *s.* न्यूनता, वैकल्यं, हीनता, दोषित्वं, ह्रासता, अपूर्णत्वं.

Defectible, *a.* न्यूनः -ना -नं, दोषिकः -की -कं, अपूर्णः -र्णा -र्णं.

Defection, *s.* त्यागः, परित्यागः, च्युतिः *f.*, भ्रंशः, भ्रष्टता, पतनं, परिवर्त्तः.

Defective, *a.* न्यूनः -ना -नं, विकलः -ला -लं, दोषी -षिणी -षि (न्), दोषवान् -वती -वत् (त्), सदोषः -षा -षं, हीनः -ना -नं, सापराधः -धा -धं, सच्छिद्रः -द्रा -द्रं, कलङ्की -ङ्किनी -ङ्कि (न्), अपूर्णः -र्णा -र्णं, अपरिपूर्णः -र्णा -र्णं, असम्पूर्णः -र्णा -र्णं, अपर्य्याप्तः -प्ता -प्तं, अङ्गहीनः -ना -नं, अत्योनः -ना -नं, ऊनः -ना -नं, असमग्रः -ग्रा -ग्रं.

Defectiveness, *s.* न्यूनता, हीनत्वं, असम्पूर्णत्वं, असमग्रता, वैकल्यं.

Defence, *s.* (Protection) रक्षणं, रक्षा, त्राणं, पालनं, रक्षणः, शरणं, आश्रयः, संश्रयः, गुप्तिः *f.*, गोपनं, अभ्युपपत्तिः *f.*, अवनं.—(Apology) उत्तरं, प्रतिवादः, व्यपदेशः, क्षमकरणं, शुद्धिः *f.*, शोधनं.—(In law) उत्तरं, प्रत्युत्तरं, निवेदनं.

Defenceless, *a.* अरक्षितः -ता -तं, रक्षाहीनः -ना -नं, अशरणः -णा -णं, निराश्रयः -या -यं, अनाश्रयः -या -यं, अप्रतिकारः -रा -रं.—(Unarmed) निरायुधः -धा -धं, अस्त्रहीनः -ना -नं, विशस्त्रः -स्त्रा -स्त्रं.

To **defend**, *v. a.* (Protect) रक्ष् (c. 1. रक्षति -क्षितुं), अभिरक्ष्, परिरक्ष्, संरक्ष्; त्रै (c. 1. त्रायते, त्रातुं), परित्रै, सन्त्रै; पा or पाल् in caus. (पालयति -यितुं or c. 2. पाति -तुं), अनुपा, परिपा, प्रतिपा, सम्पा, अभिपा; गुप् (c. 1. गोपायति, गोप्तुं or caus. गोपयति -यितुं), अनुगुप्, अभिगुप्, प्रगुप्, अभिसङ्गुप्; अव् (c. 1. अवति -वितुं), पर्य्याप् in des. (-ईप्सति -प्सितुं), परिप्राप् in des.—(Vindicate) रक्ष्, अनुपाल्, उत्तरं दा, पक्षपातं कृ; 'defend another,' परस्य सपक्षो भू, परार्थम् उत्तरं वद् (c. 1. वदति -दितुं).—(Prohibit) निवृ in caus. (-वारयति -यितुं), निषिध् (c. 1. -षेधति -षेद्धुं).

Defendable, *a.* रक्षणीयः -या -यं, रक्ष्यः -क्ष्या -क्ष्यं, गोपनीयः -या -यं, गोप्यः -प्या -प्यं, पालनीयः -या -यं, अवनीयः -या -यं.

Defendant, *s.* (Person sued) अभियुक्तः, प्रत्यर्थी *m.* (न्), प्रतिपक्षः, कार्य्यी *m.* (न्).—(Advocate) प्रतिवादी *m.* (न्), उत्तरवादी *m.* (न्), पक्षपाती *m.* (न्).

Defended, *p. p.* रक्षितः -ता -तं, अभिरक्षितः -ता -तं, पालितः -ता -तं, उपपालितः -ता -तं, गुप्तः -प्ता -प्तं, त्रातः -ता -तं, अवितः -ता -तं, गोपायितः -ता -तं.

Defender, *s.* रक्षकः, रक्षिता *m.* (तृ), रक्षी *m.* (न्), परिरक्षी *m.*, पालकः, पालः -ली *m.* (न्), पः in comp., त्राता *m.* (तृ), गोपः -पकः, गोपायकः, गोपी *m.* (न्), गोपिलः.

Defensible, *a.* रक्षणीयः -या -यं, अनुपालनीयः -या -यं, परिशुद्धिक्षमः -मा -मं.

Defensive, *a.* रक्षकः -का -कं, पालकः -का -कं, पाली -लिनी -लि (न्), वारकः -का -कं, प्रतिघाती -तिनी -ति (न्).

Defensive, *s.* आत्मरक्षा, रक्षावस्था, प्रतिघातः, परित्राणं, सावधानता.—(In war) शत्रुवारणं, युद्धनिवारणमात्रं, शत्रोः or युद्धात् सावधानता.

To **defer**, *v. a.* (Put off, delay) विलम्ब् (c. 1. -लम्बते -म्बितुं), आकालान्तरात् कार्य्यं त्यज् (c. 1. त्यजति, त्यक्तुं) or या in caus. (यापयति -यितुं).—(Refer to another) कार्य्यनिर्णयं परस्मिन् सम् in caus. (-अर्पयति -यितुं) or निक्षिप् (c. 6. -क्षिपति -क्षेप्तुं) or न्यस् (c. 4. -अस्यति -असितुं).

To **defer**, *v. n.* (Delay) विलम्ब् (c. 1. -लम्बते -म्बितुं), मन्द् (nom. मन्दायते), चिर (nom. चिरयति -रायति -यितुं), कालं या in caus. (यापयति -यितुं) or क्षिप् (c. 6. क्षिपति, क्षेप्तुं).—(Pay regard to another's opinion) परमतम् आश्रि (c. 1. -श्रयति -यितुं) or आदृ (c. 6. -द्रियते -दर्त्तुं) or प्रती (प्रति with इ, प्रत्येति -तुं) or उपगम् (c. 1. -गच्छति -गन्तुं).

Deference, *s.* (Regard) आदरः, समादरः, अनुनयः, मानं, सम्मानं, मान्यत्वं, आग्रहः, प्रश्रयः, प्रणयः, प्रतीतिः *f.*, अनुवर्त्तनं.—(Submission) अधीनता, वश्यता, नम्रता.

Deferred, *p. p.* विलम्बितः -ता -तं, आकालान्तरात् त्यक्तः -क्ता -क्तं.

Deferring, *s.* विलम्बः -म्बनं, यापनं, कालयापः, आकालान्तरात् कार्य्यत्यागः.

Defiance, *s.* युद्धार्थम् आह्वानं, समाह्वयः -ह्वानं, क्रन्दनं, क्रन्दितं, स्पर्द्धा, आस्पर्द्धा, हूतिः *f.*, हवः, अभिग्रहः, नासीरं, योधसंरावः.

Deficience, **deficiency**, *s.* न्यूनता, हीनता -त्वं, हानिः *f.*, अभावः, विरहः, रहितत्वं, अपूर्णता, असम्पूर्णत्वं, ह्रासः, ह्रसितत्वं, अल्पत्वं, क्षीणता, वैकल्यं, लोपः, लुप्तत्वं.—(Defect) दोषः, छिद्रं; 'deficiency of intellect,' बुद्धिहीनत्वं; 'of any organ of sense,' इन्द्रियवैकल्यं.

Deficient, *a.* न्यूनः -ना -नं, हीनः -ना -नं, विकलः -ला -लं, अपूर्णः -र्णा -र्णं, असम्पूर्णः -र्णा -र्णं, असमग्रः -ग्रा -ग्रं, क्षीणः -णा -णं, रहितः -ता -तं, विरहितः -ता -तं, लुप्तः -प्ता -प्तं, ह्रसितः -ता -तं, ऊनः -ना -नं; 'deficient in intellect,' न्यूनधीः -धीः -धि, विकलान्तःकरणः -णा -णं, अल्पधीः -धीः -धि; 'in any organ of sense,' न्यूनेन्द्रियः -या -यं or विकलेन्द्रियः.

Defied, *p. p.* आहूतः -ता -तं, समाहूतः -ता -तं, स्पर्द्धितः -ता -तं.

Defier, *s.* आह्वायकः, समाह्वाता *m.* (तृ), आस्पर्द्धी *m.* (न्), कृताह्वानः.

To **defile**, *v. a.* दुष् in caus. (दूषयति -यितुं), प्रतिदुष्, सन्दुष्; मलिन (nom. मलिनयति -यितुं), मलिनीकृ, कलुष (nom. कलुषयति -यितुं), अपवित्रीकृ, अमेध्यं -ध्यां -ध्यं कृ, लिप् (c. 6. लिम्पति, लेप्तुं), अनुलिप्, दिह् (c. 2. देग्धि -ग्धुं), आविल (nom. आविलयति -यितुं), मलीमसीकृ; 'defile a virgin,' कन्यां दुष्.

To **defile**, *v. n.* (March file by file) दण्डव्यूहेन or श्रेणीव्यूहेन यात्रां कृ.

Defile, *s.* (Narrow passage) सङ्कटं, सङ्कटपथः, दुर्गमार्गः, दुर्गं, सञ्चरः, सञ्चारः, कन्दरः -री, आयामः, घर्घरः, रन्ध्रं, गुहा, पर्व्वतमध्ये सङ्काथपथः.

Defiled, *p. p.* दूषितः -ता -तं, दुष्टः -ष्टा -ष्टं, मलिनितः -ता -तं, कलुषितः

-ता -तं, मलदूषितः -ता -तं, मलीमसः -सा -सं, अमेध्याक्तः -क्ता -क्तं, अमेध्यलिप्तः -प्ता -प्तं; 'virgin,' क्षतयोनिः, दूषिता.

DEFILEMENT, *s.* (The act) दूषणं.—(The state) मालिन्यं, मलिनत्वं, मलं, समलता, अशुचित्वं, अशौचं -चत्वं, अपवित्रता, कलुषं, कल्मषं, अमेध्यत्वं, दुष्टता.

DEFILER, *s.* दूषकः, दूषणः, कलुषकारी *m.* (न्), मलावहः, अशौचकृत्.

DEFINABLE, *a.* निर्वचनीयः -या -यं, निरूपणीयः -या -यं, निर्देश्यः -श्या -श्यं, उद्देश्यः -श्या -श्यं, व्याख्येयः -या -यं, निर्धारणीयः -या -यं.

To DEFINE, *v. a.* (Explain a thing by its qualities) लक्षणानि or गुणान् व्याख्या (c. 2. -ख्याति -तुं) or निरूप् (c. 10. -रूपयति -यितुं) or निर्दिश् (c. 6. -दिशति -देष्टुं) or समुद्दिश् or निर्वच् (c. 2. -वक्ति -क्तुं).—(Circumscribe) परिमा (c. 2. -माति -तुं).—(Mark out) लक्ष् (c. 10. लक्षयति -यितुं), लक्षीकृ, चिह्न् (c. 10. चिह्नयति -यितुं).—(Determine) निर्णी (c. 1. -णयति -णेतुं), निश्चि (c. 5. -चिनोति -चेतुं), निर्धृ in caus. (-धारयति -यितुं).

DEFINED, *p. p.* निरुक्तः -क्ता -क्तं, निरूपितः -ता -तं, निर्दिष्टः -ष्टा -ष्टं, समुद्दिष्टः -ष्टा -ष्टं, उद्दिष्टः -ष्टा -ष्टं, लक्षितः -ता -तं, उपलक्षितः -ता -तं, कृतलक्षणः -णा -णं, लक्षीकृतः -ता -तं, व्याख्यातः -ता -तं, परिमितः -ता -तं.

DEFINER, *s.* निर्वक्ता *m.* (क्तृ), निर्देष्टा *m.* (ष्टृ), लक्षणव्याख्याता *m.* (तृ), गुणनिरूपकः.

DEFINITE, *a.* (Settled, determined) नियतः -ता -तं, निश्चितः -ता -तं, निर्दिष्टः -ष्टा -ष्टं, निबद्धः -द्धा -द्धं, निर्णीतः -ता -तं, निर्धारितः -ता -तं, व्यवस्थापितः -ता -तं, सिद्धः -द्धा -द्धं.—(Limited) मितः -ता -तं, परिमितः -ता -तं, समर्य्यादः -दा -दं, सावधिकः -का -कं.

DEFINITION, *s.* लक्षणं, निर्वचनं, निरुक्तिः *f.*, निर्देशः, निदेशः, समुद्देशः, व्याख्या, लक्षणव्याख्या, गुणनिरूपणं.

DEFINITIVE, *a.* नियतः -ता -तं, निश्चायकः -का -कं, निर्णायकः -का -कं, लाक्षणिकः -की -कं, सावश्यकः -का -कं or अवश्यकः.

DEFINITIVELY, *adv.* नियतं, अवश्यमेव, निश्चितं, सुनिश्चितं, व्यक्तं, सुव्यक्तं.

DEFLAGRABLE, *a.* दाह्यः -ह्या -ह्यं, दहनीयः -या -यं, ज्वलनीयः -या -यं.

DEFLAGRATION, *s.* दाहः -हनं, अग्निदाहाद् अशेषेण विनाशः.

To DEFLECT, *v. a.* च्यु (c. 1. च्यवते, च्योतुं), विच्यु; भ्रंश् (c. 4. भ्रश्यति, भ्रंशितुं); पत् (c. 1. पतति -तितुं), विचल् (c. 1. -चलति -लितुं), व्यभिचर् (c. 1. -चरति -रितुं).

DEFLECTION, *s.* च्युतिः *f.*, भ्रंशः, विचलनं, व्यभिचारः, उत्क्रमः, भेदः, भ्रमः, विपथगमनं, विमार्गगमनं, उत्पथगमनं, सत्पथत्यागः.

To DEFLOUR, *v. a.* (A virgin) कुमारीं धृष् (c. 10. धर्षयति -यितुं) or अभिगम् (c. 1. -गच्छति -गन्तुं), सतीत्वं or कुमारीत्वं हृ (c. 1. हरति, हर्त्तुं) or नश् in caus. (नाशयति -यितुं), योनिक्षतिं कृ, भ्रष्टां कृ.—(Take away the beauty of any thing) शोभां or कान्तिं हृ or नश्.

DEFLOURED, *p. p.* (Virgin) क्षता, क्षतयोनिः *f.*, धर्षिता, सङ्कारी, प्रमादिका.

DEFLOURER, *s.* कुमारीगामी *m.* (न्), सतीत्वनाशकः, कन्याप्रमाथी *m.* (न्).

DEFLUOUS, *a.* अभिष्यन्दी -न्दिनी -न्दि (न्) or अवस्यन्दी, अधःप्रसारी -रिणी -रि (न्).

DEFLUXION, *s.* अभिष्यन्दः, अवस्यन्दः, प्रस्रवणं, अधःप्रवाहः, क्षरणं.

DEFŒDATION, *s.* दूषणं, मलकरणं, अशौचकरणं, अपवित्रीकरणं.

To DEFORM, *v. a.* विरूप् (c. 10. -रूपयति -यितुं), विरूपीकृ, अपरूपीकृ, कुरूपीकृ, विकलीकृ, विकृ, कदाकारीकृ, व्यङ्गीकृ.

DEFORMED, *p. p.* विरूपः -पा -पी -पं, कुरूपः -पी -पं, अपरूपः -पी -पं, विकृतः -ता -तं, विकृताङ्गः -ङ्गी -ङ्गं, विकृताकारः -रा -रं, विकृताकृतिः -तिः -ति, विकलाङ्गः -ङ्गी -ङ्गं, व्यङ्गः -ङ्गी -ङ्गं, व्याकारः -रा -रं, कदाकारः -रा -रं, कुतनुः -न्वी -नु, कुवेरः -रा -रं, पोगण्डः -ण्डा -ण्डं or अपोगण्डः, कुब्जः -ब्जा -ब्जं.

DEFORMATION, *s.* विरूपकरणं, अपरूपीकरणं, विकलीकरणं, व्यङ्गीकरणं.

DEFORMEDLY, *adv.* कुरूपेण, विकृतरूपेण, कदाकारेण, विकलं.

DEFORMITY, *s.* विरूपता, वैरूप्यं, कुरूपता, अपरूपता, वैकृत्यं, वैकृतं, व्याकारः, व्यङ्गता, कुदृश्यत्वं, पोगण्डत्वं, कुत्सितत्वं.

To DEFRAUD, *v. a.* (Cheat) वञ्च् in caus. (वञ्चयते -ति -यितुं), परिवञ्च्; प्रलभ् (c. 1. -लभते -लब्धुं), विप्रलभ्, प्रतॄ in caus. (-तारयति -यितुं), छल् (c. 10. छलयति -यितुं), अन्यायं कृ.—(Deprive by fraud) छलेन or अन्यायेन or प्रतारणाद्वारा हृ (c. 1. हरति, हर्त्तुं) or स्वत्वलोपं कृ.

DEFRAUDATION, *s.* छलेन or अन्यायेन or प्रतारणापूर्व्वं हरणं or स्वत्वलोपः.

DEFRAUDED, *p. p.* वञ्चितः -ता -तं, परिवञ्चितः -ता -तं, अतिसंहितः -ता -तं.

DEFRAUDER, *s.* वञ्चकः, वञ्चुकः, प्रतारकः, अन्यायकृत्, छली *m.* (न्).

To DEFRAY, *v. a.* धनव्ययं or व्ययशोधनं or व्ययापाकरणं स्वीकृ, परार्थे धनव्ययं कृ or व्ययशोधनं कृ, व्ययम् उपगम् (c. 1. -गच्छति -गन्तुं) or शुध् in caus. (शोधयति -यितुं) or अपाकृ or साध् in caus. (साधयति -यितुं).

DEFRAYER, *s.* व्ययशोधकः, व्ययापाकर्त्ता *m.* (र्त्तृ), परार्थे व्ययस्वीकारी *m.* (न्).

DEFRAYMENT, DEFRAYING, *s.* व्ययशोधनं, व्ययस्वीकारः, व्ययापाकरणं, व्ययमुक्तिः *f.*, व्ययमोक्षः, व्ययापनयनं, व्ययसिद्धिः *f.*, व्ययोपगमः.

DEFT, *a.* (Neat) विनीतः -ता -तं.—(Dexterous) दक्षः -क्षा -क्षं.

DEFTLY, *adv.* विनीतं, सदाक्ष्यं, सूक्ष्मं, क्षिप्रं, चतुरं, युक्तिपूर्व्वं.

DEFUNCT, *a.* मृतः -ता -तं, प्रेतः -ता -तं, परेतः -ता -तं, अतीतः -ता -तं, अपगतः -ता -तं, संस्थितः -ता -तं, विपन्नः -न्ना -न्नं, त्यक्तजीवितः -ता -तं.

DEFUNCTION, *s.* मरणं, मृत्युः *m.*, अपगमः, देहत्यागः, संस्थितिः *f.*, विपत्तिः *f.*

To DEFY, *v. a.* युद्धार्थम् आह्वे (c. 1. -ह्वयति -ते -ह्वातुं), समाह्वे; स्पर्धं (c. 1. स्पर्धते -र्धितुं), आक्रन्द् (c. 1. -क्रन्दति -न्दितुं), अभियुज् (c. 7. -युनक्ति -योक्तुं).—(Disdain, slight) अवज्ञा (c. 9. -जानाति -ज्ञातुं), कदर्थीकृ, पराकृ, लघूकृ, निराकृ.

DEFY, *s.* आह्वानं, युद्धार्थं समाह्वानं, समाह्वयः, क्रन्दितं.

DEFYER, *s.* युद्धार्थम् आह्वायकः, समाह्वाता *m.* (तृ), अभियोक्ता *m.* (क्तृ).

DEGENERACY, DEGENERATENESS, *s.* क्षीणपुण्यत्वं, कुलधर्म्मभ्रंशः, पैतृकधर्म्मच्युतिः *f.*, कुलाचारत्यागः, कुलमर्य्यादाभ्रष्टता, मर्य्यादाहानिः *f.*, सन्मार्गापगमः, धर्म्मत्यागः, दुष्टता.

DEGENERATE, *a.* क्षीणपुण्यः -ण्या -ण्यं, क्षीणधर्म्मा -र्म्मा -र्म्म or नष्टधर्म्मः, कुलधर्म्मभ्रष्टः -ष्टा -ष्टं, त्यक्तकुलमर्य्यादः -दा -दं, पैतृकाचारच्युतः -ता -तं, धर्म्मविप्लुतः -ता -तं, धर्म्मपतितः -ता -तं, परिभ्रष्टः -ष्टा -ष्टं, दुष्टः -ष्टा -ष्टं.

To DEGENERATE, *v. n.* कुलधर्म्माद् भ्रंश् (c. 4. भ्रश्यति, भ्रंशितुं) or च्यु (c. 1. च्यवते, च्योतुं) or पत् (c. 1. पतति -तितुं), दुष् (c. 4. दुष्यति, दोष्टुं).

DEGLUTITION, *s.* गरणं, निगरणं, निगारः, गरः, गीर्णिः *f.*, गिरिः *f.*, ग्रसनं.

DEGRADATION, *s.* (Deprivation or loss of office, disgrace) पदभ्रंशः, पदच्युतिः *f.*, अधिकारभ्रंशः, अधिकारनिराकरणं, अधिकारच्युतिः *f.*, पदलोपः, स्थानभ्रंशः, स्थानापकर्षः, अपकर्षः, अपमानं, अपध्वंसः, पतितत्वं, पातित्यं.—(Degeneracy, baseness) भ्रष्टता, अपकृष्टता, मर्य्यादाक्षयः, मर्य्यादानाशः, दुष्टता, वृषलत्वं, अधोगतिः *f.*, निष्क्रमः.

To DEGRADE, *v. a.* पदात् or अधिकाराद् भ्रंश् in caus. (भ्रंशयति -यितुं) or च्यु in caus. (च्यावयति -यितुं) or निराकृ or अपकृष् (c. 1. -कर्षति -क्रष्टुं).—(Lessen the value) मूल्यं or अर्घम् अल्पीकृ or ऊन (nom. ऊनयति -यितुं) or ह्रस् in caus. (ह्रासयति -यितुं) or लघ (nom. लघयति -यितुं), लघूकृ, खलीकृ.

DEGRADED, *p. p.* (Dismissed from office, disgraced) पदभ्रष्टः -ष्टा -ष्टं, पदच्युतः -ता -तं, अधिकारपतितः -ता -तं, पतितः -ता -तं, स्थानभ्रष्टः -ष्टा -ष्टं, अवज्ञोपहतः -ता -तं, खलीकृतः -ता -तं.—(Degenerate) भ्रष्टः -ष्टा -ष्टं, परिभ्रष्टः -ष्टा -ष्टं, अपकृष्टः -ष्टा -ष्टं, निकृष्टः -ष्टा -ष्टं, अधमः -मा -मं, नीचः -चा -चं, निर्विण्णः -ण्णा -ण्णं.

DEGRADING, *a.* लाघवकारी -रिणी -रि (न्) or अपमानकारी, अकीर्त्तिकरः -रा -रं, अपयशस्करः -री -रं.

DEGREE, *s.* (Station, rank) पदं, स्थानं, आस्पदं, पदविः *f.* -वी, वृत्तिः *f.*, प्रतिपत्तिः *f.*; 'high degree,' परमपदं.—(State in which a thing is) अवस्था, भावः, दशा, स्थितिः *f.*, वृत्तिः *f.*, गतिः *f.*—(Step to any thing) क्रमः, पदं.—(Order of lineage) आवलिः *f.*, श्रेणी; 'of high degree,' महाकुलप्रसूतः.—(Measure, extent) परिमाणं, प्रमाणं, पर्य्यन्तं, मात्रं; 'to what degree'? कियत् प्रमाणं, कियत् पर्य्यन्तं, किं पर्य्यन्तं; 'in some degree,' किञ्चित्, ईषत्, कतिपयेन -यात्.—(Class, order) गणः, पंक्तिः *f.*, श्रेणी, वर्गः.—(Degree of latitude, &c.) भागः, अंशः, अक्षभागः, अक्षांशः.—(In arithmetic) अङ्कत्रयं.—(By degrees) क्रमशस्, क्रमेण, क्रमे क्रमे, पदे पदे, पदशस्, प्रतिपदं, अनुपदं, पदात्पदं, शनैः, शनैः शनैः.

To DEHORT, *v. a.* उपदेशपूर्व्वं or प्रत्यादेशपूर्व्वं भयहेतुं सूचयित्वा निवृत् in caus. (-वर्त्तयति -यितुं), मैवं कार्षीः or मैवं कृथा इति मन्त्रं कृ, विपरीतम् उपदिश् (c. 6. -दिशति -देष्टुं), प्रत्यादिश्, अन्तःख्या (c. 2. -ख्याति -तुं).

DEHORTATION, *s.* विपरीतमन्त्रणं, प्रत्यादेशपूर्व्वं निवर्त्तनं, मैवं कार्षीर् इति मन्त्रकरणं, उद्यमभङ्गसाधः प्रबोधः, निषेधार्थकः परामर्शः.

DEHORTATORY, *a.* प्रत्यादेशकः -का -कं, निषेधार्थकः -का -कं, मैवं कार्षीर् इत्युपदेशकः -का -कं, निवृत्तिकारकः -का -कं.

DEHORTER, *s.* प्रत्यादेशपूर्व्वं निवर्त्तयिता *m.* (तृ), प्रत्यादेष्टा *m.* (ष्टृ).

To DEJECT, *v. a.* (Cast down) पत् in caus. (पातयति -यितुं), अधःपत् in caus.—(Dispirit, make sad) अवसद् in caus. (-सादयति -यितुं), विषण्णीकृ, अवसन्नीकृ, विषादं जन् in caus. (जनयति -यितुं), ग्लानीकृ, पीड् (c. 10. पीडयति -यितुं), व्यथ् in caus. (व्यथयति -यितुं).

DEJECT, DEJECTED, *a.* विषण्णः -ण्णा -ण्णं, अवसन्नः -न्ना -न्नं, विषादी -दिनी -दि (न्), अवसादितः -ता -तं, उद्विग्नमनाः -नाः -नः (स्) or दीनमनाः or विमनाः or दुर्मनाः or अन्तर्मनाः, अवनतः -ता -तं, निर्विण्णः -ण्णा -ण्णं, दीनमनस्कः -स्का -स्कं, दीनचेतनः -ना -नं, क्लान्तः -न्ता -न्तं, म्लानः -ना -नं, ग्लानः -ना -नं.—(In countenance) अधोमुखः -खी -खं or नतमुखः, विषण्णवदनः -ना -नं.

DEJECTEDLY, *adv.* सविषादं, सावसादं, विषण्णं, सोद्वेगं, उद्विग्नमनसा.

DEJECTEDNESS, DEJECTION, *s.* विषादः, अवसादः, विषण्णता, अवसन्नता, उद्वेगः, निर्विण्णता, क्लान्तिः *f.*, ग्लानिः *f.*, म्लानिः *f.*, दीनता.

DEJECTURE, *s.* उच्चारः, उच्चरितं, अवस्करः, शोधनं, शकृत् *m.*, पुरीषं.

DEIFICATION, *s.* (Union with Brahma) ब्रह्मत्वं, ब्रह्मभूयं, ब्रह्मनिर्व्वाणं, ब्रह्मसायुज्यं.—(Inferior deification) देवत्वं, देवभूयं, सुरभूयं.—(Act of making a god) देवकरणं, देवत्वदानं.

DEIFIED, *p. p.* देवभूतः -ता -तं, सुरभूतः -ता -तं, ब्रह्मभूतः -ता -तं, प्राप्तदेवत्वः -त्वा -त्वं, देवत्वमापन्नः -न्ना -न्नं.

DEIFORM, *a.* देवरूपी -पिणी -पि (न्), देवाकारः -रा -रं, देवाकृतिः -तिः -ति.

To DEIFY, *v. a.* देवं कृ, देवीकृ, देवं ज्ञात्वा पूज् (c. 10. पूजयति -यितुं).

To DEIGN, *v. n.* (Vouchsafe) अर्ह् (c. 1. अर्हति -र्हितुं); as, 'Deign thou to enter my house,' त्वं मम गृहं प्रवेष्टुम् अर्हसि; प्रसद् (c. 6. -सीदति -सत्तुं) or प्रसादं कृ or प्रसन्नो भूत्वा कृ; as, 'deign to cast a look on us,' प्रसीद नो दृष्टिञ्च कुरु or दृष्टिप्रसादं कुरु or प्रसन्नो भूत्वा दृष्टिं कुरु.

To DEIGN, *v. a.* अनुदा (c. 3. -ददाति -दातुं), प्रदा, अनुज्ञा (c. 9. -जानाति -ज्ञातुं), अनुग्रह् (c. 9. -गृह्णाति -ग्रहीतुं), अनुमन् (c. 4. -मन्यते -मन्तुं).

To DEINTEGRATE, *v. a.* साकल्याद् उद्धृ (c. 1. -हरति -हर्त्तुं) or अपनी (c. 2. -नयति -नेतुं), ह्रस् in caus. (ह्रासयति -यितुं), न्यूनीकृ.

DEISM, *s.* आस्तिकता, आस्तिक्यं, अद्वैतं, अद्वैतवादः, एकात्मवादः.

DEIST, *s.* आस्तिकः, अद्वैतवादी *m.* (न्), अद्वयवादी *m.*, एकात्मवादी.

DEITY, *s.* (A god) देवः, देवता, सुरः, विबुधः, ठक्कुरः, पूजिलः, नभःसद् *m.*, नाकसद् *m.*, नाकी *m.* (न्), सुचिरायुः *m.* (स्), अस्वप्नः, अनिमिषः, दैत्यारिः *m.*, दानवारिः *m.*, गीर्वाणः, निलिम्पः.—(Divine state) देवत्वं -ता.

DELACERATION, *s.* दारणं, विदारणं, खण्डं खण्डं करणं or छेदनं or कर्त्तनं.

DELACTATION, *s.* (Weaning) स्तन्यत्यागः, स्तन्यपानत्यागकरणं.

DELAPSED, *p. p.* अधःपतितः -ता -तं, अवपतितः -ता -तं, च्युतः -ता -तं.

To DELATE, *v. a.* वह् (c. 1. वहति, वोढुं), अभिवह्, आनी (c. 1. -नयति -नेतुं).—(Accuse) अभियुज् (c. 7. -युनक्ति -योक्तुं).

DELATION, *s.* वाहनं, आनयनं.—(Accusation) अभियोगः.

DELATOR, *s.* अभियोगी *m.* (न्) -योक्ता *m.* (क्तृ), अपवादकः, सूचकः.

To DELAY, *v. a.* विलम्ब् (c. 1. -लम्बते -म्बितुं or caus. -लम्बयति -यितुं), चिर (nom. चिरयति -यितुं), आकालान्तरात् त्यज् (c. 1. त्यजति, त्यक्तुं) or या in caus. (यापयति -यितुं) or क्षिप् (c. 6. क्षिपति, क्षेप्तुं) or अपनुद् in caus. (-नोदयति -यितुं), स्थगितं -तां -तं कृ, दीर्घीकृ.—(Hinder) रुध् (c. 7. रुणद्धि, रोद्धुं), निरुध्, वृ in caus. (वारयति -यितुं), निवृ; बाध् (c. 1. बाधते -धितुं), स्तम्भ् in caus. (स्तम्भयति -यितुं), विष्टम्भ्.

To DELAY, *v. n.* विलम्ब् (c. 1. -लम्बते -म्बितुं), मन्द (nom. मन्दायते), चिर (nom. चिरयति -यितुं or चिरायति), कालं या in caus. (यापयति -यितुं) or क्षिप् (c. 6. क्षिपति, क्षेप्तुं), विकॢप् (c. 1. -कल्पते -ल्पितुं), विचर् in caus. (-चारयति -यितुं), दीर्घीभू; 'he delays coming,' विलम्बेन or विलम्बाद् आगच्छति.

DELAY, *s.* विलम्बः -म्बनं, कालयापः, कालक्षेपः, क्षेपः, विकल्पः, दीर्घसूत्रता, दीर्घीकरणं; 'a short delay,' क्षणक्षेपः.—(Stay, stop) स्तम्भः, अन्तरायः, व्याघातः, बाधा; 'without delay,' अविलम्बितं, अविलम्बं -म्बेन, अचिरं -रात् -रेण, माचिरं.

DELAYED, *p. p.* विलम्बितः -ता -तं, चिरायितः -ता -तं, यापितः -ता -तं.

DELAYER, *s.* विलम्बी *m.* (न्), विलम्बकारी *m.* (न्), कालयापकः, कालक्षेपकः.

DELECTABLE, *a.* रमणीयः -या -यं, रम्यः -म्या -म्यं, सुभगः -गा -गं, मनोहरः -रा -रं, मनोरमः -मा -मं, मनोज्ञः -ज्ञा -ज्ञं, कमनीयः -या -यं, मनआपः -पा -पं, अभिरामः -मा -मं, हर्षकः -का -कं, सुनन्दः -न्दा -न्दं, मोदकः -का -कं, आह्लादजनकः -का -कं, अभिलषणीयः -या -यं, कान्तः -न्ता -न्तं.

DELECTABLENESS, *s.* रमणीयता, रम्यत्वं, कमनीयता, मनोरमत्वं, सुनन्दत्वं.

DELECTABLY, *adv.* रमणीयं, रम्यं, कमनीयं, सुभगं, मनोरमं.

DELECTATION, *s.* आह्लादः, प्रह्लादः, आनन्दः, हर्षः, प्रमोदः, अभिरुचिः *f.*

To DELEGATE, *v. a.* नियुज् (c. 7. -युनक्ति -योक्तुं or caus. -योजयति -यितुं), समादिश् (c. 6. -दिशति -देष्टुं), व्यादिश्, प्रतिसन्दिश्, प्रस्था in caus. (-स्थापयति -यितुं); प्रेर् (c. 10. -ईरयति -यितुं), न्यस् (c. 4. -अस्यति -असितुं), उपन्यस्; प्रतिपद् in caus. (-पादयति -यितुं), ऋ in caus. (अर्पयति -यितुं), समृ in caus.; परिदा.

DELEGATE, *s.* नियोगी *m.* (न्), नियुक्तः, अधिकारवान् *m.* (त्), प्रतिपुरुषः, प्रतिनिधिः *m.*, प्रतिभूः.

DELEGATED, *s.* कार्य्यनिर्वाहणे नियुक्तः -क्ता -क्तं or अधिकृतः -ता -तं, प्रेरितः -ता -तं, समादिष्टः -ष्टा -ष्टं.

DELEGATION, *s.* नियोजनं, प्रेरणं, प्रस्थापनं, समादेशः, समर्पणं.

To DELETE, *v. a.* अपमृज् (c. 2. -मार्ष्टि -ष्टुं), व्यामृज्, निर्मृज्, लोपं कृ.

DELETERIOUS, DELETORY, *a.* विनाशकः -का -कं, नाशी -शिनी -शि (न्) or प्रणाशी, घाती -तिनी -ति (न्) or विघाती, घातुकः -का -कं, क्षयकरः -री -रं, सूदनः -नी -नं, हिंस्रः -स्रा -स्रं, शारुकः -का -कं.

DELETION, *s.* व्यामर्षः, लोपः, विलोपनं, उच्छेदः, विनाशः, नाशः.

DELF, DELFE, *s.* (Mine) आकरः, खनिः *f.*, खानिः *f.*—(Earthenware) मृण्मयभाण्डं, मृद्भाण्डं, कौलालकं, मार्त्तिकभाण्डं, मृण्मयद्रव्यं.

To DELIBERATE, *v. n.* मन्त्र् (c. 10. मन्त्रयते -ति -यितुं), सम्मन्त्र्, विचर् in caus. (-चारयति -यितुं), मनसा विचर्, चिन्त् (c. 10. चिन्तयति -यितुं), सञ्चिन्त्, विचिन्त्; विगण् (c. 10. -गणयति -यितुं), वितर्क् (c. 10. -तर्कयति -यितुं); विमृश् (c. 6. -मृशति -मर्ष्टुं), परामृश्, विकॢप् (c. 1. -कल्पते -ल्पितुं, c. 10. -कल्पयति -यितुं), विनिश्चि (c. 5. -चिनोति -चेतुं), सम्भू in caus. (-भावयति -यितुं), मनसा विवेचनं कृ.

DELIBERATE, *a.* विमृश्यकारी -रिणी -रि (न्) or समीक्ष्यकारी or अक्षिप्रकारी, सावहितः -ता -तं, कृतावधानः -ना -नं, कार्य्यचिन्तकः -का -कं, अव्यग्रः -ग्रा -ग्रं, अप्रमत्तः -त्ता -त्तं, अत्वरितः -ता -तं, चतुरः -रा -रं, परिणामदर्शी -र्शिनी -र्शि (न्).

DELIBERATED, *p. p.* चिन्तितः -ता -तं, सञ्चिन्तितः -ता -तं, सुचिन्तितः -ता -तं, मन्त्रितः -ता -तं, विचारितः -ता -तं, विगणितः -ता -तं, मथितः -ता -तं.

DELIBERATELY, *adv.* विमृश्य, समीक्ष्य, सुविमृश्य, मन्त्रतस्, अवधानतस्, अवेक्षया, अत्वरितं, अव्यग्रं, असहसा, अप्रमत्तं, बुद्धिपुरःसरं, मनःपूर्व्वकं, बुद्धिपूर्व्वकं, बुद्ध्या, मतिपूर्व्वं; 'walking deliberately,' मितक्रमः.

DELIBERATENESS, *s.* समीक्ष्यकारित्वं, विमृश्यकारित्वं, अक्षिप्रकारिता, सावधानता, विचारशीलता, सतर्कता, अव्यग्रता, अप्रमादः, परिणामदर्शनं.

DELIBERATION, *s.* मन्त्रणं -णा, सम्मन्त्रणं, विचारः -रणं -णा, सुविचारः, चिन्ता, सुचिन्ता, सञ्चिन्तनं, विमर्शः, परामर्शः, विवेचना -नं, वितर्कः -र्कणं, समीक्षा -क्षणं, प्रसमीक्षा, चर्चा, विगणनं, सम्प्रधारणा, भावना, विकल्पः, समर्थनं.

DELIBERATIVE, *a.* विचारकः -का -कं, विचारी -रिणी -रि (न्), चिन्तकः -का -कं, विमर्शी -र्शिनी -र्शि (न्), मन्त्रकारः -री -रं, विचारशीलः -ला -लं.

DELICACY, *s.* (Daintiness) स्वादुता, सुस्वादुत्वं, सुरसत्वं, सौरस्यं, सुस्वादुत्वं, मिष्टता.—(Softness) सौकुमार्य्यं, सुकुमारत्वं, कोमलता, मृदुता.—(Elegance) लालित्यं, लौल्यं, लावण्यं, विलासः.—(Nicety) सूक्ष्मत्वं -ता, सौक्ष्म्यं, शुद्धता, श्लक्ष्णता.—(Slenderness, tenuity) तनुता, लघुता, लाघवं, अस्थूलता, क्षीणता.—(Scrupulousness, politeness) आदरः, सभ्यता, विनयः, सुशीलता.—(Weakness of constitution) शरीरमृदुता, अङ्गमृदुता, प्रकृतिदौर्ब्बल्यं.—(Choice food) स्वाद्वन्नं, विशिष्टान्नं, भोजनविशेषः, सुग्रासः.

DELICATE, *a.* (Dainty, of an agreeable taste) स्वादुः -दुः -द्वी -दु or सुस्वादुः, सुरसः -सा -सं, मिष्टः -ष्टा -ष्टं, सुस्वाद्यः -द्या -द्यं, स्वादुकारः -री -रं.—(Elegant) ललितः -ता -तं, चारुः -र्व्वी -रु.—(Soft) सुकुमारः -रा -रं, कोमलः -ला -लं, मृदुः -द्वी -दु.—(Nice, slender, fine, not coarse) सूक्ष्मः -क्ष्मा -क्ष्मं, तनुः -नुः -न्वी -नु or वितनुः or प्रतनुः, लघुः -घुः -घ्वी -घु, श्लक्ष्णः -क्ष्णा -क्ष्णं, पेलवः -वा -वं, क्षीणः -णा -णं, अस्थूलः -ला -लं, विरलः -ला -लं.—(Choice) विशिष्टः -ष्टा -ष्टं, उत्कृष्टः -ष्टा -ष्टं, उत्तमः -मा -मं.—(Polite) सभ्यः -भ्या -भ्यं, विनीतः -ता -तं.—(Weak in constitution) मृद्वङ्गः -ङ्गी -ङ्गं, मृदुशरीरः -रा -रं, जन्मरोगी -गिणी -गि (न्); 'a delicate woman,' तन्वी, लघ्वी, सुमध्यमा.

DELICATELY, *adv.* ललितं, सलालित्यं, सुकुमारं, कोमलं, मृदु, तनु.

DELICATES, *s.* स्वाद्वन्नं, स्वादुभोजनं, मिष्टान्नं, सुग्रासः, विशिष्टान्नं.

DELICIOUS, *a.* स्वादुः -दुः -द्वी -दु or सुस्वादुः, मधुरः -रा -रं, मिष्टः -ष्टा -ष्टं, सुस्वास्वादः -दा -दं, सुरसः -सा -सं, मनोहरः -रा -रं, मनोरमः -मा -मं, रम्यः -म्या -म्यं, रमणीयः -या -यं, मोदकः -का -कं, सुभगः -गा -गं, कमनीयः -या -यं.

DELICIOUSLY, *adv.* सुस्वादु, मधुरं, मनोरमं, रमणीयं, सुभगं.

DELICIOUSNESS, *s.* सुस्वादुता, माधुर्य्यं, सौरस्यं, रम्यता, रमणीयता.

DELIGHT, *s.* हर्षः, आनन्दः, आह्लादः, प्रह्लादः, ह्लादः, मुदा, मुद् *f.*, प्रमोदः, मोदः, आमोदः, प्रीतिः *f.*, तृप्तिः *f.*, सुखं, सौख्यं, नन्दः, नन्दथुः *m.*, मदः, प्रमदः, मादः, रतिः *f.*, परितोषः, सम्तोषः, रभसः, अभिरुचिः *f.*, कुतूहलं, चित्तप्रसन्नता, महोत्सवः; 'thrill of delight,' रोमहर्षणं, पुलकः, रोमाञ्चः.—(That which gives delight) नन्दनः -नं, आनन्दनं, आनन्ददः, हर्षकः, हर्षकरः, प्रीतिदः.

To DELIGHT, *v. a.* नन्द् in caus. (नन्दयति -यितुं), आनन्द्, अभिनन्द्; हृष् in caus. (हर्षयति -यितुं), प्रहृष्, परिहृष्; ह्लाद् in caus. (ह्लादयति -यितुं), प्रह्लाद्, आह्लाद्; सुख् (c. 10. सुखयति -यितुं), रम् in caus. (रमयति -यितुं), प्रमुद् in caus. (-मोदयति -यितुं), परितुष् in caus. (-तोषयति -यितुं), सन्तुष्; तृप् in caus. (तर्पयति -यितुं), प्री (c. 9. प्रीणाति or caus. प्रीणयति -यितुं), उल्लस् in caus. (-लासयति -यितुं), हर्षं कृ, आनन्दं दा.

To DELIGHT, *v. n.* नन्द् (c. 1. नन्दति -न्दितुं), आनन्द्, अभिनन्द्, विनन्द्; हृष् (c. 4. हृष्यति, हर्षितुं), प्रहृष्, संहृष्, सम्प्रहृष्; ह्लाद् (c. 1. ह्लादते -दितुं), रम् (c. 1. रमते, रन्तुं), अभिरम्, आरम्, संरम्, उपरम्, प्री (c. 4. प्रीयते), मुद् (c. 1. मोदते -दितुं), प्रमुद्; तुष् (c. 4. तोष्यति, तोष्टुं), परितुष्, प्रतुष्, सन्तुष्; रुच् (c. 1. रोचते -चितुं), अभिरुच्, उल्लस् (c. 1. -लसति -सितुं), विलस्; तृप् (c. 4. तृप्यति, तर्प्तुं).

DELIGHTED, *p. p.* हृष्टः -ष्टा -ष्टं, हर्षितः -ता -तं, आह्लादितः -ता -तं, प्रह्लादितः -ता -तं, ह्लादितः -ता -तं, आनन्दितः -ता -तं, आनन्दी -न्दिनी -न्दि (न्), प्रमोदितः -ता -तं, प्रमोदी -दिनी -दि (न्), मुदान्वितः -ता -तं, प्रीतिमान् -मती -मत् (त्), सन्तुष्टः -ष्टा -ष्टं, उल्लसितः -ता -तं or उल्लासितः, अभिरुचितः -ता -तं, प्रीतः -ता -तं, सुखी -खिनी -खि (न्), प्रहृष्टमनाः -नाः -नः (स्) or प्रीतमनाः, हृष्टचित्तः -त्ता -त्तं, सानन्दः -न्दा -न्दं; 'exquisitely delighted,' पुलकितः -ता -तं, परमहृष्टः -ष्टा -ष्टं, तोषरोमाञ्चितः -ता -तं.

DELIGHTFUL, *a.* रम्यः -म्या -म्यं, रमणीयः -या -यं, मनोरमः -मा -मं, मनोहरः -रा -रं, सुभगः -गा -गं, हर्षकः -का -कं, हर्षकरः -री -रं, हर्षणः -णा -णी -णं, नन्दकः -का -कं, नन्दनः -ना -नं, आनन्दनः -ना -नं, आनन्ददः -दा -दं, प्रीतिदः -दा -दं, मोदकः -का -कं, प्रमोदी -दिनी -दि (न्), रमणः -णा -णं, आनन्दमयः -यी -यं, सुखी -खिनी -खि (न्), सुखदः -दा -दं, परितोषजनकः -का -कं, रामणीयकः -का -कं, कमनीयः -या -यं, रुचिरः -रा -रं.

DELIGHTFULLY, *adv.* रम्यं, रमणीयं, मनोरमं, सुभगं, सुखेन, कमनीयं.

DELIGHTFULNESS, *s.* रम्यता, रमणीयता, मनोरमत्वं, कमनीयता, सश्रीकता.

To DELINEATE, *v. a.* (Sketch) लिख् (c. 6. लिखति, लेखितुं), आलिख्, विलिख्; रूप् (c. 10. रूपयति -यितुं); अङ्क् (c. 10. अङ्कयति -यितुं).—(Paint) चित्र् (c. 10. चित्रयति -यितुं).—(Describe) वर्ण् (c. 10. वर्णयति -यितुं), अनुवर्ण्, उपवर्ण्, संवर्ण्.

DELINEATED, *p. p.* आलिखितः -ता -तं, चित्रलिखितः -ता -तं, चित्रगतः -ता -तं, चित्रितः -ता -तं, वर्णितः -ता -तं, निरूपितः -ता -तं.

DELINEATION, *s.* आलेख्यं, आलेखनं, चित्रं, चित्रारम्भः, पाण्डुलेख्यं, वर्णनं -ना, उपवर्णनं, अङ्कनं, आदर्शः.

DELINQUENCY, *s.* दोषः, अपराधः, पापं, व्यतिक्रमः, अपक्रिया, अपकर्म्म *n.* (न्), अपचारः, दुष्कर्म्म *n.* (न्), दुष्कृतं, कुकर्म्म *n.*, दुश्चरितं, पापकर्म्म *n.*, पापकृतं.

DELINQUENT, *s.* पापी *m.* (न्), पापकारी *m.* (न्), पापकृत्, अपराधी *m.* (न्), दोषी *m.* (न्), कृतापराधः, कुकर्म्मकारी *m.* (न्), दुष्कृती *m.* (न्).

To DELIQUATE, *v. n.* विली (c. 4. -लीयते -लेतुं -लातुं), प्रविली; विद्रु (c. 1. -द्रवति -द्रोतुं), द्रवीभू, विगल् (c. 1. -गलति -लितुं), परिगल्.

DELIQUATION, *s.* द्रवः -वणं -वत्वं, विलयः -यनं, द्रवीकरणं, गलनं.

DELIQUIUM, *s.* मूर्च्छा -र्च्छनं -ना, प्रलयः, प्रमोहः, नष्टचेष्टता, निर्वेशः.

DELIRIOUS, *a.* चैतन्यरहितः -ता -तं, भ्रान्तचित्तः -त्ता -त्तं, नष्टचेतनः -ना -नं, रोगोपहतज्ञानः -ना -नं, चित्तविभ्रमात् प्रलापकारी -रिणी -रि (न्).

DELIRIUM, *s.* चित्तविभ्रमः, ज्ञानभ्रान्तिः *f.*, चैतन्यनाशः, अचैतन्यं, चित्तविप्लवः, चित्तवैकल्यं, प्रलापः.

To DELIVER, *v. a.* (Consign) प्रतिपद् in caus. (-पादयति -यितुं), ऋ in caus. (अर्पयति -यितुं), समृ, निक्षिप् (c. 6. -क्षिपति -क्षेप्तुं), न्यस् (c. 4. -अस्यति -असितुं), उपन्यस्, न्यासीकृ; निविद् in caus. (-वेदयति -यितुं), सङ्क्रम् in caus. (-क्रामयति -यितुं), प्रतिज्ञा in caus. (-ज्ञापयति -यितुं), आरुह् in caus (-रोपयति -यितुं), समाविश् in caus. (-वेशयति -यितुं).—(Give up, yield) प्रदा (c. 3. -ददाति -दातुं c. 1. -यच्छति), परिदा, सम्प्रदा, उत्सृज् (c. 6. -सृजति -स्रष्टुं), प्रोत्सृ in caus. (-सारयति -यितुं), वितृ (c. 1. -तरति -रितुं -रीतुं).—(Release, rescue) मुच् (c. 6. मुञ्चति, मोक्तुं or caus. मोचयति -यितुं), विमुच्, प्रविमुच्, मोक्ष् (c. 10. मोक्षयति -यितुं), उद्धृ (c. 1. -हरति -हर्त्तुं), समुद्धृ; निस्तृ in caus. (-तारयति -यितुं), सन्तृ, उत्तृ; त्रै (c. 1. त्रायते, त्रातुं), परित्रै, सन्त्रै; रक्ष् (c. 1. रक्षति -क्षितुं).—(Utter, pronounce) वाक्यम् ईर् (c. 10. ईरयति -यितुं), उदीर्, उच्चर् in caus. (-चारयति -यितुं), उदाहृ (c. 1. -हरति -हर्त्तुं), व्याहृ, वद् (c. 1. वदति -दितुं).—(Deliver a message, &c.) निविद् in caus. (-वेदयति -यितुं), विज्ञा in caus. (-ज्ञापयति -यितुं), आख्या (c. 2. -ख्याति -तुं).—(Assist in childbirth) सु in caus. (सावयति -यितुं), प्रसवं कृ in caus. (कारयति -यितुं).

DELIVERED, *p. p.* (Consigned) प्रतिपादितः -ता -तं, अर्पितः -ता -तं, समर्पितः -ता -तं, निक्षिप्तः -प्ता -प्तं, न्यस्तः -स्ता -स्तं, प्रणिहितः -ता -तं. —(Given up) प्रदत्तः -त्ता -त्तं, उत्सृष्टः -ष्टा -ष्टं, निसृष्टः -ष्टा -ष्टं, प्रोत्सारितः -ता -तं, वितीर्णः -र्णा -र्णं.—(Released, rescued) मुक्तः -क्ता -क्तं, मोचितः -ता -तं, उद्धृतः -ता -तं, समुद्धृतः -ता -तं, रक्षितः -ता -तं, त्रातः -ता -तं, त्राणः -णा -णं, निस्तारितः -ता -तं, उत्तीर्णः -र्णा -र्णं.—(Uttered) उच्चारितः -ता -तं.—(As a message) निवेदितः -ता -तं, निरादिष्टः -ष्टा -ष्टं.—(Of a child) प्रसूता.

DELIVERANCE, *s.* (Rescue, release) रक्षा -क्षणं, परिरक्षणं, त्राणं, परित्राणं, उद्धारः, उद्धरणं, निस्तारः, निस्तरणं, तारणं, मुक्तिः *f.*, मोक्षः, मोचनं, मोक्षणं, परिमोक्षणं.

DELIVERER, *s.* (Rescuer) त्राता *m.* (तृ), रक्षकः, मोचकः, मोक्षकः, मुक्तिदाता *m.* (तृ), उद्धर्त्ता *m.* (र्त्तृ), समुद्धर्त्ता *m.*, निस्तारकः, निस्तारयिता *m.* (तृ), तारकः.—(Announcer) निवेदकः, निवेदनकृत् *m.*, आख्यायकः, विज्ञापकः.

DELIVERY, *s.* (Rescue) मुक्तिः *f.*, त्राणं, रक्षणं. *See* DELIVERANCE. —(Consignment, giving up) अर्पणं, समर्पणं, प्रतिपादनं, निवेदनं, न्यसनं, उपन्यासः, आरोपणं, प्रदानं, परिदानं, सम्प्रदानं, विधायकत्वं. —(Of a message, &c.) निवेदनं, निरादेशः, विज्ञापनं.—(Utterance) उच्चारणं, उदाहरणं, व्याहरणं, व्याहारः.—(Childbirth) प्रसवः, प्रसूतिः *f.*, सूतिः *f.*, सूः *f.*, प्रसवकरणं, गर्भच्युतिः *f.*, जातकर्म्म *n.* (न्); 'a woman near her delivery,' आसन्नप्रसवा.

DELL, *s.* दरी -रा, कन्दरः -री, दरीभूः *f.*, द्रोणी, अद्रिद्रोणी, गुहा.

DELUDABLE, *a.* मोहनीयः -या -यं, प्रवञ्चनीयः -या -यं, प्रतारणीयः -या -यं.

To DELUDE, *v. a.* मुह् in caus. (मोहयति -यितुं), सम्मुह्, व्यामुह्, वञ्च् in caus. (वञ्चयते -यितुं), प्रवञ्च्, परिवञ्च्; प्रलभ् (c. 1. -लभते -लब्धुं); प्रतॄ in caus. (-तारयति -यितुं), प्रलुभ् in caus. (-लोभयति -यितुं).

DELUDED, *p. p.* मोहितः -ता -तं, सम्मोहितः -ता -तं, विमोहितः -ता -तं, वञ्चितः -ता -तं, प्रलब्धः -ब्धा -ब्धं, प्रतारितः -ता -तं, प्रलोभितः -ता -तं.

DELUDER, *s.* मोही *m.* (न्), वञ्चकः, प्रवञ्चकः, प्रतारकः, भ्रामकः.

DELUGE, *s.* भूतसम्प्लवः, जलाप्लावनं, जलप्लावनं, आप्लावः, जलप्रलयः, जलवेगः, तोयविप्लवः, सलिलोपप्लवः, परिप्लवः, जलोच्छ्वासः, परिवाहः, वन्या, ओघः.—(Universal deluge) एकार्णवं.—(Of rain) धारासारः, धारासम्पातः, अतिवृष्टिः *f.*, महती वृष्टिः.—(Overflow of a river) वानं.—(Sudden calamity) उत्पातः, विनिपातः.

To DELUGE, *v. a.* प्लु in caus. (प्लावयति -यितुं), आप्लु, परिप्लु, सम्प्लु; मज्ज् in caus. (मज्जयति -यितुं), निमज्ज्; 'This place is deluged by the tide,' एतत् स्थानं समुद्रवेलया प्लाव्यते.

DELUGED, *p. p.* आप्लावितः -ता -तं, आप्लुतः -ता -तं, परिप्लुतः -ता -तं, सम्प्लुतः -ता -तं, अभिप्लुतः -ता -तं, अभिपरिप्लुतः -ता -तं, समभिप्लुतः -ता -तं.

DELUSION, *s.* (Illusion, error) मोहः, माया, भ्रमः, भ्रान्तिः *f.*, व्यामोहः, विभ्रमः, मतिविभ्रमः, परिभ्रमः, आभासः, प्रपञ्चः, इन्द्रजालं, मिथ्यामतिः *f.*, विवर्त्तः, आवरणं.—(Cheating, beguiling) वञ्चना, मोहनं, प्रलोभनं, विलोभः, कूटः -टं, प्रतारणा.

DELUSIVE, DELUSORY, *a.* मोही -हिनी -हि (न्), मायी -यिनी -यि (न्), मायिकः -की -कं, मायामयः -यी -यं, जाली -लिनी -लि (न्), भ्रान्तिजनकः -का -कं, इन्द्रजालिकः -की -कं or ऐन्द्रजालिकः, भङ्गुरः -रा -रं.

To DELVE, *v. a.* खन् (c. 1. खनति -नितुं), अभिखन्, खनित्रेण गर्त्तं कृ.

DELVE, *s.* खातं -तकं, खातभूः *f.*, खेयं, गर्त्तः, विवरं, विलं, अवटः.

DELVER, *s.* खनिता *m.* (तृ), खातकः, आखनिकः, खनकः.

DEMAGOGUE, *s.* प्राकृतजननायकः, अल्पलोकनेता *m.* (तृ), पृथग्जनपुरोगमः, प्रजानायकः, प्रजोपकारकः, हीनवर्णसपक्षः, अधमवर्णपक्षपाती, उत्तमाधमवर्णमध्ये कलहकारी *m.* (न्).

DEMAIN, DEMESNE, *s.* स्वाधीना भूमिः *f.*

DEMAND, *s.* (Claim) अभियोगः, प्रार्थना, अभ्यर्थना, अर्थना, अभिमानं, याच्ञा, याचना, मार्गणं; 'false demand,' मिथ्याभियोगः.—(Question) अनुयोगः, पर्य्यनुयोगः, प्रश्नः, सम्प्रश्नः, पृच्छा, जिज्ञासा, अन्वेषणा, अनुसरणं.—(Calling for in order to purchase) क्रयार्थम् अन्वेषणा.

To DEMAND, *v. a.* (Claim) याच् (c. 1. याचति -चितुं), अर्थ् (c. 10. अर्थयति -ते -यितुं), प्रार्थ्; ममेति or मदीयमिति or मम दातव्यमिति वद् (c. 1. वदति -दितुं), स्वाधिकारं ज्ञा in caus. (ज्ञापयति -यितुं), अभियोगं कृ, स्वीकृ.—(Question) अनुयुज् (c. 7. -युनक्ति -युंक्ते -योक्तुं), ज्ञा in des. (जिज्ञासते -सितुं), प्रच्छ् (c. 6. पृच्छति, प्रष्टुं).

DEMANDABLE, *a.* अभियोक्तव्यः -व्या -व्यं, याचनीयः -या -यं, प्रार्थनीयः -या -यं.

DEMANDANT, *s.* अभियोक्ता *m.* (क्तृ), अर्थी *m.* (न्), प्रार्थयिता *m.* (तृ).

DEMANDED, *p. p.* याचितः -ता -तं, प्रार्थितः -ता -तं, अभियुक्तः -क्ता -क्तं, अनुयुक्तः -क्ता -क्तं, पृष्टः -ष्टा -ष्टं, जिज्ञासितः -ता -तं, मार्गितः -ता -तं.

DEMANDER, *s.* अभियोगी *m.* (न्), याचिता *m.* (तृ), प्रार्थकः, प्रष्टा *m.* (ष्टृ).

DEMARCATION, *s.* सीमा, परिसीमा, मर्य्यादा, अवच्छेदः, विच्छेदः.

To DEMEAN ONE'S SELF, *v. n.* व्यवहृ (c. 1. -हरति -ते -हर्त्तुं), वृत् (c. 1. वर्त्तते -र्त्तितुं), चर् (c. 1. चरति -रितुं), आचर्, समाचर्; वृत्तिम् अनुष्ठा (c. 1. -तिष्ठति -ष्ठातुं).

DEMEANOUR, *s.* वृत्तिः *f.*, व्यवहारः, आचारः, आचरणं, गतिः *f.*, स्थितिः *f.*, चलनं, रीतिः *f.*, चरितं, चरित्रं, चेष्टितं.

To DEMENTATE, *v. a.* उन्मद् in caus. (-मादयति -यितुं), मुह् in caus. (मोहयति -यितुं).

DEMENTATE, *a.* उन्मत्तः -त्ता -त्तं, नष्टचित्तः -त्ता -त्तं, मूढसंज्ञः -ज्ञा -ज्ञं.

Dementation, *s.* उन्मत्तीकरणं, मोहनं, वातुलीकरणं, भ्रान्तिकरणं.

Demerit, *s.* अगुणः -णता, वैगुण्यं, निर्गुणत्वं, दोषः, अपुण्यं, गुणाभावः.

To demerit, *v. a.* दोषं कृत्वा निन्दां or दण्डम् अर्ह् (c. 1. अर्हति -र्हितुं).

Demi, *a.* अर्द्धः -र्द्धा -र्द्धं, आर्द्धिकः -की -कं, सामि indec.

Demi-devil, *s.* अर्द्धपिशाचः, नरपिशाचः, अर्द्धेन भूतोऽर्द्धेन पिशाचः.

Demi-god, *s.* नरदेवः, देवनारकः, देवयोनिः *m.*, उपदेवता, अर्द्धदेवः. The following are different sorts of demi-gods or superhuman beings: यक्षः, सिद्धः, पिशाचः, किन्नरः, विद्याधरः, रक्षः *n.* (स्), गन्धर्व्वः, गुह्यकः.

Demi-man, *s.* अर्द्धनरः, अर्द्धपुरुषः, अर्द्धमानुषः, किन्नरः.

Demigration, *s.* देशत्यागः, स्थानत्यागः, उत्क्रमणं, देशान्तरगमनं.

Demise, *s.* (Of a king) राजमृत्युः, राजमरणं, उपरमः, उपरतिः *f.*

To demise, *v. a.* मरणकाले नियमपत्रेण प्रदा (c. 1. -यच्छति, c. 3. -ददाति -दातुं) or सम् in caus. (-अर्पयति -यितुं) or प्रतिपद् in caus. (-पादयति -यितुं).

Demission, *s.* अपकर्षः -र्षणं, अधःपातनं, अधोगतिः *f.*, अवसादनं, भङ्गः.

Democracy, *s.* सर्व्वप्रजाधिपत्यं, सर्व्ववर्णप्रभुत्वं, प्रजाप्रभुत्वं, प्रजापालितं राज्यं, राज्यविशेषो यत्र साधारण्येन सर्व्वलोकेषु न्यस्तो राज्यभारः.

Democrat, *s.* प्रजाप्रभुत्वावलम्बी *m.* (न्), प्रजाधिपत्योपकारकः, प्रजाधिपत्यानुग्राही *m.* (न्), प्रजोपकारकः, प्रजानाथः.

Democratical, *a.* प्रजाप्रभुत्वसम्बन्धी -न्धिनी -न्धि (न्), सार्व्वलौकिकः -की -कं, सार्व्ववर्णिकः -की -कं.

To demolish, *v. a.* नश् in caus. (नाशयति -यितुं), विनश्, उद्धृ (c. 1. -हरति -हर्तुं), संहृ; ध्वंस् in caus. (ध्वंसयति -यितुं), प्रध्वंस्, विध्वंस्; अधःपत् in caus. (-पातयति -यितुं); उच्छिद् (c. 7. -छिनत्ति -छेत्तुं), उन्मूल् (c. 10. -मूलयति -यितुं), साध् in caus. (साधयति -यितुं), अवसद् in caus. (-सादयति -यितुं), उत्सद्.

Demolished, *p. p.* नाशितः -ता -तं, विनाशितः -ता -तं, उद्धृतः -ता -तं, संहृतः -ता -तं, उच्छिन्नः -न्ना -न्नं, उन्मूलितः -ता -तं, भग्नः -ग्ना -ग्नं, सादितः -ता -तं, सूदितः -ता -तं, विघटितः -ता -तं, विघाटितः -ता -तं.

Demolisher, *s.* विनाशकः, विनाशकारी *m.* (न्), ध्वंसकारी, प्रलयकारी, उच्छेदकः, उन्मूलकः.

Demolition, *s.* नाशः, विनाशः, प्रलयः, ध्वंसः, प्रध्वंसः, उच्छेदः, समुच्छेदः, उद्धरणं, संहारः, समूलोद्धरणं, उत्पाटनं.

Demon, *s.* पिशाचः, भूतः, राक्षसः, असुरः, दानवः, निशाटः, निशाचरः, यज्ञारिः *m.*, यातुः *m.*, यातुधानः, विधुरः, कर्व्वुरः, कर्बुरः, कर्बूरः, प्रेतः, उपपादुकः.

Demoniac, *s.* भूताविष्टः, भूतग्रस्तः, भूतोपहतः, प्रेतवाहितः.

Demoniac, demoniacal, *a.* भौतः -ती -तं, भौतिकः -की -कं, पैशाचः -ची -चं -चिकः -की -कं, आसुरः -री -रं, राक्षसः -सी -सं; 'demoniacal possession,' भूतावेशः.

Demonology, *s.* भूतप्रेतादिविषया विद्या, वेतालपिशाचादिविषयका विद्या.

Demonstrable, *a.* साध्यः -ध्या -ध्यं, उपपादनीयः -या -यं, सूच्यः -च्या -च्यं, प्रतिपादनीयः -या -यं, प्रमेयः -या -यं, मीमांस्यः -स्या -स्यं.

Demonstrably, *adv.* प्रत्यक्षतस् -क्षेण, सुस्पष्टं, सुव्यक्तं, कोऽत्र सन्देहः.

To demonstrate, *v. a.* साध् in caus. (साधयति -यितुं), उपपद् in caus. (-पादयति -यितुं), प्रमाणीकृ, प्रमाण (nom. प्रमाणयति -यितुं) भू in caus. (भावयति -यितुं), विभू, सूच् (c. 10. सूचयति -यितुं), निर्दिश् (c. 6. -दिशति -देष्टुं), प्रदिश्, विनिर्दिश्, निर्णी (c. 1. -णयति -णेतुं); दृश् in caus. (दर्शयति -यितुं).

Demonstrated, *p. p.* सिद्धः -द्धा -द्धं, साधितः -ता -तं, उपपादितः -ता -तं, उपपन्नः -न्ना -न्नं, प्रतिपादितः -ता -तं, प्रमाणितः -ता -तं, प्रमाणीकृतः -ता -तं, विभावितः -ता -तं.

Demonstration, *s.* सिद्धिः *f.*, साधनं, सिद्धसाध्यं, उपपत्तिः *f.*, उपपादनं, सिद्धान्तः, राद्धान्तः, प्रमाणं, प्रामाण्यं, निर्देशः, निर्णयः, निर्णीतत्वं; 'ocular demonstration,' प्रत्यक्षप्रमाणं, चाक्षुषज्ञानं; 'written,' लेख्यप्रमाणं.

Demonstrative, *a.* निर्णायकः -का -कं, निश्चायकः -का -कं, निर्देशकः -का -कं, प्रामाणिकः -की -कं, सिद्धान्तकरणः -णा -णं, उपपादकः -का -कं, विभावकः -का -कं.

Demonstratively, *adv.* सप्रमाणं, सिद्धिपूर्व्वं, सुव्यक्तं, निर्व्विवादं.

Demonstrator, *s.* निर्देष्टा *m.* (ष्टृ), सिद्धान्ती *m.* (न्) प्रमाणकर्त्ता *m.* (र्त्तृ).

Demoralization, *s.* धर्म्मभ्रष्टता, धर्म्मविप्लवः, आचारदुष्टता, व्यवहारदुष्टता.

To demoralize, *v. a.* आचारान् or व्यवहारान् दुष् in caus. (दूषयति -यितुं); धर्म्माद् भ्रंश् in caus. (भ्रंशयति -यितुं) or च्यु in caus. (च्यावयति -यितुं), भ्रष्टीकृ, दुर्वृत्तं -त्तां -त्तं कृ.

Demulcent, *a.* शमकः -का -कं, शान्तिकः -की -कं, उपशायी -यिनी -यि (न्), स्निग्धः -ग्धा -ग्धं, स्नेहवान् -वती -वत् (त्), श्लिक्ष्णः -क्ष्णा -क्ष्णं.

To demur, *v. a.* or *n.* विलम्ब् (c. 1. -लम्बते -म्बितुं), शङ्क् (c. 1. शङ्कते -ङ्कितुं), विशङ्क्, आशङ्क्; विचर् in caus. (-चारयति -यितुं), विकॢप् (c. 1. -कल्पते -ल्पितुं or caus. -कल्पयति -यितुं), चिर (nom. चिरयति -यितुं), सन्दिह् (c. 2. -देग्धि -ग्धुं), मनसा आन्दोल (nom. आन्दोलयति -यितुं).

Demur, *s.* विलम्बः, सन्देहः, संशयः, विकल्पः, शङ्का, आशङ्का, वितर्कः, विचारणं; 'without demur,' अविचारितं, अविलम्बितं.

Demure, *a.* एकान्तविनीतः -ता -तं, अतिविनयवान् -वती -वत् (त्), सगौरवः -वा -वं, गम्भीरः -रा -रं, धीरः -रा -रं, शान्तः -न्ता -न्तं, व्रीडितः -ता -तं, लज्जितः -ता -तं, ह्रीमान् -मती -मत् (त्), मन्दास्यः -स्या -स्यं.

Demurely, *adv.* सविनयं, सगौरवं, एकान्तविनयेन, सलज्जं, सव्रीडं.

Demureness, *s.* विनयः, अतिविनयः, गौरवं, गाम्भीर्य्यं, धीरता, धैर्य्यं, मन्दता, शान्तिः *f.*, लज्जा, सव्रीडता, त्रपा, शालीनत्वं.

Demurrage, *s.* नौकाम् विहितकालादधिकं खाते or तीरोपान्ते धृत्वा वाणिजेन नौपतये दत्तं पारितोषिकं.

Demurrer, *s.* सन्दल्पे विषये विलम्बः or विरामः or विरतिः *f.*, अर्थनिर्णये प्राड्विवाकैर् आशल्यच्छेदनाद् विचारणत्यागः.

Den, *s.* विवरं, विलं, श्वभ्रं, गह्वरं, कन्दरः -रा, गर्त्तः, रन्ध्रं, कुहरं, गुहा, गुहागृहं, खातं, दरी, निर्व्वरिः *m.*

Deniable, *a.* प्रत्याख्येयः -या -यं, अस्वीकार्य्यः -र्य्या -र्य्यं, खण्डनीयः -या -यं.

Denial, *s.* अपह्नवः, अपह्नुतिः *f.*, निह्नवः, निह्नुतिः *f.*, प्रत्याख्यानं, अपवादः, अपलापः, प्रत्यादेशः, निरसनं, निषेधः, प्रतिषेधः, अवधीरणा, प्रणयविहतिः *f.*, अपाकृतिः *f.*, अस्वीकारः, अननुज्ञा; 'self-denial,' आत्मपरित्यागः, संयमः, संयमनं.

Denied, *p. p.* अपह्नुतः -ता -तं, निह्नुतः -ता -तं, प्रत्याख्यातः -ता -तं, अपवादितः -ता -तं, प्रत्यादिष्टः -ष्टा -ष्टं, निरस्तः -स्ता -स्तं, अननुज्ञातः -ता -तं.

Denier, *s.* अपह्नोता *m.* (तृ), निह्नोता *m.*, अपलापी *m.* (न्), अपवादी *m.* (न्).

To denigrate, *v. a.* कृष्ण (nom. कृष्णायते, कृष्णयति -यितुं), कृष्णीकृ, श्यामीकृ.

Denigration, *s.* कृष्णीकरणं, श्यामीकरणं, कालीकरणं.

Denizen, *s.* नगरस्थः, पौरः, पौरजनः, नागरः, नगरजनः, नगरवासी *m.* (न्), स्वाधीनः, स्वतन्त्रः, स्ववशः, मुक्तः, नगरस्य सामाजिकजनः.

To denizen, *v. a.* पौरीकृ, नागरीकृ, स्वाधीनीकृ, स्वतन्त्रीकृ, स्ववशीकृ.

To denominate, *v. a.* अभिधा (c. 3. -दधाति -धातुं), आख्या (c. 2. -ख्याति -तुं), कृत् (c. 10. कीर्त्तयति -यितुं), प्रकृत्, सङ्कृत्; प्रवच् (c. 2.

-चष्टे), उदाहृ (c. 1. -हरति -हर्तुं), भण् (c. 1. भणति -णितुं), नाम कृ.

DENOMINATED, *p. p.* प्रोक्तः -क्ता -क्तं, अभिहितः -ता -तं, संज्ञितः -ता -तं, स्मृतः -ता -तं, उदाहृतः -ता -तं, परिकीर्त्तितः -ता -तं, आख्यातः -ता -तं, अनूक्तः -क्ता -क्तं. The following occur at the end of compounds: अभिधः -धा -धं, अभिधानः -ना -नं, नामा -मा -म (न्), नामधेयः -या -यं, आख्यः -ख्या -ख्यं.

DENOMINATION, *s.* नाम *n.* (न्), नामधेयः -यं, अभिधा -धानं -धेयं, संज्ञा, आख्या, अभिख्या, अधिवचनं, लक्षणं, उपाधिः *m.*, ख्यातिः *f.*

DENOMINATIVE, *a.* अभिधायी -यिनी -यि (न्) -यिकः -का -कं, अभिधेयः -या -यं, नामकारी -रिणी -रि (न्), आख्यायकः -का -कं, संज्ञादायकः -का -कं.

DENOMINATOR, *s.* (Giver of a name) नामदाता *m.* (तृ), नामकृत्.—(Of a fraction) हरः, हारः -रकः, हारकाङ्कः; 'reduced to a common denominator,' सवर्णितः -ता -तं.

DENOTATION, *s.* निर्देशः -शनं, सूचनं, संसूचनं, उपलक्षणं, चिह्नकरणं.

To DENOTE, *v. a.* सूच् (c. 10. सूचयति -यितुं), संसूच्; निर्दिश् (c. 6. -दिशति -देष्टुं), उद्दिश्, प्रदिश्, विनिर्दिश्; लक्ष् (c. 10. लक्षयति -यितुं), लक्षीकृ, दृश् in caus. (दर्शयति -यितुं).

DENOTED, *p. p.* सूचितः -ता -तं, संसूचितः -ता -तं, निर्दिष्टः -ष्टा -ष्टं, लक्षितः -ता -तं, उपलक्षितः -ता -तं, दर्शितः -ता -तं, प्रदर्शितः -ता -तं.

DENOTING, DENOTATIVE, *a.* सूचकः -का -कं, दर्शकः -का -कं, वाचकः -का -कं.

DENOUEMENT, *s.* (Of a drama) कार्य्यं, निर्व्वहणं, निष्ठा.

To DENOUNCE, *v. a.* प्रकाशं भर्त्स् (c. 10. भर्त्सयति -यितुं), घोषणापूर्व्वं तर्ज् (c. 1. तर्जति -र्जितुं) or आक्रुश् (c. 1. -क्रोशति -क्रोष्टुं) or अभिशप् (c. 1. -शपति -शप्तुं); अमङ्गलं प्रकाश् in caus. (-काशयति -यितुं); अनिष्टं ख्या in caus. (ख्यापयति -यितुं) or विद् in caus. (वेदयति -यितुं).

DENOUNCEMENT, *s.* प्रकाशभर्त्सनं, प्रकाशतर्ज्जनं, घोषणापूर्व्वं तर्ज्जनं or आक्रोशनं or अभिशापः, अनिष्टख्यापनं, अमङ्गलघोषणा.

DENOUNCER, *s.* अनिष्टावेदकः, अनिष्टख्यापकः, अमङ्गलप्रकाशकः, प्रकाशं भर्त्सयिता *m.* (तृ) or तर्ज्जनकृत् or अभिशापकः.

DENSE, *a.* घनः -ना -नं, स्थूलः -ला -लं, सान्द्रः -न्द्रा -न्द्रं, पीवरः -रा -रं, सुसंहतः -ता -तं, अविरलः -ला -लं, निबिडः -डा -डं, निरन्तरः -रा -रं -रालः -ला -लं, अनन्तरः -रा -रं, दृढसन्धिः -न्धिः -न्धि, निर्विवरः -रा -रं, दृढः -ढा -ढं.

DENSITY, *s.* घनता -त्वं, स्थूलता, स्थौल्यं, सान्द्रता, पीवरत्वं, संहतत्वं, निबिडत्वं, नैबिड्यं, नैरन्तर्य्यं, दृढता, दार्ढ्यं.

DENT, *s.* प्रहारचिह्नं, आघातचिह्नं, भङ्गः, ऊर्म्मिः *f.* *See* DINT.

DENTAL, *a.* दन्त्यः -न्त्या -न्त्यं, दान्तः -न्ती -न्तं, दन्ती -न्तिनी -न्ति (न्).—(Letter) दन्त्यं, दन्तद्वारा उच्चारितम् अक्षरं.

DENTATED, DENTED, DENTICULATED, *a.* दन्ती -न्तिनी -न्ति (न्), दन्तुरः -रा -रं, अनुक्रकचः -चा -चं, भङ्गुरः -रा -रं.

DENTIFRICE, *s.* दन्तपवनं, दन्तशोधनं, दन्तधावनं, दन्तशाणं, माधवी, मिशिः *f.*

DENTIST, *s.* दन्तचिकित्सकः, दन्तवैद्यः, दन्तचिकित्सोपजीवी *m.* (न्), दन्तरोगविद्.

DENTITION, *s.* दन्तोद्भेदः, दन्तोद्भेदकालः, दन्तवृद्धिः *f.*

To DENUDATE or DENUDE, *v. a.* नग्नीकृ, विवस्त्र (nom. विवस्त्रयति -यितुं), विकोष (nom. विकोषयति -यितुं), उच्छद् (c. 10. -छादयति -यितुं) हृ (c. 1. हरति, हर्तुं), शून्यीकृ, रिक्तीकृ; 'a tree of its leaves,' निष्पत्र (nom. निष्पत्रयति -यितुं).

DENUDATION, *s.* नग्नीकरणं, विवस्त्रीकरणं, विकोषीकरणं, हरणं.

DENUDED, *p. p.* नग्नीकृतः -ता -तं, विकोषः -षा -षं, हृतः -ता -तं.

DENUNCIATION, DENUNCIATOR, *s.* *See* DENOUNCEMENT, DENOUNCER.

To DENY, *v. a.* निह्नु (c. 2. -ह्नुते -ह्नोतुं), अपह्नु, प्रत्याख्या (c. 2. -ख्याति

-तुं), अन्तःख्या, अतिख्या; अपवद् (c. 1. -वदति -दितुं), अपलप् (c. 1. -लपति -पितुं), अपवच् (c. 2. -वक्ति -क्तुं), प्रत्यादिश् (c. 6. -दिशति -देष्टुं), निरस् (c. 4. -अस्यति, असितुं), अपज्ञा (c. 9. -जानीते -ज्ञातुं), अस्वीकृ.

To DEOBSTRUCT, *v. a.* प्रतिबन्धान् हृ (c. 1. हरति, हर्तुं) or विनी (c. 1. -नयति -नेतुं), निर्विघ्न (nom. निर्विघ्नयति -यितुं), निर्विघ्नीकृ, मुच् (c. 6. मुञ्चति, मोक्तुं), विशुध् in caus. (-शोधयति -यितुं).

DEODAND, *s.* ईश्वराय देयं, देवदेयं, देवोपहारः, अपमृत्युप्रायश्चित्तं.

To DEOPPILATE, *v. a.* प्रतिबन्धं or नाडीं हृ (c. 1. हरति, हर्तुं), विशोधनं कृ.

DEOPPILATION, *s.* प्रतिबन्धहरणं, नाडहरणं, विशोधनं, निबन्धनाशनं.

DEOPPILATIVE, *a.* नाडघ्नः -घ्नी -घ्नं, प्रतिबन्धहारी -रिणी -रि (न्).

DEOSCULATION, *s.* चुम्बनं, परिरंसा, निक्षणं, निमित्तकं.

To DEPAINT, *v. a.* वर्ण् (c. 10. वर्णयति -यितुं), चित्र् (c. 10. चित्रयति -यितुं).

To DEPART, *v. n.* (Go away) अपगम् (c. 1. -गच्छति -गन्तुं), व्यपगम्, गम्; अपया (c. 2. -याति -तुं), व्यपया, प्रया, अपे (c. 2. -एति -तुं with अप, अपैति -तुं), व्यपे, विप्रे, वी (व्येति -तुं), अपसृ (c. 1. -सरति -सर्त्तुं), अपक्रम् (c. 1. -क्रामति -क्रमितुं), व्यपक्रम्, उत्क्रम्, अपसृप् (c. 1. -सर्पति -सर्प्तुं), चल् (c. 1. चलति -लितुं), प्रस्था (c. 1. -तिष्ठति -स्थातुं), विप्रस्था, सम्प्रस्था, दूरीभू, उज्झ् (c. 6. उज्झति -ज्झितुं).—(Desist from) निवृत् (c. 1. -वर्त्तते -र्त्तितुं).—(Die) प्रे (c. 2. -एति -तुं with प्र, प्रैति -तुं), देहम् उत्सृज् (c. 6. -सृजति -स्रष्टुं) or त्यज् (c. 1. त्यजति, त्यक्तुं), शरीराद् अपगम्, विपद् (c. 4. -पद्यते -पत्तुं), लोकान्तरं गम्.

To DEPART, *v. a.* उत्सृज् (c. 6. -सृजति -स्रष्टुं), त्यज् (c. 1. त्यजति, त्यक्तुं).—(Separate, distribute) वियुज् (c. 7. -युनक्ति -योक्तुं), विभज् (c. 1. -भजति -भक्तुं).

DEPART, *s.* अपगमः, व्यपगमः, विगमः, प्रयाणं.—(Death) अपगमः, संस्थितिः *f.*

DEPARTED, *p. p.* गतः -ता -तं, अपगतः -ता -तं, व्यपगतः -ता -तं, निर्गतः -ता -तं, अपेतः -ता -तं, व्यपेतः -ता -तं, प्रयातः -ता -तं, प्रस्थितः -ता -तं, अपसारितः -ता -तं, अपासृतः -ता -तं; 'one who has departed from virtue,' धर्म्मव्यपेतः -ता -तं.—(Dead) प्रेतः -ता -तं, प्रमीतः -ता -तं, व्यतीतः -ता -तं, संस्थितः -ता -तं, निर्वाणः -णा -णं, लोकान्तरगतः -ता -तं, अपविद्धलोकः -का -कं.

DEPARTER, *s.* पृथक्करणद्वारा धातुशोधकः, परिच्छेदेन धातुपरीक्षकः.

DEPARTMENT, *s.* (Allotment, division) विभागः, प्रविभागः, परिच्छेदः, विच्छेदः, भागः.—(Division of science, literature, &c.) देशः, अङ्गं, विषयः, प्रकरणं.—(Office, business) अधिकारः, नियोगः, कर्म्म *n.* (न्).—(Province) देशः, विषयः, मण्डलं, ग्रामशतं.

DEPARTURE, *s.* अपगमः, व्यपगमः, विगमः, गमनं, अपायः, प्रयाणं, अपयानं, प्रस्थानं, सम्प्रस्थानं, अपासरणं, अपसरणं, अपक्रमः -मणं, उत्क्रमणं, अत्ययः, निर्गमः, विसर्गः, वियोगः.—(Death) अपगमः, अत्ययः, संस्थितिः *f.*, तनुत्यागः, जीवोत्सर्गः, प्रयाणं.—(Abandonment) त्यागः, निवृत्तिः *f.*, प्रोज्झनं.

To DEPASTURE, *v. a.* सम्भक्ष् (c. 10. -भक्षयति -यितुं), संखाद् (c. 1. -खादति -दितुं).

To DEPAUPERATE, *v. a.* दरिद्रीकृ, कृपणीकृ, कृश (nom. कृशयति -यितुं), कृशीकृ, क्षि in caus. (क्षपयति -यितुं), क्षीणीकृ, दीनं -नां -नं कृ.

DEPECTIBLE, *a.* श्यानः -ना -नं, सान्द्रः -न्द्रा -न्द्रं, दुःखश्लेषः -षा -षं.

To DEPEND, *v. n.* (Hang from) लम्ब् (c. 1. लम्बते -म्बितुं), अवलम्ब्, प्रलम्ब्.—(Be dependent on, rest on, rely on) अवलम्ब्, समालम्ब्; आश्रि (c. 1. -श्रयति -ते -यितुं), संश्रि, समाश्रि, उपाश्रि; अधीनः -ना -नं or आयत्तः -त्ता -त्तम् अस्, वशीभू; 'The mind depends on the body,' बुद्धिः शरीरम् आश्रयति.—(Be connected with)

सम्बन्ध् in pass. (-बध्यते).—(Depend on another for support) उपजीव् (c. 1. -जीवति -वितुं), अनुजीव्.—(Be in suspense) दोल (nom. दोलायते), विलम्ब्; 'I depend entirely on you,' सर्वं त्वयि समर्पयामि.

DEPENDANCE, DEPENDENCE, *s.* (Reliance) आश्रयः, उपाश्रयः, संश्रयः, समाश्रयः, अयणं, आयः, अवलम्बनं, निष्ठा, तन्त्रता, आशयः, विश्वासः, प्रत्ययः, विश्रम्भः, समाश्वासः; 'mutual dependence,' अन्योन्याश्रयः.—(State of being at the disposal of another) पराधीनता, परायत्तत्वं, पराश्रितत्वं, परवशित्वं, परवशता, परतन्त्रत्वं, पारतन्त्र्यं, अस्वातन्त्र्यं, भक्तिः *f.*—(Connexion) सम्बन्धः -न्धित्वं, अभिसम्बन्धः, प्रबन्धः, प्रसङ्गः, प्रसक्तिः *f.*, अनुषङ्गः, समन्वयः, सम्पर्कः.—(Persons or things of which one has the disposal) भृत्यः, उपजीवी *m.* (न्), स्वद्रव्यं, स्वं.

DEPENDANT, DEPENDENT, *a.* (Depending on) आश्रितः -ता -तं, संश्रितः -ता -तं, उपाश्रितः -ता -तं, अवलम्बी -म्बिनी -म्बि (न्), अवलम्बितः -ता -तं, अधीनः -ना -नं, अभ्यधीनः -ना -नं, आयत्तः -त्ता -त्तं, वशः -शा -शं, तन्त्रः -न्त्रा -न्त्रं, निघ्नः -घ्ना -घ्नं, सक्तः -क्ता -क्तं, निबद्धः -द्धा -द्धं; 'dependent on kings,' राजसंश्रयः -या -यं; 'dependent on riches,' अर्थनिबन्धनः -ना -नं; 'a king's fortune is dependent on his minister,' सचिवायत्ता राजश्रीः.—(At the disposal of another) पराधीनः -ना -नं, पराश्रितः -ता -तं, परायत्तः -त्ता -त्तं, परतन्त्रः -न्त्रा -न्त्रं, परवशः -शा -शं, परवान् -वती -वत् (त्), उपजीवी -विनी -वि (न्), नाथवान् -वती -वत् (त्), गृह्यकः -का -कं, अस्वतन्त्रः -न्त्रा -न्त्रं.—(Hanging down) लम्बितः -ता -तं, प्रलम्बः -म्बा -म्बं, विलम्बमानः -ना -नं.

DEPENDANT, *s.* आश्रितः, अनुजीवी *m.* (न्), उपजीवी *m.*, भाक्तिकः, भृत्यः, सम्भार्य्यः, परिवारः, परायत्तजनः.

DEPERDITION, *s.* नाशः, विनाशः, क्षयः, अपायः, अपचयः, क्षतिः *f.*, ध्वंसः.

To DEPICT, *v. a.* वर्ण् (c. 10. वर्णयति -यितुं), अनुवर्ण्, उपवर्ण्, संवर्ण्; विलिख् (c. 6. -लिखति -लेखितुं), आलिख्; निर्दिश् (c. 6. -दिशति -देष्टुं), समुद्दिश्.

DEPICTED, *p. p.* वर्णितः -ता -तं, आलिखितः -ता -तं, निर्दिष्टः -ष्टा -ष्टं.

DEPILATION, *s.* लोमहरणं, रोमहरणं, निष्केशीकरणं, उल्लुञ्चनं.

DEPILATORY, *a.* लोमहृत् *m.f.n.*, रोमहारी -रिणी -रि (न्), केशनाशकः -का -कं.

DEPILOUS, *a.* रोमहीनः -ना -नं, लोमरहितः -ता -तं, अकेशः -शा -शं.

DEPLETION, *s.* शून्यीकरणं, शून्यत्वं -ता, रिक्तता, अपूर्णता, अपूरणं.

DEPLORABLE, *a.* शोचनीयः -या -यं, शोच्यः -च्या -च्यं, विलपनीयः -या -यं, अनुकम्प्यः -म्प्या -म्प्यं, क्रन्दनीयः -या -यं, शोकमयः -यी -यं, दैवोपहतः -ता -तं.

DEPLORABLENESS, *s.* शोचनीयता, शोच्यत्वं, दौर्गत्यं, दैवोपहतत्वं.

DEPLORABLY, *adv.* शोचनीयं, अनुकम्पनीयं, शोच्यप्रकारेण, कृपणं.

DEPLORATION, *s.* शोचनं, विलपनं, परिदेवनं, क्रन्दनं, रोदनं, क्रुष्टं.

To DEPLORE, *v. a.* शुच् (c. 1. शोचति -चितुं), अनुशुच्; विलप् (c. 1. -लपति -पितुं), परिदेव् (c. 1. -देवति -ते -वितुं), क्रन्द् (c. 1. क्रन्दति -न्दितुं), आक्रन्द्; रुद् (c. 2. रोदिति -तुं), अभिक्रुश् (c. 1. -क्रोशति -क्रोष्टुं).

DEPLORER, *s.* अनुशोचकः, विलापकारी *m.* (न्), परिदेवकः, रोदनकृत्.

To DEPLOY, *v. a.* (Troops) सैन्यव्यूहान् विस्तृ in caus. (-स्तारयति -यितुं).

DEPLUMATION, *s.* पक्षोत्पाटनं, पर्णोत्पाटनं, पक्षहरणं, निष्पक्षीकरणं.

To DEPLUME, *v. a.* पक्षान् or पर्णान् उत्पट् in caus. (-पाटयति -यितुं) or हृ (c. 1. हरति, हर्तुं), निष्पक्षीकृ, पक्षोल्लुञ्चनं कृ.

To DEPONE, *v. a.* न्यस् (c. 4. -अस्यति -असितुं), निक्षिप् (c. 6. -क्षिपति -क्षेप्तुं).

DEPONENT, *s.* (In law) साक्षी *m.* (न्), प्रमाता *m.* (तृ).—(Verb) अकर्त्तरि क्रिया, अकर्म्मक्रिया, आत्मनेपदे क्रिया.

To DEPOPULATE, *v. a.* निर्जनीकृ, विजनीकृ, शून्यं कृ, अरण्यं कृ, शून्यारण्यं कृ, नरशून्यं -न्यां -न्यं कृ, उपपीड् (c. 10. -पीडयति -यितुं), बाध् (c. 1. बाधते -धितुं), प्रबाध्, निर्दह् (c. 1. -दहति -दग्धुं), अभिमृद् (c. 1. -मर्दति -र्दितुं).

DEPOPULATION, *s.* निर्जनीकरणं, नरशून्यकरणं, अरण्यकरणं, विप्लवः, उपप्लवः, उपपीडनं, अवमर्द्दः, उच्छेदनं.

DEPOPULATOR, *s.* उपपीडकः, बाधकः, विप्लवकारी *m.* (न्), उच्छेदकः.

To DEPORT ONE'S SELF, *v. a.* चर् (c. 1. चरति -रितुं), आचर्, व्यवहृ (c. 1. -हरति -हर्तुं), वृत् (c. 1. वर्त्तते -र्त्तितुं), वृत्तिम् अनुष्ठा (-तिष्ठति -ष्ठातुं).

DEPORT, DEPORTMENT, *s.* वृत्तिः *f.*, व्यवहारः, आचारः, आचरणं, रीतिः *f.*, गतिः *f.*, स्थितिः *f.*, चेष्टितं, चरित्रं, चरितं, उत्साहः.

DEPORTATION, *s.* प्रवासनं, विवासनं, विवासकरणं, प्रव्राजनं.

DEPOSAL, *s.* राज्यभ्रंशः, राज्यप्रभ्रंशः, राज्यभङ्गः, राज्यपातनं.

To DEPOSE, *v. a.* (Lay down) न्यस् (c. 4. -अस्यति -असितुं), निधा (c. 3. -दधाति -धातुं), निक्षिप् (c. 6. -क्षिपति -क्षेप्तुं).—(Degrade from a high station) पदात् or अधिकाराद् भ्रंश् in caus. (भ्रंशयति -यितुं) or च्यु in caus. (च्यावयति -यितुं) or पत् in caus. (पातयति -यितुं).—(In law) स्वयं वद् (c. 1. वदति -दितुं), साक्ष्यं दा (c. 3. ददाति, दातुं), प्रमाणं दा.

DEPOSED, *p. p.* भ्रष्टराज्यः -ज्या -ज्यं, राज्यभ्रष्टः -ष्टा -ष्टं, राज्यच्युतः -ता -तं.

To DEPOSIT, *v. a.* न्यस् (c. 4. -अस्यति -असितुं), उपन्यस्, सन्न्यस्, प्रतिन्यस्; निक्षिप् (c. 6. -क्षिपति -क्षेप्तुं), उपनिक्षिप्, विनिक्षिप्; निधा (c. 3. -दधाति -धातुं), आधा, पण् (c. 1. पणते -णितुं), ऋ in caus. (अर्पयति -यितुं), स्था in caus. (स्थापयति -यितुं), न्यासीकृ, आधीकृ.

DEPOSIT, *s.* न्यासः, निक्षेपः, उपन्यासः, उपनिक्षेपः, उपनिधिः *m.*, उपनिधानं, औपनिधिकं, आधिः *m.*, आधानं, अन्वाधिः *m.*, विन्यासः, पणः; 'return of a deposit,' प्रतिदानं.—(Sediment) खलं, किट्टं, शेषः.—(Of a river) कालुष्यं.

DEPOSITARY, *s.* न्यासधारी *m.* (न्), न्यासग्राही *m.* (न्), निक्षेपधारी *m.*—(Object of trust) विश्वासस्थानं, विश्वासपात्रं, विश्वासभूमिः *f.*

DEPOSITED, *p. p.* न्यस्तः -स्ता -स्तं, निक्षिप्तः -प्ता -प्तं, उपन्यस्तः -स्ता -स्तं, विन्यस्तः -स्ता -स्तं, निहितः -ता -तं, प्रणिहितः -ता -तं, उपनिहितः -ता -तं, आहितः -ता -तं, उपहितः -ता -तं, अर्पितः -ता -तं, स्थापितः -ता -तं, अधिष्ठितः -ता -तं, आधीकृतः -ता -तं.

DEPOSITION, *s.* (In law) स्वयमुक्तिः *f.*, साक्ष्यं, साक्षित्वं, प्रमाणं.—(Degradation from sovereignty, &c.) राज्यभ्रंशः, छत्रभङ्गः, राज्यच्युतिः *f.*, पदात् or अधिकारात् प्रभ्रंशनं or पातनं.

DEPOSITOR, *s.* निक्षेप्ता *m.* (तृ), न्यासकर्त्ता *m.* (र्तृ), आधीकर्त्ता *m.*, स्थापकः.

DEPOSITORY, *s.* आधारः, निधिः *m.*, निधानं, आशयः, आस्पदं, अधिश्रयः.

DÉPÔT, *s.* आगारं, युद्धसामग्र्यागारं, सैन्यागारं, सैन्यनिवासस्थानं.

DEPRAVATION, *s.* (Act of depraving) दूषणं, भ्रष्टीकरणं.—(State) दुष्टता.

To DEPRAVE, *v. a.* दुष् in caus. (दूषयति -यितुं), सन्दुष्, प्रतिदुष्; नश् in caus. (नाशयति -यितुं), भ्रंश् in caus. (भ्रंशयति -यितुं), भ्रष्टीकृ; च्यु in caus. (च्यावयति -यितुं), शठीकृ, विकृ; 'to become depraved,' दुष् (c. 4. दुष्यति).

DEPRAVED, *p. p.* दुष्टः -ष्टा -ष्टं, अन्तर्दुष्टः -ष्टा -ष्टं, विप्रदुष्टः -ष्टा -ष्टं, भ्रष्टः -ष्टा -ष्टं, दुष्टभावः -वा -वं, दुष्टमतिः -तिः -ति, दुराचारः -रा -रं, दुरात्मा -त्मा -त्म (न्), पापचेताः -ताः -तः (स्), नष्टधीः -धीः -धि, शठः -ठा -ठं, खलः -ला -लं.

DEPRAVER, *s.* दूषकः, प्रतिदूषकः, दूषणः, नाशकः, भ्रंशकारी *m.* (न्).

DEPRAVITY, DEPRAVEDNESS, *s.* दुष्टता, विप्रदुष्टता, अन्तर्दुष्टता, दुष्टभावता,

दौरात्म्यं, भ्रष्टता, दुराचारत्वं, शाठ्यं, शठता, कुसृतिः *f.*, नष्टत्वं, दौर्जन्यं, स्वभावदौर्जन्यं, अधमाचारत्वं.

To DEPRECATE, *v. a.* प्रार्थनाद्वारेण निवृ in caus. (-वारयति -यितुं) or अपवृत् in caus. (-वर्त्तयति -यितुं) or निवृत् in caus.; मा भूयात् or मा ऽभूद् इति प्रार्थ् (c. 10. -अर्थयते -ति -यितुं), अमुकदुःखाद् मुक्तिर् भूयाद् इति प्रार्थ्.—(Beg for pardon) मे क्षन्तुम् अर्हसीति प्रार्थ्.

DEPRECATION, *s.* (Prayer against evil) दुःखनिवारणार्थं प्रार्थना or याच्ञा, मा ऽभूदिति प्रार्थना.—(Begging pardon) क्षमस्व or क्षमेथा इति प्रार्थना.

DEPRECATIVE, DEPRECATORY, *a.* दुःखनिवारणार्थप्रार्थनविशिष्टः -ष्टा -ष्टं, मा ऽभूद् इत्यर्थप्रार्थनाकारी -रिणी -रि (न्), अनिष्टनिवारकः -का -कं.

To DEPRECIATE, *v. a.* अपकृष् (c. 1. -कर्षति -क्रष्टुं), अवमन् (c. 4. -मन्यते -मन्तुं), लघु मन्, लघूकृ, मूल्यं न्यूनीकृ or न्यून (c. 10. -नयति -यितुं) or ऊन (nom. ऊनयति -यितुं), or अल्पीकृ, अल्पमूल्यं -ल्यां -ल्यं कृ.

DEPRECIATION, *s.* अपकर्षः -र्षणं, लघूकरणं, न्यूनीकरणं, अवमानं, ह्रासः.

To DEPREDATE, *v. a.* उपद्रु (c. 1. -द्रवति -द्रोतुं), अभिद्रु, उपप्लु (c. 1. -प्लवते -प्लोतुं), विप्लु, अपहृ (c. 1. -हरति -हर्तुं), लुण्ट् (c. 1. लुण्टति -ण्टितुं c. 10. लुण्टयति -यितुं), लुठ् (c. 10. लोठयति -यितुं), लोप्त्रं हृ.

DEPREDATION, *s.* उपद्रवः, विप्लवः, उपप्लवः, अपहारः, हरणं, लोप्त्रग्रहणं.

DEPREDATOR, *s.* उपद्रवी *m.* (न्), विप्लवकारी *m.* (न्), अपहारकृत्, हारकः.

To DEPREHEND, *v. a.* (Catch) ग्रह् (c. 9. गृह्णाति, ग्रहीतुं), धृ (c. 1. धरति, धर्त्तुं), अकस्माद् आसद् (c. 10. -सादयति -यितुं) or उपस्था (c. 1. -तिष्ठति -स्थातुं).—(Find out) ज्ञा (c. 9. जानाति, ज्ञातुं), विद् (c. 2. वेत्ति, वेदितुं), निरूप् (c. 10. -रूपयति -यितुं).

DEPREHENSIBLE, *a.* ग्रहणीयः -या -यं, धरणीयः -या -यं, धीगम्यः -म्या -म्यं.

DEPREHENSION, *s.* अकस्माद्धरणं, अकस्माद्ग्रहणं, अकस्मादासादनं.

To DEPRESS, *v. a.* अवनम् in caus. (-नामयति -यितुं), अपकृष् (c. 1. -कर्षति -क्रष्टुं), अवपीड् (c. 10. -पीडयति -यितुं), पत् in caus. (पातयति -यितुं), अधःपत्; अवसद् in caus. (-सादयति -यितुं), भ्रंश् in caus. (भ्रंशयति -यितुं), अपध्वंस् in caus. (-ध्वंसयति -यितुं), अधःकृ, नम्रीकृ.—(Dispirit) विषण्णीकृ, म्लानीकृ, विषद् in caus.

DEPRESSED, *p. p.* अपकृष्टः -ष्टा -ष्टं, अवनामितः -ता -तं, अवसादितः -ता -तं, पातितः -ता -तं, अवगाढः -ढा -ढं, निम्नः -म्ना -म्नं.—(In spirits) विषण्णः -ण्णा -ण्णं, अवसन्नः -न्ना -न्नं, विषादी -दिनी -दि (न्), खिन्नः -न्ना -न्नं, दीनमनस्कः -स्का -स्कं.

DEPRESSION, *s.* अपकर्षः -र्षणं, अवनामः, पातनं, अधःपातनं, अपध्वंसः, अवपीडनं.—(Of spirits) विषादः, अवसादः, अवसन्नता, उद्वेगः, खेदः, म्लानिः *f.*, ग्लानिः *f.*, औत्सुक्यं.

DEPRESSOR, *s.* अवनामकः, अपकर्षकः, अवसादकः, अवपीडकः, पातकः.

DEPRIVATION, *s.* हरणं, अपहारः, वियोगः, लोपः, भ्रंशः, हानिः *f.*, अपायः, क्षतिः *f.*, क्षयः, उपक्षयः, अपचयः, च्युतिः *f.*, ध्वंसः, परित्यागः, नाशः.

To DEPRIVE, *v. a.* हृ (c. 1. हरति, हर्त्तुं), अपहृ; भ्रंश् in caus. (भ्रंशयति -यितुं) with abl. of the thing. च्यु in caus. (च्यावयति -यितुं) with abl. c., वियुज् in caus. (-योजयति -यितुं), विप्रयुज् with abl. c.; अपनी (c. 1. -नयति -नेतुं), लुप् (c. 6. लुम्पति, लोप्तुं, caus. लोपयति -यितुं), विनाकृ; 'to be deprived of,' हा in pass. (हीयते), परिहा in pass. with inst. c., भ्रंश् (c. 4. भ्रश्यति, भ्रंशितुं) with abl. c., च्यु (c. 1. च्यवते, च्योतुं) with abl. c., वियुज् in pass. (-युज्यते) with inst. c.

DEPRIVED, *p. p.* हृतः -ता -तं, अपहृतः -ता -तं, हीनः -ना -नं, परिहीणः -णा -णं, प्रहीणः -णा -णं, वियुक्तः -क्ता -क्तं, विप्रयुक्तः -क्ता -क्तं, लुप्तः -प्ता -प्तं, रहितः -ता -तं, विरहितः -ता -तं, वर्जितः -ता -तं, विनाकृतः -ता -तं, परित्यक्तः -क्ता -क्तं; 'deprived of one's right,' हृताधिकारः -रा -रं; 'deprived of reason,' नष्टबुद्धिः -द्धिः -द्धि, अपहृतविज्ञानः -ना -नं, लुप्तप्रतिभः -भा -भं; 'deprived of life,' प्रहीणजीवितः -ता -तं.

DEPTH, *s.* गम्भीरता -त्वं, गाम्भीर्य्यं, गभीरता, अगाधता -त्वं, निम्नता, अधोगतत्वं, घनता, नीचता.—(Deep place) गम्भीरस्थानं, नीचपदं, अगाधः, उदरं, गह्वरं; 'depth of hell,' पातालोदरं.—(Abyss) अगाधदरी, अतलस्पर्शरन्ध्रं, नरकः.—(Deep sea) महोदधिः *m.*—(In measurement) वेधः -धनं; 'mean depth,' समवेधः.—(Depth of winter) शिशिरमध्यं, मध्यशिशिरं; 'in the depth of winter,' शीतकालमध्ये.

To DEPURATE, DEPURE, *v. a.* निर्म्मलीकृ, विमलीकृ, शुध् in caus. (शोधयति -यितुं), पू (c. 9. पुनाति, पवितुं), पवित्रीकृ, शुचीकृ, परिष्कृ.

DEPURATE, *a.* निर्म्मलः -ला -लं, विमलः -ला -लं, पूतः -ता -तं, पवित्रः -त्रा -त्रं, शोधितः -ता -तं, शुचिः -चिः -चि, धूतकल्मषः -षा -षं.

DEPURATION, *s.* निर्म्मलीकरणं, मलापकर्षणं, पवित्रीकरणं, शोधनं.

DEPUTATION, *s.* (Act of deputing) नियोजनं, विनियोगः, प्रेरणं.—(Persons deputed) नियोगिनः *m. pl.*, नियुक्ताः *m. pl.*, नियोगिनां समूहः or गणः.

To DEPUTE, *v. a.* नियुज् (c. 7. -युनक्ति -योक्तुं caus. -योजयति -यितुं), विनियुज्, प्रेर् (c. 10. -ईरयति -यितुं), समादिश् (c. 6. -दिशति -देष्टुं), व्यादिश्.

DEPUTED, *p. p.* नियुक्तः -क्ता -क्तं, नियोजितः -ता -तं, विनियुक्तः -क्ता -क्तं, विनियोजितः -ता -तं, प्रेरितः -ता -तं, समादिष्टः -ष्टा -ष्टं.

DEPUTY, *s.* प्रतिनिधिः *m.*, प्रतिपुरुषः, नियोगी *m.* (न्), नियुक्तः, प्रतिहस्तः -स्तकः.

To DERACINATE, *v. a.* उन्मूल् (c. 10. -मूलयति -यितुं), उत्पट् (c. 10. -पाटयति -यितुं), उच्छिद् (c. 7. -छिनत्ति -छेत्तुं), उत्खन् (c. 1. -खनति -नितुं), समूलोद्धरणं कृ.

To DERAIGN, *v. a.* प्रमाणीकृ, सत्याकृ, स्थिरीकृ, दृढीकृ, उपपद् in caus. (-पादयति -यितुं).

DERAIGNMENT, *s.* प्रमाणीकरणं, सत्यापनं, उपपादनं.—(Apostacy) धर्म्मत्यागः.

To DERANGE, *v. a.* पर्य्यस् (c. 4. -अस्यति -असितुं), व्यस्, विक्षिप् (c. 6. -क्षिपति -क्षेप्तुं), विक्षुभ् in caus. (-क्षोभयति -यितुं), क्रमं भञ्ज् (c. 7. भनक्ति, भंक्तुं) or उपहन् (c. 2. -हन्ति -न्तुं) or विलुप् (c. 6. -लुम्पति -लोप्तुं), सङ्करीकृ, आकुलीकृ, विभ्रम् in caus. (-भ्रमयति -यितुं).

DERANGED, *p. p.* व्यस्तः -स्ता -स्तं, विक्षिप्तः -प्ता -प्तं, असंस्थितः -ता -तं, अनवस्थितः -ता -तं, अव्यवस्थितः -ता -तं, व्यापन्नः -न्ना -न्नं, भग्नक्रमः -मा -मं, अस्वस्थः -स्था -स्थं, अस्तव्यस्तः -स्ता -स्तं.—(In mind) विपरीतचेताः -ताः -तः (स्), भ्रान्तमनाः -नाः -नः (स्), उन्मत्तः -त्ता -त्तं.

DERANGEMENT, *s.* उत्क्रमः, व्युत्क्रमः, भग्नप्रक्रमः, अक्रमः, असंस्थानं, अव्यवस्था, अनवस्थितत्वं, वैलक्षण्यं, व्यस्तता, विसूचता, विप्लवः, विक्षिप्तता.—(Of mind) चित्तविप्लवः, चित्तविभ्रमः, मतिविपर्य्ययः.

DERELICTION, *s.* त्यागः, परित्यागः, उत्त्यागः, विरहः, उत्सर्जनं, अपायः.

To DERIDE, *v. a.* अवहस् (c. 1. -हसति -सितुं), अपहस्, उपहस्; अपहास्यदीकृ, अवहासभूमिं कृ; भर्त्स् (c. 10. भर्त्सयते -ति -यितुं), उत्स्मि (c. 1. -स्मयते -स्मेतुं), अवगर्ह् (c. 1. -गर्हते -र्हितुं), अवज्ञा (c. 9. -जानाति -ज्ञातुं), अवक्षिप् (c. 6. -क्षिपति -क्षेप्तुं).

DERIDED, *p. p.* उपहसितः -ता -तं, अवहसितः -ता -तं, विगर्हितः -ता -तं.

DERIDER, *s.* उपहासकः, परिहासकर्त्ता *m.* (र्तृ), अवक्षेपकः.

DERIDINGLY, *adv.* परिहासेन, उपहासेन, सावक्षेपं, हास्यपुरःसरं.

DERISION, *s.* उपहासः, अवहासः, अपहासः, परिहासः, हास्यं, अवक्षेपः, उत्प्रासनं, अवज्ञा, अवहेला, अवमानं, वञ्चना, वक्रूक्ति:.

DERISIVE, *a.* परिहासकः -का -कं, हासकरः -रा -रं, अवक्षेपकः -का -कं.

DERIVABLE, *a.* प्रापणीयः -या -यं, आनयनीयः -या -यं, उत्पादनीयः -या -यं, व्युत्पादनीयः -या -यं, निष्पादनीयः -या -यं, यौगिकः -की -कं.

DERIVATION, *s.* आनयनं, उत्पत्तिः *f.*, व्युत्पत्तिः *f.*, निष्पत्तिः *f.*, अपवाहः.—(Origin) योनिः *f.*, उद्भवः, सम्भवः, प्रभवः, निर्गमः, मूलं.—(Of a word) शब्दोत्पत्तिः *f.*, धातुव्युत्पत्तिः, शब्दयोनिः *f.*

DERIVATIVE, *a.* व्युत्पन्नः -न्ना -न्नं, यौगिकः -की -कं, औत्सर्गिकः -की -कं.

DERIVATIVE, *s.* व्युत्पन्नशब्दः, उत्पन्नशब्दः, मूलाद् आनीतं यत्किञ्चित्.

To DERIVE, *v. a.* मूलाद् आनी (c. 1. -नयति -नेतुं) or निर्णी or नी or अपवह् (c. 1. -वहति -वोढुं), निष्कृष् (c. 1. -कर्षति -क्रष्टुं); उत्पत्तिं कृ, व्युत्पत्तिं कृ; निर्गम् in caus. (-गमयति -यितुं), उद्भू in caus. (-भावयति -यितुं), सम्भू in caus.; निःसृ in caus. (-सारयति -यितुं), जन् in caus. (जनयति -यितुं).—(Communicate by transmission) सञ्चर् in caus. (-चारयति -यितुं).

To DERIVE, *v. n.* उत्पद् (c. 4. -पद्यते -पत्तुं), व्युत्पद्, समुत्पद्; जन् (c. 4. जायते, जनितुं), प्रजन्; प्रभू (c. 1. -भवति -वितुं), उद्भू, सम्भू; प्रसृ (c. 1. -सरति -सर्तुं), उद्गम् (c. 1. -गच्छति -गन्तुं), निर्गम्.

DERIVED, *p. p.* उत्पन्नः -न्ना -न्नं, व्युत्पन्नः -न्ना -न्नं, आनीतः -ता -तं.

DERIVER, *s.* व्युत्पत्तिकारकः, आनयनकर्त्ता *m.* (र्त्तृ), जन्मदाता *m.* (तृ).

To DEROGATE, *v. a.* न्यूनीकृ, ऊन् (c. 10. ऊनयति -यितुं), अल्पीकृ, कन (nom. कनयति -यितुं), लघ (nom. लघयति -यितुं), लघूकृ, ह्रस् in caus. (ह्रासयति -यितुं), असूय (nom. असूयति -यितुं).

DEROGATION, *s.* न्यूनीकरणं, अल्पीकरणं, लघूकरणं, ह्रासः, अपचयः, असूया, अभ्यसूया, अपवादः, विगानं.

DEROGATORILY, *adv.* असूयया, अभ्यसूयया, सापवादं, सकीर्त्तिकरं.

DEROGATORY, *a.* लघूकारकः -का -कं, असूयकः -का -कं, अभ्यसूयकः -का -कं, अपवादकः -का -कं, अपयशस्करः -री -रं, अकीर्त्तिकरः -रा -रं, ह्रासकः -का -कं.

DERVISE, DERVISH, *s.* तुरुष्कदेशीयः सन्न्यासी or योगी *m.* (न्).

DESCANT, *s.* (Song) विगीतं, सङ्कीर्त्तं, गीतं.—(Discourse) वादः, वाक्यं, प्रवादः, प्रवचनं, वचनं, अनुकथनं, सङ्कथा, वचनक्रमः, भाषितं.

To DESCANT, *v. n.* (Sing) विगै (c. 1. -गायति -गातुं), अनुगै, सङ्गै.—(Discourse at large) सुविस्तरेण वद् (c. 1. वदति -दितुं) or प्रवद्, सुविस्तरं व्याख्या (c. 2. -ख्याति -तुं) or विवरणं कृ.

To DESCEND, *v. n.* (Come down) अवरुह् (c. 1. -रोहति -रोढुं), अवतॄ (c. 1. -तरति -रितुं -रीतुं), अवया (c. 2. -याति -तुं), अधो या, अवपत् (c. 1. -पतति -तितुं), अधो गम् (c. 1. गच्छति, गन्तुं).—(Fall) पत्, निपत्, प्रपत्, च्यु (c. 1. च्यवते, च्योतुं), प्रच्यु.—(Make hostile incursion) आक्रम् (c. 1. -क्रामति -क्रमितुं), आसद् (c. 10. -सादयति -यितुं), अभिद्रु (c. 1. -द्रवति -द्रोतुं), अभिधाव् (c. 1. -धावति -वितुं).—(Arrive, enter) आगम्, अभिगम्, उपस्था (c. 1. -तिष्ठति -स्थातुं), प्रविश् (c. 6. -विशति -वेष्टुं).—(Be derived from) उत्पद् (c. 4. -पद्यते -पत्तुं), प्रसृ (c. 1. -सरति -सर्तुं), प्रभू, निर्गम्.—(Devolve by inheritance) वंशक्रमेण or अन्वयक्रमेण आगम् or आया, पितृसकाशात् प्राप् in pass. (-आप्यते -आप्तुं).—(Descend into particulars) विस्तरशः or विभागशः or उपवर्णेन वद् (c. 1. वदति -दितुं), विस्तीर्णविवरणं कृ, समुद्देशं कृ.

To DESCEND, *v. a.* (Make to come down) अवतॄ in caus. (-तारयति -यितुं), अवरुह् in caus. (-रोहयति -यितुं), अवपत् in caus. (-पातयति -यितुं); 'he descends the tree,' द्रुमात् or तरोर् अवतरति or अवरोहति.

DESCENDANT, *s.* सन्तानः -नं, सन्ततिः *f.*, अपत्यं, प्रवरं, प्रजा, सूनुः *m.*, प्रसवः, प्रसूतिः *f.*, तन्तुः *m.*; 'descendants,' पुत्रपौत्राः *m. pl.*, कुलसन्ततिः *f.*, अपत्यानि *n. pl.*, कुलं, वंशः; 'male descendant,' पुत्रसन्तानः.

DESCENDED, *p. p.* अवतीर्णः -र्णा -र्णं, अवरूढः -ढा -ढं, अधोगतः -ता -तं; 'lineally descended or inherited,' वंशक्रमागतः -ता -तं or क्रमागतः, क्रमायातः -ता -तं, पितृप्राप्तः -प्ता -प्तं, अन्वयागतः -ता -तं.

DESCENDENT, *a.* अवरोही -हिणी -हि (न्), अधोगामी -मिनी -मि (न्), नीचगः -गा -गं, पातुकः -का -कं, अधःपाती -तिनी -ति (न्), नीचाभिमुखः -खा -खं.

DESCENSION, *s.* अवपातः, अधोगतिः *f.*, पातः, पतनं, अधःपतनं, अधःसरणं.

DESCENT, *s.* (Going downwards) अधोगतिः *f.*, अधोगमः -मनं, अवपातः, अवतारः, अवपतनं, अवतरणं, अवरोहः -हणं, अधोयानं.—(Hostile incursion) अभिक्रमः, अवस्कन्दः, आक्रान्तिः *f.*, प्रयाणं, अभिनिर्याणं.—(Transmission by succession) क्रमागमः, वंशक्रमागमः, क्रमागतत्वं, अन्वयागमः.—(Birth extraction) जन्म *n.* (न्), उत्पत्तिः *f.*, उद्भवः, सम्भवः, वंशः.—(Lineage) सन्ततिः *f.*, अन्वयः, आवलिः *f.*; 'consanguineous descent,' एकशरीरान्वयः, एकशरीरावयवत्वं.

DESCRIBABLE, *a.* वर्णनीयः -या -यं, निर्देश्यः -श्या -श्यं, निर्वचनीयः -या -यं, व्याख्येयः -या -यं, वर्णयितुं शक्यः -क्या -क्यं.

To DESCRIBE, *v. a.* वर्ण् (c. 10. वर्णयति -यितुं), अनुवर्ण्, उपवर्ण्, संवर्ण्; निर्दिश् (c. 6. -दिशति -देष्टुं), उद्दिश्, समुद्दिश्; विवृ (c. 5. -वृणोति -वरितुं -रीतुं), कथ् (c. 10. कथयति -यितुं), सङ्कथ्; कॄत् (c. 10. कीर्त्तयति -यितुं), अनुकॄत्; निर्वच् (c. 2. -वक्ति -वक्तुं); व्याख्या (c. 2. -ख्याति -तुं), विब्रू (c. 2. -ब्रवीति -वक्तुं), निरूप् (c. 10. -रूपयति -यितुं).

DESCRIBED, *p. p.* वर्णितः -ता -तं, उपवर्णितः -ता -तं, निर्दिष्टः -ष्टा -ष्टं, उद्दिष्टः -ष्टा -ष्टं, समुद्दिष्टः -ष्टा -ष्टं, निरुक्तः -क्ता -क्तं, व्याख्यातः -ता -तं, कथितः -ता -तं, निरूपितः -ता -तं, विवृतः -ता -तं.

DESCRIPTION, *s.* वर्णनं -ना, उपवर्णनं, विवरणं, विवृतिः *f.*, निर्देशः, समुद्देशः, निरुक्तिः *f.*, निर्वचनं, व्याख्या -ख्यानं, निरूपणं, कथनं, यथार्थकथनं.

DESCRIPTIVE, *a.* निर्देशकः -का -कं, समुद्देशकः -का -कं, वर्णनकृत् *m.f.n.*, वाचकः -का -कं, विवरणकारी -रिणी -रि (न्), यथार्थकथकः -का -कं.

To DESCRY, *v. a.* (Perceive at a distance, see) दूराद् आलोक् (c. 1. -लोकते, c. 10. -लोकयति -यितुं) or अवलोक्, दृश् (c. 1. पश्यति, द्रष्टुं), अनुदृश्, प्रदृश्, परिदृश्; ईक्ष् (c. 1. ईक्षते -क्षितुं), समीक्ष्, अभिवीक्ष्, प्रेक्ष्, वीक्ष्, निर्वर्ण् (c. 10. -वर्णयति -यितुं), आलक्ष् (c. 10. -लक्षयति -यितुं), उपलक्ष्.—(Find out, discover) ज्ञा (c. 9. जानाति, ज्ञातुं), अवगम् (c. 1. -गच्छति -गन्तुं), निरूप् (c. 10. -रूपयति -यितुं), सूच् (c. 10. सूचयति -यितुं).

DESCRY, *s.* दूराद् आलोकितं यत्किञ्चिद्, दूरादृष्टं वस्तु.

To DESECRATE, *v. a.* प्रतिष्ठालोपं कृ, संस्कारदूषणं कृ, संस्कारहीनं -नां -नं कृ, अपुण्यं -ण्यां -ण्यं कृ, अपवित्रीकृ, पुण्यत्वं लुप् (c. 6. लुम्पति, लोप्तुं or caus. लोपयति -यितुं), दुष् in caus. (दूषयति -यितुं), व्यभिचर् (c. 1. -चरति -रितुं), कलङ्क (nom. कलङ्कयति -यितुं), मलिनीकृ.

DESECRATED, *p.p.* लुप्तप्रतिष्ठः -ष्ठा -ष्ठं, भग्नसंस्कारः -रा -रं, भ्रष्टपुण्यत्वः -त्वा -त्वं.

DESECRATION, *s.* प्रतिष्ठालोपः, संस्कारदूषणं, पुण्यत्वदूषणं, अपवित्रीकरणं, व्यभिचारः, कलङ्ककरणं, अपुण्यकरणं.

DESERT, *s.* (A wilderness) मरुः *m.*, मरुस्थलं -ली, मरुभूमिः *f.*, जङ्गलं, अरण्यं, वनं, ईरिणं, इरिणं, धन्वा *m.* (न्), रोमशं, विदर्भः, वसुरं -सूरं.

Desert, *a.* (Wild) आरण्यः -ण्या -ण्यं -अरण्यकः -का -कं, अकूलः -ला -लं, आकुलः -ली -लं, वन्यः -न्या -न्यं, इरिणः -णा -णं, ईरिणः -णा -णं, निर्जनः -ना -नं, निर्जलः -ला -लं, निरालयः -या -यं, शून्यः -न्या -न्यं, खिलः -ला -लं.

Desert, *s.* (Merit or demerit) गुणागुणं, पुण्यापुण्यं, अर्हत्वं, धर्म्माधर्म्मं. —(Excellence, right to reward) गुणः, पुण्यं, श्रेयः *n.* (स्), सुकृतं, उपयोगः, उपयुक्तता, योग्यत्वं, पात्रता, कृतित्वं, उत्कर्षः, शस्यं, प्रशस्यं.

To desert, *v. a.* त्यज् (c. 1. त्यजति, त्यक्तुं), परित्यज्, सन्त्यज्; हा (c. 3. जहाति, हातुं), अपहा, प्रहा, विहा, अपाहा; रह् (c. 10. रहयति -यितुं), विरह्; उत्सृज् (c. 6. -सृजति -स्रष्टुं), विसृज्, अतिसृज्, उज्झ् (c. 6. उज्झति -ज्झितुं), प्रोज्झ्; परिहृ (c. 1. -हरति -हर्त्तुं).

To desert, *v. n.* (From the army) सेनां त्यक्त्वा परिवृत् (c. 1. -वर्त्तते -र्त्तितुं) or पलाय् (c. 1. पलायते -यितुं) or विपलाय्.

Deserted, *p. p.* त्यक्तः -क्ता -क्तं, परित्यक्तः -क्ता -क्तं, उत्सृष्टः -ष्टा -ष्टं, रहितः -ता -तं, विरहितः -ता -तं, उत्सृष्टः -ष्टा -ष्टं, विसर्ज्जितः -ता -तं, हीनः -ना -नं, परिहीणः -णा -णं, वर्जितः -ता -तं, शून्यः -न्या -न्यं, उज्झितः -ता -तं, प्रोज्झितः -ता -तं, विनाकृतः -ता -तं, लुप्तः -प्ता -प्तं, अपविद्धः -द्धा -द्धं.

Deserter, *s.* त्यागी *m.* (न्), त्यक्ता *m.* (क्), सेनात्यागी *m.*, विपलायी *m.* (न्), पलायी *m.* (न्), परिवर्त्ती *m.* (न्), परिवर्त्तकः, युद्धत्यागी, युद्धपराङ्मुखः.

Desertion, *s.* (Abandonment) त्यागः, परित्यागः, उत्त्यागः, विरहः, प्रोज्झनं, उत्सर्ज्जनं, विसर्ज्जनं, विसृष्टिः *f.*, परिवर्त्तः. —(From the army) सेनात्यागः, युद्धत्यागः, युद्धपलायनं, विपलायनं.

Desertless, *a.* निर्गुणः -णा -णं, अनर्हः -र्हा -र्हं, अनुपयुक्तः -क्ता -क्तं.

To deserve, *v. a.* and *n.* अर्ह् (c. 1. अर्हति -ते -र्हितुं), अर्हः -र्हा -र्हं or उपयुक्तः -क्ता -क्तं or उचितः -ता -तं or योग्यः -ग्या -ग्यम् अस् or भू; 'he deserves honour,' मानम् अर्हति; 'he deserves punishment,' दण्डम् अर्हति; 'he deserves to drink soma juice,' सोमं पातुम् अर्हति; 'does he deserve so large a salary or not?' किम् उपयुक्तो ऽयम् एतावद् वर्त्तनं गृह्णातु अनुपयुक्तो वा; 'he deserves death,' वधार्हो ऽस्ति, मरणोचितो ऽस्ति. The future pass. part. may sometimes be used in this sense; as, 'he deserves death,' वध्यो ऽस्ति; 'he deserves honour,' मान्यो ऽस्ति, पूजनीयो ऽस्ति.

Deservedly, *adv.* अर्हं, उपयुक्तं, योग्यं, उचितं, अर्हत्वेन, न्यायतस्.

Deserver, *s.* अर्हः; 'good deserver,' सत्पात्रं; 'best deserver,' अर्हत्तमः.

Deserving, *a.* (Worthy of) अर्हः -र्हा -र्हं, उपयुक्तः -क्ता -क्तं, उचितः -ता -तं, योग्यः -ग्या -ग्यं. —(Meritorious) गुणी -णिनी -णि (न्), गुणान्वितः -ता -तं.

Deserving, *s.* गुणः, उपयोगः, पुण्यं, अर्हत्वं, धर्म्मः, पात्रता, शस्यं.

Desiccants, *a.* व्रणशोषकाः *m. pl.*, क्षतशोषणार्थम् उपनाहः or उपदेहः.

To desiccate, *v. a.* शुष् in caus. (शोषयति -यितुं), उच्छुष्, उपशुष्, विशुष्, संशुष्.

To desiccate, *v. n.* शुष् (c. 4. शुष्यति, शोष्टुं), विशुष्, ओख् (c. 1. ओखति -खितुं).

Desiccation, *s.* शोषणं, परिशोषः, उच्छोषणं, शुष्ककरणं, शुष्कत्वं.

Desiccative, *a.* शोषकः -का -कं, उच्छोषणः -णी -णं, शुष्ककृत् *m. f. n.*

To desiderate, *v. a.* अप्रत्यक्षं or अविषयं किञ्चिद्वस्तु इष् (c. 6. इच्छति, एषितुं) or उत्कण्ठ् (c. 1. -कण्ठते -ण्ठितुं) or अभ्याप् in des. (-ईप्सति -प्सितुं).

Desideratum, *s.* अविद्यमानं किञ्चिद् अभीष्टं वस्तु, अवर्त्तमानो वाञ्छनीयविषयः.

To design, *v. a.* (Purpose, intend) कृ in des. (चिकीर्षति -र्षितुं), अभिप्रे (rt. इ with अभि, प्र; अभिप्रैति -तुं), उपलक्ष् (c. 10. -लक्षयति -यितुं); उद्दिश् (c. 6. -दिशति -देष्टुं), अभिसन्धा (c. 3. -दधाति -धातुं), मनः or मतिं or बुद्धिं कृ or प्रकृ with loc. or abl. case; as, 'he designs a crime,' मनः पापे करोति; 'he designs the death of the king,' राज्ञो विनाशाय मतिं करोति. —(Plan, meditate) चिन्त् (c. 10. चिन्तयति -यितुं), प्रचिन्त्, मन्त्र् (c. 10. मन्त्रयति -यितुं), घट् (c. 1. घटते -टितुं), कॢप् (c. 10. कल्पयति -यितुं), परिकॢप्, अनुसन्धा (c. 3. -दधाति -धातुं), व्यवसो (c. 4. -स्यति -सातुं). —(Devote to, apply to a particular purpose) प्रयुज् (c. 7. -युङ्क्ते -योक्तुं), उपयुज्, विनियुज्; as, 'to religious purposes,' धर्म्मार्थम् उपयुज्. —(Draw) आलिख् (c. 6. -लिखति -लेखितुं), सूत्रपातं कृ, संस्कारं कृ, संस्कृ.

Design, *s.* (Intention, purpose) चिकीर्षा -र्षितं, अभिप्रायः, अभिप्रेतं, आशयः, अर्थः, आकूतं, तात्पर्य्यं, आकांक्षा, छन्दः, छन्दः *n.* (स्), सङ्कल्पः, उद्देशः, मतिः *f.*, मतं, कार्य्यं, उपयोगः, प्रयोजनं, उपलक्षितं, अभिसन्धिः *m.* —(Plan, scheme) चिन्ता, उपायः, व्यवसितं, व्यवसायः, प्रक्रान्तं, अनुसन्धानं, कल्पना, घटनं, विधानं. —(Drawing, impression) संस्कारः, आलेख्यं, सूत्रं, सूत्रपातः; 'with the design of,' अर्थे; 'one who has not effected his design,' अकृतार्थः.

To designate, *v. a.* (Mark out, indicate) चिह्न् (c. 10. चिह्नयति -यितुं), लक्ष् (c. 10. लक्षयति -यितुं), उपलक्ष्, विशिष् in caus. (-शेषयति -यितुं), प्रदिश् (c. 6. -दिशति -देष्टुं), निर्दिश्, सूच् (c. 10. सूचयति -यितुं). —(Appoint) नियुज् (c. 10. -योजयति -यितुं), परिकॢप् (c. 10. -कल्पयति -यितुं).

Designated, *p. p.* चिह्नितः -ता -तं, लक्षितः -ता -तं, विशेषितः -ता -तं.

Designation, *s.* लक्षणं, उपलक्षणं, संलक्षणं, चिह्नं, विशेषणं, संज्ञा, अभिज्ञानं, अभिधानं, आख्या, निर्देशः, सूचनं.

Designed, *p. p.* चिकीर्षितः -ता -तं, अभिप्रेतः -ता -तं, उपलक्षितः -ता -तं, उद्दिष्टः -ष्टा -ष्टं, अर्थवान् -वती -वत् (त्), व्यवसितः -ता -तं, घटितः -ता -तं.

Designedly, *adv.* इच्छातस्, मत्ततस्, कामतस्, प्रकामं, यथाकामं, मतिपूर्व्वकं, बुद्धिपूर्व्वं, बुद्धिपुरःसरं, मनोपूर्व्वकं, मत्या, बुद्ध्या, तात्पर्य्यतस्, यथाकल्पं.

Designer, *s.* (Contriver) चिन्तकः, उपायचिन्तकः, परिकल्पकः, व्यवसायी *m.* (न्). —(Drawer) आलेखकः, संस्कारलेखकः, सूत्रपातकः.

Designing, *a.* विदग्धः -ग्धा -ग्धं, छली -लिनी -लि (न्), मायी -यिनी -यि (न्), कापटिकः -की -कं, वञ्चनशीलः -ली -लं, प्रतारकः -का -कं, सव्याजः -जा -जं.

Designless, *a.* अभिप्रायहीनः -ना -नं, निरपेक्षः -क्षा -क्षं, निष्प्रयोजनः -ना -नं.

Designment, *s.* अभिप्रायः, चिकीर्षा, आशयः, अर्थः, अर्थवत्ता, अर्थत्वं, अभिसन्धिः *m.*

Desirable, *a.* स्पृहणीयः -या -यं, स्पृह्यः -ह्या -ह्यं, अभिलषणीयः -या -यं, वाञ्छनीयः -या -यं, कमनीयः -या -यं, काम्यः -म्या -म्यं, लोभ्यः -भ्या -भ्यं, आकांक्षणीयः -या -यं, एषणीयः -या -यं, प्रार्थनीयः -या -यं, अपेक्षणीयः -या -यं, गम्यः -म्या -म्यं; 'a desirable gift,' काम्यदानं.

Desirableness, *s.* स्पृहणीयता, वाञ्छनीयत्वं, कमनीयता, काम्यत्वं, इष्टत्वं.

Desire, *s.* इच्छा, अभिलाषः, अभिलषितं, स्पृहा, वाञ्छा, ईहा, कामः, कामना, कांक्षा, आकांक्षा, अभिकांक्षा, मनोरथः, अभिमतं, समीहितं, लोभः, आशा, तृषा, तृष्णा, इच्छात्वं, इष्टिः *f.*, इष्टं, अभीष्टं, छन्दः *n.* (स्), छन्दं, रुचिः *f.*, अभिरुचिः *f.*, मनस्कामना, मनोभिमतं, अभीप्सा, लिप्सा, औत्सुक्यं, औत्कण्ठ्यं, वशः, लालसा, कौतूहलं, कान्तिः *f.*, वसारं; 'one's desire,' स्वेच्छा; 'according to one's desire,' स्वेच्छातस्, स्वेच्छया, स्ववाञ्छया, स्वरुच्या, यथेष्टं, यथाभिमतं, स्वच्छन्दं. Obs. The noun formed from the desid. base often expresses 'desire'; as, 'desire to drink,' पिपासा; 'desire to burn,' दिधक्षा.

To DESIRE, *v. a.* इष् (c. 6. इच्छति, एषितुं), अभिलष् (c. 1. -लषति, c. 4. -लष्यति -लषितुं), वाञ्छ् (c. 1. वाञ्छति -ञ्छितुं), अभिवाञ्छ्, संवाञ्छ्; कांक्ष् (c. 1. कांक्षति -क्षितुं), आकांक्ष्, अनुकांक्ष्, अभिकांक्ष्; स्पृह् (c. 10. स्पृहयति -यितुं), कम् (c. 10. कामयते -यितुं), ईह् (c. 1. ईहते -हितुं), समीह्, लुभ् (c. 4. लुभ्यति, लोब्धुं), अभिरुच् in caus. (-रोचयति -यितुं), आप् in des. (ईप्सति -प्सितुं), अभ्याप्, पर्याप्; लभ् in des. (लिप्सते -प्सितुं), अभिलभ्; आशंस् (c. 1. -शंसते -सितुं), गृध् (c. 4. गृध्यति, गर्धितुं), वश् (c. 2. वष्टि, वशितुं).—(Ask, beg for) अर्थ् (c. 10. अर्थयते -ति -यितुं), प्रार्थ्, याच् (c. 1. याचति -चितुं), वृ (c. 9. वृणीते, वरितुं -रीतुं) with 2 acc., निविद् in caus. (-वेदयति -यितुं).

DESIRED, *p. p.* इष्टः -ष्टा -ष्टं, अभीष्टः -ष्टा -ष्टं, अभिलषितः -ता -तं, वाञ्छितः -ता -तं, कांक्षितः -ता -तं, आकांक्षितः -ता -तं, अभिकांक्षितः -ता -तं, अभिमतः -ता -तं, ईहितः -ता -तं, समीहितः -ता -तं, ईप्सितः -ता -तं, अभीप्सितः -ता -तं, लिप्सितः -ता -तं, समुत्सुकः -का -कं, हृद्यः -द्या -द्यं.

DESIROUS, *a.* इच्छुः -च्छुः -च्छु, इच्छुकः -का -कं, इच्छकः -का -कं, इच्छावान् -वती -वत् (त्), इच्छान्वितः -ता -तं, अभिलाषी -षिणी -षि (न्) -षुकः -का -कं, वाञ्छी -ञ्छिनी -ञ्छि (न्), आकांक्षी -क्षिणी -क्षि (न्) or अभिकांक्षी, इच्छी -च्छिणी -च्छि (न्), अर्थी -र्थिनी -र्थि (न्), कामी -मिनी -मि (न्), कामुकः -का -कं, कामवान् -वती -वत् (त्), काम्यमानः -ना -नं, लोभी -भिनी -भि (न्), लुब्धः -ब्धा -ब्धं, स्पृहयालुः -लुः -लु, जातस्पृहः -हा -हं, सस्पृहः -हा -हं, साकांक्षः -क्षा -क्षं, ईप्सुः -प्सुः -प्सु or अभीप्सुः or प्रेप्सुः or परिप्रेप्सुः, इच्छी -च्छिनी -च्छि (न्), लिप्सुः -प्सुः -प्सु, आशंसुः -सुः -सु, आशायुक्तः -क्ता -क्तं, लालसी -सिनी -सि (न्), तृष्णकः -का -कं, वशः -शा -शं. 'Desirous' is sometimes expressed by काम affixed to the infinitive, the final of which is rejected; as, 'desirous to do,' कर्त्तुकामः -मा -मं; 'desirous to go,' गन्तुकामः -मा -मं; or by the adj. formed from the desid. base; as, 'desirous of drinking,' पिपासुः -सुः -सु; 'desirous of taking,' आदित्सुः -त्सुः -त्सु.

To DESIST, *v. n.* विरम् (c. 1. -रमति -रन्तुं), उपरम्, निवृत् (c. 1. -वर्त्तते -र्त्तितुं), निर्वृत्, विनिवृत्; शम् (c. 4. शाम्यति, शमितुं), विगम् (c. 1. -गच्छति -गन्तुं), विच्छिद् in pass. (-च्छिद्यते), विश्रम् (c. 4. -श्राम्यति -श्रमितुं), अपया (c. 2. -याति -तुं); 'he desists from wickedness,' पापाद् विरमति or निवर्त्तते.

DESISTANCE, *s.* विरतिः *f.*, विरामः, निवृत्तिः *f.*, निवर्त्तनं, निर्वृत्तिः *f.*, उपशमः.

DESISTED, *p. p.* निवृत्तः -त्ता -त्तं, विरतः -ता -तं, उपरतः -ता -तं, शान्तः -न्ता -न्तं, प्रशान्तः -न्ता -न्तं, विगतः -ता -तं, विच्छिन्नः -न्ना -न्नं.

DESK, *s.* लिखनफलकं, लिपिफलकं, लिपिसाधनाधारः, लेखसाधनाधारः.

DESOLATE, *a.* (Solitary, uninhabited) शून्यः -न्या -न्यं, शून्याकारः -रा -रं, विविक्तः -क्ता -क्तं, निर्जनः -ना -नं, निर्मनुष्यः -ष्या -ष्यं, पुरुषवर्जितः -ता -तं, अप्रजः -जा -जं, विलोकः -की -कं, निःशलाकः -का -कं, निरालयः -या -यं, वसतिहीनः -ना -नं.—(Laid waste) उच्छिन्नः -न्ना -न्नं, प्रबाधितः -ता -तं, उपपीडितः -ता -तं.

To DESOLATE, *v. a.* उपपीड् (c. 10. -पीडयति -यितुं), प्रबाध् (c. 1. -बाधते -धितुं), उच्छिद् (c. 7. -छिनत्ति -छेत्तुं), शून्यीकृ, निर्जनीकृ, निर्दह् (c. 1. -दहति -दग्धुं), वसतीः नश् in caus. (नाशयति -यितुं).

DESOLATION, *s.* (Destruction of inhabitants) शून्यीकरणं, निर्जनीकरणं, वसतिनाशः, उच्छेदः, उपपीडनं.—(State of destitution) शून्यता, निर्जनत्वं, विविक्तता, रहितत्वं, विषादः, विषण्णता.

DESPAIR, *s.* निराशा, नैराश्यं, आशाहीनता, दौर्मनस्यं, वैक्लव्यं, विषादः; 'in despair,' त्यक्ताशः, आशाहीनः, गताशः.

To DESPAIR, *v. n.* आशां हा (c. 3. जहाति, हातुं) or त्यज्, आशया हा in pass. (हीयते), नैराश्यम् उपगम् (c. 1. -गच्छति -गन्तुं) or गम्; निराशीभू, सङ्कुद् (c. 6. -कुटति -टितुं).

DESPAIRINGLY, *adv.* आशां विना, आशया विना, सनैराश्यं, नैराश्यात्.

To DESPATCH, *v. a.* (Send away hastily) सत्वरं प्रस्था in caus. (-स्थापयति -यितुं) or प्रेर् (c. 10. -ईरयति -यितुं) or प्रेष् in caus. (प्रेषयति -यितुं, rt. इष्), सम्प्रेष्, परिप्रेष्, or प्रहि (c. 5. -हिणोति -हेतुं) or प्रया in caus. (-यापयति -यितुं) or चुद् (c. 10. चोदयति -यितुं), or प्रणुद् (c. 6. -णुदति -णोत्तुं).—(Hasten, perform quickly) त्वर् in caus. (त्वरयति -यितुं), सन्त्वर्; त्वरितं कृ or सम्पद् in caus. (-पादयति -यितुं) or प्रवृत् in caus. (-वर्त्तयति -यितुं).—(Kill) व्यापद् in caus. (-पादयति -यितुं), लोकान्तरं प्राप् in caus. (-आपयति -यितुं) or प्रेर्.

DESPATCH, *s.* (Hasty execution) क्षिप्रकारित्वं, शीघ्रनिर्वाहः, त्वरा, तूर्णिः *f.*, आवेगः, अदीर्घसूत्रता.—(Official message) वाचिकं, वाचिकपत्रं, राजकीयपत्रं, राजलेखः -लेख्यं.—(Hasty messenger) धावकः, वेगी *m.* (न्), जवी *m.* (न्), लेखहारी *m.* (न्), वार्त्ताहरः, दूतः.

DESPATCHED, *p. p.* (Sent) प्रस्थापितः -ता -तं, प्रेरितः -ता -तं, प्रेषितः -ता -तं, प्रहितः -ता -तं, प्रयापितः -ता -तं, दूतः -ता -तं, प्रतिसृष्टः -ष्टा -ष्टं, नुन्नः -न्ना -न्नं, प्रणुन्नः -न्ना -न्नं, गमितः -ता -तं, प्रतिक्षिप्तः -प्ता -प्तं.

DESPATCHFUL, *a.* शीघ्रकारी -रिणी -रि (न्) or क्षिप्रकारी, अविलम्बी -म्बिनी -म्बि (न्), अदीर्घसूत्रः -त्रा -त्रं, त्वरायुक्तः -क्ता -क्तं, त्वराशीलः -ला -लं.

DESPERADO, *s.* साहसी *m.* (न्), साहसिकः, अत्याहितकर्म्मा *m.* (न्), आततायी *m.* (न्).

DESPERATE, *a.* (Without hope) निराशः -शा -शं, आशाहीनः -ना -नं, आशारहितः -ता -तं, गताशः -शा -शं, त्यक्ताशः -शा -शं, निःप्रत्याशः -शा -शं.—(Daring) साहसिकः -की -कं -सी -सिनी -सि (न्).—(Fearless) निर्भयः -या -यं, अकुतोभयः -या -यं.—(Irretrievable) निरुपायी -यिनी -यि (न्), अप्रतिकारः -रा -रं or असाध्यप्रतिकारः.—(Furious) उग्रः -ग्रा -ग्रं, संरब्धः -ब्धा -ब्धं.—(Excessive) अत्यन्तः -न्ता -न्तं, अति or सु prefixed; 'a desperate fool,' अतिमूढः; 'a desperate act,' अत्याहितं, साहसकल्पः, आततायिता.

DESPERATELY, *adv.* (Furiously) उन्मत्तवत्, साहसेन -सात्, उग्रं, संरब्धं.—(In a great degree) सु or अति prefixed; अत्यन्तं, भृशं, तीव्रं.

DESPERATENESS, *s.* (Fury, daringness) उन्मादः, संरम्भः, उग्रत्वं, साहसिकत्वं.

DESPERATION, *s.* नैराश्यं, आशाहीनता, आशाराहित्यं, निराशा.

DESPICABLE, *a.* अवमाननीयः -या -यं, अवमान्यः -न्या -न्यं or अवमान्यः, अवमन्तव्यः -व्या -व्यं, अवज्ञेयः -या -यं, अवज्ञातव्यः -व्या -व्यं, गर्ह्यः -र्ह्या -र्ह्यं, गर्हणीयः -या -यं, गर्हितः -ता -तं, अपगर्हितः -ता -तं, अतिगर्हितः -ता -तं, निन्द्यः -न्द्या -न्द्यं, निन्दनीयः -या -यं, निन्दार्हः -र्हा -र्हं, दूष्यः -ष्या -ष्यं, तुच्छः -च्छा -च्छं, कुत्सितः -ता -तं, क्षुद्रः -द्रा -द्रं, अपकृष्टः -ष्टा -ष्टं.

DESPICABLENESS, *s.* अवमान्यता, गर्ह्यत्वं, निन्द्यता, तुच्छत्वं, दूष्यता.

DESPICABLY, *adv.* गर्हणीयं, गर्हितं, कुत्सितं, अपकृष्टं, तुच्छं.

To DESPISE, *v. a.* अवज्ञा (c. 9. -जानाति -ज्ञातुं), अवमन् (c. 4. -मन्यते -मन्तुं), तृणाय मन्, अभ्यवमन्, परिमन्, गर्ह् (c. 1. गर्हते -र्हितुं), विगर्ह्, कुत्स् (c. 10. कुत्सयति -यितुं), निन्द् (c. 1. निन्दति -न्दितुं), परिभू (c. 1. -भवति -वितुं), अवधीर् (c. 10. अवधीरयति -यितुं), गुप् in des. (जुगुप्सते -प्सितुं), उपेक्ष् (c. 1. -ईक्षते -क्षितुं), अवध्यै (c. 1. -ध्यायति -ध्यातुं), बाध् in des. (बीभत्सते -त्सितुं), अवक्षिप् (c. 6. -क्षिपति -क्षेप्तुं),

कदर्थ् (c. 10. -अर्थयते -यितुं), कदर्थीकृ, तुच्छीकृ, लघूकृ.

DESPISED, *p. p.* अवमतः -ता -तं, अवमानितः -ता -तं, विमानितः -ता -तं, अपमानितः -ता -तं, अवज्ञातः -ता -तं, परिभूतः -ता -तं, गर्हितः -ता -तं, विगर्हितः -ता -तं, अवधीरितः -ता -तं, कदर्थितः -ता -तं, अवध्यातः -ता -तं, निन्दितः -ता -तं, उपेक्षितः -ता -तं, अवगणितः -ता -तं.

DESPISER, *s.* अवमन्ता *m.* (न्तृ), अवज्ञाता *m.* (तृ), अवमानकर्त्ता *m.* (र्त्तृ), निन्दकः.

DESPITE, *s.* (Malice) द्वेषः, द्रोहः, मात्सर्य्यं, ईर्ष्या, अभ्यसूया, दुर्बुद्धिः *f.*, नृशंस्यं, दौर्जन्यं, दंशः.—(Opposition) प्रतिरोधः, विरोधः, प्रतियोगः, प्रतिकारः, प्रतिकूलता; 'in despite,' अनिच्छया, विरुद्धं, प्रातिकूल्येन, or expressed by the gen. c. of the pres. part. of the root दृश् 'to see,' or मिष्; 'in despite of thee,' पश्यतस् तव; 'in despite of the princes,' मिषतां पार्थिवानां.

To DESPITE, *v. a.* कुप् in caus. (कोपयति -यितुं), रुष् in caus. (रोषयति -यितुं), तप् in caus. (तापयति -यितुं), सन्तप्; क्लिश् (c. 9. क्लिश्नाति, क्लेशुं), व्यथ् in caus. (व्यथयति -यितुं), दुःख् (c. 10. दुःखयति -यितुं).

DESPITEFUL, *a.* द्रोही -हिणी -हि (न्), द्रोहबुद्धिः -द्धिः -द्धि or दुर्बुद्धिः, ईर्ष्यी -र्ष्यिणी -र्ष्यि (न्), सासूयः -या -यं, विषहृदयः -या -यं, नृशंसः -सा -सं, मत्सरः -रा -रं, द्वेषी -षिणी -षि (न्), अहितेच्छुः -च्छुः -च्छु, हिंसाशीलः -ला -लं.

DESPITEFULLY, *adv.* सद्रोहं, सद्वेषं, हिंसापूर्व्वं, नृशंसं, साभ्यसूयं.

DESPITEFULNESS, *s.* द्रोहः, द्वेषः, मात्सर्य्यं, नृशंस्यं, दंशः, दौर्जन्यं.

To DESPOIL, *v. a.* हृ (c. 1. हरति, हर्त्तुं), अपहृ, विमुष् (c. 6. -मुष्णाति -मोषितुं), वियुज् in caus. (-योजयति -यितुं), विप्रयुज् with inst. c.; 'despoil of leaves,' निष्पत्रीकृ.

DESPOILED, *p. p.* हृतः -ता -तं, अपहृतः -ता -तं, वियुक्तः -क्ता -क्तं, वियोजितः -ता -तं; 'despoiled of all possessions,' हृतसर्व्वस्वः -स्वा -स्वं.

DESPOILER, *s.* हर्त्ता *m.* (र्त्तृ), हारकः, अपहारकः, अपहारकृत्, लुण्टाकः.

DFSPOLIATION, *s.* हरणं, अपहरणं, अभिहारः, अभ्याहारः, अभिग्रहणं.

To DESPOND, *v. n.* विषद् (c. 1. -षीदति -षत्तुं), अवसद्; निर्वेदं or विषादं or नैराश्यम् उपगम् (c. 1. -गच्छति -गन्तुं) or गम्; आशां हा (c. 3. जहाति, हातुं) or त्यज् (c. 1. त्यजति, त्यक्तुं), निर्विण्णीभू, निर्विद् (c. 4. -विद्यते -वेत्तुं), सङ्कुद् (c. 6. -कुटति -टितुं).

DESPONDENCY, *s.* विषादः, निर्वेदः, विषण्णता, निर्विण्णता, नैराश्यं, निराशा, अवसन्नता, उद्वेगः, दौर्मनस्यं, ग्लानिः *f.*, क्लान्तिः *f.*

DESPONDENT, *a.* विषण्णः -ण्णा -ण्णं, विषादी -दिनी -दि (न्), निर्विण्णः -ण्णा -ण्णं, निराशः -शा -शं, आशाहीनः -ना -नं, त्यक्ताशः -शा -शं, अवसन्नः -न्ना -न्नं, उद्विग्नमनाः -नाः -नः (स्) or दुर्मनाः or अन्तर्मनाः, ग्लानः -ना -नं.

DESPONDINGLY, *adv.* सनिर्वेदं, सविषादं, निर्वेदात्, सनैराश्यं.

To DESPONSATE, *v. a.* वाग्दत्तां कृ, वाग्दानेन विवाहार्थं प्रतिज्ञा (c. 9. -जानाति -नीते -ज्ञातुं), कन्यां प्रदा, प्रतिज्ञाविवाहितां कृ.

DESPONSATION, *s.* वाग्दानं, कन्याप्रदानं, विवाहार्थं प्रतिज्ञानं.

DESPOT, *s.* सम्राट् *m.* (ज्), अधिराजः, चक्रवर्त्ती *m.* (न्), सर्व्वेश्वरः, राजाधिराजः, एकराजः, स्वाधीनराजः, स्वयम्प्रभुः.

DESPOTIC, DESPOTICAL, *a.* अनधीनः -ना -नं, अनायत्तः -त्ता -त्तं, अधिराजकः -का -कं, स्वयम्प्रभुः -भुः -भु, साम्राज्यिकः -की -कं, स्वयम्प्रभुत्वकारी -रिणी -रि (न्).

DESPOTICALLY, *adv.* अधिराजवत्, अनायत्तं, स्वेच्छातस्, स्वकामतस्, स्वच्छन्दं.

DESPOTISM, *s.* साम्राज्यं, अधिराज्यं, ऐकपत्यं, स्वेच्छाप्रभुत्वं, अनधीनत्वं.

To DESPUMATE, *v. n.* फेन (nom. फेनायते), उत्सेचनं कृ, मण्ड (nom. मण्डायते).

DESPUMATION, *s.* फेनोत्सेचनं, मण्डोत्सेचनं, उत्सेचनं, उत्पीडः.

DESQUAMATION, *s.* त्वक्परिपुटनं, अस्थिपरिपुटनं, अध्यस्थिपरिपुटनं.

DESSERT, *s.* भोजनान्ते परिवेशितं फलमोदकादिखाद्यं, फलाहारः.

DESTINATION, *s.* (Purpose for which any thing is intended) अर्थः, अर्थत्वं, प्रयोगः, उपयोगः, प्रयोजनं, उद्देशः, आशयः, अभिप्रायः, तात्पर्य्यं.—(Place of destination) अग्रभूमिः *f.*, अग्रस्थानं, अयं, निरूपितस्थानं.

To DESTINE OF DESTINATE, *v. a.* निरूप् (c. 10. -रूपयति -यितुं), प्रक्लृप् (c. 10. -कल्पयति -यितुं), परिक्लृप्, निर्दिश् (c. 6. -दिशति -देष्टुं), उद्दिश्, प्रदिश्, समादिश्; नियुज् (c. 7. -युनक्ति -योक्तुं, c. 10. -योजयति -यितुं), प्रयुज्, उपयुज्, विनियुज्, प्रस्था in caus. (-स्थापयति -यितुं), अभिसन्धा (c. 3. -दधाति -धातुं).

DESTINED, *p. p.* निरूपितः -ता -तं, परिकल्पितः -ता -तं, निर्दिष्टः -ष्टा -ष्टं.

DESTINY, *s.* दैवं, भाग्यं, भागधेयं, कृतान्तः, विधिः *m.*, विधाता *m.* (तृ), भवितव्यता, दैविकं, अदृष्टं, नियतिः *f.*, कालनियोगः, कालधर्म्मः, दिष्टं, प्राक्तनं.

DESTITUTE, *a.* (Poor, abject, friendless) निर्धनः -ना -नं, अर्थहीनः -ना -नं, निष्किञ्चनः -ना -नं, अकिञ्चनः -ना -नं, दुर्गतः -ता -तं, निःस्वः -स्वा -स्वं, निराश्रयः -या -यं, अपाश्रयः -या -यं, अशरणः -णा -णं, बन्धुहीनः -ना -नं.—(Deprived of, in want of) हीनः -ना -नं, विहीनः -ना -नं, परिहीणः -णा -णं, रहितः -ता -तं, विरहितः -ता -तं, वर्जितः -ता -तं, विवर्जितः -ता -तं, शून्यः -न्या -न्यं, विनाकृतः -ता -तं, वियुक्तः -क्ता -क्तं, लुप्तः -प्ता -प्तं, हृतः -ता -तं, अपेतः -ता -तं; 'destitute of fruit,' फलहीनः -ना -नं or फलरहितः -ता -तं or फलापेतः -ता -तं or हृतफलः -ला -लं; 'destitute of means,' असाधनः -ना -नं.

DESTITUTION, *s.* (State of being deprived) हीनत्वं, रहितत्वं, शून्यता.—(Absence of a thing) अभावः, असम्भवः, विरहः.—(Want of money, &c., poverty) धनाभावः, वर्त्तनाभावः, निष्किञ्चनत्वं, अकिञ्चनं, दारिद्र्यं, बन्धुहीनता, असहायता, अभूमिः *f.*

To DESTROY, *v. a.* (Put an end to, ruin) नश् in caus. (नाशयति -यितुं), विनश्, प्रणश्; साध् in caus. (साधयति -यितुं), संसाध्; क्षि (c. 5. क्षिणोति, क्षेतुं or caus. क्षययति, क्षपयति -यितुं), सद् in caus. (सादयति -यितुं), लुप् (c. 6. लुम्पति, लोप्तुं or caus. लोपयति -यितुं), विलुप्; ध्वंस् in caus. (ध्वंसयति -यितुं), विध्वंस्, प्रध्वंस्; उच्छिद् (c. 7. -छिनत्ति -छेत्तुं), निर्दह् (c. 1. -दहति -दग्धुं), ग्रस् (c. 1. ग्रसते -सितुं).—(Kill) हन् (c. 2. हन्ति -न्तुं or caus. घातयति -यितुं), व्यापद् in caus. (-पादयति -यितुं), मृ in caus. (मारयति -यितुं), सूद् (c. 10. सूदयति -यितुं), अभिसूद्, निसूद्, विनिसूद्, सन्निसूद्; शद् in caus. (शातयति -यितुं), प्रमी in caus. (-मापयति -यितुं), क्षण् (c. 8. क्षणोति -णितुं).

DESTROYED, *p. p.* नष्टः -ष्टा -ष्टं, नाशितः -ता -तं, विनाशितः -ता -तं, प्रणष्टः -ष्टा -ष्टं, सादितः -ता -तं, सूदितः -ता -तं, हतः -ता -तं, घातितः -ता -तं, ध्वंसितः -ता -तं, उच्छिन्नः -न्ना -न्नं, भग्नः -ग्ना -ग्नं, व्यापादितः -ता -तं.

DESTROYER, *s.* विनाशकः, नाशी *m.* (न्), नाशकारी *m.* (न्), विनाशकारी, हन्ता *m.* (न्तृ), निहन्ता, घाती *m.* (न्), क्षयकरः, अन्तकः, अन्तकृत्, ध्वंसकः, ध्वंसकारी *m.* (न्), प्रलयकर्त्ता *m.* (र्त्तृ), सूदनः, अपहः; 'destroying angel,' कृतान्तः.

DESTRUCTIBLE, *a.* नाशनीयः -या -यं, नाश्यः -श्या -श्यं, विनश्वरः -रा -रं, ध्वंसनीयः -या -यं, अवसेयः -या -यं, क्षयी -यिणी -यि (न्).

DESTRUCTION, *s.* नाशः, विनाशः, विनष्टिः *f.*, प्रणाशः, क्षयः, ध्वंसः, प्रध्वंसः, सादनं, सूदनं, प्रलयः, संहारः, अपायः, अत्ययः, विलोपनं, लोपः, समुच्छेदः, उद्दलनं, उत्पाटनं, क्षैण्यं.—(Murder) घातः -तनं, मारणं, वधः, निहननं, प्रमापणं.—(Of the world) प्रलयः, कल्पान्तः, जहानकः, जिहानकः, संवर्त्तः, क्षयः.

DESTRUCTIVE, *a.* नाशी -शिनी -शि (न्) or प्रणाशी, विनाशकः -का -कं, क्षयकरः -री -रं, घाती -तिनी -ति (न्) or विघाती, घातुकः -का -कं, प्रध्वंसी -सिनी -सि (न्) or परिध्वंसी, अन्तकरः -री -रं, सूदनः -नी -नं, प्रमापी -पिणी -पि (न्), आत्ययिकः -की -कं, निधनकारी -रिणी-रि(न्), नाशयः -श्या -श्यं, प्राणहरः -रा -रं, अपकारकः -का -कं, घातनः -ना -नं, अभिमर्शनः -ना -नं, क्रूरः -रा -रं, अपहः -हा -हं or हः हा हं or घ्नः घ्ना घ्नं in comp.

DESTRUCTIVELY, *adv.* सनाशं, विनाशेन, विनाशकप्रकारेण, आत्ययिकं.

DESTRUCTIVENESS, *s.* नाशकत्वं, नाशित्वं, घातुकत्वं, अपकारकता.

DESUETUDE, *s.* विरतिः *f.*, उपरतिः *f.*, निवृत्तिः *f.*, निर्वृत्तिः, निवर्त्तनं, विच्छेदः.

DESULTORY, *a.* चञ्चलः -ला -लं, अस्थिरः -रा -रं, लोलः -ला -लं, तरलः -ला -लं, चपलः -ला -लं, सङ्कुसुकः -का -कं, अधीरः -रा -रं, उच्छृङ्खलः -ला -लं.

To DETACH, *v. a.* (Separate) भिद् (c. 7. भिनत्ति, भेत्तुं), विभिद्, वियुज् (c. 7. -युनक्ति -योक्तुं), विच्छिद् (c. 7. -छिनत्ति -छेत्तुं), अवच्छिद्, विश्लिष् in caus. (-श्लेषयति -यितुं), खण्ड् (c. 10. खण्डयति -यितुं), पृथक् कृ.—(Send out a party from the main army) सर्व्वसैन्यमध्यात् कतिपयसैन्यान् डमरकरणार्थं प्रस्था in caus. (-स्थापयति -यितुं).

DETACHED, *p. p.* वियुक्तः -क्ता -क्तं, विप्रयुक्तः -क्ता -क्तं, विनियुक्तः -क्ता -क्तं, भिन्नः -न्ना -न्नं, विभिन्नः -न्ना -न्नं, प्रभिन्नः -न्ना -न्नं, विच्छिन्नः -न्ना -न्नं, अवच्छिन्नः -न्ना -न्नं, विश्लिष्टः -ष्टा -ष्टं, असंलग्नः -ग्ना -ग्नं, असंसक्तः -क्ता -क्तं, असक्तः -क्ता -क्तं, व्यासक्तः -क्ता -क्तं, गतसङ्गः -ङ्गा -ङ्गं, निर्युक्तिकः -का -कं.

DETACHMENT, *s.* (Act of detaching) वियोगः, विप्रयोगः, विभेदः, विच्छेदः, अवच्छेदः, विश्लेषः, व्यासङ्गः, अनभिष्वङ्गः.—(Body of troops sent out for petty warfare) डमरकरणार्थं प्रस्थापितः सैन्यगुल्मः, सैन्यदलं.

DETAIL, *s.* विवरणं, विस्तारः, विस्तरः, वाग्विस्तारः, उपवर्णः -र्णनं, वृत्तान्तविवरणं, सर्व्ववृत्तान्तव्याख्या; 'in detail,' विस्तरेण, विस्तरशस्, सुविस्तरं, उपवर्णेन, विभागशस्.

To DETAIL, *v. a.* सुविस्तरेण कथ् (c. 10. कथयति -यितुं) or आख्या (c. 2. -ख्याति -तुं), सर्व्ववृत्तान्तं विवृ (c. 5. -वृणोति -वरितुं -रीतुं) or व्याख्या; उपवर्ण् (c. 10. -वर्णयति -यितुं), वृत्तान्तविवरणं कृ.

DETAILED, *p. p.* and *a.* उपवर्णितः -ता -तं, सविस्तरः -रा -रं, विस्तीर्णः -र्णा -र्णं.

To DETAIN, *v. a.* (Keep what belongs to another) परद्रव्यं धृ (c. 1. धरति, धर्त्तुं or caus. धारयति -यितुं) or सन्धृ or परिभुज् (c. 7. -भुनक्ति -भोक्तुं).—(Keep back, withhold) निवृ in caus. (-वारयति -यितुं), निग्रह् (c. 9. -गृह्णाति -ग्रहीतुं), विधृ in caus., उपसंहृ (c. 1. -हरति -हर्त्तुं) संहृ.—(Restrain from departure) धृ, निरुध् (c. 7. -रुणद्धि -रोद्धुं) अवरुध्.—(Hold in confinement) कारायां निरुध् or आसिध् (c. 1. -सेधति -सेद्धुं) or बन्ध् (c. 9. बध्नाति, बन्द्धुं).

DETAINED, *p. p.* धृतः -ता -तं, निरुद्धः -द्धा -द्धं, निवारितः -ता -तं.

DETAINER, *s.* धारकः, धर्त्ता *m.* (र्त्तृ), परिभोक्ता *m.* (क्तृ), निरोधकः.

To DETECT, *v. a.* ज्ञा (c. 9. जानाति, ज्ञातुं), विज्ञा, परिज्ञा, अभिज्ञा, निरूप् (c. 10. -रूपयति -यितुं), निर्णी (c. 1. -णयति -णेतुं), उपलभ् (c. 1. -लभते -लब्धुं), अवगम् (c. 1. -गच्छति -गन्तुं), अधिगम्, अभ्यागम्, धृ (c. 1. धरति, धर्त्तुं), आसद् (c. 10. -सादयति -यितुं), प्रोत्सद्, अनुसन्धा (c. 3. -दधाति -धातुं), व्यञ्ज् in caus. (-अञ्जयति -यितुं), व्यक्तीकृ, विवृ (c. 5. -वृणोति -वरितुं -रीतुं).

DETECTED, *p. p.* ज्ञातः -ता -तं, विज्ञातः -ता -तं, अभिज्ञातः -ता -तं, अवगतः -ता -तं, निरूपितः -ता -तं, धृतः -ता -तं, निर्णीतः -ता -तं, व्यञ्जितः -ता -तं, व्यक्तीकृतः -ता -तं; 'in a crime,' दृष्टदोषः -षा -षं.

DETECTION, *s.* ज्ञानं, परिज्ञानं, विज्ञानं, निरूपणं, निर्णयः, धरणं, अवगमः, अनुसन्धानं, व्यक्तीकरणं, विवृतिः *f.*

DETENTION, *s.* धरणं, धारणं, सन्धारणं, निग्रहः, निवारणं, संहरणं, संरोधः, अवरुद्धिः *f.*, अवरोधः.—(Confinement) रोधः, निरोधः -धनं, आसेधः, स्थानासेधः, सम्प्रतिरोधकः.—(Forcible detention of a debtor) बलात्कारः.

To DETER, *v. a.* भयहेतुं दर्शयित्वा निवृत् in caus. (-वर्त्तयति -यितुं) or निर्वृत् in caus., or विरम् in caus. (-रमयति -यितुं) or निवृ in caus. (-वारयति -यितुं), विभी in caus. (-भाययति -यितुं), अपभर्त्स् in caus. (-भर्त्सयति -ते -यितुं).

To DETERGE, *v. a.* मलम् अपमृज् (c. 1. -मार्जति, c. 2. -मार्ष्टि -र्ष्टुं), परिमृज्, परिष्कृ.

DETERGENT, *a.* परिमार्ज्जकः -का -कं, परिमार्ज्जिष्णुः -ष्णुः -ष्णु, शोधकः -का -कं.

To DETERIORATE, *v. n.* क्षि in pass. (क्षीयते), ह्रस् (c. 1. ह्रसते -सितुं), दुष् (c. 4. दुष्यति, दोष्टुं), भ्रंश् (c. 4. भ्रश्यति, भ्रंशितुं), विकृतीभू, अन्यथाभू, विकलीभू.

To DETERIORATE, *v. a.* दुष् in caus. (दूषयति -यितुं), विकलीकृ, विकृ, अपकृष् (c. 1. -कर्षति -क्रष्टुं), ह्रस् in caus. (ह्रासयति -यितुं).

DETERIORATED, *p. p.* क्षीणः -णा -णं, परिभ्रष्टः -ष्टा -ष्टं, विकलः -ला -लं.

DETERIORATION, *s.* (Growing worse) विकारः, विकृतिः *f.*, ह्रासः, अपचयः, क्षयः, क्षीणता, भ्रष्टता, दुष्टता, अधोगतिः *f.*, अन्यथाभावः.—(Making worse) अपकर्षः -र्षणं, विकलीकरणं.

DETERMENT, *s.* निवर्त्तनं, निवृत्तिः *f.*, उद्योगभङ्गः, उद्यमव्याघातः, विघ्नः.

DETERMINABLE, *a.* निर्णेयः -या -यं, विवेचनीयः -या -यं, निर्धारणीयः -या -यं, निर्धार्य्यः -र्य्या -र्य्यं, अवधारणीयः -या -यं, अवधार्य्यः -र्य्या -र्य्यं.

DETERMINATE, *a.* (Settled, definite) निश्चितः -ता -तं, निर्णीतः -ता -तं, नियतः -ता -तं, निर्धारितः -ता -तं, सिद्धः -द्धा -द्धं, निबद्धः -द्धा -द्धं, निर्दिष्टः -ष्टा -ष्टं, व्यवस्थापितः -ता -तं, व्यवस्थितः -ता -तं.—(Decisive) निश्चायकः -का -कं, निर्णायकः -का -कं.—(Resolved) व्यवसितः -ता -तं, कृतनिश्चयः -या -यं.

DETERMINATELY, *adv.* निश्चितं, सनिश्चयं, सनिर्णयं, निर्णयपूर्व्वं, सङ्कल्पपूर्व्वं.

DETERMINATION, *s.* निश्चयः, निर्णयः, सङ्कल्पः, व्यवसायः, कल्पः, सम्प्रधारणा, निर्धारणं, अवधारणं, सिद्धिः *f.*, निष्पत्तिः *f.*, व्यवस्थितिः *f.*, विचारः, विवेचना; 'firm determination,' दृढनिश्चयः.—(Persevering direction to an end) अभिनिवेशः, निर्बन्धः, अध्यवसायः.

DETERMINATIVE, *a.* निश्चायकः -का -कं, निर्णायकः -का -कं, निर्धारकः -का -कं.

To DETERMINE, *v. a.* (Fix, settle) स्था in caus. (स्थापयति -यितुं), अवस्था, व्यवस्था; सिध् in caus. (साधयति -यितुं), स्थिरीकृ, सिद्धीकृ, परिकॢप् (c. 10. -कल्पयति -यितुं).—(Decide) निश्चि (c. 5. -चिनोति -चेतुं), निर्णी (c. 1. -णयति -णेतुं), विचर् in caus. (-चारयति -यितुं).—(Resolve) व्यवसो (c. 4. -स्यति -सातुं), अध्यवसो, सङ्कॢप्, मनो निविश् in caus. (-वेशयति -यितुं).—(Ascertain) निरूप् in caus. (-रूपयति -यितुं), अवधृ in caus. (-धारयति -यितुं), सम्प्रधृ, निर्धृ.—(Define) निर्दिश् (c. 6. -दिशति -देष्टुं), लक्ष् (c. 10. लक्षयति -यितुं).—(Confine) परिमा (c. 2. -माति -तुं).—(Direct, influence the choice) उद्दिश्; प्रेर् in caus. (-ईरयति -यितुं), प्रयुज् in caus. (-योजयति -यितुं), प्रोत्सह् in caus. (-साहयति -यितुं).

To DETERMINE, *v. n.* (Come to a decision) निश्चयं कृ, निर्णयं कृ, सङ्कल्पं कृ.—(End, come to a conclusion) सिध् in pass. (सिध्यते or c. 4. सिध्यति), सम्पद् (c. 4. -पद्यते -पत्तुं), अवसो (c. 4. -स्यति -सातुं), व्यवसो; 'I am determined to do that,' तत् कर्त्तुं व्यवसितोऽस्मि.

DETERMINED, *p. p.* निश्चितः -ता -तं, निर्णीतः -ता -तं, कृतनिश्चयः -या -यं,

व्यवसितः -ता -तं, सिद्धः -द्धा -द्धं, व्यवस्थितः -ता -तं, निर्धारितः -ता -तं, अवधारितः -ता -तं, नियतः -ता -तं, प्रयतितः -ता -तं, निर्दिष्टः -ष्टा -ष्टं, विचारितः -ता -तं, सङ्कल्पितः -ता -तं.—(Resolute) साङ्कल्पिकः -की -कं, व्यवसायी -यिनी -यि (न्), सुस्थिरः -रा -रं, स्थिरमतिः -तिः -ति, अभिनिविष्टः -ष्टा -ष्टं; 'determined to sacrifice life,' प्राणांस् त्यक्तुं सुनिश्चितः or व्यवसितः.

DETERMINEDLY, *adv.* सुस्थिरं, स्थिरचेतसा, सुनिश्चितं, बुद्धिपुरःसरं, बुद्ध्या.

DETERMINER, *s.* निर्णेता *m.* (तृ), निश्चयकारी *m.* (न्), सङ्कल्पकृत्.

DETERSIVE, *a.* अपमार्जकः -का -कं, शोधकः -का -कं, परिष्कारकः -का -कं.

To DETEST, *v. a.* द्विष् (c. 2. द्वेष्टि -ष्टुं), प्रद्विष्, विद्विष्, गर्ह् (c. 1. गर्हते -र्हितुं), द्रुह् (c. 4. द्रुह्यति, द्रोहितुं, द्रोग्धुं), अभिद्रुह्, बाध् in des. (बीभत्सते -त्सितुं), घृण् (c. 1. घृणते -णितुं).

DETESTABLE, *a.* द्वेष्यः -ष्या -ष्यं, द्वेषणीयः -या -यं, गर्हणीयः -या -यं, गर्ह्यः -र्ह्या -र्ह्यं, गर्हितः -ता -तं, घृणार्हः -र्हा -र्हं, अभिगतः -ता -तं.

DETESTABLY, *adv.* गर्हणीयं, गर्हितं, द्वेषणीयं, विद्विष्टं, घृणार्हं.

DETESTATION, *s.* द्वेषः, विद्वेषः, विद्विष्टता, गर्हा -र्हणं, बीभत्सः, घृणा.

DETESTED, *p.p.* द्विष्टः -ष्टा -ष्टं, विद्विष्टः -ष्टा -ष्टं, गर्हितः -ता -तं, घृणितः -ता -तं, ख्यातगर्हणः -णा -णं, अवगीतः -ता -तं.

DETESTER, *s.* द्वेषी *m.* (न्), विद्वेषी *m.*, विद्वेष्टा *m.* (ष्टृ), गर्हाकारी *m.* (न्).

To DETHRONE, *v. a.* राज्यात् or सिंहासनात् पत् in caus. (पातयति -यितुं) or च्यु in caus. (च्यावयति -यितुं) or भ्रंश् in caus. (भ्रंशयति -यितुं) or उत्पट् in caus. (-पाटयति -यितुं).

DETHRONED, *p. p.* राज्यभ्रष्टः -ष्टा -ष्टं, भ्रष्टराज्यः -ज्या -ज्यं, राज्यात्प्रभ्रंशितः -ता -तं, राज्यप्रच्युतः -ता -तं, सिंहासनात्पातितः -ता -तं, राज्यादुत्पाटितः -ता -तं.

DETHRONEMENT, *s.* राज्यभ्रंशः, राज्यात्प्रभ्रंशनं, राज्यात्पातनं, राज्यादुत्पाटनं.

To DETONATE, *v. n.* स्तन् (c. 1. स्तनति -नितुं), स्फूर्ज् (c. 1. स्फूर्जति -र्जितुं), तीक्ष्णशब्दं कृ.

DETONATION, *s.* स्तनितं, स्तननं, स्फूर्जनं, विस्फूर्जितं, तीक्ष्णशब्दः, आस्फोटनशब्दः.

To DETORT, *v. a.* विकृ, साचीकृ, वक्रीकृ, विरूप् (c. 10. -रूपयति -यितुं).

To DETRACT, *v. a.* (Take away from) अपकृष् (c. 1. -कर्षति -क्रष्टुं), व्यपकृष्, अपहृ (c. 1. -हरति -हर्तुं), अपनी (c. 1. -नयति -नेतुं).— —(Diminish, lessen the value) अल्पीकृ, न्यूनीकृ, कन (nom. कनयति -यितुं), लघ (nom. लघयति -यितुं), लघूकृ, ह्रस् in caus. (ह्रासयति -यितुं).—(Disparage, calumniate) असूय (nom. असूयति -ते -यितुं), अभ्यसूय, अपवद् (c. 1. -वदति -दितुं), परिवद्; निन्द् (c. 1. निन्दति -न्दितुं), अवक्षिप् (c. 6. -क्षिपति -क्षेप्तुं), आक्षिप्.

DETRACTION, *s.* (Taking away, diminishing) अपकर्षः -र्षणं, अपनयनं, अपहरणं, अल्पीकरणं, न्यूनीकरणं, लघूकरणं, ह्रासः.—(Disparagement, calumny) असूया -यनं, अभ्यसूया, असूयुः *m.*, अपवादः, परिवादः, गणापवादः, गुणनिन्दा, गुणघातः, परगुणामत्सरः, परदोषवादः, परदोषाभिधानं, दोषाविष्करणं, पिशुनवाक्यं, पैशुन्यं, कौलीनं, विगानं, आक्षेपः, कलङ्कः, वाग्दोषः.

DETRACTOR, *s.* असूयकः, अभ्यसूयकः, अपवादी *m.* (न्), गुणापवादकः, परिवादी *m.* (न्), गुणघाती *m.* (न्), परगुणासहनः, निन्दकः, आक्षेपकः, सूचकः, खलः.

DETRACTORY, DETRACTIVE, *a.* असूयकः -का -कं, अभ्यसूयकः -का -कं, असूकः -का -कं, अपवादकः -का -कं, गुणघाती -तिनी -ति (न्), परिवादी -दिनी -दि (न्), लाघवकारी -रिणी -रि (न्), पिशुनः -ना -नं, कलङ्ककरः -री -रं, अकीर्त्तिकरः -री -रं.

DETRACTRESS, *s.* अपवादिनी, परिवादिनी, अभ्यसूयका, निन्दाकारिणी.

DETRIMENT, *s.* क्षतिः *f.*, अपायः, हानिः *f.*, अपकारः, अपचयः, हिंसा, द्रोहः, अनिष्टं, नाशः, विनाशः, विरोधः, क्षतं, अपकृतं, अपचितिः *f.*, अपहारः, क्षयः, उपक्षयः, दोषः, बाधः, भ्रंशः, ध्वंसः, प्रध्वंसः, व्ययः.

DETRIMENTAL, *a.* अपकारकः -का -कं -री -रिणी -रि (न्), घातुकः -का -कं, उपघातकः -का -कं, हिंस्रः -स्रा -स्रं, हिंसकः -का -कं, विरोधी -धिनी -धि (न्), क्षतिकारकः -का -कं, हानिजनकः -का -कं, द्रोही -हिणी -हि (न्).

To DETRUDE, *v. a.* निपत् in caus. (-पातयति -यितुं), अधःपत् in caus. or अधोऽधः पत्, अधःक्षिप् (c. 6. -क्षिपति -क्षेप्तुं), अधःकृ, प्रभ्रंश् in caus. (-भ्रंशयति -यितुं).

To DETRUNCATE, *v. a.* अवछिद् (c. 7. -छिनत्ति -छेत्तुं), अवकृत् (c. 6. -कृन्तति -कर्त्तितुं).

DETRUNCATION, *s.* छेदः, कर्त्तनं, अवच्छेदः, अवकर्त्तनं, लोपः -पनं.

DETRUSION, *s.* निपातनं, अधःपातनं, अधोऽधःपातनं, अधःक्षेपणं.

DEUCE, *s.* (Two) द्विः, द्वयं, द्विकं.—(Devil) पिशाचः, वेतालः, भूतः.

DEUTERONOMY, *s.* ईश्वरीयव्यवस्थाया द्वितीयविवरणं, मूसालिखितं पञ्चमपुस्तकं.

To DEVASTATE, *v. a.* उपपीड् (c. 10. -पीडयति -यितुं); बाध् (c. 1. बाधते -धितुं), प्रबाध्, परिबाध्; उपद्रु (c. 1. -द्रवति -द्रोतुं), अभिमृद् (c. 1. -मर्दति -र्दितुं), अवमृद्, उपप्लु (c. 1. -प्लवते -प्लोतुं), दह् (c. 1. दहति, दग्धुं), निर्दह्.

DEVASTATED, *p. p.* पीडितः -ता -तं, विप्लुतः -ता -तं, उपद्रुतः -ता -तं.

DEVASTATION, *s.* विप्लवः, उपप्लवः, उपपीडनं, पीडनं, उपद्रवः, अवमर्दः, बाधा, प्रबाधा, उच्छेदः, विनाशः, अभिसम्पातः.

To DEVELOP, *v. a.* विवृ (c. 5. -वृणोति -वृणुते -वरितुं -रीतुं), अपावृ; प्रकाश् in caus. (-काशयति -यितुं), विकाश्, प्रकटीकृ, उत्पद् in caus. (-पादयति -यितुं), विस्तृ in caus. (-स्तारयति -यितुं), प्रसृ in caus. (-सारयति -यितुं), विप्रथ् in caus. (-प्रथयति -यितुं), व्याकृ.

DEVELOPED, *p. p.* विवृतः -ता -तं, विकाशितः -ता -तं, उत्पादितः -ता -तं.

DEVELOPMENT, *s.* विवृतिः *f.*, विवरणं, विकाशनं, प्रकाशनं, प्रसारणं, उत्पत्तिः *f.*, उत्पादनं, विस्तृतिः *f.*, विस्तारणं, प्रकटीकरणं, व्याकरणं.

DEVERGENCE, *s.* अधःपतनं, अधोगतिः *f.*, च्युतिः *f.*, भ्रंशः, उत्क्रमः, वक्रता.

To DEVIATE, *v. n.* भ्रंश् (c. 4. भ्रश्यति, भ्रंशितुं), विभ्रंश्, च्यु (c. 1. च्यवते, च्योतुं), विच्यु, विचल् (c. 1. -चलति -लितुं), उत्क्रम् (c. 1. -क्रामति -क्रमितुं), व्युत्क्रम्, भ्रम् (c. 4. भ्राम्यति, भ्रमितुं), व्यभिचर् (c. 1. -चरति -रितुं) all with abl. c., त्यज् (c. 1. त्यजति, त्यक्तुं) with acc. c.

DEVIATED, *p. p.* भ्रष्टः -ष्टा -ष्टं, च्युतः -ता -तं, विचलितः -ता -तं.

DEVIATION, *s.* भ्रंशः, च्युतिः *f.*, विचलनं, उत्क्रमः, व्यभिचारः, भ्रान्तिः *f.*, भ्रमः, भेदः, विक्रिया, त्यागः.—(From the right way) सत्पथभ्रंशः, सत्पथत्यागः, उत्पथगमनं, विमार्गगमनं, कुपथगमनं, यथोचिताद्भ्रंशः.

DEVICE, *s.* (Contrivance) उपायः, व्यपदेशः, अपदेशः, व्यवसायः, प्रयोगः, कैतवप्रयोगः, प्रयुक्तिः *f.*, युक्तिः *f.*, कल्पना, चेष्टा, साधनं, प्रोत्सादनं, मन्त्रणा, छलं, माया, विधः; 'a good device,' सुयुक्तिः *f.*—(Project) अभिप्रायः, आशयः, चिन्ता.—(Emblem) चिह्नं, अङ्कः, कुलीनपदचिह्नं.

DEVIL, *s.* पिशाचः, भूतः, वेतालः, अपदेवता. *See* DEMON. The translators of the Bible have coined the word शैतान् from the Arabic.

DEVILISH, *a.* पैशाचः -ची -चं -चिकः -की -कं, भौतः -ती -तं -तिकः -की -कं.

DEVILISHLY, *adv.* पिशाचवत्, वेतालवत्.—(Greatly) अत्यर्थं, भृशं.

DEVIOUS, *a.* वक्रः -क्रा -क्रं, कुटिलः -ला -लं, अमर्यादः -दा -दं, उत्क्रान्तमर्यादः -दा -दं, व्यभिचारी -रिणी -रि (न्), अनाचारी -रिणी -रि (न्), भ्रमी -मिणी -मि (न्).

To DEVISE, *v. a.* प्रचिन्त् (c. 10. -चिन्तयति -यितुं), परिचिन्त्, मनसा क्लृप् (c. 10. कल्पयति -यितुं) or परिक्लृप्, अनुसन्धा (c. 3. -दधाति -धातुं), विधा, घट् (c. 1. घटते -टितुं), मन्त्र् (c. 10. मन्त्रयति -यितुं), व्यवसो (c. 4. -स्यति -सातुं), आलोच् (c. 10. -लोचयति -यितुं).—(Grant by will) दानपत्रेण स्वरिक्थं दायादादिभ्यः प्रदा (c. 1. -यच्छति -दातुं) or समृ in caus. (-अर्पयति -यितुं).

To DEVISE, *v. n.* उपायप्रयोगं कृ, उपायचिन्तां कृ, व्यपदेशं कृ.

DEVISE, *s.* (Bequeathing by will) दानपत्रेण दायादिभ्यो रिक्थप्रदानं.

DEVISED, *p. p.* प्रचिन्तितः -ता -तं, घटितः -ता -तं, विहितः -ता -तं, परिकल्पितः -ता -तं; 'well-devised,' सुघटितः -ता -तं.

DEVISEE, *s.* धनहारी *m.* (न्), धनाधिकारी *m.* (न्), अधिकारी, दानपात्रं.

DEVISER, *s.* (Contriver) उपायचिन्तकः, उपायज्ञः, उपेता *m.* (तृ), उपायी *m.* (न्), प्रयोजकः, परिकल्पकः, व्यवसायी *m.* (न्).

DEVISOR, *s.* दानपत्रेण रिक्थप्रदाता *m.* (तृ), सम्प्रदाता *m.*

DEVOID, *a.* (Empty) शून्यः -न्या -न्यं.—(Free from) हीनः -ना -नं, विहीनः -ना -नं, रहितः -ता -तं, विरहितः -ता -तं, शून्यः -न्या -न्यं, वर्जितः -ता -तं, विवर्जितः -ता -तं, उज्झितः -ता -तं, वीतः -ता -तं, गतः -ता -तं, or by निर्, वि and अ prefixed; as, 'devoid of fruit,' फलहीनः -ना -नं, फलरहितः -ता -तं, फलशून्यः -न्या -न्यं, वीतफलः -ला -लं, निष्फलः -ला -लं, विफलः -ला -लं, अफलः -ला -लं.

DEVOIR, *s.* सत्कारः, सत्कृतं, सत्कृतिः *f.*, आदरकर्म्म *n.* (न्), समादरः, सम्मानं, पूजा, अर्चनं -ना, स्वकर्त्तव्यं, कर्त्तव्यता, व्रतं.

To DEVOLVE, *v. a.* (Roll down) प्रवह् in caus. (-वाहयति -यितुं), प्रसृ in caus. (-सारयति -यितुं), प्रवृत् in caus. (-वर्त्तयति -यितुं), अनुवृत्, प्रपत् in caus. (-पातयति -यितुं).—(Deliver over) न्यस् (c. 4. -अस्यति -असितुं), सन्न्यस्, उपन्यस्, ऋ in caus. (अर्पयति -यितुं), समृ, प्रतिपद् in caus. (-पादयति -यितुं), निक्षिप् (c. 6. -क्षिपति -क्षेप्तुं), आरुह् in caus. (-रोपयति -यितुं), संक्रम् in caus. (-क्रामयति -यितुं).

To DEVOLVE, *v. n.* (Fall into new hands, be delivered over) आगम् (c. 1. -गच्छति -गन्तुं), आया (c. 2. -याति -तुं), संक्रम् (c. 1. -क्रमते -मितुं), न्यस् in pass. (-अस्यते), सन्न्यस् in pass., समृ in caus. pass. (-अर्प्यते), न्यस्तः -स्ता -स्तं भू.—(Roll down, fall down) अधो वृत् (c. 1. वर्त्तते -र्त्तितुं), अधो पत्, प्रपत् (c. 1. -पतति -तितुं).

DEVOLUTION, *s.* अधःपतनं, प्रवर्त्तनं, न्यसनं, सन्न्यसनं, आरोपणं.

To DEVOTE, *v. a.* (Appropriate to any use, dedicate, consecrate) विनियुज् (c. 7. -युनक्ति -योक्तुं), प्रयुज्, समृ in caus. (-अर्पयति -यितुं), निविद् in caus. (-वेदयति -यितुं), उत्सृज् (c. 6. -सृजति -स्रष्टुं), प्रणी (c. 1. -णयति -णेतुं), उपक्लृप् (c. 10. -कल्पयति -यितुं), प्रतिष्ठा in caus. (-ष्ठापयति -यितुं), सङ्कल्पं कृत्वा दा or समृ, वितॄ (c. 1. -तरति -रितुं -रीतुं).—(Addict one's self to any thing) आसञ्ज् in pass. (-सज्यते or -सज्जते -सक्तुं) with loc., भज् (c. 1. भजति -ते, भक्तुं), आसेव् (c. 1. -सेवते -वितुं), मनो निविश् in caus. (-वेशयति -यितुं), अनुरञ्ज् in pass. (-रज्यते), समायत् (c. 1. -यतते -तितुं), आसक्तः -क्ता -क्तं भू; 'he is devoted to his wife,' भार्य्यायाम् अनुरज्यते.—(Doom to destruction) नरकं गम्या इति शापं कृ.

DEVOTED, *p. p.* भक्तः -क्ता -क्तं, आसक्तः -क्ता -क्तं, प्रसक्तः -क्ता -क्तं, व्यासक्तः -क्ता -क्तं, सक्तः -क्ता -क्तं, रतः -ता -तं, निरतः -ता -तं, आरूढः -ढा -ढं, आस्थितः -ता -तं, समायत्तः -त्ता -त्तं, दृढभक्तिः -क्तिः -क्ति, भक्तियुक्तः -क्ता -क्तं, भक्तिमान् -मती -मत् (त्); 'devoted to one's master,' प्रभुभक्तः; 'to Krishna,' कृष्णाश्रितः or कृष्णाश्रितः; 'a devoted wife,' पतिव्रता, एकपत्नी, पतिसेविनी; 'a devoted husband,' पत्नीसेवी *m.* (न्), भार्य्यानुकूलः; 'a devoted friend,' स्थिरप्रेमा *m.* (न्).

DEVOTEDNESS, *s.* (Dedication, consecration) समर्पणं, उत्सर्गः, निवेदनं, विनियोगः, सङ्कल्पकरणं, प्रतिष्ठा, वितरणं.—(Addiction) भक्तिः *f.*, आसक्तिः *f.*, रक्तिः *f.*, उपसेवनं, निवेशः, अभिनिवेशः, निविष्टता, परायणता, उपासकता.

DEVOTEE, *s.* योगी *m.* (न्), सन्न्यासी *m.* (न्), तपस्वी *m.* (न्), तापसः, व्रती *m.* (न्), महाव्रती *m.* (न्), वैखानसः, मुनिः *m.*, निर्ग्रन्थः -न्थकः, धर्म्मनिबन्धी *m.* (न्), धर्म्मनिरतः, धर्म्मनिविष्टः.

DEVOTION, *s.* (Devoted attachment) भक्तिः *f.*, भक्तत्वं, अनुरागः, आसक्तिः *f.*, प्रसक्तिः *f.*, सक्तिः *f.*, अनुरक्तिः *f.*, योगः, सेवा, उपासना, उपसेवनं.—(Piety) ईश्वरभक्तिः *f.*, भजनशीलता, धर्म्मत्वं, ईश्वरसेवा, उत्सर्गः.—(Act of worship) नियमः, धर्म्मक्रिया, धर्म्मकृत्यं, तपः *n.* (स्); 'to perform austere devotion,' तपस् (nom. तपस्यति) or तपस् तप् in pass. (तप्यते); 'self-devotion,' आत्मपरित्यागः; 'devotion to a husband,' पतिसेवा, पातिव्रत्यं.

DEVOTIONAL, *a.* (Relating to religion) धर्म्मविषयकः -का -कं, ईश्वरपूजाविषयः -या -यं, तपोमयः -यी -यं.—(Religious) धर्म्मपरः -रा -रं, ईश्वरभावनः -ना -नं, भजनशीलः -ला -लं, औपासनः -नी -नं, नियमनिष्ठः -ष्ठा -ष्ठं.

To DEVOUR, *v. a.* ग्रस् (c. 1. ग्रसते -सितुं), उपग्रस्, भक्ष् (c. 10. भक्षयति -यितुं), सम्भक्ष्, खाद् (c. 1. खादति -दितुं), संखाद्, समद् (c. 2. -अत्ति -त्तुं), समश् (c. 9. -अश्नाति -अशितुं), पर्य्यश्, जक्ष् (c. 2. जक्षिति -तुं) घस् (c. 1. घसति, घस्तुं).—(Swallow up) गॄ (c. 6. गिरति, गरितुं -रीतुं), निगॄ, सङ्गॄ, ग्रस्.—(Consume) उपयुज् (c. 7. -युंक्ते -योक्तुं), नश् in caus. (नाशयति -यितुं).

DEVOURED, *p. p.* ग्रस्तः -स्ता -स्तं, जग्धः -ग्धा -ग्धं, भक्षितः -ता -तं, खादितः -ता -तं.

DEVOURER, *s.* भक्षकः, खादकः, भक्षयिता *m.* (तृ), ग्रसनकारः, ग्रसिष्णुः *m.*

DEVOUT, *a.* भक्तः -क्ता -क्तं, भक्तिमान् -मती -मत् (त्), भजनशीलः -ला -लं, धर्म्मी -र्म्मिणी -र्म्मि (न्), धार्म्मिकः -की -कं, धर्म्मिष्ठः -ष्ठा -ष्ठं, धर्म्मात्मा -त्मा -त्म (न्) or पुण्यात्मा or प्रयतात्मा, पूजकः -का -कं, व्रती -तिनी -ति (न्) or महाव्रती, ईश्वरभावनः -ना -नं, आर्त्तः -र्त्ती -र्त्तं, पुण्यशीलः -ला -लं, तपस्वी -स्विनी -स्वि (न्), ईश्वरनिष्ठः -ष्ठा -ष्ठं, श्रद्धान्वितः -ता -तं, परमेश्वरे सदाभक्तिः -क्तिः -क्ति.

DEVOUTLY, *adv.* ईश्वरभक्तिपूर्व्वं, ईश्वरभक्तत्वात्, श्रद्धापूर्व्वं.

DEVOUTNESS, *s.* ईश्वरभक्तत्वं, ईश्वरनिष्ठत्वं, नियमनिष्ठता, श्रद्धायत्त्वं.

DEW, *s.* नीहारः, तुषारः, शिशिरः, प्रालेयं, अवश्यायः, रजनीजलं, रात्रिजलं, निशाजलं, खजलं, खवारि *n.*, अवश्यायजलं, अवश्यायसलिलं, निशापुष्पं, खवाष्पः, हिमः -मं, दत्तं.

To DEW, *v. a.* नीहारेण or शिशिरेण क्लिद् in caus. (क्लेदयति -यितुं) or सिच् (c. 6. सिञ्चति, सेक्तुं) or प्रोक्ष् (c. 1. -क्षति -क्षितुं) or आर्द्रीकृ.

DEW-BESPRENT, *a.* शिशिराक्तः -क्ता -क्तं, नीहारोक्षितः -ता -तं, तुषारक्लिन्नः -न्ना -न्नं, अवश्यायावसिक्तः -क्ता -क्तं.

DEW-DROP, *s.* तुषारकणः, नीहारबिन्दुः *m.*, शिशिरबिन्दुः, अवश्यायबिन्दुः, हिमकणः, तुषारशीकरः.

DEW-LAP, *s.* गलकम्बलः, कम्बलः, सास्ना, वृषगलस्य लोलितमांसं.

DEWY, *a.* तुषारमयः -यी -यं, नीहारसिक्तः -क्ता -क्तं, सशिशिरः -रा -रं.

DEXTERITY, *s.* दक्षता, दाक्ष्यं, हस्तकौशल्यं, करदक्षता, हस्तलाघवं, हस्तपादादिक्षिप्रता, चातुर्य्यं, नैपुण्यं, युक्तिः *f.*, सुप्रयोगः -गता, पटुता, सत्वरता.

DEXTEROUS, *a.* दक्षः -क्षा -क्षं, करदक्षः -क्षा -क्षं, लघुहस्तः -स्ता -स्तं, कृतहस्तः -स्ता -स्तं, चतुरः -रा -रं, निपुणः -णा -णं, क्षिप्रः -प्रा -प्रं, युक्तिमान् -मती -मत् (त्), सुप्रयोगवान् -वती -वत् (त्), पेशलः -ला -लं,

पटुः -टुः -टु, सूत्थानः -ना -नं, उद्यः -द्या -द्यं.

DEXTEROUSLY, *adv.* सदाक्ष्यं, सलाघवं, युक्त्या, सचातुर्य्यं, सपाटवं.

DEXTRAL, *a.* दक्षिणः -णा -णं, दाक्षिणः -णी -णं, अपसव्यः -व्या -व्यं, वामेतरः -रा -रं, अवामः -मा -मं, दक्षिणस्थः -स्था -स्थं, दक्षिणपार्श्वस्थः -स्था -स्थं.

DHANWANTARI, *s.* (The physician of the gods) धन्वन्तरिः *m.*, काशिराजः.

DIABETES, *s.* बहुमूत्रमेहः, बहुमूत्ररोगः, इक्षुमेहः, प्रमेहः.

DIABOLIC, DIABOLICAL, *a.* पैशाचः -ची -चं -चिकः -की -कं, भौतिकः -की -कं, पिशाचोपमः -मा -मं, वैतालिकः -की -कं, दारुणः -णा -णं.

DIABOLICALLY, *adv.* पिशाचवत्, भूतवत्, वेतालवत्, दारुणं.

DIACOUSTICS, *s.* श्रवणविद्या, शब्दनिर्णयविद्या, ध्वनिविद्या.

DIADEM, *s.* किरीटः, मुकुटं, मौलिः *m.* -ली, वेष्टनं, शिरोवेष्टनं, अवतंसः, तिरीटं, बन्धुरं, चूडा, मस्तकाभरणं.

DIADEMED, *a.* किरीटी -टिनी -टि (न्), किरीटधारी -रिणी -रि (न्).

DIÆRESIS, *s.* स्वरविच्छेदः, पदविभेदः, अक्षरविच्छेदः, असन्धिः, यथा तितउ शब्दे.

DIAGNOSTIC, *s.* रोगलक्षणं, रोगचिह्नं, विसूचिका, प्रज्ञानं, उपसर्गः.

DIAGONAL, *a.* एककोणाद् अन्यकोणपर्य्यन्तम् अङ्कितः -ता -तं, कोणाकोणि लिखितः -ता -तं.

DIAGONAL, *s.* कर्णः, श्रुतिः *f.*, श्रवणः, एककोणाद् अन्यकोणपर्य्यन्तम् अङ्किता रेखा, कोणाकोणि लिखिता रेखा यया चतुरस्रं द्विसमीकृतं.

DIAGONALLY, *adv.* कोणाकोणि, आराग्रि, असासि.

DIAGRAM, *s.* मण्डलकं, चक्रं, कूर्म्मचक्रं, क्षेत्रं, अङ्कः, चित्रं.

DIAL, DIAL-PLATE, *s.* मुहूर्त्तदण्डादिपरिमापकं मण्डलं, अङ्कचिह्निता घटी यया मयूखद्वारेण कालः सूच्यते, शङ्कुः, यामघोषा; 'pin of a dial,' मयूखः, कीलः; 'sun-dial,' सूर्य्यघटी, प्रतोदः.

DIALECT, *s.* (Subdivision of a language) विभिन्नभाषा, देशभाषा. —(Language, speech) भाषा, भाषितं -वर्णं, वचनं, वाक्यं, वाक् *f.* (च्), उक्तिः *f.*; 'foreign dialect,' म्लेच्छभाषा.

DIALECTIC, *s.* (Logic) तर्कः, तर्कविद्या, न्यायः, आन्वीक्षिकी, अनुमानोक्तिः *f.*

DIALECTICAL, *a.* तार्किकः -की -कं, न्यायी -यिनी -यि (न्), प्रोहः -हा -हं.

DIALECTICALLY, *adv.* न्यायतस्, तर्कविद्यानुसारेण, तर्कशास्त्रवत्.

DIALECTICIAN, *s.* तर्की *m.* (न्), न्यायविद्, नैयायिकः, अक्षपादः, सांवादिकः.

DIALLING, *s.* (Science of shadow) छायाविद्या.—(Dial making) घटीनिर्म्माणं, पूर्वोक्तमण्डलनिर्म्माणशिल्पं.

DIALOGIST, *s.* कथोपकथकः, सांवादिकः, सम्भाषकः, उत्तरप्रत्युत्तरकृत्, प्रश्नोत्तरक्रमेण कथोपकथनरचकः.

DIALOGUE, *s.* कथोपकथनं, संलापः, सम्भाषा -षणं, संवादः, द्वयोः संवादः, सङ्कथा, सम्प्रवदनं, उत्तरप्रत्युत्तरं, प्रश्नोत्तरं, उक्तिप्रत्युक्तिः *f.*, परस्परालापः, वीथ्यङ्गं.

To DIALOGUE, *v. n.* सम्भाष् (c. 1. -भाषते -षितुं), संवद् (c. 1. -वदति -दितुं), संलप् (c. 1. -लपति -पितुं), संवच् (c. 2. -वक्ति -क्तुं), कथोपकथनं कृ.

DIAMETER, *s.* (Of a circle) व्यासः, विष्कम्भः, विस्तारः, विस्तृतिः *f.*

DIAMETRAL, DIAMETRICAL, *a.* व्यासक्रमेण विपरीतगतः -ता -तं, अभिमुखगतः -ता -तं.

DIAMETRICALLY, *adv.* व्यासक्रमेण विपरीतं, अभिमुखं, प्रतिकूलं, मुखामुखि.

DIAMOND, *s.* हीरं -रकः, वज्रः -ज्रं, वराटकं, अचिरं, अशिरं, दधीच्यस्थि *n.*, दृढाङ्गं, लोहजित्, सूचीमुखं, रत्नमुख्यं, भार्गवप्रियः; 'diamond-mine,' वज्राकरः.

DIAMOND-CUTTER, *s.* हीरकारः, हीरकच्छिद्, हीरमार्जकः, हीरपरिष्कारकः.

DIAPASON, *s.* स्वराष्टकं, अष्टस्वराः *m. pl.*, स्वरग्रामः, विरिञ्चाष्टकं.

DIAPER, *s.* पुष्पादिसंस्कारालङ्कृतः क्षौमपटः, चित्रपटः, वरकं.

To DIAPER, *v. a.* क्षौमपटं पुष्पादिसंस्कारेण अलङ्कृ, चित्र् (c. 10. चित्रयति -यितुं).

DIAPHANEITY, *s.* स्वच्छता, अच्छता, प्रसन्नता, प्रसत्तिः *f.*, वैशद्यं.

DIAPHANIC, DIAPHANOUS, *a.* स्वच्छः -च्छा -च्छं, अच्छः -च्छा -च्छं, प्रसन्नः -न्ना -न्नं, विशदः -दा -दं, विमलः -ला -लं, विशुद्धः -द्धा -द्धं, स्फटिकाभः -भा -भं.

DIAPHORETIC, *a.* स्वेदकरः -री -रं, स्वेदनः -ना -नं, स्वेदजनकः -का -कं, घर्म्मोत्पादकः -का -कं, प्रस्वेदितवान् -वती -वत् (त्); 'a diaphoretic,' स्वेदनं.

DIAPHRAGM, *s.* शरीरस्य मध्यदेशः, उदरवक्षःस्थलमध्ये शरीरभागः.

DIARRHŒA, *s.* अतिसारः, सारणः, प्रवाहिका, ग्रहणीरुक् *f.* (ज्), ग्रहणी, विरेकः, प्रस्कन्दनं -न्दिका, वमनः.

DIARRHŒTIC, *a.* रेचकः -की -कं, सारकः -का -कं, अधोभागहरः -रा -रं.

DIARY, *s.* आह्निकव्यवहारपुस्तकं, दैनिकवृत्तान्तपुस्तकं, आह्निकचरितलिखनं, पुस्तकं यस्मिन् दैनिकचेष्टितानि समारोप्यन्ते, पदभञ्जिका, पञ्जिका.

DIASTOLE, *s.* रूपकविशेषो येन ह्रस्वस्वरो दीर्घीक्रियते.

DIATESSERON, *s.* गान्धर्व्वविद्यायां स्वरचतुष्टयं.

DIBBLE, *s.* लघुखनित्रं, क्षुद्रखात्रं, बीजारोपणे प्रयुक्तो तीक्ष्णाग्रो दण्डः.

DICACITY, *s.* वावदूकता, अतिशयोक्तिः *f.*, जल्पः, वाचालता, अविनयः.

DICE, *s., pl.* of DIE. अक्षाः *m. pl.*, पाशकाः *m. pl.*, देवनाः *m. pl.*; 'loaded dice,' कूटाक्षाः *m. pl.*; 'player with dice,' अक्षदेवी *m.* (न्).

To DICE, *v. n.* अक्षैर् दिव् (c. 4. दीव्यति -ते, देवितुं) or प्रदिव् or प्रतिदिव् or क्रीड् (c. 1. क्रीडति -डितुं); ग्लह् (c. 1. ग्लहते -हितुं), अक्षक्रीडां कृ.

DICE-BOARD, *s.* पाशकपीठः, नयपीठी, अष्टापदं, शारिफलं.

DICE-BOX, *s.* अक्षाधारः, पाशकभाण्डं, अक्षभाजनं, अक्षसम्पुटकः.

DICER, *s.* अक्षदेवी *m.* (न्), अक्षधूर्त्तः -र्तः, अक्षक्रीडकः; 'player with unfair dice,' कूटाक्षदेवी *m.* (न्).

To DICHOTOMIZE, *v. a.* द्विधा कृ or छिद् (c. 7. छिनत्ति, छेत्तुं), पृथक्कृ.

DICKER, *s.* (Of leather) दशचर्म्माणि *n. pl.*, चर्म्मदशकं.

To DICTATE, *v. a.* आज्ञा in caus. (-ज्ञापयति -यितुं), आदिश् (c. 6. -दिशति -देष्टुं), निर्दिश्, शास् (c. 2. शास्ति, शासितुं), चुद् in caus. (चोदयति -यितुं), अभिचुद्, प्रेर् in caus. (-ईरयति -यितुं), प्रक्लृप् in caus. (-कल्पयति -यितुं).

DICTATE, *s.* आज्ञा, आदेशः, निदेशः, निर्देशः, नियमः, नियोगः, शासनं, चोदनः, विधिः *m.*, विधानं, प्रेरणं, वचनं, प्रयुक्तिः *f.*

DICTATED, *p. p.* आदिष्टः -ष्टा -ष्टं, आज्ञापितः -ता -तं, चोदितः -ता -तं.

DICTATION, *s.* आदेशः, आज्ञापनं, निर्देशः, निदेशः, नियोजनं, विज्ञापनं, चोदना.

DICTATOR, *s.* आपाततः or विनिपातसमये सर्व्वसम्मत्या परमाधिकारयुक्तो जनः, अनन्याधीनः शासिता *m.* (तृ), परमशासिता, परमप्रभुः, एकप्रभुः, एकाधिपतिः *m.*

DICTATORIAL, *a.* आज्ञापकः -का -कं, निर्देशकः -का -कं, धृष्टः -ष्टा -ष्टं.

DICTATORSHIP, *s.* पूर्व्वोक्तशासितुः पदं or अधिकारः, ऐकपत्यं, ऐकाधिपत्यं.

DICTION, *s.* वाग्व्यापारः, वाक्यव्यापारः, वाग्रीतिः *f.*, वाक्यं, उक्तिः *f.*, वचनं, भाषा, वाणी, व्याहारः, वचः *n.* (स्).

DICTIONARY, *s.* कोषः, शब्दकोषः, शब्दसङ्ग्रहः, अभिधानं, शब्दग्रन्थः, शब्दजालं, निर्वचनं, निघण्टुः *m.*; 'a dictionary compiler,' कौशिकः.

DICTUM, *s.* (Authoritative saying) वचनं, आदेशः, वक्तव्यं.

DIDACTIC, DIDACTICAL, *a.* उपदेशकः -का -कं, निर्देशकः -का -कं, शिक्षकः -का -कं, शिक्षाकरः -रा -रं, वैधिकः -की -कं, सौत्रः -त्री -त्रं.

DIDAPPER, *s.* (A diving bird) प्लवः, प्लावी *m.* (न्).

DIE, *s.* (To play with) अक्षः, पाशकः, देवनः, नयः, विस्तुलकः, दुन्दुभिः *f.* -भी, नयपुत्रकः, शारिशृङ्खला, अष्टाङ्गं; 'a loaded die,' कूटाक्षः,

दुरक्षं.—(Chance) दैवं.—(Stamp used in coinage) मुद्रा.

To DIE, *v. a.* (Colour, stain). *See To* DYE.

To DIE, *v. n.* (Lose life) मृ (c. 6. म्रियते, मर्त्तुं), सम्मृ, प्रे (c. 2. -एति -तुं, with प्र, प्रैति), परे, अती (अत्येति), व्यती; जीवनं or देहम् उत्सृज् (c. 6. -सृजति -स्रष्टुं), तनुं or शरीरं त्यज् (c. 1. त्यजति, त्यक्तुं) or न्यस् (c. 4. -अस्यति -असितुं), प्राणत्यागं कृ, प्रमी (c. 4. -मीयते), विपद् (c. 4. -पद्यते -पत्तुं), व्यापद्; पञ्चत्वं गम् (c. 1. गच्छति, गन्तुं), देहाद् अपगम्, लोकान्तरं गम् or प्राप् (c. 5. -आप्नोति -आप्तुं), संस्था (c. 1. -तिष्ठते -स्थातुं), प्रेतीभू.—(Perish, be lost) नश् (c. 4. नश्यति, नशितुं), प्रणश्, विनश्; प्रली (c. 4. -लीयते -लेतुं), क्षि in pass. (क्षीयते), प्रक्षि, संक्षि, ध्वंस् (c. 1. ध्वंसते -सितुं), विध्वंस्.—(Sink, faint) सद् (c. 1. सीदति, सत्तुं), अवसद्, विषद्; ग्लै (c. 1. ग्लायति, ग्लातुं), मुर्छ् (c. 1. मूर्च्छति -र्च्छितुं).—(Wither) शॄ in pass. (-शीर्य्यते).

DIER, *s.* (One who colours) वस्त्ररागकृत्. *See* DYER.

DIET, *s.* (Food) अन्नं, आहारः, खाद्यद्रव्यं, भोजनं, भक्ष्यं, भोज्यं; 'change of diet,' अन्नपरिवर्त्तः.—(Food regulated by the rules of medicine) पथ्यं, पथ्यान्नं, पथ्यापथ्यं.—(Assembly of princes) राजसभा, शिष्टसभा, मण्डलेश्वरसभा.

To DIET, *v. a.* (Feed by the rules of medicine) पथ्यापथ्यं निर्दिश् (c. 6. -दिशति -देष्टुं), पथ्यान्नं or पथ्यान्नेन भुज् in caus. (भोजयति -यितुं), पथ्यान्नं दा.—(Feed) भुज् in caus., पुष् (c. 10. पोषयति -यितुं), भृ (c. 3. बिभर्त्ति, भर्त्तुं).

To DIET, *v. n.* पथ्यान्नं भुज् (c. 7. भुंक्ते, भोक्तुं) or अश् (c. 9. अश्नाति, अशितुं).

DIET-DRINK, *s.* औषधीयजलं, पथ्यपानीयं, सिद्धजलं.

To DIFFER, *v. n.* (Be distinguished from) विशिष् in pass. (-शिष्यते), भिद् in pass. (भिद्यते), विभिद्, प्रभिद्, all with abl. c.; as, 'the son differs from the father,' पितुर् भिद्यते कुमारः.—(Contend, be at variance) विरुध् (c. 7. -रुणद्धि -रोद्धुं), प्रतिरुध्, प्रतिकूल (nom. प्रतिकूलयति -यितुं).—(Dissent) विपरीतं मन् (c. 4. मन्यते, मन्तुं), न सम्मन्, अन्यथा मन्, असम्मतिं कृ, विवद् (c. 1. -वदते -दितुं), न स्वीकृ, भिन्नमतः -ता -तं भू.

DIFFERENCE, *s.* (Distinction from something else) भेदः, विभेदः, प्रभेदः, भिदा, विशेषः, विशिष्टता, वैशिष्ट्यं, अन्तरं -रितं, भिन्नता, विभिन्नता, पृथक्त्वं, पार्थक्यं, अवच्छेदः, अन्यथात्वं, परत्वं, इतरत्वं.—(Contrariety) विपरीतता, वैपरीत्यं, विरोधः, विरुद्धता, विपर्य्ययः, वैलक्षण्यं, विप्रतिपत्तिः *f.*, द्वैधं, द्वैविध्यं.—(Difference of opinion, dispute) मतिप्रभेदः, मतिविपर्य्ययः, विमतिः *f.*, वैमत्यं, विवादः, विसंवादः, द्वैधं, कलहः, कलिः *m.*—(Difference of meaning) अर्थभेदः, अर्थान्तरं.—(Difference in quantity) तारतम्यं, वैषम्यं.—(Dissimilarity) असाम्यं, असादृश्यं.

To DIFFERENCE, *v. a.* विशिष् in caus. (-शेषयति -यितुं), भिद् in caus. (भेदयति -यितुं), पृथक्कृ.

DIFFERENT, *a.* (Distinct) भिन्नः -न्ना -न्नं, प्रभिन्नः -न्ना -न्नं, विभिन्नः -न्ना -न्नं, अन्यः -न्या -न्यत्, अन्यतरः -रा -रत्, इतरः -रा -रं, परः -रा -रं, विपरीतः -ता -तं, विविक्तः -क्ता -क्तं, व्यतिरिक्तः -क्ता -क्तं, विशिष्टः -ष्टा -ष्टं, त्वः त्वा त्वं.—(Dissimilar) असदृशः -शी -शं, असमानः -ना -नं, असमः -मा -मं, विषमः -मा -मं.—(Various) विविधः -धा -धं, पृथग्विधः -धा -धं, नानाविधः -धा -धं, बहुविधः -धा -धं; 'by a different road,' भिन्नमार्गेण; 'in a different way,' अन्यथा; 'different state of the case,' अन्यथात्वं. Sometimes expressed by अन्तरं affixed; as, 'a different meaning,' अर्थान्तरं.

DIFFERENTIAL, *a.* भेदकारः -री -रं, विशेषकः -का -कं.—(Differential series, dependence of larger numbers on smaller) तारतम्यं.

DIFFERENTLY, *adv.* अन्यथा, इतरथा, परतस्, अन्यतस्, इतरतस्, पृथक्, भिन्नरूपेण, अन्यप्रकारेण, विपरीतं, पृथक्त्वेन.

DIFFICULT, *a.* (Hard, not easy) कठिनः -ना -नं, दुष्करः -रा -री -रं, दुःसाध्यः -ध्या -ध्यं, दुष्चरः -रा -रं, दुर्निवहः -हा -हं, असुकरः -री -रं, असुगमः -मा -मं, विषमः -मा -मं, कष्टः -ष्टा -ष्टं, कष्टकरः -री -रं, आयासी -सिनी -सि (न्); 'difficult to be understood,' दुर्ज्ञेयः -या -यं; 'difficult to be got,' दुर्लभः -भा -भं, दुःप्राप्यः -प्या -प्यं, दुःखलभ्यः -भ्या -भ्यं, दुःखेन प्राप्यः -प्या -प्यं, दुरापः -पा -पं; 'difficult to be overcome,' दुरतिक्रमः -मा -मं; 'difficult to be cut,' दुःखच्छेद्यः -द्या -द्यं; 'difficult to be joined,' दुःसन्धानः -ना -नं; 'difficult of digestion,' दुर्जरः -रा -रं; 'difficult of ascent,' दुरारोहः -हा -हं; 'a difficult case,' सशल्योऽर्थः; 'difficult march,' संक्रमः, दुर्गसञ्चरः.—(Peevish, morose) वक्रभावः -वा -वं, दुर्धर्षः -र्षा -र्षं.

DIFFICULTLY, *adv.* दुःखेन, कष्टेन, कृच्छ्रेण, कृच्छ्रात्, कष्टं, आयासेन, कठिनं, विषमं, दुर् prefixed; as, 'difficultly attainable,' दुःप्राप्यः -प्या -प्यं.

DIFFICULTY, *s.* (Hardness, that which is hard to effect) काठिन्यं, कठिनता, दुःखं, कृच्छ्रं, कष्टं, आयासः, दुष्करत्वं, असौकर्य्यं, विषमं, वैषम्यं, दुर्गं, शल्यं, संशयः; 'difficulties,' दुर्गाणि; 'beset with difficulties,' सशल्यः -ल्या -ल्यं, सकण्टकः -का -कं; 'overcoming difficulties,' दुर्गलङ्घनः -नी -नं; 'cut with difficulty,' दुःखच्छेद्यः -द्या -द्यं or दुःखेन छेद्यः; 'without difficulty,' अनायासं -सेन; 'obtained with difficulty,' कृच्छ्राप्तः -प्ता -प्तं.—(Distress, opposition) क्लेशः, दुःखं, बाधः, विरोधः, प्रातिकूल्यं.—(Perplexity) व्यग्रता, वैक्लव्यं, विभ्रमः.—(Objection) बाधा, उद्ग्राहः.

To DIFFIDE, *v. n.* शङ्क् (c. 1. शङ्कते -ङ्कितुं), आशङ्क्, न विश्वस् (c. 2. -श्वसिति -तुं).

DIFFIDENCE, *s.* (Want of confidence in others) अविश्वासः, अप्रत्ययः, शङ्का.—(In one's self) ह्रीः, लज्जा, व्रीडा, अप्रागल्भ्यं, आशङ्का.

DIFFIDENT, *a.* (Distrustful) अविश्वासी -सिनी -सि (न्), अप्रत्ययी -यिनी -यि (न्), शङ्काशीलः -ला -लं, साशङ्कः -ङ्का -ङ्कं, सशङ्कः -ङ्का -ङ्कं.—(Modest, reserved) ह्रीमान् -मती -मत् (त्), लज्जावान् -वती -वत् (त्), अप्रगल्भः -भा -भं, अधृष्टः -ष्टा -ष्टं.

DIFFIDENTLY, *adv.* शङ्कया, शङ्कापूर्व्वं, लज्जया, अप्रगल्भं, अधृष्टं.

DIFFLUENCE, DIFFLUENCY, *s.* विद्रुतत्वं, द्रुतता, द्रवत्वं, द्राव्यत्वं, विलीनता, तरलता.

DIFFLUENT, *a.* विद्रुतः -ता -तं, द्रवः -वा -वं, विलीनः -ना -नं, तरलः -ला -लं.

To DIFFUSE, *v. a.* (Pour out) प्रस्रु in caus. (-स्रावयति -यितुं), प्रक्षिप् (c. 6. -क्षिपति -क्षेप्तुं), पत् in caus. (पातयति -यितुं).—(Spread, scatter, extend) विस्तॄ in caus. (-स्तारयति -यितुं), संस्तॄ, परिस्तॄ, प्रसृ in caus. (-सारयति -यितुं), विसृ, अतिसृ in caus., विसृप् in caus. (-सर्पयति -यितुं), प्रचर् in caus. (-चारयति -यितुं), विद्रु in caus. (-द्रावयति -यितुं), विकॄ (c. 6. -किरति -करितुं -रीतुं), प्रथ् in caus. (प्रथयति -यितुं), तन् (c. 8. तनोति -नितुं), वितन्, वृध् in caus. (-वर्धयति -यितुं), प्रवृध्, विकाश् in caus. (-काशयति -यितुं), प्रपञ्च् (c. 10. -पञ्चयति -यितुं).—(Diffuse itself, be diffused) व्याप् (c. 5. -आप्नोति -आप्तुं), विस्तॄ in pass. (-स्तीर्य्यते), विरुह् (c. 1. -रोहति -रोढुं), प्रवृध् (c. 1. -वर्धते -र्धितुं), सर्व्वत्र गम् (c. 1. गच्छति, गन्तुं), व्यश् (c. 5. -अश्नुते -अशितुं), विगाह् (c. 1. -गाहते -हितुं), प्रविश् (c. 6.

-विशति -वेष्टुं).

Diffuse, *s.* (Not concise, prolix) विस्तीर्णः -र्णा -र्णं, विस्तृतः -ता -तं, आयतः -ता -तं, अतिक्रान्तः -न्ता -न्तं, प्रपञ्चितः -ता -तं, दीर्घसूत्रः -त्रा -त्रं, असंक्षिप्तः -प्ता -प्तं, असामासिकः -की -कं.

Diffused, *p. p.* व्याप्तः -प्ता -प्तं, विस्तीर्णः -र्णा -र्णं, विस्तृतः -ता -तं, प्रसारितः -ता -तं, विसारितः -ता -तं, प्रसृतः -ता -तं, विसृतः -ता -तं, विकीर्णः -र्णा -र्णं, प्रकीर्णः -र्णा -र्णं, प्रचारितः -ता -तं, प्रकाशितः -ता -तं, प्रथितः -ता -तं, प्रवृद्धः -द्धा -द्धं, ततः -ता -तं, विततः -ता -तं, आततः -ता -तं, प्रविततः -ता -तं, प्रपञ्चितः -ता -तं, सर्व्वगतः -ता -तं, सर्व्वत्रगतः -ता -तं, परिगतः -ता -तं, दूतः -ता -तं.

Diffusely, *adv.* विस्तरशस्, विस्तरेण, सुविस्तरं, प्रपञ्चेन, वाग्विस्तारेण, असंक्षेपतस्, असमासतस्, असंक्षिप्तं, दीर्घसूत्रतया.

Diffusion, *s.* व्याप्तिः *f.*, व्यापनं, व्यापकत्वं, विस्तारः, विस्तृतिः *f.*, विस्तरः, विस्तीर्णता, प्रसारणं, प्रसरः -रणं, परिसरः, प्रततिः *f.*, विततिः *f.*, सन्ततिः *f.*, तानः, प्रतानः, प्रपञ्चः, प्रकाशः -शनं, विकाशः -शनं, व्यासः, परिक्षेपः, तन्तिः *f.*, विग्रहः.

Diffusive, *a.* व्यापकः -का -कं, व्यापी -पिनी -पि (न्), व्याप्तिमान् -मती -मत् (त्), विस्तरणशीलः -ला -लं, विस्तृतः -ता -तं, व्यश्नुवानः -ना -नं, प्रतानी -निनी -नि (न्), विसारी -रिणी -रि (न्) or प्रसारी, सान्तानिकः -की -कं, क्षिपण्युः -ण्युः -ण्यु.

Diffusively, *adv.* विस्तीर्णं, सुविस्तरं, व्याप्तं, सामान्यतस्, सर्व्वत्र, सुपर्य्याप्तं.

Diffusiveness, *s.* विस्तारः, विस्तीर्णता, विस्तृतिः *f.*, व्याप्तिः *f.*, व्यापकत्वं. —(Prolixity of style) वाग्विस्तारः, विस्तरः, प्रपञ्चः, दीर्घसूत्रता.

To dig, *v. a.* and *n.* खन् (c. 1. खनति -ते -नितुं), अभिखन्, आखन्; 'dig with a spade,' खनित्रेण खन् or खनित्रेण भूमिं भिद् (c. 7. भिनत्ति, भेत्तुं) or दृ in caus. (दारयति -यितुं) or गर्त्तं कृ.—(Dig up) उत्खन्, प्रोत्खन्.—(Pierce) निखन्, निर्भिद्, छिद्र् (c. 10. छिद्रयति -यितुं), छिद् (c. 7. छिनत्ति, छेत्तुं), व्यध् (c. 4. विध्यति, व्यद्धुं).

Digerent, *a.* अग्निवर्द्धकः -का -कं, पाचकः -का -कं, परिपाकी -किणी -कि (न्).

Digest, *s.* स्मृतिसंहिता, स्मृतिसङ्ग्रहः, धर्म्मशास्त्रसंहिता, स्मृतिशास्त्रं, स्मृतिसारः.—(Any compilation) सङ्ग्रहः, संहिता, समाहारः, संक्षेपः.

To digest, *v. a.* (Concoct in the stomach) जठरे or उदरे जॄ in caus. (जरयति -यितुं), पच् (c. 1. पचति, पक्तुं), परिपच्, क्वथ् (c. 1. क्वथति -थितुं), दह् (c. 1. दहति, दग्धुं).—(Soften by heat) निष्क्वथ्, सिद्धीकृ.—(Arrange, methodise) क्रमेण रच् (c. 10. रचयति -यितुं), विरच्, श्रेणीक्रमेण लिख् (c. 6. लिखति, लेखितुं) or ग्रन्थ् (c. 1. ग्रन्थति -न्थितुं), सङ्ग्रहं कृ.—(Prepare in the mind) मनसा विचर् in caus. (-चारयति -यितुं).—(Put up with) सह् (c. 1. सहते, सोढुं), क्षम् (c. 1. क्षमते, क्षन्तुं).

To digest, *v. n.* जठरे or उदरे जॄ (c. 4. जीर्य्यति, जरितुं -रीतुं).—(Suppurate) पूय् (c. 1. पूयते -यितुं), पूयं जन् (c. 10. जनयति -यितुं).

Digested, *p. p.* जीर्णः -र्णा -र्णं, पक्वः -क्वा -क्वं, क्वथितः -ता -तं, परिपक्वः -क्वा -क्वं, दग्धः -ग्धा -ग्धं, रूषितः -ता -तं, सिद्धः -द्धा -द्धं.

Digester, *s.* (That which strengthens digestion) जारणं, पाचकं, पाचनं, अग्निवर्धनः, रोचकः, रोचनः.—(A vessel) निष्क्वथनयन्त्रं.

Digestible, *a.* पक्तव्यः -व्या -व्यं, पचनीयः -या -यं, क्वथनीयः -या -यं.

Digestion, *s.* पाकः, परिपाकः, विपाकः, पचनं, जीर्णिः *f.*, जरणं, परिपक्वता, पुटपाकः, अग्निः *m.*, वह्निः *m.*, जठराग्निः, उदराग्निः, जठरानलः, कायाग्निः *m.*, कोष्ठाग्निः; 'slowness of digestion,' अग्निमान्द्यं; 'having a weak digestion,' मन्दाग्निः -ग्निः -ग्नि; 'having a good digestion,' दीप्ताग्निः -ग्निः -ग्नि.—(Suppuration) पूयत्वं, पाकः.

Digestive, *a.* पाचकः -का -कं, पाचनः -ना -नं, परिपाकी -किणी -कि (न्), अग्निवर्द्धकः -का -कं, अग्निदः -दा -दं, वह्निकरः -री -रं, आग्नेयः -यी -यं, रूचकः -का -कं, रोचकः -का -कं, रोचनः -ना -नं.—(Suppurative) पाकलः -ला -लं.

Digger, *s.* खनकः, खनिता *m.* (तृ), खननकारी *m.* (न्), खातकः, आखनिकः.

To dight, *v. a.* भूष् (c. 10. भूषयति -यितुं), अलङ्कृ, परिधा (c. 2. -धत्ते -धातुं).

Digit, *s.* (Of the moon) कला, इन्दुलेखा, इन्दुरेखा, शशाङ्कलेखा, इन्दुदलः.—(Arithmetical character) अङ्कः, गुणनिका.

Digitated, *a.* शाखी -खिनी -खि (न्), अङ्गुलिवद् विभिन्नः -न्ना -न्नं.

Digladiation, *s.* असियुद्धं, खड्गयुद्धं, युद्धं, कलिः *m.*, कलहः.

Dignified, *a.* उदारचरितः -ता -तं, उदारवृत्तिः -त्तिः -त्ति, मानी -निनी -नि (न्), गर्व्वितः -ता -तं, महाशयः -या -यं, महानुभावः -वा -वं, प्रतापी -पिनी -पि (न्), महाप्रतापः -पा -पं, प्रौढः -ढा -ढं, आयतिमान् -मती -मत् (त्).—(Invested with some dignity) उत्कृष्टपदयुक्तः -क्ता -क्तं, प्रवर्द्धितः -ता -तं, प्रतिपत्तिमान् -मती -मत् (त्).

To dignify, *v. a.* (Prefer) पदे वृध् in caus. (वर्धयति -यितुं), उत्कृष्टपदे नियुज् (c. 7. -युङ्क्ते -योक्तुं) or प्रतिपद् in caus. (-पादयति -यितुं).—(Honour, adorn) मन् in caus. (मानयति -यितुं), सम्मन्, भूष् (c. 10. भूषयति -यितुं), शुभ् in caus. (शोभयति -यितुं).

Dignitary, *s.* उत्कृष्टपदयुक्तः पुरोहितः, प्रतिपत्तिमान् *m.* (त्), मान्यलोकः.

Dignity, *s.* (Nobleness of mind) माहात्म्यं, औदार्य्यं, उदारता.—(Dignity of mien) प्रतापः, तेजः *n.* (स्), अनुभावः, प्रभावः, आयतिः *f.*—(Dignity of sentiments) गर्व्वः, मानं, अभिमानं, मानिता, सम्मानं, दर्पः.—(Elevation, honourable rank) उत्कृष्टता, उत्कर्षः, औत्कर्ष्यं, अभिजातता, आभिजात्यं, प्रतिपत्तिः *f.*, उत्कृष्टपदं, परमपदं, प्रधानता, उन्नतिः *f.*, अधिष्ठानं, स्थितिः *f.*, मान्यता, महार्घता, मर्य्यादा.

To digress, *v. n.* (Turn aside out of the road) उत्क्रम् (c. 1. -क्रामति -क्रमितुं), व्युत्क्रम्, विचल् (c. 1. -चलति -लितुं), विच्यु (c. 1. -च्यवते -च्योतुं), पार्श्वे गम् (c. 1. गच्छति, गन्तुं).—(Depart from the tenour of a discourse) वचनक्रमं or वाक्यप्रसङ्गं or कथायोगं त्यज् (c. 1. त्यजति, त्यक्तुं), प्रस्तुतं or प्रकृतं or मूलविषयं or प्रधानविषयं त्यक्त्वा प्रासङ्गिकम् अभिधा (c. 3. -दधाति -धातुं).

Digression, *s.* (From the tenour of a discourse) प्रस्तुतत्यागः, वचनक्रमत्यागः, वाक्यप्रसङ्गत्यागः, वाक्यक्रमभङ्गः, मूलविषयत्यागः, प्रासङ्गिकवाक्यं, प्रसङ्गः, वाक्यान्तरं, मूलविषयबहिर्गमनं.—(Deviation) उत्क्रमः, विचलनं, वक्रगमनं.

Digressive, *a.* निर्विषयः -या -यं, अनन्वितः -ता -तं, अप्रस्तुतः -ता -तं.

To dijudicate, *v. a.* विचर् in caus. (-चारयति -यितुं), निर्णी (c. 1. -णयति -णेतुं), निश्चि (c. 5. -चिनोति -चेतुं), तीर् (c. 10. तीरयति -यितुं), परिच्छेदं कृ.

Dijudication, *s.* निर्णयः, विचारः -रणं, निश्चयः, परिच्छेदः.

Dike, *s.* (Channel) कुल्या, उपकुल्या, परिखा, अखातं, खातं, नालः, प्रणालः, आधारः.—(Mound) सेतुः *m.*, सेतुबन्धः, जलसेतुः *m.*, जलबन्धकः, कूलकं, पालिः *f.*, पिण्डलः, पिण्डिलः, धरणः, संवरः, हिता.

To dilacerate, *v. a.* विदॄ (c. 9. -दृणाति -दरितुं -रीतुं, or caus. -दारयति -यितुं), विभिद् (c. 7. -भिनत्ति -भेत्तुं), निर्भिद्, विदलीकृ.

Dilaceration, *s.* विदारः -रणं, विदरः, विदलीकरणं, भिदा.

To dilapidate, *v. n.* जॄ (c. 4. जीर्य्यति, जरितुं -रीतुं), उत्सद् (c. 6. -सीदति -सत्तुं), भ्रंश् (c. 4. भ्रश्यति, भ्रंशितुं), नश् (c. 4. नश्यति, नशितुं), क्षि in pass. (क्षीयते).

To DILAPIDATE, *v. a.* नश् in caus. (नाशयति -यितुं), उत्सद् in caus. (-सादयति -यितुं), ध्वंस् in caus. (ध्वंसयति -यितुं), दुष् in caus. (दूषयति -यितुं).

DILAPIDATED, *p. p.* उत्सन्नः -न्ना -न्नं, जीर्णः -र्णा -र्णं, कृतध्वंसः -सा -सं.

DILAPIDATION, *s.* क्षयः, भङ्गः, प्रभङ्गः, ध्वंसः, नाशः, क्षतिः *f.*, दूषणं.

DILATABILITY, *s.* विवारणीयत्वं, विवारक्षमता, विकाशनीयत्वं, विस्तारणीयत्वं.

DILATABLE, *a.* विवारणीयः -या -यं, विवारक्षमः -मा -मं, विकाशनीयः -या -यं, विस्तारयितुं शक्यः -क्या -क्यं, विततीकरणीयः -या -यं.

DILATATION, *s.* विवारः, विवृतिः *f.*, विकाशः -शनं, विस्तारः, विस्तृतिः *f.*, विततिः *f.*, विततीकरणं, प्रततिः *f.*, व्यादानं, विसरणं, प्रसारणं, उत्फुल्लता, विपुलता, विजृम्भणं.

To DILATE, *v. a.* (Extend) विस्तॄ in caus. (-स्तारयति -यितुं), वितन् (c. 8. -तनोति -नितुं), व्यातन्, विततीकृ, विवृ (c. 5. -वृणोति -वरितुं -रीतुं or caus. -वारयति -यितुं), विकाश् in caus. (-काशयति -यितुं), विसृ in caus. (-सारयति -यितुं), व्यादा (c. 3. -ददाति -दातुं), द्राघ् (nom. द्राघयति -यितुं), प्रथ् (c. 10. प्रथयति -यितुं).—(Tell diffusely) सुविस्तरेण वद् (c. 1. वदति -दितुं), सुविस्तरं व्याख्या (c. 2. -ख्याति -तुं), विवरणं कृ, अनुक्तिं कृ.

To DILATE, *v. n.* वितन् in pass. (-तन्यते), विततीभू, विस्तॄ in pass. (-स्तीर्य्यते), विजृम्भ् (c. 1. -जृम्भते -म्भितुं), विवृ in caus. pass. (-वार्य्यते), विवारम् इ (c. 2. एति -तुं).

DILATED, *p. p.* विवृतः -ता -तं, विततः -ता -तं, विततीकृतः -ता -तं, विजृम्भितः -ता -तं, उज्जृम्भितः -ता -तं, व्यात्तः -त्ता -त्तं, उत्फुल्लः -ल्ला -ल्लं or फुल्लः, विकाशी -शिनी -शि (न्), विस्तृतः -ता -तं, आयतः -ता -तं, विसारितः -ता -तं, विसृतः -ता -तं, प्रवृद्धः -द्धा -द्धं.

DILATOR, *s.* विवारकृत्, विकाशकः, विततिकारः, विस्तारकः, व्यादाता *m.* (तृ).

DILATORILY, *adv.* सविलम्बं, विलम्बेन, कालक्षेपेण, मन्दं मन्दं.

DILATORINESS, *s.* दीर्घसूत्रता, चिरकारिता, अक्षिप्रकारित्वं, विलम्बः, विलम्बित्वं, कालक्षेपः, क्षेपः, मन्दः, मन्दता, मान्द्यं.

DILATORY, *a.* चिरकारी -रिणी -रि (न्) or अक्षिप्रकारी, चिरक्रियः -या -यं, दीर्घसूत्रः -त्रा -त्रं, विलम्बी -म्बिनी -म्बि (न्), मन्दः -न्दा -न्दं, मन्दायमानः -ना -नं, मन्थरः -रा -रं, दीर्घकालीनः -ना -नं, जडक्रियः -या -यं, प्रलम्बः -म्बा -म्बं, मनाक्करः -री -रं, कालक्षेपकः -का -कं.

DILECTION, *s.* स्नेहः, प्रीतिः *f.*, प्रेमा *m.* (न्), अनुरक्तिः *f.*, अनुग्रहः.

DILEMMA, *s.* उभयसम्भवः, सन्देहः.—(Doubtful choice) विकल्पः.

DILIGENCE, *s.* उद्योगः, उद्यमः, व्यवसायः, अभ्यासः, अभ्यासता, अभ्यसनं, प्रसक्तिः *f.*, अभिनिवेशः, मनोनिवेशः, अध्यवसायः, उत्साहः, यत्नः, प्रयत्नः, दीर्घप्रयत्नः, प्रवृत्तिः *f.*, अभियुक्तता, योग्यता, व्यवस्थितिः *f.*, अप्रमादः, समुत्थानं, शुश्रूषा, अनलसता.

DILIGENT, *a.* उद्योगी -गिनी -गि (न्), उद्यमी -मिनी -मि (न्), उद्युक्तः -क्ता -क्तं, व्यवसायी -यिनी -यि (न्), उत्साही -हिनी -हि (न्), सोद्योगः -गा -गं, आसक्तः -क्ता -क्तं, प्रसक्तः -क्ता -क्तं, अभिनिविष्टः -ष्टा -ष्टं, परायणः -णा -णं, प्रयत्नवान् -वती -वत् (त्), महोद्यमः -मा -मं, महोत्साहः -हा -हं, अनलसः -सा -सं, प्रसितः -ता -तं, कृतश्रमः -मा -मं.

DILIGENTLY, *adv.* प्रयत्नतस्, सोद्योगं, सव्यवसायं, मनोनिवेशेन, प्रसक्तं.

DILL, *s.* सालेयः, शालेयः, शीतशिवः, मिशी, मधुरिका, शतपुष्पा, शताह्वा.

DILUCID, *a.* (Clear) स्वच्छः -च्छा -च्छं, विमलः -ला -लं.—(Not obscure) स्पष्टः -ष्टा -ष्टं, व्यक्तः -क्ता -क्तं, भिन्नार्थः -र्था -र्थं.

To DILUCIDATE, *v. a.* स्पष्टीकृ, व्यक्तीकृ, व्याख्या (c. 2. -ख्याति -तुं), व्याकृ.

DILUCIDATION, *s.* स्पष्टीकरणं, व्यक्तीकरणं, व्याख्या, विशुद्धिः *f.*

DILUENT, *a.* विलयनः -ना -नं, क्षीणकारी -रिणी -रि (न्), तनूकरणः -णा -णं.

DILUENT, *s.* विलयनं, विद्रावणं, विलयकृत्, तनूकृत्, सूक्ष्मकृत्.

To DILUTE, *v. a.* (Attenuate) तनूकृ, क्षीणीकृ, सूक्ष्मीकृ, कृश (nom. कृशयति -यितुं), विलीनं -नां -नं कृ.—(Dilute with water) जलेन संसृज् (c. 6. -सृजति -स्रष्टुं) or मिश्र् (c. 10. मिश्रयति -यितुं).

DILUTED, *p. p.* (With water) जलसंसृष्टः -ष्टा -ष्टं, जलघटितः -ता -तं, जलमिश्रितः -ता -तं.—(Attenuated) तनूकृतः -ता -तं, प्रकृशितः -ता -तं, विलीनः -ना -नं; 'diluted decoction,' अनायासकृतं, फाण्टं.

DILUTER, *s.* जलेन मिश्रयति यो जनः, तनूकारी *m.* (न्), क्षीणकारी.

DILUTION, *s.* (Act of making thin or weak) तनूकरणं, क्षीणकरणं, कृशीकरणं, विलयनं.—(With water) जलसंसर्गः, जलमिश्रणं.

DILUVIAN, *s.* जलप्रलयसम्बन्धी -न्धिनी -न्धि (न्), जलाप्लावनविषयः -या -यं.

DIM, *a.* (Somewhat dark, obscure) मन्दच्छायः -या -यं, मन्दकान्तः -न्ता -न्तं, मलिनप्रभः -भा -भं, मलिनः -ना -नं, निष्प्रभः -भा -भं, अप्रभः -भा -भं, अतेजाः -जाः -जः (स्) or निस्तेजाः, अन्धकः -का -कं, सतिमिरः -रा -रं, अप्रकाशः -शा -शं, अस्पष्टः -ष्टा -ष्टं, अव्यक्तः -क्ता -क्तं, दुर्दृष्टः -ष्टा -ष्टं, दुर्दर्शः -र्शा -र्शं, हतज्योतीः -तीः -तिः (स्), दुरालोकः -का -कं.—(Not seeing clearly) अस्पष्टदृक् (श्), हतदृष्टिः -ष्टिः -ष्टि.—(Dull of apprehension) मन्दबुद्धिः -द्धिः -द्धि, स्थूलधीः -धीः -धि, जडमतिः -तिः -ति, अन्धधीः -धीः -धि.

To DIM, *v. a.* तिमिर (nom. तिमिरयति -यितुं), अन्धीकृ, निष्प्रभीकृ, मलिन (nom. मलिनयति -यितुं), अस्पष्टीकृ, मलिनीकृ.

DIMENSION, *s.* परिमाणं, प्रमाणं, मात्रं, मात्रा, मानं, विस्तारः, परिसरः, प्रसरः, पर्य्यन्तं, प्रपञ्चः, विशालता, विपुलता, सन्ततिः *f.*, विषयः, द्राघिमा *m.* (न्), दैर्घ्यं, आयतिः *f.*, आयामः, प्रयामः. The three dimensions are, 'length,' दैर्घ्यं; 'breadth,' विस्तारः; 'depth,' वेधः.

To DIMINISH, *v. a.* अल्पीकृ, न्यूनीकृ, ऊन् (c. 10. ऊनयति -यितुं), कन (nom. कनयति -यितुं), ह्रस् in caus. (ह्रासयति -यितुं), लघ (nom. लघयति -यितुं), लुप् (c. 6. लुम्पति, लोप्तुं).

To DIMINISH, *v. n.* अल्पीभू, न्यूनीभू, ऊनीभू, ह्रस् (c. 1. ह्रसते -सितुं), क्षि in pass. (क्षीयते), परिक्षि, अपचि in pass. (-चीयते).

DIMINISHED, *p. p.* अल्पीकृतः -ता -तं, अल्पीभूतः -ता -तं, क्षीणः -णा -णं, ह्रसितः -ता -तं, न्यूनीभूतः -ता -तं, अपचितः -ता -तं, लुप्तः -प्ता -प्तं.

DIMINUTION, *s.* (Act of making less) न्यूनीकरणं, अल्पीकरणं, ह्रासः, लोपः.—(State of growing less) क्षयः, न्यूनत्वं -ता, अल्पत्वं, अपचयः, क्षिया, क्षितिः *f.*, ह्रासः, हानिः *f.*, अवसादः.

DIMINUTIVE, *a.* अल्पः -ल्पा -ल्पं, अल्पकः -का -कं, क्षुद्रः -द्रा -द्रं, कणीकः -का -कं, स्तोकः -का -कं, सूक्ष्मः -क्ष्मा -क्ष्मं.—(In body) अल्पतनुः -नुः -नु, स्तोककायः -यी -यं, अल्पमूर्त्तिः -र्त्तिः -र्त्ति.

DIMINUTIVENESS, *s.* अल्पता, क्षुद्रता, सूक्ष्मता, सौक्ष्म्यं, स्तोकता, अणिमा *m.* (न्), लघुता, लाघवं, क्षोदिमा *m.* (न्).

DIMISH, *a.* ईषन्मलिनः -ना -नं, ईषदन्धः -न्धा -न्धं, अस्पष्टः -ष्टा -ष्टं.

DIMISSORY, *s.* गमनानुज्ञापकः -का -कं, प्रेरकः -का -कं, प्रस्थापकः -का -कं; 'letters dimissory,' अन्यधर्म्माध्यक्षाधीनदेशे गमनानुज्ञापकं पत्रं.

DIMITY, *s.* सूक्ष्मकार्पासं, सूक्ष्मतूलावस्त्रं, कार्पासाम्बरं, फालवस्त्रं.

DIMLY, *adv.* अस्पष्टं, अप्रकाशं, अव्यक्तं, निष्प्रभं, अस्फुटं, मलिनं.

DIMMED, *p. p.* हतप्रभः -भा -भं, हततेजाः -जाः -जः (स्) or क्षततेजाः, हतज्योतीः -तीः -तिः (स्), हतौजाः -जाः -जः (स्) or क्षतौजाः, मलिनितः -ता -तं.

DIMNESS, *s.* अस्पष्टता, निष्प्रभता, तिमिरं, अव्यक्तता, अप्रकाशत्वं, दुर्दर्शत्वं, दुरालोकता, प्रभाहानिः *f.*, प्रतिभाहानिः *f.*—(Stupidity) बुद्धिमान्द्यं, स्थूलता.

DIMPLE, *s.* कपोलभङ्गः, गण्डतरङ्गः, चिबुकरेखा, हनुभङ्गः, त्वगूर्म्मिका.

DIMPLY, *a.* भङ्गुरः -रा -रं, ऊर्म्मिमान् -मती -मत् (त्).

DIN, *s.* कोलाहलः, तुमुलं, घुष्टं, घोषः, उच्चैःस्वरः, झम्भा, झम्भनं, रासः, स्तनितं, ध्वनितं, क्वणितं, निःस्वनः, उद्रावः, चीत्कारः, निनादः, डिण्डिम शब्दः.

To DIN, *v. a.* डिण्डिम शब्देन or कोलाहलेन or उच्चैःशब्देन कर्णौ उपहन् (c. 2. -हन्ति -न्तुं).

To DINE, *v. n.* आहारं कृ, भोजनं कृ, मध्याह्नभोजनं कृ, माध्याह्निकाहारं कृ; 'one who has dined,' कृताहारः -रा -रं, कृतभोजनः -ना -नं.

To DINE, *v. a.* (Give a dinner to) भुज् in caus. (भोजयति -यितुं), अश् in caus. (आशयति -यितुं), प्राश्, माध्याह्निकभोजनं कृ in caus. (कारयति -यितुं).

To DING, *v. a.* (Dash) प्रसभं क्षिप् (c. 6. क्षिपति, क्षेप्तुं) or पत् in caus. (पातयति -यितुं) or अभिहन् (c. 2. -हन्ति -न्तुं) or प्रतिहन्.

To DING, *v. n.* शब्द (nom. शब्दायते), भर्त्स् (c. 10. भर्त्सयते -यितुं).

DING-DONG, *s.* घण्टाशब्दः, घण्टास्वनः, घण्टानादः.

DINGLE, *s.* दरी -रा, दरीभूः *f.*, कन्दरः -री, अद्रिद्रोणी, प्रान्तरं.

DINING-ROOM, *s.* भोजनशाला, भोजनगृहं, भोजनस्थानं, आहारस्थानं.

DINNER, *s.* मध्याह्नभोजनं, माध्याह्निकाहारः, भोजनं, आहारः; 'a dinner party,' सहभोजनं, सम्भोजनं, सग्धिः *f.*; 'invited to dinner,' भोजनार्थं निमन्त्रितः; 'to serve up dinner,' भोजनं परिविश् in caus. (-वेशयति -यितुं).

DINNER-TIME, *s.* भोजनकालः, मध्याह्नभोजनकालः, आहारकालः.

DINT, *s.* (Blow) आघातः, प्रहारः, आहतिः *f.*, अभिघातः, घातः.—(Mark made by a blow) आघातचिह्नं, भङ्गः.—(Force) बलं, शक्तिः *f.*, प्रभावः; 'by dint of,' बलेन, प्रभावात्; 'by dint of penance,' तपःप्रभावात्.

To DINT, *v. a.* आघातेन चिह्न् (c. 10. चिह्नयति -यितुं) or अङ्क् (c. 10. अङ्कयति -यितुं).

DIOCESAN, *s.* प्रधानधर्म्माध्यक्षः, धर्म्माधिपतिः *m.*, प्रधानधर्म्मोपदेशकः.

DIOCESE, *s.* प्रधानधर्म्माध्यक्षाधीनो देशः or प्रदेशः.

DIOPTRICAL, *a.* दूरदर्शनोपकारकः -का -कं, दूरदृष्टिप्रयोजकः -का -कं.

DIOPTRICS, *s. pl.* दूरस्थवस्तुदृष्टिविषयकं चाक्षुषशास्त्रप्रकरणं.

DIORTHOSIS, *s.* वक्राङ्गचिकित्सा, भग्नाङ्गसमाधानं, वक्राङ्गस्य ऋजूकरणं.

To DIP, *v. a.* (Immerge) मस्ज् in caus. (मज्जयति -यितुं), निमस्ज्, प्रमस्ज्, अवगाह् in caus. (-गाहयति -यितुं); आप्लु in caus. (-प्लावयति -यितुं).—(Moisten) क्लिद् in caus. (क्लेदयति -यितुं), सिच् (c. 6. सिञ्चति, सेक्तुं).—(Engage in) व्यापृ (c. 6. -प्रियते -पर्त्तुं), वृत् (c. 1. वर्त्तते -र्त्तितुं), प्रवृत्, आस्था (c. 1. -तिष्ठति -स्थातुं).—(Dip into a book) शास्त्रं चुम्ब् (c. 1. चुम्बति -म्बितुं) or ईषन्मनोयोगेन अधी (c. 2. अधीते, अध्येतुं).

To DIP, *v. n.* (Immerge one's self) मस्ज् (c. 6. मज्जति, मंक्तुं), निमस्ज्, अवगाह् (c. 1. -गाहते -हितुं), व्यवगाह्, विगाह्, प्लु in caus. pass. (प्लाव्यते), आप्लु (c. 1. -प्लवते -प्लोतुं).—(Enter) विश् (c. 6. विशति, वेष्टुं), प्रविश्, निविश्.—(Be engaged in) व्यापृ (c. 6. -प्रियते), व्यापृतः -ता -तं भू, निष्ठा (c. 1. -तिष्ठति -ष्ठातुं), प्रवृत्तः -त्ता -त्तं भू, आरूढः -ढा -ढं भू.—(Choose by chance) दैवम् आस्थाय ग्रह् (c. 9. गृह्णाति, ग्रहीतुं), दैवात् or अकस्माद् ग्रह्.

DIP, *s.* निमज्जनं, अवगाहः, अवनतिः *f.*, अधोगतिः *f.*, पतनं, आनतिः *f.*, नम्रता.

DIPHTHONG, *s.* द्विस्वरः, युक्तस्वरः, स्वरद्वयं, सन्ध्यक्षरं.

DIPLOMA, *s.* पददायकं or अधिकारदायकं or ख्यातिदायकं पत्रं, अधिकारपत्रं.

DIPLOMACY, *s.* (State of acting under a diploma) प्रामाधिकारस्य पदं or अवस्था.—(Privileges or customs of ambassadors) दूताधिकारः, राजदूतव्यवहारः.—(Body of ambassadors) दूतसमूहः, राजदूतमण्डलं.—(Business of an ambassador) राजदूतव्यापारः, राजप्रतिनिधिकर्म्म *n.* (न्), दौत्यकर्म्म.—(Dexterity in negotiation) माया.

DIPLOMATIC, *a.* दौतिकः -की -कं, दूतव्यवहारसम्बन्धी -न्धिनी -न्धि (न्), राजप्रतिनिधिकर्म्मविषयकः -का -कं.

DIPPER, *s.* मज्जयिता *m.* (तृ), निमज्जयिता, आप्लावकः.—(Ladle) स्रुवः.

DIRE, *a.* दारुणः -णा -णं, घोरः -रा -रं, उग्रः -ग्रा -ग्रं, भयानकः -का -कं, भयङ्करः -रा -रं, भैरवः -वी -वं, रौद्रः -द्री -द्रं, रौद्रदर्शनः -ना -नं, भीषणः -णा -णं, क्रूरः -रा -रं, भीष्मयः -यी -यं.

DIRECT, *a.* (Not crooked, not oblique) अवक्रः -क्रा -क्रं, अजिह्मः -ह्मा -ह्मं, अकुटिलः -ला -लं, ऋजुः -जुः -जु, अनुलोमः -मा -मं, अभ्रंसः -सा -सं, अविलोमः -मा -मं; 'a direct flight,' सण्डीनं.—(Not collateral) क्रमागतः -ता -तं.—(Express, plain) व्यक्तः -क्ता -क्तं, स्पष्टः -ष्टा -ष्टं, अव्यवधानः -ना -नं.

To DIRECT, *v. a.* (Aim at, point towards) अभिसन्धा (c. 3. -दधाति -धातुं), उद्दिश् (c. 6. -दिशति -देष्टुं), समुद्दिश्; 'to direct a weapon at any one,' अमुकमुद्दिश्य अस्त्रं क्षिप् (c. 6. क्षिपति, क्षेप्तुं) or प्रेर् (c. 10. -ईरयति -यितुं); 'he performed a penance directed to the deity,' देवमुद्दिश्य तपस् तेपे.—(Regulate) शास् (c. 2. शास्ति, शासितुं), अनुशास्, प्रशास्; विधृ in caus. (-धारयति -यितुं), विनियम् (c. 1. -यच्छति -यन्तुं), विधा (c. 3. -दधाति -धातुं).—(Guide, lead) नी (c. 1. नयति, नेतुं), दृश् in caus. (दर्शयति -यितुं), दिश्, प्रदिश्.—(Prescribe, point out) निर्दिश्, प्रदिश्, विनिर्दिश्; सूच् (c. 10. सूचयति -यितुं).—(Order, instruct) आदिश्, उपदिश्, आज्ञा in caus. (-ज्ञापयति -यितुं), चुद् in caus. (चोदयति -यितुं).

DIRECTED, *p. p.* (Aimed at) उद्दिष्टः -ष्टा -ष्टं, उद्दिश्य indecl., अभिसंहितः -ता -तं.—(Regulated) शासितः -ता -तं, अनुशासितः -ता -तं, विनियतः -ता -तं, व्यवस्थितः -ता -तं.—(Prescribed) निर्दिष्टः -ष्टा -ष्टं, प्रदिष्टः -ष्टा -ष्टं, देशितः -ता -तं, सूचितः -ता -तं.—(Ordered, instructed) आदिष्टः -ष्टा -ष्टं, उपदिष्टः -ष्टा -ष्टं, प्रचोदितः -ता -तं, प्रेरितः -ता -तं.—(Applied) प्रयुक्तः -क्ता -क्तं, अर्पितः -ता -तं; 'well-directed,' सुप्रयुक्तः -क्ता -क्तं.

DIRECTION, *s.* (Aim, tendency) सन्धानं, अभिसन्धानं, उद्देशः.—(Order, command) आदेशः, निदेशः, निर्देशः, आज्ञा, शासनं, शास्तिः *f.*, चोदनं, प्रेरणा, प्रयुक्तिः *f.*, मतं, वचनं.—(Management) नयः, नायः, प्रणयनं, नेतृत्वं, अधिकारः, अधिष्ठातृत्वं, सम्पादनं, निर्देशः.(Address of a letter) पत्रसंज्ञा, पत्रादेशः, पत्रोद्देशः.—(Place of abode) वासस्थानं; 'in three directions,' त्रेधा; 'in every direction,' सर्व्वपथीनः -ना -नं, चतुर्दिक्षु; 'following the natural direction,' अनुलोमनं.

DIRECTIVE, *a.* देशकः -का -कं, उद्देशकः -का -कं, आदेशी -शिनी -शि (न्), निर्देशकः -का -कं, दर्शकः -का -कं, सूचकः -का -कं.

DIRECTLY, *adv.* सद्यस्, अचिरात्, अचिरेण, सपदि, झटिति, अनन्तरं, तत्क्षणात्, क्षणान्तरे, आशु, अविलम्बितं, शीघ्रं, क्षिप्रं, तत्काले.

DIRECTOR, *s.* नायकः, अधिष्ठाता *m.* (तृ), शासिता *m.* (तृ), अनुशासकः, अध्यक्षः, आदेष्टा *m.* (ष्टृ), निर्देष्टा *m.*, आदेशी *m.* (न्), अधिकारी *m.* (न्), ईशिता *m.* (तृ), सम्पादकः, अवेक्षिता *m.* (तृ).

DIREFUL, *a.* दारुणः -णा -णं, घोरः -रा -रं, भीष्मयः -यी -यं. *See* DIRE.

DIREFULNESS, DIRENESS, *s.* दारुणत्वं, दारुणं, घोरता, उग्रता, भयानकत्वं, भीमता, क्रूरता, रौद्रता.

DIREPTION, *s.* हरणं, अपहारः, अपहरणं, अभिग्रहः, अभिहारः, विलोपनं.

DIRGE, *s.* करुणं, करुणार्थकं गीतं, कारुणिकगीतं, करुणामयं गीतं.

DIRK, *s.* कट्टारः, कृपाणी, छुरिका, शङ्कुः *m.*, कर्त्तरी, असिपुत्रिका.

DIRT, *s.* (Mud, filth) मलं, पङ्कः, कुपङ्कः, अमेध्यं, कर्द्दमः, कल्कं, जम्बालः -लं, कलुषं.—(Sordidness) कदर्यत्वं, मालिन्यं.

To DIRT, *v. a.* मलिन (nom. मलिनयति -यितुं), कलुष (nom. कलुषयति -यितुं), मलेन or पङ्केन दुष् in caus. (दूषयति -यितुं) or लिप् (c. 6. लिम्पति, लेप्तुं).

DIRTIED, *p. p.* मलिनितः -ता -तं, मलदूषितः -ता -तं, पङ्कदूषितः -ता -तं, अमेध्यलिप्तः -प्ता -प्तं, अमेध्याक्तः -क्ता -क्तं, कलुषितः -ता -तं.

DIRTILY, *adv.* समलं, मलिनं, सकर्द्दमं, सकल्कं, मलीमसं, समालिन्यं.

DIRTINESS, *s.* मालिन्यं, समलता, मलवत्त्वं, अमेध्यता -त्वं, कलुषत्वं, अशुद्धता.

DIRTY, *a.* (Filthy) मलिनः -ना -नं, समलः -ला -लं, मलवान् -वती -वत् (त्), मलदूषितः -ता -तं, मलीमसः -सा -सं, पङ्की -ङ्किनी -ङ्कि (न्) or मलपङ्की, पङ्किलः -ला -लं, कलुषः -षा -षं -षी -षिणी -षि (न्), सकर्द्दमः -मा -मं, कार्द्दमः -मी -मं, कल्की -ल्किनी -ल्कि (न्), कश्मलः -षा -षं, सजम्बालः -ला -लं, कश्मलः -ला -लं, आविलः -ला -लं, मलीयान् -यसी -यः (स्), अशुद्धः -द्धा -द्धं.—(Mean, base) नीचः -चा -चं, खलः -ला -लं, कदर्यः -र्या -र्यं, कुत्सितः -ता -तं; 'dirty clothes,' चराती.

To DIRTY, *v. a.* मलिन (nom. मलिनयति -यितुं), कलुष (nom. कलुषयति -यितुं), मलेन or अमेध्येन or पङ्केन दुष् in caus. (दूषयति -यितुं) or लिप् (c. 6. लिम्पति, लेप्तुं) or अञ्ज् (c. 7. अनक्ति, अंक्तुं), मलिनीकृ, समलं -लां -लं कृ, अमेध्यं -ध्यां -ध्यं कृ, कलङ्क (nom. कलङ्कयति -यितुं).

DIRUPTION, *s.* स्फोटनं, स्फुटनं, भेदः, विभेदः, विभङ्गः, विदारणं.

DISABILITY, *s.* अशक्तिः *f.*, असामर्थ्यं, अक्षमता, दौर्बल्यं, शक्तिहीनता, अयोग्यता, अनुपयुक्तता, निषेधः.

To DISABLE, *v. a.* अशक्तं -क्तां -क्तं कृ, अशक्तीकृ, असमर्थं -र्थां -र्थं कृ, अक्षमं -मां -मं कृ, दुर्बलीकृ, बलं or शक्तिं हृ (c. 1. हरति, हर्त्तुं), विकलीकृ, विहस्तीकृ, उपहन् (c. 2. -हन्ति -न्तुं).

DISABLED, *p. p.* हतशक्तिः -क्तिः -क्ति or उपहतशक्तिः, विहस्तीकृतः -ता -तं.

To DISABUSE, *v. a.* (Undeceive) भ्रमं or भ्रान्तिं or मोहं or मिथ्यामतिं छिद् (c. 7. छिनत्ति, छेत्तुं) or अपनी (c. 1. -नयति, नेतुं) or हृ (c. 1. हरति, हर्त्तुं), भ्रान्तेर् मुच् (c. 6. मुञ्चति, मोक्तुं), मुक्तभ्रान्तिं कृ, विगतमोहं -हां -हं कृ.

To DISACCUSTOM, *v. a.* अव्यवहारितं -तां -तं कृ, व्यवहारं or अभ्यासं लुप् (c. 6. लुम्पति, लोप्तुं) or निवृत् in caus.

DISADVANTAGE, *s.* अनर्थः, अलाभः, अहितं, अनिष्टं, अफलं, अपायः, अपचयः, अपकारः, अपचितिः *f.*, अपकृतं, अप्राप्तिः *f.*, क्षतिः *f.*, हानिः *f.*, हिंसा, क्षयः, उपक्षयः, अपहारः, नाशः, विरोधः, व्याघातः, बाधः, अनुपकारः.

To DISADVANTAGE, *v. a.* अपकृ, अपायं or अनर्थं जन् in caus. (जनयति -यितुं), अहिताय or अलाभाय भू, विरुध् (c. 7. -रुणद्धि -रोद्धुं), हिंस् (c. 1. हिंसति -सितुं).

DISADVANTAGEOUS, *a.* अपकारकः -का -कं -री -रिणी -रि (न्), अहितः -ता -तं, अनर्थः -र्था -र्थं -र्थकः -का -कं, निरर्थकः -का -कं, अफलः -ला -लं, विरोधी -धिनी -धि (न्), प्रतिकूलः -ला -लं, अनुपकारकः -का -कं, अनिष्टजनकः -का -कं, क्षतिकारकः -का -कं, उपघातकः -का -कं, हिंसकः -का -कं, अमङ्गलः -ला -लं, सापकारः -रा -रं.

DISADVANTAGEOUSLY, *adv.* अहितं, अनिष्टं, अलाभाय, अहिताय, विरोधेन, विरुद्धं, प्रतिकूलं, प्रातिकूल्येन, अनर्थकं, अमङ्गलं, सापकारं.

To DISAFFECT, *v. a.* (Cause disaffection) विरञ्ज् in caus. (-रञ्जयति -यितुं), विरक्तीकृ, वैरक्त्यं जन् (c. 10. जनयति -यितुं), उपजप् (c. 1. -जपति -पितुं), कर्णे जप् or उपजप्, भेदं or वैरं कृ.

DISAFFECTED, *p. p.* विरक्तः -क्ता -क्तं, अहितः -ता -तं, विप्रियः -या -यं, अहितैषी -षिणी -षि (न्) or अप्रियैषी, क्षीणभक्तिः -क्तिः -क्ति, अभक्तः -क्ता -क्तं, अभक्तिमान् -मती -मत् (त्), अहितबुद्धिः -द्धिः -द्धि, अहितकारी -रिणी -रि (न्).

DISAFFECTEDLY, *adv.* विरक्तं, अहितं, सवैरक्त्यं, सवैराग्यं, विप्रियं.

DISAFFECTION, *s.* विरक्तिः *f.*, वैरक्त्यं, विरागः, वैराग्यं, अपरागः, अभक्तिः *f.*, विप्रियता, अहितत्वं, अभक्तिमत्त्वं.

DISAFFIRMANCE, *s.* अपवादः, अपलापः, प्रत्याख्यानं, खण्डनं, अस्वीकारः.

To DISAGREE, *v. n.* (In opinion) विवद् (c. 1. -वदते -दितुं), विसंवद् (-वदति), न सम्मन् (c. 4. -मन्यते -मन्तुं), न अनुमन्, न स्वीकृ, असम्मतः -ता -तं भू, अन्यमतीभू.—(Differ, not to suit) भिद् in pass. (भिद्यते), असदृशः -शी -शं भू, न युज् in pass. (युज्यते).—(Be opposed to) विरुध् (c. 7. -रुणद्धि -रोद्धुं).

DISAGREEABLE, *s.* (Unpleasing) अप्रियः -या -यं, विप्रियः -या -यं, कुप्रियः -या -यं, अनभिमतः -ता -तं, अननुमतः -ता -तं, अरम्यः -म्या -म्यं, अनिष्टः -ष्टा -ष्टं, अहितः -ता -तं, अमनोज्ञः -ज्ञा -ज्ञं, अमनोहरः -रा -रं, अरुचिरः -रा -रं, अप्रीतिकरः -री -रं, अनीहितः -ता -तं, व्यलीकः -का -कं, अलीकः -का -कं, असुखदः -दा -दं, निःसुखः -खा -खं, कष्टः -ष्टा -ष्टं.—(Contrary) विरुद्धः -द्धा -द्धं, विपरीतः -ता -तं, प्रतिकूलः -ला -लं.

DISAGREEABLENESS, *s.* अप्रियता, विप्रियता, अरम्यता, अनिष्टत्वं, व्यलीकता, अलीकता, अनभिमतत्वं, अमनोज्ञत्वं, कष्टता, विरुद्धता, वैपरीत्यं.

DISAGREEABLY, *adv.* अप्रियं, अरम्यं, अनिष्टं, व्यलीकं, अरुचिरं, विरुद्धं.

DISAGREEING, *p. p.* विवदमानः -ना -नं, असम्मतः -ता -तं, परस्परविरुद्धः -द्धा -द्धं.

DISAGREEMENT, *s.* (Difference) भेदः, विभेदः, भिन्नता, असमता, असाम्यं.—(Difference of opinion) विमतिः *f.*, वैमत्यं, मतिभेदः, मतिविपर्ययः, असम्मतिः *f.*, विसंवादः, अस्वीकारः.—(Quarrel) कलहः, विप्रतिपत्तिः *f.*, विप्रयोगः.—(Contrariety) विरोधः, विरुद्धता, विपरीतता.

To DISALLOW, *v. a.* (Deny) प्रत्याख्या (c. 2. -ख्याति -तुं), निह्नु (c. 2. -ह्नुते -ह्नोतुं), प्रत्यादिश् (c. 6. -दिशति -देष्टुं), अपलप् (c. 1. -लपति -पितुं), निरस् (c. 4. -अस्यति -असितुं).—(Not to permit) न अनुज्ञा (c. 9. -जानाति -ज्ञातुं), न अनुमन् (c. 4. -मन्यते -मन्तुं), निषिध् (c. 1. -षेधति -षेद्धुं).—(Censure) निन्द् (c. 1. निन्दति -न्दितुं), गर्ह् (c. 1. गर्हते -र्हितुं).

DISALLOWABLE, *a.* प्रत्याख्येयः -या -यं, अननुज्ञेयः -या -यं, अधर्म्यः -र्म्या -र्म्यं.

DISALLOWANCE, *s.* प्रत्याख्यानं, प्रत्यादेशः, निषेधः, प्रतिषेधः, अननुज्ञा, निरसनं.

DISALLOWED, *p. p.* निषिद्धः -द्धा -द्धं, प्रतिषिद्धः -द्धा -द्धं, अननुज्ञातः -ता -तं, प्रत्याख्यातः -ता -तं, वारितः -ता -तं, निवारितः -ता -तं.

To DISANIMATE, *v. a.* निर्जीवीकृ, विचक्षीकृ, अवसद् in caus. (-सादयति -यितुं).

DISANIMATION, *s.* निर्जीवीकरणं, जीवितनाशः, प्राणहरणं, जीवितहरणं.

To DISANNUL, *v. a.* लुप् (c. 6. लुम्पति, लोप्तुं), लोपं कृ, खण्ड् (c. 10. खण्डयति -यितुं), मोघीकृ, निष्फल (nom. निष्फलयति -यितुं), अन्यथा कृ.

DISANNULLED, *p. p.* लुप्तः -प्ता -प्तं, मोघीकृतः -ता -तं, अनिष्पन्नः -न्ना -न्नं.

DISANNULMENT, *s.* लोपः, खण्डनं, मोघीकरणं, अन्यथाकरणं.

To DISAPPEAR, *v. n.* अन्तर्धा in pass. (-धीयते), तिरोधा in pass., तिरोभू, तिरस् (nom. तिरस्यति), नश् (c. 4. नश्यति, नशितुं), प्रणश्, तिरोगम् (c. 1. -गच्छति -गन्तुं), विली (c. 4. -लीयते -लेतुं), अदर्शनीभू, अदृश्यः -श्या -श्यं भू, अस्तं गम्.

DISAPPEARED, *p. p.* अन्तर्हितः -ता -तं, तिरोहितः -ता -तं, तिरोगतः -ता

-तं, नष्टः -ष्टा -ष्टं, अदृष्टः -ष्टा -ष्टं, अदृश्यः -श्या -श्यं, विलीनः -ना -नं, चक्षुरविषयः -या -यं, अप्रत्यक्षः -क्षा -क्षं, अलोकितः -ता -तं, अदृष्टिगोचरः -रा -रं, परोक्षः -क्षा -क्षं, चक्षुरतीतः -ता -तं.

DISAPPEARANCE, *s.* अन्तर्द्धा -र्द्धानं, अन्तर्द्धिः *m.*, तिरोधानं, तिरस्कारः, तिरस्क्रिया, अविषयः, अप्रत्यक्षता, अदर्शनं, अलोकनं, अपवारणं, परोक्षं, अगोचरं, अस्तमयनं, अन्तर्हितत्वं.—(Departure) अपगमः, अपायः.

To DISAPPOINT, *v. a.* आशाः खण्ड् (c. 10. खण्डयति -यितुं), सङ्कल्पं or वाञ्छाः or मनोरथान् हन् (c. 2. हन्ति -न्तुं) or प्रतिहन् or भञ्ज् (c. 7. भनक्ति, भंक्तुं), भग्नाशं -शां -शं कृ, मोघीकृ, व्यर्थीकृ, विफलीकृ, वृथा कृ, मुधा कृ, वञ्च् (c. 10. वञ्चयति -यितुं), प्रलभ् (c. 1. -लभते -लब्धुं), विप्रलभ्.

DISAPPOINTED, *p. p.* भग्नाशः -शा -शं, हताशः -शा -शं, मनोहतः -ता -तं, खण्डितः -ता -तं, खण्डिताशंसः -सा -सं, भग्नसङ्कल्पः -ल्पा -ल्पं, भग्नोद्यमः -मा -मं, आशाविभिन्नः -न्ना -न्नं, मोघाशः -शा -शं, मोघवाञ्छितः -ता -तं, अनधिगतमनोरथः -था -थं, अलब्धाभीप्सितः -ता -तं, विफलीकृतः -ता -तं, प्रतिहतः -ता -तं, अकृतार्थः -र्था -र्थं, विलधितः -ता -तं, प्रतिबद्धः -द्धा -द्धं, विप्रलब्धः -ब्धा -ब्धं, वञ्चितः -ता -तं.

DISAPPOINTMENT, *s.* आशाभङ्गः, आशाखण्डनं, उद्यमभङ्गः, सङ्कल्पभङ्गः, फलखण्डनं, विफलीकरणं, कर्म्मध्वंसः, नैराश्यं, विप्रलम्भः, विषादः, विसंवादः, प्रत्यवायः.

DISAPPROBATION, *s.* अप्रसादः, निन्दा, अप्रीतिः *f.*, विमतिः *f.*, विरागः, वैरक्त्यं, विप्रियता, असम्मतिः *f.*, अस्वीकारः, अनिच्छा, गर्हा -र्हणं, जुगुप्सा, घृणा.

To DISAPPROVE, *v. a.* निन्द् (c. 1. निन्दति -न्दितुं), गर्ह् (c. 1. गर्हते -र्हितुं), न सम्मन् (c. 4. -मन्यते -मन्तुं), न अनुमन्, न अभिमन्, न स्वीकृ, न प्रशंस् (c. 1. -शंसति -सितुं), न प्रतिनन्द् (c. 1. -नन्दति -न्दितुं), न रुच् (c. 1. रोचते -चितुं) with dat.; as, 'he disapproves of that,' तत् तस्मै न रोचते.

DISAPPROVED, *p. p.* अनभिमतः -ता -तं, असम्मतः -ता -तं, अमतः -ता -तं, अनिष्टः -ष्टा -ष्टं, अप्रशस्तः -स्ता -स्तं, गर्हितः -ता -तं, निन्दितः -ता -तं, अस्वीकृतः -ता -तं, विद्विष्टः -ष्टा -ष्टं.

To DISARM, *v. a.* शस्त्रं or अस्त्रं हृ (c. 1. हरति, हर्त्तुं), आयुधम् अपनी (c. 1. -नयति -नेतुं), निरायुधं -धां -धं कृ, निःशस्त्रं -स्त्रां -स्त्रं कृ, विशस्त्रीकृ, विसन्नीकृ.

DISARMED, *p. p.* निरायुधः -धा -धं, निरस्त्रः -स्त्रा -स्त्रं, निःशस्त्रः -स्त्रा -स्त्रं, शस्त्रवर्ज्जितः -ता -तं; 'disarmed of resentment,' क्षीणमन्युः -न्युः -न्यु.

To DISARRANGE, *v. a.* क्रमं or पर्य्यायं भञ्ज् (c. 7. भनक्ति, भंक्तुं), पर्य्यस् (c. 4. -अस्यति -असितुं), व्यस्, विक्षुभ् in caus. (-क्षोभयति -यितुं), आकुलीकृ, सङ्करीकृ.

DISARRANGEMENT, *s.* अक्रमः, उत्क्रमः, व्युत्क्रमः, क्रमभङ्गः, अपर्य्यायः, अपरिपाटिः *f.*, प्रत्यवायः, व्यस्तता, असंस्थानं.

To DISARRAY, *v. a.* (Undress) उच्छद् (c. 10. -छादयति -यितुं), अपनह् (c. 4. -नह्यति -नद्धुं), विवस्त्रीकृ.

DISARRAY, *s.* (Disorder of an army) समुत्पिञ्जः, पिञ्जलः, व्यूहभङ्गः.

DISASTER, *s.* आपद् *f.*, विपद् *f.*, व्यसनं, विपत्तिः *f.*, व्यापद् *f.*, विप्लवः, उपप्लवः, उपद्रवः, अनिष्टपातः, अत्ययः, दुर्दैवं, दुर्घटना, दौर्गत्यं, दुःखं, क्लेशः.—(From heaven) विनिपातः, उत्पातः, विनिहतः.

To DISASTER, *v. a.* पीड् (c. 10. पीडयति -यितुं), उपपीड्, अभिपीड्, बाध् (c. 1. बाधते -धितुं), उपद्रु (c. 1. -द्रवति -द्रोतुं), उपप्लु (c. 1. -प्लवते -प्लोतुं).

DISASTROUS, *a.* आत्ययिकः -की -कं, व्यसनी -निनी -नि (न्), विपद्युक्तः -क्ता -क्तं, आपन्नः -न्ना -न्नं, दुर्गतः -ता -तं, दुर्भाग्यः -ग्या -ग्यं, दैवोपहतः -ता -तं, दुःखी -खिनी -खि (न्), दुरन्तः -न्ता -न्तं, उपाकृतः -ता -तं, दारुणः -णा -णं, अशान्तिकरः -री -रं.

To DISAVOW, *v. a.* प्रत्याख्या (c. 2. -ख्याति -तुं), निह्नु (c. 2. -ह्नुते -ह्नोतुं), अपह्नु, अपलप् (c. 1. -लपति -पितुं), न स्वीकृ, न अङ्गीकृ.

DISAVOWAL, *s.* प्रत्याख्यानं, निह्नवः, अपह्नवः, निह्नुतिः *f.*, अपलापः, अस्वीकारः.

To DISAUTHORIZE, *v. a.* शक्तिं or प्रामाण्यं or प्रभुत्वं or अधिकारित्वं हृ (c. 1. हरति, हर्त्तुं) or अपहृ, लुप्तप्रमाणं -णां -णं कृ, न अनुज्ञा (c. 9. -जानाति -ज्ञातुं).

To DISBAND, *v. a.* युद्धकर्म्मणो मुच् (c. 6. मुञ्चति, मोक्तुं), सैन्यान् विसृज् (c. 6. -सृजति -स्रष्टुं), सैन्यभङ्गं कृ.

To DISBAND, *v. n.* युद्धकर्म्मणो मुच् in pass. (मुच्यते) or विसृज् in pass. (-सृज्यते).

To DISBARK, *v. a.* नौकाया अवरुह् in caus. (-रोपयति -यितुं) or अवतॄ in caus. (-तारयति -यितुं).

DISBELIEF, *s.* अविश्वासः, अप्रत्ययः, अश्रद्धा, अभक्तिः *f.*, अविश्रम्भः, प्रत्ययाभावः.

To DISBELIEVE, *v. a.* न प्रती (c. 2. प्रत्येति -तुं rt. इ), न विश्वस् (c. 2. -श्वसिति -तुं), न श्रद्धा (c. 2. -दधाति -धातुं), न प्रत्ययीकृ.

DISBELIEVER, *s.* अविश्वासी *m.* (न्), अप्रत्ययी *m.* (न्), अश्रद्दधानः, नास्तिकः.

DISBELIEVING, *a.* अश्रद्धालुः -लुः -लु, अश्रद्धावान् -वती -वत् (त्).

To DISBRANCH, *v. a.* शाखां छिद् (c. 7. छिनत्ति, छेत्तुं), निःशाखं -खां -खं कृ.

To DISBURDEN, *v. a.* भारम् उत्तॄ in caus. (-तारयति -यितु) or अवतॄ in caus., भाराद् मुच् (c. 6. मुञ्चति, मोक्तुं) or विमुच्, भारं विनी (c. 1. -नयति -नेतुं) or अपनी, निर्भारं -रां -रं कृ, रिक्तभारं -रां -रं कृ, विशुध् in caus. (-शोधयति -यितुं); 'to disburden the mind,' मनोगतं or अन्तर्गतं मनः परस्मै व्यक्तीकृ or व्याख्या (c. 2. -ख्याति -तुं).

To DISBURSE, *v. a.* व्यय् (c. 1. व्ययति, c. 10. व्यययति -यितुं root इ), व्ययीकृ, विसृज् (c. 6. -सृजति -स्रष्टुं), विनियुज् (c. 7. -युंक्ते -योक्तुं).

DISBURSED, *p. p.* व्ययितः -ता -तं, व्ययीकृतः -ता -तं, व्ययीभूतः -ता -तं, अपचितः -ता -तं, विसर्ज्जितः -ता -तं.

DISBURSEMENT, *s.* व्ययः, धनव्ययः, व्ययीकरणं, विनियोगः, विसर्गः, त्यागः, अपचितिः *f.*, अपचयः; 'receipt and disbursement,' आयव्ययौ.

DISBURSER, *s.* व्ययी *m.* (न्), व्ययकर्त्ता *m.* (र्तृ), अपचेता *m.* (तृ).

DISCALCEATED, *p. p.* निष्पादुकः -का -कं, अपपादत्रः -त्रा -त्रं, उपानद्वर्ज्जितः -ता -तं.

To DISCANDY, *v. a.* विली in caus. (-लाययति -यितुं), विद्रु in caus. (-द्रावयति -यितुं).

To DISCARD, *v. a.* अपास् (c. 4. -अस्यति -असितुं), अवमुच् (c. 6. -मुञ्चति -मोक्तुं), अवसृज् (c. 6. -सृजति -स्रष्टुं, c. 10. -सर्जयति -यितुं), विसृज्, व्यपसृज्, उत्सृज्; प्रतिक्षिप् (c. 6. -क्षिपति -क्षेप्तुं), अपाहा (c. 3. -जहाति -हातुं), अपहा, विहा; निराकृ, पराकृ; उज्झ् (c. 6. उज्झति -ज्झितुं), प्रोज्झ्, दूरीकृ, खण्ड् (c. 10. खण्डयति -यितुं).

DISCARDED, *p. p.* अपास्तः -स्ता -स्तं, अवसृष्टः -ष्टा -ष्टं, प्रतिक्षिप्तः -प्ता -प्तं, निराकृतः -ता -तं, सत्यस्तः -स्ता -स्तं, प्रोज्झितः -ता -तं, अवधूतः -ता -तं.

DISCARNATE, *a.* मांसहीनः -ना -नं, निर्मांसः -सा -सं, अमांसः -सा -सं.

To DISCERN, *v. a.* (Descry, see) दृश् (c. 1. पश्यति, द्रष्टुं), प्रदृश्, सम्प्रदृश्, प्रतिदृश्, परिदृश्, अनुदृश्, विदृश्, सन्दृश्; ईक्ष् (c. 1. ईक्षते -क्षितुं), समीक्ष्, निरीक्ष्, वीक्ष्, प्रेक्ष्, सम्प्रेक्ष्; आलोक् (c. 10. -लोकयति -यितुं, c. 1. -लोकते -कितुं), समालोक्, अवलोक्, विलोक्, लक्ष् (c. 10. लक्षयति -यितुं), आलक्ष्, समालक्ष्, संलक्ष्, आलोच् (c. 10.

-लोचयति -यितुं), निर्वर्ण् (c. 10. -वर्णयति -यितुं).—(Distinguish, judge) विविच् (c. 7. -विनक्ति -वेक्तुं or caus. -वेचयति -यितुं), विज्ञा (c. 9. -जानाति -नीते -ज्ञातुं), विचर् in caus. (-चारयति -यितुं), निर्णी (c. 1. -णयति -णेतुं), विभू in caus. (-भावयति -यितुं), परिच्छिद् (c. 7. -छिनत्ति -छेत्तुं).

DISCERNED, *p. p.* दृष्टः -ष्टा -ष्टं, ईक्षितः -ता -तं, विज्ञातः -ता -तं.

DISCERNER, *s.* द्रष्टा *m.* (ष्टृ), ईक्षिता *m.* (तृ), विज्ञः, विवेकदृश्वा *m.* (न्), विवेक्ता *m.* (क्तृ).

DISCERNIBLE, *a.* दृश्यः -श्या -श्यं, दृष्टिगोचरः -रा -रं, विज्ञेयः -या -यं, विवेचनीयः -या -यं, विभाव्यः -व्या -व्यं, विभावनीयः -या -यं, प्रत्यक्षः -क्षा -क्षं.

DISCERNIBLY, *adv.* प्रत्यक्षतस्, दृष्टिगोचरं, व्यक्तं, विशेषं, स्पष्टं.

DISCERNING, *a.* विवेकी -किनी -कि (न्), विवेकदृश्वा -श्वा -श्व (न्), विज्ञः -ज्ञा -ज्ञं, अभिज्ञः -ज्ञा -ज्ञं, दीर्घदृष्टिः -ष्टिः -ष्टि or दूरदृष्टिः, मर्म्मज्ञः -ज्ञा -ज्ञं, परिणामदर्शी -र्शिनी -र्शि (न्), बुद्धिमान् -मती -मत् (त्).

DISCERNINGLY, *adv.* सविज्ञानं, सविवेकं, विज्ञवत्, विचारेण, परिच्छेदपूर्व्वं.

DISCERNMENT, *s.* विवेकः -कता, विवेचनं, विवेकित्वं, विवेकदृश्वत्वं, विज्ञानं, परिच्छेदः, विचारः, परीक्षा, अवबोधः, अर्थज्ञानं, विभावनं, अवधारणं, विज्ञप्तिः *f.*, दूरदृष्टिः *f.*, प्रेक्षा.

To DISCERP, *v. a.* व्यवच्छिद् (c. 7. -छिनत्ति -छेत्तुं), खण्ड् (c. 10. खण्डयति -यितुं), खण्डशः कृ, खण्डं खण्डं कृ, लवशः कृ, शकलीकृ, विदॄ in caus. (-दारयति -यितुं).

DISCERPTIBLE, *a.* व्यवच्छेद्यः -द्या -द्यं, विभेद्यः -द्या -द्यं, खण्डनीयः -या -यं.

DISCERPTION, *s.* व्यवच्छेदः, विदारणं, विशसनं, शकलीकरणं.

To DISCHARGE, *v. a.* (Unload) भारम् उत्तॄ in caus. (-तारयति -यितुं) or विनी or अपनी, भाराद् मुच् (c. 6. मुञ्चति, मोक्तुं, c. 10. मोचयति -यितुं).—(Set free) मुच्, विमुच्, प्रविमुच्, मोक्ष् (c. 10. मोक्षयति -यितुं), विसृज् (c. 6. -सृजति -स्रष्टुं, c. 10. -सर्ज्जयति -यितुं), निस्तॄ in caus.—(From obligation) ऋणाद् उत्तॄ or मुच् or शुध् in caus. (शोधयति -यितुं), आनृण्यं दा.—(Pay a debt, &c.) ऋणं शुध् in caus. or अपनी or विनी or अपाकृ or अपवृज् in caus. (-वर्ज्जयति -यितुं) or अपनुद् (c. 6. -नुदति -नोत्तुं) or निरादिश् (c. 6. -दिशति -देष्टुं), आनृण्यं गम् (c. 1. गच्छति, गन्तुं) or उपगम् or आप् (c. 5. आप्नोति, आप्तुं).—(Clear, absolve) शुध् in caus., परिशुध्; पापाद् मुच्.—(Dismiss from service) पदात् or अधिकाराद् अवसृज् or विसृज् or मुच् or निराकृ, or अवरुह् in caus. (-रोपयति -यितुं) or अपास् (c. 4. -अस्यति -असितुं) or च्यु in caus. (च्यावयति -यितुं) or निःसृ in caus. (-सारयति -यितुं) or निष्क्रम् in caus. (-क्रामयति -यितुं) or बहिष्कृ.—(Perform) अनुष्ठा (c. 1. -तिष्ठति -ष्ठातुं), आस्था, सम्पद् in caus. (-पादयति -यितुं), विधा (c. 3. -दधाति -धातुं), आचर् (c. 1. -चरति -रितुं), कृ, सङ्कृ, निर्वह् in caus. (-वाहयति -यितुं).—(A missile) क्षिप् (c. 6. क्षिपति, क्षेप्तुं), प्रक्षिप्, अस् (c. 4. अस्यति, असितुं), प्रास्, मुच्, प्रमुच्, सृज्, ईर् (c. 10. ईरयति -यितुं), उदीर्, पत् in caus. (पातयति -यितुं).—(A gun) लोहगोलान् युद्धनाडेः प्रक्षिप् or निःसृ in caus., युद्धनाडिस्थम् आग्नेयचूर्णं ज्वल् in caus. (ज्वालयति -यितुं).—(Emit, pour forth) उदीर्, मुच्, प्रमुच्, उत्सृज्, उद्गॄ (c. 6. -गिरति -गरितुं -रीतुं), उद्वम् (c. 1. -वमति -मितुं), उच्चर् in caus. (-चारयति -यितुं), स्रु in caus. (स्रावयति -यितुं or c. 1. स्रवति, स्रोतुं), प्रस्रु, क्षर् (c. 1. क्षरति -रितुं), स्कन्द् in caus. (स्कन्दयति -यितुं).

To DISCHARGE, *v. n.* मुच् in pass. (मुच्यते), स्रु (c. 1. स्रवति, स्रोतुं), विली (c. 4. -लीयते).

DISCHARGE, *s.* (Unloading) भारावतरणं, उत्तरणं.—(Setting free) मोक्षः, मुक्तिः *f.*, परिमोक्षणं, उत्सर्गः, निस्तारः.—(From obligation) ऋणमोक्षः, ऋणमुक्तिः *f.*, उत्तरणं.—(Payment of a debt) ऋणशोधनं, ऋणापनयनं, ऋणापाकरणं, ऋणसिद्धिः *f.*, आनृण्यं, ऋणापनोदनं, विगणनं, निरादेशः.—(Acquittance) पापमोचनं, परिशोधः, निस्तारः, निष्कृतिः *f.*—(Dismission from office) अधिकाराद् विसर्ज्जनं or निराकरणं or अपासनं or अवरोपणं or बहिष्करणं, पदच्युतिः *f.*—(Performance) अनुष्ठानं, आचरणं, विधानं, करणं, निर्वाहः; 'discharge of one's duties,' कर्म्मानुष्ठानं.—(Voiding, emission) उत्सर्गः, विसर्गः, मोक्षणं, स्रावः, आस्रावः, आस्रवः, उच्चारः, उद्गारः.

DISCHARGED, *p. p.* (Released) मुक्तः -क्ता -क्तं, विमोचितः -ता -तं, मोक्षितः -ता -तं, विसृष्टः -ष्टा -ष्टं, उत्सृष्टः -ष्टा -ष्टं.—(From obligation) उत्तीर्णः -र्णा -र्णं, ऋणमुक्तः -क्ता -क्तं.—(Paid, as a debt) शोधितः -ता -तं, परिशुद्धः -द्धा -द्धं, सिद्धः -द्धा -द्धं, विगणितः -ता -तं, निरादिष्टः -ष्टा -ष्टं.—(Acquitted) शुद्धः -द्धा -द्धं.—(Dismissed) विसर्ज्जितः -ता -तं, विसृष्टः -ष्टा -ष्टं, अवसृष्टः -ष्टा -ष्टं, निराकृतः -ता -तं, अपविद्धः -द्धा -द्धं, अपास्तः -स्ता -स्तं, दूरीकृतः -ता -तं, प्रहितः -ता -तं, अधिकारात्भ्रंशितः -ता -तं, बहिष्कृतः -ता -तं.—(Shot) ईरितः -ता -तं, प्रक्षिप्तः -प्ता -प्तं, मुक्तः -क्ता -क्तं, निःसारितः -ता -तं, निरस्तः -स्ता -स्तं.—(Emitted) उदीरितः -ता -तं, उत्सृष्टः -ष्टा -ष्टं, उच्चारितः -ता -तं, स्कन्दितः -ता -तं.—(Performed) अनुष्ठितः -ता -तं, आचरितः -ता -तं, कृतः -ता -तं.

DISCHARGER, *s.* (Of duty) कर्म्मानुष्ठायी *m.* (न्).—(Of a missile) प्रक्षेपकः.

To DISCIND, *v. a.* द्विधा छिद् (c. 7. छिनत्ति, छेत्तुं), व्यवछिद्, द्विखण्डीकृ.

DISCIPLE, *s.* शिष्यः, अन्तेवासी *m.* (न्), अन्तेवासिजनः, छात्रः, अनुयायी *m.* (न्), विद्यार्थी *m.* (न्), अनुचरः, अनुगतिकः, आश्रितः; 'disciple of a disciple,' प्रशिष्यः.

DISCIPLESHIP, *s.* शिष्यत्वं, छात्रता, अन्तेवासित्वं, विद्यार्थित्वं, अनुयायित्वं.

DISCIPLINABLE, *a.* शासनीयः -या -यं, शास्यः -स्या -स्यं, शिक्षणीयः -या -यं.

DISCIPLINARIAN, *s.* शासिता *m.* (तृ), शिष्टिकर्त्ता *m.* (र्त्तृ), विनेता *m.* (तृ), नियामकः.

DISCIPLINARY, *a.* वैनयिकः -की -कं, शिष्टिविषयकः -का -कं.

DISCIPLINE, *s.* (Education, instruction) विनयः, शिक्षा, अभ्यासः, शासनं, शिष्टिः *f.*, शास्तिः *f.*, अनुशासनं, उपदेशः, अध्यापनं, अनुनयः, नीतिः *f.*—(Military discipline) व्यायामः, युद्धाभ्यासः, युद्धशिक्षा, युद्धनीतिः *f.*, युद्धव्यवस्था.—(Rule of government) नीतिः *f.*, नयः, राजनीतिः, व्यवस्था, नियमः, विधिः *m.*—(Chastisement) शिष्टिः *f.*, शास्तिः *f.*, शासनं, निग्रहः, साहसं, दण्डः, दमः.—(Subjection) दान्तिः *f.*

To DISCIPLINE, *v. a.* (Educate, instruct) विनी (c. 1. -नयति -नेतुं), शिक्ष् in caus. (शिक्षयति -यितुं), अनुशिक्ष्; शास् (c. 2. शास्ति, शासितुं), अनुशास्, अधी in caus. (अध्यापयति -यितुं).—(Exercise) अभ्यस् (c. 4. -अस्यति -असितुं), व्यायम् (c. 1. -यच्छति -यन्तुं).—(Regulate) विनियम्, नियम्, शास्, अनुशास्, विधृ in caus. (-धारयति -यितुं).—(Punish, chastise) शास्, अनुशास्, दण्ड् (c. 10. दण्डयति -यितुं), दम् (c. 10. दमयति -यितुं).

DISCIPLINED, *p. p.* शिष्टः -ष्टा -ष्टं, शासितः -ता -तं, विनीतः -ता -तं, अनुनीतः -ता -तं, शिक्षितः -ता -तं, कृताभ्यासः -सा -सं, दमितः -ता -तं, उद्यतः -ता -तं.

To DISCLAIM, *v. a.* निह्नु (c. 2. -ह्नुते -ह्नोतुं), अपह्नु, प्रत्याख्या (c. 2. -ख्याति -तुं), अपवद् (c. 1. -वदति -दितुं), अपलप् (c. 1. -लपति -पितुं), अपज्ञा (c. 9. -जानाति -ज्ञातुं), प्रत्यादिश् (c. 6. -दिशति -देष्टुं), निरस् (c. 4. -अस्यति -असितुं), परित्यज् (c. 1. -त्यजति -त्यक्तुं), न स्वीकृ, न अङ्गीकृ.

Disclaimer, *s.* अपह्नोता *m.* (तृ), निह्नोता *m.*, प्रत्यादेशकः, अस्वीकर्त्ता *m.* (र्तृ).

To disclose, *v. a.* (Uncover) विवृ (c. 5. -वृणोति -णुते -वरितुं -रीतुं), अपवृ, अपावृ, उच्छद् (c. 10. -छादयति -यितुं).—(Reveal) प्रकाश् in caus. (-काशयति -यितुं), विकाश्, स्पष्टीकृ, प्रकटीकृ, व्यक्तीकृ, व्यञ्ज् (c. 7. -अनक्ति -अञ्जितुं).—(Tell) निविद् in caus. (-वेदयति -यितुं), ख्या in caus. (ख्यापयति -यितुं), सूच् (c. 10. सूचयति -यितुं); 'disclose a secret,' रहस्यं भिद् (c. 7. भिनत्ति, भेत्तुं).

Disclosed, *p. p.* विवृतः -ता -तं, सूचितः -ता -तं, निवेदितः -ता -तं.

Disclosure, *s.* विवृतिः *f.*, विवरणं, प्रकाशः -शनं, स्पष्टीकरणं, व्यक्तीकरणं, प्रकटीकरणं, प्रचारणं, निवेदनं, उद्भेदः, भेदः; 'of a secret,' रहस्यभेदः.

Discoloration, *s.* (The act) विवर्णीकरणं, मलिनीकरणं, कृष्णीकरणं.—(The state) विवर्णत्वं, वैवर्ण्यं, मालिन्यं, कालुष्यं, कलङ्कः.

To discolour, *v. a.* विवर्णीकृ, विवर्ण् (c. 10. -वर्णयति -यितुं), मलिन (nom. मलिनयति -यितुं), कलुष (nom. कलुषयति -यितुं), कृष्णीकृ.

Discoloured, *p.p.* विवर्णः -र्णा -र्णं, दीनवर्णः -र्णा -र्णं, नीरक्तः -क्ता -क्तं; 'having discoloured teeth,' कृष्णदशनः -ना -नं.

To discomfit, *v. a.* पराजि (c. 1. -जयति -ते -जेतुं), पराहन् (c. 2. -हन्ति -न्तुं), परास् (c. 4. -अस्यति -असितुं), पराभू, अभिभू, विद्रु in caus. (-द्रावयति -यितुं), व्यूहान् भञ्ज् (c. 7. भनक्ति, भंक्तुं) or भिद् (c. 7. भिनत्ति, भेत्तुं), विध्वंस् in caus. (-ध्वंसयति -यितुं), पिञ्जलीकृ, स्कन्द् (c. 1. स्कन्दते -दितुं).

Discomfited, *p. p.* पराजितः -ता -तं, पराभूतः -ता -तं, पराहतः -ता -तं, परास्तः -स्ता -स्तं, प्रपलायितः -ता -तं, विद्रुतः -ता -तं, प्रतिहतोद्यमः -मा -मं, पिञ्जलः -ला -लं, समुत्पिञ्जः -ञ्जा -ञ्जं.

Discomfiture, *s.* पराजयः, अपजयः, पराभवः, व्यसनं, बलव्यसनं, भङ्गः, भेदः, विद्रवः, प्रपलायनं, हारिः *f.*, स्कन्दनं, पिञ्जलकः, समुत्पिञ्जलकः.

Discomfort, *s.* अस्वास्थ्यं, असुस्थता, दुःखं, असुखं, पीडा, व्यथा, खेदः, कष्टं, कृच्छ्रं, वेदना, चित्तवेदना, उद्वेगः, बाधा, क्लेशः, सन्तापः.

To discomfort, *v. a.* दुःख् (c. 10. दुःखयति -यितुं), पीड् (c. 10. पीडयति -यितुं), व्यथ् (c. 10. व्यथयति -यितुं), बाध् (c. 1. बाधते -धितुं), परितप् (c. 10. -तापयति -यितुं).

To discommend, *v. a.* न प्रशंस् (c. 1. -शंसति -सितुं), निन्द् (c. 1. निन्दति -न्दितुं).

To discommode, *v. a.* बाध् (c. 1. बाधते -धितुं), उपरुध् (c. 7. -रुणद्धि -रोद्धुं), क्लिश् (c. 9. क्लिश्नाति, क्लेशितुं), व्यथ् (c. 10. व्यथयति -यितुं).

Discommodious, *a.* अनुपयुक्तः -क्ता -क्तं, कष्टकरः -री -रं, अस्वास्थ्यजनकः -का -कं.

To discompose, *v. a.* क्षुभ् in caus. (क्षोभयति -यितुं), विक्षुभ्, आकुलीकृ, कातरीकृ, व्याकुलीकृ, अस्थिरीकृ, बाध् (c. 1. बाधते -धितुं), मुह् in caus. (मोहयति -यितुं), व्यामुह्, विलुप् (c. 6. -लुम्पति -लोप्तुं).

Discomposed, *p. p.* क्षोभितः -ता -तं, क्षुब्धः -ब्धा -ब्धं, आकुलितः -ता -तं. आकुलचित्तः -त्ता -त्तं, व्याकुलः -ला -लं, कातरः -रा -रं, अस्थिरः -रा -रं, अनवस्थितः -ता -तं, अनिर्वृतः -ता -तं, व्यग्रः -ग्रा -ग्रं, पारिप्लवः -वा -वं, मोहितः -ता -तं, उद्भ्रान्तः -न्ता -न्तं, विधुरः -रा -रं.

Discomposure, *s.* क्षोभः, आकुलता, व्याकुलत्वं, आकुलचित्तता, कातर्यं, अस्थिरता, अनिर्वृतिः *f.*, व्यग्रता, पारिप्लवत्वं, उद्वेगः, वैक्लव्यं, उत्कम्पः, मोहः.

To disconcert, *v. a.* (Frustrate) खण्ड् (c. 10. खण्डयति -यितुं), प्रतिहन् (c. 2. -हन्ति -न्तुं), वृथा कृ.—(Discompose) मुह् in caus. (मोहयति -यितुं), आकुलीकृ, व्यग्रीकृ.

Disconcerted, *p. p.* प्रतिहतोद्यमः -मा -मं, खण्डितः -ता -तं, मोहितः -ता -तं, आकुलितः -ता -तं, व्याकुलितः -ता -तं, विलक्षितः -ता -तं.

Disconformity, disconcruity, *s.* असादृश्यं, अयोग्यता, असङ्गतिः *f.*, विरुद्धता.

To disconnect, *v. a.* वियुज् (c. 7. -युनक्ति -योक्तुं), विश्लिष् (c. 10. -श्लेषयति -यितुं).

Disconnected, *p.p.* विप्रयुक्तः -क्ता -क्तं, असंसक्तः -क्ता -क्तं, असंलग्नः -ग्ना -ग्नं.

Disconnection, *s.* वियोगः, विप्रयोगः, असंयोगः, विश्लेषः, अनभिष्वङ्गः.

Disconsolate, *a.* विषण्णः -ण्णा -ण्णं, विषादी -दिनी -दि (न्), अवसन्नः -न्ना -न्नं, निराशः -शा -शं, हताशः -शा -शं, विमनाः -नाः -नः (स्), or क्षामनमनाः or दुर्मनाः or अन्तर्मनाः or उद्विग्नमनाः, विमनस्कः -स्का -स्कं, निरानन्दः -न्दा -न्दं, अनाश्वासनीयः -या -यं, खिद्यमानः -ना -नं, खेदान्वितः -ता -तं.

Disconsolately, *adv.* सविषादं, सखेदं, सोद्वेगं, सनैराश्यं, निरानन्दं.

Discontent, *s.* असन्तोषः, अतुष्टिः *f.*, अपरितोषः, अतृप्तिः *f.*, अरतिः *f.*, अनिर्वृतिः *f.*, अनाह्लादः, अशान्तिः *f.*, असन्तुष्टता, अतृप्तता.

Discontent, discontented, *a.* असन्तुष्टः -ष्टा -ष्टं, अतृप्तः -प्ता -प्तं, अतुष्टः -ष्टा -ष्टं, अपरितुष्टः -ष्टा -ष्टं, वितुष्टः -ष्टा -ष्टं, अरतः -ता -तं, अनिर्वृतः -ता -तं, अरतिः -तिः -ति, अशान्तः -न्ता -न्तं, अप्रीतः -ता -तं, निरानन्दः -न्दा -न्दं, अप्रशान्तकामः -मा -मं, अप्रतिलब्धकामः -मा -मं, सासूयः -या -यं.

To discontent, *v. a.* न सन्तुष् in caus. (-तोषयति -यितुं), न तृप् in caus. (-तर्पयति -यितुं), असन्तोषम् उत्पद् in caus. (-पादयति -यितुं).

Discontinuance, discontinuation, *s.* (Want of continuity) विच्छेदः, छेदः, भङ्गः, अन्तरायः, खण्डनं.—(Cessation) विरतिः *f.*, विरामः, अवरतिः *f.*, उपरतिः *f.*, निवृत्तिः *f.*, विनिवृत्तिः *f.*, निर्वृत्तिः *f.*, निवर्त्तनं, विच्छेदः, छेदः, उपशमः, अपशमः, शान्तिः *f.*, क्षयः.

To discontinue, *v. a.* and *n.* (Leave off) विरम् (c. 1. -रमति -रन्तुं), उपरम् with abl. c., निवृत् (c. 1. -वर्त्तते -र्त्तितुं), निर्वृत् with abl. c., शम् (c. 4. शाम्यति, शमितुं), विछिद् in pass. (-छिद्यते).—(Cause to cease) निवृत् in caus. (-वर्त्तयति -यितुं), विरम् in caus. (-रमयति -यितुं).—(Abandon) त्यज् (c. 1. त्यजति, त्यक्तुं), उज्झ् (c. 6. उज्झति -ज्झितुं), प्रोज्झ्.—(Interrupt, break off) विच्छिद् (c. 7. -छिनत्ति -छेत्तुं), विलुप् (c. 10. -लोपयति -यितुं), खण्ड् (c. 10. खण्डयति -यितुं).

Discontinued, *p. p.* विरतः -ता -तं, अवरतः -ता -तं, निवृत्तः -त्ता -त्तं, विच्छिन्नः -न्ना -न्नं, अवसन्नः -न्ना -न्नं, उज्झितः -ता -तं, त्यक्तः -क्ता -क्तं.

Discord, discordance, *s.* (Disagreement) भेदः, विभेदः, विभिन्नता, विरोधः, परस्परविरोधः, विमतिः *f.*, वैमत्यं, असम्मतिः *f.*, अयोग्यता, विपरीतता, वैपरीत्यं, विसंवादः, प्रातिकूल्यं, वैलक्षण्यं, विरुद्धता; 'causing discord,' भेदकरः -री -रं.—(In music) अपरवः, विस्वरशब्दः, असौम्यस्वरः, अपशब्दः.

To discord, *v. n.* विभिद् in pass. (-भिद्यते), न सम्मन् (c. 4. -मन्यते -मन्तुं), न युज् in pass. (युज्यते), विसंवद् (c. 1. -वदति -दितुं), अन्योन्यं विरुध् (c. 7. -रुणद्धि -रोद्धुं).

Discordant, *a.* (Incongruous) विरुद्धः -द्धा -द्धं, परस्परविरुद्धः -द्धा -द्धं, अयोग्यः -ग्या -ग्यं, विभिन्नः -न्ना -न्नं, असङ्गतः -ता -तं, विसङ्गतः -ता -तं, असम्मतः -ता -तं, विपरीतः -ता -तं, क्लिष्टः -ष्टा -ष्टं.—(In sound) विस्वरः -रा -रं, अस्वरः -रा -रं, असौम्यस्वरः -रा -रं, कर्कशस्वनः -ना -नं, वैतालिकः -की -कं.

Discordantly, *adv.* विरुद्धं, विपरीतं, विस्वरं, विरोधेन, अयोग्यं.

To discover, *v. a.* (Shew) दृश् in caus. (दर्शयति -यितुं), अभिदृश्, निदृश्, प्रतिदृश्.—(Reveal, make manifest) विवृ (c. 5. -वृणोति -वरितुं -रीतुं), अपवृ, प्रकाश् in caus. (-काशयति -यितुं), स्पष्टीकृ, व्यक्तीकृ, प्रकटीकृ, व्यञ्ज् (c. 7. -अनक्ति -अञ्जितुं, c. 10. -अञ्जयति -यितुं),

आविष्कृ.—(Make known) ज्ञा in caus. (ज्ञापयति -यितुं), निविद् in caus. (-वेदयति -यितुं), सूच् (c. 10. सूचयति -यितुं).—(Find out, detect) निरूप् (c. 10. -रूपयति -यितुं), ज्ञा (c. 9. जानाति -नीते, ज्ञातुं), परिज्ञा, अभिज्ञा, निर्णी (c. 1. -णयति -णेतुं), उपलभ् (c. 1. -लभते -लब्धुं), अवगम् (c. 1. -गच्छति -गन्तुं), अधिगम्, अभ्यागम्; आसद् (c. 10. -सादयति -यितुं), प्राप् (c. 5. -आप्नोति -आप्तुं), विद् (c. 6. विन्दति, वेदितुं), अभिविद्, अनुसन्धा (c. 3. -दधाति -धातुं).

Discoverable, *a.* निरूपणीयः -या -यं, ज्ञेयः -या -यं, प्रेक्षणीयः -या -यं.

Discovered, *p. p.* निरूपितः -ता -तं, ज्ञातः -ता -तं, विज्ञातः -ता -तं, अभिज्ञातः -ता -तं, निर्णीतः -ता -तं, अवगतः -ता -तं; 'in a fault,' दृष्टदोषः -षा -षं.

Discoverer, *s.* निरूपकः, निर्णेता *m.* (तृ), परिज्ञानी *m.* (न्), अवगन्ता *m.* (न्तृ).

Discovery, *s.* (Disclosing, exhibiting) विवृतिः *f.*, दर्शनं, प्रकाशनं, प्रेक्षणं.—(Finding out) ज्ञानं, परिज्ञानं, विज्ञानं, निरूपणं, प्राप्तिः *f.*, उपलब्धिः *f.*, अवगमः, अवगतिः *f.*, निर्णयः, अनुसन्धानं.

Discount, *s.* उद्धारः, उद्धृतभागः, हुण्डिकापत्राद् उद्धृतो भागः.

To discount, *v. a.* (Deduct a part) भागम् उद्धृ (c. 1. -हरति -हर्त्तुं).—(Pay a bill of exchange before hand) भागम् उद्धृत्य प्राग्विहितकालाद् हुण्डिकापत्रं शुध् in caus. (शोधयति -यितुं).

To discountenance, *v. a.* न अनुग्रह् (c. 9. -गृह्णाति -ग्रहीतुं), न अनुपाल् (c. 10. -पालयति -यितुं), न अनुकूल (nom. अनुकूलयति -यितुं), न उपकृ, लज्ज् (c. 10. लज्जयति -यितुं).

To discourage, *v. a.* (Depress, deject) अवसद् in caus. (-सादयति -यितुं), विषद् in caus., विषण्णीकृ, विषादं जन् in caus. (जनयति -यितुं), म्लानीकृ, निर्विण्णीकृ; आशाः or मनो भञ्ज् (c. 7. भनक्ति, भंक्तुं) or हन् (c. 2. हन्ति -न्तुं).—(Deter) भयहेतुं दर्शयित्वा निवृत् in caus. (-वर्त्तयति -यितुं) or निवृ in caus. (-वारयति -यितुं).

Discouraged, *p. p.* विषण्णः -ण्णा -ण्णं, अवसन्नः -न्ना -न्नं, अवसादितः -ता -तं, निर्विण्णः -ण्णा -ण्णं, भग्नोद्यमः -मा -मं, भग्नमनाः -नाः -नः (स्), मनोहतः -ता -तं, हताशः -शा -शं, खिन्नः -न्ना -न्नं, निवर्त्तितः -ता -तं, निवारितः -ता -तं.

Discouragement, *s.* मनोभङ्गः, उद्योगभङ्गः, उद्यमव्याघातः, आशाभङ्गः, निवर्त्तनं, विषादोत्पादनं, अवसादकरणं, अप्रसादः.

Discouraging, *a.* विषादोत्पादकः -का -कं, अवसादजनकः -का -कं.

Discourse, *s.* (Conversation) सम्भाषा -षणं, संलापः, सङ्कथा, आलापः, आभाषणं, संवादः, सम्प्रवदनं, कथोपकथनं, अनुकथनं, कथायोगः.—(Speech, dissertation) वचनं, वाक्यं, वचः *n.* (स्), वादः, प्रवादः, प्रवचनं, भाषितं, भाषणं, लपितं, वचनक्रमः, निगादः.

To discourse, *v. n.* (Talk, converse) भाष् (c. 1. भाषते -षितुं), सम्भाष्, सम्प्रभाष्, प्रभाष्; आलप् (c. 1. -लपति -पितुं), संलप्; वद् (c. 1. वदति -ते -दितुं), संवद्, सम्प्रवद्, वच् (c. 2. वक्ति -क्तुं), संवच्, जल्प् (c. 1. जल्पति -ल्पितुं), सञ्जल्प्.—(Treat of, talk over) व्याख्या (c. 2. -ख्याति -तुं), प्रसङ्गं कृ, कथ् (c. 10. कथयति -यितुं).

Discourser, *s.* वादी *m.* (न्), वक्ता *m.* (क्तृ), भाषी *m.* (न्), आलापी *m.* (न्), कथकः.

Discoursive, *a.* तर्की -र्किणी -र्कि (न्), ऊही -हिनी -हि (न्), सांवादिकः -की -कं.

Discourteous, *a.* असभ्यः -भ्या -भ्यं, अशिष्टः -ष्टा -ष्टं, दुर्मर्य्यादः -दा -दं, अनार्य्यः -र्य्या -र्य्यं, अविनीतः -ता -तं, अविनयः -या -यं, दुःशीलः -ला -लं, कुशीलः -ला -लं, विनयप्रमाथी -थिनी -थि (न्), अप्रसन्नः -न्ना -न्नं, दुश्चरितः -ता -तं.

Discourteously, *adv.* असभ्यं, अशिष्टं, अविनीतं, अप्रश्रितं, दुःशीलत्वात्.

Discourtesy, *s.* असभ्यता, अशिष्टता, अविनयः, दुःशीलता, अप्रसादः, अप्रश्रयः.

Discredit, *s.* अयशः *n.* (स्), अकीर्त्तिः *f.*, अख्यातिः *f.*, कुख्यातिः *f.*, अपकीर्त्तिः *f.*, अपमानं, कलङ्कः, अपकलङ्कः, अप्रतिष्ठा, मर्य्यादा हानिः *f*

To discredit, *v. a.* (Deprive of credibility) अविश्वास्यः or अश्रद्धेय इति मन् (c. 4. मन्यते, मन्तुं), प्रामाण्यं or गौरवं लघ् (nom. लघयति -यितुं) or लघूकृ, अविश्वस्तं -स्तां -स्तं कृ.—(Not to credit) न प्रती (c. 2. प्रत्येति -तुं), न विश्वस् (c. 2. -श्वसिति -तुं).—(Disgrace) अकीर्त्तिं or अयशः or अपमानं कृ or जन् (c. 10. जनयति -यितुं), लघूकृ, कलङ्कं कृ.

Discreditable, *a.* अकीर्त्तिकरः -री -रं, अयशस्करः -री -रं, कलङ्ककरः -रा -रं, अपमान्यः -न्या -न्यं, अमान्यः -न्या -न्यं, अनार्य्यः -र्य्या -र्य्यं, अयशस्यः -स्या -स्यं, मर्य्यादाविरुद्धः -द्धा -द्धं, लोकगर्हितः -ता -तं, अप्रतिष्ठः -ष्ठा -ष्ठं.

Discreet, *a.* विमृश्यकारी -रिणी -रि (न्) or समीक्ष्यकारी, विज्ञः -ज्ञा -ज्ञं, विचक्षणः -णा -णं, विचारणशीलः -ला -लं, सावहितः -ता -तं, मनस्वी -स्विनी -स्वि (न्), मतिमान् -मती -मत् (त्), कृतावधानः -ना -नं, विनीतः -ता -तं, परिणामदर्शी -र्शिनी -र्शि (न्).

Discreetly, *adv.* सुविमृश्य, सावहितं, सुविचार्य्य, विचारेण, विज्ञवत्.

Discrepance, discrepancy, *s.* विभेदः, विभिन्नता, भेदः, भिन्नता, विरोधः, विरुद्धता, विप्रतिपत्तिः *f.*, असङ्गतिः *f.*, विपरीतता, वैपरीत्यं, द्वैधं, द्वैविध्यं, विसंवादः, प्रातिकूल्यं, वैलक्षण्यं, विगीतिः *f.*

Discrepant, *a.* भिन्नः -न्ना -न्नं, विभिन्नः -न्ना -न्नं, विरुद्धः -द्धा -द्धं, विरोधी -धिनी -धि (न्), विपरीतः -ता -तं, विगीतः -ता -तं, असङ्गतः -ता -तं, विसङ्गतः -ता -तं, विसंवादी -दिनी -दि (न्), विवदमानः -ना -नं, प्रतिकूलः -ला -लं.

Discrete, *a.* भिन्नः -न्ना -न्नं, विविक्तः -क्ता -क्तं, पृथग्भूतः -ता -तं.

Discretion, *s.* (Prudence) विनयः, विनीतता, नीतिः *f.*, सुनीतिः, सुनयः, प्रसमीक्षा, समीक्षणं, समीक्ष्यकारित्वं, विमृश्यकारित्वं, चिन्ता, विज्ञता, विचक्षणता, विवेचना, विचारः.—(Liberty of acting at pleasure) स्वातन्त्र्यं, स्वाच्छन्द्यं, स्वाधीनता.—(Option) विकल्पः, अनुकल्पः; 'at one's own discretion,' स्वेच्छया, स्वरुच्या.

Discretionally, *adv.* स्वेच्छातस्, स्वेच्छानुसारेण, विकल्पतस्, कामं, अनुकामं.

Discretionary, *a.* वैकल्पिकः -की -कं, विकल्पितः -ता -तं, सविकल्पकः -का -कं, आनुकल्पिकः -की -कं, स्वाधीनः -ना -नं, स्वच्छन्दः -न्दा -न्दं, यादृच्छिकः -की -कं.

To discriminate, *v. a.* विज्ञा (c. 9. -जानाति -नीते -ज्ञातुं), विशिष् (c. 7. -शिनष्टि -शेष्टुं, c. 10. -शेषयति -यितुं), विविच् (c. 7. -विनक्ति -वेक्तुं, c. 10. -वेचयति -यितुं), लक्ष् (c. 10. लक्षयति -यितुं), परिछिद् (c. 7. -छिनत्ति -छेत्तुं), विचर् (c. 10. -चारयति -यितुं), पृथक्कृ, विज् (c. 3. वेवेक्ति, विजितुं), विभू (c. 10. -भावयति -यितुं).

Discriminated, *p. p.* विशेषितः -ता -तं, कृतलक्षणः -णा -णं, विविक्तः -क्ता -क्तं, परिछिन्नः -न्ना -न्नं, विज्ञातः -ता -तं, पृथक्कृतः -ता -तं, विचारितः -ता -तं.

Discrimination, *s.* (The act) विवेकः, विवेचनं, परिच्छेदः -दनं, विज्ञानं, अर्थविज्ञानं, अर्थज्ञानं, विभावनं, विचारः, व्यवच्छेदः, विवित्तिः *f.*, विवेकदृश्वत्वं, विवेकृत्वं, विशेषणं, पृथक्करणं, पृथगात्मता, अवधारणं.—(The state) विशिष्टता, परिच्छिन्नता, विविक्तता; 'discrimination of right and wrong,' सदसद्विवेकः; 'want of discrimination,' अविवेकः -कता.

Discriminating, *a.* विशेषज्ञः -ज्ञा -ज्ञं, विवेकदृश्वा -श्वा -श्व (न्), अर्थज्ञः -ज्ञा -ज्ञं.

Discriminative, *a.* विवेकी -किनी -कि (न्), विशेषकः -का -कं, परिच्छेदकः -का -कं, प्रभेदकारी -रिणी -रि (न्), विभावकः -का -कं, विभिता -त्री -तृ (तृ).

DISCURSIVE, *a.* (Wandering from one topic to another) बहुविषयः -या -यं, नानावस्तुविषयकः -का -कं, अनेकार्थः -र्था -र्थं, बह्वर्थः -र्था -र्थं, नानाप्रसक्तः -क्ता -क्तं, इतस्ततो भ्रमणशीलः -ला -लं, अस्थिरः -रा -रं, चपलः -ला -लं.—(Argumentative) तार्किकः -की -कं, विचारी -रिणी -रि (न्).

DISCUS, *s.* चक्रं, लौहचक्रं, चहुनं; 'of Vishnu,' शिवदत्तं.

To DISCUSS, *v. a.* विचर् in caus. (-चारयति -यितुं), वितर्क् (c. 10. -तर्कयति -यितुं), निरूप् (c. 10. -रूपयति -यितुं), विमृश् (c. 6. -मृशति -म्रष्टुं), परिमृश्, समीक्ष् (c. 1. -ईक्षते -क्षितुं), परीक्ष्, विभू (c. 10. -भावयति -यितुं), मथ् (c. 1. मथति -थितुं), वादानुवादं कृ.

DISCUSSED, *p.p.* विचारितः -ता -तं, मथितः -ता -तं, विक्तः -क्ता -क्तं, विक्तः -क्ता -क्तं.

DISCUSSION, *s.* विचारः -रणा, वितर्कः -र्कणं, वादानुवादः, वादप्रतिवादः, विमर्शः, परीक्षा, विवेचनं -ना, समीक्षा, प्रसमीक्षा, विभावनं, सम्प्रधारणा; 'topic under discussion,' प्रसङ्गः, प्रस्तावः; 'under discussion,' प्रस्तुतः -ता -तं; 'result of discussion,' मथितार्थः.—(Dispersion) विद्रावणं, विक्षेपः.

DISCUSSING, *a.* विचारकः -का -कं, विभावकः -का -कं, विमर्शी -र्शिनी -र्शि (न्).

DISCUSSIVE, *a.* दुष्टधातुनाशकः -का -कं, दुष्टरसविद्रावकः -का -कं, शोथहृत्.

DISCUTIENT, *a.* शोथघ्नः -घ्नी -घ्नं, शोथजित्, शोथहृत्, विस्फोटघ्नः -घ्नी -घ्नं.

DISDAIN, *s.* अवज्ञा -ज्ञानं, अवहेला -लनं, उपेक्षा, अवमानं, उन्मायः, गर्हा -र्हणं, घृणा, कुत्सा -त्सनं, हेलनं, निराकरणं, पराकरणं, औद्धत्यं, अवलेपः.

To DISDAIN, *v. a.* अवज्ञा (c. 9. -जानाति -ज्ञातुं), अवमन् (c. 4. -मन्यते -मन्तुं), गर्ह् (c. 1. गर्हते -र्हितुं), कुत्स् (c. 10. कुत्सयति -यितुं), उपेक्ष् (c. 1. -ईक्षते -क्षितुं), लघूकृ, तुच्छीकृ, पराकृ, निराकृ, कदर्थीकृ, प्रत्याचक्ष् (c. 2. -चष्टे).

DISDAINED, *p. p.* अवज्ञातः -ता -तं, गर्हितः -ता -तं, कुत्सितः -ता -तं, उपेक्षितः -ता -तं, कदर्थितः -ता -तं, पराकृतः -ता -तं, निराकृतः -ता -तं.

DISDAINFUL, *a.* अवमानी -निनी -नि (न्), सावहेलः -ला -लं, सावज्ञः -ज्ञा -ज्ञं, सावलेपः -पा -पं, उपेक्षकः -का -कं, सोन्मायः -या -यं, घृणी -णिनी -णि (न्).

DISDAINFULLY, *adv.* सावज्ञानं, सोन्मायं, सावहेलं, सावलेपं, अवमानेन, उपेक्षया.

DISDAINFULNESS, *s.* अवलिप्तता, सावलेपत्वं, सोन्मायता, औद्धत्यं.

DISEASE, *s.* रोगः, व्याधिः *m.*, आमयः, पीडा, रुक् *f.* (ज्), रुजा, रुग्नता, गदः, उपतापः, आर्त्तिः *f.*, कष्टं, अस्वास्थ्यं, दुःखं, विकारः, विकृतिः *f.*, विकारः, श्रमः, अमसः, मृत्युभृत्यः, क्लेशः, तापः.

To DISEASE, *v. a.* रोगेण पीड् (c. 10. पीडयति -यितुं) or व्यथ् (c. 10. व्यथयति -यितुं), दुःख् (c. 10. दुःखयति -यितुं), क्लिश् (c. 9. क्लिश्नाति, क्लेशितुं).

DISEASED, *p. p.* or *a.* रोगी -गिणी -गि (न्), रोगवान् -वती -वत् (त्), रोगार्त्तः -र्त्ता -र्त्तं, रोगग्रस्तः -स्ता -स्तं, सरोगः -गा -गं, व्याधितः -ता -तं, सामयः -या -यं, श्रमी -मिणी -मि (न्), आतुरः -रा -रं, अस्वस्थः -स्था -स्थं, विकारी -रिणी -रि (न्), विकृतः -ता -तं, अभ्यान्तः -न्ता -न्तं, अभ्यमितः -ता -तं, आमयावी -विनी -वि (न्).

To DISEMBARK, *v. a.* उत्तृ in caus. (-तारयति -यितुं), नौकायाः or पोताद् अवतृ in caus. or अवरुह् in caus. (-रोपयति -यितुं), उत्कूल (nom. उत्कूलयति -यितुं).

To DISEMBARK, *v. n.* उत्तृ (c. 1. -तरति -रितुं -रीतुं), प्रत्युत्तॄ, नौकायाः or पोताद् अवतृ or अवरुह् (c. 1. -रोहति -रोढुं).

DISEMBARKATION, *s.* उत्तरणं, प्रत्युत्तरणं, नौकाया अवतरणं or अवरोहणं.

DISEMBARKED, *p.p.* उत्तीर्णः -र्णा -र्णं, अवतीर्णः -र्णा -र्णं, अवरूढः -ढा -ढं, अतिनौः -नौः -नु, उत्कूलितः -ता -तं.

To DISEMBITTER, *v. a.* तिक्तरसं or तिक्तत्वम् अपनी (c. 1. -नयति -नेतुं), अतिक्तं -क्तां -क्तं कृ, तिक्तवर्ज्जितं -तां -तं कृ, मधुरीकृ, सुरसं -सां -सं कृ.

DISEMBODIED, *p. p.* न्यस्तदेहः -हा -हं, अङ्गहीनः -ना -नं, त्यक्तदेहः -हा -हं, देहातीतः -ता -तं, अशरीरः -रा -रं, विगतदेहः -हा -हं, कायवर्ज्जितः -ता -तं, अनङ्गः -ङ्गा -ङ्गं.

To DISEMBOGUE, *v. a.* सलिलं समुद्रे निर्गम् in caus. (-गमयति -यितुं) or प्रस्रु in caus. (-स्रावयति -यितुं) or मुच् (c. 6. मुञ्चति, मोक्तुं).

To DISEMBOGUE, *v. n.* निर्गम् (-गच्छति -गन्तुं), निःसृ (c. 1. -सरति -सर्त्तुं), अपसृ, समुद्रं विश् (c. 6. विशति, वेष्टुं) or प्रविश् or निविश्.

To DISEMBROIL, *v. a.* व्यामोहात् or उद्वेगात् or व्यस्तत्वाद् उद्धृ (c. 1. -हरति -हर्त्तुं) or मुच् (c. 6. मुञ्चति, मोक्तुं), निरुत्पातं -तां -तं कृ, निरुपद्रवं -वां -वं कृ.

To DISENCHANT, *v. a.* मन्त्रं or अभिचारं or वशक्रियां प्रतिकृ, मन्त्रप्रभावात् or अभिचारवशाद् उद्धृ (c. 1. -हरति -हर्त्तुं) or मुच् (c. 6. मुञ्चति, मोक्तुं), अभिचारभङ्गं कृ.

To DISENCUMBER, DISCUMBER, *v.a.* भारात् or विघ्नाद् उद्धृ (c. 1. -हरति -हर्त्तुं) or मुच् (c. 6. मुञ्चति, मोक्तुं), प्रतिबन्धान् अपनी (c. 1. -नयति -नेतुं), निर्विघ्नीकृ, निर्विघ्न (nom. निर्विघ्नयति -यितुं), विशुध् in caus. (-शोधयति -यितुं), निष्प्रत्यूहं -हां -हं कृ.

To DISENGAGE, *v. a.* (Separate) वियुज् (c. 7. -युनक्ति -योक्तुं), विश्लिष् in caus. (-श्लेषयति -यि ं).—(Disentangle) मुच् (c. 6. मुञ्चति, मोक्तुं, c. 10. मोचयति -यितुं), विमुच्, निर्मुच्, मोक्ष् (c. 10. मोक्षयति -यितुं), विमोक्ष्, उद्धृ (c. 1. -हरति -हर्त्तुं), विशुध् in caus. (-शोधयति -यितुं).—(Withdraw the mind) मनो निवृत् in caus. (-वर्त्तयति -यितुं).

To DISENGAGE, *v. n.* मुच् in pass. (मुच्यते), निवृत् (c. 1. -वर्त्तते -र्त्तितुं), विरञ्ज् in pass. (-रज्यते), आत्मानं निवृत् in caus. (-वर्त्तयति -यितुं); 'to be disengaged, at leisure,' प्राप्तावकाशः -शा -शं भू, सावकाशः -शा -शं भू, अवसरं प्राप् (c. 5. -आप्नोति -आप्तुं), कार्य्यरहितः -ता -तं भू, कार्य्यशून्यः -न्या -न्यं भू.

DISENGAGED, *p. p.* (Extricated) मुक्तः -क्ता -क्तं, विमुक्तः -क्ता -क्तं, उत्तीर्णः -र्णा -र्णं, समुद्धृतः -ता -तं.—(At leisure) अवकाशप्राप्तः -प्ता -प्तं, प्राप्तावसरः -रा -रं, व्यापारशून्यः -न्या -न्यं, निर्व्यापारः -रा -रं, निष्क्रियः -या -यं.

To DISENTANGLE, *v. a.* मुच् (c. 6. मुञ्चति, मोक्तुं, c. 10. मोचयति -यितुं), विमुच्, निर्मुच्, विनिर्मुच्, मोक्ष् (c. 10. मोक्षयति -यितुं), उद्धृ (c. 1. -हरति -हर्त्तुं), समुद्धृ, उत्तृ in caus. (-तारयति -यितुं), निस्तृ, विशुध् in caus. (-शोधयति -यितुं).—(Remove obstacles) विघ्नान् अपनी (c. 1. -नयति -नेतुं) or हृ (c. 1. हरति, हर्त्तुं), निर्विघ्नीकृ, निष्प्रत्यूहं -हां -हं कृ.

To DISENTHRAL, *v. a.* दास्यात् or दासभावात् or परवशात् or पराधीनत्वाद् मुच् (c. 6. मुञ्चति, मोक्तुं) or विमुच् or निस्तृ in caus. (-तारयति -यितुं) or मोक्ष् (c. 10. मोक्षयति -यितुं).

To DISENTRANCE, *v. a.* निर्भरस्वप्नात् or मूर्च्छनात् प्रबुध् in caus. (-बोधयति -यितुं).

DISESTEEM, *s.* अनादरः, असमाननं, उपेक्षा, अवमानं, अवज्ञा, अवधीरणं, असेवनं.

To DISESTEEM, *v. a.* अवमन् (c. 4. -मन्यते -मन्तुं), अवज्ञा (c. 9. -जानाति -ज्ञातुं), उपेक्ष् (c. 1. -ईक्षते -क्षितुं), अवधीर् (c. 10. -धीरयति -यितुं), कदर्थ् (c. 10. -अर्थयते -यितुं), लघूकृ, तुच्छीकृ, मन्दादरः -रा -रं भू.

DISFAVOUR, *s.* अप्रसादः, अप्रसन्नता, अननुग्रहः, निग्रहः, वैमुख्यं, अदृष्टिः *f.*, अनाश्रयः, विरक्तिः *f.*, वैरक्त्यं, अननुकूलता, अनुरोधाभावः, अनुपकारः.

To DISFAVOUR, *v. a.* न अनुग्रह् (c. 9. -गृह्णाति -ग्रहीतुं), न अनुकूल (nom. अनुकूलयति -यितुं), न प्रसद् (c. 6. -सीदति -सत्तुं), अप्रसन्नः

-ना -नं भू, अप्रसादं कृ, न उपकृ.

DISFIGURATION, *s.* विरूपकरणं, अपरूपीकरणं, कदाकारकरणं, विकृतिकरणं.

To DISFIGURE, *v. a.* विरूप् (c. 10. -रूपयति -यितुं), विरूपीकृ, अपरूपीकृ, कुरूपीकृ, विकृ, कदाकारीकृ, व्यङ्गीकृ, विकलीकृ.

DISFIGURED, *p. p.* विरूपितः -ता -तं, विरूपः -पा -पी -पं, अपरूपः -पी -पं, कुरूपः -पी -पं, विकृतः -ता -तं, विकृताङ्गः -ङ्गी -ङ्गं, विकृताकारः -रा -रं, विकृताकृतिः -तिः -ति, विकलाङ्गः -ङ्गी -ङ्गं, व्यङ्गः -ङ्गी -ङ्गं.

DISFIGUREMENT, *s.* विरूपता, वैरूप्यं, कुरूपता, अपरूपता, वैकृतं, व्यङ्गता.

To DISFRANCHISE, *v. a.* महासभायां प्रतिनिधिप्रेरणाधिकाराद् भ्रंश् in caus. (भ्रंशयति -यितुं) or च्यु in caus. (च्यावयति -यितुं), पौरजनलोपं कृ, अधिकारं हृ (c. 1. हरति, हर्तुं).

DISFRANCHISEMENT, *s.* अधिकारलोपः, अधिकाराद् भ्रंशनं, अधिकारहानिः *f.*

To DISGORGE, *v. a.* उद्गॄ (c. 6. -गिरति -गरितुं -रीतुं), वम् (c. 1. वमति -मितुं), उद्वम्, उत्क्षिप् (c. 6. -क्षिपति -क्षेप्तुं), ऊर्द्ध्वं क्षिप्, छर्द् (c. 10. छर्दयति -यितुं).

DISGORGEMENT, *s.* उद्गारः -रणं, उत्क्षिरणं, वमः -मनं, वान्तिः *f.*, ऊर्द्ध्वशोधनं.

DISGRACE, *s.* अयशः *n.* (स्), अपयशः *n.*, अकीर्त्तिः *f.*, अपकीर्त्तिः *f.*, अपमानं, अख्यातिः *f.*, कुख्यातिः, अपध्वंसः, अपकर्षः, अनादरः, कलङ्कः, अपकलङ्कः, मर्य्यादाहानिः *f.*, पराभवः, परिभवः, अभिभवः, अप्रतिष्ठा, असमर्य्यादा; 'disgrace of the family,' कुलकज्जलः, कुलाङ्गारः.

To DISGRACE, *v. a.* (Cause dishonour) अयशः कृ, अकीर्त्तिं कृ, सापमानं -नां -नं कृ, कलङ्कं कृ, कलङ्क (nom. कलङ्कयति -यितुं), कुख्यातिं जन् in caus. (जनयति -यितुं), लज्जां कृ.—(Degrade, put out of favour) पदाद् भ्रंश् in caus. (भ्रंशयति -यितुं) or च्यु in caus. (च्यावयति -यितुं) or अपकृष् (c. 1. -कर्षति -क्रष्टुं) or निराकृ.

DISGRACED, *p. p.* सापमानः -ना -नं, कलङ्कितः -ता -तं, अवज्ञोपहतः -ता -तं.

DISGRACEFUL, *a.* अकीर्त्तिकरः -री -रं, अपयशस्करः -री -रं, अयशस्यः -स्या -स्यं, कलङ्ककरः -री -रं, लज्जाकरः -री -रं, अपमानजनकः -का -कं, कलङ्की -ङ्किनी -ङ्कि (न्), अमर्य्यादाजनकः -का -कं, निन्दाकरः -री -रं.

DISGRACEFULLY, *adv.* सापमानं, अयशस्यं, अकीर्त्तिकरं, लज्जाकरं, गर्हितं.

DISGRACIOUS, *a.* अप्रसन्नः -न्ना -न्नं, अननुकूलः -ला -लं, निरनुरोधः -धा -धं, विमुखः -खी -खं, अप्रीतिकरः -री -रं, असन्तोषजनकः -का -कं.

To DISGUISE, *v. a.* (Conceal by an unusual dress) अन्यवेशेन or वेशान्तरेण छद् (c. 10. छादयति -यितुं), कपटवेशेन or छद्मवेशेन गुह् (c. 1. गूहति -हितुं, c. 10. गूहयति -यितुं), विडम्ब् (c. 10. -डम्बयति -यितुं), आकारगोपनं कृ; 'disguise one's self,' अन्यवेशं परिधा (c. 3. -दधाति -धत्ते -धातुं) or धृ in caus. (धारयति -यितुं), स्वाकारगोपनं कृ, आत्मरूपं or आत्मदेहं गुह्, आत्माकारपरिवर्त्तनं कृ.—(Conceal, cloke) छद्, गुप् in des. (जुगुप्सते -प्सितुं), प्रावृ (c. 5. -वृणोति -वरितुं -रीतुं). —(Disfigure) विरूप् (c. 10. -रूपयति -यितुं), विरूपीकृ, विकृ; 'disguise one's intentions,' स्वाभिप्रायगोपनं कृ.

DISGUISE, *s.* (Dress for concealing the person) कपटवेशः, छद्मवेशः, अन्यवेशः, वेशान्तरं, कृत्रिमवेशः, वेशः.—(Act of disguising) आकारगोपनं, वेशान्तरधारणं, विडम्बनं, अभिनयः.—(Counterfeit appearance, false show) छद्म *n.* (न्), व्यपदेशः, अपदेशः, व्याजः, छलं, लक्ष्यं, लक्षं.

DISGUISED, *p. p.* वेशधारी -रिणी -रि (न्), कपटवेशी -शिनी -शि (न्) or छद्मवेशी, कपटवेशः -शा -शं, कपटरूपी -पिणी -पि (न्), अलक्ष्यलिङ्गः -ङ्गा -ङ्गं, अलक्षितः -ता -तं; 'disguised as a Brahman,' द्विजरूपी *m.* (न्), द्विजवेशः; 'disguised censure,' व्याजनिन्दा.

DISGUISEMENT, *s.* आकारगोपनं, छद्मवेशधारणं, विडम्बनं, कपटरूपग्रहणं.

DISGUST, *s.* बीभत्सः -त्सं, घृणा, अरुचिः *f.*, गर्हा, जुगुप्सा, विकृतं, वैकृतं -त्यं, विकारः, अरतिः *f.*, वैराग्यं, विरक्तिः *f.*, वैरक्त्यं, निर्वेदः.

To DISGUST, *v. a.* बीभत्सं or अरुचिं कृ or जन् (c. 10. जनयति -यितुं), वैकृत्यम् उत्पद् in caus. (-पादयति -यितुं).

DISGUSTED, *p. p.* जातबीभत्सः -त्सा -त्सं, विकृतः -ता -तं, अरतः -ता -तं.

DISGUSTFUL, DISGUSTING, *a.* बीभत्सजनकः -का -कं, घृणोत्पादकः -का -कं, अरुचिरः -रा -रं, अरुच्युत्पादकः, अरुचिकृत् *m. f. n.*, वैराग्यकृत्, कुत्सितः -ता -तं, गर्ह्यः -र्ह्या -र्ह्यं.

DISH, *s.* शरावः, पात्रं, भाजनं, भोजनपात्रं, भाण्डं; 'made-dish,' सूदः, सिद्धान्नं.

To DISH UP, *v. a.* पात्रस्थं मांसव्यञ्जनादि परिविष् in caus. (-वेषयति -यितुं).

DISH-CLOUT, *s.* शरावमार्ज्जनः पटः, पात्रसम्मार्ज्जनार्थं चीरं.

DISH-WATER, *s.* भोजनपात्रप्रक्षालनेन घृतस्नेहादिमलिनं जलं.

DISHABILLE, *a.* दुर्वासाः -साः -सः (स्), कुचेलः -ला -लं, अविनीतवेशः -शा -शं, अनलङ्कृतः -ता -तं, अकृताभरणः -णा -णं, विवस्त्रः -स्त्रा -स्त्रं.

DISHABILLE, *s.* लघुवासः *n.* (स्), शिथिलवस्त्रं, शयनगृहे परिधेयं वसनं.

To DISHABIT, *v. a.* निर्वस् in caus. (-वासयति -यितुं), वासस्थानाद् बहिष्कृ.

To DISHEARTEN, *v. a.* आशां or मनो भञ्ज् (c. 7. भनक्ति, भंक्तुं), आशाभङ्गं कृ, अवसद् in caus. (-सादयति -यितुं), विषण्णीकृ, निर्विण्णीकृ, विषादं जन् in caus. (जनयति -यितुं), निराशीकृ.

DISHEARTENED, *p. p.* भग्नमनाः -नाः -नः (स्), भग्नाशः -शा -शं, विषण्णः -ण्णा -ण्णं, अवसादितः -ता -तं, दीनचेतनः -ना -नं, दीनमनस्कः -स्का -स्कं, ग्लानाशः -शा -शं.

DISHEVELLED, *a.* प्रविततः -ता -तं, प्रकीर्णः -र्णा -र्णं, स्रस्तः -स्ता -स्तं; 'having dishevelled hair,' विगलितकेशः -शी -शं, मुक्तकेशः -शी -शं, विस्रस्तकेशः -शी -शं, व्याममूर्द्धजः -जा -जं.

DISHONEST, *a.* (Void of probity) असाधुः -धुः -ध्वी -धु, अशुचिः -चिः -चि, अधार्म्मिकः -की -कं, अन्यायवर्त्ती -र्त्तिनी -र्त्ति (न्), अनृजुप्रकृतिः -तिः -ति, वक्रः -क्रा -क्रं, वक्री -क्रिणी -क्रि (न्), जिह्मः -ह्मा -ह्मं, कुटिलः -ला -लं, अभद्रः -द्रा -द्रं, खलः -ला -लं, दुष्टः -ष्टा -ष्टं, कपटी -टिनी -टि (न्), कापटिकः -की -कं, विषमः -मा -मं, छाद्मिकः -की -कं, कौटिकः -की -कं, कौटः -टी -टं, निकृतः -ता -तं, असरलः -ला -लं.—(Unchaste woman) भ्रष्टा, व्यभिचारिणी, असाध्वी, असती.—(Obscene) अशुद्धः -द्धा -द्धं, गर्हितः -ता -तं.

DISHONESTLY, *adv.* असाधु, अशुचि, अन्यायेन, कुटिलं, विषमं, धूर्त्तवत्.

DISHONESTY, *s.* (Want of probity) असाधुत्वं, अशुचित्वं, खलता, दुष्टता, अधर्म्मः, असरलता, असारल्यं, अनृजुता, जिह्मता, वक्रता, कौटिल्यं, कापट्यं, कौटं, अशुद्धता, अदाक्षिण्यं, माया.—(Unchastity in a woman) असतीत्वं, असाध्वीत्वं.

DISHONOUR, *s.* अपमानं, अनादरः, अवमानं -नना, विमानं, अयशः *n.* (स्), अपयशः, अकीर्त्तिः *f.*, अपकीर्त्तिः *f.*, असमर्य्यादा, अवज्ञा, परिभवः, तिरस्कारः, उपेक्षा, कलङ्कः, अपकलङ्कः, अपध्वंसः, अपकर्षः, अप्रतिष्ठा, अख्यातिः *f.*, मर्य्यादाहानिः *f.*, अङ्कनं.

To DISHONOUR, *v. a.* (Cause disgrace) अपमानं कृ, अयशः कृ, कलङ्कं कृ, कलङ्क (nom. कलङ्कयति -यितुं), अकीर्त्तिं जन् (c. 10. जनयति -यितुं), लज्जां कृ, सापमानं -नां -नं कृ.—(Dishonour a maiden) कन्यां दुष् in caus. (दूषयति -यितुं).—(Treat with dishonour) अवमन् (c. 4. -मन्यते -मन्तुं), अवज्ञा (c. 9. -जानाति -ज्ञातुं), अवधीर् (c. 10. -धीरयति -यितुं), लघूकृ.

DISHONOURABLE, *a.* अपमान्यः -न्या -न्यं, अपमाननीयः -या -यं, अनार्य्यः -र्य्या -र्य्यं, अपयशस्करः -रा -रं, अकीर्त्तिकरः -री -रं, अपमानजनकः -का -कं, कलङ्ककरः -री -रं.

DISHONOURABLY, *adv.* अनार्य्यं, अनार्य्यवत्, अयशस्यं, अपमान्यप्रकारेण.

DISHONOURED, *p. p.* अपमानितः -ता -तं, अवमानितः -ता -तं, विमानितः -ता -तं, अनर्च्चितः -ता -तं, अनादृतः -ता -तं, अनपचितः -ता -तं, खलीकृतः -ता -तं.

DISHONOURER, *s.* अपमानकर्त्ता *m.* (र्त्तृ), अनादरकृत्, उपेक्षकः, अवज्ञाता *m.* (तृ).

DISHUMOUR, *s.* प्रकृतिकटुत्वं, प्रकृतिकर्कशत्वं, स्वभाववक्रता, दुःशीलता, वक्रशीलता, अरुन्तुदत्वं.

DISINCLINATION, *s.* विरक्तिः *f.*, वैरक्त्यं, विमुखता, वैमुख्यं, अनीहा, निरीहता, अनिच्छा, अरुचिः *f.*, विमतिः *f.*, पराङ्मुखता, अप्रीतिः *f.*, निग्रहः, अस्पृहा, अप्रवृत्तिः *f.*, अप्रियत्वं.

To DISINCLINE, *v. a.* विरञ्ज् in caus. (-रञ्जयति -यितुं), वैरक्त्यं or वैमुख्यं or अनिच्छां जन् (c. 10. जनयति -यितुं) or उत्पद् in caus. (-पादयति -यितुं), पराङ्मुखं -खीं -खं कृ.

DISINCLINED, *p. p.* पराङ्मुखः -खी -खं, विमुखः -खी -खं, विरक्तः -क्ता -क्तं, विरक्तभावः -वा -वं, विमतः -ता -तं, विपरीतः -ता -तं, अनिच्छुः -च्छुः -च्छु, निरीहः -हा -हं, निःस्पृहः -हा -हं, निरभिलाषः -षा -षं, अप्रवृत्तः -त्ता -त्तं.

DISINGENUOUS, *a.* अनुदारः -रा -रं, असरलः -ला -लं, अदक्षिणः -णा -णं, वक्रभावः -वा -वं, अशुचिः -चिः -चि, सव्याजः -जा -जं, कापटिकः -की -कं, कुटिलस्वभावः -वा -वं, कृपणः -णा -णं, मलार्थकः -का -कं, कदर्य्यः -र्य्या -र्य्यं.

DISINGENUOUSLY, *adv.* अनुदारं, असरलं, अशुचि, सव्याजं, कापट्येन, कुटिलं.

DISINGENUOUSNESS, *s.* अनौदार्य्यं, असारल्यं, अशुचिता, अदाक्षिण्यं, भाववक्रता, कौटिल्यं, सव्याजत्वं, कापट्यं, कार्पण्यं, खलता, दुष्टता, माया.

DISINHERISON, *s.* (Act of disinheriting) पैतृकरिक्थच्छेदः, पैतृकरिक्थलोपः, विभागशून्यकरणं.—(The state) पैतृकाधिकारहानिः *f.*, विभागशून्यता.

To DISINHERIT or DISHERIT, *v. a.* निर्भज् in caus. (-भाजयति -यितुं), विभागशून्यं -न्यां -न्यं कृ, पैतृकधनं or पैतृकरिक्थम् अपहृ (c. 1. -हरति -हर्त्तुं), पैतृकाधिकाराद् भ्रंश् in caus. (भ्रंशयति -यितुं), गोत्ररिक्थलोपं कृ.

DISINHERITED, *p. p.* निर्भाजितः -ता -तं, विभागशून्यः -न्या -न्यं, पैतृकाधिकाराद्भ्रंशितः -ता -तं, पैतृकधनहीनः -ना -नं, अनधिकारः -रा -रं.

To DISINTER, *v. a.* शवं or मृतशरीरम् उत्खन् (c. 1. -खनति -नितुं).

DISINTERRED, *p. p.* उत्खातः -ता -तं, प्रोत्खातः -ता -तं, समाधिवहिष्कृतः -ता -तं.

DISINTERESTED, *a.* निर्ममः -मा -मं, अममः -मा -मं, अमामकः -की -कं, निष्कामः -मा -मं, अकामात्मा -त्मा -त्म (न्), अनात्मनीनः -ना -नं, मुक्तसङ्गः -ङ्गा -ङ्गं, निःसङ्गः -ङ्गा -ङ्गं, निजलाभनिवृत्ततृष्णः -ष्णा -ष्णं, स्वार्थनिरपेक्षः -क्षा -क्षं, विमलार्थकः -का -कं, विपक्षपातः -ता -तं, अपक्षपाती -तिनी -ति (न्), निःस्वार्थी -र्थिनी -र्थि (न्) or अस्वार्थार्थी, अस्वार्थलिप्सुः -प्सुः -प्सु, उदासीनः -ना -नं, अहैतुकः -का -कं, अकिञ्चनः -ना -नं, वृत्तिम्लानः -ना -नं, निरीहः -हा -हं.

DISINTERESTEDLY, *adv.* निर्ममं, निष्कामं, स्वार्थनिरपेक्षं, निर्ममत्वात्, विपक्षपातं.

DISINTERESTEDNESS, *s.* निर्ममत्वं, अममत्वं -ता, निष्कामत्वं, निःसङ्गत्वं, निरीहता, अस्वार्थार्थित्वं, विपक्षपातत्वं, अपक्षपातिता, उदासीनता, औदास्यं.

To DISJOIN, *v. a.* वियुज् (c. 7. -युनक्ति -योक्तुं), विप्रयुज्, विश्लिष् (c. 10. -श्लेषयति -यितुं).

DISJOINED, *p. p.* वियुक्तः -क्ता -क्तं, विप्रयुक्तः -क्ता -क्तं, विनियुक्तः -क्ता -क्तं, विश्लिष्टः -ष्टा -ष्टं, असंलग्नः -ग्ना -ग्नं, असंसक्तः -क्ता -क्तं, व्यवहितः -ता -तं.

To DISJOINT, *v. a.* (Put out of joint) विसन्धीकृ, सन्धित्रोटनं कृ, सन्धिं भञ्ज् (c. 7. भनक्ति, भंक्तुं), विसन्धा (c. 3. -दधाति -धातुं).—(Separate) वियुज् (c. 7. -युनक्ति -योक्तुं), विसंयुज्, विश्लिष् in caus. (-श्लेषयति -यितुं).—(Carve) अवछिद् (c. 7. -छिनत्ति -छेत्तुं), निकृत् (c. 6. -कृन्तति -कर्त्तितुं).

To DISJOINT, *v. n.* विसन्धीभू, विसंयुज् in pass. (-युज्यते).

DISJOINTED, *p. p.* विसन्धितः -ता -तं, असंश्लिष्टः -ष्टा -ष्टं, असंहतः -ता -तं.—(Not coherent) असम्बद्धः -द्धा -द्धं, अनन्वितः -ता -तं, निर्युक्तिकः -की -कं.

DISJOINTING, *s.* विसन्धीकरणं, विसन्धानं, विसंयोगः, सन्धिच्छेदः, व्यवच्छेदः.

DISJUNCT, *a.* वियुक्तः -क्ता -क्तं, विप्रयुक्तः -क्ता -क्तं, विसंयुक्तः -क्ता -क्तं, विश्लिष्टः -ष्टा -ष्टं, असंलग्नः -ग्ना -ग्नं, पृथग्भूतः -ता -तं.

DISJUNCTION, *s.* वियोगः, विसंयोगः, विप्रयोगः, निर्युक्तिः *f.*, असंयोगः, विश्लेषः, असन्धानं, विभेदः, सङ्गविच्युतिः *f.*, व्यासक्त्यं; 'of letters,' अवसानं.

DISJUNCTIVE, *a.* निर्युक्तिकः -की -कं, वियोगी -गिनी -गि (न्), विभेदकारः -री -रं.

DISJUNCTIVELY, *adv.* वियोगतस्, विसंयोगतस्, विश्लेषेण, विसंयुक्तं, पृथक्.

DISK, *s.* (Of the sun, &c.) बिम्बः -म्बं, मण्डलं, परिधिः *m.*, परिवेशः, उपसूर्य्यकं, सूर्य्यमण्डलं.—(Quoit) चक्रं.

DISLIKE, *s.* अप्रीतिः *f.*, अप्रेम *n.* (न्), अप्रियता -त्वं, विप्रियता -त्वं, विरक्तिः *f.*, वैरक्त्यं, विमतिः *f.*, द्वेषः, निग्रहः, विद्विष्टता, द्वेष्यता, अरुचिः *f.*, असौहृद्यं, विमुखता, पराङ्मुखता, वैमुख्यं, अनिच्छा, अनीहा, विद्वेषः, अनिष्टता.

To DISLIKE, *v. a.* न अभिमन् (c. 4. -मन्यते -मन्तुं), न अनुमन्, न इष् (c. 6. इच्छति, एषितुं), न अभिनन्द् (c. 1. -नन्दति -न्दितुं), न प्रतिनन्द्, न अनुरुध् (c. 4. -रुध्यते -रोद्धुं); द्विष् (c. 2. द्वेष्टि -ष्टुं), विद्विष्, विरञ्ज् in pass. (-रज्यते); न प्री (c. 9. प्रीणाति or c. 4. प्रीयते), न अनुरुच् (c. 10. -रोचयति -यितुं) or expressed by the neut. form रोचते; as, 'he dislikes that,' तत् तस्मै न रोचते.

DISLIKED, *p. p.* अप्रियः -या -यं, विप्रियः -या -यं, द्विष्टः -ष्टा -ष्टं, विद्विष्टः -ष्टा -ष्टं, अनिष्टः -ष्टा -ष्टं, अनभिमतः -ता -तं, अप्रीतिकरः -री -रं.

To DISLIKEN, *v. a.* असमानीकृ, असमीकृ, असदृशं -शीं -शं कृ, अतुल्यीकृ.

DISLIKENESS, *s.* असमानता, असाम्यं, असादृश्यं, अतुल्यता, वैषम्यं.

To DISLOCATE, *v. a.* विसन्धीकृ, सन्धित्रोटनं कृ, सन्धिं or अस्थिग्रन्थिं त्रुट् (c. 10. त्रोटयते -यितुं) or भञ्ज् (c. 7. भनक्ति, भंक्तुं), विसन्धा (c. 3. -दधाति -धत्ते -धातुं), सन्धिम् उत्सृ in caus. (-सारयति -यितुं) or स्थानान्तरीकृ.

DISLOCATED, *p. p.* विसन्धितः -ता -तं, विसन्धीकृतः -ता -तं, त्रुटितः -ता -तं, सन्धिच्युतः -ता -तं, च्युतग्रन्थिः -न्थिः -न्थि.

DISLOCATION, *s.* त्रोटनं, सन्धित्रोटनं, सन्धिभङ्गः, ग्रन्थिभङ्गः, विसन्धानं, विसन्धीकरणं, सन्धिच्युतिः *f.*; 'of hand and foot,' करपादत्रोटनं.

To DISLODGE, *v. a.* (Remove from a habitation) गृहाद् वहिष्कृ or निःसृ in caus. (-सारयति -यितुं), निर्वस् in caus. (-वासयति -यितुं), विवस्, विप्रवस्, स्थानान्तरीकृ, देशान्तरीकृ.—(Remove, drive away) अपसृ or निःसृ or उत्सृ in caus., निराकृ, दूरीकृ, अपानुद् (c. 6. -नुदति -नोत्तुं), निरस् (c. 4. -अस्यति -असितुं), विचल् in caus. (-चालयति -यितुं).

To DISLODGE, *v. n.* अपसृ (c. 1. -सरति -सर्त्तुं), स्थानान्तरं or देशान्तरं गम् (c. 1. गच्छति, गन्तुं), निवेशनस्थानं त्यज् (c. 1. त्यजति, त्यक्तुं), स्थानान्तरे निविश् (c. 6. -विशति -वेष्टुं).

DISLODGED, *p. p.* अपसारितः -ता -तं, निःसारितः -ता -तं, विवासितः -ता -तं, वहिष्कृतः -ता -तं, निष्कासितः -ता -तं, निरस्तः -स्ता -स्तं, स्थानान्तरं गमितः -ता -तं.

DISLOYAL, *a.* अभक्तः -क्ता -क्तं, अभक्तिमान् -मती -मत् (त्), क्षीणभक्तिः -क्तिः -क्ति, भक्तिहीनः -ना -नं, विश्वासघाती -तिनी -ति (न्) or विश्रम्भघाती or भक्तिघाती, शत्रुसेवी -विनी -वि (न्) or द्विट्सेवी, राजा-

भिद्रोही -हिणी -हि (न्), राजापथ्यकारी -रिणी -रि (न्), राजवैरी -रिणी -रि (न्).—(Not true to marriage) व्यभिचारी *m.* -रिणी *f.* (न्), अननुकूलः *m.*, असाध्वी *f.*, असती *f.*, अभिसारिका *f.*

DISLOYALLY, *adv.* अभक्त्या, भक्तिहीनत्वात्, अभक्तवत्, भक्तिभङ्गात्, राजद्रोहेण.

DISLOYALTY, *s.* अभक्तिः *f.*, अभक्तिमत्त्वं, भक्तिहीनता, भक्तिभङ्गः, भक्तिघातः, विश्वासभङ्गः, शत्रुसेवा, द्विड्सेवा, राजाभिद्रोहः, राजापथ्यकारित्वं.—(In love) व्यभिचारः.

DISMAL, *a.* दारुणः -णा -णं, दुःखी -खिनी -खि (न्), सशोकः -का -कं, सखेदः -दा -दं, खेदजनकः -का -कं, अनिष्टवेदी -दिनी -दि (न्), उग्रः -ग्रा -ग्रं, घोरः -रा -रं, भीरुमयः -यी -यं, रौद्रः -द्री -द्रं, निरानन्दः -न्दा -न्दं.

DISMALLY, *adv.* दारुणं, घोरं, उग्रं, सखेदं, उग्रशोकात्, भयानकं.

DISMALNESS, *s.* दारुणता, सशोकता, उग्रता, घोरत्वं, रौद्रत्वं, भयानकत्वं.

To DISMANTLE, *v. a.* (Strip of dress) विवस्त्र (nom. विवस्त्रयति -यितुं), नग्नीकृ, वस्त्रं हृ (c. 1. हरति, हर्तुं).—(Deprive a ship of rigging) नौकासज्जां or नौकोपकरणं हृ or अपहृ or अपनी (c. 1. -नयति -नेतुं).—(Deprive a town of forts) नगरपरिगतं प्राचीरादि or नगरपरिकूटं or नगरदुर्गं or नगरगुप्तिं नश् in caus. (नाशयति -यितुं).

DISMANTLED, *p.p.* विवस्त्रः -स्त्रा -स्त्रं, हृतोपकरणः -णा -णं, हृतसज्जः -ज्जा -ज्जं.

To DISMASK, *v. a.* कृत्रिममुखं or कपटवेशं or छद्मवेशम् अवतृ in caus. (-तारयति -यितुं), अपवृ (c. 5. -वृणोति -वरितुं -रीतुं), अपावृ; उच्छद् (c. 10. -च्छादयति -यितुं), स्पष्टीकृ.

To DISMAST, *v. a.* कूपकं भञ्ज् (c. 7. भनक्ति, भंक्तुं), गुणवृक्षकम् अपहृ (c. 1. -हरति -हर्तुं).

DISMASTED, *p.p.* भग्नकूपकः -का -कं, हृतगुणवृक्षकः -का -कं, निष्कूपकः -का -कं.

To DISMAY, *v. a.* त्रस् in caus. (त्रासयति -यितुं), वित्रस्, भी in caus. (भाययति or भीषयति -यितुं), विस्मि in caus. (-स्माययति -स्मापयति -यितुं), विस्मयम् उत्पद् in caus. (-पादयति -यितुं), (उद्विज् in caus. (-वेजयति -यितुं).

DISMAY, *s.* विस्मयः, साध्वसं, त्रासः, सन्त्रासः, भयं, भीषणं, उद्वेगः, दरः.

DISMAYED, *p. p.* विस्मितः -ता -तं, सन्त्रस्तः -स्ता -स्तं, भीषितः -ता -तं, त्रासितः -ता -तं, साध्वसोपहतः -ता -तं, विलक्षः -क्षा -क्षं.

To DISMEMBER, *v.a.* अङ्गाद् अङ्गम् अवच्छिद् (c. 7. -छिनत्ति -छेत्तुं), अवयवशो निकृत् (c. 6. -कृन्तति -कर्त्तितुं), गात्राणि पृथक्कृ, व्यङ्गीकृ.

DISMEMBERMENT, *s.* अङ्गव्यवच्छेदः, अवयवशो निकर्त्तनं, गात्राणां पृथक्करणं.

To DISMISS, *v. a.* (Send away) प्रस्था in caus. (-स्थापयति -यितुं), अपसृ in caus. (-सारयति -यितुं), प्रेर् (c. 10. -ईरयति -यितुं), विसृज् (c. 6. -सृजति -स्रष्टुं c. 10. -सर्जयति -यितुं), सम्प्रेष् in caus. (-प्रेषयति -यितुं).—(Give leave of departure) अनुज्ञा, (c. 9. -जानाति -ज्ञातुं).—(Discard) अपास् (c. 4. -अस्यति -असितुं), मुच् (c. 6. मुञ्चति, मोक्तुं), अवमुच्, अवसृज्, अपसृज्, उत्सृज्; हा (c. 3. जहाति, हातुं), अपाहा, अपहा, विहा; उज्झ् (c. 6. उज्झति -झितुं), प्रोज्झ्, प्रतिक्षिप् (c. 6. -क्षिपति -क्षेप्तुं), निराकृ, पराकृ, दूरीकृ; 'to dismiss from office,' अधिकारात् or पदात् or आधिपत्याद् भ्रंश् in caus. (भ्रंशयति -यितुं) or च्यु in caus. (च्यावयति -यितुं) or अवरुह् in caus. (-रोपयति -यितुं) or निराकृ.

DISMISSED, *p. p.* प्रस्थापितः -ता -तं, अपसारितः -ता -तं, सम्प्रेषितः -ता -तं, विसर्जितः -ता -तं, अवसृष्टः -ष्टा -ष्टं, निसृष्टः -ष्टा -ष्टं, अपास्तः -स्ता -स्तं, प्रतिक्षिप्तः -प्ता -प्तं, अपविद्धः -द्धा -द्धं, निष्कासितः -ता -तं, गमितः -ता -तं, निकृतः -ता -तं, दूरीकृतः -ता -तं; 'dismissed from office,' च्युताधिकारः -रा -रं, अधिकारात्भ्रंशितः -ता -तं or निराकृतः -ता -तं; 'one dismissed,' अपविद्धलोकः.

DISMISSION, DISMISSAL, *s.* प्रस्थापनं, प्रेरणं, विसर्जनं, अपसर्जनं, अवसर्जनं, अपासनं, सम्प्रेषः -षणं, त्यजनं; 'from office,' अधिकाराद् भ्रंशनं or निराकरणं or अवरोपणं.

To DISMOUNT, *v. a.* (Throw from a horse) अश्वपृष्ठात् पत् in caus. (पातयति -यितुं) or अवतृ in caus. (-तारयति -यितुं) or उत्तृ.—(Throw a cannon from its carriage) युद्धयन्त्रं स्ववाहनाद् अवतृ in caus.

To DISMOUNT, *v. n.* अश्वाद् अवरुह् (c. 1. -रोहति -रोढुं), अश्वपृष्ठाद् अवतृ (c. 1. -तरति -रितुं -रीतुं) or उत्तृ, अवया (c. 2. -याति -तुं), अधो गम् (c. 1. गच्छति, गन्तुं.)

DISMOUNTED, *p. p.* अवतीर्णः -र्णा -र्णं, उत्तीर्णः -र्णा -र्णं, अवरूढः -ढा -ढं.

DISNATURED, *p.p.* वात्सल्यरहितः -ता -तं, अवत्सलः -ला -लं, स्नेहहीनः -ना -नं.

DISOBEDIENCE, *s.* आज्ञाभङ्गः, आज्ञाव्यतिक्रमः, आज्ञालङ्घनं, अननुवर्त्तनं, असेवनं, अमाननं, अशुश्रूषा, प्रतिकूलत्वं, प्रतीपता, अवशत्वं, अननुकूलता, अननुष्ठानं, दुःशीलता.

DISOBEDIENT, *a.* आज्ञाभङ्गकरः -री -रं, आज्ञालङ्घी -ङ्घिनी -ङ्घि (न्), अनादेशकरः -री -रं, अवचनकरः -री -रं, अवचस्करः -रा -रं, अशुश्रूषुः -षुः -षु, अननुवर्त्ती -र्त्तिनी -र्त्ति (न्), अननुकूलः -ला -लं, अवशः -शा -शं, अवशवर्त्ती -र्त्तिनी -र्त्ति (न्) प्रतीपः पा -पं, अविधायी -यिनी -यि (न्) असेवी -विनी -वि (न्), प्रतिकूलः -ला -लं, दुःशीलः -ला -लं.

To DISOBEY *v. a.* आज्ञां भञ्ज् (c. 7. भनक्ति, भंक्तुं) or लङ्घ् (c. 10. लङ्घयति -यितुं) or न सेव् (c. 1. सेवते -वितुं) or न अनुवृत् (c. 1. -वर्त्तते -र्त्तितुं) or न अनुष्ठा (c. 1. -तिष्ठति -ष्ठातुं) or न श्रु in des. (शुश्रूषते -षितुं) or न प्रतीष् (c. 6. -इच्छति -एषितुं) or न अनुविधा in pass. (-धीयते) or न अभ्युपे (c. 2. अभ्युपैति -तुं); प्रतीप (nom. प्रतीपायते).

DISOBEYED, *p. p.* असेवितः -ता -तं, अशुश्रूषितः -ता -तं, अननुष्ठितः -ता -तं.

DISOBLIGATION, *s.* अप्रियं, विप्रियं, अनुपकारः, अपकारः, अपराधः, विध्वंसः.

To DISOBLIGE, *v. a.* अप्रियं or विप्रियं कृ or आचर् (c. 1. -चरति -रितुं); अपराध् (c. 4. -राध्यति c. 5. -राध्नोति -राद्धुं) with gen.; अपकृ, असन्तोषं जन् (c. 10. जनयति -यितुं), रोषं or मन्युम् उत्पद् in caus. (-पादयति -यितुं).

DISOBLIGING, *a.* अप्रियङ्करः -री -रं or अप्रियकरः, अननुरोधी -धिनी -धि (न्), अननुग्राही -हिणी -हि (न्), अननुकूलः -ला -लं, अनुपकारी -रिणी -रि (न्), अननुविधायी -यिनी -यि (न्), असन्तोषकरः -री -रं, अपकारकः -का -कं, अपराधकारी -रिणी रि (न्), व्यलीकः का -कं.

DISOBLIGINGLY, *adv.* अप्रीत्या, अननुरोधेन, अनुनयाभावात्, दुष्टभावेन.

DISOBLIGINGNESS, *s.* अननुरोधः, अननुग्रहः, अननुकूलता, अप्रियकारित्वं, अनुपकारित्वं.

DISORDER, *s.* (Irregularity, confusion) अक्रमः, उत्क्रमः, व्युत्क्रमः, क्रमभङ्गः, भग्नप्रक्रमः, व्यतिक्रमः, विसूत्रता, अपरिपाटिः *f.*, असंस्थानं, अव्यवस्था, अविधिः *m.*, अविधानं, अनवस्थितत्वं, व्यस्तता, विक्षिप्तता, सङ्करः, साङ्कर्य्यं, सङ्कीर्णत्वं, सङ्क्षोभः, व्यतिकरः.—(Tumult, disturbance) विप्लवः, तुमुलं, कोलाहलः, क्षोभः.—(Breach of law) व्यवस्थातिक्रमः.—(Disease) रोगः, व्याधिः *m.*, पीडा, व्यापद् *f.*, आमयः, वैकल्यं, अस्वास्थ्यं, असुस्थता; 'disorder of stomach,' अन्नविकारः, जठरामयः.—(Discomposure of mind) आकुलत्वं, व्याकुलत्वं, व्यग्रता, वैक्लव्यं, सम्भ्रमः; 'army in disorder,' समुत्पिञ्जः, पिञ्जलः.

To DISORDER, *v. a.* (Confuse) पर्य्यस् (c. 4. -अस्यति -असितुं), व्यस्, संक्षुभ् in caus. (-क्षोभयति -यितुं), विक्षुभ्, विक्षिप् (c. 6. -क्षिपति -क्षेप्तुं), क्रमं भञ्ज् (c. 7. भनक्ति, भंक्तुं) or विलुप् (c. 6. -लुम्पति -लोप्तुं) or उपहन् (c. 2. -हन्ति -न्तुं), सङ्करीकृ, व्यस्तव्यस्तीकृ, सङ्कुलीकृ, आकुलीकृ.—(Make sick) अस्वास्थ्यं or रोगं कृ or जन् (c. 10. जनयति

-यितुं), अस्वस्थं -स्थां -स्थं कृ, पीड् (c. 10. पीडयति -यितुं), व्यथ् (c. 10. व्यथयति -यितुं), उपहन्, उपतप् (c. 10. -तापयति -यितुं).—(Disturb the mind) व्याकुलीकृ, आकुलीकृ, व्याकुल (nom. व्याकुलयति -यितुं), व्यामुह् (c. 10. -मोहयति -यितुं), विभ्रम् (c. 10. -भ्रमयति -यितुं).

DISORDERED, *a.* (Deranged) व्यस्तः -स्ता -स्तं, अस्तव्यस्तः -स्ता -स्तं, असंस्थितः -ता -तं, अव्यवस्थितः -ता -तं, अनवस्थितः -ता -तं, भग्नक्रमः -मा -मं, क्रमहीनः -ना -नं, विक्षिप्तः -प्ता -प्तं, सङ्करीकृतः -ता -तं, सङ्कुलः -ला -लं, सङ्कीर्णः -र्णा -र्णं, व्यापन्नः -न्ना -न्नं, विगलितः -ता -तं.—(In mind) आकुलः -ला -लं, व्याकुलः -ला -लं, सम्भ्रान्तः -न्ता -न्तं, भ्रान्तमनाः -नाः -नः (स्), विपरीतचेताः -ताः -तः (स्), व्यग्रः -ग्रा -ग्रं, पारिप्लवः -वा -वं.—(In body) अस्वस्थः -स्था -स्थं, उपहतः -ता -तं, व्याधितः -ता -तं, पीडितः -ता -तं, आतुरः -रा -रं, विकारी -रिणी -रि (न्).—(As an army) विप्लुतः -ला -लं.

DISORDERLY, *a.* (Confused) अस्तव्यस्तः -स्ता -स्तं. *See* DISORDERED.—(Irregular) विधिभङ्गकः -का -कं, अनवस्थितः -ता -तं, अव्यवस्थितः -ता -तं, उन्मर्यादः -दा -दं, नियमविरुद्धः -द्धा -द्धं, विषमः -मा -मं.—(Lawless, unruly) धर्म्मरोधी -धिनी -धि (न्), अधर्म्यः -र्म्या -र्म्यं, अवशः -शा -शं, अनियतः -ता -तं, उच्छृङ्खलः -ला -लं.

DISORDERLY, *adv.* (Confusedly, without order) सङ्कुलं, सङ्कीर्णं, अक्रमेण, क्रमं विना.—(Against rule or law) अविधितस्, अधर्म्मतस्, नियमविरुद्धं.

DISORDINATE, *a.* अविधिः -धिः -धि, विधिघ्नः -घ्नी -घ्नं, निराचारः -रा -रं, अव्यवस्थितः -ता -तं, व्यभिचारी -रिणी -रि (न्).

DISORGANIZATION, *s.* निर्व्यूढिः *f.*, निर्व्यूढता, संस्थानभङ्गः, क्रमभङ्गः, रीतिखण्डनं.

To DISORGANIZE, DISORGANIZED. *See* *To* DISORDER, DISORDERED.

To DISOWN, *v. a.* निह्नु (c. 2. -ह्नुते -ह्नोतुं), अपह्नु, प्रत्याख्या (c. 2. -ख्याति -तुं), अन्तःख्या, अतिख्या, प्रत्यादिश् (c. 6. -दिशति -देष्टुं), निरस् (c. 4. -अस्यति -असितुं), अपज्ञा (c. 9. -जानीते -ज्ञातुं).

DISOWNED, *p. p.* निह्नुतः -ता -तं, अपह्नुतः -ता -तं, प्रत्याख्यातः -ता -तं.

To DISPARAGE, *v. a.* (Treat with contempt, undervalue) अवज्ञा (c. 9. -जानाति -ज्ञातुं), अपवद् (c. 1. -वदति -दितुं), परिवद्, परिभू, असूय (nom. असूयति -ते -यितुं), अभ्यसूय, उपेक्ष् (c. 1. -ईक्षते -क्षितुं), कदर्थ् (c. 10. -अर्थयते -यितुं), अवक्षिप् (c. 6. -क्षिपति -क्षेप्तुं), निन्द् (c. 1. निन्दति -न्दितुं), लघूकृ, तुच्छीकृ, तृणाय मन् (c. 4. मन्यते, मन्तुं), अवमन्, अपकृष् (c. 1. -कर्षति -क्रष्टुं), अपकृष्.—(Match unequally) अयोग्यविवाहेन सम्बन्ध् (c. 9. -बध्नाति -बन्धुं), अनुपयुक्तसम्बन्धं कृ.—(Impair by union with something inferior) अयोग्यसंसर्गेण सारताम् अपहृ (c. 1. -हरति -हर्त्तुं) or अपकृष्.

DISPARAGED, *p. p.* अवज्ञातः -ता -तं, अवमतः -ता -तं, परिभूतः -ता -तं, कदर्थितः -ता -तं, निन्दितः -ता -तं, अपकृष्टः -ष्टा -ष्टं, अवगीतः -ता -तं, लघूकृतः -ता -तं.

DISPARAGEMENT, *s.* (Detraction, dishonour) असूया -यनं, अभ्यसूया, असूयुः *m.*, अपवादः, परीवादः, परिवादः, अवज्ञा, परिभाषणं, अपमानं, निन्दा, अवहेला, परिभवः, परिभूतिः *f.*, अपकर्षः, गुणापवादः, गुणघातः, विगानं, परदोषवादः, परावज्ञा, कलङ्ककरणं, तिरस्कारः.—(Unequal match) अयोग्यसम्बन्धः, अनुपयुक्तविवाहः.

DISPARAGER, *s.* असूयकः, अभ्यसूयकः, अपवादी *m.* (न्) परिवादी *m.* गुणघाती *m.* (न्), निन्दकः; 'self-disparager,' आत्मगुणावमानी *m.* (न्).

DISPARITY, *s.* असाम्यं, असमता, असमानता, वैषम्यं, विषमता, अतुल्यत्वं, प्रभेदः, विभेदः, भेदः, भिन्नता, प्रभिन्नता, असमञ्जसं, असामञ्जस्यं, अयोग्यता, तारतम्यं, न्यूनाधिक्यं, न्यूनाधिक्यं, न्यूनातिरेकः; 'in number,' संख्यावैषम्यं, विषमसंख्यत्वं.

To DISPARK, *v. a.* वाटं सर्व्वसामान्यं कृ or निरवरोधं कृ or निरावरणं कृ.

To DISPART, *v. a.* वियुज् (c. 7. -युनक्ति -योक्तुं), विभज् (c. 1. -भजति -भक्तुं), विभिद् (c. 7. -भिनत्ति -भेत्तुं), द्विधा भिद् or कृ, द्वैधीकृ, द्विखण्डीकृ.

DISPASSION, *s.* वैराग्यं, वैरागं, विरागः, अरागत्वं, अक्रोधः, शान्तिः *f.*, शमः, शान्तता, औदास्यं, निरीहता, निरुद्वेगः, धैर्य्यं, शाम्यं.

DISPASSIONATE, *a.* विरागी -गिणी -गि (न्) or अरागी, विरक्तः -क्ता -क्तं, अरागः -गा -गं, वीतरागः -गा -गं, रागहीनः -ना -नं, शान्तः -न्ता -न्तं, समचित्तः -त्ता -त्तं, समबुद्धिः -द्धिः -द्धि, उदासी -सिनी -सि (न्), उदासीनः -ना -नं, निरञ्जनः -ना -नं, अक्रोधः -धा -धं, अपक्षपाती -तिनी -ति (न्).

DISPASSIONATELY, *adv.* शान्त्या, शान्तचेतसा, समबुद्ध्या, असम्भ्रमं, असहसा.

DISPATCH, *s.* *See* DESPATCH.

To DISPEL, *v. a.* अपनुद् (c. 6. -नुदति -नोत्तुं), अपानुद्, व्यपानुद्; निरस् (c. 4. -अस्यति -असितुं), व्यस्, अपास्, अपसृ (c. 10. -सारयति -यितुं), निःसृ, उत्सृ; निराकृ, बहिष्कृ, दूरीकृ, विचल् (c. 10. -चालयति -यितुं), विनी (c. 1. -नयति -नेतुं), अपनी, विधू (c. 5. -धूनोति -धवितुं), निर्धू, अपोह् (c. 1. -ऊहते -हितुं), विध्मा (c. 1. -धमति -ध्मातुं), हृ (c. 1. हरति, हर्त्तुं), अपहृ, परिहृ, हन् (c. 2. हन्ति -न्तुं), नश् (c. 10. नाशयति -यितुं); 'dispelling darkness,' तमोनुदः -दा -दं; 'dispelling fever,' ज्वरघ्नः -घ्नी -घ्नं, ज्वरनाशकः -का -कं, ज्वरापहः -हा -हं, ज्वरान्तकः -का -कं, 'dispelling poison,' विषघाती -तिनी -ति (न्); 'dispelling obstacles,' विघ्नहरः -रा -रं, विघ्नविनायकः -का -कं.

DISPELLED, *p. p.* निरस्तः -स्ता -स्तं. व्यस्तः -स्ता -स्तं, अपास्तः -स्ता -स्तं, निराकृतः -ता -तं, दूरीकृतः -ता -तं, अपनोदितः -ता -तं, अपसारितः -ता -तं, निर्धूतः -ता -तं, विधूतः -ता -तं, अपनीतः -ता -तं, अपोढः -ढा -ढं, अपहृतः -ता -तं.

DISPELLING, *s.* अपनुत्तिः *f.*, अपनोदः, अपसारणं, निःसारणं, निरसनं, निराकरणं.

To DISPEND, *v. a.* व्यय् (c. 10. व्यययति -यितुं c. 1. व्ययति, rt. इ), व्ययीकृ.

DISPENSARY, *s.* औषधागारं, औषधसंस्कारशाला, औषधपरिकल्पनगृहं, औषधमिश्रणस्थानं.

DISPENSATION, *s.* (Distribution) प्रणयनं, वितरणं, विभागकल्पना, परिकल्पनं, वण्टनं, प्रविभागः, क्लृप्तिः *f.*, परिनिर्वपणं, अंशनं.—(Permission to break a law) नियमभङ्गानुमतिः *f.*, विधानलङ्घनानुमतिः, व्यवस्थाभङ्गानुज्ञा, व्यवहारभङ्गानुमतिः *f.*, व्यवस्थावशाद् विमुक्तिः *f.*, आचारभङ्गोपेक्षा, मुक्तिः *f.*, विनिर्मोकः, क्षमा, मोक्षः.—(The dealing of God with men) मनुष्यान् प्रति परमेश्वरस्य गतिः *f.* or व्यवहारः or प्रवृत्तिः *f.* or क्रियाविधिः *m.*

DISPENSATOR, *s.* विभागकल्पकः, परिकल्पकः, प्रणेता *m.* (तृ), वितरणकृत्, वण्टनकृत्.

DISPENSATORY, *s.* औषधसंस्कारविषयो ग्रन्थः, वैद्यशास्त्रं.

To DISPENSE, *v. a.* क्लृप् (c. 10. कल्पयति -यितुं), परिक्लृप्, पृथक् पृथग् विभज् (c. 1. -भजति -ते -भक्तुं) or प्रविभज् or वितॄ (c. 1. -तरति -रितुं -रीतुं), निन्यस् (c. 4. -अस्यति -असितुं), विधा (c. 3. -दधाति -धातुं), अंस् (c. 10. -अंसयति -यितुं), वण्ट् (c. 10. वण्टयति -यितुं); 'to dispense justice, punishment, &c.' प्रणी (c. 1. -णयति -णेतुं) सम्प्रणी.

To DISPENSE WITH, *v. a.* अवसृज् (c. 6. -सृजति -स्रष्टुं), त्यज् (c. 1. त्यजति, त्यक्तुं), मुच् (c. 6. मुञ्चति, मोक्तुं), क्षम् (c. 1. क्षमते, क्षन्तुं), अनुज्ञा (c. 9. -जानाति -ज्ञातुं), अनुमन् (c. 4. -मन्यते -मन्तुं), उपेक्ष् (c. 1. -ईक्षते -क्षितुं).

DISPENSED, *p. p.* परिकल्पितः -ता -तं, प्रविभक्तः -क्ता -क्तं, प्रणीतः -ता -तं.

DISPENSE, *s.* नियमभङ्गानुमतिः *f.*, विधानलङ्घनक्षमा, व्यवस्थावशाद् विनिर्मोकः.

DISPENSER, *s.* परिकल्पकः, प्रणेता *m.* (तृ), वितरणकारी *m.* (न्).

To DISPEOPLE, *v. a.* निर्जनीकृ, विजनीकृ, नरशून्यं -न्यां -न्यं कृ, शून्यारण्यं कृ, निर्मनुष्यं -ष्यां -ष्यं कृ, अरण्यमिव कृ.

DISPEOPLER, *s.* नरशून्यकारी *m.* (न्), उच्छेदकः, निर्मनुष्यकारी *m.*, निर्जनकृत्.

To DISPERSE, *v. a.* विकॄ (c. 6. -किरति -करितुं -रीतुं), इतस्ततः or बहुधा or नानादिक्षु विद्रु in caus. (-द्रावयति -यितुं), विक्षिप् (c. 6. -क्षिपति -क्षेप्तुं), व्यस् (c. 4. -अस्यति -असितुं), विधू (c. 5. -धूनोति -धवितुं), निर्धू, इतस्ततो विचल् in caus. (-चालयति -यितुं) or विस्तॄ in caus. (-स्तारयति -यितुं) or अपनुद् (c. 6. -नुदति -नोत्तुं) or निरस् or गम् in caus. (गमयति -यितुं) or विसृ in caus. (-सारयति -यितुं) or प्रसृ or विध्मा (c. 1. -धमति -ध्मातुं) or अपध्मा; 'dispersing darkness,' तमोनुदः -दा -दं, तमोपहः -हा -हं, तमोहरः -रा -रं. *See* DISPERSER; 'dispersing to different quarters,' अपदिश्य.

DISPERSED, *p. p.* विकीर्णः -र्णा -र्णं, विद्रुतः -ता -तं, विक्षिप्तः -प्ता -प्तं, विगलितः -ता -तं, व्यस्तः -स्ता -स्तं, सुव्यस्तः -स्ता -स्तं, बहुधागतः -ता -तं, विधूतः -ता -तं, विनिर्धूतः -ता -तं, विभिन्नः -न्ना -न्नं, विप्रकीर्णः -र्णा -र्णं, प्रसृतः -ता -तं, प्रवृद्धः -द्धा -द्धं.

DISPERSEDLY, *adv.* विद्रुतं, असंहतं, सुव्यस्तं, सुविस्तरं, बहुधा, पृथक्.

DISPERSER, *s.* विद्रावयिता *m.* (तृ), विकिरणकृत्; 'a disperser of doubt,' संशयोच्छेदकः; also expressed by नुदः, घ्नः, घाती *m.* (न्), अपहः, नाशकः, हरः, हारी *m.* (न्), अन्तकः in comp.

DISPERSION, *s.* विद्रावणं, विक्षेपः -पणं, परिक्षेपः, विकिरः -रणं, प्रसारणं, विस्तारणं, विभेदः, बहुधागमनं.

To DISPIRIT, *v. a.* उत्साहं or मनो भञ्ज् (c. 7. भनक्ति, भंक्तुं), उत्साहभङ्गं कृ, साहसभङ्गं कृ, आशाभङ्गं कृ, मनोभङ्गं कृ, विषद् in caus. (-षादयति -यितुं), विमनीकृ, तेजो हृ (c. 1. हरति, हर्तुं), ग्लानीकृ, खिद् in caus. (खेदयति -यितुं).

DISPIRITED, *p. p.* भग्नोत्साहः -हा -हं, भग्नमनाः -नाः -नः (स्), भग्नसाहसः -सा -सं, विमनाः -नाः -नः, निरुत्साहः -हा -हं, ग्लानतेजाः -जाः -जः (स्) or निस्तेजाः, दीनमनस्कः -स्का -स्कं, दीनचेतनः -ना -नं, खिन्नः -न्ना -न्नं.

To DISPLACE, *v. a.* (Move out of place) स्वस्थानाद् विचल् in caus. (-चालयति -यितुं) or चल् in caus. or अपसृ in caus. (-सारयति -यितुं) or निःसृ in caus. or निरस् (c. 4. -अस्यति -असितुं) or अपनुद् (c. 6. -नुदति -नोत्तुं) or निराकृ or अपोह् (c. 1. -ऊहते -हितुं) or अपकृष् (c. 1. -कर्षति -क्रष्टुं), स्थानान्तरीकृ.—(Remove from office) पदात् or अधिकाराद् भ्रंश् in caus. (-भ्रंशयति -यितुं) or च्यु in caus. (च्यावयति -यितुं) or निराकृ.

DISPLACED, *p. p.* स्थानभ्रष्टः -ष्टा -ष्टं, स्थानच्युतः -ता -तं, पदनिराकृतः -ता -तं.

DISPLACING, *s.* स्वस्थानाद् अपसारणं or अपनुत्तिः *f.*, or निरसनं or निराकरणं.

To DISPLANT, *v. a.* (Remove a plant) उन्मूल् (c. 10. -मूलयति -यितुं), उत्पट् (c. 10. -पाटयति -यितुं), उत्खन् (c. 1. -खनति -नितुं).—(Eject a people) निर्वस् in caus. (-वासयति -यितुं), विवस्, वासस्थानाद् निरस् (c. 4. -अस्यति -असितुं).

To DISPLAY, *v. a.* (Spread wide) विस्तॄ in caus. (-स्तारयति -यितुं), परिस्तॄ, विकाश् in caus. (-काशयति -यितुं), वितन् (c. 8. -तनोति -नितुं), प्रसृ in caus. (-सारयति -यितुं), प्रपञ्च् (c. 10. -पञ्चयति -यितुं). —(Exhibit) प्रकाश् in caus., दृश् in caus. (दर्शयति -यितुं), प्रत्यक्षीकृ, व्यक्तीकृ, प्रकटीकृ, स्पष्टीकृ, स्फुटीकृ, व्यञ्ज् (c. 7. -अनक्ति c. 10. -अञ्जयति -यितुं), विवृ (c. 5. -वृणोति -वरितुं -रीतुं), आविष्कृ, प्रादुष्कृ, प्रकट (nom. प्रकटयति -यितुं).—(Exhibit ostentatiously) सगर्वं or सदम्भं दृश् in caus.

DISPLAY, *s.* प्रकाशनं, विकाशनं, दर्शनं, प्रपञ्चः, प्रत्यक्षीकरणं, प्रकाशीकरणं, प्रकटीकरणं, व्यञ्जनं, व्यक्तिः *f.*, विवरणं, प्रादुष्करणं, आविष्करणं.

DISPLAYED, *p. p.* प्रकाशितः -ता -तं, प्रकाशीकृतः -ता -तं, प्रकटीकृतः -ता -तं, प्रत्यक्षीकृतः -ता -तं, दर्शितः -ता -तं, विवृतः -ता -तं, व्यक्तीकृतः -ता -तं.

To DISPLEASE, *v. a.* (Offend any one) कस्यापि विप्रियं or अप्रियं or व्यलीकं कृ, असन्तोषं or अतुष्टिं जन् (c. 10. जनयति -यितुं), वितुष् in caus. (-तोषयति -यितुं), रोषम् उत्पद् in caus. (-पादयति -यितुं), कुप् in caus. (कोपयति -यितुं), रुष् in caus. (रोषयति -यितुं), अपराध् (c. 4. -राध्यति c. 5. -राध्नोति -राद्धुं).

DISPLEASED, *p. p.* वितुष्टः -ष्टा -ष्टं, असन्तुष्टः -ष्टा -ष्टं, अप्रसन्नः -न्ना -न्नं, कृतरुषः -षा -षं, रुष्टः -ष्टा -ष्टं, परिकोपितः -ता -तं, कुपितः -ता -तं, कृतव्यलीकः -का -कं, कृतमन्युः -न्युः -न्यु, आगतमन्युः -न्युः -न्यु, जातामर्षः -र्षा -र्षं.

DISPLEASING, *a.* अप्रियः -या -यं, विप्रियः -या -यं, व्यलीकः -का -कं, विरुद्धः -द्धा -द्धं, अतुष्टिकरः -री -रं, अप्रसादजनकः -का -कं, अप्रीतिकरः -री -रं, असुखावहः -हा -हं.

DISPLEASURE, *s.* (Offence, anger) अतुष्टिः *f.*, असन्तोषः, अप्रीतिः *f.*, अप्रसादः, कोपः, रोषः, मन्युः *m.*, क्रोधः, अमर्षः.—(Pain) दुःखं, असुखं, उद्वेगः.

To DISPLODE, *v. a.* महाशब्दपूर्व्वं स्फुट् in caus. (स्फोटयति -यितुं) or विदॄ in caus. (-दारयति -यितुं).

DISPLOSION, *s.* महाशब्दपूर्व्वं स्फोटनं or विदारणं, अकस्माद् भञ्जनं.

DISPORT, *s.* क्रीडा, विहारः, केलिः *m. f.*, देवनं, विलासः, विलसितं, खेला.

To DISPORT, *v. a.* विनुद् in caus. (-नोदयति -यितुं); 'disport one's self,' विहृ (c. 1. -हरति -हर्तुं), विलस् (c. 1. -लसति -सितुं), क्रीड् (c. 1. क्रीडति -डितुं), दिव् (c. 4. दीव्यति, देवितुं), खेला (nom. खेलायति -यितुं).

DISPOSAL, DISPOSE, *s.* (Orderly arrangement) विन्यासः, व्यूहनं, व्यूढिः *f.*, प्रतिविधानं, संविधानं, विधानं, रचना, विरचनं, व्यवस्थापनं, व्यवस्थितिः *f.*, क्रमेण or यथाक्रमं स्थापनं, पर्य्यायः, परिपाटिः *f.*—(Regulation) विनियमः, नियमकरणं.—(Distribution) परिकल्पनं, कल्पना, कॢप्तिः *f.*, परिनिर्व्वपणं, प्रविभागः, वण्टनं.—(Bestowing) विनियोगः, वितरणं, परहस्ते समर्पणं.—(Power of distribution, right of bestowing) परिकल्पनशक्तिः *f.*, विनियोगाधिकारः.—(Control) अधीनता, वशं, वश्यता, अधिकारः. — (Divine disposal) परमेश्वरेच्छा; 'all this kingdom is at your disposal,' सर्व्वम् इदं राज्यं युष्मदायत्तं; 'this is at my disposal,' इदं ममाधीनं.

To DISPOSE, *v. a.* (Employ to various purposes) विनियुज् (c. 7. -युनक्ति -युंक्ते -योक्तुं), नियुज्, प्रयुज्, उपयुज्.—(Give, bestow) दा (c. 3. ददाति, दातुं), वितॄ (c. 1. -तरति -रितुं -रीतुं), निक्षिप् (c. 6. -क्षिपति -क्षेप्तुं), समृ in caus. (-अर्पयति -यितुं), निधा (c. 3. -दधाति -धातुं).—(Turn to any particular purpose) अमुककर्म्मणि प्रयुज् or विनियुज् or उपयुज्.—(Adapt) युज् in caus. (योजयति -यितुं), नियुज्, प्रयुज्, कॢप् in caus. (कल्पयति -यितुं).—(Incline, give a propension) प्रवृत् in caus. (-वर्त्तयति -यितुं), प्रयुज् in caus., चेष्ट् in caus. (चेष्टयति -यितुं), प्रोत्सह् in caus. (-साहयति -यितुं).—(Regulate, arrange, adjust) विन्यस् (c. 4. -अस्यति -असितुं), विधा (c. 3. -दधाति -धातुं), संविधा, प्रतिविधा, व्यूह् (c. 1. -ऊहते -हितुं), विरच् (c. 10. -रचयति -यितुं), क्रमेण स्था in caus. (स्थापयति -यितुं), परिकॢप्.

To DISPOSE OF, *v. a.* (Apply to any purpose) प्रयुज् (c. 7. -युनक्ति -युंक्ते -योक्तुं), विनियुज्, नियुज्, उपयुज्.—(Transfer to any other person, sell to another) परहस्ते समृ in caus. (-अर्पयति -यितुं), विक्री (c. 9. -क्रीणीते -क्रेतुं); 'to dispose of one's daughter in

DIS

marriage,' कन्यादानं कृ, दारिकादानं कृ, दुहितरं दा.

Disposed, *p. p.* (Arranged, regulated) विन्यस्तः -स्ता -स्तं, प्रतिविहितः -ता -तं, विहितः -ता -तं, व्यूढः -ढा -ढं, व्यवस्थितः -ता -तं, व्यवस्थापितः -ता -तं, परिपाटीकृतः -ता -तं.—(Inclined) प्रवर्त्तितः -ता -तं, प्रयोजितः -ता -तं; 'disposed to take,' गृहयालुः -लुः -लु, ग्रहीता -त्री -तृ; 'disposed to fall,' पतयालुः -लुः -लु, पिपतिषुः -षुः -षु; or expressed by शील affixed; as, पतनशीलः -ला -लं.

Disposer, *s.* (Distributer, bestower) परिकल्पकः, दाता *m.* (तृ), प्रदाता, विनियोगकृत्.—(Regulator, director) विधाता *m.* (तृ), विनियन्ता *m.* (न्तृ), अधिष्ठाता *m.* (तृ).

Disposition, *s.* (Orderly arrangement) विन्यासः, व्यूहनं, व्यूढिः *f.* प्रतिविधानं, विधानं, संविधानं, विरचनं, व्यवस्थापनं, पर्य्यायः, क्रमेण स्थापनं.—(Temper, natural state) भावः, स्वभावः, शीलः, शीलता -त्वं, प्रकृतिः *f.*, अन्तःकरणं; 'good disposition,' सद्भावः, साधुशीलत्वं; 'bad disposition,' असद्भावः; 'an easy contented disposition,' सुखिस्वभावः; 'of a virtuous disposition,' साधुशीलः, पुण्यशीलः, सत्वशीलः; 'disposition of body,' देहस्वभावः.—(Inclination, tendency) प्रावण्यं, प्रवृत्तिः *f.*, प्रवाहः, or expressed by शीलता -त्वं or आलुता -त्वं affixed; as, 'disposition to fall,' पतनशीलता or पतयालुत्वं.

To dispossess, *v. a.* अधिकारात् or स्वत्वाद् भ्रंश् (c. 10. भ्रंशयति -यितुं) or च्यु in caus. (च्यावयति -यितुं) or पत् in caus. (पातयति -यितुं) or निराकृ, अधिकारं or स्वत्वं हृ (c. 1. हरति, हर्त्तुं) or अपहृ.

Dispossessed, *p. p.* भ्रंशितः -ता -तं, निराकृतः -ता -तं, वहिष्कृतः -ता -तं; 'dispossessed of one's right,' हृताधिकारः -रा -रं, अधिकारभ्रष्टः -ष्टा -ष्टं.

Disposure, *s.* (Disposal, power) शक्तिः *f.*, अधिकारः, परिकल्पनशक्तिः *f.*, विनियोगशक्तिः *f.*—(Posture) स्थितिः *f.*, भूमिः *f.*

Dispraise, *s.* निन्दा, अपवादः, अप्रशंसा, तिरस्कारः, उपालम्भः, अयशः *n.* (स्).

To dispraise, *v. a.* निन्द् (c. 1. निन्दति -न्दितुं), तिरस्कृ, उपालभ् (c. 1. -लभते -लब्धुं), न प्रशंस् (c. 1. -शंसते -सितुं), अपवद् (c. 1. -वदति -दितुं).

To dispread, *v. a.* बहुधा or इतस्ततः or नानादिक्षु विस्तृ in caus. (-स्तारयति -यितुं) or विक्षिप् (c. 6. -क्षिपति -क्षेप्तुं) or विद्रु in caus. (-द्रावयति -यितुं).

Disproof, *s.* अनिश्चयः, अनिर्णयः, अप्रामाण्यं, अप्रमाणं, अनुपपत्तिः *f.*, खण्डनं, आधर्षणं, पक्षाघातः, निरासः, बाधः, बाधा, अधरीकरणं, अपवादः, वितण्डा, उपमर्द्दः.

Disproportion, *s.* असाम्यं, असमता, असमानता, वैषम्यं, अतुल्यत्वं, अयोग्यता, अनुपयुक्तता, असमञ्जसं, असामञ्जस्यं.

To disproportion, *v. a.* अयुक्तं सम्बन्ध् (c. 9. -बध्नाति -बन्धुं), असमञ्जसं संयुज् (c. 7. -युनक्ति -योक्तुं), अयोग्यसम्बन्धं कृ.

Disproportionable, disproportionate, *a.* असमः -मा -मं, अयोग्यः -ग्या -ग्यं, असमानः -ना -नं, अतुल्यः -ल्या -ल्यं, अयुक्तः -क्ता -क्तं, असमञ्जसः -सा -सं, अनुपयुक्तः -क्ता -क्तं, विषमः -मा -मं.

Disproportionableness, disproportionateness, *s.* असाम्यं, अयोग्यता, अतुल्यता.

Disproportionably, disproportionately, *adv.* असमं, विषमं, अतुल्यं, अयोग्यं, अयोग्यतस्, अनुपयुक्तं, असमञ्जसं, असमानतस्.

To disprove, *v. a.* खण्ड् (c. 10. खण्डयति -यितुं), संमूष् (c. 10. -मूषयति -यितुं), अधरीकृ, निरस् (c. 4. -अस्यति -असितुं), आधृष् (c. 10. -धर्षयति -यितुं), बाध् (c. 1. बाधते -धितुं), निराकृ, अपवद् (c. 1. -वदति -दितुं).

Disproved, *p. p.* खण्डितः -ता -तं, आधर्षितः -ता -तं, अधरीकृतः -ता -तं, बाधितः -ता -तं, निरस्तः -स्ता -स्तं, निराकृतः -ता -तं, प्रत्याख्यातः -ता -तं, असिद्धः -द्धा -द्धं.

Disprover, *s.* खण्डनकृत्, आधर्षणकृत्, वितण्डाकृत्, उपमर्द्दकारी *m.* (न्).

Disputable, *a.* विवदनीयः -या -यं, विचारणीयः -या -यं, विचार्य्यः -र्य्या -र्य्यं, वितर्क्यः -र्क्या -र्क्यं, वितर्कणीयः -या -यं, प्रत्याख्येयः -या -यं.

Disputant, *s.* तर्की *m.* (न्), विवादी *m.* (न्), वादी *m.*, वादप्रतिवादकृत्, नैयायिकः, विचारणकर्त्ता *m.* (र्त्तृ), प्रोहः, शास्त्रविरोधदर्शी *m.* (न्).

Disputation, *s.* विवादः, वादानुवादः, वादप्रतिवादः, वादः, वितर्कः, तर्कः, वाक्कलहं, वादयुद्धं, वितण्डा, विसंवादः, विरोधोक्तिः *f.* विचारः, हेतुवादः.

Disputatious, *a.* विवादार्थी -र्थिनी -र्थि (न्), विवादी -दिनी -दि (न्), वादानुवादशीलः -ला -लं, वितण्डापरः -रा -रं, वितर्कप्रियः -या -यं.

To dispute, *v. a.* and *n.* विवद् (c. 1. -वदते -दितुं), विसंवद्, वादानुवादं कृ, विप्रलप् (c. 1. -लपति -पितुं), वितण्ड् (c. 1. -तण्डते -ण्डितुं), वितण्डां कृ, वितर्क् (c. 10. -तर्कयति -यितुं), कलह (nom. कलहायते), वैर (nom. वैरायते), वाक्कलहं कृ, वाग्युद्धं कृ, व्यवक्रुश् (c. 1. -क्रोशति -क्रोष्टुं).—(In law) व्यवहृ (c. 1. -हरति -हर्त्तुं), विवादास्पदीकृ.

Dispute, *s.* विवादः, वादानुवादः, वादप्रतिवादः, विसंवादः, विप्रलापः, वाग्युद्धं, वादयुद्धं, वाक्कलहः, वाक्कलिः *m.*, विरोधोक्तिः *f.*, वाक्यविरोधः, वितर्कः, वितण्डा, विप्रतिपत्तिः *f.*, वितण्डा, विचारः, वादः, वाक्यं, कलहः, विग्रहः, द्वैधं, सन्देहः; 'matter of dispute,' विवादास्पदं.

Disputed, *p.p.* विचारितः -ता -तं, सन्दिग्धः -ग्धा -ग्धं, व्याहितः -ता -तं.

Disputer, *s.* विवादी *m.* (न्), विवादकारी *m.* (न्), विवादकृत् *m.*, विचारकः, तर्की *m.* (न्), वादी *m.* (न्), हेतुवादी *m.* (न्), वितण्डाकारी *m.* (न्), न्यायी *m.* (न्), सांवादिकः.

Disqualification, *s.* अयोग्यकरणं, अपात्रीकरणं, अयोग्यत्वं -ता, अयुक्तिः *f.*, विरोधः -धित्वं, असामर्थ्यं.

Disqualified, *p. p.* अयोग्यः -ग्या -ग्यं, अपात्रीकृतः -ता -तं, विरुद्धः -द्धा -द्धं.

To disqualify, *v. a.* अपात्रीकृ, अयोग्यं -ग्यां -ग्यं कृ, अनुपयुक्तं -क्तां -क्तं कृ.

Disquiet, disquietness, disquietude, *s.* उद्वेगः, चित्तोद्वेगः, चित्तवेदना, व्यथा, अशान्तिः *f.*, कष्टं, मनोदुःखं, अनिर्वृतिः *f.*, क्लेशः, आधिः *m.*, वैक्लव्यं, मनस्तापः, उत्तापः, व्यामोहः, विडम्बना, औत्सुक्यं, मानसी व्यथा, व्यस्तता, अस्थिरता, चिन्ता.

To disquiet, *v. a.* व्यथ् (c. 10. व्यथयति -यितुं), क्लिश् (c. 9. क्लिश्नाति, क्लेष्टुं), उद्विज् in caus. (-वेजयति -यितुं), व्याकुलीकृ, आकुल (nom. आकुलयति -यितुं), बाध् (c. 1. बाधते -धितुं), क्षुभ् in caus. (क्षोभयति -यितुं), मुह् in caus. (मोहयति -यितुं), व्यामुह्, विमुह्, परिमुह्.

Disquieted, *p. p.* उद्विग्नः -ग्ना -ग्नं, व्यग्रः -ग्रा -ग्रं, व्यथितः -ता -तं, सव्यथः -था -थं, क्लिष्टः -ष्टा -ष्टं, परिक्लिष्टः -ष्टा -ष्टं, अशान्तः -न्ता -न्तं, अनिर्वृतः -ता -तं, विधुरः -रा -रं, विदुरः -रा -रं, उद्भ्रान्तः -न्ता -न्तं, मोहितः -ता -तं, जातशङ्कः -ङ्का -ङ्कं.

Disquisition, *s.* विचारः -रणा, वितर्कः, विमर्शः, विवेचना, परीक्षा, वितण्डा.

To disrank, *v. a.* पदात् or अधिकाराद् भ्रंश् in caus. (भ्रंशयति -यितुं) or च्यु in caus. (च्यावयति -यितुं) or अपकृष् (c. 1. -कर्षति -क्रष्टुं).

Disregard, *s.* उपेक्षा, अनपेक्षा, निरपेक्षता, अनादरः, अननुष्ठानं, असेवनं, अचिन्ता, अनवधानं, परित्यागः, अवक्रिया, उपात्ययः, उत्प्रेक्षा, उद्भावनं, अदर्शनं.—(Contempt) अवज्ञा, अवमानं, अवधीरणं.

To disregard, *v. a.* उपेक्ष् (c. 1. -ईक्षते -क्षितुं), समुपेक्ष्, उपप्रेक्ष्, अवज्ञा (c. 9. -जानाति -ज्ञातुं), अवमन् (c. 4. -मन्यते -मन्तुं), अवधीर् (c. 10. -धीरयति -यितुं), न अनुष्ठा (c. 1. -तिष्ठति -ष्ठातुं), न सेव् (c. 1. सेवते -वितुं), परित्यज् (c. 1. -त्यजति -त्यक्तुं).

DISREGARDED, *p. p.* उपेक्षितः -ता -तं, अनपेक्षितः -ता -तं, समुपेक्षितः -ता -तं, अवज्ञातः -ता -तं, अवधीरितः -ता -तं, अवमतः -ता -तं, अवमानितः -ता -तं, परिभूतः -ता -तं, असेवितः -ता -तं, अवगणितः -ता -तं, उज्झितः -ता -तं, अननुष्ठितः -ता -तं.

DISREGARDFUL, *a.* उपेक्षकः -का -कं, निरपेक्षः -क्षा -क्षं, निर्व्यपेक्षः -क्षा -क्षं, मन्दादरः -रा -रं, अवमानी -निनी -नि (न्), अनवधानः -ना -नं.

DISREGARDFULLY, *adv.* निरपेक्षं, अनपेक्ष्य, उपेक्षया, अवमानेन, मन्दादरं.

DISRELISH, *s.* अरुचिः *f.*, अनभिरुचिः *f.*, विरक्तिः *f.*, वैरक्त्यं, वैराग्यं, विरागः, अप्रीतिः *f.*, विप्रियता, विमतिः *f.*, विमुखता, अनिच्छा, विध्वंसः.—(Bad taste) कुस्वादः, विस्वादः.

To DISRELISH, *v. a.* न अभिमन् (c. 4. -मन्यते -मन्तुं), विद्विष् (c. 2. -द्वेष्टि -ष्टुं), अरुचिं कृ, न अभिरुच् (c. 10. -रोचयति -यितुं), or expressed by the neut. form रोचते; as, 'he disrelishes that,' तत् तस्मै न रोचते.

DISREPUTABLE, *a.* अनार्य्यः -र्य्या -र्य्यं, अपमान्यः -न्या -न्यं, अयशस्यः -स्या -स्यं, अपयशस्करः -री -रं, अकीर्त्तिकरः -री -रं, अवश्रेयः -या -यं, अप्रतिष्ठः -ष्ठा -ष्ठं, अख्यातिजनकः -का -कं, अप्रशंसनीयः -या -यं, अभिशस्तः -स्ता -स्तं.

DISREPUTABLY, *adv.* अनार्य्यं, अनार्य्यवत्, अयशस्यं, अप्रशंसनीयं.

DISREPUTATION, DISREPUTE, *s.* अयशः *n.* (स्), अपयशः *n.*, अकीर्त्तिः *f.*, अपकीर्त्तिः *f.*, दुष्कीर्त्तिः *f.*, अख्यातिः *f.*, कुख्यातिः *f.*, अनार्य्यत्वं, वाच्यता, अप्रतिष्ठा, अमर्य्यादा, मर्य्यादाहानिः *f.*, अपमानं.

DISRESPECT, *s.* अनादरः, अवज्ञा -ज्ञानं, अपमानं, अवमानं -नता, अमाननं, असम्मानं, असन्मानं, परिभवः, परिभूतिः *f.*, परिभावः, अवधीरणं, उपेक्षा -क्षणं, तिरस्कारः, तिरस्क्रिया, न्यक्कारः, अवहेलं -ला, हेलनं, धर्षणं, अमर्य्यादा, रीढा, असूर्क्षणं, असूक्षणं, सूर्क्षणं.

DISRESPECTED, *p. p.* अनादृतः -ता -तं, अवमानितः -ता -तं, अवधीरितः -ता -तं, परिभूतः -ता -तं, उपेक्षितः -ता -तं, अवज्ञातः -ता -तं, अवमतः -ता -तं.

DISRESPECTFUL, *a.* अवमानी -निनी -नि (न्), परिभावी -विनी -वि (न्) -भावुकः -का -कं, उपेक्षकः -का -कं, सावज्ञः -ज्ञा -ज्ञं, अनार्य्यः -र्य्या -र्य्यं.

DISRESPECTFULLY, *adv.* सावज्ञानं, सावमानं, अनादरात्, उपेक्षया.

To DISROBE, *v. a.* विवस्त्रीकृ, वस्त्रम् अवतॄ in caus. (-तारयति -यितुं) or उत्कृष् (c. 1. -कर्षति -क्रष्टुं) or अपनह् (c. 4. -नह्यति -नद्धुं) or उच्छद् (c. 10. -छादयति -यितुं), नग्नीकृ.

DISROBED, *p. p.* विवस्त्रः -स्त्रा -स्त्रं, वस्त्रविवृतः -ता -तं, नग्नीकृतः -ता -तं.

DISRUPTION, *s.* भङ्गः, भेदः, विभेदः, विदारः -रणं, विदरः, भिदा, विघटनं.

DISSATISFACTION, *s.* अतुष्टिः, अतृप्तिः *f.*, असन्तोषः, अपरितोषः, अशान्तिः *f.*, अतृप्तता, वितुष्टिः *f.*

DISSATISFIED, *p. p.* अतुष्टः -ष्टा -ष्टं, असन्तुष्टः -ष्टा -ष्टं, वितुष्टः -ष्टा -ष्टं, अपरितुष्टः -ष्टा -ष्टं, अतृप्तः -प्ता -प्तं, अशान्तः -न्ता -न्तं, अप्रतिलब्धकामः -मा -मं.

To DISSATISFY, *v. a.* न सन्तुष् in caus. (-तोषयति -यितुं), न परितुष्, न तृप् in caus. (तर्पयति -यितुं), अतुष्टिं जन् in caus. (जनयति -यितुं) or उत्पद् in caus. (-पादयति -यितुं).

To DISSECT, *v. a.* शरीराङ्गानि कर्त्तर्य्यादिना व्यवछिद् (c. 7. -छिनत्ति -छेत्तुं) or उच्छिद् or संछिद्, शरीरावयवान् निकृत् (c. 6. -कृन्तति -कर्त्तितुं) or विनिकृत् or पृथक्कृ or पृथक् पृथक् कृ, विशस् (c. 1. -शसति -सितुं).—(Examine minutely) सूक्ष्मं परीक्ष् (c. 1. -ईक्षते -क्षितुं).

DISSECTED, *p. p.* विशसितः -ता -तं, व्यवछिन्नः -न्ना -न्नं, विनिकृत्तः -त्ता -त्तं.

DISSECTION, *s.* विशसनं, व्यवछेदः, अङ्गछेदः, अङ्गकर्त्तनं, पृथक्करणं, सूक्ष्मपरीक्षा.

DISSECTOR, *s.* व्यवछेदकः, अङ्गछिद् *m.*, विशसिता *m.* (तृ), विशसनकृत्.

To DISSEIZE, *v. a.* अधिकाराद् भ्रंश् in caus. (भ्रंशयति -यितुं) or च्यु in caus. (च्यावयति -यितुं); हृ (c. 1. हरति, हर्त्तुं) or अपहृ.

DISSEIZING, *s.* अन्यायेन अधिकाराद् भ्रंशनं or भूमिधनादिहरणं.

To DISSEMBLE, *v. a.* and *n.* ह्नु (c. 2. ह्नुते, ह्नोतुं), अपह्नु, निह्नु, छद्म कृ, छद् (c. 10. छादयति -यितुं), गुह् (c. 1. गूहति -ते -हितुं), निगुह्, अपवृ in caus. (-वारयति -यितुं), गोपनं कृ, अपदिश् (c. 6. -दिशति -देष्टुं), व्यपदिश्, कपटं कृ, अवहित्थां कृ, अपज्ञा (c. 9. -जानाति -नीते -ज्ञातुं), प्रतारणं कृ, छल् (c. 10. छलयति -यितुं).

DISSEMBLER, *s.* छाद्मिकः, छद्मवेशी *m.* (न्), कपटवेशी *m.*, वेशधारी *m.* (न्), दाम्भिकः, गोपनकृत् *m.*, गोप्ता *m.* (प्तृ), प्रच्छादयिता *m.* (तृ).

DISSEMBLING, *s.* अपह्नवः, निह्नुतिः *f.*, निह्नवः, अवहित्था -त्थं, गोपनं, छद्म *n.* (न्), छद्मकरणं, गुप्तिः *f.*, आकारगुप्तिः *f.*, अपलापः, कापट्यं, कृत्रिमता.

DISSEMBLINGLY, *adv.* अपह्नवेन, निह्नवात्, सावहित्थं, छद्मना, मिथ्या, कृत्रिमं.

To DISSEMINATE, *v. a.* विकॄ (c. 6. -किरति -करितुं -रीतुं), प्रकॄ, विस्तॄ in caus. (-स्तारयति -यितुं), प्रचर् in caus. (-चारयति -यितुं), प्रसृ in caus. (-सारयति -यितुं), विसृ, वप् (c. 1. वपति, वप्तुं), निवप्; 'to be disseminated,' प्रचर् (c. 1. -चरति -रितुं).

DISSEMINATED, *p. p.* विकीर्णः -र्णा -र्णं, प्रचारितः -ता -तं, सुव्यस्तः -स्ता -स्तं, बहुधागतः -ता -तं, विस्तारितः -ता -तं, उप्तः -प्ता -प्तं.

DISSEMINATION, *s.* विकिरणं, व्यापनं, व्याप्तिः *f.*, विस्तारः, प्रचारणं, प्रसारणं, वपनं, उप्तिः *f.*, व्यासः.

DISSEMINATOR, *s.* विकिरणकृत् *m.*, प्रचारकः, वप्ता *m.* (प्तृ), प्रवापी *m.* (न्).

DISSENSION, *s.* भेदः, विमतिः *f.*, वैमत्यं, कलहः, कलिः *m.*, असम्मतिः *f.*, द्वन्द्वं, विरोधः, विवादः, विप्रतिपत्तिः *f.*, विसंवादः, द्वैधं, मतिविपर्य्ययः; 'a sower of dissension,' उपजापकः; 'family dissensions,' गृहछिद्रं, गृहरन्ध्रं.

To DISSENT, *v. n.* न सम्मन् (c. 4. -मन्यते -मन्तुं), विपरीतं मन्, अन्यथा मन्, असम्मतिं कृ, न स्वीकृ, विवद् (c. 1. -वदते -दितुं), विसंवद्, भिन्नमतः -ता -तं भू, मतान्तरम् अवलम्ब् (c. 1. -लम्बते -म्बितुं).

DISSENT, *s.* विमतिः *f.*, वैमत्यं, मतिप्रभेदः, मतिविपर्य्ययः, असम्मतिः *f.*, अस्वीकारः, विसंवादः, विपरीतता, भिन्नमतधारणं, मतान्तरावलम्बनं, अन्यमतधारणं, द्वैधं.

DISSENTANEOUS, *a.* असम्मतः -ता -तं, विमतः -ता -तं, विपरीतमतः -ता -तं.

DISSENTER, *s.* (One that disagrees) भिन्नमतधारी *m.* (न्), मतान्तरावलम्बी *m.* (न्), असम्मतः.—(From the church) विपथगामी *m.* (न्), अपथवर्त्ती *m.* (न्), साधारणधर्म्मविरोधी *m.* (न्), उपधर्म्मसेवी *m.* (न्), उपधर्म्मः.

To DISSERT, *v. n.* वद् (c. 1. वदति -दितुं), प्रवद्, व्याख्या (c. 2. -ख्याति -तुं), कथ् (c. 10. कथयति -यितुं), प्रसङ्गं कृ, विवरणं कृ.

DISSERTATION, *s.* वाक्यं, वादः, प्रवादः, वचनं, प्रवचनं, वचः *n.* (स्), व्याख्या, विवरणं, प्रसङ्गः, कथोपकथनं, वचनक्रमः.

To DISSERVE, *v. a.* अपकृ, न उपकृ, हिंस् (c. 7. हिनस्ति, c. 1. हिंसति -सितुं).

DISSERVICE, *s.* अपकारः, अपकृतं, क्षतिः *f.*, अपायः, अपचयः, हिंसा, अनिष्टं, द्रोहः, क्लेशः.

To DISSEVER, *v. a.* वियुज् (c. 7. -युनक्ति -युङ्क्ते -योक्तुं), विप्रयुज्, विछिद् (c. 7. -छिनत्ति -छेत्तुं), विभिद् (c. 7. -भिनत्ति -भेत्तुं), विश्लिष् in caus. (-श्लेषयति -यितुं), पृथक्कृ, द्वैधीकृ.

DISSEVERED, *p. p.* वियुक्तः -क्ता -क्तं, विप्रयुक्तः -क्ता -क्तं, विश्लिष्टः -ष्टा -ष्टं, विछिन्नः -न्ना -न्नं, गतसङ्गः -ङ्गा -ङ्गं, पृथक्कृतः -ता -तं, विगतः -ता -तं.

DISSIDENT, *a.* विमतः -ता -तं, असम्मतः -ता -तं, विपरीतमतः -ता -तं.

DISSIMILAR, *a.* असदृशः -शी -शं, असमानः -ना -नं, असमः -मा -मं, विषमः -मा -मं, अनीदृशः -शी -शं, भिन्नः -न्ना -न्नं, विभिन्नः -न्ना -न्नं, अन्यः -न्या -न्यत्, इतरः -रा -रं, परः -रा -रं.—(Heterogeneous) विजातीयः -या

-यं, भिन्नजातीयः -या -यं.

DISSIMILARITY, DISSIMILITUDE, *s.* असादृश्यं, असदृशता, असाम्यं, असमता, असमानता, अतुल्यता, वैषम्यं, भेदः, विभेदः, भिन्नता, विभिन्नता, अन्तरं, परत्वं, अन्यथात्वं, विजातीयत्वं.

DISSIMULATION, *s.* अपह्नवः, निह्नवः, निह्नुतिः *f.*, छद्मकरणं, छद्म *n.* (न्), गोपनं, गुप्तिः *f.*, आकारगुप्तिः *f.*, अवहित्था -त्थं, कापट्यं, अपलापः, कृत्रिमता, प्रतारणा, दम्भः.

To DISSIPATE, *v. a.* (Scatter) कॄ (c. 6. किरति, करितुं -रीतुं), विकॄ, प्रकॄ, विक्षिप् (c. 6. -क्षिपति -क्षेप्तुं), व्यस् (c. 4. -अस्यति -असितुं), विद्रु in caus. (-द्रावयति -यितुं), विनिर्धू (c. 5. -धूनोति -धवितुं). *See* DISPERSE. (Spend) व्यय् (c. 1. व्ययति c. 10. व्यययति -यितुं), अपचि (c. 5. -चिनोति -चेतुं).

DISSIPATED, *p. p.* कीर्णः -र्णा -र्णं, विक्षिप्तः -प्ता -प्तं, बहुधागतः -ता -तं, विनिर्धूतः -ता -तं, सुव्यस्तः -स्ता -स्तं, विगलितः -ता -तं. *See* DISPERSED. (Licentious) कामवृत्तः -त्ता -त्तं, दुराचारः -रा -रं, व्यसनी -निनी -नि (न्).

DISSIPATION, *s.* विक्षेपः, विकिरणं. *See* DISPERSION. (Prodigality) धनव्ययः, अपव्ययः, धनोत्सर्गः, मोक्षणं.—(Licentiousness) स्त्रीसम्भोगनृत्यगीतादिसेवनं, व्यसनिता.

To DISSOCIATE, *v. a.* वियुज् (c. 7. -युनक्ति -योक्तुं), विप्रयुज्, विसंयुज्, विश्लिष् (c. 10. -श्लेषयति -यितुं), पृथक्कृ, असंलग्नं -ग्नां -ग्नं कृ.

DISSOLVABLE, DISSOLUBLE, *a.* द्राव्यः -व्या -व्यं, विद्राव्यः -व्या -व्यं, विलयनीयः -या -यं, द्रवणीयः -या -यं, गलनीयः -या -यं, क्षरभावः -वा -वं, क्षरणीयः -या -यं, साध्यः -ध्या -ध्यं, आर्द्रः -र्द्रा -र्द्रं, लीनः -ना -नं, विलयनशीलः -ला -लं.

To DISSOLVE, *v. a.* (Melt) विली in caus. (-लाययति -लापयति -यितुं), विद्रु in caus. (-द्रावयति -यितुं), द्रवीकृ, आर्द्रीकृ.—(Disunite) वियुज् (c. 7. -युनक्ति -योक्तुं).—(Dissolve friendship, &c.) सौहृद्यं भिद् (c. 7. भिनत्ति, भेत्तुं) or भञ्ज् (c. 7. भनक्ति, भंक्तुं); 'dissolve a league,' संहतिभेदनं कृ; 'dissolve an assembly,' सभां विसृज् (c. 6. -सृजति -स्रष्टुं), सभाभङ्गं कृ.

To DISSOLVE, *v. n.* विली (c. 4. -लीयते -लेतुं), प्रविली, प्रली, द्रु (c. 1. द्रवति, द्रोतुं), विद्रु, गल् (c. 1. गलति -लितुं), विगल्, क्षर् (c. 1. क्षरति -रितुं), द्रवीभू, आर्द्रीभू.

DISSOLVED, *p. p.* विद्रुतः -ता -तं, द्रुतः -ता -तं, विलीनः -ना -नं, लीनः -ना -नं, परिगलितः -ता -तं, द्रवीभूतः -ता -तं, असंहतः -ता -तं.

DISSOLVENT, *a.* द्रावकरः -री -रं, विलयनः -नी -नं, विद्रावकः -का -कं.

DISSOLUTE, *a.* व्यसनी -निनी -नि (न्), अनवस्थः -स्था -स्थं, व्यभिचारी -रिणी -रि (न्), तारलः -ली -लं, तरलः -ला -लं, दुराचारः -रा -रं, कामासक्तः -क्ता -क्तं, भोगासक्तः -क्ता -क्तं, दुष्टः -ष्टा -ष्टं, विषयी -यिणी -यि (न्), अयशः -शा -शं, कामुकः -का -कं, लम्पटः.

DISSOLUTELY, *adv.* लम्पटवत्, दुष्टवत्, कामुकवत्, भोगासक्तत्वात्.

DISSOLUTENESS, *s.* लम्पटता, लाम्पट्यं, व्यसनिता, अनवस्थितिः *f.*, अनवस्थता, इन्द्रियासंयमः, दुर्वृत्तता, विषयासक्तिः *f.*, भोगासक्तिः *f.*, स्त्रीसेवा, व्यभिचारः.

DISSOLUTION, *s.* (Liquefaction) विलयः -यनं, विद्रावः, द्रावः, द्रवीकरणं.—(Destruction) प्रलयः, नाशः, विनाशः, क्षयः, परिक्षयः, ध्वंसः.—(Dissolution of an assembly) सभाभङ्गः, सभाविरामः, सभानिवृत्तिः *f.*—(Dissolution of partnership) संसर्गभेदः, संसर्गवियोगः, संसर्गित्वनिवृत्तिः *f.*

DISSONANCE, *s.* (Discord) विस्वरता -त्वं, अपस्वरः.—(Disagreement) विसंवादः.

DISSONANT, *a.* विस्वरः -रा -रं, विकृतस्वरः -रा -रं, कर्कशस्वनः -ना -नं.—(Disagreeing) परस्परविरुद्धः -द्धा -द्धं, विसङ्गतः -ता -तं.

To DISSUADE, *v. a.* मैवं कार्षीर् इति उपदिश्य निवृत् in caus. (-वर्त्तयति -यितुं), भयहेतुं दर्शयित्वा निवृत् in caus. or विरम् in caus. (-रमयति -यितुं) or निवृ in caus. (-वारयति -यितुं), मैवं कृथा इति उपदिश् (c. 6. -दिशति -देष्टुं) or प्रत्यादिश्, विपरीतम् उपदिश्, विपरीतमन्त्रणं कृ, अन्तःस्था (c. 2. -ख्याति -तुं).

DISSUADER, *s.* निवर्त्तयिता *m.* (तृ) मैवं कार्षीर् इति उपदेशकः, प्रत्यादेष्टा *m.* (ष्टृ), विपरीतमन्त्रणादाता *m.* (तृ), निषेधकर्त्ता *m.*, (र्तृ).

DISSUASION, *s.* निवर्त्तनं, प्रत्यादेशपूर्व्वं निवर्त्तनं, मैवं कार्षीर् इति प्रत्यादेशः, निषेधार्थः परामर्शः, विपरीतमन्त्रणं, उद्यमभङ्गार्थः प्रबोधः.

DISSUASIVE, *a.* निवर्त्तकः -का -कं, निवर्त्तनशीलः -ला -लं, निवृत्तिकारी -रिणी -रि (न्), निषेधार्थकः -का -कं, प्रत्यादेशकः -का -कं, भयहेतुप्रदर्शकः -का -कं, विपरीतमन्त्रणकारी -रिणी -रि (न्).

DISSUASIVE, *s.* निवृत्तिकारणं, निवृत्तिहेतुः *m.*, निवर्त्तनहेतुः *m.*

DISSYLLABIC, *a.* द्व्यक्षरः -रा -रं, अक्षरद्वयविशिष्टः -ष्टा -ष्टं.

DISSYLLABLE, *s.* द्व्यक्षरं, अक्षरद्वयविशिष्टः शब्दः, द्व्यक्षरः शब्दः.

DISTAFF, *s.* तर्कुः *f.*, तर्कुटं -टी, सूत्रतर्कुटी, सूत्रला.

To DISTAIN, *v. a.* मलिन (nom. मलिनयति -यितुं), दुष् (c. 10. दूषयति -यितुं).

DISTANCE, *s.* (Interval, space) अन्तरं, अभ्यन्तरं, अन्तरालः -लं, मार्गं, व्यवधानं, व्यवायः.—(Remoteness) दूरता, असान्निध्यं, असन्निधानं, असन्निकर्षः; 'a little distance,' किंयद्दूरं, ईषद्दूरं, नातिदूरे; 'at a distance,' दूरं, दूरे, दूरतस्, विदूरतस्.—(Haughtiness) दुर्धर्षता, दुराधर्षत्वं, अनालापः.

To DISTANCE, *v. a.* दूरीकृ, दव (nom. दवयति -यितुं), अपसृ in caus. (-सारयति -यितुं), दूरतः कृ.

DISTANCED, *p. p.* दूरीकृतः -ता -तं, अपसारितः -ता -तं.

DISTANT, *a.* (Remote) दूरः -रा -रं, विदूरः -रा -रं, दूरस्थः -स्था -स्थं, दूरस्थितः -ता -तं, दूरस्थायी -यिनी -यि (न्), अनुपस्थायी, अनुपस्थः -स्था -स्थं, दूरीभूतः -ता -तं, दूरवर्त्ती -र्त्तिनी -र्त्ति (न्), विप्रकृष्टः -ष्टा -ष्टं, असन्निकृष्टः -ष्टा -ष्टं, दविष्टः -ष्टा -ष्टं, दवीयान् -यसी -यः (स्), असन्निहितः -ता -तं, प्राध्वः -ध्वा -ध्वं.—(Haughty) दुर्धर्षः -र्षा -र्षं, दुराधर्षः -र्षा -र्षं, अनालापी -पिनी -पि (न्).

DISTASTE, *s.* (Aversion of the palate, disrelish) अरुचिः *f.*, अनभिरुचिः *f.*, विरसनं, वितृष्णा, उत्क्लेशः.—(Dislike) विरक्तिः *f.*, वैराग्यं, वैरस्यं, अरुचिः *f.*, अननुरागः, अप्रीतिः *f.*, द्वेषः, विद्वेषः, अनिच्छा, घृणा, पराङ्मुखता.

To DISTASTE, *v. a.* and *n.* (Dislike) न रुच् (c. 1. रोचते -चितुं) with dat.; as, "he distastes that,' तत् तस्मै न रोचते; न अभिनन्द् (c. 1. -नन्दति -न्दितुं), अरुचिं कृ.

DISTASTEFUL, *a.* अरुचिरः -रा -रं, अरुच्यः -च्या -च्यं, अप्रियः -या -यं, अरसः -सा -सं, विरसः -सा -सं, अरुचिजनकः -का -कं, अप्रीतिकरः -री -रं, विस्वादः -दा -दं, अस्वादुः -दुः -दु.

DISTEMPER, *s.* (Disease) रोगः, व्याधिः *m.*, आमयः, पीडा, अस्वास्थ्यं, असुस्थता, विकारः.—(Uneasiness) व्यथा, क्लेशः, दुःखं, कष्टं, आर्त्तिः *f.*, उपतापः, तापः, अनिर्वृतिः *f.*—(Bad condition) दुष्प्रकृतिः *f.*, दुःस्थितिः *f.*, असद्भावः, कुभावः, दुर्दशा, दुरवस्था.

To DISTEMPER, *v. a.* पीड् (c. 10. पीडयति -यितुं), व्यथ् (c. 10. व्यथयति -यितुं), क्लिश् (c. 9. क्लिश्नाति, क्लेशितुं), उपहन् (c. 2. -हन्ति -न्तुं), उपतप् in caus. (-तापयति -यितुं), बाध् (c. 1. बाधते -धितुं).

DISTEMPERATURE, *s.* वायुवैलक्षण्यं, वायुगुरुता, आकाशवैलक्षण्यं, गुरुतापः.

DISTEMPERED, *p. p.* व्याधितः -ता -तं, रोगी -गिणी -गि (न्), अस्वस्थः -स्था -स्थं, आर्त्तः -र्त्ता -र्त्तं, आतुरः -रा -रं, पीडितः -ता -तं, उपहतः -ता

-तं, व्याकुलः -ला -लं, उत्सिक्तः -क्ता -क्तं.

To DISTEND, *v. a.* विस्तॄ in caus. (-स्तारयति -यितुं), वितन् (c. 8. -तनोति -नितुं), स्फाय् in caus. (स्फावयति -यितुं), श्वि in caus. (श्वाययति -यितुं), आध्मा (c. 1. -धमति -ध्मातुं), प्रध्मा; 'to distend with wind,' वातेन पॄ (c. 10. -पूरयति -यितुं),

DISTENDED, *p. p.* आध्मातः -ता -तं, विततः -ता -तं, प्रवृद्धः -द्धा -द्धं, फुल्लः -ल्ला -ल्लं, शूनः -ना -नं, उच्छूनः -ना -नं, स्फातः -ता -तं, स्फीतः -ता -तं, विस्तृतः -ता -तं, प्रसारितः -ता -तं, प्रचुरीकृतः -ता -तं; 'distended with wind,' वातपूरितः -ता -तं, वातफुल्लः -ल्ला -ल्लं.

DISTENSION, DISTENTION, *s.* आध्मानं, विततिः *f.*, फुल्लता, उत्फुल्लता, विस्तारः, विस्तृतिः *f.*, स्फीतिः *f.*, स्फातिः *f.*, विजृम्भणं.

DISTICH, *s.* श्लोकः, श्लोकद्वयं, चरणयुगं, द्विचरणं, द्विपदं.

To DISTILL, *v. n.* (Fall in drops, flow gently) च्युत्, (c. 1. च्योतति -तितुं) or श्च्युत्, री (c. 4. रीयते, रेतुं), क्षर् (c. 1. क्षरति -रितुं) स्यन्द् (c. 1. स्यन्दते -न्दितुं) स्रु (c. 1. स्रवति, स्रोतुं).

To DISTILL, *v. a.* (Let fall in drops) स्रु (c. 1. स्रवति, स्रोतुं) with acc.; as, 'the clouds distill water,' तोयं स्रवन्ति मेघाः; क्षर् (c. 1. क्षरति -रितुं), जलबिन्दून् or अम्बुलवान् मुच् (c. 6. मुञ्चति, मोक्तुं), or पत्, in caus. (पातयति -यितुं), or सृज् (c. 6. सृजति, स्रष्टुं). —(Extract the spirit, as chemists) सन्धा (c. 3. -दधाति -धातुं), अभिषु (c. 5. -षुणोति -षोतुं) आसु, मद्यं निर्हृ (c. 1. -हरति -हर्त्तुं).

DISTILLATION, *s.* (Act of extracting spirit) सन्धानं -नी, मद्यसन्धानं, सन्धा, अभिषवः, आसुतिः *f.*—(Act of trickling) स्रवः, स्रावः, क्षरणं, द्रवः, द्रवणं, द्रवत्वं, निस्यन्दः, स्यन्दः -न्दनं, अभिष्यन्दः.

DISTILLATORY, *a.* सन्धानयोग्यः -ग्या -ग्यं, सन्धानसम्बन्धी -न्धिनी -न्धि (न्).

DISTILLED, *p. p.* सन्धितः -ता -तं, अभिषुतः -ता -तं, क्षारितः -ता -तं, 'distilled water,' पक्ववारि, *n.*

DISTILLER, *s.* सान्धिकः, मद्यासवनिकः, मद्यहारकः, शौण्डिकः, शुण्डी *m.* (न्) सुराकारः, सुराजीवी *m.* (न्), आसुतीवलः, कल्यपालः.

DISTILLERY, *s.* सन्धानी, मद्यसन्धानशाला, शुण्डा, मद्यनिर्हारस्थानं.

DISTINCT, *a.* (Different, separate) भिन्नः -न्ना -न्नं, विभिन्नः -न्ना -न्नं, प्रभिन्नः -न्ना -न्नं, विविक्तः -क्ता -क्तं, व्यतिरिक्तः -क्ता -क्तं, विशिष्टः -ष्टा -ष्टं, पृथग्विधः -धा -धं, विविधः -धा -धं, व्यस्तः -स्ता -स्तं, अन्यः -न्या -न्यत्, अन्यप्रकारः -रा -रं, इतरः -रा -रं; 'having distinct properties,' पृथग्गुणः -णा -णं.—(Clear) व्यक्तः -क्ता -क्तं, प्रव्यक्तः -क्ता -क्तं, स्पष्टः -ष्टा -ष्टं, स्फुटः -टा -टं, प्रत्यक्षः -क्षा -क्षं, सुप्रकाशः -शा -शं.

DISTINCTION, *s.* (Difference, separation) भेदः, विभेदः, प्रभेदः, भिन्नता, विभिन्नता, विशेषः -षणं, विशिष्टता, वैशिष्ट्यं, अन्तरं, पृथक्त्वं, पार्थक्यं, अवच्छेदः, विच्छेदः, अन्यथात्वं, भिदा, व्यासः; 'without distinction,' अविशेषः -षा -षं, निर्विशेषः -षा -षं.—(Discrimination) विवेकः, विवेचनं, परिच्छेदः, व्यवच्छेदः, पृथक्करणं; 'distinction of race,' जातित्वं.—(Eminence, superiority) विशिष्टता, वैशिष्ट्यं, उत्कृष्टता, उत्कर्षः, श्रेष्ठता, प्रमुखत्वं, समुन्नतिः *f.*, परमपदं.

DISTINCTIVE, *a.* विशेषकः -का -कं, विशेषणः -णा -णं, सविशेषः -षा -षं, अवच्छेदकः -का -कं, विच्छेदकः -का -कं, परिच्छेदकः -का -कं, पृथक्कारी -रिणी -रि (न्); 'distinctive mark,' विशेषलक्षणं.

DISTINCTIVELY, *adv.* विशेषेण, विशेषतस्, सविशेषं, पृथक् पृथक्.

DISTINCTLY, *adv.* (Separately) पृथक्.—(Clearly) व्यक्तं, सुव्यक्तं, भिन्नार्थं, स्पष्टार्थं, स्पष्टं, प्रत्यक्षतस् -क्षेण.

DISTINCTNESS, *s.* (State of being different) भिन्नता, विभिन्नभावः, पृथक्त्वं, पार्थक्यं.—(Clearness) व्यक्तिः *f.*, अभिव्यक्तिः *f.*, व्यक्तत्वं, स्पष्टता, भिन्नार्थत्वं.

To DISTINGUISH, *v. a.* and *n.* विशिष् (c. 7. -शिनष्टि -शेष्टुं, c. 10. -शेषयति -यितुं), पृथक्कृ, लक्ष् (c. 10. लक्षयति -यितुं) लक्षीकृ, परिछिद् (c. 7. -छिनत्ति -छेत्तुं), विज्ञा (c. 9. -जानाति -नीते -ज्ञातुं) विविच् (c. 7. -विनक्ति -वेक्तुं c. 10. -वेचयति -यितुं) विचर् (c. 10. -चारयति -यितुं), विभू (c. 10. -भावयति -यितुं); 'distinguish one's self, become illustrious,' विशिष् in pass. (-शिष्यते) उत्कर्षं or परमपदं प्राप् (c. 5. -आप्नोति -आप्तुं).

DISTINGUISHABLE, *a.* विशेषणीयः -या -यं, विशेष्यः -ष्या -ष्यं, विज्ञेयः -या -यं, परिच्छेदनीयः -या -यं, विभावनीयः -या -यं, विभाव्यः -व्या -व्यं, भेदनीयः -या -यं.

DISTINGUISHED, *p. p.* (Separated, discriminated) विशेषितः -ता -तं, विविक्तः -क्ता -क्तं, परिच्छिन्नः -न्ना -न्नं, पृथक्कृतः -ता -तं, विज्ञातः -ता -तं, विभावितः -ता -तं, उपलक्षितः -ता -तं.—(Marked) लक्षितः -ता -तं, उपलक्षितः -ता -तं, चिह्नितः -ता -तं, तिलकितः -ता -तं.—(Illustrious) विशिष्टः -ष्टा -ष्टं, उत्कृष्टः -ष्टा -ष्टं, ख्यातः -ता -तं, प्रसिद्धः -द्धा -द्धं, विश्रुतः -ता -तं, प्रथितः -ता -तं, स्वार्थिशब्दलक्षणोपेतः -ता -तं.

DISTINGUISHINGLY, *adv.* विशेषेण, सविशेषं, सपुरस्कारं, सविशेषमानं.

To DISTORT, *v. a.* (Make deformed) विरूप् (c. 10. -रूपयति -यितुं) विरूपीकृ, अपरूपीकृ, कुरूपीकृ, कदाकारीकृ, व्यङ्गीकृ, विकृ, वक्रीकृ, विकलीकृ.—(Twist) आकुञ्च् (c. 1. -कुञ्चति -ञ्चितुं c. 10. -कुञ्चयति -यितुं).—(Pervert) साचीकृ, वक्रीकृ.

DISTORTED, *p. p.* विकृतः -ता -तं, विरूपीकृतः -ता -तं, साचीकृतः -ता -तं, वक्रीकृतः -ता -तं; 'having the limbs distorted,' विकृताङ्गः -ङ्गी -ङ्गं, व्यङ्गः -ङ्गी -ङ्गं; 'having the face distorted,' विकृतवदनः -ना -नं.

DISTORTION, *s.* (Act of distorting) विरूपकरणं, अपरूपीकरणं, कुरूपीकरणं, विकारः, विक्रिया, साचीकरणं, वक्रीकरणं, आकुञ्चनं.—(The state) विकृतिः *f.*, वैकृत्यं, विरूपता, वैरूप्यं, व्यङ्गता, वक्रता, वक्रिमा *m.* (न्), साचीकृतं.

To DISTRACT, *v. a.* (Pull in different directions) विकृष् (c. 1. -कर्षति c. 6. -कृषति -क्रष्टुं), नानादिक्षु कृष् or आकृष् or परिकृष्, बहुधा कृ or गम् in caus. (गमयति -यितुं), विक्षिप् (c. 6. -क्षिपति -क्षेप्तुं). —(Divide, rend) विदॄ in caus. (-दारयति -यितुं), विभिद् (c. 7. -भिनत्ति -भेत्तुं), खण्ड् (c. 10. खण्डयति -यितुं), परिखण्ड्, विदलीकृ, विदल् in caus. (-दालयति -यितुं).—(Draw off from any object) अपकृष्, व्यपकृष्, अपाकृष्.—(Perplex) मुह् in caus. (मोहयति -यितुं) विमुह्, व्यामुह्, आकुलीकृ, व्याकुलीकृ.—(Make mad) उन्मद् in caus. (-मादयति -यितुं).—(Be distracted) मुह्, (c. 4. मुह्यति, मोहितुं), उन्मद् (c. 4. -माद्यति -मदितुं); 'my heart is distracted,' अस्मद् हृदयं विदीर्य्यते.

DISTRACTED, *p. p.* आकृष्टमानसः -सा -सं, विक्षिप्तः -प्ता -प्तं, विकृष्टः -ष्टा -ष्टं, मोहितः -ता -तं, विमोहितः -ता -तं, व्यग्रः -ग्रा -ग्रं, व्याकुलः -ला -लं, चित्ताकुलः -ला -लं, खण्डितः -ता -तं, उन्मत्तः -त्ता -त्तं, व्यस्तचित्तः -त्ता -त्तं.

DISTRACTEDLY, *adv.* उन्मत्तवत्, व्यग्रं, व्याकुलमनसा, विकृष्टचेतसा, मूढचेतसा.

DISTRACTEDNESS, *s.* विक्षिप्तता, व्यग्रता, उन्मत्तता, चित्तविभ्रमः, आकुलत्वं.

DISTRACTION, *s.* विकर्षः -र्षणं.—(Perturbation of mind) मोहः, विमोहः, वैचित्यं, चित्तविक्षिप्तता, आकुलचित्तता, व्यग्रता, चित्तवैकल्यं, व्याकुलता, व्यस्तता.—(Madness) उन्मत्तता.—(Separation) विभेदः, विदारणं —(Want of attention of mind) अमनोयोगः, विबोधः.—(Distraction of employment, various employment) विकर्म्म *n.* (न्).

To DISTRAIN, *v. a.* ऋणहेतोर् अधमर्णस्य द्रव्याणि भृ (c. 1. भरति भर्त्तुं) or ग्रह् (c. 9. गृह्णाति ग्रहीतुं), निरुध् (c. 7. -रुणद्धि -रोद्धुं).

DISTRESS, *s.* (Act of distraining) द्रव्यग्रहणं, द्रव्यधृतिः *f.*, अस्थाव-

रधनग्रहणं, निरोधः.—(Calamity, affliction) क्लेशः, दुःखं, दुर्दशा, दुरवस्था, दुर्गतिः *f.*, दौर्गत्यं, व्यथा, कष्टं, पीडा, शोकः, सन्तापः, उद्वेगः, वैक्लव्यं, आपद् *f.*, विपद् *f.*, विपत्तिः *f.*, व्यसनं, विप्लवः, उपप्लवः, उत्पातः, विधुरं, अरिष्टं, मन्युः *m.*, बाधः, दैन्यं, वृजिनं, विडम्बना, आदीनवः, आश्रयः.

To DISTRESS, *v. a.* क्लिश् (c. 9. क्लिश्नाति, क्लेशितुं, क्लेष्टुं), व्यथ् in caus. (व्यथयति -यितुं), पीड् (c. 10. पीडयति -यितुं), उपपीड्, अभिपीड्, बाध् (c. 1. बाधते -धितुं), तप् in caus. (तापयति -यितुं), सन्तप्, परितप्, उपतप्; उद्विज् in caus. (-वेजयति -यितुं), क्लेशं दा, व्यथां कृ, खिद् in caus. (खेदयति -यितुं).

DISTRESSED, *p. p.* क्लिष्टः -ष्टा -ष्टं, क्लेशितः -ता -तं, पीडितः -ता -तं, व्यथितः -ता -तं, दुःखितः -ता -तं, क्लिश्यमानः -ना -नं, क्लेशभाक् *m. f. n.* तापितः -ता -तं, तप्तः -प्ता -प्तं, सन्तप्तः -प्ता -प्तं, सन्तापितः -ता -तं, बाधितः -ता -तं, विपन्नः -न्ना -न्नं, आपन्नः -न्ना -न्नं, आपद्ग्रस्तः -स्ता -स्तं, दुर्दशापन्नः -न्ना -न्नं, आपद्गतः -ता -तं, कृच्छ्रगतः -ता -तं, आपत्प्राप्तः -प्ता -प्तं, दुर्गतः -ता -तं, आतुरः -रा -रं, दुःखान्वितः -ता -तं, दुःखी -खिनी -खि (न्), दुःखार्त्तः -र्त्ता -र्त्तं, कातरः -रा -रं, उपतप्यमानः -ना -नं, आतप्यमानः -ना -नं, अभ्यर्दितः -ता -तं, विधुरः -रा -रं, विदुरः -रा -रं, उद्विग्नः -ग्ना -ग्नं, विदूनः -ना -नं, दीनः -ना -नं, आधिमान् -मती -मत् (त्), आकुलितः -ता -तं, परिकर्पितः -ता -तं, आतुरचित्तः -त्ता -त्तं, आर्त्तः -र्त्ता -र्त्तं in comp.; 'friend of the distressed,' आर्त्तबन्धुः *m.*

DISTRESSFUL, DISTRESSING, *a.* क्लेशकः -का -कं, क्लेशी -शिनी -शि (न्), क्लेशदः -दा -दं, व्यथकः -का -कं, व्यथाकरः -री -रं, दुःखकरः -री -रं, दुःखमयः -यी -यं, पीडाकरः -रा -रं, उपतापनः -ना -नं, उद्वेजकः -का -कं, आत्ययिकः -की -कं.

DISTRIBUTABLE, *a.* विभाज्यः -ज्या -ज्यं, वण्टनीयः -या -यं, परिकल्पनीयः -या -यं.

To DISTRIBUTE, *v. a.* पृथक् पृथग् विभज् (c. 1. -भजति -ते -भक्तुं) or प्रविभज् or संविभज्; विभागशः or यथाविभागं or अंशांशि दा or कॢप् (c. 10. कल्पयति -यितुं), or परिकॢप् or विन्यस् (c. 4. -अस्यति -असितुं) or विधा (c. 3. -दधाति -धातुं), अंस् (c. 10. -अंसयति -यितुं), वण्ट् (c. 10. वण्टयति -यितुं), प्रकुट्ट् (c. 10. -कुट्टयति -यितुं), निक्षिप् (c. 6. -क्षिपति -क्षेप्तुं), प्रणी (c. 1. -णयति -णेतुं).—(Distribute food to a party) परिविश् or परिविष् (c. 10. -वेषयति -यितुं).

DISTRIBUTED, *p. p.* विभक्तः -क्ता -क्तं, प्रविभक्तः -क्ता -क्तं, संविभक्तः -क्ता -क्तं, पृथग् विन्यस्तः -स्ता -स्तं, परिकल्पितः -ता -तं, प्रणीतः -ता -तं.

DISTRIBUTER, *s.* विभागकर्त्ता *m.* (र्त्तृ), संविभागकृत्, विभागकल्पकः, परिकल्पकः, वण्टनकृत्, अंशयिता *m.* (तृ), अंशदः, विभक्ता *m.* (क्तृ), प्रणेता *m.* (तृ).

DISTRIBUTION, *s.* विभागः, विभागकल्पना, संविभागः, प्रविभागः, विभक्तिः *f.*, विभागकरणं, परिकल्पनं, कॢप्तिः *f.*, अंशनं, अंशकरणं, वण्टनं, परिनिर्वपणं, प्रणयनं; 'distribution of food to a party,' परिवेषः -षणं.

DISTRIBUTIVE, *a.* विभागदायी -यिनी -यि (न्), विभागकल्पकः -का -कं, अंशकारी -रिणी -रि (न्), वण्टनकारी, संविभागकृत् *m. f. n.*

DISTRIBUTIVELY, *adv.* विभागशस्, विभागतस्, भागशस्, अंशांशि, संविभागेन.

DISTRICT, *s.* मण्डलं, देशः, प्रदेशः, चक्रं, राष्ट्रं, उपवर्त्तनं, गोचरः.

To DISTRUST, *v. a.* शङ्क् (c. 1. शङ्कते -ङ्कितुं), आशङ्क्, अभिशङ्क्, परिशङ्क्; न विश्वस् (c. 2. -श्वसिति -तुं), न प्रती (c. 2. प्रत्येति -तुं rt. इ).

DISTRUST, *s.* अविश्वासः, अप्रत्ययः, अप्रतीतिः *f.*, शङ्का, आशङ्का, सन्देहः, निह्नवः, अनासक्तिः.

DISTRUSTED, *p. p.* अविश्वस्तः -स्ता -स्तं, आशङ्कितः -ता -तं, अप्रतीतः -ता -तं.

DISTRUSTFUL, *a.* अविश्वासी -सिनी -सि (न्), अप्रत्ययी -यिनी -यि (न्), शङ्काशीलः -ला -लं, आशङ्कान्वितः -ता -तं, साशङ्कः -ङ्का -ङ्कं, रोलकः -का -कं.

DISTRUSTFULLY, *adv.* अविश्वासेन, अप्रत्ययात्, शङ्कया, साशङ्कं, शङ्कापूर्व्वं.

To DISTURB, *v. a.* (Agitate, disquiet) क्षुभ् in caus. (क्षोभयति -यितुं), विक्षुभ्, संक्षुभ्, बाध् (c. 1. बाधते -धितुं), उपरुध् (c. 7. -रुणद्धि -रोद्धुं), धू (c. 5. धूनोति c. 9. धुनाति, धवितुं, धोतुं), मथ् (c. 1. मथति -थितुं) or मन्थ् (c. 1. मन्थति -न्थितुं c. 9. मथ्नाति), लुड् (c. 1. लोडति -डितुं c. 10. लोडयति -यितुं), आलुड्, समालुड्, परिलुड्, विलुड्, विलुप् (c. 6. -लुम्पति -लोप्तुं), विप्रलुप्.—(Disturb the mind) मुह् in caus. (मोहयति -यितुं), विमुह्, व्यामुह्, विप्रमुह्, सम्मुह्, परिमुह्, व्याकुल (nom. व्याकुलयति -यितुं), व्याकुलीकृ, आकुल (nom. आकुलयति -यितुं), आकुलीकृ.—(Excite anger) प्रकुप् in caus. (-कोपयति -यितुं).—(Hinder, interrupt) वृ in caus. (वारयति -यितुं), खण्ड् (c. 10. खण्डयति -यितुं), विच्छिद् (c. 7. -छिनत्ति -छेत्तुं), विहन् (c. 2. -हन्ति -न्तुं), भञ्ज् (c. 7. भनक्ति, भंक्तुं).—(Disturb slumber) निद्रां भञ्ज्; 'to be disturbed in mind,' मुह् (c. 4. मुह्यति,) विमुह्, सम्मुह्, आकुलीभू, व्याकुलीभू.

DISTURBANCE, *s.* (Agitation, disorder) क्षोभः, संक्षोभः, विक्षोभः, व्याक्षोभः, व्यस्तता, विमर्द्दः.—(Emotion of mind, perturbation) आकुलत्वं, व्याकुलत्वं, प्रकोपः, वैक्लव्यं, व्यग्रता, मोहः, आवेगः.—(Tumult) विप्लवः, आहवः, डिम्बः, तुमुलं; 'popular disturbance,' प्रकृतिक्षोभः.—(Interruption) भङ्गः, विच्छेदः, खण्डनं, बाधः.

DISTURBED, *p. p.* क्षुब्धः -ब्धा -ब्धं, क्षोभितः -ता -तं, बाधितः -ता -तं.—(In mind) आकुलः -ला -लं -लितः -ता -तं, व्याकुलः -ला -लं -लितः -ता -तं, व्याकुलीकृतः -ता -तं, आकुलचित्तः -त्ता -त्तं, मोहितः -ता -तं, विमोहितः -ता -तं, व्यस्तः -स्ता -स्तं, व्यग्रः -ग्रा -ग्रं, कातरः -रा -रं, खेदितः -ता -तं.

DISTURBER, *s.* क्षोभकरः, विक्षोभकर्त्ता *m.* (र्त्तृ), मोहकः.—(Interrupter) भञ्जकः, विच्छेदकारी *m.* (न्), विघ्नकरः, विलोपनकृत्.

DISUNION, *s.* वियोगः, विसंयोगः, विप्रयोगः, असंयोगः, निर्युक्तिः *f.*, भेदः, भिन्नता, विभेदः, विश्लेषः, अश्लेषः, असन्धानं, आसक्तत्वं, सक्तविच्युतिः *f.*, विच्छेदः, अनैक्यं, पार्थक्यं.

To DISUNITE, *v. a.* वियुज् (c. 7. -युनक्ति -योक्तुं), विप्रयुज्, विश्लिष् (c. 10. -श्लेषयति -यितुं), भिद् (c. 7. (भिनत्ति, भेत्तुं), विभिद्, विच्छिद् (c. 7. -छिनत्ति -छेत्तुं), पृथक्कृ, विगम् in caus. (-गमयति -यितुं).

To DISUNITE, *v. n.* वियुज् in pass. (-युज्यते), विप्रयुज्; विश्लिष् (c. 4. -श्लिष्यति -श्लेष्टुं); विभिद् in pass. (-भिद्यते), विगम् (c. 1. -गच्छति -गन्तुं).

DISUNITED, *p. p.* वियुक्तः -क्ता -क्तं, विप्रयुक्तः -क्ता -क्तं, विश्लिष्टः -ष्टा -ष्टं, निर्युक्तिकः -की -कं, असंलग्नः -ग्ना -ग्नं, असंसक्तः -क्ता -क्तं, असंहतः -ता -तं, विरहितः -ता -तं, द्वैधीभूतः -ता -तं.

DISUNITER, *s.* वियोगकर्त्ता *m.* (र्त्तृ), भेदकरः, पृथक्कारी *m.* (न्).

DISUSAGE, DISUSE, *s.* अव्यवहारः, अनभ्यासः, असेवनं, अनाचारः, निवृत्तिः *f.*, विरतिः *f.*, व्यवहारनिवृत्तिः *f.*, आचारत्यागः, अभ्यासविच्छेदः.

To DISUSE, *v. a.* व्यवहारं or अभ्यासं त्यज् (c. 1. त्यजति, त्यक्तुं), व्यवहाराद् विरम् (c. 1. -रमति- रन्तुं) or निवृत् (c. 1. -वर्त्तते -र्त्तितुं), न सेव् (c. 1. सेवते -वितुं).

DISUSED, *p. p.* अव्यवहारितः -ता -तं, अनभ्यस्तः -स्ता -स्तं, असेवितः -ता -तं, त्यक्तः -क्ता -क्तं; 'as words,' निरूढः -ढा -ढं.

DITCH, *s.* खातं, खातकं, परिखा, गर्त्तः, खातभूः *f.*, खेयं, अखातं, उपकुल्या, कुल्या, प्रणालः, प्रतिकूपः, निपानं.

To DITCH, *v. a.* परिखन् (c. 1. -खनति -नितुं), आखन्, परिखाकरणार्थं भूमिं खन्, परिखां कृ, गर्त्तं कृ.

DITCHER, *s.* आखनिकः, परिखाखनकः, गर्त्तखनिता *m.* (तृ), खातकः.

DITTANY, *s.* सुगन्धीय ओषधिप्रभेदः, तिक्तशाकः.

DITTO, *s.* तथा, पूर्व्वोक्तः -क्ता -क्तं, उपरिलिखितः -ता -तं.

DITTY, *s.* गीतं -तकं -तिका, गीतिः *f.*, गानं, गाथा, काव्यबन्धः.

DIURETIC, *a.* मूत्रलः -ला -लं, मूत्रवर्धकः -का -कं, मूत्रोत्पादकः -का -कं.

DIURNAL, *a.* आह्निकः -की -कं, दैनः -नी -नं -निकः -की -कं, दैनन्दिनः -नी -नं, दैवसिकः -की -कं, प्रात्यहिकः -की -कं, दिवातनः -नी -नं, अन्वाहिकः -की -कं, नैत्यिकः -की -कं, नित्यः -त्या -त्यं.

DIURNAL, *s.* पञ्जिका, पञ्जिः *f.*, पदभञ्जिका, दैनिकपुस्तकं.

DIURNALLY, *adv.* प्रतिदिनं, प्रतिदिवसं, प्रत्यहं, दिवसे दिवसे, दिने दिने.

DIUTURNAL, *a.* चिरस्थायी -यिनी -यि (न्), चिरकालिकः -की -कं.

DIVAN, *s.* (Council of state) महासभा, शिष्टसभा, तुरुष्कदेशे राजसभा. —(Saloon fitted up with sofas) केलिशयनयुक्ता शाला.

To DIVARICATE, *v. n.* द्विधा विभिद् in pass. (-भिद्यते), द्विभागीभू, द्विखण्डीभू, द्विधाभू, विगम् (c. 1. -गच्छति -गन्तुं), द्विशाखाकारेण विभिद् in pass.

To DIVARICATE, *v. a.* द्विधाकृ, द्विभागीकृ, द्विखण्डीकृ, द्विशकलीकृ.

DIVARICATION, *s.* द्विधाकरणं, द्विधाभावः, द्विखण्डीकरणं, विभिन्नता.

To DIVE, *v. a.* and *n.* मस्ज् (c. 6. मज्जति, मंक्तुं, मज्जितुं), निमस्ज्; अवगाह् (c. 1. -गाहते -हितुं -गाढुं), अवगाह्, जलमध्ये प्रविश् (c. 6. -विशति -वेष्टुं), जलान्तःप्रवेशं कृ, जलान्तःप्लवनं कृ, प्लु (c. 1. प्लवते, प्लोतुं).—(Dive after something) किञ्चिदन्वेषणार्थं जले निमस्ज्.—(Dive into any thing) अमुककर्म्मणि निविश्, निरूप् (c. 10. -रूपयति -यितुं); 'diving into books,' ग्रन्थमग्नः -ग्ना -ग्नं, ग्रन्थनिविष्टः -ष्टा -ष्टं.—(Explore) अन्विष् (c. 6. -इच्छति c. 4. -इष्यति -एषितुं), परीक्ष् (c. 1. -ईक्षते -क्षितुं).

DIVER, *s.* मंक्ता *m.* (क्तृ), निमंक्ता *m.*, गाहिता *m.* (तृ), अवगाहिता *m.*, जलेवाहः.—(Into books) शास्त्रनिष्ठः.—(Bird) प्लवः, प्लावी *m.* (न्).

To DIVERGE, *v. n.* एककेन्द्रात् पराङ्मुखः -खी -खं भू or विचल् (c. 1. -चलति -लितुं) or विगम् (c. 1. -गच्छति -गन्तुं) or विच्यु (c 1. -च्यवते -च्योतुं) or व्युत्क्रम् (c. 1. -क्रामति -क्रमितुं).

DIVERGENCE, *s.* केन्द्रपराङ्मुखता, केन्द्रापसरणं, विचलनं, विच्युतिः *f.*, विगमः, विस्तारः.

DIVERGENT, *a.* केन्द्रपराङ्मुखः -खी -खं, केन्द्रविचलः -ला -लं, विस्तृतः -ता -तं.

DIVERS, *a.* नाना indec., विविधः -धा -धं, अनेकः -का -कं, नानाप्रकारः -रा -रं, नानाविधः -धा -धं, बहुविधः -धा -धं, व्याविधः -धा -धं, नानारूपः -पी -पं.

DIVERSE, *a.* (Different) भिन्नः -न्ना -न्नं, विभिन्नः -न्ना -न्नं, अन्यः -न्या -न्यत्, असदृशः -शी -शं, असमानः -ना -नं, असमः -मा -मं, अतुल्यः -ल्या -ल्यं, विपरीतः -ता -तं, विविक्तः -क्ता -क्तं, अनीदृशः -शी -शं, इतरः -रा -रं, पृथक् indec., पृथग्विधः -धा -धं.—(Various). *See* DIVERS.

DIVERSELY, *adv.* नानारूपेण, भिन्नप्रकारेण, अनेकधा, पृथक्.

DIVERSIFICATION, *s.* नानाप्रकारकरणं, नानारूपकरणं, अनेकरूपकरणं, आकारपरिवर्त्तनं, वैचित्र्यं, विभिन्नता, विभेदः.

DIVERSIFIED, *p. p.* or *a.* नानारूपः -पी -पं, भिन्नरूपः -पी -पं, नानाप्रकारः -रा -रं, नानाविधः -धा -धं, पृथग्विधः -धा -धं, विविधः -धा -धं, व्याविधः -धा -धं, चित्रितः -ता -तं, विचित्रः -त्रा -त्रं, चित्रविचित्रः -त्रा -त्रं.

To DIVERSIFY, *v. a.* नानारूपं -पीं -पं कृ, भिन्नरूपं -पीं -पं कृ, चित्र् (c. 10. चित्रयति -यितुं), विचित्रं -त्रां -त्रं कृ, चित्रविचित्रीकृ, नानाविधं -धां -धं कृ.

DIVERSION, *s.* (Sport) विनोदः, विलासः, विलसनं, विहारः, क्रीडा, परीहासः, केलिः *m. f.*, कौतुकं.—(Act of amusing the mind) मनोविनोदः, मनोरञ्जनं, अनुरञ्जनं.—(Act of turning aside) स्वपथात् or स्वमार्गाद् भ्रंशकरणं or च्युतिकरणं or विकर्षः or विकर्षणं.

DIVERSITY, *s.* (Difference) भेदः, विभेदः, भिन्नता, विभिन्नता, असादृश्यं, असाम्यं, द्वैधं, द्वैविध्यं.—(Variety) वैचित्र्यं, विचित्रता, भेदाभेदः.

To DIVERT, *v. a.* (Turn from its course) स्वपथात् or स्वमार्गाद् भ्रंश् in caus. (भ्रंशयति -यितुं) or विचल् in caus. (-चालयति -यितुं) or विकृष् (c. 6. -कृषति c. 1. -कर्षति -क्रष्टुं) or विच्यु in caus. (-च्यावयति -यितुं).—(Amuse, please) विनुद् in caus. (-नोदयति -यितुं), विलस् in caus. (-लासयति -यितुं), नन्द् in caus. (नन्दयति -यितुं), रम् in caus. (रमयति -यितुं), रञ्ज् in caus. (रञ्जयति -यितुं).

DIVERTED, *p. p.* विकृष्टः -ष्टा -ष्टं, आकृष्टः -ष्टा -ष्टं, स्वमार्गच्यावितः -ता -तं. —(Amused) विनोदितः -ता -तं, प्रमोदितः -ता -तं, उल्लासितः -ता -तं.

DIVERTING, *a.* हासकरः -री -रं, प्रहासी -सिनी -सि (न्), हास्ययुक्तः -क्ता -क्तं, विनोदकः -का -कं, विनोदजनकः -का -कं, आनन्दकः -का -कं.

DIVERTISEMENT, *s.* (Diversion) विनोदः, विलासः.—(A ballet between the acts) अङ्कद्वयमध्ये नाटकप्रेक्षकाणां विनोदार्थं हल्लीषकं.

To DIVEST, *v. a* (Strip) विवस्त्र (nom. -वस्त्रयति -यितुं), नग्नीकृ, अवतॄ in caus. (-तारयति -यितुं), उत्कृष् (c. 1. -कर्षति -क्रष्टुं), उन्मुष् (c. 6. -मुषति -मोष्टुं), अवमुष्, विमुष्; उच्छद् (c. 10. -छादयति- यितुं), अपनह् (c. 4. -नह्यति -नद्धुं).—(Deprive of) हृ (c. 1. हरति, हर्त्तुं), अपनी (c. 1. -नयति -नेतुं), वियुज् (c. 10. -योजयति -यितुं), विनाकृ.

DIVESTURE, *s.* विवस्त्रीकरणं, नग्नीकरणं, अपनयनं, हरणं.

DIVIDABLE, *a.* विभेद्यः -द्या -द्यं, विभाज्यः -ज्या -ज्यं, खण्डनीयः -या -यं.

To DIVIDE, *v. a.* (Part, separate) भिद् (c. 7. भिनत्ति, भेत्तुं), विभिद्, छिद् (c. 7. छिनत्ति, छेत्तुं), विच्छिद्; खण्ड् (c. 10. खण्डयति -यितुं), वियुज् (c. 7. -युनक्ति -योक्तुं), विप्रयुज्, विश्लिष् (c. 10. -श्लेषयति -यितुं), पृथक्कृ, शकलीकृ.—(Divide in two) द्विधा छिद् or कृ, द्विखण्डीकृ, द्विभागीकृ, द्व्यंशीकृ.—(Make partition of) विभज् (c. 1. -भजति -भक्तुं), प्रविभज्, संविभज्, अंश् (c. 10. अंशयति -यितुं), व्यंस् (c. 10. -अंसयति -यितुं), परिकॢप् (c. 10. -कल्पयति -यितुं).

To DIVIDE, *v. n.* भिद् in pass. (भिद्यते), विभिद्, विच्छिद् in pass. (-छिद्यते), वियुज् in pass. (-युज्यते), विश्लिष् (c. 4. -श्लिष्यति -श्लेष्टुं), द्विधाभू.—(Cleave open) स्फुट् (c. 1. स्फोटति c. 6. स्फुटति -टितुं), दल् (c. 1. दलति -लितुं), विदल्.—(Divide upon a question) द्विधाभू, द्वैधीभू.

DIVIDED, *p. p.* भिन्नः -न्ना -न्नं, विभिन्नः -न्ना -न्नं, विच्छिन्नः -न्ना -न्नं, वियुक्तः -क्ता -क्तं, विश्लिष्टः -ष्टा -ष्टं, द्विधाकृतः -ता -तं, द्विधाभूतः -ता -तं, द्वैधीभूतः -ता -तं, पृथक्कृतः -ता -तं, शकलीकृतः -ता -तं, विभक्तः -क्ता -क्तं, प्रविभक्तः -क्ता -क्तं, संविभक्तः -क्ता -क्तं, अंशितः -ता -तं, द्व्यंशः -शा -शं.

DIVIDEND, *s.* (Share, interest on money, &c.) भागः, अंशः, लभ्यांशः, उद्धारः, भाज्यं, कलान्तरं.—(In arithmetic) भाज्यं.

DIVIDER, *s.* (One that separates) भेदकः, विभेदकः, भेदकरः, विच्छेदकः, छेदकरः, वियोगकृत् *m.*—(Distributer) विभागकल्पकः, संविभागकृत्, अंशयिता *m.* (तृ).

DIVINATION, *s.* गणना, गणकता, पक्षिगतिहस्तरेखादिलक्षणाद् भविष्यदनुमानं or शुभाशुभकथनं, पूर्व्वलक्षणपरीक्षा, शकुनपरीक्षणं, पूर्व्वचिह्ननिरीक्षणं, भविष्यत्सूचनं.

DIVINE, *a.* दिव्यः -व्या -व्यं, दैवः -वी -वं, देवकीयः -या -यं, देवकः -का -कं, दैविकः -की -कं, ऐश्वरः -री -रं, ईश्वरीयः -या -यं, ऐशः -शी -शं, ऐशिकः -की -कं, देवार्हः -र्हा -र्हं.—(God-like) ईश्वरतुल्यः -ल्या -ल्यं, देवरूपी -पिणी -पि (न्), ईश्वरमूर्त्तिः -र्त्तिः -र्त्ति.

DIVINE, *s.* (Clergyman) पुरोहितः, धर्म्माध्यापकः, धर्म्मोपदेशकः.—(Theologian) श्रोत्रियः, श्रुताध्ययनसम्पन्नः, परमार्थविद्.

To divine, *v. a.* and *n.* (Practice divination) गणनां कृ, पक्षिगति-चक्षुःस्पन्दादिलक्षणाद् भविष्यद् अनुमा (c. 2. -माति -तुं) or शुभाशुभं कथ् (c. 10. कथयति -यितुं) or प्रदृश् in caus. (-दर्शयति -यितुं) or सूच् (c. 10. सूचयति -यितुं), शकुनानि or पूर्व्वलक्षणानि परीक्ष् (c. 1. ईक्षते -क्षितुं).—(Conjecture) अनुमा.

Divinely, *adv.* देवरूपेण, देववत्, दिव्यरूपेण, ईश्वरीयप्रकारेण.

Diviner, *s.* (One who practices divination) दैवज्ञः, शकुनपरीक्षकः, पूर्व्वचिह्ननिरीक्षकः, निमित्तज्ञः, पक्षिगतिहस्तरेखादिलक्षणाद् भविष्यत्सूचकः.—(Conjecturer) अनुमाता *m.* (तृ).

Diving, *s.* मज्जनं, निमज्जनं, अवगाहः -हनं, विगाहः, प्लवः -वनं.

Diving-bell, *s.* वायुपूरितं घण्टाकृति यन्त्रं यत्प्रविश्य जलेवाहा गम्भीरसलिले सुचिरेण वर्त्तितुं शक्नुवन्ति.

Divinity, *s.* (State of being divine) देवत्वं -ता, भगवत्त्वं, ब्रह्मत्वं.—(A god) देवः -वी *f.*, देवता, भगवान् *m.* -वती *f.* (त्), सुरः, विबुधः, सुचिरायुः *m.* (स्).—(Theology) परमार्थविद्या, ईश्वरविषया विद्या, श्रुतिविद्या, धर्म्मशास्त्रविद्या, पारमार्थिकविद्या.

Divisibility, *s.* छेद्यत्वं, विच्छेद्यता, भेद्यत्वं, अंशनीयता, विभाज्यत्वं.

Divisible, *a.* छेद्यः -द्या -द्यं, विच्छेद्यः -द्या -द्यं, विच्छेदनीयः -या -यं, भेद्यः -द्या -द्यं, विभाज्यः -ज्या -ज्यं, अंश्यः -श्या -श्यं, अंशनीयः -या -यं, -अंशयितव्यः -व्या -व्यं.

Division, *s.* (Dividing, separating) छेदः, विच्छेदः -दनं, भेदः, विभेदः -दनं, खण्डनं, परिच्छेदः, परिच्छित्तिः *f.*, छित्तिः *f.*, पृथक्करणं, द्विधाकरणं, द्वैधीकरणं.—(Partition) भाजनं, विभागः, प्रविभागः, विभागकरणं, अंशनं, उद्धारविभागः, उद्धारः -रणं.—(Disunion) वियोगः, विसंयोगः, विप्रयोगः, विश्लेषः.—(State of being divided) भिन्नता, विभिन्नता, विच्छिन्नता, विभक्तता.—(Part, distinct portion) भागः, खण्डः, विभागः, देशः, प्रदेशः, एकदेशः.—(Division of time) कालविभक्तिः *f.*—(Of an army) गुल्मः, दलं, सैन्यव्यूहः.—(In arithmetic) भागहरः -हारः, हरणं, छेदनं.

Divisor, *s.* (In arithmetic) हरकः, हारकः, अङ्कहारकः, हरः, हारः, भाजकः.

Divorce, divorcement, *s.* निराकरणं, त्यागः, स्त्रीपुरुषविच्छेदः, धर्म्मानुसारेण or व्यवहारदर्शनानन्तरं विवाहसम्बन्धभेदः.—(From a wife) स्वभार्य्यानिराकरणं, स्वभार्य्यात्यागः; 'writing of divorce,' त्यागपत्रं.

To divorce, *v. a.* स्वभार्य्यां or स्वभर्त्तारं त्यज् (c. 1. त्यजति, त्यक्तुं) or परित्यज् or निराकृ or निरस् (c. 4. -अस्यति -असितुं), व्यवहारदर्शनानन्तरं विवाहसम्बन्धं भिद् (c. 7. भिनत्ति, भेत्तुं).

Divorced, *p. p.* त्यक्तः -क्ता -क्तं, परित्यक्तः -क्ता -क्तं, निराकृतः -ता -तं.

Divorcer, *s.* स्त्रीपुरुषयोर् विच्छेदकर्त्ता *m.* (र्त्तृ), विवाहसम्बन्धभेदकः.

To divulge, *v. a.* प्रकाश् (c. 10. -काशयति -यितुं), विकाश्, ख्या in caus. (ख्यापयति -यितुं), विख्या, प्रकटीकृ, विघुष् (c. 10. -घोषयति -यितुं), व्यक्तीकृ, व्यञ्ज् (c. 7. -अनक्ति -अञ्जितुं), विप्रथ् in caus. (-प्रथयति -यितुं), विवृ (c. 5. -वृणोति -वरितुं -रीतुं), स्पष्टीकृ, प्रचर् in caus. (-चारयति -यितुं); 'to divulge a secret,' रहस्यं भिद् (c. 7. भिनत्ति भेत्तुं); 'to divulge counsel,' मन्त्रभेदं कृ.

Divulged, *p. p.* प्रकाशितः -ता -तं, प्रकटीकृतः -ता -तं, विप्रथितः -ता -तं.

Divulger, *s.* प्रकाशकः, ख्यापकः; 'of a secret,' रहस्यभेदकरः.

Divulging, *s.* प्रकाशनं, ख्यापनं, प्रकटीकरणं, विघोषणं, विवरणं, व्यक्तीकरणं, सर्व्वत्र प्रचारणं; 'of a secret,' रहस्यभेदः; 'of counsel,' मन्त्रभेदः.

Divulsion, *s.* विदारः -रणं, विदरः, उत्पाटनं, उद्धरणं.

To dizen, *v. a.* भूष् (c. 10. भूषयति -यितुं), परिभूष्, अलङ्कृ, परिष्कृ.

Dizziness, *s.* भ्रमरं, भ्रामरं, भ्रमिः *f.*, भ्रमः, विभ्रमः, विभ्रान्तिः *f.*, घूर्णिः *f.*, घूर्णनं, चक्षुरादिचापल्यं, चक्षुरादिचाञ्चल्यं, प्रमादः.

Dizzy, *a.* (Vertiginous) भ्रामरी -रिणी -रि (न्), भ्रमी -मिणी -मि (न्), घूर्णायमानः -ना -नं.—(Causing dizziness) भ्रमरकरः -री -रं.—(Thoughtless) चपलः -ला -लं, प्रमादी -दिनी -दि (न्).

To do, *v. a.* (Act) कृ (c. 8. करोति, कुरुते, कर्त्तुं), सङ्कृ, अभिकृ; विधा (c. 3. -दधाति -धातुं), व्यवसो (c. 4. -स्यति -सातुं), चेष्ट् (c. 1. चेष्टते -ष्टितुं).—(Execute) कृ, विधा, सम्पद् in caus. (-पादयति -यितुं), घट् (c. 10. घटयति -यितुं).—(Perform) कृ, विधा, अनुष्ठा (c. 1. -तिष्ठति -ष्ठातुं), आस्था, समास्था, प्रवृत् in caus. (-वर्त्तयति -यितुं), निर्वृत्, वृत्; सम्पद् in caus., निष्पद्, उत्पद्, उपपद्.—(Practice) आचर् (c. 1. -चरति -रितुं), समाचर्, अभ्यस् (c. 4. -अस्यति -असितुं), सेव् (c. 1. सेवते -वितुं), आश्रि (c. 1. -श्रयति -ते -यितुं).—(Transact) व्यवहृ (c. 1. -हरति -हर्त्तुं) कृ, समाचर्, निर्वह् in caus. (-वाहयति -यितुं), पण् (c. 10. पणायति -यितुं), पणायां कृ.—(Carry on, effect) निर्वह् in caus., प्रवृत् in caus., प्रणी (c. 1. -णयति -णेतुं), सम्पद् in caus., तीर् (c. 10. तीरयति -यितुं), पॄ (c. 10. पारयति -यितुं).—(Exert labour) चेष्ट्, विचेष्ट्, व्यवसो, अध्यवसो, यत् (c. 1. यतते -तितुं).—(Cause) कृ, उत्पद् in caus., जन् in caus. (जनयति -यितुं), साध् in caus. (साधयति -यितुं).—(Do with, employ) प्रयुज् (c. 7. -युनक्ति -योक्तुं c. 10. -योजयति -यितुं), उपयुज्, व्यापृ in caus. (-पारयति -यितुं), प्रवृत् in caus.—(Do away, destroy) साध् in caus., विनश् in caus. (-नाशयति -यितुं), लुप् (c. 6. लुम्पति, लोप्तुं).—Do good to) उपकृ.—(Do evil to) अपकृ.—(Do one's duty) कृत्यं or कर्त्तव्यं कृ, धर्म्मं निष्पद् in caus.—(Do one's best) यथाशक्ति कृ; 'he does not know what to do,' यथाकार्य्यं न जानाति; 'one's own doing,' आत्मकृतः -ता -तं, स्वयङ्कृतः -ता -तं.

To do, *v. n.* (Act, behave) चर् (c. 1. चरति -रितुं), आचर्, समाचर्; वृत् (c. 1. वर्त्तते -र्त्तितुं), व्यवहृ.—(Fare) अस्, भू, वृत्, स्था (c. 1. तिष्ठति, स्थातुं); 'How do you do?' किं क्षेमम् अस्ति, किं कुशलं भवति, क्षेमं भवतु.—(Do well, prosper) सुस्थः -स्था -स्थम् अस्, सुस्थितः -ता -तं भू, वृध् (c. 1. वर्धते -र्धितुं).—(Do ill) दुःस्थः -स्था -स्थम् अस्, दुःस्थितिं गम् (c. 1. गच्छति, गन्तुं).—(Suit) युज् in pass. (युज्यते); 'that will do,' इत्यलं, यथेष्टं.

Do, *s.* (Ado) दुःखं, कष्टं.—(Feat) कर्म्म *n.* (न्) चेष्टितं, विचेष्टितं.

Doab, *s.* (Name of a country) अन्तर्वेदी *f.*

Do-all, *s.* सर्व्वकर्म्मी -र्म्मी -र्म्मि (न्) सर्व्वकर्म्मीणः -णा -णं, सर्व्वकार्य्यचर्चकः -का -कं.

Doat. *See* Dote.

Docible, docile, *a.* विनेयः -या -यं, प्रणेयः -या -यं, विधेयः -या -यं, वश्यः -श्या -श्यं, वशगः -गा -गं, वशानुगः -गा -गं, वश्यात्मा -त्मा -त्म (न्) अनुकूलः -ला -लं, अनायासेन शिक्षणीयः -या -यं or शिक्ष्यः -क्ष्या -क्ष्यं, गृह्यकः -का -कं, अनुविधायी -यिनी -यि (न्), अधीनः -ना -नं, आयत्तः -त्ता -त्तं, अस्वच्छन्दः -न्दा -न्दं, निघ्नः -घ्ना -घ्नं, शिक्षाशीलः -ला -लं.

Docibleness, docility, *s.* विनेयता, विधेयता, वश्यता, शिक्षणीयत्वं, शिक्षाशीलत्वं.

Dock, *s.* (The plant) लोलिका, वृक्षराजः, रक्तस्रावः, सौगन्धिकं, रक्तसौगन्धिकं.—(Tail cut short) छिन्नवालः, ह्रस्वपुच्छं.—(Station for ships) नौकावस्थानं, नौकाश्रयः, नावाश्रयः, नौकाधारः, नौकागारं, नावाधारः, नौकोद्धरणस्थानं.

To dock, *v. a.* पुच्छं छिद् (c. 7. छिनत्ति, छेत्तुं) or अवच्छिद् or ह्रस् (c. 10. ह्रासयति -यितुं), अवकृत् (c. 6. -कृन्तति -कर्त्तितुं), निकृत्, लू (c. 9. लुनाति, लवितुं).—(Lay up in a dock) नौकाश्रये निविश्

in caus. (-वेशयति -यितुं), नावम् उद्घृ (c. 1. -हरति -हर्त्तुं).

Dock-yard, *s.* नाविकभाण्डागारं, नौकानिर्म्माणस्थानं.

Docked, *p. p.* अवच्छिन्नः -न्ना -न्नं, अवकर्त्तितः -ता -तं, लूनः -ना -नं.

Docket, *s.* (Ticket on goods) अङ्कपटः, भाण्डोपरि चिह्नं or अङ्कः or अङ्कपत्रं, पत्रकं.—(Small piece of paper containing the heads of a writing) सङ्क्षेपपत्रकं, सूचिपत्रकं.—(List of those who have cases in a court) अर्थिनां or कार्य्यिणां नामावलिपत्रं.

To docket, *v. a.* (Make an abstract of a writing and enter it in a book) लिखितसङ्क्षेपं कृत्वा पुस्तके समारुह् in caus. (-रोपयति -यितुं), or अभिलिख् (c. 6. -लिखति -लेखितुं).

Doctor, *s.* (A learned man) पण्डितः, ज्ञानी *m.* (न्), व्युत्पन्नः, वैद्यः, शास्त्री *m.* (न्).—The word आचार्य्यः is affixed to the names of learned men, as 'Doctor' is prefixed: thus राघवाचार्य्यः, रामाचार्य्यः.—(Teacher) आचार्य्यः, शिक्षकः, अध्यापकः, उपदेशकः, गुरुः *m.*—(Doctor of divinity) परमार्थविद्याज्ञः, श्रुतिविद्यासम्पन्नः.—(Physician) वैद्यः, चिकित्सकः, भिषक् *m.* (ज्), आयुर्वेददृक् *m.* (श्), चिकित्साजीवी *m.* (न्), अगदङ्कारः, रोगशान्तकः, रोगहृत् *m.*, रोगहा *m.* (न्), जीवदः.

To doctor, *v. a.* कित् in des. (चिकित्सति -त्सितुं), भिषज् (nom. भिषज्यति -ज्यितुं). उपचर् (c. 1. -चरति -रितुं), उपचारं कृ, औषधीकृ.

Doctoral, *a.* आचार्य्यपदसम्बन्धी -न्धिनी -न्धि (न्), वैद्यः -द्या -द्यं.

Doctorally, *adv.* वैद्यवत्, पण्डितवत्, आचार्य्यवत्, गुरुवत्.

Doctorship, *s.* आचार्य्यता -त्वं, आचार्य्यपदं, गुरुत्वं, वैद्यपदं.

Doctrinal, *a.* तत्त्वोपदेशकः -का -कं, तत्त्वोपदेशी -शिनी -शि (न्), तत्त्वशिक्षकः -का -कं, शिक्षाविषयः -या -यं, वैधिकः -की -कं, सौत्रः -त्री -त्रं.

Doctrine, *s.* (Principle laid down) तत्त्वं, मतं, सूत्रं, न्यायः.—(System of doctrines) पथः, पन्थाः *m.* (पथिन्), मार्गः; 'a different doctrine,' परमतं; 'difference of doctrine,' शाखाभेदः; 'heretical doctrine,' असच्छास्त्रं; 'received doctrine,' आम्नायः, सम्प्रदायः; 'adhering to a doctrine,' वादरतः.—(Learning) विद्या, पाण्डित्यं.

Document, *s.* पत्रं -त्री, पत्रकं, पत्रिका, लेख्यं, लेख्यपत्रं, लेख्यप्रसङ्गः, लेख्यपत्रं, लेख्यप्रमाणं, लिखनं, लिखितं; 'a forged document,' कपटलेख्यं.

Dodecagon, *s.* द्वादशास्रं, द्वादशकोणः.

To dodge, *v. a.* and *n.* (Trick) वञ्च् (c. 10. वञ्चयते -ति -यितुं), व्यपदिश् (c. 6. -दिशति -देष्टुं), अपदिश्, प्रलभ् (c. 1. -लभते -लब्धुं), प्रतॄ in caus. (-तारयति -यितुं), छल् (c. 10. छलयति -यितुं).—(Evade) अपक्रम् (c. 1. -क्रामति -क्रमितुं), पलाय् (c. 1. पलायते -यितुं).—(Escape by suddenly shifting place) पलायमानो अकस्मात् परिवृत् (c. 1. -वर्त्तते -र्त्तितुं), विपरिवृत्, इतस्ततः परिधाव् (c. 1. -धावति -वितुं), विपरिधाव्.

Dodger, *s.* वञ्चकः, मायी *m.* (न्), कपटी *m.* (न्), व्यपदेष्टा *m.* (ष्टृ), प्रतारकः.

Doe, *s.* (She-deer) मृगी, मृगवधूः, हरिणी, एणी, रोहित् *f.*, समीची, पृषती, कन्दली; 'doe-skin,' मृगीचर्म्म *n.* (न्).

Doer, *s.* कर्त्ता *m.* (र्त्तृ), कारी *m.* (न्), कारकः, कारः, करः, कृत् in comp. विधायी *m.* (न्), अनुष्ठाता *m.* (तृ), कर्म्मकारी *m.*, कर्म्मकरः, सम्पादकः, निर्वाहकः प्रवर्त्तकः.

To doff, *v. a.* (Put off dress) वस्त्रम् अवतॄ in caus. (-तारयति -यितुं), or अपनी (c. 1. -नयति -नेतुं), अपनी, विवस्त्र (nom. -वस्त्रयति -यितुं), उत्कृष् (c. 1. -कर्षति -क्रष्टुं), अवमुच् (c. 6. -मुञ्चति -मोक्तुं), विमुच्, अपनह् (c. 4. -नह्यति -नद्धुं).

Dog, *s.* (The animal) श्वा *m.* (श्वन्), कुक्कुरः, कुकुरः, शुनकः, भषकः, मृगदंशकः, वक्रपुच्छः, वक्रवालधिः *m.*, ललजिह्वः, जिह्वालिट् *m.* (ह्), वृकारिः *m.*, ग्रामसिंहः, शीघ्रचेतनः, रात्रिजागरः, कृतज्ञः, सारमेयः, सामादः, शरत्कामी *m.* (न्), श्वकाम्यः, कौलेयकः; 'sporting-dog,' मृगयाकुशलः कुक्कुरः, आखेटकार्थं श्वा, विश्वकद्रुः *m.*; 'mad-dog,' अलर्कः; 'bite of a dog,' श्वदंशनं.—(Andiron) लोहमयः शूलाधारः. 'To go to the dogs,' शुनो गम् (c. 1. गच्छति, गन्तुं), परिक्षि in pass. (-क्षीयते), विनश् (c. 4. -नश्यति).

To dog, *v. a.* कुक्कुरवद् अन्विष् (c. 4. -इष्यति -एषितुं), पश्चाद्गम् (c. 1. -गच्छति -गन्तुं), पश्चाद्वृत् (c. 1. -वर्त्तते -र्त्तितुं), अनुवृत्, अनुसृ (c. 1. -सरति -सर्त्तुं), अनुष्ठा (c. 1. -तिष्ठति -ष्ठातुं), नित्यम् अनुसृत्य आयासं जन् (c. 10. जनयति -यितुं).

Dog-brier or dog-rose, *s.* श्वपुष्पः कण्टकगुल्मः, चोड्रपुष्पः कण्टकलतः.

Dog-cheap, *a.* श्वमांसवत् or विमांसवद् अल्पमूल्येन क्रेयः -या -यं, स्वल्पमूल्यः -ल्या -ल्यं, स्वल्पार्घः -र्घा -र्घं.

Dog-days, *s.* श्वदिनानि *n. pl.*, अत्युष्णकालः, अत्युष्णसमयः, सूर्य्यदिनानि, श्रावणात् प्रभृति भाद्रपर्य्यन्तं कालः.

Dog-fancier, *s.* श्वक्रीडी *m.* (न्), श्वगणिकः, श्वागणिकः.

Dogged, *a.* (Sullen, obstinate) वक्रभावः -वा -वं, कर्कशभावः -वा -वं, जडः -डा -डं, स्तब्धः -ब्धा -ब्धं, कठिनः -ना -नं, निष्ठुरः -रा -रं.

Doggedly, *adv.* वक्रभावेन, कर्कशभावेन, जाड्येन, निष्ठुरं, कर्कशं.

Doggedness, *s.* भाववक्रता, कार्कश्यं, जाड्यं, जडता, नैष्ठुर्य्यं, काठिन्यं.

Doggerel, *a.* (Irregular, as verses) अपरिमितचरणः -णा -णं, अपरिमितपदः -दा -दं, विषमः -मा -मं; 'doggerel verse,' कुकविता, मन्दकविता, नीचकविता.

Doggish, *a.* श्वशीलः -ला -लं, शौवः -वी -वं, कुक्कुराचारः -रा -रं, श्ववृत्तिः -त्तिः -त्ति, श्वापदः -दी -दं, शौवापदः -दी -दं; 'a doggish fellow,' श्वनरः; 'a doggish life,' श्ववृत्तिः *f.*

Doggishness, *s.* शौवं, श्वशीलता, कुक्कुराचारत्वं, श्वभावः, पशुता.

Dog-grass, *s.* तृणभेदः, तृणं, कक्षः, घासविशेषः.

Dog-hearted, *a.* श्वहृदयः -या -यं, कुक्कुरहृदयः -या -यं, कठिनहृदयः -या -यं.

Dog-hole, *s.* श्वबिलं, श्वगर्त्तः, कुक्कुरगर्त्तः, श्वविवरं, श्वभ्रं, अधमस्थानं.

Dog-keeper, *s.* श्वपोषकः, श्ववान् *m.* (त्), श्वागणिकः, श्वपचः.

Dog-kennel, *s.* कुक्कुरालयः, श्वगृहं, कुक्कुरगृहं, कुक्कुरागारं.

Dog-louse, *s.* श्वयूका, कुक्कुरयूका, श्वकीटः, कुक्कुरकीटः.

Dogma, *s.* मतं, तत्त्वं, सूत्रं, विधिः *m.*, सम्मतं, नियमः, आदेशः, निर्देशः, व्यवस्था.

Dogmatic, dogmatical, *a.* आदेशकः -का -कं or निर्देशकः, स्वमताभिमानी -निनी -नि (न्), सधर्षं स्वमतवादी -दिनी -दि (न्) or स्वमतावलम्बी -म्बिनी -म्बि (न्), मतसंस्थापनः -ना -नं, नैयमिकः -की -कं, वैधिकः -की -कं, सौत्रः -त्री -त्रं.

Dogmatically, *adv.* आदेशकप्रकारेण, सनिर्देशं, दृढनिश्चयपूर्व्वं, सधर्षं.

Dogmatism, *s.* स्वमताभिमानं, स्वमतसंस्थापनं, सधर्षं स्वमतवादः or स्वमतावलम्बनं, दृढोक्तिः *f.*

Dogmatist, dogmatiser, *s.* धर्षपूर्व्वं or गर्व्वपूर्व्वं स्वमतवादी *m.* (न्) or स्वमताभिमानी *m.* (न्) or तत्त्ववादी.

To dogmatise, *v. n.* सधर्षं or सगर्व्वं स्वमतं वद् (c. 1. वदति -दितुं), दृढोक्त्या स्वमतं संस्था in caus. (-स्थापयति -यितुं), तत्त्वानि धर्षेण वद्.

Dog's ear, *s.* कुक्कुरकर्णः, श्वकर्णः, पुस्तकपत्रकोणे श्वकर्णाकारः पुटः.

Dog-sick, *a.* कुक्कुरवद् वमनकारी -रिणी -रि (न्).

Dog's-meat, *s.* श्वमांसं, कुक्कुरमांसं, विमांसं, कुक्कुराहारः, उच्छिष्टांशं.

Dog-star, *s.* कुक्कुरसंज्ञा तारा यस्याम् उदितायाम् अत्युष्णकालो भवति.

DOG'S-TOOTH, *s.* श्वादन्तः, श्वदंष्ट्रा, कुक्कुरदन्तः.

DOG-TRICK, *s.* श्ववृत्तं, श्वचेष्टितं, श्वकर्म्म *n.* (न्), दुश्चेष्टितं, कुचेष्टा.

DOG-WEARY, *a.* कुक्कुरवत् परिश्रान्तः -न्ता -न्तं, अतिक्लान्तः -न्ता -न्तं.

DOINGS, *s. pl.* (Things done) चरितं, चरितं, चेष्टितं, विचेष्टितं, कृतं, कर्म्म *n.* (न्), विधानं, व्यापारः, चेष्टा, वृत्तं.—(Conduct) व्यवहारः, आचारः, आचरितं, चारित्र्यं, वृत्तिः *f.*, चर्य्या, प्रवृत्तिः *f.*, रीतिः *f.*

DOLE, *s.* (That which is dealt, a part, share) भागः, अंशः, विभागः, भाजितं, भाज्यं, उद्धारः, उपहारः, खण्डं, छेदः, भिन्नं, वण्टः.—(Gratuity) पारितोषिकं.—(Grief) शोकः, दुःखं.

To DOLE, *v. a.* पृथक् पृथग् विभज् (c. 1. -भजति -ते -भक्तुं), विभागशः or अंशांशि दा.

DOLEFUL, DOLESOME, *a.* सशोकः -का -कं, शोचनः -ना -नं, शोकार्त्तः -र्त्ता -र्त्तं, दुःखी -खिनी -खि (न्), समन्युः -न्युः -न्यु, विषादी -दिनी -दि (न्), उद्विग्नः -ग्ना -ग्नं, उग्रः -ग्रा -ग्रं.

DOLEFULLY, *adv.* सशोकं, सविषादं, सोद्वेगं, सदुःखं, सोत्कण्ठं, सखेदं, उग्रं.

DOLEFULNESS, DOLESOMENESS, *s.* शोकः, दुःखं, विषादः, विषण्णता, मन्युः *m.*, खेदः, उद्वेगः, अनाह्लादः, उग्रत्वं, उद्विग्नता, ग्लानिः *f.*, मनोग्लानिः *f.*, दुःखितत्वं.

DOLL, *s.* पुत्रिका, दारुपुत्रिका, पाञ्चालिका, पाञ्चलिका, पाञ्चाली, पुत्तली, दारुगर्भा, दारुस्त्री, शालभञ्जी -ञ्जिका, शालाङ्की, कुरुण्टी, पाचा, अञ्जलिकारिका.

DOLLAR, *s.* (A silver coin) रूप्यमुद्रा, रौप्यमुद्रा.

DOLORIFIC, *a.* दुःखकरः -री -रं, व्यथाकरः -री -रं, पीडाकरः -री -रं.

DOLOROUS, *a.* सशोकः -का -कं, शोकमयः -यी -यं, दुःखमयः -यी -यं, शोकान्वितः -ता -तं, समन्युः -न्युः -न्यु, खेदान्वितः -ता -तं.

DOLOUR, DOLOR, *s.* शोकः, दुःखं, खेदः, मन्युः *m.*, क्लेशः.

DOLPHIN, *s.* (Kind of sea-fish) समुद्रीयमत्स्यभेदः.—(The constellation) श्रविष्ठा, धनिष्ठा.

DOLT, *s.* स्थूलबुद्धिः *m.*, स्थूलधीः *m.*, मन्दबुद्धिः, मूर्खः, मूढः, जडः.

DOLTISH, *a.* जडबुद्धिः -द्धिः -द्धि, मन्दमतिः -तिः -ति, स्थूलः -ला -लं.

DOLTISHLY, *adv.* मूढवत्, जडवत्, मूर्खवत्, जाड्येन, बर्ब्बरवत्.

DOLTISHNESS, *s.* स्थूलबुद्धित्वं, मन्दमतित्वं, जडता -त्वं, जाड्यं, मूढता, मूर्खता, निर्बुद्धिता, अविज्ञता.

DOMAIN, *s.* (Territory governed) राष्ट्रं, विषयः, देशः, प्रदेशः.—(Empire) राज्यं.—(Estate, possession) भूमिः *f.*, अधिकारः, आधिकारत्वं, रिक्थं.

DOME, *s.* (Cupola) अर्द्धगोलाकारं प्रासादशृङ्गं or हर्म्यशिखरं.

DOMESTIC, *s.* (One who lives in the family) गृहवासी *m.* (न्), अन्तेवासी *m.* (न्), आन्तर्वेश्मिकः.—(Servant) भृत्यः, भृतकः, अनुजीवी *m.* (न्), गृहदासः, प्रेष्यः, कर्म्मकरः, सेवकः, परिचरः; 'female domestic,' दासी, प्रेष्या.

DOMESTIC, *a.* (Belonging to one's house or family) गृह्यः -ह्या -ह्यं, गृहसम्बन्धी -न्धिनी -न्धि (न्), आन्तर्वेश्मिकः -की -कं, गृहजः -जा -जं, गृहजातः -ता -तं, भृत्यः -त्या -त्यं, आवसथिकः -का -कं; 'domestic affairs,' गृहकार्य्यं, गृहव्यापारः; 'domestic chaplain,' कुलाचार्य्यः, कुलविप्रः; 'domestic contentions,' गृहच्छिद्रं, गृहभेदः, गृहकलहः; 'domestic duties,' कुलाचारः; 'domestic slave,' गृहदासः -सी; 'bewildered with domestic cares,' गृहमूढधीः.—(Not wild) गृह्यकः -का -कं, ग्राम्यः -म्या -म्यं, ग्रामवासी -सिनी -सि (न्); 'a domestic cock,' गृहकुक्कुटः, ग्रामकुक्कुटः; 'a domestic pigeon,' गृहकपोतकः.—(Staying much at home) गृहारूढचेताः *m.* (स्), गेहशूरः, गृहप्रियः, गृहवासी *m.* (न्).—(Pertaining to one's country) दैशिकः -की -कं, देश prefixed in comp., अभिजनदेशीयः -या -यं; 'intestine broil,' जनपदभेदः.

To DOMESTICATE, *v. a.* गृह्यकं -कां -कं कृ, गृहे पुष् (c. 10. पोषयति -यितुं).

DOMESTICATED, *p. p.* गृह्यकः -का -कं, गृहपुष्टः -ष्टा -ष्टं, छेकः -का -कं, ग्राम्यः -म्या -म्यं, संस्थः -स्था -स्थं.

DOMICILE, *s.* गृहं, वासस्थानं, वसतिः *f.*, निवासः, आवासः, अधिवासः, समावासः, अवस्थानं, वेश्म *n.* (न्), आलयः, निलयः, आयतनं.

DOMICILED, *p. p.* कृतवासः -सा -सं, कृतालयः -या -यं, समावासितः -ता -तं.

DOMINANT, *a.* प्रभूतः -ता -तं, प्रभवः -वा -वं, प्रभविष्णुः -ष्णुः -ष्णु, प्रधानः -ना -नं, प्रबलः -ला -लं, अतिरेकी -किणी -कि (न्), सातिशयः -या -यं, प्रकृष्टः -ष्टा -ष्टं, श्रेष्ठः -ष्ठा -ष्ठं, अधिष्ठाता -त्री -तृ (तृ), अग्रस्थः -स्था -स्थं.

To DOMINATE, *v. n.* प्रभू, अतिरिच् in pass. (-रिच्यते), उद्रिच्, व्यतिरिच्, अधिष्ठा (c. 1. -तिष्ठति -ष्ठातुं), अध्यास् (c. 2. -आस्ते -आसितुं), प्रशास् (c. 2. -शास्ति -शासितुं).

DOMINATION, *s.* प्रभुत्वं, प्रभविष्णुता, प्राधान्यं, आधिपत्यं, ईशत्वं, ऐश्वर्य्यं, अधिकारः, राजत्वं, राज्यं, शासनं, प्रशासनं, प्रबलता.

To DOMINEER, *v. n.* धर्षेण शास् (c. 2. शास्ति, शासितुं) or ईश् (c. 2. ईष्टे, ईशितुं), भर्त्सनपूर्व्वम् आधिपत्यं कृ, धृष् (c. 5. धृष्णोति, धर्षितुं).

DOMINEERING, *a.* धर्षी -र्षिणी -र्षि (न्), धृष्टः -ष्टा -ष्टं, भर्त्सनकारी -रिणी -रि (न्), मदोद्धतः -ता -तं, मदोदग्रः -ग्रा -ग्रं, उत्सिक्तः -क्ता -क्तं.

DOMINICAL, *a.* प्रभुदिवसविषयकः -का -कं, विश्रामवारसम्बन्धी -न्धिनी -न्धि (न्); 'dominical letter.' प्रभुवारलाक्षणिको वर्णः, विश्रामवारसूचकम् अक्षरं.

DOMINICAL, *s.* (The Lord's-day) ईश्वरदिवसः, प्रभुदिनं, विश्रामवारः, रविवारः, भट्टारकवारः.

DOMINICAN, *s.* डामिनिकमतावलम्बी सन्न्यासिविशेषः, योगी *m.* (न्), तपस्वी *m.* (न्).

DOMINION, *s.* ऐश्वर्य्यं, राज्यं, राजत्वं, प्रभुत्वं, ईशत्वं, अधिकारः, आधिपत्यं, शासनं.—(Country governed) राष्ट्रं, विषयः, देशः, प्रदेशः.

DOMINO, *s.* (A long cloak used as a disguise) विडम्बनयोग्यो दीर्घप्रावारः.—(An oblong piece of ivory) शलाका, दन्तादिमयो दीर्घचतुरस्रः.

DON, *s.* आर्य्यः, महाशयः, सुजनः, महानुभावः, प्रधानलोकः, शिष्टलोकः.

DONARY, *s.* धर्म्मार्थं दत्तं, ईश्वराय दत्तं वस्तु or द्रव्यं.

DONATION, *s.* दानं, प्रदानं, दत्तं, प्रदेयं, सम्प्रदानं, दायः, उपहारः, उपायनं, वितरणं, विसर्ज्जनं, उत्सर्ज्जनं, त्यागः, विश्राणनं, अंहतिः *f.*, प्रदा, दादः, दा, दं, हरणं, प्रतिपादनं, विहापितं, स्पर्शनं.

DONATIVE, *s.* दानं, प्रदानं, वितरणं, विसर्ज्जनं, पारितोषिकं.

DONE, *p. p.* कृतः -ता -तं, अनुष्ठितः -ता -तं, आचरितः -ता -तं, निष्पन्नः -न्ना -न्नं, वृत्तः -त्ता -त्तं, सम्पादितः -ता -तं.

DONEE, *s.* दानग्राही *m.* (न्), दानग्रहीता *m.* (तृ), देयी *m.* (न्).

DONGEON OR DONJON, *s.* दुर्गमध्ये सुगुप्तस्थानं, दुर्गगुप्तिः *f.*, दुर्गकोटिः *f.*; दुर्गशिखरं. *See* DUNGEON.

DONKEY, *s.* गर्द्दभः, खरः, रासभः; 'donkey-cart,' खरयानं; 'bray of a donkey,' खरनादः, खाकारः.

DONOR, *s.* दाता *m.* (तृ), प्रदाता, दायकः, दाकः, दादी *m.* (न्), दानकर्त्ता *m.* (र्तृ).

DOODLE, *s.* अल्पबुद्धिः *m.*, अल्पधीः *m.*, मूर्खः, दुर्मतिः *m.* अवज्ञभस्पी *m.* (न्).

To DOOM, *v. a.* (Condemn to punishment) दण्ड् (c. 10. दण्डयति -यितुं).—(To death) वधदण्डार्हं -र्हां -र्हं ज्ञा (c. 9. जानाति, ज्ञातुं), वधदण्डाज्ञां कृ.—(Consign) ऋ in caus. (अर्पयति -यितुं), सम्, प्रतिपद् in caus. (-पादयति -यितुं), निक्षिप् (c. 6. -क्षिपति -क्षेप्तुं), नियुज्

(c. 7. -युनक्ति -योक्तुं).—(Destine) प्रक्लृप् (c. 10. -कल्पयति -यितुं), निर्दिश् (c. 6. -दिशति -देष्टुं).—(Judge) विचर् in caus. (-चारयति -यितुं), निर्णी (c. 1. -णयति -णेतुं).

Doom, *s.* (Judgment) विचारः, अन्तिमविचारः.—(Sentence) निर्णयः, साधर्म्यं.—(Condemnation) दण्डः -ण्डनं, दण्डाज्ञा, दण्डयोगः.—(State to which one is destined) भवितव्यता, विधिः *m.*, कालनियोगः, विहितदशा, दिष्टं, नियतिः *f.*—(Ruin) नाशः, क्षयः, नाशः.

Doomed, *p. p.* दण्डितः -ता -तं, प्रकल्पितः -ता -तं, निर्दिष्टः -ष्टा -ष्टं, विचारितः -ता -तं, निर्णीतः -ता -तं, नियुक्तः -क्ता -क्तं or कालनियुक्तः.

Doomsday, *s.* विचारदिनं, महाविचारदिनं, सर्व्वलोकविचारणदिवसः.

Doomsday-book, domesday-book, *s.* पूर्व्वकाले श्वेतद्वीपराजाज्ञया लिखितं सर्व्वक्षेत्रपरिसंख्यारूपं पुस्तकं, क्षेत्रसङ्ग्रहपुस्तकं.

Door, *s.* द्वारं, द्वाः *f.* (र्), कपाटः -टं, कवाटः -टं, अररः -री -रिः *m.* वलजः, गृहमुखं, प्रतिहारः, प्रतीहारः.—(Entrance) प्रवेशः -शनं, मुखं, वेशिका, प्रतिहारणं.—(Passage) पथः; 'principal door,' सिंहद्वारं; 'private door,' अन्तर्द्वारं, प्रच्छन्नद्वारं, प्रच्छन्नं; 'back door,' पक्षद्वारं, पक्षकः; 'in doors,' गृहस्थितः; 'out of doors,' गृहबहिःस्थः, स्थानान्तरीगतः; 'next door to,' निकटस्थः -स्था -स्थं, अनन्तरवर्त्ती -र्त्तिनी -र्त्ति (न्); 'leaf of a door,' द्वारशाखा.

Door-case, *s.* द्वारपरिगतं काष्ठादि, द्वारमण्डकः.

Door-keeper, *s.* द्वारपालः, द्वारस्थः, द्वाररक्षकः, द्वारी *m.* (न्), द्वाःस्थः, द्वाःस्थितः, द्वाराध्यक्षः, प्रतिहारः, प्रतीहारः -री *f.*

Door-post, *s.* द्वारस्तम्भः, द्वारस्थूणा, द्वारकाष्ठं, द्वारदारुः *m.*

Door-sill, *s.* द्वारपिण्डी, देहलिः *f.* -ली, गृहतटी, गृहावग्रहणी, दण्डिका, उदुम्बरः, उदुम्बरः.

Doric, *a.* (Architecture) गृहनिर्म्माणे विशेषमार्गः or रीतिविशेषः.

Dormant, *a.* सुप्तः -प्ता -प्तं, प्रसुप्तः -प्ता -प्तं, शयितः -ता -तं, शयानः -ना -नं, निद्रितः -ता -तं, निद्रायणः -णा -णं.—(Concealed) प्रच्छन्नः -न्ना -न्नं, गुप्तः -प्ता -प्तं.

Dormitory, *s.* शय्यागृहं, शयनगृहं, शयनशाला, निद्राशाला, स्वप्ननिकेतनं, विश्रामशाला, शयनागारः.—(Burial-place) श्मशानं, प्रेतवनं, पितृवनं.

Dormouse, *s.* अतिनिद्रालुः क्षुद्रमूषिकभेदः, अतिस्वप्नशीलो मूषिकः.

Dorsal, *a.* पृष्ठ्यः -ष्ठ्या -ष्ठ्यं, पृष्ठसम्बन्धी -न्धिनी -न्धि (न्).

Dorsel, dorser, dosser, *s.* पृष्ठेन वाहनयोग्यः पिटकः or पेटकः or करण्डः.

Dose, *s.* यद् भेषजम् एकवारे रोगिणे देयं or रोगिणा पेयं or निगरणीयं, भेषजमात्रा, औषधमात्रा, रोगियोग्य औषधभागः, देयं, पेयं, पानं; 'a small dose of medicine,' औषधस्य अल्पभागः.

To dose, *v. a.* रोगिणा निगरणीयम् औषधभागं दा, (c. 3. ददाति, दातुं), भेषजं दा, भिषज् (nom. भिषज्यति -ज्यितुं), औषधीकृ.

Dossil, *s.* (Pledget of lint on a sore) विकेशिका.

Dot, *s.* बिन्दुः *m.*, शून्यं, विप्रुट् *f.* (ष्) or विप्रुद्, खं, कणः, अङ्कः.

To dot, *v. a.* बिन्दुना अङ्क् (c. 10. अङ्कयति -यितुं) or चिह्न् (c. 10. चिह्नयति -यितुं).

Dotage, *s.* बालिशबुद्धित्वं, बालिशता, बालिश्यं, बुद्धिनाशः, बुद्धिवैकल्यं, हतबुद्धित्वं, बुद्धिक्षीणता, ज्ञानहानिः *f.*, बुद्धिलोपः, दौर्बल्यं, जीर्णावस्था.—(Excessive fondness) अत्यन्तानुरागः, अत्यन्तप्रेम *n.* (न्).

Dotal, *a.* यौतुकसम्बन्धी -न्धिनी -न्धि (न्), औद्वाहिकः -की -कं, शौल्कः -ल्की -ल्कं, शौल्किकः -की -कं, स्त्रीधनविषयः -या -यं.

Dotard, *s.* बालिशमतिः *m.*, जरातुरः, हतबुद्धिः *m.*, क्षीणबुद्धिः *m.*, बालिशः, अतिवृद्धः.

To dote, *v. n.* (Be silly through age) अतिवृद्धत्वाद् बालिशबुद्धिः -द्धिः -द्धि भू or मुह् (c. 4. मुह्यति, मोहितुं).—(Love to excess)

अत्यनुरागवान् -वती -वत् or अत्यन्तानुरक्तः -क्ता -क्तं भू or अस्; 'I dote upon her,' तया अत्यनुरागवान् अस्मि.

Doting, *a.* अत्यनुरागवान् -वती -वत् (त्), अत्यनुरक्तः -क्ता -क्तं.

Dotingly, *adv.* अत्यनुरागेण, अत्यनुरागपूर्व्वं, सात्यनुरागं, सातिस्नेहं.

Dotted, *p. p.* चिह्नितः -ता -तं, अङ्कितः -ता -तं, चित्रितः -ता -तं.

Double, *a.* द्विगुणः -णा -णं, द्वैधः -धी -धं, द्विकः -का -कं, द्विविधः -धा -धं, द्विप्रकारः -रा -रं, द्विगुणसंख्यः -ख्या -ख्यं, द्विगुणपरिमाणः -णा -णं, उभयः -ये *sing.* and *pl.* only, द्वि in comp., as, 'having double leaves,' द्विपर्णः -र्णी -र्णं; 'having a double row of teeth,' उभयतोदन् -दती -दत् (त्) or द्विदन्; 'for a double object,' उभयार्थं.—(Deceitful) विजिह्मः -ह्मा -ह्मं, अनृजुः -जुः -जु, वञ्चकः -का -कं.

Double, *s.* (Twice the quantity) द्विगुणं, द्वैधं, द्विकं, द्विस्, द्विकृत्वस्.—(Trick) छलं, कपटः -टं, उपायः, माया, व्यपदेशः.—(A turn) विपरिवर्त्तनं.

To double, *v. a.* द्विगुणीकृ, द्विगुण (nom. द्विगुणयति -यितुं), गुणीकृ.—(Fold) पुटीकृ, पुट (nom. पुटयति -यितुं); 'to double a cape,' अन्तरीपं परितो नौकया वह् in pass. (उह्यते); 'to double the fist,' मुष्टिं बन्ध् (c. 9. बध्नाति, बन्द्धुं).

To double, *v. n.* द्विगुणीभू.—(Turn in running) विपरिवृत् (c. 1. -वर्त्तते -र्त्तितुं).—(Play tricks) मायां कृ, कुहकं कृ, कपटं कृ, व्यपदिश् (c. 6. -दिशति -देष्टुं).

Doubled, *p. p.* द्विगुणितः -ता -तं, द्विगुणीकृतः -ता -तं, गुणीकृतः -ता -तं. (Folded) पुटितः -ता -तं, पुटीकृतः -ता -तं.

Double-dealer, *s.* द्विव्यापारी *m.* (न्), द्विव्यवहारी *m.* (न्), उभयविधः, द्विकर्म्मी *m.* (न्), मायी *m.* (न्), कपटी *m.* (न्), कापटिकः, असरलः.

Double-dealing, *s.* द्विव्यापारः, द्विव्यवहारित्वं, कपटः, छलं, माया, असारल्यं, शठता, व्याजः, वैदग्ध्यं.

Double-dyed, *p. p.* द्विरञ्जितः -ता -तं, द्विरक्तः -क्ता -क्तं, द्विकषायितः -ता -तं.

Double-edged, *a.* द्विधारः -रा -रं, उभयतस् तीक्ष्णः -क्ष्णा -क्ष्णं.

Double-faced, *a.* द्विमुखः -खी -खं, द्विवदनः -नी -नं, उभयतोमुखः -खी -खं.

Double-formed, *a.* द्विरूपः -पी -पं, द्व्याकारः -रा -रं, द्विप्रकारः -रा -रं.

Double-headed, *a.* द्विशीर्षकः -का -कं, द्विशिराः -राः -रः (स्), द्विमूर्द्धः -र्द्धी -र्द्धं.

Double-meaning, *s.* द्व्यर्थः, सन्दिग्धार्थः, द्विरूपः, उपादानं.

Double-minded, *a.* द्विमनस्कः -स्का -स्कं, द्विमनाः -नाः -नः (स्).

Double-natured, *a.* द्विभावः -वा -वं, द्विधातुः -तुः -तु.

Double-tongued, *a.* द्विजिह्वः -ह्वा -ह्वं, द्विरसनः -ना -नं, मिथ्यावादी -दिनी -दि (न्) or असत्यवादी, अनृतवाक् *m. f. n.*

Doubleness, *s.* द्वैगुण्यं, द्वित्वं, द्वैतं, द्वैविध्यं, उभयत्वं.

Doubler, *s.* द्विगुणकारी *m.* (न्), द्विगुणकृत्, द्विविधकर्त्ता *m.* (र्त्तृ).

Doublet, अन्तरीयं, उरोवस्त्रं, उरश्छदः, परिधानं, उरोरक्षणी.

Doubloon, *s.* विदेशीयस्वर्णमुद्राविशेषः.

Doubly, *adv.* उभयतस्, उभयथा, द्विधा, द्विगुणं, द्विविधं.

To doubt, *v. n.* शङ्क् (c. 1. शङ्कते -ङ्कितुं), अभिशङ्क्, आशङ्क्, विशङ्क्, परिशङ्क्, सन्दिह् (c. 2. -देग्धि -ग्धुं), विक्लृप् (c. 1. -कल्पते -ल्पितुं c. 10. -कल्पयति -यितुं), संशी (c. 2. -शेते -शयितुं), विचर् in caus. (-चारयति -यितुं), मनसा दोल (nom. दोलायते -यितुं) or आन्दोल (आन्दोलयति -यितुं), सन्देहं कृ.

To doubt, *v. a.* शङ्क् (c. 1. शङ्कते -ङ्कितुं), परिशङ्क्, न विश्वस् (c. 2. -श्वसिति -तुं), न प्रती (c. 2. प्रत्येति -तुं rt. इ), उद्विज् (c. 6. -विजते -जितुं).

Doubt, *s.* सन्देहः, संशयः, शङ्का, आशङ्का, विकल्पः, विकल्पितं, वितर्कः, विशयः, द्वैधं, विचिकित्सा, द्वापरः.—(Uncertainty of mind) चित्त-

विक्षेपः, चित्तान्दोलनं, चित्तविभ्रमः, व्यस्तता, विप्रतिपत्तिः *f.*, अस्थैर्य्यं, अनिर्णयः.—(Suspicion, distrust, fear) शङ्का, अविश्वासः, अप्रत्ययः, भयं.—(Difficulty) शल्यं, दुर्गं, कृच्छ्रं, कष्टं, विषमं, बाधा.—(Objection) बाधः -धकं, उद्ग्राहः; 'case of doubt,' सन्देहपदं; 'cause of doubt,' शङ्कास्पदं; 'in doubt,' दोलायमानः -ना -नं, संशयापन्नः -न्ना -न्नं, शङ्कान्वितः -ता -तं, सशङ्कः -ङ्का -ङ्कं; 'without doubt,' असंशयं.

DOUBTED, *p. p.* सन्दिग्धः -ग्धा -ग्धं, संशयितः -ता -तं, शङ्कितः -ता -तं.

DOUBTER, *s.* संशयिता *m.* (तृ), संशयात्मा *m.* (न्), सन्दिग्धमतिः *m.*, संशयालुः *m.*, सन्देग्धा *m.* (ग्धृ), सन्देहकर्त्ता *m.* (र्त्तृ); संशयकृत्.

DOUBTFUL, *a.* सन्दिग्धः -ग्धा -ग्धं, सांशयिकः -की -कं, शङ्कनीयः -या -यं, सशङ्कः -ङ्का -ङ्कं, ससंशयः -या -यं, संशयापन्नः -न्ना -न्नं, शङ्कान्वितः -ता -तं, संशयस्थः -स्था -स्थं, संशयात्मकः -का -कं, शङ्कामयः -यी -यं, सन्दिहानः -ना -नं, वैकल्पिकः -की -कं, सविकल्पकः -का -कं, विशयी -यिनी -यि (न्).—(Ambiguous) सन्दिग्धार्थः -र्था -र्थं, अस्पष्टार्थः -र्था -र्थं.—(Questionable) आशङ्कनीयः -या -यं, वितर्क्यः -र्क्या -र्क्यं, मीमांस्यः -स्या -स्यं; 'to render doubtful,' सन्दिह् in caus. (-देहयति -यितुं).

DOUBTFULLY, *adv.* ससंशयं, सशङ्कं, सन्देहेन, शङ्कया, सविकल्पं, सवितर्कं.

DOUBTFULNESS, *s.* सन्दिग्धता, सांशयिकत्वं, ससंशयता, शङ्कनीयत्वं.

DOUBTINGLY, *adv.* साशङ्कं, शङ्कापूर्व्वं, शङ्कया, अविश्वासेन, अप्रत्ययात्.

DOUBTLESS, *a.* असंशयः -या -यं, असन्दिग्धः -ग्धा -ग्धं, निःसन्देहः -हा -हं.

DOUBTLESS, DOUBTLESSLY, *adv.* असंशयं, निःसंशयं, निःसन्देहेन, संशयं विना, कः सन्देहः, सुनिश्चितं.

DOUCEUR, *s.* पारितोषिकं, उपप्रदानं, उपायनं, उत्कोचः.

DOUGH, *s.* गुरिङ्का, जलघटितः शक्तुः *m.*, जलसंसृष्टः शक्तुः, मर्द्दितशक्तुः, पिष्टकः, अपूप्यः.

DOUGHTY, *a.* वीरः -रा -रं, शूरः -रा -रं, विक्रान्तः -न्ता -न्तं, प्रशस्तः -स्ता -स्तं,

To DOUSE, *v. a.* जले मज्ज् in caus. (मज्जयति -यितुं) or निमज्ज् or निविश् in caus. (-वेशयति -यितुं).—(Put out) निर्वा in caus. (-वापयति -यितुं).

DOVE, *s.* कपोतः, कपोतिका, पारावतः, कलरवः, कलध्वनिः *m.*, कलकण्ठः.

DOVE-COT, DOVE-HOUSE, *s.* कपोतपालिका, विटङ्कः, कपोतागारः, पारावतालयः.

DOVE-TAIL, *s.* काष्ठसन्धिः *m.*, दारुसीवनं, काष्ठग्रन्थनं, कपोतपालाकारः काष्ठसन्धिः *m.*

DOWAGER, *s.* मृतभर्त्तृधनभागिनी विधवा, निर्नाथा, रण्डा, मृतभर्त्तृका.

DOWDY, *s.* (Woman) विरूपी -पिणी, दुर्वेशिनी, दुर्वसना, स्थूलरूपी.

DOWER, DOWRY, *s.* (Jointure) स्त्रीधनं, विधवाधनं, स्त्रीवृत्तिः *f.*, स्वामिदत्तं —(Wife's portion) यौतुकं, यौतकं, युतकं, शुल्कः, औद्वाहिकं, अध्यावाहनिकं.

DOWERED, *a.* यौतुकवती, शुल्किनी, यौतुकप्राप्ता, मृतभर्त्तृधनभागिनी.

DOWERLESS, *a.* यौतुकहीनः -ना -नं, शुल्कहीनः -ना -नं, निर्धनः -ना -नं.

DOWLAS, *s.* (Coarse cloth) स्थूलपट्टं, स्थूलशाटकः, वराशिः *m.*

DOWN *s.* (Soft feather) मृदुपक्षः, सुकुमारपक्षः, स्निग्धपर्णः, सुखस्पर्शः पर्णः.—(Fine hair) मृदुलोम *n.* (न्), स्निग्धलोम, सुकुमारलोम.—(Down of the body) अङ्गरुहं, तनुरुहं, लोम *n.* (न्), रोम *n.* (न्), अङ्कुरः.—(Down of plants) तृणलोम, तृणकेशः; 'down of the gourd,' अलाबूकटं.—(Poor hilly land for pasturing sheep) अविप्रचारयोग्यं पर्व्वतीयमरुस्थलं, तृणसपर्व्वतः, निर्व्वनपर्व्वतः.

DOWN, *prep.* अव, अधस्; 'thrown down,' अवपातितः -ता -तं, अधःपातितः -ता -तं, अवक्षिप्तः -प्ता -प्तं, अधःक्षिप्तः -प्ता -प्तं; 'put down,' अधःकृतः -ता -तं; 'fallen down,' अधःपतितः -ता -तं; 'gone down,' अधोगतः -ता -तं; 'laid down,' अवतारितः -ता -तं; 'hanging down,' अवलम्बमानः -ना -नं; 'to sit down,' उपविश् (c. 6. -विशति -वेष्टुं); 'down to,' पर्य्यन्तं, यावत् affixed, as, 'down to the present time,' अधुना यावत्.

DOWN, *adv.* अधस्, अधस्तात्, नीचैः, अधोऽधस् अधोभागं प्रति.—(Tending down) अवाक्, अवाचीनं, अवकटं.—(At the bottom) अधःस्थः -स्था -स्थं; 'ups and downs,' पातोत्पाताः *m. pl.*

DOWN-CAST, *a.* अवसन्नः -न्ना -न्नं, विषण्णः -ण्णा -ण्णं, विषण्णवदनः -ना -नं, अवनतः -ता -तं, नतमुखः -खी -खं, अधोमुखः -खी -खं, अधोवदनः -नी -नं, अवाङ्मुखः -खी -खं, अधोदृष्टिः -ष्टिः -ष्टि, दीनमुखः -खी -खं, विमुखः -खा -खं, दीनमनाः -नाः नः (स्), दीनचेतनः -ना -नं.

DOWNFALL, *s.* ध्वंसः, प्रध्वंसः, क्षयः, परिक्षयः, नाशः, विनाशः, अत्ययः, व्ययः, उच्छेदः, उत्पाटनं, अधःपतनं.

DOWNFALLEN, *a.* अधःपतितः -ता -तं, परिक्षीणः -णा -णं, ध्वंसितः -ता -तं.

DOWNHEARTED, *a.* विषण्णः -ण्णा -ण्णं, दीनमनाः -नाः -नः (स्) or उद्विग्नमनाः or दुर्मनाः, दीनमनस्कः -स्का -स्कं, दीनचेतनः -ना -नं. म्लानः -ना -नं, खिद्यमानः -ना -नं, उत्साहहीनः -ना -नं.

DOWNHILL, *s.* प्रवणभूमिः *f.*, पातुकभूमिः, उत्सङ्गः, स्थानं क्रमशोऽधोगम्यं.

DOWNLOOKED, *a.* अधोदृष्टिः -ष्टिः -ष्टि, अधोमुखः -खी -खं, अधोवदनः -नी -नं, अवाङ्मुखः -खी -खं, नम्रमुखः -खी -खं, नतमूर्द्धा -र्द्धा -र्द्ध (न्).

DOWNLYING, *s.* शयनकालः, शय्यागमनसमयः, विश्रामकालः.

DOWNLYING, *a.* प्राप्तप्रसवकाला, आसन्नप्रसववेदना, प्राप्तशयनकाला.

DOWNRIGHT, *adv.* (Straight down) अवक्रं, अजिह्मं, अकुटिलं, अविलोमं, अधोऽधस्, अवाक्.—(Plainly) व्यक्तं, सुव्यक्तं, भिन्नार्थं, स्पष्टं.—(Completely) सु or अति prefixed, सम्यक्, सर्व्वतस्, अखिलेन.

DOWNRIGHT, *a.* (Plain) स्पष्टः -ष्टा -ष्टं, व्यक्तः -क्ता -क्तं, सुस्पष्टः -ष्टा -ष्टं, सुव्यक्तः -क्ता -क्तं.—(Direct) अवक्रः -क्रा -क्रं, अजिह्मः -ह्मा -ह्मं, अकुटिलः -ला -लं.

DOWNSITTING, *s.* उपवेशः -शनं, समुपवेशनं, विश्रामः.

DOWNWARD, *a.* अधस्तनः -नी -नं, अधोगामी -मिनी -मि (न्), अवाङ् -वाची -वाक् (च्), अवाचीनः -ना -नं, अवकटः -टा -टं.—(Declivous) प्रवणः -णा -णं, पातुकः -की -कं.

DOWNWARD, DOWNWARDS, *adv.* अव prefixed, अधस्, अधोऽधस्, अधस्तात्, अवाक्, अवाचीनं, अवकटं; 'looking downwards,' अधोदृष्टिः *m. f.*; 'going downwards,' अधोगामी -मिनी -मि (न्).

DOWNY, *a.* (Covered with down or soft hair) मृदुलोमवान् -वती -वत् (त्), मृदुलोमा -मा -म (न्), स्निग्धपर्णः -र्णा -र्णं.—(Soft) सुखस्पर्शः -र्शा -र्शं, कोमलः -ला -लं, मृदुः -द्वी -दु, सुकुमारः -रा -रं.

DOWRY, *s.* यौतुकं, शुल्कः. *See* DOWER.

DOWSE, *s.* आस्फोटः -टनं, चपेटिका, तलप्रहारः, कराघातः, चपेटाघातः.

To DOZE, *v. n.* निद्रा (c. 2. -द्राति -तुं), स्वप् (c. 2. स्वपिति, स्वप्तुं), प्रस्वप्, निमील् (c. 1. -मीलति -लितुं), शी (c. 2. शेते, शयितुं), निद्रां कृ, अल्पनिद्रां कृ, ईषन्निद्रां कृ.

DOZEN, *s.* and *a.* द्वादश *m. f. n.* (न्), द्वादशकः -का -कं, द्वादशसंख्यकः -का -कं.

DOZER, *s.* निद्राणः, निद्रायमाणः, ईषन्निद्राकृत् *m.*, शायी *m.* (न्).

DOZINESS, *s.* निद्रा, निद्राशीलत्वं, शिशयिषा, निद्रालुत्वं, शयालुता.

DOZY, *a.* निद्रालुः -लुः -लु, शिशयिषुः -षुः -षु, स्वप्नशीलः -ला -लं, निद्राशीलः -ला -लं, सुषुप्सुः -प्सुः -प्सु, नैद्रः -द्री -द्रं, निद्रालसः -सा -सं.

DRAB, *s.* (Low woman) बन्धकी, कुलटा, वेश्या, भ्रष्टा, व्यभिचारिणी.—(Brown cloth) कपिशवस्त्रं.

DRAB, *a.* (Dun-coloured) कपिशः -शा -शं, कपिलः -ला -लं, पिङ्गलः -ला -लं.

DRACHM, DRACHMA, s. (Silver coin) रूप्यमुद्राविशेषः.—(Eighth part of a particular weight) विशेषपरिमाणस्य पादार्द्धं.

DRAFF, s. उच्छिष्टं, शेषं, भुक्तावशेषं, शेषान्नं, मलं, खलं, किट्टं, असारः.

DRAFFISH, DRAFFY, a. मलिनः -ना -नं, खली-लिनी-लि(न्), असारः -रा -रं.

DRAFT, s. (Order for money) हुण्डिका, हुण्डिकापत्रं. *See* DRAUGHT.

To **DRAG**, v. a. कृष् (c. 1. कर्षति c. 6. कृषति, क्रष्टुं, कर्ष्टुं), आकृष्, हृ (c. 1. हरति -ते, हर्त्तुं).—(Drag off, drag away) अपकृष्, अवकृष्, व्यपकृष्, अपहृ, व्यपहृ.—(Drag out) उत्कृष्, निष्कृष्, उद्धृ, निर्हृ, उत्पट् in caus. (-पाटयति -यितुं).

To **DRAG**, v. n. कृष् in pass. (कृष्यते), आकृष्.—(Proceed slowly) विलम्ब् (c. 1. -लम्बते -म्बितुं).

DRAG, s. (Instrument for dragging) आकर्षणी, आकर्षणयन्त्रं.—(Car) रथः, क्रीडारथः, चक्रयानं.

DRAGGED, p. p. कृष्टः -ष्टा -ष्टं, आकृष्टः -ष्टा -ष्टं, अपकृष्टः -ष्टा -ष्टं, हृतः -ता -तं.

To **DRAGGLE**, v. a. पङ्केन दुष् in caus. (दूषयति -यितुं), कर्द्दमे लुठ् in caus. (लोठयति -यितुं), कर्द्दमान्तरेण कृष् (c. 1. कर्षति, क्रष्टुं).

To **DRAGGLE**, v. n. कर्द्दमे लुठ् (c. 6. लुठति -ठितुं), कर्द्दमे लोठनाद् मलिनीभू, पङ्कान्तरेण कृष् in pass. (कृष्यते).

DRAGGLE-TAIL, s. अपरिष्कृता स्त्री, अविनीतवेशिनी.

DRAG-NET, s. आकर्षकजालं, आकर्षणी, नदीतले आकर्षणयोग्यं जालं.

DRAGON, s. नागः, व्यालः, अहिः m., भुजङ्गमः, पन्नगः, पक्षयुक्तः सर्पः.

DRAGON-LIKE, a. नागरूपः -पी -पं, व्यालवद् उग्रस्वभावः -वा -वं.

DRAGOON, s. अश्वारूढः सैन्यः, अश्वारोही योद्धा m. (द्धृ), सादी m. (न्).

To **DRAGOON**, v. a. देशम् अश्वारूढसैन्येन विप्लुतं कृ.

DRAIN, s. जलनिर्गमः, जलमार्गः, नालः, प्रणालः, नाली, प्रणाली, परीवाहः, परिवाहः, सारणिः f. -णी, जलोच्छ्वासः, उदकगमनमार्गः, जलवाहनी, कर्द्दमाटकः, सङ्कुरः, भ्रमः, वाहसः; 'a village drain,' ग्रामसङ्कुरः.

To **DRAIN**, v. a. (Draw off gradually) क्रमशो निःसृ in caus. (-सारयति -यितुं) or निर्गम् in caus. (-गमयति -यितुं) or निष्कृष् (c. 1, -कर्षति -क्रष्टुं) or आकृष् or अपवह् (c. 1. -वहति -वोढुं) or परिवह् or स्रु in caus. (स्रावयति -यितुं) or निःस्रु or उत्क्षिप् (c. 6. -क्षिपति -क्षेप्तुं).—(Dry up, exhaust) शुष् in caus. (शोषयति -यितुं), उच्छुष्, विशुष्, संशुष्, शुष्कीकृ.—(Drink up) आपा (c. 1. -पिबति -पातुं), प्रपा, परिपा.

DRAINED, p. p. शोषितः -ता -तं, उच्छोषितः -ता -तं, परिवाहितः -ता -तं, आपीतः -ता -तं, शुष्कीकृतः -ता -तं, रेचितः -ता -तं, नीरसीकृतः -ता -तं.

DRAKE, s. हंसः, कलहंसः, राजहंसः, कादम्बः, वरटः, कामिकः.

DRAM, s. (A small quantity) अल्पिका, अल्पभागः.—(A draught of spirituous liquor) सुरापानं, शुण्डामात्रा, सुरामात्रा.—(Drink to give courage) वीरपाणं.—(Spirituous liquor) शुण्डा, शीधुः m. -धु n. सुरा, वारुणी, मदिरा, हाला; 'dram-shop,' शुण्डापानं; 'keeper of one,' शौण्डिकः -की f.

DRAM-DRINKER, s. सुरापः -पी f., शुण्डापायी -यिनी f. (न्), शीधुपः -पी.

DRAMA, s. नाटकः, प्रकरणं, रूपं -पकं, यात्रा. The following are various kinds: भाणः, व्यायोगः, समवाकारः, डिमः, ईहामृगः, अङ्कः, वीथी, प्रहसनं.—(Minor drama) उपरूपकं. The following are various kinds: नाटिका, त्रोटकं, गोष्ठी, सट्टकं, नाट्यरासकः, प्रस्थानं, उल्लाप्यः, काव्यं, प्रेङ्खणं, रासकं, संलापकं, श्रीगदितं, शिल्पकं, विलासिका, लासिका, दुर्मल्लिका, प्रकरणिका, हल्लीशं, भाणिका.—(The science or art of acting) नाट्यं, नटचर्य्या.

DRAMATIC, DRAMATICAL, a. नाटकीयः -या -यं, नाटकविषयः -या -यं, काव्यशास्त्रीयः -या -यं, यात्रिकः -की -कं; 'dramatic language,' नाट्योक्तिः f.; 'dramatic rules,' नाट्यधर्म्मिकः; 'dramatic representation,' नटचर्य्या.

DRAMATICALLY, adv. नाट्यधर्म्मानुसारात्, नाटकरूपेण, काव्यशास्त्रानुसारेण.

DRAMATIS-PERSONÆ, s. नटनामानि n. pl., नटानां नामावलिः f.

DRAMATIST, s. नाटकरचकः, नाटककर्त्ता m. (र्त्तृ), काव्यशास्त्रज्ञः, रूपकनिबन्धा m. (न्धृ).

DRAP, s. वस्त्रं, वसनं, पटः, चेलः -लं, चैलं, शाटकः -कं.

DRAPER, s. वस्त्रविक्रेता m. (तृ), पटविक्रयी m. (न्), वस्त्रवाणिज्यकारी m. (न्).

DRAPERY, s. (The trade) वस्त्रादिक्रयविक्रयः, वस्त्रकर्म्म n. (न्), वस्त्रवाणिज्यं.—(Cloth) वस्त्रं, पटः, वासः n. (स्).—(Dress of a picture, &c.) प्रच्छदपटः, परिच्छदः, वसनं, अम्बरं.

DRAUGHT, s. (Act of drinking) पानं.—(Quantity drunk at once) पीतं, पेयं, पानं, एकपानं; 'a draught of milk,' पयःपानं.—(Abstract) सङ्ग्रहः, सारः, वस्तु, वस्तुमात्रं.—(Delineation, sketch) आलेख्यं, आलेखनं, पाण्डुलेख्यं, चित्रारम्भः, वस्तुमात्रं.—(Picture drawn, resemblance) चित्रं, उपमा -मानं, प्रतिमानं, प्रतिमूर्त्तिः f.—(Detachment from the main army) महासैन्यमध्याद् आनीतः सैन्यगुल्मः.—(Sewer, drain) सङ्कुरः, कर्द्दमाटकः.—(Draught of a ship) यत् जलपरिमाणं नावं प्लावयति.—(Order for money), *See* DRAFT. (Act of drawing) आकर्षणं, आकृष्टिः f.; 'a draught ox,' शाकटः, प्रासङ्ग्यः, प्राग्भारः.

DRAUGHT-BOARD, s. अष्टापदं, शारिफलं -लकं, नयपीठी, पञ्चनी, पञ्चमी, पञ्चारी.

DRAUGHT-HORSE, s. शाकटः -टिकः -टीनः, रथ्यः, प्रवहणवाजी m. (न्).

DRAUGHTS, s. अष्टापदक्रीडा, शारिक्रीडा; 'a piece at draughts,' शारिः m., शारः, सारिः m., सारः, सारिका, ऋतुपुत्रकः, खेलनी -लिनी, नयः; 'moving a piece at draughts,' परिणायः, परीणायः.

DRAUGHTSMAN, s. लेखकः, आलेख्यकृत्, चित्रकारः, चित्रकरः.

To **DRAW**, v. a. (Pull along) कृष् (c. 1. कर्षति c. 6. कृषति -ते, क्रष्टुं, कर्ष्टुं), आकृष्, समाकृष्, परिकृष्, प्रतिकृष्, सङ्कृष्.—(Drag forcibly) हृ (c. 1. हरति, हर्त्तुं).—(Attract) आकृष्, समाकृष्, प्रतिकृष्, समुपकृष्; अभिप्रणी (c. 1. -णयति -णेतुं); 'she draws the eyes of all,' सर्व्वचक्षूंषि मुष्णाति.—(Lead, induce) आनी, अनुनी.—(Win conciliate) आराध् (c. 10. -राधयति -यितुं), अभिराध्, अनुरञ्ज् (c. 10. -रञ्जयति -यितुं).—(Receive, take) ग्रह् (c. 9. गृह्णाति, ग्रहीतुं), लभ् (c. 1. लभते, लब्धुं), उपलभ्, आदा, उपादा.—(Cause liquid to flow) स्रु in caus. (स्रावयति -यितुं) or मुच् (c. 6. मुञ्चति, मोक्तुं c. 10. मोचयति -यितुं) or मोक्ष् (c. 10. मोक्षयति -यितुं) or अवसिच् (c.6. -सिञ्चति -सेक्तुं); 'draw blood,' रक्तं स्रु.—(Close curtains) तिरस्करिणीं or यवनिकां संवृ (c. 5. -वृणोति -वृणुते -वरितुं -रीतुं) or सम्पुटीकृ.—(Unclose curtains) तिरस्करिणीं विवृ or विततीकृ.—(Represent, form a picture) लिख् (c. 6. लिखति, लेखितुं), आलिख्, अभिलिख्; चित्र् (c. 10. चित्रयति -यितुं).—(Describe) वर्ण् (c. 10. वर्णयति -यितुं).—(Unsheath a sword) खड्गं विकोष् (nom. -कोषयति -यितुं) or कोषाद् निःसृ in caus. (-सारयति -यितुं) or विकोषीकृ.—(Inhale) श्वस् (c. 2. श्वसिति -तुं), आश्वस्, प्राण् (c. 2. प्राणिति -तुं, rt. अन् with प्र).—(Suck the breast) स्तनं पा (c. 1. पिबति, पातुं), धे (c. 1. धयति, धातुं).—(Extract) निष्कृष्, उत्कृष्, निर्हृ.—(Extend, lengthen) तन् (c. 8. तनोति -नितुं), विस्तृ in caus. (-स्तारयति -यितुं), द्राघ् nom. (द्राघयति -यितुं).—(Utter drawlingly) दीर्घोच्चारणं कृ.—(Bend a bow) धनुर् विस्फुर् in caus. (-स्फारयति

-यितुं) or आयम् (c. 1. -यच्छति -यन्तुं).—(Derive) आनी, निष्कृष्, अपवह् (c. 1. -वहति -वोढुं).—(Cause to come out) निःसृ in caus. (-सारयति -यितुं), निर्गम् in caus. (-गमयति -यितुं), उद्भू in caus. (-भावयति -यितुं).—(Draw water) जलम् उत्तुल् (c. 10. -तोलयति -यितुं).

To DRAW-AWAY, *v. a.* अपकृष्, अपाकृष्, व्यपकृष्, व्यपाकृष्, अवकृष्, विकृष्, अपनी (c. 1. -नयति -नेतुं), व्यपनी, अपहृ (c. 1. -हरति -हर्तुं).

To DRAW-BACK, *v. a.* प्रतिकृष्, प्रत्यादा, प्रत्याहृ (c. 1. -हरति -हर्तुं), प्रतिसंहृ, प्रतिनी (c. 1. -नयति -नेतुं), प्रत्यानी.

To DRAW-DOWN, *v. a.* (Bring on, produce) आवह् (c. 1. -वहति -वोढुं), उत्पद् in caus. (-पादयति -यितुं), जन् (c. 10. जनयति -यितुं).

To DRAW-IN, *v. a.* संहृ (c. 1. -हरति -हर्तुं), प्रतिसंहृ, प्रत्याहृ, उपसंहृ.

To DRAW-OFF, *v. a.* अपकृष्, अपाकृष्, व्यपकृष्, अवकृष्, विकृष्, अपहृ, व्यपहृ, अपनी, व्यपनी, विनी.—(Cause liquid to flow) स्रु in caus. (स्रावयति -यितुं), मुच् (c. 6. मुञ्चति, मोक्तुं).

To DRAW-ON, *v. a.* आकृष्, समाकृष्, समुपकृष्, आनी, अभिप्रणी.—(Bring on, cause) आवह् (c. 1. -वहति -वोढुं), उत्पद् in caus. (-पादयति -यितुं).

To DRAW-OVER, *v. a.* (Induce) अनुनी, आकृष्, प्रोत्सह् in caus. (-साहयति -यितुं), प्रयुज् in caus. (-योजयति -यितुं).

To DRAW-OUT, *v. a.* (Extract) निष्कृष्, उत्कृष्, आकृष्, निर्हृ, उद्धृ, उद्ग्रह् (c. 9. -गृह्णाति -ग्रहीतुं), निर्दुह् (c. 2. -दोग्धि -ग्धुं).—(Extend, lengthen) तन् (c. 8. तनोति -नितुं), वितन्, व्यातन्, विततीकृ, विस्तृ in caus. (-स्तारयति -यितुं), दीर्घीकृ, द्राघ् (nom. द्राघयति -यितुं).—(Beat out metal) उद्घर्षणं कृ.—(Array an army) सैन्यं व्यूह् (c. 1. -ऊहते -हितुं), व्यूहेन रच् (c. 10. रचयति -यितुं), पंक्तिक्रमेण रच्.

To DRAW-TOGETHER, *v. a.* समाहृ, संहृ, समूह्, एकीकृ, समानी, समूह् (c. 1. ऊहते -हितुं).

To DRAW-UP, *v. a.* (Lift, raise) उत्तुल् (c. 10. -तोलयति -यितुं), उद्धृ, उत्कृष्, उद्वह् (c. 1. -वहति -वोढुं).—(Compose in writing) लिख् (c. 6. लिखति, लेखितुं), रच् (c. 10. रचयति -यितुं), विरच्, निबन्ध् (c. 9. -बध्नाति -बन्द्धुं).

To DRAW, *v. n.* (As a beast of burden) कृष् (c. 1. कर्षति c. 6. कृषति -ते, क्रष्टुं).—(As a weight) कृष्, आकृष्.—(Contract) सङ्कुच् in pass. (-कुच्यते), सङ्कोचम् इ (c. 2. एति -तुं), संहृ in pass. (-ह्रियते), संक्षिप् in pass. (-क्षिप्यते).—(Cause suppuration) पूयं or पूयत्वं or पाकं जन् in caus. (जनयति -यितुं) or उत्पद् in caus. (-पादयति -यितुं).

To DRAW-BACK, DRAW-OFF, *v. n.* अपक्रम् (c. 1. -क्रामति -क्रमितुं), व्यपक्रम्, अपसृ (c. 1. -सरति -सर्तुं), अपया (c. 2. -याति -तुं), निवृत् (c. 1. -वर्त्तते -र्त्तितुं), प्रतिनिवृत्, पार्श्वे परिवृत्, परावृत्, पलाय् (c. 1. पलायते -यितुं), अवस्था (c. 1. -तिष्ठति -स्थातुं).

To DRAW-NEAR, DRAW-ON, *v. n.* (Approach) उपस्था (c. 1. -तिष्ठति -स्थातुं), उपवृत् (c. 1. -वर्त्तते -र्त्तितुं), आगम् (c. 1. -गच्छति -गन्तुं), उपागम्, आया (c. 2. -याति -तुं).

DRAWBACK, *s.* (Deduction) उद्धारः, उद्धृतभागः, भागप्रतिदानं.—(Loss of advantage) हानिः *f.*, क्षतिः *f.*, अपचयः, अपचितिः *f.*, अपायः.

DRAW-BRIDGE, *s.* जङ्गमसेतुः *m.*, चलसेतुः *m.*, लघुसेतुः यो विक्रमम् उत्तोलयितुं वा शक्यते.

DRAWER, *s.* कर्षकः, आकर्षकः.—(A sliding case) चलकोष्ठः, चलकोष्ठकं, सम्पुटः -टकः, भाजनं.

DRAWERS, *s. pl.* (For the legs) कञ्चुकः, शाटकः, कटिवस्त्रं, कटीपटः, जङ्घापरिधानं.

DRAWING, *s.* (Act of pulling) कर्षः -र्षणं, कृष्टिः *f.*, आकर्षः -र्षणं, आकृष्टिः *f.*; 'drawing of water,' जलोत्तोलनं.—(Representation) चित्रं, चित्रलेखा -लिखनं, चित्रफलकः, आलेख्यं, वर्त्तिकारेखा, प्रतिमानं, प्रतिमा, प्रतिरूपं.—(Art of drawing) चित्रकर्म्म *n.* (न्), चित्रविद्या.

DRAWING-MASTER, *s.* चित्रकर्म्मविद् *m.* चित्रविद्योपदेशकः, चित्रलिखनविद्याज्ञः.

DRAWING-ROOM, *s.* दर्शनशाला, दर्शनगृहं, उपवेशनशाला.—(Of a king) राजदर्शनं.

To DRAWL, *v. n.* दीर्घोच्चारणेन वद् (c. 1. वदति -दितुं), दीर्घोदाहरणं कृ, मन्दं मन्दं वाक्यानि उच्चर् in caus. (-चारयति -यितुं).

DRAWLING, *s.* दीर्घोच्चारणं, दीर्घोदाहरणं, मन्दोच्चारणं, दीर्घव्याहरणं.

DRAWN, *p. p.* (Pulled) कर्षितः -ता -तं, कृष्टः -ष्टा -ष्टं, आकृष्टः -ष्टा -ष्टं.—(Delineated) आलिखितः -ता -तं, अभिलिखितः -ता -तं, चित्रितः -ता -तं.—(Unsheathed) विकोषः -षा -षं, विकोषीकृतः -ता -तं, उल्लसितः -ता -तं, कोषान्निःसारितः -ता -तं.—(Drawn up, lifted) उत्तोलितः -ता -तं, उद्वाहितः -ता -तं, उद्धृतः -ता -तं, समुद्धृतः -ता -तं.—(Drawn up in array) व्यूढः -ढा -ढं, विन्यस्तः -स्ता -स्तं, व्यूहेन रचितः -ता -तं, श्रेणीबद्धः -द्धा -द्धं.—(Equal) समानः -ना -नं, तुल्यबलः -ला -लं; 'a cart drawn by a horse,' अश्वयुक्तः or अश्वप्रयुक्तः शकटः; 'a chariot drawn by white horses,' श्वेतहयैर् युक्तो रथः.

DRAW-WELL, *s.* गम्भीरकूपः, जलकूपी, उदकाधारः.

DRAY, *s.* शकटः -टं, गन्त्री, गन्त्रीरथः, चक्रयानं, चातुरं, अहागर्य.

DRAY-HORSE, *s.* शाकटः, शाकटिकवाजी *m.* (न्), शकटाश्वः.

DRAY-MAN, *s.* शकटवाहकः, शाकटिकः, गन्त्रीवाहकः, चातुरिकः.

DREAD, *s.* त्रासः, सन्त्रासः, साध्वसं, भयं, भीतिः *f.*, भीष्मं, भीषणं.

DREAD, *a.* त्रासकरः -री -रं, भीषणः -णा -णं, भीमः -मा -मं.

To DREAD, *v. a.* and *n.* भी (c. 3. बिभेति, भेतुं) with abl. or gen. c. So also प्रभी, विभी, त्रस् (c. 4. त्रस्यति, त्रसितुं), वित्रस्, उद्विज् (c. 6. -विजते -जितुं).

DREADFUL, *a.* भयङ्करः -री -रं, भयानकः -का -कं, दारुणः -णा -णं, घोरः -रा -रं, भीमः -मा -मं, भयावहः -हा -हं, त्रासकरः -रा -रं, उग्रः -ग्रा -ग्रं, भीष्मयः -यी -यं, भैरवः -वा -वं, सुभैरवः -वा -वं, रौद्रः -द्री -द्रं, घोरदर्शनः -ना -नं, उद्वेजनीयः -या -यं.

DREADFULLY, *adv.* दारुणं, घोरं, भयानकं, उग्रं, भैरवं, रौद्रं.

DREADFULNESS, *s.* घोरत्वं, दारुणता, दारुण्यं, उग्रत्वं, रौद्रता.

DREADLESS, *a.* त्रासहीनः -ना -नं, निःसाध्वसः -सा -सं, निर्भयः -या -यं.

DREAM, *s.* स्वप्नः, स्वप्नदर्शनं, स्वप्नसृष्टिः *f.*, स्वप्नप्रपञ्चः, सुप्तज्ञानं, सुप्तविज्ञानं, स्वापः, दर्शनं, स्वप्नकल्पितं, निद्रा, संवेशः.—(Vain fancy) मृषार्थकं, वृथावासना, अनर्थकवासना, मिथ्यावासना, असम्भवकल्पना, दुर्वासना, अनर्थकचिन्ता, आभासः, अनर्थकभावना; 'like a dream,' स्वप्नवत्.

To DREAM, *v. n.* (See images in sleep) स्वप्नं दृश् (c. 1. पश्यति, द्रष्टुं), स्वप्न (nom. स्वप्नायते), उत्स्वप्न, स्वप्नकल्पितं दृश्.—(Imagine, think) चिन्त् (c. 10. चिन्तयति -यितुं), भू in caus. (भावयति -यितुं), मनसि or मनसा क्लृप् (c. 10. कल्पयति -यितुं).—(Think idly) अनर्थकचिन्तां कृ, वृथावासनां कृ, असम्भवकल्पनां कृ.

To DREAM, *v. a.* (See in a dream) स्वप्ने दृश् (c. 1. पश्यति, द्रष्टुं).

DREAMER, *s.* स्वप्नदर्शकः.—(A fanciful man) वृथावासनाकारी *m.* (न्), दुर्वासनाकृत्, अनर्थकचिन्ताकरः, असम्भवकल्पयिता *m.* (तृ).

DREAMY, *a.* स्वप्नवान् -वती -वत् (त्), स्वप्नमयः -यी -यं.

DREARINESS, *s.* शून्यता, निर्जनत्वं, निर्मनुष्यता, निरानन्दता, घोरता.

DREARY, DREAR, *a.* (Uninhabited, gloomy, wild) निर्जनः -ना -नं,

निर्भेनुषः -षा -षं, शून्यः -न्या -न्यं, तमस्वी -स्विनी -स्वि (न्), तामसः -सी -सं, निष्प्रभः -भा -भं, आकुलः -ली -लं, आरण्यकः -का -कं.—(Joyless) निरानन्दः -न्दा -न्दं.

DREDGE, *s.* (Drag-net) आकर्षणजालं, आकर्षणी, आकर्षणयन्त्रं.

To DREDGE, *v. a.* (Catch with a dredge) आकृष् (c. 1. -कर्षति -क्रष्टुं).—(Scatter flour on meat when roasting) पच्यमानमांसे चूर्णं क्षिप् (c. 6. क्षिपति, क्षेप्तुं).

DREGGISH, DREGGY, *a.* मलिनः -ना -नं, समलः -ला -लं, खली -लिनी -लि (न्).

DREGS, *s.* मलं, खलं, किट्टं, उच्छिष्टं, शेषं, कलङ्कः, अमेध्यं, अवस्करः, अपस्करः, कल्कं, असारः, विनीयः.

To DRENCH, *v. a.* क्लिद् in caus. (क्लेदयति -यितुं), सिच् (c. 6. सिञ्चति सेक्तुं), समुक्ष् (c. 1. -उक्षति -क्षितुं), अभ्युक्ष्, जलेन मु in caus. (प्लावयति -यितुं), समाप्लु.

DRENCH, *s.* (A draught) पानं, पेयं.—(Medicine for horses, &c.) अश्वादिना निगरणीयम् औषधं.

DRENCHED, *p. p.* सिक्तः -क्ता -क्तं, समाप्लुतः -ता -तं, प्रक्लिन्नः -न्ना -न्नं.

DRESS, *s.* वेशः, वेषः, वस्त्रं, वासः *n.* (स्), वसनं, परिधानं, भरणं, आभरणं, परिच्छदः, अम्बरं, भूषणं, विभूषणं, अलङ्कारः, प्रसाधनं, आच्छादनं, प्रतिकर्म्म *n.* (न्), सज्जा, संस्कारः, नेपथ्यं, आकल्पः.

To DRESS, *v. a.* (Clothe) वेष्ट् (c. 1. वेष्टते -ष्टितुं), परिवेष्ट्, प्रवेष्ट्; आच्छद् (c. 10. -छादयति -यितुं), प्रवृ (c. 5. -वृणोति -वरितुं -रीतुं), संव्ये (c. 1. -व्ययति -व्यातुं), वस्त्र (nom. वस्त्रयति -यितुं), परिधा in caus. (-धापयति -यितुं), प्रसाध् in caus. (-साधयति -यितुं), वस् in caus. (वासयति -यितुं), विवस्, प्रतिवस्.—(Clothe one's self) वस् (c. 2. वस्ते, वसितुं), प्रवस्, विवस्, परिधा (c. 3. -धत्ते -धातुं), वस्त्राणि परिधा or आच्छद् or आमुच् (c. 6. -मुञ्चति -मोक्तुं).—(Adorn) भूष् (c. 1. भूषति -षितुं c. 10. भूषयति -यितुं); विभूष्, परिभूष्, अलङ्कृ, समलङ्कृ, परिष्कृ.—(Prepare) कॢप् (c. 10. कल्पयति -यितुं), उपकॢप्; संस्कृ, उपस्कृ सज्जीकृ.—(Prepare food) अन्नं or मांसं पच् (c. 1. पचति, पक्तुं) or संस्कृ, or श्रा in caus. (श्रपयति -यितुं) or सिद्धीकृ or सन्धा (c. 3. -दधाति -धातुं).—(Dress the hair) केशान् रच् (c. 10. रचयति -यितुं).—(Trim, put in order) रच्, विरच्, विधा, सज्जीकृ, विन्यस् (c. 4. -अस्यति -असितुं).—(Curry a horse) अश्वलोम मृज् (c. 2. मार्ष्टि -र्ष्टुं) or सम्मृज्.—(Dress leather) चर्म्म परिष्कृ.—(Cleanse) शुध् in caus. (शोधयति -यितुं), प्रक्षल् (c. 10. -क्षालयति -यितुं), निर्णिज् (c. 3. -नेनेक्ति -नेक्तुं).—(Dress a wound) क्षतं परिष्कृ, औषधं प्रतिसृ in caus. (-सारयति -यितुं).

DRESSED, *p. p.* (Clothed) आच्छादितः -ता -तं, परिच्छन्नः -न्ना -न्नं, वेष्टितः -ता -तं, वस्त्रवेष्टितः -ता -तं, वासितः -ता -तं, सवेशः -शा -शं, सचेलः -ला -लं, सवासाः -साः -सः (स्), संवीतः -ता -तं, प्रावृतः -ता -तं, परिहितः -ता -तं, वेशी -शिनी -शि (न्), वस्त्रान्वितः -ता -तं, अनग्नः -ग्ना -ग्नं, अलङ्कृतः -ता -तं, भूषितः -ता -तं; 'well-dressed,' सुवेशः -शा -शं, सुवसनः -ना -नं, सुवः *m. f. n.* (स्); 'ill-dressed,' दुर्वासाः -साः -सः (स्); 'dressed as a herdsman,' गोपवेशः or गोपवासाः; 'dressed as a hermit,' मुनिवेशः; 'dressed in yellow,' पीताम्बरः -रा -रं.—(Cooked) पक्वः -क्वा -क्वं, सिद्धः -द्धा -द्धं, संस्कृतः -ता -तं, श्राणः -णा -णं, शृतः -ता -तं, श्रपितः -ता -तं, प्रणीतः -ता -तं, उपसम्पन्नः -न्ना -न्नं, राद्धः -द्धा -द्धं; 'dressed food,' सिद्धान्नं; 'half dressed,' आपक्वः -क्वा -क्वं; 'half-dressed grain,' पौलिः *m.*, अभ्युषः, अभ्यूषः, अभ्योषः.—(As a wound) प्रतिसारितः -ता -तं.

DRESSER, *s.* (One who dresses) आच्छादकः, प्रसाधकः -का, परिधानकृत्, कल्पकः.—(Of hair) केशरचकः.—(Table for dressing food) अन्नसंस्कारफलकं, पाकफलकः.

DRESSING, *s.* (Putting on clothes) वस्त्राच्छादनं, वस्त्रपरिधानं, अङ्गसंस्कारः, कल्पना, वस्त्रमाल्यादिविन्यासः.—(Of food) अन्नसंस्कारः, पाकः, पाकनिष्पत्तिः *f.*—(Of a wound) प्रतिसारणं, लेपः, प्रलेपः, विलेपः, उपदेहः, उपनाहः.—(Chastisement) शास्तिः *f.*, दण्डनं, वेत्राघातः.

DRESSING-GOWN, *s.* अङ्गसंस्कारकाले भृतो लघुप्रावारः.

DRESSING-ROOM, *s.* वस्त्रपरिधानशाला, आच्छादनशाला, विभूषणागारः, नेपथ्यं, अङ्गसंस्कारगृहं.

DRESS-MAKER, *s.* स्त्रीवेशकारिणी, स्त्रीवस्त्रकृत् *f.*, स्त्रीवेशनिर्म्माणोपजीविनी.

DRESSY, *a.* दर्शनीयः -या -यं, दर्शनीयवेशी -शिनी -शि (न्).

To DRIB, *v. a.* उद्धृ (c. 1. -हरति -हर्तुं), अवछिद् (c. 7. -छिनत्ति -छेत्तुं).

To DRIBBLE, *v. n.* लवशः or विन्दुक्रमेण स्यन्द् (c. 1. स्यन्दते -न्दितुं) or प्रस्यन्द्, शनैः शनैः क्षर् (c. 1. क्षरति -रितुं) or री (c. 4. रीयते, रेतुं) or स्रु (c. 1. स्रवति, स्रोतुं).

To DRIBBLE, *v. a.* लवशः or विन्दुक्रमेण स्रु in caus. (स्रावयति -यितुं).

DRIBBLET, *s.* कणः, कणिका, लवः, लेशः, स्तोकः, खण्डं, अल्पभागः; 'in dribblets,' लवशस्, अल्पाल्पं, स्तोकशस्.

DRIED, *p. p.* शुष्कः -ष्का -ष्कं, शोषितः -ता -तं, विशोषितः -ता -तं, उच्छुष्कः -ष्का -ष्कं, गतरसः -सा -सं, म्लानः -ना -नं, वसुः -सुः -सु; 'dried flesh,' शुष्कमांसं, वल्लूरं; 'dried fruit,' चिप्रदहः; 'dried up,' उच्छोषितः -ता -तं.

DRIER, *s.* शोषणः, शोषकः, उच्छोषणः -णी -णं, शुष्ककृत्.

DRIFT, *s.* (Tendency, aim) प्रवृत्तिः *f.*, प्रवाहः, तात्पर्य्यं, अन्वयः, अभिप्रायः, अभिप्रेतं, आशयः, उद्देशः, प्रायणं, अभिसन्धिः *m.*, आकांक्षा.—(Impulse) वेगः, प्रेरणं, प्रणोदः.—(Heap) राशिः *m. f.*, पुञ्जः, चितिः *f.*, सञ्चयः, निकरः; 'of snow,' हिमपुञ्जः, हिमसंहतिः *f.*—(Shower of any thing) सम्पातः, पातः, वर्षः.

To DRIFT, *v. a.* प्रवह् in caus. (-वाहयति -यितुं), सम्पत् in caus. (-पातयति -यितुं), प्रेर् (c. 10. प्रेरयति -यितुं rt. ईर्), राशीकृ, पुञ्जीकृ, पिण्डीकृ, एकौघीकृ.

To DRIFT, *v. n.* वातबलेन राशीभू, वायुवेगात् पुञ्जीभू.—(Be carried away by the current) सलिलवेगेन संवह् in pass. (समुह्यते) or अपवह् in pass.

DRIFTED, *p. p.* वातप्रेरितः -ता -तं, वायुवेगराशीकृतः -ता -तं.

To DRILL, *v. a.* (Perforate) व्यध् (c. 4. विध्यति, व्यद्धुं), छिद्र् (c. 10. छिद्रयति -यितुं), शुषिरीकृ.—(Exercise troops) सैन्यान् अभ्यस् (c. 4. -अस्यति -असितुं), सैन्यान् रणशिक्षां or अस्त्रशिक्षां शिक्ष् (c. 10. शिक्षयति -यितुं), युद्धविद्यां शिक्ष्, सैन्यव्यायामं कृ.—(Sow seed in rows) पंक्तिक्रमेण बीजानि वप् (c. 1. वपति, वप्तुं).

DRILL, *s.* (Boring tool) आविधः, वेधनी, वेधनिका, आस्फोटनी.—(Act of training soldiers) शस्त्राभ्यासः, अस्त्रशिक्षा, सैन्यव्यायामः.—(Baboon) वानरः, कपिः *m.*

To DRINK, *v. a.* पा (c. 1. पिबति, पातुं), आपा, निपा, परिपा, चम् (c. 1. चमति -मितुं), आचम् (c. 1. आचामति); 'to drink up,' आपा; 'drink in,' निपा; 'drink together,' सम्पा; 'drink after,' अनुपा; 'to give to drink,' पा in caus. (पाययति -यितुं).

To DRINK, *v. n.* पा (c. 1. पिबति, पातुं).—(Be a drunkard) पानरतः -ता -तम् अस्.—(Feast with liquors) सम्पीतिं कृ, सपीतिं कृ.—(Salute in drinking) चषकग्रहणकाले मङ्गलप्रार्थनां कृ or शुभं भूयाद् इति वद् (c. 1. वदति -दितुं).

Drink, *s.* पानं, पानीयं, पेयं, पयः *n.* (स्), आचमनीयं, मद्यं, मदिरा.

Drinkable, *a.* पेयः -या -यं, पानीयः -या -यं, प्रपाणीयः -या -यं, आचमनीयः -या -यं, पानयोग्यः -ग्या -ग्यं, पानोपयुक्तः -क्ता -क्तं.

Drinker, *s.* पाता *m.* (तृ), पायी *m.* (न्), पानरतः, पानप्रसक्तः, मद्यपीतः.

Drinking, *s.* पानं, पीतिः *f.*, निपानं, आचमनं; 'drinking together,' सम्पीतिः *f.*, सपीतिः *f.*

Drinking-vessel, *s.* पानपात्रं, पानभाजनं, पानयोग्यभाजनं, आचमनोपयुक्तपात्रं, चषकः, सरकः, अनुतर्षः -र्षणं.

To **drip**, *v. n.* कणशः or लवशः or बिन्दुक्रमेण स्यन्द् (c. 1. स्यन्दते -न्दितुं) or प्रस्यन्द्, शनैः शनैः क्षर् (c. 1. क्षरति -रितुं) or री (c. 4. रीयते, रेतुं) or स्रु (c. 1. स्रवति, स्रोतुं).

To **drip**, *v. a.* कणशः or शनैः शनैः स्रु in caus. (स्रावयति -यितुं).

Drip, *s.* (Edge of a roof) पटलप्रान्तः, वलिकः -कं, नीध्रं.

Dripping, *part.* (Trickling) स्यन्दी -न्दिनी -न्दि (न्), स्यन्नः -न्ना -न्नं, निस्यन्दमानः -ना -नं, क्षरन् -रन्ती -रत् (त्), रीणः -णा -णं, स्रुतः -ता -तं.

Dripping, *s.* (Act of trickling) क्षरणं, स्रवणं, स्रवणं, प्रस्रवणं, स्रवः, स्रवः, स्रावः, स्यन्दनं.—(Fat which falls from roasting meat) पच्यमानमांसघृतं, मांसवसा, मांसस्नेहः, मांसनिर्गतसारः.

Dripping-pan, *s.* पच्यमानमांसात् प्रस्रुतघृतस्य भाजनं, मांसस्नेहाधारः.

To **drive**, *v. a.* (Impel, compel) प्रेर् (c. 10. -ईरयति -यितुं), प्रणुद् (c. 6. -णुदति -णोत्तुं), प्रचुद् (c. 10. -चोदयति -यितुं), प्रवृत् in caus. (-वर्त्तयति -यितुं), चल् in caus. (चालयति -यितुं) नियुज् in caus. (-योजयति -यितुं), कृष् (c. 1. कर्षति, क्रष्टुं), समाकृष्.—(Urge or guide horses) अश्वान् प्रेर् or प्रणुद् or प्रचुद् or यम् (c. 1. यच्छति, यन्तुं).—(Drive a carriage) रथं वह् in caus. (वाहयति -यितुं), or चल् in caus.—(Drive a nail) कीलम् आहत्य प्रविश् in caus. (-वेशयति -यितुं).—(Drive away) अपानुद्, व्यपानुद्, निराकृ, अपाकृ, निरस् (c. 4. -अस्यति -असितुं), अपास्, अपवह् (c. 1. -वहति -वोढुं), व्यपवह्, अपवह् in caus., निर्धू (c. 5. -धूनोति -धवितुं), विधू, निःसृ in caus. (-सारयति -यितुं), बाध् (c. 1. बाधते -धितुं), हृ (c. 1. हरति, हर्त्तुं), अपहृ, परिहृ.

To **drive**, *v. n.* (Be impelled) प्रेरितः -ता -तं भू, अपवह् in pass. (अपोह्यते rt. वह्), संवह् in pass. चल् in caus. pass. (चाल्यते) कृष् in pass. (कृष्यते).—(Rush against) आपत् (c. 1. -पतति -तितुं), अभिपत्.—(In a carriage) क्रीडारथेन विहारं कृ.—(Aim at) अभिसन्धा (c. 3. -दधाति -धातुं), उद्दिश् (c. 6. -दिशति -देष्टुं), अभिप्रे (c. 2. अभिप्रैति -तुं rt. इ).

Drive, *s.* क्रीडारथेन भ्रमणं or विहारः or परिक्रमः.

To **drivel**, *v. n.* लालां or श्लेष्माणं मुखात् स्रु in caus. (स्रावयति -यितुं) or पत् in caus. (पातयति -यितुं) or निःसृ in caus. (-सारयति -यितुं).—(Be idiotic, childish) बुद्धिविकलः -ला -लं भू, बालिशीभू, जडीभू.

Drivel, *s.* लाला, मुखस्रावः, वक्त्रासवः, वदनासवः, स्यन्दिनी, द्राविका, सृणिका, लसिका, मुखनिःसारितं जलं.

Driveller, *s.* लालास्रावकः.—(Idiot) जडः, मूढः, बुद्धिविकलः.

Driven, *p. p.* प्रेरितः -ता -तं, प्रणोदितः -ता -तं, प्रणुन्नः -न्ना -न्नं, प्रवर्त्तितः -ता -तं, प्रचोदितः -ता -तं; 'driven away,' अपनोदितः -ता -तं, निराकृतः -ता -तं, अपाकृतः -ता -तं, निरस्तः -स्ता -स्तं, निर्धूतः -ता -तं, विधूतः -ता -तं, अवधूतः -ता -तं, अपोढः -ढा -ढं, व्यपोढः -ढा -ढं, व्यावितः -ता -तं.

Driver, *s.* प्रेरकः, प्रणोदकः.—(Of a carriage) रथवाहकः, यन्ता *m.* (न्तृ), नियन्ता *m.*, प्राजकः, प्राजिता *m.* (तृ), प्रचेता *m.* (तृ), याता *m.* (तृ).—(Of horses) अश्वप्रणोदकः, हयङ्कषः.—(Of an elephant) महामात्रः, आधोरणः, हस्तिपः -पकः.—(Of cattle) पशुप्रेरकः.

Driving, *s.* प्रेरणं, प्रणोदः.—(Of cattle) पशुप्रेरणं, उदजः; 'driving away,' अपनोदनं, निरसनं, निराकरणं.

To **drizzle**, *v. n.* शीकर (nom. शीकरायते), शीक् (c. 1. शीकते -कितुं).

To **drizzle**, *v. a.* शीकरं वृष् (c. 1. वर्षति -र्षितुं), सूक्ष्मविन्दून् वृष्.

Drizzling, *s.* शीकरवर्षः, शीकरपातः, सूक्ष्मविन्दुवर्षः.

Drizzly, *a.* शीकरौघः -घा -घं, शीकरविशिष्टः -ष्टा -ष्टं.

Droll, *a.* हासकरः -री -रं, हास्यः -स्या -स्यं, उपहास्यः -स्या -स्यं, रसिकः -का -कं, विनोदी -दिनी -दि (न्), कौतुकी -किनी -कि (न्), असङ्कृतः -ता -तं, अपरूपः -पा -पं.

Droll, *s.* परिहासवेदी *m.* (न्), वैहासिकः, विदूषकः, भण्डः, नर्म्मसचिवः.

To **droll**, *v. n.* भण्ड् (c. 1. भण्डते -ण्डितुं), भण्डवत् परिहासं कृ.

Drollery, *s.* हास्यत्वं, हास्यं, परिहासः, नर्म्म *n.* (न्), उपहास्यता, विहासः, वैहासिककर्म्म *n.* (न्), भाण्डं, लालिका, विनोदः.

Dromedary, *s.* एककुकुद्, द्विककुद्मान् *m.* (त्), उष्ट्रविशेषः, क्रमेलः.

Drone, *s.* (Male bee) पुम्मधुकरः, पुम्भृङ्गः.—(Idler) अलसः, निष्कर्म्मा *m.* (न्), निरुत्साहः, आलस्यशीलः, मन्दगतिः *m.*, तन्द्रालुः.

To **drone**, *v. n.* अलसः -सा -सम् अस्, आलस्यं कृ, मन्दीभू.

Dronish, *a.* आलस्यशीलः -ला -लं, तन्द्रालुः -लुः -लु, निरुद्योगः -गा -गं.

To **droop**, *v. n.* ग्लै (c. 1. ग्लायति, ग्लातुं), परिग्लै, सद् (c. 1. सीदति, सत्तुं), अवसद्, विषद्, व्यवसद्, क्षि in pass. (क्षीयते), म्लै (c. 1. म्लायति, म्लातुं), ध्वंस् (c. 1. ध्वंसते -सितुं), विध्वंस्, क्लम् (c. 4. क्लाम्यति, क्लमितुं), परिक्लम्, स्रंस् (c. 1. स्रंसते -सितुं), विस्रंस्, गल् (c. 1. गलति -लितुं), तम् (c. 4. ताम्यति, तमितुं), शिथिलीभू.

Drooping, *a.* ग्लानः -ना -नं, परिम्लानः -ना -नं, सन्नः -न्ना -न्नं, अवसन्नः -न्ना -न्नं, स्रंसमानः -ना -नं, स्रंसी -सिनी -सि (न्), विषादी -दिनी -दि (न्), म्लायन् -यन्ती -यत् (त्), ध्वंसी -सिनी -सि (न्) or विध्वंसी, क्लान्तः -न्ता -न्तं, शिथिलः -ला -लं, आगलितः -ता -तं.

Drop, *s.* बिन्दुः *m.*, कणः, विप्रुट् *f.* (ष्), विप्रुद्, पृषत् *n.*, पृषतः, पृषन्ति *n.* लवः, लेशः, स्तोकः, गडः, धारा, कणिका, शीकरः, स्फटकः, पुष्वा; 'drop of water,' जलबिन्दुः *m.*, अम्बुकणः -णा, अम्बुलवः, जलरण्डः, पयोगडः.—(Ear-ring) लोलकः, कुण्डलं; 'drop by drop,' लवशस्, बिन्दुक्रमेण.

To **drop**, *v. a.* (Pour out in drops) लवशस् or बिन्दुक्रमेण स्रु in caus. (स्रावयति -यितुं) or पत् in caus. (पातयति -यितुं).—(Let fall) पत् in caus., स्रंस् in caus. (स्रंसयति -यितुं), भ्रंश् in caus. (भ्रंशयति -यितुं), च्यु in caus. (च्यावयति -यितुं), ध्वंस् in caus. (ध्वंसयति -यितुं).—(Let go) मुच् (c. 6. मुञ्चति, मोक्तुं), सृज् (c. 6. सृजति, स्रष्टुं, c. 10. सर्ज्जयति -यितुं), विसृज्.—(Leave off) त्यज् (c. 1. त्यजति, त्यक्तुं), अपास् (c. 4. -अस्यति -असितुं), निवृत् (c. 1. -वर्त्तते -र्त्तितुं) with abl.—(Utter a word casually) अकस्मात् or अनपेक्षितं वाक्यं वद् (c. 1. वदति -दितुं).

To **drop**, *v. n.* (Distill in drops) स्यन्द् (c. 1. स्यन्दते -न्दितुं), प्रस्यन्द्, स्रु (c. 1. स्रवति, स्रोतुं), प्रस्रु, च्युत् or श्च्युत् (च्योतति, श्च्योतति -तितुं), क्षर् (c. 1. क्षरति -रितुं), री (c. 4. रीयते, रेतुं).—(Fall) स्रंस् (c. 1. स्रंसते -सितुं), आस्रंस्, विस्रंस्, पत् (c. 1. पतति -तितुं), भ्रंश् (c. 4. भ्रश्यति, c. 1. भ्रंशते, भ्रंशितुं), परिभ्रंश्, गल् (c. 1. गलति -लितुं), अवगल्, समागल्, विगल्, च्यु (c. 1. च्यवते, च्योतुं), ध्वंस् (c. 1. ध्वंसते -सितुं), लष् (c. 1. लषते -षितुं).—(Die) मृ (c. 6. म्रियते, मर्त्तुं).—(Sink) सद् (c. 1. सीदति, सत्तुं), अवसद्, विषद्, ग्लै (c. 1. ग्लायति, ग्लातुं).—(Faint) मुर्छ्

(c. 1. मूर्च्छति -र्च्छितुं).

Droplet, *s.* सूक्ष्मबिन्दुः *m.*, क्षुद्रबिन्दुः, सूक्ष्मकणः, कणिका.

Dropped, *p. p.* स्रस्तः -स्ता -स्तं, पतितः -ता -तं, निपतितः -ता -तं, भ्रष्टः -ष्टा -ष्टं, गलितः -ता -तं, विगलितः -ता -तं, च्युतः -ता -तं, ध्वस्तः -स्ता -स्तं.

Dropping, *s.* स्यन्दः, स्यन्दनी, स्रावः, स्रवणं, सुतं, स्रुतं, रीणं.

Dropping, *part.* or *a.* स्यन्दी -न्दिनी -न्दि (न्), स्यन्दमानः -ना -नं, स्रवन् -वन्ती -वत् (त्), स्रुतः -ता -तं, क्षरन् -रन्ती -रत् (त्), स्रावः -वा -वं, रीणः -णा -णं.

Dropsical, *a.* जलोदरी -रिणी -रि (न्) or उदरी, जठरामयग्रस्तः -स्ता -स्तं.

Dropsy, *s.* जलोदरं -री, उदरी, उदकोदरं, जठरामयः.

Dross, *s.* (Of metals) मलं, धातुमलं, अयोमलं, कलङ्कः, अयोमलं, धातुमलं, मण्डूरं, किट्टालः, सिंहाणं, सिंहानं, धूर्त्तं.—(Refuse matter) मलं, खलं, किट्टं, अमेध्यं, कल्कं, उच्छिष्टं, अवस्करः, अपस्करः, असारः.

Drossy, *a.* समलः -ला -लं, मलिनः -ना -नं, कलङ्की -ङ्किनी -ङ्कि (न्).

Drought, *s.* अनावृष्टिः *f.*, अवर्षणं, जलशोषः, अवग्रहः -ग्राहः, शुष्ककालः, वृष्टेरभावः, जलाभावः, पानीयाभावः.

Droughty, *a.* अनावृष्टिः -ष्टिः -ष्टि, निर्वृष्टिः -ष्टिः -ष्टि, वृष्टिशून्यः -न्या -न्यं, निर्जलः -ला -लं, शुष्कः -ष्का -ष्कं, जलशून्यः -न्या -न्यं, निरुदकः -का -कं.

Drove, *s.* (Collection of cattle driven) गोपालेन प्रेरितः पशुगणः or पशुसमूहः.—(Any herd) कदम्बकं, यूथं, गणः, सङ्घः, वृन्दं, कुलं, सङ्घातः, संहतिः *f.*

Drover, *s.* पशुप्रेरकः, पशुप्रणोदकः, गोचारकः, पशुपालः.

To **drown**, *v. a.* (Immerge in water) जले or अम्भसि मस्ज् in caus. (मज्जयति -यितुं) or निमस्ज् or प्रविश् in caus. (-वेशयति -यितुं).—(Kill by immersion) जले मज्जयित्वा व्यापद् in caus. (-पादयति -यितुं).—(Deluge, inundate) प्लु in caus. (प्लावयति -यितुं), आप्लु, परिप्लु, सम्प्लु.

To **drown**, *v. n.* जले मस्ज् (c. 1. मज्जति -ज्जितुं or मंक्तुं) or निमस्ज् or प्रमस्ज्, जले मंक्त्वा नश् (c. 4. नश्यति, नशितुं) or व्यापद् (c. 4. -पद्यते -पत्तुं) or पञ्चत्वं गम् (c. 1. गच्छति, गन्तुं).

Drowned, *p. p.* मग्नः -ग्ना -ग्नं, निमग्नः -ग्ना -ग्नं, प्रमग्नः -ग्ना -ग्नं, जलेमग्नः -ग्ना -ग्नं, प्लावितः -ता -तं, आप्लावितः -ता -तं, परिप्लुतः -ता -तं, समाप्लुतः -ता -तं.

Drowner, *s.* मंक्ता *m.* (क्तृ), निमंक्ता *m.*, मज्जयिता *m.* (तृ), प्लावकः.

Drowning, *s.* मज्जनं, निमज्जनं, आप्लावः, प्लावनं, परिप्लवः.

To **drowse**, *v. n.* निद्रा (c. 2. -द्राति -तुं), स्वप् (c. 2. स्वपिति, स्वप्तुं), निमील् (c. 1. -मीलति -लितुं), स्वप् in des. (सुषुप्सति -प्सितुं).

Drowsily, *adv.* सुषुप्सुवत्, निद्रालुवत्, निद्रालसवत्, आलस्येन.

Drowsiness, *s.* निद्रा, निद्रालुत्वं, तन्द्रा, तन्द्रिः *f.*, तन्द्रिका, सुषुप्सुत्वं, शिशयिषा, आलस्यं, अलसत्वं, परासुता, स्वापः, स्वप्नशीलत्वं, शयालुता.

Drowsy, *a.* निद्रालुः -लुः -लु, सुषुप्सुः -प्सुः -प्सु, शिशयिषुः -षुः -षु, तैन्द्रः -न्द्री -न्द्रं, निद्राशीलः -ला -लं, निद्रालसः -सा -सं, स्वप्नशीलः -ला -लं.

To **drub**, *v. a.* वेत्रेण तड् (c. 10. ताडयति -यितुं) or प्रहृ (c. 1. -हरति -हर्त्तुं).

Drubbing, *s.* ताडनं, आघातः, वेत्राघातः, यष्ट्याघातः.

To **drudge**, *v. n.* अविरतं or अतिदेहक्लेशेन आयस् (c. 4. -यस्यति -यसितुं) or श्रम् (c. 4. श्राम्यति, श्रमितुं) or परिश्रम्, निरन्तरायासं कृ, अतिशरीरायासेन नीचकर्म्म कृ or व्रातं कृ.

Drudge, *s.* निरन्तरायासी *m.* (न्), अविरतायासी *m.*, अतिक्लेशेन नीचकर्म्मकारी *m.* (न्), अपकर्म्मकृत्, श्रमणः, व्रातीनः, हीनवृत्तिः *m.*, कृतायासः.

Drudgery, *s.* निरन्तरायासः, अविरतायासः, शरीरायासः, कायक्लेशः, नित्यश्रमः, नित्यक्लेशः, नित्यकष्टं, नीचकर्म्म *n.* (न्), दास्यं, दासत्वं, व्रातं.

Drudgingly, *adv.* अतिक्लेशेन, अतिश्रमेण, नित्यकष्टपूर्व्वं, साविरतायासं.

Drug, *s.* औषधं, भेषजं, अगदः, औषधीयद्रव्यं, रसः, भैषज्यं, रोगिवल्लभः, व्यवायी *m.* (न्), जायुः *m.*, जारी, जाली.—(Unsaleable commodity) अपण्यं, अविक्रेयं, अविक्रेयद्रव्यं.

To **drug**, *v. a.* (Tincture with drugs, &c.) औषधादिना मिश्र् (c. 10. मिश्रयति -यितुं) or संसृज् (c. 6. -सृजति -स्रष्टुं).—(With something unwholesome) अपथ्यद्रव्येण or विरुद्धद्रव्येण मिश्र्.—(Dose with drugs) औषधीकृ, भिषज् (nom. भिषज्यति).

Drugget, *s.* स्थूलपटः, स्थूलपट्टः, स्थूलशाटकः -टिका -टिः *m.* वराशिः *m.*, चित्रास्तरणार्थं, चित्रपटावरणं.

Druggist, *s.* औषधविक्रेता *m.* (तृ), भेषजविक्रयी *m.* (न्), औषधीयद्रव्यक्रयविक्रयिकः, औषधकारः, भेषजकारः.

Drum, *s.* मृदङ्गः, पटहः, मर्द्दलः, दुन्दुभिः *m.*, डिण्डिमः, मुरजः, भेरी, आनकः, झल्लरी, झर्झरी, आनद्धं, अवनद्धं, ढक्का, आडम्बरः, मड्डुः *m.*; 'military drum,' सङ्ग्रामपटहः, विजयमर्द्दलः, महादुन्दुः *m.*—(Of the ear) कर्णोदरं, श्रवणोदरं, कर्णदुन्दुभिः *m.*

To **drum**, *v. n.* मर्द्दलं or डिण्डिमं तड् (c. 10. ताडयति -यितुं), पटहम् आहन् (c. 2. -हन्ति -न्तुं).—(Beat) स्पन्द् (c. 1. स्पन्दते -न्दितुं).

Drummer, *s.* मार्द्दङ्गिकः, मार्द्दङ्गः, मौरजिकः, पटहताडकः, पाणिवादः, पाणिघः, माड्डुकः, झाल्लरिः.

Drumstick, *s.* कोणः, शारिका, रणः, मृदङ्गताडनार्थं काष्ठं.

Drunk, drunken, *a.* मत्तः -त्ता -त्तं, पानादिना उन्मत्तः -त्ता -त्तं, मदोन्मत्तः -त्ता -त्तं, मद्यपीतः -ता -तं, क्षीबः -बा -बं, शौण्डः -ण्डा -ण्डं, परिक्षीबः -बा -बं, मदयित्नुः -त्नुः -त्नु, मदोद्धतः -ता -तं, सुमदः -दा -दं, प्रक्षीबितः -ता -तं, उत्कटः -टा -टं.—(Drenched) सिक्तः -क्ता -क्तं; 'to be drunk,' मद् (c. 4. माद्यति, मदितुं); 'to make drunk,' मद् in caus. (मादयति -यितुं).

Drunkard, *s.* पानरतः, पानप्रसक्तः, मद्यपानासक्तः, पानशौण्डः.

Drunkenness, *s.* मत्तत्वं, उन्मत्तता, मद्योन्मत्तत्वं, मादः, मदः, क्षैब्यं, क्षीबता, शौण्डत्वं, परिक्षीबता, उत्कटः, मद्यपानजन्योऽवस्थाविशेषः.

Dry, *a.* शुष्कः -ष्का -ष्कं, परिशुष्कः -ष्का -ष्कं, संशुष्कः -ष्का -ष्कं, उच्छुष्कः -ष्का -ष्कं, निर्जलः -ला -लं, निरुदकः -का -कं, नीरसः -सा -सं, निःसलिलः -ला -लं, अतिमितः -ता -तं, अक्लिन्नः -न्ना -न्नं, अपरिक्लिन्नः -न्ना -न्नं, अस्निग्धः -ग्धा -ग्धं, निःस्नेहः -हा -हं, निस्नेहः -हा -हं, स्नेहरहितः -ता -तं, अनार्द्रः -र्द्रा -र्द्रं, वानः -ना -नं, जाङ्गलः -ला -लं, रूक्षः -क्षा -क्षं, रूक्षः -क्षा -क्षं.—(Flat as style) अरसिकः -का -कं, अरसः -सा -सं.—(Sarcastic) अरुन्तुदः -दा -दं.—(Thirsty) उदकार्थी -र्थिनी -र्थि (न्), तृषार्त्तः -र्त्ता -र्त्तं; 'dry soil,' मरुः *m.*, मरुस्थलं -ली; 'the dry ground,' स्थलं; 'dry flesh,' शुष्कमांसं.

To **dry**, *v. a.* शुष् in caus. (शोषयति -यितुं), विशुष्, संशुष्, परिशुष्, उपशुष्, शुष्कीकृ, निर्जलीकृ, नीरसीकृ; स्नेहं or क्लेदं or रसं हृ (c. 1. हरति, हर्त्तुं) or अपनी (c. 1. -नयति -नेतुं) or निष्कृष् (c. 1. -कर्षति -क्रष्टुं); ओल् in caus. (ओलयति -यितुं); 'to dry up,' उच्छुष् in caus. (उच्छोषयति -यितुं rt. शुष्).

To **dry**, *v. n.* शुष् (c. 4. शुष्यति, शोष्टुं), परिशुष्, विशुष्, संशुष्, उपशुष्, शुष्कीभू, निर्जलीभू, नीरसीभू; ओल् (c. 1. ओलति -लितुं), व्यय् (c. 1. व्ययते -यितुं), आश्यै (c. 1. -श्यायते -श्यातुं).

Dryad, *s.* वनदेवता, वनाधिष्ठात्री देवता, वन्यस्त्री.

Dryer, *s.* शोषकः, शोषणः, उच्छोषणः, परिशोषकः, शुष्ककृत्.

Dry-eyed, *a.* निरश्रुलोचनः -ना -नं, निःसलिलनयनः -ना -नी -नं.

Drying, *s.* शोषः -षणं, परिशोषणं, विशोषणं, उच्छोषणं, शुष्ककरणं.

DRYLY, *adv.* शुष्कं, परिशुष्कं, शुष्कतया, अरसं.—(Sarcastically) अरुन्तुदत्वेन.

DRYNESS, *s.* शुष्कता -त्वं, परिशुष्कता, संशुष्कता, शोषः, निर्जलत्वं, नीरसत्वं, निःस्नेहता, अस्निग्धता, स्नेहराहित्यं.—(Of style, expression) अरसिकत्वं, अरुन्तुदत्वं.

DRY-NURSE, *s.* स्तन्यदानव्यतिरेकेण बालकप्रतिपालिका, बालकपोष्ट्री, अङ्कपाली, शिशुपालिका.

To DRY-NURSE, *v. a.* स्तन्यदानव्यतिरेकेण बालकं पाल् (c. 10. पालयति -यितुं) or प्रतिपाल् or पुष् (c. 10. पोषयति -यितुं) or उपचर् (c. 1. -चरति -रितुं).

DRY-SHOD, *a.* शुष्कपादः -दा -दं -दुकः -का -कं, शुष्कचरणः -णा -णं.

DUAL, *a.* द्विवाचकः -का -कं, द्विकः -का -कं, द्विवचनात्मकः -का -कं, द्विसंख्यकः -का -कं; 'the dual number,' द्विवचनं.

DUALITY, *s.* द्वित्वं, द्वैतं, द्वैधं, द्वैगुण्यं.

To DUB, *v. a.* नवपदे नियुज् (c. 7. -युनक्ति -योक्तुं), नवोपाधिं दा, नवनाम दा, नूतनपदवीं दा; 'dub a knight,' सादिपदं दा.

DUBIOUS, *a.* सन्दिग्धः -ग्धा -ग्धं, संशयी -यिनी -यि (न्), संशयस्थः -स्था -स्थं, ससंशयः -या -यं, सांशयिकः -की -कं, संशयापन्नः -न्ना -न्नं, शङ्कनीयः -या -यं, शङ्कान्वितः -ता -तं, सशङ्कः -ङ्का -ङ्कं, शङ्कामयः -यी -यं, संशयालुः -लुः -लु, संशयापन्नमानसः -सा -सं, सन्दिहानः -ना -नं, वैकल्पिकः -की -कं, विशयी -यिनी -यि (न्), अनिश्चितः -ता -तं, अस्थिरः -रा -रं.—(Not clear) अस्पष्टः -ष्टा -ष्टं, अव्यक्तः -क्ता -क्तं, अप्रकाशः -शी -शं, अप्रत्यक्षः -क्षा -क्षं.

DUBIOUSLY, *adv.* सन्दिग्धं, ससंशयं, सशङ्कं, सन्देहेन, शङ्कया, शङ्कापूर्वं.

DUBIOUSNESS, *s.* सन्दिग्धता, ससंशयत्वं, सांशयिकत्वं, अनिश्चयः, अनैश्चित्यं.

DUBITABLE, *a.* वितर्क्यः -र्क्या -र्क्यं, मीमांस्यः -स्या -स्यं, आशङ्कनीयः -या -यं.

DUBITATION, *s.* सन्देहः, संशयः, शङ्का, आशङ्का, विकल्पः, वितर्कः.

DUCAL, *a.* प्रधानकुलीनपदसम्बन्धी -न्धिनी -न्धि (न्), परमपदसम्बन्धी.

DUCAT, *s.* प्रधानकुलीनजनमुद्राङ्कितो मुद्राविशेषः.

DUCHESS, *s.* प्रधानकुलीनजनस्य पत्नी or भार्य्या.

DUCK, *s.* (Bird) हंसः, वरटः -टा -टी, प्लवः, कलहंसः, चक्रवाकः, कादम्बः; 'wild duck,' कामिकः.—(Sudden inclination of the head) अकस्मात् शिरोनमीकरणं or मस्तकानतिः *f.*—(Stone thrown obliquely on the water) जले तिर्य्यक्क्षिप्तः प्रस्तरः.—(Word of endearment) प्रियः -या, दयितः -ता, वत्सः -त्सा, हृदयप्रियः -या.

To DUCK, *v. a.* (Plunge in water) जले मज्ज् in caus. (मज्जयति -यितुं) or निमज्ज् or अवगाह् in caus. (-गाहयति -यितुं) or आप्लु in caus. (-प्लावयति -यितुं) or निक्षिप् (c. 6. -क्षिपति -क्षेप्तुं).—(Bow the head suddenly) मस्तकम् अकस्माद् नम् in caus. (नामयति, नमयति -यितुं) or नम्रीकृ.

To DUCK, *v. n.* (Dip) मज्ज् (c. 6. मज्जति, मंक्तुं, मज्जितुं), निमज्ज्, अवगाह् (c. 1. -गाहते -हितुं).—(Bow the head suddenly) मस्तकम् अकस्माद् नम् (c. 1. नमति, नन्तुं), अकस्माद् नम्रीभू.

DUCKED, *p. p.* जलेमग्नः -ग्ना -ग्नं, जलाप्लुतः -ता -तं, प्रमग्नः -ग्ना -ग्नं.

DUCKER, *s.* मज्जयिता *m.* (तृ), मंक्ता *m.* (क्तृ), आप्लावकः, प्लवः.

DUCKING, *s.* मज्जनं, निमज्जनं, अवगाहः, प्लावः, प्लवनं, आप्लावः -प्लवनं.

DUCKLING, *s.* हंसशावकः, वरटशावकः, वरटशिशुः *m.*

DUCT, *s.* (Canal, passage) नाली, प्रणालः -ली -लिका, सारणिः *f.*, पथः, मार्गः, सङ्क्रमः, गमनागमनपथः.—(Of the body) नालः -ली -ला, नाडिः *f.*, नाडिः *f.* -डी, शिरा, सिरा, धमनिः *f.* -नी, तन्त्री.

DUCTILE, *a.* (Tractable) सुविनेयः -या -यं, सुप्रयोज्यः -या -यं, विधेयः -या -यं, वश्यः -श्या -श्यं, आकर्षणीयः -या -यं, सुखकर्षणीयः -या -यं.—(Pliable) आयम्यः -म्या -म्यं, आनम्यः -म्या -म्यं, मृदुः -द्वी -दु, द्रवः -वा -वं.—(As metal) उद्वर्त्तनीयः -या -यं, उद्वर्त्तनयोग्यः -ग्या -ग्यं.

DUCTILENESS, DUCTILITY, *s.* सुविनेयत्वं, आयम्यता, आनम्यता, मृदुत्वं, द्रवत्वं, सुकर्षणीयता.—(Of metals) सुखोद्वर्त्तनीयता, उद्वर्त्तनयोग्यता.

DUDGEON, *s.* (Anger) मन्युः *m.*, कोपः, क्रोधः, रोषः, अमर्षः, द्वेषः, दुर्भावः.—(Small dagger) क्षुद्रकृपाणी, असिपुत्रिका.

DUE, *a.* (That ought to be paid or received) देयः -या -यं, प्रतिदेयः -या -यं, दानीयः -या -यं, दातव्यः -व्या -व्यं, शोध्यः -ध्या -ध्यं, शोधनीयः -या -यं, संशोध्यः -ध्या -ध्यं, परिशोधनीयः -या -यं, प्राप्यः -प्या -प्यं, प्राप्तव्यः -व्या -व्यं, ग्राह्यः -ह्या -ह्यं.—(Fit, becoming) योग्यः -ग्या -ग्यं, युक्तः -क्ता -क्तं, यथायोग्यः -ग्या -ग्यं, उचितः -ता -तं, यथोचितः -ता -तं, उपयुक्तः -क्ता -क्तं, यथार्हः -र्हा -र्हं, अनुरूपः -पा -पं; 'in due time,' उपयुक्ते समये, समया; 'in due form,' विधिवत्, यथाविधि.

DUE, *s.* (That which ought to be paid or received) देयं, प्रतिदेयं, दानीयं, शोधनीयं, ग्राह्यं, प्राप्यं, प्राप्तव्यं.—(Debt) ऋणं.—(That which ought to be done) कर्त्तव्यं; 'respect is due to parents,' मातापितरौ पूजनीयौ.—(Tribute) शुल्कः -ल्कं, करः, तारिकं, तार्य्यं, राजग्राह्यभागः.—(Right) अधिकारः, स्वाधिकारः.

DUE, *adv.* (Directly) अवक्रं, अजिह्मं, अविलोमं, समरेखं.

DUEL, *s.* द्वन्द्वयुद्धं, द्वन्द्वसम्प्रहारः, द्वन्द्वं, नियुद्धं, मल्लयुद्धं.

To DUEL, *v. n.* द्वन्द्वयुद्धं कृ, द्वन्द्वसम्प्रहारं कृ, द्वन्द्वं कृ.

DUELLER, DUELLIST, *s.* द्वन्द्वयोद्धा *m.* (द्धृ), मल्लयोद्धा *m.*, द्वन्द्वकृत्.

DUG, *s.* (Of an animal) स्तनः, कुचः, कुचतटं; 'of a cow,' गोस्तनः.

DUG, *p. p.* खातः -ता -तं, खनितः -ता -तं, निखातः -ता -तं, उत्खातः -ता -तं.

DUKE, *s.* कुलीनपदानां मध्ये प्रधानपदभाक् *m.* (ज्), उत्तमकुलीनपदस्थः.—(Chief, prince) अधिपतिः *m.*, राजा *m.* (न्), ईश्वरः.

DUKEDOM, *s.* उत्तमकुलीनपदं, पूर्वोक्तकुलीनजनस्य आधिपत्यं or अधिकारः.

DULCET, *a.* (Sweet to the taste) स्वादुः -द्वी -दु, मिष्टः -ष्टा -ष्टं, सुरसः -सा -सं.—(To the ear) श्रुतिसुखः -खा -खं, सुस्वरः -रा -रं, मधुरः -रा -रं.

DULCIFICATION, *s.* मधुरीकरणं, मधुसात्करणं, निरम्लीकरणं.

To DULCIFY or DULCORATE, *v. a.* मधुरीकृ, मधुसात्कृ, स्वादूकृ, मिष्टीकृ.

DULCIMER, *s.* वाद्ययन्त्रविशेषः, तन्त्री *m.* (न्), वल्लकी, विपञ्चिका.

DULL, *a.* (Stupid) मन्दः -न्दा -न्दं, मन्दबुद्धिः -द्धिः -द्धि, स्थूलधीः -धीः -धि, जडः -डा -डं, मूढः -ढा -ढं.—(Blunt) अतीक्ष्णः -क्ष्णा -क्ष्णं, अतीव्रः -व्रा -व्रं, अतेजाः -जाः -जः (स्) or निस्तेजाः, तेजोहीनः -ना -नं, धाराहीनः -ना -नं.—(Not bright) मन्दकान्तः -न्ता -न्तं, मन्दतेजाः -जाः -जः (स्), मन्दद्युतिः -तिः -ति, मन्दच्छायः -या -यं, निस्तेजाः -जाः -जः (स्), निष्प्रभः -भा -भं, अप्रभः -भा -भं, मलिनः -ना -नं.—(Sluggish) मन्दः -न्दा -न्दं, मन्थरः -रा -रं, मन्दगतिः -तिः -ति, मन्दगामी -मिनी -मि (न्), मन्थरः -रा -रं, अलसः -सा -सं.—(Gross) स्थूलः -ला -लं, घनः -ना -नं.—(Sad) विषण्णः -ण्णा -ण्णं, विषादी -दिनी -दि (न्), क्लान्तः -न्ता -न्तं, ग्लानः -ना -नं, दीनमनाः -नाः -नः (स्).—(Flat, insipid) अरसः -सा -सं, अरसिकः -का -कं.—(Tedious, troublesome) कष्टकरः -रा -रं, विषमः -मा -मं.—(Cheerless) निरानन्दः -न्दा -न्दं.—(Dull of hearing) श्रोत्रविकलः -ला -लं, श्रवणेन्द्रियविकलः -ला -लं; 'a dull day,' दुर्दिनं; 'a dull boil,' दुष्टव्रणः.

To DULL, *v. a.* (Stupefy) जडीकृ, मूढीकृ, मन्दीकृ, मुह् in caus. (मोहयति -यितुं).—(Blunt) अतीक्ष्णीकृ, अतीव्रं -व्रां -व्रं कृ, घनीकृ, स्थूलीकृ.—(Make dim) मन्दीकृ, निष्प्रभीकृ, मलिन (nom. मलिनयति -यितुं), तेजो हृ (c. 1. हरति, हर्तुं).—(Dispirit) मनो खण्ड् (c. 10.

सवइयति -यितुं), ग्लानीकृ, विषण्णीकृ, विषद् in caus. (-षादयति -यितुं).

Dull-witted, *a.* मन्दमतिः -तिः -ति, मन्दबुद्धिः -द्धिः -द्धि, स्थूलबुद्धिः -द्धिः -द्धि, स्थूलधीः -धीः -धि, जडमतिः &c., जडबुद्धिः &c., दुर्मतिः &c.

Dully, *adv.* मन्दं, मन्दं मन्दं, तेजो विना, सविषादं, रसं विना.

Dulness, *s.* (Stupidity) मन्दता, मान्द्यं, स्थूलता, बुद्धिमान्द्यं, स्थूलबुद्धित्वं, मूढता, अविदग्धता.—(Bluntness) अतीक्ष्णता, घनत्वं, अतीव्रता, धाराहीनता.—(Sluggishness) गतिमन्दता, आलस्यं.—(Dimness) तेजोमान्द्यं, निष्प्रभता, प्रभाहानिः *f.*, प्रतिभाहानिः *f.*, अप्रकाशत्वं, अप्रतापः, अतेजः *n.* (स्), अस्पष्टता.

Duly, *adv.* (Fitly) यथायोग्यं, युक्तं, यथार्हं -र्हतस्, यथोचितं, सम्यक्, यथातथं, यथान्याय्यं.—(In proper time) उपयुक्तसमये, समया.

Dumb, *a.* मूकः -का -कं, अडवाक् *m.f.n.* (च्), स्तब्धवाक् *m.f.n.*, जडः -डा -डं, अवाक् *m.f.n.*, वाग्रहितः -ता -तं, वागिन्द्रियविकलः -ला -लं, वाक्शक्तिहीनः -ना -नं, मुद्रितमुखः -खा -खं, निःशब्दः -ब्दा -ब्दं, निर्वचनः -ना -नं, अनालापः -पा -पं.

Dumbly, *adv.* मूकं, जडं, निःशब्दं, मौक्यपूर्वं, तूष्णीं.

Dumbness, *s.* मूकता, मौक्यं, वाक्स्तम्भः, वाग्जडता, वाग्जाड्यं, वाक्स्तब्धता, वागिन्द्रियवैकल्यं, वाग्राहित्यं, अवाक्त्वं, नीरवता.

Dumb-show, *s.* वाग्व्यतिरेकेण हस्तपादादिसञ्चालनं.

To dumfounder, *v. a.* मुह् in caus. (मोहयति -यितुं), विमुह्, आकुलीकृ, व्याकुलीकृ.

Dumpish, *a.* विषादी -दिनी -दि (न्), उद्विग्नमनाः -नाः -नः (स्) or दुर्मनाः.

Dumpling, *s.* (Apple) आम्रफलगर्भः क्षुद्रपोलिका.—(Currant) पिष्टापूपः.

Dumps, *s. pl.* विषादः, विषण्णता, चित्तोद्वेगः, खेदः, ग्लानिः *f.*, ग्लानिः *f.*

Dumpy, *a.* ह्रस्वस्थूलः -ला -लं, सङ्घनः -ना -नं, दृढसन्धिः -न्धी -न्धि.

Dun, *a.* (Dark-coloured) कपिशः -शा -शं, श्यावः -वा -वं, श्यामः -मा -मं, पिङ्गलः -ला -लं, ताम्रवर्णः -र्णा -र्णं, कृष्णवर्णः -र्णा -र्णं.

To dun, *v. a.* (For a debt) अतिनिर्बन्धेन ऋणदानं प्रार्थ् (c. 10. -र्थयति -ते -यितुं).

Dun, *s.* अतिनिर्बन्धेन ऋणप्रार्थकः, सनिर्बन्धो धनार्थी *m.* (न्).

Dunce, *s.* दुर्बुद्धिः *m.*, अनभिज्ञः, अज्ञः, निर्बोधः, अव्युत्पन्नः, मेधाहीनः.

Dunderhead, *s.* स्थूलबुद्धिः *m.*, स्थूलमतिः *m.*, बटुकः, बर्बरः.

Dung, *s.* पुरीषं, शकृत् *n.*, विष्ठा, विट् *f.* (ष्), पशुचरितं, पशुचारः, गूथः -थं, अमेध्यं, शोधनं, पूतिकं, अवस्करः, अपस्करः, शारीरं, शमलं, वर्चस्कः -स्कं, दूष्यं, कल्कं, मलं, सारः, भूमिलेपनं; 'cow-dung,' गोमयः -यं, गोकृतं, गोहल्लं.

To dung, *v. a.* पुरीषेण लिप् (c. 6. लिम्पति, लेप्तुं) or अञ्ज् (c. 7. अनक्ति, अंक्तुं).

To dung, *v. n.* पुरीषम् उत्सृज् (c. 6. -सृजति -स्रष्टुं), पुरीषोत्सर्गं कृ.

Dungeon, *s.* कारा, कारागारं, कारावेश्म *n.* (न्), बन्धनागारं, गुप्तिः *f.*, अन्धकूपः.

Dunghill, *s.* पुरीषराशिः *m.f.*, शकृद्राशिः, अमेध्यस्थानं, अशुचिस्थानं.

Dunghill, *a.* कलुषयोनिः -निः -नि, विहीनयोनिः -निः -नि, हीनजातिः -तिः -ति.

Dupe, *s.* सुखवञ्चनीयः, सुप्रतारणीयः, वञ्चितः, दम्भास्पदं, कपटास्पदं.

To dupe, *v. a.* वञ्च् in caus. (वञ्चयति -ते -यितुं), परिवञ्च्, प्रलभ् (c. 1. -लभते -लब्धुं), विप्रलभ्; छल् (c. 10. छलयति -यितुं), प्रतॄ in caus. (-तारयति -यितुं), दम्भ् (c. 5. दभ्नोति, दम्भितुं).

Duped, *p. p.* वञ्चितः -ता -तं, विप्रलब्धः -ब्धा -ब्धं, प्रतारितः -ता -तं.

Duplicate, *a.* द्विगुणः -णा -णं; 'a duplicate,' प्रतिरूपं, प्रतिलिपिः *f.*

To duplicate, *v. a.* (Double) द्विगुणीकृ.—(Fold) पुटीकृ, पुट (nom. पुटयति -यितुं).

Duplication, *s.* द्विगुणीकरणं, पुटीकरणं, द्वैगुण्यं, द्वैतं.

Duplicature, *s.* (Fold) पुटः, व्यावर्त्तनं, उर्म्मिका, भङ्गः.

Duplicity, *s.* वैदग्ध्यं, विदग्धता, कपटः, माया, छलं, असारल्यं.

Durability, *s.* चिरस्थायित्वं, स्थिरता, ध्रौव्यं, ध्रुवता, अक्षयता, स्थायित्वं, स्थितिः *f.*, संस्थितिः *f.*, स्थावरत्वं, अनपायः.

Durable, *a.* स्थायी -यिनी -यि (न्) or चिरस्थायी or दीर्घकालस्थायी, स्थिरः -रा -रं, स्थावरः -रा -रं, चिरकालिकः -का -कं, ध्रुवः -वा -वं, अक्षयः -या -यं, स्थितिमान् -मती -मत् (त्), संस्थः -स्था -स्थं, नित्यः -त्या -त्यं, अनपायः -या -यं -यी -यिनी -यि (न्), अजरः -रा -रं.

Durably, *adv.* स्थिरं, ध्रुवं, ध्रौव्येण, अक्षयं, अनपायेन.

Dura mater, *s.* मस्तिष्कस्य वाह्यवेष्टनं or आवेष्टनत्वक् *f.* (च्).

Durance, *s.* आसेधः, स्थानासेधः, रोधः, निरोधनं, सम्प्रतिरोधकः, बन्धनं, प्रतिबन्धनं, कारागारे निरोधः or बन्धनं.

Duration, *s.* स्थितिः *f.*, संस्थितिः *f.*; 'duration of an eclipse,' उपसर्गस्थितिः *f.*—(Space of time) परिमाणं, प्रमाणं; 'duration of day and night,' अहोरात्रस्य परिमाणं.—(Long duration) स्थायित्वं, स्थिरता, स्थावरत्वं, ध्रुवता, ध्रौव्यं, अविरामः.

Durgá, *s.* (The goddess) दुर्गा, जगन्माता *f.* (तृ), दक्षजा, श्यामा. *See* Bhavání.

During, *prep.* यावत्, पर्य्यन्तं, मध्ये, अन्तरे affixed; 'during life,' जीवनपर्य्यन्तं or यावज्जीवं or by prefixing आ with abl.; as, आजीवनान्तात्, आमरणात् (*i. e.* 'until death'); 'during the performance of the vow,' आसमापनाद् व्रतस्य (*i. e.* 'until the completion of the vow'); 'during three fortnights,' पक्षत्रयमध्ये.

Dusk, *a.* ईषत्तामसः -सी -सं, तमस्कल्पः -ल्पा -ल्पं, ईषत्तमस्वी -स्विनी -स्वि (न्), ईषत्तिमिरावृतः -ता -तं, प्रादोषिकः -की -कं, वैकालिकः -की -कं, सान्ध्यः -न्ध्यी -न्ध्यं.—(A little black) आकालः -ला -लं, ईषत्कृष्णः -ष्णा -ष्णं, आनीलः -ला -लं.

Dusk, *s.* (Twilight) सन्ध्या, सन्ध्याकालः -लं, सन्ध्यासमयः, विकालः, अभ्यान्तं, प्रदोषः, सायङ्कालः.

Duskily, *adv.* ईषदन्धकारेण, ईषत्तमसा, अस्पष्टं, अप्रकाशं.

Duskiness, *s.* ईषदन्धकारः, ईषत्तमिस्रं, ईषत्तिमिरं, अवतमसं.

Dusky or duskish, *a.* ईषत्तामसः -सी -सं, ईषत्तमस्वी -स्विनी -स्वि (न्), ईषदन्धकारयुक्तः -क्ता -क्तं, अस्पष्टः -ष्टा -ष्टं, ईषत्कृष्णः -ष्णा -ष्णं, श्यामः -मा -मं. *See* Dusk.

Dust, *s.* रेणुः *m.f.*, पांशुः *m.*, रजः *n.* (स्), धूलिः *m.f.* -ली *f.*, क्षोदः -दितं, भूरेणुः *m.f.*, अवकरः, अवस्करः, सङ्करः, सङ्कारः, वातकेतुः *m.*, वायुकेतुः *m.*, क्षितिकणः -णा, परागः, मेदिनीद्रवः, तुस्तं, तूस्तं, पांसुः *m.*, रजः *m.*; 'dust of the feet,' चरणजं, पदारः; 'dust of a flower,' परागः, पुष्परेणुः *m.*, सुमनोरजः *n.* (स्); 'dust of gold,' काञ्चनभूः *f.*; 'free from dust,' नीरजाः -जाः -जः (स्), नीरजस्कः -स्का -स्कं, निर्धूलिः -लिः -लि.

To dust, *v. a.* (Free from dust) नीरजीकृ, निर्धूलीकृ, रेणुम् अपमृज् (c. 2. -मार्ष्टि -र्ष्टुं, c. 1. -मार्जति -र्जितुं) or अवमृज्, रेणुदूषितं यत्किञ्चित् शुध् (c. 10. शोधयति -यितुं), पांशुपरिष्कारं कृ.

Dusted, *p. p.* नीरजीकारितः -ता -तं, मार्ज्जितः -ता -तं, सम्मृष्टः -ष्टा -ष्टं, हृतपांशुः -शुः -शु, नीरेणुः -णुः -णु, निष्पांशूकृतः -ता -तं.

Duster, *s.* नक्तकः, मार्ज्जनी, मार्ज्जनपटः, अवस्करकः, रेणुपरिष्कारकः.

Dust-hole, *s.* अवस्करः, गृहमार्ज्जितपांश्वादिनिचयस्थानं, सङ्करस्थानं, उच्छिष्टप्रक्षेपणार्थं गर्त्तः.

DUST-MAN, *s.* अवस्करकः, मलाकर्षी *m.* (न्), मलपूः *m.*, अमेध्यहारी *m.* (न्).

DUSTY, *a.* पांशुलः -ला -लं, पांशुरः -रा -रं, रेणुदूषितः -ता -तं, रेणुरूषितः -ता -तं, भूरेणुरूक्षः -क्षा -क्षं, रजस्वलः -ला -लं, धूल्यवलुण्ठितः -ता -तं.

DUTCH, *a.* हल्लण्डदेशसम्बन्धी -न्धिनी -न्धि (न्).

DUTIFUL, *a.* भक्तः -क्ता -क्तं, भक्तिमान् -मती -मत् (त्), भक्तियुक्तः -क्ता -क्तं, दृढभक्तिः -क्तिः -क्ति, वश्यः -श्या -श्यं, वशवर्त्ती -र्त्तिनी -र्त्ति (न्), धर्म्मचारी -रिणी -रि (न्), धर्म्मज्ञः -ज्ञा -ज्ञं, धर्म्मपालकः -का -कं, धर्म्मसेवी -विनी -वि (न्), आज्ञापालकः -का -कं, वशानुगः -गा -गं, शुश्रूषुः -षुः -षु, दृढव्रतः -ता -तं, विदितधर्म्मा -र्म्मा -र्म्म (न्), आदृतः -ता -तं, उपयुक्तः -क्ता -क्तं.—(To a parent) पितृभक्तः -क्ता -क्तं, पैतृकधर्म्मपालकः, पितृवशाधीनः-ना-नं.—(To a husband) पतिव्रता.—(To a master) प्रभुभक्तः.

DUTIFULLY, *adv.* भक्तवत्, भक्त्या, धर्म्मपालकवत्, सधर्म्मपालनं.

DUTIFULNESS, *s.* भक्तिः *f.*, भक्तिमत्त्वं, वश्यता, धर्म्मपालनं, आज्ञानुवर्त्तनं, शुश्रूषा, अधीनता, आदरः, प्रणिपातः; 'to parents,' पितृभक्तिः *f.*, पितृसम्मानं, पितृसेवा; 'to a husband,' पतिसेवा.

DUTY, *s.* (That which a person is bound to do) धर्म्मः, स्वधर्म्मः, कर्त्तव्यं, स्वकर्त्तव्यं, कर्त्तव्यता, कार्य्यं, कृत्यं, क्रिया, स्वकर्म्म *n.* (न्), न्याय्यकर्म्म, नियमः, यमः, व्रतं, धूः *f.* (धुर्), धुरा, तपः *n.* (स्).—(Appointed duty, office) नियोगः, अधिकारः, पदं, स्थानं, आस्पदं; 'perpetual duty,' नित्यकृत्यं, नित्यकर्म्म *n.* (न्), यमः; 'voluntary duty,' नियमः; 'fulfilment of duty,' धर्म्मनिष्पत्तिः *f.*, कृतकृत्यता; 'one who has done his duty,' कृतकृत्यः, कृतक्रियः; 'morning duty,' प्रातःकृत्यं; 'a woman's peculiar duty,' स्त्रीनिबन्धनं; 'charged with weighty duties,' धुरीणः, धुरीयः, धुर्वहः.—(Reverence) भक्तिः *f.*, मानं, सम्मानं, नमस्कारः, आदरः.—(Impost) शुल्कः -ल्कं, करः, तारिकं, तार्य्यं, राजग्राह्यभागः; 'duty paid at ferries, &c.,' घट्टादिदेयं.

DWARF, *s.* वामनः -नी *f.*, खर्व्वः -र्व्वा, खर्व्वः -र्व्वा, ह्रस्वकायः, अतनुकृशरीरः, अतुङ्गः, कुब्जः, खट्टेरकः.

To DWARF, *v. a.* ह्रस् in caus. (ह्रासयति -यितुं), वामनीकृ, खर्व्वीकृ.

DWARFISH, *a.* वामनः -ना -नं, ह्रस्वः -स्वा -स्वं, खर्व्वः -र्व्वा -र्व्वं or निखर्व्वः, अतुङ्गः -ङ्गा -ङ्गं, वामनाकृतिः -तिः -ति, खर्व्वाकारः -रा -रं, ह्रस्वमूर्त्तिः -र्त्तिः -र्त्ति, वामनतनुः -नुः -नु, क्षुद्रतनुः -नुः -नु, स्तोककायः -या -यं, खट्टेरकः -का -कं.

DWARFISHLY, *adv.* वामनवत्, खर्व्ववत्, अतुङ्गवत्, वामनरूपेण.

DWARFISHNESS, *s.* वामनता -त्वं, खर्व्वता, ह्रस्वता, क्षुद्रता, अतुङ्गता.

To DWELL, *v. n.* वस् (c. 1. वसति, वस्तुं), निवस्, अधिवस्, आवस्, प्रतिवस्, अध्यावस्, समावस्, अधिनिवस्, सन्निवस्; वृत् (c. 1. वर्त्तते -र्त्तितुं), स्था (c. 1. तिष्ठति -ते, स्थातुं), अधिष्ठा, आस् (c. 2. आस्ते, आसितुं), अध्यास्, आश्रि (c. 1. -श्रयति -ते -यितुं) with acc., सेव् (c. 1. सेवते -वितुं), निषेव्, उपसेव् with acc., जुष् (c. 6. जुषते, जोषितुं) with acc., निली (c. 4. -लीयते -लेतुं), संली, अधिशी (c. 2. -शेते-शयितुं), वासं कृ.—(Dwell together) संवस्.—(Dwell abroad) प्रवस्.—(Dwell on a subject) अतिप्रसङ्गं कृ, प्रपञ्चं कृ, दीर्घसूत्रतां कृ; 'on a note in singing,' दीर्घस्वरं कृ.

DWELLER, *s.* वासी *m.* -सिनी *f.* (न्), निवासी *m.* -सिनी *f.* (न्), निलायी *m.* -यिनी *f.*, वासकृत्.

DWELLING, *s.* वासः, वासस्थानं, वसतिः *f.*, निलयः -यनं, आलयः, गृहं, गेहः -हं, वेश्म *n.* (न्), निवेशनं, आयतनं, निकेतः -तनं, आगारः, भवनं, वसितं, निवासः, निवसतिः *f.*, समावासः, अवस्थानं, संवासः, आवसथः, वास्तुः *m.*, स्थानं, ओकः *n.* (स्), धाम *n.* (न्).

DWELLING, *part.* (Residing) वासी -सिनी -सि (न्), निवासी, &c., वर्त्ती -र्त्तिनी -र्त्ति (न्), स्थः स्था स्थं, स्थायी -यिनी -यि (न्), कृतालयः -या -यं, आश्रितः -ता -तं, समाश्रितः -ता -तं, सेवी -विनी -वि (न्), अधिशयानः -ना -नं.

DWELLING-HOUSE, *s.* निवासगृहं, वासगेहः -हं, वासागारः, निवासवेश्म *n.* (न्).

DWELLING-PLACE, *s.* वासस्थानं, निवासस्थानं, निवासभूमिः *f.*, निवासभूयं.

DWELT, *p. p.* उषितः -ता -तं, अध्युषितः -ता -तं, आश्रितः -ता -तं.

To DWINDLE, *v. n.* अल्पीभू, न्यूनीभू, ह्रस् (c. 1. ह्रसते -सितुं), क्षि in pass. (क्षीयते), परिक्षि, अपक्षि in pass. (-क्षीयते), सद् (c. 1. सीदति, सत्तुं).

To DWINDLE, *v. a.* अल्पीकृ, न्यूनीकृ, ह्रस् in caus. (ह्रासयति -यितुं).

DWINDLED, *p. p.* अल्पीभूतः -ता -तं, अल्पीकृतः -ता -तं, क्षीणः -णा -णं, न्यूनीभूतः -ता -तं, ह्रसितः -ता -तं, अपचितः -ता -तं, विशीर्णः -र्णा -र्णं.

DYE, *s.* रागः, रङ्गः, वर्णः, कषायः -यं; 'red dye,' लाक्षा, राक्षा; 'blue dye,' नीलं; 'plants used for dye,' लोध्रः, कुसुम्भं, कुङ्कुमः, कषायकृत्.

To DYE, *v. a.* रञ्ज् in caus. (रञ्जयति -यितुं), अभिरञ्ज्, वर्ण् (c. 10. वर्णयति -यितुं), चित्र् (c. 10. चित्रयति -यितुं), सरागं -गां -गं कृ, कषाय (nom. कषायति), कषायीकृ, कुङ्कुमादिना अञ्ज् (c. 7. अनक्ति, अंक्तुं); 'to dye clothes,' कुसुम्भादिना वस्त्राणि रञ्ज् or वस्त्ररागं कृ.

DYED, *p. p.* रञ्जितः -ता -तं, रक्तः -क्ता -क्तं, रागी -गिणी -गि (न्), सरागः -गा -गं, रागान्वितः -ता -तं, कषायितः -ता -तं, कषायचित्रः -त्रा -त्रं, चित्रितः -ता -तं, वर्णितः -ता -तं; 'with saffron,' कुङ्कुमाक्तः -क्ता -क्तं; 'dyed red,' अरुणितः -ता -तं.

DYEING, *s.* रञ्जनं, रागकरणं, वर्णनं, चित्रकरणं, कषायीकरणं; 'of clothes,' वस्त्ररागकरणं, वस्त्ररञ्जनं.

DYER, *s.* रञ्जकः, रागकृत् *m.*, वस्त्ररागकृत्, रागी *m.* (न्), रजकः, वस्त्राणां नीलकुसुम्भादिना रागकारकः.

DYING, *part.* (About to die) म्रियमाणः -णा -णं, मुमूर्षुः -र्षुः -र्षु, आसन्नमृत्युः -त्युः -त्यु, मृतकल्पः -ल्पा -ल्पं, मृतप्रायः -या -यं, कण्ठगतप्राणः -णा -णं, गतायूः -यूः -युः (स्); 'dying first,' पूर्व्वमारी -रिणी -रि (न्).

DYKE, *s.* सेतुः *m.*, जलसेतुः, जलबन्धकः. *See* DIKE.

DYNASTY, *s.* आवलिः *f.*—(Of kings) राजावलिः *f.* -ली, राजवंशः, राजसन्ततिः *f.*, राजकुलं, राजश्रेणी; 'former dynasty,' प्राग्वंशः.

DYSENTERIC, *a.* (Having dysentery) अतिसारी -रिणी -रि (न्), सातिसारः -रा -रं.

DYSENTERY, *s.* अतिसारः, आमातिसारः, सारणः, प्रवाहिका, ग्रहणी, विरेकः, आमरक्तः, प्रस्कन्दनं -न्दिका, उदरामयः, उदरभङ्गः, घसन्तः.

DYSPEPSIA, *s.* अजीर्णं, अजीर्णिः *f.*, अजीर्णता, अपक्तिः *f.*, अपाकः, पाककृच्छ्रं, मन्दाग्निः *m.*, तीक्ष्णाग्निः, अप्रदीप्ताग्निः, अवक्षाथः, कुपित्तं, अन्नविकारः, आमयावित्वं, परिणामशूलः.

DYSPEPTIC, *a.* मन्दाग्निपीडितः -ता -तं, आमयावी -विनी -वि (न्).

DYSPNŒA, *s.* दुःश्वासः, श्वासावरोधः, श्वासकृच्छ्रं, श्वासस्तम्भः.

E

EACH, *a.* (All) सर्व्वः -र्व्वा -र्व्वं, विश्वः -श्वा -श्वं, सकलः -ला -लं; 'Each' is usually expressed by प्रति or अनु prefixed; as, 'each day,' प्रतिदिनं, प्रतिदिवसं, अनुदिनं, अन्वहं; 'each night,' प्रतिरात्रं; 'each month,' प्रतिमासं; 'each one,' प्रत्येकं. 'Or by doubling the word; as, 'each day,' दिने दिने, दिवसे दिवसे, अहरहः; 'in each house,' गृहे गृहे; 'each one,' एकैकः -का -कं, एकैकशस्, पृथक् पृथक्; 'each other,' परस्परं -रां, अन्योन्यं, इतरेतरं; 'each man,' एकैकजनः, प्रतिजनं; 'in each direction,' प्रतिदिशं, सर्व्वदिक्षु; 'each man related his own dream,' एकैको जनः स्वं स्वं स्वप्नम् अकथयत्.

Eager, *a.* अतीच्छः -च्छा -च्छं, अत्यभिलाषी -षिणी -षि (न्), अत्याकांक्षी -क्षिणी -क्षि (न्), कुतूहली -लिनी -लि (न्), कौतूहलान्वितः -ता -तं, व्यग्रः -ग्रा -ग्रं, उत्सुकः -का -कं, तीक्ष्णः -क्ष्णा -क्ष्णं, सरभसः -सा -सं, उद्युक्तः -क्ता -क्तं, सचेष्टः -ष्टा -ष्टं, व्यवसितः -ता -तं, आसक्तः -क्ता -क्तं, अवसक्तः -क्ता -क्तं, रतः -ता -तं, उत्कः -त्का -त्कं, शीघ्रकर्म्मा -र्म्मा -र्म्म (न्), उच्चण्डः -ण्डा -ण्डं, प्रचण्डः -ण्डा -ण्डं, उत्तमः -मा -मं.

Eagerly, *adv.* अत्यभिलाषेण, अतीच्छया, अतिस्पृहातस्, कौतूहलेन, कुतूहलात्, कौतुकेन, अतिवाञ्छया, ईहातस्, सतैक्ष्ण्यं, सरभसं, व्यवसितं.

Eagerness, *s.* कौतूहलं, कुतूहलं, कौतुकं, अत्यभिलाषः, अतिस्पृहा, अतिवाञ्छा, अतिशयेच्छा, तैक्ष्ण्यं, तीक्ष्णता, उत्तापः, उच्चण्डता, प्रचण्डता, व्यग्रता, औत्सुक्यं, उद्योगः, प्रौढिः *f.*, रभसः, आग्रहः, गर्द्धः, उष्मः.

Eagle, *s.* उत्क्रोशः, कुररः -रा -री, गृध्रः, खरः, समुत्क्रोशः, पक्षिराजः, राजपक्षी *m.* (न्).

Eagle-eyed, *a.* उत्क्रोशदृष्टिः -ष्टिः -ष्टि, सूक्ष्मदृष्टिः -ष्टिः -ष्टि.

Eaglet, *s.* उत्क्रोशशावकः, कुररशावकः, उत्क्रोशपोतकः, कुररशिशुः *m.*

Ear, *s.* कर्णः, श्रोत्रं, श्रुतिः *f.*, श्रवः -वणं, श्रोतः *n.* (स्), श्रवणपथः, शब्दग्रहः, ध्वनिग्रहः, शब्दाधिष्ठानं, पैञ्जूषः, कुहरं.—(Organ of hearing) श्रवणेन्द्रियं; 'outer ear,' श्रुतिमण्डलं, वेष्टनं; 'tip of the ear,' पालिः *f.*; 'lobe of the ear,' कर्णलतिका; 'root of the ear,' श्रुतिमूलं, कर्णजाहं; 'hollow of the ear,' श्रवणोदरं; 'ringing in the ear,' कर्णनादः, कर्णक्ष्वेडः; 'boring the ear,' कर्णवेधः; 'having the ears pricked up,' स्तब्धकर्णः -र्णा -र्णं; 'this noise splits the ear,' अयं शब्दः श्रुतिं छिनत्ति; 'he gives ear,' कर्णं ददाति.—(Ear of corn) कणिशः -शं, धान्यशीर्षकं, शस्यमञ्जरी.—(Handle) कर्णः, वारङ्गः.

Ear-ache, *s.* कर्णशूलं, कर्णवेदना, कर्णव्यथा.

Ear-bored, *a.* विद्धकर्णः -र्णा -र्णं, छिद्रितकर्णः -र्णा -र्णं, छिन्नकर्णः -र्णा -र्णं.

Ear-borer, *s.* कर्णवेधनिका -नी, कर्णारा.

Eared, *a.* (Having ears) कर्णी -र्णिनी -र्णि (न्), कर्णवान् -वती -वत् (त्), कर्णिलः -ला -लं -र्णिकः -का -कं.—(Having spikes) मञ्जरितः -ता -तं, सकणिशः -शा -शं.

Earlap, *s.* कर्णपालिः *f.*, श्रवणपालिः *f.*, कर्णलतिका, कर्णशष्कुली.

Ear-pick, *s.* कर्णकण्डूयनकः, कर्णनिर्घर्षणकः, कर्णशोधनी.

Ear-piercing, *a.* कर्णवेधी -धिनी -धि (न्), कर्णभेदी -दिनी -दि (न्).

Ear-ring, *s.* कुण्डलं, कर्णिका, अवतंसः, कर्णालङ्कारः, कर्णालङ्कृतिः *f.*, कर्णाभरणं, कर्णवेष्टनं, कर्णवेष्टकं, कर्णेन्दुः *f.*, उत्तंसः, कर्णान्दुः *f.*, तुड्डुः *m.*; 'wearing ear-rings,' कुण्डली -लिनी -लि (न्), कुण्डलधारी -रिणी -रि (न्), अवतंसितः -ता -तं.

Ear-shot, *s.* कर्णगोचरः -रा -रं, कर्णविषयः -या -यं, श्रुतिपर्य्यन्तं.

Ear-wax, *s.* कर्णमलः -लं, कर्णगूथः, कर्णविट् *f.* (ष्), तोक्मं, वारुण्डः -ण्डं.

Ear-wig, *s.* कर्णकीटी, कर्णजलूका, कर्णजलौका *f.* -काः *f.* (स्), कर्णदुन्दुभिः *f.*

Ear-witness, *s.* श्रुतसाक्षी *m.* (न्), स्वकर्णेन श्रुत्वा साक्ष्यं ददाति यः.

Earl, *s.* कुलीनपदानां मध्ये तृतीयपदभाक् *m.* (ज्), तृतीयकुलीनपदस्थः.

Earldom, *s.* तृतीयकुलीनपदं, तृतीयकुलीनपदस्थितस्य आधिपत्यं or अधिकारः.

Earliness, *s.* शीघ्रता, क्षिप्रता, अविलम्बः, पूर्व्वत्वं, प्राक्त्वं, प्राग्भावः, अग्रत्वं, प्रत्यग्रत्वं, सद्यस्त्वं, अचिरत्वं.—(Early maturity) प्राग्विहितकालात् पक्कता or परिणतत्वं.—(Of the day) सुप्रभातं, अतिप्रभातं, अतिप्रत्यूषः.

Early, *a.* (Forward, prior in time) पूर्व्वः -र्व्वा -र्व्वं, अग्रः -ग्रा -ग्रं, प्रत्यग्रः -ग्रा -ग्रं, प्राक्तनः -ना -नं, सद्यस्कः -स्का -स्कं, सद्यस्कालीनः -ना -नं, अचिरः -रा -रं.—(Mature before the time) अपूर्णकालः -ला -लं, प्राग्विहितकालात् or नियमितकालात् पूर्व्वं परिणतः -ता -तं or पक्कः -क्का -क्कं; 'early decrepitude,' युवजरा.—(Early in the day) प्रगेतनः -नी -नं, अतिप्रगेतनः -नी -नं, पूर्व्वाह्णेतनः -नी -नं, प्रातःकालीनः -ना -नं, प्रभातीयः -या -यं, औषिकः -की -कं, उषस्यः -स्या -स्यं, औषसः -सी -सं, वैयुष्टः -ष्टी -ष्टं.

Early, *adv.* (Soon) सद्यस्, अचिरेण, आशु, झटिति.—(In advance) अग्रे, प्राक्, पूर्व्वं, पूर्व्वे.—(Betimes in the morning) प्रभाते, अतिप्रभाते, प्रगे, अतिप्रगे, प्रत्यूषे, अतिप्रत्यूषे, प्रातर्, प्रातःकाले, सकाले, उषा, प्राह्णे, पूर्व्वाह्णे, प्राक्, व्युष्टं, समया, समये, वेलायां.

To earn, *v. a.* अर्ज् (c. 10. अर्जयति -यितुं), उपार्ज्, लभ् (c. 1. लभते, लब्धुं), उपलभ्, प्राप् (c. 5. -आप्नोति -आप्तुं), अवाप्, अधिगम् (c. 1. -गच्छति -गन्तुं), अश् (c. 5. अश्नुते, अशितुं), उपाश्; आदा (c. 3. -ददाति -दत्ते -दातुं), उपादा, निर्व्विश् (c. 6. -विशति -वेष्टुं), कॢप् (c. 10. कल्पयति -यितुं); 'to earn money by labour,' श्रमेण धनम् उपार्ज्; 'earn wages,' वेतनम् अर्ह् (c. 1. अर्हति -र्हितुं).

Earned, *p. p.* अर्जितः -ता -तं, उपार्ज्जितः -ता -तं, श्रमेणोपार्ज्जितः -ता -तं, लब्धः -ब्धा -ब्धं, उपात्तः -त्ता -त्तं, निर्व्विष्टः -ष्टा -ष्टं.

Earnest, *a.* (Zealous) व्यग्रः -ग्रा -ग्रं, उद्युक्तः -क्ता -क्तं, उद्योगी -गिनी -गि (न्), आसक्तचेताः -ताः -तः (स्), समुद्यतः -ता -तं, उत्सुकः -का -कं, प्रयत्नवान् -वती -वत्, महोद्यमः -मा -मं, कृतप्रयत्नः -त्ना -त्नं, सचेष्टः -ष्टा -ष्टं, प्रचण्डः -ण्डा -ण्डं, उच्चण्डः -ण्डा -ण्डं, उत्साही -हिनी -हि (न्), व्यवसायी -यिनी -यि (न्), तीक्ष्णः -क्ष्णा -क्ष्णं, अत्यनुरागी -गिणी -गि (न्).—(Intent) निविष्टः -ष्टा -ष्टं, अभिनिविष्टः -ष्टा -ष्टं, निविष्टमनाः -नाः -नः (स्), आसक्तः -क्ता -क्तं, कृतनिश्चयः -या -यं, अनन्यविषयात्मा -त्मा -त्म (न्), एकाग्रचित्तः -त्ता -त्तं; 'earnest desire,' अतिस्पृहा, कौतूहलं, गाढाभिलाषः, अतिशयेच्छा.

Earnest, *s.* (Seriousness, not jest) गौरवं, अलाघवं, धीरत्वं, अपरिहासः; 'in earnest,' अपरिहासेन, सगौरवं, अलाघवेन, सधैर्य्यं.—(Part paid beforehand) पूर्व्वदत्तभागः, पूर्व्वदत्तमूल्यं.—(Foretaste) पूर्व्वभुक्तिः *f.*—(Pledge) उपनिधिः *m.*, उपन्यासः, आधिः *m.*, निक्षेपः.

Earnestly, *adv.* यत्नतस्, यत्नात्, सोत्साहं, महायत्नपूर्व्वं, महोद्यमपूर्व्वं, आसक्तचेतसा, व्यग्रं, निविष्टमनसा, अभिनिवेशेन, निर्बन्धेन, सोद्योगं, उत्सुकं, ईहातस्, अत्यनुरागेण; 'earnestly desiring,' अतीच्छः -च्छा -च्छं, अत्यभिलाषी -षिणी -षि (न्).

Earnestness, *s.* व्यग्रता, निवेशः, अभिनिवेशः, मनोनिवेशः, चित्तासक्तिः *f.*, उद्युक्तता, उद्योगः, मनोनिर्बन्धः, उच्चण्डता, औत्सुक्यं, उत्साहः, चेष्टा, अनुरागः, उग्रत्वं, तैक्ष्ण्यं, आत्मैकाग्र्यं, अभियुक्तता.

Earnings, *s. pl.* उपार्ज्जनं, उपार्ज्जितं, अर्ज्जनं, लब्धिः *f.*, लभ्यं, लभ्यांशः, वेतनं, वर्त्तनं, निर्वेशः, कर्म्मण्या, भरण्यं, निष्क्रयः.

Earth, *s.* (The globe) पृथिवी, पृथ्वी, भूः *f.*, धरणी, मही, वसुधा, धरित्री, धरा, मेदिनी, भूमिः *f.*, क्षितिः *f.*, अवनिः *f.* -नी, जगती, उर्व्वी, क्ष्मा, क्षोणी -णिः *f.*, क्षौणिः *f.*, वसुन्धरा, वसुमती, धारिणी, धात्री, भूगोलः, भूमण्डलं, भूलोकः, भूर्लोकः, रसा, गौः *f.* (गो), ज्या, स्थिरा, अचला, निश्चला, अनन्ता, कुः *f.*, मर्त्यः, काश्यपी, विश्वम्भरा, भूतधात्री, विश्वधारिणी, धारयित्री, सर्व्वसहा, संसारः, गोत्रा, इला, इलिका, भुरिक् or भूरिक् *f.* (ज्), भुवनं, विष्टपः -पं, विश्वं, सागरमेखला, उदधिमेखला, समुद्राम्बरा, इलागोलं, खस्तनी, व्योमस्थली, रत्नगर्भा, गिरिकर्णिका, धीजसूः *f.* (-सू), नराधारा, दैत्यमेदजा, विश्वगन्धा, नृतुः *m.*

—(Ground, surface of the earth) भूमिः *f.*, भूतलं, पृथिवीतलं, क्षितितलं, महीतलं, क्ष्मातलं.—(Particles of earth, soil) मृत् *f.* मृत्तिका, मृदा, मृत्खण्डं, क्षितिखण्डः.

To EARTH, *v. a.* भूमौ निविश् in caus. (-वेशयति -यितुं) or निधा (c. 3. -दधाति -धातुं) or सम् in caus. (-र्पयति -यितुं), भूमिगुप्तं -प्तां -प्तं कृ.

To EARTH, *v. n.* भूमिं निविश् (c. 6. -विशति -वेष्टुं), भूमौ गर्त्तं or विवरं कृ.

EARTH-BORN, *a.* भूमिजः -जा -जं, क्षितिजः -जा -जं, भूमिसम्भवः -वा -वं, स्थलजः -जा -जं, महीजः -जा -जं.

EARTHEN, *a.* (Made of earth) मार्त्तिकः -की -कं, मृण्मयः -यी -यं, मृत्तिकामयः-यी-यं, मृत्तिकानिर्म्मितः-ता-तं, महीमयः-यी-यं, माहेयः-यी-यं.

EARTHEN-WARE, *s.* मृण्मयभाण्डं, मृद्भाण्डानि *n. pl.*, कौलालकं, मार्त्तिकं.

EARTHINESS, *s.* मार्त्तिकत्वं, भौमत्वं, पार्थिवत्वं, माहेयता, स्थूलता.

EARTHLING, *s.* मर्त्यः, पृथिवीस्थः, पृथिवीवासी *m.* (न्), संसारी *m.* (न्), विषयी *m.* (न्), भूजन्तुः *m.*

EARTHLY, *a.* पार्थिवः -वी -वं, भौमः -मी -मं -मिकः -की -कं, लौकिकः -की -कं, ऐहलौकिकः -की -कं, माहेयः -यी -यं, सांसारिकः -की -कं, ऐहिकः -की -कं.

EARTHLY-MINDED, *a.* विषयासक्तचेताः -ताः -तः (स्), संसारासक्तमनाः -नाः -नः (स्), विषयोपभोगव्यग्रः -या -यं.

EARTHQUAKE, *s.* भूकम्पः, भूमिकम्पः, धरणीचलनं, भूमिचलनं, भूचलं, भूच्छायितं; 'to quake, as the earth,' छ्माय् (c. 1. छ्मायते -यितुं).

EARTH-WORM, *s.* भूजन्तुः *m.*, क्षितिजन्तुः *m.*, भूलता, महीलता, कुसूः *m.*, वैराटः, किञ्चुलुकः.—(Mean person) नीचजनः, तुच्छजनः.

EARTHY, *a.* पार्थिवः -वी -वं, भौमः -मी -मं. *See* EARTHEN, EARTHLY.

EASE, *s.* सुखं, सौख्यं, अनायासः, विश्रामः, विश्रान्तिः *f.*, शमः, उपशमः, निर्वृत्तिः *f.*, निवृत्तिः *f.*, विरतिः *f.*, शान्तिः *f.*, स्वास्थ्यं, सुस्थता, सुस्थितिः *f.*; अकष्टं, अदुःखं, अक्लेशः, निरुद्वेगः, प्रसादः.—(Facility) सौकर्य्यं, सुकरत्वं, अनायासः, सौगम्यं; 'love of ease,' सुखेच्छा; 'at ease,' सुखेन, यथासुखं, निर्वृतः -ता -तं, निरुद्विग्नः -ग्ना -ग्नं.

To EASE, *v. a.* (Free from pain) दुःखं हृ (c. 1. हरति, हर्त्तुं) or शम् (c. 10. शमयति -यितुं), क्लेशं or उद्वेगं हृ.—(Alleviate) शम्, प्रशम्, उपशम्; शान्त्व् or सान्त्व् (c. 10. सान्त्वयति -यितुं), उपसान्त्व्; लघ (nom. लघयति -यितुं), लघूकृ, शान्तिं दा.—(Free from labour, remove a burden) निरायासं -सां -सं कृ, भारं हृ or उद्धृ or अपनी (c. 1. -नयति -नेतुं).—(Free from any thing) मुच् (c. 6. मुञ्चति, मोक्तुं).

EASEL, *s.* चित्रफलकः, चित्रमञ्चः, चित्राधारः, चित्रलेखापादपः.

EASEMENT, *s.* सुखं, सौख्यं, उपकारः -करणं, साहाय्यं.—(Evacuation) मलविसर्गः, मलशुद्धिः *f.*

EASILY, *adv.* (Without difficulty) सुखेन, सुखं, यथासुखं, अनायासेन, अनायासं, निरायासं, सुकरं, सौकर्य्येण, अयत्नेन, अयत्नतस्, अदुःखेन, अकष्टेन, अक्लेशेन, अश्रमेण, दुःखं विना, क्लेशं विना, हेलया. Often expressed by सु or सुख prefixed; as, 'easily borne,' सुसहः -हा -हं; 'easily obtained,' सुलभः -भा -भं; 'easily cut,' सुखच्छेद्यः -द्या -द्यं; 'easily attained,' सुखसाध्यः -ध्या -ध्यं; 'easily done,' अनायासकृतः -ता -तं; 'doing easily,' सुखकरः -रा -रं.—(With tranquillity) सविश्रामं, शान्त्या, शमेन, निरुद्विग्नं, स्वास्थ्येन.—(Leisurely) सावकाशं.—(Readily) कामं.

EASINESS, *s.* (Facility) सौकर्य्यं, सुकरत्वं -ता, सौगम्यं, सुगमत्वं, सुखत्वं, सुसाध्यता, अनायासः, निरायासत्वं.—(Readiness to comply) अनुकूलता, आनुकूल्यं, अनुरोधः.—(Freedom from pain) स्वास्थ्यं, शान्तिः *f.*, सुस्थता, अक्लेशः; 'easiness of circumstances,' द्रव्यानुकूल्यं.

EAST, *s.* (Eastern quarter) पूर्व्वदिक् *f.* (श्), प्राची, पूर्व्वा, प्राचीनदिक् *f.* (श्), पूर्व्वकाष्ठा, पूर्व्वाशा, सूर्य्योदयस्थानं; 'the eastern country,' प्राच्यः, प्राग्देशः, पूर्व्वदेशः.

EAST, EASTERLY, EASTERN, *a.* प्राङ् प्राची प्राक् (च्), प्राच्यः -च्या -च्यं, पूर्व्वः -र्व्वा -र्व्वं, प्राचीनः -ना -नं, पूर्व्वदिश्यः -श्या -श्यं, पूर्व्वदेशीयः -या -यं, पूर्व्वदिक्स्थः -स्था -स्थं, पूर्व्वदेशजः -जा -जं, पूर्व्वजः -जा -जं; 'facing the east,' प्राङ्मुखः -खा -खी -खं, पूर्व्वमुखः -खा -खं; 'Madhyadesha is east of Vinashana,' मध्यदेशो विनशनात् पूर्व्वः; 'as far as the eastern ocean,' आपूर्व्वसमुद्रात्; 'the eastern mountain,' उदयः, उदयगिरिः *m.*, उदयाचलः, उदयशैलः, पूर्व्वपर्व्वतः, पूर्व्वाद्रिः *m.*, दिनमूर्द्धा *m.* (न्), पूर्व्वाचलः.

EASTER, *s.* ख्रीष्टपुनरुत्थानदिवसमुद्दिश्य महोत्सवः, ख्रीष्टपुनरुत्थानपर्व्व *n.* (न्).

EASTERLY, EASTWARD, *adv.* पुरस्तात्, पूर्व्वेण, पुरस्, प्राक्, पूर्व्वं, पूर्व्वदिशं, पूर्व्वदेशे, सूर्य्योदयं प्रति, पुरा, पूर्व्वपार्श्वे.

EASY, *a.* (Not difficult to be done) निरायासः -सा -सं, निरायासकृतः -ता -तं, अनायासी -सिनी -सि (न्), सुखः -खा -खं, सुकरः -रा -री -रं, सुसाध्यः -ध्या -ध्यं or सुखसाध्यः, सुगमः -मा -मं, लघुः -घुः -घ्वी -घु, अकष्टः -ष्टा -ष्टं, अकठिनः -ना -नं, अविषमः -मा -मं, सुखेन कार्य्यः -र्य्या -र्य्यं.—(Intelligible) सुबोधः -धा -धं, सुगम्यः -म्या -म्यं, सुग्राह्यः -ह्या -ह्यं, अव्याख्येयः -या -यं.—(Free from pain, quiet) स्वस्थः -स्था -स्थं, सुस्थः -स्था -स्थं, शान्तः -न्ता -न्तं, सुखी -खिनी -खि (न्), दुःखहीनः -ना -नं, निरुद्वेगः -गा -गं, निर्वृतः -ता -तं; 'an easy, happy character,' सुखिस्वभावः.—(Complying) अनुकूलः -ला -लं; 'easy of utterance,' सुखोच्चार्य्यः -र्य्या -र्य्यं; 'easy of acquisition,' सुलभः -भा -भं, सुप्राप्यः -प्या -प्यं, सुखलभ्यः -भ्या -भ्यं or सुखेन लभ्यः; 'easy in its paces,' सुखायनः -ना -नं, सुखचारः -रा -रं; 'an easy case,' निश्शल्योऽर्थः.

To EAT, *v. a.* and *n.* खाद् (c. 1. खादति -दितुं), सङ्खाद्; अद् (c. 2. अत्ति -त्तुं), समद्; भक्ष् (c. 10. भक्षयति -यितुं), सम्भक्ष्, अश् (c. 9. अश्नाति, अशितुं), समश्, पर्य्यश्, प्राश्, भुज् (c. 7. भुंक्ते, भोक्तुं), उपभुज्, जक्ष् (c. 2. जक्षिति -तुं), ग्रस् (c. 1. ग्रसते -सितुं), घस् (c. 1. घसति, घस्तुं), प्सा (c. 2. प्साति -तुं), चम् (c. 1. चमति -मितुं), आस्वद् or आस्वाद् (c. 1. -स्वदति -स्वादति -दितुं), गॄ (c. 6. गिरति, गरितुं -रीतुं), निगॄ, चर्व् (c. 1. चर्वति -र्वितुं), अभ्यवहृ (c. 1. -हरति -हर्त्तुं), अभ्याहृ, प्रत्यालिह् (c. 2. -लेढि -ढुं), प्रत्यवसो (c. 4. -स्यति -सातुं), उपयुज् (c. 7. -युनक्ति -युंक्ते -योक्तुं), वल्भ् (c. 1. वल्भते -ल्भितुं), आहारं कृ; 'he bid them eat and drink,' अश्नीत पिबतेति तान् अवदत्.

EATABLE, *a.* खाद्यः -द्या -द्यं, खादनीयः -या -यं, भक्ष्यः -क्ष्या -क्ष्यं, भक्षणीयः -या -यं, भोज्यः -ज्या -ज्यं, भोजनीयः -या -यं, आद्यः -द्या -द्यं, अदनीयः -या -यं, आहार्य्यः -र्य्या -र्य्यं, अभ्यवहरणीयः -या -यं, अभ्याहार्य्यः -र्य्या -र्य्यं.

EATABLE, *s.* भक्ष्यं, भोज्यं, भोजनं, खाद्यद्रव्यं, भक्ष्यवस्तु *n.*, खाद्यं, प्राशित्रं, अशितम्भवं, आहार्य्यं, अभ्याहार्य्यं -र्य्यं.

EATEN, *p. p.* भक्षितः -ता -तं, खादितः -ता -तं, भुक्तः -क्ता -क्तं, अन्नः -न्ना -न्नं, जग्धः -ग्धा -ग्धं, अशितः -ता -तं, प्राशितः -ता -तं, आशितः -ता -तं, अभ्यवहृतः -ता -तं, प्सातः -ता -तं, आस्वादितः -ता -तं, स्वदितः -ता -तं, चर्वितः -ता -तं, गिलितः -ता -तं, प्रत्यवसितः -ता -तं, लिप्तः -प्ता -प्तं, प्रत्यालीढः -ढा -ढं, ग्रसितः -ता -तं, उपयुक्तः -क्ता -क्तं, वल्भितः -ता -तं.

EATER, *s.* खादकः, भक्षकः, अत्ता *m.* (त्तृ), भोक्ता *m.* (क्तृ), भक्षयिता *m.* (तृ), भोजी *m.* (न्), आशी *m.* (न्); 'great eater,' बह्वाशी *m.* बहुभुक् *m.* (ज्).

EATING, *s.* (Act of) भक्षणं, खादनं, भोजनं, चर्वणं, अशनं, प्राशनं,

अभ्यवहरणं, अभ्यवहारः, अभ्याहारः, ग्रसनं, भक्षणं, जग्धिः f., आस्वादः -दनं, प्रत्यवसानं, गिलनं, प्सा, प्सानं, वल्भनं; 'eating together,' सहभोजनं, सग्धिः f.; 'eating of every thing,' सर्व्वान्नभोजी -जिनी -जि (न्), सर्व्वान्नीनः -ना -नं.

Eating-house, s. पक्वान्नविक्रयस्थानं, सिद्धान्नागारः, पक्वान्नपण्यशाला.

Eaves, s. पटलप्रान्तः, वलिकः -कं, नीध्रं, पटलान्तः.

Eaves-dropper, s. गूढश्रोता m. (तृ), प्रच्छन्ने स्थित्वा द्वयोः संलापं कौतुकभावात् शृणोति यः, प्रच्छन्नश्रावी m. (न्).

Ebb, s. पश्चाद्वेला, विपरीतवेला, परावेला, पश्चात्प्रवाहः, विपरीतप्रवाहः, समुद्रवेलाया विपरीतगतिः f., समुद्रजलस्य पुनरावर्त्तः or प्रत्यावर्त्तनं or परावर्त्तः or विपरिवर्त्तनं, वेलापरिवर्त्तनं; 'ebb and flow,' वेला.

To ebb, v. n. वेलावत् परावृत् (c. 1. -वर्त्तते -र्त्तितुं) or विपरिवृत् or परिवृत् or पुनरावृत्, विपरीतं गम् (c. 1. गच्छति, गन्तुं), पश्चात्प्रवाहं कृ.—(Decline) क्षि in pass. (क्षीयते); 'a place whence water has ebbed,' परापः -पा -पं.

Ebony, s. कोविदारः, कुद्दालः, क्षितिसारकः, केन्दुः m., युगपत्रकः, स्फूर्जकः, तिन्दुकः, कालस्कन्धः, कुलकः, चमरिकः.

Ebriety, s. मादः, उन्मादः, उन्मत्तता, मद्यपानजोऽवस्थाविशेषः.

Ebriosity, s. उन्मादशीलता, सदोन्मत्तता, क्षीवता, नित्यक्षीवता.

Ebullition, s. उत्सेचनं, उत्सेकः, फुत्कारः, फेनकरणं, फेनता.—(Internal agitation) अन्तर्वेगः, अन्तःक्षोभः.

Eccentric, a. (Deviating from the centre) केन्द्रापगामी -मिनी -मि (न्) or मध्यस्थानाद् अपगामी, केन्द्रभ्रष्टः -ष्टा -ष्टं.—(From usual custom) लोकाचारविरुद्धः -द्धा -द्धं, व्यवहारविरुद्धः -द्धा -द्धं, नियमबहिर्गतः -ता -तं, उत्क्रान्तमर्य्यादः -दा -दं, विपथगामी -मिनी -मि (न्), उत्सूत्रः -त्रा -त्रं, व्यभिचारी -रिणी -रि (न्), अव्यवस्थितः -ता -तं, विषमः -मा -मं, विलक्षणः -णा -णं, लोकबाह्यः -ह्या -ह्यं, त्यक्तलोकमार्गः -र्गा -र्गं.

Eccentricity, s. लोकाचारविरोधः, उत्क्रमः, विधिविरुद्धता, लोकमर्य्यादाव्यभिचारः, वैषम्यं, उत्सूत्रता.

Ecclesiastic, a. पौरोहितः -ती -तं, मण्डलीसम्बन्धी -न्धिनी -न्धि (न्) or पौरोहित्यसम्बन्धी, धर्म्मोपदेशविषयः -या -यं, याजकीयः -या -यं.

Ecclesiastic, s. पुरोहितः, धर्म्माध्यापकः, धर्म्मशास्त्रोपदेशकः, आचार्य्यः, याजकः, धर्म्मशास्त्रव्यवसायी m. (न्).

Echo, s. प्रतिध्वनिः f., प्रतिशब्दः, प्रतिस्वनः, प्रतिरवः, प्रतिश्रुत् f., प्रतिध्वानः, प्रतिवचनं, ग्रहणं, अनुनादः, प्रतिगर्जनं, व्यनुनादः, ध्वनिः f., स्वानं.

To echo, v. n. and a. ध्वन् (c. 1. ध्वनति -नितुं), प्रध्वन्, प्रतिध्वन्, स्वन् (c. 1. स्वनति -नितुं), प्रतिस्वन्, स्तन् (c. 1. स्तनति -नितुं), प्रतिध्वनिं कृ, प्रतिशब्दं कृ, प्रतिरवं कृ; 'to cause to echo,' अनुनद् in caus. (-नादयति -यितुं), व्यनुनद्.

Echoing, part. अनुनादयन् -यन्ती -यत् (त्), प्रतिगर्जन् -र्जन्ती -र्जत् (त्); 'echoing with,' अनुनादः -दा -दं, निर्घुष्टः -ष्टा -ष्टं, परिसङ्कुष्टः -ष्टा -ष्टं; 'with the sound of the lute,' सवीणानुनादः -दा -दं.

Eclaircissement, s. परिशोधनं, विवरणं, विवृतिः f., व्याख्या, स्पष्टीकरणं.

Eclat, s. प्रशंसा, स्तुतिः f., श्लाघा, कीर्त्तिः f., ख्यातिः f., सुख्यातिः f., यशः n. (स्), विश्रुतिः f., विश्रावः, प्रतिष्ठा, शोभा, प्रभा; 'causing eclat,' कीर्त्तिकरः -री -रं.

Eclectic, a. उद्धारकः -का -कं, उद्धरणः -णा -णं, वरणकृत्, चूर्णिकृत्.

Eclipse, s. ग्रहः -हणं, उपरागः, उपसर्गः, उपप्लवः, राहुग्राहः, ग्रहपीडनं, राहुसंस्पर्शः, औपग्रहिकः, औपग्रस्तिकः, विमर्द्दनं, परागः; 'solar eclipse,' सूर्य्यग्रहः, सूर्य्योपरागः; 'lunar eclipse,' चन्द्रग्रहणं.

To eclipse, v. a. (Darken) तिमिर (nom. तिमिरयति -यितुं), तिमिरीकृ,

अन्धीकृ, मलिनीकृ, प्रछद् (c. 10. -छादयति -यितुं), आछद्.—(To be eclipsed as the sun, &c.) उपरञ्ज् in pass. (-रज्यते), उपसृज् in pass. (-सृज्यते); 'Ráhu eclipsed the sun,' राहुः सूर्य्यम् उपाग्रसत्.

Eclipsed, p. p. (As the sun, &c.) उपसृष्टः -ष्टा -ष्टं, उपरक्तः -क्ता -क्तं, ग्रस्तः -स्ता -स्तं, राहुग्रस्तः -स्ता -स्तं, राहुयुक्तः -क्ता -क्तं, उपप्लुतः -ता -तं, सोपप्लवः -वा -वं.—(Obscured) तिमिरावृतः -ता -तं, तमोवृतः -ता -तं, आच्छन्नः -न्ना -न्नं, प्रच्छन्नः -न्ना -न्नं, उपच्छन्नः -न्ना -न्नं, मलिनः -ना -नं, मलिनप्रभः -भा -भं.

Ecliptic, s. क्रान्तिमण्डलं, क्रान्तिः f., क्रान्तिकक्षः, रविमार्गः.

Eclogue, s. गोमेषपशुपालनादिविषयं क्षुद्रकाव्यं, ग्राम्यकविता.

Economic, economical, a. (Pertaining to the management of household concerns) गृहकर्म्मनिर्वाहसम्बन्धी -न्धिनी -न्धि (न्).—(Frugal) परिमितव्ययः -या -यं, स्वल्पव्ययः -या -यं, अव्ययः -या -यं, अमुक्तहस्तः -स्ता -स्तं, व्ययपराङ्मुखः -खी -खं, अबहुदः -दा -दं.

Economically, adv. परिमितव्ययेन, स्वल्पव्ययेन, अमुक्तहस्तेन.

Economics, s. गृहकार्य्यं, गृहव्यापारः, गृहकर्म्मनिर्व्वाहविद्या.

Economist, s. परिमितव्ययी m. (न्).—(Political economist) नीतिज्ञः, नीतिविद्याकुशलः, नीतिशास्त्रविद् m.

To economize, v. n. परिमितव्ययेन गृहकार्य्याणि निर्वह् in caus. (-वाहयति -यितुं).

Economy, s. (Management of a household) गृहकार्य्यनिर्वाहः, गृहकर्म्मनयः, गार्हस्थ्यं.—(Frugality) परिमितव्ययः, स्वल्पव्ययः, अमुक्तहस्तत्वं.—(Management) नयः, नीतिः f., प्रणयनं, निर्वाहः.—(Arrangement) विन्यासः, विरचनं, संविधानं, कल्पना.—(System) स्थितिः f., संस्थानं, मार्गः.—(Political economy) नीतिः f., नीतिविद्या, राजनीतिः f., राज्यकर्म्मनिर्वाहविद्या.

Ecstasied, a. सम्मोहितः -ता -तं, हर्षमोहितः -ता -तं, हर्षोन्मत्तः -त्ता -त्तं, प्रहर्षितः -ता -तं, आनन्दमग्नः -ग्ना -ग्नं, पुलकितः -ता -तं, रोमाञ्चितः -ता -तं.

Ecstasy, s. प्रमदः, उन्मदः, मादः, प्रहर्षः, मोहः, सम्मोहः, आनन्दः, परमानन्दः, हर्षोन्मत्तता, रोमहर्षः, अत्यन्ताह्लादः, अत्यानन्दः.

Ecstatic, ecstatical, a. मादनः -ना -नी -नं, उन्मादनः -ना -नं, मोहनः -ना -नी -नं, सम्मोही -हिनी -हि (न्), परमानन्ददः -दा -दं, परमाह्लादजनकः -का -कं, पुलकजनकः -का -कं.

Ecstatically, adv. सपरमानन्दं, सानन्दं, समादं, परमाह्लादेन.

Ecumenical, a. सार्व्वलौकिकः -की -कं, सर्व्वसाधारणः -णी -णं.

Edacious, a. भक्षकः -का -कं, खादकः -का -कं, भोजी -जिनी -जि (न्), घस्मरः -रा -रं, घस्मरः -री -रं, प्रघसः -सा -सं, बहुभुक् m. (ज्), बह्वाशी -शिनी -शि (न्), भोजनलुब्धः -ब्धा -ब्धं.

Edacity, s. घस्मरता, अतिभोजनं, गृध्नता, जिघृक्षा.

Eddy, s. जलावर्त्तः, जलगुल्मः, आवर्त्तिका, आवर्त्तिनी, भृमिः m., भ्रमः, भ्रमरकः, अवघूर्णः, दरणिः m., आरणिः m., कूलहुण्डकः, कूलन्धयः, तालूरः.

Edentated, a. निर्दशनः -ना -नं, नीरदः -दा -दं, अदंष्ट्री -ष्ट्रिणी -ष्ट्रि (न्).

Edge, s. (Border, margin) प्रान्तः, अन्तः -न्तं, उपान्तं, समन्तः, पर्य्यन्तं, सीमा, परिसरः, कच्छः, उत्सङ्गः, कोटिः f., धारः.—(Edge or point of a blade) धारा -रं, कोटिः f., अश्रिः f., पालिः f., पाली, पालिका, अणिः m., आणिः m. f., शिखरः -रं, कोणः, अग्रं.—(Edge of a brook) कच्छः, तीरं, तटं, कूलं, कच्छान्तः; 'edge of a wood,' वनान्तं; 'edge of a mountain,' उत्सङ्गः, टङ्का, धारा; 'edge of a roof,' पटलप्रान्तः, वलिकः, नीध्रं; 'two-edged,' द्विधारः -रा -रं, उभयतस् तीक्ष्णः -क्ष्णा -क्ष्णं; 'red-edged,' रक्तकोटिः -टिः -टि; 'state of being set on edge (the teeth),' दन्तहर्षः.—(Keenness) तैक्ष्ण्यं, तीक्ष्णता, तेजः n. (स्); 'of appetite,' अग्निः m., रुचिः f.

To EDGE, *v. a.* (Border) प्रान्त (nom. प्रान्तयति -यितुं), समन्त, (समन्तयति -यितुं), पर्य्यन्तं कृ.—(Sharpen) तिज् (c. 10. तेजयति -यितुं), तीक्ष्णीकृ, निशो (c. 4. -श्यति -शातुं).

EDGED, *a.* (Having an edge) धारी -रिणी -रि (न्), धाराधरः -रा -रं, कोटिमान् -मती -मत् (त्).—(Sharp-edged) तीक्ष्णधारः -रा -रं, शितधारः -रा -रं, तीक्ष्णाग्रः -ग्रा -ग्रं, लविः -विः -वि; 'two-edged sword,' द्विधारखड्गः.

EDGELESS, *a.* धाराहीनः -ना -नं, कोटिरहितः -ता -तं, अतीक्ष्णः -क्ष्णा -क्ष्णं.

EDGING, *s.* कोटिः f.—(Of a garment) अञ्चलः, वस्त्राञ्चलः -लं.

EDIBLE, *a.* खाद्यः -द्या -द्यं, खादनीयः -या -यं, भोज्यः -ज्या -ज्यं, भक्ष्यः -क्ष्या -क्ष्यं, भक्षणीयः -या -यं, भोजनीयः -या -यं, आद्यः -द्या -द्यं, अदनीयः -या -यं, आहार्य्यः -र्य्या -र्य्यं.

EDICT, *s.* राजाज्ञा, राजशासनं, शासनं, धर्म्मकीलः; 'written order,' आज्ञापत्रं, शासनपत्रं, पट्टः.

EDIFICATION, *s.* ज्ञाननिष्ठा, निष्ठा, ज्ञानवृद्धिः f., ज्ञानप्राप्तिः f., शिक्षा, समुत्थानं, उपदेशः, ज्ञानदानं.

EDIFICE, *s.* हर्म्म्यं, शाला, भवनं, मन्दिरं, धाम n. (न्), सौधं, अट्टालिका, प्रासादः, सदनं, गृहं, वरणः, वास्त्रं, प्राकारः.

EDIFIED, *p. p.* शिक्षितः -ता -तं, प्राप्तज्ञानः -ना -नं, वृद्धज्ञानः -ना -नं, लब्धज्ञानः -ना -नं, गृहीतज्ञानः -ना -नं, उपदिष्टः -ष्टा -ष्टं.

To EDIFY, *v. a.* निष्ठां कृ or जन् (c. 10. जनयति -यितुं), शिक्ष् (c. 10. शिक्षयति -यितुं), उपदिश् (c. 6. -दिशति -देष्टुं), ज्ञानं वृध् in caus. (वर्धयति -यितुं).

EDIFYING, *a.* निष्ठावर्धकः -का -कं, ज्ञानवर्धकः -का -कं, उपदेशकः -का -कं.

To EDIT, *v. a.* ग्रन्थं शोधयित्वा प्रकाश् (c. 10. -काशयति -यितुं), प्रकटीकृ.

EDITED, *p. p.* प्रकाशितः -ता -तं, शोधितः -ता -तं, शुद्धीकृतः -ता -तं.

EDITION, *s.* (Publication) प्रकाशनं, प्रकाशकरणं, प्रकटीकरणं.—(Number of copies printed at once) एकवारे मुद्रितो ग्रन्थसमूहः.

EDITOR, *s.* प्रकाशकः, ग्रन्थप्रकाशकः, ग्रन्थशोधकः.

To EDUCATE, *v. a.* विनी (c. 1. -नयति -नेतुं), अनुनी, शिक्ष् (c. 10. शिक्षयति -यितुं), अनुशिक्ष्, शास् (c. 2. शास्ति, शासितुं), अनुशास्, अधी in caus. (अध्यापयति -यितुं, rt. इ), उपदिश् (c. 6. -दिशति -देष्टुं), पुष् (c. 10. पोषयति -यितुं), पाल् (c. 10. पालयति -यितुं), प्रतिपाल्, अभ्यस् (c. 4. -अस्यति -असितुं), संवृध् in caus. (-वर्धयति -यितुं), विद्यां दा.

EDUCATED, *p. p.* शिक्षितः -ता -तं, कृतविद्यः -द्या -द्यं, लब्धविद्यः -द्या -द्यं, गृहीतविद्यः -द्या -द्यं, कृताभ्यासः -सा -सं, कृतबुद्धिः -द्धिः -द्धि, कृतधीः -धीः -धि, अनुनीतः -ता -तं, विनीतः -ता -तं, शिष्टः -ष्टा -ष्टं, संवर्धितः -ता -तं, पोषितः -ता -तं, व्युत्पन्नः -न्ना -न्नं, संस्कृतः -ता -तं; 'well-educated,' सुशिक्षितः -ता -तं.

EDUCATION, *s.* शिक्षा, अध्यापनं, विनयः, अनुनयः, शिष्टिः f., शास्तिः f., शासनं, अनुशासनं, उपदेशः, विद्यादानं, अभ्यासः, पोषः -षणं, पुष्टिः f., पालनं, प्रतिपालनं, संवर्धनं, विद्याप्राप्तिः f., विद्यालब्धिः f., विद्याग्रहणं, विद्यार्ज्जनं, व्युत्पत्तिः f.

EEL, *s.* जलव्यालः, कुञ्चिका, अन्धाहिः m. f., पङ्कगतिः f.

EFFABLE, *a.* कथनीयः -या -यं, वाच्यः -च्या -च्यं, निर्वचनीयः -या -यं.

To EFFACE, *v. a.* अपमृज् (c. 2. -मार्ष्टि -र्ष्टुं), व्यामृज्, प्रमृज्, अवमृज्, उन्मृज्; व्यामृश् (c. 6. -मृशति -म्रष्टुं), अवमृश्; अवमृद् (c. 9. -मृद्नाति -मर्दितुं), उच्छिद् (c. 7. -छिनत्ति -छेत्तुं), विनश् in caus. (-नाशयति -यितुं), उद्धृ (c. 1. -हरति -हर्तुं), समुद्धृ, उन्मूल् (c. 10. -मूलयति -यितुं), लुप् (c. 6. लुम्पति, लोप्तुं), लोपं कृ, अवमर्षणं कृ, व्यामर्षं कृ.

EFFACED, *p. p.* अपमृष्टः -ष्टा -ष्टं, उन्मृष्टः -ष्टा -ष्टं, व्यामृष्टः -ष्टा -ष्टं, उच्छिन्नः -न्ना -न्नं, अवमृदितः -ता -तं, मृदितः -ता -तं, लुप्तः -प्ता -प्तं.

EFFACEMENT, *s.* मार्जना, अपमार्जना, व्यामर्षः, अवमर्षणं, लोपः.

EFFECT, *s.* (That which is produced by an agent) उत्पन्नं, निष्पन्नं, उद्भूतं, सिद्धिः f., उत्पत्तिः f., कार्य्यं, वृत्तं, अनुवृत्तं, घटना.—(Consequence) फलं, कर्म्मफलं, फलमुत्तरं, प्रयोगः, प्रयुक्तिः f., उत्तरं, अनुसारः, परिणामः, अन्तः -न्तं, वृत्तान्तः, शेषः, अनुषङ्गः, कार्य्यं, अन्वयः, योगः, अनुभवः, भव्यं, फलोदयः, प्रतिफलं, उदर्कः, प्रत्ययः.—(Purpose) अर्थः, प्रयोजनं, अभिप्रायः; 'to what effect?' किमर्थं; 'he spoke to that effect,' इत्युवाच.—(Advantage, validity) फलं, प्रयोजनं, अर्थः, प्रभावः; 'of no effect,' निष्फलः -ला -लं, निरर्थकः -का -कं, निष्प्रयोजनः -ना -नं; 'to destroy the effect of any thing,' निष्फल (nom. निष्फलयति -यितुं), मोघीकृ.—(Completion) निष्पत्तिः f., सिद्धिः f.—(Fact) वस्तु n., अर्थः; 'in effect,' वस्तुतस्, अर्थतस्, तत्त्वतस्.—(Effects, goods) द्रव्याणि n. pl., वस्तूनि n. pl., सामग्र्यं, सामग्री, विभवः, रिक्थं.

To EFFECT, *v. a.* उत्पद् in caus. (-पादयति -यितुं), सम्पद्, निष्पद्, उपपद्, समुत्पद्; साध् in caus. (साधयति -यितुं), संसाध्, सिद्धीकृ, जन् in caus. (जनयति -यितुं), सञ्जन्; कृ (c. 8. करोति, कर्तुं), सकृ, तन् (c. 8. तनोति -नितुं), निर्मा (c. 2. -माति -तुं).

EFFECTED, *p. p.* सिद्धः -द्धा -द्धं, सम्पादितः -ता -तं, उत्पादितः -ता -तं, उपपादितः -ता -तं, निष्पादितः -ता -तं, समुत्पादितः -ता -तं, निष्पन्नः -न्ना -न्नं, सम्पन्नः -न्ना -न्नं, उत्पन्नः -न्ना -न्नं, उपपन्नः -न्ना -न्नं, कृतः -ता -तं, साधितः -ता -तं, सिद्धीकृतः -ता -तं, राद्धः -द्धा -द्धं, अनुराद्धः -द्धा -द्धं; 'one who has effected his object,' कृतार्थः, कृतार्थीभूतः.

EFFECTIBLE, *a.* साध्यः -ध्या -ध्यं, साधनीयः -या -यं, प्रसाध्यः -ध्या -ध्यं, निष्पाद्यः -द्या -द्यं, उपपाद्यः -द्या -द्यं, सम्पादनीयः -या -यं, करणीयः -या -यं, कर्तुं or उत्पादयितुं शक्यः -क्या -क्यं.

EFFECTIVE, *a.* साधकः -का -कं, साधिकः -का -कं, कार्य्यसाधकः -का -कं, प्रसाधकः -का -कं, सम्पादकः -का -कं, निष्पादकः -का -कं, प्रतिपादकः -का -कं, उत्पादकः -का -कं, निष्पादनः -ना -नं, कारकः -का -कं, कारी -रिणी -रि (न्), फलोत्पादकः -का -कं.

EFFECTIVELY, *adv.* अमोघं, सफलं, निष्पत्तिपूर्वं, निष्पादकप्रकारेण, अव्यर्थं, सबलं, प्रभावेन.

EFFECTLESS, *a.* निष्फलः -ला -लं, व्यर्थः -र्था -र्थं, मोघः -घा -घं, अनुपपन्नः -न्ना -न्नं, निर्बलः -ला -लं, निर्गुणः -णा -णं, निष्प्रयोजनः -ना -नं.

EFFECTUAL, *a.* अमोघः -घा -घं, फलोत्पादकः -का -कं, सफलः -ला -लं, अव्यर्थः -र्था -र्थं, अव्यर्थयत्नः -त्ना -त्नं, प्रबलः -ला -लं, बलवान् -वती -वत् (त्), शक्तिमान् -मती -मत् (त्), सप्रयोजनः -ना -नं, सार्थकः -का -कं, अनिरर्थकः -का -कं, समर्थः -र्था -र्थं, उपयोगी -गिनी -गि (न्).

EFFECTUALLY, *adv.* अमोघं, अव्यर्थं, सफलं, सप्रयोजनं, बलवत्.

To EFFECTUATE, *v. a.* साध् (c. 10. साधयति -यितुं), सम्पद् (c. 10. -पादयति -यितुं).

EFFEMINACY, *s.* स्त्रीत्वं, स्त्रीता, स्त्रैणं, क्लैब्यं, क्लीवता, सौकुमार्य्यं, कोमलता, मृदुता, स्त्रीव्यवहारित्वं, स्त्रीधर्म्मसेवा.

EFFEMINATE, *a.* स्त्रैणः -णी -णं, स्त्रीधर्म्मा -र्म्मा -र्म्म (न्), स्त्रीधर्म्मी -र्म्मिणी -र्म्मि (न्), स्त्रीव्यवहारी -रिणी -रि (न्), स्त्रीसदाचारी -रिणी -रि (न्), क्लीवः -वा -वं, सुकुमारः -रा -रं, कोमलः -ला -लं; 'an effeminate person,' निष्पुरुषः, कापुरुषः, गेहशूरः.

To EFFEMINATE, *v. a.* क्लीबीकृ, स्त्रीवत् कृ, निष्पुरुषीकृ, कोमलीकृ.

EFFEMINATELY, *adv.* स्त्रीवत्, निष्पुरुषवत् कापुरुषवत्, क्लीबवत्, नारीरूपेण, स्त्रीधर्म्मानुसारात्.

To EFFERVESCE, *v. n.* फेन (nom. फेनायते) उत्सेचनं कृ, फेनलः -ला -लं भू, फेनलीभू, फुल् कृ, बुद्बुद (nom. बुद्बुदायते), फुत्कारेण वृध् (c. 1. वर्धते -र्धितुं) or उच्छूनीभू, or उष्णीभू or आलोडितः -ता -तं भू.

EFFERVESCENCE, *s.* फेनता, फेनलत्वं, फेनवत्त्वं, उत्सेकः, उत्सेचनं, उच्छूनीभावः, फेनभावः, उष्णत्वं, उत्तापः, अन्तःक्षोभः, आलोडनं.

EFFERVESCING, *a.* फेनलः -ला -लं, फेनायमानः -ना -नं, फेनवान् -वती -वत् (त्), फेनिलः -ला -लं, बुद्बुदायमानः -ना -नं.

EFFETE, *a.* (Barren) वन्ध्यः -न्ध्या -न्ध्यं, अप्रसवी -विनी -वि (न्), निष्फलः -ला -लं, शुष्कः -ष्का -ष्कं.—(Worn out) जीर्णः -र्णा -र्णं.

EFFICACIOUS, *a.* प्रबलः -ला -लं, बलवान् -वती -वत् (त्), सप्रभावः -वा -वं, प्रभविष्णुः -ष्णुः -ष्णु, शक्तिमान् -मती -मत् (त्), प्रतापी -पिनी -पि (न्), समर्थः -र्था -र्थं, क्षमः -मा -मं, गुणवान् -वती -वत् (त्), अलम्मः -मा -मं, कार्य्यसाधकः -का -कं, सिद्धिकरः -री -रं, गुणकारी -रिणी -रि (न्), अमोघः -घा -घं, अव्यर्थः -र्था -र्थं, फलवान् -वती -वत् (त्), तेजोवान् -वती -वत् (त्).

EFFICACIOUSLY, *adv.* प्रभावेण, अमोघं, प्रबलं, अलमर्थं, अलमर्थं, सफलं.

EFFICACY, *s.* प्रभावः, प्राबल्यं, बलं, शक्तिः *f.*, सामर्थ्यं, तेजः *n.* (स्), प्रभविष्णुता, प्रतापः, बलवत्त्वं, अमोघता, फलवत्त्वं, फलोत्पादनं.

EFFICIENCY, *s.* कार्य्यसिद्धिक्षमता, कार्य्यसम्पादकत्वं, कार्य्यकारित्वं, कर्म्मक्षमता, कर्म्मसामर्थ्यं, कार्य्योपयुक्तता. *See* EFFICACY.

EFFICIENT, *a.* कार्य्यसाधकः -का -धिका -कं, कार्य्यसम्पादकः -का -कं, कार्य्यसिद्धिक्षमः -मा -मं, कार्य्योपयुक्तः -क्ता -क्तं, कार्य्यक्षमः -मा -मं, कर्म्मक्षमः -मा -मं, अलङ्कर्म्मीणः -णा -णं, फलोत्पादकः -का -कं. *See* EFFICACIOUS.

EFFICIENTLY, *adv.* सिद्धिपूर्व्वं, अमोघं, सप्रभावं, यथा कर्म्म सिध्यते तथा.

EFFIGY, *s.* प्रतिमा -मानं, मूर्त्तिः *f.*, प्रतिकायः, प्रतिरूपं, प्रतिकृतिः *f.*, रूपं, आकृतिः *f.*, आकारः, वपुः *n.* (स्).

EFFLORESCENCE, *s.* पुष्पोत्पादनं, पुष्पोत्पत्तिः *f.*, प्रस्फोटनं.—(Eruption on the skin) दद्रुः *m.*, उदर्दः, पुष्पाकारस्फोटोत्पत्तिः *f.*

EFFLUENCE, *s.* निःसारः -रणं, निःस्रावः, प्रस्रवः -वणं, प्रवृत्तिः *f.*, प्रवाहः, उत्पत्तिः *f.*, निर्गमः.

EFFLUVIUM, EFFLUVIA, *s.* उद्गारः, वासः, वाष्पः.—(Bad odour) दुर्गन्धः, कुत्सितगन्धः, पूतिगन्धः.

EFFLUX, EFFLUXION, *s.* निःस्रावः, प्रस्रावः, प्रस्रवणं, उत्सेकः, प्रसेकः, निःसारः -रणं, संस्रावः, प्रवाहः, प्रवृत्तिः *f.*, उत्पत्तिः *f.*

EFFORT, *s.* यत्नः, प्रयत्नः, चेष्टा, चेष्टितं, विचेष्टितं, उत्साहः, उद्यमः, उद्योगः, व्यवसायः, अध्यवसायः, चेष्टनं, प्रवृत्तिः *f.*, व्यापारः, आयासः, प्रयासः, घटनं -ना, घटा, ग्रहः, गुरणं, गूरणं, गोरणं, उपक्रमः, कर्म्मयोगः, प्रयोगः, व्यायामः; 'to make effort,' यत् (c. 1. यतते -तितुं), प्रयत्, चेष्ट् (c. 1. चेष्टते -ष्टितुं), विचेष्ट्, व्यवसो (c. 4. -स्यति -सातुं), उद्यम् (c. 1. -यच्छति -यन्तुं).

EFFRONTERY, *s.* धार्ष्ट्यं, धृष्टता, प्रागल्भ्यं, प्रगल्भता, निर्लज्जत्वं, प्रतिभानं.

EFFULGENCE, *s.* उज्ज्वलता, तेजः *n.* (स्), दीप्तिः *f.*, द्युतिः *f.*, बृहद्द्युतिः *f.*, प्रतापः, प्रभा.

EFFULGENT, *a.* तेजस्वी -स्विनी -स्वि (न्), उज्ज्वलः -ला -लं, अतिशोभनः -ना -नं, सुप्रभः -भा -भं, अतिदीप्तिमान् -मती -मत् (त्), तैजसः -सी -सं.

To EFFUSE, *v. a.* पत् in caus. (पातयति -यितुं), उत्सृज् (c. 6. -सृजति -स्रष्टुं), विसृज्, स्कन्द् in caus. (स्कन्दयति -यितुं), उत्सिच् (c. 6. -सिञ्चति -सेक्तुं), अवसिच्, निषिच्, मुच् (c. 6. मुञ्चति, मोक्तुं), प्रमुच्, स्रु in caus. (स्रावयति -यितुं), प्रस्रु, आवृत् in caus. (-वर्त्तयति -यितुं).

EFFUSED, *p. p.* स्कन्दितः -ता -तं, उत्सृष्टः -ष्टा -ष्टं, स्रावितः -ता -तं.

EFFUSION, *s.* उत्सर्गः, निषेकः, उत्सेकः, स्कन्दनं, स्रावः, अवसेचनं, पातः -तनं, मोचनं, मोक्षणं, विसर्गः, निक्षेपः.

EGG, *s.* अण्डं, डिम्बः, डिम्भः, कोशः, कोषः -षकः, पेशिः *f.*, पेशी; 'fowl's egg,' कुक्कुटाण्डं; 'egg-born,' अण्डजः -जा -जं.

To EGG ON or EDGE, *v. a.* प्रेर् (c. 10. प्रेरयति -यितुं, rt. ईर्), उत्सह् in caus. (-साहयति -यितुं), प्रोत्सह्, चुद् (c. 10. चोदयति -यितुं), उत्तिज् (c. 10. -तेजयति -यितुं).

EGG-PLANT, *s.* हिङ्गुलीरः, हिङ्गुली, वङ्गनः, वार्त्ताकुः *m.* -की, भण्टाकी, वातिगः, दुःप्रधर्षिणी, चित्रफला, कुकुटं.

EGLANTINE, *s.* जवापुष्पो वन्यलताभेदः, वरजवा.

EGOTISM, *s.* अहङ्कारः, अहङ्क्रिया, अहङ्कृतिः *f.*, अहन्ता, अहमहमिका, अहम्मतिः *f.*, ममता, आत्माभिमानं, आत्मश्लाघा, आत्मस्तुतिः *f.*

EGOTIST, *s.* अहङ्कारी *m.* (न्), अहंयुः *m.*, आत्माभिमानी *m.* (न्), ममतायुक्तः.

EGOTISTICAL, *a.* अहङ्कारी -रिणी -रि (न्), अहङ्कारवान् -वती -वत् (त्) or अहङ्क्रियावान्, अहंयुः -युः -यु, मामकः -की -कं, आत्मनीनः -ना -नं.

EGREGIOUS, *a.* (Eminent) विशिष्टः -ष्टा -ष्टं, ख्यातः -ता -तं, प्रसिद्धः -द्धा -द्धं, उत्कृष्टः -ष्टा -ष्टं, अधिकः -का -कं, प्रमुखः -खा -खं, उत्तमः -मा -मं. —(Great) परमः -मा -मं, अति prefixed; 'an egregious fool,' अतिमूर्खः, प्रतिनिविष्टमूर्खः, अयमविनष्टचित्तः; 'an egregious rascal,' ख्यातगर्हणः, अत्यन्तदुष्टः, अतिगर्हितः.

EGREGIOUSLY, *adv.* परमं, अति, अतीव, अतिशयेन, भृशं, अतिमात्रं.

EGRESS, EGRESSION, *s.* निःसारः -रणं, निःसरणं, अपसारः, निर्गमः, निर्गतिः *f.*, बहिर्गमनं, निष्क्रमणं, निर्याणं, विनिर्गमः.

EGYPT, *s.* (The country) मिसरदेशः.

EGYPTIAN, *s.* and *a.* मिसरदेशजः, मिसरदेशीयः -या -यं.

EIGHT, *a.* अष्ट or अष्टौ *m.f.n.* (अष्टन्), अष्टकः -का -कं, अष्टसंख्यकः -का -कं.

EIGHTEEN, *a.* अष्टादश *m.f.n.* (न्), अष्टादशसंख्यकः -का -कं.

EIGHTEENTH, *a.* अष्टादशः -शी -शं.

EIGHTFOLD, *a.* अष्टगुणः -णा -णं, अष्टविधः -धा -धं, अष्टकः -का -कं, अष्टाङ्गः -ङ्गा -ङ्गं, अष्टप्रकारः -रा -रं, अष्टधा.

EIGHTH, *a.* अष्टमः -मी -मं, अष्टकः -का -कं; 'one-eighth,' अष्टमांशः, अष्टमभागः, पादार्द्धं.

EIGHTIETH, *a.* अशीतः -ती -तं, अशीतितमः -मा -मं.

EIGHTHLY, *adv.* अष्टमस्थले, अष्टमपदे, अष्टमस्थाने.

EIGHTY, *a.* अशीतिः *f. sing.*, अशीतिसंख्यकः -का -कं; 'eighty years old,' आशीतिकः -का -कं; 'eighty-one,' एकाशीतिः *f.*; 'eighty-two,' द्व्यशीतिः *f.*; 'eighty-three,' त्र्यशीतिः *f.*

EITHER, *pron. distrib.* (Of two) अन्यतरः -रा -रत्.—(Of many) अन्यतमः -मा -मत्; 'either of two days,' अन्यतरेद्युस्.

EITHER, *conj.* वा placed after a word, अथवा, वापि, किंवा; 'either a friend or an enemy,' मित्रं वा अथवा शत्रुः.

To EJACULATE, *v. a.* उत्क्षिप् (c. 6. -क्षिपति -क्षेप्तुं), उद्गॄ (c. 6. -गिरति -गरितुं -रीतुं).—(Utter a sudden prayer) आकस्मिकप्रार्थनाम् उदीर् (c.10. -ईरयति -यितुं), अकस्मात्, प्रार्थनाम् उदाहृ (c.1. -हरति -हर्त्तुं).

EJACULATION, *s.* उद्गारः, उद्गिरणं, उत्क्षेपः, उदीरणं, उदाहरणं.—(Utterance of a sudden prayer) आकस्मिकप्रार्थनोदीरणं.

EJACULATORY *a.* उत्क्षेपकः -का -कं, अकस्माद् उदीरितः -ता -तं, आकस्मिकः -की -कं.

To EJECT, *v. a.* अपास् (c. 4. -अस्यति -असितुं), निःसृ in caus. (-सार-

यति -यितुं), निराकृ, बहिष्कृ, बहिःकृ, दूरीकृ, उत्क्षिप् (c. 6. -क्षिपति -क्षेप्तुं), प्रतिक्षिप्, समाक्षिप्, निष्कस् in caus. (-कासयति -यितुं).—(From office) अधिकारात् or साचिव्याद् भ्रंश् in caus. (भ्रंशयति -यितुं) or च्यु in caus. (च्यावयति -यितुं).—(Vomit up) उत्क्षिप्, उद्गृ (c. 6. -गिरति -गरितुं -रीतुं).

Ejected, *p. p.* निःसारितः -ता -तं, निरस्तः -स्ता -स्तं, अपास्तः -स्ता -स्तं, निराकृतः -ता -तं, बहिष्कृतः -ता -तं, बहिःकृतः -ता -तं, उत्क्षिप्तः -प्ता -प्तं, अपसारितः -ता -तं, अपविद्धः -द्धा -द्धं.—(From office) च्युताधिकारः -रा -रं, अधिकारात्प्रभ्रंशितः -ता -तं, निर्भिन्नः -न्ना -न्नं.

Ejection, *s.* निरसनं, निःसारणं, अपसारणं, उत्क्षेपः, बहिष्करणं, अपासनं, निर्वासनं, निराकरणं, अपसर्जनं, प्रयापणं, निष्कासनं.

Ejectment, *s.* राजाज्ञापत्रेण क्षेत्रगृहादेर् निराकरणं.

Ejulation, *s.* विलपनं, परिदेवनं, कोलाहलः, क्रुष्टं, क्रन्दनं, हाहाकारः, आर्त्तनादः, हा हतोऽस्मीति उत्क्रोशनं.

To eke, *v. a.* (Enlarge) वृध् in caus. (वर्धयति -यितुं), विस्तृ in caus. (-स्तारयति -यितुं), प्रसृ in caus. (-सारयति -यितुं).—(Lengthen) द्राघ (nom. द्राघयति -यितुं), तन् (c. 8. तनोति -नितुं), दीर्घीकृ.

To elaborate, *v. a.* संस्कृ, परिष्कृ, महायत्नेन or बहुश्रमेण साध् in caus. (साधयति -यितुं) or सिद्धीकृ or निष्पद् in caus. (-पादयति -यितुं) or निर्मा (c. 2. -माति -तुं) or क्लृप् (c. 10. कल्पयति -यितुं) or विधा (c. 3. -दधाति -धातुं).

Elaborate, elaborated, *a.* or *p. p.* संस्कृतः -ता -तं, परिष्कृतः -ता -तं, महायत्नेन कल्पितः -ता -तं or विरचितः -ता -तं or सिद्धीकृतः -ता -तं.

Elaborately, *adv.* महायत्नेन, महायासेन, सपरिष्कारं, बहुश्रमेण, बहुप्रयासेन, परिष्कारपूर्व्वं.

Elaboration, *s.* परिष्कारः, परिष्कृतिः *f.*, संस्कारः, महायत्नेन साधनं or निष्पादनं or निर्माणं or कल्पनं or विरचनं.

To elance, *v. a.* अस् (c. 4. अस्यति, असितुं), प्रास्, क्षिप् (c. 6. क्षिपति, क्षेप्तुं), प्रक्षिप्, सृज् (c. 6. सृजति, स्रष्टुं), मुच् (c. 6. मुञ्चति, मोक्तुं), प्रमुच्.

To elapse, *v. n.* अती (c. 2. अत्येति -तुं, rt. इ), व्यती, अतिक्रम् (c. 1. -क्रामति -क्रमितुं), व्यतिक्रम्, अतिवृत् (c 1. -वर्त्तते -र्त्तितुं), गम् (c. 1. गच्छति, गन्तुं); 'a long time elapsed,' अतिचक्राम सुमहान् कालः; 'ten days having elapsed,' अतिक्रान्ते दशाहे.

Elapsed, *p. p.* अतीतः -ता -तं, व्यतीतः -ता -तं, अतिक्रान्तः -न्ता -न्तं, गतः -ता -तं, भूतः -ता -तं.

Elastic, *a.* स्थितिस्थापकः -का -कं, प्रकृतिप्रापकः -का -कं, वर्द्धनक्षमः -मा -मं, सुखाकुञ्चनीयः -या -यं, विततीकरणीयः -या -यं, विस्तारयितुं शक्यः -क्या -क्यं, स्वप्रकृतिं प्रति निवर्त्तनशीलः -ला -लं.

Elasticity, *s.* स्थितिस्थापकं -कत्वं -कता, वर्धनक्षमता, प्रकृतिप्रापकत्वं, स्वप्रकृतिं प्रति निवर्त्तनशीलता, सुखाकुञ्चनीयता.

Elate, elated, *a.* उन्नतः -ता -तं, समुन्नतः -ता -तं, उन्नतमनस्कः -स्का -स्कं, प्रहृष्टमनाः -नाः -नः (स्), हृष्टचित्तः -त्ता -त्तं, उल्लासितः -ता -तं, उन्नद्धचेताः -ताः -तः (स्), समुन्नतचित्तः -त्ता -त्तं, प्रमुदितः -ता -तं, प्रफुल्लः -ल्ला -ल्लं, दर्पाध्मातः -ता -तं; 'elated with victory,' जयगर्व्वितः -ता -तं.

To elate, *v. a.* दृप् in caus. (दर्पयति -यितुं), प्रहृष् in caus. (-हर्षयति -यितुं), उल्लस् in caus. (-लासयति -यितुं), प्रमुद् in caus. (-मोदयति -यितुं).

Elation, *s.* उन्नतिः *f.*, चित्तसमुन्नतिः *f.*, उन्नतमनस्कत्वं, हर्षः, प्रहर्षः, दर्पः, प्रमोदः, गर्व्वः; 'from conquest,' जयगर्व्वः.

Elbow, *s.* अरत्निः *m.*, कफोणिः *m. f.* -णी, कूर्परः, कफणिः *m. f.* -णी, कीलः.—(Of a river) वङ्कः, वक्रं, भङ्गुरः, पुटभेदः.—(Corner) कोणः.

To elbow, *v. a.* अरत्निना ताडयित्वा बहिष्कृ, अरत्निना आहन् (c. 2. -हन्ति -न्तुं).

Elbow-chair, *s.* अरत्निधारणयोग्यः पीठविशेषः.

Elbow-room, *s.* (Room for motion) प्रसरः, अवकाशः.

Elder, *a.* ज्यायान् -यसी -यः (स्), ज्येष्ठः -ष्ठा -ष्ठं, वयोज्येष्ठः -ष्ठा -ष्ठं, पूर्व्वजः -जा -जं, अग्रजः -जा -जं, वरः -रा -रं, वरीयान् -यसी -यः (स्), वरिष्ठः -ष्ठा -ष्ठं, अधिकवयाः -याः -यः (स्), वरवयाः &c., अधिकवयस्कः -स्का -स्कं, वर्षीयान् -यसी -यः (स्), वर्षिष्ठः -ष्ठा -ष्ठं, अग्रिमः -मा -मं, अग्रियः -या -यं, अकनिष्ठः -ष्ठा -ष्ठं.

Elder, *s.* (Venerable person) गुरुः *m.*, गुरुजनः, आर्य्यजनः, वृद्धः; 'elders,' वृद्धाः *m. pl.*, प्राचीनाः *m. pl.*, प्राचीनलोकाः *m. pl.*, पूर्व्वपुरुषाः *m. pl.*, प्राञ्चः *m. pl.*

Elderly, *a.* अधिकवयाः -याः -यः (स्), मध्यमवयस्कः -स्का -स्कं, अतिक्रान्तयौवनः -ना -नं, ईषद्वृद्धः -द्धा -द्धं.

Eldership, *s.* ज्येष्ठता -त्वं, ज्यैष्ठ्यं, अधिकवयस्कता, गुरुत्वं.

Eldest, *a.* ज्येष्ठः -ष्ठा -ष्ठं or सर्व्वज्येष्ठः, अग्रिमः -मा -मं, श्रेष्ठः -ष्ठा -ष्ठं, सर्व्वश्रेष्ठः -ष्ठा -ष्ठं. *See* Elder.

To elect, *v. a.* वृ (c. 5. वृणोति -णुते, c. 9. वृणाति -णीते, c. 1. वरति -रितुं -रीतुं, c. 10. वरयति -यितुं), आवृ, उद्वृ, प्रवृ; उद्धृ (c. 1. -हरति -हर्त्तुं), व्यावृत् (c. 4. व्यावृत्यते), अनुरुच् in caus. (-रोचयति -यितुं), मनोनीतं -तां -तं कृ.—(Take) ग्रह् (c. 9. गृह्णाति, ग्रहीतुं), उद्ग्रह्, आदा.—(Appoint) नियुज् (c. 10. -योजयति -यितुं), निरूप् (c. 10. -रूपयति -यितुं).—(Prefer) पुरोधा (c. 3. -दधाति -धातुं); 'they elect a god to rule over them,' देवं राज्ये वरयन्ति; 'she elects him as a husband,' सा तं पतित्वे वरयति.

Elect, elected, *a.* and *p. p.* मनोनीतः -ता -तं, वृतः -ता -तं, व्यावृत्तः -त्ता -त्तं, वृत्तः -त्ता -त्तं, उद्धृतः -ता -तं, गृहीतः -ता -तं, उद्गृहीतः -ता -तं, पुरोहितः -ता -तं; 'to any office,' पदे नियुक्तः -क्ता -क्तं.

Election, *s.* वृतिः *f.*, वरः -रणं, उद्धारः, उद्धरणं, उद्ग्रहणं, ग्रहणं, आदानं, नियोजनं, मनोनयः.

Electioneering, *s.* पदप्रेप्सुसंवर्द्धनार्थं पराश्रयप्रार्थनं.

Elective, *a.* पराश्रयाधीनः -ना -नं, पराग्रहाधीनः -ना -नं, वरणाधिकारविशिष्टः -ष्टा -ष्टं, वरणकारी -रिणी -रि (न्).

Elector, *s.* वरणकारी *m.* (न्), वरयिता *m.* (तृ), वरणकृत् *m.*, वरणाधिकारवान् *m.* (त्).

Electoral, *a.* वरणाधिकारसम्बन्धी -न्धिनी -न्धि (न्), वरयितृपदसम्बन्धी.

Electorate, *s.* वरयितुः or वरणकारिणः पदं or अधिकारः.

Electre, electrum, *s.* (Amber) तैलस्फटिकः, शूकापुष्टः.—(Mixed metal) मिश्रितधातुः *m.*, कांस्यं, पीतलोहं.

Electric, electrical, *a.* वैद्युतः -ती -तं, विद्युत्वान् -त्वती -त्वत् (त्), तडित्वान् -त्वती -त्वत् (त्), विद्युन्मयः -यी -यं, विद्युद्विषयः -या -यं.

Electricity, *s.* विद्युत् *f.*, तडित् *f.*, विद्युद्वस्तु *n.*, वैद्युतशक्तिः *f.*, वज्रस्फुलिङ्गः.—(The science) विद्युद्विद्या, वज्रस्फुलिङ्गविद्या.

Electuary, *s.* लेह्यं, अवलेह्यं, अवलेहः, अवलेह्यौषधं.

Eleemosynary, *a.* भिक्षादानसम्बन्धी -न्धिनी -न्धि (न्), दरिद्रपालनार्थः -र्था -र्थं, दरिद्रोपकारी -रिणी -रि (न्), दरिद्रपोषणार्थं दत्तः -त्ता -त्तं.

Elegance, elegancy, *s.* चारुता, सौन्दर्य्यं, विनीतत्वं, विलासः, लावण्यं, शोभा, लालित्यं; 'of form,' रूपलावण्यं; 'of speech,' वाग्विलासः.

Elegant, *a.* विलासी -सिनी -सि (न्), चारुः -र्व्वी -रु, सुललितः -ता -तं, ललितः -ता -तं, विनीतः -ता -तं, लावण्यवान् -वती -वत् (त्), लीला-

वान् &c., सुन्दरः -रा -री -रं, सुरूपः -पी -पं, रोचिष्णुः -ष्णुः -ष्णु, सुरेखः -खा -खं, भाजिष्णुः -ष्णुः -ष्णु, विभ्राट् *m.f.n.* (ज्), सुशीलः -ला -लं, शुभगः -गा -गं, अग्राम्यः -म्या -म्यं; 'an elegant woman,' रूपवती, सुमध्यमा.—(As composition) सुरसः -सा -सं.

Elegantly, *adv.* सविलासं, विलासवत्तया, सलावण्यं, सुललितं, चारु.

Elegiac, *a.* कारुणिकः -की -कं, करुणामयः -यी -यं, शोकसूचकः -का -कं.

Elegy, *s.* करुणं, कारुणिकगीतं, शोकगानं, शोकसूचकगीतं.

Element, *s.* (First or constituent principle) मूलवस्तु *n.*, मूलं, भूतं, बीजं, अधिभूतं, मात्रं, विषयः, भूतमात्रं -त्रा, तन्मात्रं, अवयवः; 'the five elements,' पञ्चभूतं, पृथिव्यादि *n.*—(Of a science, &c.) तत्त्वं, सूत्रं.—(Letter) अक्षरं.—(Rudiments) आरम्भः, प्रारम्भः.—(Outline) वस्तुमात्रं, वस्तु.—(Ingredient) अंशः, भागः, अवयवः; 'elementary substance,' अव्याकृतं; 'elementary property,' कारणगुणः.

Elemental, *a.* भौतः -ती -तं, भौतिकः -की -कं, आधिभौतिकः -की -कं, भूतभावः -वा -वं, पाञ्चभौतिकः -की -कं.

Elementary, *a.* (Simple, uncompounded) अव्याकृतः -ता -तं, निरवयवः -वा -वं.—(Primary) मूलिकः -की -कं, मौलः -ली -लं.—(Rudimental) आरम्भकः -का -कं, प्रारम्भकः -का -कं.

Elephant, *a.* हस्ती *m.* (न्), गजः, करी *m.* (न्), दन्ती *m.* (न्), द्विपः, वारणः, मातङ्गः, मतङ्गः, कुञ्जरः, नागः, द्विरदः, इभः, रदी *m.* (न्), द्विपायी *m.* (न्), अनेकपः, विषाणी *m.* (न्), करेणुः *m.f.*, लम्बकर्णः, पद्मी *m.* (न्), शुण्डालः, कर्णिकी *m.* (न्), दन्तावलः, स्तम्बेरमः, दीर्घवक्त्रः, द्रुमारिः *m.*, दीर्घमारुतः, विलोमजिह्वः, शुण्डी *m.* (न्), पीलुः *m.*, महामृगः, मतङ्गजः, षष्टिहायनः; 'female elephant,' हस्तिनी, करिणी, पद्मिनी, धेनुका, वशा, 'young elephant,' कलभः -भी *f.*, करिशावकः, करेणुशिशुः *m.*, दिक्कः; 'a large elephant,' गजपुङ्गवः, करेणुवर्य्यः; 'wild elephant,' वनगजः; 'furious elephant,' मत्तः, प्रभिन्नः, गर्जितः; 'rutting elephant,' मदोत्कटः, मदकलः; 'elephant out of rut,' उद्वान्तः, निर्मदः; 'leader of a herd of elephants,' यूथनाथः, यूथपः; 'herd of elephants,' यूथः -थं, हास्तिकं, गजता, गजव्रजं; 'troop of war-elephants,' घटा, घटना; 'elephants of the quarters,' ऐरावतः, पुण्डरीकः, वामनः, कुमुदः, अञ्जनः, पुष्पदन्तः, सार्वभौमः, सुप्रतीकः; 'their females,' अभ्रमुः *f.*, कपिला, पिङ्गला, अनुपमा, ताम्रकर्णी, शुभ्रदन्ती, अङ्गना, अञ्जनावती; 'elephant's trunk,' शुण्डा; 'his temples,' गण्डः, कटः; 'his frontal globes,' कुम्भौ; 'the hollow between them,' विदुः; 'his forehead,' ललाटं, अवग्रहः; 'his eye-ball,' इषीका, ईषिका; 'corner of his eye,' निर्य्याणं, निर्याणं; 'root of his ear,' चूलिका; 'of his tail,' पेचकः; 'his withers,' स्कन्धदेशः, आसनं; 'his side,' पक्षभागः, पार्श्वभागः; 'his thigh,' गात्रं, अवरं; 'juice from his temples,' मदः, दानं; 'water emitted from his trunk,' वमथुः *m.*, करशीकरः; 'his roaring,' करिगर्ज्जितं, बृंहितं; 'elephant-breaking,' हस्तिशिक्षा; 'elephant-breaker,' हस्तिशिक्षाजीवी *m.* (न्); 'elephant-stable,' वारणशाला; 'master of the elephants,' गजाध्यक्षः.

Elephant-driver, *s.* हस्तिपः -पकः -पालः, महामात्रः, हस्तिचारी *m.* (न्), हस्त्यारोहः, निषादी *m.* (न्), आधोरणः.

Elephantiasis, *s.* (Disease of the skin) वल्मीकः, त्वग्रोगः, दुश्चर्म्मत्वं.

Elephantine, *a.* हास्तेयकः -की -कं, ऐभः -भी -भं; 'as big as an elephant,' हस्तिद्वयसः -सी -सं, गजमात्रः -त्री -त्रं.

To elevate, *v. a.* उन्नम् in caus. (-नमयति -यितुं), उच्छ्रि (c. 1. उच्छ्रयति -यितुं, rt. श्रि), समुच्छ्रि, प्रोच्छ्रि, उद्यम् (c. 1. -यच्छति -यन्तुं), उच्चीकृ, ऊर्द्ध्वीकृ, उत्था in caus. (-थापयति -यितुं, rt. स्था), उत्क्षिप् (c. 6. -क्षिपति -क्षेप्तुं), उन्नी (c. 1. -नयति -नेतुं), उद्धन् (c. 2. -हन्ति -न्तुं), उद्धृ (c. 1. -हरति -हर्त्तुं), अधिरुह् in caus. (-रोपयति -यितुं), उन्नतिं कृ.—(To a high office) उत्कृष्टपदे नियुज् (c. 7. -युंक्ते -योक्तुं) or प्रतिपद् in caus. (-पादयति -यितुं).

Elevated, *p. p.* उन्नतः -ता -तं, समुन्नतः -ता -तं, उच्छ्रितः -ता -तं, समुच्छ्रितः -ता -तं, अभ्युच्छ्रितः -ता -तं, उत्कृष्टः -ष्टा -ष्टं, उद्गतः -ता -तं, समुद्गतः -ता -तं, उत्थापितः -ता -तं, उद्धृतः -ता -तं, समुद्धृतः -ता -तं, अभ्युत्थितः -ता -तं, उद्यतः -ता -तं, अधिरोपितः -ता -तं, अधिरूढः -ढा -ढं, आरूढः -ढा -ढं, अध्यारूढः -ढा -ढं, उन्नतः -ता -तं, उद्वृत्तः -त्ता -त्तं, उद्ग्रहितः -ता -तं, उत्तुङ्गः -ङ्गा -ङ्गं, सोच्छ्रायः -या -यं, आहितगौरवः -वा -वं, कृतोच्चैस् ind., उच्छ्रायी -यिणी -यि (न्).

Elevation, *s.* उन्नतिः *f.*, समुन्नतिः *f.*, उत्कर्षः, उत्कृष्टता, उच्छ्रयः, समुच्छ्रयः, उच्छ्रायः, समुच्छ्रायः, उच्छ्रितिः *f.*, उत्थापनं, अभ्युत्थानं, उत्थितिः *f.*, उत्सेधः, समुत्सेधः, उद्गतिः *f.*, उत्तुङ्गता, औत्कर्ष्यं, उन्नतता, उत्तोलनं, ऊर्द्ध्वत्वं, अधिरोहः, उन्नयः -यनं, उन्नामः, उन्नमनं, उपचयः, प्रतिपत्तिः *f.*, उच्चता, उदयः.

Eleven, *a.* एकादश *m. f. n. pl.* (न्), एकादशसंख्यकः -का -कं.

Eleventh, *a.* एकादशः -शी -शं.

Elf, *s.* विद्याधरः, अपदेवता, वेतालः, भूतः, राक्षसः, पिशाचः.

Elf-lock, *s.* जटा, जटिः *f.*, सटा.

Elfish, *a.* पैशाचिकः -की -कं, भौतिकः -की -कं, राक्षसः -सी -सं.

To elicit, *v. a.* निर्णी (c. 1. -णयति -णेतुं), निष्कृष् (c. 1. -कर्षति -क्रष्टुं), उत्कृष्; निर्हृ (c. 1. -हरति -हर्त्तुं), उद्धृ, उत्पद् in caus. (-पादयति -यितुं), उत्पत्तिं कृ, निर्गम् in caus. (-गमयति -यितुं), निःसृ in caus. (-सारयति -यितुं), उद्भू in caus. (-भावयति -यितुं), निर्दुह् (c. 2. -दोग्धि -ग्धुं), उद्ग्रह् (c. 9. -गृह्णाति -ग्रहीतुं), अपवह् (c. 1. -वहति -वोढुं).

Elicitation, *s.* निर्हारः, उद्धारः, उत्पादनं, निष्कर्षणं, निर्णयनं.

Elicited, *p. p.* निर्हृतः -ता -तं, उद्धृतः -ता -तं, उत्पादितः -ता -तं.

To elide, *v. a.* (Cut off a syllable) लुप् (c. 6. लुम्पति, लोप्तुं).

Eligibility, *s.* वरणीयता, वार्य्यत्वं, ग्राह्यत्वं, ग्रहणीयता, योग्यता.

Eligible, *a.* वरणीयः -या -यं, वार्य्यः -र्य्या -र्य्यं, वृत्यः -त्या -त्यं, ग्राह्यः -ह्या -ह्यं, ग्रहणीयः -या -यं, आदेयः -या -यं, योग्यः -ग्या -ग्यं, उपयुक्तः -क्ता -क्तं.

Elimination, *s.* (Turning out of doors) गृहाद् बहिष्करणं or निराकरणं.—(In algebra) नाशः, मध्यमनाशः, मध्यमाहरणं, मध्यमापनयनं.

Elision, *s.* (Cutting off of a syllable) लोपः, अक्षरत्यागः.

Elixir, *s.* (Medicine prolonging life) रसायनं, तेजोवर्धनं.

Elk, *s.* चतुष्पदजन्तुविशेषः, हरिणप्रभेदः.

Ell, *s.* वस्त्रमापने प्रयुक्तः परिमाणविशेषः.

Ellipse, *s.* (An oval figure) अण्डाकारः, अण्डाकृतिः *m.*

Ellipsis, *s.* (Figure of rhetoric) श्लेषः, व्यञ्जना -नं, व्यङ्ग्यः, लक्षणा, उपलक्षणं, व्यञ्जकः; 'supplying an ellipsis,' अध्याहारः, अभ्यूहः, ऊहः.

Elliptic, elliptical, *a.* (Oval) अण्डाकारः -रा -रं, अण्डाकृतिः -तिः -ति.—(Requiring something to be supplied) अध्याहार्य्यः -र्य्या -र्य्यं, ऊह्यः -ह्या -ह्यं, अभ्यूह्यः -ह्या -ह्यं, आनुषङ्गिकः -की -कं.

Elm, *s.* वनपादपविशेषः, वन्यवृक्षप्रभेदः.

Elocution, *s.* (Pronunciation) उच्चारणं, उदाहरणं, व्याहारः, वाणी.—(In rhetoric) शब्दचातुर्य्यं, वाङ्मयं, वक्तृता, वक्तृत्वशक्तिः *f.*, वाक्पटुता.

To elongate, *v. a.* दीर्घीकृ, द्राघ (nom. द्राघयति -यितुं), प्रसृ in caus. (-सारयति -यितुं), प्रतन् (c. 8. -तनोति -नितुं), वितन्, विततीकृ.

ELONGATED, *p. p.* प्रसृतः -ता -तं, आयामितः -ता -तं, आयतः -ता -तं, व्यायतः -ता -तं, आयतिमान् -मती -मत् (त्), लम्बितः -ता -तं.

ELONGATION, *s.* आयतिः *f.*, दीर्घीकरणं, तानं, प्रसारणं, द्राघिमा *m.* (न्).

To ELOPE, *v. n.* गूढविवाहार्थं मातृपितृस्वजनाद्यगोचरेण पलाय् (c. 1. पलायते -यितुं) or मातृपितृस्वजनादीनाम् आश्रयं त्यज् (c. 1. त्यजति, त्यक्तुं), अपसृप् (c. 1. -सर्पति -सर्प्तुं).

ELOPEMENT, *s.* गूढविवाहार्थं मातृपितृस्वजनाद्यगोचरेण पलायनं or विपलायनं or मातृपिताश्रयत्यागः.

ELOQUENCE, *s.* वाक्पटुता, वाक्पाटवं, पटुत्वं, पाटवं, वाग्विभवः, वक्तृत्वं, वक्तृत्वशक्तिः *f.*, वाक्शक्तिः *f.*, सद्वक्तृता, वाग्मित्वं, वाग्विदग्धता, शब्दचातुर्य्यं, सुप्रलापः, सुभाषितं, सुवचनं, वाचाशक्तिः *f.*

ELOQUENT, *a.* वाक्पटुः -टुः -टु, वाग्मी -ग्मिनी -ग्मि (न्), वाक्यविशारदः -दा -दं, वाग्विद् *m. f. n.*, प्रवचनपटुः -टुः -टु, पटुः -टुः -टु, सद्वक्ता -क्त्री -क्तृ (तृ), वागीशः -शा -शं, वाक्पतिः -तिः -ति, सुवचाः -चाः -चः (स्), वाग्विदग्धः -ग्धा -ग्धं, शब्दचतुरः -रा -रं, सारस्वतः -ती -तं, सुमुखः -खी -खं.

ELOQUENTLY, *adv.* पाटवेन, सपाटवं, वाग्विभवेन, शब्दचातुर्य्येण.

ELSE, *a.* अन्यः -न्या -न्यत्, इतरः -रा -रं, परः -रा -रं, व्यतिरिक्तः -क्ता -क्तं, भिन्नः -न्ना -न्नं, प्रभिन्नः -न्ना -न्नं, अपरः -रा -रं; 'any thing else,' किञ्चिद् अन्यत्; 'what else can he do,' पुनः किं करोति; 'any thing else but this,' एतद्भिन्नं किञ्चित्, अस्मात् परं किञ्चित्, or एतद्व्यतिरिक्तं किञ्चित्.

ELSE, *conj.* (Otherwise) अन्यथा, अथवा, नो चेत्, न चेत्, इतरथा, इतरतस्, अन्यतस्, परतस्, अन्यत्, किंवा, एतद्विना, एतद्व्यतिरेकेण.

ELSEWHERE, *adv.* अन्यत्र, इतरत्र, परत्र, अन्यतस्, अपरतस्, इतरतस्, स्थानान्तरे, अन्यस्थाने, भिन्नस्थाने; 'gone elsewhere,' स्थानान्तरं गतः -ता -तं.

To ELUCIDATE, *v. a.* स्पष्टीकृ, सुस्पष्टीकृ, स्पष्ट (nom. स्पष्टयति -यितुं), प्रकाश् in caus. (-काशयति -यितुं), व्याख्या (c. 2. -ख्याति -तुं), व्यक्तीकृ, व्याकृ, परिशुध् in caus. (-शोधयति -यितुं), दृष्टान्तीकृ, दृष्टान्तेन or निदर्शनेन व्याख्या.

ELUCIDATED, *p. p.* स्पष्टीकृतः -ता -तं, व्याख्यातः -ता -तं, प्रकाशितः -ता -तं.

ELUCIDATION, *s.* स्पष्टीकरणं, व्याख्या, प्रकाशनं, दृष्टान्तेन व्याकरणं.

ELUCIDATOR, *s.* प्रकाशकः, व्याख्याता *m.* (तृ), उद्देशकः, निदर्शनकारकः.

To ELUDE, *v. a.* छलेन अपक्रम् (c. 1. -क्रामति -क्रमितुं) or व्यपक्रम् or पलाय् (c. 1. पलायते -यितुं) or व्यपसृप् (c. 1. -सर्पति -सर्प्तुं), निर्गम् (c. 1. -गच्छति -गन्तुं), पलायित्वा परिहृ (c. 1. -हरति -हर्त्तुं), निस्तॄ (c. 1. -तरति -रितुं -रीतुं); 'It eludes the grasp by reason of its subtilty,' सूक्ष्मत्वाद् ग्रहीतुं न शक्यते; 'eluding the senses,' इन्द्रियागोचरः -रा -रं.

ELUMBATED, *a.* श्रोणिविकलः -ला -लं, क्षीणकटिबलः -ला -लं.

ELUSION, *s.* छलेन पलायनं or अपक्रमः -मणं, निर्गतिः *f.*, निर्गमः.

ELUSIVE, *a.* पलायनपरायणः -णा -णं, विपलायी -यिनी -यि (न्).

ELUSORY, *a.* छली -लिनी -लि (न्), मायी -यिनी -यि (न्), छाद्मिकः -की -कं.

ELYSIAN, *a.* स्वर्गीयः -या -यं, स्वर्ग्यः -र्ग्या -र्ग्यं, परमानन्ददः -दा -दं.

ELYSIUM, *s.* नन्दनं, स्वर्गः, आनन्दस्थानं, सुखाधारः, सुखदं, वैकुण्ठं.

To EMACIATE, *v. a.* कृश (nom. कृशयति -यितुं), क्षि in caus. (क्षपयति -यितुं), क्षीणं -णां -णं कृ, ग्लै in caus. (ग्लपयति -यितुं), मांसक्षयं कृ, शुष्कीकृ.

To EMACIATE, *v. n.* क्षि in pass. (क्षीयते), कृशीभू, विशॄ in pass. (-शीर्य्यते), क्षै (c. 1. क्षायति, क्षातुं), ग्लै (c. 1. ग्लायति, ग्लातुं), शुष् (c. 4. शुष्यति, शोष्टुं), शुष्कीभू.

EMACIATED, *p. p.* or *a.* कृशः -शा -शं, परिकृशः -शा -शं, कृशाङ्गः -ङ्गी -ङ्गं, क्षीणशरीरः -रा -रं, क्षीणमांसः -सा -सं, शुष्कमांसः -सा -सं, शुष्काङ्गः -ङ्गी -ङ्गं, क्षामः -मा -मं, ग्लानः -ना -नं, शीर्णः -र्णा -र्णं, विशीर्णः -र्णा -र्णं, अमांसः -सा -सं, ग्लास्नुः -स्नुः -स्नु; 'by hunger,' क्षुत्क्षामः -मा -मं.

EMACIATION, *s.* कार्श्यं, कृशत्वं -ता, कृशाङ्गत्वं, क्षामता, शीर्णता, शरीरक्षीणता, शरीरशोषणं, शरीरपाकः, मांसशुष्कता, मांसक्षयः, शोषः.

EMANANT, EMANATIVE, *a.* प्रसृतः -ता -तं, निःसृतः -ता -तं, विनिःसृतः -ता -तं, उत्पन्नः -न्ना -न्नं, उद्भूतः -ता -तं, प्रवृत्तः -त्ता -त्तं, निर्गतः -ता -तं.

To EMANATE, *v. n.* (Flow from) स्रु (c. 1. स्रवति, स्रोतुं), प्रस्रु, निःस्रु, विस्रु.—(Proceed from) उत्पद् in pass. (-पद्यते), निःसृ (c. 1. -सरति -सर्त्तुं), विनिःसृ, प्रसृ; निर्गम् (c. 1. -गच्छति -गन्तुं), बहिर्गम्, उद्गम्, उदि (c. 1. -अयति -एतुं), उद्भू, प्रभू.

EMANATION, *s.* निःस्रावः, निःसारः -सरणं, उत्पत्तिः *f.*, निर्गमः -मनं, उद्गमः, उद्भवः, उद्भावः, उदयनं, प्रवृत्तिः *f.*

To EMANCIPATE, *v. a.* मुच् (c. 6. मुञ्चति, मोक्तुं, c. 10. मोचयति -यितुं), विमुच्, निर्मुच्, मोक्ष् (c. 10. मोक्षयति -यितुं), विमोक्ष्, उद्धृ (c. 1. -हरति -हर्त्तुं), विसृज् (c. 6. -सृजति -स्रष्टुं, c. 10. -सर्जयति -यितुं), निस्तॄ in caus. (-तारयति -यितुं), त्रै (c. 1. त्रायते, त्रातुं), परित्रै.

EMANCIPATED, *p. p.* मुक्तः -क्ता -क्तं, विमोचितः -ता -तं, मोक्षितः -ता -तं, उद्धृतः -ता -तं, निस्तारितः -ता -तं, विसृष्टः -ष्टा -ष्टं, परित्राणः -णा -णं, रक्षितः -ता -तं, उत्तीर्णः -र्णा -र्णं.—(From worldly existence) मुक्तः -क्ता -क्तं, निर्वृतः -ता -तं, निर्वाणः -णा -णं, सिद्धः -द्धा -द्धं.

EMANCIPATION, *s.* मुक्तिः *f.*, मोचनं, मोक्षः -क्षणं, विमोक्षः -क्षणं, विमुक्तिः *f.*, विमोचनं, परिमोक्षणं, वैमुक्तं, उद्धारः, उद्धरणं, निस्तारः, त्राणं, परित्राणं, विसर्गः, तारणं.—(From worldly existence) मुक्तिः *f.*, निर्वाणं, निर्वृतिः *f.*, अपवर्गः -वर्जनं, सिद्धिः *f.*, सद्गतिः *f.*, परमागतिः *f.*, श्रेयः *n.* (स्), निःश्रेयः *n.* (स्), निःश्रेयसं, निर्याणं, पुनर्जन्मक्षयः, कैवल्यं; 'desirous of it,' मुमुक्षुः -क्षुः -क्षु, तितीर्षुः -र्षुः -र्षु.

EMANCIPATOR, *s.* मोचकः, मोक्षकः, उद्धर्त्ता *m.* (र्त्तृ), त्राता *m.* (तृ).

To EMASCULATE, *v. a.* वृषणौ or वृषणद्वयम् उत्कृत् (c. 6. -कृन्तति -कर्त्तितुं) or छिद् (c. 7. छिनत्ति, छेत्तुं), अण्डच्छेदं कृ, पुंस्त्वं हृ (c. 1. हरति, हर्त्तुं), विफलीकृ, शण्डीकृ, निष्पुरुषीकृ, क्लीबीकृ.

EMASCULATED, *p. p.* छिन्नवृषणः -णा -णं, मुष्कशून्यः -न्या -न्यं, विफलीकृतः -ता -तं, विफलः -ला -लं, हृतपौरुषः -षा -षं, शण्डः, षण्ढः, क्लीबः, नपुंसकः.

EMASCULATION, *s.* वृषणच्छेदः, वृषणोत्पाटनं, पुंस्त्वहरणं, शण्डता.

To EMBALE, *v. a.* द्रव्यकूर्चं कृ, कूर्चीकृ, भाण्डं कृ, पोटलिकां कृ.

To EMBALM, *v. a.* मृतशरीरं तद्रक्षणाय सुगन्धिद्रव्याक्तं कृ or तद्रक्षार्थं तिक्तौषधव्यञ्जनादिना पॄ in caus. (पूरयति -यितुं).

EMBANKMENT, *s.* सेतुः *m.*, सेतुबन्धः, मृत्तिकाचयः, धरणः, पिण्डनः, वप्रः.

To EMBAR, *v. a.* निरुध् (c. 7. -रुणद्धि -रोद्धुं), निवृ in caus. (-वारयति -यितुं).

EMBARGO, *s.* निषेधः, निरोधः, अवरोधः, बाधा, वारणं, नावां गमनागमननिषेधः or वाणिज्यकर्म्मनिषेधः.

To EMBARK, *v. a.* नौकाम् आरुह् in caus. (-रोपयति -यितुं) or प्रविश् in caus. (-वेशयति -यितुं) or निविश् in caus., नौकायां समॄ in caus. (-अर्पयति -यितुं).

To EMBARK, *v. n.* नौकां or पोतम् आरुह् (c. 1. -रोहति -रोढुं) or प्रविश् (c. 6. -विशति -वेष्टुं) or निविश्.—(Undertake) आरभ् (c. 1. -रभते -रब्धुं).

EMBARKATION, *s.* नौकारोहणं, नौकारोपणं, नौकाप्रवेशनं, पोतनिवेशनं, नौकासमर्पणं.

EMBARKED, *p. p.* नौकारूढः -ढा -ढं, तरणिम् आरूढः -ढा -ढं, पोतारोपितः -ता -तं, नौकाप्रविष्टः -ष्टा -ष्टं, पोतनिवेशितः -ता -तं, नौकासमर्पितः -ता -तं.

To EMBARRASS, *v. a.* मुह् in caus. (मोहयति -यितुं), विमुह्, व्यामुह्, व्याकुलीकृ, व्याकुलीकृ, व्याकुल (nom. व्याकुलयति -यितुं), व्यग्रीकृ, सङ्कटीकृ, बाध् (c. 1. बाधते -धितुं), क्लिश् (c. 9. क्लिश्नाति, क्लेशितुं), क्लेशं दा, दुःखं दा, शल्यं कृ, रुध् (c. 7. रुणद्धि, रोद्धुं).

EMBARRASSED, *p. p.* मोहितः -ता -तं, विमोहितः -ता -तं, व्याकुलः -ला -लं, आकुलितः -ता -तं, व्यग्रः -ग्रा -ग्रं, समाकुलः -ला -लं, कातरः -रा -रं, कृच्छ्रगतः -ता -तं, बाधितः -ता -तं, क्लिष्टः -ष्टा -ष्टं, विपन्नः -न्ना -न्नं, आपन्नतः -ता -तं, उपरुद्धः -द्धा -द्धं, दुःस्थः -स्था -स्थं.

EMBARRASSMENT, *s.* व्याकुलता, आकुलत्वं, व्यग्रता, मोहः, व्यामोहः, कातरता, व्यस्तता, सम्भ्रमः, क्लेशः, दुःखं, शल्यं, बाधः -धा, कार्य्यसन्देहः.

EMBASSADOR, *s.* दूतः, राजदूतः, राजप्रेरितः, राजप्रस्थापितः, राजप्रतिनिधिः *m.*, राजकर्म्मकरः, राजकार्य्यकृत्.

EMBASSADRESS, *s.* दूती -तिः *f.*, दूतिका, राजदूती, राजदूतस्य पत्नी or भार्य्या.

EMBASSAGE, EMBASSY, *s.* दूत्यं, दौत्यं, दूतक्रिया, दूतधर्म्मः; 'sent on an embassy,' प्रस्थापितः -ता -तं, प्रेरितः -ता -तं, दूतः -ता -तं.

To EMBATTLE, *v. a.* व्यूह् (c. 1. -ऊहते -हितुं), सैन्यं युद्धार्थं व्यूहेन रच् (c. 10. रचयति -यितुं) or सज्जीकृ or अवस्था in caus. (-स्थापयति -यितुं).

EMBEDDED, *p. p.* or *a.* निहितः -ता -तं, न्यस्तः -स्ता -स्तं, निविष्टः -ष्टा -ष्टं.

To EMBELLISH, *v. a.* भूष् (c. 10. भूषयति -यितुं), विभूष्, अलङ्कृ, समलङ्कृ, परिष्कृ, संस्कृ, शुभ् in caus. (शोभयति -यितुं), उपशुभ्, मण्ड् (c. 10. मण्डयति -यितुं), परिकर्म्म (nom. परिकर्म्मयति -यितुं), रञ्ज् (c. 10. रञ्जयति -यितुं).

EMBELLISHED, *p. p.* भूषितः -ता -तं, विभूषितः -ता -तं, अलङ्कृतः -ता -तं, परिष्कृतः -ता -तं, संस्कृतः -ता -तं, शोभितः -ता -तं, उपशोभितः -ता -तं, कृतशोभः -भा -भं, मण्डितः -ता -तं, प्रसाधितः -ता -तं, सालङ्कारः -रा -रं, कृतालङ्कारः -रा -रं.

EMBELLISHMENT, *s.* अलङ्कारः, अलङ्करणं, अलङ्क्रिया, भूषणं, विभूषणं, भरणं, आभरणं, परिष्कारः, परिष्कृतिः *f.*, संस्कारः, अङ्गसंस्कारः, परिकर्म्म *n.* (न्), प्रतिकर्म्म, प्रसाधनं, मण्डनं, शोभा -भनं, कल्पना, सज्जा, रञ्जनं, आकल्पः, वेशः.—(Of a book) पत्ररञ्जनं.—(Theatrical dress) नेपथ्यं, वर्णः, आहार्य्यः.

EMBER-DAYS, *s. pl.* यथापर्य्यायं वत्सरे वत्सरे चत्वार उपवाससमयाः, पुण्यदिनानि, पुण्याहानि.

EMBERS, *s. pl.* भस्म *n.* (न्), भसितं, तप्ताङ्गारोच्छिष्टं, अग्नेरुच्छिष्टं, अङ्गारशेषं, भूतिः *f.*

To EMBEZZLE, *v. a.* ग्रस् (c. 1. ग्रसते -सितुं), निक्षिप्तद्रव्यं निह्नवेन स्वीयं कृ or स्वीकृ, न्यस्तधनादि छलेन स्वकीयं कृत्वा उपयुज् (c. 7. -युनक्ति -युङ्क्ते -योक्तुं), परवित्तम् अपह्नवेन स्वाधीनं कृत्वा हृ (c. 1. हरति, हर्त्तुं) or अपहृ, अपह्नु (c. 2. -ह्नुते -ह्नोतुं), निह्नु.

EMBEZZLED, *p. p.* ग्रस्तः -स्ता -स्तं, निह्नुतः -ता -तं, अपह्नवेन or छलेन स्वीकृतः -ता -तं or उपयुक्तः -क्ता -क्तं or हृतः -ता -तं or अपहृतः -ता -तं.

EMBEZZLEMENT, *s.* ग्रसनं, अपह्नवेन or निह्नवेन हरणं or अपहारः, निक्षिप्तधनादेः or परवित्तस्य छलेन उपयोगः or प्रयोगः, अपह्नवः, निह्नवः, अभिलाषः.

To EMBLAZE or EMBLAZON, *v. a.* कुलीनपदचिह्नानि लिखित्वा शुभ् in caus. (शोभयति -यितुं), कुलीनपदचिह्नैर् अलङ्कृ, रञ्ज् (c. 10. रञ्जयति -यितुं).

EMBLAZONED, *p. p.* कुलीनपदचिह्नशोभितः -ता -तं, उद्योतितः -ता -तं.

EMBLEM, *s.* चिह्नं, लक्षणं, व्यञ्जनं, लिङ्गं, लाञ्छनं, निदर्शनं, आदर्शः, दृष्टान्तः, संज्ञा, प्रतिमा, प्रतिरूपं, सङ्केतः, केतुः *m.*, ध्वजः, पताका.

EMBLEMATIC, EMBLEMATICAL, *a.* उद्बोधकः -का -कं, लाक्षणिकः -की -कं, चिह्नकारी -रिणी -रि (न्) or निदर्शनकारी, लिङ्गी -ङ्गिनी -ङ्गि (न्).

EMBLEMATICALLY, *adv.* निदर्शनक्रमेण, लाक्षणिकप्रकारेण, उद्बोधनार्थं.

EMBLIC MYROBALAN, *s.* (A plant) तिष्यफला, आमलकः -की, अमृता, वयस्था, वयःस्था, कायस्था.

EMBODIED, *p. p.* शरीरी -रिणी -रि (न्), शरीरवान् -वती -वत् (त्), देही -हिनी -हि (न्), देहवान् -वती -वत् (त्), सविग्रहः -हा -हं, सशरीरः -रा -रं, सवपुष्कः -ष्की -ष्कं, जातरूपः -पी -पं, जातशरीरः -रा -रं, सन्निपतितः -ता -तं.

EMBODIMENT, *s.* शरीरवत्त्वं, देहवत्त्वं, सशरीरता, सन्निपातः, समाहारः, एकशरीरीकरणं.

To EMBODY, *v. a.* सशरीरं -रां -रं कृ, एकशरीरीकृ, एकाङ्गीकृ, देहवन्तं -वतीं -वत् कृ.—(Collect into a mass) सङ्ग्रह् (c. 9. -गृह्णाति -ग्रहीतुं), एकौघीकृ, एकत्र कृ, एकीकृ.

To EMBOLDEN, *v. a.* आश्वस् in caus. (-श्वासयति -यितुं), समाश्वस्, निर्भयं -यां -यं कृ.

EMBOLDENED, *p. p.* आश्वासितः -ता -तं, गतभीः -भीः -भि, वीतभयः -या -यं.

To EMBOSS, *v. a.* राजतभाण्डादीनि उच्चरेखादिना अलङ्कृ or उपस्कृ or गण्डाकारेण परिष्कृ or समुत्सेधेन तक्ष् (c. 1. तक्षति -क्षितुं).

EMBOSSMENT, *s.* राजतभाण्डादीनाम् उच्चरेखादिना अलङ्करणं, गण्डाकारेण or उच्चैःप्रकारेण तक्षणं, समुत्सेधेन तक्षणं, प्रतिच्छाया.

To EMBOWEL, *v. a.* नाडीः or अन्त्राणि बहिष्कृ or निर्हृ (c. 1. -हरति -हर्त्तुं).

To EMBRACE, *v. a.* आलिङ्ग् (c. 1. -लिङ्गति -ङ्गितुं), समालिङ्ग्; आश्लिष् (c. 4. -श्लिष्यति -श्लेष्टुं), संश्लिष्, समाश्लिष्, उपश्लिष्; स्वञ्ज् (c. 1. स्वजते, स्वंक्तुं), परिष्वञ्ज्, सम्परिष्वञ्ज्, उपगुह् (c. 1. -गूहति -हितुं), परिरभ् (c. 1. -रभते -रब्धुं), पीड् (c. 10. पीडयति -यितुं), क्रोडीकृ, क्रोडे कृ.—(Comprise) परिग्रह् (c. 9. -गृह्णाति -ग्रहीतुं), परिसमाप् (c. 5. -आप्नोति -आप्तुं), प्रतिसंहृ (c. 1. -हरति -हर्त्तुं).—(Encompass) परिवेष्ट् (c. 1. -वेष्टते -ष्टितुं), परिवृ (c. 5. -वृणोति -वरितुं -रीतुं).

EMBRACE, *s.* आलिङ्गनं -ङ्गितं, आश्लेषः, संश्लेषः, श्लेषः, परिष्वङ्गः, परिरम्भः, उपगूढं, उपगूहनं, अवगूहनं, अङ्कपाली -लिका, अङ्कपालिः *m.*, श्लिषा, लीः *f.*, अङ्कः, कोलः, लयः, क्रोडीकरणं, क्रोडीकृतिः *f.*

EMBRACED, *p. p.* आलिङ्गितः -ता -तं, श्लिष्टः -ष्टा -ष्टं, आश्लिष्टः -ष्टा -ष्टं, संश्लिष्टः -ष्टा -ष्टं, परिष्वक्तः -क्ता -क्तं, परिरब्धः -ब्धा -ब्धं, परिगूढः -ढा -ढं, उपगूढः -ढा -ढं, पीडितः -ता -तं, अभिलीनः -ना -नं, लीनः -ना -नं, निलीनः -ना -नं, क्रोडीकृतः -ता -तं.

EMBRASURE, *s.* प्राकारे छिद्रं or रन्ध्रं, आकाशजननी *m.* (न्), जालकः.

To EMBROCATE, *v. a.* अङ्गम् औषधीयजलेन लिप् (c. 6. लिम्पति, लेप्तुं) or आलिप् or उपलिप् or अनुलिप् or औषधीयजलेन आर्द्रीकृत्य मृद् (c 9. मृद्नाति, मर्द्दितुं) or सम्मृद् or घृष् (c. 1. घर्षति -र्षितुं).

EMBROCATION, *s.* आलेपनं, लेपः, विलेपः, उपदेहः, औषधीयजलं, पूरणः.

To EMBROIDER, *v. a.* सूचीद्वारेण पुष्पाद्यलङ्कारान् सिव् (c. 4. सीव्यति, सेवितुं) or निषिव् or चित्र् (c. 10. चित्रयति -यितुं), कार्म्मिकवस्त्रं कृ.

EMBROIDERED, *p. p.* सूचिकर्म्मद्वारेण पुष्पाद्यलङ्कृतः -ता -तं, चित्रितः -ता -तं, कार्म्मिकः -की -कं; 'embroidered cloth,' कार्म्मिकवस्त्रं.

EMBROIDERER, *s.* सूचीशिल्पवित् *m. f.*, सूचीशिल्पोपजीवी *m.* -विनी *f.* (न्), कार्म्मिकवस्त्रकृत् *m. f.*

EMBROIDERY, *s.* सुवर्णसूत्रादिना पुष्पाद्यलङ्कारसीवनं, सूचिता, सूचीकर्म्म *n.* (न्), सूचीशिल्पं; 'embroidered cloth,' कार्म्मिकवस्त्रं.

To EMBROIL, *v. a.* सङ्कटीकृ, सङ्कुलीकृ, संक्षुभ् in caus. (-क्षोभयति -यितुं), सङ्कॄ (c. 6. -किरति -करितुं -रीतुं), अस्तव्यस्तीकृ, आकुलीकृ, व्याकुलीकृ,

भेदं or वैरक्यं जन् (c. 10. जनयति -यितुं) or कृ.

EMBROILED, *p. p.* संक्षुब्धः -ब्धा -ब्धं, जातभेदः -दा -दं, जातविरागः -गा -गं.

EMBROILMENT, *s.* सङ्कुलीकरणं, संक्षोभः, साङ्कर्य्यं, विप्रतिपत्तिः *f.*, भेदकरणं.

EMBRYO, EMBRYON, *s.* भ्रूणः, गर्भः, कललं, कललः -लं, वं, गर्भस्थबालकस्य प्रथमावयवः, पुलकः.—(Rudiments of any thing) आरम्भः, प्रारम्भः.

EMENDABLE, *a.* शोधनीयः -या -यं, संशोध्यः -ध्या -ध्यं, समाधेयः -या -यं.

EMENDATION, *s.* शोधनं, शुद्धिः *f.*, संशुद्धिः *f.*, विशोधनं, समाधानं, प्रतिसमाधानं.

EMENDATOR, *s.* शोधकः, संशोधकः, शोधनकृत्, समाधाता *m.* (तृ).

EMENDED, *p. p.* शोधितः -ता -तं, शुद्धीकृतः -ता -तं, संशुद्धः -द्धा -द्धं.

EMERALD, *s.* मरकतः, अश्मगर्भं, हरिन्मणिः *m.*, रौहिणेयं, गारुत्मत् *n.*, गारुडः, गरुडाश्मा *m.* (न्), गरुडाङ्कितं, गरुडोत्तीर्णं, राजनीलः, सुनीलकः, मसारः, आपनिकः; 'of the colour of an emerald,' मारकतः -ती -तं.

To EMERGE, *v. n.* (From the water, &c.) सलिलाद् उन्मज्ज् (c. 6. -मज्जति -मंक्तुं -मज्जितुं) or उत्था (c. 1. -तिष्ठति -थातुं, rt. स्था) or वहिर्गम् (c. 1. -गच्छति -गन्तुं) or निर्गम् or निःसृ (c. 1. -सरति -सर्त्तुं) or उन्नह् (c. 4. -नह्यति -नद्धुं).—(Rise into view) उदि (c. 1. उदयति, उदेतुं, rt. इ), प्रादुर्भू, आविर्भू, वहिर्भू, प्रभू, उत्पद् (c. 4. -पद्यते -पत्तुं), प्रकाश् (c. 1. -काशते -शितुं), प्रकाशं निर्गम्, उद्भा (c. 2. -भाति -तुं), निर्भा, प्रकाशं or प्रत्यक्षं दृश् in pass. (दृश्यते), दृष्टिगोचरः -रा -रं भू.—(Re-appear) पुनर्दृश् in pass.

EMERGENCE, EMERGENCY, *s.* प्रयोजनं, अवसरः, प्रस्तावः, समयः, कार्य्यं, अवश्यकता, आवश्यकत्वं, अकस्मादुत्पन्नं, अकस्माद्वृत्तं, अकस्माद्भूतं, आकस्मिकसम्भवः, अनिश्चितविषयः, अभ्युदयः, समुच्चयः, समुत्पत्तिः *f.*, आपद् *f.*, विपद् *f.*; 'according to the emergency,' यथावसरं, यथाप्रयोजनं, प्रस्तावसदृशं, कार्य्यवशात्, यथाकार्य्यं, यथासम्भवं, प्रसङ्गवशात्; 'in this emergency,' इहसमये.

EMERGENT, *a.* उन्मज्जन् -ज्जन्ती -ज्जत् (त्).—(Unexpected) अकस्मादुत्पन्नः -न्ना -न्नं, आकस्मिकः -की -कं.—(Urgent) आवश्यकः -की -कं.

EMERY, *s.* महालोहं, उत्तमलोहः, अयस्कान्तः, लोहपरिष्कारको धातुः.

EMETIC, *s.* वमनं, वान्तिकृत्, वमनोत्पादकम् औषधं.

EMETIC, EMETICAL, *a.* वान्तिदः -दा -दं, वमनकारी -रिणी -रि (न्).

EMIGRANT, *s.* स्वदेशं त्यक्तुकामः, देशान्तरम् अधिविवत्सुः, दूरदेशे विवत्सुः.

To EMIGRATE, *v. n.* स्वदेशं त्यक्त्वा देशान्तरे or दूरदेशे or प्रदेशे वस् (c. 1. वसति, वस्तुं) or अधिवस् with acc. c., or अध्यास् (c. 2. -आस्ते -आसितुं) with acc. c., दूरदेशे विवत्सया स्वदेशं त्यज् (c. 1. त्यजति, त्यक्तुं).

EMIGRATION, *s.* दूरदेशाधिवासनार्थं स्वदेशत्यागः, देशान्तराधिवासनं, प्रदेशाधिवासनं, देशत्यागः.

EMINENCE, *s.* (Exaltation, distinction) उत्कर्षः, उत्कृष्टता, प्रमुखत्वं, सौत्कर्ष्यं, विशिष्टता, वैशिष्ट्यं, उन्नतिः *f.*, समुन्नतिः *f.*, प्रधानत्वं, प्रकर्षः, प्रकृष्टत्वं, परमपदं, परपदं, अधिकत्वं, आधिक्यं, शिष्टता, श्रेष्ठत्वं, महोदयः, सुख्यातिः *f.*, विख्यातिः *f.*, सेव्यता.—(Height) उच्छ्रयः, उच्छ्रायः, समुच्छ्रयः, उत्सेधः, समुत्सेधः, उच्चत्वं, उत्तुङ्गता, ऊर्द्धत्वं; 'a rising ground,' उन्नतभूभागः, उच्चस्थानं.

EMINENT, *a.* उत्कृष्टः -ष्टा -ष्टं, प्रमुखः -खा -खं, विशिष्टः -ष्टा -ष्टं, शिष्टः -ष्टा -ष्टं, उन्नतः -ता -तं, समुन्नतः -ता -तं, उत्तमः -मा -मं, परमः -मा -मं, परः -रा -रं, श्रेष्ठः -ष्ठा -ष्ठं, अधिकः -का -कं, मुख्यः -ख्या -ख्यं, अग्रियः -या -यं, प्रधान prefixed in comp., प्रवरः -रा -रं, वरेण्यः -ण्या -ण्यं, प्रवर्हः -र्हा -र्हं, उच्चः -च्चा -च्चं, उच्छ्रितः -ता -तं.—(Celebrated) विश्रुतः -ता -तं, ख्यातः -ता -तं, महायशस्कः -स्का -स्कं, प्रथितः -ता -तं; 'of eminent endowments,' महाभागः -गा -गं, गुणाढ्यः -ढ्या -ढ्यं; 'to be eminent,' विशिष् in pass. (-शिष्यते). *See* EXCELLENT.

EMINENTLY, *adv.* अत्यन्तं, अतिशयेन, अत्यर्थं, भृशं, अधिकं, निर्भरं, अति prefixed.

EMISSARY, *s.* दूतः, वार्त्तायनः, चारः, चरः, वार्त्ताहरः, सन्देशहरः, कार्य्यङ्करः, प्रयोज्यः, आख्यायकः.—(Secret agent) गूढपुरुषः, गुप्तदूतः, गुप्तचरः -चारी *m.* (न्), गुप्तगतिः *m.*, रहस्याख्यायी *m.* (न्), प्रणिधिः *m.*, प्रतिष्कः -ष्कशः -ष्कसः.

EMISSION, *s.* निरसनं, उत्सर्गः, उत्सर्जनं, उत्क्षेपः -पणं, विसर्गः, उद्गारः, उच्चारः, स्रावः, आस्रावः, मोक्षणं, मोचनं, प्रमोचनं, उदीरणं, उद्गमनं, उत्तारः, ऊर्द्ध्वशोधनं.

To EMIT, *v. a.* उत्सृज् (c. 6. -सृजति -स्रष्टुं), विसृज्, निरस् (c. 4. -अस्यति -असितुं), निःसृ in caus. (-सारयति -यितुं), मुच् (c. 6. मुञ्चति, मोक्तुं), प्रमुच्, उत्क्षिप् (c. 6. -क्षिपति -क्षेप्तुं), उद्गॄ (c. 6. -गिरति -गरितुं -रीतुं), उदीर् (c. 10. -ईरयति -यितुं), समुदीर्, समीर्, उच्चर् in caus. (-चारयति -यितुं), उद्वम् (c. 1. -वमति -मितुं), स्रु in caus. (स्रावयति -यितुं), प्रस्रु, स्कन्द् (c. 10. स्कन्दयति -यितुं), निर्गम् in caus. (-गमयति -यितुं); 'to emit blood,' रक्तं स्रु in caus.; 'to emit saliva,' श्लेष्मनिरसनं कृ; 'to emit heat,' उष्माणम् उद्वम्.

EMITTED, *p. p.* उत्सृष्टः -ष्टा -ष्टं, उत्क्षिप्तः -प्ता -प्तं, उदीरितः -ता -तं, निरस्तः -स्ता -स्तं, स्कन्दितः -ता -तं, उच्चारितः -ता -तं, उद्वान्तः -न्ता -न्तं.

EMMENAGOGUE, *s.* स्त्रीणाम् ऋतुवर्धकम् औषधं.

EMMET, *s.* पिपीलिका, पुत्तिका.

To EMMEW, *v. a.* पिञ्जरे or सङ्कटस्थाने निरुध् (c. 7. -रुणद्धि -रोद्धुं).

EMOLLIENT, *a.* स्नेही -हिनी -हि (न्), स्निग्धः -ग्धा -ग्धं, स्नेहवान् -वती -वत्, चिक्कणः -णा -णं, शान्तिकरः -री -रं, शान्तिदः -दा -दं, स्निग्धकारी -रिणी -रि (न्).

EMOLLIENT, *s.* स्नेहनं, अभ्यञ्जनं, अभ्यङ्गः, आलेपः, उपदेहः.

EMOLUMENT, *s.* लाभः, फलं, लब्धिः *f.*, प्राप्तिः *f.*, फलोदयः, आयः, प्रतिपत्तिः *f.*, अर्थः, लभ्यं, आगमः, उदयः, वेतनं, वर्त्तनं.

EMOTION, *s.* (Passion, feeling) रसः, भावः, विकारः, मनोविकारः, रागः, चित्तवृत्तिः *f.*, चित्तविकारः, विभ्रमः.—(Agitation of mind) उत्कम्पः, उत्तापः, अन्तःक्षोभः, चित्तक्षोभः, अन्तर्वेगः, अभितापः, मनस्तापः; 'under emotion,' अन्यथावृत्तिः -त्तिः -त्ति.

To EMPALE, *v. a.* (Enclose with a row of stakes or stockade) युद्धे सैन्यरक्षार्थं वाटेन or शङ्कुपंक्त्या परिवृ (c. 5. -वृणोति -वरितुं -रीतुं). —(Put to death by fixing on a stake) शूले or कीले or तीक्ष्णशूले आरुह् in caus. (-रोपयति -यितुं) or समारुह् in caus., or निविश् in caus. (-वेशयति -यितुं), कील (nom. कीलयति -यितुं).

EMPALED, *p. p.* कीलितः -ता -तं, शूलारोपितः -ता -तं, शूलनिवेशितः -ता -तं, प्रोतः -ता -तं.

EMPALEMENT, *s.* शूलारोपः -पणं, शूलनिवेशनं; 'deserving empalement,' शूल्यः -ल्या -ल्यं; 'stake for empalement,' शूलः, कीलः.

To EMPANNEL, EMPARLANCE, EMPASSION. *See To* IMPANNEL, &c.

EMPEROR, *s.* राजाधिराजः, महाराजाधिराजः, अधिराजः, अधीश्वरः, राजराजः, महाराजः, सम्राट् *m.* (ज्) or अधिराट् *m.*, मण्डलेश्वरः, चक्रवर्त्ती *m.* (न्), सार्वभौमः, सर्वेश्वरः, अधिराज्यभाक् *m.* (ज्).

EMPHASIS, *s.* अवधारणं, गुरूच्चारणं, दीर्घोच्चारणं, गौरवं.

EMPHATIC, *a.* (Impressive) गुरुः -र्वी -रु.—(Requiring emphasis) अवधारणीयः -या -यं, अवधार्य्यः -र्य्या -र्य्यं.—(Uttered with emphasis) गौरवेण or अवधारणेन उच्चारितः -ता -तं.

EMPHATICALLY, *adv.* अवधारणेन, सावधारणं, गौरवेण, सगौरवं.

EMPIRE, *s.* आधिराज्यं, अधिराज्यं, साम्राज्यं, राज्यं, राजत्वं, आधिपत्यं,

ऐश्वर्य्यं,ईशत्वं, राजाधिकारः, प्रभुत्वं.—(Region governed) राष्ट्रं, विषयः.

EMPIRIC, *s.* (A quack) दुश्चिकित्सकः, मिथ्याचिकित्सकः, छद्मवैद्यः, आयुर्वेदानभिज्ञः.—(One who makes experiments) परीक्षकः.

EMPIRICAL, *a.* (Charlatanical) आयुर्वेदविरुद्धः -द्धा -द्धं, मिथ्याचिकित्सासम्बन्धी -न्धिनी -न्धि (न्), छाद्मिकः -की -कं, कापटिकः -की -कं.—(Experimental) परीक्षकः -का -कं.

EMPIRICALLY, *adv.* आयुर्वेदविरुद्धं, दुश्चिकित्सकवत्, परीक्षाक्रमेण.

EMPIRICISM, *s.* मिथ्याचिकित्सा, दुश्चिकित्सा -त्सनं, आयुर्वेदानभिज्ञता, आयुर्वेदविरुद्धा चिकित्सा, परीक्षा -क्षणं.

EMPLASTIC, *a.* लेप्यः -प्या -प्यं, श्यानः -ना -नं, पिच्छिलः -ला -लं, सान्द्रः -न्द्रा -न्द्रं.

To EMPLOY, *v. a.* (Use) प्रयुज् (c. 7. -युनक्ति -युंक्ते -योक्तुं, c. 10. -योजयति -यितुं), उपयुज्, सेव् (c. 1. सेवते -वितुं), विधा (c. 3. -दधाति -धातुं), उपभुज् (c. 7. -भुनक्ति -भुंक्ते -भोक्तुं), अभ्यस् (c. 4. -अस्यति -असितुं), व्यवहृ in caus. (-हारयति -यितुं), धृ in caus. (धारयति -यितुं), वाह् in caus. (वाहयति -यितुं).—(Occupy, give employment) व्यापृ in caus. (-पारयति -यितुं), प्रवृत् in caus. (-वर्त्तयति -यितुं), प्रयुज्.—(Engage, appoint) नियुज्, विनियुज्, अधिकृ, प्रकृ; 'is employed,' विधीयते; 'having employed,' अधिकृत्य, आस्थाय, आश्रित्य; 'employing,' वाहयन् -यन्ती -यत् (त्).

EMPLOYED, *p. p.* (Used) प्रयुक्तः -क्ता -क्तं, प्रयोजितः -ता -तं, उपयुक्तः -क्ता -क्तं, व्यवहृतः -ता -तं, व्यवहारितः -ता -तं, उपभुक्तः -क्ता -क्तं, सेवितः -ता -तं.—(Appointed) नियुक्तः -क्ता -क्तं, विनियुक्तः -क्ता -क्तं, युक्तः -क्ता -क्तं.—(Occupied) व्यापृतः -ता -तं, व्यापारितः -ता -तं, व्यापारी -रिणी -रि (न्), व्यवसायी -यिनी -यि (न्).

EMPLOYER, *s.* प्रयोजयिता *m.* (तृ), प्रयोजकः, व्यापारयिता *m.* (तृ), प्रवर्त्तकः.

EMPLOYMENT, *s.* (Use) प्रयोगः, प्रयोजनं, उपयोगः, उपभोगः, व्यवहारः, अभ्यासः.—(Occupation, business, profession) व्यापारः, कार्य्यं, कर्म्म *n.* (न्), व्यवसायः, व्यवहारः, वृत्तिः *f.*, प्रवृत्तिः *f.*, प्रवर्त्तनं, कार्य्योद्योगः, वर्त्तनं, वृत्तं, वृत्तिता, जीविका.—(Appointment) नियोगः, नियोजनं, नियुक्तिः *f.*, विनियोगः; 'out of employment,' निर्वृत्तिः -त्तिः -त्ति, क्षीणवृत्तिः -त्तिः -त्ति.

To EMPOISON, *v. a.* (Administer poison) विषं or तीक्ष्णरसं दा, विषप्रयोगं कृ, विषप्रयोगेण नश् in caus. (नाशयति -यितुं).—(Taint with poison) विषेण दिह् (c. 2. देग्धि -ग्धुं) or अञ्ज् (c. 7. अनक्ति, अंक्तुं).

EMPOISONED, *p. p.* विषदिग्धः -ग्धा -ग्धं, विषाक्तः -क्ता -क्तं, विषयुक्तः -क्ता -क्तं.

EMPOISONMENT, *s.* विषप्रयोगः, विषदानं, विषेण नाशनं or मारणं.

EMPORIUM, *s.* वाणिज्यस्थानं, लोकयात्रायोग्या or महाजनकर्म्मयोग्या नगरी.

To EMPOVERISH, EMPOVERISHMENT. *See* IMPOVERISH, &c.

To EMPOWER, *v. a.* शक्तिं or सामर्थ्यं or अधिकारित्वं दा, नियुज् (c. 7. -युनक्ति -युंक्ते -योक्तुं, c. 10. -योजयति -यितुं), समर्थं -र्थां -र्थं कृ, अनुमन् (c. 4. -मन्यते -मन्तुं), क्षमताम् ऋ in caus. (अर्पयति -यितुं).

EMPRESS, *s.* राजाधिराजस्य पत्नी, राज्ञी, अधीश्वरी, महाराजपत्नी.

EMPTIED, *p. p.* रेचितः -ता -तं, विरेचितः -ता -तं, शून्यीकृतः -ता -तं, गततोयः -या -यं, गतजलः -ला -लं; 'poured out,' पातितः -ता -तं, अवतारितः -ता -तं.

EMPTINESS, *s.* शून्यत्वं -ता, रिक्तता -त्वं, रिक्तं, असारता, निःसारता, विरसता, नीरसता, रसाभावः, अपूर्णत्वं, वितानत्वं, तुच्छत्वं, फल्गुता.

EMPTION, *s.* क्रयः, क्रयणं, क्रयकरणं.

EMPTY, *a.* रिक्तः -क्ता -क्तं, रिक्तकः -का -कं, शून्यः -न्या -न्यं, शून्यमध्यः -ध्या -ध्यं, विरसः -सा -सं, नीरसः -सा -सं, असारः -रा -रं, निःसारः -रा -रं, निःसत्त्वः -त्त्वा -त्त्वं, सारहीनः -ना -नं, वितानः -ना -नं, अपूर्णः -र्णा -र्णं, वशिकः -का -कं, तुच्छः -च्छा -च्छं.

To EMPTY, *v. a.* रिच् (c. 7. रिणक्ति, रेक्तुं), विरिच्, रिक्तीकृ, शून्यीकृ विरसीकृ, निःसारीकृ, सारं हृ (c. 1. हरति, हर्त्तुं).—(Pour out water, &c.) तोयम् अवतृ in caus. (-तारयति -यितुं) or पत् in caus. (पातयति -यितुं) or प्रस्रु in caus. (-स्रावयति -यितुं); 'the river empties itself into the sea,' नदी समुद्रं विशति.

EMPTY-HANDED, *a.* रिक्तहस्तः -स्ता -स्तं, रिक्तपाणिः -णिः -णि, शून्यहस्तः -स्ता -स्तं.

EMPTY-HEADED, *a.* शून्यमस्तकः -का -कं, निर्बोधः -धा -धं, अल्पबुद्धिः -द्धिः -द्धि.

To EMPURPLE, *v. a.* धूम्रीकृ, लोहितीकृ, अरुणीकृ, धूम्रवर्णं -र्णां -र्णं कृ, धूम्रवर्णेन रञ्ज् in caus. (रञ्जयति -यितुं).

EMPYREAL, *a.* आग्नेयः -यी -यं, उपर्य्युपरिगगणसम्बन्धी -न्धिनी -न्धि (न्).

EMPYREAN, *s.* उपर्य्युपरिस्थगगणं, उत्तमस्वर्गः, सूक्ष्माग्निस्थानं.

To EMULATE, *v. a.* स्पर्द्ध् (c. 1. स्पर्द्धते -र्द्धितुं), विस्पर्द्ध्, आस्पर्द्ध्, प्रतिस्पर्द्ध् with inst. c.; जि in des. (जिगीषति -षितुं), संघृष् (c. 1. -घर्षति -र्षितुं), परम् अभिभवितुं यत् (c. 1. यतते -तितुं), पराभिभवनाय उद्योगं कृ, अहम्पूर्व्वम् अहम्पूर्व्वमिति वद् (c. 1. वदति -दितुं); 'he emulates Indra,' शक्रेण सह स्पर्द्धते.

EMULATION, *s.* स्पर्द्धा, आस्पर्द्धा, प्रतिस्पर्द्धा, जिगीषा, विजिगीषा, सङ्घर्षः, पराभिभवेच्छा, पराभिभवनाय उद्योगः, अहम्पूर्व्विका, सापत्न्यं.

EMULATIVE, EMULOUS, *a.* स्पर्द्धी -र्द्धिनी -र्द्धि (न्), प्रतिस्पर्द्धी &c., जिगीषुः -षुः -षु, जिगीषन् -षन्ती -षत् (त्), विजिगीषुः -षुः -षु, जयेच्छुः -च्छुः -च्छु, पराभिभवेच्छुः -च्छुः -च्छु, बीभत्सुः -त्सुः -त्सु.

EMULATOR, *s.* स्पर्द्धाकारी *m.* (न्), जिगीषुः *m.*, सङ्घर्षकारी *m.*, सपत्नः.

To EMULGE, *v. a.* निर्दुह् (c. 2. -दोग्धि -ग्धुं, c. 10. -दोहयति -यितुं), नीरसीकृ.

EMULGENT, *a.* निर्दोहनकारी -रिणी -रि (न्), निर्दोग्धा -ग्ध्री -ग्धृ (ग्धृ).

EMULSION, *s.* पायसिकम् औषधं, पायसं, पयस्यं.

EMUNCTORY, *s.* शरीरमलद्वारं, शरीरमलपथः, देहोत्सर्गपथः.

To ENABLE, *v. a.* शक्तिं or सामर्थ्यं or क्षमतां दा, समर्थं -र्थां -र्थं कृ, शक्तं -क्तां -क्तं कृ, क्षमं -मां -मं कृ, समर्थीकृ, क्लृप् in caus. (कल्पयति -यितुं).

To ENACT, *v. a.* (Act, perform) कृ, विधा (c. 3. -दधाति -धातुं), प्रयुज् (c. 7. -युंक्ते -योक्तुं), निष्पद् in caus. (-पादयति -यितुं), सम्पद् in caus.—(Decree) व्यवस्थाद्वारेण or शासनद्वारेण निष्पन्नं कृ or सिद्धं कृ, व्यवस्थां कृ, शासनं कृ, व्यवस्था in caus. (-स्थापयति -यितुं), प्रशास् (c. 2. -शास्ति -शासितुं), प्रक्लृप् (c. 10. -कल्पयति -यितुं).—(Represent in action) नट् (c. 10. नाटयति -यितुं), अभिनी (c. 1. -नयति -नेतुं).

ENACTED, *p. p.* व्यवस्थापितः -ता -तं, निष्पन्नः -न्ना -न्नं, प्रशासितः -ता -तं.

ENACTMENT, *s.* शासनं, प्रशासनं, व्यवस्था -स्थापनं, नियमः, शासनपत्रं, आज्ञापत्रं, राजाज्ञा, विधानं, निदेशः, आदेशः.

ENAMEL, *s.* सुवर्णालङ्कारचित्रकरणे प्रयुक्तं काचवत् सुविलयं मणिवत् सुतेजनीयं स्निग्धद्रव्यं.

To ENAMEL, *v. a.* पूर्व्वोक्तस्निग्धद्रव्येण सुवर्णालङ्कारान् चित्र् (c. 10. चित्रयति -यितुं) or चित्रविचित्रीकृ.

To BE ENAMOURED, *v. n.* अनुरागवान् -वती -वत् or अनुरक्तः -क्ता -क्तं or आसक्तः -क्ता -क्तं भू or अस् with inst. c. or loc. c., अनुरञ्ज् in pass. (-रज्यते) आसञ्ज् in pass. (-सज्यते), with loc. c., मुह्

(c. 4. मुह्यति, मोहितुं); 'he is enamoured with her,' तया अनुरागवान् अस्ति.

ENAMOURED, *p. p.* अनुरागवान् -वती -वत् (त्), अनुरागी -गिणी -गि (न्), अनुरक्तः -क्ता -क्तं, आसक्तः -क्ता -क्तं, कामासक्तः -क्ता -क्तं, आत्तमन्मथः -था -थं.

To ENCAGE, *v. a.* पिञ्जरे प्रविश् in caus. (-वेशयति -यितुं) or निरुध् (c. 7. -रुणद्धि -रोद्धुं) or अवरुध् or बन्ध् (c. 9. बध्नाति, बन्धुं).

To ENCAMP, *v. n.* निविश् (c. 6. -विशते -वेष्टुं), उपविश् (-विशति), बलेन or सैन्येन उपविश्, कटके or शिविरे वस् (c. 1. वसति, वस्तुं) or समावस् or अध्यास् (c. 2. -आस्ते -आसितुं).

To ENCAMP, *v. a.* सैन्यं निविश् in caus. (-वेशयति -यितुं), कटके समावस् in caus. (-वासयति -यितुं), शिविरे स्था in caus. (स्थापयति -यितुं).

ENCAMPED, *p. p.* निविष्टः -ष्टा -ष्टं, उपविष्टः -ष्टा -ष्टं, समावासितः -ता -तं, समावासितकटकः -का -कं, निवेशितसैन्यः -न्या -न्यं, अध्यासितः -ता -तं.

ENCAMPMENT, *s.* (Act of encamping) निवेशनं, वाहिनीनिवेशनं, बलोपवेशनं, समावासः.—(Camp) निवेशः, शिविरं, कटकः, मन्दिरं, स्कन्धावारः, बलस्थितिः *f.*, पटकः.

To ENCASE, *v. a.* *See* INCASE.

To ENCAVE, *v. a.* कन्दरे or कुहरे or विवरे गुह् (c. 1. गूहति, गोढुं), गर्त्ते गोपनं कृ.

ENCEINTE, *a.* गर्भिणी, गर्भवती, पूर्णगर्भा, ससत्त्वा, आपन्नसत्त्वा.

To ENCHAFE, *v. a.* तप् in caus. (तापयति -यितुं), परितप्, कुप् in caus. (कोपयति -यितुं), प्रकुप्, रुष् in caus. (रोषयति -यितुं), बाध् (c. 1. बाधते -धितुं).

To ENCHAIN, *v. a.* निगडेन or शृङ्खलया बन्ध् (c. 9. बध्नाति, बन्धुं), निगड (nom. निगडयति -यितुं), शृङ्खल (nom. शृङ्खलयति -यितुं).

To ENCHANT, *v. a.* (Subdue by spells) मन्त्रद्वारेण वशीकृ or मुह् in caus. (मोहयति -यितुं), अभिमन्त्र् (c. 10. -मन्त्रयते -यितुं), अनुमन्त्र्; अभिचर् (c. 10. -चारयति -यितुं), मायां कृ.—(Charm the mind) मनो हृ (c. 1. हरति, हर्त्तुं) or रम् (c. 10. रमयति -यितुं), हृष् (c. 10. हर्षयति -यितुं), प्रहृष्, परमहर्षं जन् (c. 10. जनयति -यितुं).

ENCHANTED, *p. p.* (With joy) हृष्टमानसः -सी -सं, हृतमानसः -सी -सं, परमहृष्टः -ष्टा -ष्टं, हृष्टचित्तः -त्ता -त्तं, परमानन्दितः -ता -तं, पुलकितः -ता -तं.—(By spells) अभिमन्त्रितः -ता -तं, मन्त्रमोहितः -ता -तं. *See* CHARMED.

ENCHANTER, *s.* मायी *m.* (न्), अभिचारी *m.* (न्), अभिचारविद्, मायाकारः, मायाकृत् *m.*, मायिकः, मोही *m.* (न्), ऐन्द्रजालिकः, योगी *m.* (न्), योगेश्वरः.

ENCHANTING, *a.* मनोहरः -रा -रं, परमहर्षकरः -री -रं, परमानन्ददः -दा -दं, मोही -हिनी -हि (न्). *See* CHARMING.

ENCHANTINGLY, *adv.* मायया, सुरमणीयं, यथा परमहर्षो जायते तथा.

ENCHANTMENT, *s.* माया, अभिचारः, वशक्रिया, योगः, सम्प्रयोगः, अभिमन्त्रणं, इन्द्रजालं, जालं, कुहकः, मोहः, मन्त्रमोहनं, संवदनं -ना, मूलकर्म्म *n.* (न्), चित्रकर्म्म *n.*, कार्म्मणं, कुसृतिः *f.*

ENCHANTRESS, *s.* मायिनी, योगिनी, अभिचारिणी, मोहिनी, कुहककारी.

To ENCHASE, *v. a.* (A gem in gold) मणिं सुवर्णे प्रणिधा (c. 3. -दधाति -धातुं) or खच् (c. 10. खचयति -यितुं).—(Adorn silver vessels, &c., by embossed work) राजतभाण्डादीनि उत्करेखादिना अलङ्कृ or उपस्कृ.

To ENCIRCLE, *v. a.* परिवेष्ट् (c. 1. -वेष्टते -ष्टितुं, c. 10. -वेष्टयति -यितुं), उपवेष्ट्, संवेष्ट्, परिवृ (c. 5. -वृणोति -वरितुं -रीतुं), परिष्ठा (c. 1. -तिष्ठति -ष्ठातुं), परिगम् (c. 1. -गच्छति -गन्तुं), परिसृ (c. 1. -सरति -सर्त्तुं), मण्डल (nom. मण्डलयति -यितुं).—(Embrace) परिष्वञ्ज् (c. 1. -ष्वजते -ष्वंक्तुं).

ENCIRCLED, *p. p.* वलयितः -ता -तं, मण्डलितः -ता -तं, परिमण्डलितः -ता -तं, परिगतः -ता -तं, परिवेष्टितः -ता -तं, आवृतः -ता -तं, व्याप्तः -प्ता -प्तं.

ENCIRCLET, *s.* वलयः, मण्डलं, परिमण्डलं, चक्रवालं, परिवेष्टनं.

To ENCLOSE, ENCLOSED, ENCLOSURE. *See* INCLOSE, &c.

ENCOMIAST, *s.* स्तुतिपाठकः, मङ्गलपाठकः, बन्दी *m.* (न्), वर्णकः, गुणोत्कीर्त्तनकृत्, गुणकथकः, गुणप्रशंसकः, गुणप्रशंसाकारी *m.* (न्).

ENCOMIASTIC, ENCOMIASTICAL, *a.* प्रशंसाकरः -री -रं, स्तुतिमयः -यी -यं, श्लाघामयः -यी -यं, वन्दारुः -रुः -रु, गुणप्रकाशकः -का -कं, कीर्त्तिप्रकाशकः -का -कं.

ENCOMIUM, *s.* प्रशंसा, स्तुतिः *f.*, श्लाघा, गुणप्रशंसा, गुणश्लाघा, गुणस्तुतिः *f.*, स्तुतिवाक्यं, प्रशंसावाक्यं, स्तुतिवादः, गुणोत्कीर्त्तनं, गुणगानं, वन्दना, वर्णना, यशोवर्णना, स्तोत्रं, स्तवः, वन्दिपाठः.

To ENCOMPASS, *v. a.* परिवेष्ट् (c. 1. -वेष्टते -ष्टितुं, c. 10. -वेष्टयति -यितुं), संवेष्ट्, उपवेष्ट्, प्रवेष्ट्; परिवृ (c. 5. -वृणोति -वरितुं -रीतुं), परिगम् (c. 1. -गच्छति -गन्तुं), परिष्ठा (c. 1. -तिष्ठति -ष्ठातुं), पर्युपस्था, परिसृ (c. 1. -सरति -सर्त्तुं), परी (c. 2. पर्य्येति -तुं, rt. इ), परिवी, व्याप् (c. 5. -आप्नोति -आप्तुं), संवल् (c. 1. -वलते -लितुं), रुध् (c. 7. रुणद्धि, रोद्धुं).

ENCOMPASSED, *p. p.* वेष्टितः -ता -तं, परिवेष्टितः -ता -तं, परिवृतः -ता -तं, आवृतः -ता -तं, वृतः -ता -तं, परिगतः -ता -तं, परीतः -ता -तं, अभिपरीतः -ता -तं, परिवीतः -ता -तं, परिवारितः -ता -तं, संवीतः -ता -तं, वलयितः -ता -तं, संवलितः -ता -तं, व्याप्तः -प्ता -प्तं, परिक्षिप्तः -प्ता -प्तं, परिप्लुतः -ता -तं, अभिपरिप्लुतः -ता -तं, निलीनः -ना -नं, गुम्फितः -ता -तं, रुद्धः -द्धा -द्धं; 'having encompassed,' परीत्य.

ENCOMPASSMENT, *s.* परिवेष्टनं, वेष्टनं, परिवृतिः *f.*, वृतिः *f.*, परिवेशः -वेषः, परिगमः, परिसर्पः, परिक्रिया.—(Circumlocution) वक्रोक्तिः *f.*

ENCORE, *s.* पुनर्, पुनर्वारं, नाटकसङ्गीतादिशालायां प्रशंसासूचनार्थं प्रेक्षकाणां पुनरिति सांराविणं or पुनर् गीयतां पुनर् अभिनीयतामिति बहुभिः कृता संहूतिः *f.*

To ENCORE, *v. a.* प्रशंसासूचनार्थं पुनरिति उत्क्रुश् (c. 1. -क्रोशति -क्रोष्टुं), पुनरिति संहूतिं कृत्वा पुनरभिनयं प्रार्थ् (c. 10. -अर्थयति -ते -यितुं).

ENCOUNTER, *s.* (Meeting) समागमः, समागतिः *f.*, सङ्गः, सङ्गमः, सङ्गतं, मेलनं, मेलकः, मिलनं, समासादनं.—(Conflict, collision) समाघातः, संयुगः, समरः, सङ्ग्रामः, युद्धं, विग्रहः, सम्प्रहारः, अभिसम्पातः, सम्पराय:, सङ्घट्टः -ट्टनं, सम्मर्द्दः, प्रतिघातः, सम्फेटः.

To ENCOUNTER, *v. a.* and *n.* (Meet) समागम् (c. 1. -गच्छति -गन्तुं), सङ्गम्, मिल् (c. 6. मिलति, मेलितुं), सम्मिल्, समे (c. 2. समैति -तुं, rt. इ), आसद् (c. 10. -सादयति -यितुं), समासद्, प्रतिमुखं or अभिमुखं गम्, सम्मुखीभू.—(In a hostile manner) प्रतियुध् (c. 4. -युध्यते -योद्धुं), विग्रह् (c. 9. -गृह्णाति -ग्रहीतुं), सङ्घट्ट् (c. 1. -घट्टते -ट्टितुं), समाहन् (c. 2. -हन्ति -न्तुं), समाघातं कृ.

ENCOUNTERED, *p. p.* समागतः -ता -तं, सङ्गतः -ता -तं, समुपागतः -ता -तं, मिलितः -ता -तं, प्रतिमुखागतः -ता -तं, अभिमुखागतः -ता -तं, आसादितः -ता -तं, समासादितः -ता -तं, आक्रान्तः -न्ता -न्तं, विगृहीतः -ता -तं.

To ENCOURAGE, *v. a.* आश्वस् in caus. (-श्वासयति -यितुं), समाश्वस्, विश्वस्, उच्छ्वस्; प्रोत्सह् in caus. (-साहयति -यितुं), समुत्सह्, परिशान्त्व् (c. 10. -शान्त्वयति -यितुं), प्रहृष् in caus. (-हर्षयति -यितुं), उत्तिज् in caus. (-तेजयति -यितुं), अनुग्रह् (c. 9. -गृह्णाति -ग्रहीतुं), सङ्गृह्, प्रदिश् in caus. (-देशयति -यितुं), तेजः or विश्वासं or आशां कृ or दा or वृध् in caus. (वर्धयति -यितुं) or संवृध्; प्रवृत् in caus. (-वर्त्तयति -यितुं).

ENCOURAGED, *p. p.* आश्वासितः -ता -तं, समाश्वासितः -ता -तं, उच्छ्वासितः

-ता -तं, प्रोत्साहितः -ता -तं, उत्तेजितः -ता -तं, अनुगृहीतः -ता -तं.

ENCOURAGEMENT, *s.* (Act of encouraging) आश्वासनं, समाश्वासनं, उल्लासः, प्रोत्साहः -हनं, प्रवर्त्तः, प्ररोचनं, उत्तेजनं, समुत्तेजनं, तेजोवर्धनं, वर्धनं, संवर्धनं.—(Favor) अनुग्रहः, आग्रहः, अनुग्रहः, ग्रहः, साहाय्यं, उपकारः, अनुपालनं, आनुकूल्यं, अभ्युपपत्तिः *f.*, अनुरागः.

ENCOURAGER, *s.* आश्वासकः, प्रोत्साहकः, प्रवर्त्तकः, अनुग्रहीता *m.* (तृ).

ENCOURAGING, *a.* आश्वासकः -सिका -कं, आशावर्धकः -का -कं, तेजस्करः -री -रं, सान्त्वदः -दा -दं, प्ररोचनदः -दा -दं.

To ENCROACH, *v. n.* क्रमे क्रमे प्रसृप् (c. 1. -सर्पति -सर्प्तुं), पदे पदे प्रसृप्य पराधिकारं or परभूमिम् आविश् (c. 6. -विशति -वेष्टुं) or प्रविश् or समाविश्; क्रमे क्रमे स्वाधिकारमर्य्यादाम् अतिक्रम्य पराधिकारं or परभूमिम् आक्रम् (c.1. -क्रामति -क्रमितुं) or अभिक्रम् or अध्याक्रम्; पराधीनं किञ्चिद् द्रव्यम् अधर्म्मेण or अन्यायतो ग्रह् (c. 9. गृह्णाति, ग्रहीतुं) or अभिग्रह् or ग्रस् (c. 1. ग्रसते -सितुं) or स्वीकृ or आत्मीयं कृ.

ENCROACHER, *s.* पदे पदे प्रसर्पकः or पराधिकारग्रसकः or पराधिकाराक्रामकः or स्वभूमिमर्य्यादातिक्रामकः or पराधीनद्रव्यग्राहकः.

ENCROACHING, ENCROACHMENT, *s.* पदे पदे प्रसर्पणं or पराधिकारप्रवेशः; क्रमे क्रमे पराधिकाराक्रमणं or परभूम्यभिक्रमः or स्वाधिकारातिक्रमणं or स्वाधिकारोल्लङ्घनं or पराधीनद्रव्यग्रसनं or पराधिपत्याक्रान्तिः *f.* or स्वाधिपत्यातिक्रान्तिः *f.*

To ENCRUST, *v. a.* *See To* INCRUST.

To ENCUMBER, *v. a.* (Load, clog) भारं दा or न्यस् (c. 4. -अस्यति -असितुं), भारवन्तं -वतीं -वत् कृ, भाराक्रान्तं -न्तां -न्तं कृ, भारेण परिबाध् (c. 1. -बाधते -धितुं) or गतिपरिबाधां कृ or उपरुध् (c. 7. -रुणद्धि -रोद्धुं) or प्रतिरुध् or प्रतिबन्ध् (c. 9. -बध्नाति -बन्धुं) or स्तम्भ् in caus. (स्तम्भयति -यितुं) or विघ्न (nom. विघ्नयति -यितुं) or आयस् in caus. (-यासयति -यितुं) or क्लिश् (c. 9. क्लिश्नाति, क्लेशितुं).—(Load with debts) ऋणभारग्रस्तं -स्तां -स्तं कृ.

ENCUMBERED, *p. p.* भारवान् -वती -वत् (त्), भारी -रिणी -रि (न्), भारयुक्तः -क्ता -क्तं, भाराक्रान्तः -न्ता -न्तं, भारग्रस्तः -स्ता -स्तं, बाधितः -ता -तं, प्रतिरुद्धः -द्धा -द्धं, विघ्नितः -ता -तं.

ENCUMBRANCE, *s.* (Load) भारः, धुरा.—(Impediment) बाधा -धकः, प्रतिबन्धः, प्रतिरोधः, उपरोधः, विघ्नः, स्तम्भः, प्रतिष्टम्भः, विष्टम्भः, प्रत्यूहः, अन्तरायः.—(Useless addition) अनुबन्धः.—(Debt) ऋणभारः, ऋणं, भारत्वं.

ENCYCLICAL, *a.* चाक्रिकः -की -कं, चाक्रेयः -यी -यं, मण्डली -लिनी -लि (न्), वर्त्तुलः -ला -लं; 'letter,' बहुजनानुद्दिश्य पत्रं, बहुसाधारणपत्रं.

ENCYCLOPÆDIA, *s.* विद्याचक्रं, विद्यामण्डलं, विद्यामुक्तावलिः *f.*, विद्याहारावलिः *f.*, विद्यावलिः *f.*, विद्यापर्य्यायः.

END, *s.* (Extremity) अन्तः -न्तं, पर्य्यन्तं, प्रान्तः, सन्तः, पारः -रं.—(Termination) अवसानं, पर्य्यवसानं, अवसायः, अवसादः, अवसन्नता, समाप्तिः *f.*, सायः, अन्तः -न्तं, शेषः, पर्य्यवशेषः, परिणामः, क्षयः, गतिः *f.*, निधनं, अत्ययः.—(Conclusion) समाप्तिः *f.*, निष्पत्तिः *f.*, सिद्धिः *f.*, निर्वृत्तिः *f.*, निष्ठा.—(Cessation) विरतिः *f.*, विरामः, अवरतिः *f.*, उपरतिः *f.*, निवृत्तिः *f.*, विनिवृत्तिः *f.*, विच्छेदः, उपशमः.—(Limit, term) अवधिः *m.*, सीमा, अन्तरं.—(Last stage) परिणामः.—(Death) अन्तकालः, अन्तः, अन्तकः, निधनं, अत्ययः, अपगमः, अपायः, मरणं, नाशः, विनाशः, देहक्षयः, उपसंहारः.—(Extreme point) अग्रं, अग्रभागः, मुखं, शिखा, शिखरं, अवधिः *m.*—(Consequence) अन्तः, फलं, फलमुत्तरं, उत्तरं, परिणामः.—(Object, scope) अर्थः, आशयः, अभिप्रायः, तात्पर्य्यं, उद्देशः, अभिसन्धिः *m.*, कार्य्यं, कार्य्यवस्तु *n.*; 'end of the world,' प्रलयः, क्षयः, कल्पः, कल्पान्तः, संवर्त्तः, उपसंयमः; 'end of day,' दिवसात्ययः, दिनावसानं; 'end of night,' निशावसानं, क्षपात्ययः; 'end of a garment,' अञ्चलः, पटाञ्चलः -लं, तरी, तरिः *f.*, दशा, वस्तिः *m.*; 'hear my speech to the end,' मद्वचनम् अवसानपर्य्यन्तं or शेषं यावत् शृणु.

To END, *v. a.* अवसो (c. 4. -स्यति -सातुं), समाप् in caus. (-आपयति -यितुं), सम्पॄ in caus. (-पूरयति -यितुं), निवृत् in caus. (-वर्त्तयति -यितुं) or निवृत् with abl. c. (c. 1. -वर्त्तते -र्त्तितुं), निर्वृत्, विनिवृत्, विरम् in caus. (-रमयति -यितुं) or विरम् with abl. c. (c. 1. -रमति -रन्तुं), उपरम्, व्युपरम्, निष्पद् in caus. (-पादयति -यितुं), साध् in caus. (साधयति -यितुं), प्रतियत् (c. 10. -यातयति -यितुं). Often rendered by अन्त as the last member of a compound; as, 'death ends life,' मरणान्तं जीवितं.—(Get to the end) पार् (c. 10. पारयति -यितुं), तीर् (c. 10. तीरयति -यितुं).

To END, *v. n.* विरम् (c. 1. -रमति -रन्तुं), उपरम्, व्युपरम्; निवृत् (c. 1. -वर्त्तते -र्त्तितुं), विनिवृत्, निर्वृत्, समाप् in pass. (-आप्यते), निष्पद् in pass. (-पद्यते), विगम् (c. 1. -गच्छति -गन्तुं), अपया (c. 2. -याति -तुं), विच्छिद् in pass. (-छिद्यते), अवसद् (c. 1. -सीदति -सत्तुं), शम् (c. 4. शाम्यति, शमितुं). Often expressed by अन्तः -न्ता -न्तं or पर्य्यन्तः -न्ता -न्तं as the last member of a compound; as, 'a name which ends in a long vowel,' दीर्घवर्णान्तं नाम; 'ending at the ocean,' सागरपर्य्यन्तः -न्ता -न्तं.

To ENDANGER, *v. a.* संशयस्थं -स्थां -स्थं कृ, शङ्कास्थं -स्थां -स्थं कृ, सन्देहस्थं -स्थां -स्थं कृ, भयस्थं -स्थां -स्थं कृ, सन्देहदोलस्थं -स्थां -स्थं कृ, संशयापन्नं -न्नां -न्नं कृ, शङ्कास्पदं कृ; 'one who endangers his life,' संशयितजीवितः.

To ENDEAR, *v. a.* प्रियं -यां -यं कृ, हृदयप्रियं -यां -यं कृ, दयितं -तां -तं कृ, प्रीतं -तां -तं कृ, अभीष्टं -ष्टां -ष्टं कृ, इष्टं -ष्टां -ष्टं कृ, स्नेहपात्रं कृ.

ENDEARING, *a.* प्रियङ्करः -री -रं, प्रियकारः -री -रं, प्रीतिकरः -री -रं.

ENDEARMENT, *s.* प्रेमकारणं, स्नेहकारणं, प्रियता -त्वं, प्रेमहेतुः *m.*, प्रेमकर्म्म *n.* (न्), शृङ्गारकर्म्म *n.*, ललितं, हावः, विलासः; 'word of endearment,' प्रियवाक्यं.

ENDEAVOR, *s.* यत्नः, प्रयत्नः, उद्यमः, उद्योगः, उत्साहः, चेष्टा -ष्टनं, व्यवसायः, अध्यवसायः, समुद्यमः, प्रवृत्तिः *f.*, आरम्भः, उपक्रमः, आयासः, प्रयासः, गुरणं, विचेष्टितं, उत्थानं, ग्रहः, व्यापारः, घटना.

To ENDEAVOR, *v. n.* यत् (c. 1. यतते -तितुं), प्रयत्, चेष्ट् (c. 1. चेष्टते -ष्टितुं), विचेष्ट्, सचेष्ट्, व्यवसो (c. 4. -स्यति -सातुं), अध्यवसो, उद्यम् (c. 1. -यच्छति -यन्तुं), व्यायम्, घट् (c. 1. घटते -टितुं), उपक्रम् (c. 1. -क्रमते -मितुं), आयस् (c. 4. -यस्यति -यसितुं), प्रयस्, आरभ् (c. 1. -रभते -रब्धुं), समारभ्, वाह् (c. 1. वाहते -हितुं), प्रवृत् (c. 1. -वर्त्तते -र्त्तितुं), उद्योगं कृ, प्रयासं कृ.

ENDEAVORED, *p. p.* व्यवसितः -ता -तं, अध्यवसायितः -ता -तं, चेष्टितः -ता -तं, कृतप्रयत्नः -त्ना -त्नं, समुद्यतः -ता -तं, कृतोत्साहः -हा -हं, घाहितः -ता -तं.

ENDED, *p. p.* अवसितः -ता -तं, अवसन्नः -न्ना -न्नं, पर्य्यवसितः -ता -तं, सन्नः -न्ना -न्नं, सितः -ता -तं, निवृत्तः -त्ता -त्तं, निर्वृत्तः -त्ता -त्तं, वृत्तः -त्ता -त्तं, समाप्तः -प्ता -प्तं, परिणतः -ता -तं, गतः -ता -तं, विगतः -ता -तं, अस्तङ्गतः -ता -तं, अस्तङ्गमितः -ता -तं.

ENDING, *s.* अन्तः -न्तं, शेषः, समाप्तिः *f.*; 'of a word,' पदान्तं, पदस्य शेषवर्णः.

ENDICT, ENDICTMENT, ENDITE. *See* INDICT, &c.

ENDIVE, *s.* शाकप्रभेदः, शुक्तैलादिना सह खादनीयः शाकः.

ENDLESS, *a.* अनन्तः -न्ता -न्तं -न्तकः -का -कं, अत्यन्तः -न्ता -न्तं, अपर्य्यन्तः -न्ता -न्तं, अशेषः -षा -षं, निरवधिः -धिः -धि, अपारः -रा -रं, निरन्तरः -रा -रं, अविरतः -ता -तं, अनवरतः -ता -तं, अमितः -ता -तं, अतिदीर्घः -र्घा -र्घं.

ENDLESSLY, *adv.* अत्यन्तं, अविरतं, अनारतं, निरन्तरं, अशेषतस्.

ENDLESSNESS, *s.* आनन्त्यं, अनन्तता -त्वं, अत्यन्तत्वं, अविरामः, अविरतिः *f.*, अविच्छेदः, आनन्तर्य्यं, नित्यता.

ENDORSE, ENDORSEMENT. *See* INDORSE, INDORSEMENT.

To ENDOW, *v. a.* (With a portion) यौतुकं or शुल्कं or वृत्तिं दा, प्रतिष्ठां कृ, प्रतिष्ठा in caus. (-ष्ठापयति -यितुं).—(Furnish with any thing) युज् (c. 10. योजयति -यितुं), समायुज्, सम्पन्नं -न्नां -न्नं कृ, युक्तं -क्तां -क्तं कृ, दा; 'to be endowed with,' युज् in pass. (युज्यते); 'he is endowed with all good qualities,' सर्व्वगुणोपेतोऽस्ति.

ENDOWED, *p. p.* (With a portion, &c.) प्रतिष्ठितः -ता -तं, गृहीतशुल्कः -ल्का -ल्कं.—(Furnished with any thing) युक्तः -क्ता -क्तं, संयुक्तः -क्ता -क्तं, उपेतः -ता -तं, सम्पन्नः -न्ना -न्नं, उपपन्नः -न्ना -न्नं, अन्वितः -ता -तं, प्रयुक्तः -क्ता -क्तं, शीलः -ला -लं, शीलितः -ता -तं.—(With a grant of property) निबद्धः -द्धा -द्धं.

ENDOWMENT, *s.* (Settling a dower on a woman) यौतुकदानं, प्रतिष्ठा.—(Settling property for religious purposes) देवस्वदानं, अग्रहारदानं, प्रतिष्ठा.—(The property so settled) देवस्वं, अग्रहारः.—(Grant of money for support) निबन्धः -न्धनं.—(Quality, gift of nature) गुणः, शक्तिः *f.*

To ENDUE, *v. a.* सम्पन्नं -न्नां -न्नं कृ, युक्तं -क्तां -क्तं कृ, युज् (c. 10. योजयति -यितुं), समायुज्, दा; 'to be endued,' सम्पन्नः -न्ना -न्नं भू, युज् in pass. (युज्यते). *See* ENDOW.

ENDUED, *p. p.* सम्पन्नः -न्ना -न्नं, उपेतः -ता -तं, युक्तः -क्ता -क्तं, संयुक्तः -क्ता -क्तं, समायुक्तः -क्ता -क्तं, अन्वितः -ता -तं, आपन्नः -न्ना -न्नं, उपपन्नः -न्ना -न्नं.

ENDURANCE, *s.* (Bearing with patience) सहनं, सहत्वं, सहता, साहनं, सहिष्णुता -त्वं, सहनशीलता, क्षमा, तितिक्षा, क्षान्तिः *f.*, मर्षः -र्षणं, धैर्य्यं, धृतिः *f.*, धीरत्वं, स्थैर्य्यं, उत्साहः; 'of austerities,' दमः.—(Continuance) संस्थितिः *f.*, स्थितिः *f.*, स्थायित्वं.

To ENDURE, *v. a.* (Bear) सह् (c. 1. सहते, सोढुं), विषह्, क्षम् (c. 1. क्षमते, क्षन्तुं), संक्षम्, तिज् in des. (तितिक्षते -क्षितुं), मृष् (c. 4. मृष्यति -ते, मर्षितुं, c. 10. मर्षयति -यितुं), धृ in caus. (धारयति -यितुं), उपागम् (c. 1. -गच्छति -गन्तुं), भुज् (c. 7. भुंक्ते, भोक्तुं), धैर्य्यम् आलम्ब् (c. 1. -लम्बते -म्बितुं) or अवलम्ब्. Sometimes expressible by शक्; as, 'I cannot endure to see him,' तं द्रष्टुं न शक्नोमि.

To ENDURE, *v. n.* (Last, continue) स्था (c. 1. तिष्ठति -ते, स्थातुं), चिरस्थायी -यिनी -यि भू.

ENDURED, *p. p.* सोढः -ढा -ढं, विसोढः -ढा -ढं, क्षान्तः -न्ता -न्तं, तितिक्षितः -ता -तं, मर्षितः -ता -तं; 'not to be endured,' न सह्यः -ह्या -ह्यं, न क्षन्तव्यः -व्या -व्यं.

ENDURER, *s.* सोढा *m.* (ढृ), विसोढा *m.*, क्षन्ता *m.* (न्तृ), सहः in comp.

ENDURING, *a.* (Lasting) स्थायी -यिनी -यि (न्), चिरस्थायी &c., दीर्घकालस्थायी &c., संस्थः -स्था -स्थं, अविसर्गी -र्गिणी -र्गि (न्).—(Patient) सहिष्णुः -ष्णुः -ष्णु, सहनशीलः -ला -लं, तितिक्षुः -क्षुः -क्षु, सहनः -ना -नं, क्षमः -मा -मं, सहः -हा -हं.

ENDWISE, *adv.* अग्रे, अग्रतस्, अध्यग्रं, अग्रम् उपधाय or अवलम्ब्य.

ENEMY, *s.* शत्रुः *m.*, रिपुः *m.*, अरिः *m.*, अरातिः *m.*, विपक्षः, वैरी *m.* (न्), अमित्रः, प्रतिपक्षः, अपकारी *m.* (न्), अपकर्त्ता *m.* (र्तृ), द्वेषी *m.* (न्), द्वेष्टा *m.* (ष्टृ), द्वेषणः, द्विषन् *m.* (त्), द्विट् *m.* (ष्), विद्विट्, विद्वेषी *m.* (न्), अहितः, विरोधी *m.* (न्), प्रतिरोधी *m.* -रोधकः, सपत्नः, दुर्हृद् *m.*, अभिघाती *m.* (न्), प्रत्यवस्थाता *m.* (तृ), परः, पारक्यः, परिपन्थी *m.* (न्) -न्थकः, प्रत्यर्थी *m.* (न्), शात्रवः, प्रतिबन्धकः, विजिगीषुः *m.*; 'enemy in the rear,' पार्ष्णिग्राहः; 'having no enemies,' अभूतशत्रुः -त्रुः -त्रु.

ENERGETIC, *a.* उत्साही -हिनी -हि (न्), उद्योगी -गिनी -गि (न्), व्यवसायी -यिनी -यि (न्), उद्यमी -मिनी -मि (न्), उत्साहयुक्तः -क्ता -क्तं, सोत्साहः -हा -हं, सोद्योगः -गा -गं, उद्युक्तः -क्ता -क्तं, तेजोवान् -वती -वत् (त्), तेजस्वी -स्विनी -स्वि (न्), कृतप्रयत्नः -त्ना -त्नं, प्रयत्नवान् -वती -वत् (त्), सयत्नः -त्ना -त्नं, कर्म्मोद्युक्तः -क्ता -क्तं, तीक्ष्णकर्म्मा -र्म्मा -र्म्म (न्), कर्म्मशीलः -ला -लं, कर्म्मी -र्म्मिणी -र्म्मि (न्), शक्तिमान् -मती -मत् (त्), शक्तिरूपः -पा -पं, अनलसः -सा -सं, अतन्द्रः -न्द्रा -न्द्रं, अतन्द्रितः -ता -तं, आलस्यशून्यः -न्या -न्यं, प्रगल्भः -ल्भा -ल्भं, वीर्य्यवान् -वती -वत् (त्).

ENERGETICALLY, *adv.* सोत्साहं, सोद्योगं, सव्यवसायं, उद्यमेन, सयत्नं, शक्त्या, प्रयत्नतस्, सवीर्य्यं, ससत्त्वं, पौरुषेण.

ENERGY, *s.* (Power) तेजः *n.* (स्), वीर्य्यं, शक्तिः *f.*, सत्त्वं, प्रभावः, पौरुषं.—(Activity) उद्योगः, व्यवसायः, उद्यमः, उत्साहः, सत्त्वोत्साहः, कर्म्मोद्योगः, सयत्नता, प्रवृत्तिः *f.* The divine energies or mothers of the gods are ब्राह्मी, महेश्वरी, ऐन्द्री, वाराही, वैष्णवी, कौमारी, कौवेरी, चामुण्डा.

To ENERVATE, *v. a.* दुर्बलीकृ, शिथिलीकृ, तेजः or शक्तिं or वीर्य्यं हृ (c. 1. हरति, हर्त्तुं), क्लीव् in caus. (क्लीवयति -यितुं), क्षीणीकृ, क्षीणं -णां -णं कृ, क्लीवीकृ.

ENERVATED, *p. p.* हततेजाः -जाः -जः (स्), क्षीणवीर्य्यः -र्य्या -र्य्यं, शिथिलशक्तिः -क्तिः -क्ति.

ENERVATION, *s.* दुर्बलीकरणं, शिथिलीकरणं, तेजोहरणं, तेजोहानिः *f.*, वीर्य्यक्षयः, शक्तिहानिः *f.*, क्लीवभावः, क्लीवत्वं, प्रमीला.

To ENFEEBLE, *v. a.* दुर्बलीकृ, अल्पबलीकृ, तेजः or सत्त्वं हृ (c. 1. हरति, हर्त्तुं).

ENFEEBLED, *p. p.* क्षीणशक्तिः -क्तिः -क्ति, शिथिलबलः -ला -लं, हततेजाः -जाः -जः (स्), क्षीणसत्त्वः -त्त्वा -त्त्वं, गतवीर्य्यः -र्य्या -र्य्यं, सामर्थ्यहीनः -ना -नं, दुर्बलः -ला -लं; 'by age,' जरितः -ता -तं, जरातुरः -रा -रं.

To ENFORCE, *v. a.* (Give strength to) दृढीकृ, स्थिरीकृ, दृढ (nom. दृढयति -यितुं), संस्तम्भ् (c. 5. -स्तभ्नोति -स्तम्भितुं, c. 10. -स्तम्भयति -यितुं), सबलं -लां -लं कृ, तेजः or शक्तिं दा.—(Put in act by force) बलेन or बलात्कारेण कृ in caus. (कारयति -यितुं) or प्रवृत् in caus. (-वर्त्तयति -यितुं) or प्रणी (c. 1. -णयति -णेतुं) or निर्वह् in caus. (-वाहयति -यितुं) or निष्पद् in caus. (-पादयति -यितुं). The causal form of a verb may express the sense of enforce; as, 'to enforce payment,' दा in caus. (दापयति -यितुं).

ENFORCED, *p. p.* बलेन प्रवर्त्तितः -ता -तं or निष्पादितः -ता -तं or प्रणीतः -ता -तं, दृढीकृतः -ता -तं, स्थिरीकृतः -ता -तं, संस्तब्धः -ब्धा -ब्धं; 'payment must be enforced,' दाप्यः (*i.e.* he must be made to pay).

ENFORCEMENT, *s.* (Putting in act by force) बलात्कारः, बलेन प्रवर्त्तनं or प्रणयनं or निष्पादनं.—(Corroboration) दृढीकरणं, स्थिरीकरणं, संस्तम्भः, दृढप्रमाणं.—(Urgent evidence) दृढप्रमाणं, गुरुप्रमाणं.

To ENFRANCHISE, *v. a.* (Free from slavery or confinement) दास्यात् or बन्धनाद् मुच् (c. 6. मुञ्चति, मोक्तुं, c. 10. मोचयति -यितुं) or विमुच् or मोक्ष् (c. 10. मोक्षयति -यितुं) or विसृज् (c. 6. -सृजति -स्रष्टुं).—(Admit to the privileges of citizens) स्वाधीनीकृ, स्वतन्त्रीकृ, स्ववशीकृ, पौरजनानाम् अधिकारान् दा or प्रदा.

ENFRANCHISEMENT, *s.* (Liberation from slavery or custody) दास्यमोक्षः, बन्धनमोक्षः, दासभावाद् विमोक्षः or विमुक्तिः *f.*—(Admission to the privileges of citizen, &c.) पौरजनाधिकारदानं, स्वाधीनीकरणं.

To ENGAGE, *v. a.* (Occupy, employ) व्यापृ in caus. (-पारयति -यितुं), प्रवृत् in caus. (-वर्त्तयति -यितुं), प्रयुज् in caus. (-योजयति -यितुं); 'be occupied in,' व्यापृ in pass. (-प्रियते) with loc. c., वृत् (c. 1. वर्त्तते -र्त्तितुं), प्रवृत् with loc. c., आस्था (c. 1. -तिष्ठति -स्थातुं) with acc. c., सेव् (c. 1. सेवते -वितुं), निरतः -ता -तं भू.—(Appoint to any business) नियुज्, विनियुज्, अधिकृ, प्रकृ, वृ (c. 10. वरयति -यितुं).—(Bind by contract) नियमपत्रेण or नियमेन बन्ध् (c. 9. बध्नाति, बन्धुं), प्रतिज्ञापत्रेण बन्ध्.—(Encounter, attack) युद्धं कृ, सङ्ग्रामं कृ, समाघातं कृ, संयुध् (c. 4. -युध्यते -योद्धुं), आक्रम् (c. 1. -क्रामति -क्रमितुं).—(Win, draw) आराध् (c. 10. -राधयति -यितुं), अनुरञ्ज् (c. 10. -रञ्जयति -यितुं), आकृष् (c. 1. -कर्षति -क्रष्टुं), अनुनी (c. 1. -नयति -नेतुं).—(Pledge, pawn) पण् (c. 1. पणते -णितुं), आधीकृ.

To ENGAGE, *v. n.* (In battle) संयुध् (c. 4. -युध्यते -योद्धुं), युद्धारम्भं कृ, रणाभियोगं कृ.—(Undertake) आरभ् (c. 1. -रभते -रब्धुं), उपक्रम् (c. 1. -क्रमते -मितुं), व्यवसो (c. 4. -स्यति -सातुं).—(Promise, make a contract) प्रतिज्ञा (c. 9. -जानीते -ज्ञातुं), सम्प्रतिज्ञा, नियमं कृ, समयाकृ, पणं कृ, अङ्गीकृ, पण् (c. 1. पणते -णितुं), उपगम् (c. 1. -गच्छति -गन्तुं); 'make a contract of marriage,' विवाहप्रतिज्ञां कृ, विवाहसम्बन्धं कृ, वाग्दानं कृ, वाग्निश्चयं कृ; 'better die than engage in such an act as this,' वरं मरणं न च ईदृशे कर्म्मणि प्रवृत्तिः.

ENGAGED, *p. p.* (Occupied in) व्यापृतः -ता -तं, निरतः -ता -तं, रतः -ता -तं, प्रवृत्तः -त्ता -त्तं, परः -रा -रं, निष्ठः -ष्ठा -ष्ठं, निष्ठितः -ता -तं, आस्थितः -ता -तं, अवस्थितः -ता -तं, वृत्तः -त्ता -त्तं, निविष्टः -ष्टा -ष्टं, निवेशितः -ता -तं; 'engaged in business,' कर्म्मनिष्ठः -ष्ठा -ष्ठं, कर्म्मोद्युक्तः -क्ता -क्तं, कार्य्यवान् -वती -वत् (त्), क्रियावान् &c., कर्म्मी -र्म्मिणी -र्म्मि (न्), व्यापारी -रिणी -रि (न्), व्यवसायी -यिनी -यि (न्), कर्म्मसूद्यतः -ता -तं; 'being engaged in,' प्रवर्त्तमानः -ना -नं; 'engaged in devotion,' योगारूढः -ढा -ढं; 'engaged in reading,' अध्ययनरतः -ता -तं, अध्ययनाभिमुखः -खा -खं; 'engaged in meditation,' ध्यानपरः -रा -रं, ध्यानतत्परः -रा -रं; 'engaged in one's own duties,' स्वधर्म्मे निरतः -ता -तं; 'engaged in a quarrel,' कलहायितः -ता -तं.—(By contract, promised) प्रतिज्ञातः -ता -तं, संविदितः -ता -तं, उपगतः -ता -तं, अभ्युपगतः -ता -तं, अभ्युपेतः -ता -तं, अङ्गीकृतः -ता -तं, प्रज्ञप्तः -प्ता -प्तं, कृतसङ्केतः -ता -तं, कृतसमयः -या -यं, कृतसम्बन्धः -न्धा -न्धं.—(Engaged to be married) प्रतिज्ञाविवाहितः -ता, वाग्दत्ता -त्ता, प्रज्ञप्ता -प्ता.

ENGAGEMENT, *s.* (Occupation) व्यापारः, कार्य्यं, कर्म्म *n.* (न्), प्रवृत्तिः *f.*, प्रवर्त्तनं, वृत्तिः *f.*, व्यवसायः, व्यवहारः.—(Agreement, contract) प्रतिज्ञा -ज्ञानं, सङ्केतः, संविद् *f.*, समयः, नियमः, संस्कारः, उपगमः, अभ्युपगमः, अभ्युपायः, पणः, परिपणनं, व्यवस्था, प्रज्ञप्तिः *f.*, समाधिः *m.*; 'to make an engagement,' समयं कृ, समयाकृ. *See To* ENGAGE, *v. n.* 'To keep an engagement,' प्रतिज्ञातं पाल् (c. 10. पालयति -यितुं); 'to break an engagement,' समयं भिद् (c. 7. भिनत्ति, भेत्तुं), समयभेदं कृ, विसंवादं कृ; 'one who has fulfilled his engagement,' कृतप्रतिज्ञः.—(Marriage-contract) वाग्निश्चयः, विवाहप्रतिज्ञा.—(Battle) युद्धं, रणाभियोगः, समाघातः, सङ्ग्रामः, सम्प्रहारः.—(Obligation) अवश्यकर्त्तव्यं.

ENGAGING, *a.* (Attractive, pleasing) मनोहरः -रा -रं, हृदयग्राही -हिणी -हि (न्), हृदयकर्षी -र्षिणी -र्षि (न्), मित्रयुः -युः -यु, मित्रवत्सलः -ला -लं, अनुरञ्जकः -का -कं, हृदयङ्गमः -मा -मं, अनुरागजनकः -का -कं.

ENGAGINGLY, *adv.* मनोहरं, सप्रणयं, यथा हृदयम् आकृष्यते तथा.

To ENGENDER, *v. a.* (Beget) जन् in caus. (जनयति -यितुं), सञ्जन्, विजन्, प्रसू (c. 2. -सूते, c. 4. -सूयते -सोतुं).—(Produce) उत्पद् in caus. (-पादयति -यितुं), जन् in caus.

ENGENDERED, *p. p.* जातः -ता -तं, जनितः -ता -तं, उपजातः -ता -तं, उत्पादितः -ता -तं, प्रसूतः -ता -तं, प्ररूढः -ढा -ढं, उद्भवः -वा -वं, in comp.

ENGINE, *s.* यन्त्रं, उपकरणं, साधनं, विलालः; 'military engine,' युद्धयन्त्रं, युद्धास्त्रं; 'fire-engine,' अग्निनिर्वापणयन्त्रं.

ENGINEER, *s.* यन्त्रकारः -रकः, यन्त्रनिर्म्माणशिल्पविद्, यन्त्रविद्, कलाज्ञः.

ENGINEERING, *s.* यन्त्रकारस्य व्यापारः or कर्म्म *n.* (न्).

To ENGIRD, *v. a.* परिवेष्ट् (c. 1. -वेष्टते -ष्टितुं), मण्डल (nom. मण्डलयति -यितुं).

ENGLAND, *s.* श्वेतद्वीपः, इङ्गलण्डनामको देशः.

To ENGORGE, *v. a.* ग्रस् (c. 1. ग्रसते -सितुं), निगॄ (c. 6. -गिरति -गरितुं -रीतुं).

To ENGRAPPLE, *v. n.* बाहूबाहवि or हस्ताहस्ति युध् (c. 4. युध्यते, योद्धुं).

To ENGRASP, *v. a.* ग्रह् (c. 9. गृह्णाति, ग्रहीतुं), धृ (c. 1. धरति, धर्त्तुं).

To ENGRAVE, *v. a.* तक्ष् (c. 1. तक्षति -क्षितुं, c. 5. तक्ष्णोति), त्वक्ष् (c. 1. त्वक्षति -क्षितुं), रेखादिना अलङ्कृ or उपस्कृ or मुद्रीकृ or मुद्र् (nom. मुद्रयति -यितुं).

ENGRAVED, *p. p.* तष्टः -ष्टा -ष्टं, रेखादिना मुद्रितः -ता -तं or मुद्रीकृतः -ता -तं.

ENGRAVER, *s.* तक्षकः, तष्टा *m.* (ष्टृ), त्वष्टा *m.* (ष्टृ), मुद्राकरः.

ENGRAVING, *s.* तक्षणं, तक्षणकर्म्म *n.* (न्).—(A print) मुद्रा.

To ENGROSS, *v. a.* (Thicken) स्थूलीकृ, घनीकृ, सान्द्रीकृ, निविडीकृ.—(Fatten) पुष् in caus. (पोषयति -यितुं), प्यै in caus. (प्याययति -यितुं).—(Take the whole) सर्व्वं ग्रह् (c. 9. गृह्णाति, ग्रहीतुं), पूर्व्वं ग्रह्, समुदायं ग्रह्; 'to engross the mind,' चित्तैकाग्र्यं जन् (c. 10. जनयति -यितुं), चित्तम् अनन्यविषयं कृ or एकप्रवणं कृ.—(Purchase the whole of a commodity with a view to sell at a higher price) अधिकमूल्येन विक्रयार्थं सर्व्वभाण्डानि पूर्व्वं क्री (c. 9. क्रीणाति -णीते, क्रेतुं), पूर्व्वक्रयं कृ, प्रख्या (c. 2. -ख्याति -तुं).—(Copy in a large distinct hand) सुव्यक्ताक्षरैः or स्पष्टरूपेण लिख् (c. 6. लिखति, लेखितुं), सुस्पष्टाक्षराणि लिखित्वा उत्तॄ (c. 1. -तरति -रितुं -रीतुं).

ENGROSSED, *p. p.* (Absorbed) निविष्टः -ष्टा -ष्टं, अभिनिविष्टः -ष्टा -ष्टं, आविष्टः -ष्टा -ष्टं, निमग्नः -ग्ना -ग्नं, आसक्तचेताः -ताः -तः (स्), अनन्यविषयः -या -यं, एकप्रवणः -णा -णं, एकाग्रः -ग्रा -ग्रं, परायणः -णा -णं; 'by fear,' भयैकप्रवणः -णा -णं.—(Forestalled) पूर्व्वं गृहीतः -ता -तं or क्रीतः -ता -तं.

ENGROSSER, *s.* (Forestaller) पूर्व्वक्रेता *m.* (तृ), सर्व्वभाण्डक्रेता, पूर्व्वग्राहकः, प्रख्याता *m.* (तृ).—(Copier) सुस्पष्टरूपेण लेखकः, सुव्यक्तलिपिकारः.

To ENGULPH, *v. a.* जलावर्त्ते or जलगुल्मे निक्षिप् (c. 6. -क्षिपति -क्षेप्तुं), अवघूर्णेन ग्रस् (c. 1. ग्रसते -सितुं), उपग्रस्.

To ENHANCE, *v. a.* वृध् in caus. (वर्धयति -यितुं), उपचि (c. 5. -चिनोति -चेतुं), अधिकीकृ, अधिकं -कां -कं कृ, गर (nom. गरयति -यितुं), प्रचुरीकृ; 'is enhanced,' उपचीयते.

ENHANCED, *p. p.* वर्धितः -ता -तं, अधिकीकृतः -ता -तं, उपचितः -ता -तं.

ENHANCEMENT, *s.* वृद्धिः *f.*, वर्धनं, उपचयः, विवर्धनं, उन्नतिः *f.*, अभ्युदयः.

ENIGMA, *s.* गूढं, गूढवाक्यं, गूढप्रश्नः, प्रवह्लिः *f.* -ह्लिका, प्रहेलिका, प्रश्नदूती,

खेयः, खेयोक्तिः *f.*

Enigmatical, *a.* गूढः -ढा -ढं, गूढार्थः -र्था -र्थं, निगूढार्थः -र्था -र्थं, सन्दिग्धार्थः -र्था -र्थं, अस्पष्टार्थः -र्था -र्थं, द्व्यर्थः -र्था -र्थं, दुर्ज्ञेयः -या -यं, बोधागम्यः -म्या -म्यं, अव्याख्येयः -या -यं, व्याख्यागम्यः -म्या -म्यं, वक्रः -क्रा -क्रं.

Enigmatically, *adv.* गूढं, सगूढार्थं, निगूढार्थतस्, अस्पष्टं, अव्यक्तं, वक्रोक्त्या.

To **Enjoin**, *v. a.* आदिश् (c. 6. -दिशति -देष्टुं), निर्दिश्, प्रदिश्, विनिर्दिश्, समादिश्, सन्दिश्, व्यादिश्, उपदिश्; आज्ञा in caus. (-ज्ञापयति -यितुं), समाज्ञा, नियुज् (c. 7. -युनक्ति -योक्तुं, c. 10. -योजयति -यितुं), विनियुज्, सन्नियुज्, चुद् (c. 10. चोदयति -यितुं), प्रचुद्, सञ्चुद्, शास् (c. 2. शास्ति, शासितुं), विधा (c. 3. -दधाति -धातुं).

Enjoined, *p. p.* आदिष्टः -ष्टा -ष्टं, निर्दिष्टः -ष्टा -ष्टं, उद्दिष्टः -ष्टा -ष्टं, प्रचोदितः -ता -तं, सञ्चोदितः -ता -तं, विहितः -ता -तं; 'by the vedas,' वेदविहितः -ता -तं.

To **Enjoy**, *v. a.* भुज् (c. 7. भुनक्ति, भुंक्ते, भोक्तुं), उपभुज्, अनुभुज्, परिभुज्, अभिभुज्; अश् (c. 5. अश्नुते, c. 9. अश्नाति, अशितुं), समश्, उपाश्; अनुभू (c. 1. -भवति -वितुं), आस्वद् or आस्वाद् (c. 1. -स्वदति or -स्वादते -दितुं), पुष् (c. 4. पुष्यति, पोष्टुं) with acc. c.—(Delight in) रम् (c. 1. रमते, रन्तुं), अभिरम्, नन्द् (c. 1. नन्दति -न्दितुं), अभिनन्द्, रुच् (c. 1. रोचते -चितुं).—(Possess with satisfaction) सुखेन or सन्तोषेण उपयुज् (c. 7. -युनक्ति -युंक्ते -योक्तुं) or धृ (c. 10. धारयति -यितुं) or धा (c. 3. धत्ते, धातुं) or सेव् (c. 1. सेवते -वितुं).

Enjoyable, *a.* भोग्यः -ग्या -ग्यं, उपभोग्यः -ग्या -ग्यं, सुभोगीनः -ना -नं, भोगवान् -वती -वत् (त्), रम्यः -म्या -म्यं, रमणीयः -या -यं, सुभगः -गा -गं, आनन्ददः -दा -दं, सुखदः -दा -दं, मनोरमः -मा -मं, कमनीयः -या -यं, आस्वादनीयः -या -यं.

Enjoyably, *adv.* सभोगं, सोपभोगं, रमणीयं, सुभगं, जोषं.

Enjoyed, *p. p.* भुक्तः -क्ता -क्तं, उपभुक्तः -क्ता -क्तं, कृतोपभोगः -गा -गं, अनुभूतः -ता -तं, अशितः -ता -तं, आस्वादित -ता -तं.

Enjoyment, *s.* (Fruition) भोगः, भुक्तिः *f.*, उपभोगः, परिभोगः, अनुभवः, आस्वादः -दनं, फलभोगः, सुखास्वादः, निर्वेशः.—(Pleasure) सुखं, सौख्यं, रतिः *f.*, रतं, आनन्दः, हर्षः, आह्लादः, आमोदः, प्रमोदः, सन्तोषः, मदः.

To **Enkindle**, *v. a.* उद्दीप् in caus. (-दीपयति -यितुं), उत्तप् in caus. (-तापयति -यितुं), उत्तिज् in caus. (-तेजयति -यितुं), समिन्ध् (c. 7. -इन्द्धे -न्धितुं), प्रज्वल् in caus. (-ज्वलयति -यितुं), संज्वल्, सन्धुक्ष् (c. 10. -धुक्षयति -यितुं).

Enkindled, *p. p.* उद्दीप्तः -प्ता -प्तं, समिद्धः -द्धा -द्धं, उत्तेजितः -ता -तं, उत्तापितः -ता -तं, सन्तप्तः -प्ता -प्तं, ज्वलितः -ता -तं, सन्धुक्षितः -ता -तं.

To **Enlarge**, *v. a.* (Extend, make large) विस्तॄ in caus. (-स्तारयति -यितुं), वितन् (c. 8. -तनोति -नितुं), प्रथ् (c. 10. प्रथयति -यितुं), विशालीकृ, विपुलीकृ, प्रचुरीकृ, प्रसृ in caus. (-सारयति -यितुं).—(Augment) वृध् in caus. (वर्धयति -यितुं), संवृध्; ऋध् in caus. (ऋधयति -यितुं), आप्यै in caus. (-प्याययति -यितुं), समाप्यै, स्फाय् in caus. (स्फावयति -यितुं), स्फीतीकृ, वृद्धिं नी (c. 1. नयति, नेतुं), बृंह् (c. 10. बृंहयति -यितुं), उपबृंह्.

To **Enlarge**, *v. n.* (Grow large) वृध् (c. 1. वर्धते -र्धितुं), अभिवृध्, विवृध्, प्रवृध्; विशालीभू, विपुलीभू, प्रचुरीभू, प्यै (c. 1. प्यायते, प्यातुं), उपचि in pass. (-चीयते), स्फाय् (c. 1. स्फायते -यितुं), आस्फाय्, वितन् in pass. (-तन्यते), विस्तॄ in pass. (-स्तीर्य्यते), वृद्धिम् इ (c. 2. एति -तुं), प्ररुह् (c. 1. -रोहति -रोढुं).—(Describe at large) वर्ण् (c. 10. वर्णयति -यितुं), उपवर्ण्, संवर्ण्, सुविस्तरेण वद् (c. 1. वदति -दितुं), वाग्विस्तारेण or वाक्प्रपञ्चेन व्याख्या (c. 2. -ख्याति -तुं), प्रपञ्च् (c. 10. -पञ्चयति -यितुं), बहुक्तिं कृ.

Enlarged, *p. p.* प्रवृद्धः -द्धा -द्धं, प्रथितः -ता -तं, उपचितः -ता -तं, वर्धितः -ता -तं, प्ररूढः -ढा -ढं, प्लूनः -ना -नं, स्फीतः -ता -तं, स्फातः -ता -तं, आप्यायितः -ता -तं, बृंहितः -ता -तं.

Enlargement, *s.* वृद्धिः *f.*, वर्धनं, प्रवृद्धिः *f.*, विवृद्धिः *f.*, स्फातिः *f.*, स्फीतिः *f.*, विस्तारः, आप्यायनं, बृंहणं, विपुलता, विशालता, स्फारः, प्रपञ्चः, बाहुल्यं.

Enlarger, *s.* वृद्धिकरः, स्फीतिकरः, विस्तारकः, संवर्धकः.

To **Enlighten**, *v. a.* विकाश् in caus. (-काशयति -यितुं), प्रकाश्, द्युत् in caus. (द्योतयति -यितुं), प्रद्युत्, उद्द्युत्, दीप्, in caus. (दीपयति -यितुं), विदीप्, उद्दीप्; विराज् in caus. (-राजयति -यितुं), भास in caus. (भासयति -यितुं), प्रभास्, उद्भास्, भाज् in caus. (भाजयति -यितुं), विमल (nom. विमलयति -यितुं).—(Instruct) उपदिश् (c. 6. -दिशति -देष्टुं).

Enlightened, *p. p.* प्रकाशितः -ता -तं, प्रद्योतितः -ता -तं, उद्द्योतितः -ता -तं, दीपितः -ता -तं, सुप्रभातः -ता -तं.—(Instructed) गृहीतार्थः -र्था -र्थं, प्राप्तबुद्धिः -द्धिः -द्धि, उपदिष्टः -ष्टा -ष्टं.

To **Enlist**, *v. a.* (Enter names on a list) नामावलिपत्रे or नामपरिसंख्यापत्रे नामानि समारुह् in caus. (-रोपयति -यितुं) or आरुह् or अभिलिख् (c. 6. -लिखति -लेखितुं) or लिख्.—(Enlist soldiers) सैन्यमध्ये समारुह् in caus. or सैन्यनामावलिमध्ये आरुह् or अभिलिख्, युद्धकर्म्मणि व्यापृ in caus. (-पारयति -यितुं) or प्रवृत् in caus. (-वर्त्तयति -यितुं), अस्त्राणि ग्रह् in caus. (ग्राहयति -यितुं).—(Gain over to one's own party) स्वपक्षीकृ, आत्मपक्षीकृ, आत्मसात्कृ.

Enlisted, *p. p.* सैन्यनामावलिमध्ये समारोपितः -ता -तं, अभिलिखितः -ता -तं.

Enlisting, *s.* सैन्यनामावलिमध्ये समारोपणं or आरोपणं or नामाभिलेखनं, युद्धे प्रवर्त्तनं.

To **Enliven**, *v. a.* आश्वस् in caus. (-श्वासयति -यितुं), समाश्वस्, विश्वस्, उत्तिज् in caus. (-तेजयति -यितुं), तेजः कृ or दा.—(Make cheerful) हृष् in caus. (हर्षयति -यितुं), ह्लाद् in caus. (ह्लादयति -यितुं), आह्लाद्, उल्लस् in caus. (-लासयति -यितुं).

Enmity, *s.* वैरं, वैरिता, शत्रुता, रिपुता, अरिता, शात्रवं, विपक्षता, द्वेषः -षणं, विद्वेषः, विरोधः, वैरभावः, प्रतिद्वन्द्वं, प्रतिपक्षता, विद्विष्टता, अप्रीतिः *f.*, परता.

To **Ennoble**, *v. a.* (Raise to nobility) कुलीनपदे नियुज् (c. 7. -युंक्ते -योक्तुं) or प्रतिपद् in caus. (-पादयति -यितुं).—(Dignify) शुभ् in caus. (शोभयति -यितुं), सम्मन् in caus. (-मानयति -यितुं), उत्कर्षं कृ, उन्नतिं कृ, यशः कृ.

Ennoblement, *s.* प्रतिपत्तिः *f.*, उत्कर्षः, पदवृद्धिः *f.*, कुलीनता, पदसमुन्नतिः *f.*

Ennui, *s.* ग्लानिः *f.*, क्लान्तिः *f.*, आन्तिः *f.*, विषादः, विषण्णता, विमर्द्दः.

Enormity, *s.* (Atrocious crime) अतिपातकं, अतिपापं, महापातकं, महापापं, अघोरपातकं.—(Atrociousness) अतिदुष्टता, अघोरता, घोरता.

Enormous, *a.* (Beyond measure, exceeding) अतिमात्रः -त्रा -त्रं, अप्रमः -मा -मं, अपरिमितः -ता -तं.—(Very large) अतिमहान् -हती -हत् (त्), सुमहान् &c., अतिबृहन् -हती -हत् (त्).—(In body) अतिकायः -या -यं, बृहत्कायः -या -यं, बृहच्छरीरः -रा -रं, भीमविग्रहः -हा -हं.

Enormously, *adv.* अत्यन्तं, अतिमात्रं, अतिशयेन, सुमहत्, अतिमहत्.

Enough, *adv.* अलं, यथेष्टं, इत्यलं, पर्य्याप्तं, प्रचुरं, प्रचुरतरं, उपयुक्तं, कृतं, यथावत्; 'quite enough,' अलन्तरां; 'enough of this,' अलम् अनेन; 'enough of ceremony,' कृतम् आदरेण; 'to be enough for,' क्लृप् (c 1. कल्पते -ल्पितुं).

Enough, *a.* यथेष्टः -ष्टा -ष्टं, उपयुक्तः -क्ता -क्तं, उचितः -ता -तं, समर्थः -र्था

-र्यं, पर्याप्तः -प्ता -प्तं, प्रचुरः -रा -रं -रतरः -रा -रं, सम्पूर्णः -र्णा -र्णं, बहुलः -ला -लं; 'just food enough to satisfy hunger,' तृप्तिमात्रोचितम् अन्नं; 'food enough for a year,' संवत्सरनिर्वाहसमर्थम् अन्नं.

ENOUGH, *s.* यथेष्टत्वं, पर्याप्तिः *f.*, प्राचुर्य्यं, उपयुक्तत्वं, बाहुल्यं, निर्वाहः; 'having enough for subsistence,' अलञ्जीविकः -का -कं.

ENQUIRE, ENQUIRY. *See* INQUIRE, &c.

To ENRAGE, *v. a.* कुप् in caus. (कोपयति -यितुं), प्रकुप्, संकुप्; क्रुध् in caus. (क्रोधयति -यितुं), रुष् in caus. (रोषयति -यितुं), क्रोधं or कोपं जन् (c. 10. जनयति -यितुं).

To be ENRAGED, *v. n.* क्रुध् (c. 4. क्रुध्यति, क्रोद्धुं), संक्रुध्, अभिसंक्रुध्; कुप् (c. 4. कुप्यति, कोपितुं), प्रकुप्, सङ्कुप्; रुष् (c. 4. रुष्यति, रोषितुं), with dat. c.

ENRAGED, *p. p.* क्रुद्धः -द्धा -द्धं, कुपितः -ता -तं, प्रकोपितः -ता -तं, प्रकुपितः -ता -तं, संक्रुद्धः -द्धा -द्धं, कोपाकुलः -ला -लं, रुषितः -ता -तं, रुष्टः -ष्टा -ष्टं, संरब्धः -ब्धा -ब्धं, उपजातकोपः -पा -पं, जातामर्षः -र्षा -र्षं, आगतमन्युः -न्युः -न्यु, जातरोषः -षा -षं, इद्धमन्युः -न्युः -न्यु, रुषान्वितः -ता -तं.

To ENRAPTURE, ENRAVISH, *v. a.* परमहर्षेण मुह् in caus. (मोहयति -यितुं) or सम्मुह्, अतिशयेन प्रहृष् in caus. (-हर्षयति -यितुं) or परिहृष्; 'to be enraptured,' अत्यन्तं हृष् (c. 4. हृष्यति, हर्षितुं), पुलकितः -ता -तम् अस्, परमहर्षेण मुह् (c. 4. मुह्यति, मोहितुं).

ENRAPTURED, *p. p.* हर्षमोहितः -ता -तं, सम्मोहितः -ता -तं, प्रहर्षितः -ता -तं, सम्प्रहृष्टः -ष्टा -ष्टं, पुलकितः -ता -तं, रोमाञ्चितः -ता -तं, परमानन्दितः -ता -तं, विस्मितः -ता -तं, हर्षोन्मत्तः -त्ता -त्तं.

ENRAVISHMENT, *s.* परमहर्षजो मोहः, सम्मोहः, प्रहर्षः, हर्षावेशः, परमानन्दः, अत्यन्ताह्लादः, विस्मयः, उन्मदः.

To ENRICH, *v. a.* (Make rich) सधनं -नां -नं कृ, आढ्यं -ढ्यां -ढ्यं कृ, समृद्धीकृ, वृध् in caus. (वर्धयति -यितुं), धनं or अर्थं वृध्.—(Make fertile) आप्यै in caus. (-प्याययति -यितुं), स्फाय् in caus. (स्फावयति -यितुं), स्फीतीकृ, सफल (nom. सफलयति -यितुं).—(Adorn) शुभ् in caus. (शोभयति -यितुं), उपशुभ्.

ENRICHED, *p.p.* संवर्धितः -ता -तं, आप्यायितः -ता -तं, स्फीतीकृतः -ता -तं.

ENRICHING, *a.* अर्थकरः -री -रं, अर्थजनकः -का -कं, शोभकृत् *m. f. n.*

To ENROLL, *v. a.* नामावलिपत्रे or नामपरिसंख्यापत्रे नामानि समारुह् in caus. (-रोपयति -यितुं) or आरुह् or अभिलिख् (c. 6. -लिखति -लेखितुं) or लिख्.

ENROLLED, *p. p.* नामावलिपत्रे समारोपितः -ता -तं or अभिलिखितः -ता -तं, अभिलिखितनामा -मा -म (न्), आरोपितनामा -मा -म (न्).

ENROLLER, *s.* नामलेखकः, नामाभिलेखकः, नामसमारोपकः, नामारोपकः.

ENROLMENT, *s.* नामाभिलेखनं, नामसमारोपणं, नामारोपणं, नामलिखनं, नामलेखनं.

ENS, *s.* (Being) भूतं, अधिभूतं, सत्त्वं, भावः, सत्ता, सम्भवः.

ENSAMPLE, *s.* *See* EXAMPLE.

To ENSANGUINE, *v. a.* रक्तेन or शोणितेन लिप् (c. 6. लिम्पति, लेप्तुं), रक्ताक्तं -क्तां -क्तं कृ.

To ENSCONCE, *v. a.* छद् (c. 10. छादयति -यितुं), संछद्, प्रछद्, रक्ष् (c. 1. रक्षति -क्षितुं), गुप् (c. 1. गोपायति, गोप्तुं), अभिगुप्, गुह् (c. 1. गूहति -हितुं); 'ensconce one's self,' आश्रि (c. 1. -श्रयति -यितुं), समाश्रि, संश्रि, आत्मानं गुप् or गुह्.

ENSCONCED, *p.p.* समाश्रितः -ता -तं, गुप्तः -प्ता -प्तं, प्रच्छन्ने स्थापितः -ता -तं.

To ENSEAR, *v. a.* दह् in caus. (दाहयति -यितुं), आरम् ऋ in caus. (अर्पयति -यितुं).

To ENSHIELD, *v. a.* आछद् (-छादयति -यितुं), गुप् (c. 1. गोपायति, गोप्तुं).

To ENSHRINE, *v. a.* पवित्रद्रव्यं सुगहनाधारे or सुगहनभाण्डे or सुप्रतिष्ठितभाजने निविश् in caus. (-वेशयति -यितुं) or रक्ष् (c. 1. रक्षति -क्षितुं).

ENSHRINED, *p. p.* सुप्रतिष्ठितभाण्डे or सुगहनाधारे रक्षितः -ता -तं.

ENSIFORM, *a.* अस्याकारः -रा -रं, खड्गाकृतिः -तिः -ति, खड्गाकारः -रा -रं.

ENSIGN, *s.* (Banner) पताका, ध्वजः, ध्वजपटः, केतनं, केतुः *m.*, वैजयन्ती, केतुवसनः, जयन्तः, कदली -लिका, उच्छूलः.—(Badge) चिह्नं, लिङ्गं, ध्वजः, व्यञ्जनं, लक्षणं.—(Officer). *See* the next word.

ENSIGN-BEARER, *s.* ध्वजी *m.* (न्), ध्वजवान् *m.* (त्), पताकी *m.* (न्), वैजयन्तिकः, ध्वजधारी *m.* (न्), पताकाधारी *m.* (न्), पताकावाहकः.

To ENSLAVE, *v. a.* दासीकृ, वशीकृ, करदीकृ, दास (nom. दासयति -यितुं), दास्ये or दासत्वे नियुज् (c. 7. -युनक्ति -योक्तुं), दास्यं गम् in caus, (गमयति -यितुं).

ENSLAVED, *p. p.* दासीकृतः -ता -तं, दास्यं गमितः -ता -तं, दास्यगतः -ता -तं.

ENSLAVEMENT, *s.* दास्यं, दासत्वं, दासभावः, परप्रेष्यत्वं, बन्धनं.

To ENSNARE, *v. a.* *See* INSNARE.

To ENSUE, *v. n.* अनुवृत् (c. 1. -वर्त्तते -र्त्तितुं), प्रवृत्, अनुसृ (c. 1. -सरति -सर्त्तुं), उत्पद् in pass. (-पद्यते), जन् in pass. (जायते), अन्वि (c. 2. अन्वेति -तुं rt. इ), अनुया (c. 2. -याति -तुं), उपस्था (c. 1. -तिष्ठति -स्थातुं), अनुस्था, पश्चाद् आगम् (c. 1. -गच्छति -गन्तुं), सम्भू, प्रभू, उद्भू.

ENSUED, *p.p.* उत्पन्नः -न्ना -न्नं, प्रवृत्तः -त्ता -त्तं, वृत्तः -त्ता -त्तं, जातः -ता -तं.

ENSUING, *a.* आगामी -मिनी -मि (न्), भावी -विनी -वि (न्), उत्तरकालीनः -ना -नं, अनुवर्त्ती -र्त्तिनी -र्त्ति (न्), अनागतः -ता -तं; 'in the ensuing year,' आगामिवत्सरे.

To ENSURE, *v. a.* *See* INSURE.

ENTABLATURE, ENTABLEMENT, *s.* गृहस्य यो भागः स्तम्भाग्रेऽवलम्बते.

ENTAIL, *s.* (An estate inherited lineally) क्रमागतरिक्थं, क्रमायातरिक्थं.—(Rule of descent) क्रमागमविधिः *m.*, अन्वयागमविधिः *m.*, बद्धत्वं, नियुक्तता.

To ENTAIL, *v. a.* (An estate) रिक्थं or स्थावरधनादि विशेषक्रमागमानुसारेण दायादिभ्यः प्रदा (c. 3. -ददाति -दातुं), रिक्थाधिकारित्वं विशेषक्रमागमानुसारात् स्थिरीकृ or बन्ध् (c. 9. बध्नाति, बन्द्धुं).—(Bring on) आवह् (c. 1. -वहति -वोढुं) or उत्पद् in caus. (-पादयति -यितुं) or जन् in caus. (जनयति -यितुं).

To ENTANGLE, *v. a.* संश्लिष् in caus. (-श्लेषयति -यितुं), आश्लिष्, परिश्लिष्, श्लिष्टीकृ, संलग्नीकृ, ग्रन्थ् (c. 1. ग्रन्थति -न्थितुं), ग्रन्थिलीकृ, सङ्कुलीकृ, आकुलीकृ, आकुञ्च् (c. 1. -कुञ्चति -ञ्चितुं), आवृत् in caus. (-वर्त्तयति -यितुं), सङ्कीर्णीकृ, सग्रन्थ् (c. 9. -ग्रथ्नाति -ग्रन्थुं), सम्मिश्र् (c. 10. -मिश्रयति -यितुं); 'to be entangled, as the hair,' जट् or झट् (c. 1. जटति, झटति -टितुं); 'to disentangle,' उद्ग्रन्थ्, समुद्ग्रन्थ्.

ENTANGLED, *p. p.* (Caught) श्लिष्टः -ष्टा -ष्टं, आश्लिष्टः -ष्टा -ष्टं, संश्लिष्टः -ष्टा -ष्टं, परिश्लिष्टः -ष्टा -ष्टं, परिलग्नः -ग्ना -ग्नं, संलग्नः -ग्ना -ग्नं, सक्तः -क्ता -क्तं, सम्बद्धः -द्धा -द्धं.—(Confused) सङ्कीर्णः -र्णा -र्णं, सङ्कुलः -ला -लं, ग्रन्थिलः -ला -लं.—(Twisted) आकुञ्चितः -ता -तं; 'entangled in the teeth,' दन्तश्लिष्टः -ष्टा -ष्टं, दन्तसक्तः -क्ता -क्तं; 'entangled in the branches,' विटपपरिलग्नः -ग्ना -ग्नं, शाखासु सक्तः -क्ता -क्तं; 'entangled hair,' जटा, जुटकं, जूटः; 'having entangled hair,' जटावान् -वती -वत् (त्), जटिलः -ला -लं; 'entangled in a net,' जालबद्धः -द्धा -द्धं.

ENTANGLEMENT, *s.* आश्लिष्टता, संलग्नता, ग्रन्थिलत्वं, जटिलत्वं, सङ्कुलता, सङ्कीर्णत्वं, सङ्करः, सङ्कर्य्यं, व्यतिकरः, आकुलत्वं, व्याकुलत्वं.

To ENTER, *v. a.* and *n.* विश् (c. 6. विशति, वेष्टुं), प्रविश्, निविश्, आविश्, समाविश्, आगम् (c. 1. -गच्छति -गन्तुं), अभिगम्, अभ्यागम्, अन्तर्गम्, आया (c. 2. -याति -तुं), अभिया, उपस्था (c. 1. -तिष्ठति -स्थातुं), श्रि (c. 1. श्रयति -यितुं), आश्रि, गाह् (c. 1. गाहते -हितुं), विगाह्.—(Set down in writing) अभिलिख् (c. 6. -लिखति -लेखितुं), पुस्तके समारुह् in caus. (-रोपयति -यितुं) or आरुह्.—(Enter upon a business) प्रवृत् (c. 1. -वर्त्तते -र्त्तितुं), प्रक्रम् (c. 1. -क्रमते -मितुं), उपक्रम्.—(Enter into another's views) परमतम् अनुमन् (c. 4. -मन्यते -मन्तुं) or ग्रह् (c. 9. गृह्णाति, ग्रहीतुं).

ENTERED, *p. p.* प्रविष्टः -ष्टा -ष्टं, निविष्टः -ष्टा -ष्टं, आविष्टः -ष्टा -ष्टं.—(In writing) अभिलिखितः -ता -तं, आरोपितः -ता -तं, लेख्यारूढः -ढा -ढं, समारोपितः -ता -तं.

ENTERPRISE, *s.* (Undertaking) प्रवृत्तिः *f.*, उद्योगः, उत्साहः, आरम्भः, उपक्रमः, व्यवसायः, उद्यमः, चेष्टा, चेष्टितं, कर्म्म *n.* (न्), प्रौढिः *f.*, ग्रहः, साध्यं.—(Bold undertaking) महोत्साहः, दुर्गकर्म्म *n.* (न्), अद्भुतकर्म्म *n.*, आश्चर्य्यकर्म्म *n.*, कठिनकर्म्म *n.*

To ENTERPRISE, *v. a.* उपक्रम् (c. 1. -क्रमते -मितुं), आरभ् (c. 1. -रभते -रब्धुं), समारभ्, व्यवसो (c. 4. -स्यति -सातुं), प्रवृत् (c. 1. -वर्त्तते -र्त्तितुं).

ENTERPRISER, *s.* कठिनकर्म्मप्रवृत्तः, दुर्गकर्म्मव्यवसायी *m.* (न्), महोत्साहः.

ENTERPRISING, *a.* व्यवसायी -यिनी -यि (न्), व्यवसायकारी -रिणी -रि (न्), उद्योगी -गिनी -गि (न्), सोद्योगः -गा -गं, कठिनकर्म्मव्यवसायी &c., साहसिकः -की -कं.

To ENTERTAIN, *v. a.* (A guest with hospitality) अतिथिं सत्कृ or सेव् (c. 1. सेवते -वितुं) or पूज् (c. 10. पूजयति -यितुं), आतिथ्यं कृ, सत्कारं कृ; 'with choice food,' स्वाद्वन्नैः or भोजनविशेषैः सन्तुष् in caus. (-तोषयति -यितुं) or तृप् in caus. (तर्पयति -यितुं) or भुज् in caus. (भोजयति -यितुं).—(Amuse) विनुद् (c. 10. -नोदयति -यितुं), विलस् (c. 10. -लासयति -यितुं), रम् (c. 10. रमयति -यितुं).—(Hold in the mind) मनसि or मनसा धृ (c. 1. धरति, धर्त्तुं) or उपलभ् (c. 1. -लभते -लब्धुं) or ग्रह् (c. 9. गृह्णाति, ग्रहीतुं).

ENTERTAINED, *p. p.* (Hospitably) सत्कृतः -ता -तं.—(Amused) विनोदितः -ता -तं.

ENTERTAINER, *s.* सत्कारी *m.* (न्), सत्कृत् *m.*, आमन्त्रयिता *m.* (तृ), निमन्त्रणकृत्.

ENTERTAINING, *a.* विनोदकः -का -कं, विनोदजनकः -का -कं, हास्ययुक्तः -क्ता -क्तं.

ENTERTAINMENT, *s.* (Amusement) विनोदः, विलासः.—(Of guests) सत्कारः, सत्कर्म्म *n.* (न्), अतिथिसत्क्रिया, अतिथिसेवा, अतिथिपूजनं, आतिथ्यं, अतिथिक्रिया, सङ्ग्रहः.—(Feast) उत्सवः, सहभोजनं, सम्भोजनं.

To ENTHRALL. *See* INTHRALL.

To ENTHRONE, *v. a.* राजासने or सिंहासने उपविश् in caus. (-वेशयति -यितुं) or अध्यास् in caus. (-आसयति -यितुं), राज्ये अभिषिच् (c. 6. -षिञ्चति -षेक्तुं).

ENTHRONED, *p. p.* सिंहासनोपविष्टः -ष्टा -ष्टं, सिंहासनाध्यासितः -ता -तं, अध्यासीनः -ना -नं, राज्ये अभिषिक्तः -क्ता -क्तं.

ENTHRONEMENT, *s.* सिंहासनोपवेशनं, सिंहासनाध्यासः, अभिषेकः.

ENTHUSIASM, *s.* (Religious) अतिशयदेवभक्तिजन्यो मादविशेषः or उन्मादः or मदः or उन्मदः, अतिश्रद्धाप्रयुक्ता उन्मत्तता, भक्तिव्यग्रता, श्रद्धाव्यग्रता, भक्तिचण्डता, मिथ्याभक्तिः *f.*—(Warmth, zeal) उत्तापः, उष्णता, उष्मः, चण्डता, उग्रचण्डता, प्रचण्डता, व्यग्रता, उग्रता, औत्सुक्यं, तैक्ष्ण्यं, तीक्ष्णता, अत्यन्तानुरागः, बुद्धिव्यग्रता.

ENTHUSIAST, *s.* (In religion) अतिशयदेवभक्तिवाद उन्मत्तो जनः, देवभक्तिव्यग्रः, मिथ्याभक्तिमान् *m.* (त्).—(In any thing) उग्रप्रबुद्धिः *m.*, व्यग्रबुद्धिः *m.*, प्रमदजनः, तीक्ष्णजनः.

ENTHUSIASTIC, ENTHUSIASTICAL, *a.* व्यग्रः -ग्रा -ग्रं, उत्तप्तः -प्ता -प्तं, चण्डः -ण्डा -ण्डं, उग्रचण्डः -ण्डा -ण्डं, प्रचण्डः -ण्डा -ण्डं, उष्णः -ष्णा -ष्णं, उग्रः -ग्रा -ग्रं, अत्यनुरागी -गिणी -गि (न्), उत्सुकः -का -कं, तीक्ष्णः -क्ष्णा -क्ष्णं, तीक्ष्णकर्म्मा -र्म्मा -र्म्म (न्), उद्युक्तः -क्ता -क्तं, उन्मादवान् -वती -वत् (त्).

ENTHUSIASTICALLY, *adv.* अतिव्यग्रं, उत्तापेन, अत्यनुरागेण, सकुतूहलं.

ENTHYMEME, *s.* न्यूनैकावयवः or न्यूनैकपक्षो न्यायविशेषः, लुप्तन्यायः.

To ENTICE, *v. a.* आकृष् (c. 1. -कर्षति -क्रष्टुं), लुभ् in caus. (लोभयति -यितुं), प्रलुभ्, परिलुभ्, मुह् in caus. (मोहयति -यितुं), भ्रान्तिं जन् (c. 10. जनयति -यितुं), प्रलभ् (c. 1. -लभते -लब्धुं), लल् (c. 10. लालयति -यितुं), दुष्कर्म्मणि प्रवृत् in caus. (-वर्त्तयति -यितुं) or नियुज् (c. 10. -योजयति -यितुं).

ENTICED, *p. p.* आकृष्टः -ष्टा -ष्टं, प्रलोभितः -ता -तं, लालितः -ता -तं.

ENTICEMENT, *s.* आकर्षणं, आकृष्टिः *f.*, प्रलोभनं, विलोभनं, मोहनं, विमोहनं, मोहः, लोभः, लालनं, लोभदर्शनं, वञ्चनं, प्रलम्भः.

ENTICER, *s.* प्रलोभकः, आकर्षकः, विमोही *m.* (न्), लाली *m.* (न्), लोभदर्शकः.

ENTICING, *a.* प्रलोभकः -का -कं, आकर्षकः -का -कं, आकर्षी -र्षिणी -र्षि (न्), विमोहनः -ना -नी -नं, मोही -हिनी -हि (न्), भ्रान्तिजनकः -का -कं.

ENTICINGLY, *adv.* सप्रलोभनं, आकृष्ट्या, प्रलोभनेन, आकर्षकप्रकारेण.

ENTIRE, *a.* (Complete, whole, not defective) कृत्स्नः -त्स्ना -त्स्नं, सकलः -ला -लं, सर्व्वः -र्व्वा -र्व्वं, विश्वः -श्वा -श्वं, सम्पूर्णः -र्णा -र्णं, पूर्णः -र्णा -र्णं, समग्रः -ग्रा -ग्रं, निखिलः -ला -लं, अखिलः -ला -लं, समस्तः -स्ता -स्तं, पर्य्याप्तः -प्ता -प्तं, अशेषः -षा -षं, निःशेषः -षा -षं, निरवशेषः -षा -षं, अन्यूनः -ना -नं, अनूनः -ना -नं, अविकलः -ला -लं, अखण्डः -ण्डा -ण्डं, अभग्नः -ग्ना -ग्नं, अभिन्नः -न्ना -न्नं, अक्षतः -ता -तं, साद्यन्तः -न्ता -न्तं, आत्यन्तिकः -की -कं, न्यक्षः -क्षा -क्षं, सिमः *m.* only. (Of perfect integrity) अभेद्यः -द्या -द्यं, अहार्य्यः -र्य्या -र्य्यं, सरलः -ला -लं.—(An entire horse) सवृषणोऽश्वः, वीजाश्वः.

ENTIRELY, *adv.* अशेषतस्, अशेषेण, निःशेषेण, निरवशेषं, कृत्स्नशस्, कार्त्स्न्येन, साकल्येन, अखिलेन, निखिलेन, सर्व्वतस्, सर्व्वशस्, विश्वतस्, आमूलं, सम्यक्, पर्य्याप्तं, साद्यन्तं, अन्यूनं, अखण्डतस्; 'entirely around,' समन्ततस्, अभितस्.

ENTIRENESS, ENTIRETY, *s.* कार्त्स्न्यं, कार्त्स्नं, साकल्यं आखिल्यं, सामग्र्यं, सम्पूर्णता, समुदायः, समस्तता, समस्तिः *f.*, अभिन्नता, अखण्डत्वं, अन्यूनता, अवैकल्यं.—(Integrity) अभेद्यता, सारल्यं, मायाहीनता.

To ENTITLE, *v. a.* (Give a title or name) नाम कृ or दा, उपाधिं or संज्ञां दा, नामधेयं कृ, अभिधा (c. 3. -दधाति -धातुं), आख्या (c. 2. -ख्याति -तुं), कृत् (c. 10. कीर्त्तयति -यितुं), उदाहृ (c. 1. -हरति -हर्त्तुं).—(Give a claim) अधिकारं or अधिकारित्वं or स्वत्वं दा; 'to be entitled,' अर्ह् (c. 1. अर्हति -ते -र्हितुं), अर्हः -र्हा -र्हं or उपयुक्तः -क्ता -क्तं अस्; 'he is entitled to honour,' मानम् अर्हति; 'he is entitled to receive so much salary,' उपयुक्तोऽयम् एतावद् वर्त्तनं गृह्णाति; 'knowledge entitles to respect,' विद्या मान्यत्वकारणं; 'a good man is entitled to reverence,' साधुजनः पूजनीयः.

ENTITLED, *p. p.* (Named) प्रोक्तः -क्ता -क्तं, अभिहितः -ता -तं, स्मृतः -ता -तं, संज्ञितः -ता -तं, उदाहृतः -ता -तं, आख्यातः -ता -तं. *See* CALLED. (Having a claim) अधिकारी -रिणी -रि (न्), अर्हः -र्हा -र्हं; 'entitled to honour,' पूजार्हः -र्हा -र्हं; 'entitled to a sixth,'

षड्भागभाक् *m, f. n.* (ज्).

ENTITY, *s.* भूतं, अधिभूतं, सत्त्वं, सत्ता, भावः, वस्तु *n.*, वर्त्तनं.

To ENTOMB, *v. a.* श्मशाने or समाधौ स्था in caus. (स्थापयति -यितुं) or निधा (c. 3. -दधाति -धातुं) or निखन् (c. 1. -खनति -नितुं) or समृ in caus. (-अर्पयति -यितुं).

ENTOMBED, *p. p.* निखातः -ता -तं, समाधिनिखातः -ता -तं, भूमिनिखातः -ता -तं.

ENTRAIL, ENTRAILS, *s.* अन्त्रं, अन्त्राणि *n. pl.*, पुरीतत् *m. n.*, नाडिः -डी *f.*, धमनी, कोष्ठः.

ENTRANCE, *s.* (Act of entering) प्रवेशः -शनं, निवेशः -शनं, आवेशः -शनं, समावेशः, वेशः -शनं, वेषणं, वेशिका, प्रतिहारणं.—(Door, gate) द्वारं, द्वारवर्त्म *n.* (न्), मुखं, गृहमुखं, निःसरणं, प्रतीहारः, पथः; 'principal entrance,' सिंहद्वारं; 'private entrance,' प्रच्छन्नद्वारं.

ENTRANCED, *p. p.* (Put in a trance) मूर्च्छितः -ता -तं, मूर्च्छापन्नः -न्ना -न्नं.—(Enraptured) सम्मोहितः -ता -तं, मोहप्राप्तः -प्ता -प्तं, परमहर्षमोहितः -ता -तं.

To ENTRAP, *v. a.* उन्माथे or पाशे पत् in caus. (पातयति -यितुं), जाले पातयित्वा बन्ध् (c. 9. बध्नाति, बन्द्धुं) or धृ (c. 1. धरति, धर्त्तुं) or ग्रह् (c. 9. गृह्णाति, ग्रहीतुं), प्रलुभ् in caus. (-लोभयति -यितुं).

ENTRAPPED, *p. p.* उन्माथे पातितः -ता -तं, पाशबद्धः -द्धा -द्धं, जालबद्धः -द्धा -द्धं.

To ENTREAT, *v. a.* अञ्जलिं कृत्वा प्रार्थ् (c. 10. -अर्थयति -ते -यितुं), सम्प्रार्थ्, अभ्यर्थ्; विनयेन or कृताञ्जलिवत् प्रार्थ् or याच् (c. 1. याचति -चितुं), अभियाच्, प्रयाच्, सम्प्रयाच्; प्रसद् (c. 10. -सादयते -ति -यितुं), विनी (c. 1. -नयति -नेतुं), विनयेन स्वार्थं निविद् (c. 10. -वेदयति -यितुं).

ENTREATED, *p. p.* अञ्जलिकर्म्मपूर्व्वं प्रार्थितः -ता -तं or अभ्यर्थितः -ता -तं, विनयेन याचितः -ता -तं, प्रसादितः -ता -तं, अनुनीतः -ता -तं.

ENTREATY, *s.* प्रार्थनं -ना, अभ्यर्थना, अर्थः, अर्थित्वं -ता, याचना, विनतिः *f.*, मार्गणं, विनयेन निवेदनं.

ENTRY, *s.* (Passage for entrance) द्वारं, द्वारवर्त्म *n.* (न्), गमनागमनपथः.—(Ingress) प्रवेशः -शनं.—(Committing to writing) अभिलिखनं, लेख्यारोपणं, पुस्तकारोपणं, समारोपणं.

To ENUCLEATE, *v. a.* स्पष्टीकृ, व्यक्तीकृ, विशुध् in caus. (-शोधयति -यितुं), परिशुध्.

To ENUMERATE, *v. a.* संख्या (c. 2. -ख्याति -तुं), सम्परिख्या, परिसंख्या, प्रसंख्या; परिगण् (c. 10. -गणयति -यितुं), विगण्, प्रगण्, गण्; अनुपूर्व्वशस् or एकैकशस् or यथाक्रमं or पृथक् पृथक् ख्या, उद्दिश् (c. 6. -दिशति -देष्टुं), समुद्दिश् निर्दिश्.

ENUMERATED, *p. p.* परिसंख्यातः -ता -तं, परिगणितः -ता -तं, उद्दिष्टः -ष्टा -ष्टं, समुद्दिष्टः -ष्टा -ष्टं, एकैकशः or प्रत्येकं कथितः -ता -तं or निर्दिष्टः -ष्टा -ष्टं, अनुक्रान्तः -न्ता -न्तं.

ENUMERATION, *s.* परिसंख्या -ख्यानं, संख्या, गणनं -ना, परिगणना, समुद्देशः, एकैकशो निर्देशः.

To ENUNCIATE, *v. a.* उच्चर् in caus. (-चारयति -यितुं), उदीर् (c. 10. -ईरयति -यितुं), समुदीर्, उदाहृ (c. 1. -हरति -हर्त्तुं), प्रख्या (c. 2. -ख्याति -तुं), कॄत् (c. 10. कीर्त्तयति -यितुं), प्रकॄत्.

ENUNCIATED, *p. p.* उच्चारितः -ता -तं, उदीरितः -ता -तं, उदाहृतः -ता -तं.

ENUNCIATION, *s.* उच्चारणं, उदीरणं, उदाहरणं, व्याहारः -हरणं, समुदाहरणं, ख्यापनं, विज्ञापनं, प्रकीर्त्तनं, प्रकाशनं, घोषणा.

ENUNCIATIVE, *a.* उच्चारकः -का -कं, ख्यापकः -का -कं, आवेदकः -का -कं.

To ENVELOP, *v. a.* आवेष्ट् (c. 1. -वेष्टते -ष्टितुं), परिवेष्ट्, संवेष्ट्, आछद् (c. 10. -छादयति -यितुं), परिछद्, समाछद्, प्रछद्, प्रतिछद्, संछद्; परिवृ (c. 5. -वृणोति -वरितुं -रीतुं), आवृ; पिधा (c. 3. -दधाति -धातुं), कोशेन परिवेष्ट्.

ENVELOPE, *s.* कोशः, कोषः, आवेष्टनं, परिवेष्टनं, वेष्टनं, प्रच्छदपटः, प्रावारः, प्रावरणं, वासनं, पिधानं, पुटः, आच्छादनं, निचोलः, अवगुण्ठनं.

ENVELOPED, *p. p.* वेष्टितः -ता -तं, आवेष्टितः -ता -तं, परिवेष्टितः -ता -तं, कोशस्थः -स्था -स्थं, वासनस्थः -स्था -स्थं, परीतः -ता -तं, अवगुण्ठितः -ता -तं.

To ENVENOM, *v. a.* विषेण लिप् (c. 6. लिम्पति, लेप्तुं) or दिह् (c. 2. देग्धि -ग्धुं) or अञ्ज् (c. 7. अनक्ति, अंक्तुं) or संसृज् (c. 6. -सृजति -स्रष्टुं), सविषं -षां -षं कृ.

ENVENOMED, *p. p.* विषाक्तः -क्ता -क्तं, विषलिप्तः -प्ता -प्तं, विषप्रदिग्धः -ग्धा -ग्धं, सविषः -षा -षं, गरली -लिनी -लि (न्); 'envenomed shaft,' दिग्धः.

ENVIABLE, *a.* ईर्षणीयः -या -यं, ईर्ष्योत्पादकः -का -कं, लोभ्यः -भ्या -भ्यं, स्पृहणीयः -या -यं, प्रार्थनीयः -या -यं, आकांक्षणीयः -या -यं.

ENVIED, *p. p.* ईर्षितः -ता -तं, ईर्ष्यितः -ता -तं, अभिलषितः -ता -तं, स्पर्धितः -ता -तं.

ENVIER, *s.* ईर्ष्यी *m.* (न्), असूयकः, अभ्यसूयकः, परकल्याणासहनः.

ENVIOUS, *a.* ईर्ष्यी -र्ष्यिणी -र्ष्यि (न्), ईर्ष्यालुः -लुः -लु, ईर्षकः -का -कं, सेर्ष्यः -र्ष्या -र्ष्यं, मत्सरः -रा -रं -री -रिणी -रि (न्), समत्सरः -रा -रं, परधनमत्सरः -रा -रं, परधनाभिलाषुकः -का -कं, परगुणमत्सरः -रा -रं, परोत्कर्षासहनः -ना -नं, परप्रशंसासहिष्णुः -ष्णुः -ष्णु, स्पर्धी -र्धिनी -र्धि (न्), साभ्यसूयः -या -यं, कृतेर्ष्यः -र्ष्या -र्ष्यं, सञ्जातेर्ष्यः -र्ष्या -र्ष्यं, कुहनः -ना -नं, बीभत्सुः -त्सुः -त्सु, स्पृहयालुः -लुः -लु, अभिलाषी -षिणी -षि (न्), परशुभामर्षणः -णा -णं.

ENVIOUSLY, *adv.* सेर्ष्यं, सासूयं, समत्सरं, समात्सर्य्यं, साभ्यसूयं.

To ENVIRON, *v. a.* परिवेष्ट् (c. 1. -वेष्टते -ष्टितुं), परिवृ (c. 5. -वृणोति -वरितुं -रीतुं), आवृ, परिष्ठा (c. 1. -तिष्ठति -ष्ठातुं). *See* ENCOMPASS.

ENVIRONED, *p. p.* परिवेष्टितः -ता -तं, परिवृतः -ता -तं, आवृतः -ता -तं, परिगतः -ता -तं, परीतः -ता -तं, वलयितः -ता -तं, व्याप्तः -प्ता -प्तं.

ENVIRONS, *s.* (Of a town) नगरोपान्तं, उपनगरं, उपपुरं, परिसरः.

ENVOY, *s.* दूतः, राजदूतः, सखी *m.* (न्), सन्देशहरः, वार्त्ताहरः, निसृष्टार्थः, कार्य्यङ्करः, राजचारः, राजप्रतिनिधिः *m.*

To ENVY, *v. a.* ईर्ष्य् (c. 1. ईर्ष्यति -र्ष्यितुं), ईर्क्ष्य् (c. 1. ईर्क्ष्यति -क्ष्यितुं), स्पृह् (c. 10. स्पृहयति -यितुं), स्पर्ध् (c. 1. स्पर्धते -र्धितुं), असूय (nom. असूयति -ते -यितुं), अभ्यसूय, परद्रव्यम् अभिलष् (c. 1. -लषति, c. 4. -लष्यति -षितुं), परोत्कर्षं न सह् (c. 1. सहते, सोढुं) or न मृष् (c. 4. मृष्यति, मर्षितुं), मात्सर्य्यं कृ.

ENVY, *s.* ईर्ष्या, असूया, मात्सर्य्यं, मत्सरः -रता, स्पर्धा, स्पर्धिता, अक्षान्तिः *f.*, अमर्षः, परिमर्षः, रागः, द्वेषः, ईर्षा, स्पृहा, परधनाभिलाषः, परोत्कर्षासहिष्णुता, अन्यगुणासहिष्णुता, अन्यशुभद्वेषः, परप्रशंसाया असहिष्णुता.

EOLUS, *s.* (God of the winds) पवनदेवता, वायुदेवता.

EPACT, *s.* कालगणकभाषायां सौरवत्सरावसाने अमावस्याः प्रभृति तिथिसंख्यासूचकः शब्दः or शब्दो येन चान्द्रवत्सरात् सौरवत्सराधिक्यं सूच्यते.

EPAULET, *s.* स्कन्धाभरणं, सैनिकजनैः स्कन्धदेशे भृतः पदसूचको-लङ्कारः, अंशालङ्कारः, अंशाभरणं.

EPHEMERAL, *a.* ऐकाहिकः -की -कं, क्षणविध्वंसी -सिनी -सि (न्), उत्पन्नविनाशी -शिनी -शि (न्), क्षणभङ्गुरः -रा -रं, एकाहमात्रस्थायी -यिनी -यि (न्).

EPHEMERIS, *s.* आह्निकव्यवहारपुस्तकं, दैवसिकवृत्तान्तपुस्तकं.—(In astronomy) पुस्तकं यस्मिन् नक्षत्राणां गतिभावादि प्रतिदिनम् आरोप्यते.

EPIC, *a.* ऐतिहासिकः -की -कं, वीरचरित्रकथकः -का -कं, काथिकः -की -कं, शूरवृत्तान्तविषयः -या -यं, महाकाव्यसम्बन्धी -न्धिनी -न्धि (न्).

EPIC, *s.* (Poem) महाकाव्यं, इतिहासः, वीरचरित्रविषयं काव्यं.

EPICENE, *a.* सामान्यलिङ्गः -ङ्गा -ङ्गं, साधारणलिङ्गः -ङ्गा -ङ्गं.

EPICURE, *a.* मिष्टान्नव्यञ्जनादिषु प्रसक्तः, सर्व्वान्नरसज्ञः, स्वाद्वन्नाभिलाषी *m.* (न्), उदरपरायणः, कुक्षिम्भरिः *m.*, लोलुपः, अतिलोभी *m.* (न्), रसिकः, वैषयिकः, विषयासक्तः, विषयसेवी *m.* (न्), पात्रेसमितः.

EPICUREAN, *a.* विषयी -यिणी -यि (न्), शारीरिकसुखसेवी -विनी -वि (न्), वैषयिकः -की -कं, भोगपरायणः -णा -णं.

EPICURISM, *s.* विषयोपसेवा, विषयासक्तिः *f.*, शारीरिकसुखानुरागः.

EPICYCLE, *s.* (In astronomy) प्राक् चक्रं, परिधिः *m.*

EPIDEMIC, EPIDEMICAL, *a.* देशसाधारणः -णा -णी -णं, सर्व्वगः -गा -गं, बहुजनसामान्यः -न्या -न्यं; 'disease,' मारी, मारिः -रिः *f.*, महामारी, मरकः, मारकः, आतङ्कनं, सन्निपातकः, उपसर्गः.

EPIDERMIS, *s.* बाह्यत्वक् *f.* (च्), बहिस्त्वक्, बाह्यचर्म्म *n.* (न्), अवभासिनी.

EPIGLOTTIS, *s.* उपजिह्वा, अलिजिह्वा, प्रतिजिह्वा, घण्टिका, शुण्डिका.

EPIGRAM, *s.* अबहुश्लोकपरिमाणं रसिककाव्यं, सरसं लघुकाव्यं.

EPIGRAMMATICAL, *a.* पूर्व्वोक्तलघुकवितायोग्यः -ग्या -ग्यं, रसिककवितासम्बन्धी -न्धिनी -न्धि (न्).—(Pointed) रसिकः -का -कं, रसवान् -वती -वत् (त्), सरसः -सा -सं.

EPIGRAMMATIST, *s.* पूर्व्वोक्तरसिककविताकर्त्ता *m.* (र्तृ), लघुकाव्यरचकः.

EPILEPSY, *s.* अपस्मारः, ग्रहामयः, भामरं, भूतविक्रिया, प्रतानः, मूर्च्छावायुः *m.*

EPILEPTIC, *a.* अपस्मारी -रिणी -रि (न्), भामरी -रिणी -रि (न्), वातग्रस्तः -स्ता -स्तं, वायुग्रस्तः -स्ता -स्तं, ग्रहामयपीडितः -ता -तं, आकृष्टः -ष्टा -ष्टं.

EPILOGUE, *s.* अन्तवाक्यं, शेषवाक्यं, अन्त्यवचनं, समापकवाक्यं, समापनवचनं.

EPINICION, *s.* जयगीतं, जयशब्दः.

EPIPHANY, *s.* ख्रीष्टप्रकाशनं, ख्रीष्टप्रकाशनमुद्दिश्य ख्रीष्टजन्मपर्व्वणः परं द्वादशदिने सेवितो महोत्सवः, ख्रीष्टप्रकाशनपर्व्व *n.* (न्).

EPISCOPACY, *s.* धर्म्माध्यक्षता -त्वं, धर्म्माध्यक्षाधिपत्यं, धर्म्माध्यक्षाधिकारः, धर्म्माध्यक्षकर्तृका ख्रीष्टीयसमाजनीतिः *f.*

EPISCOPAL, EPISCOPALIAN, *a.* धर्म्माध्यक्षसम्बन्धी -न्धिनी -न्धि (न्), धर्म्माध्यक्षशासितः -ता -तं, धर्म्माध्यक्षपालितः -ता -तं.

EPISCOPATE, *s.* धर्म्माध्यक्षाधिकारः, धर्म्माध्यक्षाधिपत्यं, धर्म्माध्यक्षपदं.

EPISODE, *s.* उपाख्यानं, उपकथा, प्रसङ्गवाक्यं, प्रासङ्गिकवाक्यं, पताका, मूलविषयबहिर्गता कथा.

EPISODIC, EPISODICAL, *a.* प्रासङ्गिकः -की -कं, मूलविषयानन्वितः -ता -तं, प्रस्तुतविषयबहिर्गतः -ता -तं, अनन्वितः -ता -तं, अप्रस्तुतः -ता -तं.

EPISPASTIC, *a.* त्वक्स्फोटोत्पादकः -का -कं, स्फोटकारी -रिणी -रि (न्).

EPISTLE, *s.* पत्रं, लेखः, लेख्यं, पत्रिका, पत्री, संवादपत्रं, सन्देशपत्रं, लिपिः *f.*

EPISTOLARY, *a.* पत्री -त्रिणी -त्रि (न्), पत्रीयः -या -यं, लेख्यकः -का -कं.

EPITAPH, *s.* चैत्यस्य उपरिलिखितं मृतजनमुद्दिश्य स्तुतिवाक्यं, चैत्योपरि लिखिता तत्रैव निखातजनमुद्दिश्य गुणस्तुतिः, चैत्यलिपिः *f.*, चैत्योपरिस्था लिपिः.

EPITHALAMIUM, *s.* वैवाहिकगीतं, औद्वाहिकगीतं, विवाहसमये माङ्गलिकगीतं.

EPITHEM, *s.* उत्कारिका, उपदेहः, उपनाहः, प्रलेपः, लेपः.

EPITHET, *s.* विशेषणं -षकः -कं, संज्ञाविषयः, सम्बुद्धिः *f.*, उपाधिः *m.*, गुणागुणवाचकः शब्दः.

EPITOME, *s.* संक्षेपः -पणं, सङ्ग्रहः, सारसङ्ग्रहः, सारः, संहिता, प्रत्याहारः, समाहारः, समाहृतिः *f.*, समसनं.

To EPITOMIZE, *v. a.* संक्षिप् (c. 6. -क्षिपति -क्षेप्तुं), संहृ (c. 1. -हरति -हर्त्तुं), उपसंहृ.

EPITOMIZED, *p. p.* संक्षिप्तः -प्ता -प्तं, सांक्षेपिकः -की -कं, समस्तः -स्ता -स्तं, सामासिकः -की -कं, संहृतः -ता -तं, उपसंहृतः -ता -तं, चुम्बकः -का -कं.

EPITOMIZER, EPITOMIST, *s.* संक्षेप्ता *m.* (प्तृ), सङ्ग्रहकर्त्ता *m.* (र्तृ), सारलेखकः.

EPOCH, EPOCHA, *s.* (A fixed era from which computation of years begin) शकः, शाकः, शकः, संवत् indec. The era of Śáliváhana is called शाकः, that of Vikramáditya, संवत्.—(Any period or fixed time) कालः, कालावधिः *m.*, अवधिः *m.*, निर्णीतकालः.

EPODE, *s.* उपगीतं, उपगानं, अधिगीतं, अपरगीतं, गीतानुबन्धः.

EPOPEE, *s.* महाकाव्यं, वीरचरित्रविषयं काव्यं.

EPULATION, *s.* उत्सवकरणं, उत्सवः, मिष्टान्नभोजनं.

EQUABLE, *a.* समानः -ना -नं, निर्विकारः -रा -रं.—(In motion) समानगतिः -तिः -ति.—(In temper) समभावः -वी -वं, समवृत्तिः -त्तिः -त्ति, समचित्तः -त्ता -त्तं.

EQUAL, *a.* समः -मा -मं, समानः -ना -नं, तुल्यः -ल्या -ल्यं, समीयः -या -यं, सदृशः -शी -शं, ईदृशः -शी -शं.—(Not inferior) अनवरः -रा -रं, अनवमः -मा -मं.—(Even, uniform) समानः -ना -नं, समस्थः -स्था -स्थं, निर्विकारः -रा -रं, अव्रसः -सा -सं; 'of equal extent or size,' सम्मितः -ता -तं, सममात्रः -त्रा -त्रं, तुल्यपरिमाणः -णा -णं; 'equal to all,' सर्व्वसमः -मा -मं; 'of equal strength,' तुल्यबलः -ला -लं; 'equal in glory,' समानतेजाः -जाः -जः (स्); 'this is equal to a sixteenth part of that,' एतत् तस्य षोडशांशेन समं.

EQUAL, *s.* (Of the same age) समानवयस्कः, समवयस्कः, सवयाः *m.* (स्), तुल्यवयाः *m.* (स्), समानजन्मा *m.* (न्), वयस्यः.—(Of the same rank) समानपदस्थः, तुल्यपदस्थः.

To EQUAL, *v. a.* समीकृ, समानीकृ, तुल्यीकृ, समान (nom. समानयति -यितुं), समानं -नां -नं कृ, तुल्यं -ल्यां -ल्यं कृ.

EQUALITY, *s.* समता, साम्यं, समानता, तुल्यता -त्वं, सामान्यं, साम्यता, प्रतियोगिता.—(In rank) समानपदं, तुल्यपदं.—(In tribe) सवर्णता.

EQUALIZATION, *s.* समीकरणं, समानीकरणं, तुल्यत्वं, समानता.

To EQUALIZE, *v. a.* समीकृ, समानीकृ, तुल् (c. 10. तुलयति -यितुं). *See To* EQUAL.

EQUALIZED, *p. p.* समीकृतः -ता -तं, समानीकृतः -ता -तं, तुलितः -ता -तं.

EQUALLY, *adv.* समं, समानं, समानतस्, तुल्यवत्, साम्यतस्, सामान्येन.

EQUANIMITY, *s.* समचित्तत्वं, समबुद्धिता, समभावः, समानवृत्तिः *f.*, सर्व्वसमता, सत्त्वसम्पन्नता, सत्त्वं, सम्पदापदोर् हर्षविषादराहित्यं.

EQUANIMOUS, *a.* समचित्तः -त्ता -त्तं, समबुद्धिः -द्धिः -द्धि, समभावः -वी -वं, समवृत्तिः -त्तिः -त्ति, सत्त्वसम्पन्नः -न्ना -न्नं, सत्यसम्पन्नः -न्ना -न्नं, सम्पदापदोर् हर्षविषादरहितः -ता -तं, निर्विकारः -रा -रं.

EQUATION, *s.* (In algebra) समीक्रिया, समीकरणं, साम्यं, फलं; 'of unknown quantity,' अव्यक्तसाम्यं; 'unlimited equation,' एकवर्णसमीकरणं.

EQUATOR, *s.* निरक्षः, भूचक्रं, भूपरिधिः *m.*, भूगोलरेखा; 'equatorial region,' निरक्षदेशः; 'celestial equator,' नाडिमण्डलं, नाडीमण्डलं. *See* EQUINOCTIAL LINE.

EQUATORIAL, *a.* निरक्षसम्बन्धी -न्धिनी -न्धि (न्), भूचक्रसम्बन्धी, &c.

EQUERY, EQUERRY, *s.* राजाश्वपालः, राजाश्वशालारक्षणे नियुक्तो जनः.—(Stable for horses) अश्वशाला, वाजिशाला.

EQUESTRIAN, *a.* आश्वः -श्वी -श्वं, आश्विकः -की -कं, अश्वीयः -या -यं, तुरगी -गिणी -गि (न्); 'person on horseback,' अश्वारूढः, अश्वारोही *m.* (न्).

EQUIANGULAR, *a.* समकोणः -णा -णं, समानास्रः -स्रा -स्रं, तुल्यकोणः -णा -णं.

EQUIDISTANT, *a.* समान्तरः -रा -रं, तुल्यान्तरः -रा -रं, समान्तरस्थः -स्था -स्थं.

EQUILATERAL, *a.* समभुजः -जा -जं, समानबाहुः -हुः -हु, समपार्श्वः -र्श्वा -र्श्वं ; 'an equilateral triangle,' समत्रिभुजः.

EQUILIBRIUM, *s.* तुल्यता, भारतुल्यता, समतोलत्वं, तुल्यबलत्वं, परिमाणतुल्यता, समता, साम्यं.

EQUINOCTIAL, *a.* विषुवीयः -या -यं, विषुवसम्बन्धी -न्धिनी -न्धि (न्); 'equinoctial line,' विषुवच्चक्रं, विषुवमण्डलं, विषुवद्वृत्तं, विषुवरेखा, भूचक्रं, भूपरिधिः *m.*, नाडीमण्डलं; 'equinoctial point,' अयनं.

EQUINOX, *s.* विषुवं, विषुवत् *n.*, विष्वक् *n.*, विषुपं; 'the vernal equinox,' महाविषुवं, हरिपदं; 'autumnal,' विषुपदं; 'day of the equinox,' विषुवदिनं.

EQUINUMERANT, *a.* समसंख्यः -ख्या -ख्यं, समानसंख्यः -ख्या -ख्यं.

To EQUIP, *v. a.* सज्जीकृ, सज्ज् (c. 1. सज्जति -ज्जितुं), ससज्जं -ज्जां -ज्जं कृ, सर्व्वोपकरणैः or सोपकारद्रव्यैः समायुज् in caus. (-योजयति -यितुं) or युज्, सर्व्वसोपकारद्रव्याणि उपक्लृप् (c. 10. -कल्पयति -यितुं) or सम्प्रक्लृप् or उपस्था in caus. (-स्थापयति -यितुं), or उपपद् in caus. (-पादयति -यितुं) or सम्भृ (c. 1. -भरति -भर्त्तुं) or उपस्कृ or पुरस्कृ or सिद्धीकृ or प्रस्तुतीकृ, द्रव्यसम्भारं कृ, उपकरणसम्भारं कृ.—(With arms) अस्त्रैः or शस्त्रैः सज्जीकृ, सन्नह् (c. 4. -नह्यति -नद्धुं), संवर्म्म् (nom. -वर्म्मयति -यितुं).—(Fit out a ship) नावं समुद्रयानार्थं or युद्धार्थं सज्जीकृ.—(With clothes) वस्त्रैर् वेष्ट् (c. 1. वेष्टते -ष्टितुं) or भूष् (c. 10. भूषयति -यितुं) or अलङ्कृ.

EQUIPAGE, *s.* (Implements, materials) उपकरणं, साधनं, सामग्र्यं -ग्री, सम्भारः, उपस्करः.—(Paraphernalia) सज्जा, परिच्छदः, सन्नाहः, अलङ्क्रिया.—(Of war) युद्धसज्जा, युद्धोपकरणं, वाहिनी.—(Retinue) परिवर्हः, वर्हः, तन्त्रं.—(Vehicle) वाहनं, विमानं.

EQUIPMENT, *s.* (Act of equipping) सज्जीकरणं, सज्जनं -ना, सज्जकर्म्म *n.* (न्), सज्जा, साधनं, सम्भारः, सम्भृतिः *f.*, आयोजनं, उपाकर्म्म *n.* (न्), पुरस्कारः, पुरस्करणं. *See* EQUIPAGE.

EQUIPOISE, *s.* तुल्यता, भारतुल्यता, तुल्यभारत्वं, समतोलत्वं, तुल्यबलत्वं, समता, साम्यं, तुल्यपरिमाणं, परिमाणतुल्यता.

To EQUIPOISE, *v. a.* समीकृ, तुल्यीकृ, तुल्यबलीकृ, समतोलीकृ.

EQUIPOISED, *p. p.* तुलितः -ता -तं, समीकृतः -ता -तं, समतोलः -ला -लं.

EQUIPOLLENCE, *s.* तुल्यबलत्वं, बलसमता, तुल्यशक्तित्वं, शक्तिसाम्यं.

EQUIPOLLENT, *a.* तुल्यबलः -ला -लं, तुल्यशक्तिः -क्तिः -क्ति, तुल्यौजाः -जाः -जः (स्).

EQUIPONDERANCE, *s.* तुल्यता, भारतुल्यता, समतोलत्वं, तुल्यबलत्वं.

EQUIPONDERANT, *a.* समतोलः -ला -लं, तुल्यबलः -ला -लं, तुल्यपरिमाणः -णा -णं.

EQUIPPED, *p. p.* सज्जीकृतः -ता -तं, सज्जितः -ता -तं, सज्जः -ज्जा -ज्जं, सोपकारद्रव्ययुक्तः -क्ता -क्तं, संयुक्तः -क्ता -क्तं, समायुक्तः -क्ता -क्तं, समन्वितः -ता -तं, सोपकारः -री -रं, सन्नद्धः -द्धा -द्धं, पिनद्धः -द्धा -द्धं, संहितः -ता -तं.

EQUITABLE, *a.* समदर्शी -र्शिनी -र्शि (न्), धर्म्मकारी -रिणी -रि (न्), न्यायकारी &c., न्यायी -यिनी -यि (न्), धार्म्मिकः -की -कं, न्यायवर्त्ती -र्त्तिनी -र्त्ति (न्), यथान्यायः -या -यं, अपक्षपाती -तिनी -ति (न्), विपक्षपातः -ता -तं, पक्षपातरहितः -ता -तं, सर्व्वसमः -मा -मं, उभयसाधारणः -णा -णी -णं, निरपेक्षी -क्षिणी -क्षि (न्).

EQUITABLENESS, *s.* साम्यं, समता, सर्व्वसमता, अपक्षपातः, न्यायता.

EQUITABLY, *adv.* न्यायतस्, यथान्यायं, न्यायवत्, पक्षपातं विना, साम्येन.

EQUITY, *s.* न्यायः, धर्म्मः, न्यायता, अपक्षपातः, साम्यं, समता, उभयसामान्यं, सर्व्वसमता, युक्तिः *f.*, याथार्थ्यं, विचारः.—(Qualification of the severity of law) दण्डनैष्ठुर्य्यशमनं, धर्म्मनैष्ठुर्य्यशमनं; 'court of equity,' दण्डनैष्ठुर्य्यशमका महाविचारणसभा.

EQUIVALENT, *a.* सममूल्यः -ल्या -ल्यं, तुल्यमूल्यः -ल्या -ल्यं, समानमूल्यः -ल्या -ल्यं, तुल्यबलः -ला -लं, तुल्यार्थः -र्था -र्थं, समार्थः -र्था -र्थं, समानबलः -ला -लं, समशक्तिः -क्तिः -क्ति, तुल्यशक्तिः -क्तिः -क्ति, तुल्यः -ल्या -ल्यं, समः -मा -मं, समानः -ना -नं.

EQUIVALENT, *s.* समानमूल्यकं द्रव्यं, तुल्यद्रव्यं, तुल्यवस्तु *n.*, प्रतिक्रिया, प्रतीकारः, प्रतिकृतिः *f.*, प्रत्युपकारः, निस्तारः, प्रतिफलं, परिवर्त्तः, तुल्यत्वं, साम्यं, समानत्वं.

EQUIVOCAL, *a.* सन्दिग्धार्थः -र्था -र्थं, अस्पष्टार्थः -र्था -र्थं, द्व्यर्थः -र्था -र्थं, वक्रः -क्रा -क्रं, वक्रार्थः -र्था -र्थं, अस्पष्टः -ष्टा -ष्टं, विकल्पार्थकः -का -कं.

EQUIVOCALLY, *adv.* सन्दिग्धार्थतस्, द्व्यर्थतस्, वक्रोक्त्या, अस्पष्टं, अव्यक्तं.

EQUIVOCALNESS, *s.* सन्दिग्धार्थः, द्व्यर्थः, अर्थसन्देहः, अर्थसन्दिग्धता, अर्थवक्रिमा *m.* (न्), अस्पष्टता, सन्दिग्धता, वक्रता.

To EQUIVOCATE, *v. n.* वक्रं or सवक्रार्थं or अर्थवक्रतया or द्व्यर्थतो वद् (c. 1. वदति -दितुं), वक्रोक्तिं कृ, अस्पष्टं वद्.

EQUIVOCATING, *a.* वक्रोक्तिमान् -मती -मत् (त्), वाक्छलान्वितः -ता -तं.

EQUIVOCATION, *s.* वक्रोक्तिः *f.*, वक्रवाक्यं, वक्रभणितं, वक्रवचनं, वाक्यवक्रता, वाक्छलं, वक्रता, वक्रिमा *m.* (न्), अर्थवैकल्यं, अपदेशः, व्यपदेशः.

EQUIVOCATOR, *s.* द्व्यर्थवक्ता *m.* (क्तृ), द्व्यर्थवादी *m.* (न्), वक्रवाक्यवादी *m.*

EQUIVOQUE, *s.* वक्रोक्तिः *f.*, कूटोक्तिः *f.*, कैतववादः, लालिका, अर्थापत्तिः *f.*

ERA, *s.* कालः, युगः, शाकः, शकः, संवत् indec. The era of Śálivàhana is called शाकः, that of Vikramáditya, संवत्.

To ERADIATE, *v. a.* स्फुर् (c. 6. स्फुरति -रितुं), रश्मीन् or किरणान् पत् in caus. (पातयति -यितुं) or मुच् (c. 6. मुञ्चति, मोक्तुं) or निक्षिप् (c. 6. -क्षिपति -क्षेप्तुं).

ERADICABLE, *a.* उन्मूल्यः -ल्या -ल्यं, उन्मूलनीयः -या -यं, उत्पाटनीयः -या -यं, मूल्यः -ल्या -ल्यं.

To ERADICATE, *v. a.* उन्मूल् (c. 10. -मूलयति -यितुं), समुन्मूल्, उत्पट् (c. 10. -पाटयति -यितुं), मूलात् or आमूलं or समूलम् उद्धृ (c. 1. -हरति -हर्त्तुं) or समुद्धृ or उच्छिद् (c. 7. -छिनत्ति -छेत्तुं) or उत्खन् (c. 1. -खनति -नितुं), व्यपरुह् in caus. (-रोपयति -यितुं), उद्बृह् (c. 6. -बृहति -बर्हितुं).

ERADICATED, *p. p.* उन्मूलितः -ता -तं, उत्पाटितः -ता -तं, उच्छिन्नः -न्ना -न्नं, उद्धृतः -ता -तं, उत्खातः -ता -तं, व्यपरोपितः -ता -तं, आवर्हितः -ता -तं, उद्बर्हितः -ता -तं.

ERADICATION, *s.* उत्पाटनं, उच्छेदः, उद्धरणं, उन्मूलनं, समूलोत्पाटनं, समूलोद्धरणं, मूलादुद्धरणं, व्यपरोपणं, समूलघातं, निष्कोषणं, विनाशः.

ERADICATIVE, *a.* उच्छेदी -दिनी -दि (न्), उत्पाटनकारी -रिणी -रि (न्).

ERADICATOR, *s.* उद्धर्त्ता *m.* (र्तृ), उन्मूलयिता *m.* (तृ), उच्छेदी *m.* (न्).

To ERASE, *v. a.* (Rub out) व्यामृज् (c. 2. -मार्ष्टि -र्ष्टुं), अपमृज्, उन्मृज्, व्यामृश् (c. 6. -मृशति -म्रष्टुं), लुप् (c. 6. लुम्पति, लोप्तुं), विलुप् (c. 10. -लोपयति -यितुं), लोपं कृ.—(Destroy) उच्छिद् (c. 7. -छिनत्ति -छेत्तुं), उद्धृ (c. 1. -हरति -हर्त्तुं), विनश् in caus. (-नाशयति -यितुं).

ERASED, *p. p.* व्यामृष्टः -ष्टा -ष्टं, लुप्तः -प्ता -प्तं, उच्छिन्नः -न्ना -न्नं.

ERASTIAN, *s.* ख्रीष्टीयसमाजो राज्यरीतिसम्बद्धो भवति or राज्यरीत्यधीनो भवति इति मन्यते यो जनः.

ERASURE, *s.* व्यामर्षः, लोपः, विलोपनं, उच्छेदः, विनाशः.

ERE, *adv.* or *prep.* प्राक्, पूर्व्वं, पुरा, अग्रे; 'ere he could come,' तस्य आगमनात् पूर्व्वं or पुरा; 'ere the time appointed,' प्राग् विहितकालात्; 'ere twelve years are over,' प्राग् द्वादशसमाः; or, expressed by loc. absolute; as, 'ere my child die,' मम पुत्रे न मृते सति.

ERELONG, *adv.* अचिरेण, अचिरात्, न चिरेण, न चिरात्, पुरा.

ERENOW, *adv.* अधुना पूर्व्वं, अद्य पूर्व्वं, प्राग् इहसमयात्.

To ERECT, *v. a.* (Set up) स्था in caus. (स्थापयति -यितुं), प्रतिष्ठा, अवस्था, संस्था, अधिष्ठा, अधिरुह् in caus. -रोपयति -यितुं), निरुह्, रुह्.—(Raise, elevate) उत्था (rt. स्था with उत्), उन्नम् in caus. (-नमयति -यितुं), उच्छ्रि (c. 1. -च्छ्रयति -यितुं, rt. श्रि), समुच्छ्रि, प्रोच्छ्रि; उत्क्षिप् (c. 6. -क्षिपति -क्षेप्तुं), उद्यम् (c. 1. -यच्छति -यन्तुं), उद्धृ (c. 1. -हरति -हर्त्तुं), उन्नी (c. 1. -नयति -नेतुं), उद्बृह् (c. 6. -बृहति -बर्हितुं), उन्नीकृ, ऊर्द्ध्वीकृ, उच्चैः कृ; 'to erect the hair,' पुलक (nom. पुलकयति -यितुं).

ERECT, *a.* उन्नतः -ता -तं, समुन्नतः -ता -तं, अनतः -ता -तं, ऋजुः -जुः -जु, उच्छ्रितः -ता -तं, उत्तानः -ना -नं, अजिह्मः -ह्मा -ह्मं, उच्चः -च्चा -च्चं, उच्छ्रितः -ता -तं.—(Having the head or countenance erect) उन्नतशिराः -राः -रः (स्), प्रकटशीर्षः -र्षा -र्षं, ऊर्द्ध्वमुखः -खी -खं, उत्फलमलः -ला -लं; 'having the hair erect,' पुलकितः -ता -तं, रोमाञ्चितः -ता -तं.

ERECTED, *p. p.* प्रतिष्ठापितः -ता -तं, प्रतिष्ठितः -ता -तं, अधिष्ठितः -ता -तं, उत्थापितः -ता -तं, उच्छ्रितः -ता -तं, उन्नमितः -ता -तं, उन्नतः -ता -तं, उद्धृतः -ता -तं, उद्यतः -ता -तं, उद्बर्हितः -ता -तं, उन्नीकृतः -ता -तं, उद्गूर्णः -र्णा -र्णं, उद्वृतः -त्ता -त्तं, उद्वर्त्तितः -ता -तं.

ERECTION, *s.* (Establishing) प्रतिष्ठापनं, संस्थापनं, अवस्थापनं.—(Raising) उत्थापनं, उच्छ्रयः, उच्छ्रायः, उच्छ्रितिः *f.*, समुच्छ्रयः, उन्नतिः *f.*, उन्नमनं, उद्यमः -यनं, उद्यामः, उन्नायः, उत्क्षेपः, उद्ग्रमः, उद्धर्षणं; 'of the hair of the body,' पुलकः, पुलकोद्गमः, उद्धर्षणं, रोमहर्षणं, रोमाञ्चः -ञ्चनं, रोमोद्गमः, रोमोद्भेदः, उद्धूषणं.

ERECTNESS, *s.* अनतता, उन्नतता, उत्तानत्वं, उच्चता, ऋजुता.

EREMITE, *s.* अरण्यवासी *m.* (न्), वनवासी *m.*, वनस्थायी *m.* (न्), वानप्रस्थः

ERMINE, *s.* नकुलजातीयो हिमवद्देशजः शुक्ललोमा क्षुद्रजन्तुः.

EROTIC, *a.* कामी -मिनी -मि (न्), शृङ्गारी -रिणी -रि (न्), कामविषयः -या -यं.

To ERR, *v. n.* भ्रम् (c. 4. भ्राम्यति, भ्रमितुं), विभ्रम्, परिभ्रम्, भ्रान्तिं कृ, अपराध् (c. 4. -राध्यति, c. 5. -राध्नोति -राद्धुं), अपराधं कृ, दोषं कृ, प्रमद् (c. 4. -माद्यति -मदितुं), सत्पथात् or यथोचिताद् भ्रंश् (c. 4. भ्रश्यति, भ्रंशितुं) or च्यु (c. 1. च्यवते, च्योतुं) or विच्यु or विचल् (c. 1. -चलति -लितुं), उत्क्रम् (c. 1. -क्रामति -क्रमितुं), व्युत्क्रम्, व्यभिचर् (c. 1. -चरति -रितुं); उत्पथेन or उन्मार्गेण गम् (c. 1. गच्छति, गन्तुं), मुह् (c. 4. मुह्यति, मोहितुं), प्रमादं कृ.

ERRAND, *s.* सन्देशः, सन्दिष्टं, शासनं, शास्तिः *f.*, आदेशः, आज्ञा, निर्देशः, समाचारः, वाचिकं, दूत्यं, दौत्यं, कार्य्यं, कृत्यं, कर्त्तव्यं; 'sending on an errand,' प्रतिशासनं.

ERRANT, *a.* भ्रमी -मिणी -मि (न्), परिभ्रमी &c., पर्य्यटनकारी -रिणी -रि (न्), इतस्ततो भ्रमणकारी &c., अवनिचरः -रा -रं.

ERRANTRY, *s.* भ्रमणं, परिभ्रमणं, अटनं, पर्य्यटनं, चक्राटनं.

ERRATA-LIST, *s.* शुद्धिपत्रं, शोधनपत्रं, अशुद्धशोधनपत्रं.

ERRATIC, *a.* परिभ्रमी -मिणी -मि (न्), भ्रमणशीलः -ला -लं, चरः -रा -रं, चलनः -ना -नं, जङ्गमः -मा -मं, अस्थिरः -रा -रं, चञ्चलः -ला -लं. *See* ERRANT.

ERRATUM, *s.* अशुद्धं, अशुद्धिः *f.*, अशोधनं.

ERRHINE, *a.* नस्यः -स्या -स्यं, क्षुत्करः -री -रं, छिक्कः -का -कं.

ERRONEOUS, *a.* भ्रान्तिमान् -मती -मत् (त्), अशुद्धः -द्धा -द्धं, अयथार्थः -र्था -र्थं, अतथ्यः -थ्या -थ्यं, वितथः -था -थं, अनृतः -ता -तं, असत्यः -त्या -त्यं, भ्रमजनकः -का -कं, भ्रमात्मकः -का -कं, भ्रमोत्पादकः -का -कं, प्रमादी -दिनी -दि (न्), प्रमादवान् -वती -वत् (त्). Often expressed by मिथ्या or मृषा prefixed; as, 'an erroneous opinion,' मिथ्यामतिः *f.*; 'an erroneous statement,' मिथ्यावादः, मृषावादः; 'erroneous conclusion,' अपसिद्धान्तः.

ERRONEOUSLY, *adv.* मिथ्या, मृषा, अन्यथा, अयथार्थं, अयथावत्, वृथा, अतथ्यं, वितथं, अनृतं, असत्यं, प्रमादेन, सप्रमादं.

ERRONEOUSNESS, *s.* अयाथार्थ्यं, असत्यता, अयथार्थता, अतथ्यता, वितथत्वं, भ्रान्तिमत्त्वं, प्रमादवत्त्वं.

ERROR, *s.* (Mistake) भ्रमः, भ्रान्तिः *f.*, मतिभ्रमः, मतिभ्रान्तिः *f.*, विभ्रमः, मतिविभ्रमः, प्रमादः, मिथ्यामतिः *f.*, परिभ्रमः, भ्रामः, प्रपञ्चः, मोहः, व्यामोहः, विवर्त्तः, विचिकित्सा.—(Irregular course, deviation) उन्मार्गः, उन्मार्गगमनं, विमार्गगमनं, उत्पथः, सत्पथभ्रंशः, यथोचितभ्रंशः, उत्क्रमः, व्यतिक्रमः, व्यभिचारः, भ्रेषः.—(Fault, sin) दोषः, अपराधः, पापं; 'in error,' अपराधी -धिनी -धि (न्), अपराद्धः -द्धा -द्धं; 'I am not in error,' नाहम् अपराद्धः.

ERST, *adv.* पुरा, पूर्व्वं, पूर्व्वतस्, पूर्व्वकाले, प्राक्, प्राक्काले.

ERUBESCENCE, *s.* अरुणीभावः, अरुणिमा *m.* (न्), मुखारुणिमा *m.*, कपोलरागः.

ERUBESCENT, *a.* ईषद्रक्तवदनः -नी -नं, ईषदरुणितकपोलः -ला -लं.

To ERUCT, *v. a.* उद्गॄ (c. 6. -गिरति -गरितुं -रीतुं), उद्वम् (c. 1. -वमति -मितुं).

ERUCTATION, *s.* उद्गारः, उद्गिरणं, उद्वमः -मनं, उत्क्षेपः -पणं, उद्भ्रमः, उद्गारः; 'sour eructation,' अम्लोद्गारः.

ERUDITE, *a.* पण्डितः -ता -तं, विद्यावान् -वती -वत् (त्), ज्ञानवान् &c., कृतधीः -धीः -धि, व्युत्पन्नः -न्ना -न्नं, विपश्चित् *m. f. n.*, शिक्षितः -ता -तं.

ERUDITION, *s.* पाण्डित्यं, विद्या, ज्ञानं, व्युत्पत्तिः *f.*, शिक्षा, वैदुष्यं.

ERUGINOUS, *a.* ताम्रमलसमभावः -वी -वं, ताम्रकलङ्करूपः -पी -पं.

ERUPTION, *s.* (Bursting forth, emission) उद्भेदः, प्रोद्भेदः, उद्गारः, उद्गिरणं, उत्सर्गः, उत्क्षेपः, उद्गमः, स्फोटनं, निःसरणं, निर्गमः.—(On the skin) दद्रुः *m.*, खर्ज्जूः *f.*, स्फोटोत्पत्तिः *f.*, विस्फोटः, वरटी, वरण्डकः.

ERUPTIVE, *a.* उद्भेदी -दिनी -दि (न्), स्फोटविशिष्टः -ष्टा -ष्टं.

ERYSIPELAS, *s.* उदर्दः, विसर्पः, दद्रुः *m.*, दद्रूः *m.*

ESCALADE, *s.* लङ्घनं, दुर्गलङ्घनं, अवस्कन्दः -न्दनं, उल्लङ्घनं.

To ESCAPE, *v. n.* and *a.* पलाय् (c. 1. पलायते -यितुं, rt. इ), विपलाय्, प्रपलाय्, सम्पलाय्; निस्तॄ (c. 1. -तरति -रितुं -रीतुं), उत्तॄ; अपक्रम् (c. 1. -क्रामति -क्रमितुं), निर्गम् (c. 1. -गच्छति -गन्तुं), प्रद्रु (c. 1. -द्रवति -द्रोतुं), विद्रु, विप्रद्रु; प्रधाव् (c. 1. -धावति -वितुं), अपधाव्, उत्पत् (c. 1. -पतति -तितुं), निष्पत्, अपसृप् (c. 1. -सर्पति -सर्प्तुं), क्षेमं or त्राणं or रक्षां लभ् (c. 1. लभते, लब्धुं) or प्राप् (c. 5. -आप्नोति -आप्तुं).—(Avoid) परिहृ (c. 1. -हरति -हर्त्तुं), प्रोञ्छ् (c. 6. -उञ्छति -ञ्छितुं), त्यज् (c. 1. त्यजति, त्यक्तुं), परित्यज्; 'escaping,' निस्तीर्य्य, पलायित्वा, पलायमानः -ना -नं; 'one who has escaped danger,' भयमुक्तः -क्ता -क्तं, भयविमुक्तः -क्ता -क्तं, भयत्रातः -ता -तं, क्षेमप्राप्तः -प्ता -प्तं; 'he escapes blame,' दोषेण विमुच्यते.

ESCAPE, *s.* निस्तारः, निस्तरणं, उत्तरणं, निर्गमः, निर्गतिः *f.*, पलायनं, प्रपलायनं, विपलायनं, अपक्रमः, अपयानं, प्रद्रावः, विद्रवः, उद्द्रावः, अत्ययः, अपायः, क्षेमप्राप्तिः *f.*, त्राणं, मोक्षः, मुक्तिः *f.*, शेषः; 'from punishment,' दण्डभङ्गः, दण्डमोक्षः; 'desire of escaping with life,' प्राणपरीप्सा.

ESCAPED, *p. p.* निस्तीर्णः -र्णा -र्णं, उत्तीर्णः -र्णा -र्णं, पलायितः -ता -तं, निर्गतः -ता -तं, द्रुतः -ता -तं, परिभ्रष्टः -ष्टा -ष्टं, प्रभ्रष्टः -ष्टा -ष्टं.

ESCHALOT, *s.* लशुनजातीयः क्षुद्रकन्दः, तीक्ष्णकन्दभेदः.

ESCHAROTIC, *a.* मांसदाहकः -का -कं, मांसविलयनकृत्.

ESCHAROTIC, *s.* विलयनं, अवसादनं, मांसदाहकः प्रलेपः.

Escheat, *s.* उत्तराधिकारिणो ऽभावाद् भूस्वामिहस्तगतं भूमिक्षेत्रादि or भूस्वामिना प्राप्तं क्षेत्रादि.

To escheat, *v. n.* उत्तराधिकारिणाम् अभावाद् भूस्वामिन आधिकारत्वे परावृत् (c. 1. -वर्त्तते -र्त्तितुं) or भूस्वामिहस्तं गम् (c. 1. गच्छति, गन्तुं) or भूस्वामिना पुनः प्राप् in pass. (प्राप्यते).

To eschew, *v. a.* वृज् (c. 10. वर्जयति -यितुं), हा (c 3. जहाति, हातुं), उत्सृज् (c. 6. -सृजति -स्रष्टुं), त्यज् (c. 1. त्यजति, त्यक्तुं), प्रोज्झ् (c. 6. -उज्झति -ज्झितुं).

Escort, *s.* (Body of men for protection) रक्षार्थं सैनिकगुल्मः or सैन्यदलं, रक्षकाः *m. pl.*, परिचराः *m. pl.*, अनुचराः *m. pl.*, परिवारः.—(Protection, safeguard) रक्षा -क्षणं, आश्रयः, शरणं.—(Attendance for defence) रक्षार्थम् अनुव्रजनं, अनुव्रज्या.

To escort, *v. a.* (Attend by way of defence) रक्षार्थम् अनुव्रज् (c. 1. -व्रजति -जितुं) or अनुया (c. 2. -याति -तुं), अध्वनि रक्ष् (c. 1. रक्षति -क्षितुं), सञ्चर् in caus. (-चारयति -यितुं).

Escorted, *p. p.* अनुयातः -ता -तं, अध्वनि रक्षितः -ता -तं, सञ्चारितः -ता -तं.

Escritoir, *s.* लिपिसज्जाधारः, लेखसाधनाधारः.

Esculent, *a.* खाद्यः -द्या -द्यं, खादनीयः -या -यं, भक्षणीयः -या -यं.

Escutcheon, *s.* कुलचिह्नपत्रं, वंशमर्य्यादालक्षणपत्रं.

Esophagus, *s.* अन्नवाहिस्रोतः *n.* (स्), निगरणस्रोतः *n.* (स्).

Esoteric, *a.* गूढः -ढा -ढं, अलौकिकः -की -कं, अन्तर्भूतः -ता -तं.

Espalier, *s.* वातावरणार्थम् उद्यानपरितो रोपिता क्षुद्रवृक्षपंक्तिः *f.*, वृक्षशालं.

Especial, *a.* (Particular) विशेषकः -का -कं, सविशेषः -षा -षं, विशेष्यः -ष्या -ष्यं, विशेष in comp., as, 'especial duty,' विशेषधर्म्मः.—(Principal) उत्तमः -मा -मं, परमः -मा -मं, मुख्यः -ख्या -ख्यं, अधिकः -का -कं.

Especially, *adv.* विशेषतस्, सविशेषं, प्रधानतस्, मुख्यशस्, परमं.

Espied, *p. p.* दृष्टः -ष्टा -ष्टं, आलोकितः -ता -तं, आलक्षितः -ता -तं.

Espionage, *s.* पैशुन्यं, चारकर्म्म *n.* (न्), गूढावेक्षणं, चारचक्षुः *n.* (स्).

Esplanade, *s.* तृणास्तीर्णः समभूभागः, तृणविशिष्टः समस्थलीकृतः क्रीडाप्रदेशः.

Espousal, *s.* वाग्दानं, कन्याप्रदानं, वाग्निश्चयः, विवाहसम्बन्धः.—(Adoption) परिग्रहः, सङ्ग्रहः, ग्रहणं, अनुपालनं; 'of another's cause,' पक्षपातः.

To espouse, *v. a.* (Betroth) वाग्दानं कृ, विवाहप्रतिज्ञां कृ.—(Marry a wife) कन्यां विवह् (c. 1. -वहति -वोढुं) or उद्वह् or परिणी (c. 1. -णयति -णेतुं) or परिग्रह् (c. 9. -गृह्णाति -ग्रहीतुं).—(Take to one's self, adopt, maintain) स्वीकृ, आत्मसात्कृ, अङ्गीकृ, सङ्ग्रह्, परिग्रह्, संवृध् in caus. (-वर्धयति -यितुं), अनुपाल् (c. 10. -पालयति -यितुं); 'the cause of another,' परस्य सपक्षो भू or पक्षपातं कृ or पक्षपाती भू; 'of a follower,' भक्ताभिमानं कृ.

Espoused, *p. p.* वाग्दत्तः -त्ता -त्तं, प्रदत्तः -त्ता -त्तं, प्रत्तः -त्ता -त्तं, प्रतिज्ञाविवाहितः -ता -तं, विवाहितः -ता -तं, परिणीतः -ता -तं, उपोढः -ढा -ढं.

To espy, *v. a.* (See at a distance) दूराद् आलोक् (c. 1. -लोकते, c. 10. -लोकयति -यितुं) or अवलोक् or दृश् (c. 1. पश्यति, द्रष्टुं) or ईक्ष् (c. 1. ईक्षते -क्षितुं) or समीक्ष् or प्रेक्ष् or आलक्ष् (c. 10. -लक्षयति -यितुं), निरूप् (c. 10. -रूपयति -यितुं).

Esquire, *s.* (Armour-bearer) सान्नहनिकः.—(Gentleman) महाशयः, आर्य्यः. In cases where esquire is affixed to a name out of respect, श्री may be prefixed.

To essay, *v. a.* परीक्ष् (c. 1. -ईक्षते -क्षितुं), परीक्षां कृ, यत् (c. 1. यतते -तितुं), चेष्ट् (c. 1. चेष्टते -ष्टितुं), उद्यम् (c. 1. -यच्छति -यन्तुं), उपक्रम् (c. 1. -क्रमते -मितुं), व्यवसो (c. 4. -स्यति -सातुं), आरभ् (c. 1. -रभते -रब्धुं).

Essay, *s.* परीक्षा -क्षणं, उद्योगः, चेष्टा, उद्यमः, समुद्यमः, आरम्भः, प्रवृत्तिः *f.*, उपक्रमः.—(A composition on any thesis) अमुकपक्षविषयो लेख्यबन्धः or निबन्धः or लेख्यप्रसङ्गः, लेख्यं, लेख्यपत्रं.

Essayist, *s.* लेख्यनिबन्धा *m.* (न्धृ), निबन्धकृत् *m.*, लेखकः.

Essence, *s.* (Constituent substance or nature) सारः -रता, वस्तु *n.*, मूलवस्तु *n.*, भावः, पदार्थः, मूलं, अधिभूतं.—(Pith, extract) सारः, निष्कर्षः, निर्यासः, कषायः, निर्गलितार्थः, मण्डः, रसः.—(Perfume) वासः, आमोदः, सुगन्धिद्रव्यं, सौरभं.

Essential, *a.* (Constituent) वास्तवः -वी -वं, सारः -रा -रं, सारभूतः -ता -तं, सारवान् -वती -वत् (त्), स्वाभाविकः -की -कं; 'essential nature,' सारता.—(Important or necessary in the highest degree) आवश्यकः -की -कं, अत्यवश्यकः -का -कं, गुर्व्वर्थः -र्था -र्थं, बह्वर्थः -र्था -र्थं, अतिप्रयोजनार्हः -र्हा -र्हं.

Essential, *s.* (First principle) तत्त्वं.—(Constituent principle) वस्तु, मूलं, पदार्थः.—(Important point) परमार्थः, गुर्व्वर्थः, प्रधानार्थः.

Essentially, *adv.* सारतस्, वस्तुतस्, अर्थतस्, भावतस्, भावेन, तत्त्वतस्, पदार्थतस्; 'essentially necessary to be done,' अवश्यकार्य्यः -र्य्या -र्य्यं.

To establish, *v. a.* (Set up, settle) स्था in caus. (स्थापयति -यितुं), प्रतिष्ठा, अवस्था, संस्था, रुह् in caus. (रोपयति -यितुं), निरुह्; प्रतिनिधा (c. 3. -दधाति -धातुं).—(Ordain, enact) व्यवस्था in caus. विधा, प्रक्लृप् (c. 10. -कल्पयति -यितुं), परिक्लृप्, प्रतिपद् in caus. (-पादयति -यितुं), नियुज् (c. 7. युंक्ते -योक्तुं).—(Make firm, ratify) स्थिरीकृ, दृढीकृ, सुस्थिरं -रां -रं कृ, संस्तम्भ् (c. 5. -स्तभ्नोति -स्तम्भितुं, c. 10. -स्तम्भयति -यितुं); 'by fresh evidence,' प्रमाणीकृ, भू in caus. (भावयति -यितुं), विभू, उपपद् in caus. सत्याकृ.

Established, *p. p.* स्थापितः -ता -तं, प्रतिष्ठापितः -ता -तं, प्रतिष्ठितः -ता -तं, संस्थापितः -ता -तं, व्यवस्थितः -ता -तं, व्यवस्थापितः -ता -तं, स्थितः -ता -तं, स्थावरः -रा -रं, विहितः -ता -तं, प्रकल्पितः -ता -तं, प्रतिपादितः -ता -तं, निश्चितः -ता -तं, स्थिरीकृतः -ता -तं, उपन्यस्तः -स्ता -स्तं.—(Proved) प्रमाणीकृतः -ता -तं, निर्णीतः -ता -तं, सिद्धः -द्धा -द्धं, उपपन्नः -न्ना -न्नं; 'established custom,' कृतानुसारः.

Establishment, *s.* (Act of establishing) प्रतिष्ठापनं, संस्थापनं, अवस्थापनं, स्थापनं, व्यवस्थापनं, नियोजनं.—(Confirmation) स्थिरीकरणं, दृढीकरणं, संस्तम्भः, सत्यापनं, सत्याकृतिः *f.*—(System) स्थितिः *f.*, संस्थानं.

Estate, *s.* (Condition) अवस्था, स्थितिः *f.*, भावः, दशा, वृत्तिः *f.*—(Property, possession) रिक्थं, दायः, धनं, अधिकारः, भूमिः *f.*; 'paternal estate,' पैतृकभूमिः *f.*—(Rank) पदं, स्थानं, पदविः *f.*—(Degree, order) वर्गः, गणः.

To esteem, *v. a.* (Value) मन् (c. 4. मन्यते, मन्तुं, c. 10. मानयति -यितुं), सम्मन्, प्रतिमन्; पूज् (c. 10. पूजयति -यितुं), सम्पूज्, अभिपूज्, आदृ (c. 6. -द्रियते -दर्त्तुं); 'to esteem highly,' बहु मन्.—(Consider, think) मन्, भू in caus. (भावयति -यितुं), विभू, विगण् (c. 10. -गणयति -यितुं).

Esteem, *s.* (Opinion) मतं, मतिः *f.*—(Regard, respect) मानं, सम्मानं, आदरः, पूजा, मान्यत्वं; 'high esteem,' बहुमानं, बहुमतिः *f.*

Esteemed. *p. p.* मतः -ता -तं, सम्मानितः -ता -तं, आदृतः -ता -तं, पूजितः -ता -तं; esteemed highly,' बहुमतः -ता -तं.—(Considered) स्मृतः -ता -तं.

Estimable, *a.* मान्यः -न्या -न्यं, सम्मान्यः -न्या -न्यं, अर्घ्यः -र्घ्या -र्घ्यं, अर्घार्हः -र्हा -र्हं, आदरणीयः -या -यं, पूजनीयः -या -यं; 'highly estimable,' परमभान्यः -न्या -न्यं.—(To be reckoned) गणनीयः -या -यं, अनुमेयः -या -यं.

To ESTIMATE, *v. a.* विगण् (c. 10. -गणयति -यितुं), परिगण्, प्रगण्, गण्; संख्या (c. 2. -ख्याति -तुं), परिसंख्या, कल् (c. 10. कलयति -यितुं), सङ्कल्, अर्घं or मूल्यं संख्या or निर्णी (c. 1. -णयति -णेतुं) or निरूप् (c. 10. -रूपयति -यितुं); विभू in caus. (-भावयति -यितुं); 'to estimate worth,' गुणं ग्रह् (c. 9. गृह्णाति, ग्रहीतुं); 'to estimate highly,' बहु मन् (c. 4. मन्यते, मन्तुं).

ESTIMATE, *s.* (Computation) विगणनं -ना, परिसंख्यानं, गणना.—(Valuation) मूल्यपरिसंख्या, मूल्यनिरूपणं, मूल्यविज्ञापनं, अर्घविज्ञप्तिः *f.*; 'rough estimate,' स्थूलमानं, आकारः.

ESTIMATED, *p. p.* विगणितः -ता -तं, विभावितः -ता -तं, निर्णीतमूल्यः -ल्या -ल्यं, निरूपितमूल्यः -ल्या -ल्यं, सङ्कलितः -ता -तं, परिसंख्यातः -ता -तं.

ESTIMATION, *s.* (Calculation) विगणना, गणना, संख्या, परिसंख्यानं.—(Esteem, regard) मानं, सम्मानं, आदरः; 'high estimation,' बहुमानं, बहुमतिः *f.*

ESTIMATOR, *s.* गणकः, विगणकः, गुणकारः, संख्याता *m.* (तृ), मूल्यनिरूपकः.

ESTIVAL, *a.* नैदाघः -घी -घं, ग्रीष्मकालसम्बन्धी -न्धिनी -न्धि (न्).

ESTRADE, *s.* समभूमिः *f.*, समानभूमिः, समस्थलं, समस्थानं.

To ESTRANGE, *v. a.* विरञ्ज् in caus. (-रञ्जयति -यितुं), वैरक्तं जन् (c. 10. जनयति -यितुं), विरक्तीकृ, स्नेहं निवृत् in caus. (-वर्त्तयति -यितुं) or भिद् (c. 7. भिनत्ति, भेत्तुं), स्नेहच्छेदं कृ, स्नेहविच्छेदं कृ, स्नेहभेदं कृ, द्वैधीकृ, द्वैधं जन्, विश्लिष् in caus. (-श्लेषयति -यितुं), दूरीकृ.

ESTRANGED, *p. p.* विरक्तः -क्ता -क्तं, जातविरागः -गा -गं, विकृतः -ता -तं, विकारितः -ता -तं, विकृतबुद्धिः -द्धिः -द्धि, निवृत्तस्नेहः -हा -हं, दूरीभूतः -ता -तं.

ESTRANGEMENT, *s.* विरक्तिः *f.*, वैरक्त्यं, विरागः, वैराग्यं, विकृतिः *f.*, विकारः, बुद्धिविकारः, स्नेहनिवृत्तिः *f.*, स्नेहविच्छेदः, स्नेहभेदः, स्नेहच्छेदः, वियोगः, विप्रयोगः, विश्लेषः, दूरीभावः, पृथग्भावः.

ESTUARY, *s.* समुद्रशाखा, समुद्रवक्त्रः.—(Mouth of a river) सम्भेदः, सङ्गमः.

To ESTUATE, *v. n.* फेन (nom. फेनायते), उत्सेचनं कृ, वेला (nom. वेलायते).

ET-CÆTERA. Expressed by आदिः -दि in the *m.* or *n.* gender and in the *plur.* or *sing.* numb.; as, 'parrots, starlings, &c.,' शुकसारिकादयः; 'Indra, Kuvera, &c.,' इन्द्रकुवेरादयः; 'Of Agni, Pavana, &c.,' अग्निपवनादीनां; 'the nose, eyes, &c.,' नासचक्षुरादीनि; 'peace, war, &c.' सन्धिविग्रहादि; 'by liberality, &c.,' दानादिना; 'from liberality, &c.,' दानादेः (for दानादिनः). Sometimes इति is prefixed to आदि; as, 'the word chitralig, &c.,' चित्रलिगित्यादि. Sometimes आदिकः -का -कं, आद्यः -द्या -द्यं and प्रभृति are used for आदि; as, 'gifts, &c.,' दानादिकं; 'Indra, &c.,' इन्द्राद्याः, or इन्द्रप्रभृतयः *pl.*

To ETCH, *v. a.* लिख् (c. 6. लिखति, लेखितुं), आलिख्, चित्र् (c. 10. चित्रयति -यितुं).

ETCHING, *s.* चित्रलिखनं, चित्रं, आलेख्यं, वर्त्तिकारेखा.

ETERNAL, *a.* नित्यः -त्या -त्यं, अनन्तः -न्ता -न्तं -न्तकः -का -कं, सनातनः -नी -नं, शाश्वतः -ती -तं, अनादिः -दिः -दि, अनाद्यन्तः -न्ता -न्तं, अनाद्यः -द्या -द्यं, सदातनः -नी -नं, अनन्तकालस्थायी -यिनी -यि (न्), सर्व्वकालीनः -ना -नं, नैत्यिकः -की -कं, अनन्यः -न्या -न्यं, ध्रुवः -वा -वं, सन्ततः -ता -तं, सततः -ता -तं, अभीक्ष्णः -क्ष्णा -क्ष्णं, निरपायः -या -यं, निरन्तरः -रा -रं, अविच्युतः -ता -तं, अविसर्गी -र्गिणी -र्गि (न्), अविरतः -ता -तं, अमरः -रा -रं.

ETERNALLY, *adv.* नित्यं, नित्यदा, नित्यशस्, शाश्वतं, शश्वत्, सततं, सन्ततं, अनन्तं, अनाद्यन्तं, सना, अजस्रं, अनिशं, अभीक्ष्णं, निरन्तरं, अविरतं, अश्रान्तं, अनारतं, सर्व्वकालं.

ETERNITY, *s.* नित्यता, नैत्यं, अनन्तता -त्वं, आनन्त्यं, अनन्त्यं, अनन्तकालः, अनाद्यन्तता, ध्रुवता, ध्रौव्यं, अनन्तभावः, नैरन्तर्य्यं, अमरता.

To ETERNIZE, *v. a.* अनन्त (nom. अनन्तयति -यितुं), अनन्तीकृ, शाश्वतीकृ.

ETESIAN, *a.* सांवत्सरिकः -की -कं, प्रतिवार्षिकः -की -कं, सामयिकः -की -कं.

ETHER, *s.* आकाशः, खं, शून्यं, वायुः *m.*, निर्म्मलवायुः, अन्तरीक्षोपरिस्थः सूक्ष्मवायुः, नभः *n.* (स्), गगणं, विहायः *n.* (स्).

ETHERIAL, *a.* आकाशीयः -या -यं, आकाशजः -जा -जं, आकाशसम्भवः -वा -वं, आकाशस्थः -स्था -स्थं, खसम्भवः -वा -वं, वायवः -वी -वं, वैहायसः -सी -सं.

ETHIC, ETHICAL, *a.* वैनयिकः -की -कं, नीतिविषयः -या -यं, नीतिविद्याविषयकः -का -कं, नीतिशास्त्रसम्बन्धी -न्धिनी -न्धि (न्), नीतिशास्त्रीयः -या -यं.

ETHICALLY, *adv.* नीतिशास्त्रवत्, नीतिशास्त्रानुसारेण.

ETHICS, *s.* नीतिविद्या, नीतिः *f.*, नीतिशास्त्रं, विनयः, विनयविद्या, अर्थशास्त्रं, दण्डनीतिः *f.*, शीलविद्या, आन्वीक्षिकी.—(As invented by Vrihaspati) बार्हस्पत्यं.

ETHNIC, ETHNICAL, *a.* (Relating to the Gentiles) अन्यदेशीयः -या -यं, भिन्नदेशीयः -या -यं, देवार्च्चकसम्बन्धी -न्धिनी -न्धि (न्), देवपूजकसम्बन्धी &c.

ETHNOLOGY, *s.* नृकुलविद्या, नृजातिविद्या, नृवंशविद्या.

ETIQUETTE, *s.* सदाचारविधिः *m.*, आर्य्यव्यवहारविधिः, सुजनाचारविधिः, विनयविधिः, विनयरीतिः *f.*, आदरविधिः *m.*, सौजन्यं, मर्य्यादा, सुनीतिः *f.*, सभ्यता, सच्चरित्रं, न्यायः.

ETYMOLOGICAL, *a.* शब्दव्युत्पत्तिविषयः -या -यं, पदभञ्जनविषयः -या -यं, शब्दशास्त्रसम्बन्धी -न्धिनी -न्धि (न्), शब्दसाधनविद्यासम्बन्धी &c.

ETYMOLOGIST, *s.* शब्दव्युत्पत्तिकुशलः, पदभञ्जनविद्याज्ञः, शब्दशास्त्रज्ञः.

To ETYMOLOGIZE, *v. n.* शब्दव्युत्पत्तिं कृ, पदभञ्जनं कृ, शब्दसाधनं कृ.

ETYMOLOGY, *s.* व्युत्पत्तिः *f.*, शब्दव्युत्पत्तिः *f.*, शब्दव्युत्पत्तिविद्या, पदभञ्जनं, शब्दसाधनं, शब्दसाधनविद्या.

EUCHARIST, *s.* ख्रीष्टमृत्युस्मरणार्थकं भोजनं, ख्रीष्टभोजनं, ख्रीष्टप्रकल्पितभोजनं.—(Giving thanks to God) ईश्वरस्य धन्यवादकरणं or कुशलवादः.

EULOGIST, *s.* प्रशंसकः, गुणस्तावकः, स्तुतिपाठकः, वन्दी *m.* (न्).

EULOGISTIC, *a.* स्तुतिमयः -यी -यं, प्रशंसाकरः -री -रं, वन्दारुः -रुः -रु.

To EULOGIZE, *v. a.* प्रशंस् (c. 1. -शंसति -सितुं), स्तु (c. 2. स्तौति, स्तोतुं), अभिष्टु, संस्तु, श्लाघ् (c. 1. श्लाघते -घितुं), गुणान् कृत् (c. 10. कीर्त्तयति -यितुं) or उत्कृत्.

EULOGIZED, *p. p.* प्रशंसितः -ता -तं, प्रशस्तः -स्ता -स्तं, श्लाघितः -ता -तं, स्तुतः -ता -तं.

EULOGY, *s.* प्रशंसा -सनं, गुणप्रशंसा, स्तुतिः *f.*, गुणस्तुतिः *f.*, स्तवः, श्लाघा, गुणश्लाघा, स्तुतिवादः, स्तुतिवाक्यं, गुणोत्कीर्त्तनं, स्तोत्रं, शंसा, यशोवर्णना, वर्णना, वन्दना, वन्दिपाठः, गुणगानं, भोगावली.

EUNUCH, *s.* क्लीवः, षण्ढः, षण्डः, शण्ढः, शण्डः, मुष्कशून्यः, छिन्नवृषणः, छिन्नमुष्कः, निष्पुरुषः, नपुंसकः, पोगण्डः, षण्डः, तृतीयप्रकृतिः *m.*, तृतीयाप्रकृतिः, अफलः, विफलः, वर्षवरः, तूवरः.—(Guard of the women's apartments) स्थापत्यः, कञ्चुकी *m.* (न्), शुद्धान्तपालकः, शुद्धान्तजनः.

EUPHONIC, *a.* सुस्वरः -रा -रं, सुशब्दः -ब्दा -ब्दं, सुश्राव्यः -व्या -व्यं, श्रुतिसुखः -खा -खं, सुखारुस्वनः -ना -नं, अकर्कशः -शा -शं.

EUPHONY, *s.* सुस्वरः, सुशब्दः, सुस्वनः, सुश्राव्यशब्दः, अकटुत्वं, अकर्कशत्वं.

EUPHORBIA, *s.* बहुदुग्धिका, समन्तदुग्धा, सीहुण्डः, वज्रद्रुः *m.*, स्नुक् *f.* (ह्).

खुही, गुडा.

EUROPEAN, *s.* अरोपीयः, अरोपनामकदेशजः, तावमुखः,

To EVACUATE, *v. a.* शून्यीकृ, उत्सृज् (c. 6. -सृजति -स्रष्टुं), विसृज्, विरिच् (c. 7. -रिणक्ति -रिंक्ते -रेक्तुं), रिच्, उच्चर् (c. 1. -चरति -रितुं), निश्चर् in caus. (-चारयति -यितुं), शुध् (c. 10. शोधयति -यितुं), ; 'the bowels,' मलोत्सर्गं कृ, मलविसर्गं कृ, मलशुद्धिं कृ.

EVACUATED, *p. p.* रेचितः -ता -तं, विरेचितः -ता -तं, शोधितः -ता -तं, रिक्तः -क्ता -क्तं, विरिक्तः -क्ता -क्तं, विसृष्टः -ष्टा -ष्टं.

EVACUATION, *s.* (Of the bowels) मलविसर्गः, मलोत्सर्गः, समुत्सर्गः, मलशुद्धिः *f.*, मलशोधनं, विरेकः, विरेचनं, रेकः, रेचनं, मलोच्चारः, उच्चारः, शोधनं, उत्थानं, निर्हारः, निश्चारकः, अधोभागहरं.

To EVADE, *v. a.* छलेन पलायित्वा परिहृ (c. 1. -हरति -हर्त्तुं) or प्रोज्झ् (c. 6. -उज्झति -ज्झितुं).—(Elude by sophistry) वक्रोक्त्या छल् (c. 10. छलयति -यितुं), अपलप् (c. 1. -लपति -पितुं), अपह्नु (c. 2. -ह्नुते -ह्नोतुं), निह्नु, अपदिश् (c. 6. -दिशति -देष्टुं), व्यपदिश्.

To EVADE, *v. n.* (Escape) छलेन पलाय् (c. 1. पलायते -यितुं, rt. इ) or निस्तॄ (c. 1. -तरति -रितुं -रीतुं) or अपक्रम् (c. 1. -क्रामति -क्रमितुं) or अपधाव् (c. 1. -धावति -वितुं) or अपसृप् (c. 1. -सर्पति -सर्प्तुं), or उत्पत् (c. 1. -पतति -तितुं) or निष्पत्.—(Practice artifice) वाक्छलं कृ, वक्रोक्तिं कृ, व्यपदेशं कृ, अपह्नवं कृ.

EVADED, *p. p.* छलेन or अपदेशेन परिहृतः -ता -तं or प्रोज्झितः -ता -तं, निह्नुतः -ता -तं, अपह्नुतः -ता -तं, निस्तीर्णः -र्णा -र्णं.

EVAGATION, *s.* भ्रमणं, परिभ्रमणं, विभ्रान्तिः *f.*, भ्रान्तिः *f.*, विचलनं, व्यभिचारः,

EVANESENCE, *s.* अन्तर्द्धानं, तिरोधानं, अन्तर्हितत्वं, अदर्शनं.

EVANESCENT, *a.* तिरोधेयः -या -यं, अन्तर्हितः -ता -तं, अदृश्यरूपः -पी -पं, अदृश्यः -श्या -श्यं, अप्रत्यक्षः -क्षा -क्षं, परोक्षः -क्षा -क्षं.—(Fleeting) भङ्गुरः -रा -रं, क्षणभङ्गुरः -रा -रं, क्षणमात्रस्थायी -यिनी -यि (न्), अशाश्वतः -ती -तं.

EVANGELICAL, *a.* सुसंवादानुसारी -रिणी -रि (न्), ख्रीष्टीयधर्म्मानुयायी -यिनी -यि (न्), ख्रीष्टप्रचारितः -ता -तं, ख्रीष्टीयधर्म्मपुस्तकान्तर्गतः -ता -तं.

EVANGELIST, *s.* (Writer of the life of Christ) ख्रीष्टचरित्ररचकः, ख्रीष्टसमाचाररचकः, सुसंवादलेखकः, मङ्गलसमाचारलेखकः.—(Preacher of the Gospel) सुसंवादप्रचारकः, ख्रीष्टीयधर्म्मप्रवक्ता *m.* (क्तृ).

To EVANGELIZE, *v. a.* and *n.* सुसंवादं प्रचर् in caus. (-चारयति -यितुं), ख्रीष्टीयधर्म्मं प्रवच् (c. 2. -वक्ति -क्तुं) or उपदिश् (c. 6. -दिशति -देष्टुं) or ग्रह् in caus. (-ग्राहयति -यितुं), ख्रीष्टीयधर्म्मे प्रवृत् in caus. (-वर्त्तयति -यितुं).

To EVAPORATE, *v. n.* वाष्प (nom. वाष्पायते), धूम (nom. धूमायते) वाष्पसाद्भू, वाष्पीभू, वाष्परूपेण उत्पत् (c. 1. -पतति -तितुं) or उद्गम् (c. 1. -गच्छति -गन्तुं), धूमरूपेण विद्रु (c. 1. -द्रवति -द्रोतुं) or नश् (c. 4. नश्यति, नशितुं) or प्रणश् or अन्तर्धा in pass. (-धीयते) or क्षि in pass. (क्षीयते).—(Dry up) आतपेन परिशुष् (c. 4. -शुष्यति -शोष्टुं), शुष्कीभू.

To EVAPORATE, *v. a.* वाष्पसात्कृ, धूमसात्कृ, वाष्पीकृ, वाष्परूपेण विद्रु in caus. (-द्रावयति -यितुं), आतपेन परिशुष् in caus. (-शोषयति -यितुं) or शुष्कीकृ.

EVAPORATED, *p. p.* आतपशुष्कः -ष्का -ष्कं, परिशुष्कः -ष्का -ष्कं, शोषितरसः -सा -सं, वाष्परूपेण उद्गतरसः -सा -सं, वाष्पसात्कृतः -ता -तं, वाष्पीभूतः -ता -तं.

EVAPORATION, *s.* (Drying up) परिशोषः -षणं, शोषः -षणं, उच्छोषणं. —(Conversion to vapour) वाष्पसात्करणं, धूमसात्करणं, वाष्पभावः, वाष्परूपेण उत्पतनं or उद्गमः or नाशः, वाष्पीभूतत्वं.

EVASION, *s.* (Artifice to elude) अपदेशः, व्यपदेशः, छद्म *n.* (न्), छलं, कपटः -टं, अपह्नवः, निह्नवः.—(Equivocation) वक्रोक्तिः *f.*, वक्रता, वक्रवाक्यं, वाक्छलं, अपलापः, कैतववादः, प्रतीपवचनं.—(Escape) निस्तारः, उत्तरणं, निर्गमः, निर्गतिः *f.*, पलायनं, अपक्रमः.

EVASIVE, *a.* छली -लिनी -लि (न्), छलान्वितः -ता -तं, व्यपदेशकः -का -कं, वञ्चकः -का -कं, निह्नवकारी -रिणी -रि (न्),—(Equivocating) वक्रः -क्रा -क्रं, वाक्छलान्वितः -ता -तं; 'an evasive answer,' निह्नवोत्तरं, वक्रोत्तरं,

EVASIVELY, *adv.* वाक्छलेन, वक्रोक्त्या, निह्नवेन, सनिह्नवं, वक्रं.

EVE, *s.* (The fast to be observed on the evening before a holiday) महापर्व्वणः पूर्व्वदिनान्ते सेवनीय उपवासः, पुण्यदिवसस्य पूर्व्वप्रदोषः. —(Decline of day). *See* EVENING.—'To be on the eve of happening,' उपस्था (c. 1. -तिष्ठति -स्थातुं).

EVEN, *s.* सायः, सायङ्कालः, प्रदोषः, प्रदोषकालः. *See* EVENING.

EVEN-TIDE, *s.* सन्ध्याकालः, सन्ध्यासमयः, सायङ्कालः, प्रदोषकालः, प्रदोषसमयः.

EVEN, *a.* (Level, flat) समः -मा -मं, समानः -ना -नं, समस्थः -स्था -स्थं, सपाटः -टा -टं, घनाघनः -ना -नं; 'even ground,' समभूमिः *f.*, समस्थलं, आजिः *f.*, पाटः.—(Straight) समरेखः -खा -खं, अवक्रः -क्रा -क्रं, अभुग्नः -ग्ना -ग्नं, निर्भुग्नः -ग्ना -ग्नं, ऋजुः -जुः -जु, अञ्जसः -सा -सं.—(Smooth) श्लक्ष्णः -क्ष्णा -क्ष्णं, अरूक्षः -क्षा -क्षं.—(Uniform, equal) तुल्यः -ल्या -ल्यं, समतुल्यः -ल्या -ल्यं, उभयपार्श्वयोः समानः -ना -नं, निर्विकारः -रा -रं; 'in temper,' समभावः -वी -वं, समवृत्तिः -त्तिः -त्ति.—(Not odd) युग्मः -ग्मा -ग्मं, युगलः -ला -लं, समः -मा -मं; 'an even number,' युग्मं, युगलं; 'with both feet even,' समपदं.

To EVEN, *v. a.* समस्थलीकृ, समीकृ, समानीकृ, समान (nom. समानयति -यितुं).

EVEN, *adv.* अपि, एव, वा, वापि, सत्यं; 'even though,' यद्यपि, यद्यपि स्यात्, तथापि; 'even so,' एवं, एवमेव, तथा, तथापि, तथैव; 'even as,' यथैव, यद्वदेव, यत्प्रकारेण; 'even now,' अद्यापि, अद्यैव; 'not even,' नापि, नैव.

EVEN-HANDED, *a.* उभयसमः -मा -मं, समदर्शी -र्शिनी -र्शि (न्), विपक्षपातः -ता -तं.

EVENING, *s.* प्रदोषः, प्रदोषकालः, सायः, सायङ्कालः, सायाह्नः, अपराह्णः, सन्ध्या, सन्ध्याकालः, विकालः -लकः, वैकालः, दिनान्तः, दिनावसानं, दिवसावसानं, दिवसात्ययः, अहःशेषः, दिनशेषः, रजनीमुखं, निशादिः *f.*, रात्र्यारम्भः, उत्सूरः, अह्नः पञ्चमो भागः; 'in the evening,' सायं, सायं, दिनान्ते, अभिसायं, अनुसन्ध्यं; 'good evening to you,' शुभस् ते प्रदोषः.

EVENING, *a.* प्रादोषिकः -की -कं, वैकालिकः -की -कं, सान्ध्यः -न्ध्यी -न्ध्यं, सायन्तनः -नी -नं, अपराह्णेतनः -नी -नं or अपराह्णतनः.

EVENLY, *adv.* समं, समानं, समानतस्, अञ्जसा, तुल्यं; 'evenly matched,' तुल्यबलः -ला -लं, तुल्यवीर्य्यः -र्य्या -र्य्यं, समतोलः -ला -लं.

EVEN-MINDED, *a.* समचित्तः -त्ता -त्तं, समबुद्धिः -द्धिः -द्धि, समभावः -वा -वं, सत्त्वसम्पन्नः -न्ना -न्नं, सात्त्वसम्पन्नः -न्ना -न्नं, सम्पदापदोर् हर्षविषादरहितः -ता -तं.

EVENNESS, *s.* समता, समानता -त्वं, साम्यं, साम्यता, सामञ्जस्यं, तुल्यता, ऋजुता, निर्भुग्नता; 'of temper,' समचित्तत्वं, समानवृत्तिः *f.*, समभावः.

EVENT, *s.* वृत्तं, सम्भवः, उत्पन्नं, समुत्पत्तिः *f.*, समुत्पन्नं, समुदयः, सङ्गतं, गतं, सङ्गतिः *f.*, घटना, समुपागतं, उपागमः, समुपस्थितं.—(Consequence, conclusion) उद्भूतं, अनुवृत्तं, अनुवर्त्तनं, परिणामः, निष्पत्तं, सिद्धिः *f.*

To EVENTERATE, *v. a.* निरन्त्रीकृ, अन्त्राणि भिद् in caus. (-दारयति -यितुं).

EVENTFUL, *a.* गुरुघटनाविशिष्टः -ष्टा -ष्टं, गुरुसङ्कटविशिष्टः -ष्टा -ष्टं, बहुवृत्तविशिष्टः -ष्टा -ष्टं, बहुसमुदायवान् -वती -वत् (त्), बहुघटनामयः -यी -यं.

To EVENTILATE, *v. a.* वीज् (c. 10. वीजयति -यितुं), विधू (c. 5. -धूनोति, c. 6. -धुवति -धवितुं), निष्पावं कृ.

EVENTUAL, *a.* (Consequential) अनुवर्त्ती -र्त्तिनी -र्त्ति (न्), आनुषङ्गिकः -की -कं, अनुसारी -रिणी -रि (न्), अनुभूतः -ता -तं, परः -रा -रं.—(Ultimate) अन्तिमः -मा -मं, अन्त्यः -न्त्या -न्त्यं.

EVENTUALLY, *adv.* अन्ततस्, अन्ते, शेषे, शेषतस्, परतस्, प्रयोगतस्.

EVER, *adv.* (At any time) कदाचित्, कदापि, कदाचन, कर्हिचित्, जातु.—(Always, at all times) सदा, सर्व्वदा, सततं, नित्यदा, अनुक्षणं, प्रतिक्षणं; 'for ever,' नित्यं, सर्व्वकालं, अनन्तकालं, शाश्वतीः समाः, अजस्रं, शश्वत्, निरन्तरं, सना; 'ever and anon,' वारं वारं, काले काले, अनुकालं; 'ever since,' यतः प्रभृति; 'ever so little,' मनाक्, ईषत्, किञ्चित्, कियत्.—(As a word of enforcement) एव; 'ever young,' नित्ययौवनः -ना -नं; 'ever happy,' सदानन्दः -न्दा -न्दं.

EVERGREEN, *a.* अशीर्णपत्रः -त्रा -त्रं, अम्लानपर्णः -र्णा -र्णं, अशुष्कपर्णः -र्णा -र्णं.

EVERLASTING, *a.* अनन्तः -न्ता -न्तं, अनन्तकालस्थायी -यिनी -यि (न्), नित्यस्थायी &c., शाश्वतः -ती -तं, अक्षयः -या -यं, अनाश्यः -श्या -श्यं, अजरः -रा -रं. *See* ETERNAL.

EVERLASTINGLY, *adv.* शाश्वतं, अनन्तकालं, शाश्वतीः समाः, नित्यं, अजस्रं.

EVERLIVING, *a.* नित्यजीवी -विनी -वि (न्), अनन्तकालजीवी &c. *See* ETERNAL.

EVERMORE, *s.* अनन्तकालं, सर्व्वकालं, शाश्वतीः समाः, शाश्वतं, शश्वत्, नित्यं, नित्यकालं, सततं, अजस्रं, सना. *See* ETERNALLY.

EVER-RESTLESS, *a.* नित्यगतिः -तिः -ति, सदागतिः -तिः -ति, सततगतिः -तिः -ति.

EVERSION, *s.* पर्य्यासः, पराक्षेपः, परिवर्त्तनं, नाशः, विनाशः.

To EVERT, *v. a.* पर्य्यस् (c. 4. -अस्यति -असितुं), पराक्षिप् (c. 6. -क्षिपति -क्षेप्तुं), अधः कृ.

EVERY, *a.* सर्व्वः -र्व्वा -र्व्वं, विश्वः -श्वा -श्वं, सकलः -ला -लं, सर्व्वकः -का -कं; 'every art,' सर्व्वकर्म्म *n.* (न्); 'knowing every thing,' सर्व्वज्ञः; 'every road,' सर्व्वपथः; 'the maker of every thing,' सर्व्वभूतकृत्, सर्व्वकर्त्ता *m.* (र्तृ), विश्वकृत्; 'enduring every thing,' सर्व्वंसहः, विश्वसहः; 'every one,' सर्व्वजनाः *m. pl.*, विश्वजनं; 'dear to every one,' सर्व्वप्रियः; 'sustaining every thing,' विश्वम्भरः. 'Every,' may often be expressed by प्रति or अनु prefixed; as, 'every day,' प्रतिदिनं, प्रतिदिवसं, अनुदिनं, अन्वहं, प्रत्यहं; 'every night,' प्रतिरात्रं; 'every month,' प्रतिमासं; 'every moment,' अनुक्षणं; 'to every one,' प्रत्येकं. Or by doubling the word; as, 'every day,' दिने दिने, दिवसे दिवसे, अहरहः; 'in every house,' गृहे गृहे; 'every one,' एकैकः -का -कं, एकैकशस्, पृथक् पृथक्; 'every man,' एकैकजनः, प्रतिजनं; 'in every direction,' प्रतिदिशं, सर्व्वदिक्षु, सर्व्वपथीनः -ना -नं; 'on every side,' सर्व्वतस्, समन्ततस्, समन्तात्, विश्वतस्, परितस्.

EVERYWHERE, *adv.* सर्व्वत्र, सर्व्वतस्, विश्वतस्, विष्वक्, सर्व्वके, प्रतिदिशं; 'going everywhere,' सर्व्वत्रगः -गा -गं, सर्व्वगः -गा -गं, विश्वव्यापी -पिनी -पि (न्).

To EVICT, *v. a.* निर्णयपादानन्तरं or व्यवहारदर्शनानन्तरम् अधिकाराद् भ्रंश् (c. 10. भ्रंशयति -यितुं) or निराकृ or बहिष्कृ or अधिकारं or स्वत्वं हृ (c. 1. हरति, हर्तुं).

EVICTED, *p. p.* व्यवहारसभासकाशाद् आज्ञया हृताधिकारः -रा -रं, साधितः -ता -तं.

EVICTION, *s.* व्यवहारमण्डपसकाशाद् आज्ञानुसारेण अधिकारनिराकरणं or बहिष्करणं or स्वत्वहरणं, साधनं.

EVIDENCE, *s.* (Testimony) साक्ष्यं, साक्षिता, प्रमाणं, साधनं, प्रामाण्यं, प्रमाता *m.* (तृ), क्रियानिर्देशः, साधननिर्देशः; 'written evidence,' लेख्यप्रमाणं, लिखितं, साधनपत्रं; 'ocular evidence,' प्रत्यक्षप्रमाणं, साक्षात्प्रमाणं, चाक्षुषज्ञानं; 'false evidence,' कौटसाक्ष्यं, कूटसाक्ष्यं; 'want of evidence,' साक्ष्यभावः, प्रमाणाभावः.—(Witness) साक्षी *m.* (न्), प्रमाता *m.* (तृ); 'having evidence,' साक्षिमान् -मती -मत् (त्).

To EVIDENCE, *v. a.* प्रमाण (nom. प्रमाणयति -यितुं), प्रमाणीकृ, साक्षिणा or साक्ष्येण or प्रमाणेन साध् (c. 10. साधयति -यितुं) or भू in caus. (भावयति -यितुं) or निर्दिश् (c. 6. -दिशति -देष्टुं) or उपपद् in caus. (-पादयति -यितुं).

EVIDENCED, *p. p.* साक्षिभावितः -ता -तं, साक्षिलक्षणः -णा -णं, स्पष्टीकृतः -ता -तं.

EVIDENT, *a.* स्पष्टः -ष्टा -ष्टं, सुस्पष्टः -ष्टा -ष्टं, व्यक्तः -क्ता -क्तं or प्रव्यक्तः or अभिव्यक्तः, प्रत्यक्षः -क्षा -क्षं, प्रकाशः -शा -शं, सुप्रकाशः -शा -शं, समक्षः -क्षी -क्षं, स्फुटः -टा -टं, उल्बणः -णा -णं; 'to make evident,' स्पष्टीकृ, व्यक्तीकृ, प्रकाश् (c. 10. -काशयति -यितुं), प्रकटीकृ, प्रत्यक्षीकृ, आविष्कृ, प्रादुष्कृ; 'to be evident,' स्पष्टीभू, आविर्भू, प्रादुर्भू, प्रादुरस्, प्रकाश् (c. 1. -काशते -शितुं); 'made evident,' स्पष्टीकृतः -ता -तं, प्रादुष्कृतः -ता -तं, प्रकाशितः -ता -तं, प्रत्यक्षभूतः -ता -तं.

EVIDENTLY, *adv.* व्यक्तं, सुव्यक्तं, स्पष्टं, स्पष्टरूपेण, प्रत्यक्षतस्, प्रत्यक्षेण, साक्षात्, प्रकाशं, स्फुटं, प्रादुस्, समक्षं, नाम.

EVIL, *a.* दुष्टः -ष्टा -ष्टं, पापः -पा -पं, पापी -पिनी -पि (न्), खलः -ला -लं, अभद्रः -द्रा -द्रं, असाधुः -धुः -धु, असन् -सती -सत् (त्), निर्गुणः -णा -णं, शठः -ठा -ठं, मन्दः -न्दा -न्दं, अधमः -मा -मं, कुत्सितः -ता -तं, कदर्य्यः -र्य्या -र्य्यं, अधार्म्मिकः -की -कं. 'Evil,' is often expressed by दुर् or कु, or अप prefixed; as, 'an evil man,' दुर्जनः; 'evil thought,' कुचिन्ता, अपध्यानं; 'evil conduct,' दुर्णयः; 'evil deed,' कुकर्म्म *n.* (न्), दुष्कर्म्म *n.*, अपकर्म्म *n.*, पापकर्म्म *n.*, असत्कर्म्म *n.*, दुष्कृतं; 'evil course,' कुमार्गः, उन्मार्गः, विमार्गः; 'evil destiny,' दुर्भाग्यं, दुर्दैवं.

EVIL, *s.* (Wickedness) पापं, दुष्टता, दोषः, व्यसनं -निता, शाठ्यं, दौष्ट्यं, असाधुता, अधर्म्मः, व्यभिचारः, दौरात्म्यं, दौर्जन्यं, कुसृतिः *f.*, निकारः.—(Injury) अपकारः, अपकृतं, अपायः, द्रोहः, हिंसा, क्षतिः *f.*—(Misfortune, distress) अपायः, अशुभं, दुर्गतिः *f.*, दौर्गत्यं, अकुशलं, अभद्रं, अरिष्टं, अनिष्टं, अहितं, दुःखं, दुरवस्था, दुर्दशा, व्यसनं, उत्पातः, आपद् *f.*, विपद् *f.*, विपत्तिः *f.*, अनिष्टपातः, अनयः, क्लेशः, कष्टं.

EVIL, *adv.* दुष्ठु; expressed by दुर्, वि, दुष्ट, पाप &c., prefixed; 'evil-intentioned,' दुष्टबुद्धिः -द्धिः -द्धि, दुराशयः -या -यं, पापाशयः -या -यं; 'evil-affected,' विरक्तः -क्ता -क्तं, अहितः -ता -तं; 'evil-natured,' दुष्प्रकृतिः -तिः -ति; 'evil-fated,' दैवोपहतः -ता -तं, उपहतकः -का -कं, दुर्दैवग्रस्तः -स्ता -स्तं; 'evil-favoured,' कुरूपः -पी -पं.

EVIL-DOER, *s.* पापकारी *m.* (न्), पापकर्त्ता *m.* (र्तृ), पापकरः, पापकृत् *m.*, पापकर्म्मा *m.* (न्), असत्कर्म्मा, कुकर्म्मा, दुष्कृती *m.* (न्), कुकर्म्मकारी *m.*, मन्दचरितः, मन्दकारी *m.*, दुर्वृत्तः, दुष्टचारी *m.* (न्), अधर्म्मचारी *m.* (न्), व्यसनी *m.* (न्).

EVIL-EYE, *s.* कुदृष्टिः *f.*, अदृष्टिः *f.*, दुरीक्षणा, क्रूरदृष्टिः *f.*; evil-eyed,' क्रूरदृक् *m. f. n.* (श्), असदृक् *m. f. n.* पापदृष्टिः -ष्टिः -ष्टि.

EVIL-MINDED, *a.* पापमतिः -तिः -ति, पापबुद्धिः -द्धिः -द्धि, पापचेतनः -ना -नं, दुष्टचित्तः -त्ता -त्तं, दुष्टबुद्धिः -द्धिः -द्धि, दुष्टमतिः -तिः -ति, दुरात्मा

-त्मा -त्म (न्), अधर्म्मात्मा &c., पापात्मा &c., पापस्वभावः -वा -वं, दुष्टान्तःकरणः -णा -णं, दुर्हृदयः -या -यं.

Evil-speaking, *s.* दुरालापः, अपवादः, वाग्दोषः, पिशुनवाक्यं, मौखर्य्यं.

To evince, *v. a.* स्पष्टीकृ, व्यक्तीकृ, प्रकाश् (c. 10. -काशयति -यितुं), सूच् (c. 10. सूचयति -यितुं), निर्दिश् (c. 6. -दिशति -देष्टुं), प्रदिश्, दृश् in caus. (दर्शयति -यितुं), प्रमाणीकृ.

Evincible, *a.* सूच्यः -च्या -च्यं, साध्यः -ध्या -ध्यं, निर्देशनीयः -या -यं.

Evincibly, *adv.* स्पष्टं, सुस्पष्टं, सुव्यक्तं, असंशयं, अत्र न सन्देहः.

To eviscerate, *v. a.* निरन्त्रीकृ, निरन्त्र (nom. निरन्त्रयति -यितुं), नाडीर् वहिष्कृ.

Evitable, *a.* परिहरणीयः -या -यं, हेयः -या -यं, वर्ज्जनीयः -या -यं.

Evocation, *s.* (Calling upon) आह्वानं, प्रह्वायः, अनुकर्षणं.—(Appealing) पुनराह्वानं, पुनर्विचारप्रार्थना, अन्यप्राड्विवाकसाक्षाद् आह्वानं.

To evoke, *v. a.* आह्वे (c. 1. -ह्वयति -ह्वातुं), प्रह्वे, अनुकृष् (c. 1. -कर्षति -क्रष्टुं).—(From one tribunal to another) अन्यविचारसभासाक्षाद् आह्वे.

Evolution, *s.* (Unfolding) विस्तारः -रणं, प्रसारणं, प्रकटीकरणं, विवारः, विवृतिः *f.*—(In arithmetic) प्रादुर्भावः.—(Series) श्रेणी, श्रेढी.

To evolve, *v. a.* विस्तृ in caus. (-स्तारयति -यितुं), प्रसृ in caus. (-सारयति -यितुं), विवृ (c. 5. -वृणोति -वरितुं -रीतुं), अपावृ, वितन् (c. 8. -तनोति -नितुं), विततीकृ.

Evolved, *p. p.* विस्तारितः -ता -तं, प्रसारितः -ता -तं, विवृतः -ता -तं.

Evulsion, *s.* उत्पाटनं, उत्कर्षणं, विकर्षणं, उल्लुञ्चनं, अवलुञ्चनं.

Ewe, *s.* मेषी -षिका, एडका, उरणी, भेडी, अविला; 'ewe's milk,' अविसोढं, अविदूसं, अविमरीसं.

Ewer, *s.* घटी, उदकपात्रं, उदपात्रं, कुम्भः, पुटग्रीवः, कमण्डलुः *m.*

To exacerbate, *v. a.* प्रकुप् in caus. (-कोपयति -यितुं), उत्तिज् in caus. (-तेजयति -यितुं), तीक्ष्णीकृ, तिग्मतरं -रां -रं कृ, तीव्रतरं -रां -रं कृ, उग्रतरं -रां -रं कृ.

Exacerbation, *s.* प्रकोपः -पणं, उत्तेजनं, समुत्तेजनं, उग्रत्वं, कोपज्वलनं, कोपवर्धनं, रोगवृद्धिः *f.*

Exact, *a.* (Accurate, correct) यथार्थः -र्था -र्थं, याथार्थिकः -की -कं, समञ्जसः -सा -सं, अञ्जसः -सा -सं, सत्यः -त्या -त्यं, ऋतः -ता -तं, तथ्यः -थ्या -थ्यं, यथातथः -था -थं, शुचिः -चिः -चि, शुद्धः -द्धा -द्धं, निर्दोषः -षा -षं, दोषरहितः -ता -तं, स्पष्टः -ष्टा -ष्टं.—(Careful) सयत्नः -त्ना -त्नं, अवहितः -ता -तं, अप्रमादी -दिनी -दि (न्).—(Nice, precise) सूक्ष्मः -क्ष्मा -क्ष्मं.—(Not different) समानः -ना -नं, निर्विशेषः -षा -षं, अनन्यः -न्या -न्यं -न्यत्, समसमानः -ना -नं.—(Neither more nor less) नाधिको न च न्यूनः; 'the exact state,' तारतम्यं; 'exact measurement,' सूक्ष्ममानं.

To exact, *v. a.* (Compel to pay) दा in caus. (दापयति -यितुं), विहा in caus. (-हापयति -यितुं); 'exact tribute,' बलिं or शुल्कम् आहृ in caus. (-हारयति -यितुं) or अवहृ.—(Take forcibly) बलात् or बलेन ग्रह् (c. 9. गृह्णाति, ग्रहीतुं) or आदा (c. 3. -ददाति -दत्ते -दातुं).—(Demand) याच् (c. 1. याचति -चितुं), प्रार्थ् (c. 10. -अर्थयति -ते -यितुं).—(Enforce) कृ in caus. (कारयति -यितुं) with 2 acc.; 'exact punishment,' दण्डं प्रणी (c. 1. -णयति -णेतुं).

To exact, *v. n.* बाध् (c. 1. बाधते -धितुं), बाधं कृ, उपद्रवं कृ, उपधिं कृ.

Exacted, *p. p.* बलाद्गृहीतः -ता -तं, अवहारितः -ता -तं, आहारितः -ता -तं, आकारितः -ता -तं, विहापितः -ता -तं.

Exacter, *s.* बलात्कारपूर्व्वं परस्वादायी *m.* (न्) or परस्वग्राहकः, उपधिकः, औपधिकः, बाधकः, आहारकः, अवहारकः, हारकः.

Exacting, *a.* बाधकः -का -कं, विप्रलुम्पकः -का -कं, प्रार्थकः -का -कं.

Exaction, *s.* बलेन ग्रहणं or आदानं or हरणं, भर्त्सनपूर्व्वं प्रार्थनं or याचना, बाधः -धनं, उपद्रवः, विप्लवः, उपधिकरणं, परस्वादानं, अर्कव्रतं.

Exactly, *adv.* यथार्थं, यथावत्, सम्यक्, अञ्जसा, समञ्जसं, यथातथं, तथ्यं, सत्यं, ऋतं, सूक्ष्मत्वेन, सूक्ष्मतया; 'neither more nor less,' नाधिकं न च न्यूनं; 'exactly so,' एवमेव, तथैव; 'exactly alike,' समसमानः -ना -नं.

Exactness, *s.* (Accuracy) याथार्थ्यं, यथार्थता, सम्यक्त्वं, याथातथ्यं, सत्यता, तथ्यं, सामञ्जस्यं, शुद्धता.—(Niceness, precision) सूक्ष्मता, सौक्ष्म्यं.—(Carefulness) अवहितत्वं, अप्रमादः, यत्नः, आस्था.—(Regularity, method) पारिपाट्यं, समता, अनुक्रमणं, क्रमानुसारः, न्यायः.

To exaggerate, *v. a.* अत्युक्त्या or अतिशयोक्त्या वृध् (c. 10. वर्धयति -यितुं) or विस्तृ in caus. (-स्तारयति -यितुं) or अधिकीकृ, or उपचि (c. 5. -चिनोति -चेतुं), अतिशयेन वर्ण् (c. 10. वर्णयति -यितुं), अतिवर्णनं कृ, अत्युक्तिं कृ, वाग्विस्तारं कृ.

Exaggerated, *p. p.* वर्धितः -ता -तं, अधिकीकृतः -ता -तं, विस्तारितः -ता -तं, उपचितः -ता -तं, अत्युक्तिपूर्व्वं वर्णितः -ता -तं or प्रपञ्चितः -ता -तं.

Exaggeration, *s.* अत्युक्तिः *f.*, अतिशयोक्तिः *f.*, अधिकं, वागाधिक्यं, अधिकीकरणं, वागुपचयः, वाक्यबाहुल्यं, चित्रोक्तिः, अतिवर्णना, अतिप्रपञ्चः.

To exagitate, *v. a.* विक्षुभ् in caus. (-क्षोभयति -यितुं). *See* Agitate.

To exalt, *v. a.* उन्नम् in caus. -नमयति -यितुं), उच्छ्रि (c. 1. उच्छ्रयति -यितुं, rt. श्रि), समुच्छ्रि, उच्चीकृ, ऊर्द्ध्वीकृ, उन्नी (c. 1. -नयति -नेतुं), उन्नतिं कृ, समुन्नतिं कृ, उद्धृ (c. 1. -हरति -हर्त्तुं), अधिरुह् in caus. (-रोपयति -यितुं). *See* Elevate.

Exaltation, *s.* उन्नतिः *f.*, समुन्नतिः *f.*, उत्कर्षः, उत्कृष्टता, औत्कर्ष्यं, उच्छ्रयः, समुच्छ्रयः, उत्सेधः, उद्धृतिः *f.*, उदयः, उच्चता, ऊर्द्ध्वत्वं, अधिरोहः. *See* Elevation.

Exalted, *p. p.* उन्नतः -ता -तं, समुन्नतः -ता -तं, उच्छ्रितः -ता -तं, उत्कृष्टः -ष्टा -ष्टं, उद्धतः -ता -तं, उद्यतः -ता -तं, अधिरोपितः -ता -तं, अधिरूढः -ढा -ढं, उद्धृतः -ता -तं, आभ्युदयिकः -की -कं. *See* Elevated.

Examination, *s.* (Investigation) परीक्षा -क्षणं, निरूपणं, अनुसन्धानं, विचारः -रणं -णा, जिज्ञासा, अन्वेषणा -णं, अनुयोगः, समीक्षणं, संवीक्षणं, प्रसमीक्षा, निर्णयः, चर्च्चा, निरूपत्वं, विमर्शः, निश्चयः. परीष्टिः *f.*, विवेचना, शोधनं.—(By question) प्रश्नेन परीक्षा, प्रश्नोत्तरक्रमेण जिज्ञासा or परीक्षा.—(Inspection) निरीक्षणं, आलोचनं, अवेक्षा -क्षणं, दर्शनं, सन्दर्शनं.—(Judicial) विचारः, व्यवहारदर्शनं, आह्वानदर्शनं; 'examination of a witness,' साक्षिपरीक्षा.

To examine, *v. a.* (Investigate) परीक्ष् (c. 1. -ईक्षते -क्षितुं), निरूप् (c. 10. -रूपयति -यितुं), अनुसन्धा (c. 3. -दधाति -धातुं), ज्ञा in des. (जिज्ञासते -सितुं), अन्विष् (c. 4. -इष्यति -एषितुं) or अन्वेष् (c. 1. -एषते -षितुं), अनुयुज् (c. 7. -युनक्ति -युंक्ते -योक्तुं), विचर् in caus. (-चारयति -यितुं), चर्च् (c. 1. चर्चति -र्चितुं), विमृश् (c. 6. -मृशति -म्रष्टुं), निर्णी (c. 1. -णयति -णेतुं), निश्चि (c. 5. -चिनोति -चेतुं), विनिश्चि, विचि, अभिनिध्यै (c. 1. -ध्यायति -ध्यातुं), मार्ग् (c. 10. मार्गयति -यितुं).—(Inspect) निरीक्ष्, अवेक्ष्, समीक्ष्, वीक्ष्, अभिवीक्ष्, दृश् (c. 1. पश्यति द्रष्टुं), अनुदृश्, परिदृश्, सन्दृश्, प्रतिदृश्, आलोच् (c. 10. -लोचयति -यितुं), आलोक् (c. 10. -लोकयति -यितुं).—(Interrogate) अनुप्रच्छ् (c. 6. -पृच्छति -प्रष्टुं), परिप्रच्छ्, समनुप्रच्छ्, प्रश्नेन परीक्ष्, प्रश्नोत्तरक्रमेण परीक्ष् or अनुयुज्.—(Judicially) विचर् in caus. विचारं कृ; 'examine witnesses,' साक्षिणः परीक्ष्.

Examined, *p. p.* निरूपितः -ता -तं, परीक्षितः -ता -तं, निरीक्षितः -ता -तं, अवेक्षितः -ता -तं, जिज्ञासितः -ता -तं, विचारितः -ता -तं, अनुयुक्तः -क्ता -क्तं, चर्चितः -ता -तं, अन्वेषितः -ता -तं, निर्णीतः -ता -तं, आलोचितः -ता -तं.

Examiner, *s.* परीक्षकः, विचारकः, विचारकर्त्ता *m.* (र्त्तृ), अनुसन्धाता *m.* (तृ), निरूपकः, अनुयोक्ता *m.* (क्तृ), निर्णेता *m.* (तृ), जिज्ञासाकृत्.

Example, *s.* (Pattern for imitation) प्रमाणं, प्रमा, आदर्शः, प्रतिरूपं, प्रतिमा -मानं; 'to follow an example,' अनुकृ; 'following an example,' अनुकरणं; 'whatever example he sets, the world follows,' यत् प्रमाणं स कुरुते लोकस् तद् अनुवर्त्तते; 'men follow my example,' मम वर्त्म मनुष्या अनुवर्त्तन्ते or अनुगच्छन्ति.—(Person fit for an example) प्रमाणं, प्रमाता *m.* (तृ).—(Instance serving for illustration) दृष्टान्तः, निदर्शनं, उदाहारः -हरणं, उपोद्घातः; 'for example,' दृष्टान्तरूपेण, दृष्टान्तक्रमेण, यथा, तथाहि.

Exanimate, *a.* निर्जीवः -वा -वं, अजीवः -वा -वं, विचेतनः -ना -नं, निस्तेजाः -जाः -जः (स्), भग्नमनाः -नाः -नः (स्), निरुत्साहः -हा -हं, प्राणहीनः -ना -नं.

To exanimate, *v. a.* निर्जीवीकृ, मनोभङ्गं कृ, तेजो हृ (c. 1. हरति, हर्त्तुं).

Exanimation, *s.* प्राणहत्या, मनोभङ्गः, उत्साहभङ्गः, तेजोहरणं.

To exasperate, *v. a.* कुप् in caus. (कोपयति -यितुं), प्रकुप्, सङ्कुप्, कोपं or क्रोधं जन् (c. 10. जनयति -यितुं), क्रुध् in caus. (क्रोधयति -यितुं).

Exasperated, *p. p.* प्रकोपितः -ता -तं, प्रकुपितः -ता -तं, उपजातकोपः -पा -पं, जातक्रोधः -धा -धं, संरब्धः -ब्धा -ब्धं, जातामर्षः -र्षा -र्षं, इद्धमन्युः -न्युः -न्यु.

Exasperation, *s.* प्रकोपः -पणं, क्रोधकरणं, कोपकरणं, संरम्भः.

To exauctorate, *v. a.* पदात् or अधिकाराद् भ्रंश् (c. 10. भ्रंशयति -यितुं). *See* Dismiss.

To excavate, *v. a.* खन् (c. 1. खनति -ते -नितुं), उत्खन्, निखन्, अभिखन्, प्रोत्खन्, खनित्रेण भूमिं भिद् (c. 7. भिनत्ति, भेत्तुं) or दॄ in caus. (दारयति -यितुं) or भूमौ गर्त्तं or विवरं कृ, शुषिरीकृ, शून्यीकृ.

Excavated, *p. p.* निखातः -ता -तं, उत्खातः -ता -तं, खातः -ता -तं, खनितः -ता -तं, शुषिरीकृतः -ता -तं, शून्यीकृतः -ता -तं, पुटितः -ता -तं.

Excavation, *s.* (Act of digging out) खननं, उत्खननं.—(A cavity) खातं, गर्त्तः, रन्ध्रं, कुहरं, अवटः -टिः *m.*, बिलं, शुषिरं.

Excavator, *s.* खनकः, खनिता *m.* (तृ), आखनिकः, खातकः.

To excecate, *v. a.* अन्धीकृ, तिमिरीकृ, तिमिर (nom. तिमिरयति -यितुं).

To exceed, *v. a.* and *n.* अतिक्रम् (c. 1. -क्रामति -क्रमितुं), अतिभू (c. 1. -भवति -वितुं), अभिभू, अती (c. 2. अत्येति -तुं rt. इ), अतिशी (c. 2. -शेते -शयितुं), अधिशी, अतिचर् (c. 1. -चरति -रितुं), अतिगम् (c. 1. -गच्छति -गन्तुं), अतिरिच् in pass. (-रिच्यते), with abl. c. अतिरिक्तः -क्ता -क्तं भू, अधिकीभू, लङ्घ् (c. 10. लङ्घयति -यितुं), अत्यस् (c. 2. अत्यस्ति).

Exceeded, *p. p.* अतिक्रान्तः -न्ता -न्तं, उत्क्रान्तः -न्ता -न्तं, अतीतः -ता -तं, अत्ययितः -ता -तं, अतिशायितः -ता -तं, लङ्घितः -ता -तं.

Exceeding, *a.* (Surpassing) अतिक्रामकः -का -कं, अतिचरः -रा -रं, अतिगः -गा -गं, अतिरेकी -किणी -कि (न्), अतिशयी -यिनी -यि (न्), अतिरिक्तः -क्ता -क्तं, अधिकः -का -कं -कतरः -रा -रं, समधिकः -का -कं -कतरः -रा -रं, अभ्यधिकः -का -कं.—(In a great degree, very) अत्यन्तः -न्ता -न्तं, अति or सु or अतिशय prefixed, भूरिः -रिः -रि, गाढः -ढा -ढं, बाढः -ढा -ढं, परमः -मा -मं, परः -रा -रं, अतिमितः -ता -तं, अपरिमितः -ता -तं, पुरुः -रुः -रु; 'exceeding large,' अतिमहान् -हती -हत् (त्), सुमहान् &c.; 'exceeding bounds,' अतिमर्य्यादः -दा -दं, अतिभूमिः -मिः -मि; 'exceeding human power,' अतिमानुषः -षा -षं, मनातिगः -गा -गं; 'exceeding orders,' उल्लङ्घितशासनः -ना -नं.

Exceedingly, *adv.* अति or सु or अतिशय prefixed, अतिशयं -येन, सातिशयं, भृशं, अत्यन्तं, निर्भरं, अत्यर्थं, अतीव, नितान्तं, परं, गाढं, बाढं, प्रगाढं, एकान्ततस्, अतितरां, सुतरां, अतिमात्रं, अधिकं, निकामं, सुमहत्.

To excel, *v. a.* and *n.* विशिष् in pass. (-शिष्यते), with abl. c., अतिरिच् in pass. (-रिच्यते), with abl. c., अतिशी (c. 2. -शेते -शयितुं), अतिक्रम् (c. 1. -क्रामति -क्रमितुं), अती (c. 2. अत्येति -तुं rt. इ), अतिचर् (c. 1. -चरति -रितुं), अतिगम् (c. 1. -गच्छति -गन्तुं), अतिभू, अभिभू, जि (c. 1. जयति, जेतुं), विजि, पराजि, प्रशंस् in pass. (-शस्यते); 'one whose eyes excel the lotus,' अधिक्षिप्तपद्मनेत्रः -त्री.

Excelled, *p. p.* अतीतः -ता -तं, अतिक्रान्तः -न्ता -न्तं, अतिशायितः -ता -तं.

Excellence, excellency, *s.* (State of excelling or possessing good qualities) विशिष्टता, वैशिष्ट्यं, श्रेष्ठता -त्वं, उत्कृष्टता, उत्कर्षः, औत्कर्ष्यं, प्रकर्षः, प्रकृष्टत्वं, प्राशस्त्यं, प्रशस्तिः *f.*, उत्तमता, गुणवैशेष्यं, गुणोत्कर्षः, गुणप्रकर्षः, गुणिता, गुणता, गुणवत्ता -त्वं, सारत्वं, कौशलं, सौष्ठवं, सारत्वं, मतल्लिका, मचर्चिका, उद्घः, तल्लजः, प्रकाण्डः -ण्डं.—(Any valuable quality) गुणः, उत्कृष्टगुणः, परभागः; 'your excellency,' आर्य्य.

Excellent, *a.* विशिष्टः -ष्टा -ष्टं, उत्कृष्टः -ष्टा -ष्टं, श्रेष्ठः -ष्ठा -ष्ठं, उत्तमः -मा -मं, अनुत्तमः -मा -मं, प्रशस्तः -स्ता -स्तं, प्रशस्यः -स्या -स्यं, शस्तः -स्ता -स्तं, शस्यः -स्या -स्यं, श्रेयान् -यसी -यः (स्), सत्तमः -मा -मं, शिष्टः -ष्टा -ष्टं, परमः -मा -मं, अग्रियः -या -यं, अग्र्यः -ग्र्या -ग्र्यं, परः -रा -रं, वरः -रा -रं, प्रवरः -रा -रं, वरेण्यः -ण्या -ण्यं, प्रवर्हः -र्हा -र्हं, पुष्कलः -ला -लं, अतिशोभनः -ना -नं, सारवान् -वती -वत् (त्), अर्घ्यः -र्घ्या -र्घ्यं, भट्टारकः -का -कं, अपीव्यः -व्या -व्यं.—(Having excellent qualities) गुणी -णिनी -णि (न्), गुणवान् -वती -वत् (त्), गुणोत्कृष्टः -ष्टा -ष्टं, गुणोपेतः -ता -तं, गुणमयः -यी -यं, गुणवत्तमः -मा -मं, अधिगुणः -णा -णं; 'having numberless good qualities,' अपरिमितगुणगणः -णा -णं. Excellent may be expressed by ऋषभः or पुङ्गवः or व्याघ्रः or सिंहः or शार्दूलः or इन्द्रः or प्रकाण्डः in comp.; as, 'an excellent or eminent man,' पुरुषर्षभः, पुरुषव्याघ्रः, नरपुङ्गवः &c.; 'an excellent woman,' उत्तमा, वरारोहा, वरवर्णिनी, मत्तकाशिनी, कुमारीतल्लजः.

Excellently, *adv.* उत्तमं, अनुत्तमं, प्रशस्तं, श्रेष्ठं, सु, सुष्ठु, भद्रं.

To except, *v. a.* वृज् (c. 10. वर्ज्जयति -यितुं), अपास् (c. 4. -अस्यति -असितुं), पर्य्युदस्, व्युदस्, अपहा (c. 3. -जहाति -हातुं), विहा, त्यज् (c. 1. त्यजति, त्यक्तुं), मुच् (c. 6. मुञ्चति, मोक्तुं), उपसंहृ (c. 1. -हरति -हर्त्तुं).

Except, *prep.* वर्ज्जयित्वा, अपास्य, अपहाय, मुक्त्वा all with acc. c., विना with inst. or acc. c., ऋते with abl. or acc. c., अन्तरेण, अन्तरा, व्यतिरेकेण, व्यतिरिक्तं, वर्ज्जं, अन्यत्र, पृथक्.—(Unless) यदि न. Sometimes expressed by the loc. absolute; as, 'except ye eat flesh,' आमिषे न भुक्ते or by the indecl. part.; as, 'except ye see,' न दृष्ट्वा.

Excepted, *p. p.* वर्ज्जितः -ता -तं, पर्य्युदस्तः -स्ता -स्तं, विनिर्मुक्तः -क्ता -क्तं, व्यतिरिक्तः -क्ता -क्तं, उपसंहृतः -ता -तं, व्यावृत्तः -त्ता -त्तं, व्यावृतः -ता -तं, अपास्तः -स्ता -स्तं.—(In grammar) निपातितः -ता -तं, विधिसङ्कोचितः -ता -तं.

Excepting, *part.* वर्ज्जयित्वा, अपास्य, मुक्त्वा, अपहाय, हित्वा, त्यक्त्वा.

EXCEPTION, *s.* (Act of excepting) वर्ज्जः -र्ज्जनं, अपासनं, पर्युदासः, व्युदासः, अपहानिः *f.*, विनिर्मोकः, परिहारः -हरणं, व्यतिरेकः, व्यावृतिः *f.*, अपवादः, निषेधः.—(In grammar) निपातनं, ग्रहणं, विपक्षः, विधिसङ्कोचः, विधिभङ्गकः.—(That which is to be excepted) वर्ज्जनीयं, वर्ज्यं.—(Objection) बाधः -धा, अपवादः, उद्ग्राहः.

EXCEPTIONABLE, *a.* बाध्यः -ध्या -ध्यं, परिहरणीयः -या -यं, परिहार्य्यः -र्य्या -र्य्यं, वर्ज्यः -र्ज्या -र्ज्यं, वर्ज्जनीयः -या -यं, अप्रशस्तः -स्ता -स्तं.

EXCERPTED, *p.p.* उद्धृतः -ता -तं, निर्हृतः -ता -तं, व्यवस्थितः -ता -तं.

EXCERPTION, *s.* उद्धारः, निर्हारः, व्यवस्थितिः *f.*, चूर्णिः *m.*, चूर्णिकरणं.

EXCESS, *s.* अधिकता, आधिक्यं, आतिरेक्यं, आतिशय्यं, उद्रेकः, उपचयः, अतिरिक्तता, उत्सेकः, भृशता, भाढ्यं, भूमिमा *m.* (न्), उत्कर्षः, गाढता, आत्यन्तिकता, समभिहारः, एकान्तत्वं, अपरिमितत्वं, बाहुल्यं, प्राचुर्य्यं.—(Transgression of due limits) मर्य्यादातिक्रमः, अमर्य्यादा, अतिक्रमः, अत्याचारः, अत्ययः.—(Intemperance in eating, &c.) आहारादिविषये असंयमः.

EXCESSIVE, *a.* अति or अतिशय or सु prefixed, अत्यन्तः -न्ता -न्तं, गाढः -ढा -ढं, भूरिः -रिः -रि, अधिकः -का -कं, अतिमात्रः -त्रा -त्रं, अपरिमितः -ता -तं, अमितः -ता -तं, अतिमितः -ता -तं, नितान्तः -न्ता -न्तं, आत्यन्तिकः -की -कं, प्रगाढः -ढा -ढं, उद्गाढः -ढा -ढं, उद्रिक्तः -क्ता -क्तं, अतिमर्य्यादः -दा -दं, एकान्तः -न्ता -न्तं, भृशः -शा -शं, सुभृशः -शा -शं, निर्भरः -रा -रं, भरः -रा -रं, उत्कटः -टा -टं, अतिशयी -यिनी -यि (न्), अतिशायनः -ना -नं, अतिरिक्तः -क्ता -क्तं, परमः -मा -मं, परः -रा -रं; 'excessive heat,' अतिदाहः, गुरुतापः; 'excessive speaking,' अतिशयोक्तिः *f.*; 'excessive sleep,' सुनिद्रा, निर्भरनिद्रा; 'excessive rain,' भूरिवृष्टिः *f.*; 'excessive pain,' तीव्रवेदना.

EXCESSIVELY, *adv.* भृशं, सुभृशं, निर्भरं, अत्यन्तं, अतिशयं -येन, सातिशयं, गाढं, प्रगाढं, उद्गाढं, नितान्तं, अतिमात्रं, एकान्ततस्, अत्यर्थं, निर्दयं, अतिमर्य्यादं, अतितरां, सुतरां, तीव्रं, बलवत्, अतिवेलं. Often expressed by अति or सु or अतिशय prefixed; as, 'excessively sharp,' अतितीक्ष्णः -क्ष्णा -क्ष्णं.

To EXCHANGE, *v. a.* परिवृत् in caus. (-वर्त्तयति -यितुं), निमे (c. 1. -मयते -मातुं), विनिमे, विमे, all with acc. and inst. c., प्रतिदा, परिवर्त्तं कृ, विनिमयं कृ, व्यतिहृ (c. 1. -हरति -हर्त्तुं), प्रतिपण् (c. 10. -पणयति -यितुं). 'To exchange' may be expressed by the phrase 'having given one thing to take another,' अन्यद् दत्त्वा अन्यद् आदा, or अन्यत् दत्त्वा अन्यद् ग्रह् (c. 9. गृह्णाति, ग्रहीतुं); 'he exchanges beans for sesamum seeds,' तिलैर् माषान् परिवर्त्तयति or तिलेभ्यः प्रति माषान् ददाति; 'liquids to be exchanged for liquids,' रसा रसैर् निमातव्याः; 'not to be exchanged,' अपरिवर्त्तनीयः -या -यं, अप्रतिपण्यः -ण्या -ण्यं.

EXCHANGE, *s.* परिवर्त्तः -र्त्तनं, परिवृत्तिः *f.*, परीवर्त्तः, विनिमयः, विमयः, निमयः, निमेयः, नैमेयः, वैमेयः, प्रतिदानं, परिदानं, परावर्त्तः, परावृत्तिः *f.*, व्यतिहारः, व्यतीहारः, निमया.—(Barter) भाण्डविनिमयः.—(Place where merchants meet) श्रेष्ठिचत्वरं, वणिक्समागमचत्वरं; 'exchange of civilities,' प्रतिपूजनं; 'exchange of favours,' परस्परोपकारः; 'exchange of blows,' अन्योन्यघातः, व्यतिहारः; 'in exchange for,' प्रति, विनिमयेन; 'in exchange for one's life,' स्वप्राणविनिमयेन.

EXCHANGEABLE, *a.* परिवर्त्तनीयः -या -यं, निमातव्यः -व्या -व्यं, प्रतिपण्यः -ण्या -ण्यं.

EXCHANGED, *p.p.* परिवर्त्तितः -ता -तं, परिवृत्तः -त्ता -त्तं, परावृत्तः -त्ता -त्तं.

EXCHANGER, *s.* परिवर्त्तकः, परिवर्त्तनकृत्, विनिमयकर्त्ता *m.* (र्त्तृ), विमयकारी *m.* (न्).

EXCHEQUER, *s.* (Treasury) राजकोषः, राजधनागारः, राजधनगृहं, राजस्वकोषः; 'chancellor of the exchequer,' कोषाध्यक्षः, कोषाधीशः, कोशाधीशः, राजधनाधिकारी *m.* (न्), राजस्वपालकः, गञ्जाधिपः.—(Court). *See* CHANCERY.

EXCISABLE, *a.* (article) शुल्कस्थानं, करस्थानं.

EXCISE, *s.* स्वदेशनिर्म्मितद्रव्याणां राजग्राह्यभागः or राजदेयो भागः, शुल्कः -ल्कं, करः, स्वविषयनिर्म्मितद्रव्येषु राजनिरूपितः करः.

To EXCISE, *v. a.* स्वदेशनिर्म्मितद्रव्याणां or -द्रव्येषु राजग्रहणीयं भागं निरूप् (c. 10. -रूपयति -यितुं) or राजदेयभागं निरूप्, करं or शुल्कं निरूप् or स्था in caus. (स्थापयति -यितुं).

EXCISEMAN, *s.* स्वदेशनिर्म्मितद्रव्याणां राजग्राह्यभागनिरूपकः, शुल्काध्यक्षः, कराध्यक्षः, करनिरूपकः, करग्राही *m.* (न्), करग्रहः.

EXCISION, *s.* उच्छेदः, उच्छित्तिः *f.*, उत्कर्त्तनं, कर्त्तनं, विच्छेदः, विच्छित्तिः *f.*, उत्पाटनं, उद्धरणं, विनाशः.

EXCITABILITY, *s.* उत्तेजनीयता, उद्दीपनीयता, उत्तेजनक्षमता, उत्तापनीयता, प्रकोपणीयता, शीघ्रकोपित्वं.

EXCITABLE, *a.* उत्तेजनीयः -या -यं, उत्तापनीयः -या -यं, उद्दीपनीयः -या -यं, प्रवर्त्तनीयः -या -यं, प्रकोपणीयः -या -यं, शीघ्रकोपी -पिनी -पि (न्), चित्तवेगी -गिनी -गि (न्).

EXCITANT, *s.* रुचकं, प्ररोचनं, दीपकं, तेजनं, तेजोवर्धनं.

EXCITATION, *s.* उत्तेजनं, समुत्तेजनं, उत्तापः -पनं, उद्दीपनं, दीपनं, प्ररोचनं, प्रोत्साहः -हनं.

To EXCITE, *v. a.* उत्तिज् in caus. (-तेजयति -यितुं), समुत्तिज्, उत्तप् in caus. (-तापयति -यितुं), उद्दीप् (c. 10. -दीपयति -यितुं), दीप्, उत्था in caus. (-थापयति -यितुं, rt. स्था), व्युत्था, उद्युज् in caus. (-योजयति -यितुं), उत्सह् in caus. (-साहयति -यितुं), प्रोत्सह्, प्ररुच् in caus. (-रोचयति -यितुं), प्रवृत् in caus. (-वर्त्तयति -यितुं), चुद् (c. 10. चोदयति -यितुं), प्रचुद्, सञ्चुद्, परिचुद्, सन्धुक्ष् (c. 10. -धुक्षयति -यितुं), उद्धन् (c. 2. -हन्ति -न्तुं).—(Create, cause) जन् (c. 10. जनयति -यितुं), उत्पद् (c. 10. -पादयति -यितुं); 'to excite divisions,' भेदं जन्.

EXCITED, *p. p.* उत्तेजितः -ता -तं, तेजितः -ता -तं, समुत्तेजितः -ता -तं, उत्तापितः -ता -तं, उत्तप्तः -प्ता -प्तं, उद्दीप्तः -प्ता -प्तं, उद्युक्तः -क्ता -क्तं, प्रवर्त्तितः -ता -तं, उत्थापितः -ता -तं, उद्धतः -ता -तं, विनिवृत्तः -त्ता -त्तं, चोदितः -ता -तं, उद्धुरो -रा -रं, कृतोद्यमः -मा -मं, संरब्धः -ब्धा -ब्धं, उज्जृम्भितः -ता -तं.—(Caused) जनितः -ता -तं, जातः -ता -तं, उत्पन्नः -न्ना -न्नं.—(Under emotion) चित्तवेगवान् -वती -वत् (त्), अन्यथावृत्तिः -त्तिः -त्ति, गतशान्तिः -न्तिः -न्ति, गतधृतिः -तिः -ति.

EXCITEMENT, *s.* उत्तापः, उत्तप्तता, उत्तेजनं, उद्दीपः -पनं, उद्दीप्तिः *f.*, दीपनं, प्ररोचनं, उत्थापनं, प्रोत्साहः -हनं, प्रवर्त्तः -र्त्तनं, प्रवृत्तिः *f.*, अभितापः, उन्मदः, उद्धतिः *f.*, उद्योगः, संरम्भः.—(Emotion) चित्तवेगः, उत्कम्पः, चित्तोत्तापः.

EXCITER, *s.* उत्तापकः, उद्दीपकः, दीपकः, उत्थापकः, उत्तेजकः, प्रोत्साहकः, प्रवर्त्तकः.

EXCITING, *a.* उद्दीपकः -का -कं, चित्तोत्तापकारी -रिणी -रि (न्).

To EXCLAIM, *v. n.* उत्क्रुश् (c. 1. -क्रोशति -क्रोष्टुं), विक्रुश्, प्रक्रुश्, उच्चैःस्वरेण घुष् in caus. (घोषयति -यितुं), उद्घुष्, विघुष्, उच्चैः or प्रकाशं वद् (c. 1. वदति -दितुं) or भाष् (c. 1. भाषते -षितुं), उच्चैःस्वरं कृ, उच्चैर्घुष्टं कृ, उच्चभाषणं कृ, उच्चवाक्यम् उदीर् (c. 10. -ईरयति -यितुं),

प्रक्ष्विड् (c. 1. -क्ष्वेडति -डितुं).

EXCLAIMED, *p. p.* उत्क्रुष्टः -ष्टा -ष्टं, विक्रुष्टः -ष्टा -ष्टं, उद्घुष्टः -ष्टा -ष्टं.

EXCLAMATION, *s.* उत्क्रोशः, उत्क्रुष्टं, घोषणं -णा, उद्घोषणं, उद्गारः, उच्चैर्घुष्टं, उद्घुष्टं, उच्चभाषणं, उच्चैःस्वरः, रासः, प्रक्ष्वेडनं, चीत्कारः.

EXCLAMATORY, *a.* उत्क्रोशकः -का -कं, उद्घोषणः -णा -णं, विक्रोशनः -ना -नं.

To EXCLUDE, *v. a.* (Thrust out) वहिःकृ, वहिष्कृ, निराकृ, अपाकृ, निःसृ in caus. (-सारयति -यितुं), अपास्, निरस् (c. 4. -अस्यति -असितुं), अपास्, अपानुद् (c. 6. -नुदति -नोत्तुं), निष्कस् in caus. (-कासयति -यितुं).—(Debar) बाध् (c. 1. बाधते -धितुं), निषिध् (c. 1. -षेधति -षेद्धुं), वृ in caus. (-वारयति -यितुं), निरुध् (c. 7. -रुणद्धि -रोद्धुं), विरुध्, अवरुध्.—(Except, not include) वृज् (c. 10. वर्ज्जयति -यितुं), अपास्, पर्य्युदस्, व्युदस्, उपसंहृ, उपसंहरणं कृ, न परिग्रह् (c. 9. -गृह्णाति -ग्रहीतुं); 'is excluded,' परिहीयते.

EXCLUDED, *p. p.* वहिष्कृतः -ता -तं, वहिःकृतः -ता -तं, निराकृतः -ता -तं, निरस्तः -स्ता -स्तं, उदस्तः -स्ता -स्तं, अपास्तः -स्ता -स्तं, निःसारितः -ता -तं, निषिद्धः -द्धा -द्धं, बाधितः -ता -तं, निवारितः -ता -तं, विहीनः -ना -नं, परिहीणः -णा -णं.—(Excepted) वर्ज्जितः -ता -तं, पर्य्युदस्तः -स्ता -स्तं, व्यतिरिक्तः -क्ता -क्तं, उपसंहृतः -ता -तं, व्यावृत्तः -त्ता -त्तं, व्यावृतः -ता -तं; 'excluded from society,' अपांक्तः -क्ता -क्तं.

EXCLUSION, *s.* वहिष्करणं, वहिःकरणं, निराकरणं, निरासः, निरसनं, अपासनं, अपसारणं, निःसारणं, निष्कासनं, निषेधः, प्रतिषेधः, निवारणं, वारणं, अवरोधनं, निरोधः, विरोधः, विरुद्धत्वं, वहिर्भावः.—(Exception) वर्ज्जनं, पर्य्युदासः, व्युदासः, उपसंहारः -हरणं, व्यावृत्तिः *f.*, व्यतिरेकः.

EXCLUSIVE, *a.* (Debarring) निवारकः -का -कं, बाधकः -का -कं, निषेधकः -का -कं.—(Possessed to the exclusion of others) असामान्येन भुक्तः -क्ता -क्तं, पृथग्भुक्तः -क्ता -क्तं, अन्यव्यतिरेकेण भुक्तः -क्ता -क्तं, अनन्यः -न्या -न्यं -न्यत्, केवलः -ला -लं.—(In logic) वैशेषिकः -की -कं.—(Not including, not taking into the account) वर्ज्जयित्वा, अपास्य, अपहाय, हित्वा, अपरिगणय्य; or expressed by रहितः -ता -तं, हीनः -ना -नं in comp.

EXCLUSIVELY, *adv.* (To the exclusion of others, apart) असामान्येन, असाधारण्येन, पृथक्, एकान्ततस्, एकान्ते, अन्यव्यतिरेकेण, केवलं, विजने.—(Without including) वर्ज्जयित्वा, अपास्य, अपरिगणय्य.

EXCLUSIVENESS, *s.* कैवल्यं, केवलत्वं, अनन्यता, असामान्येन परिभोगः.

To EXCOGITATE, *v. a.* प्रचिन्त् (c. 10. -चिन्तयति -यितुं), परिचिन्त्, विचिन्त्, मनसा क्लृप् (c. 10. कल्पयति -यितुं), परिक्लृप्.

EXCOGITATED, *p. p.* प्रचिन्तितः -ता -तं, मनःकल्पितः -ता -तं, परिकल्पितः -ता -तं.

EXCOGITATION, *s.* उपायचिन्तनं, परिचिन्ता, मनसा परिकल्पनं.

To EXCOMMUNICATE, *v. a.* ख्रीष्टीयसमाजाद् वहिष्कृ or निराकृ or निरस् (c. 4. -अस्यति -असितुं), ख्रीष्टीयधर्म्माधिकाराद् भ्रंश् (c. 10. भ्रंशयति -यितुं) or च्यु in caus. (च्यावयति -यितुं), अपांक्तीकृ, अपात्रीकृ.

EXCOMMUNICATED, *p. p.* ख्रीष्टीयसमाजाद् वहिष्कृतः -ता -तं or निराकृतः -ता -तं, अपांक्तः -क्ता -क्तं, अपात्रीकृतः -ता -तं.

EXCOMMUNICATION, *s.* ख्रीष्टीयसमाजाद् वहिष्करणं or निराकरणं or निरसनं, अपांक्तीकरणं, अपात्रीकरणं; 'by edict,' अपांक्तपत्रं.

To EXCORIATE, *v. a.* त्वक्छेदं कृ, त्वग्भेदं कृ, चर्म्मक्षतं कृ, त्वगुल्लेखनं कृ, चर्म्म लिख् (c. 6. लिखति, लेखितुं) or उल्लिख् or दॄ in caus. (दारयति -यितुं) or विदॄ, त्वच (nom. त्वचयति -यितुं), चर्म्म घृष् (c. 1. घर्षति -र्षितुं) or निर्घृष्, निस्त्वचीकृ.

EXCORIATED, *p. p.* क्षतचर्म्मा -र्म्मा -र्म्म (न्), उल्लिखितचर्म्मा &c., विदारितत्वक् *m. f. n.*, निघृष्टचर्म्मा &c., घर्षितचर्म्मा &c., निस्त्वचः -चा -चं.

EXCORIATION, *s.* त्वक्क्षतिः *f.*, चर्म्मक्षतिः *f.*, त्वक्परिक्षतिः *f.*, चर्म्मोल्लिखनं, त्वक्छेदः, त्वग्भेदः, त्वगुल्लिखनं, त्वग्दारणं, चर्म्मदारणं, चर्म्मनिर्घर्षणं.

EXCORTICATION, *s.* निस्त्वचीकरणं, निर्वल्कलीकरणं, त्वक्परिपुटनं.

EXCREMENT, *s.* शकृत् *n.*, पुरीषं, उच्चारः, उच्चरितं, अमेध्यं, मलं, शरीरमलं, विष्ठा, विष्ठा, विट् *f.*, (ष्), गूथः -थं, शारीरं, शमलं, अवस्करः, अपस्करः, वर्च्चस्कः -स्कं, कल्कं, हन्नं, हूयं, पूतिकं, शोधनं, किट्टं; 'excrement and urine,' विण्मूत्रं; 'to void excrement,' पुरीषोत्सर्गं कृ, विण्मूत्रोत्सर्गं कृ, गु (c. 6. गुवति -वितुं).

EXCREMENTAL, *a.* उच्चरितः -ता -तं, उत्सर्जितः -ता -तं, हन्नः -न्ना -न्नं.

EXCREMENTITIOUS, *a.* मली -लिनी -लि (न्), पुरीषमयः यी -यं, विण्मयः -यी -यं.

EXCRESCENCE, *s.* गण्डः -ण्डका, स्फोटः -टकः, अर्बुदः, आभोगः; 'fleshy excrescence,' अधिमांसं; 'on the tongue,' अधिजिह्वः; 'on the bone,' अध्यस्थि *n.*

To EXCRETE, *v. a.* उत्सृज् (c. 6. -सृजति -स्रष्टुं), मूत्रपुरीषोत्सर्गं कृ, उच्चर् (c. 1. -चरति -रितुं), गु (c. 6. गुवति -वितुं), हद् (c. 1. हदते, हत्तुं).

EXCRETED, *p. p.* उच्चरितः -ता -तं, हन्नः -न्ना -न्नं, गूनः -ना -नं.

EXCRETION, *s.* (Act of excreting) उत्सर्गः, उत्सर्जनं, उच्चरणं.—(That which is excreted) उच्चारः, उच्चरितं, मलं. *See* EXCREMENT.

EXCRETIVE, EXCRETORY, *a.* उत्सर्गकारी -रिणी -रि (न्), उच्चारकः -का -कं, मलवहिष्कारकः -का -कं, मलरेचकः -का -कं.

To EXCRUCIATE, *v. a.* व्यथ् (c. 10. व्यथयति -यितुं), तप् in caus. (तापयति -यितुं), सन्तप्, परितप्, यत् in caus. (यातयति -यितुं), कृष् in caus. (कर्षयति -यितुं), तिग्मयातनां दा or कृ.

EXCRUCIATED, *p. p.* व्यथितः -ता -तं, सन्तप्तः -प्ता -प्तं, कर्षितः -ता -तं.

EXCRUCIATING, *a.* व्यथकः -का -कं, व्यथाकरः -री -रं, उद्वेजनकरः -री -रं, सन्तापकः -का -कं, तिग्मयातनाकारी -रिणी -रि (न्), अरुन्तुदः -दा -दं, प्रमाथी -थिनी -थि (न्).

EXCRUCIATION, *s.* तिग्मयातना, तीव्रवेदना, यातना, व्यथा -थनं.

To EXCULPATE, *v. a.* दोषात् or अपराधात् शुध् in caus. (शोधयति -यितुं) or विशुध् or परिशुध् or मुच् (c. 6. मुञ्चति, मोक्तुं), निर्दोषीकृ, निरपराधीकृ, अनपराधिनं -धिनीं -धि कृ.

EXCULPATED, *p. p.* दोषमुक्तः -क्ता -क्तं, विशोधितः -ता -तं, विशुद्धः -द्धा -द्धं, निर्दोषः -षा -षं, निरपराधः -धा -धं, विगतदोषः -षा -षं, गतकलङ्कः -ङ्का -ङ्कं.

EXCULPATION, *s.* विशोधनं, विशुद्धिः *f.*, परिशोधः -धनं, दोषमुक्तिः *f.*, दोषमोचनं, निर्दोषीकरणं, निरपराधीकरणं, दोषप्रक्षालनं, दोषमार्जनं.

EXCULPATORY, *a.* शोधकः -का -कं, शोधनः -ना -नं, विशोधकः -का -कं, विशोधनः -ना -नं, परिशोधनः -ना -नं, दोषमोचकः -का -कं, निर्दोषकारी -रिणी -रि (न्).

EXCURSION, *s.* (Ramble) भ्रमणं, परिभ्रमः -मणं, विहारः, विहरणं.—(Deviation) उत्क्रमः, विचलनं, व्यभिचारः, भ्रान्तिः *f.*, पथत्यागः, पथभ्रंशः, पथोल्लङ्घनं, पथातिक्रमः.

EXCURSIVE, *a.* भ्रमी -मिणी -मि (न्), भ्रमणकारी -रिणी -रि (न्), उत्क्रान्तमर्य्यादः -दा -दं, व्यभिचारी -रिणी -रि (न्), विहारी -रिणी -रि (न्), त्यक्तमार्गः -र्गा -र्गं.

EXCUSABLE, *a.* क्षमणीयः -या -यं, क्षमतव्यः -व्या -व्यं, क्षमार्हः -र्हा -र्हं, सह्यः -ह्या -ह्यं, शोधनीयः -या -यं, मार्जनीयः -या -यं, मोचनीयः -या -यं, सहनीयः -या -यं.

To EXCUSE, *v. a.* (Pardon) क्षम् (c. 1. क्षमते -ति, क्षन्तुं), संक्षम्, मृष् (c. 4. मृष्यति, मर्षितुं, मर्ष्टुं, c. 10. मर्षयति -यितुं).—(Free from fault) दोषात् or अपराधात् शुध् (c. 10. शोधयति -यितुं) or विशुध् or परिशुध् or मुच् (c. 6. मुञ्चति, मोक्तुं), निर्दोषीकृ.—(Extenuate a fault or crime) दोषं or पापं क्षम् or छद् (c. 10. छादयति -यितुं) or आछद् or मृज् (c. 2. मार्ष्टि -र्ष्टुं), दोषक्षालनं कृ.—(Remit) अवसृज् (c. 6. -सृजति -स्रष्टुं), मुच्, विमुच्.—(Excuse one's self) उत्तरं कृ or दा, अपदेशं कृ, व्यपदेशं कृ, छद्म कृ, आत्मदोषं छद्, आत्मानं शुध्, आत्मदोषमार्जनं कृ, छलं कृ, अपदिश् (c. 6. -दिशति -देष्टुं), व्यपदिश्; 'excuse me,' प्रसीदतु भवान्.

Excuse, *s.* उत्तरं, उत्तरदानं, अपदेशः, व्यपदेशः, छद्म *n.* (न्), दोषछादनं, पापाच्छादनं, आच्छादनं, शुद्धिः *f.*, विशुद्धिः *f.*, शोधनं, पापशोधनं, निमित्तं, दोषमार्जना, दोषक्षालनं, दोषप्रक्षालनं, अनुनयः, उपदेशः, प्रत्यवस्कन्दः, कैतवं, छलं, क्षमाप्रार्थनं.

Excused, *p. p.* क्षान्तः -न्ता -न्तं, मुक्तः -क्ता -क्तं, विमोचितः -ता -तं, अवसृष्टः -ष्टा -ष्टं.

Excuseless, *a.* निरुत्तरः -रा -रं, अक्षमणीयः -या -यं, अक्षमार्हः -र्हा -र्हं.

Excuser, *s.* (One who pleads for another) परार्थम् उत्तरवादी *m.* (न्), पक्षपाती *m.* (न्), क्षमाकारी *m.* (न्).—(One who forgives) क्षन्ता *m.* (न्).

Execrable, *a.* गर्हणीयः -या -यं, गर्ह्यः -र्ह्या -र्ह्यं, गर्हितः -ता -तं, शापार्हः -र्हा -र्हं, घृणार्हः -र्हा -र्हं, द्वेष्यः -ष्या -ष्यं, द्वेषणीयः -या -यं, आक्रोशनीयः -या -यं.

Execrably, *adv.* गर्हणीयं, गर्ह्यं, गर्हितं, गर्ह्यप्रकारेण, द्वेषणीयं.

To execrate, *v. a.* शप् (c. 1. शपति -ते, c. 4. शप्यति, शप्तुं), अभिशप्, परिशप्; गर्ह् (c. 1. गर्हते -र्हितुं), आक्रुश् (c. 1. -क्रोशति -क्रोष्टुं), अमङ्गलं or अनिष्टम् आशंस् (c. 1. -शंसते -सितुं), भर्त्स् (c. 10. भर्त्सयति -यितुं), धिक्कृ, घृण् (c. 1. घृणते -णितुं), बाध् in des. (बीभत्सते -त्सितुं).

Execrated, *p. p.* शप्तः -प्ता -प्तं, अभिशप्तः -प्ता -प्तं, गर्हितः -ता -तं, आक्रुष्टः -ष्टा -ष्टं, धिक्कृतः -ता -तं, निर्भर्त्सितः -ता -तं, अभिशस्तः -स्ता -स्तं.

Execration, *s.* शापः, अभिशापः, शपः -पनं, शपथः, परिशापः, आक्रोशः -शनं, अवक्रोशः, उपक्रोशः, भर्त्सनं, निर्भर्त्सनं, तर्ज्जनं, अभिषङ्गः, अभीषङ्गः, गालिः *m.*

To execute, *v. a.* कृ, विधा (c. 3. -दधाति -धातुं), निर्वह् in caus. (-वाहयति -यितुं), सम्पद् in caus. (-पादयति -यितुं), निष्पद्, अनुष्ठा (c. 1. -तिष्ठति -ष्ठातुं), आस्था, समास्था, साध् (c. 10. साधयति -यितुं), संसाध्, सिद्धीकृ, वृत् in caus. (वर्त्तयति -यितुं), निर्वृत्, निवृत्, संवृत्, प्रवृत्, प्रणी (c. 1. -णयति -णेतुं), सम्प्रणी, घट् (c. 10. घटयति -यितुं), आचर् (c. 1. -चरति -रितुं), समाचर्, प्रयुज् (c. 7. -युनक्ति -योक्तुं). (Inflict capital punishment) धर्म्मसभाविचारानुसारेण वधदण्डार्हं हन् (c. 2. हन्ति -न्तुं), वधदण्डं कृ, प्राणदण्डं कृ.

Executed, *p. p.* कृतः -ता -तं, अनुष्ठितः -ता -तं, निष्पादितः -ता -तं, निष्पन्नः -न्ना -न्नं, सम्पादितः -ता -तं, विहितः -ता -तं, निर्वाहितः -ता -तं, आचरितः -ता -तं, सिद्धीकृतः -ता -तं, साधितः -ता -तं, प्रणीतः -ता -तं, घटितः -ता -तं.—(Put to death by judicial sentence) धर्म्मसभाविचारानुसारेण हतः -ता -तं or व्यापादितः -ता -तं.

Execution, *s.* (Performance) करणं, विधानं, अनुष्ठानं, आचरणं, निर्वहणं, निर्वाहः, निष्पादनं, सम्पादनं, निर्वर्त्तनं, साधनं, सिद्धिः *f.*, निष्पत्तिः *f.*—(Putting to death by judicial sentence) धर्म्मसभाविचारानुसारेण प्राणघातः or प्राणहननं or प्राणदण्डः, वधदण्डार्हघातः, वधः, हत्या, व्यापादनं, मारणं; 'place of execution,' वध्यभूमिः *f.*, वधस्थानं, घातस्थानं, वधस्थली.

Executioner, *s.* घातुकपुरुषः, घातकजनः, वध्यपुरुषः, वधकर्म्माधिकारी *m.*

(न्), मृतपाः *m.*, दण्डपाशिकः.

Executive, *a.* सम्पादकः -का -कं, निर्वाहकः -का -कं, साधकः -का -कं, विधायकः -का -कं, प्रवर्त्तकः -का -कं, निष्पादकः -का -कं, प्रणायकः -का -कं.

Executor, *s.* मृतपत्त्रनिरूपणाधिकृतः, मृतलेखाधिकारी *m.* (न्), मृतकर्म्माधिकारी *m.*, मृतकर्म्मनिर्वाहकः, मृतकर्म्मसम्पादकः, मृतपत्त्रानुसारेण तद्विषयनिर्वाहकः.

Executorship, *s.* मृतजनकर्म्माधिकारिणः पदं or कर्म्म *n.* (न्).

Executrix, *s.* मृतलेखाधिकारिणी स्त्री, मृतकर्म्माधिकारिणी.

Exegesis, *s.* व्याख्या -ख्यानं, विवरणं, व्याकरणं, विवृतिः *f.*, उद्देशः.

Exegetical, *a.* वाचकः -का -कं, उद्देशकः -का -कं, प्रकाशकः -का -कं.

Exegetically, *adv.* व्याख्याक्रमेण, प्रकाशनार्थं, उद्दिश्य, विवरणार्थं.

Exemplar, *s.* प्रमाणं, प्रतिमा -मानं, उपमा, प्रतिरूपं, आदर्शः, प्रतिकृतिः *f.*, न्यायाधारः, दृष्टान्तः.

Exemplarily, *adv.* प्रमाणतस्, प्रमाणवत्, प्रमाणम् इव, प्रमाणरूपेण, प्रामाणिकप्रकारेण, दृष्टान्तरूपेण, अनुकरणीयप्रकारेण, अनुकरणीयं.

Exemplariness, *s.* अनुकरणीयता, अनुकरणयोग्यता, अनुगम्यत्वं, अनुवर्त्तनीयत्वं, प्रामाणिकत्वं, प्रमाणयोग्यता, प्रामाण्यं, दृष्टान्तता.

Exemplary, *a.* प्रमाणयोग्यः -ग्या -ग्यं, अनुकरणयोग्यः -ग्या -ग्यं, अनुकरणीयः -या -यं, अनुकरणार्हः -र्हा -र्हं, अनुगम्यः -म्या -म्यं, अनुवर्त्तनीयः -या -यं, दृष्टान्तयोग्यः -ग्या -ग्यं, प्रामाणिकः -की -कं, दार्ष्टान्तिकः -की -कं.

Exemplification, *s.* उदाहरणं, उदाहारः, समुदाहरणं, उद्देशः, निदर्शनं, प्रदर्शनं, दृष्टान्तः, दृष्टान्तीकरणं, उत्प्रेक्षा.

Exemplified, *p. p.* उदाहृतः -ता -तं, समुदाहृतः -ता -तं, प्रदर्शितः -ता -तं, उद्दिष्टः -ष्टा -ष्टं, दृष्टान्तेन स्पष्टीकृतः -ता -तं or प्रकाशितः -ता -तं.

To exemplify, *v. a.* दृष्टान्तेन स्पष्टीकृ or प्रकाश् (c. 10. -काशयति -यितुं) or प्रदृश् (c. 10. -दर्शयति -यितुं) or उद्दिश् (c. 6. -दिशति -देष्टुं), दृष्टान्तीकृ, उदाहृ (c. 1. -हरति -हर्त्तुं), व्याहृ.

To exempt, *v. a.* मुच् (c. 6. मुञ्चति, मोक्तुं, c. 10. मोचयति -यितुं), विमुच्, निर्मुच्, विनिर्मुच्; मोक्ष् (c. 10. मोक्षयति -यितुं), विमोक्ष्; विसृज् (c. 6. -सृजति -स्रष्टुं, c. 10. -सर्जयति -यितुं), अवसृज्; 'to exempt from taxes,' अकरीकृ, निष्करीकृ, स्वाधीनीकृ.

Exempt, exempted, *a.* and *p. p.* (Free from) वर्जितः -ता -तं, विवर्जितः -ता -तं, मुक्तः -क्ता -क्तं, विनिर्मुक्तः -क्ता -क्तं, निर्मुक्तः -क्ता -क्तं, शून्यः -न्या -न्यं, रहितः -ता -तं, हीनः -ना -नं, विनाकृतः -ता -तं, वियुक्तः -क्ता -क्तं, विगतः -ता -तं, वीतः -ता -तं; 'exempt from bias,' मुक्तसङ्गः -ङ्गा -ङ्गं, सङ्गमुक्तः -क्ता -क्तं, सङ्गवर्जितः -ता -तं, सङ्गहीनः -ना -नं, विगतसङ्गः -ङ्गा -ङ्गं; 'exempt from passion,' वीतरागः -गा -गं. Or expressed by अ or निर् prefixed; as, 'exempt from tax,' अकरः -रा -रं, निष्करः -रा -रं.—(Not liable) अनधीनः -ना -नं, अनायत्तः -त्ता -त्तं.

Exemption, *s.* (Freedom from) मुक्तिः *f.*, मोक्षः, विनिर्मोकः, निर्मोकः, विमोक्षः, विरहः, राहित्यं, रहितत्वं, शून्यता, अभावः, असम्भवः, व्यावृत्तिः *f.*; 'exemption from war,' युद्धाभावः. Or expressed by अ prefixed; as, 'exemption from fear,' अभयं; 'exemption from exertion,' अनायासः; 'exemption from taxes,' अकरत्वं.

To exenterate, *v. a.* निरन्त्रीकृ, नाडीः or अन्त्राणि वहिष्कृ.

Exequial, *a.* और्द्ध्वदेहिकः -की -कं, अन्त्येष्टिक्रियासम्बन्धी -न्धिनी -न्धि (न्), अन्त्यसत्क्रियासम्बन्धी &c., श्राद्धादिकर्म्मसम्बन्धी &c.

Exequies, *s.* और्द्ध्वदेहिकं, और्द्ध्वदेहिकक्रिया, अन्त्येष्टिक्रिया, अन्त्येष्टिः *f.*,

अमतसत्क्रिया, मृतशरीरसत्कर्म्म n. (न्), प्रेतकर्म्म n. अन्त्यकर्म्म n. शवकर्म्म n.

EXERCISE, s. (Habitual practice) अभ्यासः, अभ्यसनं, अभ्यासता, चर्य्या, आवृत्तिः f.—(Performance) आचरणं, प्रवृत्तिः f., व्यापारः, निषेवनं, अनुष्ठानं.—(Employment) प्रयोगः, उपयोगः, सेवनं.—(Exertion) व्यवसायः, उद्यमः, आयासः, उद्योगः, चेष्टा, उत्थानं.—(Discipline) शिक्षा.—(Bodily exercise) व्यायामः, परिश्रमः, शरीरपरिश्रमः.—(Exercise of mind) मनोव्यापारः, मनोव्यवसायः.—(Military exercise) सैन्यव्यायामः, अस्त्रशिक्षा, शस्त्राभ्यासः, युद्धाभ्यासः, योग्या; 'daily exercises,' नित्यकृत्यं; 'taking exercise,' व्यायामी -मिनी -मि (न्).

To EXERCISE, v. a. (Practice habitually) अभ्यस् (c. 4. -अस्यति -असितुं), आचर् (c. 1. -चरति -रितुं), समाचर्, अभ्यासं कृ.—(Employ, use) प्रयुज् (c. 7. -युनक्ति -युंक्ते -योक्तुं), उपयुज्, व्यापृ in caus. (-पारयति -यितुं).—(Perform) कृ, आचर्, आस्था, (c. 1. -तिष्ठति -स्थातुं), अनुष्ठा, सेव् (c. 1. सेवते -वितुं), निषेव्, आसेव्, उपसेव्.—(Discipline) शिक्ष् in caus. (शिक्षयति -यितुं).—(Exercise the body, troops, &c.) व्यायम् (c. 10. -यमयति -यामयति -यितुं, c. 1. -यच्छति -यन्तुं).—(Exercise one's self) चेष्ट् (c. 1. चेष्टते -ष्टितुं), आत्मानं चेष्ट् (c. 10. चेष्टयति -यितुं), उद्यम् (c. 1. -यच्छति -यन्तुं), व्यायम्, व्यवसो (c. 4. -स्यति -सातुं), उद्योगं कृ; 'having exercised,' व्यायाम्य.

To EXERCISE, v. n. (Use bodily exercise for health) शरीरव्यायामं कृ, आरोग्यार्थं विहारं कृ or परिश्रमं कृ.

EXERCISED, p. p. अभ्यस्तः -स्ता -स्तं, कृताभ्यासः -सा -सं, उद्यतः -ता -तं, व्यायतः -ता -तं, कृतोद्यमः -मा -मं, शिक्षितः -ता -तं, शीलितः -ता -तं.

To EXERT, v. a. (Bring into action) प्रयुज् (c. 7. -युनक्ति -युंक्ते -योक्तुं, c. 10. -योजयति -यितुं), उपयुज्, उद्युज्, चेष्ट् in caus. (चेष्टयति -यितुं), व्यापृ in caus. (-पारयति -यितुं) वृत् in caus. (वर्त्तयति -यितुं), प्रवृत्, वाह् (c. 10. वाहयति -यितुं), उत्सह् in caus. (-साहयति -यितुं).—(Exert one's self) चेष्ट् (c. 1. चेष्टते -ष्टितुं), आत्मानं चेष्ट् in caus., विचेष्ट्, यत् (c. 1. यतते -तितुं), प्रयत्, व्यवसो (c. 4. -स्यति -सातुं), उद्यम् (c. 1. -यच्छति -यन्तुं), व्यायम्, आयस् (c. 4. -यस्यति -यसितुं), घट् (c. 1. घटते -टितुं, c. 10. घटयति -यितुं), उद्योगं कृ, यत्नं कृ.

EXERTED, p. p. चेष्टितः -ता -तं, उद्यतः -ता -तं, उद्युक्तः -क्ता -क्तं, प्रयुक्तः -क्ता -क्तं, व्यवसितः -ता -तं, यत्तः -त्ता -त्तं, वाहितः -ता -तं, प्रवर्त्तितः -ता -तं.

EXERTION, s. चेष्टा -ष्टनं, उद्योगः, उद्यमः, उत्साहः, यत्नः, व्यवसायः, चेष्टितं, विचेष्टितं, प्रयत्नः, अध्यवसायः, आयासः, प्रयासः, प्रवृत्तिः f., घटनं -ना, घटा, गुरणं, गूरणं, गोरणं, व्यापारः, ग्रहः, कर्म्मयोगः, उत्थानं, प्रयोगः, व्यायामः.

EXEUNT OMNES, निष्क्रान्ताः सर्व्वे.

To EXFOLIATE, v. n. अध्यस्थिवद् वल्करूपेण गल् (c. 1. गलति -लितुं) or विगल्, दुष्टास्थिवत् or गलितास्थिवद् वल्कलपपरिपुटनं कृ.

EXFOLIATION, s. अध्यस्थि n., अध्यस्थिपरिपुटनं, अध्यस्थिगलनं.

EXHALATION, s. (Act or process of exhaling) उद्गारः, निश्वासः, प्रश्वासः, निःश्वासः, निःश्वसनं, उत्क्षेपः.—(Rising of vapour, &c.) वाष्पोद्गारः, वाष्पोन्नतिः f., धूमोन्नतिः f.—(The vapour exhaled) वाष्पः, धूमः -मिका; 'sending forth exhalations,' उद्गारी -रिणी -रि (न्).

To EXHALE, v. a. उद्गॄ (c. 6. -गिरति -गरितुं -रीतुं), निश्वस् (c. 2. -श्वसिति -तुं), निःश्वस्, प्रश्वस्, प्रवा (c. 2. -वाति -तुं), मुच् (c. 6. मुञ्चति, मोक्तुं), प्रमुच्, उदीर् (c. 10. -ईरयति -यितुं), उत्क्षिप् (c. 6. -क्षिपति -क्षेप्तुं), उद्गम् in caus. (-गमयति -यितुं), निर्गम्.

EXHALED, p. p. उद्गीर्णः -र्णा -र्णं, निश्वसितः -ता -तं, उदीरितः -ता -तं.

EXHALEMENT, s. उद्गारः, उद्गीर्णं, वाष्पः, धूमः -मिका.

To EXHAUST, v. a. (Drain off, dry up) शुष् in caus. (शोषयति -यितुं), उच्छुष्, विशुष्, संशुष्, शुष्कीकृ.—(Empty, draw out all the contents) शून्यीकृ, विरसीकृ, निःसारीकृ, सर्व्वसारं हृ (c. 1. हरति, हर्त्तुं), निःशेषीकृ, निरवशेषीकृ.—(Consume) क्षि (c. 1. क्षयति, c. 5. क्षिणोति or caus. क्षपयति -यितुं), क्षीणीकृ, नश् in caus. (नाशयति -यितुं), क्षयीकृ.—(Weary, fatigue) खिद् in caus. (खेदयति -यितुं), ग्लै in caus. (ग्लपयति -यितुं), परिग्लै, क्लम् in caus. (क्लमयति -यितुं), सद् in caus. (सादयति -यितुं), अवसद्.—(Drink up) आपा (c. 1. -पिबति -पातुं), परिपा.

EXHAUSTED, p. p. (Drained) शोषितः -ता -तं, उच्छोषितः -ता -तं, शुष्कीकृतः -ता -तं.—(Consumed) क्षीणः -णा -णं, परिक्षीणः -णा -णं.—(Fatigued, wearied) श्रान्तः -न्ता -न्तं, परिश्रान्तः -न्ता -न्तं, क्लान्तः -न्ता -न्तं, अवसन्नः -न्ना -न्नं, खिन्नः -न्ना -न्नं, ग्लानः -ना -नं, परिग्लानः -ना -नं, क्लमी -मिनी -मि (न्), आहितक्लमः -मा -मं, क्षतः -ता -तं.—(Expended) व्ययितः -ता -तं; 'exhausted of strength,' गतसत्त्वः -त्त्वा -त्त्वं, गततेजाः -जाः -जः (स्), च्युतोत्साहः -हा -हं.

EXHAUSTION, s. (Act of draining, emptying) शोषणं, उच्छोषणं, शून्यीकरणं, सर्व्वसारहरणं.—(Consumption) क्षयः, परिक्षयः, नाशः, व्ययः.—(Fatigue) श्रान्तिः f., क्लान्तिः f., क्लमः, श्रमः, क्लमथः, अवसादः, ग्लानिः f., खेदः, परिश्रान्तिः f., क्लमित्वं.—(State of being empty) शून्यता -त्वं.

EXHAUSTLESS, a. अक्षयः -या -यं, अक्षयी -यिणी -यि (न्), अनाश्यः -श्या -श्यं.

To EXHIBIT, v. a. दृश् in caus. (दर्शयति -यितुं), प्रदृश्, प्रकाश् in caus. (-काशयति -यितुं), सूच् (c. 10. सूचयति -यितुं), व्यक्तीकृ, प्रकटीकृ, प्रादुष्कृ, आविष्कृ, व्यञ्ज् (c. 7. -अनक्ति -अंक्तुं, c. 10. -अञ्जयति -यितुं), निर्दिश् (c. 6. -दिशति -देष्टुं), प्रदिश्, प्रसृ in caus. (-सारयति -यितुं), आहृ in caus. (-हारयति -यितुं), प्रत्यक्षीकृ.

EXHIBITED, p. p. दर्शितः -ता -तं, प्रकाशितः -ता -तं, व्यक्तीकृतः -ता -तं.

EXHIBITER, s. दर्शकः, दर्शयिता m. (तृ), प्रदर्शकः, प्रकाशकः, निर्देष्टा m. (ष्टृ).

EXHIBITION, s. दर्शनं, प्रदर्शनं, प्रकाशनं, निर्देशः, सूचनं, व्यक्तीकरणं, व्यञ्जनं, व्यक्तिः f., विवरणं, प्रकटीकरणं, प्रादुष्करणं, आविष्करणं, प्रकाशीकरणं; प्रेक्षणं.—(Maintenance in the university) राजविद्यालये वृत्तिः f.

EXHIBITIONER, s. राजविद्यालये वृत्तिभाक् m. (ज्) or वृत्तिभुक् m. (ज्).

To EXHILARATE, v. a. हृष् in caus. (हर्षयति -यितुं), प्रहृष्, परिहृष्, ह्लाद् in caus. (ह्लादयति -यितुं), आह्लाद्, प्रह्लाद्, नन्द् in caus. (नन्दयति -यितुं), अभिनन्द्; मुद् in caus. (मोदयति -यितुं), प्रमुद्, उल्लस् in caus. (-लासयति -यितुं), मद् in caus. (मादयति, मदयति -यितुं), रम् in caus. (रमयति -यितुं).

EXHILARATED, p. p. प्रहर्षितः -ता -तं, आनन्दितः -ता -तं, प्रमुदितः -ता -तं.

EXHILARATING, a. प्रहर्षकः -का -कं, आनन्दकारी -रिणी -रि (न्).

EXHILARATION, s. हर्षः, प्रहर्षः, आनन्दः, प्रह्लादः, आह्लादः, प्रमोदः, उल्लासः, प्रफुल्लता, चित्तप्रसन्नता, मादः, प्रमदः.

To EXHORT, v. a. (Advise) उपदिश् (c. 6. -दिशति -देष्टुं), प्रबुध् (c. 10. -बोधयति -यितुं), प्रदिश् (c. 10. -देशयति -यितुं), मन्त्रणां दा.—(Animate) आश्वस् in caus. (-श्वासयति -यितुं), समाश्वस्.—(Instigate) उत्सह् in caus. (-साहयति -यितुं), प्रोत्सह्, समुत्सह्, चुद् (c. 10. चोदयति -यितुं), प्रचुद्, चेष्ट् in caus. (चेष्टयति -यितुं), प्रवृत् in caus. (-वर्त्तयति -यितुं), प्रयुज् (c. 10. -योजयति -यितुं), उद्युज्, प्रोत्सृ in caus. (-सारयति -यितुं), ईह् in caus. (ईहयति -यितुं).

EXHORTATION, s. उपदेशः, उपदेशवाक्यं, प्रबोधनं, प्रचोदनं, प्रबोधवाक्यं.

मन्त्रणं -णा, प्रवर्त्तकवाक्यं, विनयवाक्यं, प्रोत्साहः -हनं, प्रवर्त्तनं, प्रयोजनं, प्रेरणा.

EXHORTATIVE, EXHORTATORY, *a.* उपदेशकः -का -कं, प्रबोधकः -का -कं, प्रचोदनः -ना -नं.

EXHORTED, *p. p.* प्रबोधितः -ता -तं, प्रचोदितः -ता -तं, उपदिष्टः -ष्टा -ष्टं.

EXHORTER, *s.* उपदेष्टा *m.* (ष्टृ), उपदेशी *m.* (न्), प्रचोदकः, प्रवर्त्तकः, प्रयोजकः, प्रोत्साहकः, उत्साहहेतुकः, प्रेरकः.

EXHUMATION, *s.* शवोत्खननं, मृतशरीरोत्खननं.

To EXHUME, *v. a.* शवं or मृतशरीरम् उत्खन् (c. 1. -खनति -नितुं).

EXHUMED, *p. p.* उत्खातः -ता -तं, प्रोत्खातः -ता -तं, श्मशानबहिष्कृतः -ता -तं.

EXIGENCE, EXIGENCY, *s.* (Urgent need) प्रयोजनं, अवश्यकता, आवश्यकत्वं, कार्य्यवशः,—(Occasion) अवसरः, समयः, प्रस्तावः.—(Distress) आपद् *f.*, विपद् *f.*, विपत्तिः *f.*; 'according to the exigency,' यथाप्रयोजनं, प्रयोजनवत्, अर्थवत्, यथासमयं, यथावसरं, प्रस्तावसदृशं; 'in this exigency,' इह समये.

EXILE, *s.* प्रवासः -सनं, विवासः -सनं, निर्वासनं, विप्रवासः -सनं, उद्वासः -सनं, प्रव्राजनं, गृहभङ्गः, स्वदेशाद् दूरीभावः or निरसनं or निराकरणं, दूरसंस्थानं; 'the person exiled,' प्रवासी *m.* (न्), विप्रवासी *m.*

To EXILE, *v. a.* विवस् in caus. (-वासयति -यितुं), प्रवस्, निर्वस्, विप्रवस्; प्रव्रज् in caus. (-व्राजयति -यितुं), स्वदेशाद् बहिष्कृ or निराकृ or दूरीकृ or निरस् (c. 4. -अस्यति -असितुं) or अपानुद् (c. 6. -नुदति -नोत्तुं) or निःसृ in caus. (-सारयति -यितुं), देशान्तरीकृ.

EXILED, *p. p.* प्रवासितः -ता -तं, विवासितः -ता -तं, स्वदेशदूरीकृतः -ता -तं.

To EXIST, *v. n.* (Be) अस् (c. 2. अस्ति), भू (c. 1. भवति -वितुं), सम्भू, वृत् (c. 1. वर्त्तते -र्त्तितुं), प्रवृत्, विद् in pass. (विद्यते), जन् (c. 4. जायते), उत्पद् (c. 4. -पद्यते -पत्तुं).—(Live) जीव् (c. 1. जीवति -वितुं), प्राण् (c. 2. प्राणिति -तुं, rt. अन्).—(Remain) स्था (c. 1. तिष्ठति, स्थातुं), वृत्, आस् (c. 2. आस्ते).

EXISTENCE, *s.* जीवनं, जीवितं, जीवः -वा, वृत्तिः *f.*, वर्त्तनं, भवः, भावः, सम्भवः, वृत्तिता, अस्ति ind., सत्त्वं, सत्ता, प्राणपरिग्रहः, प्राणधारणं, असुधारणं, निश्वसनप्रश्वसनं, सद्भावः, अवस्था, स्थितिः *f.*

EXISTENT, *a.* जीवी -विनी -वि (न्), जीवन् -वन्ती -वत् (त्), वर्त्तमानः -ना -नं, विद्यमानः -ना -नं, वर्त्तिष्णुः -ष्णुः -ष्णु, भविष्णुः -ष्णुः -ष्णु, ध्रियमाणः -णा -णं, सन् सती सत् (त्).

EXIT, *s.* निष्क्रमः -मणं, निर्गमः, विनिर्गमः, निर्याणं, निष्क्रान्तिः *f.*, अपगमः, अपक्रमः -मणं, अपयानं.—(In dramatic language) निष्क्रामः -मा -मं.

To EXONERATE, *v. a.* (Unload) भाराद् मुच् (c. 6. मुञ्चति, मोक्तुं) or विमुच्; भारम् उत् in caus. (-तारयति -यितुं) or अपनी (c. 1. -नयति -नेतुं), निर्भारं -रां -रं कृ.—(Clear) शुध् (c. 10. शोधयति -यितुं), विशुध्; दोषाद् मुच्, निर्दोषं -षां -षं कृ.

EXONERATED, *p. p.* भारमुक्तः -क्ता -क्तं, दोषमुक्तः -क्ता -क्तं, विशोधितः -ता -तं.

EXORABLE, *a.* वरदः -दा -दं, सुप्रसादितः -ता -तं, सान्त्वनीयः -या -यं.

EXORBITANCE, EXORBITANCY, *s.* अपरिमितत्वं, अमर्य्यादा, मर्य्यादातिक्रमः, निर्मध्यस्थ्यं, अमाध्यस्थ्यं, अमितत्वं, आधिक्यं, आतिरेक्यं, अधिकता, उद्रेकः, वैषम्यं, उत्क्रमः.

EXORBITANT, *a.* अपरिमितः -ता -तं, अमितः -ता -तं, अतिमर्य्यादः -दा -दं, अमर्य्यादः -दा -दं, अतिमात्रः -त्रा -त्रं, अतिरिक्तः -क्ता -क्तं, उद्रिक्तः -क्ता -क्तं, अमध्यस्थः -स्था -स्थं, निर्मध्यस्थः -स्था -स्थं, उत्क्रान्तमर्य्यादः -दा -दं, अधिकः -का -कं, विषमः -मा -मं.

EXORBITANTLY, *adv.* अपरिमितं, अतिमर्य्यादं, अतिमात्रं, विषमं.

To EXORCISE, *v. a.* भूतोपहतजनात् शपनमन्त्रादिना भूतम् अपसृ in caus. (-सारयति -यितुं), अमुकजनं त्यक्त्वा दूरम् अपेहि इति शपथपूर्व्वं भूतं वद् (c. 1. वदति -दितुं).

EXORCISM, *s.* भूतोपहतजनात् शापमन्त्रादिना भूतापसारणं.

EXORCIST, *s.* शपनमन्त्रादिना भूतापसारी *m.* (न्) or भूतापसारकः.

EXORDIUM, *s.* वाक्मुखं, वाक्यारम्भः, आभाषः, परिभाषा, प्रकरणं, प्रस्तावः -वना, उपोद्घातः, प्रारम्भः, वन्दना.

EXOSSATED, EXOSSEOUS, *a.* निरस्थीकृतः -ता -तं, अस्थिरहितः -ता -तं.

EXOTERIC, *a.* बाह्यः -ह्या -ह्यं, साधारणः -णा -णी -णं, सुव्यक्तः -क्ता -क्तं.

EXOTIC, *a.* विदेशीयः -या -यं, विदेशी -शिनी -शि (न्), वैदेशिकः -की -कं, विदेशजः -जा -जं, परदेशी -शिनी -शि (न्), पारदेशिकः -की -कं, अन्यदेशीयः -या -यं, अन्यदेशोद्भवः -वा -वं, बहिर्भवः -वा -वं.

EXOTIC, *s.* (Plant) विदेशीयवृक्षः, अन्यदेशीयवृक्षः.

To EXPAND, *v. a.* विस्तृ in caus. (-स्तारयति -यितुं), वितन् (c. 8. -तनोति -नितुं), व्यातन्, प्रतन्, विततीकृ; विसृ in caus. (-सारयति -यितुं), प्रसृ, विकाश् in caus. (-काशयति -यितुं), प्रकाश्, प्रथ् (c. 10. प्रथयति -यितुं), विवृ (c. 5. -वृणोति -वरितुं -रीतुं, or caus. -वारयति -यितुं), विकस् in caus. (-कासयति -यितुं), वृध् in caus. (वर्धयति -यितुं), प्रवृध्, प्रपञ्च् (c. 10. -पञ्चयति -यितुं), व्यादा (c. 3. -ददाति -दातुं), कठोर (nom. कठोरयति -यितुं); 'expand itself,' व्याप् (c. 5. -आप्नोति -आप्तुं).

To EXPAND, *v. n.* विस्तॄ in pass. (-स्तीर्य्यते), वितन् in pass. (-तन्यते), विततीभू, विजृम्भ् (c. 1. -जृम्भते -म्भितुं), विवृ in caus. pass. (-वार्य्यते), प्रवृध् (c. 1. -वर्धते -र्धितुं), प्रसृप् (c. 1. -सर्पति -सर्प्तुं).—(As flowers) विकस् (c. 1. -कसति -सितुं), प्रविकस्, स्फुट् (c. 6. स्फुटति -टितुं), फुल्ल् (c. 1. फुल्लति -ल्लितुं).

EXPANDED, *p. p.* विततः -ता -तं, प्रविततः -ता -तं, ततः -ता -तं, सन्ततः -ता -तं, विस्तारितः -ता -तं, विस्तीर्णः -र्णा -र्णं, विस्तृतः -ता -तं, विवृतः -ता -तं, विसारितः -ता -तं, प्रसारितः -ता -तं, विसृतः -ता -तं, प्रसृतः -ता -तं, व्याप्तः -प्ता -प्तं, प्रथितः -ता -तं, प्रवृद्धः -द्धा -द्धं, व्यात्तः -त्ता -त्तं, विततीकृतः -ता -तं, विजृम्भितः -ता -तं, उज्जृम्भितः -ता -तं, प्रपञ्चितः -ता -तं.—(As a flower) विकसितः -ता -तं, फुल्लः -ल्ला -ल्लं, उत्फुल्लः -ल्ला -ल्लं, स्फुटितः -ता -तं.

EXPANDING, *a.* or *part.* विकाशी -शिनी -शि (न्) or विकासी, विकस्वरः -रा -रं -स्वरः -रा -रं, विकसन् -सन्ती -सत् (त्), प्रसारी -रिणी -रि (न्).

EXPANSE, *s.* (A spreading, extent) प्रपञ्चः, विकाशः, विस्तारः, प्रसरः, वितानकं, सन्ततिः *f.*, तानं, प्रतानः, पाटः; 'expanse of heaven,' व्योम *n.* (न्), व्योमविस्तृतं, शून्यं; 'of water,' वारिविस्तरः.

EXPANSIBILITY, *a.* विस्तारणीयता, विकाशनीयता, विस्तारक्षमता, व्यापकत्वं.

EXPANSIBLE, *a.* विस्तारयितुं or विततितुं शक्यः -क्या -क्यं, विस्तारणीयः -या -यं, विस्तारक्षमः -मा -मं, विततीकरणीयः -या -यं.

EXPANSION, *s.* विस्तारः, विस्तृतिः *f.*, विस्तरः, विततिः *f.*, प्रततिः *f.*, सन्ततिः *f.*, ततिः *f.*, विकाशः -शनं, प्रकाशः -शनं, प्रसारः -रणं, प्रसरः, परिसरः, विवृतिः *f.*, विचारः, विसरणं, व्यादानं, विसर्पणं, प्रसर्पणं, प्रपञ्चः, व्याप्तिः *f.*, व्यापनं, व्यापकत्वं, विजृम्भणं, विहृतिः *f.*, व्यासः, परिक्षेपः, अतिरिक्तता.

EXPANSIVE, *a.* व्यापकः -का -कं, व्याप्तिमान् -मती -मत् (त्), विस्तारकः -का -कं, प्रसारी -रिणी -रि (न्), विसर्पी -र्पिणी -र्पि (न्), सामानिकः -की -कं.

To EXPATIATE, *v. n.* सुविस्तरं or प्रपञ्चेन वद् (c. 1. वदति -दितुं) or व्याख्या (c. 2. -ख्याति -तुं), वाग्विस्तारं कृ, बहुक्तिं कृ.—(Rove at large) विहृ (c. 1. -हरति -हर्त्तुं), परिभ्रम् (c. 1. -भ्रमति, c. 4. -भ्राम्यति -भ्रमितुं).

To EXPATRIATE, *v. a.* प्रवस् in caus. (-वासयति -यितुं), विवस्, स्वदेशाद् वहिष्कृ or दूरीकृ or निराकृ or निःसृ in caus. (-सारयति -यितुं), देशान्तरीकृ.

EXPATRIATED, *p.p.* प्रवासितः -ता -तं, विवासितः -ता -तं, स्वदेशवहिष्कृतः -ता -तं.

EXPATRIATION, *s.* प्रवासः -सनं, विवासनं, प्रव्राजनं, स्वदेशवहिष्करणं.

To EXPECT, *v. a.* प्रतीक्ष् (c. 1. -ईक्षते -क्षितुं), अपेक्ष्, व्यपेक्ष्, सम्प्रतीक्ष्, उदीक्ष्, निरीक्ष्, प्रतिपाल् (c. 10. -पालयति -यितुं), आकांक्ष् (c. 1. -कांक्षति -क्षितुं), प्रत्याकांक्ष्, उद्दृश् (c. 1. -पश्यति -द्रष्टुं).

To EXPECT, *v. n.* प्रतीक्षां कृ, प्रत्याशां कृ, प्रतीक्षी -क्षिणी -क्षि भू.

EXPECTABLE, *a.* अपेक्ष्यः -क्ष्या -क्ष्यं, अपेक्षणीयः -या -यं, प्रतीक्ष्यः -क्ष्या -क्ष्यं.

EXPECTANT, *a.* प्रतीक्षी -क्षिणी -क्षि (न्), प्रतीक्षकः -का -कं, अपेक्षी -क्षिणी -क्षि (न्), अपेक्षकः -का -कं, व्यपेक्षः -क्षा -क्षं, प्रत्याशी -शिनी -शि (न्), आकांक्षी -क्षिणी -क्षि (न्), सप्रत्याशः -शा -शं, अर्थी -र्थिनी -र्थि (न्).

EXPECTATION, *s.* अपेक्षा, प्रतीक्षा -क्षणं, व्यपेक्षा, उदीक्षणं, सम्प्रतीक्षा, निरीक्षा, प्रत्याशा, आशा, व्यपाश्रयः, अभिनन्दा; 'in expectation,' अपेक्षया.

EXPECTED, *p. p.* अपेक्षितः -ता -तं, प्रतीक्षितः -ता -तं, आकांक्षितः -ता -तं, चित्तकलितः -ता -तं; 'to be expected,' अपेक्षणीयः -या -यं, आकांक्षणीयः -या -यं.

To EXPECTORATE, *v. a.* श्लेष्माणं or श्लेष्मकं निरस् (c. 4. -अस्यति -असितुं) or उत्क्षिप् (c. 6. -क्षिपति -क्षेप्तुं) or उद्गॄ (c. 6. -गिरति -गरितुं -रीतुं) or मुखाद् निःसृ in caus. (-सारयति -यितुं), श्लेष्मनिरसनं कृ, निष्ठीव् (c. 1. -ष्ठीवति -ष्ठेवितुं), उत्कास् (c. 1. -कासते -सितुं).

EXPECTORATED, *p.p.* निष्ठ्यूतः -ता -तं, मुखनिरस्तः -स्ता -स्तं, मुखनिःसारितः -ता -तं.

EXPECTORATION, *s.* श्लेष्मनिरसनं, निष्ठ्यूतिः *f.*, निष्ठेवनं, उत्कासनं, श्लेष्मोत्क्षेपः.

EXPECTORATIVE *a.* श्लेष्मवर्धकः -का -कं, कफवर्धकः -का -कं, कफकरः -री -रं.

EXPEDIENCE, EXPEDIENCY. *s.* युक्तता, युक्तिः *f.*, योग्यता, उपयुक्तत्वं, उपयोगिता, उपयोगः, औचित्यं, उपपत्तिः *f.*, याथातथ्यं, याथार्थ्यं, सफलता, सोपकारत्वं, सार्थत्वं.

EXPEDIENT, *a.* उपयोगी -गिनी -गि (न्), उपयुक्तः -क्ता -क्तं, सोपकारः -रा -रं, अर्थयुक्तः -क्ता -क्तं, अर्थकरः -री -रं, सार्थकः -का -कं, हितः -ता -तं, योग्यः -ग्या -ग्यं, उपकारकः -का -कं, सफलः -ला -लं.

EXPEDIENT, *s.* (Means) उपायः, अभ्युपायः, गतिः *f.*, साधनं, कर्म्मसाधनं, गुणः, अङ्गं, विधानं, उपकरणं, सम्भवः, योगः, उपपत्तिः *f.*, उपक्रमः. The six expedients of defence are सन्धिः, विग्रहः, यानं, आसनं, द्वैधं, आश्रयः. The four expedients for reducing an enemy are भेदः, दण्डः, साम, दानं.

EXPEDIENTLY, *adv.* युक्तं, यथायोग्यं, यथोचितं, सोपकारं, सफलं, स्थाने.

To EXPEDITE, *v. a.* त्वर् in caus. (त्वरयति -यितुं), सन्त्वर्, त्वरितं or सत्वरं कृ or विधा (c. 3. -दधाति -धातुं), or सम्पद् in caus. (-पादयति -यितुं) or साध् (c. 10. साधयति -यितुं) or प्रवृत् in caus. -वर्त्तयति -यितुं), क्षेप (nom. क्षेपयति -यितुं), शीघ्र (nom. शीघ्रयति -यितुं). —(Despatch) सत्वरं प्रस्था in caus. (-स्थापयति -यितुं).

EXPEDITED, *p.p.* त्वरितं कृतः -ता -तं or सम्पादितः -ता -तं, वेगितः -ता -तं.

EXPEDITION, *s.* (Haste, speed) त्वरा, तूर्णिः *f.*, सत्वरता, त्वरणं, शीघ्रता, शैघ्र्यं, क्षिप्रता, द्रुतत्वं, वेगः -गिता, आवेगः, जवः, प्रजवः, लघुता, लाघवं, अविलम्बः, उद्योगः, क्षिप्रकारित्वं, शीघ्रनिर्वाहः, त्वरितगतिः *f.*, शीघ्रगमनं, आशुगमनं.—(March of an army, &c.) प्रस्थानं, प्रयाणं, यानं, गमनं, गतिः *f.*, यात्रा, अभिषेणनं, अभिनिर्याणं.—(Enterprise) प्रवृत्तिः *f.*, उपक्रमः.

EXPEDITIOUS, *a.* त्वरितः -ता -तं, सत्वरः -रा -रं, त्वरावान् -वती -वत् (त्), त्वरान्वितः -ता -तं, शीघ्रः -घ्रा -घ्रं, क्षिप्रः -प्रा -प्रं, शीघ्रकारी -रिणी -रि (न्), क्षिप्रकारी &c., अविलम्बः -म्बा -म्बं -म्बी -म्बिनी -म्बि (न्), अविलम्बितः -ता -तं, अप्रलम्बः -म्बा -म्बं, द्रुतः -ता -तं, लघुः -घुः -घु, वेगी -गिनी -गि (न्), वेगवान् -वती -वत् (त्), जवी -विनी -वि (न्), तूर्णः -र्णा -र्णं, धावकः -का -कं, अदीर्घसूत्रः -त्रा -त्रं, शीघ्रगामी -मिनी -मि (न्), त्वरितगतिः -तिः -ति; 'being expeditious,' शीघ्रायमाणः -णा -णं, त्वरमाणः -णा -णं.

EXPEDITIOUSLY, *adv.* त्वरितं, सत्वरं, क्षिप्रं, शीघ्रं, अविलम्बितं, आशु, वेगतस्.

To EXPEL, *v. a.* (Banish) विवस् in caus. (-वासयति -यितुं), प्रवस्, निर्वस्, विप्रवस्; प्रव्रज् in caus. (-व्राजयति -यितुं), स्वदेशाद् वहिष्कृ or निराकृ or दूरीकृ.—(Drive away, eject, dismiss) निरस् (c. 4. -अस्यति -असितुं), अपास्, उदस्, निःसृ in caus. (-सारयति -यितुं), उत्सृ, अपसृ, निःसरणं कृ, अपानुद् (c. 6. -नुदति -नोत्तुं), निष्कस् in caus. (-कासयति -यितुं), निराकृ, वहिष्कृ, वहिःकृ, दूरीकृ, निष्क्रम् in caus. (क्रामयति -यितुं), उत्क्षिप् (c. 6. -क्षिपति -क्षेप्तुं), प्रतिक्षिप्, निर्धू (c. 5. -धूनोति -धवितुं), भ्रंश् in caus. (भ्रंशयति -यितुं) च्यु in caus. (च्यावयति -यितुं).

EXPELLED, *p. p.* निर्वासितः -ता -तं, विवासितः -ता -तं, प्रवासितः -ता -तं, स्वदेशवहिष्कृतः -ता -तं, निरस्तः -स्ता -स्तं, अपास्तः -स्ता -स्तं, निःसारितः -ता -तं, निष्क्रामितः -ता -तं, वहिष्कृतः -ता -तं, वहिःकृतः -ता -तं, निःकासितः -ता -तं, उदस्तः -स्ता -स्तं, अवकृष्टः -ष्टा -ष्टं, निर्धूतः -ता -तं, अवधूतः -ता -तं, च्यावितः -ता -तं; 'from society,' अपपात्रितः -ता -तं, अवपात्रितः -ता -तं, अपांक्तः -क्ता -क्तं.

EXPELLER, *s.* निर्वासनकारी *m.* (न्), अपसारकः, अपनोदकः, नुदः in comp.

To EXPEND, *v. a.* (Disburse) व्यय् (c. 1. व्ययति, c. 10. व्यययति -यितुं, rt. इ), व्ययीकृ, त्यज् (c. 1. त्यजति, त्यक्तुं), विसृज् (c. 6. -सृजति -स्रष्टुं), विनियुज् (c. 7. -युंक्ते -योक्तुं), अपचि (c. 5. -चिनोति -चेतुं).—(Lay out, consume) उपयुज् (c. 7. -युनक्ति -युंक्ते), प्रयुज्.—(Waste) विक्षिप् (c. 6. -क्षिपति -क्षेप्तुं), क्षि (c. 1. क्षयति, c. 5. क्षिणोति or caus. क्षपयति -यितुं), उपक्षि, क्षयं कृ.

EXPENDED, *p. p.* व्ययितः -ता -तं, व्ययीकृतः -ता -तं, व्ययीभूतः -ता -तं, अपचितः -ता -तं, विसर्ज्जितः -ता -तं, क्षपितः -ता -तं, विनियुक्तः -क्ता -क्तं, प्रयुक्तः -क्ता -क्तं.

EXPENDITURE, EXPENSE, *s.* व्ययः, धनव्ययः, अपव्ययः, व्ययीकरणं, अपचयः, अपचितिः *f.*, विसर्गः, उत्सर्गः -र्ज्जनं, त्यागः, परित्यागः, अर्थोत्सर्गः, अर्थत्यागः, क्षयः, उपक्षयः, संक्षयः, अवक्षयः, मोक्षणं, क्षेपः, विनियोगः, अपहारः, व्ययः; 'income and expenditure,' आयव्ययौ.

EXPENSELESS, *a.* निर्मूल्यः -ल्या -ल्यं, निर्व्ययः -या -यं, अल्पमूल्यः -ल्या -ल्यं.

EXPENSIVE, *a.* (Costly) बहुमूल्यः -ल्या -ल्यं, बहुव्ययः -या -यं, बहुधनव्ययेन or बहुमूल्येन क्रेयः -या -यं or साध्यः -ध्या -ध्यं, महार्घः -र्घा -र्घं, दुर्मूल्यः -ल्या -ल्यं, महार्हः -र्हा -र्हं, महाधनः -ना -नं, अर्घ्यः -र्घ्या -र्घ्यं.—(Extravagant) व्ययी -यिनी -यि (न्), अतिव्ययी &c., अपरिमितव्ययी &c., व्ययशीलः -ला -लं, अर्थनाशी -शिनी -शि (न्), अपचेता -त्री -तृ (तृ).

EXPENSIVELY, *adv.* बहुधनव्ययेन, बहुमूल्येन, बहुव्ययपूर्व्वं.

EXPENSIVENESS, *s.* बहुमूल्यता, दुर्मूल्यता, महार्घता, माहार्घ्यं.—(Extravagance) अतिव्ययः, महाव्ययः, बहुव्ययः, अर्थदूषणं.

EXPERIENCE, *s.* (Trial) परीक्षा -क्षणं, अनुभवः.—(Use, practice) अभ्यासः, पूर्व्वाभ्यासः, अभ्यसनं, उपभोगः, भोगः, भुक्तिः *f.*, आचारः.—

(Knowledge derived from trials) अनुभूतिः *f.*, अनुभवः, वेदनं, संवेदः, वेदित्वं, बोधः, प्रतीतिः *f.* दर्शनं, ऊहा, परिपाकः, पाकः, परिपक्कता; 'by experience,' अनुभवेन, अनुभवात्, कार्य्यतस्; 'one's own experience,' स्वानुभवः; 'universal experience,' सर्व्वानुभूतिः *f.*

To EXPERIENCE, *v. a.* (Suffer, feel) अनुभू (c. 1. -भवति -वितुं), भुज् (c. 7. भुंक्ते, भोक्तुं), उपभुज्, अश् (c. 5. अश्नुते, अशितुं), उपाश्, समश्, उपागम् (c. 1. -गच्छति -गन्तुं), उपगम्, प्राप् (c. 5. -आप्नोति -आप्तुं), विद् (c. 10. वेदयते -यितुं), आसद् (c. 10. -सादयति -यितुं), दृश् (c. 1. पश्यति, द्रष्टुं).—(Make trial of) परीक्ष् (c. 1. -ईक्षते -क्षितुं), ; 'one who has not experienced a battle,' अनासादितविग्रहः.

EXPERIENCED, *p. p.* (Suffered) अनुभूतः -ता -तं, उपागतः -ता -तं, उपगतः -ता -तं, उपभुक्तः -क्ता -क्तं, अनुभूयमानः -ना -नं.—(Skilful by reason of much observation) बहुदृष्टः -ष्टा -ष्टं, बहुदृश्वा -श्वा -श्व (न्), बहुदर्शी -र्शिनी -र्शि (न्), परिपक्कबुद्धिः -द्धिः -द्धि, अविपक्कबुद्धिः &c., पक्कः -क्का -क्कं, कोविदः -दा -दं, व्युत्पन्नः -न्ना -न्नं, अनुभवी- विनी -वि (न्), ऊहिवानः -ना -नं.

EXPERIMENT, *s.* परीक्षा -क्षणं, परीक्षितं, ऊहिः *f.*, अनुभूतिः *f.*, अनुभवः.

To EXPERIMENT, *v. a.* परीक्ष् (c. 1. -ईक्षते -क्षितुं), जिज्ञा in des. (जिज्ञासते -सितुं), अनुभू.

EXPERIMENTAL, *a.* परीक्षकः -का -कं, अनुभवी -विनी -वि (न्).—(Derived from experience) परीक्षालब्धः -ब्धा -ब्धं, परीक्षामूलः -ला -लं, अनुभूतिमूलः -ला -लं.

EXPERIMENTALLY, *adv.* अनुभवेन -वात्, स्वानुभवेन, परीक्षापूर्व्वं, कार्य्यतस्.

EXPERIMENTER, EXPERIMENTALIST, *s.* परीक्षकः, परीक्षणकारी *m.* (न्), अनुभावी *m.* (न्).

EXPERT, *a.* कुशलः -ला -लं, निपुणः -णा -णं, दक्षः -क्षा -क्षं, विज्ञः -ज्ञा -ज्ञं, अभिज्ञः -ज्ञा -ज्ञं, प्रवीणः -णा -णं, चतुरः -रा -रं, पक्कः -क्का -क्कं, परिपक्कः -क्का -क्कं, सुप्रयोगवान् -वती -वत् (त्), पटुः -टुः -ट्वी -टु, विचक्षणः -णा -णं, कृती -तिनी -ति (न्), पेशलः -ला -लं, युक्तिमान् -मती -मत् (त्), विशारदः -दा -दं, विदग्धः -ग्धा -ग्धं, चञ्चुरः -रा -रं; 'expert in arms,' शस्त्रकुशलः -ला -लं, शस्त्रविद् *m. f. n.*, शस्त्रज्ञः -ज्ञा -ज्ञं.

EXPERTLY, *adv.* निपुणं, चतुरं, सुप्रयोगेण, युक्त्या, सपाटवं, विज्ञवत्.

EXPERTNESS, *s.* दक्षता, दाक्ष्यं, चातुर्य्यं, चतुरता, नैपुण्यं, निपुणता, पटुत्वं, पाटवं, कौशल्यं, प्रवीणता, प्रावीण्यं, युक्तिः *f.*, सुप्रयोगः -गता, विज्ञता, अभिज्ञता, वैचक्षण्यं, योग्यता, विदग्धता, वैदग्ध्यं; 'of hand,' हस्तकौशल्यं, हस्तलाघवं, करदक्षता; 'of hands, feet, &c.,' हस्तपादादिक्षिप्रता.

EXPIABLE, *a.* शोधनीयः -या -यं, शोध्यः -ध्या -ध्यं, निष्करणीयः -या -यं, मोचनीयः -या -यं, मार्ज्जनीयः -या -यं, क्षमणीयः -या -यं, क्षन्तव्यः -व्या -व्यं, प्रायश्चेतः -त्या -त्यं.

To EXPIATE, *v. a.* पापप्रायश्चित्तं कृ, पापनिष्कृतिं कृ, पापं निष्कृ or अपनुद् (c. 6. -नुदति -नोत्तुं) or शम् (c. 10. शमयति -यितुं) or हृ (c. 1. हरति, हर्त्तुं) or मृज् (c. 2. मार्ष्टि -र्ष्टुं), प्रायश्चित्तेन पापात् शुध् (c. 10. शोधयति -यितुं) or परिशुध् or विशुध् or मुच् (c. 6. मुञ्चति, मोक्तुं) or पू (c. 9. पुनाति, पवितुं) or पवित्रीकृ, पापकर्म्म साध् (c. 10. साधयति -यितुं); 'it is expiated,' प्रायश्चित्तीयते.

EXPIATED, *p. p.* निष्कृतः -ता -तं, शोधितः -ता -तं, मृष्टः -ष्टा -ष्टं, निर्णिक्तः -क्ता -क्तं, पवित्रीकृतः -ता -तं, पावितः -ता -तं, परिपूतः -ता -तं, शान्तः -न्ता -न्तं.

EXPIATION, *s.* प्रायश्चित्तं, निष्कृतिः *f.*, शुद्धिः *f.*, शोधनं, मुक्तिः *f.*, मोचनं, शान्तिः *f.*, उपशान्तिः *f.*, प्रतीकारः, पावनं, अपनुत्तिः *f.*, अपनोदनं, पापशोधनं, पापविशुद्धिः *f.*, पापशान्तिः *f.*, पापनिर्हरणं, अघनाशनं, पापापनुत्तिः *f.*, पापप्रक्षालनं, पापनिर्णेजनं, पापमार्जना, निमित्तधर्म्मः.

EXPIATORY, *a.* शोधकः -का -कं, पावकः -का -कं, पापघ्नः -घ्नी -घ्नं, अघमर्षणः -णी -णं, अघनाशकः -का -कं, अघनाशनः -ना -नं, शमकः -का -कं, शामिकः -की -कं.

EXPIRATION, *s.* (Breathing out) निश्वासः, निःश्वसनं, निःश्वासः, प्रश्वासः, प्राणोद्गारः, प्राणोत्क्षेपः, प्राणत्यागः.—(Exhalation) उद्गारः.—(Cessation, close) अवसानं, अन्तः, निर्वृत्तिः *f.*, विरतिः *f.*, उपरमः, समाप्तिः *f.*, शेषः, पर्य्यवसानं, अत्ययः, क्षयः.

To EXPIRE, *v. a.* (Breathe out) निःश्वस् (c. 2. -श्वसिति -तुं), निश्वस्, प्रश्वस्, प्राणं or श्वासम् उत्क्षिप् (c. 6. -क्षिपति -क्षेप्तुं) or उद्गम् in caus. (-गमयति -यितुं) or निर्गम् or उदीर् (c. 10. -ईरयति -यितुं).—(Exhale) उद्गॄ (c. 6. -गिरति -गरितुं -रीतुं), प्रवा (c. 2. -वाति -तुं), प्रमुच् (c. 6. -मुञ्चति -मोक्तुं).

To EXPIRE, *v. n.* (Breathe the last, die) प्राणत्यागं कृ, प्राणान् हा (c. 3. जहाति, हातुं) or त्यज् (c. 1. त्यजति, त्यक्तुं), श्वासत्यागं कृ, शेषप्राणं कृ, मृ (c. 6. म्रियते, मर्त्तुं), जीवनोत्सर्गं कृ, पञ्चत्वं गम् (c. 1. गच्छति, गन्तुं), नश् (c. 4. नश्यति, नशितुं).—(Close, end) निवृत् (c. 1. -वर्त्तते -र्त्तितुं), निर्वृत्, विरम् (c. 1. -रमति -रन्तुं), उपरम्, समाप् in pass. (-आप्यते), विगम्, अपया (c. 2. -याति -तुं), अवसद् (c. 1. -सीदति -सत्तुं).

EXPIRED, *p. p.* गतप्राणः -णा -णं, गतासुः -सुः -सु, उत्क्रान्तासुः -सुः -सु, परासुः -सुः -सु, प्राप्तपञ्चत्वः -त्वा -त्वं, प्रेतः -ता -तं, परेतः -ता -तं, संस्थितः -ता -तं.

EXPIRING, *part.* and *a.* कण्ठगतप्राणः -णा -णं, म्रियमाणः -णा -णं, मुमूर्षुः -र्षुः -र्षु, आसन्नमृत्युः -त्युः -त्यु.—(As a lamp) निर्वास्यन् -स्यन्ती -स्यत् (त्).

To EXPLAIN, *v. a.* व्याख्या (c. 2. -ख्याति -तुं), व्यक्तीकृ, स्पष्टीकृ, व्याकृ, विवृ (c. 5. -वृणोति -वरितुं -रीतुं), प्रकाश् (c. 10. -काशयति -यितुं), स्पष्ट (nom. स्पष्टयति -यितुं), व्याहृ (c. 1. -हरति -हर्त्तुं), समुद्दिश् (c. 6. -दिशति -देष्टुं), उद्दिश्, प्रबुध् (c. 10. -बोधयति -यितुं), सम्बुध्, विब्रू (c. 2. -ब्रवीति), प्रवच् (c. 2. -वक्ति -क्तुं), प्रवद् (c. 1. -वदति -दितुं), व्याचक्ष् (c. 2. -चष्टे), निरूप् (c. 10. -रूपयति -यितुं), परिशुध् (c. 10. -शोधयति -यितुं), वर्ण् (c. 10. वर्णयति -यितुं), कथ् (c. 10. कथयति -यितुं), प्रदृश् in caus. (-दर्शयति -यितुं), प्रकॄत् (c. 10. -कीर्त्तयति -यितुं), विवरणं कृ.

EXPLAINABLE, *a.* व्याख्येयः -या -यं, उद्देश्यः -श्या -श्यं, प्रवक्तव्यः -व्या -व्यं.

EXPLAINED, *p. p.* व्याख्यातः -ता -तं, व्याकृतः -ता -तं, स्पष्टीकृतः -ता -तं, विवृतः -ता -तं, प्रकाशितः -ता -तं, निरूपितः -ता -तं, द्योतितः -ता -तं, वर्णितः -ता -तं.

EXPLAINER, *s.* व्याख्याता *m.* (तृ), प्रवक्ता *m.* (क्तृ), प्रकाशकः, उद्देशकः.

EXPLANATION, *s.* व्याख्या -ख्यानं, विवृतिः *f.*, विवरणं, व्याकरणं, व्याकृतिः *f.*, स्पष्टीकरणं, प्रकाशनं, उद्देशः, समुद्देशः, निरूपणं, समाधानं.

EXPLANATORY, *a.* वाचकः -का -कं, उद्देशकः -का -कं, समुद्देशकः -का -कं, व्याख्याकारी -रिणी -रि (न्), विवरणकारी &c., अर्थकथकः -का -कं, प्रकाशकः -का -कं.

EXPLETIVE, *s.* पादपूरणं, उपाक्षरं, वाक्यालङ्कारः, पादपूरकः शब्दः.

EXPLICABLE, *a.* See EXPLAINABLE.

To EXPLICATE, *v. a.* विवृ (c. 5. -वृणोति -वरितुं -रीतुं), व्याख्या (c. 2. -ख्याति -तुं), प्रकटीकृ.

EXPLICATION, *s.* विवृतिः *f.*, विवरणं, व्याख्या -ख्यानं, व्यक्तीकरणं, प्रकटीकरणं.

EXPLICATIVE, *a.* विवरणार्थकः -का -कं, प्रकाशकः -का -कं, वाचकः -का -कं.

EXPLICIT, *s.* व्यक्तः -क्ता -क्तं, सुव्यक्तः -क्ता -क्तं, स्पष्टः -ष्टा -ष्टं, सुस्पष्टः -ष्टा -ष्टं, सुप्रकाशः -शा -शं, स्पष्टार्थः -र्था -र्थं, भिन्नार्थः -र्था -र्थं, स्फुटः -टा -टं, अवक्रः -क्रा -क्रं.

EXPLICITLY, *adv.* व्यक्तं, सुव्यक्तं, स्पष्टं, सुस्पष्टं, सुप्रकाशं, स्पष्टार्थं, भिन्नार्थं, स्फुटं; 'explicitly shews,' स्पष्टयति.

EXPLICITNESS, *s.* व्यक्तत्वं -ता, सुव्यक्तता, स्पष्टता, सुस्पष्टता, सुप्रकाशता, स्पष्टार्थत्वं, भिन्नार्थत्वं, अवक्रता, वाचकता.

To EXPLODE, *v. n.* अकस्मादग्निपाताद्विबलाद् महाशब्देन or महाशब्दपूर्व्वं विभिद् in pass. (-भिद्यते) or विदृ in pass. (-दीर्य्यते) or स्फुट् (c. 6. स्फुटति -टितुं) or विदल् (c. 1. -दलति -लितुं).

To EXPLODE, *v. a.* (Decry with noise, shew disapprobation) उच्चैःस्वरेण निन्द् (c. 1. निन्दति -न्दितुं), कर्कशशब्देन अप्रसादं or अस्वीकारं सूच् (c. 10. सूचयति -यितुं) or अवज्ञास्पदं कृ.

EXPLODED, *p. p.* (Burst) महाशब्देन विदीर्णः -र्णा -र्णं or विभिन्नः -न्ना -न्नं or स्फुटितः -ता -तं, निरस्तः -स्ता -स्तं.—(Brought into dispute) अधुनातनव्यवहारविरुद्धः -द्धा -द्धं, नूतनाचारविरुद्धः -द्धा -द्धं, अवज्ञातः -ता -तं, परिभूतः -ता -तं.

EXPLOIT, *s.* कर्म्म *n.* (न्), महाकर्म्म *n.*, चेष्टितं, चेष्टा, विचेष्टितं, चरित्रं, प्रवृत्तिः *f.*, अद्भुतकर्म्म *n.*, आश्चर्य्यकर्म्म *n.*

EXPLORATION, *s.* अन्वेषणा -णं, पर्य्येषणं, अनुसन्धानं, जिज्ञासा, अनुसरणं, परीक्षा -क्षणं, निरूपणं, समीक्षणं, संवीक्षणं, मार्गः -र्गणं, अनुयोगः, शोधनं.

To EXPLORE, *v. a.* अन्विष् (c. 4. -इष्यति, c. 6. -इच्छति -एषितुं -एष्टुं), अनुसन्धा (c. 3. -दधाति -धातुं), निरूप् (c. 10. -रूपयति -यितुं), ज्ञा in des. (जिज्ञासते -सितुं), मार्ग् (c. 1. मार्गति, c. 10. मार्गयति -यितुं), मृग् (c. 10. मृगयते -ति -यितुं), परीक्ष् (c. 1. -ईक्षते -क्षितुं), निरीक्ष्, संवीक्ष्.

EXPLORED, *p. p.* अन्वेषितः -ता -तं, अन्विष्टः -ष्टा -ष्टं, निरूपितः -ता -तं.

EXPLORER, *s.* अन्वेष्टा *m.* (ष्टृ), अन्वेषी *m.* (न्), अनुसन्धाता *m.* (तृ), परीक्षकः.

EXPLOSION, *s.* महाशब्दपूर्व्वं विदारणं or स्फोटनं or स्फुटनं or अकस्माद् विभङ्गः, समहाशब्दो विदारः, आकस्मिकविदारशब्दः, आकस्मिकविभङ्गशब्दः, ध्माशब्दः.

EXPLOSIVE, *a.* आकस्मिकविदारणकारी -रिणी -रि (न्), महाशब्दपूर्व्वविभङ्गकारी &c., ध्माशब्दकारी &c,. विदारकः -का -कं, शीघ्रदाह्यः -ह्या -ह्यं.

To EXPORT, *v. a.* (Goods to a foreign country) वाणिज्यद्रव्याणि or वस्तूनि विदेशे or देशान्तरे or वहिर्देशे वह् (c. 1. वहति, वोढुं or caus. वाहयति -यितुं) or आवह् or उपवह् or निर्विवह् or तॄ in caus. (तारयति -यितुं) or सन्तॄ in caus. or आनी (c. 1. -नयति -नेतुं or caus. -नाययति -यितुं) or उपनी or प्रेर् (c. 10. -ईरयति -यितुं).

EXPORTABLE, *a.* देशान्तरे or वहिर्देशे वाह्यः -ह्या -ह्यं or उपवाह्यः &c.

EXPORTATION, *s.* देशान्तरे or वहिर्देशे वाहनं or उपवाहनं or अभिवाहनं or तारणं or प्रेरणं.

EXPORTED, *p. p.* विदेशे or वहिर्देशे वाहितः -ता -तं or तारितः -ता -तं or सन्तारितः -ता -तं or प्रेरितः -ता -तं, देशान्तरीकृतः -ता -तं.

EXPORTS, *s. pl.* विदेशे or वहिर्देशे वाह्यानि वाणिज्यद्रव्याणि or वस्तूनि.

To EXPOSE, *v. a.* (Uncover) विवृ (c. 5. -वृणोति -णुते -वरितुं -रीतुं), अपवृ, अपावृ, उच्छद् (c. 10. -छादयति -यितुं).—(Make public) प्रकाश् (c. 10. -काशयति -यितुं), विकाश्, प्रकाशीकृ, प्रकटीकृ, व्यक्तीकृ, प्रत्यक्षीकृ, प्रादुष्कृ, आविष्कृ.—(Expose to view) प्रत्यक्षीकृ, सर्व्वदृग्गोचरं -रां -रं कृ.—(For sale) पण्यवीथिकायां प्रसृ in caus. (-सारयति -यितुं).—(Make liable) अधीनं -नां -नं कृ.—(To the air) वायुव्याप्यं -प्यां -प्यं कृ.—(To the sun) सूर्य्यव्याप्यं -प्यां -प्यं कृ. (To contempt, ridicule) अवमानास्पदं कृ, अवहासस्थानं कृ, हास्यं -स्यां -स्यं कृ.—(To danger) भयस्थानं कृ, शङ्कास्पदं कृ; 'to expose the failings of others,' परच्छिद्राणि विवृ or अपवृ.

EXPOSED, *p. p.* विवृतः -ता -तं, अपावृतः -ता -तं, अनावृतः -ता -तं, अनाच्छादितः -ता -तं, प्रकाशीकृतः -ता -तं, प्रकटीकृतः -ता -तं, प्रसारितः -ता -तं; 'caught out in a crime,' दृष्टदोषः -षा -षं; 'exposed to the weather,' अभावकाशिकः -की -कं; 'exposed for sale,' क्रये प्रसारितः -ता -तं, क्रय्यः -य्या -य्यं, पण्यः -ण्या -ण्यं, पण्यवीथिकायां प्रसारितः -ता -तं.

EXPOSITION, *s.* विवृतिः *f.*, विवरणं, व्याख्या -ख्यानं, स्पष्टीकरणं, प्रकाशनं, व्याकृतिः *f.*, व्याकरणं, व्यक्तीकरणं, चूर्णकं.

EXPOSITOR, *s.* व्याख्याता *m.* (तृ), प्रकाशकः, प्रवक्ता *m.* (क्तृ), अर्थपरिशोधकः, अर्थविज्ञापकः, चूर्णिकृत् *m.*

EXPOSITORY, *a.* वाचकः -का -कं, प्रकाशकः -का -कं, उद्देशकः -का -कं.

To EXPOSTULATE, *v. a.* आपत्तिं कृ, अन्यायेन or असम्यक् or अनुचितं करोषि or अन्याय्यकर्म्म त्वया कृतम् इत्यादिनिन्दावाक्यैर् अकृत्यकारिणं कञ्चिज्जनं निवृ in caus. (-वारयति -यितुं), मैवं कार्षीः or मैवं कृथाः or नैतत् त्वया करणीयम् इत्यादिवाक्यैर् अन्यायकारिणा सह विचर् (c. 10. -चारयति -यितुं) or अन्याय्यकर्म्मणः कञ्चिज्जनं निवृत् in caus. (-वर्त्तयति -यितुं), प्रत्यादिश् (c. 6. -दिशति -देष्टुं).

EXPOSTULATION, *s.* आपत्तिः *f.*, अन्याय्यकर्म्म or असम्यक्कर्म्म or अयुक्तकर्म्म करोषि or कुकर्म्म त्वया कृतम् इत्यादिनिन्दार्थकं वाक्यं or इत्यादिवाक्यैर् अन्यायकारिणा सह विचारणं, निवर्त्तनार्थं वाक्यं, निषेधार्थकं प्रबोधवाक्यं, प्रतिवादः, प्रत्यादेशः.

EXPOSTULATORY, *a.* आपत्तिमयः -यी -यं, निन्दामयः -यी -यं, प्रत्यादेशकः -का -कं.

EXPOSURE, *s.* विवृतिः *f.*, विवरणं, प्रकाशनं, विकाशनं, व्यक्तीकरणं, प्रकटीकरणं, प्रत्यक्षीकरणं, दृग्गोचरीकरणं, प्रसारणं; 'to the air,' वायुव्याप्यकत्वं.

To EXPOUND, *v. a.* व्याख्या (c. 2. -ख्याति -तुं), व्याकृ, प्रवद् (c. 1. -वदति -दितुं), प्रवच् (c. 2. -वक्ति -क्तुं), स्पष्टीकृ, व्याहृ (c. 1. -हरति -हर्त्तुं), व्याचक्ष् (c. 2. -चष्टे), विवृ (c. 5. -वृणोति -वरितुं -रीतुं), प्रकाश् (c. 10. -काशयति -यितुं), निरूप् (c. 10. -रूपयति -यितुं), विब्रू (c. 2. -ब्रवीति).

EXPOUNDED, *p. p.* व्याख्यातः -ता -तं, व्याकृतः -ता -तं, विवृतः -ता -तं, प्रकाशितः -ता -तं, निरूपितः -ता -तं, स्पष्टीकृतः -ता -तं, व्याहृतः -ता -तं.

EXPOUNDER, *s.* व्याख्याता *m.* (तृ), प्रवक्ता *m.* (क्तृ), वक्ता *m.*, वादी *m.* (न्), प्रकाशकः, वाचकः, अर्थशोधकः; 'of the law,' धर्म्मप्रवक्ता *m.*

To EXPRESS, *v. a.* (Press out) निष्पीड् (c. 10. -पीडयति -यितुं), निपीड्, निष्कृष् (c. 1. -कर्षति -क्रष्टुं), निर्हृ (c. 1. -हरति -हर्त्तुं), निर्दुह् (c. 2. -दोग्धि -ग्धुं).—(Utter, declare) वद् (c. 1. वदति -दितुं), कथ् (c. 10. कथयति -यितुं), उदाहृ (c. 1. -हरति -हर्त्तुं), व्याहृ, उच्चर् (c. 10. -चारयति -यितुं), ज्ञा in caus. (ज्ञापयति -यितुं), विज्ञा, आविद् in caus. (-वेदयति -यितुं), कृत् (c. 10. कीर्त्तयति -यितुं), प्रकाश् (c. 10. -काशयति -यितुं), सूच् (c. 10. सूचयति -यितुं), बुध् (c. 10. बोधयति -यितुं).—(Represent, exhibit) सूच्, दृश् in caus. (दर्शयति -यितुं); 'by gestures, &c.,' नट् (c. 10. नाटयति -यितुं), अभिनी (c. 10. -नयति -नेतुं), रूप् (c. 10. रूपयति -यितुं); 'they express love,' शृङ्गारभावं नाटयन्ति; 'he expresses delight,' हर्षं नाटयति; 'in painting, &c.,' प्रतिरूपं कृ, प्रतिमूर्त्तिं कृ, प्रतिमानं कृ.—(Indicate) सूच्, उद्दिश् (c. 6. -दिशति -देष्टुं), निर्दिश्, लक्ष् (c. 10. लक्षयति -यितुं).

EXPRESS, *a.* (Clear) व्यक्तः -क्ता -क्तं, सुव्यक्तः -क्ता -क्तं, स्पष्टः -ष्टा -ष्टं, स्पष्टार्थः -र्था -र्थं, अवक्रः -क्रा -क्रं, अवक्रार्थः -र्था -र्थं, भिन्नार्थः -र्था -र्थं, असन्दिग्धार्थः -र्था -र्थं; 'in express terms,' स्पष्टार्थतस्.

EXPRESS, *s.* (Courier) वेगी *m.* (न्), प्रजवी *m.* (न्), जवी *m.*, तरस्वी *m.* (न्), उद्वेगः, त्वरितः, जवनः, जवः, धावकः, अध्वगः, वार्त्ताहरः.

EXPRESSED, *p. p.* (In words) उक्तः -क्ता -क्तं, कथितः -ता -तं, आवेदितः -ता -तं, अभिहितः -ता -तं.—(Shewn, indicated) दर्शितः -ता -तं,

सूचितः -ता -तं.

Expressible, *a.* कथनीयः -या -यं, कथ्यः -थ्या -थ्यं, निर्वचनीयः -या -यं, व्याख्येयः -या -यं.—(To be pressed out) निष्कर्षणीयः -या -यं, निर्हरणीयः -या -यं.

Expression, *s.* (Declaration) वादः, कथनं, ज्ञापनं, विज्ञापनं, ख्यापनं, आवेदनं, अभिधानं, बोधनं, कीर्त्तनं, प्रवचनं.—(Utterance) उदाहरणं, व्याहरणं, उच्चारणं.—(Phrase, word) उक्तिः *f.*, वाक्यं, वचनं, उक्तं, वाक् *f.* (च्), शब्दः, अभिधेयं, वचः *n.* (स्), पदं; 'authorized expression,' आप्तोक्तिः.—(Style, manner) रीतिः *f.*, मार्गः, व्यापारः; 'style of expression,' वाग्व्यापारः.—(Feeling, tone) रसः.

Expressive, *a.* वाचकः, -का -कं, सूचकः -का -कं, उद्बोधकः -का -कं, अभिप्रायिकः -का -कं, उद्देशकः -का -कं, अर्थः -र्था -र्थं or अर्थकः -का -कं in comp.; as, 'expressive of tenderness,' करुणार्थकः -का -कं.—(Full of meaning) पूर्णार्थः -र्था -र्थं, अर्थवान् -वती -वत् (त्), सार्थः -र्था -र्थं, गुर्वर्थः -र्था -र्थं, साकूतः -ता -तं.

Expressively, *adv.* पूर्णार्थतस्, व्यक्तार्थतस्, सार्थं, साकूतं, सगौरवं.

Expressiveness, *s.* वाचकत्वं, पूर्णार्थत्वं, अर्थवत्त्वं, सार्थत्वं, गौरवं.

Expressly, *adv.* व्यक्तं, सुव्यक्तं, सुस्पष्टं, स्पष्टार्थतस्, व्यक्तार्थतस्, अवक्रं, असन्दिग्धार्थतस्.

To **Exprobate**, *v. a.* निन्द् (c. 1. निन्दति -न्दितुं), गर्ह् (c. 1. गर्हते -र्हितुं), विगर्ह्, कुत्स् (c. 10. कुत्सयति -यितुं), उपालभ् (c. 1. -लभते -लब्धुं), तिरस्कृ.

Exprobation, *s.* निन्दा, गर्हा, तिरस्कारः, दुर्वाक्यं, भर्त्सनवाक्यं, उपक्रोशः.

To **Expugn**, *v. a.* दुर्गं लङ्घ् (c. 10. लङ्घयति -यितुं), विजि (c. 1. -जयते -ति -जेतुं).

Expugnable, *a.* लङ्घनीयः -या -यं, आक्रमणीयः -या -यं, विजेतव्यः -व्या -व्यं.

Expugnation, *s.* दुर्गलङ्घनं, दुर्गाक्रमणं, विजयः, जयः.

Expulsion, *s.* अपसारणं, निःसारणं, निरसनं, निराकरणं, अपनोदः -दनं, निर्वासनं, विवासनं, प्रवासनं, प्रव्राजनं, बहिष्करणं, निष्कासनं, निःकासनं, प्रयापणं.—(The state) प्रवासः, विवासः.

Expulsive, *a.* अपनोदनः -ना -नं, निरसनः -ना -नं, निराकरिष्णुः -ष्णुः -ष्णु.

Expunction, *s.* लोपः, विलोपः -पनं, उच्छेदः, अपमार्जना, व्यामर्दः, विनाशः.

To **Expunge**, *v. a.* लुप् (c. 6. लुम्पति, लोप्तुं, c. 10. लोपयति -यितुं), विलुप्, उच्छिद् (c. 7. -छिनत्ति -छेत्तुं), व्यामृज् (c. 2. -मार्ष्टि -र्ष्टुं), अपमृज्, उन्मृज्, व्यामृश् (c. 6. -मृशति -म्रष्टुं), विनश् in caus. (-नाशयति -यितुं), उद्धृ (c. 1. -हरति -हर्त्तुं).

Expunged, *p. p.* उच्छिन्नः -न्ना -न्नं, लुप्तः -प्ता -प्तं, व्यामृष्टः -ष्टा -ष्टं, उद्धृतः -ता -तं.

To **Expurgate**, *v. a.* शुध् (c. 10. शोधयति -यितुं), विशुध्, पू (c. 9. पुनाति -नीते, पवितुं), विपू, परिपू, निर्म्मलीकृ, मलं हृ (c. 1. हरति, हर्त्तुं), पवित्रीकृ, शुचीकृ, परिष्कृ.

Expurgated, *p. p.* विशोधितः -ता -तं, पावितः -ता -तं, पवित्रीकृतः -ता -तं.

Expurgation, *s.* शोधनं, विशोधनं, पावनं, पवित्रीकरणं, मलापकर्षणं, निर्म्मलीकरणं, परिष्करणं.

Expurgatory, *a.* शोधकः -का -कं, पावकः -का -कं, पावनः -ना -नं.

Exquisite, *a.* (Choice) उत्तमः -मा -मं, शिष्टः -ष्टा -ष्टं, विशिष्टः -ष्टा -ष्टं, उत्कृष्टः -ष्टा -ष्टं.—(Nice, accurate) सूक्ष्मः -क्ष्मा -क्ष्मं, समञ्जसः -सा -सं, शुद्धः -द्धा -द्धं.—(Highest) परमः -मा -मं, उत्तमः -मा -मं; 'exquisite delight,' परमानन्दः, परमहर्षः, रोमहर्षणं, पुलकः; 'causing exquisite pleasure,' परमानन्ददः -दा -दं, हृषितस्रुट् *m. f. n.*—(Keen) तीक्ष्णः -क्ष्णा -क्ष्णं, तीव्रः -व्रा -व्रं; 'exquisite pain,' तीव्रवेदना.

Exquisitely, *adv.* (Nicely) सूक्ष्मं, सूक्ष्मत्वेन, ससौक्ष्म्यं, अञ्जसा.—(In a high degree) परमं, उत्तमं; 'exquisitely delighted,' परमहृष्टः -ष्टा -ष्टं, पुलकितः -ता -तं, हर्षरोमाञ्चितः -ता -तं.

Exquisiteness, *s.* (Nicety) सूक्ष्मता, सौक्ष्म्यं, सामञ्जस्यं.—(Keenness) तीक्ष्णता, तैक्ष्ण्यं, तीव्रता.—(Choiceness) उत्तमता, उत्कृष्टता.

To **Exsiccate**, *v. a.* शुष् in caus. (शोषयति -यितुं), उच्छुष्, विशुष्.

Exsiccation, *s.* शोषः -षणं, उच्छोषणं, परिशोषः, विशोषणं, नीरसीकरणं.

Exsiccant, **exsiccative**, *a.* शोषकः -का -कं, उच्छोषणः -णी -णं, विशोषणः -णी -णं.

Exspuition, *s.* निष्ठीवः -वनं, निष्ठेवनं, श्लेष्मनिरसनं, उद्गिरणं.

Extant, *a.* (Protruding) बहिःस्थः -स्था -स्थं, बहिर्भूतः -ता -तं.—(In existence) विद्यमानः -ना -नं, वर्त्तमानः -ना -नं, प्रकाशः -शा -शं.

Extasy, **extatic**. *See* **Ecstacy**, **ecstatic**.

Extemporaneous, **extemporary**, *a.* अचिन्तापूर्व्वः -र्व्वा -र्व्वं, अपूर्व्वचिन्तः -न्ता -न्तं, अचिन्तितः -ता -तं, अयत्नपूर्व्वः -र्व्वा -र्व्वं, अयत्नकृतः -ता -तं, अयत्नभूतः -ता -तं, आकस्मिकः -की -कं, अविचारितः -ता -तं, अकल्पितः -ता -तं, अध्यानपूर्व्वः -र्व्वा -र्व्वं, प्रस्तुतः -ता -तं, समयोपयुक्तः -क्ता -क्तं, प्रस्तावयोग्यः -ग्या -ग्यं.

Extempore, *adv.* पूर्व्वचिन्ताम् or पूर्व्वयत्नम् अकृत्वा, चिन्तां विना, पूर्व्वध्यानं विना, अचिन्तितं, अविचारितं, अनायासेन, द्रुतं.

To **Extemporize**, *v. n.* पूर्व्वचिन्ताम् अकृत्वा वद् (c. 1. वदति -दितुं), अकस्मात् or पूर्व्वविचारं विना वद्.

To **Extend**, *v. a.* तन् (c. 8. तनोति -नितुं), वितन्, व्यातन्, प्रतन्, विततीकृ, प्रसृ in caus. (-सारयति -यितुं), अतिसृ, विसृ; विस्तृ or विस्तॄ (c. 5. -स्तृणोति, c. 9. -स्तृणाति -स्तरितुं -रीतुं, c. 10. -स्तारयति -यितुं), प्रथ् (c. 10. प्रथयति -यितुं), आयम् (c. 1. -यच्छति -यन्तुं), प्रपञ्च् (c. 10. -पञ्चयति -यितुं), प्रचर् in caus. (-चारयति -यितुं).—(Extend the hand, &c.) हस्तं प्रसृ in caus. or प्रग्रह् (c. 9. -गृह्णाति -ग्रहीतुं).—(Enlarge) वृध् in caus. (वर्धयति -यितुं), संवृध्, विवृध्, विशालीकृ, विपुलीकृ, प्रचुरतरं -रां -रं कृ.—(Grant, impart) दा (c 3. ददाति, दातुं), प्रदा, अनुदा, प्रयम्.—(Prolong) द्राघ (nom. द्राघयति -यितुं), दीर्घीकृ, दीर्घतरं -रां -रं कृ.

To **Extend**, *v. n.* तन् in pass. (तन्यते), वितन्, विततीभू, प्रसृ (c. 1. -सरति -सर्त्तुं), प्रसृप् (c. 1. -सर्पति -सर्प्तुं), विसृप्, आया (c. 2. -याति -तुं), आयम् (c. 1. -यच्छते -यन्तुं), प्रथ् (c. 1. प्रथते -थितुं), विप्रथ्, प्ररुह् (c. 1. -रोहति -रोढुं), विरुह्, विस्तॄ in pass. (-स्तीर्य्यते), व्याप् (c. 5. -आप्नोति -आप्तुं), विप्रस्था (c. 1. -तिष्ठति -स्थातुं), प्रवृध् (c. 1. -वर्धते -र्धितुं), विजृम्भ् (c. 1. -जृम्भते -म्भितुं).

Extended, *p. p.* विततः -ता -तं, प्रविततः -ता -तं, आततः -ता -तं, सन्ततः -ता -तं, आयतः -ता -तं, समायतः -ता -तं, आयामितः -ता -तं, व्यायतः -ता -तं, प्रथितः -ता -तं, प्रसारितः -ता -तं, प्रसृतः -ता -तं, विसृतः -ता -तं, विस्तृतः -ता -तं, विस्तीर्णः -र्णा -र्णं, बहुविस्तीर्णः -र्णा -र्णं, आयतिमान् -मती -मत् (त्), विरूढः -ढा -ढं, प्ररूढः -ढा -ढं, प्रवृद्धः -द्धा -द्धं, परिगतः -ता -तं, विजृम्भितः -ता -तं.—(As the hand, &c.) प्रसारितः -ता -तं, उच्छ्रितः -ता -तं; 'having the fingers extended,' उत्थिताङ्गुलिः -लिः -लि.

Extendible, **extensible**, *a.* विस्तारयितुं or वितनितुं शक्यः -क्या -क्यं, विस्तारणीयः -या -यं, प्रसारणीयः -या -यं, विस्तारणक्षमः -मा -मं, आयाम्यः -म्या -म्यं.

Extensibility, *s.* विस्तारणीयता, वितननक्षमता, आयाम्यता.

Extension, *s.* विस्तारः, विस्तृतिः *f.*, विस्तीर्णता, विस्तरः, विततिः *f.*, प्रततिः *f.*, आयतिः *f.*, आयामः, वितानः -नं, तानः, सन्ततिः *f.*, प्रसारणं, प्रसरणं, प्रसरः, विसरणं, प्रसर्पणं, विसर्पणं, प्रपञ्चः, व्याप्तिः *f.*, व्यापनं, वृद्धिः *f.*,

प्रवृद्धिः *f.*, प्रपञ्चः, व्यासः, विपुलता.

EXTENSIVE, *a.* विस्तीर्णः -र्णा -र्णं, विपुलः -ला -लं, विशालः -ला -लं, सुपर्य्याप्तः -प्ता -प्तं, बृहन् -हती -हत् (त्), पृथुः -थ्वी -थु, पृथुलः -ला -लं, प्रचुरः -रा -रं, विकटः -टा -टं, आयतः -ता -तं, आयतिमान् -मती -मत् (त्), असम्बाधः -धा -धं, अनल्पः -ल्पा -ल्पं.

EXTENSIVELY, *adv.* सुविस्तीर्णं, सुविस्तरं, सुविस्तरेण, विस्तरशस्, अतिमात्रं, विपुलं, प्रचुरं, सामान्यतस्.

EXTENSIVENESS, *s.* विस्तीर्णता, विस्तारः, विस्तृतिः *f.*, विपुलता, विशालता, पृथुत्वं, बृहत्त्वं, परिसरः, आयतिः *f.*, व्याप्तिः *f.*, व्यापकत्वं.

EXTENT, *s.* (Bulk, width, length) विस्तारः, विशालता, विपुलता, बृहत्त्वं, आयतिः *f.*, आयामः, प्रपञ्चः, सन्ततिः *f.*, वितानकं, पाटः.—(Compass) परिमाणं, परिणाहः, परिसरः, परिधिः *m.*—(Degree, measure) मात्रं, परिमाणं, प्रमाणं, मानं.—(Limit) पर्य्यन्तं.—(Range) विषयः; 'to what extent?' कियत्पर्य्यन्तं, किम्पर्य्यन्तं, कियत्प्रमाणं; 'to such extent,' एतावत्; 'such an extent,' एतावत्त्वं; 'to a slight extent,' ईषत्, किञ्चित्, अल्पमात्रं, स्तोकं.

To EXTENUATE, *v. a.* (Lessen) न्यूनीकृ, न्यून् (c. 10. -नयति -यितुं), लघ (nom. लघयति -यितुं), कन (nom. कनयति -यितुं), अल्पीकृ, क्षीणीकृ, ह्रस् (c. 10. ह्रासयति -यितुं).—(A crime) शम् (c. 10. शमयति -यितुं), उपशम्, पापापनुत्तिं कृ, पापक्षालनं कृ.

EXTENUATED, *p. p.* उपशान्तः -न्ता -न्तं, शमितः -ता -तं, न्यूनीकृतः -ता -तं.

EXTENUATION, *s.* पापोपशान्तिः *f.*, पापशान्तिः *f.*, उपशमः, पापापनोदनं, पापापनुत्तिः *f.*, पापमार्जना, पापप्रक्षालनं, पापापेक्षा.

EXTERIOR, *a.* बाह्यः -ह्या -ह्यं, बाहीकः -का -कं, बहिःस्थः -स्था -स्थं, बहिर्भूतः -ता -तं, बहिर्भवः -वा -वं, बहिस् in comp.; as, 'an exterior object,' बहिरङ्गः.

EXTERIOR, *s.* बहिर्भागः, बाह्यभागः, बहिर्भावः, उपरिस्थभागः.

To EXTERMINATE, *v. a.* उच्छिद् (c. 7. -छिनत्ति -छेत्तुं), समूलं or आमूलम् उद्धृ (c. 1. -हरति -हर्त्तुं) or समुद्धृ or उत्पट् (c. 10. -पाटयति -यितुं), उन्मूल् (c. 10. -मूलयति -यितुं), नश् in caus. (नाशयति -यितुं), विनश्.

EXTERMINATED, *p. p.* उच्छिन्नः -न्ना -न्नं, विनाशितः -ता -तं, उद्धृतः -ता -तं, उत्पाटितः -ता -तं, उन्मूलितः -ता -तं, सादितः -ता -तं.

EXTERMINATION, *s.* उच्छेदः, समुच्छेदः, उच्छित्तिः *f.*, सर्व्वनाशः, उद्धरणं, समूलोत्पाटनं, मूलादुद्धरणं, उन्मूलनं, समूलघातः, विनाशः, प्रलयः, लोपः, शोधनं.

EXTERMINATOR, *s.* उद्धर्त्ता *m.* (र्त्तृ), विनाशकः, उच्छेदी *m.* (न्).

EXTERMINATORY, *a.* उच्छेदी -दिनी -दि (न्), सर्व्वनाशकः -का -कं.

EXTERNAL, *a.* बाह्यः -ह्या -ह्यं, बाहीकः -का -कं, बहिःस्थः -स्था -स्थं, बहिर्वर्त्ती -र्त्तिनी -र्त्ति (न्), बहिर्भूतः -ता -तं, बहिर्भवः -वा -वं, बहिस् in comp.; as, 'an external part,' बहिरङ्गः.

EXTERNALLY, *adv.* बाह्यतस्, बहिस्, बहिर्भागे, उपरिभागे; 'produced externally,' बहिर्भवः -वा -वं.

EXTINCT, *a.* (Extinguished) शान्तः -न्ता -न्तं, शमितः -ता -तं, निर्वाणः -णा -णं.—(Abolished, at an end) नष्टः -ष्टा -ष्टं, विनष्टः -ष्टा -ष्टं, निवृत्तः -त्ता -त्तं, निर्वृत्तः -त्ता -त्तं, विगतः -ता -तं, निर्गतः -ता -तं, अवसितः -ता -तं, अवसन्नः -न्ना -न्नं, क्षीणः -णा -णं, परिक्षीणः -णा -णं, उच्छिन्नः -न्ना -न्नं, लुप्तः -प्ता -प्तं; 'becomes extinct,' शाम्यति.

EXTINCTION, EXTINGUISHMENT, *s.* (Quenching) निर्वाणं, निर्वापणं, शान्तिः *f.*—(Abolition, destruction) नाशः, विनाशः, प्रणाशः, उच्छेदः, समुच्छेदः, उद्धरणं, लोपः, विलोपनं, क्षयः, संहारः; 'of race,' निर्वंशः.

To EXTINGUISH, *v. a.* (Quench) निर्वा in caus. (-वापयति -यितुं), शम् in caus. (शमयति -यितुं), उपशम्, प्रशम्.—(Destroy, put an end to) नश् in caus. (नाशयति -यितुं), विनश्, निवृत् in caus. (-वर्त्तयति -यितुं), उच्छिद् (c. 7. -छिनत्ति -छेत्तुं), निर्दह् (c. 1. -दहति -दग्धुं), लुप् (c. 6. लुम्पति, लोप्तुं, c. 10. लोपयति -यितुं), सद् in caus. (सादयति -यितुं); 'to be extinguished,' शम् (c. 4. शाम्यति, शमितुं), निर्वा (c. 4. -वायति).

EXTINGUISHABLE, *a.* शाम्यः -म्या -म्यं, शमनीयः -या -यं, निर्वाप्यः -प्या -प्यं, निर्वापणीयः -या -यं, नाश्यः -श्या -श्यं, नाशनीयः -या -यं, विलोपनीयः -या -यं.

EXTINGUISHED, *p. p.* (Quenched) निर्वाणः -णा -णं, निर्वापितः -ता -तं, शान्तः -न्ता -न्तं, संशान्तः -न्ता -न्तं, शमितः -ता -तं, प्रशमितः -ता -तं, शान्ताग्निः -ग्निः -ग्नि, शान्तार्च्चिः -र्च्चिः -र्च्चि.—(Destroyed) नष्टः -ष्टा -ष्टं, विनष्टः -ष्टा -ष्टं.

EXTINGUISHER, *s.* निर्वापकः, निर्वाणकारी *m.* (न्).—(Of a candle) दीपनिर्वापकः.

To EXTIRPATE, *v. a.* उन्मूल् (c. 10. -मूलयति -यितुं), समुन्मूल्, मूलात् or समूलम् उद्धृ (c. 1. -हरति -हर्त्तुं), समुद्धृ, उच्छिद् (c. 7. -छिनत्ति -छेत्तुं), उत्पट् (c. 10. -पाटयति -यितुं), व्यपरुह् in caus. (-रोपयति -यितुं), उद्बृह् (c. 6. -वृहति -वर्हितुं), निष्कुष् (c. 9. -कुष्णाति -कोषुं).

EXTIRPATED, *p. p.* उन्मूलितः -ता -तं, उत्पाटितः -ता -तं, उच्छिन्नः -न्ना -न्नं, उद्धृतः -ता -तं, व्यपरोपितः -ता -तं, आवर्हितः -ता -तं, आवृहितः -ता -तं, निष्कुषितः -ता -तं, निर्बीजः -जा -जं.

EXTIRPATION, *s.* उन्मूलनं, उत्पाटनं, उच्छेदः, उद्धरणं, समूलोत्पाटनं, समूलोद्धरणं, उच्छित्तिः *f.*, व्यपरोपणं, निष्कोषणं, नाशः, विनाशः.

EXTIRPATOR, *s.* उद्धर्त्ता *m.* (र्त्तृ), उन्मूलयिता *m.* (तृ), उच्छेदी *m.* (न्).

To EXTOL, *v. a.* प्रशंस् (c. 1. -शंसति -सितुं), अभिप्रशंस्, स्तु (c. 2. स्तौति, स्तोतुं), अभिष्टु, संस्तु, विष्टु, परिसंस्तु, श्लाघ् (c. 1. श्लाघते -घितुं, c. 10. श्लाघयति -यितुं), कृत् (c. 10. कीर्त्तयति -यितुं), प्रथ् (c. 10. प्रथयति -यितुं), विख्या (c. 2. -ख्याति -तुं), प्रख्या.

EXTOLLED, *p. p.* प्रशंसितः -ता -तं, कीर्त्तितः -ता -तं, अभिष्टुतः -ता -तं.

EXTOLLER, *s.* प्रशंसकः, कीर्त्तयिता *m.* (तृ), अनुकीर्त्तनकृत् *m.*, स्तावकः.

EXTORSIVE, *a.* बाधकः -का -कं, उपद्रवी -विणी -वि (न्), सबाधः -धा -धं.

To EXTORT, *v. a.* and *n.* बलात् or बलेन ग्रह् (c. 9. गृह्णाति, ग्रहीतुं), अन्यायेन आदा (c. 3. -दत्ते -ददाति -दातुं), दा in caus. (दापयति -यितुं), विहा in caus. (-हापयति -यितुं), आहृ in caus. (-हारयति -यितुं), बाध् (c. 1. बाधते -धितुं), परिबाध्, उपधिं कृ.

EXTORTED, *p. p.* बलाद्गृहीतः -ता -तं, दापितः -ता -तं, विहापितः -ता -तं.

EXTORTER, EXTORTIONER, *s.* अन्यायेन परस्वादायी *m.* (न्), बलेन परस्वग्राहकः, बाधकः, उपद्रवी *m.* (न्), उपधिकः, औपधिकः, दुर्वृत्तः, दुरात्मा *m.* (न्), दस्युः *m.*, लोठयिता *m.* (तृ).

EXTORTION, *s.* अन्यायेन or बलेन परस्वग्रहणं, बाधः -धनं, उपद्रवः, विप्लवः, अभिद्रोहः, उपधिकरणं, उपधिः *m.*, बलात्कारः, निष्ठुरता, दौरात्म्यं, हठः.

EXTRA, *s.* अधिकं, आधिक्यं, आतिरेक्यं, अति in comp.—(Beyond the usual quantity) अधिकः -का -कं, अतिरिक्तः -क्ता -क्तं, निरूपितपरिमाणातिरिक्तः -क्ता -क्तं.

To EXTRACT, *v. a.* निष्कृष् (c. 1. -कर्षति -क्रष्टुं), उत्कृष्, आकृष्; उद्धृ (c. 1. -हरति -हर्त्तुं), निर्हृ, उद्ग्रह् (c. 9. -गृह्णाति -ग्रहीतुं), निर्दुह् (c. 2. -दोग्धि -ग्धुं), निष्कुष् (c. 9. -कुष्णाति -कोषुं), उत्खन् (c. 1. -खनति -नितुं), उद्बृह् (c. 6. -वृहति -वर्हितुं), उत्पद् in caus. (-पादयति -यितुं), निर्गम् in caus. (-गमयति -यितुं); 'the teeth,' दन्तान् उद्धृ.

EXTRACT, *s.* (That which is extracted) उद्धृतं, उद्धारः, निष्कर्षः,

चूर्णिः *m.*—(Essence) रसः, निर्यासः, निर्व्यूहः, कषायः, अवलेहः; 'of flowers,' पुष्पनिर्यासः.—(Epitome) सङ्ग्रहः, सारः, संक्षेपः.

EXTRACTED, *p. p.* उद्धृतः -ता -तं, निष्कर्षितः -ता -तं, निर्हृतः -ता -तं, निष्कुषितः -ता -तं, निर्गतः -ता -तं, उद्गृहीतः -ता -तं, व्यवस्थितः -ता -तं; 'having the teeth extracted,' उद्धृतदंष्ट्रः -ष्ट्रा -ष्ट्रं.

EXTRACTION, *s.* उद्धारः, निर्हारः, निष्कर्षणं, अभ्यवकर्षणं, आकर्षणं, निष्कोषणं, व्यवस्थितिः *f.*—(Birth, lineage) जन्म *n.* (न्), जातिः *f.*, उत्पत्तिः *f.*, उद्भवः, सम्भवः, वंशः, कुलं; 'of high extraction,' महाकुलः -ला -लं; 'of royal extraction,' राजवंश्यः -श्या -श्यं.

EXTRA-JUDICIAL, *a.* व्यवहारविधिबहिर्भूतः -ता -तं, व्यवहारबाह्यः -ह्या -ह्यं, व्यवहारातिरिक्तः -क्ता -क्तं, व्यवहारातिचरः -रा -रं, व्यवहारातिक्रान्तः -न्ता -न्तं.

EXTRA-JUDICIALLY, *adv.* व्यवहारविधिव्यतिरेकेण, व्यवहारम् अतिक्रम्य.

EXTRA-MUNDANE, *a.* लोकबहिर्भूतः -ता -तं, लोकबाह्यः -ह्या -ह्यं, अतिसंसारः -रा -रं, अलौकिकः -की -कं, असांसारिकः -की -कं.

EXTRANEOUS, *a.* बाह्यः -ह्या -ह्यं, वाहीकः -का -कं, बहिर्भवः -वा -वं, बहिर्भूतः -ता -तं, बहिःस्थः -स्था -स्थं, भिन्नः -न्ना -न्नं, विभिन्नः -न्ना -न्नं, अन्यः -न्या -न्यत्, परः -रा -रं, विविक्तः -क्ता -क्तं, असहजः -जा -जं, असम्बन्धी -न्धिनी -न्धि (न्), विदेशीयः -या -यं.

EXTRAORDINARILY, *adv.* अपूर्व्वप्रकारेण, अद्भुतप्रकारेण, अद्भुतं, असाधारण्येन, वैलक्षण्येन, विचित्रं, आश्चर्य्यप्रकारेण, अप्रसिद्धं.

EXTRAORDINARINESS, *s.* अद्भुतत्वं, आश्चर्य्यत्वं, अपूर्व्वत्वं, अप्रसिद्धत्वं, वैलक्षण्यं, वैलक्षण्यं, असाधारण्यं, विचित्रता.

EXTRAORDINARY, *a.* अपूर्व्वः -र्व्वा -र्व्वं, अदृष्टपूर्व्वः -र्व्वा -र्व्वं, असाधारणः -णी -णं, असामान्यः -न्या -न्यं, अप्रसिद्धः -द्धा -द्धं, आश्चर्य्यः -र्य्या -र्य्यं, महाद्भुतः -ता -तं, अद्भुतः -ता -तं, अप्रकृतः -ता -तं, विचित्रः -त्रा -त्रं, विलक्षणः -णा -णं, अधिकः -का -कं, लोकोत्तरः -रा -रं, अधिकोत्तरः -रा -रं, विरलः -ला -लं.

EXTRAVAGANCE, *s.* (In expenditure) अतिव्ययः, अपव्ययः, महान् व्ययः, धनव्ययः, धनोत्सर्गः, अर्थोत्सर्गः, धनमोक्षणं, अर्थदूषणं, व्ययापरिमितता, —(Excess in general) अतिक्रमः, उत्क्रमः, मर्य्यादातिक्रमः, नियमातिक्रमः, अमर्य्यादा, अपरिमितता, अत्ययः, अत्याचारः, अभिचारः.

EXTRAVAGANT, *a.* (Prodigal) अतिव्ययी -यिनी -यि (न्), अपव्ययी &c., व्ययशीलः -ला -लं, अपरिमितव्ययः -या -यं, अर्थघ्नः -घ्नी -घ्नं, धनापचेता -त्री -तृ (तृ), मुक्तहस्तः -स्ता -स्तं.—(Exceeding bounds) मर्य्यादातिक्रमी -मिणी -मि (न्), अतिक्रान्तमर्य्यादः -दा -दं, उत्क्रान्तमर्य्यादः -दा -दं, अमर्य्यादः -दा -दं, अतिमर्य्यादः -दा -दं, अपरिमितः -ता -तं, अत्याचारी -रिणी -रि (न्), अभिचारी -रिणी -रि (न्).

EXTRAVAGANTLY, *adv.* (Prodigally) अतिव्ययेन, महाव्ययेन, मुक्तहस्तेन. —(Beyond all bounds) अतिमर्य्यादं, अत्यन्तं, अतिमात्रं, अतिशयेन, अपरिमितं.

To EXTRAVAGATE, *v. a.* मर्य्यादाम् अतिक्रम् (c. 1. -क्रामति -क्रमितुं), उत्क्रम्, व्युत्क्रम्.

EXTRAVAGATION, *s.* मर्य्यादातिक्रमः, नियमातिक्रमः, उत्क्रमः, उल्लङ्घनं.

EXTRAVASATED, *a.* नाडिबहिर्भूतः -ता -तं, नाडिबहिष्कृतः -ता -तं, शिराबहिर्गतः -ता -तं.

EXTRAVASATION, *s.* नाडिबहिष्करणं, रक्तोत्सर्गः, रक्तमोक्षणं.

EXTREME, *a.* (Outermost) बाह्यः -ह्या -ह्यं.—(Greatest, utmost) परमः -मा -मं, महान् -हती -हत् (त्), अत्यन्तः -न्ता -न्तं, आत्यन्तिकः -की -कं, उत्तमः -मा -मं, परः -रा -रं, अतिशय or अति prefixed; as, 'extreme pain,' अतिव्यथा.—(Last) अन्त्यः -न्त्या -न्त्यं, अन्तिमः -मा -मं, अन्त or शेष in comp.; 'extreme part,' शेषभागः; 'extreme limit,' परमावधिः *m.*

EXTREME, *s.* अन्तः -न्तं, पर्य्यन्तं, पारः -रं, उत्तमावधिः *m.*, परमावधिः *m.*,

शेषभागः.—(Excess) अत्यन्तता, आधिक्यं, आतिशय्यं.

EXTREMELY, *adv.* अत्यन्तं, अतिशयेन, अतिमात्रं, नितान्तं, अत्यर्थं, एकान्तं -न्ततस्, परमं, परं, अतीव, बहु, अति or अतिशय prefixed; as, 'extremely passionate,' अत्यन्तकोपनः -ना -नं.

EXTREMITY, *s.* (Utmost point) अन्तः -न्तं, अग्रं, अग्रभागः, पर्य्यन्तं, प्रान्तः, सीमा, अवधिः *m.*, पारः -रं, उत्तमावधिः *m.*, परमावधिः *m.*, शेषावधिः *m.*, शेषभागः; 'the lower extremities,' अधःकायः, शरीरस्य अधोभागः.—(Utmost distress) अतिकृच्छ्रं, अत्यन्तक्लेशः, अत्यन्तदुःखं.

EXTRICABLE, *a.* उद्धरणीयः -या -यं, उद्धार्य्यः -र्य्या -र्य्यं, मोचनीयः -या -यं.

To EXTRICATE, *v. a.* उद्धृ (c. 1. -हरति -हर्तुं), समुद्धृ, मुच् (c. 6. मुञ्चति, मोक्तुं, c. 10. मोचयति -यितुं), विमुच्, प्रविमुच्, उत्तॄ in caus. (-तारयति -यितुं), निस्तॄ, सन्तॄ; मोक्ष् (c. 10. मोक्षयति -यितुं), त्रै (c. 1. त्रायते, त्रातुं), परित्रै, सन्त्रै, रक्ष् (c. 1. रक्षति -क्षितुं), विशुध् (c. 10. -शोधयति -यितुं).

EXTRICATED, *p. p.* उद्धृतः -ता -तं, समुद्धृतः -ता -तं, उत्तीर्णः -र्णा -र्णं, निस्तारितः -ता -तं, तारितः -ता -तं, मुक्तः -क्ता -क्तं, मोचितः -ता -तं, त्राणः -णा -णं.

EXTRICATION, *s.* उद्धारः, उद्धरणं, समुद्धरणं, मुक्तिः *f.*, मोचनं, विमोचनं, मोक्षः -क्षणं, रक्षा, परिरक्षणं, त्राणं, निस्तारः, निस्तरणं, उत्तारः, उत्तरणं, तारणं, विशोधनं, शुद्धिः *f.*

EXTRINSIC, EXTRINSICAL, *a.* बाह्यः -ह्या -ह्यं, वाहीकः -का -कं, बहिःस्थः -स्था -स्थं, बहिर्भवः -वा -वं, असहजः -जा -जं, असम्बन्धी -न्धिनी -न्धि (न्).

EXTRINSICALLY, *adv.* बाह्यतस्, बहिस्, बहिर्भागे, अनभ्यन्तरात्.

To EXTRUDE, *v. a.* बहिष्कृ, निरस् (c. 4. -अस्यति -असितुं), उत्सृ (c. 10. -सारयति -यितुं).

EXTRUSION, *s.* बहिष्करणं, निःसारणं, अपसारणं, उत्सारणं, निरसनं.

EXTUBERANCE, *s.* अधिमांसं, स्फोटः, शोथः, गडुः, उच्चभागः.

EXUBERANCE, *s.* समृद्धिः *f.*, सामृद्ध्यं, परिपूर्णता, बाहुल्यं, बहुत्वं, प्राचुर्य्यं, स्फीतिः *f.*, स्फातिः *f.*, उत्सेकः, उद्रेकः, उपचयः, वृद्धिः *f.*, आधिक्यं.

EXUBERANT, *a.* समृद्धः -द्धा -द्धं, बहुलः -ला -लं, परिपूर्णः -र्णा -र्णं, प्रचुरः -रा -रं, वर्धिष्णुः -ष्णुः -ष्णु, स्फीतः -ता -तं, उत्सिक्तः -क्ता -क्तं, उद्रिक्तः -क्ता -क्तं, पीनः -ना -नं, पुष्कलः -ला -लं, अतिरिक्तः -क्ता -क्तं, उपचितः -ता -तं.

EXUBERANTLY, *adv.* बाहुल्येन, बहुशस्, प्रचुरं, पुष्कलं, उद्रेकेण.

To EXUBERATE, *v. n.* बहुलीभू, प्रचुरीभू, समृध् (c. 5. -ऋध्नोति -अर्धितुं).

EXUDATION, *s.* स्वेदः, प्रस्वेदः, स्वेदजलस्रावः, स्वेदबिन्दुस्रावः, रसः, रसस्रावः, स्यन्दनं, स्रवः -वणं, प्रस्रवणं, स्रावः, निर्यासः, स्रुतिः *f.*, घर्म्मपयः *n.* (स्), कषायः, वेष्टकः.

To EXUDE, *v. n.* स्विद् (c. 4. स्विद्यति, स्वेत्तुं), प्रस्विद्, स्वेदवत् प्रस्रु (c. 1. -स्रवति -स्रोतुं) or स्यन्द् (c. 1. स्यन्दते -न्दितुं).

To EXUDE, *v. a.* स्वेदं प्रस्रु in caus. (-स्रावयति -यितुं) or निःसृ in caus. (-सारयति -यितुं).

EXUDED, *p. p.* प्रस्रुतः -ता -तं, स्यन्नः -न्ना -न्नं, निःसृतः -ता -तं, निर्गतः -ता -तं.

To EXULCERATE, *v. a.* व्रणीकृ, व्रणं or क्षतं कृ or उत्पद् in caus. (-पादयति -यितुं).

EXULCERATION, *s.* व्रणकरणं, क्षतकरणं, व्रणोत्पत्तिः *f.*, व्रणोत्पादनं.

To EXULT, *v. n.* अत्यन्तं or अतिशयेन नन्द् (c. 1. नन्दति -न्दितुं) or आनन्द् or हृष् (c. 4. हृष्यति, हर्षितुं) or ह्लाद् (c. 1. ह्लादते -दितुं), उल्लस् (c. 1. -लसति -सितुं), परमहर्षम् इ (c. 2. एति -तुं), मद् (c. 4. माद्यति, मदितुं).

EXULTATION, *s.* परमानन्दः, परमहर्षः, परमाह्लादः, अत्यन्ताह्लादः, मादः, अत्यानन्दः, महोत्सवः.

EXULTING, *a.* परमहृष्टः -ष्टा -ष्टं, उल्लसितः -ता -तं, अत्यानन्दी -न्दिनी -न्दि (न्), सगर्व्वः -र्व्वा -र्व्वं, सदर्पः -र्पा -र्पं.

EXUPERABLE, *a.* लङ्घनीयः -या -यं, अधिगम्यः -म्या -म्यं, अतिक्रमणीयः -या -यं.

EXUSTION, *s.* निर्दाहः, निर्दहनं, परिदहनं, भस्मसात्करणं.

EYE, *s.* चक्षुः *n.* (स्), नयनं, लोचनं, नेत्रं, विलोचनं, अक्षि *n.*, ईक्षणं, प्रेक्षणं, दृष्टिः *f.*, दृक् *f.* (श्), दृशा, दृशिः *f.*, अक्षं, दैवदीपः, विचक्षुरः; 'pupil of the eye,' तारका, कनीनिका; 'corner of the eye,' अपाङ्गः, नयनोपान्तः; 'mind's eye,' ज्ञानचक्षुः *n.* (स्), ज्ञानदृष्टिः *f.*; 'evil-eye,' कुदृष्टिः *f.*; 'long eyes,' आकर्णलोचने; 'having good eyes,' सुलोचनः -ना -नी -नं, वामलोचनः -ना -नं, स्वक्षः -क्षी -क्षं; 'having large eyes,' फुल्लनयनः -ना -नी -नं, फुल्ललोचनः -ना -नी -नं; 'having sharp eyes,' सूक्ष्माक्षः -क्षी -क्षं; 'having red eyes,' अरुणेक्षणः -णा -णं; 'doing what is right in one's own eyes,' स्वेच्छाचारी -रिणी -रि (न्); 'before one's eyes,' प्रत्यक्षे, प्रत्यक्षेण, प्रत्यक्षतस्, समक्षं, साक्षात्, पश्यतस् ind. or expressed by the pres. part. of दृश्; as, 'he steals my goods before my eyes,' पश्यतो मम द्रव्याणि हरति; 'visible to the eye,' चक्षुर्ग्राह्यः -ह्या -ह्यं, दृष्टिगोचरः -रा -रं; 'with one's own eye,' स्वचक्षुषा; 'glance of the eye,' दृष्टिपातः, नयनपातः; 'in my eyes,' मां प्रति.—(View, regard) दृष्टिः *f.*, दर्शनं, प्रेक्षितं, वीक्षितं, निरीक्षा.—(Aperture) छिद्रं, रन्ध्रं; 'eye of a needle,' सूचीछिद्रं, सूचिरन्ध्रं.—(Catch for a book) कुडुपः.—(Bud) मुकुलं, कुड्मलं, जालकं.

To EYE, *v. a.* निरीक्ष् (c. 1. -ईक्षते -क्षितुं), आलोक् (c. 10. -लोकयति -यितुं, c. 1. -लोकते -कितुं); 'to eye askance,' कटाक्षेण or अपाङ्गेन दृश् (c. 1. पश्यति, द्रष्टुं) or अवेक्ष्.

EYE-BALL, *s.* तारा, चक्षुःपिण्डः, नेत्रपिण्डः, नेत्रकोषः -षं, अक्षिगोलः, अक्षिकूटकः, विडालः; 'of an elephant,' इषीका.

EYE-BEAM, *s.* (Glance) नयनपातः, दृष्टिपातः, दृष्टिनिपातः, दृष्टिबाणः.

EYE-BROW, *s.* भ्रूः *f.*, भ्रूलता, कोदण्डः, चक्षुर्भ्रूः *f.*; 'the two eye-brows,' भ्रुवौ du.; 'space between them,' कूर्चः, भ्रुवोर्मध्यं; 'wrinkled eye-brow,' लोचकः.

EYED, *p. p.* and *a.* (Viewed) निरीक्षितः -ता -तं, आलोकितः -ता -तं; 'eyed askance,' कटाक्षितः -ता -तं.—(Having eyes) used in comp.; as, 'black-eyed,' कृष्णनयनः -नी -नं, असितनयनः -नी -नं, नीलाक्षः -क्षी -क्षं; 'fiery-eyed,' ज्वलितनयनः -नी -नं; 'one-eyed,' एकाक्षः -क्षा -क्षं, काणः -णा -णं, एकाक्षिविकलः -ला -लं.

EYE-DROP, *s.* वाष्पविन्दुः *m.*, नयनविन्दुः, अश्रुविन्दुः, नेत्रजलं, नेत्राम्बु *n.*, नेत्रजं, नयनसलिलं, नयनवारि *n.* अश्रु *n.*

EYE-GLASS, *s.* उपनेत्रं, उपनयनं, सुलोचनं —(Lens) दीप्तोपलः, अर्कोश्मा *m.* (न्).

EYE-LASH, *s.* पक्ष्म *n.* (न्), अक्षिपक्ष्म *n.*, नेत्रच्छदलोम *n.* (न्), रश्मिः *m.*, रश्मकः, उदानः.

EYE-LESS, *a.* अचक्षुः -क्षुः -क्षुः (स्), विचक्षुः -क्षुः -क्षुः (स्), अनक्षः -क्षा -क्षं, अनयनः -ना -नं, गताक्षः -क्षा -क्षं, दृष्टिहीनः -ना -नं, अदृक् *m. f. n.* (श्), नेत्रेन्द्रियविकलः -ला -लं.

EYELET, EYELET-HOLE, *s.* गवाक्षः, छिद्रं, रन्ध्रं.

EYE-LID, *s.* नेत्रच्छदः, नयनच्छदः, अक्षिपुटः, पुटः, नयनवर्त्म *n.* (न्), वर्त्म *n.*, आडम्बरः.

EYE-SALVE, *s.* चक्षुरञ्जनं, नेत्राञ्जनं, चक्षुर्विलेपनं, नयनलेपः.

EYE-SERVICE, *s.* केवलं प्रभुप्रत्यक्षेण कृता शुश्रूषा or परिचर्य्या.

EYE-SHOT, *s.* चक्षुर्विषयः, नयनविषयः, दृष्टिगोचरः -रं.

EYE-SIGHT, *s.* दृष्टिः *f.*, नयनदृष्टिः *f.*, नेत्रेन्द्रियं, चक्षुरिन्द्रियं, दर्शनशक्तिः *f.*

EYE-SORE, *s.* चक्षुःपीडा, नेत्रपीडाकरं or नयनक्लेशकं वस्तु.

EYE-SPOTTED, *p. p.* नयनाकारचिह्नैर् विचित्रितः -ता -तं.

EYE-TOOTH, *s.* पार्श्वदन्तः, नयनदन्तः, चक्षुर्दन्तः.

EYE-WINK, *s.* अक्षिसंज्ञा, नेत्रसङ्केतः, अक्षिसङ्कोचसंज्ञा, कटाक्षः.

EYE-WITNESS, *s.* स्वचक्षुषा साक्षी *m.* (न्), प्रत्यक्षदर्शी *m.* (न्), प्रत्यक्षदर्शनः, साक्षाद्द्रष्टा *m.* (ऋ), साक्षाद्दर्शी *m.*, देश्यः.

EYRIE, *s.* श्येनादिनीडः, श्येनकुलायः, प्रतुदादिपक्षिस्थानं.

F.

FABACEOUS, *a.* मौद्गीनः -ना -नं, माषीणः -णा -णं, शिम्बासगुणः -णा -णं.

FABLE, *s.* (Feigned story) पुरावृत्तकथा, पुरावृत्तोपाख्यानं, कूटार्थोपाख्यानं, उपाख्यानं, आख्यानं, आख्यायिका, कथा, परिकथा, इतिहासः.—(Fiction) कल्पनासृष्टिः *f.*, प्रबन्धकल्पना, मनःकल्पितं, व्यपदेशः.

To FABLE, *v. a.* and *n.* पुरावृत्तकथां रच् (c. 10. रचयति -यितुं), विरच्, मनसा क्लृप् (c. 10. कल्पयति -यितुं) or सृज् (c. 6. सृजति, स्रष्टुं), मिथ्याकथा रच्.

FABLED, *p. p.* मनःकल्पितः -ता -तं, काल्पनिकः -की -कं, कूटार्थः -र्था -र्थं.

FABRIC, *s.* (Structure) निर्म्माणं, निर्म्मितिः *f.*, कल्पना.—(Edifice) हर्म्यं, शाला, भवनं, मन्दिरं, प्रासादः, धाम *n.* (न्), अट्टालिका.—(Form, texture) आकारः, आकृतिः *f.*, ऊतिः *f.*

To FABRICATE, *v. a.* (Construct) निर्मा (c. 2. -माति -तुं, c. 3. -मिमीते, c. 4. -मीयते caus. -मापयति -यितुं), कृ (c. 8. करोति, कर्त्तुं caus. कारयति -यितुं), क्लृप् (c. 10. कल्पयति -यितुं), विरच् (c. 10. -रचयति -यितुं), सृज् (c. 6. सृजति, स्रष्टुं), घट् (c. 1. घटते -टितुं).—(Invent) मनसा क्लृप्, मिथ्या क्लृप् or कृ.

FABRICATED, *p. p.* (Constructed) निर्म्मितः -ता -तं, रचितः -ता -तं, विरचितः -ता -तं, घटितः -ता -तं, कल्पितः -ता -तं.—(Invented) मनःकल्पितः -ता -तं, कृत्रिमः -मा -मं.

FABRICATION, *s.* (Construction) निर्म्माणं, निर्म्मितिः *f.*, रचना, विरचना, कल्पनं -ना, घटनं.—(Falsehood, forgery) मनःकल्पितं, मिथ्याकथा.

FABRICATOR, *s.* निर्म्माता *m.* (ऋ), निर्म्माणकारी *m.* (न्), रचकः, विरचकः.

FABULIST, *s.* पुरावृत्तकथाविरचकः, इतिहासरचकः, ऐतिहासिकः.

FABULOUS, *a.* (Fictitious) कृत्रिमः -मा -मं, मनःकल्पितः -ता -तं, काल्पनिकः -की -कं, अप्रसिद्धः -द्धा -द्धं, कूटार्थः -र्था -र्थं.—(Relating to fable) पुरावृत्तकथासम्बन्धी -न्धिनी -न्धि (न्), ऐतिहासिकः -की -कं, काथिकः -की -कं.

FABULOUSLY, *adv.* कृत्रिमप्रकारेण, कल्पनापूर्व्वं, इतिहासानुसारेण.

FAÇADE, *s.* (Of a building) हर्म्यमुखं, प्रासादमूर्द्धा *m.* (न्).

FACE, *s.* (Visage) मुखं, वदनं, आननं, वक्त्रं, आस्यं, वन्दनं, तुण्डं, इमन् indec.; 'face like the moon,' वदनचन्द्रः, वदनेन्दुः *m.*—(Air, look) वदनं, दृष्टिः *f.*, आकारः, आभा.—(Surface) तलं, मुखं, पृष्ठं, पीठं; 'face of the earth,' भूतलं, पृथिवीतलं, क्षितिपीठं.—(State) अवस्था, स्थितिः *f.*, दशा, भावः, रूपं; 'before the face,' प्रतिमुखं, सम्मुखं -खे, अभिमुखं, साक्षात्, समक्षं, प्रत्यक्षं -क्षेण -क्षतस्, अग्रे, अग्रतस्; 'face to face,' सम्मुखं, मुखामुखि; 'in face of,' सम्मुखः -खा -खी -खं, सम्मुखीनः -ना -नं, अभिमुखः -खा -खी -खं; 'having the face averted,' विमुखः -खी -खं, पराङ्मुखः -खी -खं; 'to turn away the face,' विमुखीभू; 'to stand face to face,' सम्मुखीभू; 'to fall with one's face on the ground,' भूमौ न्यङ्मुखः or अधोमुखः

पत् (c. 1. पतति -तितुं); 'a wry face,' विकृताननं.

To FACE, *v. a.* सम्मुखीभू, अभिमुखीभू, प्रतिमुखीभू.—(Meet, oppose) अभिमुखं गम् (c. 1. गच्छति, गन्तुं), अभिवृत् (c. 1. -वर्त्तते -र्त्तितुं), पर्य्यवस्था (c. 1. -तिष्ठति -स्थातुं); 'one who faces the foe,' अभ्यमित्रीणः, अभ्यमित्रीयः, अभ्यमित्र्यः.—(Be opposite to) expressed by मुख or अभिमुख in comp.; 'to face the south,' दक्षिणामुखः -खी -खं भू; 'the north,' उदङ्मुखः -खी -खं भू, उत्तराभिमुखः -खी -खं भू; 'the east,' प्राङ्मुखः -खी -खं भू.—(Covered with additional cloth) अधिवस्त्रेण or अधिकपटेन छद् (c. 10. छादयति -यितुं).

FACED, *a.* अधिवस्त्रोपेतः -ता -तं, उत्तरवस्त्रान्वितः -ता -तं.—(Having a face) used in comp.; as, 'lovely faced,' सुमुखः -खी -खं, मुग्धाननः -नी -नं; 'lotus-faced,' आननाब्जः -ब्जा -ब्जं; 'moon faced,' चन्द्रमुखः -खी -खं.

FACELESS, *s.* निर्मुखः -खा -खी -खं, निर्वदनः -ना -नं, मुखहीनः -ना -नं.

FACET, *s.* (Small surface of a gem) कणः.

FACETIOUS, *a.* रसिकः -का -कं, रसी -सिनी -सि (न्), रसवान् -वती -वत् (त्), सरसः -सा -सं, परिहासशीलः -ला -लं, परिहासवेदी -दिनी -दि (न्), प्रहासी -सिनी -सि (न्), विनोदी -दिनी -दि (न्), विदूषकः -का -कं; 'facetious conversation,' सरसालापः, चित्रं.

FACETIOUSLY, *adv.* सरसं, हासकरणार्थं, विनोदार्थं, रसिकप्रकारेण.

FACETIOUSNESS, *s.* रसिकत्वं, रसवत्त्वं, सरसता, परिहासशीलता, विनोदकत्वं, हास्यता, हासोत्पादकत्वं, उज्ज्वलता.

FACILE, *a.* सुखः -खा -खं, सुकरः -रा -रं, निरायासः -सा -सं, अनायासी -सिनी -सि (न्), सुसाध्यः -ध्या -ध्यं, सुगमः -मा -मं, सुखेन कार्य्यः -र्य्या -र्य्यं, अकठिनः -ना -नं.—(Complying) अनुकूलः -ला -लं.—(Easy of access) अभिगम्यः -म्या -म्यं.

To FACILITATE, *v. a.* सुकरं -रां -रं कृ, निरायासीकृ, सुखीकृ, दुःखानि or दुर्गाणि or विघ्नान् or शल्यानि विनी (c. 1. -नयति -नेतुं) or अपनी or हृ (c. 1. हरति, हर्त्तुं) or नश् (c. 10. नाशयति -यितुं), निर्विघ्नीकृ, निष्प्रत्यूहीकृ.

FACILITATED, *p. p.* सुकरीकृतः -ता -तं, हृतविघ्नः -घ्ना -घ्नं, हृतप्रत्यूहः -हा -हं.

FACILITY, *s.* सौकर्य्यं, सुकरत्वं, सौख्यं, सौगम्यं, सुगमत्वं, सुसाध्यता, अनायासः, निरायासत्वं, अकाठिन्यं, अकष्टत्वं, अवैषम्यं.

FACING, *part.* (Opposite to) अभिमुखः -खा -खी -खं, सम्मुखः -खा -खं, सम्मुखीनः -ना -नं, अभिमुखगतः -ता -तं, प्रतिमुखः -खा -खं; 'facing the north,' उत्तराभिमुखः -खा -खं, or expressed by मुख; as, 'facing the east,' प्राङ्मुखः -खा -खं; 'the west,' प्रत्यङ्मुखः; 'the south,' दक्षिणामुखः; 'the north,' उदङ्मुखः; 'with the head facing the east,' प्राक्शिरसः -सा -सं.

FACING, *s.* (Additional covering in front of a garment) वस्त्राग्रभागे स्यूतम् अधिकांशुकं or अधिवसनं.—(End of a sleeve) पिप्पलान्तं.—(Of a fortification) दुर्गमुखं.

FAC-SIMILE, *s.* प्रतिलिपिः *f.*, हस्ताक्षरप्रतिरूपं.

FACT, *s.* वस्तु *n.* भूतं, अर्थः, वृत्तं, कर्म्म *n.* (न्), कृतं, कृतवस्तु *n.*—(Reality) तत्त्वं, सत्त्वं, सत्ता, सत्यता, यथार्थता, याथार्थ्यं, प्रकृतत्वं; 'in fact,' वस्तुतस्, अर्थतस्, तत्त्वतस्, परमार्थतस्.

FACTION, *s.* (A party) पक्षः, शाखा, गणः, दलं; 'one of the opposite faction,' विपक्षः; 'one's own faction,' आत्मपक्षः; 'following a faction,' पक्षपातः -तिता, पक्षपातकृतस्नेहः, गणता.—(Political dissension) भेदः, द्वैधं, द्वन्द्वं, विरोधः, राजद्रोहः.

FACTIOUS, *a.* (Relating to faction) पाक्षः -क्षी -क्षं.—(Promoting faction, seditious) राज्यभेदकरः -री -रं, राजद्रोही -हिणी -हि (न्), कलहकारी -रिणी -रि (न्), भेत्ता -त्त्री -तृ (तृ), उपजापकः -का -कं, उपद्रवी -विणी -वि (न्).

FACTIOUSLY, *adv.* भेदकरणार्थं, कलहकरणार्थं, सोपजापं, उपजापकवत्.

FACTIOUSNESS, *s.* भेदकरणशीलता, राजद्रोहः, कलहकारित्वं, उपजापः.

FACTITIOUS, *a.* कृत्रिमः -मा -मं, कृतकः -का -कं, कल्पितः -ता -तं, काल्पनिकः -की -कं, रचितः -ता -तं, घटितः -ता -तं, शिल्पिकः -का -कं, शिल्पनिर्म्मितः -ता -तं, यौक्तिकः -की -कं.

FACTITIOUSLY, *adv.* कृत्रिमप्रकारेण, शिल्पेन, कल्पनापूर्व्वं.

FACTOR, *s.* वणिक्प्रतिनिधिः *m.*, देशान्तरे वाणिज्यकर्म्मनिर्वाहणे नियुक्तो जनः, नियोगी *m.* (न्), नियुक्तः, प्रतिपुरुषः.

FACTORAGE, *s.* वणिक्प्रतिनिधिगृहीतः शुल्कः, वणिक्कर्म्मनिर्वाहणार्थं नियोगिणे देयं पारितोषिकं.

FACTORY, *s.* (Manufactory) शिल्पगृहं, शिल्पशाला, यन्त्रगृहं, आवेशनं, प्रावेशनं, अन्वासनं, पण्यनिर्म्माणशाला, वाणिज्यद्रव्यनिर्म्माणगृहं.

FACTOTUM, *s.* सर्व्वकर्म्मी *m. f.* (न्), सर्व्वकर्म्मकरः -री, सर्व्वकर्म्मीणः -णा.

FACULTY, *s.* (Power) शक्तिः *f.*, बलं, क्षमता, सामर्थ्यं, प्रभावः, आशक्तिः.—(Faculty of the mind) धीशक्तिः *f.*, मनःशक्तिः *f.*, निष्क्रमः, संस्कारः, चित्तसंस्कारः.—(Facility of performance) योग्यता, युक्तिः *f.*, सुप्रयोगता, कौशल्यं, पाटवं.—(Privilege) अधिकारः.—(The body of doctors) वैद्यगणः, चिकित्सकवर्गः.

FACUND, *a.* वाक्पटुः -टुः -टु, वाग्मी -ग्मिनी -ग्मि (न्). *See* ELOQUENT.

FACUNDITY, *s.* वाक्पटुता, वाक्पाटवं, पटुत्वं, वाग्विदग्धता.

To FADDLE, *v. n.* रम् (c. 1. रमते, रन्तुं), खेल् (c. 1. खेलति -लितुं), खेलां कृ.

To FADE, *v. n.* (Decay, wither) म्लै (c. 1. म्लायति, म्लातुं), परिम्लै, विशृ in pass. (-शीर्य्यते), क्षि in pass. (क्षीयते), सद् (c. 1. सीदति, सत्तुं), अवसद्, व्यवसद्, जृ (c. 4. जीर्य्यति, जरितुं -रीतुं), नश् (c. 4. नश्यति, नशितुं), प्रणश्, विनश्, ध्वंस् (c. 1. ध्वंसते -सितुं), विध्वंस्, शद् (c. 1. शीयते, शत्तुं), ग्लै (c. 1. ग्लायति, ग्लातुं), म्ली (c. 4. -लीयते -लेतुं), गल् (c. 1. गलति -लितुं).—(Lose colour) विवर्णीभू, नीरक्तीभू.

To FADE, *v. a.* (Cause to wither) क्षि in caus. (क्षपयति, क्षययति -यितुं), अवसद् in caus. (-सादयति -यितुं), ध्वंस् in caus. (ध्वंसयति -यितुं), म्लै in caus. (म्लपयति -यितुं), म्लानीकृ, विशीर्णीकृ, तेजो हृ (c. 1. हरति, हर्त्तुं).—(Deprive of colour) विवर्णीकृ, वर्णं दुष् in caus. (दूषयति -यितुं) or नश् in caus. (नाशयति -यितुं).

FADED, *p. p.* म्लानः -ना -नं, परिम्लानः -ना -नं, शीर्णः -र्णा -र्णं, विशीर्णः -र्णा -र्णं, क्षीणः -णा -णं, ध्वस्तः -स्ता -स्तं, अवसन्नः -न्ना -न्नं, जीर्णः -र्णा -र्णं, तान्तः -न्ता -न्तं.—(In colour) विवर्णः -र्णा -र्णं, हीनवर्णः -र्णा -र्णं, वीतरागः -गा -गं, गतवर्णः -र्णा -र्णं, नीरक्तः -क्ता -क्तं.

FADING, *s.* म्लानिः *f.*, शीर्णता, विशीर्णता, क्षयः, ध्वंसः, अवसादः, जीर्णिः *f.*, तेजोहानिः *f.*, शोषः, शुष्कता.—(Loss of colour) वर्णहानिः *f.*, वैवर्ण्यं.

FADING, *part.* or *a.* म्लायन् -यन्ती -यत् (त्), म्लायमानः -ना -नं, विशीर्य्यमाणः -णा -णं, क्षीयमाणः -णा -णं, म्लायमानः -ना -नं, क्षयी -यिणी -यि (न्), क्षयिष्णुः -ष्णुः -ष्णु, विनश्वरः -रा -रं, विध्वंसी -सिनी -सि (न्).

FÆCAL, FÆCES. *See* FECAL, FECES.

To FAG, *v. a.* अतिकायक्लेशेन नीचकर्म्म कृ in caus. (कारयति -यितुं) or दास्यं कृ in caus. खिद् in caus. (खेदयति -यितुं), आयस् in caus. (-यासयति -यितुं).

To FAG, *v. n.* अतिकायक्लेशेन श्रम् (c. 4. श्राम्यति, श्रमितुं), or आयस् (c. 4. -यस्यति -यसितुं), खिद् (c. 4. खिद्यते, खेत्तुं), निरन्तरायासं कृ.

FAG, *s.* दासः, निरन्तरायासी *m.* (न्), अतिश्रमेण नीचकर्म्मकारी *m.* (न्).

Fag-end, *s.* अन्तः -न्तं, अग्रं, अग्रभागः, शेषभागः.—(Refuse) शेषः, अवशिष्टं, उच्छिष्टं, परभागः.

Fagged, *p.p.* खिन्नः -न्ना -न्नं, अतिशरीरायासेन परिश्रान्तः -न्ता -न्तं.

Fagging, *s.* निरन्तरायासः, शरीरायासः, कायक्लेशः, नित्यश्रमः, नित्यक्लेशः.

Fagot, *s.* काष्ठभारः, काष्ठकूर्चः, काष्ठखण्डभारः, दारुखण्डपिण्डः.

To fagot, *v. a.* काष्ठभारं कृ, कूर्चीकृ, काष्ठखण्डानि एकत्र बन्ध् (c. 9. बध्नाति, बन्द्धुं) or एकपिण्डीकृ or एकगुच्छीकृ.

To fail, *v. n.* (Decay, decline) क्षि in pass. (क्षीयते), परिक्षि, सद् (c. 1. सीदति, सत्तुं), अवसद्, ध्वंस् (c. 1. ध्वंसते -सितुं), विध्वंस्, परिहा in pass. (-हीयते), प्रहा, भ्रंश् (c. 4. भ्रश्यति, भ्रंशितुं), विस्रंस् (c. 1. -स्रंसते -सितुं), म्लै (c. 1. म्लायति, म्लातुं).—(Cease, be extinct) निवृत् (c. 1. -वर्त्तते -र्त्तितुं), नश् (c. 4. नश्यति, नशितुं).—(Become deficient) न्यूनीभू, ह्रस् (c. 1. ह्रसते -सितुं), क्षि in pass. अपचि in pass. (-चीयते).—(Miss, not to succeed) न सिध् (c. 4. सिध्यति, सेद्धुं), विफलीभू, न उपपद् (c. 4. -पद्यते -पत्तुं), न सम्पद्, वृथाभू, मोघीभू, भग्नाशः -शा -शं भू, प्रतिहन् in pass. (-हन्यते).—(Omit, neglect) हा (c. 3. जहाति, हातुं), प्रमद् (c. 4. -माद्यति -मदितुं), न कृ, न अनुष्ठा (c. 1. -तिष्ठति -ष्ठातुं), न सेव् (c. 1. सेवते -वितुं).—(Become bankrupt) परिक्षि in pass. परिक्षीणः -णा -णं भू.

To fail, *v. a.* (Desert) हा (c. 3. जहाति, हातुं), अपहा, विहा, त्यज् (c. 1. त्यजति, त्यक्तुं), परित्यज्; 'one who fails in his efforts,' भग्नोद्यमः.

Fail, *s.* परित्यागः, अननुष्ठानं, असेवनं, अकरणं, अपक्रिया, उपात्ययः, हानिः *f.*; 'without fail,' अवश्यं, अवश्यमेव, नूनं, सुनिश्चितं, असंशयं, नियतं.

Failed, *p. p.* अनुपपन्नः -न्ना -न्नं, अप्रतिपन्नः -न्ना -न्नं, अकृतः -ता -तं, अननुष्ठितः -ता -तं.

Failing, *part.* सीदन् -दन्ती -दत् (त्), क्षीयमाणः -णा -णं, विकलः -ला -लं.

Failing, *s.* (Fault) दोषः, अपराधः, छिद्रं, अगुणः, मन्तुः *m.*, वैकल्यं.

Failure, *s.* (Want, deficience) अभावः, असम्भवः, विरहः, अविषयः, अप्राप्तिः *f.*, हानिः *f.*, हीनता, न्यूनता, रहितत्वं, ह्रासः, क्षीणता, वैकल्यं, लोपः; 'on failure,' अभावे, अविषये.—(Decay) क्षयः, परिक्षयः, ध्वंसः, नाशः, विनाशः, भ्रंशः; 'failure of intellect,' बुद्धिविनाशः; 'failure of memory,' स्मृतिभ्रंशः.—(Miscarriage, want of success) असिद्धिः *f.*, अनुपपत्तिः *f.*, असम्पत्तिः *f.*, विपत्तिः *f.*, अप्रतिपत्तिः *f.*, कार्य्यविपत्तिः *f.*, भङ्गः, अकरणिः *f.*—(Omission, non-performance) परित्यागः, अननुष्ठानं, असेवनं, अकरणं, अपक्रिया, उपात्ययः; 'in performance of duty,' अतिपातः; 'in a promise,' संविद्व्यतिक्रमः; 'in a vow,' व्रतलोपनं.—(Becoming insolvent) परिक्षयः, परिक्षीणता, गृहभङ्गः.

Fain, *a.* सकामः -मा -मं, इच्छुः -च्छुः -च्छु, अभिलाषी -षिणी -षि (न्).

Fain, *adv.* प्रकामं, कामं, सकामं, इच्छातस्, सानन्दं, सानुरागं; 'he would fain have filled (his) belly,' उदरं पूरयितुम् अकांक्षत् or ऐच्छत्.

To faint, *v. n.* मुर्छ् (c. 1. मूर्छति -र्छितुं), मूर्छां गम् (c. 1. गच्छति, गन्तुं), मुह् (c. 4. मुह्यति, मोहितुं), नष्टचेतनः -ना -नं भू, चेतनां or चैतन्यं हा (c. 3. जहाति, हातुं), ग्लै (c. 1. ग्लायति, ग्लातुं), परिग्लै, म्लै (c. 1. म्लायति, म्लातुं), परिम्लै, क्लम् (c. 4. क्लाम्यति, क्लमितुं), तम् (c. 4. ताम्यति, तमितुं), आतम्, प्रतम्, प्रली (c. 4. -लीयते -लेतुं).—(Sink, be dejected) सद् (c. 1. सीदति, सत्तुं), अवसद्, विषण्णीभू, क्षि in pass. (क्षीयते), स्रंस् (c. 1. स्रंसते -सितुं).

Faint, *a.* (Languid) ग्लानः -ना -नं, परिग्लानः -ना -नं, म्लानः -ना -नं, परिम्लानः -ना -नं, क्लान्तः -न्ता -न्तं, क्लमी -मिनी -मि (न्), तान्तः -न्ता -न्तं, विषण्णः -ण्णा -ण्णं, शिथिलाङ्गः -ङ्गी -ङ्गं, अवसन्नाङ्गः -ङ्गी -ङ्गं, स्रस्ताङ्गः -ङ्गी -ङ्गं, विश्लथाङ्गः -ङ्गी -ङ्गं.—(Feeble) शिथिलबलः -ला -लं, निर्बलः -ला -लं, सत्त्वरहितः -ता -तं.—(As colour) पाण्डुः -ण्डुः -ण्डु, मन्दच्छायः -या -यं; 'faint red,' ईषद्रक्तः -क्ता -क्तं, श्वेतरक्तः -क्ता -क्तं.—(As sound) मन्दः -न्दा -न्दं.

Fainted, *p. p.* मूर्च्छितः -ता -तं, मूर्छागतः -ता -तं, कश्मलगतः -ता -तं, नष्टचेतनः -ना -नं, चैतन्यरहितः -ता -तं, प्रमुग्धः -ग्धा -ग्धं, प्रलीनः -ना -नं.

Faint-hearted, *a.* भीतहृदयः -या -यं, भीरुहृदयः -या -यं, हरिणहृदयः -या -यं, चकितहृदयः -या -यं, भयाक्रान्तमनाः -नाः -नः (स्).

Faint-heartedly, *adv.* भीरुवत्, भीतवत्, कापुरुषवत्, कातर्य्येण, चकितं.

Faint-heartedness, *s.* हृदयभीरुता, हृदयकातर्य्यं, कातरता.

Fainting, *s.* मूर्छा, मूर्छनं -ना, मोहः, सम्मोहः, प्रमोहः, कश्मलं, कस्मलं, नष्टचेष्टता, चेतनाहानिः *f.*, चैतन्यहानिः, चैतन्यनाशः, चित्तवैकल्यं, प्रलयः, निर्वेशः, मूः *f.*, (मुर्).

Fainting, *part.* or *a.* मूर्च्छितः -ता -तं, मूर्छालः -ला -लं, मूर्त्तः -र्त्ता -र्त्तं, स्रस्ताङ्गः -ङ्गी -ङ्गं; 'from sorrow,' शोकमूर्च्छितः -ता -तं. *See* Fainted.

Faintly, *adv.* अल्पबलेन, मन्दं, ईषत्, कियत्, मनाक्, अबलवत्.

Faintness, *s.* ग्लानिः *f.*, म्लानिः *f.*, क्लान्तिः *f.*, क्लमित्वं, अवसादः, अवसन्नता, दीनता, दौर्बल्यं, अङ्गशैथिल्यं, सत्त्वराहित्यं, मान्द्यं, मन्दता.

Fair, *a.* (Beautiful) सुन्दरः -रा -री -रं, चारुः -र्व्वी -रु, चारुदर्शनः -ना -नं, शोभनः -ना -नं, शुभः -भा -भं, शुभः -भा -भं, कान्तः -न्ता -न्तं, सौम्यः -म्या -म्यं, वामः -मा -मं, सुमुखः -खी -खं, रूपवान् -वती -वत् (त्), सुरूपः -पी -पं, सुदृश्यः -श्या -श्यं, रुचिरः -रा -रं, शुभाननः -ना -नं, श्रीमान् -मती -मत् (त्).—(Clear) विमलः -ला -लं, निर्म्मलः -ला -लं, विशदः -दा -दं, स्वच्छः -च्छा -च्छं, दीप्रः -प्रा -प्रं, शुद्धः -द्धा -द्धं; 'fair weather,' निर्म्मलदिनं, सुदिनं.—(Free from clouds) अनभ्रः -भ्रा -भ्रं, निरभ्रः -भ्रा -भ्रं, व्यभ्रः -भ्रा -भ्रं, गततोयदः -दा -दं, वितिमिरः -रा -रं.—(Just, honest) धर्म्यः -र्म्या -र्म्यं, न्याय्यः -य्या -य्यं, यथान्यायः -या -यं, न्यायवर्त्ती -र्त्तिनी -र्त्ति (न्), समः -मा -मं, सरलः -ला -लं, शुचिः -चिः -चि, शुद्धमतिः -तिः -ति, विमलात्मा -त्मा -त्म (न्), निष्कपटः -टा -टं, निर्व्याजः -जा -जं, सात्त्विकः -की -कं, ऋजुः -जुः -जु.—(Favourable) अनुकूलः -ला -लं, प्रसन्नः -न्ना -न्नं.—(Middling) मध्यमः -मा -मं, न स्थूलो न सूक्ष्मः, नाधिको न च न्यूनः; 'the fair sex,' रमणीगणः, प्रमदागणः.

Fair, *adv.* (Civilly) अनुनयेन, सुशीलवत्, अनुकूलं.—(Honestly) यथान्यायं, समं; 'he bids fair,' उपपद्यते, युज्यते.

Fair, *s.* (Annual market) मेला, निगमः, क्रयारोहः, निवेटः -टं, हट्टः, अवटङ्कः, निषद्या, सांवत्सरिकः क्रेतृविक्रेतृसमागमः, लोकयात्रा.

Fair-complexioned, *a.* विमलवर्णः -र्णा -र्णं, विशदवर्णः -र्णा -र्णं, सुवर्णः -र्णा -र्णं.

Fair-dealing, *s.* शुचिता, सारल्यं, न्यायः, समता, अव्याजः, अकापट्यं.

Fair-faced, *a.* सुमुखः -खी -खं, चारुमुखः -खी -खं, शुभाननः -ना -नं.

Fair-haired, *a.* सुकेशी -शिनी -शि (न्), सुकेशवान् -वती -वत् (त्).

Fairing, *s.* मेलासमये क्रीतं प्रीतिदानं.

Fairly, *adv.* (Justly) धर्म्मतस्, धर्म्मेण, न्यायतस्, न्यायेन, यथान्यायं, न्याय्यं, समं, सम्यक्, सारल्येन, कपटं विना, अमायया.

Fairness, *s.* (Beauty) सौन्दर्य्यं, चारुता, शोभा, कान्तिः *f.*, रूपं, श्रीः *f.*—(Clearness) विमलता, निर्म्मलता, वैमल्यं, वैशद्यं, प्रसन्नता, शुद्धिः *f.*, दीप्तिः *f.*—(Honesty, candour) सारल्यं, सरलता, शुचिता, समता, साम्यं, न्यायता, दाक्षिण्यं, ऋजुता, आर्जवं, अव्याजः, धर्म्यता, धर्म्मः.

Fair-spoken, *a.* प्रियवादी -दिनी -दि (न्), प्रियंवदः -दा -दं, वन्दारुः -रुः -रु.

Fairy, *s.* विद्याधरी, पिशाची, योगिनी, राक्षसी, नायिका, मायिनी, दैत्या, भती.

FAIRY, *a.* पैशाचिकः -की -कं, भौतिकः -की -कं, राक्षसः -सी -सं.

FAITH, *s.* श्रद्धा, भक्तिः *f.*, प्रत्ययः, विश्वासः, विश्रम्भः, आस्था, निष्ठा, आस्तिक्यबुद्धिः *f.*, आस्तिकता, भक्तता; 'of one faith,' एकभक्तिः -क्तिः -क्ति; 'to have faith in,' श्रद्धा (c. 3. -दधाति -धातुं), विश्वस् (c. 2. -श्वसिति -तुं).—(Veracity, honesty) सत्यता, सत्यवादित्वं, विश्वास्यता, सारल्यं; 'done with faith,' श्रद्धाकृतः -ता -तं.

FAITH, *exclam.* सत्यं, नूनं, खलु, एवं, आश्चर्य्यं, चित्रं.

FAITHFUL, *a.* (Firm in adherence) भक्तः -क्ता -क्तं, भक्तिमान् -मती -मत् (त्), दृढभक्तिः -क्तिः -क्ति, भक्तियुक्तः -क्ता -क्तं, आप्तः -प्ता -प्तं, अव्यभिचारी -रिणी -रि (न्); 'faithful to one's master,' प्रभुभक्तः -क्ता -क्तं; 'a faithful friend,' स्थिरप्रेमा *m.* (न्), दृढप्रेमा *m.*, दृढसौहृदः. —(True to obligations) सत्यप्रतिज्ञः -ज्ञा -ज्ञं, सत्यसन्धः -न्धा -न्धं, संशितव्रतः -ता -तं, अस्कन्दितव्रतः -ता -तं, अलङ्घितव्रतः -ता -तं, अनुव्रतः, -ता -तं, प्रतिज्ञापालकः -का -कं.—(Full of faith, having faith) श्रद्धालुः -लुः -लु, श्रद्धावान् -वती -वत् (त्), श्रद्दधानः -ना -नं, श्रद्दधत् -धती -धत् (त्), श्रद्धामयः -यी -यं, विश्वासी -सिनी -सि (न्), प्रत्ययी -यिनी -यि (न्).—(To be trusted, confided in) विश्वास्यः -स्या -स्यं, विश्वसनीयः -या -यं, विश्वस्तः -स्ता -स्तं, विश्रब्धः -ब्धा -ब्धं; 'faithful wife,' पतिव्रता, साध्वी, सती, सुचरित्रा, स्वीया, एकपत्नी; 'faithful lover,' अनुकूलः.

FAITHFULLY, *adv.* भक्त्या, दृढभक्त्या, भक्तवत्, सत्यं, सारल्येन, कपटं विना.

FAITHFULNESS, *s.* (Firm adherence) भक्तिः *f.*, दृढा भक्तिः, भक्तत्वं, भक्तिमत्त्वं, दृढभक्तित्वं, आसक्तिः *f.*, अनुरक्तिः *f.*, दृढं सौहृदं.—(Veracity) सत्यता, सत्यवादित्वं.—(Performance of promises) प्रतिज्ञापालनं -लकत्वं.—(In a wife) पातिव्रत्यं, सतीत्वं, साध्वीत्वं; 'in a lover,' अनुकूलता.

FAITHLESS, *a.* (Unbelieving) अश्रद्दधानः -ना -नं, श्रद्धारहितः -ता -तं, अविश्वासी -सिनी -सि (न्), अप्रत्ययी -यिनी -यि (न्).—(Disloyal, perfidious) अभक्तः -क्ता -क्तं, अभक्तिमान् -मती -मत् (त्), भक्तिहीनः -ना -नं, विश्वासघाती -तिनी -ति (न्), विश्रम्भघाती &c., छिद्रसेवी -विनी -वि (न्), कुटिलाचारः -रा -रं.—(Not to be trusted) अविश्वास्यः -स्या -स्यं.—(Not true to engagements) भग्नप्रतिज्ञः -ज्ञा -ज्ञं, असत्यसन्धः -न्धा -न्धं, मिथ्याप्रतिज्ञः -ज्ञा -ज्ञं, विसंवादी -दिनी -दि (न्).—(Not truc to marriage) व्यभिचारी *m.* रिणी *f.* (न्), असाध्वी *f.*, असती *f.*

FAITHLESSLY, *adv.* अभक्त्या, अभक्तवत्, भक्तिभङ्गात्, प्रतिज्ञाभङ्गात्, मिथ्या.

FAITHLESSNESS, *s.* (Unbelief) अश्रद्धा, अविश्वासः, अप्रत्ययः, अविश्रम्भः. —(Disloyalty) अभक्तिः *f.*, भक्तिहीनता, भक्तिभङ्गः, विश्वासभङ्गः, विश्वासघातः, शत्रुसेवा.—(Violation of promises, &c.) प्रतिज्ञाभङ्गः, प्रतिज्ञातिक्रमः, व्रतलोपनं, संविद्व्यतिक्रमः.

FALCATED, *a.* दात्राकृतिः -तिः -ति, लवित्राकारः -रा -रं, वक्रः -क्रा -क्रं.

FALCHION, *s.* वक्रखड्गः, चन्द्रहासः, निस्त्रिंशः, खड्गः, मण्डलाग्रः, कृपाणः -णकः.

FALCON, *s.* श्येनः, कपोतारिः *m.*, घातिपक्षी *m.* (न्), खगान्तकः, शशादनः, पत्री *m.* (न्), नीलपिच्छः, कपोताद्यनुसरणे शिक्षितः श्येनः.

FALCONER, *s.* श्येनजीवी *m.* (न्), श्येनपोषकः, श्येनपालकः, श्येनशिक्षकः.

FALCONRY, *s.* श्यैनम्पाता, श्येनशिक्षा, श्येनपोषः, श्येनपालनं.

FALD-STOOL, *a.* इतस्ततो वहनयोग्यो लघुपीठः, धर्म्माध्यक्षपीठः -ठं.

To FALL, *v. n.* पत् (c. 1. पतति -तितुं), निपत्, परिपत्, भ्रंश् (c. 4. भ्रश्यति, c. 1. भ्रंशते -शितुं), परिभ्रंश्, च्यु (c. 1. च्यवते, च्योतुं), ध्वंस् (c. 1. ध्वंसते -सितुं), विध्वंस्, स्रंस् (c. 1. स्रंसते -सितुं), आस्रंस्, विस्रंस्, गल् (c. 1. गलति -लितुं), अवगल्, विगल्, समागल्, लम्ब् (c. 1. लम्बते -म्बितुं), स्खल् (c. 1. स्खलति -लितुं).—(Die) मृ (c. 6. म्रियते, मर्त्तुं). —(Sink) सद् (c. 6. सीदति, सत्तुं), अवसद्.—(Fall away) 'become lean,' क्षि in pass. (क्षीयते), कृशीभू; 'apostatize,' स्वधर्म्माद् भ्रंश् or च्यु or विच्यु; 'decline, fade,' ग्लै (c. 1. ग्लायति, ग्लातुं), म्ली (c. 4. -लीयते -लेतुं).—(Fall back) अवस्था (c. 1. -तिष्ठते -स्थातुं), अपसृ (c. 1. -सरति -सर्त्तुं).—(Fall calm) निर्वातीभू.—(Fall down) अवपत्, निपत्, प्रपत्; 'prostrate one's self in worship,' प्रणिपत्, अवनिं गम् (c. 1. गच्छति, गन्तुं), अष्टाङ्गपातं कृ; 'fall down with one's face on the ground,' भूमौ न्यङ्मुखः or अधोमुखः पत्; 'fall down at one's feet,' पादयोः or चरणयोः पत्.—(Fall foul) आक्रम् (c. 1. -क्रामति -क्रमितुं).—(Fall from) भ्रंश्, प्रभ्रंश् or च्यु with abl. c.—(Fall into) निपत्; 'fall into the hands of the enemy,' शत्रुहस्ते पत्.—(Fall in with) सम्मन् (c. 4. -मन्यते -मन्तुं), उपगम्.—(Fall off) 'withdraw,' पलाय् (c. 1. पलायति -यितुं, rt. इ), चल् (c. 1. चलति -लितुं), अवस्था, अपसृ; 'abandon one's duty,' स्वधर्म्मं त्यज् (c. 1. त्यजति, त्यक्तुं).—(Fall on) आपत्, आक्रम्, आसद् (c. 10. -सादयति -यितुं), अभिद्रु, (c. 1. -द्रवति -द्रोतुं). —(Fall out) 'quarrel,' विवद् (c. 1. -वदते -दितुं), कलहं कृ; 'befall,' निपत्, आपत्, उपस्था (c. 1. -तिष्ठति -स्थातुं), सम्भू.—(Fall short) न्यूनीभू, ह्रस् (c. 1. ह्रसते -सितुं), क्षि in pass., हा in pass. (हीयते). (Fall sick) रोगग्रस्तः -स्ता -स्तं भू, पीडितः -ता -तं भू.—(Fall to) उपक्रम्, प्रक्रम्.—(Fall under) अन्तर्गण् in pass. (-गण्यते).—(Fall upon). *See To* FALL ON. (Fall into misfortune) आपद्ग्रस्तः -स्ता -स्तं भू, आपद् (c. 4. -पद्यते -पत्तुं).

To FALL, *v. a.* (Drop, let fall) पत् in caus. (पातयति -यितुं), भ्रंश् in caus. (भ्रंशयति -यितुं), स्रंस् in caus. (स्रंसयति -यितुं).—(Diminish) न्यूनीकृ.

FALL, *s.* (Act of falling and dropping) पातः, पतनं, अवपातः, निपातः, निपतनं, सम्पातः, प्रपतनं, भ्रंशः, प्रभ्रंशः, च्युतिः *f.*, ध्वंसः -सनं, विध्वंसः, प्रध्वंसः, अधोगतिः *f.*, अधःपतनं, विस्रंसा.—(Death, ruin) क्षयः, परिक्षयः, ध्वंसः, परिध्वंसः, नाशः.—(Degradation) पदभ्रंशः, पदच्युतिः *f.*, स्थानप्रभ्रंशः, अपकर्षः, अपध्वंसः, अधोगमः -मनं, मर्य्यादाक्षयः.—(Declension, sinking) च्युतिः *f.*, क्षयः, अवक्षयः, सादः, अवसादः.—(Diminution) न्यूनता, ह्रासः, अपचयः, क्षयः.—(Declivity) पातुकः, पातुकभूमिः *f.*, प्रवणभूमिः *f.*, निम्नभूमिः.—(Cascade) प्रपातः, प्रस्रवणं, वारिप्रवाहः, निर्झरः.—(Fall of the leaf) पर्णध्वंसः, पत्रापगमः, शरद् *f.*—(Fall of snow) हिमवर्षः.—(Fall of rain) धारासम्पातः, धारासारः, धारा, आसारः, अभ्रावकाशः.—(Fall from a vehicle) वाहनभ्रंशः, वाहभ्रंशः.

FALLACIOUS, *a.* मोही -हिनी -हि (न्), मोहनः -ना -नी -नं, भ्रान्तिजनकः -का -कं, भ्रमजनकः -का -कं, भ्रान्तिमान् -मती -मत् (त्), मायी -यिनी -यि (न्), वञ्चकः -का -कं, अविश्वसनीयः -या -यं, असत्यः -त्या -त्यं, मिथ्या in comp.; 'a fallacious opinion,' मिथ्यामतिः *f.*; a fallacious argument,' मिथ्याहेतुः *m.*

FALLACIOUSLY, *adv.* मिथ्या, मोहनार्थं, सव्याजं, मायया, वञ्चनार्थं.

FALLACIOUSNESS, *s.* भ्रान्तिजनकत्वं, भ्रान्तिमत्त्वं, वञ्चकता, असत्यता, सव्याजत्वं; 'of an argument,' हेत्वाभासः.

FALLACY, *s.* (Deceitfulness) वञ्चकत्वं, कूटता.—(Mistake) भ्रमः, भ्रान्तिः *f.*, मिथ्यामतिः *f.*—(False argument) मिथ्याहेतुः *m.*, आभासः, हेत्वाभासः, पक्षाभासः, फक्किका.

FALLEN, *p. p.* पतितः -ता -तं, निपतितः -ता -तं, प्रपतितः -ता -तं, भ्रष्टः -ष्टा -ष्टं, प्रभ्रष्टः -ष्टा -ष्टं, च्युतः -ता -तं, स्रस्तः -स्ता -स्तं, ध्वस्तः -स्ता -स्तं,

गलितः -ता -तं, विगलितः -ता -तं, पन्नः -न्ना -न्नं, स्खन्नः -न्ना -न्नं; 'fallen down,' अधःपतितः -ता -तं; 'fallen asleep,' सुप्तः -प्ता -प्तं, प्रसुप्तः -प्ता -प्तं; 'fallen into distress,' विपद्ग्रस्तः -स्ता -स्तं, आपन्नः -न्ना -न्नं, आपदम्प्राप्तः -प्ता -प्तं.

FALLIBILITY, s. भ्रान्तिमत्त्वं, मोहयोग्यता, मोहाधीनता, भ्रमजनकता, मोहवत्त्वं, वञ्चनीयता, वञ्चकता, प्रमादवत्त्वं, असत्यता.

FALLIBLE, a. भ्रान्तिजनकः -का -कं, भ्रमजनकः -का -कं, भ्रान्तिमान् -मती -मत् (त्), मोही -हिनी -हि (न्), भ्रमणशीलः -ला -लं, वञ्चनीयः -या -यं, भ्रमयोग्यः -ग्या -ग्यं.

FALLING, part. पातुकः -का -कं, पाती -तिनी -ति (न्), पतयालुः -लुः -लु, स्रंसी -सिनी -सि (न्), ध्वंसी -सिनी -सि (न्), पित्सन् -त्सती -त्सत् (त्), पिपतिषुः -षुः -षु.

FALLING, s. (Indenture) भङ्गः, निम्नता.—(Falling away) धर्मभ्रंशः, धर्मच्युतिः f., धर्मत्यागः.—(Falling off) भ्रंशः, भ्रेषः, क्षयः, उत्क्रमः.

FALLING-SICKNESS, s. भ्रमरं, ग्रहामयः, अपस्मारः, भूतविक्रिया, प्रतानः.

FALLOW, a. (Unsowed) अनुप्तः -प्ता -प्तं, अनुप्तसस्यः -स्या -स्यं, अनुप्तिमः -मा -मं, अवापितः -ता -तं.—(Untilled) अप्रहतः -ता -तं, अकृष्टः -ष्टा -ष्टं, अफालकृष्टः -ष्टा -ष्टं, अकृतः -ता -तं, अहलः -ला -लं, अहल्यः -ल्या -ल्यं, खिलः -ला -लं; 'fallow land,' अनुप्तभूमिः f., अप्रहतभूमिः f.—(Pale red) ईषद्रक्तः -क्ता -क्तं, श्वेतरक्तः -क्ता -क्तं.

To FALLOW, v. a. बीजारोपणव्यतिरेकेण or बीजानि अनुप्त्वा भूमिं हलेन कृष् (c. 1. कर्षति, क्रष्टुं) or भूमिलोष्टान् भिद् (c. 7. भिनत्ति, भेत्तुं).

FALLOWING, s. बीजवपनव्यतिरेकेण भूमिकर्षणं or लोष्टभेदनं or भूमिहतिः f.

FALLOWNESS, s. अनुप्तत्वं, अकृष्टता, अहल्यता, वन्ध्यता, निष्फलता, वैफल्यं.

FALSE, a. (Not true) असत्यः -त्या -त्यं, निःसत्यः -त्या -त्यं, अनृतः -ता -तं, अतथ्यः -थ्या -थ्यं, वितथः -था -थं, अयथार्थः -र्था -र्थं, असन् -सती -सत् (त्), अप्रकृतः -ता -तं, अलीकः -का -कं, मिथ्या or मृषा or अन्यथा in comp.; as, 'a false accusation,' मिथ्याभियोगः, मिथ्यापवादः; 'a false opinion,' मिथ्यामतिः f.; 'a false reply,' मिथ्योत्तरं; 'false speaking,' मृषावादः, मिथ्यावादः, असत्यभाषणं; 'false accuser,' मृषापवादी m. (न्).—(Fictitious) कृत्रिमः -मा -मं, कल्पितः -ता -तं, काल्पनिकः -की -कं, विडम्बितः -ता -तं, कपटी -टिनी -टि (न्), कूट or कपट or छद्म in comp.; as, 'false coin,' कूटस्वर्णं; 'false dice,' कूटाक्षः; 'false document,' कपटलेख्यं; 'false balances,' कूटतुला; 'false measure,' कूटमानं; 'a false ascetic,' छद्मतापसः, बकव्रती m. (न्); 'in a false dress,' छद्मवेशी m. (न्).—(Unfaithful, treacherous) विश्वासघाती -तिनी -ति (न्), रहस्यभेदी -दिनी -दि (न्), मन्त्रभेदी &c., क्षीणभक्तिः -क्तिः -क्ति, व्यभिचारी -रिणी -रि (न्); 'to vows, engagements,' खण्डितव्रतः -ता -तं, उल्लङ्घितव्रतः -ता -तं, असत्यसन्धः -न्धा -न्धं, लुप्तव्रतः -ता -तं; 'a false wife,' अपतिव्रता.—(Hypocritical) कुहकः -का -कं, दम्भी -म्भिनी -म्भि (न्); 'false worship,' धर्मविडम्बनं.—(Vain, groundless) वृथा or मिथ्या in comp. मोघः -घा -घं; 'a false alarm,' वृथाक्रोशः; 'false hope,' मोघाशा.—(Dishonest) कापटिकः -की -कं.

FALSE-HEARTED, a. विश्वासघाती -तिनी -ति (न्), अस्थिरप्रेमा -मा -म (न्).

FALSEHOOD, s. (Want of truth) असत्यता, निःसत्यता, अतथ्यता, अनृतता, वितथता, अलीकता, अयाथार्थ्यं.—(A lie) अनृतं, असत्यं, वितथं, अतथ्यं, अलीकं, अश्लीलं, मृषोद्यं.—(Speaking falsehood) मिथ्यावादः, मृषावादः, मिथ्याकथनं, मृषाभाषिता, असत्यभाषणं, मृषाभिधानं, कैतववादः; 'one who tells a falsehood,' अनृतवादी m. (न्), मिथ्यावादी, मृषावादी; 'devoted to falsehood,' अनृतव्रतः -ता -तं.

FALSELY, adv. मिथ्या, मृषा, अन्यथा, असत्यं, निःसत्यं, अनृतं; 'acting falsely,' मिथ्याचारः -रा -रं; 'speaking falsely,' अनृतवादी -दिनी -दि (न्), अनृतवाच् m. f. n. (च्); 'falsely modest,' मिथ्याविनीतः -ता -तं, कपटविनयवान् -वती -वत् (त्).

FALSENESS, s. (Want of truth) असत्यता, निःसत्यता.—(Fictitiousness) कूटता, कृत्रिमता, कापट्यं.—(Duplicity) कपटता, व्याजः, कैतवं, शठता.—(Perfidy) विश्वासभङ्गः, विश्वासघातः, मन्त्रभेदः.

FALSE-PROPHET, s. भविष्यद्वादिनो वेशधारी m. (न्), मिथ्याभविष्यद्वादी m.

FALSE-WITNESS, s. कूटसाक्षी m. (न्), मिथ्यासाक्षी m., कूटकारकः, कौटसाक्ष्यं, मिथ्यासाक्ष्यं, अतथ्यसाक्ष्यं.

FALSIFICATION, s. कूटकरणं, कपटकरणं, छद्मकरणं, कृत्रिमकरणं, मिथ्याकरणं, अन्यथाकरणं.

FALSIFIER, s. कूटकः, कूटकृत्, कपटकारी m. (न्), मिथ्याकारी m.—(Disprover) खण्डनकृत्, प्रत्याख्याता m. (तृ), अपरीकारी m.

To FALSIFY, v. a. (Counterfeit) कूटं कृ, कपटं कृ, छल् (c. 10. छलयति -यितुं), अन्यथा कृ, मिथ्या कृ.—(Disprove) खण्ड् (c. 10. खण्डयति -यितुं), अपरीकृ, असत्यम् इति सूच् (c. 10. सूचयति -यितुं).—(Violate, break) अतिक्रम् (c. 1. -क्रामति -क्रमितुं), भिद् (c. 7. भिनत्ति, भेत्तुं), लुप् (c. 6. लुम्पति, लोप्तुं).

To FALSIFY, v. n. असत्यं वद् (c. 1. वदति -दितुं), मिथ्या or मृषा वद्.

FALSITY, s. असत्यता, निःसत्यता, अनृतता, अयाथार्थ्यं, वितथत्वं, अलीकता.

To FALTER, v. n. (Speak with broken utterance) स्वरभङ्गेन or भग्नस्वरेण or स्खलद्वाक्येन वद् (c. 1. वदति -दितुं), स्खलितं वद्, स्वरेण स्खल् (c. 1. स्खलति -लितुं, c. 10. स्खलयति -यितुं), गद्गदया वाचा वद्, अस्पष्टवाचा वद्, गद्गद (nom. गद्गदति).—(Tremble, totter) स्खल्, प्रस्खल्, स्खलनं कृ, कम्प् (c. 1. कम्पते -म्पितुं), वेप् (c. 1. वेपते -पितुं).

FALTERING, part. or a. स्खलितवाक्यः -क्या -क्यं, भग्नस्वरः -रा -रं, भिन्नस्वरः -रा -रं.

FALTERING, s. स्खलनं, वाक्यस्खलनं, स्खलद्वाक्यं, स्वरभङ्गः, स्वरभेदः, गद्गदवाच् f. (च्), अस्पष्टवचनं.

FALTERINGLY, adv. स्खलत्स्वरेण, स्खलद्वाक्येन, स्वरभङ्गेन, गद्गदवाचा.

FAME, s. कीर्त्तिः f., यशः n. (स्), ख्यातिः f., सुख्यातिः f., परिख्यातिः f., विश्रुतिः f., प्रतिष्ठा, विश्रावः, प्रसिद्धिः f., प्रकीर्त्तिः f., कीर्त्तना -नं, प्रथा, प्रथितिः f., सम्प्रथा, समाख्या, समाज्ञा, प्रतिपत्तिः f., विख्यातिः f., प्रविख्यातिः f., प्रतिख्यातिः f., रूढिः.—(Rumour) जनश्रुतिः f., जनप्रवादः, जनोदाहरणं.

FAMED, a. ख्यातः -ता -तं, विख्यातः -ता -तं, प्रसिद्धः -द्धा -द्धं, विश्रुतः -ता -तं, प्रथितः -ता -तं, कीर्त्तितः -ता -तं, समाख्यातः -ता -तं, लोकविश्रुतः -ता -तं.

FAME-GIVING, a. कीर्त्तिकरः -री -रं, यशस्करः -री -रं, कीर्त्तिदः -दा -दं.

FAMILIAR, a. (Domestic) गृहजः -जा -जं -जातः -ता -तं, आगारवेश्मिकः -की -कं, कौलिकः -की -कं, कुल in comp.—(Well acquainted with, intimate) परिचितः -ता -तं, सुविद् m. f. n., सुसंसर्गी -र्गिणी -र्गि (न्), संस्तुतः -ता -तं; 'with the scriptures,' शास्त्रज्ञः, स्वधीतशास्त्रः; 'with law,' स्मृतिकुशलः.—(Accustomed to) अभ्यस्तः -स्ता -स्तं.—(Well-known) सुविदितः -ता -तं, सुज्ञातः -ता -तं, प्रसिद्धः -द्धा -द्धं.—(Unceremonious) आदरहीनः -ना -नं, निर्गौरवः -वा -वं, निरादरः -रा -रं.—(Ordinary) प्राकृतः -ती -तं, लौकिकः -की -कं, लोकसिद्धः -द्धा -द्धं, प्रसिद्धः -द्धा -द्धं; 'familiar conversation,' विस्रम्भालापः.

FAMILIAR, s. (Friend) सुपरिचितः सुहृद् m.; दृढसुहृद् m., सुसंसर्गी m.

(न्), चिरमित्रं, चारः.

FAMILIARITY, *s.* (Intimate association) सुसंसर्गः, दृढसंसर्गः, संसर्गित्वं, संसक्तिः *f.*, आसक्तः, संयोगः.—(Intimate acquaintance) परिचयः, सुपरिचयः, परिज्ञानं, संस्तवः.—(Freedom from ceremony, affability) अनादरः, आदरहीनता, गौरवहीनता, अभिगम्यता.

To FAMILIARIZE, *v. a.* अभ्यस् (c. 4. -अस्यति -असितुं), अभ्यासेन सुगमं -मां -मं or सुकरं -रां -रं कृ, निरन्तराभ्यासं कृ, परिचयं कृ.

FAMILIARIZED, *p.p.* अभ्यस्तः -स्ता -स्तं, कृताभ्यासः -सा -सं, कृतपरिचयः -या -यं.

FAMILIARLY, *adv.* निर्गौरवं, गौरवं विना, निरादरं, अनादरेण, चिरमित्रवत्, सुपरिचितवत्; 'familiarly conversing,' विश्रब्धप्रलापी -पिनी -पि(न्).

FAMILY, *s.* (Race) कुलं, वंशः, कुटुम्बः, जातिः *f.*, गोत्रं, सन्तानः, प्रवरं.—(Lineage) अन्वयः, सन्ततिः *f.*, जननं, आवलिः *f.*, अन्ववायः.—(Household) गृहजनः, अभिजनः, स्वजनः, परिजनः, कुटुम्बकं, स्त्रीपुत्रकन्यादि; 'head of a family,' कुटुम्बी, कौटुम्बिकः, कुलपतिः *m.*, कुलोद्वहः; 'of the same family,' सकुलः -ला -लं, सकुल्यः -ल्या -ल्यं; 'relating to a family,' कौलः -ली -लं -लिकः -की -कं, कुल in comp.; 'of good or noble family,' महाकुलः -ला -लं -लीनः -ना -नं, कुलीनः -ना -नं, कौलेयः -यी -यं, कुलिकः -का -कं, कुलोद्गतः -ता -तं; 'of low family,' दुष्कुलीनः -ना -नं, अकुलीनः -ना -नं; 'a woman of good family,' कुलनारी, कुलकन्या; 'of royal family,' राजवंश्यः -श्या -श्यं; 'family honour,' कुलमर्य्यादा; 'family pride,' कुलाभिमानं, कुलोन्नतिः *f.*; 'family disgrace,' कुलनिन्दा; 'family respectability,' कुलोत्कर्षः; 'family duty,' कुलधर्म्मः, कुलाचारः; 'family priest,' कुलाचार्य्यः; 'family party,' गृहोत्सवः; 'family feuds,' गृहच्छिद्रं; 'family connexions,' गोष्ठी, कुलसन्धिः *f.*; 'of ancient family,' दीर्घवंशः -शा -शं; 'attentive in supporting one's family,' कुटुम्बव्यापृतः, कुलालम्बी *m.* (न्), अभ्यागारिकः, उपाधिः *m.*; 'cruelty to one's family,' अनात्म्यं.

FAMINE, *s.* दुर्भिक्षं, दुष्कालः, दुर्भक्ष्यं, अन्नाकालं, अकालः, प्रयामः, नीवाकः, अनाहारकालः, आहारविरहः, आहाराभावः, अन्नाभावः, आहारासम्भवः, दुर्मूल्यं.

To FAMISH, *v. a.* क्षुधया पीड् (c. 10. पीडयति -यितुं) or व्यापद् (c. 10. -पादयति -यितुं) or अवसद् in caus. (-सादयति -यितुं) or कृशीकृ, क्षुधार्त्तं -र्त्तां -र्त्तं कृ.

To FAMISH, *v. n.* आहारविरहाद् अवसद् (c. 6. -सीदति -सत्तुं) or क्षि in pass. (क्षीयते) or क्षीणशरीरः -रा -रं भू or कृशाङ्गीभू or व्यापद् (c. 4. -पद्यते).

FAMISHED, *p.p.* or *a.* क्षुत्पीडितः -ता -तं, क्षुधार्त्तः -र्त्ता -र्त्तं, क्षुधापीडितः -ता -तं, क्षुत्क्षामः -मा -मं, क्षुत्परिकृशः -शा -शं, क्षुधार्दितः -ता -तं, बुभुक्षितः -ता -तं, निरन्नः -न्ना -न्नं.

FAMISHMENT, *s.* क्षुत्पीडा, क्षुत्क्षामता, अनाहारः, अन्नाभावः, बुभुक्षा.

FAMOUS, *a.* ख्यातः -ता -तं, सुख्यातः -ता -तं, यशस्वी -स्विनी -स्वि (न्), महायशाः -शाः -शः (स्) -यशस्कः -स्का -स्कं, कीर्त्तिमान् -मती -मत् (त्), विश्रुतः -ता -तं, प्रथितः -ता -तं, प्रसिद्धः -द्धा -द्धं, विख्यातः -ता -तं, परिख्यातः -ता -तं, कीर्त्तितः -ता -तं, प्रतीतः -ता -तं, प्रतिपत्तिमान् -मती -मत् (त्), पृथुप्रथः -था -थं, लोकविश्रुतः -ता -तं, 'rendering famous,' यशस्करः -री -रं, यशस्यः -स्या -स्यं, कीर्त्तिकरः -री -रं.

FAMOUSLY, *adv.* महायशसा, महाकीर्त्तिपूर्व्वं, परमं, उत्तमप्रकारेण.

FAMOUSNESS, *s.* कीर्त्तिमत्त्वं, यशस्विता, ख्यातिमत्त्वं, विश्रुतिः *f.*

FAN, *s.* व्यजनं, तालवृन्तः -न्तं, वीजनं, प्रकीर्णकं, चामरं, मरुदान्दोलः, उत्क्षेपणं, व्यजः.—(For winnowing) सूर्प्पः -र्प्पं, शूर्प्पः -र्प्पं.

To FAN, *v. a.* वीज् c. 10. वीजयति -यितुं), उपवीज्, अनुवीज्, उद्वीज्, व्यजनवायुना विधू (c. 5. -धूनोति, c. 6. -धुवति -धवितुं), व्यजनवातेन शीतल (nom. शीतलयति -यितुं).

FANATIC, FANATICAL, *a.* देवभक्तिव्ययः -ग्रा -ग्रं or अतिश्रद्धाव्ययः, स्वकामतदेवभक्तिवाद् उन्मत्तः -त्ता -त्तं or उन्मत्तबुद्धिः -द्धिः -द्धि or उच्छ्वसद्बुद्धिः -द्धिः -द्धि or भ्रान्तबुद्धिः -द्धिः -द्धि.

FANATIC, *s.* अतिशयदेवभक्तिवाद् उन्मत्तजनः or उन्मादी *m.* (न्), मिथ्याभक्तिमान् *m.* (त्), क्षपणकः.

FANATICALLY, *adv.* देवभक्तिव्ययवत्, स्वकामदेवभक्त्या, उन्मत्तवत्.

FANATICISM, *s.* स्वकामदेवभक्तिजन्यो मादविशेषः or उन्मादः or उन्मदः or उन्मत्तबुद्धित्वं, अतिश्रद्धाप्रयुक्ता उन्मत्तता, अतिभक्तिव्ययता, अतिश्रद्धाव्ययता, भक्तिबुद्धता, मिथ्याभक्तिः *f.*

FANCIED, *p. p.* भावितः -ता -तं, विभावितः -ता -तं, मतः -ता -तं.

FANCIFUL, *a.* (Formed in the imagination) मानसिकः -की -कं, मनोजः -जा -जं, मनसिजः -जा -जं, मनोगतः -ता -तं, मायामयः -यी -यं, वासनाकल्पितः -ता -तं, काल्पनिकः -की -कं, मनःकल्पितः -ता -तं, मनोरथसृष्टः -ष्टा -ष्टं, सङ्कल्पजः -जा -जं, अमूलकः -का -कं.—(Fanciful man) वृथावासनाकारी *m.* (न्), दुर्वासनाकृत् *m.*, अनर्थकचिन्ताकरः, असम्भवकल्पकः, चपलबुद्धिः *m.*, मनोलौल्यवान् *m.* (त्), लोलमतिः *m.*

FANCIFULLY, *adv.* वृथावासनापूर्व्वं, अनर्थकचिन्तापूर्व्वं, काल्पनिकप्रकारेण, मनोलौल्यात्, बुद्धिचापल्यात्.

FANCIFULNESS, *s.* मनोलौल्यं, बुद्धिचापल्यं, लोलबुद्धित्वं, मायावत्त्वं, बुद्धिविलासिता, मिथ्यासङ्कल्पवत्त्वं.

FANCY, *s.* (The faculty of imagination) कल्पनाशक्तिः *f.*, भावना -नं, विभावना -नं, वासना, कल्पना.—(Idea) बुद्धिः *f.*, मतिः *f.*, सङ्कल्पः, मनोमतं, चिन्ता, मनोरथसृष्टिः *f.*—(Caprice, whim) मनोलौल्यं, बुद्धिविलासः, बुद्धिचापल्यं, चापलं, भासः, आभासः, निर्बन्धः, लहरी, तरङ्गः, अवहित्थः *m.*, छन्दः *n.* (स्).—(Strange fancy) वृथावासना, असम्भवकल्पना, अनर्थकवासना, मिथ्यावासना, दुर्वासना, अनर्थकचिन्ता, मनोमाया, मृषार्थकं.—(Liking) रुचिः *f.*, अभिरुचिः *f.*

To FANCY, *v. n.* (Imagine, think) मन् (c. 4. मन्यते, मन्तुं), भू (c. 10. भावयति -यितुं), विभू, सम्भू, चिन्त् (c. 10. चिन्तयति -यितुं). 'To fancy one's self,' is sometimes expressed by the adj. मन्यः -न्या -न्यं; as, 'one who fancies himself learned,' पण्डितम्मन्यः; 'one who fancies himself good,' साधुम्मन्यः; 'one who fancies herself beautiful,' सुन्दरीम्मन्या.

To FANCY, *v. a.* (Form in the mind) मनसा क्लृप् (c. 10. कल्पयति -यितुं) or भू in caus. (भावयति -यितुं) or कृ.—(Like) अभिनन्द् (c. 1. -नन्दति -न्दितुं), रुच् (c. 1. रोचते -चितुं) with dat. of the person; as, 'he fancies that,' तत् तस्मै रोचते; 'doing what one fancies,' कामकारी *m.* (न्); 'eating what one fancies,' कामभक्षः.

FANCY-FRAMED, *a.* मनःकल्पितः -ता -तं, वासनाकल्पितः -ता -तं, मनोजः -जा -जं, मनसिजः -जा -जं, मनोरथसृष्टः -ष्टा -ष्टं, मानसिकः -की -कं.

FANCY-SICK, *a.* विकृतबुद्धिः -द्धिः -द्धि; 'one who fancies himself sick,' रोगिम्मन्यः.

FANE, *s.* देवतागारः, देवागारः, देवालयः, देवतायतनं, देवभवनं, देवप्रासादः, देवगृहं, देववेश्म *n.* (न्), देवतामन्दिरं, देवतावासः.

FANG, *s.* दंष्ट्रा, दशनः -नं, रदः -दनः, दन्तः, उदग्रदन्तः, दीर्घदन्तः, विषाक्तः

-ष्टं, दाढा, दाढकः, राक्षसी; 'of a serpent,' विषदन्तः, आशीः *f.* (स्).—(Claw) नखः.

FANGED, *a.* दंष्ट्री -ष्ट्रिणी -ष्ट्रि (न्), दन्ती -न्तिनी -न्ति (न्), दीर्घदन्तवान् -वती -वत् (त्).

FANGLESS, *a.* निर्दशनः -ना -नं, भग्नदंष्ट्रः -ष्ट्रा -ष्ट्रं, गलितदन्तः -न्ता -न्तं, निर्दन्तः -न्ता -न्तं, दशनोच्छिष्टः -ष्टा -ष्टं.

FAN-LIGHT, *s.* व्यजनाकारो गवाक्षः or गृहाक्षः.

FANNED, *p. p.* वीजितः -ता -तं, उपवीजितः -ता -तं, वीज्यमानः -ना -नं, उद्वीज्यमानः -ना -नं, व्यजनेन विधूयमानः -ना -नं or विधुतः -ता -तं.

FANNER, *s.* वीजयिता *m.* (तृ), वीजनकर्त्ता *m.* (र्त्तृ), विधविता *m.* (तृ).

FANTASM, *s.* मिथ्यावासना, मनोरथसृष्टिः *f.*, आभासः, अपच्छाया.

FANTASTIC, FANTASTICAL, *a.* (Existing in the imagination) मनःकल्पितः -ता -तं, मनसिजः -जा -जं, वासनाकल्पितः -ता -तं, मानसिकः -की -कं.—(Capricious, whimsical) चपलः -ला -लं, लोलः -ला -लं.—(Odd) विषमः -मा -मं, असङ्गतः -ता -तं, अपरूपः -पा -पी -पं, विलक्षणः -णा -णं.

FANTASTICALLY, *adv.* चपलं, चापल्येन, मनोलौल्यात्, विषमं, असङ्गतं.

FANTASTICALNESS, *s.* चापल्यं, मनोलौल्यं, वैषम्यं, अपरूपता, असङ्गतत्वं.

FANTASY, *s.* *See* FANCY.

FAR, *a.* दूरः -रा -रं, विदूरः -रा -रं, दूरस्थः -स्था -स्थं -स्थायी -यिनी -यि (न्), दूरवर्त्ती -र्त्तिनी -र्त्ति (न्), दूरीभूतः -ता -तं, अनुपस्थायी -यिनी -यि (न्), अनुपस्थः -स्था -स्थं, असन्निकृष्टः -ष्टा -ष्टं, विप्रकृष्टः -ष्टा -ष्टं, असन्निहितः -ता -तं; 'very far,' सुदूरः -रा -रं, दविष्ठः -ष्ठा -ष्ठं, दवीयान् -यसी -यः (स्).

FAR, *adv.* (At a distance) दूरं, दूरे, दूरतस्, विदूरतस्, आरात्.—(To a distance) दूरं, दूरपर्य्यन्तं.—(By a distance) दूरेण.—(From far) दूरात्, दूरतस्.—(To a great extent) अत्यन्तं, भृशं, बहु, सु or अति or अतिशय prefixed.—(As far as) expressed by आ prefixed governing the abl. c., or by पर्य्यन्तं or अन्त affixed; as, 'the earth as far as the ocean,' आसमुद्रात् or समुद्रपर्य्यन्तं or सागरान्ता पृथिवी.—(By far) दूरेण; 'action is by far inferior to devotion,' कर्म्म दूरेण अवरं योगात्.—(How far?) किं पर्य्यन्तं, कियत् पर्य्यन्तं, कियत् प्रमाणं.—(So far) तदन्तं, तत्पर्य्यन्तं.—(Far off) दूरस्थः -स्था -स्थं, दूरसंस्थः -स्था -स्थं, दूरीभूतः -ता -तं; 'the day being far spent,' अतिक्रान्ते दिवसे; 'a woman far gone in love,' दूरगतमन्मथा.

FAR-EXTENDED, *a.* बहुविस्तीर्णः -र्णा -र्णं, सर्व्वत्रव्यापी -पिनी -पि (न्).

FAR-FAMED, *a.* पृथुप्रथः -था -थं, पृथुयशाः -शाः -शः (स्), महायशाः &c.

FAR-FETCHED, *a.* क्लिष्टः -ष्टा -ष्टं, यत्नकृतः -ता -तं; 'far-fetched idea,' क्लिष्टकल्पना.

FAR-SEEING, *a.* दूरदर्शी -र्शिनी -र्शि (न्), दीर्घदर्शी -र्शिनी -र्शि (न्).

FAR-SIGHTED, *a.* दूरदृष्टिः -ष्टिः -ष्टि, दीर्घदृष्टिः -ष्टिः -ष्टि, पारदृश्वा -श्वा -श्व (न्).

FARCE, *s.* प्रहसनं, विलासिका, दुर्म्मल्लिका, हास्योत्पादको नाटकः, परिहासजनकम् उपरूपकं.

FARCICAL, *a.* प्रहसनसम्बन्धी -न्धिनी -न्धि (न्).—(Droll) हासकरः -री -रं, हास्यः -स्या -स्यं, उपहास्यः -स्या -स्यं, रसिकः -का -कं, विनोदी -दिनी -दि (न्), हास्योत्पादकः -का -कं, असङ्गतः -ता -तं, अपरूपः -पा -पं.

FARCY, *s.* अश्वानां चर्म्मरोगविशेषः or दुश्चर्म्मत्वं or चर्म्मदूषिका.

FARDEL, *s.* कूर्चः, गुच्छः -च्छकः, पोटलिका, पोट्टली, भारः.

To FARE, *v. n.* (Be in any state) वृत् (c. 1. वर्त्तते -र्त्तितुं), अस् (c. 2. अस्ति), भू (c. 1. भवति -वितुं), स्था (c. 1. तिष्ठति, स्थातुं); 'to fare well,' सुस्थः -स्था -स्थं or सुस्थितः -ता -तं भू or अस्; 'to fare badly,' दुःस्थः -स्था -स्थं भू or अस्; 'faring well,' भविष्णुः -ष्णुः -ष्णु, भूष्णुः -ष्णुः -ष्णु, भविता -त्री -तृ (तृ).—(Feed) भोजनं कृ, भुज् (c. 7. भुंक्ते, भोक्तुं), आहारं कृ; 'to fare well,' स्वाद्वन्नानि or उत्तमान्नानि or परमान्नानि भुज्.

FARE, *s.* (Passage-money) आतारः, आतरः, तरपण्यं, तरमूल्यं, तारिकं, तार्य्यं, अनुत्तरं.—(Food) भोजनं, आहारः, अन्नं, भक्ष्यं; 'good fare,' उत्तमाहारः, परमान्नं, उत्तमान्नं; 'bad fare,' कदन्नं.

FAREWELL, *adv.* (To bid farewell) आमन्त्र् (c. 10. -मन्त्रयते -यितुं), अनुमन्त्र्, आप्रच्छ् (c. 6. -पृच्छते -ति -प्रष्टुं).—(Bidding farewell) आमन्त्रणं, आप्रच्छनं, प्रस्थानकाले कुशलवादः or प्रणामः or नमस्कारः; 'farewell!' कुशलं भूयात्, सुखं भूयात्, कल्याणं भूयात्, सुखम् आस्तां.

FARINA, *s.* परागः, सुमनोरजः *n.* (स्), पुष्परेणुः *m.*, सुमनःपांशुः *m.*, पुरुः *m.*

FARINACEOUS, *a.* शस्यमयः -यी -यं, धान्यमयः -यी -यं, गोधूमचूर्णमयः -यी -यं.

FARM, *s.* क्षेत्रं, भूमिः *f.*, क्षेत्रभूमिः, भूः *f.*, कृषिक्षेत्रं, कर्षणभूमिः *f.*, सीत्यं.

To FARM, *v. a.* (Let out the collection of the revenue or any other work at a certain rate per cent.) शते शते निरूपितमूल्यं प्रतिज्ञाय or शते शते नियमितभागो मया दातव्य इति सन्धिं कृत्वा अमुकजनं शुल्ककरादिग्रहणे or किञ्चित्कर्म्मनिर्वहणे नियुज् (c. 7. -युनक्ति -योक्तुं, c. 10. -योजयति -यितुं).—(Undertake any work for another at a certain rate per cent.) शते शते नियमितभागो मद्वेतनार्थम् उद्धरणीयं or शते शते निरूपितमूल्यं मया ग्रहणीयम् इति सन्धिं कृत्वा अमुकजनस्थाने किञ्चित् कर्म्म निर्वह् in caus. (-वाहयति -यितुं) or नियमितमूल्यम् अपेक्ष्य परस्थाने किञ्चित् कर्म्म व्यवसो (c. 4. -स्यति -सातुं) or अध्यवसो.—(Farm the tolls) निरूपितमूल्यं दत्त्वा राजस्थाने घट्टनदीतरादिदेयशुल्कान् ग्रह् (c. 9. गृह्णाति, ग्रहीतुं).—(Cultivate land) क्षेत्रं or भूमिं कृष् (c. 6. कृषति, c. 1. कर्षति, क्रष्टुं).

FARM-HOUSE, *s.* क्षैत्रिकगृहं, कर्षकगृहं, क्षैत्रिकवेश्म *n.* (न्), क्षेत्रपतिगृहं.

FARM-YARD, *s.* क्षैत्रिकगृहोपान्ते वाटी or वाटिका or चत्वरं.

FARMER, *s.* क्षेत्रकर्षकः, क्षैत्रिकः, क्षेत्री *m.* (न्), कर्षकः, कृषिकः, कृषकः, क्षेत्राजीवः, कृषिजीवी *m.* (न्), कृषीवलः, कार्षकः, क्षेत्रपतिः *m.*—(Of the revenue) शते शते नियमितभागो मद्वेतनार्थम् उद्धरणीय इति सन्धिं कृत्वा शुल्ककरादि गृह्णाति यो जनः.

FARMING, *s.* कृषिकर्म्म *n.* (न्), कृषिः *f.*, कार्षिः *f.*, क्षैत्रिकव्यापारः, अनृतं.

FARRAGINOUS, *a.* सान्निपातिकः -की -कं, सन्निपतितः -ता -तं, प्रकीर्णः -र्णा -र्णं, बहुद्रव्यनिर्म्मितः -ता -तं, नानाद्रव्यघटितः -ता -तं.

FARRAGO, *s.* सन्निपातः, प्रकीर्णकं, नानाद्रव्यसम्मिश्रणं.

FARRIER, *s.* अश्वचिकित्सकः, अश्ववैद्यः.—(Shoer of horses) अश्वपादुकाबन्धा *m.* (न्धृ), अश्वपादुकाकारः.

FARRIERY, *s.* अश्वचिकित्सा, अश्वरोगचिकित्सनविद्या.

FARROW, *s.* शूकरशावकगणः, शूकरपोतकगणः, शूकरापत्यं.

To FARROW, *v. n.* शूकरीप्रकारेण शावकगणं सु (c. 2. सूते, c. 4. सूयते, सोतुं) or प्रसु.

FART, *s.* पर्दः -र्दनं, गुदरवः, पायुशब्दः, शर्द्धः.

FARTHER, *adv.* दूरतरं, विदूरतरं, अधिकदूरे, अग्रे, अग्रतरं, अग्रतस्, पुरतस्, पुरस्.—(Moreover) अपरं, अपरञ्च, अधिकं, अधिकन्तु, अन्यच्च, अपिच, किञ्च, परन्तु. *See* the more correct word *further.*

FARTHER, *a.* दूरतरः -रा -रं, विदूरतरः -रा -रं, दवीयान् -यसी -यः (स्), अधिकदूरस्थः -स्था -स्थं, अपरः -रा -रं; 'the farther side,' पारः; 'on the farther side,' पारे.

FARTHEST, *a.* दूरतमः -मा -मं, विदूरतमः -मा -मं, दविष्ठः -ष्ठा -ष्ठं, सुदूरः

-रा -रं, अत्यन्तदूरस्थः -स्था -स्थं.

FARTHING, *s.* ताम्रमुद्रा, कपर्द्दकः, वराटकः.

FASCES, *s.* धर्म्माध्यक्षलक्षणं, दण्डनायकचिह्नं, पूर्व्वकाले रोमनगरे दण्डलाक्षणिकः काष्ठखण्डसम्बद्धः परशुः.

FASCIA, *s.* पट्टः, पट्टकः, बन्धनं, वेष्टनं, आवेष्टनं, कवलिका.

FASCIATION, *s.* पट्टबन्धनं, कवलिकाबन्धनं, अनुवेल्लितं.

To FASCINATE, *v. a.* (Bewitch) मुह् in caus. (मोहयति -यितुं), मोहं कृ, मायां कृ, मन्त्रद्वारेण वशीकृ or अभिमन्त्र् (c. 10. -मन्त्रयते -यितुं) or अनुमन्त्र् or अभिचर् (c. 10. -चारयति -यितुं).—(Captivate) चित्तं or मनो हृ (c. 1. हरति, हर्त्तुं) or रम् in caus. (रमयति -यितुं) or आकृष् (c. 1. -कर्षति -क्रष्टुं), हृदयं ग्रह् (c. 9. गृह्णाति, ग्रहीतुं).

FASCINATED, *p. p.* मोहितः -ता -तं, विमोहितः -ता -तं, सम्मोहितः -ता -तं, परिमूढः -ढा -ढं, सम्मुग्धः -ग्धा -ग्धं, आकृष्टचित्तः -त्ता -त्तं, हृतमानसः -सी -सं, वशीकृतः -ता -तं, वशीभूतः -ता -तं.

FASCINATING, *a.* चित्तहारी -रिणी -रि (न्), चित्तापहारी &c., मनोहरः -रा -रं, मोहनः -ना -नी -नं, विमोहनः &c., मोही -हिनी -हि (न्), परिमोही &c., आकर्षकः -की -कं, आकर्षिकः -की -कं, आकृष्टवान् -वती -वत् (त्), हृदयग्राही -हिणी -हि (न्); 'a fascinating woman,' मुग्धा, प्रमदा, मदिरेक्षणा.

FASCINATION, *s.* मोहः -हनं, परिमोहनं, विमोहनं, सम्मोहः, आकर्षः, माया, वशक्रिया, अभिमन्त्रणं, अभिचारः, इन्द्रजालं, कार्म्मणं -णत्वं.

FASCINE, *s.* युद्धे व्यवहारितः काष्ठभारः or काष्ठकूर्चः.

FASHION, *s.* (Form) आकारः, आकृतिः *f.*, रूपं, संस्कारः, मूर्त्तिः *f.*, विधानं, संस्थानं.—(Cut, shape) आकारः, आकृतिः *f.*, रीतिः *f.*—(Prevailing custom) लौकिकाचारः, लोकाचारः, लोकव्यवहारः, लोकरीतिः *f.*, लोकमार्गः, लोकव्यापारः, धारा, लोकमतं.—(Manner, mode) प्रकारः, विधः, विधिः *m.*, रीतिः *f.*, मार्गः; 'after this fashion,' अनेन प्रकारेण, एवंविधं; 'after one's own fashion,' स्वानुरूपं.

To FASHION, *v. a.* (Form) निर्मा (c. 2. -माति, c. 3. -मिमीते, c. 4. -मायते -मातुं), विनिर्मा, रच् (c. 10. रचयति -यितुं), विरच्, क्लृप् (c. 10. कल्पयति -यितुं), विधा (c. 3. -दधाति -धातुं), घट् (c. 10. घटयति -यितुं), कृ, सङ्कृ.—(Adapt) युज् (c. 10. योजयति -यितुं), सन्धा, समाधा.

FASHIONABLE, *a.* लौकिकः -की -कं, व्यावहारिकः -की -कं, आचारिकः -की -कं, लोकसिद्धः -द्धा -द्धं, लोकप्रसिद्धः -द्धा -द्धं, व्यवहारसिद्धः -द्धा -द्धं, लोकाचारानुसारी -रिणी -रि (न्), लोकव्यवहारानुसारी &c., लोकमतानुसारी &c., लौकिकाचारानुरूपः -पा -पं, लौकिकरीत्यनुरूपः -पा -पं, लोकमार्गानुयायी -यिनी -यि (न्).

FASHIONABLY, *adv.* लोकाचारानुसारेण, लोकव्यवहारानुसारात्, लोकरीतिवत्.

FASHIONED, *p. p.* निर्म्मितः -ता -तं, रचितः -ता -तं, विरचितः -ता -तं, कल्पितः -ता -तं, क्लृप्तः -प्ता -प्तं, घटितः -ता -तं, कारितः -ता -तं.

FAST, *a.* (Firm, close) दृढः -ढा -ढं, स्थिरः -रा -रं, स्थावरः -रा -रं, स्तब्धः -ब्धा -ब्धं, अचलः -ला -लं, निश्चलः -ला -लं, दृढसन्धिः -न्धिः -न्धि, गाढः -ढा -ढं.—(Fixed) बद्धः -द्धा -द्धं, सन्निबद्धः -द्धा -द्धं; 'a fast colour,' स्थिररङ्गः; 'a fast friend,' दृढसौहृदः, दृढभक्तिः *m*; 'a fast sleep,' सुषुप्तिः *f.*, सुनिद्रा, अतिशयनिद्रा, अघोरनिद्रा.—(Quick in motion) त्वरितगतिः -तिः -ति, शीघ्रगामी -मिनी -मि (न्), द्रुतगतिः -तिः -ति, शीघ्रः -घ्रा -घ्रं, महावेगः -गा -गं, वेगवान् -वती -वत् (त्)

FAST, *adv.* (Firmly) दृढं, गाढं, स्थिरं; 'fast-rooted,' बद्धमूलः -ला -लं; 'held fast,' सुगृहीतः -ता -तं, सुधृतः -ता -तं, कररुद्धः -द्धा -द्धं; 'fast bound,' दृढबद्धः -द्धा -द्धं; 'shut fast,' दृढसंवृतः -ता -तं, दृढपिहितः -ता -तं; 'fast asleep,' सुषुप्तः -प्ता -प्तं, सुनिद्रितः -ता -तं, अतिशयनिद्रितः -ता -तं, सुखसुप्तः -प्ता -प्तं or सुखं सुप्तः -प्ता -प्तं.—(Swiftly) शीघ्रं, त्वरितं, द्रुतं, क्षिप्रं, सत्वरं, आशु, अविलम्बितं, अशनैः; 'going fast,' त्वरितगतिः -तिः -ति; 'spoken fast,' त्वरितोदितः -ता -तं.

To FAST, *v. n.* उपवस् (c. 1. -वसति -वस्तुं), लङ्घ् (c. 1. लङ्घते -ङ्घितुं), निरूपितकालपर्य्यन्तं भोजनात् or आहाराद् निवृत् (c. 1. -वर्त्तते -र्त्तितुं), उपवासं कृ, अनशनं कृ, आहारनिवृत्तिं कृ; 'to death,' प्रायोपवेशनं कृ.

FAST, *s.* उपवासः, उपवस्तं, उपोषितं, उपोषणं, औपवस्तं, अनशनं, अनाहारः, अभोजनं, लङ्घनं, आक्षपणं.

FAST-DAY, *s.* उपवासदिनं, उपोषणदिनं, अनाहारदिवसः, लङ्घनदिवसः.

FASTED, *p. p.* उपोषितः -ता -तं, कृतोपवासः -सा -सं.

To FASTEN, *v. a.* (Make fast) बन्ध् (c. 9. बध्नाति, बन्द्धुं), सम्बन्ध्, निबन्ध्, अनुबन्ध्.—(Shut up) पिधा (c. 3. -दधाति -धातुं), निरुध् (c. 7. -रुणद्धि -रोद्धुं).—(Bar) अर्गलेन बन्ध्, कील (nom. कीलयति -यितुं).—(Unite together) सम्बन्ध्, संयुज् (c. 7. -युनक्ति -योक्तुं), संश्लिष् in caus. (-श्लेषयति -यितुं), सन्धा, संलग्नीकृ.—(Tie) योक्त्र (nom. योक्त्रयति -यितुं), ग्रन्थ् (c. 9. ग्रथ्नाति, c. 1. ग्रन्थति -न्थितुं).—(Tie on) पिनह् (c. 4. -नह्यति -नद्धुं), आनह्, आबन्ध्, अनुबन्ध्.—(Impress) प्रणिधा.—(Make firm) दृढीकृ, स्थिरीकृ, संस्तम्भ् (c. 5. -स्तभ्नोति -स्तम्भितुं, c. 10. -स्तम्भयति -यितुं).

FASTENED, *p. p.* बद्धः -द्धा -द्धं, पिहितः -ता -तं, पिधानवान् -वती -वत् (त्), सपिधानः -ना -नं, निरुद्धः -द्धा -द्धं, युक्तः -क्ता -क्तं, संयुक्तः -क्ता -क्तं, संयोजितः -ता -तं, संलग्नीकृतः -ता -तं, लग्नः -ग्ना -ग्नं, पिनद्धः -द्धा -द्धं, आनद्धः -द्धा -द्धं, कीलायितः -ता -तं, कीलितः -ता -तं.

FASTENING, *s.* (Any thing that binds) बन्धनं -नी, बन्धनग्रन्थिः *m.*—(Joining) सन्धिः *m.*—(Of a bracelet) कुडुपः, सन्धिः *m.*

FASTER, *s.* उपवासी *m.* (न्), उपवासकर्त्ता *m.* (र्तृ), कृतोपवासः, सोपवासः.

FASTER, *adv.* (More rapidly) शीघ्रतरं, अधिकवेगेन, लघुतरं.

FASTIDIOUS, *a.* उपेक्षकः -का -कं, अवमानी -निनी -नि (न्), सावहेलः -ला -लं, सावज्ञः -ज्ञा -ज्ञं, घृणी -णिनी -णि (न्), दुस्तोषणीयः -या -यं, दुःखतोषणीयः -या -यं, दुःखेन सन्तोषणीयः -या -यं or तर्पणीयः -या -यं.

FASTIDIOUSLY, *adv.* सावज्ञानं, उपेक्षया, सावहेलं, सावमानं, दुस्तोषणीयं.

FASTIDIOUSNESS, *s.* अवमानशीलता, उपेक्षकत्वं, सावहेलत्वं, दुस्तोषणीयता, दुस्तर्पणीयता, अवमानिता.

FASTING, *s.* उपवासः, उपोषणं -षितं, अनशनं, निरशनं, अभोजनं, अभक्षणं, अनाहारः, लङ्घनं, आक्षपणं, अपतर्पणं; 'to death,' प्रायः -यणं, प्रायोपवेशनं -शनिका.

FASTING, *part.* or *a.* उपवासी -सिनी -सि (न्), निराहारः -रा -रं, अनशनः -ना -नं, अभक्षः -क्षा -क्षं, अनाशकः -का -कं, अकृताहारः -रा -रं; 'to death,' प्रायोपविष्टः -ष्टा -ष्टं.

FASTNESS, *s.* (Firmness) दृढता, स्थिरता, स्तब्धता, अचलता, निश्चलता.—(Strong-hold) दुर्गं, कोटिः *f.*, शिखरी *m.* (न्).

FASTUOUS, *a.* गर्व्वी -र्व्विणी -र्व्वि (न्), सावलेपः -पा -पं, उद्धतः -ता -तं.

FAT, *a.* पीवरः -रा -री -रं, पीनः -ना -नं, मेदस्वी -स्विनी -स्वि (न्), पुष्टः -ष्टा -ष्टं, पुष्टाङ्गः -ङ्गी -ङ्गं, मांसलः -ला -लं, स्थूलः -ला -लं, स्थूलकायः -या -यं, प्यानः -ना -नं, आप्यानः -ना -नं, प्रप्यानः -ना -नं, स्फीतः -ता -तं, स्फातः -ता -तं, पीवा -वा -व (न्), तुन्दी -न्दिनी -न्दि (न्), तुन्दिकः -का -कं, उच्छूनः -ना -नं, कुक्षकः -क्षी -क्षं.—(Fertile) स्फीतः -ता -तं; 'fat land,' उर्व्वरा.

FAT, *s.* मेदः *n.* (स्), वसा, वपा, मांससारः, मांसस्नेहः, घृतं.

To FAT, *v. a.* प्यै in caus. (प्याययति -यितुं), आप्यै, पुष् in caus. (पोष-

यति -यितुं), स्फाय् in caus. (स्फावयति -यितुं), स्थूलीकृ, पीवरीकृ, पुष्टीकृ.

To FAT, *v. n.* आप्यै (c. 1. -प्यायते -प्यातुं), पुष् (c. 4. पुष्यति, पोष्टुं), पीवरीभू.

FAT. *s.* (tub) भाण्डं. *See* VAT.

FATAL, *a.* (Proceeding from fate, relating to it) दैवः -वी -वं -विकः -की -कं, दैष्टिकः -की -कं, कार्त्तान्तिकः -की -कं, दैवप्रयुक्तः -क्ता -क्तं, दैववशः -शा -शं, नियतः -ता -तं, आवश्यकः -की -कं.—(Deadly, calamitous) प्राणघातकः -का -कं, प्राणहरः -रा -रं, प्राणान्तिकः -की -कं or प्राणान्तकः, प्राणनाशकः -की -कं, मृत्युजनकः -का -कं, मारात्मकः -का -कं, साङ्घातिकः -की -कं, मारकः -का -कं, अन्तकरः -रा -रं, व्यापादकः -का -कं, आत्ययिकः -की -कं, अनायुष्यः -ष्या -ष्यं, मर्म्मान्तिकः -की -कं, मर्म्मभेदी -दिनी -दि (न्), दुरन्तः -न्ता -न्तं, दुर्विपाकः -का -कं.

FATALISM, *s.* दैवायत्तता, दैवाधीनता, दैववशित्वं, दैवचिन्ता, दैविकता, दैष्टिकता.

FATALIST, *s.* दैवपरः, दैवाधीनः, दैवायत्तः, दैवपरायणः, दैवचिन्तकः.

FATALITY, *s.* आवश्यकता, अवश्यकत्वं, भवितव्यता, कृतान्तः, नियतिः *f.*

FATALLY, *adv.* (By necessity) दैवात्, दैववशात्, दैवनियोगात्.—(Mortally) प्राणनाशेन, सनाशं, आत्ययिकं.

FATE, *s.* दैवं, कृतान्तः, विधाता *m.* (तृ), विधिः *m.*, भागधेयं, भाग्यं, नियतिः *f.*, भवितव्यता, दिष्टं, दैविकं, अदृष्टं, कालनियोगः, कालः, कालधर्म्मः, गतिः *f.*, व्यसनं, कर्म्म *n.* (न्), कर्म्मवशः, कार्य्यवशः, प्राक्तनं.—(Death) मृत्युः *m.*, नाशः, विनाशः, क्षयः; 'ill-fate,' दुर्दैवं, दौर्भाग्यं; 'good-fate,' सौभाग्यं.

FATED, *a.* दैवनियुक्तः -क्ता -क्तं, कालनियुक्तः -क्ता -क्तं, दैवनिर्दिष्टः -ष्टा -ष्टं, नियतः -ता -तं, दैविकः -की -कं, दैष्टिकः -की -कं, भवितव्यः -व्या -व्यं; 'one whose fated time is come,' प्राप्तकालः -ला -लं; 'well-fated,' सुभाग्यः -ग्या -ग्यं, सौभाग्यवान् -वती -वत् (त्), पुण्यवान् &c.; 'ill-fated,' दुर्दैवग्रस्तः -स्ता -स्तं, दैवोपहतः -ता -तं.

FATHER, *s.* पिता *m.* (तृ), जनकः, जननः, जनिता *m.* (तृ), जनयिता *m.* (तृ), जन्मदः, तातः, प्रसविता *m.* (तृ), प्रजावान् *m.* (त्), धाता *m.* (तृ), वप्ता *m.* (प्तृ), वापिः, देहकृत् *m.*, सम्भूः *m.*; 'of a family,' कुलपतिः *m.*; 'of a son,' पुत्री *m.* (न्), सुती *m.* (न्); 'father and mother,' मातापितरौ *m.* du. or मातरपितरौ, तातजनयित्र्यौ *f.* du.; 'father of all,' विश्वधाता *m.* (तृ).—(Title of respect) गुरुः, आचार्य्यः.

FATHER-IN-LAW, *s.* श्वशुरः, धर्म्मपिता *m.* (तृ), पूज्यः; 'father and mother-in-law,' श्वश्रूश्वशुरौ *m.* du.

To FATHER, *v. a.* पुत्रं ग्रह् (c. 9. गृह्णाति, ग्रहीतुं), पोष्यपुत्रं or कृत्रिमपुत्रं ग्रह्.—(Acknowledge as one's own) स्वीकृ.—(Ascribe to another as his offspring, or production) पुत्रारोपणं कृ, किञ्चित् परस्मै आरुह् in caus. (-रोपयति -यितुं), तेन प्रसूतं or तेन विरचितम् इति विज्ञा in caus. (-ज्ञापयति -यितुं).

FATHERHOOD, *s.* पितृत्वं -ता, जनकत्वं -ता, पितृभावः, प्रजावत्त्वं, पितृधर्म्मः.

FATHER-LAND, *s.* पैतृकभूमिः *f.*, पैतृकदेशः, पैतृकविषयः, जन्मभूमिः *f.*, मूलभूमिः.

FATHERLESS, *a.* अपितृकः -का -कं, पितृहीनः -ना -नं, तातहीनः -ना -नं, छमण्डः or छेमण्डः *m.* only, अनाथः -था -थं, निर्णाथः -था -थं.

FATHERLINESS, *s.* पितृतुल्यता, ताततुल्यता, पैतृकत्वं, वात्सल्यं.

FATHERLY, *a.* पितृसन्निभः -भा -भं, पितृतुल्यः -ल्या -ल्यं, ताततुल्यः -ल्या -ल्यं, तातलः -ला -लं, पैतृकः -की -कं or पैत्रिकः, पैत्रः -त्री -त्रं, पितृनिर्विशेषः -षा -षं, मनोजवः -वा -वं.

FATHERLY, *adv.* पितृवत्, जनकवत्, तातवत्, पितृरूपेण, जनकरूपेण.

FATHOM, *s.* (Measure of length) व्यामः, व्यायामः, न्यग्रोधः.—(Penetration) वेधः -धनं, मर्म्मवेधः.

To FATHOM, *v. a.* (Sound the depth) वेधं or गाम्भीर्य्यं or तलं परीक्ष् (c. 1. -ईक्षते -क्षितुं) or निरूप् (c. 10. -रूपयति -यितुं) or मा in caus. (मापयति -यितुं).—(Penetrate) व्यध् (c. 4. विध्यति, व्यद्धुं); 'one's designs,' मर्म्म व्यध्, अभिप्रायं परीक्ष् or निरूप्.

FATHOMLESS, *a.* अतलस्पर्शः -र्शा -र्शं, अगाधः -धा -धं, अनवगाह्यः -ह्या -ह्यं, अगम्यः -म्या -म्यं, अगम्यतलः -ला -लं.

FATIDICAL, *a.* भविष्यद्वाचकः -का -कं, भविष्यत्प्रदर्शकः -का -कं.

FATIGUE, *s.* क्लान्तिः *f.*, श्रान्तिः *f.*, क्लमः, श्रमः, आयासः, परिश्रमः, परिश्रान्तिः *f.*, खेदः, क्लेशः, क्लमित्वं, क्लमथः, अवसादः, ग्लानिः *f.*, कष्टं, व्यायामः, कायक्लेशः, तन्द्रा; 'inured to fatigue,' जितश्रमः -मा -मं.

To FATIGUE, *v. a.* खिद् in caus. (खेदयति -यितुं), क्लम् in caus. (क्लमयति -यितुं), परिक्लम्, आयस् in caus. (-यासयति -यितुं), श्रम् in caus. (श्रमयति -यितुं), परिश्रम्, सद् in caus. (सादयति -यितुं), अवसद्, ग्लै in caus. (ग्लपयति -यितुं), परिग्लै, क्लिश् (c. 9. क्लिश्नाति, क्लेशितुं), श्रान्तिं जन् in caus. (जनयति -यितुं).

FATIGUED, *p. p.* श्रान्तः -न्ता -न्तं, परिश्रान्तः -न्ता -न्तं, क्लान्तः -न्ता -न्तं, श्रमार्त्तः -र्त्ता -र्त्तं, जातश्रमः -मा -मं, खिन्नः -न्ना -न्नं, खेदितः -ता -तं, क्लिष्टः -ष्टा -ष्टं, क्लिशितः -ता -तं, क्लेशितः -ता -तं, ग्लानः -ना -नं, परिग्लानः -ना -नं, क्लमी -मिनी -मि (न्), श्रमी -मिणी -मि (न्), अवसन्नः -न्ना -न्नं, अवसादितः -ता -तं, सश्रमः -मा -मं; 'to be fatigued,' श्रम् (c. 4. श्राम्यति, श्रमितुं), आयस् (c. 4. -यस्यति -यसितुं), खिद् (c. 4. खिद्यते, खेत्तुं), क्लम् (c. 4. क्लाम्यति, क्लमितुं), कष्ट (nom. कष्टायते).

FATIGUING, *a.* श्रमकरः -री -रं, श्रमजनकः -का -कं, क्लेशकः -की -कं.

FATNESS, *s.* स्थूलता, स्थौल्यं, मेदस्विता, पुष्टता, पुष्टिः *f.*, पीनता, पीवरत्वं, स्फीतिः *f.*, मेदोवृद्धिः *f.*, स्फातिः *f.*, उन्मेदा, शरीरस्थूलता, स्थूलकायत्वं, आप्यायनं.

To FATTEN, *v. a.* पै in caus. (प्याययति -यितुं), आप्यै, पुष् in caus. (पोषयति -यितुं), स्थूलीकृ, पीवरीकृ, पुष्टीकृ, स्फाय् in caus. (स्फावयति -यितुं), संवृध् in caus. (वर्धयति -यितुं).

To FATTEN, *v. n.* आप्यै (c. 1. -प्यायते -प्यातुं), पुष् (c. 4. पुष्यति, पोष्टुं), स्थूलीभू, पीवरीभू, संवृध् (c. 1. -वर्धते -र्धितुं), स्फाय् (c. 1. स्फायते -यितुं).

FATTENED, *p. p.* पुष्टः -ष्टा -ष्टं, पुष्टाङ्गः -ङ्गी -ङ्गं, आप्यायितः -ता -तं, बृंहितः -ता -तं, स्थूलीकृतः -ता -तं, संवर्धितमांसः -सा -सं.

FATTENING, *a.* पौष्टिकः -की -कं, पुष्टिदः -दा -दं, बृंहणः -णा -णं.

FATTY, *a.* मेदस्वी -स्विनी -स्वि (न्), मांसलः -ला -लं, सस्नेहः -हा -हं.

FATUITY, *s.* मूर्खता, मौर्ख्यं, मूढता, मोहः, बालिशता, मुग्धता.

FATUOUS, *a.* मूर्खः -र्खा -र्खं, मूढः -ढा -ढं, बालिशमतिः -तिः -ति, दुर्बुद्धिः -द्धिः -द्धि, दुर्मतिः -तिः -ति, अल्पधीः -धीः -धि.

FAUCET, *s.* भाण्डनिवेशितो जलनिर्गमयोग्यो नाडिविशेषः.

FAULT, *s.* दोषः, अपराधः, मन्तुः *m.*, भ्रमः, छिद्रं, अगुणः, पापं, दूषणं, प्रमादः, कर्म्मदोषः, व्यतिक्रमः, परवाच्यं.—(Find fault with) निन्द् (c. 1. निन्दति -न्दितुं), उपालभ् (c. 1. -लभते -लब्धुं), दोषीकृ.

FAULT-FINDER, *s.* दोषग्राही -हिणी -हि (न्), दोषग्राहकः -का -कं, निन्दकः -का -कं, पापदर्शी -र्शिनी -र्शि (न्), छिद्रानुसारी -रिणी -रि (न्), छिद्रान्वेषी -षिणी -षि (न्).

FAULTILY, *adv.* दोषेण, अपराधेन, सदोषं, सापराधं, प्रमादेन, अन्यथा.

FAULTINESS, *s.* अपराधिता -त्वं, दोषिता -त्वं, दोषवत्त्वं, सापराधता, सदोषत्वं, दुष्टता, वाच्यता.

FAULTLESS, *a.* निर्दोषः -षा -षं, निरपराधः -धा -धं, अपराधहीनः -ना -नं, अपापः -पा -पं, अनघः -घा -घं, अनवद्यः -द्या -द्यं, अकल्मषः -षा -षं, अनेनाः -नाः -नः (स्), निरागाः -गाः -गः (स्), निश्छिद्रः -द्रा -द्रं, विशुद्धः -द्धा -द्धं, निर्म्मलः -ला -लं; 'in form,' अव्यङ्गः -ङ्गी -ङ्गं,

शुद्धरूपः -पी -पं.

FAULTLESSNESS, *s.* निर्दोषत्वं, निरपराधत्वं, दोषहीनता, विशुद्धता.

FAULTY, *a.* दोषी -षिणी -षि (न्), अपराधी -धिनी -धि (न्), दोषवान् -वती -वत् (त्), निन्दनीयः -या -यं, निन्दार्हः -र्हा -र्हं, सापराधः -धा -धं, सदोषः -षा -षं, दोषिकः -की -कं, वाच्यः -च्या -च्यं, प्रामादिकः -की -कं, प्रमादी -दिनी -दि (न्), प्रमादवान् -वती -वत् (त्), अशुद्धः -द्धा -द्धं, प्राप्तदोषः -षा -षं, अयथार्थः -र्था -र्थं, वितथः -था -थं, अनृतः -ता -तं; 'full of faults,' बहुदोषः -षा -षं; 'a faulty statement,' मिथ्यावादः, मृषावादः; 'a faulty conclusion,' अपसिद्धान्तः.

FAUN, *s.* (Sylvan deity) वनदेवता, स्थलीदेवता, वनेचरः.

To FAVOR, *v. a.* अनुग्रह् (c. 9. -गृह्णाति -ग्रहीतुं), अनुकूल (nom. अनुकूलयति -यितुं), उपकृ, उपकारं कृ, साहाय्यं कृ, प्रसादं कृ, अनुपाल् (c. 10. -पालयति -यितुं), प्रतिपाल्, भज् (c. 1. भजति -ते, भक्तुं), अनुरुध् (c. 4. -रुध्यति -रोद्धुं), जुष् (c. 6. जुषते, जोषितुं), रक्षां कृ, प्रसन्नो भू or अस्, स्नेहं कृ, कृपां कृ, परप्रियं or परहितम् इष् (c. 6. इच्छति, एषितुं).—(Resemble) सरूपः -पी -पं भू or अस्; 'a child that favors his father,' पितृरूपः पुत्रः; 'fortune favors the brave,' साहसे श्रीः प्रतिवसति.

FAVOR, *s.* (Kind regard, friendly disposition) प्रसादः, अनुग्रहः, अनुकूलता, आनुकूल्यं, प्रसन्नता, प्रीतिः *f.*, प्रियता, स्नेहः, अनुरोधः, हितेच्छा, हितेप्सा.—(Support, countenance) आग्रहः, संग्रहः, ग्रहः, आश्रयः, संश्रयः, आधारः, अनुपालनं, साहाय्यं, उपकारः, पुरस्कारः, संवर्धनं, वर्धनं, शरण्यता, अभ्युपपत्तिः *f.*—(Kind act) उपकृतं, उपकारः, सुकृतं, सुकृतिः *f.*, उपचारः, प्रियं, हितं.—(Leave, permission) अनुमतिः *f.*, अनुज्ञा; 'to ask a favour,' प्रसद् (c. 10. -सादयते -यितुं), with acc. of person, उपकारं प्रार्थ् (c. 10. -अर्थयते -यितुं); 'I ask you as a favor not to be angry with me,' प्रसादये त्वां न मे क्रोद्धुम् अर्हसि; 'conciliate the favor,' आराध् (c. 10. -राधयति -यितुं), अनुरञ्ज् in caus. (-रञ्जयति -यितुं).

FAVORABLE, *a.* प्रसन्नः -न्ना -न्नं, सुप्रसन्नः -न्ना -न्नं, अनुग्राही -हिणी -हि (न्), अनुकूलः -ला -लं, आनुग्राहकः -की -कं, हितैषी -षिणी -षि (न्), प्रियैषी &c., हितकामः -मा -मं, हितेप्सुः -प्सुः -प्सु, हितः -ता -तं, सुहितः -ता -तं, प्रियकारः -री -रं, प्रियङ्करः -री -रं, हितबुद्धिः -द्धिः -द्धि, अर्थकृत्, उपकारकः -का -कं.—(Tending to promote) उत्पादकः -का -कं; 'favorable to wealth,' अर्थोत्पादकः -का -कं; 'to longevity,' आयुष्यः -ष्या -ष्यं; 'to be favorable,' प्रसद् (c. 1. -सीदति -सत्तुं); 'I am favorable to you,' प्रसन्नोऽस्मि तव.

FAVORABLENESS, *s.* प्रसन्नता, अनुकूलता, आनुकूल्यं, हितबुद्धित्वं.

FAVORABLY, *adv.* प्रसन्नं, प्रसादेन, अनुग्रहेण, सानुग्रहं, सानुकूल्यं, प्रियं.

FAVORED, *p.p.* अनुगृहीतः -ता -तं, उपकृतः -ता -तं, प्रतिपालितः -ता -तं.

FAVORER, *s.* अनुग्राही *m.* (न्), अनुग्राहकः, उपकारकः, अनुपालकः.

FAVORITE, *s.* प्रियः -या, सुप्रियः -या, वल्लभः -भा, सुभगः -गा, हृदयप्रियः -या, स्नेहपात्रं, प्रीतिपात्रं; 'general favorite,' सर्वप्रियः; 'a royal favorite,' नृपवल्लभः, राजवल्लभः; 'a favorite wife,' सुभगा.

FAVORITE, *a.* प्रियः -या -यं, प्रियतमः मा -मं, हृदयप्रियः -या -यं, दयितः -ता -तं, इष्टतमः -मा -मं, अभीष्टः -ष्टा -ष्टं, हृद्यः -द्या -द्यं.

FAVORITISM, *s.* पक्षपातिता, पक्षानुग्रहः, पक्षोत्साहित्वं, पक्षता, स्नेहः.

FAWN, *s.* मृगशावकः, मृगपोतकः, हरिणशिशुः *m.*, हरिणवत्सः, कुरङ्गः; 'fawn-eyed,' कुरङ्गनयनः -ना -नी -नं.

To FAWN, *v. n.* (Bring forth a fawn) मृगशावकं or कुरङ्गं सु (c. 2. सूते, c. 4. सूयते, सोतुं) or प्रसु or जन् (c. 10. जनयति -यितुं).

To FAWN UPON, *v. n.* साष्टाङ्गपातं प्रणम्य सान्त्व् or शान्त्व् (c. 10. सान्त्वयति -यितुं), अभिशान्त्व्, उपसान्त्व्, परिशान्त्व् or लल् (c. 10. लालयति -यितुं).

FAWNER, *s.* साष्टाङ्गपातं प्रणम्य सान्त्वकारः, लाली *m.* (न्), चाटुकारः.

FAWNING, *s.* अष्टाङ्गप्रणामपूर्वं सान्त्वनं or लालनं, अतिचाटुकारः.

FAWNINGLY, *adv.* साष्टाङ्गपातं, कृताञ्जलिकर्म्मपूर्वं, एकान्तचाटुकारेण.

FAY, *s.* विद्याधरी, पिशाची, योगिनी, राक्षसी. *See* FAIRY.

FEALTY, *s.* भक्तिः *f.*, प्रभुभक्तिः *f.*, भक्तता, प्रभुभक्तता, आसक्तिः *f.*, अनुषक्तः.

FEAR, *s.* भयं, भीतिः *f.*, भीरुता, त्रासः, सन्त्रासः, परित्रासः, साध्वसं, शङ्का, आशङ्का, दरः -रं, भीष्मं, भीषणं; 'removal of fear,' भयप्रतीकारः; 'causing fear,' भयङ्करः -रा -रं, भयकारकः -का -कं, भयदः -दा -दं, भयप्रदः -दा -दं; 'cause of fear,' भयहेतुः *m.*; 'agitated by fear,' भयविह्वलः -ला -लं; 'through fear,' भयात्, त्रासात्, भीत्या, भीतेः, शङ्कया; 'through fear of punishment,' दण्डभयात्.

To FEAR, *v. a.* भी (c. 3. बिभेति, भेतुं) with abl. or gen. c. So also प्रभी, विभी, त्रस् (c. 4. त्रस्यति, त्रसितुं), वित्रस्, उद्विज् (c. 6. -विजते -जितुं), व्यथ् (c. 1. व्यथते -थितुं), प्रव्यथ् all with abl. c., शङ्क् (c. 1. शङ्कते -ङ्कितुं), आशङ्क् with acc. c., तर्क् (c. 10 तर्कयति -यितुं).

To FEAR, *v. n.* त्रस् (c. 4. त्रस्यति, त्रसितुं), व्यथ् (c. 1. व्यथते -थितुं), उद्विग्नीभू, भयार्त्तः -र्त्ता -र्त्तं भू or अस्; 'do not fear,' मा भैषीः, मा त्रासीः or मा त्रसीः.

FEARFUL, *a.* (Affected by fear, timid) भयार्त्तः -र्त्ता -र्त्तं, भयातुरः -रा -रं, भीरुः -रुः -रु -रुकः -का -कं, सभयः -या -यं, भीतः -ता -तं, ससाध्वसः -सा -सं, सशङ्कः -ङ्का -ङ्कं, शङ्कितः -ता -तं, त्रस्तः -स्ता -स्तं, सन्त्रस्तः -स्ता -स्तं, दीनः -ना -नं, त्रसुः -सुः -सु, भीलुकः -का -कं, दरितः -ता -तं.—(Terrible) भयङ्करः -रा -रं, भयानकः -की -कं, भयावहः -हा -हं, त्रासकरः -री -रं, भीरुमयः -यी -यं, दारुणः -णा -णं, रौद्रः -द्री -द्रं, घोरः -रा -रं, भीमः -मा -मं, भीषणः -णा -णं, भीष्मः -ष्मा -ष्मं, भैरवः -वी -वं.

FEARFULLY, *adv.* (With fear) सभयं, सत्रासं, भयेन, ससाध्वसं, सशङ्कं.—(Terribly) दारुणं, घोरं, भैरवं, भयानकं.

FEARFULNESS, *s.* भीरुता, भीतत्वं, सभयत्वं, सन्त्रस्तता, रौद्रता.

FEARLESS, *a.* निर्भयः -या -यं, अभयः -या -यं, अभीतः -ता -तं, विभीतः -ता तं, अशङ्कः -ङ्का -ङ्कं, निःशङ्कः -ङ्का -ङ्कं, विशङ्कः -ङ्का -ङ्कं, निर्विशङ्कः -ङ्का -ङ्कं, अभीरुः -रुः -रु, अपभीः -भीः -भि, अपशङ्कः -ङ्का -ङ्कं, निःसाध्वसः -सा -सं, विगतभयः -या -यं, अकुतोभयः -या -यं, निःसंशयः -या -यं, साहसिकः -की -कं.

FEARLESSLY, *adv.* निर्भयं, अभयं, निःशङ्कं, अभीतवत्, साहसेन; 'acting fearlessly,' निर्धार्य्यः -र्य्या -र्य्यं.

FEARLESSNESS, *s.* निर्भयत्वं, अभीतिः *f.*, अभीतता, अभयं -यत्वं, शौर्य्यं.

FEASIBILITY, *s.* शक्यता, साध्यता, करणीयता, सम्भाव्यता, उपपाद्यत्वं.

FEASIBLE, *a.* साध्यः -ध्या -ध्यं, करणीयः -या -यं, शक्यः -क्या -क्यं, कर्त्तुं शक्यः -क्या -क्यं, सुकरः -रा -रं, सम्भाव्यः -व्या -व्यं, सम्भावनीयः -या -यं, उपपाद्यः -द्या -द्यं, कार्य्यः -र्य्या -र्य्यं, सुगमः -मा -मं, लभ्यः -भ्या -भ्यं, सुलभः -भा -भं.

FEAST, *s.* (Festival) उत्सवः, महः, पर्व्व *n.* (न्), यात्रा, यात्रोत्सवः, उद्धर्षः, उद्धवः, पर्व्वरीणः, अभ्युदयः, क्षणः, चर्च्चरी; 'a great feast,' महोत्सवः.—(Entertainment) सत्क्रिया, सहभोजनं, सम्भोजनं, उत्तमान्नसम्भारः, परमान्नसम्भारः; 'feast of lanterns,' दीपोत्सवः; 'feast to the eye,' नयनोत्सवः.

To FEAST, *v. n.* परमान्नानि भुज् (c. 7. भुङ्क्ते, भोक्तुं), उत्तमाहारं कृ, उत्तमभोजनं कृ, उत्तमान्नेन तृप् (c. 4. तृप्यति), उत्सवं कृ, महोत्सवं कृ.

To feast, *v. a.* उत्सवान्नैः or भोजनविशेषैः सन्तृप् (c. 10. -तर्पयति -यितुं) or सन्तुष् in caus. (-तोषयति -यितुं), परमान्नानि भुज् in caus. (भोजयति -यितुं), सत्कृ.

Feasted, *p. p.* सत्कृतः -ता -तं, परमान्नसन्तर्पितः -ता -तं.

Feasting, *s.* उत्सवकरणं, परमान्नभोजनं, उत्सवाहारकरणं, सहभोजनं.

Feat, *s.* कर्म्म *n.* (न्), चरित्रं, चेष्टितं, अद्भुतकर्म्म *n.*, आश्चर्य्यकर्म्म *n.*

Feather, *s.* पक्षः, पर्णः, गरुत् *m.*, पिच्छं, पतत्रं, पत्रं, पक्ष्म *n.* (न्), वाजः, तनुरुहः; 'of a peacock,' मयूरपिच्छं; 'of an arrow,' पुङ्खः, शरपुङ्खा, शरपक्षः, पत्रं, वाजः, मणिकाचः.

Feather-bed, *s.* पक्षपूरितं शयनं, पक्षशय्या, मृदुशयनं, कोमलपर्य्यङ्कः, सुखस्पर्शप्रस्तरः.

Feathered, *a.* पक्षी -क्षिणी -क्षि (न्), पक्षवान् -वती -वत् (त्), पक्षाच्छादितः -ता -तं, पक्षयुक्तः -क्ता -क्तं, सपक्षः -क्षा -क्षं, गरुत्मान् -त्मती -त्मत् (त्), पत्री -त्रिणी -त्रि (न्), पतत्री -त्रिणी -त्रि (न्).

Feathery, *a.* पक्षतुल्यः -ल्या -ल्यं, पक्षसदृशः -शी -शं, पक्षसगुणः -णा -णं.

Feature, *s.* (Form of the face) वदनाकृतिः *f.*, वदनाकारः, वदनरेखा, मुखरेखा, मुखावयवः, वदनावयवः.—(Form, cast) आकारः, आकृतिः *f.*, संस्कारः, संस्थानं, रूपं, मूर्त्तिः *f.*

To feaze, *v. a.* उद्ग्रन्थ् (c. 1. -ग्रन्थयति -न्थितुं, c. 9. -ग्रथ्नाति), समुद्ग्रन्थ्.

Febriculose, *a.* ईषज्ज्वरी -रिणी -रि (न्), ईषज्ज्वरातुरः -रा -रं.

Febrifacient, *a.* ज्वरकरः -रा -रं, ज्वरोत्पादकः -का -कं.

Febrifuge, *a.* ज्वरघ्नः -घ्नी -घ्नं, ज्वरनाशकः -का -कं, ज्वरान्तकः -का -कं, ज्वरहन्ता -न्त्री -न्तृ (न्तृ), ज्वरनिवारकः -का -कं; 'a febrifuge,' ज्वरनाशकम् औषधं, ज्वरापहा.

Febrile, *a.* ज्वरी -रिणी -रि (न्), ज्वरितः -ता -तं, ज्वरजः -जा -जं.

February, *s.* फाल्गुनः, माघः, तपस्यः, फाल्गुनिकः, वत्सरस्य द्वितीयमासः.

Fecal, *a.* मलमयः -यी -यं, शकृन्मयः -यी -यं, विण्मयः -यी -यं, मलिनः -ना -नं, अमेध्यः -ध्या -ध्यं, मली -लिनी -लि (न्).

Feces, *s.* मलं, पुरीषं, विष्ठा, विट् *f.* (ष्), उच्चारः, उच्चरितं, शमलं, गूथः, अवस्करः, अपस्करः, वर्च्चस्कः, दूष्यं.—(Dregs) मलं, खलं, कल्कं, किट्टं, उच्छिष्टं, शेषं, कलङ्कः; 'to discharge feces,' पुरीषोत्सर्गं कृ, विण्मूत्रोत्सर्गं कृ.

Feculence, *s.* मालिन्यं, समलता, अमेध्यता, मलवत्त्वं, कलुषता, मलं.

Feculent, *a.* समलः -ला -लं, मलवान् -वती -वत् (त्), मलिनः -ना -नं, मलीमसः -सा -सं, मलदूषितः -ता -तं, अमेध्यः -ध्या -ध्यं, खली -लिनी -लि (न्), कल्की -ल्किनी -ल्कि (न्), कलुषः -षा -षं -षी -षिणी -षि (न्), विड्भवः -वा -वं, कलङ्की -ङ्किनी -ङ्कि (न्).

Fecund, *a.* बहुप्रजः -जा -जं, बह्वपत्यः -त्या -त्यं, अवन्ध्यः -न्ध्या -न्ध्यं, बहुफलदः -दा -दं, प्रजनिष्णुः -ष्णुः -ष्णु; 'fecund soil,' उर्व्वरा.

To fecundate, *v. a.* सफलीकृ, बहुफलदीकृ, रेतः or परागं सिच् (c. 6. सिञ्चति, सेक्तुं).

Fecundation, *s.* सफलीकरणं, अवन्ध्यीकरणं, परागसेकः, रेतःसेचनं.

Fecundity, *s.* साफल्यं, सफलता, फलवत्त्वं, जनकता, अवन्ध्यता, स्फीतिः *f.*, प्रसवनं, प्रसवित्वं, सावकत्वं, प्रजनिष्णुता.

Fed, *p. p.* पुष्टः -ष्टा -ष्टं, पुषितः -ता -तं, पोषितः -ता -तं, भृतः -ता -तं, पालितः -ता -तं, सन्तोषितः -ता -तं, समर्पितः -ता -तं, अशितः -ता -तं, आशितः -ता -तं; 'well-fed,' सुपुष्टः -ष्टा -ष्टं, हृष्टपुष्टः -ष्टा -ष्टं, स्वाशितः -ता -तं; 'ill-fed,' विपुष्टः -ष्टा -ष्टं; 'fed on by cattle,' आशितङ्गवीनः -ना -नं; 'having fed,' भोजयित्वा.

Federal, *a.* साङ्घातिकः -की -कं, सामयिकः -की -कं, सहितः -ता -तं.

Federate, *a.* सन्धितः -ता -तं, कृतसन्धिः -न्धिः -न्धि, कृतसम्बन्धः -न्धा -न्धं, संहतः -ता -तं, सहितः -ता -तं, सङ्घातवान् -वती -वत् (त्), संयुक्तः -क्ता -क्तं.

Fee, *s.* (Recompense) शुल्कः -ल्कं, पारितोषिकं, वेतनं, भाटिः *f.*, भाटकः, दक्षिणा, उपप्रदानं, उपायनं, निस्तारः, प्रतिफलं.—(Land granted by a lord) भूस्वामिना स्वपरिचरहस्ते समर्पिता भूमिः; 'fee-simple,' स्वाधीनभूमिः *f.*

To fee, *v. a.* पारितोषिकं दा, वेतनं दा, उपप्रदानेन परितुष् in caus. (-तोषयति -यितुं) or सन्तुष्, उत्कोचं दा.

Feeble, *a.* अल्पबलः -ला -लं, दुर्बलः -ला -लं, अल्पशक्तिः -क्तिः -क्ति, अल्पवीर्य्यः -र्य्या -र्य्यं, अल्पसत्त्वः -त्त्वा -त्त्वं, अल्पतेजाः -जाः -जः (स्), शिथिलबलः -ला -लं, शिथिलशक्तिः -क्तिः -क्ति, निर्बलः -ला -लं, बलहीनः -ना -नं, सामर्थ्यहीनः -ना -नं, क्षीणबलः -ला -लं, असमर्थः -र्था -र्थं, शिथिलः -ला -लं, फल्गुः -ल्गुः -ल्गु, विस्रस्ततेजाः -जाः -जः (स्), क्षीणः -णा -णं, अवसन्नः -न्ना -न्नं, क्षामः -मा -मं, क्लीवः -वा -वं, छातः -ता -तं, शातः -ता -तं, अमांसः -सा -सं.

Feeble-minded, *a.* अल्पबुद्धिः -द्धिः -द्धि, दुर्मतिः -तिः -ति, अल्पधीः -धीः -धि.

Feebleness, *s.* दौर्बल्यं, अल्पशक्तित्वं, अल्पबलं, बलशैथिल्यं, शक्तिशैथिल्यं, शिथिलता, क्षीणता, क्षीणशक्तित्वं, वीर्य्यहानिः *f.*, शक्तिहीनता, सत्त्वहानिः *f.*, तेजोहीनता, अतेजः *n.* (स्), अशक्तिः *f.*, असामर्थ्यं, सामर्थ्यहीनता, अवसादः, विस्रंसा, क्लैव्यं.

Feebly, *adv.* अल्पबलेन, अल्पशक्त्या, दुर्बलं, निर्बलं, दौर्बल्येन.

To feed, *v. a.* (Give to eat) भुज् in caus. (भोजयति -यितुं), अश् in caus. (आशयति -यितुं), प्राश् in caus., भोजनं or अन्नं दा.—(Nourish) पुष् (c. 1. पोषति -षितुं, c. 9. पुष्णाति, c. 10. पोषयति -यितुं), परिपुष्, पाल् (c. 10. पालयति -यितुं), प्रतिपाल्, भृ (c. 3. बिभर्त्ति, भर्त्तुं), सम्भृ, अन्नेन सन्तुष् in caus. (-तोषयति -यितुं) or सन्तृप् in caus. (-तर्पयति -यितुं) or संवृध् (c. 10. -वर्धयति -यितुं).—(Pasture) चर् in caus. (चारयति -यितुं).—(Supply) उपस्था in caus. (-स्थापयति -यितुं), उपक्लृप् (c. 10. -कल्पयति -यितुं); 'to be plentifully fed,' आपॄ in pass. (-पूर्य्यते).

To feed, *v. n.* (Eat) भुज् (c. 7. भुङ्क्ते, भोक्तुं), उपभुज्, अश् (c. 9. अश्नाति, अशितुं), समश्, पर्य्यश्, प्राश्, खाद् (c. 1. खादति -दितुं), अद् (c. 2. अत्ति -त्तुं), भक्ष् (c. 10. भक्षयति -यितुं), अन्नेन पॄ in pass. (पूर्य्यते) or पुष् (c. 4. पुष्यति, पोष्टुं).—(Graze) चर् (c. 1. चरति -रितुं), तृण् (c. 8. तृणोति, तर्णोति -र्णितुं) तृणं भुज्.

Feed, *s.* (Provender, fodder) भक्ष्यं, भोज्यं, विधा, विधानं, विधिः *m.*, गवादनं, अश्वादनं.—(Quantity of corn, &c. eaten by a horse at once) यत् तृणधान्यादि एकवारे अश्वेन भुज्यते; 'day's feed for a cow,' गवाह्निकं.

Feeder, *s.* (Giver of food) भोजयिता *m.* (तृ), आशयिता *m.* (तृ), पोष्टा *m.* (ष्टृ), पोषयिता *m.* (तृ), आहारदाता *m.* (तृ), अन्नदाता *m.*—(One that eats) भक्षकः, खादकः, अत्ता *m.* (त्तृ), भोक्ता *m.* (क्तृ), भक्षयिता *m.* (तृ), भोजी *m.* (न्), आशी *m.* (न्); 'on grain,' शस्यभक्षकः, शस्यादः, शस्याद्; 'on grass,' तृणजम्भः; 'on flesh,' मांसभक्षः, पिशिताशनः, क्रव्यादः, क्रव्याद्, मांसभुक् *m.* (ज्); 'on fruit,' फलाशी *m.* (न्), फलाशनः.

Feeding, *s.* (Giving food) आहारदानं, अन्नदानं, पोषणं, पालनं, भरणं.—(Eating) भक्षणं, खादनं, भोजनं, अशनं, प्राशनं, भक्षणं, ग्रसनं, अभ्यवहरणं; 'upon grain,' शस्यभक्षणं.

To feel, *v. a.* (Perceive by the touch) स्पृश् (c. 6. स्पृशति, स्प्रष्टुं), संस्पृश्, परिस्पृश्, हस्तेन or पाणिना परामृश् (c. 6. -मृशति -म्रष्टुं) or परिमृश् or मृश् or आलभ् (c. 1. -लभते -लब्धुं).—(Try by touch)

स्पर्शेन or हस्तसम्पर्केण परीक्ष् (c. 1. -ईक्षते -क्षितुं) or निरूप् (c. 10. -रूपयति -यि-); 'to feel the pulse,' नाडीं परीक्ष्, नाडीपरीक्षां कृ. —(Suffer, experience) अनुभू, उपगम् (c. 1. -गच्छति -गन्तुं), उपागम्, विद् (c. 10. वेदयते -यितुं), सूच् (c. 10. सूचयति -यितुं); 'one who feels pain,' अनुभूतव्यथः, जातव्यथः, आहितव्यथः.—(Be affected with) उपहतः -ता -तं भू or अस्.—(Know) ज्ञा (c. 9. जानाति, ज्ञातुं).—(Feel for the woes of another) परस्य समदुःखः -खा -खं भू or अस्, परदुःखमुपलभ्य कारुण्यं सूच् or कृ, अनुकम्प् (c. 1. -कम्पते -म्पितुं).

Feel, *s.* स्पर्शः, स्पृष्टिः *f.*, संस्पर्शः, सम्पर्कः, परिमर्शः.

Feeler, *s.* (Of an insect) कीटमस्तकाग्रे परामर्शयोग्यं सूक्ष्मशृङ्गं.

Feeling, *s.* (Sense of touch) स्पर्शः, स्पर्शज्ञानं, स्पर्शेन्द्रियं, स्पृष्टिः *f.*, संस्पर्शः, परिमर्शः, परामर्शः, सम्पर्कः.—(Sensation, perception) संवेदः, वेदनं, बोधः, ज्ञानं, चेतना, चैतन्यं, चित् *f.*, चित्तवृत्तिः *f.*, उपगमः, उपागमः, उपलम्भः, उपलब्धिः *f.*—(Emotion, sentiment) रसः, भावः, चित्तवृत्तिः *f.*, रागः, चित्तरागः, चित्तविकारः.—(Feeling for others) कृपा, दया, अनुकम्पा, करुणा, समदुःखत्वं; 'the feelings,' चेतः *n.* (स्), चित्तं, चैतन्यं, हृदयं.

Feeling, *part.* or *a.* (Sentient) चेतनः -ना -नं, चेतकः -की -कं, चेतनावान् -वती -वत् (त्).—(Impassioned, affecting) रसिकः -का -की -कं, रसी -सिनी -सि (न्), रसवान् -वती -वत् (त्), भाविकः -का -की -कं, रागी -गिणी -गि (न्), हृदयङ्गमः -मा -मं.

Feelingly, *adv.* सरसं, सरागं, हृदयङ्गमप्रकारेण, कृपापूर्वं, सानुकम्पं.

Feet, *s. pl.* पादौ m. du., चरणौ n. du.; 'ornament for the feet,' नूपुरः.

To feign, *v. a.* (Invent) मनसा क्लृप् (c. 10. कल्पयति -यितुं) or परिक्लृप् or सृज् (c. 6. सृजति, स्रष्टुं).—(Pretend) छद्म कृ, छल् (c. 10. छलयति -यितुं), कपटं कृ, व्याजं कृ, अलीकृ, कूटं कृ; 'to feign one's self asleep,' आत्मानं प्रसुप्तम् इव दृश् in caus. (दर्शयति -यितुं) or मिथ्याप्रसुप्तः -प्ता -प्तं भू or अस्; 'feigning himself dead,' आत्मानं मृतवत् सन्दर्श्य; 'feigning himself just,' साधुवेशधारी *m.* (न्).

Feigned, *p. p.* or *a.* कल्पितः -ता -तं, मनःकल्पितः -ता -तं, काल्पनिकः -की -कं, कृत्रिमः -मा -मं, कृतकः -का -कं, कूटार्थः -र्था -र्थं, विडम्बितः -ता -तं; 'a feigned dress,' कपटवेशः, छद्मवेशः; 'in a feigned dress,' छद्मवेशी *m.* (न्); 'a feigned ascetic,' छद्मतापसः, वैडालव्रतिकः, बकव्रती *m.* (न्); 'feigned kindness,' मिथ्योपचारः.

Feignedly, *adv.* मिथ्या, सकपटं, सकूटं, सव्याजं, छलेन, छद्मना, असत्यं.

Feigner, *s.* परिकल्पकः, कूटकः, छद्मवेशी *m.* (न्), कपटिकः, छली *m.* (न्), प्रतारकः; 'of madness,' उन्मत्तलिङ्गी *m.* (न्).

Feint, *s.* अपदेशः, व्यपदेशः, छद्म *n.* (न्), कूटः -टं, छलं, मिषं, कैतवं, निमित्तं, व्याजः, कपटः, उपधा; 'mock attack,' मिथ्याक्रमणं, मिथ्याघातः.

To felicitate, *v. a.* मङ्गलवचनं or कल्याणवचनं वद् (c. 1. वदति -दितुं), कल्यं वद्, कुशलवादं कृ, मङ्गलं or कुशलं भूयाद् इति वद्, आनन्द् (c. 10. -नन्दयति -ते -यितुं), अभिवन्द् (c. 1. -वन्दते -न्दितुं), संवन्द्, अभिवद् (c. 10. -वादयते -यितुं), अभिनन्द् (c. 1. -नन्दति -न्दितुं).

Felicitated, *p. p.* अभिवन्दितः -ता -तं, अभिनन्दितः -ता -तं, आनन्दितः -ता -तं.

Felicitation, *s.* अभिवन्दनं, कल्यवादः, कल्याणवचनं, मङ्गलवाक्यं, कल्यं, कल्या, कुल्यं, कुशलवादः, आशीर्वादः, धन्यवादः, अभिवादनं.

Felicitous, *a.* परमानन्दितः -ता -तं, परमसुखी -खिनी -खि (न्), अतिकल्याणः -णा -णं.

Felicitously, *adv.* परमसुखेन, परमानन्देन, अतिकल्याणं, अतिसुखेन.

Felicity, *s.* परमसुखं, परमानन्दः, परमाह्लादः, सुखं, सौख्यं, अत्यन्तसुखं, हर्षः, धन्यता, कल्याणं, शर्म्म *n.* (न्), प्रह्लादः, श्रेयः *n.* (स्), निःश्रेयसं, सौभाग्यं.—(Heavenly) सद्गतिः *f.*, स्वर्गगतिः, परमागतिः *f.*, सिद्धिः *f.*, परमपदं, अपवर्गः, मोक्षः.

Feline, *a.* वैडालः -ली -लं -लिकः -की -कं, मार्जारीयः -या -यं.

Fell, *a.* (Cruel, savage) क्रूरः -रा -रं, रौद्रः -द्री -द्रं, दारुणः -णा -णं, उग्रः -ग्रा -ग्रं, निष्ठुरः -रा -रं, शौवापदः -दी -दं, व्यालः -ला -लं.

Fell, *s.* चर्म्म *n.* (न्), अजिनं, दृतिः *m.*, कृत्तिः *f.*, पशुचर्म्म *n.*

To fell, *v. a.* पत् in caus. (पातयति -यितुं), अवपत्, निपत्, अवछिद् (c. 7. -छिनत्ति -छेत्तुं), छिद्; अवकृत् (c. 6. -कृन्तति -कर्त्तितुं), प्रकृत्, अवभञ्ज् (c. 7. -भनक्ति -भंक्तुं), निभञ्ज्, प्रभञ्ज्, भंश् in caus. (भ्रंशयति -यितुं), आघातेन or प्रहारेण भूमौ पत् in caus.

Felled, *p. p.* पातितः -ता -तं, निपातितः -ता -तं, अवपातितः -ता -तं, छिन्नः -न्ना -न्नं, अवछिन्नः -न्ना -न्नं, प्रभग्नः -ग्ना -ग्नं, भ्रंशितः -ता -तं.

Feller, *s.* अवपातकः, निपातकः, छेत्ता *m.* (तृ), अवछेत्ता *m.*

Fellifluous, *a.* पित्तस्रावी -विणी -वि (न्), पित्तमयः -यी -यं, पित्तपूर्णः -र्णा -र्णं.

Fellmonger, *s.* पशुचर्म्मविक्रेता *m.* (तृ), दृतिक्रयविक्रयिकः, चर्म्मकारः.

Fellness, *s.* क्रूरता, दारुण्यं, दारुणता, रौद्रता, उग्रत्वं, नैष्ठुर्य्यं, पशुत्वं.

Felloe, *s.* (Of a wheel) नेमिः *f.* *See* Felly.

Fellow, *s.* (Companion) सहायः, सहचरः, सङ्गी *m.* (न्), अनुषङ्गी *m.*, सहभावी *m.* (न्), सहवर्त्ती *m.* (न्), बन्धुः *m.*, सखा *m.* (स), मित्रं.—(Equal) वयस्यः, सवयाः *m.* (स्), समवयस्कः, तुल्यपदस्थः.—(One of the same kind) सजातिः *m.*, सजातीयः, सविधः.—(One of two or a pair) यमः -मा -मं, यमकः -का -कं, युग्मकः, एकतरः -रा -रं.—(Of a college) विद्यालये लाभालाभभागी *m.* (न्) or आयभाक् *m.* or आयभागी *m.* (न्).—(Of a learned body) पण्डितगणाभ्यन्तरः, आचार्य्यपंक्त्यभ्यन्तरः.—(Of any association) गणाभ्यन्तरः, श्रेण्यभ्यन्तरः, पांसुः, पांसेयः.—(Appellation of contempt) माणवकः, मनुष्यकः, जाल्मः; 'poor fellow,' तपस्वी *m.* (न्); 'my good fellow,' भद्र, सौम्य.

To fellow, *v. a.* समायुज् (c. 7. -युनक्ति -योक्तुं, c. 10. -योजयति -यितुं), संयुज्, समाधा (c. 3. -दधाति -धातुं), सन्धा, एकयुक्, एकीकृ, तुल्यीकृ.

Fellow-citizen, *s.* एकपौरः, एकपुरवासी *m.* (न्), एकनगरस्थः, एकग्रामीणः, एकग्रामनिवासी *m.* (न्), सांस्थानिकः.

Fellow-citizenship, *s.* पौरसख्यं, पौरसाहाय्यं, पौरसाहित्यं, एकपौरत्वं.

Fellow commoner, *s.* विद्यालये आचार्य्यगणसहभोजी कुलीनछात्रः.

Fellow-councilor, *s.* सहमन्त्री *m.* (न्), समन्त्री *m.*, समसचिवः.

Fellow-countryman, *s.* स्वदेशजः, स्वदेशीयः, एकदेशीयः, एकदेशवासी *m.* (न्), एकस्थानजः, सांस्थानिकः, संस्थः.

Fellow-creature, *s.* सजातिः *m.*, सजातीयः, समानजातिः *m.*, समानजातीयः, समभूतं, समभावः, समजः.

Fellow-feeling, *s.* समदुःखत्वं, समदुःखसुखत्वं, समभावः, कृपा, अनुकम्पा.

Fellow-heir, *s.* समांशी *m.* (न्), समाधिकारी *m.* (न्), समांशभाक् *m.* *See* Co-heir.

Fellow-helper, *s.* सहकारी *m.* (न्), सहकृत् *m.*, साहाय्यकृत् *m.*, सहायः.

Fellow-laborer, *s.* सहकर्म्मी *m.* (न्), एककर्म्मकारी *m.*, सम्भूयकारी *m.*

Fellow-prisoner, *s.* सहबन्दिः *f.*, एककारास्थायी *m.* (न्), एककारागुप्तः.

Fellow-scholar, *s.* सहाध्यायी *m.* (न्), सहाध्येता *m.* (तृ), सहशिष्यः, सहछात्रः.

Fellow-servant, *s.* सहदासः, सहभृत्यः, एकप्रभुसेवकः, सहसेवकः.

Fellowship, *s.* सहायता -त्वं, साहाय्यं, साहित्यं, साहं, संसर्गः, संसर्गिता, सङ्गः, सङ्गतिः *f.*, साङ्गत्यं, सङ्गित्वं, सङ्गमः, सङ्घातः, संयोगः, साहचर्य्यं, समागमः, संवासः, मैत्र्यं, मैत्री, मित्रत्वं, सख्यं, सौहृदं.—(In a college) विद्यालये आयभागित्वं or आयसंविभागिनः पदं or अधिकारः or वृत्तिः *f.*

FELLOW-SOLDIER, *s.* सहयुध्वा *m.* (न्), सहयुध्वानः, सहयोद्धा *m.* (द्धृ), सहसैन्यः.

FELLOW-STUDENT, *s.* सहाध्यायी *m.* (न्), सहपाठकः, सहशिष्यः, सहछात्रः, समछात्रः, सब्रह्मचारी *m.* (न्), सतीर्थः, सतीर्थ्यः.

FELLOW-SUBJECT, *s.* एकराजभक्तः, एकराजाधीनः, एकराज्यवासी *m.* (न्).

FELLOW-SUFFERER, *s.* सहदुःखी *m.* (न्), समदुःखी *m.*, समदुःखभागी *m.* (न्), सहदुःखभाक् *m.* (ज्), समदुःखोपेतः, सहभोगी *m.* (न्).

FELLOW-TRAVELLER, *s.* समध्वः -ध्वा, समपथगः, सहयायी *m.* (न्), सहपथिकः, सहगामी *m.* (न्), समाध्वनि वर्त्तमानः, सममार्गेण यायी *m.* (न्).

FELLOW-WORKER, *s.* सहकर्म्मी *m.* (न्), एककर्म्मकारी *m.* (न्), सहकारः, सहकृत्वा *m.* (न्).

FELLY, *adv.* दारुणं, क्रूरं, निष्ठुरं, उग्रं, रौद्रतया, पशुवत्, श्वापदवत्.

FELLY, *s.* (Of a wheel) नेमिः *f.*, चक्रनेमिः, चक्रपरिधिः *m.*, प्रधिः *m.*, प्रधिमण्डलं, नीध्रं, नीव्रः.

FELO-DE-SE, *s.* आत्महा *m.* (न्), आत्मघाती *m.* (न्), आत्मत्यागी *m.* (न्), कृतजीवितत्यागः, आत्मव्यापादकः.

FELON, *s.* आततायी *m.* (न्), महापातकी *m.* (न्), महापापी *m.* (न्), महापराधी *m.* (न्), साहसिकः.—(Whitlow) नखसम्भवः, चिप्यं.

FELONIOUS, *a.* आततायी -यिनी -यि (न्), जिघांसुः -सुः -सु, घाती -तिनी -ति (न्), साहसिकः -की -कं, साहसी -सिनी -सि (न्), दुराचारः -रा -रं, दुर्वृत्तः -त्ता -त्तं, दुष्टः -ष्टा -ष्टं, पापिष्ठः -ष्ठा -ष्ठं, वधोद्यतः -ता -तं, सदुष्टः -ष्टा -ष्टं, द्रोहबुद्धिः -द्धिः -द्धि.

FELONIOUSLY, *adv.* द्रोहबुद्ध्या, द्रोहचेतसा, द्रोहभिमानपूर्व्वं, दुष्टमतिपूर्व्वं.

FELONY, *s.* आततायिता, महापातकं, महापापं, महापराधः, साहसं.

FELT, *p. p.* अनुभूतः -ता -तं, ज्ञातः -ता -तं, उपगतः -ता -तं, विदितः -ता -तं, ज्ञातः -ता -तं, चित्तभवः -वा -वं, आहितः -ता -तं.

FELT, *s.* ऊर्णा, और्णवस्त्रं, उर्णा, और्णकं, ऊर्णायुः *m.*, कम्बलः.

To FELT, *v. a.* ऊर्णालोमादि संहत्य व्यूतिव्यतिरेकेण स्थूलवस्त्रं कृ.

FELUCCA, *s.* अग्रे पश्चाच्च कर्णयुक्ता लघुनौका or लघुनौका यस्याः कर्णः कदापि पश्चात् कदापि अग्रे युज्यते.

FEMALE, *s.* स्त्री, नारी, मानुषी, मनुषी, अङ्गना, योषित् -ता, योषा, महिला, वनिता, अबला, स्त्रीजनः, अङ्गनाजनः, अबलाजनः, वधूः, सीमन्तिनी, वामा; 'female friend,' सखी; 'female apartments,' शुद्धान्तः.

FEMININE, *a.* स्त्रैणः -णी -णं, स्त्रीसम्बन्धी -न्धिनी -न्धि (न्), निष्पुरुषः -षा -षं, स्त्रीधर्म्मा -र्म्मा -र्म्म (न्).—(Soft, delicate) सुकुमारः -री -रं, कोमलः -ला -लं, पेलवः -वा -वं, मृदुः -द्वी -दु; 'the feminine gender,' स्त्रीलिङ्गं.

FEN, *s.* अनूपः, अनूपभूः *f.*, कच्छः, कच्छभूः *f.*, पङ्कः, कर्द्दमः.

FENCE, *s.* आवरणं, वृतिः *f.*, प्रान्ततो वृतिः, प्रावृतिः *f.*, प्राकारः, प्राचीरं, अवरोधकं, वेष्टकः, वेष्टनं, वेष्टः, आवेष्टकः, प्रावरः, आवारः, वारणं -णी, वरणः, स्तम्भकरः, मत्तवारणं, मत्तालम्बः, गडः, नेमः, मोघः, मोघाली.—(Defence) रक्षा -क्षणं, गुप्तिः *f.*, त्राणं.

To FENCE, *v. a.* (Inclose with a hedge) प्राचीरेण परिवेष्ट् (c. 1. -वेष्टते -ष्टितुं, c. 10. -वेष्टयति -यितुं) or आवृ (c. 5. -वृणोति -वरितुं -रीतुं) or परिवृ or अवरुध् (c. 7. -रुणद्धि -रोद्धुं) or निरुध् or वृ in caus. (वारयति -यितुं).—(Fortify) परिखाप्राकारादिना परिवृ or आवृ or संवेष्ट्.—(Defend) रक्ष् (c. 1. रक्षति -क्षितुं), परिरक्ष्.

To FENCE, *v. n.* (Practise the art of fencing) यष्टिद्वारेण शस्त्रविद्यां or आयुधविद्याम् अभ्यस् (c. 4. -अस्यति -असितुं) or शिक्ष् (c. 1. शिक्षते -क्षितुं), त्सरुमार्गान् कृ, यष्टिमार्गान् कृ.—(Fight with foils) यष्टियुद्धं कृ, दण्डादण्डि युद्धं कृ, यष्टिक्रीडां कृ, दण्डक्रीडां कृ.

FENCED, *p. p.* or *a.* प्राचीरेण वृतः -ता -तं, सावरणः -णा -णं, प्राकारावृतः -ता -तं, प्रावृतः -ता -तं, प्राकारीयः -या -यं, अवरुद्धः -द्धा -द्धं.

FENCELESS, *a.* अनावृतः -ता -तं, अरक्षितः -ता -तं, अरुद्धः -द्धा -द्धं.

FENCER, *s.* यष्टियुद्धकर्त्ता *m.* (र्त्तृ), आयुधविद्याभ्यासी *m.* (न्), यष्टिक्रीडाशिक्षकः.

FENCING, *s.* आयुधविद्या, शस्त्रविद्या, यष्टियुद्धं, दण्डयुद्धं, यष्टिक्रीडा.

FENCING-MASTER, *s.* आयुधविद्योपदेशकः, यष्टिक्रीडोपदेशी *m.* (न्).

FENCING-SCHOOL, *s.* आयुधविद्यावेश्म *n.* (न्), आयुधशिक्षाशाला, शस्त्रविद्याशिक्षालयः, यष्टिक्रीडाशिक्षाशाला.

To FEND, *v. a.* वृ in caus. (वारयति -यितुं), निवृ, प्रतिहन् (c. 2. -हन्ति -न्तुं).

FENDER, *s.* अङ्गारगुप्तिः *f.*, अङ्गारवारणी -णं, अङ्गारावरोधकं, अङ्गारस्तम्भकः.—(Of a carriage) वरूथः, रथगुप्तिः *f.*

FENNEL, *s.* शालेयः, सालेयः, शतपुष्पा, भूरिपुष्पा, स्कन्धबन्धना, छत्रा, शीतशिवः, मधुरिका, मिशी, मिश्रेया, कारवी, घोषा.

FENNY, *a.* अनूपः -पा -पं, आनूपः -पी -पं, कच्छः -च्छा -च्छं, जलाढ्यः -ढ्या -ढ्यं, आप्यः -प्या -प्यं, सजलः -ला -लं, पङ्किलः -ला -लं.

FEOD, *s.* युद्धे ममोपकारी भवेति सन्धिं कृत्वा भूस्वामिना परहस्ते समर्पिता भूमिः or परस्मै विसर्ज्जितः क्षेत्राधिकारः.

FEODAL, FEODARY. *See* FEUDAL, FEUDATORY.

To FEOFF, *v. a.* पूर्व्वोक्तसन्धिना क्षेत्राद्यधिकारं परहस्ते or परस्मै सम् in caus. (-अर्पयति -यितुं) or परं क्षेत्राद्यधिकारे नियुज् (c. 10. -योजयति -यितुं).

FEOFFEE, *s.* पूर्व्वोक्तसन्धिपुरःसरं भूस्वामिना क्षेत्राद्यधिकारे नियुक्तः or क्षेत्राद्यधिकारवान् *m.* (त्).

FEOFFER, *s.* पूर्व्वोक्तसन्धिपुरःसरं परस्मै क्षेत्राद्यधिकारसमर्पकः.

FEOFFMENT, *s.* पूर्व्वोक्तसन्धिपुरःसरं परस्मै समर्पितो भूम्यधिकारः.

FERACIOUS, *a.* स्फीतः -ता -तं, फली -लिनी -लि (न्), अवन्ध्यः -न्ध्या -न्ध्यं.

FERACITY, *s.* फलवत्त्वं, साफल्यं, स्फीतता, अवन्ध्यता, उर्व्वरात्वं.

FERINE, *a.* पाशवः -वी -वं, शौवापदः -दी -दं, श्वापदः -दी -दं, पशुशीलः -ला -लं, पशुव्यवहारः -रा -रं, पशुधर्म्मा -र्म्मा -र्म्म (न्), वन्यः -न्या -न्यं.

FERITY, *s.* पशुता -त्वं, पशुशीलता, क्रूराचारत्वं, निष्ठुरता.

To FERMENT, *v. a.* अन्तःक्षोभं or अन्तर्ज्वलनं or अन्तस्तापं or उद्भावं जन् (c. 10. जनयति -यितुं), उत्सेचनं जन्, अन्तः क्षुभ् (c. 10. क्षोभयति -यितुं), उत्तप् (c. 10. -तापयति -यितुं).

To FERMENT, *v. n.* अन्तःक्षुभ् (c. 4. क्षुभ्यति, क्षोभितुं), अन्तःक्षोभं or अन्तस्तापम् उपगम् (c. 1. -गच्छति -गन्तुं) or गम् or इ (c. 2. एति -तुं), उत्तप्तः -प्ता -प्तं भू or अस्, उद्धू, फेन (nom. फेनायते).

FERMENT, *s.* (Intestine motion, heat) अन्तःक्षोभः, अन्तस्तापः, अन्तर्दाहः, अन्तर्वेगः, अन्तरुत्सेकः, उत्तापः, अन्तरालोडनं, अन्तरुष्मः, उष्णत्वं, प्रचण्डता.—(That which causes fermentation, yeast) नग्नहूः *m.*, किण्वः -ण्वं, मण्डः -ण्डं, सुरामण्डः, अभिषवः, कारोत्तरः, कारोत्तमः, कादम्बरीबीजं.

FERMENTABLE, *a.* अन्तरुत्सेकयोग्यः -ग्या -ग्यं, अन्तरुत्सेचनक्षमः -मा -मं, अन्तःक्षोभणीयः -या -यं.

FERMENTATION, *s.* सन्धानं, सन्धिका, अन्तर्दहनं, अन्तःक्षोभः, अन्तस्तापः, अन्तर्दाहः, अन्तरुत्सेकः, उत्सेकः, उत्सेचनं, उद्भावः, उत्तापः, उष्णत्वं, अन्तरुष्मः, उच्चण्डता, अन्तश्चण्डता, अन्तरालोडनं, विकारः.

FERMENTATIVE, *a.* उद्भावकारी -रिणी -रि (न्), अन्तःक्षोभकारी &c., उत्सेकजनकः -का -कं, मण्डजनकः -का -कं.

FERMENTED, *a.* विकृतः -ता -तं, विकारितः -ता -तं, सन्धितः -ता -तं, सन्धानोपगतः -ता -तं, अन्तःक्षुब्धः -ब्धा -ब्धं, उत्सिक्तः -क्ता -क्तं; 'fermented liquor,' सुरासवः, यवसुरं.

FERN, *s.* समङ्गा, गुप्तपुष्प ओषधिभेदः, बहुपत्रकः.

FERNY, *a.* समज्ञाविशिष्टः -ष्टा -ष्टं, समज्ञावृतः -ता -तं, समज्ञामयः -यी -यं.

FEROCIOUS, *a.* रौद्रः -द्री -द्रं, क्रूरः -रा -रं, अतिक्रूरः -रा -रं, मारात्मकः -का -कं, उग्रः -ग्रा -ग्रं, शौवापदः -दी -दं, श्वापदः -दी -दं, व्यालः -ला -लं, साहसिकः -की -कं, दारुणः -णा -णं, क्रूरचरितः -ता -तं, क्रूरकर्म्मा -र्म्मा -र्म्म (न्), रौरवः -वी -वं, व्यालतमः -मा -मं.

FEROCIOUSLY, *adv.* अतिक्रूरवत्, अतिक्रौर्य्येण, श्वापदवत्, व्यालवत्, उग्रं.

FEROCITY, *s.* रौद्रता, क्रूरता, अतिक्रूरता, क्रौर्य्यं, उग्रत्वं, व्यालत्वं.

FERREOUS, *a.* लौहः -ही -हं, आयसः -सी -सं, लोहलः -ला -लं, लोहमयः -यी -यं, अयोमयः -यी -यं, लोहस्वभावः -वा -वं.

FERRET, *s.* बभ्रुः *m.*, नकुलः, अक्रूषः, नकुलजातीयो जन्तुः.

To FERRET, *v. a.* शशकादिबिलेवासिनो क्षुद्रजन्तून् बभ्रुभिर् गर्त्तेभ्यो निःसृ in caus. (-सारयति -यितुं) or गर्त्तेभ्यो बहिष्कृत्य अनुसृ, इन्दुरादीन् गर्त्ताश्रयान् निःसृ in caus.

FERRUGINOUS, *a.* लोहकलङ्कमयः -यी -यं, अयोमलवान् -वती -वत् (त्).

FERRULE, *s.* लोहवलयः, लोहबन्धनी -नं, लौहरक्षणी, दण्डाग्रबन्धनी.

To FERRY OVER, *v. a.* नावा or नौकया नदीं or नदीपारं तॄ in caus. (तारयति -यितुं).

To FERRY OVER, *v. n.* नौकया नदीं or नदीपारं तॄ (c. 1. तरति -रितुं -रीतुं) or सन्तॄ.

FERRY, *s.* (Place of passing over rivers) नदीतरस्थानं, तरस्थानं, तरणस्थानं, उत्तरणस्थानं, तरः, घट्टः -ट्टी, उत्तरः.

FERRY-BOAT, *s.* तरणनौका, तरणिः -णिः *f.*, तारणिः -णिः *f.*, तरित्री, तरिः *f.*, तरिकं -का, तारकः -कं, तरण्डः -ण्डा -ण्डी, तरालुः *m.*, तरान्धुः *m.*, वहित्रं, उडुपः -पं.

FERRY-MAN, *s.* तारकः, तरिकः -की *m.* (न्), तारणः, तरिता *m.* (तृ).

FERTILE, *a.* बहुफलः -ला -ली -लं, बहुफलदः -दा -दं -दायी -यिनी -यि (न्), बहुफलोत्पादकः -का -कं, बहुशस्यदः -दा -दं, प्रचुरशस्योत्पादकः -का -कं, फली -लिनी -लि (न्), फलवान् -वती -वत् (त्), सफलः -ला -लं, स्फीतः -ता -तं, पीनः -ना -नं, अवन्ध्यः -न्ध्या -न्ध्यं; 'fertile soil,' उर्व्वरा or अर्व्वरा.

FERTILELY, *adv.* सफलं, सबहुफलं, स्फीतं, स्फीतया, यथा बहुफलम् उत्पद्यते तथा, अवन्ध्यं.

FERTILENESS, FERTILITY, *s.* फलवत्त्वं, सफलता, फलिता, साफल्यं, स्फीतिः *f.*, बहुफलोत्पादकत्वं, अवन्ध्यत्वं, उर्व्वरात्वं, अर्व्वरत्वं.

To FERTILIZE, *v. a.* सफल (nom. सफलयति -यितुं), सफलीकृ, स्फीतीकृ, स्फाय् in caus. (स्फावयति -यितुं), आप्यै in caus. (-प्याययति -यितुं).

FERTILIZED, *p. p.* सफलीकृतः -ता -तं, स्फीतीकृतः -ता -तं, आप्यायितः -ता -तं.

FERULE, FERULA, *s.* काष्ठफलकविशेषो येन हस्ततले शिष्यताडनं क्रियते.

To FERULE, *v. a.* पूर्व्वोक्तकाष्ठफलकेन करतले शिष्यं तड् (c. 10. ताडयति -यितुं).

FERVENCY, *s.* व्यग्रता, चण्डता, उच्चण्डता, प्रचण्डता, उष्णता, उष्मः, उत्तापः, तैक्ष्ण्यं, तीक्ष्णता, उद्योगः, उद्युक्तता, उग्रता, औत्सुक्यं, अनुरागः, आसक्तिः *f.*, चित्तासक्तिः *f.*, मनोनिर्बन्धः, उत्साहः; 'pious ardour,' अतिशयभक्तिः *f.*, भक्तिव्यग्रता.

FERVENT, *a.* व्यग्रः -ग्रा -ग्रं, चण्डः -ण्डा -ण्डं, प्रचण्डः -ण्डा -ण्डं, उच्चण्डः -ण्डा -ण्डं, उत्तप्तः -प्ता -प्तं, उष्णः -ष्णा -ष्णं, उद्योगी -गिनी -गि (न्), उद्युक्तः -क्ता -क्तं, सोद्योगः -गा -गं, तीक्ष्णः -क्ष्णा -क्ष्णं, अनुरक्तः -क्ता -क्तं, अत्यनुरागी -गिणी -गि (न्), उत्सुकः -का -कं, आसक्तः -क्ता -क्तं, समुद्यतः -ता -तं, उग्रः -ग्रा -ग्रं; 'in piety,' अतिभक्तः -क्ता -क्तं, भक्तिव्यग्रः -ग्रा -ग्रं.

FERVENTLY, *adv.* व्यग्रं, अत्यनुरागेण, सतैक्ष्ण्यं, उत्तापेन, सोद्योगं, औत्सुक्येन, उत्सुकं, उग्रं, सानुरागं, प्रचण्डं, व्यवसितं, अतिकुतूहलेन.

FERVID, *a.* तप्तः -प्ता -प्तं, सन्तप्तः -प्ता -प्तं, उपतप्तः -प्ता -प्तं, अभितप्तः -प्ता -प्तं, उत्तप्तः -प्ता -प्तं, चण्डः -ण्डा -ण्डं, प्रचण्डः -ण्डा -ण्डं, उष्णः -ष्णा -ष्णं, तीक्ष्णः -क्ष्णा -क्ष्णं, तीव्रः -व्रा -व्रं, तिग्मः -ग्मा -ग्मं.

FERVOUR, *s.* तापः, उत्तापः, सन्तापः, उपतापः, अभितापः, उष्णता, औष्ण्यं, दाहः, चण्डता, तीक्ष्णता, तैक्ष्ण्यं, तिग्मता, तीव्रता. *See* FERVENCY.

FESTAL, *a.* पार्व्वः -र्व्वी -र्व्वं, औत्सविकः -की -कं, यात्रिकः -की -कं.

To FESTER, *v. n.* पूय् (c. 1. पूयते -यितुं), पाकं कृ, पक्वः -क्वा -क्वं भू, सपूयः -या -यं भू, पूतीभू, व्रणवद् दुष् (c. 4. दुष्यति, दोष्टुं).

FESTIVAL, *s.* उत्सवः, पर्व्व *n.* (न्), पर्व्वाहः, पर्व्वरीणं, उत्सवदिनं, महः, महः *n.* (स्), उद्धर्षः, यात्रा, उद्धवः, क्षणः, अभ्युदयः, चर्चरी; 'great festival,' महोत्सवः; 'public festival,' यात्रोत्सवः; 'fixed,' नैश्चित्यं; 'completion of a festival,' पर्व्वपूर्णता.

FESTIVE, *a.* आनन्दी -न्दिनी -न्दि (न्), सानन्दः -न्दा -न्दं, आनन्दसूचकः -का -कं, सोत्सवः -वा -वं, उत्सवकारी -रिणी -रि (न्), हर्षणः -णा -णं.

FESTIVITY, *s.* समुत्सवः, उत्सवः, महोत्सवः, उत्सवकालः, हर्षः, आनन्दः, आह्लादः, आमोदः, प्रमोदः, विश्रम्भः.

FESTOON, *s.* माला, हारः, प्रालम्बिका; 'of flowers,' कुसुममाला.

FETAL, *a.* गार्भः -र्भी -र्भं, गार्भिकः -की -कं, भ्रूणसम्बन्धी -न्धिनी -न्धि (न्).

To FETCH, *v. a.* (Bring) आनी (c. 1. -नयति -नेतुं), उपानी, आहृ (c. 1. -हरति -हर्तुं).—(Derive) आनी, निर्णी, नी, अपवह् (c. 1. -वहति -वोढुं).—(Draw, cause to appear) निष्कृष् (c. 1. -कर्षति -क्रष्टुं), स्रु in caus. (स्रावयति -यितुं), उत्पद् in caus. (-पादयति -यितुं), जन् in caus. (जनयति -यितुं); 'draw blood,' शोणितम् उत्पद् in caus., रक्तं स्रु in caus.; 'fetch a sigh,' दीर्घं निःश्वस् (c. 2. -श्वसिति -तुं) or निश्वस्.—(Perform) कृ.—(Fetch a price) अमुकमूल्येन विक्री in pass. (-क्रीयते); 'what price does it fetch?' कियता मूल्येन विक्रीयते.

FETCH, *s.* उपायः, व्यपदेशः, अपदेशः, छलं -लना, कपटः, व्याजः.

FETCHED, *p. p.* आनीतः -ता -तं, उपानीतः -ता -तं, आहृतः -ता -तं.

FETE, *s.* उत्सवः, महोत्सवः, उत्सवदिनं, उद्धर्षदिनं.

FETID, *a.* दुर्गन्धः -न्धा -न्धं, दुर्गन्धी -न्धिनी -न्धि (न्), असुगन्धः -न्धा -न्धं, उग्रगन्धिः -न्धिः -न्धि, पूतिगन्धिकः -की -कं, असुरभिः -भिः -भि, पूतः -ता -तं.

FETIDNESS, *s.* दुर्गन्धत्वं, दौर्गन्धिः *m.*, पूतिगन्धता, पूतिः *f.*, पूतत्वं.

FETLOCK, *s.* अश्वानां पादजङ्घासन्धिः *m.* or चरणजङ्घापर्व्व *n.* (न्) or पादजङ्घासन्धिरूढो लोमपिण्डः or लोमगुच्छकः.

FETOR, *s.* दुर्गन्धः, पूतिगन्धः, कुत्सितगन्धः, उग्रगन्धः, असुगन्धः.

FETTER, *s.* निगडः -डं, बन्धनं, बन्धः, पाशः, शृङ्खलः -ला -लं, यन्त्रणा, यन्त्रं, योक्त्रं, चारः, प्रसितिः *f.*; 'for the feet,' पादपाशः -शी, चरणपाशः, पादबन्धनं; 'of iron,' लौहबन्धः -न्धं -न्धनं, शृङ्खला.

To FETTER, *v. a.* निगडेन or पाशेन or शृङ्खलया बन्ध् (c. 9. बध्नाति, बन्द्धुं), निगड (nom. निगडयति -यितुं), पाश (nom. पाशयति -यितुं), शृङ्खल (nom. शृङ्खलयति -यितुं), योक्त्र (nom. योक्त्रयति -यितुं), यन्त्र् (c. 10. यन्त्रयति -यितुं), पाशीकृ, पाशेन यम् (c. 1. यच्छति, यन्तुं) or संयम्.

FETTERED, *p. p.* निगडितः -ता -तं, निगडेन बद्धः -द्धा -द्धं, पाशितः -ता -तं, पाशीकृतः -ता -तं, शृङ्खलितः -ता -तं, यन्त्रितः -ता -तं, संयमितचरणः -णा -णं, बद्धपादः -दा -दं.

FETUS, *s.* भ्रूणः, गर्भः, कललं, कललः -लं, पिण्डः, -ण्डं, गर्भस्थबालकः, जरायुस्थो बालकः, उदरस्थः शिशुः *m.*, जठरस्थशिशुः *m.*, अन्तरापत्यं.

FEUD, *s.* (Quarrel) कलहः -हं, कलिः *m.*, विरोधः, विग्रहः, विपक्षता, युद्धं, द्वन्द्वं; 'family feud,' कुटुम्बकलहः, गृहच्छिद्रं, गृहरन्ध्रं.—(Right to land). *See* FEOD.

FEUDAL, *a.* पूर्व्वकाले क्षेत्राधिकारविषये यो नियमस् तत्सम्बन्धी -न्धिनी -न्धि (न्) or क्षेत्रस्वामिक्षेत्राधिकारिणोर् मध्ये यः समयस् तद्विषयकः -का -कं.

FEUDATORY, s. पूर्व्वकाले भूस्वाम्यधीनः क्षेत्राधिकारी m. (न्), उपजीवी m. (न्).

FEVER, s. ज्वरः, संज्वरः, तापः, शरीरतापः, शरीरदाहः, देहदाहः, अन्तर्दाहः, जूर्त्तिः f., महागदः; 'common fever,' प्राकृतज्वरः; 'bilious fever,' पित्तज्वरः; 'continued fever,' सततज्वरः; 'remittent,' सन्ततज्वरः; 'slow fever,' प्रलेपकः; 'ill of fever,' see FEVERISH. 'To be ill of fever,' ज्वर् (c. 1. ज्वरति -रितुं), संज्वर्; 'attack of fever,' ज्वरावतरणं, ज्वराक्रमणं, आतपलङ्घनं.

To FEVER, v. a. ज्वर् in caus. (ज्वरयति -यितुं), संज्वर्, in caus. ज्वरं कृ, तप् in caus. (तापयति -यितुं), सन्तप्, दह् (c. 1. दहति, दग्धुं).

FEVERISH, a. (Ill with fever) ज्वरी -रिणी -रि (न्), ज्वरितः -ता -तं, सज्वरः -रा -रं, संज्वारी -रिणी -रि (न्), ज्वरातुरः -रा -रं, संज्वरातुरः -रा -रं, ज्वरपीडितः -ता -तं, ज्वरग्रस्तः -स्ता -स्तं.—(Having a slight fever) ईषज्ज्वरी -रिणी -रि (न्).—(Producing fever) ज्वरजनकः -का -कं, ज्वरोत्पादकः -का -कं.

FEVERISHNESS, s. सज्वरत्वं, ईषज्ज्वरग्रस्तता, ज्वरभावः, ज्वरित्वं.

FEW, a. अल्पः -ल्पा -ल्पं, स्वल्पः -ल्पा -ल्पं, स्वल्पकः -का -कं, अबहुः -हुः -ह्वी -हु, कतिपयः -या -यं, अप्रचुरः -रा -रं, स्तोकः -का -कं, अल्पसंख्यकः -का -कं, अबृंहितः -ता -तं, अनेकः -का -कं, मितः -ता -तं, परिमितः -ता -तं, अभूशः -शा -शं; 'a few,' अल्पे, स्वल्पे, कतिचित्, अनेके, कतिपयजनाः m. pl., कतिचिज्जनाः m. pl., स्तोकाः m. pl., कति कति; 'a few paces,' कतिचित्पदानि n. pl.; 'fewest,' न्यूनः -ना -नं, अवरः -रा -रं.

FEWNESS, s. अल्पता, स्वल्पता, अबहुत्वं, अप्राचुर्य्यं, स्तोकत्वं.

FIAT, s. आज्ञा, आदेशः, निदेशः, नियोगः, शासनं, व्यवस्था.

FIB, s. असत्यं, अनृतं, वितथं, अलीकं, मिथ्यावादः, मृषावादः.

To FIB, v. n. असत्यं वद् (c. 1. वदति -दितुं), मृषा or मिथ्या वद्.

FIBBER, s. असत्यवादी m. (न्), मिथ्यावादी m., मृषावादी m., अनृती m. (न्).

FIBRE, s. (Thread) तन्तुः m., तन्त्रं, सूत्रं, गुणः.—(Filament) केशरः, पक्ष्म n. (न्), अंशुः m.—(Fibre of the body) शिरा, सिरा, नाडी, स्नायुः m., वसा, वहीरुः m.—(Of a leaf) पत्रशिरा, पत्रनाडिका, दलस्नसा.—(Of the lotus) मृणालः -लं, बिशं, बिसं, विसं, तन्तुलं.

FIBRED, a. मृणाली -लिनी -लि (न्), तन्तुमान् -मती -मत् (त्), अंशुमान् &c.

FIBRIL, s. सूक्ष्मतन्तुः m., सूक्ष्मतन्त्रं, सूक्ष्मकेशरः, सूक्ष्मशिरा.

FIBROUS, a. तन्त्री -न्त्रिणी -न्त्रि (न्), तन्तुमान् -मती -मत् (त्), तन्तुमयः -यी -यं, केशरी -रिणी -रि (न्), सूत्री -त्रिणी -त्रि (न्), सूक्ष्मनाडिविशिष्टः -ष्टा -ष्टं, शिरालः -ला -लं.

FIBULA, s. जङ्घाया बहिरस्थि n., जङ्घाबाह्यास्थि.—(Clasp) कुडुपः.

FICKLE, a. चञ्चलः -ला -लं, चञ्चलहृदयः -या -यं, चञ्चलबुद्धिः -द्धिः -द्धि, चपलः -ला -लं, चपलात्मकः -का -कं, चलचित्तः -त्ता -त्तं, सङ्कसुकः -का -कं, अस्थिरः -रा -रं, अनवस्थः -स्था -स्थं, अनवस्थानः -ना -नं, अनवस्थितः -ता -तं, लोलः -ला -लं, तरलः -ला -लं, प्रकृतितरलः -ला -लं, अधीरः -रा -रं, अन्यमनाः -नाः -नः (स्), नैकभावाश्रयः -या -यं, सञ्चारी -रिणी -रि (न्).

FICKLENESS, s. चञ्चलत्वं, चाञ्चल्यं, चपलता, चापल्यं, अस्थिरता, अस्थैर्य्यं, चलचित्तता, लोलता, लौल्यं, मनोलौल्यं, तरलता, तारल्यं, सङ्कसुकत्वं, अनवस्थितिः f., अधीरत्वं, अधृतिः f.

FICKLY, adv. चञ्चलं, चपलं, तरलं, अस्थिरं, अस्थैर्य्येण, मनोलौल्यात्.

FICTION, s. (Feigning, invention) कल्पना -नं, कॢप्तिः f., परिकल्पनं -ना, रचना, सृष्टिः f., मनःसृष्टिः f., कल्पनासृष्टिः f., कृत्रिमकरणं.—(That which is feigned, false story) मनःकल्पिता कथा, कूटार्थोपाख्यानं, कूटार्थभाषिता, परिकथा, मिथ्याकथा, मिथ्यावाक्यं, प्रबन्धकल्पना, अनृतं; 'a poetical fiction,' प्रकरणं.

FICTITIOUS, a. कल्पितः -ता -तं, परिकल्पितः -ता -तं, काल्पनिकः -की -कं, मनःकल्पितः -ता -तं, कृत्रिमः -मा -मं, कृतकः -का -कं, कूटार्थः -र्था -र्थं, मिथ्यार्थकः -का -कं, मृषार्थकः -का -कं, असत्यः -त्या -त्यं, अप्रकृतः -ता -तं, विडम्बितः -ता -तं, कपटी -टिनी -टि (न्), मिथ्या in comp.; 'fictitious coin,' कूटस्वर्णं.

FICTITIOUSLY, adv. मिथ्या, असत्यं, सकपटं, सकूटं, सव्याजं, मृषा, कृत्रिमं, काल्पनिकप्रकारेण, सविडम्बनं.

FIDDLE, s. (Violin) सारङ्गी, शारङ्गी, पिनाकी.

To FIDDLE, v. n. सारङ्गीं वद् in caus. (वादयति -यितुं) or संवद्, शारिकां सृ in caus. (सारयति -यितुं).—(Trifle, fidget) चपलः -ला -लं भू, तुच्छकर्म्म कृ, तृणादि सृ in caus.

FIDDLE-FADDLE, s. मृषार्थकं, वृथाकथा, आलस्यवचनं, असम्बद्धवाक्यं.

FIDDLE-FADDLE, a. तृणप्रायः -या -यं, असम्बद्धः -द्धा -द्धं, तुच्छः -च्छा -च्छं.

FIDDLER, s. सारङ्गीवादकः, पिनाकीवादकः, सारङ्गीपाणिः m.

FIDDLESTICK, s. शारिका, कोणः, रणः, परिवादः, घर्षरिका.

FIDDLE-STRING, s. तन्त्री, तन्त्रं, सारङ्गीतन्तुः m., सारङ्गीसूत्रं.

FIDELITY, s. भक्तिः f., भक्तिमत्त्वं, भक्तता, विश्वास्यत्वं, धीरत्वं, अभेद्यता, विश्वस्तता, विश्वासता, सेवा; 'to a master,' प्रभुभक्तिः f.; 'to a husband,' पतिव्रतं, पातिव्रत्यं, पतिसेवा.

To FIDGET, v. n. चपलः -ला -लं भू, चञ्चलः -ला -लं भू, चापल्यं कृ; 'with the hands,' पाणिचापल्यं कृ.

FIDGET, s. (Restlessness) चापल्यं, चञ्चलत्वं, अशान्तिः f., सदाचलत्वं.

FIDGETY, a. चपलः -ला -लं, चञ्चलः -ला -लं, सदाचलः -ला -लं, सततगतिः -तिः -ति, अशान्तः -न्ता -न्तं, असुस्थः -स्था -स्थं.

FIDUCIAL, a. विश्वासी -सिनी -सि (न्), विश्वस्तः -स्ता -स्तं, असन्दिग्धः -ग्धा -ग्धं.

FIDUCIARY, a. प्रत्ययी -यिनी -यि (न्), दृढविश्वासः -सा -सं.

FIDUCIARY, s. (Trustee) न्यासधारी m. (न्), निक्षेपधारी m. (न्), विश्वस्तजनः.

FIE, exclam. धिक्, शान्तं, हा, अपेहि, अपसर.

FIEF, s. क्षेत्रं, भूमिः f. See FEOD.

FIELD, s. क्षेत्रं, केदारः, भूमिः f., वप्रिः m., तटं, मालं, वाटं, पाटीरः 'of corn,' शस्यक्षेत्रं; 'ploughed field,' सीत्यक्षेत्रं, कृष्टभूमिः f.; 'field of battle,' रणभूमिः f., युद्धक्षेत्रं, रणक्षेत्रं, समराङ्गनं, रणाङ्गनं, रङ्गभूमिः f., रणाजिरं, रणः -णं, आयोधनं, मल्लभूमिः f., हल्लिका; 'relating to a field,' कैदारः -री -रं, क्षेत्रिकः -की -कं, क्षेत्री -त्रिणी -त्रि (न्).—(Space for action) प्रसरः.

FIELD-DAY, s. युद्धाभ्यासदिवसः, युद्धशिक्षादिवसः, सैन्यव्यायामदिनं.

FIELD-MARSHAL, s. बलाध्यक्षः, सेनाध्यक्षः, सेनाधिपः, सेनापतिः m.

FIELD-MOUSE, s. क्षेत्रवासी क्षुद्रमूषिकविशेषः, ग्राम्यमूषिकः.

FIELD-PIECE, s. रणभूमौ प्रयोजनीयं लघुयुद्धयन्त्रं.

FIELD-SPORTS, s. वनक्रीडा, जङ्गलक्रीडा, मृगयाविहारः, मृगव्यं, मृगया.

FIEND, s. पिशाचः, भूतः, वेतालः, राक्षसः, असुरः, दानवः, दैत्यः, दैतेयः, निशाटः, निशाचरः, रात्रिचरः, रजनीचरः, नक्तचरः, क्षणदाचरः, कौणपः, यातुः m., यातुधानः, यज्ञारिः m., प्रेतः, विपुरः, कर्बुरः.

FIENDISH, FIEND-LIKE, a. पैशाचः -ची -चं -चिकः -की -कं, भौतः -ती -तं -तिकः -की -कं, राक्षसः -सी -सं, वैतालिकः -की -कं, आसुरः -री -रं, पिशाचसन्निभः -भा -भं, दारुणः -णा -णं, पिशाचवद् अतिदुष्टः -ष्टा -ष्टं.

FIERCE, a. (Savage) क्रूरः -रा -रं, रौद्रः -द्री -द्रं, उग्रः -ग्रा -ग्रं, दारुणः -णा -णं, रौरवः -वी -वं, व्यालः -ला -लं, श्वापदः -दी -दं, श्वापदः -दी -दं.—(With anger) कोपज्वलितः -ता -तं, कोपोन्मत्तः -त्ता -त्तं, कोपाकुलः -ला -लं, संरब्धः -ब्धा -ब्धं, संरम्भी -म्भिणी -म्भि (न्), समन्युः -न्युः -न्यु.

—(Violent) तीक्ष्णः -क्ष्णा -क्ष्णं, तीव्रः -व्रा -व्रं, चण्डः -ण्डा -ण्डं, प्रचण्डः -ण्डा -ण्डं, प्रखरः -रा -रं, साहसिकः -की -कं, घोरः -रा -रं.

FIERCELY, *adv.* क्रूरं, क्रौर्य्येण, रौद्रं, उग्रं, श्वापदवत्, व्यालवत्, तीव्रं, तीक्ष्णं, सतैक्ष्ण्यं, प्रचण्डं.

FIERCENESS, *s.* (Savageness) क्रूरता, रौद्रता, क्रौर्य्यं, उग्रत्वं, व्यालत्वं.—(Furiousness) संरम्भः, संरब्धता, प्रतिरम्भः, कोपोन्मत्तता.—(Violence) तीक्ष्णता, तैक्ष्ण्यं, तीव्रता, चण्डता, प्रचण्डता, प्राखर्य्यं.

FIERY, *a.* (Consisting of fire) आग्नेयः -यी -यं, अग्निमयः -यी -यं, अग्निमान् -मती -मत् (त्), काशानवः -वी -वं.—(Vehement, hot) तीक्ष्णः -क्ष्णा -क्ष्णं, तैजसः -सी -सं, चण्डः -ण्डा -ण्डं, प्रचण्डः -ण्डा -ण्डं, उच्चण्डः -ण्डा -ण्डं, उष्णः -ष्णा -ष्णं, उग्रः -ग्रा -ग्रं.—(Irascible) शीघ्रकोपी -पिनी -पि (न्), सुलभकोपः -पा -पं, पित्तवेगी -गिनी -गि (न्).

FIFE, *s.* वेणुः *m.*, वंशः, विवरनालिका, ध्वनिनाला.

FIFER, *s.* वेणुध्मः, वेणुवादः -दकः, वांशिकः, वंशवादकः.

FIFTEEN, *a.* पञ्चदश *m. f. n. pl.* (न्), पञ्चदशसंख्यकः -का -कं.

FIFTEENTH, *a.* पञ्चदशः -शी -शं.

FIFTH, *a.* पञ्चमः -मी -मं, पञ्चकः -का -कं; 'one-fifth,' पञ्चमांशः.

FIFTHLY, *adv.* पञ्चतस्, पञ्चमतस्, पञ्चमस्थाने, पञ्चमपदे.

FIFTIETH, *a.* पञ्चाशः -शी -शं, पञ्चाशत्तमः -मी -मं.

FIFTY, *a.* पञ्चाशत् *f. sing.*, अर्द्धशतः -ता -तं; 'one hundred and fifty,' सार्द्धशतं.

FIG, *s.* अञ्जीरं, उडुम्बरफलं, न्यग्रोधफलं, पिप्पलफलं.

FIG-TREE, *s.* उडुम्बरः, उदुम्बरः, वटः, न्यग्रोधः, पर्कटी, पिप्पलः, गजभक्षकः, अञ्जीरं.

To FIGHT, *v. a.* and *n.* युध् (c. 4. युध्यते, योद्धुं, c. 10. योधयति -यितुं), प्रतियुध्, संयुध्, आयुध्, प्रायुध्, विग्रह् (c. 9. -गृह्णाति -ह्णीते -ग्रहीतुं), with inst. or sometimes acc. c.; as, 'he fights with his enemies,' शत्रुभिः or शत्रुभिः सह युध्यते or विगृह्णाति or अरीन् प्रतियुध्यते or योधयति; सम्प्रहृ (c. 1. -हरति -हर्त्तुं), युद्धं कृ, सङ्ग्रामं कृ, कलह (nom. कलहायते), वैर (nom. वैरायते); 'to desire to fight,' रणकाम (nom. -काम्यति), युध् in des. (युयुत्सते -त्सितुं).

FIGHT, *s.* युद्धं, सङ्ग्रामः, आयोधनं, प्रयुद्धं, रणः -णं, समरः -रं, संयुगः, संख्यं, आहवः, सङ्करः, समाघातः, समित् *f.*, समितिः *f.*, सम्प्रहारः, विग्रहः, कलिः *m.*; 'close fight,' नियुद्धं.

FIGHTER, *s.* योद्धा *m.* (द्धृ), योधी *m.* (न्), नियोद्धा *m.*, नियोधकः, युध्वा *m.* (न्), युयुत्सुः *m.*, प्रयुयुत्सुः *m.*, युधानः, प्रहारी *m.* (न्), प्रहर्त्ता *m.* (र्त्तृ), प्रहरन् *m.* (त्).

FIGHTING, *part.* युध्यमानः -ना -नं, योधयन् -यन्ती -यत् (त्), युद्धकारी -रिणी -रि (न्).—(Qualified for war) युद्धोपयुक्तः -क्ता -क्तं, युद्धकर्म्मयोग्यः -ग्या -ग्यं.

FIGMENT, *s.* कल्पितकथा, कल्पितवाक्यं, मिथ्याकथा. *See* FICTION.

FIGURANTE, *s.* नर्त्तकी, लासकी, लासिका, नर्त्तनवृत्तिः *f.*, नृत्यकुशली.

FIGURATE, *a.* आकारवान् -वती -वत् (त्), आकृतिमान् -मती -मत् (त्), साकारः -रा -रं, रूपवान् -वती -वत् (त्), मूर्त्तिमान् -मती -मत् (त्), अवयवी -विनी -वि (न्), रूपभृत् *m. f. n.*, रूपभृत्, *m. f. n.* आकारधारी -रिणी -रि (न्).

FIGURATION, *s.* रूपकरणं, आकारविधानं, मूर्त्तिकरणं, संस्कारः, आकृतिः *f.*

FIGURATIVE, *a.* रूपकः -का -कं, व्यञ्जकः -का -कं, लाक्षणिकः -की -कं, उपलक्षितः -ता -तं, ध्वनितः -ता -तं, गौणः -णी -णं; 'figurative style,' व्यञ्जनं -ना, व्यञ्जनावृत्तिः *f.*, व्यङ्ग्यः, उपक्षेपः.

FIGURATIVELY, *adv.* सव्यञ्जनं, व्यञ्जनापूर्व्वं, सरूपकं, सोपलक्षणं.

FIGURATIVENESS, *s.* रूपकत्वं, व्यञ्जकत्वं, गौणत्वं, लाक्षणिकत्वं.

FIGURE, *s.* (Form) आकारः, आकृतिः *f.*, मूर्त्तिः *f.*, रूपं, संस्कारः, संस्थानं, विधानं, विग्रहः, प्रतिकृतिः *f.*, वरिमा *m.* (न्), अङ्कः.—(Image) प्रतिमा, प्रतिरूपं, प्रतिकृतिः *f.*, प्रतिकायः.—(Figure of speech) रूपकं, व्यञ्जनं -ना, व्यञ्जकः, ध्वनिः *m.*, उपलक्षणं, लक्षणा, उपक्षेपः, आरोपः, निदर्शनं.—(Shape, body) वपुः *n.* (स्), कायः, देहः, शरीरं, गात्रं, अङ्गं, संहननं; 'having a handsome figure,' सुरूपः -पी -पं, सुगात्रः -त्री -त्रं, रूपवान् -वती -वत् (त्), आकारवान् &c., सिंहसंहननः -ना -नं, सुमध्यमा *f.*

To FIGURE, *v. a.* (Form into a shape) कृ, संस्कृ, क्लृप् (c. 10. कल्पयति -यितुं), सङ्क्लृप्, विधा (c. 3. -दधाति -धातुं), विरच् (c. 10. -रचयति -यितुं).—(Delineate, depict) रूप् (c. 10. रूपयति -यितुं), लिख् (c. 6. लिखति, लेखितुं), आलिख्, विलिख्, अङ्क् (c. 10. अङ्कयति -यितुं), चित्र् (c. 10. चित्रयति -यितुं), वर्ण् (c. 10. वर्णयति -यितुं).—(Diversify) नानारूपं -पीं -पं कृ, भिन्नरूपं -पीं -पं कृ, चित्र्, विचित्रीकृ, चित्रविचित्रीकृ.—(Adorn with figures) नानाचिह्नैर् अलङ्कृ or चित्रविचित्रीकृ, नानारेखाभिः or नानाप्रकाराङ्कैः शुभ् (c. 10. शोभयति -यितुं).—(Figure to one's self) मनसा क्लृप् or भू (c. 10. भावयति -यितुं), विभू.

FIGURED, *p. p.* or *a.* (Adorned with figures) नानारेखालङ्कृतः -ता -तं, नानारेखाचिह्नितः -ता -तं, अङ्कितः -ता -तं, अङ्की -ङ्किनी -ङ्कि (न्), चित्रितः -ता -तं.

FILACEOUS, *s.* सूत्री -त्रिणी -त्रि (न्), तन्तुमयः -यी -यं, तन्त्री -न्त्रिणी -न्त्रि (न्).

FILAMENT, *s.* केशरः, तन्तुः *m.*, तन्त्रं, पक्ष्म *n.* (न्), अंशुः *m.*, सूक्ष्मसूत्रं; 'of the lotus,' मृणालः -लं, बिशं, बिसं, बिसं, किञ्जल्कः, मकरन्दः, तन्तुलं, अलिमकः.

FILBERT, *s.* स्वाद्यबीजगर्भम् अण्डाकृति फलं.

To FILCH, *v. a.* मुष् (c. 9. मुष्णाति, मोषितुं), परिमुष्, प्रमुष्, चुर् (c. 10. चोरयति -यितुं), स्तेन् (c. 10. स्तेनयति -यितुं), अपहृ (c. 1. -हरति -हर्त्तुं).

FILCHED, *p. p.* मूषितः -ता -तं, चौरहृतः -ता -तं, अपहृतः -ता -तं.

FILCHER, *s.* मोषकः, मोषी *m.* (न्), आमोषी *m.*, मुमुषिषुः *m.*, स्तेयकृत् *m.*

FILCHING, *s.* मोषः -षणं, मुष्टिः *f.*, मुष्टं, स्तेयं, चौरिका, अपहारः.

FILE, *s.* (Thread) सूत्रं, तन्त्रं, तन्त्री, तन्तुः *m.*, गुणः.—(A wire on which papers are strung) पत्रारोपणयोग्या शलाका, लोहतारा यस्यां लेख्यपत्रादीनि क्रमेण समारोप्यन्ते.—(The whole number of papers arranged on a wire) शलाकारोपितो लेख्यपत्रसमूहः, लेख्यपत्रावलिः *f.*, लेख्यपत्रश्रेणी, श्रेणीभूतो लेख्यपत्रसमूहः.—(Row of soldiers) सैन्यश्रेणिः *f.*, सूचिः *f.*, दण्डव्यूहः.—(Instrument for polishing) अनुक्रकचं लोहमार्ज्जनयन्त्रं, उच्चरेखाविशिष्टं लोहघर्षणयन्त्रं, लोहमार्ज्जनी.

To FILE, *v. a.* (To arrange papers on a wire) लेख्यपत्रादीनि शलाकायां or लोहतारायां यथाक्रमम् आरुह् in caus. (-रोपयति -यितुं), लेख्यपत्राणि श्रेणीकृ or विरच् (c. 10. -रचयति -यितुं).—(Rub with a file) लोहमार्ज्जनेन घृष् (c. 1. घर्षति -र्षितुं) or परिमृज् or मृज् (c. 2. मार्ष्टि -र्ष्टुं) or चूर्ण् (c. 10. चूर्णयति -यितुं).

To FILE, *v. n.* (March in file) दण्डव्यूहेन or सूचिव्यूहेन or श्रेणिव्यूहेन यात्रां कृ.

FILIAL, *a.* पुत्र्यः -त्र्या -त्र्यं, पुत्रीयः -या -यं, पौत्रः -त्री -त्रं, पौत्रिकः -की -कं, पुत्रसम्बन्धी -न्धिनी -न्धि (न्), पुत्रयोग्यः -ग्या -ग्यं, पुत्रोपयुक्तः -क्ता -क्तं; 'filial affection,' पितृभक्तिः *f.*; 'filial duty,' पुत्रधर्म्मः.

FILIALLY, *adv.* पुत्रवत्, सुतवत्, पुत्रधर्म्मवत्, पितृभक्त्या.

FILIATION, *s.* पुत्रत्वं, सुतत्वं.—(Adoption) पुत्रीकरणं.

FILIGREE, *s.* सूक्ष्मरेखारूपेण राजताभाण्डादीनां तक्षणकर्म्म *n.* (न्).

FILINGS, *s pl.* लोहचूर्णं, कृष्णचूर्णं, लोहजं, लोहकिट्टं, लोहं, शूलघातनं, गैरिलः, लोहखण्डं.

To FILL, *v. a.* पॄ in caus. (पूरयति -यितुं), आपॄ, परिपॄ, सम्पॄ, समापॄ, पूर्णीकृ, परिपूर्णीकृ, सम्पूर्णीकृ, सङ्कुलीकृ, आकीर्णीकृ, सङ्कीर्णीकृ, पर्य्याकुलीकृ, आकॄ (c. 6. -किरति -करितुं -रीतुं), संकॄ, समाकॄ, आप् (c. 5. -आप्नोति -आप्तुं), आवृ (c. 5. -वृणोति -वरितुं -रीतुं), उभ् or उम्भ् (c. 6. उभति, उम्भति -म्भितुं).—(Make abundant) प्रचुरीकृ, बहुलीकृ.—(Supply, store) सम्भृ (c. 3. -बिभर्त्ति, c. 1. -भरति -भर्तुं), सञ्चितं -तां -तं कृ.—(Satisfy, glut) अत्यादिना पॄ or सन्तुष् (c. 10. -तोषयति -यितुं) or सन्तृप् (c. 10. -तर्पयति -यितुं).

To FILL, *v. n.* (Become full) पॄ in pass. (पूर्य्यते), आपॄ, सम्पॄ, समापॄ, परिपॄ, प्रपॄ, पूर्णीभू, सम्पूर्णीभू, परिपूर्णीभू, सङ्कुलीभू, सङ्कीर्णीभू.

FILLED, *p. p.* पूरितः -ता -तं, पूर्णः -र्णा -र्णं, परिपूर्णः -र्णा -र्णं, सम्पूर्णः -र्णा -र्णं, अभिपूर्णः -र्णा -र्णं, पूर्य्यमाणः -णा -णं, आकीर्णः -र्णा -र्णं, सङ्कीर्णः -र्णा -र्णं, अनुकीर्णः -र्णा -र्णं, सङ्कुलः -ला -लं, समाकुलः -ला -लं, पर्य्याकुलः -ला -लं, व्याप्तः -प्ता -प्तं, आवृतः -ता -तं, आविष्टः -ष्टा -ष्टं, चितः -ता -तं, आचितः -ता-तं, समाचितः -ता-तं, निचितः -ता -तं, सञ्चितः -ता -तं, सम्भृतः -ता -तं, भरितः -ता -तं, प्रोम्भितः -ता -तं, गर्भः -र्भा -र्भं, in comp.; as, 'a tube filled with powder,' चूर्णगर्भा नाडिः.

FILLER, *s.* पूरयिता *m.* (तृ), पूरकः -का, पूरणकारी *m.* (न्).

FILLET, *s.* पट्टः, ललाटपट्टः -ट्टं, मूर्द्धवेष्टनं, ललाटवेष्टनं, बन्धनी, केशवेशः; 'binding the head with fillets,' पट्टबन्धनं.

To FILLET, *v. a.* पट्टेन बन्ध् (c. 9. बध्नाति, बन्द्धुं) or वेष्ट् (c. 1. वेष्टते -ष्टितुं).

FILLING, *part.* पूरकः -का -कं, पूरणः -णा -णी -णं.

FILLING, *s.* पूरणं, आपूरणं, पूर्त्तिः *f.*, आपूर्त्तिः *f.*, पूर्णीकरणं.

To FILLIP, *v. a.* अङ्गुलिनखेन तड् (c. 10. ताडयति -यितुं), अङ्गुलिघातं कृ.

FILLIP, *s.* अङ्गुलिघातः, अङ्गुलिप्रहारः, अङ्गुलिताडनं, अङ्गुलिध्वनिः *m.*, अङ्गुलिस्फोटनं, छोटिका.

FILLY, *s.* किशोरी, बालवाजिनी, बालतुरगी, बालघोटिका.

FILM, *s.* पटलं, पुटः, सूक्ष्मत्वक् *f.* (च्), सूक्ष्मचर्म्म *n.* (न्); 'over the eye,' अक्षिपटलं, अमर्षानं.

FILMY, *a.* पटलावृतः -ता -तं, पटलमयः -यी -यं, सूक्ष्मत्वग्विशिष्टः -ष्टा -ष्टं.

To FILTER, *v. a.* सम्मार्जनयन्त्रद्वारा जलं शुध् (c. 10. शोधयति -यितुं) or सम्मृज् (c. 2. -मार्ष्टि -ष्टुं) or निर्म्मलीकृ or पवित्रीकृ, जलोत्पवनं कृ.

To FILTER, *v. n.* जलसम्मार्जनयन्त्रात् निर्गल् (c. 1. -गलति -लितुं) or शनैः शनैर् निःसृत्य शुध् (c. 4. शुध्यति, शोद्धुं) or लवशः स्यन्दमानः शुद्धीभू.

FILTERED, *p. p.* शोधितः -ता -तं, सम्मृष्टः -ष्टा -ष्टं, निर्गलितः -ता -तं.

FILTH, *s.* मलं, अमेध्यं, अमेध्यत्वं, मालिन्यं, कुत्सितत्वं, कलुषं -षत्वं, कालुष्यं, पङ्कः, कुपङ्कः, कर्द्दमः, कल्कं, खलता, विड्डादि *n.*, अवस्करः, अपस्करः, वर्च्चस्कं.

FILTHILY, *adv.* अमेध्यं, अपवित्रं, अशुद्धं, कुत्सितं, कुत्सितप्रकारेण.

FILTHINESS, *s.* अमेध्यता, अपवित्रत्वं, मलिनता, कुत्सितत्वं, अशुद्धता.

FILTHY, *a.* मलिनः -ना -नं, समलः -ला -लं, मलदूषितः -ता -तं, मलीमसः -सा -सं, अमेध्यः -ध्या -ध्यं, अपवित्रः -त्रा -त्रं, अशुद्धः -द्धा -द्धं, कलुषः -षा -षं -षी -षिणी -षि (न्), कश्मरः -रा -रं, पङ्की -ङ्किनी -ङ्कि (न्), पङ्किलः -ला -लं, कश्मलः -ला -लं, कुत्सितः -ता -तं; 'filthy conversation,' कुत्सितवाक्यं.

FILTRATION, *s.* जलोत्पवनं, उत्पवनं, जलशोधनं, जलसम्मार्जनं, निर्गलनं.

FIN, *s.* मत्स्यपक्षः, मत्स्यदेहधिः *m.*, मत्स्यतनुरुहः, मत्स्यवाजः; 'fin-footed,' जालपादः -दा -दं, जालपाद् *m. f. n.*

FINABLE, *a.* दाप्यः -प्या -प्यं, दण्ड्यः -ण्ड्या -ण्ड्यं, दण्डनीयः -या -यं.

FINAL, *a.* अन्त्यः -न्त्या -न्त्यं, अन्तिमः -मा -मं, आन्तः -न्ती -न्तं, समाप्तिकः -की -कं, चरमः -मा -मं, पश्चिमः -मा -मं, जघन्यः -न्या -न्यं, अन्त or शेष in comp.

FINALLY, *adv.* अन्ततस्, शेषे, अवशेषे, शेषतस्, अन्ते, अवसाने.

FINANCE, FINANCES, *s.* आयः, बलिः *m.*, करः, धनं, शुल्कः -ल्कं, उदयः, आगमः, धनागमः, कारः, राजस्वं, राजधनं, नृपांशः; 'control of the finance,' धनाधिकारः; 'superintendant of,' धनाधिकारी *m.*

FINANCIAL, *a.* बालेयः -यी -यं, शौल्कः -ल्की -ल्कं, राजधनसम्बन्धी -न्धिनी -न्धि (न्).

FINANCIER, *s.* धनाधिकारी *m.* (न्), राजकोशाध्यक्षः, राजस्वपालकः.

To FIND, *v. a.* (Meet with, obtain) अधिगम् (c. 1. -गच्छति -गन्तुं), अध्यागम्, गम्, आसद् (c. 10. -सादयति -यितुं), प्राप् (c. 5. -आप्नोति -आप्तुं), आप्, अवाप्, समाप्; लभ् (c. 1. लभते, लब्धुं), उपलभ्, विद् (c. 6. विन्दति, वेदितुं), अभिविद्, प्रतिपद् (c. 4. -पद्यते -पत्तुं), आविश् (c. 6. -विशति -वेष्टुं), इ (c. 2. एति -तुं), ऋच्छ् (c. 1. ऋच्छति), अव् (c. 1. अवति -वितुं), उद्देशं कृ.—(Find out, discover) ज्ञा (c. 9. जानाति -नीते, ज्ञातुं), परिज्ञा, अभिज्ञा, परिज्ञानं कृ, निरूप् (c. 10. -रूपयति -यितुं), अनुसन्धा (c. 3. -दधाति -धातुं), अन्विष् (c. 6. -इच्छति -एषितुं), निर्णी (c. 1. -णयति -णेतुं), उपलभ् (c. 1. -लभते -लब्धुं), अवगम्.—(Find out, invent) परिकॢप् (c. 10. -कल्पयति -यितुं).—(Find out, solve) परिशुध् (c. 10. शोधयति -यितुं), व्याख्या (c. 2. -ख्याति -तुं), व्याकृ, स्पष्टीकृ, व्यक्तीकृ, उच्छिद् (c. 7. -छिनत्ति -छेत्तुं).

FINDER, *s.* अधिगन्ता *m.* (न्तृ), आसादयिता *m.* (तृ), प्रापकः, अवाप्ता *m.* (प्तृ).

To FIND FAULT WITH, *v. a.* दोषीकृ, निन्द् (c. 1. निन्दति -न्दितुं), प्रतिनिन्द्, उपालभ् (c. 1. -लभते -लब्धुं), तिरस्कृ, दोषम् आरुह् in caus. (-रोपयति -यितुं), दोषं ग्रह् (c. 9. गृह्णाति, ग्रहीतुं).

FINDING, *s.* अधिगमः, आसादनं, प्राप्तिः *f.*, लब्धिः *f.*, अवगतिः *f.*, परिज्ञानं.

FINE, *a.* (Subtile, thin, minute) सूक्ष्मः -क्ष्मा -क्ष्मं, तनुः -नुः -न्वी -नु, प्रतनुः -नुः -नु, वितनुः -न्वी -नु, क्षीणः -णा -णं, श्लक्ष्णः -क्ष्णा -क्ष्णं, कणीकः -का -कं, अल्पः -ल्पा -ल्पं, दहरः -रा -रं; 'in discerning minute beauties, &c.,' कुशाग्रीयमतिः -तिः -ति, मार्म्मिकः -की -कं.—(Delicate) पेलवः -वा -वं, कोमलः -ला -लं, सुकुमारः -री -रं.—(Not coarse) अस्थूलः -ला -लं, सूक्ष्मः -क्ष्मा -क्ष्मं, विरलः -ला -लं; 'fine cloth,' सूक्ष्मवस्त्रं, सुचेलकं, अंशुकं, दुकूलं, —(Keen) तीक्ष्णः -क्ष्णा -क्ष्णं.—(Clear, pure) शुद्धः -द्धा -द्धं, विशुद्धः -द्धा -द्धं, विमलः -ला -लं.—(Excellent) उत्कृष्टः -ष्टा -ष्टं, उत्तमः -मा -मं, परमः -मा -मं.—(Handsome, elegant) शोभनः -ना -नं, सुन्दरः -री -रं, कान्तः -न्ता -न्तं, विनीतः -ता -तं, रूपवान् -वती -वत् (त्), सुरूपः -पी -पं; 'having fine eyes,' वामलोचनः -ना -नं, सुलोचनः -ना -नं; 'having fine teeth,' सुदन् -दती -दत् (त्); 'having fine hair,' सुकेशी -शिनी -शि (न्), केशवः -वा -वं; 'a fine woman,' रूपवती, प्रमदा, सुन्दरी; 'a fine lady,' सुन्दरीम्मन्या, सुवेशिनीम्मन्या; 'a fine day,' सुदिनं, उत्तमाहः; 'fine night,' सुरात्रिः *f.* —(Fine art) कला.

FINE, *s.* (Mulct) दण्डः, धनदण्डः, अर्थदण्डः, पणः; 'small fine,' दण्डलेशः -शं; 'in fine,' शेषे, अन्ततस्, वस्तुतस्.

To FINE, *v. a.* (Punish with a fine) दण्ड् (c. 10. दण्डयति -यितुं), दा in caus. (दापयति -यितुं), साध् (c. 10. साधयति -यितुं), अपहृ (c. 1. -हरति -हर्त्तुं).—(Refine, clarify) शुध् (c. 10. शोधयति -यितुं), परिशुध्, विशुध्, पवित्रीकृ, परिष्कृ, विमलीकृ, निर्म्मलीकृ, मलं हृ (c. 1. हरति, हर्त्तुं), प्रसन्नीकृ, पू (c. 9. पुनाति, पवितुं).

FINED, *p. p.* दण्डितः -ता -तं, दापितः -ता -तं, साधितः -ता -तं, अपहृतः -ता -तं.

To FINEDRAW, *v. a.* अतिसौक्ष्म्येण or अतिशुद्धतया वस्त्रछिद्रं सिव् (c. 4. सीव्यति, सेवितुं) or सूच्या सन्धा (c. 3. -धत्ते -धातुं).

FINEDRAWER, *s.* अतिसौक्ष्म्येण वस्त्रछिद्रसीवनकृत्, अतिसूक्ष्मसूचिकर्म्मविद्.

FINEDRAWING, *s.* अतिसूक्ष्मत्वेन वस्त्रछिद्रसीवनं, अतिसूक्ष्मसूचिकर्म्म *n.* (न्).

FINE-FINGERED, *a.* करदक्षः -क्षा -क्षं, लघुहस्तः -स्ता -स्तं, युक्तिमान् -मती -मत् (त्).

FINELY, *adv.* (Minutely, nicely) सूक्ष्मं, सौक्ष्म्येण, सूक्ष्मत्वेन.—(Elegantly, excellently) चारु, सुन्दरं, सुष्ठु, उत्तमं, सु prefixed; as, 'finely dressed,' सुवेशः -शा -शं.

FINENESS, *s.* (Minuteness, thinness) सूक्ष्मता -त्वं, सौक्ष्म्यं, तानवं, तनुता, श्लक्ष्णता, क्षीणता, अल्पत्वता.—(Absence of coarseness) अस्थूलता, विरलता.—(Clearness) शुद्धता, विशुद्धता, विमलत्वं.—(Keenness) तीक्ष्णता, तैक्ष्ण्यं.—(Elegance, beauty) शोभा, कान्तिः *f.*, सौन्दर्य्यं, चारुता, रम्यता, विनीतता.—(Excellence) उत्कृष्टता, उत्तमता, श्रेष्ठता; 'of gold,' वर्णिका.

FINER, *s.* धातुशोधकः, धातुपरिष्कारकः, मलापकर्षकः.

FINERY, *s.* (Show, splendor) शोभा, प्रतिभा, तेजः *n.* (स्), प्रतापः, आडम्बरः.—(Decorations, &c.) अलङ्कारः, अलङ्क्रिया, भूषणं, विभूषणं, आभरणं, प्रसाधनं, परिकर्म्म *n.* (न्), प्रतिकर्म्म *n.*, परिष्कारः, मण्डनं, रञ्जनं, अङ्करागादि; 'fond of finery,' अलङ्कारिष्णुः -ष्णुः -ष्णु, प्रियमण्डना *f.*, अलङ्कारप्रियः -या -यं.

FINE-SPUN, *a.* सूक्ष्मीकृतः -ता -तं, सूक्ष्मीभूतः -ता -तं, सूक्ष्मतन्त्रीकृतः -ता -तं.

FINESSE, *s.* माया, सूक्ष्मोपाययोगः, सूक्ष्मं, सूक्ष्मता, व्यपदेशः.

FINGER, *s.* अङ्गुलिः *f.* -ली, अङ्गुरिः *f.* -री, करपल्लवः, करशाखा, कराग्रपल्लवः, करकुड्मलं, अभीशुः *f.*, शक्करी, धयुः *f.*; 'the fore-finger,' प्रदेशिनी; 'little-finger,' कनीनी -निका, कनिष्ठाङ्गुली; 'like a finger,' आङ्गुलिकः -की -कं; 'talking with the fingers,' अङ्गुलिसन्देशः; 'the five fingers,' अङ्गुलीपञ्चकं; 'six-fingered,' षडङ्गुलिः -लिः -लि.

To FINGER, *v. a.* अङ्गुल्या परामृश् (c. 6. -मृशति -म्रष्टुं) or स्पृश् (c. 6. स्पृशति, स्प्रष्टुं) or आलभ् (c. 1. -लभते -लब्धुं) or समालभ्.

FINGERED, *p. p.* अङ्गुलिस्पृष्टः -ष्टा -ष्टं, अङ्गुलिपरिघट्टितः -ता -तं.

FINGER-NAIL, *s.* नखः, कररुहः, करजः, करकण्टकः, पाणिजः, अङ्गुलीसम्भूतः.

FINGER-RING, *s.* अङ्गुरीयः -यं -यकं, अङ्गुलीयकं, अङ्गुलीकः -कं, अङ्गुलिमुद्रा, ऊर्म्मिका.

FINICAL, *a.* एकान्तविनीतः -ता -तं, एकान्तसूक्ष्मः -क्ष्मा -क्ष्मं, एकान्तपेलवः -वा -वं, एकान्तकोमलः -ला -लं, अतिशोभनः -ना -नं, अत्युत्कृष्टः -ष्टा -ष्टं.

FINICALNESS, *s.* एकान्तविनीतता, अतिसूक्ष्मता, एकान्तपेलवता.

FINIKIN, *a.* एकान्तसूक्ष्मः -क्ष्मा -क्ष्मं, अतिलघुः -घुः -घ्वी -घु, स्वल्पविषयेषु or सुलघुविषयेषु कृतावधानः -ना -नं.

FINING, *s.* (Imposing a fine) दण्डनं, साधनं, अवहरणं.

To FINISH, *v. a.* समाप् (c. 10. -आपयति -यितुं), सम्पॄ (c. 10. -पूरयति -यितुं), निर्वृत् (c. 10. -वर्त्तयति -यितुं), निवृत्, संवृत्, अवसो (c. 4. -स्यति -सातुं), निष्पद् (c. 10. -पादयति -यितुं), सम्पद्, साध् (c. 10. साधयति -यितुं), संसाध्, विरम् (c. 10. -रमयति -यितुं), तीर् (c. 10. तीरयति -यितुं), पार् (c. 10. पारयति -यितुं).—(Polish up, elaborate) संस्कृ, परिष्कृ, महायत्नेन साध् or सिद्धीकृ.

FINISHED, *p. p.* समाप्तः -प्ता -प्तं, समापितः -ता -तं, सम्पूर्णः -र्णा -र्णं, समापन्नः -न्ना -न्नं, सम्पन्नः -न्ना -न्नं, निष्पन्नः -न्ना -न्नं, अवसितः -ता -तं, सितः -ता -तं, अवसन्नः -न्ना -न्नं, पर्य्यवसितः -ता -तं, सिद्धः -द्धा -द्धं, निर्वृत्तः -त्ता -त्तं, निवृत्तः -त्ता -त्तं, वृत्तः -त्ता -त्तं, साधितः -ता -तं, विपर्य्यस्तः -स्ता -स्तं, अपनीतः -ता -तं, सुविहितः -ता -तं.—(Polished) संस्कृतः -ता -तं, परिष्कृतः -ता -तं.

FINISHER, *s.* समापकः, समापयिता, साधकः, निष्पादकः, सिद्धिदाता *m.* (तृ).

FINISHING, FINISH, *s.* समाप्तिः *f.*, समापनं, सिद्धिः *f.*, साधनं, निष्पत्तिः *f.*, निर्वृत्तिः *f.*, निर्वर्त्तनं, अन्तः -न्तं.

FINITE, *a.* अन्तवान् -वती -वत् (त्), आद्यन्तवान् &c., साद्यन्तः -न्ता -न्तं, समर्य्यादः -दा -दं, मितः -ता -तं, परिमितः -ता -तं, प्रमेयः -या -यं, परिमेयः -या -यं, नियतः -ता -तं, निरूपितः -ता -तं.

FINITELY, *adv.* परिमितं, साद्यन्तं, समर्य्यादं, नियतं.

FINITENESS, *s.* परिमितता, प्रमेयता, अन्तवत्त्वं, साद्यन्तत्वं.

FINLESS, *a.* पक्षहीनः -ना -नं, पक्षरहितः -ता -तं, पक्षवर्ज्जितः -ता -तं.

FINNY, *a.* पक्षवान् -वती -वत् (त्), पक्षविशिष्टः -ष्टा -ष्टं.

FIR, *s.* देवदारुः *m.*, इन्द्रदारुः, इन्द्रवृक्षः, देवकाष्ठं, किलिमः.

FIRE, *s.* अग्निः *m.*, वह्निः *m.*, अनलः, पावकः, पावनः, ज्वलनः, दहनः, तेजः *n.* (स्), कृष्णवर्त्मा *m.* (न्), कृशानुः *m.*, हुतभुक् *m.* (ज्), हविरशनः, हुताशः -शनः, हविर्भुक् *m.*, हव्यवाहनः, हव्याशनः, कव्यवाहनः, तनूनपात् *m.* (द्), आशयाशः, आश्रयाशः, आश्रयभुक् *m.* (ज्), आश्रयध्वंसी *m.* (न्), बर्हिः *m.* (स्), दमुनाः *m.* (स्), शुष्मा *m.* (न्), धासिः *m.*, दावः, पचनः, पाचनः, पाचकः, जुहुवान् *m.* (त्), वाशिः *m.* शिखी *m.* (न्), शिखावान् *m.* (त्), अर्चिष्मान् *m.* (त्), प्रभाकरः, छिदिरः, शुन्ध्युः *m.*, जगनुः *m.*, जागृविः *m.*, अपाम्पित्तः, अप्पित्तं, जलपित्तः, हिमारातिः *m.*, वायुसखः -खा *m.*, धूमकेतुः, शुक्रः, आशरः, शुचिः *m.*, समिधः, वैश्वानरः, वीतिहोत्रः, अग्निहोत्रः, धनञ्जयः, कृपीटयोनिः *m.*, जातवेदाः *m.* (स्), शोचिष्केशः, उषर्बुधः, बृहद्भानुः *m.*, रोहिताश्वः, आशुशुक्षणिः *m.*, चित्रभानुः *m.*, हिरण्यरेताः *m.* (स्), ज्वालाजिह्वः, सप्तार्चिः *m.* (स्), विभावसुः *m.*, वृषाकपिः *m.*, स्वाहापतिः *m.*, स्वाहाप्रियः, स्वाहाभुक् *m.* (ज्); 'the god of fire,' अग्निदेवः -वता; 'his wife,' स्वाहा, अग्नायी, वृषाकपायी; 'on fire,' अग्निदीप्तः -प्ता -प्तं; 'placed on the fire,' अग्निस्थः -स्था -स्थं; 'a forest-fire,' वनवह्निः *m.*, दावः, दवाग्निः *m.*, दावानलः; 'fire-temple,' अग्न्यागारः, अग्निगृहं; 'cooked with fire,' अग्निपक्वः -क्वा -क्वं.—(Conflagration) दाहः -हनं, ज्वालः; 'of a house,' गृहदाहः.—(Vigour) तेजः *n.* (स्), सत्त्वं; 'submarine fire,' और्वः, वाडवाग्निः *m.*, समुद्रवह्निः *m.*

To FIRE, *v. a.* दह् (c. 1. दहति, दग्धुं), निर्दह्, प्रदह्, सम्प्रदह्, परिदह्, आदह्, अनुदह्, ज्वल् in caus. (ज्वालयति, ज्वलयति -यितुं), प्रज्वल्, दीप् in caus. (दीपयति -यितुं), प्रदीप्, समिन्ध् (c. 7. -इन्द्धे -इन्धितुं), सन्धुक्ष् (c. 10. -धुक्षयति -यितुं), तप् (c. 10. तापयति -यितुं), अग्निसात्कृ, ज्योतिस्सात्कृ.—(Animate) उत्तिज् (c. 10. -तेजयति -यितुं), प्रोत्सह् in caus. (-साहयति -यितुं).—(Fire off a gun) लोहगोलान् युद्धनाडेः प्रक्षिप् (c. 6. -क्षिपति -क्षेप्तुं) or निःसृ in caus. (-सारयति -यितुं), युद्धनाडिस्थम् आग्नेयचूर्णं ज्वल् in caus.

To FIRE, *v. n.* (Take fire) दह् (c. 4. दह्यति -ते, दग्धुं), दीप् (c. 4. दीप्यते, दीपितुं), सन्दीप्, आदीप्, प्रदीप्, ज्वल् (c. 1. ज्वलति -लितुं), प्रज्वल्, समिन्ध् in pass. (-इध्यते), समिद्धीभू, सन्धुक्ष् (c. 1. -धुक्षते -क्षितुं), अग्निदीप्तः -प्ता -प्तं भू.

FIRE-ARMS, *s.* अग्न्यस्त्रं -स्त्राणि *n. pl.*, आग्नेयास्त्रं -स्त्राणि *n. pl.*, भुशुण्डी, अन्तरग्निबलेन गुलिकाप्रक्षेपणी लोहनाडिः.

FIRE-ARROW, *s.* अग्निबाणः, आग्नेयबाणः, अग्निशरः, अग्निसायकः.

FIRE-BALL, *s.* अग्निगोलः -लकः, शीघ्रदाह्यचूर्णगर्भो लोहगोलो यो युद्धे विदीर्णो भूत्वा रिपुनाशं करोति.

FIRE-BRAND, *s.* उल्का, उल्मुकं, अङ्गारः -रं, अलातं, आलातं, अग्निकाष्ठं, अग्निकुक्कुटः, कुकूटः, कुलुङ्गुञ्जा, अग्नियुद्धकाष्ठं, ज्वलनकाष्ठं; 'a number of fire-brands,' आङ्गारं.—(Incendiary) अग्निदः.

FIRED, *p. p.* ज्वलितः -ता -तं, प्रज्वालितः -ता -तं, समिद्धः -द्धा -द्धं, प्रदीप्तः -प्ता -प्तं, उद्दीप्तः -प्ता -प्तं, सन्तप्तः -प्ता -प्तं, सन्धुक्षितः -ता -तं.

FIRE-ENGINE, *s.* अग्निनिर्वापणयन्त्रं, गृहदाहनिर्वाणकरणार्थं यन्त्रं.

FIRE-EYED, *a.* ज्वलितनयनः -ना -नं, ज्वलितचक्षुः -क्षुः -क्षुः (स्).

FIRE-FLY, *s.* खद्योतः, खज्योतिः *m.* (स्), ज्योतिरिङ्गः -ङ्गणः, प्रभाकीटः, ज्योतिर्वीजं, गुह्यदीपकः, ध्वान्तोन्मेषः, चिल्लमीलिका.

FIRE-MAN, *s.* गृहदाहनिर्वापणे नियुक्तो जनः, अग्निनिर्वाणकारी *m.* (न्).

FIRE-PAN, *s.* अग्न्याधारः, अङ्गारिणी, अङ्गारधानिका, अङ्गारशकटी, अग्निपात्रं, हसनी, हसन्ती -न्तिका.

FIRE-PLACE, *s.* चुल्लिः *f.* -ल्ली, अङ्गारिणी, वितानं, अश्मन्तं -न्तकं, अश्मन्तं, अन्तिका, अन्दिका, उद्धानं, उध्मानं, उद्धारं, अधिश्रयणी, दूडकः, अग्निकुण्डं.

FIRE-PROOF, *a.* अदाह्यः -ह्या -ह्यं, अदहनीयः -या -यं, अग्निनास्पृश्यः -श्या -श्यं.

FIRE-SHIP, *s.* अग्निनौका, आग्नेयनौका, शीघ्रदाह्यवस्तुपूरिता युद्धनौका.

FIRE-SHOVEL, *s.* अङ्गारधारणयोग्यो लोहकुद्दालः.

FIRE-SIDE, *s.* गृहाग्निस्थानं, अग्निसमीपं, गृहाग्निनिकटे, गृहाग्न्युपान्तं, वितानं.

FIRE-STONE, *s.* अग्निप्रस्तरः, अग्निपाषाणः, आग्नेयाश्मा *m.* (न्).

FIRE-TONGS, *s.* अङ्गारधारणयोग्यो लौहसन्दंशकविशेषः.

FIRE-WOOD, *s.* अग्निकाष्ठं, दाह्यकाष्ठं, इन्धनं, इध्मं, समित् *f.* (ध्).

FIRE-WORKS, *s.* अग्निक्रीडा, धूपादिक्रीडा, अग्नितारादिक्रीडा.

FIRING, *s.* दाह्यं, इध्मं, समिन्धनं, अङ्गारकाष्ठतृणादीनि दाह्यवस्तूनि.

FIRKIN, *s.* मानविशेषः, आढकः, अर्द्धाढकः, द्रोणः, अर्द्धद्रोणः.

FIRM, *a.* दृढः -ढा -ढं, स्थिरः -रा -रं, निश्चलः -ला -लं, अचलः -ला -लं, अविचलितः -ता -तं, धीरः -रा -रं, धृतिमान् -मती -मत् (त्), धैर्य्यवान् -वती -वत् (त्), स्थाणुः -णुः -णु, स्थास्नुः -स्नुः -स्नु, स्थावरः -रा -रं, स्थेयान् -यसी -यः (स्), स्थेष्ठः -ष्ठा -ष्ठं, अकम्पितः -ता -तं, अक्षुब्धः -ब्धा -ब्धं, अस्खलितः -ता -तं, अव्यभिचारी -रिणी -रि (न्), व्यवस्थितः -ता -तं, स्थितः -ता -तं, स्थितिमान् -मती -मत् (त्), गाढः -ढा -ढं, प्रगाढः -ढा -ढं.—(Compact) घनः -ना -नं, दृढः -ढा -ढं, संहतः -ता -तं, अशिथिलः -ला -लं, दृढसन्धिः -न्धिः -न्धि, निर्भेटः -टा -टं; 'firm in mind,' स्थिरमतिः -तिः -ति, निश्चलमतिः -तिः -ति, स्थितधीः -धीः -धि, स्थिरात्मा -त्मा -त्म (न्), अभिन्नात्मा &c.; 'in friendship,' दृढसौहृदः; 'in allegiance,' दृढभक्तिः *m.*; 'in battle,' दृढायुधः; 'firm as a rock,' शिलाघनः -ना -नं, शैलसारः -रा -रं; 'firm step,' अस्खलितगतिः; 'a firm, compact breast,' घनपयोधरः; 'firm-footed,' स्थिरपदः -दा -दं.

FIRM, *s.* (Partnership) अनेकवाणिज्यजनसंसर्गः, सहव्यापारिणां बहुजनानाम् आख्या or उपाधिः *m.*

To FIRM, *v. a.* दृढीकृ, स्थिरीकृ, द्रढ (nom. द्रढयति -यितुं).

FIRMAMENT, *s.* आकाशः, आकाशवर्त्म *n.* (न्), व्योम *n.* (न्), व्योमविस्तृतं, नभोमण्डलं, नभस्तलः -लं, गगणं, खं, अन्तरीक्षं, नक्षत्रमण्डलं, ज्योतिश्चक्रं, तारापथः, खगोलः, उडुपथः, शून्यं, शून्यत्वं, घनाश्रयः, मेघवर्त्म *n.* (न्).

FIRMAMENTAL, *a.* आकाशीयः -या -यं, आन्तरीक्षः -क्षी -क्षं, वैहायसः -सी -सं, विहायसीयः -या -यं, गगणीयः -या -यं, गगणस्थः -स्था -स्थं, नभःस्थः -स्था -स्थं.

FIRMLY, *adv.* दृढं, स्थिरं, निश्चलं, धैर्य्येण, स्थैर्य्येण, गाढं, प्रगाढं, दार्ढ्येन; 'firmly rooted,' बद्धमूलः -ला -लं; 'firmly devoted,' दृढभक्तिः -क्तिः -क्ति; 'firmly tied,' दृढबद्धः -द्धा -द्धं; 'firmly united,' दृढसन्धिः -न्धिः -न्धि.

FIRMNESS, *s.* दृढता, दार्ढ्यं, द्रढिमा *m.* (न्), द्राढ्यं, स्थिरता, स्थैर्य्यं, धीरत्वं, धैर्य्यं, धृतिः *f.*, निश्चलता, अचलत्वं, स्थितिः *f.*, व्यवस्थितिः *f.*, स्थास्नुता, धृतिमत्त्वं, स्थितिमत्त्वं, गाढता, प्रगाढता, स्थेमा *m.* (न्), अक्षोभः, अकम्पः, अस्खलनं, स्थावरत्वं, धारणा.—(Compactness) घनत्वं -ता, संहतिः *f.*, संहतता, सन्धिः *m.*, सान्द्रता, दृढत्वं.

FIRST, *a.* प्रथमः -मा -मं, पूर्व्वः -र्व्वा -र्व्वं, आद्यः -द्या -द्यं, आदिमः -मा -मं, अग्र्यः -ग्र्या -ग्र्यं, अग्रिमः -मा -मं, आदिः *m.*, पौरस्त्यः -स्त्या -स्त्यं, प्राक्तनः -नी -नं.—(Chief) मुख्यः -ख्या -ख्यं, प्रमुखः -खा -खं, अग्र्यः -ग्र्या -ग्र्यं, प्राग्र्यः -ग्र्या -ग्र्यं, अग्रियः -या -यं, अग्रीयः -या -यं, प्रधानः -ना -नं, प्रष्ठः -ष्ठा -ष्ठं, प्रवरः -रा -रं, पुरोगमः -मा -मं; 'first and last,' पूर्व्वापरः -रा -रं; 'first half,' पूर्व्वार्द्धः; 'first part of the night,' पूर्व्वरात्रः; 'first attack' (of disease), पूर्व्वावतारः; 'dying first,' पूर्व्वमारी -रिणी -रि (न्); 'first of all,' सर्व्वप्रधानः -ना -नं, सर्व्वाग्र्यः -ग्र्या -ग्र्यं.

FIRST, *adv.* प्रथमं, पूर्व्वं, अग्रे, आदितस्, आदौ, पुरस्, पुरस्तात्; 'at first, in the first place,' प्रथमं, प्रथमतस्, पूर्व्वं; 'first and last,' आद्यन्तं.

FIRST-BEGOTTEN, *a.* पूर्व्वप्रसूतः -ता -तं, पूर्व्वजनितः -ता -तं, पूर्व्वजः -जा -जं, प्रथमजातः -ता -तं, प्रथमप्रसूतः -ता -तं, अग्रजातः -ता -तं.

FIRST-BORN, *s.* पूर्व्वजः, अग्रजः, अग्रियः, अग्रिमः, अग्र्यः, अग्रजन्मा *m.* (न्), ज्येष्ठः, वयोज्येष्ठः, अधिकवयाः *m.* (स्), सर्व्वपुत्रज्येष्ठः, प्रधानसन्तानः.

FIRST-FRUITS, *s.* प्रथमफलं, आदिफलं, प्रथमजातं फलं, अग्रफलं, प्रथमोत्पन्नं फलं, प्रथमोत्पन्नं, नवशस्यं; 'sacrifice of first-fruits,' आग्रायणं.

FIRSTLING, *s.* पशोः प्रथमजातसन्तानः or प्रथमप्रसूतसन्ततिः *f.*

FIRSTLY, *adv.* प्रथमतस्, प्रथमं, पूर्व्वं, आदितस्.

FIRST-RATE, *a.* परमः -मा -मं, श्रेष्ठः -ष्ठा -ष्ठं, उत्कृष्टः -ष्टा -ष्टं.

FISCAL, *a.* बालेयः -यी -यं, शौल्कः -ल्की -ल्कं, राजायसम्बन्धीयः -या -यं.

FISH, *s.* मत्स्यः, मीनः, झषः, मत्सः, विसारः -री *m.* (न्), वैसारी *m.* (न्), वैसारिणः, अण्डजः, शकली *m.* (न्), शल्की *m.* (न्), शल्कली *m.*, कण्टकी *m.* (न्), आम्भसिकः, जलजः, जलप्रियः, जलजन्तुः *m.*, जलेचरः, जलचारी *m.* (न्), पाठीनः, अनिमिषः, अनिमेषः, स्थिरजिह्वः, षडक्षीणः, पृथुरोमा *m.* (न्), आत्माशी *m.* (न्), मत्सी *f.*, मत्सः; 'fish-bone,' कण्टकः; 'fish-sauce,' मत्स्यगण्डः, मीनाक्षीणः; 'fish-bannered god,' मीनकेतनः, मकरध्वजः, मकरकेतुः *m.*, झषकेतनः.

To FISH, *v. a.* and *n.* मत्स्यान् ग्रह् (c. 9. गृह्णाति, ग्रहीतुं) or धृ (c. 1. धरति, धर्त्तुं) or बन्ध् (c. 9. बध्नाति, बन्धुं), मत्स्यघातं कृ, झष् (c. 1. झषति -षितुं).—(Search) अन्विष् (c. 1. -इच्छति -एषितुं), अनुसृ (c. 1. -सरति -सर्त्तुं).

FISH-BASKET, *s.* मत्स्यधानी, मत्स्यबन्धिनी, कुवेणी, मत्स्यभाजनं.

FISHER, FISHERMAN, *s.* धीवरः, कैवर्त्तः, मात्स्यिकः, मैनिकः, निषादः, मत्स्यधारी *m.* (न्), मत्स्यजीवी *m.* (न्), मत्स्यबन्धी *m.* (न्), मीनघाती *m.* (न्), मत्स्यघातोपजीवी *m.* (न्), जालिकः, जाली *m.* (न्), कुपिनी *m.* (न्), शाफरिकः, तीवरः, छोटी *m.* (न्), दासः, दाशः, धीवा *m.* (न्).

FISHERY, *s.* धीवरकर्म्म *n.* (न्), मत्स्यबन्धनं, मत्स्यग्रहणं.—(Place for catching fish) मत्स्यग्रहणस्थानं.

FISH-HOOK, *s.* बडिशं -शा -शी, वडिशी, वलिशं -शी, मत्स्यवेधनं -नी.

FISHING, *s.* मत्स्यबन्धनं, मत्स्यग्रहणं, मत्स्यवधः, मत्स्यघातः.

FISHING-BOAT, *s.* धीवरनौका, कैवर्त्तनौका, निषादनौका, मात्स्यिकपोतः.

FISHING-NET, *s.* मत्स्यजालं, मत्स्यग्रहणार्थं जालं, कुपिनी.

FISHING-TACKLE, *s.* मत्स्यग्रहणोपकरणं, मत्स्यबन्धनसाधनं.

FISH-KETTLE, *s.* मत्स्यपचनयोग्या दीर्घस्थाली, मत्स्यपचनी.

FISH-MARKET, *s.* मत्स्यविक्रयस्थानं, मीनविक्रयशाला, निषद्या.

FISHMONGER, *s.* मत्स्यविक्रेता *m.* (तृ), मत्स्यविक्रयोपजीवी *m.* (न्).

FISH-POND, *s.* मत्स्यपूर्णं सरः *n.* (स्), मीनाश्रयः, मत्स्यालयः, मीनालयः.

FISH-SPAWN, *s.* मीनाण्डं, मत्स्याण्डं, झषाण्डं, मत्स्यडिम्बः.

FISH-WOMAN, *s.* मत्स्यविक्रेत्री, मत्स्यविक्रयोपजीविनी.

FISHY, *a.* मात्स्यः -त्स्यी -त्स्यं, मात्स्यिकः -की -कं, मात्सिकः -की -कं, मैनिकः -की -कं, मीनरः -रा -रं, मत्स्यगुणोपेतः -ता -तं.

FISSILE, *a.* विदलः -ला -लं, भिदुरः -रा -रं, छिदुरः -रा -रं, भिदेलिमः -मा -मं.

FISSURE, *s.* छिद्रं, रन्ध्रं, सन्धिः *m.*, भित्तिः *f.*, भङ्गः, दरी -रा, विदरः.

To FISSURE, *v. a.* विद् (c. 10. -दारयति -यितुं), विदल् (c. 10. -दलयति -यितुं).

FIST, *s.* मुष्टिः *m. f.* -ष्टी, हस्तमुष्टिः, मुस्तुः *m.*, खटः -टकः -टिकः, रत्निः *m.* -त्नी *f.*, जितकाशिः *m.*; 'doubling or clenching the fist,' मुष्टिबन्धः, मुष्टिसङ्ग्राहः, हस्तसङ्ग्राहः.

To FIST, *v. a.* मुष्टिना or मुष्ट्या तड् (c. 10. ताडयति -यितुं) or प्रहृ (c. 1. -हरति -हर्त्तुं), मुष्टिसङ्ग्राहेण पीड् (c. 10. पीडयति -यितुं).

FISTICUFFS, *s.* मुष्टिप्रहारः, मुष्टिपातः, मुष्टियुद्धं, मौष्टा, मुष्टीमुष्टि युद्धं, बाहुयुद्धं, मल्लयुद्धं, पाणिघातः.

FISTULA, *s.* नाडिः *f.* -डी, नालिः -ली, नाडीव्रणः, नालीव्रणः, नालीघातं; 'in ano,' शतपोनकः, भगन्दरः; 'lachrymalis,' अश्रुनाली.

FISTULOUS, *a.* नाड्याकारः -रा -रं, नाडिरूपः -पा -पं; 'fistulous sore,' नाडीव्रणः.

FIT, *s.* (Paroxysm of any disease) आवेशः, अवतारः -तरणं, आक्रमः -मणं; 'fit of the gout,' वातरोगावेशः; 'fit of fever,' ज्वरावतारः; 'of ague,' कम्पज्वराक्रमः, शीतज्वरावेशः; 'fit of anger,' क्रोधावेशः; 'fit of lust,' कामावेशः; 'of madness,' उन्मादावेशः.—(Fit of fainting, epilepsy, &c.) मूर्छा -र्छनं -ना, भ्रमरं, भ्रमिः *f.*, घूर्णिः *f.*

FIT, FITTING, *a.* युक्तः -क्ता -क्तं, योग्यः -ग्या -ग्यं, उपयुक्तः -क्ता -क्तं, उपयोगी -गिनी -गि (न्), यथायोग्यः -ग्या -ग्यं, उचितः -ता -तं, समुचितः -ता -तं, यथोचितः -ता -तं, समञ्जसः -सा -सं, उपपन्नः -न्ना -न्नं, पर्य्याप्तः -प्ता -प्तं, न्याय्यः -य्या -य्यं, सम्भाव्यः -व्या -व्यं, सम्भावितः -ता -तं, अनुरूपः -पा -पं, अर्हः -र्हा -र्हं, यथार्हः -र्हा -र्हं, सङ्गतः -ता -तं, सङ्गतार्थः -र्था -र्थं, पथ्यः -थ्या -थ्यं, औपयिकः -की -कं, अभिनीतः -ता -तं, लभ्यः -भ्या -भ्यं, भजमानः -ना -नं.—(Qualified) क्षमः -मा -मं, कर्म्मक्षमः -मा -मं, अलङ्कर्म्मीणः -णा -णं; 'fit for a man,' अलम्पुरुषीणः -णा -णं; 'fit for sacrifice,' यज्ञियः -या -यं, यज्ञार्हः -र्हा -र्हं; 'a field fit for growing rice,' शाल्युद्भवोचितं क्षेत्रं. Sometimes expressed by the fut. pass. part.; as, 'fit to be eaten,' खाद्यः -द्या -द्यं, खादनीयः -या -यं; 'fit to be done,' कार्य्यः -र्य्या -र्य्यं, करणीयः -या -यं.

To FIT, *v. a.* (Adapt, accommodate) युज् (c. 10. योजयति -यितुं, c. 7. युनक्ति, योक्तुं), समायुज्, आयुज्, सन्धा (c. 3. -दधाति -धातुं), समाधा, योग्यं -ग्यां -ग्यं or उपयुक्तं -क्तां -क्तं कृ.—(Fit out, equip) सज्जीकृ, सज्ज् (c. 1. सज्जति -ज्जितुं), सोपकारद्रव्यैः समायुज्, उपयुक्तद्रव्याणि सम्प्रकॢप् (c. 10. -कल्पयति -यितुं) or उपकॢप् or उपपद् (c. 10. -पादयति -यितुं) or पुरस्कृ or उपस्कृ or प्रस्तुतीकृ सर्व्वोपकारद्रव्ययुक्तं -क्तां -क्तं कृ, उपयुक्तद्रव्यसाधनं कृ; 'fit out a ship,' समुद्रयानार्थं or युद्धार्थं नावं सज्जीकृ.

To FIT, *v. n.* (Be proper, suitable) युज् in pass. (युज्यते), उपपद् in pass. (-पद्यते), योग्यः -ग्या -ग्यं भू or अस्, उपयुक्तः -क्ता -क्तं भू, अर्ह् (c. 1. अर्हति -र्हितुं); 'it is not fit that you should grieve,' न शोचितुम् अर्हसि; 'it is not fit that I should go,' न गन्तुम् अर्हामि.—(Be qualified) कॢप् (c. 1. कल्पते -ल्प्तुं), उपकॢप्, क्षमः -मा -मं भू, उचितः -ता -तं भू; 'he is fit for immortality,' अमृतत्वाय कल्पते.

FITCH, *s.* (A chick-pea) चणकः, हरिमन्थः -न्थकः.

FITFUL, *a.* चञ्चलः -ला -लं, चलः -ला -लं, विषमः -मा -मं, लोलः -ला -लं, चपलः -ला -लं, अनित्यः -त्या -त्यं.

FITLY, *adv.* युक्तं, योग्यं, यथायोग्यं, उचितं, यथोचितं, उपयुक्तं, योगतस्, यथार्हं -र्हतस्, सम्यक्, यथार्थं, यथायथं, यथातथं, अनुरूपं, साम्प्रतं, स्थाने.

FITNESS, *s.* युक्तता, योग्यता, युक्तिः *f.*, उपयोगः, उपयुक्तता, उपयोगिता, उचितत्वं, औचित्यं, सामञ्जस्यं, समञ्जसं, उपपत्तिः *f.*, सम्भावना, न्यायः -य्यता, सङ्गतत्वं, पर्य्याप्तिः *f.*, यथार्हता, याथार्थ्यं, कल्पः, अभेषः, देशरूपं, कर्त्तव्यता.—(Qualification) पात्रता -त्वं, क्षमता.

FITTING, *s.* (Adaptation) समायोजनं, समाधानं.—(Equipping) सज्जीकरणं, सज्जनं, सज्जकर्म्म *n.* (न्), साधनं, पुरस्करणं.—(Suitable) *see* FIT.

FIVE, *a.* पञ्च *m. f. n.* (न्), पञ्चकः -का -कं, दशार्द्धः, पञ्चतयः -या -यं, पञ्चत् *m. f. n.*, पञ्चसंख्यकः -का -कं; 'aggregate of five,' पञ्चतं -ता, पञ्चकत्वं; 'having five claws,' पञ्चनखः -खा -खं; 'having five fingers,' पञ्चाङ्गुलिः -लिः -लि; 'five times,' पञ्चकृत्वस्; 'having five parts,' पञ्चाङ्गः -ङ्गी -ङ्गं; 'five-hundred,' पञ्चशतं.

FIVE-FOLD, *a.* पञ्चगुणः -णा -णं, पञ्चविधः -धा -धं, पञ्चधा.

FIVE-LEAVED, *a.* पञ्चपर्णः -र्णी -र्णं, पञ्चपत्रः -त्रा -त्रं, पञ्चदलः -ला -लं.

FIVES, *a.* कन्दुकक्रीडा, कन्दुकलीला, गुलिकाक्रीडाविशेषः.

To FIX, *v. a.* (Establish) स्था in caus. (स्थापयति -यितुं), प्रतिष्ठा, अवस्था, संस्था, धा (c. 3. दधाति, धातुं), विधा, प्रतिनिधा, रुह् in caus. (रोपयति -यितुं), आरुह्, निरुह्.—(Make firm) स्थिरीकृ, दृढीकृ, सुस्थिरं -रां -रं कृ.—(Fasten) बन्ध् (c. 9. बध्नाति, बन्द्धुं).—(Determine, ascertain) निश्चि (c. 5. -चिनोति -चेतुं), निर्णी (c. 1. -णयति -णेतुं), उन्नी, निरूप् (c. 10. -रूपयति -यितुं), परिकॢप् (c. 10. -कल्पयति -यितुं).—(Fix the gaze or eye) लक्षं बन्ध्, अनिमिषेण or अनिमेषेण or अनन्यदृष्ट्या or स्तिमितलोचनेन दृश् (c. 1. पश्यति, द्रष्टुं), दृष्टिं निविश् in caus. (-वेशयति -यितुं).—(Fix the mind) मनो निविश् in caus., or युज् (c. 7. युनक्ति, योक्तुं, c. 10. योजयति -यितुं), अनन्यमनस्कः -स्का -स्कं भू, एकाग्रः -ग्रा -ग्रं भू; 'on any object,' अर्थे धृतिं बन्ध्.

To FIX, *v. n.* (Be fixed) निष्ठा (c. 1. -तिष्ठति -ष्ठातुं), प्रणिधा in pass. (-धीयते), प्रतिनिधा, स्था in caus. pass. (स्थाप्यते), प्रतिष्ठा, बन्ध् in pass. (बध्यते), स्थिरीभू.

FIXED, *p. p.* (Established) स्थापितः -ता -तं, प्रतिष्ठापितः -ता -तं, प्रतिष्ठितः -ता -तं, संस्थापितः -ता -तं, संस्थितः -ता -तं, स्थितः -ता -तं, अवस्थापितः -ता -तं, अवस्थितः -ता -तं, निहितः -ता -तं, रोपितः -ता -तं, कृतावस्थः -स्था -स्थं, स्थिरीकृतः -ता -तं, विहितः -ता -तं.—(Certain, determined) नियतः -ता -तं, निश्चितः -ता -तं, सुनिश्चितः -ता -तं, निष्पन्नः -न्ना -न्नं.—(Firm) स्थिरः -रा -रं, स्थायी -यिनी -यि (न्), स्थावरः -रा -रं, स्थाणुः -णुः -णु, स्थास्नुः -स्नुः -स्नु, दृढः -ढा -ढं, निश्चलः -ला -लं, अकम्पितः -ता -तं, अस्पन्दः -न्दा -न्दं, नैष्ठिकः -की -कं.—(Attached) लग्नः -ग्ना -ग्नं, अनुलग्नः -ग्ना -ग्नं, आसक्तः -क्ता -क्तं, संसक्तः -क्ता -क्तं.—(Fastened) बद्धः -द्धा -द्धं; 'firmly fixed,' दृढबद्धः -द्धा -द्धं, दृढरोपितः -ता -तं, बद्धमूलः -ला -लं; 'having the eye or look fixed,' बद्धदृष्टिः -ष्टिः -ष्टि, अनिमिषनयनः -ना -नं, स्तिमितलोचनः -ना -नं, स्थिरदृष्टिः -ष्टिः -ष्टि; 'having the mind fixed,' अवस्थितमतिः -तिः -ति, निवेशितमनाः -नाः -नः (स्), आसक्तमनाः &c., आसक्तचित्तः -त्ता -त्तं, अनन्यमनस्कः -स्का -स्कं, अकुण्ठमेधाः -धाः -धः (स्); 'fixed in the mind,' चित्तीकृतः -ता -तं; 'of fixed intent,' बद्धानुशयः -या -यं; 'fixed as to time,' कृतकालः -ला -लं.

FIXEDLY, *adv.* दृढं, स्थिरं, स्थैर्य्येण, अवस्थितचेतसा, स्थिरदृष्ट्या.

FIXEDNESS, *s.* स्थिरता, स्थैर्य्यं, स्थितिः *f.*, व्यवस्थितिः *f.*, अवस्थितिः *f.*, संस्थितिः *f.*, स्थायित्वं, निष्ठा, धृतिः *f.*, धैर्य्यं, दृढता, दार्ढ्यं, स्थावरत्वं,

स्थाणुता, निश्चलत्वं, स्थेमा *m.* (न्), स्थितिमत्त्वं, अकम्पः.

FIXITY, *s.* संलग्नत्वं, अनुलग्नता, संसक्तिः *f.*, संश्लेषः, संहतिः *f.*, समासञ्जनं.

FIXTURE, *s.* स्थावरं, स्थावरद्रव्यं, स्थितद्रव्यं; 'fixtures,' स्थावरराशि.

FLABBINESS, *s.* शिथिलता, शैथिल्यं, मृदुता, कोमलत्वं, लालित्यं.

FLABBY, *a.* शिथिलः -ला -लं, ललितः -ता -तं, कोमलः -ला -लं, स्निग्धः -ग्धा -ग्धं, मेदुरः -रा -रं, अकठिनः -ना -नं.

FLACCID, *a.* शिथिलः -ला -लं, श्लथः -था -थं, प्रश्लथः -था -थं, म्लानः -ना -नं, आर्द्रः -र्द्रा -र्द्रं, असंहतः -ता -तं, वलिनः -ना -नं, वलिभः -भा -भं, वलिमान् -मती -मत् (त्).

FLACCIDITY, *s.* शैथिल्यं, शिथिलता, श्लथता, प्रश्रयः, श्रन्थः, म्लानता, आर्द्रता, विस्रंसः, असंहतत्वं, वलिमत्त्वं.

FLAG, *s.* (Ensign, banner) पताका, ध्वजः, ध्वजपटः, ध्वजांशुकः, केतनं, केतुः *m.*, केतुवसनः, वैजयन्ती -न्तिका, जयन्तः, कदली -लिका, उच्छलः.—(Stone) शिला, परिस्तरः, प्रस्तरः.—(Plant) गोलोमी, भूतकेशः, श्वेतदूर्वा.

To FLAG, *v. n.* ग्लै (c. 1. ग्लायति, ग्लातुं), परिग्लै, सद् (c. 1. सीदति, सत्तुं), अवसद्, म्लै (c. 1. म्लायति, म्लातुं), ध्वंस् (c. 1. ध्वंसते -सितुं), विध्वंस्, स्रंस् (c. 1. स्रंसते -सितुं), विस्रंस्, क्षि in pass. (क्षीयते), शिथिलीभू, शिथिलबलः -ला -लं भू, शिथिलतेजाः -जाः -जः भू, खिद् (c. 4. खिद्यते, खेत्तुं), खिन्नः -न्ना -न्नं भू.

To FLAG, *v. a.* (Pave with flag-stones) परिस्तरेण or प्रस्तरैः or शिलाभिर् आस्तॄ (c. 5. -स्तृणोति, c. 9. -स्तृणाति -स्तरितुं -रीतुं).

FLAG-OFFICER, *s.* नौकासमूहपतिः *m.*, युद्धनौकासमूहाधिपतिः *m.*

FLAG-STAFF, *s.* ध्वजस्तम्भः, केतुयष्टिः *m. f.*, ध्वजः, यष्टिः, पताकायष्टिः.

FLAG-STONE, *s.* शिला, शिलापट्टः, शिलाफलकं, परिस्तरः, प्रस्तरः.

To FLAGELLATE, *v. a.* रज्ज्वा or रज्जुना or चर्म्मदण्डेन तड् (c. 10. ताडयति -यितुं) or आहन् (c. 2. -हन्ति -न्तुं) or प्रहृ (c. 1. -हरति -हर्त्तुं).

FLAGELLATION, *s.* कशाघातः, कशाताडनं, कशा, चर्म्मदण्डताडनं.

FLAGEOLET, *s.* वंशः, वेणुः *m.*, विवरनालिका, सानेयी -यिका.

FLAGGED, *p. p.* प्रस्तरास्तीर्णः -र्णा -र्णं, शिलास्तीर्णः -र्णा -र्णं.

FLAGGING, *part.* म्लानः -ना -नं, स्रंसी -सिनी -सि (न्), खिन्नः -न्ना -न्नं.

FLAGGY, *a.* शिथिलः -ला -लं, श्लथः -था -थं, प्रश्लथः -था -थं.

FLAGITIOUS, *a.* अतिपापी -पिनी -पि (न्), महापापी &c., अतिपातकी -किनी -कि (न्), महापातकी &c., अतिदुर्वृत्तः -त्ता -त्तं, अतिपापिष्ठः -ष्ठा -ष्ठं, अतिदुष्टः -ष्टा -ष्टं, अतिदोषी -षिणी -षि (न्), दारुणः -णा -णं, घोरः -रा -रं.

FLAGITIOUSLY, *adv.* समहापापं, अतिपापिष्ठवत्, अतिदुर्वृत्तवत्, दारुणं.

FLAGITIOUSNESS, *s.* अतिदुष्टता, महापातकं, महापापं, पापिष्ठता, दौरात्म्यं, दुर्वृत्तता, घोरता, दारुणता.

FLAGON, *s.* पुटग्रीवः, सुराभाजनं, पानभाजनं, पानपात्रं.

FLAGRANCY, *s.* सर्व्वप्रकाशता, सर्व्वप्राकट्यं, वाच्यता, अतिदुष्टता, घोरता.

FLAGRANT, *a.* प्रकाशः -शा -शं, सर्व्वप्रकाशः -शा -शं, सर्व्वप्रसिद्धः -द्धा -द्धं, लोकविदितः -ता -तं, अतिदुष्टः -ष्टा -ष्टं, घोरः -रा -रं, पुरःस्फुरन् -रन्ती -रत् (त्).

FLAGRANTLY, *adv.* प्रकाशं, सुप्रकाशं, सर्व्वप्रसिद्धं, अतिदुष्टं.

FLAGRATION, *s.* दाहः, दहनं, दाहनं, ज्वलनं, ज्वालः, प्लोषः.

FLAIL, *s.* धान्यमर्द्दनयष्टिः *m. f.*, शस्यकण्डनयन्त्रं, कण्डनी, शस्यमर्द्दनी, शिथिलदण्डविशेषो यदाघातेन धान्यादि निस्तुषीक्रियते.

FLAKE, *s.* (Of snow) हिमलवः, हिमकणः, तुषारघनः, नीहारघनः, हिमतूलं, हिमाङ्कुरः, तुषारगडः, तूलोपमो हिमानीलवः.—(Layer) फलकः -कं.—(Scale, loose piece) वल्कं, शल्कं, शकलं.

To FLAKE, *v. n.* शकलीभू, शकलानि बन्ध् (c. 9. बध्नाति, बन्धुं).

FLAKY, *a.* सशल्कः -ल्का -ल्कं, शकली -लिनी -लि (न्), फलकी -किनी -कि (न्).

FLAM, *s.* अनर्थकं, मृषार्थकं, माया, छलं, प्रतारणा, छद्म *n.* (न्).

FLAMBEAU, *s.* उल्का, उल्मुकं, ज्वलनकाष्ठं, अग्निकाष्ठं, अलातं.

FLAME, *s.* शिखा, अग्निशिखा, अर्च्चिः *f.* (स्), अर्च्चिः *f.*, ज्वालः -ला, अग्निज्वाला, ज्वलः -लका, ज्वालाग्निः *m.*, अग्निजिह्वा, शिखिशिखा, कीलः -ला, अग्निकीलः, हेतिः *f.*, उल्का, तेजः *n.* (स्); 'in flames,' ज्वलन् -लन्ती -लत् (त्), ज्योतिस्सात्.

To FLAME, *v. a.* ज्वल् in caus. (ज्वालयति, ज्वलयति -यितुं), प्रज्वल्, सम्प्रज्वल्.

To FLAME, *v. n.* ज्वल् (c. 1. ज्वलति -लितुं), प्रज्वल्, उज्ज्वल्, सम्प्रज्वल्, ज्वल् in freq. (जाज्वल्यते), दीप् (c. 4. दीप्यते -पितुं), प्रदीप्, आदीप्.

FLAME-COLOURED, *a.* अग्निवर्णः -र्णा -र्णं, वह्निवर्णः -र्णा -र्णं, पीतः -ता -तं.

FLAMING, *part.* and *a.* ज्वलन् -लन्ती -लत् (त्), ज्वलयन् -यन्ती -यत् (त्), ज्वलः -ला -लं, ज्वली -लिनी -लि (न्), ज्वाली &c., ज्वालः -ली -लं, ज्वलितः -ता -तं, उज्ज्वलः -ला -लं, जाज्वल्यमानः -ना -नं, प्रज्वलितः -ता -तं, उज्ज्वलः -ला -लं, प्रदीप्तः -प्ता -प्तं, अर्च्चिष्मान् -ष्मती -ष्मत् (त्).

FLAMINGO, *s.* राजहंसः, हंसकः, रक्तपक्षः, अग्निवर्णः पक्षिभेदः.

FLAMY, *a.* शिखी -खिनी -खि (न्), शिखावलः -ला -लं, आग्नेयः -यी -यं.

FLANK, *s.* पार्श्वः -र्श्वं, पार्श्वभागः, पार्श्वाङ्कं, पक्षः, पक्षभागः, उत्सङ्गः, कुक्षिः *m.*, अङ्कः, कोलः, कृत्वं, तः; 'of a horse,' कक्ष्यं; 'on the flank,' पार्श्वतस्.

To FLANK, *v. a.* and *n.* (Attack the flank) पार्श्वं or पार्श्वभागम् आक्रम् (c. 1. -क्रामति -क्रमितुं).—(Guard on the flank) पार्श्वतो रक्ष् (c. 1. रक्षति -क्षितुं).—(Border, be posted on the side) पार्श्वतः or निकटे or पार्श्वभागे स्था (c. 1. तिष्ठति स्थातुं) or वृत् (c. 1. वर्त्तते -र्त्तितुं), स्पृश् (c. 6. स्पृशति, स्प्रष्टुं).

FLANNEL, *s.* कम्बलः, ऊर्णायुः *m.*, और्णपटः, औरभ्रं, ऊर्णानिर्म्मितं or मेषलोममयं विरलवस्त्रं, सहस्ररोम *n.* (न्), साशूकः, कुतपः.

FLAP, *s.* (Any thing that hangs loose) लम्बिका, लोला, लोलकः, लम्बमानवस्तु *n.*, प्रलम्बवस्तु, प्रलम्बितं.—(The motion of it) आस्फालः -लनं -लितं.

To FLAP, *v. a.* (The wings) पक्षौ स्फल् in caus. (स्फालयति -यितुं) or आस्फल् or चल् in caus. (चालयति -यितुं) or उत्क्षिप् (c. 6. -क्षिपति -क्षेप्तुं).

To FLAP, *v. n.* आस्फालितं कृ, आस्फल् (c. 1. -स्फलति -लितुं), झलज्झला (nom. झलज्झलायते).

FLAPPED, *p. p.* आस्फालितः -ता -तं, चालितः -ता -तं, लोलितः -ता -तं.

FLAPPING, *s.* (Of wings) आस्फालनं, पक्षास्फालनं, पक्षस्फालनं, पक्षोत्क्षेपः, झलज्झला.—(Of ears) कर्णतालः.

To FLARE, *v. n.* चञ्चलशिखया or सचञ्चलशिखं or चञ्चलरूपेण ज्वल् (c. 1. ज्वलति -लितुं) or उज्ज्वल् or ज्वल् in freq. (जाज्वल्यते).

FLARE, *s.* चञ्चलशिखा, चञ्चलज्वालः, कम्पितज्वाला, स्फुरद्द्युतिः *f.*

FLARING, *a.* चञ्चलशिखया जाज्वल्यमानः -ना -नं or उज्ज्वलः -ला -लं.

FLASH, *s.* ज्वाला, स्फुरितं, स्फुरणं, द्युतिस्फुरणं, प्रभाकम्पः, अकस्मात्स्फुरणं, अकस्माद्दीप्तिः *f.*, क्षणप्रभा, क्षणद्युतिः *f.*, अचिरप्रभा, अचिरद्युतिः *f.*—(Of lightning) विद्युत्स्फुरणं, सौदामिनीस्फुरणं, विद्युत्प्रकाशः, विद्युत्कम्पः, विद्युद्दाम *n.* (न्), मेघज्योतिः *n.* (स्), विद्युज्ज्वाला, इरम्मदः.

To FLASH, *v. n.* स्फुर् (c. 6. स्फुरति -रितुं), विद्युत् (c. 1. -द्योतते -तितुं), अकस्मात् प्रकाश् (c. 1. -काशते -शितुं) or ज्वल् (c. 1. ज्वलति -लितुं) or उज्ज्वल् or प्रज्वल्, विद्युद्वत् कम्प् (c. 1. कम्पते -म्पितुं).

FLASHING, *a.* or *part.* स्फुरन् -रन्ती -रत् (त्), स्फुरितः -ता -तं, विद्योत-

मानः -ना -नं, द्योतमानः -ना -नं, कम्पमानः -ना -नं, कम्पितप्रभः -भा -भं, क्षणप्रकाशन् -शन्ती -शत् (त्).

FLASHY, *a.* क्षणमात्रद्योती -तिनी -ति (न्), मिथ्याद्योती &c., मिथ्यातैजसः -सी -सं, मिथ्यातेजोमयः -यी -यं.—(Unsubstantial) असारः -रा -रं, निस्सत्त्वः -त्त्वा -त्त्वं.

FLASK, *s.* कूपी, पुटग्रीवः, काचपात्रं, काचभाजनं; 'of wine,' मद्यभाजनं.

FLASKET, *s.* अन्नभाजनं, अन्नपात्रं, खाद्यद्रव्यभाजनं.

FLAT, *a.* (Even) समः -मा -मं, समानः -ना -नं, समस्थः -स्था -स्थं, सपाटः -टा -टं, समरेखः -खा -खं, निर्भुग्नः -ग्ना -ग्नं, अभुग्नः -ग्ना -ग्नं.—(Not elevated) अनुच्चः -च्चा -च्चं, अनुन्नतः -ता -तं, निम्नः -म्ना -म्नं, नतः -ता -तं.—(Prostrate, lying flat) दण्डवत्पतितः -ता -तं, भूमौ क्षिप्तदेहः -हा -हं, अवनिकृतः -ता -तं.—(Vapid, tasteless) विरसः -सा -सं, नीरसः -सा -सं, अरसिकः -का -कं, फल्गुः -ल्गुः -ल्गु, असारः -रा -रं, निस्सारः -रा -रं, अलवणः -णा -णं, सारहीनः -ना -नं, लवणहीनः -ना -नं, निस्तेजाः -जाः -जः (स्), तेजोहीनः -ना -नं, क्लीवः -वा -वं, निःस्वादुः -दुः -दु, विस्वादः -दा -दं.—(Plain) अवक्रः -क्रा -क्रं; 'flat roof,' पृष्ठं; 'flat surface,' समपृष्ठं, समतलं.

FLAT, *s.* (A plain) समभूमिः *f.*, समस्थलं -ली, समभूभागः, समस्थानं, आजिः *f.*, पाटः, समं.—(Low ground) निम्नभूमिः *f.*—(Shoal) सैकतं.—(Of a sword, &c.) फलकः -कं, पत्रं.—(In music) अनुदात्तः, मन्दः, मन्द्रः, उदात्तेतरः शब्दः.—(Flat-bottomed boat) तरालुः *m.*, तरान्धुः *m.*—(Stupid fellow) मन्दबुद्धिः *m.*, स्थूलधीः *m.*

To FLAT, *v. a.* समीकृ, समानीकृ, समस्थलीकृ, निम्नीकृ.

FLAT-BOTTOMED, *a.* समतलः -ला -लं, समाधोभागः -गा -गं, समाधःस्थानः -ना -नं.

FLAT-NOSED, *a.* नतनासिकः -का -कं, अवनाटः -टा -टं, अवटीटः -टा -टं, अवभ्रटः -टा -टं, खुरणसः -सा -सं or -णाः -णाः -णः (स्).

FLATLY, *adv.* समं, समानतस्.—(Plainly) अवक्रं, सुव्यक्तं.

FLATNESS, *s.* (Evenness) समता, साम्यं, समानता -त्वं, साम्यता, पाटः, निर्भुग्नता, अभुग्नता.—(Want of elevation) अनुच्चता, अनुन्नतिः *f.*, निम्नता, नतत्वं.—(Insipidity, dulness) अरसिकत्वं, नारस्यं, फल्गुता, असारता, निःस्वादुता, अलावण्यं, नालवण्यं, अतेजः *n.* (स्), तेजोहीनता.

To FLATTEN, *v. a.* समीकृ, समानीकृ, समस्थलीकृ, निम्नीकृ, वामनीकृ.—(Depress) अवनम् in caus. (-नामयति -नमयति -यितुं), नतीकृ.—(Lay flat) दण्डवत् पत् in caus. (पातयति -यितुं).—(Make vapid) रसं हृ (c. 1. हरति, हर्तुं), फल्गूकृ, विरसीकृ.

To FLATTEN, *v. n.* समीभू, निम्नीभू, अवनतीभू, नतीभू, विरसीभू.

FLATTENED, *p. p.* अवनामितः -ता -तं, निम्नीकृतः -ता -तं, नतीकृतः -ता -तं.

FLATTENING, *s.* अवनामः, निम्नीकरणं, नतीकरणं, समीकरणं.

FLATTER, *s.* अवनामकः, समकरणयन्त्रं, मुद्गरविशेषः.

To FLATTER, *v. a.* (Soothe by praise, &c.) सान्त्व् or शान्त्व् (c. 10. सान्त्वयति -यितुं), परिशान्त्व्, अभिशान्त्व्, अतिप्रशंसया or स्तुतिवाक्यैः or चाटूक्त्या or मधुरैर्वचोभिः सान्त्व् or प्रलुभ् (c. 10. -लोभयति -यितुं) or सन्तुष् (c. 10. -तोषयति -यितुं) or लल् (c. 10. लालयति -यितुं).—(Speak what is agreeable) प्रियं or प्रियाणि or चाटुवाक्यानि वद् (c. 1. वदति -दितुं).—(Praise falsely) मिथ्या प्रशंस् (c. 1. -शंसति -सितुं) or श्लाघ् (c. 1. श्लाघते -घितुं).—(Gratify) आराध् (c. 10. -राधयति -यितुं), प्रमुद् (c. 10. -मोदयति -यितुं), सभाज् (c. 10. सभाजयति -यितुं).—(Raise false hopes) मिथ्या आशावृद्धिं कृ.

FLATTERED, *p. p.* प्रशंसितः -ता -तं, मिथ्याप्रशस्तः -स्ता -स्तं, लालितः -ता -तं, कृतसान्त्वनः -ना -नं, चाटूक्त्याराधितः -ता -तं, सभाजितः -ता -तं, आश्वासितः -ता -तं.

FLATTERER, *s.* प्रशंसकः, प्रियवादी *m.* (न्), प्रियंवदः, चाटुवादी *m.* सान्त्ववादः, सान्त्वनकारी *m.* (न्), चाटुकारः, लाली *m.* (न्), मिथ्याप्रशंसकः, शंस्ता *m.* (स्तृ), कपटप्रशंसाकृत् *m.*, मिथ्याश्वासकः, आश्वासनशीलः, कापटिकः.

FLATTERING, *a.* परितोषकः -का -कं, सन्तोषणः -णा -णं, सान्त्वनः -ना -नं, स्तुतिमयः -यी -यं, प्रशंसाकरः -री -रं, प्रीतिकरः -रा -रं, आश्वासकः -का -कं.

FLATTERINGLY, *adv.* अतिप्रशंसया, चाटूक्त्या, अतिशयस्तुत्या, सान्त्वनपूर्वं.

FLATTERY, *s.* अतिप्रशंसा -सनं, मिथ्याप्रशंसा -सनं, सान्त्वः -न्त्वं -न्त्वनं -ना, सान्त्ववाक्यं, सान्त्वोक्तिः *f.*, सान्त्वकारः, चाटूक्तिः *f.*, चाटुकारः, चाटुः *m.*, -टु *n.*, लालनं, प्रियवाक्यं, मधुरवाक्यं, मधुरवचः *n.* (स्), कोमलवाक्यं, कोमलत्वं, आश्वासनं, चालोकः, चालोकशब्दः, अनुनयः, आराधनं.

FLATTISH, *a.* ईषत्समः -मा -मं, ईषत्समानः -ना -नं, ईषन्निम्नः -म्ना -म्नं.

FLATULENCE, FLATULENCY, *s.* वायुपूर्णता, वायुरोगः, वातफुल्लता, वातफुल्लान्त्रं, वातिकत्वं, कोष्ठाश्रितवायुः *m.*, वायुः *m.*, वातः, वायुगण्डः, अन्त्राध्मानं, उदराध्मानं, आध्मातः, पुप्फुलः -लं.

FLATULENT, *a.* वायुग्रस्तः -स्ता -स्तं, वायुरोगग्रस्तः -स्ता -स्तं, वातफुल्लः -ल्ला -ल्लं, वातफुल्लान्त्रः -न्त्रा -न्त्रं, वातिकः -की -कं, वातबद्धः -द्धा -द्धं, वायुबद्धः -द्धा -द्धं.

FLATUS, *s.* वायुः *m.*, वातः, अन्त्रस्थवायुः, उदरजवातः, उदरजो वातः.

To FLAUNT, *v. n.* सगर्वं or सदम्भं चल् (c. 1. चलति -लितुं), गर्व्वितगत्या चल् or चर् (c. 1. चरति -रितुं).

FLAUNTING, *a.* गर्व्वेण चारी -रिणी -रि (न्), गर्व्वितगतिः -तिः -ति, खेलगामी -मिनी -मि (न्), दर्शनीयमानी -निनी -नि (न्).

FLAVOR, *s.* रसः, आस्वादः, स्वादः, रुचिः *f.*, अभिरुचिः *f.*, लालित्यं, लावण्यं.

To FLAVOR, *v. a.* रसं दा (c. 3. ददाति, दातुं), सरसं -सां -सं कृ, सुरसीकृ.

FLAVORED, *p. p.* or *a.* रसितः -ता -तं, सरसः -सा -सं, रसिकः -का -कं; 'well-flavored,' सुरसः -सा -सं, सुस्वास्वादः -दा -दं, सुललितः -ता -तं, सुस्वादुः -द्वी -दु.

FLAVORLESS, *a.* अरसः -सा -सं -सिकः -की -कं, विरसः -सा -सं, निरसः -सा -सं, नीरसः -सा -सं, निःस्वादुः -दुः -दु, विस्वादः -दा -दं, अस्वादुः -दुः -दु.

FLAVOROUS, *a.* सुरसः -सा -सं, रसिकः -का -कं, रसवान् -वती -वत् (त्), स्वादुः -द्वी -दु, सुस्वास्वादः -दा -दं, मिष्टः -ष्टा -ष्टं.

FLAW, *s.* (Crack) छिद्रं, रन्ध्रं, भित्तिः *f.*, खण्डः, भेदः, छेदः, भङ्गः, सन्धिः *m.*—(Defect) दोषः, अपराधः, छिद्रं, कलङ्कः.—(In a gem) पुलकः, खण्डः, रक्तबिन्दुः *m.*; 'without a flaw,' निश्छिद्रः -द्रा -द्रं, नीरन्ध्रः -न्ध्रा -न्ध्रं.—(Sudden gust of wind) प्रभञ्जनः, निर्घातः, व्योममुद्गरः.

To FLAW, *v. a.* छिद्र् (c. 10. छिद्रयति -यितुं), खण्ड् (c. 10. खण्डयति -यितुं).

FLAWLESS, *a.* निश्छिद्रः -द्रा -द्रं, नीरन्ध्रः -न्ध्रा -न्ध्रं, निर्दोषः -षा -षं.

FLAWY, *a.* सच्छिद्रः -द्रा -द्रं, सरन्ध्रः -न्ध्रा -न्ध्रं, सदोषः -षा -षं, दर्दरः -रा -रं.

FLAX, *s.* अतसी, उमा, क्षुमा, क्षौमी, शणं, मसीना, मसृणा, सुवर्चला, मालिका.

FLAX-COMB, *s.* अतसीमार्जकः, उमामार्जनी, उमाशोधनी, शणप्रसाधनी.

FLAX-DRESSER, *s.* अतसीशोधकः, उमापरिष्कारकः, शणप्रसाधकः.

FLAXEN, *a.* क्षौमः -मी -मं, क्षौमकः -की -कं, क्षौमः -मी -मं, शाणः -णी -णं.

To FLAY, *v. a.* त्वच (nom. त्वचयति -यितुं), निस्त्वचीकृ, चर्म्म निष्कृष् (c. 1. -कर्षति -क्रष्टुं) or उत्कृष् or निर्हृ (c. 1. -हरति -हर्तुं), निश्चर्म्म (nom. निश्चर्म्मयति -यितुं), त्वक्ष् (c. 1. त्वक्षति -क्षितुं).

FLAYED, *p. p.* निस्त्वचीकृतः -ता -तं, निस्त्वकः -चा -चं, निश्चर्म्मा -र्म्मा -र्म्म (न्).

FLAYER, *s.* चर्म्मनिष्कर्षकः, चर्म्मोत्पाटी *m.* (न्), त्वग्विदारकः.

FLAYING, *s.* निस्त्वचीकरणं, चर्म्मनिष्कर्षणं, निश्चर्म्मीकरणं, त्वकपरिपुटनं.

FLEA, *s.* देहिका, मत्कुणः, मक्षिका, तल्पकीटः, रक्तपायी *m.* (न्).

To FLEA, *v. a.* देहिका or तल्पकीटान् अपनी (c. 1. -नयति -नेतुं) or दूरीकृ.

FLEA-BITE, *s.* देहिकादंशः, मत्कुणदंशनं, देहिकादशनाङ्कः, मक्षिकादंशः.

Flea-bitten, *a.* देहिकादष्टः -ष्टा -ष्टं, देहिकादंशितः -ता -तं, मक्षिकादष्टः -ष्टा -ष्टं

Fleam, *s.* पशुचिकित्सकादिभिः सिराव्यधे or रक्तमोक्षणे प्रयुक्तं तीक्ष्णाग्रयन्त्रं.

Fled, *p. p.* पलायितः -ता -तं, विपलायितः -ता -तं, विद्रुतः -ता -तं.

To fledge, *v. a.* सपक्षं -क्षां -क्षं कृ, पक्षैर् युज् (c. 10. योजयति -यितुं).

Fledged, *p. p.* पक्षयुक्तः -क्ता -क्तं, पक्षवान् -वती -वत् (त्), गरुत्मान् -त्मती -त्मत् (त्मत्).

To flee, *v. n.* पलाय् (c. 1. पलायते -यितुं, rt. इ), विपलाय्, प्रपलाय्, सम्पलाय्, द्रु (c. 1. द्रवति, द्रोतुं), विद्रु, विप्रद्रु, प्रद्रु, प्राद्रु; प्रधाव् (c. 1. -धावति -वितुं), अपधाव्, निष्पत् (c. 1. -पतति -तितुं), उत्पत्, अपक्रम् (c. 1. -क्रामति -क्रमितुं), निर्गम् (c. 1. -गच्छति -गन्तुं), अपगम्, अपसृप् (c. 1. -सर्पति -सर्प्तुं), व्यपसृप्, भज् (c. 1. भजति -ते, भक्तुं) with दिशः or ककुभः.—(Avoid) वृज् (c. 10. वर्जयति -यितुं), विवृज् परिवृज्, परिहृ (c. 1. -हरति -हर्त्तुं), त्यज् (c. 1. त्यजति, त्यक्तुं).

Fleece, *s.* मेषलोम *n.* (न्), अविलोम *n.* (न्), मेषरोम *n.* (न्), मेषाङ्गरुहं, यन् मेषलोमपरिमाणम् एकवारे अवछिद्यते, मेषस्य छिन्नलोम *n.* (न्).

To fleece, *v. a.* मेषलोम छिद् (c. 7. छिनत्ति, छेत्तुं) or लू (c. 9. लुनाति, लवितुं).—(Strip, plunder) हृ (c. 1. हरति, हर्त्तुं), अपहृ, प्रबाध् (c. 1. -बाधते -धितुं).

Fleeced, *p. p.* हृतसर्व्वस्वः -स्वा -स्वं, अपहृतस्वः -स्वा -स्वं, बाधितः -ता -तं.

Fleecy, *a.* लोमशः -शा -शं, रोमशः -शा -शं, बहुलोमा -मा -म (न्), बहुरोमा &c., लोमावृतः -ता -तं, बहुलोमवान् -वती -वत् (त्), मेषलोममयः -यी -यं.

To fleer, *v. a.* अवहस् (c. 1. -हसति -सितुं), अपहस्, कु स्मि (c. 1. स्मयते, स्मेतुं), उत्स्मि, विकृतदृष्ट्या स्मि, तिरस्कृ, मुखरीकृ, अवक्षिप् (c. 6. -क्षिपति -क्षेप्तुं).

Fleer, *s.* अवहासः, अवहेला, अवक्षेपः, कुस्मयः, कुस्मितं, दृष्टिविक्षेपः.

Fleerer, *s.* उपहासकः, अवक्षेपकः, मुखरजनः, कुस्मितः.

Fleet, *s.* बृहन्नौकासमूहः, महानौकासमूहः, बृहन्नौसङ्घः, युद्धनौसमूहः.

Fleet, *a.* शीघ्रगामी -मिनी -मि (न्), द्रुतगामी &c., द्रुतगतिः -तिः -ति, लघुगतिः -तिः -ति, महावेगः -गा -गं, महाजवः -वा -वं, वेगवान् -वती -वत् (त्), जवी -विनी -वि (न्), शीघ्रजवः -वा -वं, प्रतूर्णः -र्णा -र्णं, त्वरितः -ता -तं, त्वरितगतिः -तिः -ति, ससौष्ठवः -वा -वं.—(As the wind) वायुवेगः -गा -गं, वायुवेगसमः -मा -मं, वायुगतिः -तिः -ति, वायव्यः -व्या -व्यं.

To fleet, *v. n.* (Go swiftly) द्रुतगत्या or महावेगेन चल् (c. 1. चलति -लितुं), त्वर् (c. 1. त्वरते -रितुं), शीघ्र (nom. शीघ्रायते), द्रुतं गम् (c. 1. गच्छति, गन्तुं).

To fleet, *v. a.* (Skim over) लघुगत्या अतिक्रम् (c. 1. -क्रामति -क्रमितुं) or विसृप् (c. 1. -सर्पति -सर्प्तुं).—(Skim milk) दुग्धफेनम् अपनी (c. 1. -नयति -नेतुं).

Fleeting, *a.* क्षणमात्रस्थायी -यिनी -यि (न्), अचिरस्थायी &c., अध्रुवः -वा -वं, क्षणभूतः -ता -तं, क्षणभङ्गुरः -रा -रं, क्षणिकः -का -की -कं.

Fleetly, *adv.* शीघ्रं, द्रुतं, त्वरितं, महावेगेन, महाजवेन, द्रुतगत्या, लघुगत्या, लघु, क्षिप्रं, सरभसं, ससौष्ठवं.

Fleetness, *s.* शीघ्रता, द्रुतत्वं, शीघ्रगामित्वं, त्वरितगतिः *f.*, वेगः, प्रजवः, जवः, सत्वरता, तूर्णिः *f.*, आशुगमनं, रभसः.

Flesh, *s.* मांसं, आमिषं, पललं, क्रव्यं, पिशितं usually in plural, तरसं, पलं, असृजं, शुक्तं, मेदस्कृत् *n.*, काश्यपं, उत्तसं; 'dried flesh,' शुष्कलः -ला -ली -लं, शुष्कमांसं, उत्तप्तं, वल्लूरं; 'game,' जाङ्गलं, जाङ्गलं.—(Body) शरीरं.—(Carnality) शरीरोपसेवा, विषयासक्तिः *f.*, आमिषं.

To flesh, *v. a.* अभ्यस् (c. 4. -अस्यति -असितुं), निर्दयीकृ, क्रूरकर्म्माभ्यस्तं -स्तां -स्तं कृ.

Flesh-broth, *s.* मांसशूषं, मांसयूषं, मांसनिष्क्वाथः, मांसक्वाथः, सूपः.

Flesh-brush, *s.* त्वगाघर्षणी, चर्म्मनिर्घर्षणकः, चर्म्ममार्जनी.

Flesh-color, *s.* मांसवर्णः, आमिषवर्णः, क्रव्यवर्णः, मांसरागः.

Flesh-colored, *a.* मांसवर्णः -र्णा -र्णं, आमिषवर्णः -र्णा -र्णं, क्रव्यसवर्णः -र्णा -र्णं.

Flesh-diet, *s.* मांसाहारः, मांसभोजनं, आमिषाहारः.

Fleshiness, *s.* मांसत्वं, मांसलत्वं, पुष्टता, पुष्टाङ्गत्वं, पीनता, पीवरता, मेदस्विता, मेदोवृद्धिः *f.*, शरीरस्थूलता.

Fleshless, *a.* अमांसः -सा -सं, निर्मांसः -सा -सं, विमांसः -सा -सं, विपुष्टः -ष्टा -ष्टं, अपुष्टः -ष्टा -ष्टं, मांसहीनः -ना -नं.

Fleshliness, *s.* शरीरोपसेवा, विषयोपसेवा, विषयासक्तिः *f.*, शारीरिकविषयसङ्गः, कामासक्तिः *f.*

Fleshly, *a.* (Carnal) शारीरिकः -की -कं, शरीरजः -जा -जं, दैहिकः -की -कं, कायिकः -की -कं, वापुषिकः -की -कं, विषयी -यिणी -यि (न्), ऐहिकः -की -कं, सांसारिकः -की -कं.

Flesh-meat, *s.* मांसाहारः, मांसभोजनं, खाद्यमांसं, भोजनार्थम् आमिषं.

Fleshmonger, *s.* मांसविक्रयी *m.* (न्), सौनिकः.—(Pimp) विटः.

Fleshy, *a.* मांसलः -ला -लं, मांसशीलः -ला -लं, पुष्टः -ष्टा -ष्टं, पुष्टाङ्गः -ङ्गी -ङ्गं, क्रव्यमयः -यी -यं, पीनः -ना -नं, पीवरः -रा -रं, मेदस्वी -स्विनी -स्वि (न्).

Flexibility, *s.* आनम्यता, नम्यता, नमनीयत्वं, कुञ्चनीयता, अवकुञ्चनीयत्वं. आयम्यत्वं, मृदुता, कोमलता, शैथिल्यं.

Flexible, *a.* आनम्यः -म्या -म्यं, नम्यः -म्या -म्यं, नमनीयः -या -यं, कुञ्चनीयः -या -यं, अवकुञ्चनीयः -या -यं, आयम्यः -म्या -म्यं, नमनशीलः -ला -लं, कुञ्चनशीलः -ला -लं, मृदुः -दुः -द्वी -दु, कोमलः -ला -लं, शिथिलः -ला -लं, अदृढः -ढा -ढं.

Flexion, *s.* नतिः *f.*, नमनं, आनतिः *f.*, आनमनं, कुञ्चनं, अवकुञ्चनं, भङ्गः -ङ्गी.

Flexuous, *a.* वक्रः -क्रा -क्रं, वक्रिमः -मा -मं, भङ्गुरः -रा -रं, कुटिलः -ला -लं, जिह्मः -ह्मा -ह्मं, विसर्पी -र्पिणी -र्पि (न्).

Flexure, *s.* नतिः *f.*, आनतिः *f.*, वक्रता, वक्रिमा *m.* (न्), कुञ्चनं, अवकुञ्चनं, जिह्मता, भङ्गः -ङ्गी, पुटः.

To flicker, *v.n.* (With the wings) विहायसा or व्योममध्ये पक्षास्फालनं कृ.—(As a flame, &c.) इतस्ततश् चल् (c. 1. चलति -लितुं), चञ्चलीभू, चपलीभू, चञ्चलरूपेण ज्वल् (c. 1. ज्वलति -लितुं).

Flickering, *a.* (With the wings) व्योममध्ये पक्षास्फालनकारी -रिणी -रि (न्).—(Unsteady) चञ्चलः -ला -लं, विचलः -ला -लं, चलः -ला -लं, चपलः -ला -लं.

Flier, *s.* पलायी *m.* (न्), विपलायी *m.*, प्रपलायी *m.*, पलायनकृत् *m.*

Flight, *s.* (Act of fleeing, running away) पलायनं, विपलायनं, प्रपलायनं, द्रावः, द्रवः, विद्रवः, प्रद्रावः, उद्द्रावः, सन्द्रावः, सन्दावः, अपक्रमः, अपयानं, अपायः, अपगमः, डमरं, शृगाली -लिका; 'to put to flight,' विद्रु in caus. (-द्रावयति -यितुं), द्रु; 'put to flight,' भयद्रुतः -ता -तं, विद्रुतः -ता -तं, कान्दिशीकः -का -कं, प्रपलायितः -ता -तं, पलायितः -ता -तं.—(Flying of a bird) डीनं, डयनं, प्रडीनं, निडीनं; 'upward flight of a bird,' उड्डीनं, उड्डयनं, प्रडीनं; 'downward flight,' अवडीनं; 'indirect flight,' विडीनं; 'direct flight,' अविडीनं.—(Number of birds flying) पक्षिमाला, पक्षिश्रेणी, डीयमानपक्षिगणः; 'of geese,' हंसमाला; 'of pigeons,' कापोतं; 'of parrots,' शौकं.—(Flight of an arrow) शरवेगः, शरपातः.—(Elevation or excursion of thought) बुद्धिसमुन्नतिः *f.*, बुद्धिविलासः.—(Flight of stairs) सोपानपद्धतिः *f.*, सोपानश्रेणिः *f.*, निःश्रेणी -णिः *f.*

FLIGHTINESS, *s.* बुद्धिभ्रान्तिः *f.*, बुद्धिविभ्रमः, बुद्धिविलासः, मतिचापल्यं, उच्छृङ्खलता.

FLIGHTY, *a.* भ्रान्तबुद्धिः -द्धिः -द्धि, विभ्रान्तमनाः -नाः -नः (स्), चपलमतिः -तिः -ति, उच्छृङ्खलबुद्धिः -द्धिः -द्धि, अस्थिरबुद्धिः -द्धिः -द्धि, पारिप्लवः -वा -वं.

FLIMSINESS, *s.* असारता, निःसारता, निर्बलता, तेजोहीनता, तुच्छत्वं, शैथिल्यं.

FLIMSY, *a.* असारः -रा -रं, निःसारः -रा -रं, सारहीनः -ना -नं, निस्तेजाः -जाः -जः (स्), अवास्तवः -वी -वं -विकः -की -कं, निर्बलः -ला -लं, तुच्छः -च्छा -च्छं, तनुः -नुः -न्वी -नु, शिथिलः -ला -लं.

To FLINCH, *v. n.* निवृत् (c. 1. -वर्त्तते -र्त्तितुं), परिवृत्, परावृत् with abl. c., उद्विज् (c. 6. -विजते -जितुं) with abl. c., विकम्प् (c. 1. -कम्पते -म्पितुं), अवस्था (c. 1. -तिष्ठते -स्थातुं), पलाय् (c. 1. पलायते -यितुं, rt. इ), पराङ्मुखीभू, विमुखीभू, त्यज् (c. 1. त्यजति, त्यक्तुं).

FLINCHER, *s.* परिवर्त्तकः, परिवर्त्ती *m.* (न्), कर्म्मनिवृत्तः, कर्म्मत्यागी *m.* (न्), पराङ्मुखः, विकम्पितः -म्पकः.

FLINCHING, *s.* विकम्पः -म्पनं, विकम्पितं, निवृत्तिः *f.*, निवर्त्तनं, पराङ्मुखता.

To FLING, *v. a.* क्षिप् (c. 6. क्षिपति, क्षेप्तुं), प्रक्षिप्, अस् (c. 4. अस्यति -सितुं), प्रास्, अभ्यस्, मुच् (c. 6. मुञ्चति, मोक्तुं), प्रमुच्, सृज् (c. 6. सृजति, स्रष्टुं), ईर् (c. 10. ईरयति -यितुं), पत् in caus. (पातयति -यितुं).—(Fling away) अपास्, अवमुच्, प्रमुच्, अवसृज्, विसृज्, व्यपसृज्, प्रतिक्षिप्, अपहा (c. 3. -जहाति -हातुं).

To FLING, *v. n.* क्रोधसंरम्भात् पादादिक्षेपं कृ or खुरक्षेपं कृ, अवक्षिप् (c. 6. -क्षिपति -क्षेप्तुं).

FLING, *s.* क्षेपः -पणं, प्रक्षेपः, निःक्षेपः, असनं, पातः -तनं.—(Gibe) क्षेपः, अवक्षेपः.

FLINT, *s.* अग्निप्रस्तरः, अरणिः *m.*, वह्निप्रस्तरः, आग्नेयप्रस्तरः.

FLINTY, *a.* अग्निप्रस्तरमयः -यी -यं.—(Cruel, hard-hearted) पाषाणहृदयः -या -यं, अयोहृदयः -या -यं, कठिनहृदयः -या -यं.

FLIP, *s.* (A beverage) मद्ययवसुरादिनिर्म्मितं पानीयं.—(Stroke) आघातः, आस्फालनं.

FLIPPANCY, *s.* (Of speech) वाक्चापल्यं, वावदूकता.—(Pertness) चापल्यं, चपलत्वं, चाचल्यं, अस्थिरता, लोलता, लौल्यं, अनवस्थितिः *f.*, प्रगल्भता.

FLIPPANT, *a.* (In speech) वाक्चपलः -ला -लं, वाक्चञ्चलः -ला -लं, वाचालः -ला -लं.—(Pertness) चपलः -ला -लं, चञ्चलः -ला -लं, अस्थिरः -रा -रं, लोलः -ला -लं, अनवस्थितः -ता -तं, प्रगल्भः -ल्भा -ल्भं.

FLIPPANTLY, *adv.* चपलं, चापल्यात्, लौल्यात्, चञ्चलं, अस्थैर्य्यात्.

To FLIRT, *v. a.* (Toss suddenly) अकस्मात् or सहसा क्षिप् (c. 6. क्षिपति, क्षेप्तुं).

To FLIRT, *v. n.* (Jeer) क्षिप् (c. 6. क्षिपति, क्षेप्तुं), अवक्षिप्.—(Act with giddiness) चपलः -ला -लं भू, चञ्चलः -ला -लं भू.—(Coquet) विलस् (c. 1. -लसति -सितुं), लल् (c. 1. ललति -लितुं), खेला (nom. खेलायति -यितुं), विलासं कृ, हावं कृ, प्रेमललितं कृ, प्रेमखेलां कृ.

FLIRT, *s.* (Quick throw) अकस्मात्क्षेपः, आकस्मिकक्षेपः.—(Coquette) रसिका स्त्री, प्रगल्भा स्त्री, धृष्टा स्त्री, चपला स्त्री, विलासिनी, लालिनी, लीलावती, प्रेमखेलाकारिणी.

FLIRTATION, *s.* (Playing at courtship) प्रेमखेला, प्रेमललितं, लीला, खेला, विलासः, हावः, लालसा, रमस्यं.

To FLIT, *v. n.* (Fly away, move rapidly) प्रडी (c. 4. -डीयते, c. 1. -डयते -यितुं), द्रुतगत्या or लघुगत्या or लघु चल् (c. 1. चलति -लितुं) or सृप् (c. 1. सर्पति, सर्प्तुं).—(Rove on the wing, flutter) विपति or आकाशे विसृप्, व्योममध्ये पक्षास्फालनं कृ.—(Be unstable) अस्थिरः -रा -रं भू, चञ्चलीभू, चपलीभू.—(Migrate, move about) उत्क्रम् (c. 1. -क्रामति -क्रमितुं), देशान्तरं गम् (c. 1. गच्छति, गन्तुं), स्थानात् स्थानं गम्, इतस्ततो भ्रम् (c. 4. भ्राम्यति, भ्रमितुं).

FLITCH, *s.* लवणीकृतं शूकरपार्श्वमांसं, शूकरस्य शुष्कमांसं, वल्लूरं.

FLITTER, *s.* वस्त्रखण्डः -ण्डं, चीरं, कर्पटः, लक्तकं, कन्था.

FLITTER-MOUSE, *s.* जतुका -तूका, अजिनपत्रा, चर्म्मचटका, चर्म्मचटी.

FLITTING, *s.* लघुचलनं, विसर्पणं, सर्पणं, अस्थैर्य्यं, भ्रमणं.

To FLOAT, *v. n.* (Be borne on the surface, not to sink) प्लु (c. 1. प्लवते, प्लोतुं), भास् (c. 1. भासते -सितुं), उन्मज्ज् (c. 6. -मज्जति -मंक्तुं), उत्पत् (c. 1. -पतति -तितुं).—(Swim) तॄ (c. 1. तरति -रितुं -रीतुं), जले विसृ (c. 1. -सरति -सर्त्तुं).

To FLOAT, *v. a.* प्लु in caus. (प्लावयति -यितुं), वह् in caus. (वाहयति -यितुं).

FLOAT, *s.* (Raft) प्लवः, प्लवाका, तरण्डः -ण्डी, तरण्डः, तरत् *n.*, तर्षिः *m.*, तारणः, वहित्रं, कोलः, उडुपः -पं, वारितरः.—(Of a fishing-line) तरण्डः.

FLOATING, *part.* or *a.* प्लवमानः -ना -नं, भासमानः -ना -नं.

FLOCCULENT, *a.* घनीभूतः -ता -तं, श्यानः -ना -नं.—(Seeds) ग्रीष्महासं, वंशकर्पं.

FLOCK, *s.* (Collection of animals) यूथं, गणः, समूहः, सङ्घः, सङ्घातः, व्रजः, कुलं, वृन्दं, संहतिः *f.*, ओघः, कदम्बकं, निवहः, समुदायः, समुदयः, समाहारः, पाशवं, निकरः, समवायः, सञ्चयः, चयः, निकुरुम्बं -म्बकं, वारः, विसरः, व्रातः, सन्दोहः, समजः, सार्थः, निकायः.—(Flock of sheep) मेषयूथं, अविगणः, अविकुलं, अविकटः, आविकं, औरभ्रकं; 'of goats,' आजकं; 'of goats and sheep,' अजाविकं; 'of cattle,' पशुगणः, गोकुलं, गोवृन्दं; 'of pigeons,' कापोतं; 'of parrots,' शौकं; 'of peacocks,' मायूरं; 'of geese,' हंसमाला, हंसश्रेणी; 'of partridges,' तैत्तिरं; 'in flocks,' यूथशस्.—(Flock of cotton) तूलं -लिका, इन्द्रतूलं; 'flock-mattress,' तूलिका.

To FLOCK TOGETHER, *v. n.* एकत्र मिल् (c. 6. मिलति, मेलितुं), यूथशः or पशुयूथवत् सङ्गम् (c. 1. -गच्छति -गन्तुं) or समागम् or समे (c. 2. समैति -तुं, rt. इ) or अनुसृ (c. 1. -सरति -सर्त्तुं), एकीभू, एकत्रभू, एकौघीभू, समूहीभू, सङ्कुलीभू.

To FLOG, *v. a.* चर्म्मदण्डेन or कशया or वेत्रेण तड् (c. 10. ताडयति -यितुं) or आहन् (c. 2. -हन्ति -न्तुं) or प्रहृ (c. 1. -हरति -हर्त्तुं) or दण्ड् (c. 10. दण्डयति -यितुं).

FLOGGED, *p. p.* कशाताडितः -ता -तं, कशादण्डितः -ता -तं, वेत्राहतः -ता -तं.

FLOGGING, *s.* कशाताडनं, कशाघातः, कशा, रज्जुताडनं, वेत्राघातः, चर्म्मदण्डप्रहारः; 'deserving it,' कश्यः -श्या -श्यं, कशार्हः -र्हा -र्हं.

FLOOD, *s.* (Deluge, inundation) जलाप्लावनं, जलप्लावनं, आप्लावः, जलप्रलयः, जलवेगः, तोयविप्लवः, सलिलोपप्लवः, जलोच्छ्वासः, जलौघः, आप्लावजलं, परीवाहः, विदारः, वन्या.—(Universal flood) भूतसम्प्लवः, एकार्णवं.—(Stream) स्रोतः *n.* (स्), प्रवाहः.—(Tide) वेला, रयः.—(Overflow of a river) वानं.—(Flood of tears) अश्रुप्रवाहः, अश्रुपातः, अश्रुवर्षः, वाष्पवर्षः, धाराश्रु *n.*, अश्रुकलाम्बुः *m.*

To FLOOD, *v. a.* प्लु in caus. (प्लावयति -यितुं), आप्लु, सम्प्लु; 'is flooded,' प्लाव्यते.

FLOODED, *p. p.* प्लावितः -ता -तं, आप्लावितः -ता -तं, परिप्लुतः -ता -तं, अभिप्लुतः -ता -तं, सम्प्लुतोदकः -का -कं, अभिपरिप्लुतः -ता -तं.

FLOOD-GATE, *s.* जलद्वारं, जलपथः, जलवर्त्म *n.* (न्), जलनिर्गमः, जलनिःसरणं.

FLOOK, *s.* लङ्गरदन्तः, लङ्गरभुजः, लङ्गराकर्षणी, नौबन्धनयन्त्रकीलः.

FLOOR, *s.* (Bottom of a building, part on which one walks) तलं, गृहतलं, हर्म्यतलं, गृहभूमिः *f.*, गृहभूः *f.*, वेश्मभूः *f.*, कुट्टिमं, तलिमं, भूतलः, गृहपीठः, गृहपोतकः, पोतः, वास्तुः *m.*, प्रतिष्ठानं, गृहमूलं, भूमिः *f.*, भूतलं, पृष्ठं.—(Story of a house) भूमिः, कोष्ठः -ष्ठं, मञ्चः; 'second floor,' द्वितीयभूमिः *f.*, द्वितीयकोष्ठं; 'upper floor,' उपरिभूमिः *f.*

—(Platform of boards) फलकः -कं, फलकास्तरः -रणं, दीर्घकाष्ठास्तरः -रणं, फलकास्तरिमा m. (न्), फलकसंस्तरः, मञ्चः -ञ्चकः.

To FLOOR, *v. a.* फलकैः or दीर्घकाष्ठैः or काष्ठफलकैर् आस्तॄ (c. 9. -स्तृणाति -स्तरितुं -रीतुं), फलक (nom. फलकयति -यितुं), सफलकीकृ.—(Strike down) भूमौ पत् in caus. (पातयति -यितुं).

FLOORING, *s.* फलकास्तरणं, फलकास्तरः, फलकास्तरिमा m. (न्), परिस्तरः.

To FLOP, *v. a.* आस्फोटनशब्देन तड् (c. 10. ताडयति -यितुं), आस्फल् (c. 10. -स्फालयति -यितुं).

FLORA, *s.* (The goddess) सीता, पुष्पदेवता.—(Catalogue of plants) ओषधिपरिसंख्या.

FLORAL, *a.* पौष्पः -ष्पी -ष्पं -ष्पिकः -की -कं, कौसुमः -मी -मं, सौमनसः -सी -सं.

FLORID, *a.* (In colour or complexion) रक्तवर्णः -र्णा -र्णं, अरुणवर्णः -र्णा -र्णं, पुष्पवर्णः -र्णा -र्णं.—(As style) पुष्पितः -ता -तं, अलङ्कृतः -ता -तं, वागलङ्कारमयः -यी -यं, व्यञ्जनामयः -यी -यं, शोभितः -ता -तं.

FLORIDITY, FLORIDNESS, *s.* (Of complexion) कपोलरागः, वदनरक्तता, मुखारुणिमा m. (न्).—(Of style) अलङ्कारः, सालङ्कारत्वं, वागलङ्कारः, वागलङ्क्रिया, वाक्शोभा.

FLORIFEROUS, *a.* पुष्पोत्पादकः -का -कं, पुष्पजनकः -का -कं, पुष्पदः -दा -दं.

FLORILEGIUM, *s.* पुष्पचयः, पुष्पावचयः, पुष्पप्रचायः, कुसुमावचयः.

FLORIN, *s.* विदेशीयमुद्राविशेषः, रूप्यमुद्राविशेषः.

FLORIST, *s.* पुष्पादिविज्ञः, पुष्पलावः, ओषधिविज्ञः, मालाकारः, मालिकः, माली m. (न्).

FLOTA, *s.* बृहन्नौकासमूहः, महावाणिज्यनौकासमूहः.

FLOTILLA, *s.* क्षुद्रनौकासमूहः, क्षुद्रनौकासङ्ग्रहः.

To FLOUNCE, *v. n.* सम्भ्रमोपहतत्वात् or संरम्भाविष्टत्वात् शरीराङ्गानि or शरीरम् इतस्ततः क्षिप् (c. 6. क्षिपति, क्षेप्तुं) or विक्षिप् or चल् in caus. (चालयति -यितुं) or विचल्.

FLOUNCE, *s.* (Sudden jerk of the body) अकस्माद् अङ्गविक्षेपः or शरीरविक्षेपः.—(A piece of cloth sewed round a gown with the lower border loose) स्त्रीवेशपरितः स्यूतः शिथिलाधोभागो वस्त्रखण्डः, स्त्रीवेशोपरि शोभार्थम् अधिकवस्त्रविन्यासः.

FLOUNCED, *p. p.* अधिकवस्त्रपंक्तिशोभितः -ता -तं, वेशोपरिस्थपटपंक्तिशोभितः -ता -तं.

FLOUNDER, *s.* समुद्रजः क्षुद्रमत्स्यभेदः.

To FLOUNDER, *v. n.* यथा वाजी पङ्के तथा पादादिविक्षेपेण लुट् (c. 6. लुठति -ठितुं), पङ्कपतितवद् निर्गमेच्छया शरीराङ्गानि इतस्ततः क्षिप् (c. 6. क्षिपति, क्षेप्तुं), विप्लु (c. 1. -प्लवते -प्लोतुं).

FLOUR, *s.* शक्तुः m., गोधूमचूर्णं, गोधूमक्षोदः, चूर्णं, क्षोदः, अपूपः, पिष्टं, गुण्डिकः -का, समीदः, समिता.

To FLOURISH, *v. n.* (Thrive) ऋध् (c. 5. ऋध्नोति, c. 4. ऋध्यति, अर्धितुं), समृध्, एध् (c. 1. एधते -धितुं), समेध्, वृध् (c. 1. वर्धते -र्धितुं), विवृध्, संवृध्, समृद्धीभू.—(Use lofty language) गर्व्वितवाक्यम् आक्षि (c. 1. -अयति -यितुं).

To FLOURISH, *v. a.* (Embellish with flowers, &c.) पुष्पाद्यलङ्कारेण शुभ् (c. 10. शोभयति -यितुं) or रञ्ज् (c. 10. रञ्जयति -यितुं), अलङ्कृ, समलङ्कृ, चित्र् (c. 10. चित्रयति -यितुं).—(Brandish) भ्रम् in caus. (भ्रमयति, भ्रामयति -यितुं), उद्भ्रम्.

FLOURISH, *s.* (Show, embellishment) शोभा, अलङ्कारः, अलङ्क्रिया, रञ्जनं.—(Lofty language) गर्व्वितवाक्यं, दर्पवाक्यं.—(Brandishing) भ्रान्तिः *f.*, उद्भ्रमः, उद्भ्रान्तिः *f.*

FLOURISHED, *p. p.* (Embellished) अलङ्कृतः -ता -तं.—(Brandished) उद्भ्रान्तः -न्ता -न्तं.

FLOURISHING, *a.* समृद्धः -द्धा -द्धं, वर्धमानः -ना -नं, वर्द्धिष्णुः -ष्णुः -ष्णु, अधिकर्द्धिः -र्द्धिः -र्द्धि, उदयी -यिनी -यि (न्), शुभान्वितः -ता -तं, सुस्थः -स्था -स्थं.

To FLOUT, *v. a.* अवहस् (c. 1. -हसति -सितुं), अवक्षिप् (c. 6. -क्षिपति -क्षेप्तुं), गर्ह् (c. 1. गर्हते -र्हितुं), अवज्ञा (c. 9. -जानाति -ज्ञातुं), तिरस्कृ, मुखरीकृ.

FLOUTED, *p. p.* अवज्ञातः -ता -तं, मुखरीकृतः -ता -तं, गर्हितः -ता -तं.

To FLOW, *v. n.* (Run as water) स्रु (c. 1. स्रवति, स्रोतुं), प्रस्रु, परिस्रु, स्यन्द् (c. 1. स्यन्दते -न्दितुं), प्रस्यन्द्, सृ (c. 1. सरति, सर्तुं), प्रसृ, संसृ, क्षर् (c. 1. क्षरति -रितुं), री (c. 4. रीयते, रेतुं), गल् (c. 1. गलति -लितुं), जलं प्रवह् (c. 1. -वहति -वोढुं), पयस् (nom. पयस्यति).—(Glide along) प्रसृप् (c. 1. -सर्पति -सर्प्तुं), विसृप्, संसृप्, सृप्, विसृ, प्रसृ.—(As the tide) वेलावत् प्रस्रु, वेला (nom. वेलायते).—(Proceed) प्रवृत् (c. 1. -वर्त्तते -र्त्तितुं), प्रसृ, प्रगम् (c. 1. -गच्छति -गन्तुं), प्रया (c. 2. -याति -तुं), प्रचल् (c. 1. -चलति -लितुं).—(Arise from) उत्पद् (c. 4. -पद्यते -पत्तुं), जन् (c. 4. जायते, जनितुं), प्रभू, प्रवृत्.—(Hang loose, as hair, &c.) विगलितः -ता -तं भू, प्रविततः -ता -तं भू, प्रलम्बः -बा -बं भू, विस्रंस् (c. 1. -स्रंसते -सितुं), शिथिलीभू.

FLOW, *s.* (Stream, course) स्रवः -वणं, प्रवाहः, स्रोतः *n.* (स्), प्रस्रवः, प्रस्रवणं, प्रस्रावः, स्रावः, संसृतिः *f.*, प्रवृत्तिः *f.*, जलवाहनं, स्यन्दः -न्दनं, निस्यन्दः, अभिष्यन्दः, गलनं, गालः, क्षरणं, उदकप्रवाहः.—(Current) वेला, वेगः, रयः, धारः -रा, ओघः, पात्रसंस्कारः, अनुपद्धतिः *f.*, पात्रकङ्कारः, रायभाटी, ऊर्म्मी.—(Tide) वेला, समुद्रवेला, समुद्ररयः.—(Flow of words) वाक्सरणिः *f.*, वाक्चापल्यं; 'flow of tears,' अश्रुपातः, अश्रुप्रवाहः, धाराश्रु *n.*; 'flow of blood,' असृक्पातः, असृग्धारा.

FLOWER, *s.* पुष्पं, कुसुमं, सुमनाः *m.* -नः *n.* -नसः *f. pl.* (स्), फुल्लं, प्रसवः, प्रसूनं, प्रसूतं, सूनं; 'flower-gathering,' पुष्पचयः, पुष्पावचयः, पुष्पप्रचयः, पुष्पप्रचायः, कुसुमावचयः; 'flower-gatherer,' पुष्पचायी *m.* (न्), पुष्पावचायी *m.* (न्), पुष्पलावः; 'flower-seller,' पुष्पाजीवी *m.* (न्), मालाकारः, मालिकः.—(Prime, best part) सारः, उत्तमभागः, श्रेष्ठभागः; 'flower of age,' यौवनावस्था; 'flower of youth,' यौवनप्रौढिः *f.*, नवयौवनं, अक्षतयौवनं; 'of corn,' धान्यस्य सारभागः; 'in the flower of youth,' प्रौढयौवनः -ना -नं.—(Catamenia) पुष्पं, कुसुमं.

To FLOWER, *v. n.* (Blossom) पुष्प् (c. 4. पुष्प्यति, पुष्पितुं), कुसुम (nom. कुसुमयति -यितुं), फुल्ल् (c. 1. फुल्लति -ल्लितुं), स्फुट् (c. 6. स्फुटति -टितुं, c. 1. स्फोटते -टितुं), विकस् (c. 1. -कसति -सितुं).—(Be in the prime) प्रौढयौवनः -ना -नं भू.—(Froth) फेन (nom. फेनायते) मण्ड (nom. मण्डायते).

To FLOWER, *v. a.* पुष्पाद्यलङ्कारेण शुभ् (c. 10. शोभयति -यितुं).

FLOWER-ARMED, *a.* (The Hindu Cupid) कुसुमायुधः, कुसुमेषुः *m.*, पुष्पास्त्रः, पुष्पचापः.

FLOWER-DE-LUCE or FLOWER-DE-LIS, *s.* उत्पलभेदः, पद्मविशेषः.

FLOWERED, *p. p.* or *a.* पुष्पितः -ता -तं, कुसुमितः -ता -तं, विकसितः -ता -तं, फुल्लः -ल्ला -ल्लं.—(Embellished with flowers) पुष्पाद्यलङ्कारशोभितः -ता -तं.

FLOWERET, *s.* पुष्पकः -कं, क्षुद्रपुष्पं, क्षुद्रकुसुमं.

FLOWER-GARDEN, *s.* पुष्पोद्यानं, कुसुमोद्यानं, पुष्पवाटी -टिका, उद्यानं, कुसुमाकरः.

FLOWERING, *a.* फुल्लवान् -वती -वत् (त्), प्रफुल्लः -ल्ला -ल्लं, पुष्पी -ष्पिणी -ष्पि (न्), पुष्पवान् -वती -वत् (त्), पुष्पितः -ता -तं, कुसुमितः -ता -तं, कुसुमवान् -वती -वत् (त्), स्फुटितपुष्पः -ष्पा -ष्पं, विकासी -सिनी -सि

(न्), पुष्पदः -दा -दं.

FLOWERLESS, *a.* अपुष्पः -ष्पा -ष्पं, अपुष्पकः -का -कं, अपुष्पदः -दा -दं.

FLOWER-STALK, *s.* मञ्जरी, पुष्पवृन्तं, प्रसवबन्धनं.

FLOWERY, *a.* (Having flowers) पौष्पः -ष्पी -ष्पं, पुष्पी -ष्पिणी -ष्पि (न्), सपुष्पः -ष्पा -ष्पं, पुष्पितः -ता -तं, पुष्पशाली -लिनी -लि (न्), पुष्पमयः -यी -यं, कौसुमः -मी -मं, सौमनसः -सी -सं, सकुसुमः -मा -मं. —(As style) पुष्पितः -ता -तं, अलङ्कृतः -ता -तं, वागलङ्कारमयः -यी -यं, व्यञ्जनामयः -यी -यं.

FLOWING, *part.* or *a.* स्रुतः -ता -तं, स्रवन् -वन्ती -वत् (त्), प्रस्रुतः -ता -तं, स्यन्नः -न्ना -न्नं, स्यन्दी -न्दिनी -न्दि (न्), विसारी -रिणी -रि (न्), प्रसारी &c., विसृत्वरः -रा -रं, विसृमरः -रा -रं, रीणः -णा -णं, स्रुतः -ता -तं.

FLOWING, *s.* स्रवः -वणं, प्रस्रवः -वणं, प्रस्रावः, स्रावः, उदकप्रवाहः, वेला.

FLOWINGLY, *adv.* वाक्सरणिपूर्व्वं, वाक्चापल्येन, द्रुतं, द्रुतवाक्येन, अस्खलितवाक्येन, अविलम्बितं, अविलम्बितवाक्येन.

FLUCTUANT, *a.* ऊर्म्मिवद् इतस्ततो लोलमानः -ना -नं or विचलः -ला -लं.

To FLUCTUATE, *v. n.* (Roll or move to and fro) इतस्ततो लुट् (c. 6. लुठति -ठितुं) or लुल् (c. 1. लोलति -ते -लितुं) or चल् (c. 1. चलति -लितुं) or विचल्.—(Be unsteady, irresolute) दोल (nom. दोलायते -यितुं), विचल्, विचलीभू, अस्थिरः -रा -रं भू, अस्थिरीभू, अनवस्थितः -ता -तं भू, चञ्चलीभू, पातोत्पातं कृ, विक्लृप् (c. 1. -कल्पते -ल्पितुं, c. 10. -कल्पयति -यितुं).

FLUCTUATING, *a.* दोलायमानः -ना -नं, विचलः -ला -लं, अप्रतिष्ठः -ष्ठा -ष्ठं, अनवस्थितः -ता -तं, अस्थिरः -रा -रं, चलः -ला -लं, चञ्चलः -ला -लं, लोलः -ला -लं, लोलमानः -ना -नं, चपलः -ला -लं, तरलायितः -ता -तं.

FLUCTUATION, *s.* अस्थैर्य्यं, अस्थिरता, अनवस्थितिः *f.*, विचलनं, चञ्चलता, चाञ्चल्यं, चलता, आन्दोलनं, दोलायमानता, अप्रतिष्ठा, चपलता, पातोत्पातः.

FLUE, *s.* (Passage for smoke) धूमपथः, धूममार्गः, धूमवर्त्म *n.* (न्), धूमनिर्गमपथः.—(Soft down) मृदुलोम *n.* (न्), मृदुपक्षः.

FLUENCY, *s.* (Of speech) वाक्सरणिः *f.*, वाग्द्रुतता, वाक्चापल्यं, वाक्क्षिप्रता, वाग्विभवः, वाक्पटुता, वाक्चातुर्य्यं, शब्दचातुर्य्यं, वाक्कौशलं, वाक्शीघ्रता, वाग्बाहुल्यं.

FLUENT, *a.* (In speech) वाग्द्रुतः -ता -तं, द्रुतवाक् *m. f. n.* (च्), वाक्क्षिप्रः -प्रा -प्रं, वाक्त्वरितः -ता -तं, त्वरितवाक् *m. f. n.*, वाक्पटुः -टुः -टु, अस्खलितवाक्यः -क्या -क्यं, अस्खलद्वाक्यः -क्या -क्यं, अविलम्बितवाक्यः -क्या -क्यं, शब्दचतुरः -रा -रं.

FLUENTLY, *adv.* द्रुतवाक्येन, क्षिप्रवाक्येन, वाक्चापल्येन, अविलम्बितवाचा, अस्खलितवाचा, त्वरितवाचा, वाग्विभवेन, द्रुतं, शीघ्रं, अस्खलितं, अविलम्बितं.

FLUID, *a.* द्रवः -वा -वं, द्रुतः -ता -तं, विद्रुतः -ता -तं, द्राव्यः -व्या -व्यं, विलीनः -ना -नं, तरलः -ला -लं, पयस्यः -स्या -स्यं, विभाजनीयः -या -यं.

FLUID, *s.* द्रवः, रसः, द्रवद्रव्यं, द्रववस्तु *n.*, जलवद्द्रव्यं, वारि *n.*, जलं, पयः *n.* (स्).

FLUIDITY, *s.* द्रवता -त्वं, द्राव्यत्वं, द्रुतत्वं, विद्रुतत्वं, विलीनता, तारल्यं.

FLUKE, *s.* लङ्गरदन्तः, लङ्गरभुजः. *See* FLOOK.

FLUMMERY, *s.* मिथ्याप्रशंसा, मिथ्यास्तुतिः *f.*, कल्पितप्रशंसा, अनर्थकस्तुतिः *f.*

FLUNG, *p. p.* क्षिप्तः -प्ता -प्तं, प्रक्षिप्तः -प्ता -प्तं, अस्तः -स्ता -स्तं; 'flung aside,' अपास्तः -स्ता -स्तं, अपसारितः -ता -तं, समाक्षिप्तः -प्ता -प्तं.

FLUNKEY, *s.* दासः, नीचकर्म्मकरः, तुच्छकर्म्मकरः, कापुरुषः, लटकः.

FLURRIED, *p. p.* आकुलितः -ता -तं, आकुलीकृतः -ता -तं, व्याकुलः -ला -लं -लितः -ता -तं, सम्भ्रान्तः -न्ता -न्तं, ससम्भ्रमः -मा -मं, विभ्रान्तमनाः -नाः -नः (स्), विक्षिप्तचित्तः -त्ता -त्तं, व्यग्रः -ग्रा -ग्रं, समाकुलः -ला -लं, चित्तवेगवान् -वती -वत् (त्), व्यस्तः -स्ता -स्तं, कातरः -रा -रं.

FLURRY, *s.* आकुलत्वं, व्याकुलता, सम्भ्रमः, विभ्रमः, चित्तभ्रान्तिः *f.*, चित्तवेगः, व्यग्रता, आवेगः, संवेगः, व्यस्तता, कातरता, वैक्लव्यं, विस्मयः, मोहः.

To FLURRY, *v. a.* आकुलीकृ, व्याकुलीकृ, व्याकुल (nom. व्याकुलयति -यितुं), कातरीकृ, मुह् (c. 10. मोहयति -यितुं), विमुह्, चित्तवेगं जन् (c. 10. जनयति -यितुं).

To FLUSH, *v. n.* (Become suddenly red) अकस्माद् रक्तोद्गमत्वाद् अरुणमुखीभू or लोहिताननः -ना -नं भू or रक्तवदनः -ना -नं भू, अरुणीभू, रक्तीभू, लोहित (nom. लोहितायते), रञ्ज् in pass. (रज्यते) संरञ्ज्.

To FLUSH, *v. a.* (Redden suddenly) अकस्माद् अरुणीकृ or रक्तीकृ or अरुण (nom. अरुणयति -यितुं), सरागं -गां -गं कृ, रञ्ज् in caus. (रञ्जयति -यितुं).—(Elate) दृप् in caus. (दर्पयति -यितुं), उन्नतीकृ, गर्व्वितीकृ.

FLUSH, *a.* (Vigorous) प्रौढतेजाः -जाः -जः (स्), तेजस्वी -स्विनी -स्वि (न्), प्रौढः -ढा -ढं.—(Affluent) धनाढ्यः -ढ्या -ढ्यं, समृद्धः -द्धा -द्धं.—(Liberal) धनव्ययशीलः -ला -लं, मुक्तहस्तः -स्ता -स्तं.

FLUSH, *s.* कपोलरागः, कपोलरक्तता, मुखारुणिमा *m.* (न्), वदनरागः, नववर्णः.—(Abundance, affluence) बाहुल्यं, धनबाहुल्यं, समृद्धिः *f.*

FLUSHED, *p. p.* (Colored) अरुणितः -ता -तं, अरुणीकृतः -ता -तं, रञ्जितः -ता -तं, रक्तः -क्ता -क्तं, रागी -गिणी -गि (न्), कपोलरागवान् -वती -वत् (त्).—(Elated) उन्नतः -ता -तं, दर्पाध्मातः -ता -तं, दृप्तः -प्ता -प्तं; 'with victory,' जयगर्व्वितः -ता -तं.

FLUSHING, *s.* अरुणीभावः, वदनरक्तत्वं, रक्तवर्णः, लोहितवर्णः.

To FLUSTER, *v. a.* पानादिना मद् in caus. (मादयति -यितुं) or उन्मत्तीकृ or विमुह् (c. 10. -मोहयति -यितुं) or चित्तविभ्रमं जन् (c. 10. जनयति -यितुं).

FLUSTER, *s.* चित्तविभ्रमः, मद्यपानजः सम्भ्रमः, व्यग्रता, मोहः, व्याकुलता.

FLUTE, *s.* (Instrument) वेणुः *m.*, वंशः -शी, मुरली, सानेयी -यिका, सानिका, विवरनालिका, दर्दुरः, नन्दः; 'sound of the flute,' वेणुशब्दः, वेणुध्वनिः *m.*, क्षोभनं.—(Channel of a column) स्तम्भरेखा, स्तम्भसीता.

To FLUTE, *v. n.* (Play on the flute) वेणुं or वंशीं ध्मा (c. 1. धमति, ध्मातुं) or प्रध्मा or वद् in caus. (वादयति -यितुं) or संवद् or प्रवद्.

To FLUTE, *v. a.* स्तम्भपरितो दीर्घरेखाः कृ or निखन् (c. 1. -खनति -नितुं).

FLUTE-PLAYER, *s.* वेणुध्मः, वांशिकः, वैणविकः, मुरलीवादकः.

FLUTED, *p. p.* or *a.* स्तम्भवद् दीर्घरेखायुक्तः -क्ता -क्तं or रेखार्पितयुक्तः -क्ता -क्तं.

To FLUTTER, *v. n.* (Flap the wings in mid air) विहायसा or व्योममध्ये पक्षास्फालनं कृ or पक्षस्पन्दनं कृ or पक्षौ स्फल् (c. 10. स्फालयति -यितुं) or आस्फल्, प्रडीनम् अकृत्वा आकाशमध्ये पक्षौ विचल् in caus. (-चालयति -यितुं) or चल्.—(Move about with bustle) इतस्ततश् चल् or धाव् (c. 1. धावति -वितुं).—(Vibrate, beat, be agitated) स्पन्द् (c. 1. स्पन्दते -न्दितुं), कम्प् (c. 1. कम्पते -म्पितुं), विकम्प्, स्फुर् (c. 6. स्फुरति -रितुं), क्षुभ् (c. 4. क्षुभ्यति, क्षोभितुं), उच्छ्वस् (c. 2. -श्वसिति -तुं, rt. श्वस्), दोल् (nom. दोलायते -यितुं).

FLUTTER, *s.* (Vibration) स्पन्दनं, प्रतिस्पन्दनं, स्फुरणं, कम्पः -म्पनं, विकम्पः, उच्छ्वासः, उच्छ्वसनं, इतस्ततो विचलनं or चलनं.—(Hurry, agitation) सम्भ्रमः, वेगः, संवेगः, आवेगः, चित्तवेगः, क्षोभः.

FLUTTERING, *s.* पक्षास्फालनं, पक्षस्पन्दनं, पक्षकम्पनं, पक्षचालनं, स्फालः -लनं.

FLUTTERING, *part.* or *a.* आस्फालितः -ता -तं, स्पन्दमानः -ना -नं, कम्पमानः -ना -नं, विचलः -ला -लं, विचलन् -लन्ती -लत् (त्), उच्छ्वासी -सिनी -सि (न्); 'in the breeze,' अनिलोद्धतः -ता -तं, पवनाहतः -ता -तं, पवनक्षिप्तः -प्ता -प्तं.

FLUVIAL, FLUVIATIC, *a.* नादेयः -यी -यं, नदीसम्बन्धी -न्धिनी -न्धि (न्).

FLUX, *s.* (Flow) स्रवः -वणं, प्रस्रवः -वणं, प्रस्रावः, प्रवाहः, स्यन्दः, क्षरणं, गलनं, गालः.—(Of the tide) वेला.—(Confluence) सङ्गमः, समागमः.—(Bloody flux) आमातिसारः, आमरक्तं.

To FLUX, *v. a.* विली in caus. (-लाययति -लापयति -यितुं), द्रवीकृ, द्रु in caus. (द्रावयति -यितुं), विद्रु, गल् in caus. (गालयति -यितुं), विलीनीकृ.

FLUXIBILITY, FLUXILITY, *s.* द्रवत्वं, द्राव्यत्वं, गलनीयता, विलीनता.

FLUXIBLE, *a.* द्राव्यः -व्या -व्यं, गलनीयः -या -यं, सुविलयः -या -यं.

FLUXION, *s.* स्रवः -वणं, प्रस्रवः -वणं, स्रावः, प्रवाहः, गलनं, क्षरणं.

To FLY, *v. n.* (As a bird in the air) डी (c. 4. डीयते, c. 1. डयते -यितुं), प्रडी, उड्डी, खे or वियति विसृप् (c. 1. -सर्पति -सर्प्तुं) or सृप्, आकाशेन गम् (c. 1. गच्छति, गन्तुं) or या (c. 2. याति -तुं), पत् (c. 1. पतति -तितुं), उत्पत्, प्रोत्पत्, समुत्पत्, सम्पत्.—(Move along swiftly) त्वरितं or सत्वरं or शीघ्रं गम् or चल् (c. 1. चलति -लितुं) or सृ (c. 1. सरति, सर्तुं) or प्रसृ.—(Run away) पलाय् (c. 1. पलायते -यितुं, rt. इ), विपलाय्, प्रपलाय्, सम्पलाय्, प्रद्रु (c. 1. -द्रवति -द्रोतुं), विद्रु, विप्रद्रु, प्रधाव् (c. 1. -धावति -वितुं), अपधाव्, अपक्रम् (c. 1. -क्रामति -क्रमितुं), अपगम्, निर्गम्, अपसृप् (c. 1. सर्पति -सर्प्तुं), अपया (c. 2. -याति -तुं), अपसृ (c. 1. -सरति -सर्तुं), अपे (c. 2. अपैति -तुं, rt. इ).—(Pass rapidly) शीघ्रम् अतिक्रम् or अती (c. 2. अत्येति -तुं, rt. इ) or अतिवृत् (c. 1. -वर्त्तते -र्त्तितुं); 'to fly away,' उड्डी, प्रडी, प्रोड्डी, निष्पत्; 'he flew away,' पलायितः; 'to fly at,' अभिपत्, आपत्, उपपत्, अभिद्रु, आद्रु, उपद्रु, अभिधाव्, आधाव्, प्रतिधाव्; 'to fly up,' उड्डी, उत्पत्, अधिरुह् (c. 1. -रोहति -रोढुं); 'to let fly,' मुच् (c. 6. मुञ्चति, मोक्तुं), सृज् (c. 6. सृजति, स्रष्टुं), पत् in caus. (पातयति -यितुं).

To FLY, *v. a.* (Avoid) वृज् (c. 10. वर्जयति -यितुं), विवृज्, त्यज् (c. 1. त्यजति, त्यक्तुं), परिहृ (c. 1. -हरति -हर्तुं).—(Cause to float in the air) आकाशे विसृप् in caus. (-सर्पयति -यितुं) or विसृ in caus. (-सारयति -यितुं).

FLY, *s.* (Insect) मक्षिका, मशकः, मक्षीका, माचिका, भम्भः, भम्भराली, बम्भराली.

FLY-BITTEN, *a.* मक्षिकादष्टः -ष्टा -ष्टं, मक्षिकादंशाङ्कितः -ता -तं.

To FLY-BLOW, *v. a.* मक्षिकावद् अण्डप्रसवेन स्वामांसं दुष् (c. 10. दूषयति -यितुं).

FLY-BOAT, *s.* प्रणालीप्लवनयोग्या लघुनौका, द्रुतगामिनी दीर्घनौका.

FLY-CATCHER, *s.* मक्षिकाखादकः पक्षिभेदः, मक्षिकाभुज् *m.* (क्), मक्षिकानाशकः.

To FLY-FISH, *v. n.* मक्षिकां वडिशे निवेश्य मत्स्यान् ग्रह् (c. 9. गृह्णाति, ग्रहीतुं).

FLY-FLAP, *s.* मक्षिकानिवारणार्थं चामरं, अवचूलकं, रोमगुच्छः.

FLY-LEAF, *s.* मलपृष्ठं, पुस्तकस्य आद्यन्तयोः शून्यपत्रं.

FLYER, *s.* डीयमानः, खविसर्पी *m.* (न्), आकाशगामी. *See* FLIER.—(Wheel) तुलाचक्रं.

FLYING, *s.* (Act of) डीनं, डयनं, प्रडीनं, विसर्पणं, आकाशगमनं, पतनं; 'flying up and down,' डीनावडीनं.

FLYING, *part.* डीयमानः -ना -नं, खविसर्पी -र्पिणी -र्पि (न्), आकाशगतिः -तिः -ति, आकाशगामी -मिनी -मि (न्), आकाशयायी -यिनी -यि (न्), पतन् -न्ती -तत् (त्), नभोगतिः -तिः -ति; 'flying up,' उड्डीयमानः -ना -नं.

FLYING-BRIDGE, *s.* नौसेतुः *m.*, चलसेतुः *m.*, जङ्गमसेतुः.

FLYING-FISH, *s.* आकाशगमनशीलो मत्स्यभेदः.

FOAL, *s.* अश्वशावः -वकः, किशोरः, घोटकवत्सः, बालः, बालघोटकः, अश्वरोधः.

To FOAL, *v. n.* किशोरं or अश्वशावकं सु (c. 2. सूते, c. 4. सूयते, सोतुं) or प्रसु or जन् (c. 10. जनयति -यितुं) or प्रजा (c. 4. -जायते -जनितुं).

FOAM, *s.* फेनः, मण्डः -ण्डं, पराङ्गः, परङ्गः, कारुजः, उत्पीडः, उत्सेकः, उत्सेचनं.

To FOAM, *v. n.* फेन (nom. फेनायते -यितुं), मण्ड (nom. मण्डायते -यितुं), उत्सेचनं कृ, उत्पीडं कृ, फेनम् उत्पद् in caus. (-पादयति -यितुं) or निर्गम् in caus. (-गमयति -यितुं).

FOAMING, *part.* फेनायमानः -ना -नं, उत्सेचनकारी -रिणी -रि (न्).

FOAMY, *a.* फेनलः -ला -लं, फेनिलः -ला -लं, फेनवान् -वती -वत् (त्), फेनी -निनी -नि (न्), फेनोत्पादकः -का -कं.

FOB, *s.* घटीकोषः, घटीपिधानं, क्षुद्रघटीधारकः, कटिवस्त्रपार्श्वे कालमापनयन्त्राधारः or -कोषः.

To FOB, *v. a.* छल् (c. 10. छलयति -यितुं), वञ्च् in caus. (वञ्चयते -यितुं), छलं कृ.

FOCUS, *s.* अग्रांशुः *m.*, अग्रकरः, केन्द्रं, बिन्दुः *m.*, अक्षः, तेजःसङ्घप्रदेशः, नाभिः *m. f.*

FODDER, *s.* पशुभोजनं, गवादनं, गवादिभोजनं, अश्वादनं, पशुखादनीयं शुष्कतृणादि, विघः -घा -घानं, विघिः *m.*

To FODDER, *v. a.* शुष्कतृणादि दा (c. 3. ददाति, दातुं) or भुज् (c. 10. भोजयति -यितुं).

FOE, *s.* शत्रुः *m.*, रिपुः *m.*, अरिः *m.*, अरातिः *m.*, वैरी *m.* (न्), विपक्षः, अमित्रः, प्रतिपक्षः, विरोधी *m.* (न्), प्रतिद्वन्द्वः, सपत्नः, अपकारी *m.* (न्), अहितः.

FŒTAL, FŒTUS, FŒCES. *See* FETAL, &c.

FOG, *s.* (Mist) धूमिका, धूलिका, धूपिका, शीकरः, सबाष्पः, मृगतृष्णा -तृषा -ष्णिका, मृगतृट् *f.* (ष्), कूहा, कुहेडिका, कुज्झटिका, कुज्झटिः *f.* -टी -टिका, हिमझटिः *f.*, रुझेटिः *f.*, धूममहिषी.—(After grass) द्वितीयतृणं.

FOGGINESS, *s.* सधूमिकत्वं, धूमलता, सशीकरत्वं, कुज्झटिकावस्था, कुज्झटिकाकीर्णता, सान्धकारत्वं, शीकराकीर्णता.

FOGGY, *a.* सधूमिकः -का -कं, धूमिकावृतः -ता -तं, धूमलः -ला -लं, सशीकरः -रा -रं, शीकरीयः -या -यं, शीकरौघः -घा -घं, कुज्झटिकाच्छन्नः -न्ना -न्नं, सान्धकारः -रा -रं, सकुज्झटिकः -का -कं, अभियः -या -यं.—(Dull) स्थूलः -ला -लं.

FOH, *exclam.* धिक्, शान्तं, अपैहि, अपसर.

FOIBLE, *s.* छिद्रं, दोषः, कलङ्कः, अपराधः, वैकल्यं, हानिः *f.*, हीनता.

To FOIL, *v. a.* (Frustrate) प्रतिहन् (c. 2. -हन्ति -न्तुं), व्याहन्, परास् (c. 4. -अस्यति -असितुं), खण्ड् (c. 10. खण्डयति -यितुं), उद्यमभङ्गं कृ, विफलीकृ, वृथा कृ.—(Blunt) रुग्नीकृ, विरुग्नीकृ; 'one who foils one's designs,' कार्य्यहन्ता *m.* (न्तृ).

FOIL, *s.* (Defeat, frustration) प्रतिहतिः *f.*, खण्डनं, भङ्गः.—(Blunt sword) धाराहीनः खड्गः, क्रीडाखड्गः, युद्धक्रीडायां प्रयुक्तो लोहयष्टिः.—(Leaf of metal) धातुपत्रं; 'tin-foil,' त्रपुपत्रं.—(Foil of a jewel) रत्नप्रभावर्धकं, मणितेजोवर्धको धातुपत्रखण्डः.—(Any thing which sets off) प्रकाशकः -का -कं, कान्तिवर्धकः -का -कं, शोभकृत् *m. f. n.*

FOILED, *p. p.* प्रतिहतः -ता -तं, परास्तः -स्ता -स्तं, भग्नोद्यमः -मा -मं, विफलीकृतः -ता -तं, खण्डिताशंसः -सा -सं, अकृतार्थः -र्था -र्थं, हताशः -शा -शं, मनोहतः -ता -तं, विक्षिप्तः -प्ता -प्तं, विनिवृत्तकामः -मा -मं, तिरस्कृतः -ता -तं.

FOILER, *s.* कार्य्यहन्ता *m.* (न्तृ), उद्यमभङ्गकारी *m.* (न्), कर्म्मध्वंसकारी *m.*

FOIN, *s.* यष्टिक्रीडायां यष्ट्याघातः or यष्टिप्रहारः, खड्गाघातः.

To FOIN, *v. a.* यष्टिक्रीडायां यष्टिना प्रहृ (c. 1. -हरति -हर्तुं) or आहन् (c. 2. -हन्ति -न्तुं).

To FOIST, *v. a.* छलेन or कपटेन निविश् in caus. (-वेशयति -यितुं) or अभिलिख् (c. 6. -लिखति -लेखितुं), मिथ्या कॢप् (c. 10. कल्पयति

-यितुं), कृत्रिमं -मां -मं कृ.

Foisted, *p. p.* छलेन निवेशितः -ता -तं or अभिलिखितः -ता -तं.

Foistiness, *s.* पर्य्युषितत्वं, विरसत्वं, ईषत्पूतत्वं, पूतिगन्धिता, कुरसत्वं.

Fold, *s.* (For sheep or cattle) मेषस्थानं -नकं, व्रजः, व्रजाजिरं, मेषव्रजः, मेषशाला, गोष्ठं, गोस्थानकं.—(A double in cloth, &c.) पुटः, वस्त्रपुटः, ऊर्म्मिः *m. f.* -र्म्मिका -र्म्मी, भङ्गः, वस्त्रभङ्गः, तरङ्गः, व्यावर्त्तनं, चूणः. 'Fold,' in comp. is expressed by the affix धा; as, 'two-fold,' द्विधा, or by गुण; as, द्विगुणः -णा -णं.

To fold, *v. a.* (Double) पुटीकृ, पुट (nom. पुटयति -यितुं), द्विगुण (nom. द्विगुणयति -यितुं), द्विगुणीकृ, व्यावृत् (c. 10. -वर्त्तयति -यितुं) विपरिवृत्, व्यावर्त्तनं कृ, संवृ (c. 5. -वृणोति, c. 1. -वरति -रितुं -रीतुं), सम्पीड् (c. 10. -पीडयति -यितुं); 'fold the arms,' भुजौ सम्पीड्; 'in the arms,' भुजापीडं कृ.—(Confine sheep in a fold) मेषान् व्रजे निविश् in caus. (-वेशयति -यितुं) or निरुध् (c. 7. -रुणद्धि -रोद्धुं).

Folded, *p. p.* पुटितः -ता -तं, पुटीकृतः -ता -तं, द्विगुणितः -ता -तं, संवृतः -ता -तं, सम्पीडितः -ता -तं, व्यावर्त्तितः -ता -तं; 'folded or wrapped up,' वेष्टितः -ता -तं, वासनस्थः -स्था -स्थं; 'folded leaf,' दलकपाटः.

Folding, *s.* पुटीकरणं, व्यावर्त्तनं, संवृतिः *f.*; 'folding in the arms,' भुजापीडं कृ.

Folding-doors, *s.* द्विकपाटयुक्तं or द्विशालायुक्तं द्वारं.

Foliage, *s.* पत्रं -त्राणि *n. pl.*, पर्णं, दलं, वृक्षपत्रं, तरुच्छदः, तरुजं.

To foliate, *v. a.* मुद्गराघातेन धातुं सूक्ष्मपत्राकारं कृ or धातुपत्रं कृ, उद्घर्त्तनं कृ.

Foliation, *s.* मुद्गराघातेन धातुपत्रकरणं, उद्घर्त्तनं.

Folio, *s.* पुस्तकपत्रं, महापत्रं, पृथुपत्रं, बृहत्पत्रं, विशालपत्रं, द्विपत्रं.

Folk, *s.* लोकः, जनः, मनुष्यजातिः *f.*, नृजातिः *f.*, प्रजा, जगती.

To follow, *v. a.* (Go after) अनुगम् (c. 1. -गच्छति -गन्तुं), अन्वागम्, पश्चाद् गम्, अनुया (c. 2. -याति -तुं), समनुया, अन्वि (c. 2. -एति -तुं), अनुवृत् (c. 1. -वर्त्तते -र्त्तितुं), समनुवृत्, अनुसृ (c. 1. -सरति -सर्त्तुं), अनुव्रज् (c. 1. -व्रजति -जितुं), समनुव्रज्, अनुक्रम् (c. 1. -क्रामति -क्रमितुं), अनुचर् (c. 1. -चरति -रितुं), अन्वग्या, पुरस्कृ.—(Imitate) अनुकृ, अनुवृत्, अनुगम्.—(Observe, practise) अनुष्ठा (c. 1. -तिष्ठति -ष्ठातुं), आस्था, सेव् (c. 1. सेवते -वितुं), उपसेव्, निषेव्, समासेव्, आश्रि (c. 1. -श्रयति -यितुं), विधा (c. 3. -दधाति -धातुं).—(Adhere to, serve, honour) आश्रि, श्रु in des. (शुश्रूषते -षितुं), उपास् (c. 2. -आस्ते -आसितुं), भज् (c. 1. भजते, भक्तुं), परिचर्.—(Result from) उत्पद् (c. 4. -पद्यते -पत्तुं), जन् in pass. (जायते), अनुवृत्, उद्भू, अनुभू.

Followed, *p. p.* अनुगतः -ता -तं, अनुयातः -ता -तं, अनुगम्यमानः -ना -नं, अन्वीयमानः -ना -नं.—(Observed) अनुष्ठितः -ता -तं, सेवितः -ता -तं, आश्रितः -ता -तं.

Follower, *s.* (One who goes after) अनुगामी *m.* (न्), पश्चाद्गामी, अनुगः -गतः, अनुयायी *m.* (न्), अनुवर्त्ती *m.* (न्), अनुचरः -चारी *m.* (न्), अनुगतिकः, अनुयायिकः, अभिसरः, पार्श्वपरिवर्त्ती *m.* (न्), पार्ष्णिग्राहः, उपधावनः.—(Adherent, disciple) अनुषङ्गी, भक्तः, आश्रितः, भाक्तिकः, शिष्यः; 'follower of Krishna,' कृष्णाश्रितः.—(Attendant, defendant) परिजनः, अनुचरः, सेवकः, अनुजीवी *m.* (न्) -विकः, उपजीवी *m.*, परिवारः.—(Companion, associate) सहायः, सहचरः, सङ्गी *m.* (न्).

Following, *part.* (Going after) अनुगः -गा -गं, अनुयायी -यिनी -यि (न्), अनुसारी -रिणी -रि (न्), अनुवर्त्ती -र्त्ती -र्त्ति (न्), अनुपथः -था -थं, अन्वक्षः -क्षा -क्षं, अन्वङ् अनूची अन्वक् (च्), अनुपदं.—(Next after) परः -रा -रं.—(Succeeding) अनुयायी &c.

Following, *s.* (Act of) अनुगमः -मनं, अनुसरणं, अनुवर्त्तनं, अनुव्रजनं.

Folly, *s.* मूर्खता, मौर्ख्यं, मूढता -त्वं, मोहः, मौढ्यं, बुद्धिहीनता, निर्बुद्धिता, अज्ञता, अविज्ञता, अनभिज्ञता, अज्ञानं, ज्ञानाभावः, प्रज्ञाहीनता.

To foment, *v. a.* (Heat with warm lotions) स्विद् in caus. (स्वेदयति -यितुं), प्रस्विद्, घर्म्मोदकादिना or उष्णोदकादिना लिप् (c. 6. लिम्पति, लेप्तुं) or अनुलिप् or अञ्ज् (c. 7. अनक्ति, अंक्तुं) or दिह् (c. 2. देग्धि -ग्धुं) or सिच् (c. 6. सिञ्चति, सेक्तुं) or निषिच्.—(Encourage, excite) वृध् in caus. (वर्धयति -यितुं), संवृध् in caus., प्रवृत् in caus. (-वर्त्तयति -यितुं), तेजो दा, तेजोवृद्धिं कृ, उत्तिज् (c. 10. -तेजयति -यितुं), उत्तप् (c. 10. -तापयति -यितुं), उद्दीप् (c. 10. -दीपयति -यितुं); 'foment dissensions,' उपजप् (c. 1. -जपति -पितुं), कर्णे जप्, उपजापेन भेदं वृध् in caus.

Fomentation, *s.* (Act of heating with warm lotions, &c.) स्वेदनं, प्रस्वेदनं, घर्म्मोदकादिना विलेपनं or अनुलेपनं or सेचनं.—(The lotion itself) घर्म्मलेपः, घर्म्मानुलेपनं, उष्णोपदेहः.—(Encouragement) उद्दीपनं, उत्तेजनं, उत्तापः, संवर्धनं.

Fomented, *p. p.* स्वेदितः -ता -तं.—(Encouraged) उद्दीप्तः -प्ता -प्तं, संवर्धितः -ता -तं.

Fomenter, *s.* (Of dissension) उपजापकः, कर्णेजपः, भेदकरः, कलिकारकः.

Fond, *a.* (Loving) अनुरक्तः -क्ता -क्तं, अनुरागवान् -वती -वत् (त्), अनुरागी -गिणी -गि (न्), सानुरागः -गा -गं, स्नेही -हिनी -हि (न्), स्नेहितः -ता -तं, कामी -मिनी -मि (न्), प्रणयी -यिनी -यि (न्).—(Attached to, delighting in) आसक्तः -क्ता -क्तं, प्रसक्तः -क्ता -क्तं, परः -रा -रं, तत्परः -रा -रं, रतः -ता -तं, सेवी -विनी -वि (न्), अभिलाषी -षिणी -षि (न्), आनन्दी -न्दिनी -न्दि (न्) -न्दितः -ता -तं, प्रमोदी -दिनी -दि (न्); 'fond of one's ease,' सुखाभिलाषी -षिणी -षि (न्); 'fond of embracing,' आलिङ्गनतत्परः -रा -रं; 'fond of noise,' स्वनमोदी &c. Often expressed by प्रिय in comp.; as, 'fond of water,' जलप्रियः -या -यं; 'fond of mountains,' गिरिप्रियः -या -यं; 'fond of ornament,' प्रियमण्डनः -ना -नं; or by काम in comp.; as, 'fond of flesh,' मांसकामः -मा -मं; 'to be fond of,' अनुरागवान् -वती -वद् अस् or भू, सेव् (c. 1. सेवते -वितुं), अभिलष् (c. 1. -लषति -षितुं), रुच् (c. 1. रोचते -चितुं), with dat. of the person; अभिनन्द् (c. 1. -नन्दति -न्दितुं).—(Doting) अत्यनुरक्तः -क्ता -क्तं.—(Silly) मूढः -ढा -ढं, मुग्धः -ग्धा -ग्धं.

To fondle, *v. a.* आलिङ्ग् (c. 1. -लिङ्गति -ङ्गितुं), समालिङ्ग्, परिष्वञ्ज् (c. 1. -ष्वजते -ष्वंक्तुं), परिमृश् (c. 6. -मृशति -म्रष्टुं), लल् (c. 10. लालयति -यितुं), क्रोडीकृ, भुजापीडितं -तां -तं कृ, प्रेम कृ, अनुरागं कृ, अङ्कीकृ, अङ्के कृ, अङ्के पाल् (c. 10. पालयति -यितुं).

Fondled, *p. p.* लालितः -ता -तं, क्रोडीकृतः -ता -तं, भुजापीडितः -ता -तं.

Fondling, *s.* (Caressing) आलिङ्गनं, परिष्वङ्गः, लालनं, क्रोडीकरणं, अङ्कपाली -लिका -लिः *m.*, भुजापीडः.—(The person or thing fondled) प्रेमपात्रं, प्रेमभूमिः *f.*, अनुरागपात्रं.

Fondly, *adv.* सानुरागं, वात्सल्येन, अतिस्नेहेन, अतिप्रीतिपूर्वं.—(Foolishly) मूढवत्.

Fondness, *s.* स्नेहः, प्रीतिः *f.*, अनुरक्तिः *f.*, अनुरागः, प्रेम *n.* (न्), प्रियता, वात्सल्यं, वत्सलता, प्रणयः, अभिरुचिः *f.*, रुचिः *f.*, सन्तोषः.

Font, *s.* पूजाशालामध्ये जलसंस्कारकरणे प्रयुक्तः प्रस्तरमयो जलाधारः.—(Complete assortment of printing types of one size) समपरिमाणमुद्राक्षरपरिसंख्या.

Food, *s.* भोजनं, आहारः, भोज्यं, भक्ष्यं, खाद्यं, अन्नं, आद्यं, अदनं, खादनं,

आहार्य्यं, अभ्याहार्य्यं, आमिषं, जग्धिः *f.*, अशनं, भक्षणं, भक्ष्यं, खाद्यं, जेमनं, जमनं, अन्नः *n.* (स्), वल्भिः *m.*, निघसः, विघसः, ग्रासः, प्सानं, प्रत्यदनं, खाद्यः, देहयात्रा, जीवनकः, शरीरयात्रा, न्यादः, लेपः, लेहः; 'choice food,' परमान्नं, उत्तमान्नं, भोजनविशेषः; 'bad food,' कदन्नं; 'food and raiment,' ग्रासाच्छादनं, अन्नाच्छादनं, अशनाच्छादनं or -ने n. du., अन्नवस्त्रं, कशिपू m. du.; 'food of the gods,' अमृतं, पीयूषं, पेयूषं, सुधा, लेह्यं; 'to eat food,' आहारं कृ. Food is divided by the Hindús into five kinds, भक्ष्यं, भोज्यं, लेह्यं, चोष्यं, पेयं.

Fool, *s.* मूर्खः, मूढः, अज्ञः, निर्बुद्धिः *m.*, निर्बोधः, अबुद्धिः *m.* -द्धिमान् *m.* (त्), अबुधः, अप्राज्ञः, अविज्ञः, अविद्वान् *m.* (स्), प्रमूढः, प्रज्ञाहीनः, अज्ञानी *m.* (न्), जडः, जडमतिः *m.*, अल्पधीः *m.*, मन्दबुद्धिः *m.*, मन्दः, बर्बरः, कुक्कुटः, लटः.—(Buffoon, jester) विदूषकः, नर्म्मसचिवः, भण्डः.

To fool, *v. n.* खेला (nom. खेलायति), कुड् (c. 6. कुडति -डितुं), परिहासं कृ, लड् (c. 1. लडति -डितुं).

To fool, *v. a.* मुह् (c. 10. मोहयति -यितुं), सम्मुह्, वञ्च् (c. 10. वञ्चयते -यितुं), प्रलभ् (c. 1. -लभते -लब्धुं), छल् (c. 10. छलयति -यितुं).

Foolery, *s.* मूर्खकर्म्म *n.* (न्), मूर्खक्रिया, मूर्खता, बालकर्म्म *n.*, बालिश्यं.

Fool-hardiness, *s.* असमीक्ष्य साहसं, अविचारेण प्रगल्भता, अतिसाहसिकत्वं, धाष्टर्त्वं, अविमृश्यकारित्वं, अत्याहितं, दर्पः, प्रमत्तता.

Fool-hardy, *a.* असमीक्ष्य साहसी -सिनी -सि (न्), अविमृश्य प्रगल्भः -ल्भा -ल्भं, धाष्टर्ः -ष्टा -ष्टं, प्रमत्तवीरः -रा -रं, प्रमत्तशूरः -रा -रं.

Foolish, *a.* मूर्खः -र्खा -र्खं, मूढः -ढा -ढं, अज्ञः -ज्ञा -ज्ञं, अनभिज्ञः -ज्ञा -ज्ञं, निर्बुद्धिः -द्धिः -द्धि, निर्बोधः -धा -धं, अबुद्धिमान् -मती -मत् (त्), अप्राज्ञः -ज्ञा -ज्ञं, अल्पबुद्धिः &c., दुर्बुद्धिः &c., अल्पधीः -धीः -धि, बुद्धिहीनः -ना -नं, प्रज्ञाहीनः -ना -नं, दुर्मेधाः -धाः -धः (स्), दुर्मतिः -तिः -ति, अज्ञानः -ना -नं -नी -निनी -नि (न्), अकोविदः -दा -दं, बालिशः -शा -शं, बालिशमतिः -तिः -ति, अल्पधीः -धीः -धि, वैधेयः -यी -यं, असत्कृतः -ता -तं.

Foolishly, *adv.* मूर्खवत्, मूढवत्, अज्ञवत्, अज्ञानात्, मौर्ख्यात्, अल्पबुद्ध्या.

Foolishness, *s.* मूर्खता, मौर्ख्यं, मूढता, मौढ्यं, अज्ञता, अनभिज्ञता, निर्बुद्धित्वं, मोहः, बुद्धिहीनता, अबोधता, अज्ञानं, ज्ञानाभावः, बालिशता, बालिश्यं.

Foolscap, *s.* मूर्खशिरोवेष्टनसंज्ञकः कार्पासविशेषः or पत्रविशेषः.

Foot, *s.* (Part of the body) पादः, पदं, चरणं -णः, अंह्रिः *m.*, अङ्घ्रिः *m.*, अधमाङ्गं, लग्नः; 'both feet,' पादौ du., चरणौ du., चरणयुगं; 'point of the foot,' पादाग्रं, पदिकं; 'foot and knee,' पदष्ठीवं.—(Bottom, base) तलं, अधोभागः, अधःस्थानं, मूलं, उपस्थः; 'foot of a tree,' तरुतलं, वृक्षतलं, वृक्षाङ्घ्रिः *m.*, पादः; 'foot of a mountain,' उपत्यका, शैलोपशल्यं, पर्व्वततलं, गिरिपादः, पर्व्वताधोभागः.—(Measure) मनुष्यपादपरिमाणं, सार्द्धचतुरङ्गुलिपरिमाणं; 'ornament for the feet,' नूपुरः, पादाङ्गदं, चरणाभरणं, पादकटकः, तुलाकोटिः *f.*, मञ्जीरं; 'water for ablution of the feet,' पाद्यं, पादोदकं; 'to go on foot,' पद्भ्यां or पादाभ्यां व्रज् (c. 1. व्रजति -जितुं) or चर् (c. 1. चरति -रितुं); 'going on foot,' पादचारः; 'foot by foot,' पादशस्, पदे पदे, पच्छस्; 'at the foot,' पादतस्; 'to set on foot,' प्रवृत् (c. 10. -वर्त्तयति -यितुं); 'set on foot,' प्रवर्त्तितः -ता -तं, उपक्रान्तः -न्ता -न्तं.

To foot, *v. a.* (Kick) पादेन प्रहृ (c. 1. -हरति -हर्त्तुं) or आहन् (c. 2. -हन्ति -न्तुं), पादाघातं कृ.—(Tread) क्रम् (c. 1. क्रामति, क्रमितुं), चरणपातं कृ.

To foot it, *v. n.* नृत् (c. 4. नृत्यति, नर्त्तितुं), पादादि सञ्चल् in caus. (-चालयति -यितुं).

Foot-ball, *s.* वाताध्मातो गोचर्म्मगोलः यः सक्रीडमानजनपादाघातेन इतस्ततो विक्षिप्यते, पादाहतकन्दुकक्रीडा.

Foot-board, *s.* पादफलकं, चरणफलकं, पादकाष्ठं.

Foot-boy, *s.* बालसेवकः, युवसेवकः, बालभृत्यः, युवप्रेष्यः.

Foot-bridge, *s.* सङ्क्रमः, सङ्क्रामः, सङ्क्रमसेतुः *m.*, दुर्गसञ्चरः -सञ्चारः.

Footed, *p. p.* पादाहतः -ता -तं.—(Having feet) पादी -दिनी -दि (न्), पदी &c.

Foot-fall, *s.* पदपातः, पादपातः, चरणपातः, पदन्यासः, पदविष्टम्भः.—(Trip) स्खलनं.

Foot-fight, *s.* पादातियुद्धं, पदातियुद्धं, पदिकयुद्धं, पदगयुद्धं.

Foot-guard, *s.* पादातिकसैन्यः, पदातिकसैनिकः, पदगरक्षकः.

Footing, *s.* (Ground for the feet) पादन्यासस्थानं, पादनिक्षेपस्थानं, पदविष्टम्भस्थानं, पदं, स्थानं, भूमिः *f.*, स्थलं, आस्पदं, वर्त्म *n.* (न्), पदवी -विः *f.*, अयनं, सरणिः *f.*, वर्त्तनं; 'firm footing,' प्रतिष्ठानं; 'place with no firm footing,' अस्थानं.—(Basis, foundation) मूलं, उपष्टम्भः, तलं.—(Support) उपस्तम्भः, उपघ्नः, आश्रयः, अवलम्बनं. (Condition, position) अवस्था, स्थितिः *f.*, भावः, संस्थानं, वृत्तिः *f.*

Footless, *a.* पादहीनः -ना -नं, निष्पादः -दा -दं, चरणहीनः -ना -नं.

Foot-licker, *s.* पादसेवकः, चरणसेवकः, पदानुरागः, पीठमर्द्दः.

Foot-man, *s.* (Foot-soldier) पदातिः *m.* -तिकः, पादातिः *m.* -तिकः, पादातः, पदातः, पादात्, पत्तिः *m.*, पदगः, पद्गः, पदिकः, पादचारः -री *m.* (न्), पादाविकः, पदाजिः *m.*—(Running footman) जाङ्घिकः.—(Servant) सेवकः, प्रेष्यः, कुलसेवकः, परिचरः, किङ्करः.

Foot-mark, *s.* पादचिह्नं, पदचिह्नं, पदाङ्कः, पदपङ्क्तिः *f.*, पादमुद्रा, चरणपदवी, पदवी, पदं; 'of a horse,' खुरपदवी.

Foot-pace, *s.* पदपातः, पादगतिः *f.*, पदक्रमः, चरणक्रमः,

Foot-pad, *s.* मार्गस्थितचौरः, पादचारचौरः, परिपन्थी *m.* (न्), होडा *m.* (ढृ).

Foot-pan, *s.* पाद्यपात्रं, पाद्यभाजनं, पाद्याधारः, पादोदकपात्रं.

Foot-path, *s.* पदविः *f.* -वी, पदगपथः, पदिकमार्गः, पादचारयोग्यः क्षुद्रपथः.

Foot-soldier, *s.* पदातिः *m.*, पत्तिः *m.*, पदातिकसैन्यः, पादातिकयोद्धा *m.* (द्धृ). *See* Foot-man.

Foot-stalk, *s.* प्रसवबन्धनं, वृन्तं, मञ्जरी.

Foot-step, *s.* (Mark of the foot) पादचिह्नं, पदाङ्कः, पदपङ्क्तिः *f.*, पादमुद्रा, चरणपदवी.—(Tread) पदपातः, पादपातः, पादन्यासः, चरणपातः, पदविक्षेपः, पदविष्टम्भः.—(Course, track) पदविः -वी *f.*, अनुपदं, पद्धतिः *f.*, पथः, मार्गः, अयनं, वर्त्म *n.* (न्).—(Token) चिह्नं, लक्षणं.

Foot-stool, *s.* पादपीठं, चरणपीठं, पादासनं, पादपः, पदासनं.

Fop, *s.* दर्शनीयमानी *m.* (न्), दम्भी *m.* (न्), गर्व्वी *m.* (न्), आत्माभिमानी, रूपगर्व्वितः, सुवेशमानी *m.*, सुवेशिनम्मन्यः, छेकः.

Foppery, *s.* सुवेशमानिता, रूपमानिता, मूर्खता, मूर्खकर्म्म *n.* (न्).

Foppish, *a.* दम्भी -म्भिनी -म्भि (न्), वेशाभिमानी -निनी -नि (न्).

Foppishness, *s.* वेशाभिमानता, दम्भः, दाम्भिकत्वं, रूपगर्व्वितत्वं.

For, *conj.* (Because) यतस्, यत्, येन, यस्मात्, हि, इति हेतोः, तदर्थं, अनेन हेतुना. *See* Because.—(For as much as) यतस्, यत्, or expressed by the abl. c. of the abst. noun; as, 'for as much as he was a good man,' सज्जनत्वात्.

For, *prep.* (In exchange for) प्रति with abl. c., विनिमयेन; 'he exchanges beans for sesamum seed,' तिलेभ्यः प्रति माषान् ददाति; or expressed by the inst. c., as, तिलैर् माषान् परिवर्त्तयति; 'in exchange for one's life,' स्वप्राणविनिमयेन.—(Instead of, in place of) स्थाने, प्रति.—(Toward) प्रति, उद्दिश्य with acc. c.—(On account of, by reason of) अर्थं, अर्थे, हेतोः, हेतौ, कृते, निमित्ते, कारणात् all affixed to the crude; as, 'for this cause,' तदर्थं, or expressed by उद्दिश्य with acc. c., or by the abl. c.; as, 'for anger he did it,' कोपात् तत् कृतवान्; 'for want of money,' धनाभावात्.—(Conducive to) अर्थं, अर्थे, or expressed by the dat. c., as, 'for the good of the world,' भूतये भुवः; 'for one's own advantage,' आत्मविवृद्धये.—(For the sake of) अर्थं, अर्थे, हेतोः, कृते, or by dat. c., as, 'for the satisfying of hunger,' क्षुधाशान्तये; 'for thy enjoyment,' तव भोगाय.—(In order to obtain) अर्थं, अर्थे or by dat. c., as, 'for fame,' प्रतिपत्तये, or even by inst. c., as, 'for hire,' भाटकेन.—(In return for) प्रति, or more usually expressed by the indec. part.; as, 'for so doing,' तत् कृत्वा.—(During a certain time) यावत्, पर्य्यन्तं; 'for life,' पुरुषस्यायुर् यावत्, यावज्जीवं, जीवनपर्य्यन्तं, or by prefixing आ with abl. c., as, आमरणात्, आजीवनान्तात् (*i. e.* until death); 'lasting for life,' आमरणान्तिकः -का -कं; 'for three days,' दिनत्रयपर्य्यन्तं; 'for a hundred years,' वर्षशतं यावत्. Sometimes expressed by the acc. c., as, 'for one month,' एकं मासं; 'for two months,' द्वौ मासौ; 'for a hundred years,' वर्षशतं, or even by the instr. c., as, 'for twelve years,' द्वादशभिर् वर्षैर्; 'for a few days,' कतिपयदिवसैः; 'for a long time,' चिरकालं, अनेककालं, चिरात्, चिरेण, चिराय; 'food for a year,' वर्षोपभोग्यम् अन्नं.—(In proportion to, considering) अपेक्ष्य, उद्दिश्य, प्रतीक्ष्य, अवेक्ष्य, all with acc. c.—(On the part of) अपेक्ष्य, उद्दिश्य, कृते; 'as for me,' मामपेक्ष्य, मामुद्दिश्य, मत्कृते.—(On the side of) सपक्षः -क्षा -क्षं; 'he is for us,' अस्माकं सपक्षो भवति.—(Notwithstanding, for all that) तथापि.—(As if) वत् affixed, इव; 'he shewed himself for dead,' मृतवत् or मृतम् इव आत्मानम् अदर्शयत्.—(According to) यथा, अनुसारेण, अनुरूपेण; 'for one's ability,' यथाशक्ति. 'For,' may be expressed by the acc. c. in such phrases as 'looking for,' 'waiting for,' &c.; as, 'he looks for me,' माम् अपेक्षते, or by other cases; as, 'we depend on God for success,' ईश्वराधीना सिद्धिः; 'I have great affection for her,' तस्याम् अनुरागवान् अस्मि or तया सह महान् स्नेहः, or by गत, as, 'through love for him,' तद्गतेन अनुरागेण, or by the crude form, as, 'search for money,' धनान्वेषणं, or even by the affix सात्, as, 'he built a house for the Brahman,' गृहं चकार द्विजातिसात्.—(For the most part) प्रायेण, प्रायस्, प्रायशस्, भूयिष्ठं.

FORAGE, *s.* (Food for horses and cattle) अश्वादनं, गवादनं, अश्वादिभोजनं.—(Provisions) यात्रिकं, पाथेयं, खाद्यद्रव्यं, भोज्यं, भोजनसम्भारः.—(Search for food) खाद्यद्रव्यान्वेषणं; 'going to forage,' प्रसारः -रणं, प्रसरणं.

To FORAGE, *v. n.* परिभ्रमणं कृत्वा खाद्यद्रव्याणि or अश्वादनम् अन्विष् (c. 4. -इष्यति -एषितुं), प्रसारं or अवस्कन्दं or उपद्रवं कृत्वा धान्यादिभोज्यम् अपहृ (c. 1. -हरति -हर्तुं).

FORAGER, *s.* भोजनार्थं परिभ्रमणकारी *m.* (न्) or अवस्कन्दकारी or प्रसारी *m.* (न्), युद्धसमये खाद्यद्रव्यान्वेषी *m.* (न्), or अश्वादिभोजनार्थं धान्यादिहारकः.

FORAGING, *s.* भोजनान्वेषणार्थं परिभ्रमणं or प्रसारणं or प्रसरणं or अवस्कन्दः or उपद्रवः, युद्धसमये खाद्यद्रव्यान्वेषणं; 'foraging army,' प्रचक्रं.

FORAY, *s.* उपद्रवः, अवस्कन्दः, विप्लवः, लोप्त्रार्थम् उपप्लवः.

To FORBEAR, *v. a.* and *n.* (Cease from) निवृत् (c. 1. -वर्त्तते -र्त्तितुं), विरम् (c. 1. -रमति -रन्तुं).—(Delay, pause) विलम्ब् (c. 1. -लम्बते -म्बितुं), विरम्, आकालान्तरात् त्यज् (c. 1. त्यजति, त्यक्तुं).—(Avoid) वृज् (c. 10. वर्जयति -यितुं), परिहृ (c. 1. -हरति -हर्तुं).—(Be patient) सह् (c. 1. सहते, सोढुं), क्षम् (c. 1. क्षमते -मितुं, क्षन्तुं).

FORBEARANCE, *s.* (Çessation from, avoidance) निवृत्तिः *f.*, विनिवृत्तिः *f.*, सन्निवृत्तिः *f.*, विरतिः *f.*, विरामः, उपरतिः *f.*, वर्जनं, त्यागः, परिहारः.—(Patience) क्षमा, क्षान्तिः *f.*, तितिक्षा, सहनं, सहनशीलता, सहिष्णुता, मर्षः, परामर्षः, अपकारेऽपि चित्तस्याविकारः.—(Restraint) संयमः, यमः, यामः, संयामः, वियामः, वियमः, दमः.

FORBEARING, *a.* सहनशीलः -ला -लं, सहिष्णुः -ष्णुः -ष्णु, तितिक्षुः -क्षुः -क्षु, क्षमी -मिणी -मि (न्), संयामवान् -वती -वत् (त्).

To FORBID, *v. a.* (Prohibit) प्रतिषिध् (c. 1. -षेधति -षेद्धुं, c. 10. -षेधयति -यितुं), निषिध्, प्रत्याख्या (c. 2. -ख्याति -तुं), अन्तःख्या, परिभाष् (c. 1. -भाषते -षितुं), मैवं कुरु or मैवं कार्षीर् इति आज्ञा in caus. (-ज्ञापयति -यितुं) or आदिश् (c. 6. -दिशति -देष्टुं).—(Prevent) वृ in caus. (वारयति -यितुं), निवृ, निरुध् (c. 7. -रुणद्धि -रोद्धुं), बाध् (c. 1. बाधते -धितुं); 'heaven forbid!' इत्थं न भूयात्, एतादृशं न भवतु, शान्तं.

FORBIDDANCE, *s.* निषेधः, प्रतिषेधः, प्रतिषेधोक्तिः *f.*, प्रत्याख्यानं, वारणं, निवारणं, निरोधः, बाधः, बाधकता.

FORBIDDEN, *p. p.* निषिद्धः -द्धा -द्धं, प्रतिषिद्धः -द्धा -द्धं, निवारितः -ता -तं.

FORBIDDING, *a.* बीभत्सजनकः -का -कं, घृणोत्पादकः -का -कं, अनिष्टः -ष्टा -ष्टं.

FORCE, *s.* (Strength) बलं, शक्तिः *f.*, सामर्थ्यं, समर्थता.—(Energy might) तेजः *n.* (स्), वीर्य्यं, विक्रमः, पराक्रमः, ऊर्जः, शौर्य्यं.—(Violence) बलात्कारः, साहसं, प्रमाथः, प्रसभं.—(Momentum) वेगः, आपातः.—(Efficacy) प्रभावः, प्राबल्यं, गौरवं, सामर्थ्यं, प्रतापः.—(Validity) सिद्धिः *f.*, निष्पत्तिः *f.*; 'of force,' सिद्धः -द्धा -द्धं, निष्पन्नः -न्ना -न्नं; 'of no force,' असिद्धः -द्धा -द्धं, मोघः -घा -घं, निष्फलः -ला -लं; 'put in force,' प्रवर्त्तितः -ता -तं.—(Force of a word) शब्दशक्तिः *f.*, शब्दसामर्थ्यं -समर्थता, निरूढः, लक्षणा.—(Forces, troops) बलं, सैन्यं, सेना, सैन्याः *m. pl.*, अनीकं -कानि *n. pl.*, अनीकिनी, दण्डः; 'by force,' बलात्, बलेन, बलात्कारेण; 'taken by force,' बलाद्गृहीतः -ता -तं, बलहापहृतः -ता -तं.

To FORCE, *v. a.* (Compel). Expressed by the causal form usually in conjunction with बलात् or बलेन or बलात्कारेण or यत्नेन; as, 'to force a man to do any thing,' बलेन पुरुषं किञ्चित् कृ in caus. (कारयति -यितुं) or प्रवृत् in caus. (-वर्त्तयति -यितुं); 'to force to give,' दा in caus. (दापयति -यितुं); 'to force to go,' बलेन गम् in caus. (गमयति -यितुं).—(Impel, drive) प्रेर् (c. 10. प्रेरयति -यितुं), कृष् (c. 1. कर्षति, क्रष्टुं), समाकृष्, प्रणुद् (c. 6. -णुदति -णोत्तुं).—(Use force) बलात्कारं कृ, साहसं कृ, विक्रमं कृ, यत्नं कृ, प्रतियत्नं कृ.—(Force a town, storm) दुर्गं लङ्घ् (c. 10. लङ्घयति -यितुं) or भञ्ज् (c. 7. भनक्ति, भंक्तुं) or बलेन प्रविश् (c. 6. -विशति -वेष्टुं).—(Violate) धृष् (c. 10. धर्षयति -यितुं), बलात्कारेण अभिगम् (c. 1. -गच्छति -गन्तुं).—(Cause to produce fruit prematurely) प्राक्पूर्णकालात् फलोत्पत्तिं जन् (c. 10. जनयति -यितुं).

FORCED, *p. p.* (To do) बलात् कारितः -ता -तं.—(To pay) दापितः -ता -तं.—(Done by force) बलात्कृतः -ता -तं, बलात्कारितः -ता -तं, यत्नकृतः -ता -तं, यत्नपूर्णः -र्णा -र्णं.—(Strained, unnatural, affected)

क्लिष्टः -ष्टा -ष्टं, प्रतियत्नपूर्व्वः -र्व्वा -र्व्वं, विलक्षः -क्षा -क्षं, कृत्रिमः -मा -मं; 'a forced idea,' क्लिष्टकल्पना; 'a forced smile,' वैलक्ष्यस्मितं.

FORCEDLY, *adv.* बलात्, यत्नपूर्व्वं, प्रतियत्नपूर्व्वं, वैलक्ष्येण, सवैलक्ष्यं.

FORCEFUL, *a.* बलवान् -वती -वत् (त्), शक्तः -क्ता -क्तं, साहसी -सिनी -सि (न्).

FORCELESS, *a.* निर्बलः -ला -लं, शक्तिहीनः -ना -नं, अशक्तः -क्ता -क्तं.

FORCE-MEAT, *s.* वुस्तं, निस्तनी, मिष्टान्नं, उपस्करः, व्यञ्जनं.

FORCEPS, *s.* सन्दंशः -शकं -शका, खड्गधारा, शल्योद्धरणयन्त्रं.

FORCIBLE, *a.* (Powerful) प्रबलः -ला -लं, बलवान् -वती -वत् (त्), शक्तिमान् -मती -मत् (त्), समर्थः -र्था -र्थं, तेजोवान् -वती -वत् (त्), —(Efficacious) सप्रभावः -वा -वं, प्रभविष्णुः -ष्णुः -ष्णु, अमोघः -घा -घं, अव्यर्थः -र्था -र्थं.—(Impressive) निर्बन्धेन or दार्ढ्येन or गौरवेण or सगौरवम् उक्तः -क्ता -क्तं, तीक्ष्णः -क्ष्णा -क्ष्णं.—(Violent, done by force) साहसिकः -की -कं, बलेन कृतः -ता -तं; 'forcible entry,' बलप्रवेशः or बलात्प्रवेशः; 'forcible removal,' बलापकर्षः.

FORCIBLENESS, *s.* बलवत्त्वं, शक्तिमत्त्वं, प्राबल्यं, सामर्थ्यं, तैक्ष्ण्यं, गौरवं.

FORCIBLY, *adv.* बलात्, बलेन, बलात्कारेण, बलवत्, प्रसभं, प्रसह्य, अभिभूय, प्रमथ्य, बलापकर्षं, अवगृह्य.—(Impressively) निर्बन्धेन, दार्ढ्येन, गौरवेण, सगौरवं.

FORD, *s.* नदीतरस्थानं, नदीतरस्थलं, तरणस्थानं, उत्तरणस्थानं, ईषज्जलो नदीभागः, घट्टः.

To FORD, *v. a.* पद्भ्यां or पादाभ्यां or अश्वगजादिवाहनेन नदीम् ईषज्जलस्थाने तॄ (c. 1. तरति -रितुं -रीतुं) or नदीपारं तॄ.

FORDABLE, *a.* पद्भ्यां or पादाभ्यां or अश्वगजादिवाहनेन तार्य्यः -र्य्या -र्य्यं, सुतरः -रा -रं, पादस्पृश्यतलः -ला -लं, अल्पजलः -ला -लं.

FORDING, *s.* पद्भ्यां or पादाभ्यां or अश्वादिवाहनेन नदीतरणं or उत्तरणं.

FORE, *a.* पूर्व्वः -र्व्वा -र्व्वं, अग्रः -ग्रा -ग्रं, पूर्व्ववर्त्ती -र्त्तिनी -र्त्ति (न्), अग्रगामी -मिनी -मि (न्), पूर्व्वगतः -ता -तं; 'fore-part,' अग्रभागः, अग्रांशः; 'fore part of the thigh,' अग्रजङ्घा.

FORE, *adv.* पूर्व्वं, पूर्व्वे, अग्रे, अग्रतस्, पूर्व्वतस्, प्राक्; 'fore and aft,' नावोऽग्रभागात्प्रभृति पश्चिमभागपर्य्यन्तं.

To FORE-ADMONISH, *v. a.* अग्रे प्रबुध् (c. 10. -बोधयति -यितुं) or उपदिश् (c. 6. -दिशति -देष्टुं).

FORE-ARM, *s.* प्रकोष्ठः, प्रवेष्टः, कलाचिका, अग्रबाहुः *m.*, अग्रभुजः.

To FORE-ARM, *v. a.* अग्रे or पूर्व्वं सन्नह् (c. 4. -नह्यति -नद्धुं) or युद्धार्थं सज्जीकृ.

To FORE-BODE, *v. a.* अनिष्टघटनां पूर्व्वं सूच् (c. 10. सूचयति -यितुं) or अग्रे ज्ञा (c. 9. जानाति, ज्ञातुं) or प्रदृश् (c. 1. -पश्यति -द्रष्टुं), पूर्व्वलक्षणं दा, पूर्व्वचिह्नं दा, पूर्व्वलक्षणेन अनिष्टम् अनुमा (c. 2. -माति -तुं) or अवगम् (c. 1. -गच्छति -गन्तुं).

FOREBODER, *s.* अनिष्टसूचकः, अनिष्टप्रदर्शकः, पूर्व्वलक्षणज्ञः, पूर्व्वलिङ्गज्ञः, अग्रसूचकः.

FOREBODING, *s.* अनिष्टसूचनं -ना, अनिष्टप्रदर्शनं, पूर्व्वलक्षणाद् अनिष्टानुमानं.

To FORECAST, *v. a.* and *n.* अग्रे or पूर्व्वं चिन्त् (c. 10. चिन्तयति -यितुं) or प्रचिन्त् or निरूप् (c. 10. -रूपयति -यितुं) or उपायम् अनुसन्धा, (c. 3. -दधाति -धातुं), अग्रविवेचनां कृ, अग्रकल्पनां कृ.

FORECAST, *s.* अग्रचिन्तनं, अग्रनिरूपणं, पूर्व्वविवेचनं, पूर्व्वकल्पना, दीर्घदृष्टिः *f.*

FORECASTLE, *s.* नावः पूर्व्वभागः or अग्रभागः, अग्रकूपकपुरतो नौभागः.

To FORECLOSE, *v.* प्रतिबन्ध् (c. 9. -बध्नाति -बन्धुं), प्रतिषिध् (c. 1. -षेधति -षेद्धुं).—(Foreclose a mortgage) न्यासकारिण ऋणमोक्षणक्षमताम् अपनी (c. 1. -नयति -नेतुं).

FORECLOSURE, *s.* प्रतिबन्धनं, प्रतिषेधः, अवरोधनं, ऋणमोक्षणक्षमताहरणं.

FOREDECK, *s.* नौकापृष्ठस्य पूर्व्वभागः or अग्रभागः, पूर्व्वपृष्ठं, अग्रपृष्ठं.

To FORE-DETERMINE, *v. a.* अग्रे निश्चि (c. 5. -चिनोति -चेतुं) or निर्णी (c. 1. -णयति -णेतुं).

FORE-DETERMINED, *p. p.* पूर्व्वनिश्चितः -ता -तं, पूर्व्वनिर्णीतः -ता -तं, अग्रविचारितः -ता -तं.

To FOREDOOM, *v. a.* अग्रे or पूर्व्वं निर्दिश् (c. 6. -दिशति -देष्टुं) or प्रकॢप् (c. 10. -कल्पयति -यितुं) or विचर् in caus. (-चारयति -यितुं).

FOREFATHERS, *s. pl.* पूर्व्वाः *m. pl.*, पूर्व्वपुरुषाः *m. pl.*, पूर्व्वजाः *m. pl.*, पितृलोकः, पितरः *m. pl.*, पितृपितामहादि *n.*, वृद्धाः *m. pl.*; 'practice of forefathers,' वृद्धाचारः.

To FOREFEND, *v. a.* निवृ (c. 10. -वारयति -यितुं), प्रतिहन् (c. 2. -हन्ति -न्तुं), प्रतिकृ.

FOREFINGER, *s.* प्रदेशिनी, प्रदेशनी, देशिनी, देशी *m.* (न्), तर्ज्जनी, तरिता.

FOREFOOT, *s.* अश्वादिचतुष्पदजन्तूनां पूर्व्वपादः or सम्मुखीनपादः.

To FOREGO, *v. a.* अवसृज् (c. 6. -सृजति -स्रष्टुं), उत्सृज्, त्यज् (c. 1. त्यजति, त्यक्तुं), परित्यज्, हा (c. 3. जहाति, हातुं), उज्झ् (c. 6. उज्झति -ज्झितुं), प्रोज्झ्.

FOREGONE, *s.* त्यक्तः -क्ता -क्तं, परित्यक्तः -क्ता -क्तं, अवसृष्टः -ष्टा -ष्टं.

FOREGROUND, *s.* चित्रगतभूमेर् अग्रभागः or पूर्व्वभागः.

FOREHEAD, *s.* ललाटं, अलिकं, अलीकं, भालं, गोधिः *m.*, मुखः -खं, ललाटतटं, ललाटपट्टं, लकं, निटलं, गण्डशैलः, महाशङ्खः; 'having a high forehead.' उच्चललाटः -टा -टं; 'the open forehead,' ललाटफलकं.

FOREIGN, *a.* विदेशीयः -या -यं, वैदेशिकः -की -कं, विदेशी -शिनी -शि (न्), पारदेशिकः -की -कं, परदेशी -शिनी -शि (न्), विदेशजः -जा -जं, अन्यदेशीयः -या -यं, अन्यदेशजः -जा -जं, अन्यदेशोद्भवः -वा -वं, भिन्नदेशीयः -या -यं; 'a foreign country,' विदेशः, वहिर्देशः, देशान्तरं, अन्यदेशः.—(Extraneous) वहिर्भवः -वा -वं, वहिर्भूतः -ता -तं, वहिःस्थः -स्था -स्थं, वाह्यः -ह्या -ह्यं.—(Not pertaining) असम्बन्धी -न्धिनी -न्धि (न्), अनन्वितः -ता -तं, असम्पर्कीयः -या -यं.

FOREIGNER, *s.* विदेशी *m.* (न्), विदेशीयः, वैदेशिकः, परदेशी *m.* (न्), पारदेशिकः, पारदेश्यः, भिन्नदेशीयः, वहिर्देशजः, विदेशादागतः, देशान्तरादागतः, वहिर्देशोद्भवः, वैदेश्यः.

FOREIGNNESS, *s.* वाह्यत्वं, वहिर्भूतत्वं, दूरत्वं, असम्बन्धः, असम्पर्कः.

To FORE-IMAGINE, *v. a.* अग्रे मन् (c. 4. मन्यते, मन्तुं) or चिन्त् (c. 10. चिन्तयति -यितुं).

To FORE-JUDGE, *v. a.* अग्रे or पूर्व्वं विचर् (c. 10. -चारयति -यितुं) or निर्णी (c. 1. -णयति -णेतुं).

To FORE-KNOW, *v. a.* अग्रे or पूर्व्वं ज्ञा (c. 9. जानाति, ज्ञातुं) or विद् (c. 2. वेत्ति, वेदितुं) or निरूप् (c. 10. -रूपयति -यितुं) or बुध् (c. 4. बुध्यते, बोद्धुं), भविष्यद् ज्ञा, प्रवेक्ष् (c. 1. -ईक्षते -क्षितुं), प्रदृश् (c. 1. -पश्यति -द्रष्टुं), पूर्व्वं लक्ष्यीकृ.

FOREKNOWLEDGE, *s.* अग्रज्ञानं, पूर्व्वज्ञानं, अग्रनिरूपणं, भविष्यज्ज्ञानं, भाविज्ञानं, प्रवेक्षणं, प्रदर्शनं, पूर्व्वलक्ष्यं, अग्रदृष्टिः *f.*, पूर्व्वदृष्टिः *f.*

FOREKNOWN, *p. p.* पूर्व्वज्ञातः -ता -तं, अग्रज्ञातः -ता -तं, अग्रनिरूपितः -ता -तं.

FORELAND, *s.* अन्तरीपः -पं, समुद्रमध्ये महाद्वीपवहिःस्थो भूमिभागः, उदग्रभूमिः *f.*, उदग्रभूः *f.*, उदग्रस्थलं, महाद्वीपनासिका, समुद्रनासिका.

FORELOCK, *s.* ललाटरुहः -हं, ललाटजः -जं, केशपाशी, ललाटकेशः, मस्तकाग्रकेशः, मस्तकाग्ररुहः केशपाशः or केशपक्षः.

FOREMAN, *s.* (Of a jury) द्वादशप्रमाणपुरुषप्रधः, द्वादशमध्यस्थपुरुषमुख्यं, प्रधानमध्यस्थः, मुख्यप्रमाणपुरुषः.—(Superintendant) कार्य्याधिष्ठाता *m.* (तृ), अधिकर्म्मिकः, कार्य्याधीशः, कार्य्याध्यक्षः, कार्य्याधिकृतः, श्रेष्ठी *m.* (न्), कर्म्म कुर्व्वताम् अधिष्ठाता *m.*

FOREMAST, *s.* नौकाग्रस्थः कूपकः, नौकाग्रभागे गुणवृक्षकः, अग्रकूपकः.

FORE-MENTIONED, *a.* पूर्व्वोक्तः -क्ता -क्तं, पूर्व्वोदितः -ता -तं, प्रागुक्तः -क्ता -क्तं.

FOREMOST, *a.* अग्रः -ग्रा -ग्रं, मुख्यः -ख्या -ख्यं, प्रमुखः -खा -खं, अग्र्यः -ग्र्या -ग्र्यं, अग्रीयः -या -यं, प्राग्र्यः -ग्र्या -ग्र्यं, प्रधानः -ना -नं, प्रथमः -मा -मं, उत्तमः -मा -मं, उत्कृष्टः -ष्टा -ष्टं, श्रेष्ठः -ष्ठा -ष्ठं, सर्व्वश्रेष्ठः -ष्ठा -ष्ठं, सर्व्वाग्रस्थः -स्था -स्थं; 'first in rank,' प्रथमपदस्थः -स्था -स्थं.

FORENAMED, *a.* पूर्व्वोक्तः -क्ता -क्तं, पूर्व्वाभिहितः -ता -तं, पूर्व्वोदाहृतः -ता -तं.

FORENOON, *s.* पूर्व्वाह्नः, प्राह्णः, पूर्व्वाह्णकालः; 'in the forenoon,' प्राह्णे, पूर्व्वाह्णे, प्राह्णेतमां; 'relating to it,' प्राह्णेतनः -नी -नं, पूर्व्वाह्णेतनः -नी -नं.

FORENSIC, *a.* व्यावहारिकः -की -कं or व्यवहारिकः, व्यवहारी -रिणी -रि (न्), विचारसभासु व्यवहारितः -ता -तं, विचारस्थानसम्बन्धीयः -या -यं.

To FORE-ORDAIN, *v. a.* अग्रे or पूर्व्वं निरूप् (c. 10. -रूपयति -यितुं) or प्रक्लृप् (c. 10. -कल्पयति -यितुं) or निर्दिश् (c. 6. -दिशति -देष्टुं) or नियुज् (c. 7. -युनक्ति -योक्तुं) or विधा (c. 3. -दधाति -धातुं).

FORE-ORDAINED, *p. p.* अग्रनिरूपितः -ता -तं, पूर्व्वनिर्दिष्टः -ष्टा -ष्टं, पूर्व्वप्रकल्पितः -ता -तं.

FOREPART, *s.* अग्रभागः, पूर्व्वभागः, आदिभागः, प्रथमभागः, सम्मुखभागः.

FORERANK, *s.* अग्रपदं, प्रथमपदं, प्रधानपदं, मुख्यपदं, श्रेष्ठपदविः *f.*

To FORE-RUN, *v. a.* अग्रे or अग्रतः or पुरः or प्राक् सृ (c. 1. सरति, सर्त्तुं) or गम् (c. 1. गच्छति, गन्तुं) or या (c. 2. याति -तुं) or वृत् (c. 1. वर्त्तते -र्त्तितुं).

FORE-RUNNER, *s.* अग्रेसरः, अग्रसरः, अग्रगः -गामी *m.* (न्), पुरोगः -गामी *m.*, प्राग्गामी *m.*, अग्रवर्त्ती *m.* (न्), अग्रगतः, पूर्व्वपुरुषः.

FORESAID, *p. p.* पूर्व्वोक्तः -क्ता -क्तं, पूर्व्वोदितः -ता -तं, प्रागुक्तः -क्ता -क्तं.

FORESAIL, *s.* नौकाग्रस्थकूपकालम्बितं वायुवसनं or वातवसनं.

To FORESAY, *v. a.* अग्रे or पूर्व्वं वद् (c. 1. वदति -दितुं) or प्रवद्, भविष्यद् वद्.

To FORESEE, *v. a.* प्रदृश् (c. 1. -पश्यति -द्रष्टुं), उद्दृश्, प्रवेक्ष् for प्रावेक्ष् (c. 1. -ईक्षते -क्षितुं), अग्रे or पूर्व्वं दृश्, अनागतं or परिणामं or भविष्यद् दृश् or समीक्ष्, अग्रे ज्ञा (c. 9. जानाति, ज्ञातुं) or निरूप् (c. 10. -रूपयति -यितुं).

FORESEEING, *part.* प्रपश्यन् -श्यन्ती -श्यत् (त्), अग्रदर्शी -र्शिनी -र्शि (न्), अनागतदर्शी &c., पूर्व्वदर्शी &c., भविष्यद्दर्शी &c., दूरदर्शी &c., अन्तरज्ञः -ज्ञा -ज्ञं, प्रवेक्षन् &c. for प्रावेक्षन् &c.

FORESEEN, *p. p.* प्रवेक्षितः -ता -तं, प्रदृष्टः -ष्टा -ष्टं, सन्दृष्टः -ष्टा -ष्टं, सन्दृश्यमानः -ना -नं, अग्रनिरूपितः -ता -तं.

To FORESHADOW, *v. a.* पूर्व्ववर्णनं कृ, पूर्व्वमूर्त्तिं कृ, अग्रे रूप् (c. 10. रूपयति -यितुं).

To FORESHAME, *v. a.* लज्ज् in caus. (लज्जयति -यितुं), कलङ्क (nom. कलङ्कयति -यितुं).

FORE-SHIP, *s.* नावः पूर्व्वभागः or अग्रभागः, नौकाग्रभागः.

To FORESHORTEN, *v. a.* मूर्त्तिं चित्रसमर्पणात् सम्मुखभागे ह्रस् (c. 10. ह्रासयति -यितुं) or संहृ (c. 1. -हरति -हर्त्तुं) or संक्षिप् (c. 6. -क्षिपति -क्षेप्तुं).

To FORESHOW, *v. a.* प्रदृश् in caus. (-दर्शयति -यितुं), अग्रे or पूर्व्वं दृश or सूच् (c. 10. सूचयति -यितुं), भविष्यत् सूच् or वद् (c. 1. वदति -दितुं).

FORESHOWN, *p. p.* प्रदर्शितः -ता -तं, अग्रसूचितः -ता -तं, पूर्व्वसूचितः -ता -तं.

FORESIGHT, *s.* पूर्व्वदृष्टिः *f.*, अग्रदृष्टिः *f.*, प्रवेक्षणं, प्रदर्शनं, परिणामदृष्टिः *f.*, अग्रनिरूपणं, भविष्यद्दर्शनं, दूरदृष्टिः *f.*, दूरदर्शनं, दीर्घदृष्टिः *f.*, परिवेदना.

FORESKIRT, *s.* अग्रस्थो वस्त्राञ्चलः, परिधानस्य अग्राञ्चलः, अग्रतो वसनान्तं.

To FORESPEAK, *v. a.* अग्रे वद् (c. 1. वदति -दितुं), प्रवद्, प्रव्याहृ (c. 1. -हरति -हर्त्तुं).

FORESPENT, *a.* क्षीणबलः -ला -लं, श्रान्तः -न्ता -न्तं, खिन्नः -न्ना -न्नं.

FORESPOKEN, *a.* पूर्व्वोक्तः -क्ता -क्तं, पूर्व्वोदितः -ता -तं, प्रागुक्तः -क्ता -क्तं.

FOREST, *s.* अरण्यं -ण्यी -ण्यानी, वनं -नी, अटविः -वी *f.*, गहनं, गहः, काननं, विपिनं, जङ्गलः -लं, दावः, दवः, कान्तारः -रं, कुञ्जं, रिक्तं, तल्लं; 'forest on fire,' दावः, दावाग्निः *m.*, मुखाग्निः, मल्लिलुः.

FOREST, *a.* वन्यः -न्या -न्यं, आरण्यः -ण्यी -ण्यं -ण्यकः -का -कं, जङ्गलः -ला -लं, जाङ्गलः -ली -लं; 'produced in a forest,' वनोद्भवः -वा -वं, अरण्यजः -जा -जं -जातः -ता -तं, अरण्यभवः -वा -वं, अरण्योत्पन्नः -न्ना -न्नं, अरण्यसम्भवः -वा -वं, अरण्य or वन in comp.; as, 'a forest tree,' वनपादपः, अरण्यवृक्षः, वनराजिः *m.*, वनस्पतिः *m.*, वन्यतरुः *m.*

To FORESTALL, *v. a.* (Take beforehand) अग्रे or पूर्व्वं or पूर्व्वतो ग्रह् (c. 9. गृह्णाति, ग्रहीतुं) or आदा (c. 3. -दत्ते -दातुं), अग्रे गृहीत्वा निवृ (c. 10. -वारयति -यितुं) or निषिध् (c. 1. -षेधति -षेद्धुं).—(Buy beforehand) पूर्व्वं क्री (c. 9. क्रीणाति, क्रेतुं), पूर्व्वक्रयं कृ, प्रख्या (c. 2. -ख्याति -तुं).

FORESTALLED, *p. p.* पूर्व्वगृहीतः -ता -तं, पूर्व्वक्रीतः -ता -तं, प्रख्यातः -ता -तं.

FORESTALLER, *s.* पूर्व्वक्रेता *m.* (तृ), अग्रक्रयी *m.* (न्), सर्व्वपण्यानि विक्रयस्थानानयनात् पूर्व्वं क्रीत्वा मूल्यवर्षकः.

FORESTER, *s.* (Inhabitant of a forest) वनवासी *m.* (न्), अरण्यवासी *m.*, वनस्थायी *m.* (न्), वनस्थः, वनेचरः, वनचरः, वनचारी *m.* (न्), वनवर्त्ती *m.* (न्), वनौकाः *m.* (स्), अरण्यौकाः *m.* (स्), वनाश्रयः, वनव्यवहारी *m.* (न्), आरण्यकः, अरण्यसद् *m.*—(Overseer of the forests) अरण्याध्यक्षः, अरण्यरक्षकः.

FORETASTE, *s.* पूर्व्वभुक्तिः *f.*, अग्रभुक्तिः *f.*, पूर्व्वभोजनं, पूर्व्वास्वादनं, अग्रोपभोगः, पूर्व्वोपभोगः, पूर्व्वानुभवः, पूर्व्वज्ञानं, अग्रज्ञानं.

To FORETASTE, *v. a.* अग्रे or पूर्व्वं or अग्रतो भुज् (c. 7. भुंक्ते, भोक्तुं) or उपभुज् or अनुभू or आस्वाद् (c. 1. -स्वादति -दितुं), पूर्व्वभुक्तिं कृ, पूर्व्वस्वादनं कृ.

FORETASTED *p. p.* पूर्व्वभुक्तः -क्ता -क्तं, पूर्व्वास्वादितः -ता -तं, पूर्व्वानुभूतः -ता -तं.

To FORETELL, *v. a.* अग्रे or अग्रतः or पूर्व्वं वद् (c. 1. वदति -दितुं) or प्रवद्, भविष्यद् वद् or वच् (c. 2. वक्ति -क्तुं), प्रदृश् in caus. (-दर्शयति -यितुं) अग्रे दृश्, अनागतं ज्ञा in caus. (ज्ञापयति -यितुं).

FORETELLER, *s.* अग्रवादी *m.* (न्), भविष्यद्वक्ता *m.* (क्तृ), भविष्यद्वादी *m.*, भाविवक्ता *m.*, अनागतज्ञापकः, प्रदर्शकः, भाविदर्शकः, दैवज्ञः.

To FORETHINK, *v. a.* पूर्व्वं or अग्रे चिन्त् (c. 10. चिन्तयति -यितुं) or प्रचिन्त् or विमृश् (c. 6. -मृशति -म्रष्टुं) or निरूप् (c. 10. -रूपयति -यितुं), पूर्व्वविवेचनं कृ.

FORETHOUGHT, *s.* पूर्व्वचिन्ता, अग्रचिन्ता, पूर्व्वविवेचनं -ना, अग्रविवेचनं, पूर्व्वविचारणं -णा, अग्रनिरूपणं, पूर्व्वविमर्शः, प्रसमीक्षा, प्रवेक्षणं, पूर्व्वदृष्टिः *f.*, दीर्घदृष्टिः *f.*, परिणामदृष्टिः, परिवेदना.

To FORETOKEN, *v. a.* अग्रे or पूर्व्वं दृश् (c. 10. दर्शयति -यितुं) or सूच् (c. 10. सूचयति -यितुं), प्रदृश्, पूर्व्वलक्षणं or पूर्व्वचिह्नं दा, पूर्व्वलक्षणेन भविष्यत् सूच्.

FORETOKEN, *s.* पूर्व्वलक्षणं, पूर्व्वचिह्नं, पूर्व्वलिङ्गं, भाविलक्षणं, भाविचिह्नं, भविष्यल्लक्षणं, भविष्यल्लिङ्गं.

FORETOLD, *p. p.* पूर्व्वकथितः -ता -तं, प्रदर्शितः -ता -तं, प्राक्सम्भवादुक्तः -क्ता -क्तं.

FORE-TOOTH, *s.* अग्रदन्तः, राजदन्तः, सम्मुखदन्तः, मुख्यदन्तः.

FORETOP, *s.* मस्तकाग्रकेशः.—(Of a ship) कूपकाग्रे मञ्चकः.

FOR EVER, *adv.* नित्यं, सर्व्वकालं, अनन्तकालं, शाश्वतीः समाः.

FORE-WARD, *s.* सेनामुखं, ध्वजिनीमुखं, सेनाग्रं, रणमूर्द्धा *m.* (न्), शिरः *n.* (स्).

To FORE-WARN, *v. a.* अग्रे or पूर्व्वं बुध् (c. 10. बोधयति -यितुं) or प्रबुध् or प्रत्यादिश् (c. 6. -दिशति -देष्टुं) or उपदिश् or सन्दिश् or ज्ञा in caus. (ज्ञापयति -यितुं), पूर्व्वलक्षणं दा.

FORE-WARNED, *p. p.* पूर्व्वबोधितः -ता -तं, अग्रविज्ञापितः -ता -तं, पूर्व्वोपदिष्टः -ष्टा -ष्टं.

Fore-warning, *s.* अग्रप्रत्यादेशः, पूर्व्वबोधनं, पूर्व्वोपदेशः, पूर्व्वविज्ञप्तिः *f.*

To **forfeit**, *v. a.* दण्ड् in pass. (दण्ड्यते), दण्डं दा; 'he forfeits the eighth part of his property,' स्ववित्तस्य अष्टमांशं दण्ड्यते.—(Lose one's right) स्वाधिकारात् or स्वस्वत्वाद् भ्रंश् (c. 4. भ्रश्यति, भ्रंशितुं) or परिभ्रंश् or प्रभ्रंश् or च्यु (c. 1. च्यवते, च्योतुं) or प्रच्यु, हा in pass. (हीयते) with instr. or abl. c., प्रहा; 'he forfeits his right,' तस्मात् स्वत्वम् अपवर्त्तते; 'his kingdom,' राज्यात् प्रभ्रश्यति.

Forfeit, *s.* दण्डः, धनदण्डः, अर्थदण्डः, हारितं, विहापितं, निक्षेपः, न्यासः.

Forfeitable, *a.* दण्ड्यः -ण्ड्या -ण्ड्यं, दण्डनीयः -या -यं, हेयः -या -यं.

Forfeited, *p. p.* दण्डितः -ता -तं, भ्रष्टः -ष्टा -ष्टं, हीनः -ना -नं, च्युतः -ता -तं; 'one who has forfeited his right,' हृताधिकारः -रा -रं, च्युताधिकारः -रा -रं, अधिकाराद्भ्रष्टः -ष्टा -ष्टं; 'all his property,' सर्व्वस्वदण्डः -ण्डा -ण्डं, हृतसर्व्वस्वः -स्वा -स्वं; 'his kingdom,' राज्यात्प्रभ्रष्टः -ष्टा -ष्टं.

Forfeiture, *s.* हानिः *f.*, भ्रंशः, अपहारः, च्युतिः *f.*, नाशः, अपवर्त्तनं, वृद्धिः *f.*, दण्डदानं; 'of right,' स्वत्वहानिः *f.*, अधिकारहानिः, अधिकारभ्रंशः; 'of property,' वित्तहानिः *f.*, दायापवर्त्तनं.

Forge, *s.* कुटिलिका, उध्मानं, अग्निकुण्डं, ताम्रलोहघटनस्थानं, निर्म्माणस्थानं.

To **forge**, *v. a.* (Metals) ताम्रलोहादि मुद्गरादिना ताडयित्वा नानारूपेण घट् (c. 10. घटयति -यितुं) or कुटिलिकायां विलाप्य घट् or निर्म्मा (c. 2. -माति -तुं).—(Make) घट्, निर्म्मा, कॢप् (c. 10. कल्पयति -यितुं), विधा (c. 3. -दधाति -धातुं), विरच् (c. 10. -रचयति -यितुं).—(Counterfeit) छलेन or कपटेन कॢप् or निर्म्मा, कूटं कृ, कपटं कृ; 'forge a writing,' कपटलेख्यं कृ, कूटलेखं कृ.

Forged, *p. p.* (Fabricated) घटितः -ता -तं, कल्पितः -ता -तं, रचितः -ता -तं, निर्म्मितः -ता -तं.—(Counterfeit) काल्पनिकः -की -कं, कृत्रिमः -मा -मं, कपटी -टिनी -टि (न्), कूट or कपट in comp.; as, 'a forged document,' कपटलेख्यं, कूटलेखः; 'a forged decree,' कूटशासनं; 'forged coin,' कूटस्वर्णं.

Forger, *s.* कूटकः, कूटकृत् *m.* -कारः, कपटलेख्यकारी *m.* (न्), कूटलेख्यकारकः, कपटिकः, कपटकारी *m.*, कृत्रिमलेखकृत्.

Forgery, *s.* कूटकरणं, कपटकरणं, कपटलेख्यकरणं, कूटलेख्यकरणं, कृत्रिमलेखकरणं, कूटता.—(That which is counterfeited) कपटलेखः.

To **forget**, *v. a.* विस्मृ (c. 1. -स्मरति -ते -स्मर्त्तुं), न स्मृ, अपस्मृ, स्मृतेर् भ्रंश् (c. 4. भ्रश्यति, भ्रंशितुं) with nom. of thing forgotten, स्मृत्यपेतः -ता -तं भू, विस्मरणात् परित्यज् (c. 1. -त्यजति -त्यक्तुं), अवमर्षणं कृ.

Forgetful, *a.* विस्मरणशीलः -ला -लं, विस्मारकः -का -कं, नष्टसंस्मृतिः -तिः -ति, नष्टस्मृतिः -तिः -ति, अपस्मृतिः -तिः -ति, अनवहितः -ता -तं, प्रमत्तः -त्ता -त्तं.

Forgetfulness, *s.* विस्मृतिः *f.*, विस्मरणं, विस्मरणशीलता, अस्मृतिः *f.*, अस्मरणं, अपस्मारः, प्रस्मृतिः *f.*, स्मृतिभ्रंशः, स्मृतिहानिः *f.*, स्मृतिनाशः, भ्रमः.

Forging, *s.* घटनं -ना, निर्म्माणं, कल्पनं, रचना, कूटकरणं.

To **forgive**, *v. a.* क्षम् (c. 1. क्षमते -ति, क्षन्तुं), संक्षम्, मुच् (c. 6. मुञ्चति, मोक्तुं), विमुच्, अवसृज् (c. 6. -सृजति -स्रष्टुं), त्यज् (c. 1. त्यजति, त्यक्तुं), मृष् (c. 4. मृष्यति, मर्षितुं, मर्ष्टुं, c. 10. मर्षयति -यितुं), मृज् (c. 2. मार्ष्टि -र्ष्टुं), अनुज्ञा (c. 9. -जानाति -ज्ञातुं), समनुज्ञा, सह् (c. 1. सहते, सोढुं), निर्यत् (c. 10. -यातयति -यितुं); 'forgive injuries,' अपराधान् क्षम्; 'forgive sins,' पापानि मृज् or अवसृज्; 'forgive a debt,' ऋणं त्यज्.

Forgiven, *p. p.* क्षान्तः -न्ता -न्तं, दोषमुक्तः -क्ता -क्तं, पापमुक्तः -क्ता -क्तं, विमोचितः -ता -तं, अवसृष्टः -ष्टा -ष्टं, पापमार्ज्जितः -ता -तं.

Forgiveness, *s.* क्षमा, क्षान्तिः *f.*, पापमोचनं, पापमुक्तिः *f.*, दोषमुक्तिः *f.*, अपराधसहिष्णुता, पापमार्जनं, विमोचनं, कृपा, दया, मर्षणं; 'of a debt,' ऋणत्यागः.

Forgiving, *a.* क्षमी -मिणी -मि (न्), क्षमावान् -वती -वत् (त्), क्षमान्वितः -ता -तं, क्षमायुक्तः -क्ता -क्तं, अपराधसहिष्णुः -ष्णुः -ष्णु, दयालुः -लुः -लु, कृपालुः -लुः -लु.

Forgotten, *p. p.* विस्मृतः -ता -तं, अस्मृतः -ता -तं, स्मृतिभ्रष्टः -ष्टा -ष्टं, स्मृत्यपेतः -ता -तं, स्मरणगतः -ता -तं.

Fork, *s.* खाद्यमांसाद्युत्तोलनार्थं शूलविशेषः, कण्टकः; 'two-pronged,' द्विशिखशूलः, द्व्यग्रशूलः; 'three-pronged,' त्रिशिखशूलः, त्र्यग्रशूलः.

To **fork**, *v. n.* (Divide in two) द्विशिखः -खा -खं भू, द्विशिखारूपेण भिन्नीभू or विभिद् in pass. (-भिद्यते), द्विशिखीभू.

To **fork**, *v. a.* पूर्व्वोक्तशूलेन उत्तुल् (c. 10. -तोलयति -यितुं) or उत्क्षिप् (c. 6. -क्षिपति -क्षेप्तुं).

Forked, forky, *a.* द्विशिखः -खा -खं, द्व्यग्रः -ग्रा -ग्रं, वक्रः -क्रा -क्रं, कण्टकाकारः -रा -रं; 'having a forked tongue,' द्विजिह्वः -ह्वा -ह्वं, द्विरसनः -ना -नं; 'forked lightning,' विद्युल्लता, तडिल्लता, ध्रौत्रं.

Forlorn, *a.* गतिहीनः -ना -नं, अगतिकः -का -कं, अशरणः -णा -णं, निःशरणः -णा -णं, सहायहीनः -ना -नं, निःसहायः -या -यं, असहायः -या -यं, अनाथः -था -थं, निराश्रयः -या -यं, एकाकी -किनी -कि (न्), निरवलम्बः -म्बा -म्बं; 'on the forlorn hope,' त्यक्तजीवितः -ता -तं, त्यक्तप्राणः -णा -णं.

Form, *s.* (Shape) आकारः, आकृतिः *f.*, रूपं, मूर्त्तिः *f.*, संस्कारः, संस्थानं, धरिमा *m.* (न्), विग्रहः, वपुः *n.* (स्), वर्पः *n.* (स्); 'in the form of a man,' नररूपेण; 'of regular form,' आकारशुद्धः -द्धा -द्धं.—(Manner, fashion) प्रकारः, रीतिः *f.*, विधः, विधिः *m.*, मार्गः, विधानं, प्रकृतिः *f.*, भेदः.—(Established rule) विधिः *m.*, नियमः, स्थितिः *f.*, सूत्रं, धर्म्मः, मर्य्यादा, व्यवस्था, क्रमः, आचारः, चर्य्या, व्यवहारः.—(Method) क्रमः.—(Ceremony) नियमः, विधिः *m.* संस्कारः.—(Arrangement) विन्यासः, पर्य्यायः, प्रतिविधानं, विरचना.—(Long seat) दीर्घासनं, दीर्घपीठं, फलकं.—(Class of scholars) सहाध्यायिनां पंक्तिः *f.*, छात्रपदं.—(Bed of a hare) शशकशय्या, शशकासनं; 'in due form,' यथाविधि, यथावत्, विधिवत्, विधितस्.

To **form**, *v. a.* कृ (c. 8. करोति, कुरुते, कर्त्तुं), संस्कृ, अभिकृ, निर्म्मा (c. 2. -माति, c. 3. -मिमीते, c. 4. -मायते -मातुं), विनिर्म्मा, कॢप् (c. 10. कल्पयति -यितुं), सङ्कॢप्, विधा (c. 3. -दधाति -धातुं), रच् (c. 10. रचयति -यितुं), विरच्, घट् (c. 10. घटयति -यितुं); 'to form a plan,' उपायं प्रचिन्त् (c. 10. -चिन्तयति -यितुं) or मनसा कॢप्; 'to form in clots, as blood,' रक्तगुल्मान् बन्ध् (c. 9. बध्नाति, बन्धुं); 'to form an alliance,' सन्धा, सन्धिं कृ.

Formal, *a.* (Agreeable to established rule) नैयमिकः -की -कं, वैधिकः -की -कं, नियमानुसारी -रिणी -रि (न्), रीत्यनुसारी &c., व्यावहारिकः -की -कं.—(Strictly ceremonious) अत्याचारः -रा -रं, आचारसेवी -विनी -वि (न्), सभ्याचारनिष्ठः -ष्ठा -ष्ठं, नियमनिष्ठः -ष्ठा -ष्ठं, नियमशीलः -ला -लं.—(Exact) यथार्थः -र्था -र्थं, याथार्थिकः -की -कं, समञ्जसः -सा -सं.—(Constituent) वास्तवः -वी -वं.

Formalist, *s.* नियममात्रसेवी *m.* -विनी *f.* (न्), धर्म्मक्रियामात्रनिष्ठः *m.* -ष्ठा *f.*, धर्म्मकृत्यमात्रावलम्बी *m.* -म्बिनी *f.* (न्), यमान् अकुर्व्वाणो नियमान् केवलान् भजन् *m.* (त्).

Formality, *s.* (Observance of forms) नियममात्रसेवनं, धर्म्मक्रियामात्रनिष्ठा.—(Ceremoniousness) अत्याचारसेवनं, अत्यादरः, सभ्यरीतिनिष्ठा, एकान्ततः सभ्यनियमसेवनं; 'enough of this formality,' कृतं कृतम् आदरेण.

FORMALLY, *adv.* (According to established rule) विधिवत्, यथाविधि, नियमानुसारेण, रीत्यनुसारात्.—(Ceremoniously) सत्कारादरेण, सत्कारादरपूर्व्वं, आचाराचारसेवनात्, सभ्यनियमानुसारात्.

FORMATION, *s.* निर्म्माणं, निर्म्मितिः *f.*, रचना, विरचनं -ना, कल्पनं -ना, विधानं, करणं, घटनं, उत्पादनं, उत्पत्तिः *f.*, जननं, उद्भवः, सम्भवः, सृष्टिः *f.*, सर्ज्जनं.

FORMED, *p. p.* (Made) निर्म्मितः -ता -तं, रचितः -ता -तं, विरचितः -ता -तं, घटितः -ता -तं, कल्पितः -ता -तं, क्लृप्तः -प्ता -प्तं, कारितः -ता -तं, विहितः -ता -तं, उत्पादितः -ता -तं, सृष्टः -ष्टा -ष्टं, सम्भृतः -ता -तं, मयः -यी -यं in comp.; 'formed of wood,' काष्ठमयः -यी -यं, काष्ठनिर्म्मितः -ता -तं, काष्ठघटितः -ता -तं.—(Shaped) रूपी -पिणी -पि (न्), साकारः -रा -रं, आकार or आकृति in comp.; 'well-formed,' सुरूपः -पी -पं; 'formed like the moon,' चन्द्राकारः -रा -रं.

FORMER, *s.* (He that forms) कर्त्ता *m.* (र्तृ), कारकः, कारी *m.* (न्), निर्म्माता *m.* (तृ), विधायी *m.* (न्), रचकः, विरचकः, स्रष्टा *m.* (ष्टृ), उत्पादकः.

FORMER, *a.* (Before in time, preceding) पूर्व्वः -र्व्वा -र्व्वं, पौर्व्विकः -की -कं, पूर्व्वतनः -नी -नं, प्राक्तनः -नी -नं, प्रथमः -मा -मं, आद्यः -द्या -द्यं, अग्रः -ग्रा -ग्रं, प्राग्गामी -मिनी -मि (न्), प्राक् in comp.; as, 'former time,' प्राक्कालं, पूर्व्वकालं.—(Ancient, belonging to past time) प्राक्कालीनः -ना -नं, पूर्व्वकालीनः -ना -नं, गतकालीनः -ना -नं, अतीतकालीनः -ना -नं, अग्रकालीनः -ना -नं, प्राचीनः -ना -नं; 'former and latter,' पूर्व्वापरं; 'belonging to a former existence) पौर्व्वदेहिकः -की -कं.

FORMERLY, *adv.* पूर्व्वं, पूर्व्वे, पूर्व्वकाले, प्राक्काले, पूर्व्वतस्, पुरा, प्राक्, भूतपूर्व्वं, भूतकाले, अतीतकाले, गतकाले, अग्रे, पुरस्तात्, पुरस्; 'as formerly,' यथापूर्व्वं; 'done formerly,' पूर्व्वकृतः -ता -तं; 'formerly stated,' पूर्व्वोक्तः -क्ता -क्तं, पूर्व्वचोदितः -ता -तं; 'formerly seen,' पूर्व्वदृष्टः -ष्टा -ष्टं; 'formerly informed,' विज्ञापितपूर्व्वः -र्व्वा -र्व्वं.

FORMIDABLE, *a.* भयङ्करः -रा -रं, भयानकः -की -कं, भयावहः -हा -हं, त्रासकरः -री -रं, भीरुमयः -यी -यं, भयजनकः -का -कं, भयदः -दा -दं, शङ्काकरः -रा -रं, प्रतिभयः -या -यं, भीषणः -णा -णं, भैरवः -वी -वं, दारुणः -णा -णं.

FORMIDABLENESS, *s.* भयानकत्वं, भयजनकता, भीषणता, दारुण्यं.

FORMIDABLY, *adv.* भयानकं, दारुणं, भैरवं, भयङ्करप्रकारेण.

FORMLESS, *a.* अरूपः -पी -पं -पी -पिणी -पि (न्), नीरूपः -पा -पं, अनाकारः -रा -रं, निराकारः -रा -रं, निराकृतिः -तिः -ति, आकृतिहीनः -ना -नं, अमूर्त्तः -र्त्ता -र्त्तं.

FORMULA, FORMULARY, FORMULE, *s.* (Prescribed rule) विधिः *m.*, सूत्रं, नियमः, रीतिः *f.*, व्यवस्था, स्थितिः *f.*, विधः -धा -धानं; 'book of forms,' विधिग्रन्थः, नियमग्रन्थः, सूत्रग्रन्थः.

To FORNICATE, *v. n.* वेश्यां गम् (c. 1. गच्छति, गन्तुं) or अभिगम् or सेव् (c. 1. सेवते -वितुं), व्यभिचर् (c. 1. -चरति -रितुं), व्युच्चर्, पण्यस्त्रीभिः सह सम्भोगं कृ.

FORNICATION, *s.* वेश्यागमनं, वेश्यासेवा, पण्यस्त्र्यभिगमनं, स्त्रीसेवा, पण्यस्त्रीसम्भोगः, व्यभिचारः, व्यभिचारकर्म्म *n.* (न्), जारकर्म्म *n.*, लम्पटता.

FORNICATOR, *s.* वेश्यागामी *m.* (न्), गणिकासेवी *m.* (न्), पण्यस्त्रीसम्भोगी, व्यभिचारी *m.* (न्), लम्पटः.

FORNICATRESS, *s.* पुंश्चली, पुरुषगामिनी, परपुरुषगामिनी, व्यभिचारिणी, बन्धकी, अभिसारिका, निशाचरी.

To FORSAKE, *v. a.* त्यज् (c. 1. त्यजति, त्यक्तुं), परित्यज्, सन्त्यज्, हा (c. 3. जहाति, हातुं), अपहा, विहा, प्रहा, अपाहा, उत्सृज् (c. 6. -सृजति -स्रष्टुं), विसृज्, अतिसृज्, व्यपसृज्, रह् (c. 10. रहयति -यितुं), विरह्, उज्झ् (c. 6. उज्झति -ज्झितुं), प्रोज्झ्, परिहृ (c. 1. -हरति -हर्त्तुं).

FORSAKEN, *p. p.* त्यक्तः -क्ता -क्तं, परित्यक्तः -क्ता -क्तं, उत्सृष्टः -ष्टा -ष्टं, विसर्ज्जितः -ता -तं, रहितः -ता -तं, विरहितः -ता -तं, प्रोज्झितः -ता -तं.

FORSAKER, *s.* त्यागी *m.* (न्), त्यक्ता *m.* (क्तृ), परित्यागी *m.* (न्).

FORSAKING, *s.* त्यागः, परित्यागः, उत्सर्गः, प्रोज्झनं, विसर्ज्जनं, विरहः.

FORSOOTH, *s.* नाम, किल, सत्यं, सत्यमेव, नूनं, खलु, अवश्यं.

To FORSWEAR, *v. a.* (Renounce with oath) शपथेन or शपथपूर्व्वं त्यज् (c. 1. त्यजति, त्यक्तुं) or प्रत्याख्या (c. 2. -ख्याति -तुं) or निह्नु (c. 2. -ह्नुते -ह्नोतुं).

To FORSWEAR, *v. n.* (Swear falsely) मिथ्याशपथं कृ, मृषा शपथं कृ, मिथ्या शप् (c. 1. शपति -ते, c. 4. शप्यति, शप्तुं), असत्यं शपथं कृ, मिथ्यादिव्यं कृ.

FORSWEARER, *s.* (One that renounces on oath) शपथपूर्व्वं त्यागी *m.* (न्).—(False swearer) मिथ्याशपथकारी *m.* (न्).

FORSWORN, *p. p.* (Renounced on oath) शपथपूर्व्वं त्यक्तः -क्ता -क्तं or परित्यक्तः -क्ता -क्तं.—(Perjured) असत्यशपथः -था -थं.

FORT, *s.* (Fortified place) दुर्गं, कोट्टिः *f.*, कोटः, कूटः, कुटः, शिखरी *m.* (न्), गुल्मः, मन्थरः.

FORTE, *s.* (Strong point) अग्रगुणः, उत्कृष्टगुणः, श्रेष्ठगुणः.

FORTH, *s.* (A way) मार्गः, पथः, वर्त्म *n.* (न्), अयनं.

FORTH, *adv.* (Forward, out). Expressed by अग्रे, प्रकाशं, प्र, निर्, बहिस्, उत्; as, 'to go forth,' निर्गम् (c. 1. -गच्छति -गन्तुं), बहिर्गम्; 'call forth,' प्रवृत् (c. 10. -वर्त्तयति -यितुं), प्रोत्सह् (c. 10. -साहयति -यितुं); 'set forth,' प्रकाश् (c. 10. -काशयति -यितुं), प्रादुष्कृ, प्रकटीकृ, निर्दिश् (c. 6. -दिशति -देष्टुं); 'draw forth,' निष्कृष् (c. 1. -कर्षति -क्रष्टुं), उत्कृष्, निःसृ in caus. (-सारयति -यितुं); 'burst forth,' उद्भिद् (c. 7. -भिनत्ति -भेत्तुं), प्रोद्भिद्.—(From that time forth) तदाप्रभृति, ततःप्रभृति, तत्कालादारभ्य, तद्दिनादारभ्य; 'from this time forth,' अद्यप्रभृति, अद्यारभ्य, अद्यावधि.

FORTH, *prep.* निर्, बहिस्, प्र, उत्; 'going forth,' निर्याणं, प्रयाणं, बहिर्गमनं, प्रस्थानं.

FORTHCOMING, *a.* आगामी -मिनी -मि (न्), आगमनार्हः -र्हा -र्हं, उपस्थायी -यिनी -यि (न्).

FORTHWITH, *s.* सद्यस्, अचिरात्, अचिरेण, सपदि, झटिति, तदनन्तरं, अतःपरं, अनन्तरं, ततस्, तत्क्षणात्, आशु, क्षिप्रं, अविलम्बितं, तत्काले.

FORTIETH, *a.* चत्वारिंशः -शी -शं, चत्वारिंशत्तमः -मा -मं.

FORTIFICATION, *s.* (The act) दुर्गकरणं, परिखाप्राचीरादिनिर्म्माणं, परिक्रिया.—(The works themselves) दुर्गं, प्राचीरं, परिखा, नगरपरिगतं परिखाप्राचीरादि, परिकूटं, गुप्तिः *f.*, कुटः, कूटः, कोटः.

FORTIFIED, *p. p.* परिखाप्राचीरादिवेष्टितः -ता -तं, प्राचीरावृतः -ता -तं, गुप्तः -प्ता -प्तं, सन्नद्धः -द्धा -द्धं, दृढीकृतः -ता -तं; 'a fortified city,' दुर्गपुरं, दुर्गनगरं, प्राचीरावृतं नगरं.

FORTIFIER, *s.* दुर्गकारी *m.* (न्), प्राचीरकर्त्ता *m.* (र्तृ), संस्तम्भकः.

To FORTIFY, *v. a.* (Surround with a wall, ditch, &c.) परिखाप्राचीरादिना परिवेष्ट् (c. 10. -वेष्टयति -यितुं) or परिवृ (c. 5. -वृणोति -वरितुं -रीतुं), दुर्गं कृ.—(Confirm, strengthen) दृढीकृ, स्थिरीकृ, संस्तम्भ् (c. 5. -स्तभ्नोति -स्तम्भितुं).

FORTIORI A. (Argument) दण्डापूपन्यायेन वितर्कः.

FORTITUDE, *s.* स्थैर्य्यं, धैर्य्यं, धीरत्वं, धृतिः *f.*, स्थिरता, मनःस्थैर्य्यं, चित्तस्य स्थैर्य्यं, वीर्य्यं, वीरता, शौर्य्यं, शूरता, साहसं, पौरुषं, निर्भयता.

Fortnight, *s.* पक्षः, द्विसप्ताहः, मासार्द्धं, अर्द्धमासः.

Fortress, *s.* दुर्गं, कोटिः *f.*, कोटः, कूटः, कुटः, शिखरी *m.* (न्), गुल्मः, मन्थरः ; 'governor of a fortress,' दुर्गाधिकारी *m.* (न्), दुर्गाध्यक्षः, कोटिपालः.

Fortuitous, *a.* आकस्मिकः -की -कं, दैविकः -की -कं, दैवाधीनः -ना -नं, दैवायत्तः -त्ता -त्तं, आपतिकः -की -कं, अदृष्टः -ष्टा -ष्टं, अचिन्तितः -ता -तं, अकस्माद्घटितः -ता -तं, अकस्मादुत्पन्नः -न्ना -न्नं.

Fortuitously, *adv.* अकस्मात्, दैवात्, दैवयोगात्, दैववशात्, अदृष्टवशात्.

Fortuity, *s.* दैवयोगः, दैवं, दैवाधीनता, अदृष्टं, आकस्मिकत्वं.

Fortunate, *a.* सौभाग्यवान् -वती -वत् (त्) or भाग्यवान्, धन्यः -न्या -न्यं, पुण्यवान् -वती -वत् (त्), शर्म्मवान् &c., श्रीमान् -मती -मत् (त्), मङ्गलः -ला -लं, कल्याणः -णा -णं -णी -णिनी -णि (न्), शुभः -भा -भं, कुशलः -ला -लं, कुशलशाली -लिनी -लि (न्), सुखभागी -गिनी -गि (न्), महाभागः -गा -गं, सुभगः -गा -गं, सुकृती -तिनी -ति (न्), लक्ष्मीवान् &c., श्रीयुक्तः -क्ता -क्तं, भद्रः -द्रा -द्रं, शिवः -वा -वं.

Fortunately, *adv.* सौभाग्येन -ग्यात्, कल्याणात्, कौशल्यात्, माङ्गल्येन, दिष्ट्या, श्रिया, सुभगं.

Fortunateness, *s.* सौभाग्यवत्त्वं, पुण्यवत्त्वं, धन्यता, कल्याणता, माङ्गल्यं.

Fortune, *s.* (Goddess) लक्ष्मीः, श्रीः.—(Chance, destiny) दैवं, भाग्यं, भागधेयं, भवितव्यता, दैवयोगः, दैवदशा, अदृष्टं, कृतान्तः, नियतिः *f.*, विधिः *m.*, गतिः *f.*, दैविकं, दिष्टं, रिष्टं, कालनियोगः.—(Good fortune) सौभाग्यं, कल्याणं, भद्रं, शुभं, शिवं, मङ्गलं, माङ्गल्यं, कुशलं -लता, कौशल्यं, श्रीः, लक्ष्मीः, सम्पत्तिः *f.*, सम्पद् *f.*, शर्म्म *n.* (न्), भयः, पुण्योदयः ; 'bad fortune,' दुर्भाग्यं, दुर्दैवं.

To fortune, *v. n.* दैवाद् घट् (c. 1. घटते -टितुं) or सम्पद् (c. 4. -पद्यते -पत्तुं),

Fortune-hunter, *s.* विवाहार्थं धनवतीं स्त्रीम् अन्विष्यति यो जनः.

Fortune-teller, *s.* दैवज्ञः -ज्ञा, विप्रश्निका, गणकः -की, मङ्गलादेशवृत्तः, मङ्गलामङ्गलादेशी *m.* (न्), आदेशी *m.*, शुभाशुभदर्शनाजीवः, कार्तान्तिकः.

Fortune-telling, *s.* दैवप्रश्नः, शुभाशुभदर्शनं, मङ्गलादेशः, जातकं.

Forty, *s.* चत्वारिंशत् *f.* sing. ; 'forty-one,' एकचत्वारिंशत् ; 'forty-two,' द्वाचत्वारिंशत् ; 'forty-three,' त्रयश्चत्वारिंशत् ; 'forty-four,' चतुश्चत्वारिंशत्.

Forward, *a.* (At the fore-part) अग्रस्थः -स्था -स्थं, सम्मुखस्थः -स्था -स्थं, सम्मुखीनः -ना -नं, प्रष्ठः -ष्ठा -ष्ठं.—(Prompt, eager) उद्युक्तः -क्ता -क्तं, उद्यतः -ता -तं, प्रत्युत्पन्नः -न्ना -न्नं, अविलम्बः -म्बा -म्बं, प्रस्तुतः -ता -तं, व्यग्रः -ग्रा -ग्रं, प्रगल्भः -ल्भा -ल्भं, प्रचण्डः -ण्डा -ण्डं.—(Bold) निर्लज्जः -ज्जा -ज्जं, प्रगल्भः -ल्भा -ल्भं, सप्रतिभः -भा -भं, प्रतिभानवान् -वती -वत् (त्).—(Before its time) अपूर्णकालः -ला -लं, आकालिकः -की -कं, आकालभवः -वा -वं, प्राक्पूर्णकालात् पक्वः -क्वा -क्वं.—(Advanced in learning) कृतागमः -मा -मं, कृतविद्यागमः -मा -मं.—(Anterior) अग्र्यः -ग्र्या -ग्र्यं.

Forward, *adv.* (In front) अग्रं, अग्रतस्, पुरस्, पुरतस्, पुरस्तात्, अभितस्, अभिमुखं, प्रतिमुखं, सम्मुखं, or expressed by प्र or आ ; 'going forward,' प्रगमनं, प्रस्थानं, अग्रगमनं ; 'to go forward and backward,' प्रतिगतागतं कृ, गतागतं कृ, गमनागमने कृ, यातायातं कृ ; 'from this day forward,' अद्यारभ्य, अद्यप्रभृति, अधुनारभ्य, अद्यावधि.

To forward, *v. a.* (Advance, promote) पुरस्कृ, उपकृ, साहाय्यं कृ, सहायत्वं कृ, प्रयुज् (c. 10. -योजयति -यितुं), उद्युज्, प्रवृध् (c. 10. -वर्धयति -यितुं), प्रवृत् (c. 10. -वर्त्तयति -यितुं), उद्योगं कृ.—(Accelerate) त्वर् in caus. (त्वरयति -यितुं), सन्त्वर्. —(Send forward) प्रेर् (c. 10. -ईरयति -यितुं), पुरस्कृ.

Forwarded, *p. p.* पुरस्कृतः -ता -तं, प्रेरितः -ता -तं, सञ्चारितः -ता -तं.

Forwardness, *s.* (Promptness) प्रत्युत्पन्नता, उद्योगः, उद्यमः, उत्साहः, उद्युक्तता, सयत्नता, प्रवृत्तिः *f.*, अविलम्बः.—(Eagerness) प्रचण्डता, व्यग्रता, तीक्ष्णता.—(Boldness) प्रगल्भता, प्रागल्भ्यं, निर्लज्जत्वं, प्रतिभा -भानं.—(Advance before the usual time) प्राक्पूर्णकालात् पक्वता.—(In learning, &c.) विद्यागमः, आगमः.

Fosse, *s.* परिखा, खातं -तकं, खातभूः *f.*, खेयं, अखातं, अवटः.

Fossil, *s.* धातुः *m.*, धातुद्रव्यं, उपधातुः *m.*, शिलाजं, शिलाभवं, शिलोत्पन्नं, शिलोद्भवं, उत्खातद्रव्यं, प्रस्तरः.

Fossil, *a.* शिलाजः -जा -जं, शिलोद्भवः -वा -वं, उत्खातः -ता -तं.

Fossilist, *s.* शिलाजद्रव्यगुणधर्म्मादितत्त्वज्ञः, धातुविद्याज्ञः.

To foster, *v. a.* पुष् (c. 1. पोषति, c. 9. पुष्णाति, पोषितुं, c. 10. पोषयति -यितुं), परिपुष्, पाल् (c. 10. पालयति -यितुं), प्रतिपाल्, वृध् in caus. (वर्धयति -यितुं), संवृध्, प्रवृध्, भृ (c. 1. भरति -ते, भर्त्तुं), अनुग्रह् (c. 9. -गृह्णाति -ग्रहीतुं), लल् (c. 10. लालयति -यितुं), तेजो वृध्, उपकृ.

Foster-brother, *s.* धात्रीपुत्रः, एकस्तनपायी भ्राता *m.* (तृ).

Foster-child, *s.* पोष्यपुत्रः -त्री, परिस्कन्नः -स्कन्दः, परिष्कन्दः -ष्कन्नः, परभृतः -ता.

Foster-dam, *s.* धात्री, धात्रेयिका, प्रतिपालिका, अङ्कपाली.

Foster-earth, *s.* धात्री मृत्तिका, पोषणभूमिः *f.*, प्रतिपालकभूमिः *f.*

Foster-father, *s.* धाता *m.* (तृ), पालकपिता *m.* (तृ), प्रतिपालकः, अन्नदाता *m.* (तृ).

Foster-mother, *s.* धात्री, धात्रेयिका, पयुः *f.*, अङ्कपाली, मातृका.

Foster-sister, *s.* धात्रेयिका, धात्रेयी, एकस्तनपायिनी स्वसा *f.* (सृ).

Foster-son, *s.* पोष्यपुत्रः, पोष्यसुतः, पोष्यसन्तानः, परिस्कन्नः.

Fostered, *p. p.* पोषितः -ता -तं, पुष्टः -ष्टा -ष्टं, पालितः -ता -तं, प्रतिपालितः -ता -तं, वर्धितः -ता -तं, संवर्धितः -ता -तं, भर्त्रिमः -मा -मं—(By another) परभृतः -ता -तं, परपुष्टः -ष्टा -ष्टं, अन्यवर्धितः -ता -तं.

Fosterer, *s.* पालकः, प्रतिपालकः, पालयिता *m.* (तृ), पोषकः, पोष्टा *m.* (ष्टृ).

Foul, *a.* (Filthy, impure) मलिनः -ना -नं, समलः -ला -लं, मलवान् -वती -वत् (त्), मलीमसः -सा -सं, मलीयान् -यसी -यः (स्), मलदूषितः -ता -तं, कलुषः -षा -षं -षी -षिणी -षि (न्), अमेध्यः -ध्या -ध्यं, कुत्सितः -ता -तं, कश्मलः -ला -लं, आविलः -ला -लं, अपवित्रः -त्रा -त्रं, अशुद्धः -द्धा -द्धं.—(Muddy) मलपङ्की -ङ्किनी -ङ्कि (न्), पङ्किलः -ला -लं, कार्द्दमः -मी -मं.—(Detestable) गर्हितः -ता -तं, गर्ह्यः -र्ह्या -र्ह्यं.—(Wicked) दुष्टः -ष्टा -ष्टं.—(Obscene) अवाच्यः -च्या -च्यं.—(Unfair) कूटकः -का -कं, विषमः -मा -मं, कूट in comp. ; 'foul play,' कूटता.—(Unfavourable) अननुकूलः -ला -लं.—(Foul weather) दुर्द्दिनं.—(Foul air) पूतिवातः ; 'foul smell,' पूतिगन्धः ; 'to fall foul of each other,' प्रतिमुखम् आगत्य परस्परं शरीरसमाघातं कृ.

To foul, *v. a.* मलिन (nom. मलिनयति -यितुं), दुष् in caus. (दूषयति -यितुं), कलुष (nom. कलुषयति -यितुं), आविल (nom. आविलयति -यितुं), समलीकृ.

Foul-feeding, *a.* मलभुक् *m. f. n.*, मलभोजी -जिनी -जि (न्), कुत्सिताहारभुक्.

Foully, *adv.* मलिनं, समलं, अमेध्यं, कुत्सितं, गर्हितं, अतिदुष्टं.

Foul-mouthed, *a.* दुर्मुखः -खी -खं, वाग्दुष्टः -ष्टा -ष्टं, मुखरः -रा -रं, अबद्धमुखः -खा -खं, मुखशफः -फा -फं, मुखशीलः -ला -लं, कटुभाषी -षिणी -षि (न्).

Foulness, *s.* मालिन्यं, समलता, मलवत्त्वं, कलुषत्वं, कालुष्यं, अमेध्यता -त्वं, अशुद्धता, अपवित्रत्वं, अशुचित्वं, कुत्सितत्वं, गर्ह्यता, पूतित्वं.

Found, *p. p.* आसादितः -ता -तं, समासादितः -ता -तं, अधिगतः -ता -तं, प्राप्तः -प्ता -प्तं, प्रपन्नः -न्ना -न्नं, निरूपितः -ता -तं ; 'having found,' आसाद्य.

To FOUND, *v. a.* (Lay the foundation) मूलं न्यस् (c. 4. -न्यस्यति -न्यसितुं) or धा (c. 3. दधाति, धातुं) or रुह् in caus. (रोपयति -यितुं). —(Build) निर्मा (c. 2. -माति -तुं or in caus. मापयति -यितुं), कृ in caus. (कारयति -यितुं).—(Establish) स्था in caus. (स्थापयति -यितुं), प्रतिष्ठा, व्यवस्था, संस्था, रुह् in caus., प्रतिनिधा.

FOUNDATION, *s.* (Of a house) भित्तिमूलं, भित्तिः *f.*, गृहभूमिः *f.*, वेश्मभूः *f.*, वास्तुः *m.* -स्तु *n.*, गृहपोतकः, पोतः, पोटः, कुट्टिमं, सुतलः, तलिमं, गृहप्रतिष्ठा.—(Basis of any thing) मूलं, वस्तु *n.*, उपष्टम्भः, अधोभागः. —(Endowment) प्रतिष्ठा; 'to lay the foundation of a house,' इष्टकान्यासं कृ, भित्तिन्यासं कृ.

FOUNDED, *p. p.* प्रतिष्ठापितः -ता -तं, रोपितः -ता -तं, न्यस्तमूलः -ला -लं, स्थापितः -ता -तं, निर्म्मितः -ता -तं, मूलः -ला -लं; as, 'founded on knowledge,' ज्ञानमूलः -ला -लं.

FOUNDER, *s.* स्थापकः, प्रथमस्थापकः, प्रतिष्ठापकः, निर्म्माता *m.* (तृ), प्रयोजकः, प्रवर्त्तकः, आरम्भकः, आदिकर्त्ता *m.* (र्तृ); 'of a religion,' प्रवर्त्तकाचार्य्यः.—(Caster of metals) व्योकारः.

To FOUNDER, *v. n.* समुद्रमध्ये जलाविष्टत्वाद् मज्ज् (c. 6. मज्जति -ज्जितुं).

FOUNDERED, *p. p.* समुद्रमध्ये जलाविष्टत्वात् प्रमग्नः -ग्ना -ग्नं or मग्नः.

FOUNDERY, FOUNDRY, *s.* सन्धानी, कुप्यशाला, लोहादिविलयनशाला.

FOUNDLING, *s.* त्यक्तबालकः, उज्झितबालकः, मातृपितृविरहितो बालः, उत्सृष्टबालः, अनुद्दिष्टपितृको बालकः.

FOUNDRESS, *s.* स्थापकी, प्रथमस्थापका, निर्म्मात्री, प्रवर्त्तिका, आरम्भकर्त्री.

FOUNT, FOUNTAIN, *s.* प्रस्रवणं, निर्झरः, झरः -रा -री, स्रवः, जलाकरः, उत्सः, प्रपा, कूपः; 'artificial,' शृङ्गं.—(Source, original) मूलं, योनिः *m. f.*, आदिः *m.*, हेतुः *m.*—(Of types). *See* FONT.

FOUR, *a.* चत्वारः *m. pl.* चतस्रः *f. pl.* चत्वारि *n. pl.* (चतुर्), चतुष्टयः -यी -यं. The neut. of this last word expresses 'the aggregate of four,' and sometimes 'four' itself; as, 'four hours,' दण्डचतुष्टयं; 'in four ways,' चतुर्विधः -धा -धं, चतुर्धा; 'four times,' चतुः ind., चतुःकृत्वस् ind.

FOUR-CORNERED, *a.* चतुरस्रः -स्रा -स्रं, चतुष्कोणः -णा -णं.

FOUR-FACED, *a.* (Brahmá) चतुर्मुखः, चतुराननः, चतुर्वदनः, चतुर्वक्त्रः.

FOUR-FOLD, *a.* चतुर्गुणः -णा -णं, चतुर्विधः -धा -धं, चतुःप्रकारः -रा -रं, चतुष्टयः -यी -यं, चतुरङ्गी -ङ्गिणी -ङ्गि (न्), चतुर्धा.

FOUR-FOOTED, *a.* चतुष्पादः -दा -दं, चतुष्पदः -दा -दं, चतुष्पाद् *m. f. n.*

FOURSCORE, *a.* अशीतिः *f. sing.*, अशीतिसंख्यकः -का -कं, विंशतिचतुष्टयं; 'fourscore years of age,' आशीतिकः -का -कं.

FOURSQUARE, *a.* चतुरस्रः -स्रा -स्रं, चतुष्कोणः -णा -णं.

FOURTEEN, *a.* चतुर्दश *m. f. n.* (न्), चतुर्दशसंख्यकः -का -कं, समद्वयं.

FOURTEENTH, *a.* चतुर्दशः -शी -शं.

FOURTH, *a.* चतुर्थः -र्थी -र्थी -र्थं, तुरीयः -या -यं -यकः -का -कं, तुर्य्यः -र्य्या -र्य्यं, पादिकः -की -कं; 'a fourth part,' चतुर्भागः, चतुर्थांशः, पादः, पादिनः.

FOURTHLY, *adv.* चतुर्थतस्, तुरीयतस्, चतुर्थस्थाने, चतुर्थपदे.

FOUR-WHEELED, *a.* चतुश्चक्रः -क्रा -क्रं, चतुश्चक्रयुक्तः -क्ता -क्तं.

FOWL, *s.* (A winged animal) पक्षी *m.* -क्षिणी *f.* (न्), खगः, विहगः, विहङ्गमः, पतगः, पतत्री *m.* (न्), शकुनः, शकुनिः *m.*—(Gallinaceous or domestic fowl) कुक्कुटः -टी, चरणायुधः, कृकवाकुः *m.*, ताम्रचूडः; 'wild-fowl,' रज्जुदालकः.

To FOWL, *v. n.* पक्षिणो ग्रह् (c. 9. गृह्णाति, ग्रहीतुं) or धृ (c. 1. धरति, धर्त्तुं) or बन्ध् (c. 9. बध्नाति, बन्धुं), शकुन (nom. शकुनयति -यितुं), पक्षिवधेन उपजीव् (c. 1. -जीवति -वितुं).

FOWLER, *s.* व्याधः, शाकुनिकः, लुब्धकः, जालिकः, वागुरिकः, पक्षिग्राहकः, पक्षिबन्धी *m.* (न्), पक्षिवधजीवी *m.* (न्).

FOWLING, *s.* पक्षिधरणं, पक्षिग्रहणं, पक्षिघातः, पक्षिवधः, पक्षिमारणं.

FOWLING-PIECE, *s.* पक्षिमारणे प्रयुक्ता लघ्वी आग्नेयनाडी.

FOX, *s.* लोमशा -शी, लोमालिका, उल्कामुखी, शृगालः -ली -लिका, किंकिः *f.*, खिंखिः *f.*, खिङ्खिरः -रा, क्रोष्टा *m.* (ष्टु), भूरिमायः; 'flying-fox,' वातुलिः *f.*, वल्गुलः.

FOX-GLOVE, *s.* रक्तपुष्पो विषवीर्य्य ओषधिभेदः.

FOX-HOUND, *s.* शृगालाखेटिकः, लोमशाखेटकः, शृगालाद्यनुसरणे शिक्षितो मृगव्यकुक्कुरः, शृगालारिः *m.*

FOX-HUNT, *s.* शृगालानुसरणं, शृगालाखेटः, लोमशाद्यनुधावनं.

FOX-HUNTER, *s.* शृगालाखेटकः, शृगालानुसारी *m.* (न्), लोमशानुधावकः.

FOX-LIKE, *a.* बहुमायः -या -यं, शृगालधर्म्मा -र्म्मा -र्म्म (न्), विदग्धः -ग्धा -ग्धं.

FRACTION, *s.* (In arithmetic) भिन्नं, भागः, अंशः, राशिः *m. f.*, राशिभागः, अपूर्णः; 'multiplication of fractions,' भिन्नगुणनं; 'addition,' भिन्नसङ्कलितं; 'subtraction,' भिन्नव्यवकलितं; 'division,' भिन्नभागहरः; 'square of a fraction,' भिन्नवर्गः; 'cube,' भिन्नघनं; 'assimilation of fractions,' भागजातिः *f.*

FRACTIONAL, *a.* भागिकः -की -कं, भागी -गिनी -गि (न्), अपूर्णः -र्णा -र्णं.

FRACTIOUS, *a.* कलहकारी -रिणी -रि (न्), सुलभकोपः -पा -पं, प्रतीपः -पा -पं.

FRACTIOUSLY, *adv.* कलहकारिवत्, कलहकरणार्थं, प्रतीपवत्.

FRACTURE, *s.* भङ्गः, भेदः, विभङ्गः, भञ्जनं, भेदनं, विभेदः, भक्तिः *f.*, प्रभङ्गः, खण्डनं, विदारणं.—(Of a bone) अस्थिभङ्गः, अस्थिभेदः, अस्थित्रोटनं.

To FRACTURE, *v. a.* भञ्ज् (c. 7. भनक्ति, भंक्तुं), प्रभञ्ज्, विभञ्ज्, भिद् (c. 7. भिनत्ति, भेत्तुं), विभिद्, खण्ड् (c. 10. खण्डयति -यितुं), विदृ (c. 10. -दारयति -यितुं), शकलीकृ.—(A bone) अस्थि भञ्ज् or भिद् or त्रुट् (c. 10. त्रोटयते -यितुं).

FRACTURED, *p. p.* भग्नः -ग्ना -ग्नं, भिन्नः -न्ना -न्नं, खण्डितः -ता -तं, विभिन्नः -न्ना -न्नं, रुग्णः -ग्णा -ग्णं, विदीर्णः -र्णा -र्णं, शकलीकृतः -ता -तं, त्रुटितः -ता -तं.

FRAGILE, *a.* भङ्गुरः -रा -रं, भिदुरः -रा -रं, सुभङ्गः -ङ्गा -ङ्गं, सुभेद्यः -द्या -द्यं, सुखभेद्यः -द्या -द्यं, सुखखण्डनीयः -या -यं, विनश्वरः -रा -रं.

FRAGILITY, *s.* भङ्गुरत्वं -ता, भिदुरता, सुभङ्गत्वं, सुभेद्यता, सुखखण्डनीयता, विनश्वरत्वं, कोमलता, क्षयिता, क्षीणता.

FRAGMENT, *s.* खण्डः -ण्डं -ण्डकः, भिन्नं, भित्तं, भित्तिः *f.*, दलं, विदलं, भागः, अंशः, शकलः -लं, अपूर्णः, पिण्डं, पिण्ड् *f.*, विकिरः, छः, आदिष्टं; 'in fragments,' खण्डशस्, खण्डं खण्डं, भागशस्; 'in a thousand fragments,' सहस्रखण्डशः, सहस्रधा.

FRAGMENTARY, *a.* खण्डी -ण्डिनी -ण्डि (न्), भागी -गिनी -गि (न्), खण्डमयः -यी -यं.

FRAGRANCE, FRAGRANCY, *s.* सुगन्धः, सुगन्धिः *m.* -न्धिता, सौगन्ध्यं, गन्धः, उपगन्धः, आमोदः, मोदः, सुरभिः *m.*, सौरभ्यं, सुवासः, वासः, परिमलः, तिक्तः, निर्हारः.

FRAGRANT, *s.* सुगन्धः -न्धा -न्धं -न्धिः -न्धिः -न्धि, सौगन्धिकः -की -कं, गन्धी -न्धिनी -न्धि (न्), सगन्धः -न्धा -न्धं, गन्धवहः -हा -हं, गन्धवान् -वती -वत् (त्), सुरभिः -भिः -भि, सुवासितः -ता -तं, सवासः -सा -सं, आमोदी -दिनी -दि (न्), सामोदः -दा -दं, तिक्तः -क्ता -क्तं, कषायः -या -यं.

FRAGRANTLY, *adv.* सगन्धं, सुगन्धेन, सामोदं, सवासं, सुरभि, तिक्तं.

FRAIL, *a.* भङ्गुरः -रा -रं, क्षणभङ्गुरः -रा -रं, क्षयी -यिणी -यि (न्), नश्वरः -रा -रं, विनश्वरः -रा -रं, द्रुतापायः -या -यं, क्षणविध्वंसी -सिनी -सि

(न्), सद्यःपाती -तिनी -ति (न्), अनित्यः -त्या -त्यं, अस्थायी -यिनी -यि (न्).

FRAIL, *s.* (Basket made of rushes) दर्ब्भमयः or नलमयः पेटकः.

FRAILTY, *s.* भङ्गुरता -त्वं, अस्थैर्य्यं, अधैर्य्यं, धृतिहीनता, दौर्बल्यं, अल्पशक्तित्वं, क्षयिता, नश्वरत्वं, अनित्यता, अस्थायिता.

To FRAME, *v. a.* (Fabricate, form) कृ, संस्कृ, निर्मा (c. 2. -माति -तुं, c. 3. -मिमीते, c. 4. -मायते), कॢप् (c. 10. कल्पयति -यितुं), घट् (c. 10. घटयति -यितुं), विधा (c. 3. -दधाति -धातुं), रच् (c. 10. रचयति -यितुं). —(Adjust, shape) विरच्, संविधा, समाधा, विन्यस् (c. 4. -अस्यति -असितुं).—(Compose) रच्, विरच्, निबन्ध् (c. 9. -बध्नाति -बन्धुं), सङ्ग्रह् (c. 9. -गृह्णाति -ग्रहीतुं).—(Conform) सादृश्यं कृ, आनुरूप्यं कृ, सदृशीकृ; 'frame a plan in the mind,' उपायं मनसा कॢप्.

FRAME, *s.* (Fabric) निर्म्माणं, कल्पनं -ना, घटनं.—(Form) आकारः, आकृतिः *f.*, रूपं.—(Body) शरीरं, देहः, गात्रं, गात्रकं, कायः, मूर्त्तिः *f.*, अङ्गं, वपुः *n.* (स्); 'of a hardy frame,' वज्रदेही -हिनी -हि (न्), वज्रशरीरी -रिणी -रि (न्).—(Stand, support) मञ्चः -ञ्चकः, वृक्षः -क्षकः, तलः, उपस्तम्भः.—(Of a picture) चित्रकोशः, चित्रावरणं, चित्रावेष्टनं, चित्रपरिगतं काष्ठादि.—(Of a window) वातायनपरिगतं काष्ठादि.—(State) स्थितिः *f.*, भावः, अवस्था, वृत्तिः *f.*, दशा; 'frame of mind,' मनोभावः, मनःस्थितिः *f.*, चित्तवृत्तिः *f.*; 'frame of body,' शरीरस्थितिः *f.*—(Structure, system) संस्थानं, संस्थितिः *f.*, स्थितिः *f.*, रीतिः *f.*, प्रवृत्तिः *f.*, व्यूहः -हनं.

FRAMED, *p.p.* रचितः -ता -तं, विरचितः -ता -तं, कल्पितः -ता -तं, घटितः -ता -तं, निर्म्मितः -ता -तं, कृतः -ता -तं, विहितः -ता -तं.

FRAMER, *s.* रचकः, विरचकः, कर्त्ता *m.* (र्त्तृ), कारकः, निबन्धा *m.* (न्धृ).

FRANCHISE, *s.* पौरजनाधिकारः.—(Freedom from burden) मुक्तिः *f.*, विमुक्तिः *f.*, मोचनं, विमोचनं, मोक्षः, अकरत्वं, निष्करत्वं, स्वाधीनता.

To FRANCHISE, *v. a.* मुच् (c. 6. मुञ्चति, मोक्तुं, c. 10. मोचयति -यितुं), विमुच्. *See* ENFRANCHISE.

FRANGIBILITY, *s.* भङ्गुरत्वं -ता, भिदुरता, सुभङ्गत्वं, सुभेद्यता, खण्डनीयता.

FRANGIBLE, *a.* भङ्गुरः -रा -रं, खण्डनीयः -या -यं, भेद्यः -द्या -द्यं.

FRANK, *a.* (Ingenuous, candid) अकपटः -टा -टं, निष्कपटः -टा -टं, अमायः -या -यं, अमायिकः -की -कं, मायाहीनः -ना -नं, विमलात्मा -त्मा -त्म (न्), विमलार्थकः -का -कं, अवक्रः -क्रा -क्रं, अगूढभावः -वा -वं, सरलः -ला -लं, दक्षिणः -णा -णं, निर्व्यलीकः -का -कं.—(Generous) उदारः -रा -रं.

FRANK, *s.* (Coin) रूप्यमुद्राविशेषः.—(Letter carried without postage) मूल्यं विना वाहनीयं पत्रं.—(The mark which makes it free) इदं पत्रं मूल्यं विना वाह्यम् इति पत्रोपरि सूचकं चिह्नं.

To FRANK, *v. a.* इदं पत्रं मूल्यं विना वाहनीयम् इति पत्रस्योपरिलिखितचिह्नेन सूच् (c. 10. सूचयति -यितुं).

FRANK-HEARTED, *a.* उदारचेताः -ताः -तः (स्), उदारधीः -धीः -धि, विमलात्मा -त्मा -त्म (न्).

FRANKINCENSE, *s.* कुन्दुरुः *m.f.* -रूकः, कुन्दुः *f.*, रसालं, कुम्भधूपः, खोटीरसः.

FRANKLY, *adv.* निष्कपटं, कपटं विना, अवक्रं, अमायया, व्यक्तं, निर्व्याजं, निर्व्यलीकं, सरलं, दाक्षिण्येन, उदारवत्.

FRANKNESS, *s.* उदारत्वं, औदार्य्यं, सरलता, सारल्यं, अवक्रता, कपटहीनता, निष्कपटत्वं, मायाहीनता, दाक्षिण्यं, भावागूढता, अमाया, निर्व्यलीकता, विमलात्मता, अकापट्यं.

FRANTIC, *a.* उन्मत्तः -त्ता -त्तं, उन्मादः -दा -दं, उन्मादसंरब्धः -ब्धा -ब्धं, मदोत्कटः -टा -टं, मदविक्षिप्तः -प्ता -प्तं, व्यस्तचित्तः -त्ता -त्तं, प्रमदः -दा -दं.

FRANTICLY, *adv.* उन्मत्तवत्, उन्मादवत्, उन्मादविक्षिप्तवत्, वातुलवत्.

FRANTICNESS, *s.* उन्मत्तता, उन्मादः, उन्मादसंरब्धता, चित्तविक्षिप्तता, चित्तव्यस्तता, चित्तविभ्रमः, विमोहः, सोन्मादत्वं, वातुलता.

FRATERNAL, *a.* भ्रात्रीयः -या -यं, भ्रातृकः -का -कं, भ्रातृसन्निभः -भा -भं.

FRATERNALLY, *adv.* भ्रातृवत्, भ्रातृरूपेण, सोदरवत्, भ्रात्रीयप्रकारेण.

FRATERNITY, *s.* (Brotherhood) भ्रातृत्वं, सौभ्रात्रं.—(Association) संसर्गः, संसर्गित्वं, साहित्यं, बन्धुता.—(Body of men associated) सहकारिजनसमूहः.

To FRATERNIZE, *v. a.* भ्रातृवत् सहितः -ता -तं भू or सह मिल् (c. 6. मिलति -ते, मेलितुं) or संयुक्तः -क्ता -क्तं भू or सङ्गतवान् -वती -वद् भू.

FRATRICIDE, *s.* भ्रातृहत्या, भ्रातृवधः, भ्रातृघातः.—(One who murders a brother) भ्रातृघातकः, भ्रातृहा *m.* (न्), भ्रातृघाती *m.* (न्).

FRAUD, *s.* कपटः -टं, व्याजः, छलं -लना, कैतवं, कूटः -टं, कौटं, माया, दम्भः, उपधिः *m.*, वञ्चनं -ना, प्रवञ्चना, प्रलम्भः, विप्रलम्भः, अतिसन्धानं, अभिसन्धिः *m.* -न्धानं, प्रपञ्चः, प्रतारणं -णा, कुहकः, व्याकूतिः, संघातः, निमीलिका, दाक्षाजिनं, स्खलितं.

FRAUDFUL, *a.* कपटी -टिनी -टि (न्), मायी -यिनी -यि (न्). *See* FRAUDULENT.

FRAUDULENCE, *s.* कपटता, कापट्यं, कूटता, सव्याजता, धूर्त्तता, शठता.

FRAUDULENT, *a.* कपटी -टिनी -टि (न्), कापटिकः -की -कं, छली -लिनी -लि (न्), मायी -यिनी -यि (न्), वञ्चकः -का -कं, प्रवञ्चकः -का -कं, कूटकः -का -कं, कौटः -टी -टं -टिकः -की -कं, छाद्मिकः -की -कं, दाम्भिकः -की -कं, धूर्त्तः -र्त्ता -र्त्तं, प्रतारकः -का -कं, सव्याजः -जा -जं, उपधिकः -का -कं, प्रलम्भकः -का -कं, शठः -ठा -ठं, दाक्षाजिनिकः -की -कं, तस्किलः -ला -लं, स्थगः -गा -गं, कूट in comp.

FRAUDULENTLY, *adv.* सकपटं, सव्याजं, सकूटं, छलेन, सकैतवं, धूर्त्तवत्, वञ्चनार्थं, कितववत्, शठवत्, दम्भात्, मायया, समायं.

FRAUGHT, *a.* (Laden) धुरीणः -णा -णं, धुरीयः -या -यं, भारवान् -वती -वत् (त्).—(Filled) पूर्णः -र्णा -र्णं, अभिपूर्णः -र्णा -र्णं, परिपूर्णः -र्णा -र्णं, पूर्य्यमाणः -णा -णं, आकीर्णः -र्णा -र्णं, सङ्कीर्णः -र्णा -र्णं, सङ्कुलः -ला -लं, गर्भः -र्भा -र्भं in comp.; 'fraught with happiness,' सुखावहः -हा -हं.

FRAY, *s.* कलहः, कलिः *m.*, युद्धं, तुमुलं, द्वन्द्वं, सङ्ग्रामः, समरः, संयुगः, डिम्बः, डमरः, डामरः, विरोधः, व्यवक्रोशनं.

To FRAY, *v. a.* (Rub) वस्त्राञ्चलवद् घर्षणेन जर्जरीभू or रूक्षीभू.

FRAYED, *p.p.* वस्त्राञ्चलवद् घर्षणेन जर्जरीकः -का -कं or जर्जरीभूतः -ता -तं.

FREAK, *s.* चापलं, लौल्यं, मनोलौल्यं, बुद्धिचापल्यं, छन्दः *n.* (स्), लीला, खेला, केलिः *m. f.*, विलासः, विहारः, लहरी, तरङ्गः, अवहित्थः *m.*

To FREAK, *v. a.* चित्र् (c. 10. चित्रयति -यितुं), चित्रीकृ, चित्रविचित्रीकृ.

FREAKISH, *a.* चपलः -ला -लं, लोलः -ला -लं, केलिकः -का -कं, लीलाखेलः -ला -लं.

FREAKISHLY, *adv.* चपलं, चापल्यात्, लौल्यात्, मनोलौल्यात्, सलीलं.

FREAKISHNESS, *s.* चापल्यं, चपलता, लौल्यं, लीलावत्त्वं, विलासिता.

FRECKLE, *s.* जडुलः, कालकः, विप्रुः *m.*, तिलकः, तिलः, तिलकालकः, चिह्नं.

FRECKLED, *a.* जडुलचिह्नितः -ता -तं, तिलकी -किनी -कि (न्), तिलकः -का -कं.

FREE, *a.* (Set at liberty) मुक्तः -क्ता -क्तं, विमुक्तः -क्ता -क्तं, मोचितः -ता -तं, विमोचितः -ता -तं, मोक्षितः -ता -तं, विमोक्षितः -ता -तं, निर्मुक्तः -क्ता -क्तं, विसृष्टः -ष्टा -ष्टं.—(Not subject to the will of others) स्वाधीनः -ना -नं, अनधीनः -ना -नं, अपराधीनः -ना -नं, अनायत्तः -त्ता -त्तं, स्वतन्त्रः -न्त्रा -न्त्रं, आत्मतन्त्रः -न्त्रा -न्त्रं, विवशः -शा -शं, स्वैरचारी -रिणी -रि (न्), स्वेच्छाचारी &c., स्वच्छन्दः -न्दा -न्दं, अनुपाश्रयः -या -यं, अभुजिष्यः -ष्या -ष्यं.—(Unshackled) अबद्धः -द्धा -द्धं, निर्यन्त्रणः -णा -णं, विशृङ्खलः -ला -लं, उच्छृङ्खलः -ला -लं. (Unrestrained)

अयतः -ता -तं, अनियतः -ता -तं, अवशः -शा -शं, निर्यन्त्रितः -ता -तं, अयन्त्रितः -ता -तं, निरवग्रहः -हा -हं.—(Unimpeded) निर्विघ्नः -घ्ना -घ्नं, अविघ्नः -घ्ना -घ्नं -घ्नितः -ता -तं, अविरोधितः -ता -तं, निरवरोधः -धा -धं, अविहतः -ता -तं, निष्प्रत्यूहः -हा -हं, असम्बाधः -धा -धं.—(Free in expenses) मुक्तहस्तः -स्ता -स्तं, त्यागशीलः -ला -लं.—(Not decorous) अमर्य्यादः -दा -दं, मर्य्यादातिक्रान्तः -न्ता -न्तं.—(Gratuitous) मूल्यं विना दत्तः -त्ता -त्तं or लब्धः -ब्धा -ब्धं, अक्रीतः -ता -तं, धर्म्मार्थकः -का -कं.—(Open to all) सर्व्वसामान्यः -न्या -न्यं, सर्व्वसाधारणः -णी -णं.—(Free in speech) अयन्त्रितकथः -था -थं, अयतवाक् *m.f.n.* (च्).—(Free from, exempt) वर्ज्जितः -ता -तं, विवर्ज्जितः -ता -तं, मुक्तः -क्ता -क्तं, रहितः -ता -तं, हीनः -ना -नं, शून्यः -न्या -न्यं, विगतः -ता -तं, वीतः -ता -तं or expressed by निर् or स्व prefixed; 'free from bias,' मुक्तसङ्गः -ङ्गा -ङ्गं, सङ्गवर्ज्जितः -ता -तं, सङ्गहीनः -ना -नं; 'free from desire,' वीतकामः -मा -मं, विगतकामः -मा -मं; 'free from debt,' अनृणः -णा -णं, अनृणी -णिनी -णि (न्), अवतीर्णर्णः -र्णा -र्णं; 'free from motive,' निष्कारणः -णा -णं; 'free choice,' स्वेच्छा; 'free course,' प्रसरः.

To Free, *v. a.* (Set at liberty) मुच् (c. 6. मुञ्चति, मोक्तुं, c. 10. मोचयति -यितुं), विमुच्, निर्मुच्, मोक्ष् (c. 10. मोक्षयति -यितुं), विमोक्ष्, विसृज् (c. 6. -सृजति -स्रष्टुं, c. 10. -सर्ज्जयति -यितुं), निस्तॄ in caus. (-तारयति -यितुं), त्रै (c. 1. त्रायते, त्रातुं).—(Free from confinement) बन्धनात् मुच्.—(From encumbrance) मुच्, विशुध् in caus. (-शोधयति -यितुं), विघ्नान् or भारम् अपनी (c. 1. -नयति -नेतुं) or विनी or हृ (c. 1. हरति, हर्त्तुं) or उद्धृ, निर्विघ्नीकृ, निष्कण्टकं -कां -कं कृ, निष्प्रत्यूहीकृ.—(From doubt) संशयम् अपनी.—(From blame) निर्दोषीकृ.—(From taxes) अकरीकृ, निष्करीकृ.

Free-agency, *s.* स्वेच्छा, स्वैरता, स्वातन्त्र्यं, स्वाच्छन्द्यं, स्वतन्त्रता.

Free-booter, *s.* दस्युः, साहसिकः, प्रसह्यचौरः, परिपन्थी *m.* (न्), लुण्ठाकः.

Free-booting, *s.* अपहरणं, चौर्य्यं, चौरत्वं, अभ्याहारः, साहसं.

Free-born, *a.* अदासजः -जा -जं, अदासेयजातिः -तिः -ति, अदासीपुत्रः, उदारयोनिः -निः -नि, उदारजातिः -तिः -ति, कुलीनजः -जा -जं.

Freed, *p. p.* or *a.* मुक्तः -क्ता -क्तं, विमुक्तः -क्ता -क्तं, विमोचितः -ता -तं, मोक्षितः -ता -तं, वर्ज्जितः -ता -तं; 'freed from confinement,' मुक्तबन्धनः -ना -नं or बन्धनमुक्तः -क्ता -क्तं; 'from desire,' विगतकामः -मा -मं, कामातीतः -ता -तं.

Freedman, *s.* मुक्तजनः, दास्यमुक्तः, दास्यमोक्षितः, दास्याद्विमोचितः.

Freedom, *s.* (Liberty) मुक्तिः *f.*, विमुक्तिः *f.*, मोक्षः, विमोक्षः -क्षणं, विमोचनं, वैमुक्त्यं, परिमोक्षणं.—(Freedom from slavery) दास्यमुक्तिः *f.*, दास्यमोक्षः, अदास्यं, अदासत्वं.—(From confinement) बन्धनमुक्तिः *f.*—(From obstacle or restraint) निर्विघ्नता, विघ्नमुक्तिः *f.*, निर्यन्त्रणं -णत्वं, निरवरोधता, उच्छृङ्खलता, अयन्त्रितत्वं.—(Independence) स्वाधीनता, स्वतन्त्रता, अवशता, स्वातन्त्र्यं, अनधीनता.—(Freedom of will) स्वेच्छा, स्वाच्छन्द्यं, स्वैरता.—(Want of decorum) अमर्य्यादा, अविनयः, मर्य्यादातिक्रमः.—(Freedom of a city) स्वाधीनपुराधिकारः, पौरजनाधिकारः.—(Exemption from) मुक्तिः *f.*, विरहः, राहित्यं, शून्यता, अभावः, असम्भवः; 'freedom from taxes,' अकरत्वं, निष्करत्वं; 'from war,' युद्धाभावः.

Free-hearted, *a.* उदारचेताः -ताः -तः (स्), अगूढभावः -वा -वं.

Freehold, *s.* स्वाधीनभूमिः *f.*, अपराधीनभूमिः *f.*, आत्माधीनक्षेत्रं.

Freeholder, *s.* स्वाधीनभूमिधारी *m.* (न्), आत्माधीनभूमिधारी, स्वाधीनक्षेत्रधारी.

Freely, *adv.* (Without restraint) निर्विघ्नं, निर्यन्त्रणं, निष्प्रत्यूहं, निर्यन्त्रितं, निरवरोधेन, अनिवारितं, असम्बाधं.—(Voluntarily) कामं, प्रकामं, कामतस्, स्वच्छन्दात्, स्वेच्छया.—(Copiously) बाहुल्येन, बहुशस्.—(Without persuasion) अयाचितं.—(Gratuitously) मूल्यं विना.

Free-liver, *s.* बह्वाशी -शिनी -शि (न्), अत्याहारी -रिणी -रि (न्), कुक्षिम्भरिः -रिः -रि.

Freeman, *s.* अदासः, स्वाधीनः, अपराधीनः, अपरवशः, स्वतन्त्रः.

Freemason, *s.* परस्परोपकारार्थं संसर्गिणां जनानां गणाभ्यन्तरः.

Free-minded, *a.* अव्याकुलचित्तः -त्ता -त्तं, चिन्ताशून्यमनाः -नाः -नः (स्).

Freeness, *s.* (Freedom from restraint) निर्विघ्नता, निर्यन्त्रणं -णत्वं, निरवरोधता, उच्छृङ्खलत्वं.—(Of speech) वागयतत्वं.—(Frankness, openness) अगूढशीलता, निष्कपटता.—(Liberality) मुक्तहस्तत्वं, त्यागशीलता.

Free-spoken, *a.* अयन्त्रितकथः -था -थं, अयतवाक् *m.f.n.* (च्), स्वच्छवाक् *m.f.n.*

Free-stone, *s.* गृहनिर्म्माणे प्रयुक्तः सुच्छेद्यप्रस्तरविशेषः.

Free-thinker, *s.* नास्तिकः, धर्म्मादेर् निन्दकः, देवनिन्दकः, धर्म्मावमानी *m.* (न्).

Free-will, *s.* स्वेच्छा, स्वच्छन्दता, स्वाच्छन्द्यं, स्वकामः, यदृच्छा.

Free-woman, *s.* अदासी, स्वाधीना स्त्री, अनधीना, स्वैरचारिणी.

To Freeze, *v. n.* अतिशीतलत्वाद् घनीभू or संहतीभू or संहन् in pass. (-हन्यते), अतिशीतोदकवत् शीनीभू or श्यै (c. 1. श्यायते, श्यातुं) or हिमपिण्डान् बन्ध् (c. 9. बध्नाति, बन्द्धुं), हिमपिण्डीभू, शीतीभू, शीनीभू, श्यानीभू, जडीभू.

To Freeze, *v. a.* अतिशीतलत्वाद् घनीकृ or संहतीकृ or हिमपिण्डरूपेण संहन् (c. 2. -हन्ति -न्तुं) or श्यै in caus. (श्यापयति -यितुं) or श्यानीकृ, शीतीकृ, जड (nom. जडयति -यितुं).

Freight, *s.* (Cargo of a ship) नौकाभारः, नौभारः, नौकास्थद्रव्याणि, पोतस्थं भाण्डं, नाविकं, पौतिकं.—(Fare) आतरः, तरपण्यं, तारिकं, तार्य्यं, अनुतरं.

To Freight, *v. a.* नौकायां द्रव्याणि निविश् in caus. (-वेशयति -यितुं) or आरुह् in caus. (-रोपयति -यितुं) or द्रव्यैः पृ (c. 10. पूरयति -यितुं).

Freighted, *p. p.* द्रव्यपूरितः -ता -तं, आरोपितभाण्डः -ण्डा -ण्डं or गृहीतभाण्डः.

Freighter, *s.* नौकायां भाण्डनिवेशकः or द्रव्यनिवेशकः, नौकापूरकः.

Frenetic, *a.* *See* Frantic.

Frenum, *s.* (In anatomy) सेवनं, सीवनी.

Frenzied, *a.* उन्मादवान् -वती -वत् (त्), विक्षिप्तचित्तः -त्ता -त्तं.

Frenzy, *s.* उन्मादः, चित्तविप्लवः, चित्तविभ्रमः, प्रामाद्यं, आवेशः.

Frequence, frequency, *s.* बहुत्वं -ता, बाहुल्यं, नित्यता -त्वं, अभीक्ष्णता, पौनःपुन्यं, पुनःपुनस्त्वं, अविरतिः *f.*, अविरामः, नैरन्तर्य्यं.

Frequent, *a.* नित्यः -त्या -त्यं, नैत्यिकः -की -कं, अभीक्ष्णः -क्ष्णा -क्ष्णं, पुनःपुनर् वर्त्तमानः -ना -नं, बहुशः or बहुवारं or अनेकशः or मुहुर्मुहुर् घटमानः -ना -नं, सततः -ता -तं, अविरतः -ता -तं.

To Frequent, *v. a.* सेव् (c. 1. सेवते -वितुं), निषेव्, नित्यम् आश्रि (c. 1. -श्रयति -ते -यितुं), पुनःपुनः or बहुवारम् अभिगम् (c. 1. -गच्छति -गन्तुं) or अभ्यागम्, जुष् (c. 6. जुषते, जोषितुं), गाह् (c. 1. गाहते -हितुं).

Frequentative, *s.* (Verb in grammar) यङ्लुगन्तः, यङन्तः.

Frequented, *p. p.* सेवितः -ता -तं, निषेवितः -ता -तं, आश्रितः -ता -तं, जुष्टः -ष्टा -ष्टं, आकीर्णः -र्णा -र्णं, आचरितः -ता -तं.

Frequenting, *s.* सेवनं, निषेवणं, आश्रयणं, मुहुर् अभ्यागमनं, सङ्गतिः *f.*

Frequently, *adv.* बहुशस्, भूयस्, भूयोभूयः, मुहुस्, मुहुर्मुहुस्, असकृत्, अनेकशस्, बहुवारं, बहुकृत्वस्, अनेककृत्वस्, नित्यं, पुनःपुनर्, वारंवारं,

अभीक्ष्णं, प्रायस्, प्रायेण, प्रायशस्, वारेण, शश्वत्, सततं.

Fresco, *s.* (Coolness) शीतलता.—(Painting) मज्जोदकं, मज्जोदकचित्रं.

Fresh, *a.* (New, recent) नवः -वा -वं, अभिनवः -वा -वं, प्रतिनवः -वा -वं, नूतनः -ना -नं, प्रत्यग्रः -ग्रा -ग्रं, सद्यस्कः -स्का -स्कं, सद्यस्कालीनः -ना -नं, नवीनः -ना -नं, अप्राचीनः -ना -नं.—(Not faded) अम्लानः -ना -नं, विम्लानः -ना -नं, अविकलः -ला -लं, अशुष्कः -ष्का -ष्कं.—(Recently obtained) सद्यःप्राप्तः -प्ता -प्तं.—(Cool) शीतलः -ला -लं.—(Somewhat strong) ईषत्तीक्ष्णः -क्ष्णा -क्ष्णं, ईषत्प्रबलः -ला -लं.—(With unimpaired vigor) अक्षतवीर्य्यः -र्य्या -र्य्यं, अविकलतेजाः -जाः -जः (स्), अश्रान्तः -न्ता -न्तं, अक्लान्तः -न्ता -न्तं.—(Fresh colored) नववर्णः -र्णा -र्णं, रक्तवर्णः -र्णा -र्णं.—(Not salt) अलवणः -णा -णं.—(Full of spirit) सरसः -सा -सं, रसिकः -का -कं, रसी -सिनी -सि (न्); 'fresh butter,' नवनी -नीतं.

To freshen, *v. a.* नवीकृ, शीतलीकृ, सरसीकृ, लावण्यं हृ (c. 1. हरति, हर्त्तुं).

To freshen, *v. n.* (Grow brisk) ईषत्तीक्ष्णीभू, ईषत्तीव्रीभू, ईषत्प्रबलीभू.

Freshly, *adv.* (Newly) सद्यस्, नवं, अभिनवं, प्रत्यग्रं.—(Briskly) ईषत्तीक्ष्णं, ईषत्तीव्रं, ईषद्बलवत्.—(Coolly) शीतलं; 'freshly heated,' सद्यस्तप्तः -प्ता -प्तं.

Freshman, *s.* नवशिष्यः, नवच्छात्रः, नूतनशिष्यः, प्राथमकल्पिकः.

Freshness, *s.* (Newness) नवता -त्वं, अभिनवत्वं, नूतनता -त्वं, नवीनता, प्रत्यग्रता.—(Vigor) अम्लानिः *f.*, वीर्य्यं, तेजः *n.* (स्), अविक्लमः, अश्रान्तिः *f.*, अक्लान्तिः *f.*—(State of not being withered or impaired) अशीर्णता, अम्लानता, अक्षीणता, अक्षतत्वं, अवैकल्यं.—(Freedom from salt) अलावण्यं.—(Briskness) ईषत्तीक्ष्णता, सबलता.—(Of color) नववर्णः, रक्तवर्णः, अरुणवर्णः.

Fret, *s.* (Of the sea) समुद्रक्षोभः, इतस्ततो वीचिप्रलोठनं or ऊर्म्मिप्रलोठनं.—(Vexation of mind) आत्मद्रोहः, आत्मक्लेशः, आत्मपीडा, स्वमनस्तापः, स्वचित्तक्षोभः, अशान्तिः *f.*, उद्वेगः.

To fret, *v. a.* (Vex) व्यथ् (c. 10. व्यथयति -यितुं), तप् (c. 10. तापयति -यितुं), परितप्, सन्तप्, बाध् (c. 1. बाधते -धितुं), क्लिश् (c. 9. क्लिश्नाति, क्लेशितुं), क्षुभ् (c. 10. क्षोभयति -यितुं).—(Chafe) घृष् (c. 1. घर्षति -र्षितुं), आघृष्, घर्षणेन तप् or क्षतीकृ or व्रणीकृ.

To fret, *v. n.* (Be vexed) व्यथ् (c. 1. व्यथते -थितुं), तप् in pass. (तप्यते), परितप्, सन्तप्, आतप्, क्लिश् (c. 4. क्लिश्यते, क्लेशितुं), उद्विज् (c. 6. -विजते -जितुं), शुच् (c. 1. शोचति -चितुं), ज्वर् (c. 1. ज्वरति -रितुं), सञ्ज्वर्, दुर्म्मनस् (nom. दुर्म्मनायते), आत्मानं तप् (c. 10. तापयति -यितुं), क्षुभ् (c. 4. क्षुभ्यति, क्षोभितुं).—(Wear away by friction) घर्षणेन क्षि in pass. (क्षीयते) or परिक्षतीभू.

Fretful, *a.* आत्मद्रोही -हिणी -हि (न्), शीघ्रकोपी -पिनी -पि (न्), आत्मतापी -पिनी -पि (न्), वक्रभावः -वा -वं, दुष्प्रकृतिः -तिः -ति, दुर्म्मनाः -नाः -नः (स्).

Fretfully, *adv.* वक्रभावेन, वक्रप्रकृतित्वात्, दुष्प्रकृतित्वात्, समनस्तापं.

Fretfulness, *s.* आत्मद्रोहः, आत्मक्लेशः, आत्मपीडा, स्वमनस्तापः, स्वचित्तक्षोभः, भाववक्रता, प्रकृतिवक्रता, प्रतीपता, सदाप्रतीपत्वं, उद्वेगः, अशान्तिः *f.*

Fretted, *p. p.* व्यथितः -ता -तं, क्लिष्टः -ष्टा -ष्टं, सन्तापितः -ता -तं, पीडितः -ता -तं, बाधितः -ता -तं.—(Rubbed) घर्षितः -ता -तं.

Fretty, *a.* व्यत्यस्तरेखालङ्कृतः -ता -तं, व्यत्यस्तरेखारूपेण तष्टः -ष्टा -ष्टं.

Fretwork or fret, *s.* व्यत्यस्तरेखारूपं तक्षणकर्म्म *n.* (न्).

Friability, *s.* चूर्णयोग्यता, सुचूर्णनीयता, भङ्गुरत्वं, भिदुरता.

Friable, *a.* सुचूर्णनीयः -या -यं, चूर्णयोग्यः -ग्या -ग्यं, भिदुरः -रा -रं, भङ्गुरः -रा -रं, सुभेद्यः -द्या -द्यं, सुखखण्डनीयः -या -यं.

Friar, *s.* सन्न्यासी *m.* (न्), तपस्वी *m.* (न्), योगी *m.* (न्), मुनिः *m.*, वैरागी *m.* (न्).

Friary, *s.* मठः, सन्न्यासिनां मठः, आश्रमः, तपोवनं, विहारः.

Fricassee, *s.* पक्षिशशकादिमांसनिष्क्वथितं सरसभोजनं or सव्यञ्जनभोजनं, रसकः, मांसव्यञ्जनं.

To fricassee, *v. a.* पक्षिशशकादिमांसं रसादिना सह or व्यञ्जनादिना सह निष्क्वथ् (c. 1. -क्वथति -थितुं).

Friction, *s.* घर्षणं, आघर्षः -र्षणं, सङ्घर्षः, उद्घर्षणं, अभिघर्षणं, निर्घर्षणं, उपघर्षणं, परस्परघर्षणं, मर्द्दनं, अभिमर्द्दः, परिमर्द्दनं, परिमर्शः, आघट्टनं, विघट्टनं, उद्घट्टनं, मार्ज्जनं, परिमार्ज्जनं.

Friday, *s.* शुक्रवारः, कुलवारः, भृगुवारः, सप्ताहस्य षष्ठवारः.

Fried, *p. p.* भृष्टः -ष्टा -ष्टं, भर्ज्जितः -ता -तं, भ्रष्टः -ष्टा -ष्टं, कन्दुपक्वः -क्वा -क्वं; 'fried meat,' शूल्यं, भरुटकं; 'fried grain,' लाजाः *m. pl.*, अक्षतं -ताः *m. pl.*, धानाः *f. pl.*, भृष्टयवः.

Friend, *s.* मित्रं, सुहृत् *m.* (द्), सखा *m.* (खि), बन्धुः *m.*, वयस्यः, स्निग्धः, स्नेही *m.* (न्), बान्धवः, सहायः, अनुरागी *m.* (न्), प्रणयी *m.* (न्), सुहृत्तमः, हितः, हितकारी *m.* (न्), प्रियकृत् *m.*, सध्रू *m.* (स्), अनुकूलः, विभावः, केलिकरः, सङ्गी *m.* (न्), आर्य्यः; 'friend of the same age,' सवयाः *m.* (स्), वयस्यः; 'female friend,' सखी *f.*; 'an old friend,' चिरमित्रं; 'a true friend,' सन्मित्रं; 'my friend,' सखे voc. c. *m.*, सखि voc. c. *f.*

To friend, *v. a.* मित्र (nom. मित्रीयते -यितुं), सखिवृत्तिं कृ or आस्था (c. 1. -तिष्ठति -स्थातुं), उपकृ, अनुग्रह् (c. 9. -गृह्णाति -ग्रहीतुं).

Friendless, *a.* मित्रहीनः -ना -नं, बन्धुहीनः -ना -नं, अबन्धुः -न्धुः -न्धु, अबान्धवः -वी -वं, असहायः -या -यं, निःसहायः -या -यं, अनाथः -था -थं, अलब्धनाथः -था -थं, निराश्रयः -या -यं, अशरणः -णा -णं, निरवलम्बः -म्बा -म्बं, बान्धवोज्झितः -ता -तं.

Friendlessness, *s.* मित्रहीनता, बन्धुहीनता, असहायता, निराश्रयत्वं.

Friendliness, *s.* मित्रत्वं, सौहृद्यं, बन्धुता, प्रीतिः *f.*, सखित्वं, प्रणयः, प्रेम *n.* (न्), प्रियता, अनुरागः, अनुकूलता, उपकारशीलता, हितता, हितेच्छा, हितकाम्या.

Friendly, *a.* हितः -ता -तं, हितैषी -षिणी -षि (न्), हितवान् -वती -वत् (त्), हितकामः -मा -मं, हितप्रेप्सुः -प्सुः -प्सु, सुहितः -ता -तं, मैत्रः -त्री -त्रं, मित्रः -त्रा -त्रं, साखेयः -यी -यं, सुहृत्तमः -मा -मं, कृतमैत्रः -त्रा -त्रं, अनुरागी -गिणी -गि (न्), प्रणयी -यिनी -यि (न्), सप्रणयः -या -यं, स्नेही -हिनी -हि (न्), स्निग्धः -ग्धा -ग्धं, स्नेहशीलः -ला -लं, प्रीतिमान् -मती -मत् (त्), सानुरागः -गा -गं, प्रियङ्करः -रा -रं, प्रियकृत् *m. f. n.*, हितकरः -री -रं, अनुकूलः -ला -लं, अनुग्राही -हिणी -हि (न्), उपकारशीलः -ला -लं, सुहृदयः -या -यं, प्रियतमः -मा -मं; 'friendly-minded,' हितबुद्धिः -द्धिः -द्धि; 'friendly to all creatures,' कृतभूतमैत्रः; 'friendly dispute,' प्रीतिकलहः, प्रीतिवादः.

Friendly, *adv.* मित्रवत्, बन्धुवत्, हितवत्, स्निग्धवत्, मित्रत्वात्, प्रियं.

Friendship, *s.* मित्रत्वं -ता, मैत्र्यं, मैत्री, सौहृद्यं, सौहार्द्दं, सुहृत्ता, सख्यं, साख्यं, सखित्वं, बन्धुता, स्नेहः, प्रणयः, प्रीतिः *f.*, प्रेम *n.* (न्), प्रियता, साहाय्यं, सहायता, अनुरागः, साप्तपदीनं; 'to form friendship with another,' अन्यस्मिन् प्रीतिं कृ.

Frieze, *s.* (Coarse cloth) स्थूलपट्टं, स्थूलशाटकः, वराशिः *m.*—(In architecture) महाभवनस्य यो दीर्घचतुरस्रो भागः स्तम्भाग्रम् अवलम्बते स च उच्चप्रकारेण तक्षितैर् नानामनुष्यप्रतिमानैर् अलङ्क्रियते.

Frigate, *s.* युद्धनौका, महायुद्धनौका, बृहद्युद्धनौः *f.*

Fright, *s.* त्रासः, सन्त्रासः, भयं, साध्वसं, शङ्का, भीतिः *f.*, परिकम्पः,

उद्वेगः, आतङ्कः, भीषणं, दरः.

To FRIGHT, FRIGHTEN, *v. a.* भी in caus. (भाययति -यितुं or भीषयति -यितुं), त्रस् in caus. (त्रासयति -यितुं), सन्त्रस्, वित्रस्, उत्त्रस्, उद्विज् in caus. (-वेजयति -यितुं), कम्प् in caus. (कम्पयति -यितुं), विकम्प्.

FRIGHTENED, *p.p.* भीतः -ता -तं, त्रासितः -ता -तं, त्रस्तः -स्ता -स्तं, सन्त्रस्तः -स्ता -स्तं, वित्रस्तः -स्ता -स्तं, भीषितः -ता -तं, भयार्त्तः -र्त्ता -र्त्तं, भयातुरः -रा -रं, भयाक्रान्तः -न्ता -न्तं, शङ्कितः -ता -तं, अभिशङ्कितः -ता -तं, दरितः -ता -तं, ससाध्वसः -सा -सं, चकितः -ता -तं, तर्जितः -ता -तं.

FRIGHTFUL, *a.* दारुणः -णा -णं, भयानकः -का -कं, भयङ्करः -रा -रं, भयावहः -हा -हं, घोरः -रा -रं, भीमः -मा -मं, भैरवः -वी -वं, सुभैरवः -वी -वं, भीष्मः -ष्मा -ष्मं, भीरुमयः -यी -यं, रौद्रः -द्री -द्रं, त्रासकरः -रा -रं, विकटः -टा -टं, उग्रः -ग्रा -ग्रं, करालः -ला -लं, शङ्काजनकः -का -कं, उद्वेजनीयः -या -यं; 'in appearance,' भीमदर्शनः -ना -नं, रौद्रदर्शनः -ना -नं, करालवदनः -ना -नं.

FRIGHTFULLY, *adv.* दारुणं, घोरं, भयानकं, उग्रं, भैरवं, सुभैरवं, रौद्रं.

FRIGHTFULNESS, *s.* दारुणता -त्वं, घोरता -त्वं, दारुण्यं, उग्रता -त्वं, रौद्रता.

FRIGID, *a.* (Cold) शीतलः -ला -लं, शीतः -ता -तं, शिशिरः -रा -रं, हिमः -मा -मं, अनुष्णः -ष्णा -ष्णं, जडः -डा -डं, सुषीमः -मा -मं.—(Wanting in affection) निःस्नेहः -हा -हं, स्नेहशून्यः -न्या -न्यं.

FRIGIDITY, *s.* (Coldness) शीतता, शीतलता, शीतं, शैत्यं, हिमं, जडता, जाड्यं, सुषीमः.—(Of affection) निःस्नेहता, नैःस्नेह्यं.

FRIGIDLY, *adv.* शीतलं, शिशिरं, शैत्येन, जाड्येन, जडं, स्नेहं विना.

FRILL, *s.* विरलांशुकमय ऊर्म्मिवद् उत्तानतो वस्त्रालङ्कारः, वस्त्राञ्चलं, अञ्चलः, वस्त्रकोटिः *f.*, ऊर्म्याकारांशुकमयो वस्त्रालङ्कारः, ऊर्म्मिमदंशुकमयो वस्त्रानुबन्धः.

FRINGE, *s.* अञ्चलः, वस्त्राञ्चलः -लं, तरी, तरिः *f.*, वस्तिः *m.*, दशा, शिथिलतन्तुमयो वस्त्राद्यलङ्कारः or वस्त्राद्यनुबन्धः.

To FRINGE, *v. a.* पूर्व्वोक्ताञ्चलेन अलङ्कृ, शिथिलतन्तुभिर् वस्त्रादिकोटिम् अलङ्कृ.

FRIPPERER, *s.* जीर्णवस्त्रक्रयविक्रयिकः, चीरवस्त्रव्यापारी *m.* (न्).

FRIPPERY, *s.* (Old clothes) जीर्णवस्त्रं, चीरवस्त्रं, चीराणि *n. pl.*, वस्त्रखण्डाः *m. pl.*, उच्छिष्टवस्त्रं.—(Useless matter) निरर्थकं, मुधार्थकं, उच्छिष्टं.

To FRISK, *v. n.* चित्तप्रहर्षात् क्रीड् (c. 1. क्रीडति -ते -डितुं) or प्रक्रीड् or विक्रीड्, or इतस्ततः प्लु (c. 1. प्लवते, प्लोतुं) or नृत् (c. 4. नृत्यति, नर्त्तितुं) or रम् (c. 1. रमते, रन्तुं) or खेला (nom. खेलायति) or हस्तपादादि सञ्चल् in caus. (-चालयति -यितुं).

FRISKER, *s.* चित्तप्रसन्नत्वाद् इतस्ततः प्लवकः or नर्त्तकः or खेलाकारी *m.* (न्).

FRISKY, *a.* हृष्टः -ष्टा -ष्टं, चित्तप्रहर्षाद् इतस्ततः क्रीडमानः -ना -नं or प्लवनशीलः -ला -लं, प्रहृष्टः -ष्टा -ष्टं, प्रफुल्लः -ल्ला -ल्लं, आनन्दी -न्दिनी -न्दि (न्), खेलाकारी -रिणी -रि (न्).

FRITH, *s.* समुद्रस्य सङ्कटपथः, सङ्कटं, सम्भेदः, सङ्गमः.

FRITTER, *s.* भृष्टपिष्टकविशेषः, भृष्टापूपः.—(Fragment) खण्डः -ण्डकः, शकलः -लं, विदलं.

To FRITTER, *v. a.* खण्ड् (c. 10. खण्डयति -यितुं), खण्डशः कृ, शकलीकृ; 'fritter away,' अल्पम् अल्पं or खण्डं खण्डं क्षिप्त्वा न्यूनीकृ or क्षीणीकृ or क्षि in caus. (क्षपयति -यितुं).

FRIVOLITY, FRIVOLOUSNESS, *s.* लघुता, लाघवं, लघुवृत्तित्वं -ता, लघुकर्म्मकारित्वं, तुच्छवृत्तित्वं, तुच्छता, चपलता, चापल्यं, चपलवृत्तित्वं, आनर्थक्यं, निरर्थकता.

FRIVOLOUS, *a.* लघुः -घुः -घु, लघुवृत्तिः -त्तिः -त्ति, लघुकर्म्मा -र्म्मा -र्म्म (न्), चपलः -ला -लं, चपलवृत्तिः -त्तिः -त्ति, तुच्छकर्म्मा &c., अनर्थकवृत्तिः -त्तिः -त्ति, निरर्थककर्म्मकारी -रिणी -रि (न्); 'in mind,' लघुचेताः -ताः -तः (स्).

FRIVOLOUSLY, *adv.* लघु, लाघवेन, लघुवृत्तित्वात्, चपलं, निरर्थकं.

To FRIZ, FRIZZLE, *v. a.* कुञ्च् (c. 1. कुञ्चति -ञ्चितुं, c. 10. कुञ्चयति -यितुं), आकुञ्च्, व्यावृत् in caus. (-वर्त्तयति -यितुं), बन्धुरीकृ, उत्तानतीकृ.

FRO, *adv.* (To and fro) इतस्ततस्, इतश्चेतस्, अग्रे पश्चात्; 'going to and fro,' गमनागमनं, गतागतं, प्रतिगतागतं, यातायातं.

FROCK, *s.* (Upper garment) उत्तरीयं.—(Gown) शाटः -टी -टकः, स्त्रीकटीवस्त्रं.

FROG, *s.* भेकः, मण्डूकः, प्लवः, प्लवगः, प्लवगतिः *m.*, प्लवङ्गमः, दर्दुरः, व्यङ्गः, वर्षाभूः *m.*, वर्षाघोषः, वृष्टिभूः *m.*, दर्दरीकः, गूढवर्च्चाः *m.* (स्), अलिमकः, अजिह्वः, शल्लः, शालूरः, सालूरः; 'female,' भेकी, मण्डूकी.—(Of a horse's foot) अश्वखुरमध्यं.

FROGGY, *a.* भेकपूर्णः -र्णा -र्णं, मण्डूकपूर्णः -र्णा -र्णं, दार्दुरः -री -रं.

FROLIC, *s.* क्रीडा, खेला, विहारः, लीला, क्रीडाकौतुकं, कौतुकं, विलासः, विलसनं, परीहासः, केलिः *m.f.*, छन्दः *n.* (स्); 'of a calf,' आलीढकं.

To FROLIC, *v. n.* क्रीड् (c. 1. क्रीडति -ते -डितुं), प्रक्रीड्, विक्रीड्, सङ्क्रीड्, परिक्रीड्, विलस् (c. 1. -लसति -सितुं), रम् (c. 1. रमते, रन्तुं), विहृ (c. 1. -हरति -हर्त्तुं), खेला (nom. खेलायति), लल् (c. 1. ललति -लितुं).

FROLICSOME, *a.* विलासी -सिनी -सि (न्), लीलावान् -वती -वत् (त्), क्रीडावान् &c., केलिकः -का -कं, क्रीडापरः -रा -रं, केलिपरः -रा -रं, खेलापरः -रा -रं, उल्लसः -सा -सं, उल्लासितः -ता -तं, समुल्लसितः -ता -तं, विहारी -रिणी -रि (न्), कलाकेलिः -लिः -लि.

FROM, *prep.* In phrases where it denotes procession, derivation, deliverance, extraction, separation, distance, emission, removal, the reason or motive of any act, and the ground or cause of any thing, it is usually expressed by the abl. case. It is also expressed in some phrases by such words as सकाशात्, मध्यात्, प्रभृति, आरभ्य, or even by the prep. आ with the abl. c. The following are examples; 'coming out from his house,' निःसृत्य गृहात्; 'from avarice anger arises,' लोभात् क्रोधः प्रभवति; 'even from poison nectar may be taken,' विषाद् अप्य् अमृतं ग्राह्यं; 'he delivers me from danger,' त्रायते मां भयात्; 'Krishna is a hundred kos from Somanáth,' कृष्णाः शतं क्रोशाः सोमनाथात्; 'he separates the good from the bad,' साधून् दुष्टेभ्यः पृथक्करोति; 'having discharged an arrow from the bow,' बाणं धनुषः प्रक्षिप्य; 'he rises from his seat,' आसनाद् उत्तिष्ठति; 'from fear of punishment,' दण्डभयात्; 'from unsteadiness of mind,' अनवस्थितचित्तत्वात्; 'from being founded on observation,' प्रत्यक्षमूलत्वात्. The abl. c. is also used to express 'from' in the sense of *since*; as, 'from childhood,' बाल्यात् or बाल्यतः; 'from the earliest period of the world,' जगदारम्भकालात्, but in these cases प्रभृति or आरभ्य or अवधि are often added, or आ may sometimes, but very rarely, be prefixed; as, 'from childhood,' बाल्यात् प्रभृति, आबाल्यात्, आबाल्यकालात्; 'from birth,' जन्मतः प्रभृति, जन्मत आरभ्य, आजन्मतः, जन्मावधि; 'from the very first glance,' प्रथमदर्शनक्षणात् प्रभृति. The word सकाशात् is used in such phrases as, 'from the presence of the king,' राजसकाशात्; 'an order from the council,' सभासकाशाद् आज्ञा. The word मध्यात् in such phrases as, 'from among the soldiers,' सैन्यमध्यात्. Other examples of the modes of expressing 'from' are, 'from the top to the bottom,' ऊर्द्ध्वाद् अधःपर्य्यन्तं; 'from the hole of the weasel to the hole of the serpent,' नकुलविवराद् आरभ्य सर्पविवरं यावत्; 'from birth to death,' जन्मावधि मृत्युपर्य्यन्तं; 'from that time forth,' तदाप्रभृति, तत्कालात् प्रभृति; 'from this day,' अद्यारभ्य, अद्यप्रभृति, अद्यावधि; 'from city to city,' पुरात् पुरं; 'from the beginning to the end,' प्रथमात्प्रभृति or आप्रथमाद् अन्तं यावत्, अनुपूर्व्वशस्; 'Let them be told from me,' उच्यन्तां मम वचनात्; 'from any one soever,' यतःकुतश्चित्; 'from above,' ऊर्द्ध्वात्, उपरिष्टात्; 'from below,' अधस्तात्, अधःस्थानात्; 'from behind,' पश्चिमभागात्; 'from far,' दूरात्, दूरतस्; 'from hence,' इतस्, अतस्; 'from without,' बहिर्देशात्; 'from within,' अभ्यन्तरात्.

FRONT, *s.* (Face) मुखं, वदनं, आननं, आस्यं.—(Forehead) मूर्द्धा *m.* (न्), शिरः *n.* (स्), ललाटं.—(Fore part of any thing) अग्रं, अग्रभागः, अग्रदेशः, अग्रांशः, मुखं, मूर्द्धा; 'in front,' अग्रे, अग्रतस्, पुरस्, पुरतस्, पुरस्तात्, सम्मुखे -खं, अभिमुखे -खं, प्रतिमुखे -खं, अभितस्, साक्षात्, समक्षं, प्रत्यक्षं; 'in front of the assembly,' सभासाक्षात्; 'in front of the army,' अनीकस्य पुरस्; 'in the front, at the head,' अग्रे, मूर्द्ध्नि, धुरि; 'the front of the army,' रणमूर्द्धा, समरमूर्द्धा, सेनामुखं, सेनाग्रं; 'front ranks,' अग्रानीकं; 'to place in front,' पुरस्कृ.

To FRONT, *v. a.* and *n.* सम्मुखीभू, अभिमुखीभू, प्रतिमुखीभू, सम्मुखे वृत् (c. 1. वर्त्तते -र्त्तितुं).—(Be opposite to) expressed by मुख or अभिमुख in comp.; as, 'to front the south,' दक्षिणामुखः -खी -खं भू; 'to front the east,' प्राङ्मुखः -खी -खं भू.

FRONTAGE, *s.* गृहस्य or गृहसमूहस्य सम्मुखभागः or अग्रभागः, सम्मुखस्थितिमुखं.

FRONTAL, *a.* लालाटिकः -की -कं, ललाटसम्बन्धी -न्धिनी -न्धि (न्).

FRONTAL, *s.* (Fillet) ललाटपट्टः -ट्टं, ललाटवेष्टनं, मूर्द्धवेष्टनं, मस्तकबन्धनी; 'of an elephant,' कुम्भः, घटः.

FRONTIER, *s.* सीमा, देशान्तः -न्तं, समन्तः, सामन्तं, प्रान्तः, देशसमन्तः, देशप्रान्तः, पर्य्यन्तः -न्तं, उपान्तः -न्तं; 'dwelling on the frontier,' सामन्तवासी -सिनी -सि (न्), पर्य्यन्तस्थः -स्था -स्थं.

FRONTIER, *a.* सामन्तः -न्ती -न्तं, सीमावर्त्ती -र्त्तिनी -र्त्ति (न्).

FRONTING, *part.* सम्मुखः -खा -खी -खं, सम्मुखीनः -ना -नं, अभिमुखः -खा -खी -खं, प्रतिमुखः -खा -खं, अभिमुखगतः -ता -तं; 'fronting the north,' उत्तराभिमुखः -खा -खं, उदङ्मुखः -खी -खं.

FRONTISPIECE, *s.* (Of a book) अलङ्करणार्थं पुस्तकस्य प्रथमपृष्ठसम्मुखे मुद्रिता वस्तुप्रासङ्गिकी प्रतिमा, ग्रन्थाग्रे प्रतिमा or मुद्रा.—(Of a building) गृहस्य अग्रभागः, गृहमुखं.

FRONTLESS, *a.* निर्लज्जः -ज्जा -ज्जं, लज्जाहीनः -ना -नं, धृष्टः -ष्टा -ष्टं.

FRONTLET, *s.* ललाटपट्टः -ट्टं, ललाटवेष्टनं, मूर्द्धवेष्टनं, शिरोबन्धनी.

FROST, *s.* हिमं, तुषारः, नीहारः, अवश्यायः, प्रालेयं, निहारः, तौषारं, हिमानी, हिमसंहतिः *f.*, हिमिका, तुहिनं, शिशिरं, मिहिका, महिका, खजलं, दर्सं, इन्द्राग्निधूमः, भस्मतूलं, कुज्झटिः *f.* -टिका; 'hoar-frost,' तुषारकणाः.

FROST-BITTEN, *a.* हिमोपहतः -ता -तं, तुषारोपहतः -ता -तं, शीतोपहतः -ता -तं.

FROSTED, *a.* (In cookery) तुषारकणसदृशशर्करान्वितः -ता -तं.

FROSTY, *a.* हिमः -मा -मं, हिमवान् -वती -वत् (त्), हैमः -मी -मं, हिम्यः -म्या -म्यं, नीहारवान् &c., तुषारः -रा -रं, तौषारः -री -रं, तुषारवान् &c.

FROTH, *s.* फेनः, मण्डः -ण्डं, सुरामण्डः, कारोत्तरः, काहलः, उत्पीडः, परञ्जः.

To FROTH, *v. n.* फेन (nom. फेनायते), मण्ड (nom. मण्डायते), उत्सेकं कृ, उत्सेचनं कृ.

FROTHINESS, *s.* फेनता, फेनलता, फेनिलत्वं, फेनवत्त्वं.—(Emptiness) शून्यता -त्वं, असारता, निःसारता, अनर्थकता.

FROTHY, *a.* फेनलः -ला -लं, फेनिलः -ला -लं, फेनी -निनी -नि (न्), फेनवान् -वती -वत् (त्), फेनमयः -यी -यं.—(Empty) शून्यः -न्या -न्यं, असारः -रा -रं, निःसारः -रा -रं, सारहीनः -ना -नं, तुच्छः -च्छा -च्छं, लघुः -घुः -घु.

FROUZY, *a.* दुर्गन्धः -न्धा -न्धं, पूतिगन्धः -न्धा -न्धं, उग्रगन्धिः -न्धिः -न्धि.

FROWARD, *a.* प्रतीपः -पा -पं, विप्रतीपः -पा -पं, विपरीतकारी -रिणी -रि (न्), प्रतिकूलः -ला -लं, अवश्यः -श्या -श्यं, अविनेयः -या -यं, अदम्यः -म्या -म्यं, अदमनीयः -या -यं, वक्रभावः -वा -वं, कर्कशभावः -वा -वं, उच्छृङ्खलः -ला -लं, विलोमः -मा -मं, उल्लङ्घितशासनः -ना -नं.

FROWARDLY, *adv.* प्रतीपं, प्रतिकूलं, वक्रभावेन, कर्कशभावेन, प्रतीपशीलत्वात्.

FROWARDNESS, *s.* प्रतीपता, प्रतिकूलता -त्वं, अवश्यत्वं, अविनेयता, अदम्यत्वं, भाववक्रता, वक्रशीलता, कार्कश्यं.

To FROWN, *v. n.* भ्रूभङ्गं कृ, भ्रूकुटिं कृ, कटाक्षेण or भ्रूभङ्गेन दृश् (c. 1. पश्यति, द्रष्टुं), भ्रुवौ सङ्कुच् (c. 1. -कोचति -चितुं), भ्रूक्षेपं कृ, भ्रूसङ्कोचं कृ.

FROWN, *s.* भ्रूभङ्गः, भ्रूकुटिः *f.* -टी, भ्रुकुटिः *f.* -टी, भृकुटी, भ्रूक्षेपः, काक्षं, भ्रूसङ्कोचः -चनं, कटाक्षः.

FROWNED UPON, *p. p.* कटाक्षितः -ता -तं, भ्रूभङ्गेन निरीक्षितः -ता -तं.

FROWNING, *a.* नतभ्रूः -भ्रूः -भ्रु, संहतभ्रूः -भ्रूः -भ्रु, सभ्रूभङ्गः -ङ्गा -ङ्गं, सभ्रूक्षेपः -पा -पं, सभृकुटीमुखः -खी -खं, सकटाक्षः -क्षा -क्षं, काक्षः -क्षा -क्षं.

FROWNINGLY, *adv.* सभ्रूभङ्गं, भ्रूभङ्गेन, सभ्रूक्षेपं, भ्रूक्षेपेण, कटाक्षेण, सकटाक्षं.

FROZEN, *a.* or *p. p.* अतिशीतत्वाद् घनीभूतः -ता -तं or संहतीभूतः -ता -तं or श्यानीभूतः -ता -तं, हिमसंहतः -ता -तं, अवश्यानः -ना -नं, अवशीतः -ता -तं, अवशीनः -ना -नं, शीतः -ता -तं, शीनः -ना -नं, जडीभूतः -ता -तं, जडीकृतः -ता -तं.

FRUCTIFEROUS, *a.* फलदः -दा -दं, फलदायी -यिनी -यि (न्), फली -लिनी -लि (न्).

FRUCTIFICATION, *s.* सफलीकरणं, फलदीकरणं, अवन्ध्यीकरणं, आधानं.

To FRUCTIFY, *v. a.* सफल (nom. सफलयति -यितुं), सफलीकृ, बहुफलदीकृ, फलितं -तां -तं कृ, स्फीतीकृ, अवन्ध्यीकृ.

FRUCTUOUS, *a.* फली -लिनी -लि (न्), फलवान् -वती -वत् (त्), फलदः -दा -दं.

FRUGAL, *a.* परिमितव्ययः -या -यं, मितव्ययी -यिनी -यि (न्), स्वल्पव्ययः -या -यं, अव्ययः -या -यं, व्ययपराङ्मुखः -खी -खं, अबहुप्रदः -दा -दं, अबहुदः -दा -दं, अमुक्तहस्तः -स्ता -स्तं, परिमितः -ता -तं, कृपणः -णा -णं.

FRUGALITY, *s.* परिमितव्ययः, मितव्ययः, स्वल्पव्ययः, अमुक्तहस्तत्वं, व्ययपराङ्मुखता, परिमितत्वं, कृपणत्वं.

FRUGALLY, *adv.* परिमितव्ययेन, मितव्ययेन, स्वल्पव्ययेन, अमुक्तहस्तेन, अल्पव्ययपूर्व्वं, परिमितं, कृपणं, सकार्पण्यं.

FRUIT, *s.* (Produce of a tree or plant) फलं, वृक्षादिफलं, प्रसवः, वृक्षोत्पन्नं.—(Offspring) अपत्यं, सन्तानः, सन्ततिः *f.*, प्रजा, प्रसूतिः *f.*, उत्पत्तिः *f.*—(Effect, consequence) उत्पन्नं, उत्पत्तिः *f.*, उद्भूतं, कार्य्यं, वृत्तं, फलं, कर्म्मफलं.—(Profit) फलं, लाभः, अर्थः; 'moist fruit,' शलाटुः *m. f. n.*; 'dry fruit,' वानः -ना -नं; 'collection of fruit,' फलोच्चयः; 'fruit season,' फलकालः, फलसमयः; 'fruit-stalk,' शस्यमञ्जरी, प्रसवबन्धनं; 'to bear fruit,' फल् (c. 1. फलति -लितुं), फलं दा; 'bearing fruit,' फलनिष्पत्तिः *f.*

FRUIT-BEARER, *s.* फलदाता *m.* (तृ), फलग्राही *m.* (न्), फलेग्राही *m.*, फलदः.

FRUIT-BEARING, *a.* फलदः -दा -दं -दायी -यिनी -यि (न्), फलग्रहिः -हिः

-हि, फलेग्रहिः -हिः -हि, फली -लिनी -लि (न्), फलवान् -वती -वत् (त्), फलशाली -लिनी -लि (न्).

FRUITERER, *s.* फलविक्रेता *m.* (तृ), फलक्रयविक्रयिकः, फलादिविक्रयी *m.* (न्).

FRUITERY, *s.* (Fruit collectively) फलत्वं, फलानि *n. pl.*, फलोच्चयः. —(Fruit-loft) फलस्थानं, फलागारं.

FRUITFUL, *a.* फली -लिनी -लि (न्), फलवान् -वती -वत् (त्), बहुफलः -ला -ली -लं, फलितः -ता -तं, सफलः -ला -लं, प्रचुरफलः -ला -लं, फलदः -दा -दं -दायी -यिनी -यि (न्), बहुफलदः -दा -दं, फलोत्पादकः -का -कं, फलेग्रहिः -हिः -हि, कृतफलः -ला -लं, फलोपेतः -ता -तं, अवन्ध्यः -न्ध्या -न्ध्यं.—(Prolific) बहुप्रजः -जा -जं, बहुप्रजावान् -वती -वत् (त्), बहुपत्यः -त्या -त्यं, प्रजनिष्णुः -ष्णुः -ष्णु.—(Productive of) उत्पादकः -का -कं, जनकः -का -कं, सावकः -विका -कं.

FRUITFULLY, *adv.* सफलं, सबहुफलं, फलबाहुल्येन, बहुशस्, प्रचुरं.

FRUITFULNESS, *s.* साफल्यं, सफलता, फलवत्त्वं, फलिता, फलबाहुल्यं, फलप्राचुर्य्यं, फलोत्पादकत्वं. —(Fecundity) प्रजनिष्णुता, बहुप्रजावत्त्वं, बहुपत्यत्वं, स्फीतिः *f.*, प्रसवित्वं, सावकत्वं.—(Productiveness) उत्पादकता, जनकता.

FRUITION, *s.* भोगः, भुक्तिः *f.*, उपभोगः, परिभोगः, फलभोगः, अनुभवः, आस्वादः -दनं, सुखभोगः, सुखास्वादः.

FRUITIVE, *a.* फलभोगी -गिनी -गि (न्), उपभोगी &c., परिभोक्ता -क्त्री -क्तृ (क्तृ).

FRUITLESS, *a.* निष्फलः -ला -लं, विफलः -ला -लं, अफलः -ला -लं, फलहीनः -ना -नं, फलापेतः -ता -तं, मोघः -घा -घं, अनर्थः -र्था -र्थं -र्थकः -का -कं, व्यर्थः -र्था -र्थं, निरर्थकः -का -कं, अपार्थः -र्था -र्थं, अनुपयुक्तः -क्ता -क्तं, निष्प्रयोजनः -ना -नं, वन्ध्यः -न्ध्या -न्ध्यं.

FRUITLESSLY, *adv.* निष्फलं, विफलं, मोघं, व्यर्थं, वृथा, मुधा.

FRUITLESSNESS, *s.* निष्फलता, विफलता, वैफल्यं, अफलत्वं, फलहीनता, व्यर्थता, वैयर्थ्यं, अनर्थकत्वं, मोघता, अनुपयोगः, वन्ध्यत्वं.

FRUIT-TIME, *s.* फलकालः, फलसमयः, फलावचयकालः, फलसङ्ग्रहकालः.

FRUIT-TREE, *s.* फलदः, फलग्राही *m.* (न्), सफलवृक्षः.

FRUITY, *a.* फलसरसः -सा -सं, फलरसोपेतः -ता -तं, फलोपमः -मा -मं.

FRUMENTACEOUS, *a.* गोधूममयः -यी -यं, धान्यमयः -यी -यं, शस्यमयः -यी -यं.

FRUMENTY, *s.* *See* FURMENTY.

To FRUSTRATE, *v. a.* खण्ड् (c. 10. खण्डयति -यितुं), प्रतिहन् (c. 2. -हन्ति -न्तुं), व्याहन्, विफलीकृ, निष्फलीकृ, मोघीकृ, व्यर्थीकृ, सङ्कल्पं हन् or भञ्ज् (c. 7. भनक्ति, भंक्तुं), वृथा कृ, मुधा कृ, यत्नं or आशां खण्ड्, भग्नाशं -शां -शं कृ, विफलं -लां -लं कृ, तिरोभू in caus. (-भावयति -यितुं); 'to be frustrated,' वृथा भू, मुधा भू, तिरोभू.

FRUSTRATE, *a.* निष्फलः -ला -लं, विफलः -ला -लं, मोघः -घा -घं, व्यर्थः -र्था -र्थं, निष्प्रयोजनः -ना -नं, अनिष्पन्नः -न्ना -न्नं.

FRUSTRATED, *p. p.* खण्डितः -ता -तं, प्रतिहतः -ता -तं, व्याहतः -ता -तं, विफलीकृतः -ता -तं, मोघीकृतः -ता -तं, वृथाभूतः -ता -तं, व्यर्थीकृतः -ता -तं, मनोहतः -ता -तं; 'in one's efforts,' भग्नोद्यमः -मा -मं, खण्डितयत्नः -त्ना -त्नं, व्यर्थयत्नः -त्ना -त्नं, भग्नसङ्कल्पः -ल्पा -ल्पं; 'in one's expectations,' भग्नाशः -शा -शं, हताशः -शा -शं, खण्डिताशंसः -सा -सं, आशाविभिन्नः -न्ना -न्नं, मोघवाञ्छितः -ता -तं, अनधिगतमनोरथः -था -थं, अकृतार्थः -र्था -र्थं, भग्नसङ्कल्पः -ल्पा -ल्पं.

FRUSTRATION, *s.* खण्डनं, भङ्गः, विफलीकरणं, निष्फलीकरणं, मोघीकरणं, व्यर्थीकरणं, वृथाकरणं, व्याघातः.—(Of expectation) आशाखण्डनं, आशाभङ्गः.—(Of effort) यत्नखण्डनं, यत्नव्याघातः, कर्म्मध्वंसः.

FRUSTRATIVE, FRUSTRATORY, *a.* व्यर्थकारी -रिणी -रि (न्), विफलकारी &c., मोघकारी &c., वृथाकारी &c., खण्डनकारी &c., घाती -तिनी -ति (न्), भञ्जकः -का -कं, व्याघातजनकः -का -कं.

FRUTESCENT, *a.* गुल्मी -ल्मिनी -ल्मि (न्), स्तम्बकारः -री -रं.

FRUTICANT, *a.* अङ्कुरितः -ता -तं, पल्लवितः -ता -तं, पल्लवी -विनी -वि (न्).

FRY, *s.* (Swarm of fish) मत्स्यसङ्घातः, मत्स्यसङ्घः, क्षुद्रमत्स्यसमूहः, क्षुद्राण्डमत्स्यसङ्घातः, पोताधानं.—(Spawn) मत्स्याण्डकः, मीनाण्डं.—(Any thing fried) भृष्टान्नं.

To FRY, *v. a.* भ्रस्ज् (c. 6. भृज्जति -ते, भ्रष्टुं, भर्ष्टुं), भृज् (c. 1. भर्जते -र्जितुं), अम्बरीषे पच् (c. 1. पचति, पक्तुं).

To FRY, *v. n.* भृज् in pass. (भृज्यते), भृष्टः -ष्टा -ष्टं भू, पच् in pass. (पच्यते).

FRYING, *s.* भर्ज्जनं, भृज्जनं or अम्बरीषे पचनं or पाकः.

FRYING-PAN, *s.* अम्बरीषं, भ्राष्ट्रः, ऋजीषं, भृज्जनं, भर्ज्जनयन्त्रं, कटाहः, कन्दुः -न्दूः *m. f. n.*, स्वेदनी, स्वेदनिका.

FUCATED, *a.* चित्रितः -ता -तं, मिथ्यारागान्वितः -ता -तं, कपटरागान्वितः &c.

To FUDDLE, *v. a.* मद् in caus. (मदयति, मादयति -यितुं) or उन्मद्, मद्यदानेन मुह् in caus. (मोहयति -यितुं) or मूढीकृ.

To FUDDLE, *v. n.* मद् (c. 4. माद्यति, मदितुं), मत्तीभू, मद्यपानेन मूढीभू.

FUDDLED, *p. p.* मत्तः -त्ता -त्तं, मद्यपानेन उन्मत्तः -त्ता -त्तं or मूढः -ढा -ढं, मदोन्मत्तः -त्ता -त्तं, मूढबुद्धिः -द्धिः -द्धि.

FUDDLER, *s.* पानरतः, पानप्रसक्तः, मद्यपानासक्तः, पानशौण्डः.

FUDGE, *s.* अनर्थकं, आनर्थक्यं, असम्बद्धं, मृषार्थकं.

FUEL, *s.* इन्धनं, इध्मं, समित् *f.* (ध्), समिन्धनं, एधः *n.* (स्), दारुकाष्ठं, अरणिः *m. f.*, दारुं, ज्वलनार्थम् अङ्गारकाष्ठादि.

To FUEL, *v. a.* इन्धनं दा, काष्ठादीनि दारुवस्तूनि उपस्था in caus. (-स्थापयति -यितुं) or अग्नौ क्षिप् (c. 6. क्षिपति, क्षेप्तुं).

FUGACIOUS, *a.* पलायी -यिनी -यि (न्), प्रपलायी &c., विपलायी &c., पलायनशीलः -ला -लं, पलायमानः -ना -नं, अस्थायी -यिनी -यि (न्).

FUGACIOUSNESS, FUGACITY, *s.* पलायनशीलता, अस्थायित्वं, चञ्चलत्वं.

FUGITIVE, *a.* (Apt to flee away) प्रपलायी -यिनी -यि (न्), पलायनपरायणः -णा -णं.—(Unstable, fleeting) अस्थिरः -रा -रं, अचिरस्थायी -यिनी -यि (न्), चञ्चलः -ला -लं, चपलः -ला -लं, अशाश्वतः -ती -तं, क्षणिकः -की -कं, अनियतः -ता -तं, असुरक्षः -क्षा -क्षं, याप्यधर्म्मकः -का -कं, तरलः -ला -लं.

FUGITIVE, *s.* पलायी *m.* (न्), विपलायी *m.*, युद्धत्यागी *m.* (न्), सेनात्यागी *m.* -त्यक्ता *m.* (क्तृ), युद्धपराङ्मुखः.

FUGITIVENESS, *s.* चाञ्चल्यं, चञ्चलता, अस्थैर्य्यं, अस्थिरता, चापल्यं, तरलता, अचिरस्थायित्वं.

FULCRUM, *s.* उपस्तम्भः, आधारः, धारणं, अवलम्बनं, आलम्बः, आश्रयः.

To FULFIL, *v. a.* (Complete) सम्पृ in caus. (-पूरयति -यितुं), पृ, समभिपृ, सम्पूर्णीकृ, सम्पद् in caus. (-पादयति -यितुं), निष्पद्, समाप् in caus. (-आपयति -यितुं).—(Accomplish, carry into effect) साध् (c. 10. साधयति -यितुं), संसाध्, निर्वह् in caus. (-वाहयति -यितुं), सफलं -लां -लं कृ, सफलीकृ, तीर् (c. 10. तीरयति -यितुं); 'to fulfil a promise,' प्रतिज्ञां शुध् (c. 10. शोधयति -यितुं) or अपवृज् (c. 10. -वर्जयति -यितुं) or तॄ (c. 1. तरति, तरितुं -रीतुं, तर्त्तुं); 'is fulfilled,' सिध्यति.

FULFILLED, *p. p.* सम्पूर्णः -र्णा -र्णं, पूर्णीभूतः -ता -तं, सम्पन्नः -न्ना -न्नं, निष्पन्नः -न्ना -न्नं, सिद्धः -द्धा -द्धं, साधितः -ता -तं, कृतार्थीभूतः -ता -तं, निर्वृत्तः -त्ता -त्तं; 'one whose wishes are fulfilled,' पूर्णकामः -मा -मं, कृतार्थः -र्था -र्थं.

FULFILLER, *s.* पूरकः, पूरयिता *m.* (तृ), सम्पूरकः, परिपूरकः, सम्पादकः, साधकः.

FULFILLING, *part.* पूरयन् -यन्ती -यत् (त्), पूरणः -णा -णी -णं, सम्पादकः

-का -कं, निष्पादनः -ना -नं, समापकः -का -कं; 'fulfilling the desires,' कामपूरः -रा -रं.

Fulfilment, *s.* पूरणं, साधनं, सिद्धिः *f.*, संसिद्धिः *f.*, समाप्तिः *f.*, निष्पत्तिः *f.*, सम्पूर्णता, परिपूर्णता; 'of one's wishes,' इच्छापूरणं, कामसिद्धिः *f.*, साध्यसिद्धिः *f.*, इच्छासम्पत् *f.*, कृतार्थता.

Fulgency, *s.* द्युतिः *f.*, दीप्तिः *f.*, तेजस् *n.*, प्रभा, उज्ज्वलता, दीप्रता.

Fulgent, *a.* दीप्तिमान् -मती -मत् (त्), द्युतिमान् &c., प्रभावान् &c., द्योती -तिनी -ति (न्), उज्ज्वलः -ला -लं, अतितेजसः -सी -सं.

Fuliginous, *a.* कज्जलमयः -यी -यं, धूम्रः -म्रा -म्रं, सधूमः -मा -मं.

Full, *a.* (Replete) पूर्णः -र्णा -र्णं, सम्पूर्णः -र्णा -र्णं, परिपूर्णः -र्णा -र्णं, पूरितः -ता -तं, आकीर्णः -र्णा -र्णं, सङ्कीर्णः -र्णा -र्णं, सङ्कुलः -ला -लं, व्याप्तः -प्ता -प्तं, आढ्यः -ढ्या -ढ्यं, संवलितः -ता -तं, सम्भृतः -ता -तं, मयः -यी -यं in comp.; 'a jar full of ghee,' घृतपूर्णो घटः; 'full of nectar,' अमृतमयः -यी -यं.—(Complete, entire) सकलः -ला -लं, निखिलः -ला -लं, कृत्स्नः -त्स्ना -त्स्नं, समग्रः -ग्रा -ग्रं, अशेषः -षा -षं, अविकलः -ला -लं, अखण्डः -ण्डा -ण्डं, अन्यूनः -ना -नं, सिद्धः -द्धा -द्धं; 'full two years old,' पूर्णद्विवर्षः -र्षी -र्षं.—(Mature) पक्कः -क्का -क्कं, परिपक्कः -क्का -क्कं, परिणतः -ता -तं, सम्पन्नः -न्ना -न्नं.—(As the moon) पूर्णः -र्णा -र्णं, प्रौढः -ढा -ढं, कठोरः -रा -रं; 'at full length,' विस्तरेण, सुविस्तरं.

Full, *s.* पूर्णता -त्वं, सम्पूर्णता, पूर्त्तिः *f.*, साकल्यं; 'to the full,' सर्व्वतस्.

Full, *adv.* सर्व्वथा, साकल्येन, अशेषतस्, अशेषेण, कृत्स्नशस्.

To full, *v. a.* वस्त्रं पेषणयन्त्रेण घनीकृ or स्थूलीकृ or संहत्य निर्णिज् (c. 3. -णेनेक्ति -णेक्तुं) or प्रक्षल् (c. 10. -क्षालयति -यितुं) or सम्मृज् (c. 2. -मार्ष्टि -ष्टुं).

Full-blown, *a.* फुल्लः -ल्ला -ल्लं, उत्फुल्लः -ल्ला -ल्लं, प्रफुल्लः -ल्ला -ल्लं, स्फुटितः -ता -तं, प्रस्फुटः -टा -टं, विकचः -चा -चं, विकसितः -ता -तं.

Full-bodied, *a.* स्थूलशरीरः -रा -रं, प्रौढकायः -या -यं, पुष्टाङ्गः -ङ्गी -ङ्गं.

Full-bosomed, *a.* पीनस्तनः -ना -नं, स्तनाभोगवान् -वती -वत् (त्), पीनकुचकुड्मलः -ला -लं.

Full-bottomed, *a.* स्थूलाधोभागः -गा -गं, बृहदधोभागः -गा -गं.

Full-eyed, *a.* फुल्लनयनः -ना -नं, फुल्ललोचनः -ना -नं.

Full-fed, *a.* पुष्टाङ्गः -ङ्गी -ङ्गं, हृष्टपुष्टः -ष्टा -ष्टं, परितृप्तः -प्ता -प्तं.

Full-grown, *a.* प्रवृद्धः -द्धा -द्धं, प्रौढः -ढा -ढं, एधितः -ता -तं, प्ररूढः -ढा -ढं, उन्नतः -ता -तं, गतशैशवः -वा -वं, पूर्णवृद्धिः -द्धिः -द्धि, कठोरः -रा -रं.

Full-growth, *s.* प्रवृद्धिः *f.* -द्धता, प्रौढिः *f.*, प्रौढता, पूर्णवृद्धिः *f.*

Full-laden, *a.* सुभारवान् -वती -वत् (त्), पूर्णगर्भः -र्भा -र्भं.

Full-moon, *s.* पूर्णेन्दुः *m.*, सकलेन्दुः *m.*, पूर्णिमा, राका, कठोरचन्द्रः, अखण्डकलः; 'day of full moon,' पौर्णमासी, पूर्णिमा, पौर्णिमा.

Fuller, *s.* रजकः, वस्त्रनिर्णेजकः, वस्त्रधावकः, चेलधावः, वस्त्रमार्जकः.

Fuller's-earth, *s.* रजकादिभिर् वस्त्रमार्जने प्रयुक्तो मृत्तिकाविशेषः.

Fuller's-thistle, *s.* रजकादिभिर् वस्त्रपरिष्करणे प्रयुक्तो बहुतीक्ष्णशूकवान् क्षुरभेदः.

Fullery, *s.* वस्त्रनिर्णेजनस्थानं, वस्त्रधावनगृहं, वस्त्रमार्जनशाला.

Fulling-mill, *s.* वस्त्रनिर्णेजने प्रयुक्तं पेषणयन्त्रं, वस्त्रमार्जनयन्त्रं.

Fully, *adv.* सर्व्वतस्, सर्व्वशस्, अशेषतस्, अशेषेण, निःशेषेण, निरवशेषं -षतस्, कृत्स्नशस्, सम्यक्, साकल्येन, अखिलेन, अखण्डतस्, सम्पूर्णं, अशून्यं; 'at full length,' विस्तरेण -रशस्, सुविस्तरं.

Fulminant, *a.* स्फूर्ज्जन् -र्ज्जन्ती -र्ज्जत् (त्), स्फूर्ज्जवान् -वती -वत् (त्), वज्रनिर्घोषकारी -रिणी -रि (न्), स्तनितकारी &c.

To fulminate, *v. n.* स्फूर्ज्ज् (c. 1. स्फूर्ज्जति -र्ज्जितुं), स्तन् (c. 1. स्तनति -नितुं), वज्रनिर्घोषवत् or वज्रनिष्पेषवत् शब्दं कृ.—(Issue threatenings as if with the force of thunder) वज्रनिर्घोषेण इव भर्त्सनानि उदीर् (c. 10. -ईरयति -यितुं).

Fulmination, *s.* स्फूर्ज्जनं, मेघनिर्घोषः, वज्रनिर्घोषेण इव आक्रोशनं.

Fulness, *s.* पूर्णता -त्वं, सम्पूर्णता, परिपूर्णता -त्वं, पूर्त्तिः *f.*, आपूर्त्तिः *f.*, आकीर्णता, सङ्कीर्णता, व्याप्तिः *f.*, सम्भारः.—(Satiety) परिपूर्णता, सौहित्यं.—(Perfection) सिद्धिः *f.*, संसिद्धिः *f.*, प्रौढिः *f.*, सम्पन्नता, सम्पद् *f.*—(Maturity) परिणामः, परिणतिः *f.*, परिपाकः.—(Plenty) बाहुल्यं, प्राचुर्य्यं; 'fulness of consequences,' फलपाकः.

Fulsome, *a.* बीभत्सजनकः -का -कं, विरसः -सा -सं, अरुचिरः -रा -रं, घृणाजनकः -का -कं, कुत्सितः -ता -तं, गर्ह्यः -र्ह्या -र्ह्यं, वैराग्यकृत् *m. f. n.*

Fulsomely, *adv.* विरसं, अरुचिरं, कुत्सितं, यथा बीभत्सः or घृणा जायते तथा.

Fulsomeness, *s.* विरसता, वैरस्यं, कुत्सितत्वं, गर्ह्यता, अरुचिरता.

To fumble, *v. a.* and *n.* परामृश् (c. 6. -मृशति -म्रष्टुं), परिमृश्, अदक्षप्रकारेण कर्म्म कृ or विधा (c. 3. -दधाति -धातुं), समालभ् (c. 1. -लभते -लब्धुं).

Fumbler, *s.* अदक्षप्रकारेण परिमर्शकारी *m.* (न्) or कर्म्मविधायी *m.* (न्).

Fumbling, *s.* अदक्षपरिमर्शः, तमःप्रवेशः, अदक्षप्रकारेण कर्म्मकरणं.

Fumblingly, *adv.* अदक्षपरिमर्शेन, अदक्षं, अपटु, अनाप्तं, अक्षिप्रं.

Fume, *s.* (Smoke, vapor) धूमः -मिका, धूपः -पिका, वाष्पः.—(Exhalation) धूमोद्गारः, धूमोद्गतिः *f.*—(Rage) कोपः, क्रोधः, संरम्भः.

To fume, *v. n.* (Smoke) धूम (nom. धूमायते -ति), धूप (nom. धूपायति -ते), धूमोद्गारं कृ.—(Be angry) क्रुध् (c. 4. क्रुध्यति, क्रोद्धुं), कुप् (c. 4. कुप्यति, कोपितुं), संरब्धः -ब्धा -ब्धं भू.

To fume, *v. a.* धूम (nom. धूमयति -यितुं), धूप (nom. धूपायति, धूपयति -यितुं), धूस (nom. धूसयति-यितुं), वास् (c. 10. वासयति -यितुं), अनुवास्, अधिवास्.

Fumid, *a.* सधूमः -मा -मं, धूम्रः -म्रा -म्रं, धौमीयः -यी -यं.

To fumigate, *v. a.* धूप (nom. धूपायति or धूपयति -यितुं), धूम (nom. धूमयति-यितुं), वास् (c. 10. वासयति -यितुं), अनुवास्, धूमव्याप्तं -प्तां -प्तं कृ.

Fumigated, *p. p.* धूपितः -ता -तं, धूपायितः -ता -तं, अवधूपितः -ता -तं, वासितः -ता -तं, अनुवासितः -ता -तं, धूमव्याप्तः -प्ता -प्तं.

Fumigation, *s.* वासनं, अनुवासनं, अधिवासनं, सधूमीकरणं, धूमव्याप्यकरणं.

Fuming, *part.* धूमायमानः -ना -नं.—(Angry) क्रुध्यन् -ध्यन्ती -ध्यत् (त्).

Fumingly, *adv.* सक्रोधं, सकोपं, सरोषं, संरम्भात्, संरब्धवत्.

Fumitory, *s.* क्षुद्रपुष्पस्तवकविशिष्ट ओषधिप्रभेदः.

Fumous, fumy, *a.* धूममयः -यी -यं, सधूमः -मा -मं, सधूपः -पा -पं.

Fun, *s.* परिहासः -स्यं, परीहासः, खेला, क्रीडा, कौतुकं, क्रीडाकौतुकं, नर्म्म *n.* (न्), केलिः *m. f.*, प्रहसनं, हासिका, उज्ज्वलता, मुदा; 'in fun,' परिहास्येन.

Funambulist, *s.* रज्जुचारी *m.* (न्), रज्जुनर्त्तकः, रज्जुनृत्यकारी *m.* (न्), प्लवकः.

Function, *s.* (Performance) करणं, निर्वाहः, अनुष्ठानं, आचरणं.—(Office, employment) कर्म्म *n.* (न्), कार्य्यं, कृत्यं, क्रिया, व्यापारः, व्यवसायः, व्यवहारः, वृत्तिः *f.*, प्रवृत्तिः *f.*, वृत्तं, नियोगः, पदं, अधिकारः.—(Duty, property) धर्म्मः, गुणः, व्रतं.—(Faculty) इन्द्रियं, कर्म्मेन्द्रियं, शक्तिः *f.*

Functional, *a.* ऐन्द्रियिकः -की -कं, शक्तिसम्बन्धीयः -या -यं.

Functionary, *s.* नियोगी *m.* (न्), नियुक्तः, अधिकारी *m.* (न्), अधिकारवान् *m.* (त्), कर्म्मकारी *m.* (न्), कर्म्मकरः, कर्म्मनिर्वाहकः.

Fund, *s.* (Stock) सञ्चयः, सञ्चितं, पुञ्जः, समुदायः, सङ्ग्रहः, सम्भारः, संयोगः, सन्निपातः, समयः, चायः, निचयः, संहारः, समाहारः, समवायः, कोषः,

संस्थितिः *f.*, संस्थानं.—(Capital) मूलधनं, नीविः -वी *f.*, परिणतं, परिपणं.—(Money lent to government and bearing interest) राजकोषे निक्षिप्तं सवृद्धिकं धनं.

To FUND, *v. a.* सञ्चितं कृ, पुञ्जं कृ, मूलधनं सञ्चि (c. 5. -चिनोति -चेतुं).

FUND-HOLDER, *s.* राजधनार्थी *m.* (न्), राजकोषे सवृद्धिकधननिक्षेप्ता *m.* (तृ).

FUNDAMENT, *s.* गुदं, पायुः *m.* मैत्रः, अपानं, अपानद्वारं, मार्गः, मलद्वारं, सीमं, गुह्यं, शकृद्देशः, अधोङ्गं, अधोभागः, अधोदेशः, अधोपथः.

FUNDAMENTAL, *a.* मौलः -ली -लं, मूलिकः -की -कं, मूली -लिनी -लि (न्), आवश्यकः -की -कं, गुर्वर्थः -र्था -र्थं, प्रधानार्थः -र्था -र्थं, पारमार्थिकः -की -कं, सारः -रा -रं, वास्तवः -वी -वं.

FUNDAMENTAL, *s.* (Principle) तत्त्वं, मूलतत्त्वं, गुरुतत्त्वं, सारः, मूलं, परमार्थः, प्रधानं, प्रधानतत्त्वं.

FUNDAMENTALLY, *adv.* मूलतस्, वस्तुतस्, सारतस्, प्रधानतस्, तत्त्वतस्.

FUNERAL, *s.* अन्त्येष्टिः *f.*, अन्त्येष्टिक्रिया, प्रेतकर्म्म *n.* (न्), प्रेतकार्य्यं, प्रेतकृत्यं, और्द्धदेहिका -कं, और्द्धदेहिकक्रिया, अन्त्यकर्म्म *n.* (न्), अन्तकर्म्म *n.*, शवकर्म्म *n.*, मृतशरीरसत्कर्म्म *n.* उत्तरक्रिया, अन्तसत्क्रिया, सत्क्रिया, प्रेतनिर्हारः, शवानुगमनं, श्मशानयापनं, श्मशाने स्थापनकर्म्म *n.* (न्), श्राद्धादिकर्म्म, शवदाहादि कर्म्म *n.*

FUNERAL, *a.* और्द्धदेहिकः -की -कं, आन्तकर्म्मिकः -की -कं, अन्त्येष्टिसम्बन्धी -न्धिनी -न्धि (न्); 'funeral rite,' श्राद्धं, प्रेतकर्म्म *n.* (न्), अन्त्येष्टिः *f.*, कटोदकं; 'funeral fire,' चितानिनः *m.*, श्मशानाग्निः *m.*; 'funeral hymn,' यमगाथा.

FUNERAL-PILE, *s.* चिता, चितिः *f.* -ती, चित्या, श्मशानाग्निः *m.*

FUNEREAL, *s.* अन्त्येष्टियोग्यः -ग्या -ग्यं, शोकसूचकः -का -कं, विलापी -पिनी -पि (न्), श्माशानिकः -की -कं, निरानन्दः -न्दा -न्दं.

FUNGOUS, *a.* छत्राकरूपेण or गोमयछत्रवद् रोही -हिणी -हि (न्), छत्राकोपमः -मा -मं, छत्राकस्वभावः -वा -वं, छत्रकगुणविशिष्टः -ष्टा -ष्टं.

FUNGUS, *s.* गोमयछत्रं, विड्जछत्रं, विड्जं, गोमयजं, छत्रं -त्रा, छत्राकं, छत्रकः, शिलीन्ध्रं -न्ध्रकं, उच्छिलीन्ध्रं -न्ध्रकं, अतिच्छत्रः -त्रकः, अर्य्याङ्गं.

FUNICLE, *s.* रज्जुकः, क्षुद्ररज्जुः *m. f.*, क्षुद्रगुणः, सूत्रं, तन्तुः *m.*

FUNK, *s.* अतिभयात् कृतो दुर्गन्धः or कुत्सितगन्धः or पूतिगन्धः, पूतिः *f.*

To FUNK, *v. n.* अतिभयाद् दुर्गन्धं कृ or कुत्सितगन्धं कृ.

FUNNEL, *s.* (For smoke) धूमपथः, धूममार्गः, धूमद्वारं.—(Tube, pipe) सूच्याकारा नाली, प्रणाली -लिका, नाडिः *f.* -डी, सुषिरनालिः *f.*

FUNNY, *a.* (Droll) हास्यः -स्या -स्यं, उपहास्यः -स्या -स्यं, हासकरः -री -रं, रसिकः -का -कं, सरसः -सा -सं, विनोदी -दिनी -दि (न्), कौतुकी -किनी कि (न्), अपरूपः -पा -पं.

FUNNY, *s.* (Light boat) लघुनौकाविशेषः.

FUR, *s.* लोम *n.* (न्), पशुलोम *n.* (न्), रोम *n.* (न्), अङ्गरुहं, तनुरुहं, तनुजं, पश्वादेर् लोमशचर्म्म *n.* (न्), लोमचर्म्म *n.*—(On the tongue) कुलुकं, कुल्वकः, जिह्वामलं.

FUR, *a.* पशुलोममयः -यी -यं, लोमनिर्म्मितः -ता -तं.

To FUR, *v. a.* लोमावृतं -तां -तं कृ, वस्त्रं लोमान्वितं or लोमोपेतं कृ.

FURBELOW, *s.* ऊर्म्याकारांशुकमयो वस्त्राञ्चलः or वस्त्रसम्बन्धी अलङ्कारः, स्त्रीवस्त्रपरितः स्यूतम् ऊर्म्याकारम् अधिकांशुकं.

To FURBISH, *v. a.* तिज् (c. 10 तेजयति -यितुं), निष्टप् (c. 10. निष्टापयति -यितुं, rt. तप्), मृज् (c. 2. मार्ष्टि -र्ष्टुं), कान्तिं दा, धाव् (c. 10. धावयति -यितुं), परिष्कृ.

FURBISHED, *p. p.* तेजितः -ता -तं, सुनिष्टप्तः -प्ता -प्तं, मार्जितः -ता -तं, मृष्टः -ष्टा -ष्टं, प्रमृष्टः -ष्टा -ष्टं, निर्धौतः -ता -तं, धौतः -ता -तं, परिष्कृतः -ता -तं.

FURBISHER, *s.* तेजकः, मार्जनकृत्, सम्मार्जकः, धावकः, निर्णेजकः, कान्तिदायकः.—(Of weapons) अस्त्रमार्ज्जः, असिधावः.

FURBISHING, *s.* तेजनं, मार्जनं, मार्ष्टिः *f.*, धावनं, परिष्कारः.

FURCATED, *a.* द्व्यग्रः -ग्रा -ग्रं, अग्रद्वयविशिष्टः -ष्टा -ष्टं, वक्रः -क्रा -क्रं.

FURIOUS, *a.* (Mad) उन्मत्तः -त्ता -त्तं, उन्मादः -दा -दं, मदोत्कटः -टा -टं, उन्मादसंरब्धः -ब्धा -ब्धं, मदोदग्रः -ग्रा -ग्रं, मत्तः -त्ता -त्तं, समदः -दा -दं, उत्कटः -टा -टं.—(Violent) उग्रः -ग्रा -ग्रं, साहसिकः -की -कं, प्रबलः -ला -लं, महावेगवान् -वती -वत् (त्), उच्चण्डः -ण्डा -ण्डं.—(With rage) कोपाकुलः -ला -लं, क्रोधाकुलः -ला -लं, संरब्धः -ब्धा -ब्धं, संरम्भी -म्भिणी -म्भि (न्), रोषणः -णा -णं, रोषवेगाकुलः -ला -लं.

FURIOUSLY, *adv.* उग्रं, उन्मत्तवत्, संरम्भेण, कोपाकुलवत्, महावेगेन.

FURIOUSNESS, *s.* उन्मत्तता, उग्रता, संरब्धत्वं, संरम्भः, कोपाकुलत्वं.

To FURL, *v. a.* नौकावसनं or वातवसनं सम्पुटीकृ or संवेष्ट् (c. 10. -वेष्टयति -यितुं) or संहृ (c. 1. -हरति -हर्त्तुं) or संवृ (c. 1. -वरति, c. 5. वृणोति -वरितुं -रीतुं).

FURLED, *p. p.* संवृतः -ता -तं, सम्पुटीकृतः -ता -तं, संवेष्टितः -ता -तं.

FURLONG, *s.* नल्वः, किष्कुचतुःशतं, अर्द्धक्रोशस्य अष्टमभागः.

FURLOUGH, *s.* निरूपितकालं यावत् कर्म्मत्यागानुज्ञा or कर्म्मविरामानुज्ञा or कर्म्मनिवृत्तिः *f.*, or कर्म्मावकाशः or अवकाशः or कर्म्मावसरः.

FURMENTY, *s.* दुग्धेन सह क्वथितं गोधूमधान्यादि भोजनं.

FURNACE, *s.* उष्मानं, उद्धानं, उद्धारं, चुल्लिः *f.* -ल्ली, अश्मन्तं, अस्मन्तं, अन्तिका, अन्दिका, अधिश्रयणी, अग्निकुण्डं, वह्निकुण्डं, भीरुरन्ध्रः, मुषा; 'a portable furnace,' अङ्गारधानिका, अङ्गारशकटी, हसन्ती, हसनी.

To FURNISH, *v. a.* (Supply with all things necessary) सर्व्वोपकरणैः समायुज् (c. 10. -योजयति -यितुं) or संयुज् or युज्, सर्व्वोपकारद्रव्याणि उपक्लृप् (c. 10. -कल्पयति -यितुं) or परिक्लृप् or सम्प्रक्लृप् or उपस्था in caus. (-स्थापयति -यितुं) or उपपद् in caus. (-पादयति -यितुं) or सम्भृ (c. 1. -भरति -भर्त्तुं) or पुरस्कृ or प्रस्तुतीकृ or विधा (c. 3. -दधाति -धातुं), द्रव्यसम्भारं कृ, उपकरणसम्भारं कृ; 'furnish a house,' गृहम् उपस्करादिना समायुज् or पीठशयनभाण्डाद्युपेतं कृ; 'furnish with arms,' अस्त्रैः or शस्त्रैः सज्जीकृ, सन्नह् (c. 4. -नह्यति -नद्धुं).—(Equip) सज्जीकृ, सज्ज् (c. 1. सज्जति -ज्जितुं), ससज्जं -ज्जां -ज्जं कृ.

FURNISHED, *p. p.* युक्तः -क्ता -क्तं, संयुक्तः -क्ता -क्तं, समायुक्तः -क्ता -क्तं, समन्वितः -ता -तं, अन्वितः -ता -तं, उपेतः -ता -तं, उपक्लृप्तः -प्ता -प्तं, परिक्लृप्तः -प्ता -प्तं, सम्प्रक्लृप्तः -प्ता -प्तं, संहितः -ता -तं, सम्भृतः -ता -तं.—(With necessaries) सोपकारद्रव्ययुक्तः -क्ता -क्तं, सोपकारः -रा -रं, सोपकरणः -णा -णं, सोपस्करः -रा -रं; 'a furnished house,' उपस्करादियुक्तं गृहं, सोपस्करगृहं.—(Equipped) सज्जीकृतः -ता -तं.

FURNITURE, *s.* उपकरणं, उपस्करः, परिच्छदः, पारिणाह्यं, परीभाण्डं, सामग्र्यं -ग्री, सम्भारः, सज्जा; 'household furniture,' गृहोपस्करः, गृहपारिणाह्यं.—(Appendages) अनुबन्धाः *m. pl.*

FURRED, *p. p.* or *a.* लोमावृतः -ता -तं, लोमवान् -वती -वत् (त्), लोमान्वितः -ता -तं; 'as the tongue,' मलवान् -वती -वत् (त्), समलः -ला -लं.

FURRIER, *s.* पशुलोमविक्रेता *m.* (तृ), लोमक्रयविक्रयिकः, लोमव्यवसायी *m.* (न्).

FURROW, *s.* (Made by a plough) सीता, हलिः *m.*, लाङ्गलपद्धतिः *f.*, हलरेखा, वृहद्धलं, लेखा.—(Groove) शुषिरं, रेखा.—(Wrinkle) रेखा, वदनरेखा, बहुरेखाः *pl.*

To FURROW, *v. a.* सीतां कृ, विलेखनं कृ, लाङ्गलेन पद्धतिं कृ or लेखां कृ or भूमौ रेखाः कृ, हल् (c. 1. हलति -लितुं), भूमिं कृष् (c. 1. कर्षति, क्रष्टुं).

FURROWED, *p. p.* सीत्यः -त्या -त्यं, रेखाचिह्नितः -ता -तं, रेखान्वितः -ता -तं.

FURRY, *a.* लोमशः -शा -शं, लोमवान् -वती -वत् (त्), लोममयः -यी -यं.

FURTHER, *a.* (More distant) दूरतरः -रा -रं, विदूरतरः -रा -रं, दवीयान्

-यसी -यः (स्), अधिकदूरस्थः -स्था -स्थं.—(Additional) अधिकः -का -कं, अधिकतरः -रा -रं, अपरः -रा -रं, परः -रा -रं. *See* FARTHER.

FURTHER, *adv.* दूरतरं, विदूरतरं, अधिकदूरे, अग्रे, अग्रतरं, अग्रतस्, पुरतस्, ऊर्द्ध्वं; 'further and further,' उत्तरोत्तरं, अधिकाधिकं; 'move off a little further,' स्तोकम् अन्तरं or किञ्चिद् अपरतोऽपसर.—(Moreover) अपरं, अपरञ्च, अधिकन्तु, किञ्च, अन्यच्च.

To FURTHER, *a.* उपकृ, पुरस्कृ, साहाय्यं कृ, प्रवृत् (c. 10. -वर्त्तयति -यितुं), प्रवृध् (c. 10. -वर्धयति -यितुं), संवृध्, प्रयुज् (c. 10. -योजयति -यितुं), अनुग्रह् (c. 9. -गृह्णाति -ग्रहीतुं), उपग्रह्, त्वर् (c. 10. त्वरयति -यितुं), उपकारं कृ, पक्षपातं कृ.

FURTHERANCE, *s.* उपकारः -रिता, उपकरणं, साहाय्यं, वर्धनं, प्रवर्धनं, वृद्धिः *f.*, संवर्धना, उपग्रहः, अनुग्रहः, सङ्ग्रहः, प्रवर्त्तनं, पक्षपातः.

FURTHERED, *p. p.* प्रवर्धितः -ता -तं, संवर्धितः -ता -तं, प्रवर्त्तितः -ता -तं, कृतसाहाय्यः -य्या -य्यं, उपकृतः -ता -तं, कृतोपकारः -रा -रं.

FURTHERER, *s.* उपकारी *m.* (न्), उपकारकः, साहाय्यकर्त्ता *m.* (र्तृ), प्रवर्धकः, प्रवर्त्तकः, संवर्धनकारी *m.*, उत्तरसाधकः, प्रयोजकः.

FURTHERMORE, *s.* अपरञ्च, अपरं, अपरन्तु, परन्तु, अधिकन्तु, अन्यच्च, अपिच, किञ्च.

FURTHEST, FURTHERMOST, *a.* दूरतमः -मा -मं, विदूरतमः -मा -मं, दविष्ठः -ष्ठा -ष्ठं, सुदूरः -रा -रं, अत्यन्तदूरः -रा -रं, अतिदूरस्थः -स्था -स्थं.

FURTHEST, *adv.* दूरतमं, विदूरतमं, सुदूरं, अत्यन्तदूरं, दविष्ठं.

FURTIVE, *a.* चौरहृतः -ता -तं, छलेन हृतः -ता -तं or गृहीतः -ता -तं, चौर्य्येण अपहृतः -ता -तं, मुषितः -ता -तं.

FURTIVELY, *adv.* छलेन, निभृतं, सुनिभृतं, रहसि, उपांशु, चौरवत्.

FURUNCLE, *s.* व्रणः -णं, नालीव्रणः, स्फोटः -टकः, विस्फोटः, गण्डः.

FURY, *s.* (Madness) उन्मादः, उन्मत्तता, प्रामाद्यं, मदोत्कटत्वं, मदोदग्रता.—(Rage) संरम्भः, संरब्धता, उग्रता -त्वं, कोपः, क्रोधः, सौत्कट्यं, चण्डता, उग्रचण्डता.—(Impetuous motion) अत्यन्तवेगः, महावेगः, आपातः.—(Goddess of vengeance) चण्डा -ण्डी, दुर्गा.—(Furious woman) चण्डी.

FURZE, *s.* प्रचुरकण्टकः पीतपुष्पः सदाहरितवर्णो गुल्मभेदः.

FURZY, *a.* पूर्व्वोक्तगुल्मावृतः -ता -तं, सकण्टकस्तम्बपूर्णः -र्णा -र्णं.

FUSCATION, *s.* तिमिरीकरणं, तिमिरं, कलुषीकरणं, अन्धकारकरणं.

FUSCOUS, *a.* आकृष्णः -ष्णा -ष्णं, श्यामः -मा -मं, कपिशवर्णः -र्णा -र्णं.

To FUSE, *v. a.* विली in caus. (-लाययति -लापयति -यितुं), विद्रु in caus. (-द्रावयति -यितुं), द्रवीकृ, गल् in caus. (गालयति -यितुं), गलितीकृ, जलसात्कृ, आर्द्रीकृ, विलीनीकृ.

To FUSE, *v. n.* विली (c. 4. -लीयते -लेतुं), प्रविली, प्रली, द्रु (c. 1. द्रवति, द्रोतुं), विद्रु, गल् (c. 1. गलति -लितुं), विगल्, द्रवीभू, विलीनीभू, जलसाद्भू, क्षर् (c. 1. क्षरति -रितुं).

FUSED, *p. p.* द्रुतः -ता -तं, विद्रुतः -ता -तं, विद्रावितः -ता -तं, विलीनः -ना -नं, लीनः -ना -नं, निलीनः -ना -नं, द्रवीकृतः -ता -तं, द्रवीभूतः -ता -तं, गलितः -ता -तं, गालितः -ता -तं, परिगलितः -ता -तं, तप्तः -प्ता -प्तं.

FUSEE, *s.* (Of a watch) घटीमध्यवर्त्ती सूची यत्परितः शृङ्खलम् आवेष्टितं तिष्ठति.—(Small firelock) क्षुद्रपरिमाणा युद्धनाडी or आग्नेयनाडिः *f.*

FUSIBILITY, *s.* द्राव्यत्वं -ता, विद्राव्यता, द्रवत्वं, गलनीयता, विलयनीयता.

FUSIBLE, *a.* द्राव्यः -व्या -व्यं, विद्राव्यः -व्या -व्यं, विलयनीयः -या -यं, गलनीयः -या -यं, द्रवणीयः -या -यं, सुविलयः -या -यं, क्षरणीयः -या -यं, क्षरभावः -वा -वं, याव्यः -व्या -व्यं, विलयनशीलः -ला -लं.

FUSIL, *s.* क्षुद्रपरिमाणा लघुयुद्धनाडी or आग्नेयनाडिः *f.*

FUSILEER, *s.* पूर्व्वोक्तशस्त्रधारी or पूर्व्वोक्तशस्त्रभृत् सैन्यः or योद्धा *m.* (द्धृ).

FUSING, *part.* द्रवमाणः -णा -णं, गाली -लिनी -लि (न्).

FUSION, *s.* द्रावः, द्रवत्वं, विलयनं, विलयः, विद्रावः, गलनं, गालनं, लयः -यं, गलितत्वं, प्रतीवापः, द्रवीकरणं, विलीनता.

FUSS, *s.* सम्भ्रमः, व्यग्रता, आकुलत्वं, वैक्लव्यं, व्यस्तता, तुमुलं, कोलाहलः.

FUSSY, *a.* सम्भ्रमशीलः -ला -लं, व्यग्रशीलः -ला -लं.

FUST, *s.* (Of a column) स्तम्भदण्डः, स्तम्भः, स्थूणास्तम्भः, स्तम्भयष्टिः *f.*—(Strong smell) दुर्गन्धः, कुत्सितगन्धः, पूतिगन्धः, उग्रगन्धः.

FUSTIAN, *s.* (Cloth) स्थूलकार्पासं, स्थूलवस्त्रं, स्थूलशाटकः, वराशिः *m.*—(Inflated style of writing) गर्व्वितवाग्वृत्तिः *f.*, दर्पवाक्यं, अतिशयोक्तिः *f.*

FUSTIAN, *a.* कार्पासिकः -की -कं, स्थूलकार्पासमयः -यी -यं.—(Inflated) अतिगर्व्वितः -ता -तं, आध्मातः -ता -तं.

FUSTINESS, *s.* पूतिः *f.*, कुत्सितत्वं, पूतिगन्धता, दुर्गन्धः, विरसता, वैरस्यं.

FUSTY, *a.* दुर्गन्धः -न्धा -न्धं, पूतिगन्धः -न्धा -न्धं, उग्रगन्धिः -न्धिः -न्धि, कुत्सितगन्धः -न्धा -न्धं, विरसः -सा -सं, पूतः -ता -तं, पर्य्युषितः -ता -तं.

FUTILE, *a.* लघ्वर्थः -र्था -र्थं, तृणप्रायः -या -यं, निरर्थकः -का -कं, अनर्थकः -का -कं, मोघः -घा -घं, असारः -रा -रं, क्लीवः -वा -वं, मन्दः -न्दा -न्दं.

FUTILITY, *s.* अनर्थकत्वं, लाघवं, मोघता, असारता, क्लीवता, निर्गुणत्वं.

FUTURE, *a.* भावी -विनी -वि (न्), भविष्यन् -ष्यन्ती -ष्यत् (त्), आगामी -मिनी -मि (न्), अनागतः -ता -तं, भाविकः -का -कं, उत्तरकालीनः -ना -नं, कालान्तरीयः -या -यं, श्वौवस्तिकः -की -कं, श्वस्तनः -नी -नं.—(Belonging to another world) पारलौकिकः -की -कं, पारत्रिकः -की -कं, आमुष्मिकः -की -कं, अमुत्रत्यः -त्या -त्यं; 'future event,' भाविघटना; 'future tense,' भविष्यत्कालः.

FUTURE, FUTURITY, *s.* भविष्यत्कालः, भाविकालः, उत्तरकालः, आगामिकालः, परकालः, भावि *n.* (न्), भविष्यत् *n.*, आयतिः *f.*, आयत्तिः *f.*, उदर्कः; 'knowledge of futurity,' भविष्यज्ज्ञानं; 'ignorant of the future,' अश्वस्तनवित् *m. f. n.*

FUZZBALL, *s.* रेणुपूरितो गोमयच्छत्रप्रभेदः, बहुपांशुगर्भं विड्जच्छत्रं.

FY, *exclam.* धिक्, अपैहि, अपेहि, शान्तं, उम्, अये, अरे, कित्.

G.

GABARDINE, *s.* स्थूलशाटकः, स्थूलशाटी, ग्राम्यजनभृतं शिथिलोत्तरीयं.

To GABBLE, *v. n.* जल्प् (c. 1. जल्पति -ल्पितुं), उपजल्प्, प्रलप् (c. 1. -लपति -पितुं), अनर्थकवाक्यम् उदीर् (c. 10. -ईरयति -यितुं), अनर्थकशब्दं कृ, वृथाशब्दं कृ.

GABBLE, *s.* जल्पः -ल्पना -ल्पितं, प्रजल्पः, प्रलापः, निरर्थकशब्दः, चीत्कारः.

GABBLER, *s.* जल्पकः, जल्पाकः, उपजल्पी *m.* (न्), अनर्थकशब्दकारी *m.* (न्).

GABEL, *s.* शुल्कः -ल्कं, करः, राजग्राह्यभागः, राजदेयो भागः, राजस्वं.

GABION, *s.* युद्धे शत्रुप्रक्षिप्तगोलनिवारको मृत्तिकागर्भः करण्डविशेषः.

GABLE, GABLE-END, *s.* गृहशृङ्गं, प्रासादशृङ्गं, गृहशिखरं, वडभिः *f.*

GAD, *s.* (Head of a spear or arrow) शूलाग्रं, वाणाग्रं.—(Wedge of steel or iron) तीक्ष्णायसकीलः, लोहकीलः.

To GAD ABOUT, *v. n.* अट् (c. 1. अटति -टितुं), पर्य्यट्, भ्रम् (c. 1. भ्रमति, c. 4. भ्राम्यति, भ्रमितुं), परिभ्रम्, अट् in freq. (अटाट्यते), इतस्ततो विचर् (c. 1. -चरति -रितुं).

GADDER, *s.* अटनकारी *m.* (न्), पर्य्यटनकृत्, भ्रमणकारी *m.*, अवनिचरः.

GADDING ABOUT, *s.* अटनं, पर्य्यटनं, भ्रमणं, परिभ्रमणं, व्रज्या, विहरणं.

GADFLY, *s.* दंशः -शी, दंशकः, वनमक्षिका, अरण्यमक्षिका, गोमक्षिका, नीलाङ्कुः *m.*, पांशुरः.

GAFF, *s.* (Light spear used by fishermen) लघुशूलः, धीवरी.—(For extending sails) नौकावसनप्रसारणार्थं यष्टिः *m. f.*

GAFFER, *s.* साधुजनः, आर्य्यकः, आर्य्यमाणवकः, तपस्वी *m.* (न्),

To GAG, *v. a.* मुखं बन्ध् (c. 9. बध्नाति, बन्धुं) or प्रतिबन्ध् or रुध् (c. 7. रुणद्धि, रोद्धुं) or निरुध् or प्रतिरुध् or पिधा (c. 3. -दधाति -धातुं).

GAG, *s.* मुखरोधनं, मुखबन्धनी, मुखप्रतिबन्धकं, मुखपिधानं.

GAGE, *s.* (Pledge) पणः, परिपणनं, प्रतिपाणं, आधिः *m.*, बन्धकः.—(Challenge) आह्वानं.—(Measure) परिमाणं, परिमाणविधिः *m.*, परिमाणरीतिः *f.*, प्रमाणं, मानं.—(Instrument for measuring) मापनयन्त्रं, परिमापनयन्त्रं; 'rain-gage,' वृष्टिमापनयन्त्रं.

To GAGE, *v. a.* (Pledge) पण् (c. 1. पणते -णितुं), पणं कृ, प्रतिज्ञा (c. 9. -जानीते -ज्ञातुं), अङ्गीकृ.—(Bind by pledge) पणेन बन्ध् (c. 9. बध्नाति, बन्धुं).—(Measure). *See* GUAGE.

To GAGGLE, *v. n.* हंसनादं कृ, हंसवत् कूज् (c. 1. कूजति -जितुं).

GAGGLING, *s.* हंसनादः, हंसरुतं, हंसकूजनं, कूजनं.

GAIETY, *s.* *See* GAYETY.

GAILY, *adv.* (Joyfully) सहर्षं, सानन्दं, हृष्टमनसा, प्रफुल्लमनसा, प्रसन्नचेतसा, प्रमोदेन.—(Splendidly) अतिशोभनं, शोभनं, सशोभं; 'gaily dressed,' शोभनवेशी -शिनी -शि (न्), उज्ज्वलवेशधारी -रिणी -रि (न्).

GAIN, *s.* लाभः, लब्धिः *f.*, प्राप्तिः *f.*, फलं, अर्ज्जनं, उपार्ज्जनं, लभ्यं, लभ्यांशः, प्रतिपत्तिः *f.*, आयः, फलोदयः, अर्थः, उत्पन्नं, पण्यफलत्वं, योगक्षेमः, वृद्धिः *f.*, विवृद्धिः *f.*, प्रयोगः.

To GAIN, *v. a.* (Obtain, acquire) अर्ज् (c. 10. अर्जयति -यितुं), उपार्ज्; लभ् (c. 1. लभते, लब्धुं), उपलभ्, आप् (c. 5. आप्नोति, आप्तुं), प्राप् सम्प्राप्, अवाप्, समाप्; आसद् (c. 10. -सादयति -यितुं), समासद्, अधिगम् (c. 1. -गच्छति -गन्तुं), गम्, प्रतिपद् (c. 4. -पद्यते -पत्तुं), आपद्, आविश् (c. 6. -विशति -वेष्टुं), समाविश्, अश् (c. 5. अश्नुते, अशितुं), समश्, उपाश्, विद् (c. 6. विन्दति, वेत्तुं, वेदितुं), अभिविद्, प्रतिविद्, इ (c. 2. एति -तुं), स्वीकृ.—(Gain by conquest) निर्जि (c. 1. -जयति -जेतुं).—(Gain over) अनुरञ्ज् (c. 10. -रञ्जयति -यितुं), प्रसाध् (c. 10. -साधयति -यितुं); 'to one's own party,' आत्मपक्षीकृ.—(Gain ground) वृध् (c. 1. वर्धते -र्धितुं), प्रभू.

To GAIN, *v. n.* (Have advantage) लाभं कृ, फलं कृ.—(Grow rich, prosper) समृद्धीभू, समृध् (c. 5. -ऋध्नोति -अर्धितुं), वृध् (c. 1. वर्धते -र्धितुं).—(Advance on, encroach) क्रमे क्रमे प्रसृप् (c. 1. -सर्पति -सप्तुं) or प्रगम् (c. 1. -गच्छति -गन्तुं).—(Prevail against) अतिरिच् in pass. (-रिच्यते), अभिभू, प्रभू, जि (c. 1. जयति, जेतुं).

GAINABLE, *a.* प्राप्यः -प्या -प्यं, लभ्यः -भ्या -भ्यं, आसादनीयः -या -यं.

GAINED, *p. p.* प्राप्तः -प्ता -प्तं, आप्तः -प्ता -प्तं, अवाप्तः -प्ता -प्तं, लब्धः -ब्धा -ब्धं, अर्ज्जितः -ता -तं, उपार्ज्जितः -ता -तं, आसादितः -ता -तं, समासादितः -ता -तं, अधिगतः -ता -तं, आपन्नः -न्ना -न्नं, उपात्तः -त्ता -त्तं, कलितः -ता -तं; 'gained with difficulty,' कृच्छ्राप्तः -प्ता -प्तं.

GAINER, *s.* अर्जयिता *m.* (तृ), अर्जकः, उपार्जकः, प्रापकः, फलप्रापकः, लब्धा (ब्धृ).

GAINFUL, *a.* फली -लिनी -लि (न्), फलदः -दा -दं, सफलः -ला -लं, अर्थकरः -री -रं, अर्थदः -दा -दं, लाभजनकः -का -कं, प्राप्तिजनकः -का -कं.

GAINFULLY, *adv.* सफलं, सलाभं, सार्थं, लाभेन, फलोदयेन.

GAINFULNESS, *s.* सफलता, सलाभता, सार्थत्वं, लाभः, लब्धिः *f.*, प्राप्तिः *f.*

GAINLY, *adv.* दक्षं, सदाक्ष्यं, युक्त्या, सपाटवं, चतुरं, पर्य्याप्तं.

To GAINSAY, *v. a.* विपरीतं वद् (c. 1. वदति -ते -दितुं), विवद्, अपवद्, प्रत्याख्या (c. 2. -ख्याति -तुं), अन्तःख्या, अपलप् (c. 1. -लपति -पितुं), विरुध् (c. 7. -रुणद्धि -रोद्धुं), अधरीकृ, बाध् (c. 1. बाधते -धितुं).

GAINSAYED, *p. p.* प्रत्याख्यातः -ता -तं, अपह्नुतः -ता -तं, बाधितः -ता -तं.

GAINSAYER, *s.* विपरीतवादी *m.* (न्), प्रत्याख्याता *m.* (तृ), अपवादकः, विवादी *m.* (न्), प्रतिवादी *m.*, विरोधी *m.* (न्), विघ्नकारी *m.* (न्).

GAIRISH, *a.* अतिशोभनः -ना -नं, एकान्तशोभनः -ना -नं, शोभामात्रसेवी -विनी -वि (न्), अलङ्करिष्णुः -ष्णुः -ष्णु, दाम्भिकः -की -कं, रूपाध्मातः -ता -तं.

GAIRISHLY, *adv.* अतिशोभनं, एकान्तशोभापूर्व्वं, रूपाध्मातवत्, सदम्भं, दाम्भिकवत्.

GAIRISHNESS, *s.* अतिशोभा, एकान्तशोभा, दम्भः, दाम्भिकत्वं, रूपाध्मातत्वं.

GAIT, *s.* गतिः *f.*, गमनं, गतं, चारः, चरणं, चलनं, सरणं, व्रजनं, अयनं; 'graceful in gait,' सुगः -गा -गं -गामी -मिनी -मि (न्), शुभगः -गा -गं, हंसगामी &c., चारचणः -णा -णं.

GAITER, *s.* स्थूलवस्त्रमयं जङ्घात्राणं or जङ्घारक्षणं, जङ्घोत्तरीयं.

GALA, *s.* उत्सवः -वदिनं, महोत्सवः, पर्व्व *n.* (न्), पर्व्वाहः, उद्धर्षः.

GALACTOPHAGIST, *s.* क्षीरपः -पायी *m.* (न्), दुग्धपः, पयस्यः, क्षीरादः, क्षीराशी *m.* (न्).

GALAXY, *s.* (Milky way) मन्दाकिनी, आकाशगङ्गा, स्वर्गङ्गा, नागवीथी, हरिताली.—(Assemblage of splendid objects) शोभनवस्तुमण्डलं, सुप्रभवस्तुसमूहः.

GALE, *s.* प्रबलवायुः *m.*, प्रचण्डवायुः *m.*, अतिवातः, वात्या, वात्यावेगः, चण्डवातः, वाताली, वातरूपः, वातगुल्मः, झञ्झावातः, झञ्झा, पवनः, पवनाघातः, भवानिलः, भ्राजिः *f.*, व्राजिः *f.*, करीषङ्कषा, फः; 'tossed by gales,' पवनक्षिप्तः -प्ता -प्तं, पवनवेगक्षिप्तः -प्ता -प्तं.

GALIOT, *s.* शीघ्रगामी लघुनौकाविशेषः.

GALL, *s.* (Bitter fluid, bile) पित्तं, तिक्तपित्तं, मायुः *m.*—(Rancour) विषं, विषहृदयत्वं, कालकूटं, दंशः, दुष्टभावः, दुर्बुद्धिः *f.*, द्रोहः, द्वेषः, कटुता, तीक्ष्णता, तिग्मता, उग्रत्वं, अरुन्तुदत्वं, कठोरता, क्रोधः.—(Excrescence on a tree) वृक्षफेनः -नकः.

GALL-BLADDER, *s.* पित्ताधारः, तिक्तपित्ताधारः, तिक्तपित्ताशयः.

GALL-STONE, *s.* पित्ताशयजा शर्करा.

To GALL, *v. a.* (Excoriate by friction) घर्षणेन चर्म्मक्षतं कृ or त्वक्छेदं कृ or त्वगुल्लेखनं कृ, चर्म्म घृष् (c. 1. घर्षति -र्षितुं) or कृष् (c. 10. कर्षयति -यितुं).—(Vex, harass) तप् (c. 10. तापयति -यितुं), परितप्, सन्तप्, पीड् (c. 10. पीडयति -यितुं), अभिपीड्, आपीड्, क्लिश् (c. 9. क्लिश्नाति, क्लेष्टुं), बाध् (c. 1. बाधते -धितुं), अर्द् (c. 10. अर्दयति -यितुं), समर्द्, मर्म्मपीडां कृ, अरुन्तुदः -दा -दं भू.

To GALL, *v. n.* (Vex one's self) आत्मानं तप् (c. 10. तापयति -यितुं), or पीड् (c. 10. पीडयति -यितुं) or बाध् (c. 1. बाधते -धितुं), परितप् in pass. (-तप्यते).

GALLANT, *a.* (Brave, heroic) वीरः -रा -रं, प्रवीरः -रा -रं, महावीर्य्यः -र्य्या -र्य्यं, शूरः -रा -रं, पराक्रान्तः -न्ता -न्तं, विक्रान्तः -न्ता -न्तं, विक्रमी -मिणी -मि (न्), साहसिकः -की -कं, माहात्मिकः -की -कं, उदारचेताः -ताः -तः (स्).—(Courteous, inclined to courtship) सभ्यः -भ्या -भ्यं, सभ्यशीलः -ला -लं, सुशीलः -ला -लं, स्त्र्युपासनशीलः -ला -लं, स्त्र्युपचारशीलः -ला -लं, सुजनः -ना -नं, प्रेमशीलः -ला -लं.

GALLANT, *s.* (Courtly man) सभ्यजनः, सुजनः.—(One attentive to ladies) स्त्र्युपासकः, स्त्र्युपचारकः -चारपरः.—(Lover) प्रणयी *m.* (न्), कामिजनः, कामी *m.* (न्), कामुकः, नायकः, रमकः.—(Paramour) जारः, रमणः, उपपतिः *m.*, पापपतिः *m.*, विटः, चेटकः.

GALLANTLY, *adv.* (Bravely) सवीर्य्यं, महावीर्य्येण, महावीरवत्, शूरवत्, समहाशौर्य्यं, सपराक्रमं, सविक्रमं, उदारवत्, प्रसभं.—(Like one inclined to courtship) स्त्र्युपासकवत्, स्त्र्युपचारकवत्, रमणवत्.

GALLANTRY, *s.* (Bravery) वीर्य्यं, महावीर्य्यं, शौर्य्यं, वीरता, शूरता,

पौरुषं, विक्रमः, पराक्रमः, धाम *n.* (न्).—(Nobleness) उदारता, औदार्य्यं, माहात्म्यं.—(Courtliness, attention to ladies) सभ्यता, सुशीलता, सुजनता, स्त्र्युपासनं, स्त्र्युपचारः.

GALLED, *p. p.* (Having the skin torn by friction) क्षतचर्म्मा -र्म्मा -र्म्म (न्), घर्षितचर्म्मा &c., छिन्नत्वक् *m. f. n.*—(Harassed) सन्तापितः -ता -तं, क्लिष्टः -ष्टा -ष्टं, पीडितः -ता -तं, बाधितः -ता -तं.

GALLEON, *s.* सुवर्णरूप्यसन्तारणे प्रयुक्ता बृहती विदेशीयनौका.

GALLERY, *s.* (Covered way) छन्नपथः, छन्नमार्गः.—(In a building) हर्म्ये or महाभवने इतस्ततो भ्रमणयोग्यः पथः.—(Elevated floor furnished with seats) दीर्घासनयुक्तो मञ्चः or मञ्चकः.—(Covered terrace outside a house) बहिर्द्वारप्रकोष्ठकं, वरण्डः, निष्काशः.

GALLEY, *s.* (Long, light boat) दीर्घपरिमाणा लघुनौका, मद्गुः *m.*—(Cook-room of a ship of war) युद्धनौकायाः पाकस्थानं.

GALLEY-SLAVE, *s.* आमृत्योर् मद्गुदण्डसञ्चारणे नियुक्तो महापातकी *m.* (न्).

GALLIARD, *a.* हृष्टः -ष्टा -ष्टं, प्रफुल्लः -ल्ला -ल्लं, उल्लसः -सा -सं, रसिकः -का -कं.

GALLICISM, *s.* फ्रान्सीयरीत्यनुसारी वाग्व्यापारः.

GALLIGASKINS, *s.* नीचभाषायां स्थूलवस्त्रमयं जङ्घोत्तरीयं or जङ्घापरिधानं.

GALLIMATIA, *s.* असम्बद्धप्रलापः, अनर्थकवाक्यं, वृथाकथा, प्रलपितं.

GALLIMAUFRY, *s.* सन्निपातः, सान्निपातिकं, प्रकीर्णकं, सङ्कीर्णकं.

GALLINACEOUS, *a.* गृह्यकुक्कुटसम्बन्धी -न्धिनी -न्धि (न्) or -वाचकः -का -कं; 'a gallinaceous fowl,' कुक्कुटः -टी, कृकवाकुः *m.*, ताम्रचूडः, चरणायुधः.

GALLING, *s.* घर्षणेन चर्म्मक्षतिः *f.* or त्वक्परिक्षतिः *f.*, चर्म्मदारणं, चर्म्मनिर्घर्षणं.

GALLINULE, *s.* कालकण्ठः -ण्ठकः, नीलकण्ठः, दात्यूहः, आत्यूहः, नत्यूहः, जलरङ्कुः, पीतमुण्डः, मञ्जुलः, मासक्षः, डाहुकः, खेगमनः, हुडुक्कः, मादकः.

GALLIPOT, *s.* भेषजविक्रेतृभिः प्रयुक्तं मृण्मयम् औषधपात्रं, चलुकः, चुलुकः.

GALL-NUT, *s.* मसीजलकरणे प्रयुक्तः फलाकारो वृक्षफेनः.

GALLON, *s.* द्रवद्रव्याणां परिमाणविशेषः, अर्द्धप्रस्थः.

GALLOON, *s.* स्वर्णरूप्यसूत्रमयस् तान्तवालङ्कारविशेषः.

To GALLOP, *v. n.* प्लु (c. 1. प्लवते, प्लोतुं), वल्ग् (c. 1. वल्गति -ल्गितुं), आवल्ग्, धोर् (c. 1. धोरति -रितुं), धाव् (c. 1. धावति -वितुं), पुलायितं कृ, प्लुतगत्या or वल्गितेन चल् (c. 1. चलति -लितुं).

GALLOP, *s.* वल्गितं, पुलायितं, पुला, प्लुतः -तं, प्लवः -वनं, विप्लावः, विक्रान्तिः *f.*, तरङ्गः, धोरणं, धोरितं -तकं, धौरितकं.

GALLOPADE, *s.* द्रुतनृत्यविशेषो यत्र नर्त्तकाः प्लुतगत्या चलन्ति.

GALLOPER, *s.* प्लवगः -गतिः *m.*, प्लवकः, वल्गितकारी *m.* (न्), पुलायितकृत्.

To GALLOW, *v. a.* त्रस् in caus. (त्रासयति -यितुं), भी in caus. (भाययति -यितुं).

GALLOWAY, *s.* मध्यमपरिमाणो न बृहन् न क्षुद्रस् तुरङ्गभेदः.

GALLOWS, *s.* उद्बन्धनकाष्ठं, उद्बन्धनवृक्षः, बधस्थानं, घातस्थानं.

GALOCHE, GALOSHE, *s.* काष्ठपादुका, उत्तरपादुका, उपपादुका.

GALVANIC, *a.* वक्ष्यमाणवैद्युतशक्तिसम्बन्धी -न्धिनी -न्धि (न्).

GALVANISM, *s.* गल्वाणिनाम्ना विदेशीयविदुषा परिकल्पिता विद्युतीयशक्तिः or वैद्युतशक्तिः or आकर्षकशक्तिः, विद्युत्क्रियाङ्गं.

GALVANIST, *s.* पूर्व्वोक्तविद्युत्क्रियाशास्त्रातत्त्वज्ञः.

To GALVANIZE, *v. a.* पूर्व्वोक्तविद्युतीयशक्त्या आकृष् (c. 1. -कर्षति -क्रष्टुं) or उपहन् (c. 2. -हन्ति -न्तुं).

GALVANIZED, *p. p.* पूर्व्वोक्तवैद्युतशक्त्युपहतः -ता -तं.

To GAMBLE, *v. n.* (With dice, &c.) अक्षैः or अक्षान् दिव् (c. 4. दीव्यति -ते, देवितुं) or प्रदिव् or प्रतिदिव्, अक्षैः क्रीड् (c. 1. क्रीडति -डितुं), अक्षादिक्रीडां कृ, द्यूतक्रीडां कृ, अक्षद्यूतं कृ.

GAMBLER, *s.* द्यूतकरः -कारः, अक्षद्यूतः, अक्षद्यूः *m.*, अक्षदेवी *m.* (न्), अक्षधूर्त्तः, धूर्त्तः, कितवः, द्यूतक्रीडकः, आक्षिकः. *See* GAMESTER.

GAMBLING, *s.* अक्षद्यूतं, द्यूतं, द्यूतक्रीडा, अक्षादिक्रीडा, देवनं, अक्षवती, द्यूतसेवा, कैतवं, ग्लहः, पणः, दुरोदरं.

GAMBOGE, *s.* पीतवर्णः पूर्व्वदेशीयवृक्षनिर्यासः.

To GAMBOL, *v. n.* (Frolic) क्रीड् (c. 1. क्रीडति -डितुं), विक्रीड्, परिक्रीड्, दिव् (c. 4. दीव्यति -ते, देवितुं), चित्तप्रहर्षाद् इतस्ततः प्लु (c. 1. प्लवते, प्लोतुं) or नृत् (c. 4. नृत्यति, नर्त्तितुं), खेला (nom. खेलायति -यितुं), कुमार (nom. कुमारयति -यितुं).

GAMBOL, *s.* क्रीडा -डनं, देवनं, खेला, केलिः *m. f.*, लीला, नृत्यं, लास्यं.

GAMBOLING, *part.* क्रीडन् -डन्ती -डत् (त्), क्रीडमानः -ना -नं, दीव्यन्, व्यती -व्यत् (त्).

GAME, *s.* (Sport) क्रीडा, खेला, केलिः *m. f.*, लीला, नर्म्म *n.* (न्), परीहासः, कूर्द्दनं, विलासः.—(Game of play) रासः, रासेरसः.—(Wild animals) जाङ्गलं, जङ्गलपक्ष्यादि, वन्यपश्वादि, आरण्यपशुपक्ष्यादि.—(The chase) मृगव्यं, मृगया.—(Scheme) सङ्कल्पः, निश्चितं, व्यवसितं, व्यवसायः, कल्पना.

To GAME, *v. n.* क्रीड् (c. 1. क्रीडति -डितुं), दिव् (c. 4. दीव्यति -ते, देवितुं).—(With dice, &c.) अक्षैः क्रीड् or दिव् द्यूतक्रीडां कृ.

GAME-COCK, *s.* चरणायुधः, नखायुधः, युद्धे शिक्षितः कृकवाकुः.

GAMEKEEPER, *s.* वन्यपक्षिरक्षकः, जाङ्गलपक्षिप्रतिपालकः, वन्यजन्तुपोषकः.

GAME-LEG, *s.* खञ्जजङ्घा, पङ्गुजङ्घा, गतिविकलः पादः, पङ्गुपादः.

GAMESOME, *a.* क्रीडापरः -रा -रं, क्रीडावान् -वती -वत् (त्), लीलावान् &c., खेलापरः -रा -रं, विलासी -सिनी -सि (न्), केलिकः -का -कं.

GAMESOMENESS, *s.* क्रीडापरत्वं, खेलापरत्वं, सविलासता, लीलावत्त्वं, उल्लसता.

GAMESTER, *s.* द्यूतकरः -कारः, द्यूतकृत् *m.*, अक्षदेवी *m.* (न्), अक्षद्यूतः, अक्षद्यूः *m.*, अक्षधूर्त्तः, द्यूतवृत्तिः *m.*, द्यूतसेवी *m.* (न्), द्यूतप्रसक्तः, अक्षक्रीडकः, धूर्त्तः, कितवः, अक्षादिसेवी *m.*, दुरोदरः, कृष्णकोहलः.

GAMING, *s.* अक्षद्यूतं, द्यूतं -तः, द्यूतकर्म्म *n.* (न्), द्यूतक्रीडा, द्यूतसेवा, अक्षादिक्रीडा, अक्षवती, देवनं, कैतवं, ग्लहः, पणः, दुरोदरं.

GAMING-HOUSE, *s.* द्यूतसभा, द्यूतस्थानं, द्यूतशाला, द्यूतगृहं; 'keeper of one,' द्यूतसभाधिकारी *m.* (न्), सभिकः, द्यूताधिकारी *m.*, द्यूतकारकः, द्यूतवृत्तिः *m.*

GAMMON, *s.* (Dried hog's flesh) वल्लूरं, शूकरस्य शुष्कमांसं or वासितमांसं.—(Game) चर्म्मपट्टिकाक्रीडा, शारिक्रीडा.—(Imposition, hoax) छलं, वञ्चनं, कपटः, दम्भः.

To GAMMON, *v. a.* शूकरमांसं शुष्कीकृ or लवणीकृ, वल्लूरं कृ.—(Hoax) प्रलभ् (c. 1. -लभते -लब्धुं), अभिसन्धा (c. 3. -दधाति -धातुं), वञ्च् (c. 10. वञ्चयति -यितुं).

GAMUT, *s.* (Musical scale) ग्रामः. The seven musical notes of the Hindú gamut are called निषादः, ऋषभः, गान्धारः, षड्जः, मध्यमः, धैवतः, पञ्चमः.

GANDER, *s.* वरटः, हंसः, राजहंसः, कलहंसः, चक्रः, चक्रवाकः, चक्राङ्गः.

GANDHARBA, *s.* (A celestial musician. These are demigods who inhabit heaven, and form the orchestra at the banquets of the gods) गन्धर्व्वः, हाहाः (स्), हुहुः *m.*, हुहूः *m.*, हहाः *m.*

GANESHA, *s.* (Son of Siva and Párvatí, the god of wisdom, and remover of difficulties and obstacles, addressed at the commencement of all undertakings, and at the opening of all compositions. He is called 'Ganesha,' as presiding over the troop of deities attendant on Siva) गणेशः, गणनाथः, गणाधिपः, गणनायकः, गणपतिः *m.*, गणाग्रणीः *m.*,

गणः, हेमाङ्गः, हेरम्बः, हस्तिमल्लः,—(As remover of obstacles) विघ्नेशः, विघ्नराजः, विघ्ननाशकः -शनः, विघ्नविनायकः, विनायकः, विघ्नहारी *m.* (न्).—(Elephant-faced) गजाननः, गजवदनः, गजास्यः. —(Elephant-toothed) गजदन्तः.—(One-toothed) एकदन्तः.—(Big-bellied) लम्बोदरः.—(Two-bodied) द्विदेहः.—(Having two mothers) द्वैमातुरः.

GANG, *s.* (Company of persons) गणः, जनसमूहः, जनसंसर्गः, जननिवहः, सङ्घः, सङ्गः; 'of thieves,' चौरगणः.

GANG-BOARD, *s.* नौकारोहणावरोहणार्थं दीर्घकाष्ठफलकं.

GANG-DAYS, *s.* भ्रमणदिवसाः *m. pl.*, परिक्रमदिवसाः, पर्य्यटनकालः.

GANGES, *s.* (The River) गङ्गा, गङ्गाका, गङ्गिका. The name Gangá is derived from the root *gam*, 'to go,' *i. e.* 'that which goes or flows on the earth,' whence also the name भवायना, 'going in the world.' (Daughter of Jahnu. The Ganges in its course from heaven disturbed the devotions of this saint, upon which he drank up its waters, but released them again at the intercession of the sage Bhagíratha. Hence the following names) जाह्नवी, जह्नुतनया, जह्नुसुता, भागीरथी, (Crest of Siva. The Ganges, in its descent from heaven, alighted on the head of Siva, where it wandered for a time in the tresses of his hair) हरशेखरा. (River of heaven) स्वर्णदी, सुरनदी, सुरनिम्नगा, स्वरापगा, स्वर्गगङ्गा, स्वर्वापी, खापगा, सिद्धापगा.—(Flowing in heaven, earth, and hell) त्रिपथगा, त्रिस्रोताः *f.* (स्).—(Flowing from the foot of Vishnu) विष्णुपदी.—(Mother of Bhíshma) भीष्मसूः *f.*—(The very auspicious one) महाभद्रा.

GANGLION, *s.* स्नायुस्फोटः -टकः, शिरास्फोटकः, नाडीविस्फोटः.

GANGRENE, *s.* कोथः, पूतिमांसं, विद्रधिः *m.*, क्षतं, नालीव्रणः, मांसपाकः, रक्तविद्रधिः *m.*, मांसपूतिः, शरीरस्य परभागे स्वस्थे सति एकभागस्य पूतीभावः.

To GANGRENE, *v. n.* मांसैकदेशे पूतीभू, पूतमांसीभू, कोथीभू.

GANGRENOUS, *a.* कोथवान् -वती -वत् (त्), कोथीयः -या -यं, पूतिमांसवान् &c.

GANGWAY, *s.* नौकायां गमनागमनपथः or आरोहणावरोहणपथः.

GANTLET, GANTLOPE, *s.* सेनायां दण्डार्हस्य दण्डविशेषः; 'to run the gantlet,' महापातकिवत् सैन्यानां यष्टिपाणीनां द्विपंक्तिमध्ये धाव् (c. 1. धावति -ते -वितुं) यावद् एकैकेन यष्ट्याघातः क्रियते.

GAOL, *s.* कारा, कारागारं, कारावेश्म *n.* (न्), बन्धनागारं, बन्धनालयः, बन्धनगृहं, बन्धनस्थानं, गुप्तिः *f.*

To GAOL, *v. a.* कारायां बन्ध् (c. 9. बध्नाति, बन्द्धुं) or निरुध् (c. 7. -रुणद्धि -रोद्धुं).

GAOL-DELIVERY, *s.* काराशुद्धिः *f.*, कारागारशोधनं, बन्धनागारविशोधनं.

GAOLER, *s.* कारागाराध्यक्षः, कारारक्षकः, बन्धनालयरक्षकः.

GAP, *s.* (In a wall) सन्धिः *m.*, गृहरन्ध्रं, सुरङ्गा, कुड्यच्छेदः.—(Breach, chasm) भङ्गः, भेदः, छेदः, रन्ध्रं, छिद्रं, विवरं, विच्छेदः, गर्त्तः, खण्डः -ण्डनं.

To GAPE, *v. n.* जृम्भ् (c. 1. जृम्भते -म्भितुं), विजृम्भ्, प्रजृम्भ्, जभ् or जम्भ् (c. 1. जभते, जम्भते -म्भितुं), मुखं व्यादा (c. 3. -ददाति -दातुं) or विस्तॄ in caus. (-स्तारयति -यितुं), जृम्भं कृ, ग्लै (c. 1. ग्लायति, ग्लातुं).—(Open in fissures) स्फुट् (c. 6. स्फुटति -टितुं), विदल् (c. 1. -दलति -लितुं), विदॄ in pass. (-दीर्य्यते).

GAPER, *s.* जृम्भी *m.* (न्), जृम्भकः, जृम्भणकारी *m.* (न्), मुखव्यादानकारी.

GAPING, GAPE, *s.* जृम्भः -म्भा -म्भणं -म्भिका, जृम्भितं, विजृम्भितं, विजृम्भणं, ह्म्मं *n.* (न्), हाफिका, उपपुष्पिका.—(Opening the mouth) मुखव्यादानं, मुखविवृतिः *f.*

GAPING, *part.* जृम्भः -म्भा -म्भं, जृम्भमाणः -णा -णं, जृम्भी -म्भिणी -म्भि (न्), जृम्भावान् -वती -वत् (त्), जृम्भितः -ता -तं, विजृम्भितः -ता -तं, व्यात्तमुखः -खा -खं, विवृतमुखः -खा -खं.

GAP-TOOTHED, *a.* विरलदन्ती -न्तिनी -न्ति (न्), विच्छिन्नदन्ती &c.

GARB, *s.* वेशः, वेषः, वासः *n.* (स्), परिधानं, परिच्छदः, अम्बरं, वस्त्रं, वसनं, आच्छादनं, सज्जा, प्रसाधनं.

GARBAGE, *s.* उच्छिष्टं, उच्छिष्टान्नं, शेषान्नं, पशोर् अन्त्रादि, मलं.

To GARBLE, *v. a.* (Pick out the best parts of a book to serve a purpose) छलार्थं or वचनार्थं ग्रन्थस्य उत्तमवचनानि or उत्तमदेशान् उद्धृ (c. 1. -हरति -हर्त्तुं) or समुद्धृ or ग्रन्थचूर्णिं कृ, ग्रन्थं खण्ड् (c. 10. खण्डयति -यितुं).—(Pervert) साचीकृ, वक्रीकृ, विकृ, विकलीकृ.

GARBLED, *p.p.* साचीकृतः -ता -तं, छलेन विकलीकृतः -ता -तं or खण्डितः -ता -तं.

GARBOIL, *s.* कोलाहलः, तुमुलं, हलहलाशब्दः, हाहाकारः.

GARDEN, *s.* उद्यानं, आरामः, उपवनं, पुष्पवाटी -टिका, पुष्पवनं, वाटिका, वृक्षवाटिका, कुसुमाकरः, वेलं, तेपनं, पुष्पफलोपचयहेतुर् भूभागः; 'pleasure-garden,' क्रीडार्था भूमिः, क्रीडावाटिका, क्रीडावनं; 'garden near a house,' गृहवाटिका, गृहारामः; 'kitchen-garden,' शाकशाकटं, शाकशाकिनं, शाकवाटिका.

To GARDEN, *v. n.* उद्यानं कृ, पुष्पफलोत्पत्तियोग्यं भूमिभागं कृष् (c. 6. कृषति, क्रष्टुं), उद्यानकर्म्म कृ.

GARDENER, *s.* उद्यानपालः -लकः, उद्यानरक्षकः, उद्यानसेवकः, मालिकः, माली *m.* (न्).

GARDENING, *s.* उद्यानकरणं, उद्यानकर्म्म, उद्यानसेवनं, पुष्पफलोत्पत्तिकर्म्म *n.* (न्).

GARDEN-PLOT, *s.* पुष्पफलोत्पत्तियोग्यो भूमिभागः, पुष्पस्थलं, स्थलं -ली.

GARDEN-STUFF, *s.* उद्यानजं, उद्यानोद्भिद् *m.f.n.*, उद्यानजं शाकादि.

GARDEN-WALL, *s.* उद्यानपरिसरः, वाटिकापरिसरः, उद्यानप्राकारः.

GARGARISM, *s.* आचाम्यं, आचमनीयं, कवलः, मुखमार्जनजलं.

To GARGARIZE, *v. a.* आचम् (c. 1. -चामति -चमितुं), जलम् उपस्पृश् (c. 6. -स्पृशति -स्प्रष्टुं).

GARGLE, *s.* आचाम्यं, आचमनीयं, कवलः, मुखधावनार्थं जलादि.

To GARGLE, *v. a.* जलम् आचम् (c. 1. -चामति -चमितुं) or उपस्पृश् (c. 6. -स्पृशति -स्प्रष्टुं), आचमनं कृ, उपस्पर्शं कृ, जलोपस्पर्शं कृ, जलादिना मुखं मृज् (c. 2. मार्ष्टि -र्ष्टुं) or धाव् (c. 10. धावयति -यितुं).

GARGLED, *p. p.* आचान्तः -न्ता -न्तं, उपस्पृष्टः -ष्टा -ष्टं.

GARISH, *a.* *See* GAIRISH.

GARLAND, *s.* माला, माल्यं, स्रक् *f.* (ज्), दाम *n.* (न्), हारः, आवलिः -ली *f.*, प्रालम्बः -म्बिका; 'of flowers,' कुसुममाला, पुष्पावली, कुसुमस्तबकः, कुसुमावतंसकं; 'of pearls,' मुक्तावली, देवच्छन्दः, शतयष्टिकः; 'other kinds of garlands,' गुत्सः, गुत्सार्द्धः, गोस्तनः.

To GARLAND, *v. a.* मालया or स्रजा अलङ्कृ, मालायुक्तं -क्तां -क्तं कृ.

GARLANDED, *p. p.* माली -लिनी -लि (न्), स्रग्वी -ग्विणी -ग्वि (न्), स्रग्धरः -रा -रं.

GARLIC, *s.* लशुनं, रशुनं, लशूनं, लसुनः, रसुनः, रसोनः -नकः, गृञ्जनः, महौषधं, महाकन्दः, अरिष्टः, सोनहः, उग्रगन्धः, दीर्घपत्रः, ग्रन्थिमूलं, श्रीमस्तकः, मुखदूषणः, राहूच्छिष्टः, तरिता.

GARLIC-EATER, *s.* लशुनाशी *m.* (न्), लशुनभोजी *m.* (न्), लशुनादः.

GARLICKY, *a.* लशुनीयः -या -यं, रशुनीयः -या -यं.

GARMENT, *s.* वस्त्रं, वेशः, वेषः, वासस् *n.*, वसनं, परिधानं, परिच्छदः, अम्बरं, आच्छादनं, प्रच्छादनं, प्रसाधनं, संव्यानं, प्रवारः, अम्बरः; 'undergarment,' अन्तरीयं, अन्तर्वासस्, अधोवसनं; 'upper,' उत्तरीयं, प्रावारः.

Garner, s. कुशूलः, धान्यागारं, अन्नकोष्ठः, कोष्ठः -ष्ठकं, भाण्डागारं, व्रीह्यगारं, कण्डोलः -लकः, काण्डालः, पिटः, कुदरः.

To garner, v. a. कुशूले निविश् (c. 10. -वेशयति -यितुं) or सञ्चि (c. 5. -चिनोति -चेतुं).

Garnered, p. p. कुशूलभूतः -ता -तं, कोष्ठभूतः -ता -तं, कुशूलीकृतः -ता -तं.

Garnet, s. रक्तवर्णो मणिविशेषः, पद्मरागविशेषः, सर्पमणिः m.f.

To garnish, v. a. शुभ् (c. 10. शोभयति -यितुं), उपशुभ्, भूष् (c. 10 भूषयति -यितुं), विभूष्, अलङ्कृ, समलङ्कृ, परिष्कृ, रञ्ज् (c. 10. रञ्जयति -यितुं).

Garnish, s. अलङ्कारः, अलङ्क्रिया, शोभा -भनं, भूषणं, विभूषणं, आभरणं. सज्जा, प्रसाधनं. See Garnishment.

Garnished, p. p. शोभितः -ता -तं, उपशोभितः -ता -तं, अलङ्कृतः -ता -तं, भूषितः -ता -तं, विभूषितः -ता -तं, परिष्कृतः -ता -तं, प्रसाधितः -ता -तं, कृतशोभः -भा -भं.

Garnishment, garniture, s. सज्जा, उपकरणानि n. pl., शोभार्थम् अनुबन्धाः m. pl.

Garret, s. उपरिस्थः कोष्ठः, क्षोमः -मं, क्षौमः -मं, अट्टः, अट्टालः, कूटागारं, चन्द्रशाला -लिका, चूला.

Garrison, s. दुर्गनिवासिनः सैन्याः m. pl., दुर्गस्थाः सैन्याः, दुर्गस्थसैन्यं, दुर्गसैन्यं, दुर्गबलं, दुर्गरक्षिणः m. pl., दुर्गरक्षकाः m. pl., रक्षिणः m. pl., रक्षकाः m. pl., रक्षिवर्गः.

To garrison, v. a. नगररक्षार्थं दुर्गे सैन्यान् or रक्षकान् निविश् in caus. (-वेशयति -यितुं), नगररक्षणे सैन्यगुल्मं नियुज् (c. 7. युनक्ति -योक्तुं).

Garrisoned, p. p. रक्षकयुक्तः -क्ता -क्तं, रक्षार्थं सैन्ययुक्तः -क्ता -क्तं.

Garrulity, s. वावदूकता, वाचालता, बहुवादित्वं, बहुभाषिता, अतिशयोक्तिः f. जल्पकता, जल्पाकत्वं, वाग्मित्वं, अतिभाषणं, अत्यालापः, अतिवादः.

Garrulous, a. वावदूकः -का -कं, वाचालः -ला -लं, बहुभाषी -षिणी -षि (न्), बहुवादी -दिनी -दि (न्), जल्पकः -का -कं, जल्पाकः -का -कं, वाग्मी -ग्मिनी -ग्मि (न्), गदयित्नुः -त्नुः -त्नु, मुखरः -रा -रं, वक्ता -क्त्री -क्तृ (क्तृ).

Garter, s. जङ्घाबन्धनी, पादबन्धनी, जङ्घाबन्धः, जङ्घावस्त्ररक्षणी.

Garuda, s. (The bird on which the god Vishnu is carried, represented as being something between a man and a bird, and considered as the lord of the feathered tribe. He is the son of Kasyapa by Vinatá, and younger brother of Aruna) गरुडः, गरुत्मान् m. (-त्मत्), तार्क्ष्यः, खगेश्वरः, सुपर्णः, विष्णुरथः, वैनतेयः, विनतासूनुः m., नागान्तकः, पन्नगाशनः, भुजगदारणः, सिताननः, रुक्माङ्गः. The son of Garuda is called सम्पातिः -तिकः.

Gas, s. वायुः m., वाष्पः, वातः, धूमः, धूमिका, अङ्गारजो वायुः m.

Gash, s. दीर्घच्छेदः, गम्भीरच्छेदः, दीर्घक्षतं, गम्भीरक्षतं, दीर्घगम्भीरस् त्वग्भेदः or त्वक्छेदः.

To gash, v. a. दीर्घच्छेदं कृ, गम्भीरच्छेदं कृ, दीर्घगम्भीरं त्वग्भेदं कृ.

Gasometer, s. वायुमापनयन्त्रं, अङ्गारजवायुनिर्म्माणस्थानं.

To gasp, v. n. मुखं व्यादाय कृच्छ्रेण श्वासप्रश्वासं कृ, कृच्छ्रेण श्वस् (c. 2. श्वसिति -तुं) or प्राण् (c. 2. प्राणिति -तुं), दुःश्वासं कृ, प्राणकृच्छ्रोपहतः -ता -तं भू.

Gasp, s. दुःश्वासः, श्वासः, श्वसितं, दुःश्वसितं, उच्छ्वासः, उच्छ्वसितं, प्राणः.

Gasping, part. उच्छ्वसन् -सन्ती -सती -सत् (त्), कृच्छ्रेण श्वसन् &c., उच्छ्वसितः -ता -तं, काशश्वासः -सा -सं, दुःश्वासी -सिनी -सि (न्), श्वासकृच्छ्रोपहतः -ता -तं, यष्टिप्राणः -णा -णं.

Gastric, a. जाठरः -री -रं, औदरिकः -की -कं, उदरीयः -या -यं, जठरीयः -या -यं; 'gastric juice,' कोष्ठाग्निः m., अग्निः.

Gastronome, s. उदरपरायणः, उदरसेवी m. (न्), कुक्षिम्भरिः m., सद्व्यञ्जनरसज्ञः.

Gastronomy, s. सद्व्यञ्जनरसविद्या, परमान्नरसविद्या, उदरसेवा.

Gastrotomy, s. उदरच्छेदः -दनं, जठरच्छेदः -दनं.

Gate, s. द्वारं, द्वाः f. (र्), प्रतीहारः, प्रतिहारः, वररः -री -रं, गृहमुखं, द्वारकण्टकः; 'back-gate,' पक्षद्वारं; 'private-gate,' प्रच्छन्नद्वारं, प्रच्छन्नद्वारं; 'city-gate,' पुरद्वारं, नगरद्वारं, गोपुरं; 'raised place over it,' हस्तिनखः; 'outer-gate,' बहिर्द्वारं.

Gate-post, s. द्वारस्तम्भः, द्वारस्थूणा, द्वारदारुः m.; 'its ornament,' तोरणः.

Gate-way, s. द्वारवर्त्म n. (न्), द्वारपथः, निःसरणं.

To gather, v. a. (Collect) चि (c. 5. चिनोति, चेतुं), अवचि, समाचि, सञ्चि, आचि, प्रचि, समानी (c. 1. -नयति -नेतुं), समुपानी, समादा (c. 3. -ददाति -दातुं), समाहृ (c. 1. -हरति -हर्तुं), उपसंहृ, समूह् (c. 1. -ऊहते -हितुं), सङ्ग्रह् (c. 9. -गृह्णाति -ग्रहीतुं), ग्रह्, सम्भृ (c. 1. -भरति, c. 3. -बिभर्त्ति -भर्तुं), संवृ (c. 5. -वृणोति, c. 1. -वरति -रितुं), एकीकृ, एकत्र कृ.—(Gather flowers, &c.) पुष्पाणि चि or अवचि or लू (c. 9. लुनाति, लवितुं).—(Select) उद्धृ, समुद्धृ, वृ, उद्धृ.—(Deduce, infer) अनुमा (c. 2. -माति -तुं, c. 3. -मिमीते), ऊह् (c. 1. ऊहते -हितुं), अपोह्, अवगम् (c. 1. -गच्छति -गन्तुं).

To gather, v. n. (Congregate) सङ्गम् (c. 1. -गच्छति -गन्तुं), समागम्, समे (सम् and आ with rt. इ, समैति -तुं), एकत्र मिल् (c. 6. मिलति, मेलितुं), सम्मिल्, एकत्र आगम्.—(Increase) वृध् (c. 1. वर्धते -र्धितुं), उपचि in pass. (-चीयते).—(Form matter) पूय् (c. 1. पूयते -यितुं), पूयं बन्ध् (c. 9. बध्नाति, बन्द्धुं), पूयपूर्णः -र्णा -र्णं भू.

Gather, s. (Fold) वस्त्रपुटः, ऊर्म्मिः m.f., ऊर्म्मिका, व्यावर्त्तनं, चूणः.

Gathered, p. p. चितः -ता -तं, सञ्चितः -ता -तं, अवचितः -ता -तं, उपचितः -ता -तं, समूढः -ढा -ढं, सङ्गृहीतः -ता -तं, लूनः -ना -नं.

Gatherer, s. अवचायी m. (न्), सञ्चयी m. (न्), सङ्ग्रहीता m. (तृ), सङ्ग्राहकः; 'gatherer of taxes,' करग्रहः, शुल्कग्राही m. (न्); 'of flowers,' पुष्पावचायी m.

Gathering, s. (Act of collecting) चयनं, सञ्चयनं, चायः, अवचयः, अवचायः, लावः, सङ्ग्रहः -हणं, एकत्रकरणं; 'of flowers,' पुष्पचयः, कुसुमावचयः, पुष्पप्रचायः.—(Crowd, assembly) समूहः, सङ्घः, सञ्चयः, सङ्घातः, समागमः, समवायः, समाहारः, समयः; 'of people,' जनसमूहः, जननिवहः, लोकसङ्घः.—(Abscess) विद्रधिः m., पूयसम्पूर्णः स्फोटः. —(Gathering of clouds) घनचयः, घनौघः, घनजालं, घनघनौघः.

Gaudery, s. अलङ्कारः, चित्रविचित्राभरणानि n. pl., शोभाकरद्रव्याणि n. pl.

Gaudily, adv. सचित्रालङ्कारं, शोभाकरणार्थं, एकान्तशोभनं, चित्रविचित्रं; 'gaudily dressed,' उज्ज्वलवेशधारी -रिणी -रि (न्).

Gaudiness, s. रक्तता, सरागत्वं, रागः, रङ्गः, चित्रता, चित्रविचित्रता, शोभा, एकान्तशोभा, अतिशोभा, वर्णः, नानावर्णत्वं, कर्बुरता, वाह्यदृष्टिः f.

Gaudy, a. बहुवर्णः -र्णा -र्णं, नानावर्णः -र्णा -र्णं, चित्रः -त्रा -त्रं, चित्रविचित्रः -त्रा -त्रं, अतिशोभनः -ना -नं, एकान्तशोभनः -ना -नं, रक्तः -क्ता -क्तं, अतिरागी -गिणी -गि (न्), चित्रालङ्कारवान् -वती -वत् (त्), उज्ज्वलः -ला -लं.

Gaudy, s. (A feast) उत्सवः, उत्सवदिनं, पर्व्वाहः, उद्धर्षः.

To gauge, v. a. प्रमाणदण्डेन भाण्डभरकं मा (c. 2. माति -तुं, c. 10. मापयति -यितुं).

Gauge, s. (Measure) परिमाणं, प्रमाणं, मानं, परिमाणविधिः m., परिमाणरीतिः f.—(Instrument for measuring) मापनयन्त्रं, परिमापनदण्डः, प्रमाणदण्डः, भाण्डपूरकमापनार्थं यष्टिः m. See Gage.

GAUGER, *s.* प्रमाणदण्डद्वारेण भाण्डभरकमापकः, परिमाणकर्त्ता *m.* (र्तृ).

GAUGING, *s.* प्रमाणदण्डेन भाण्डभरकमापनं or भाण्डपूरकपरिमापणं.

GAUNT, *a.* कृशः -शा -शं, परिकृशः -शा -शं, कृशाङ्गः -ङ्गी -ङ्गं, क्षीणशरीरः -रा -रं, क्षीणमांसः -सा -सं, क्षामः -मा -मं, शुष्काङ्गः &c., क्षुत्क्षामः &c.

GAUNTLET, *s.* लोहनिर्म्मितं हस्ताच्छादनं or हस्तवारं; 'to throw the gauntlet,' पूर्व्वोक्तहस्ताच्छादनं भूमौ प्रक्षिप्य युद्धार्थम् आह्वे (c. 1. -ह्वयति -ह्वातुं).

GAUR, *s.* (The country) गौडः; 'its inhabitants,' गौडाः *m. pl.*

GAUZE, *s.* विरलतन्तुः सूक्ष्मवस्त्रविशेषः, विरलांशुकं, सूक्ष्मांशुकं.

GAVOT, *s.* गवोतसंज्ञको लघुनृत्यविशेषः.

GAWK, *s.* मूर्खः, मूढः, स्थूलबुद्धिः *m.*, स्थूलधीः *m.*, जडधीः *m.*

GAWKY, *a.* स्थूलः -ला -लं, स्थूलशरीरः -रा -रं, दीर्घस्थूलः -ला -लं, दीर्घदेहः -हा -हं, अदक्षः -क्षा -क्षं, विरूपः -पी -पं.

GAY, *a.* (Merry) उल्लसः -सा -सं -सितः -ता -तं, आनन्दी -न्दिनी -न्दि (न्), हृष्टः -ष्टा -ष्टं, प्रहृष्टः -ष्टा -ष्टं, हृष्टहृदयः -या -यं, प्रफुल्लः -ल्ला -ल्लं, उल्लासितः -ता -तं, समुल्लसितः -ता -तं, विलासी -सिनी -सि (न्), केलिकः -का -कं, मुदितः -ता -तं, प्रमोदी -दिनी -दि (न्), ललितः -ता -तं, परिहासशीलः -ला -लं, हासी -सिनी -सि (न्).—(Showy) नानावर्णः -र्णा -र्णं, बहुवर्णः -र्णा -र्णं, चित्रविचित्रः -त्रा -त्रं, अतिशोभनः -ना -नं.

GAYETY, *s.* उल्लसता, उल्लासः, आनन्दः, आह्लादः, सानन्दता, हर्षः, प्रहर्षः, प्रफुल्लता, मुदा, प्रमोदः, चित्तप्रसन्नता, प्रहसनं.—(Merry making) उत्सवः, महोत्सवः, उत्सवकरणं.

GAYLY, *adv.* सानन्दं, सहर्षं, प्रमोदेन, उल्लासेन, प्रहृष्टवत्.—(Showily) बहुवर्णं, चित्रविचित्रं, अतिशोभनं; 'gayly dressed,' उज्ज्वलवेशधारी -रिणी -रि (न्).

To GAZE, *v. a.* and *n.* ईक्ष् (c. 1. ईक्षते -क्षितुं), प्रेक्ष्, निरीक्ष्, वीक्ष्, अभिवीक्ष्, समीक्ष्, आलोक् (c. 10. -लोकयति -यितुं, c. 1. -लोकते -कितुं), बद्धदृष्ट्या or स्थिरदृष्ट्या or अनिमिषनयनाभ्यां निरीक्ष् or दृश् (c. 1. पश्यति, द्रष्टुं), स्थिरदृष्टिं कृ, दृष्टिं or लक्ष्यं बन्ध् (c. 9. बध्नाति, बन्द्धुं).

GAZE, *s.* स्थिरदृष्टिः *f.*, बद्धदृष्टिः *f.*, अनिमिषदृष्टिः *f.*, दृष्टिः *f.*, आलोकनं, ईक्षणं, निरीक्षा, वीक्षणं, वीक्षितं, प्रेक्षणं, प्रेक्षितं, दर्शनं, लक्षः -क्षणं; 'with fixed gaze,' बद्धदृष्टिः -ष्टिः -ष्टि, अनिमिषनयनः -ना -नं.

GAZEHOUND, *s.* दृष्टिमात्रेण शशकाद्यनुसरणशीलो मृगव्यकुक्कुरः.

GAZELLE, *s.* तनुशरीरो हरिणभेदः, मृगः -गी; 'gazelle-eyed,' मृगीदृक् *m.f.n.* (श्).

GAZETTE, *s.* वार्त्तिकपत्रं, समाचारपत्रं, संवादपत्रं, सन्देशपत्रं.

To GAZETTE, *v. a.* वार्त्तिकपत्रेण प्रकाश् (c. 10. -काशयति -यितुं).

GAZETTEER, *s.* अमुकदेशे यत्किञ्चिद् नगरग्राममार्गादि विद्यते तदाकारना-मादिवाचकं पुस्तकं.

GAZING, *part.* स्थिरदृष्ट्या प्रेक्षमाणः -णा -णं or आलोकयन् -यन्ती -यत् (त्); 'gazing up to heaven,' नभोदृष्टिः -ष्टिः -ष्टि; 'in various directions,' इतस्ततो दत्तदृष्टिः.

GAZING-STOCK, *s.* तिरस्कारविषयः, अवहासभूमिः *f.*, परिभवास्पदं, कौतुकं.

GEAR, *s.* उपकरणं, सामग्री -ग्र्यं, सज्जा, परिच्छदः, पारिणाह्यं, आभरणं, प्रसाधनं, प्रतिकर्म्म *n.* (न्); 'plough-gear,' हलोपकरणं.

GEESE, *s. pl.* हंसाः *m. pl.* *See* GOOSE.

GELATIN, *s.* क्वथितमांसनिर्म्मितं घनीभूतं or श्यानीभूतं स्वच्छद्रव्यं.

GELATINOUS, *a.* पूर्व्वोक्तश्यानद्रव्यगुणविशिष्टः -ष्टा -ष्टं, श्यानः -ना -नं, शीनः -ना -नं, सान्द्रः -न्द्रा -न्द्रं, संलग्नशीलः -ला -लं, अपलेह्यः -ह्या -ह्यं.

To GELD, *v. a.* वृषणाद् उत्कृत् (c. 6. -कृन्तति -कर्त्तितुं) or छिद् (c. 7. छिनत्ति, छेत्तुं), वृषणाद्वयम् उत्पट् (c. 10. -पाटयति -यितुं).

GELDED, *p. p.* छिन्नवृषणः -णा -णं, छिन्नमुष्कः -ष्का -ष्कं, मुष्कशून्यः -न्या -न्यं.

GELDING, *s.* (Horse) अवृषणो -षः, छिन्नवृषणो वाजी *m.* (न्).

GELID, *a.* अतिशीतलः -ला -लं, अत्यन्तशिशिरः -रा -रं, हिमः -मा -मं.

GELIDITY, GELIDNESS, *s.* अतिशीतलता, अतिशैत्यं, शीतता, शिशिरत्वं.

GELLY, *s.* क्वथितमांसनिर्म्मितो घनीभूतः or श्यानीभूतः स्वच्छरसः.

GEM, *s.* (Precious stone) मणिः *m.f.* -णी, रत्नं, चारुशिला, प्रस्तरः, मणिरत्नं; 'necklace of gems,' मणिमाला, मणिसरः, रत्नावलिः *f.*; 'its central gem,' तरलः; 'mine of gems,' रत्नाकरः.—(Bud) मुकुलं, जालकं, पल्लवः -वं, कुड्मलं.

To GEM, *v. a.* मणिभिः or रत्नैर् अलङ्कृ or भूष् (c. 10. भूषयति -यितुं).

To GEM, *v. n.* (Bud) मुकुल् (c. 1. मुकुलति -लितुं), अङ्कुर (nom. अङ्कुरयति -यितुं).

To GEMINATE, *v. a.* द्विगुणीकृ, द्विगुण (nom. द्विगुणयति -यितुं), द्वैधीकृ, द्विकं -कां -कं कृ.

GEMINATION, *s.* द्विगुणीकरणं, द्वैगुण्यं, द्विरावृत्तिः *f.*, पुनरुक्तिः *f.*

GEMINI, *s. pl.* (Twins) यमौ m. du., यमजौ m. du.—(Constellation) द्वन्द्वः, मिथुनः, त्रियामः.

GEMINOUS, *a.* द्विगुणः -णा -णं, द्विकः -का -कं, द्वैधः -धी -धं, द्विविधः -धा -धं, यमः -मा -मं, यमकः -का -कं.

GEMINY, *s.* मिथुनं, द्वन्द्वं, यमकं, यमलं, युगं, युग्मं, युगलं, द्वयं.

GEMMATE, *a.* मुकुलितः -ता -तं, मुकुलवान् -वती -वत् (त्), पल्लवितः -ता -तं.

GEMMED, *p. p.* रत्नवान् -वती -वत् (त्), मणिमान् -मती -मत् (त्), रत्नमयः -यी -यं, रत्नानुविद्धः -द्धा -द्धं, रत्नालङ्कृतः -ता -तं, मणिभूषितः -ता -तं.

GEMMY, *a.* मणिशः -शा -शं, रत्नज्योती -तिनी -ति (न्), मणिमयः -यी -यं.

GENDER, *s.* लिङ्गं, प्रकृतिः *f.*; 'masculine gender,' पुंलिङ्गं, पुरुषः; 'feminine gender,' स्त्रीलिङ्गं; 'a noun of invariable gender,' अजहल्लिङ्गः

To GENDER, *v. a.* जन् in caus. (जनयति -यितुं), सञ्जन्, प्रभू or प्रसु (c. 2. -सूते, c. 4. -सूयते -सोतुं), उत्पद् in caus. (-पादयति -यितुं).

To GENDER, *v. n.* स्त्रीपुरुषवत् सङ्गम् (c. 1. -गच्छति -गन्तुं) or मैथुनं कृ.

GENEALOGICAL, *a.* वंशावलीविषयः -या -यं, वंशान्वयविषयकः -का -कं, वंशक्रमसम्बन्धी -न्धिनी -न्धि (न्).

GENEALOGIST, *s.* अन्वयज्ञः, वंशावलिज्ञः, पाठकः, कुलाचार्य्यः, वंशावलिलेखकः, वंशपरम्पराज्ञः.

GENEALOGY, *s.* वंशावली -लिः *f.*, आवलिः *f.*, वंशान्वयः, अन्वयः, वंशश्रेणी, वंशक्रमः, वंशपरम्परा, वंशानुचरितं, वंशविततिः *f.*, वंशविवरणं; 'of kings,' राजावलिः *f.*, नृपावलिः, पार्थिवावलिः.

GENERAL, *a.* (Common to many, or all) साधारणः -णा -णी -णं, सामान्यः -न्या -न्यं, सर्व्वसामान्यः -न्या -न्यं, बहुसामान्यः -न्या -न्यं, सर्व्वसाधारणः -णी -णं, सर्व्वः -र्व्वा -र्व्वं, सार्व्वः -र्व्वी -र्व्वं, सार्व्विकः -की -कं, सर्व्वीयः -या -यं, सर्व्वजनीयः -या -यं, सार्व्वजनिकः -की -कं, सर्व्वजनीनः -ना -नं, विश्वजनीनः -ना -नं, विश्वजनीयः -या -यं, विश्वजन्यः -न्या -न्यं, सार्व्वलौकिकः -की -कं, लौकिकः -की -कं, व्यापकः -का -कं, सर्व्वव्यापकः -का -कं, सर्व्वमयः -यी -यं, औत्सर्गिकः -की -कं.—(Not particular) अविशेषकः -का -कं, अवच्छेदावच्छेदकः -का -कं.—(Usual) प्रायिकः -की -कं, लोकसिद्धः -द्धा -द्धं, आचारिकः -की -कं, सर्व्वत्र प्रचलः -ला -लं or प्रचलितः -ता -तं; 'general practice,' जनरीतिः *f.*, लोकव्यवहारः; 'general order,' सामान्यशासनं; 'general opinion,' बहुमतं; 'general collection,' सर्व्वसङ्ग्रहः; 'general reader,' पुस्तकः, प्रघटाविद् *m.*; 'in general,' प्रायेण, प्रायशस्, बहुशस्. *See* GENERALLY.

GENERAL, *s.* (Of an army) सेनापतिः *m.*, वाहिनीपतिः *m.*, सेनानीः *m.*, सेनाधिपः, सेनाग्रगः, चमूपतिः *m.*, योधमुख्यः, सेनाध्यक्षः, सैन्याध्यक्षः, बलाध्यक्षः, दण्डनायकः, महासेनः; 'skilful general,' सांयुगीनः.—(Total, whole) साकल्यं, सामान्यं, साधारण्यं, समुदायः.

GENERALISSIMO, *s.* प्रधानसेनापतिः *m.*, अग्रसेनानीः *m.*, प्रधानसैन्याध्यक्षः.

GENERALITY, *s.* (State of being general) सामान्यं -न्यत्वं, साधारण्यं, साधारणत्वं.—(Greatest part) प्रधानभागः, अधिकभागः, बहुतरभागः, प्रधानांशः.

GENERALIZATION, *s.* अवच्छेदावच्छेदः, व्यापकत्वं, जातिनिर्देशः, बहुसामान्यकरणं, गणीकरणं.

To GENERALIZE, *v. a.* अवच्छेदावच्छेदं कृ, बहुव्यापकं -कां -कं कृ, बहुसामान्यं -न्यां -न्यं कृ, गणीकृ, जातिनिर्देशं कृ.

GENERALLY, *adv.* प्रायस्, प्रायशस्, प्रायेण, भूयस्, बहुशस्, बाहुल्येन, भूयिष्ठं, बहुतरं, साधारण्येन, सामान्यतस्, साकल्येन.

GENERALNESS, *s.* साधारणत्वं, सामान्यत्वं, व्यापकत्वं, बाहुल्यं, प्रसिद्धत्वं.

GENERALSHIP, *s.* सैनापत्यं, सेनापतित्वं.—(Skill in tactics) व्यूहपाण्डित्यं, रणपाण्डित्यं, सेनाव्यूहनैपुण्यं, बलविन्यासकौशल्यं, सेनानयप्रवीणता.

GENERALTY, *s.* साकल्यं, समस्तत्वं, सामान्यं, कार्त्स्न्यं, आखिल्यं, समुदायः.

To GENERATE, *v. a.* जन् in caus. (जनयति -यितुं), सञ्जन्, प्रसू or प्रसु (c. 1. -सवति, c. 2. -सूते, c. 4. -सूयते -सोतुं), सू, उत्पद् in caus. (-पादयति -यितुं).

GENERATED, *p. p.* जातः -ता -तं, जनितः -ता -तं, उपजातः -ता -तं, सञ्जातः -ता -तं, उत्पादितः -ता -तं, समुत्पादितः -ता -तं, प्रसूतः -ता -तं, प्ररूढः -ढा -ढं, कृतजन्मा -न्मा -न्म (न्), उद्भवः -वा -वं, प्रभवः -वा -वं; 'generated in water,' जलोद्भवः -वा -वं.

GENERATION, *s.* (Production) जननं, प्रजननं, जन्म *n.* (न्), उत्पादनं, उत्पत्तिः *f.*, प्रसूतिः *f.*, प्रसवः, सम्भवः, उद्भवः, प्रभवः.—(Race) जातिः *f.*, वंशः, सन्तानः, सन्ततिः *f.*, कुलं, अन्वयः, प्रवरं.—(The people living at the same time) समवयस्काः or समकालजीविनः पुरुषाः *m. pl.*—(Series of descendants) वंशावली, वंशपरम्परा, वंशश्रेणी; 'extending to seven generations,' साप्तपौरुषः -षी -षं; 'organ of generation,' उपस्थः.

GENERATIVE, *a.* जनकः -का -कं, उत्पादकः -का -कं, सावकः -विका -कं.

GENERATOR, *s.* जनयिता *m.* (तृ), जनिता *m.* (तृ), जननः, जनकः, जन्मदः -दाता *m.* (तृ), बीजप्रदः, बीजी *m.* (न्), उत्पादकः.

GENERIC, GENERICAL, *a.* सामान्यः -न्या -न्यं, साधारणः -णा -णी -णं, वर्गीयः -या -यं, जातीयः -या -यं, जातिसम्बन्धीयः -या -यं, व्यापकः -का -कं; 'generic property,' जातित्वं, जातिधर्म्मः, जातिस्वभावः, सामान्यं, समानाधिकरणं; 'generic characteristic,' जातिलक्षणं, सामान्यलक्षणं.

GENERICALLY, *adv.* जातिमुद्दिश्य, वर्गमुद्दिश्य, जातितस्, सामान्यतस्.

GENEROSITY, *s.* (Liberality) औदार्य्यं, उदारता, दानशीलता, त्यागशीलता -त्वं, त्यागः, त्यागिता, बहुप्रदत्वं, अतिसर्ज्जनं, अतिदानं, वदान्यता, अकार्पण्यं, विलम्भः.—(Nobleness of soul) माहात्म्यं, औदार्य्यं, उदारता.

GENEROUS *a.* (Liberal) उदारः -रा -री -रं, दानशीलः -ला -लं, त्यागशीलः -ला -लं, बहुप्रदः -दा -दं, बहुदः -दा -दं, अतिदाता -त्री -तृ (तृ), दायकः -का -कं, दानरतः -ता -तं, वदान्यः -न्या -न्यं, अकृपणः -णा -णं, स्थूललक्ष्यः -क्ष्या -क्ष्यं, उदात्तः -त्ता -त्तं.—(Noble-minded) उदारचेताः -ताः -तः (स्), उदारधीः -धीः -धि, उदारचरितः -ता -तं, माहात्मिकः -की -कं, महामनाः -नाः -नः (स्), महानुभावः -वा -वं, महेच्छः -च्छा -च्छं, उदीर्णः -र्णा -र्णं.—(Of honourable birth) सत्कुलीनः -ना -नं, महाकुलः -ला -लं.

GENEROUSLY, *adv.* उदारवत्, वदान्यवत्, औदार्य्येण, दानशीलत्वात्, माहात्म्येन.

GENEROUSNESS, *s.* औदार्य्यं, उदारता, माहात्म्यं. *See* GENEROSITY.

GENESIS, *s.* धर्म्मग्रन्थानां मध्यात् प्रथमग्रन्थः, जगत्सृष्टिविषयकं मूसालिखितम् आदिपुस्तकं.

GENET, *s.* (Horse) सुरूपी विदेशीयः क्षुद्रवाजी *m.* (न्).—(Civet) गन्धमार्जारः.

GENETHLIAC, *s.* (Birthday poem) जन्मदिवसमुद्दिश्य काव्यं.

GENIAL, *a.* (Contributing to propagation) सावकः -का -कं, प्रसवकारी -रिणी -रि (न्), प्रसूतिवर्धकः -का -कं.—(Contributing to life and cheerfulness) जीवदः -दा -दं, तेजोवर्धकः -का -कं, आनन्दकरः -रा -रं, रम्यः -म्या -म्यं, रमणीयः -या -यं, मनोरमः -मा -मं, सुखकरः -री -रं, प्रसन्नः -न्ना -न्नं, सुभगः -गा -गं, प्रसादकरः -रा -रं, हृषिरः -रा -रं.

GENIALLY, *adv.* प्रसन्नं, प्रसादेन, सप्रसादं, सानन्दं, प्रमोदेन, सहर्षं.

GENIALNESS, *s.* सुनन्दता, रम्यता, रमणीयत्वं, प्रसन्नता, सानन्दता.

GENICULATED, *a.* जानुपर्व्वाकारग्रन्थियुक्तः -क्ता -क्तं, ग्रन्थिलः -ला -लं.

GENITAL, *a.* प्रसवसम्बन्धी -न्धिनी -न्धि (न्), जननसम्बन्धी &c., यौनः -नी -नं.

GENITALS, *s. pl.* उपस्थः, शिश्नादि *n.*, भगादि *n.*, अधोऽङ्गं, जननाङ्गं.

GENITIVE, *a.* or *s.* (In grammar) सम्बन्धः, शेषः, षष्ठी विभक्तिः *f.*

GENITOR, *s.* जनयिता *m.* (तृ), जनिता *m.* (तृ), जनकः, जननः, जन्मदः.

GENIUS, *s.* (Natural disposition) स्वभावः, प्रकृतिः *f.*, शीलः, गुणः.—(Strength of mind, power of intellect) धीशक्तिः *f.*, बुद्धिशक्तिः *f.*, मनःशक्तिः *f.*, मनोयुक्तिः *f.*, बुद्धिसामर्थ्यं, बुद्धिप्रभावः, मतिसुप्रयोगता.—(Power of invention) कल्पनाशक्तिः *f.*—(Man endowed with talent) गुणी *m.* (न्), गुणवान् *m.* (त्), धीशक्तियुक्तः, बुद्धिशक्तिमान् *m.* (त्), युक्तबुद्धिः *m.*, बुद्धिमान् *m.* (त्), धीमान् *m.* (त्).—(Peculiar characteristic) विशेषणं, लक्षणं, स्वभावः, स्वधर्म्मः, वृत्तिः *f.*; 'poetical genius,' कविताशक्तिः *f.*

GENIUS, *s.* (Demon) भूतः, असुरः, दैत्यः, दानवः, प्रेतः, पिशाचः; 'evil genius,' दुर्दैवं; 'good genius,' सुदैवं, शुभदैवं.

GENTEEL, *a.* सभ्यः -भ्या -भ्यं, सभ्याचारी -रिणी -रि (न्), आर्य्यः -र्य्या -र्य्यं, आर्य्यव्यवहारः -रा -रं, आर्य्यवृत्तः -त्ता -त्तं, सद्वृत्तः -त्ता -त्तं, सुजनः -ना -नं, साधुवृत्तः -त्ता -त्तं, साधुव्यवहारः -रा -रं, सुशीलः -ला -लं, अग्राम्यः -म्या -म्यं, शिष्टाचारी -रिणी -रि (न्), महानुभावः -वा -वं.—(Elegant) विनीतः -ता -तं, चारुः -र्व्वी -रु, ललितः -ता -तं.

GENTEELLY, *adv.* सभ्यवत्, सुशीलवत्, आर्य्यवत्, सुजनवत्, सभ्याचारानुसारेण.

GENTEELNESS, *s.* सभ्यता, आर्य्यत्वं, सभ्याचारत्वं, आर्य्यवृत्तत्वं, सुशीलता, शिष्टाचारत्वं, सौजन्यं, सुजनता, साधुता, विनीतत्वं.

GENTIAN, *s.* (Plant) किरातः, किराततिक्तः, अनार्य्यतिक्तः, चिरातिक्तः, चिरतिक्तः, काण्डतिक्तकः, कैरातं, भूनिम्बः, भूतीकः.

GENTILE, *s.* अन्यदेशीयः, भिन्नदेशीयः, भिन्नदेशीयलोकः, अन्यदेशीयलोकः, देवतार्च्चकः, देवताभ्यर्च्चकः, देवार्च्चकः.—(Kindred) गोत्रजः; 'in grammar,' ज्ञातिवाचकः.

GENTILE, *a.* अन्यदेशीयः -या -यं, भिन्नदेशीयः -या -यं, जातीयः -या -यं.

GENTILISM, *s.* देवार्च्चकत्वं, देवतार्च्चनं -ना, देवताभ्यर्च्चनं, भिन्नदेशीयता.

GENTILITIAL, *a.* कौलिकः -की -कं, कुलजः -जा -जं, वंशिकः -की -कं, वंश्यः -श्या -श्यं, जातीयः -या -यं, दैशिकः -की -कं.

GENTILITY, *s.* (Politeness of manners) सभ्यता, सभ्याचारत्वं, सुशीलता, शिष्टाचारत्वं, आर्य्यत्वं, आर्य्यवृत्तत्वं, सौजन्यं, सुजनता, साधुवृत्तत्वं, सुविनीतता, महानुभावता.—(Good birth) कुलीनता, महाकुलत्वं, वंशविशुद्धता, कुलोत्कर्षः.

GENTLE, *a.* (Well-born) कुलीनः -ना -नं, सत्कुलीनः -ना -नं, महाकुलः

-ला -लं, महाकुलप्रसूतः -ता -तं, साधुजः -जा -जं, साधुवंशजः -जा -जं, आर्य्यवंशजः -जा -जं, सुजन्मा -न्मा -न्म (न्); 'a maid of gentle birth,' कुलकन्यका.—(Mild, soft, bland) मृदुः -द्वी -दु, मृदुलः -ला -लं, मन्दः -न्दा -न्दं, कोमलः -ला -लं, सौम्यः -म्या -म्यी -म्यं, स्निग्धः -ग्धा -ग्धं, सुकुमारः -रा -री -रं, मसृणः -णा -णं, अनुग्रः -ग्रा -ग्रं, अकर्कशः -शा -शं, अपरुषः -षा -षं, अचण्डः -ण्डा -ण्डी -ण्डं, अक्रूरः -रा -रं, असाहसिकः -की -कं, सुकरः -रा -री -रं; 'of a gentle disposition,' मृदुभावः -वा -वं, मृदुस्वभावः -वा -वं.—(Quiet, tame) शान्तः -न्ता -न्तं, उपशान्तः -न्ता -न्तं, शमी -मिनी -मि (न्), दान्तः -न्ता -न्तं; 'a gentle breeze,' मन्दानिलः, मृदुवातः; 'a gentle laugh,' मन्दहास्यं, मन्दस्मितं, ईषद्धासः; 'gentle remedy,' सौम्योपचारः, सामोपचारः; 'by gentle means,' साम्ना; 'gentle speech,' प्रियवाक्यं, प्रियोदितं.

GENTLE, *s.* (Maggot) अलिः *m.*, अली *m.* (न्), कोषकारी *m.* (न्).

GENTLEFOLK, *s.* आर्य्यलोकाः *m. pl.*, साधुजनाः *m. pl.*, आर्य्यमिश्राः *m. pl.*, कुलीनलोकः.

GENTLEMAN, *s.* आर्य्यः, आर्य्यजनः, आर्य्यमिश्रः, साधुः *m.*, साधुजनः, महाशयः, महानुभावः, कुलीनः, कुलीनजनः, सत्कुलीनः, सुजनः, सुजन्मा *m.* (न्), सज्जनः, सज्जातिः *m.*, महाजनः, सत्कुलजातः, सुविनीतः, श्री prefixed.

GENTLEMAN-COMMONER, *s.* राजविद्यालये अन्तेवासिनां मध्यात् प्रथमपदस्थः.

GENTLEMANLIKE, GENTLEMANLY, *a.* आर्य्यव्यवहारानुसारी -रिणी -रि (न्), सभ्याचारानुसारी &c., सभ्यः -भ्या -भ्यं, आर्य्यवृत्तः -त्ता -त्तं, सुशीलः -ला -लं, सुविनीतः -ता -तं, शिष्टाचारयोग्यः -ग्या -ग्यं; 'gentlemanly deportment,' आर्य्यवृत्तिः *f.*, सौजन्यं.

GENTLEMANLINESS, *s.* आर्य्यत्वं, सुशीलता, सौजन्यं, सुविनीतता.

GENTLENESS, *s.* मृदुता, म्रदिमा *m.* (न्), मार्द्दवं, मन्दता, कोमलता, सौम्यता -त्वं, स्निग्धता, सौकुमार्य्यं, सुकुमारता, अनुग्रता, अकार्कश्यं, अकर्कशत्वं, अपरुषता, अपारुष्यं, अचण्डता, असाहसं; 'of disposition,' भावमृदुता.

GENTLEWOMAN, *s.* आर्य्या, कुलीना स्त्री, सुशीला स्त्री, सुविनीता स्त्री.

GENTLY, *adv.* शनैस्, शनैः शनैस्, शनकैस्, मन्दं मन्दं, मृदु, अनुग्रं, अकर्कशं, अपरुषं, अचण्डं, साहसं विना.

GENTRY, *s.* आर्य्यलोकाः *m. pl.*, आर्य्याः *m. pl.*, साधुलोकाः *m. pl.*, कुलीनलोकाः *m. pl.*, कुलीनवर्गः, सुजनवर्गः, सुजनता, सौजन्यं.

GENUFLEXION, *s.* पूजार्थं जानुभ्यां नतिः *f.* or आनतिः *f.*, जानुनतिः *f.*

GENUINE, *a.* सत्यः -त्या -त्यं, प्रकृतः -ता -तं, वास्तवः -वी -वं -विकः -की -कं, अकल्पितः -ता -तं, अकृत्रिमः -मा -मं, अकपटः -टा -टं, निष्कपटः -टा -टं, निर्व्याजः -जा -जं, निर्व्यलीकः -का -कं, यथार्थः -र्था -र्थं, सारः -रा -रं.

GENUINELY, *adv.* सत्यं, निष्कपटं, कपटं विना, निर्व्याजं, निर्व्यलीकं, यथार्थं.

GENUINENESS, *s.* सत्यता, प्रकृतत्वं, अकृत्रिमता, अकल्पितत्वं, याथार्थ्यं, यथार्थता, निर्व्यलीकता, निर्व्याजत्वं, वास्तविकता, सारता.

GENUS, *s.* (In logic) परं.—(A class) जातिः *f.*, गणः, वर्गः, जातिमात्रं, गोत्रं.

GEOGRAPHER, *s.* भूपृष्ठविद्याज्ञः, भूगोलविद्याज्ञः, भूगोलशास्त्रज्ञः, भूपृष्ठलेखकः, भूगोलज्ञानी *m.* (न्), भूगोलस्य यत् किञ्चिद् देशसमुद्रनगरादि विद्यते तदाकारनामादिलेखकः, भूपृष्ठस्य देशसमुद्रपर्व्वतनद्यादिव्याख्याता *m.* (ृ), भूपृष्ठविवरणकृत्.

GEOGRAPHICAL, *a.* भूगोलविषयः -या -यं, भूपृष्ठविषयकः -का -कं, भूगोलशास्त्रविषयः -या -यं, भूपृष्ठसम्बन्धी -न्धिनी -न्धि (न्), भूगोलशास्त्रीयः -या -यं.

GEOGRAPHICALLY, *adv.* भूगोलशास्त्रानुसारेण, भूगोलशास्त्रवत्.

GEOGRAPHY, *s.* भूपृष्ठविद्या, भूगोलविद्या, भूपृष्ठविषयकं ज्ञानं, भूगोलस्य यत् किञ्चिद् देशसमुद्रनगरादि विद्यते तदाकारनामादिव्याख्या, भूपृष्ठस्य देशसमुद्रपर्व्वतनद्यादीनां ज्ञानं or विवरणं, भूगोलशास्त्रं.

GEOLOGICAL, *a.* पार्थिवांशविषयः -या -यं, पृथिवीविद्यासम्बन्धी -न्धिनी -न्धि (न्), पृथिवीसंस्थानविषयकः -का -कं.

GEOLOGIST, *s.* पार्थिवांशविद्याज्ञः, पृथिवीविद्याज्ञः, पृथिवीसंस्थानव्याख्याता *m.* (ृ), मृत्तिकाभावगुणादिविवरणकृत् *m.*

GEOLOGY, *s.* पार्थिवांशानां ज्ञानं or विद्या, पार्थिवांशविषयं ज्ञानं, पृथिवीविद्या, पार्थिवांशानां प्राचीनेतिहासः, पृथिवीसंस्थानविद्या, मृत्तिकासंस्थानविद्या, मृत्तिकाभावगुणादिविवरणविद्या.

GEOMETRAL, GEOMETRIC, GEOMETRICAL, *a.* क्षैत्रः -त्री -त्रं, क्षेत्रपरिमाणविषयः -या -यं, क्षेत्रगतः -ता -तं, क्षेत्रविद्यानुसारी -रिणी -रि (न्), रेखागणितसम्बन्धी -न्धिनी -न्धि (न्); 'geometrical proof,' क्षेत्रगतोपपत्तिः *f.*

GEOMETRICALLY, *adv.* क्षेत्रविद्यानुसारेण, रेखागणितशास्त्रवत् or -तस्.

GEOMETRICIAN, *s.* क्षेत्रविद्याज्ञः, रेखागणितविद् *m.*, क्षैत्रज्ञः, रेखागणितशास्त्रदर्शी *m.* (न्), क्षेत्रपरिमाणविद्यावान् *m.* (त्).

GEOMETRY, *s.* क्षैत्रं, क्षेत्रं, क्षेत्रविद्या, क्षेत्रपरिमाणविद्या, क्षेत्रपरिमाणविषया विद्या, रेखागणितं, रेखागणितशास्त्रं, रेखागणनाविद्या; 'proof by geometry,' क्षेत्रगतोपपत्तिः *f.*

GEORGIC, *s.* गोमेषादिविषयं गीतं, कृषिविद्याविषयकं काव्यं.

GERANIUM, *s.* बकमुखाकारबीजकोषः सुपुष्पवान् ओषधिभेदः.

GERFALCON, *s.* श्येनभेदः, कपोतारिः *m.*, घातिपक्षी *m.* (न्).

GERM, GERMEN, GERMIN, *s.* (The embryo of fruit, a bud) पल्लवः -वं, अङ्कुरः, अभिनवोद्भिद् *m.*, जालकं, क्षारकः, जोषिका, कुन्दुकं; 'of leaves,' नाडिः *f.*—(Origin, that from which any thing springs) बीजं, योनिः *m.f.*, आदिः *m.*, आरम्भः, गर्भः, मूलं.

GERMAN, *a.* (Related) सम्बन्धी -न्धिनी -न्धि (न्), सम्पर्की -र्किणी -र्कि (न्); 'cousin german,' पितृव्यपुत्रः -त्री, मातुलपुत्रः -त्री.—(Belonging to Germany) जर्म्मणिदेशसम्बन्धी &c., जर्म्मणिदेशजः -जा -जं; 'language,' जर्म्मणिदेशभाषा.

GERMANDER, *s.* अनेकौषधीनां सामान्यनाम *n.* (न्), ओषधिगणसंज्ञा.

GERMANISM, *s.* जर्म्मणिदेशभाषासम्बन्धी सम्प्रदायः.

To GERMINATE, *v. n.* स्फुट् (c. 6. स्फुटति -टितुं), फुल्ल् (c. 1. फुल्लति -ल्लितुं), अङ्कुर (nom. अङ्कुरयति -यितुं), विकस् (c. 1. -कसति -सितुं), उद्भिद् in pass. (-भिद्यते), प्रोद्भिद्, प्ररुह् (c. 1. -रोहति -रोढुं), वृध् (c. 1. वर्धते -र्धितुं).

GERMINATING, *part.* उद्भिज्जः -ज्जा -ज्जं, उद्भिद् *m.f.n.*, उद्भिदः -दा -दं, प्ररोही -हिणी -हि (न्), अङ्कुरितः -ता -तं, फुल्लवान् -वती -वत्, प्रस्फुटः -टा -टं, स्फुटन् -टन्ती -टत् (त्).

GERMINATION, *s.* स्फुटनं, स्फुटता, उद्भेदः, प्रोद्भेदः, प्ररोहः, उद्वर्त्तनं.

GERUND, *s.* लाटीनभाषाव्याकरणे क्रियावाचकः शब्दः.

GESTATION, *s.* गर्भधारणं, गर्भपोषणं, गर्भवहनं, गर्भिणीभावः.

To GESTICULATE, *v. n.* अङ्गानि विक्षिप् (c. 6. -क्षिपति -क्षेप्तुं), हस्तादि विक्षिप् or सञ्चल् in caus. (-चालयति -यितुं), अङ्गविक्षेपं कृ, इङ्ग् (c. 1. इङ्गति -ङ्गितुं), नट् (c. 10. नाटयति -यितुं), अभिनयं कृ, आङ्गिककर्म्म कृ.

GESTICULATION, *s.* अङ्गविक्षेपः -पणं, हस्तादिविक्षेपः, अङ्गहारः, इङ्गितं, इङ्गितकरणं, अङ्गसञ्चालनं, हस्तादिसञ्चालनं, सङ्केतकरणं, शाणी, सूचा -चना, भावकरणं, आङ्गिककर्म्म *n.* (न्).

GESTICULATOR, *s.* अङ्गविक्षेपकः, हस्तादिविक्षेपकः, अङ्गसञ्चालकः, इङ्गितकारी *m.* (न्), सङ्केतकारी *m.* (न्).

GESTURE, *s.* इङ्गितं, अङ्गविक्षेपः, हस्तादिविक्षेपः, सङ्केतः, अङ्गहारः -रिः *m.*, चेष्टा, भावः, इङ्गः, अभिनयः, अभिनीतिः *f.*, सूचना.

To GESTURE, *v. a.* साङ्गविक्षेपं कृ, सहस्तविक्षेपं कृ, साभिनयं कृ.

To GET, *v. a.* (Obtain) आप् (c. 5. आप्नोति, आप्तुं), प्राप्, अवाप्,

सम्प्राप्, समवाप्; लभ् (c. 1. लभते, लब्धुं), उपलभ्, अर्ज् (c. 1. अर्जति -र्जितुं, c. 10. अर्जयति -यितुं), उपार्ज्, आसद् (c. 10. -सादयति -यितुं), समासद्, अधिगम् (c. 1. -गच्छति -गन्तुं), गम्, प्रतिपद् (c. 4. -पद्यते -पत्तुं), आपद्, अभिपद्, आविश् (c. 6. -विशति -वेष्टुं), इ (c. 2. एति -तुं), अश् (c. 5. अश्नुते, अशितुं), उपाश्, समश्.—(Have) धा (c. 3. दधाति, धत्ते, धातुं), धृ in caus. (धारयति -यितुं), भृ (c. 3. बिभर्त्ति, भर्तुं), आप्.—(Beget) जन् (c. 10. जनयति -यितुं).—(Learn) शिक्ष् (c. 1. शिक्षते -क्षितुं), अधी (c. 2. अधीते, अध्येतुं rt. इ), अधिगम्.—(Induce, persuade) अनुनी (c. 1. -नयति -नेतुं), प्रोत्सह् (c. 10. -साहयति -यितुं), or expressed by the causal; as, 'he got him to return,' निवर्त्तयामास.—(Earn) उपार्ज्, लभ्.—(Receive, take) आदा (c. 3. -दत्ते -दातुं), ग्रह् (c. 9. गृह्णाति, ग्रहीतुं), उपलभ्.—(Procure, get ready) क्लृप् (c. 10. कल्पयति -यितुं), परिक्लृप्, सज्जीकृ, उत्पद् (c. 10. -पादयति -यितुं).—(Get together) समानी (c. 1. -नयति -नेतुं), सञ्चि (c. 5. -चिनोति -चेतुं), समादा, सङ्ग्रह्, एकीकृ, एकत्र कृ.—(Get over, get through, surmount) आरुह् (c. 1. -रोहति -रोढुं), अधिरुह्, अतिक्रम् (c. 1. -क्रामति -क्रमितुं), तीर् (c. 10. तीरयति -यितुं), पार् (c. 10. पारयति -यितुं), तॄ (c. 1. तरति -रितुं -रीतुं), निस्तॄ; 'get over a difficulty,' दुःखम् आरुह्, दुःखपारं गम् (c. 1. गच्छति, गन्तुं), दुःखस्यान्तं गम्.—(Get up, prepare) उपस्कृ, संस्कृ, पुरस्कृ, विरच् (c. 10. -रचयति -यितुं), सज्जीकृ.—(Get into debt) ऋणं कृ, ऋणग्रस्तः -स्ता -स्तं भू, ऋणवान् -वती -वत् भू.

To GET, *v. n.* (Arrive at) आगम् (c. 1. -गच्छति -गन्तुं), उपगम्, अभिगम्, प्राप् (c. 5. -आप्नोति -आप्तुं), अवाप्, आया (c. 2. -याति -तुं), उपस्था (c. 1. -तिष्ठति -स्थातुं).—(Get away) अपगम्, अपया, अपे (c. 2. अपैति -तुं, rt. इ), अपसृ (c. 1. -सरति -सर्त्तुं), अपक्रम् (c. 1. -क्रामति -क्रमितुं), चल्, (c. 1. चलति -लितुं), प्रस्था.—(Get before) अग्रे or पूर्व्वं or पूर्व्वम् आगम् or प्राप्.—(Get clear) मुच् in pass. (मुच्यते).—(Get down) अवरुह् (c. 1. -रोहति -रोढुं), अवतॄ (c. 1. -तरति -रितुं -रीतुं), अधो या or गम्.—(Get in) विश् (c. 6. विशति, वेष्टुं), प्रविश्, निविश्, आविश्.—(Get off, escape) पलाय् (c. 1. पलायते -यितुं, rt. इ), विपलाय्, निस्तॄ, अपक्रम्, निर्गम्.—(Get off, alight) अवतॄ, अवरुह्.—(Get out) अपगम्, अपसृ, अपे.—(Get up) उत्था for उत्स्था.—(Get quit of) मुच् in pass.—(Get on) प्रगम्, प्रवृत् (c. 1. -वर्त्तते -र्त्तितुं), प्रसृ, प्रया, प्रचल्.—(Get drunk) मत्तः-त्ता-त्तं भू, उन्मत्तीभू; 'get out with you,' अपसर, अपैहि, अपेहि.

GETTER, *s.* प्रापकः, अवाप्ता *m.* (प्तृ), लब्धा *m.* (ब्धृ), अर्जकः, उपार्जकः, अधिगन्ता *m.*(न्तृ), लाभकृत् *m.*, आदाता *m.*(तृ), ग्राहकः, जनकः, उत्पादकः.

GETTING, *s.* लाभः, लब्धिः *f.*, आप्तिः *f.*, प्राप्तिः *f.*, प्रापणं, अवाप्तिः *f.*, सम्प्राप्तिः *f.*, अर्जनं, उपार्जनं, आसादनं, अधिगमः, आगमः, ग्रहणं.

GEWGAW, *s.* स्वल्पमूल्यकम् आभरणं, अल्पार्थं क्रीडाद्रव्यं, क्रीडनकं, कन्दुकं, खेलाद्रव्यं, कदर्थद्रव्यं.

GHASTFULLY, *adv.* पिशाचवत्, भूतवत्, प्रेतवत्, दारुणं, भयानकं, घोरं.

GHASTLINESS, *s.* रूपदारुण्यं, वदनघोरता, मुखरौद्रता, भूतसरूपता, भौतत्वं, करालत्वं, विकटत्वं.

GHASTLY, *a.* (Like a ghost) भूतसरूपः -पी -पं, प्रेतसरूपः -पी -पं, भौतिकः -की -कं, पैशाचिकः -की -कं, शवसवर्णः -र्णा -र्णं, प्रेतसवर्णः -र्णा -र्णं.—(Frightful) घोररूपः -पी -पं, घोराकृतिः -तिः -ति, दारुणः -णा -णं, भयानकः -का -कं, रौद्रः -द्री -द्रं, भीमदर्शनः -ना -नं, उग्रम्पश्यः -श्या -श्यं, करालमुखः -खी -खं.

GHAUT, *s.* (Landing-place) घट्टः -ट्टी, सञ्जनं, गुल्मः.—(Malaya range of mountains) मलयः, मलयाचलः, मलयपर्व्वतः, मलयाद्रिः *m.*, दक्षिणाचलः, दक्षिणपर्व्वतः.

GHEE, *s.* घृतं, हविस् *n.*, सर्पिस् *n.*, हव्यं, हवनीयं, हविष्यं, आज्यं, तनूनपं, तृप्तं.

GHOST, *s.* (Soul) आत्मा *m.* (न्), अन्तरात्मा *m.* (न्).—(Disembodied spirit) प्रेतः, प्रेतनरः, परेतः, नारकः, नरकवासी *m.* (न्), नरकामयः.—(Goblin) वेतालः, रात्रिचरः, निशाचरः, निशाटः, भूतः -तं, श्मशानवासी *m.* (न्), राक्षसः; 'to give up the ghost,' प्राणत्यागं कृ, ईश्वरहस्ते जीवनं or प्राणं समृ in caus. (-अर्पयति -यितुं).

GHOSTLIKE, *s.* प्रेतसरूपः -पा -पी -पं, भूतसरूपः -पा -पी -पं.

GHOSTLINESS, *s.* प्रेतत्वं, भूतत्वं, परेतत्वं, आत्मता, पारमार्थिकत्वं.

GHOSTLY, *a.* (Spiritual) आत्मिकः -की -कं, आत्मविषयः -या -यं, पारमार्थिकः -की -कं, अशारीरिकः -की -कं, पारत्रिकः -की -कं.—(Pertaining to ghosts) भौतिकः -की -कं, प्रेतसम्बन्धी -न्धिनी -न्धि (न्).

GIANT, *s.* (A man of extraordinary size) बृहत्कायः, बृहच्छरीरः, विकटशरीरः, भीमविग्रहः, प्रकाण्डशरीरः, अखर्वः.—(A titan) दैत्यः, असुरः, राक्षसः, दानवः, दैतेयः, रक्षस् *n.*, इन्द्रारिः *m.*, सुरद्विट् *m.* (ष्), दितिसुतः, दनुजः, यातु *n.*, यातुधानः, पूर्व्वदेवः, शुक्रशिष्यः, कौणपः, नैर्ऋतः, निकषात्मजः, क्रव्याद् *m.*, निशाचरः.

GIANTESS, *s.* बृहत्काया, बृहच्छरीरा, विकटशरीरा स्त्री, राक्षसी.

GIANT-LIKE, GIANTLY, *a.* बृहत्कायः -या -यं, बृहच्छरीरः -रा -रं.

To GIBBER, *v. n.* जल्प् (c. 1. जल्पति -ल्पितुं), अस्पष्टं वद् (c. 1. वदति -दितुं).

GIBBERISH, *s.* अनर्थकवाक्यं, असम्बद्धवाक्यं, वृथाकथा, मृषार्थकवचनं, जल्पितं; 'one who talks it,' अनिबद्धप्रलापी *m.* (न्).

GIBBET, *s.* उद्बन्धनकाष्ठं, उद्बन्धनवृक्षः, वधस्थानं, घातस्थानं.

To GIBBET, *v. a.* रज्जुपाशेन उद्बन्ध् (c. 9. -बध्नाति -बन्धुं), उद्बन्धनं कृ.

GIBBOSITY, *s.* कुब्जता, न्युब्जता, कूर्म्मपृष्ठाकारत्वं, पिण्डाकारता, आभोगः, खण्डमण्डलत्वं.

GIBBOUS, *a.* (Convex, protuberant) न्युब्जः -ब्जा -ब्जं, पिण्डाकारः -रा -रं, कूर्म्मपृष्ठाकारः -रा -रं, गण्डाकारः -रा -रं, आभोगी -गिनी -गि (न्); 'as the moon,' खण्डमण्डलः -ला -लं.—(Hump-backed) कुब्जः -ब्जा -ब्जं, गडुरः -रा -रं.

GIBBOUSNESS, *s.* न्युब्जता, कूर्म्मपृष्ठाकारता, साभोगता. *See* GIBBOSITY.

GIB-CAT, *s.* जीर्णमार्जारः, अतिवृद्धो बिडालः.

To GIBE, *v. a.* and *n.* क्षिप् (c. 6. क्षिपति, क्षेप्तुं), अवक्षिप्, परिक्षिप्, अवहस् (c. 1. -हसति -सितुं), अवज्ञा (c. 9. -जानाति -ज्ञातुं), तिरस्कृ, मुखरीकृ.

GIBE, *s.* क्षेपः, अवक्षेपः, तिरस्कारः, अवहासः, दुर्वाक्यं, दुरुक्तं, कटुवाक्यं.

GIBER, *s.* क्षेपकः, अवक्षेपकः, दुर्मुखः, मुखरः, दुर्वक्ता *m.* (क्तृ).

GIBLETS, *s. pl.* हंसादेर् यत् पादमस्तकयकृदादि प्राक्शूलारोपणाद् अवच्छिन्नीभूय पृथक् पच्यते, हंसस्य पचनयोग्यं शुक्रकृदन्त्रादि, हंसखण्डकाः *m. pl.*

GIDDILY, *adv.* भ्रामररोगग्रस्तवत्, सभ्रामरं, चपलं, मनोलौल्यात्.

GIDDINESS, *s.* (Of the head, &c.) भ्रमरं, भ्रामरं, भ्रमिः *f.*, भ्रमः, विभ्रमः, विभ्रान्तिः *f.*, घूर्णिः *f.*, घूर्णनं, चक्षुरादिचापल्यं -चापलं, चक्षुरादिविभ्रान्तिः *f.*, प्रमादः.—(Of character) चपलता, चापल्यं, चञ्चलत्वं, चाञ्चल्यं, चलचित्तता, अस्थिरता, अस्थैर्य्यं, लोलता, अनवस्थितिः *f.*, अधीरत्वं, लौल्यं, मनोलौल्यं, विभ्रान्तिः *f.*, विभ्रान्तशीलता, तरलता, प्रमत्तता.

GIDDY, *a.* (In the head) भ्रामरी -रिणी -रि (न्), भ्रमी -मिणी -मि (न्), घूर्णरोगी -गिणी -गि (न्), भ्रामररोगी &c., विभ्रान्तः -न्ता -न्तं.—(Causing giddiness) भ्रमकरः -री -रं.—(In character) चपलः -ला -लं, चञ्चलः -ला -लं, विभ्रान्तशीलः -ला -लं, अस्थिरः -रा -रं, अनवस्थः -स्था -स्थं, अनवस्थितः -ता -तं, अधीरः -रा -रं, चपलबुद्धिः -द्धिः -द्धि, चपलात्मकः -का -कं, चलचित्तः -त्ता -त्तं, लोलः -ला -लं, लोलमनाः

-नाः -नः (स्), प्रमत्तः -त्ता -त्तं, प्रमादी -दिनी -दि (न्).—(Elated) उद्धतः -ता -तं, मत्तः -त्ता -त्तं; 'with power,' ऐश्वर्य्यमत्तः -त्ता -त्तं.

GIFT, s. दानं, प्रदानं, दत्तं, प्रदेयं, सम्प्रदानं, दायः, उपहारः, उपायनं, वितरणं, त्यागः, उत्सर्ज्जनं, विसर्गः, विसर्ज्जनं, विश्राणनं, अंहतिः f., उपग्राह्यं, उपढौकनं, उपदा -दानकं, प्रदा, दादः, दा, दं, विहापितं, प्रतिपादनं, निर्वपणं, स्पर्शनं, प्रादेशनं, प्रदेशनं, अपवर्ज्जनं, उपचारः, प्रीतिदानं, प्राभृतं; 'a special gift,' सदायः, सुदायः, हरणं; 'nuptial gift,' यौतकं; 'desirable gift,' प्रवारणं, प्रहारणं; 'gift to deceased ancestors,' पितृदानं.—(Endowment) गुणः, शक्तिः f.

GIFTED, p. p. or a. (Endowed) सम्पन्नः -न्ना -न्नं, उपपन्नः -न्ना -न्नं, युक्तः -क्ता -क्तं, संयुक्तः -क्ता -क्तं, उपेतः -ता -तं, अन्वितः -ता -तं, शीलितः -ता -तं.—(With talents) गुणी -णिनी -णि (न्), गुणवान् -वती -वत् (त्), इष्टगुणसम्पन्नः -न्ना -न्नं, सद्गुणोपेतः -ता -तं.

GIG, s. (Any thing that whirls round in play) भ्रमरं, भ्रमरक्रीडनकं.—(A light carriage) द्विचक्रयुक्तं लघुयानं, लघुरथः.—(Boat) उपनौका, लघुनौका, क्षुद्रनौका.

GIGANTIC, a. वृहत्कायः -या -यं, वृहच्छरीरः -रा -रं -री -रिणी -रि (न्), भीमविग्रहः -हा -हं, अतिकायः -या -यं, विकटशरीरः -रा -रं, अतिमहान् -हती -हत् (त्), अतिवृहन् -हती -हत् (त्), राक्षसपरिमाणः -णा -णं, दैत्यपरिमाणः -णा -णं.

GIGGLE, s. असभ्यपरिहासः, अनर्थकहासः, कुहसितं, मूर्खहसितं.

To GIGGLE, v. n. असभ्यपरिहासं कृ, अनर्थकहासं कृ, मूर्खवत् or असभ्यं or कु हस् (c. 1. हसति -सितुं), कक्ष् (c. 1. कक्षति -क्षितुं), कख् (c. 1. कखति -खितुं).

GIGGLER, s. असभ्यपरिहासशीलः, निरर्थकहासकारी m. (न्).

To GILD, v. a. (Overlay with gold) सुवर्ण (nom. सुवर्णयति -यितुं), स्वर्णपत्रपिनद्धं -द्धां -द्धं कृ, सुवर्णोपेतं -तां -तं कृ.—(Illuminate) रञ्ज् (c. 10. रञ्जयति -यितुं), द्युत् (c. 10. द्योतयति -यितुं), विराज् (c. 10. -राजयति -यितुं), प्रकाश् (c. 10. -काशयति -यितुं).

GILDED, p. p. सुवर्णितः -ता -तं, रसितः -ता -तं, स्वर्णपत्रपिनद्धः -द्धा -द्धं, स्वर्णमण्डितः -ता -तं, स्वर्णपत्रसंवीतः -ता -तं or -प्रतिबद्धः -द्धा -द्धं, राजतान्वितः -ता -तं, रञ्जितः -ता -तं, राजितः -ता -तं, प्रद्योतितः -ता -तं.

GILDER, s. स्वर्णपत्रादिना रञ्जकः, स्वर्णपत्रपिनद्धकारी m. (न्).

GILDING, s. स्वर्णरञ्जनं, सुवर्णीकरणं, स्वर्णमण्डनं; 'of the leaves of a book,' पत्ररञ्जनं.

GILL, s. (Organ of respiration in fishes) मत्स्यानां श्वासेन्द्रियं, मत्स्यानां श्वासप्रश्वासार्थं मस्तकरन्ध्रं or शिरोरन्ध्रद्वयं.—(Of a fowl) कुक्कुटस्य मुखकम्बलः or मुखस्याधःस्थं लोलमांसं.—(Flesh on the lower part of the cheek) अधोगण्डमांसं, अधोगण्डः, अधःकपोलः, चिबुकमांसं.—(Measure) द्रवद्रव्याणां परिमाणविशेषः.

GILLY-FLOWER, s. अनेकौषधीनां सामान्यनाम n. (न्), ओषधिगणसंज्ञा.

GILT, p. p. or a. सुवर्णितः -ता -तं, रसितः -ता -तं, राजतान्वितः -ता -तं. *See* GILDED.

GILT, s. सुवर्णरञ्जनं, स्वर्णपत्रं; 'silver-gilt,' विमलं.

GILT-HEAD, s. (Fish) गडकः, शकुलगडकः, शकुलार्भकः, शालः, कुम्भिलः.

GIMCRACK, s. निरर्थकयन्त्रं, क्रीडायन्त्रं, क्रीडाद्रव्यं, क्रीडनकं.

GIMLET, s. वेधनिका, आस्फोटनी, लास्फोटनी, आविधः.

GIMP, s. कौशिकसूत्रनिर्म्मितः सुतनुचेलकः.

GIN, s. (Spirit) शुण्डा, सुरा -री, वारुणी, शीधुः m. -धु n., मदिरा, हाला, आसवं; 'gin-drinker,' सुरापः -पी, शुण्डापायी m. -यिनी; 'gin-drinking,' सुरापानं; 'gin-shop,' शुण्डापानं, पानगोष्ठिका.—(Snare, trap) पाशः, उन्माथः, जालं, कूटयन्त्रं, वागुरा, पाशबन्धं.

GINGER, s. आर्द्रकं, शृङ्गवेरं, अकुलोमः, गुल्ममूलं, अपाकशाकं; 'dry ginger,' शुष्कार्द्रं, शुण्ठिः f. -ण्ठी -शठ्यं, विश्वभेषजं, विश्वं -श्वा, महौषधं, नागरं.

GINGER-BEER, s. आर्द्रकपानं, आर्द्रकरसः, आर्द्रकपानीयं, आर्द्रकसुरा.

GINGER-BREAD, s. आर्द्रकपिष्टकः, आर्द्रकपूपः, आर्द्रकमयं मिष्टान्नं.

GINGER-WINE, s. आर्द्रकमद्यं, आर्द्रकमदिरा, आर्द्रकसुरा.

GINGERLY, adv. सावधानं, अवधानेन, शनैः शनैस्, असहसा.

GINGHAM, s. रेखाविचित्रितं कार्पासाम्बरं or तूलावस्त्रं.

GINGIVAL, a. दन्तमांससम्बन्धी -न्धिनी -न्धि (न्), दन्तशिरासम्बन्धी &c.

To GINGLE, v. n. शिञ्ज् (c. 2. शिंक्ते, c. 1. शिञ्जते -ञ्जितुं), विशिञ्ज्, क्वण् (c. 1. क्वणति -णितुं), किङ्किण (nom. किङ्किणायते), झञ्झनं कृ.

GINGLE, GINGLING, s. शिञ्जः -ञ्जा, शिञ्जितं, आशिञ्जितं, क्वणितं, किङ्किणिशब्दः, झञ्झनं, झनत्कारः.

GINGLING, part. क्वणन् -णन्ती -णत् (त्), शिञ्जी -ञ्जिनी -ञ्जि (न्).

GINNET, s. अश्वकः. *See* JENNET.

GIPSY, s. हस्तरेखानिरीक्षणानन्तरं दैवकथनाद्युपजीवी चक्राटः, अवनिचरः -रा f., धूर्त्तः -र्त्ता f., काकचरित्रः -त्रा.

GIRAFFE, s. तरक्षुरूपेण चित्रित उष्ट्रजातीयो दीर्घग्रीवो जन्तुभेदः.

To GIRD, v. a. (Bind round) बन्ध् (c. 9. बध्नाति, बन्धुं), परिबन्ध्.—(Bind on) आबन्ध्, पिनह् (c. 4. -नह्यति -नद्धुं), अवनह्, सन्नह्, पिनद्धं -द्धां -द्धं कृ, आकच् (c. 1. -कचते -चितुं); 'gird the loins,' कटिं बन्ध्.—(Encircle, invest) परिवेष्ट् (c. 1. -वेष्टते -ष्टितुं, c. 10. -वेष्टयति -यितुं), परिधा (c. 3. -दधाति -धत्ते -धातुं), परिवृ (c. 5. -वृणोति -वरितुं -रीतुं).

To GIRD, v. n. (Gibe) क्षिप् (c. 6. क्षिपति, क्षेप्तुं), अवक्षिप्, अवहस् (c. 1. -हसति -सितुं).

GIRD, s. आकर्षः, शूलं, अपतानकः, अपतन्त्रकः, आक्षेपकः, वेगाघातः.

GIRDED, p. p. बद्धः -द्धा -द्धं, पिनद्धः -द्धा -द्धं, आनद्धः -द्धा -द्धं, अवनद्धः -द्धा -द्धं, आबद्धः -द्धा -द्धं, परिवेष्टितः -ता -तं, परिहितः -ता -तं.

GIRDER, s. गृहतले वृहत्काष्ठं or अग्रकाष्ठं or महादारुः m.

GIRDLE, s. (Belt) मेखला, रसना, कटिसूत्रं, कटिबन्धनं -नी, काञ्ची, कलापः, कक्षा, कक्ष्या, परिकरः, सारसं -सनं, वलनं, सप्तकी, शृङ्खरी, रशना, शृङ्खला.—(Inclosure, circumference) वेष्टनं, परिवेष्टनं, आवेष्टनं, मण्डलं, वलयः, चक्रवालं.—(Zodiac) राशिचक्रं.

To GIRDLE, v. a. मेखलया बन्ध् (c. 9. बध्नाति, बन्धुं), वेष्ट् (c. 1. वेष्टते -ष्टितुं, c. 10. वेष्टयति -यितुं), परिवेष्ट्, परिवृ (c. 5. -वृणोति -वरितुं -रीतुं).

GIRDLER, s. मेखलाकारः, रसनाकर्त्ता m. (र्त्तृ), कटिसूत्रकारी m. (न्).

GIRL, s. कन्या, कुमारी, तरुणी, बाला, बालिका, पुत्री, दारिका, अनागतार्त्तवा, लग्निका, नग्निका, गौरी, वासूः f.

GIRLHOOD, s. कन्यात्वं, कुमारीत्वं, तरुणीत्वं, कौमार्य्यं, तारुण्यं.

GIRLISH, a. कन्यायोग्यः -ग्या -ग्यं, कुमारीयोग्यः -ग्या -ग्यं.

GIRLISHLY, adv. कन्यावत्, कुमारीवत्, तरुणीवत्, कन्यारूपेण.

GIRT, p.p. बद्धः -द्धा -द्धं, पिनद्धः -द्धा -द्धं, वेष्टितः -ता -तं, परिवेष्टितः -ता -तं; 'girt with a falchion,' बद्धनिस्त्रिंशः -शा -शं; 'sea-girt,' समुद्रमेखलः -ला -लं.

GIRTH, s. उदरत्राणं, अधोबन्धनं -नी, वरत्रा, वर्द्ध्रं, वर्द्ध्री, नद्ध्री, चूषा, कक्षा, कक्ष्या.

To GIRTH, v. a. वरत्रया बन्ध् (c. 9. बध्नाति, बन्धुं), उदरत्राणं पिनह् (c. 4. -नह्यति -नद्धुं).

GIST, s. अर्थः, मुख्यार्थः, परमार्थः, उत्तमार्थः, अग्रविषयः.

To GIVE, v. a. दा (c. 3. ददाति, दत्ते, दातुं), प्रदा, प्रादा, अभिदा, सम्प्रदा,

निदा, अनुदा, सम्दा, यम् (c. 1. यच्छति -ते, दातुं), प्रयम्, संयम्, प्रतियम्, सम्प्रयम्, दद् (c. 1. ददते -दितुं), प्रतिपद् (c. 10. -पादयति -यितुं), उपपद्, ऋ in caus. (अर्पयति -यितुं), सम्, निक्षिप् (c. 6. -क्षिपति -क्षेप्तुं), वितॄ (c. 1. -तरति -रितुं -रीतुं), विश्रण् (c. 10. -श्राणयति -यितुं), त्यज् (c. 1. त्यजति, त्यक्तुं), विसृज् (c. 10. -सर्जयति -यितुं), ग्रह् in caus. (ग्राहयति -यितुं), आहृ (c. 1. हरति -हर्तुं), उपहृ, सङ्क्रम् in caus. (-क्रामयति -यितुं), दिश् (c. 6. दिशति, देष्टुं).—(Give away) प्रदा, प्रयम्.—(Give back) प्रतिदा, प्रतिपद्, प्रत्यर्प् (caus. of ऋ with प्रति), निर्यत् (c. 10. -यातयति -यितुं), प्रतिनिर्यत्, प्रतिरुह् in caus. (-रोपयति -यितुं).—(Give chase) अनुधाव् (c. 1. धावति -वितुं), अनुसृ (c. 1. -सरति -सर्तुं).—(Give forth) प्रकाश् (c. 10. -काशयति -यितुं), ख्या in caus. (ख्यापयति -यितुं), निविद् (c. 10. -वेदयति -यितुं).—(Give the hand for support) करालम्बनं कृ.—(Give in) अनुदा, अनुज्ञा (c. 9. -जानाति -नीते -ज्ञातुं), त्यज्.—(Give over) त्यज्, उत्सृज् (c. 6. -सृजति -स्रष्टुं), विरम् (c. 1. -रमति -रन्तुं) with abl. c., निवृत् (c. 1. -वर्त्तते -र्त्तितुं) with abl. c. 'To give over a sick man,' असाध्य इति परित्यज्य रोगातुरं मुच् (c. 6. मुञ्चति, मोक्तुं).—(Give out) निविद्, प्रकाश्, विघुष् (c. 10. -घोषयति -यितुं); 'emit,' उत्सृज्, मुच्, निःसृ in caus. (-सारयति -यितुं).—(Give up) त्यज्, परित्यज्, सन्त्यज्; हा (c. 3. जहाति, हातुं), विहा; उत्सृज्, विमुच्, उज्झ् (c. 6. उज्झति -ज्झितुं), प्रोज्झ्, प्रत्यादिश्.—(Give one's self up to) आसञ्ज् in pass. (-सज्यते or -सज्जते), सेव् (c. 1. सेवते -वितुं), आसेव्, आसक्तः -क्ता -क्तं भू, निरतः -ता -तं भू.—(Give ground) अपक्रम् (c. 1. -क्रामति -क्रमितुं), अवस्था (c. 1. -तिष्ठते -स्थातुं), परावृत्, निवृत्.—(Give way) पन्थानं दा, त्यज्, अवसृ (c. 1. -सरति -सर्तुं); 'give way,' अवसरत, पन्थानं त्यजत.—(Give in marriage) दा, प्रदा, उपादिश्; 'the girl is given in marriage to a husband,' कन्या वोढुः प्रदीयते.—(Give thanks) धन्यवादं कृ, धन्यं वद् (c. 1. वदति -दितुं), कुशलं वद्.—(Give ear) कर्णं दा.—(Give power) शक्तिं दा, क्षमताम् ऋ, नियुज् (c. 7. -युनक्ति -योक्तुं).—(Give utterance) उदीर् (c. 10. -ईरयति -यितुं), उच्चर् (c. 10. -चारयति -यितुं), उदाहृ.—(Give suck) धे in caus. (धापयति -यितुं), उपधे, पा in caus. (पाययति -यितुं).—(Give offence) रुष् in caus. (रोषयति -यितुं), विप्रियं कृ.

To GIVE, *v. n.* (Give way, sink) सद (c. 1. सीदति, सत्तुं), अवसद्.—(Relent, be mitigated) शम् (c. 4. शाम्यति, शमितुं), प्रशम्, शान्तिं or सान्त्वनं या (c. 2. याति -तुं), शान्तीभू, शिथिलीभू.—(Recede) अपसृ (c. 1. -सरति -सर्तुं), निवृत् (c. 1. -वर्त्तते -र्त्तितुं), अपया.—(Cease) विरम् (c. 1. -रमति -रन्तुं), निवृत्, शम्.—(Give in to) अनुज्ञा (c. 9. -जानाति -ज्ञातुं), अनुमन् (c. 4. -मन्यते -मन्तुं).

GIVEN, *p. p.* दत्तः -त्ता -त्तं, प्रदत्तः -त्ता -त्तं, प्रत्तः -त्ता -त्तं, नीत्तः -त्ता -त्तं, निहितः -ता -तं, निक्षिप्तः -प्ता -प्तं, प्रतिपादितः -ता -तं, उपपादितः -ता -तं, विश्राणितः -ता -तं, अर्पितः -ता -तं, समर्पितः -ता -तं, वितीर्णः -र्णा -र्णं, विसर्जितः -ता -तं, विसृष्टः -ष्टा -ष्टं, उपन्यस्तः -स्ता -स्तं; 'well given,' सूत्तः -त्ता -त्तं; 'given and taken,' दत्तादत्तः -त्ता -त्तं, दत्तापहृतः -ता -तं.—(Given up) त्यक्तः -क्ता -क्तं, परित्यक्तः -क्ता -क्तं, उत्सृष्टः -ष्टा -ष्टं.—(Addicted to) आसक्तः -क्ता -क्तं, रतः -ता -तं, निरतः -ता -तं; 'given quantity,' दृश्यः.

GIVER, *s.* दाता *m.* (तृ), प्रदाता, दायकः, दायी *m.* (न्), दानकर्त्ता *m.* (र्तृ), दाकः, दादी *m.* (न्), प्रदः or दः in comp., त्यागी *m.* (न्); 'giver and receiver,' दातृग्राहकौ m. du., दातृप्रतीच्छकौ m. du.

GIVING, *s.* दानं, प्रदानं, सम्प्रदानं, त्यागः, वितरणं, विसर्ज्जनं.

GIZZARD, *s.* कुक्कुटादीनां जठरः or उदरं or अमाजठरं or पक्वाशयः.

GLACIAL, *a.* हिम्यः -म्या -म्यं, हैमः -मी -मं, हिमरूपः -पा -पं.

To GLACIATE, *v. n.* हिमीभू, हिमवत् संहतीभू or शीतीभू.

GLACIATION, *s.* शीतीकरणं, शीतीभावः, हिमीकरणं, हिमसंहतिः *f.*

GLACIER, *s.* हिमपर्व्वतोत्सङ्गे सुविस्तीर्णा हिमसंहतिः.

GLACIS, *s.* दुर्गबहिर्भागे प्रवणभूमिः *f.* or निम्नभूमिः or स्थानं क्रमशो ऽधोगम्यं.

GLAD, *a.* हृष्टः -ष्टा -ष्टं, प्रहृष्टः -ष्टा -ष्टं, हृष्टहृदयः -या -यं, हृष्टमानसः -सा -सं, हर्षयुक्तः -क्ता -क्तं, आनन्दी -न्दिनी -न्दि (न्), आनन्दितः -ता -तं, सानन्दः -न्दा -न्दं, प्रीतः -ता -तं, आह्लादितः -ता -तं, प्रह्लादितः -ता -तं, प्रह्लन्नः -न्ना -न्नं, तुष्टः -ष्टा -ष्टं, परितुष्टः -ष्टा -ष्टं, तृप्तः -प्ता -प्तं, प्रसादितः -ता -तं, प्रफुल्लः -ल्ला -ल्लं, उल्लसः -सा -सं -सितः -ता -तं, अभिरूषितः -ता -तं, मत्तः -त्ता -त्तं.—(Making glad) हर्षकः -का -कं, नन्दकः -का -कं, मोदकः -का -कं, आनन्दकरः -री -रं, हर्षकरः -री -रं, सुभगः -गा -गं, रमणीयः -या -यं.

To GLAD, GLADDEN, *v. a.* हृष् (c. 10. हर्षयति -यितुं), प्रहृष्, परिहृष्, नन्द् (c. 10. नन्दयति -यितुं), अभिनन्द्, ह्लाद् (c. 10. ह्लादयति -यितुं), आह्लाद्, प्रह्लाद्, रम् (c. 10. रमयति -यितुं), उल्लस् (c. 10. -लासयति -यितुं), तुष् (c. 10. तोषयति -यितुं), तृप् (c. 10. तर्पयति -यितुं), प्रमुद् (c. 10. -मोदयति -यितुं), प्री (c. 9. प्रीणाति, c. 10. प्रीणयति -यितुं).

GLADDENED, *p. p.* आह्लादितः -ता -तं, आनन्दितः -ता -तं, प्रमोदितः -ता -तं.

GLADDENING, *a.* हर्षकः -का -कं, हर्षणः -णा -णं, हर्षकरः -री -रं, नन्दकः -का -कं, आनन्दनः -ना -नं, आनन्ददः -दा -दं, प्रीतिदः -दा -दं.

GLADDER, GLADDENER, *s.* आनन्दकारी *m.* (न्), आनन्दकः, सुखदः.

GLADE, *s.* जङ्गलमध्ये or वनमध्ये पथः, वनपथः, वनमार्गः, वृक्षावृतः पथः, तरुगुल्मावृतो मार्गः.

GLADIATE, *a.* खड्गाकारः -रा -रं, असाकारः -रा -रं, खड्गाकृतिः -तिः -ति.

GLADIATOR, *s.* मल्लः, मल्लः, आसिकः, असिक्रीडकः, खड्गक्रीडकः, अस्त्रक्रीडकः, नैस्त्रिंशिकः.

GLADIATORIAL, *a.* मल्लसम्बन्धी -न्धिनी -न्धि (न्), असिक्रीडासम्बन्धी &c., आसिकः -की -कं.

GLADIATURE, *s.* असियुद्धं, खड्गयुद्धं, असिक्रीडा, खड्गक्रीडा.

GLADLY, *adv.* सानन्दं, सहर्षं, हर्षेण, हृष्टमनसा, हृष्टवत्, साह्लादं, आह्लादेन, प्रह्लादेन, प्रमोदेन, सन्तोषेण.

GLADNESS, *s.* हर्षः, आनन्दः, आह्लादः, प्रह्लादः, प्रमोदः, आमोदः, हृष्टिः *f.*, मुदा, हृष्टता, प्रहृष्टता, प्रफुल्लता, उल्लासः, उल्लसत्वं, चित्तप्रसन्नता, प्रीतिः *f.*, प्रीतता, तुष्टिः *f.*, सन्तुष्टिः *f.*, मोदः, उत्सवः.

GLADSOME, *a.* आनन्दी -न्दिनी -न्दि (न्), रम्यः -म्या -म्यं, सुभगः -गा -गं.

GLAIR, *s.* अण्डशुक्लं, अण्डगर्भपरिगतः शुक्लरसः, अण्डपयस् *n.*

GLANCE, *s.* (Of the eye) दृष्टिपातः, दृष्टिनिपातः, नयनपातः, दृष्टिविक्षेपः, कटाक्षः, नेत्रकटाक्षः, अपाङ्गदृष्टिः *f.*, अपाङ्गदर्शनं, वीक्षितं, प्रेक्षितं, अवलोकनं, काक्षः, दृष्टिबाणः.—(Slight view) ईषद्दर्शनं, ईषद्दृष्टिः *f.*, अर्द्धवीक्षणं, अर्द्धदृष्टिः *f.*; 'glance in return,' प्रतिसमीक्षणं.—(A shoot of light) स्फुरितं, स्फुरणं, द्युतिपातः, रश्मिः *m.*

To GLANCE, *v. n.* (As light) स्फुर् (c. 6. स्फुरति -रितुं), परिस्फुर्, लस् (c. 1. लसति -सितुं).—(Strike lightly and pass by) लघु हत्वा or ताडयित्वा अतिक्रम् (c. 1. -क्रामति -क्रमितुं) or अती (c. 2. अत्येति -तुं, rt. इ), द्रुतम् अतिक्रम्य घृष् (c. 1. घर्षति -र्षितुं).—(Glance with the eye) दृष्टिं पत् (c. 10. पातयति -यितुं) or विक्षिप् (c. 6. -क्षिपति -क्षेप्तुं), दृष्टिबाणं पत्, कटाक्ष (nom. कटाक्षयति -यितुं).—(Glance at, inspect slightly) ईषद् दृश् (c. 1. पश्यति, द्रष्टुं) or निरीक्ष् (c. 1. -ईक्षते -क्षितुं), अर्द्धवीक्षणं कृ.

GLANCING, *part.* स्फुरन् -रन्ती -रत् (त्), लसन् -सन्ती -सत् (त्), स्फुरितः -ता -तं.

GLANCINGLY, *adv.* लघु, ईषत्, अल्पमात्रं, सार्द्धदर्शनं, लाघवेन, तिर्य्यक्, तिरस्, वक्रगत्या.

GLAND, *s.* शरीराभ्यन्तरे ग्रन्थिसंज्ञकः पित्तश्लेष्माद्याशयो मृदुमांसपिण्डः, मांसग्रन्थिः *m.*

GLANDERS, *s.* अश्वानाम् उग्ररोगविशेषो यत्र नासिकारन्ध्रेण दुर्गन्धश्लेष्म or दुर्गन्धमलम् उत्सृज्यते.

GLANDULE, *s.* शरीराभ्यन्तरे श्लेष्माद्याशयो मृदुमांसपिण्डकः.

GLANDULOUS, GLANDULAR, *a.* पूर्व्वोक्तमांसपिण्डसम्बन्धी -न्धिनी -न्धि (न्).

GLANS, *s.* (Penis) मणिः *m.f.*

GLARE, *s.* तेजस् *n.*, अतितेजस्, अतिद्युतिः *f.*, द्युतिः *f.*, अतिप्रभा, भाः *f.* (स्), दृष्टिसन्तापका द्युतिः, नयनोपघातिनी प्रभा, हेतिः *f.*, उज्ज्वलद्युतिः *f.*, प्रखरदीप्तिः *f.*, खरदीप्तिः *f.*—(Fierce look) उग्रदृष्टिः *f.*, तीक्ष्णदृष्टिः, कोपज्वलिता दृष्टिः.

To GLARE, *v. n.* अतितेजसा द्युत् (c. 1. द्योतते -तितुं), उज्ज्वल् (c. 1. -ज्वलति -लितुं), ज्वल् in freq. (जाज्वल्यते), दीप् in freq. (देदीप्यते), अतितेजसा दृष्टिं सन्तप् (c. 10. -तापयति -यितुं) or उपहन् (c. 2. -हन्ति -न्तुं), स्फुर् (c. 6. स्फुरति -रितुं).—(Look with fierce eyes) तीक्ष्णदृष्टिं or कोपज्वलितां दृष्टिं पत् (c. 10. -पातयति -यितुं), रोषप्रदीप्ताक्षः -क्षा -क्षं भू.

GLAREOUS, *a.* अण्डशुक्लसगुणः -णा -णं, अण्डशुक्लधर्म्मी -र्म्मी -र्म्मि (न्).

GLARING, *part.* or *a.* अतितैजसः -सी -सं, उज्ज्वलः -ला -लं, अतिद्योती -तिनी -ति (न्), अतितेजसा दृष्टिसन्तापकः -का -कं or नयनोपघाती -तिनी -ति (न्), भास्वान् -स्वती -स्वत् (त्), कार्शानवः -वी -वं.—(Clear, notorious) सर्व्वप्रकाशः -शा -शं, सुप्रकाशः -शा -शं, पुरःस्फुरन् -रन्ती -रत् (त्); 'having eyes glaring with anger,' रोषदीप्ताक्षः -क्षा -क्षं.

GLARINGLY, *adv.* सुप्रकाशं, सर्व्वप्रकाशं, सर्व्वप्रसिद्धं, अतितेजसा.

GLASS, *s.* (Transparent substance formed by fusing sand with alkalies) काचः, क्षारः, सिध्मं, अभ्रं -भ्रकं, स्फटिकः.—(Glass drinking-vessel) काचभाजनं, काचपात्रं, काचकूपी, पलिघः, पुलकः, पारी; 'glass jar,' काचघटी.—(Looking-glass, mirror) दर्पणः, मुकुरः, आदर्शः.

GLASS, *a.* काचमयः -यी -यं, काचनिर्म्मितः -ता -तं, काच in comp.

To GLASS, *v. a.* See *To* GLAZE.

GLASS-BLOWER, *s.* काचधमकः, क्षारधमकः, काचध्माकारः, काचनिर्म्माणकृत्.

GLASSFUL, *s.* काचपात्रपूरणं, काचभाण्डभरकः, काचभाण्डपूरकः.

GLASS-GRINDER, *s.* काचपरिष्कारकः, काचमार्ज्जकः, काचतेजस्कारी *m.* (न्).

GLASS-HOUSE, *s.* काचनिर्म्माणशाला, क्षारनिर्म्माणगृहं, काचशाला.

GLASSINESS, *s.* स्वच्छता, प्रसन्नता, प्रसत्तिः *f.*, विमलता, श्लक्ष्णता.

GLASS-LIKE, *a.* काचोपमः -मा -मं, काचसगुणः -णा -णं.

GLASS-MAN, *s.* काचविक्रेता *m.* (तृ), काचद्रव्यविक्रयी *m.* (न्), काचव्यवसायी *m.* (न्).

GLASS-WORK, *s.* काचनिर्म्माणं, काचनिर्म्माणशिल्पं, काचकर्म्म *n.* (न्).

GLASSY, *a.* काचोपमः -मा -मं, काचवत्प्रसन्नः -न्ना -न्नं, काचवद्विमलः -ला -लं, स्वच्छः -च्छा -च्छं, स्फटिकप्रभः -भा -भं, श्लक्ष्णः -क्ष्णा -क्ष्णं.

GLAUCOUS, *a.* समुद्रवर्णः -र्णा -र्णं, श्यामहरित् *m.f.n.*, घननीलः -ला -लं.

GLAVE, *s.* पृथुपत्रः खड्गः, कृपाणः, निस्त्रिंशः, असिः *m.*

To GLAZE, *v. a.* काच (nom. काचयति -यितुं), काचेन आच्छद् (c. 10. -च्छादयति -यितुं), काचान्वितं -तां -तं कृ, काचोपेतं -तां -तं कृ.—(Make smooth) श्लक्ष्ण (nom. श्लक्ष्णयति -यितुं), स्निग्धीकृ, श्लक्ष्णीकृ.

GLAZED, *p.p.* काचितः -ता -तं, काचान्वितः -ता -तं, काचाच्छादितः -ता -तं.

GLAZIER, *s.* काचव्यवसायी *m.* (न्), काचबन्धकः, काचबन्धा *m.* (न्धृ).

GLAZING, *s.* काचबन्धनं, काचाच्छादनं, काचकर्म्म *n.* (न्).

GLEAM, *s.* (Sudden shoot of light) द्युतिस्फुरणं, स्फुरितं, अकस्मात्स्फुरणं, प्रभास्फुरणं, क्षणप्रभा, क्षणद्युतिः *f.*, क्षणज्योतिस् *n.*, अचिरप्रभा, अचिरद्युतिः *f.*, अकस्माद्दीप्तिः *f.* द्युतिज्वाला.—(Beam) रश्मिः *m.*, किरणः, अंशुः *m.*—(Brightness) उज्ज्वलता, प्रभा, तेजस् *n.*

To GLEAM, *v. n.* स्फुर् (c. 6. स्फुरति -रितुं), प्रस्फुर्, परिस्फुर्, लस् (c. 1. लसति -सितुं), विद्युत् (c. 1. -द्योतते -तितुं), अकस्मात् or क्षणमात्रं प्रकाश् (c. 1. -काशते -शितुं) or ज्वल् (c. 1. ज्वलति -लितुं) or उज्ज्वल्.

GLEAMING, *part.* स्फुरन् -रन्ती -रत् (त्), लसन् -सन्ती -सत् (त्), स्फुरितः -ता -तं.

GLEAMY, *a.* क्षणमात्रद्योतमानः -ना -नं, क्षणप्रभः -भा -भं, कम्पितप्रभः -भा -भं, चञ्चलप्रभः -भा -भं, चञ्चलद्योती -तिनी -ति (न्), प्रकाशमानः -ना -नं, उज्ज्वलः -ला -लं.

To GLEAN, *v. a.* and *n.* उञ्छ् (c. 1. 6. उञ्छति -ञ्छितुं), शिल् or सिल् (c. 6. शिलति, सिलति -लितुं), ग्रस् or उग्रस् (c. 9. ग्रसाति, c. 10. ग्रासयति, उग्रसाति, उग्रासयति -यितुं), शेषधान्यानि or शस्यशेषं or अवशिष्टकणिशान् or लूनशस्यावशिष्टं चि (c. 5. चिनोति, चेतुं) or अवचि or उद्धृ (c. 1. -हरति -हर्तुं) or हृ or सङ्ग्रह् (c. 9. गृह्णाति -ग्रहीतुं).

GLEAN, *s.* धान्यशेषं, अवशिष्टकणिशसङ्ग्रहः, शेषधान्यसञ्चयः, लूनशस्यावशिष्टं.

GLEANED, *p.p.* हृतधान्यशेषः -षा -षं, हृतशस्यावशेषः -षा -षं, उद्धृतसर्व्वकणिशः -शा -शं, सङ्गृहीतसर्व्वशस्यः -स्या -स्यं.

GLEANER, *s.* शिलोञ्छवृत्तिः *m.f.*, उञ्छवृत्तिः *m.f.*, उञ्छशीलः -ला -लं, शिलोञ्छकारी *m.* (न्), शेषधान्यसङ्ग्राहकः, अवशिष्टकणिशसञ्चयी *m.* (न्), उच्छिष्टशस्यावचायी *m.* (न्).

GLEANING, *s.* (The act) उञ्छः, उञ्छनं, शिलोञ्छः, उञ्छशिलं, उञ्छसिलं, शिलोञ्छवृत्तिः *f.*, उञ्छवृत्तिः *f.*, शिलं, ऋतं, कटभङ्कः, अवशिष्टशस्यसङ्ग्रहः -हणं, लूनक्षेत्रशेषधान्यावचयः, उच्छिष्टकणिशचयः, शस्यशेषापहरणं, धान्यशादानं.—(That which is gleaned) शस्यशेषं, शस्यावशिष्टं, लूनशस्योच्छिष्टं, लूनकेदारशेषधान्यानि *n. pl.*, कणिशावशेषः.

GLEBE, *s.* (Soil, ground) मृद् *f.*, मृत्तिका, स्थलं -ली, भूमिः *f.*, लोष्टं, मृल्लोष्टं.—(Land belonging to a beneficed clergyman) धर्म्माध्यापकभूमिः *f.*, धर्म्माध्यापकक्षेत्रं.

GLEBY, *a.* मृल्लोष्टमयः -यी -यं, भृत्पूर्णः -र्णा -र्णं, मार्त्तिकः -की -कं.

GLEE, *s.* हर्षः, आह्लादः, प्रह्लादः, आनन्दः, मुदा, प्रमोदः, आमोदः, मदः, उल्लासः, उत्सवः, महोत्सवः.

GLEEFUL, *a.* हृष्टः -ष्टा -ष्टं, आनन्दी -न्दिनी -न्दि (न्), हृष्टचित्तः -त्ता -त्तं.

To GLEEK, *v. n.* अवक्षिप् (c. 6. -क्षिपति -क्षेप्तुं), अवहस् (c. 1. -हसति -सितुं).

GLEET, *s.* मूत्रमार्गरोगः, मूत्रमार्गदोषः, मेहविकारः, प्रमेहविकारः, इक्षुमेहः, मूत्रमार्गनिर्गतं पूयशोणितं, धातुप्रस्रावः.

To GLEET, *v. n.* शनैर् मूत्रमार्गात् स्रु (c. 1. स्रवति, स्रोतुं) or प्रस्रु.

GLEN, *s.* दरी -रा, कन्दरः -री, दरीभूः *f.*, अद्रिद्रोणी, निम्नभूमिः *f.*, प्रान्तरं.

GLENE, *s.* अक्षिपात्रं, अक्षिरन्ध्रं, नयनपात्रं, नयनकोषः.

GLIB, *a.* (Smooth, slippery) स्निग्धः -ग्धा -ग्धं, श्लक्ष्णः -क्ष्णा -क्ष्णं, चिक्कणः -णा -णं.—(In speech) वाग्द्रुतः -ता -तं, वाक्चपलः -ला -लं, द्रुतवाक् *m.f.n.*, वाक्क्षिप्रः -प्रा -प्रं, वाक्पटुः -टुः -टु, त्वरितवाक् *m.f.n.*

To GLIB, *v. a.* (Castrate) वृषणद्वयम् उत्कृत् (c. 6. -कृन्तति -कर्त्तितुं).—(Make smooth) श्लक्ष्ण (nom. श्लक्ष्णयति -यितुं).

GLIBLY, *adv.* द्रुतं, श्लक्ष्णं, क्षिप्रं, वाक्चापल्येन, द्रुतवाचा, अविलम्बितं, अस्खलितवाक्येन, अस्खलितं.

GLIBNESS, *s.* (Smoothness) श्लक्ष्णता, स्निग्धता, चिक्कणत्वं.—(In speech)

वाक्चापल्यं, वाग्द्रुतता, वाक्क्षिप्रता, वाक्पटुता, वाक्सरणिः *f.*

To glide, *v. n.* सृप् (c. 1. सर्पति, स्रप्तुं), प्रसृप्, विसृप्, संसृप्, विसृ (c. 1. -सरति -सर्तुं), प्रसृ, संसृ, चल् (c. 1. चलति -लितुं).—(As a river) स्रु (c. 1. स्रवति, स्रोतुं), प्रस्रु, स्यन्द् (c. 1. स्यन्दते -न्दितुं), प्रस्यन्द्, री (c. 4. रीयते, रेतुं).—(Move slowly) शनैः शनैः सृ or चल्.

Glide, *s.* सर्पणं, संसर्पः, विसर्पणं, विसारः, स्रवः -वणं, प्रस्रवणं.

Glider, *s.* विसर्पी *m.* (न्), संसर्पी *m.*, विसारी *m.* (न्), विसर्पणकृत् *m.*

Gliding, *part.* विसर्पन् -र्पन्ती -र्पत् (त्), विसर्पी -र्पिणी -र्पि (न्), संसर्पी &c., विसारी -रिणी -रि (न्), प्रसारी &c., विसृत्वरः -रा -रं, स्रवन् -वन्ती -वत् (त्), स्यन्दी -न्दिनी -न्दि (न्); 'in the air,' वियति विसर्पी &c.

Gliding, *s.* सर्पणं, विसर्पः -र्पणं, संसर्पः -र्पणं, विसारः, संसृतिः *f.*, स्रवः -वणं, शनैः सरणं; 'in the air,' खसर्पणं, वियति विसर्पणं; 'gliding up,' उत्सर्पणं.

Glidingly, *adv.* द्रुतं, अविलम्बितं, शनैः शनैः, विसृत्वरं.

Gliff, *s.* ईषद्दर्शनं, ईषद्दृष्टिः *f.*, अर्द्धवीक्षणं, अर्द्धदृष्टिः *f.*

Glike, *s.* अवहासः, अवक्षेपः, तिरस्कारः, गर्हा, अवज्ञा.

Glim, *s.* दीपः -पकः, दीपिका, प्रदीपः, दीपद्युतिः *f.*

To glimmer, *v. n.* मन्दतेजसा or मन्दप्रभया दीप् (c. 4. दीप्यते, दीपितुं) or प्रकाश् (c. 1. -काशते -शितुं) or द्युत् (c. 1. द्योतते -तितुं), ईषत् or मन्दं द्युत् or स्फुर् (c. 6. स्फुरति -रितुं), प्रस्फुर्, ईषत्स्फुरणं कृ, मन्दप्रभः -भा -भं भू, पाण्डुकिरणान् पत् (c. 10. पातयति -यितुं).

Glimmer, *s.* मन्दतेजस् *n.*, मन्दद्युतिः *f.*, मन्दप्रभा, मन्ददीप्तिः *f.*, स्फुरणं, स्फुरितं, ईषत्स्फुरणं, ईषत्प्रभा, पाण्डुप्रभा.

Glimmering, *part.* ईषत्स्फुरितः -ता -तं, मन्दप्रभः -भा -भं, मन्दच्छायः -या -यं, मन्दतेजाः -जाः -जः (स्), पाण्डुद्युतिः -तिः -ति, पाण्डुरश्मिः -श्मिः -श्मि, पाण्डुकिरणः -णा -णं.

Glimpse, *s.* (Short or slight view) ईषद्दर्शनं, ईषद्दृष्टिः *f.*, अर्द्धदृष्टिः *f.*, अर्द्धवीक्षणं, क्षणदर्शनं, अचिरदर्शनं, मुहूर्त्तदर्शनं.—(Flash) क्षणप्रभा, अचिरप्रभा.

To glisten, *v. n.* द्युत् (c. 1. द्योतते -तितुं), स्फुर् (c. 6. स्फुरति -रितुं).

Glistening, *part.* or *a.* स्फुरन् -रन्ती -रत् (त्), स्फुरितः -ता -तं.

To glister, *v. n.* *See To* glisten.

To glitter, *v. n.* द्युत् (c. 1. द्योतते -तितुं), प्रकाश् (c. 1. काशते -शितुं), स्फुर् (c. 6. स्फुरति -रितुं), दीप् (c. 4. दीप्यते, दीपितुं), राज् (c. 1. राजति -ते -जितुं), भा (c. 2. भाति -तुं), भ्राज् (c. 1. भ्राजते -जितुं), विभ्राज्, भास् (c. 1. भासते -सितुं), आभास्, प्रभास्, अवभास्, चकास् (c. 2. चकास्ति, चकासितुं), रुच् (c. 1. रोचते -चितुं), वर्चस् (nom. वर्चायते).

Glitter, *s.* द्युतिः *f.*, दीप्तिः *f.*, प्रभा, तेजस् *n.*, ज्योतिस् *n.*, कान्तिः *f.*, रुचिः *f.*, द्युतिमत्त्वं, दीप्तिमत्त्वं, आभा, वर्चस् *n.*, छविः *f.*, छाया, उज्ज्वलता.

Glittering, *part.* or *a.* द्योती -तिनी -ति (न्), द्योतमानः -ना -नं, दीप्तिमान् -मती -मत् (त्), प्रभावान् -वती -वत् (त्), देदीप्यमानः -ना -नं, तेजोमयः -यी -यं, प्रकाशमानः -ना -नं, वर्चस्वी -स्विनी -स्वि (न्), धौतः -ता -तं, उज्ज्वलः -ला -लं, कान्तिमान् -मती -मत् (त्), सितः -ता -तं, स्फुरितप्रभः -भा -भं.

Glitteringly, *adv.* दीप्त्या, तेजसा, वर्चसा, स्फुरत्तेजसा, स्फुरितं, उज्ज्वलं.

To gloat, *v. n.* अत्यभिलाषात् or अतिलोभाद् विवृताक्षो निरीक्ष् (c. 1. -ईक्षते -क्षितुं) or शून्यदृष्ट्या निरीक्ष् or विवृतनयनः -ना -नं भू.

Gloating, *part.* or *a.* अतिलोभेन विवृताक्षः -क्षी -क्षं, लोभोत्फुल्लनयनः -ना -नं, अत्यभिलाषात् शून्यदृष्टिः -ष्टिः -ष्टि.

Globate, globated, *a.* गोलाकारः -रा -रं, गोलाकृतिः -तिः -ति, मण्डलाकारः -रा -रं, वर्त्तुलः -ला -लं, वर्त्तुलाकृतिः -तिः -ति, मण्डली -लिनी -लि (न्).

Globe, *s.* (A sphere) गोलः -ला -लं -लकः, मण्डलं, परिमण्डलं, वर्त्तुलः, पिण्डः, चक्रं.—(Earth) भूगोलः, भूमण्डलं, क्षितिमण्डलं, अवनिमण्डलं, इलागोलं, ब्रह्माण्डः.

To globe, *v. a.* गोलीकृ, एकमण्डलीकृ, परिमण्डलीकृ, वर्त्तुलीकृ.

Globose, globous, *a.* मण्डली -लिनी -लि (न्), वर्त्तुलः -ला -लं.

Globosity, *s.* गोलत्वं, गोलाकारत्वं, वर्त्तुलता, मण्डलत्वं, परिमण्डलता.

Globular, *a.* गोलाकारः -रा -रं, गोलाकृतिः -तिः -ति, मण्डलाकारः -रा -रं, मण्डली -लिनी -लि (न्), वर्त्तुलः -ला -लं, वृत्तः -त्ता -त्तं, गुडः -डा -डं, घटी -टिनी -टि (न्), निस्तलः -ला -लं.

Globularly, *adv.* गोलवत्, मण्डलवत्, गोलाकारेण, मण्डलरूपेण, वर्त्तुलं.

Globule, *s.* गुलिका, गुली, बिन्दुः *m.*, अणुः *m.*, रेणुः *m.f.*, परमाणुः *m.*, क्षुद्रगोलः.

Globy, *a.* मण्डलाकारः -रा -रं, गोलाकारः -रा -रं, वर्त्तुलः -ला -लं.

To glomerate, *v. a.* गोलीकृ, मण्डलीकृ, परिमण्डल (nom. परिमण्डलयति -यितुं), वर्त्तुलीकृ, पिण्डीकृ, एकौघीकृ, एकत्र कृ.

Glomerate, glomerated, *a.* or *p. p.* पिण्डीभूतः -ता -तं, एकौघीभूतः -ता -तं, एकगोलीकृतः -ता -तं, एकत्रीभूतः -ता -तं.

Glomeration, *s.* (The act) पिण्डीकरणं, राशीकरणं.—(A collection) राशिः *m.f.*, पिण्डः, ओघः, सन्निपातः, सञ्चयः.

Glomerous, *a.* पिण्डी -ण्डिनी -ण्डि (न्), पिण्डितः -ता -तं, पिण्डाकृतिः -तिः -ति.

Gloom, *s.* अवतमसं, अन्धकारः, ईषदन्धकारः, तमस् *n.*, तिमिरं, तमिस्रं, तामिस्रं, तमसं, निष्प्रभता, सान्धकारता, ध्वान्तं, अन्धं, भूच्छाया.

To gloom, *v. n.* तिमिरीभू, अन्धीभू, तमस्वी -स्विनी -स्वि भू.

To gloom, *v. a.* तिमिर (nom. तिमिरयति -यितुं), तिमिरीकृ, कलुषीकृ.

Gloomily, *adv.* (Dimly) सावतमसं, सान्धकारं, निष्प्रभं, अप्रकाशं.—(Not cheerfully) सविषादं, सावसादं, विषण्णमनसा, सोद्वेगं.

Gloominess, *s.* अवतमसं, ईषत्तिमिरं, ईषत्तमस्विता, निष्प्रभता, अप्रकाशत्वं, सान्धकारत्वं.—(Of mind) विषादः, विषण्णता, अवसन्नता, चित्तोद्वेगः, निरानन्दता.

Gloomy, *a.* तमस्वी -स्विनी -स्वि (न्), ईषत्तमस्वी &c., तामसः -सी -सं, ईषत्तामसः -सी -सं, ईषदन्धकारः -रा -रं, सान्धकारः -रा -रं, सतिमिरः -रा -रं, तमोयुक्तः -क्ता -क्तं, तमस्कल्पः -ल्पा -ल्पं, तमोवृतः -ता -तं, तमोमयः -यी -यं, निष्प्रभः -भा -भं or निःप्रभः, निरालोकः -का -कं, अप्रकाशः -शा -शं, अस्पष्टः -ष्टा -ष्टं, अप्रभः -भा -भं, मलिनप्रभः -भा -भं, दुर्दर्शः -र्शा -र्शं, मलिनः -ना -नं, अरोकः -का -कं, विगतः -ता -तं.—(Dejected, melancholy) विषण्णः -ण्णा -ण्णं, अवसन्नः -न्ना -न्नं, दीनचेतनः -ना -नं, निरानन्दः -न्दा -न्दं, म्लानः -ना -नं.

Glorification, *s.* (Act of giving glory) गुणप्रशंसा -सनं, गुणोत्कीर्त्तनं, उत्कीर्त्तनं, यशःकीर्त्तनं, अनुकीर्त्तनं, यशोवर्णना, स्तुतिवादः, गुणश्लाघा, धन्यवादः, वन्दना, प्रशंसाकरणं.—(Elevation to glory) ऊर्द्ध्वगतिः *f.*, स्वर्गारोहणं, स्वर्गगतिः *f.*, परमपदप्राप्तिः *f.*

Glorified, *p. p.* उत्कीर्त्तितः -ता -तं, प्रशंसितः -ता -तं, कृतधन्यवादः -दा -दं.—(Elevated to glory) ऊर्द्ध्वगतः -ता -तं, स्वर्गारूढः -ढा -ढं.

To glorify, *v. a.* गुणान् कृत् (c. 10. कीर्त्तयति -यितुं) or उत्कृत्, प्रशंस् (c. 1. -शंसति -सितुं), श्लाघ् (c. 1. श्लाघते -घितुं), स्तु (c. 2. स्तौति, स्तोतुं), धन्यं वद् (c. 1. वदति -दितुं), धन्यवादं कृ, यशः or कीर्त्तिं or महिमानं वर्ण् (c. 10. वर्णयति -यितुं) or प्रकाश् (c. 10. -काशयति -यितुं).—(Elevate to celestial glory) स्वर्गम् आरुह् in caus. (-रोपयति -यितुं), परमपदं प्राप् in caus. (-आपयति -यितुं).

Glorious, *a.* (Illustrious) महायशाः -शाः -शः (स्), कीर्त्तिमान् -मती

-मत् (त्), यशस्वी -स्विनी -स्वि (न्) यशस्वान् -स्वती -स्वत् (त्), महोदयः, -या -यं, श्रीमान् -मती -मत् (त्), विश्रुतः -ता -तं, ख्यातः -ता -तं.—(Of great splendour) प्रतापवान् -वती -वत् (त्), प्रतापी -पिनी -पि (न्), तेजोमयः -यी -यं, तेजस्वी -स्विनी -स्वि (न्), ओजस्वी &c., वर्चस्वी &c., सुप्रभः -भा -भं, अतिशोभनः -ना -नं, तैजसः -सी -सं.—(Excellent, noble) उत्कृष्टः -ष्टा -ष्टं, उत्तमः -मा -मं, प्रशस्तः -स्ता -स्तं, 'conferring glory,' यशस्करः -री -रं, कीर्त्तिकरः -री -रं.

GLORIOUSLY, *adv.* प्रतापेन, सप्रतापं, सुप्रभं, उत्कृष्टं, उत्तमं, प्रशस्तं.

GLORY, *s.* (Splendour) तेजस् *n.*, द्युतिः *f.*, बृहद्द्युतिः *f.*, प्रतापः, तेजस्विता, ओजस्विता, प्रभा, शोभा, उज्ज्वलता.—(Praise) प्रशंसा, श्लाघा, स्तुतिः *f.*, स्तुतिवाक्यं, स्तोत्रं.—(Honour) मानं, पूजा.—(Fame, renown) कीर्त्तिः *f.*, यशस् *n.*, ख्यातिः *f.*, सुख्यातिः *f.*, विश्रुतिः *f.*, कीर्त्तनं, प्रथा, प्रतिपत्तिः *f.*, महिमा *m.* (न्), जनोदाहरणं.—(Celestial bliss) स्वर्गगतिः *f.*, स्वर्गभोगः, सद्गतिः *f.*, परमागतिः *f.*, परमपदं, अपवर्गः, सिद्धिः *f.*, मोक्षः.—(Of victory) जयश्रीः.—(Vain-glory) आत्मश्लाघा, दर्पः, गर्व्वः, अहङ्कारः, विकत्था.

To GLORY, *v. n.* (Boast) आत्मानं श्लाघ् (c. 1. श्लाघते -घितुं), दृप् (c. 4. दृप्यति, द्रप्तुं), गर्व्व् (c. 1. गर्व्वति -र्व्वितुं), विकत्थ् (c. 1. -कत्थते -त्थितुं), दम्भं कृ.—(Exult) अत्यन्तं नन्द् (c. 1. नन्दति -न्दितुं) or आनन्द्.

GLORYING, *s.* आत्मश्लाघा, विकत्था, अहङ्कारः, दर्पः, दम्भः, दर्पकरणं.

GLOSS, *s.* (Comment) टीका, भाष्यं, भाष्यं, व्याख्या, विवरणं, वार्त्तिकं, टिप्पनी.—(Superficial lustre) वाह्यशोभा, कल्पितशोभा, वाह्यस्निग्धता, वाह्यकान्तिः *f.*, वाह्यरुचिः *f.*, आभा, छविः *f.*

To GLOSS, *v. a.* and *n.* (Explain, write a comment) टीकया व्याख्या (c. 2. -ख्याति -तुं) or व्याकृ or स्पष्टीकृ or व्याहृ (c. 1. -हरति -हर्त्तुं), टीकां लिख् (c. 6. लिखति, लेखितुं), टीकां कृ.—(Give a superficial lustre) वाह्यशोभां दा, वाह्यकान्तिं दा, स्निग्धीकृ, उपरिभागं शुभ् (c. 10. शोभयति -यितुं).

GLOSSARIAL, *a.* शब्दकोषविषयकः -का -कं, परिभाषाप्रकाशकः -का -कं.

GLOSSARIST, GLOSSATOR, GLOSSER, *s.* शब्दकोषलेखकः, शब्दसङ्ग्रहकारी *m.* (न्), कौशिकः, निर्व्वचनकृत् *m.*

GLOSSARY, *s.* कोषः, शब्दकोषः, शब्दसङ्ग्रहः, शब्दग्रन्थः, शब्दजालं, निर्व्वचनं, निघण्टुः *m.*, अभिधानं, परिभाषाप्रकाशको ग्रन्थः.

GLOSSINESS, *s.* वाह्यशोभा, वाह्यकान्तिः *f.* वाह्यरुचिः *f.*, स्निग्धता, स्नैग्ध्यं, चिक्कणता, कल्पितशोभा.

GLOSSOGRAPHER, *s.* टीकालेखकः, भाष्यलेखकः, टिप्पनीलेखकः.

GLOSSOGRAPHY, *s.* टीकालेखनं, शब्दकोषलेखनं, शब्दकोषरचनं.

GLOSSY, *a.* स्निग्धः -ग्धा -ग्धं, चिक्कणः -णा -णं, श्लक्ष्णः -क्ष्णा -क्ष्णं, वहिर्भागे शोभनः -ना -नं or रुचिरः -रा -रं or तेजितः -ता -तं or परिष्कृतः -ता -तं.

GLOTTIS, *s.* उपजिह्वा, प्रतिजिह्वा, अलिजिह्वा.

GLOVE, *s.* हस्ताच्छादनं, हस्तत्राणं, हस्तपरिधानं, पाणिवस्त्रं, पाणिवेष्टनं, करवेष्टनं, हस्ताभरणं.

To GLOVE, *v. a.* हस्तं पूर्व्वोक्तवस्त्रेण आछद् (c. 10. -छादयति -यितुं).

GLOVER, *s.* हस्ताच्छादनकृत् *m.*, पाणिवस्त्रविक्रयी *m.* (न्).

To GLOW, *v. n.* दीप् (c. 4. दीप्यते, दीपितुं) or in freq. (देदीप्यते) ज्वल् (c. 1. ज्वलति -लितुं), दह् (c. 4. दह्यति, दग्धुं or in pass. दह्यते), तप् in pass. (तप्यते or c. 1. तपति, तप्तुं), सन्तप्, प्रतप्, अभितप्.—(Become red) अरुणीभू, रक्तीभू, रञ्ज् in pass. (रज्यते), संरञ्ज्; 'the east glows,' प्राची संरज्यते.

GLOW, *s.* तापः, उत्तापः, दीप्तिः *f.*, तेजस्, द्युतिः *f.*, दाहः, चण्डता, उष्णता, उज्ज्वलता.—(Redness of colour) रक्तता, अरुणिमा *m.* (न्), रागः; 'glow in the cheek,' कपोलरागः, मुखरागः.

GLOWING, *part.* or *a.* दीप्तः -प्ता -प्तं, दीप्यमानः -ना -नं, देदीप्यमानः -ना -नं, तप्तः -प्ता -प्तं, सन्तप्तः -प्ता -प्तं, उपतप्तः -प्ता -प्तं, अभितप्तः -प्ता -प्तं, उत्तप्तः -प्ता -प्तं, तापी -पिनी -पि (न्), तैजसः -सी -सं, चण्डः -ण्डा -ण्डं, प्रचण्डः -ण्डा -ण्डं, उज्ज्वलः -ला -लं, ज्वाली -लिनी -लि (न्), दह्यमानः -ना -नं; 'glowing with anger,' रोषप्रदीपितः -ता -तं, कोपज्वलितः -ता -तं; 'having glowing cheeks,' रक्तकपोलः -ला -लं; 'having glowing eyes,' दीप्ताक्षः -क्षा -क्षं.

GLOWINGLY, *adv.* तापेन, उत्तापेन, तेजसा, दीप्त्या, प्रचण्डं, उष्णं.

GLOW-WORM, *s.* प्रभाकृमिः *m.*, प्रभाकीटः, द्युतिमत्कीटः, खद्योतः.

To GLOZE, *v. a.* लल् (c. 10. लालयति -यितुं), सान्त्व् (c. 10. सान्त्वयति -यितुं).

GLOZE, *s.* लालनं, सान्त्वनं -ना, सान्त्ववाक्यं, चाटुः *m.*, मधुरवाक्यं.

GLOZER, *s.* लाली *m.* (न्), सान्त्ववादः, चाटुकारः, चाटुवादी *m.* (न्).

GLUE, *s.* लेपः, विलेपः, संलग्नीकरणार्थम् अतिश्यानद्रव्यं, सुधा.

To GLUE, *v. a.* पूर्व्वोक्तलेपद्वारेण संलग्नीकृ or संयुज् (c. 7. -युनक्ति -योक्तुं) or संश्लिष् (c. 10. -श्लेषयति -यितुं).

GLUED, *p. p.* संलग्नीकृतः -ता -तं, संयुक्तः -क्ता -क्तं, संश्लिष्टः -ष्टा -ष्टं.

GLUEY, *a.* श्यानः -ना -नं, सान्द्रः -न्द्रा -न्द्रं, चिक्कणः -णा -णं.

GLUM, *a.* वक्रभावः -वा -वं, सदावक्रः -क्रा -क्रं, प्रतीपः -पा -पं.

To GLUT, *v. a.* (Satiate) अत्यन्तं तृप् (c. 10. तर्पयति -यितुं) or सन्तृप् or पॄ in caus. (पूरयति -यितुं) or परिपॄ, अतितृप्तिं or अतिसौहित्यं जन् (c. 10. जनयति -यितुं).—(Swallow, gorge) ग्रस् (c. 1. ग्रसते -सितुं), उपग्रस्, गॄ (c. 6. गिरति, गरितुं -रीतुं).

GLUT, *s.* (More than enough) अतिरेक्यं, अतिरिक्तता, आधिक्यं, आतिशय्यं, उत्सेकः, उद्रेकः, उत्कर्षः.—(Too great plenty) अतिबाहुल्यं.—(Satiety) अतितृप्तिः *f.*, अतिसौहित्यं.

To GLUTINATE, *v. a.* लेपद्वारेण संलग्नीकृ or संयुज् (c. 7. -युनक्ति -योक्तुं).

GLUTINATION, *s.* लेपादिना संलग्नीकरणं or संयोजनं or संश्लेषणं.

GLUTINOUS, *a.* श्यानः -ना -नं, चिक्कणः -णा -णं, सान्द्रः -न्द्रा -न्द्रं, स्निग्धः -ग्धा -ग्धं, संलग्नशीलः -ला -लं, अनुलग्नशीलः -ला -लं.

GLUTINOUSNESS, *s.* श्यानता, सान्द्रता, स्निग्धता, स्नैग्ध्यं, संलग्नशीलता.

GLUTTED, *p. p.* अतितृप्तः -प्ता -प्तं, अतिपूरितः -ता -तं, अतिपूर्णः -र्णा -र्णं.

GLUTTON, *s.* अत्याहारी *m.* (न्), अपरिमिताहारी *m.*, अत्यन्तभोजी *m.* (न्), कुक्षिम्भरिः *m.*, उदरम्भरिः *m.*, औदरिकः, अतिलोभी *m.* (न्), गृध्नजनः, सर्व्वभुक् *m.*, वर्व्वरः *m.*

To GLUTTONIZE, *v. n.* अत्यन्तं भुज् (c. 7. भुंक्ते, भोक्तुं), अत्याहारं कृ, गृध् (c. 4. गृध्यति, गर्धितुं), अतिभोजनं कृ.

GLUTTONOUS, GLUTTONISH, *a.* अत्याहारी -रिणी -रि (न्), बह्वाशी -शिनी -शि (न्), अतिभोजी -जिनी -जि (न्), अतिबुभुक्षुः -क्षुः -क्षु, बहुभोक्ता -क्त्री -क्तृ (क्तृ), अपरिमिताहारी &c., भक्षकः -का -कं, घस्मरः -रा -रं, अद्मरः -रा -रं, प्रघसः -सा -सं, कुक्षिम्भरिः -रिः -रि, उदरम्भरिः -रिः -रि, देहम्भरः -री -रं, औदरिकः -की -कं, लोलुभः -भा -भं, गृध्नः -ध्ना -ध्नं, गर्धी -र्धिनी -र्धि (न्), लोलः -ला -लं, आद्यूनः -ना -नं.

GLUTTONOUSLY, *adv.* अत्याहारेण, गृध्नजनवत्, औदरिकवत्, सातिभोजनं.

GLUTTONY, *s.* अत्याहारः, अतिभोजनं, अतिबुभुक्षा, अधिकभोजनं, अपरिमिताहारः, घस्मरता, गृध्नता, लोलता, लौल्यं, अतृप्तिः *f.*, उदरभरणं.

GLYPH, *s.* गृहनिर्म्माणे स्तम्भोपरि रेखाकारेण तक्षितो ऽलङ्कारः.

GLYPTOGRAPHY, *s.* रत्नोपरि तक्षणशिल्पं or तक्षणकर्म्म *n.* (न्) or लिखनं.

To GNARL, *v. n.* गर्ज् (c. 1. गर्जति -र्जितुं), रै (c. 1. रायति, रातुं), घुर्घुरां कृ.

GNARLED, *a.* ग्रन्थिलः -ला -लं, बहुग्रन्थिः -न्थिः -न्थि, पर्व्वविशिष्टः -ष्टा -ष्टं.

To GNASH, *v. a.* and *n.* क्ष्विड् or क्ष्विद् (c. 1. क्ष्वेडति, क्ष्वेदति -डितुं -दितुं), दन्तान् दन्तैर् घृष् (c. 1. घर्षति -र्षितुं) or निष्पिष् (c. 7. -पिनष्टि -पेष्टुं), सन्दंश (c. 1. -दशति -दंष्टुं), कटकट (nom. कटकटापयति -यितुं), क्ष्वेडनं कृ, दन्तघर्षणं कृ.

GNASHING, *s.* दन्तघर्षणं, क्ष्वेडनं, क्ष्वेडितं, कटकटशब्दः.

GNAT, *s.* मशकः, मसकः, सूक्ष्ममक्षिका, दंशकः; भम्भरालिका, सूचिवदनः, रणरणः, प्राक्षिका, रात्रिजागरदः.

GNAT-SNAPPER, *s.* मशकखादकः पक्षिभेदः, मशकनाशकः.

To GNAW, *v. a.* and *n.* चर्व् (c. 1. चर्वति -र्वितुं, c. 10. चर्वयति -यितुं), दंश् (c. 1. दशति, दंष्टुं), विदंश्, सन्दंश्, सम्मुखदन्तैर् अल्पाल्पं खाद् (c. 1. खादति -दितुं) or अश् (c. 9. अश्नाति, अशितुं) or भक्ष् (c. 10. भक्षयति -यितुं), क्रमशः खाद् or चर्वणं कृ or कर्त्तनं कृ.

GNAWED, *p. p.* चर्वितः -ता -तं, सम्मुखदन्तैः क्रमशः खादितः -ता -तं, विदश्यमानः -ना -नं, गलितः -ता -तं.

GNAWER, *s.* चर्वणकारी *m.* (न्), दंशनकृत् *m.*, सम्मुखदन्तैः खादकः.

GNAWING, *s.* चर्वणं, दंशनं, सम्मुखदन्तैर् अल्पाल्पखादनं or कर्त्तनं.

GNOME, *s.* पृथिव्यभ्यन्तरे वासी अल्पाकारादिरहितो भूतविशेषः.

GNOMON, *s.* (Of a dial) कीलः, मयूखः, शङ्कुः *m.*, नरः, ना *m.* (न्).

GNOMONIC, *s.* घटीकीलनिर्म्माणसम्बन्धी -न्धिनी -न्धि (न्).

GNOMONICS, *s.* घटीकीलनिर्म्माणविद्या, कालमापकमण्डलनिर्म्माणशिल्पं, मुहूर्त्तदण्डादिपरिमापकमण्डलसम्बन्धिनी विद्या.

GNOSTIC, *s.* ग्नास्तिकसंज्ञकः प्राचीननास्तिकविशेषः.

To GO, *v. n.* गम् (c. 1. गच्छति, गन्तुं), या (c. 2. याति -तुं), इ (c. 2. एति -तुं), सृ (c. 1. सरति, सर्त्तुं), चर् (c. 1. चरति -रितुं), पद् (c. 4. पद्यते, पत्तुं), व्रज् (c. 1. व्रजति -जितुं), ऋ (c. 1. ऋच्छति, अर्त्तुं), चल् (c. 1. चलति -लितुं), गा (used only in 3d pret. अगात्), इङ्ग् (c. 1. इङ्गति -ङ्गितुं), अंह् (c. 1. अंहते -हितुं).—(Walk) क्रम् (c. 1. क्रामति, c. 4. क्राम्यति, क्रमितुं), पादाभ्यां गम् or चर्.—(Flow) सु (c. 1. स्रवति, स्रोतुं), स्यन्द् (c. 1. स्यन्दते -न्दितुं), री (c. 4. रीयते, रेतुं).—(Glide along) सृप् (c. 1. सर्पति, सप्तुं).—(Pass current, circulate) प्रचल्, प्रचर्.—(Fare) वृत् (c. 1. वर्त्तते -र्त्तितुं), स्था (c. 1. तिष्ठति, स्थातुं); 'How goes it with you?' कीदृशी स्थितिर् भवतः.—(Be about to do) expressed by काम with the infin.; as, 'What were you going to say?' किम् असि वक्तुकामः; 'What are you going to do?' किं कर्त्तुकामो ऽसि, or by the desid. form, as किं विवक्षसि, किं चिकीर्षसि.—(Go about, attempt) यत् (c. 1. यतते -तितुं), उद्यम् (c. 1. -यच्छति -यन्तुं), व्यवसो (c. 4. -स्यति -सातुं), उपक्रम्.—(Go against) आक्रम्, अभिक्रम्, अभिप्रया.—(Go aside) पार्श्वे चल्.—(Go astray) भ्रम् (c. 4. भ्राम्यति, भ्रमितुं), विभ्रम्, सत्पथात् च्यु (c. 1. च्यवते, च्योतुं) or भ्रंश् (c. 4. भ्रश्यति, भ्रंशितुं), उत्क्रम्, व्युत्क्रम्, व्यभिचर्, उन्मार्गेण गम्.—(Go away) अपगम्, व्यपगम्, विगम्, अपया, व्यपया, प्रया, अपे (c. 2. अपैति -तुं, rt. इ), व्यपे, अपसृ, अपक्रम्, व्यपक्रम्, अपसृप्, चल्, प्रस्था, विप्रस्था, सम्प्रस्था.—(Go between) अन्तश्चर्, अन्तरि, अन्तर्वृत्, मध्ये वृत्, मध्ये स्था, मध्यस्थः -स्था -स्थं भू, मध्यवर्त्ती -र्त्तिनी -र्त्ति भू.—(Go by) अतिक्रम्, अती, व्यती, अतिवृत्; 'to go by sea,' समुद्रेण या.—(Go down) अधो गम्, अधो या, अवया, अवरुह् (c. 1. -रोहति -रोढुं).—(Go for nothing) तृणप्रायः -या -यं भू.—(Go forth) निर्गम्, निर्या, विनिर्या, निःसृ, विनिःसृ, निष्क्रम्, निरि, निश्चर्.—(Go forward) प्रगम्, अग्रे गम्, पुरो गम्, प्रया, प्रसृ, प्रस्था.—(Go in) विश् (c. 6. विशति, वेष्टुं), निविश्, प्रविश्, आविश्, आगम्, अन्तर्गम्, आया, उपस्था.—(Go in and out) गमनागमनं कृ.—(Go off, depart) अपगम्, अपया.—(Go off, die) प्रे, परे, अती, देहाद् अपगम्, लोकान्तरं गम्.—(Go off, explode) अन्तरग्निबलेन विभिद् in pass. (-भिद्यते), विदृ in pass. (-दीर्य्यते).—(Go on, proceed) प्रगम्, प्रया, प्रसृ, प्रसृप्, प्रवृत्; 'the work goes on,' प्रसर्पति कर्म्म; 'the laugh goes on,' प्रवर्त्तते हासः.—(Go out, issue) निर्गम्, विनिर्गम्, निःसृ, विनिःसृ, निर्या, विनिर्या, अभिनिर्या, निष्क्रम्, विनिष्क्रम्, अभिनिष्क्रम्, निश्चर्, विनिश्चर्, निरि, बहिर्गम्.—(Go out, as a fire or light) निर्वै (c. 4. -वायति -वातुं) or in caus. pass. (-वाप्यते), शम् (c. 4. शाम्यति, शमितुं).—(Go over, read) अधी (c. 2. अधीते, rt. इ), अधिगम्, अधिगा used only in 3d pret. atm. (अध्यगीष्ट).—(Go over from one party to another) स्वपक्षं त्यक्त्वा परपक्षम् आश्रि (c. 1. -श्रयति -यितुं), स्वधर्म्मात् भ्रंश् (c. 4. भ्रश्यति, भ्रंशितुं).—(Go through, execute) निर्वह् (c. 10. -वाहयति -यितुं), प्रवृत् in caus. (-वर्त्तयति -यितुं), साध् (c. 10. साधयति -यितुं).—(Go through, undergo) उपगम्, उपागम्, सह् (c. 1. सहते, सोढुं), अनुभू.—(Go through, penetrate) प्रविश्, निविश्, विश्, व्यध् (c. 4. विध्यति, व्यद्धुं), निर्भिद् (c. 7. -भिनत्ति -भेत्तुं).—(Go to, go towards) आगम्, उपगम्, उपागम्, समुपगम्, अधिगम्, अभिगम्, आया, अभिया, उपया, उपाया, प्रत्याया, समाया, समुपया, उपस्था, अभिसृ, आवृत्, अभिवृत्, प्रतिवृत्, उपावृत्, अभ्यावृत्, आव्रज्, प्रतिव्रज्, अभिपद्, समापद्, प्रतिपद्, समुपपद्, ए (c. 2. एति -तुं, rt. इ with आ), अभ्ये, उपे, अभी, (अभ्येति), प्रती, आक्रम्, उपक्रम्, अभ्यृ.—(Go up) ऊर्द्ध्वं गम्, उदि (c. 1. -अयति -एतुं), उच्चैर् व्रज्.—(Go with) अनुया, समनुया, अन्वि, सह गम् or चर्, सहायीभू.—(Go on horseback) अश्ववाहनेन भ्रम्.—(Go on foot) पादाभ्यां गम्.—(Go to bed) शय्यां गम्.—(Go to law) विवद् (c. 1. -वदते -दितुं).—(Go to sea) नौकाम् आरुह्.—(Go ashore) नौकाया उत्तॄ (c. 1. -तरति -रितुं -रीतुं) or अवरुह्.

GO-BETWEEN, *s.* मध्यस्थः, मध्यवर्त्ती *m.* (न्), सन्धिजीवकः.—(Female) दूती, सञ्चारिका, सुरतताली.

GO-BY, *s.* पलायनं, अपक्रमः, निर्गमः, अपयानं, व्यपदेशः.

GO TO, *interj.* अपैहि, अपसर, एहि, यातु, धिक्.

GO-CART, *s.* शकटिका, बालकानां पादचारशिक्षार्थं चक्रयानविशेषः, क्रीडाशकटः.

GOAD, *s.* तोदनं, तोत्रं, प्रतोदः, अङ्कुशः, प्राजनं, सृणिः *f.*, प्रवयणं.

To GOAD, *v. a.* प्रतोदेन तुद् (c. 6. तुदति, तोत्तुं) or वितुद् or आतुद्.—(Incite) प्रेर् (c. 10. ईरयति -यितुं), प्रचुद् (c. 10. -चोदयति -यितुं), प्रणुद् (c. 6. -णुदति -णोत्तुं), प्रवृत् (c. 10. -वर्त्तयति -यितुं), प्रोत्सह् (c. 10. -साहयति -यितुं), उत्तिज् (c. 10. -तेजयति -यितुं).

GOADED, *p. p.* प्रतुन्नः -न्ना -न्नं, प्रेरितः -ता -तं, प्रोत्साहितः -ता -तं.

GOAL, *s.* अग्रं, अग्रभूमिः *f.*, अग्रस्थानं.—(Final end) अभिप्रायः, शेषाभिप्रायः, आशयः, उद्देशः, अर्थः, अन्तः, उत्तरं, फलमुत्तरं, परिणामः.

GOAT, *s.* छागः -गलः, छगलः, अजः, वस्तः, स्तुभकः, पर्णभोजनः, लम्बकर्णः, पयस्वलः, शिवाप्रियः, देवानाम्प्रियः; 'wild-goat,' वनाजः, वनच्छागः, अरण्यछागः; 'she-goat,' छागी, अजा; 'excrescence on a goat's neck,' मणिः *m. f.*; 'flock of goats,' आजकं; 'relating to a goat,' वास्तः -स्ती -स्तं.

GOAT-HERD, *s.* जाबालः, अजजीविकः, अजाजीवः -वी *m.* (न्), अजापालकः, छागपालकः, अजपः -पालकः, छागपोषकः.

GOATISH, *a.* अजवत् कामुकः -का -कं, अजगन्धः -न्धा -न्धं, छागगन्धः &c.

GOATISHLY, *adv.* अजवत्, छागवत्, कामुकवत्, कामुकं.

GOATSKIN, *s.* अजचर्म्म *n.* (न्), छागचर्म्म *n.*, छागाजिनं, अजाजिनं.

GOB, *s.* कवलिका, अल्पपिण्डः, अल्पग्रासः, मुखपूरणं, कवलः.

To GOBBLE, *v. a.* ग्रस् (c. 1. ग्रसते -सितुं), उपग्रस्, गृध्रवत् सत्वरं भक्ष् (c. 10. भक्षयति -यितुं) or खाद् (c. 1. खादति -दितुं), गॄ (c. 6. गिरति, गरितुं -रीतुं).

To GOBBLE, *v. n.* शीघ्रनिगरणशब्दं कृ, दीर्घकण्ठपक्षिवत् शब्दं कृ.

GOBBLER, *s.* शीघ्रभोजी *m.* (न्), शीघ्राशी *m.* (न्), बह्वाशी *m.*, भक्षकः, घस्मरः.

GOBLET, *s.* कांस्यं, कंसः -सं, कंशः -शं, पानभाजनं, पानपात्रं; 'relating to one,' कंसीयः -या -यं.

GOBLIN, *s.* वेतालः, रात्रिचरः, रात्रिचारः, रजनीचरः, क्षपाचरः, नक्तञ्चरः -चारी *m.* (न्), निशाटः, भूतः, राक्षसः, पिशाचः, असुरः, प्रेतः, अपदेवता, क्रव्याद् *m.*, यज्ञारिः *m.*, विधुरः, कर्बुरः, कौणपः.

GOD, *s.* (The Supreme Being) ईश्वरः, परमेश्वरः, परेश्वरः, परमात्मा *m.* (न्).—(A god) देवः -वता, सुरः, अमरः, विबुधः, अनिमिषः, अजरः, चिरायुः *m.* (स्), सुचिरायुः *m.* (स्), भगवान् *m.* (त्).—(The Creator) सर्व्वस्रष्टा *m.* (ष्टृ), धाता *m.* (तृ), विधाता *m.*, जगत्कर्त्ता *m.* (र्तृ), विश्वसृक् *m.*, भूतादिः *m.*, सात् *n.*—(God of gods) ईश्वरेश्वरः; 'city god,' नगरदेवता.—(Self-existent) स्वयम्भूः *m.*

GODAVERÍ, *s.* (River) गोदावरी, तपनी, तपनात्मजा.

GOD-CHILD, *s.* धर्म्मपुत्रः -त्री, धर्म्मसुतः -ता.

GOD-DAUGHTER, *s.* धर्म्मपुत्री, धर्म्मसुता, जलसंस्कारकाले ख्रीष्टीयधर्म्मशिक्षणार्थं स्वीकृता पुत्री.

GODDESS, *s.* देवी, सुरी, अमरा -री, अजरा -री, देवपत्नी, देवाङ्गना, भगवती.

GODFATHER, *s.* धर्म्मपिता *m.* (तृ), धर्म्मप्रतिभूः *m.*, जलसंस्कारकाले ख्रीष्टीयधर्म्मशिक्षणाय प्रतिजानीते यो बालस्य कृत्रिमपिता.

GODHEAD, *s.* देवत्वं -ता, ईश्वरत्वं -ता, देवभूयं, भगवत्त्वं, ब्रह्मत्वं, ब्रह्मभूयं.

GODLESS, *a.* अनीश्वरः -रा -रं, अनीश्वरवादी -दिनी -दि (न्), नास्तिकः, अनीश्वररोचितः -ता -तं.—(Impious) निर्धर्म्मः -र्म्मा -र्म्मं, अधार्म्मिकः -की -कं, अतिदुष्टः -ष्टा -ष्टं.

GODLESSLY, *adv.* नास्तिकवत्, पापण्डवत्, अतिदुष्टं, धर्म्मव्यतिरेकेण.

GODLESSNESS, *s.* अनीश्वरत्वं, नास्तिकत्वं, निर्धर्म्मता, अतिदुष्टता.

GODLIKE, *a.* देवतुल्यः -ल्या -ल्यं, देवोपमः -मा -मं, देवरूपी -पिणी -पि (न्), दिव्यः -व्या -व्यं, देवार्हः -र्हा -र्हं, ईश्वरीयः -या -यं, ईश्वरमूर्त्तिः -र्त्तिः -र्त्ति.

GODLINESS, *s.* ईश्वरसेवा -वनं, ईश्वरभक्तिः *f.*, देवभक्तिः *f.*, ईश्वरश्रद्धा, ईश्वरपूजा, धर्म्मत्वं, धार्म्मिकता, धर्म्मसेवा, ब्रह्मण्यता, पुण्यशीलता.

GODLY, *a.* ईश्वरसेवी -विनी -वि (न्), ईश्वरभक्तः -क्ता -क्तं, ईश्वरपूजकः -का -कं, देवपूजकः -का -कं, पुण्यशीलः -ला -लं, पुण्यात्मा -त्मा -त्म (न्), भजनशीलः -ला -लं, भक्तिमान् -मती -मत् (त्), धर्म्मी -र्म्मिणी -र्म्मि (न्), धार्म्मिकः -की -कं, धर्म्मचारी -रिणी -रि (न्), ब्रह्मण्यः -ण्या -ण्यं.

GODLY, *adv.* ईश्वरभक्तवत्, देवपूजकवत्, धार्म्मिकवत्, पुण्यं.

GODMOTHER, *s.* धर्म्ममाता *f.* (तृ), जलसंस्कारकाले ख्रीष्टीयधर्म्मशिक्षणाय प्रतिजानीते या बालकस्य कृत्रिममाता.

GODSEND, *s.* देवदत्तं, ईश्वरदत्तं, लक्ष्मीदत्तं, श्रीदत्तं, सौभाग्यं.

GODSHIP, *s.* ईश्वरत्वं -ता, देवत्वं -ता, देवभावः, देवभूयं, भगवत्त्वं.

GODSON, *s.* धर्म्मपुत्रः, धर्म्मसुतः, जलसंस्कारकाले ख्रीष्टीयधर्म्मशिक्षणार्थं स्वीकृतः पुत्रः.

GODWIT, *s.* दीर्घमुखः पक्षिभेदः, दीर्घचञ्चुः *m.*, दीर्घजङ्घः, दीर्घपाद् *m.*

GOER, *s.* गामी *m.* (न्), गन्ता *m.* (न्तृ), यायी *m.* (न्), सरः, सारी *m.* (न्), क्रमिता *m.* (तृ), चलः, गमनकारी *m.* (न्); 'a quick goer,' अविलम्बितक्रमः, द्रुतक्रमः.

To GOGGLE, *v. n.* चक्षुषी इतस्ततो लुल् (c. 1. लोलति -लितुं, c. 10. लोलयति -यितुं), विवृताक्षः -क्षा -क्षं भू, तिर्य्यग्दृष्टिः -ष्टिः -ष्टि भू.

GOGGLE-EYE, *s.* लोलनयनं, लोलनेत्रं, फुल्लनयनं, विवृतचक्षुस् *n.*

GOGGLE-EYED, *a.* लोलनयनः -ना -नं, लोलाक्षिः -क्षिः -क्षि, उत्फुल्लनयनः -ना -नं, फुल्ललोचनः -ना -नं, तिर्य्यग्दृष्टिः -ष्टिः -ष्टि, वक्रदृष्टिः -ष्टिः -ष्टि, उद्भेक्षः -क्षा -क्षं, उद्ग्रनयनः -ना -नं.

GOING, *part.* चरन् -रन्ती -रत् (त्), चलन् -लन्ती -लत् (त्), क्रामन् -मन्ती -मत् (त्), सरन् -रन्ती -रत् (त्), गामी -मिनी -मि (न्), सरः -रा -रं, सरणः -णा -णं, चरः -रा -रं; 'going in a straight line,' सरलयायी -यिनी -यि (न्).

GOING, *s.* गमः -मनं, सरणं, चरणं, चारः, चलनं, व्रजनं, गतिः *f.*, गतं, अयनं, क्रमः -मणं; 'going away,' अपगमः, व्यपगमः, अपयानं, अपसरणं, अपायः, प्रस्थानं; 'going out,' निष्क्रमः -मणं, निष्क्रान्तिः *f.*, निर्गमः, निर्याणं, बहिर्गमनं; 'going and coming,' गमागमः, गमनागमनं, गतागतं, यातायातं.

GOITRE, *s.* गडुः *m.*, गण्डिः *m.*; 'having it,' गडुकण्ठः -ण्ठी -ण्ठं.

GOITROUS, *a.* गडुपीडितः -ता -तं, गडुकण्ठः -ण्ठी -ण्ठं.

GOLD, *s.* सुवर्णं, स्वर्णं, कनकं, काञ्चनं, हिरण्यं, हेम *n.* (न्), हेमं, रुक्मं, रुग्मं, भर्म *n.* (न्), भर्मं, जातरूपं, जाम्बूनदं, शातकुम्भं, शातकुम्भः, शातकौम्भं, चामीकरं, निष्कं, हाटकं, हिरणं, तपनीयं, महारजतं, कलधौतं, कलधूतं, कार्त्तस्वरं, अष्टापदः -दं, कर्बुरं, कर्ब्बूरं, गाङ्गेयं, गौरं, दीप्तं, भास्करं, जाम्बवं, तेजस्, शतसाहं, महाधातुः *m.*, सौमेरुकं, लोहोत्तमं, पिङ्गानं, सुराहं, दाक्षायणं, मानसिः *m.*, पुरटं, पुरुदं, वह्निबीजं, अकुप्यं, मृदुत्वकं; 'pure gold,' कुमारं; 'virgin gold,' पिङ्गाशं; 'false gold,' कूटस्वर्णं; 'gold for ornaments,' शृङ्गिकनकं; 'a heap of gold,' काञ्चनचयः; 'a piece of gold,' कनकभङ्गः; 'a gold coin,' सुवर्णमुद्रा; 'a weight of gold,' कनकपलः, सुवर्णः -र्णं.

GOLD, *a.* सुवर्ण or स्वर्ण or कनक or काञ्चन &c. in comp.; as, 'a gold bracelet,' सुवर्णकङ्कणं; 'gold stick,' कनकदण्डः; 'gold-mine,' कनकस्थली, काञ्चनकन्दरः; 'gold necklace,' हेमसूत्रकं, कनकसूत्रं. *See* GOLDEN.

GOLD-BEATER, *s.* स्वर्णपत्रकारः -कृत्, सुवर्णकारविशेषो यो मुद्गरादिना सुवर्णम् अतिसूक्ष्मीकरोति or अतिशयेन तनूकरोति or उद्वर्त्तयति.

GOLD-DRAWER, *s.* सुवर्णोद्वर्त्तनकारी *m.* (न्), कनकोद्वर्त्तनकृत् *m.*

GOLD-DUST, *s.* कनकपरागः, काञ्चनभूः *f.*, कनकरेणुः *m.*

GOLDEN, *a.* सौवर्णः -र्णी -र्णं, स्वर्णमयः -यी -यं, स्वर्णनिर्म्मितः -ता -तं, स्वर्णिकः -का -कं, सुवर्णवान् -वती -वत् (त्), काञ्चनः -नी -नं, काञ्चनमयः -यी -यं, कनकमयः -यी -यं, सुवर्णकृतः -ता -तं, रुक्मवान् -वती -वत् (त्), तापनीयः -यी -यं; 'golden ornament,' कनकभूषणं. *See* GOLD, *a.*

GOLDFINCH, *s.* कनकवर्णपक्षयुक्तो मधुररुतविशिष्टः क्षुद्रपक्षी *m.* (न्).

GOLD-FISH, *s.* चीनदेशजः कनकवर्णो मत्स्यभेदः.

GOLD-LEAF, *s.* स्वर्णपत्रं, कनकपत्रं, अष्टापदपत्रं, पत्रं.

GOLDSMITH, *s.* स्वर्णकारः, सुवर्णकारः, हेमकारः, रुक्मकारकः, नाडिन्धमः, हेमलः, कलादः, कणादः, गौञ्जिकः, सुवर्णस्य विकारान्तरकृत् *m.*

GOLD-THREAD, *s.* कनकसूत्रं, हेमसूत्रं, सुवर्णतन्तुः *m.*

GOLF, *s.* कन्दुकक्रीडा, कन्दुकलीला, गुलिकाक्रीडा.

GONDOLA, *s.* वेनिशनगरवासिभिः प्रयुक्तो लघुनौकाविशेषः.

GONDOLIER, *s.* पूर्व्वोक्तनौकावाहकः, पूर्व्वोक्तनौकादण्डधरः.

GONE, *p. p.* गतः -ता -तं, यातः -ता -तं, चलितः -ता -तं, सृतः -ता -तं, चरितः -ता -तं, क्रमितः -ता -तं, इतः -ता -तं, पन्नः -न्ना -न्नं; 'gone away,' अपगतः -ता -तं, व्यपगतः -ता -तं; 'gone out,' निर्गतः -ता

-तं, निष्क्रान्तः -न्ता -न्तं, बहिर्गतः -ता -तं.—(Past) वृत्तः -त्ता -त्तं, भूतः -ता -तं, अतीतः -ता -तं, अतिक्रान्तः -न्ता -न्तं.

GONFALON, GONFANON, *s.* पताका, ध्वजः, केतुः *m.*, वैजयन्ती.

GONG, *s.* कांस्यं, घनं, गभीरिका.

GONIOMETER, *s.* कोणपरिमापकयन्त्रं, असमापनयन्त्रं.

GONORRHŒA, *s.* रक्तपीरकः, रक्तस्रावकः, धातुक्षरणं, मूत्रमार्गरोगः.

GOOD, *a.* (Not bad, excellent) साधुः -धुः -ध्वी -धु, भद्रः -द्रा -द्रं, उत्तमः -मा -मं, प्रशस्तः -स्ता -स्तं, प्रशस्यः -स्या -स्यं, शस्तः -स्ता -स्तं, शस्यः -स्या -स्यं, शिष्टः -ष्टा -ष्टं, शुभः -भा -भं, कुशलः -ला -लं, कल्याणः -णा -णं, सन् सती सत् (त्), सत्तमः -मा -मं, श्रेष्ठः -ष्ठा -ष्ठं, सारः -रा -रं, सारवान् -वती -वत् (त्), आर्य्यः -र्य्या -र्य्यं, वरः -रा -रं, निर्दोषः -षा -षं, अदुष्टः -ष्टा -ष्टं, often expressed by सु prefixed; as, 'a good action,' सुक्रिया; 'a good man,' साधुजनः, सज्जनः; 'a good road,' सुपथः, सन्मार्गः.—(Virtuous) धार्म्मिकः -की -कं, सच्चरितः -ता -तं, सदाचारः -रा -रं, साधुवृत्तः -त्ता -त्तं, आर्य्यवृत्तः -त्ता -त्तं, शुभाचारः -रा -रं, सुकर्म्मा -र्म्मा -र्म्म (न्), सुकृती -तिनी -ति (न्), सुकृत् *m. f. n.*, सुचरितः -ता -तं, कुशली -लिनी -लि (न्), पुण्यः -ण्या -ण्यं, पुण्यकर्म्मा -र्म्मा -र्म्म (न्), पुण्यशीलः -ला -लं, पुण्यात्मा -त्मा -त्म (न्), वृत्तवान् -वती -वत् (त्).—(Suitable, fit) योग्यः -ग्या -ग्यं, युक्तः -क्ता -क्तं, उपयुक्तः -क्ता -क्तं, उचितः -ता -तं, समुचितः -ता -तं, हितः -ता -तं, सुहितः -ता -तं, sometimes expressed by the fut. pass. part.; as, 'good to eat,' खाद्यः -द्या -द्यं, खादनीयः -या -यं.—(Wholesome) पथ्यः -थ्या -थ्यं.—(Useful) उपयोगी -गिनी -गि (न्), सोपकारः -रा -रं.—(Kind) हितः -ता -तं, हितकामः -मा -मं, सुजनः -ना -नं, प्रियङ्करः -रा -रं, प्रियकारः -रा -रं, उपकारकः -का -कं.—(Tending to promote) उत्पादकः -का -कं.—(Sound, undamaged) अक्षतः -ता -तं, अदूषितः -ता -तं.—(Entire, complete) सम्पूर्णः -र्णा -र्णं, सकलः -ला -लं, कृत्स्नः -त्स्ना -त्स्नं.—(Considerable, great) बहुः -ह्वी -हु, अनल्पः -ल्पा -ल्पं, महान् -हती -हत् (त्), भूरिः -रिः -रि, प्रचुरः -रा -रं, सु or अति prefixed; as, 'a good deal vexed,' सुदुःखितः -ता -तं, अतिदुःखितः -ता -तं; 'a good distance,' सुदूरं; 'a good while ago,' सुदीर्घकाले गते.—(Valid) धर्म्यः -र्म्या -र्म्यं, अविशुद्धः -द्धा -द्धं. 'Good quality,' गुणः; 'endowed with good qualities,' गुणी -णिनी -णि (न्), सद्गुणः -णा -णं; 'good wishes,' कल्याणवचनं, आशीर्वचनं; 'good and bad,' शुभाशुभः -भा -भं, हिताहितः -ता -तं, सारासारः -रा -रं; 'beloved by the good,' आर्य्यजुष्टः -ष्टा -ष्टं; 'to make good,' सम्पद् (c. 10. -पादयति -यितुं), सम्पॄ (c. 10. -पूरयति -यितुं), साध् (c. 10. साधयति -यितुं); 'make good a promise,' प्रतिज्ञाम् अपवृज् (c. 10. -वर्जयति -यितुं); 'make good a debt,' ऋणं शुध् (c. 10. शोधयति -यितुं) or अपाकृ; 'a good fellow,' भद्रः; 'in good time,' उपयुक्तकाले.

GOOD, *s.* (Benefit, welfare) हितं, श्रेयस् *n.*, भद्रं, शुभं, कल्याणं, कुशलं, क्षेमं, मङ्गलं, भूतिः *f.*; 'for the good of the world,' लोकहिताय, भूतये भुवः; 'good and evil,' हिताहितं, शुभाशुभं, भद्राभद्रं, मङ्गलामङ्गलं; 'good and bad,' सारासारं.—(Utility) उपयोगः, अर्थः, फलं, लाभः.—(Virtue) पुण्यं, सुकृतं, सुचरितं, साधुवृत्तं, धर्म्मः; 'to do good,' हितं कृ, क्षेमं कृ, उपकृ.

GOOD, *adv.* सु prefixed, सुष्ठु; 'as good as,' समं; 'this is as good as a sixteenth part,' एतत् षोडशांशेन समं.

GOOD, *interj.* भद्रं, वाढं, कामं, भवतु, अस्तु, एवमस्तु, तथेति.

GOOD-BREEDING, *s.* सभ्यता, विनयः, सुविनयः, सुशीलता; 'a man of good breeding,' सुविनीतः, सुशीलः.

GOOD-CONDITIONED, *a.* सुस्थः -स्था -स्थं, सुस्थितः -ता -तं, सुवृत्तः -त्ता -त्तं.

GOOD-FELLOW, *s.* भद्रः, भद्रजनः, साधुजनः, सहपायी *m.* (न्), रसिकजनः.

GOOD-FELLOWSHIP, *s.* उत्सवकारिणां संसर्गः, सुसङ्गः, सुसाहित्यं, सुमैत्र्यं.

GOOD-FORTUNE, *s.* सौभाग्यं, भाग्यं, कल्याणं, भद्रं, शुभं, मङ्गलं, माङ्गल्यं, कुशलं, कौशल्यं, दैवं, सुदैवं, श्रीः *f.*, लक्ष्मीः *f.*, शर्म्म *n.* (न्), सम्पद्, सम्पत्तिः *f.*, पुण्योदयः.

GOOD-FRIDAY, *s.* ख्रीष्टस्य क्रूशारोपणमुद्दिश्य महोपवासदिनं.

GOOD-HUMOUR, *s.* सद्भावः, सुस्वभावः, सुशीलता, चित्तप्रसन्नता, सत्प्रकृतिः *f.*

GOOD-HUMOURED, *a.* सुप्रकृतिः -तिः -ति, सत्प्रकृतिः -तिः -ति, हृष्टभावः -वा -वं, हृष्टचित्तः -त्ता -त्तं, प्रसन्नस्वभावः -वा -वं.

GOOD-HUMOUREDLY, *adv.* सद्भावेन, सुस्वभावात्, सुशीलवत्, हृष्टवत्.

GOOD-LOOKING, *a.* सुदृश्यः -श्या -श्यं, सुदर्शनः -ना -नं, सुरूपः -पी -पं.

GOOD-LUCK, *s.* सौभाग्यं. *See* GOOD-FORTUNE.

GOOD-MANNERS, *s.* विनयः, विनीतता, मर्य्यादा, सुशीलता, सभ्यता, सदाचारता, सुनीतिः *f.*, सुचरितं, सच्चरित्रं.

GOOD-NATURE, *s.* सद्भावः, सुस्वभावः, सुप्रकृतिः *f.*, सत्प्रकृतिः *f.*, सुशीलता, साधुशीलत्वं, साधुत्वं, आर्य्यता.

GOOD-NATURED, *a.* सुप्रकृतिः -तिः -ति, सत्प्रकृतिः -तिः -ति, सुशीलः -ला -लं, सुभाववान् -वती -वत् (त्), साधुशीलः -ला -लं, सुहृदयः -या -यं, सुहृदयवान् &c.

GOOD-SENSE, *s.* सुविवेकः, सुबोधः, बुद्धिमत्त्वं, विज्ञता, प्रज्ञता.

GOOD-WILL, *s.* हितता, सुहितता, हितेच्छा, प्रीतिः *f.*, हितकाम्या, सौहृद्यं प्रियता, अनुकूलता.

GOOD-WOMAN, *s.* गृहिणी, गृहमेधिनी, गृहव्यापारकुशला or -दक्षा.

GOODLINESS, *s.* रूपलावण्यं, सौन्दर्य्यं, शोभा, चारुता, रूपवत्त्वं.

GOODLY, *a.* (Graceful) सुन्दरः -रा -री -रं, चारुः -र्वी -रु, सुदृश्यः -श्या -श्यं, सुदर्शनः -ना -नं, सुरूपः -पी -पं, लावण्यवान् -वती -वत् (त्).—(Pleasant) रम्यः -म्या -म्यं, रमणीयः -या -यं, रुचिरः -रा -रं.

GOODMAN, *s.* गृही *m.* (न्), गेही *m.* (न्), कुटुम्बी *m.* (न्), स्वामी *m.* (न्).

GOODNESS, *s.* (Excellence) साधुता -त्वं, सत्त्वं, प्रशस्तता, प्राशस्त्यं, प्रशस्तिः *f.*, उत्तमता, श्रेष्ठता, उत्कृष्टता, सारत्वं, प्रकृष्टता, विशिष्टता, कौशलं, सौष्ठवं, आर्य्यता.—(Virtue, piety) पुण्यता, पुण्यशीलता, साधुशीलता, धर्म्मत्वं, सदाचारता, साधुवृत्तत्वं, धार्म्मिकत्वं, देवभक्तिः *f.*—(Kindness) सुजनत्वं, सौजन्यं, प्रियता, दया, कृपा.

GOODS, *s. pl.* (Property, effects) द्रव्यं, द्रव्याणि *n. pl.*, वस्तूनि *n. pl.*, विभवः, सामग्री -ग्र्यं, रिक्थं.—(Moveable household furniture) अस्थावरद्रव्याणि *n. pl.*, गृहोपस्करादि *n.*, गृहोपकरणानि.—(Merchandise) भाण्डानि *n. pl.*, भाण्डकं, पण्यं, पण्यानि *n. pl.*, विट्पण्यं.

GOOSE, *s.* हंसः -सी, राजहंसः -सी, वरटः -टा -टी, वरला, चक्राङ्गः -ङ्गी, श्वेतपत्रः, श्वेतच्छदः, श्वेतगरुत् *m.*, सितपक्षः, शितिच्छदः, शितिपक्षः, जालपाद् *m.*, नीलाक्षः, मानसालयः, मानसौकाः *m.* (स्), मन्दगमना, धार्त्तराष्ट्रः, पुरुदंशकः, मल्लिकः, शकवः, सरःकाकः -की, कलहंसः -सी; 'ruddy goose,' चक्रः, चक्रवाकः, रथाङ्गः, कोकः, द्वन्द्वचरः -चारी; 'wild goose,' चक्राङ्गी; 'tame goose,' ग्राम्यहंसः.—(Fool) मूर्खः, निर्बुद्धिः *m.*

GOOSEBERRY, *s.* कण्टकितगुल्मोत्पन्नम् अम्लफलं.

GOOSEBERRY-FOOL, *s.* क्षीरेण सह क्वथितः पूर्व्वोक्तफलरसः.

GOR-BELLIED, *a.* महोदरः -रा -रं, स्थूलोदरः -रा -रं, लम्बोदरः -रा -रं, तुन्दी -न्दिनी -न्दि (न्), बृहत्कुक्षिः -क्षिः -क्षि, वृद्धनाभिः -भिः -भि.

GOR-BELLY, *s.* महोदरं, स्थूलोदरं, बृहत्तुन्दं, बृहत्कुक्षिः *m.*

GORE, *s.* (Blood) रक्तं, असृक् *n.* (ज्), लोहितं, रुधिरं, शोणितं, क्षतजं. —(Clotted blood) घनरक्तं, घनलोहितं, रक्तगुल्मः.—(Triangular piece of cloth sewed into a garment to widen it) वस्त्रपृथूकरणार्थं तन्निवेशितस् त्र्यस्राकारः पटखण्डः.

To GORE, *v. a.* (Pierce with a pointed instrument) शूलादिना त्वचं भिद् (c. 7. भिनत्ति, भेत्तुं) or निर्भिद् or छिद् (c. 7. छिनत्ति, छेत्तुं) or व्यध् (c. 4. विध्यति, व्यद्धुं).—(With the point of a horn) शृङ्गाग्रेण त्वचं निर्भिद् or व्यध्.

GORED, *p. p.* छिन्नत्वक् *m.f. n.*, क्षतचर्म्मा -र्म्मा -र्म्म (न्), विदारितत्वक् *m. f. n.*, उच्छिन्नितचर्म्मा &c., विद्धः -द्धा -द्धं.

GORGE, *s.* (Gullet) निगरणः, अन्नवाहिस्रोतस् *n.*, गलः, कण्ठः.—(Defile between mountains) सङ्कटं, सङ्कटपथः, दुर्गमार्गः, कन्दरः -री, पर्व्वतरन्ध्रं, रन्ध्रं, सञ्चरः, सञ्चारः, पर्व्वतमध्ये सञ्चारपथः.

To GORGE, *v. a.* (Swallow) गृ (c. 6. गिरति, गरितुं -रीतुं), निगृ, ग्रस् (c. 1. ग्रसते -सितुं).—(Fill with food) अन्नेन पृ (c. 10. पूरयति -यितुं), or परिपृ or अत्यन्तं तृप् (c. 10. तर्पयति -यितुं).

To GORGE, *v. n.* अन्नेन पृ in pass. (पूर्य्यते) or अत्यन्तं पृ.

GORGED, *p. p.* अन्नपूरितः -ता -तं, अतिपूरितः -ता -तं, अतितृप्तः -प्ता -प्तं.

GORGEOUS, *a.* तेजस्वी -स्विनी -स्वि (न्), तैजसः -सी -सं, महाप्रतापः -पा -पं, प्रतापी -पिनी -पि (न्), प्रतापवान् -वती -वत् (त्), अतिशोभनः -ना -नं, सुप्रभः -भा -भं, शुभः -भा -भं, उज्ज्वलः -ला -लं, स्पर्धी -र्धिनी -र्धि (न्).

GORGEOUSLY, *adv.* अतितेजसा, महाप्रतापेन, अतितैजसं, सुप्रभं.

GORGEOUSNESS, *s.* अतितेजस् *n.*, सुप्रतापः, अतिशोभा, सुप्रभा, उज्ज्वलता.

GORGET, *s.* ग्रीवात्राणं, गलत्राणं, कण्ठावरणं, अर्द्धचन्द्राकृति कवचं.

GORGING, *s.* निगरणं, ग्रसनं, अत्याहारः, अतिभोजनं, अन्नपूरणं.

GORGON, *s.* सर्पाकारकेशविशिष्टा भयङ्करमूर्त्तिः स्त्री.

GORMAND, *s.* अत्याहारी *m.* (न्), अतिभोजी *m.* (न्). *See* GOURMAND.

To GORMANDIZE, *v. n.* अत्यन्तं भुज् (c.7. भुंक्ते, भोक्तुं), अत्याहारं कृ, अतिभोजनं कृ.

GORMANDIZER, *s.* अत्याहारी *m.* (न्), बह्वाशी *m.* (न्), अतिभोजी *m.* (न्), अतिबुभुक्षुः *m.*, भक्षकः, घस्मरः, अस्मरः, कुक्षिम्भरिः *m.*, उदरम्भरिः *m.*, पात्रेसमितः.

GORMANDIZING, *s.* अत्याहारः, अतिभोजनं, घस्मरता, बह्वाशित्वं, गृध्नता.

GORY, *a.* रक्तविलिप्तः -प्ता -प्तं, रक्ताक्तः -क्ता -क्तं, असृग्लिप्तः -प्ता -प्तं, रक्तगुल्ममयः -यी -यं, रक्तमलिनः -ना -नं.

GOSHAWK, *s.* अतिगृध्नशीलः श्येनभेदः, श्येनकः.

GOSLING, *s.* हंसशावकः, वरटशावकः, हंसशिशुः *m.*

GOSPEL, *s.* सुसंवादः, मङ्गलसंवादः, मङ्गलसमाचारः, सुवार्त्ता, शुभवार्त्ता.

GOSPELER, *s.* ख्रीष्टसमाचाररचकः, सुसंवादलेखकः, सुसंवादप्रचारकः, ख्रीष्टीयधर्म्मप्रवक्ता *m.* (क्तृ).

To GOSPELIZE, *v. a.* सुसंवादं प्रचर् in caus. (-चारयति -यितुं).

GOSSAMER, *s.* ग्रीष्मसमये वायुप्रेरिता मर्कटवासतन्तवः *m. pl.*, वाततूलं.

GOSSIP, *s.* (Tattler) जल्पकः, जल्पाकः, उपजल्पी *m.* (न्), परार्थवादी *m.* (न्), परकार्य्यचर्च्चकः, वावदूकः, प्रलापी *m.* (न्), गायनः.—(Tattle) जल्पितं, जल्पः, प्रजल्पः, प्रलापः.—(Tippling companion) सहपायी *m.* (न्), पानमित्रं.

To GOSSIP, *v. n.* जल्प् (c. 1. जल्पति -ल्पितुं), प्रलप् (c. 1. -लपति -पितुं), संलप्, अनर्थककथां कृ, वृथाकथां कृ, कथोपकथनं कृ.

GOSSIPING, *s.* जल्पः -ल्पनं, जल्पितं, प्रजल्पः, संलापः, वाक्चापल्यं, आलस्यवचनं, गायनं, निरर्थककथा, वावदूकता, वाचालता.

GOT, GOTTEN, *p. p.* प्राप्तः -प्ता -प्तं, अवाप्तः -प्ता -प्तं, लब्धः -ब्धा -ब्धं, अधिगतः -ता -तं, आसादितः -ता -तं, आपन्नः -न्ना -न्नं, प्रपन्नः -न्ना -न्नं.

GOUGE, *s.* अर्द्धचन्द्राकारफलको व्रश्चनविशेषः, तक्षणी.

To GOUGE, *v. a.* (The eye) लोचनम् उत्पट् (c. 10. -पाटयति -यितुं).

GOURD, *s.* अलाबूः *f.*, अलाबुः *f.*, आलाबुः, लाबुः, तुम्बी -म्बिः *f.*, तुम्बः -म्बकः -कं, चिच्चिका, तुम्बरी, कुष्माण्डकः, कूष्माण्डकः, कर्कारुः *m.*, कर्कटः; 'bitter gourd,' तिक्तिका, कटुतुम्बी, इक्ष्वाकुः *f.*

GOURMAND, *s.* अत्याहारी *m.* (न्), बहुभक्षकः, बहुभोजी *m.* (न्), भक्षकः, कुक्षिम्भरिः *m.*, उदरम्भरिः *m.*, औदरिकः.

GOUT, *s.* वातः, वातरोगः, वातव्याधिः *m.*, वातगुल्मः, वातरक्तं, वातपुडा, वातशोणितं, पादशोथः, पादगण्डिरः, पादवल्मीकं.

GOUTINESS, *s.* वातुलता, वातूलत्वं, वातिकत्वं, सवातत्वं.

GOUTY, *a.* वातकी -किनी -कि (न्), वातरोगी -गिणी -गि (न्), वातुलः -ला -लं, वातूलः -ला -लं, वातग्रस्तः -स्ता -स्तं, वातिकः -की -कं, वातासहः -हा -हं.

To GOVERN, *v. a.* शास् (c. 2. शास्ति, शासितुं), अनुशास्, प्रशास्, समनुशास्, यम् (c. 1. यच्छति, यन्तुं), नियम्, संयम्, विनियम्, सन्नियम्, ईश् (c. 2. ईष्टे, ईशितुं), पाल् (c. 10. पालयति -यितुं), परिपाल्, विनी (c. 1. -नयति -नेतुं), प्रणी, वशीकृ, विधा (c. 3. -दधाति -धातुं), अध्यास् (c. 2. -आस्ते -आसितुं), गुप् (c. 1. गोपायति, c. 10. गोपयति -यितुं).—(Keep in subjection, restrain) वशीकृ, यम्, विनियम्, संयम्, निग्रह्, (c. 9. -गृह्णाति -ग्रहीतुं), विनिग्रह्, संहृ (c. 1. -हरति -हर्त्तुं), दम् (c. 10. दमयति -यितुं), यन्त्र् (c. 10. यन्त्रयति -यितुं), नियन्त्र्; 'to govern a country well,' राष्ट्रं सम्यक् पाल्; 'governing noun,' अन्वयी *m.* (न्).

To GOVERN, *v. n.* राज्यं कृ, राज्याधिकारं कृ, राज्यपालनं कृ, राज्यशासनं कृ, राजकार्य्यं कृ, राज्यव्यवहारं कृ, आधिपत्यं कृ.

GOVERNABLE, *a.* शास्यः -स्या -स्यं, शासनीयः -या -यं, वश्यः -श्या -श्यं, विधेयः -या -यं, प्रणेयः -या -यं, विनेयः -या -यं, विनीतः -ता -तं, आज्ञाधीनः -ना -नं.

GOVERNANCE, *s.* शासनं, शास्तिः *f.*, अनुशासनं, पालनं, प्रतिपालनं, आधिपत्यं, अधिकारः, नीतिः *f.*, विनयः, वशः, वशिता, संयमः, विनियमः, यमः.

GOVERNED, *p. p.* शासितः -ता -तं, अनुशासितः -ता -तं, प्रशासितः -ता -तं, पालितः -ता -तं, वशीकृतः -ता -तं, संयतः -ता -तं, विनियतः -ता -तं, नियमितः -ता -तं, निगृहीतः -ता -तं; 'governed by another,' पराधीनः -ना -नं, परतन्त्रः -न्त्रा -न्त्रं.

GOVERNESS, *a.* बालाध्यापिका, बालोपदेशिका, बालोपदेशिनी, शिक्षाकरी.

GOVERNMENT, *s.* (Administration of government) राज्यं, राज्याधिकारः, राज्यधुरा, राजधुरा, राज्यनीतिः *f.*, राज्यपालनं, राज्यव्यवहारः, नीतिः *f.*, वैशस्त्रं.—(Control, regulation) शासनं, शास्तिः *f.*, अनुशासनं, वशः -शं, यमः, संयमः, विनियमः, निग्रहः, दमः -मनं, यन्त्रणं.—(Authority) अधिकारः, अधीकारः, आधिपत्यं, प्रभुत्वं, ईशत्वं, ऐश्वर्य्यं.—(Empire) राज्यं, राजत्वं, आधिपत्यं.—(The king's ministers) राजधुर्वहाः *m. pl.*, राजमन्त्रिणः *m. pl.*, राजसचिवाः *m. pl.*; 'form of government,' राज्यरीतिः *f.*, राज्यविधिः *m.*; 'government affairs,' राज्यव्यवहारः, राजकार्य्यं; 'good government,' सम्यक् पालनं; 'bad government,' असम्यक् पालनं.

GOVERNOR, *s.* अधिपतिः *m.*, अधिष्ठाता *m.* (तृ), अधिकारी *m.* (न्), अध्यक्षः, अधिपः, शासिता *m.* (तृ), प्रशासिता *m.*, शास्ता *m.*, शासकः, अनुशासकः, अधिकृतः, ईशिता *m.* (तृ), ईश्वरः, ईशः, पालयिता *m.* (तृ), नियन्ता *m.* (न्तृ), राष्ट्रियः.

GOVERNORSHIP, *s.* आधिपत्यं, अधिष्ठातृत्वं, अध्यक्षता, अधिकारिता.

GOWN, *s.* शाटी, शाटकः, स्त्रीकटीवस्त्रं, कटिवस्त्रं, कटीपटः, पटवासः, चोटी, चलनकं.

GOWNED, *a.* सञ्चाटकः -का -कं, कटिवस्त्रवेष्टितः -ता -तं.

GOWNSMAN, *s.* पण्डितवेशधारी *m.* (न्), पण्डितवेशः.—(In an university) राजविद्यालये अन्तेवासिवेशधारी *m.* (न्).

GRAB, *s.* ग्रहः, ग्रहणं, सङ्ग्रहः -हणं, सङ्ग्राहः, धरणं, धृतिः *f.*

GRABBED, *p. p.* अकस्मात् सङ्गृहीतः -ता -तं or धृतः -ता -तं.

To GRABBLE, *v. n.* (Grope) परामृश् (c. 6.- मृशति -मर्ष्टुं).—(Lie prostrate on the belly) उदरेण भूमिं गम् (c. 1. गच्छति, गन्तुं), खिन्नदेहः -हा -हं भू, अधमूर्द्धशयः -या -यं भू.

GRACE, *s.* (Favor) प्रसादः, अनुग्रहः, दया, कृपा, अनुकम्पा, प्रसन्नता, अनुकूलता, अनुरोधः.—(Good-will, kindness) प्रीतिः *f.*, प्रियता, हितता, हितेच्छा.—(Beauty, elegance) शोभा, लावण्यं, विलासः, चारुता, सौन्दर्य्यं, विनीतता, लालित्यं, श्रीः *f.*—(Pardon) क्षमा, पापशोधनं, पापमार्जनं, निष्कृतिः *f.*—(Blessing before or after meat) भोजनात् पूर्व्वं परं वा धन्यवादः.—(Goddess of beauty) श्रीदेवता, श्रीः *f.*

To GRACE, *v. a.* शुभ् (c. 10. शोभयति -यितुं), उपशुभ्, अलङ्कृ, समलङ्कृ, भूष् (c. 10. भूषयति -यितुं), विभूष्, शोभां कृ or दा, मन् (c. 10. मानयति -यितुं).

GRACED, *p. p.* शोभितः -ता -तं, उपशोभितः -ता -तं, कृतशोभः -भा -भं.

GRACEFUL, *a.* विलासी -सिनी -सि (न्), चारुः -र्व्वी -रु, लावण्यवान् -वती -वत् (त्), सुन्दरः -रा -री -रं, सुरूपः -पी -पं, सुललितः -ता -तं, ललितः -ता -तं, विनीतः -ता -तं, लीलावान् -वती -वत् (त्), शुभगः -गा -गं, सुगः -गा -गं; 'graceful walk,' शुभगतिः *f.*, सुगतिः *f.*; 'graceful speech,' वाग्विलासः; 'having a graceful gait,' शुभगतिः -तिः -ति.

GRACEFULLY, *adv.* सविलासं, विलासेन, विलासतया, सलावण्यं, लावण्येन, सुन्दरं, सौन्दर्य्येण, सुललितं, विनीतं, चारु.

GRACEFULNESS, *s.* चारुता, सौन्दर्य्यं, लावण्यं, रूपलावण्यं, विलासः -सिता, लालित्यं, सुलालित्यं, विनीतता -त्वं, रूपवत्त्वं, शोभा, श्रीः *f.*, वामता, सुरूपत्वं.

GRACELESS, *a.* अमर्त्यदुष्टभावः -वा -वं, दुराचारः -रा -रं, मन्दचरित्रः -त्रा -त्रं, नष्टभावः -वा -वं, अतिदुष्टः -ष्टा -ष्टं, ईश्वरप्रसादबहिष्कृतः -ता -तं.

GRACELESSNESS, *s.* अमर्त्यदुष्टता, अतिदुष्टता, दुराचारता, नष्टता.

GRACIOUS, *a.* प्रसन्नः -न्ना -न्नं, सुप्रसन्नः -न्ना -न्नं, अनुग्राही -हिणी -हि (न्), अनुकूलः -ला -लं, आनुग्राहकः -की -कं, प्रसादितः -ता -तं, अनुकम्पी -म्पिनी -म्पि (न्), दयावान् -वती -वत् (त्), दयाशीलः -ला -लं, दयालुः -लुः -लु, कृपावान् &c., सानुकम्पः -म्पा -म्पं, हितः -ता -तं, हितबुद्धिः -द्धिः -द्धि, सानुक्रोशः -शा -शं, कृपालुः -लुः -लु, उपकारी -रिणी -रि (न्), उपकारकः -का -कं, भक्तवत्सलः -ला -लं; 'be thou gracious,' प्रसीद.

GRACIOUSLY, *adv.* प्रसन्नं, सुप्रसन्नं, प्रसादेन, सप्रसादं, अनुग्रहेण, सानुग्रहं, अनुकूलं, सानुकूल्यं, सानुकम्पं, कृपया, दयया, हितेच्छया.

GRACIOUSNESS, *s.* प्रसन्नता, सुप्रसन्नता, प्रसादः, अनुग्रहः, अनुकूलता, आनुकूल्यं, अनुकम्पा, दयालुत्वं, कृपालुत्वं -ता, हितता, हितबुद्धित्वं, सानुकम्पता.

GRADATION, *s.* क्रमः -मणं, अनुक्रमः -मणं, पर्य्यायः, आनुपूर्व्यं, आनुपूर्व्वी -र्व्वी-र्व्वकं, परम्परा, अन्वयः, समन्वयः, उत्तरोत्तरं, अल्पाल्पता, अनुयायित्वं; 'in regular gradation,' यथाक्रमं, क्रमशस्, अनुपूर्व्वशस्, क्रमे क्रमे, पर्य्यायेण.

GRADE, *s.* क्रमः, पदं, पदविः *f.* -वी, आस्पदं, अवस्था; 'highest grade,' परमपदं.

GRADIENT, *a.* (Moving by steps) क्रामन् -मन्ती -मत् (त्), क्रममाणः -णा -णं.—(Rising and descending) उन्नतानतः -ता -तं; 'gradients,' पातोत्पाताः *m. pl.*

GRADUAL, *a.* क्रमकः -का -कं, क्रमिकः -का -कं, अल्पाल्पः -ल्पा -ल्पं, उत्तरोत्तरः -रा -रं, आनुक्रमिकः -की -कं, आनुपदिकः -की -कं, अनुपूर्व्वः -र्व्वा -र्व्वं, आनुपूर्व्विकः -की -कं.

GRADUALLY, *adv.* क्रमशस्, क्रमतस्, क्रमेण, क्रमे क्रमे, पदे पदे, पदशस्, प्रतिपदं, अनुपदं, पदात्पदं, शनैः, शनैः शनैः.

To GRADUATE, *v. a.* राजविद्यालये पदं प्राप् in caus. (-आपयति -यितुं) or पदे नियुज् (c. 7. -युंक्ते -योक्तुं).—(Mark with degrees) आनुक्रमिकचिह्नैर् अङ्क् (c. 10. अङ्कयति -यितुं), अनुक्रमेण चिह्नैर् अङ्क्, क्रमकच्छेदैर् अङ्क्.

To GRADUATE, *v. n.* (Receive a degree at an university) राजविद्यालये पदं प्राप् (c. 5. -आप्नोति -आप्तुं).

GRADUATE, *a.* महाविद्यालये पदप्राप्तः or पदयुक्तः or पदवान् *m.* (त्).

GRADUATED, *p. p.* राजविद्यालये पदयुक्तः -क्ता -क्तं.—(Marked with degrees) आनुक्रमिकचिह्नैर् अङ्कितः -ता -तं, आनुक्रमिकच्छेदाङ्कितः -ता -तं.

GRADUATION, *s.* अनुक्रमः -मणं, क्रमः -मणं, पर्य्यायः, आनुपूर्व्यं.—(Marking with degrees) आनुक्रमिकचिह्नाङ्कनं, आनुक्रमिकच्छेदाङ्कनं.

GRAFT, *s.* वृक्षशाखानिवेशितो भिन्नवृक्षपल्लवः -वं or भिन्नवृक्षकिसलयः.

To GRAFT, *v. a.* एकवृक्षशाखायां भिन्नवृक्षपल्लवं निविश् (c. 10. -वेशयति -यितुं), एकवृक्षपल्लवं भिन्नवृक्षपल्लवेन संयुज् (c. 10. -योजयति -यितुं) or संलग्नीकृ.

GRAFTED, *p. p.* भिन्नवृक्षशाखानिवेशितः -ता -तं, भिन्नवृक्षविटपसंयुक्तः -क्ता -क्तं.

GRAFTING, *s.* एकवृक्षशाखायां भिन्नवृक्षपल्लवनिवेशनं.

GRAIN, *s.* (Seed of corn) धान्यं, धान्यादि *n.*—(Corn in general) शस्यं, सीत्यं, गारित्रः, स्तम्बकरिः *m.*, बीजरुहः, जीवसाधनं.—(Seed) बीजं -जकं.—(A particle) कणः -णिकः -का, लवः, लेशः, अणुः *m.*, रेणुः *m.*; 'a grain of rice,' तण्डुलकणः.—(Seed used as a weight) काकिणी.—(Vein of wood) काष्ठरेखा, काष्ठलेखा, काष्ठशिरा; 'against the grain,' प्रतिलोमः -मा -मं, प्रतीपः -पा -पं; 'with the grain,' अनुलोमः -मा -मं; 'grain freed from chaff,' धान्यास्थि; 'fried grain,' लाजा -जाः *m. pl.*, अक्षतं; 'wetted grain,' लाजः.

To GRAIN, *v. a.* काष्ठरेखानुकारेण चित्र् (c. 10. चित्रयति -यितुं) or चित्रीकृ.

GRAINED, *p. p.* or *a.* (Painted in imitation of the fibres of wood) काष्ठरेखासमवर्णेन चित्रितः -ता -तं or लिखितः -ता -तं, दारुरेखानुकृतवर्णः -र्णा -र्णं.

GRAINY, *a.* धान्यमयः -यी -यं, शस्यमयः -यी -यं, धान्यवान् -वती -वत् (त्).

GRAMINEOUS, *a.* तृणमयः -यी -यं, तृणसः -सा -सं, शाद्वलः -ला -लं.

GRAMINIVOROUS, *a.* तृणभक्षकः -का -कं, तृणखादकः -का -कं, तृणभोजी -जिनी -जि (न्), तृणभक्ष्यः -क्ष्या -क्ष्यं, घासादः -दा -दं, घासाहारी -रिणी -रि (न्).

GRAMMAR, *s.* व्याकरणं, व्याकृतिः *f.*, व्याकरणशास्त्रं, शब्दशास्त्रं, शास्त्रचक्षुस् *n.*, व्युत्पत्तिः *f.*, व्युत्पत्तिवादः, शब्दव्युत्पत्तिः *f.*, शब्दशुद्धिः *f.*

GRAMMAR-SCHOOL, *s.* व्याकरणशिक्षाशाला, व्याकरणपाठशाला.

GRAMMARIAN, *s.* वैयाकरणः, वैयाकरणीयः, व्याकरणशास्त्रज्ञः, शब्दशास्त्रज्ञः, व्याकरणज्ञः, व्याकरणाध्यापकः, शाब्दिकः, व्याकरणव्युत्पन्नः.

GRAMMATICAL, *a.* वैयाकरणः -णी -णं -णीयः -या -यं, शाब्दिकः -की -कं, व्याकरणसम्बन्धी -न्धिनी -न्धि (न्).—(According to grammar) व्याकरणानुसारी -रिणी -रि (न्), व्याकरणाविरुद्धः -द्धा -द्धं; 'grammatical accuracy,' शब्दशुद्धिः *f.*

GRAMMATICALLY, *adv.* व्याकरणानुसारेण, व्याकरणाविरोधेन, शब्दशास्त्रवत्.

GRANARY, *s.* कुशूलः, धान्यागारं, शस्यागारं, बीजागारं, धान्यकोष्ठः -ष्ठकं, कोष्ठकं, कण्डोलः -लकः, काण्डालः, पिटः, कुदरः, मरारः.

GRAND, *a.* (Great) महान् -हती -हत् (त्), बृहन् -हती -हत् (त्).—(Splendid) प्रतापी -पिनी -पि (न्), प्रतापवान् -वती -वत् (त्), सुप्रभः -भा -भं, तैजसः -सी -सं, तेजस्वी -स्विनी -स्वि (न्), उज्ज्वलः -ला -लं.—(Principal) प्रधान in comp., प्रमुखः -खा -खं, मुख्यः -ख्या -ख्यं, अग्रः -ग्रा -ग्रं, अग्र्यः -ग्र्या -ग्र्यं, अग्रीयः -या -यं, उत्तमः -मा -मं.—(Noble) उत्कृष्टः -ष्टा -ष्टं.

GRANDAM, *s.* मातामही, पितामही.—(Old woman) वृद्धा स्त्री, जरिणी.

GRANDCHILD, *s.* पुत्रसुतः -ता, पुत्रात्मजः -जा, पौत्रः -त्री, दौहित्रः -त्री.

GRANDDAUGHTER, *s.* पौत्री, नप्त्री, पुत्रसुता, पुत्रपुत्री, सुतात्मजा, पुत्रात्मजा.—(Daughter's daughter) दौहित्री, पुत्रिकासुता; 'great granddaughter,' प्रपौत्री, प्रतिनप्त्री.

GRANDEE, *s.* कुलीनजनः, कुलश्रेष्ठी *m.* (न्), राजन्यः, उच्चपदस्थः, उत्कृष्टपदस्थः, सत्कुलीनः, अभिजनवान् *m.* (त्).

GRANDEUR, *s.* (Greatness) महत्त्वं, महिमा *m.* (न्), बृहत्त्वं.—(Splendor, dignity) प्रतापः, विभूतिः *f.*, वैभवं, तेजस् *n.*, उज्ज्वलता, सुप्रभता, ओजस्विता, प्रभावः, ऐश्वर्य्यं, सम्पत्तिः *f.*—(Nobleness, elevation) माहात्म्यं, औदार्य्यं, उदारता, उत्कर्षः, उत्कृष्टता, श्रेष्ठत्वं.

GRANDEVITY, *s.* चिरजीवः -वा -वितं, दीर्घवयस्कत्वं, वृद्धता.

GRANDEVOUS, *a.* चिरजीवी -विनी -वि (न्), दीर्घजीवी &c., दीर्घायुः -युः -युः (स्).

GRANDFATHER, *s.* (Paternal) पितामहः, पितृपिता *m.* (तृ).—(Maternal) मातामहः, मातृपिता *m.* (तृ), आर्य्यकः; 'great grandfather,' प्रपितामहः, प्रमातामहः; 'great great grandfather,' वृद्धप्रपितामहः, 'great great grandmother,' वृद्धप्रमातामहः.

GRANDILOQUENCE, *s.* गर्व्वितवाक्यं, अतिशयोक्तिः *f.*, अत्युक्तिः *f.*, चित्रोक्तिः *f.*, दर्पवाक्यं, दर्पोन्मत्तवचनं.

GRANDILOQUENT, *a.* गर्व्वितवाक्यः -क्या -क्यं, उच्चवादी -दिनी -दि (न्).

GRANDINOUS, *a.* करकामयः -यी -यं, शिलावृष्टिमान् -मती -मत् (त्).

GRANDLY, *adv.* तेजसा, प्रतापेन, सप्रतापं, सुप्रभं, विभूत्या, वैभवेन, ऐश्वर्य्येण, उज्ज्वलं, उत्कर्षेण, उत्कृष्टं, श्रेष्ठं, प्रभावेण.

GRANDMOTHER, *s.* (Paternal) पितामही, पितृमाता *f.* (तृ), पितृप्रसूः *f.*—(Maternal) मातामही, मातृमाता *f.* (तृ); 'great grandmother,' प्रपितामही, प्रमातामही.

GRAND-NEPHEW, *s.* भ्रातृपौत्रः, भ्रातृनप्ता *m.* (तृ), स्वसृपौत्रः, स्वसृनप्ता *m.*

GRANDNESS, *s.* महत्त्वं, महिमा *m.* (न्), वैभवं, प्रतापः. *See* GRANDEUR.

GRAND-NEICE, *s.* भ्रातृपौत्री, भ्रातृनप्त्री, स्वसृनप्त्री, स्वसृपौत्री.

GRANDSIRE, *s.* पितामहः, मातामहः, आर्य्यकः, पितृपिता *m.* (तृ).

GRANDSON, *s.* (Son's son) पौत्रः, नप्ता *m.* (तृ), पुत्रसुतः, पुत्रपुत्रः, सुतात्मजः, पुत्रात्मजः.—(Daughter's son) दौहित्रः, पुत्रिकापुत्रः, पुत्रिकासुतः; 'great grandson,' प्रपौत्रः, प्रतिनप्ता *m.* (तृ); 'great great grandson,' परप्रपौत्रः, परप्रतिनप्ता *m.* (तृ), परम्परः.

GRANGE, *s.* क्षेत्रं, भूमिः *f.*, क्षेत्रभूमिः *f.*, क्षेत्रिकगृहादि *n.*

GRANITE, *s.* ग्राणित्संज्ञकः सुदृढप्रस्तरविशेषः.

GRANIVOROUS, *a.* शस्यभक्षकः -का -कं, शस्यादः -दा -दं, धान्यभुक् *m.f.n.*

GRANT, *s.* प्रदानं, सम्प्रदानं, दानं, दत्तं, प्रदा, वितरणं, विसर्ज्जनं, उत्सर्गः, उत्सर्ज्जनं, दायः, विहापितं; 'grant of maintenance,' वृत्तिदानं; 'a written grant,' लेख्यपत्रं, समर्पणपत्रं; 'a royal grant,' शासनं, शासनपत्रं, पट्टः; 'grant of property,' निबन्धः -न्धनं; 'grant of safe conduct,' अभयप्रदानं.

To GRANT, *v. a.* (Give, confer) दा (c. 3. ददाति, c. 1. यच्छति, दातुं), प्रदा, अनुदा, वितॄ (c. 1. -तरति -रितुं -रीतुं), प्रतिपद् (c. 10. -पादयति -यितुं), दिश् (c. 6. दिशति, देष्टुं), उपाकृ, उपाकृ.—(Admit) स्वीकृ, स्वीकारं कृ, अङ्गीकृ, ग्रह् (c. 9. गृह्णाति, ग्रहीतुं), अनुग्रह्.—(Allow) अनुज्ञा (c. 9. -जानाति -नीते -ज्ञातुं), अभ्यनुज्ञा, अनुमन् (c. 4. -मन्यते -मन्तुं).

GRANTED, *p. p.* प्रदत्तः -त्ता -त्तं, प्रत्तः -त्ता -त्तं, दत्तः -त्ता -त्तं, वितीर्णः -र्णा -र्णं, स्वीकृतः -ता -तं, अङ्गीकृतः -ता -तं, अनुज्ञातः -ता -तं, अनुमतः, -ता -तं; 'be it so,' भवतु, एवमस्तु, अस्त्वेवं.

GRANTEE, *s.* दानग्रहीता *m.* (तृ), आदाता *m.* (तृ), दानभोगी *m.* (न्).

GRANTOR, *s.* दाता *m.* (तृ), दानकर्त्ता *m.* (र्तृ), उत्सर्गकर्त्ता *m.*

GRANULAR, GRANULARY, *a.* बीजमयः -यी -यं, शस्यबीजाकारः -रा -रं.

To GRANULATE, *v. a.* बीजाकारं -रां -रं कृ, क्षुद्रपिण्डीकृ, शस्यबीजाकारेण घनीकृ or सान्द्रीकृ or संहतीकृ or खण्डीकृ.

To GRANULATE, *v. n.* बीजाकारपिण्डान् बन्ध् (c. 9. बध्नाति, बन्द्धुं), बीजाकारीभू, सूक्ष्मपिण्डीभू, शस्यबीजाकारेण घनीभू.

GRANULATED, *p. p.* शस्यबीजाकारः -रा -रं.—(Sugar) खण्डमोदकः, शर्करा.

GRANULATION, *s.* बीजाकारपिण्डबन्धनं, क्षुद्रपिण्डबन्धनं.—(Of flesh) उत्पादनं, अङ्कुरं.

GRANULE, *s.* कणिका, बीजकं, लवः, अणुः *m.*, गुटिका, क्षुद्रगुटिका.

GRAPE, *s.* द्राक्षा, मृद्वीका, मृद्वी, स्वाद्वी, स्वादुरसा, मधुरसा, गोस्तनी -ना, रसा, रसाला, चारुफला, कापिशायनी, साद्वी, हरहूरा; 'made of grapes,' मार्द्वीकः -की -कं; 'juice of grapes,' द्राक्षारसः.

GRAPERY, *s.* द्राक्षारोहणयोग्यं गृहं, द्राक्षावाटिका.

GRAPE-SHOT, *s.* युद्धनाडेः प्रक्षेपणीयो द्राक्षास्तवककल्पेण पिण्डीभूतो गुलिकासमूहः.

GRAPE-STONE, *s.* द्राक्षाबीजं -जकं, द्राक्षाफलस्य अष्टिः *f.* or अष्ठीला.

GRAPHIC, GRAPHICAL, *a.* सुचित्रितः -ता -तं, सुवर्णितः -ता -तं, सुनिर्द्दिष्टः -ष्टा -ष्टं, सुलिखितः -ता -तं, सुकल्पितः -ता -तं, सुनिर्देशकः -का -कं.

GRAPHICALLY, *adv.* सुवर्णनेन, सुनिर्देशेन, सुविवरणेन, सुचित्रितं, सुनिर्द्दिष्टं.

GRAPNEL, *s.* चतुर्दन्तयुक्तो लङ्गरविशेषः, चतुर्दन्तयुक्तम् आकर्षणयन्त्रं, आकर्षणी -र्षिणी.

To GRAPPLE, *v. a.* (Lay hold of, seize) सङ्ग्रह् (c. 9. -गृह्णाति -ग्रहीतुं), उपसङ्ग्रह्, धृ (c. 1. धरति, धर्त्तुं), आकृष् (c. 1. -कर्षति, c. 6. -कृषति -क्रष्टुं).

To GRAPPLE WITH, *v. n.* बाहूबाहवि or हस्ताहस्ति युध् (c. 4. युध्यते, योद्धुं), बाहुयुद्धे सङ्गम् (c. 1. -गच्छति -गन्तुं).

GRAPPLE, *s.* (Hold) सङ्ग्राहः, आग्रहः, धृतिः *f.*—(Close fight) बाहुयुद्धं.—(Hook) आकर्षणी -र्षिणी.

GRAPPLED, *p. p.* सङ्गृहीतः -ता -तं, धृतः -ता -तं, आकर्षितः -ता -तं.

GRAPPLING-IRONS, *s. pl.* लोहमयम् आकर्षणयन्त्रं, आकर्षणी -र्षिणी.

GRAPY, *a.* द्राक्षामयः -यी -यं, द्राक्षारसः -सा -सं, द्राक्षोपमः -मा -मं.

GRASHOPPER, *s.* *See* GRASSHOPPER.

To GRASP, *v. a.* and *n.* ग्रह् (c. 9. गृह्णाति, ग्रहीतुं), सङ्ग्रह्, परिग्रह्, अभिग्रह्, उपसङ्ग्रह्, मुष्टिना ग्रह् or सङ्ग्रह्, धृ (c. 1. धरति, धर्त्तुं), ग्रस् (c. 1. ग्रसते -सितुं), परामृश् (c. 6. -मृशति -म्रष्टुं), अवलम्ब् (c. 1. -लम्बते -म्बितुं), सङ्ग्राहं कृ.—(Grasp at, try to seize) ग्रह् in des. (जिघृक्षति -ते -क्षितुं), हृ (c. 1. हरति, हर्त्तुं), संहृ, अपहृ, हृ in des. (जिहीर्षति -ते -र्षितुं); 'one who has grasped his sword,' गृहीतखड्गः.

GRASP, *s.* मुष्टिसङ्ग्राहः, ग्रहः -हणं, मुष्टिग्रहणं, सङ्ग्रहः, सङ्ग्राहः, हस्तग्रहः, आग्रहः, धृतिः *f.*, हस्तधृतिः *f.*, धरणं, अवलम्बनं, करालम्बनं; 'tightness of grasp,' दृढमुष्टिता; 'within the grasp,' ग्राह्यः -ह्या

-ह्यं, ग्रहणीयः -या -यं.

GRASPED, *p. p.* गृहीतः -ता -तं, मुष्टिसङ्गृहीतः -ता -तं, मुष्टिसङ्ग्राहपीडितः -ता -तं, धृतः -ता -तं, ग्रस्तः -स्ता -स्तं, लुस्तः -स्ता -स्तं, कुञ्चितः -ता -तं.

GRASPER, *s.* ग्राहकः, मुष्टिसङ्ग्राहकृत्, सङ्ग्रहीता *m.* (तृ), हर्त्ता *m.* (र्त्तृ).

GRASPING, *s.* ग्रहणं, सङ्ग्राहः, सङ्ग्रहः, धृतिः *f.*, धरणं, हरणं.

GRASPING, *part.* or *a.* जिघृक्षुः -क्षुः -क्षु, जिहीर्षुः -र्षुः -र्षु, पुरोभागी -गिनी -गि (न्), ग्रहणशीलः -ला -लं.

GRASS, *s.* तृणं, घासः, यवसः, शष्पः, शादः, अर्ज्जुनं -नी, खटः, खेटं; 'sacrificial grass,' कुशः -शः, दर्भः, कुथः, पवित्रं; 'young grass,' बालतृणं, शष्पं; 'fragrant grass,' कतृणं, सौगन्धिकं, देवजग्धं -ग्धकं, पौरं, ध्यामं, रौहिषं; 'abounding with grass,' तृणपूर्णः -र्णा -र्णं, बहुतृणः -णा -णं, महाघासः -सा -सं.

To GRASS, *v. a.* तृणेन आछद् (c. 10. -छादयति -यितुं), सतृणं -णां -णं कृ.

GRASSHOPPER, *s.* शरभः, शलभः, पतङ्गः, चिशाङ्गः *m.*

GRASSINESS, *s.* सतृणत्वं, सघासत्वं, शाड्वलता, बहुघासत्वं.

GRASSLESS, *a.* तृणहीनः -ना -नं, अतृणः -णा -णं, तृणवर्ज्जितः -ता -तं.

GRASS-PLOT, *s.* तृणावृतो भूमिभागः or भूप्रदेशः, सतृणस्थलं.

GRASSY, *a.* तृणसः -सा -सं, तृणमयः -यी -यं, सतृणः -णा -णं, तृणावृतः -ता -तं, तृणाच्छादितः -ता -तं, घासमयः -यी -यं, बहुघासः -सा -सं, बहुतृणः -णा -णं, महाघासः -सा -सं, शाड्वलः -ला -लं, शाद्वलः -ला -लं.—(Green, verdant) हरितः -ता -तं, शादहरितः -ता -तं.

GRATE, *s.* (Fire-place) इध्मगुप्तिः *f.*, अङ्गारगुप्तिः *f.*, अङ्गारिणी, अग्निकुण्डं, चुल्ली, इध्मधारणी, अङ्गारधारणी, वितानं.—(Iron-lattice) लोहजालं, लोहजालकः, आयसलोहदण्डयुक्तम् अवरोधकं or व्यवधानं.

To GRATE, *v. a.* (Rub) घृष् (c. 1. घर्षति -र्षितुं), पिष् (c. 7. पिनष्टि, पेष्टुं), निष्पिष्, मृद् (c. 9. मृद्नाति, मर्द्दितुं), सङ्घट्ट् (c. 10. -घट्टयति -यितुं); 'to grate the teeth,' दन्तान् दन्तैर् घृष् or निष्पिष्.—(Fret, irritate) व्यथ् (c. 10. व्यथयति -यितुं), बाध् (c. 1. बाधते -धितुं), तप् (c. 10. तापयति -यितुं), मर्म्माणि तुद् (c. 6. तुदति, तोत्तुं) or स्पृश् (c. 6. स्पृशति, स्प्रष्टुं).—(Furnish with an iron lattice) लोहजालेन युज् (c. 10. योजयति -यितुं), आयसलोहदण्डैर् युज्.—(Reduce to powder by rubbing) घर्षणेन चूर्णीकृ or क्षोदीकृ.

To GRATE, *v. n.* परस्परघर्षणं कृ, परस्परघर्षणजं कर्कशशब्दं कृ.

GRATED, *p. p.* (Rubbed) घर्षितः -ता -तं, आघर्षितः -ता -तं, पिष्टः -ष्टा -ष्टं, चूर्णीकृतः -ता -तं, क्षोदितः -ता -तं.—(Furnished with a grating) लोहजालयुक्तः -क्ता -क्तं.

GRATEFUL, *a.* (Having a due sense of benefits) कृतज्ञः -ज्ञा -ज्ञं, कृतवेदी -दिनी -दि (न्), कृत्यवेदी -दिनी -दि (न्), उपकृतज्ञः -ज्ञा -ज्ञं, उपकारस्मर्त्ता -र्त्री -र्त्तृ (र्त्तृ), कृतोपकारस्य स्मर्त्ता &c., उपकृतस्मरन् -रन्ती -रत् (त्).—(Agreeable) रम्यः -म्या -म्यं, रमणीयः -या -यं, सुभगः -गा -गं, हृद्यः -द्या -द्यं.—(To the taste) सुखास्वादः -दा -दं, सुरसः -सा -सं.

GRATEFULLY, *adv.* कृतज्ञवत्, उपकारस्मरणात्.—(Agreeably) रम्यं, सुभगं.

GRATEFULNESS, *s.* (Gratitude) कृतज्ञता, उपकृतज्ञता, उपकारस्मरणं, कृतोपकारस्मरणं.—(Agreeableness) रम्यता, रमणीयता, सुभगता.

GRATER, *s.* घर्षणी, घर्षणयन्त्रं, निघर्षणकः, घर्षणालुः, आघट्टकः.

GRATIFICATION, *s.* (Act of pleasing, indulging) सन्तोषणं, तोषः -षणं, तुष्टिकरणं, तुष्टिदानं, तर्पणं, प्रीतिकरणं, आराधनं, अनुरोधः -धनं, अनुवर्त्तनं, प्रसादनं, आनमनं, आनतिः *f.*; 'gratification of an humour,' छन्दोनुवर्त्तनं, छन्दोनुवृत्तं; 'of a wish,' मनोरथसिद्धिः *f.*, इच्छासाधनं, इच्छादानं.—(Pleasure, satisfaction) तुष्टिः *f.*, सन्तोषः, परितोषः, तोषः, प्रीतिः *f.*, तृप्तिः *f.*, सुखं, सौख्यं, आनन्दः, आह्लादः, रतिः *f.*, अभिरुचिः *f.*

GRATIFIED, *p. p.* तुष्टः -ष्टा -ष्टं, सन्तोषितः -ता -तं, परितुष्टः -ष्टा -ष्टं, सन्तुष्टः -ष्टा -ष्टं, प्रीतः -ता -तं, तृप्तः -प्ता -प्तं, तर्पितः -ता -तं, आराधितः -ता -तं, प्रसादितः -ता -तं, आनन्दितः -ता -तं, प्रमोदितः -ता -तं, प्रतिग्राहितः -ता -तं; 'in mind,' प्रीतमनाः -नाः -नः (स्); 'having every wish gratified,' सर्व्वसिद्धार्थः -र्था -र्थं, पूर्णकामः -मा -मं, कृतार्थः -र्था -र्थं, चरितार्थः -र्था -र्थं.

To GRATIFY, *v. a.* (Please) सुख् (c. 10. सुखयति -यितुं), सन्तुष् (c. 10. -तोषयति -यितुं), परितुष्, नन्द् (c. 10. नन्दयति -यितुं), आनन्द्, प्री (c. 9. प्रीणाति, c. 10. प्रीणयति -यितुं), तृप् (c. 10. तर्पयति -यितुं), प्रमुद् (c. 10. -मोदयति -यितुं), रम् (c. 10. रमयति -यितुं), ह्लाद् (c. 10. ह्लादयति -यितुं), हृष् (c. 10. हर्षयति -यितुं), सभाज् (c. 10. सभाजयति -यितुं), रुच् (c. 1. रोचते -चितुं) with dat. of person, सुखं कृ, प्रीतिं दा.—(Indulge, humour, soothe) अनुवृत् (c. 1. -वर्त्तते -र्त्तितुं), आराध् (c. 10. -राधयति -यितुं), प्रसद् (c. 10. -सादयति -यितुं), अनुरञ्ज् (c. 10. -रञ्जयति -यितुं), अनुरुध् (c. 4. -रुध्यते -रोद्धुं), लल् (c. 10. लालयति -यितुं).

GRATIFYING, *part.* or *a.* परितोषकः -का -कं, सन्तोषकः -का -कं, तुष्टिकरः -रा -रं, तुष्टिदः -दा -दं, परितोषजनकः -का -कं, तुष्टिजननः -नी -नं, सुखकरः -रा -रं, सुखदः -दा -दं, प्रीतिकरः -री -रं, प्रीतिदः -दा -दं, आनन्ददः -दा -दं, नन्दकः -का -कं, तर्पी -र्पिणी -र्पि (न्), रमणः -णा -णं, आराधकः -का -कं, अनुरञ्जकः -का -कं.

GRATING, *part.* or *a.* कर्कशः -शा -शं, निष्ठुरः -रा -रं, खरः -रा -रं, अरुन्तुदः -दा -दं, कटुः -टुः -ट्वी -टु; 'to the ears,' कर्णकटुः -टुः -टु.

GRATING, *s.* परस्परघर्षणं, परस्परघर्षणजः कर्कशशब्दः.—(Partition of iron bars) लोहजालं, लोहजालकः, आयसलोहदण्डयुक्तम् अवरोधकं or व्यवधानं.

GRATINGLY, *adv.* कर्कशं, निष्ठुरं, अरुन्तुदं, कटु, कार्कश्येन.

GRATIS, *adv.* मूल्यं विना, मूल्यव्यतिरेकेण, निर्मूल्यं, धर्म्मार्थं.

GRATITUDE, *s.* कृतज्ञता, उपकारज्ञता, उपकृतज्ञता, उपकारस्मरणं, कृतोपकारस्मरणं, प्रत्युपकारकरणेच्छा.

GRATUITOUS, *a.* मूल्यं विना दत्तः -त्ता -त्तं, निर्मूल्यः -ल्या -ल्यं, प्रकामं or स्वेच्छातो दत्तः -त्ता -त्तं, धर्म्मार्थकः -का -कं; 'gratuitous labour,' विष्टिः *f.*—(Groundless) अहेतुकः -का -कं, निर्निमित्तः -त्ता -त्तं, निष्कारणः -णा -णं.

GRATUITOUSLY, *adv.* मूल्यं विना, मूल्यव्यतिरेकेण, धर्म्मार्थं, निर्मूल्यं.

GRATUITY, *s.* पारितोषिकं, शुल्कः -ल्कं, उपायनं, प्रदानं, दानं.

To GRATULATE, *v. a.* अभिनन्द् (c. 1. -नन्दति -न्दितुं), अभिवन्द् (c. 1. -वन्दते -न्दितुं), कल्याणवचनं वद् (c. 1. वदति -दितुं), कल्यं वद्, कुशलवादं कृ. *See* CONGRATULATE.

GRATULATION, *s.* अभिनन्दा -न्दनं, अभिवन्दनं, कल्याणवादः, कल्यवादः.

GRATULATORY, *a.* कल्यवादी -दिनी -दि (न्), अभिनन्दकः -का -कं.

GRAVE, *s.* (Place for the dead) समाधिः *m.*, अवटः, श्मशानं, मृतशरीरस्थानं, स्तुकं, सन्धिः *m.*, शववासः, शवगर्त्तः.

GRAVE, *a.* (Serious) गुरुः -र्व्वी -रु, अलघुः -घुः -घु, मन्दः -न्दा -न्दं, जडः -डा -डं.—(Momentous) गुर्व्वर्थः -र्था -र्थं, बह्वर्थः -र्था -र्थं, गम्भीरार्थः -र्था -र्थं.—(Deep in sound) गम्भीरः -रा -रं, गभीरः -रा -रं, मन्द्रः -न्द्रा -न्द्रं, मन्दः -न्दा -न्दं, मन्थरः -रा -रं, आमन्द्रः -न्द्रा -न्द्रं, धीरः -रा -रं, घनः -ना -नं.—(In grammar) प्लुतः -तं; 'the grave accent,' अनुदात्तः.

To GRAVE, *v. a.* and *n.* तक्ष् (c. 1. तक्षति -क्षितुं, c. 5. तक्ष्णोति), त्वक्ष् (c. 1.

त्वचति -चितुं), मुद्र (nom. मुद्रयति -यितुं), मुद्रीकृ.

GRAVE-CLOTHES, *s.* शववस्त्रं, शवाच्छादनं, मृतशरीरपरिधानं.

GRAVE-DIGGER, *s.* समाधिखनकः, अवटखनिता *m.* (तृ), शवगर्त्तखनकः.

GRAVE-STONE, *s.* चित्यं, चैत्यं, चैत्यः, चितापूडकं, मृतजनस्मरणप्रस्तरः, श्मशानप्रस्तरः, समाधिप्रस्तरः.

GRAVEL, *s.* शर्करा, वालुका, चूर्णखण्डः, चूर्णः -र्णं, शिलाखण्डः, पाषाणखण्डः, शिलाचूर्णं, पाषाणचूर्णं.—(The disease) शर्करा, अश्मरी, अश्मरीः -रं, मूत्रखण्डः, पांशुशर्करा.

To GRAVEL, *v. a.* सशर्करं -रां -रं कृ, शर्करान्वितं -तां -तं कृ, शर्करावृतं -तां -तं कृ, शर्करीकृ.—(Perplex) विमुह् (c. 10. -मोहयति -यितुं), शल्यं कृ.

GRAVELLY, *a.* शार्करीयः -यी -यं, शार्करः -री -रं, शार्करकः -का -कं, शर्करावान् -वती -वत् (त्), शर्करिकः -की -कं, शर्करिलः -ला -लं, सशर्करः -रा -रं.

GRAVEL-WALK, *s.* शर्करावृतः पथः, शर्करावान् उद्यानमार्गः.

GRAVELY, *adv.* गुरु, अलघु, गौरवेण, सगौरवं, गम्भीरं, भावगम्भीरं, गाम्भीर्य्येण, धीरं, मन्दं.

GRAVEN, *p. p.* तष्टः -ष्टा -ष्टं, तक्षितः -ता -तं, मुद्रितः -ता -तं.

GRAVENESS, *s.* गुरुता -त्वं, गौरवं, गरिमा *m.* (न्), गम्भीरता, गाम्भीर्य्यं, धीरत्वं -ता, अलघुता, अलाघवं, जडता, जाड्यं.

GRAVEOLENCE, *s.* दुर्गन्धः, कुत्सितगन्धः, दौर्गन्धि *n.*, पूतिगन्धः.

GRAVEOLENT, *a.* दुर्गन्धी -न्धिनी -न्धि (न्), कुत्सितगन्धः -न्धा -न्धं.

GRAVER, *s.* तक्षकः, तष्टा *m.* (ष्टृ), तक्षणकर्त्ता *m.* (र्त्तृ), मुद्राकरः.

GRAVID, *a.* गर्भिणी, गर्भवती, पूर्णगर्भा, गृहीतगर्भा, अन्तरापत्या.

GRAVING, *s.* तक्षणं, तक्षणकर्म्म *n.* (न्), तक्षणकार्य्यं.

To GRAVITATE, *v. n.* स्वभारगुरुत्वाद् भूमिं प्रति पत् (c. 1. पतति -तितुं) or पत् in des. (पिपतिषति -षितुं, पित्सति) or अधः पत्, or अधो गम् (c. 1. गच्छति, गन्तुं) or अन्यमूर्त्तिं प्रति आकृष् in pass. (-कृष्यते).

GRAVITATION, *s.* स्वभारगुरुत्वाद् भूमिं प्रति पतनशीलता or पातुकत्वं or पिपतिषा or अधःपातुकता or अन्यमूर्त्तिं प्रति आकर्षणशीलता.

GRAVITY, *s.* (Weight) गुरुत्वं, गौरवं, गरिमा *m.* (न्), भारः, भारगुरुता.—(Seriousness) गुरुता, गौरवं, गम्भीरता, गाम्भीर्य्यं, धीरत्वं -ता, अलघुता, अलाघवं, जडता, जाड्यं, मन्दता.—(Tendency of a body towards the earth, or towards another body) स्वभारगुरुत्वाद् भूमिं प्रति पातुकत्वं or अन्यमूर्त्तिं प्रति आकर्षणशीलता.—(Specific gravity) भारमानं.

GRAVY, *s.* मांसयूषं, मांसजूषं, मांसव्यञ्जनं, व्यञ्जनं, उपस्करः, तेमनं, लालसीकं, प्रहितं, मिष्टान्नं, प्रदिग्धः.

GRAY, *a.* धूसरः -री -रं, धूम्रः -री -रं, पांशुवर्णः -र्णा -र्णं, भस्मवर्णः -र्णा -र्णं, ईषत्पाण्डुः -ण्डुः -ण्डु, ईषद्धवलः -ला -लं, आशुक्लः -क्ला -क्लं, शुक्लकृष्णः -ष्णा -ष्णं.—(As the hair) पलितः -ता -तं, धवलः -ला -लं, पक्वः -क्वा -क्वं; 'gray hair,' पलितं.—(Old) जीर्णः -र्णा -र्णं, वृद्धः -द्धा -द्धं, पक्वः -क्वा -क्वं.

GRAY, *s.* (The colour) धूसरः, धूम्रः, धूसरवर्णः, पांशुवर्णः.

GRAY-BEARD, *s.* शुक्लश्मश्रुः *m.*, धवलश्मश्रुः *m.*, जीर्णकूर्चः.

GRAY-EYED, *a.* पाण्डुनयनः -ना -नं, धूसरनेत्रः -त्रा -त्रं.

GRAY-HAIRED, *a.* पलितः -ता -तं, पलिक्नी *f.*, धवलकेशः -शी -शं, शुक्लकेशः -शी -शं, पक्वकेशः -शी -शं.

GRAY-HEADED, *a.* पलितशिराः -राः -रः (स्), पलितमस्तकः -का -कं.

GRAY-HOUND, *s.* *See* GREY-HOUND.

GRAYISH, *a.* ईषद्धूसरः -रा -रं, आधूसरः -रा -रं, ईषत्पांशुवर्णः -र्णा -र्णं.

GRAYLING, *s.* स्वच्छनदीजो मत्स्यप्रभेदः.

GRAYNESS, *s.* धूसरत्वं, धूसरवर्णत्वं, पांशुवर्णत्वं.—(Of the hair) पलितं, केशधावल्यं, केशशुक्लता, केशपक्वता.—(Oldness) वृद्धत्वं, जीर्णता, पक्वता.

To GRAZE, *v. a.* (Touch lightly, rub) घृष् (c. 1. घर्षति -र्षितुं), लघु तड् (c. 10. ताडयति -यितुं), लघुगत्या अतिक्रम्य घृष्.—(Feed cattle with grass) चर् in caus. (चारयति -यितुं), तृणम् अश् in caus. (आशयति -यितुं) or भुज् in caus. (भोजयति -यितुं) or खाद् in caus. (खादयति -यितुं), तृणं दा.

To GRAZE, *v. n.* (Feed on grass) चर् (c. 1. चरति -रितुं), तृण् (c. 8. तर्णोति, तृणोति, तर्णितुं), तृणं खाद् (c. 1. खादति -दितुं) or अश् (c. 9. अश्नाति, अशितुं) or भक्ष् (c. 10. भक्षयति -यितुं).

GRAZED, *p. p.* (Rubbed) घृष्टः -ष्टा -ष्टं, घर्षितः -ता -तं, लघु ताडितः -ता -तं.—(Eaten by cattle) गोचरितः -ता -तं, गोभक्षितः -ता -तं, आशितङ्गवीनः -ना -नं, अशितङ्गवीनः -ना -नं.

GRAZER, *s.* तृणखादकः, तृणभक्षकः, तृणाशी *m.* (न्), चरिता *m.* (तृ).

GRAZIER, *s.* गोचारकः, गवादिचारकः, गोपालकः, पशुपोषकः.

GRAZING, *s.* गोचरः -रणं, गोप्रचारः, प्रचारः, तृणखादनं.

GREASE, *s.* वसा, घृतं, मेदस् *n.*, स्नेहः, मांसस्नेहः, मांससारः, वपा, तैलं, तिलस्नेहः, अभ्यञ्जनं.

To GREASE, *v. a.* वसया or घृतेन or स्नेहेन लिप् (c. 6. लिम्पति, लेप्तुं) or अञ्ज् (c. 7. अनक्ति, अंक्तुं, c. 10. अञ्जयति -यितुं) or दिह् (c. 2. देग्धि -ग्धुं), घृताक्तं -क्तां -क्तं कृ, स्निग्धीकृ, स्नेहाक्तीकृ.

GREASED, *p. p.* वसालिप्तः -प्ता -प्तं, घृताभ्यक्तः -क्ता -क्तं, स्नेहाक्तः -क्ता -क्तं, वसाभ्यक्तः -क्ता -क्तं, घृतोक्षितः -ता -तं, अभ्यक्तः -क्ता -क्तं.

GREASILY, *adv.* पिच्छिलं, स्निग्धं, वसया, सस्नेहं, सघृतं, घृतेन.

GREASINESS, *s.* पिच्छिलता -त्वं, स्निग्धता, स्नैग्ध्यं, घृताक्तत्वं, घृतवत्त्वं, स्नेहवत्त्वं, सस्नेहत्वं, मेदस्विता, वसालिप्तता.

GREASY, *a.* वसामयः -यी -यं, घृतवान् -वती -वत् (त्), घृताक्तः -क्ता -क्तं, वसाभ्यक्तः -क्ता -क्तं, पिच्छिलः -ला -लं, स्निग्धः -ग्धा -ग्धं, स्नेहवान् -वती -वत् (त्), सस्नेहः -हा -हं, स्नेही -हिनी -हि (न्), स्नेहाक्तः -क्ता -क्तं, मेदस्वी -स्विनी -स्वि (न्), प्रमेदितः -ता -तं, वसायुक्तः -क्ता -क्तं, सतैलः -ला -लं.

GREAT, *a.* (Large) महान् -हती -हत् (त्), बृहन् -हती -हत् (त्), विशालः -ला -लं, विपुलः -ला -लं, पृथुः -थुः -थ्वी -थु, पृथुलः -ला -लं, उरुः -रुः -रु, स्थूलः -ला -लं, विकटः -टा -टं, करालः -ला -लं, विशङ्कटः -टा -टी -टं, वङ्कुः -ङ्कुः -ङ्कु, अक्षितः -ता -तं.—(Great in number, a great many) बहुः -हुः -ह्वी -हु, बहुलः -ला -लं, बहुसंख्यकः -का -कं, भूरिः -रिः -रि, प्रचुरः -रा -रं.—(Extensive) विस्तीर्णः -र्णा -र्णं, पृथुपरिमाणः -णा -णं.—(Noble, eminent) महात्मा -त्मा -त्म (न्), विश्रुतः -ता -तं, महायशस्कः -स्का -स्कं, प्रसिद्धः -द्धा -द्धं, उत्कृष्टः -ष्टा -ष्टं, श्रेष्ठः -ष्ठा -ष्ठं, महाभागः -गा -गं, प्रतिष्ठः -ष्ठा -ष्ठं.—(Chief, principal) प्रधान in comp., मुख्यः -ख्या -ख्यं, अग्र्यः -ग्र्या -ग्र्यं, परमः -मा -मं.—(Important) गुरुः -र्व्वी -रु, परमः -मा -मं, अलघुः -घुः -घु.—(Expressing a great degree of any thing) अति or सु or महा prefixed, अत्यन्तः -न्ता -न्तं, गाढः -ढा -ढं, अतिमात्रः -त्रा -त्रं, अधिकः -का -कं, नितान्तः -न्ता -न्तं, एकान्तः -न्ता -न्तं, भृशः -शा -शं, अतिरिक्तः -क्ता -क्तं, परः -रा -रं; 'great fear,' महाभयं, अतिभयं; 'great vigour,' सुवीर्य्यं; 'great heat,' अतिदाहः, सुदाहः, गुरुतापः; 'great rain,' भूरिवृष्टिः *f.*; 'to a great distance,' सुदूरं -रे -रतस्, अतिदूरं -रे; 'to a great degree,' अत्यन्तं, अत्यर्थं, अतिमात्रं, भृशं, अतिशयं -येन, निर्भरं, गाढं, बहु; 'great grandson,' प्रपौत्रः; 'great grandfather,' प्रपितामहः; 'a great many people' बहुजनाः *m. pl.*

GREAT, *s.* (The whole) साकल्यं, समुदायः, समासः, समस्तिः *f.*, सामग्र्यं.—(Great people) कुलीनजनाः *m. pl.*, सेव्यजनाः *m. pl.*, उत्कृष्टपदस्थाः *m. pl.*, महाजनाः *m. pl.*; 'fit for the great,' माहाजनिकः -की -कं.

GREAT-COAT, *s.* उत्तरीयं, उत्तरीयवस्त्रं, प्रावारः -रकः, निचोलः -ली.

GREAT-HEARTED, GREAT-MINDED, *a.* महात्मा -त्मा -त्म (न्), महामनाः -नाः -नः (स्), उदारचेताः -ताः -तः (स्), महासत्त्वः -त्त्वा -त्त्वं, महेच्छः -च्छा -च्छं.

GREATER, *a.* महत्तरः -रा -रं, विशालतरः -रा -रं, बृहत्तरः -रा -रं, गुरुतरः -रा -रं, गरीयान् -यसी -यः (स्), उत्तरः -रा -रं.—(Greater number) बहुतरः -रा -रं, भूयान् -यसी -यः (स्), भूयिष्ठः -ष्ठा -ष्ठं, अधिकः -का -कं, अधिकतरः -रा -रं, परः -रा -रं, परतरः -रा -रं, अपरः -रा -रं; 'greater and greater,' अधिकाधिकं, उत्तरोत्तरं.

GREATEST, *a.* महत्तमः -मा -मं, बृहत्तमः -मा -मं, सुमहान् -हती -हत् (त्). गुरुतमः -मा -मं, गरिष्ठः -ष्ठा -ष्ठं, अधिकतमः -मा -मं; 'in the greatest degree,' सुभृशं, सुमहत्, अतिमहत्, सुतरां, अतितरां.

GREATLY, *adv.* (In a great degree) सु or अति or अतिशय prefixed, भृशं, सुभृशं, अत्यन्तं, निर्भरं, अतिशयं -येन, अतिमात्रं, अत्यर्थं, भूरि, गाढं, नितान्तं, सुतरां, अतितरां, अधिकं, अतीव, परं, बलवत्; 'greatly grieved,' सुदुःखितः -ता -तं.—(Nobly) माहात्म्येन, उदारवत्.

GREATNESS, *s.* (Largeness) महत्त्वं, महिमा *m.* (न्), बृहत्त्वं, विशालता, विपुलता, पृथुता -त्वं, प्रथिमा *m.* (न्), पार्थवं, स्थूलता, स्थौल्यं, उरुता -त्वं, विकटता, वैकट्यं, म्रदिमा *m.* (न्), परिम्रदिमा *m.*—(Extent) विस्तीर्णता, सुविस्तीर्णता.—(Bulk) परिमाणं.—(Eminence) उत्कर्षः, उत्कृष्टता, प्रसिद्धता, श्रेष्ठत्वं, यशस्विता, विभूतिः *f.*, आधिक्यं.—(Grandeur) विभूतिः *f.*, वैभवं, प्रभावः, ऐश्वर्यं.—(Greatness of mind) माहात्म्यं, उदारता, औदार्यं.—(Of rank) कुलीनता, कुलोत्कर्षः, अभिजातता, सेव्यता.

GREAVES, *s. pl.* जङ्घात्राणं, जंघत्रं, जंघत्राणं, जङ्घाकवचं, जङ्घारक्षणी, ऊरुत्राणं, ऊरुवर्म्म *n.* (न्).

GRECIAN, *a.* ग्रीकदेशीयः -या -यं, ग्रीकदेशजः -जा -जं, यावनः -नी -नं, यवनीयः -या -यं, यवनदेशीयः -या -यं.

GRECIAN, *s.* ग्रीकदेशवासी *m.* (न्), यवनः, यवनदेशजः.

GRECISM, *s.* ग्रीकभाषानुसारिणी वाग्वृत्तिः, ग्रीकभाषासम्प्रदायः.

GREECE, *s.* ग्रीकदेशः, यवनः, यवनदेशः.

GREEDILY, *adv.* अतिलोभेन -भात्, अतिलौल्यात्, लुब्धजनवत्, गृध्रवत्, अतिशयलिप्सया, अतिशयजिघृक्षया, लोभावेशात्, अत्यभिलाषेण, अतीच्छया, अतिस्पृहातस्.

GREEDINESS, *s.* लुब्धता, लोभवत्त्वं, लोभः, अतिभोजनं, अत्याहारः, गृध्नता, गृधुता, अतिबुभुक्षा, अधिकभोजनं, घस्मरता, लोलता, लौल्यं, अस्मरता, अतृप्तिः *f.*, अपरितोषः, अत्याकांक्षा, अतिलिप्सा, लिप्सातिशयः, उदरभरणं, जिघृक्षा, गर्द्धः, भक्षकत्वं, अत्यभिलाषः, अतिस्पृहा.

GREEDY, *a.* (Voracious) लुब्धः -ब्धा -ब्धं, आहारलुब्धः -ब्धा -ब्धं, लोभी -भिनी -भि (न्), भक्षकः -का -कं, बहुभक्षकः -का -कं, बह्वाशी -शिनी -शि (न्), बहुभुक् *m. f. n.*, घस्मरः -रा -रं, अस्मरः -रा -रं, गृध्नः -ध्ना -ध्नं, गृध्नुः -ध्नुः -ध्नु, गर्धी -र्धिनी -र्धि (न्), गर्धनः -ना -नं, जिघृक्षुः -क्षुः -क्षु, बुभुक्षुः -क्षुः -क्षु, अतिभोजी -जिनी -जि (न्), अत्याहारी -रिणी -रि (न्), अपरिमिताहारी &c., कुक्षिम्भरिः -रिः -रि, उदरम्भरिः -रिः -रि, आत्मम्भरिः -रिः -रि, औदरिकः -की -कं, स्वोदरपूरकः -का -कं, उदरपिशाचः -ची -चं, लोलुभः -भा -भं, लोलः -ला -लं, लोलुपः -पा -पं, लोभाविष्टः -ष्टा -ष्टं.—(Eager after) अत्यभिलाषी -षिणी -षि (न्), अभिलाषकः -का -कं, अतीच्छः -च्छा -च्छं, तृष्णकः -का -कं, अत्याकांक्षी -क्षिणी -क्षि (न्), मत्सरः -रा -रं; 'to be greedy,' गृध् (c. 4. गृध्यति, गर्धितुं), लुभ् (c. 4. लुभ्यति, लोब्धुं).

GREEK, *a.* ग्रीकदेशीयः -या -यं, यवनदेशीयः -या -यं.

GREEK, *s.* ग्रीकदेशजः, यवनदेशवासी *m.* (न्), यवनः.—(Language of Greece) ग्रीकभाषा.

GREEN, *a.* हरितः -ता -रिणी -तं, हरित् *m. f. n.*, हरितवर्णः -र्णा -र्णं, हरिद्वर्णः -र्णा -र्णं, हरिः -रिः -रि, पलाशः -शी -शं, पालाशः -शी -शं, श्यामः -मा -मं, भरितः -ता -तं, तालकाभः -भा -भं, श्यामवर्णः -र्णा -र्णं; 'green wood,' आर्द्रकाष्ठं; 'to make green,' हरितीकृ; 'to become green,' हरित (nom. हरितायते).

GREEN, *s.* (The colour) हरित् *m.*, हरितः, हरिः *m.*, पालाशः, तालकाभः.—(Grassy plat) हरिततृणावृतो भूमिभागः, हरितस्थानं, हरितस्थलं -स्थानं.

GREENED, *p. p.* हरितीकृतः -ता -तं, हरितीभूतः -ता -तं.

GREEN-FINCH, *s.* हरितपक्षयुक्तः पक्षिभेदः.

GREENGAGE, *s.* हरितवर्णः फलविशेषः.

GREEN-GROCER, *s.* शाकफलादिविक्रेता *m.* (तृ), शाकादिविक्रयी *m.* (न्).

GREENHORN, *s.* अविपक्वबुद्धिः *m.*, अपक्वधीः *m.*, अकोविदः.

GREEN-HOUSE, *s.* बालवृक्षादिरक्षणार्थं काचपटलं गृहं.

GREENISH, *a.* ईषद्धरितः -ता -तं, ईषत्पलाशः -शी -शं, आश्यामः -मा -मं.

GREEN-LEAVED, *a.* हरितच्छदः -दा -दं, हरित्पर्णः -र्णा -र्णं, हरितपत्रः -त्रा -त्रं.

GREENNESS, *s.* हरितत्वं, हरित्त्वं, पलाशता, पालाशता, श्यामता -त्वं.—(Immaturity) अपक्वता, अविपक्वता; 'of mind,' अपक्वबुद्धित्वं.

GREEN-ROOM, *s.* शाणी, नेपथ्यं, नेपथ्यशाला.

GREENS, *s. pl.* शाकादि *n.*, हरितकं, खादनीयशाकाः *m. pl.*

GREEN-SICKNESS, *s.* स्त्रीरोगविशेषो यस्मिन् मुखं श्यामवर्णं भवति देहस्य चावसादो जायते.

GREEN-SWARD, *s.* घासावृता भूमिः, हरितभूमिः, सतृणस्थलं.

To GREET, *v. a.* अभिनन्द् (c. 1. -नन्दति -न्दितुं), अभिवन्द् (c. 1. -वन्दते -न्दितुं), वन्द्, अभिवद् (c. 10. -वादयते -ति -यितुं), कुशलवाक्यैर् अभिवद् or अभिभाष् (c. 1. -भाषते -षितुं), अर्च् (c. 1. अर्चति -र्चितुं, c. 10. अर्चयति -यितुं), अभ्यर्च्, नमस्कृ, नमस्कारं कृ, सत्कृ, कुशलवादं कृ, प्रणम् (c. 1. -णमति -णन्तुं), प्रणतिं कृ; 'to greet in return,' प्रत्यभिवद्, प्रत्यर्च्.

GREETED, *p. p.* अभिनन्दितः -ता -तं, अभिवादितः -ता -तं, कुशलवाक्यैः सम्भाषितः -ता -तं or अभिभाषितः -ता -तं, नमस्कृतः -ता -तं, सत्कृतः -ता -तं.

GREETER, *s.* अभिवादयिता *m.* (तृ), अभिवादकः, अभिनन्दकः.

GREETING, *s.* अभिनन्दा -न्दनं, अभिवादः -दनं, वन्दनं, अभिवन्दनं, कुशलवाक्यैः सम्भाषणं or अभिभाषणं, कुशलप्रश्नः, सत्कारः, सत्कृतिः *f.*, नमस्कारः, नमस्क्रिया, कौशलं -ली, कुशलवादः; 'greeting in return,' प्रत्यभिवादः -दनं.

GREGARIOUS, *a.* यूथचारी -रिणी -रि (न्), अनेकचरः -रा -रं, सङ्घचारी &c.

GREGARIOUSLY, *adv.* यूथशस्, सङ्घशस्, अनेकशस्, गणशस्.

GREGARIOUSNESS, *s.* यूथचारित्वं, सङ्घचारित्वं, अनेकचारित्वं.

GRENADE, *s.* युद्धे हस्तप्रक्षेपणीया आग्नेयचूर्णगर्भा लोहगुली या अग्निबलेन शतखण्डशो विदीर्णा भूत्वा रिपुनाशं करोति.

GRENADIER, *s.* दीर्घशिरस्त्रभृत् पूर्वोक्ताग्नेयास्त्रपाणिः सैन्यविशेषः.

GREY, *a.* *See* GRAY.

GREYHOUND, *s.* दृष्टिगोचरशशकानुसरणे शिक्षितः सुतनुशरीरो मृगयाकुक्कुरः.

GRICE, *s.* शूकरशावकः, शूकरशिशुः *m.*, वराहशावकः.

To GRIDE, *v. a.* कर्कशशब्दपूर्वं छिद् (c. 7. छिनत्ति, छेत्तुं).

GRIDELIN, *a.* शुक्लरक्तः -क्ता -क्तं, धवलरक्तः -क्ता -क्तं.

GRIDIRON, *s.* विरलाधोभागो भर्ज्जनयन्त्रविशेषः, ऋजरीषं, भ्राष्ट्रः -ष्ट्रं, भृज्जनं, ऋजीषं.

GRIEF, *s.* शोकः, खेदः, दुःखं, सन्तापः, क्लेशः, शुक् *f.* (च्), मन्युः *m.*, व्यथा, विषादः, पीडा, मनोदुःखं, मनस्तापः, मनःपीडा, मनोव्यथा, निर्वेदः, आधिः *m.*, उद्वेगः, परितापः, अनिर्वृतिः *f.*, कृच्छ्रं, मनःकृच्छ्रं, मनोवेदना, आर्त्तिः *f.*; 'grief for the loss of any one,' उत्कण्ठा, औत्कण्ठ्यं, उद्वेगः, उत्सुकता, उत्कः.

GRIEVANCE, *s.* कष्टं, क्लिष्टिः *f.*, क्लेशः, दुःखं, पीडा, बाधा, आबाधा, बाधकं, क्लेशकं, आर्त्तिः *f.*, द्रोहः, कष्टकरं किञ्चित्; 'infantine grievance,' शिशुक्रन्दः.

To GRIEVE, *v. a.* दुःख् (c. 10. दुःखयति -यितुं), शुच् (c. 10. शोचयति -यितुं), पीड् (c. 10. पीडयति -यितुं), आपीड्, उपपीड्, अभिपीड्, परिपीड्, व्यथ् (c. 10. व्यथयति -यितुं), क्लिश् (c. 9. क्लिश्नाति, क्लेशितुं, क्लेष्टुं), संक्लिश्, खिद् (c. 10. खेदयति -यितुं), तप् (c. 10. तापयति -यितुं), परितप्, सन्तप्, अनुतप्, अभितप्, उपतप्, उद्विज् (c. 10. -वेजयति -यितुं), आयस् (c. 10. -यासयति -यितुं), दु (c. 5. दुनोति, दोतुं), विदु, शोकं दा or जन् (c. 10. जनयति -यितुं), क्लेशं कृ, व्यथां कृ, मनोदुःखं कृ.

To GRIEVE, *v. n.* शुच् (c 1. शोचति -चितुं), अनुशुच्, परिशुच्, अनुप्रशुच्, शोकार्त्तीभू, खिद् (c. 4. खिद्यते, खेत्तुं), परिखिद्, दुःख (nom. दुःखायते or दुःखीयते), तप् in pass. (तप्यते), परितप्, सन्तप्, अनुतप्, अभितप्, उपतप्, उद्विज् (c. 6. -विजते -जितुं), व्यथ् (c. 1. व्यथते -थितुं), प्रव्यथ्, सम्प्रव्यथ्, क्लिश् (c. 4. क्लिश्यते -ति, क्लेशितुं), परिक्लिश्, संक्लिश्, दु (c. 5. दुनोति, c. 4. दूयते, दोतुं), विदु, दुर्मनस् (nom. दुर्मनायते), उन्मनस्, कृच्छ्र (nom. कृच्छ्रायते), मन्तु (nom. मन्तूयते), शोचनं कृ; 'to grieve for,' अनुशुच्.

GRIEVED, *p. p.* दुःखितः -ता -तं, दुःखी -खिनी -खि (न्), दुःखार्त्तः -र्त्ता -र्त्तं, शोचितः -ता -तं, शोकार्त्तः -र्त्ता -र्त्तं, शोकातुरः -रा -रं, पीडितः -ता -तं, पीड्यमानः -ना -नं, सन्तप्तः -प्ता -प्तं, सन्तापितः -ता -तं, अभिसन्तप्तः -प्ता -प्तं, तापितः -ता -तं, खेदितः -ता -तं, क्लेशितः -ता -तं, क्लिष्टः -ष्टा -ष्टं, क्लिश्यमानः -ना -नं, व्यथितः -ता -तं, उद्वेजितः -ता -तं, उद्विग्नः -ग्ना -ग्नं, दूनः -ना -नं, विदूनः -ना -नं, बाधितः -ता -तं, अनुभूतशोकः -का -कं, आर्त्तः -र्त्ता -र्त्तं or आतुरः -रा -रं in comp.

GRIEVING, *part.* शोचमानः -ना -नं, शोचनः -ना -नं, खिद्यमानः -ना -नं, क्लिश्यमानः -ना -नं, परितप्यमानः -ना -नं, विदूयमानः -ना -नं.

GRIEVINGLY, *adv.* सशोकं, सखेदं, सदुःखं, सक्लेशं, सोद्वेगं, शोकेन, उद्वेगेन.

GRIEVOUS, *a.* दुःखकरः -री -रं, दुःखमयः -यी -यं, दुःखी -खिनी -खि (न्), शोकजनकः -का -कं, क्लेशकः -का -कं, क्लेशी -शिनी -शि (न्), क्लेशदः -दा -दं, उग्रः -ग्रा -ग्रं, पीडाकरः -रा -रं, व्यथकः -का -कं, व्यथाकरः -री -रं, कष्टकरः -री -रं -कारकः -का -कं, शोचनीयः -या -यं, शोच्यः -च्या -च्यं, सशोकः -का -कं, उपतापनः -ना -नं, उद्वेजकः -का -कं, सवेदनः -ना -नं, बाधकः -का -कं, गुरुः -र्वी -रु, आत्ययिकः -की -कं, दुर् दुश्, दुष्, दुस् or दुः in comp.

GRIEVOUSLY, *adv.* उग्रं, शोचनीयं, सशोकं, यथा शोकः or क्लेशो जायते तथा.

GRIEVOUSNESS, *s.* उग्रत्वं -ता, शोच्यता, शोचनीयता, सशोकत्वं, क्लेशः, क्लिष्टता, दुःखं, दुःखिता, घोरता, कष्टं.

GRIFFIN, GRIFFON, *s.* कविकल्पित उत्क्रोशोर्द्धकायः सिंहाधःकायो जन्तुविशेषः.

GRIFFIN-LIKE, *a.* पूर्व्वोक्तजन्तुसरूपः -पी -पं or -समभावः -वा -वं.

GRIG, *s.* चञ्चलशीलः क्षुद्रजलव्यालः, कुञ्चिकाभेदः.

To GRILL, *v. a.* भ्रज्ज् (c. 6. भृज्जति, भ्रष्टुं), भृज् (c. 1. भर्जते -र्जितुं), ऋञ्ज् (c. 1. ऋञ्जते -ञ्जितुं), तप् (c. 10. तापयति -यितुं), पच् (c. 1. पचति, पक्तुं)

GRILLED, *p. p.* भृष्टः -ष्टा -ष्टं, भर्जितः -ता -तं, तापितः -ता -तं.

GRIM, *a.* घोरः -रा -रं, उग्रः -ग्रा -ग्रं, दारुणः -णा -णं, भयानकः -का -कं, रौद्रः -द्री -द्रं, करालः -ला -लं, विकटः -टा -टं, कुत्सितः -ता -तं; 'in appearance' घोराकृतिः -तिः -ति, उग्राकारः -रा -रं, उग्रम्पश्यः -श्या -श्यं, उग्रदर्शनः -ना -नं, रौद्रदर्शनः -ना -नं, कुरूपः -पी -पं, अपरूपः -पी -पं, कदाकारः -रा -रं, दुर्दर्शनः -ना -नं, कुदृश्यः -श्या -श्यं.

GRIM-FACED, *a.* उग्रमुखः -खी -खं, घोरवदनः -ना -नं, करालवदनः -ना -नं.

GRIMACE, *s.* वदनविकृतिः *f.*, मुखविकृतिः *f.*, मुखविकारः, मुखवैरूप्यं, मुखविरूपता, मुखवक्रता, वक्रमुखं, विकृतमुखं, वक्रास्यं, कुमुखं.

GRIMALKIN, *s.* वृद्धविडालः, वृद्धमार्जारः, जीर्णविडालः.

GRIME, *s.* मलं, किट्टं, कल्कं, अमेध्यं, कलुषं, मालिन्यं.

To GRIME, *v. a.* मलिन (nom. मलिनयति -यितुं), कलुष (nom. कलुषयति -यितुं), मलेन दुष् (c. 10. दूषयति -यितुं).

GRIMED, *p. p.* मलिनितः -ता -तं, मलदूषितः -ता -तं, अमेध्यलिप्तः -प्ता -प्तं.

GRIMLY, *adv.* उग्रं, घोरं, दारुणं, भयानकं, रौद्रं, घोराकारेण.

GRIMNESS, *s.* घोरता, उग्रता -त्वं, रौद्रता, दारुण्यं, उग्राकारत्वं, करालता, उग्रमुखत्वं, करालमुखत्वं, कुदृश्यत्वं, कुरूपत्वं.

GRIMY, *a.* समलः -ला -लं, अमेध्याक्तः -क्ता -क्तं, कल्की -ल्किनी -ल्कि (न्).

To GRIN, *v. n.* कुस्मि (c. 1. -स्मयते -यितुं -स्मेतुं), कुस्मितं कृ, कु हस् (c. 1. हसति -सितुं), कुहासं कृ, विकृतं स्मि or हस्, विकृतमुखेन स्मि, मुखविकारेण हस्, कुस्मितं कृत्वा दन्तान् दृश् (c. 10. दर्शयति -यितुं), दन्तान् घृष् (c. 1. घर्षति -र्षितुं).

GRIN, *s.* कुस्मितं, कुहासः, कुहसितं, कुविहसितं, विकृतस्मितं, विकृतहासः, वक्रस्मितं, दन्तदर्शनं, दन्तघर्षणं.

To GRIND, *v. a.* (Comminute by attrition) चूर्ण् (c. 10. चूर्णयति -यितुं), प्रचूर्ण्, विचूर्ण्, चूर्णीकृ, पिष् (c. 7. पिनष्टि, पेष्टुं), निष्पिष्, विनिष्पिष्, प्रतिपिष्, उत्पिष्, मृद् (c. 9. मृद्नाति, मर्द्दितुं, c. 10. मर्दयति -यितुं), अवमृद्, विमृद्, प्रमृद्, अभिमृद्, क्षुद् (c. 7. क्षुणत्ति, क्षोत्तुं), क्षोदीकृ, खण्ड् (c. 10. खण्डयति -यितुं), गुण्ड् (c. 1. गुण्डति, c. 10. गुण्डयति -यितुं), कुट्ट् (c. 10. कुट्टयति -यितुं).—(Sharpen by friction) घर्षणेन निशो (c. 4. -श्यति -शातुं) or तिज् (c. 10. तेजयति -यितुं) or तीक्ष्णीकृ or तीक्ष्णधारीकृ.—(Rub one against another) घृष् (c. 1. घर्षति -र्षितुं), परस्परघर्षणं कृ; 'to grind the teeth,' दन्तान् दन्तैर् निष्पिष् or घृष्, दन्तघर्षणं कृ, क्ष्विड् (c. 1. क्ष्वेडति -डितुं), दन्तक्ष्वेडनं कृ.—(Oppress) बाध् (c. 1. बाधते -धितुं), पीड् (c. 10. पीडयति -यितुं).

To GRIND, *v. n.* पेषणं कृ, चूर्णीभू, क्षोदीभू, सम्पिष्टीभू, खण्डीभू.

GRINDER *s.* (One who grinds) पेषणकारी *m.* (न्), पेषकः, पेष्टरः.—(Instrument for grinding) पेषणं -णी, पेषणयन्त्रं.—(Tooth that chews) दाढा, चर्वणदन्तः, महादन्तः.

GRINDING, *s.* पेषणं, निष्पेषणं, चूर्णीकरणं, मर्दनं, विमर्दनं, कुट्टनं, अवहननं, घर्षणं; 'of the teeth,' दन्तघर्षणं, क्ष्वेडनं.

GRINDSTONE, *s.* (For grinding) पेषणं -णी -णिः *f.*, पेषणशिला, पेषणप्रस्तरः, पेषाकः, शिला, शिलापट्टः, क्षोदः.—(For sharpening) शाणः -णी, शानः, भ्रमः -मिः *f.*, शाणप्रस्तरः.

GRINNER, *s.* कुस्मितकारी *m.* (न्), कुस्मेरः, कुहासी *m.* (न्), विकृतहासी *m.*, विकृतमुखः, दन्तदर्शकः.

GRIPE, *s.* (Grasp) सङ्ग्राहः, ग्रहः -हणं, मुष्टिसङ्ग्राहः, मुष्टिबन्धः, हस्तग्रहः, दुर्मोचहस्तग्रहः, धृतिः *f.*, हस्तधृतिः *f.*—(Squeeze, pressure) पीडा -डनं, निपीडनं.—(Handful) मुष्टिः *f.*

To GRIPE, *v. a.* (Grasp) ग्रह् (c. 9. गृह्णाति, ग्रहीतुं), सङ्ग्रह्, मुष्टिना ग्रह् or सङ्ग्रह्, हस्तेन धृ (c. 1. धरति, धर्तुं), सङ्ग्राहं कृ.—(Close the fist) मुष्टिं or हस्तं बन्ध् (c. 9. बध्नाति, बन्धुं), मुष्टिबन्धं कृ.—(Squeeze) पीड् (c. 10. पीडयति -यितुं), सम्पीड्.—(Pain in the bowels) अन्त्रवेदनां कृ or जन् (c. 10. जनयति -यितुं).

GRIPED, *p. p.* मुष्टिसङ्ग्राहपीडितः -ता -तं, हस्तधृतः -ता -तं.

GRIPER, *s.* ग्राहकः, मुष्टिसङ्ग्राहकृत् *m.*—(Oppressor) परस्वग्राहकः, बाधकः, पीडकः.

GRIPES, *s. pl.* अन्त्रशूलं, नाडिशूलं, अन्त्रवेदना, जठरव्यथा.

GRISETTE, *s.* वणिक्पुत्री, वणिजः स्त्री or दुहिता *f.* (तृ), कन्या.

GRISLINESS, *s.* उग्रता -त्वं, घोरता, दारुणता, रौद्रता, क्रूरता.

GRISLY, *a.* उग्रः -ग्रा -ग्रं, घोरः -रा -रं, दारुणः -णा -णं, भयानकः -का -कं, क्रूरः -रा -रं, करालः -ला -लं, घोराकृतिः -तिः -ति, उग्रम्पश्यः -श्या -श्यं, उग्रदर्शनः -ना -नं, करालवदनः -ना -नं, कुदृश्यः -श्या -श्यं.

GRIST, *s.* (Corn ground) गोधूमचूर्णं, गोधूमक्षोदः, पिष्टधान्यं, पिष्टं.—(Corn for grinding) पेषणाय धान्यं, पेषणयोग्यं शस्यं, पेषणीयधान्यं, यत्शस्यम् एकवारे पेष्टुं शक्यते.

GRISTLE, *s.* तरुणास्थि *n.*, कोमलास्थि *n.*, उपास्थि *n.*, शिथिलास्थि *n.*, सन्धिबन्धनं, दृढमांसं.

GRISTLY, *a.* तरुणास्थिमयः -यी -यं, कोमलास्थिमान् -मती -मत् (त्), उपास्थिसमभावः -वा -वं.

GRIT, *s.* (Sand, gravel) शर्करा, चूर्णखण्डः, शिलाखण्डः, चूर्णः -र्णं, वालुका.—(Coarse part of meal) शक्तुशर्करा, घनशक्तुः *m.*, शक्तुघनः.

GRITTINESS, *s.* शार्करीयता, शर्करावत्त्वं, सशर्करत्वं.

GRITTY, *a.* शार्करीयः -यी -यं, शर्करावान् -वती -वत् (त्), शार्करिकः -की -कं, शर्करिलः -ला -लं, सशर्करः -रा -रं.

GRIZZLE, *s.* (Gray colour) धूसरः, धूसरवर्णः, पांशुवर्णः.

GRIZZLY, *a.* ईषद्धूसरः -रा -रं, ईषत्पांशुवर्णः -र्णा -र्णं, ईषत्पाण्डुः -ण्डुः -ण्डु, शुक्लकृष्णः -ष्णा -ष्णं; 'grizzly bear,' पूर्व्वोक्तवर्णविशिष्टो वृहदृक्षः.

To GROAN, *v. n.* वेदनोपहतत्वाद् दीर्घनादं कृ or दीर्घरावं कृ or दीर्घं निःश्वस् or निश्वस् (c. 2. -श्वसिति -तुं) or दीर्घं रु (c. 2. रौति, रवितुं) or नद् (c. 1. नदति -दितुं) or क्रुश् (c. 1. क्रोशति, क्रोष्टुं), दुःखार्त्तत्वाद् दीर्घचित्कारं कृ, आर्त्तनादं कृ, आर्त्तरावं कृ, आर्त्तवद् दीर्घं नद् or स्तन् (c. 1. स्तनति -नितुं) or विस्तन्, or निष्टन्, स्तननं कृ, दीर्घनिश्वासं कृ, गम्भीरनादं कृ, गम्भीरनिश्वासं कृ.

GROAN, *s.* आर्त्तनादः, आर्त्तरावः, दुःखार्त्तस्य दीर्घनादः or दीर्घरावः or दीर्घचित्कारः, दीर्घनिश्वासः, दीर्घनिःश्वासः, सदीर्घनिश्वासो गम्भीरनादः, सीत्कारः, सीत्कृतं, चीत्कारः, स्तननं, परिदेवनं -वितं.

GROANING, *part.* वेदनोपहतत्वाद् दीर्घनादी -दिनी -दि (न्) or दीर्घनिश्वासी &c.

GROANING, *s.* दीर्घनादकरणं, आर्त्तनादः, दीर्घनिश्वसितं, स्तननं.

GROAT, *s.* ताम्रमुद्राविशेषः.

GROCER, *s.* उपस्करादिविक्रेता *m.* (तृ), मिष्टान्नादिविक्रयी *m.* (न्), शुष्कफलादिविक्रेता *m.*, शर्करादिविक्रयी *m.*

GROCERY, *s.* मिष्टान्नादि *n.*, उपस्करादिद्रव्यं, शुष्कफलादि *n.*, शर्करादिद्रव्यं.

GROG, *s.* मदिरा, सुरा -री, वारुणी, शीधुः *m.* -धु *n.*, शुण्डा.

GROG-DRINKER, *s.* सुरापः -पी, शुण्डापायी *m.* -यिनी *f.*, शीधुपः.

GROIN, *s.* वंक्षणः -णं, वाटः, ऊरुसन्धिः *m.*, सक्थिसन्धिः *m.*

GROOM, *s.* अश्वपालः -लकः, सादी *m.* (न्), पालकः, भोगपालः, भोगिकः, चारकः, अश्वरक्षः -क्षकः, अश्वसेवकः, किरातः.

To GROOM, *v. a.* अश्वलोम मृज् (c. 2. मार्ष्टि -र्ष्टुं), अश्वं पाल् (c. 10. पालयति -यितुं).

GROOVE, *s.* शुषिरं, दीर्घशुषिरं, दीर्घरेखारूपेण खनितं शुषिरं, दीर्घगर्त्तः, दीर्घकुहरं, दीर्घशून्यं, खातरेखा, खातसीता.

To GROOVE, *v. a.* शुषिरीकृ, दीर्घरेखारूपेण खन् (c. 1. खनति -नितुं) or उत्खन्, दीर्घशुषिरं कृ, दीर्घरेखां कृ, सीतां कृ.

To GROPE, *v. a.* and *n.* तमसि or अन्धकारे परामृश् (c. 6. -मृशति -म्रष्टुं) or परिमृश्, तमसि परीक्ष् (c. 1. -ईक्षते -क्षितुं) or अन्विष् (c. 4. -इष्यति, c. 1. -इच्छति -एषितुं) or निरूप् (c. 10. -रूपयति -यितुं), तमः प्रविश्य हस्तेन परीक्ष् or निरूप्, निरूपणार्थं or हस्तपरामर्शार्थं तमः प्रविश् (c. 6. -विशति -वेष्टुं) or तमःप्रवेशं कृ.

GROPER, *s.* अन्धकारे हस्तपरामर्शकारी *m.* (न्), तमसि परीक्षकः or निरूपकः, तमःप्रवेशकः.

GROPING, *s.* अन्धकारे हस्तद्वारेण परामर्शः, तमसि हस्तेन जिज्ञासा or अन्वेषणं or निरूपणं.

GROSS, *a.* (Bulky) स्थूलः -ला -लं, स्थूलकायः -या -यं, वृहन् -हती -हत् (त्), वृहदङ्गः -ङ्गी -ङ्गं.—(Fat, corpulent) पीनः -ना -नं, पीवरः -रा -रं, मेदस्वी -स्विनी -स्वि (न्), वृहत्कुक्षिः -क्षिः -क्षि.—(Coarse, thick, not fine) घनः -ना -नं, स्थूलः -ला -लं, असूक्ष्मः -क्ष्मा -क्ष्मं, सान्द्रः -न्द्रा -न्द्रं, निबिडः -डा -डं, निरन्तरः -रा -रं, नीरन्ध्रः -न्ध्रा -न्ध्रं, स्त्यानः -ना -नं.—(Indelicate, vulgar) अशुद्धः -द्धा -द्धं, अवाच्यः -च्या -च्यं, गर्ह्यः -र्ह्या -र्ह्यं, कुत्सितः -ता -तं, असभ्यः -भ्या -भ्यं, ग्राम्यः -म्या -म्यं, नीचः -चा -चं.—(Unrefined, impure) अशिष्टः -ष्टा -ष्टं, अविनयः -या -यं, अविनीतः -ता -तं, अपरिष्कृतः -ता -तं, दुर्मर्य्यादः -दा -दं, अमेध्यः -ध्या -ध्यं, मलीमसः -सा -सं.—(Great, excessive) अत्यन्तः -न्ता -न्तं, अति or सु or महा prefixed; as, 'a gross blunder,' अतिदोषः.—(Disgraceful) अयशस्करः -री -रं, लज्जाकरः -री -रं.—(Dull) मन्दः -न्दा -न्दं, मूढः -ढा -ढं, जडः -डा -डं; 'gross measurement,' स्थूलमानं; 'gross ignorance,' घनाज्ञानं; 'gross darkness,' अन्धतमस, अन्धतामसं.

GROSS, *s.* (The bulk, chief part) प्रधानभागः, प्रधानांशः, अधिकभागः, स्थूलांशः, बहुतरभागः, साकल्यं, सामग्र्यं, समुदायः, समासः, समस्तिः *f.*; 'in the gross,' साकल्येन.—(Twelve dozen) द्वादशद्वादशकं, एकशतं चतुश्चत्वारिंशत्.

GROSSLY, *adv.* (Coarsely, not finely) स्थूलं, घनं, सान्द्रं, निबिडं.—(Not delicately) अशुद्धं, असभ्यं, अशिष्टं, अविनीतं, विनयविरोधेन, मर्य्यादाविरुद्धं.—(Greatly, enormously) अत्यन्तं, अतिशयेन, अतिमात्रं, अति or महा prefixed; as, 'grossly indecent,' अतिगर्हितः -ता -तं; 'grossly criminal,' महापातकी *m.* (न्).

GROSSNESS, *s.* (Bulkiness) स्थूलता, स्थौल्यं, वृहत्त्वं.—(Fatness) शरीरस्थूलता, स्थूलकायत्वं, पीनता, मेदस्विता.—(Density) घनता, सान्द्रता, स्थूलत्वं, नैबिड्यं, नैरन्तर्य्यं, स्त्यानं, स्त्यानता.—(Coarseness, want of refinement) अशुद्धता, अशुद्धिः *f.*, अशिष्टता, असभ्यता, अविनयः, अविनीतत्वं, अमर्य्यादा, गर्ह्यता, अमेध्यता.—(Enormity) अत्यन्तता, अतिरिक्तता, आधिक्यं, गाढता, महत्त्वं.

GROT, GROTTO, *s.* (Cave) कन्दरः -रा, गह्वरं -री, कुहरं, शैलरन्ध्रं, गुहा, शैलविवरं.—(Natural grotto) देवखातं -तकं, देवखातबिलं.—(Artificial) क्रीडाकन्दरः, क्रीडागह्वरं, कुञ्जः, कुञ्जकुटीरः.

GROTESQUE, *a.* अपरूपः -पा -पी -पं, असङ्गतरूपः -पा -पं, हास्यरूपः -पा -पं, असङ्गताकारः -रा -रं, कदाकारः -रा -रं, हास्यः -स्या -स्यं, विषमः -मा -मं, विलक्षणः -णा -णं.

GROTESQUELY, *adv.* असङ्गतरूपेण, हास्यरूपेण, विषमं, असङ्गतं.

GROTESQUENESS, *s.* अपरूपता, असङ्गतत्वं, हास्यता, वैषम्यं.

GROUND, *s.* (Earth) भूमिः *f.*, भूः *f.*, मही, पृथिवी, पृथ्वी, धरणी, धरा.

वसुधा, क्षिति: *f.*, अवनि: *f.* -नी, उर्व्वी, मेदिनी, वसुमती, वसुन्धरा, धारिणी, क्षोणी -णि: *f.*, क्षौणि: *f.*—(Surface of the earth) भूतलं, महीतलं, महीपृष्ठं, भूपृष्ठं, पृथिवीतलं, क्षितितलं, क्षौणितलं, क्षितिपीठं, धरोपस्थ:.—(Land, estate) भूमि: *f.*, क्षेत्रं.—(Foundation, basis of any thing) मूलं, उपष्टम्भ:, उपस्तम्भ:, वस्तु.—(Fundamental cause, reason) हेतु: *m.*, आदिहेतु: *m.*, कारणं, आदिकारणं, निमित्तं, निदानं, प्रयोजनं, उपपत्ति: *f.*—(First principle) तत्त्वं.—(Ground for the site of a house) गृहभूमि: *f.*, वेश्मभू: *f.*, भित्तिमूलं, तलिमं, कुट्टिमं, वास्तु: *m.*, पोत:, गृहपोतक:, गृहप्रतिष्ठा.—(Soil) मृत् *f.*, मृत्तिका, मृदा, मृत्खण्ड:.—(Field of action) रणभूमि: *f.*, रणक्षेत्रं.—(First colour) आदिवर्ण:.—(First form) प्रथमसंस्कार:; 'to gain ground,' वृध् (c. 1. वर्धते -र्धितुं), प्रवृध्, उत्तरोत्तरं वृध्; 'lose ground,' क्षि in pass. (क्षीयते), अपचि in pass. (-चीयते), शनै: शनैर् निवृत् (c. 1. -वर्त्तते -र्त्तितुं).

To GROUND, *v. a.* (Lay on the ground) भूमौ न्यस् (c. 4. -अस्यति -असितुं) or निधा (c. 3. -दधाति -धातुं).—(Fix, found) मूलं न्यस् or स्था in caus. (स्थापयति -यितुं) or प्रतिष्ठा; often expressed by मूल: -ला -लं in comp.; as, 'faith grounded on knowledge,' ज्ञानमूल: प्रत्यय:.—(Settle in rudiments of knowledge) विद्यारम्भान् or विद्यातत्त्वानि शिक्ष् (c. 10. शिक्षयति -यितुं); 'in grammar,' व्याकरणारम्भान् शिक्ष्.

To GROUND, *v. n.* (As a ship) उत्कूल (nom. उत्कूलयति -यितुं), उत्कूलीभू.

GROUND, *p. p.* (Reduced to powder) चूर्णित: -ता -तं, चूर्णीकृत: -ता -तं, पिष्ट: -ष्टा -ष्टं, निष्पिष्ट: -ष्टा -ष्टं, सम्पिष्ट: -ष्टा -ष्टं, मर्दित: -ता -तं, विमर्दित: -ता -तं, मृदित: -ता -तं, परिमृदित: -ता -तं, क्षोदित: -ता -तं, क्षोदीकृत: -ता -तं, क्षुण्ण: -ण्णा -ण्णं, खण्डित: -ता -तं, गुण्डित: -ता -तं, रूषित: -ता -तं, घर्षित: -ता -तं, घृष्ट: -ष्टा -ष्टं.

GROUNDED, *p. p.* (Run aground) उत्कूलित: -ता -तं; 'grounded on the rudiments of knowledge,' सुशिक्षितविद्यारम्भ: -म्भा -म्भं; 'in grammar,' स्वधीतव्याकरण: -णा -णं.

GROUND-FLOOR, *s.* गृहस्य अध:कोष्ठा: *m. pl.* or भूमिष्ठा: शाला: *f. pl.* or भूमिष्ठो भाग: or भूमिष्ठभाग:, गृहतलं, गृहतलिमं, गृहकुट्टिमं.

GROUND-IVY, *s.* नीलपुष्प: क्षुद्रलताविशेष:.

GROUNDLESS, *a.* निर्मूल: -ला -लं, अमूल: -ला -लं -लक: -का -कं, निर्हेतु: -तु: -तु, अहेतुक: -का -कं, निष्प्रयोजन: -ना -नं, निर्निमित्त: -त्ता -त्तं, निष्कारण: -णा -णं, अनर्थक: -का -कं; 'groundless charge,' मिथ्याभियोग:; 'groundless enmity,' शुष्कवैरं.

GROUNDLESSLY, *adv.* निष्कारणं, अकारणं, हेतुना विना, हेतुं विना, निष्प्रयोजनं, कारणं विना, प्रयोजनं विना, मिथ्या.

GROUNDLESSNESS, *s.* अहेतुता, निर्हेतुता, निष्कारणत्वं, अकारणं, निर्मूलत्वं, निर्निमित्तत्वं.

GROUND-PLOT, *s.* गृहभूमि: *f.*, वेश्मभू: *f.*, वास्तु: *m.* -स्तु, कुट्टिमं, तलिमं.

GROUND-RENT, *s.* भूमिकर:, भूमिशुल्क: -ल्कं, भूस्वामिग्राह्य: शुल्क:.

GROUNDS, *s. pl.* (Dregs) मलं, किट्टं, उच्छिष्टं, शेषं, खलं, कल्कं, कलङ्क:, असार:.

GROUNDSEL, *s.* क्षुद्रपत्रविशिष्ट ओषधिभेद:.

GROUNDSIL, *s.* देहली, गृहावग्रहणी, गृहतटी.

GROUNDWORK, *s.* मूलं -लत्वं, आरम्भ:, प्रारम्भ:, आदिकर्म्म *n.* (न्), मूलकर्म्म *n.*

GROUP, *s.* सङ्घ:, समूह:, सङ्घात:, समुदाय:, समवाय:, सञ्चय:, गण:, गुल्म:, गुच्छ: -च्छक:, गुत्स:, स्तबक:, ओघ:, वृन्दं; 'a group of people,' जनसमूह:, जनौघ:, जनसङ्घ:, जननिवह:, जनता; 'of houses,' सङ्घवनं, समनिचिति: *f.*, चतु:शालं; 'of flowers,' पुष्पगुत्स:; 'in groups,' सङ्घशस्, गुल्मशस्.

To GROUP, *v. a.* सङ्घश: कृ, एकत्र कृ, एकीकृ, सङ्घीकृ, समूहीकृ, गुल्मीकृ, वृन्दीकृ, गणीकृ, सञ्चि (c. 5. -चिनोति -चेतुं).

GROUPED, *p. p.* कृतसङ्घ: -घा -घं, कृतसमूह: -हा -हं, गणीभूत: -ता -तं.

GROUSE, *s.* वन्यपक्षिभेद:, जङ्गलप्रिय: कृष्णवर्ण: पक्षिभेद:.

GROUT, *s.* (Coarse meal) घनशक्तु: *m.*—(Lees) उच्छिष्टं, शेषं, किट्टं, असार:.

GROVE, *s.* वनं, उपवनं, काननं, विपिनं, वृक्षवाटिका, वृक्षजालं, वनिका, वनान्त:, आराम:, गहनं, अरण्यं, अटवि: *f.* -वी, वृक्षखण्डं, वृक्षछाया, प्रपावनं; 'a grove near a house,' गृहाराम:, निष्कुट:; 'a number of groves,' वन्या, वनसमूह:.

To GROVEL, *v. n.* कीटवद् भूमौ सृप् (c. 1. सर्पति, स्रप्तुं), सर्पवद् उरसा चल् (c. 1. चलति -लितुं), उरोगमनं कृ.—(Act in a mean manner) नीचवत् or अधमवत् or अपकृष्टवत् or निकृष्टवद् आचर् (c. 1. -चरति -रितुं), तुच्छीभू.

GROVELING, *part.* or *a.* (Creeping) भूमौ सर्पी -र्पिणी -र्पि (न्).—(Abject) नीच: -चा -चं, अधम: -मा -मं, निकृष्ट: -ष्टा -ष्टं, अपकृष्ट: -ष्टा -ष्टं, कृपण: -णा -णं, अधमाचार: -रा -रं, क्षुद्र: -द्रा -द्रं, तुच्छ: -च्छा -च्छं.

To GROW, *v. n.* (As a plant) रुह् (c. 1. रोहति, रोढुं), प्ररुह्, संरुह्, स्फुट् (c. 6. स्फुटति -टितुं), फुल्ल् (c. 1. फुल्लति -ल्लितुं); 'the lotus does not grow on the top of mountains,' न पर्वताग्रे नलिनी प्ररोहति.—(Increase) वृध् (c. 1. वर्धते -र्धितुं), विवृध्, संवृध्, अभिवृध्, प्रवृध्, परिवृध्, संविवृध्, एध् (c. 1. एधते -धितुं), समेध्, ऋध् (c. 5. ऋध्नोति, c. 4. ऋध्यति, अर्धितुं), उपचि in pass. (-चीयते), प्यै (c. 1. प्यायते, प्यातुं), आप्यै, पुष् (c. 4. पुष्यति, पोष्टुं), स्फाय् (c. 1. स्फायते -यितुं), आस्फाय्, वृद्धिम् इ (c. 2. एति -तुं) or या (c. 2. याति -तुं), स्फीतीभू.—(Extend) विस्तृ in pass. (-स्तीर्य्यते), व्याप् (c. 5. -आप्नोति -आप्तुं), विततीभू.—(Improve) आगमं कृ; 'in knowledge,' विद्यागमं कृ, विद्याप्राप्तिं कृ.—(Become) भू, सम्भू, जन् (c. 4. जायते); 'to grow fat,' स्थूलीभू, पीवरीभू, पुष्टीभू; 'to grow lean,' कृशीभू, कृशाङ्ग: -ङ्गी -ङ्गं भू.—(Proceed from, arise) जन्, उपजन्, प्रजन्, सञ्जन्, विजन्, अभिजन्, उत्पद् (c. 4. -पद्यते -पत्तुं), उदि (c. 1. -अयति -एतुं), उद्भू, प्रभू, सम्भू.—(Grow up, arrive at manhood) प्रौढीभू, अतीतशैशव: -वा -वं भू.—(Grow old) जॄ (c. 4. जीर्य्यति, जरितुं -रीतुं), जीर्णीभू.

To GROW, *v. a.* (Cause to grow) रुह् in caus. (रोपयति -यितुं), निरुह्, संरुह्, वृध् in caus. (वर्धयति -यितुं).

GROWER, *s.* रोपयिता *m.* (तृ), वर्धक:; 'of trees,' वृक्षरोपयिता *m.*

GROWING, *part.* (As a plant, &c.) रोही -हिणी -हि (न्), रुह: -हा -हं, प्रजनिष्णु: -ष्णु: -ष्णु, उद्भव: -वा -वं or प्रभव: -वा -वं or भव: -वा -वं or ज: जा जं or उत्थ: -त्था -त्थं or जात: -ता -तं or भू: भू: भु in comp.; as, 'growing in water,' जलरुह: -हा -हं, जलरुट् *m. f. n.* (ह्), जलोद्भव: -वा -वं, जलज: -जा -जं -जात: -ता -तं, जलभू: -भू: -भु; 'growing on the rocks,' शिलाभव: -वा -वं, शिलोत्थ: -त्था -त्थं, शिलाज: -जा -जं; 'growing on the head,' शिरोरुह: -हा -हं.—(Increasing) वर्धमान: -ना -नं, वर्धी -र्धिनी -र्धि (न्), वर्धन: -नी -नं, वर्धिष्णु: -ष्णु: -ष्णु, एधमान: -ना -नं, उपचीयमान: -ना -नं, विस्तीर्य्यमाण: -णा -णं, विजृम्भमाण: -णा -णं; 'growing in size,' वर्धमानशरीर: -रा -रं, प्रवर्धमानावयव: -वा -वं; 'growing old,' जीर्य्यन् -र्य्यन्ती -र्य्यत् (त्).

GROWL, *s.* गर्जनं, गर्जितं, घुर्घुरा, घर्घरितं, भषणं, रायणं, रुतं.

To GROWL, *v. n.* गर्ज् (c. 1. गर्जति -र्जितुं), अभिगर्ज्, परिगर्ज्, गर्जनं कृ, घुर्घुरां कृ, भष् (c. 1. भषति -षितुं), रै (c. 1. रायति, रातुं), घुर् (c. 6. घुरति -रितुं).

GROWN, *p. p.* रूढः -ढा -ढं, वर्धितः -ता -तं, प्ररूढः -ढा -ढं, संवर्धितः -ता -तं, प्रवृद्धः -द्धा -द्धं, उपचितः -ता -तं, एधितः -ता -तं, समेधितः -ता -तं, समृद्धः -द्धा -द्धं, स्फीतः -ता -तं, आप्यायितः -ता -तं, बृंहितः -ता -तं.—(Produced) जातः -ता -तं, उत्पन्नः -न्ना -न्नं, उपजातः -ता -तं. —(Grown in size) वर्धितदेहः -हा -हं, प्ररूढकायः -या -यं.—(Full grown) प्रौढः -ढा -ढं, प्रौढशरीरः -रा -रं, प्रवृद्धः -द्धा -द्धं, गतशैशवः -वा -वं, अतीतशैशवकालः -ला -लं, वयःप्राप्तः -प्ता -प्तं, वृद्धः -द्धा -द्धं.

GROWTH, *s.* रूढिः *f.*, प्ररूढिः *f.*—(Increase) वृद्धिः *f.*, वर्धनं, विवृद्धिः *f.*, विवर्धनं, प्रवृद्धिः *f.*, ऋद्धिः *f.*, उपचयः, स्फातिः *f.*, स्फीतिः *f.*, अभ्युदयः, समुत्थानं, आप्यायनं, विस्तारः, व्याप्तिः *f.*—(Production) उत्पत्तिः *f.*, उत्पादनं, जन्म *n.* (न्), जननं, प्रजननं, उद्भवः, प्रभवः.—(Improvement) वृद्धिः, आगमः.—(Full growth) प्रौढिः *f.*, प्रौढता, प्रवृद्धता.

To GRUB, *v. n.* खन् (c. 1. खनति -नितुं); 'grub up,' उत्खन्, प्रोत्खन्.

GRUB, *s.* कीटः, कृमिः *m.*, कीटडिम्भः, कीटाण्डजं, कोशस्थः.—(Dwarf, short, thick man) वामनः, खर्वः, ह्रस्वस्थूलः.

GRUBBER, *s.* खनकः, खनिता *m.* (तृ).—(Instrument) खनित्रं, खात्रं.

To GRUBBLE, *v. n.* अन्धकारे हस्तेन परामृश् (c. 6. -मृशति -म्रष्टुं) or आलभ् (c. 1. -लभते -लब्धुं) or स्पर्शेन निरूप् (c. 10. -रूपयति -यितुं).

To GRUDGE, *v. a.* and *n.* (Envy) असूय (nom. असूयति -ते -यितुं), ईर्ष्य् (c. 1. ईर्ष्यति -र्ष्यितुं), स्पृह् (c. 10. स्पृहयति -यितुं), अभिलष् (c. 1. -लषति, c. 4. -लष्यति -षितुं), न सह् (c. 1. सहते, सोढुं), न मृष् (c. 4. मृष्यति, मर्षितुं), मात्सर्यं कृ.—(Give or take unwillingly) अकामतस् or अकामेन or अनिच्छातो दा or ग्रह् (c. 9. गृह्णाति, ग्रहीतुं).—(Do any thing reluctantly or grudgingly) अकामतस् or अनिच्छातस् or दुःखेन or कृच्छ्रेण or सासूयं or असूयया किञ्चित् कृ.—(Refuse) प्रत्याख्या (c. 2. -ख्याति -तुं).—(Complain, murmur) विलप् (c. 1. -लपति -पितुं).

GRUDGE, *s.* (Malice, ill-will) मात्सर्यं, असूया, अभ्यसूया, ईर्ष्या, द्रोहः, द्रोहचिन्तनं, दुष्टभावः.—(Enmity) वैरं, वैरिता, वैरभावः.—(Hatred) द्वेषः, विद्वेषः, विद्विष्टता, दीर्घद्वेषः, चिरद्वेषः, द्वेष्यता.

GRUDGINGLY, *adv.* सासूयं, असूयया, अभ्यसूयया, मात्सर्येण, समात्सर्यं, दुष्टभावेन, अकामतस्, अकामं -मेन, अनिच्छातस्, दुःखेन, कृच्छ्रेण, कातर्येण.

GRUEL, *s.* काञ्जिकः.—(Rice-gruel) यवागूः *f.*, श्राणा, तरला, विलेपी, उष्णिका, सिद्धजलं.—(Sour gruel) आरनालं -लकं, सौवीरं, कुल्माषं, कुल्माषः, कुल्माषाभिषुतं, अभिषवं, अभिषुतं, काञ्जिका -कं, काञ्जिकं, काञ्जीकं, कुञ्जलं, धान्याम्लं, अवन्तिसोमं.

GRUFF, *a.* कर्कशस्वभावः -वा -वं, कर्कशः -शा -शं, रूक्षः -क्षा -क्षं, परुषः -षा -षं, निष्ठुरः -रा -रं, कटुः -टुः -ट्वी -टु, कठोरः -रा -रं, कठिनः -ना -नं.—(As tone) मन्द्रः -न्द्रा -न्द्रं, आमन्द्रः -न्द्रा -न्द्रं, गम्भीरः -रा -रं; 'a gruff voice,' गम्भीरस्वरः.

GRUFFLY, *adv.* कर्कशं, रूक्षं, परुषं, निष्ठुरं, कठिनं, कठोरं, मन्द्रं.

GRUFFNESS, *s.* कर्कशत्वं -ता, कार्कश्यं, रूक्षता, रौक्ष्यं, परुषता, निष्ठुरत्वं, नैष्ठुर्यं, कटुत्वं, कठोरता, काठिन्यं, स्वभावकटुता.—(Of tone) मन्द्रता, गम्भीरता, गाम्भीर्यं.

To GRUMBLE, *v. n.* (Make a low, harsh sound) गर्ज् (c. 1. गर्जति -र्जितुं), परिगर्ज्, गर्जनं कृ, स्तन् (c. 1. स्तनति -नितुं), स्तनितं कृ, घुर् (c. 6. घुरति -रितुं), गुञ्ज् (c. 1. गुञ्जति -ञ्जितुं), मन्द्रशब्दं कृ, गम्भीरशब्दं कृ. —(Complain discontentedly) असन्तुष्टत्वाद् विलप् (c. 1. -लपति -पितुं) or परिदेव् (c. 1. -देवते -वितुं).

GRUMBLER, *s.* असन्तुष्टत्वात् सदापरिदेवी *m.* (न्), असन्तुष्टजनः.

GRUMBLING, *s.* गर्जनं, गर्जितं, परिगर्जनं, स्तनितं, स्तननं, मन्द्रशब्दः, गम्भीरशब्दः, गम्भीरनादः, गम्भीरध्वनिः *m.*, गभीरशब्दः.—(Sound of complaint) परिदेवनं -वितं, विलपनं.

GRUMBLING, *part.* गम्भीरनादी -दिनी -दि (न्), मन्द्रशब्दकारी -रिणी -रि (न्).

GRUME, *s.* गुल्मः, पिण्डः -ण्डं, घनता; 'of blood,' रक्तगुल्मः, घनलोहितं.

GRUMOUS, *a.* पिण्डीभूतः -ता -तं, घनीभूतः -ता -तं, श्यानः -ना -नं, सान्द्रः -न्द्रा -न्द्रं, गुल्मी -ल्मिनी -ल्मि (न्); 'grumous blood,' घनलोहितं.

To GRUNT, *v. n.* शूकरवद् घर्घरितं कृ or कण्ठनादं कृ or गम्भीरनादं कृ, गर्ज् (c. 1. गर्जति -र्जितुं), घुर्घुराशब्दं कृ.

GRUNT, GRUNTING, *s.* घर्घरितं, शूकरनादः, शूकरगर्जितं, शूकरस्य कण्ठनादः or गम्भीरनादः.

GRUNTLING, *s.* शूकरशावकः, शूकरशिशुः *m.*, बालशूकरः.

GUARANTEE, *s.* (One who is surety for another) प्रतिभूः *m.*, प्रतिनिधिः *m.*, मध्यस्थः.—(Security) प्रातिभाव्यं, पारिभाव्यं, प्रात्ययिकः, प्रत्ययकारिणी, लग्नकः, बन्धकः.

To GUARANTEE, *v. a.* प्रतिभूः or प्रतिनिधिः भू, प्रातिभाव्यं कृ, पारिभाव्यं कृ, लग्नकं or प्रात्ययिकं or बन्धकं दा, प्रत्ययं कृ.

To GUARD, *v. a.* and *n.* रक्ष् (c. 1. रक्षति -क्षितुं), अभिरक्ष्, परिरक्ष्, संरक्ष्, प्रतिरक्ष्, पाल् or पा (c. 10. पालयति -यितुं, c. 2. पाति -तुं), अनुपाल्, परिपाल्, प्रतिपाल्, सम्पाल्, अभिपाल्, उपपाल्, गुप् (c. 1. गोपायति, गोप्तुं, c. 10. गोपयति -यितुं), अनुगुप्, अभिगुप्, प्रगुप्, अभिसङ्गुप्, त्रै (c. 1. त्रायते, त्रातुं), परित्रै, सन्त्रै, अव् (c. 1. अवति -वितुं), पर्याप् in des. (-ईप्सति -प्सितुं), परिप्राप्.—(Ward off) वृ (c. 10. वारयति -यितुं), निवृ.—(Guard against) अवधा (c. 3. -धत्ते -धातुं), अवहितः -ता -तं भू, सावधानः -ना -नं भू, अवधानं कृ; 'guard against avarice,' लोभात् सावधानो भव.—(Keep guard) रक्षां कृ, रक्षार्थं जागृ (c. 2. जागर्त्ति, जागरितुं).

GUARD, *s.* (Act of guarding) रक्षणं, रक्षा, रक्षणः, पालनं, त्राणं, गुप्तिः *f.*, गोपनं, अवनं.—(A sentry) रक्षकः, रक्षी *m.* (न्), सैन्यः, सैनिकः, सेनारक्षः, परिचरः, उपरक्षणं, परिधिस्थः, रक्षिवर्गः, अनीकस्थः, सज्जनं; 'captain of the guards,' गुल्मस्थानाधिकारी *m.* (न्), गुल्मस्थानाधिपः, रक्षाधिकृतः.—(That which protects any part of the body from injury) त्राणं, त्रं affixed, वारणं; 'a finger-guard,' अङ्गुलित्राणं, अङ्गुलित्रं; 'guard for the arm in shooting,' गोधा, तलं -ला, ज्याघातवारणं; 'to stand on one's guard,' सावधानः -ना -नं or सचेतनः -ना -नं स्था or भू; 'be on your guard,' सावधानो भव, सावहितो भव.

GUARD-ROOM, *s.* उद्वाटः, रक्षकाणां वासागारं, सैन्यस्थानं, सैनिकशाला.

GUARDABLE, *a.* रक्षणीयः -या -यं, रक्ष्यः -क्ष्या -क्ष्यं, पालनीयः -या -यं.

GUARDED, *p. p.* रक्षितः -ता -तं, अभिरक्षितः -ता -तं, पालितः -ता -तं, उपपालितः -ता -तं, गुप्तः -प्ता -प्तं, गोपायितः -ता -तं, त्रातः -ता -तं, त्राणः -णा -णं, अवितः -ता -तं.—(Cautious) अवहितः -ता -तं, स्ववहितः -ता -तं, सावधानः -ना -नं.

GUARDEDLY, *adv.* सावधानं, अवधानेन, अवहितं, स्ववहितं, सुविमृश्य.

GUARDEDNESS, *s.* अवधानता, सावधानता, स्ववहितत्वं, समीक्ष्यकारित्वं.

GUARDER, *s.* रक्षकः, रक्षी *m.* (न्), परिरक्षी *m.*, रक्षिता *m.* (तृ), पालयिता *m.* (तृ), पालकः, पालः -ली *m.* (न्), गोप्ता *m.* (प्तृ), गोपः -पकः, गोपायकः, गोपी *m.* (न्), गोपिलः, त्राता *m.* (तृ), पः in comp.

GUARDFUL, *a.* सावधानः -ना -नं, अवहितः -ता -तं, स्ववहितः -ता -तं.

GUARDIAN, *s.* पालकः, प्रतिपालकः, रक्षकः, गोप्ता *m.* (प्तृ), पालः, नाथः, अध्यक्षः.—(Of an orphan) पितृस्थानः -नीयः, मातृपितृस्थानः, नाथः; 'guardian deity,' लोकपालः -लकः.

GUARDIANSHIP, *s.* रक्षणं, रक्षा, रक्षकत्वं, पालकत्वं, रक्षितृपदं.

GUARDSHIP, *s.* रक्षणं, रक्षा, पालनं, त्राणं, गुप्तिः *f.*, गोपनं.

GUDGEON, *s.* वडिशद्वारेण सुग्रहणीयः क्षुद्रमत्स्यभेदः.—(A person easily cheated) सुवञ्चनीयः, सुप्रतारणीयः.

GUERDON, *s.* फलं, प्रतिफलं, पारितोषिकं, वेतनं.

To GUESS, *v. a.* and *n.* अनुमा (c. 2. -माति, c. 4. -मायते, c. 3. -मिमीते -मातुं), तर्क् (c. 10. तर्कयति -यितुं), वितर्क्, ऊह् (c. 1. ऊहते -हितुं), अवगम् (c. 1. -गच्छति -गन्तुं), शङ्क् (c. 1. शङ्कते -ङ्कितुं), अनिर्णयपूर्व्वम् अनुभू, अनिश्चयपूर्व्वं निरूप् (c. 10. -रूपयति -यितुं) or प्रदृश् (c. 1. -पश्यति -द्रष्टुं) or विवेचनां कृ or मन् (c. 4. मन्यते, मन्तुं).

GUESS, *s.* अनुमानं, अनुमितिः *f.*, अनुमानोक्तिः *f.*, वितर्कः -र्कणं, ऊहा -हनं, शङ्का, अनुभवः, अनुभूतिः *f.*, अनिश्चयपूर्व्वं निरूपणं, अनिर्णयपूर्व्वा विवेचना, अदृढप्रमाणः परामर्शः, अवगतिः, उपलब्धिः *f.*, उपलक्ष्यः.

GUESSED, *p. p.* अनुमितः -ता -तं, वितर्कितः -ता -तं, शङ्कितः -ता -तं.

GUESSER, *s.* अनुमाता *m.* (तृ), अनुमानकर्त्ता *m.* (र्त्तृ), वितर्ककः.

GUEST, *s.* अतिथिः *m. f.* -थी *f.*, अभ्यागतः, अभ्यागतजनः, गृहाभ्यागतः, गृहागतः, आगन्तुः *m. f.*, आगान्तुः, आगन्तुकः -का -कं, आवेशिकः -की -कं, प्राघुणः, प्राघुणिकः, प्रघूर्णः, साङ्केतिकः; 'proper for a guest,' आतिथ्यः -थ्यी -थ्यं, आतिथेयः -यी -यं.

GUEST-CHAMBER, *s.* अतिथिशाला, अतिथिसत्कारयोग्या शाला.

GUEST-RITE, *s.* अतिथिसत्कारः -सत्क्रिया, अतिथिक्रिया, अतिथिसेवा.

To GUGGLE, *v. n.* *See* GURGLE.

GUIDANCE, *s.* नयः, नायः, नीतिः *f.*, प्रणयनं, नेतृत्वं, विनियमः, पथदर्शनं.—(Direction) निर्देशः, निदेशः, उपदेशः, शास्तिः *f.*, शासनं, अनुशास्तिः *f.*, अनुशासनं, विधानं; 'good guidance,' सुनयः, सुनीतिः *f.*

To GUIDE, *v. a.* नी (c. 1. नयति, नेतुं), आनी, समानी, मार्गं or पथं दृश् (c. 10. दर्शयति -यितुं), गम् (c. 10. गमयति -यितुं).—(Direct) निर्दिश् (c. 6. -दिशति -देष्टुं), उपदिश्, उद्दिश्, शास् (c. 2. शास्ति, शासितुं), अनुशास्, समनुशास्, प्रणी, विनियम् (c. 1. -यच्छति -यन्तुं), विधृ (c. 10. -धारयति -यितुं), विधा (c. 3. -दधाति -धातुं).

GUIDE, *s.* नेता *m.* (तृ), नायकः, नेत्रः, विनेता *m.* (तृ), पथदर्शकः, मार्गदर्शकः, दर्शकः, दर्शयिता *m.* (तृ), प्रदर्शकः, निर्देष्टा *m.* (ष्टृ), निर्देशकः, उद्देशकः, उपदेशी *m.* (न्), उपदेशकः, देशकः, उपदेष्टा *m.* (ष्टृ), आदेष्टा *m.*, पथिकः, सञ्चारकः, शासिता *m.* (तृ), शास्ता *m.*, अनुशासकः, अध्यक्षः.

GUIDED, *p. p.* नीतः -ता -तं, आनीतः -ता -तं, समानीतः -ता -तं, नीयमानः -ना -नं, गमितः -ता -तं, शासितः -ता -तं, अनुशासितः -ता -तं, निर्दिष्टः -ष्टा -ष्टं.

GUIDE-POST, *s.* पथदर्शनार्थं or मार्गसूचनार्थं स्थूणा.

GUILD, *s.* श्रेणी -णिः *m.*, सहकारिजनसमूहः, नगरकार्य्यसम्पादनार्थं जनसंसर्गः, नागरसमाजः, वणिक्समाजः, निगमः, नैगमः, महाजनसंसर्गः.

GUILD-HALL, *s.* सहकारिणां वाणिज्यजनानां समागमशाला, निगमशाला, नगरकार्य्यसम्पादनार्थं महाचत्वरं.

GUILE, *s.* माया, कपटः -टं, छलं -लना, शठता, शाठ्यं, खलता, धूर्त्तता, व्याजः, विदग्धता, वैदग्ध्यं, छद्म *n.* (न्), कूटः -टं, कौटिल्यं, कैतवं, वक्रता, कापट्यं, वञ्चनं -ना, असारल्यं.

GUILEFUL, *a.* मायावान् -वती -वत् (त्), मायी -यिनी -यि (न्), मायामयः -यी -यं, मायान्वितः -ता -तं, मायावी -विनी -वि (न्), छली -लिनी -लि (न्), छलान्वितः -ता -तं, विदग्धः -ग्धा -ग्धं, कापटिकः -की -कं, वञ्चकः -का -कं, वञ्चनशीलः -ला -लं, शठः -ठा -ठं, खलः -ला -लं, कुटिलः -ला -लं, विजिह्मः -ह्मा -ह्मं, सव्याजः -जा -जं, धूर्त्तः -र्त्ता -र्त्तं, वक्रः -क्रा -क्रं, वक्रभावः -वा -वं.

GUILEFULLY, *adv.* मायया, समायं, शाठ्येन, छलेन, खलवत्, शठवत्, धूर्त्तवत्, सव्याजं, कितववत्, कैतवेन, विदग्धं.

GUILEFULNESS, *s.* मायावत्त्वं, शठता, शाठ्यं, कौटिल्यं, वक्रता, विजिह्मता, विदग्धता, सव्याजत्वं, असारल्यं.

GUILELESS, *a.* अमायी -यिनी -यि (न्), अमायिकः -की -कं, मायाहीनः -ना -नं, निष्कपटः -टा -टं, कपटहीनः -ना -नं, निर्व्याजः -जा -जं, छलरहितः -ता -तं, शुद्धमतिः -तिः -ति, सरलः -ला -लं, अजिह्मः -ह्मा -ह्मं, अवक्रः -क्रा -क्रं, अकुटिलः -ला -लं, विमलात्मा -त्मा -त्म (न्), निर्व्यलीकः -का -कं, दक्षिणः -णा -णं, अकृत्रिमः -मा -मं, अकूटः -टा -टं.

GUILELESSLY, *adv.* मायां विना, मायया विना, मायाव्यतिरेकेण, कपटं विना, निष्कपटं, निर्व्याजं, सरलवत्.

GUILELESSNESS, *s.* मायाहीनता, सारल्यं, अवक्रता, अजिह्मता, शुद्धता.

GUILLOTINE, *s.* शिरश्छेदनयन्त्रं, अतितीक्ष्णयन्त्रं यदाघातेन निमेषमात्रेण शीर्षच्छेदः क्रियते.

To GUILLOTINE, *v. a.* पूर्व्वोक्तयन्त्रेण मस्तकं छिद् (c. 7. छिनत्ति, छेत्तुं).

GUILT, *s.* (Criminality) अपराधिता -त्वं, सापराधता, पापित्वं, सपापत्वं, अपराद्धता, दोषिता -त्वं, सदोषता, पापवत्त्वं, दोषवत्त्वं.—(Crime) पापं, अपराधः, दोषः, पातकं, दुष्कृतं, दुष्कर्म्म *n.* (न्), पापकर्म्म *n.*, कल्मषं, एनस् *n.*, आगस् *n.*, अघं, दुरितं, मन्तुः *m.*

GUILTILY, *adv.* सापराधं, सपापं, सदोषं, सपातकं, अपराद्धवत्.

GUILTINESS, *s.* अपराधिता, अपराद्धता, सापराधत्वं, पापित्वं, सपापता, दोषिता -त्वं, सदोषता, पापवत्ता, दोषवत्ता.

GUILTLESS, *a.* निष्पापः -पा -पं -पी -पिनी -पि (न्), अपापः -पा -पं, निरपराधः -धा -धं, अनपराधी -धिनी -धि (न्), निर्दोषः -षा -षं -षी -षिणी -षि (न्), पापहीनः -ना -नं, शुद्धः -द्धा -द्धं, शुद्धमतिः -तिः -ति, अनघः -घा -घं.

GUILTLESSLY, *adv.* निष्पापं, पापं विना, निरपराधं, अपराधेन विना.

GUILTLESSNESS, *s.* निष्पापत्वं, निर्दोषत्वं, निरपराधिता, शुद्धता.

GUILTY, *adv.* अपराधी -धिनी -धि (न्), अपराद्धः -द्धा -द्धं, सापराधः -धा -धं, कृतापराधः -धा -धं, प्राप्तापराधः -धा -धं, पापी -पिनी -पि (न्), पापवान् -वती -वत् (त्), पापकर्म्मा -र्म्मा -र्म्म (न्), सपापः -पा -पं, दोषी -षिणी -षि (न्), दोषवान् -वती -वत् (त्), सदोषः -षा -षं, पातकी -किनी -कि (न्), दुष्कृती -तिनी -ति (न्), एनस्वी -स्विनी -स्वि (न्), कृतैनाः -नाः -नः (स्), अनिष्कृतैनाः &c., कृतागाः -गाः -गः (स्), अभिपन्नः -न्ना -न्नं; 'rashly guilty,' चिकुरः -रा -रं, चपलः -ला -लं.

GUINEA, *s.* सुवर्णमुद्राविशेषः, सुवर्णः.

GUINEA-HEN, *s.* चित्रशरीरविशिष्टा विदेशीयकुक्कुटी.

GUINEA-PIG, *s.* अल्पशरीरो विदेशीयशूकरभेदः.

GUISE, *s.* वेशः, वेषः, वासस् *n.*, परिधानं, अम्बरं, वस्त्रं, वसनं, आकारः, रूपं, व्यवहारः, रीतिः *f.*; 'in the guise of a herdsman,' गोपवेशः; 'of a Brahmin,' द्विजरूपी *m.* (न्).

GUITAR, *s.* वीणा, वल्लकी, विपञ्ची -ञ्चिका, तन्त्री, रुद्री, सारङ्गी, शारङ्गी, पिनाकी, ततं, परिवादिनी.

GULF, *s.* (A bay) खातं, खातं, समुद्रखण्डः, पुटभेदः.—(Abyss) अगाधदरी, अगाधरन्ध्रं, अतलस्पर्शखातं, गम्भीररन्ध्रं, नरकः.—(Whirlpool) आवर्त्तः, जलावर्त्तः, जलगुल्मः, अवघूर्णः, घूर्णः, घूर्णजलं.

GULFY, *a.* घूर्णजलपूर्णः -र्णा -र्णं, जलगुल्ममयः -यी -यं.

To GULL, *v. a.* वञ्च् (c. 10. वञ्चयते -ति -यितुं), परिवञ्च्, छल् (c. 10

छलयति -यितुं), प्रतृ (c. 10. -तारयति -यितुं).

GULL, s. (Bird) जलकुक्कुटः -टी, विष्किरा, गङ्गाचिल्ली, देवट्टी, क्षांक्षः. —(One easily cheated) सुवञ्चनीयः, सुप्रतारणीयः.

GULL-CATCHER, s. वञ्चकः, प्रतारकः, छली m. (न्), कूटकारः.

GULLED, p. p. वञ्चितः -ता -तं, प्रलब्धः -ब्धा -ब्धं, प्रतारितः -ता -तं.

GULLERY, s. वञ्चनं, छलं, कपटः -टं, प्रतारणा, व्याजः, कैतवं.

GULLET, s. निगरणस्रोतस् n., निगरणः, अन्नवाहिस्रोतस् n.

GULLIBILITY, s. सुवञ्चनीयता, सुखवञ्चनीयत्वं, सुप्रतारणीयता.

GULLIBLE, a. सुवञ्चनीयः -या -यं, सुखेन प्रतारणीयः -या -यं.

GULLY, s. नालः, प्रणालः -ली -लिका, खातं, कुल्या, जलमार्गः, उदकगमनमार्गः, जलवाहनी, परीवाहः, सारणिः -णी f.

To GULLY, v. a. भूमिम् उत्खन् (c. 1. -खनति -नितुं), प्रणालिकां कृ, कुल्यां कृ.

GULLY-HOLE, s. कर्दमाटकरन्ध्रं, प्रणालिकारन्ध्रं, प्रणालीविवरं.

GULOSITY, s. अतिभोजनं, अत्याहारः, घस्मरता, अतृप्तिः f.

To GULP, v. a. जलं बहुशो गॄ (c. 6. गिरति, गरितुं -रीतुं) or निगॄ or अवगॄ or ग्रस् (c. 1. ग्रसते -सितुं).—(Disgorge) उद्गॄ, उत्क्षिप् (c. 6. -क्षिपति -क्षेप्तुं).

GULP, s. गरणं, गरा, गीर्णिः f., गिरिः f., निगारः, निगरणं, ग्रसनं, ग्रासः, एकवारे निगीर्णं यत्किञ्चित्.—(Disgorging) उद्गारः -रणं, उद्गिरणं, उद्वमः -मनं.

GUM, s. (Fleshy covering of the teeth) दन्तमांसं, दन्तवेष्टः -ष्टनं, दन्तशिरा, दन्तमूलं, वेला.—(Exudation from trees) निर्यासः, वृक्षनिर्यासः, वृक्षरसः.—(Adhesive substance) श्यानद्रव्यं, सान्द्रद्रव्यं.

To GUM, v. a. पूर्व्वोक्तनिर्यासेन or श्यानद्रव्येण लिप् (c. 6. लिम्पति, लेप्तुं) or संयुज् (c. 7. -युनक्ति -योक्तुं) or संलग्नीकृ.

GUM-ARABIC, s. सूक्ष्मपत्रः, सूक्ष्मपत्ररसः.

GUM-BOIL, s. दन्तविस्फोटः, दन्तस्फोटः -टकः, दन्तव्रणः -णं, दन्तार्बुदः, द्विजव्रणः, वैदर्भः, उपकुशः.

GUMMINESS, s. सान्द्रत्वं, श्यानत्वं, स्निग्धता, संलग्नशीलता.

GUMMY, a. वृक्षनिर्यासमयः -यी -यं, श्यानः -ना -नं, सान्द्रः -न्द्रा -न्द्रं.

GUN, s. अन्तरग्निबलेन गुलिकाप्रक्षेपणी लोहनाडिः or -डी, गुलिप्रक्षेपणी सुषिरनाली, गुलिकाप्रक्षेपार्थं शुषिरयन्त्रं, लोहसुषिः f.

GUNNER, s. पूर्व्वोक्तनाडिद्वारा गुलिकाप्रक्षेपकः, लोहनाडिधारी m. (न्), अग्न्यस्त्रधारी m., आग्नेयास्त्रप्रक्षेपकः.

GUNNERY, s. अग्न्यस्त्रविद्या, लोहनाडिद्वारेण गुलिकाप्रक्षेपणविद्या.

GUNPOWDER, s. आग्नेयचूर्णं, शीघ्रदाहचूर्णं, आग्नेयक्षोदः, महाशब्दपूर्व्वम् अग्निसम्पर्कात् सद्योदाहचूर्णं.

GUN-SHOT, s. लोहगुलिकागोचरं, लोहगुलिविषयः, युद्धनाडिक्षेपणं.

GUN-SMITH, s. अग्न्यस्त्रकारः, आग्नेयशस्त्रकारः, आग्नेयनाडिनिर्म्माता m. (तृ), युद्धनाडिनिर्म्माणशिल्पज्ञः.

GUN-STOCK, s. आग्नेयनाडिदण्डः, लोहनाडिदारुः m., नाडिधारकः.

GUNWALE, GUNNEL, s. नौपार्श्वधारा -रः, नौपार्श्वस्य उपरिकाष्ठं, नावुत्तरकः.

GURGE, s. जलावर्त्तः, जलभ्रमः, जलावघूर्णः, जलगुल्मः, घूर्णजलं.

To GURGLE, v. n. जलवद् घर्घरशब्देन सु (c. 1. स्रवति, स्रोतुं), घर्घरशब्दं कृ, घर्घ or गर्ग (nom. घर्घायते, गर्गायते), गर्घ् (c. 1. गर्घति -र्घितुं).

GURGLING, s. घर्घरशब्देन जलप्रस्रावः, घर्घरा.

To GUSH, v. n. प्रपत् (c. 1. -पतति -तितुं), निपत्, बहुशः प्रसु (c. 1. -स्रवति -स्रोतुं) or प्रस्यन्द् (c. 1. -स्यन्दते -न्दितुं) or क्षर् (c. 1. क्षरति -रितुं), वेगेन or वेगतो निःसृ (c. 1. -सरति -सर्त्तुं); 'tears gushed from (her) eyes,' जलं नेत्राभ्यां प्रापतत्.

GUSH, GUSHING, s. बहुप्रस्रावः, जलप्रपातः, उत्सेकः, उत्सेचनं, उत्पीडः.

GUSSET, s. वस्त्रनिवेशित उपवस्त्रखण्डः or अधिकवस्त्रखण्डः.

GUST, s. (Blast of wind) निर्घातः, प्रभञ्जनः, व्योममुद्गरः, वातरूपः, वायुगुल्मः, वायुवेगः, वात्या, प्रबलवायुः m., प्रचण्डवायुः m., चण्डवातः, तीव्रवातः, पवनाघातः, जवानिलः.—(Taste) स्वादः, आस्वादः, रसनेन्द्रियं, रुचिः f., अभिरुचिः f.

GUSTATION, s. स्वादनं, आस्वादनं, प्राशनं, लेहनं.

GUSTFUL, a. हृद्यः -द्या -द्यं, रुचिरः -रा -रं, सरसः -सा -सं.

GUSTLESS, a. विरसः -सा -सं, निःस्वादुः -दुः -दु, अस्वादुः -दुः -दु.

GUSTO, s. रुचिः f., अभिरुचिः f., रसः, सुरसः, आस्वादः.

GUSTY, a. वातलः -ला -लं, वातवान् -वती -वत् (त्), वातीयः -या -यं, वातमयः -यी -यं, बहुपवनः -ना -नं, पवनक्षिप्रः -प्रा -प्रं.

GUT, s. नाडिः -डी f., अन्तर्नाडी, नाली -लिः f., धमनी -निः f., शिरा, सिरा, अन्त्रं, पुरीतत् m. n., कोष्ठः.—(Stomach) उदरं, जठरः -रं.

To GUT, v. a. निरन्त्रीकृ, निरन्त्र (nom. निरन्त्रयति -यितुं), नाडीः or अन्त्राणि बहिष्कृ.—(Plunder) द्रव्याणि अपहृ (c. 1. -हरति -हर्त्तुं).

GUTTA SERENA, s. तिमिरं; 'an eye affected with it,' तिमिरदोषहतं चक्षुस्.

GUTTED, p. p. निरन्त्रीकृतः -ता -तं, हृतसर्व्वद्रव्यः -व्या -व्यं.

GUTTER, s. प्रणालः -ली -लिका, नालः, जलनिर्गमः, जलमार्गः, परीवाहः, जलवाहनी, सारणिः f. -णी, उदकगमनमार्गः.

To GUTTER, v. a. प्रणालीरूपेण उत्खन् (c. 1. -खनति -नितुं) or शुषिरीकृ.

To GUTTER, v. n. प्रणालीरूपेण उत्खन् in pass. (-खन्यते) or शुषिरीभू, प्रणालिकां कृ, ज्वलद्दीपिकारूपेण लघशः स्यन्द् (c. 1. स्यन्दते -न्दितुं).

GUTTLER, s. बहुभक्षकः, अतिभोजी m. (न्), कुक्षिम्भरिः m.

GUTTURAL, a. कण्ठ्यः -ण्ठ्या -ण्ठ्यं, कण्ठस्थः -स्था -स्थं, ग्रैवः -वी -वं, ग्रैवेयः -यी -यं; 'guttural letter,' कण्ठ्यं; 'guttural sound,' कुहरं.

GUZARAT, s. (The country) गुर्ज्जरः.—(The people) गुर्ज्जराः m. pl.

To GUZZLE, v. a. बहुशो गॄ (c. 6. गिरति, गरितुं -रीतुं) or निगॄ or ग्रस् (c. 1. ग्रसते -सितुं) or पा (c. 1. पिबति, पातुं), पानरतः -ता -तं भू.

GUZZLER, s. अतिपायी m. (न्), अतिभोजी m. (न्), पानरतः.

GYMNASIUM, s. व्यायामशाला, मल्लयुद्धशाला, मल्लशाला, विहारः.

GYMNASTIC, a. व्यायामी -मिनी -मि (न्), व्यायामसम्बन्धी -न्धिनी -न्धि (न्), मल्लयुद्धसम्बन्धी &c., व्यायामशीलः -ला -लं.

GYMNASTICS, s. pl. व्यायामः, मल्लयुद्धं, व्यायामविद्या.

GYPSY, GYPSEY. *See* GIPSY.

To GYRATE, v. n. परिवृत् (c. 1. -वर्त्तते -र्त्तितुं), भ्रम् (c. 4. भ्राम्यति, c. 1. भ्रमति -मितुं), घूर्ण् (c. 6. 1. घूर्णति -ते -र्णितुं), परिघूर्ण्, विघूर्ण्, व्याघूर्ण्.

GYRATION, s. परिवर्त्तनं, आवर्त्तः, भ्रमः -मणं, भ्रमिः f., घूर्णिः f., घूर्णनं; 'of a bird,' परिडीनकं.

GYRE, s. चक्रावर्त्तः, चक्रगतिः f., आवृत्तिः f., मण्डलं, परिमण्डलं.

To GYRE, v. a. निगडेन बन्ध् (c. 9. बध्नाति, बन्द्धुं), निगड (nom. निगडयति -यितुं), पाश (nom. पाशयति -यितुं).

GYVES, s. pl. निगडः -डं, पाशः, बन्धनं -नानि n. pl., पादपाशः, शृङ्खला.

H.

HA, *interj.* हा, हहा, आहा, अहो, आहो, अहहः, अहोवत्, ह, अह, आ, अयि, साश्चर्य्यं.

HABEAS CORPUS, s. मिथ्यानिरोधनिषेधार्थकं पूर्व्वकालीनशासनपत्रं.

HABERDASHER, s. वस्त्रादिविक्रेता m. (तृ), वसनादिविक्रेता m., अंशुकादिविक्रयी m. (न्), क्षुद्रद्रव्यविक्रेता m.

HABERDASHERY, s. पूर्व्वोक्तव्यापारिणा विक्रीता वस्त्रादिद्रव्यसामग्री.

HABERGEON, *s.* वक्षस्त्राणं, उरस्त्राणं, उरश्छदः, कक्षस्यकवचं.

HABILIMENT, *s.* वेशः, परिधानं, परिच्छदः, वसनं, वस्त्रं, आभरणं, अम्बरं, वासस् *n.*, प्रसाधनं, आच्छादनं, सज्जा.

HABIT, *s.* (Dress) वेशः, वेषः, वसनं, वस्त्रं, वासस् *n.*, परिधानं, परिच्छदः, अम्बरं.—(State, condition) अवस्था, स्थितिः *f.*, भावः, वृत्तिः *f.*, दशा, संस्थितिः *f.*, स्वभावः; 'habit of body,' शरीरस्थितिः *f.*, देहस्वभावः; 'habit of mind,' चित्तवृत्तिः *f.*—(Temperament, disposition) प्रकृतिः *f.*, शीलः -लता, स्वभावः, अन्तःकरणं.—(Custom, practice, established manner) आचारः, अभ्यासः, व्यवहारः, समाचारः, नित्यकृत्यं, नित्यक्रिया, रीतिः *f.*, व्यवहृतिः *f.*, शीलः, प्रचारः, चरितं, चर्य्या, क्रमः, नियमः, आवृत्तिः *f.*, व्यापारः, प्रवृत्तिः *f.*, मार्गः, अनुशीलनं; 'bad habit,' व्यसनं; 'having bad habits,' दुराचारः -रा -रं, पापसमाचारः -रा -रं, पापचर्य्यः -र्य्या -र्य्यं, दुर्वृत्तः -त्ता -त्तं, दुश्चरितः -ता -तं, व्यसनी -निनी -नि (न्).

To HABIT, *v. a.* वेष्ट् (c. 1. वेष्टते -ष्टितुं), परिवेष्ट्, आच्छद् (c. 10. -छादयति -यितुं), वस्त्र (nom. वस्त्रयति -यितुं), परिधा in caus. (-धापयति -यितुं).

HABITABLE, *a.* वासतेयः -यी -यं, वास्तव्यः -व्या -व्यं, वासयोग्यः -ग्या -ग्यं, वासक्षमः -मा -मं, आजीव्यः -व्या -व्यं, उपजीव्यः -व्या -व्यं.

HABITANT, *s.* वासी *m.* (न्), निवासी *m.*, निलायी *m.* (न्), वासकृत्.

HABITATION, *s.* वासः, वासस्थानं, निवासः, वसतिः *f.*, निवसतिः *f.*, गृहं, गेहः -हं, वेश्म *m.* (न्), निलयः -यनं, आलयः, आयतनं, निवेशनं, निकेतः -तनं, आगारः, भवनं, वसितं, समावासः, अवस्थानं, आवसथः, स्थानं, ओकस् *n.*, धाम *n.* (न्).

HABITUAL, *a.* आभ्यासिकः -की -कं, अभ्यस्तः -स्ता -स्तं, आचारिकः -की -कं, आचरितः -ता -तं, व्यावहारिकः -की -कं, व्यवहारिकः -की -कं, नित्यः -त्या -त्यं, स्वाभाविकः -की -कं, अनुशीलितः -ता -तं, नैयमिकः -की -कं, प्रायिकः -की -कं.

HABITUALLY, *adv.* नित्यं, नियमशस्, यथाव्यवहारं, यथारीति, साभ्यासं, अभ्यासेन, अभ्यासपूर्व्वं, यथाभ्यासं.

To HABITUATE, *v. a.* अभ्यस् (c. 4. -अस्यति -असितुं), अभ्यासं कृ, अभ्यस्तं -स्तां -स्तं कृ, शिक्ष् (c. 10. शिक्षयति -यितुं), शील् (c. 10. शीलयति -यितुं); 'to be habituated,' अभ्यस्तः -स्ता -स्तं भू.

HABITUATED, *p. p.* अभ्यस्तः -स्ता -स्तं, शिक्षितः -ता -तं, कृताभ्यासः -सा -सं, शीलितः -ता -तं, अनुशीलितः -ता -तं, शीलः -ला -लं in comp.

HABITUDE, *s.* (Custom) व्यवहारः, आचारः, रीतिः *f.*, चरितं, चर्य्या, नित्यकृत्यं.—(Relation) सम्बन्धः, सम्पर्कः, प्रतीक्षा.—(Intercourse) संसर्गः.

To HACK, *v. a.* (Mangle) व्यवछिद् (c. 7. -छिनत्ति -छेत्तुं), व्रश्च् (c. 6. वृश्चति, व्रश्चितुं), प्रव्रश्च्, विदृ (c. 10. -दारयति -यितुं), बहुलवशः खण्ड् (c. 10. खण्डयति -यितुं) or छिद्, बहुखण्डशः कृ, खण्डं खण्डं कृ, बहुखण्डीकृ, क्षतविक्षतीकृ.

To HACK, *v. n.* (For hire) अतिशरीरायासेन नीचकर्म्म कृ, निरन्तरायासं कृ, पण्यः -ण्या -ण्यं भू, सर्व्वप्रयोज्यः -ज्या -ज्यं भू, सर्व्वसाधारणीभू.

HACK, *s.* (Cut) प्रहारः, छेदः, आघातः, क्षुरिकाघातः.—(Horse kept for hire, worn out horse) कदश्वः, पण्याश्वः, भाटकीयवाजी *m.* (न्), साधारणवाजी *m.*, सर्व्वप्रयोज्यवाजी *m.*, पण्यघोटकः, अश्वकः; 'hack-carriage,' पण्यवाहनं, साधारणरथः.—(Drudge) निरन्तरायासी *m.* (न्), अतिदेहक्लेशेन नीचकर्म्मकारी *m.* (न्), हीनवृत्तिः *m.*, व्रातीनः.

HACKED, *p. p.* व्यवछिन्नः -न्ना -न्नं, क्षतविक्षतः -ता -तं, वृक्णः -क्णा -क्णं.

To HACKLE, *v. a.* वस्त्रनिर्म्माणयोग्यं शणं or अतसीं मृज् (c. 2. मार्ष्टि -र्ष्टुं) or सम्मृज्, or परिष्कृ or शुध् (c. 10. शोधयति -यितुं) or पृथक्कृ.

HACKLE, *s.* अतसीमार्जनी, शणमार्जकः, उमाशोधनी.

HACKNEY, *s.* (Horse) कदश्वः, अश्वकः, पण्याश्वः, पण्यघोटकः, साधारणवाजी *m.* (न्), भाटकीयवाजी *m.*—(Any thing much used, a drudge, a hireling) नीचकर्म्मणि नियुक्तः, नीचकर्म्मकारी *m.* (न्), निरन्तरायासी *m.* (न्), हीनवृत्तिः *m.*, वैतनिकः, पण्यः, साधारणः, सर्व्वप्रयोज्यः.—(Prostitute) पण्यस्त्री, साधारणस्त्री.

To HACKNEY, *v. a.* नीचकर्म्मणि नियुज् (c. 7. -युनक्ति -योक्तुं, c. 10. -योजयति -यितुं), पण्यीकृ, साधारणीकृ, सर्व्वप्रयोज्यं -ज्यां -ज्यं कृ, जीर्णीकृ.

HACKNEY-COACH, *s.* साधारणरथः, पण्यरथः, पण्यवाहनं, सर्व्वप्रयोज्यरथः.

HACKNEYED, *p. p.* सर्व्वप्रयुक्तः -क्ता -क्तं, सर्व्वसाधारणः -णा -णी -णं, सर्व्वपण्यः -ण्या -ण्यं, अपकर्म्मनियुक्तः -क्ता -क्तं, जीर्णः -र्णा -र्णं.

HADDOCK, *s.* हड्डकसंज्ञकः समुद्रीयमत्स्यभेदः.

HADES, *s.* प्रेतलोकः, अधोलोकः, अधोभुवनं, नरकः, पातालं.

HAFT, *s.* (Handle) त्सरुः *m.*, तलः, वारङ्गः, मुष्टिः *m.* -ष्टी *f.*, दण्डः, कर्णः.

To HAFT, *v. a.* त्सरौ or तले or वारङ्गे निविश् (c. 10. -वेशयति -यितुं).

HAG, *s.* कुरूपी -पिणी, कुट्टिनी, डाकिनी, वृद्धा स्त्री, जरिणी.

HAGGARD, *a.* कृशाननः -ना -नं, क्षीणवदनः -ना -नं, क्षामवदनः -ना -नं, शुष्कवदनः -ना -नं, उग्रमुखः -खा -खं, उग्रदर्शनः -ना -नं.

HAGGISH, *a.* कुरूपिणी, अपरूपिणी, विरूपिणी, जरापरिणता.

To HAGGLE, *v. a.* व्यवछिद् (c. 7. -छिनत्ति -छेत्तुं), क्षतविक्षतीकृ, खण्डशः कृ.

To HAGGLE, *v. n.* (In bargaining) क्रयकाले विलप् (c. 1. -लपति -पितुं) or विचर् (c. 10. -चारयति -यितुं) or एतावत् दातुम् इच्छामीति वादानुवादं कृ or न्यूनमूल्यं दिप्सामीति वद् (c. 1. वदति -दितुं).

HAGGLER, *s.* क्रयकाले विलापी *m.* (न्) or एतावन्मूल्यं न दातुम् इच्छामीति वादानुवादकारी *m.* (न्).

HAGIOGRAPHA, *s.* धर्म्मग्रन्थः, धर्म्मशास्त्रसंहिता, धर्म्मपुस्तकं.

HAH, *interj.* हा, अहो, अहोवत्, अहह, हाहा, आ, अयि, आश्चर्य्यं.

HAIL, *s.* (Frozen rain) करका, करकावृष्टिः *f.*, शिला, शिलावृष्टिः *f.*, वर्षोपलः, पयोघनः, पयोगडः, घनकफः, मेघास्थि *n.*, मेघकफः, मेघगर्भः, धारा, तोयडिम्भः, महत्फलं, पिण्डाभं, धाराङ्कुरः, मटची, शिलीन्ध्रं, वार्भिला.

HAIL, *exclam.* नमस्, स्वस्ति, कुशलं, कुशलं भूयात्, सुखं भूयात्, कल्याणं भूयात्, क्षेमं भवतु, शेवं, अभिवादये, अभिवन्दे.

To HAIL, *v. n.* (Pour down hail) करकासारं वृष् (c. 1. वर्षति -र्षितुं), शिला वृष्, उपलान् वृष् or पत् (c. 10. पातयति -यितुं).

To HAIL, *v. a.* (Call from a distance) दूरात् आह्वे (c. 1. -ह्वयति -ह्वातुं) or ह्वे or सम्बोधनं कृ or आक्रन्द् (c. 1. -क्रन्दति -न्दितुं) or आमन्त्र् (c. 10. -मन्त्रयते -यितुं) or समामन्त्र् or अभिभाष् (c. 1. -भाषते -षितुं) or आभाष्.—(Salute) वन्द् (c. 1. वन्दते -न्दितुं), अभिवन्द्, अभिवद् (c. 10. -वादयति -ते -यितुं), नमस्कृ, आमन्त्र्, उपास् (c. 2. -आस्ते -आसितुं).

HAILED, *p. p.* दूरात् आहूतः -ता -तं or अभिहितः -ता -तं or आमन्त्रितः -ता -तं, सम्बोधितः -ता -तं, आक्रन्दितः -ता -तं.

HAIL-STONE, *s.* शिला, वर्षोपलः, पयोघनः, करका, पयोगडः.

HAIL-STORM, *s.* करकासारः, करकावृष्टिः *f.*, शिलासारः.

HAILY, *a.* करकामयः -यी -यं, शिलामयः -यी -यं, वर्षोपलमयः &c.

HAIR, *s.* केशः, बालः, कचः, चिकुरः, वृजनः -जिनः, कुन्तलः.—(Of the head) केशः, शिरोरुहः, शिरोरुट् *m.*, शिरसिजः, मूर्द्धजः, कृशला.—(Of the body) लोम *n.* (न्), रोम *n.* (न्), तनुरुहः -हं, तनूरुहः -हं, तनुरुट् *m.* (ह्), तनुजं, अङ्कुरः; 'a head of hair,' कैश्यं, कैशिकं; 'a quantity of hair,' केशकलापः, केशपक्षः, केशोच्चयः, केशपाशः, कचपाशः, कचपक्षः, कचहस्तः, चिकुरपाशः, चिकुरपक्षः, चिकुरहस्तः; 'having much or fine hair,' केशी -शिनी -शि (न्), केशवान् -वती -वत् (त्), केशवः -वा -वं, केशिकः -की -कं; 'a fine head of hair,' केशभारः, कवरीभारः -भरः; 'a braid of hair,' कवरी, केशगर्भः -र्भकः, केशवेशः; 'braided hair,' धम्मिल्लः, वेणिः -णी *f.*, वेणिका, प्रवेणिः -णी *f.*; 'a lock of hair,' अलकः -कं, चूर्णकुन्तलः, भ्रमरकः, काकपक्षः, शिखण्डः -ण्डकः, केशपाशी, चूडा, शिखा; 'clotted hair,' जटा, सटा; 'unentangled hair,' शीर्षण्यः, शिरस्यः; 'covered with hair,' लोमशः -शा -शं, बहुलोमा -मा -म (न्), रोमाक्रान्तः -न्ता -न्तं; 'point of hair,' वालाग्रं; 'erection of the hair,' रोमहर्षणं, उद्धर्षणं. *See* Erection.—(Filament of a plant) केशरः, केसरः.

Hair-bell, *s.* घण्टाकारपुष्पविशिष्ट ओषधिभेदः.

Hair-breadth, *s.* एककेशान्तरं, एककचपरिमाणं, अत्यल्पान्तरं.

Hair-broom, *s.* केशनिर्म्मिता मार्जनी, लोममयी शोधनी.

Hair-brush, *s.* केशमार्जनी, केशशोधनी, केशनिर्घर्षणकः.

Hair-cloth, *s.* लोमनिर्म्मितं वस्त्रं, केशमयः पटः.

Hair-cutter, *s.* केशच्छिद् *m.* -छेत्ता *m.* (तृ), शिरोरुहच्छेदकः.

Hair-dresser, *s.* केशरचकः, केशविरचकः, केशसंस्कारकृत् *m.*

Hair-dressing, *s.* केशरचना, केशविरचनं -ना, केशसंस्कारः.

Haired, *a.* केशी -शिनी -शि (न्), केशवान् -वती -वत् (त्).

Hairiness, *s.* लोमशत्वं, रोमशत्वं, बहुलोमत्वं, लोमप्राचुर्य्यं.

Hairless, *a.* अकेशः -शा -शं, विकेशः -शा -शं, केशहीनः -ना -नं, निर्लोमा -मा -म (न्), लोमरहितः -ता -तं, अविद्यमानलोमा &c.

Hairy, *a.* लोमशः -शा -शं, रोमशः -शा -शं, बहुलोमा -मा -म (न्), प्रचुरलोमा &c., बहुकेशः -शा -शं, केशी -शिनी -शि (न्), केशकः -का -कं, केशिकः -की -कं, केशवः -वा -वं, बहुकेशवान् -वती -वत् (त्), लोमवान् &c., लोममयः -यी -यं, लोमपूर्णः -र्णा -र्णं.

Hake, *s.* समुद्रीयमत्स्यभेदः.

Halberd, *s.* युद्धे प्रयुक्तः काष्ठदण्डो लोहाग्रः शूलविशेषः, प्रासः, शक्तिः *f.*

Halberdier, *s.* पूर्व्वोक्तशूलधरः, शक्तिग्रहः, शाक्तीकः, प्रासिकः.

Halcyon, *s.* (Kingfisher) मत्स्यरङ्कः -ङ्कः, सुचित्रकः, कुट्टकः.

Halcyon, *a.* प्रसन्नः -न्ना -न्नं, शान्तः -न्ता -न्तं, प्रशान्तः -न्ता -न्तं, निर्वेगः -गा -गं, निराकुलः -ला -लं, निर्वृतः -ता -तं, निर्वातः -ता -तं, सुखी -खिनी -खि (न्).

Hale, *a.* निरामयः -या -यं, नीरोगः -गा -गं, नीरुजः -जा -जं, नीरुक् *m. f. n.* (ज्), कल्यः -ल्या -ल्यं, आधिव्याधिरहितः -ता -तं, अक्षतः -ता -तं.

To hale, *v. a.* कृष् (c. 1. कर्षति, क्रष्टुं), आकृष्, अपकृष्, अपहृ (c. 1. -हरति -हर्त्तुं).

Half, *s.* अर्द्धं -र्द्धः, अर्द्धभागः, अर्द्धांशः; 'half an hour,' अर्द्धदण्डः; 'half a league,' अर्द्धक्रोशः; 'half a hundred,' अर्द्धशतं; 'half the body,' अर्द्धाङ्गं; 'a year and a half,' सार्द्धवत्सरः; 'a hundred and a half,' सार्द्धशतं; 'the best half,' उत्तमार्द्धं -र्द्धः; 'the last half,' अपरार्द्धं, पश्चार्द्धं; 'sharing a half,' अर्द्धभागी -गिनी -गि (न्), अर्द्धांशी -शिनी -शि (न्), अर्द्धी -र्द्धिनी -र्द्धि (न्); 'lasting half a month,' सार्द्धमासिकः -की -कं.

Half, *a.* अर्द्धः -र्द्धा -र्द्धं, आर्द्धिकः -की -कं, अर्द्धिकः -का -कं; 'half assent,' अर्द्धाङ्गीकारः; 'half moon,' अर्द्धचन्द्रः.

Half, *adv.* अर्द्धं, अर्द्धेन, सामि; 'half-man, half-woman,' अर्द्धेन पुरुषोऽर्द्धेन स्त्री; 'half-eaten,' अर्द्धभुक्तः -क्ता -क्तं, जग्धार्द्धः -र्द्धा -र्द्धं, सामिभुक्तः -क्ता -क्तं; 'half-drank,' अर्द्धपीतः -ता -तं, सामिपीतः -ता -तं; 'half-read,' अर्द्धवाचितः -ता -तं; 'half-spoken,' अर्द्धोक्तः -क्ता -क्तं; 'half-closed,' अर्द्धसंवृतः -ता -तं, मुकुलितः -ता -तं, निमीलितः -ता -तं.

Half-blood, *s.* or *a.* भिन्नोदरः -रा -रं, भिन्ननाभिः -भिः -भि, भिन्नगर्भः -र्भा -र्भं, असमानोदरः -रा -रं, भिन्नोदर्य्यः, अन्योदर्य्यः, भिन्नशरीरान्वयः.

Half-brother, *s.* वैमात्रः -त्रेयः, भ्राता द्वैमातुरः, अन्योदर्य्यः, सापत्नः.

Half-dead, *a.* मृतकल्पः -ल्पा -ल्पं, मृतप्रायः -या -यं, मुमूर्षुः -र्षुः -र्षु, आसन्नमृत्युः -त्युः -त्यु, मरणोन्मुखः -खी -खं, अर्द्धमृतः -ता -तं, कण्ठगतप्राणः -णा -णं.

Half-heard, *a.* अर्द्धश्रुतः -ता -तं, ईषच्छ्रुतः -ता -तं.

Half-holiday, *s.* अर्द्धोत्सवः, अर्द्धमहोत्सवः, अर्द्धानध्यायः.

Half-learned, *a.* अल्पज्ञानी -निनी -नि (न्), किञ्चिज्ज्ञः -ज्ञा -ज्ञं, चुञ्चुकः.

Half-lost, *a.* नष्टप्रायः -या -यं, आसन्ननाशः -शा -शं, नाशोन्मुखः -खी -खं.

Half-moon, *s.* अर्द्धचन्द्रः, चन्द्रार्द्धं, अर्द्धेन्दुः *m.*; 'shaped like a half-moon,' अर्द्धचन्द्राकारः -रा -रं, अर्द्धचन्द्राकृतिः -तिः -ति.

Half-pay, *s.* निवृत्तयुद्धस्य सैन्यस्य प्रकल्पितम् अर्द्धवेतनं.

Half-penny, *s.* ताम्रमुद्रार्द्धं, ताम्रमुद्राविशेषः.

Half-pike, *s.* लघुशूलः -लं, अदीर्घपरिमाणः शूलविशेषः, परिघः.

Half-seas-over, *s.* ईषन्मत्तः -त्ता -त्तं, ईषदुन्मत्तः -त्ता -त्तं, ईषत्क्षीवः -वा -वं.

Half-sister, *s.* वैमात्री, वैमात्रेयी, स्वसा द्वैमातुरी, अन्योदर्य्या.

Half-sphere, *s.* अर्द्धमण्डलं, अर्द्धगोलः, मण्डलार्द्धं, भूगोलार्द्धं.

Half-starved, *a.* अनाहारेण म्रियमाणः -णा -णं or मृतप्रायः -या -यं, क्षुधावसन्नः -न्ना -न्नं.

Half-uttered, *a.* अर्द्धोक्तः -क्ता -क्तं, अर्द्धोदितः -ता -तं, अर्द्धकथितः -ता -तं.

Half-way, *adv.* अर्द्धमार्गे, अर्द्धपथे, मध्यमार्गे, मध्यपथे.

Half-witted, *a.* अल्पबुद्धिः -द्धिः -द्धि, अल्पधीः -धीः -धि, अल्पमेधाः -धाः -धः (स्).

Half-year, *s.* अर्द्धवत्सरः, वत्सरार्द्धं, अब्दार्द्धं, षण्मासः, अयनं.

Half-yearly, *a.* षाण्मासिकः -की -कं, आर्द्धवर्षिकः -की -कं.

Halibut, *s.* बृहत्कायः समुद्रीयमत्स्यभेदः.

Halidom, *s.* शापः, शपथः, दिव्यं, सत्यं, प्रत्ययः.

Halituous, *a.* प्राणसमभावः -वा -वं, वाष्पोपमः -मा -मं, धूमलः -ला -लं.

Hall, *s.* (Large room at the entrance of a house) शाला, वहिर्द्वारशाला, द्वारोपान्ते महाशाला, वासकोष्ठः, कक्षा, कक्ष्या, किर्म्मी; 'a temporary hall,' मण्डपः -पा, जनाश्रयः; 'a judgment-hall,' विचारशाला.

Halleluiah, hallelujah, *exclam.* ईश्वरस्य धन्यवादं or स्तुतिवादं कुरुत.

Halleluiah, *s.* ईश्वरस्य धन्यवादः or स्तुतिवादः or स्तुतिगानं.

Halliard, halyard, *s.* नौरज्जुः *m.*, नौगुणः, वातवसनोत्तोलनार्थं रज्जुः.

Halloo, *interj.* भोः, भो, भोभो, हे, है, अये, अयि, अरे, रे, अहो, हंहो, हलहलाशब्दः.

To halloo, *v. n.* हलहलाशब्दं कृ, हलहला (nom. हलहलायते), भोः, हे, है इत्यादिशब्दैर् उत्क्रुश् (c. 1. -क्रोशति -क्रोष्टुं) or दूराद् आह्वे (c. 1. -ह्वयति -ह्वातुं), उच्चैःस्वरेण घुष् (c. 10. घोषयति -यितुं).

To halloo, *v. a.* (Set on by shouts) हे, है, हलहला इत्यादिशब्दैः कुक्कुरादीन् प्रचुद् (c. 10. -चोदयति -यितुं).

To hallow, *v. a.* (Make holy) पवित्रीकृ, पवित्रं -त्रां -त्रं कृ, पुण्यीकृ, पुण्यं -ण्यां -ण्यं कृ, पूज्यं -ज्यां -ज्यं कृ, शुद्धीकृ.—(Consecrate) संस्कृ, अभिसंस्कृ, अभिषिच् (c. 6. -षिञ्चति -षेक्तुं), प्रोक्ष् (c. 1. -उक्षति -क्षितुं), प्रतिष्ठा in caus. (-ष्ठापयति -यितुं), धर्म्मार्थं विनियुज् (c. 7. -युनक्ति -योक्तुं) or निर्दिश् (c. 6. -दिशति -देष्टुं).

Hallowed, *p. p.* (Made holy, reverenced) पवित्रीकृतः -ता -तं, पवित्रितः -ता -तं, पूजितः -ता -तं, पूज्यः -ज्या -ज्यं, अर्चितः -ता -तं.—(Consecrated) संस्कृतः -ता -तं, कृतसंस्कारः -रा -रं, प्रतिष्ठितः -ता -तं, सुप्रतिष्ठितः -ता -तं, प्रोक्षितः -ता -तं, प्रणीतः -ता -तं, अभिषिक्तः -क्ता

-क्तं, धर्म्मार्थं विनियोजितः -ता -तं.

Hallucination, *s.* मोहः, व्यामोहः, माया, भ्रमः, भ्रान्तिः *f.*, मतिविभ्रमः, मिथ्यामतिः *f.*, इन्द्रजालं, वञ्चना.

Halm, *s.* (Straw) तृणं, पलालः -लं -ली, पलः, धान्यकल्कं.

Halo, *s.* द्युतिमाला, अंशुमाला, सूर्य्यपरिगतं or चन्द्रपरिगतं द्युतिमण्डलं or दीप्तिमण्डलं or रक्तवर्णमण्डलं, दीप्तिचक्रं, द्युतिवलयः, परिधिः *m.*, परिवेशः.

Halser, *s.* नौरज्जुः *m.*, नौगुणः, नौबन्धनरज्जुः, नौबन्धनार्थं महागुणः.

Halt, *s.* (Stopping) अयानं, पथमध्ये स्थितिः *f.* or अवस्थितिः *f.*, स्थानं, आसनं, विश्रामः, यानविरतिः *f.*, विरामः, अवरतिः *f.*, स्तम्भः, यतिः *f.* —(Limping) लङ्गः.

Halt, *a.* (Lame) पङ्गुः -ङ्गुः -ङ्गु, खञ्जः -ञ्जा -ञ्जं, स्रोरः -रा -रं, गतिविकलः -ला -लं, पादविकलः -ला -लं.

To halt, *v. n.* (Stop) पथमध्ये स्था (c. 1. तिष्ठति -ते, स्थातुं), संस्था, विष्ठा, अवस्था, or विरम् (c. 1. रमति -रन्तुं) or विश्रम् (c. 4. -श्राम्यति -श्रमितुं), स्तम्भ् (c. 1. स्तम्भते -म्भितुं).—(Limp) लङ्ग् (c. 1. लङ्गति -ङ्गितुं), खञ्जीभू, गतिविकलः -ला -लम् अस्.

Halted, *p. p.* निवृत्तयानः -ना -नं, अवस्थितः -ता -तं, सन्निषण्णः -ण्णा -ण्णं.

Halter, *s.* (Rope) कण्ठपाशः -शकः, कण्ठरज्जुः *m.*, पाशः, कण्ठलता, पलापः, प्रग्रहः, प्रग्राहः.

To halter, *v. a.* कण्ठपाशेन बन्ध् (c. 9. बध्नाति, बन्द्धुं), पाश (nom. पाशयति -यितुं).

To halve, *v. a.* अर्द्धीकृ, द्विसमभागीकृ, द्विधा कृ, द्विखण्डीकृ, द्व्यंशीकृ.

Halved, *a.* अर्द्धीकृतः -ता -तं, सामिकृतः -ता -तं, द्विसमभागीकृतः -ता -तं.

Halves, *s. pl.* (To go halves) अर्द्धभागी -गिनी -गि भू, अर्द्धांशी -शिनी -शि भू.—(To cry halves) अर्द्धभागो ममेति वद् (c. 1. वदति -दितुं).

Ham, *s.* (Back of the knee) मन्दिरः, जङ्घोरुसन्धेः पश्चिमभागः.—(Thigh) सक्थि *n.*, जङ्घा, जाङ्गनी; 'seated on the hams,' कृतावसक्थिकः -का -कं.—(Dried hog's flesh) वल्लूरं, शूकरस्य शुष्कमांसं.

Hamadryad, *s.* वनदेवता, तरुदेवता, वृक्षाधिष्ठात्री देवता, वन्यस्त्री.

Hamlet, *s.* ग्रामः, क्षुद्रग्रामः, पल्लिः *f.*, पल्ली, पद्रः, खेटकः, निवसथः.

Hammer, *s.* मुद्गरः, घनः, अयोघनः, अयोग्रं, मुषलः, मुसलः.

To hammer, *v. a.* मुद्गरेण आहन् (c. 2. -हन्ति -न्तुं) or तड् (c. 10. ताडयति -यितुं) or प्रहृ (c. 1. -हरति -हर्त्तुं).

To hammer, *v. n.* (Labour, work hard) महायासं कृ, महाकष्टेन मुहुर् मुहुर् उद्योगं कृ, पुनः पुनर् उत्साहं कृ or श्रम् (c.4. श्राम्यति, श्रमितुं).

Hammer-cloth, *s.* रथोपस्थवस्त्रं, सूतासनाच्छादनं.

Hammerer, *s.* मुद्गरेण ताडयिता *m.* (तृ), मुद्गरादिना कर्म्मकारी *m.* (न्).

Hammering, *s.* मुद्गरताडनं, मुद्गरप्रहरणं, मुद्गराघातः.

Hammock, *s.* दोला -ली, दोलिका, प्रेङ्खा, खट्वा, प्रेङ्खोलनं.

Hamper, *s.* पेटा -टी, पेटिका, पेटकः, करण्डः, डल्लकः.

To hamper, *v. a.* रुध् (c. 7. रुणद्धि, रोद्धुं), प्रतिरुध्, निरुध्, विरुध्, विहन् (c. 2. -हन्ति -न्तुं), व्याहन्, विघ्न (nom. विघ्नयति -यितुं), बाध् (c. 1. बाधते -धितुं), क्लेशं दा, शल्यं कृ.

Hampered, *p. p.* विरुद्धः -द्धा -द्धं, विघ्नितः -ता -तं, बाधितः -ता -तं.

Hamstring, *s.* मन्दिरशिरा, मन्दिरस्नायुः *m.*, जङ्घोरुसन्धिबन्धनं, ऊरुपर्व्व-बन्धनस्नायुः *m.*, जङ्घोरुबन्धनं.

To hamstring, *v. a.* मन्दिरशिरां छिद् (c. 7. छिनत्ति, छेत्तुं), जङ्घोरुपर्व्वबन्धनं छित्त्वा गतिविकलं -लां -लं कृ.

Hamstrung, *p. p.* छिन्नमन्दिरस्नायुः -युः -यु, छिन्नजङ्घोरुबन्धनः -ना -नं.

Hanaper, *s.* कोषः, राजकोषः, राजस्वकोषः, धनकोषः.

Hand, *s.* (Palm with the fingers) हस्तः, करः, पाणिः *m.*, पञ्चशाखः, भुजादलः, शयः, शमः, कुलिः *m.*, हरणः; 'the right hand,' अग्रहस्तः, अग्रकरः, अग्रपाणिः *m.*; 'the left hand,' वामहस्तः; 'the palm of the hand,' हस्ततलं, करतलं; 'the open hand,' प्रहस्तः, प्रपाणिः *m.*, चपेटः; 'back of the hand,' करपृष्ठं, अवहस्तः; 'hollow of the hand,' करपुटं, करकोषः, करपार्श्वं; 'both hands,' हस्तौ *m.* du., हस्तद्वयं, करद्वयं; 'a beautiful hand,' करकमलं, करपद्मं, करपल्लवः, करपङ्कजं; 'the hand below the wrist,' करभः, हस्तपुच्छं; 'the clenched hand,' मुष्टिः *m. f.*, हस्तमुष्टिः; 'part of the hand sacred to the gods,' देवतीर्थं, दैवं; 'to the manes,' पितृतर्पणं, पितृतीर्थं, पित्र्यं; 'the hands and feet,' पाणिपादं; 'bound hand and foot,' संयमितकरचरणः -णा -णं; 'hand to hand,' हस्ताहस्ति, मुष्टीमुष्टि, बाहूबाहवि; 'hand in hand,' सहितं, सह, समं, योगतस्, सम्भूय, एकीभूय; 'with joined hands,' अभिगृहीतपाणिः -णिः -णि; 'with hands across,' व्यत्यस्तपाणिः -णिः -णि; 'with one's own hand,' स्वहस्तेन; 'at hand,' उपस्थितः -ता -तं, आसन्नः -न्ना -न्नं, सन्निहितः -ता -तं; 'in hand, in one's possession,' हस्तस्थः -स्था -स्थं, हस्तस्थितः -ता -तं, हस्तवर्त्ती -र्त्तिनी -र्त्ति (न्), हस्तगतः -ता -तं; 'held in the hand,' करधृतः -ता -तं, करतलधृतः -ता -तं, करनिहितः -ता -तं, करग्राह्यः -ह्या -ह्यं; 'in hand, ready to hand,' प्रस्तुतः -ता -तं, प्रत्युत्पन्नः -न्ना -न्नं, सिद्धः -द्धा -द्धं; 'matter in hand,' प्रस्तुतं; 'sword in hand,' खड्गपाणिः *m.*; 'staff in hand,' लगुडहस्तः; 'off hand,' अचिरेण, अविलम्बितं, आकस्मिकः -की -कं, प्रत्युत्पन्नः -न्ना -न्नं, अचिन्तापूर्व्वः -र्व्वा -र्व्वं; 'out of hand,' तत्काले, तत्क्षणात्, सपदि, सद्यस्; 'living from hand to mouth,' उत्पन्नभक्षी -क्षिणी -क्षि (न्); 'to take in hand,' आरभ् (c. 1. -रभते -रब्धुं), व्यवसो (c. 4. -स्यति -सातुं), अध्यवसो; 'to lend a hand,' उपकृ, साहाय्यं कृ, सहायत्वं कृ; 'to lay hands on,' धृ (c. 1. धरति, धर्त्तुं), ग्रह् (c. 9. गृह्णाति, ग्रहीतुं), हृ (c. 1. हरति, हर्त्तुं); 'to shake hands,' परस्परं पाणिं ग्रह्, अन्योन्यं हस्तं or हस्तौ स्पृश् (c. 6. स्पृशति, स्प्रष्टुं); 'to have a hand in,' सहकारी -रिणी -रि भू or अस्; 'to get the upper hand,' अभिभू, प्रभू; 'to clap the hands,' करतालं कृ; 'to support with the hand,' करालम्बनं कृ; 'under-hand,' तिरस्, रहस्, छलेन.—(A measure) हस्तपरिमाणं, करतलपरिमाणं.—(Side, part) पार्श्वः, पक्षः, भागः; 'on the one hand,' एकतस्, एकत्र; 'on the other hand,' अन्यत्र, पुनर्; 'on all hands,' सर्व्वतस्, सर्व्वत्र.—(Action, performance) करणं, विधानं, प्रवृत्तिः *f.*, चेष्टा, क्रिया.—(Power, possession) शक्तिः *f.*, अधिकारः, आधिकारण्यं; 'fallen into one's hand,' हस्तगतः -ता -तं.—(Agent) कर्त्ता *m.* (र्तृ), कारः, कारकः, कर्म्मकारः.—(Index of a dial) कीलः, देशिनी, प्रदेशिनी, सूचिः *f.*, सूचिनी.—(Form of writing) स्वाक्षरं, स्वहस्ताक्षरं, लिपिः *f.*

To hand, *v. a.* (Give with the hand) हस्तेन गृहीत्वा परहस्ते दा (c. 3. ददाति, दातुं) or प्रदा or ऋ in caus. (अर्पयति -यितुं) or समृ or प्रतिपद् (c. 10. -पादयति -यितुं).—(Guide or lead with the hand) हस्तेन नी (c. 1. नयति, नेतुं) or समानी or गम् in caus. (गमयति -यितुं).—(Support with the hand) परालम्बनार्थं हस्तं दा, करालम्बनं कृ.—(Hand down, transmit) क्रमागतं -तां -तं कृ, क्रमायातं -तां -तं, क्रमेण or पारम्पर्य्येण सञ्चर् (c. 10. -चारयति -यितुं) or सङ्क्रम् (c. 10. -क्रामयति -यितुं) or प्रतिपद्.

Hand-barrow, *s.* हस्तसञ्चालितं वाहनं or यानं.

Hand-bell, *s.* हस्तेन वादिता क्षुद्रघण्टा, घण्टिका, हस्तघण्टा.

HAND-BREADTH, *s.* एकहस्तपरिमाणं, एककरपरिमाणं, पाणितलं.

HANDCUFF, *s.* हस्तपाशः, पाणिबन्धनं, हस्तबन्धः, करबन्धनं.

To HANDCUFF, *v. a.* हस्तौ पाशेन बन्ध् (c. 9. बध्नाति, बन्द्धुं), पाणिबन्धनं कृ.

HANDCUFFED, *p. p.* बद्धहस्तः -स्ता -स्तं, यन्त्रितकरः -रा -रं, संयमितकरः -रा -रं.

HANDED, *p. p.* (Given into the hand) हस्ते दत्तः -त्ता -त्तं or अर्पितः -ता -तं.—(Led with the hand) हस्तेन नीतः -ता -तं.—(Supported with the hand) दत्तहस्तः -स्ता -स्तं, आलम्बितकरः -रा -रं.—(Handed down) पारम्पर्य्यक्रमागतः -ता -तं, क्रमायातः -ता -तं, पारम्पर्य्येण सञ्चारितः -ता -तं.

HANDFUL, *s.* मुष्टिः *m. f.*, हस्तपूरणं, पाणिपूरणं, गण्डूषः -षा, मुष्टिपरिमितं द्रव्यं; 'a handful of grass,' तृणमुष्टिः.

HAND-GALLOP, *s.* ईषत्पुलायितं, अर्द्धपुलायितं, ईषद्वल्गितं, अर्द्धवल्गितं.

HAND-GUN, *s.* हस्तद्वारेण प्रयुक्ता आग्नेयनाडिः, हस्तनाडिः.

HANDICRAFT, *s.* शिल्पं, शिल्पकर्म्म *n.* (न्), शिल्पिकं, शिल्पविद्या, हस्तकर्म्म *n.*, हस्तव्यापारः, हस्तव्यवसायः.

HANDICRAFTSMAN, *s.* शिल्पी *m.* (न्), शिल्पकारः, कर्म्मकारः, हस्तव्यापारी *m.* (न्), हस्तव्यवसायी *m.* (न्), पाणिघः.

HANDILY, *adv.* सदाक्ष्यं, दाक्ष्येण, दक्षं, करदाक्ष्येण, हस्तकौशल्येन, हस्तलाघवेन, कुशलं, निपुणं, चतुरं, सलाघवं, युक्त्या.

HANDINESS, *s.* दक्षता, दाक्ष्यं, हस्तकौशल्यं, करदक्षता, हस्तलाघवं, हस्तपादादिक्षिप्रता, युक्तिः *f.*, कौशल्यं, कुशलता, सुप्रयोगः -गता, नैपुण्यं, चातुर्य्यं, चतुरता, पटुता, क्षिप्रता.

HANDIWORK, *s.* हस्तकर्म्म *n.* (न्), हस्तव्यापारः, हस्तकृतं कर्म्म.

HANDKERCHIEF, *s.* नक्तकः, चरकं, मुखमार्जनी, गात्रमार्जनी; 'neck-handkerchief,' कण्ठवेष्टनं, गलावेष्टनं, कण्ठवस्त्रं.

To HANDLE, *v. a.* (Feel with the hand) स्पृश् (c. 6. स्पृशति, स्प्रष्टुं), संस्पृश्, परिस्पृश्, हस्तेन परामृश् (c. 6. -मृशति -म्रष्टुं) or परिमृश् or आलभ् (c. 1. -लभते -लब्धुं) or समालभ् or घट्ट् (c. 10. घट्टयति -यितुं) or परिघट्ट्.—(Manage) प्रणी (c. 1. -णयति -णेतुं), विधा (c. 3. -दधाति -धातुं).—(Use) प्रयुज् (c. 7. -युनक्ति -युंक्ते -योक्तुं), उपयुज्.—(Treat) आचर् (c. 1. -चरति -रितुं), व्यवहृ (c. 1. -हरति -हर्त्तुं).—(Discuss) विचर् (c. 10. -चारयति -यितुं), विमृश्.

HANDLE, *s.* मुष्टिः *m. f.*, धारकः, दण्डः, तलः, तालः, नालः, कर्णः.—(Of a sword, &c.) त्सरुः *m.*, सरुः *m.*, तलः, तालः.—(Of a plough) ईषादण्डः; 'become a handle,' नालायितः -ता -तं.

HANDLED, *p. p.* स्पृष्टः -ष्टा -ष्टं, संस्पृष्टः -ष्टा -ष्टं, परामृष्टः -ष्टा -ष्टं, परिमृष्टः -ष्टा -ष्टं, परिघट्टितः -ता -तं, करघट्टितः -ता -तं, करपरिघट्टितः -ता -तं.

HANDLESS, *a.* अहस्तः -स्ता -स्तं, विहस्तः -स्ता -स्तं, अकरः -रा -रं.

HAND-MAID, *s.* दासी, दासिका, चेटी, सेविका, परिचारिका.

HAND-MILL, *s.* यन्त्रपेषणी, हस्तेन सञ्चालिता पेषणी.

HAND-RAIL, *s.* (Of a staircase) सोपाने उभयतः स्थापिता क्षुद्रस्तम्भपंक्तिः.

HAND-SAW, *s.* हस्तसञ्चारितं करपत्रं, हस्तसञ्चालितः क्रकचः.

HANDSEL, *s.* प्रथमविक्रयः, आदिविक्रयः, प्रथमप्रयोगः, प्रथमव्यवहारः, प्रथमकर्म्म *n.* (न्), आदिक्रिया.

To HANDSEL, *v. a.* प्रथमं कृ or प्रयुज् (c. 7. -युनक्ति -युंक्ते -योक्तुं), प्रथमप्रयोगं कृ.

HANDSOME, *a.* (Beautiful) सुरूपः -पी -पं, रूपवान् -वती -वत् (त्), रूपी -पिणी -पि (न्), रूपोपेतः -ता -तं, सुगात्रः -त्री -त्रं, स्वङ्गः -ङ्गी -ङ्गं, वराङ्गः -ङ्गी -ङ्गं, दर्शनीयः -या -यं, सुदृश्यः -श्या -श्यं, चारुः -र्व्वी -रु, चारुदर्शनः -ना -नं, सौम्यः -म्या -म्यी -म्यं, सुन्दरः -रा -री -रं, शोभनः -ना -नं, कान्तः -न्ता -न्तं, लावण्यवान् -वती -वत् (त्), वामः -मा -मं, वामिलः -ला -लं, पुष्कलः -ला -लं, सिंहसंहननः -ना -नं; 'having a handsome countenance,' शुभाननः -ना -नं, चारुवदनः -ना -नं, सुमुखः -खा -खी -खं, आननाब्जः -ब्जा -ब्जं; 'a handsome woman,' रूपवती, प्रमदा. Often expressed by सु; as, 'having handsome teeth,' सुदन् -दती -दत् (त्); 'having handsome eyes,' सुनयनः -ना -नं, सुदृक् *m. f. n.* (श्); 'having a handsome waist,' सुमध्यमा.—(Generous, liberal) उदारः -रा -रं, वदान्यः -न्या -न्यं, स्थूललक्ष्यः -क्ष्या -क्ष्यं, अकृपणः -णा -णं.—(Ample, large) विपुलः -ला -लं, विशालः -ला -लं, प्रचुरः -रा -रं, बृहन् -हती -हत् (त्).

HANDSOMELY, *adv.* (With beauty or grace) चारु, सुन्दरं, सौन्दर्य्येण, लावण्येन, सलावण्यं, शोभनं, शोभया.—(Generously) उदारवत्, वदान्यवत्, अकृपणं.

HANDSOMENESS, *s.* सुरूपता, रूपवत्त्वं, रूपं, रूपलावण्यं, दर्शनीयता, सुदृश्यता, चारुता, सौम्यता, सौन्दर्य्यं, कान्तता, शोभा, वामता.

HAND-STROKE, *s.* कराघातः, हस्ताघातः, पाणिघातः, हस्तप्रहारः, हस्तपातः.

HAND-WEAPON, *s.* हस्तायुधं, हस्तशस्त्रं, हस्तास्त्रं, हस्तप्रहरणं.

HAND-WRITING, *s.* स्वहस्ताक्षरं, हस्ताक्षरं, स्वाक्षरं, हस्तलिखनं, हस्तलेखा.—(In general) लेखः -खा, लिखनं, लिपिः *f.*, लिबिः *f.*, अक्षरसंस्थानं.

HANDY, *a.* दक्षः -क्षा -क्षं, करदक्षः -क्षा -क्षं, लघुहस्तः -स्ता -स्तं, चतुरः -रा -रं, कुशलः -ला -लं, निपुणः -णा -णं, क्षिप्रः -प्रा -प्रं, युक्तिमान् -मती -मत् (त्), सुप्रयोगवान् -वती -वत् (त्), पटुः -टुः -टु, लघुः -घुः -घु.—(Convenient, ready, near) उपयुक्तः -क्ता -क्तं, प्रस्तुतः -ता -तं, प्रत्युत्पन्नः -न्ना -न्नं, आसन्नः -न्ना -न्नं, निकटः -टा -टं, समीपस्थः -स्था -स्थं.

HANDY-BLOW, *s.* कराघातः, हस्ताघातः, पाणिघातः; 'handy-blows,' मुष्टीमुष्टि.

To HANG, *v. a.* उद्बन्ध् (c. 9. -बध्नाति -बन्द्धुं), उद्बन्धनं कृ, उद्बद्धं -द्धां -द्धं कृ, ऊर्द्ध्वं or उच्चैः or विहायसा बन्ध्, आन्दोल (nom. आन्दोलयति -यितुं); 'by a loop,' काच (nom. काचयति -यितुं).—(Put to death by hanging) रज्जुपाशेन उद्बन्ध्, उद्बन्धनेन हन् (c. 2. हन्ति -न्तुं or caus. घातयति -यितुं) or प्राणदण्डं कृ.—(With curtains, &c.) यवनिकादिना परिवेष्ट् (c. 1. -वेष्टते -ष्टितुं) or प्रच्छद् (c. 10. -छादयति -यितुं).

To HANG, *v. n.* (Be suspended) उद्बन्ध् in pass. (-बध्यते), ऊर्द्ध्वं or उच्चैर् बन्ध्.—(Dangle) लम्ब् (c. 1. लम्बते -म्बितुं), अवलम्ब्, प्रलम्ब्, लुल् (c. 1. लोलति -ते -लितुं), लुठ् (c. 6. लुठति -ठितुं), चञ्च् (c. 1. चञ्चति -ञ्चितुं).—(Swing) दोल (nom. दोलायते -यितुं), प्रेङ्ख् (c. 1. प्रेङ्खति -ङ्खितुं).—(Depend) अवलम्ब्, समालम्ब्, आश्रि (c. 1. -श्रयति -ते -यितुं), अधीनः -ना -नं भू.—(Cling to) अवलम्ब्, समालम्ब्, संलग्नीभू, अनुलग्नीभू, लग्नीभू, अनुबन्ध् in pass., सञ्ज् in pass. (सज्यते, सज्जते).—(Hang back) विलम्ब्.—(Hang by) अवलम्ब्; 'hanging by the mouth,' मुखेन अवलम्ब्य.—(Hang down) अवलम्ब्, प्रलम्ब्, अधो लम्ब्.—(Hang over, impend) उपस्था (c. 1. -तिष्ठति -स्थातुं). प्रत्युपस्था.—(Hang over, project) बहिर्लम्ब्.—(Hang one's self) आत्मदेहम् उद्बन्ध्, रज्जुपाशेन आत्मघातं कृ.—(Hang the head) शिरो नम् (c. 10. नामयति, नमयति -यितुं) or अवनम्.

HANGER, *s.* (One who hangs) उद्बन्धा *m.* (न्धृ), उद्बन्धनकृत्.—(Sort of sword) हस्तपत्रः खड्गविशेषः, हस्तकृपाणः.

HANGER-ON, *s.* उपजीवी *m.* (न्), अनुजीवी *m.*, परान्नभोजी *m.* (न्), परपिण्डादः, पराधीनः, पात्रेसमितः, पीठमर्द्दः.

HANGING, *s.* उद्बन्धनं, ऊर्द्ध्वबन्धनं.—(Tapestry, drapery) जवनिका, चित्रजवनिका, यवनिका, प्रच्छदपटः, अपटी, परिच्छदः, वसनं, अम्बरं.

HANGING, *part.* (Dangling, being suspended) लम्बमानः -ना -नं.

लम्बः -म्बा -म्बं, प्रलम्बः -म्बा -म्बं, लम्बितः -ता -तं, अवलम्बितः -ता -तं, अवलम्बः -म्बा -म्बं, अवलम्बी -म्बिनी -म्बि (न्), विलम्बमानः -ना -नं; 'hanging the head,' नतमूर्द्धा-र्द्धा-र्द्ध (न्), अवनतशिराः -राः -रः (स्).

HANGMAN, *s.* दण्डपाशिकः, मृतपाः *m.*, घातुकपुरुषः, उद्बन्धनकर्म्माधिकृतः.

HANG-NAIL, *s.* नखाङ्कुरः, नखमूलाङ्कुरः, नखकीलः.

HANK, *s.* (A bundle of skeins) पञ्जिकासमूहः.—(Wooden ring) काष्ठवलयः.—(Check) संयमः, नियहः, यन्त्रणं, निरोधः.

To HANKER AFTER, *a.* अभिलष् (c. 1. -लषति, c. 4. -लष्यति -लषितुं), वाञ्छ् (c. 1. वाञ्छति -ञ्छितुं), अभिवाञ्छ्, स्पृह् (c. 10. स्पृहयति -यितुं), कांक्ष् (c. 1. कांक्षति -क्षितुं), आकांक्ष्, अनुकांक्ष्, उत्कण्ठ् (c. 1. -कण्ठते -ण्ठितुं), लुभ् (c. 4. लुभ्यति, लोब्धुं), कम् (c. 10. कामयते -यितुं), लभ् in des. (लिप्सते -प्सितुं), गृध् (c. 4. गृध्यति, गर्धितुं).

HANKERING, *s.* स्पृहा, अभिलाषः, वाञ्छा, उत्कण्ठा, आकांक्षा.

HAP, HAP-HAZARD, *s.* दैवं, दैवयोगः, दैवगतिः *f.*, दैवघटना, अदृष्टं, सङ्गतिः *f.*, दैवसङ्गतं, नियतिः *f.*

HAPLESS, *a.* दुर्भाग्यः -ग्या -ग्यं, अभाग्यः -ग्या -ग्यं, मन्दभाग्यः -ग्या -ग्यं, दैवहीनः -ना -नं, निर्दैवः -वा -वं, अधन्यः -न्या -न्यं, हतभाग्यः -ग्या -ग्यं.

HAPLY, *adv.* दैवात्, दैववशात्, दैवयोगेन, अदृष्टवशात्, अकस्मात्, अनिश्चितं, अचिन्तितं, अपिनाम, किल.

To HAPPEN, *v. n.* घट् (c. 1. घटते -टितुं), निपत् (c. 1. -पतति -तितुं), आपत्, सम्पद् (c. 4. -पद्यते -पत्तुं), उपपद्, समापद्, उत्पद्, उपस्था (c. 1. -तिष्ठति -स्थातुं), समुपस्था, सम्भू (c. 1. -भवति -वितुं), संवृत् (c. 1. -वर्त्तते -र्त्तितुं), वृत्, आगम् (c. 1. -गच्छति -गन्तुं), उपागम्, दैवात् or अकस्माद् भू.

HAPPENED, *p. p.* घटितः -ता -तं, उपस्थितः -ता -तं, समुपस्थितः -ता -तं, समापन्नः -न्ना -न्नं, उपपन्नः -न्ना -न्नं, उत्पन्नः -न्ना -न्नं, निपतितः -ता -तं, आपतितः -ता -तं, वृत्तः -त्ता -त्तं, संवृत्तः -त्ता -त्तं, आगतः -ता -तं, उपागतः -ता -तं, सम्भूतः -ता -तं.

HAPPILY, *adv.* (Fortunately) सौभाग्येन -ग्यात्, कल्याणात्, दिष्ट्या, सुभगं.—(In a state of happiness) सुखं, सुखेन, यथासुखं, सौख्येन, स्वास्थ्येन.

HAPPINESS, *s.* सुखं, सौख्यं, सुखित्वं, आनन्दः, आह्लादः, धन्यता, हर्षः, कल्याणं, शर्म्म *n.* (न्), श्रेयस्, निःश्रेयसं, क्षेमं -मं, स्वास्थ्यं, कुशलं, शुभं, मङ्गलं, माङ्गल्यं, कौशल्यं, भद्रं, सौभाग्यं, सम्मतिः *f.*, सम्पद् *f.*, निर्वृतिः *f.*, निवृतिः *f.*, श्रीः *f.*, पुण्योदयः, शस्तं, मतल्लिका, मचर्चिका, प्रकाण्डं, उद्धः, तल्लजः.

HAPPY, *a.* सुखी -खिनी -खि (न्), सुखयुक्तः -क्ता -क्तं, सुखभागी -गिनी -गि (न्), आनन्दी -न्दिनी -न्दि (न्), हृष्टः -ष्टा -ष्टं, प्रीतः -ता -तं, तुष्टः -ष्टा -ष्टं, प्रहृष्टः -ष्टा -ष्टं, प्रमोदी -दिनी -दि (न्), प्रमुदितः -ता -तं, विशोकः -का -कं, शोकहीनः -ना -नं, सुस्थः -स्था -स्थं, निर्वृतः -ता -तं, अकातरः -रा -रं, तृप्तः -प्ता -प्तं, मत्तः -त्ता -त्तं.—(Fortunate, prosperous) धन्यः -न्या -न्यं, सौभाग्यवान् -वती -वत् (त्), भाग्यवान् &c., पुण्यवान् &c., पुण्यः -ण्या -ण्यं, शर्म्मवान् &c., क्षेमवान् &c., क्षेमः -मा -मं, क्षेम्यः -म्या -म्यं, कुशली -लिनी -लि (न्), कुशलः -ला -लं, कल्याणः -णा -णं -णी -णिनी -णि (न्), शुभः -भा -भं, शुभान्वितः -ता -तं, शुभंयुः -युः -यु, भद्रः -द्रा -द्रं, श्रीमान् -मती -मत् (त्), श्रीयुक्तः -क्ता -क्तं, लक्ष्मीवान् &c., मङ्गलः -ला -लं, शिवः -वा -वं, भावुकः -का -कं, भविकः -का -कं, भव्यः -व्या -व्यं, श्वःश्रेयसः -सा -सं, शस्तः -स्ता -स्तं, लक्षणः -णा -णं, श्रीलः -ला -लं, समृद्धः -द्धा -द्धं, अधिकर्द्धिः -र्द्धिः -र्द्धि, वर्द्धिष्णुः -ष्णुः -ष्णु, निरापद् *m. f. n.*; 'a happy moment,' शुभलग्नः; 'a happy result,' शुभफलं, स्वन्तं; 'having a happy result,' स्वन्तः -न्ता -न्तं; 'to be happy,' सुख (nom. सुखायते).

HARANGUE, *s.* वाक्यं, अलङ्कारमयं वाक्यं, रसिकवाक्यं.

To HARANGUE, *v. n.* बहुजनसमाजे अलङ्कारमयं वाक्यं वद् (c. 1. वदति -दितुं), अभिवद्, अभिभाष् (c. 1. -भाषते -षितुं).

HARANGUER, *s.* बहुजनसमाजे अलङ्कारमयवाक्यवक्ता *m.* (क्तृ), वागीशः, वागीश्वरः, प्रवचनपटुः, वाक्यद्वारेण विस्मयोत्पादकः or इन्द्रियमोहकः.

To HARASS, *v. a.* (Fatigue) खिद् (c. 10. खेदयति -यितुं), आयस् (c. 10. -यासयति -यितुं), सद् (c. 10. सादयति -यितुं), अवसद्, क्लम् (c. 10. क्लमयति -यितुं), परिक्लम्, श्रम् (c. 10. श्रमयति -यितुं), परिश्रम्, ग्लै in caus. (ग्लपयति -यितुं).—(Vex) बाध् (c. 1. बाधते -धितुं), प्रबाध्, परिबाध्, क्लिश् (c. 9. क्लिश्नाति, क्लेशितुं), संक्लिश्, पीड् (c. 10. पीडयति -यितुं), परिपीड्, उपपीड्, प्रपीड्, अभिपीड्, अभिनिपीड्, निपीड्, सम्पीड्, आपीड्, व्यथ् (c. 10. व्यथयति -यितुं), अर्द् (c. 10. अर्दयति -यितुं), समर्द्, दु (c. 5. दुनोति, दोतुं), प्रदु, तप् (c. 10. तापयति -यितुं), परितप्, सन्तप्, कृष् (c. 10. कर्षयति -यितुं), अभिकृष्, उपरुध् (c. 7. -रुणद्धि, रोद्धुं), मथ् (c. 1. मथति, c. 9. मथ्नाति, मन्थितुं), प्रमथ्, क्षि (c. 5. क्षिणोति, क्षेतुं), रध् (c. 10. रन्धयति -यितुं), उपहन् (c. 2. -हन्ति -न्तुं).

HARASSED, *p. p.* खेदितः -ता -तं, खिन्नः -न्ना -न्नं, श्रान्तः -न्ता -न्तं, परिश्रान्तः -न्ता -न्तं, क्लान्तः -न्ता -न्तं, बाधितः -ता -तं, क्लिष्टः -ष्टा -ष्टं, क्लिशितः -ता -तं, क्लेशितः -ता -तं, परिक्लिष्टः -ष्टा -ष्टं, पीडितः -ता -तं, अर्दितः -ता -तं, अभ्यर्दितः -ता -तं, समर्दितः -ता -तं, अवसादितः -ता -तं, दूनः -ना -नं, उपहतः -ता -तं, व्यथितः -ता -तं, विडम्बितः -ता -तं, दुर्मनायमानः -ना -नं; 'to be harassed,' खिद् (c. 4. खिद्यते).

HARASSER, *s.* खेदकरः, श्रमकरः, बाधकः, क्लेशकः, पीडकः, पीडाकरः.

HARASSING, *a.* खेदजनकः -का -कं, क्लेशकरः -री -रं, दुःखकरः -री -रं.

HARBINGER, *s.* अग्रेसरः, अग्रसरः, अग्रगः, अग्रगामी *m.* (न्), पुरोगः -गामी *m.* (न्), प्राग्गामी *m.*, अग्रवर्त्ती *m.* (न्), अग्रगतः, दूतः, वार्त्तावाहकः, वार्त्ताहरः, सन्देशहरः; 'harbinger of spring,' वसन्तदूतः.

HARBOR, *s.* (For ships) खातं, नौबन्धनयोग्यं खातं, नौबन्धनखातं, नौरक्षणस्थानं, नौकाश्रयः.—(Shelter, place of rest) आश्रयः, समाश्रयः, संश्रयः, प्रतिश्रयः, आशयः, अवस्थानं, अवकाशः, वासस्थानं, निवासस्थानं, आवासस्थानं.

To HARBOR, *v. a.* आश्रयं कृ or दा, अवकाशं दा, वासस्थानं दा, वस् in caus. (वासयति -यितुं), निवस्, सत्कृ.—(Entertain in the mind) मनसि or मनसा धृ (c. 1. धरति, धर्त्तुं) or उपलभ् (c. 1. -लभते -लब्धुं) or ग्रह् (c. 9. गृह्णाति, ग्रहीतुं).

To HARBOR, *v. n.* आश्रि (c. 1. -श्रयति -यितुं), समाश्रि, वस् (c. 1. वसति, वस्तुं), निवस्.

HARBORAGE, *s.* आश्रयः, समाश्रयः, संश्रयः, अवस्थानं, अवकाशः.

HARBORER, *s.* आश्रयकर्त्ता *m.* (र्त्तृ), आश्रयः, आशयिता *m.* (तृ), अवस्थापकः, ग्रहीता *m.* (तृ).

HARBORLESS, *a.* निराश्रयः -या -यं, आश्रयहीनः -ना -नं, निर्वासः -सा -सं.

HARD, *a.* (Firm, solid, compact) दृढः -ढा -ढं, घनः -ना -नं, कठिनः -ना -नं, कर्कशः -शा -शं, कठोरः -रा -रं, संहतः -ता -तं, अशिथिलः -ला -लं, अमसृणः -णा -णं, वज्रः -ज्रा -ज्रं, ग्रावा -वा -व (न्), वज्रमयः -यी -यं, दृढसन्धिः -न्धिः -न्धि, कर्कैरः -रा -रं, जरठः -ठा -ठं, गाढः -ढा -ढं, प्रगाढः -ढा -ढं, कीकसः -सा -सं, कक्खटः -टा -टं, कठोलः -ला -लं, क्रूरः -रा -रं, निष्ठुरः -रा -रं, द्रवेतरः -रा -रं.—(Hard to be understood) दुर्ज्ञेयः -या -यं.—(Difficult, not easy to be done) कठिनः -ना -नं, दुष्करः -रा -री -रं, दुःसाध्यः -ध्या -ध्यं, दुष्करः -रा -रं, असुकरः -री -रं, असुगमः -मा -मं, विषमः -मा -मं, कष्टः -ष्टा -ष्टं,

दुर्निवहः -हा -हं, आयासकृतः -ता -तं, दुःखसाध्यः -ध्या -ध्यं, दुःखेन कार्य्यः -र्य्या -र्य्यं or साध्यः -ध्या -ध्यं. Often expressed by दुर् or दुःख in comp.; as, 'hard to be borne,' दुःसहः -हा -हं; 'hard to obtain,' दुर्लभः -भा -भं, दुःखलभ्यः -भ्या -भ्यं, दुष्प्रापः -पा -पं, दुःखेन प्राप्यः -प्या -प्यं; 'hard to be crossed,' दुस्तरः -रा -रं, दुस्तार्य्यः -र्य्या -र्य्यं; 'hard to be broken,' दुर्भेद्यः -द्या -द्यं, दुःखभेद्यः -द्या -द्यं; 'hard to be relinquished,' दुस्त्यजः -जा -जं.—(Fatiguing, painful, laborious) कष्टकरः -री -रं, दुःखी -खिनी -खि (न्), दुःखकरः -रा -रं, क्लेशी -शिनी -शि (न्), क्लेशकः -का -कं.—(Severe, harsh) कठोरः -रा -रं, निष्ठुरः -रा -रं, उग्रः -ग्रा -ग्रं, उग्रदण्डः -ण्डा -ण्डं, तीक्ष्णः -क्ष्णा -क्ष्णं, क्रूरः -रा -रं, कर्कशः -शा -शं, रूक्षः -क्षा -क्षं.—(Unfavorable) अननुकूलः -ला -लं; 'hard fate,' दुर्दैवं.—(Sour, acid) अम्लरसः -सा -सं, शुक्तः -क्ता -क्तं.

HARD, *adv.* (Near, hard by) समीपं, निकटे, उपान्ते, आरात्, आसन्नः -न्ना -न्नं, सन्निकृष्टः -ष्टा -ष्टं.—(With difficulty) दुःखेन, कष्टेन, कृच्छ्रेण, आयासेन, कठिनं, विषमं, दुर् prefixed. (Violently, with force) बलेन, बलात्, बलवत्, तीव्रं, तीक्ष्णं, प्रसभं.—(Hard) शीघ्रं, सत्वरं, त्वरितं.

HARD-BOUND, *a.* दृढबद्धः -द्धा -द्धं, दृढसन्धिः -न्धिः -न्धि, बद्धकोष्ठः -ष्ठा -ष्ठं.

HARD-DRINKER, *s.* मद्यपानप्रसक्तः, पानरतः, अतिपायी *m.* (न्).

HARD-EARNED, *a.* श्रमेणोपार्ज्जितः -ता -तं, कृच्छ्रोपार्ज्जितः -ता -तं, कृच्छ्राप्तः -प्ता -प्तं.

To HARDEN, *v. a.* कठिनीकृ, घनीकृ, कठोरीकृ, दृढीकृ, कर्कशीकृ, स्तब्धीकृ, कठिनं -नां -नं कृ.

To HARDEN, *v. n.* कठिनीभू, घनीभू, कठोरीभू, दृढीभू, कर्कशीभू.

HARDENED, *p.p.* कठिनीकृतः -ता -तं, घनीकृतः -ता -तं, दृढीभूतः -ता -तं.

HARD-FEATURED, *a.* कठिनवदनः -ना -नं, कठिनमुखः -खी -खं, दुर्मुखः -खी -खं.

HARD-FISTED, *a.* कठिनमुष्टिः -ष्टिः -ष्टि, दृढमुष्टिः -ष्टिः -ष्टि.

HARD-HEARTED, *a.* कठिनहृदयः -या -यं, कठिनान्तःकरणः -णा -णं, पाषाणहृदयः -या -यं, अयोहृदयः -या -यं, निर्दयः -या -यं, निरनुक्रोशः -शा -शं, दुर्हृदयः -या -यं, अक्लिन्नहृदयः -या -यं, वज्रमयः -यी -यं.

HARD-HEARTEDNESS, *s.* कठिनहृदयता, हृदयकाठिन्यं, निरनुक्रोशता.

HARDIHOOD, *s.* वीर्य्यं, वीरता, धीरत्वं, धृतिः *f.*, धैर्य्यं, शौर्य्यं, शूरता, साहसं, निर्भयत्वं, प्रगल्भता, प्रागल्भ्यं, स्थैर्य्यं, स्थिरता.

HARDILY, *adv.* शूरवत्, वीरवत्, धीरवत्, धैर्य्येण, साहसेन, धीरं.

HARDINESS, *s.* (Boldness) शौर्य्यं, धीरत्वं, धैर्य्यं, धृतिः *f.*, वीरता.—(Of body) देहकाठिन्यं, शरीरदृढता, दृढदेहत्वं.

HARDLY, *adv.* (With difficulty) दुःखेन, कष्टेन, कृच्छ्रेण, कठिनं, कष्टं, आयासेन, दुर् prefixed.—(Scarcely, barely) कष्टं, कष्टेन, कृच्छ्रेण.—(Severely) निष्ठुरं, कठोरं, उग्रं, तीक्ष्णं, नैष्ठुर्य्येण.

HARD-MOUTHED, *a.* कठिनमुखः -खा -खं, दृढमुखः -खा -खं, कठोरमुखः -खा -खं.

HARDNESS, *s.* (Firmness, solidity) दृढता, दार्ढ्यं, द्रढिमा *m.* (न्), कठिनता, काठिन्यं, घनता, कठोरता, द्राढ्यं, कर्कशता, कार्कश्यं, निष्ठुरता.—(Difficulty to be understood) दुर्ज्ञेयता, अस्पष्टता.—(Difficulty to be effected) दुःसाध्यता, दुष्करत्वं, काठिन्यं, कठिनता, असौकर्य्यं, कष्टत्वं.—(Severity) निष्ठुरता, नैष्ठुर्य्यं, कठोरता, उग्रता, तीक्ष्णता, कर्कशता, कार्कश्यं.

HARDS, *s. pl.* शणोच्छिष्टं, शणावशिष्टं, शणशेषं, अतसीशणादेः शेषभागः.

HARDSHIP, *s.* क्लेशः, कायक्लेशः, देहक्लेशः, शरीरक्लेशः, श्रमः, आयासः, शरीरायासः, कष्टं, खेदः, परिश्रमः.—(Oppression) बाधः -धा, अभिद्रोहः, निष्ठुरता, उत्पातः.

HARDWARE, *s.* पिठरकटाहादीनि लौहभाण्डानि, लोहमयभाण्डं -ण्डानि *n.pl.*, लोहादिनिर्म्मितभाण्डानि.

HARDWAREMAN, *s.* लौहभाण्डविक्रयी *m.* (न्), पिठरकटाहादिभाण्डविक्रेता *m.* (तृ).

HARDY, *a.* (Bold, brave) शूरः -रा -रं, वीरः -रा -रं, प्रवीरः -रा -रं, प्रगल्भः -ल्भा -ल्भं, साहसी -सिनी -सि (न्), प्रतिभानवान् -वती -वत् (त्), प्रतिभावान् &c.—(In body) दृढदेहः -हा -हं, कठिनदेहः -हा -हं, दृढशरीरः -रा -रं.

HARE, *s.* शशः, शशकः, लम्बकर्णः, लोमकर्णः -र्णकः, मृदुलोमकः, मृदुरोमवान् *m.* (त्).

HAREBRAINED, *a.* चपलबुद्धिः -द्धिः -द्धि, चञ्चलबुद्धिः -द्धिः -द्धि, विभ्रान्तशीलः -ला -लं.

HAREHUNTING, *s.* शशकाखेटः, शशकानुसरणं.

HARELIP, *s.* शशकौष्ठः, छिन्नौष्ठः, शशकौष्ठरूपेण छिन्नौष्ठः.

HAREM, *s.* (Women's apartments) अन्तःपुरं, अवरोधः -धनं, अवरोधगृहं, अवरोधायनं, स्त्रीगृहं, स्त्र्यगारं, शुद्धान्तः, भोगगृहं, भोगावासः, कलत्रावासः, सुविदल्लं; 'guard of the harem,' शुद्धान्तपालकः.

HARESKIN, *s.* शशोर्णः, शशलोम *n.* (न्), शशचर्म्म *n.* (न्), शशकाजिनं.

HARICOT, *s.* शाकमूलादिना सह सिद्धं मांसं.

HARK, *interj.* शृणु, कर्णं देहि, अवधीयतां, निशामय.

HARLEQUIN, *s.* चित्रवेशो भण्डविशेषः, वैहासिकः, परिहासवेदी *m.* (न्).

HARLOT, *s.* वेश्या, गणिका, पण्यस्त्री, पण्याङ्गना, पण्याजनः, पणाङ्गना, वारस्त्री, वाराङ्गना, वारविलासिनी, वारसुन्दरी, पुंश्चली, भोग्या, बन्धकी, दारिका, भष्टा, साधारणस्त्री, सामान्या स्त्री, व्यभिचारिणी, कुलटा, निशाचरी, ग्रामणीः, वेश्या, रूपाजीवा, कुम्भा, लञ्जिका, झर्झरा, बन्धुरा, चपारण्डा; 'a company of harlots,' गाणिक्यं.

HARLOTRY, *s.* वेश्यात्वं, वेश्यावृत्तिः *f.*, वेश्याव्यवसायः, वैशिकं, पौंश्चल्यं, वारसेवा, वेश्यासेवा.

HARM, *s.* हिंसा -सनं, क्षतिः *f.*, परिक्षतिः *f.*, घातं, द्रोहः, अभिद्रोहः, अपायः, नाशः, अपकारः, अपकृतं, पीडा, व्यथा, अपचयः, अपचितिः *f.*, विहेठः -ठनं, हानिः *f.*, दूषणं, दोषः, अनिष्टं, अपहारः, क्षयः, अर्दना.

To HARM, *v. a.* हिंस् (c. 7. हिनस्ति, c. 1. हिंसति -सितुं), उपहिंस्, विहिंस्, आहिंस्; अपकृ; अर्द् (c. 10. अर्दयति -यितुं), समर्द्, पीड् (c. 10. पीडयति -यितुं), व्यथ् (c. 10. व्यथयति -यितुं), क्षण् (c. 8. क्षणोति -णितुं), परिक्षण्, क्षतिं कृ, परिक्षतिं कृ, दुष् (c. 10. दूषयति -यितुं), द्रुह् (c. 4. द्रुह्यति, द्रोग्धुं), उपहन् (c. 2. -हन्ति -न्तुं), बाध् (c. 1. बाधते -धितुं), रिष् (c. 1. रेषति, c. 4. रिष्यति, रेष्टं).

HARMED, *p. p.* हिंसितः -ता -तं, विहिंसितः -ता -तं, क्षतः -ता -तं, परिक्षतः -ता -तं, विक्षतः -ता -तं, अर्दितः -ता -तं, पीडितः -ता -तं, निपीडितः -ता -तं, व्यथितः -ता -तं, दूषितः -ता -तं, अपकृतः -ता -तं, कृतापकारः -रा -रं, विहतः -ता -तं, रिष्टः -ष्टा -ष्टं.

HARMFUL, *a.* हिंस्रः -स्रा -स्रं, हिंसकः -का -कं, हिंसात्मकः -का -कं, हिंसाजनकः -का -कं, हिंसाकरः -री -रं, क्षतिकारकः -का -कं, क्षतिजनकः -का -कं, अपकारकः -का -कं, द्रोही -हिणी -हि (न्), भूतधुक् *m. f. n.* (ह्), नृशंसः -सा -सं, शारुकः -का -कं, शरारुः -रुः -रु, घातुकः -का -कं, उपघातकः -का -कं, सबाधः -धा -धं, रिष्वः -ष्वा -ष्वं.

HARMFULLY, *adv.* हिंसापूर्व्वं, क्षतिपूर्व्वं, सद्रोहं, सापकारं, सदूषणं.

HARMLESS, *a.* अहिंसकः -का -कं, अहिंस्रः -स्रा -स्रं, हिंसारहितः -ता -तं, अनपकारी -रिणी -रि (न्), अद्रोही -हिणी -हि (न्), अनुपघातकः -का -कं.—(Innocent) निर्दोषः -षा -षं, अदुष्टः -ष्टा -ष्टं, निष्पापः -पा -पं.

HARMLESSLY, *adv.* अहिंसया, अहिंसापूर्व्वं, अद्रोहेण, दोषं विना.

HARMLESSNESS, *s.* अहिंसा, अनपकारः, अद्रोहः, हिंसात्यागः, अहिंसकत्वं,

अनपकारकता.—(Innocence) निर्दोषत्वं, अदुष्टता, शुद्धत्वं, पापहीनता.

HARMONIC, HARMONICAL, *a.* एकतालः -ला -लं, एकस्वरः -रा -रं, एकतानः -ना -नं, समस्वरः -रा -रं, मधुरस्वरः -रा -रं, सङ्गतस्वरः -रा -रं.

HARMONICA, *s.* (Musical glasses) जलतरङ्गः.

HARMONICS, *s.* मधुरस्वराः *m. pl.*, सुस्वरविद्या, चारुस्वनविद्या.

HARMONIOUS, *a.* (Symphonious) एकतालः -ला -लं, एकस्वरः -रा -रं, सङ्गतस्वरः -रा -रं, समस्वरः -रा -रं, एकस्वनः -ना -नं, एकलयः -या -यं, एकतानः -ना -नं.—(Melodious) सुस्वरः -रा -रं, मधुरस्वरः -रा -रं, मधुरस्वनः -ना -नं, सुचारुस्वनः -ना -नं, श्रोत्राभिरामः -मा -मं, श्रोत्रसुखः -खा -खं, श्रुतिसुखः -खा -खं, सुखश्रवः -वा -वं, सुश्राव्यः -व्या -व्यं, सुशब्दः -ब्दा -ब्दं, मधुरः -रा -रं, मधुकः -का -कं.—(Consonant, agreeing) सदृशः -शी -शं, अविरुद्धः -द्धा -द्धं, अनुगुणः -णा -णं, अनुसारी -रिणी -रि (न्), तुल्यः -ल्या -ल्यं.

HARMONIOUSLY, *adv.* (With symphony) स्वरैक्येन, तालैक्येन, एकस्वरेण, स्वरसङ्गेन, सङ्गतस्वरेण.—(Melodiously) सुस्वरं, मधुरस्वरेण.—(Agreeably, in concord) सदृशं, अविरुद्धं, अनुसारेण.

HARMONIOUSNESS, *s.* तालैक्यं, स्वरैक्यं, स्वरसङ्गः, सुस्वरता, सुश्राव्यता, माधुर्य्यं, सादृश्यं, सदृशता, अविरुद्धता.

To HARMONIZE, *v. n.* (Agree) सदृशीभू, सदृशः -शी -शम् अस्, एकीभू, तुल्यीभू, अनुगुणीभू, न विरुध् (c. 7. -रुणद्धि -रोद्धुं).

To HARMONIZE, *v. a.* सदृशीकृ, सदृशं -शीं -शं कृ, एकीकृ, तुल्यीकृ.—(Make musical) तालैक्यं कृ, स्वरैक्यं कृ, सुस्वरीकृ, सुश्राव्यं -व्यां -व्यं कृ.

HARMONY, *s.* (Of sound, musical concord) तालैक्यं, स्वरैक्यं, स्वरसङ्गः, स्वरैकता, एकतालः, एकतानः, एकलयः; 'of singing, dancing, and music,' तौर्य्यत्रिकं, सङ्गीतं.—(Melody) सुस्वरता, सुश्राव्यता, स्वरमाधुर्य्यं, कलता, तालः.—(Agreement, concord) ऐक्यं, एकता, सङ्गः, योग्यता, सादृश्यं, अविरोधः, आनुकूल्यं, अनुसारिता, संयोगः, सन्धिः *m.*, दाक्षिण्यं; 'of sentiment,' सम्मतिः *f.*, एकचित्तता, चित्तैक्यं, मतैक्यं, परस्परानुमतिः *f.*, संवादः.—(Friendship, love) प्रीतिः *f.*, मैत्र्यं, स्नेहः, सौहृद्यं.

HARNESS, *s.* (Of a horse) अश्वसज्जा, अश्वपरिच्छदः, अश्वाभरणं, अश्वप्रसाधनं, रथ्यसज्जा.—(Accoutrements) सज्जा, सन्नाहः, परिच्छदः, परिधानं, पारिणाह्यं, प्रसाधनं.

To HARNESS, *v. a.* (Fix a horse to a chariot) अश्वं रथे नियुज् (c. 7. -युनक्ति -योक्तुं, c. 10. -योजयति -यितुं) or युज् or आयुज्; रथम् अश्वेन संयुज्.—(Put on the furniture of a horse) अश्वं सज्जीकृ or ससज्जं कृ, अश्वसज्जनं कृ.—(Accoutre) सज्ज् (c. 1. सज्जति -ज्जितुं), सन्नह् (c. 4. -नह्यति -नद्धुं), पिनह्.

HARNESSED, *p. p.* रथनियुक्तः -क्ता -क्तं, रथसंयोजितः -ता -तं, आयुक्तः -क्ता -क्तं, संसक्तयुगः -गा -गं, संयुक्तः -क्ता -क्तं, सज्जीकृतः -ता -तं, सज्जितः -ता -तं, ससज्जः -ज्जा -ज्जं.

HARNESS-MAKER, *s.* अश्वसज्जाकर्त्ता *m.* (र्त्तृ), अश्वपरिच्छदकारी *m.* (न्).

HARP, *s.* वल्लकी, वीणा, विपञ्ची -ञ्चिका, तन्त्री, रुद्री.

To HARP, *v. n.* (Play on the harp) वल्लकीं or वीणां वद् (c. 10. वादयति -यितुं); 'celebrate on the harp,' उपवीण (nom. उपवीणयति -यितुं); 'harp on a subject,' अतिप्रसङ्गं कृ, पुनरुक्तिं कृ, प्रपञ्चं कृ, दीर्घसूत्रः -त्रा -त्रं भू.

HARPER, *s.* वीणावादः -दकः, वैणिकः, वीणापाणिः, वल्लकीवादः.

HARPOON, *s.* तिमिवेधनार्थं शूलः, धीवरी, तिमिवेधनी, मकरवेधनी.

HARPOONER, *s.* तिमिवेधकः, मकरवेधकः, मीनराघाती *m.* (न्).

HARPSICHORD, *s.* तालवाद्यविशेषः, तन्त्री, वल्लकी, विपञ्चिका.

HARPY, *s.* कविकल्पितः स्त्रीमुखो गृध्रपक्षिशरीरः लुलुब्धशीलो जन्तुभेदः.—(Plunderer) अपहारकः, साहसिकः, विप्रलुम्पकः, उपद्रवी *m.* (न्).

HARRIDAN, *s.* वृद्धबन्धकी, जीर्णवेश्या, वृद्धा गणिका.

HARRIER, *s.* शशकाखेटकः कुक्कुरभेदः, शशकाखेटे शिक्षितो मृगव्यश्वा *m.* (न्).

HARROW, *s.* कोटिशः, कोटीशः, लोष्टभेदनः, लोष्टघ्नः, आकर्षणी, जित्यः.

To HARROW, *v. a.* कोटिशेन भूमिं कृष् (c. 6. कृषति, क्रष्टुं), पूर्व्वोक्तयन्त्रेण मृल्लोष्टानि भिद् (c. 7. भिनत्ति, भेत्तुं) or दॄ in caus. (दारयति -यितुं).—(Lacerate, torment) विदॄ in caus., सन्तप् (c. 10. -तापयति -यितुं), कृष् (c. 10. कर्षयति -यितुं).

HARROWER, *s.* कोटिशेन भूमिकर्षकः or मृल्लोष्टभेदकः.

HARROWING, *a.* विदारकः -का -कं, अरुन्तुदः -दा -दं, सन्तापकः -का -कं.

To HARRY, *v. a.* बाध् (c. 1. बाधते -धितुं), पीड् (c. 10. पीडयति -यितुं), क्लिश् (c. 9. क्लिश्नाति, क्लेशितुं), व्यथ् (c. 10. व्यथयति -यितुं).

HARSH, *a.* (Rough to the touch) रूक्षः -क्षा -क्षं, रुक्षः -क्षा -क्षं, परुषः -षा -षं, दुःखस्पर्शः -र्शा -र्शं, कर्कशः -शा -शं, विषमः -मा -मं, असमसृणः -णा -णं.—(Rough to the ear) कर्णकटुः -टुः -टु, कर्कशस्वनः -ना -नं, कर्कशस्वरः -रा -रं, विस्वरः -रा -रं, कुश्राव्यः -व्या -व्यं, विकृतस्वरः -रा -रं.—(Rough to the taste, sour) शुक्तः -क्ता -क्तं, अम्लरसः -सा -सं, कषायः -या -यं, कषायान्वितः -ता -तं.—(Austere, severe, crabbed) निष्ठुरः -रा -रं, कर्कशः -शा -शं, उग्रः -ग्रा -ग्रं, कठिनः -ना -नं, क्रूरः -रा -रं, कटुः -टुः -टु, कठोरः -रा -रं, शठः -ठा -ठं, कीटकः -का -कं, जाल्मः -ल्मा -ल्मं; 'harsh words,' कर्कशवाक्यं, परुषवचनं, परुषोक्तिः *f.*, शुक्तं, विकृतवचनं.

HARSHLY, *adv.* (Roughly) रूक्षं, परुषं, कर्कशं, विषमं.—(Discordantly) विस्वरं, कर्कशं, कर्कशस्वरेण, विकृतस्वरं.—(Severely, austerely) निष्ठुरं, नैष्ठुर्य्येण, कर्कशं, कार्कश्येन, सकार्कश्यं, कठिनं, काठिन्येन, उग्रं, कठोरं, कटु.

HARSHNESS, *s.* (Roughness to the touch) रूक्षता, रौक्ष्यं, परुषता, पारुष्यं, कार्कश्यं, वैषम्यं, दुःखस्पर्शत्वं.—(Roughness to the ear) कर्णकटुता, कर्कशता, विस्वरता, कुश्राव्यता.—(Roughness to the taste) शुक्तता, अम्लता, कषायत्वं, कटुता.—(Severity, austerity) निष्ठुरता, नैष्ठुर्य्यं, कर्कशता, कार्कश्यं, उग्रता, कठिनता, काठिन्यं, क्रूरता, कठोरता, कटुता, पारुष्यं, शुक्तता, व्यलीकता, जाल्मता.

HARSLET, HASLET, *s.* शूकरान्त्राणि *n. pl.*, शूकरस्य हृद्यकृदन्त्रादि.

HART, *s.* मृगः, हरिणः, कुरङ्गः -ङ्गकः -ङ्गमः, कृष्णसारः, एणः.

HARTSHORN, *s.* मृगशृङ्गं, मृगविषाणः; 'spirits of hartshorn,' मृगशृङ्गादिनिर्यासः, मृगशृङ्गादिनिष्कर्षितो रसः.

HARAM-SCARUM, *a.* चपलः -ला -लं, अस्थिरः -रा -रं, प्रमादी -दिनी -दि (न्).

HARVEST, *s.* (The season of gathering the corn) शस्यसङ्ग्रहकालः, शस्यच्छेदनकालः, शस्यकर्त्तनसमयः, शस्यलवनकालः, गोधूमकर्त्तनकालः, शस्यसञ्चयकालः, शस्यसङ्ग्रहः.—(Gathered corn) सङ्गृहीतशस्यं, लूनशस्यं, छिन्नशस्यं.

To HARVEST, *v. a.* शस्यसङ्ग्रहं कृ, शस्यं सङ्ग्रह् (c. 9. -गृह्णाति -ग्रहीतुं) or छिद् (c. 7. छिनत्ति, छेत्तुं) or लू (c. 9. लुनाति, लवितुं) or चि (c. 5. चिनोति, चेतुं), शस्यसञ्चयं कृ.

HARVEST-HOME, *s.* शस्यसङ्ग्रहकालमुद्दिश्य ग्राम्यजनसेवितो महोत्सवः.

HARVEST-LORD, *s.* शस्यच्छेत्तॄणां मध्यात् प्रधानच्छेत्ता *m.* (त्तृ), श्रेष्ठः शस्यसङ्ग्राहकः or शस्यसङ्ग्रहीता *m.* (तृ), प्रधानलवकः.

HARVEST-MAN, HARVESTER, *s.* शस्यच्छेत्ता *m.* (त्तृ), शस्यसङ्ग्राहकः, शस्यसङ्ग्रहीता *m.* (तृ), शस्यसञ्चयी *m.* (न्), शस्यलवकः, धान्यादिसञ्चयकारी *m.* (न्).

To HASH, *v. a.* खण्डं खण्डं कृ, खण्डशः कृ or छिद् (c. 7. छिनत्ति, छेत्तुं) or विच्छिद्, शकलीकृ, खण्डीकृ.

HASH, *s.* (Hashed meat) व्यञ्जनादिना सह सिद्धं छिन्नमांसं or खण्डमांसं.

HASP, *s.* कुडुपः, सन्धिः *m.*, बन्धनी, बन्धनकुडुपः.

To HASP, *v. a.* पूर्व्वोक्तकुडुपेन बन्ध् (c. 9. बध्नाति, बन्द्धुं).

HASSOCK, *s.* भजनशालायां पीठविशेषो यस्मिन् ईश्वरपूजको जानुद्वयं न्यस्य पूजां करोति, पादपः, विष्टरः.

HASTE, *s.* त्वरा, तूर्णिः *f.*, त्वरणं, त्वरितं, सत्वरता, सम्भ्रमः, शीघ्रता, शैघ्र्यं, क्षिप्रता, द्रुतत्वं, वेगः -गिता, आवेगः, जवः, प्रजवः, जूतिः *f.*, जूर्णिः *f.*, तरस् *n.*, रभसः, अविलम्बः, आशुकारित्वं, क्षिप्रकारित्वं, त्वरितगतिः *f.*, आशुगमनं, रंहतिः *f.*; 'in haste,' ससम्भ्रमं, सत्वरं; 'to make haste,' त्वर् (c. 1. त्वरते -रितुं); 'make haste,' त्वर्य्यतां.

To HASTE, HASTEN, *v. a.* त्वर् in caus. (त्वरयति -यितुं), सन्त्वर्, क्षेप (nom. क्षेपयति -यितुं), क्षिप्रीकृ, द्रुततरं -रां -रं कृ.

To HASTE, HASTEN, *v. n.* त्वर् (c. 1. त्वरते -रितुं), सन्त्वर्, अतित्वर्, शीघ्र (nom. शीघ्रायते), तरण (nom. तरण्यति); 'to move with haste,' आशु or सत्वरं or त्वरितं गम् (c. 1. गच्छति, गन्तुं) or चल् (c. 1. चलति -लितुं), द्रु (c. 1. द्रवति, द्रोतुं), धाव् (c. 1. धावति -वितुं); 'to hasten towards,' अभिद्रु, आद्रु, समाद्रु, समुपद्रु, प्रतिद्रु, अभिधाव्.

HASTILY, *adv.* सत्वरं, त्वरितं, क्षिप्रं, शीघ्रं, आशु, तूर्णं, ससम्भ्रमं, सरभसं, सहसा, द्रुतं, वेगतस्, अविलम्बितं, सपदि, झटिति.—(Passionately) क्रोधात्, कोपात्, क्रोधाविष्टत्वात्.

HASTINAPUR, *s.* (The city) हस्तिनापुरं, हस्तिनीपुरं, गजाह्वं -ह्वयं.

HASTINESS, *s.* (Haste, speed) सत्वरता -त्वं, शीघ्रता, शैघ्र्यं, क्षिप्रता, द्रुतता, आशुता.—(Precipitation) क्षिप्रकारिता, आशुकारित्वं, साहसं.—(Of temper) शीघ्रकोपित्वं.

HASTINGS, *s. pl.* प्रथमसतीलकः, प्राक्पूर्णकालात् खादनीयः सातिलकः.

HASTY, *a.* (Quick, expeditious) त्वरितः -ता -तं, त्वरावान् -वती -वत् (त्), त्वरायुक्तः -क्ता -क्तं, सत्वरः -रा -रं, त्वरान्वितः -ता -तं, तूर्णः -र्णा -र्णं, शीघ्रः -घ्रा -घ्रं, क्षिप्रः -प्रा -प्रं, द्रुतः -ता -तं, शीघ्रकारी -रिणी -रि (न्), क्षिप्रकारी &c., आशुकारी &c., अविलम्बः -म्बा -म्बं -म्बी -म्बिनी -म्बि (न्), अविलम्बितः -ता -तं.—(Rash) साहसी -सिनी -सि (न्).—(In temper) शीघ्रकोपी -पिनी -पि (न्), सुलभकोपः -पा -पं.

HAT, *s.* ऊर्णामयं शिरस्कं or शिरस्त्रं or शिरस्त्राणं or मस्तकाभरणं.

HAT-BAND, *s.* शिरस्कबन्धनं -नी, शिरस्कवेष्टनं.

HAT-BOX, HAT-CASE, *s.* शिरस्काधारः, शिरस्कभाण्डं, शिरस्कधारकः.

To HATCH, *v. a.* कुलायनिलायेन पक्षिशावकान् अण्डाद् उत्पद् (c. 10. -पादयति -यितुं) or जन् (c. 10. जनयति -यितुं) or डिम्बाद् निर्गम् (c. 10. -गमयति -यितुं) or उद्भू in caus. (-भावयति -यितुं), कुलायनिलायं कृ.—(Contrive) प्रचिन्त् (c. 10. -चिन्तयति -यितुं), परिचिन्त्, घट् (c. 1. घटते -टितुं).

To HATCH, *v. n.* अण्डात् or डिम्बाद् उत्पद् (c. 4. -पद्यते) or जन् (c. 4. जायते) or उद्भू or समुद्भू.

HATCH, *s.* (A brood) यः पक्षिशावकगण एकवारे डिम्बाद् उत्पद्यते or जायते, पक्षिशावकगणः.—(Contrivance, discovery) परिकल्पनं -ना, घटनं, विवृतिः *f.*—(Opening in a ship's deck) नौपृष्ठे द्वारं, नौकामुखं, नौकोदरनिःसरणपथः, नौकोदरद्वारं.

HATCHEL, *s.* अतसीमार्जकः, उमामार्जनी, उमाशोधनी, शणप्रसाधनी.

To HATCHEL, *v. a.* पूर्व्वोक्तमार्जकयन्त्रेण अतसीं शुध् (c. 10. शोधयति -यितुं).

HATCHER, *s.* परिकल्पकः, प्रचिन्तकः, परिचिन्तकः, घटकः.

HATCHET, *s.* टङ्कः, तङ्कः, कुठारः -री, वृक्षभिद् *f.*, वृक्षभेदी *m.* (न्), परशुः *m.f.*, पर्शुः, परश्वधः, छिदिः *f.*, स्वधितिः *m.f.*, इध्मप्रव्रश्चनं, पाषाणदारकः.

HATCHET-FACE, *s.* टङ्कमुखं, टङ्कधारोपमम् अतिक्षीणवदनं.

HATCHING, *s.* कुलायनिलायेन डिम्बात् or अण्डाद् शावकोत्पादनं or पक्षिशावकोत्पत्तिः *f.*, पक्षिशावकोद्भवः.

HATCHMENT, *s.* गृहस्योपरि स्थापितं मृतजनस्य कुलचिह्नफलकं.

HATCHWAY, *s* नौपृष्ठे द्वारं, नौकोदरद्वारं, नौकोदरनिःसरणपथः, नौकोदरगमनागमनपथः.

To HATE, *v. a.* द्विष् (c. 2. द्वेष्टि -ष्टुं), विद्विष्, प्रद्विष्, गर्ह् (c. 1. गर्हते -र्हितुं), घृण् (c. 6. घृणते -णितुं), घृणां कृ, कुत्स् (c. 10. कुत्सयति -यितुं), गुप् in des. (जुगुप्सते -प्सितुं), ऋत् (irreg. ऋतीयते -यितुं), द्रुह् (c. 4. द्रुह्यति, द्रोहितुं, द्रोग्धुं), अभिद्रुह्, बाध् in des. (बीभत्सते -त्सितुं), द्वेषं कृ; 'he hates his enemy,' रिपुं द्वेष्टि, or रिपुं प्रति द्वेषं करोति.

HATE, *s.* द्वेषः, विद्वेषः, विद्विष्टता, घृणा, अप्रीतिः *f.*

HATED, *p.p.* द्विष्टः -ष्टा -ष्टं, विद्विष्टः -ष्टा -ष्टं, घृणितः -ता -तं, गर्हितः -ता -तं.

HATEFUL, *a.* द्वेष्यः -ष्या -ष्यं, द्वेषणीयः -या -यं, विद्विष्टः -ष्टा -ष्टं, गर्ह्यः -र्ह्या -र्ह्यं, गर्हणीयः -या -यं, गर्हितः -ता -तं, कुत्सितः -ता -तं, घृणार्हः -र्हा -र्हं, अप्रियतः -ता -तं.

HATEFULLY, *adv.* द्वेषणीयं, गर्हणीयं, गर्हितं, कुत्सितं, घृणार्हं.

HATEFULNESS, *s.* द्वेष्यता, द्वेषणीयता, गर्ह्यता, घृणार्हत्वं, कुत्सितत्वं.

HATER, *s.* द्वेषी *m.* (न्), विद्वेषी *m.*, विद्वेष्टा *m.* (ष्टृ), प्रद्वेष्टा *m.*, द्विट् *m.* (ष्), विद्विट् *m.*, प्रद्विट् *m.*, द्वेषणः, विरोधी *m.* (न्), घृणाकारी *m.* (न्).

HATRED, *s.* द्वेषः, विद्वेषः, प्रद्वेषः, विद्विष्टता, घृणा, गर्हा -र्हणं, कुत्सा -त्सनं, अप्रीतिः *f.*, ऋतीया, विरोधः, द्वेष्यता, जुगुप्सा, बीभत्सः.

HATTER, *s.* ऊर्णामयशिरस्ककारः, शिरस्कविक्रेता *m.* (तृ).

HAUBERK, *s.* कञ्चुकः, कवचः, तनुत्रं, वारबाणः, वाणवारः.

HAUGHTILY, *adv.* सदर्पं, साटोपं, समानं, सगर्व्वं, सोन्मायं, सोन्मादं, प्रगल्भं, उद्धतं, सावहेलं, सावलेपं, दर्पेण, गर्व्वेण, धर्षेण.

HAUGHTINESS, *s.* मानं, अभिमानं -नता, मानिता, अभिमानिता, दर्पः, गर्व्वः, प्रगल्भता, प्रागल्भ्यं, अहङ्कारः, उद्धतिः *f.*, औद्धत्यं, उन्मायः, उन्मादः, अवहेला -लनं, अवलेपः, अवलिप्तता, सावलेपत्वं, चित्तसमुन्नतिः *f.*, चित्तोन्नतिः *f.*, उत्सिक्तता, आटोपः, साटोपत्वं, धर्षः, प्रतिभानं, शौटीर्य्यं.

HAUGHTY, *a.* मानी -निनी -नि (न्), मानवान् -वती -वत् (त्), अभिमानी &c., अभिमानवान् &c., गर्व्वी -र्व्विणी -र्व्वि (न्), गर्व्वितः -ता -तं, सदर्पः -र्पा -र्पं, साटोपः -पा -पं, दृप्तः -प्ता -प्तं, दृप्रः -प्रा -प्रं, प्रगल्भः -ल्भा -ल्भं, अहङ्कारी -रिणी -रि (न्), उद्धतः -ता -तं, मदोद्धतः -ता -तं, मदोदग्रः -ग्रा -ग्रं, उत्सिक्तः -क्ता -क्तं, शौटीरः -रा -रं, अवलिप्तः -प्ता -प्तं, प्रधर्षितः -ता -तं, प्रधृष्टः -ष्टा -ष्टं, ऊर्द्धदृष्टिः -ष्टिः -ष्टि, सावहेलः -ला -लं, सोन्मायः -या -यं; 'to be haughty,' दृप् (c. 4. दृप्यति, दर्प्तुं, द्रप्तुं), प्रगल्भ् (c. 1. -गल्भते -ल्भितुं).

To HAUL, *v. a.* कृष् (c. 1. कर्षति, c. 6. कृषति, क्रष्टुं, कर्ष्टुं), आकृष्, हृ (c. 1. हरति -ते, हर्त्तुं).

HAUL, *s.* आकर्षः -र्षणं, कर्षः -र्षणं, आकृष्टिः *f.*, हरणं.

HAULED, *p.p.* कृष्टः -ष्टा -ष्टं, आकृष्टः -ष्टा -ष्टं, आकर्षितः -ता -तं, हृतः -ता -तं.

HAUM, *s.* शस्यनालः -ली, पलः, पलालः -लं, तृणं.

HAUNCH, *s.* उत्सङ्गः, कटिः *m.* -टी, जघनं, नितम्बः, क्रोडः, पालिः *f.*, प्रोथः, अङ्कः, श्रोणिः *f.* -णी, पश्चाद्भागः; 'haunch of venison,' मृगजघनं.

To HAUNT, *v. a.* and *n.* पुनःपुनः or वारं वारम् अभिगम् (c. 1. -गच्छति -गन्तुं) or अभ्यागम् or अभिसृ (c. 1. -सरति -सर्त्तुं, c. 10. -सारयति -यितुं) or अभिसारणं कृ, मुहुर्मुहुर् गमनागमनं कृ, नित्यगमनं कृ, नित्यम् आश्रि (c. 1. -श्रयति -ते -यितुं).

HAUNT, *s.* स्थानं यत्र पुनःपुनर् अभिगमः or अभिसरणं क्रियते, गमनागमनस्थानं, नित्यगमनस्थानं, आश्रयः, समाश्रयः, आशयः, आयतनं, आलयः, निलयः.

HAUNTED, *p. p.* or *a.* पुनःपुनर् आश्रितः -ता -तं or अभिसारितः -ता -तं; 'by ghosts,' रात्रिचरसेवितः -ता -तं, प्रेतनरजुष्टः -ष्टा -ष्टं, वेतालनिषेवितः -ता -तं.

HAUNTER, *s.* अभिसारी *m.* (न्), गमनागमनकारी *m.*, पुनःपुनर् अभ्यागमकारी *m.*

HAUNTING, *s.* अभिसरणं, पुनःपुनर् अभिगमः or अभ्यागमः or गमनागमनं, नित्यगमनं.

HAUTBOY, *s.* शुषिरवाद्यविशेषः, वृहद्वंशः, सानेयी.

HAUTEUR, *s.* मानं, अभिमानं, अहङ्कारः, उद्धतिः *f.*, औद्धत्यं, चित्तोन्नतिः *f.*, चित्तसमुन्नतिः *f.*, दर्पः, गर्व्वः.

To HAVE, *v. a.* (Hold in possession, possess) धा (c. 3. दधाति, धत्ते, धातुं), विधा, धृ (c. 10. धारयति -यितुं, c. 1. धरति, धर्त्तुं), भुज् (c. 7. भुंक्ते, भोक्तुं), परिभुज्, भृ (c. 3. बिभर्त्ति, भर्त्तुं), शील् (c. 10. शीलयति -यितुं), दध् (c. 1. दधते -धितुं), परिभोगं कृ.—(Obtain, gain) आप् (c. 5. आप्नोति, आप्तुं), प्राप्, अवाप्, लभ् (c. 1. लभते, लब्धुं), उपलभ्.—(Receive) ग्रह् (c.9. गृह्णाति, ग्रहीतुं), आदा.—(Be urged by obligation) expressed by the fut. pass. part.; as, 'I have to go,' मया गन्तव्यं; 'I have to write a letter,' मया पत्रं लेखनीयं.—(Have in esteem) मन् (c. 10. मानयति -यितुं), सम्मन्.—(Have in contempt) अवज्ञा (c. 9. -जानाति -ज्ञातुं), अवमन्.—(Have on, wear) धृ, भृ, परिधा.—(Have a care) अवधानं कृ, सावधानः -ना -नं भू.

HAVEN, *s.* (For ships) नौबन्धनयोग्यं स्थानं, नौबन्धनस्थानं, नौरक्षणस्थानं, नौकाश्रयः.—(Shelter) आश्रयः, समाश्रयः, संश्रयः, आशयः, अवस्थानं, रक्षास्थानं.

HAVING, *part.* (Possessing) दधत् -धती -धत् (त्), दधानः -ना -नं, विदधत् -धती -धत् (त्), धारयन् -यन्ती -यत् (त्), धारी -रिणी -रि (न्), दधः -धा -धं, शाली -लिनी -लि (न्): often expressed by the affixes वत्, मत्, इन्, विन्, मिन्, वल; as, 'having wealth,' धनवान् -वती -वत् (त्), धनी -निनी -नि (न्); 'having wisdom,' धीमान् -मती -मत् (त्): also expressible by उपेतः -ता -तं, अन्वितः -ता -तं, युक्तः -क्ता -क्तं in comp.; as, 'having wealth,' धनोपेतः &c.

HAVING, *s.* (Possession) धरणं, धारणं, शालिता, अधिकारः, भुक्तिः *f.*, परिभोगः.—(Goods) विभवः, द्रव्यं, रिक्थं.

HAVOC, *s.* महानाशः, महाक्षयः, संहारः, महाप्रलयः, महोत्पातः, सर्व्वनाशः, उच्छेदः, महाविप्लवः, विनाशः.

To HAVOC, *v. a.* महानाशं कृ, महाक्षयं कृ, महोत्पातं कृ, अत्यन्तं नश् (c. 10. नाशयति -यितुं), उच्छिद् (c. 7. -छिनत्ति -छेत्तुं).

HAW, *s.* हासंज्ञकं बीजगर्भं गुटिकाकारं क्षुद्रफलं.

To HAW, *v. n.* (Hesitate in speaking) भिन्नस्वरेण or स्खलितस्वरेण वद् (c. 1. वदति -दितुं).

HAWK, *s.* (Bird) श्येनः, पत्री *m.* (न्), शशादनः, कपोतारिः *m.*, खगान्तकः, घातिपक्षी *m.* (न्), नीलपिच्छः, सत्काण्डः, कपोताद्यनुसरणे शिक्षितः श्येनः.—(Forcing up phlegm) उत्कासनं, श्लेष्मोत्क्षेपः.

To HAWK, *v. a.* (Catch birds by means of hawks) श्येनादिभिः पक्षिणो ग्रह् (c. 9. गृह्णाति, ग्रहीतुं) or पक्ष्यनुसरणं कृ, श्यैनम्पातां कृ.—(Force up phlegm) उत्कास् (c. 1. -कासते -सितुं), श्लेष्माणम् उत्क्षिप् (c. 6. -क्षिपति -क्षेप्तुं) or निरस् (c. 4. -अस्यति -असितुं), श्लेष्मनिरसनं कृ.—(Sell goods by outcry in the streets) नगरमार्गेषु भ्रमणं कृत्वा घोषणपूर्व्वं द्रव्याणि विक्री (c. 9. -क्रीणाति -णीते -क्रेतुं).

HAWKER, *s.* (Seller of goods by outcry in the streets of a town) नगरमार्गेषु घोषणपूर्व्वं तुच्छद्रव्यविक्रेता *m.* (तृ).—(Falconer) श्येनजीवी *m.* (न्), श्येनशिक्षकः, श्येनपोषकः, श्येनपालकः.

HAWK-EYED, *a.* श्येननयनः -ना -नं, सूक्ष्मदृष्टिः -ष्टिः -ष्टि, सूक्ष्मदर्शी -र्शिनी -र्शि (न्), दूरदर्शी &c.

HAWKING, *s.* (Falconry) श्यैनम्पाता, श्येनादिभिः पक्षिग्रहणं, श्येनशिक्षा, श्येनपालनं.—(Forcing up phlegm) उत्कासनं, श्लेष्मोत्क्षेपः.—(Selling goods by outcry in the streets of a town) नगरमार्गेषु घोषणपूर्व्वं तुच्छद्रव्यविक्रयः.

HAWSER, *s.* नौरज्जुः *m.*, क्षुद्ररज्जुः. *See* HALSER.

HAWTHORN, *s.* हासंज्ञकफलविशिष्टः कण्टकितगुल्मभेदः.

HAY, *s.* शुष्कतृणं, शुष्कघासः, शुष्कशष्पं, तृणं, घासः.

HAYCOCK, *s.* शुष्कतृणचितिः *f.*, शुष्कघासस्तूपः, तृणचयः.

HAY-HARVEST, *s.* शुष्कतृणसङ्ग्रहः, शुष्कतृणसञ्चयकालः.

HAY-LOFT, *s.* शुष्कतृणसङ्ग्रहकोष्ठकं, शुष्कघासरक्षागारं.

HAY-MAKER, *s.* शुष्कतृणसङ्ग्राहकः, शुष्कतृणसञ्चयी *m.* (न्).

HAY-MAKING, *s.* शुष्कतृणसङ्ग्रहः, शुष्कघाससञ्चयः -यनं.

HAY-MARKET, *s.* तृणविक्रयस्थानं, घासविक्रयचत्वरं.

HAY-RICK, HAY-STACK, *s.* शुष्कतृणराशिः *m.*, शुष्कतृणोत्करः, शुष्कघासचितिः *f.*, शुष्कतृणविस्तरः.

HAZARD, *s.* (Chance) दैवं, दैवयोगः, दैवगतिः *f.*, दैवघटना, दैवसङ्गतं, दैववशः, अदृष्टं.—(Risk, danger) संशयः, शङ्का, सन्देहः, विकल्पः; 'a condition of hazard,' शङ्कास्पदं, संशयस्थानं; 'hazard of life,' जीवितसंशयः.—(Game at dice) द्यूतक्रीडा, अक्षादिक्रीडा, द्यूतकर्म्म *n.* (न्), द्यूतव्यवहारः, द्यूतं.

To HAZARD, *v. a.* संशयस्थं -स्थां -स्थं कृ, सन्देहस्थं -स्थां -स्थं कृ, सन्देहदोलस्थं -स्थां -स्थं कृ, शङ्कास्थं -स्थां -स्थं कृ, संशयापन्नं -न्नां -न्नं कृ, दैवाधीनं -नां -नं कृ, दैववशं -शां -शं कृ, शङ्कास्पदं कृ; 'one who hazards his life,' संशयितजीवितः.

HAZARDABLE, *a.* दैवाधीनः -ना -नं, दैवायत्तः -त्ता -त्तं, संशयस्थः -स्था -स्थं.

HAZARDED, *p. p.* संशयितः -ता -तं, दैववशङ्गमितः -ता -तं.

HAZARDER, *s.* किञ्चित् संशयस्थं करोति यो जनः; 'a hazarder of life,' संशयितजीवितः.

HAZARDOUS, *a.* सन्दिग्धः -ग्धा -ग्धं, सांशयिकः -की -कं, संशयस्थः -स्था -स्थं, सन्देहस्थः -स्था -स्थं, शङ्काक्रान्तः -न्ता -न्तं, भयाक्रान्तः -न्ता -न्तं, संशयापन्नः -न्ना -न्नं, भयहेतुकः -का -कं, दैवाधीनः -ना -नं, दैववशः -शा -शं, भयानकः -का -कं; 'a hazardous situation,' संशयस्थानं, भयस्थानं, शङ्कास्पदं.

HAZARDOUSLY, *adv.* शङ्कया, सन्देहेन, संशयेन, ससंशयं, अनिष्टशङ्कया.

HAZARDOUSNESS, *s.* सन्दिग्धता, भयाक्रान्तता, दैवाधीनता, दैवायत्तत्वं.

HAZE, *s.* धूमिका, अवाष्पः, मृगतृष्णा, कुहेडिका, कुहेली, कुज्झटिका.

To HAZE, *v. n.* कुज्झटिका (nom. कुज्झटिकायते), धूमिका (nom. धूमिकायते).

HAZEL, *s.* ईषत्कपिशफलविशिष्टो गुल्मभेदः.

HAZEL, *a.* वक्ष्यमाणफलसवर्णः -र्णा -र्णं, ईषत्कपिशः -शा -शं.

HAZEL-NUT, *s.* ईषत्पाण्डवर्णे दृढत्वक्परिवृतं पूर्व्वोक्तगुल्मफलं.

HAZINESS, *s.* सधूमिकत्वं, कुज्झटिकावस्था, सान्धकारत्वं, साभ्रता.

HAZY, *a.* सधूमिकः -का -कं, धूमिकावृतः -ता -तं, सकुज्झटिकः -का -कं, कुज्झटिकामयः -यी -यं, सान्धकारः -रा -रं, अभ्रियः -या -यं, साभ्रः -भ्रा -भ्रं, सन्धकः -का -कं.

HE, *s.* सः (तद्), एषः (एतद्), असौ *m.* (अदस्), सकः; 'so and so,'

अमुकनामा *m.* (न्). Obs. The visarga of सः and श्यः is dropped before *any consonant*.

Head, *s.* (Uppermost part of the human body) शिरस् *n.*, शीर्षं -र्षकं, मूर्द्धा *m.* (न्), मस्तकः -कं, मुण्डः -ण्डं -ण्डकं, मौलिः -ली *m. f.*, केनारः, चूडालं, वराङ्गं, उत्तमाङ्गं, सीमन्तः -न्तं, केशभूः *m.*—(A chief, leader) नायकः, मुखरः, अग्रगः, पतिः *m.*, अधिपतिः *m.*, अधिपः, अधिष्ठाता *m.* (तृ), श्रेष्ठः, श्रेष्ठी *m.* (न्), शिष्टः, प्रष्ठः, शिरोवर्त्ती *m.* (न्), मुख्य or प्रधान in comp.; as, 'head-minister,' मुख्यमन्त्री *m.* (न्), प्रधानमन्त्री *m.*; 'head-merchant,' विट्पतिः *m.*; 'head-scholar,' पट्टशिष्यः, श्रेष्ठशिष्यः; 'head of the police,' दण्डनायकः, दण्डपालकः; 'with Karna at their head,' कर्णमुखाः *m. pl.*, कर्णपुरोगमाः *m. pl.*—(Division of a subject) पदं, स्थानं, मार्गः, विषयः, अधिकरणं.—(Top, forepart) अग्रं, शिरस् *n.*, शीर्षकं; 'head of a spear,' शूलाग्रं; 'head of a boat,' मङ्गः; 'at the head of,' अग्रे or expressed by धुरि in such phrases as, 'a father at the head of all who possess sons,' पिता धुरि पुत्रिणां.—(The first place) अग्रस्थानं, उत्तमस्थानं.—(Source) प्रभवः, उद्भवः, उद्गमः, मूलं, हेतुः *m.*; 'of a river,' सरिन्मुखं, सरित्प्रभवः.—(Head of hair) कैशिकं, कैश्यं, केशपाशः, केशपक्षः; 'belonging to the head,' शीर्षण्यः -ण्या -ण्यं; 'to cut off the head,' शिरः or मस्तकं छिद् (c. 7. छिनत्ति, छेत्तुं); 'to be over head and ears in debt,' ऋणग्रस्तः -स्ता -स्तं भू, ऋणमग्नः -ग्ना -ग्नं भू; 'to get ahead of,' अतिक्रम् (c. 1. -क्रामति -क्रमितुं); 'to make head against,' प्रतिकूल (nom. प्रतिकूलयति -यितुं), पर्य्युपस्था (c. 1. -तिष्ठति -स्थातुं), प्रस्था, प्रया (c. 2. -याति -तुं).

To head, *v. a.* (Lead, act as a leader) नी (c. 1. नयति, नेतुं), अग्रे or पुरो गम् (c. 1. गच्छति, गन्तुं), अधिष्ठा (c. 1. -तिष्ठति -ष्ठातुं); 'headed by Karna,' कर्णमुखः -खा -खं or कर्णपुरोगमः -मा -मं.—(Cut off the head) शिरः or मस्तकं छिद् (c. 7. छिनत्ति, छेत्तुं), विमस्तक (nom. विमस्तकयति -यितुं), शीर्षच्छेदं कृ.—(Oppose) प्रतिकूल (nom. प्रतिकूलयति -यितुं).

Headache, *s.* शिरोवेदना, शीर्षवेदना, शीर्षव्यथा, शिरःपीडा, शिरोर्त्तिः *f.*, शिरःशूलं, शिरोरोगः; 'afflicted with it,' शीर्षवेदनः -ना -नं.

Head-band, *s.* मूर्द्धवेष्टनं, शिरोवेष्टनं, शिरोबन्धनं -नी, ललाटवेष्टनं, ललाटपट्टः -ट्टं, मस्तकबन्धनी.

Head-borough, *s.* गर्द्धाटः.

Head-dress, *s.* मस्तकाभरणं, मस्तकभूषणं, मुकुटं, मकुटं, किरीटः, शेखरः, मौलिः *m. f.*, चूडा.

Headed, *p. p.* मुखः -खा -खं or पुरोगमः -मा -मं in comp.; as, 'headed by Karna,' कर्णमुखः -खा -खं; 'two-headed,' द्विशीर्षकः -का -कं; 'three-headed,' त्रिशिराः -राः -रः (स्).

Head-foremost, *a.* अवाक्शिराः -राः -रः (स्), अधःशिराः &c., अधोमुखः -खा -खं, अवाङ्मुखः -खा -खं.

Headiness, *s.* साहसं, विषमसाहसं, गमकारित्वं, क्षिप्रकारिता, मदः.

Headland, *s.* अन्तरीपः -पं, समुद्रमध्ये महाद्वीपवहिःस्थो भूमिभागः, उदग्रभूमिः *f.*, महाद्वीपनासिका, भूमिनासिका, उदग्रस्थलं.

Headless, *a.* अशिरस्कः -स्का -स्कं, अशिराः -राः -रः (स्), मस्तकहीनः -ना -नं, अपमूर्द्धा -र्द्धा -र्द्ध (न्); 'a headless trunk,' कबन्धः -न्धं, अपमूर्द्धकलेवरं.

Headlong, *a.* (Head-foremost) अधोमुखः -खी -खं, अवाङ्मुखः -खी -खं, अवाङ् -वाची -वाक् (च्), अवाक्शिराः -राः -रः (स्), अधःशिराः &c.—(Rash) साहसी -सिनी -सि (न्), गमकारी -रिणी -रि (न्), क्षिप्रकारी &c.—(Precipitous) प्रवणः -णा -णं, पातुकः -का -कं.

Headlong, *adv.* अधोमुखेन, अवाङ्मुखं -खेन, अवाक्शिरसा, अवाक्.—(Rashly) साहसेन, सहसा, अनालोचितं.

Headmost, *a.* अग्रस्थः -स्था -स्थं, सर्वाग्रस्थः -स्था -स्थं, अग्र्यः -ग्र्या -ग्र्यं, प्राग्र्यः -ग्र्या -ग्र्यं, मुख्यः -ख्या -ख्यं, प्रमुखः -खा -खं, प्रधान in comp.

Headpiece, *s.* (Armour for the head) शिरस्त्राणं, शिरस्त्रं, शीर्षकं, शीर्षण्यं, शीर्षरक्षं.—(Force of understanding) धीशक्तिः *f.*, बुद्धिसामर्थ्यं.

Headship, *s.* मुख्यता, प्रमुखता -त्वं, प्रधानता, प्राधान्यं, श्रेष्ठता.

Headsman, *s.* घातुकपुरुषः, घातकजनः, वध्यपुरुषः, वधकर्म्माधिकारी *m.* (न्), मृतपाः *m.*, दण्डपाशिकः, शिरश्छेदी *m.* (न्).

Headstall, *s.* अश्वस्य शिरोबन्धनी or मस्तकबन्धनं.

Headstrong, *a.* साहसी -सिनी -सि (न्), आत्मः -त्मा -त्मं, गमकारी -रिणी -रि (न्), क्षिप्रकारी &c., चपलः -ला -लं, प्रमत्तः -त्ता -त्तं, अस्थिरः -रा -रं, प्रतीपः -पा -पं, धीरः -रा -रं, अवशः -शा -शं, निर्यन्त्रणः -णा -णं, उच्छृङ्खलः -ला -लं, दुर्दमः -मा -मं.

Heady, *a.* साहसी -सिनी -सि (न्), तीक्ष्णकर्म्मा -र्म्मा -र्म्म (न्), संरम्भी -म्भिणी -म्भि (न्), उच्चण्डः -ण्डा -ण्डं, शीघ्रकोपी -पिनी -पि (न्), अमर्षी -र्षिणी -र्षि (न्).

To heal, *v. a.* शम् (c. 10. शमयति -यितुं), प्रशम्, उपशम्, कित् in des. (चिकित्सति -त्सितुं), स्वस्थं -स्थां -स्थं कृ or सुस्थं कृ, निरामयं -यां -यं कृ, नीरोगं -गां -गं कृ, प्रतिकृ, भिषज् (nom. भिषज्यति), रोगाद् मुच् (c. 6. मुञ्चति, मोक्तुं), समुत्था in caus. (-थापयति -यितुं, rt. स्था), साध् (c. 10. साधयति -यितुं); 'heal a wound,' व्रणं रुह् in caus. (रोपयति -यितुं), व्रणरोपणं कृ.—(Reconcile) समाधा (c. 3. -दधाति -धातुं), सन्धा, प्रतिसमाधा.

To heal, *v. n.* शम् (c. 4. शाम्यति, शमितुं), उपशम्, स्वस्थः -स्था -स्थं भू, सुस्थः -स्था -स्थं भू.

Healed, *p. p.* शमितः -ता -तं, शान्तः -न्ता -न्तं, शान्तरोगः -गा -गं, उपशान्तः -न्ता -न्तं, प्रशान्तः -न्ता -न्तं, रोगमुक्तः -क्ता -क्तं, चिकित्सितः -ता -तं, सुस्थः -स्था -स्थं, स्वस्थः -स्था -स्थं, समुत्थितः -ता -तं, प्रतिकृतः -ता -तं; 'as a sore or wound,' रोपितः -ता -तं, रूढः -ढा -ढं, रूढव्रणः -णा -णं, शुष्कः -ष्का -ष्कं.

Healer, *s.* चिकित्सकः, रोगशान्तकः, रोगहृत् *m.*, भिषक् *m.* (ज्).

Healing, *a.* रोगशमकः -का -कं, शान्तिकरः -री -रं, शान्तिदः -दा -दं, शान्तिकः -की -कं, रोगहरः -रा -रं, रोगघ्नः -घ्नी -घ्नं.

Healing, *s.* (The act) चिकित्सा -त्सनं, शमः, शान्तिः *f.*, उपशमः, रोगशान्तिः *f.*, रोगशमः, रुक्प्रतिक्रिया, प्रतीकारः, सुस्थकरणं, समुत्थानं, भेषजं; 'of a sore,' व्रणरोपणं.

Health, *s.* स्वास्थ्यं, स्वस्थता, अरोगः, आरोग्यं, अरोगिता, सुस्थता, सुस्थितिः *f.*, अनामयं, निरामयता, रोगाभावः, कल्यत्वं -ता, कुशलं, शरीरकुशलं, शरीरसुखं, वार्त्तः, उत्पाली.—(Bad health) अस्वास्थ्यं, असुस्थता, शरीरदुःस्थितिः *f.*, रोगिता, सरोगता; 'health to you,' स्वस्ति, कुशलं ते.

Healthful, *a.* अरोगी -गिणी -गि (न्), नीरोगः -गा -गं, आरोग्यः -ग्यी -ग्यं, सुस्थः -स्था -स्थं, स्वस्थः -स्था -स्थं, निरामयः -या -यं. *See* Healthy.

Healthfully, *adv.* अरोगेण, सारोग्यं, निरामयं, स्वास्थ्येन, कुशलं.

Healthfulness, *s.* अरोगिता -त्वं, स्वास्थ्यं, निरामयता, कल्यत्वं.

Healthily, *adv.* सारोग्यं, सानामयं, शरीरस्वास्थ्येन, स्वस्थवत्.

Healthiness, *s.* स्वास्थ्यं, स्वस्थता, आरोग्यं, अरोगिता, सुस्थता, शरीरसुस्थितिः *f.*, निरामयत्वं, अनामयत्वं, कल्यत्वं -ता, रोगाभावः.

HEALTHLESS, *a.* अस्वस्थः -स्था -स्थं, असुस्थशरीरः -रा -रं, सरोगः -गा -गं.

HEALTHSOME, *a.* स्वास्थ्यजनकः -का -कं, रोगनिवर्त्तकः -का -कं, रोगघ्नः -घ्नी -घ्नं.

HEALTHY, *a.* सुस्थः -स्था -स्थं, सुस्थितः -ता -तं, अरोगी -गिणी -गि (न्), नीरोगः -गा -गं, नीरुजः -जा -जं, नीरुक् *m. f. n.* (ज्), निरामयः -या -यं, स्वस्थः -स्था -स्थं, सहारोग्यः -ग्या -ग्यं, कल्यः -ल्या -ल्यं, कुशली -लिनी -लि (न्), निर्व्याधिः -धिः -धि, व्याधिहीनः -ना -नं, रोगहीनः -ना -नं, चङ्गः -ङ्गा -ङ्गं, वार्त्तः -र्त्ता -र्त्तं, निष्पीडः -डा -डं.—(Causing health) स्वास्थ्यजनकः -का -कं, आरोग्यकरः -री -रं, अनामयकरः -री -रं.

HEAP, *s.* राशिः *m.* -शी *f.*, सञ्चयः, निचयः, चयः, चितिः *f.*, प्रचयः, पिण्डः, प्रकरः, उत्करः, निकरः, ओघः, पुञ्जः, पूगः, स्तूपः, स्तोमः, वृन्दं, समूहः, समवायः, सङ्घः, समुदायः, चायः, संस्थानं, सङ्कूहः, कूटः; 'a heap of grass,' तृणराशिः *m.*, तृणविस्तरः, तृण्या.

To HEAP, *v. a.* राशीकृ, आचि (c. 5. -चिनोति -चेतुं), समाचि, सञ्चि, समाक्षिप् (c. 6. -क्षिपति -क्षेप्तुं), पिण्डीकृ, पिण्ड् (c. 1. पिण्डते, c. 10. पिण्डयति -यितुं), ओघीकृ, वृन्दीकृ, एकत्रीकृ, एकत्र कृ, पुञ्जीकृ, पूगीकृ.

HEAPED, *p. p.* राशीकृतः -ता -तं, राशीभूतः -ता -तं, आचितः -ता -तं, उपचितः -ता -तं, समुपचितः -ता -तं, सञ्चितः -ता -तं, पिण्डितः -ता -तं, पिण्डीकृतः -ता -तं, पिण्डीभूतः -ता -तं, एकौघभूतः -ता -तं, पुञ्जितः -ता -तं, पूगीकृतः -ता -तं, सङ्कुलितः -ता -तं, सङ्कूढः -ढा -ढं, पुञ्जिष्ठः -ष्ठा -ष्ठं, एकपिण्डीभूतः -ता -तं, एकत्रीभूतः -ता -तं, समूढः -ढा -ढं, पर्य्यस्तः -स्ता -स्तं; 'heaped with flowers,' कुसुमचितः -ता -तं.

HEAPER, *s.* राशिकर्त्ता *m.* (र्तृ), पिण्डकर्त्ता *m.*, सञ्चयकारी *m.* (न्).

HEAPY, *a.* पिण्डी -ण्डिनी -ण्डि (न्), निचयी -यिनी -यि (न्), उत्करीयः -या -यं.

To HEAR, *v. a.* and *n.* श्रु (c. 5. शृणोति, श्रोतुं), उपश्रु, समुपश्रु, अनुश्रु, परिश्रु, आकर्ण् (c. 10. -कर्णयति -यितुं), निशम् (c. 10. -शामयति -यितुं, c. 4. -शाम्यति -शमितुं), विनिशम्, सन्निशम्, श्रवणेन्द्रियेण or कर्णद्वारेण उपलभ् (c. 1. -लभते -लब्धुं) or बुध् (c. 1. बोधति -धितुं) or ग्रह् (c. 9. गृह्णाति, ग्रहीतुं), श्रवणं कृ; 'having heard,' श्रुत्वा, निशाम्य.

HEARD, *p. p.* श्रुतः -ता -तं, आकर्णितः -ता -तं; 'as heard,' यथाश्रुतं.

HEARER, *s.* श्रोता *m.* (तृ), श्रवणकर्त्ता *m.* (र्तृ), आकर्णयिता *m.* (तृ).

HEARING, *s.* श्रवणं, श्रुतिः *f.*, आकर्णनं, निशमनं, निशामनं; 'sense of hearing,' श्रोत्रं, श्रवणेन्द्रियं; 'out of hearing,' असंश्रवः -वा -वं, कर्णागोचरः -रा -रं; 'out of the hearing of the master,' गुरोर् असंश्रवे; 'within hearing,' कर्णगोचरः -रा -रं, कर्णश्रवः -वा -वं.

To HEARKEN, *v. n.* श्रु (c. 5. शृणोति, श्रोतुं), आकर्ण् (c. 10. -कर्णयति -यितुं), निशम् (c. 10. -शामयति -यितुं), श्रवणं कृ.

HEARKENER, *s.* श्रोता *m.* (तृ), श्रवणकारी *m.* (न्), निशमनकारी *m.*

HEARSAY, *s.* किंवदन्ती, जनश्रुतिः *f.*, जनवादः, जनरवः.

HEARSE, *s.* शववाहनं, शवयानं, प्रेतवहनार्थं खट्वा, प्रेतवहनसाधनं, कटः.

HEART, *s.* (The seat of life in an animal) हृदयं, हृद् *n.*, हृत्पिण्डं, रक्ताशयः, अग्रमांसं, बुक्काग्रमांसं, मर्म्म *n.* (न्), बुक्कः -क्का -क्कं, बृक्कः, कन्तुः *m.*, रिक्थं, भयत् *m.*—(Seat of feeling) चित्तं, चेतस्, हृदयं, अन्तःकरणं, अन्तःप्रकृतिः *f.*, अन्तरात्मा *m.* (न्), आत्मा *m.*, मनस् *n.*, अन्तर्भावः, मानसं, स्वान्तं.—(The breast) वक्षस् *n.*, वक्षस्स्थलं, वक्षःस्थलं.—(Vital part) मर्म्म *n.* (न्), मर्म्मस्थानं -स्थलं, हृदयस्थानं -स्थलं.—(Inner part of any thing) गर्भः, उदरं, अभ्यन्तरं or expressed by अन्तर् prefixed; as, 'the heart of the city,' अन्तर्नगरं.—(Courage, spirit) वीर्य्यं, शौर्य्यं, तेजस्, सत्त्वं, पौरुषं.—(Affection) स्नेहः, प्रणयः, हार्द्दं, भावः, रागः; 'my heart beats,' स्पन्दते or कम्पते हृदयं मे; 'it goes to my heart,' मर्म्म भिनत्ति or स्पृशति; 'to take heart,' आश्वस् (c. 2. -श्वसिति -तुं), समाश्वस्; 'to learn by heart,' अभ्यस् (c. 4. -अस्यति -असितुं), कण्ठं कृ; 'learnt by heart,' कण्ठस्थः -स्था -स्थं, अभ्यस्तः -स्ता -स्तं; 'learning by heart,' कण्ठं; 'to be out of heart,' दीनमनस्कः -स्का -स्कं भू; 'pure in heart,' निर्म्मलान्तःकरणः -णा -णं; 'with all one's heart,' कामं, प्रकामं; 'heart's desire,' मनोवाञ्छितं; 'from the heart,' अन्तःकरणेन; 'heart-searching,' चित्तज्ञः -ज्ञा -ज्ञं.

HEART-ACHE, *s.* हृदयव्यथा, हृदयवेदना, चित्तवेदना, अन्तःकरणवेदना, मनोदुःखं, मनःपीडा, हृदयशल्यं, मानसी व्यथा.

HEART-APPALLING, *a.* मर्म्मभेदी -दिनी -दि (न्), चित्तशङ्काजनकः -का -कं.

HEART-BREAKING, *a.* हृदयभेदी -दिनी -दि (न्), मर्म्मभिद् *m. f. n.*, हृदयाविध् *m. f. n.* (ध्), मर्म्मस्पृक् *m. f. n.* (श्).

HEART-BROKEN, *p. p.* भिन्नहृदयः -या -यं, विद्धहृदयः -या -यं.

HEART-BURN, *s.* तीक्ष्णाग्निः *m.*, आम्लपित्तं, हृदयवेदना, हृद्रोगः.

HEART-DEAR, *a.* हृदयप्रियः -या -यं, हृद्यः -द्या -द्यं, हृदयङ्गमः -मा -मं.

HEART-EASE, *s.* हृदयसुखं, मनःसुखं, हृदयशान्तिः *f.*, हृत्सुखं, मनोनिर्वृतिः *f.*, चित्तनिर्वृतिः *f.*, मनोविश्रान्तिः *f.*, हृदयस्वास्थ्यं.

HEART-EASING, *a.* हृदयसुखजनकः -का -कं, मनःशान्तिकरः -री -रं.

HEART-FELT, *a.* हृद्गतः -ता -तं, हृदयजातः -ता -तं, चित्तभवः -वा -वं.

HEART-RENDING, *a.* मर्म्मभेदी -दिनी -दि (न्), मर्म्मच्छेदी &c., हृदयभेदी &c., हृदयभिद् *m. f. n.*, हृदयाविध् *m. f. n.* (ध्), मर्म्मस्पृक् *m. f. n.* (श्), मर्म्मपीडाकरः -री -रं, चित्तपीडाजनकः -का -कं, चित्तोद्वेगजनकः -का -कं, मनोदुःखकारी -रिणी -रि (न्).

HEART-ROBBING, *a.* मनोहरः -रा -रं, मनोहारी -रिणी -रि (न्), चित्तहारी &c., चित्तापहारी &c., चित्तहृत् *m. f. n.*, हृदयग्राही -हिणी -हि (न्).

HEART-SICK, *a.* आतुरचित्तः -त्ता -त्तं, उद्विग्नमनाः -नाः -नः (स्), विमनाः &c.

HEART'S-EASE, *s.* त्रिवर्णपुष्पविशिष्ट ओषधिभेदः.

HEART-SORE, *s.* मनोव्यथा, मनःपीडा, हृदयपीडा, मनोदुःखं.

HEART-STRINGS, *s.* हृत्पिण्डपरिगतं शिरादि.

HEART-STRUCK, *a.* हतचित्तः -त्ता -त्तं, विद्धहृदयः -या -यं, हृद्विद्धः -द्धा -द्धं.

HEART-SWELLING, *a.* चित्तक्षोभकारी -रिणी -रि (न्), हृदयकम्पकारी &c.

HEART-WHOLE, *a.* अक्षतहृदयः -या -यं, अभिन्नहृदयः -या -यं, अविकलचित्तः -त्ता -त्तं.

HEART-WOUNDED, *a.* क्षतहृदयः -या -यं, भिन्नहृदयः -या -यं, भिन्नमर्म्मा -र्म्मा -र्म्म (न्), विद्धमर्म्मा &c., विद्धहृदयः -या -यं.

HEART-WOUNDING, *a.* मर्म्मभेदी -दिनी -दि (न्), हृदयभेदी &c., हृदयाविध् *m. f. n.* (ध्).

To HEARTEN, *v. a.* आश्वस् (c. 10. -श्वासयति -यितुं), तेजः or विश्वासं or आशां कृ or दा or वृध् (c. 10. वर्धयति -यितुं).

HEARTH, *s.* अग्निकुण्डं, वितानं, चुल्लिः *f.* -ल्ली, अश्मन्तं, अन्तिका, उपचाय्यः, पक्षः.

HEARTILY, *adv.* कामं, प्रकामं, कामतस्, सर्व्वान्तःकरणेन, सद्भावेन, चित्तसन्तोषेण, सन्तुष्टचेतसा, इच्छातस्, स्वेच्छातस्, निर्व्यलीकं, निष्कपटं.—(With vigour) सवीर्य्यं, हृष्टपुष्टवत्.

HEARTINESS, *s.* (Sincerity) सारल्यं, सरलता, सत्यशीलता, अमाया, अकापट्यं, चित्तनिर्म्मलता.—(Vigour, strength) तेजस् *n.*, सत्त्वं, वीर्य्यं, पौरुषं, सारता.

HEARTLESS, *a.* (Spiritless, without vigour) निस्तेजाः -जाः -जः (स्), निर्वीरः -रा -रं, निर्वीर्य्यः -र्य्या -र्य्यं, निःसत्त्वः -त्त्वा -त्त्वं, भीरुहृदयः -या -यं, क्लीबहृदयः -या -यं.—(Hard-hearted) कठिनहृदयः -या -यं, निर्दयः -या -यं, दयाहीनः -ना -नं, निष्करुणः -णा -णं.

HEARTLESSLY, *adv.* (In a spiritless manner) निर्वीर्य्यं, निर्वीरवत्,

सत्त्वं विना, क्लीववत्, भीरुहृदयेन.—(In a cruel manner) निर्दयं, निष्करुणं, हृदयकाठिन्यात्.

HEARTLESSNESS, *s.* (Want of spirit) निर्वीर्य्यं, वीर्य्यहीनता, तेजोहीनता, अपौरुषं, हृदयभीरुता, क्लीवता.—(Cruelty) दयाहीनता, हृदयकाठिन्यं, निष्करुणता, कृपाराहित्यं.

HEARTY, *a.* (Sincere) सरलः -ला -लं, निर्म्मलचित्तः -त्ता -त्तं, सत्यशीलः -ला -लं, मायाहीनः -ना -नं, निष्कपटः -टा -टं, निर्व्यलीकः -का -कं, —(Vigorous, in full health) वीर्य्यवान् -वती -वत् (त्), तेजोवान् &c., हृष्टपुष्टः -ष्टा -ष्टं, सुस्थः -स्था -स्थं, कल्यः -ल्या -ल्यं, सपौरुषः -षा -षं.

HEAT, *s.* घर्म्मः, तापः, अभितापः, उपतापः, उत्तापः, सन्तापः, आतपः, दाहः, उष्णता, औष्ण्यं, उष्मः, उष्मा *m.* (न्), औष्म्यं, निदाघः, चण्डता, तिग्मता, तिग्मं, तैग्म्यं, अग्निः *m.*, अशिशिरता, ग्रीष्मः, इद्धं, तीक्ष्णं, खरं.—(Hot weather) ग्रीष्मः, निदाघः, घर्म्मः.—(Ardour, vehemence) उत्तापः, उच्चण्डता, प्रचण्डता, उग्रता, व्यग्रता, तीक्ष्णता, तैक्ष्ण्यं, उष्मः.—(Anger) चण्डता, तिग्मता, संरम्भः, मदः, उष्मः, क्रोधः, उग्रता. —(Course at a race) चर्य्या.—(Flush on the face) कपोलरागः. —(Heat of youth) यौवनदर्पः, यौवनमदः.—(As of a bitch, &c.) मदः.—(Morbid heat) स्पर्शः, तापकः; 'it emits heat,' उष्मायते.

To HEAT, *v. a.* तप् (c. 10. तापयति -यितुं, c. 1. तपति, तप्तुं), उत्तप्, प्रतप्, सन्तप्, उष्णीकृ, दीप् (c. 10. दीपयति -यितुं), ज्वल् (c. 10. ज्वलयति -यितुं), सन्धुक्ष् (c. 10. -धुक्षयति -यितुं), स्विद् (c. 10. स्वेदयति -यितुं), दह् (c. 1. दहति, दग्धुं).

HEATED, *p. p.* तप्तः -प्ता -प्तं, सन्तप्तः -प्ता -प्तं, उपतप्तः -प्ता -प्तं, उत्तप्तः -प्ता -प्तं, तापी -पिनी -पि (न्), तापितः -ता -तं, दीप्तः -प्ता -प्तं, जाततापः -पा -पं, स्वेदितः -ता -तं.

HEATER, *s.* जलादितापनार्थं तप्तलोहपिण्डः.

HEATH, *s.* (Plant) जङ्गलरुहः क्षुद्रौषधिभेदः.—(Wild ground) जङ्गलभूमिः *f.*—(Common ground) सर्व्वसामान्यभूमिः *f.*

HEATH-COCK, *s.* जङ्गलदेशसेवी कुक्कुटभेदः.

HEATHEN, *s.* देवतार्च्चकः, देवार्च्चकः, देवताभ्यर्च्चकः, देवपूजकः, देवप्रतिमापूजकः, देवतोपासकः, देवतासेवकः, प्रतिमापूजकः, प्रतिमासेवकः.

HEATHEN, *a.* देवार्च्चकसम्बन्धी -न्धिनी -न्धि (न्), प्रतिमापूजकसम्बन्धी &c.

HEATHENISH, *a.* देवार्च्चकयोग्यः -ग्या -ग्यं, देवार्च्चकव्यवहारः -रा -रं, देवार्च्चकधर्म्मा -र्म्मा -र्म्म (न्), प्रतिमापूजकयोग्यः -ग्या -ग्यं, देवार्च्चकाचारः -रा -रं.—(Barbarous) क्रूराचारः -रा -रं, दुराचारः -रा -रं.

HEATHENISM, *s.* देवार्च्चा -र्च्चनं, देवतार्च्चनं -ना, देवताभ्यर्च्चा -र्च्चनं, प्रतिमापूजा, देवपूजा, देवार्च्चकाचारत्वं.

HEATHY, *a.* जङ्गलः -ला -लं, जाङ्गलः -ली -लं, जङ्गलवृक्षावृतः -ता -तं.

HEATING, *s.* तापनं, तपनं, सन्तापनं, उष्णीकरणं, दीपनं, घर्म्मकरणं.

HEATING, *a.* तापकः -का -कं, तापनः -नी -नं, दीपनः -ना -नं.

To HEAVE, *v. a.* (Lift, raise) उत्तुल् (c. 10. -तोलयति -यितुं), उद्धृ (c. 1. -हरति -हर्त्तुं), उन्नम् (c. 10. -नमयति -यितुं), उत्था in caus. (-थापयति -यितुं, rt. स्था), उन्नी (c. 1. -नयति -नेतुं), उद्यम् (c. 1. -यच्छति -यन्तुं), उच्छ्रि (c. 1. -श्रयति -यितुं, rt. श्रि), उच्चीकृ.

To HEAVE, *v. n.* (Palpitate) स्पन्द् (c. 1. स्पन्दते -न्दितुं), कम्प् (c. 1. कम्पते -म्पितुं), स्फुर् (c. 6. स्फुरति -रितुं).—(Swell gently) लुठ् (c. 6. लुठति -ठितुं), प्रलुठ्, उत्सृप् (c. 1. -सर्पति -सर्प्तुं).—(Pant) कृच्छ्रेण श्वासप्रश्वासं कृ, उच्छ्वसं कृ; 'to heave a sigh,' दीर्घं निःश्वस् (c. 2. -श्वसिति -तुं), दीर्घनिश्वासं कृ or त्यज् (c. 1. त्यजति, त्यक्तुं); 'heaving a sigh,' दीर्घं निःश्वस्य.

HEAVE, *s.* उत्तोलनं, उद्धरणं, उन्नमनं, उच्चयः -यनं, उत्क्षेपः, उद्गारः.

HEAVEN, *s.* (Region of the blessed) स्वर्गः, स्वर् indecl., स्वर्लोकः, पुण्यलोकः, सुरलोकः, देवलोकः, त्रिदिवः -वं, दिवं, द्यौः *f.* (दिव्), द्यौ *f.* (द्यो), नाकः, देवनिकायः, देवालयः, सुरवर्त्म *n.* (न्), सुरपथं, शाश्वतं, सौरिकः, त्रिपिष्टपं, शक्रभवनं, सुखाधारः, सुखदं, त्रिदशालयः, त्रिदशावासः, अकुण्ठधिष्ण्यं; 'the heaven of Vishnu,' वैकुण्ठं.—(The sky) आकाशः, गगणं, नभस् *n.*, व्योम *n.* (न्), खं, अन्तरीक्षं, अम्बरं, दिगन्तरं, तारापथः, मेघवर्त्म *n.* (न्), ज्योतिश्चक्रं, ज्योतिषचक्रं; 'heaven and earth,' द्यावापृथिव्यौ *f. du.*, द्यावाभूम्यौ *f. du.*, दिवस्पृथिव्यौ *f. du.*, आकाशपृथिव्यौ *f. du.*, द्योभूम्यौ, स्वर्गमर्त्यौ, द्यावाक्षमे *f. du.*, रोदसी *n. du.* (स्), रोदस्यौ *f. du.*

HEAVEN-BORN, *a.* दिविजः -जा -जं, स्वर्गजातः -ता -तं, स्वर्गोत्पन्नः -न्ना -न्नं.

HEAVENLY, *a.* स्वर्गीयः -या -यं, स्वर्ग्यः -र्ग्या -र्ग्यं, दिव्यः -व्या -व्यं, दिविजः -जा -जं, दिविष्ठः -ष्ठा -ष्ठं, खस्थः -स्था -स्थं, नभःस्थः -स्था -स्थं, नभसीयः -या -यं, आन्तरीक्षः -क्षी -क्षं, वैहायसः -सी -सं; 'heavenly voice,' वैहायसी वाक्; 'heavenly bodies,' खस्थपदार्थाः *m.pl.*; 'heavenly nymph,' सुराङ्गना, स्वर्वेश्या.—(Excellent) परमः -मा -मं.

HEAVENLY, *adv.* दिव्यं, स्वर्गस्थवत्, स्वर्गीयप्रकारेण, दिव्यरूपेण.

HEAVENWARDS, *s.* स्वर्गं प्रति, स्वर्गाभिमुखं, त्रिदिवं प्रति.

HEAVILY, *adv.* (With great weight) गौरवेण, सगौरवं, महाभारेण, अतिभारेण, सुभरं, गुरुभारेण.—(Slowly) मन्दं, विलम्बेन, शनैः शनैस्, विलम्बितं, मान्द्येन.—(Sorrowfully) विषादेन, सविषादं, विषण्णमनसा. —(Vehemently) अति or सु prefixed, भृशं, तीव्रं, तीक्ष्णं; 'heavily laden,' गुरुभारवान् -वती -वत् (त्), अतिभारी -रिणी -रि (न्), सुभरः -रा -रं.

HEAVINESS, *s.* (Ponderousness) गुरुत्वं, गौरवं, गरिमा *m.* (न्), भारवत्त्वं. भारित्वं, भारः.—(Slowness, dulness) मन्दता, मान्द्यं, जडता, जाड्यं, स्थूलता.—(Dejection) विषादः, विषण्णता, अवसादः, दीनता.

HEAVING, *s.* (Palpitation) स्पन्दनं, कम्पनं, स्फुरणं.—(Swelling, undulation) उत्सर्पः -र्पणं, प्रलोठनं, लोठनं, लुठनं, लुलितं; 'of a wave,' ऊर्म्मिप्रलोठनं, ऊर्म्मिविभ्रमः.

HEAVING, *part.* (Palpitating) स्पन्दमानः -ना -नं, कम्पमानः -ना -नं, स्फुरन् -रन्ती -रत् (त्), स्फुरितः -ता -तं.—(Swelling gently) प्रलोठितः -ता -तं, उत्सर्पी -र्पिणी -र्पि (न्), उत्सर्पितः -ता -तं, लुलितः -ता -तं, लोलः -ला -लं, लोलमानः -ना -नं.

HEAVY, *a.* (Ponderous) गुरुः -र्व्वी -रु, भारी -रिणी -रि (न्), भारवान् -वती -वत् (त्), धुरीणः -णा -णं, धौरेयः -यी -यं, उद्गुरः -रा -रं; 'very heavy,' गरिष्ठः -ष्ठा -ष्ठं, गरीयान् -यसी -यः (स्).—(Slow) मन्दः -न्दा -न्दं, मन्थरः -रा -रं, मन्दगतिः -तिः -ति, विलम्बी -म्बिनी -म्बि (न्), विलम्बितः -ता -तं, अलसः -सा -सं.—(Dull, stupid) जडः -डा -डं, मन्दबुद्धिः -द्धिः -द्धि, स्थूलः -ला -लं, स्थूलधीः -धीः -धि.—(Dejected, sad) विषण्णः -ण्णा -ण्णं, विषादी -दिनी -दि (न्), अवसन्नः -न्ना -न्नं, दीनमनस्कः -स्का -स्कं.—(Grievous) गुरुः -र्व्वी -रु, क्लेशी -शिनी -शि (न्), दुःखी -खिनी -खि (न्), दुःखकरः -री -रं.—(Vehement) गुरुः -र्व्वी -रु, तीक्ष्णः -क्ष्णा -क्ष्णं, तीव्रः -व्रा -व्रं, उग्रः -ग्रा -ग्रं, गाढः -ढा -ढं. अति or सु prefixed; as, 'heavy rain,' अतिवृष्टिः *f.*; 'heavy displeasure,' गुरुकोपः; 'a heavy sea,' वातं, ऊर्म्मिप्रलोठनं, ऊर्म्मिविभ्रमः.

HEAVY-HEADED, *a.* स्थूलबुद्धिः -द्धिः -द्धि, मन्दमतिः -तिः -ति, जडधीः -धीः -धि.

HEAVY-LADEN, *a.* सुभारवान् -वती -वत् (त्), गुरुभारवान् &c., अतिभारी -रिणी -रि (न्), सुभरः -रा -रं, सुधुरन्धरः -रा -रं.

HEBDOMAD, *s.* (Week) सप्ताहं, सप्तदिनं, दिनसप्तकं.

HEBDOMADAL, *a.* साप्ताहिकः -की -कं, सप्तदिनः -ना -नं.

To HEBETATE, *v. a.* घनीकृ, स्थूलीकृ, अतीक्ष्णीकृ, धाराहीनं -नां -नं

कृ, तेजो हृ (c. 1. हरति, हर्तुं), जडीकृ, मन्दीकृ, मूढीकृ.

HEBETUDE, s. अतीक्ष्णता, घनता, स्थूलता, धाराहीनता, जडता, जाड्यं, मन्दता, मान्द्यं, आलस्यं.

HEBRAISM, s. यिहुदीयभाषानुसारी वाग्व्यापारः.

HEBRAIST, s. यिहुदीयभाषाव्युत्पन्नः, यिहुदीयभाषानिपुणः.

HEBREW, s. (The language) यिहुदीयभाषा.—(A Jew) यिहुदीयः.

HECATOMB, s. एकशतबलिदानं, शतगोबलिकरणं, शतगोमेधः.

HECTIC, a. ज्वरसूचकः -का -कं, अन्तर्दाहसूचकः -का -कं, ज्वरी -रिणी -रि (न्), ज्वरितः -ता -तं.

HECTIC, s. (Fever) ज्वरविशेषः, प्रलेपकः.

HECTOR, s. शूरम्मन्यः, शूरमानी m. (न्), पिञ्जशूरः, दम्भी m. (न्), कुम्भः, विटः, भर्त्सनकारी m. (न्), कलहकारः, विकत्थी m. (न्), आत्मश्लाघी m. (न्).

To HECTOR, v. n. भर्त्स् (c. 10. भर्त्सयति -ते -यितुं), विकत्थ् (c. 1. -कत्थते -त्थितुं), तर्ज् (c. 1. तर्जति -र्जितुं), तिरस्कृ, भुक्करीकृ, आत्मानं श्लाघ् (c. 1. श्लाघते -घितुं).

HECTORING, s. भर्त्सनकरणं, विकत्था -त्थनं, अहङ्कारोक्तिः f., आहोपुरुषिका, अहमहमिका, शूरमानं, आत्मश्लाघा, गर्व्वितवाक्यं.

HEDGE, s. वृतिः f., क्षेत्रवृतिः f., क्षेत्रप्रान्ततो वृतिः f., प्रावृतिः f., प्राचीरं, क्षेत्रप्राचीरं, क्षेत्रसीमा, प्राकारः, प्रावरः, आवरणं, आवारः, वारणं -णी, वरणः, धारा, क्षेत्रधारा, अवरोधकं, क्षेत्रावरोधकं, वेष्टनं, क्षेत्रवेष्टनं, मत्तवारणं, वेष्टः, आवेष्टकः, स्तम्भकरः, मत्तालम्बः, नेमः, गडः, मोषः, मोषाली.

To HEDGE, v. a. प्राचीरादिना परिवेष्ट् (c. 1. -वेष्टते -ष्टितुं, c. 10. -वेष्टयति -यितुं) or आवृ (c. 5. -वृणोति -वरितुं -रीतुं) or परिवृ or अवरुध् (c. 7. -रुणद्धि -रोद्धुं).

HEDGE-BORN, a. अन्त्यजः -जा -जं, अन्त्यजातीयः -या -यं, नीचजातीयः -या -यं, अधमजातीयः -या -यं, हीनवर्णः -र्णा -र्णं.

HEDGE-HOG, s. शल्यः -ल्यकः, शल्यकण्टः, शल्लकी, श्वाविध् m. (ध्).

HEDGE-SPARROW, s. कलविङ्कः -ङ्ककः, कलिङ्ककः, कलाविकलः, चटकः.

HEDGER, s. प्राचीरकारी m. (न्), क्षेत्रसीमारचकः.

HEDGING-BILL, s. क्षेत्रसीमारचनार्थं दात्रविशेषः.

To HEED, v. a. अवधा (c. 3. -धत्ते -धातुं), मनो धा सावधानः -ना -नं भू, अवहितः -ता -तं भू or अस्.—(Respect, regard) सेव् (c. 1. सेवते -वितुं), निषेव्, भज् (c. 1. भजति -ते, भक्तुं), अवेक्ष् (c. 1. -ईक्षते -क्षितुं), अपेक्ष्, मन् (c. 10. मानयति -यितुं), प्रतिमन्, आदृ (c. 6. -द्रियते -दर्त्तुं), अभिनन्द् (c. 1. -नन्दति -न्दितुं).

HEED, s. अवधानं -नता, अवहितता, सावधानता, अवेक्षा, अपेक्षा, अभिनिवेशः, मनोनिवेशः, मनःप्रवेशः, मनोयोगः, अप्रमादः; 'to take heed,' अवधानं कृ, अवधा (c. 3. -धत्ते -धातुं), मनो धा, सावधानः -ना -नं भू; 'take thou heed,' सावधानो भव.

HEEDFUL, a. सावधानः -ना -नं, अवहितः -ता -तं, कृतावधानः -ना -नं, दत्तावधानः -ना -नं, अप्रमत्तः -त्ता -त्तं, अप्रमादी -दिनी -दि (न्), सचेतनः -ना -नं, अर्पितचेतनः -ना -नं, समीक्ष्यकारी -रिणी -रि (न्), विमृश्यकारी &c., प्रमादरहितः -ता -तं.

HEEDFULLY, adv. सावधानं, अवधानेन, अवहितं, प्रमादं विना, अप्रमत्तं.

HEEDFULNESS, s. अवधानता, सावधानता, अवहितत्वं, अप्रमादित्वं.

HEEDLESS, a. अनवधानः -ना -नं, असावधानः -ना -नं, अनवहितः -ता -तं, प्रमत्तः -त्ता -त्तं, प्रमादी -दिनी -दि (न्), प्रमादवान् -वती -वत् (त्), निरपेक्षः -क्षा -क्षं, असमीक्ष्यकारी -रिणी -रि (न्).

HEEDLESSLY, adv. अनवधानेन, अनवहितं, अवधानं विना, प्रमादेन, प्रमत्तं, सप्रमादं, निरपेक्षं, अनपेक्षया, असमीक्ष्य.

HEEDLESSNESS, s. अनवधानं -नता, असावधानता, प्रमादः, अनपेक्षा, अनवेक्षा.

HEEL, s. पार्ष्णिः m. f., पादमूलं, घुटिकास्कन्धः, कूर्च्चशिरस् n., गोहिरं, पादस्य पश्चिमो भागः.—(Of a shoe) पादुकायाः पश्चाद्भागः, पादुकामूलं; 'to be at one's heels,' पार्ष्णिं ग्रह् (c. 9. गृह्णाति, ग्रहीतुं), वर्त्म अनुगम् (c. 1. -गच्छति -गन्तुं) or पश्चाद् गम्; 'to take to one's heels,' पलाय् (c. 1. पलायते -यितुं, rt. इ); 'heels upwards,' ऊर्द्ध्वपादः -दा -दं, ऊर्द्ध्वचरणः -णा -णं, ऊर्द्ध्वपार्ष्णिः -र्ष्णिः -र्ष्णि.

To HEEL, v. n. (Fall over on one side) एकपार्श्वे पत् (c. 1. पतति -तितुं) or परिवृत् (c. 1. -वर्त्तते -र्त्तितुं) or प्रलम्ब् (c. 1. -लम्बते -म्बितुं) or प्रणतः -ता -तं भू or अस्.

To HEEL, v. a. (A shoe) पादुकामूलं कृ, पादुकायाः पश्चाद्भागं कृ.

HEELED, p. p. (Having heels) पार्ष्णिलः -ला -लं, पार्ष्णियुक्तः -क्ता -क्तं.

HEEL-PIECE, s. पादुकादेः पश्चाद्भागः, पादुकामूलं.

HEFT, s. (Effort) चेष्टा -ष्टितं, विचेष्टितं, उद्योगः, उत्साहः, यत्नः.—(Handle) वारङ्गः, त्सरुः, मुष्टिः m. -ष्टी.

HEGIRA, s. यावनशाकः, यावनिकशाकः, मुसलमानीयशाकः.

HEIFER, s. गोवत्सा, वत्सा; 'of one year old,' एकहायनी, एकाब्दा, एकवर्षिका; 'of two years,' द्विहायनी; 'of three years,' त्रिहायणी, त्र्यब्दा; 'of four years,' चतुर्हायणी, चतुरब्दा.

HEIGH-HO, *interj.* अहो, अहोवत, अहह, हा, हन्त, हाहा.

HEIGHT, s. (Elevation) उन्नतत्वं -ता, उन्नतिः f., समुन्नतिः f., उत्कर्षः, उत्कृष्टता, उच्छ्रयः, समुच्छ्रयः, उच्छ्रायः, समुच्छ्रायः, उच्छ्रितिः f., उत्सेधः, समुत्सेधः, उन्नतिः f., तुङ्गता, उत्तुङ्गता, औन्नत्यं, उच्चता, ऊर्द्ध्वत्वं -ता, उन्नयः, प्रोन्नता, उत्साहः.—(High place, hill) उन्नतभूभागः, उच्चस्थानं, पर्व्वतः, गिरिः m., तुङ्गशेखरः.—(Summit) अग्रं, शिखा, शिखरं, शृङ्गं.—(Elevation of rank) कुलोत्कर्षः, कुलोत्कृष्टता, उच्चपदं, परमपदं, प्रधानता, प्रकृष्टत्वं, श्रेष्ठत्वं.—(Utmost degree) उत्तमावधिः m., परमावधिः m.; 'the height of summer,' ग्रीष्ममध्यं, महाग्रीष्मः; 'in the height of summer,' ग्रीष्ममध्ये, मध्यग्रीष्मे.

To HEIGHTEN, v. a. (Exalt) उच्चीकृ, ऊर्द्ध्वीकृ, उन्नी (c. 1. -नयति -नेतुं), उन्नतिं कृ.—(Increase, aggravate) वृध् (c. 10. वर्धयति -यितुं), उपचि (c. 5. -चिनोति -चेतुं), अधिकीकृ, अधिकतरं -रां -रं कृ.

HEIGHTENED, p. p. वर्धितः -ता -तं, उपचितः -ता -तं, लम्भितः -ता -तं.

HEINOUS, a. घोरः -रा -रं, अघोरः -रा -रं, दारुणः -णा -णं, गर्हितः -ता -तं, गर्ह्यः -र्ह्या -र्ह्यं, पापिष्ठः -ष्ठा -ष्ठं, अतिपातकी -किनी -कि (न्), अतिपापी -पिनी -पि (न्), महापापी &c., अतिदुष्टः -ष्टा -ष्टं, दुष्टतमः -मा -मं, उत्कटः -टा -टं; 'a heinous crime,' महापातकं, अतिपातकं, अघोरपातकं.

HEINOUSLY, *adv.* दारुणं, घोरं, गर्हितं, पापिष्ठं, अतिदुष्टं.

HEINOUSNESS, s. घोरता, अघोरता, दारुणता, अतिदुष्टता, पापिष्ठत्वं, अतिगर्ह्यता, गर्हितत्वं.

HEIR, s. उत्तराधिकारी m. (न्), अधिकारी m., धनाधिकारी m. (न्), दायादः, दायादवः, रिक्थी m. (न्), रिक्थहारी m. (न्), रिक्थभागी m. (न्), ऋक्थहारी m. (न्), ऋक्थभागी m. (न्), अंशभाक् m. (ज्), अंशहरः, अंशहारी m. (न्), अंशी m. (न्), अंशकः.

To HEIR, v. a. अधिकृ, अधिकारी -रिणी -रि भू, दायादो भू.

HEIR-APPARENT, s. युवराजः; 'state of one,' युवराजत्वं.

HEIRESS, s. उत्तराधिकारिणी, दायादी -दा, धनाधिकारिणी.

HEIRLESS, s. अदायिकः -का -कं, दायादहीनः -ना -नं.

HEIR-LOOM, s. वंशक्रमेण पितृप्राप्तं किञ्चिद् अस्थावरद्रव्यं.

HEIRSHIP, s. उत्तराधिकारिता -त्वं, धनाधिकारिता -त्वं, अधिकारिता.

HELD, p. p. (Grasped, taken in the hand) गृहीतः -ता -तं, धृतः

-ता -तं, ग्रस्तः -स्ता -स्तं, हितः -ता -तं, निहितः -ता -तं; 'held fast,' सुगृहीतः -ता -तं; 'held in the hand,' हस्तगृहीतः -ता -तं, हस्तधृतः -ता -तं, हस्तस्थः -स्था -स्थं, हस्तस्थितः -ता -तं, हस्तगतः -ता -तं.—(Esteemed, considered) स्मृतः -ता -तं, मतः -ता -तं, अभिहितः -ता -तं; 'is held,' अभिधीयते.—(Detained, stopped) धृतः -ता -तं, स्तम्भितः -ता -तं.—(Restrained) निवारितः -ता -तं, निरुद्धः -द्धा -द्धं.—(Contained) धारितः -ता -तं, अन्तर्गतः -ता -तं, परिगृहीतः -ता -तं.—(Kept, solemnized) सेवितः -ता -तं, पालितः -ता -तं, चरितः -ता -तं, आचरितः -ता -तं.—(Held out) प्रसारितः -ता -तं.—(Held up) उच्छ्रितः -ता -तं, उद्धृतः -ता -तं, उद्यतः -ता -तं, उन्नमितः -ता -तं, उत्थितः -ता -तं, उद्गूर्णः -र्णा -र्णं.

HELIOTROPE, *s.* सूर्य्यकमलं, श्रीहस्तिनी, भूरुण्डी.

HELL, *s.* नरकः, नारकः, निरयः, अधोलोकः, अधोगतिः *f.*, अधोभुवनं, पातालं, बलिसद्म *n.* (न्), रसातलं, दुर्गतिः *f.*, प्रमथालयं, नागलोकः. The following are different hells, वाडवाग्निः *m.*, संहातः, संहारः, धूमप्रभा, पङ्कधूमः, पङ्कप्रभा, तामिस्रं, तमःस्थितं, प्रतापनः, तपनः, महातमप्रभा, तप्तपाषाणकुण्डं, लोहशङ्कुः *m.*, सकाकोलः, सम्प्रतापनं, महारौरवः, रौरवः, पूयदः, अयःपानं, पर्य्यावर्त्तनं, प्राणरोधः, तप्तशूर्म्मिः *m.f.*, दन्दशूकः, अन्धकूपः, अवीचिः *f.*, अवटनिरोधनः, कृमिभोजनं, कालसूत्रं, क्षारकर्द्दमः, पुत् *n.*; 'pains of hell,' यातना, कारणा; 'river of hell,' वैतरणी.

HELL-DOOMED, *a.* नैरयः -यी -यं, नारकी -किणी -कि (न्), नरकगामी -मिनी -मि (न्).

HELL-FIRE, *s.* नरकाग्निः *m.*, नारकाग्निः *m.*, नरकानलः, यातना.

HELL-HOUND, *s.* नरककुक्कुरः, नरकश्वा *m.* (न्), नरकीयश्वा *m.*

HELLEBORE, *s.* औषधीयवृक्षभेदः.

HELLENISM, *s.* ग्रीकभाषानुसारी वाग्व्यापारः, ग्रीकवाक्यं.

HELLISH, *a.* नारकः -की -कं, नारकी -किणी -कि (न्), नरकीयः -या -यं, नारकीयः -यी -यं, नरकस्थः -स्था -स्थं, नैरयः -यी -यं.

HELLISHLY, *adv.* नरकवासिवत्, पिशाचवत्, राक्षसवत्, नरके यथा पापिष्ठप्रकारेण

HELLISHNESS, *s.* नारकत्वं, नारकीयत्वं, पापिष्ठत्वं, अतिगर्हता.

HELM, *s.* (Rudder) कर्णः, अरित्रं, केनिपातः -तकः, पोतरक्षः.—(Helmet) शिरस्त्राणं, शीर्षरक्षं, मस्तकरक्षणी.

To HELM, *v.a.* कर्णं धृ (c. 10. धारयति -यितुं) or ग्रह् (c. 9. गृह्णाति, ग्रहीतुं).

HELMET, *s.* शिरस्त्राणं, शिरस्त्रं, शिरस्कं, शीर्षकं, शीर्षण्यं, शीर्षरक्षं, मस्तकरक्षणी, मस्तकावरणी, खोलकः.

HELMSMAN, *s.* कर्णधारः, कर्णग्राहः, कर्णिकः, कर्णी *m.* (न्), नाविकः.

HELOT, *s.* दासः, क्रीतदासः, पूर्व्वकालीनो दासः.

To HELP, *v. a.* (Assist) उपकृ (c. 8. -करोति -कर्त्तुं), उपकारं कृ, साहाय्यं कृ, सहायत्वं कृ, उपचर् (c. 1. -चरति -रितुं), उपग्रह् (c. 9. -गृह्णाति -ग्रहीतुं), अनुग्रह्, अभिरक्ष् (c. 1. रक्षति -क्षितुं), आनुकूल्यं कृ, पक्षपातं कृ.—(Further) पुरस्कृ, प्रवृत् (c. 10. -वर्त्तयति -यितुं), संवृध् (c. 10. -वर्धयति -यितुं), प्रवृध्, प्रयुज् (c. 10. -योजयति -यितुं), उद्योगं कृ.—(Forbear, restrain one's self) निवृत् (c. 1. -वर्त्तते -र्त्तितुं), आत्मानं निग्रह्, or rather expressed by the fut. pass. part. with अवश्यं; as, 'I cannot help going,' अवश्यं मया गन्तव्यं; 'how can I help it,' का गतिः.—(Help at table) परिविष् or परिविश् (c. 10. -वेषयति -यितुं).

To HELP, *v. n.* साहाय्यं कृ, सहायो भू, उपकारी -रिणी -रि भू or अस् or साहाय्यकारी भू, अनुकूलः -ला -लं भू or अस्.

HELP, *s.* उपकारः -रिता, उपकृतं, साहाय्यं, सहायत्वं -ता, साहित्यं, उपग्रहः, अनुग्रहः, आग्रहः, सङ्ग्रहः, उपचारः, अभिरक्षा, आनुकूल्यं, अनुकूलता, संवर्धनं, अनुपालनं.—(Resource) गतिः *f.*, आश्रयः, शरणं, उपायः; 'a helping hand,' करालम्बनं; 'Help! Help!' त्राहि, त्राहि, परित्रायध्वं, परित्रायध्वं.

HELPED, *p. p.* उपकृतः -ता -तं, कृतोपकारः -रा -रं, कृतसाहाय्यः -य्या -य्यं.

HELPER, *s.* उपकारी *m.* (न्), उपकर्त्ता *m.* (र्तृ), उपकारकः, साहाय्यकारी *m.* (न्), सहकारी *m.*, सहायः, उत्तरसाधकः.

HELPFUL, *a.* उपकारकः -का -कं, उपकारकारी -रिणी -रि (न्), सोपकारः -रा -रं, उपयोगी -गिनी -गि (न्), साहाय्यकारी -रिणी -रि (न्).

HELPFULNESS, *s.* उपकारिता, उपकारकत्वं, उपयोगिता, सोपकारत्वं.

HELPLESS, *a.* निरुपायः -या -यं, उपायहीनः -ना -नं, गतिहीनः -ना -नं, गतघ्नः -ना -नं, निराश्रयः -या -यं, अपाश्रयः -या -यं, अशरणः -णा -णं, निरवलम्बः -म्बा -म्बं, अनुपकृतः -ता -तं, निःसहायः -या -यं, असहायः -या -यं, विवशः -शा -शं, विहस्तः -स्ता -स्तं.

HELPLESSLY, *adv.* निरुपायं, निराश्रयं, उपायव्यतिरेकेण, उपायं विना.

HELPLESSNESS, *s.* निरुपायत्वं, उपायहीनता, गतिहीनता, निराश्रयत्वं.

HELPMATE, *s.* सहकारी *m.* (न्), साहाय्यकारी *m.*, सम्भूयकारी *m.*

HELTER-SKELTER, *adv.* सङ्कुलं, सङ्कीर्णं, साङ्कर्य्येण, क्रमेण विना, अक्रमेण.

HELVE, *s.* परशुदण्डः, दण्डः, त्सरुः, तलः, मुष्टिः *m.* -ष्टी.

To HELVE, *v. a.* परशुं दण्डेन युज् (c. 10. योजयति -यितुं).

HEM, *s.* (Of a garment) अञ्चलः, वस्त्राञ्चलः -लं, दशा, वसनदशा, वस्तिः *m.*, तरी, माढिः *f.*, चीरी, शुल्कं, वसनग्रन्थिः *m.*, वसनप्रान्तः, वसनान्तः.—(Clearing the throat) उत्कासनं.

To HEM, *v. a.* अञ्चल (nom. अञ्चलयति -यितुं), अञ्चलं सिव् (c. 4. सीव्यति, सेवितुं), अञ्चलं कृ.—(Clear the throat) उत्कास् (c. 1. -कासते -सितुं), उत्कासनं कृ.

To HEM IN, *v. a.* परिवेष्ट् (c. 1. -वेष्टते -ष्टितुं, c. 10. -वेष्टयति -यितुं), परिवृ (c. 5. -वृणोति -वरितुं -रीतुं), निरुध् (c. 7. -रुणद्धि -रोद्धुं), प्रतिरुध्.

HEMMED IN, *a.* परिवेष्टितः -ता -तं, परिवृतः -ता -तं, प्रतिरुद्धः -द्धा -द्धं, निरुद्धः -द्धा -द्धं, प्रतिबद्धः -द्धा -द्धं, सङ्कुलः -ला -लं.

HEMICYCLE, *s.* अर्द्धचक्रं, अर्द्धगोलः, अर्द्धावृत्तिः *f.*

HEMIPLEGY, *s.* पक्षाघातः, अर्द्धाङ्गाघातः, अर्द्धाङ्गवायुः *m.*

HEMISPHERE, *s.* अर्द्धगोलः, अर्द्धमण्डलं, भूगोलस्य अर्द्धभागः, अर्द्धभुवनं.

HEMISPHERICAL, *a.* अर्द्धगोलाकारः -रा -रं, अर्द्धमण्डली -लिनी -लि (न्).

HEMISTICH, *s.* अर्द्धश्लोकः, श्लोकार्द्धं, अर्द्धपद्यं.

HEMLOCK, *s.* पूर्व्वकाले प्रसिद्धो विषविधाने प्रयुक्तस् तीक्ष्णौषधिभेदः.

HEMORRHAGE, HEMORRHAGY, *s.* रक्तस्रावः, रुधिरस्रावः, रक्तातीसारः, असृक्स्रावः, रक्तक्षरणं.

HEMORRHOIDS, *s.* अर्शस् *n.*, अर्शं, अर्शोरोगः, गुदाङ्कुरः, गुदकीलः, गुदरोगः.

HEMP, *s.* शणं, भङ्गा, मातुलानी, इन्द्राशनः, अभया, मत्कुणारिः *m.*

HEMPEN, *a.* शाणः -णी -णं, भाङ्गीनः -ना -नं, शणमयः -यी -यं, शणसूत्रमयः -यी -यं; 'a hempen cord,' शणसूत्रं.

HEMP-FIELD, *s.* भङ्ग्यं, भाङ्गीनक्षेत्रं, शणक्षेत्रं, भङ्गाक्षेत्रं.

HEMP-SEED, *s.* शणबीजं, भाङ्गीनबीजं, पक्षिखाद्यं क्षुद्रबीजं.

HEN, *s.* कुक्कुटी, कुक्कुटवधूः *f.*, पक्षिणी, ग्राम्यकुक्कुटी.

HEN-COOP, *s.* ग्राम्यकुक्कुटादिरक्षणार्थं पिञ्जरं or वीतंसः, कुक्कुटपालिका, कुक्कुटपिञ्जरं.

HEN-HEARTED, *a.* भीरुहृदयः -या -यं, कुक्कुटीव भयशीलः -ला -लं.

HEN-HOUSE, *s.* कुक्कुटपालिका, कुक्कुटगृहं, कुक्कुटागारं.

HEN-PECKED, *a.* स्त्रीजितः -ता -तं, स्त्रीवशः -शा -शं, स्त्रीवशवर्त्ती -र्त्तिनी

-र्त्ति (न्), दयिताधीनः -ना -नं, स्त्रीविधेयः -या -यं, भार्य्याटिकः, काकरूकः, कावरूकः -की -कं.

Hen-roost, *s.* कुक्कुटालयः, कुक्कुटनिलयः, कुक्कुटनिवासस्थानं.

Hence, *adv.* (From this place) इतस्; 'begone hence!' अपेहि, अपसर, दूरम् अपसर.—(From this time) अद्यारभ्य, अतःपरं, एतत्कालादारभ्य, अत ऊर्द्ध्वं.—(From this cause) तस्मात्, अतस्, अस्मात्, अतएव, अमुतस्.—(For this reason) अतःकारणात्, अनेन हेतुना, तस्य हेतोः.—(In another place) अन्यतस्, अन्यत्र, अपरतस्, इतरतस्.

Henceforth, henceforward, *adv.* अद्य प्रभृति, अद्यारभ्य, अद्यावधि, अधुनारभ्य, एतत्कालादारभ्य, एतद्दिनादारभ्य, अतःपरं, अतःप्रभृति, इतःपरं.

Heptagon, *s.* सप्तास्रं -स्री, सप्तकोणः -णं, सप्तभुजः, सप्तकोणा मूर्त्तिः.

Heptagonal, *a.* सप्तास्रः -स्रा -स्रं, सप्तकोणः -णा -णं, सप्तभुजः -जा -जं.

Her, *pron.* तां acc. c. *f.* (तद्), इमां acc. c. *f.* (इदं); 'of her,' तस्याः, अस्याः; as, 'her house,' तस्या गृहं; 'her own,' expressed by स्व; as, 'her own house,' स्वगृहं.

Herald, *s.* वन्दी *m.* (न्), राजदूतः, सन्दिष्टार्थः, राजसन्देशहरः, राजवार्त्ताहरः, अग्रेसरः -री *m.* (न्), अग्रगामी *m.* (न्), राजपाठकः.

Heraldick, *a.* वंशावलीसूचकः -का -कं, कुलीनपदचिह्नविषयः -या -यं.

Heraldry, *s.* कुलीनपदचिह्नविषया विद्या, वंशावलीविषयका विद्या.

Herb, *s.* ओषधिः -धी *f.*, शाकः, तृणं, लता, हरितकं, अर्भः, कन्दः.

Herbaceous, *a.* (Relating to herbs) शाकतृणादिविषयः -या -यं, तृणसः -सा -सं.—(Eating herbs) शाकतृणादिभोजी -जिनी -जि (न्).

Herbage, *s.* तृणं, घासः, यवसः, गवादनं, गवादिखाद्यं, क्षेत्रियं.

Herbal, *s.* शुष्कौषधिपुस्तकं, शुष्कतृणादिपुस्तकं, वृक्षतृणादिविवरणपुस्तकं, शुष्कतृणादिविषयो ग्रन्थः, वृक्षायुर्वेदः.

Herbalist, *s.* शाकतृणादिविषयशास्त्रज्ञः, ओषधितृणादिनामगुणादितत्त्वज्ञः, शुष्कौषधिसङ्ग्राहकः, वृक्षायुर्वेदज्ञः.

Herbarium, *s.* शुष्कौषधिपुस्तकं, शुष्कौषधिसङ्ग्रहः, शुष्कौषधयः *f. pl.*

To herbalize, *v. n.* शुष्कौषधिसङ्ग्रहं कृ, ओषधितृणाद्यन्वेषणार्थं भ्रमणं कृ.

Herbelet, *s.* ओषधिका, क्षुद्रौषधिः *f.*, क्षुद्रलता.

Herbescent, *a.* ओषधिरूपेण रोही -हिणी -हि (न्), ओषधितृणादिमध्ये जातः -ता -तं.

Herbid, *a.* तृणावृतः -ता -तं, तृणादिविशिष्टः -ष्टा -ष्टं.

Herbous, *a.* तृणादिमयः -यी -यं, ओषधिशाकादिमयः -यी -यं.

Herb-woman, *s.* शाकादिविक्रेत्री स्त्री, शाकादिविक्रयिणी.

Herby, *a.* शाकतृणादिसगुणः -णा -णं, शाकादिगुणविशिष्टः -ष्टा -ष्टं.

Herculean, *a.* अत्यन्तबलवान् -वती -वत् (त्), अतिशक्तिमान् -मती -मत् (त्), अतिप्रबलः -ला -लं, अतिबृहन् -हती -हत् (त्), अतिदुष्करः -री -रं.

Herd, *s.* (Collection of animals) यूथं, गणः, सङ्घः, सङ्घातः, समूहः, कुलं, वृन्दं, व्रजः, संहतिः *f.*, कदम्बकं, ओघः, निवहः, समुदायः, समुदयः, समाहारः, निकरः, समवायः, सञ्चयः, सार्थः, विसरः, वारः, निकायः, निकुरुम्बं -म्बकं, समजः, सन्दोहः; 'herd of cattle,' पशुगणः, गोकुलं, गोवृन्दं, गव्या, गोत्रा, पाशवं; 'herd of swine,' शूकरगणः, शूकरनिवहः, वराहव्रजः; 'a herd of elephants,' हास्तिकं; 'a herd of calves,' वात्सकं; 'of oxen,' औक्षकं, उक्ष्णां संहतिः; 'of milch cows,' धैनुकं, 'rich in herds of cattle,' गोमान् -मती -मत् (त्), गोमी -मिनी -मि (न्).—(Company of men) जनसमूहः, पुरुषगणः.

To herd, *v. n.* पशुयूथवद् एकत्र मिल् (c. 6. मिलति, मेलितुं), यूथशः सङ्गम् (c. 1. -गच्छति -गन्तुं) or समागम् or समे (c. 2. समैति -तुं, rt. इ), एकीभू, एकत्र भू, एकीकृभू, समूहीभू, सङ्कुलीभू.

Herdsman, *s.* गोपालः, पशुपालः, गोरक्षः -क्षकः, पशुरक्षी *m.* (न्), गोचारकः, यूथपतिः *m.*, गोपः, गोसंख्यः; 'his business,' पाशुपाल्यं, पशुपालनं, पशुरक्षणं; 'herdsman's wife,' गोपी.

Here, *adv.* (In this place) अत्र, इह, इहस्थाने, अस्मिन् देशे.—(In this world) इह, इहलोके, इहकाले; 'in this world and the next,' इहामुत्र; 'on this occasion,' इहसमये; 'here am I,' सोऽहं, एषोऽस्मि; 'here we are,' इमे स्मः; 'here and there,' इतस्ततस्, इतश्चेतस्, प्रतिदेशं.

Hereabouts, *adv.* अत्र, इह, इहसमीपे, इहस्थानसमीपे, अत्रोपान्ते, अत्रान्तिके, इहस्थानोपान्ते.

Hereafter, *adv.* अतःपरं, अत ऊर्द्ध्वं, ततः परं, इतःपरं, परं, परम्, परतस्, अपरं, अनन्तरं, एतदनन्तरं, तदनन्तरं, परस्तात्, पश्चात्, तत्पश्चात्, एतत्पश्चात्, उत्तरतस्, उत्तरत्र, परकाले, अपरकाले, अतस्, ततस्, पुरा; 'in the next world,' परत्र, अमुत्र, प्रेत्य, परलोके; 'in the sequel,' अग्रे.

Hereafter, *s.* परकालः, अपरकालः, उत्तरकालः, भविष्यत्कालः, भाविकालः, आगामिकालः.

Hereat, *adv.* अतस्, ततस्, तदनन्तरं, अत्रान्तरे.

Hereby, *adv.* तेन, एतेन, तद्द्वारा, तद्द्वारेण, तस्मात्.

Hereditament, *s.* दायः, पैतृकं रिक्थं, गोत्ररिक्थं, अधिकारः.

Hereditarily, *adv.* पारम्पर्य्येण, क्रमागमेन, वंशक्रमेण, परम्परतस्, परम्परं.

Hereditary, *a.* परम्परीणः -णा -णं, पारम्परीयः -या -यं, परम्परः -रा -रं, परम्परागतः -ता -तं, क्रमागतः -ता -तं, क्रमायातः -ता -तं, पैतृकः -की -कं, कौलिकः -की -कं, कुलजः -जा -जं, परम्परप्राप्तः -प्ता -प्तं.—(As disease) सञ्चारी -रिणी -रि (न्), शुक्रशोणितद्वारेणानुप्रविशन् -शन्ती -शत् (त्); 'hereditary estate,' पैतृकभूमिः *f.*, वंशभोज्यं; 'hereditary succession,' क्रमागतत्वं; 'hereditary servant,' मूलभृत्यः.

Herefrom, *adv.* अतस्, अतःकारणात्, तस्मात्, अस्य हेतोः.

Herein, *adv.* अत्र, इह, इहविषये, अस्मिन् विषये, अस्मिन् अर्थे.

Hereon, *adv.* अत्रोपरि, तत्रोपरि, अतस्, अत्रान्तरे.

Heresiarch, *s.* विधर्म्मनायकः, वैधर्म्यपतिः *m.*, स्वधर्म्मपरित्यागं कारयित्वा परधर्म्मावलम्बनं कारयति यो जनः, धर्म्मत्यागप्रवर्त्तकः.

Heresy, *s.* विधर्म्मः, वैधर्म्यं, उपधर्म्मः, विधर्म्मसेवा, अपपथः, विपथः, अपपथगमनं, मिथ्यादृष्टिः *f.*, कुदृष्टिः *f.*, स्वधर्म्मपरित्यागपूर्व्वं परधर्म्मावलम्बनं or परधर्म्माश्रयः or परमतग्रहणं or मतान्तरप्रवेशः, नास्तिक्यं, नास्तिकता, देवनिन्दा, असच्छास्त्रानुशंसनं.

Heretic, *s.* पाषण्डः -ण्डकः -ण्डी *m.* (न्), अपपथगामी *m.* (न्), अपपथवर्त्ती *m.* (न्), विधर्म्मसेवी *m.* (न्), उपधर्म्मसेवी *m.*, उपधर्म्मः, विधर्म्मावलम्बी *m.* (न्), परधर्म्मावलम्बी *m.*, स्वधर्म्मभ्रष्टः, स्वधर्म्मच्युतः, मतान्तरावलम्बी *m.*, नास्तिकः, देवनिन्दकः, वृषिणः *m.*

Heretical, *a.* वैधर्म्मिकः -की -कं, पाषण्डधर्म्मी -र्म्मिणी -र्म्मि (न्), अपपथगामी -मिनी -मि (न्), विपथगामी &c., अपपथवर्त्ती -र्त्तिनी -र्त्ति (न्), धर्म्मविरुद्धः -द्धा -द्धं.

Heretically, *adv.* पाषण्डवत्, नास्तिकवत्, धर्म्मविरुद्धं, देवनिन्दकवत्.

Heretofore, *adv.* पूर्व्वं, पूर्व्वे, पूर्व्वकाले, प्राक्काले, पूर्व्वतस्, पुरा, प्राक्, भूतकाले, अतीतकाले, गतकाले, वर्त्तमानकालात् पूर्व्वं, इहसमयात् पूर्व्वं, इतःप्राक्.

Hereupon, *adv.* अतस्, ततस्, अत्रोपरि, तत्रोपरि, अत्रान्तरे.

Herewith, *adv.* अनेन सह, एतेन सह, तेन सह, एतत्सहितं, एतेन समं.

Heriot, *s.* भूस्वामिने देयो दण्डः or शुल्कविशेषः.

Heriotable, *a.* पूर्व्वोक्तशुल्काधीनः -ना -नं.

Heritable, *a.* पितृप्राप्यः -प्या -प्यं, औत्तराधिकः -की -कं, दाययोग्यः -ग्या -ग्यं.

Heritage, *s.* पैतृकधनं, पैतृकं रिक्थं, अधिकारः, पैतृकाधिकारः, दायः.

दायत्वं, गोचरिक्थं, पैतृकं, औद्धारिकं.

HERMAPHRODITE, s. षण्ढः, शण्ढः, षण्डः, क्लीवः, अर्द्धेन पुरुषोऽर्द्धेन स्त्री.

HERMETICAL, a. रसायनीयः -या -यं, रसायनज्ञः -ज्ञा -ज्ञं.

HERMETICALLY, adv. रसायनानुसारात्, रसायनरीत्यनुसारेण.—(Closely) सुदृढं, अतिदृढं, सुगाढं.

HERMIT, s. अरण्यवासी m. (न्), वनवासी m. (न्), वनस्थायी m. (न्), वनस्थः, वानप्रस्थः, योगी m. (न्), यती m. (न्), तपस्वी m. (न्), मुनिः m., सन्न्यासी m. (न्), यतिः m., वैखानसः, वनी m. (न्), उदासीनः, संसारत्यागी m. (न्), लोकत्यागी m.

HERMITAGE, s. आश्रमः, मुनिवासः, मुनिस्थानं, अरण्यवासः, पर्णशाला.

HERNIA, s. अन्त्रवृद्धिः f., अन्त्रवृद्धिरोगः; 'umbilical hernia,' नाभिवर्द्धनः, नाभिगुडकः, नाभिगोलकः.

HERO, s. वीरः, शूरः, विक्रान्तः, महावीरः, प्रवीरः, दृढायुधः, युद्धवीरः, भटः, सुभटः, महौजाः m. (स्), औजसिकः, अतिरथः, रथी m. (न्), रथारोही m. (न्), युयुत्सुः m., प्रयुत्सुः m., शौटीरः, गम्भीरः, जेता m. (तृ), दमनः, चारभटः, वागरः, पत्तिः m., त्यागी m. (न्), जन्यः.—(Of a drama, &c.) नायकः.

HEROIC, HEROICAL, a. वीर्य्यवान् -वती -वत् (त्), महावीर्य्यः -र्य्या -र्य्यं, वीरः -रा -रं, शूरः -रा -रं, प्रवीरः -रा -रं, विक्रान्तः -न्ता -न्तं, पराक्रान्तः -न्ता -न्तं, शौर्य्यवान् -वती -वत् (त्), शूरयोग्यः -ग्या -ग्यं, धामवान् &c., साहसिकः -की -कं; 'heroic poem,' वीरचरित्रविषयं काव्यं.

HEROICALLY, adv. शूरवत्, वीरवत्, सवीर्य्यं, महावीर्य्येण, शौर्य्येण, सशौर्य्यं, सपराक्रमं, सविक्रमं.

HEROINE, s. वीरा, शूरा, विक्रान्ता स्त्री, पराक्रान्ता स्त्री, वीर्य्यवती.—(Of a poem, &c.) नायिका, दिव्यादिव्या.

HEROISM, s. वीर्य्यं, शौर्य्यं, वीरत्वं, सुवीर्य्यं, शूरत्वं -ता, प्रवीरत्वं, विक्रमः, सुविक्रमः, पराक्रमः, वीर्य्यवत्त्वं, धाम n. (न्), वीरश्रीः f., शौटीर्य्यं, शुटीर्य्यं, प्राधानिकं, प्राधान्यं, पौरुषं, साहसं, रणोत्साहः, महौजस् n., उत्साहवर्धनः, वीरः.

HERON, s. क्रौञ्चः, कङ्कः, कङ्कपक्षी m. (न्), वकः, दीर्घपाद् m., आमिषप्रियः, लोहपृष्ठः, मत्स्यहारी m. (न्), प्रेयोपत्यः.

HERRING, s. हेरिङ्नामा समुद्रीयमत्स्यभेदः.

HERS, pron. तस्याः gen. c. (तद्), अस्याः gen. c. (इदं), तदीयः -या -यं, or expressed by स्व in comp.

HERSELF, pron. सा स्वयं.

HESITANCY, s. सन्देहः, संशयः, विकल्पः, शङ्का, आशङ्का, चित्तास्थैर्य्यं, चलचित्तता.

To HESITATE, v. n. विकॢप् (c. 1. -कल्पते -ल्पितुं, c. 10. -कल्पयति -यितुं), शङ्क् (c. 1. शङ्कते -ङ्कितुं), अभिशङ्क्, आशङ्क्, विशङ्क्, परिशङ्क्, विलस् (c. 1. -लसते -सितुं), विचर् (c. 10. -चारयति -यितुं), मनसा दोल (nom. दोलायते -यितुं) or आन्दोल (आन्दोलयति -यितुं), चिर (nom. चिरायति -ते, चिरयति -यितुं), सन्देहं कृ.

HESITATION, s. विकल्पः, शङ्का, सन्देहः, संशयः, आशङ्का, विकल्पितं, विचारणं, वितर्कः, चिन्ता, विशयः, द्वैधं, विचिकित्सा.—(In speaking) स्वरभेदः, स्वरभङ्गः, वाक्यस्खलनं, स्खलद्वाक्यं, गद्गदवाक् f., गद्गदपदं, अस्पष्टवचनं; 'having a hesitation in the speech,' स्खलितवाक् m.f.n. (च्), स्खलितवाक्यः -क्या -क्यं, स्खलद्वाक्यः -क्या -क्यं, भिन्नस्वरः -रा -रं, भग्नस्वरः -रा -रं.

HETEROCLITE, a. भिन्नविभक्तिः -क्तिः -क्ति, साधारणनियमबहिर्भूतः -ता -तं, विधिनिपातितः -ता -तं, साधारणविधिविपरीतः -ता -तं.

HETERODOX, a. विधर्म्मी -र्म्मिणी -र्म्मि (न्), वैधर्म्मिकः -की -कं, धर्म्मविपरीतः -ता -तं, धर्म्मविरुद्धः -द्धा -द्धं, सच्छास्त्रविरुद्धः -द्धा -द्धं, सत्पथविपरीतः -ता -तं, भिन्नधर्म्मा -र्म्मा -र्म्म (न्), भिन्नमतः -ता -तं, अशास्त्रीयः -या -यं, अवैधः -धी -धं, अपथगामी -मिनी -मि (न्), विपथगामी &c., अपथवर्त्ती -र्त्तिनी -र्त्ति (न्), वृषिणः -णिः -णि.

HETERODOXY, s. कुदृष्टिः f., मिथ्यादृष्टिः f., कुपथः, विपथः, अपथः, कापथः, विधर्म्मः, असच्छास्त्रं.

HETEROGENEITY, s. विजातीयता, जातिभेदः, गुणविभिन्नता, वैवर्ण्यं, वैविध्यं.

HETEROGENEOUS, a. विजातीयः -या -यं, भिन्नजातीयः -या -यं, विविधः -धा -धं, नानाविधः -धा -धं, पृथग्विधः -धा -धं, विवर्णः -र्णा -र्णं.

To HEW, v. a. छिद् (c. 7. छिनत्ति, छेत्तुं), अवछिद्, कृत् (c. 6. कृन्तति, कर्त्तितुं), निकृत्, विकृत्, लू (c. 9. लुनाति, लवितुं), विशस् (c. 1. -शसति -सितुं); 'to hew in pieces,' खण्डं खण्डं छिद्, खण्डशः कृ or छिद्.

HEWED, p. p. छिन्नः -न्ना -न्नं, छिद्यमानः -ना -नं, छिन्नभिन्नः -न्ना -न्नं, व्यवछिन्नः -न्ना -न्नं, विशसितः -ता -तं, खनितः -ता -तं.

HEWER, s. छेत्ता m. (तृ), छेदी m. (न्), छेदकारः, विशसिता m. (तृ), छिद् in comp.; 'hewer of wood,' वनछिद्, काष्ठछिद् m.

HEXAGON, s. षट्कोणं -णः, षड्भुजः, षडस्रं -स्री, षट्कोणा मूर्त्तिः.

HEXAGONAL, a. षड्भुजः -जा -जं, षट्कोणः -णा -णं, षडस्रः -स्रा -स्रं.

HEXAMETER, s. षट्पदी श्लोकः, षट्पदविशिष्टः श्लोकः.

HEY, interj. किं, किमुत, किंस्वित्, ननु, स्वित्, अहो, आहा, हा.

HEYDAY, interj. हा, हाहा, आहा, अहो, आ, अहह.

HEYDAY, s. (Joy, hilarity) उल्लसता, परिहासः, हासिका, मुदा; 'heyday of youth,' यौवनप्रौढिः f., अक्षतयौवनं, नवयौवनं.

HIATUS, s. विच्छेदः, छेदः, छिद्रं, भेदः, भङ्गः, अन्तरं.

HIBERNAL, a. हैमन्तः -न्ती -न्तं -न्तिकः -की -कं, हैमनः -नी -नं, शीतकालसम्बन्धी -न्धिनी -न्धि (न्).

HICCOUGH OR HICCUP, s. हेक्का, हिक्का, प्राणघ्नी, श्वासकाशः, हृल्लासः, यमला, गम्भीरा, अनुबन्धी.

To HICCOUGH OR HICCUP, v. n. हिक्क् (c. 1. हिक्कति -ते -क्कितुं), हेक्कां कृ, हिक्कां कृ.

HID, HIDDEN, p. p. गुप्तः -प्ता -प्तं, गूढः -ढा -ढं, निगूढः -ढा -ढं, छन्नः -न्ना -न्नं, प्रच्छन्नः -न्ना -न्नं, छादितः -ता -तं, अन्तर्हितः -ता -तं, अन्तरितः -ता -तं, अपवारितः -ता -तं, निवारितः -ता -तं, निभृतः -ता -तं, स्थगितः -ता -तं, संवृतः -ता -तं, तिरोहितः -ता -तं, तिरस्कृतः -ता -तं; 'to be hidden,' गुह् in pass. (गुह्यते), गुप् in pass. (गुप्यते), तिरस्कृ in pass. (-क्रियते), रहस् (nom. रहायते); 'hidden behind the bushes,' विटपान्तरितः -ता -तं.

To HIDE, v. a. गुह् (c. 1. गूहति -ते, गूहितुं, गोढुं), निगुह्, विनिगुह्, छद् (c. 10. छादयति -यितुं), आच्छद्, समाच्छद्, प्रच्छद्, प्रतिच्छद्, सञ्छद्, गुप् (c. 1. गोपायति, गोप्तुं or in des. जुगुप्सते -प्सितुं), स्थग् (c. 10. स्थगयति -यितुं), अन्तर्धा (c. 3. -दधाति -धातुं), तिरोधा, अपिधा, पिधा, उपनिधा, अपवृ (c. 10. -वारयति -यितुं), संवृ, गोपनं कृ, निह्नु (c. 2. -ह्नुते -ह्नोतुं).

To HIDE, v. n. गुप्तः -प्ता -प्तं भू, अन्तरितः -ता -तं भू, गुप् in pass. (गुप्यते), तिरस्कृ in pass. (-क्रियते); 'he hides behind the bushes,' विटपान्तरितो भवति.

HIDE, s. (Skin of an animal) चर्म्म n. (न्), अजिनं, दृतिः m., कृत्तिः f., त्वक् f. (च्), पशुत्वक् f., पशुचर्म्म n. (न्), पशुलोम n. (न्).

HIDE-AND-SEEK, s. बालानां क्रीडाविशेषो यत्र एकतमे गुप्तशरीरे सति तदन्वेषणार्थं बालकगणः इतस्ततो धावति.

HIDE-BOUND, *a.* (Niggardly) दृढमुष्टिः -ष्टिः -ष्टि, गाढमुष्टिः -ष्टिः -ष्टि, स्वल्पव्ययी -यिनी -यि (न्), कृपणः -णा -णं.—(Harsh, untractable) कर्कशः -शा -शं, कठिनः -ना -नं, प्रतीपः -पा -पं, अवश्यः -श्या -श्यं.

HIDEOUS, *a.* करालवदनः -ना -नं, करालमुखः -खी -खं, करालाननः -ना -नं, करालः -ला -लं, उग्रदर्शनः -ना -नं, उग्रम्पश्यः -श्या -श्यं, भीमदर्शनः -ना -नं, घोरदर्शनः -ना -नं, घोराकृतिः -तिः -ति, घोररूपः -पी -पं, रौद्रदर्शनः -ना -नं, कुत्सितः -ता -तं, दुर्दर्शनः -ना -नं, कुरूपः -पी -पं, कदाकारः -रा -रं.

HIDEOUSLY, *adv.* सकरालवदनं, घोररूपेण, उग्ररूपेण, उग्रं.

HIDEOUSNESS, *s.* करालता, उग्रता, घोरत्वं, रौद्रता, कुत्सितत्वं.

HIDER, *s.* गोपनकर्त्ता *m.* (र्तृ), गोपः -पकः, गोप्ता *m.* (प्तृ), छादयिता *m.* (तृ).

HIDING, *s.* गोपनं, गुप्तिः *f.*, सङ्गोपनं, छादनं, प्रच्छादनं, अन्तर्धानं, तिरोधानं, स्थगनं, अपवारणं, अपिधानं, पिधानं.

HIDING-PLACE, *s.* गुप्तिः *f.*, गुप्तिस्थानं, निभृतस्थानं, गूढस्थानं.

To HIE, *v. n.* त्वर् (c. 1. त्वरते -रितुं), सन्त्वर्, सत्वरं गम् (c. 1. गच्छति, गन्तुं) or आश्रि (c. 1. -श्रयति -ते -यितुं), अभिश्रि, संश्रि.

HIERARCH, *s.* पौरोहित्यवर्गाधिपतिः *m.*, आचार्य्यवर्गाधिपतिः *m.*, पुरोहितगणपतिः *m.*, पुरोहितेश्वरः.

HIERARCHICAL, *a.* पुरोहिताधिपत्यसम्बन्धी -न्धिनी -न्धि (न्), पुरोहिताधिकारसम्बन्धी &c.

HIERARCHY, *s.* पुरोहिताधिपत्यं, पुरोहिताधिकारः, आचार्य्याधिपत्यं, धर्म्माध्यापकैश्वर्य्यं.

HIEROGLYPHIC, *s.* गूढाक्षरं, निगूढाक्षरं, बीजाक्षरं, गूढवर्णः, शब्दसूचकं निगूढचिह्नं.

HIEROGLYPHICAL, *a.* गूढाक्षरसम्बन्धी -न्धिनी -न्धि (न्), गूढाक्षरीयः -या -यं.

HIEROPHANT, *s.* महापुरोहितः, महायाजकः, महागुरुः *m.*, आचार्य्यः.

To HIGGLE, *v. n.* (Chaffer) पण् (c. 1. पणते -णितुं or पणायति -यितुं), पणं कृ, पणीकृ, तुच्छप्रकारेण क्रयविक्रयं कृ, क्षुद्रवाणिज्यं कृ.—(Hang back in bargaining) नैतावद् दित्सामीति क्रयसमये विलस्ब् (c. 1. -लम्बते -म्बितुं).

HIGGLEDY-PIGGLEDY, *adv.* अस्तव्यस्तः -स्ता -स्तं, अधरोत्तरः -रा -रं, छिन्नभिन्नः -न्ना -न्नं, आदिपश्चात्.

HIGGLER, *s.* क्षुद्रवाणिज्यकारी *m.* (न्), क्षुद्रवणिक् *m.* (ज्), दरिद्रसार्थवाहः.

HIGH, *a.* (Lofty) उच्चः -च्चा -च्चं, उन्नतः -ता -तं, उच्छ्रितः -ता -तं, समुन्नतः -ता -तं, समुच्छ्रितः -ता -तं, अभ्युच्छ्रितः -ता -तं, सोच्छ्रायः -या -यं, उच्छ्रायी -यिणी -यि (न्), प्रांशुः -शुः -शु, तुङ्गः -ङ्गा -ङ्गं, उत्तुङ्गः -ङ्गा -ङ्गं, उदग्रः -ग्रा -ग्रं, उन्नतः -ता -तं, उच्चयः -या -यं, ऊर्द्ध्वः -र्द्ध्वा -र्द्ध्वं, उत्तरः -रा -रं, उत्तमः -मा -मं, दीर्घः -र्घा -र्घं; 'a high tree,' उन्नततरुः *m.*, दीर्घतरुः.—(Elevated in rank) उत्कृष्टः -ष्टा -ष्टं, उत्कृष्टपदस्थः -स्था -स्थं, प्रतिपत्तिमान् -मती -मत् (त्), उत्तमपदस्थः -स्था -स्थं, अनवमः -मा -मं, अनीचः -चा -चं.—(Noble, of high family) महाकुलः -ला -लं -लीनः -ना -नं.—(Haughty) गर्व्वी -र्व्विणी -र्व्वि (न्), गर्व्वोद्धतः -ता -तं, उन्नतचेताः -ताः -तः (स्), उच्चचेताः &c., उद्धतः -ता -तं, समुद्धतः -ता -तं, उत्सिक्तः -क्ता -क्तं.—(Capital, great, chief) उत्तमः -मा -मं, परमः -मा -मं, मुख्यः -ख्या -ख्यं, श्रेष्ठः -ष्ठा -ष्ठं, प्रधान in comp., महा in comp.—(As sound) उदात्तः -त्ता -त्तं, उच्चालः -ला -लं, कलोत्तालः -ला -लं; 'a high tone,' उदात्तः, उच्चस्वरः, तारः; 'in a high tone,' उदात्तस्वरेण, उच्चैःस्वरेण; 'high and low,' उत्तमाधमः -मा -मं, उत्कृष्टापकृष्टः -ष्टा -ष्टं, उत्तराधरः -रा -रं, उच्चावचः -चा -चं, उन्नतानतः -ता -तं, निम्नोन्नतः -ता -तं; 'the high and low,' उत्तमाधमौ *m.* du., उत्कृष्टापकृष्टौ *m.* du.; 'very high,' अत्युच्चः -च्चा -च्चं; 'higher and higher,' उत्तरोत्तरं; 'highest,' उत्तमः -मा -मं, परमः -मा -मं; 'a high price,' दुर्मूल्यं; 'a high wind,' प्रबलवायुः *m.*, प्रचण्डवायुः, अतिवातः; 'high ground,' उन्नतभूभागः; 'as high as an elephant,' गजद्वयसः -सी -सं, गजमात्रः -त्री -त्रं, गजदघ्नः -घ्नी -घ्नं, गजपरिमाणः -णा -णं.

HIGH, *adv.* उच्चैस्, उच्चकैस्, उच्चैस्तमां, उच्चं; 'on high,' ऊर्द्ध्वं, ऊर्द्धं, उपरि; 'from on high,' उपरिष्टात्; 'to carry one's self high,' दृप् (c. 4. दृप्यति, दर्प्तुं).

HIGH-BIRTH, *s.* कुलोत्कर्षः, कुलोत्कर्षं, कुलीनता, अभिजातता, आभिजात्यं.

HIGH-BLEST, *a.* अतिपुण्यवान् -वती -वत् (त्), अतिधन्यः -न्या -न्यं, महाभागः -गा -गं, परमसुखी -खिनी -खि (न्), सौभाग्यवान् &c.

HIGH-BLOWN, *a.* अत्याध्मातः -ता -तं, अतिस्फीतः -ता -तं, अत्युच्छूनः -ना -नं.

HIGH-BORN, *a.* महाकुलजः -जा -जं, महाकुलप्रसूतः -ता -तं, सत्कुलजातः -ता -तं, सत्कुलीनः -ना -नं, कुलीनः -ना -नं, विशुद्धकुलभवः -वा -वं, श्रेष्ठकुलोद्भूतः -ता -तं, कुलश्रेष्ठी -ष्ठिनी -ष्ठि (न्), सद्वंशः -शा -शं, सद्वंशजातः -ता -तं, प्रधानवंशोद्भवः -वा -वं, महावंशीयः -या -यं, उत्तमवंशजातः -ता -तं, अभिजातः -ता -तं, अभिजनवान् -वती -वत् (त्).

HIGH-BUILT, *a.* उच्चैर्निर्म्मितः -ता -तं, उच्छ्रायी -यिणी -यि (न्).

HIGH-COLOURED, *a.* अतिरागी -गिणी -गि (न्), अतिरञ्जितः -ता -तं.

HIGH-DAY, *s.* उत्सवदिनं, उद्धर्षदिनं, शुभदिनं, पर्व्वाहः, सुदिनं.

HIGH-FED, *a.* अतिपुष्टः -ष्टा -ष्टं, सुपुष्टः -ष्टा -ष्टं, हृष्टपुष्टः -ष्टा -ष्टं.

HIGH-FLOWN, *a.* अतिगर्व्वितः -ता -तं, महागर्व्वी -र्व्विणी -र्व्वि (न्), स्फीतः -ता -तं.

HIGH-FLYING, *a.* अपरिमितः -ता -तं, अतिक्रान्तमर्य्यादः -दा -दं.

HIGH-HEAPED, *a.* अतिसञ्चितः -ता -तं, अत्याचितः -ता -तं, महाराशीभूतः -ता -तं.

HIGH-HUNG, *a.* ऊर्द्ध्वबद्धः -द्धा -द्धं, उच्चैर्बद्धः -द्धा -द्धं.

HIGH-METTLED, *a.* अदीनसत्त्वः -त्त्वा -त्त्वं, महासत्त्वः -त्त्वा -त्त्वं, महातेजाः -जाः -जः (स्), तेजोवान् -वती -वत् (त्), गर्व्वितः -ता -तं, अतिमादवान् &c.

HIGH-MINDED, *a.* महामनाः -नाः -नः (स्), महामनस्कः -स्का -स्कं, महात्मा -त्मा -त्म (न्), महामतिः -तिः -ति, उदारचेताः -ताः -तः (स्), उदारचरितः -ता -तं, गर्व्वी -र्व्विणी -र्व्वि (न्).

HIGH-PRIEST, *s.* महायाजकः, महापुरोहितः.

HIGH-PRINCIPLED, *a.* धर्म्मशीलः -ला -लं, पुण्यशीलः -ला -लं, पुण्यात्मा -त्मा -त्म (न्).

HIGH-PRIZED, *a.* महामूल्यः -ल्या -ल्यं, महार्घः -र्घा -र्घं, बहुमतः -ता -तं.

HIGH-RED, *a.* अतिरक्तः -क्ता -क्तं, घनरक्तः -क्ता -क्तं, घनारुणः -णा -णं.

HIGH-ROAD, *s.* महापथः, महामार्गः, राजमार्गः, रथ्या, घण्टापथः.

HIGH-SEASONED, *a.* सुवासितः -ता -तं, सुप्रयस्तः -स्ता -स्तं, सुसंस्कृतः -ता -तं.

HIGH-SPIRITED, *a.* अदीनसत्त्वः -त्त्वा -त्त्वं, महासत्त्वः -त्त्वा -त्त्वं, महातेजाः -जाः -जः (स्), महेच्छः -च्छा -च्छं, ऊर्ज्जिताश्रयः -या -यं; 'high-spirited speech,' ऊर्ज्जिताश्रयं वचनं.

HIGH-STREET, *s.* राजमार्गः, महामार्गः, प्रतोली, रथ्या, विशिखा; 'a town having a high street,' प्रतोलीकः.

HIGH-TREASON, *s.* राजशरीराभिद्रोहः, राजापथ्यकारित्वं.

HIGH-WROUGHT, *a.* महायत्नेन संस्कृतः -ता -तं or परिष्कृतः -ता -तं or कल्पितः -ता -तं.

HIGHEST, *a.* (Most lofty) उच्चतमः -मा -मं.—(Greatest) परमः -मा -मं, उत्तमः -मा -मं; 'a criminal in the highest degree,' महापातकी *m.* (न्).

HIGHLAND, *s.* पर्व्वतीयदेशः, अधित्यका, उन्नतदेशः.

HIGHLAND, *a.* पर्व्वतीयः -या -यं, पार्व्वतः -ती -तं.

HIGHLANDER, *s.* पार्व्वतीयजनः, पर्व्वतवासी *m.* (न्), पर्व्वतीयः.

HIGHLY, *adv.* (With elevation) उच्चैस्, उच्चं.—(In a great degree, very) परमं, परं, भृशं, अत्यन्तं, अतीव, अति or सु prefixed; 'highly indignant,' अत्यमर्षी -र्षिणी -र्षि (न्); 'highly delighted,' परमानन्दी -न्दिनी -न्दि (न्); 'highly respectable,' परममान्यः -न्या -न्यं.

HIGHMOST, *a.* उत्तमः -मा -मं, उच्चतमः -मा -मं, उच्चैस्तमः -मा -मं, सर्व्वोपरिस्थः -स्था -स्थं.

HIGHNESS, *s.* (Elevation) उच्चता, उन्नतिः *f.*, ऊर्द्धत्वं.—(A title, your highness) भवान् *m.* (त्), भगवान् *m.* (त्), कुमारः.

HIGHWAY, *s.* राजमार्गः, राजपथः, महापथः, महामार्गः, नरपतिपथः, महावर्त्म *n.* (न्), वर्त्म *n.*, रथ्या, विशिखा, संसरणं, साधारणपथः, घण्टापथः; 'highway police,' मार्गपालः.

HIGHWAYMAN, *s.* परिपन्थी *m.* (न्), पारिपन्थिकः, सारणिकघ्नः, पादविकघ्नः, दस्युः *m.*, होडा *m.* (ड्).

HIJJAL, *s.* (Tree) निचुलः, हिज्जलः, इज्जलः, अम्बुजः.

HILARITY, *s.* आह्लादः, उल्लसता, उल्लासः, हर्षः, प्रहर्षः, आनन्दः, सानन्दता, प्रफुल्लता, मुदा, प्रहसनं, हासिका, आमोदः, कौतुकं, उत्सवः.

HILL, *s.* पर्व्वतः, गिरिः *m.*, शैलः, अद्रिः *m.*, भूधरः, अचलः, महीधरः, सानुमान् *m.* (त्); 'hill near a mountain,' पादः, प्रत्यन्तपर्वतः.

HILLOCK, *s.* क्षुद्रपर्व्वतः, वल्मीकं, वप्रः -प्री, मृत्तिकाचयः, वामलूरः, नाकुः *m.*, उन्नतभूभागः.

HILLY, *a.* पर्व्वतीयः -या -यं, पार्व्वतीयः -यी -यं, सपर्व्वतः -ता -तं, सगिरिः -रिः -रि, उच्चनीचः -चा -चं, विषमः -मा -मं.

HILT, *s.* (Of a sword, &c.) त्सरुः *m.*, मुष्टिः *m.*, खड्गमुष्टिः, तलः, तालः, वारङ्गः.

HILTED, *a.* त्सरुमान् -मती -मत् (त्), मुष्टिविशिष्टः -ष्टा -ष्टं, दृढमुष्टिः -ष्टिः -ष्टि.

HIM, *pron.* तं acc. *m.* (तद्), एतं acc. *m.* (एतद्), एनं acc. *m.* (इदं).

HIMÁLAYA, *s.* (Mountain) हिमालयः, हिमाद्रिः *m.*, हिमवान् *m.* (त्), हिमप्रस्थः, हिमः, तुषाराद्रिः *m.*, उदगद्रिः *m.*, गिरीशः, तुहिनशैलः.

HIND, *s.* (Female of a deer) मृगी, हरिणी, कुरङ्गी, एणी, मृगवधूः *f.*, समीची, रोहित् *f.*, पृषती.—(A boor) ग्राम्यजनः, वृषलः.—(A servant) दासः, भृत्यः.

HIND, HINDER, *a.* पश्चिमः -मा -मं, जघन्यः -न्या -न्यं, अवरः -रा -रं, अपरः -रा -रं, पाश्चात्यः -त्या -त्यं, पश्चातीयः -या -यं.—(The hinder part) पृष्ठदेशः, पश्चाद्देशः, पश्चाद्भागः, पश्चिमभागः, पृष्ठं, नितम्बः; 'in the hinder part,' पश्चाद्भागे, अवरतस्, अवरस्तात्; 'hind quarter of an elephant,' अपरं; 'of a ship,' नावः पश्चिमभागः or पश्चाद्भागः.

To HINDER, *v. a.* वृ (c. 10. वारयति -यितुं), निवृ, विनिवृ, प्रतिवृ, आवृ, रुध् (c. 7. रुणद्धि, रोद्धुं), प्रतिरुध्, निरुध्, संरुध्, अवरुध्, उपरुध्; बाध् (c. 1. बाधते -धितुं), विहन् (c. 2. -हन्ति -न्तुं), व्याहन्, प्रतिहन्, विघ्न (nom. विघ्नयति -यितुं), स्तम्भ् (c. 10. स्तम्भयति -यितुं), विष्टम्भ्, प्रतिबन्ध् (c. 9. -बध्नाति -बन्धुं), प्रतिषिध् (c. 1. -षेधति -षेद्धुं).

HINDERANCE, *s.* विघ्नः, प्रत्यूहः, अन्तरायः, व्याघातः, विघातः, बाधः -धा, बाधकः -कता, विरोधः, अवरोधः, निरोधः, संरोधः, प्रतिरोधः, उपरोधः, रोधः -धनं, वारणं, निवारणं, आवरणं, स्तम्भः -म्भनं, विष्टम्भः, प्रतिष्टम्भः, प्रतिबन्धः -न्धकं -न्धकता, विष्कम्भः, प्रतिषेधः, हेठः.

HINDERED, *p.p.* वारितः -ता -तं, निवारितः -ता -तं, रुद्धः -द्धा -द्धं, विरुद्धः -द्धा -द्धं, निरुद्धः -द्धा -द्धं, उपरुद्धः -द्धा -द्धं, अवरुद्धः -द्धा -द्धं, बाधितः -ता -तं, विघ्नितः -ता -तं, विहतः -ता -तं, व्याहतः -ता -तं, प्रतिहतः -ता -तं, पराहतः -ता -तं, स्तम्भितः -ता -तं, स्तब्धः -ब्धा -ब्धं, विष्टब्धः -ब्धा -ब्धं, प्रतिबद्धः -द्धा -द्धं, प्रतिषिद्धः -द्धा -द्धं, सार्गलः -ला -लं.

HINDERER, *s.* विरोधी *m.* (न्), वारकः, निवारकः, बाधकः, विघ्नकारी *m.* (न्), प्रतिबन्धकः, स्तम्भकरः -कारी *m.*, प्रतिबन्धकः.

HINDERING, *part.* रुन्धन् -न्धती -न्धत् (त्), विरुन्धानः -ना -नं, रोधनः -नी -नं.

HINDERMOST, *a.* पश्चिमः -मा -मं, जघन्यः -न्या -न्यं, पाश्चात्यः -त्या -त्यं, पश्चातीयः -या -यं, अवरः -रा -रं, अवरतमः -मा -मं, अवरतस् indec., अवरस्तात् indec.

HINDRANCE, *s.* *See* HINDERANCE.

HINGE, *s.* द्वारसन्धिः *m.*, सन्धिः *m.*, द्वारग्रन्थिः *m.*, केन्द्रं.

To HINT, *v. a.* इङ्गितं कृ, सङ्केतं कृ, उद्दिश् (c. 6. -दिशति -देष्टुं), समुद्दिश्, सूच् (c. 10. सूचयति -यितुं), आकूतं कृ.—(Suggest) उपन्यस् (c. 4. -अस्यति -असितुं).

HINT, *s.* इङ्गितं, इङ्गः, सङ्केतः, आकारः, आकूतं, मीलितं, अङ्गवैकृतं, भावः, सूचना, सूचितं.—(Suggestion) उपन्यासः; 'understanding a hint,' इङ्गितकोविदः.

HINTED, *p. p.* उद्दिष्टः -ष्टा -ष्टं, सूचितः -ता -तं.

HIP, *s.* (Joint of the thigh) कटिः *m.* -टी, कटः, श्रोणिः *f.* -णी, श्रोणिफलकं, कलत्रं, अङ्कः, जघनं, प्रोथः, क्रोडः, पालिः *f.*, वरारोहा, ककुद्मती, मेखलापदं.—(Lowness of spirits) विषादः, अवसादः.

HIPPISH, *a.* विषादी -दिनी -दि (न्), विषण्णः -ण्णा -ण्णं, दुर्मनाः -नाः -नः (स्).

HIPPOGRIFF, *s.* कविकल्पितः पक्षवान् अश्वविशेषः.

HIPPOPOTAMUS, *s.* विदुः *m.*, वारियादस् *n.*, शुण्डा, ग्राहः, अवहारः.

HIPSHOT, *s.* त्रुटितश्रोणिः -णिः -णि, विसन्धितकटिः -टिः -टि.

To HIRE, *v. a.* निरूपितकालं यावद् वेतनेन or मूल्येन ग्रह् (c. 9. गृह्णाति, ग्रहीतुं), मूल्यं or वेतनं दत्त्वा सन्दिष्टकालं यावद् ग्रह् or प्रयुज् (c. 7. -युनक्ति -युङ्क्ते -योक्तुं, c. 10. -योजयति -यितुं) or उपभुज् (c. 7. -भुनक्ति -भुङ्क्ते -भोक्तुं) or सेव् (c. 1. सेवते -वितुं), भट् (c. 1. भटति, टितुं), भृ (c. 1. भरति -ते, भर्त्तुं), भाटक (nom. भाटकयति -यितुं), परिक्री (c. 9. -क्रीणाति -क्रेतुं), आनिर्दिष्टकालाद् भृतिं दा.—(Hire labourers) मूल्यं दत्त्वा or प्रतिज्ञाय आविहितकालात् कर्म्मणि नियुज् or प्रयुज् or व्यापृ (c. 10. -पारयति -यितुं), कर्म्मकरान् उपनी (c. 1. -नयते -नेतुं).

HIRE, *s.* (Act of hiring) निरूपितकालं यावद् वेतनेन or मूल्येन ग्रहणं, मूल्यं दत्त्वा आसन्दिष्टकालाद् ग्रहणं, प्रयोगः, वेतनदानं.—(Wages) भृतिः *f.*, भृत्या, भरणं, भरण्यं, भाटिः *f.*, भाटकः, वेतनं, मूल्यं, निर्वेशः, कर्म्मण्या, वर्णं, निष्क्रयः, भर्म्म *n.* (न्), भर्म्मं, विधा, विष्टिः *f.*, पणः, हार्यं, विरहिणी, वेधा; 'for hire,' निरूपितमूल्येन ग्रहणीयः -या -यं or प्रयोज्यः -ज्या -ज्यं, पण्यः -ण्या -ण्यं, साधारणः -णी -णं; 'working for hire,' भृतिभुक् *m. f. n.*, भरण्यभुक्.

HIRED, *p. p.* आनिरूपितकालाद् वेतनेन गृहीतः -ता -तं, भृतः -ता -तं, कृतवेतनः -ना -नं, प्रकल्पितवेतनः -ना -नं, भाटकितः -ता -तं, भाटकीयः -या -यं; 'hired labourer,' भृतकः, भृतिभुक् *m.* (ज्); 'teacher,' भृतकाध्यापकः.

HIRELING, *s.* भृतकः, भृतिभुक् *m.* (ज्), भरण्यभुक् *m.*, भृत्यः, वैतनिकः, वेतनार्थी *m.* (न्), वर्णिकः, कर्म्मकरः.

HIRER, *s.* भृतिदाता *m.* (तृ), वेतनदाता *m.* (तृ), मूल्यदाता *m.*

HIRSUTE, *a.* प्रचुरलोमा -मा -म (न्), बहुलोमा -मा -म (न्), लोमशः -शा -शं.

HIS, *pron. poss.* तस्य gen. c. (तद्), अस्य gen. c. (इदं), तदीयः -या -यं or expressed by स्व in comp.; as, 'his house,' स्वगृहे.

To HISS, *v. a.* and *n.* (As a serpent, &c.) सर्पवत् श्वस् (c. 2. श्वसिति -तुं), सर्पनादं कृ, सर्पशब्दं कृ, सीत्कारं कृ, शीशृशब्दं कृ.—(Hiss off, show disapprobation by hissing) कर्कशशब्देन अप्रसादं सूच् (c. 10. सूचयति -यितुं) or अवज्ञास्पदं कृ.

HISS, HISSING, *s.* श्वासः, सर्पश्वासः, सर्पनादः, सर्पशब्दः, कर्कशशब्दः, सीत्कारः, सीत्कृतं, शीशृशब्दः, कर्कशशब्देन अप्रसादसूचनं.

HIST, *adv.* तूष्णीं भव, मौनीभव, निःशब्दो भव, वाचं यम.

HISTORIAN, *s.* ऐतिहासिकः, इतिहासरचकः, इतिहासलेखकः, पुरावृत्तरचकः, वृत्तरचकः, भूतरचकः, पुराभूतलेखकः, पुराणरचकः, पुराणोपाख्यानरचकः, शिष्टसमाचाररचकः, चरित्रलेखकः.

HISTORIC, HISTORICAL, *a.* ऐतिहासिकः -की -कं, इतिहासविषयः -या -यं, इतिहाससम्बन्धी -न्धिनी -न्धि (न्), पुरावृत्तविषयः -या -यं, वृत्तरचनासम्बन्धी &c., शिष्टसमाचारसम्बन्धी &c., पौराणिकः -की -कं.

HISTORICALLY, *adv.* इतिहासक्रमेण, इतिहासानुसारेण, पुराणोपाख्यानक्रमेण.

To HISTORIFY, *v. a.* इतिहासं लिख् (c. 6. लिखति, लेखितुं) or रच् (c. 10. रचयति -यितुं), पुरावृत्तानि रच्.

HISTORIOGRAPHER, *s.* इतिहासरचकः, इतिहासलेखकः, पुराणोपाख्यानरचकः, पुरावृत्तरचकः.

HISTORY, *s.* इतिहासः, पुरावृत्तं, उपाख्यानं, पुराणोपाख्यानं, पुरावृत्तोपाख्यानं, शिष्टसमाचारः, उदन्तः; 'writing of history,' इतिहासरचना, पुरावृत्तरचना, पुराभूतविवरणं, शिष्टसमाचारविरचना, उपाख्यानरचना, चरित्रलिखनं.

HISTRIONIC, HISTRIONICAL, *a.* नाटकीयः -या -यं, नाट्यसम्बन्धी -न्धिनी -न्धि (न्), रङ्गसम्बन्धी &c., रङ्गयोग्यः -ग्या -ग्यं, नाट्यशालायोग्यः -ग्या -ग्यं.

HIT, *s.* (Blow, stroke) आघातः, घातः, अभिघातः, प्रहारः, हतिः *f.*, आहतिः *f.*, ताडनं, पातः.—(Chance) दैवं, सङ्गतिः *f.*; 'good hit,' सुदैवं, शुभगतिः *f.*, सौभाग्यं, सम्पद् *f.*

To HIT, *v. a.* तड् (c. 10. ताडयति -यितुं), वितड्, प्रहृ (c. 1. -हरति -हर्तुं), हन् (c. 2. हन्ति -न्तुं), अभिहन्, निहन्, विहन्, आहन्, समाहन्, अभ्याहन्, तुद् (c. 6. तुदति -ते, तोत्तुं), आतुद्, वितुद्, व्यध् (c. 4. विध्यति -ते, व्यद्धुं), प्रतिव्यध्; 'to hit the mark,' लक्ष्यं व्यध्.—(Attain) प्राप् (c. 5. -आप्नोति -आप्तुं), गम् (c. 1. गच्छति, गन्तुं), या (c. 2. याति -तुं), इ (c. 2. एति -तुं), स्पृश् (c. 6. स्पृशति, स्प्रष्टुं), आविश् (c. 6. -विशति -वेष्टुं); 'to hit upon,' आसद् (c. 10. -सादयति -यितुं), उपगम्, उपागम्.

To HIT, *v. n.* (Clash) परस्परं सङ्घट्ट् (c. 1. -घट्टते -ट्टितुं), परस्परसमाघातं कृ.—(Succeed) सिध् (c. 4. सिध्यति, सेद्धुं), सम्पद् (c. 4. -पद्यते -पत्तुं).

HIT, *p. p.* ताडितः -ता -तं, हतः -ता -तं, आहतः -ता -तं, समाहतः -ता -तं, अभिहतः -ता -तं, प्रहृतः -ता -तं; 'hit upon,' आसादितः -ता -तं, विहितः -ता -तं; 'hit off,' उपपन्नः -न्ना -न्नं.

To HITCH, *v. n.* (Lay hold) ग्रह् (c. 9. गृह्णाति, ग्रहीतुं), धृ (c. 1. धरति, धर्तुं), अनुबन्ध् (c. 9. -बध्नाति -बन्द्धुं), आकृष् (c. 1. -कर्षति -क्रष्टुं).—(Be caught, held) धृतः -ता -तं भू, रुद्धः -द्धा -द्धं भू, बन्ध् in pass. (बध्यते), अनुबन्ध्, बद्धः -द्धा -द्धं भू, स्तम्भितः -ता -तं भू.

HITHE, *s.* घट्टः, उमः, गुल्मः, तरस्थानं, उत्तरणस्थानं.

HITHER, *adv.* इतस्, अत्र, इह, इहस्थाने, अस्मिन् देशे; 'come hither,' उपैहि, इत इतस्; 'hither and thither,' इतस्ततस्, इतश्चेतस्.

HITHER, *a.* ऐहिकः -की -कं, ऐहस्थानिकः -की -कं, उपस्थः -स्था -स्थं, उपगमः -मा -मं, आसन्नतरः -रा -रं, नेदीयान् -यसी -यः (स्).

HITHERMOST, *s.* आसन्नतमः -मा -मं, समीपतमः -मा -मं, निकटस्थः -स्था -स्थं, सन्निहितः -ता -तं, अन्तिकः -का -कं, उपस्थः -स्था -स्थं, नेदिष्ठः -ष्ठा -ष्ठं.

HITHERTO, *adv.* अद्य यावत्, अद्यपर्य्यन्तं, तात्कालपर्य्यन्तं, एतत्कालपर्य्यन्तं, वर्त्तमानकालपर्य्यन्तं, आवर्त्तमानकालात्, तत्क्षणपर्य्यन्तं, एतत्क्षणपर्य्यन्तं, अद्यावधि.

HITHERWARD, *adv.* इतस्, इह, अत्र, इहस्थानं प्रति.

HIVE, *s.* मधुकोषः, करण्डः, छत्रकः, चषालः, मधुमक्षिकाधारः, मधुकरवासः, मधुकरालयः, मधुकरपोषणस्थानं.

To HIVE, *v. a.* मधुकोषे निविश् (c. 10. -वेशयति -यितुं), करण्ड (nom. करण्डयति -यितुं).

To HIVE, *v. n.* मधुकोषं निविश् (c. 6. -विशति, वेष्टुं), सङ्कुशः करण्डं निविश्.

HO, HOA, *interj.* हो, अहो, हंहो, हं, हे, हौ, होहौ, है, अरे, अररे.

HOAR, *a.* धवलः -ला -लं, शुक्लः -क्ला -क्लं, श्वेतः -ता -तं, शुभ्रः -भ्रा -भ्रं, गौरः -रा -री -रं, विशदः -दा -दं.

HOARD, *s.* अतिसञ्चयः, निभृतसञ्चयः, गूढसञ्चयः, सञ्चयः, निचयः, चयः, प्रचयः, समुच्चयः, समुदायः, सङ्घातः, समयः, पुञ्जः, पूगः, गणः, समूहः, संहारः, सङ्ग्रहः, समाहारः, निर्हारः, निधानं. निधिः *m.*, राशिः *m.*; 'hoard of barbarians,' म्लेच्छगणः.

To HOARD, *v. a.* निभृतं सञ्चि (c. 5. -चिनोति -चेतुं) or समाचि, गूढसञ्चयं कृ, अतिसञ्चयं कृ, पुञ्जीकृ, राशीकृ.

HOARDED, *p. p.* सञ्चितः -ता -तं, समाचितः -ता -तं, पुञ्जीकृतः -ता -तं.

HOARDER, *s.* सञ्चयी *m.* (न्), अतिसञ्चयकारी *m.* (न्), गूढचयकारी *m.*

HOAR-FROST, *s.* नीहारः, तुषारः, तुषारकणः, प्रालेयं, हिमं, हिमानी, हैमं, तुहिनं, खजलं, अवश्यायः.

HOARINESS, *s.* धावल्यं, धवलता, शुक्लता, गौरता, वैशद्यं, शुक्लिमा *m.* (न्); 'of the hair,' केशधावल्यं, केशशुक्लता, केशपक्वता, पलितं, पलितत्वं.

HOARSE, *a.* रूक्षस्वरः -रा -रं, रूक्षाभिभाषी -षिणी -षि (न्), स्वरभग्नः -ग्ना -ग्नं, भग्नस्वरः -रा -रं, गम्भीरस्वरः -रा -रं, कलः -ला -लं.

HOARSELY, *adv.* रूक्षस्वरेण, गम्भीरस्वरेण, भग्नस्वरेण, रूक्षं, गभीरं.

HOARSENESS, *s.* स्वररूक्षता, स्वरगम्भीरता, स्वरभङ्गः, स्वरभग्नता, स्वरभेदः, कलत्वं -ता.

HOARY, *a.* शुक्लः -क्ला -क्लं, धवलः -ला -लं, श्वेतः -ता -तं, गौरः -रा -री -रं, शुभ्रः -भ्रा -भ्रं, विशदः -दा -दं.—(Gray-haired) पलितः -ता -क्नी -तं, पलितकेशः -शी -शं, शुक्लकेशः -शी -शं, धवलकेशः -शी -शं, पक्वकेशः -शी -शं.

HOAX, *s.* वञ्चनं -ना, प्रवञ्चना, छल *n.* (न्), कपटः -टं, प्रतारणं -णा.

To HOAX, *v. a.* वञ्च् (c. 10. वञ्चयते -ति -यितुं), प्रवञ्च्, प्रलभ् (c. 1. -लभते -लब्धुं), छल् (c. 10. छलयति -यितुं), प्रतॄ, c. 10. (-तारयति -यितुं), व्यपदिश् (c. 6. -दिशति -देष्टुं).

HOAXED, *p. p.* वञ्चितः -ता -तं, विप्रलब्धः -ब्धा -ब्धं, मोहितः -ता -तं.

HOB, *s.* (A clown) वृषलः, ग्राम्यजनः, प्राकृतजनः, जानपदः.

To HOBBLE, *v. n.* (Limp) खञ्ज् (c. 1. खञ्जति -ञ्जितुं), लङ्ग् (c. 1. लङ्गति -ङ्गितुं), वङ्ग् (c. 1. वङ्गति -ङ्गितुं), खोर् (c. 1. खोरति -रितुं), खोल् (c. 1. खोलति -लितुं), खोड् (c. 1. खोडति -डितुं), खोट् (c. 1. खोटति -टितुं), गतिविकलः -ला -लं भू.

HOBBLE *s.* (Limping) लङ्गः, खञ्जता, पङ्गुता.—(Evil plight) दुर्दशा.

HOBBLER, *s.* खञ्जः, लङ्गगतिः, लङ्गगामी *m.* (न्), गतिविकलः.

HOBBLING, *s.* खञ्जत्वं, पङ्गुता, खोरता, लङ्गः, गतिवैकल्यं.

HOBBLINGLY, *adv.* खञ्जवत्, पङ्गुवत्, खोरवत्, लङ्गगत्या.

HOBBY, *s.* (Species of hawk) श्येनभेदः, उत्क्रोशभेदः.—(Fancy) छन्दस् *n.*, चापलं, बुद्धिचापल्यं, निर्बन्धः, लहरी, अबहिः *m.*, रुचिः *f.*, अभिरुचिः *f.*, मनोरथः, प्रियद्रव्यं, प्रियवस्तु *n.*—(A stupid fellow) मूढः, मूर्खः, जडः, स्थूलजनः.

HOBBY-HORSE, *s.* क्रीडामृगः, क्रीडाश्वः, चर्म्ममृगः, क्रीडनकं, क्रीडाद्रव्यं.

HOBGOBLIN, *s.* रात्रिचरः, रात्रिचारः, रजनीचरः, क्षणदाचरः, नक्तञ्चरः -चारी *m.* (न्), निशाटः, भूतः, वेतालः, प्रेतः, पिशाचः, राक्षसः, असुरः, क्रव्याद् *m.*, कर्बुरः, अपदेवता.

HOBNAIL, *s.* अश्वपादुकाकीलः, अश्वपादुकाशङ्कुः *m.*, बृहत्कीलः.

HOBSON'S CHOICE, *s.* विकल्पाभावः, अविकल्पः, विकल्पं विना.

HOCK, *s.* (Kind of wine) मद्यविशेषः.—(Of quadrupeds) चतुष्पदानां पश्चिमजङ्घाया मध्यसन्धिः or अरत्निरूपः सन्धिः.

To HOCK, *v. a.* पूर्व्वोक्तसन्धिशिरां छिद् (c. 7. छिनत्ति, छेत्तुं), पश्चिमजङ्घाशिरां छिद्.

HOCUS-POCUS, *s.* तन्त्रमन्त्रं, माया, कुहकः, जालं, मूलकर्म्म *n.* (न्).

HOD, *s.* लेपकारिभिः स्कन्धेन धृतं काष्ठमयं लेपपात्रं, लेपाधारः, विलेपभाजनं.

HODGE-PODGE, *s.* सन्निपातः, प्रकीर्णकं, सङ्कीर्णकं, नानाद्रव्यसमूहः.

HODIERNAL, *a.* अद्यतनः -नी -नं, वर्त्तमानदिवसीयः -या -यं.

HOE, *s.* खनित्रं, खात्रं, खनाग्रः, खनघनः, खनघातः, खनहननं -नी, खनहा *m.* (न्), आखनः -निकः, आखानं.

To HOE, *v. a.* खनित्रेण खन् (c. 1. खनति -ते -नितुं), खात्रेण भूमिं भिद् (c. 7. भिनत्ति, भेत्तुं) or दृ (c. 10. दारयति -यितुं), खनित्रेण कक्षान् उद्धृ (c. 1. -हरति -हर्त्तुं) or उत्खन्.

HOG, *s.* शूकरः, सूकरः, वराहः, कोलः, दंष्ट्री *m.* (न्), वक्रदंष्ट्रः, चक्रदंष्ट्रः, चक्रदंष्ट्रः, पक्रपक्रः, पोत्री *m.* (न्), स्थूलनासः, दीर्घरदः, मुखलाङ्गलः, भूदारः, किरः, किरिः *m.*, किटिः *m.*, बहुप्रजः, बहुपत्यः, घृष्टिः *m.*, गृष्टिः *m.*, घोणी *m.* (न्), स्तब्धरोमा *m.* (न्), क्रोडः; 'village hog,' ग्राम्यः, विड्चरः.

HOG-HERD, *s.* शूकरपालः -लकः, शूकरपोषकः, वराहरक्षी *m.* (न्).

HOGGISH, *a.* शूकरीयः -या -यं, सौकरः -री -रं, वाराहः -ही -हं, शूकरोपमः -मा -मं, शूकरसगुणः -णा -णं, वराहसगुणः -णा -णं.

HOGGISHNESS, *s.* शूकरीयता, सौकर्य्यं, शौकर्य्यं, पशुत्वं, अतिलोभः.

HOGO, *s.* अतिस्वादः, तीक्ष्णस्वादः, सूक्ष्मस्वादः.

HOGSHEAD, *s.* द्रवद्रव्याणां परिमाणविशेषः.

HOGSTY, *s.* शूकरस्थानं, शूकरालयः, शूकरगृहं, शूकरवासः.

HOGWASH, *s.* शूकरखाद्यं भुक्तावशेषं or उच्छिष्टान्नं.

HOGWEED, *s.* पुनर्नवा, शोथघ्नी.

HOIDEN, *s.* प्रगल्भा स्त्री, निर्लज्जा स्त्री, पुंश्चली, स्वैरिणी, बन्धकी, असभ्या स्त्री, ग्रामिणी.

To HOIDEN, *v. n.* पूर्व्वोक्त स्त्री यत्प्रकारेण तत्प्रकारेण चर् (c. 1. चरति -रितुं) or आचर् or वृत् (c. 1. वर्त्तते -र्त्तितुं).

To HOIST, *v. a.* उत्तुल् (c. 10. -तोलयति -यितुं), तुल्, उद्धृ (c. 1. -हरति -हर्त्तुं), उन्नी (c. 1. -नयति -नेतुं), उद्धट् (c. 10. -घाटयति -यितुं), उच्छ्रि (c. 1. -श्रयति -यितुं, rt. श्रि), उद्यम् (c. 1. -यच्छति -यन्तुं), उत्था in caus. (-थापयति -यितुं, rt. स्था), उच्चीकृ, ऊर्द्ध्वीकृ.

HOISTED, *p.p.* उत्तोलितः -ता -तं, उद्धृतः -ता -तं, उच्छ्रितः -ता -तं, उद्घाहितः -ता -तं, उद्वाहितः -ता -तं, उद्घाटितः -ता -तं, उद्यतः -ता -तं.

To HOLD, *v. a.* (Keep) धृ (c. 1. धरति, धर्त्तुं, c. 10. धारयति -यितुं), धा (c. 3. धत्ते, धातुं), रक्ष् (c. 1. रक्षति -क्षितुं); 'hold in the hand,' हस्तेन धृ.—(Maintain) भृ (c. 1. भरति, c. 3. बिभर्त्ति, भर्त्तुं), भृ, सम्भृ, पाल् (c. 10. पालयति -यितुं); 'hold an opinion,' मतं धृ (c. 10. धारयति), मतम् अवलम्ब् (c. 1. -लम्बते -म्बितुं) or समालम्ब्.—(Possess) धा (c. 3. दधाति, धत्ते, धातुं), विधा, आधा, भृ, धृ (c. 10.), शील् (c. 10. शीलयति -यितुं), आप् (c. 5. आप्नोति, आप्तुं).—(Esteem) मन् (c. 4. मन्यते, मन्तुं); 'hold in high estimation,' बहु मन्; 'hold in contempt,' अवमन्, तृणाय मन्, लघूकृ, तुच्छीकृ, कदर्थीकृ.—(Detain) धृ, सन्धृ, रुध् (c. 7. रुणद्धि, रोद्धुं), निरुध्, अवरुध्.—(Hold in confinement) कारायां निरुध् or बन्ध् (c. 9. बध्नाति, बन्द्धुं) or धृ.—(Hold back, withhold) निवृ (c. 10. -वारयति -यितुं), निग्रह् (c. 9. -गृह्णाति -ग्रहीतुं), विनिग्रह्, सन्निग्रह्, उपसंहृ (c. 1. -हरति -हर्त्तुं), संहृ, विधृ.—(Contain) धा, आधा, धृ, भृ, आदा (c. 3. -ददाति -दत्ते -दातुं), ग्रह्, परिग्रह्; 'room to hold all,' सर्व्वेषां धारणे स्थानं.—(Take hold, lay hold) ग्रह्, परिग्रह्, सङ्ग्रह्, हस्तेन ग्रह्, धृ, हस्तेन धृ, परामृश् (c. 6. -मृशति -म्रष्टुं), हस्तेन अवलम्ब् (c. 1. -लम्बते -म्बितुं) or समालम्ब्.—(Celebrate as a festival) सेव् (c. 1. सेवते -वितुं), विधिवत् कृ, यथाविधि अनुष्ठा (c. 1. -तिष्ठति -ष्ठातुं) or पाल्.—(Carry on, perform) कृ, विधा, सम्पद् (c. 10. -पादयति -यितुं), निर्वह् (c. 10. -वाहयति -यितुं), अनुष्ठा.—(Hold out, extend) प्रसृ (c. 10. -सारयति -यितुं), प्रग्रह्.—(Hold out, offer) प्रयम् (c. 1. -यच्छति -यन्तुं), उपनी (c. 1. -नयति -नेतुं), उपन्यस् (c. 4. -अस्यति -असितुं), उपस्था in caus. (-स्थापयति -यितुं), उपढौ.—(Hold up, raise aloft) उच्चीकृ, उच्चैः कृ, ऊर्द्ध्वीकृ, उन्नम् (c. 10. -नमयति -यितुं), उच्छ्रि (c. 1. -श्रयति -यितुं), उद्यम्.—(Hold up, sustain) धृ, सन्धृ, आलम्ब् (c. 1. -लम्बते, c. 10. -लम्बयति -यितुं), अवलम्ब्, समवलम्ब्, उत्तम्भ् (c. 10. -तम्भयति -यितुं, rt. स्तम्भ्), भृ.—(Hold one's tongue) जिह्वां रक्ष् or धृ.

To HOLD, *v. n.* (Stand, remain firm) स्था (c. 1. तिष्ठति, स्थातुं), स्थिरीभू.—(Last, endure) स्था, संस्था, चिरस्थायी -यिनी -यि भू, ध्रुवीभू.—(Refrain) आत्मानं संयम् (c. 1. -यच्छति -यन्तुं), आत्मानं यम्, विरम् (c. 1. -रमति -रन्तुं) with abl. c., निवृत् (c. 1. -वर्त्तते -र्त्तितुं) with abl. c., परिहृ (c. 1. -हरति -हर्त्तुं), संहृ.—(Adhere) अनुबन्ध् (c. 9. -बध्नाति -बन्द्धुं or in pass. -बध्यते), अनुलग्नीभू, संलग्नीभू, अवलम्ब् (c. 1. -लम्बते -म्बितुं), अवलम्बी -म्बिनी -म्बि भू.—(Be dependent on) अधीनः -ना -नं भू, आश्रितः -ता -तं भू, अवलम्ब्.—(Hold off) विलम्ब्.—(Hold on) संस्था, पर्य्यवस्था, निर्बन्धं कृ.—(Hold out, resist) चिरेण सह् (c. 1. सहते, सोढुं), चिरकालेन प्रतिकृ.—(Hold together) संलग्नीभू, सम्बन्ध् in pass. (-बध्यते).

HOLD, *s.* (Act of holding) धृतिः *f.*, धरणं, धारणं, ग्रहणं, आग्रहः, सङ्ग्राहः.—(Taking hold) ग्रहणं, सङ्ग्रहणं, सङ्ग्राहः, ग्रहः, हस्तेन ग्रहणं, हस्तेन धृतिः *f.* or धरणं; 'letting go the hold,' स्रस्तहस्तः -स्ता -स्तं.—(Place of holding) धारकः.—(Place of custody) कारा, कारागारं, बन्धनस्थानं, निरोधस्थानं, गुप्तिः *f.*—(Fortified place) दुर्गं, कोटिः *f.*—(Support) आलम्बः -म्बनं, अवलम्बनं, धारणं, आधारः, उपस्तम्भः, आग्रहः, सङ्ग्रहः.—(Influence) अधिकारः, भारः, गौरवं, वशः -शं.—(Hold of a ship) गुप्तिः *f.*, नौगुप्तिः *f.*, नौकोदरं, नौकाधोभागः.

HOLDER, *s.* धारी *m.* (न्), धारकः, धरः, धारणकर्त्ता *m.* (र्तृ), धारयः, ग्राहकः, ग्राही *m.* (न्).

HOLDFAST, *s.* (Any thing that takes hold) ग्राहकः -कं, ग्रहणी, धरः -री -रं, बन्धनी, कुडुपः.—(Parsimonious man) दृढमुष्टिः *m.*, गाढमुष्टिः *m.*, बद्धमुष्टिः *m.*, अमुक्तहस्तः.

HOLDING, *s.* धरणं, धारणं, ग्रहणं, आधानं, आदानं, रक्षणं.

HOLDING, *part.* धारी -रिणी -रि (न्), धारयन् -यन्ती -यत् (त्), धरः -रा -री -रं, आददानः -ना -नं, आदधानः -ना -नं; 'holding' may be expressed by हस्त in comp.; as, 'holding a stick,' दण्डहस्तः -स्ता -स्तं; 'holding a sword,' खड्गहस्तः -स्ता -स्तं.

HOLE, *s.* विवरं, बिलं, गर्त्तः, रन्ध्रं, छिद्रं, कुहरं, शुषिरं, शुषिः *f.* -षी, कूपः, अवटः -टिः *m.*, गुहा, विरोकं, रोकं, रुहकं, रोपं, सङ्कुः *m.*, मर्कारा, भूकं, दूकं, निर्व्यथनं.—(Cave) गह्वरं, कन्दरः -रं, दरी, खातं, निर्दरिः *m.*, गुहा, शैलरन्ध्रं.—(Of a beast) श्वभ्रं, विवरं; 'of a serpent,' सर्पविवरं; 'rat-hole,' मूषिकविवरं; 'full of holes,' अनेकरन्ध्रः -न्ध्रा -न्ध्रं, सरन्ध्रः &c., बहुविवरः -रा -रं, बहुबिलः -ला -लं; 'one who picks holes in the character of others,' छिद्रान्वेषी -षिणी -षि (न्), छिद्रानुसारी -रिणी -रि (न्).

HOLIDAY, *s.* *See* HOLYDAY.

HOLILY, *adv.* पुण्यं, पुण्यवत्, पुण्यशीलवत्, पवित्रं, पवित्रवत्, धर्म्मेण्ठी-

लघवत्, शुचिवत्, शौचेन.

HOLINESS, *s.* पुण्यता -त्वं, पुण्यशीलता, पवित्रता -त्वं, शुचिता -त्वं, शौचं, धर्म्मशीलता, साधुत्वं -ता, धर्म्मत्वं -ता, देवभक्तिः *f.*, पुण्यवत्त्वं, ब्रह्मवर्च्चसं, ब्रह्मण्यता, वृत्ताध्ययनर्द्धिः *f.*; 'his holiness,' भगवान् *m.* (त्).

HOLLO, *interj.* भो, भोः, भोस्, भोभो, हलहला, हे, है, अहो, हं, हंहो.

To HOLLO, *v. n.* हे, है, भो, हलहला इत्यादिशब्दान् कृ or इत्यादिशब्दैर् दूरस्थजनम् आह्वे (c. 1. -ह्वयति -ह्वातुं), उच्चैःस्वरेण दूरस्थं कञ्चिज्जनम् आह्वे, हलहला (nom. हलहलायते).

HOLLAND, *s.* (Country) हलन्दसंज्ञको देशः.

HOLLANDER, *s.* हलन्दीयः, हलन्दीयजनः, हलन्ददेशजः.

HOLLANDS, *s.* (Spirits) शुण्डा, सुरा -री, वारुणी, हाला.

HOLLOW, *a.* (Empty within) शून्यः -न्या -न्यं, शून्यमध्यः -ध्या -ध्यं, शून्यगर्भः -र्भा -र्भं, शून्योदरः -रा -रं, शुषिरः -रा -रं, रिक्तमध्यः -ध्या -ध्यं, रिक्तगर्भः -र्भा -र्भं, उत्तानः -ना -नं, वितानः -ना -नं, पुटाकारः -रा -रं, गर्भाकारः -रा -रं, उदराकृतिः -तिः -ति.—(In sound) मन्दः -न्दा -न्दं, मन्थरः -रा -रं, मन्द्रः -न्द्रा -न्द्रं, गभीरः -रा -रं, गम्भीरः -रा -रं.—(Worthless, unsubstantial) निःसारः -रा -रं, असारः -रा -रं, सारहीनः -ना -नं, निःसत्त्वः -त्त्वा -त्त्वं.—(Vain) मोघः -घा -घं, निरर्थकः -का -कं.—(False) असत्यः -त्या -त्यं, निःसत्यः -त्या -त्यं, वितथः -था -थं, कृत्रिमः -मा -मं, मिथ्या in comp.; 'a hollow reed,' शून्या.

HOLLOW, *s.* (Cavity, hole) विवरं, विलं, कुहरं, गर्त्तः, कोटः, शुषिरं, शून्यः, अवटः -टिः *m.*, कूपः, गुहा.—(Inner part) गर्भः, उदरं, अभ्यन्तरं, क्रोडं.—(Hollow ground) दरा -री, दरीभूः *f.*, कन्दरः -री, निम्नभूमिः *f.*, द्रोणी, अद्रिद्रोणी.—(Excavation) खातं, खातभूः *f.*—(Natural hollow) देवखातं.—(Cavern) गह्वरं, कन्दरः, गुहा, कुहरं.—(Canal) कुल्या, प्रणाली, सारणिः *f.*—(Hollow of a tree) कोटरः -रं, वृक्षभवनं, तरुक्रोडं, प्रान्तरं, निर्गूढः, आलवालः, निष्कुहः; 'hollow of the hand,' पुटः, पुटितं, करकोषः; 'hollow of the ear,' चुषुभः; 'hollow of the loins,' गर्त्तः, जघनकूपकौ *m.* du.; 'hollow of a boiler,' स्थालीविलं.

To HOLLOW, *v. a.* शून्यीकृ, शुषिरीकृ, खन् (c. 1. खनति -ते -नितुं), उत्खन्, पुट् (c. 10. पुटयति -यितुं), पुटीकृ.

HOLLOWED, *p. p.* खातः -ता -तं, उत्खातः -ता -तं, पुटितः -ता -तं, शून्यीकृतः -ता -तं, शुषिरीकृतः -ता -तं.

HOLLOWNESS, *s.* शून्यता -त्वं, शुषिरता -त्वं, रिक्तता.—(Of sound) मन्दता, मन्द्रता, गभीरता, गम्भीरता -त्वं, गाम्भीर्य्यं.—(Worthlessness) निःसारता, असारता, मोघता, फल्गुता.—(Falsity) असत्यता, निःसत्यता, कृत्रिमता, कूटता, कापट्यं.

HOLLY, *s.* कण्टकितपत्रविशिष्टः सदाहरितो गुल्मभेदः.

HOLLYHOCK, *s.* नानावर्णपुष्पविशिष्ट ओषधिभेदः.

HOLM-OAK, *s.* चिरस्थायी महावृक्षभेदः.

HOLOCAUST, *s.* होमः, हुतं, हव्यं, हुतहोमं, आहुतं, आहवनीयं.

HOLPEN, *p. p.* उपकृतः -ता -तं, कृतोपकारः -रा -रं, कृतसाहाय्यः -य्या -य्यं.

HOLY, *a.* पुण्यः -ण्या -ण्यं, पुण्यवान् -वती -वत् (त्), पुण्यशीलः -ला -लं, पुण्यात्मा -त्मा -त्म (न्), पवित्रः -त्रा -त्रं, धर्म्मशीलः -ला -लं, शुचिः -चिः -चि, शुचिमनाः -नाः -नः (स्), शुचिव्रतः -ता -तं, विमलः -ला -लं, अमलात्मा -त्मा -त्म (न्), निर्म्मलान्तःकरणः -णा -णं, शुद्धमतिः -तिः -ति, पवित्रमतिः -तिः -ति, शुद्धात्मा &c., शुद्धहृदयः -या -यं, धार्म्मिकः -की -कं, साधुः -धुः -ध्वी -धु; 'holy land,' पुण्यभूमिः *f.*, पुण्यभूः *f.*; 'holy writ,' श्रुतिः *f.*; 'holy place of pilgrimage,' तीर्थः -र्थं, पुण्यतीर्थं, क्षेत्रं, पुण्यस्थानं.

HOLYDAY, *s.* (Sacred day) पुण्याहं, पुण्यदिनं, पुण्यदिवसः.—(Festival) उत्सवः, उत्सवदिनं, पर्व्वाहः, उद्धर्षदिनं, आनन्ददिवसः, यात्रा, रासेरसः.—(Day on which there is intermission of study) अनध्यायः, अनध्यायदिवसः, अनध्यायमहोत्सवः, अस्वाध्यायतिथिः *m. f.*, विश्रामदिवसः; 'holyday folk,' यात्राजनः, यात्रालोकः.

HOLY-WATER, *s.* पुण्यजलं, पुण्योदकं, पुण्याम्बु *n.*, पुण्यवारि *n.*

HOMAGE, *s.* पूजा, प्रणामः, प्रणतिः *f.*, प्रणिपातः -पतनं, अर्च्चनं -ना, अर्च्चा, अभ्यर्च्चा, अभ्यर्च्चनं, नमस्कारः, मानं, सम्मानं, सत्कारः, पादवन्दनं, सेवा, सेवाञ्जलिः *m.*, आदरः, भक्तिः *f.*, प्रभुभक्तिः *f.*, प्रतीतिः *f.*, विनीतिः *f.*, उपासना, श्रेयं.

To HOMAGE, *v. a.* पूज् (c. 10. पूजयति -यितुं), सम्पूज्, अर्च्च् (c. 1. अर्च्चति -र्च्चितुं, c. 10. अर्च्चयति -यितुं), प्रणिपत् (c. 1. -पतति -तितुं), उपास् (c. 2. -आस्ते -आसितुं), प्रणम् (c. 1. -णमति -णन्तुं), सत्कृ; 'he paid homage,' प्रणतवान्.

HOMAGER, *s.* पूजकः, प्रणामकृत् *m.*, प्रणिपातकारी *m.* (न्), सम्मानकृत् *m.*

HOME, *s.* स्वगृहं, गृहं, स्वस्थानं, स्वदेशः, स्ववासः, स्वविषयः, स्वगेहः, स्ववेश्म *n.* (न्), निजगृहं, निजालयः, निजगेहः, स्वभवनं, स्वनिलयः; 'devoted to home,' गृहासक्तचेताः -ताः -तः (स्).

HOME, *adv.* गृहं प्रति, स्वगृहं प्रति; 'he went home,' गृहं ययौ.—(Close) निकटे; 'speech that strikes home,' सङ्गतवाक्यं, हृदयङ्गमवाक्यं.

HOME-BORN, *a.* गृहजातः -ता -तं, स्वगृहजः -जा -जं, स्वदेशजः -जा -जं; 'home-born slave,' गृहजातो दासः, ज्ञातिदासः.

HOME-BRED, *a.* गृहजः -जा -जं, गृह्यः -ह्या -ह्यं, आत्मवैश्मिकः -की -कं.

HOME-FELT, *a.* अन्तरस्थः -स्था -स्थं, अन्तरतमः -मा -मं, अन्तर्भूतः -ता -तं.

HOMELESS, *a.* निरालयः -या -यं, निरास्पदः -दा -दं, निराश्रयः -या -यं.

HOMELINESS, *s.* ग्राम्यता, ग्रामीयत्वं, गृह्यता, असभ्यता, नीचता, अश्लीलता, अशुद्धत्वं, अशिष्टत्वं.

HOMELY, *a.* ग्राम्यः -म्या -म्यं, ग्रामिकः -की -कं, ग्रामीयः -या -यं, ग्रामीणः -णा -णं, गृह्यः -ह्या -ह्यं, गृहजः -जा -जं, प्राकृतः -ता -तं, असभ्यः -भ्या -भ्यं, अश्लीलः -ला -लं, नीचः -चा -चं, अधमः -मा -मं, अशुद्धः -द्धा -द्धं, अशिष्टः -ष्टा -ष्टं, असंस्कृतः -ता -तं, अपरिष्कृतः -ता -तं; 'homely speech,' ग्राम्यं.

HOMELY, *adv.* ग्राम्यं, ग्राम्यप्रकारेण, असभ्यं, नीचं, गृह्यवत्.

HOME-MADE, *a.* गृहनिर्म्मितः -ता -तं, गृहकृतः -ता -तं, गृहोत्पन्नः -न्ना -न्नं.

HOME-SPUN, *a.* गृहजातः -ता -तं, गृहजः -जा -जं, गृह्यः -ह्या -ह्यं.

HOME-STALL or HOME-STEAD, *s.* गृहं, वासस्थानं, वसतिः *f.*, आवासः.

HOMEWARD, *adv.* गृहं प्रति, स्ववासं प्रति, स्वस्थानं प्रति.

HOMICIDAL, *a.* नृहत्याकारी -रिणी -रि (न्), मनुष्यघाती -तिनी -ति (न्).

HOMICIDE, *s.* नृहत्या, मनुष्यहत्या, मनुष्यवधः, मनुष्यघातः.—(One who kills a man) नृहन्ता *m.* (न्तृ), मनुष्यघातकः.

HOMILY, *s.* पूजाशालासु श्रावणीयं धर्म्मविषयं वाक्यं.

HOMOGENEAL, HOMOGENEOUS, *a.* समानजातीयः -या -यं, सजातीयः -या -यं, समानजातिः -तिः -ति, सजातिः -तिः -ति, समभावः -वा -वं, समानभावः -वा -वं, समधर्म्मा -र्म्मा -र्म्म (न्), एकजातिः -तिः -ति, एकधर्म्मा &c., स्वभावीयः -या -यं.

HOMOGENEALNESS, HOMOGENEITY, HOMOGENEOUSNESS, *s.* समानजातिता, सजातिता, भावसमता, भावसमानता, जातिसमता.

HOMOLOGOUS, *a.* तुल्याकारः -रा -रं, तुल्यपरिमाणः -णा -णं, समपरिमाणः -णा -णं.

HOMONYMOUS, *a.* भिन्नार्थः -र्था -र्थं, सन्दिग्धार्थः -र्था -र्थं, द्व्यर्थः -र्था -र्थं,

समसंज्ञकः -का -कं, समनामा -मा -म (न्).

HOMONYMY, *s.* भिन्नार्थता, विभिन्नार्थता, अर्थभेदः, द्व्यर्थता, नामसमता.

HONE, *s.* शाणः -णी, शाणाश्म *n.* (न्), शानः, क्षुरधारातेजनप्रस्तरः.

HONEST, *a.* (Upright, just) सरलः -ला -लं, दक्षिणः -णा -णं, शुचिः -चिः -चि, न्यायाचारः -रा -रं, न्यायवर्त्ती -र्त्तिनी -र्त्ति (न्), न्याय्यः -य्या -य्यं, ऋजुः -जुः -जु, सच्चरितः -ता -तं, सात्त्विकः -की -कं, शुद्धमतिः -तिः -ति, शुद्धात्मा -त्मा -त्म (न्), अजिह्मः -ह्मा -ह्मं, अकुटिलः -ला -लं, अशठः -ठा -ठं, अशठधीः -धीः -धि, मायाहीनः -ना -नं, अमायः -या -यं -यिकः -की -कं, अकपटः -टा -टं, निष्कपटः -टा -टं, कपटहीनः -ना -नं, निर्व्याजः -जा -जं, विमलात्मा -त्मा -त्म (न्), निर्व्यलीकः -का -कं, अवक्रः -क्रा -क्रं, धार्म्मिकः -की -कं, दम्भरहितः -ता -तं, धर्म्मकारी -रिणी -रि (न्), भद्रः -द्रा -द्रं, साधुः -धुः -ध्वी -धु, सन् सती -सत् (त्), उत्तमः -मा -मं, सरलयायी -यिनी -यि (न्), स्वच्छः -च्छा -च्छं, प्राञ्जलः -ला -लं, प्रगुणः -णा -णं.—(True) सत्यः -त्या -त्यं, सत्यकः -का -कं, सत्यशीलः -ला -लं, सत्यवृत्तः -त्ता -त्तं, सत्यवादी -दिनी -दि (न्).

HONESTLY, *adv.* सरलं, सारल्येन, न्यायेन, न्यायतस्, न्याय्यं, निष्कपटं, कपटं विना, निर्व्याजं, निर्व्यलीकं, अमायया, मायां विना, सरलवत्, शुचिवत्, अजिह्मं, सदाक्षिण्यं.

HONESTY, *s.* सारल्यं, सरलता, दाक्षिण्यं, शुचिता -त्वं, ऋजुता, आर्जवं, अमाया, मायाहीनता, अकपटः, अकापट्यं, कपटहीनता, अव्याजः, न्यायिता, न्यायाचारता, अजिह्मता, अकौटिल्यं, अशठता, निर्व्यलीकता, अवक्रता, अस्तेयं, अपैशुनं, भद्रता, साधुता, शुद्धत्वं, धार्म्मिकत्वं, सत्यता, सत्यशीलता, सत्यवादित्वं, नैर्मल्यं, विमलता, अदत्तानुपादानं.

HONEY, *s.* मधु *n.*, क्षौद्रं, पुष्पनिर्यासः, पुष्परसः, पुष्पसारः, पुष्पासवं, कुसुमासवं, माक्षिकं, क्षारं -वकं, सारघं, कापिशायनं; 'honey of flowers,' मरं; 'become honey,' मधुसाद्भूतः -ता -तं.

To HONEY, *v. n.* मधुरवचोभिः or मधुरवाक्यैः सान्त्व् (c. 10. सान्त्वयति -यितुं).

HONEY-COMB, *s.* मधुकोषः, मधुवासः, मधुचक्रं, माक्षिकाश्रयं, मधुक्रमः, करण्डः.

HONEY-MOON, *s.* आनन्दमासः, विवाहात् परं प्रथममासो यस्मिन् स्त्रीपुरुषौ प्रेममात्रं कुरुतः.

HONEY-SUCKLE, *s.* सुरभिगन्धविशिष्टो लताविशेषः.

HONEY-SWEET, *a.* मधुरः -रा -रं, मधुवत् स्वादुः -दुः -द्वी -दु, मधुसात् ind.

HONEY-TONGUED, *a.* मधुरभाषी -षिणी -षि (न्), मधुरवादी -दिनी -दि (न्).

HONIED, *a.* मधुमान् -मती -मत् (त्), मधुमयः -यी -यं, मधुरः -रा -रं.

HONORARY, *a.* सम्मानकरः -रा -रं, मानदः -दा -दं, यशस्यः -स्या -स्यं, यशस्वी -स्विनी -स्वि (न्), कीर्त्तिकरः -रा -रं, यशस्करः.—(Conferring honour only, without gain) सम्मानमात्रदः -दा -दं, कीर्त्तिमात्रकरः -री -रं, अलाभकरः -री -रं.

HONOUR, *s.* (Fame, reputation) कीर्त्तिः *f.*, यशस् *n.*, ख्यातिः *f.*, सुख्यातिः *f.*, विख्यातिः *f.*, प्रतिष्ठा, विश्रुतिः *f.*, समाख्या, प्रतिपत्तिः *f.* —(Reverence) सम्मानं, मानं, पूजा, अर्चनं -ना, अर्चा, अभ्यर्चा -र्चनं, नमस्कारः, सेवा, अर्हा, अर्हणं -णा, आदरः, सम्भावना, सत्कारः, आराधनं, पुरस्कारः, सम्भ्रमः, श्लाघा.—(Dignity, honourable rank) उत्कर्षः, उत्कृष्टता, उत्कृष्टपदं, कुलीनपदं, प्रतिपत्तिः *f.*, प्रधानपदं, प्रधानता, प्राधान्यं, श्रेष्ठत्वं, उन्नतिः *f.*, मर्य्यादा, अभिजातता, पूज्यता, मान्यता -त्वं, अभ्यर्हणीयता.—(Family honour) मर्य्यादा, कुलमर्य्यादा.

To HONOUR, *v. a.* पूज् (c. 10. पूजयति -यितुं), सम्पूज्, अभिपूज्, मन् (c. 10. मानयति -यितुं), सम्मन्, प्रतिमन्, अर्च् (c. 1. अर्चति -र्चितुं, c. 10. अर्चयति -यितुं), अभ्यर्च्, समभ्यर्च्, समर्च्, सेव् (c. 1. सेवते -वितुं, c. 10. सेवयति -यितुं), अर्ह् (c. 10. अर्हयति -यितुं), सम्भू (c. 10. -भावयति -यितुं), आदृ (c. 6. -द्रियते -दर्त्तुं), नमस्कृ, सत्कृ, पुरस्कृ, आराध् (c. 10. -राधयति -यितुं), श्रु in des. (शुश्रूषते -षितुं), अर्ह् (c. 1. अर्हति -र्हितुं), मह् (c. 1. महति -हितुं), अनुग्रह् (c. 9. -गृह्णाति -ग्रहीतुं), पूजां कृ, सम्मानं कृ.—(Accept a bill) लेख्यपत्रं ग्रह् or स्वीकृ or आदृ.

HONOURABLE, *a.* पूज्यः -ज्या -ज्यं, पूजनीयः -या -यं, पूजयितव्यः -व्या -व्यं, सम्पूजनीयः -या -यं, सम्मान्यः -न्या -न्यं, मान्यः -न्या -न्यं, मानी -निनी -नि (न्), पूजार्हः -र्हा -र्हं, अर्चार्हः -र्हा -र्हं, अर्ह्यः -र्ह्या -र्ह्यं, अर्हणीयः -या -यं, श्लाघ्यः -घ्या -घ्यं, आदरणीयः -या -यं, पुरस्करणीयः -या -यं, मर्य्यादावान् -वती -वत् (त्), मर्य्यादान्वितः -ता -तं.—(Illustrious) ख्यातः -ता -तं, सुख्यातः -ता -तं, यशस्वी -स्विनी -स्वि (न्), महायशाः -शाः -शः (स्), कीर्त्तिमान् -मती -मत् (त्), प्रतिपत्तिमान् -मती -मत् (त्), विश्रुतः -ता -तं, प्रसिद्धः -द्धा -द्धं.—(Conferring honour) कीर्त्तिकरः -री -रं, यशस्करः -री -रं, यशस्यः -स्या -स्यं.—(Upright, equitable) सच्चरितः -ता -तं, न्यायाचारः -रा -रं, धार्म्मिकः -की -कं, शुचिः -चिः -चि, दक्षिणः -णा -णं, सात्त्विकः -की -कं, शुद्धात्मा -त्मा -त्म (न्), निर्व्यलीकः -का -कं, निष्कपटः -टा -टं, विमलात्मा -त्मा -त्म (न्), अवक्रः -क्रा -क्रं, ऋजुः -जुः -जु, साधुः -धुः -ध्वी -धु.—(Noble) कुलीनः -ना -नं, उदारः -रा -रं, उदारचेताः -ताः -तः (स्).

HONOURABLY, *adv.* समानं, सम्मानपूर्व्वं, शुचिवत्, धार्म्मिकवत्, साधुवत्, उदारवत्, औदार्य्येण, सत्कारपूर्व्वं, नमस्कारपूर्व्वं, श्लाघ्यप्रकारेण, सुकीर्त्तिपूर्व्वं, सुयशसा, निर्व्यलीकं, सम्पूजनीयं.

HONOURED, *p. p.* पूजितः -ता -तं, सम्पूजितः -ता -तं, अर्चितः -ता -तं, अभ्यर्चितः -ता -तं, सम्मानितः -ता -तं, पुरस्कृतः -ता -तं, सेवितः -ता -तं, अर्हितः -ता -तं, सेव्यमानः -ना -नं, निषेव्यमाणः -णा -णं, आदृतः -ता -तं, अञ्चितः -ता -तं, सत्कृतः -ता -तं, महितः -ता -तं, आराधितः -ता -तं, शुश्रूषितः -ता -तं, अनिन्दितः -ता -तं.—(Accepted as a bill) गृहीतः -ता -तं, स्वीकृतः -ता -तं, आदृतः -ता -तं; 'to be honoured,' पूज् in pass. (पूज्यते), मह् (nom. महीयते).

HOOD, *s.* स्त्रीवस्त्रानुबद्धं मस्तकाच्छादनं or मस्तकावरणं or मस्तकपिधानं, फणाकारं मस्तकाच्छादनं, शिरस्कं, शिरस्त्रं -स्त्राणं, शिरोवस्त्रं; 'of a snake,' फणः -णा -णं, भोगः, स्फोटा.

To HOOD, *v. a.* पूर्व्वोक्तपिधानेन मस्तकम् आछद् (c. 10. -छादयति -यितुं), मस्तकावरणेन पिधा (c. 3. -दधाति -धातुं).

To HOODWINK, *v. a.* चक्षुषी वस्त्रेण रुध् (c. 7. रुणद्धि, रोद्धुं), नयने पिधानेन आवृ (c. 5. -वृणोति -वरितुं -रीतुं) or आछद् (c. 10. -छादयति -यितुं), नयनरोधं कृ.

HOOF, *s.* खुरः, क्षुरः, शफः -फं, वर्त्तकः -का, मिषृम्यः, पुटः, पिञ्जः, रिङ्खः; 'hoof of a cow,' गोखुरं, गोष्पदं; 'mark of a hoof,' खुरपदवी, खुरचिह्नं.

HOOFED, *a.* खुरी -रिणी -रि (न्), क्षुरी -रिणी -रि (न्), खुरयुक्तः -क्ता -क्तं.

HOOK, *s.* (Any thing bent that catches hold) आकर्षी -र्षिणी, अङ्कुशः, आकर्षणार्थं वक्रपत्रं or वक्रलोहः, ग्रहणी, धरणी.—(Fish-hook) वडिशं -शा -शी, बडिशी, बलिशं -शी, मत्स्यवेधनं -नी.—(Hook for driving an elephant) अङ्कुशः -शं, अङ्कुषः -षं, शृणिः *f.*—(Bill-hook) दात्रं.

To HOOK, *v. a.* (Fish) वडिशेन मत्स्यान् व्यध् (c. 4. विध्यति, व्यद्धुं) or धृ (c. 1. धरति, धर्त्तुं) or ग्रह् (c. 9. गृह्णाति, ग्रहीतुं) or बन्ध् (c. 9. बध्नाति, बन्द्धुं), धरणं कृ, ग्रहणं कृ.

HOOKED, *a.* (Bent in the form of a hook) वक्रः -क्रा -क्रं, अङ्कुशाकारः -रा -रं, अङ्कुशी -शिनी -शि (न्), अनृजुः -जुः -जु, कुञ्चितः -ता -तं.

HOOP, *s.* (Any thing circular) चक्रं, चक्रवालं, वलयः -यं.—(For playing with) क्रीडाचक्रं, क्रीडावलयः.

To hoop, *v. a.* (Bind with hoops) लोहवलयान् बन्ध् (c. 9. बध्नाति, बन्द्धुं), लोहचक्रादिभिर् युज् (c. 10. योजयति -यितुं).—(Shout out) चित्कारं कृ, चित्कारशब्दं कृ, उच्चैःस्वरेण उद्घुष् (c. 10. -घोषयति -यितुं).

Hooper, *s.* (A cooper) लोहवलयबन्धा *m.* (न्धृ), काष्ठभाण्डकारः.

Hooping-cough, *s.* आक्षेपककाशः, हूपशब्दपूर्व्वकः काशः, बालकानां काशः.

To hoot, *v. n.* रु (c. 2. रौति, रवितुं), विरु, दीर्घरुतं कृ, दीर्घरावं कृ, घूत्कृ, घूत्कारं कृ, चित्कारं कृ, उच्चैःस्वरेण उद्घुष् (c. 10. -घोषयति -यितुं); 'to hoot at,' हे, रे, अरे, धिक्, हुम्, घूत् इत्यादिशब्दैर् अवमानं or अवज्ञां or अप्रसादं सूच् (c.10. सूचयति -यितुं) or इत्यादिशब्दैर् अवज्ञास्पदं कृ.

Hoot, hooting, *s.* दीर्घरुतं, दीर्घरावः, रावः, घूत्कारः, घूत्कृतं, चित्कारः, हे, रे, धिक्, घूत् इत्यादिशब्दैर् अवमानसूचनं or अप्रसादसूचनं.

To hop, *v. n.* प्लु (c. 1. प्लवते, प्लोतुं), वल्ग् (c. 1. वल्गति -ल्गितुं), नृत् (c. 4. नृत्यति, नर्त्तितुं), एकपादेन प्लु or वल्ग्.

Hop, *s.* (The plant) लताविशेषो यस्य पुष्पाणि यवरसेन सह संसृज्यन्ते तेन च यवसुरा उत्पाद्यते.—(Jump) प्लवः, प्लुतं, वल्गितं, स्कन्दः, नृत्यं, नर्त्तनं, एकपादेन प्लुतं, वल्गितं.

Hope, *s.* आशा, प्रत्याशा, आशंसा, आकांक्षा, आशाबन्धः, मनोरथः, अपेक्षा, व्यपेक्षा, प्रतीक्षा, सम्प्रतीक्षा, स्पृहा, निरीक्षा, उदीक्षणं, ईप्सितं, मनस्विता; 'hope of a good issue,' फलाकांक्षा; 'having one's hopes fulfilled,' पूर्णमनोरथः, आशाप्राप्तः; 'hopes whose fulfilment is delayed,' विलम्बितफला मनोरथाः; 'hope-inspiring,' आशाजननः -ना -नं.

To hope, *v. a.* and *n.* आशंस् (c. 1. -शंसते -सितुं), आकांक्ष् (c. 1. -कांक्षति -क्षितुं), प्रत्याकांक्ष्, प्रतीक्ष् (c. 1. -ईक्षते -क्षितुं), अपेक्ष्, व्यपेक्ष्, उदीक्ष्, स्पृह् (c. 10. स्पृहयति -यितुं), वाञ्छ् (c. 1. वाञ्छति -ञ्छितुं), अभिवाञ्छ्, आशां कृ, प्रत्याशां कृ, आशंसां कृ, आशास् (c. 2. शास्ते -शासितुं); 'I hardly hoped to see you again,' न खलु म आसीद् आशंसा यथा पुनरपि त्वां प्रेक्षिष्ये; 'I hope' may be expressed by the particle कच्चित्; as, 'I hope the fever does not pain you much,' कच्चित् त्वां नातिबाधते ज्वरः.

Hopeful, *a.* (Full of hope) आशावान् -वती -वत् (त्), आशान्वितः -ता -तं, आशायुक्तः -क्ता -क्तं, आशाविष्टः -ष्टा -ष्टं, आशाबद्धः -द्धा -द्धं, स्पृहयालुः -लुः -लु, आकांक्षी -क्षिणी -क्षि (न्), सप्रत्याशः -शा -शं, प्रत्याशी -शिनी -शि (न्), अपेक्षी -क्षिणी -क्षि (न्), अपेक्षकः -का -कं.—(Promising, exciting hope) आशाजननः -ना -नं, आशाकारी -रिणी -रि (न्).

Hopefully, *adv.* सप्रत्याशं, साशंसं, आशापूर्व्वं, आशंसापूर्व्वं.

Hopefulness, *s.* आशावत्त्वं, आशाविष्टत्वं, सप्रत्याशत्वं.

Hopeless, *a.* आशाहीनः -ना -नं, निराशः -शा -शं, आशारहितः -ता -तं, गताशः -शा -शं, त्यक्ताशः -शा -शं, निःप्रत्याशः -शा -शं, हताशः -शा -शं.

Hopelessly, *adv.* निराशं, निःप्रत्याशं, आशां विना, गताशं.

Hopelessness, *s.* नैराश्यं, निराशता, आशाहीनता, आशाराहित्यं.

Hopper, *s.* (One who hops) एकपादेन प्लुतकारी *m.* (न्), एकपादेन नर्त्तकः.—(In a mill) शस्याधारः, शस्यपात्रं.

Hopping, *s.* एकपादेन नर्त्तनं or नृत्यं or प्लुतकरणं or वल्गितकरणं.

Horal, horary, *a.* मौहूर्त्तिकः -की -कं, घटिकाविषयः -या -यं.

Horde, *s.* अस्थिरवासिनां or पर्य्यटनकारिणां म्लेच्छपुरुषाणां समूहः or सङ्घः or बृहत्कुलं or बृहद्गणः, शबरगणः, किरातगणः.

Horizon, *s.* दिङ्मण्डलं, मण्डलं, चक्रवालं, चक्रं, दिगन्तः, आकाशकक्षा, अम्बरान्तं -न्तः, चक्रपालः. 'The eastern horizon,' प्राची दिक्, प्राचीमूलं.

Horizontal, *a.* अनुप्रस्थः -स्था -स्थं, अन्वायतनः -ना -नं, दिगन्तसमः -मा -मं, समः -मा -मं, समरेखः -खा -खं, समस्थः -स्था -स्थं, सपाटः -टा -टं; 'a horizontal line,' तिर्य्यग्मार्गः, समरेखा; 'plane,' समानभूभागः.

Horizontally, *adv.* अनुप्रस्थं, अन्वायतनं, समं, समरेखं, समानरूपेण.

Horn, *s.* (Of an animal) शृङ्गं, विषाणः -णी -णं, कूणिका, काहलः -ला -लिका; 'of a buffalo,' गवलं.—(Wind-instrument) शङ्खः, काहलः -ला; 'to blow a horn,' शङ्खं ध्मा (c. 1. धमति, ध्मातुं) or प्रध्मा.—(Of the moon) चन्द्रशिखा, चन्द्रशृङ्गं, चन्द्राग्रं.

Horn-book, *s.* बालकस्य आरम्भपुस्तकं or आदिपुस्तकं or प्रथमपाठग्रन्थः.

Horned, *a.* शृङ्गी -ङ्गिणी -ङ्गि (न्), शृङ्गिणः -णा -णं, विषाणी -णिनी -णि (न्), शृङ्गविशिष्टः -ष्टा -ष्टं; 'in the form of a horn,' शृङ्गाकारः -रा -रं; 'horned moon,' सिनीवाली.

Hornet, *s.* बृहद्वरलभेदः, बृहद्भ्रमरोलः, विषशृङ्गी *m.* (न्), विषशूकः.

Hornless, *s.* अशृङ्गः -ङ्गा -ङ्गं, शृङ्गहीनः -ना -नं; 'hornless bull,' तूबरः.

Horn-owl, *s.* उलूकभेदः, शृङ्गिणपेचकः, शृङ्गिकौशिकः.

Horn-pipe, *s.* नृत्यविशेषः यस्मिन् नर्त्तको हस्तपादादि इतस्ततः क्षिप्रं सञ्चालयति, नाविकनृत्यं.

Horny, *a.* शार्ङ्गः -र्ङ्गी -र्ङ्गं, शृङ्गमयः -यी -यं, शृङ्गगुणः -णा -णं.

Horologe, horology, *s.* घटी, यामघोषा, कालमापनयन्त्रं.

Horoscope, *s.* जन्मपत्रं -त्रिका, जन्मनक्षत्रपत्रं, जन्मयोगपत्रं, जन्मकालग्रहः.

Horrible, *a.* दारुणः -णा -णं, घोरः -रा -रं, सुभैरवः -वी -वं, भैरवः -वी -वं, रौद्रः -द्री -द्रं, भयङ्करः -री -रं, सुभयानकः -की -कं, भयानकः -की -कं, भीमः -मा -मं, उग्रः -ग्रा -ग्रं, भीषणः -णा -णं, त्रासकरः -रा -रं, भयावहः -हा -हं, विकटः -टा -टं, करालः -ला -लं, भीष्मः -ष्मा -ष्मं.—(In appearance) घोरदर्शनः -ना -नं, रौद्रदर्शनः -ना -नं, भीमदर्शनः -ना -नं.

Horribly, *adv.* दारुणं, घोरं, भयानकं, सुभैरवं, रौद्रं, उग्रं, विकटं.

Horrid, *a.* घोरः -रा -रं, दारुणः -णा -णं, उग्रः -ग्रा -ग्रं, कुत्सितः -ता -तं, भयानकः -का -कं, भयङ्करः -री -रं, भीमः -मा -मं, भीषणः -णा -णं, रौद्रः -द्री -द्रं, भैरवः -वी -वं, विकटः -टा -टं, करालः -ला -लं.

Horridly, *adv.* घोरं, दारुणं, उग्रं, कुत्सितं, अतिकुत्सितं, रौद्रं.

Horridness, *s.* घोरता, दारुणता, उग्रता, कुत्सितत्वं, भयानकत्वं, रौद्रता.

Horrific, *a.* भैरवकारकः -का -कं, भैरवजनकः -का -कं, सुभयङ्करः -री -रं, सुभयानकः -का -कं, साध्वसकारी -रिणी -रि (न्).

Horrified, *p. p.* भयसंहृष्टरोमा -मा -म (न्), साध्वसोपहतः -ता -तं.

To horrify, *v. a.* भैरवं जन् (c. 10. जनयति -यितुं), ससाध्वसं -सां -सं कृ.

Horripilation, *s.* रोमहर्षः -र्षणं, लोमहर्षणं, संहर्षः, उद्धर्षणं, रोमाञ्चः -ञ्चनं, रोमोद्गमः, रोमोद्भेदः, पुलकः, पुलकोद्गमः, उद्धूषणं.

Horror, *s.* भैरवं, भयसंहर्षः, भयकम्पः, साध्वसं, भीषणं, भीष्मं, भीमं, घोरं, भयानकं, भयङ्करं, त्रासः, सन्त्रासः, परिकम्पः.

Horse, *s.* अश्वः, हयः, तुरङ्गः -ङ्गमः, तुरगः, वाजी *m.* (न्), घोटकः, वाहः, तार्क्ष्यः, अर्व्वा *m.* (न्), सैन्धवः, सप्तिः *m.*, किल्की *m.* (न्), प्रचेलकः, अभिगाता *m.* (तृ), पीतिः *m.*, पीती *m.* (न्), वीतिः *m.*, पलङ्कारः, मुद्गभुक् *m.* (ज्), मुद्गभोजी *m.* (न्), गन्धर्व्वः; 'a well-bred horse,' आजानेयः, कुलीनः, सिन्धुवारः, भूमिपक्षः, भूमिरक्षकः; 'a well-trained horse,' विनीतः, साधुवाही *m.* (न्); 'a white horse,' कर्कः; 'a bay horse,' उकनाहः, कियाहः; 'a fleet horse,' जवनः, जवाधिकः, प्रजवी *m.* (न्); 'a good horse,' वल्लभः, हयोत्तमः; 'a chariot horse,' रथ्यः; 'a pack-horse,' पृष्ठ्यः, स्थौरी *m.* (न्), स्थूरी *m.*, स्थोरी *m.*; 'a horse for sacrifice,' ययुः *m.*, अश्वमेधीयः; 'four-horsed carriage,' चतुरश्वो रथः.—

(Cavalry) आश्वं, आश्विकं, अश्वारूढाः m. pl.—(Support for towels, &c.) मार्ज्जनपटाधारः, वस्त्राधारः; 'relating to a horse,' अश्वीयः -या -यं, आश्विकः -की -कं, आश्वः -श्वी -श्वं.—(A number of horses,' अश्वीयं, आश्वं.

To HORSE, *v. a.* अश्वम् आरुह् in caus. (-रोपयति-यितुं), अश्वारूढं-ढां-ढं कृ.

HORSE-BACK, *s.* अश्वपृष्ठं, ऊर्द्ध्वस्थितिः *f.*; 'on horse-back,' अश्वपृष्ठे loc. c.; 'going on horse-back,' तुरङ्गयायी *m.* (न्).

HORSE-BEAN, *s.* क्षुद्रशिम्बिकभेदः, शिम्बा, मुद्गः, माषः.

HORSE-BOAT, *s.* अश्ववहनं, अश्ववहनयोग्या नौका.

HORSE-BREAKER, *s.* अश्वदमकः, अश्वविनेता *m.* (तृ), अश्वशिक्षकः, अश्वशिक्षाजीवी *m.* (न्).

HORSE-BREAKING, *s.* अश्वदमनं, अश्वशिक्षा, अश्वविनयः.

HORSE-CHESTNUT, *s.* (Tree) श्यामफलविशिष्टो वृक्षभेदः.

HORSE-CLOTH, *s.* अश्वास्तरणं, आस्तरः, अश्वपरिस्तोमः.

HORSE-COMB, *s.* अश्वमार्जनी, अश्वलोमशोधनी.

HORSE-DEALER, *s.* अश्वव्यापारी *m.* (न्), हयज्ञः, हेडावुक्कः, हेलावुक्कः, हयविद्याविशारदः.

HORSE-DRIVING, *s.* अश्वसारथ्यं, अश्वप्रेरणं, हयप्रेरणं.

HORSE-DUNG, *s.* अश्वशकृत् *n.*, अश्वपुरीषं, अश्वमलं, अश्वहन्नं.

HORSE-FACED, *a.* अश्वमुखः -खी -खं, अश्ववदनः -ना -नं, हयमुखः -खी -खं, तुरङ्गवक्त्रः -क्त्रा -क्त्रं, तुरङ्गाननः -ना -नं, तुरङ्गास्यः -स्या -स्यं.

HORSE-FLESH, *s.* अश्वमांसं, घोटकमांसं, तुरगमांसं.

HORSE-FLY, *s.* अश्वदंशकः, हयदंशी, अश्वमक्षिका.

HORSE-GUARDS, *s.* अश्वारूढसैनिकाः *m. pl.*, राजशरीररक्षकम् अश्वारूढसैन्यं.

HORSE-HAIR, *s.* अश्वलोम *n.* (न्), अश्वरोम *n.* (न्), अश्वबालः.

HORSE-LAUGH, *s.* अट्टहासः, अतिहासः, अतिहसितं, महाहासः, आच्छुरितं, सोत्प्रासः.

HORSE-LEECH, *s.* अश्वदंशका जलौका, अश्वरक्तपायिनी.—(Farrier) अश्वचिकित्सकः, अश्ववैद्यः.

HORSEMAN, *s.* अश्वारूढः, अश्वारोहः -ही *m.* (न्), हयारूढः, हयारोहः, सादी *m.* (न्), अश्वसादी *m.* (न्), तुरगी *m.* (न्), तुरङ्गी *m.* (न्), अश्ववहः, अश्ववारः, सायी *m.* (न्), हयविद्याविशारदः.

HORSEMANSHIP, *s.* अश्वविद्या, हयविद्या, अश्वारोहणविद्या, हयज्ञता, हयारोहः, अश्वहृदयं.

HORSE-MEAT, *s.* अश्वाहारः, अश्वभोजनं, अश्वखाद्यं, पशुखाद्यद्रव्यं.

HORSE-POND, *s.* अश्वतडागः, अश्वपुष्करिणी, अश्ववापी.

HORSE-RACE, *s.* अश्वचर्य्या, अश्वमार्गः, अश्वधावनं.

HORSE-RADISH, *s.* कुरुकन्दकः -कं, कन्दमूलभेदः.

HORSE-SHOE, *s.* अश्वखुरत्रं, अश्वखुरत्राणं, अश्वखुरबन्धनं, अश्वपादुका.

HORSE-STEALER, *s.* अश्वहारकः, वाजिहर्त्ता *m.* (र्तृ), अश्वमुक् *m.* (ष्).

HORSE-TRAPPINGS, *s.* आदानं, अश्वपरिस्तोमः, अश्वसज्जा, अश्वास्तरणं.

HORSE-WAY, *s.* अश्वपथः, अश्वमार्गः, अश्ववर्त्म *n.* (न्).

HORSE-WHIP, *s.* कशा, अश्वकशा, अश्वताडनी, अश्वप्रतोदः, प्रतिष्कशः, प्रतिष्कषः, चर्म्मदण्डः.

To HORSE-WHIP, *v. a.* कशया or चर्म्मदण्डेन तड् (c. 10. ताडयति -यितुं) or आहन् (c. 2. -हन्ति -न्तुं) or प्रहृ (c. 1. -हरति -हर्त्तुं), कशाघातं कृ.

HORTATION, *s.* उपदेशः, उपदेशवाक्यं, प्रबोधनं, प्रबोधवाक्यं, मन्त्रणं.

HORTATORY, *a.* उपदेशकः -का -कं, प्रबोधकः -का -कं, आदेशकः -का -कं.

HORTICULTURAL, *a.* उद्यानविद्यासम्बन्धी -न्धिनी -न्धि (न्), उद्यानविषयः -या -यं.

HORTICULTURE, *s.* उद्यानविद्या, उद्यानकर्म्मविद्या, उद्यानकर्म्म, उद्यानकरणविद्या, उद्यानकरणं, उद्यानकृषिकर्म्म *n.* (न्), पुष्पफलोत्पत्तिकर्म्म *n.* (न्).

HORTICULTURIST, *s.* उद्यानविद्याज्ञः, उद्यानकर्म्मकः, उद्यानकर्म्मोपजीवी *m.* (न्).

HORTULAN, *a.* उद्यानसम्बन्धी -न्धिनी -न्धि (न्).

HORTUS SICCUS, *s.* शुष्कोद्यानं, शुष्कौषधिपुस्तकं, शुष्कौषधिसङ्ग्रहः, शुष्कतृणादिसङ्ग्रहः, शुष्कौषधयः *f. pl.*

HOSE, *s.* ऊर्णामयं पादत्राणं, और्णपादत्रं, पादरक्षणं, जङ्घापरिधानं.

HOSIER, *s.* पूर्व्वोक्तपादत्रविक्रेता *m.* (तृ), और्णपादत्रविक्रयी *m.* (न्).

HOSPITABLE, *a.* आतिथ्यः -थ्या -थ्यं, आतिथेयः -यी -यं, अतिथिसेवकः -का -कं, अतिथिपूजकः -का -कं, आतिथ्यकारी -रिणी -रि (न्), प्रियातिथिः -थिः -थि, वत्सलातिथिः -थिः -थि, सत्कारशीलः -ला -लं.

HOSPITABLY, *adv.* आतिथ्यपूर्व्वं, सातिथ्यं, सत्कारेण, सत्कारपूर्व्वं, आतिथेयं; 'to receive hospitably,' सत्कृ, आतिथ्यं कृ.

HOSPITAL, *s.* आरोग्यशाला, चिकित्साशाला, चिकित्सागारं, रोगप्रतीकारशाला, रोगोपचारशाला, रोगार्त्तलोकपोषणस्थानं, दरिद्रलोकानां रोगचिकित्सनशाला, धर्म्मशाला.

HOSPITALITY, *s.* आतिथ्यं, अतिथित्वं, अतिथिक्रिया, आतिथ्यकर्म्म *n.* (न्), अतिथिसत्कारः, अतिथिसत्क्रिया, सत्कारः, सत्क्रिया, सत्कर्म्म *n.* (न्), सत्कृतिः *f.*, सत्कृतं, अतिथिसेवा, अतिथिपूजनं, मनुष्ययज्ञः, नृयज्ञः.

HOST, *s.* (Entertainer) सत्कारी *m.* (न्), सत्कृत् *m.*, आमन्त्रयिता *m.* (तृ), निमन्त्रणकृत् *m.*, निमन्त्रकः, भोजनदाता *m.* (तृ), आतिथ्यकृत् *m.* —(Army) चमूः *f.*, सेना, अनीकं, वाहिनी, अनीकिनी, वरूथिनी, योधसमूहः.—(A great number) समूहः, सङ्घः, सङ्घातः, गणः, कुलं, समवायः, समुदायः, निवहः, निकायः; 'a host of persons,' जनसमूहः, लोकसङ्घः, जनौघः; 'a host of enemies,' शत्रुनिकायः; 'a host of excellencies,' गुणग्रामः.

To HOST, *v. n.* (Lodge) वस् (c. 1. वसति, वस्तुं), निवस्, अतिथिर् भू or अस्.—(Encounter in battle) युद्धे समागम् (c. 1. -गच्छति -गन्तुं) or सङ्गम्.

HOSTAGE, *s.* शरीरबन्धकः, बन्धकः, सन्धिनियमस्योपरि विश्वासार्थं त्यक्तः शरीरबन्धकः.

HOSTEL, HOSTELRY, *s.* उत्तरणस्थानं, उत्तरणगृहं, उपकारी -रिका.

HOSTESS, *s.* आतिथ्यकारिणी, सत्कारिणी, निमन्त्रणकारिणी, भोजनदात्री.

HOSTILE, *a.* वैरी -रिणी -रि (न्), विरुद्धः -द्धा -द्धं, विरोधी -धिनी -धि (न्), विपक्षः -क्षा -क्षं, प्रतिकूलः -ला -लं, विपरीतः -ता -तं, अहितः -ता -तं, अहितकारी -रिणी -रि (न्), प्रातिपक्षः -क्षी -क्षं, विद्वेषी -षिणी -षि (न्), द्वेषी &c., द्वेषणः -णा -णं, विद्विषः -षा -षं, शात्रवीयः -यी -यं, द्रोहवृत्तिः -त्तिः -त्ति, अपकारी -रिणी -रि (न्), प्रतिरोधी -धिनी -धि (न्), पर्य्यवस्थाता -त्री -तृ (तृ), सवैरः -रा -रं; 'a hostile invasion,' शत्रुविग्रहः; 'to be hostile,' विपक्षीभू, प्रतिकूल (nom. प्रतिकूलयति -यितुं), विरुध् (c. 7. -रुणद्धि -रोद्धुं), वैर (nom. वैरायते), शत्रु (nom. शत्रूयति), द्विष् (c. 2. द्वेष्टि -ष्टुं), विद्विष्, पर्य्यवस्था (c. 1. -तिष्ठति -स्थातुं).

HOSTILELY, *adv.* शत्रुवत्, रिपुवत्, विरोधेन, विरुद्धं, विपरीतं, विपक्षवत्.

HOSTILITY, *s.* वैरिता, वैरभावः, वैरं, शत्रुता, रिपुता, विपक्षता, विरोधः, विरुद्धता, विद्वेषः, द्वेषः, शात्रवं, अरिता, प्रतिपक्षता, विद्विष्टता, अप्रीतिः *f.*, प्रतिद्वन्द्वं, परता -त्वं; 'natural hostility,' जातिवैरं.—(War, state of war) युद्धं, युद्धभावः, युद्धावस्था, विग्रहः, संग्रामः.

HOSTLER, *s.* अश्वपालः -लकः, अश्वरक्षकः, उत्तरणस्थाने अभ्यागतान् अश्वान् पालयति यो जनः.

HOT, *a.* (Contrary to cold) उष्णः -ष्णा -ष्णं, तप्तः -प्ता -प्तं, चण्डः -ण्डा -ण्डं, प्रचण्डः -ण्डा -ण्डं, उच्चण्डः -ण्डा -ण्डं, सन्तप्तः -प्ता -प्तं, उपतप्तः -प्ता -प्तं, तापी -पिनी -पि (न्), कोष्णः -ष्णा -ष्णं, सोष्मः -ष्मा -ष्मं, सोष्मा

-ष्मा -ष्म (न्), नैदाघः -घी -घं, अशिशिरः -रा -रं, अशीतः -ता -तं, तिग्मः -ग्मा -ग्मं, तीव्रः -व्रा -व्रं, तीक्ष्णः -क्ष्णा -क्ष्णं, खरः -रा -रं, ग्रीष्मः -ष्मा -ष्मं, घर्म्म in comp.; 'hot season, hot weather,' उष्णकालः, उष्णसमयः, ग्रीष्मः, ग्रीष्मकालः, निदाघः, निदाघकालः, उष्णागमः; 'hot water,' उष्णोदकं, घर्म्मोदकं, घर्म्माम्बु *n.*—(Hot to the taste) तिग्मः -ग्मा -ग्मं, तीक्ष्णः -क्ष्णा -क्ष्णं, तीव्रः -व्रा -व्रं, खरः -रा -रं, कटुः -टुः -टु, उग्रः -ग्रा -ग्रं.—(Passionate) चण्डः -ण्डा -ण्डं, चण्डवान् -वती -वत् (त्), तीक्ष्णः -क्ष्णा -क्ष्णं, तिग्मः -ग्मा -ग्मं, उग्रः -ग्रा -ग्रं, शीघ्रकोपी -पिनी -पि (न्), रागी -गिणी -गि (न्), उष्णः -ष्णा -ष्णं.—(Impetuous) तीक्ष्णकर्म्मा -र्म्मा -र्म्म (न्), संरम्भी -म्भिणी -म्भि (न्), उत्तप्तः -प्ता -प्तं; 'to make hot,' तप् (c. 10. तापयति -यितुं); 'to be hot,' उष्णीभू, उष्म (nom. उष्मायते).

HOTBED, *s.* गोहयशकृदादिप्रक्षेपेण तप्तीकृतम् उद्यानस्थलं, उष्णस्थलं.

HOTCH-POTCH, *s.* नानाखाद्यद्रव्यसंयोगः, नानाशाकादिसम्मिश्रणं, सन्निपातः, प्रकीर्णकं.

HOTEL, *s.* उत्तरणशाला, उत्तरणगृहं, उत्तरणस्थानं, उपकारी -रिका, उपकार्य्या, औपकार्य्यं, प्रवासीयगृहं.

HOT-HEADED, *a.* साहसिकः -की -कं, साहसी -सिनी -सि (न्), उच्चण्डः -ण्डा -ण्डं, उत्तप्तः -प्ता -प्तं, संरम्भी -म्भिणी -म्भि (न्), शीघ्रकोपी -पिनी -पि (न्), तीक्ष्णकर्म्मा -र्म्मा -र्म्म (न्); 'hot-headed zeal,' उत्तापः.

HOT-HOUSE, *s.* उद्याने विदेशीयवृक्षरक्षणार्थं काचाच्छादितं तप्तगृहं or उष्णागृहं.

HOTLY, *adv.* तीक्ष्णं, तीव्रं, तिग्मं, सतैक्ष्ण्यं, चण्डं, प्रचण्डं, उच्चण्डं, उग्रं, उग्रतया, उत्तापेन, सोष्मं, उत्तप्तं, उष्णं.

HOT-MOUTHED, *a.* तीक्ष्णवादी -दिनी -दि (न्), उग्रमुखः -खी -खं, दुर्मुखः -खी -खं.

HOTNESS, *s.* उष्णता, औष्ण्यं, तापः, तप्तत्वं, चण्डता, प्रचण्डता, अशिशिरता, तिग्मता, तैग्म्यं, तीक्ष्णता, निदाघः.—(To the taste) तिग्मता, तीक्ष्णता, तीव्रता, कटुता, उग्रता -त्वं.—(Ardor, vehemence) उत्तापः, उच्चण्डता, व्यग्रता, तीक्ष्णता, उष्मः, संरम्भः.—(Of temper) चण्डता, शीघ्रकोपित्वं.

HOTSPUR, *s.* साहसिकजनः, तीक्ष्णस्वभावो जनः, संरम्भी *m.* (न्).

HOVEL, *s.* कुटीरः, कुटेरः, कुटी, तृणकुटी, उटजः, मण्डपः, गोष्ठं.

To HOVEL, *v. a.* कुटीरे वस् (c. 1. वसति, वस्तुं) or निवस्, कुटीरम् अधिवस्.

HOVEN, *a.* उच्छूनः -ना -नं, प्रस्फुरितः -ता -तं, उत्थितः -ता -तं.

To HOVER, *v. n.* विहायसा or व्योममध्ये वृत् (c. 1. वर्त्तते -र्त्तितुं) or व्यावृत्, आकाशमध्ये मस्तकोपरि वृत्, प्रडीनम् अकृत्वा ऊर्द्ध्वंपतति विसृप् (c. 1. -सर्पति -सृप्तुं) or विचल् (c. 1. -चलति -लितुं), व्योममध्ये पक्षास्फालनं कृत्वा निश्चलो वृत्.—(Hesitate, waver) विलम्ब् (c. 1. -लम्बते -म्बितुं), दोल (nom. दोलायते), आन्दोल (nom. आन्दोलयति -यितुं), विक्लृप् (c. 1. -कल्पते -ल्पितुं), विचर् (c. 10. -चारयति -यितुं), विशङ्क् (c. 1. -शङ्कते -ङ्कितुं).

HOUGH, *s.* जङ्घास्थिशिरा, जङ्घास्थिस्नायुः *m.* जङ्घासन्धिबन्धनं.

To HOUGH, *v. a.* जङ्घास्थिशिरां छिद् (c. 7. छिनत्ति, छेत्तुं).

HOUND, *s.* मृगयाकुक्कुरः, मृगव्यकुक्कुरः, मृगयार्थं कुक्कुरः, आखेटकार्थं श्वा *m.* (न्), आखेटिकः, मृगारिः *m.*, मृगदंशकः, वृकारिः *m.*, विश्वकद्रुः *m.*

To HOUND, *v. a.* मृगव्यकुक्कुरैर् अनुसृ (c. 1. -सरति -सर्त्तुं).

HOUR, *s.* घटिका, होरा, केरली, दिवसस्य चतुर्विंशभागः or चतुर्विंशतितमांशः, दिनांशः; 'an hour of forty eight minutes,' मुहूर्त्तः -र्त्तं; 'a space of twenty-four minutes,' दण्डः; 'half-an-hour,' अर्द्धघटिका; 'an hour and a half,' अर्द्धयामः.

HOUR-GLASS, *s.* यामनाली, वालुकायन्त्रं, कालपरिमापकयन्त्रं.

HOURI, *s.* दिव्याङ्गना, दिव्यकन्या, देवकन्या, स्वर्गकन्या, स्वर्वेश्या.

HOURLY, *adv.* प्रतिमुहूर्त्तं, मुहूर्त्ते मुहूर्त्ते, दण्डे दण्डे, प्रतिदण्डं.

HOUR-PLATE, *s.* मुहूर्त्तदण्डादिपरिमापकं मण्डलं, यामघोषा, घटीमुखं.

HOUSE, *s.* गृहं, गेहं -हः, वेश्म *n.* (न्), भवनं, आलयः, निलयः, आयतनं, निकेतः -तनं -तकं, निवेशनं, सदनं, मन्दिरं, वासः, संवासः, वासस्थानं, आगारः -रं, अगारः -रं, निवासः, निवासस्थानं, निवसतिः *f.*, वसितं, समावासः, आवसथः, निकाय्यः, अवस्थानं, वरूथं, उदवसितं, वास्तुः *m.* ओकस् *n.*, धाम *n.* (न्), छत्वरः, निशान्तं, कुटः -टी, शाला, सभा, स्थानं; 'house and land,' गृहक्षेत्रादि; 'a number of houses,' सन्निचितिः *f.*; 'house of confinement,' बन्धनगृहं, बन्धनागारं, बन्धनालयः; 'confined to the house,' गृहानुबद्धः -द्धा -द्धं.—(Family, race) कुलं, वंशः, कुटुम्बः, जातिः *f.*—(Family, household) गृहजनः, परिजनः, परिवारः, स्वजनः, कुटुम्बकं, स्त्रीपुत्रकन्यादि.

To HOUSE, *v. a.* गृहे निविश् (c. 10. -वेशयति -यितुं), गृहं प्रविश् (c. 10. -वेशयति -यितुं), वेश्मनि वस् (c. 10. वासयति -यितुं), आश्रयं दा, वासस्थानं दा.

HOUSE-BREAKER, *s.* गृहभेदकः, आगारभेदकः, भित्तिचौरः, सन्धिचौरः सन्धिचौरः, कारुचौरः, कुड्यच्छेदी, कपाटघ्नः, खानिलः, कुजम्भलः -म्भिलः.

HOUSE-BUILDER, *s.* गृहकारकः, गृहकारी *m.* (न्), गृहकर्म्मी *m.* (न्), गृहनिर्म्माता *m.* (तृ).

HOUSE-BURNER, *s.* गृहदाहकः, आगारदाहकः, गृहदाहनकृत् *m.*

HOUSE-BURNING, *s.* गृहदाहः -हनं, गृहदहनं, गृहप्लोषः, आगारदाहः.

HOUSEDOG, *s.* गृहकुक्कुरः, गृहरक्षकः श्वा *m.* (न्).

HOUSEDOOR, *s.* गृहद्वारं, गेहद्वारं.

HOUSEHOLD, *s.* गृहजनः, परिजनः, गृहपरिजनः, गृहपरिवारः, स्वजनः, परिवारः, अभिजनः, कुटुम्बकं.

HOUSEHOLD, *a.* गृह्यः -ह्या -ह्यं, गृहसम्बन्धी -न्धिनी -न्धि (न्), आवसथिकः -की -कं or expressed by गृह in comp.; as, 'household affairs,' गृहकार्य्यं, गृहकरणं, गृहव्यापारः; 'household utensils,' गृहोपस्करः; 'household gods,' गृह्या देवताः *f. pl.*, कुलदेवताः *f. pl.*; 'household bread,' गृहापूपः.

HOUSEHOLDER, *s.* गृहस्थः, गृहस्वामी *m.* (न्), गृहपतिः *m.*, गृहाधिकारी *m.* (न्), गृही *m.* (न्), गेही *m.* (न्), कुटुम्बी *m.* (न्), कौटुम्बिकः, गृहमेधी *m.* (न्), स्नातकः, ज्येष्ठाश्रमी *m.* (न्).

HOUSEHOLD-STUFF, *s.* गृहोपस्करः, गृहोपकरणं, गृहसामग्री -ग्र्यं.

HOUSEKEEPER, *s.* (Householder) गृही *m.* (न्), गेही *m.* (न्), गृहस्वामी *m.* (न्), गृहाधिकारी *m.* (न्), कुटुम्बी *m.* (न्).—(A woman who has the care of a family) गृहिणी, गेहिनी, कुटुम्बिनी, गृहमेधिनी.

HOUSEKEEPING, *s.* गृहव्यापारः, गृहकार्य्यं, गृहकरणं, गृहकर्म्म *n.* (न्), गार्हस्थ्यं, गृहस्थता.

HOUSELEEK, *s.* कुतृणं, गृहभित्तिरुह ओषधिभेदः.

HOUSELESS, *a.* गृहहीनः -ना -नं, गृहशून्यः -न्या -न्यं, निरालयः -या -यं, अनिकेतनः -ना -नं, अकेतनः -ना -नं, अलयः -या -यं, निराश्रयः -या -यं, अशरणः -णा -णं, निर्वासः -सा -सं.

HOUSEMAID, *s.* गृहदासी, गृहपरिष्कारिणी, गृहमार्ज्जनी, दासी.

HOUSE-ROOM, *s.* गृहावस्थानं, वासस्थानं, निवासस्थानं, आवासः, वासः.

HOUSE-TOP, *s.* गृहपृष्ठं, गृहाग्रं, गृहशिखरं, गृहशृङ्गं.

HOUSE-WARMING, *s.* गृहप्रवेशः, नवगृहप्रवेशकाले उत्सवः, वास्तुप्रवेशः, वास्तुसंशमनं -नीयं.

HOUSEWIFE, *s.* गृहमेधिनी, गृहव्यापारकुशला, गृहकार्य्यदक्षा, गृहकर्म्मनिपुणा, गृहिणी, गेहिनी.

HOUSEWIFERY, *s.* गृहव्यापारकुशलता, गृहकार्य्यदक्षता, गृहकर्म्मनिपुणता, गृहमेधित्वं, परिमितव्ययः.

Housing, *s.* (House-room) वासस्थानं, निवासस्थानं.—(Of a horse or elephant) आस्तरः -रणं, परिस्तोमः, वर्णः, आदानं.

How, *adv.* कथं, किं, केन प्रकारेण, केन रूपेण, किमु, कुतस्, किमुत; 'how much, how many, how little, how long, &c.,' कियान् -यती -यत् (त्) or कियत् indec., कतिः -तिः -ति or कति in comp.; as, 'how long?' कियत्कालं, कियन्तं कालं, कियता कालेन, कतिकालं; 'how long!' कियच्चिरं; 'how many sorts?' कतिविधः -धा -धं; 'how many times?' कतिकृत्वस्; 'for how much?' कियता मूल्येन; 'how far?' कियत्पर्य्यन्तं, किम्पर्य्यन्तं, कियदवधि; 'how much more,' किम्पुनर्, किमुत, किमु, किम्, कुतःपुनर्; 'how much less,' किमुत, किमु; 'how so?' किमिति, किमिव; 'how else,' अथकिम्; 'how wonderful,' किमाश्चर्य्यं; 'how do you do?' किं क्षेमम् अस्ति भवतः, किं कुशलम् अस्ति भवतः, कीदृशी स्थितिर् भवतः; 'how are we to act?' किम् अस्माभिः करणीयं; 'he knows not how to act,' यथाकार्य्यं न जानाति; 'how great is that darkness!' सोऽन्धकारः कियान् महान्; 'any how,' यथाकथञ्चित्, यथातथा, कथञ्चन, कथञ्चित्.

Howbeit, *adv.* तथापि, तथैव, तथाच, किञ्च, अपि, अपितु, किन्तु.

Howdah, *s.* (On the back of an elephant) वरण्डकः.

However, *adv.* तथापि, किञ्च, अपितु, किन्तु, तु, परन्तु, पुनर्; 'in whatever manner,' यत्प्रकारेण.

Howitzer, *s.* अलतरग्निबलेन लोहगुलिकाप्रक्षेपकं युद्धयन्त्रं.

To howl, *v. n* रु (c. 2. रौति, रवितुं), विरु, दीर्घरावं कृ, दीर्घरुतं कृ, गर्ज् (c. 1. गर्जति -र्जितुं), भष् (c. 1. भषति -षितुं), रै (c. 1. रायति रातुं), रस् (c. 1. रसति -सितुं), रट् (c. 1. रटति -टितुं), वाश् (c. 1. वाशते -शितुं).

Howl, howling, *s.* रावः, रुतं, दीर्घरावं, दीर्घरुतं, गर्जनं, रायणं, भाषः, भषणं, बुक्कनं, वाशितं, भुलभुल्ला; 'making a howling,' दीर्घरावः -वी -वं.

Howsoever, *adv.* यत्प्रकारेण, येन प्रकारेण, यथा यथा, यथातथा, तथापि

To hox, *v. a.* जङ्घास्थिशिरां छिद् (c. 7. छिनत्ति, छेत्तुं).

Hoy, *s.* बृहन्नौकाविशेषः, विशालनौका.

Hubbub, *s.* कोलाहलः, कलकलः, कलरवः, रासः, हलहलाशब्दः, कालकीलः, तुमुलं, विप्लवः, कलहः.

Huckaback, *s.* नानारेखाङ्कितः क्षौमपटविशेषः.

Hucklebacked, *a.* न्युब्जः -ब्जा -ब्जं, कुब्जः -ब्जा -ब्जं, वक्रकन्धरः -रा -रं

Hucklebone, *s.* कट्यस्थि *n.*, कटास्थि *n.*, श्रोण्यस्थि *n.*, जघनास्थि.

Huckster, *s.* क्षुद्रवाणिज्यकारी *m.* (न्), तुच्छवाणिज्यकृत्, कुत्सितवणिक् *m.* (ज्).

To huckster, *v. n.* तुच्छवाणिज्यं कृ, तुच्छप्रकारेण or नीचप्रकारेण or कुत्सितप्रकारेण वाणिज्यं कृ.

To huddle, *v.a.* सम्मिश्रीकृ, अस्तव्यस्तीकृ, सङ्कुलीकृ, सङ्करीकृ, सम्मिश्र् (c. 10. -मिश्रयति -यितुं), सम्बाध् (c. 1. -बाधते -धितुं), अधरोत्तरीकृ, संक्षुभ्.

To huddle, *v. n.* सम्मिश्रीभू, सङ्कुलीभू, सङ्कीर्णीभू, सङ्करीभू, अस्तव्यस्तीभू, अधरोत्तरीभू, सम्बाधीभू.

Huddle, *s.* अस्तव्यस्तता -त्वं, अधरोत्तरं, सङ्करः, साङ्कर्य्यं, सङ्क्षोभः.

Hue, *s.* (Dye, colour) वर्णः, रागः, रङ्गः, छाया, छविः *f.*—(Hue and cry) जनरवः, बहुभिः कृता संहूतिः, जनघोषणा.

Huff, *s.* (Anger) क्रोधावेशः, क्रोधः, कोपः, रोषः, संरम्भः.—(Arrogance) दर्पः, दर्पावेशः, औद्धत्यं.—(One inflated with arrogance) दर्पाध्मातः, अतिगर्वितः, उद्धतः.

To huff, *v. a.* रुष् (c. 10. रोषयति -यितुं), कुप् (c. 10. कोपयति -यितुं).

To huff, *v. n.* दृप् (c. 4. दृप्यति, द्रप्तुं), धृष् (c. 5. धृष्णोति, धर्षितुं), दर्पाध्मातः -ता -तं भू, भर्त्स् (c. 10. भर्त्सयति -ते -यितुं), विकत्थ् (c. 1. -कत्थते -त्थितुं).

Huffer, *s.* दाम्भिकः, भर्त्सनकारः, विकत्थी *m.* (न्), दर्पी *m.* (न्), शूरम्मन्यः.

Huffish, *a.* (Angry) क्रोधाविष्टः -ष्टा -ष्टं, कोपी -पिनी -पि (न्), सरोषः -षा -षं, सकोपः -पा -पं.—(Arrogant) दृप्तः -प्ता -प्तं, गर्व्वी -र्व्विणी -र्व्वि (न्), उद्धतः -ता -तं, दर्पी -र्पिणी -र्पि (न्), आत्मश्लाघी -घिनी -घि (न्).

Huffishly, *adv.* सकोपं, सरोषं, सदर्पं, धृष्टवत्, गर्व्वितवत्.

Huffishness, *s.* सकोपत्वं, सरोषत्वं, क्रोधाविष्टता, गर्व्वितत्वं, अहङ्कारः.

To hug, *v. a.* आलिङ्ग् (c. 1. -लिङ्गति -ङ्गितुं), समालिङ्ग्, आश्लिष् (c. 4. -श्लिष्यति -श्लेष्टुं), संश्लिष्, समाश्लिष्, परिष्वञ्ज् (c. 1. ष्वजते -ष्वंक्तुं), परिरभ् (c. 1. -रभते -रब्धुं), बाहुभ्यां पीड् (c. 10. पीडयति -यितुं) or परिग्रह् (c. 9. -गृह्णाति -ग्रहीतुं).

Hug, *s.* आलिङ्गनं -ङ्गितं, आश्लेषः, परिष्वङ्गः, बाहूपपीडः, अङ्कपाली.

Hugged, *p. p.* आलिङ्गितः -ता -तं, आश्लिष्टः -ष्टा -ष्टं, पीडितः -ता -तं.

Huge, *a.* बृहन् -हती -हत् (त्), अतिबृहन् &c., सुबृहन् &c., महान् -हती -हत् (त्), अतिमहान् &c., सुमहान् &c., स्थूलः -ला -लं, अतिविशालः -ला -लं, बृहत्परिमाणः -णा -णं, अपरिमितः -ता -तं, वरीयान् -यसी -यः (स्), वरिष्ठः -ष्ठा -ष्ठं, गरिष्ठः -ष्ठा -ष्ठं.—(In body) महाकायः -या -यं, अतिकायः -या -यं, बृहत्कायः -या -यं, बृहच्छरीरः -रा -रं.

Hugely, *adv.* सुमहत्, अतिमहत्, सुबृहत्, अत्यन्तं, अतिमात्रं, अपरिमितं.

Hugeness, *s.* सुबृहत्त्वं, बृहत्त्वं, महत्त्वं, सुमहत्त्वं, अतिमहत्त्वं, स्थूलता, अतिविशालता, अपरिमितत्वं, सुविपुलता, कायबृहत्त्वं, बृहत्कायत्वं.

Hugger-mugger, *s.* रहस् *n.*, गूढता, प्रच्छन्नता; 'in huggermugger,' रहसि, रहस्यं, निभृतं, प्रच्छन्नं, गुप्तं, उपांशु.

Hulk, *s.* जीर्णनौका, गुणकूपकादिरहिता नौका, रज्जुकूपकादिहीनो नौकायाः स्थूलभागः.

Hull, *s.* (Integument) कञ्चुकः, आवेष्टनं, परिवेष्टनं, कोशः, कोषः, पुटः, त्वक् *f.* (च्).—(Of a ship) गुणकूपकादिभिन्नो नौकाभागः, नौकायाः स्थूलभागः or कायः.

Hully, *a.* कोशवान् -वती -वत् (त्), तुषवान् &c., त्वग्युक्तः -क्ता -क्तं.

To hum, *v. n.* गुञ्ज् (c. 1. गुञ्जति -ञ्जितुं), रु (c. 2. रौति, रवितुं), विरु, रणरणं कृ; 'to hum and haw,' भिन्नस्वरेण or स्खलितवाचा वद् (c. 1. वदति -दितुं).

Hum! *interj.* हुम्, हूम्, आ, आस्, हा, अहो, अहोवत्, तावत्, किं.

Hum, *s.* (Buzzing sound) कलः, कलरवः, कलकलः, कलस्वरः, रुतं, विरुतं, रावः, विरावः, गुञ्जनं, गुञ्जितं, मर्मरः, झङ्कारः, रणत्कारः; 'of bees,' अलिविरावः, अलिविरुतं.

Human, *a.* मानुषः -षी -षं -षिकः -की -कं, मानवीनः -ना -नं, मानवीयः -या -यं, पौरुषः -षी -षं, पौरुषेयः -यी -यं, जनकीयः -या -यं, नारः -री -रं, मनुष्यजातीयः -या -यं, लौकिकः -की -कं; 'human nature,' पुरुषत्वं -ता, मनुष्यत्वं -ता, मानुष्यं, मानुषत्वं; 'human race,' मनुष्यजातिः *f.*, मनुष्यवर्गः, नृजातिः *f.*; 'human form,' नररूपं; 'human art,' मनुष्यकला; 'a human brute,' पुरुषपशुः *m.*

Humane, *a.* परोपकारशीलः -ला -लं, परोपकारी -रिणी -रि (न्), परहितैषी -षिणी -षि (न्), परहितः -ता -तं, परहितकामः -मा -मं, उपकारपरः -रा -रं, दयालुः -लुः -लु, कृपालुः -लुः -लु, कारुणिकः -की -कं, सकरुणः -णा -णं, दयाशीलः -ला -लं, करुणाशीलः -ला -लं, करुणात्मा -त्मा -त्म (न्), करुणार्द्रः -र्द्रा -र्द्रं, अनुकम्पी -म्पिनी -म्पि (न्), सानुकम्पः -म्पा -म्पं, सर्व्वभूतानुकम्पकः -का -कं, आपद्रक्षणशीलः -ला -लं, दया-

वान् -वती -वत् (त्), सुहृदयः -या -यं, सुशीलः -ला -लं, दीनानुकम्पनः -ना -नं, सदयः -या -यं, सानुक्रोशः -शा -शं, क्षमावान् -वती -वत् (त्), अनृशंसः -सा -सं, करुणावेदी -दिनी -दि (न्).

Humanely, *adv.* सकरुणं, सकारुण्यं, सानुकम्पं, सदयं, दयाशीलत्वात्, सुशीलवत्, परहितेच्छया.

Humanist, *s.* शास्त्रज्ञः, शास्त्रव्युत्पन्नः, शब्दशास्त्रविद् *m.*, विद्वज्जनः.

Humanity, *s.* (Benevolence, compassion) दया, दयाशीलता, दयालुता, कारुण्यं, करुणा, करुणाशीलत्वं, अनुकम्पा, कृपा, परहितेच्छा, परोपकारशीलता, हितकाम्या, उपकारपरता, करुणार्द्रता, सानुकम्पता, आपन्नरक्षणं.—(Nature of man) पुरुषता -त्वं, मानुषता, मनुष्यता -त्वं, मानुष्यं, मानवत्वं, मानव्यं.

To humanize, *v. a.* शिष्टाचारान् or आर्य्यव्यवहारान् शिक्ष् (c. 10. शिक्षयति -यितुं) or शास् (c. 2. शास्ति, शासितुं), शिष्टीकृ, सुशीलीकृ, विनीतं -तां -तं कृ, सभ्यं -भ्यां -भ्यं कृ.

Humankind, *s.* मनुष्यजातिः *f.*, नृजातिः *f.*, मनुष्यवर्गः, पुरुषवर्गः.

Humanly, *adv.* पुरुषवत्, मनुष्यवत्, नरवत्, मानुषवत्, मानुषप्रकारेण.

Humbird or humming bird, *s.* कलरवकारी नानावर्णो सूक्ष्मपक्षिभेदः.

Humble, *a.* नम्रबुद्धिः -द्धिः -द्धि, नम्रचेताः -ताः -तः (स्), नम्रः -म्रा -म्रं, विनम्रः -म्रा -म्रं, नम्रशीलः -ला -लं, विनतचेताः &c., विनतः -ता -तं, विनयी -यिनी -यि (न्), विनीतः -ता -तं, सविनयः -या -यं, निर्विण्णः -ण्णा -ण्णं, निर्विण्णचेताः &c., अगर्व्वः -र्व्वा -र्व्वं, गर्व्वहीनः -ना -नं, दर्पहीनः -ना -नं, दर्परहितः -ता -तं, दम्भरहितः -ता -तं, वीतदम्भः -म्भा -म्भं, निरहङ्कारः -रा -रं, अनहङ्कारी -रिणी -रि (न्), अनहङ्कृतः -ता -तं, निरहङ्कारी &c., निरभिमानः -ना -नं, अभिमानहीनः -ना -नं, अभिमानशून्यः -न्या -न्यं, अनभिमानी -निनी -नि (न्), अनुद्धतः -ता -तं, वश्यात्मा -त्मा -त्म (न्).—(Low) अपकृष्टः -ष्टा -ष्टं, नीचः -चा -चं, अधमः -मा -मं, प्राकृतः -ती -तं, कृपणः -णा -णं.

To humble, *v. a.* अपकृष् (c. 1. -कर्षति, c. 6. -कृषति -क्रष्टुं), नम् (c. 10. नमयति -यितुं), अवनम्, नम्रीकृ, पत् (c. 10. -पातयति -यितुं), भ्रंश् (c. 10. भ्रंशयति -यितुं), अभिभू (c. 1. -भवति -वितुं), तिरोभू (c. 10. -भावयति -यितुं), दर्पं or गर्व्वं भञ्ज् (c. 7. भनक्ति, भंक्तुं) or हृ (c. 1. हरति, हर्त्तुं).

Humble-bee, *s.* गुञ्जकृत् *m.*, स्वनमोदी *m.* (न्), भृङ्गराजः, भ्रमरः.

Humbled, *p. p.* भग्नदर्पः -र्पा -र्पं, आत्तगर्व्वः -र्व्वा -र्व्वं, हृतगर्व्वः -र्व्वा -र्व्वं, अभिभूतः -ता -तं, पराभूतः -ता -तं, पातितः -ता -तं, नम्रीकृतः -ता -तं, आनतः -ता -तं.

Humbleness, *s.* बुद्धिनम्रता, नम्रता, विनम्रता, नम्रशीलता, विनयः, विनीतिः *f.*, विनतिः *f.*, वश्यता, अनहङ्कारः, अगर्व्वः, गर्व्वहीनता, दर्पहीनता, अनभिमानता, अपकृष्टता.

Humbling, *s.* अभिभवः, अभिभूतिः *f.*, अपकर्षः -र्षणं, दर्पभङ्गः, मानभङ्गः, दर्पहरणं, नम्रीकरणं.

Humbling, *a.* दर्पहः -हा -हं, दर्पहरः -रा -रं, मानहरः -रा -रं.

Humbly, *adv.* सविनयं, नम्रचेतसा, नम्रं, विनम्रं, दर्पं विना, गर्व्वं विना, अगर्व्वेण, निरभिमानेन, अहङ्कारं विना, सनिर्वेदं, निर्विण्णं, अनुद्धतं, कृपणं.

Humbug, *s.* प्रतारणं -णा, कपटः -टं, व्याजः, प्रवञ्चना, छलं, कैतवं.

To humbug, *v. a.* प्रतॄ (c. 10. -तारयति -यितुं), छल् (c. 10. छलयति -यितुं), मुह् (c. 10. मोहयति -यितुं), प्रलभ् (c. 1. -लभते -लब्धुं), अभिसन्धा (c. 3. -दधाति -धातुं).

Hum-drum, *a.* मन्दः -न्दा -न्दं, विरसः -सा -सं, अरसिकः -का -कं, फल्गुः -ल्गुः -ल्गु, कष्टकरः -रा -रं, जडः -डा -डं.

Humectation, *s.* क्लेदनं, आर्द्रीकरणं, आप्लावनं, तेमनं, समुन्दनं.

To humectate, *v. a.* क्लिद् (c. 10. क्लेदयति -यितुं), आप्लु (c. 10. -प्लावयति -यितुं), आर्द्रीकृ, उन्द् (c. 7. उनत्ति, उन्दितुं), समुन्द्, सरसीकृ.

Humerus, *s.* प्रगण्डः.

Humid, *a.* आर्द्रः -र्द्रा -र्द्रं, सार्द्रः -र्द्रा -र्द्रं, तिमितः -ता -तं, स्तिमितः -ता -तं, सरसः -सा -सं, क्लिन्नः -न्ना -न्नं, उन्नः -न्ना -न्नं, समुन्नः -न्ना -न्नं, चोदः -दा -दं.

Humidity, *s.* आर्द्रता, सार्द्रता, क्लेदः, संक्लेदः, क्लिन्नता, सरसता, तेमः, स्तेमः, तेमनं, समुन्दनं, समुन्नता.

Humiliating, *a.* दर्पहः -हा -हं, दर्पहरः -रा -रं, मानहरः -रा -रं.

Humiliation, *s.* मानभङ्गः, मानहानिः *f.*, दर्पभङ्गः, दर्पहरणं, अपकर्षः -र्षणं, अभिभवः, अभिभूतिः *f.*, नम्रता, नम्रीकरणं, विनतिः *f.*, दान्तिः *f.*, नियमनं, दमनं.

Humility, *s.* विनयः, विनीतिः *f.*, विनतिः *f.*, नम्रता, विनम्रता, नम्रशीलता, बुद्धिनम्रता, अनहङ्कारः, अगर्व्वः, गर्व्वहीनता, दर्पहीनता, अनभिमानं, वश्यता, दैन्यं, दीनता, निर्वेदः, निर्विण्णता, अनौद्धत्यं, आनतिः *f.*, सन्नतिः *f.*, अपकृष्टता, कृपणता, कार्पण्यं.

Humorist, *s.* परिहासवेदी *m.* (न्), परिहासशीलः, रसिकः, रसज्ञः, वैहासिकः, हासकरः, विदूषकः, भण्डः, नर्म्मसचिवः, रागी *m.* (न्).

Humorous, *a.* रसिकः -का -कं, रसी -सिनी -सि (न्), रसवान् -वती -वत् (त्), सरसः -सा -सं, परिहासशीलः -ला -लं, हासकरः -री -रं, हासजनकः -का -कं, हास्यः -स्या -स्यं, उपहास्यः -स्या -स्यं, प्रहासी -सिनी -सि (न्), विनोदी -दिनी -दि (न्), कौतुकी -किनी -कि (न्).

Humorously, *adv.* सरसं, रसिकप्रकारेण, हास्यप्रकारेण, रसिकं, हास्यं, विनोदार्थं, परिहासपूर्व्वं.

Humorousness, *s.* रसिकत्वं, रसवत्त्वं, सरसत्वं, परिहासशीलता, हास्यता, उपहास्यता, हासजनकता, विनोदकत्वं.

Humoursome, *s.* (Peevish) वक्रभावः -वा -वं, वक्रशीलः -ला -लं.—(Full of whims) चपलप्रकृतिः -तिः -ति, चपलभावः -वा -वं, चलचित्तः -त्ता -त्तं, छन्दोवान् -वती -वत् (त्), नैकभावाश्रयः -या -यं.

Humour, *s.* (Moisture) क्लेदः -दं, संक्लेदः, स्तेमः, तेमः, जलावसेकः, चिक्लिदं, समुन्दनं, स्नेहः, आर्द्रता.—(Fluid) रसः, जलं; 'of the body,' धातुः *m.*; 'disorder of the humours,' दोषः; 'vitiation of the three humours,' दोषत्रयं.—(Temper of mind) भावः, स्वभावः, शीलः, शीलता -त्वं, प्रकृतिः *f.*; 'good humour,' सद्भावः सत्प्रकृतिः *f.*, सुशीलता, सुप्रकृतिः *f.*; 'bad humour,' असद्भावः, वक्रभावः; 'in a bad humour,' दुष्प्रकृतिः -तिः -ति, दुःशीलः -ला -लं, वक्रभावः -वा -वं.—(Whim) छन्दस् *n.*, छन्दं, मनोलौल्यं, बुद्धिलौल्यं, बुद्धिविलासः, बुद्धिचापल्यं, चापलं, तरङ्गः, लहरी, अवहित्थः *m.*—(Wit) रसः, रसिकता, रसिता, चित्रं, वैदग्ध्यं, कौतुकं.

To humour, *v. a.* अनुवृत् (c. 1. -वर्त्तते -र्त्तितुं), अनुकूल् (c. 10. -कूलयति -यितुं), सन्तुष् (c. 10. -तोषयति -यितुं), परितुष्, अनुरुध् (c. 4. -रुध्यते -ति -रोद्धुं), आराध् (c. 10. -राधयति -यितुं), अनुग्रह् (c. 9. -गृह्णाति -ग्रहीतुं), प्रसद् (c. 10. -सादयति -यितुं), अनुरञ्ज् (c. 10. -रञ्जयति -यितुं), भज् (c. 1. भजति -ते, भक्तुं), लल् (c. 10. लालयति -यितुं), 'to humour one's inclination,' छन्दोऽनुवृत्.—(Suit) युज् (c. 4. युज्यते, c. 10. योजयति -यितुं).

Humoured, *p. p.* अनुवृत्तः -त्ता -त्तं, अनुरुद्धः -द्धा -द्धं, अनुगृहीतः -ता -तं, आराधितः -ता -तं, प्रसादितः -ता -तं, सन्तोषितः -ता -तं.

Humouring, *s.* (Indulging) अनुवर्त्तनं, अनुवृत्तिः *f.*, छन्दोनुवृत्तं, अनुरोधः -धनं, सन्तोषणं, तुष्टिकरणं, तुष्टिदानं, आराधनं, प्रसादनं, प्रीतिकरणं, तर्पणं.

Hump, *s.* गडुः *m.*, स्यगुः *m.*, पृष्ठग्रन्थिः *m.*; 'of a bull, &c.,' ककुद् *f.*, ककुदः -दं, अंसकूटः; 'having a hump,' ककुद्मान् -द्मती -द्मत् (त्), ककुद्मी -द्मिनी -द्मि (न्), न्युब्जः -ब्जा -ब्जं.

HUMP-BACKED, *a.* कुब्जः -ब्जा -ब्जं, कुब्जकः -का -कं, गडुः -डुः -डु, गडुरः -रा -रं, गडुलः -ला -लं, वक्रपृष्ठः -ष्ठा -ष्ठं, उन्नतस्कन्धः -न्धा -न्धं.

HUNCH, *s.* (A hump) गडुः *m.*, स्वगुः *m.*—(A lump) पिण्डः, गण्डका, घनः.

To HUNCH, *v. a.* करागिना तड् (c. 10. ताडयति -यितुं) or आहन् (c. 2. -हन्ति -न्तुं).

HUNCH-BACKED, *a.* गडुपृष्ठः -ष्ठा -ष्ठं. *See* HUMP-BACKED.

HUNDRED, *a.* शतं, शतसंख्यकः -का -कं, एकशतसंख्यकः -का -कं, शतकः -का -कं, दशतिः *f.* The word शतं may be used with the nom. pl. or gen. pl.; as, 'a hundred ancestors,' शतं पितरः or शतं पितॄणां; or in comp., as, 'a hundred years,' वर्षशतं, शतवर्षं; 'a hundred and fifty,' सार्द्धशतं; 'a hundred thousand,' लक्षं -क्षा; 'a hundred millions,' अर्बुदं; 'a hundred years old,' शतायूः -यूः -युः (स्).

HUNDRED, *s.* शतं, शतकः, दशतिः *f.*; 'by hundreds,' शतशस्.

HUNDREDTH, *a.* शततमः -मी -मं, शतः -ती -तं.

HUNGER, *s.* क्षुधा, क्षुत् *f.* (ध्), बुभुक्षा, जिघत्सा, अन्नलिप्सा, आहारलिप्सा, अशनाया -यितं, अन्नायी, क्षारिका; 'hunger and thirst,' क्षुत्पिपासा or -से *f.* du.

To HUNGER, *v. n.* क्षुध् (c. 4. क्षुध्यति, क्षोद्धुं), भुज् in des. (बुभुक्षति -ते -क्षितुं), घस् in des. (जिघत्सति -त्सितुं), अशन (nom. अशनायति -यितुं), अन्नं or आहारं लभ् in des. (लिप्सते -प्सितुं); 'to hunger after righteousness,' धर्म्माय क्षुध्.

HUNGER-BIT, HUNGER-BITTEN, *a.* क्षुधार्त्तः -र्त्ता -र्त्तं, क्षुत्पीडितः -ता -तं.

HUNGERED, *a.* क्षुधितः -ता -तं, बुभुक्षितः -ता -तं, क्षुधार्त्तः -र्त्ता -र्त्तं.

HUNGERLY, *a.* अन्नार्थी -र्थिनी -र्थि (न्), भोजनार्थी &c., आहारार्थी &c.

HUNGER-STARVED, *a.* क्षुदवसन्नः -न्ना -न्नं, क्षुधावसन्नः -न्ना -न्नं, क्षुधार्दितः -ता -तं.

HUNGRY, *a.* क्षुधार्त्तः -र्त्ता -र्त्तं, क्षुधितः -ता -तं, क्षुत्पीडितः -ता -तं, क्षुधापीडितः -ता -तं, क्षुधातुरः -रा -रं, बुभुक्षितः -ता -तं, बुभुक्षुः -क्षुः -क्षु, जिघत्सुः -त्सुः -त्सु, आहारार्थी -र्थिनी -र्थि (न्), अन्नार्थी &c., अन्नलिप्सुः -प्सुः -प्सु, आहारलिप्सुः -प्सुः -प्सु, अशनायितः -ता -तं, क्षुधाव्याकुलः -ला -लं; 'hungry and thirsty,' क्षुत्पिपासितः -ता -तं, क्षुत्तृष्णोपपीडितः -ता -तं.—(Lean) कृशः -शा -शं, अपुष्टः -ष्टा -ष्टं, विपुष्टः -ष्टा -ष्टं.

HUNKS, *s.* कृपणः, कदर्य्यः, धनलोभी *m.* (न्), मितम्पचः.

To HUNT, *v. a.* and *n.* (Chase) मृग् (c. 10. मृगयते -यितुं), मृगयां कृ, आखिट् (c. 1. -खेटति -टितुं), परिकल् (c. 10. -कालयति -यितुं).—(Pursue, follow after, search for) अनुसृ (c. 1. -सरति -सर्त्तुं), अनुधाव् (c. 1. -धावति -वितुं), पश्चाद्धाव्, अनुवृत् (c. 1. -वर्त्तते -र्त्तितुं), पश्चाद्वृत्, अन्विष् (c. 4. -इष्यति -एषितुं).

HUNT, *s.* (Chase) मृगया, मृगव्यं, खेटः -टं, आखेटः, आक्षोदनं, आच्छोदनं, पापर्द्धिः *f.*, पराधिः *f.*—(Pursuit, search) अनुसरणं, अनुधावनं, अन्वेषणं -णा, पर्य्येषणा, मृगणं, मार्गणं.

HUNTED, *p. p.* मृगितः -ता -तं, अनुसृतः -ता -तं, अनुधावितः -ता -तं, आखेटितः -ता -तं, अन्विष्टः -ष्टा -ष्टं, अन्वेषितः -ता -तं.

HUNTER, *s.* (One who pursues wild animals) व्याधः, मृगयुः *m.*, लुब्धकः, मृगवधाजीवः, मृगजीवनः, आखेटकः, मृगादिपशुहन्ता *m.* (न्तृ), सौकरिकः, अन्ध्रः, खड्गिकः; 'with nets,' जालिकः.—(Horse) मृगयाश्वः.

HUNTING, *s.* मृगया, मृगव्यं, खेटः -टं, आखेटः, आक्षोदनं, आच्छोदनं, पापर्द्धिः *f.*, पराधिः *f.*; 'hunting-knife,' कर्त्तरिका; 'hunting-dog,' आखेटकः श्वा *m.* (न्), मृगयाकुक्कुरः; 'hunting appointments,' मृगयावेशः.—(Pursuit, search) अनुसरणं, अनुधावनं, अन्वेषणं -णा, पर्य्येषणा, मृगणं, मार्गणं.

HUNTING-HORN, *s.* मृगयाशङ्खः, मृगव्यशङ्खः, व्याधवादितं शृङ्गं or विषाणं.

HUNTRESS, *s.* व्याधी *f.*, व्याधस्त्री, आखेटकी, मृगयाकारिणी.

HUNTSMAN, *s.* मृगयाकारी *m.* (न्), मृगव्यकारी *m.*, मृगयुः *m.*, आखेटकः.

HUNTSMANSHIP, *s.* मृगयाविद्या, मृगव्यविद्या, आखेटविद्या.

HURDLE, *s.* काष्ठशलाकानिर्म्मितम् अवरोधकं or आवरणं, स्तम्भकरः.

HURDY-GURDY, *s.* कर्कशशब्दः सतन्त्रीवाद्यविशेषः.

To HURL, *v. a.* क्षिप् (c. 6. क्षिपति, क्षेप्तुं), प्रक्षिप्, अस् (c. 4. अस्यति, असितुं), प्रास्, ईर् (c. 10. ईरयति, -यितुं), उदीर्, समीर्, मुच् (c. 6. मुञ्चति, मोक्तुं), प्रमुच्, सृज् (c. 6. सृजति, स्रष्टुं), व्यवसृज्, पत् (c. 10. पातयति -यितुं), प्रहृ (c. 1. -हरति -ते -हर्त्तुं), प्रेष् (c. 10. प्रेषयति -यितुं, rt. इष्), उद्गुर् (c. 6. -गुरते -रितुं); 'to hurl stones,' शिलाप्रहरणं कृ; 'is hurled down,' निपात्यते.

HURL, *s.* (Throw) क्षेपः -पणं, असनं, पातनं.—(Tumult) तुमुलं, कोलाहलः, विप्लवः, डिम्बः.

HURLED, *p. p.* क्षिप्तः -प्ता -प्तं, प्रक्षिप्तः -प्ता -प्तं, अस्तः -स्ता -स्तं, प्रास्तः -स्ता -स्तं, पातितः -ता -तं, ईरितः -ता -तं, विसृष्टः -ष्टा -ष्टं.

HURLER, *s.* क्षेपकः, क्षेप्ता *m.* (प्तृ), असिता *m.* (तृ), प्रासकः.

HURLING, *s.* क्षेपणं, असनं, पातनं; 'of stones,' शिलाप्रहरणं.

HURLY-BURLY, *s.* कोलाहलः, हलहलाशब्दः, कालकीलः -लकः, तुमुलं.

HURRAH, *exclam.* जयशब्दः, प्रशंसाशब्दः, आनन्दशब्दः.

HURRICANE, *s.* चक्रवातः, प्रभञ्जनः, उत्पातवातः, अतिवातः, वात्या, वात्यावेगः, चण्डवातः, प्रचण्डवायुः *m.*, वाताली, वातरूषः, वातगुल्मः, झञ्झावातः, झञ्झा, जवानिलः, भूमिः *m.*, निर्घातः, पवनाघातः.

HURRIED, *a.* त्वरितः -ता -तं; 'spoken fast,' त्वरितोदितः -ता -तं, निरस्तः -स्ता -स्तं.

HURRIEDLY, *adv.* त्वरितं, सत्वरं, द्रुतं, शीघ्रं, अविलम्बितं, सरभसं.

To HURRY, *v. a.* त्वर् (c. 10. त्वरयति -यितुं), सन्त्वर्.—(Hurry along, drive, impel) कृष् (c. 1. कर्षति, क्रष्टुं), समाकृष्, प्रेर् (c. 10. -ईरयति -यितुं), प्रणुद् (c. 6. -णुदति -णोत्तुं).

To HURRY, *v. n.* त्वर् (c. 1. त्वरते -रितुं), सन्त्वर्, अतित्वर्, शीघ्र (nom. शीघ्रायते), सत्वरं or शीघ्रं गम् (c. 1. गच्छति, गन्तुं) or चर् (c. 1. चरति -रितुं).

HURRY, *s.* त्वरा, सम्भ्रमः, संवेगः, आवेगः, वेगः, रभसः, क्षिप्रकारिता, त्वरितगतिः *f.*, आशुगमनं, शीघ्रता.—(Bustle) सम्भ्रमः, आकुलत्वं, व्यग्रता, व्यस्तता; 'in a hurry,' त्वरितः -ता -तं, सम्भ्रमी -मिणी -मि (न्), सम्भ्रान्तः -न्ता -न्तं, आकुलः -ला -लं.

HURRY-SKURRY, *adv.*ससम्भ्रमं, सरभसं, सावेगं, व्याकुलं, सम्भ्रमेण.

To HURT, *v. a.* हिंस् (c. 7. हिनस्ति, c. 1. हिंसति -सितुं), विहिंस्, उपहिंस्, आहिंस्, क्षतं कृ, क्षतिं कृ, क्षण् (c. 8. क्षणोति -णितुं), परिक्षण्, अपकृ, द्रोहं कृ, अर्द् (c. 10. अर्दयति -यितुं), समर्द्, पीड् (c. 10. पीडयति -यितुं), व्यथ् (c. 10. व्यथयति -यितुं), रिष् (c. 1. रेषति, c. 4. रिष्यति, रेषितुं, रेष्टुं), क्षि (c. 5. क्षिणोति, c. 1. क्षयति, क्षेतुं), हन् (c. 2. हन्ति -न्तुं), विहन्, उपहन्, तुद् (c. 6. तुदति, तोत्तुं), नश् (c. 10. नाशयति -यितुं), दुष् (c. 10. दूषयति -यितुं), द्रुह् (c. 4. द्रुह्यति, द्रोग्धुं); 'you hurt me by your sharp words,' तुदसि मे मर्म्माणि वाक्शरैः.

HURT, *s.* क्षतं, क्षतिः *f.*, परिक्षतं, हिंसा -सनं, अपकारः, अपकृतं, द्रोहः, अभिद्रोहः, अपायः, क्षयः, उपक्षयः, पीडा, व्यथा, आघातः, बाधः, नाशः, दोषः, विहेठः -ठनं, हानिः *f.*, रिष्टं.

HURT, *p. p.* क्षतः -ता -तं, परिक्षतः -ता -तं, विक्षतः -ता -तं, हिंसितः -ता -तं, विहिंसितः -ता -तं, अपकृतः -ता -तं, कृतापकारः -रा -रं, अर्दितः

-ता -तं, पीडितः -ता -तं, निपीडितः -ता -तं, व्यथितः -ता -तं, विहतः -ता -तं, दूषितः -ता -तं, रिष्टः -ष्टा -ष्टं.

HURTER, *s.* क्षतकारी *m.* (न्), अपकारी *m.*, हिंसकः, रेष्टा *m.* (ष्टृ).

HURTFUL, *a.* हिंस्रः -स्रा -स्रं, हिंसालुः -लुः -लु -लुकः -का -कं, हिंसात्मकः -का -कं, अपकारी -रिणी -रि (न्), अपकारकः -का -कं, आपकरः -री -रं, क्षतिकारी &c., क्षतिजनकः -का -कं, अहितः -ता -तं, नृशंसः -सा -सं, शरारुः -रुः -रु, शारुकः -का -कं, घातुकः -का -कं, उपघातकः -का -कं, हानिजनकः -का -कं, बाधकः -का -कं, सबाधः -धा -धं, रिष्वः -ष्वा -ष्वं, अनिष्टजनकः -का -कं, द्रोही -हिणी -हि (न्).

HURTFULLY, *adv.* हिंसापूर्व्वं, हिंसया, क्षतपूर्व्वं, सक्षतं, हिंस्रं, हिंस्रप्रकारेण, अहितं, यथा हिंसा क्रियते तथा, यथा क्षतं जायते तथा.

HURTFULNESS, *s.* हिंस्रता -त्वं, हिंसालुता, क्षतिकारिता, अहितत्वं.

To HURTLE, *v. a.* समाहन् (c. 2. -हन्ति -न्तुं), परस्परसमाघातं कृ.—(Whirl) भ्रम् (c. 10. भ्रमयति -यितुं).

HURTLESS, *a.* अहिंस्रः -स्रा -स्रं, अनपकारी -रिणी -रि (न्).

HUSBAND, *s.* (Man married to a woman) पतिः *m.*, भर्त्ता *m.* (र्तृ), स्वामी *m.* (न्), वरः, वोढा *m.* (ढृ), विवोढा *m.*, वरयिता *m.* (तृ), कान्तः, परिणेता *m.* (तृ), परिणायकः, नाथः, दयितः, इष्टः, प्रियः -यतमः, धवः, उपयन्ता *m.* (न्तृ), परिग्रहीता *m.* (तृ), क्षेत्रिकः, हृदयेशः, प्राणेशः, जीवितेशः, प्राणनाथः, प्राणाधिनाथः, वेत्ता *m.* (त्तृ); 'husband and wife,' दम्पती *m.* du., जम्पती *m.* du., भार्य्यापती *m.* du., जायापती *m.* du.; 'a husband's brother,' देवा *m.* (वृ), देवः, देवरः, देवलः; 'a second husband,' दिधिषुः *m.* -षूः *m.*—(Economist) परिमितव्ययी *m.* (न्), अल्पव्ययी *m.*—(Cultivator) कृषकः, कृषिकारी *m.* (न्).

To HUSBAND, *v. a.* (Economize) परिमितव्ययं कृ, न व्ययीकृ, न विक्षिप् (c. 6. -क्षिपति -क्षेप्तुं); 'to husband one's time,' न कालक्षेपं कृ.—(Cultivate) कृष् (c. 6. कृषति, क्रष्टुं).

HUSBANDLESS, *a.* पतिहीना, भर्तृहीना, भर्तृरहिता, निर्णाथा, अनाथा.

HUSBANDLY, *a.* परिमितव्ययः -या -यं, गृहव्यापाराभिज्ञः -ज्ञा -ज्ञं.

HUSBANDMAN, *s.* (Cultivator, farmer) कृषकः, कृषिकः, कर्षकः, कार्षकः, कार्षिकः, कृषीवलः, क्षेत्रकर्षकः, क्षेत्रिकः, क्षेत्री *m.* (न्). क्षेत्राजीवः, कृषिजीवी *m.* (न्), हालिकः, क्षेत्रपतिः *m.*, कृषाणः, कीनाशः, आर्द्धिकः.—(Man of the third tribe) वैश्यः, विट् *m.* (श्), ऊरुजः, अरव्यः, अर्य्यः, भूमिस्पृक् *m.* (श्).

HUSBANDRY, *s.* (Agriculture) कृषिः *f.*, कार्षिः *f.*, कृषिकर्म्म *n.* (न्), कृषिविद्या, अनृतं, वैश्यक्रिया, वैश्यवृत्तिः *f.*, हलभृतिः *f.*, कर्षणं, कृष्टिः *f.*, प्रमृतं.—(Frugality, economy) परिमितव्ययः, गृहकर्म्मनयः, गृहकर्म्मनिर्वाहविद्या.

HUSH, *exclam.* शान्तं, शान्तं शान्तं, शब्दं मा कुरु, तूष्णीम्भव, मौनीभव, निःशब्दो भव, वाचं यम, वाग्रोधं कुरु, हूम्, नीचैस्.

To HUSH, *v. a.* शम् (c. 10. शमयति -यितुं), प्रशम्, उपशम्, सान्त्व् (c. 10. सान्त्वयति -यितुं), शब्दशान्तिं कृ, शब्दरोधं कृ, निःशब्दीकृ.

To HUSH, *v. n.* शम् (c. 4. शाम्यति, शमितुं), उपशम्, प्रशम्, प्रसद् (c. 1. -सीदति -सत्तुं), शान्तीभू, निःशब्दीभू, मौनीभू, तूष्णीम्भू.

HUSHED, *p. p.* शान्तः -न्ता -न्तं, शमितः -ता -तं, प्रशमितः -ता -तं.

HUSK, *s.* तुषः -षा, तुसः, त्वक् *f.* (च्), कञ्चुकः, कोशः, पुटः, आवेष्टनं; 'of corn,' धान्यत्वक् *f.* (च्), धान्यतुषः.—(Chaff) बुसं, बुषं, तुच्छं, तुच्छधान्यकं, धान्यकल्कं; 'rice in husk,' शुष्काक्षं.

To HUSK, *v. a.* निस्तुष (nom. निस्तुषयति -यितुं), निस्तुषीकृ, तुषीकृ, निस्त्वच (nom. निस्त्वचयति -यितुं), निस्त्वचीकृ, त्वच (nom. त्वचयति -यितुं), तुषं or त्वचं हृ (c. 1. हरति, हर्त्तुं).

HUSKED, *p. p.* (Stripped of the husk) निस्तुषितः -ता -तं, निस्तुषः -षा -षं, निस्त्वचः -चा -चं, तुषीकृतः -ता -तं.—(Having a husk) तुषरः -रा -रं, तुषवान् -वती -वत् (त्), त्वग्युक्तः -क्ता -क्तं.

HUSKY, *a.* (Having husks, consisting of husks) सतुषः -षा -षं, बहुतुषवान् -वती -वत् (त्), तुषमयः -यी -यं, त्वङ्मयः -यी -यं.—(Rough, harsh) रूक्षः -क्षा -क्षं, कर्कशः -शा -शं; 'in sound,' रूक्षस्वरः -रा -रं.

HUSSAR, *s.* अश्वारूढः सैन्यः, अश्वारोही *m.* (न्), सादी *m.* (न्).

HUSSY, *s.* पापीयसी, दासीपुत्री, बन्धकी, दुष्टा स्त्री.

HUSTINGS, *s.* काष्ठनिर्म्मितो मञ्चविशेषो यत्र नगरप्रतिनिधिवरणं क्रियते.

To HUSTLE, *v. a.* निरस् (c. 4. -अस्यति -असितुं), निःसृ (c. 10. -सारयति -यितुं), निराकृ, बहिष्कृ, सबाध् (c. 1. -बाधते -धितुं), संक्षुभ् (c. 10. -क्षोभयति -यितुं).

HUSWIFE, *s.* गृहिणी, कुटुम्बिनी, गेहिनी, स्वामिनी, गृहमेधिनी, गृहव्यापारकुशला.

HUSWIFERY, *s.* गृहव्यापारकुशलता, गृहकार्य्यदक्षता, गृहकर्म्मनिपुणता, गृहमेधित्वं, परिमितव्ययः.

HUT, *s.* उटजः, कुटीरः, पर्णशाला, कुटेरः, कुटिरं, सहोटजः, तृणौकस् *n.*, तृणकुटी, कुट्टिमः, वेश्म *n.* (न्), कायमानं.

HUTCH, *s.* (Bin) धान्यकोष्ठकं, कुशूलः, पिटः.—(For rabbits) शशकागारः, शशकरक्षणी.

HUZZA, *s.* जयशब्दः, जयनादः, आनन्दशब्दः, प्रणादः, जयध्वनिः *m.*, जयकोलाहलः, जयारवः, प्रशंसानादः.

To HUZZA, *v. n.* जयशब्दं कृ, प्रणादं कृ, जयप्रणादं कृ.

HYACINTH, *s.* सुगन्धपुष्प ओषधिभेदः, सुगन्धिकुसुमा.

HYBRID, *a.* सङ्कीर्णजातिः -तिः -ति, सङ्कीर्णजातीयः -या -यं, सङ्करजातः -ता -तं, सङ्कीर्णः -र्णा -र्णं.

HYDRA, *s.* जलव्यालः, जलभुजङ्गमः, कविकल्पितो बहुमस्तकविशिष्टो वृहन् जलव्यालः.

HYDRAULIC, HYDRAULICAL, *a.* जलचलनविषयः -या -यं, चलनजलसम्बन्धी -न्धिनी -न्धि (न्), जङ्गमजलसम्बन्धी &c.

HYDRAULICS, *s.* चलनजलविद्या, जङ्गमजलविद्या, जलचलनविषया विद्या.

HYDROCELE, *s.* कोषवृद्धिः *f.*, मुष्कवृद्धिः *f.*, कुरण्डः.

HYDROCEPHALUS, *s.* जलमस्तकः, उदकमस्तकः, मस्तकाध्मानं.

HYDRODYNAMICS, *s.* जलगुणविषया विद्या, जलशक्तिविषया विद्या.

HYDROGEN, *s.* जलकरः, जलजं, जलजो वायुः, जलजो वाष्पः.

HYDROGRAPHER, *s.* समुद्रवेलादिपत्रलेखकः, नदीसमुद्रादिपत्रलेखकः, समुद्रलेखकः, समुद्रालेख्यकृत् *m.*, वेलालेख्यकृत् *m.*

HYDROGRAPHICAL, *a.* समुद्रलिखनसम्बन्धी -न्धिनी -न्धि (न्).

HYDROGRAPHY, *s.* समुद्रलिखनं, समुद्रलिखनविद्या, नदीसमुद्रादिपत्रलिखनं, समुद्रवेलादिविवरणं.

HYDROMANCY, *s.* जलादिलक्षणात् शुभाशुभदर्शनं or भविष्यदनुमानं or अनागतवृत्तसूचनं or भाविविषयप्रदर्शनं.

HYDROMEL, *s.* जलसंसृष्टं मधु, जलमधु *n.*, जलमाक्षिकं, मधु *n.*

HYDROMETER, *s.* जलपरिमापकयन्त्रं, जलमापनी.

HYDROPATHY, *s.* शीतजलप्रयोगेण रोगचिकित्सा, जलोपचारः.

HYDROPHOBIA, *s.* अलर्करोगः, जलभयं, अलर्कदंशनप्रयुक्तो जलभयरोगः.

HYDROPIC, HYDROPICAL, *a.* जलोदरी -रिणी -रि (न्), जलोदरीयः -या -यं.

HYDROPSY, *s.* जलोदरं -री, उदरी, उदकोदरं, आध्मानं, जठरामयः.

HYDROSTATICS, *s.* स्थावरजलविषया or अजङ्गमजलविषया विद्या, जलादिद्रवद्रव्यधर्म्मविषया विद्या.

HYEMAL, *a.* शीतकालीनः -ना -नं, हैमनः -नी -नं -निकः -की -कं.

Hyena, *s.* तरक्षुः *m.*, तरक्षुकः, तरक्षः, तर्क्षुः *m.*, मृगाजीवः, मृगादनः, युयुक्खुरः.

Hygrometer, *s.* क्लेदपरिमापकयन्त्रं, तेमपरिमापकः.

Hymen, *s.* विवाहाधिष्ठात्री देवता, विवाहाधिष्ठाता *m.* (तृ).

Hymeneal, *a.* वैवाहिकः -की -कं, विवाहीयः -या -यं, उद्वाहिकः -की -कं, पाणिग्रहणिकः -की -कं.

Hymn, *s.* स्तुतिगीतं, ईश्वरस्तुतिगीतं, स्तुतिगानं, गीतं, सङ्कीर्तं, गानं, भक्तिगानं, गाथा, गेयं, खेलिः *f.*, स्तोत्रं, सूक्तं; 'a chanter of hymns,' सुम्नयुः *m.*, गायकः, उद्गाता *m.* (तृ).

To hymn, *v. a.* (Celebrate in song) सङ्कीर्तद्वारेण स्तु (c. 2. स्तौति, स्तोतुं) or स्तुतिं कृ or प्रशंस् (c. 1. -शंसति -सितुं), उपवीण (nom. उपवीणयति -यितुं).

To hymn, *v. n.* गै (c. 1. गायति, गातुं), उद्गै, प्रगै, सुम्न (nom. सुम्नायते), स्तुतिं पठ् (c. 1. पठति -ठितुं), स्तुतिपाठं कृ.

Hymned, *p. p.* उपगीतः -ता -तं, उपगीयमानः -ना -नं, स्तुतः -ता -तं, संस्तुतः -ता -तं, स्तूयमानः -ना -नं.

Hyp, *s.* विषादः, अवसादः, अवसन्नता, उद्वेगः, ग्लानिः *f.*, खेदः.

To hyp, *v. a.* विषद् (c. 10.-षादयति -यितुं), विषण्णीकृ, ग्लानीकृ, उद्विग्नीकृ.

Hyperbole, *s.* अत्युक्तिः *f.*, अतिशयोक्तिः *f.*, चित्रोक्तिः *f.*, अधिकोक्तिः *f.*, अधिकं, वागाधिक्यं, वागुपचयः, वाक्यबाहुल्यं, अतिवर्णना, सत्यातिक्रमः, याथार्थ्यातिक्रमः, यथार्थोल्लङ्घनं, सत्यातिरिक्ता कथा.

Hyperbolic, hyperbolical, *a.* अत्युक्तिपूर्व्वः -र्व्वा -र्व्वं, अत्युक्तिमान् -मती -मत् (त्), अधिकः -का -कं, अधिकवाङ्मयः -यी -यं, अतिक्रान्तसत्यः -त्या -त्यं, उल्लङ्घितसत्यः -त्या -त्यं.

Hyperbolically, *adv.* अत्युक्त्या, अत्युक्तिपूर्व्वं, अतिशयोक्त्या, सत्यातिक्रमेण.

To hyperbolize, *v. n.* अत्युक्तिं कृ, अतिशयोक्तिं कृ, अतिवर्णनं कृ, अतिशयोक्त्या वद् (c. 1. वदति -दितुं).

Hyperborean, *a.* उत्तरः -रा -रं, उत्तरदिश्यः -श्या -श्यं, उत्तरीयः -या -यं, उदङ् -दीची -दक् (च्), उदीचीनः -ना -नं, उत्तरदिक्सम्बन्धी -न्धिनी -न्धि (न्); 'a hyperborean,' उत्तरदेशजः.

Hypercritic, *s.* अतिशयेन गुणदोषपरीक्षकः, एकान्ततो गुणदोषनिरूपकः or दोषग्राही *m.* (न्), वितण्डकः.

Hypercriticism, *s.* अतिशयेन गुणदोषपरीक्षा or गुणदोषनिरूपणं, वितण्डा, अतिवितण्डा.

Hyphen, *s.* सम्बन्धचिह्नं, संयोगचिह्नं, सम्बन्धसूचकं चिह्नं or अङ्कः.

Hypochondres, hypochondria, *s.* कुपितवायुः *m.*, वायुरोगः, विषादः, विषण्णता, अवसादः, उद्वेगः.

Hypochondriac, hypochondriacal, *a.* कुपितवायुग्रस्तः -स्ता -स्तं, विषादी -दिनी -दि (न्), विषण्णः -ण्णा -ण्णं, अन्यमनाः -नाः -नः (स्), चिन्ताकुलः -ला -लं, उद्विग्नः -ग्ना -ग्नं.

Hypocrisy, *s.* कुहना -निका, दम्भः, कुहकवृत्तिः *f.*, धर्म्मोपधा, मिथ्याधर्म्मः -र्म्मत्वं, कपटधर्म्मः, धर्म्मविषये छद्म *n.* (न्), छद्मवेशः or कापट्यं, कुक्कुटिः *f.* -टी, काल्पनिकता, धर्म्मध्वजमात्रं, आर्य्यरूपता, आर्य्यवेशधारणं, मघः, मक्षः.

Hypocrite, *s.* दम्भी *m.* (न्), दाम्भिकः, कुहकः, कुहकवृत्तिः *m.*, कपटधर्म्मी *m.* (न्), कपटी *m.* (न्), आर्य्यवेशधारी *m.* (न्), वेशधारी *m.*, धर्म्मध्वजी *m.* (न्), आर्य्यरूपः, आर्य्यलिङ्गी *m.* (न्), छद्मतापसः, कपटतपस्वी *m.* (न्), कपटव्रती *m.* (न्), लिङ्गवृत्तिः *m.*, छद्मवेशी *m.* (न्), कपटवेशी *m.* (न्), बकव्रती *m.* (न्), वैडालव्रतिकः, कौक्कुटिकः, कुयोगी *m.* (न्), छन्दपातनः, लोकरञ्जनार्थम् आर्य्यकर्म्मानुष्ठायी *m.* (न्), साधुम्मन्यः.

Hypocritical, *a.* दाम्भिकः -की -कं, दम्भी -म्भिनी -म्भि (न्), कुहनः -ना -नं, कपटी -टिनी -टि (न्), कापटिकः -की -कं, छद्मवेशी -शिनी -शि (न्), छाद्मिकः -की -कं, धर्म्मोपधः -धा -धं, काल्पनिकः -की -कं.

Hypocritically, *adv.* कुहकवत्, दाम्भिकवत्, सदम्भं, सकपटं, मिथ्याधर्म्मेण.

Hypogastric, *a.* वास्तेयः -यी -यं; 'hypogastric region,' वस्तिः *m.-f.*

Hypothenuse, *s.* कर्णः, विषमकर्णः.

Hypothesis, *s.* उपन्यासः, प्रतिज्ञा, कल्पना, प्रमेयं, निष्प्रमाणेन उपन्यासः अप्रमाणपूर्व्वं उपन्यासः, अनुमानं, अनुभवः.

Hypothetic, hypothetical, *a.* अप्रमाणपूर्व्वम् उपन्यस्तः -स्ता -स्तं, आनुमानिकः -की -कं, काल्पनिकः -की -कं, सोपन्यासः -सा -सं, निष्प्रमाणः -णा -णं.

Hypothetically, *adv.* उपन्यासक्रमेण, प्रतिज्ञाक्रमेण, सोपन्यासं, निष्प्रमाणेन.

Hyssop, *s.* हिस्सप्संज्ञकः कटुरसविशिष्ट ओषधिभेदः.

Hysteric, hysterical, *a.* मूर्च्छालः -ला -लं, मूर्च्छावान् -वती -वत् (त्), गर्भरोगोपहतत्वाद् मूर्च्छाग्रस्तः -स्ता -स्तं, मूर्च्छनोपहतः -ता -तं.

Hysterics, *s.* जरायुरोगजाता मूर्च्छना or मूर्च्छा, गर्भरोगजात उपसर्गः or आवेशः.

I.

I, *pron.* अहम् (अस्मद्); 'I myself,' सो ऽहं.

Iambic, *s.* ध्वजं, द्व्यक्षरं पदं यस्य पूर्व्वाक्षरं लघु पश्चिमाक्षरं गुरु.

Ibex, *s.* पर्व्वतवासी छागभेदः, अजः, वस्तः, पर्णभोजनः.

Ibis, *s.* पूर्व्वं मिसरदेशे महापूजापुरःसरं पालितः पक्षिभेदः.

Ice, *s.* हिमं, हिमानी, हिमसंहतिः *f.*, हिमसंहतम् उदकं, शीतमुदकं, घनजलं, संहतजलं, घनीकृतजलं, तुषारः, नीहारः, प्रालेयं, अवश्यायः.

To ice, *v. a.* हिमीकृ, तुषारीकृ, हिमरूपं -पां -पं कृ.—(Cool with ice) हिमद्वारेण or तुषारद्वारेण शीतलीकृ or शिशिरीकृ or शीतल (nom. शीतलयति -यितुं).

Iceberg, *s.* हिमपर्व्वतः, हिमराशिः *m.*, तुषारपर्व्वतः, तुषारराशिः *m.*, घनजलराशिः.

Ice-bound, *a.* हिमबद्धः -द्धा -द्धं, हिमपरिवेष्टितः -ता -तं.

Ice-house, *s.* ग्रीष्मकाले हिमरक्षणयोग्यं गृहं, हिमगृहं, हिमगुप्तिः *f.*

Ichneumon, *s.* अङ्गूषः, नकुलः, बभ्रुः *m.*

Ichor, *s.* पूयरक्तं, पूयशोणितं.

Ichthyology, *s.* मत्स्यविद्या, मत्स्यजातिगुणादिविषया विद्या.

Ichthyosaurus, *s.* मत्स्यमकरः.

Icicle, *s.* हिमकणः -णिका, तुषारकणः, नीहारकणः, हिमविन्दुः *m.*

Iciness, *s.* हिमता, हिम्यता, हिमवत्त्वं, हैमता, हैमं, शीतता, शैत्यं.

Iconoclasm, *s.* देवताप्रतिमाभङ्गः, देवतामूर्त्तिभञ्जनं.

Iconoclast, *s.* देवताप्रतिमाभञ्जकः, देवतामूर्त्तिभङ्गकरः.

Iconography, *s.* प्रतिमालिखनं, मूर्त्तिविवरणं, प्रतिमूर्त्तिव्याख्या.

Iconology, *s.* प्रतिमाविद्या, देवतादिप्रतिमानविषया विद्या.

Icy, *a.* हिमः -मा -मं, हिम्यः -म्या -म्यं, हैमः -मी -मं, हिमवान् -वती -वत् (त्), तुषारवान् &c., तौषारः -री -रं, नीहारवान् &c.—(Frigid) शीतः -ता -तं, शीतलः -ला -लं, शिशिरः -रा -रं, जडः -डा -डं.—(Wanting in affection) निःस्नेहः -हा -हं, स्नेहशून्यः -न्या -न्यं.

Idea, *s.* बुद्धिः *f.*, मतिः *f.*, सङ्कल्पः, मनोगतं, मनसिजं, चिन्ता, मनःकल्पितं, मनःकल्पना, कल्पना, वासना, भावना, बोधः; 'with the idea that,' 'under the idea of,' is expressed by the inst. c. of बुद्धिः; as, 'with the idea that he was a tiger,' व्याघ्रबुद्ध्या; 'with the idea of reaching,' प्रापणबुद्ध्या; 'from an idea of (his) incapacity,' अपात्रबुद्ध्या.—(Abstract idea) भावः.

Ideal, *a.* मनसिजः -जा -जं, मनोगतः -ता -तं, मनोजः -जा -जं, मानसिकः

-की -कं, मानसः -सी -सं, मनोभवः -वा -वं, चिन्तोद्भूतः -ता -तं, चिन्ताभवः -वा -वं, काल्पनिकः -की -कं, मनःकल्पितः -ता -तं, मायामयः -यी -यं, मायिकः -की -कं.

IDEALISM, *s.* माया, विषयाभावबुद्धिः *f.*, अमूर्त्तिवादः, अविद्या.

IDEALIST, *s.* मायिकमतावलम्बी *m.* (न्), विषयाभाववादी *m.* (न्).

IDEALLY, *adv.* मनसा, मनसि, बुद्ध्या, बुद्धिमात्रेण, चिन्तया, चिन्तामात्रेण.

IDENTICAL, *a.* अनन्यः -न्या -न्यं, अभिन्नः -न्ना -न्नं, अविभिन्नः -न्ना -न्नं, अनन्यरूपः -पा -पं, अभिन्नरूपः -पा -पं, समः -मा -मं, समानः -ना -नं, समसमानः -ना -नं, तुल्यः -ल्या -ल्यं, अभेदः -दा -दं, अपरः -रा -रं, अविपरीतः -ता -तं, निरस्तभेदः -दा -दं, निर्विशेषः -षा -षं; 'identical with the world,' जगत्समः -मा -मं, जगदात्मकः -का -कं.

IDENTICALLY, *adv.* अनन्यं, अभिन्नं, समं, समानं, समसमानं, अपृथक्.

IDENTIFICATION, *s.* समीकरणं, एकीकरणं, सायुज्यं; 'with Brahma,' ब्रह्मसायुज्यं, ब्रह्मभूयं.

IDENTIFIED, *p. p.* समीकृतः -ता -तं, समानीकृतः -ता -तं, समीभूतः -ता -तं, समानीभूतः -ता -तं, एकीकृतः -ता -तं, सरूपीकृतः -ता -तं.

To IDENTIFY, *v. a.* समीकृ, समानीकृ, एकीकृ, सरूपीकृ, तुल्यीकृ, अनन्यीकृ.

To IDENTIFY, *v. n.* समीभू, समानीभू, एकीभू, सरूपीभू, संयुक्तः -क्ता -क्तं भू.

IDENTITY, *s.* समता, समानता, साम्यं, अभिन्नता, अनन्यता, अभेदः, अविभेदः, अविभिन्नता, सारूप्यं, सरूपता, सात्मता, स्वरूपता, तादात्म्यं; 'identity of class,' सावर्ण्यं, सजातित्वं.

IDES, *s.* रोमीयपञ्जिकायां मासस्य त्रयोदशो दिवसः or पञ्चदशो दिवसः.

IDIOCY, *s.* जडता, जाड्यं, मूढता, मूर्खता, बुद्धिवैकल्यं, बुद्धिन्यूनता, अज्ञता, मेधाभावः, बुद्ध्यभावः, बोधाभावः.

IDIOM, *s.* वाग्रीतिः *f.*, वाग्वृत्तिः *f.*, वाग्व्यापारः, वाग्व्यवहारः, वाग्धारा, विशेषवाक्यं, विशेषवचनं, सविशेषवाक्यं, भाषाविशेषणं, विशेषभाषा, विशिष्टवचनं, विशिष्टवाक्यं, विशिष्टभाषा, भाषालक्षणं, भाषावच्छेदः, अवच्छेदकवाक्यं, सम्प्रदायः.

IDIOMATIC, *a.* भाषाविशेषकः -का -कं, भाषालाक्षणिकः -की -कं, विशेषवाग्रीत्यनुसारी -रिणी -रि (न्), भाषारीत्यनुसारी &c.

IDIOSYNCRASY, *s.* प्रकृतिस्वभावः, शरीरस्वभावः, देहस्वभावः, जातिस्वभावः.

IDIOT, *s.* जडः, मूढः, न्यूनबुद्धिः *m.*, न्यूनधीः *m.*, बुद्धिविकलः, विकलबुद्धिः *m.*, निर्बुद्धिः *m.*, बुद्धिहीनः, हतबुद्धिः *m.*, हतज्ञानः, मूर्खः, अज्ञः, निर्बोधः, न्यूनपञ्चाशद्भावः, पामरः, बर्बरः, वैधेयः, बालिशः, यथाजातः.

IDIOTCY, *s.* *See* IDIOCY.

IDIOTIC, *a.* जडः -डा -डं, मूढः -ढा -ढं, मूर्खः -र्खा -र्खं, न्यूनबुद्धिः -द्धिः -द्धि, न्यूनधीः -धीः -धि, निर्बुद्धिः -द्धिः -द्धि, अल्पबुद्धिः -द्धिः -द्धि, निर्बोधः -धा -धं, बुद्धिविकलः -ला -लं, बालिशः -शा -शं, वैधेयः -यी -यं.

IDIOTISM, *s.* (Peculiarity of expression) विशेषवाक्यं, विशेषभाषा, भाषाविशेषणं, वाग्रीतिः *f.*, विशेषवाग्रीतिः *f.*—(Idiotcy) जडता, जाड्यं, मूढता, बुद्धिवैकल्यं, बुद्धिन्यूनता.

IDLE, *a.* (Averse to labour, doing nothing) अलसः -सा -सं, आलस्यः -स्या -स्यं, निष्कर्म्मा -र्म्मा -र्म्म (न्), निष्कर्म्मकः -का -कं, अकर्म्मशीलः -ला -लं, अकर्म्मा &c., कर्म्मरहितः -ता -तं, कार्य्यशून्यः -न्या -न्यं, निर्व्यापारः -रा -रं, अव्यापारी -रिणी -रि (न्), अक्रियः -या -यं, निरुद्योगः -गा -गं -गी -गिनी -गि (न्), निरुत्साहः -हा -हं, अनुद्योगः -गा -गं, निरुद्यमः -मा -मं, निश्चेष्टः -ष्टा -ष्टं, कार्य्यपराङ्मुखः -खा -खं, अकर्म्मकृत् *m. f. n.*, कर्म्मविमुखः -खा -खं, उदासीनः -ना -नं, सावकाशः -शा -शं, कर्म्मद्वेषी -षिणी -षि (न्); 'to be idle,' उदास् (c. 2. -आस्ते -आसितुं), अलसीभू.—(Vain, useless) निरर्थकः -का -कं, अनर्थकः -का -कं, व्यर्थः -र्था -र्थं, मोघः -घा -घं, निष्प्रयोजनः -ना -नं, किमर्थः -र्था -र्थं, असद्वद्यः -द्या -द्यं; 'idle talk,' आलस्यवचनं, वृथाकथा; 'idle talker,' असद्वद्यभाषकः.

To IDLE, *v. n.* आलस्यं कृ, अलसीभू, कालक्षेपं कृ, कालहरणं कृ, कालव्ययं कृ, कालं क्षिप् (c. 6. क्षिपति, क्षेप्तुं), उदास् (c. 2. -आस्ते -आसितुं).

IDLENESS, *s.* आलस्यं, अलसता -त्वं, अकर्म्मशीलता, कार्य्यप्रद्वेषः, कार्य्यपराङ्मुखता, कर्म्मविमुखता, अनुद्योगः, अव्यापारः, कार्य्यशून्यता, निष्कर्म्मत्वं, उदासीनता, कालक्षेपः.

IDLER, *s.* अलसजनः, आलस्यकारी *m.* (न्), निष्कर्म्मकः, निर्व्यापारः, अव्यापारी *m.* (न्), मुखनिरीक्षकः, लालाटिकः, कालक्षेपकः, कार्य्यपुटः.

IDLY, *adv.* अलसवत्, अलसं, आलस्येन, सालस्यं, उदासीनवत्.—(Vainly) वृथा, मुधा, असद्वद्यं, निरर्थकं.

IDOL, *s.* देवताप्रतिमा -मानं, देवप्रतिमा, देवतामूर्त्तिः *f.*, देवमूर्त्तिः *f.*, देवता, दैवतः -तं, प्रतिमा -मानं, विग्रहः, देवताविग्रहः, देवताप्रतिमूर्त्तिः *f.*, ठक्कुरः, पुत्तलिका; 'attendant on an idol,' देवलः, देवाजीवी *m.* (न्), देवाजीवः, प्रतिमापरिचारकः.

IDOLATER, *s.* देवतार्च्चकः, देवताभ्यर्च्चकः, देवार्च्चकः, देवतापूजकः, प्रतिमापूजकः, देवप्रतिमापूजकः, देवतोपासकः, देवतासेवी *m.* (न्), विग्रहसेवी, प्रतिमासेवी *m.* (न्) -सेविता *m.* (तृ).

IDOLATRESS, *s.* देवतार्च्चिका, देवताभ्यर्च्चिका, प्रतिमापूजयित्री, देवतापूजका, देवतोपासिका, प्रतिमासेविनी, प्रतिमासेविणी.

To IDOLATRIZE, *v. n.* देवताः पूज् (c. 10. पूजयति -यितुं), प्रतिमाः पूज् or अर्च् (c. 1. अर्चति -र्चितुं) or अभ्यर्च्, देवतार्चनं कृ, प्रतिमापूजां कृ.

IDOLATROUS, *a.* देवतार्च्चकः -का -कं, प्रतिमापूजकः -का -कं, देवप्रतिमापूजकः -का -कं, प्रतिमापूजाविशिष्टः -ष्टा -ष्टं, प्रतिमापूजासम्बन्धी -न्धिनी -न्धि (न्).

IDOLATRY, *s.* देवतार्च्चनं -ना, देवताभ्यर्च्चनं -ना, देवताभ्यर्च्चा, देवार्च्चा, देवतापूजा, प्रतिमापूजा, देवप्रतिमापूजा, देवतोपासना, प्रतिमासेवा, विग्रहपूजा, मूर्त्तिसेवा, देवताराधना -नं, देवतोपचर्य्या.

IDOLIST, *s.* प्रतिमापूजकः, मूर्त्तिपूजयिता *m.* (तृ), प्रतिमानसेवी *m.* (न्).

To IDOLIZE, *v. a.* अतिप्रेम कृ, अत्यनुरागवान् -वती -वत् or अत्यन्तानुरक्तः -क्ता -क्तं भू or अस्, अतिशयेन or एकान्ततः प्री (c. 4. प्रीयते, प्रेतुं) all with instr. or loc. c., देववत् पूज् (c. 10. पूजयति -यितुं) or भज् (c. 1. भजते, भक्तुं).

IDONEOUS, *a.* युक्तः -क्ता -क्तं, उपयुक्तः -क्ता -क्तं, योग्यः -ग्या -ग्यं.

IDYL, *s.* पशुपालनादिविषयम् अबहुश्लोकं क्षुद्रकाव्यं.

IF, *conj.* यदि, चेत् usually used with the indicative; as, 'if he live he will behold prosperity,' यदि जीवति भद्राणि पश्यति; 'if there be need of me,' यदि मया प्रयोजनम् अस्ति; 'if avarice were abandoned, who would be poor?' तृष्णा चेत् परित्यक्ता को दरिद्रः.—(As if) इव.—(If so) यद्येवं.—(If not) यदि न, न चेत्, नो चेत्, न वा.

IGNEOUS, *a.* आग्नेयः -यी -यं, अग्निमयः -यी -यं, अग्निमान् -मती -मत् (त्), अग्नितुल्यः -ल्या -ल्यं, अग्निस्वभावः -वा -वं, कार्शानवः -वी -वं.

To IGNIFY, *v. a.* अग्निसात्कृ, अग्निरूपं -पां -पं कृ, अग्निवत् कृ.

IGNIS-FATUUS, *s.* मिथ्याग्निः *m.*, मिथ्यादीप्तिः *f.*, मिथ्याद्युतिः *f.*, पिशाचदीपिका.

To IGNITE, *v. a.* ज्वल् (c. 10. ज्वालयति, ज्वलयति -यितुं), प्रज्वल्, संज्वल्, समिन्ध् (c. 7. -इन्द्धे -इन्धितुं), दीप् (c. 10. दीपयति -यितुं), प्रदीप्, सन्दीप्, आदीप्, उद्दीप्, सन्धुक्ष् (c. 10. -धुक्षयति -यितुं), दह् (c. 1. दहति, दग्धुं), तप् (c. 10. तापयति -यितुं), समिद्धीकृ, ज्योतिस्सात्कृ.

To IGNITE, *v. n.* समिन्ध् in pass. (-इध्यते), समिद्धीभू, दीप् (c. 4. दीप्यते, दीपितुं), सन्दीप्, प्रदीप्, ज्वल् (c. 1. ज्वलति -लितुं), प्रज्वल्, दह् (c. 4. दह्यति, दग्धुं), सन्धुक्ष् (c. 1. -धुक्षते -क्षितुं), अग्निदीप्तः -प्ता -प्तं भू.

IGNITED, *p. p.* समिद्धः -द्धा -द्धं, इद्धः -द्धा -द्धं, ज्वलितः -ता -तं, प्रज्वालितः -ता -तं, दीपितः -ता -तं, उद्दीप्तः -प्ता -प्तं, प्रदीप्तः -प्ता -प्तं, सन्धुक्षितः -ता -तं, सन्तप्तः -प्ता -प्तं.

IGNITIBLE, *a.* दीपनीयः -या -यं, दीप्यः -प्या -प्यं, ज्वलनीयः -या -यं, ज्वलनशीलः -ला -लं, दाह्यः -ह्या -ह्यं.

IGNITION, *s.* इन्धनं, समिन्धनं, ज्वलनं, दीपनं, उद्दीपनं, दहनं, तापः.

IGNOBLE, *a.* (Of low birth) अकुलीनः -ना -नं, दुष्कुलीनः -ना -नं, अकुलः -ला -लं, हीनजातिः -तिः -ति, न्यग्जातिः -तिः -ति, अपकृष्टजातिः -तिः -ति.—(Mean, base) नीचः -चा -चं, अपकृष्टः -ष्टा -ष्टं, निकृष्टः -ष्टा -ष्टं, अधमः -मा -मं, खलः -ला -लं, अनार्य्यः -र्य्या -र्य्यं, कदर्य्यः -र्य्या -र्य्यं, कृपणः -णा -णं, कुत्सितः -ता -तं, तुच्छः -च्छा -च्छं, दीनः -ना -नं, जघन्यः -न्या -न्यं, प्राकृतः -ती -तं, हीनः -ना -नं.—(Disgraceful) अकीर्त्तिकरः -री -रं.

IGNOBLY, *adv.* अकुलीनवत्, अपकृष्टवत्, नीचवत्, हीनजातिवत्, अनार्य्यवत्, अनार्य्यं, खलवत्, कृपणवत्, अधमजनवत्, अपकृष्टं, कृपणं, कुत्सितं, सदैन्यं, कदर्य्यं.

IGNOMINIOUS, *a.* अकीर्त्तिकरः -री -रं, अपयशस्करः -री -रं, अयशस्यः -स्या -स्यं, अयशस्वी -स्विनी -स्वि (न्), गर्हितः -ता -तं, गर्ह्यः -र्ह्या -र्ह्यं, कलङ्ककरः -री -रं, कलङ्की -ङ्किनी -ङ्कि (न्), लज्जाकरः -री -रं, अपमानकरः -री -रं, वाच्यः -च्या -च्यं, कुत्सितः -ता -तं, कदर्य्यः -र्य्या -र्य्यं, अपकृष्टः -ष्टा -ष्टं, अनार्य्यः -र्य्या -र्य्यं.

IGNOMINIOUSLY, *adv.* गर्हितं, अयशस्यं, सापमानं, कदर्य्यं, कुत्सितं, अनार्य्यं.

IGNOMINY, *s.* अकीर्त्तिः *f.*, अयशस् *n.*, अपकीर्त्तिः *f.*, अपयशस्, अपमानं, अख्यातिः *f.*, कुख्यातिः *f.*, यशोहानिः *f.*, कीर्त्तिहानिः *f.* मर्य्यादाहानिः *f.*, तेजोहानिः *f.*, कलङ्कः, अपकलङ्कः, अपकर्षः, अपध्वंसः, अवमानं, अवज्ञा, परिभवः, तिरस्कारः, अप्रतिष्ठा, अमर्य्यादा.

IGNORAMUS, *s.* अज्ञः, अज्ञानी *m.* (न्), निर्बुद्धिः *m.*, निर्बोधः, अबुद्धिमान् *m.* (त्).

IGNORANCE, *s.* अज्ञानं -नता, अज्ञता, अनभिज्ञता -त्वं, अनभिज्ञानं -नत्वं, अविज्ञता, ज्ञानाभावः, प्रज्ञाहीनता, ज्ञानहीनता, अबोधः -धता, अबुद्धिः *f.*, अविद्या, अज्ञानित्वं, निर्बुद्धिता, बुद्धिहीनता; 'spiritual ignorance,' मोहः, अज्ञानं, अविद्या, अहम्मतिः *f.*

IGNORANT, *a.* अज्ञानः -ना -नं, अज्ञानी -निनी -नि (न्), अज्ञः -ज्ञा -ज्ञं, अनभिज्ञः -ज्ञा -ज्ञं, अविज्ञः -ज्ञा -ज्ञं, अप्राज्ञः -ज्ञा -ज्ञं, अबोधः -धा -धं, अबुधः -धा -धं, ज्ञानहीनः -ना -नं, प्रज्ञाहीनः -ना -नं, विद्याहीनः -ना -नं, विद्याविहीनः -ना -नं, विद्यारहितः -ता -तं, विद्याशून्यः -न्या -न्यं, बोधहीनः -ना -नं, निर्बोधः -धा -धं, निर्बुद्धिः -द्धिः -द्धि, दुर्बुद्धिः -द्धिः -द्धि, अबुद्धिमान् -मती -मत् (त्), दुर्मतिः -तिः -ति, अविपश्चिद्, अविद्वान् -दुषी -द्वत् (स्), अविद्यः -द्या -द्यं, अकोविदः -दा -दं, अव्युत्पन्नः -न्ना -न्नं, अश्रुतः -ता -तं, वैधेयः -यी -यं.

IGNORANTLY, *adv.* अज्ञानतस्, अज्ञानात्, अज्ञानेन, अज्ञानपूर्व्वं, अबोधपूर्व्वं.

IGUANA, *s.* गौधारः, गौधेयः, गौधेरः, गोधा, गोधिका, गोधिः *m.*, गोधिकात्मजः, निहाका, नक्रः.

ILIAC, *a.* आन्त्रिकः -की -कं, नाडिसम्बन्धी -न्धिनी -न्धि (न्); 'iliac-passion,' उदावर्त्तः, शूलव्याधिः *m.*, शूलरोगः, अन्त्रशूलं.

ILL, *a.* (Bad, evil) दुष्टः -ष्टा -ष्टं, पापः -पा -पं, खलः -ला -लं, मन्दः -न्दा -न्दं, कदर्य्यः -र्य्या -र्य्यं, निर्गुणः -णा -णं, कुत्सितः -ता -तं, नीचः -चा -चं, अधमः -मा -मं, शठः -ठा -ठं, अभद्रः -द्रा -द्रं, असाधुः -धुः -धु, असन् -सती -सत् (त्), असारः -रा -रं, अधार्म्मिकः -की -कं; 'ill,' as a general word, is often expressed by दुर्, कु, अप or वि; as, 'ill conduct,' दुर्णयः, कुकर्म्म *n.* (न्), अपकर्म्म *n.*, विकर्म्म *n.*; 'an ill road,' दुरध्वः, कुपथं, विमार्गः, कदध्वा *m.* (न्); 'ill policy,' अनीतिः *f.*, दुर्णीतिः *f.*; 'ill luck,' दुर्भाग्यं, दुर्दैवं.—(Unwell, sick) अस्वस्थः -स्था -स्थं, अस्वस्थशरीरः -रा -रं, असुस्थशरीरः -रा -रं, असुस्थः -स्था -स्थं, असुस्थितः -ता -तं, रोगी -गिणी -गि (न्), सरोगः -गा -गं, रोगग्रस्तः -स्ता -स्तं, रोगान्वितः -ता -तं, रोगवान् -वती -वत् (त्), रोगार्त्तः -र्त्ता -र्त्तं, व्याधितः -ता -तं, व्याधियुक्तः -क्ता -क्तं, आमयः -या -यं, आमी -मिनी -मि (न्), विकारी -रिणी -रि (न्). Expressed also by पीडितः -ता -तं, आतुरः -रा -रं, आर्त्तः -र्त्ता -र्त्तं, ग्रस्तः -स्ता -स्तं in comp.; as, 'ill with fever,' ज्वरपीडितः -ता -तं, ज्वरातुरः -रा -रं, ज्वरग्रस्तः -स्ता -स्तं, सज्वरः -रा -रं.

ILL, *s.* (Evil, wickedness) दुष्टता, पापं, दोषः, व्यसनं -निता, दौष्ट्यं, शाठ्यं, शठता, खलता, मन्दता, असाधुता, अधर्म्मः, दुराचारत्वं, भ्रष्टता, कुसृतिः *f.*—(Distress, calamity) अपायः, अनिष्टं, दुःखं, अशुभं, अकुशलं, दुर्गतिः *f.*, दौर्गत्यं, अभद्रं, अरिष्टं, अहितं, व्यसनं, उत्पातः, विपद् *f.*, आपद् *f.*, विपत्तिः *f.*, अनिष्टपातः, क्लेशः, कष्टं, दुर्दशा, दुरवस्था.—(Disadvantage, loss, injury) अनर्थः, अपायः, अहितं, अपचयः, अपकारः, अपकृतं, क्षतिः *f.*, हानिः *f.*, क्षयः, नाशः.—(Disease, pain) रोगः, व्याधिः *m.*, आमयः, पीडा, दुःखं, क्लेशः, कष्टं, आर्त्तिः *f.*, उपतापः, तापः, अस्वास्थ्यं; 'boding ill,' अनिष्टसूचकः -का -कं; 'designing ill,' द्रोहचिन्तकः -का -कं.

ILL, *adv.* (Not well, badly) दुष्टु, दुष्टं, असम्यक्, अभद्रं, अयुक्तं or expressed by दुर्, वि, अ, कु, अप, दुष्ट, पाप &c. prefixed; as, 'ill-intentioned,' दुराशयः -या -यं, दुष्टबुद्धिः -द्धिः -द्धि, पापाशयः -या -यं; 'ill-done,' दुष्कृतः -ता -तं, अपकृतः -ता -तं; 'ill-behaved,' दुःशीलः -ला -लं, कुशीलः -ला -लं, दुर्वृत्तः -त्ता -त्तं; 'ill-natured,' दुष्प्रकृतिः -तिः -ति; 'ill-fated,' दुर्दैवग्रस्तः -स्ता -स्तं, दुर्दैवोपहतः -ता -तं, दुर्भाग्यः -ग्या -ग्यं; 'ill-managed,' दुर्णीतः -ता -तं; 'ill-conditioned,' दुःस्थः -स्था -स्थं, दुःस्थितः -ता -तं; 'ill at ease,' अनिर्वृतः -ता -तं; 'ill-grounded,' अमूलः -ला -लं -लकः -का -कं; 'ill-ordered,' दुष्क्रमः -मा -मं, अक्रमः -मा -मं; 'ill-regulated,' अव्यवस्थितः -ता -तं; 'ill-qualified,' अयुक्तः -क्ता -क्तं, अयोग्यः -ग्या -ग्यं; 'ill-shaped,' कुरूपः -पा -पं, अपरूपः -पा -पं, विरूपः -पा -पी -पं; 'ill-sounding,' विस्वरः -रा -रं, अस्वरः -रा -रं; 'ill-treated,' अपकृतः -ता -तं; 'ending ill, turning out ill,' दुरन्तः -न्ता -न्तं, दुष्परिणामः -मा -मं.—(Not well in health) अस्वस्थं, अस्वास्थ्येन, असुस्थं; 'to be ill,' अस्वस्थः -स्था -स्थं भू. *See* ILL, *a.* (Not easily) दुःखेन, कष्टेन, कष्टं, कृच्छ्रेण, कठिनं, विषमं.

ILL-ADVISED, *a.* असमीक्ष्य कृतः -ता -तं, अनालोचितः -ता -तं, अपरीक्षितः -ता -तं.

ILL-AFFECTED, *a.* अहितः -ता -तं, विरक्तः -क्ता -क्तं, द्रोहबुद्धिः -द्धिः -द्धि, अहितैषी -षिणी -षि (न्), अपकारार्थी -र्थिनी -र्थि (न्); 'to be ill-affected,' विरक्तीभू, अभिद्रुह् (c. 4. -द्रुह्यति -द्रोग्धुं).

ILLACERABLE, *s.* अविदार्य्यः -र्य्या -र्य्यं, अविदारणीयः -या -यं, अछेदनीयः -या -यं.

ILLAPSE, *s.* निपतनं, प्रपतनं, प्रवेशः, अकस्माद् आक्रमणं.

To ILLAQUEATE, *v. a.* उन्माथे or पाशे पत् (c. 10. पातयति -यितुं), जाले पातयित्वा बन्ध् (c. 9. बध्नाति, बन्धुं), पाश (nom. पाशयति -यितुं), पाशीकृ.

ILLAQUEATION, *s.* उन्माथे पातनं, जाले बन्धनं, पाशीकरणं.

ILL-ARRANGED, *a.* दुष्क्रमः -मा -मं, दुर्विरचितः -ता -तं, दुर्विहितः -ता -तं.

ILLATION, *s.* अनुमानं, अनुमितिः *f.*, अपवाहः, अपोहः -हनं, अभ्यूहः.

ILLATIVE, *a.* आनुमानिकः -की -कं, आनुषङ्गिकः -की -कं, यौक्तिकः -की -कं.

ILLATIVELY, *adv.* अनुमानेन, अनुमानतस्, प्रयोगतस्, अपवाहेन.

Illaudable, *a.* अप्रशंसनीयः -या -यं, अश्लाघ्यः -घ्या -घ्यं, अश्लाघनीयः -या -यं.

Ill-behaved, *a.* *See* Ill-bred.

Ill-bred, *a.* दुर्विनीतः -ता -तं, अविनीतः -ता -तं, अनीतः -ता -तं, दुर्विनयः -या -यं, अविनयः -या -यं, विनयरोधी -धिनी -धि (न्), विनयप्रमाथी -थिनी -थि (न्), विनयापेतः -ता -तं, अशिष्टः -ष्टा -ष्टं, विशीलः -ला -लं, कुशीलः -ला -लं, दुःशीलः -ला -लं, असभ्यः -भ्या -भ्यं, दुराचारः -रा -रं, दुश्चेष्टितः -ता -तं, दुर्वृत्तः -त्ता -त्तं, व्यभिचारी -रिणी -रि (न्), असम्यक्कारी &c.

Ill-breeding, *s.* अविनयः, दुर्विनीतता, कुशीलता, दुःशीलता, अशिष्टता, असभ्यता, विनयभङ्गः, शीलवञ्चना.

Ill-contrived, *a.* दुर्घटितः -ता -तं, दुर्णीतः -ता -तं, अपक्वः -क्वा -क्वं.

Ill-conditioned, *a.* दुःस्थः -स्था -स्थं, दुःस्थितः -ता -तं, दुर्वृत्तिः -त्तिः -त्ति.

Ill-conducted, *a.* दुर्णीतः -ता -तं, दुर्घटितः -ता -तं, असम्यग् घटितः -ता -तं.

Ill-dressed, *a.* दुर्वासाः -साः -सः (स्), कुवेष्टितः -ता -तं, कुप्रावृतः -ता -तं.

Illegal, *a.* स्मृतिविरुद्धः -द्धा -द्धं, व्यवहारविरुद्धः -द्धा -द्धं, नियमविरुद्धः -द्धा -द्धं, व्यवस्थाविरुद्धः -द्धा -द्धं, स्मृत्यपेतः -ता -तं, असमार्त्तः -र्त्ती -र्त्तं, शास्त्रविरुद्धः -द्धा -द्धं, धर्म्मरोधी -धिनी -धि (न्), अधर्म्यः -र्म्या -र्म्यं, निषिद्धः -द्धा -द्धं, अव्यवस्थितः -ता -तं, अशास्त्रिकः -का -कं, अशास्त्रीयः -या -यं, अवैधः -धी -धं, अविधिः -धिः -धि, विधिभञ्जकः -का -कं.

Illegality, *s.* स्मृतिविरोधः -विरुद्धता, व्यवहारविरोधः, नियमविरोधः, शास्त्रविरोधः, अस्मृतिः *f.*, अधर्म्यता, धर्म्मविरोधः, व्यवस्थाविरोधः, अव्यवस्था, विकर्म्म *n.* (न्), विकर्म्मक्रिया, व्यवस्थातिक्रमः, व्यवहारातिक्रमः, नियमभङ्गः, विधिभङ्गः, व्यवस्थाभङ्गः.

Illegally, *adv.* स्मृतिविरोधेन, व्यवहारविरुद्धं, नियमविरुद्धं, शास्त्रविरोधेन, धर्म्मविरुद्धं; 'acting illegally,' विकर्म्मकृत् *m.f.n.*, विकर्म्मिकः -की -कं.

Illegibility, *s.* अस्पष्टता, अव्यक्तत्वं, अस्पष्टाक्षरत्वं, दुर्वाच्यता.

Illegible, *a.* अस्पष्टाक्षरः -रा -रं, अव्यक्ताक्षरः -रा -रं, दुर्वाच्यः -च्या -च्यं, अस्पष्टवर्णः -र्णा -र्णं.

Illegitimacy, *s.* अनौरसता, विजातता, विजन्म *n.* (न्), वैजात्यं, अनभिजातत्वं, जारजत्वं, जारजातता, उपपत्नीजातत्वं, दासीजातत्वं, जन्मवैलक्षण्यं.

Illegitimate, *a.* विजातः -ता -तं, विजनितः -ता -तं, विजन्मा -न्मा -न्म (न्), विजातीयः -या -यं, अधर्म्मजः -जा -जं, अनभिजातः -ता -तं, उपपत्नीजातः &c., जारजातः &c., जारजः -जा -जं, असतीप्रसूतः -ता -तं, कृष्णपक्षजः -जा -जं, कृष्णपक्षीयः -या -यं; 'an illegitimate child,' अनौरसः -सी, कुण्डः -ण्डी *m.* (न्), उपपत्नीसुतः -ता, उपपत्नीपुत्रः -त्री, जारजः -जा, दासीपुत्रः, कौलटेरः -रा, कौलटेयः -यी, कौलटिनेयः -यी, बन्धुलः, बान्धकिनेयः; 'of a widow,' गोलकः.—(Spurious) कृत्रिमः -मा -मं, कल्पितः -ता -तं.—(Unlawful) व्यवहारविरुद्धः -द्धा -द्धं, अव्यवहारिकः -की -कं, नियमविरुद्धः -द्धा -द्धं, अधर्म्यः -र्म्या -र्म्यं, निषिद्धः -द्धा -द्धं.

Illegitimately, *adv.* विजन्मना, जन्मवैलक्षण्येन, वैजात्येन, कुण्डवत्, अधर्म्मेण.—(Unlawfully) व्यवहारविरुद्धं, नियमविरुद्धं.

Ill-fame, *s.* अपयशस् *n.*, अयशस् *n.*, अकीर्त्तिः *f.*, अख्यातिः *f.*, अप्रतिष्ठा.

Ill-fated, *a.* दैवोपहतः -ता -तं, हतदैवः -वी -वं, दुर्दैवग्रस्तः -स्ता -स्तं, दुर्भाग्यः -ग्या -ग्यं, उपहतकः -का -कं.

Ill-favored, *a.* कुरूपः -पा -पी -पं, अपरूपः -पी -पं, कदाकारः -रा -रं, कुत्सितरूपः -पी -पं, असुन्दरः -री -रं, दुर्दर्शनः -ना -नं, अपलक्षणी -णिनी -णि (न्).

Ill-fitted, *a.* अयोग्यः -ग्या -ग्यं, अयुक्तः -क्ता -क्तं, अक्षमः -मा -मं.

Ill-formed, *a.* कुरूपी -पिणी -पि (न्), विरूपः -पी -पं, अपरूपः -पी -पं.

Ill-gotten, *a.* द्रोहार्ज्जितः -ता -तं, अन्यायोपार्ज्जितः -ता -तं, वृजिनार्ज्जितः -ता -तं.

Illiberal, *a.* अनुदारः -रा -रं, कृपणः -णा -णं, अदानशीलः -ला -लं, अत्यागशीलः -ला -लं, अदाता -त्री -तृ (तृ), अवदान्यः -न्या -न्यं, कुत्सितः -ता -तं, मत्सरी -रिणी -रि (न्), कृपणबुद्धिः -द्धिः -द्धि, कृपणधीः -धीः -धि, कृपणचेताः -ताः -तः (स्), कृपणस्वभावः -वा -वं, दीनचेताः &c., नीचमनाः -नाः -नः (स्).

Illiberality, *s.* कार्पण्यं, कृपणता, अनौदार्य्यं, अनुदारता, अदानशीलता, बुद्धिकार्पण्यं, स्वभावकार्पण्यं, कृपणबुद्धित्वं, स्वभावदीनता, स्वभावदैन्यं, बुद्धिनीचता, अत्यागशीलता, अवदान्यता, मात्सर्य्यं.

Illiberally, *adv.* अनुदारं, कृपणं, कार्पण्येन, सकार्पण्यं, कृपणवत्.

Illicit, *a.* निषिद्धः -द्धा -द्धं, प्रतिषिद्धः -द्धा -द्धं, अधर्म्यः -र्म्या -र्म्यं, धर्म्मविरुद्धः -द्धा -द्धं, धर्म्मरोधी -धिनी -धि (न्), नियमविरुद्धः -द्धा -द्धं, व्यवहारविरुद्धः -द्धा -द्धं, अव्यवहारिकः -की -कं, निवारणीयः -या -यं, निवार्य्यः -र्य्या -र्य्यं.

Illimitable, *a.* अनन्तः -न्ता -न्तं, अनन्तः -न्ता -न्तं, अनन्तवान् -वती -वत् (त्), अप्रमेयः -या -यं, अमेयः -या -यं.

Illimited, *a.* अनन्तः -न्ता -न्तं -न्तकः -का -कं, अमितः -ता -तं, अपरिमितः -ता -तं, निरवधिः -धिः -धि, अपर्य्यन्तः -न्ता -न्तं, अमर्य्यादः -दा -दं, अशेषः -षा -षं, असीमकः -का -कं.

Illiterate, *a.* निरक्षरः -रा -रं, अनक्षरः -रा -रं, अशिक्षितः -ता -तं, विद्याहीनः -ना -नं, ज्ञानहीनः -ना -नं, अपण्डितः -ता -तं, अप्राज्ञः -ज्ञा -ज्ञं, अकृतबुद्धिः -द्धिः -द्धि, असंस्कृतबुद्धिः -द्धिः -द्धि, अकृतः -ता -तं, अविज्ञः -ज्ञा -ज्ञं.

Illiterateness, *s.* अपाण्डित्यं, विद्याहीनता, विद्याभावः, अप्राज्ञता, अविद्या, अशिक्षितत्वं, अकृतबुद्धित्वं.

Ill-judged, *a.* अविचार्य्य or अविमृश्य or अविवेचनपूर्व्वं कृतः -ता -तं.

Ill-judging, *a.* विवेकशून्यः -न्या -न्यं, अविवेकी -किनी -कि (न्).

Ill-looking, *a.* दुर्दर्शनः -ना -नं, कुदर्शनः -ना -नं, कुरूपः -पी -पं.

Ill-luck, *s.* दुर्दैवं, दुर्भाग्यं, दौर्भाग्यं, दुर्गतिः *f.*, दौर्गत्यं, अमङ्गलं, अकुशलं, अभद्रं, अरिष्टं, व्यसनं -निता, विपत् *f.*, दुरदृष्टं, दुर्जातं, अनिष्टपातः, अश्रीकं.

Ill-mannered, *a.* कुशीलः -ला -लं, वामशीलः -ला -लं, दुःशीलः -ला -लं, विशीलः -ला -लं, दुर्विनीतः -ता -तं, दुर्विनयः -या -यं, दुराचारः -रा -रं, असत्कृतः -ता -तं.

Ill-nature, *s.* भावदुष्टता, कुशीलता, वामशीलता, दुःशीलता, दौःशील्यं, भावप्रतीपता, भावकार्कश्यं, स्वभाववक्रता, कर्कशभावत्वं, निकृतिः *f.*, प्रकृतिवक्रता.

Ill-natured, *a.* दुष्प्रकृतिः -तिः -ति, दुष्टप्रकृतिः -तिः -ति, दुष्टस्वभावः -वा -वं, कर्कशभावः -वा -वं, प्रतीपस्वभावः -वा -वं, वक्रप्रकृतिः -तिः -ति, दुःशीलः -ला -लं, कुशीलः -ला -लं, वामशीलः -ला -लं, कटुस्वभावः -वा -वं, नैकृतिकः -की -कं.

Ill-naturedly, *adv.* स्वभावकार्कश्यात्, प्रकृति दुष्टत्वात्, कर्कशं, वामशीलत्वात्.

Illness, *s.* रोगः, व्याधिः *m.*, रोगिता, आमयः, रुक् *f.* (ज्), रुजा, पीडा, अस्वास्थ्यं, अस्वस्थता, असुस्थता, क्लेशः, दुःखं, रुग्णता, आर्त्तिः *f.*, उपतापः, कष्टं, विकारः, विकृतिः *f.*, विकरः, अमः, अमसः, तापः; 'dangerous illness,' सन्निपातकः.

Illogical, *a.* न्यायविरुद्धः -द्धा -द्धं, न्यायविपरीतः -ता -तं, अन्यायी -यिनी -यि (न्), अन्याय्यः -य्या -य्यं, अन्यायानुसारी -रिणी -रि (न्), अन्यायसिद्धः -द्धा -द्धं, अयुक्तिसिद्धः -द्धा -द्धं, अनानुमानिकः -की -कं, अतार्किकः -की -कं; 'illogical conclusion,' अविनिगमः.

Illogically, *adv.* न्यायविरुद्धं, न्यायविरोधेन, अन्यायानुसारेण, अयुक्त्या.

Ill-omened, *a.* अनिष्टलक्षणः -णा -णं, अनिष्टशकुनः -ना -नं, अशस्तः -स्ता -स्तं.

ILL-STARRED, *a.* हतदैवः -वा -वं, दैवोपहतः -ता -तं, उपहतकः -का -कं, दुर्भाग्यः -ग्या -ग्यं, मन्दभाग्यः -ग्या -ग्यं.

ILL-TEMPERED, *a.* दुष्प्रकृतिः -तिः -ति, कर्कशभावः -वा -वं. *See* ILL-NATURED.

ILL-TIMED, *a.* अप्राप्तावसरः -रा -रं, अप्राप्तकालः -ला -लं, अकालिकः -की -कं, असामयिकः -की -कं, अप्राप्तसमयः -या -यं, अनवसरः -रा -रं.

ILL-TRAINED, *a.* दुर्विनीतः -ता -तं, अविनीतः -ता -तं, अशिक्षितः -ता -तं.

To ILL-TREAT, *v. a.* अपकृ, अपकारं कृ, द्रोहं कृ, अर्द् (c. 10. अर्दयति -यितुं).

ILL-TREATED, *p. p.* अपकृतः -ता -तं, कृतापकारः -रा -रं, पीडितः -ता -तं, अर्दितः -ता -तं.

ILL-TURN, *s.* अपकृतं, अपकारः, अप्रियं, अहितं, हिंसा, द्रोहः, क्षतिः *f.*

To ILLUDE, *v. a.* वञ्च् (c. 10. वञ्चयते -यितुं), प्रवञ्च्, मुह् (c. 10. मोहयति -यितुं), छल् (c. 10. छलयति -यितुं), प्रतॄ (c. 10. -तारयति -यितुं), प्रलभ् (c. 1. -लभते -लब्धुं), प्रलुभ् (c. 10. -लोभयति -यितुं).

ILLUDED, *p. p.* मोहितः -ता -तं, विमोहितः -ता -तं, वञ्चितः -ता -तं.

To ILLUME, ILLUMINE, ILLUMINATE, *v. a.* द्युत् (c. 10. द्योतयति -यितुं), प्रद्युत्, उद्द्युत्, विद्युत्, प्रकाश् (c. 10. -काशयति -यितुं), विकाश्, दीप् (c. 10. दीपयति -यितुं), विदीप्, उद्दीप्, प्रदीप्, विराज् (c. 10. -राजयति -यितुं), भास् (c. 10. भासयति -यितुं), प्रभास्, उद्भास्, अवभास्, भ्राज् (c. 10. भ्राजयति -यितुं), रञ्ज् (c. 10. रञ्जयति -यितुं), तेजसा रञ्ज्, विमल (nom. विमलयति -यितुं), विमलीकृ.—(Illuminate a manuscript) पत्रं रञ्ज्.

ILLUMINATED, ILLUMINED, *p. p.* द्योतितः -ता -तं, प्रद्योतितः -ता -तं, उद्द्योतितः -ता -तं, प्रकाशितः -ता -तं, विकाशितः -ता -तं, दीपितः -ता -तं, आदीपितः -ता -तं, उद्दीपितः -ता -तं, प्रदीपितः -ता -तं, राजितः -ता -तं, विराजितः -ता -तं, उज्ज्वलितः -ता -तं, भासितः -ता -तं, अवभासितः -ता -तं, उद्भासितः -ता -तं, चकासितः -ता -तं, रञ्जितः -ता -तं.

ILLUMINATION, *s.* द्योतनं, प्रद्योतनं, उद्द्योतः, द्युतिः *f.*, प्रकाशनं, विकाशनं, दीपनं, दीप्तिः *f.*, प्रदीपनं, प्रदीप्तिः *f.*, उद्दीपनं, उज्ज्वलनं, उज्ज्वलता, उद्भासः, भ्राजिष्णुता, प्रकाशता.—(Rows of lights displayed in token of joy) उत्सवकाले हर्षसूचका दीपमाला -लिका or दीपशृङ्खला or दीपसमूहः.—(Of a manuscript) पत्ररञ्जनं, कलधौतलिपिः *f.*

ILLUMINATOR, *s.* दीपकः, प्रदीपकः, प्रकाशकः, द्युतिकरः, दीप्तिकर्त्ता *m.* (र्त्तृ); 'of a manuscript,' पत्ररञ्जकः.

ILLUSION, *s.* माया, मोहः, व्यामोहः, भ्रमः, भ्रान्तिः *f.*, विभ्रमः, मतिविभ्रमः, आभासः, प्रपञ्चः, इन्द्रजालं, जालं, अलीकता, कूटः, अजया, आवरणं, अविद्या; 'power of illusion,' मायाशक्तिः *f.*, आवरणशक्तिः *f.*

ILLUSIVE, ILLUSORY, *a.* मायी -यिनी -यि (न्), मायिकः -की -कं, मायावी -विनी -वि (न्), मायामयः -यी -यं, मोही -हिनी -हि (न्), जाली -लिनी -लि (न्), इन्द्रजालिकः -की -कं, ऐन्द्रजालिकः -की -कं, भ्रमी -मिणी -मि (न्), भ्रान्तिजनकः -का -कं, वञ्चकः -का -कं, अलीकः -का -कं.

To ILLUSTRATE, *v. a.* (Make clear, brighten) प्रकाश् (c. 10. -काशयति -यितुं), विकाश्, शुभ् (c. 10. शोभयति -यितुं), विमल (nom. विमलयति -यितुं), विमलीकृ, द्युत् (c. 10. द्योतयति -यितुं), दीप् (c. 10. दीपयति -यितुं).—(Elucidate, explain) व्याख्या (c. 2. -ख्याति -तुं), स्पष्टीकृ, व्यक्तीकृ, व्याकृ, सुस्पष्टीकृ, स्पष्ट (nom. स्पष्टयति -यितुं), व्याहृ (c. 1. -हरति -हर्त्तुं), उदाहृ, परिशुध् (c. 10. -शोधयति -यितुं), विवृ (c. 5. -वृणोति -वरितुं -रीतुं), विवरणं कृ, प्रकाश्, दृष्टान्तीकृ, दृष्टान्तेन or निदर्शनेन व्याख्या or प्रकाश्.

ILLUSTRATED, *p. p.* प्रकाशितः -ता -तं, स्पष्टीकृतः -ता -तं, व्याख्यातः -ता -तं, उदाहृतः -ता -तं, समुदाहृतः -ता -तं, द्योतितः -ता -तं, व्याकृतः -ता -तं, निरूपितः -ता -तं, वर्णितः -ता -तं, दार्ष्टान्तिकः -की -कं, उपमितः -ता -तं.

ILLUSTRATION, *s.* उदाहरणं, उदाहारः, समुदाहरणं, निदर्शनं, दृष्टान्तः, उत्प्रेक्षा, उद्देशः, उपोद्घातः, व्याख्या, प्रदर्शनं; 'for an illustration,' निदर्शनार्थं, प्रदर्शनार्थं.

ILLUSTRATIVE, *a.* प्रकाशकः -का -कं, उद्देशकः -का -कं, दार्ष्टान्तिकः -की -कं.

ILLUSTRATIVELY, *adv.* निदर्शनार्थं, प्रदर्शनार्थं, दृष्टान्तक्रमेण, उदाहरणार्थं.

ILLUSTRATOR, *a.* प्रकाशकः, अर्थप्रकाशकः, उद्देशकः, अर्थव्याख्याता *m.* (तृ), अर्थप्रदर्शकः, निदर्शनकृत्, दृष्टान्तकारी *m.* (न्), उदाहर्त्ता *m.* (र्त्तृ).

ILLUSTRIOUS, *a.* विश्रुतः -ता -तं, ख्यातः -ता -तं, विख्यातः -ता -तं, सुख्यातः -ता -तं, यशस्वी -स्विनी -स्वि (न्), महायशाः -शाः -शः (स्), महायशस्कः -स्का -स्कं, प्रथितः -ता -तं, प्रसिद्धः -द्धा -द्धं, कीर्त्तिमान् -मती -मत् (त्), कीर्त्तितः -ता -तं, श्रीमान् -मती -मत् (त्), दीप्तिमान् &c., यशस्वान् -स्वती -स्वत् (त्), पृथुप्रथः -था -थं, प्रतिपत्तिमान् -मती -मत् (त्), प्रतिष्ठः -ष्ठा -ष्ठं, प्रतिष्ठान्वितः -ता -तं, सुप्रतिष्ठः -ष्ठा -ष्ठं, लोकविश्रुतः -ता -तं, परिख्यातः -ता -तं, लोकप्रथितः -ता -तं, विशालः -ला -लं, प्रतीतः -ता -तं, विज्ञातः -ता -तं, द्वात्रिंशल्लक्षणोपेतः -ता -तं, लब्धनामा -मा -म (न्).—(Eminent) उत्कृष्टः -ष्टा -ष्टं, प्रमुखः -खा -खं, महाभागः -गा -गं, विशिष्टः ष्टा -ष्टं, महान् -हती -हत् (त्), श्रिष्टः -ष्टा -ष्टं; 'rendering illustrious,' यशस्करः -री -रं, यशस्यः -स्या -स्यं, कीर्त्तिकरः -री -रं.

ILLUSTRIOUSLY, *adv.* महायशसा, महाकीर्त्तिपूर्व्वं, उत्कृष्टं, विशिष्टं, विश्रुतं, प्रथितं, प्रसिद्धं, यशस्यं.

ILLUSTRIOUSNESS, *s.* विश्रुतिः *f.*, कीर्त्तिमत्त्वं, ख्यातिमत्त्वं, यशस्विता, उत्कृष्टता.

ILL-WILL, *s.* दुष्टभावः, दुष्टबुद्धिः *f.*, द्रोहबुद्धिः *f.*, दुर्बुद्धिः *f.*, द्रोहचिन्तनं, द्रोहः, मात्सर्य्यं, असूया, अभ्यसूया, द्वेषः, अहितत्वं, अप्रीतिः *f.*

IMAGE, *s.* प्रतिमा, प्रतिमानं, प्रतिरूपं, प्रतिमूर्त्तिः *f.*, मूर्त्तिः *f.*, प्रतिकृतिः *f.*, प्रतिकायः, उपमा -मानं, प्रतियातना, प्रतिच्छन्दः, प्रतिनिधिः *m.*, अर्चा, विग्रहः.—(Reflected image) प्रतिबिम्बं, प्रतिच्छाया, बिम्बः -म्बं, प्रतिच्छन्दः -न्दकं.—(Idol) देवताप्रतिमा.—(Iron image) लोहप्रतिमा, सूर्म्मी, स्थूणा.—(Mental image) मनःकल्पना, मनःसङ्कल्पः, मनसिजं, 'image maker,' प्रतिमाकारः, उपमाता *m.* (तृ); 'a son the image of his father,' पितृरूपः पुत्रः.

To IMAGE, *v. a.* (Form an image of) बिम्ब (nom. बिम्बयति -यितुं), प्रतिबिम्ब, प्रतिमानं कृ, प्रतिरूपं कृ, प्रतिमूर्त्तिं कृ.—(In the mind) मनसा कॢप् (c. 10. कल्पयति -यितुं) or संकॢप्.

IMAGED, *p. p.* बिम्बितः -ता -तं, प्रतिबिम्बितः -ता -तं, बिम्बगतः -ता -तं, बिम्बागतः -ता -तं, कल्पितः -ता -तं; 'in the water,' जलप्रतिबिम्बितः -ता -तं; 'in the mind,' मनःकल्पितः -ता -तं.

IMAGERY, *s.* (Forms of the fancy) मनःकल्पना, मनःकल्पितं, कल्पना, मनःसङ्कल्पः, मनोवासना, मनःसृष्टिः *f.*, मनःपरिकल्पनं, मनोवासना, वासनाकल्पितं.—(Figurative style) व्यञ्जनावृत्तिः *f.*, व्यञ्जनं, व्यङ्ग्यः, उपलक्षणं, लक्षणा, निदर्शनं.

IMAGE-WORSHIP, *s.* प्रतिमापूजा, देवताभ्यर्चा, प्रतिमासेवा, मूर्त्तिसेवा.

IMAGINABLE, *a.* विभावनीयः -या -यं, विभाव्यः -व्या -व्यं, भावनीयः -या -यं, मन्तव्यः -व्या -व्यं, बोध्यः -ध्या -ध्यं, बोधनीयः -या -यं, मनःकल्पनीयः -या -यं, मनसा कल्पनीयः -या -यं, चिन्तनीयः -या -यं, चिन्त्यः -न्त्या -न्त्यं, बोधगम्यः -म्या -म्यं, अन्तर्भावनीयः -या -यं.

IMAGINARY, *a.* मनःकल्पितः -ता -तं, वासनाकल्पितः -ता -तं, बुद्धिकल्पितः -ता -तं, मनसा कल्पितः -ता -तं, काल्पनिकः -की -कं, मनसिजः -जा -जं, मनोजः -जा -जं, मनोभवः -वा -वं, मानसिकः -की -कं, मनोगतः -ता -तं, सङ्कल्पजः -जा -जं, मनःसृष्टः -ष्टा -ष्टं, मनोरथसृष्टः -ष्टा -ष्टं,

चिन्तामात्रकल्पितः -ता -तं, चिन्तामात्रेण परिकल्पितः -ता -तं, चिन्ताभवः -वा -वं, अमूलकः -का -कं, मायामयः -यी -यं, असत्यः -त्या -त्यं.

Imagination, *s.* भावना -नं, विभावना -नं, सङ्कल्पः, कल्पना, मनःकल्पना, वासना, चिन्ता.—(Idea) बुद्धिः *f.*, मतिः *f.*, मनोगतं, मनःकल्पितं, मनसिजं, मनोजं, बोधः.—(Faculty of conception) कल्पनाशक्तिः *f.*, भावनाशक्तिः *f.*, विभावनाशक्तिः *f.*, उपलब्धिः *f.*, अनुभवः.

Imaginative, *a.* विभावकः -का -कं, कल्पकः -का -कं, परिकल्पकः -का -कं, काल्पनिकः -की -कं, भावनापरः -रा -रं, वासनापरः -रा -रं, विभावनशीलः -ला -लं.

To imagine, *v. a.* (Form in the mind) मनसा क्लृप् (c. 10. कल्पयति -यितुं) or संक्लृप् or परिक्लृप् or भू (c. 10. भावयति -यितुं) or विभू or सम्भू, मनसा सृज् (c. 6. सृजति, स्रष्टुं) or कृ.

To imagine, *v. n.* (Think, conceive) मन् (c. 4. मन्यते, मन्तुं), चिन्त् (c. 10. चिन्तयति -यितुं), भू (c. 10. भावयति -यितुं), विभू, सम्भू, बुध् (c. 1. बोधति -धितुं), तर्क् (c. 10. तर्कयति -यितुं), ध्यै (c. 1. ध्यायति, ध्यातुं), अवगम् (c. 1. -गच्छति -गन्तुं), उपलभ् (c. 1. -लभते -लब्धुं), अवे (c. 2. अवैति -तुं, rt. इ), अनुभू; 'I imagine,' मन्ये; 'don't imagine,' मैवं मंस्थाः.

Imagined, *p. p.* चिन्तितः -ता -तं, भावितः -ता -तं, विभावितः -ता -तं, मतः -ता -तं, मनःकल्पितः -ता -तं, मनसा कल्पितः -ता -तं, वासनाकल्पितः -ता -तं, मनःसृष्टः -ष्टा -ष्टं, बुद्धः -द्धा -द्धं, उपलब्धः -ब्धा -ब्धं, अवगतः -ता -तं, मनोगतः -ता -तं, अनुभूतः -ता -तं.

Imbalm, imbargo, imbark. *See* Embalm, &c.

Imbecile, *a.* दुर्बलः -ला -लं, अल्पबलः -ला -लं, कृपणः -णा -णं, क्षीणबलः -ला -लं, अल्पशक्तिः -क्तिः -क्ति, क्लीबः -बा -बं.—(In mind) न्यूनबुद्धिः -द्धिः -द्धि, न्यूनधीः -धीः -धि, अल्पबुद्धिः -द्धिः -द्धि, बालिशमतिः -तिः -ति, कृपणबुद्धिः &c.

Imbecility, *s.* दौर्बल्यं, दुर्बलता, कार्पण्यं, कृपणता, क्लीबता, क्लैब्यं, अतेजस् *n.*, अयोग्यता, बालिश्यं.—(Mental) बुद्धिन्यूनता, न्यूनबुद्धित्वं, अल्पबुद्धित्वं, बालिशमतित्वं, बुद्धिकार्पण्यं.

Imbedded, *a.* अन्तर्गतः -ता -तं, निहितः -ता -तं, निविष्टः -ष्टा -ष्टं; 'in rocks,' पाषाणान्तर्गतः -ता -तं.

To imbibe, *v. a.* निपा (c. 1. -पिबति -पातुं), उत्पा, आपा, शुष् (c. 10. शोषयति -यितुं), उच्छुष्, ग्रस् (c. 1. ग्रसते -सितुं); 'water is imbibed,' पयो निपीयते.—(Receive in the mind) मनसा ग्रह् (c. 9. गृह्णाति, ग्रहीतुं) or उपलभ् (c. 1. -लभते -लब्धुं).

Imbibed, *p. p.* निपीतः -ता -तं, आपीतः -ता -तं, उपलब्धः -ब्धा -ब्धं.

To imbitter, *v. a.* दुःख् (c. 10. दुःखयति -यितुं), दुःखं जन् (c. 10. जनयति -यितुं), निरानन्दं -न्दां -न्दं कृ, सदुःखं -खां -खं कृ, दुःखमयं -यीं -यं कृ, उग्रीकृ, कटूकृ, तिग्मीकृ, तीव्रीकृ, कठोरीकृ, निष्ठुरीकृ.

Imbodied, imbody, imbolden. *See* Embodied, &c.

To imborder, *v. a.* प्रान्त (nom. प्रान्तयति -यितुं), पर्य्यन्तं कृ, सीमां कृ.

To imbosom, *v. a.* (Hold in the bosom) क्रोडीकृ, क्रोडे कृ, अङ्के कृ or रक्ष् (c. 1. रक्षति -क्षितुं) or पाल् (c. 10. पालयति -यितुं), भुजाभ्यां पीड् (c. 10. पीडयति -यितुं), भुजापीडं कृ.—(Inclose, surround) परिवेष्ट् (c. 1. -वेष्टते -ष्टितुं, c. 10. -वेष्टयति -यितुं), परिगम् (c. 1. -गच्छति -गन्तुं), परिसृ (c. 1. -सरति -सर्त्तुं).

Imbosomed, *p. p.* क्रोडीकृतः -ता -तं, अन्तर्गतः -ता -तं, परिवृतः -ता -तं.

To imbrown, *v. a.* कपिश (nom. कपिशयति -यितुं), कपिशीकृ, श्यावीकृ, पिङ्गलीकृ, ताम्रीकृ, ताम्रवर्णं -र्णां -र्णं कृ, ताम्रं -म्रां -म्रं कृ.

Imbrowned, *p.p.* कपिशितः -ता -तं, कपिशीकृतः -ता -तं, पिङ्गलीकृतः -ता -तं.

To imbrue, *v. a.* सिच् (c. 6. सिञ्चति, सेक्तुं), क्लिद् (c. 10. क्लेदयति -यितुं), उक्ष् (c. 1. उक्षति -क्षितुं), समुक्ष्, अभ्युक्ष्, लिप् (c. 6. लिम्पति, लेप्तुं), अञ्ज् (c. 7. अनक्ति, अंक्तुं).

Imbrued, *p. p.* (In blood) असृग्लिप्तः -प्ता -प्तं, शोणिताक्तः -क्ता -क्तं, शोणितोक्षितः -ता -तं, रक्तक्लिन्नः -न्ना -न्नं, रक्ताक्तः -क्ता -क्तं.

To imbue, *v. a.* (Dye) रञ्ज् (c. 10. रञ्जयति -यितुं), अभिरञ्ज्.—(Cause to learn) उपदिश् (c. 6. -दिशति -देष्टुं), शिक्ष् (c. 10. शिक्षयति -यितुं).

Imbued, *p. p.* रञ्जितः -ता -तं, शिक्षितः -ता -तं, उपदिष्टः -ष्टा -ष्टं.

Imitable, *a.* अनुकरणीयः -या -यं, अनुगम्यः -म्या -म्यं, अनुगमनीयः -या -यं, अनुकार्य्यः -र्य्या -र्य्यं, अनुवर्त्तनीयः -या -यं, अनुवृत्यः -त्या -त्यं.

To imitate, *v. a.* अनुकृ (c. 8. -करोति -कुरुते -कर्त्तुं), अनुगम् (c. 1. -गच्छति -गन्तुं), अनुवृत् (c. 1. -वर्त्तते -र्त्तितुं), समनुवृत्, अनुया (c. 2. -याति -तुं), समनुया, अनुसृ (c. 1. -सरति -सर्त्तुं), अनुव्रज् (c. 1. -व्रजति -जितुं), अनुहृ (c. 1. -हरति -ते -हर्त्तुं), अनुष्ठा (c. 1. -तिष्ठति -ष्ठातुं), अनुचर् (c. 1. -चरति -रितुं), अन्वि (c. 2. -एति -तुं), विडम्ब् (c. 10. -डम्बयति -यितुं).

Imitated, *p.p.* अनुकृतः -ता -तं, अनुगतः -ता -तं, अनुवृत्तः -त्ता -त्तं.

Imitation, *s.* अनुकारः, अनुकरणं, अनुक्रिया, अनुकृतिः *f.*, अनुकर्म्म *n.* (न्), अनुगमः, अनुगतिः *f.*, अनुवृत्तिः *f.*, अनुवर्त्तनं, अनुसरणं, अनुहारः, अनुसृतिः *f.*, अनुष्ठानं, विडम्बनं -ना.—(A copy, resemblance) प्रतिरूपं, अनुरूपं, आदर्शः, सादृश्यं, औपम्यं, उपमा, प्रतिमानं.

Imitative, *a.* अनुकारी -रिणी -रि (न्), अनुकरणशीलः -ला -लं, अनुगामी -मिनी -मि (न्), अनुगमनशीलः -ला -लं, अनुगतिकः -की -कं, गतानुगतिकः -की -कं.

Imitator, *s.* अनुकारी *m.* (न्), अनुकारकः, अनुकर्त्ता *m.* (र्त्तृ), अनुगामी *m.* (न्), अनुगतिकः, अनुयायी *m.* (न्), अनुवर्त्ती *m.* (न्), अनुचारी *m.* (न्), गतानुगतिकः.

Immaculate, *a.* अनघः -घा -घं, निष्कल्मषः -षा -षं, अकल्मषः -षा -षं, निष्कलङ्कः -ङ्का -ङ्कं, अनेनाः -नाः -नः (स्), निर्मलः -ला -लं, विमलः -ला -लं, निर्दोषः -षा -षं, निरपराधः -धा -धं, अनिन्द्यः -न्द्या -न्द्यं.

Immanent, *a.* निष्ठः -ष्ठा -ष्ठं, अन्तर्भवः -वा -वं, अन्तरस्थः -स्था -स्थं.

Immanity, *s.* क्रूरता, दारुणता, क्रौर्य्यं, दारुण्यं, निष्ठुरता, नैष्ठुर्य्यं.

Immarcessible, *a.* अम्लानी -निनी -नि (न्), अम्लानिः -निः -नि, अनश्वरः -रा -रं, अविनश्वरः -रा -रं, अक्षयः -या -यं, अनाश्यः -श्या -श्यं, अजरः -रा -रं.

To immask, *v. a.* कपटवेशेन or छद्मवेशेन छद् (c. 10. छादयति -यितुं), or आकारगोपनं कृ, विडम्ब् (c. 10. -डम्बयति -यितुं).

Immaterial, *a.* (Incorporeal, not consisting of matter) अमूर्त्तिकः -का -कं, अमूर्त्तः -र्त्ता -र्त्तं, अमूर्त्तिमान् -मती -मत् (त्), अमूर्त्तिमयः -यी -यं, अशरीरी -रिणी -रि (न्), अशारीरिकः -की -कं, अदैहिकः -की -कं, अदेही -हिनी -हि (न्), अवास्तवः -वी -वं, आत्मीयः -या -यं, आत्मिकः -की -कं, निरवयवः -वा -वं.—(Unimportant) अगुरुः -र्वी -रु, लघुः -घुः -घु, अल्पार्थः -र्था -र्थं, अगुर्वर्थः -र्था -र्थं, लघ्वर्थः -र्था -र्थं, अनावश्यकः -की -कं, अल्पप्रभावः -वा -वं, निष्प्रयोजनः -ना -नं.

Immaterialism, *s.* देहभिन्नात्मवादः, आत्मास्तित्ववादः, आत्मास्तित्वमतं.

Immaterialist, *s.* अमूर्त्तिवादी *m.* (न्), निराकारवादी *m.*, आत्मवादी.

Immateriality, *s.* अमूर्त्तिः *f.*, अमूर्त्तिमत्त्वं, मूर्त्तिहीनता, अशरीरिता, निरवयवत्वं, आत्मता -त्वं, अपाञ्चभौतिकता, निराकारत्वं, अनावश्यकत्वं.

Immaterially, *adv.* अनावश्यकं, अल्पप्रभावेण, लघु, निष्प्रयोजनं.

Immature, *a.* अपक्वः -क्वा -क्वं, अपरिपक्वः -क्वा -क्वं, अपक्विमः -मा -मं, अविपक्विमः -मा -मं, अपरिणतः -ता -तं, अपाकः -का -कं, अप्रौढः -ढा -ढं, अपूर्णः -र्णा -र्णं, अपूर्णकालः -ला -लं, असम्पूर्णः -र्णा -र्णं, असम्पूर्ण-

काल: -ला -लं, असम्पन्न: -न्ना -न्नं, असिद्ध: -द्धा -द्धं, आपक्व: -क्वा -क्वं, अतिशीघ्र: -घ्रा -घ्रं, अपुष्कल: -ला -लं, अप्राप्तयौवन: -ना -नं.

IMMATURELY, *adv.* अपक्वं, अपरिपक्वं, प्राक्परिपाकात्, परिपाकात्पूर्व्वं, प्राक्पूर्णकालात्, पूर्णकालात्पूर्व्वं, अतिशीघ्रं.

IMMATURENESS, IMMATURITY, *s.* अपक्वता, अपरिपक्वता, अपक्वि: *f.*, अपाक:, अपरिपाक:, अविपाक:, अपरिणतत्वं, अपरिणाम:, अपरिणति: *f.*, अप्रौढता, अपूर्णता, असम्पूर्णता, असिद्धता, असिद्धि: *f.*, असम्पन्नता, अपुष्कलता, अपौष्कल्यं.

IMMEASURABLE, *a.* अप्रमेय: -या -यं, अपरिमेय: -या -यं, अमेय: -या -यं, दुष्प्रमेय: -या -यं, अपरिमाण: -णा -णं, अपरिमित: -ता -तं, अमित: -ता -तं.

IMMEASURABLENESS, *s.* अप्रमेयता, अपरिमेयत्वं, अमेयता, दुष्प्रमेयत्वं.

IMMEASURABLY, *adv.* अप्रमेयं, अपरिमेयं, अपरिमितं, अत्यन्तं.

IMMEDIATE, *a.* (Proximate) उपस्थ: -स्था -स्थं, उपस्थायी -यिनी -यि (न्), उपस्थित: -ता -तं, सन्निहित: -ता -तं, अन्तिक: -का -कं, आसन्न: -न्ना -न्नं, निकट: -टा -टं.—(Without a medium or intervention) अनन्तर: -रा -रं, अव्यवहित: -ता -तं, अव्यवधान: -ना -नं, निरन्तर: -रा -रं.—(Without the intervention of time, instant) साद्यस्क: -स्की -स्कं, सद्यस्क: -स्का -स्कं, तात्कालिक: -की -कं, साम्प्रतिक: -की -कं, वर्त्तमान: -ना -नं, आकालिक: -की -कं, अचिर: -रा -रं, शीघ्र: -घ्रा -घ्रं, क्षणान्तर: -रा -रं.—(Direct) अवक्र: -क्रा -क्रं, अजिह्म: -ह्मा -ह्मं, अकुटिल: -ला -लं.

IMMEDIATELY, *adv.* सद्यस्, सपदि, आपाततस्, अनन्तरं, तत्क्षणात्, तत्काले, तत्क्षणे, झटिति, क्षणान्तरे, सम्प्रति, वर्त्तमानकाले, द्राक्, शीघ्रं, आशु, अकालक्षेपेण, अविलम्बितं; 'immediately after,' अनन्तरं, समनन्तरं; 'immediately on,' is expressed by मात्रात्; as, 'immediately on leaving the ship,' नौकातो निर्गममात्रात्; 'immediately on laying hands,' हस्तार्पणमात्रात्.

IMMEDIATENESS, *s.* आनन्तर्य्यं, नैरन्तर्य्यं, साद्यस्कता, सद्यस्कत्वं, शीघ्रता.

IMMEDICABLE, *a.* अचिकित्स्य: -त्स्या -त्स्यं, दुरुपचार: -रा -रं, ओषधिपथातिग: -गा -गं.

IMMELODIOUS, *a.* विस्वर: -रा -रं, अस्वर: -रा -रं, कुस्वर: -रा -रं.

IMMEMORABLE, *a.* अस्मरणीय: -या -यं, असंस्मर्त्तव्य: -व्या -व्यं, स्मरणायोग्य: -ग्या -ग्यं.

IMMEMORIAL, *a.* (Beyond memory) स्मरणातिग: -गा -गं, स्मृत्यतिग: -गा -गं, स्मरणातिक्रान्त: -न्ता -न्तं, अतिस्मृति: -ति: -ति, अस्मार्त्त: -र्त्ती -र्त्तं, जनश्रुत्यतिग: -गा -गं, अतिप्राचीन: -ना -नं, विस्मरणीय: -या -यं; 'immemorial succession,' अनादिपरम्परा, अनागम:.

IMMENSE, *a.* (Unlimited) अत्यन्त: -न्ता -न्तं, अनन्त: -न्ता -न्तं, अपरिमित: -ता -तं, अपरिमाण: -णा -णं, अमित: -ता -तं, अप्रमेय: -या -यं, अपरिमेय: -या -यं, अमेय: -या -यं, दुष्प्रमेय: -या -यं, अतिमर्य्याद: -दा -दं, अतिमात्र: -त्रा -त्रं, आत्यन्तिक: -की -कं, नितान्त: -न्ता -न्तं.—(Very great) सुमहान् -हती -हत् (त्), अतिमहान् &c., अतिबृहन् -हती -हत् (त्); 'in bulk,' बृहच्छरीर: -रा -रं, बृहत्काय: -या -यं, अपरिमितशरीर: -रा -रं.

IMMENSELY, *adv.* अत्यन्तं, अतिमात्रं, अपरिमितं, नितान्तं, अतिशयेन, सुमहत्.

IMMENSITY, *s.* (Unlimited extension) अमितता, अपरिमितत्वं, अपरिमाणत्वं, अप्रमेयता, अमेयता.—(Infinity) अत्यन्तता, अनन्तता, आनन्त्यं, आत्यन्तिकत्वं.—(Vastness of size) सुमहत्त्वं, सुबृहत्त्वं, शरीरबृहत्त्वं.—(Infinite space) महाकाशं.

To IMMERGE, *v. a.* निमज्ज् (c. 10. -मज्जयति -यितुं), मज्ज्, अवगाह् (c. 10. -गाहयति -यितुं), आप्लु (c. 10. -प्लावयति -यितुं), स्ना in caus. (स्नापयति, स्नपयति -यितुं), जलं प्रविश् (c. 10. -वेशयति -यितुं), जले निविश्.

To IMMERGE, *v. n.* (Immerse one's self) निमज्ज् (c. 6. -मज्जति -ज्जितुं -मंक्तुं), मज्ज्, अवगाह् (c. 1. -गाहते -हितुं -गाढुं), व्यवगाह्, विगाह्, आप्लु (c. 1. -प्लवते -प्लोतुं), स्ना (c. 2. स्नाति -तुं), जलं प्रविश् (c. 6. -विशति -वेष्टुं).

To IMMERSE, *v. a.* See *To* IMMERGE.

IMMERSED, *p. p.* मग्न: -ग्ना -ग्नं, निमग्न: -ग्ना -ग्नं, प्रमग्न: -ग्ना -ग्नं, निमज्जमान: -ना -नं, अवगाहित: -ता -तं, अवगाढ: -ढा -ढं, विगाढ: -ढा -ढं, गाहित: -ता -तं, आप्लुत: -ता -तं, निष्णात: -ता -तं, निवेशित: -ता -तं, निविष्ट: -ष्टा -ष्टं, अभिनिविष्ट: -ष्टा -ष्टं, अभिनिवेशित: -ता -तं, लीन: -ना -नं, निष्ठ: -ष्ठा -ष्ठं, निषित: -ता -तं, निष्ण: -ष्णा -ष्णं; 'immersed in sorrow,' शोकसागरमग्न: -ग्ना -ग्नं, शोकमग्न: -ग्ना -ग्नं; 'immersed in business,' कार्य्यनिष्ठ: -ष्ठा -ष्ठं, कर्म्मनिविष्ट: -ष्टा -ष्टं.

IMMERSION, *s.* निमज्जनं, मज्जनं, प्रमज्जनं, अवगाहनं, विगाह: -हनं, आप्लव:, आप्लाव: -वनं, स्नानं, जलप्रवेश:, जलान्त:प्रवेश:, अभिषेक:, निष्णानं.

IMMETHODICAL, *a.* अक्रमक: -का -कं -मिक: -का -कं, अव्यवस्थित: -ता -तं, क्रमहीन: -ना -नं, क्रमविरुद्ध: -द्धा -द्धं, अपर्य्याय: -या -यं.

IMMETHODICALLY, *adv.* अक्रमेण, क्रमेण विना, क्रमविरुद्धं, अक्रमतस्, अपर्य्यायतस्.

IMMETHODICALNESS, *s.* अक्रम:, क्रमहीनता, अव्यवस्थितत्वं, अपर्य्याय:.

IMMIGRANT, *s.* एकदेशत्यागानन्तरं देशान्तराधिविवस्तु: *m.* or देशान्तराधिवासी *m.* (न्), अन्यदेशविवस्तु: *m.*

To IMMIGRATE, *v. n.* एकदेशं त्यक्त्वा देशान्तरे वस् (c. 1. वसति, वस्तुं) or अधिवस् with acc. c., or अध्यास् (c. 2. -आस्ते -आसितुं), अन्यदेशाधिवासनार्थम् एकदेशं त्यज् (c. 1. त्यजति, त्यक्तुं).

IMMIGRATION, *s.* देशान्तराधिवासनं, प्रदेशाधिवासनं, देशत्याग:.

IMMINENT, *a.* उपस्थायी -यिनी -यि (न्), उपस्थित: -ता -तं, उपस्थ: -स्था -स्थं, समुपस्थित: -ता -तं, समुपगत: -ता -तं, समीपवर्त्ती -र्त्तिनी -र्त्ति (न्), निकटवर्त्ती &c., आसन्नवर्त्ती &c., उपनत: -ता -तं; 'imminent death,' कुपितान्तक: -का -कं.

To IMMINGLE, *v. a.* मिश्र् (c. 10. मिश्रयति -यितुं), विमिश्र्, सम्मिश्र्, मिश्रीकृ, एकीकृ.

IMMINGLED, *p.p.* मिश्रित: -ता -तं, सन्निपतित: -ता -तं, संसृष्ट: -ष्टा -ष्टं.

IMMINUTION, *s.* ह्रास:, क्षय:, हानि: *f.*, न्यूनता, अपचय:.

IMMISCIBILITY, *s.* अमिश्रणीयता, अयोजनीयता, अयाव्यता, मिश्रणाक्षमता.

IMMISCIBLE, *a.* अमिश्रणीय: -या -यं, अयोजनीय: -या -यं, अयाव्य: -व्या -व्यं.

IMMISSION, *s.* निक्षेपणं, न्यसनं, प्रवेशनं, निवेशनं, प्रवेशकरणं.

To IMMIT, *v. a.* निक्षिप् (c. 6. -क्षिपति -क्षेप्तुं), निविश् (c. 10. -वेशयति -यितुं).

IMMITIGABLE, *a.* अशमनीय: -या -यं, अशाम्य: -म्या -म्यं, अनुपशम्य: -म्या -म्यं.

IMMITTED, *p. p.* निक्षिप्त: -प्ता -प्तं, निवेशित: -ता -तं, प्रवेशित: -ता -तं.

To IMMIX, *v. a.* मिश्र् (c. 10. मिश्रयति -यितुं), विमिश्र्, मिश्रीकृ, सम्मिश्रीकृ.

IMMOBILITY, *s.* निश्चलत्वं, अचलत्वं, स्थिरता, स्थैर्य्यं, स्थावरत्वं, व्यवस्थिति: *f.*, अवस्थिति: *f.*, संस्थिति: *f.*, स्थायित्वं, स्थाणुता, अकम्प:.

IMMODERATE, *a.* अपरिमित: -ता -तं, अत्यन्त: -न्ता -न्तं, अतिमात्र: -त्रा -त्रं, अतिमर्य्याद: -दा -दं, अमित: -ता -तं, अपरिमाण: -णा -णं, नितान्त: -न्ता -न्तं, अतिमित: -ता -तं, अधिक: -का -कं, अमर्य्याद: -दा -दं, आत्यन्तिक: -की -कं, सु or अति or अतिशय prefixed.

IMMODERATELY, *adv.* अपरिमितं, अत्यन्तं, अतिमात्रं, नितान्तं, अतिशयेन, अतिमर्य्यादं, अत्यर्थं, अति or सु or अतिशय prefixed.

IMMODERATION, *s.* अपरिमितत्वं, अमितत्वं, मर्य्यादातिक्रम:, अमर्य्यादा.

IMMODEST, *a.* निर्लज्जः -ज्जा -ज्जं, लज्जाहीनः -ना -नं, त्रपाहीनः -ना -नं, व्रीडाहीनः -ना -नं, अविनीतः -ता -तं, अलज्जः -ज्जा -ज्जं, विलज्जः -ज्जा -ज्जं, अनिभृतः -ता -तं, वियातः -ता -तं, प्रगल्भः -ल्भा -ल्भं, धृष्टः -ष्टा -ष्टं.—(Impure, obscene) अशुद्धः -द्धा -द्धं, अशुचिः -चिः -चि, अवाच्यः -च्या -च्यं, गर्ह्यः -र्ह्या -र्ह्यं.—(Unchaste) असद्वृत्तः -त्ता -त्तं, असाधुवृत्तः -त्ता -त्तं, व्यसनी -निनी -नि (न्), व्यभिचारी -रिणी -रि (न्), पांशुलः -ला -लं; 'an immodest woman,' बन्धकी, असती, पुंश्चली, असाध्वी, कुलटा, अभिसारिका, धर्षिणी.

IMMODESTLY, *adv.* अविनीतं, निर्लज्जं, वैयात्येन, अशुद्धं, प्रगल्भं, विनयविरोधेन, धृष्टवत्, अशुचि.

IMMODESTY, *s.* निर्लज्जत्वं, लज्जाहीनता, अलज्जा, अविनयः, अविनीतत्वं, वैयात्यं, प्रगल्भता, प्रागल्भ्यं, धृष्टता, अशुद्धता, अशुचिता, गर्ह्यता; 'in a woman,' पौंश्चल्यं, असतीत्वं, असाध्वीत्वं.

To IMMOLATE, *v. a.* क्रतौ हन् (c. 2. हन्ति -न्तुं), उपहारार्थं हन्, उत्सर्गार्थं हन् or शस् (c. 1. शसति -सितुं) or विशस् or प्रमी in caus. (-मापयति -यितुं), or उपहृ or उपहारीकृ or प्रोक्ष् (c. 1. -उक्षति -क्षितुं), उत्सर्गपूर्व्वं हन्, घातयित्वा उत्सर्गं कृ, हत्वा उत्सृज् (c. 6. -सृजति -स्रष्टुं), बलिं कृ, बलिदानं कृ.

IMMOLATED, *p. p.* उपहारार्थं हतः -ता -तं or प्रमीतः -ता -तं or शसितः -ता -तं, उपहृतः -ता -तं, उपहारीकृतः -ता -तं, प्रोक्षितः -ता -तं.

IMMOLATION, *s.* उपहारार्थं घातः or घातनं or निहननं, उत्सर्गार्थं मारणं or प्रमापणं or विशसनं or शसनं, शमनं, ससनं, प्रोक्षणं, परम्पराकं, उपहारः, उपहरणं, उत्सर्गकरणं, बलिदानं.

IMMORAL, *a.* निर्धर्म्मः -र्म्मा -र्म्मं -र्म्मा -र्म्मा -र्म्म (न्), अधार्म्मिकः -की -कं, धर्म्मविरुद्धः -द्धा -द्धं, धर्म्मापेतः -ता -तं, धर्म्मरोधी -धिनी -धि (न्), अधर्म्मी -र्म्मिणी -र्म्मि (न्), कुधर्म्मा -र्म्मा -र्म्म (न्), अपुण्यः -ण्या -ण्यं, असाधुः -ध्वी -धु, अशुचिः -चिः -चि, कुशीलः -ला -लं, विशीलः -ला -लं, दुःशीलः -ला -लं, दुश्चरित्रः -त्रा -त्रं, असच्चरित्रः -त्रा -त्रं, असत्कर्म्मा -र्म्मा -र्म्म (न्), दुष्टः -ष्टा -ष्टं, कर्म्मदुष्टः -ष्टा -ष्टं, दुर्वृत्तः -त्ता -त्तं, व्यभिचारी -रिणी -रि (न्), पापी -पिनी -पि (न्), पापकर्म्मा &c., व्यसनी -निनी -नि (न्), कुचरितः -ता -तं, अधर्म्मचारी -रिणी -रि (न्).

IMMORALITY, *s.* अधर्म्मः, अधर्म्मत्वं -ता, निर्धर्म्मत्वं, अधार्म्मिकत्वं, असाधुत्वं, अपुण्यता, अशुचिता, दुष्टता, दुर्वृत्तत्वं, व्यसनिता, व्यसनं, कुशीलता, दुश्चरित्रता, अधर्म्मचारित्वं, दुःशीलता, दौःशील्यं, व्यभिचारः.

IMMORTAL, *a.* (Exempt from death) अमरः -री -रं, अमर्त्यः -र्त्या -र्त्यं, सदाजीवी -विनी -वि (न्), सदास्थायी -यिनी -यि (न्), मरणरहितः -ता -तं.—(Imperishable) निर्जरः -रा -रं, अजरः -रा -रं, अक्षयः -या -यं, अनश्वरः -रा -रं, अनाश्यः -श्या -श्यं, अविनाशी -शिनी -शि (न्), निरपायः -या -यं.—(Eternal) अनन्तः -न्ता -न्तं, नित्यः -त्या -त्यं, सनातनः -नी -नं, सदातनः -नी -नं, शाश्वतः -ती -तं, अनाद्यन्तः -न्ता -न्तं, सर्व्वकालीनः -ना -नं, अनन्तकालस्थायी -यिनी -यि (न्).

IMMORTALITY, *s.* अमरता -त्वं, अमर्त्यता, निर्जरता -त्वं, अजरता -त्वं, अक्षयता, अनश्वरता, अनाश्यता, अनन्तता, आनन्त्यं, अनन्त्यं, सदास्थायित्वं, नित्यता.

To IMMORTALIZE, *v. a.* अमरीकृ, निर्जरीकृ, अनश्वरीकृ, अक्षयीकृ, शाश्वतीकृ, नित्यीकृ, आनन्त्यं कृ or जन् (c. 10. जनयति -यितुं).

IMMORTALLY, *adv.* अमरं, अमरत्वेन, अमरवत्, अमर्त्यवत्, निर्जरं, अजरं, अक्षयं, अनश्वरं, अनन्तकाले -लं, अनन्तं, आनन्त्येन, सनातनं, शाश्वतं, निरपायं, अविनाशेन.

IMMOVABILITY, *s.* अचलता -त्वं, निश्चलत्वं, स्थावरत्वं, स्थिरता, अचरिष्णुता, स्तब्धता.

IMMOVABLE, *a.* अचलः -ला -लं, निश्चलः -ला -लं, स्थावरः -रा -रं, अचरः -रा -रं, अचरिष्णुः -ष्णुः -ष्णु, अजङ्गमः -मा -मं, अस्पन्दः -न्दा -न्दं, अच्युतः -ता -तं, स्थिरः -रा -रं, स्थायी -यिनी -यि (न्), स्तब्धः -ब्धा -ब्धं, स्थाणुः -णुः -णु, स्थास्नुः -स्नुः -स्नु, जङ्गमेतरः -रा -रं, स्तिमितः -ता -तं, अनेतन -ना -न (न्); 'immovables,' स्थावराणि.

IMMOVABLY, *adv.* अचलं, निश्चलं, स्थावरं, स्थिरं, स्तब्धं, स्थाणुवत्.

IMMUND, *a.* अशुचिः -चिः -चि, अपवित्रः -त्रा -त्रं, अशौची -चिनी -चि (न्).

IMMUNDICITY, *s.* अशुचिता -त्वं, अशौचं, आशौचं, अपवित्रता -त्वं, अशोधनं.

IMMUNITY, *s.* मुक्तिः *f.*, मोक्षः, विमोक्षः, विनिर्मोकः, निर्मोकः, विरहः, राहित्यं, रहितत्वं, शून्यता, अभावः, असम्भवः, or expressed by अ prefixed; as, 'immunity from danger,' अभयं; 'from exertion,' अनायासः; 'from taxes,' अकरत्वं.

To IMMURE, *v. a.* निरुध् (c. 7. -रुणद्धि -रोद्धुं), अवरुध्, रुध्; 'in a prison,' कारायां निरुध् or बन्ध् (c. 9. बध्नाति, बन्द्धुं), कारागुप्तं -प्तां -प्तं कृ.—(Inclose) परिवृ (c. 5. -वृणोति -वरितुं -रीतुं), परिवेष्ट् (c. 1. -वेष्टते -ष्टितुं, c. 10. -वेष्टयति -यितुं), संवेष्ट्, उपवेष्ट्.—(Surround with a wall) प्राकारेण परिवृ, प्राकारीयं -यां -यं कृ.

IMMURED, *p. p.* निरुद्धः -द्धा -द्धं, अवरुद्धः -द्धा -द्धं, अन्तर्गतः -ता -तं.

IMMUTABILITY, *s.* अविकार्य्यता -त्वं, अविकारत्वं, निर्विकारत्वं, अविकारः, स्थिरता, अमोघता, अपरिवर्त्तनं, नित्यता.

IMMUTABLE, *a.* अविकार्य्यः -र्य्या -र्य्यं, अविकारः -रा -रं, अविक्रियः -या -यं, निर्विकारः -रा -रं, विकाराक्षमः -मा -मं, विकारहीनः -ना -नं, स्थिरः -रा -रं, अमोघः -घा -घं, निर्विकल्पः -ल्पा -ल्पं, नित्यः -त्या -त्यं, अपरिवर्त्तनीयः -या -यं.

IMMUTABLY, *adv.* अविकार्य्यं, अविकारेण, अविकार्य्यत्वेन, स्थिरं, नित्यं, निर्विकारं, निर्विकल्पं, अमोघं.

IMMUTATION, *s.* विकारः, विक्रिया, विकृतिः *f.*, वैकृत्यं, विपर्य्ययः, परिवर्त्तः.

IMP, *s.* पिशाचः, भूतः, राक्षसः, असुरः, दैत्यः, दानवः, ग्रहः, यातुः *m.*, यातुधानः, विधुरः, क्रव्याद् *m.*, निशाटः, निशाचरः, कर्बुरः, कर्व्वुरः.

To IMP, *v. a.* (Graft) एकवृक्षशाखायां भिन्नवृक्षपल्लवं निविश् (c. 10. -वेशयति -यितुं).—(Lengthen) दीर्घतरं -रां -रं कृ, दीर्घीकृ.

IMPACABLE, *a.* अशाम्यः -म्या -म्यं, असान्त्वनीयः -या -यं, अतोषणीयः -या -यं.

IMPACT, *s.* स्पर्शः, संस्पर्शः, सम्पर्कः, उपघातः, आघातः, प्रतिघातः.

To IMPAIR, *v. a.* न्यूनीकृ, ह्रस् (c. 10. ह्रासयति -यितुं), अल्पीकृ, विकलीकृ, ऊन (nom. ऊनयति -यितुं), ऊन् (c. 10. ऊनयति -यितुं), न्यून्, क्षण् (c. 8. क्षणोति -णितुं), परिक्षण्, क्षीणीकृ, क्षतिं कृ, परिक्षतिं कृ, दुष् (c. 10. दूषयति -यितुं), उपहन् (c. 2. -हन्ति -न्तुं), लघ (nom. लघयति -यितुं), लुप् (c. 6. लुम्पति, लोप्तुं), लघूकृ, नश् (c. 10. नाशयति -यितुं), विनश्.—(Enfeeble) शिथिलीकृ, अल्पबलीकृ, दुर्बलीकृ, बलं or तेजः or सत्त्वं हृ (c. 1. हरति, हर्त्तुं).

IMPAIRED, *p. p.* विकलः -ला -लं, विकलीभूतः -ता -तं, विकलीकृतः -ता -तं, अल्पीभूतः -ता -तं, अल्पीकृतः -ता -तं, न्यूनीकृतः -ता -तं, न्यूनीभूतः -ता -तं, क्षीणः -णा -णं, ह्रसितः -ता -तं, अपचितः -ता -तं, लुप्तः -प्ता -प्तं, शिथिलीकृतः -ता -तं, उपहतः -ता -तं, विशीर्णः -र्णा -र्णं; 'impaired in strength,' शिथिलबलः -ला -लं, क्षीणबलः -ला -लं, हृतबलः -ला -लं, हृतसत्त्वः -त्त्वा -त्त्वं.

IMPAIRING, IMPAIRMENT, *s.* न्यूनता -त्वं, न्यूनीकरणं, क्षयः, ह्रासः, हानिः *f.*, अल्पत्वं -ता, वैकल्यं, विकलीकरणं, शैथिल्यं, शिथिलीकरणं, अपचयः, क्षिया, अवसादः.

To IMPALE, *v. a.* IMPALED, IMPALEMENT. *See* EMPALE, &c.

IMPALPABILITY, *s.* अस्पृश्यता, अस्पर्शनीयता, दुःस्पृश्यता, अग्राह्यता,

अग्रहणीयत्वं, अव्यक्तता, अव्यक्ति f., अतिसूक्ष्मता.

IMPALPABLE, *a.* अस्पृश्यः -श्या -श्यं, अस्पर्शनीयः -या -यं, दुःस्पर्शः -र्शा -र्शं, दुःस्पृश्यः -श्या -श्यं, अग्राह्यः -ह्या -ह्यं, अग्रहणीयः -या -यं, दुरभिग्रहः -हा -हं, दुरालभः -भा -भं, स्पर्शाव्यक्तः -क्ता -क्तं, अव्यक्तः -क्ता -क्तं, अप्रत्यक्षः -क्षा -क्षं, इन्द्रियैरग्राह्यः -ह्या -ह्यं, इन्द्रियाग्राह्यः -ह्या -ह्यं, इन्द्रियागोचरः -रा -रं, अतिसूक्ष्मः -क्ष्मा -क्ष्मं.

IMPALPABLY, *adv.* अस्पर्शनीयं, अस्पृश्यं, अव्यक्तं, अप्रत्यक्षं.

To IMPANNEL, *v. a.* (A jury) नामावलिपत्रे or नामपरिसंख्यापत्रे द्वादशप्रमाणपुरुषाणां or द्वादशमध्यस्थपुरुषाणां नामानि समारुह् in caus. (-रोपयति -यितुं) or अभिलिख् (c. 6. -लिखति -लेखितुं).

IMPARASYLLABIC, *a.* असमानाक्षरः -रा -रं, अतुल्याक्षरः -रा -रं.

IMPARITY, *s.* असाम्यं, असमता, असमानता, असामान्यं, वैषम्यं, विषमता, विषमं, अतुल्यत्वं -ता, असमञ्जसं, असामञ्जस्यं, तारतम्यं.

To IMPARK, *v. a.* वाटं कृ, वाटिकां कृ, भूमिभागं प्राचीरेण परिवृ (c. 5. -वृणोति -वरितुं -रीतुं) or वृतिपरिगतं कृ.

To IMPART, *v. a.* प्रदा (c. 3. -ददाति -दातुं), अभिदा, सम्प्रदा, निदा, दा, यम् (c. 1. यच्छति, दातुं), प्रयम्, सम्प्रयम्, प्रतिपद् (c. 10. -पादयति -यितुं), उपपद्, वितृ (c. 1. -तरति -रितुं -रीतुं), आहृ (c. 1. -हरति -हर्तुं), उपहृ, ऋ in caus. (अर्पयति -यितुं), समृ, निक्षिप् (c. 6. -क्षिपति -क्षेप्तुं), सङ्क्रम् in caus. (-क्रामयति -यितुं), ग्रह् in caus. (ग्राहयति -यितुं), प्रदानं कृ.—(Impart information, make known) विज्ञा in caus. (-ज्ञापयति -यितुं), निविद् (c. 10. -वेदयति -यितुं), समाविद्, संवद् (c. 1. -वदति -दितुं), संवादं कथ् (c. 10. कथयति -यितुं), समाचारं कथ्; 'impart a secret,' रहस्यं प्रकाश् (c. 10. -काशयति -यितुं).

IMPARTED, *p. p.* प्रदत्तः -त्ता -त्तं, प्रत्तः -त्ता -त्तं, निदत्तः -त्ता -त्तं, नीत्तः -त्ता -त्तं, प्रतिपादितः -ता -तं, उपपादितः -ता -तं, वितीर्णः -र्णा -र्णं, अर्पितः -ता -तं, समर्पितः -ता -तं, निक्षिप्तः -प्ता -प्तं, निहितः -ता -तं, संक्रान्तः -न्ता -न्तं.—(Made known) निवेदितः -ता -तं, विज्ञापितः -ता -तं, विज्ञप्तः -प्ता -प्तं.—(As a secret, &c.) प्रकाशितः -ता -तं.—(As a disease) संचारितः -ता -तं, संक्रान्तः -न्ता -न्तं.

IMPARTER, *s.* दाता *m.* (तृ), प्रदाता *m.*, दायी *m.* (न्), प्रतिपादकः.

IMPARTIAL, *a.* अपक्षपाती -तिनी -ति (न्), विपक्षपातः -ता -तं, पक्षपातरहितः -ता -तं, पक्षपातहीनः -ना -नं, समदर्शी -र्शिनी -र्शि (न्), सर्व्वसमः -मा -मं, समः -मा -मं, निःसङ्गः -ङ्गा -ङ्गं, सङ्गहीनः -ना -नं, मुक्तसङ्गः -ङ्गा -ङ्गं, न्यायी -यिनी -यि (न्), न्यायवर्त्ती -र्त्तिनी -र्त्ति (न्), उदासीनः -ना -नं, उदासी -सिनी -सि (न्), उभयसाधारणः -णा -णी -णं, उभयसमः -मा -मं, उभयसामान्यः -न्या -न्यं, मध्यस्थः -स्था -स्थं, धार्म्मिकः -की -कं, निरपेक्षः -क्षा -क्षं, समानवृत्तिः -त्तिः -त्ति.

IMPARTIALITY, *s.* अपक्षपातः, पक्षपातहीनता, साम्यं, समता, सर्व्वसमता, उभयसमता, औदास्यं, उदासीनता, निःसङ्गता, सङ्गहीनता, न्यायः, धर्म्मन्यायः.

IMPARTIALLY, *adv.* अपक्षपातेन, पक्षपातं विना, समं, साम्येन, असङ्गेन, सङ्गं विना, न्यायेन, न्यायतस्, उदासीनं, उदासीनवत्.

IMPARTIBLE, *a.* अविभाज्यः -ज्या -ज्यं, अवघट्टनीयः -या -यं, अनंश्यः -श्या -श्यं.

IMPASSABLE, *a.* अतरणीयः -या -यं, अतार्य्यः -र्य्या -र्य्यं, दुस्तरः -रा -रं, दुस्तार्य्यः -र्य्या -र्य्यं, सुदुस्तरः -रा -रं, दुरुत्तरः -रा -रं, दुर्गः -र्गा -र्गं, दुर्गमः -मा -मं, अगम्यः -म्या -म्यं, अगमनीयः -या -यं, दुरत्ययः -या -यं, गहनः -ना -नं, सङ्कटः -टा -टं, सबाधः -धा -धं, गत्नूनः -ना -नं.

IMPASSABLENESS, *s.* अतार्य्यत्वं, दुस्तार्य्यत्वं, अगम्यता, दुर्गम्यता.

IMPASSIBLE, *a.* अचेतनः -ना -नं, निश्चेतनः -ना -नं, शोकदुःखाक्षमः -मा -मं, क्लेशदुःखादिहीनः -ना -नं, रागहीनः -ना -नं, अरागी -गिणी -गि (न्).

IMPASSIBLENESS, *s.* अचैतन्यं, शोकदुःखाक्षमता, क्लेशदुःखादिहीनता.

To IMPASSION, *v. a.* संरक्तीकृ, सरागीकृ, रागवन्तं -वतीं -वत् कृ.

IMPASSIONED, *p. p.* संरक्तः -क्ता -क्तं, रागवान् -वती -वत् (त्), रागी -गिणी -गि (न्), रागान्वितः -ता -तं, सरागः -गा -गं, सानुरागः -गा -गं, अनुरागी -गिणी -गि (न्), सरसः -सा -सं, रसी -सिनी -सि (न्), रसिकः -का -कं, शृङ्गारी -रिणी -रि (न्), शृङ्गारितः -ता -तं.

IMPATIENCE, *s.* अमर्षः, अक्षमता, अक्षमा, अक्षान्तिः *f.*, असहिष्णुता -त्वं, विमर्षः, असहनं, असहत्वं, अतितिक्षा, अनुत्साहः.

IMPATIENT, *a.* असहिष्णुः -ष्णुः -ष्णु, असहनः -ना -नं, असहः -हा -हं, असहमानः -ना -नं, असहनशीलः -ला -लं, अक्षमः -मा -मं, अक्षामिमान् -मती -मत् (त्), अक्षमी -मिणी -मि (न्), अक्षन्ता -न्त्री -न्तृ (न्तृ), अमर्षणः -णा -णं, विमर्षी -र्षिणी -र्षि (न्), जातामर्षः -र्षा -र्षं, अतितिक्षुः -क्षुः -क्षु, उत्सुकः -का -कं, उत्कः -त्का -त्कं.

IMPATIENTLY, *adv.* सामर्षं, सविमर्षं, अमर्षेण, विमर्षेण, असहिष्णुवत्, अक्षान्त्या, असहनशीलत्वात्, सावेगं.

To IMPAWN, *v. a.* आधीकृ, पण् (c. 1. पणते -णितुं), परिपण्, निक्षिप् (c. 6. -क्षिपति -क्षेप्तुं), न्यस् (c. 4. -अस्यति -असितुं).

To IMPEACH, *v. a.* अभियुज् (c. 7. -युनक्ति -योक्तुं), व्यवहारसभायां or व्यवहारानुसारेण अभियुज् or अभिशंस् (c. 1. -शंसति -सितुं) or अभियोगं कृ or अभिशंसनं कृ or अपवद् (c. 1. -वदति -दितुं), दोषीकृ, उपालभ् (c. 1. -लभते -लब्धुं).

IMPEACHABLE, *a.* अभियोक्तव्यः -व्या -व्यं, व्यवहारसभायाम् अभियोज्यः -ज्या -ज्यं.

IMPEACHED, *a.* व्यवहाराभियुक्तः -क्ता -क्तं, अभियुक्तः -क्ता -क्तं, व्यवहाराभिशस्तः -स्ता -स्तं.

IMPEACHER, *s.* अभियोगी *m.* (न्), अभियोक्ता *m.* (क्तृ), अभियोगकृत् *m.*, अपवादकः.

IMPEACHMENT, *s.* अभियोगः, व्यवहाराभियोगः, अभिशंसनं, व्यवहाराभिशंसनं, अपवादः, संशयः.

IMPECCABILITY, *s.* निष्पापत्वं, पापहीनता, पापाभावः, पापाक्षमता.

IMPECCABLE, *a.* अपापः -पा -पं, निष्पापः -पा -पं, पापाक्षमः -मा -मं.

To IMPEDE, *v. a.* रुध् (c. 7. रुणद्धि, रोद्धुं), प्रतिरुध्, निरुध्, उपरुध्, संरुध्, विरुध्; विहन् (c. 2. -हन्ति -न्तुं), व्याहन्, प्रतिहन्, प्रतिबन्ध् (c. 9. -बध्नाति -बन्द्धुं), वृ (c. 10. वारयति -यितुं), निवृ, विनिवृ, आवृ, समावृ, प्रतिवृ, विघ्न (nom. विघ्नयति -यितुं), बाध् (c. 1. बाधते -धितुं), स्तम्भ् (c. 10. स्तम्भयति -यितुं, c. 9. स्तभ्नाति, स्तम्भितुं), विष्टम्भ्, प्रत्यूहीकृ, निषिध् (c. 1. -षेधति -षेद्धुं).

IMPEDED, *p. p.* रुद्धः -द्धा -द्धं, विरुद्धः -द्धा -द्धं, प्रतिरुद्धः -द्धा -द्धं, निरुद्धः -द्धा -द्धं, उपरुद्धः -द्धा -द्धं, विहतः -ता -तं, प्रतिहतः -ता -तं, पराहतः -ता -तं, वारितः -ता -तं, निवारितः -ता -तं, विघ्नितः -ता -तं, बाधितः -ता -तं, स्तम्भितः -ता -तं, स्तब्धः -ब्धा -ब्धं, विष्टब्धः -ब्धा -ब्धं, अन्तरितः -ता -तं, सार्गलः -ला -लं.

IMPEDIMENT, *s.* विघ्नः, व्याघातः, अन्तरायः, प्रत्यूहः, प्रतिबन्धः, विष्टम्भः, प्रतिष्टम्भः, स्तम्भः -म्भनं, रोधः, संरोधः, विरोधः, अवरोधः, उपरोधः, निरोधः, विघातः -तं, विहननं, विहतिः *f.*, बाधा -धकः, वारणं, निवारणं, आवरणं.—(Impediment in speech) वाक्स्खलनं, वाग्भेदः, वाग्वैकल्यं; 'having an impediment in one's speech,' स्खलद्वाक् -क्वा -क्वं, वाग्विकलः -ला -लं, भिन्नवाक् *m. f. n.*, कद्वदः -दा -दं.

IMPEDIMENTAL, *a.* (Causing impediment) व्याघातकः -का -कं, विघाती -तिनी -ति (न्), विघ्नकरः -री -रं, विघ्नकारी -रिणी -रि (न्), विरोधी -धिनी -धि (न्), प्रतिरोधी &c., औपरोधिकः -की -कं, विष्टम्भी -म्भिनी -म्भि (न्), निवारकः -का -कं.

To IMPEL, *v. a.* (Drive, urge forward) प्रेर् (c. 10. -ईरयति -यितुं)

प्रणुद् (c. 6. -णुदति -णोत्तुं), प्रचुद् (c. 10. -चोदयति -यितुं), सञ्चुद्, परिचुद्, चुद्, कृष् (c. 1. कर्षति, क्रष्टुं), समाकृष्.—(Incite to action) प्रवृत् (c. 10. -वर्त्तयति -यितुं), प्रयुज् (c. 10. -योजयति -यितुं), नियुज्, उद्युज्, उत्सह् (c. 10. -साहयति -यितुं), प्रोत्सह्, प्ररुच् (c. 10. -रोचयति -यितुं), चेष्ट् (c. 10. चेष्टयति -यितुं), उत्तप् (c. 10. -तापयति -यितुं).

IMPELLED, *p. p.* प्रेरितः -ता -तं, प्रणोदितः -ता -तं, प्रणुन्नः -न्ना -न्नं, प्रचोदितः -ता -तं, प्रवर्त्तितः -ता -तं, प्रवृत्तः -त्ता -त्तं, नियोजितः -ता -तं, प्रयोजितः -ता -तं, प्रोत्साहितः -ता -तं, प्ररोचितः -ता -तं, समाकृष्टः -ष्टा -ष्टं, आकृष्टः -ष्टा -ष्टं.

IMPELLENT, *s.* प्रेरकः, प्रेरयिता *m.* (तृ), प्रणोदकः, प्रवर्त्तकः, प्रयोजकः, प्रोत्साहकः, प्रचोदकः.

To IMPEND, *v. n.* (Be near) उपस्था (c. 1. -तिष्ठति -ते -स्थातुं), प्रत्युपस्था, समुपस्था, समीपे स्था or वृत् (c. 1. वर्त्तते -र्त्तितुं), निकटे स्था or वृत्, उपगम् (c. 1. -गच्छति -गन्तुं), उपागम्, समुपगम्, उपनतः -ता -तं भू.—(Hang over) आलम्ब् (c. 1. -लम्बते -म्बितुं), प्रलम्ब्, अवलम्ब्, लम्ब्.—(Be about to fall) पत् in des. (पिपतिषति -षितुं, पित्सति -त्सितुं), आपत् (c 1. -पतति -तितुं).

IMPENDENT, IMPENDING, *a.* उपस्थायी -यिनी -यि (न्), उपस्थितः -ता -तं, उपस्थः -स्था -स्थं, समुपस्थितः -ता -तं, समीपवर्त्ती -र्त्तिनी -र्त्ति (न्), निकटवर्त्ती &c., आसन्नवर्त्ती &c., उपनतः -ता -तं, समुपगतः -ता -तं, पतनोन्मुखः -खा -खं, पिपतिषुः -षुः -षु, पित्सुः -त्सुः -त्सु.

IMPENETRABILITY, *s.* अवेध्यता, अव्यध्यता, अभेद्यता, अच्छेद्यत्वं, अप्रवेश्यत्वं, वज्रता -त्वं, गहनत्वं; 'impenetrability,' as a property of matter, is expressed in scientific treatises by the word विरोधः.

IMPENETRABLE, *a.* (Not to be pierced) अवेध्यः -ध्या -ध्यं, अव्यध्यः -ध्या -ध्यं, अभेद्यः -द्या -द्यं, अभेदनीयः -या -यं, अच्छेद्यः -द्या -द्यं, अच्छेदनीयः -या -यं, अव्याप्यः -प्या -प्यं, अच्छिद्रणीयः -या -यं, कलिलः -ला -लं.—(Not to be entered) अप्रवेश्यः -श्या -श्यं, अप्रवेष्टव्यः -व्या -व्यं, गहनः -ना -नं.—(Very hard) वज्रमयः -यी -यं, वज्रः -ज्रा -ज्रं.

IMPENETRABLY, *adv.* अभेद्यं, अवेध्यं, अच्छेदनीयं, गहनं, वज्रवत्.

IMPENITENCE, IMPENITENCY. *s.* अननुतापः, अपश्चात्तापः, पश्चात्तापहीनता, पश्चात्तापाभावः, अननुशोकः, अखेदः, खेदहीनता, खेदराहित्यं, अप्रायश्चित्तं, अननुशयः, स्तब्धचित्तत्वं.

IMPENITENT, *a.* अननुतापी -पिनी -पि (न्), अननुतप्तः -प्ता -प्तं, पश्चात्तापहीनः -ना -नं, अननुतापशीलः -ला -लं, खेदहीनः -ना -नं, खेदरहितः -ता -तं, अननुशयी -यिनी -यि (न्), स्तब्धचित्तः -त्ता -त्तं, कठिनचित्तः -त्ता -त्तं.

IMPERATIVE, *a.* आज्ञापकः -का -कं, आदेशकः -का -कं, आदेशी -शिनी -शि (न्), नियोजकः -का -कं, प्रबोधकः -का -कं, अवश्यकर्त्तव्यः -व्या -व्यं; 'imperative mood,' विधिः *m.*, आज्ञावाचकः -कं.

IMPERCEPTIBLE, *a.* अव्यक्तः -क्ता -क्तं, अप्रत्यक्षः -क्षा -क्षं, अविभाव्यः -व्या -व्यं, अविभावनीयः -या -यं, अगम्यः -म्या -म्यं, अगोचरः -रा -रं.—(To the senses) अतीन्द्रियः -या -यं, इन्द्रियागोचरः -रा -रं, इन्द्रियागम्यः -म्या -म्यं, इन्द्रियातीतः -ता -तं.—(To the eye) परोक्षः -क्षा -क्षं, अलोकनीयः -या -यं, नयनागोचरः -रा -रं.—(To the ear) कर्णागोचरः -रा -रं.

IMPERCEPTIBLY, *adv.* अव्यक्तं, अप्रत्यक्षं -क्षेण, अविभावनीयं, अगोचरं; 'going imperceptibly,' अव्यक्तगतिः -तिः -ति.

IMPERFECT, *a.* (Not complete) असम्पूर्णः -र्णा -र्णं, अपूर्णः -र्णा -र्णं, अपरिपूर्णः -र्णा -र्णं, असम्पन्नः -न्ना -न्नं, असमाप्तः -प्ता -प्तं, असिद्धः -द्धा -द्धं, असमग्रः -ग्रा -ग्रं, अनिखिलः -ला -लं, अनिष्पन्नः -न्ना -न्नं, अपर्य्याप्तः -प्ता -प्तं, असंसिद्धः -द्धा -द्धं, अपक्वः -क्वा -क्वं, खण्ड in comp.—(Defective) न्यूनः -ना -नं, विकलः -ला -लं, हीनः -ना -नं, लुप्तः -प्ता -प्तं, दोषी -षिणी -षि (न्), सच्छिद्रः -द्रा -द्रं, ऊनः -ना -नं.—(Wanting some organ) अङ्गहीनः -ना -नं, न्यूनेन्द्रियः -या -यं, विकलेन्द्रियः -या -यं, विकलाङ्गः -ङ्गा -ङ्गं.—(Tense) अद्यतनभूतः, अनद्यतनः; the grammatical symbols are घी, लङ्; 'imperfect comparison,' लुप्तोपमा.

IMPERFECTION, *s.* (Defect) दोषः, छिद्रं, अगुणः, अपराधः, कलङ्कः, दूषणं, वैकल्यं, हानिः *f.*, हीनता, क्षतिः *f.*, न्यूनता, अपर्य्याप्तिः *f.*, अशुद्धता; 'in a gem,' पुलकः, त्रसः.

IMPERFECTLY, *adv.* असम्पूर्णं, असमग्रं, खण्डशस्, अनिखिलेन, असम्पन्नं, असम्यक्, अपर्य्याप्तं, विकलं, वैकल्येन.

IMPERFECTNESS, *s.* असम्पूर्णता, अपूर्णता, असम्पन्नता, असिद्धिः *f.*, असमग्रता.

IMPERFORATE, *a.* नीरन्ध्रः -न्ध्रा -न्ध्रं, निश्छिद्रः -द्रा -द्रं, अच्छिद्रितः -ता -तं.

IMPERIAL, *a.* माहाराजिकः -की -कं, आधिराजिकः -की -कं, महाराजकीयः -या -यं, महाराजयोग्यः -ग्या -ग्यं, साम्राजिकः -की -कं, महेश्वरीयः -या -यं.

IMPERIALIST, *s.* महाराजाधीनः, अधिराजाधीनः, महाराजानुचरः, महाराजानुभक्ती *m.* (न्); 'imperialist army,' महाराजसैन्यं.

To IMPERIL, *v. a.* संशयस्थं -स्थां -स्थं कृ, सन्देहस्थं -स्थां -स्थं कृ.

IMPERIOUS, *a.* (Commanding) आज्ञापकः -का -कं, आदेशकः -का -कं.—(Overbearing, haughty) धृष्टः -ष्टा -ष्टं, धर्षी -र्षिणी -र्षि (न्), भर्त्सनकारी -रिणी -रि (न्), उद्धतः -ता -तं, अवलिप्तः -प्ता -प्तं, सावहेलः -ला -लं, सोन्माथः -था -थं, प्रगल्भः -ल्भा -ल्भं, दृप्तः -प्ता -प्तं.

IMPERIOUSLY, *adv.* धर्षेण, प्रगल्भं, सावहेलं, सावलेपं, सोन्माथं, साटोपं.

IMPERIOUSNESS, *s.* धृष्टता, धर्षः, अवलिप्तता, अवलेपः, सावलेपत्वं, अवहेला, उद्धतिः *f.*, चित्तसमुन्नतिः *f.*, प्रगल्भता, प्रागल्भ्यं, उत्सिक्तता, साटोपत्वं.

IMPERISHABLE, *a.* अक्षयः -या -यं, अक्षय्यः -य्या -य्यं, अक्षयी -यिणी -यि (न्), अनश्वरः -रा -रं, अविनश्वरः -रा -रं, अविनाशी -शिनी -शि (न्), अनाश्यः -श्या -श्यं, अव्ययः -या -यं, अजरः -रा -रं, निर्जरः -रा -रं, अजर्य्यः -र्य्या -र्य्यं, अक्षरः -रा -रं, अक्षयणीयः -या -यं.

IMPERISHABLENESS, *s.* अक्षयता -त्वं, अनश्वरता, अनाश्यत्वं, अविनाश्यता, अजरत्वं, निर्जरत्वं, अव्ययीभावः.

IMPERMEABLE, *a.* अव्याप्यः -प्या -प्यं, अप्रवेश्यः -श्या -श्यं, अप्रवेशनीयः -या -यं.

IMPERMEABLENESS, *s.* अव्याप्यता, अप्रवेश्यता, अभेद्यत्वं.

IMPERSONAL, *a.* अकर्त्तृकः -का -कं, कर्त्तृवाचहीनः -ना -नं, अकर्त्तृवाच्यः -च्या -च्यं, भाववाचकः -का -कं; 'impersonal verb,' भाववाच्यं, अकर्त्तृवाचका क्रिया.

IMPERSONALLY, *adv.* अकर्त्तृकं, अकर्त्तृवाच्यक्रमेण, भाववाच्यानुसारेण.

IMPERTINENCE, IMPERTINENCY, *s.* (Rudeness) अविनयः, अविनीतता, अशिष्टता, परुषवचनं, दुरुक्तिः *f.*, वाक्पारुष्यं, कुशीलता, दुःशीलता, अशीलता, वामशीलता, धृष्टता, धर्षः, प्रगल्भता, चापल्यं, क्लेशदायकत्वं, उत्तरदायकत्वं.—(Meddling with others' affairs) पराधिकारचर्चा, पराधिकारप्रवेशः.—(State of not relating to the subject) निर्विषयता -त्वं, अप्रासङ्गिकत्वं, अप्रस्तुतत्वं, असम्बन्धः.—(Nonsense) आनर्थक्यं, अनर्थकता, असङ्गतत्वं.

IMPERTINENT, *a.* (Rude) अविनीतः -ता -तं, अशिष्टः -ष्टा -ष्टं, धृष्टः -ष्टा -ष्टं, प्रगल्भः -ल्भा -ल्भं, दुःशीलः -ला -लं, अशीलः -ला -लं, कुशीलः -ला -लं, वामशीलः -ला -लं, चपलः -ला -लं, परुषवाक् *m. f. n.*, परुषवादी -दिनी -दि (न्), क्लेशदायकः -का -कं; 'giving impertinent answers,' उत्तरदायकः -का -कं.—(Meddling with others' affairs) पराधिकारचर्चकः -का -कं.—(Irrelevant) अप्रासङ्गिकः -की -कं, अप्रस्तुतः -ता -तं, निर्विषयः -या -यं, असम्बन्धी -न्धिनी -न्धि (न्),

असम्पर्कीयः -या -यं, निष्प्रयोजनः -ना -नं, प्रस्तुतवहिर्भूतः -ता -तं.—(Nonsensical) अनर्थकः -का -कं, असङ्गतः -ता -तं.

IMPERTINENTLY, *adv.* (Rudely) अविनयेन, अविनीतवत्, धृष्टवत्, प्रगल्भवत्, अशिष्टवत्, कुशीलवत्, परुषोक्त्या.—(Officiously) अतिचर्चापूर्व्वं.—(Irrelevantly) असङ्गतं, अप्रस्तुतं, अप्रासङ्गिकं, निष्प्रयोजनं.

IMPERTURBABLE, *a.* अक्षोभ्यः -भ्या -भ्यं, अक्षोभणीयः -या -यं, अवस्थितमतिः -तिः -ति, स्थिरमतिः -तिः -ति, समबुद्धिः -द्धिः -द्धि, अनाकुलचित्तः -त्ता -त्तं, अपारिप्लवः -वी -वं, अकातरः -रा -रं, अविचलितमनाः -नाः -नः (स्), निर्विकारः -रा -रं.

IMPERTURBATION, *s.* अक्षोभ्यता, अनाकुलचित्तता, अपारिप्लवत्वं, अव्यग्रता.

IMPERVIOUS, *a.* (Not to be penetrated or entered) अप्रवेश्यः -श्या -श्यं, अप्रवेशनीयः -या -यं, अगम्यः -म्या -म्यं, गहनः -ना -नं, सुगहनः -ना -नं, गह्वरः -या -यं, गभीरः -रा -रं, गम्भीरः -रा -रं, कलिलः -ला -लं, सङ्कटः -टा -टं, सबाधः -धा -धं, काढः -ढा -ढं.—(Compact, without interstice) निबिडः -डा -डं, अविरलः -ला -लं, निर्विवरः -रा -रं, नीरन्ध्रः -न्ध्रा -न्ध्रं.—(Not to be pierced) अवेध्यः -ध्या -ध्यं, अव्याप्यः -प्या -प्यं, अभेद्यः -द्या -द्यं, अच्छेदनीयः -या -यं.

IMPERVIOUSNESS, *s.* अप्रवेश्यता, गम्भीरत्वं, गहनत्वं, अव्याप्यता, अगम्यता, अवेध्यता, नीरन्ध्रता, नैबिड्यं.

IMPETRABLE, *a.* अभ्यर्थनीयः -या -यं, प्रार्थनेन प्राप्यः -प्या -प्यं.

To IMPETRATE, *v. a.* प्रार्थनेन or अभ्यर्थनाद्वारेण प्राप् (c. 5. -आप्नोति -आप्तुं).

IMPETRATION, *s.* प्रार्थनया or याञ्चाद्वारेण प्राप्तिः *f.* or प्रापणं.

IMPETUOSITY, *s.* वेगः, आवेगः, महावेगः, संवेगः, अत्यन्तवेगः, संरम्भः, संरब्धत्वं, आपातः, तीक्ष्णता, तैक्ष्ण्यं, साहसं, उग्रता, उच्चण्डता, अमर्षः, क्षिप्रता, रभसः, कुतूहलं, तीव्रता.

IMPETUOUS, *a.* वेगवान् -वती -वत् (त्), वेगी -गिनी -गि (न्), महावेगः -गा -गं, भीमवेगः -गा -गं, उद्दीर्णवेगः -गा -गं, संरम्भी -म्भिणी -म्भि (न्), चण्डः -ण्डा -ण्डं, उच्चण्डः -ण्डा -ण्डं, तीक्ष्णः -क्ष्णा -क्ष्णं, तीक्ष्णकर्म्मा -र्म्मा -र्म्म (न्), अमर्षी -र्षिणी -र्षि (न्), अमर्षणः -णा -णं, अमर्षवान् -वती -वत् (त्), साहसी -सिनी -सि (न्), साहसिकः -की -कं, उग्रः -ग्रा -ग्रं, तीव्रः -व्रा -व्रं, प्रबलः -ला -लं, रोषणः -णा -णं, कुतूहली -लिनी -लि (न्).

IMPETUOUSLY, *adv.* महावेगेन, भीमवेगेन, अत्यन्तवेगेन, वेगतस्, सवेगं, संरम्भेण, आपाततस्, तीक्ष्णं, सामर्षं, उच्चण्डं, उग्रं, सरभसं, साहसेन, संरब्धवत्, सकुतूहलं, कौतूहलेन.

IMPETUOUSNESS, *s.* *See* IMPETUOSITY.

IMPETUS, *s.* वेगः, आवेगः, संवेगः, आपातः, अत्यन्तवेगः, गतिशक्तिः *f.*

IMPIETY, *s.* अधर्म्मः -र्म्मत्वं, वैधर्म्यं, निर्धर्म्मत्वं, धर्म्मलोपः, धर्म्महीनता, अभक्तिः *f.*, भक्तिहीनता, अभक्तत्वं, देवनिन्दा, दुष्टता, अपुण्यत्वं, असाधुता, पापिष्ठत्वं, सपापत्वं, पापं, दुष्कृतं, कुकर्म्म *n.* (न्).

To IMPINGE, *v. a.* आहन् (c. 2. -हन्ति -न्तुं), अभिहन्, अभ्याहन्, आपत् (c. 1. -पतति -तितुं), प्रपत्, संघट्ट् (c. 1. -घट्टते -ट्टितुं).

IMPIOUS, *a.* अधर्म्मी -र्म्मिणी -र्म्मि (न्), अधार्म्मिकः -की -कं, निर्धर्म्मः -र्म्मा -र्म्मं, धर्म्महीनः -ना -नं, धर्म्मालीकः -का -कं, अभक्तः -क्ता -क्तं, देवनिन्दकः -का -कं, भक्तिहीनः -ना -नं, दुष्टः -ष्टा -ष्टं, अपुण्यः -ण्या -ण्यं, असाधुः -ध्वी -धु, पापी -पिनी -पि (न्), पापिष्ठः -ष्ठा -ष्ठं, अनीश्वररोचितः -ता -तं.

IMPIOUSLY, *adv.* अधर्म्मतस्, अधर्म्मेण, अपुण्यवत्, पापिष्ठवत्, देवनिन्दकवत्.

IMPIOUSNESS, *s.* *See* IMPIETY.

IMPLACABILITY, IMPLACABLENESS, *s.* अशाम्यता, असान्त्वनीयता, अतोषणीयता, अप्रसाद्यत्वं.

IMPLACABLE, *a.* अशाम्यः -म्या -म्यं, अतोषणीयः -या -यं, अशमनीयः -या -यं, असान्त्वनीयः -या -यं, अनाराध्यः -ध्या -ध्यं, अप्रसाद्यः -द्या -द्यं, दुःखेन शाम्यः -म्या -म्यं or आराध्यः -ध्या -ध्यं.—(Constant in hatred) दीर्घद्वेषी -षिणी -षि (न्), अतिद्वेषी &c.; 'implacable hatred,' दीर्घद्वेषः, बद्धवैरं.

IMPLACABLY, *adv.* अशमनीयं, अशाम्यं, अतोषणीयं, अनाराधनीयं.

To IMPLANT, *v. a.* निरुह् in caus. (-रोपयति -यितुं), निष्ठा in caus. (-ष्ठापयति -यितुं), प्रतिष्ठा, निष्ठं -ष्ठां -ष्ठं कृ, निधा (c. 3. -दधाति -धातुं), प्रणिधा, उपनिधा, निखन् (c. 1. -खनति -नितुं).

IMPLANTED, *p. p.* निष्ठः -ष्ठा -ष्ठं, निष्ठितः -ता -तं, प्रतिष्ठितः -ता -तं, सुप्रतिष्ठितः -ता -तं, निरूढः -ढा -ढं, निखातः -ता -तं, निहितः -ता -तं.

To IMPLEAD, *v. a.* अभियुज् (c. 7. -युनक्ति -योक्तुं), व्यवहारसभायाम् उत्तरप्रत्युत्तरे कृ.

IMPLEMENT, *s.* यन्त्रं, उपकरणं, साधनं, भाण्डं, कार्य्यसाधनं, सामग्र्यं -ग्री, द्रव्यं, पात्रं, उपस्करः, सम्भारः.

To IMPLICATE, *v. a.* सम्बन्ध् (c. 9. -बध्नाति -बन्द्धुं), अनुबन्ध्, संश्लिष् (c. 10. -श्लेषयति -यितुं), आश्लिष्, परिश्लिष्, संसृज् (c. 6. -सृजति -स्रष्टुं); 'he is implicated in many crimes,' बहुपापैः सम्बध्यते.

IMPLICATED, *p. p.* सम्बद्धः -द्धा -द्धं, अनुबद्धः -द्धा -द्धं, संश्लिष्टः -ष्टा -ष्टं, संसृष्टः -ष्टा -ष्टं, ग्रस्तः -स्ता -स्तं, अनुषङ्गी -ङ्गिणी -ङ्गि (न्), लिप्तः -प्ता -प्तं.

IMPLICATION, *s.* (Involution, connection) सम्बन्धः, अनुबन्धः, अभिसम्बन्धः, अनुषङ्गः, समन्वयः, सम्पर्कः, संसर्गः.—(Implying) विवक्षा, अर्थापत्तिः *f.*, अनुमानं, अपवाहः, उपलक्ष्यः.

IMPLICIT, *a.* अनाशङ्कितः -ता -तं, अवितर्कितः -ता -तं, अवैकल्पिकः -की -कं, अविचार्य्य कृतः -ता -तं, अवितर्क्य कृतः -ता -तं, अशङ्कात्मकः -का -कं, असांशयिकः -की -कं, असन्दिग्धः -ग्धा -ग्धं.

IMPLICITLY, *adv.* अवितर्क्य, अविचार्य्य, अनाशङ्कापूर्व्वं, अशङ्कया, अवितर्केण, असंशयपूर्व्वं, अविकल्पेन.

IMPLIED, *p. p.* or *a.* विवक्षितः -ता -तं, अर्थसम्बद्धः -द्धा -द्धं, उपलक्षितः -ता -तं, आनुषङ्गिकः -की -कं; 'implied meaning,' विवक्षितार्थः, फलितार्थः, ध्वनितार्थः, ध्वनिः *m.*

To IMPLORE, *v. a.* प्रार्थ् (c. 10. -अर्थयते -ति -यितुं), अभ्यर्थ्, सम्प्रार्थ्, अर्थ्, विनयेन or अञ्जलिं कृत्वा प्रार्थ्, कृताञ्जलिः or निर्बन्धेन याच् (c. 1. याचति -चितुं), अभियाच्, संयाच्, प्रयाच्, सम्प्रयाच्, प्रसद् (c. 10. -सादयते -ति -यितुं), विनी (c. 1. -नयति -नेतुं), अनुनी, विनयेन स्वार्थं निविद् (c. 10. -वेदयति -यितुं), नाथ् (c. 1. नाथति -थितुं).

IMPLORED, *p. p.* अञ्जलिकर्म्मपूर्व्वं प्रार्थितः -ता -तं or अभ्यर्थितः -ता -तं, विनयेन or निर्बन्धेन याचितः -ता -तं or अभियाचितः -ता -तं, प्रसादितः -ता -तं, अनुनीतः -ता -तं.

IMPLORER, *s.* कृताञ्जलिः प्रार्थकः or प्रार्थयिता *m.* (तृ), निर्बन्धेन याचकः.

To IMPLY, *v. a.* वच् in des. (विवक्षति -क्षितुं), सूच् (c. 10. सूचयति -यितुं), संसूच्. Often expressed by अर्थ in comp., as, 'a speech which implies censure,' निन्दार्थो वादः.

IMPOLICY, *s.* कुनीतिः *f.*, दुर्नीतिः *f.*, दुर्णयः, अनीतिः *f.*, दुर्णीतं, अनयः.

IMPOLITE, *a.* अशिष्टः -ष्टा -ष्टं, असभ्यः -भ्या -भ्यं, अविनीतः -ता -तं, अशीलः -ला -लं, कुशीलः -ला -लं, विशीलः -ला -लं, दुःशीलः -ला -लं, दुर्मर्य्यादः -दा -दं, नष्टविनयः -या -यं, ग्राम्यः -म्या -म्यं, असुजनः -ना -नं, अनार्य्यः -र्य्या -र्य्यं.

IMPOLITENESS, *s.* अशिष्टता, असभ्यता, अविनयः, कुशीलता, दुःशीलता.

IMPOLITIC, *a.* (Not acquainted with good policy, not prudent)

अनीतिज्ञः -ज्ञा -ज्ञं, अनीतिवित् *m.f.n.*, अनीतिमान् -मती -मत् (त्), अनीतिकुशलः -ला -लं, दुर्णीतः -ता -तं, अविनीतः -ता -तं, अमतिमान् -मती -मत् (त्), अबुद्धिमान् &c., अबुधः -धा -धं, अविज्ञः -ज्ञा -ज्ञं, अविवेचकः -का -कं, अकोविदः -दा -दं.—(Not politic, adapted to injure the public interest) अहितः -ता -तं, नीतिविरुद्धः -द्धा -द्धं, प्रजार्थविरोधी -धिनी -धि (न्), अर्थविरोधी &c., अनर्थकरः -रा -रं, अनर्थजनकः -का -कं, अनिष्टकरः -री -रं, असमीक्ष्य कृतः -ता -तं, अपकारः -रा -रं, अयौक्तिकः -की -कं.

IMPOLITICLY, *adv.* नीतिविरुद्धं, अहितं -ताय, अर्थविरोधेन, असमीक्ष्य.

IMPONDERABLE, IMPONDEROUS, *a.* निर्भारः -रा -रं, अभारी -रिणी -रि (न्), अतोलनीयः -या -यं, अगुरुः -र्वी -रु, अतिसूक्ष्मः -क्ष्मा -क्ष्मं, अतिलघुः -घुः -घु.

To IMPORT, *v. a.* (Bring goods from a foreign country) वाणिज्यद्रव्याणि or वाणिज्यवस्तूनि विदेशात् or देशान्तरात् or वहिर्देशाद् आनी (c. 1. -नयति -नेतुं) or उपनी or आवह् (c. 1. -वहति -वोढुं) or उपवह् or आहृ (c. 1. -हरति -हर्तुं).—(Convey a meaning, imply) सूच् (c. 10. सूचयति -यितुं), संसूच्, उद्दिश् (c. 6. -दिशति -देष्टुं), वच् in des. (विवक्षति -क्षितुं), उद्बुध् (c. 10. -बोधयति -यितुं), or expressed by अर्थ in comp.; as, 'a speech which imports censure,' निन्दार्थो वादः.—(Be of weight or consequence) गुर्वर्थः -र्था -र्थं भू.

IMPORT, *s.* (Goods brought from a foreign country) विदेशात् or देशान्तरात् or वहिर्देशाद् आनीतानि वाणिज्यद्रव्याणि *n. pl.* or वाणिज्यवस्तूनि *n. pl.*, विदेशीयवस्तूनि *n. pl.*, विदेशजद्रव्याणि *n. pl.*, वहिर्देशवस्तूनि.—(Meaning) अर्थः, अभिप्रायः, अभिप्रेतं, विवक्षा, उद्देशः, आशयः; 'of like import,' समानार्थः -र्था -र्थं.—(Importance) गौरवं, गुरुत्वं, प्रभावः.

IMPORTABLE, *a.* विदेशाद् आनेयः -या -यं or आनेतव्यः -व्या -व्यं.

IMPORTANCE, *s.* (Consequence) गौरवं, गुरुत्वं -ता, गुर्वर्थत्वं, प्रभावः, भारः; 'of a thing,' द्रव्यगुरुता; 'of an act,' कार्यगुरुता.—(Of a person) उत्कर्षः, औत्कर्ष्यं, प्रधानता, सेव्यता, प्रतिपत्तिः *f.*, प्रागल्भ्यं, गर्वः, मानं.

IMPORTANT, *a.* गुरुः -र्वी -रु, गुर्वर्थः -र्था -र्थं, बह्वर्थः -र्था -र्थं, महार्थः -र्था -र्थं, परमार्थः -र्था -र्थं, गुरुप्रभावः -वा -वं, महाप्रभावः -वा -वं, बहुप्रभावः -वा -वं, परमप्रभावः -वा -वं, परमः -मा -मं, अलघुः -घुः -घु, महोपकारी -रिणी -रि (न्), भारी -रिणी -रि (न्), भारवान् -वती -वत् (त्), आवश्यकः -की -कं; 'important object,' गुर्वर्थः, परमार्थः, महार्थः; 'most important,' गरिष्ठः -ष्ठा -ष्ठं, गुरुतमः -मा -मं; 'more important,' गरीयान् -यसी -यः (स्).

IMPORTANTLY, *adv.* गुरु, परमप्रभावेण, परमं, अलघु.

IMPORTATION, *s.* (Act of bringing from a foreign country) विदेशात् or वहिर्देशात् or देशान्तरात् आनयः -यनं or उपनयः -यनं or आवाहनं or आवहनं or उपवाहनं.—(The commodities imported) विदेशाद् आनीतानि द्रव्याणि, देशान्तराद् आनीतवस्तूनि, विदेशीयवस्तुसमूहः.

IMPORTED, *p.p.* विदेशात् or वहिर्देशाद् आनीतः -ता -तं or उपनीतः -ता -तं.

IMPORTER, *s.* विदेशात् or वहिर्देशाद् वाणिज्यद्रव्यानेता *m.* (तृ).

IMPORTUNACY, *s.* निर्बन्धः, अतिनिर्बन्धः, अतियाचना -नं, अतिप्रार्थनं -ना, आग्रहः, अतिनिर्बन्धेन याचना or प्रार्थनं, वारं वारं प्रार्थना, नित्यप्रार्थनं, नित्ययाचना, नित्ययाचनेन परोद्वेजनं or परायासकरणं.

IMPORTUNATE, *a.* निर्बन्धशीलः -ला -लं, अतिनिर्बन्धशीलः -ला -लं, आग्रही -हिणी -हि (न्), आग्रहशीलः -ला -लं, अतियाचकः -का -कं, अतिप्रार्थकः -का -कं, निर्बन्धेन याचकः -का -कं, नित्यप्रार्थकः -का -कं, नित्यं याचनेन परोद्वेजकः -का -कं or परायासकरः -री -रं, वारं वारं प्रार्थकः -का -कं; 'importunate solicitation,' निर्बन्धः, आग्रहः.

IMPORTUNATELY, *adv.* निर्बन्धेन, अतिनिर्बन्धेन, आग्रहेण, साग्रहं, प्रसभं, मुहुर्मुहुः, पुनःपुनर्.

IMPORTUNATENESS, *s.* *See* IMPORTUNACY.

To IMPORTUNE, *v. a.* अतिनिर्बन्धेन or निर्बन्धेन प्रार्थ् (c. 10. -अर्थयति -यितुं) or अभ्यर्थ् or याच् (c. 1. याचति -चितुं) or अभियाच्, आग्रहेण प्रार्थ्, वारं वारं प्रार्थ्, अतियाचनेन परम् उद्विज् (c. 10. -वेजयति -यितुं), नित्यप्रार्थनेन परम् आयस् (c. 10. -यासयति -यितुं).

IMPORTUNED, *p.p.* निर्बन्धेन प्रार्थितः -ता -तं or याचितः -ता -तं, अतियाचितः -ता -तं.

IMPORTUNER, *s.* अतिप्रार्थकः, अतियाचकः, निर्बन्धेन प्रार्थकः, अतियाञ्चया परोद्वेजकः.

IMPORTUNITY, *s.* निर्बन्धः, अतिनिर्बन्धः, अतियाचना -नं, आग्रहः, वारं वारं प्रार्थना, पुनःपुनः प्रार्थनं, अतियाचनेन परोद्वेजनं. *See* IMPORTUNACY.

To IMPOSE, *v. a.* (Lay on) न्यस् (c. 4. -अस्यति -असितुं), निविश् (c. 10. -वेशयति -यितुं), समाविश्, नियुज् (c. 10. -योजयति -यितुं, c. 7. -युनक्ति -योक्तुं), धा (c. 3. दधाति, धातुं), निधा, विधा, आरुह् in caus. (-रोपयति -यितुं), स्था in caus. (स्थापयति -यितुं), उपस्था, अवस्था.—(Set over) अधिकृ, उपधिकृ, नियुज्, विनियुज्.—(Impose upon, deceive) प्रलभ् (c. 1. -लभते -लब्धुं), विप्रलभ्, वञ्च् (c. 10. वञ्चयते -ति -यितुं), परिवञ्च्, छल् (c. 10. छलयति -यितुं), अभिसन्धा, अतिसन्धा, दम्भ् (c. 5. दभ्नोति, दम्भितुं).

IMPOSED, *p.p.* न्यस्तः -स्ता -स्तं, निवेशितः -ता -तं, नियुक्तः -क्ता -क्तं, नियोजितः -ता -तं, विहितः -ता -तं, अधिकृतः -ता -तं; 'imposed upon,' वञ्चितः -ता -तं, प्रलब्धः -ब्धा -ब्धं, विप्रलब्धः -ब्धा -ब्धं, अतिसंहितः -ता -तं.

IMPOSING, *a.* विस्मयोत्पादकः -का -कं, आश्चर्यकरः -रा -रं, विस्मापकः -का -कं, अद्भुतः -ता -तं, गुरुः -र्वी -रु, महातेजाः -जाः -जः (स्).

IMPOSITION, *s.* (Act of laying on) न्यासः, न्यसनं, निवेशनं, आरोपणं, स्थापनं; 'of hands,' हस्तन्यासः.—(That which is imposed, a tax) करः, शुल्कः -ल्कं.—(Task given as a punishment) साहसं, व्रतं, शिष्येण दण्डार्थम् अधिककर्त्तव्यं किञ्चित्.—(Fraud, deception) दम्भः, वञ्चनं -ना, छलं, प्रलम्भः, विप्रलम्भः अभिसन्धिः *m.*, अतिसन्धानं.

IMPOSSIBILITY, *s.* अशक्यता, असाध्यता, अकर्त्तव्यता, अकरणीयता, अकार्यता.—(An impossibility, an absurdity) असाध्यं, असम्भवः, मृषार्थकं, शशविषाणं, शशशृङ्गं, खपुष्पं, गगणपुष्पं, गगणकुसुमं; 'impossibilities,' असाध्यानि *n. pl.*

IMPOSSIBLE, *a.* अशक्यः -क्या -क्यं, असाध्यः -ध्या -ध्यं, असाधनीयः -या -यं, असम्भवः -वा -वं, अकर्त्तव्यः -व्या -व्यं, अकरणीयः -या -यं, अकार्य्यः -र्य्या -र्य्यं, असङ्कृतः -ता -तं, अघटितः -ता -तं, अघटमानः -ना -नं, अघटनीयः -या -यं, अगम्यः -म्या -म्यं, अप्राप्यः -प्या -प्यं, अपार्य्यः -र्य्या -र्य्यं, अपारणीयः -या -यं, अक्षमः -मा -मं.

IMPOST, *s.* करः, शुल्कः -ल्कं, राजकरं, कारः, राजग्राह्यभागः, राजस्वं, राजदेयं, राजधनं, शाल्किकः, तारिकं, तार्य्यं.

IMPOSTHUME, *s.* विद्रधिः *m.*, पूयसम्पूर्णः स्फोटः or विस्फोटः, सपूयव्रणं.

IMPOSTOR, *s.* (Deceiver) दम्भी *m.* (न्), दाम्भिकः, दम्भकः, कुहकः, कूटकारः, कूटकः, वञ्चकः, कपटी *m.* (न्), कापटिकः, धूर्त्तः, कितवः, प्रतारकः, छद्मवेशी *m.* (न्).—(In religion) धर्म्मध्वजी *m.* (न्), धार्म्म-

लिङ्गी m. (न्), आर्य्यरूपः, धर्म्मोपधः, पाषण्डः, पाखण्डः, लिङ्गवृत्तिः m., सर्व्वलिङ्गी m. (न्), छद्मतापसः, कपटधर्म्मी m. (न्).

IMPOSTURE, s. दम्भः, वञ्चनं -ना, प्रवञ्चना, प्रलम्भः, विप्रलम्भः, कूटः -टं, कपटः -टं, व्याजः, छलं -लना, कैतवं, कौटं, उपधिः m., प्रतारणं -णा, कुहकः, अभिसन्धिः m., अतिसन्धानं, छद्म n. (न्).

IMPOTENCE, IMPOTENCY, s. (Want of strength or power) वीर्य्यहानिः f., शक्तिहीनता, अशक्तिः f., अशक्तता, अवीर्य्यं, निर्बलता, बलहीनता, सत्त्वहानिः f., निःसत्त्वं, सत्त्वाभावः, वीर्य्याभावः, असामर्थ्यं, असमर्थत्वं, अतेजस् n., तेजोहीनता, क्लीबता, दौर्बल्यं, दुर्बलता, शक्तिवैकल्यं.—(Absence of virility) क्लीवत्वं, क्लैब्यं, अपुंस्त्वं, निष्पुरुषत्वं, अपौरुषं, नपुंसकत्वं, ध्वजभङ्गः, निर्वीजता, निष्फलत्वं, अजनकता.

IMPOTENT, a. (Without power) निर्बलः -ला -लं, बलहीनः -ना -नं, शक्तिहीनः -ना -नं, अशक्तः -क्ता -क्तं, अबलः -ला -लं, असमर्थः -र्था -र्थं, सामर्थ्यहीनः -ना -नं, निर्वीर्य्यः -र्य्या -र्य्यं, वीर्य्यहीनः -ना -नं, अवीरः -रा -रं, निःसत्त्वः -त्त्वा -त्त्वं, सत्त्वहीनः -ना -नं, निस्तेजाः -जाः -जः (स्), तेजोहीनः -ना -नं, गततेजाः &c., अकल्पः -ल्पा -ल्पं, दुर्बलः -ला -लं, अक्षमः -मा -मं, अपारगः -गा -गं.—(Wanting virility) क्लीवः -वा -वं, पुंस्त्वहीनः -ना -नं, पुंशक्तिहीनः -ना -नं, निष्पुरुषः -षा -षं, पुरुषशक्तिवर्जितः -ता -तं, नपुंसकः -का -कं, निर्वीजः -जा -जं, भग्नध्वजः -जा -जं, निष्फलः -ला -लं.

IMPOTENTLY, adv. निर्बलं, अबलं, दुर्बलं, अवीरवत्, निर्वीर्य्यवत्, क्लीववत्, निर्वीर्य्यं, बलं विना, वीर्य्यं विना, निःसत्त्वेन.

To IMPOUND, v. a. यूथपरिभ्रष्टपश्वादि अवरोधस्थाने निरुध् (c. 7. -रुणद्धि -रोद्धुं) or रक्ष् (c. 1. रक्षति -क्षितुं).

To IMPOVERISH, v. a. दरिद्रीकृ, निर्धनीकृ, क्षीणीकृ, धनं नश् (c. 10. नाशयति -यितुं), क्षीणधनं -नां -नं कृ.—(Enfeeble, exhaust strength) कृश (nom. क्रशयति -यितुं), कृशीकृ, तेजः or सत्त्वं or वीर्य्यं हृ (c. 1. हरति, हर्त्तुं) or नश्, दुर्बलीकृ, क्षि in caus. (क्षपयति -यितुं).

IMPOVERISHED, p. p. (Reduced to poverty) क्षीणधनः -ना -नं, निर्धनः -ना -नं, दरिद्रितः -ता -तं, दरिद्रीकृतः -ता -तं, दारिद्र्यगतः -ता -तं, धनच्युतः -ता -तं, क्षीणार्थः -र्था -र्थं, नष्टार्थः -र्था -र्थं, नष्टधनः -ना -नं, गतविभवः -वा -वं, प्रचलितविभवः -वा -वं, शिथिलवसुः -सुः -सु, विगतश्रीकः -का -कं, विनष्टलक्ष्मीकः -का -कं, निष्किञ्चनः -ना -नं, अकिञ्चनः -ना -नं.—(Exhausted of energy) क्षीणसत्त्वः -त्त्वा -त्त्वं, कृशीभूतः -ता -तं, गतवीर्य्यः -र्य्या -र्य्यं, च्युतोत्साहः -हा -हं.

IMPOVERISHMENT, s. दरिद्रता, दारिद्र्यं, दरिद्रीकरणं, धननाशः, धनहानिः f., धनच्युतिः f., सत्त्वहानिः f., क्षीणता.

IMPRACTICABILITY, s. असाध्यता -त्वं, असाधनीयता, अकर्त्तव्यता, अकरणीयता, अकार्य्यता, अशक्यता -त्वं, कर्त्तुम् अशक्यता, असम्भवत्वं, असम्भाव्यता, अनुपपाद्यता, अघटनीयत्वं, अगम्यत्वं, दुष्करत्वं.

IMPRACTICABLE, a. असाध्यः -ध्या -ध्यं, असाधनीयः -या -यं, अकर्त्तव्यः -व्या -व्यं, अकरणीयः -या -यं, अकार्य्यः -र्य्या -र्य्यं, अशक्यः -क्या -क्यं, कर्त्तुम् अशक्यः -क्या -क्यं, अकृत्यः -त्या -त्यं, अघटनीयः -या -यं, असम्भवः -वा -वं, असम्भाव्यः -व्या -व्यं, असम्भावनीयः -या -यं, अनुपपाद्यः -द्या -द्यं, दुष्करः -रा -रं, अगम्यः -म्या -म्यं, अपार्य्यः -र्य्या -र्य्यं.

IMPRACTICABLY, adv. असाधनीयं, अकरणीयं, असम्भवेन, असम्भावनीयं.

To IMPRECATE, v. a. शप् (c. 1. शपति -ते, c. 4. शप्यति, शप्तुं), अभिशप्, परिशप्, आक्रुश् (c. 1. -क्रोशति -क्रोष्टुं), अमङ्गलं or अनिष्टम् आशंस् (c. 1. -शंसते -सितुं) or प्रार्थ् (c. 10. -अर्थयते -यितुं), गर्ह् (c. 1. गर्हते -र्हितुं), भर्त्स् (c. 10. भर्त्सयति -यितुं), धिक्कृ.

IMPRECATED, p. p. अभिशप्तः -प्ता -प्तं, आक्रुष्टः -ष्टा -ष्टं, धिक्कृतः -ता -तं.

IMPRECATION, s. शापः, अभिशापः, आक्रोशनं, अपक्रोशः, अभीषङ्गः, अभिषङ्गः, अनिष्टाशंसनं, अनिष्टप्रार्थना, मन्दप्रार्थना, मन्दवाञ्छा, भर्त्सनं, गालिः m., धिक्करणं.

IMPRECATORY, a. अभिशापार्थकः -का -कं, आक्रोशकः -की -कं, अनिष्टाशंसकः -का -कं, अनिष्टप्रार्थकः -का -कं.

IMPREGNABLE, a. अलङ्घनीयः -या -यं, अलंघ्यः -ङ्घ्या -ङ्घ्यं, अनाक्रमणीयः -या -यं, अनाक्रम्यः -म्या -म्यं, दुराक्रमः -मा -मं, दुराक्रामः -मा -मं, अगम्यः -म्या -म्यं, दुर्गमः -मा -मं.—(Invincible) अजेयः -या -यं, दुर्जयः -या -यं, अपराजितः -ता -तं.

To IMPREGNATE, v. a. (Infuse the principle of conception, make pregnant) सिच् (c. 6. सिञ्चति, सेक्तुं), निषिच्, आसिच्, रेतः सिच्, गर्भं ग्रह् in caus. (ग्राहयति -यितुं) or उत्पद् (c. 10. -पादयति -यितुं), गर्भवतीं कृ, ससत्त्वां कृ, आपन्नसत्त्वां कृ, अन्तरापत्नीं कृ, सञ्जातगर्भां कृ, गर्भाधानं कृ, निषेकं कृ.—(Infuse particles of one thing into another) प्रक्षिप् (c. 6. -क्षिपति -क्षेप्तुं), निषिच्, प्रक्षेपं कृ, व्याप् (c. 5. -आप्नोति -आप्तुं), व्याप्तं -प्तां -प्तं कृ.

IMPREGNATED, p. p. सिक्तः -क्ता -क्तं, गृहीतगर्भा, उत्पन्नगर्भा, ससत्त्वा, आपन्नसत्त्वा, सञ्जातगर्भा.—(Infused) व्याप्तः -प्ता -प्तं.

IMPREGNATING, part. गर्भदः -दा -दं, सेचकः -का -कं, गर्भोत्पादकः -का -कं.

IMPREGNATION, s. सेकः, सेचनं, निषेकः, आसेकः, आसेचनं, गर्भग्रहणं, गर्भोत्पादनं, गर्भाधानं, गर्भधारणं, भ्रूणः.

IMPREGNATOR, s. सेक्ता m. (कृ), सेचकः, निषेककारी m. (न्), गर्भदः, गर्भोत्पादकः.

To IMPRESS, v. a. (Imprint, stamp, make a mark by pressure) मुद्र (nom. मुद्रयति -यितुं), मुद्रीकृ, अङ्क् (c. 10. अङ्कयति -यितुं), चिह्न (nom. चिह्नयति -यितुं), मुद्रितं -तां -तं कृ, लक्ष् (c. 10. लक्षयति -यितुं), प्रणिधा (c. 3. -दधाति -धातुं), न्यस् (c. 4. -अस्यति -असितुं), निविश् (c. 10. -वेशयति -यितुं), निपीड् (c. 10. -पीडयति -यितुं) अङ्कितं -तां -तं कृ.—(Fix deep in the mind, &c.) हृदये सुनिश्चितं -तां -तं कृ, चित्तनिष्ठं -ष्ठां -ष्ठं कृ, हृत्स्थं -स्थां -स्थं कृ, हृद्गतं -तां -तं कृ, हृदयगतं -तां -तं कृ, हृदये कृ, हृदये निविश् or निष्ठा in caus. (-ष्ठापयति -यितुं); 'to be impressed,' निष्ठा (c. 1. -तिष्ठति -ष्ठातुं).—(Impress seamen) राजाज्ञया बलात्कारेण धृत्वा नाविकादिकर्म्मणि व्यापृ (c. 10. -पारयति -यितुं).

IMPRESS, s. मुद्रा, अङ्कः, चिह्नं, न्यासः, लक्षणं; 'having the impress of knowledge) ज्ञानमुद्रः -द्रा -द्रं.

IMPRESSED, p. p. (Imprinted) मुद्रितः -ता -तं, मुद्रीकृतः -ता -तं, कृतमुद्रः -द्रा -द्रं, मुद्राङ्कितः -ता -तं, अङ्कितः -ता -तं, कृताङ्कः -ङ्का -ङ्कं, चिह्नितः -ता -तं, समुद्रः -द्रा -द्रं, लक्षितः -ता -तं.—(Infixed) निष्ठितः -ता -तं, निष्ठः -ष्ठा -ष्ठं, न्यस्तः -स्ता -स्तं, निहितः -ता -तं, प्रणिहितः -ता -तं, निवेशितः -ता -तं; 'in the mind,' हृदयनिष्ठितः -ता -तं, चित्तनिष्ठः -ष्ठा -ष्ठं, हृदयगतः -ता -तं, हृद्गतः -ता -तं, हृदयनिवेशितः -ता -तं, हृत्स्थः -स्था -स्थं.

IMPRESSIBLE, s. अङ्कनीयः -या -यं, अङ्क्यः -ङ्क्या -ङ्क्यं, चिह्नक्षमः -मा -मं.

IMPRESSION, s. (Mark, stamp) मुद्रा, अङ्कः, चिह्नं.—(Act of impressing) अङ्कनं.—(Impression on the mind) संस्कारः, चित्तसंस्कारः, मनःसंस्कारः.—(Idea, image in the mind) बुद्धिः f., मतिः f., अनुभवः, मनोगतं, मनसिजं, आभासः, भासः.—(Sensible effect) उदयं, निष्पन्नं, उत्पत्तिः f., सम्पन्नं.—(Indentation) आघातचिह्नं, अभिघातचिह्नं, भङ्गः, छेदः.—(Number of books printed at once) एकवारे मुद्रितो ग्रन्थसमूहः.

IMPRESSIVE, a. हृदयङ्गमः -मा -मं, हृद्गमः -मा -मं, हृदयग्राही -हिणी -हि

(न्), चित्तहारी -रिणी -रि (न्), हृदयस्पृक् *m.f.n.* (श्), मर्म्मस्पृक् *m.f.n.*, विस्मयोत्पादकः -का -कं, हृद्वेदकः -का -कं, भावोत्पादकः &c.

IMPRESSIVELY, *adv.* हृदयङ्गमप्रकारेण, यथा हृदयं स्पृश्यते इति प्रकारेण.

IMPRESSIVENESS, *s.* हृदयङ्गमत्वं, हृद्गमत्वं, हृदयस्पृक्त्वं, विस्मयोत्पादकत्वं.

IMPRESSMENT, *s.* राजाज्ञया बलात्कारधरणानन्तरं नाविकादिकर्म्मणि प्रवर्त्तनं.

To IMPRINT, *v. a.* मुद्र् (nom. मुद्रयति -यितुं), मुद्रीकृ, मुद्रितं -तां -तं कृ, अङ्क् (c. 10. अङ्कयति -यितुं), चिह्न् (nom. चिह्नयति -यितुं), प्रणिधा (c. 3. -दधाति -धातुं), न्यस् (c. 4. -अस्यति -असितुं), निविश् (c. 10. -वेशयति -यितुं); 'on the mind,' हृदयनिष्ठं -ष्ठां -ष्ठं कृ, हृदये मुद्रितमिव किञ्चित् कृ, हृदये निविश्.

IMPRINTED, *p. p.* मुद्रितः -ता -तं, मुद्रीकृतः -ता -तं, अङ्कितः -ता -तं, मुद्राङ्कितः -ता -तं, कृतमुद्रः -द्रा -द्रं.—(Infixed) निहितः -ता -तं, न्यस्तः -स्ता -स्तं, निहितः -ता -तं, प्रणिहितः -ता -तं, निवेशितः -ता -तं; 'on the mind,' हृदयनिष्ठः -ष्ठा -ष्ठं, हृदयगतः -ता -तं, हृद्गतः -ता -तं, हृदयनिवेशितः -ता -तं.

To IMPRISON, *v. a.* कारायां or कारागारे निरुध् (c. 7. -रुणद्धि -रोद्धुं) or बन्ध् (c. 9. बध्नाति, बन्द्धुं), कारागृहं प्रविश् (c. 10. -वेशयति -यितुं), बन्धनालये रक्ष् (c. 1. रक्षति -क्षितुं) or अवरुध् or आसिध् (c. 1. -सेधति -सेद्धुं), कारागुप्तं -प्तां -प्तं कृ.

IMPRISONED, *p. p.* कारागुप्तः -प्ता -प्तं, कारानिरुद्धः -द्धा -द्धं, कारायां बद्धः -द्धा -द्धं, काराबद्धः -द्धा -द्धं, कारागारप्रवेशितः -ता -तं, अवरुद्धदेहः -हा -हं, निरुद्धः -द्धा -द्धं, आसिद्धः -द्धा -द्धं, प्रतिबद्धः -द्धा -द्धं.

IMPRISONMENT, *s.* कारानिरोधः, निरोधः -धनं, काराबन्धनं, बन्धनं, प्रतिबन्धनं, कारागारप्रवेशनं, कारागृहप्रवेशः, कारागोपनं, कारागृहगुप्तिः *f.*, आसेधः, स्थानासेधः, रोधः, सम्प्रतिरोधकः, प्रग्रहः.

IMPROBABILITY, *s.* असम्भवः -वता -त्वं, असम्भाव्यता, असम्भावनीयता, असम्भावना, अनुपपत्तिः *f.*, अनुपपाद्यता, असङ्गतिः *f.*, असङ्गतत्वं, अघटनीयता, अभवनीयत्वं, अप्रमेयता, असाध्यता.

IMPROBABLE, *a.* असम्भवः -वा -वं, असम्भाव्यः -व्या -व्यं, असम्भावनीयः -या -यं, असम्भावितः -ता -तं, असङ्गतः -ता -तं, अनुपपन्नः -न्ना -न्नं, असत्यसन्निभः -भा -भं, असत्यसङ्काशः -शा -शं, अभवनीयः -या -यं, असाध्यः -ध्या -ध्यं, असाधनीयः -या -यं, अघटनीयः -या -यं, अघटितः -ता -तं, अघटमानः -ना -नं, अप्रमेयः -या -यं; 'it is improbable,' न उपपद्यते.

IMPROBABLY, *adv.* असम्भवेन, असम्भावनीयं, असङ्गतं, असाध्यं, अन्यथा.

IMPROBITY, *s.* असाधुत्वं -ता, अशुचित्वं, अधर्म्मः, असरलता, असारल्यं, अनृजुता, अदाक्षिण्यं, अशुद्धता, दुष्टता, अभद्रता, नीचत्वं, खलता, जिह्मता, कौटिल्यं, कापट्यं, कौटं, वक्रता.

IMPROMPTU, *adv.* पूर्व्वचिन्ताम् अकृत्वा, पूर्व्वचिन्तां विना, अचिन्तितं, अनायासेन.

IMPROMPTU, *a.* अचिन्तापूर्व्वः -र्व्वा -र्व्वं, अपूर्व्वचिन्तः -न्ता -न्तं, अयत्नपूर्व्वः -र्व्वा -र्व्वं, आकस्मिकः -की -कं, प्रस्तुतः -ता -तं, पूर्व्वविचारहीनः -ना -नं.

IMPROPER, *a.* अयुक्तः -क्ता -क्तं, अयोग्यः -ग्या -ग्यं, अनुचितः -ता -तं, अन्याय्यः -य्या -य्यं, असङ्गतः -ता -तं, अनुपयुक्तः -क्ता -क्तं, असमञ्जसः -सा -सं, अनुपपन्नः -न्ना -न्नं, अनर्हः -र्हा -र्हं, असदृशः -शी -शं, अपथ्यः -थ्या -थ्यं, असमीचीनः -ना -नं, असम्भाव्यः -व्या -व्यं, असम्भावनीयः -या -यं, अपथ्यः -थ्या -थ्यं, अयथार्थः -र्था -र्थं; sometimes expressed by कु prefixed; as, 'an improper marriage,' कुविवाहः.—(Improper to be done) अकर्त्तव्यः -व्या -व्यं, अकरणीयः -या -यं, अकार्य्यः -र्य्या -र्य्यं, अननुष्ठेयः -या -यं, मानुष्ठेयः -या -यं, अननुष्ठातव्यः -व्या -व्यं; 'to be spoken,' अवचनीयः -या -यं.

IMPROPERLY, *adv.* अयुक्तं, अयोग्यं, अनुपयुक्तं, अनुचितं -तेन, असाम्प्रतं -ति, असम्यक्, अन्यायेन, अन्यायतस्, असङ्गतं, अयथार्थं, अयोगतस्, अकार्य्यतस्, दुःधर्मं, निःधर्मं, असम्भावनीयं; 'acting improperly,' अकृत्यकारी -रिणी -रि (न्), व्यभिचारी &c.

IMPROPRIETY, *s.* अयुक्तिः *f.*, अयुक्तता, निर्युक्तिः *f.*, अन्यायः -यत्वं, अनुपयुक्तता, अविनयः, अविनीतता, अनौचित्यं, अनुचितत्वं, अनौचित्यं, अयोग्यता, असमञ्जसं, असामञ्जस्यं, अनुपपत्तिः *f.*, असङ्गतत्वं, व्यलीकता, असम्यक्त्वं, अयाथार्थ्यं; 'of conduct,' अमर्य्यादा, कुचर्य्या, कुचरितं, कुचेष्टितं, दुश्चरितं, दुश्चेष्टितं, अपचारः, अकार्य्यं, अकर्त्तव्यता, भ्रेषः, व्यभिचारः, अनियमः, मर्य्यादातिक्रमः; 'of speech,' अवचनीयता, अवाच्यता.

IMPROSPERITY, *s.* असमृद्धिः *f.*, अकल्याणं, अकुशलं, अशुभं, असम्पत्तिः *f.*

IMPROSPEROUS, *a.* असमृद्धः -द्धा -द्धं, अकल्याणः -णा -णं, अक्षेमवान् -वती -वत् (त्).

IMPROVABILITY, *s.* वर्धनीयता, संवर्धनीयता, वृंहणीयता, श्रेयस्त्वक्षमता.

IMPROVABLE, *a.* वर्धनीयः -या -यं, संवर्धनीयः -या -यं, वृंहणीयः -या -यं, श्रेयस्त्वक्षमः -मा -मं, भद्रतरभावक्षमः -मा -मं, वृद्धिम् आनेयः -या -यं, भद्रतरीकरणीयः -या -यं.

To IMPROVE, *v. a.* (Make better, advance in good qualities) भद्रतरं -रां -रं कृ, अधिकतरं -रां -रं कृ, भद्रतरीकृ, अधिकीकृ, वृध् (c. 10. वर्धयति -यितुं), संवृध्, परिवृध्, वृंह् (c. 10. वृंहयति -यितुं), वृद्धिं नी (c. 1. नयति, नेतुं) or प्राप् in caus. (-आपयति -यितुं), श्रेयस्त्वं or भद्रतरत्वं or भद्रतरभावं नी or प्राप्, श्रेयांसं -यसीं -यः कृ.—(Make productive, turn to good account) सफलं -लां -लं कृ, सफलीकृ, सु प्रयुज् (c. 7. -युनक्ति -युंक्ते -योक्तुं).

To IMPROVE, *v. n.* (Grow better, advance in goodness or any excellence) भद्रतरः -रा -रं भू, भद्रतरीभू, वृध् (c. 1. वर्धते -र्धितुं), अभिवृध्, विवृध्, प्रवृध्, संवृध्, वृद्धिं गम् (c. 1. गच्छति, गन्तुं) or प्राप् (c. 5. -आप्नोति -आप्तुं), श्रेयान् -यसी -यो भू, अधिकः -का -कं भू, अधिकतरः -रा -रं भू, अधिकीभू, अधिकतरीभू, उपचि in pass. (-चीयते), अभ्युदयं or उपचयं गम् or इ (c. 2. एति -तुं); 'improve in knowledge,' विद्यागमं कृ, विद्याप्राप्तिं कृ, विद्यार्ज्जनं कृ.

IMPROVED, *p. p.* वर्धितः -ता -तं, प्रवृद्धः -द्धा -द्धं, उपचितः -ता -तं, वृंहितः -ता -तं, परिवृंहितः -ता -तं, भद्रतरीभूतः -ता -तं, अधिकीभूतः -ता -तं, समुत्थितः -ता -तं.—(Employed profitably) सफलीकृतः -ता -तं, सुप्रयुक्तः -क्ता -क्तं.

IMPROVEMENT, *s.* (Advancement in any excellence) वृद्धिः *f.*, प्रवृद्धिः *f.*, वर्धनं, उपचयः, समुत्थानं, अभ्युदयः, वृंहणं, परिवृंहणं, आधिक्यं, प्राप्तिः *f.*, आगमः.—(State of being better) श्रेयस्त्वं, भद्रतरत्वं, श्रेष्ठता, श्रैष्ठ्यं.—(Advancement in knowledge) विद्यागमः, विद्याप्राप्तिः *f.*, विद्यार्ज्जनं.—(Progression) प्रगमनं, अग्रगमनं.—(Employment to beneficial purposes) सुप्रयोगः, सफलीकरणं.

IMPROVIDENCE, *s.* अपूर्व्वदृष्टिः *f.*, अदीर्घदृष्टिः *f.*, अपरिणामदृष्टिः *f.* -दर्शनं, अदूरदृष्टिः *f.*, अपूर्व्वचिन्ता, अपूर्व्वविवेचनं, अपूर्व्वनिरूपणं, अप्रसमीक्षा, असमीक्ष्यकारिता, पूर्व्वविवेचनाभावः, पूर्व्वचिन्ताभावः, अपूर्व्वविचारणं -णा, असावधानता.

IMPROVIDENT, *a.* अदीर्घदर्शी -र्शिनी -र्शि (न्), अदूरदर्शी &c., अपूर्व्वदृष्टिः -ष्टिः -ष्टि, अदीर्घदृष्टिः -ष्टिः -ष्टि, अपरिणामदर्शी &c., अपूर्व्वविवेकी -किनी -कि (न्), असमीक्ष्यकारी -रिणी -रि (न्), अभविष्यद्दर्शी &c.

IMPROVIDENTLY, *adv.* पूर्व्वचिन्तां विना, अग्रविवेचनां विना, अग्रनिरूपणं विना, पूर्व्वविचारणां विना, अपरिणामदृष्ट्या, असमीक्षापूर्व्वं, अप्रसमीक्ष्य, अप्रविमृश्य.

IMPROVING, *part.* or *a.* (Growing better) वर्धमानः -ना -नं, वर्धी

-र्धिनी -र्धि (न्), वर्धनः -नी -नं, उपचीयमानः -ना -नं.—(Making better) वर्धकः -का -कं, वृद्धिकरः -री -रं, बृंहणः -णा -णी -णं.

IMPRUDENCE, *s.* अविनयः, अविनीतता, अनीतिः *f.*, दुर्विनीतता, दुर्णीतिः *f.*, दुर्णयः, असमीक्षा, असमीक्ष्यकारित्वं, अविज्ञता, अप्रज्ञता, अप्राज्ञत्वं, अविवेचना, अविचारः -रणा, अविचक्षणता, अवैचक्षण्यं, असावधानता, अमनस्विता.

IMPRUDENT, *a.* अविज्ञः -ज्ञा -ज्ञं, अप्रज्ञः -ज्ञा -ज्ञं, अविचक्षणः -णा -णं, अविनीतः -ता -तं, दुर्विनीतः -ता -तं, अनभिज्ञः -ज्ञा -ज्ञं, अनीतिमान् -मती -मत् (त्), अनीतिज्ञः -ज्ञा -ज्ञं, अविमृश्यकारी -रिणी -रि (न्), असमीक्ष्यकारी &c., अमनस्वी -स्विनी -स्वि (न्), अमतिमान् -मती -मत् (त्), अविवेकी -किनी -कि (न्), अविवेचकः -का -कं, अविचारशीलः -ला -लं, अकार्य्यचिन्तकः -का -कं, अबुधः -धा -धं, असावधानः -ना -नं.

IMPRUDENTLY, *adv.* अविज्ञवत्, अविनीतवत्, अविमृश्य, असमीक्ष्य, असमीक्षापूर्व्वं, अविचारपूर्व्वं, अविचार्य्य, अनालोचितं, अविचारितं, अबुधवत्.

IMPUDENCE, *s.* निर्लज्जता -त्वं, लज्जाहीनता, अलज्जता, अलज्जा, धृष्टता, धार्ष्ट्यं, प्रगल्भता, प्रागल्भ्यं, वैयात्यं, त्रपाहीनता, अनपत्रपत्वं, निस्त्रपत्वं, निरपत्रपत्वं, अव्रीडता, व्रीडाहीनता, अविनयः, अविनीतता.

IMPUDENT, *a.* निर्लज्जः -ज्जा -ज्जं, लज्जाहीनः -ना -नं, अलज्जः -ज्जा -ज्जं, विलज्जः -ज्जा -ज्जं, अविनीतः -ता -तं, दुर्विनीतः -ता -तं, धृष्टः -ष्टा -ष्टं, अत्रपः -पा -पं, त्रपाहीनः -ना -नं, निस्त्रपः -पा -पं, निरपत्रपः -पा -पं, अनपत्रपः -पा -पं, वियातः -ता -तं, प्रगल्भः -ल्भा -ल्भं, व्रीडाहीनः -ना -नं, स्वल्पव्रीडः -डा -डं, अल्पलज्जः -ज्जा -ज्जं, अनिभृतः -ता -तं, धर्षितः -ता -तं, धृष्णक् *m.f.n.* (ज्), धृष्णुः -ष्णुः -ष्णु, त्यक्तलज्जः -ज्जा -ज्जं, प्रौढः -ढा -ढं.

IMPUDENTLY, *adv.* धृष्टवत्, अविनीतवत्, दुर्विनीतवत्, अविनीतं, धार्ष्ट्येन, प्रगल्भं, प्रगल्भवत्, लज्जां विना, वैयात्येन, प्रौढवत्, वियातवत्.

To IMPUGN, *v. a.* विपरीतं वद् (c. 1. वदति -दितुं), अपवद्, विवद्, प्रत्याख्या (c. 2. -ख्याति -तुं), अधरीकृ, विरुध् (c. 7. -रुणद्धि -रोद्धुं), प्रतिरुध्, प्रतिकूल (nom. प्रतिकूलयति -यितुं).

IMPUGNED, *p. p.* अपवादितः -ता -तं, प्रत्याख्यातः -ता -तं, अधरीकृतः -ता -तं, विरुद्धः -द्धा -द्धं, बाधितः -ता -तं, विप्रतिपन्नः -न्ना -न्नं.

IMPUGNER, *s.* विपरीतवादी *m.* (न्), अपवादकः, प्रतिवादी *m.* (न्).

IMPULSE, *s.* वेगः, आवेगः, मनोवेगः, प्रेरणं -णा, प्रणोदः, प्रवर्त्तः -र्त्तनं, प्रोत्साहः -हनं, प्ररोचनं, शक्तिः *f.*—(Motive) हेतुः *m.*, प्रयोगः, प्रयोजनं, निमित्तं, निबन्धनं, कारणं.—(Mental impression) मनःसंस्कारः.

IMPULSION, *s.* प्रेरणं -णा, प्रणोदः -दनं, प्रचोदनं, आकर्षः -र्षणं, प्रवर्त्तनं.

IMPULSIVE, *a.* प्रेरकः -का -कं, प्रणोदकः -का -कं, प्रचोदकः -का -कं.—(Actuated by impulse) वेगी -गिनी -गि (न्), वेगवान् -वती -वत् (त्), वेगशीलः -ला -लं.

IMPUNCTUAL, *a.* असमयपालकः -का -कं, असामयिकः -की -कं, अकालिकः -की -कं.

IMPUNITY, *s.* (Exemption from punishment) अदण्डः -ण्डः, दण्डाभावः, असाहसं, अशिष्टिः *f.*—(Exemption from injury or hurt) अक्षतिः *f.*, अक्षतं, अहिंसा, हिंसाभावः, अपीडा, अनाशः, अनपकारः; 'with impunity to one's self,' स्वयमक्षतेन.

IMPURE, *a.* अशुद्धः -द्धा -द्धं, अशुचिः -चिः -चि, अपवित्रः -त्रा -त्रं, अमेध्यः -ध्या -ध्यं, अपूतः -ता -तं, अशुद्धिः -द्धिः -द्धि, अशौची -चिनी -चि (न्), आशौची &c., अनिर्मलः -ला -लं, समलः -ला -लं, मलवान् -वती -वत् (त्), मलिनः -ना -नं, अपुण्यः -ण्या -ण्यं, अपवनः -ना -नं, शौचहीनः -ना -नं.—(Obscene) गर्हितः -ता -तं, गर्ह्यः -र्ह्या -र्ह्यं, कुत्सितः -ता -तं, अवाच्यः -च्या -च्यं.—(Unchaste) लम्पटः -टा -टं, पांशुलः -ला -लं.

IMPURELY, *adv.* अशुद्धं, अपवित्रं, अपुण्यं, समलं, साशौचं, अशुचिवत्, अमेध्यं, अशुद्धवत्, मलिनं, लम्पटवत्, गर्हितं.

IMPURENESS, IMPURITY, *s.* अशुद्धिः *f.*, अशुद्धत्वं -ता, अशोधनं, अशुचित्वं -ता, अशुचिः *f.*, अशौचं -चत्वं, आशौचं, अपवित्रत्वं -ता, अमेध्यता, अपुण्यता, अपूतता, अपूतिः *f.*, समलता, मलवत्त्वं, मालिन्यं, मलं, कलुषत्वं, कालुष्यं, शौचहीनता, अप्रायत्यं.—(Obscenity) गर्हितत्वं, कुत्सितत्वं, अवाच्यता.—(Unchastity) लम्पटत्वं, लाम्पट्यं, पांशुलता; 'an impure thing,' अपद्रव्यं.

To IMPURPLE, *v. a.* धूम्रीकृ, धूम्रलीकृ, धूम्रल (nom. धूम्रलयति -यितुं). *See* EMPURPLE.

IMPUTABLE, *a.* आरोपणीयः -या -यं, अध्यारोपणीयः -या -यं, सम्बन्धनीयः -या -यं, अभिसम्बन्धनीयः -या -यं.

IMPUTATION, *s.* (Act of imputing) आरोपः -पणं, अध्यारोपः -पणं, अभिसम्बन्धनं, सम्बन्धनं, प्रसङ्गः; 'imputation of a crime,' दोषारोपः, दोषकल्पनं, दोषप्रसङ्गः.—(Charge) अभियोगः, अपवादः, अभिशंसनं, संशयः.—(Reproach) अवक्षेपः, क्षेपः, अभिवादः, परीवादः, दुर्वाक्यं, दुरुक्तं, तिरस्कारवाक्यं, कलङ्कः.

To IMPUTE, *v. a.* (Attribute) आरुह् in caus. (-रोपयति -यितुं), अध्यारुह्, अभिसम्बन्ध् (c. 9. -बध्नाति -बन्द्धुं), सम्बन्ध्.—(Impute a crime to any one) कस्मिंश्चिद् दोषम् आरुह् or क्षिप् (c. 6. क्षिपति, क्षेप्तुं), दोषारोपणं कृ, दोषप्रसङ्गं कृ, दोषकल्पनं कृ.—(Cast imputations) अवक्षिप्, अधिक्षिप्, क्षिप्, अपवद् (c. 1. -वदति -दितुं).

IMPUTED, *p. p.* आरोपितः -ता -तं, आरूढः -ढा -ढं, अध्यारोपितः -ता -तं.

IMPUTER, *s.* आरोपकः, आरोपयिता *m.* (तृ), आरोपणकृत् *m.*, अवक्षेपकः.

IN, *prep.* नि prefixed to roots may give the sense of 'in;' as, 'to enter in,' निविश्; 'to dwell in,' निवस्. When 'in' is used for 'within,' or 'in the midst,' it may be expressed by अन्तर्, अन्तरा, अन्तरे, मध्ये. But the most frequent use of 'in' is expressed in Sanskrit by the locative case, without any preposition; as, 'in the city,' नगरे; 'in the night,' रात्रौ; 'a tree planted in the earth,' पृथिव्यां रोपितो वृक्षः; 'confidence in you,' त्वयि विश्वासः; 'engaging in the acquisition of wealth,' अर्थार्जने प्रवृत्तिः *f.*; 'the sun in the east,' प्राचि सूर्य्यः; 'he sinks in the mud,' पङ्के मज्जति; 'he delights in the good of others,' परहिते रमते; 'in the front of the fight,' रणमूर्द्ध्नि. In cases where 'in' refers to any division of time, or the manner in which any thing is done, it is usually expressed in Sanskrit by the instr. case; as, 'in three years,' त्रिभिर् वर्षैः; 'in twelve months,' द्वादशभिर् मासैः; 'in hundreds of years,' वर्षशतैः; 'in an instant,' क्षणेन; 'in process of time,' कालपर्य्यायेण; 'in how long time?' कियता कालेन; 'in a short time,' अचिरेण; 'in this manner,' अनेन प्रकारेण; 'in abundance,' बाहुल्येन; 'in the form of a man,' नररूपेण; 'in joke,' परिहासेन; 'written in Sanskrit,' संस्कृतेन रचितं. Certain adverbial affixes and prefixes may often express 'in;' as, 'in front,' अग्रतस्; 'in the first place,' प्रथमतस्; 'in another place,' अन्यत्र; 'in one place,' एकत्र; 'in many places,' बहुत्र; 'in the next world,' अमुत्र; 'in every way,' सर्व्वथा; 'in another way,' अन्यथा; 'in one way,' एकधा; 'in a hundred ways,' शतधा; 'in many ways,' बहुधा; 'in some way,'

कथञ्चित्, कथमपि; 'in small quantities,' अल्पशस्; 'in large quantities,' बहुशस्; 'in proper order,' क्रमशस्, क्रमतस्, अनुक्रमं; 'in every direction,' प्रतिदेशं; 'in three directions,' त्रेधा; 'in like manner,' तथैव, तद्वत्; 'in vain,' वृथा, मुधा. Sometimes 'in' may be expressed by a participle; as, 'he has pleasure in calumniating others,' अन्यान् परिवदन् स तुष्यति or पराभिशंसनं कृत्वा तुष्टो भवति; 'what bravery is there in killing a sleeping man?' किं पौरुषं हत्वा सुप्तं; 'he said that to me in joke,' उपहस्य माम् तद् अवदत्. The sense of 'in,' may be inherent in a noun; as, 'to go in and out,' गमनागमने कृ. 'In as much as,' is expressed by यस्मात्, येन, or by the abl. or instr. case of the abstract noun; as, 'in as much as it is founded on observation,' प्रत्यक्षमूलत्वात् or प्रत्यक्षमूलतया.

INABILITY, *s.* अशक्तिः *f.*, अशक्तता -त्वं, असामर्थ्यं, असमर्थत्वं, अक्षमता -त्वं, शक्तिहीनता, अबलत्वं, निर्बलत्वं, दौर्बल्यं, बलहीनता, शक्तिवैकल्यं, अयोग्यता -त्वं.

INABSTINENCE, *s.* असंयमः -मनं, असंयामः, अयतेन्द्रियत्वं, अयताहारत्वं, अनिवृत्तिः *f.*

INACCESSIBILITY, *s.* अगम्यता, अनभिगम्यता, दुर्गम्यता, दौर्ग्यं, अप्राप्यता, अलङ्घनीयत्वं, अलभ्यता, गहनत्वं.

INACCESSIBLE, *a.* अगम्यः -म्या -म्यं, अनभिगम्यः -म्या -म्यं, अगमनीयः -या -यं, दुर्गम्यः -म्या -म्यं, दुर्गमः -मा -मं, दुर्गः -र्गा -र्गं, अप्राप्यः -प्या -प्यं, दुष्प्राप्यः -प्या -प्यं, दुरासदः -दा -दं, दुरारोहः -हा -हं, सुदुरारुहः -हा -हं, दुरुपक्रमः -मा -मं, अलङ्घनीयः -या -यं, गहनः -ना -नं, विषमस्थः -स्था -स्थं.—(Not to be obtained) अलभ्यः -भ्या -भ्यं, दुर्लभः -भा -भं, अप्रापणीयः -या -यं.—(Forbidding access, haughty) दुर्धर्षः -र्षा -र्षं.

INACCURACY, *s.* अशुद्धिः *f.*, अशुद्धता -त्वं, अशोधनं, अयाथार्थ्यं, असम्यक्त्वं, असङ्गतत्वं, अतथ्यं, असामञ्जस्यं, भ्रमः, प्रमादः, अन्यथात्वं.

INACCURATE, *a.* अशुद्धः -द्धा -द्धं, अशोधितः -ता -तं, अयथार्थः -र्था -र्थं, असम्यङ् -मीची -म्यक् (क्), असङ्गतः -ता -तं, अतथ्यः -थ्या -थ्यं, असमञ्जसः -सा -सं, अनञ्जसः -सा -सं, अयाथार्थिकः -की -कं, अनृतः -ता -तं.

INACCURATELY, *adv.* अशुद्धं, अयथार्थं, असम्यक्, अतथ्यं, असङ्गतं, असमञ्जसं, अन्यथा, अनञ्जसा, अनृतं.

INACTION, *s.* अकर्म्म *n.* (न्), अक्रिया, अक्रियत्वं -ता, अप्रवृत्तिः *f.*, नैष्कर्म्यं, अचेष्टा, अनुद्योगः, आलस्यं, अलसता, अव्यवसायः, निर्व्यापारः, औदासीन्यं, औदास्यं, निर्वृत्तिः *f.*

INACTIVE, *a.* अकर्म्मा -र्म्मा -र्म्म (न्), अकर्म्मकृत् *m. f. n.*, निष्कर्म्मा -र्म्मा -र्म्म (न्), अक्रियः -या -यं, क्रियाशून्यः -न्या -न्यं, निश्चेष्टः -ष्टा -ष्टं, निरुद्योगः -गा -गं, निरुत्साहः -हा -हं, निरुद्यमः -मा -मं, अप्रवर्त्तकः -का -कं, अयत्नः -त्ना -त्नं, अप्रयत्नः -त्ना -त्नं, प्रयत्नशून्यः -न्या -न्यं, अयत्नकारी -रिणी -रि (न्), अयत्नवान् -वती -वत् (त्), लघुप्रयत्नः -त्ना -त्नं, अव्यवसायी -यिनी -यि (न्), निर्व्यापारः -रा -रं, वृत्तिरहितः -ता -तं, अलसः -सा -सं, उदासीनः -ना -नं, अनुद्यतः -ता -तं; 'to remain inactive,' अलसीभू, अलसो वृत्, उदास् (c. 2. -आस्ते -आसितुं).

INACTIVELY, *adv.* निरुद्योगं, निरुत्साहं, उद्योगम् अकृत्वा, यत्नं विना, प्रयत्नम् अकृत्वा, अलसवत्, उदासीनवत्.

INACTIVITY, *s.* अक्रिया -यत्वं, अकर्म्म *n.* (न्), अनुद्योगः, अनुत्साहः, अप्रवृत्तिः *f.*, अव्यवसायः, अयत्नः, अप्रयत्नता, अचेष्टा, निर्व्यापारः, नैष्कर्म्यं, क्रियाशून्यता, आलस्यं, अलसता, औदासीन्यं, औदास्यं, कार्य्यप्रद्वेषः.

INADEQUACY, *s.* अक्षमता -त्वं, असामर्थ्यं, असमर्थता, अयोग्यता, अनुपयुक्तत्वं.

INADEQUATE, *a.* अक्षमः -मा -मं, असमर्थः -र्था -र्थं, अयोग्यः -ग्या -ग्यं, अनुपयुक्तः -क्ता -क्तं, अपर्य्याप्तः -प्ता -प्तं, अनुचितः -ता -तं, अप्रभूतः -ता -तं, कार्य्याक्षमः -मा -मं, अनलम् indec.

INADEQUATELY, *adv.* अपर्य्याप्तं, अनुपयुक्तं, अयोग्यं, अनलम्, अक्षमं.

INADMISSIBLE, *a.* अनादेयः -या -यं, अग्राह्यः -ह्या -ह्यं, अग्रहणीयः -या -यं, अनुपादेयः -या -यं, अस्वीकरणीयः -या -यं, अस्वीकार्य्यः -र्य्या -र्य्यं, अमन्तव्यः -व्या -व्यं; 'into society,' अपाङ्क्तेयः -या -यं, अपाङ्क्त्यः -क्त्या -क्त्यं, अपाङ्क्तः -क्ता -क्तं.

INADVERTENCE, INADVERTENCY, *s.* प्रमादः, प्रमाद्यं, अनवधानं -नता, असावधानता, अमनोयोगः, अनपेक्षा, अनवेक्षा, उपेक्षा.

INADVERTENT, *a.* प्रमादी -दिनी -दि (न्), प्रमादवान् -वती -वत् (त्), प्रमत्तः -त्ता -त्तं, अनवधानः -ना -नं, असावधानः -ना -नं, अनवहितः -ता -तं, उपेक्षकः -का -कं, निरपेक्षः -क्षा -क्षं, अमनोयोगी -गिनी -गि (न्).

INADVERTENTLY, *adv.* प्रमादेन -दात्, प्रमत्तं, सप्रमादं, प्रमाद्यात्, अनवधानेन -नात्, अनवहितं, अमनोयोगात्, अनपेक्षया, निरपेक्षं, असमीक्ष्य.

INALIENABLE, *a.* अविभेद्यः -द्या -द्यं, अविभेदनीयः -या -यं, अविच्छेदनीयः -या -यं, परवशे कर्त्तुम् अशक्यः -क्या -क्यं, परवशे स्थापयितुम् अशक्यः -क्या -क्यं, अदेयः -या -यं, अनन्यादेयः -या -यं, अनन्यहार्य्यः -र्य्या -र्य्यं, अनन्यसमर्पणीयः -या -यं, परादेयः -या -यं, वंशमात्रोपभोग्यः -ग्या -ग्यं; 'inalienable property,' पराधीनं कर्त्तुं न शक्यते यद् द्रव्यं.

INALIENABLENESS, *s.* अविभेद्यता, अविभेदनीयता, अनन्यादेयता, अनन्यहार्य्यता.

INALTERABLE, *a.* अविकार्य्यः -र्य्या -र्य्यं, अविकरणीयः -या -यं.

INAMISSIBLE, *a.* अहेयः -या -यं, अहार्य्यः -र्य्या -र्य्यं, अत्याज्यः -ज्या -ज्यं, अहरणीयः -या -यं, अनाश्यः -श्या -श्यं, अविनाश्यः -श्या -श्यं.

INAMORATA, *s.* प्रिया, कान्ता, कामिनी, अनुरागवती, प्रणयिनी, रागिणी.

INAMORATO, *s.* प्रियः, कान्तः, कामी *m.* (न्), अनुरागवान् *m.* (त्), प्रणयी *m.* (न्), रागी *m.* (न्).

INANE, *a.* शून्यः -न्या -न्यं, रिक्तः -क्ता -क्तं, असारः -रा -रं, निःसारः -रा -रं, सारहीनः -ना -नं, वितानः -ना -नं, तुच्छः -च्छा -च्छं.

INANIMATE, *a.* निर्जीवः -वा -वं, विचेतनः -ना -नं, अचेतनः -ना -नं, अप्राणी -णिनी -णि (न्), प्राणहीनः -ना -नं, निष्पन्दः -न्दा -न्दं; 'animate and inanimate,' चेतनाचेतनं.

INANITION, *s.* शून्यता, असारता, सारहीनता, अपूर्णता, अवसादः, निरन्नत्वं.

INANITY, *s.* शून्यत्वं, रिक्तता -त्वं, निःसारत्वं, साराभावः, रिक्तं.

INAPPETENCY, *s.* अलोभः, अनभिलाषः, अनभिरुचिः *f.*, अनिच्छा, अवाञ्छा.

INAPPLICABLE, *a.* अयोग्यः -ग्या -ग्यं, अनुपयुक्तः -क्ता -क्तं, अनुपयोगी -गिनी -गि (न्), अनुपपन्नः -न्ना -न्नं, अप्रयोक्तव्यः -व्या -व्यं, अप्रयोज्यः -ज्या -ज्यं.

INAPPLICATION, *s.* अनभिनिवेशः, अमनःप्रवेशः, अमनोयोगः, अनभ्यासः, अनुद्योगः, अप्रवृत्तिः *f.*, अप्रवृत्तत्वं, अव्यवसायः, आलस्यं, अलसता -त्वं.

INAPPOSITE, *a.* अयुक्तः -क्ता -क्तं, असङ्गतः -ता -तं, अयोग्यः -ग्या -ग्यं, प्रस्तुतबहिर्भूतः -ता -तं, प्रस्तुतविरुद्धः -द्धा -द्धं.

INAPPOSITELY, *adv.* असङ्गतं, अयुक्तं, अयोग्यं, अनुपयुक्तं, अनुपपन्नं.

INAPPREHENSIBLE, *a.* अग्राह्यः -ह्या -ह्यं, अगम्यः -म्या -म्यं, अनुपलभ्यः -भ्या -भ्यं.

INAPPREHENSIVE, *a.* अशङ्की -ङ्किनी -ङ्कि (न्), अशङ्कान्वितः -ता -तं.

INAPPROACHABLE, *a.* अनभिगम्यः -म्या -म्यं, अनुपगम्यः -म्या -म्यं, अगम्यः -म्या -म्यं.

INAPPROPRIATE, *a.* अयोग्यः -ग्या -ग्यं, अयुक्तः -क्ता -क्तं, असङ्गतः -ता -तं, असङ्गतार्थः -र्था -र्थं, अनुपयोगी -गिनी -गि (न्), निर्युक्तिकः -की -कं.

INAPPROPRIATELY, *adv.* अयोग्यं, अयुक्तं, असङ्गतं, अनुपयुक्तं, अस्थाने.

INAPTITUDE, *s.* अयोग्यता, अनुपयुक्तत्वं, अनुपयोगिता, अपात्रता -त्वं, अयुक्तिः *f.*, निर्युक्तिः *f.*, अनुचितत्वं.

INAPTLY, *adv.* अयुक्तं, अयोग्यं, अनुपयुक्तं, अयुक्त्या, अस्थाने.

INARABLE, *a.* अकर्षणीयः -या -यं, अकृषियोग्यः -ग्या -ग्यं, असीत्यः -त्या -त्यं.

INARTICULATE, *a.* अव्यक्तः -क्ता -क्तं, अस्पष्टः -ष्टा -ष्टं, अव्यक्तपदः -दा -दं, अस्पष्टाक्षरः -रा -रं, सन्दिग्धाक्षरः -रा -रं, अव्यक्ताक्षरः -रा -रं, अव्यक्तवर्णः -र्णा -र्णं, अस्फुटः -टा -टं, अपरिस्फुटः -टा -टं, मदकलः -ला -लं, क्ष्विष्टः -ष्टा -ष्टं, क्ष्वेडितः -ता -तं, गद्गदः -दा -दं; 'inarticulate speech,' गद्गदवाक् *f.* (च्), गद्गदपदं, क्ष्विष्टं, क्ष्वेडितं, सीत्कृतं, हिक्का; 'with a voice inarticulate from weeping,' बाष्पसन्दिग्धया गिरा.

INARTICULATELY, *adv.* अव्यक्तं, अस्पष्टं, अस्फुटं, गद्गदवाचा, सन्दिग्धाक्षरया गिरा, सन्दिग्धवाचा, अस्पष्टोच्चारणेन.

INARTICULATENESS, *s.* अव्यक्तता, अस्पष्टता, वागस्पष्टता, उच्चारणास्पष्टत्वं.

INARTIFICIAL, *a.* अकृत्रिमः -मा -मं, अकृतकः -का -कं, अकाल्पनिकः -की -कं.

INARTIFICIALLY, *adv.* अकृत्रिमं, अकृत्रिमप्रकारेण, अकल्पनापूर्व्वं, अप्रतियत्नपूर्व्वं, स्वयकृतं.

IN AS MUCH AS, *adv.* यस्मात्, येन. *See* IN.

INATTENTION, *s.* अनवधानं -नता, असावधानता, अनवहितत्वं, अमनोयोगः, उपेक्षा, अनवेक्षा, अनपेक्षा, प्रमादः, प्रमत्तता, प्रमाद्यं, अनभिनिवेशः, अमनोनिवेशः, अमनःप्रवेशः, अनिविष्टचित्तता, अनासक्तचित्तता, विबोधः, अननुष्ठानं, अननुशातृत्वं, अनादरः, उज्झानं, शून्यहृदयत्वं, असतर्कत्वं, विरक्तत्वं, अननुरागः.

INATTENTIVE, *a.* असावधानः -ना -नं, अनवधानः -ना -नं, अनवहितः -ता -तं, अमनोयोगी -गिनी -गि (न्), प्रमत्तः -त्ता -त्तं, प्रमादी -दिनी -दि (न्), प्रमादवान् -वती -वत् (त्), निरपेक्षः -क्षा -क्षं, उपेक्षकः -का -कं, अनिविष्टचित्तः -त्ता -त्तं, अनासक्तः -क्ता -क्तं, अनासक्तचित्तः -त्ता -त्तं, विबुद्धः -द्धा -द्धं, मन्दादरः -रा -रं, विरक्तः -क्ता -क्तं.

INATTENTIVELY, *adv.* अनवधानेन -नतस्, अनवहितं, अवधानं विना, सप्रमादं.

INAUDIBLE, *a.* अश्राव्यः -व्या -व्यं, अश्रवणीयः -या -यं, अश्रोतव्यः -व्या -व्यं, कर्णागोचरः -रा -रं, अकर्णश्रवः -वा -वं, श्रोत्राग्राह्यः -ह्या -ह्यं, श्रोतुम् अशक्यः -क्या -क्यं.

INAUDIBLY, *adv.* अश्रवणीयं, अश्राव्यं, यथा श्रोतुं न शक्यते तथा.

INAUGURAL, *a.* (As an address) अभिषेककाले or प्रतिष्ठाकाले or अधिकारप्रवेशकाले भाषितः -ता -तं or भाषणीयः -या -यं.

To INAUGURATE, *v. a.* अभिषिच् (c. 6. -षिञ्चति -षेक्तुं) with loc. c., अभिषेकादिसंस्कारेण नवाधिकारं प्रविश् (c. 10. -वेशयति -यितुं) or नवाधिकारप्रवेशनं कृ, प्रतिष्ठा in caus. (-ष्ठापयति -यितुं), अभिमन्त्र् (c. 10. -मन्त्रयति -यितुं), उपनिमन्त्र्.

INAUGURATED, *p. p.* अभिषिक्तः -क्ता -क्तं, कृताभिषेकः -का -कं, प्रतिष्ठितः -ता -तं, कृतसंस्कारः -रा -रं, अभिसंस्कृतः -ता -तं, अभिषेकादिना नवपदप्रवेशितः -ता -तं.

INAUGURATION, *s.* अभिषेकः, अभिषेचनं, प्रतिष्ठा, संस्कारः, अधिकारप्रवेशसंस्कारः, अभिमन्त्रणं.

INAURATION, *s.* स्वर्णाञ्जनं, सुवर्णाञ्जनं, स्वर्णपत्राच्छादनं, सुवर्णीकरणं.

INAUSPICIOUS, *a.* अशुभः -भा -भं, अकल्याणः -णा -णं, अमङ्गलः -ला -लं, अमङ्गल्यः -ल्या -ल्यं, अकुशलः -ला -लं, अभद्रः -द्रा -द्रं, अशकुनः -ना -नं, अनिष्टसूचकः -का -कं, अमङ्गलजनकः -का -कं, अधन्यः -न्या -न्यं, अनिष्टः -ष्टा -ष्टं, अक्षेमः -मा -मं, अक्षेम्यः -म्या -म्यं, अक्षेमवान् -वती -वत् (त्), दुर्भाग्यः -ग्या -ग्यं, अभाग्यः -ग्या -ग्यं.—(Unfavorable) अननुकूलः -ला -लं.

INAUSPICIOUSLY, *adv.* अशुभं, अकल्याणं, अमङ्गलं, अकुशलं, अभद्रं, अक्षेमेण, अदिष्ट्या, अशुभलग्ने, अननुकूलं.

INAUSPICIOUSNESS, *s.* अकल्याणं, अमाङ्गल्यं, अकौशल्यं, अशुभत्वं, अक्षेमः.

INAVERTIBLE, *a.* अनिवार्य्यः -र्य्या -र्य्यं, अनिवारणीयः -या -यं, अनिवारयितव्यः -व्या -व्यं, अपरिहार्य्यः -र्य्या -र्य्यं, दुरत्ययः -या -यं.

INBEING, *s.* अन्तर्भावः, अन्तर्वृत्तिः *f.*, निष्ठा, योगः.

INBORN, INBRED, *a.* अन्तर्जातः -ता -तं, अन्तर्जनितः -ता -तं, अन्तर्भवः -वा -वं, निजः -जा -जं, सहजः -जा -जं, सहजातः -ता -तं, निष्ठः -ष्ठा -ष्ठं, स्वाभाविकः -की -कं, स्वभावजः -जा -जं, अन्तर्वर्त्ती -र्त्तिनी -र्त्ति (न्), अन्तरजातः -ता -तं, नैसर्गिकः -की -कं.

To INCAGE, *v. a* पिञ्जरे or वीतंसे निरुध् (c. 7. -रुणद्धि -रोद्धुं) or अवरुध्.

INCALCULABLE, *a.* अगणनीयः -या -यं, अगण्यः -ण्या -ण्यं, अविगण्यः -ण्या -ण्यं, अविगणनीयः -या -यं, असंख्येयः -या -यं.

INCALCULABLY, *adv.* अगणनीयं, अविगणनीयं, यथा गणना कर्त्तुं न शक्यते.

INCANDESCENCE, *s.* अत्युष्मा *m.* (न्), अत्युष्णता, अत्यौष्ण्यं, अत्यन्तचकता.

INCANTATION, *s.* मन्त्रः, अभिमन्त्रणं, मन्त्रमोहनं, अभिचारः, वशक्रिया, वशीकरणं, योगः, सम्प्रयोगः, चित्रकर्म्म *n.* (न्), मूलकर्म्म *n.*, माया, हुङ्कृतं, संवदनं -ना, हिंसाकर्म्म *n.* (न्), जालं, कुसृतिः *f.*; 'to use incantations,' अभिमन्त्र् (c. 10. -मन्त्रयते -यितुं), अनुमन्त्र्, मन्त्रद्वारेण वशीकृ or मुह् (c. 10. मोहयति -यितुं), अभिचर् (c. 10. -चारयति -यितुं), मायां कृ.

INCANTATORY, *a.* आभिचारिकः -की -कं, अभिचारिकः -की -कं, मान्त्रिकः -की -कं.

INCAPABILITY, INCAPABLENESS, *s.* अक्षमता, असामर्थ्यं, असमर्थता, अशक्तिः *f.*, अशक्तता, अयोग्यता, अयुक्तिः *f.*, अनुपयोगिता, अपात्रता, अनर्हता.

INCAPABLE, *a.* अक्षमः -मा -मं, असमर्थः -र्था -र्थं, अशक्तः -क्ता -क्तं, अयोग्यः -ग्या -ग्यं, अनुपयुक्तः -क्ता -क्तं, अनुपयोगी -गिनी -गि (न्), शक्तिहीनः -ना -नं, अपात्रिकः -की -कं, अनुचितः -ता -तं, अनर्हः -र्हा -र्हं. *See* CAPABLE.

INCAPACIOUS, *a.* अविस्तीर्णः -र्णा -र्णं, अविस्तृतः -ता -तं, अविशालः -ला -लं, अपृथुः -थुः -थु, अविपुलः -ला -लं, सबाधः -धा -धं, सङ्कटः -टा -टं, अविवृतः -ता -तं.

INCAPACIOUSNESS, *s.* अविस्तीर्णता, अविशालत्वं, अपृथुता, सबाधत्वं.

To INCAPACITATE, *v. a.* अक्षमीकृ, अशक्तीकृ, अक्षमं -मां -मं कृ, अशक्तं -क्तां -क्तं कृ, असमर्थीकृ, असमर्थं -र्थां -र्थं कृ, अपात्रीकृ, अयोग्यं -ग्यां -ग्यं कृ, अनुपयुक्तं -क्तां -क्तं कृ, शक्तिं हृ (c. 1. हरति, हर्त्तुं).

INCAPACITATED, *p. p.* अपात्रीकृतः -ता -तं, अक्षमीभूतः -ता -तं, हृतशक्तिः -क्तिः -क्ति.

INCAPACITY, *s.* अशक्तिः *f.*, असामर्थ्यं, अक्षमता, असमर्थता, अयोग्यता -त्वं, अयुक्तिः *f.*, शक्तिहीनता, अनुपयुक्तता, अनुपयोगित्वं, अपात्रता -त्वं.—(Mental incapacity) बोधशक्तिहीनता, बुद्धिहीनता, धीशक्तिहीनता, मेधाभावः.

To INCARCERATE, *v. a.* कारागारे or कारागृहे निरुध् (c. 7. -रुणद्धि -रोद्धुं) or अवरुध् or बन्ध् (c. 9. बध्नाति, बन्द्धुं), निरोधगृहं or बन्धनालयं प्रविश् (c. 10. -वेशयति -यितुं), आसिध् (c. 1. -सेधति -सेद्धुं).

INCARCERATED, *p. p.* कारागारे निरुद्धः -द्धा -द्धं, अवरुद्धदेहः -हा -हं.

INCARCERATION, *s.* कारागारप्रवेशनं, कारागृहप्रवेशः, कारानिरोधः, काराबन्धनं, कारागोपनं, कारागृहगुप्तिः *f.*

INCARNATE, *a.* शरीरी -रिणी -रि (न्), सशरीरः -रा -रं, शरीरवान् -वती -वत् (त्), देही -हिनी -हि (न्), सदेहः -हा -हं, देहवान् -वती -वत् (त्), मूर्त्तिमान् -मती -मत् (त्), वपुष्मान् -ष्मती -ष्मत् (त्), सवपुषः -षी -षं, शरीरधारी -रिणी -रि (न्), गृहीतशरीरः -रा -रं, गृहीतदेहः -हा -हं, मनुष्यशरीरेण अवतीर्णः -र्णा -र्णं, शरीरगतः -ता -तं, देहगतः -ता -तं, देहतन्त्रः -न्त्रा -न्त्रं, अवरुद्धदेहः -हा -हं, अवतारी -रिणी -रि (न्).

INCARNATION, *s.* अवतारः, शरीरग्रहणं, शरीरधारणं, मनुष्यशरीरधारणं, देहग्रहणं, देहधारणं, मूर्त्तिमत्त्वं, सशरीरता. *See* VISHNU.

To incase, *v. a.* (Put in a case) भाण्डे or आधारे निविश् (c. 10. -वेशयति -यितुं) or निधा (c. 3. -दधाति -धातुं).—(Cover, inclose) पिधा, आवृ (c. 5. -वृणोति -वरितुं -रीतुं), परिवृ, परिवेष्ट् (c. 1. -वेष्टते -ष्टितुं, c. 10. -वेष्टयति -यितुं), आच्छद् (c. 10. -छादयति -यितुं), परिच्छद्.

Incased, *p. p.* आवृतः -ता -तं, पिहितः -ता -तं, कोशस्थः -स्था -स्थं, परिवेष्टितः -ता -तं, परिवृतः -ता -तं, परिच्छन्नः -न्ना -न्नं.

Incaution, *s.* अनवधानं -नता, असावधानता, अनपेक्षा, अनवेक्षा, असमीक्षा, अविवेचनं, प्रमादं, प्रमादः.

Incautious, *a.* अनवधानः -ना -नं, असावधानः -ना -नं, अनवहितः -ता -तं, प्रमत्तः -त्ता -त्तं, प्रमादी -दिनी -दि (न्), प्रमादवान् -वती -वत् (त्), निरपेक्षः -क्षा -क्षं, असमीक्ष्यकारी -रिणी -रि (न्), अविमृश्यकारी &c., साहसी -सिनी -सि (न्).

Incautiously, *adv.* अनवधानतस्, अनवधानेन, अनवहितं, अवधानं विना, सप्रमादं, प्रमादात्, प्रमादतस्, प्रमाद्यतस्, प्रमत्तं, प्रमत्तवत्, निरपेक्षं, अनपेक्षया, असमीक्ष्य, अविमृश्य.

Incautiousness, *s.* अनवधानता, असावधानता, प्रमादं, अपरिणामदृष्टिः *f.*

Incendiarism, *s.* गृहदाहः -हनं, आगारदाहः -हनं, गृहज्वलनं, गृहप्रोषः.

Incendiary, *s.* गृहदाहकः, आगारदाही *m.* (न्), अग्निदः, आततायी *m.* (न्), महापातकी *m.* (न्), तामसः.

Incense, *s.* धूपः, यक्षधूपः, सुगन्धिकः, वह्निगन्धः, सिह्लः -ह्लकः, शिह्लः, तुरुष्कः, यावनः, पिण्डकः, पिण्डातः, कपिजः, कप्याख्यः, मेरुकः, पालङ्की, कृत्रिमः, तैलपर्णी.

To incense, *v. a.* (Perfume with incense) धूप् (c. 1. धूपायति, c. 10. धूपयति -यितुं), अवधूप्, परिधूप्, धूपेन वास् (c. 10. वासयति -यितुं) or सुरभीकृ.—(Provoke to anger) कुप् (c. 10. कोपयति -यितुं), प्रकुप्, सकुप्, कोपं or क्रोधं जन् (c. 10. जनयति -यितुं), क्रुध् (c. 10. क्रोधयति -यितुं), कोपेन ज्वल् (c. 10. ज्वलयति -यितुं) or उद्दीप् (c. 10. -दीपयति -यितुं) or उत्तिज् (c. 10. -तेजयति -यितुं), संरब्धीकृ.

Incensed, *p. p.* (Perfumed with incense) धूपितः -ता -तं, धूपायितः -ता -तं.—(Exasperated) कुपितः -ता -तं, कोपितः -ता -तं, प्रकोपितः -ता -तं, प्रकुपितः -ता -तं, कोपदीप्तः -प्ता -प्तं, कोपज्वलितः -ता -तं, समिद्धकोपः -पा -पं, इद्धकोपः -पा -पं, संरब्धः -ब्धा -ब्धं, संरक्तः -क्ता -क्तं.

Incensement, *s.* प्रकोपः -पनं, कोपकरणं, क्रोधकरणं, कोपज्वलनं, संरम्भः.

Incensory, *s.* धूपाधारः, धूपपात्रं, धूपभाजनं, गन्धद्रव्यपात्रं.

Incentive, *s.* प्रोत्साहः -हनं, प्ररोचनं, प्रवर्त्तः -र्त्तनं, उत्तेजनं, समुत्तेजनं, प्रेरणं -णा, प्रणोदः -दनं, प्रचोदनं, प्रयोजनं, हेतुः *m.*, कारणं, निमित्तं, निबन्धनं, उत्तेजकं, उद्बोधकं.

Incentive, *a.* (Inciting) प्रोत्साहकः -का -कं, प्रवर्त्तकः -का -कं, उत्तेजकः -का -कं, प्रेरकः -का -कं, प्रयोजकः -का -कं, प्रणोदकः -का -कं.

Inception, *s.* आरम्भः, प्रारम्भः, समारम्भः, उपक्रमः, प्रक्रमः.

Inceptive, *a.* आरम्भकः -का -कं, आरम्भोद्बोधकः -का -कं.

Incertitude, *s.* अनिर्णयः, अनियमः, अनिश्चयः, शङ्का, विकल्पः, सन्दिग्धता.

Incessant, *a.* अविरतः -ता -तं, अनवरतः -ता -तं, निरन्तरः -रा -रं, नित्यः -त्या -त्यं, नैत्यिकः -की -कं, अत्यन्तः -न्ता -न्तं, अनन्तः -न्ता -न्तं, अनारतः -ता -तं, अविरलः -ला -लं, अविश्रान्तः -न्ता -न्तं, अश्रान्तः -न्ता -न्तं, अनिवृत्तः -त्ता -त्तं, अविच्छिन्नः -न्ना -न्नं, अपरिच्छिन्नः -न्ना -न्नं, शाश्वतः -ती -तं, नियतः -ता -तं, अभीक्ष्णः -क्ष्णा -क्ष्णं, सर्व्वकालीनः -ना -नं, सर्व्वक्षणीयः -या -यं, अविसर्गी -र्गिणी -र्गि (न्), प्रसक्तः -क्ता -क्तं, अखण्डितः -ता -तं.

Incessantly, *adv.* अविरतं, अनवरतं, निरन्तरं, नित्यं, नित्यदा, नित्यशस्, प्रतिक्षणं, अनुक्षणं, अनारतं, अजस्रं, अनिशं, शाश्वतं, अभीक्ष्णं, अविश्रान्तं, अश्रान्तं, नियतं, सततं, सन्ततं, सर्व्वदा, सर्व्वकालं, प्रसक्तं, अत्यन्तं, वारं वारं, मुहुस्, मुहुर्मुहुस्, अनन्तकालं.

Incest, *s.* अगम्यागमनं, अगम्यगमनं, गोत्रगमनं, गोत्राभिगमनं, व्यभिचारः.—(With a mother) मातृगमनं.—(With a sister) स्वसृगमनं.—(With a daughter) दुहितृगमनं.—(With a father's wife) गुरुतल्पगमनं, गुरुतल्पं.

Incestuous, *a.* अगम्यागामी *m.* (न्), अगम्यगामिनी *f.*, गोत्रगामी *m.*, गोत्राभिगामी *m.* (न्), व्यभिचारी *m.* (न्); 'an incestuous son,' मातृगामी *m.* (न्), गुरुतल्पगः, गुरुतल्पी *m.* (न्).

Inch, *s.* अङ्गुलः, अङ्गुलपरिमाणं, अङ्गुष्ठपर्व्वपरिमाणं; 'a line eight inches long,' अष्टाङ्गुलपरिमिता रेखा; 'an inch long,' अङ्गुलपरिमितः -ता -तं, अङ्गुलमितः -ता -तं.

Inchmeal, *s.* अङ्गुलपरिमाणः खण्डः, अङ्गुष्ठपर्व्वभरः.

To inchoate, *v. a.* आरभ् (c. 1. -रभते -रब्धुं), प्रारभ्, प्रक्रम् (c. 1. -क्रमते -मितुं).

Inchoate, *a.* आरब्धः -ब्धा -ब्धं, समारब्धः -ब्धा -ब्धं, प्रारब्धः -ब्धा -ब्धं.

Inchoation, *s.* आरम्भः, प्रारम्भः, समारम्भः, प्रारब्धिः *f.*, उपक्रमः, प्रक्रमः, अभ्यादानं, उपोद्घातः.

Inchoative, *a.* आरम्भकः -का -कं, प्रारम्भकः -का -कं, आरम्भसूचकः -का -कं.

Incidence, *s.* पतनं, आपतनं, अभिपतनं, आपातः, निपातः, समुत्पत्तिः *f.*; 'angle of incidence,' पतनकोणः, आपतनकोणः.

Incident, *a.* (Happening) आपतिकः -की -कं, आपतनशीलः -ला -लं, उपस्थायी -यिनी -यि (न्), उपस्थितः -ता -तं.

Incident, *s.* (An event) वृत्तं, भूतं, सम्भवः, उत्पन्नं, समुत्पत्तिः *f.*, समुत्पन्नं, सङ्गतं, सङ्गतिः *f.*, समुपागतं, समुपस्थितं, आगन्तुः *m.*, घटना -नं.—(Episode) उपाख्यानं, उपकथा, प्रसङ्गवाक्यं.

Incidental, *a.* (Casual, accidental, occasional) आपतिकः -की -कं, आगन्तुः -न्तुः -न्तु, आगन्तुकः -का -की -कं, आहार्य्यः -र्य्या -र्य्यं, आकस्मिकः -की -कं, प्रासङ्गिकः -की -कं, सहजेतरः -रा -रं, कादाचित्कः -त्का -त्कं, अनित्यः -त्या -त्यं, नैमित्तिकः -की -कं, विरलागतः -ता -तं; 'incidental cause,' कार्य्यकारणं.

Incidentally, *adv.* (Casually) आगन्तुकप्रकारेण, अकस्मात्, दैवात्, हठात्, सङ्गत्या, दैवयोगेन.—(Beside the main design) मूलविषयबहिस्, प्रस्तुतविषयव्यतिरेकेण; 'from some incidental cause,' कार्य्यकारणतस्.

To incinerate, *v. a.* भस्मीकृ, भस्मसात्कृ, भस्मराशीकृ.

Incinerated, *p. p.* भस्मीभूतः -ता -तं, भस्मसात्कृतः -ता -तं, भस्मराशीभूतः -ता -तं.

Incineration, *s.* भस्मीकरणं, भस्मसात्करणं, भस्मराशीकरणं.

Incipiency, *s.* आरम्भः, प्रारम्भः, समारम्भः, प्रारब्धिः *f.*, उपक्रमः.

Incipient, *a.* आरम्भकः -का -कं, आरब्धः -ब्धा -ब्धं, प्रारब्धः -ब्धा -ब्धं.

Incircumspection, *s.* असमीक्षा -क्षणं, असमीक्ष्यकारित्वं, अनवधानं -नता, असावधानता.

To incise, *v. a.* छिद् (c. 7. छिनत्ति, छेत्तुं), निश्छिद्, कृत् (c. 6. कृन्तति, कर्त्तितुं), निकृत्, तक्ष् (c. 1. तक्षति, c. 5. तक्ष्णोति -क्षितुं).

Incised, *a.* निकृत्तः -त्ता -त्तं, निश्छिन्नः -न्ना -न्नं, तष्टः -ष्टा -ष्टं.

Incision, *s.* छेदः -दनं, निश्छेदः, कर्त्तनं, निकर्त्तनं, व्रश्चनं, लूनिः *f.*, लावः, छित्तिः *f.*, छिदा, खण्डनं; 'in the flesh,' मांसच्छेदः, त्वक्छेदः, त्वग्भेदः, मांसक्षतं.

Incisor, *s.* छेदकदन्तः, अग्रदन्तः, राजदन्तः, सम्मुखदन्तः, मुख्यदन्तः.

Incisory, *a.* छेदकः -का -कं, छित्वरः -रा -रं, छेदकरः -री -रं.

INCITATION, *s.* प्रोत्साहनं, प्रेरणं, उत्तेजनं, समुत्तेजनं, प्रवर्त्तनं, प्ररोचनं, प्रचोदनं, प्रणोदः -दनं.

To INCITE, *v. a.* उत्सह् in caus. (-साहयति -यितुं), प्रोत्सह्, समुत्सह्, प्रवृत् (c. 10. -वर्त्तयति -यितुं), प्रेर् (c. 10. प्रेरयति -यितुं), चुद् (c. 10. चोदयति -यितुं), प्रचुद्, सञ्चुद्, सम्प्रचुद्, परिचुद्, प्रणुद् (c. 6. -णुदति -णोत्तुं), प्ररुच् (c. 10. -रोचयति -यितुं), उद्युज् (c. 10. -योजयति -यितुं), प्रयुज्, नियुज्, चेष्ट् (c. 10. चेष्टयति -यितुं), आकृ (c. 10. -कारयति -यितुं), उद्दीप् (c. 10. -दीपयति -यितुं), उत्तप् (c. 10. -तापयति -यितुं), सन्धुक्ष् (c. 10. -धुक्षयति -यितुं), प्रदिश् (c. 10. -देशयति -यितुं), उत्स्था in caus. (-थापयति -यितुं, rt. स्था), ईह् (c. 10. ईहयति -यितुं). The loc. or dat. c. is required of the thing to which one is incited; as, 'he incited them to murder their mother,' तान् मातुर् वधे or वधाय प्राचोदयत्.—(Encourage) आश्वस् (c. 10. -श्वासयति -यितुं), तेजः or विश्वासं कृ or वृध् (c. 10. वर्धयति -यितुं).

INCITED, *p. p.* प्रोत्साहितः -ता -तं, प्रवर्त्तितः -ता -तं, प्रेरितः -ता -तं, प्रचोदितः -ता -तं, चोदितः -ता -तं, प्रवृत्तः -त्ता -त्तं, प्रयोजितः -ता -तं, नियोजितः -ता -तं, उद्युक्तः -क्ता -क्तं, प्रणोदितः -ता -तं, प्रणुन्नः -न्ना -न्नं, उत्तेजितः -ता -तं, उत्थापितः -ता -तं, प्ररुचितः -ता -तं, उत्तप्तः -प्ता -प्तं, उद्दीप्तः -प्ता -प्तं.

INCITEMENT, *s.* प्रोत्साहः -हनं, प्रवर्त्तः -र्त्तनं, प्रेरणं -णा, प्रलोभनं, प्ररोचनं, उत्तेजनं, समुत्तेजनं, प्रणोदः -दनं, प्रचोदनं.—(Motive) प्रयोजनं, हेतुः *m.*, उत्साहहेतुः, कारणं, प्रयोगः, निमित्तं, निबन्धनं.

INCITING, *a.* प्रोत्साहकः -का -कं, प्रवर्त्तकः -का -कं, प्रेरकः -का -कं, प्रचोदकः -का -कं, प्रणोदकः -का -कं, प्रयोजकः -का -कं.

INCIVIL, *a.* असभ्यः -भ्या -भ्यं, अशिष्टः -ष्टा -ष्टं, अदक्षिणः -णा -णं, दुर्मर्य्यादः -दा -दं, दुःशीलः -ला -लं, कुशीलः -ला -लं.

INCIVILITY, *s.* अशिष्टता, दुःशीलता, कुशीलता, अविनयः, असभ्यता, अमर्य्यादा, दुर्मर्य्यादता, अननुनयः, अदाक्षिण्यं, अनार्य्यता.

INCIVILLY, *adv.* असभ्यवत्, अशिष्टवत्, कुशीलवत्, विनयविरुद्धं, विनयं विना, अमर्य्यादापूर्व्वं, मर्य्यादाविरोधेन.

INCLEMENCY, *s.* (Want of clemency) अदया, निर्दयता, अदयता, निष्करुणता, अकारुण्यं, अकृपा, कृपाहीनता, दयाहीनता, अननुकम्पा, अनुकम्पाहीनता.—(Severity, roughness as of the weather, &c.) निष्ठुरता, नैष्ठुर्य्यं, उग्रता, कठोरता, क्रूरता, क्रौर्य्यं, कटुता, कर्कशता, कार्कश्यं, रूक्षता, रौक्ष्यं, अमृदुता, पारुष्यं, प्रचण्डता, दुर्दिनं.—(Boisterousness, rainyness) वातलता, बहुवातवृष्टित्वं.

INCLEMENT, *a.* निर्दयः -या -यं, अदयः -या -यं, दयाहीनः -ना -नं, निष्करुणः -णा -णं, अकरुणः -णा -णं, निष्कृपः -पा -पं, कृपाहीनः -ना -नं, दयारहितः -ता -तं, अनुकम्पाहीनः -ना -नं.—(Severe, rough as weather, &c.) उग्रः -ग्रा -ग्रं, निष्ठुरः -रा -रं, कठोरः -रा -रं, कटुः -टुः -टु, क्रूरः -रा -रं, कर्कशः -शा -शं, रूक्षः -क्षा -क्षं, अमृदुः -द्वी -दु, प्रचण्डः -ण्डा -ण्डं.—(Boisterous, rainy) वातलः -ला -लं, वृष्टिमान् -मती -मत् (त्), बहुवातवृष्टिः -ष्टिः -ष्टि.

INCLINATION, *s.* (Disposition, tendency) प्रावण्यं, प्रवणता, प्रवाहः, प्रवृत्तिः *f.*, or more usually expressed by शीलः or शीलता -त्वं or by आलुता -त्वं affixed, or by the desid. form; as, 'inclination to fall,' पतनशीलता -त्वं or पतयालुता -त्वं or पिपतिषा.—(Desire) अभिलाषः, इच्छा, कांक्षा, आकांक्षा, छन्दं, छन्दस्.—(Bending) नवता, नतिः *f.*, आनतिः *f.*; 'inclination of a planet,' परमापमः; 'greatest inclination of a planet,' विक्षेपभुजः; 'following one's inclination,' कामकारी -रिणी -रि (न्), कामचारः -रा -रं.

To INCLINE, *v. n.* (Bend, lean) नम् (c. 1. नमति, नन्तुं), अवनम्, आनम्, नम्रीभू, अवलम्ब् (c. 1. -लम्बते -म्बितुं), आलम्ब्, प्रलम्ब्.—(Be disposed) प्रवणः -णा -णं भू, expressed by शीलः -ला -लं; as, 'to be inclined to give,' दानशीलः -ला -लं भू.—(Have a wish or desire) इष् (c. 6. इच्छति, एषितुं), अभिलष् (c. 1. -लषति, c. 4. -लष्यति -षितुं), कांक्ष् (c. 1. कांक्षति -क्षितुं), आकांक्ष्, अभिकांक्ष्.

To INCLINE, *v. a.* (Cause to bend) नम् (c. 10. नमयति, नामयति -यितुं), आनम्, अवनम्, आवृज् (c. 10. -वर्जयति -यितुं), नम्रीकृ.—(Give a propension, or tendency) प्रवणीकृ, प्रवृत् (c. 10. -वर्त्तयति -यितुं), प्रयुज् (c. 10. -योजयति -यितुं), नियुज्, उद्युज्, प्रोत्सह् (c. 10. -साहयति -यितुं), अभिलाषं or इच्छां or आकांक्षां दा.

INCLINED, *p. p.* (Disposed) प्रवणः -णा -णं, प्रवर्त्तितः -ता -तं, or more usually expressed by शीलः -ला -लं or आलुः -लुः -लु affixed, or by the desid. form; as, 'inclined to fall,' पतनशीलः -ला -लं, पतयालुः -लुः -लु, पिपतिषुः -षुः -षु; 'inclined to give,' दानशीलः -ला -लं, दित्सुः -त्सुः -त्सु.—(Bent) नतः -ता -तं, नामितः -ता -तं, आनतः -ता -तं, प्रणतः -ता -तं, नम्रः -म्रा -म्रं.

INCLINING, *part.* आनतः -ता -तं, प्रणतः -ता -तं, अवलम्बनः -ना -नं, अवलम्बी -म्बिनी -म्बि (न्), प्रवणः -णा -णं; 'inclining to the south,' दक्षिणप्रवणः -णा -णं.

To INCLOSE, *v. a.* परिवृ (c. 5. -वृणोति -वरितुं -रीतुं), आवृ, परिवेष्ट् (c. 1. -वेष्टते -ष्टितुं, c. 10. -वेष्टयति -यितुं), संवेष्ट्, उपवेष्ट्, प्रवेष्ट्, संवल् (c. 1. -वलते -लितुं), अवरुध् (c. 7. -रुणद्धि -रोद्धुं), निरुध्, संरुध्, रुध्.—(With a fence) प्राचीरेण परिवेष्ट् or आवृ or वृ (c. 10. वारयति -यितुं) or अवरुध्.—(Cover with a wrapper or envelope) आवेष्ट्, आच्छद् (c. 10. -छादयति -यितुं), परिच्छद्, समाच्छद्, प्रतिच्छद्, संछद्, पिधा (c. 3. -दधाति -धातुं), कोशेन परिवेष्ट्, कोशस्थं -स्थां -स्थं कृ, अन्तर्गतं -तां -तं कृ.

INCLOSED, *p. p.* परिवृतः -ता -तं, परिवेष्टितः -ता -तं, आवृतः -ता -तं, परिगतः -ता -तं, परिवारितः -ता -तं, संवलितः -ता -तं, रुद्धः -द्धा -द्धं.—(With a fence, &c.) प्राचीरेण वृतः -ता -तं, प्राकारावृतः -ता -तं, सावरणः -णा -णं, प्राकारीयः -या -यं, अवरुद्धः -द्धा -द्धं.—(In a wrapper, &c.) आवेष्टितः -ता -तं, कोशान्तर्गतः -ता -तं, कोशस्थः -स्था -स्थं, वासनस्थः -स्था -स्थं, अन्तर्गतः -ता -तं, पिहितः -ता -तं, परिच्छन्नः -न्ना -न्नं, प्रतिच्छन्नः -न्ना -न्नं, अवगुण्ठितः -ता -तं.

INCLOSURE, *s.* (That which incloses, a fence) वृतिः *f.*, प्राचीरं, आवरणं, प्राकारः, वेष्टनं, आवेष्टनं, अवरोधकं, वेष्टकः, आवेष्टकः, वेष्टः, प्रावृतिः *f.*, प्रावरः, आधारः, वारणं -णी, वरणः, मत्तवारणं, लम्भकरः, वलयः.—(Ground inclosed) वाटः, वाटी, वाटिका.—(Paper inclosed) अन्तर्गतपत्रं, वासनस्थपत्रं; 'inclosure of an edifice,' कक्षा, कक्ष्या; 'inclosure for a sacrifice,' चत्वरं, सुगहना, कुम्बा, स्थण्डिलं.

To INCLOUD, *v. a.* अभ्रं कृ, मेघं कृ, तिमिर (nom. तिमिरयति -यितुं), तिमिरीकृ, मलिनीकृ, मेघावृतं -तां -तं कृ, तमोवृतं -तां -तं कृ.

To INCLUDE, *v. a.* (Comprise, comprehend) परिग्रह् (c. 9. -गृह्णाति -ग्रहीतुं), परिसमाप् (c. 5. -आप्नोति -आप्तुं), अन्तर्गण् (c. 10. -गणयति -यितुं), अन्तर्गतं -तां -तं कृ, अन्तर्गम् (c. 10. -गमयति -यितुं), बन्ध् (c. 9. बध्नाति, बन्द्धुं), निबन्ध्, प्रतिसंहृ (c. 1. -हरति -हर्तुं); 'excluding this, including that,' एतद्वर्ज्जं तत्सहितं.—(Contain, hold) धा (c. 3. दधाति, धातुं), आधा, आदा (c. 3. -ददाति -दातुं), धृ (c. 1. धरति, c. 10. धारयति -यितुं), प्रविश् (c. 10. -वेशयति -यितुं).

INCLUDED, *p. p.* अन्तर्गतः -ता -तं, अन्तर्गणितः -ता -तं, अन्तर्वर्त्ती -र्त्तिनी

-र्त्ति (न्), आन्तर्गणिकः -की -कं, परिगृहीतः -ता -तं, समाविष्टः -ष्टा -ष्टं, प्रविष्टः -ष्टा -ष्टं, आकलितः -ता -तं, प्रतिसंहृतः -ता -तं, अधिश्रितः -ता -तं, सहितः -ता -तं, अवान्तरः -रा -रं, गर्भः -र्भा -र्भं in comp., गर्भितः -ता -तं, बद्धः -द्धा -द्धं, निबद्धः -द्धा -द्धं; 'included space,' अभ्यन्तरं, अन्तरालं.

INCLUSION, *s.* परिग्रहः, ग्रहणं, परिसमाप्तिः *f.*, अन्तर्गणना, प्रतिसंहारः, समावेशः, निबन्धः, समासक्तिः *f.*, व्याप्तिः *f.*, संवरः, अधिकरणं.

INCLUSIVE, *a.* परिसमापकः -का -कं, परिग्राही -हिणी -हि (न्), आन्तर्गणिकः -की -कं, अन्तर्गणितः -ता -तं, अन्तर्गतः -ता -तं, व्यापी -पिनी -पि (न्), व्यापकः -का -कं; 'inclusive of,' सहितः -ता -तं.

INCLUSIVELY, *adv.* सर्व्वमपेक्ष्य, अशेषतस्, अशेषेण, निःशेषेण, निरवशेषं, साकल्येन, साद्यन्तं, पर्य्याप्तं, सहितं.

INCOAGULABLE, *a.* अश्यानीयः -या -यं, अश्येयः -या -यं.

INCOERCIBLE, *a.* अयन्त्रणीयः -या -यं, अनियन्तव्यः -व्या -व्यं.

INCOGITABLE, *a.* अचिन्तनीयः -या -यं, अध्यानीयः -या -यं, अभावनीयः -या -यं.

INCOGITANCE, INCOGITANCY, *s.* अचिन्ता, चिन्ताशून्यत्वं, अध्यानं, अविचारणं, अभावना, भावनाशून्यत्वं, चिन्ताभावः.

INCOGITANT, *a.* निश्चिन्तः -न्ता -न्तं, चिन्तारहितः -ता -तं, विचारहीनः -ना -नं.

INCOGNITO, *a.* or *adv.* गुप्तरूपः -पा -पं, प्रच्छन्नरूपः -पा -पं, अलक्षितः -ता -तं, अलक्ष्यरूपः -पा -पं, अलक्ष्यलिङ्गः -ङ्गा -ङ्गं, अप्रकाशरूपः -पा -पं, गुप्तरूपेण, प्रच्छन्नरूपेण, अलक्ष्यरूपेण, अप्रकाशरूपेण, अलक्षितं.

INCOGNIZABLE, *a.* अलक्ष्यः -क्ष्या -क्ष्यं, अज्ञेयः -या -यं, अविज्ञेयः -या -यं.

INCOHERENCE, INCOHERENCY, *s.* असम्बन्धः, अनन्वयः, असङ्गतिः *f.*, असक्रमः, असंस्थितिः *f.*, असम्पर्कः, विरोधः, विरुद्धता, अयोग्यता, अयुक्तिः *f.*, असन्दर्भः, अनिर्वाहः, असामञ्जस्यं, अननुषङ्गः.

INCOHERENT, *a.* असम्बद्धः -द्धा -द्धं, अबद्धः -द्धा -द्धं, अनन्वितः -ता -तं, अन्वयहीनः -ना -नं, असङ्गतः -ता -तं, असंस्थितः -ता -तं, विरुद्धः -द्धा -द्धं, सन्दर्भविरुद्धः -द्धा -द्धं, अयोग्यः -ग्या -ग्यं, असमञ्जसः -सा -सं, असमवेतः -ता -तं, अघटमानः -ना -नं, आकुलः -ला -लं, व्याकुलः -ला -लं.—(As speech) अव्यक्तः -क्ता -क्तं, अस्फुटः -टा -टं, भिन्नः -न्ना -न्नं, भग्नः -ग्ना -ग्नं, स्खलितः -ता -तं.

INCOHERENTLY, *adv.* असम्बद्धं, असम्बद्धप्रकारेण, असङ्गतं, अयोग्यं, असमञ्जसं, सन्दर्भविरोधेन, असमवेतरूपं, आकुलं, आकुलवत्; 'talking incoherently,' अव्यक्तवाक् *m.f.n.* (च्), अस्फुटवाक्, भिन्नवाक्, भिन्नजल्पः -ल्पा -ल्पं.

INCOMBUSTIBILITY, *s.* अदाह्यता -त्वं, अदहनीयता, अज्वलनीयता.

INCOMBUSTIBLE, *a.* अदहनीयः -या -यं, अदाह्यः -ह्या -ह्यं, अज्वलनीयः -या -यं, दुर्दाह्यः -ह्या -ह्यं, दुर्ज्वलनीयः -या -यं, दुःसञ्ज्वलनीयः -या -यं.

INCOME, *s.* आयः, आगमः, धनागमः, अर्थागमः, उदयः, धनोदयः, उत्पन्नं, प्राप्तिः *f.*; 'income and expenditure,' आयव्ययौ *m.* du.

INCOMMENSURABLE, INCOMMENSURATE, *a.* असमः -मा -मं, असमानः -ना -नं, असमपरिमाणः -णा -णं, अतुल्यपरिमाणः -णा -णं, असदृशः -शी -शं, अननुरूपः -पा -पं.

INCOMMENSURABLENESS, *s.* असमता, असमानता, असादृश्यं, असमपरिमाणत्वं.

INCOMMENSURABLY, *adv.* अननुरूपेण, अननुसारेण, असदृशं, असमं.

To INCOMMODE, *v. a.* पीड् (c. 10. पीडयति -यितुं), उपपीड्, अभिपीड्, आयस् (c. 10. -यासयति -यितुं), बाध् (c. 1. बाधते -धितुं), परिबाध्, प्रबाध्, अधिबाध्, रुध् (c. 7. रुणद्धि, रोद्धुं), उपरुध्, अभिरुध्, क्लिश् (c. 9. क्लिश्नाति, क्लेशितुं), व्यथ् (c. 10. व्यथयति -यितुं), आकुलीकृ, व्याकुलीकृ, समाकुलीकृ; 'don't incommode yourself,' अलम् आयासेन.

INCOMMODED, *p. p.* पीडितः -ता -तं, अभिपीडितः -ता -तं, बाधितः -ता -तं, उपरुद्धः -द्धा -द्धं, क्लेशितः -ता -तं, क्लिष्टः -ष्टा -ष्टं, व्यथितः -ता -तं, आकुलः -ला -लं, समाकुलः -ला -लं.

INCOMMODIOUS, *a.* अयोग्यः -ग्या -ग्यं, अयुक्तः -क्ता -क्तं, अनुपयुक्तः -क्ता -क्तं, अनुपयोगी -गिनी -गि (न्), अहितः -ता -तं, अनुपकारी -रिणी -रि (न्); 'giving trouble,' क्लेशकरः -री -रं, क्लेशकः -का -कं, कष्टकरः -री -रं, पीडाकरः -री -रं, उपरोधी -धिनी -धि (न्).

INCOMMODIOUSLY, *adv.* अयोग्यं, अयुक्तं, अनुपयुक्तं, यथा कष्टं or क्लेशः or उपरोधः or पीडा जायते तथा.

INCOMMODIOUSNESS, *s.* अयोग्यता, अयुक्तता, सक्लेशत्वं, सकष्टत्वं, उपरोधः.

INCOMMUNICABLE, *a.* अदेयः -या -यं, अप्रतिपादनीयः -या -यं, असंवदनीयः -या -यं, अनिवेद्यः -द्या -द्यं, अन्यादेयः -या -यं, अनन्यदेयः -या -यं.

INCOMMUNICABLENESS, *s.* अदेयता, अप्रदेयता, अप्रतिपादनीयता, असंवदनीयता.

INCOMMUNICATIVE, *a.* असंवादशीलः -ला -लं, परिमितकथः -था -थं, वाग्यतः -ता -तं, कथाविरक्तः -क्ता -क्तं, भाषणविरक्तः -क्ता -क्तं.

INCOMMUTABLE, *a.* अपरिवर्त्तनीयः -या -यं, अप्रतिपण्यः -ण्या -ण्यं, अप्रतिदेयः -या -यं.

INCOMPACT, *a.* अघनः -ना -नं, असंहतः -ता -तं, अदृढः -ढा -ढं, असान्द्रः -न्द्रा -न्द्रं.

INCOMPARABLE, *a.* अतुल्यः -ल्या -ल्यं, अतुलनीयः -या -यं, अतुलः -ला -लं, अनुपमः -मा -मं, निरुपमः -मा -मं, अनुपमेयः -या -यं, अप्रतिमेयः -या -यं, अप्रतिमः -मा -मं, असाधारणः -णा -णी -णं, असामान्यः -न्या -न्यं, असदृशः -शी -शं, अद्वितीयः -या -यं, अप्रतिरूपः -पा -पं, अनुत्तमः -मा -मं, सर्व्वश्रेष्ठः -ष्ठा -ष्ठं, सर्व्वजित् *m.f.n.*, उपादेयः -या -यं.

INCOMPARABLENESS, *s.* अतुल्यता, अनुपमेयता, अनुपमत्वं, अप्रतिमेयता.

INCOMPARABLY, *adv.* अतुल्यं, अनुपमेयं, अप्रतिमेयं, निरुपमं.

INCOMPASSIONATE, *a.* निर्दयः -या -यं, अदयः -या -यं, दयाहीनः -ना -नं, निष्करुणः -णा -णं, निष्कृपः -पा -पं, निर्घृणः -णा -णं, वीतदयः -या -यं.

INCOMPASSIONATELY, *adv.* निर्दयं, दयां विना, निष्करुणं, अकृपया, अकरुणं.

INCOMPATIBILITY, *s.* अयोग्यता, विरुद्धता, विरोधः, विपरीतता, वैपरीत्यं, असङ्गतत्वं, असङ्गतिः *f.*, असाङ्गत्यं, अयुक्तता, असम्भवः, असम्भाव्यता, अनुपयुक्तता, वैलक्षण्यं.

INCOMPATIBLE, *a.* विरुद्धः -द्धा -द्धं, विरोधी -धिनी -धि (न्), अयोग्यः -ग्या -ग्यं, असङ्गतः -ता -तं, विसङ्गतः -ता -तं, असम्भाव्यः -व्या -व्यं, असम्भवः -वा -वं, असंस्थितः -ता -तं, विपरीतः -ता -तं, अनुपयुक्तः -क्ता -क्तं, अयुक्तः -क्ता -क्तं, विलक्षणः -णा -णं, परस्परविरुद्धः -द्धा -द्धं.

INCOMPATIBLY, *adv.* विरोधेन, असङ्गतं, अयोग्यं, असम्भाव्यं, विपरीतं.

INCOMPETENCE, INCOMPETENCY, *s.* अयोग्यता, अक्षमता -त्वं, असामर्थ्यं, असमर्थता, अशक्तिः *f.*, अशक्तता, बलहीनता, अयुक्तता, अनुपयुक्तत्वं, अपर्य्याप्तिः *f.*, अनुचितत्वं.

INCOMPETENT, *a.* अक्षमः -मा -मं, असमर्थः -र्था -र्थं, अयोग्यः -ग्या -ग्यं, अशक्तः -क्ता -क्तं, अनुपयुक्तः -क्ता -क्तं, अपर्य्याप्तः -प्ता -प्तं, अनुचितः -ता -तं, अपारकः -का -कं, अपारगः -गा -गं, अकृती -तिनी -ति (न्); 'incompetent witness,' हीनः, हीनवादी *m.* (न्).

INCOMPETENTLY, *adv.* अक्षमवत्, अशक्तवत्, असामर्थ्येन, अनुपयुक्तं, अपर्य्याप्तं, अयोग्यं, अनुचितं, हीनवत्.

INCOMPLETE, *a.* असमाप्तः -प्ता -प्तं, असम्पन्नः -न्ना -न्नं, असम्पूर्णः -र्णा -र्णं, अपूर्णः -र्णा -र्णं, अपरिपूर्णः -र्णा -र्णं, असिद्धः -द्धा -द्धं, अनिष्पन्नः -न्ना -न्नं, असमग्रः -ग्रा -ग्रं, अपर्य्याप्तः -प्ता -प्तं, अनिखिलः -ला -लं, अकृतः -ता -तं, कृताकृतः -ता -तं, अपूर्य्यमाणः -णा -णं, असमस्तः -स्ता -स्तं,

अपक्व: -क्वा -क्वं, सावशेषः -षा -षं.—(Defective) विकलः -ला -लं, न्यूनः -ना -नं, हीनः -ना -नं, लुप्तः -प्ता -प्तं, खण्डितः -ता -तं, विकलाङ्गः -ङ्गी -ङ्गं, अङ्गविकलः -ला -लं, न्यूनाङ्गः -ङ्गी -ङ्गं.

INCOMPLETELY, *adv.* असम्पूर्णं, असम्यक्तं, असमग्रं, अपर्य्याप्तं, असम्यक्, सावशेषं, खण्डतस्, अनिखिलेन, विकलं, वैकल्येन.

INCOMPLETENESS, *s.* अपूर्णता, असम्पूर्णता, अपरिपूर्णता -त्वं, अपूर्त्तिः *f.*, असमाप्तिः *f.*, असमाप्तत्वं, असिद्धिः *f.*, असंसिद्धिः, अपक्वता, अपरिपक्वता, वैकल्यं, न्यूनता, हीनता, स्थूलोच्चयः.

INCOMPLEX, *a.* असङ्कीर्णः -र्णा -र्णं, अमिश्रितः -ता -तं, असमस्तः -स्ता -स्तं.

INCOMPOSED, *a.* अशान्तः -न्ता -न्तं, अस्थिरः -रा -रं, व्याकुलः -ला -लं.

INCOMPOSITE, *a.* असमस्तः -स्ता -स्तं, अमिश्रितः -ता -तं, निरवयवः -वा -वं.

INCOMPREHENSIBLE, *a.* अज्ञेयः -या -यं, अग्राह्यः -ह्या -ह्यं, अग्रहणीयः -या -यं, अबोधगम्यः -म्या -म्यं, अमनोगम्यः -म्या -म्यं, बोधागम्यः -म्या -म्यं, अबोधनीयः -या -यं, अभावनीयः -या -यं, अविभाव्यः -व्या -व्यं, अचिन्त्यः -न्त्या -न्त्यं, अचिन्तनीयः -या -यं, अनुपलभ्यः -भ्या -भ्यं, अतर्क्यः -र्क्या -र्क्यं, अप्रतर्क्यः -र्क्या -र्क्यं, बोधातीतः -ता -तं, इन्द्रियागोचरः -रा -रं, मनसा ग्रहीतुम् अशक्यः -क्या -क्यं.

INCOMPREHENSIBLENESS, *s.* अज्ञेयता, अग्राह्यता, बोधागम्यत्वं, अचिन्तनीयत्वं.

INCOMPREHENSIBLY, *adv.* अचिन्तनीयं, यथा मनसा ग्रहीतुं न शक्यते.

INCOMPRESSIBILITY, *s.* असंक्षेपणीयता, असंहरणीयता, स्थितिस्थापकहीनता.

INCOMPRESSIBLE, *a.* असंक्षेपणीयः -या -यं, असंहरणीयः -या -यं, असङ्कोचनीयः -या -यं, असम्पीडनीयः -या -यं, स्थितिस्थापकहीनः -ना -नं, संवरितुम् अशक्यः -क्या -क्यं.

INCONCEALABLE, *a.* अगोपनीयः -या -यं, अगोप्यः -प्या -प्यं, अगुह्यः -ह्या -ह्यं, अप्रच्छादनीयः -या -यं, प्रकाशनीयः -या -यं.

INCONCEIVABLE, *a.* अचिन्त्यः -न्त्या -न्त्यं, अचिन्तनीयः -या -यं, अविचिन्त्यः -न्त्या -न्त्यं, अभावनीयः -या -यं, अविभाव्यः -व्या -व्यं, दुर्विभाव्यः -व्या -व्यं, असम्भावनीयः -या -यं, अबोधनीयः -या -यं, अबोध्यः -ध्या -ध्यं, बोधागम्यः -म्या-म्यं, अमनोगम्यः -म्या-म्यं, अधीगम्यः -म्या-म्यं, अमन्तव्यः -व्या -व्यं, अज्ञानविषयः -या -यं, इन्द्रियागोचरः -रा -रं, अतीन्द्रियः -या -यं; 'of inconceivable beauty,' अचिन्त्यरूपः -पा -पं.

INCONCEIVABLENESS, *s.* अचिन्त्यता, अविचिन्त्यत्वं, अविभाव्यता, बोधागम्यत्वं.

INCONCEIVABLY, *adv.* अचिन्तनीयं, अभावनीयं, अचिन्त्यप्रकारेण, अतीन्द्रियं.

INCONCLUSIVE, *a.* अप्रमाणः -णा -णं, निष्प्रमाणः -णा -णं, अप्रामाणिकः -की -कं, प्रमाणहीनः -ना -नं, अनिश्चायकः -का -कं, अनिर्णीतः -ता -तं, अनिर्णायकः -का -कं, अनिश्चयकारी -रिणी -रि (न्), अनिर्दिष्टः -ष्टा -ष्टं.

INCONCLUSIVELY, *adv.* अप्रमाणेन, प्रमाणं विना, अप्रामाण्येन, निष्प्रमाणं, अनिश्चितं, अनिर्णीतं, असिद्धान्तपूर्वं, निश्चयं विना.

INCONCLUSIVENESS, *s.* अप्रामाण्यं, अप्रमाणं, प्रमाणहीनता, अनिश्चायकत्वं, अनिर्णायकत्वं, अनिर्णेतृत्वं, अनिर्णीतत्वं, अनिश्चितत्वं, अनिर्देष्टृत्वं, निदर्शनहीनता.

INCONDITE, *a.* अपरिष्कृतः -ता -तं, अनुपस्कृतः -ता -तं, असंस्कृतः -ता -तं.

INCONFORMABLE, *a.* अननुरूपः -पा -पं, असदृशः -शी -शं, अननुगुणः -णा -णं.

INCONFORMITY, *s.* अननुरूपता, अनानुरूप्यं, असादृश्यं, अननुसारित्वं.

INCONGENIAL, *a.* अस्वाभाविकः -की -कं, स्वभावविरुद्धः -द्धा -द्धं, अननुगुणः -णा -णं.

INCONGRUENCE, INCONGRUITY, *s.* अयोग्यता, अयुक्तता, अयुक्तिः *f.*, असङ्गतिः *f.*, असङ्गतत्वं, असाङ्गत्यं, अननुरूपता, अनानुरूप्यं, असादृश्यं, असमञ्जसं, असामञ्जस्यं, विरुद्धता, विरोधनं, अयथार्थता, अयाथार्थ्यं, अनुचितत्वं, अनौचित्यं, अनुपपत्तिः *f.*, अनुपयुक्तता, अननुसारिता, असम्बद्धता.

INCONGRUOUS, *a.* अयोग्यः -ग्या -ग्यं, अयुक्तः -क्ता -क्तं, असङ्गतः -ता -तं, विरुद्धः -द्धा -द्धं, विरोधी -धिनी -धि (न्), असमञ्जसः -सा -सं, अनुपयुक्तः -क्ता -क्तं, असदृशः -शी -शं, अयथार्थः -र्था -र्थं, अयाथार्थिकः -की -कं, अनुचितः -ता -तं, असम्भवः -वा -वं, अननुसारी -रिणी -रि (न्), अनुपपन्नः -न्ना -न्नं, असम्बद्धः -द्धा -द्धं.

INCONGRUOUSLY, *adv.* अयोग्यं, अयुक्तं, असङ्गतं, विरोधेन, असमञ्जसं, असदृशं, अनुचितं, अनुपयुक्तं, अयथार्थं, असम्बद्धं.

INCONNEXEDLY, *adv.* असंयोगेन, अयोगतस्, असम्बन्धेन, असम्पर्केण, असम्बद्धं.

INCONNEXION, *s.* असंयोगः, अयोगः, असम्बन्धः, असङ्गः, असंसर्गः, असम्पर्कः.

INCONSCIONABLE, *a.* अन्याय्यः -य्या -य्यं, अयथार्थः -र्था -र्थं, अयाथार्थिकः -की -कं.

INCONSEQUENCE, *s.* अप्रयुक्तिः *f.*, अयुक्तिः *f.*, अनन्वयः, अपरिणामः.

INCONSEQUENT, *a.* अप्रयुक्तः -क्ता -क्तं, अप्रयोगी -गिणी -गि (न्), अयौक्तिकः -की -कं.

INCONSIDERABLE, *a.* अगुरुः -र्वी -रु, लघुः -घुः -घु, अल्पः -ल्पा -ल्पं, स्वल्पः -ल्पा -ल्पं, अत्यल्पः -ल्पा -ल्पं, क्षुद्रः -द्रा -द्रं, तुच्छः -च्छा -च्छं, अगण्यः -ण्या -ण्यं, अबहुः -ह्वी -हु, अमहान् -हती -हत् (त्), अल्पार्थः -र्था -र्थं, लघ्वर्थः -र्था -र्थं, अमान्यः -न्या -न्यं, मितः -ता -तं.

INCONSIDERATE, *a.* असमीक्ष्यकारी -रिणी -रि (न्), अविमृश्यकारी &c., निश्चिन्तः -न्ता -न्तं, अपरिणामदर्शी -र्शिनी -र्शि (न्), अविचारी -रिणी -रि (न्), अविवेकी -किनी -कि (न्), अविवेचकः -का -कं, नष्टविवेकः -का -कं, असावधानः -ना -नं, साहसी -सिनी -सि (न्), अनालोचितः -ता -तं, अपरीक्षितः -ता -तं, आलसः -ला -लं, अकार्य्यचिन्तकः -का -कं, अमनस्वी -स्विनी -स्वि (न्), प्रमत्तः -त्ता -त्तं.

INCONSIDERATELY, *adv.* असमीक्ष्य, अविचार्य्य, अविमृश्य, अविचारेण, विचारं विना, विवेचनं विना, सहसा, चिन्तया विना, अनवेक्षया, अनालोचितं, अनवधानतस्, प्रमत्तवत्, आलस्यवत्, सप्रमादं, निरपेक्षं, निश्चिन्तं.

INCONSIDERATENESS, INCONSIDERATION, *s.* अविचारः -रणं -णा, असमीक्षा -क्षणं, अविवेचनं -ना, अविवेकता, अविवेचकता, अचिन्ता, अविमर्शः, असावधानता, अपरिणामदर्शनं, अचर्चा, अमनोयोगः, अवितर्कः, अनालोचनं.

INCONSISTENCE, INCONSISTENCY, *s.* असङ्गतिः *f.*, असङ्गमः, असङ्गतता, असाङ्गत्यं, असंस्थितिः *f.*, विरोधः -धनं, विरुद्धता, विपरीतता, वैपरीत्यं, अयोग्यता, असम्भवता, भेदः, विभेदः, असादृश्यं, विपर्य्ययः, अनन्वयः.—(Inconsistence in argument or narration, self contradiction) पूर्व्वापरविरोधः, पूर्व्वापरवैपरीत्यं, वचनविरोधः, विपरीतवचनं, विरोधोक्तिः *f.*, वचनभेदः, चित्तभेदः, विगीतिः *f.*, विसंवादः, बाधः -धा.

INCONSISTENT, *a.* असङ्गतः -ता -तं, असंस्थितः -ता -तं, विरुद्धः -द्धा -द्धं, विपरीतः -ता -तं, विरोधी -धिनी -धि (न्), परस्परविरुद्धः -द्धा -द्धं, परस्परविरोधी -धिनी -धि (न्), परस्परपराहतः -ता -तं, विसङ्गतः -ता -तं, अयोग्यः -ग्या -ग्यं, असम्भवः -वा -वं, अनन्वितः -ता -तं, क्लिष्टः -ष्टा -ष्टं, सङ्कुलः -ला -लं, विगीतः -ता -तं, असदृशः -शी -शं, पूर्व्वापरविरुद्धः -द्धा -द्धं, बाधितः -ता -तं; 'to make an inconsistent assertion,' विपरीतं वद् (c. 1. वदति -दितुं), विसंवद्, विप्रवद्.

INCONSISTENTLY, *adv.* असङ्गतं, विरोधेन, विरुद्धं, अयोग्यं, विपरीतं, वैपरीत्येन, परस्परविरुद्धं, विसङ्गतं, असदृशं, अयथा.

INCONSOLABLE, *a.* निर्विनोदः -दा -दं, दुर्विनोदः -दा -दं, असान्त्वनीयः -या -यं, असन्तोषणीयः -या -यं, अप्रबोधनीयः -या -यं, अनाश्वासनीयः -या -यं, अविनोदनीयः -या -यं, अशरणः -णा -णं, निःशरणः -णा -णं, शोकाकुलः -ला -लं, अत्युत्कण्ठितः -ता -तं.

INCONSONANCE, *s.* अयोग्यता, अननुसारः, अनानुरूप्यं, असादृश्यं, विरोधः.

INCONSONANT, *a.* अयोग्यः -ग्या -ग्यं, अननुसारी -रिणी -रि (न्), असदृशः -शी -शं, अननुरूपः -पा -पं, विरुद्धः -द्धा -द्धं, विरोधी -धिनी -धि (न्),

INCONSPICUOUS, *a.* अप्रकाश: -शा -शं, अव्यक्त: -क्ता -क्तं, अप्रत्यक्ष: -क्षा -क्षं.

INCONSTANCY, *s.* अस्थिरता -त्वं, अस्थैर्य्यं, अधीरता, अधैर्य्यं, अधृति: *f.*; चञ्चलत्वं -ता, चपलता, चाञ्चल्यं, चापल्यं, चलचित्तता, अस्थायित्वं, लोलता, लौल्यं, तारल्यं, सङ्कसुकत्वं, अनवस्थिति: *f.*, अस्थेमा *m.* (न्), अनियतता.

INCONSTANT, *a.* अस्थिर: -रा -रं, अस्थायी -यिनी -यि (न्), अस्थावर: -रा -रं, चञ्चल: -ला -लं, चपल: -ला -लं, अधीर: -रा -रं, चलचित्त: -त्ता -त्तं, चपलात्मक: -का -कं, सङ्कसुक: -का -कं, चञ्चलहृदय: -या -यं, लोल: -ला -लं, तरल: -ला -लं, प्रकृतितरल: -ला -लं, अनवस्थ: -स्था -स्थं, अनवस्थित: -ता -तं, अधृतिमान् -मती -मत् (त्), अनित्य: -त्या -त्यं.

INCONSTANTLY, *adv.* अस्थिरं, अस्थिरवत्, चञ्चलं, चञ्चलवत्, चपलं, चापल्येन, चपलवत्, अधीरं, अधीरवत्, लोलवत्, तरलं.

INCONSUMABLE, *a.* अनाश्य: -श्या -श्यं, अविनाश्य: -श्या -श्यं, अक्षय: -या -यं.

INCONTAMINATE, *a.* अदुष्ट: -ष्टा -ष्टं, अदूषित: -ता -तं, अकलङ्कित: -ता -तं.

INCONTESTABLE, *a.* अविवदनीय: -या -यं, निर्विवाद: -दा -दं, अप्रत्याख्येय: -या -यं, अविचार्य्य: -र्य्या -र्य्यं, अवितर्क्य: -र्क्या -र्क्यं, अवितर्कणीय: -या -यं, अबाध्य: -ध्या -ध्यं, असन्दिग्ध: -ग्धा -ग्धं, नि:सन्देह: -हा -हं, निश्चित: -ता -तं, सुनिश्चित: -ता -तं, नियत: -ता -तं.

INCONTESTABLY, *adv.* निर्विवादं, सुनिश्चितं, असन्दिग्धं, असंशयं, नि:संशयं, अत्र न संशय:, सुनियतं.

INCONTINENCE, INCONTINENCY, *s.* असंयम:, अयतेन्द्रियत्वं, असंयतेन्द्रियता, अजितेन्द्रियत्वं, अनवस्था, अनवस्थता, अनवस्थिति: *f.*, अनियति: *f.*, अयम:, अदम:, अदान्ति: *f.*, व्यभिचार:, उपस्थासंयम:, लम्पटता, लाम्पट्यं, प्रतिषिद्धविषयेष्व् अतिप्रसङ्ग:.

INCONTINENT, *a.* असंयत: -ता -तं, असंयतेन्द्रिय: -या -यं, अयती -तिनी -ति (न्), अयतेन्द्रिय: -या -यं, अजितेन्द्रिय: -या -यं, अयतमैथुन: -ना -नं, असंयतोपस्थ: -स्था -स्थं, अनवस्थित: -ता -तं, अनवस्थ: -स्था -स्थं, व्यभिचारी -रिणी -रि (न्), व्यसनी -निनी -नि (न्), लम्पट: -टा -टं, निषिद्धविषयेष्व् अतिप्रसक्त: -क्ता -क्तं.

INCONTINENTLY, *adv.* असंयमेन, संयमं विना, लम्पटवत्, अजितेन्द्रियत्वात्.

INCONTROLLABLE, *a.* असंयमनीय: -या -यं, अदमनीय: -या -यं, अनिग्रहणीय: -या -यं, अवश्य: -श्या -श्यं, अनिवार्य्य: -र्य्या -र्य्यं, अशासनीय: -या -यं.

INCONTROVERTIBLE, *a.* अप्रत्याख्येय: -या -यं, अविवदनीय: -या -यं, अविचारणीय: -या -यं, अविवदनीय: -या -यं, निर्विवाद: -दा -दं, अविचार्य्य: -र्य्या -र्य्यं, अवितर्क्य: -र्क्या -र्क्यं, अवितर्कणीय: -या -यं, अबाध्य: -ध्या -ध्यं, अखण्डनीय: -या -यं, अविग्रह: -हा -हं, सुनिश्चित: -ता -तं, असन्दिग्ध: -ग्धा -ग्धं.

INCONTROVERTIBLY, *adv.* निर्विवादं, सुनिश्चितं, असंशयं, नि:संशयं, अवितर्कणीयं.

INCONVENIENCE, INCONVENIENCY, *s.* (That which gives trouble or impedes) क्लेश:, कष्टं, पीडा, बाधा -धक:, व्यथा, कृच्छ्रं, दु:खं, शल्यं, उपरोध:, रोध:, विरोध:, आयास:, कण्टक: -कं, विडम्बनं -ना, अनिष्टं, असुखं, आयासहेतु: *m.*, क्लेशहेतु: *m.*, पीडाहेतु: *m.*, कष्टकारणं.—(Unsuitableness) अयोग्यता, अयुक्ति: *f.*, निर्युक्ति: *f.*, अयुक्तता, अनुपयुक्तता, अनुपयोगिता, अनुपपत्ति: *f.*, अनुचितता.

To INCONVENIENCE, *v. a.* क्लेशं दा or कृ, कष्टं कृ, दु:खं कृ, शल्यं कृ, उपरोधं कृ, बाध् (c. 1. बाधते -धितुं), पीड् (c. 10. पीडयति -यितुं), रुध् (c. 7. रुणद्धि, रोद्धुं), उपरुध्.

INCONVENIENT, *a.* अयोग्य: -ग्या -ग्यं, अनुपयुक्त: -क्ता -क्तं, अनुपयोगी -गिनी -गि (न्), अयुक्त: -क्ता -क्तं, अनुचित: -ता -तं, अनुपपन्न: -न्ना -न्नं, अहित: -ता -तं, अनुपकारी -रिणी -रि (न्), असमञ्जस: -सा -सं.—(Causing trouble or uneasiness) क्लेशकर: -री -रं, क्लेशद: -दा -दं, क्लेशक: -का -कं, कष्टकर: -री -रं, दु:खद: -दा -दं, पीडाकर: -री -रं, उपरोधी -धिनी -धि (न्), बाधक: -का -कं, आयासहेतुक: -का -कं, क्लेशहेतुक: -का -कं, कष्टकारक: -का -कं.

INCONVENIENTLY, *adv.* अयोग्यं, अयुक्तं, अनुपयुक्तं, अनुचितं, अनुपपन्नं, असमञ्जसं, असाम्प्रतं, यथा कष्टं or क्लेश: or उपरोध: or पीडा जायते तथा.

INCONVERSABLE, *a.* असंवादशील: -ला -लं, अनालापी -पिनी -पि (न्), असंलापी &c., असंवादी &c., परिमितकथ: -था -थं, वाग्यत: -ता -तं.

INCONVERSANT, *a.* अविज्ञ: -ज्ञा -ज्ञं, अनभिज्ञ: -ज्ञा -ज्ञं, असम्पन्न: -न्ना -न्नं.

INCONVERTIBILITY, *s.* अपरिवर्त्तनीयता, अपरिवर्त्तनयोग्यता, अविकार्य्यता.

INCONVERTIBLE, *a.* अपरिवर्त्तनीय: -या -यं, अपरिवर्त्तनयोग्य: -ग्या -ग्यं.

INCORPORAL, *a.* *See* INCORPOREAL.

To INCORPORATE, *v. a.* एकशरीरीकृ, एकीकृ, एकत्र कृ, सम्मिश्र् (c. 10. -मिश्रयति -यितुं), संयुज् (c. 7. -युनक्ति -योक्तुं), संश्लिष् (c. 10. -श्लेषयति -यितुं), संसृज् (c. 6. -सृजति -स्रष्टुं).

To INCORPORATE, *v. n.* एकशरीरीभू, एकीभू, एकत्र भू, सम्मिश्रीभू, संयुज् in pass. (-युज्यते).

INCORPORATE, *a.* शारीरिक: -की -कं, शरीरी -रिणी -रि (न्).

INCORPORATED, *p. p.* संयुक्त: -क्ता -क्तं, संश्लिष्ट: -ष्टा -ष्टं, एकीकृत: -ता -तं, सहित: -ता -तं, कृतसंसर्ग: -र्गा -र्गं, संसृष्ट: -ष्टा -ष्टं, संहत: -ता -तं, सङ्घातवान् -वती -वत् (त्), एकत्रीभूत: -ता -तं.

INCORPORATION, *s.* संयोग:, संयोजनं, संसर्ग:, सम्मिश्रणं, संश्लेष:.

INCORPOREAL, *a.* अशरीरी -रिणी -रि (न्), अशरीरवान् -वती -वत् (त्), अदेहवान् -वती -वत् (त्), विदेह: -हा -हं, अमूर्त्तिमान् -मती -मत् (त्), अनङ्ग: -ङ्गा -ङ्गं, निरवयव: -वा -वं, अशारीरिक: -की -कं, देहशून्य: -न्या -न्यं, निराकार: -रा -रं, अदैहिक: -की -कं.

INCORPOREALLY, *adv.* अशरीरेण, निराकारेण, निरवयवं, विदेहं.

INCORPOREITY, *s.* अशरीरित्वं, अशरीरवत्त्वं, देहशून्यता, निरवयवता.

INCORRECT, *a.* अशुद्ध: -द्धा -द्धं, अशोधित: -ता -तं, अयथार्थ: -र्था -र्थं, असम्यङ् -मीची -म्यक् (च्), असमीचीन: -ना -नं, असमञ्जस: -सा -सं, अयाथार्थिक: -की -कं, अतथ्य: -थ्या -थ्यं, अनञ्जस: -सा -सं, वितथ: -था -थं, अनृत: -ता -तं, असङ्गत: -ता -तं, अप्रकृत: -ता -तं, दोषी -षिणी -षि (न्), सदोष: -षा -षं, दोषवान् -वती -वत् (त्), अशुचि: -चि: -चि, असत्य: -त्या -त्यं.—(In conduct) दुर्वृत्त: -त्ता -त्तं, असाधुवृत्त: -त्ता -त्तं, दुराचार: -रा -रं, अधार्मिक: -की -कं, अशुचिकर्म्मा -र्म्मा -र्म्म (न्).

INCORRECTLY, *adv.* अशुद्धं, अयथार्थं, अयथावत्, वृथा, असम्यक्, अन्यथा, अनञ्जसा, असमञ्जसं, अशुचि, वितथं, अतथ्यं, अनृतं, असत्यं, असमीचीनं, असङ्गतं, असाधु, सदोषं.

INCORRECTNESS, *s.* अशुद्धि: *f.*, अशुद्धता, अविशुद्धि: *f.*, अशोधनं, अयथार्थता, अयाथार्थ्यं, असम्यक्त्वं, असमीचीनता, असामञ्जस्यं, अतथ्यता, असत्यता, वितथत्वं, अनृतं, अनृतत्वं, अशुचिता, अन्यथात्वं, अयाथातथ्यं, सदोषता, दोषवत्त्वं, असाधुता.

INCORRIGIBLE, *a.* असाध्य: -ध्या -ध्यं, अशोधनीय: -या -यं, अशोध्य: -ध्या -ध्यं, असाधनीय: -या -यं, समाधातुम् अशक्य: -क्या -क्यं, साधयितुम् अशक्य: -क्या -क्यं, अशासनीय: -या -यं, अप्रतिसमाधेय: -या -यं, अतिदुष्ट: -ष्टा -ष्टं, शिक्षातीत: -ता -तं.

INCORRIGIBLENESS, INCORRIGIBILITY, *s.* असाध्यता, असाधनीयता, अशोधनीयता.

INCORRIGIBLY, *adv.* असाधनीयं, यथा समाधातुं न शक्यते तथा.

INCORRODIBLE, *a.* अगलनीय: -या -यं, अक्षयणीय: -या -यं, अनाश्य: -श्या -श्यं.

INCORRUPT, INCORRUPTED, *a.* अदुष्ट: -ष्टा -ष्टं, अदूषित: -ता -तं, अविकृत: -ता -तं, अविकारित: -ता -तं, शुचि: -चि: -चि, शुद्ध: -द्धा -द्धं, पवित्र:

-ष्टा -ष्टं, अभ्रष्टः -ष्टा -ष्टं.

INCORRUPTIBILITY, *s.* अक्षयता -त्वं, अनश्वरता -त्वं, अनाश्यता, अदूष्यता, अजर्य्यता -त्वं, अभेद्यता, अहार्य्यता.

INCORRUPTIBLE, *a.* अक्षयः -या -यं, अक्षयणीयः -या -यं, अनश्वरः -रा -रं, अनाश्यः -श्या -श्यं, अदूष्यः -ष्या -ष्यं, अदूषणीयः -या -यं, अजर्य्यः -र्य्या -र्य्यं, अविकार्य्यः -र्य्या -र्य्यं.—(By bribe) अभेद्यः -द्या -द्यं, अहार्य्यः -र्य्या -र्य्यं.

INCORRUPTION, *s.* अदूषणं, अदुष्टता, अक्षयः, अनश्वरता, अविकारः, अनाशः.

INCORRUPTNESS, *s.* अदुष्टता, अक्षयता, अभ्रष्टता, अविकार्य्यता.—(Integrity) अभेद्यता, अहार्य्यता, शुचिता, सारल्यं, सच्चरित्रता.

To INCRASSATE, *v. a.* घनीकृ, स्थूलीकृ, सान्द्रीकृ, असूक्ष्मीकृ, पीवरीकृ.

To INCRASSATE, *v. n.* घनीभू, स्थूलीभू, सान्द्रीभू, पीवरीभू.

INCRASSATION, *s.* घनीकरणं, स्थूलीकरणं, सान्द्रीकरणं, पीवरीकरणं, स्थूलता.

To INCREASE, *v. n.* वृध् (c. 1. वर्धते -र्धितुं), विवृध्, संवृध्, प्रवृध्, अभिवृध्, परिवृध्, संविवृध्, वृद्धिम् इ (c. 2. एति -तुं) or या (c. 2. याति -तुं) or प्राप् (c. 5. -आप्नोति -आप्तुं), एध् (c. 1. एधते -धितुं), समेध्, ऋध् (c. 4. ऋध्यति, c. 5. ऋध्नोति, अर्धितुं), समृध्, उपचि in pass. (-चीयते), प्रचि, परिचि, प्यै (c. 1. प्यायते, प्यातुं), आप्यै, स्फाय् (c. 1. स्फायते -यितुं), आस्फाय्, स्फीतीभू, प्रचुरीभू, अधिकीभू, अधिकतरीभू, बहुतरीभू, उपचयं or अभ्युदयम् इ.—(Extend) विस्तॄ in pass. (-स्तीर्य्यते), वितन् in pass. (-तन्यते), प्रसृ (c. 1. -सरति -सर्तुं), प्रसृप् (c. 1. -सर्पति -सर्प्तुं), विजृम्भ् (c. 1. -जृम्भते -म्भितुं), विस्तारम् इ.—(Grow) रुह् (c. 1. रोहति, रोढुं), प्ररुह्; 'increase in knowledge,' विद्यागमं कृ, विद्याप्राप्तिं कृ.

To INCREASE, *v. a.* वृध् (c. 10. वर्धयति -यितुं), परिवृध्, संवृध्, विवृध्, वृद्धिं नी (c. 1. नयति, नेतुं), एध् (c. 10. एधयति -यितुं), समेध्, बृंह् (c. 10. बृंहयति -यितुं), परिबृंह्, उपबृंह्, समुपबृंह्, आप्यै (c. 10. -प्याययति -यितुं), समाप्यै, स्फाय् (c. 10. स्फावयति -यितुं), आस्फाय्, स्फीतीकृ, बंह् (nom. बंहयति -यितुं), सबंह्, प्रचुरीकृ, प्रचुरतरं -रां -रं कृ, अधिकीकृ, अधिकतरं -रां -रं कृ, बहुतरीकृ, अधिकतरीकृ.—(Extend) विस्तॄ (c. 10. -स्तारयति -यितुं), वितन् (c. 8. -तनोति -नितुं), तन्, विततीकृ, प्रसृ (c. 10. -सारयति -यितुं), विसृ.

INCREASE, *s.* वृद्धिः *f.*, विवृद्धिः *f.*, प्रवृद्धिः *f.*, वर्धनं, विवर्धनं, संवर्धनं, ऋद्धिः *f.*, समृद्धिः *f.*, स्फातिः *f.*, स्फीतिः *f.*, उपचयः, अभ्युदयः, बृंहणं, परिबृंहणं, उपबृंहणं, उत्सेकः, समुत्थानं, उन्नतिः *f.*, समुन्नतिः *f.*, आप्यायनं, विस्तारः, प्ररूढिः *f.*, आधिक्यं, अधिकता, प्रपञ्चः, बाहुल्यं.

INCREASED, *p. p.* वृद्धः -द्धा -द्धं, प्रवृद्धः -द्धा -द्धं, विवृद्धः -द्धा -द्धं, वर्धितः -ता -तं, विवर्धितः -ता -तं, संवर्धितः -ता -तं, उपचितः -ता -तं, एधितः -ता -तं, समेधितः -ता -तं, ऋद्धः -द्धा -द्धं, समृद्धः -द्धा -द्धं, स्फीतः -ता -तं, स्फातः -ता -तं, आप्यायितः -ता -तं, प्ररूढः -ढा -ढं, बृंहितः -ता -तं, परिबृंहितः -ता -तं, परिवृहितः -ता -तं, उपबृंहितः -ता -तं, प्रथितः -ता -तं, प्रचुरीकृतः -ता -तं, विततः -ता -तं, विस्तीर्णः -र्णा -र्णं, विस्तृतः -ता -तं, विरूढः -ढा -ढं, प्रसारितः -ता -तं, विजृम्भितः -ता -तं.

INCREASING, *part.* वर्धमानः -ना -नं, वर्धी -र्धिनी -र्धि (न्), वर्धनः -ना -नं, वर्धिष्णुः -ष्णुः -ष्णु, एधमानः -ना -नं, समेधमानः -ना -नं, उपचीयमानः -ना -नं, प्रचीयमानः -ना -नं, विजृम्भमाणः -णा -णं, विस्तीर्य्यमाणः -णा -णं; 'increasing in bulk,' वर्धमानशरीरः -रा -रं, प्रचीयमानावयवः -वा -वं.

INCREASINGLY, *adv.* अधिकाधिकं, उत्तरोत्तरं, वर्धमानप्रकारेण.

INCREATE, INCREATED, *a.* असृष्टः -ष्टा -ष्टं, अभूतः -ता -तं, अजनितः -ता -तं.

INCREDIBILITY, *s.* अश्रद्धेयता, अविश्वास्यता, अविश्वसनीयत्वं, अप्रत्येतव्यता, अविश्वासपात्रता, अप्रामाणिकत्वं, प्रत्ययातीतत्वं, विश्वासातिगत्वं, विश्वासातीतता, अतिप्रत्ययता.

INCREDIBLE, *a.* अश्रद्धेयः -या -यं, अविश्वास्यः -स्या -स्यं, अविश्वसनीयः -या -यं, अप्रत्येतव्यः -व्या -व्यं, अप्रामाणिकः -की -कं, विश्वासातिगः -गा -गं, विश्वासपथातिगः -गा -गं, प्रत्ययातीतः -ता -तं, अतीतप्रत्ययः -या -यं, अतिप्रत्ययः -या -यं, अतिविश्वासः -सा -सं, विश्वासायोग्यः -ग्या -ग्यं, अतिकथः -था -थं.

INCREDIBLY, *adv.* अतिप्रत्ययं, अतिविश्वासं, अश्रद्धेयं, अविश्वसनीयं.

INCREDULITY, *s.* अश्रद्धा, अप्रत्ययः, अविश्वासः, अप्रतीतिः *f.*, अभक्तिः *f.*, अश्रद्धालुता, अप्रत्ययशीलता, अविश्वासशीलता, प्रत्ययाभावः.

INCREDULOUS, *a.* अप्रत्ययी -यिनी -यि (न्), अप्रत्ययशीलः -ला -लं, अविश्वासी -सिनी -सि (न्), अविश्वासशीलः -ला -लं, अविश्रम्भशीलः -ला -लं, अश्रद्धालुः -लुः -लु, अश्रद्धधानः -ना -नं, अश्रद्धावान् -वती -वत् (त्), शङ्काशीलः -ला -लं.

INCREDULOUSLY, *adv.* अप्रत्ययेन -यात्, अविश्वासेन, विश्वासं विना, साशङ्कं.

INCREMENT, *s.* वृद्धिः *f.*, वर्धनं, उपचयः, अभ्युदयः, उन्नतिः *f.*, आधिक्यं.

To INCREPATE, *v. a.* निन्द् (c. 1. निन्दति -न्दितुं), प्रतिनिन्द्, धिक्कृ.

INCREPATION, *s.* निन्दा, परीवादः, परिभाषणं, उपालम्भः, उपक्रोशः, धिक्कारः.

To INCRIMINATE, *v. a.* अभियुज् (c. 7. -युनक्ति -योक्तुं), दोषम् आरुह् in caus. (-रोपयति -यितुं), दोषारोपणं कृ.

To INCRUST, *v. a.* बाह्यत्वचा or त्वगूपपटलेन or घनपटलेन आच्छद् (c. 10. -च्छादयति -यितुं) or आवेष्ट् (c. 10. -वेष्टयति -यितुं), बाह्यभागे or बहिर्भागे or उपरिभागे घनीकृ or श्यानीकृ or संहतीकृ.

INCRUSTATION, *s.* त्वक् *f.* (च्), त्वगूपपटलं, बाह्यपटलं, बाह्यकोशः, बहिरावेष्टनं, बहिर्भागे घनता, वल्कं, शल्कं.

INCRUSTED, *p. p.* सपटलः -ला -लं, त्वगुपेतः -ता -तं, बहिर्भागे घनीभूतः -ता -तं.

To INCUBATE, *v. n.* कुलायनिलायं कृ, नीडनिलायं कृ, अण्डप्रसवानन्तरम् आपक्षिशावकोत्पत्तेर् नीडे निली (c. 4. -लीयते -लेतुं) or अण्डोपरि उपविश् (c. 6. -विशति -वेष्टुं).

INCUBATION, *s.* कुलायनिलायः -यिता, नीडनिलायः, अण्डोपरि or डिम्बोपरि उपवेशः -शनं.

INCUBUS, *s.* (Nightmare) कुस्वप्नः, दुःस्वप्नः, अजीर्णप्रयुक्तस्वप्नः, स्वप्नकल्पितो हृदयदेशोपरिस्थो महाभारः.

To INCULCATE, *v. a.* निर्बन्धेन or मुहुर्मुहुर् उपदिश् (c. 6. -दिशति -देष्टुं) or शिक्ष् (c. 10. शिक्षयति -यितुं) or हृदये निविश् (c. 10. -वेशयति -यितुं) or विनिविश् or चित्तनिष्ठं -ष्ठां -ष्ठं कृ.

INCULCATED, *p. p.* निर्बन्धेन or मुहुर्मुहुर् उपदिष्टः -ष्टा -ष्टं, मुहुरुपदेशेन मनोनिवेशितः -ता -तं or चित्तविनिवेशितः -ता -तं or चित्तनिष्ठितः -ता -तं.

INCULCATION, *s.* निर्बन्धेन उपदेशः, मुहुरुपदेशः, मुहुरुपदेशेन चित्तनिवेशनं or मनोनिवेशनं.

INCULPABLE, *a.* निर्दोषः -षा -षं, निरपराधः -धा -धं, अनिन्द्यः -न्द्या -न्द्यं.

To INCULPATE, *v. a.* निन्द् (c. 1. निन्दति -न्दितुं), दोषम् आरुह् in caus. (-रोपयति -यितुं), दोषीकृ.

INCULTURE, *s.* अपरिष्कारः, असंस्कारः, अपरिष्कृतिः *f.*, अकर्षणं, अकृषिः *f.*

INCUMBENT, *a.* (Lying on, resting on) अवलम्बी -म्बिनी -म्बि (न्), अवलम्बितः -ता -तं, आश्रितः -ता -तं, उपाश्रितः -ता -तं, उपस्थः -स्था -स्थं, उपस्थायी -यिनी -यि (न्), उपरिस्थः -स्था -स्थं.—(Obligatory, indispensable) अवश्यकर्तव्यः -व्या -व्यं, अवश्यकः -का -कं, आवश्यकः -की -कं, अवश्यकरणीयः -या -यं, sometimes expressed by the fut. pass. part. alone; as, 'it is incumbent upon you to go,' त्वया गन्तव्यं, or by the use of the verb अर्ह् (c. 1. अर्हति); as, 'it is incumbent upon you to marry the damsel,' त्वं

कन्यां वोढुम् अर्हसि.

INCUMBENT, *s.* (The person in possession of a benefice) धर्म्मवृत्तिभोगी *m.* (न्), धर्म्मवृत्तिधारी *m.* (न्), वृत्तिभोगी *m.*

To INCUR, *v. a.* आप् (c. 5. आप्नोति, आप्तुं), प्राप्, अवाप्, सम्प्राप्, समाप्, उपगम् (c. 1. -गच्छति -गन्तुं), उपागम्, अधिगम्, गम्, इ (c. 2. एति -तुं), ऋ (c. 1. ऋच्छति), आसद् (c. 10. -सादयति -यितुं), प्रतिपद् (c. 4. -पद्यते -पत्तुं), लभ् (c. 1. लभते, लब्धुं), अनुभू.—(Bring on) आवह् (c. 1. -वहति -वोढुं), उत्पद् (c. 10. -पादयति -यितुं).—(Be liable to) अधीनः -ना -नं भू, अर्हः -र्हा -र्हं भू, योग्यः -ग्या -ग्यं भू, or expressed by the fut. pass. part.; as, 'he incurs a penalty,' दण्ड्यः or दण्डनीयः or दण्डार्हः or दण्डयोग्यो भवति.

INCURABILITY, *s.* असाध्यता, अचिकित्स्यत्वं, अप्रतिसमाधेयता, अप्रतिकार्य्यता, दुरुपचारत्वं, निरुपचारत्वं, निरुपायत्वं, अनुपायत्वं, उपायहीनता, अशमनीयता, अनुपशमनीयता, अपरिहार्य्यता, साध्यताभावः.

INCURABLE, *a.* असाध्यः -ध्या -ध्यं, असाधनीयः -या -यं, अचिकित्स्यः -त्स्या -त्स्यं, अचिकित्सनीयः -या -यं, अचिकित्सितव्यः -व्या -व्यं, अचिकित्सः -त्सा -त्सं, अप्रतीकार्य्यः -र्य्या -र्य्यं, अप्रतिसमाधेयः -या -यं, अशमनीयः -या -यं, अनुपशमनीयः -या -यं, दुरुपचारः -रा -रं, निरुपचारः -रा -रं, निरुपायः -या -यं, अनुपायः -या -यं, चिकित्सितुम् अशक्यः -क्या -क्यं, ओषधिपथातिगः -गा -गं, अपरिहार्य्यः -र्य्या -र्य्यं.

INCURABLY, *adv.* अचिकित्सनीयं, असाधनीयं, दुरुपचारं, निरुपायं, अप्रतिसमाधेयं, यथा चिकित्सितुं न शक्यते तथा.

INCURIOSITY, *s.* अकौतुकं, अकौतूहलं, अकुतूहलं, अजिज्ञासा, अनुत्सुकता, अनौत्सुक्यं.

INCURIOUS, *a.* विकौतुकः -का -कं, अकुतूहली -लिनी -लि (न्), अनुत्सुकः -का -कं, अजिज्ञासुः -सुः -सु.

INCURRED, *p. p.* प्राप्तः -प्ता -प्तं, उपागतः -ता -तं, उपगतः -ता -तं, आसादितः -ता -तं, लब्धः -ब्धा -ब्धं, अनुभूतः -ता -तं.

INCURSION, *s.* अवस्कन्दः -न्दनं, उपद्रवः, अभिद्रवः, उपप्लवः, विप्लवः, अभिक्रमः -मणं, आक्रमः, अभिमर्द्दः, अभिग्रहः, अभिनिर्य्याणं; 'to make incursions,' अवस्कन्द् (c. 1. -स्कन्दति -स्कन्तुं), समवस्कन्द्, उपद्रु (c. 1. -द्रवति -द्रोतुं), अभिद्रु, समाद्रु, समुपद्रु, अभिधाव् (c. 1. -धावति -वितुं).

INCURSIVE, *a.* उपद्रवी -विणी -वि (न्), अवस्कन्दकारी -रिणी -रि (न्).

To INCURVATE, *v. a.* नम् (c. 10. नामयति -यितुं), आनम्, अवनम्, नम्रीकृ, वक्रीकृ, कुच् (c. 1. कुचति -चितुं), आवृज् (c. 10. -वर्जयति -यितुं), कुटिलीकृ.

INCURVATED, *p. p.* नामितः -ता -तं, वक्रीकृतः -ता -तं, कुचितः -ता -तं.

INCURVATION, *s.* वक्रीकरणं, आनतिः *f.*, नतिः *f.*, आकुञ्चनं, अवकुञ्चनं.

INDEBTED, *a.* (In debt) ऋणी -णिनी -णि (न्), ऋणवान् -वती -वत् (त्), ऋणबद्धः -द्धा -द्धं, ऋणग्रस्तः -स्ता -स्तं, कृतर्णः -र्णा -र्णं.—(Obliged by something received) अनुगृहीतः -ता -तं, उपकृतः -ता -तं, उपकारबद्धः -द्धा -द्धं; 'I am indebted to you for your advice,' अनुगृहीतोऽहं तवोपदेशेन.

INDECENCY, *s.* अविनयः, अविनीतत्वं -ता, अमर्य्यादा, मर्य्यादातिक्रमः, विनयातिक्रमः, अयुक्तिः *f.*, अयोग्यता, अकर्त्तव्यता, अनुपयुक्तता, अनुपपत्तिः *f.*, अनुचितत्वं, अनौचित्यं, अशिष्टता, असभ्यता, अयाथार्थ्यं, भ्रेषः, भ्रंशः.—(In language) गर्ह्यता, गर्हितत्वं, अवाच्यता.

INDECENT, *a.* अविनीतः -ता -तं, अविनयवान् -वती -वत् (त्), विनयापेतः -ता -तं, अतिक्रान्तविनयः -या -यं, अतिक्रान्तमर्य्यादः -दा -दं, मर्य्यादाविरुद्धः -द्धा -द्धं, विनयविरुद्धः -द्धा -द्धं, अविनयः -या -यं, अमर्य्यादः -दा -दं, अयुक्तः -क्ता -क्तं, अयोग्यः -ग्या -ग्यं, अनुपयुक्तः -क्ता -क्तं, अकर्त्तव्यः -व्या -व्यं, अनुचितः -ता -तं, अनुपपन्नः -न्ना -न्नं, शिष्टाचारविरुद्धः -द्धा -द्धं, अशिष्टः -ष्टा -ष्टं, निर्लज्जः -ज्जा -ज्जं, लज्जाकरः -री -रं, अन्याय्यः -य्या -य्यं, न्यायविरुद्धः -द्धा -द्धं, असत्कृतः -ता -तं, असमञ्जसः -सा -सं, अयथार्थः -र्था -र्थं.—(In language) गर्ह्यः -र्ह्या -र्ह्यं, गर्हितः -ता -तं, अवाच्यः -च्या -च्यं, अवचनीयः -या -यं, दुरुक्तः -क्ता -क्तं, कुश्राव्यः -व्या -व्यं.

INDECENTLY, *adv.* अविनयेन, विनयविरोधेन, विनयविरुद्धं, मर्य्यादाविरुद्धं, विनयं विना, अविनीतवत्, अयुक्तं, अयोग्यं, अनुपयुक्तं, अन्यायतस्, अनुचितं, असत्कृतं, शिष्टाचारविरुद्धं, गर्हितं, गर्हणीयं.

INDECISION, *s.* अनिश्चयः, अनिर्णयः, सन्देहः, विकल्पः, संशयः, आशङ्का, शङ्का, वितर्कः.—(Indecision of character) अस्थिरमतित्वं, सन्दिग्धमतित्वं, विकल्पशीलता, सन्देहशीलता, अनिर्णयशीलता, चञ्चलता, चञ्चलमतित्वं, चलचित्तता, अनवस्थितिः *f.*, अधीरत्वं, आन्दोलितचित्तत्वं.

INDECISIVE, *a.* अनिश्चायकः -का -कं, अनिर्णायकः -का -कं, अनिर्णयनः -ना -नं, अनिश्चितः -ता -तं, अनिर्णीतः -ता -तं, सन्दिग्धः -ग्धा -ग्धं, संशयस्थः -स्था -स्थं, वैकल्पिकः -की -कं, सविकल्पः -ल्पा -ल्पं.—(Vacillating in character) अस्थिरमतिः -तिः -ति, सन्दिग्धमतिः -तिः -ति, चञ्चलशीलः -ला -लं, चलचित्तः -त्ता -त्तं, अनवस्थितमतिः -तिः -ति, आन्दोलितचित्तः -त्ता -त्तं, दोलायमानमतिः -तिः -ति.

INDECISIVELY, *adv.* अनिश्चयपूर्व्वं, अनिर्णयपूर्व्वं, अनिश्चितं, अनिर्णयेन.

INDECLINABLE, *a.* अव्ययः -या -यं, अव्ययी -यिनी -यि (न्), अविकार्य्यः -र्य्या -र्य्यं, अविभक्तिकः -का -कं; 'an indeclinable word,' अव्ययः -यं, अव्ययशब्दः; 'an indeclinable compound,' अव्ययीभावः.

INDECOROUS, *a.* अविनीतः -ता -तं, अविनयः -या -यं, विनयविरुद्धः -द्धा -द्धं, विनयापेतः -ता -तं, अयुक्तः -क्ता -क्तं, अन्याय्यः -य्या -य्यं, अयोग्यः -ग्या -ग्यं, अनुपयुक्तः -क्ता -क्तं, अनुचितः -ता -तं, मर्य्यादाविरुद्धः -द्धा -द्धं, अमर्य्यादः -दा -दं, असत्कृतः -ता -तं, अनियमः -मा -मं, शिष्टाचारविरोधी -धिनी -धि (न्), सभ्याचारविरोधी &c., अतिक्रान्तविनयः -या -यं.

INDECOROUSLY, *adv.* अविनीतवत्, अविनयेन, विनयविरुद्धं, मर्य्यादाविरोधेन, अशिष्टवत्, असभ्यवत्, दुःशीलवत्, कुशीलवत्, अयुक्तं, अयोग्यं, अनुपयुक्तं, अनुचितं, अन्यायतस्, अन्यायेन, असम्यक्, असत्कृतं.

INDECORUM, *a.* अविनयः, अविनीतता -त्वं, अमर्य्यादा, मर्य्यादातिक्रमः, विनयविरोधः, अन्यायः -य्यत्वं, अयुक्तिः *f.*, अयुक्तता, अनुपयुक्तता, अनुचितत्वं, अनौचित्यं, अयोग्यता, असत्कृतत्वं, असम्यक्त्वं, अनुपपत्तिः *f.*, असमञ्जसं, अयाथार्थ्यं, सदाचारविरोधः, शिष्टाचारातिक्रमः, असभ्यता, अशिष्टत्वं, कुशीलता, दुःशीलता, कुरीतिः *f.*, अनीतिः *f.*, कुनीतिः *f.*, अनयः, कुचर्य्या, व्यभिचारः, अनियमः, अपचारः, अकर्त्तव्यता.

INDEED, *adv.* खलु, नूनं, एवं, एव, सत्यं, सत्यमेव, अवश्यं, अर्थतस्, वस्तुतस्, तत्त्वतस्, परमार्थतस्, किल, वै, नाम, ध्रुवं, तावत्.

INDEFATIGABLE, *a.* अश्रान्तः -न्ता -न्तं, अविश्रान्तः -न्ता -न्तं, अपरिश्रान्तः -न्ता -न्तं, अक्लान्तः -न्ता -न्तं, अतन्द्रितः -ता -तं, निस्तन्द्रिः -न्द्रिः -न्द्रि, अविषादः -दा -दं, बहुश्रमः -मा -मं -मी -मिणी -मि (न्), महोत्साही -हिनी -हि (न्).

INDEFATIGABLENESS, *s.* अश्रान्तता, अश्रान्तिः *f.*, अक्लान्तिः *f.*, अतन्द्रा.

INDEFATIGABLY, *adv.* अश्रान्तं, अतन्द्रितं, अतन्द्रितस्, अक्लान्तमनसा.

INDEFEASIBLE, *a.* अलोप्यः -प्या -प्यं, अलोपनीयः -या -यं, अविनाश्यः -श्या -श्यं.

INDEFENSIBLE, *a.* अरक्षणीयः -या -यं, अप्रतिपालनीयः -या -यं, अपक्षपातक्षमः -मा -मं, अशोधनीयः -या -यं, अशोध्यः -ध्या -ध्यं, अपरिशुद्धिक्षमः -मा -मं, अप्रतिपादनीयः -या -यं, अव्यवस्थाप्यः -प्या -प्यं, अनुत्तरः -रा -रं.

INDEFINITE, *a.* अलक्षण्यः -ण्या -ण्यं, अलक्षितः -ता -तं, अनियतः -ता -तं, अनियमितः -ता -तं, अनिर्दिष्टः -ष्टा -ष्टं, अनिश्चितः -ता -तं, अव्यवस्थितः -ता -तं,

अपरिमितः-ता-तं, उपलक्षणः-णा-णं; 'indefinite tense,' अनद्यतनभूतः.

INDEFINITELY, *adv.* अपरिमितं, अमितं, अनियतं, अनिर्दिष्टं, अनिश्चितं.

INDELIBLE, *a.* अनाश्यः -श्या -श्यं, अविनाश्यः -श्या -श्यं, अलोप्यः -प्या -प्यं, अलोपनीयः -या -यं, अमार्ष्टव्यः -व्या -व्यं, अनपमृज्यः -ज्या -ज्यं, अक्षरः -रा -रं, अक्षय्यः -य्या -य्यं.

INDELIBLY, *adv.* अलोपनीयं, अनाश्यं, यथा अपमार्ष्टुं न शक्यते तथा.

INDELICACY, *s.* अविनयः, अविनीतता -त्वं, असभ्यता, अशिष्टता, अमर्य्यादा, मर्य्यादातिक्रमः, मर्य्यादाविरोधः, अशुद्धता, कुशीलता, दुःशीलता, सदाचारविरोधः, असूक्ष्मत्वं -ता.

INDELICATE, *a.* अविनीतः -ता -तं, विनयविरुद्धः -द्धा -द्धं, मर्य्यादाविरुद्धः -द्धा -द्धं, असभ्यः -भ्या -भ्यं, अशिष्टः -ष्टा -ष्टं, अयुक्तः -क्ता -क्तं, अनुपयुक्तः -क्ता -क्तं, असङ्गतः -ता -तं, अनुचितः -ता -तं, असमञ्जसः -सा -सं, अयथार्थः -र्था -र्थं.—(Offensive to good manners) सदाचारविरुद्धः -द्धा -द्धं, शिष्टाचारविरुद्धः -द्धा -द्धं.—(In language) अवाच्यः -च्या -च्यं.

INDELICATELY, *adv.* अविनीतं, विनयविरुद्धं, मर्य्यादाविरोधेन, असभ्यवत्, अविनीतवत्, अशिष्टवत्, अयुक्तं, सदाचारविरुद्धं, दुःशीलवत्, असङ्गतं.

INDEMNIFIED, *p. p.* परितोषितः -ता -तं, प्रत्युपकृतः -ता -तं, रक्षितः -ता -तं.

To INDEMNIFY, *v. a.* (Secure against loss) अग्निचौरादिभ्यो रक्ष् (c. 1. रक्षति -क्षितुं), योगक्षेमं कृ, क्षेमप्रतिविधानं कृ.—(Make good loss, compensate) क्षतिं पृ (c. 10. पूरयति -यितुं) or सम्पृ, क्षतिपूरणं कृ, परितुष् (c. 10. -तोषयति -यितुं), पारितोषिकं दा, क्षतिपारितोषिकं कृ, क्षतिनिष्कृतिं दा, क्षतिं निष्कृ or अपाकृ or प्रतिकृ or शुध् (c. 10. शोधयति -यितुं) or परिशुध्, अपकारमपेक्ष्य प्रत्युपकृ.

INDEMNITY, *s.* योगक्षेमः, अग्निचौरादिभ्यो रक्षारूपं क्षेमप्रतिविधानं, विधायकत्वं.—(Compensation) क्षतिपूरणं, क्षतिसम्पूरणं, हानिपूरणं, क्षतिमपेक्ष्य परितोषः, क्षतिपारितोषिकं, क्षतिनिष्कृतिः *f.*, दण्डनिष्कृतिः *f.*, दण्डनिस्तारः, प्रत्युपकारः, प्रत्युपकृतं, क्षतिशोधनं, अपकारशुद्धिः *f.*, उपहारः; 'paper of indemnity,' हानिपूरणपत्रं, दण्डाभयपत्रं, अदण्डपत्रं, अभयपत्रं.

INDEMONSTRABLE, *a.* असाध्यः -ध्या -ध्यं, अनुपपादनीयः -या -यं, असूच्यः -च्या -च्यं.

To INDENT, *v. a.* क्रकचरूपेण or दन्तपंक्तिरूपेण भङ्गुरं -रां -रं कृ, दन्तुरं -रां -रं कृ, सदन्तं -न्तां -न्तं कृ, सदन्तीकृ, भङ्गं कृ, भङ्गुरीकृ, सभङ्गं -ङ्गां -ङ्गं कृ, छेदं कृ, अवच्छेदं कृ, क्रकचदन्तरूपेण छिद् (c. 7. छिनत्ति, छेत्तुं) or विछिद्, ऊर्म्मिरूपं -पां -पं कृ, अङ्क् (c. 10. अङ्कयति -यितुं).

INDENTATION, *s.* भङ्गः, छेदः, अवच्छेदः, विच्छेदः, दन्तः, क्रकचदन्तरूपो भङ्गः, भङ्गकरणं, भङ्गुरीकरणं, अङ्कः, अङ्कनं.

INDENTED, *p. p.* or *a.* भङ्गुरः -रा -रं, सभङ्गः -ङ्गा -ङ्गं, दन्तुरः -रा -रं, दन्ती -न्तिनी -न्ति (न्), अनुक्रकचः -चा -चं, क्रकचदन्तरूपेण विच्छिन्नः -न्ना -न्नं, ऊर्म्मिमान् -मती -मत् (त्), अङ्कितः -ता -तं, क्रकचाकारः -रा -रं.

INDENTURE, *s.* नियमपत्रं, लेखपत्रं, लेख्यपत्रं, पत्रं, लेख्यं, प्रतिज्ञापत्रं.

INDEPENDENCE, *s.* अनधीनता, अनायत्तता, स्वाधीनता, स्वतन्त्रता, स्वातन्त्र्यं, स्वच्छन्दता, स्वाच्छन्द्यं, स्वैरिता, स्वैरता, आत्माधीनता, आत्मायत्तता, आत्मतन्त्रता, आत्माश्रयः, आत्माश्रितत्वं, आत्मसंश्रयः, अनायत्तवृत्तिता, स्वैरवृत्तित्वं, स्वच्छन्दवृत्तिता, यदृच्छा, अपराधीनता, अपरायत्तता, अपरवशत्वं, विवशत्वं, अवशत्वं, अपारतन्त्र्यं, अनवलम्बत्वं, व्युत्थानं.

INDEPENDENT, *a.* अनधीनः -ना -नं, अनायत्तः -त्ता -त्तं, स्वाधीनः -ना -नं, स्वतन्त्रः -न्त्रा -न्त्रं, स्वच्छन्दः -न्दा -न्दं, आत्माधीनः -ना -नं, आत्मायत्तः -त्ता -त्तं, आत्मतन्त्रः -न्त्रा -न्त्रं, आत्माश्रितः -ता -तं, आत्मसंश्रितः -ता -तं, अनुपाश्रितः -ता -तं, अनाश्रितः -ता -तं, अनपाश्रयः -या -यं, स्वैरी -रिणी -रि (न्), स्वैरवृत्तिः -त्तिः -त्ति, स्वैरः -री -रं, स्वैरचारी -रिणी -रि (न्), स्वच्छन्दवृत्तिः -त्तिः -त्ति, अनायत्तवृत्तिः -त्तिः -त्ति, अवशः -शा -शं, विवशः -शा -शं, अपरवशः -शा -शं, अपराधीनः -ना -नं, अपरायत्तः -त्ता -त्तं, अपरतन्त्रः -न्त्रा -न्त्रं, अनवलम्बः -म्बा -म्बं -म्बी -म्बिनी -म्बि (न्), यादृच्छिकः -की -कं, स्वेच्छाचारी -रिणी -रि (न्), यथेष्टचारी &c., अनपेक्षः -क्षा -क्षं, निरपेक्षः -क्षा -क्षं, अभुजिष्यः -ष्या -ष्यं; 'independent of any written title,' आगमनिरपेक्षः -क्षा -क्षं; 'independent woman,' स्वैरिणी, अवीरा.

INDEPENDENTLY, *adv.* अनधीनं, अनुपाश्रितं, अनाश्रितं, स्वाधीनवत्, स्वतन्त्रवत्, स्वातन्त्र्येण, स्वैरवत्, स्वच्छन्दवत्, विवशं, यदृच्छया, स्वेच्छया, यथेष्टं, यथाकामं; 'independently of any written title,' आगमनिरपेक्षं.

INDESCRIBABLE, *a.* अवर्णनीयः -या -यं, अनिर्देश्यः -श्या -श्यं, अव्याख्येयः -या -यं, अनिर्वचनीयः -या -यं, वर्णयितुम् अशक्यः -क्या -क्यं; 'this is indescribable,' तद् वर्णयितुं न शक्यते.

INDESIRABLE, *a.* अस्पृहणीयः -या -यं, अस्पृह्यः -ह्या -ह्यं, अप्रार्थनीयः -या -यं.

INDESTRUCTIBILITY, *s.* अनाश्यता, अविनश्वरत्वं, अक्षयता, अजरत्वं.

INDESTRUCTIBLE, *a.* अनाश्यः -श्या -श्यं, अविनाश्यः -श्या -श्यं, अविनश्वरः -रा -रं, अनश्वरः -रा -रं, अविनाशी -शिनी -शि (न्), अनाशनीयः -या -यं, अक्षयः -या -यं, अक्षयी -यिणी -यि (न्), अक्षय्यः -य्या -य्यं, अध्वंसनीयः -या -यं, अविध्वंसनीयः -या -यं, अजरः -रा -रं.

INDETERMINATE, *a.* अनियतः -ता -तं, अनिश्चितः -ता -तं, अनिर्णीतः -ता -तं, अनिर्धारितः -ता -तं, अनिर्दिष्टः -ष्टा -ष्टं, अव्यवस्थितः -ता -तं, अलक्षितः -ता -तं, अलक्षणः -णा -णं, अपरिमितः -ता -तं, वैकल्पिकः -की -कं, सन्दिग्धः -ग्धा -ग्धं, अविवक्षितः -ता -तं.

INDETERMINATELY, *adv.* अनियतं, अनिश्चितं, अनिश्चयपूर्व्वं, अनिर्णयपूर्व्वं.

INDETERMINATION, *s.* अनिश्चयः, अनिर्णयः, अनिर्धारणं, अनिष्पत्तिः *f.*, अनवधारणं.

INDEX, *s.* (That which points out, as the forefinger) देशी *m.* (न्), प्रदेशिनी, प्रदेशनी, देशकः, प्रदर्शकः, दर्शयिता *m.* (तृ), दर्शकः, प्रकाशकः.—(Table of contents) सूचीपत्रं, सूचिः *f.* -ची, अनुक्रमणिका, पत्रपञ्जी, निर्वचनं, निघण्टुः; 'index of names,' नामावलिः *f.*; 'index of a letter, in algebra,' घातमापकः.

INDIA, *s.* (The country) भारतवर्षं, भरतवर्षं, भारतं, भारतदेशः, जम्बुः, जम्बु *n.*, जम्बुद्वीपः.

INDIAN, *a.* भारतवर्षीयः -या -यं, भारतदेशीयः -या -यं, भारतदेशजः -जा -जं, भारतवर्षसम्बन्धी -न्धिनी -न्धि (न्).

INDIAN-RUBBER, *s.* अतिस्थितिस्थापकविशिष्टो भारतदेशीयवृक्षनिर्यासः.

To INDICATE, *v. a.* सूच् (c. 10. सूचयति -यितुं), संसूच्, प्रदिश् (c. 6. -दिशति -देष्टुं), निर्दिश्, विनिर्दिश्, उद्दिश्, सन्दिश्, अपदिश्, आदिश्, दृश् (c. 10. दर्शयति -यितुं), अभिदृश्, निदृश्, प्रतिदृश्, लक्षीकृ, प्रकटीकृ, व्यक्तीकृ, आविष्कृ, बुध् (c. 10. बोधयति -यितुं), उद्बुध्, निरूप् (c. 10. -रूपयति -यितुं), प्रकाश् (c. 10. -काशयति -यितुं), आविद् (c. 10. -वेदयति -यितुं), निविद्, लक्ष् (c. 10. लक्षयति -यितुं).

INDICATED, *p. p.* सूचितः -ता -तं, निर्दिष्टः -ष्टा -ष्टं, उद्दिष्टः -ष्टा -ष्टं, दर्शितः -ता -तं, वेदितः -ता -तं, आवेदितः -ता -तं, लक्षितः -ता -तं.

INDICATION, *s.* लक्षणं, चिह्नं, लिङ्गं, सूचना, पूर्व्वलक्षणं, पूर्व्वलिङ्गं, पूर्व्वचिह्नं, पूर्व्वरूपं, रूपकं, व्यञ्जनं, प्रज्ञानं, अभिज्ञानं, संज्ञा, आकूतं, आकारः, इङ्गः, इङ्गितं, सङ्केतः, अवगतिः *f.*, अनुभवः, प्रमाणं.

INDICATIVE, *a.* सूचकः -का -कं, अनुसूचकः -का -कं, दर्शकः -का -कं, लाक्षणिकः -की -कं, लाक्षण्यः -ण्या -ण्यं, बोधकः -का -कं, उद्बोधकः -का -कं, वाचकः -का -कं, अभिव्यञ्जकः -का -कं, उद्देशकः -का -कं,

निर्देशकः -का -कं, देशकः -का -कं, देशी -शिनी -शि (न्), गमकः -का -कं, ज्ञापकः -का -कं, निवेदकः -का -कं; 'indicative mode,' कर्तृवाच्यं, स्वार्थः.

To INDICT, *v. a.* अभियोगपत्रेण or अपवादपत्रेण अभियुज् (c. 7. -युनक्ति -योक्तुं) or अभिशंस् (c. 1. -शंसति -सितुं) or अपवद् (c. 1. -वदति -दितुं).

INDICTABLE, *a.* अभियोक्तव्यः -व्या -व्यं, अभियोज्यः -ज्या -ज्यं, अभियोजनीयः -या -यं.

INDICTED, *p. p.* अपवादपत्रद्वारा अभियुक्तः -क्ता -क्तं or अभिशस्तः -स्ता -स्तं, लेख्याभियुक्तः -क्ता -क्तं.

INDICTER, *s.* अभियोक्ता *m.* (क्तृ), अभियोगपत्रलेखकः.

INDICTMENT, *s.* अभियोगपत्रं, अपवादपत्रं, अभियोगलेख्यं, लेख्यं, अभियोगः, अभिशंसनं.

INDIFFERENCE, *s.* (Unconcernedness) उदासीनता, औदास्यं, औदासीन्यं, निरुत्सुकता, अनुत्सुकता, अनौत्सुक्यं, विरक्तिः *f.*, विरक्तता, वैराग्यं, वैरक्त्यं, अनभिलाषः, अनीहा, निरीहता -त्वं, अनपेक्षा, अनवेक्षा, अनादरः, निरादरः, निःस्पृहता, अस्पृहा, निःस्नेहता, नैःस्नेह्यं, जडता, जाड्यं, निःसक्तत्वं, असक्तता, सङ्गहीनता, स्नेहहीनता, वितृष्णा, अमनोयोगः, प्रमादः, निर्वृतिः.—(Impartiality) अपक्षपातः -तिता, विपक्षपातत्वं, अपक्षता, स्नेहराहित्यं, असङ्गः.—(State in which there is no difference) अविशेषत्वं, निर्विशेषत्वं, अभिन्नता -त्वं.—(Neutrality) मध्यस्थता.

INDIFFERENT, *a.* (Unconcerned) उदासीनः -ना -नं, उदासी -सिनी -सि (न्), निरुत्सुकः -का -कं, अनुत्सुकः -का -कं, विरक्तः -क्ता -क्तं, निरीहः -हा -हं, अनपेक्षः -क्षा -क्षं, निरपेक्षः -क्षा -क्षं, अनभिलाषः -षा -षं, निरादरः -रा -रं, निःस्पृहः -हा -हं, विगतस्पृहः -हा -हं, निःस्नेहः -हा -हं, स्नेहहीनः -ना -नं, निःसङ्गः -ङ्गा -ङ्गं, सङ्गशून्यः -न्या -न्यं, गतसङ्गः -ङ्गा -ङ्गं, अनिच्छुकः -का -कं, विकौतुकः -का -कं, अव्यग्रः -ग्रा -ग्रं, जडः -डा -डं, समबुद्धिः -द्धिः -द्धि, समभावः -वा -वं, अमनोयोगी -गिनी -गि (न्), निर्वृतः -ता -तं.—(Impartial) विपक्षपातः -ता -तं, अपक्षपाती -तिनी -ति (न्), समदर्शी -र्शिनी -र्शि (न्), समदृष्टिः -ष्टिः -ष्टि, निःसङ्गः -ङ्गा -ङ्गं, गतसङ्गः -ङ्गा -ङ्गं.—(Having no difference, not different) निर्विशेषः -षा -षं, अविशेषः -षा -षं, अविशिष्टः -ष्टा -ष्टं, अभिन्नः -न्ना -न्नं.—(Neutral) मध्यस्थः -स्था -स्थं, मध्यवर्त्ती -र्त्तिनी -र्त्ति (न्), तटस्थः -स्था -स्थं, समपक्षः -क्षा -क्षं.—(Of a middling quality, bad) विगुणः -णा -णं, निर्गुणः -णा -णं, मध्यमः -मा -मं, सामान्यः -न्या -न्यं; 'an indifferent person,' उदासः, उदासिता *m.* (तृ), उदासी *m.* (न्), बहिरङ्गः.

INDIFFERENTLY, *adv.* निर्विशेषं -षेण, अविशेषेण, अविशिष्टं, निरपेक्षं, अनपेक्षया.—(Badly) विगुणं, निर्गुणं, यावत्तावत्.

INDIGENCE, INDIGENCY, *s.* दरिद्रता, दारिद्र्यं, दारिद्रं, निर्धनता -त्वं, अधनता, निष्किञ्चनत्वं, कार्पण्यं, दीनता, दैन्यं, दुर्गतिः *f.*, निःस्वता.

INDIGENOUS, *a.* स्वदेशीयः -या -यं, स्वदेशजः -जा -जं, स्वदेशजातः -ता -तं, देशजः -जा -जं, दैशिकः -की -कं, स्वदेशोद्भवः -वा -वं.

INDIGENT, *a.* दरिद्रः -द्रा -द्रं, निर्धनः -ना -नं, अधनः -ना -नं, अल्पधनः -ना -नं, निष्किञ्चनः -ना -नं, निष्कञ्चनः -ना -नं, दीनः -ना -नं, कृपणः -णा -णं, दुर्गतः -ता -तं, वित्तहीनः -ना -नं, अर्थहीनः -ना -नं, निःस्वः -स्वा -स्वं, दरिद्रायकः -का -कं.

INDIGENTLY, *adv.* दरिद्रवत्, निर्धनवत्, दारिद्र्येण, कृपणं, दीनं, सदैन्यं.

INDIGESTED, *a.* अजीर्णः -र्णा -र्णं, अपक्वः -क्वा -क्वं, अपरिपक्वः -क्वा -क्वं, अजातपाकः -का -कं, अक्वथितः -ता -तं, अदग्धः -ग्धा -ग्धं, असिद्धः -द्धा -द्धं, अरुचितः -ता -तं.—(Not regularly arranged) अव्यवस्थितः -ता -तं.

INDIGESTIBLE, *a.* अपाच्यः -च्या -च्यं, दुष्पाच्यः -च्या -च्यं, दुष्पचः -चा -चं, अपाक्यः -क्या -क्यं, अपक्तव्यः -व्या -व्यं, अपचनीयः -या -यं, दुर्जरः -रा -रं, अजर्य्यः -र्य्या -र्य्यं, अक्लपनीयः -या -यं, अपाकयोग्यः -ग्या -ग्यं.

INDIGESTION, *s.* अजीर्णिः *f.*, अजीर्णं, अजीर्णता, अजरणं, अपक्तिः *f.*, अपाकः, अपरिपाकः, पाककृच्छ्रं, मन्दाग्निः *m.*, तीक्ष्णाग्निः *m.*, अप्रदीप्ताग्निः *m.*, अग्नितीक्ष्णता, अवक्वाथः, अक्वाथः, अपक्वता, अपरिपक्वता, कुपित्तं, अरुचिः *f.*, अरोचकः, अन्नविकारः, अजीर्णविकारः, आमयावित्वं, परिणामशूलः.

INDIGNANT, *a.* समन्युः -न्युः -न्यु, अतिक्रुद्धः -द्धा -द्धं, अतिक्रोधी -धिनी -धि (न्), अतिकोपी -पिनी -पि (न्), कुपितः -ता -तं, कोपाकुलः -ला -लं, कृतमन्युः -न्युः -न्यु, कृतकोपः -पा -पं, आगतमन्युः -न्युः -न्यु, अतिरुष्टः -ष्टा -ष्टं, सरोषः -षा -षं, जातामर्षः -र्षा -र्षं, सामर्षः -र्षा -र्षं, जातरोषः -षा -षं, जनितरोषः -षा -षं, उपजातकोपः -पा -पं, इद्धमन्युः -न्युः -न्यु, संरम्भी -म्भिणी -म्भि (न्).

INDIGNANTLY, *adv.* सकोपं, सरोषं, सक्रोधं, सामर्षं, क्रोधेन, कोपाकुलवत्.

INDIGNATION, *s.* मन्युः *m.*, रोषः, क्रोधः, कोपः, अमर्षः, संरम्भः, अत्यन्तक्रोधः, गुरुकोपः, अतिरोषः, अवज्ञापूर्व्वः क्रोधः, अवहेलापूर्व्वः कोपः, गर्ज्जनं.

INDIGNITY, *s.* अपमानं, अवमानं, अवज्ञा -ज्ञानं, परिभवः, अनादरः, अवहेला -लं -लनं, परावज्ञा, उपेक्षा -क्षणं, गर्हा -र्हणं, अवधीरणं, कुत्सा -त्सनं, हेलनं, तिरस्कारः, न्यक्कारः.

INDIGO, *s.* नीलं.—(The plant) नीली, नीलिनी, नीलिका, काला, रञ्जनी, तूली, तूणी, द्रोणिका, द्रोणी, स्यमीका, स्थिररङ्गा, दोला, श्रीफली, ग्रामीणा, मधुपर्णिका, क्लीतकिका, तुत्था, पुक्कसी, नीलपुष्पिका; 'indigo vat,' नीलपाचनभाण्डं, नीलसन्धानभाण्डं; 'maceration of indigo,' नीलपाचनं, नीलीसन्धानं.

INDIRECT, *a.* वक्रः -क्रा -क्रं, कुटिलः -ला -लं, जिह्मः -ह्मा -ह्मं, विजिह्मः -ह्मा -ह्मं, अनृजुः -जुः -जु, वक्रिमः -मा -मं, असरलः -ला -लं, तिर्य्यङ् तिरश्ची तिर्य्यक् (च्), वक्री -क्रिणी -क्रि (न्), विषमः -मा -मं; 'indirect flight,' विडीनं; 'indirect speech,' वक्रभणितं, वक्रोक्तिः *f.*

INDIRECTLY, *adv.* वक्रं, कुटिलं, जिह्मं, विजिह्मं, अनृजु, असरलं, तिर्य्यक्, तिरस्, विषमं,—(Not expressly) अव्यक्तं, वक्रोक्त्या.

INDIRECTNESS, *s.* वक्रता, कुटिलता, कौटिल्यं, जिह्मता, अनृजुता, असरलत्वं, असारल्यं, तिर्य्यक्त्वं, विषमता, वैषम्यं.

INDISCERNIBLE, *a.* अदृश्यः -श्या -श्यं, अदर्शनीयः -या -यं, अदृष्टिगोचरः -रा -रं, अविज्ञेयः -या -यं, अप्रत्यक्षः -क्षा -क्षं, अलक्ष्यः -क्ष्या -क्ष्यं, अप्रेक्ष्यः -क्ष्या -क्ष्यं, अप्रेक्षणीयः -या -यं, अलोकनीयः -या -यं, अविभाव्यः -व्या -व्यं, अव्यक्तः -क्ता -क्तं.

INDISCERPTIBILITY, *s.* अच्छेद्यता, अव्यवच्छेद्यत्वं, अभेद्यता, अविभेद्यता, अखण्डनीयता.

INDISCERPTIBLE, *a.* अच्छेद्यः -द्या -द्यं, अविभेद्यः -द्या -द्यं, अखण्डनीयः -या -यं.

INDISCOVERABLE, *a.* अनिरूपणीयः -या -यं, अज्ञेयः -या -यं, अविज्ञेयः -या -यं.

INDISCREET, *a.* अविनीतः -ता -तं, दुर्विनीतः -ता -तं, अविनयः -या -यं, अविनयवान् -वती -वत् (त्), अनीतिज्ञः -ज्ञा -ज्ञं, अविज्ञः -ज्ञा -ज्ञं, अविचक्षणः -णा -णं, अविचारी -रिणी -रि (न्), अविचारणशीलः -ला -लं, अविमृश्यकारी -रिणी -रि (न्), असमीक्ष्यकारी &c., अविवेचकः -का -कं, अबुद्धिमान् -मती -मत् (त्), अमतिमान् &c., अमनस्वी -स्विनी -स्वि (न्), अपरिणामदर्शी -र्शिनी -र्शि (न्), अनवहितः -ता -तं, विचारशून्यः -न्या -न्यं.

INDISCREETLY, *adv.* अविनयेन, विनयविरुद्धं, अविनीतवत्, अविज्ञवत्, अविमृश्य, असमीक्ष्य, अविचार्य्य, असमीक्षापूर्व्वं, अविचारपूर्व्वं, अविचारितं, अविवेचनापूर्व्वं, अनालोचितं, अविचक्षणवत्.

INDISCRETE, *a.* अविविक्तः -क्ता -क्तं, अभिन्नः -न्ना -न्नं, अविच्छिन्नः -न्ना -न्नं.

INDISCRETION, *s.* अविनयः, अविनीतता -त्वं, अनीतिः *f.*, दुर्णीतिः *f.*, दुर्णयः, अविज्ञता, असमीक्षा, असमीक्ष्यकारित्वं, अविचारः -रणा, अविवेचना, अविचक्षणता, अवैचक्षण्यं, अबुद्धिमत्त्वं, अमनस्विता, अनवेक्षा, असावधानता, बाल्यता, प्रमादः; 'indiscretion of youth,' यौवनदर्पः.

INDISCRIMINATE, *a.* अविविक्तः -क्ता -क्तं, निर्विशेषः -षा -षं, अविशेषः -षा -षं -षकः -का -कं, अविशेषणः -णा -णं, अविशेषणीयः -या -यं, विशेषहीनः -ना -नं, अपरिच्छिन्नः -न्ना -न्नं, अपरिच्छेदितः -ता -तं. अपृथक्कृतः -ता -तं, अकृतलक्षणः -णा -णं, अलक्षितः -ता -तं, अभेदः -दा -दं, अपरिच्छेदकः -का -कं, अव्यवस्थितः -ता -तं.—(Confused) सङ्कुलः -ला -लं, सङ्कीर्णः -र्णा -र्णं, अस्तव्यस्तः -स्ता -स्तं.

INDISCRIMINATELY, *adv.* अविशेषेण, निर्विशेषं -षेण, अविविक्तं, अभेदेन.—(Confusedly) सङ्कुलं, सङ्कीर्णं, क्रमं विना, अक्रमेण.

INDISCRIMINATING, INDISCRIMINATIVE, *a.* अविवेकी -किनी -कि (न्), निर्विवेकः -का -कं, अविशेषज्ञः -ज्ञा -ज्ञं, अविवेकदृश्वा -श्वा -श्व (न्), अविशेषणः -णा -णं, अपरिच्छेदकः -का -कं, अविभावकः -का -कं.

INDISCRIMINATION, *s.* अविवेकः, अविवेचना, अविज्ञता, अपरिच्छेदः, अविज्ञानं, अविभावनं, अविचारः, अव्यवच्छेदः, अविवेकत्वं.

INDISPENSABLE, *a.* अवश्यकः -का -कं, आवश्यकः -की -कं, अवश्यकर्त्तव्यः -व्या -व्यं, अवश्यकार्य्यः -र्य्या -र्य्यं, अवश्यकरणीयः -या -यं, अवश्यः -श्या -श्यं, अपरित्याज्यः -ज्या -ज्यं, अपरिहार्य्यः -र्य्या -र्य्यं, अपरिहरणीयः -या -यं, अत्याज्यः -ज्या -ज्यं, अवश्यभवितव्यः -व्या -व्यं, सर्व्वथा करणीयः -या -यं, नैत्यिकः -की -कं; 'indispensable act,' अवश्यकर्त्तव्यं, नित्यकृत्यं, नित्यकर्म्म *n.* (न्).

INDISPENSABLENESS, *s.* अवश्यकत्वं, आवश्यकता, अवश्यकर्त्तव्यता, अत्याज्यत्वं, अपरिहार्य्यता.

INDISPENSABLY, *adv.* अवश्यं, अवशं, विवशं, अत्यवश्यं, अपरिहरणीयं.

To INDISPOSE, *v. a.* वैरक्त्यं or अनिच्छां or अरुचिं जन् (c. 10. जनयति -यितुं) or उत्पद् (c. 10. -पादयति -यितुं), पराङ्मुखं -खां -खं कृ, विरञ्ज् (c. 10. -रञ्जयति -यितुं), विमुखीकृ, न प्रवृत् (c. 10. -वर्त्तयति -यितुं), प्रतिकूलं -लां -लं कृ, अननुकूलं -लां -लं कृ.—(Make unfit) अयोग्यं -ग्यां -ग्यं कृ, अनुपयुक्तं -क्तां -क्तं कृ.—(Disorder the health) अस्वस्थीकृ.

INDISPOSED, *p. p.* (Disinclined) पराङ्मुखः -खी -खं, विमुखः -खी -खं, विरक्तः -क्ता -क्तं, विरक्तभावः -वा -वं, विपरीतः -ता -तं, अनिच्छुः -च्छुः -च्छु, विमतः -ता -तं, अनभिलाषी -षिणी -षि (न्), प्रतिकूलः -ला -लं, अननुकूलः -ला -लं, अप्रवृत्तः -त्ता -त्तं.—(In health) अस्वस्थः -स्था -स्थं, अस्वस्थशरीरः -रा -रं, असुस्थः -स्था -स्थं, असुस्थशरीरः -रा -रं, अस्वास्थ्यः -स्थ्या -स्थ्यं, ईषद्रोगी -गिणी -गि (न्), ईषद्रोगार्त्तः -र्त्ता -र्त्तं.

INDISPOSITION, *s.* (Disinclination) विरक्तिः *f.*, विरागः, वैरक्त्यं, विमुखता, वैमुख्यं, पराङ्मुखता, अनिच्छा, अरुचिः *f.*, विमतिः *f.*, अनीहा, निरीहता, अस्पृहा, अप्रीतिः *f.*, प्रतिकूलता, विपरीतता, अप्रवृत्तिः *f.*—(Slight disorder of the health) अस्वास्थ्यं, अस्वस्थता, असुस्थता, शरीरास्वास्थ्यं, ईषद्रोगः, अल्परोगः, रोगः, ईषत्पीडा.

INDISPUTABLE, *a.* अविवदनीयः -या -यं, निर्विवादः -दा -दं, अविचारणीयः -या -यं, अविचार्य्यः -र्य्या -र्य्यं, अवितर्क्यः -र्क्या -र्क्यं, अवितर्कणीयः -या -यं, अप्रत्याख्येयः -या -यं, अबाध्यः -ध्या -ध्यं, अखण्डनीयः -या -यं, अनाशङ्कनीयः -या -यं, असन्दिग्धः -ग्धा -ग्धं, अविसंवादी -दिनी -दि (न्), सुनिश्चितः -ता -तं.

INDISPUTABLY, *adv.* निर्विवादं, अविवदनीयं, असंशयं, सुनिश्चितं.

INDISSOLUBILITY, *s.* (State of being not to be broken) अभेद्यता, दुर्भेद्यता, अलंघ्यता.—(State of being not to be melted) अद्राव्यता, अद्रवणीयत्वं, अगलनीयता, अक्षरणीयत्वं, अयाप्यता.

INDISSOLUBLE, *a.* (Not to be broken or violated) अभेद्यः -द्या -द्यं, दुर्भेद्यः -द्या -द्यं, अखण्डनीयः -या -यं, अलंघ्यः -घ्या -घ्यं, अनतिक्रमणीयः -या -यं.—(Not to be melted) अद्राव्यः -व्या -व्यं, अविद्राव्यः -व्या -व्यं, अविलयनीयः -या -यं, अविलयनशीलः -ला -लं, अगलनीयः -या -यं, अक्षरणीयः -या -यं, अयाप्यः -प्या -प्यं, अद्रवणीयः -या -यं.—(Very firm) सुदृढः -ढा -ढं, वज्रप्रायः -या -यं.

INDISSOLUBLY, *adv.* अभेद्यप्रकारेण, अलंघनीयं, सुदृढं, अतिदृढं, दृढबन्धनपूर्व्वं, यथा भेत्तुं न शक्यते तथाप्रकारेण.

INDISTINCT, *a.* अव्यक्तः -क्ता -क्तं, अनभिव्यक्तः -क्ता -क्तं, अस्पष्टः -ष्टा -ष्टं, अविस्पष्टः -ष्टा -ष्टं, अस्फुटः -टा -टं, अपरिस्फुटः -टा -टं, अप्रत्यक्षः -क्षा -क्षं, अप्रकाशः -शा -शं, अव्यञ्जनः -ना -नं, अभिन्नः -न्ना -न्नं.—(As speech) अस्पष्टः -ष्टा -ष्टं, अविस्पष्टः -ष्टा -ष्टं, क्लिष्टः -ष्टा -ष्टं, मदकलः -ला -लं; 'indistinct speech,' अविस्पष्टं, क्लिष्टं, म्लेच्छः.—(Confused) सङ्कीर्णः -र्णा -र्णं, व्यस्तः -स्ता -स्तं, सङ्कुलः -ला -लं.—(Imperfect) विकलः -ला -लं.

INDISTINCTION, *s.* अभेदः, अविभेदः, अभिन्नता, अविच्छेदः, अपृथक्त्वं, अपरिच्छेदः, व्यस्तता, सङ्कीर्णता.

INDISTINCTLY, *adv.* अव्यक्तं, अस्पष्टं, अस्पष्टार्थं, अस्फुटं, अपरिस्फुटं, अप्रत्यक्षं -क्षतस् -क्षेण, अस्पष्टत्वेन, अव्यक्तत्वेन.

INDISTINCTNESS, *s.* अव्यक्तता -त्वं, अव्यक्तिः *f.*, अनभिव्यक्तिः *f.*, अस्पष्टता -त्वं, अस्फुटता, अपरिस्फुटता, अभिन्नता, अप्रत्यक्षता -त्वं, अप्रकाशत्वं.—(Confusion) व्यस्तता, सङ्कीर्णता.

INDISTINGUISHABLE, *a.* अव्यक्तः -क्ता -क्तं, अविज्ञेयः -या -यं, अविभावनीयः -या -यं, अविभाव्यः -व्या -व्यं, अदृश्यः -श्या -श्यं, अपरिच्छेदनीयः -या -यं, परिच्छेत्तुम् अशक्यः -क्या -क्यं, अदृष्टिगोचरः -रा -रं, अप्रत्यक्षः -क्षा -क्षं, अलक्ष्यः -क्ष्या -क्ष्यं, अलोकनीयः -या -यं.

To INDITE, *v. a.* लिख् (c. 6. लिखति, लेखितुं), अभिलिख्, लेखनं कृ, अभिलेखनं कृ.

INDITED, *p. p.* लिखितः -ता -तं, अभिलिखितः -ता -तं, रचितः -ता -तं.

INDIVIDUAL, *a.* अव्यापी -पिनी -पि (न्), अव्यापकः -का -कं, अव्याप्तः -प्ता -प्तं, अविभक्तः -क्ता -क्तं, व्यक्तः -क्ता -क्तं, एकः -का -कं.

INDIVIDUAL, *s.* (A single person) व्यक्तिः, एकजनः, जनः, लोकः.

INDIVIDUALITY, *s.* व्यक्तिता, व्यक्तिः *f.*, व्यक्तता -त्वं, अव्याप्तिः *f.*, अव्याप्तत्वं, अव्यापकत्वं, अविभक्तिः *f.*, अविभक्तता, पृथक्त्वं, पार्थक्यं, पृथगात्मिका, ममता, एकता, ऐक्यं.

INDIVIDUALLY, *adv.* पृथक्, पृथक् पृथक्, प्रत्येकं, एकैकं, एकतस्, एकैकशस्.

To INDIVIDUATE, *v. a.* पृथक्कृ, पृथक् पृथग् विभिद् (c. 7. -भिनत्ति -भेत्तुं).

INDIVISIBILITY, *s.* अच्छेद्यता, अविच्छेद्यत्वं, अभेद्यता, अविभाज्यता, अनंश्यता, असावयवत्वं, अवयवहीनता, निरवयवत्वं, छेत्तुम् अशक्यता.

INDIVISIBLE, *a.* अच्छेद्यः -द्या -द्यं, अविच्छेद्यः -द्या -द्यं, अविच्छेदनीयः -या -यं, अभेद्यः -द्या -द्यं, अविभाज्यः -ज्या -ज्यं, अनंश्यः -श्या -श्यं, अनंशनीयः -या -यं, अपृथक्करणीयः -या -यं, छेत्तुम् अशक्यः -क्या -क्यं, परिच्छेत्तुम् अयोग्यः -ग्या -ग्यं, निरवयवः -वा -वं.

INDIVISIBLY, *adv.* अच्छेदनीयं, अविच्छेद्यं, यथा छेत्तुं न शक्यते तथाप्रकारेण.

INDOCILE, *a.* अविनेयः -या -यं, अवश्यः -श्या -श्यं, अशिक्ष्यः -क्ष्या -क्ष्यं, अशिक्षणीयः -या -यं, अप्रणेयः -या -यं, अविधेयः -या -यं, अवशगः -गा -गं, अशिक्षणीयः -या -यं, अनायत्तः -त्ता -त्तं, अनधीनः -ना -नं, दुःशास्यः -स्या -स्यं, दुःशासनः -ना -नं, दुर्निग्रहः -हा -हं, दुर्दमः -मा -मं, दुर्दान्तः -न्ता -न्तं, प्रतीपः -पा -पं, स्वच्छन्दः -न्दा -न्दं, स्वैरी -रिणी -रि (न्), स्वैरचारी -रिणी -रि (न्), स्वेच्छाचारी &c., अगृह्यकः -का -कं.

INDOCILITY, *s.* अविनेयता, अविधेयता, अवश्यत्वं, अनायत्तत्वं, अनधीनता, प्रतीपता, दुर्दान्तता, अशिक्ष्यता, अशिक्षणीयत्वं, स्वैरिता, स्वाच्छन्द्यं.

To INDOCTRINATE, *v. a.* उपदिश् (c. 6. -दिशति -देष्टुं), शिक्ष् (c. 10. शिक्षयति -यितुं), ज्ञा in caus. (ज्ञापयति -यितुं), शास् (c. 2. शास्ति, शासितुं), अनुशास्.

INDOCTRINATED, *p. p.* शिक्षितः -ता -तं, उपदिष्टः -ष्टा -ष्टं, अध्यापितः -ता -तं.

INDOCTRINATION, *s.* उपदेशः -शनं, शिक्षा, शासनं, अनुशासनं, प्रतिबोधः.

INDOLENCE, *s.* आलस्यं, अलसता -त्वं, आलस्यशीलता, तन्द्रा -न्द्रिः *f.* -द्री, तन्द्रिका, तन्द्रालुता, मन्दता, मान्द्यं, जडता, जाड्यं, अनुद्योगः, अनुत्साहः, अध्यवसायः, अप्रवृत्तिः *f.*, कार्य्यविमुखता, कार्य्यप्रद्वेषः, अनुत्सुकता, कुण्ठता, मिद्धं.

INDOLENT, *a.* अलसः -सा -सं, आलस्यः -स्या -स्यं, आलस्यशीलः -ला -लं, तन्द्रालुः -लुः -लु, मन्दः -न्दा -न्दं, क्रियासु मन्दः -न्दा -न्दं, अनुद्योगी -गिनी -गि (न्), निरुद्योगः -गा -गं -गी -गिनी -गि (न्), निरुत्साहः -हा -हं, निरुद्यमः -मा -मं, अप्रयत्नः -त्ना -त्नं, प्रयत्नशून्यः -न्या -न्यं, लघुप्रयत्नः -त्ना -त्नं, अध्यवसायी -यिनी -यि (न्), जडः -डा -डं, कुण्ठः -ण्ठा -ण्ठं, कार्य्यद्वेषी -षिणी -षि (न्), कार्य्यविमुखः -खा -खं, उदासीनः -ना -नं, निश्चेष्टः -ष्टा -ष्टं; 'indolent tumour,' अर्बुदः -दं, मेदोर्बुदं.

INDOLENTLY, *adv.* अलसवत्, अलसं, आलस्येन, मन्दं, अनुद्योगेन.

INDOMITABLE, *a.* अदमनीयः -या -यं, अदम्यः -म्या -म्यं, दुर्दम्यः -म्या -म्यं, दुर्दमः -मा -मं, दुर्दान्तः -न्ता -न्तं, अशृष्यः -ष्या -ष्यं, अदीनचेताः -ताः -तः (स्).

To INDORSE, *v. a.* (Write on the back of a paper or bill) पत्रपृष्ठे or पत्रविपरीतभागे लिख् (c. 6. लिखति, लेखितुं), हुण्डिकापत्रदृढीकरणार्थं विपरीतभागे स्वनामाक्षराणि लिख्, लेख्यपत्रसत्याकरणार्थं पृष्ठभागे स्वाक्षरं लिख्.—(Corroborate, sanction) दृढीकृ, सत्याकृ, सत्यं कृ, प्रमाणीकृ, प्रमाणं दा, सप्रमाणं -णां -णं कृ.

INDORSED, *p. p.* पृष्ठभागे or विपरीतभागे लिखितः -ता -तं, सत्याकृतः -ता -तं, सत्यीकृतः -ता -तं, प्रमाणीकृतः -ता -तं, सप्रमाणः -णा -णं.

INDORSEMENT, *s.* पत्रदृढीकरणार्थं विपरीतभागे स्वनामाक्षरलिखनं, लेख्यपत्रप्रमाणीकरणार्थं पृष्ठभागे स्वाक्षरलिखनं.

INDRA, *s.* (The Hindu Jove or Jupiter Tonans, chief of the secondary deities. He presides over Swarga or Paradise, and is more particularly the god of the atmosphere and winds. He is also regent of the east quarter of the sky) इन्द्रः, महेन्द्रः, शक्रः, मघवा *m.* (न्), मघवान् *m.* (त्), ऋभुक्षी *m.* (न्), ऋभुक्षः, तुराषाद् *m.* (-षाह्), सङ्क्रन्दनः, देवः, वैकुण्ठः.—(As chief of the deities, he is called) देवपतिः *m.*, देवदेवः, देवराजः, देवताधिपः, सुरपतिः *m.*, सुराधिपः, सुरराजः, सुरेन्द्रः, अमरेशः -रेश्वरः, सुरप्रियः, सुरग्रामणीः, अमरभर्त्ता *m.* (र्तृ), अमराधिपतिः *m.*—(As lord of the atmosphere) दिवस्पतिः *m.*, वृषा *m.* (न्), आकाशेशः.—(As lord of the winds) मरुत्वान् *m.* (त्), मरुत्पालः, मरुतां भर्त्ता *m.* (र्तृ), मरुत्सखः.—(As lord of the eight Vasus or demigods Wind, Fire, &c.) वासवः.—(As the Thunderer) वज्री *m.* (न्), वज्रधरः, वज्रपाणिः *m.*, कुलिशभृत् *m.*—(As splitting mountains with his thunderbolt, or as clipping their wings) गोत्रभिद् *m.*, अद्रिभिद् *m.*, नगभिद् *m.*, गिरिभिद् *m.*, गिरिच्छिद् *m.*, पर्व्वतारिः *m.*—(As breaking cities, &c., into fragments) पुरन्दरः, पुरन्दः, आखण्डलः, विहोजाः *m.* (स्), विडौजाः.—(As ruling or destroying demons) पाकशासनः, वृत्रहा *m.* (न्), बलारातिः *m.*, बलभिद्, जम्भद्वेषी *m.* (न्), जम्भद्विट् *m.* (ष्), नमुचिद्विट् *m.*, नमुचिसूदनः, पुरुदंशाः *m.* (स्).—(As lord of paradise) स्वर्गपतिः *m.*, स्वर्गभर्त्ता *m.* (र्तृ), स्वाराट् *m.* (ज्), स्वर्गराजः, इन्द्रलोकेशः, नाकनाथः, नाकनायकः, नाकवेधकः.—(As borne on the clouds, cloud-compeller) मेघवाहनः, घनवाहनः, घनाघनः, जीमूतवाहनः, पर्जन्यः.—(As lord of a hundred sacrifices; the performance of a hundred aśwamedhas elevating the sacrificer to the rank of Indra) शतक्रतुः *m.*, शतमखः, शतमन्युः *m.*—(As having a thousand eyes, in consequence of the curse of Gautama, who covered him over with a thousand disgraceful marks, and afterwards changed them to eyes) सहस्राक्षः, सहस्रनयनः, सहस्रदृक् *m.* (श्), सहस्रनेत्रः.—(As husband of Sachí) शचीपतिः *m.*—(As destroyer of his own father-in-law Puloma, to prevent his curse for the violation of his daughter) पुलोमभिद् *m.*, पुलोमद्विट् *m.* (ष्), पुलोमजित् *m.*, पुलोमारिः *m.*—(As the victorious leader of the celestial armies) जिष्णुः *m.*, सुनासीरः.—(As the good preserver) सुत्रामा *m.* (न्), सूत्रामा.—(As the best of deities) लेखर्षभः.—(As much invoked) पुरुहूतः.—(As having green horses) हरिहयः.—(As borne on a white horse) श्वेतवाः *m.* (ह्), श्वेतवाहः.—(As presiding over the site of a house) वास्तोष्पतिः *m.*—(As suffering from the curse of the saint Chyavana) दुश्च्यवनः.—(As listening to the old) वृद्धश्रवाः *m.* (स्).—(His wife is called) शची -चिः, इन्द्राणी, शक्राणी, मघोनी, इन्द्रशक्तिः *f.*, पुलोमजा, पौलोमी.—(His son) जयन्तः, पाकशासनिः *m.*, ऐन्द्रिः *m.*—(His daughter) देवसेना.—(His paradise) स्वर्गः, इन्द्रलोकः, सुरलोकः, सुरसद्म *m.* (न्), सुरेन्द्रलोकः, अमर्त्यभुवनं, नाकः, ऋभुक्षः.—(His pleasure garden or elysium) नन्दनं, नन्दनवनं.—(His city) अमरावती, देवपुः *f.* (र्).—(His palace) वैजयन्तः.—(His car) विमानः, व्योमयानं, सहस्रहयेश्वः.—(His horse) उच्चैःश्रवाः *m.* (स्), देवाश्वः, श्वेतहयः.—(His charioteer) मातलिः, मातुलिः, शक्रसारथिः *m.*—(One of his doorkeepers) देवनन्दी *m.* (न्).—(His thunderbolt) वज्रः -ज्रं, कुलिशं, अशनिः *m. f.*, वज्राशनिः *m.*, भिदुरं, ह्रादिनी, पविः *m.*, शतकोटिः *m.*, शम्बः, शम्भः, दम्भोलिः *m.*, स्वरुः *m.*, इन्द्रप्रहरणं, अभ्रोत्थं.—(His elephant) ऐरावतः, ऐरावणः, अभ्रमातङ्गः, अभ्रमुप्रियः, अभ्रमुवल्लभः, श्वेतहस्ती *m.* (न्), इन्द्रकुञ्जरः.—(His bent bow, visible to mortals as the rainbow) शक्रधनुस्, इन्द्रायुधं, शक्रशरासनं.—(His unbent bow, invisible to mortals) रोहितं.—(His musicians) गन्धर्व्वाः *m. pl.*; 'their chief,' चित्ररथः.

INDUBITABLE, *a.* असंशयः -या -यं, निःसंशयः -या -यं, असन्दिग्धः -ग्धा -ग्धं, निःसन्देहः -हा -हं, सुनिश्चितः -ता -तं, अशङ्कितः -ता -तं, अनाशङ्कनीयः -या -यं.

INDUBITABLY, *adv.* असंशयं, असन्दिग्धं, सुनिश्चितं, अत्र न संशयः.

To INDUCE, *v. a.* अनुनी (c. 1. -नयति -नेतुं), आनी, नी.—(Incite to any action by argument, &c.) सुहेतुवादेन or चाटूक्त्या कस्मिंश्चित् कर्म्मणि प्रवृत् (c. 10. -वर्त्तयति -यितुं) or नियुज् (c. 10. -योजयति -यितुं) or प्रयुज्, प्रोत्सह् (c. 10. -साहयति -यितुं), उत्सह्, समुत्सह्, आकृष् (c. 1. -कर्षति -क्रष्टुं), प्रलुभ् (c. 10. -लोभयति -यितुं). Sometimes the sense of 'induce' may be expressed by the causal form; as, 'to induce to return,' निवृत् in caus. (-वर्त्तयति -यितुं); 'he induces her to go home,' तां गृहं गमयति.—(Bring on, produce) आवह् (c. 1. -वहति -वोढुं), उत्पद् (c. 10. -पादयति -यितुं), जन् (c. 10. जनयति -यितुं).

INDUCED, *p. p.* अनुनीतः -ता -तं, प्रवर्त्तितः -ता -तं, प्रवृत्तः -त्ता -त्तं, प्रोत्साहितः -ता -तं, आकृष्टः -ष्टा -ष्टं, आकर्षितः -ता -तं.—(Brought on) उत्पादितः -ता -तं.

INDUCEMENT, *s.* प्रोत्साहः -हनं, प्रलोभनं, प्रवर्त्तः -र्त्तनं, प्रवर्त्तकं, प्ररोचनं, उत्तेजनं, प्रेरणं -णा, अभ्युपायनं.—(Motive) हेतुः *m.*, प्रयोजनं -जकं, प्रयोगः, कारणं, निमित्तं -त्तकं, निदानं, निबन्धनं, करणं.

To INDUCT, *v. a.* नियमानुसारेण नवाधिकारं प्रविश् (c. 10. -वेशयति -यितुं), दीक्षाकर्म्मपूर्व्वं नवाधिकारे नियुज् (c. 10. -योजयति -यितुं).

INDUCTED, *p. p.* नियमानुसारेण or दीक्षाकर्म्मपूर्व्वं नवपदप्रवेशितः -ता -तं.

INDUCTION, *s.* (A kind of argument) अनुमानं, अनुमा, अनुमितिः *f.*, ऊहनं, अभ्यूहः, अपवाहः, व्याप्तिः *f.*, सिद्धान्तः, अर्थापत्तिः *f.*, परामर्शः, कल्पनं -ना, उपलक्ष्यः, अनुभवः, अवगमः.—(Reasoning from particulars to generals) विशेषपरीक्षापूर्व्वं साधारणानुमानं or साधारणनिश्चयः.—(Introduction into a new office) नियमानुसारेण or दीक्षाकर्म्मपूर्व्वं नवाधिकारप्रवेशनं or नवपदप्रवेशकरणं.

INDUCTIVE, *a.* आनुमानिकः -की -कं, व्यापकः -का -कं; 'reasoning,' अनुमानोक्तिः *f.*

To INDUE, *v. a.* *See* ENDUE.

To INDULGE, *v. a.* (Gratify, yield to humour) अनुवृत् (c. 1. -वर्त्तते -र्त्तितुं), अनुरुध् (c. 4. -रुध्यते -रोद्धुं), अनुकूल (nom. अनुकूलयति -यितुं) लल् (c. 10. लालयति -यितुं), अनुविधा in pass. (-धीयते), अनुकूलीभू.—(Favour) अनुग्रह् (c. 9. -गृह्णाति -ग्रहीतुं), अनुकूल.—(Permit) अनुज्ञा (c. 9. -जानाति -ज्ञातुं), अनुमन् (c. 4. -मन्यते -मन्तुं), अनुमुद् (c. 1. -मोदते -दितुं), क्षम् (c. 1. क्षमते, क्षन्तुं), क्षान्तिं कृ.—(Permit to be, not to oppose) न विरुध् (c. 7. -रुणद्धि -रोद्धुं), न प्रतिरुध्, न प्रतिकूल (nom. प्रतिकूलयति -यितुं), न प्रतिकृ, न यम् (c. 1. यच्छति यन्तुं), न निग्रह्, न निषिध् (c. 1. -षेधति -षेद्धुं), उपेक्ष् (c. 1. -ईक्षते -क्षितुं); 'indulge one's humour,' छन्दो ऽनुवृत्; 'one's passions, इन्द्रियाणि न संयम् or न निग्रह्.

INDULGED, *p. p.* अनुवृत्तः -त्ता -त्तं, अनुरुद्धः -द्धा -द्धं, अनुगृहीतः -ता -तं, लालितः -ता -तं, अविरुद्धः -द्धा -द्धं, अप्रतिरुद्धः -द्धा -द्धं, अयतः -ता -तं, असंयतः -ता -तं, अनिगृहीतः -ता -तं, अयन्त्रितः -ता -तं, अनिषिद्धः -द्धा -द्धं, उपेक्षितः -ता -तं, अनुज्ञातः -ता -तं, अनुमतः -ता -तं, दत्तानुज्ञः -ज्ञा -ज्ञं, क्षान्तः -न्ता -न्तं.

INDULGENCE, *s.* अनुवर्त्तनं, अनुवृत्तिः *f.*, अनुरोधः -धनं, छन्दोनुवृत्तं, छन्दोनुवर्त्तनं, छन्दोनुरोधः, अनुविधानं, अनुविधायित्वं, क्षमा, क्षान्तिः *f.*, अनुग्रहः, अनुज्ञा -ज्ञानं, अनुमतिः *f.*, स्वीकारः, उपेक्षा.—(Not restraining) असंयमः, अविरोधः, अप्रतिरोधः, अनवरोधः, अनिग्रहः, अदमः, अनिषेधः; 'indulgence of one's passions,' इन्द्रियासंयमः; 'in sorrow,' शोकचर्चा.

INDULGENT, *a.* छन्दोनुवर्त्ती -र्त्तिनी -र्त्ति (न्), छन्दोनुरोधी -धिनी -धि (न्), अनुरोधकः -का -कं, अनुविधायी -यिनी -यि (न्), अनुग्राही -हिणी -हि (न्), छन्दोनुसारी -रिणी -रि (न्), छन्दोनुयायी -यिनी -यि (न्), आनुग्राहकः -की -कं, अनुकूलः -ला -लं, क्षमी -मिणी -मि (न्), क्षमावान् -वती -वत् (त्), अनुकम्पकः -का -कं, करुणात्मा -त्मा -त्म (न्), कारुणिकः -की -कं, प्रियकारः -री -रं, प्रियङ्करः -री -रं, स्निग्धः -ग्धा -ग्धं.

INDULGENTLY, *adv.* अनुरोधेन, अनुग्रहेण, क्षमापूर्व्वं, क्षान्तिपूर्व्वं, सानुरोधं, सानुग्रहं, अनुकूलं, अनुकूलवत्, सदयं, सकारुण्यं, कृपया.

To INDURATE, *v. n.* (Grow hard) घनीभू, कठिनीभू, कठोरीभू, दृढीभू.

To INDURATE, *v. a.* घनीकृ, कठिनीकृ, दृढीकृ, कठोरीकृ, कर्कशीकृ.

INDURATED, *p. p.* घनीभूतः -ता -तं, दृढीभूतः -ता -तं, कठोरीभूतः -ता -तं.

INDURATION, *s.* घनीकरणं, दृढीकरणं, घनीभावः, दृढीभावः, काठिन्यं, कठिनता, घनता, कठोरता, कर्कशता.

INDUS, *s.* (The river) सिन्धुः *m.*

INDUSTRIAL, *a.* कार्म्मिकः -की -कं, कार्म्मः -र्म्मी -र्म्मं, कर्म्मी -र्म्मिणी -र्म्मि (न्).

INDUSTRIOUS, *a.* कर्म्मशीलः -ला -लं, उद्योगशीलः -ला -लं, कर्म्मासक्तः -क्ता -क्तं, कर्म्मप्रसक्तः -क्ता -क्तं, कर्म्मनिष्ठः -ष्ठा -ष्ठं, बहुकर्म्मा -र्म्मा -र्म्म (न्), बहुकरः -रा -रं, कर्म्मी -र्म्मिणी -र्म्मि (न्), कर्म्मोद्युक्तः -क्ता -क्तं, क्रियावान् -वती -वत् (त्), उद्योगी -गिनी -गि (न्), सदोद्योगी &c. सोद्योगः -गा -गं, उद्युक्तः -क्ता -क्तं, प्रयत्नवान् -वती -वत् (त्), सयत्नः -त्ना -त्नं, दीर्घप्रयत्नः -त्ना -त्नं, उत्साही -हिनी हि (न्), सोत्साहः -हा -हं, व्यवसायी -यिनी -यि (न्), उद्यमी -मिनी -मि (न्), अनलसः -सा -सं, निरालस्यः -स्या -स्यं, अनालस्यः -स्या -स्यं, आलस्यहीनः -ना -नं, कार्म्मः -र्म्मी -र्म्मं, कर्म्मशूरः -रा -रं, क्रियाभिनिविष्टः -ष्टा -ष्टं, कर्म्मपरायणः -णा -णं, कृतश्रमः -मा -मं, परिश्रमी -मिणी -मि (न्), बहुश्रमः -मा -मं, श्रमसहः -हा -हं, कर्म्मप्रसितः -ता -तं, आयासी -सिनी -सि (न्), सक्रियः -या -यं, अतन्द्रितः -ता -तं, तन्द्राहीनः -ना -नं.

INDUSTRIOUSLY, *adv.* सोद्योगं, सोत्साहं, सयत्नं, यत्नतस्, प्रयत्नतस्, व्यवसायेन, सव्यवसायं, अनलसवत्, अनालस्येन, अतन्द्रितस्, अतन्द्रितं, अभिनिवेशेन, श्रमेण, परिश्रमेण, प्रसक्तं.

INDUSTRY, *s.* कर्म्मशीलता, उद्योगः, व्यवसायः, उद्यमः, कर्म्मासक्तिः *f.*, कर्म्मप्रसक्तिः *f.*, कर्म्माभिनिवेशः, क्रियानिवेशः, उत्साहः, यत्नः, प्रयत्नः, सयत्नता, दीर्घप्रयत्नत्वं, अध्यवसायः, कर्म्मोद्योगः, प्रवृत्तिः *f.*, प्रवर्त्तनं, चेष्टा, अभ्यासः -सता, अभ्यसनं, समुत्थानं, अनलसता, अनालस्यं, आलस्यहीनता, प्रयासः, आयासः, श्रमः, परिश्रमः, क्रिया, कर्म्म *n.* (न्), सोद्योगता.

INDWELLING, *a.* निष्ठः -ष्ठा -ष्ठं, अन्तर्भवः -वा -वं, अन्तर्वर्त्ती -र्त्तिनी -र्त्ति (न्).

To INEBRIATE, *v. a.* मद् (c. 10. मादयति, मदयति -यितुं), मत्तीकृ, उन्मत्तीकृ, मत्तं -त्तां -त्तं कृ, मादं जन् (c. 10. जनयति -यितुं).

INEBRIATED, *p. p.* मत्तः -त्ता -त्तं, उन्मत्तः -त्ता -त्तं, उन्मदः -दा -दं, मदोन्मत्तः -त्ता -त्तं, क्षीवः -वा -वं, परिक्षीवः -वा -वं, प्रक्षीवितः -ता -तं, मद्यपीतः -ता -तं, शौण्डः -ण्डा -ण्डं.

INEBRIATION, *s.* मादः, मदः, उन्मादः, मत्तत्वं, उन्मत्तता, क्षैव्यं, क्षीवता, परिक्षीवता, शौण्डत्वं, प्रामाद्यं.

INEFFABLE, *a.* अकथनीयः -या -यं, अकथ्यः -थ्या -थ्यं, अवर्णनीयः -या -यं, अनिर्वचनीयः -या -यं, अवचनीयः -या -यं, अवाच्यः -च्या -च्यं, अवक्तव्यः -व्या -व्यं, अतिकथः -था -थं, वाग्विभवातिगः -गा -गं, वाग्विभवातिवृत्तः -त्ता -त्तं, अनिरुक्तः -क्ता -क्तं.

INEFFABLENESS, *s.* अकथनीयता, अकथ्यता, अवर्णनीयता, अवचनीयता.

INEFFABLY, *adv.* अकथनीयं, अवर्णनीयं, अनिर्वचनीयं, अतिकथं.

INEFFACEABLE, *a.* अनपमृज्यः -ज्या -ज्यं, अलोपनीयः -या -यं, अनाश्यः -श्या -श्यं.

INEFFECTIVE, *a.* निष्फलः -ला -लं, विफलः -ला -लं, व्यर्थः -र्था -र्थं, व्यर्थयत्नः -त्ना -त्नं, असाधकः -का -कं, निरर्थकः -का -कं, अनर्थकः -का -कं, अपार्थः -र्था -र्थं, दुर्बलः -ला -लं, निर्बलः -ला -लं, अप्रबलः -ला -लं, असमर्थः -र्था -र्थं, मोघः -घा -घं, अक्षमः -मा -मं, असिद्धिकरः -री -रं, अशक्तिमान् -मती -मत् (त्), प्रभावहीनः -ना -नं, शिथिलः -ला -लं, शिथिलबलः -ला -लं, दुर्बलायासः -सा -सं, निष्प्रयोजनः -ना -नं, अनुपयुक्तः -क्ता -क्तं, अनुपयोगी -गिनी -गि (न्).

INEFFECTIVELY, *adv.* निष्फलं, विफलं, व्यर्थं, मोघं, अप्रबलं, निर्बलं.

INEFFECTUAL, *a.* निष्फलः -ला -लं, अफलजनकः -का -कं, अफलोत्पादकः -का -कं, फलहीनः -ना -नं, मोघः -घा -घं, शक्तिहीनः -ना -नं, अप्रबलः

-ला -लं, असमर्थः -र्था -र्थं. See INEFFECTIVE.

INEFFECTUALLY, *adv.* निष्फलं, मोघं, व्यर्थं, निर्बलं, वृथा, मुधा.

INEFFICACIOUS, *a.* अप्रबलः -ला -लं, निष्प्रभावः -वा -वं, अकिञ्चित्करः -री -रं, अप्रभविष्णुः -ष्णुः -ष्णु, अफलवान् -वती -वत् (त्), तेजोहीनः -ना -नं, अक्षमः -मा -मं, अगुणवान् &c., अशक्तिमान्, असमर्थः -र्था -र्थं, अनुपकारी -रिणी -रि (न्). See INEFFECTUAL.

INEFFICACIOUSLY, *adv.* अप्रबलं, अप्रभावेण, मोघं, निष्फलं, अफलं, अक्षमं, मुधा.

INEFFICACY, *s.* निष्फलता, अफलता, वैफल्यं, अप्राबल्यं, अप्रबलता, अप्रभावः, प्रभावहीनता, शक्तिहीनता, असामर्थ्यं, असमर्थता, बलहीनता, निर्बलता, प्रतापहीनता, तेजोहीनता, मोघत्वं, अक्षमता, व्यर्थता, अनर्थकत्वं, शैथिल्यं, शिथिलता, अनुपयुक्तत्वं.

INEFFICIENCY, *s.* अक्षमता -त्वं, असामर्थ्यं, असमर्थता, अशक्तिः *f.*, अशक्तता, बलहीनता, अयुक्तता, अयोग्यत्वं, अनुपयुक्तत्वं, कार्य्याक्षमता, कार्य्यसिद्ध्यक्षमता, कार्य्याकारित्वं. See INEFFICACY.

INEFFICIENT, *a.* अक्षमः -मा -मं, कार्य्याक्षमः -मा -मं, असमर्थः -र्था -र्थं, अशक्तः -क्ता -क्तं, अयोग्यः -ग्या -ग्यं, अनुपयुक्तः -क्ता -क्तं, अप्रबलः -ला -लं, दुर्बलः -ला -लं, बलहीनः -ना -नं, शक्तिहीनः -ना -नं, असाधकः -का -कं, कर्म्मासाधकः -का -कं, कार्य्यासाधकः -का -कं, कार्य्यसिद्ध्यक्षमः -मा -मं, अपारकः -का -कं, अकार्य्यकारी -रिणी -रि (न्), अकृती -तिनी -ति (न्). See INEFFICACIOUS.

INEFFICIENTLY, *adv.* असिद्धिपूर्व्वं, अक्षमं, अयोग्यं, अप्रबलं, अनुपयुक्तं, व्यर्थं.

INELASTIC, *a.* अस्थितिस्थापकविशिष्टः -ष्टा -ष्टं, स्थितिस्थापकहीनः -ना -नं.

INELEGANCE, *s.* असौन्दर्य्यं, अलावण्यं, आलावण्यं, अचारुता, अशोभा.

INELEGANT, *s.* असुन्दरः -रा -री -रं, अलावण्यवान् -वती -वत् (त्), अविनीतः -ता -तं, अशोभनः -ना -नं, कुरूपः -पी -पं, अश्लीलः -ला -लं, अप्रशस्तः -स्ता -स्तं.

INELEGANTLY, *adv.* असुन्दरं, अविनीतं, अलावण्येन, अप्रशस्तं, अशोभापूर्व्वं.

INELIGIBLE, *a.* अवरणीयः -या -यं, अवार्य्यः -र्य्या -र्य्यं, अयोग्यः -ग्या -ग्यं.

INELOQUENT, *a.* अवाग्मी -ग्मिनी -ग्मि (न्), असद्वक्ता -क्त्री -क्तृ (क्तृ), दुर्मुखः -खा -खं, मुखदुर्बलः -ला -लं, हीनवाक् *m. f. n.*, वागपटुः -टुः -टु, वाग्जडः -डा -डं.

INEPT, *a.* अयुक्तः -क्ता -क्तं, अयोग्यः -ग्या -ग्यं, अनभिज्ञः -ज्ञा -ज्ञं.

INEPTLY, *adv.* अयुक्तं, अयोग्यं, अनुपयुक्तं, अनभिज्ञवत्, अज्ञवत्.

INEQUALITY, *s.* असमता, असाम्यं, असमानता, विषमता, वैषम्यं, विषमं, असामान्यं, असाम्यता, अतुल्यता -त्वं.—(Diversity) असादृश्यं, असदृशता -त्वं, भिन्नता, विभिन्नता, भेदः, विभेदः, असमञ्जसं.—(Of number) विषमसंख्यत्वं, तारतम्यं.

INEQUITABLE, *a.* अन्याय्यः -य्या -य्यं, अन्यायी -यिनी -यि (न्), अधार्म्मिकः -की -कं.

INERRABILITY, *s.* अभ्रमणशीलता, अभ्रान्तिशीलता, भ्रमायोग्यता, अभ्रान्तिः *f.*

INERRABLE, *a.* अभ्रमणशीलः -ला -लं, अभ्रान्तिशीलः -ला -लं, भ्रमायोग्यः -ग्या -ग्यं.

INERT, *a.* जडः -डा -डं, अचेष्टः -ष्टा -ष्टं, नष्टचेष्टः -ष्टा -ष्टं, निश्चेष्टः -ष्टा -ष्टं, अचेतनः -ना -नं, चेष्टाहीनः -ना -नं, गतिहीनः -ना -नं, अचलः -ला -लं, निश्चलः -ला -लं, कुण्ठः -ण्ठा -ण्ठं.—(Slow to act) अनुद्योगी -गिनी -गि (न्), अनुद्योगशीलः -ला -लं, अप्रवर्त्तकः -का -कं, प्रवृत्तिशून्यः -न्या -न्यं, मन्दः -न्दा -न्दं, आलस्यशीलः -ला -लं, तन्द्रालुः -लुः -लु, अल्पचेष्टितः -ता -तं.

INERTIA, *s.* जडता -त्वं, जाड्यं, अचलता, निश्चलता, कुण्ठता.

INERTLY, *adv.* जडवत्, जडं, जाड्येन, सजाड्यं, आलस्येन, अलसवत्, मन्दं.

INERTNESS, *s.* जडता, जाड्यं, अचेष्टा, चेष्टाशून्यता, चेष्टाविमुखता, गतिहीनता, अनुद्योगः, अप्रवृत्तिः *f.*, अप्रवर्त्तनं, मन्दता, मान्द्यं, अलसत्वं, आलस्यं, तन्द्रिका, कुण्ठता.

INESTIMABLE, *a.* अनर्घ्यः -र्घ्या -र्घ्यं, अनर्घः -र्घा -र्घं, अमूल्यः -ल्या -ल्यं, मूल्यातीतः -ता -तं, मूल्यातिगः -गा -गं, अतिमूल्यः -ल्या -ल्यं, अनुत्तमः -मा -मं, अनुत्कृष्टः -ष्टा -ष्टं.

INEVITABLE, *a.* अपरिहार्य्यः -र्य्या -र्य्यं, अपरिहरणीयः -या -यं, अनिवार्य्यः -र्य्या -र्य्यं, अवारणीयः -या -यं, अवश्यकः -का -कं, आवश्यकः -की -कं, अवश्यः -श्या -श्यं, अनतिक्रमणीयः -या -यं, अहार्य्यः -र्य्या -र्य्यं, अवर्ज्जनीयः -या -यं, अनिवारः -रा -रं, अवशः -शा -शं, भवितव्यः -व्या -व्यं, अवश्यभवनीयः -या -यं, नियतः -ता -तं, आनुषङ्गिकः -की -कं.

INEVITABLENESS, *s.* अपरिहार्य्यता, अनिवार्य्यता, अवश्यकता, आवश्यकत्वं, निवारणाशक्यता, अनतिक्रमणीयता; 'inevitable act,' अवश्यकर्त्तव्यं, आवश्यं -श्यकं.

INEVITABLY, *adv.* अवश्यं, अवशं, नियतं, ध्रुवं, अनिवारणीयं.

INEXCITABLE, *a.* अनुत्तेजनीयः -या -यं, अक्षोभणीयः -या -यं, अक्षोभ्यः -भ्या -भ्यं.

INEXCUSABLE, *a.* अक्षमणीयः -या -यं, अक्षन्तव्यः -व्या -व्यं, अक्षम्यः -म्या -म्यं, असहव्यः -व्या -व्यं, अमार्ज्जनीयः -या -यं, अमार्ष्टव्यः -व्या -व्यं, अमृज्यदोषः -षा -षं, निरुत्तरः -रा -रं, निरुत्तरीयः -या -यं, उत्तरशून्यः -न्या -न्यं, अमोचनीयः -या -यं, अशोधनीयः -या -यं, असहनीयः -या -यं, असोढव्यः -व्या -व्यं, अनिवार्य्यदोषः -षा -षं.

INEXCUSABLENESS, *s.* अक्षमणीयता, अक्षम्यता, अमार्ज्जनीयता, निरुत्तरत्वं.

INEXCUSABLY, *adv.* अक्षमणीयं, निरुत्तरं, यथा उत्तरं न शक्यते दातुं तथा.

INEXHAUSTED, *a.* अक्षीणः -णा -णं, अव्ययितः -ता -तं, अशून्यः -न्या -न्यं.

INEXHAUSTIBLE, *a.* अक्षयः -या -यं, अक्षयी -यिणी -यि (न्), अक्षयणीयः -या -यं, अशक्यक्षयः -या -यं, अव्ययः -या -यं, अशक्यव्ययः -या -यं, अनाश्यः -श्या -श्यं, अविनाशी -शिनी -शि (न्), अनन्तः -न्ता -न्तं.

INEXHAUSTIBLENESS, *s.* अक्षयता -त्वं, अक्षयित्वं, अनाश्यता, अनन्तता.

INEXORABLE, *a.* अनाराध्यः -ध्या -ध्यं, अनाराधनीयः -या -यं, दुराराध्यः -ध्या -ध्यं, असान्त्वनीयः -या -यं, अप्रसादनीयः -या -यं, अननुनेयः -या -यं, अविनेयः -या -यं, निर्दयः -या -यं, कठिनहृदयः -या -यं, पाषाणहृदयः -या -यं, अयोहृदयः -या -यं, कठोरचित्तः -त्ता -त्तं.

INEXORABLY, *adv.* निर्दयं, निर्दयवत्, अनाराधनीयं, पाषाणचित्तत्वात्.

INEXPECTATION, *s.* अनपेक्षा, अप्रतीक्षा, अनिरीक्षा, अप्रत्याशा, अनाशा.

INEXPEDIENCE, INEXPEDIENCY, *s.* अयोग्यता, अयुक्तता -त्वं, अयुक्तिः *f.*, अनुपयुक्तता -त्वं, अनुपयोगिता, अनौचित्यं, अनुपपत्तिः *f.*, अनर्हत्वं, अयाथार्थ्यं, अकर्त्तव्यता, अकार्य्यता.

INEXPEDIENT, *a.* अयोग्यः -ग्या -ग्यं, अनुपयुक्तः -क्ता -क्तं, अनुपयोगी -गिनी -गि (न्), अनुचितः -ता -तं, अनर्थकरः -री -रं, अनुपकारकः -का -कं, अकर्त्तव्यः -व्या -व्यं, अकरणीयः -या -यं, अकार्य्यः -र्य्या -र्य्यं.

INEXPERIENCE, *s.* अननुभूतिः *f.*, अननुभवः, अपाकः, अपरिपाकः, अपक्वता, अपरिपक्वता, अपक्वबुद्धित्वं, अप्रतीतिः *f.*, अप्रत्ययः, अव्यापारः, अदर्शनं, अव्युत्पन्नता, बालिशता, बालिश्यं, व्यवहाराज्ञता, अज्ञता, अनभिज्ञता, अपटुता.

INEXPERIENCED, *a.* अविपक्वबुद्धिः -द्धिः -द्धि, अपरिपक्वबुद्धिः -द्धिः -द्धि, अपक्वः -क्वा -क्वं, अकोविदः -दा -दं, अव्युत्पन्नः -न्ना -न्नं, अव्यापारः -रा -रं, बालिशः -शा -शं, अल्पज्ञः -ज्ञा -ज्ञं, अल्पदृश्वा -श्वा -श्व (न्), अनभिज्ञः -ज्ञा -ज्ञं, अज्ञः -ज्ञा -ज्ञं, व्यवहाराज्ञः -ज्ञा -ज्ञं.

INEXPERT, *a.* अकुशलः -ला -लं, अदक्षः -क्षा -क्षं, अनिपुणः -णा -णं, अपटुः -टुः -टु, अपेशलः -ला -लं, अचतुरः -रा -रं, कौशल्यहीनः -ना -नं, अविचक्षणः -णा -णं, अविदग्धः -ग्धा -ग्धं, अयुक्तिमान् -मती -मत् (त्), अविज्ञः -ज्ञा -ज्ञं, अनभिज्ञः -ज्ञा -ज्ञं.

INEXPERTNESS, *s.* अदक्षता, अदाक्ष्यं, अकुशलता, अकौशल्यं, आकौशलं,

अकौशलं, अनिपुणता, अनैपुण्यं, अपटुत्वं, अप्रवीणता, अयुक्तिः *f.*, अनभिज्ञता, अविदग्धता.

INEXPIABLE, *a.* अशोधनीयः -या -यं, अशोध्यः -ध्या -ध्यं, अमोचनीयः -या -यं, प्रायश्चित्तायोग्यः -ग्या -ग्यं, प्रायश्चित्तानर्हः -र्हा -र्हं, अनिष्कारणीयः -या -यं, असमार्ज्जनीयः -या -यं, अपरिमार्ज्जनीयः -या -यं, निष्कृतयोग्यः -ग्या -ग्यं, अशक्यनिष्कृतिः -तिः -ति.

INEXPIABLY, *adv.* यथा प्रायश्चित्तं कर्त्तुं न शक्यते तथाप्रकारेण.

INEXPLICABLE, *a.* अव्याख्येयः -या -यं, अविवरणीयः -या -यं, अनिर्देश्यः -श्या -श्यं, अनुद्देश्यः -श्या -श्यं, अवर्णनीयः -या -यं, अनिर्वचनीयः -या -यं, दुर्बोधः -धा -धं, असुबोध्यः -ध्या -ध्यं, गहनः -ना -नं, अशक्यार्थः -र्था -र्थं.

INEXPLICABLY, *adv.* यथा व्याख्यातुं न शक्यते तथाप्रकारेण, अविवरणीयं.

INEXPRESSIBLE, *a.* अकथनीयः -या -यं, अकथ्यः -थ्या -थ्यं, अनिर्वचनीयः -या -यं, अनिर्वाच्यः -च्या -च्यं, अनाख्येयः -या -यं, अव्याख्येयः -या -यं, अनिवेद्यः -द्या -द्यं, अनिवेदनीयः -या -यं, अनुच्चारणीयः -या -यं, अनुच्चार्य्यः -र्य्या -र्य्यं, वाग्विभवातिगः -गा -गं.

INEXPRESSIBLY, *adv.* अकथनीयं, यथा निर्देष्टुं न शक्यते तथाप्रकारेण.

INEXPUGNABLE, *a.* अलङ्घनीयः -या -यं, अनाक्रमणीयः -या -यं, दुर्गम्यः -म्या -म्यं.

INEXTINGUISHABLE, *a.* अशमनीयः -या -यं, अप्रशमनीयः -या -यं, अशाम्यः -म्या -म्यं, अनिर्वाप्यः -प्या -प्यं, अनिर्वाणीयः -या -यं, अनिर्वाणयोग्यः -ग्या -ग्यं.

INEXTRICABLE, *a.* अनुद्धरणीयः -या -यं, अनुद्धार्य्यः -र्य्या -र्य्यं, अमोचनीयः -या -यं, दुस्तार्य्यः -र्य्या -र्य्यं, दुस्तरः -रा -रं, सुदुस्तरः -रा -रं.

INFALLIBILITY, *s.* अभ्रान्तिमत्त्वं, अभ्रान्तिशीलता, अभ्रमाधीनता, अमोहाधीनता, अभ्रमयोग्यता, अभ्रान्तिः *f.*, अस्खलितमतित्वं, स्खलनासम्भवः, अमोघता, अव्यर्थता, प्रमादाक्षमता.

INFALLIBLE, *a.* अभ्रान्तिशीलः -ला -लं, अभ्रमाधीनः -ना -नं, अभ्रान्तिमान् -मती -मत् (त्), भ्रमायोग्यः -ग्या -ग्यं, अभ्रान्तः -न्ता -न्तं, अमोहाधीनः -ना -नं, अस्खलितमतिः -तिः -ति, अस्खलितबुद्धिः -द्धिः -द्धि, अप्रमादी -दिनी -दि (न्), प्रमादहीनः -ना -नं, प्रमादाक्षमः -मा -मं, अमोघः -घा -घं, अव्यर्थः -र्था -र्थं, निश्चितः -ता -तं.

INFALLIBLY, *adv.* सुनिश्चितं, निश्चितं, अमोघं, अव्यर्थं, अवश्यं, असंशयं.

INFAMOUS, *a.* ख्यातगर्हणः -णा -णं, दुष्कीर्त्तिः -र्त्तिः -र्त्ति, अकीर्त्तिमान् -मती -मत् (त्), अयशस्वी -स्विनी -स्वि (न्), अयशस्यः -स्या -स्यं, कुख्यातिः -तिः -ति, वाच्यः -च्या -च्यं, अभिशस्तः -स्ता -स्तं, गर्हितः -ता -तं, गर्ह्यः -र्ह्या -र्ह्यं, कुयशस्कः -स्का -स्कं, अपयशस्कः -स्का -स्कं, अपयशस्वी &c., कुख्यातः -ता -तं, अख्यातः -ता -तं, अतिदुष्टः -ष्टा -ष्टं, कलङ्की -ङ्किनी -ङ्कि (न्), पिशुनः -ना -नं, दुर्वृत्तः -त्ता -त्तं, पांसनः -ना -नं.—(Causing infamy) अकीर्त्तिकरः -री -रं, अपयशस्करः -री -रं, कलङ्ककरः -रा -रं, लज्जाकरः -री -रं, निन्दाकरः -री -रं.

INFAMOUSLY, *adv.* ख्यातगर्हणं, गर्हणीयं, गर्हितं, अतिदुष्टं, अतिदुष्टवत्, अयशस्यं, अकीर्त्तिकरं, वाच्यप्रकारेण.

INFAMY, INFAMOUSNESS, *s.* अकीर्त्तिः *f.*, अपकीर्त्तिः *f.*, कुकीर्त्तिः *f.*, अयशस् *n.*, अपयशस् *n.*, अख्यातिः *f.*, कुख्यातिः *f.*, अप्रतिष्ठा, वाच्यता, अमर्य्यादा, मर्य्यादाहानिः *f.*, कलङ्कः, अपकलङ्कः, अपकर्षः, अपध्वंसः.

INFANCY, *s.* बालत्वं, बाल्यं, बालकत्वं, बाल्यभावः, बाल्यकालः, बाल्यावस्था, बालावस्था, शैशवं, शिशुकालः, शिशुभावः.—(Beginning or early period of any thing) आरम्भः, प्रारम्भः, प्रथमकालः, आदिकालः.

INFANT, *s.* बालः -ला, स्तनपः -पा *f.*, स्तनपाः *m.*, स्तनपायी *m.* -यिनी *f.*, स्तनन्धयः -या -यी, क्षीरपः -पा, क्षीरादः -दा, क्षीरपायी -यिनी, क्षीरादः, बालकः, अतिबालकः, डिम्भः -म्भा, डिम्बः -म्बा, दारकः, उत्तानशयः -या, शिशुः *m.*; 'infant offspring,' बालापत्यं.—(Minor) अप्राप्तव्यवहारः, अज्ञातव्यवहारः, व्यवहारायोग्यः, किशोरः.

INFANT, *a.* *See* INFANTILE.

INFANTA, *s.* राजवंशीयकन्या, राजकन्या, राजपुत्री, राजकुमारी.

INFANTICIDE, *s.* बालहत्या, बालकहत्या, शिशुहत्या, शिशुवधः, बालकवधः, बालघातः.—(The agent) बालहा *m.* (न्), बालहन्ता *m.* (न्तृ), बालघातकः -ती *m.* (न्).

INFANTILE, INFANTINE, *a.* बालकीयः -या -यं, बालः -ला -लं, बालेयः -यी -यं, बालकः -का -कं, अतिबालकः -का -कं, किशोरः -रा -रं, बालसम्बन्धी -न्धिनी -न्धि (न्), बालयोग्यः -ग्या -ग्यं, शिशुसम्बन्धी &c.

INFANTRY, *s.* पादातं, पदातिः *m.*, पदातयः *m. pl.*, पत्तिः *m.*, पत्तयः *m. pl.*, पादातिकसैन्यं, पदातिकसैन्याः *m. pl.*, पदगसैन्यं, पदातिकाः *m. pl.*, पत्ताः *m. pl.*; 'a body of infantry,' पत्तिसंहतिः *f.*, पत्तिसमूहः; 'a line of infantry,' पत्तिपङ्क्तिः *f.*, पत्तिश्रेणी.

To INFATUATE, *v. a.* मुह् (c. 10. मोहयति -यितुं), सम्मुह्, मोहेन उपहन् (c. 2. -हन्ति -न्तुं), मूढीकृ, ज्ञानलोपं कृ, बुद्धिभ्रंशं कृ, हतबुद्धिं -द्धिं -द्धि कृ.

INFATUATED, *a.* मूढः -ढा -ढं, सम्मूढः -ढा -ढं, मोहितः -ता -तं, विमोहितः -ता -तं, सम्मोहितः -ता -तं, प्रमूढसंज्ञः -ज्ञा -ज्ञं, परिमूढः -ढा -ढं, मोहोपहतः -ता -तं, हतबुद्धिः -द्धिः -द्धि, उपहतबुद्धिः -द्धिः -द्धि, उपहतः -ता -तं, प्रमुदितेन्द्रियः -या -यं, हतज्ञानः -ना -नं, नष्टज्ञानः -ना -नं, नष्टबुद्धिः -द्धिः -द्धि, भ्रष्टबुद्धिः -द्धिः -द्धि, बुद्धिभ्रष्टः -ष्टा -ष्टं, नष्टविवेकः -का -कं, दुर्मदान्धः -न्धा -न्धं; 'by lust,' काममूढः -ढा -ढं.

INFATUATING, *a.* मनमोही -हिनी -हि (न्), परिमोही &c., मोहनः -ना -नी -नं, विमोहनः &c., मोहकारी &c.

INFATUATION, *s.* मोहः, सम्मोहः, मूढता -त्वं, मौढ्यं, मूर्खता -त्वं, मौर्ख्यं, मूढग्राहः, बुद्धिहीनता, बुद्धिभ्रंशः, ज्ञानभ्रंशः, बुद्धिलोपः, ज्ञानलोपः, बुद्धिनाशः, नष्टविवेकता, मोहोपहतत्वं, मोहाविष्टत्वं.

INFEASIBILITY, *s.* असाध्यता, असाधनीयता, अकरणीयता, अशक्यता, असम्भाव्यता, दुःसाध्यता, अनुपपाद्यत्वं.

INFEASIBLE, *a.* असाध्यः -ध्या -ध्यं, दुःसाध्यः -ध्या -ध्यं, अकरणीयः -या -यं, अशक्यः -क्या -क्यं, कर्त्तुम् अशक्यः -क्या -क्यं, दुष्करः -रा -रं, असम्भाव्यः -व्या -व्यं, असम्भावनीयः -या -यं, अनुपपाद्यः -द्या -द्यं, दुर्लभः -भा -भं.

To INFECT, *v. a.* दुष् (c. 10. दूषयति -यितुं), स्वरोगम् अन्यस्मिन् सञ्चर (c. 10. -चारयति -यितुं) or संक्रम् (c. 10. -क्रमयति -क्रामयति -यितुं), स्वरोगदूषितं -तां -तं कृ, रोगदूषितं -तां -तं कृ, रोगाक्रान्तं -न्तां -न्तं कृ, रोगसंसृष्टं -ष्टां -ष्टं कृ, संसर्गदूषितं -तां -तं कृ, रोगसम्पर्केण or रोगसंसर्गेण दुष्.

INFECTED, *p. p.* or *a.* दूषितः -ता -तं, रोगदूषितः -ता -तं, रोगाक्रान्तः -न्ता -न्तं, रोगसंसर्गदूषितः -ता -तं, रोगसम्पर्कदूषितः -ता -तं, संसृष्टः -ष्टा -ष्टं, रोगसंसृष्टः -ष्टा -ष्टं, रोगसञ्चारदूषितः -ता -तं, सञ्चारदुष्टः -ष्टा -ष्टं, सञ्चारितरोगग्रस्तः -स्ता -स्तं, सङ्क्रामदोषग्रस्तः -स्ता -स्तं, रोगदोषप्राप्तः -प्ता -प्तं.

INFECTION, *s.* सञ्चारः, सञ्चारदोषः, रोगसञ्चारः, रोगसञ्चारदोषः, रोगसङ्क्रमः, स्पर्शसञ्चारः, रोगसम्पर्कः, सम्पर्कदोषः, स्पर्शदोषः, रोगसंसर्गः, संसर्गदोषः, दोषः, दूषणं, संस्रवः.

INFECTIOUS, INFECTIVE, *a.* सञ्चारी -रिणी -रि (न्), स्पर्शसञ्चारी &c., सञ्चारकः -का -कं, सङ्क्रमिता -त्री -तृ (तृ), साङ्क्रामिकः -की -कं, सम्पर्कीयः -या -यं, संसर्गी -र्गिणी -र्गि (न्), संसर्गीयः -या -यं, सांसर्गिकः -की -कं, स्पर्शाक्रामकः -का -कं, दूषकः -का -कं, दूषणः -णा -णं, दूषयिष्णुः -ष्णुः -ष्णु.

INFECTIOUSNESS, *s.* सञ्चारित्वं, स्पर्शसञ्चारित्वं -ता, सञ्चारकत्वं, साङ्क्रामिकत्वं, सांसर्गिकत्वं, सम्पर्काक्रामकत्वं.

INFECUND, *a.* वन्ध्यः -न्ध्या -न्ध्यं, निष्फलः -ला -लं, अफलः -ला -लं, अप्रजः -जा -जं, अनपत्यः -त्या -त्यं, असुती -तिनी -ति (न्), अप्रसवी -विणी -वि (न्), शुष्कः -ष्का -ष्कं.

INFECUNDITY, *s.* वन्ध्यता, निष्फलता, अफलता, अनपत्यत्वं, अप्रजायत्वं, फलहीनता; 'in a female,' वन्ध्यात्वं.

INFELICITY, *s.* असुखं, असौख्यं, दुःखं, अकल्याणं, अकुशलं, अशर्म्म *n.* (न्), अधन्यता, अक्षेमः, अश्रेयस्, अस्वास्थ्यं, अनिर्वृतिः *f.*

To INFER, *v. a.* अनुमा (c. 2. -माति -तुं, c. 3. -मिमीते), प्रमा, ऊह् (c. 1. ऊहते -हितुं), अपोह्, निर्णी (c. 1. -णयति -णेतुं), अवगम् (c. 1. -गच्छति -गन्तुं), तर्क् (c. 10. तर्कयति -यितुं), अनुतर्क्, प्रतर्क्, अपवह् (c. 1. -वहति -वोढुं), उन्नी (c. 1. -नयति -नेतुं), उन्नयनं कृ, अनुमानं कृ.

INFERABLE, *a.* अनुमेयः -या -यं, आनुमानिकः -की -कं, ऊहनीयः -या -यं, अपोहनीयः -या -यं, अवगम्यः -म्या -म्यं, समधिगम्यः -म्या -म्यं, उपलक्ष्यः -क्ष्या -क्ष्यं, अनुमानसाध्यः -ध्या -ध्यं, अनुमानगम्यः -म्या -म्यं, तर्कसाध्यः -ध्या -ध्यं, अनुमानवेद्यः -द्या -द्यं, उन्नयनसाध्यः -ध्या -ध्यं, यौक्तिकः -की -कं.

INFERENCE, *s.* अनुमानं, अनुमितिः *f.*, अनुमा, ऊहनं, ऊहा, अपोहः -हनं, अभ्यूहः, अपवाहः, युक्तिः *f.*, प्रयुक्तिः *f.*, तर्कः, तर्कनिश्चयः, तर्कनिर्णयः, अनुमाननिर्णयः, अनुमानसिद्धान्तः, तर्कसिद्धान्तः, उन्नयनं, कल्पनं -ना, अनुषङ्गः, उपलक्ष्यः, अन्वयः, परामर्शः, व्याप्तिः *f.*, अनुभूतिः *f.*, अनुभवः, लिङ्गं, वितर्कः; 'an inference from circumstances,' अर्थापत्तिः *f.*; 'subject of an inference,' व्याप्यं; 'leading to one,' उन्नायकः -का -कं, अनुमापकः -का -कं. Strictly, the process of 'inference' is अनुमानं, and the result अनुमितिः.

INFERENTIAL, *a.* आनुमानिकः -की -कं, अनुमानसिद्धः -द्धा -द्धं, ऊही -हिनी -हि (न्), उन्नायकः -का -कं, यौक्तिकः -की -कं, तर्कसिद्धः -द्धा -द्धं.

INFERIOR, *a.* (Lower or low in place) अधःस्थः -स्था -स्थं, अधरस्थः -स्था -स्थं, अधरः -रा -रं, नीचस्थः -स्था -स्थं, निम्नः -म्ना -म्नं, अधस्तनः -नी -नं.—(Lower or low in station, rank, value) नीचः -चा -चं, अपकृष्टः -ष्टा -ष्टं, निकृष्टः -ष्टा -ष्टं, प्रतिकृष्टः -ष्टा -ष्टं, अधमः -मा -मं, अवरः -रा -रं, अवमः -मा -मं, हीनः -ना -नं, अनुत्तमः -मा -मं, कुत्सितः -ता -तं, जघन्यः -न्या -न्यं, दुष्टः -ष्टा -ष्टं, खलः -ला -लं, न्यङ् नीची न्यक् (च्), अर्व्वा -र्व्वती -र्व्वत् (न्), चरमः -मा -मं, गर्ह्यः -र्ह्या -र्ह्यं, रेफः -फा -फं, रेपः -पा -पं, रेफाः -फाः -फः (स्), रेपाः &c., याप्यः -प्या -प्यं, खेटः -टा -टं, अवद्यः -द्या -द्यं, अणकः -का -कं, अनकः -का -कं, आणकः -का -कं, कुपूयः -या -यं, अनार्य्यः -र्य्या -र्य्यं, अल्पः -ल्पा -ल्पं; 'of inferior rank,' अपरपदभाक् *m. f. n.* (ज्), अवरपदस्थः -स्था -स्थं, हीनजातिः -तिः -ति. Sometimes expressed by दुर् in comp.; as, 'of inferior family,' दुष्कुलीनः -ना -नं.—(Inferior in age) कनीयान् -यसी -यः (स्), कनिष्ठः -ष्ठा -ष्ठं, अवरजः -जा -जं, अनुजः -जा -जं.—(Secondary) अप्रधानः -ना -नं, अमुख्यः -ख्या -ख्यं, अप्राग्र्यः -ग्र्या -ग्र्यं, गौणः -णी -णं.—(Less) ऊनः -ना -नं, न्यूनः -ना -नं, अल्पीयान् -यसी -यः (स्).

INFERIOR, *s.* (A person in a lower station) अवरपदस्थः, अवरः, अनुजीवी *m.* (न्), हीनपदस्थः.

INFERIORITY, *s.* अवरत्वं, नीचत्वं -ता, अपकर्षः -र्षता, अपकृष्टता -त्वं, निकृष्टता, हीनता, जघन्यत्वं -ता, अनुत्कर्षः, हीमता, दुष्टता, खलता, अप्रधानता, अप्राधान्यं, अमुख्यता, गौणता.

INFERNAL, *a.* नारकः -की -कं, नारकी -किणी -कि (न्), नरकीयः -या -यं, नारकीयः -यी -यं, नरकस्थः -स्था -स्थं, पातालीयः -या -यं, पातालसम्बन्धी -न्धिनी -न्धि (न्), नरकसम्बन्धी &c., नैरयः -यी -यं, पैशाचः -ची -चं -चिकः -की -कं, आसुरः -री -रं, राक्षसः -सी -सं, अधोभुवनसम्बन्धी &c.—(Infernal regions) नरकः -कं, पातालं, अधोभुवनं, अधोलोकः, प्रेतलोकः, बलिसद्म *n.* (न्), बलिमन्दिरं, रसातलं, नागलोकः, निरयः.

INFERNAL, *s.* (Inhabitant of hell) नरकवासी *m.* (न्), पातालवासी *m.*, नरकस्थः, नरकसंस्थः, पातालस्थः.

INFERNALLY, *adv.* नरकीयप्रकारेण, पिशाचवत्, राक्षसवत्, नरके यथा.

INFERRED, *p. p.* अनुमितः -ता -तं, अनुमानसिद्धः -द्धा -द्धं, अपोहितः -ता -तं, अपोढः -ढा -ढं, अवगतः -ता -तं, तर्कसिद्धः -द्धा -द्धं, अनुभूतः -ता -तं.

INFERTILE, *a.* वन्ध्यः -न्ध्या -न्ध्यं, निष्फलः -ला -लं, अफलः -ला -लं, अफलदः -दा -दं, अफलवान् -वती -वत् (त्), अस्फीतः -ता -तं, अल्पफलः -ला -लं, अल्पफलदः -दा -दं; 'infertile soil,' अनुर्व्वरा, अनूर्व्वरा.

INFERTILITY, *s.* वन्ध्यात्वं -ता, निष्फलता, अफलता, अफलवत्त्वं, अस्फीतिः *f.*, अस्फीतता; 'of the soil,' अनुर्व्वरात्वं.

To INFEST, *v. a.* बाध् (c. 1. बाधते -धितुं), प्रबाध्, उपरुध् (c. 7. -रुणद्धि -रोद्धुं), आयस् (c. 10. -यासयति -यितुं), क्लिश् (c. 9. क्लिश्नाति, क्लेशितुं), पीड् (c. 10. पीडयति -यितुं), तप् (c. 10. तापयति -यितुं), परितप्, उपद्रु (c. 1. -द्रवति -द्रोतुं), समुपद्रु, उपसृज् (c. 6. -सृजति -स्रष्टुं), उपप्रु (c. 1. -प्रवते -प्रोतुं), उपद्रवं कृ, उपसर्गं कृ, उपप्लवं कृ.

INFESTED, *p. p.* उपद्रुतः -ता -तं, समुपद्रुतः -ता -तं, उपप्रुतः -ता -तं, उपसृष्टः -ष्टा -ष्टं, बाधितः -ता -तं, उपरुद्धः -द्धा -द्धं, पीडितः -ता -तं.—(Frequented) सेवितः -ता -तं, आश्रितः -ता -तं, आचरितः -ता -तं, जुष्टः -ष्टा -ष्टं; 'by beasts of prey,' श्वापदाचरितः -ता -तं, श्वापदोपसृष्टः -ष्टा -ष्टं.

INFIDEL, *s.* नास्तिकः, अविश्वासी *m.* (न्), अश्रद्धधानः, अश्रद्धः, शास्त्राविश्वासी *m.*, शास्त्राश्रद्धः, धर्म्मनिन्दकः, धर्म्मोदेर् निन्दकः, अनीश्वरवादी *m.* (न्).—(Disbeliever in Christianity) ख्रीष्टीयधर्म्मनिन्दकः, ख्रीष्टीयशास्त्राविश्वासी *m.* (न्).

INFIDEL, *a.* अश्रद्धः -द्धा -द्धं, अश्रद्धालुः -लुः -लु, अश्रद्धधानः -ना -नं, अश्रद्धावान् -वती -वत् (त्), अविश्वासी -सिनी -सि (न्), अविश्वासशीलः -ला -लं, नास्तिकवृत्तिः -त्तिः -त्ति, नास्तिकधर्म्मा -र्म्मा -र्म्म (न्), भक्तिहीनः -ना -नं, देवनिन्दकः -का -कं.

INFIDELITY, *s.* अश्रद्धा, अविश्वासः, नास्तिक्यं, नास्तिकता -त्वं, शास्त्राविश्वासः, शास्त्राश्रद्धा, धर्म्मनिन्दा, अनीश्वरवादः, परलोकाभावबुद्धिः *f.*, अभक्तिः *f.*, अप्रत्ययः, विश्वासाभावः, शास्त्रनिन्दा, देवनिन्दा.—(Disbelief in Christianity) ख्रीष्टीयधर्म्माविश्वासः, ख्रीष्टीयधर्म्मनिन्दा.—(Conjugal infidelity) व्यभिचारः, विवाहसंविद्व्यतिक्रमः, विवाहसमयभङ्गः, विवाहप्रतिज्ञाभङ्गः, असाधुता, जारकर्म्म *n.* (न्); 'on the part of the wife,' अपातिव्रत्यं, असाध्वीत्वं, असतीत्वं.

INFINITE, *a.* अनन्तः -न्ता -न्तं -न्तकः -का -कं, अत्यन्तः -न्ता -न्तं, अपर्य्यन्तः -न्ता -न्तं, अनाद्यन्तः -न्ता -न्तं, अमितः -ता -तं, अपरिमितः -ता -तं, अपरिमेयः -या -यं, अप्रमेयः -या -यं, निरवधिः -धिः -धि, अपारः -रा -रं, अमर्य्यादः -दा -दं, निर्म्मर्य्यादः -दा -दं, अतिमर्य्यादः -दा -दं, अशेषः -षा -षं, निरन्तरः -रा -रं, असीमकः -का -कं; 'of infinite splendour,' अमितद्युतिः -तिः -ति, अमिततेजाः -जाः -जः (स्); 'any infinite number,' परार्द्धं.

INFINITELY, *adv.* अत्यन्तं, अनन्तं, अमितं, अपरिमितं, अतिमर्य्यादं, अशेषतस्.

INFINITENESS, *s.* अनन्तता, आनन्त्यं, अनन्त्यं, अमितता, अपरिमितत्वं.

INFINITESIMAL, *a.* अतिसूक्ष्मः -क्ष्मा -क्ष्मं, अत्यन्तसूक्ष्मः &c., अल्पिष्ठः -ष्ठा -ष्ठं.

INFINITIVE, *s.* (In grammar) साधारणरूपं, सामान्यरूपं, भाववचनं. The grammatical symbol for the infinitive mood is तुम्.

INFINITIVELY, *adv.* साधारणरूपेण, सामान्यरूपेण, भाववचनरूपेण.

INFINITY, INFINITUDE, *s.* अनन्तता, आनन्त्यं, अनन्त्यं, अत्यन्तता, अनाद्यन्तता -त्वं, अमितता -त्वं, अपरिमितता -त्वं, अप्रमेयता, अपारता, सीमाभावः, असीमत्वं, अवधिहीनता, निरवधिभावः, अमर्य्यादभावः, आनन्तर्य्यं, नित्यता.

INFIRM, *s.* (Feeble) दुर्बलः -ला -लं, क्षीणबलः -ला -लं, क्षीणः -णा -णं,

शिथिलबलः -ला -लं, अल्पबलः -ला -लं, निर्बलः -ला -लं, अशक्तः -क्ता -क्तं, क्षीणशक्तिः -क्तिः -क्ति, अल्पशक्तिः -क्तिः -क्ति, शिथिलशक्तिः -क्तिः -क्ति, क्षीणवीर्य्यः -र्य्या -र्य्यं, क्षीणसत्त्वः -त्त्वा -त्त्वं, अल्पवीर्य्यः &c., असमर्थः -र्था -र्थं, अवसन्नः -न्ना -न्नं, क्लीवः -वा -वं.—(Not firm) अस्थिरः -रा -रं, अधीरः -रा -रं, अदृढः -ढा -ढं, अध्रुवः -वा -वं.—(From age) जरी -रिणी -रि (न्), जीर्णः -र्णा -र्णं, जरातुरः -रा -रं, जरापरिणतः -ता -तं, जराग्रस्तः -स्ता -स्तं, जरणः -णा -णं, जरद्धः -द्धा -द्धं, जरठः -ठा -ठं, जीर्णवान् -वती -वत् (त्).

INFIRMARY, *s.* आरोग्यशाला, रोगिशाला, चिकित्साशाला, रोग्यालयः, रोग्याश्रयः, चिकित्सालयः, स्वास्थ्यालयः, रोगप्रतीकारशाला, रोगार्त्तलोकचिकित्सनस्थानं.

INFIRMITY, *s.* (Feebleness) दौर्बल्यं, दुर्बलता, बलहीनता, बलशैथिल्यं, शिथिलता, अल्पशक्तित्वं, क्षीणता, क्षीणशक्तित्वं, अशक्तिः *f.*, अशक्तता, वीर्य्यहानिः *f.*, सत्त्वहानिः *f.*—(Foible, failing) छिद्रं, दोषः, अपराधः, अगुणः, वैकल्यं, हानिः *f.*, हीनता.—(Malady, disorder) रोगः, व्याधिः *m.*, आमयः, पीडा, अस्वास्थ्यं.

INFIRMNESS, *s.* जरा, जीर्णिः *f.*, जीर्णता, ज्यानिः *f.*, जीर्णावस्था, क्लैव्यं.

To INFIX, *v. a.* निक्षि in caus. (-क्षापयति -यितुं), निक्षिप्तं -प्तां -प्तं कृ, निधा (c. 3. -दधाति -धातुं), प्रणिधा, निबन्ध् (c. 9. -बध्नाति -बन्द्धुं), निखन् (c. 1. -खनति -ते -नितुं), निरुह् in caus. (-रोपयति -यितुं), निविश् (c. 10. -वेशयति -यितुं).

INFIXED, *p. p.* निक्षिप्तः -प्ता -प्तं, निखातः -ता -तं, निहितः -ता -तं, प्रणिहितः -ता -तं, निबद्धः -द्धा -द्धं, निरूढः -ढा -ढं, निविष्टः -ष्टा -ष्टं, निवेशितः -ता -तं.

To INFLAME, *v. a.* तप् (c. 10. तापयति -यितुं, c. 1. तपति, तप्तुं), सन्तप्, दीप् (c. 10. दीपयति -यितुं), प्रदीप्, आदीप्, सन्दीप्, उपदीप्, ज्वल् (c. 10. ज्वालयति, ज्वलयति -यितुं), दह् (c. 1. दहति, दग्धुं), प्रदह्, सम्प्रदह्, परिदह्, आदह्, समिन्ध् (c. 7. -इन्द्धे -इन्धितुं), सन्धुक्ष् (c. 10. -धुक्षयति -यितुं), अग्निसात्कृ.—(Excite) उद्दीप्, उत्तप्, उत्तिज् (c. 10. -तेजयति -यितुं), समुत्तिज्, उत्सह् (c. 10. -साहयति -यितुं), प्रोत्सह्, प्ररुच् (c. 10. -रोचयति -यितुं).—(Irritate) कुप् (c. 10. कोपयति -यितुं), प्रकुप्, क्रुध् (c. 10. क्रोधयति -यितुं), कोपं जन् (c. 10. जनयति -यितुं).

INFLAMED, *p. p.* तप्तः -प्ता -प्तं, तापितः -ता -तं, सन्तप्तः -प्ता -प्तं, सन्तापितः -ता -तं, दीप्तः -प्ता -प्तं, दीपितः -ता -तं, प्रदीप्तः -प्ता -प्तं, उद्दीप्तः -प्ता -प्तं, ज्वलितः -ता -तं, प्रज्वालितः -ता -तं, समिद्धः -द्धा -द्धं, दग्धः -ग्धा -ग्धं, सन्धुक्षितः -ता -तं.—(Excited) उत्तेजितः -ता -तं, समुत्तेजितः -ता -तं.—(Provoked) प्रकोपितः -ता -तं, प्रकुपितः -ता -तं; 'inflamed with wrath,' कोपज्वलितः -ता -तं, कोपदीप्तः -प्ता -प्तं; 'inflamed with pride' समिद्धदर्पः -र्पा -र्पं; 'to be inflamed,' दह् (c. 4. दह्यति -ते, दग्धुं), दीप् (c. 4. दीप्यते, दीपितुं), ज्वल् (c. 1. ज्वलति -लितुं), समिन्ध् in pass. (-इध्यते).

INFLAMMABILITY, *s.* दाह्यता -त्वं, दहनीयता -त्वं, ज्वलनशीलता, आशुज्वलनीयता, शीघ्रज्वलनीयता, सुखज्वलनीयत्वं, दहनशीलता.

INFLAMMABLE, *a.* दाह्यः -ह्या -ह्यं, दहनीयः -या -यं, ज्वलनीयः -या -यं, ज्वलनशीलः -ला -लं, दहनशीलः -ला -लं, आशुज्वलनीयः -या -यं, शीघ्रज्वलनीयः -या -यं, सुखज्वलनीयः -या -यं, दीपनीयः -या -यं, दीप्यः -प्या -प्यं, ज्वलनार्हः -र्हा -र्हं, दाहात्मकः -का -कं.

INFLAMMATION, *s.* (The act) तापनं, सन्तापनं, दीपनं, प्रदीपनं, उद्दीपनं, दहनं, दाहनं, ज्वलनं.—(State of heat) दाहः, तापः, सन्तापः, उपतापः, अभितापः, उत्तापः, विदाहः, शोषः, प्लोषः.—(Internal heat) अन्तर्दाहः, अन्तर्ज्वलनं; 'he died of inflammation,' जातदाहो व्यपद्यत.—(Morbid heat) उपतापः, दाहः, उपतप्ता *m.* (प्तृ), तापकः, स्पर्शः; 'inflammation of the glands of the neck,' गलगण्डमाला; 'of the eye,' सिरोत्पातः.

INFLAMMATORY, *a.* (Inflaming) तापकः -का -कं, तापी -पिनी -पि (न्), उपतापी &c., तापनः -नी -नं, दाहकः -का -कं, दीपकः -का -कं, दीपनः -ना -नं, प्रदीपनः -नी -नं, उद्दीपकः -का -कं, दाहजनकः -का -कं, दाहोत्पादकः -का -कं, दाहकारकः -का -कं, तापजनकः -का -कं, तापकरः -री -रं.—(Accompanied with inflammation) दाहवान् -वती -वत् (त्), सदाहः -हा -हं, दाहयुक्तः -क्ता -क्तं, दाहविशिष्टः -ष्टा -ष्टं, दाहिकः -की -कं, सतापः -पा -पं, तापी -पिनी &c., उपतापी &c., दाह in comp.; as, 'inflammatory fever,' दाहज्वरः.

To INFLATE, *v. a.* ध्मा (c. 1. धमति, ध्मातुं), आध्मा, समाध्मा, प्रध्मा, उपध्मा.—(Distend with air) वातेन पृ (c. 10. पूरयति -यितुं), वातफुल्लं -ल्लां -ल्लं कृ, वायुपूरितं -तां -तं कृ, श्वासेन पृ.—(Swell) स्फाय् (c. 10. स्फावयति -यितुं), श्वि (c. 10. श्वाययति -यितुं), विस्तृ (c. 10. -स्तारयति -यितुं), स्फीतीकृ.—(Puff up) दर्पाध्मातं -तां -तं कृ, उद्धतीकृ, उन्मत्तीकृ.

INFLATED, *p. p.* ध्मातः -ता -तं, आध्मातः -ता -तं, समाध्मातः -ता -तं, वातपूरितः -ता -तं, वायुपूर्णः -र्णा -र्णं, श्वासपूरितः -ता -तं, वातफुल्लः -ल्ला -ल्लं, स्फीतः -ता -तं; 'inflated with pride,' दर्पाध्मातः -ता -तं, मदाध्मातः -ता -तं, दर्पोद्धतः -ता -तं, मदोद्धतः -ता -तं; 'to be inflated,' ध्मा in pass. (ध्मायते), आध्मा, वातेन पृ in pass. (पूर्य्यते).

INFLATION, *s.* (The act) आध्मानं, समाध्मानं, ध्मानं, वातपूरणं, श्वासपूरणं.—(State) ध्मातत्वं, आध्मातत्वं, वायुध्मातता, वातपूर्णता, वातफुल्लता.—(State of being puffed up with pride) दर्पाध्मातत्वं, मदाध्मातत्वं, मदोद्धतिः *f.*

To INFLECT, *v. a.* (Bend) नम् (c. 10. नामयति -यितुं), अवनम्, आनम्, नम्रीकृ, आवृज् (c. 10. -वर्जयति -यितुं), वक्रीकृ.—(In grammar) आख्या (c. 2. -ख्याति -तुं), शब्दरूपं कृ, रूप् (c. 10. रूपयति -यितुं), विभक्तिं कृ.

INFLECTED, *p. p.* नतः -ता -तं, नामितः -ता -तं, आनतः -ता -तं, अवभुग्नः -ग्ना -ग्नं, विभुग्नः -ग्ना -ग्नं.—(In grammar) आख्यातः -ता -तं, सविभक्तिः -क्तिः -क्ति, कृतविभक्तिः -क्तिः -क्ति.

INFLECTION, *s.* (Act of bending) नतिः *f.*, आनतिः *f.*, नम्रीकरणं, वक्रीकरणं, अवकुञ्चनं.—(In grammar) विभक्तिः *f.*, विभक्तिकार्य्यं, व्यक्तिः *f.*, रूपं, रूपान्तरं, अवगृह्यं, लिङ्गकार्य्यं, कार्य्यं; 'series of inflections,' रूपावलिः *f.*

INFLECTIVE, *a.* नम्रीकरणक्षमः -मा -मं, वक्रीकरणक्षमः -मा -मं.

INFLEXIBILITY, INFLEXIBLENESS, *s.* अनमनीयता, सुदृढता, काठिन्यं, कठोरता, धीरता, धैर्य्यं, दृढसङ्कल्पत्वं, हृदयकाठिन्यं, निर्विकल्पता, संहननं, आग्रहः.

INFLEXIBLE, *a.* (That cannot be bent) अनमनीयः -या -यं, अनाम्यः -म्या -म्यं, अकुञ्चनीयः -या -यं.—(Firm, hard) दृढः -ढा -ढं, सुदृढः -ढा -ढं, कठिनः -ना -नं, कठोरः -रा -रं, संहतः -ता -तं.—(In mind, purpose, &c.) दृढसङ्कल्पः -ल्पा -ल्पं, स्थिरनिश्चयः -या -यं, स्थिरमतिः -तिः -ति, अनाराधनीयः -या -यं, कठिनहृदयः -या -यं, पाषाणहृदयः -या -यं, निर्विकल्पः -ल्पा -ल्पं, आग्रही -हिणी -हि (न्), धीरः -रा -रं.

INFLEXIBLY, *adv.* सुदृढं, दृढचेतसा, सुस्थिरं, दृढनिश्चयपूर्व्वं, निर्विकल्पं.

To INFLICT, *v. a.* प्रणी (c. 1. -णयति -णेतुं), सम्प्रणी, प्रवृत् (c. 10. -वर्त्तयति -यितुं), प्रयुज् (c. 10. -योजयति -यितुं), आचर् (c. 1. -चरति -रितुं), विधा (c. 3. -दधाति -धातुं), कृ (c. 8. करोति, कर्त्तुं), पत् (c. 10.

पातयति -यितुं); 'to inflict punishment,' दण्डं प्रणी, दण्डं कृ.

INFLICTED, *p. p.* प्रणीतः -ता -तं, सम्प्रणीतः -ता -तं, प्रवर्त्तितः -ता -तं, प्रयुक्तः -क्ता -क्तं, आचरितः -ता -तं, विहितः -ता -तं, कृतः -ता -तं.

INFLICTER, *s.* (Of punishment) दण्डप्रणेता *m.* (तृ), दण्डप्रवर्त्तकः, दण्डभृत् *m.*

INFLICTION, *s.* प्रणयनं, प्रवर्त्तनं, प्रयोगः, आचरणं, विधानं, करणं; 'of punishment,' दण्डप्रणयनं, दण्डयोगः, दण्डप्रयोगः, दण्डप्रवर्त्तनं, दण्डाधानं, दण्डोपधानं, दण्डपातनं, दण्डकरणं.

INFLUENCE, *s.* प्रभावः, अधिकारः, गौरवं, वशं, शक्तिः *f.*, बलं, भारः, प्रभवः, प्रभुता, कर्तृत्वं, क्षमता, प्रतापः, सामर्थ्यं, गुणः, कार्य्यकारित्वं, गुणकारिता, व्यापकता, व्याप्तिः *f.*; 'the influence of love,' कामाधिकारः; 'under the influence of love,' कामवशः -शा -शं, कामाधिष्ठितः -ता -तं, कामोपहतः -ता -तं; 'through the influence of love,' कामवशात्; 'through the influence of alarm,' साध्वसवशात्; 'planetary influence,' ग्रहावेशः.

To INFLUENCE, *v. a.* अधिकृ, प्रभू, अधिष्ठा (c. 1. -तिष्ठति -ष्ठातुं), उपहन् (c. 2. -हन्ति -न्तुं), वशीकृ.—(Induce, move to action) प्रवृत् (c. 10. -वर्त्तयति -यितुं), प्रेर् (c. 10. -ईरयति -यितुं), नियुज् (c. 10. -योजयति -यितुं), प्रयुज्, अनुनी (c. 1. -नयति -नेतुं), आकृष् (c. 1. -कर्षति -क्रष्टुं), प्रोत्सह् (c. 10. -साहयति -यितुं).

INFLUENCED, *p. p.* अधिष्ठितः -ता -तं, अधिकृतः -ता -तं, उपहतः -ता -तं, प्रेरितः -ता -तं, प्रवर्त्तितः -ता -तं, नियुक्तः -क्ता -क्तं, नियोजितः -ता -तं, आकृष्टः -ष्टा -ष्टं, प्रोत्साहितः -ता -तं, वशः -शा -शं in comp.; 'influenced by love,' कामाधिष्ठितः -ता -तं, कामोपहतः -ता -तं, कामवशः -शा -शं; 'influenced by avarice,' लोभाकृष्टः -ष्टा -ष्टं.

INFLUENTIAL, *a.* गुरुः -र्व्वी -रु, सगौरवः -वा -वं, गुरुप्रभावः -वा -वं, सप्रभावः -वा -वं, प्रभविष्णुः -ष्णुः -ष्णु, भारी -रिणी -रि (न्), प्रबलः -ला -लं, शक्तिमान् -मती -मत् (त्), अधिकारी -रिणी -रि (न्), प्रतापी -पिनी -पि (न्).

INFLUENTIALLY, *adv.* प्रभावेण, सप्रभावं, गौरवेण, सगौरवं, सभारं.

INFLUENZA, *s.* साधारणपीनसरोगः, साधारणश्लेष्मरोगः, सन्निपातकः.

INFLUX, *s.* आगमः -मनं, प्रवाहः, अन्तःप्रवाहः, अन्तर्वहनं, प्रस्रवणं, अन्तःस्रवणं, अन्तर्गमनं.

To INFOLD, *v. a.* वेष्ट् (c. 1. वेष्टते -ष्टितुं), आवेष्ट्, परिवेष्ट्, संवेष्ट्, आछद् (c. 10. -छादयति -यितुं), परिछद्, पिधा (c. 3. -दधाति -धातुं), कोशेन परिवेष्ट्, कोशस्थं -स्थां -स्थं कृ, वासनस्थं -स्थां -स्थं कृ.—(Clasp with the arms, embrace) भुजाभ्यां पीड् (c. 10. पीडयति -यितुं), आलिङ्ग् (c. 1. -लिङ्गति -ङ्गितुं), समालिङ्ग्, आश्लिष् (c. 4. -श्लिष्यति -श्लेष्टुं).

INFOLDED, *p. p.* आवेष्टितः -ता -तं, वेष्टितः -ता -तं, परिवेष्टितः -ता -तं, आछन्नः -न्ना -न्नं, कोशस्थः -स्था -स्थं, वासनस्थः -स्था -स्थं, अवगुण्ठितः -ता -तं.

To INFOLIATE, *v. a.* सपत्रीकृ, सपर्णीकृ, सदलीकृ, पत्रान्वितं -तां -तं कृ.

To INFORM, *v. a.* (Make known, tell) ज्ञा in caus. (ज्ञापयति, ज्ञपयति -यितुं), विज्ञा, निविद् (c. 10. -वेदयति -यितुं), आविद्, समाविद्, विद्, बुध् (c. 10. बोधयति -यितुं), प्रबुध्, प्रतिबुध्, अवबुध्, सूच् (c. 10. सूचयति -यितुं), संसूच्, आख्या (c. 2. -ख्याति -तुं or caus. -ख्यापयति -यितुं), समाख्या, ख्या, कथ् (c. 10. कथयति -यितुं), अवगम् (c. 10. -गमयति -यितुं), शंस् (c. 1. शंसति -सितुं), प्रत्यादिश् (c. 6. -दिशति -देष्टुं), सन्दिश्, आदिश्, श्रु (c. 10. श्रावयति -यितुं), कर्णगोचरीकृ.—(Inform against) अपराधं सूच्, प्राड्विवाकसाक्षाद् आह्वे (c. 1. -ह्वयति -ह्वातुं), उपनिधा (c. 3. -दधाति -धातुं), पैशुन्यं कृ, पिशुनो भू.

INFORMAL, *a.* विधिविरुद्धः -द्धा -द्धं, अविधिः -धिः -धि, विधिघ्नः -घ्नी -घ्नं, अवैधिकः -की -कं, नियमविरुद्धः -द्धा -द्धं, रीतिविरुद्धः &c., अव्यवस्थितः -ता -तं, उत्सूत्रः -त्रा -त्रं, अमर्य्यादः -दा -दं, अयोग्यः -ग्या -ग्यं, अयथार्थः -र्था -र्थं.

INFORMALITY, *s.* अविधिः *m.*, विधिविरोधः, विध्यतिक्रमः, अव्यवस्था, उत्क्रमः, अविधानं, अनियमः, अरीतिः *f.*, विधिभङ्गः, नियमभङ्गः, अमर्य्यादा, विसूत्रता.

INFORMALLY, *adv.* अविधिवत्, अविधितस्, अविधानतस्, विधिविरुद्धं, अयथाविधि, नियमविरोधेन, अक्रमेण, अविधिपूर्व्वं.

INFORMANT, *s.* ज्ञापकः, विज्ञापकः, आवेदकः, निवेदकः, बोधकः, प्रबोधकः, सूचकः, सूची *m.* (न्), ख्यापकः, आख्यायकः.

INFORMATION, *s.* विज्ञप्तिः, विज्ञापनं, ज्ञप्तिः, ज्ञापनं, ज्ञाप्तिः *f.*, विज्ञाप्तिः *f.*, निवेदनं, आवेदनं, विदितं, बोधः -धनं, प्रबोधः -धनं, सूचनं, संसूचनं, आख्यानं, ख्यापनं, प्रत्यादेशः.—(Intelligence, news) वार्त्ता, समाचारः, वृत्तान्तः, सन्देशः, सन्दिष्टं, संवादः, सूचना.—(Knowledge) ज्ञानं, विज्ञानं, बोधः, अवगमः.—(In law, intelligence of crime) अपराधसूचनं -ना, अन्यायसूचनं -ना, स्वयमुक्तिः *f.*, पैशुन्यं, उपनिधानं.

INFORMED, *p. p.* विज्ञप्तः -प्ता -प्तं, विज्ञापितः -ता -तं, ज्ञापितः -ता -तं, ज्ञप्तः -प्ता -प्तं, ज्ञपितः -ता -तं, अनुज्ञापितः -ता -तं, आवेदितः -ता -तं, निवेदितः -ता -तं, बोधितः -ता -तं, प्रबोधितः -ता -तं, सूचितः -ता -तं, संसूचितः -ता -तं, आख्यातः -ता -तं, समाख्यातः -ता -तं, प्रत्यादिष्टः -ष्टा -ष्टं, सन्दिष्टः -ष्टा -ष्टं, गृहीतार्थः -र्था -र्थं.

INFORMER, *s.* सूचकः, सूची *m.* (न्), पिशुनः, कर्णजपः, कर्णेजपः, बोधकः, उपनिधाता *m.* (तृ), अपराधसूचकः, अन्यायसूचकः.—(Conveyer of intelligence) वार्त्तिकः, वार्त्तायनः.

INFORMITY, *s.* निराकारत्वं, अनाकारत्वं, अरूपता, विरूपता, वैरूप्यं, निरवयवत्वं.

INFRACTION, *s.* भङ्गः, भञ्जनं, खण्डनं, भेदः, अतिक्रमः, व्यतिक्रमः -मणं, लङ्घनं, उल्लङ्घनं; 'of an agreement,' संविद्व्यतिक्रमः; 'of a law,' व्यवस्थालङ्घनं.

INFRANGIBLE, *a.* अभेद्यः -द्या -द्यं, अभेदनीयः -या -यं, अखण्डनीयः -या -यं, अलङ्घ्यः -ङ्घ्या -ङ्घ्यं, अनतिक्रमणीयः -या -यं, अलङ्घनीयः -या -यं.

INFREQUENCY, *s.* विरलता, वैरल्यं, अबहुत्वं, अनभीक्ष्णता, अनाभीक्ष्ण्यं, अनित्यता, कादाचित्कत्वं, क्षाणिकत्वं, अपौनःपुन्यं, असामान्यं.

INFREQUENT, *a.* विरलः -ला -लं, विरलागतः -ता -तं, अनभीक्ष्णः -क्ष्णा -क्ष्णं, अबहुशो वर्त्तमानः -ना -नं, अनित्यः -त्या -त्यं, अनैत्यिकः -की -कं, कादाचित्कः -त्का -त्कं, क्षाणिकः -का -कं, अपौनःपुनिकः -की -कं, असततः -ता -तं, असामान्यः -न्या -न्यं.

INFREQUENTLY, *adv.* अबहुशस्, अनभीक्ष्णं, अनित्यं, विरलं, कदाचित्.

To INFRINGE, *v. a.* (Break) भञ्ज् (c. 7. भनक्ति, भंक्तुं), खण्ड् (c. 10. खण्डयति -यितुं), भिद् (c. 7. भिनत्ति, भेत्तुं), भङ्गं कृ.—(Violate) अतिक्रम् (c. 1. -क्रामति -क्रमितुं), व्यतिक्रम्, लङ्घ् (c. 10. लङ्घयति -यितुं), उल्लङ्घ्, विलङ्घ्, लुप् (c. 10. लोपयति -यितुं), विलुप्, अतिचर् (c. 1. -चरति -रितुं), अतिवृत् (c. 1. -वर्त्तते -र्त्तितुं).

INFRINGED, *p. p.* भग्नः -ग्ना -ग्नं, लङ्घितः -ता -तं, उल्लङ्घितः -ता -तं, अतिक्रान्तः -न्ता -न्तं, लुप्तः -प्ता -प्तं, खण्डितः -ता -तं, विच्छिन्नः -न्ना -न्नं.

INFRINGER, *s.* भङ्गकरः, भञ्जकः, भङ्गकारी *m.* (न्), लङ्घनकारी, अतिक्रमी *m.* (न्), विच्छेदकः, लोपकरः, अतिवर्त्ती *m.* (न्).

INFRINGEMENT, *s.* भङ्गः, भञ्जनं, भेदः, खण्डनं, अतिक्रमः -मणं, व्यतिक्रमः -मणं, लङ्घनं, उल्लङ्घनं, लोपः -पनं, विच्छेदः, अतिवर्त्तनं; 'of a compact,' संविद्व्यतिक्रमः, नियमातिक्रमः, नियमभङ्गः; 'of a law,' व्यवस्थालङ्घनं, व्यवस्थालोपः.

INFURIATE, *a.* कोपाकुलः -ला -लं, क्रोधाकुलः -ला -लं, रोषवेगाकुलः -ला -लं, संरब्धः -ब्धा -ब्धं, क्रोधान्धः -न्धा -न्धं, उन्मादसंरब्धः -ब्धा -ब्धं, मदोत्कटः

-टा -टं, क्रोधविक्षिप्तः -प्ता -प्तं.

To INFURIATE, *v. a.* कोपाकुलीकृ, रोषवेगेन व्याकुलीकृ, संरब्धीकृ.

To INFUSCATE, *v. a.* तिमिर (nom. तिमिरयति -यितुं), तिमिरीकृ, कृष्णीकृ, श्यामीकृ.

To INFUSE, *v. a.* (Pour in, mix) आसिच् (c. 6. -सिञ्चति -सेक्तुं), निषिच्, सिच्, प्रक्षिप् (c. 6. -क्षिपति -क्षेप्तुं), निक्षिप्, मिश्र् (c. 10. मिश्रयति -यितुं), सम्मिश्र् संसृज् (c. 6. -सृजति -स्रष्टुं), मिश्रीकृ, मिश्रणं कृ.—(Introduce) निविश् (c. 10. -वेशयति -यितुं), प्रविश्, आविश्; 'infuse into the mind,' चित्ते निविश्, उपदिश् (c. 6. -दिशति -देष्टुं), उपदेशं कृ.—(Steep) वास् (c. 10. वासयति -यितुं), क्वथ् (c. 1. क्वथति -थितुं), भू (c. 10. भावयति -यितुं).

INFUSED, *p. p.* आसिक्तः -क्ता -क्तं, सिक्तः -क्ता -क्तं, प्रक्षिप्तः -प्ता -प्तं, निक्षिप्तः -प्ता -प्तं, मिश्रितः -ता -तं, व्याप्तः -प्ता -प्तं, संसृष्टः -ष्टा -ष्टं, निवेशितः -ता -तं, विलीनः -ना -नं.—(Steeped) वासितः -ता -तं, भावितः -ता -तं.

INFUSIBLE, *a.* (That may be infused) प्रक्षेपणीयः -या -यं, मिश्रणीयः -या -यं, निवेशनीयः -या -यं.—(Incapable of fusion) अद्राव्यः -व्या -व्यं, अद्रवणीयः -या -यं.

INFUSION, *s.* (Act of pouring in) आसेकः, आसेचनं, प्रक्षेपः -पणं, मिश्रणं, मिश्रीकरणं, सम्मिश्रणं.—(Act of introducing) निवेशनं, प्रवेशनं.—(Suggestion, instruction) उपन्यासः, प्रबोधः -धनं, उपदेशः.—(Process of steeping) वासनं, भावनं, क्वथनं, निष्क्वाथः.—(The liquor in which plants are steeped) कषायः -यं, रसः, निर्यासः, निर्यूहः, क्वाथः.

INGATHERING, *s.* शस्यसङ्ग्रहः, शस्यसञ्चयः, शस्यसङ्ग्रहकालः.

INGELABLE, *a.* अघनीकरणीयः -या -यं, घनीकरणाशक्यः -क्या -क्यं.

To INGEMINATE, *v. a.* द्विगुणीकृ, द्विगुण (nom. द्विगुणयति -यितुं), पुनःपुनः कृ, वारं वारं कृ, द्विवारं कृ, मुहुर्मुहुः कृ, असकृत् कृ.

INGEMINATE, *a.* द्विगुणितः -ता -तं, पुनःपुनः कृतः -ता -तं.

INGEMINATION, *s.* द्विगुणीकरणं, पुनःपुनःकरणं, द्विवारकरणं, असकृत्करणं.

INGENERATE, INGENERATED, *a.* अन्तर्जातः -ता -तं, सहजः -जा -जं, निजः -जा -जं.

INGENIOUS, *a.* (Possessed of invention, prompt to invent) युक्तिमान् -मती -मत् (त्), यौक्तिकः -की -कं, उपायज्ञः -ज्ञा -ज्ञं, उपायी -यिनी -यि (न्), कल्पकः -का -कं, परिकल्पकः -का -कं, विज्ञः -ज्ञा -ज्ञं, चतुरः -रा -रं, निपुणः -णा -णं, सुप्रयोगवान् -वती -वत् (त्), विदग्धः -ग्धा -ग्धं, प्रवीणः -णा -णं, सूक्ष्मबुद्धिः -द्धिः -द्धि, तीक्ष्णबुद्धिः -द्धिः -द्धि, पटुः -टुः -टु, उपकारकः -का -कं, व्यवसायी -यिनी -यि (न्), विचक्षणः -णा -णं, दक्षः -क्षा -क्षं.—(Of curious design or structure) सुयुक्तिकृतः -ता -तं, सुयुक्तिनिष्पन्नः -न्ना -न्नं, सुप्रयोगकृतः -ता -तं, सुप्रयुक्तः -क्ता -क्तं.

INGENIOUSLY, *adv.* युक्त्या, सुयुक्त्या, सुप्रयोगेन, विज्ञवत्, चातुर्य्येण, चतुरं, निपुणं, निपुणवत्, विचक्षणवत्, सपाटवं, दाक्ष्येण, दक्षवत्.

INGENUITY, INGENIOUSNESS, *s.* युक्तिः *f.*, सुयुक्तिः *f.*, सुप्रयोगः, युक्तिमत्त्वं, कल्पना, कल्पनाशक्तिः *f.*, कल्पकत्वं, विज्ञता, उपायज्ञता, चतुरता, चातुर्य्यं, निपुणता, नैपुण्यं, सूक्ष्मता, बुद्धिसूक्ष्मता, बुद्धितीक्ष्णता, पटुता, पाटवं, विदग्धता, वैदग्ध्यं, प्रवीणता, वैचक्षण्यं, दक्षता, दाक्ष्यं, कला, मनुष्यकला, व्यवसायः.

INGENUOUS, *a.* निष्कपटः -टा -टं, अकपटः -टा -टं, विमलात्मा -त्मा -त्म (न्), विमलार्थकः -का -कं, मायाहीनः -ना -नं, अमायः -या -यं, अमायिकः -की -कं, निर्व्याजः -जा -जं, अवक्रः -क्रा -क्रं, सरलः -ला -लं, शुद्धमतिः -तिः -ति, अजिह्मः -ह्मा -ह्मं, ऋजुः -जुः -जु, निर्व्यलीकः -का -कं, दक्षिणः -णा -णं, अगूढभावः -वा -वं, शुचिः -चिः -चि, शुचिमनाः -नाः -नः (स्), निर्म्मलचित्तः -त्ता -त्तं, अकृपणः -णा -णं.—(Generous, noble) उदारः -रा -रं, उदारचेताः -ताः -तः (स्), महानुभावः -वा -वं.

INGENUOUSLY, *adv.* निष्कपटं, कपटं विना, अवक्रं, अमायया, सरलं, सरलवत्, सारल्येन, निर्व्यलीकं, निर्व्याजं, दाक्षिण्येन, उदारवत्.

INGENUOUSNESS, *s.* उदारत्वं, औदार्य्यं, कपटहीनता, निष्कपटत्वं, निष्कापट्यं, अकापट्यं, अमाया, मायाहीनता, सरलता, सारल्यं, अवक्रता, अजिह्मता, ऋजुता, आर्जवं, निर्व्यलीकता, दाक्षिण्यं, शुचिता, विमलात्मता, चित्तनिर्म्मलत्वं, भावागूढता, शुद्धमतित्वं, भावशुद्धत्वं, अव्याजः, अकापेक्ष्यं, उदीर्णता.

INGLORIOUS, *a.* अयशस्वी -स्विनी -स्वि (न्), अयशस्यः -स्या -स्यं, अकीर्त्तिमान् -मती -मत् (त्), अकीर्त्तिकरः -री -रं, अकीर्त्तिदः -दा -दं, अयशस्करः -री -रं, अपयशस्करः -री -रं, अख्यातः -ता -तं, अश्रीमान् -मती -मत् (त्), निःश्रीकः -का -कं, अपमानजनकः -का -कं, कलङ्ककरः -री -रं, निःप्रतापः -पा -पं, लज्जाकरः -री -रं.

INGLORIOUSLY, *adv.* अयशस्यं, सापमानं, सकलङ्कं, अकीर्त्तिपूर्व्वं.

INGOT, *s.* तूलिकाविलीनः सुवर्णादिपिण्डः, तूलिकाकारः सुवर्णरूप्यादिपिण्डः, सुवर्णादिकीलः; 'ingot mould,' तूलिका, तुलिका, ईषीका, ईषिका.

To INGRAFT, *v. a.* एकवृक्षशाखायाम् अन्यवृक्षपल्लवं निविश् (c. 10. -वेशयति -यितुं), एकवृक्षपल्लवम् अन्यवृक्षपल्लवेन संयुज् (c. 10. -योजयति -यितुं).

INGRAFTED, *p. p.* निवेशितः -ता -तं, निहितः -ता -तं, संलग्नीकृतः -ता -तं.

INGRAFTMENT, *s.* एकवृक्षशाखायाम् अन्यवृक्षपल्लवनिवेशनं, संलग्नीकरणं.

INGRATE, *a.* अकृतज्ञः -ज्ञा -ज्ञं, कृतघ्नः -घ्नी -घ्नं, अकृतवेदी -दिनी -दि (न्), अनुपकृतज्ञः -ज्ञा -ज्ञं, उपकारविस्मर्त्ता -र्त्री -र्त्तृ (र्त्तृ), कृतनाशकः -की -कं.

To INGRATIATE, *v. a.* (Conciliate favor for one's self) आराध् (c. 10. -राधयति -यितुं), अनुरञ्ज् (c. 10. -रञ्जयति -यितुं), सान्त्व् (c. 10. सान्त्वयति -यितुं), प्रसद् (c. 10. -सादयति -यितुं), प्रसाध् (c. 10. -साधयति -यितुं), लल् (c. 10. लालयति -यितुं), अनुग्रहं प्राप् (c. 5. -आप्नोति -आप्तुं), अनुरागं कृ, स्नेहं कृ, अनुरुध् (c. 4. -रुध्यति -रोद्धुं).

INGRATITUDE, *s.* अकृतज्ञता, कृतघ्नता, उपकृतघ्नता, उपकारविस्मृतिः *f.*, उपकारविस्मरणं, उपकृतविस्मृतिः *f.*, कृतपूर्व्वनाशनं, कृतनाशनं, उपकारनाशनं, कृतपूर्व्वविस्मृतिः *f.*, अनुपकारिता, निरुपकारिता, प्रत्युपकाराभावः.

INGREDIENT, *s.* भागः, अंशः, द्रव्यं, साधनद्रव्यं, उपकरणं, अङ्गं, वस्तु; 'any thing mixed as an ingredient in drugs in the course of decoction,' प्रक्षिप्तं, भावितं.

INGRESS, *s.* प्रवेशः -शनं, निवेशः -शनं, आवेशः -शनं, समावेशः, वेशः -शनं, वेषणं, वेशिका, सन्निवेशः, सञ्चारः; 'of the sun into a sign,' संक्रान्तिः *f.*, संक्रमः; 'of a luminary at an eclipse,' वेधः.

INGUINAL, *a.* वंक्षणसम्बन्धी -न्धिनी -न्धि (न्), वंक्षणीयः -या -यं.

To INGULF, *v. a.* *See To* ENGULPH.

To INGURGITATE, *v. a.* जलादि बहुशो गॄ (c. 6. गिरति, गरितुं -रीतुं) or निगॄ or अवगॄ or ग्रस् (c. 1. ग्रसते -सितुं).

INGUSTABLE, *a.* रसनेन्द्रियातीतः -ता -तं, रसनेन्द्रियाविषयः -या -यं.

To INHABIT, *v. a.* वस् (c. 1. वसति, वस्तुं), निवस्, प्रतिवस् all with loc. c., आवस्, समावस्, अधिवस्, अधिनिवस्, अध्यावस्, उपवस्, सन्निवस् with acc. c. or loc. c., अध्यास् (c. 2. -आस्ते -आसितुं), समध्यास् with acc. c., आस् with loc. c., आश्रि (c. 1. -श्रयति -ते -यितुं) with acc. c., सेव् (c. 1. सेवते -वितुं), निषेव्, उपसेव् with acc. c., अधिष्ठा (c. 1. -तिष्ठति -ष्ठातुं) with acc. c. or loc. c., स्था with loc. c., जुष् (c. 6. जुषते, जोषितुं) with acc. c., निली (c. 4. -लीयते -लेतुं), वासं कृ.

INHABITABLE, *a.* वस्तव्यः -व्या -व्यं, वास्तव्यः -व्या -व्यं, वासतेयः -यी -यं.

वसनीयः -या -यं, आवसनीयः -या -यं, निवसनीयः -या -यं, वासयोग्यः -ग्या -ग्यं, वासक्षमः -मा -मं, वासार्हः -र्हा -र्हं, आजीव्यः -व्या -व्यं, उपजीव्यः -व्या -व्यं.

INHABITANT, *s.* वासी *m.* (न्), निवासी *m.*, वासकारी *m.* (न्), निवासकारी *m.*, निलायी *m.* (न्), स्थायी *m.* (न्), अवस्थायी *m.*, स्थः or संस्थः in comp.

INHABITATION, *s.* वासः, निवासः, निवसनं, वसतिः *f.*, निवसतिः *f.*, निलयः -यनं.

INHABITED, *p. p.* उषितः -ता -तं, अध्युषितः -ता -तं, अध्यासितः -ता -तं, सेवितः -ता -तं, अधिष्ठितः -ता -तं, निषेवितः -ता -तं, जुष्टः -ष्टा -ष्टं; 'formerly inhabited by cattle,' उषितङ्गवीनः -ना -नं; 'an inhabited country,' जनपदः, जानपदः.

INHABITING, *part.* वसन् -सन्ती -सती -सत् (त्), निवसन् -सन्ती -सत् (त्), निवासी -सिनी -सि (न्), कृतालयः -या -यं, आश्रितः -ता -तं, समाश्रितः -ता -तं, सेवी -विनी -वि (न्), अधिशयानः -ना -नं.

To INHALE, *v. a.* श्वस् (c. 2. श्वसिति -तुं), निश्वस्, उरःस्थानं or वक्षःस्थानं or हृदयस्थानं श्वासेन पृ (c. 10. पूरयति -यितुं) or वायुना पृ, श्वासं कृ, निपा (c. 1. -पिबति -पातुं).

INHARMONIOUS, *a.* विस्वरः -रा -रं, अपस्वरः -रा -रं, कर्कशस्वनः -ना -नं.

To INHERE, *v. n.* निष्ठा (c. 1. -तिष्ठति -ष्ठातुं), अन्तःस्था, अधिष्ठा, अन्तर्भू, अन्तर्वृत् (c. 1. -वर्त्तते -र्त्तितुं), अन्तर् ज्ञा in pass. (ज्ञायते), सहजः -जा -जं भू.

INHERENCE, INHERENCY, *s.* निष्ठा -ष्ठानं, निष्ठितिः *f.*, अन्तःस्थितिः, अधिष्ठितिः *f.*, अधिष्ठानं, संस्था, संस्थितिः *f.*, स्थितिः *f.*, अन्तर्भावः, अन्तर्वर्त्तनं, अन्तर्वृत्तिः *f.*, अनुषङ्गः -ङ्गिका, निरूढिः *f.*, समवायः, समवायसम्बन्धः.

INHERENT, *a.* निष्ठः -ष्ठा -ष्ठं, निष्ठितः -ता -तं, अन्तर्भवः -वा -वं, अन्तर्भूतः -ता -तं, अन्तर्जातः -ता -तं, अन्तरस्थः -स्था -स्थं, अन्तःस्थः -स्था -स्थं, अन्तःस्थायी -यिनी -यि (न्), अन्तर्वर्त्ती -र्त्तिनी -र्त्ति (न्), निजः -जा -जं, सहजः -जा -जं, निरूढः -ढा -ढं, अनुषङ्गी -ङ्गिनी -ङ्गि (न्), अनुषङ्गिकः -की -कं, आनुषङ्गिकः -की -कं, प्रासङ्गिकः -की -कं, आवेशिकः -की -कं, समवायी -यिनी -यि (न्), समवेतः -ता -तं, व्यस्तः -स्ता -स्तं, समस्तः -स्ता -स्तं; 'inherent in the body,' देहनिष्ठः -ष्ठा -ष्ठं.—(Naturally pertaining to) स्वाभाविकः -की -कं, स्वभावजः -जा -जं, प्रकृतिस्थः -स्था -स्थं, नैसर्गिकः -की -कं, औत्सर्गिकः -की -कं, सांसिद्धिकः -की -कं; 'inherent nature,' अन्तर्भावः, स्वभावः.

To INHERIT, *v. a.* अधिकृ, उत्तरेण or उत्तरम् अधिकृ, वंशक्रमागमेन प्राप् (c. 5. -आप्नोति -आप्तुं) or ग्रह् (c. 9. गृह्णाति, ग्रहीतुं), पितुः प्राप्, पितृतः प्राप्, क्रमागतेन प्राप्, अन्वयागमेन प्राप्, वंशाधिकारेण प्राप्, पारम्पर्य्येण प्राप्, वंशक्रमेण पितुः प्राप्, पैतृकाधिकारं प्राप्, अधिकारी -रिणी -रि भू, उत्तराधिकारी भू, दायादो भू; 'to inherit property,' पैतृकरिक्थं प्राप्, गोत्ररिक्थं प्राप्, क्रमागतरिक्थं प्राप्.

INHERITABLE, *a.* पितृप्राप्यः -प्या -प्यं, पितृपुत्रपरम्पराभोग्यः -ग्या -ग्यं, उत्तराधिकारोपभोग्यः -ग्या -ग्यं, औद्धारिकः -की -कं, दाययोग्यः -ग्या -ग्यं.

INHERITANCE, *s.* (Act of receiving an inheritance) पैतृकरिक्थग्रहणं, रिक्थप्राप्तिः *f.*, अधिकारप्राप्तिः *f.*, रिक्थहरणं, अंशहरणं, रिक्थभागग्रहणं, दायभागप्राप्तिः *f.*—(Right of inheritance) उत्तराधिकारः -रिता, अधिकारः -रिता -त्वं, रिक्थाधिकारः, दायत्वं, दायाधिकारः.—(Heritage, estate, patrimony) पैतृकरिक्थं, पैतृकं रिक्थं or ऋक्थं, गोत्ररिक्थं, पैतृकधनं, गोत्रधनं, दायः, ऋक्थभागः, पैतृकं, औद्धारिकं, क्रमागतरिक्थं, क्रमागतधनं.—(Portioning of inheritance) दायविभागः, दायभागः, रिक्थविभागः, उद्धारविभागः, रिक्थवण्टनं; 'to divide an inheritance,' पैतृकरिक्थं भज् (c. 1. भजति -ते, भक्तुं) or विभज्.—(Share of an inheritance) भागः, अंशः, उद्धारः.

INHERITED, *p. p.* पितृप्राप्तः -प्ता -प्तं, पितृगृहीतः -ता -तं, क्रमागमेन प्राप्तः -प्ता -प्तं, क्रमागतः -ता -तं, क्रमायातः -ता -तं, क्रमाद् आगतः -ता -तं, अन्वयागतः -ता -तं, परम्पराप्राप्तः -प्ता -प्तं, परम्परायातः -ता -तं, पारम्पर्य्येणागतः -ता -तं, परम्परीणः -णा -णं.

INHERITOR, *s.* अधिकारी *m.* (न्), उत्तराधिकारी *m.*, दायादः, भागी *m.* (न्), भाक् in comp. (ज्), अंशी *m.* (न्); 'inheritor of property,' धनाधिकारी *m.*, रिक्थभागी *m.* (न्). *See* HEIR.

INHERITRESS, INHERITRIX, *s.* अधिकारिणी, उत्तराधिकारिणी, दायादी.

To INHIBIT, *v. a.* नियम् (c. 1. -यच्छति -यन्तुं), संयम्, निग्रह् (c. 9. -गृह्णाति -ग्रहीतुं), निरुध् (c. 7. -रुणद्धि -रोद्धुं), अवरुध्, वृ (c. 10. वारयति -यितुं), निवृ, निषिध् (c. 1. -षेधति -षेद्धुं).

INHIBITION, *s.* संयमः, निग्रहः, निवारणं, निरोधः, संरोधः, निषेधः.

INHOSPITABLE, *a.* अनातिथेयः -यी -यं, अनातिथ्यः -थ्यी -थ्यं, अतिथिद्वेषी -षिणी -षि (न्), अभ्यागतद्वेषी &c., आतिथ्यविमुखः -खा -खं, सत्कारद्वेषी &c., सत्कारविमुखः -खा -खं, असत्कारशीलः -ला -लं, अभ्यागताननुपकारी -रिणी -रि (न्), अभ्यागताशरणः -णा -णं, अभ्यागताहितः -ता -तं, अभ्यागतानादरी -रिणी -रि (न्).

INHOSPITABLENESS, INHOSPITALITY, *s.* अनातिथ्यं, अनातिथेयत्वं, अनतिथित्वं, असत्कारः, असत्कर्म्म *n.* (न्), अतिथिद्वेषः, अभ्यागतद्वेषः, अतिथ्यनादरः, अतिथ्यसत्कारः.

INHOSPITABLY, *adv.* अनातिथेयं, अनातिथ्यपूर्व्वं, असत्कारेण, असत्कारपुरःसरं, अतिथिद्वेषिवत्.

INHUMAN, *a.* अमनुष्यः -ष्या -ष्यं, अमनुष्यधर्म्मा -र्म्मा -र्म्म (न्), मनुष्यविधर्म्मा &c.—(Cruel) निर्दयः -या -यं, दयाहीनः -ना -नं, क्रूरः -रा -रं, क्रूरकर्म्मा -र्म्मा -र्म्म (न्), निष्ठुरः -रा -रं, निष्कृपः -पा -पं, निष्करुणः -णा -णं, निर्घृणः -णा -णं, राक्षसधर्म्मा &c., कठिनहृदयः -या -यं.

INHUMANITY, *s.* अमनुष्यत्वं, निर्दयता -त्वं, क्रूरता, क्रौर्य्यं, दयाहीनता, निष्ठुरता, नैष्ठुर्य्यं, निष्करुणता, कृपाहीनता, दौरात्म्यं.

INHUMANLY, *adv.* अमनुष्यवत्, निर्दयं, निष्ठुरं, नैष्ठुर्य्येण, क्रूरवत्, क्रौर्य्येण, निष्करुणं, राक्षसवत्, निष्कृपं, दुरात्मवत्.

INHUMATION, *s.* भूमिखननं, निखननं, निखातत्वं, भूमौ निखननं, भूमिसमर्पणं, भूमिनिक्षेपः, भूमिनिवेशनं, क्षितिन्यासः.

To INHUME, *v. a.* भूमौ निखन् (c. 1. -खनति -नितुं) or निधा (c. 3. -दधाति -धातुं) or स्था in caus. (स्थापयति -यितुं) or समृ in caus. (-अर्पयति -यितुं) or निक्षिप् (c. 6. -क्षिपति -क्षेप्तुं) or न्यस् (c. 4. -अस्यति -असितुं).

INIMICAL, *a.* वैरी -रिणी -रि (न्), अहितः -ता -तं, अहितकारी -रिणी -रि (न्), द्वेषी -षिणी -षि (न्), द्वेषणः -णा -णं, विद्वेषी &c., विद्वेष्टा -ष्ट्री -ष्टृ (ष्टृ), सवैरः -रा -रं, अपथ्यकारी &c., अपकारी &c., प्रतिकूलः -ला -लं, विरोधी -धिनी -धि (न्), विपक्षः -क्षा -क्षं, प्रतिपक्षः -क्षा -क्षं, द्रोहबुद्धिः -द्धिः -द्धि, द्रोहवृत्तिः -त्तिः -त्ति, शात्रवः -वी -वं, शात्रवीयः -यी -यं, अहितमनाः -नाः -नः (स्), अहितशीलः -ला -लं, अमित्रः -त्रा -त्रं, अस्निग्धः -ग्धा -ग्धं, असुहृद् *m. f. n.*, अनुपकारी -रिणी -रि (न्), अननुकूलः -ला -लं, विपरीतः -ता -तं.

INIMICALLY, *adv.* शत्रुवत्, अहितवत्, सवैरं, अमित्रवत्, अस्निग्धवत्, शत्रुबुद्ध्या, द्रोहबुद्ध्या, प्रतिकूलं, विरोधेन, विरुद्धं, विपक्षवत्, अननुकूलं, विपरीतं, रिपुवत्.

INIMITABILITY, *s.* अनुपमेयता, अननुकार्य्यता, अनन्यसाम्यत्वं, अद्वितीयता.

INIMITABLE, *a.* अनुपमेयः -या -यं, अननुकार्य्यः -र्य्या -र्य्यं, अननुकरणीयः

-या -यं, अनुपमः -मा -मं, अप्रतिमः -मा -मं, उपमातीतः -ता -तं, अनुकरणातिगः -गा -गं, अनन्यसाध्यः -ध्या -ध्यं, अनन्यशक्यः -क्या -क्यं, अन्यासाध्यः -ध्या -ध्यं, अन्याशक्यः -क्या -क्यं, अतुल्यः -ल्या -ल्यं, अद्वितीयः -या -यं, असाधारणः -णा -णी -णं.

INIMITABLY, *adv.* अनुपमेयं, अननुकरणीयं, अतुल्यं, अनुपमं.

INIQUITOUS, *a.* अन्यायी -यिनी -यि (न्), अन्याय्यः -य्या -य्यं, अयथान्यायः -या -यं, न्यायविरुद्धः -द्धा -द्धं, अधार्म्मिकः -की -कं, अधर्म्मी -र्म्मिणी -र्म्मि (न्), धर्म्मापेतः -ता -तं, पापः -पा -पं, पापी -पिनी -पि (न्), पापिष्ठः -ष्ठा -ष्ठं, खलः -ला -लं, दुर्वृत्तः -त्ता -त्तं, दुराचारः -रा -रं, कुकर्म्मा -र्म्मा -र्म्म (न्), दुष्टः -ष्टा -ष्टं, किल्बिषी -षिणी -षि (न्).

INIQUITOUSLY, *adv.* अन्यायतस्, अयथान्यायं, न्यायविरुद्धं, न्यायविरोधेन, अधर्म्मतस्, अधर्म्मेण, पापिष्ठवत्, दुष्टवत्, खलवत्, दुराचारवत्.

INIQUITY, *s.* अधर्म्मः -र्म्मता -त्वं, अन्यायः, अन्याय्यत्वं -ता, अन्यायिता, धर्म्मविरोधः, न्यायविरोधः, न्यायविरुद्धता, धर्म्मापेतत्वं, पापं, दुष्टता, पापिष्ठता, खलता, दुर्वृत्तिः *f.*, दुर्वृत्तत्वं, अनीतिः *f.*, नीतिविरोधः, कुकर्म्म *n.* (न्), दुष्कर्म्म *n.*, कुक्रिया, दुराचारत्वं, अपकर्म्म *n.*, अपचारः, शठता, दौरात्म्यं, कुसृतिः *f.*, व्यसनं.

INITIAL, *a.* आदि in comp., आद्यः -द्या -द्यं, आदिकः -का -कं, आदिमः -मा -मं, आदिस्थः -स्था -स्थं, आदिवर्त्ती -र्त्तिनी -र्त्ति (न्), प्राथमिकः -की -कं, प्रथमः -मा -मं, पूर्व्वः -र्व्वा -र्व्वं, पौर्व्विकः -की -कं, पौरस्त्यः -स्त्या -स्त्यं, आरम्भकः -का -कं, आरम्भस्थः -स्था -स्थं.

INITIAL, *s.* (First letter of a name) नामादिवर्णः, नामाक्षरं, आद्यवर्णः, प्रथमवर्णः.

To INITIATE, *v. a.* (Instruct in rudiments or principles) विद्यारम्भान् or विद्यातत्त्वानि or प्रथमतत्त्वानि उपदिश् (c. 6. -दिशति -देष्टुं), प्रथमोपदेशं कृ, प्रथमशिक्षां कृ, विद्याप्रवेशं कृ, विद्याभिनिवेशं कृ, विद्योपक्रमं कृ.—(Introduce by initiatory ceremonies) दीक्ष् (c. 1. दीक्षते -क्षितुं), उपनी (c. 1. -नयति -नेतुं), दीक्षापूर्व्वम् उपनी, दीक्षाकर्म्मपूर्व्वं or संस्कारपूर्व्वं or अभिमन्त्रणपूर्व्वं or मन्त्रपूर्व्वं प्रविश् (c. 10. -वेशयति -यितुं), दीक्षां कृ, दीक्षाकर्म्म कृ.—(Instruct in initiatory ceremonies) दीक्षाकर्म्म उपदिश्, संस्कारमन्त्रान् or दीक्षामन्त्रान् उपदिश्.

INITIATED, *p. p.* दीक्षितः -ता -तं, कृतदीक्षः -क्षा -क्षं, संस्कृतः -ता -तं, कृतसंस्कारः -रा -रं, जातसंस्कारः -रा -रं, संस्कारितः -ता -तं, अभिसंस्कृतः -ता -तं, अभिमन्त्रितः -ता -तं, मन्त्रवान् -वती -वत् (त्), उपनीतः -ता -तं, उपनीयमानः -ना -नं, कृताभिषेकः -का -कं, राद्धः -द्धा -द्धं, उपदिष्टः -ष्टा -ष्टं, कृतविद्यारम्भः -म्भा -म्भं, कृतविद्योपक्रमः -मा -मं, कृतविद्याप्रवेशः -शा -शं, विद्याप्रविष्टः -ष्टा -ष्टं.

INITIATION, *s.* (Instruction in rudiments or principles) विद्यारम्भोपदेशः, विद्यातत्त्वोपदेशः, प्रथमतत्त्वोपदेशः, प्रथमोपदेशः, प्रथमशिक्षा, विद्याप्रवेशः -शनं, विद्याभिनिवेशः -शनं.—(Introduction by initiatory ceremonies, &c.) दीक्षा, दीक्षाकरणं, दीक्षाकर्म्म *n.* (न्), उपनयः -यनं, उपनायः, दीक्षापूर्व्वम् उपनयनं, दीक्षापूर्व्वं प्रवेशनं, संस्कारः, अभिमन्त्रणं, अभिषेकः.—(Instruction in initiatory ceremonies) दीक्षाकर्म्मोपदेशः, मन्त्रोपदेशः, उपदेशः.

INITIATIVE, *s.* (Introductory step) आरम्भः, प्रत्युत्क्रमः, प्रत्युत्क्रान्तिः *f.*

INITIATIVE, INITIATORY, *a.* आरम्भकः -का -कं, प्रारम्भकः -का -कं, आद्यः -द्या -द्यं, आदिमः -मा -मं, आदिकः -का -कं.—(Relating to introductory ceremonies) दीक्षाकर्म्मसम्बन्धी -न्धिनी -न्धि (न्).

To INJECT, *v. a.* अन्तःक्षिप् (c. 6. -क्षिपति -क्षेप्तुं), अन्तःप्रक्षिप्, निक्षिप्, अन्तःक्षेपं कृ, अन्तःप्रक्षेपं कृ, अन्तःकृ.—(With a syringe) वस्तिद्वारेण अन्तःक्षिप् or अन्तःप्रक्षिप्.

INJECTED, *p. p.* अन्तःक्षिप्तः -प्ता -प्तं, अन्तःप्रक्षिप्तः -प्ता -प्तं, निक्षिप्तः -प्ता -प्तं.

INJECTION, *s.* अन्तःक्षेपः -पणं, अन्तःप्रक्षेपः -पणं, निक्षेपणं.—(Clyster) वस्तिः *m. f.*

To INJOIN. See *To* ENJOIN.

INJUDICIOUS, *a.* अविवेकी -किनी -कि (न्), अविवेचकः -का -कं, विवेकशून्यः -न्या -न्यं, विवेचनाशून्यः -न्या -न्यं, अविवेकदृश्वा -श्वा -श्व (न्), अविज्ञः -ज्ञा -ज्ञं, अविचक्षणः -णा -णं, अबुद्धिमान् -मती -मत् (त्), अविचारी -रिणी -रि (न्), अविचारकः -का -कं, विचारशून्यः -न्या -न्यं, अपरिच्छेदी -दिनी -दि (न्).

INJUDICIOUSLY, *adv.* अविवेकेन, अविवेचकवत्, विवेकं विना, अविज्ञवत्, अविचारेण, विचारं विना, अविचक्षणवत्.

INJUDICIOUSNESS, *s.* अविवेकः -कता -कित्वं, अविवेचकत्वं, विवेकशून्यता, अविवेचना, अविज्ञता, अविचारः, विचारशून्यता, अविचक्षणता, अवैचक्षण्यं, अबुद्धिमत्त्वं, अपरिच्छेदः, परिच्छेदहीनता.

INJUNCTION, *s.* आज्ञा, आदेशः, निदेशः, निर्देशः, नियोगः, चोदनं -ना, नियमः, निदर्शनं, विधानं, शासनं, वचनं; 'sacred injunction,' विधिः *m.*, कल्पः; 'chief injunction,' मुख्यः; 'secondary,' अनुकल्पः.

To INJURE, *v. a.* हिंस् (c. 7. हिनस्ति, c. 1. हिंसति -सितुं), विहिंस्, उपहिंस्, आहिंस्, अपकृ, क्षतिं कृ, क्षतं कृ, क्षण् (c. 8. क्षणोति -णितुं), परिक्षण्, विक्षण्, पीड् (c. 10. पीडयति -यितुं), अर्द् (c. 10. अर्दयति -यितुं), समर्द्, व्यथ् (c. 10. व्यथयति -यितुं), रिष् (c. 1. रेषति, c. 4. रिष्यति, रेषितुं, रेष्टुं), क्षि (c. 5. क्षिणोति, c. 1. क्षयति, क्षेतुं), दुष् (c. 10. दूषयति -यितुं), नश् (c. 10. नाशयति -यितुं), हन् (c. 2. हन्ति -न्तुं), विहन्, उपहन्, धृष् (c. 10. धर्षयति -यितुं), द्रोहं कृ, द्रुह् (c. 4. द्रुह्यति, द्रोग्धुं), अपराध् (c. 5. -राध्नोति, c. 4. -राध्यति -राद्धुं) with gen. c., रिह् (c. 1. रेहति, रेढुं), अतिवृत् (c. 1. -वर्त्तते -र्त्तितुं), अपकारं कृ, अपायं कृ, हिंसां कृ, अहितं कृ, अन्यायं कृ, हानिं कृ, ध्वंसं कृ, दुःखं दा, क्लेशं दा, अनिष्टं कृ.

INJURED, *p. p.* हिंसितः -ता -तं, विहिंसितः -ता -तं, अपकृतः -ता -तं, प्राप्तापकारः -रा -रं, कृतापकारः -रा -रं, क्षतः -ता -तं, परिक्षतः -ता -तं, विक्षतः -ता -तं, अर्दितः -ता -तं, पीडितः -ता -तं, निपीडितः -ता -तं, व्यथितः -ता -तं, रिष्टः -ष्टा -ष्टं, कृतध्वंसः -सा -सं, दूषितः -ता -तं, विहतः -ता -तं, जातापायः -या -यं, प्राप्तहानिः -निः -नि, व्यापन्नः -न्ना -न्नं, व्यापादितः -ता -तं.

INJURER, *s.* हिंसकः, हिंसाकारी *m.* (न्), अपकारी *m.*, अपकारकः, क्षतिकारकः, अन्यायकारी *m.*, परापकारी *m.*, अनिष्टकारी *m.*, अहितकारी *m.*, द्रोहकारी *m.*, रेष्टा *m.* (ृ), नशिता *m.* (ृ), नंष्टा *m.* (ृ), द्रोही *m.* (न्), द्वेषी *m.* (न्), विहेठकः.

INJURIOUS, *a.* हिंसकः -का -कं, हिंस्रः -स्रा -स्रं, हिंसालुः -लुः -लु -लुकः -का -कं, हिंसात्मकः -का -कं, अपकारी -रिणी -रि (न्), अपकारकः -का -कं, आपकरः -री -रं, क्षतिकरः -री -रं, क्षतिजनकः -का -कं, हानिकरः -री -रं -जनकः -का -कं, अहितकरः -री -रं, अनिष्टकरः -री -रं, अहितः -ता -तं, नृशंसः -सा -सं, शरारुः -रुः -रु, शारुकः -का -कं, रिष्वः -ष्वा -ष्वं, घातुकः -का -कं, उपघातकः -का -कं, नंशुकः -का -कं, बाधकः -का -कं, द्रोही -हिणी -हि (न्), भूतद्रुक् *m. f. n.* (ह्).

INJURIOUSLY, *adv.* हिंसापूर्व्वं, हिंसया, सापकारं, सापायं, अपकारेण, अहितं, क्षतिपूर्व्वं, द्रोहपूर्व्वं, क्षतपूर्व्वं, द्रोहेण, हिंसाप्रकारेण, नृशंसं, यथा हिंसा क्रियते तथा, यथा क्षतं or अपायो जायते तथा, सद्रोहं, सदर्पणं.

INJURY, *s.* (Wrong) हिंसा -सनं, अपकारः, अपकृतं, अपकृतिः *f.*, अपक्रिया, द्रोहः, अभिद्रोहः, अन्यायः, अपराधः, हिंसाकर्म्म *n.* (न्), निकारः,

विप्रकारः, पीडा -डनं, प्राणिपीडा, अहितं, अनिष्टं, व्यापादः -दनं, विहेठः -ठनं.—(Hurt, harm, detriment) क्षतिः *f.*, क्षतं, परिक्षतिः *f.*, परिक्षतं, अपकारः, अपकृतं, अपायः, हानिः *f.*, नाशः, ध्वंसः, अपचयः, अपचितिः *f.*, दूषणं, अर्दना, क्षयः, उपक्षयः, बाधः, दुःखं, दोषः, भंशः.

INJUSTICE, *s.* अधर्म्मः -र्म्मता -त्वं, अन्यायः -यता -त्वं, अन्याय्यता, अन्यायिता, धर्म्मविरोधः, धर्म्मविरुद्धता, धर्म्मापेतता, न्यायविपर्य्ययः, न्यायविरोधः, न्यायविरुद्धता, अनीतिः *f.*, अनयः, दुर्णीतिः.

INK, *s.* मसिः *f.* -सी, मषिः *f.* -षी, मसिका, मसीजलं, मलिनाम्बु *n.*, पत्राञ्जनं, अञ्जनं, कालिका, काली, वर्णिका, मेला, गोला; 'red ink,' अलक्तरसः, अलक्तः -क्तकं.

To INK, *v. a.* मस्या लिप् (c. 6. लिम्पति, लेप्तुं) or मलिन (nom. मलिनयति -यितुं) or दुष् (c. 10. दूषयति -यितुं), मसिदूषितं -तां -तं कृ, कालीकृ.

INK-HORN, *s.* मसिधानी, मसिकूपी, मसिभाजनं, मसिपात्रं, मस्याधारः.

INKLING, *s.* ईषज्ज्ञानं, किञ्चिज्ज्ञानं, ईषद्बोधनं, ईषत्सूचना -नं, किञ्चित्सूचितं, इङ्गितं, सङ्केतः, भासः, आभासः, वासना.

INKSTAND, *s.* मसिधानी -नं, मसिकूपी, मसिभाजनं, मस्याधारः, मसिपात्रं, मेलान्धुः *m.*, वार्ह्लः -लं, लिपिसज्जापात्रं, लेखसाधनपात्रं, लिपिसामग्र्यभाजनं.

INKY, *a.* मसिमयः -यी -यं, मसिवर्णः -र्णा -र्णं, समसिः -सिः -सि, मसीयः -या -यं, मसिलिप्तः -प्ता -प्तं, मसिदूषितः -ता -तं.

INLAID, *p. p.* खचितः -ता -तं, अनुविद्धः -द्धा -द्धं, प्रतिबद्धः -द्धा -द्धं, प्रणिहितः -ता -तं, छुरितः -ता -तं, पिनद्धः -द्धा -द्धं, मण्डितः -ता -तं, करस्थः -स्था -स्थं -खितः -ता -तं; 'is inlaid,' प्रणिधीयते.

INLAND, *a.* मध्यदेशीयः -या -यं, मध्यदेशी -शिनी -शि (न्), मध्यदेशस्थः -स्था -स्थं, देशमध्यस्थः -स्था -स्थं, देशमध्यवर्त्ती -र्त्तिनी -र्त्ति (न्), समुद्रदूरस्थः -स्था -स्थं, समुद्रदूरवर्त्ती -र्त्तिनी -र्त्ति (न्), समुद्रानिकटवर्त्ती &c., असमुद्रतीरस्थः -स्था -स्थं.—(Not foreign, domestic) अविदेशीयः -या -यं, देशीयः -या -यं, दैशिकः -की -कं, देश in comp.

INLANDER, *s.* समुद्रदूरवासी *m.* (न्), मध्यदेशजः, मध्यदेशवासी *m.*

To INLAPIDATE, *v. a.* पाषाणीकृ, प्रस्तरीकृ, पाषाणवत् कठिनीकृ.

To INLAY, *v. a.* नानावर्णद्रव्यैः खच् (c. 10. खचयति -यितुं) or अनुव्यध् (c. 4. -विध्यति -व्यद्धुं) or छुर् (c. 6. छुरति -रितुं) or बन्ध् (c. 9. बध्नाति, बन्द्धुं), निधा (c. 3. -दधाति -धातुं), प्रणिधा, चित्रविचित्रीकृ, करम्बीकृ, नानाविधद्रव्यैः खचितं -तां -तं कृ or मण्डितं कृ.

INLAYER, *s.* प्रणिधाता *m.* (तृ), नानावर्णद्रव्यनिबन्धा *m.* (न्धृ), प्रणिधायी *m.* (न्).

INLAYING, *s.* नानावर्णद्रव्यनिबन्धनं, प्रणिधानं, विचित्रीकरणं.

INLET, *s.* (Entrance, place of ingress) द्वारं, प्रवेशद्वारं, प्रवेशमार्गः, पथः, मार्गः.—(Creek, or recess in the shore of the sea) समुद्रवङ्कः, वङ्कः, खञ्जः, तटभङ्गः, तीरभङ्गः, तीरभेदः, पुटभेदः, खातं.

To INLIST, *v. a.* *See* ENLIST.

INLY, *a.* आन्तरिकः -की -कं, अन्तरस्थः -स्था -स्थं. *See* INTERNAL, INWARD.

INMATE, *s.* सहवासी *m.* (न्), निवासी *m.* (न्), सहवर्त्ती *m.* (न्), सहस्थायी *m.*, एकगृहवासी *m.*, एकगृहस्थायी *m.*

INMOST, *a.* अन्तरतमः -मा -मत्, अन्तरतमस्थः -स्था -स्थं, अत्यभ्यन्तरः -रा -रं, अत्यभ्यन्तरस्थः -स्था -स्थं, अत्यन्तरस्थः &c., अत्यभ्यन्तरवर्त्ती -र्त्तिनी -र्त्ति (न्), अत्यान्तरिकः -की -कं, अत्यन्तर्गतः -ता -तं, अत्यन्तर्भूतः -ता -तं.

INN, *s.* (House for the lodging of travellers) उत्तरणगृहं, उत्तरणशाला, उत्तरणस्थानं, उत्तरणीयगेहं, उपकारी -रिका, उपकारिकागृहं, उपकार्य्या, औपकार्य्या -र्य्यं, प्रवासीयगृहं.—(Tavern) गञ्जा -ञ्जिका, मदिरागृहं, मदिराशाला.—(Residence of lawyers) स्मृतिशास्त्रज्ञमठः, स्मृतिशास्त्रज्ञवेश्म *n.* (न्).

To INN, *v. n.* उत्तरणगृहे वस् (c. 1. वसति, वस्तुं), उत्तरणशालां निविश् (c. 6. -विशति -वेष्टुं), अध्वमध्ये रथाद् अवतीर्य्य पूर्ष्ठीकगृहं निविश्.

To INN, *v. a.* उत्तरणगृहे वस् (c. 10. वासयति -यितुं), उत्तरणशालां निविश् (c. 10. -वेशयति -यितुं).

INN-KEEPER, *s.* उत्तरणगृहपतिः *m.*, उत्तरणशालास्वामी *m.* (न्), उपकारिकागृहाधिकारी *m.* (न्), शौण्डिकः.

INNATE, *a.* सहजः -जा -जं, सहजातः -ता -तं, अन्तर्जातः -ता -तं, निजः -जा -जं, अन्तर्भवः -वा -वं, अन्तरुत्पन्नः -न्ना -न्नं, अन्तर्भूतः -ता -तं, अन्तर्वर्त्ती -र्त्तिनी -र्त्ति (न्), अन्तरस्थः -स्था -स्थं, स्वाभाविकः -की -कं, स्वभावजः -जा -जं, नैसर्गिकः -की -कं, निसर्गजः -जा -जं, औत्सर्गिकः -की -कं, प्रकृतिस्थः -स्था -स्थं, प्राकृतिकः -की -कं, औत्पत्तिकः -की -कं, अन्तरीयः -या -यं.

INNATELY, *adv.* स्वभावात् -वेन, स्वभावतस्, सहजं, निजभावेन.

INNATENESS, *s.* स्वाभाविकत्वं, सहजत्वं, अन्तर्भावः, अन्तर्जातत्वं, नैसर्गिकत्वं.

INNAVIGABLE, *a.* अनौतार्य्यः -र्य्या -र्य्यं, अनाव्यः -व्या -व्यं, नावतार्य्यः -र्य्या -र्य्यं, नावगम्यः -म्या -म्यं, अनौगम्यः -म्या -म्यं, नौगमनाशक्यः -क्या -क्यं.

INNER, *a.* अन्तरस्थः -स्था -स्थं, आन्तरिकः -की -कं, आन्तरः -री -रं, अन्तरीयः -या -यं, आभ्यन्तरः -री -रं, अभ्यन्तर or अन्तर or अन्तर् in comp., अन्तर्भवः -वा -वं, अन्तर्गतः -ता -तं, अन्तर्भूतः -ता -तं, अन्तर्वर्त्ती -र्त्तिनी -र्त्ति (न्), अन्तरतमः -मा -मत्, अन्तःस्थितः -ता -तं, मध्यस्थः -स्था -स्थं, गर्भस्थः -स्था -स्थं, अन्तरङ्गः -ङ्गा -ङ्गं; 'inner apartments,' अन्तर्गृहं, अन्तर्भवनं, भवनोदरं, वासगृहं.

INNERMOST, *a.* अन्तरतमः -मा -मत्. *See* INMOST.

INNOCENCE, INNOCENCY, *s.* (Freedom from guilt) शुचिता, शुद्धता -त्वं, निष्पापत्वं, निरपराधता -धिता, अनपराधता, निर्दोषत्वं, अपापत्वं, दोषहीनता, अपराधहीनता, अपराधशून्यता, निष्कलङ्कता -त्वं, अनघता, निर्म्मलता, शुद्धमतित्वं, विमलचित्तत्वं, मतिशुद्धता, चित्तशुद्धिः *f.*, शुद्धिः *f.*—(Guilelessness) निष्कापट्यं, अकापट्यं, मायाहीनता, छलहीनता, सारल्यं, अदुष्टता; 'innocence and guilt,' गुणदोषौ *m.* du.

INNOCENT, *a.* शुचिः -चिः -चि, निरपराधः -धा -धं, अनपराधः -धा -धं -धी -धिनी -धि (न्), निर्दोषः -षा -षं -षी -षिणी -षि (न्), अदोषः -षा -षं, निष्पापः -पा -पं -पी -पिनी -पि (न्), अपापः -पा -पं, पापहीनः -ना -नं, अपराधहीनः -ना -नं -शून्यः -न्या -न्यं, पापरहितः -ता -तं, शुद्धः -द्धा -द्धं, शुद्धमतिः -तिः -ति, शुचिमनाः -नाः -नः (स्), शुचिकर्म्मा -र्म्मा -र्म्म (न्), शुक्लकर्म्मा &c., अकृष्णकर्म्मा &c., शिष्टिदानः -ना -नं, निष्कलङ्कः -ङ्का -ङ्कं, अनघः -घा -घं, अकृतापराधः -धा -धं, अकृतैनाः -नाः -नः (स्), अकृतपापः -पा -पं, निर्म्मलः -ला -लं, निर्म्मलचित्तः -त्ता -त्तं, विमलचित्तः -त्ता -त्तं, अदृष्टदोषः -षा -षं, अदृष्टापराधः -धा -धं, अहेतुकः -का -कं.—(Guileless) निष्कपटः -टा -टं, निर्व्याजः -जा -जं, छलरहितः -ता -तं, निर्व्यलीकः -का -कं, विमलात्मा -त्मा -त्म (न्), मायाहीनः -ना -नं, सरलः -ला -लं, निष्कृत्रिमः -मा -मं, अकृत्रिमः -मा -मं, अदुष्टः -ष्टा -ष्टं.

INNOCENT, *s.* (A guiltless person) शुचिजनः, निरपराधी *m.* (न्).

INNOCENTLY, *adv.* अनपराधेन, निरपराधं, पापं विना, निष्पापं, शुचि, शुचिवत्, शुचिमनसा, निर्म्मलचेतसा, अनघं, अनघवत्, निर्व्यलीकं, निष्कपटं.

INNOCUOUS, *a.* अहिंसकः -का -कं, अहिंस्रः -स्रा -स्रं, हिंसारहितः -ता -तं, अहिंसाकरः -री -रं, अनपकारी -रिणी -रि (न्), अनपकारकः -का -कं, अक्षतिकारकः -का -कं, अद्रोही -हिणी -हि (न्).

INNOCUOUSLY, *adv.* अहिंसया, अहिंसापूर्व्वं, अक्षतिपूर्व्वं, अद्रोहेण.

INNOCUOUSNESS, *s.* अहिंसा, अनपकारः -रकता, अहिंसकत्वं, अद्रोहः.

To INNOVATE, *v. a.* (Introduce new customs) नूतनरीतिं or नवव्यवहारान् स्था in caus. (स्थापयति -यितुं) or संस्था or प्रवृत् (c. 10. -वर्त्तयति -यितुं) or कॢप् (c. 10. कल्पयति -यितुं) or प्रकॢप्, व्यवहारान्तराणि स्था, कुलव्यवहारभिन्नान् नवाचारान् स्था, कुलाचारभिन्नान् नवीनव्यवहारान् कॢप्, देशव्यवहारभिन्नान् नूतनव्यवहारान् प्रकॢप्, देशाचारान् परिवृत् or नवीकृ, नूतनसम्प्रदायान् or मतान्तराणि स्था, अन्यसम्प्रदायान् कृ or कॢप्, नूतनकर्म्माणि प्रवृत् (c. 10. -वर्त्तयति -यितुं).

INNOVATION, *s.* (The act) नवव्यवहारस्थापनं, नूतनरीतिसंस्थापनं, व्यवहारान्तरकल्पनं, नवीनाचारसंस्थापनं, नूतनसम्प्रदायकल्पनं, देशाचारपरिवर्त्तनं, कुलाचारपरिवर्त्तनं, नूतनकर्म्मप्रवर्त्तनं, नवीकरणं.—(The change made) नूतनरीतिः *f.*, नवरीतिः *f.*, नवीनव्यवहारः, व्यवहारान्तरं, रीत्यन्तरं, नवाचारः, नवाचरितं, नवचरितं, नवमार्गः, नवधारा.

INNOVATOR, *s.* नवरीतिस्थापकः, नूतनव्यवहारस्थापकः, व्यवहारान्तरप्रकल्पकः, नवव्यवहारप्रवर्त्तकः, देशव्यवहारपरिवर्त्तकः, कुलाचारपरिवर्त्तकः, नवसम्प्रदायप्रवर्त्तकः, मतान्तरस्थापकः.

INNOXIOUS, *a.* अहिंसकः -का -कं, अहिंस्रः -स्रा -स्रं, अनपकारी -रिणी -रि (न्), अक्षतिकरः -री -रं, अघातुकः -का -कं, अद्रोही -हिणी -हि (न्), अरिष्टः -ष्टा -ष्टं, अशारुकः -की -कं.

INNOXIOUSLY, *adv.* अहिंसया, अनपकारेण, अद्रोहेण, अक्षतिपूर्व्वं.

INNOXIOUSNESS, *s.* अहिंसता -त्वं, अनपकारः -रकत्वं, अहिंसकत्वं -ता, अघातुकत्वं, अशारुकत्वं, हिंसात्यागः.

INNUENDO, *s.* वक्रोक्तिः *f.*, व्यंग्योक्तिः *f.*, व्यंग्यः -ग्यं, भङ्गिः *f.*, भंगयुक्तिः *f.*, श्लेषोक्तिः *f.*, पर्य्यायोक्तिः *f.*

INNUMERABLE, *a.* अगणनीयः -या -यं, अगण्यः -ण्या -ण्यं, असंख्येयः -या -यं, असंख्यः -ख्या -ख्यं, अत्यसंख्यः -ख्या -ख्यं, गणनातीतः -ता -तं, गणनाशक्यः -क्या -क्यं, संख्यातीतः -ता -तं, लक्षगुणः -णा -णं, कोटिगुणः -णा -णं, अगणितः -ता -तं; 'in innumerable numbers,' कोटिशस्.

INNUMERABLENESS, *s.* अगणनीयता, अगण्यता, असंख्येयता, असंख्यता.

INNUTRITION, *s.* अपुष्टिः *f.*, अपोषणं, पोषणाभावः, अभरणं.

INNUTRITIOUS, *a.* अपुष्टिदः -दा -दं, अपुष्टिकरः -री -रं, अपोषकः -का -कं.

INOBSERVABLE, *a.* अलक्ष्यः -क्ष्या -क्ष्यं, दुर्लक्ष्यः &c., अदृश्यः -श्या -श्यं.

To INOCULATE, *v. a.* (A tree) एकवृक्षशाखायां भिन्नवृक्षपल्लवं निविश् (c. 10. -वेशयति -यितुं), कलमं निविश्.—(Insert infectious matter in the flesh) विस्फोटरसबिन्दुं बाहुमांसे निविश् (c. 10. -वेशयति -यितुं), रक्तवरटीजपूयलवम् अन्यमांसे निविश् or त्वक्छेदनानन्तरं बाहुमांसे निविश्, विस्फोटजरसनिवेशनेन रक्तवरटीरोगम् अन्यस्मिन् संक्रम् (c. 10. -क्रामयति -यितुं) or सञ्चर् (c. 10. -चारयति -यितुं).

INOCULATED, *p. p.* (Budded) भिन्नवृक्षशाखानिवेशितः -ता -तं.—(Infected by inoculation with small-pox, &c.) स्फोटजरसनिवेशनेन रक्तवरटीरोगदूषितः -ता -तं.

INOCULATION, *s.* (Budding) एकवृक्षशाखायां भिन्नवृक्षपल्लवनिवेशनं.—(Inserting infectious matter in the flesh) सुस्थजनमांसे विस्फोटपूयलवनिवेशनं, स्फोटजरसनिवेशनेन रक्तवरटीरोगदूषणं or रक्तवटीरोगसञ्चारणं.

INOCULATOR, *s.* (Of plants) वृक्षशाखायां भिन्नवृक्षपल्लवनिवेशकः.—(Of infectious matter) विस्फोटपूयलवनिवेशकः, रक्तवरटीरोगसञ्चारकः.

INODOROUS, *a.* निर्गन्धः -न्धा -न्धं, अगन्धः -न्धा -न्धं, गन्धहीनः -ना -नं.

INOFFENSIVE, *a.* अनपकारी -रिणी -रि (न्), अनपकारकः -का -कं, अनपकारशीलः -ला -लं, अनपराधी -धिनी -धि (न्), निरपराधः -धा -धं, अहिंसकः -का -कं, अहिंस्रः -स्रा -स्रं, हिंसारहितः -ता -तं, अहिंसाकरः -री -रं, अपरद्रोही -हिणी -हि (न्), अद्रोहशीलः -ला -लं, निर्द्रोही &c., अपरदुःखदः -दा -दं, अपरक्लेशदः -दा -दं, अघातुकः -का -कं, अबाधकः -का -कं, अविरोधी -धिनी -धि (न्), निर्दोषी -षिणी -षि (न्), निरुपद्रवी -विणी -वि (न्), सात्त्विकः -की -कं, सत्त्वशीलः -ला -लं, अप्रतिभुक् *m. f. n.* (ज्).

INOFFENSIVELY, *adv.* अनपकारेण, अहिंसया, अद्रोहेण, अनपराधेन, निरपराधं.

INOFFENSIVENESS, *s.* अहिंसा, अनपकारः -रिता -रकता, अनपकारशीलता, अहिंसाशीलता, अहिंसा, अद्रोहः, अद्रोहशीलता, अबाधकता, सत्त्वशीलता, अनपराधिता, हिंसात्यागः.

INOFFICIAL, *a.* अनाधिकारिकः -की -कं, अनधिकारप्रयुक्तः -क्ता -क्तं.

INOPERATIVE, *a.* असाधकः -का -कं, अकार्य्यसाधकः -का -कं, अकार्य्यकारकः -का -कं -री -रिणी -रि (न्), अकिञ्चित्करः -री -रं, अफलोत्पादकः -का -कं.

INOPPORTUNE, *a.* अकालिकः -की -कं, आकालिकः -की -कं, अप्राप्तकालः -ला -लं, अकालीनः -ना -नं, अनवसरः -रा -रं, अप्राप्तावसरः -रा -रं, असामयिकः -की -कं, असमयोचितः -ता -तं, असमयोपयुक्तः -क्ता -क्तं, अप्रसङ्गोचितः -ता -तं, अप्राप्तप्रसङ्गः -ङ्गा -ङ्गं, अप्रास्ताविकः -की -कं, अकालसदृशः -शी -शं, अप्रस्तावसदृशः -शी -शं, अप्रस्तावयोग्यः -ग्या -ग्यं, असमयानुरूपः -पा -पं, अयथाकालः -ला -लं, अस्थानः -ना -नं, अयोग्यः -ग्या -ग्यं.

INOPPORTUNELY, *adv.* अकाले -लेन, अस्थाने -नं, अनवसरं -रेण, असमयेन, अकालसदृशं, असमयानुरूपेण, अयोग्यं, अयथाकालं, अप्रसङ्गवत्, अपदं, असाम्प्रतं, असम्प्रति.

INOPPORTUNENESS, *s.* अकालिकत्वं, आकालिकत्वं, अकालीनता, असामयिकत्वं, अनवसरः, असमयः, अयोग्यता.

INORDINATE, *a.* अपरिमितः -ता -तं, अत्यन्तः -न्ता -न्तं, आत्यन्तिकः -की -कं, अतिमर्य्यादः -दा -दं, अमर्य्यादः &c., उन्मर्य्यादः &c., मर्य्यादातीतः -ता -तं, अतिक्रान्तमर्य्यादः -दा -दं, मर्य्यादातीतः -ता -तं, अतिमात्रः -त्रा -त्रं, अमितः -ता -तं, अपरिमाणः -णा -णं, अतिमितः -ता -तं, अनियमितः -ता -तं, लंघितमर्य्यादः -दा -दं, लंघितनियमः -मा -मं, उद्रिक्तः -क्ता -क्तं, अतिरिक्तः -क्ता -क्तं.

INORDINATELY, *adv.* अपरिमितं, अत्यन्तं, अतिमर्य्यादं, अतिमात्रं, अतिशयेन, नितान्तं, सातिशयं, अतितरां, सुतरां, अत्यर्थं, तीव्रं, सुभृशं.

INORDINATENESS, *s.* अपरिमितता -त्वं, अपरिमाणं, अमितत्वं, मर्य्यादातिक्रमः, नियमातिक्रमः, आत्यन्तिकत्वं, अमर्य्यादा, उद्रिक्तता, अतिरिक्तता.

INORGANIC, *a.* अप्राणी -णिनी -णि (न्), निर्जीवः -वा -वं, जीवितसाधनहीनः -ना -नं, प्राणवायुसञ्चारहीनः -ना -नं, जडः -डा -डं, निरवयवः -वा -वं, अङ्गरहितः -ता -तं.

INOSCULATION, *s.* अग्रद्वयसन्धिः *m.* -सन्धानं, पार्श्वद्वयसंयोगः.

INQUEST, *s.* (Judicial inquiry) विचारः -रणं -णा, व्यवहारपरीक्षा, व्यवहारदर्शनं.—(Inquiry into the cause of a sudden death) अपमृत्युपरीक्षा, अपमृत्युकारणविचारः, अपमृत्युवृत्तान्तविचारः.

INQUIETUDE, *s.* अशान्तिः *f.*, अशान्तचित्तता, चित्ताशान्तिः *f.*, चित्तोद्वेगः, उद्वेगः, उद्विग्नता, अनिर्वृतिः *f.*, चित्तानिर्वृतिः *f.*, मनस्तापः, चित्तवेदना, चित्तव्यथा, मनोदुःखं, मनःपीडा, कष्टं, अस्वास्थ्यं, अस्वस्थता, असमाधानं, आधिः *m.*, क्लेशः, व्याकुलता, व्यामोहः, मानसी व्यथा, व्यस्तता, अस्थिरता, अस्थैर्य्यं, औत्सुक्यं, वैक्लव्यं.

To INQUINATE, *v. a.* दुष् (c. 10. दूषयति -यितुं), मलिन (nom. मलिनयति -यितुं).

To INQUIRE, *v. a.* (Ask a question) प्रच्छ् (c. 6. पृच्छति, प्रष्टुं), अनुप्रच्छ्, परिप्रच्छ्, समनुप्रच्छ्, प्रश्नं कृ, पृच्छनं कृ, अनुयुज् (c. 7. -युनक्ति

-युंक्ते -योक्तुं), अनुयोगं कृ, अभिचुद् (c. 10. -चोदयति -यितुं).—(Investigate, examine into) परीक्ष् (c. 1. -ईक्षते -क्षितुं), निरूप् (c. 10. -रूपयति -यितुं), अनुसन्धा (c. 3. -दधाति -धातुं), ज्ञा in des. (जिज्ञासते -सितुं), अन्विष् (c. 4. -इष्यति -एषितुं), अन्वेष् (c. 1. -एषते -षितुं), विचर् (c. 10. -चारयति -यितुं), विमृश् (c. 6. -मृशति -म्रष्टुं), चर्च् (c. 1. चर्चति -र्चितुं), निर्ध्यै (c. 1. -ध्यायति -ध्यातुं), निश्चि (c. 5. -चिनोति -चेतुं), विनिश्चि, मार्ग् (c. 1. मार्गति, c. 10. मार्गयति -यितुं), मृग् (c. 10. मृगयते -यितुं), गवेष् (c. 10. गवेषयति -यितुं), अभिनिर्ध्यै (c. 1. -ध्यायति -ध्यातुं), जिज्ञासां कृ, अन्वेषणं कृ.—(Inquire about one's health, &c.) कुशलप्रश्नं कृ, कुशलसम्प्रश्नं कृ, सम्प्रश्नं कृ.

INQUIRED, *p. p.* पृष्टः -ष्टा -ष्टं, अनुयुक्तः -क्ता -क्तं, परीक्षितः -ता -तं, जिज्ञासितः -ता -तं, निर्णीतः -ता -तं, चर्चितः -ता -तं, निरूपितः -ता -तं.

INQUIRER, *s.* (One who asks a question) प्रष्टा *m.* (ष्टृ), पृच्छकः, प्रश्नकारी *m.* (न्), अनुयोक्ता *m.* (क्तृ), अनुयोगकृत् *m.*—(One who investigates) परीक्षकः, निरूपकः, विचारकः, अनुसन्धाता *m.* (तृ), निर्णेता *m.* (तृ), जिज्ञासुः *m.* -सकः, अन्वेषकः, जिज्ञासाकृत् *m.*—(Inquirer after knowledge) ज्ञानेप्सुः *m.*, ज्ञानेच्छुः *m.*

INQUIRING, *a.* जिज्ञासुः -सुः -सु, ज्ञानेप्सुः -प्सुः -प्सु, ज्ञानेच्छुः -च्छुः -च्छु.

INQUIRY, *s.* (Question, interrogation) प्रश्नः, सम्प्रश्नः, पृच्छा -च्छनं, अनुयोगः -योजनं.—(Investigation) परीक्षा -क्षणं, निरूपणं, अनुसन्धानं, जिज्ञासा, विचारः -रणं -णा, अन्वेषणं -णा, चर्चा, समीक्षा -क्षणं, निर्णयः, पर्येषणा, गवेषणं -णा, परीष्टिः *f.*, निश्चयः, अनुसरणं, विमर्शः, विवेचना, शोधः -धनं; 'spirit of inquiry,' ज्ञानेच्छा, ज्ञानेप्सा; 'friendly inquiry respecting health,' &c. कुशलप्रश्नः, सम्प्रश्नः, सान्त्वना.

INQUISITION, *s.* (Examination) परीक्षा -क्षणं, अनुसन्धानं, जिज्ञासा, अनुयोगः, समीक्षणं, संवीक्षणं.—(Judicial) विचारः -रणा.—(Court for religious inquiry) धर्म्मपरीक्षणसभा, धर्म्मविचारणसभा.

INQUISITIVE, *a.* पिपृच्छिषुः -षुः -षु, पृच्छकः -का -कं, प्रश्नशीलः -ला -लं, पृच्छनशीलः -ला -लं, कुतूहली -लिनी -लि (न्), कौतूहलपरः -रा -रं, कौतूहलान्वितः -ता -तं, कौतुकाविष्टः -ष्टा -ष्टं, जिज्ञासुः -सुः -सु, अनुसन्धानेच्छुः -च्छुः -च्छु, अनुसन्धानशीलः -ला -लं, अन्वेषणशीलः -ला -लं, अन्वेषणासक्तः -क्ता -क्तं.—(Inclined to seek knowledge) ज्ञानेच्छुः -च्छुः -च्छु, ज्ञानेप्सुः -प्सुः -प्सु.

INQUISITIVELY, *adv.* कौतूहलेन -लात्, कुतूहलेन, जिज्ञासया, अन्वेषणशीलत्वात्, कौतुकेन, सकौतुकं.

INQUISITIVENESS, *s.* कौतूहलं, कुतूहलं, जिज्ञासाकुतूहलं, ज्ञानकुतूहलं, अनुसन्धानेच्छा, पिपृच्छिषा, जिज्ञासा, कौतुकं, कुतुकं, निरूपणेच्छा, ज्ञानेच्छा, अन्वेषणाकांक्षा, अन्वेषणासक्तिः *f.*, अन्वेषणशीलता, पृच्छनशीलता, अनुसन्धानशीलत्वं, असति प्रयोजने किमेतदिति जिज्ञासा.

INQUISITOR, *s.* परीक्षकः, विचारकः, अनुसन्धाता *m.* (तृ), निरूपकः.—(Member of court of inquisition) धर्म्मपरीक्षासभासद् *m.*, धर्म्मविचारसभासद्.

INQUISITORIAL, *a.* परीक्षकः -का -कं, अतिपरीक्षकः -का -कं, अनुसन्धायी -यिनी -यि (न्), निरूपकः -का -कं, चर्चकः -का -कं, परीक्षासम्बन्धी -न्धिनी -न्धि (न्).

INQUISITORIALLY, *adv.* अतिपरीक्षापूर्व्वं, अत्यनुसन्धानपूर्व्वं, अतिचर्चया.

To INRAIL, *v. a.* शङ्कुपंक्त्या परिवेष्ट् (c. 10. -वेष्टयति -यितुं) or आवृ (c. 5. -वृणोति -वरितुं -रीतुं) or अवरुध् (c. 7. -रुणद्धि -रोद्धुं).

INROAD, *s.* उपद्रवः, अभिद्रवः, अवस्कन्दः -न्दनं, उपप्लवः, विप्लवः, अभिक्रमः -मणं, अकस्माद् आक्रमणं, अभिमर्द्दः, अभिनिर्याणं; 'to make inroads,' अवस्कन्द् (c. 1. -स्कन्दति -स्कन्तुं), उपद्रु (c. 1. -द्रवति -द्रोतुं).

INSALUBRIOUS, *a.* अनारोग्यः -ग्या -ग्यं, अनारोग्यकरः -री -रं, रोगकरः &c., रोगजनकः -का -कं, व्याधिकरः &c., अस्वास्थ्यकारकः -का -कं, अक्षेम्यः -म्या -म्यं, अक्षेमकरः -रा -रं, बाधकः -का -कं.

INSALUBRITY, *s.* अनारोग्यं, रोगजनकत्वं, व्याधिजनकत्वं, अक्षेम्यता.

INSALUTARY, *a.* अहितः -ता -तं, अक्षेमकरः -रा -रं, अक्षेमङ्करः -री -रं, अक्षेम्यः -म्या -म्यं, अहितकरः -री -रं, अनिष्टकरः &c.

INSANABLE, *a.* अचिकित्स्यः -त्स्या -त्स्यं, अशमनीयः -या -यं. *See* INCURABLE.

INSANE, *a.* उन्मत्तः -त्ता -त्तं, उन्मादवान् -वती -वत् (त्), उन्मादः -दा -दं -दी -दिनी -दि (न्), सोन्मादः -दा -दं, उन्मदः -दा -दं, उन्मदिष्णुः -ष्णुः -ष्णु, प्रमदः -दा -दं, मत्तः -त्ता -त्तं, विक्षिप्तबुद्धिः -द्धिः -द्धि -मनस्कः -स्का -स्कं, हतबुद्धिः &c., नष्टबुद्धिः &c., भ्रष्टबुद्धिः &c., बुद्धिभ्रष्टः -ष्टा -ष्टं, नष्टमतिः -तिः -ति, विक्षिप्तमतिः &c., नष्टेन्द्रियः -या -यं, भ्रान्तचित्तः -त्ता -त्तं, विप्लुतचित्तः -त्ता -त्तं, मूढचेताः -ताः -तः (स्), हतज्ञानः -ना -नं, वातुलः -ला -लं, वातूलः -ला -लं, क्षीबः -बा -बं.

INSANELY, *adv.* उन्मत्तवत्, मत्तवत्, सोन्मादं, वातुलवत्, उन्मादेन.

INSANENESS, INSANITY, *s.* उन्मत्तता, मत्तता, सोन्मादत्वं, बुद्धिभ्रंशः, बुद्धिविक्षिप्तता, चित्तविभ्रमः, चित्तविप्लवः, बुद्धिनाशः, इन्द्रियनाशः, प्रामाद्यं, वातुलता.

INSATIABLE, INSATIATE, *a.* अतर्पणीयः -या -यं, अतर्प्यः -र्प्या -र्प्यं, अनातृप्यः -प्या -प्यं, अशक्यतृप्तिः -प्तिः -प्ति, तर्पणाशक्यः -क्या -क्यं, दुष्पूरः -रा -रं, अशमनीयः -या -यं, अतोषणीयः -या -यं, अतृप्तः -प्ता -प्तं.—(Very greedy) अतिलुब्धः -ब्धा -ब्धं, अतिलोभी -भिनी -भि (न्), लोलुपः -पा -पं, बह्वाशः -शा -शं, बहुभक्षकः -का -कं, मत्सरः -रा -रं.

INSATIABLENESS, *s.* अतर्पणीयता -त्वं, अतर्प्यत्वं, अतृप्तिः *f.*, अतिलुब्धता.

INSATIABLY, *adv.* अतर्पणीयं, यथा तृप्तिः or तुष्टिर् न जायते तथाप्रकारेण.

INSATISFACTION, *s.* अतुष्टिः *f.*, असन्तोषः, अपरितोषः, अतृप्तिः *f.*, असमाधानं.

To INSCRIBE, *v. a.* अभिलिख् (c. 6. -लिखति -लेखितुं), लिख्, पत्रे or लेख्ये सम् ऋ in caus. (-अर्पयति -यितुं) or निविश् (c. 10. -वेशयति -यितुं) or आरुह् in caus. (-रोपयति -यितुं) or न्यस् (c. 4. -अस्यति -असितुं), अक्षराणि पत्रे निविश् or सम् ऋ or न्यस्, पत्रारूढं -ढां -ढं कृ, पत्रान्तर्गतं -तां -तं कृ.—(Mark with letters) वर्णाङ्कितं -तां -तं कृ, वर्णैर् अङ्क् (c. 10. अङ्कयति -यितुं), अक्षराङ्कितं -तां -तं कृ.—(Dedicate a book) नामलिखनपूर्व्वं or नामाङ्कनपूर्व्वं ग्रन्थं सम् ऋ in caus., or निविद् (c. 10. -वेदयति -यितुं).

INSCRIBED, *p. p.* अभिलिखितः -ता -तं, लिखितः -ता -तं, न्यस्ताक्षरः -रा -रं, निवेशिताक्षरः -रा -रं, समर्पिताक्षरः -रा -रं, लेख्यारूढः -ढा -ढं, लेख्यारोपितः -ता -तं, पत्रनिवेशितः -ता -तं, पत्रान्तर्गतः -ता -तं, अङ्कितः -ता -तं.

INSCRIPTION, *s.* (Writing) अभिलेखनं, अभिलिखितं, लिखितं, लिखनं, लेखनं, लेखः -खा, लेख्यं, लिपिः *f.*, लिपिका.—(Writing on a stone) पाषाणलेखः, शिलालेखः, अङ्कितलेखः, मुद्रितलेखः.—(Dedication of a book) नामलिखनपूर्व्वं ग्रन्थसमर्पणं, नामाङ्कनपूर्व्वं ग्रन्थनिवेदनं.

INSCRUTABLE, *a.* अतर्क्यः -र्क्या -र्क्यं, दुर्ज्ञेयः -या -यं, बोधागम्यः -म्या -म्यं, बुद्ध्यतीतः -ता -तं, अबोधगम्यः -म्या -म्यं, अप्रतर्क्यः -र्क्या -र्क्यं, अज्ञेयः -या -यं, अलक्ष्यः -क्ष्या -क्ष्यं, दुर्लक्ष्यः -क्ष्या -क्ष्यं, अचिन्त्यः -न्त्या -न्त्यं, अचिन्तनीयः -या -यं, अनुपलभ्यः -भ्या -भ्यं, इन्द्रियागोचरः -रा -रं, गहनः -ना -नं, परमगहनः -ना -नं, अगाधः -धा -धं; 'whose ways are inscrutable,' अनुपलक्ष्यवर्त्मा -र्त्मा -र्त्म (न्).

INSCRUTABLY, *adv.* परमगहनं, दुर्ज्ञेयं, अचिन्तनीयं, अतर्क्यप्रकारेण.

To INSCULP, *v. a.* तक्ष् (c. 1. तक्षति -क्षितुं), उपस्कृ, मुद्रीकृ, तक्षणं कृ.

INSECT, *s.* कीटः -टकः, कृमिः *m.*, क्रिमिः *m.*, नीलङ्गुः *m.*, नीलाङ्गुः, सर्पः -र्पी -र्पिणी.

INSECTILE, *a.* कीटजातीयः -या -यं, कीटधर्म्मा -र्म्मा -र्म्म (न्).

INSECTIVOROUS, *a.* कीटभोजी -जिनी -जि (न्), कीटभक्षकः -का -कं, कीटाशी &c.

INSECURE, *a.* सशङ्कः -ङ्का -ङ्कं, शङ्कनीयः -या -यं, शंक्यः -क्या -क्यं, शङ्कान्वितः -ता -तं, सभयः -या -यं, संशयापन्नः -न्ना -न्नं, शङ्कापन्नः -न्ना -न्नं, संशयस्थः -स्था -स्थं, संशयात्मकः -का -कं, भययुक्तः -क्ता -क्तं, शङ्कास्पदं.

INSECURITY, *s.* सभयता, सशङ्कता -त्वं, शङ्कनीयता, संशयापन्नता, भयशङ्का, भयसंशयः, भयं, शङ्का, संशयः, अक्षेमः -मं.

INSENSATE, *a.* निर्बोधः -धा -धं, निर्बुद्धिः -द्धिः -द्धि, अबुद्धिमान् -मती -मत् (त्), प्रमूढः -ढा -ढं, प्रमुग्धः -ग्धा -ग्धं, अचेतनः -ना -नं.

INSENSIBILITY, INSENSIBLENESS, *s.* (Want of corporeal sensibility) अचैतन्यं, अचेतना, इन्द्रियस्वापः, इन्द्रियसुप्तिः *f.*, सुप्तिः *f.*, स्पर्शाज्ञानं, स्पर्शानभिज्ञता, नष्टेन्द्रियता, इन्द्रियनाशः.—(Want of emotion or tenderness) रागहीनता, विकाराभावः, भावहीनता, रसहीनता, दयाहीनता, कृपाहीनता.—(Dullness, torpor) जडता, जडिमा *m.* (न्), जाड्यं, अचिन्ता, कुण्ठता.—(Loss of consciousness, fainting) चेतनाहानिः *f.*, चैतन्यहानिः *f.*, चैतन्यनाशः, नष्टचेष्टता, संज्ञाहानिः *f.*, संज्ञानाशः, चित्तवैकल्यं, मोहः, प्रमोहः, प्रलयः, मूर्च्छा -र्च्छना.

INSENSIBLE, *a.* (Imperceptible) अगोचरः -रा -रं, इन्द्रियागोचरः -रा -रं, इन्द्रियाग्राह्यः -ह्या -ह्यं, इन्द्रियाविषयः -या -यं, अतीन्द्रियः -या -यं, अलक्ष्यः -क्ष्या -क्ष्यं.—(Wanting corporeal sensibility) अचेतनः -ना -नं, विचेतनः -ना -नं, विसंज्ञः -ज्ञा -ज्ञं, नष्टेन्द्रियः -या -यं, सुप्तेन्द्रियः -या -यं, सुप्तः -प्ता -प्तं, स्पर्शानभिज्ञः -ज्ञा -ज्ञं.—(Void of emotion, feeling, or tenderness) रागहीनः -ना -नं, रसहीनः -ना -नं, दयाहीनः -ना -नं, निर्दयः -या -यं, कृपारहितः -ता -तं, अनार्द्रचित्तः -त्ता -त्तं, अद्रवचित्तः -त्ता -त्तं.—(Dull, torpid) जडः -डा -डं, कुण्ठः -ण्ठा -ण्ठं, अचिन्तः -न्ता -न्तं.—(Void of consciousness, fainted) नष्टचेतनः -ना -नं, गतचेतनः -ना -नं, चैतन्यरहितः -ता -तं, अचेतनः -ना -नं, विचेतनः -ना -नं, निश्चेतनः -ना -नं, गतचेताः -ताः -तः (स्), नष्टसंज्ञः -ज्ञा -ज्ञं, निःसंज्ञः -ज्ञा -ज्ञं, संज्ञाहीनः -ना -नं, नष्टचेष्टः -ष्टा -ष्टं, निश्चेष्टितः -ता -तं, असंज्ञः -ज्ञा -ज्ञं, गतसंज्ञः -ज्ञा -ज्ञं, मृतकल्पः -ल्पा -ल्पं, प्रमूढः -ढा -ढं, प्रमुग्धः -ग्धा -ग्धं, मोहितः -ता -तं, प्रमोहितः -ता -तं, प्रलीनः -ना -नं, मूर्च्छितः -ता -तं.

INSENSIBLY, *adv.* (Imperceptibly) इन्द्रियागोचरं, अव्यक्तं, अलक्ष्यप्रकारेण, दुर्लक्ष्यं.—(Gradually) क्रमे क्रमे, क्रमशस्, क्रमेण, शनैः, पदशस्, पदे पदे, शनैः शनैः.

INSENTIENT, *a.* अचेतनः -ना -नं, विचेतनः -ना -नं, अप्राणभृत्. *See* INSENSIBLE.

INSEPARABLE, *a.* अवियोज्यः -ज्या -ज्यं, अवियोजनीयः -या -यं, अभेद्यः -द्या -द्यं, अभेदनीयः -या -यं, अविभेद्यः -द्या -द्यं, वियोजनाशक्यः -क्या -क्यं, अविभजनीयः -या -यं, अपृथक्करणीयः -या -यं, अद्वैधीकरणीयः -या -यं, नित्यसम्बन्धी -न्धिनी -न्धि (न्), नित्यसहवर्त्ती -र्त्तिनी -र्त्ति (न्), समवायसम्बन्धी &c., समवायी &c.; 'inseparable relation,' समवायसम्बन्धः, समवायिकरणं.

INSEPARABLENESS, *s.* अवियोज्यता, अभेद्यता, अविभेद्यता, नित्यसम्बन्धः.

INSEPARABLY, *adv.* अविभेदनीयं, अवियोजनीयं, नित्यसम्बन्धेन, दृढसम्बन्धेन, समवायसम्बन्धेन, यथा वियोक्तुं न शक्यते तथाप्रकारेण.

To INSERT, *v. a.* निविश् (c. 10. -वेशयति -यितुं), प्रविश्, आविश्, समाविश्, अन्तर्गतं -तां -तं कृ, अन्तरस्थं -स्थां -स्थं कृ, अन्तःस्थितं -तां -तं कृ, अन्तः स्था in caus. (स्थापयति -यितुं), निधा (c. 3. -दधाति -धातुं), न्यस् (c. 4. -अस्यति -असितुं); 'insert in writing,' अभिलिख् (c. 6. -लिखति -लेखितुं), पत्रे or लेख्ये समृ in caus. (-अर्पयति -यितुं) or आरुह् in caus. (-रोपयति -यितुं).

INSERTED, *p. p.* निवेशितः -ता -तं, प्रवेशितः -ता -तं, समावेशितः -ता -तं, निविष्टः -ष्टा -ष्टं, अन्तर्गतः -ता -तं, अन्तरस्थः -स्था -स्थं, निहितः -ता -तं, प्रत्याकलितः -ता -तं; 'in writing,' अभिलिखितः -ता -तं, लेख्यारूढः -ढा -ढं, लेख्यारोपितः -ता -तं.

INSERTION, *s.* निवेशः -शनं, प्रवेशः -शनं, आवेशनं, समावेशनं, अन्तःस्थापनं, निधानं, आरोपणं, समर्पणं; 'in writing,' अभिलिखनं, लेख्यारोपणं, लेख्यसमर्पणं.

To INSHRINE, *v. a.* *See To* ENSHRINE.

INSIDE, *s.* (Interior of any thing) अभ्यन्तरं, अन्तरं, गर्भः, उदरं, क्रोडं, अन्तःभागः, अभ्यन्तरभागः, विलं, विवरं, कुहरं; 'the inside of a house,' गृहाभ्यन्तरं, अन्तर्गृहं, अन्तर्भवनं, भवनोदरं; 'the inside of a boiler,' स्थालीविलं; 'the inside of a tree,' तरुकोटरः -रं, तरुक्रोडं.

INSIDE, *adv.* अभ्यन्तरे, अन्तर्, अन्तरे; 'inside the house,' गृहाभ्यन्तरे.

INSIDIOUS, *a.* छली -लिनी -लि (न्), छलनापरः -रा -रं, कपटी -टिनी -टि (न्), कापटिकः -की -कं, मायी -यिनी -यि (न्), बहुमायः -या -यं, भूरिमायः -या -यं, मायान्वितः -ता -तं, मायाकरः -री -रं, मायापटुः -टुः -टु, कौटिकः -की -कं, सव्याजः -जा -जं, छाद्मिकः -की -कं, प्रतारकः -का -कं, उपजापकः -का -कं, वञ्चकः -का -कं, मोही -हिनी -हि (न्), प्रलोभकः -का -कं.

INSIDIOUSLY, *adv.* छलेन, सकपटं, समायं, मायया, सव्याजं, उपजापकवत्, प्रलोभनार्थं, सकूटं, छद्मपूर्व्वं, वञ्चनार्थं, कितववत्, धूर्त्तवत्.

INSIDIOUSNESS, *s.* सकपटत्वं, कापट्यं, कूटता, सकूटता, सव्याजता, कापटिकत्वं, वञ्चकत्वं, कौटिकत्वं, छाद्मिकत्वं, उपजापः.

INSIGHT, *s.* अभिनिवेशः, निवेशः, प्रवेशः, परिज्ञानं, अभिज्ञानं, ज्ञानं, परिचयः, निरीक्षणं, अवेक्षणं, आलोचना.

INSIGNIA, *s.* चिह्नं, लक्षणं, लिङ्गं, व्यञ्जनं, उपकरणं; 'insignia of royalty,' राजलक्षणं, राजचिह्नं, नृपलक्ष्म *n.* (न्); these are 'the parasol,' छत्रं, and 'the fan,' चामरं; 'bearing of royal insignia,' प्रक्रिया, अधिकारः.

INSIGNIFICANCE, INSIGNIFICANCY, *s.* (Want of meaning) अनर्थकत्वं, निरर्थकत्वं, आनर्थक्यं, अर्थहीनता, अर्थशून्यता, अर्थाभावः, अनर्थकत्वं.—(Unimportance) लघुता, लाघवं, लघिमा *m.* (न्), प्रभावहीनता, अल्पप्रभावत्वं, अल्पत्वं, अगुरुता, अगौरवं, गौरवहीनता.—(Meanness) लाघवं, लघुवृत्तिता, क्षुद्रता, कदर्य्यता, तुच्छत्वं, अपकृष्टता, अपकर्षः, कुत्सितत्वं, दीनता, निःसत्त्वं, सत्त्वहीनता, क्षुद्रकत्वं.

INSIGNIFICANT, *a.* (Void of meaning) अनर्थकः -का -कं, निरर्थकः -का -कं, निरर्थः -र्था -र्थं, अर्थहीनः -ना -नं, अर्थशून्यः -न्या -न्यं, अर्थावाचकः -का -कं, अवाचकः -का -कं.—(Unimportant) लघुः -घुः -घ्वी -घु, अगुरुः -रुः -र्व्वी -रु, अल्पप्रभावः -वा -वं, प्रभावहीनः -ना -नं, गौरवहीनः -ना -नं, अल्पः -ल्पा -ल्पं, स्वल्पः -ल्पा -ल्पं, अकिञ्चित्करः -री -रं.—(Mean) क्षुद्रः -द्रा -द्रं, कदर्य्यः -र्य्या -र्य्यं, लघुवृत्तिः -त्तिः -त्ति, तुच्छः -च्छा -च्छं, अपकृष्टः -ष्टा -ष्टं, कुत्सितः -ता -तं, निःसत्त्वः -त्त्वा -त्त्वं, सत्त्वहीनः -ना -नं, तृणप्रायः -या -यं, अल्पिष्ठकीर्त्तिः -र्त्तिः -र्त्ति, किम्वान् -म्वती -म्वत् (त्); 'insignificant person,' क्षुद्रजनः, अजनः.

INSIGNIFICANTLY, *adv.* (Without meaning) अर्थं विना, अनर्थकं, निरर्थकं.—(Without importance) लघु, अगुरु, अगौरवेण, लाघवेन, अल्पप्रभावेण.

INSINCERE, *a.* असत्यः -त्या -त्यं, निःसत्यः -त्या -त्यं, असरलः -ला -लं, कृत्रिमः -मा -मं, कल्पितः -ता -तं, काल्पनिकः -की -कं, कृतकः -का -कं, कूटार्थः -र्था -र्थं, मिथ्यार्थकः -का -कं, मृषार्थकः -का -कं, कपटी -टिनी -टि (न्), कापटिकः -की -कं, छाद्मिकः -की -कं, अनृजुः -जुः -जु, जिह्मः -ह्मा -ह्मं, वक्रः -क्रा -क्रं, कुटिलः -ला -लं, मायी -यिनी -यि (न्), मायिकः -की -कं, अयथार्थः -र्था -र्थं, अनृतः -ता -तं, अलीकः -का -कं, वितथः -था -थं, अतात्त्विकः -की -कं, असात्त्विकः -की -कं, अशुद्धः -द्धा -द्धं, अनिर्म्मलः -ला -लं, मिथ्या or मृषा in comp.

INSINCERELY, *adv.* असरलं, असत्यं, निःसत्यं, कृत्रिमं, अनृतं, अयथार्थं, मायया, समायं, अशुद्धं, मिथ्या, मृषा.

INSINCERITY, *s.* निःसत्यता, असत्यता, असारल्यं, असरलता, कृत्रिमता, काल्पनिकत्वं, कूटार्थत्वं, कापट्यं, सकपटत्वं, कपटता, अनृजुता, जिह्मता, वक्रता, अनृतत्वं; कुटिलता, माया, कौटिल्यं *m.*, मायिकत्वं, कुहना, छद्म *n.* (न्), छाद्मिकत्वं, छद्मवेशः, दम्भः, दाम्भिकत्वं, कुहकवृत्तिः *f.*, अयथार्थता, अलीकता, वितथता, अपह्नवः, निह्नवः.

To INSINUATE, *v. a.* (Introduce gently) शनैः शनैः or क्रमे क्रमे प्रविश् (c. 10. -वेशयति -यितुं) or निविश् or आविश्.—(Work one's self into favor by gentle means) शनैः शनैः सान्त्वादिना or लालनादिकर्म्मणा परानुग्रहं प्राप् (c. 5. -आप्नोति -आप्तुं) or सम्पद् (c. 10. -पादयति -यितुं), परानुग्रहसम्पादनार्थं सामादिना लल् (c. 10. लालयति -यितुं) or सान्त्व् (c. 10. सान्त्वयति -यितुं) or आराध् (c. 10. -राधयति -यितुं) or अनुरञ्ज् (c. 10. -रञ्जयति -यितुं), मन्दं मन्दं लालनाद्युपायैः परप्रीतिं गम् (c. 1. गच्छति, गन्तुं) or अधिगम्.—(Hint by oblique allusion) वक्रोक्त्या उद्दिश् (c. 6. -दिशति -देष्टुं) or सूच् (c. 10. सूचयति -यितुं) or उपन्यस् (c. 4. -अस्यति -असितुं) वक्रोक्तिं कृ, छेकोक्तिं कृ, छेकोक्त्या सूच्, सङ्केतं कृ अवक्षिप् (c. 6. -क्षिपति -क्षेप्तुं), उपक्षिप्.

To INSINUATE, *v. n.* (Creep in) मन्दं मन्दं निविश् (c. 6. -विशति -वेष्टुं) or प्रविश् or सृप् (c. 1. सर्पति, सर्प्तुं) or उपसृप् or आगम् (c. 1. -गच्छति -गन्तुं) or अभ्यागम्.

INSINUATED, *p. p.* (Introduced gently) शनैः शनैः or मन्दं मन्दं निवेशितः -ता -तं or प्रवेशितः -ता -तं.—(Hinted) वक्रोक्त्या सूचितः -ता -तं or उद्दिष्टः -ष्टा -ष्टं, अवक्षिप्तः -प्ता -प्तं, उपक्षिप्तः -प्ता -प्तं.

INSINUATING, INSINUATIVE, *a.* (Stealing gradually on the affections) शनैः शनैः परानुग्रहसम्पादकः -का -कं or परानुरागोत्पादकः -का -कं, लाली -लिनी -लि (न्), लालनशीलः -ला -लं.—(Using oblique allusion) वक्रोक्त्या सूचकः -का -कं, अवक्षेपकः -का -कं, निह्नुवानः -ना -नं.

INSINUATION, *s.* (Act of stealing on the affections) शनैः शनैः सान्त्वादिना or लालनादिना परानुग्रहसम्पादनं or परानुरागसम्प्राप्तिः *f.*, लालनं, सान्त्वनं -ना, सामादिना प्रीतिकरणं.—(Oblique allusion, hint) वक्रोक्तिः *f.*, छेकोक्तिः *f.*, व्यङ्ग्योक्तिः *f.*, व्यङ्ग्यं, वक्रभणितं, वक्रवाक्यं, वक्रसूचितं, निह्नुतिः *f.*, निह्नवः, अवक्षेपः, पर्य्यायोक्तिः *f.*—(Creeping in gradually) मन्दं मन्दम् उपसर्पणं or अभ्यन्तरनिवेशः.

INSIPID, *a.* विरसः -सा -सं, अरसः -सा -सं, नीरसः -सा -सं, अरसिकः -का -कं, निरसः -सा -सं, रसहीनः -ना -नं, अलवणः -णा -णं, लवणहीनः -ना -नं, विस्वादः -दा -दं, निःस्वादुः -दुः -दु, स्वादहीनः -ना -नं, अस्वादुः -दुः -दु, असारः -रा -रं, निस्सारः -रा -रं, सारहीनः -ना -नं, फल्गुः -ल्गुः -ल्गु, निःसत्त्वः -त्त्वा -त्त्वं, सत्त्वहीनः -ना -नं, निस्तेजाः -जाः -जः (स्).

INSIPIDITY, INSIPIDNESS, *s.* विरसता -त्वं, वैरस्यं, अरसता, आरस्यं, अरसिकत्वं, नीरसता, निरसः, रसहीनता, अलवणता, अलावण्यं, आलवण्यं, लवणहीनता, अस्वादुता, विस्वादत्वं, असारता -त्वं, सारहीनता, फल्गुता.

INSIPIDLY, *adv.* विरसं, वैरस्येन, रसादृते, रसं विना, विस्वादं.

To INSIST, *v. n.* (Insist upon, urge with firmness) निर्बन्धं कृ, अतिनिर्बन्धं कृ, आग्रहं कृ; धैर्य्यं or स्थैर्य्यम् अवलम्ब् (c. 1. -लम्बते -म्बितुं), अतिनिर्बन्धेन पर्य्यवस्था (c. 1. -तिष्ठति -स्थातुं); 'to insist on a thing's being done,' इदम् अवश्यं करणीयम् इति दृढोक्त्या वद् (c. 1. वदति -दितुं) or इति निर्बन्धेन वद्.

INSITIENCY, *s.* अतृष्णा, अतृषा, तृष्णाभावः, अपिपासा, पिपासाभावः.

To INSNARE, *v. a.* पाशे or उन्माथे or वागुरायां पत् (c. 10. पातयति -यितुं), जाले पातयित्वा बन्ध् (c. 9. बध्नाति, बन्धुं), जालबद्धं -द्धां -द्धं कृ, प्रलुभ् (c. 10. -लोभयति -यितुं).

INSNARED, *p. p.* उन्माथपातितः -ता -तं, पाशबद्धः -द्धा -द्धं, जालबद्धः &c.

INSOBRIETY, *s.* अतिपानं, मद्यपानासक्तिः *f.*, मत्तता, उन्मत्तता.

INSOCIABLE, *a.* संलापविमुखः -खी -खं, सम्भाषणविमुखः -खी -खं, संलापपराङ्मुखः &c., असंलापी -पिनी -पि (न्), अनालापी &c., असंलापशीलः -ला -लं.

To INSOLATE, *v. a.* सूर्य्यव्याप्तं -प्तां कृ, सूर्य्यतेजोव्याप्तं -प्तां कृ, सूर्य्यकिरणव्याप्तं -प्तां कृ, सूर्य्यव्याप्यं -प्यां कृ.

INSOLENCE, INSOLENCY, *s.* धर्षः -र्षणं, धृष्टता, धार्ष्ट्यं, दर्पः, प्रगल्भता प्रागल्भ्यं, उद्धतिः *f.*, औद्धत्यं, अवहेला -लनं, अवलेपः, अवलिप्तता, सावलेपत्वं, गर्व्वः, उन्मादः, प्रतिभानं, वैयात्यं, निर्लज्जत्वं, अविनयः, उन्मायः, उत्सिक्तता, उत्सेकः.

INSOLENT, *a.* धृष्टः -ष्टा -ष्टं, धर्षितः -ता -तं, प्रधृष्टः -ष्टा -ष्टं, धर्षी -र्षिणी -र्षि (न्), प्रधर्षितः -ता -तं, दृप्तः -प्ता -प्तं, सदर्पः -र्पा -र्पं, प्रगल्भः -ल्भा -ल्भं, उद्धतः -ता -तं, मदोद्धतः -ता -तं, गर्व्वी -र्व्विणी -र्व्वि (न्), गर्व्वितः -ता -तं, अवलिप्तः -प्ता -प्तं, सावलेपः -पा -पं, सावहेलः -ला -लं, उत्सिक्तः -क्ता -क्तं, उन्मत्तः -त्ता -त्तं, अविनीतः -ता -तं, अविनयः -या -यं, प्रतिभामुखः -खी -खं, प्रतिभानवान् -वती -वत् (त्), प्रतिभावान् &c., प्रतिभान्वितः -ता -तं, वियातः -ता -तं, निर्लज्जः -ज्जा -ज्जं, लज्जाहीनः -ना -नं, मदोदग्रः -ग्रा -ग्रं.

INSOLENTLY, *adv.* धृष्टवत्, धर्षेण, सधर्षं, सदर्पं, दर्पेण, प्रगल्भं, प्रगल्भवत्, प्रागल्भ्येन, सावलेपं, सावहेलं, अविनयेन, प्रसह्य, अभिषह्य, प्रमथ्य.

INSOLIDITY, *s.* अघनता -त्वं, अकाठिन्यं, अदृढता, अन्तःशून्यता.

INSOLUBILITY, INSOLVABLENESS, *s.* (Indissolvable) अद्राव्यता, अद्रवणीयता, अगलनीयता, द्रावणाशक्यता, अविलयनीयता.

INSOLUBLE, INSOLVABLE, *a.* (Indissolvable) अद्राव्यः -व्या -व्यं, अद्रवणीयः -या -यं, अभेद्यः -द्या -द्यं, अगलनीयः -या -यं.—(Not to be solved) अपरिशोधनीयः -या -यं, अव्याख्येयः -या -यं.

INSOLVENCY, *s.* परिक्षीणता, ऋणशोधनाशक्तिः *f.*, ऋणमोचनाशक्तिः *f.*, ऋणमोचनासमर्थ्यं, ऋणापकरणाशक्तिः *f.*, ऋणशोधनाक्षमता, निर्धनता.

INSOLVENT, *a.* परिक्षीणः -णा -णं, ऋणशोधनाक्षमः -मा -मं, ऋणशोधनाशक्तः -क्ता -क्तं, ऋणमोचनाशक्तः -क्ता -क्तं, ऋणापकरणाशक्तः -क्ता -क्तं, ऋणापकरणासमर्थः -र्था -र्थं, ऋणपरिशोधनाक्षमः -मा -मं, निर्धनः -ना -नं, गतविभवः -वा -वं.

IN SO MUCH THAT, *adv.* (To such a degree) एतत्पर्य्यन्तं, एतावत्पर्य्यन्तं, एतावत्, एतदवधि, एतावदवधि, यथा तथा.

To INSPECT, *v. a.* निरीक्ष् (c. 1. -ईक्षते -क्षितुं), परीक्ष्, अवेक्ष्, वीक्ष्,

अभिवीक्ष्, समीक्ष्, निरूप् (c. 10. -रूपयति -यितुं), दृश् (c. 1. पश्यति, द्रष्टुं), अनुदृश्, परिदृश्, अभिदृश्, प्रतिदृश्, सन्दृश्, अनुसन्धा (c. 3. -दधाति -धातुं), आलोच् (c. 10. -लोचयति -यितुं), आलोक् (c. 10. -लोकयति -यितुं), कार्य्यदर्शनं कृ, कार्य्येक्षणं कृ, कार्य्यावेक्षणं कृ.

INSPECTED, *p. p.* निरीक्षितः -ता -तं, अवेक्षितः -ता -तं, निरूपितः -ता -तं, परीक्षितः -ता -तं, आलोचितः -ता -तं, समीक्षितः -ता -तं.

INSPECTION, *s.* (Looking into, examination) निरीक्षणं, निरीक्षा, परीक्षा -क्षणं, अवेक्षणं, अवेक्षा, समीक्षा -क्षणं, प्रसमीक्षा, वीक्षणं, संवीक्षणं, निरूपणं, अनुसन्धानं, आलोचनं -ना, आलोकनं, दर्शनं, सन्दर्शनं, कार्य्यदर्शनं, कार्य्येक्षणं, कार्य्यावेक्षणं, अनुसन्धानं.—(Superintendence) अध्यक्षता -त्वं, कार्य्याधीशता, अधिकारः, अधिकर्म्म *n.* (न्).

INSPECTOR, *s.* (One who looks into, examines) निरीक्षकः, निरीक्षिता *m.* (तृ), अवेक्षकः, अवेक्षिता *m.*, परीक्षकः, समीक्षकः, निरूपकः, निरूपयिता *m.* (तृ), अनुसन्धाता *m.* (तृ), द्रष्टा *m.* (ष्टृ), उपद्रष्टा.—(Superintendent of affairs) अध्यक्षः, कार्य्याध्यक्षः, कार्य्यद्रष्टा *m.* (ष्टृ), कार्य्याधीशः, कार्य्यावेक्षिता *m.* (तृ), कार्य्येक्षिता *m.*, अधिकारी *m.* (न्), कर्म्माधिकारी *m.*, अधिकर्म्मिकः; 'inspector of morals,' धर्म्माध्यक्षः, व्यवहारद्रष्टा *m.* (ष्टृ); 'of the coinage,' रूप्याध्यक्षः; 'of a district,' गोपः.

INSPECTORSHIP, *s.* अध्यक्षता -त्वं, कार्य्याध्यक्षत्वं, कार्य्याधीशता, प्रभुत्वं.

INSPERSION, *s.* निषेकः, निषेचनं, अभिषेकः, अभिषिञ्चनं, प्रोक्षणं, अभिप्रोक्षणं, अभ्युक्षणं, समुक्षणं.

INSPIRATION, *s.* (Breath inspired) श्वासः, श्वसनं, श्वसितं, प्राणः, निश्वासः, उच्छ्वासः, आनः, आहरः.—(Act of drawing air into the lungs) श्वासग्रहणं, प्राणग्रहणं, श्वासादानं, प्राणादानं, श्वसनं, निश्वसनं, निश्वासग्रहणं; 'inspiration and expiration,' श्वासप्रश्वासं, श्वासनिःश्वासं.—(Breathing into any thing) श्वासपूरणं, प्राणपूरणं, श्वासेन पूरणं, श्वासप्रक्षेपणं.—(Infusion) प्रक्षेपः -पणं, निक्षेपः.—(Supernatural infusion into the mind) ईश्वरप्रेरणा, ईश्वरसञ्चारणं, ईश्वरसूचना, ईश्वरोपदेशः, ईश्वरप्रबोधः, ईश्वरात्मावेशः, ईश्वरात्मव्याप्तिः *f.*, ईश्वरप्रयुक्तज्ञानं, दैवज्ञानं, गोत्रं; 'poetical inspiration,' प्राणः.

To INSPIRE, *v. a.* (Breathe into) श्वासेन पृ (c. 10. पूरयति -यितुं), श्वासपूरितं -तां -तं कृ.—(Draw into the lungs) श्वासग्रहणं कृ, श्वासादानं कृ, श्वस् (c. 2. श्वसिति -तुं), निश्वस्, उरःस्थानं श्वासेन पृ, श्वासमार्गेण प्राणम् आकृष् (c. 1. -कर्षति -क्रष्टुं); 'to inspire and expire,' श्वासप्रश्वासं कृ, श्वासनिःश्वासं कृ.—(Infuse into the mind, suggest) चित्ते निविश् (c. 10. -वेशयति -यितुं), प्रबुध् (c. 10. -बोधयति -यितुं), उपन्यस् (c. 4. -अस्यति -असितुं), उपनिधा (c. 3. -दधाति -धत्ते -धातुं); 'inspire with fear,' भयम् उपनिधा or जन् (c. 10 जनयति -यितुं) or उत्पद् (c. 10. -पादयति -यितुं), सभयं -यां कृ.—(Inspire with courage, incite) आश्वस् (c. 10. -श्वासयति -यितुं), समाश्वस्, उच्छ्वस्, विश्वस्, उत्तिज् (c. 10. -तेजयति -यितुं), प्रोत्सह्, (c. 10. -साहयति -यितुं), समुत्सह्, प्रेर् (c. 10. -ईरयति -यितुं), नियुज् (c. 10. -योजयति -यितुं), प्रयुज्, प्रवृत् (c. 10. -वर्त्तयति -यितुं), तेजः or विश्वासं कृ or जन् or उत्पद्.—(Inspire supernaturally) ईश्वरप्रेरितं -तां कृ, ईश्वरोपदिष्टं -ष्टां कृ.

INSPIRED, *p. p.* (Breathed) श्वसितः -ता -तं, निश्वसितः -ता -तं, उच्छ्वसितः -ता -तं.—(Infused) व्याप्तः -प्ता -प्तं, भावितः -ता -तं, निवेशितः -ता -तं.—(Supernaturally inspired) ईश्वरप्रेरितः -ता -तं, ईश्वरोपदिष्टः -ष्टा -ष्टं, ईश्वरसूचितः -ता -तं, ईश्वरसञ्चारितः -ता -तं, ईश्वरप्रबोधितः -ता -तं, ईश्वरात्मव्याप्तः -प्ता -प्तं.—(Inspired with courage) आश्वासितः -ता -तं, जातविश्वासः -सा -सं, उत्तेजितः -ता -तं; 'inspired with,' is often expressed by जात in comp.; as, 'inspired with fear,' जातभयः -या -यं.

To INSPIRIT, *v. a.* आश्वस् (c. 10. -श्वासयति -यितुं), समाश्वस्, विश्वस्, उत्तिज् (c. 10. -तेजयति -यितुं), तेजः or विश्वासं or समाश्वासं कृ or दा or जन् (c. 10. जनयति -यितुं) or उत्पद् (c. 10. -पादयति -यितुं), प्रोत्सह् (c. 10. -साहयति -यितुं), उत्सह्, हृष् (c. 10. हर्षयति -यितुं), प्रहृष्, उल्लस् (c. 10. -लासयति -यितुं), जीव् (c. 10. जीवयति -यितुं).

INSPIRITED, *p. p.* आश्वासितः -ता -तं, समाश्वासितः -ता -तं, उच्छ्वसितः -ता -तं, उत्तेजितः -ता -तं, प्रोत्साहितः -ता -तं, उत्साहितः -ता -तं, जातोत्साहः -हा -हं, जाततेजाः -जाः -जः (स्).

INSPIRITING, *a.* आश्वासकः -सिका -कं, उत्तेजकः -का -कं, प्रोत्साहकः -का -कं, उत्साहजनकः -का -कं, उत्साहकारकः -का -कं, तेजस्करः -री -रं, तेजोवर्धकः -का -कं, हर्षकः -का -कं.

To INSPISSATE, *v. a.* घनीकृ, स्थूलीकृ, सान्द्रीकृ, स्त्यव (nom. स्त्यवयति -यितुं).

INSPISSATE, INSPISSATED, *a.* or *p. p.* घनः -ना -नं, घनीभूतः -ता -तं, स्थूलः -ला -लं, स्थूलीभूतः -ता -तं, सान्द्रः -न्द्रा -न्द्रं, स्त्यानः -ना -नं, निबिडः -डा -डं.

INSPISSATION, *s.* घनता -त्वं, घनीकरणं, स्थूलता, स्थूलीकरणं, सान्द्रता, सान्द्रीभावः, नैबिड्यं, गाढता.

INSTABILITY, *s.* अस्थिरता, अस्थैर्य्यं, अधैर्य्यं, अधृतिः *f.*, अधीरता, अस्थायित्वं, अनवस्थितिः *f.*, अनवस्था, चञ्चलता, चाञ्चल्यं, चापल्यं.

INSTABLE, *a.* अस्थिरः -रा -रं, अधीरः -रा -रं. *See* UNSTABLE.

To INSTALL, *v. a.* अभिषिच् (c. 6. -षिञ्चति -षेक्तुं), with loc. c. of the office in which one is installed, अभिषेकादिसंस्कारेण नवाधिकारं प्रविश् (c. 10. -वेशयति -यितुं), संस्कारपूर्व्वं नवाधिकारप्रवेशनं कृ, यथाविधि प्रतिष्ठा in caus. (-ष्ठापयति -यितुं) or अधिकारारूढं कृ, अभिमन्त्र् (c. 10. -मन्त्रयति -यितुं), उपनिमन्त्र्, पदस्थं कृ.

INSTALLATION, *s.* अभिषेकः, अभिषेचनं, अभिषेकादिसंस्कारेण नवाधिकारप्रवेशः, संस्कारपूर्व्वं नवाधिकारप्रवेशनं, अधिकारप्रवेशसंस्कारः, प्रतिष्ठापनं, संस्कारः, अधिकारस्थापनं, अधिकारप्रतिष्ठापनं, पदस्थापनं.

INSTALLED, *p. p.* अभिषिक्तः -क्ता -क्तं, कृताभिषेकः -का -कं, प्राप्ताभिषेकः -का -कं, कृतसंस्कारः -रा -रं, प्राप्तसंस्कारः -रा -रं, संस्कारपूर्व्वं नवाधिकारप्रवेशितः -ता -तं or नवाधिकारप्रतिष्ठापितः -ता -तं or नवपदप्रतिष्ठापितः -ता -तं, प्रतिष्ठितः -ता -तं, प्रतिष्ठापितः -ता -तं, कृतप्रतिष्ठः -ष्ठा -ष्ठं, लब्धप्रतिष्ठः -ष्ठा -ष्ठं, अधिकारस्थः -स्था -स्थं, पदारूढः -ढा -ढं, अधिकारारूढः -ढा -ढं, अभिसंस्कृतः -ता -तं.

INSTALMENT, *s.* (Act of installing). *See* INSTALLATION. (Part of a large sum of money to be paid) कालान्तरेण देयस्य बहुधनस्य भागः or विभागः or अंशः, ऋणभागः, ऋणविभागः; 'by instalments,' भागशस्, विभागशस्, विभागतस्, शनैः.

INSTANCE, *s.* (Urgency, urgent solicitation) निर्बन्धः, प्रार्थनं -ना, निर्बन्धेन प्रार्थनं, आग्रहः, प्रेरणा.—(Example) दृष्टान्तः, निदर्शनं, उदाहरणं, उदाहारः, उपोद्घातः, प्रतीकं, लक्ष्यं; 'for instance,' दृष्टान्तरूपेण, दृष्टान्ततस्, यथा, तथाहि, तथा.—(Case) स्थलं, पदं.—(Occasion) प्रस्तावः, समयः, वारः, स्थानं; 'in the first instance,' प्रथमसमये, प्रथमं -मतस्, अग्रे.

To INSTANCE, *v. n.* दृष्टान्तं कृ, दृष्टान्तीकृ, दृष्टान्तं दा, दृष्टान्त (nom. दृष्टान्तयति -यितुं), दृष्टान्तक्रमेण कथ् (c. 10. कथयति -यितुं).

INSTANT, *a.* (Urgent) निर्बन्धशीलः -ला -लं, आग्रही -हिणी -हि (न्), आग्रहशीलः -ला -लं, अतियाचकः -का -कं, अतिप्रार्थकः -का -कं.—

(Immediate, without intervening time) अनन्तरकालीनः -ना -नं, अनन्तरकालिकः -की -कं, तात्कालिकः -की -कं, साद्यस्कः -स्की -स्कं, सद्यस्कः -स्का -स्कं, अव्यवहितकालः -ला -लं, साम्प्रतिकः -की -कं, क्षणान्तरः -रा -रं.—(Quick) शीघ्रः -घ्रा -घ्रं, अचिरः -रा -रं.—(Current) वर्त्तमानः -ना -नं.

INSTANT, *s.* (A moment) क्षणः, विपलं, पलं, निमेषः, निमिषः, मात्रा, त्रुटिः *f.*; 'the current moment,' आपातः; 'in an instant,' क्षणात्, निमेषमात्रेण, क्षणमात्रेण, क्षणान्तरे, एकपदे; 'for an instant,' क्षणं -णेन -णात्, क्षणमात्रं, निमेषमात्रं; 'for that very instant,' तत्क्षणादेव; 'at that instant,' तत्क्षणात् -णे, तत्काले, तदानीमेव; 'at this very instant,' इदानीमेव, एतत्काले; 'every instant,' प्रतिक्षणं, अनुक्षणं; 'the next instant,' क्षणान्तरं; 'the instant,' may often be expressed by मात्रं, in such phrases as 'the instant of birth,' जातमात्रं; 'from the instant of birth,' जातमात्रात्.

INSTANTANEOUS, *a.* तत्क्षणिकः -की -कं, तत्कालिकः -की -कं, तात्कालिकः -की -कं, क्षणिकः -का -की -कं, अव्यवहितकालीनः -ना -नं, अव्यवहितकालिकः -की -कं, आकालिकः -की -कं, क्षणभूतः -ता -तं, अचिरः -रा -रं, क्षणान्तरः -रा -रं.

INSTANTANEOUSLY, *adv.* तत्क्षणे, तत्क्षणेन, क्षणात्, क्षणेन, सद्यस्, तत्काले, सपदि, क्षणमात्रेण, निमेषमात्रेण, क्षणान्तरे, झटिति, आपाततस्.

INSTANTLY, *adv.* तत्क्षणात् -णेन -णं, क्षणात् -णेन, सद्यस्, सपदि, अनन्तरं, झटिति, द्राक्, प्रतिक्षणं, अञ्जसा, सम्प्रति, आपाततस्, अशनैः, अविलम्बितं, अव्यवहितकाले, अचिरेण.—(Urgently) निर्बन्धेन, आग्रहेण.

To INSTATE, *v. a.* प्रतिष्ठा in caus. (-ष्ठापयति -यितुं), संस्था, स्था, रुह् in caus. (रोपयति -यितुं), पदं प्रविश् (c. 10. -वेशयति -यितुं), पदस्थं कृ, पदप्रतिष्ठितं कृ, पदारूढं कृ.

IN STATU QUO, (Former state) प्रत्यवस्थानं, पूर्व्वावस्था.

INSTAURATION, *s.* प्रतिष्ठापनं, प्रत्यवस्थापनं, सन्धानं, प्रतिसमाधानं.

INSTEAD OF, *adv.* or *prep.* प्रति usually following a word in the abl. c., स्थाने, विनिमयात् -येन, स्थले, भूमौ; 'Kāma instead of Krishna,' प्रद्युम्नः केशवात् प्रति; 'instead of me,' मत्स्थाने; 'instead of thee,' त्वद्विनिमयेन.

To INSTEEP, *v. a.* वास् (c. 10. वासयति -यितुं), सिच् (c. 6. सिञ्चति, सेक्तुं), चिरकालेन जलेन समाप्लु (c. 10. -प्लावयति -यितुं) or जलसमाप्लुतं कृ, आर्द्रीकृ.

INSTEP, *s.* पिचिण्डिका, पिचण्डिका, पिण्डिका, पिण्डिः *f.*, पिण्डी, पादपिण्डः, पादोपरिभागः, पादाग्रं.

To INSTIGATE, *v. a.* प्रोत्सह् (c. 10. -साहयति -यितुं), उत्सह्, समुत्सह्, नियुज् (c. 10. -योजयति -यितुं), प्रयुज्, उद्युज्, प्रेर् (c. 10. प्रेरयति -यितुं, rt. ईर्), चुद् (c. 10. चोदयति -यितुं), प्रचुद्, सञ्चुद्, प्रवृत् (c. 10. -वर्त्तयति -यितुं), चेष्ट् (c. 10. चेष्टयति -यितुं), प्रणुद् (c. 6. -णुदति -णोत्तुं), प्ररुच् (c. 10. -रोचयति -यितुं), उत्तिज् (c. 10. -तेजयति -यितुं), उत्था in caus. (-थापयति -यितुं, rt. स्था), उद्दीप् (c. 10. -दीपयति -यितुं). The loc. or dat. c. is required of the thing to which one is instigated. *See* INCITE.

INSTIGATED, *p. p.* प्रोत्साहितः -ता -तं, नियोजितः -ता -तं, प्रयोजितः -ता -तं, प्रयुक्तः -क्ता -क्तं, उद्युक्तः -क्ता -क्तं, प्रेरितः -ता -तं, चोदितः -ता -तं, प्रचोदितः -ता -तं, प्रवर्त्तितः -ता -तं, प्रवृत्तः -त्ता -त्तं, प्रणोदितः -ता -तं, उत्तेजितः -ता -तं, प्ररुचितः -ता -तं, उत्थापितः -ता -तं.

INSTIGATION, *s.* प्रोत्साहः -हनं, प्रेरणं -णा, नियोजनं, प्रवर्त्तनं, प्रचोदनं, उत्तेजनं, समुत्तेजनं, प्रणोदः -दनं, प्ररोचनं, सञ्चारणं, नियोगः, प्रयोजनं, प्रयोजककर्तृत्वं.

INSTIGATOR, *s.* प्रोत्साहकः, प्रेरकः, नियोजकः, प्रयोजकः, प्रवर्त्तकः, सञ्चारकः, प्रचोदकः, उत्तेजकः, प्रणोदकः, उत्साहहेतुकः, प्रयोजककर्त्ता *m.* (र्त्तृ), प्रवर्त्तनकारी *m.* (न्); 'to an evil act,' कुप्रवर्त्तकः.

To INSTIL, *v. a.* (Infuse by drops) लवशः or कणशो निषिच् (c. 6. -षिञ्चति -षेक्तुं) or आसिच् or निक्षिप् (c. 6. -क्षिपति -क्षेप्तुं) or प्रक्षिप्.—(Infuse gradually into the mind) अल्पशः or अल्पाल्पं or शनैः शनैर् उपदिश् (c. 6. -दिशति -देष्टुं or चित्ते निविश् (c. 10. -वेशयति -यितुं) or प्रविश् with acc. c.

INSTILLATION, *s.* लवशो निषेकः or निषेचनं or प्रक्षेपणं, शनैर् उपदेशनं.

INSTILLED, *p. p.* लवशः or शनैः शनैः or क्रमे क्रमे निषिक्तः -क्ता -क्तं or निक्षिप्तः -प्ता -प्तं or निवेशितः -ता -तं or प्रवेशितः -ता -तं, क्रमेणोपदिष्टः -ष्टा -ष्टं.

INSTINCT, *s.* (Natural knowledge) सहजज्ञानं, सहजबुद्धिः *f.*, उपज्ञा, स्वाभाविकबुद्धिः *f.*, स्वाभाविकज्ञानं, प्राकृतिकबुद्धिः *f.*, अन्तर्गतबुद्धिः *f.*, नैसर्गिकबुद्धिः *f.*, पशुबुद्धिः *f.*

INSTINCT, *a.* (Excited, animated) उत्तेजितः -ता -तं, उद्दीप्तः -प्ता -प्तं, दीप्तः -प्ता -प्तं, दीपितः -ता -तं, उद्दीपितः -ता -तं, तेजितः -ता -तं, जीवितः -ता -तं, सजीवीकृतः -ता -तं.

INSTINCTIVE, *a.* (Prompted by instinct, spontaneous) सहजः -जा -जं, सहजज्ञानप्रयुक्तः -क्ता -क्तं, सहजज्ञानसिद्धः -द्धा -द्धं, स्वाभाविकः -की -कं, साहजिकः -की -कं, प्राकृतिकः -की -कं, उपज्ञासूचितः -ता -तं, स्वाभाविकबुद्धिसूचितः -ता -तं, प्रकृतिसिद्धः -द्धा -द्धं, नैसर्गिकः -की -कं, स्वभावप्रेरितः -ता -तं, सांसिद्धिकः -की -कं.

INSTINCTIVELY, *adv.* स्वभावतस्, स्वभावेन, सहजज्ञानात्, स्वाभाविकज्ञानात्, प्राकृतिकज्ञानात्, निसर्गतस्, स्वतस्, स्वयं.

To INSTITUTE, *v. a.* (Establish, ordain, enact) स्था in caus. (स्थापयति -यितुं), प्रतिष्ठा, संस्था, अवस्था, व्यवस्था, विधा (c. 3. -दधाति -धातुं), प्रतिनिधा, क्लृप् (c. 10. कल्पयति -यितुं), प्रक्लृप्, परिक्लृप्, आदिश् (c. 6. -दिशति -देष्टुं), सन्दिश्, निर्दिश्, प्रचुद् (c. 10. -चोदयति -यितुं), प्रतिपद् (c. 10. -पादयति -यितुं), नियुज् (c. 7. -युनक्ति -योक्तुं); 'is instituted,' कल्प्यते, प्रकल्प्यते.—(Instruct) उपदिश्, निर्दिश्.—(Begin, set on foot) प्रवृत् (c. 10. -वर्त्तयति -यितुं), आरभ् (c. 1. -रभते -रब्धुं).

INSTITUTE, *s.* (Established law, ordinance, precept) व्यवस्था, विधिः *m.*, विधानं, नियमः, शास्त्रविधानं, कल्पः, सूत्रं, निदर्शनं, शास्त्रनिदर्शनं, शास्त्रमर्य्यादा, नियोगः, चोदना, चरितं -त्रं.—(Institutes of religion or law) शास्त्रं, धर्म्मशास्त्रं.—(Compendium of institutes) धर्म्मसंहिता, संहिता.

INSTITUTED, *p. p.* प्रकल्पितः -ता -तं, कल्पितः -ता -तं, विहितः -ता -तं, स्थापितः -ता -तं, प्रतिष्ठापितः -ता -तं, संस्थापितः -ता -तं, प्रचोदितः -ता -तं, निर्दिष्टः -ष्टा -ष्टं, प्रवर्त्तितः -ता -तं.

INSTITUTION, *s.* (Act of establishing) कल्पनं, प्रकल्पनं, स्थापनं, प्रतिष्ठापनं, संस्थापनं, व्यवस्थापनं, अवस्थापनं, विधानं, नियोजनं.—(Law enjoined by authority) विधिः *m.*, विधानं, व्यवस्था, नियमः, कल्पः, निदर्शनं, नियोगः, सूत्रं.—(Organised society) मठः, सभा, श्रेणी -णिः *m. f.*, संसर्गः; 'literary institution,' विद्यालयः, विद्यावेश्म *n.* (न्), विद्याशाला; 'religious institution,' धर्म्मशाला.—(System) स्थितिः *f.*, संस्थितिः *f.*, संस्थानं, मार्गः, रीतिः *f.*

INSTITUTIONAL, *a.* वैधिकः -की -कं, नैयमिकः -की -कं, शास्त्रीयः -या -यं.

INSTITUTOR, *s.* स्थापकः, संस्थापकः, प्रतिष्ठापकः, व्यवस्थापकः, प्रयोजकः,

प्रवर्त्तकः, विधायकः, विधायी *m.* (न्), विधाता *m.* (तृ), आरम्भकः, स्थापनकारी *m.* (न्).

To INSTRUCT, *v. a.* (Teach) उपदिश् (c. 6. -दिशति -देष्टुं), शिक्ष् (c. 10. शिक्षयति -यितुं), अनुशिक्ष्, अभिशिक्ष्, अधी in caus. (अध्यापयति -यितुं rt. इ), शास् (c. 2. शास्ति, शासितुं), अनुशास्, पठ् (c. 10. पाठयति -यितुं), निदृश् (c. 10. -दर्शयति -यितुं), उपदेशं कृ, विद्यां दा.—(Educate) विनी (c. 1. -नयति -नेतुं), अनुनी.—(Inform) ज्ञा in caus. (ज्ञापयति, ज्ञपयति -यितुं), विज्ञा, निविद् (c. 10. -वेदयति -यितुं), बुध् (c. 10. बोधयति -यितुं), सूच् (c. 10. सूचयति -यितुं), अनुसूच्.—(Direct, enjoin) आदिश्, निर्दिश्, समादिश्, प्रदिश्, सन्दिश्, आज्ञा in caus., समाज्ञा, नियुज् (c. 7. -युनक्ति -योक्तुं, c. 10. -योजयति -यितुं), चुद् (c. 10. चोदयति -यितुं), प्रचुद्, सञ्चुद्.

INSTRUCTED, *p. p.* (Taught) उपदिष्टः -ष्टा -ष्टं, शिक्षितः -ता -तं, अध्यापितः -ता -तं, शासितः -ता -तं, अनुशासितः -ता -तं, शिष्टः -ष्टा -ष्टं, अनुशिष्टः -ष्टा -ष्टं, लब्धविद्यः -द्या -द्यं, प्राप्तविद्यः -द्या -द्यं, गृहीतविद्यः -द्या -द्यं, पाठितः -ता -तं.—(Informed) ज्ञापितः -ता -तं, विज्ञापितः -ता -तं, विज्ञप्तः -प्ता -प्तं, बोधितः -ता -तं.—(Directed) आदिष्टः -ष्टा -ष्टं, निर्दिष्टः -ष्टा -ष्टं, प्रचोदितः -ता -तं, आज्ञप्तः -प्ता -प्तं.

INSTRUCTION, *s.* (Teaching) उपदेशः -शनं, शिक्षा -क्षणं, अध्यापनं, शासनं, अनुशासनं, पाठः -ठनं, विद्यादानं, बोधनं, प्रतिबोधः.—(Direction, order) आज्ञा, आदेशः, निदेशः, निर्देशः, शासनं, शास्तिः *f.*, चोदनं -ना, नियोगः.—(Precept) विधिः *m.*, विधानं, नियमः, सूत्रं, कल्पः, निदर्शनं.

INSTRUCTIVE, *a.* उपदेशकः -का -कं, उपदेशी -शिनी -शि (न्), उपदेशकरः -रा -रं, उपदेशावहः -हा -हं, उपदेशप्रदः -दा -दं, बोधकः -का -कं, निदेशी -शिनी -शि (न्), शिक्षाकरः -रा -रं, ज्ञानोत्पादकः -का -कं, उपदेश in comp.

INSTRUCTOR, *s.* उपदेशकः, उपदेशी *m.* (न्), उपदेष्टा *m.* (ष्टृ), अध्यापकः, शिक्षकः, शिक्षाकरः, उपाध्यायः, गुरुः *m.*, शिक्षागुरुः *m.*, आचार्य्यः, उपदेशकृत् *m.* -कारी *m.* (न्), शिक्षादाता *m.* (तृ), विद्यादाता *m.*, ज्ञापकः.

INSTRUCTRESS, *s.* उपदेशिका, उपदेष्ट्री, उपदेशिनी, अध्यापिका, आचार्य्या, शिक्षिका, उपदेशकर्त्री, शिक्षाकर्त्री, शिक्षादात्री.

INSTRUMENT, *s.* (Tool, implement) यन्त्रं, उपकरणं, साधनं, कर्म्मसाधनं, कार्य्यसाधनं, सामग्र्यं -ग्री, द्रव्यं, उपस्करः, विलालः; 'astronomical instrument,' ज्योतिषयन्त्रं.—(Means, instrumental cause) कारणं, करणं, हेतुः *m.*, निमित्तं -त्तकं, निमित्तकारणं, प्रयोजनं.—(Agent, doer) कारकः, कर्त्ता *m.* (र्त्तृ), साधकः, प्रयोजकः, प्रयोज्यः, कार्य्यसाधकः, हेतुकः, कारकहेतुः *m.*—(Musical instrument) वादित्रं, वाद्यं, तूर्य्यं, आतोद्यं, तालितं; 'a wind instrument,' शुषिरं, शुषिरवाद्यं, शङ्खः -ङ्खं; 'stringed instrument,' ततं, तन्तुवाद्यं; 'instrument for martial music,' रणवाद्यं; 'sounded by the mouth,' मुखवाद्यं; 'covered with skin,' चर्म्मवाद्यं. *See* DRUM. (Deed, writing) साधनपत्रं, लेखः, लेखपत्रं, पत्रं, पत्रकं, लेख्यं, लेख्यप्रसङ्गः, करणं.

INSTRUMENTAL, *a.* (Serving to effect some end) कारणिकः -की -कं, हेतुकः -का -कं, हैतुकः -की -कं, कारकः -रिका -कं, साधकः -धिका -कं, साधिकः -का -कं, कार्य्यसाधकः &c., कारणभूतः -ता -तं, साधनभूतः -ता -तं, साधनीभूतः -ता -तं, कारणीभूतः -ता -तं, प्रसाधकः -का -कं, प्रयोजकः -का -कं, उपकारी -रिणी -रि (न्), कारी &c., कारकवान् -वती -वत् (त्), सम्पादकः -का -कं.—(Not vocal) वाद्यजः -जा -जं, वाद्यजनितः -ता -तं, वाद्यसिद्धः -द्धा -द्धं, वाद्यसम्बन्धी -न्धिनी -न्धि (न्), वाद्योत्पन्नः -न्ना -न्नं.—(Instrumental case in grammar) करणं, तृतीया विभक्तिः.

INSTRUMENTALITY, *s.* कारणत्वं -ता, कारकत्वं, हेतुता -त्वं, निमित्तत्वं, साधकत्वं, साधनत्वं, कर्तृत्वं, कर्तृकत्वं, करणत्वं, प्रयोजकत्वं.

INSTRUMENTALLY, *adv.* कारणतस्, हेतुतस्, कारणत्वेन, निमित्ततस्, करणतस्.

INSUAVITY, *s.* असृदुता, असौम्यता, अस्निग्धता, कर्कशत्वं, परुषता, चण्डता.

INSUBJECTION, *s.* अनधीनता, अनायत्तता, अवज्ञता, अविधेयता, अवश्यत्वं.

INSUBORDINATE, *a.* अवशः -शा -शं, अविनीतः -ता -तं, अविधेयः -या -यं.

INSUBORDINATION, *s.* अविनयः, अविनीतता, अविधेयता, आज्ञाभङ्गः, आज्ञाव्यतिक्रमः, शासनभङ्गः, अवशत्वं, स्वाम्यनधीनता, दुःशीलता.

INSUBSTANTIAL, *a.* अवास्तवः -वी -वं -विकः -की -कं, निःसारः -रा -रं, असारः -रा -रं, सारहीनः -ना -नं, निःसत्त्वः -त्त्वा -त्त्वं, सत्त्वहीनः -ना -नं, असन् -सती -सत् (त्), वायुसमः -मा -मं, असत्यः -त्या -त्यं.

INSUBSTANTIALITY, *s.* अवस्तुता, अवास्तवत्वं, अवस्तु *n.*, वस्त्वभावः, असारत्वं, सारहीनता, सत्त्वहीनता, असत्यता.

INSUFFERABLE, *a.* असह्यः -ह्या -ह्यं, असहनीयः -या -यं, दुःसहः -हा -हं, निःसहः -हा -हं, अक्षन्तव्यः -व्या -व्यं, अक्षमणीयः -या -यं, सहनाशक्यः -क्या -क्यं.

INSUFFERABLENESS, *s.* असह्यता, असहनीयता, निःसहत्वं, दौःसह्यं.

INSUFFERABLY, *adv.* असहनीयं, यथा सोढुं न शक्यते तथाप्रकारेण.

INSUFFICIENCY, *s.* (Deficiency, state of not being enough) न्यूनता, हीनता, क्षीणता, अल्पत्वं, विरहः, अयथेष्टता, अप्राचुर्य्यं, अपर्य्याप्तिः *f.*, अबाहुल्यं, अभावः, अनिर्वाहः.—(Inadequateness) अनुपयुक्तत्वं, अयोग्यता, अक्षमता -त्वं, अनौचित्यं, अनुचितत्वं, अपर्य्याप्तिः *f.*, असमर्थता, असामर्थ्यं.

INSUFFICIENT, *a.* (Not enough, deficient) अनलम् indec., अयथेष्टः -ष्टा -ष्टं, अपर्य्याप्तः -प्ता -प्तं, न्यूनः -ना -नं, हीनः -ना -नं, क्षीणः -णा -णं, अपूर्णः -र्णा -र्णं, अप्रचुरः -रा -रं, निर्वाहाक्षमः -मा -मं, निर्वाहासमर्थः -र्था -र्थं.—(Inadequate) अनुपयुक्तः -क्ता -क्तं, अयोग्यः -ग्या -ग्यं, अक्षमः -मा -मं, असमर्थः -र्था -र्थं, अपर्य्याप्तः -प्ता -प्तं, अनुचितः -ता -तं.

INSUFFICIENTLY, *adv.* (Not enough) अनलं, अयथेष्टं, अप्रचुरं.—(Inadequately) अनुपयुक्तं, अयोग्यं, अक्षमं, अपर्य्याप्तं, अनुचितं, अपर्य्याप्तं.

INSUFFLATION, *s.* (Act of breathing on) श्वासप्रक्षेपः, प्राणप्रक्षेपः, श्वासन्यासः.

INSULAR, *a.* (Belonging to an island) द्वीप्यः -प्या -प्यं, द्वैप्यः -प्यी -प्यं, द्वैपः -पी -पं, द्वीपी -पिनी -पि (न्), द्वीपीयः -या -यं, द्वीपसम्बन्धी &c., उपद्वीपसम्बन्धी &c.—(Surrounded by water) द्वीपाकारः -रा -रं, उपद्वीपाकारः -रा -रं, द्वीपरूपः -पा -पं, जलवेष्टितः -ता -तं, जलपरिगतः -ता -तं.

INSULARITY, *s.* द्वीपाकारत्वं, द्वीपरूपता, द्वीपता -त्वं, जलवेष्टितत्वं.

To INSULATE, *v. a.* पृथक् स्था in caus. (स्थापयति -यितुं), पृथक्कृ, अन्यवियुक्तं -क्तां कृ, अन्यविच्छिन्नं -न्नां कृ, अन्यविश्लिष्टं -ष्टां कृ.

INSULATED, *p. p.* or *a.* अनन्यसंलग्नः -ग्ना -ग्नं, अनन्यसंसक्तः -क्ता -क्तं, अनन्यसंयुक्तः -क्ता -क्तं, अन्यविश्लिष्टः -ष्टा -ष्टं, अन्यविभिन्नः -न्ना -न्नं, पृथक्स्थितः -ता -तं.

INSULATION, *s.* अन्यवियोगः, अन्यविभेदः, अनन्यसंयोगः, अन्यविच्छेदः.

INSULT, *s.* अधिक्षेपः, अपमानवाक्यं, अवमानवाक्यं, तिरस्कारवाक्यं, तिरस्कारः, अपमानं, अवज्ञा -ज्ञानं, परिभवः, अपमानक्रिया, अवलेपः, अवहेला -लनं, अपवादः, परीवादः, वाक्पारुष्यं, परिभाषणं, निन्दा, दुर्वचस् *n.*, धर्षणं, अनार्य्यं, खलोक्तिः *f.*, अनादरः, अनादरक्रिया, भर्त्सना, निर्भर्त्सना, क्षेपः.

To INSULT, *v. a.* अवज्ञा (c. 9. -जानाति -ज्ञातुं), अवमन् (c. 4. -मन्यते

-मन्तुं), अपमन्, अपमानं कृ, अवज्ञां कृ, अनार्य्यं कृ, तिरस्कृ, परिभू, लघूकृ, तुच्छीकृ, कदर्थीकृ, अवक्षिप् (c. 6. -क्षिपति -क्षेप्तुं), अधिक्षिप्, परिक्षिप्, आक्षिप्, अवगुर् (c. 6. -गुरते -रितुं), आक्षर् (c. 10. -क्षारयति -यितुं), अपवद् (c. 1. -वदति -ते -दितुं), परिवद्, कुत्स् (c. 10. कुत्सयति -यितुं); 'he insulted her,' तेन तस्या अनार्य्यं कृतं.

INSULTED, *p. p.* परिभूतः -ता -तं, अवज्ञातः -ता -तं, अवमानितः -ता -तं, अपमानितः -ता -तं, विमानितः -ता -तं, क्षिप्तः -प्ता -प्तं, अवक्षिप्तः -प्ता -प्तं, आक्षिप्तः &c., गर्हितः -ता -तं, अवधीरितः -ता -तं, तिरस्कृतः -ता -तं, निन्दितः -ता -तं, धर्षितः -ता -तं.

INSULTER, *s.* अपमानकर्त्ता *m.* (र्त्तृ), अवमन्ता *m.* (न्तृ), अवज्ञानकृत्, अनार्य्यकृत्.

INSULTING, *a.* अपमानकारी -रिणी -रि (न्), अपमानसूचकः -का -कं, अपमानार्थकः -का -कं, अवमानी -निनी -नि (न्), परिभवी -विणी -वि (न्), परिभावी &c., परिभावुकः -का -कं, अवक्षेपकः -का -कं, तिरस्कारमयः -यी -यं, निन्दार्थः -र्था -र्थं, कुत्सावादी -दिनी -दि (न्).

INSULTINGLY, *adv.* सापमानं, सतिरस्कारं, सावक्षेपं, अवज्ञापूर्व्वं.

INSUPERABLE, *a.* अनतिक्रमणीयः -या -यं, अनतिक्रम्यः -म्या -म्यं, दुरतिक्रमः -मा -मं, अलंघनीयः -या -यं, अलंघ्यः -घ्या -घ्यं, दुर्लंघ्यः -घ्या -घ्यं, अनधिगम्यः -म्या -म्यं, दुरधिगम्यः &c., दुरधिगमः -मा -मं, दुरत्ययः -या -यं, दुस्तरः -रा -रं, दुःसाध्यः -ध्या -ध्यं, दुरारोहः -हा -हं, अजेयः -या -यं, दुर्जेयः -या -यं.

INSUPERABLENESS, *s.* अलंघ्यता, अनतिक्रम्यता, अनधिगम्यता, अजेयता.

INSUPERABLY, *adv.* अलंघनीयं, अनतिक्रमणीयं, दुर्जेयं, दुरारोहं.

INSUPPORTABLE, *a.* असह्यः -ह्या -ह्यं, असहनीयः -या -यं, दुःसहः -हा -हं, दुःसहनीयः -या -यं, अक्षमाप्यः -प्या -प्यं, न क्षमाप्यः -प्या -प्यं, निःसहः -हा -हं, दुर्वहः -हा -हं, दुरुद्वहः -हा -हं.

INSUPPORTABLENESS, *s.* असह्यता, असहनीयता, दुःसह्यता, अक्षमाप्यता.

INSUPPORTABLY, *adv.* असहनीयं, दुःसहनीयं, यथा सोढुं न शक्यते तथा.

INSUPPRESSIBLE, *a.* अनिग्रहीतव्यः -व्या -व्यं, दुर्निग्रहः -हा -हं, दुर्निवारः -रा -रं.

INSURANCE, *s.* योगक्षेमः, क्षेमप्रतिविधानं, क्षेमकरणं, क्षेमविधानं, विधायकत्वं, सत्याकरणं, सत्याकृतिः *f.*, सत्यापनं; 'against fire,' अग्निजनाशात् क्षेमप्रतिविधानं; 'against thieves, &c.,' चौरादिभ्यः क्षेमप्रतिविधानं or क्षेमकरणं or रक्षा -क्षणं or अहार्य्यत्वं or अनाश्यत्वं.

To INSURE, *v. a.* योगक्षेमं कृ, क्षेमं कृ or विधा (c. 3. -दधाति -धातुं) or प्रतिविधा, सत्याकृ, सत्यीकृ, स्थिरीकृ, दृढीकृ, अहार्य्यत्वं कृ, अनाश्यत्वं कृ, अभेद्यत्वं कृ; 'the merchant insures his goods,' वणिग् द्रव्याणि सत्याकरोति.

INSURED, *p. p.* सत्याकृतः -ता -तं, क्षेमयुक्तः -क्ता -क्तं, रक्षितः -ता -तं.

INSURGENT, *s.* राजप्रतियोधी *m.* (न्), राजयुध्वा *m.* (न्), राजविरोधी *m.* (न्), राजप्रतिरोधी *m.*, उपद्रवी *m.* (न्), विप्लवकृत् *m.*, राजद्रोही *m.* (न्), उपद्रवकारी *m.* (न्), प्रजाविप्लवकारी *m.*, प्रकृतिक्षोभकारी *m.*

INSURMOUNTABLE, *a.* दुरारोहः -हा -हं, अनारोहः -हा -हं, अलंघनीयः -या -यं, अनधिगम्यः -म्या -म्यं, दुरधिगमः -मा -मं, अनतिक्रम्यः -म्या -म्यं, दुस्तरः -रा -रं. *See* INSUPERABLE.

INSURMOUNTABLENESS, *s.* दुरारोहत्वं, अलंघनीयता, अनधिगम्यत्वं, दौस्तर्य्यं.

INSURRECTION, *s.* राजयुद्धं, उपद्रवः, उपप्लवः, प्रजाविप्लवः, राज्योपद्रवः, राजप्रकोपः, प्रकोपः, प्रकृतिक्षोभः, राज्यक्षोभः, प्रजाक्षोभः, राजद्रोहः, राजविरुद्धसम्भूयसमुत्थानं.

INSURRECTIONARY, *a.* उपद्रवी -विणी -वि (न्), राजविरुद्धः -द्धा -द्धं, राजप्रतीपः -पा -पं, राजप्रतिकूलः -ला -लं, राजविपरीतः -ता -तं, विप्लवसम्बन्धी -न्धिनी -न्धि (न्).

INSUSCEPTIBILITY, *a.* अग्राहकत्वं, अग्रहणशीलता, ग्रहणाक्षमता, वेदनाशक्तिः *f.*

INSUSCEPTIBLE, *a.* अग्राही -हिणी -हि (न्), अग्राहकः -का -कं, अग्रहणशीलः -ला -लं, ग्रहणाक्षमः -मा -मं, ग्रहणशक्तिरहितः -ता -तं, वेदनशक्तिहीनः -ना -नं.

INTANGIBLE, *s.* अस्पृश्यः -श्या -श्यं, अस्पर्शनीयः -या -यं, अस्प्रष्टव्यः -व्या -व्यं, दुःस्पर्शः -र्शा -र्शं, दुःस्पृश्यः -श्या -श्यं, अस्पर्शवेद्यः -द्या -द्यं, स्पर्शागम्यः -म्या -म्यं, स्पर्शागोचरः -रा -रं, स्पर्शायोग्यः -ग्या -ग्यं, दुरालभः -भा -भं, अनालभ्यः -भ्या -भ्यं.

INTANGIBLENESS, *s.* अस्पृश्यता, अस्पर्शनीयता, स्पर्शावेद्यता, स्पर्शागम्यता.

INTEGER, INTEGRAL, *s.* (A whole number) पूर्णाङ्कः, अभिन्नाङ्कः, अभिन्नः, सम्पूर्णाङ्कः, रूपं.

INTEGRAL, *a.* अभिन्नः -न्ना -न्नं, पूर्णः -र्णा -र्णं, सम्पूर्णः -र्णा -र्णं, अविकलः -ला -लं, अखण्डः -ण्डा -ण्डं, अन्यूनः -ना -नं, अत्रुटितः -ता -तं, साङ्गः -ङ्गा -ङ्गं.—(In algebra) पूरितः -ता -तं, पूर्णः -र्णा -र्णं; 'integral calculus,' पूरितगणितं; 'differential and integral calculus,' चैलक्षणपूरितगणितं; 'integral existence,' अधिकरणं.

To INTEGRATE *v. a.* सम्पूर्णीकृ, सम्पूर् (c. 10. -पूरयति -यितुं), प्रतिसङ्कृ.

INTEGRATION, *s.* (In algebra) पूरितं, पूर्णीकरणं, सम्पूर्णीकरणं.

INTEGRITY, *s.* (Entireness) सम्पूर्णता, पूर्णता, अभिन्नता, अभिन्नभावः, अखण्डता, अवैकल्यं, अन्यूनता, साकल्यं, सामग्र्यं, समस्तता, समस्तिः *f.*, समुदायः, साङ्गता.—(Probity, soundness, incorruptness) अभेद्यता, सारल्यं, सरलता, शुचिता, मायाहीनता, ऋजुता, शुद्धता, अदुष्टता, न्यायिता, अजिह्मता, अवक्रता, अशठता, सत्यता, सत्यशीलता, विमलता, नैर्मल्यं, साधुता; 'of strict integrity,' अभेद्यः -द्या -द्यं, सरलः -ला -लं, अहार्य्यः -र्य्या -र्य्यं. *See* HONEST.

INTEGUMENT, *s.* वेष्टनं, आवेष्टनं, परिवेष्टनं, पटलं, कञ्चुकः, आच्छादनं, छादनं, छदनं, आवरणं, प्रावरणं, वासनं, शिरा, पुटः -टं, कोशः, पिधानं, शरीरावरणं.

INTELLECT, *s.* बुद्धिः *f.*, धीः *f.*, मेधा, मतिः *f.*, मनस् *n.*, प्रज्ञा, चित् *f.*, चेतना, चेतस् *n.*, चित्तं, ज्ञानं, बोधः, संवित् *f.*, संवित्तिः *f.*, मनीषा, उपलब्धिः *f.*, प्रतिभा, ज्ञप्तिः *f.*, प्रतिपद् *f.*, शेमुषी, धिषणा, प्रेक्षा, ज्ञानदृष्टिः *f.*, ध्यानं, बोधशक्तिः *f.*, चिच्छक्तिः *f.*, ज्ञानशक्तिः *f.*, संज्ञा.

INTELLECTION, *s.* बोधः -धनं, ज्ञानं, ग्रहणं, बुद्धिग्रहः, आकलनं.

INTELLECTUAL, INTELLECTIVE, *a.* (Relating to the understanding) मानसिकः -की -कं, मानसः -सी -सं, बुद्धिसम्बन्धी -न्धिनी -न्धि (न्), बुद्धिविषयः -या -यं, चित्तसम्बन्धी &c., ज्ञानसम्बन्धी &c.—(Existing in the intellect, perceived by it) मनसिजः -जा -जं, मनोजः -जा -जं, मनोगतः -ता -तं, मनोभवः -वा -वं, चित्तभवः -वा -वं, चित्तगतः -ता -तं, मानसिकः &c., बुद्धिगम्यः -म्या -म्यं, धीगम्यः -म्या -म्यं.—(Endowed with intellect) बुद्धिमान् -मती -मत् (त्), धीमान् &c., मतिमान् &c., मेधावी -विनी -वि (न्), मनीषी -षिणी -षि (न्), सुबुद्धिः -द्धिः -द्धि, मेधिरः -रा -रं, चिच्छक्तिविशिष्टः -ष्टा -ष्टं; 'possessing all intellectual qualities,' सर्व्वधीगुणः -णा -णं, अखिलधीगुणः &c.; 'intellectual faculty,' धीशक्तिः *f.*, निष्क्रमः. *See* INTELLIGENT.

INTELLECTUALLY, *adv.* बुद्ध्या, बोधेन, मनसा, ज्ञानतस्, बुद्धिपूर्व्वं.

INTELLIGENCE, *s.* (Understanding, skill, cleverness) बुद्धिः *f.*, ज्ञानं, धीः *f.*, मेधा, चेतना, चैतन्यं, चित् *f.*, चिच्छक्तिः *f.*, विज्ञता, कुशलता, कौशल्यं, चातुर्य्यं, वैचक्षण्यं, विदग्धता, वैदग्ध्यं.—(Information, tidings) वार्त्ता, समाचारः, सन्देशः, वृत्तान्तः, संवादः, वाचिकं, उदन्तः, किंवदन्ती, सूचना; 'good intelligence' सुवार्त्ता, शुभवार्त्ता; 'secret intelligence,' गूढभावितं.—(A spiritual being) चेतनः, सचेतनव्यक्तिः f., बुद्धिरूपव्यक्तिः.

INTELLIGENCER, s. (Messenger) वार्त्तिकः, वार्त्तायनः, वार्त्ताहरः, वार्त्तावहः, सन्देशहरः, आख्यायकः.—(Newspaper) वार्त्तिकपत्रं, समाचारपत्रं.

INTELLIGENT, a. बुद्धिमान् -मती -मत् (त्), धीमान् &c., मतिमान् &c., मेधावी -विनी -वि (न्), मनस्वी &c., सबुद्धिः -द्धिः -द्धि, सुबुद्धिः &c., कुशलबुद्धिः &c., सुधीः -धीः -धि, शुद्धधीः &c., कृतधीः &c., सुबोधः -धा -धं, मेधिरः -रा -रं, सज्ञानः -ना -नं, ज्ञानी -निनी -नि (न्), ज्ञानवान् &c., प्रज्ञावान् &c., प्राज्ञः -ज्ञा -ज्ञं, मनीषी -षिणी -षि (न्), प्रेक्षावान् &c., कोविदः -दा -दं, ज्ञाता -त्री -तृ (तृ), विदुरः -रा -रं, विन्दुः -न्दुः -न्दु, मर्म्मज्ञः -ज्ञा -ज्ञं.—(Clever) विज्ञः -ज्ञा -ज्ञं, विचक्षणः -णा -णं, कुशलमतिः -तिः -ति, निपुणमतिः &c., चतुरः -रा -रं, चतुरबुद्धिः &c., अभिज्ञः -ज्ञा -ज्ञं, विदग्धः -ग्धा -ग्धं, विदग्धबुद्धिः &c., कल्याणबुद्धिः &c.

INTELLIGENTLY, adv. विज्ञवत्, सुबुद्ध्या, सुबुद्धिपूर्व्वं, बुद्धिकौशल्येन, विदग्धवत्, विचक्षणवत्, अभिज्ञवत्, चतुरं, वैचक्षण्येन, सवैचक्षण्यं, सचातुर्य्यं.

INTELLIGIBLE, a. बोध्यः -ध्या -ध्यं, बोधनीयः -या -यं, बुद्धिगम्यः -म्या -म्यं, बुद्धिग्राह्यः -ह्या -ह्यं, सुगम्यः -म्या -म्यं, सुग्राह्यः -ह्या -ह्यं, स्पष्टः -ष्टा -ष्टं, विस्पष्टः -ष्टा -ष्टं, सुस्पष्टः -ष्टा -ष्टं, स्पष्टार्थः -र्था -र्थं, ज्ञेयः -या -यं, संवेद्यः -द्या -द्यं, भिन्नार्थः -र्था -र्थं.

INTELLIGIBLENESS, INTELLIGIBILITY, s. बोध्यता, बोधनीयता, बुद्धिगम्यता, सुगम्यता, सुग्राह्यता, स्पष्टत्वं, सुस्पष्टत्वं, सुज्ञेयता.

INTELLIGIBLY, adv. स्पष्टं, सुस्पष्टं, विस्पष्टं, स्पष्टार्थतस्, भिन्नार्थतस्.

INTEMPERANCE, s. असंयमः -मनं, अयमः, असंयतत्वं, मर्य्यादातिक्रमः, अमर्य्यादा, अपरिमितत्वं, अमितत्वं, अनियमः, नियमातिक्रमः, अतिक्रमः, अत्याचारः, अदमः, अनिग्रहः, आधिक्यं, उद्रेकः, उत्सेकः, अतिरिक्तता, आतिशय्यं.—(In pleasures, enjoyments, or habits) भोगामितत्वं, अपरिमितभोगित्वं, असंयताचारत्वं, अनियतवृत्तिता, अजितेन्द्रियत्वं, अयतेन्द्रियत्वं.—(In eating) अत्याहारः, अतिभोजनं, अतिभक्षणं, भोजनासक्तिः f., अयताहारत्वं, असंयताहारत्वं, आहारादिविषये असंयमः.—(In drinking) अतिपानं, पानासक्तता, पानप्रसक्तत्वं.

INTEMPERATE, a. (Not moderate or restrained within limits) असंयतः -ता -तं, असंयमी -मिनी -मि (न्), असंयमशीलः -ला -लं, अमितः -ता -तं, अपरिमितः -ता -तं, अतिमर्य्यादः -दा -दं, अमर्य्यादः -दा -दं, अयतः -ता -तं, अतिक्रान्तमर्य्यादः -दा -दं, अतिक्रान्तनियमः -मा -मं, अनियमवान् -वती -वत् (त्), अतिमितः -ता -तं, अपरिमाणः -णा -णं, अधिकः -का -कं, उद्रिक्तः -क्ता -क्तं, अतिरिक्तः -क्ता -क्तं, अतिशयी -यिनी -यि (न्), अदान्तः -न्ता -न्तं.—(In pleasures or habits) अमितभोगी -गिनी -गि (न्), अपरिमितभोगः -गा -गं, असंयताचारः -रा -रं, अयताचारः -रा -रं, अयतवृत्तिः -त्तिः -त्ति, असंयतवृत्तिः -त्तिः -त्ति, अत्याचारी -रिणी -रि (न्), अयतेन्द्रियः -या -यं, अजितेन्द्रियः -या -यं, अनियतेन्द्रियः -या -यं.—(In eating) अतिभोजी -जिनी -जि (न्), अमितभोजी &c., अत्याहारी &c., अयताहारः -रा -रं, अपरिमिताहारः -रा -रं. See GLUTTONOUS. (In drinking) अतिपायी -यिनी -यि (न्), पानासक्तः -क्ता -क्तं, पानप्रसक्तः -क्ता -क्तं.

INTEMPERATELY, adv. असंयमेन, असंयतं, अपरिमितं, अमितं, अतिमर्य्यादं, मर्य्यादातिक्रमेण, नियमातिक्रमेण, अपरिमाणेन, अतिशयेन, अतिरिक्तं, आधिक्येन.

INTEMPERATURE, s. गुणवैषम्यं, गुणाधिक्यं, गुणातिरेकं, अपरिमितत्वं, वैषम्यं.

INTENABLE, a. अप्रतिपादनीयः -या -यं, अव्यवस्थापनीयः -या -यं, अरक्षणीयः -या -यं.

To INTEND, v. a. (Mean, purpose) अभिप्रे (अभिप्रैति -तुं), अभिप्रायं कृ, कृ in des. (चिकीर्षति -र्षितुं), उद्दिश् (c. 6. -दिशति -देष्टुं), मनसा उद्दिश्, अभिसन्धा (c. 3. -दधाति -धातुं), इष् (c. 6. इच्छति, एषितुं), उपलक्ष् (c. 10. -लक्षयति -यितुं), परिकॢप् (c. 10. -कल्पयति -यितुं), मनः or मतिं or बुद्धिं कृ or प्रकृ, with loc. or dat. case; as, 'he intends going,' मनो गमनाय करोति. Sometimes expressible by the des. form of a verb; as, 'to intend to go,' गम् in des. (जिगमिषति -षितुं); 'to intend to do,' कृ in des.; 'to intend to say,' वच् in des. (विवक्षति -क्षितुं).

INTENDANCY, s. अध्यक्षता -त्वं, अधिष्ठातृत्वं, अधिकारिता, अधीशता.

INTENDANT, s. अध्यक्षः, अधिष्ठाता m. (तृ), अधिकारी m. (न्), उपद्रष्टा m. (ष्टृ).

INTENDED, p. p. अभिप्रेतः -ता -तं, चिकीर्षितः -ता -तं, उद्दिष्टः -ष्टा -ष्टं, मनसोद्दिष्टः -ष्टा -ष्टं, उपलक्षितः -ता -तं, सङ्कल्पितः -ता -तं, इष्टः -ष्टा -ष्टं, कृताभिप्रायः -या -यं, परिकल्पितः -ता -तं; 'intended to be said,' विवक्षितः -ता -तं; 'not intended,' अनभिप्रेतः -ता -तं.

INTENDING, part. अभिप्रेत्य, उद्दिश्य, मनसोद्दिश्य, अभिसन्धाय.

INTENDMENT, s. अभिप्रायः, अभिप्रेतं, आशयः, अर्थः, उद्देशः, अभिसन्धिः m.

INTENSE, a. अत्यन्तः -न्ता -न्तं, आत्यन्तिकः -की -कं, गाढः -ढा -ढं, तीव्रः -व्रा -व्रं, तीक्ष्णः -क्ष्णा -क्ष्णं, उग्रः -ग्रा -ग्रं, चण्डः -ण्डा -ण्डं, प्रचण्डः -ण्डा -ण्डं, उच्चण्डः -ण्डा -ण्डं, प्रकृष्टः -ष्टा -ष्टं, प्रबलः -ला -लं, प्रगाढः -ढा -ढं, नितान्तः -न्ता -न्तं, भृशः -शा -शं, सुभृशः -शा -शं, निर्भरः -रा -रं, अतिशयी -यिनी -यि (न्), अतिशायनः -ना -नं, कठोरः -रा -रं, परमः -मा -मं, महान् -हती -हत् (त्), परः -रा -रं, उदीर्णः -र्णा -र्णं, उद्धतः -ता -तं, कठिनः -ना -नं, तैजसः -सी -सं, व्यग्रः -ग्रा -ग्रं, भूरिः -रिः -रि, अति or अतिशय or सु prefixed; 'intense darkness,' घनतिमिरं; 'intense heat,' अतिदाहः, गुरुतापः, बलधूष्मा m. (न्); 'intense pain,' तीव्रवेदना; 'intense study,' अत्यन्ताभिनिवेशः, अतिप्रवेशः, व्यासक्तिः.

INTENSELY, adv. अत्यन्तं, अतिशयेन, तीव्रं, तीक्ष्णं, अतितैक्ष्ण्येन, प्रचण्डं, नितान्तं, भृशं, सुभृशं, निर्भरं, कठोरं, गाढं, अतिशयेन, उग्रं, परमं, अतीव, अति or अतिशय or सु prefixed; 'intensely passionate,' अत्यन्तकोपनः -ना -नं, अतिकोपनः -ना -नं.

INTENSITY, INTENSENESS, s. अत्यन्तता, आत्यन्तिकत्वं, तीव्रता, तीक्ष्णता, तैक्ष्ण्यं, उग्रता, चण्डता, प्रचण्डता, गाढता, प्रगाढता, नितान्तत्वं, प्रबलता, प्राबल्यं, कठोरता, भृशता, भ्रशिमा m. (न्), प्रकृष्टता, प्रकर्षः, तैजसं, काठिन्यं, व्यग्रता, उद्रेकः, उदीर्णता, उत्कर्षः, अतिभूमिः f., आतिशय्यं, 'intensity of application to study,' अभिनिवेशः, अत्यन्ताभिनिवेशः, व्यासक्तिः.

INTENSION, s. विततिः f., आततिः f., वृद्धिः f., प्रकर्षः, उत्कर्षः, प्रकृष्टता.

INTENSIVE, a. (Serving to give force or emphasis) शक्तिकरः -रा -रं, प्रकर्षकरः -रा -रं, उत्कर्षज्ञापकः -का -कं, अर्थविशेषकारकः -का -कं, वर्धकः -का -कं, वृद्धिकरः &c.

INTENT, a. (Having the mind fixed closely on one object) एकाग्रः -ग्रा -ग्रं, एकचित्तः -त्ता -त्तं, एकतानः -ना -नं, एकाग्रचित्तः -त्ता -त्तं, एकनिष्ठः -ष्ठा -ष्ठं, अनन्यमनाः -नाः -नः (स्), अनन्यवृत्तिः -त्तिः -त्ति, अनन्यविषयः -या -यं, अनन्यविषयात्मा -त्मा -त्म (न्), अनन्यमनस्कः -स्का -स्कं, एकायनः -ना -नं.—(Intent on any object) आसक्तः -क्ता -क्तं, आसक्तचित्तः -त्ता -त्तं, आसक्तचेताः -ताः -तः (स्), अभिनिविष्टः -ष्टा -ष्टं, अभिनिवेशी -शिनी -शि (न्), निविष्टः -ष्टा -ष्टं, प्रविष्टः -ष्टा -ष्टं, परायणः -णा -णं, परः -रा -रं, तत्परः -रा -रं, रतः -ता -तं, निरतः -ता -तं, अभियुक्तः -क्ता -क्तं, आयुक्तः -क्ता -क्तं, सक्तः -क्ता -क्तं, संसक्तः -क्ता -क्तं,

निष्ठः -ष्ठा -ष्ठं, निष्ठितः -ता -तं, आविष्टः -ष्टा -ष्टं, आविष्टचित्तः -त्ता -त्तं, आविष्टमना: &c., अभिमुखः -खा -खं, नियतः -ता -तं, व्यग्रः -ग्रा -ग्रं, व्यग्रमना: &c., तन्मनस्कः -स्का -स्कं, आहितः -ता -तं, कृतनिश्चयः -या -यं; 'intent on reading,' अध्ययनपरः -रा -रं, अध्ययनाभिमुखः -खा -खं.

INTENT, *s.* अभिप्रायः, अभिप्रेतं, आशयः, उद्देशः, अर्थः, तात्पर्य्यं; 'with what intent?' किमुद्दिश्य; 'to all intents,' सर्व्वार्थतस्.

INTENTION, *s.* (Design) अभिप्रायः, अभिप्रेतं, चिकीर्षितं, चिकीर्षा, आशयः, सङ्कल्पः, उद्देशः, आकांक्षा, बुद्धिः *f.*, मतिः *f.*, मतं, इङ्गितं, छन्दः, तात्पर्य्यं, आकूतं, इच्छा, चेष्टा, कल्पना, परिकल्पना, परिकल्पितं, उपलक्षितं, निश्चितं.—(End, aim, object) अर्थः, आशयः, अभिसन्धिः *m.*, कार्य्यं, कार्य्यवस्तु *n.*, प्रयोजनं, अर्थवत्ता.—(Meaning) विवक्षितं, विवक्षा; 'purity of intention,' चित्तशुद्धिः *f.*, अन्तःकरणशुद्धिः *f.*; 'change of intention,' बुद्धिभेदः, मतिभेदः; 'declared intention,' ईरिताकूतं; 'with what intention?' किमुद्दिश्य.—(Fixedness of attention) एकाग्रता. *See* INTENTNESS.

INTENTIONAL, *a.* मतिपूर्व्वः -र्व्वा -र्व्वं, बुद्धिपूर्व्वः &c., ज्ञानपूर्व्वः &c., बुद्धिपुरःसरः -रा -रं, अभिप्रायपूर्व्वः &c., ऐच्छिकः -की -कं, बुद्धिकृतः -ता -तं, कामकृतः -ता -तं, कामिकः -की -कं, काम्यः -म्या -म्यं, यथाकामः -मा -मं, साभिप्रायः -या -यं, सङ्कल्पकृतः -ता -तं, साङ्कल्पिकः -की -कं, यथाकल्पः -ल्पा -ल्पं, ज्ञानकृतः -ता -तं, अर्थवान् -वती -वत् (त्), सार्थः -र्था -र्थं, चिकीर्षितः -ता -तं, अभिप्रेतः -ता -तं.

INTENTIONALLY, *adv.* बुद्धिपूर्व्वं, बुद्धिपुरःसरं, मतिपूर्व्वं, अभिप्रायपूर्व्वं, साभिप्रायं, ज्ञानपूर्व्वं, बुद्ध्या, इच्छातस्, कामतस्, यथाकामं, प्रकामं, मत्या, मनःपूर्व्वकं, तात्पर्य्यतस्, यथाकल्पं, ज्ञानतस्, इच्छापूर्व्वं.

INTENTIONED, *a.* (In composition). Expressed by आशय, बुद्धि &c. in comp.; as, 'well-intentioned,' शुभाशयः -या -यं; 'ill-intentioned,' दुराशयः -या -यं, द्रोहबुद्धिः -द्धिः -द्धि.

INTENTIVE, *a.* कृतावधानः -ना -नं, अवहितः -ता -तं, समाहितः -ता -तं.

INTENTLY, *adv.* एकाग्रं, एकाग्रचेतसा, अनन्यमनसा, आसक्तचेतसा, निविष्टमनसा, अभिनिवेशेन, अभिनिवेशपूर्व्वं, साभिनिवेशं, निष्ठापूर्व्वं, निर्बन्धेन, सैकाग्र्यं, मनोयोगेन, समनोयोगं, व्यग्रं, व्यग्रवत्.

INTENTNESS, *s.* एकाग्रता, एकचित्तता -त्वं, अनन्यचित्तता, अभिनिवेशः, चित्ताभिनिवेशः, अभिनिविष्टता, आसक्तिः *f.* -क्तता, निवेशः, प्रवेशः, निविष्टता, ऐकाग्र्यं, अभियुक्तता, परता, निष्ठा, निष्ठितत्वं, एकनिष्ठता, आविष्टत्वं, अनन्यवृत्तिः *f.*, मनोयोगः; 'intentness of soul,' आत्मैकाग्र्यं, चित्तैकाग्र्यं.

To INTER, *v. a.* भूमौ or श्मशाने निखन् (c. 1. -खनति -नितुं -खातुं) or स्था in caus. (स्थापयति -यितुं) or समृ in caus. (-अर्पयति -यितुं) or निधा (c. 3. -दधाति -धातुं), भूमिगतं -तां -तं कृ.

INTERCALAR, INTERCALARY, *a.* अधिकः -का -कं, निवेशितः -ता -तं, सौराब्दपूरकः -का -कं; 'intercalary month,' अधिकमासः, अधिमासः, मलमासः, मलिम्लुचः, अनामकः, अधिमासशेषः, पुरुषोत्तममासः, असंक्रान्तिकमासः; 'intercalary day,' अधिकदिवसः, अधिदिवसः; 'intercalary verse,' अधिकश्लोकः.

To INTERCALATE, *v. a.* (A month) अधिकमासं निविश् (c. 10. -वेशयति -यितुं), अधिमासं निविश्.—(A day) अधिकदिवसं निविश्.

INTERCALATION, *s.* (Of a month) अधिकमासनिवेशनं.—(Of a day) अधिकदिवसनिवेशनं, अधिदिवसनिवेशनं.

To INTERCEDE, *v. n.* (Intervene, pass between) अन्तर्गम् (c. 1. -गच्छति -गन्तुं), अन्तर्वृत् (c. 1. -वर्त्तते -र्त्तितुं), अन्तःस्था (c. 1. -तिष्ठति -स्थातुं), मध्ये वृत्, मध्ये स्था, उपस्था.—(Mediate between two parties) मध्यस्थो भू or अस्, मध्यवर्त्ती भू, माध्यस्थ्यं कृ, मध्यस्थवृत्तिम् आस्था, सन्धा (c. 3. -दधाति -धातुं), सन्धानं कृ.—(Plead in favor of another) परार्थे प्रार्थ् (c. 10. -अर्थयते -ति -यितुं), परार्थप्रार्थनं कृ, परार्थे वद् (c. 1. वदति -दितुं) or प्रतिवद्, परार्थविनतिं कृ, परार्थे विनी (c. 1. -नयति -नेतुं) or अनुनी or निवेदनं कृ, परार्थनिवेदनं कृ.

INTERCEDER, *s.* मध्यस्थः, मध्यवर्त्ती *m.* (न्), परार्थप्रार्थकः, परार्थप्रार्थनकृत् *m.*, परार्थवादी *m.* (न्), परार्थे निवेदनकृत् *m.*

To INTERCEPT, *v. a.* रुध् (c. 7. रुणद्धि, रोद्धुं), अवरुध्, विरुध्, प्रतिरुध्, उपरुध्, निरुध्, संरुध्, गतिरोधं कृ, गतिभङ्गं कृ, विच्छिद् (c. 7. -छिनत्ति -छेत्तुं), गतिविच्छेदं कृ, गतिच्छेदं कृ, वियुज् (c. 10. -योजयति -यितुं), निवृ (c. 10. -वारयति -यितुं), व्यवह् (c. 10. व्यवहयति -यितुं), प्रतिबन्ध् (c. 9. -बध्नाति -बन्धुं).

INTERCEPTED, *p. p.* रुद्धः -द्धा -द्धं, अवरुद्धः -द्धा -द्धं, विच्छिन्नः -न्ना -न्नं.

INTERCEPTER, *s.* रोधकः, गतिभङ्गकारी *m.* (न्), विच्छेदकारी *m.*

INTERCEPTION, *s.* गतिरोधः -धनं, गतिभङ्गः, गतिविच्छेदः, गतिच्छेदः, रोधः -धनं, अवरोधः, विच्छेदः, निवारणं, प्रतिबन्धः, स्तम्भनं, विघ्नः.

INTERCESSION, *s.* (Mediation between two parties) माध्यस्थ्यं, माध्यस्थं, मध्यस्थत्वं, सन्धानकरणं.—(Pleading in favor of another) परार्थप्रार्थना -नं, परार्थे प्रार्थनं, परार्थवादः, परार्थनिवेदनं, परार्थे निवेदनं; 'to make intercession.' *See To* INTERCEDE.

INTERCESSOR, *s.* (Mediator) मध्यस्थः, मध्यवर्त्ती *m.* (न्), मध्यस्थायी *m.* (न्), मध्यस्थितः.—(Pleader for another) परार्थप्रार्थकः, परार्थे प्रार्थयिता *m.* (तृ), परार्थे प्रार्थनकृत् *m.*, परार्थवादी *m.* (न्), परार्थे निवेदनकारी *m.*

INTERCESSORY, *a.* परार्थप्रार्थकः -का -कं, परार्थप्रार्थनविषयः -या -यं.

To INTERCHANGE, *v. a.* परस्परं परिवृत् (c. 10. -वर्त्तयति -यितुं) or विनिमे (c. 1. -मयते -मातुं) or निमे or विनिमयं कृ, परस्परपरिवर्त्तनं कृ, परस्परविनिमयं कृ, व्यतिकरं कृ, परस्परं दानप्रतिदानं कृ or आदानप्रदानं कृ, व्यतिहृ (c. 1. -हरति -हर्त्तुं).

INTERCHANGE, *s.* परिवर्त्तनं, परस्परपरिवर्त्तनं, विनिमयः, परस्परविनिमयः, परिवृत्तिः *f.*, परीवर्त्तः, निमयः, विमयः, निमेयः, वैमेयः, व्यतिकरः, व्यतिहारः, व्यतीहारः, परावृत्तिः *f.*, विपर्य्ययः, परस्परं दानप्रतिदानं, आदानप्रदानं.

INTERCHANGEABLE, *a.* परिवर्त्तनीयः -या -यं, विनिमातव्यः -व्या -व्यं, विनिमयार्हः -र्हा -र्हं.—(Following each other in succession) परस्परानुगामी -मिनी -मि (न्), अन्योन्यपृष्ठानुगामी &c.

INTERCHANGEABLY, *adv.* विनिमयेन, विपर्य्ययेण, पर्य्यायेण, परिवर्त्तनेन, परिवृत्य.

INTERCISION, *s.* विच्छेदः, छेदः, अवच्छेदः, भङ्गः, रोधः, अवरोधः.

To INTERCLUDE, *v. a.* अवरुध् (c. 7. -रुणद्धि -रोद्धुं), विच्छिद् (c. 7. -छिनत्ति -छेत्तुं).

INTERCOSTAL, *a.* पञ्जरमध्यस्थः -स्था -स्थं, पंक्तिमध्यवर्त्ती -र्त्तिनी -र्त्ति (न्), पर्शुकाभ्यन्तरस्थः -स्था -स्थं.

INTERCOURSE, *s.* संसर्गः, परस्परसंसर्गः, अन्योन्यसंसर्गः, संसर्गिता, सङ्गतिः *f.*, साङ्गत्यं, सङ्गमः, सङ्गः, समागमः, उपगमः, गमनागमनं, परस्परालापः, आलापः, सम्भाषः, सम्पर्कः, साहित्यं, आनुगत्यं, साहचर्य्यं, सङ्घट्टनं, परिचयः; 'intercourse of society,' लोकव्यवहारः, लोकसंसर्गः, लोकयात्रा; 'of the sexes,' स्त्रीपुरुषसङ्गः, मिथुनीभावः, मैथुनं.

INTERCUTANEOUS, *a.* त्वगन्तर्भूतः -ता -तं, त्वगन्तर्गतः -ता -तं, त्वगन्तःस्थः -स्था -स्थं.

To INTERDICT, *v. a.* अन्तःख्या (c. 2. -ख्याति -तुं), प्रत्याख्या, निषिध् (c. 1. -षेधति -षेद्धुं, c. 10. -षेधयति -यितुं), प्रतिषिध्, निवृ (c. 10.

-वारयति -यितुं), निषेधं कृ, बाध् (c. 1. बाधते -धितुं).

INTERDICT, INTERDICTION, *s.* निषेधः, प्रतिषेधः, आसेधः, प्रत्याख्यानं, वारणं, निवारणं, निरोधः, विरोधनं, बाधः, निषिद्धत्वं.

INTERDICTED, *p.p.* निषिद्धः -द्धा -द्धं, प्रतिषिद्धः -द्धा -द्धं, अन्तःस्यातः -ता -तं.

INTERDICTORY, *a.* निषेधकः -का -कं, निषेधार्थकः -का -कं, निषेधकरः -रा -रं.

INTEREST, *s.* (Advantage, good) अर्थः, हितं, लाभः, फलं, कल्याणं, कुशलं, मङ्गलं, क्षेमः -मं, श्रेयस्, भूतिः *f.*; 'for the public interest,' लोकहिताय; 'one's own interest,' स्वार्थः, स्वहितं, स्वलाभः, स्वकार्य्यं, आत्महितं, आत्मवृद्धिः; 'for one's own interest,' आत्महिताय, आत्मविवृद्धये; 'regard to one's own interest,' स्वार्थापेक्षा, स्वार्थदृष्टिः *f.*, स्वहितावलोकनं, स्वार्थलिप्सा; 'regardful of one's own interest,' स्वार्थपरः -रा -रं, स्वार्थसाधनतत्परः -रा -रं, स्वार्थपरायणः -णा -णं, स्वार्थलिप्सुः -प्सुः -प्सु, स्वार्थार्थी -र्थिनी -र्थि (न्), स्वहितैषी -षिणी -षि (न्), स्वलाभपरायणः -णा -णं; 'regardless of it.' *See* DISINTERESTED.—(Concern, lively feeling about) स्नेहः, अवेक्षा, अपेक्षा, प्रतीक्षा, अनुरागः, रागः, स्पृहणीयत्वं, स्पृहा, सम्बन्धः, अभिसम्बन्धः, अभिसन्धानं.—(Partiality for, bias in favor of) सङ्गः, पक्षपातः, स्नेहः; 'void of all interest in,' वीतसङ्गः -ङ्गा -ङ्गं, मुक्तसङ्गः &c., निःसङ्गः &c., विपक्षपातः -ता -तं.—(Gratification) विनोदः.—(Power to interest or please) विनोदकत्वं, मनोरञ्जकता, हृद्गमत्वं, रसः.—(Influence) गौरवं, गुरुत्वं, प्रभावः, प्राबल्यं, अधिकारः, भारः.—(Share, portion, participation in loss or gain) भागः, अंशः, विभागः, लाभालाभविभागित्वं, लाभालाभसम्बन्धः.—(Interest on money, usury) वृद्धिः *f.*, वार्धुष्यं, भागः, कलान्तरं, कारिका, कारिता, कुसीदवृद्धिः *f.*; 'compound interest,' चक्रवृद्धिः *f.*; 'simple interest,' सरलवृद्धिः *f.*; 'bearing interest,' सवृद्धिकः -का -कं, भागिकः -की -कं, भाग्यः -ग्या -ग्यं; 'bearing no interest,' अवृद्धिकः -की -कं; 'interest at the rate of five per cent.,' शते विंशभागः, पञ्चकं शतं, पञ्चोत्तरं; 'at four per cent.,' शते पञ्चविंशभागः; 'at two per cent.,' द्विकं शतं.

To INTEREST, *v.a.* (Excite interest, partiality, or concern) स्नेहं or अनुरागं or स्पृहां or पक्षपातम् उत्पद् (c. 10. -पादयति -यितुं) or जन् (c. 10. जनयति -यितुं), अनुरञ्ज् (c. 10. -रञ्जयति -यितुं), अनुरक्तं -क्तां कृ, सानुरागं -गां कृ, सङ्गम् उत्पद्.—(Engage the attention, amuse) विनुद् (c. 10. -नोदयति -यितुं), मनः or चित्तं विनुद् or रञ्ज् (c. 10. रञ्जयति -यितुं), हृदयं गम् (c. 1. गच्छति, गन्तुं), चित्तविनोदं कृ.—(Give a share in) भागं or अंशं दा, संविभागित्वं or समांशित्वं दा, भागिनं -गिनीं कृ, अंशिनं -शिनीं कृ.—(Have a share in) भागं or अंशं लभ् (c. 1. लभते, लब्धुं) or प्राप् (c. 5. -आप्नोति -आप्तुं), भागी -गिनी -गि भू or अस्.—(Have concern in) सम्बन्ध् in pass. (-बध्यते), सम्बद्धः -द्धा -द्धं भू.—(Interest one's self for another) परहितैषी -षिणी -षि भू or अस्, परहितेप्सुः -प्सुः -प्सु भू, परहितार्थी -र्थिनी -र्थि भू.

INTERESTED, *p.p.* or *a.* (Having one's affections or concern excited) जातस्नेहः -हा -हं, जातानुरागः -गा -गं, अनुरञ्जितः -ता -तं, अनुरक्तः -क्ता -क्तं, विरक्तः -क्ता -क्तं, अभिसंहितः -ता -तं.—(Having partiality for) सङ्गी -ङ्गिनी -ङ्गि (न्), पक्षपाती -तिनी -ति (न्), सपक्षपातः -ता -तं, सङ्गयुक्तः -क्ता -क्तं.—(Having the attention engaged) आसक्तः -क्ता -क्तं, निविष्टः -ष्टा -ष्टं, अभिनिविष्टः -ष्टा -ष्टं, निरतः -ता -तं.—(Amused) विनोदितः -ता -तं.—(Made a sharer in) भागी -गिनी -गि (न्), संविभागी &c.—(Concerned in a cause or in consequences) सम्बन्धी -न्धिनी -न्धि (न्), सम्बद्धः -द्धा -द्धं, अर्थसम्बद्धः -द्धा -द्धं, लाभालाभसम्बद्धः -द्धा -द्धं, अभिसम्बद्धः &c.—(Self-interested) स्वलाभासक्तः -क्ता -क्तं, स्वफलासक्तः -क्ता -क्तं, सकामः -मा -मं, सार्थः -र्था -र्थं, स्वार्थदर्शी -र्शिनी -र्शि (न्), कामात्मा -त्मा -त्म (न्), स्वार्थापेक्षकः -का -कं.

INTERESTING, *a.* (Engaging the attention, exciting the passions, amusing) विनोदकः -का -कं, विनोददः -दा -दं, हृदयङ्गमः -मा -मं, हृद्गमः -मा -मं, अनुरागजनकः -का -कं, मनोरञ्जकः -का -कं, चित्तवेधकः -का -कं, मनोहरः -रा -रं, हृदयग्राही -हिणी -हि (न्), हृदयस्पृक् *m.f.n.* (श्).

To INTERFERE, *v. n.* (Intermeddle) परव्यापारान् or परकार्य्याणि प्रविश् (c. 6. -विशति -वेष्टुं) or चर्च् (c. 1. चर्चति -र्चितुं), परव्यापारचर्चां कृ, परकार्य्यप्रवेशं कृ, परनियोगचर्चां कृ, पराधिकारचर्चां कृ, परकार्य्यनिरूपणं कृ, परकार्य्येषु व्यापृ in pass. (-प्रियते) or व्यापृतः -ता -तम् अस्.—(Clash, come into collision) परस्परं विरुध् (c. 7. -रुणद्धि -रोद्धुं) or संघट्ट् (c. 1. -घट्टते -ट्टितुं), परस्परविरोधं कृ, परस्परविपर्य्यासं कृ.

INTERFERENCE, *s.* (Intermeddling) परव्यापारप्रवेशः, परकार्य्यप्रवेशः, परव्यापारचर्चा, पराधिकारचर्चा, परनियोगचर्चा, परकार्य्यनिरूपणं.—(Mediation, interposition) माध्यस्थ्यं, मध्यस्थत्वं, अन्तर्गमनं, अन्तरागमनं.—(Clashing, collision) परस्परविरोधः, परस्परसमाघातः.

INTERFLUENT, *s.* मध्यस्रवन् -वन्ती -वत् (त्), मध्यस्यन्दी -न्दिनी -न्दि (न्).

INTERFUSED, *a.* मध्यविस्तीर्णः -र्णा -र्णं, मध्यप्रसारी -रिणी -रि (न्).

INTERIM, *s.* मध्यकालः, अन्तर्गतकालः, अन्तरितकालः, अन्तरं, कालान्तरं, कालाभ्यन्तरं; 'in the interim,' अत्रान्तरे.

INTERIOR, *a.* अन्तरस्थः -स्था -स्थं, आन्तरिकः -की -कं, आन्तरः -री -रं, अन्तर्भूतः -ता -तं, अन्तर्गतः -ता -तं, अन्तःस्थः -स्था -स्थं, अन्तर्वर्त्ती -र्त्तिनी -र्त्ति, अन्तर्भवः -वा -वं, आभ्यन्तरः -री -रं, अन्तरङ्गः -ङ्गा -ङ्गं, अन्तरतमः -मा -मत्, गर्भस्थः -स्था -स्थं, अन्तर् in comp.—(Inland) मध्यदेशस्थः -स्था -स्थं.

INTERIOR, *s.* (The inside) अभ्यन्तरं, अन्तर्भागः, अन्तःप्रदेशः, अन्तरङ्गं, गर्भः, उदरं, मध्यभागः, विलं, विवरं; 'interior of a boiler,' स्थालीविलं; 'interior of a house,' गृहाभ्यन्तरं, अन्तर्गृहं, अन्तर्भवनं, भवनोदरं, गर्भागारं; 'interior of a country,' देशमध्यं, मध्यदेशः.

INTERJACENCY, *s.* मध्यस्थितिः *f.*, मध्यवर्त्तनं, मध्यवर्त्तित्वं, अन्तर्वर्त्तनं.

INTERJACENT, *a.* मध्यस्थितः -ता -तं, मध्यवर्त्ती -र्त्तिनी -र्त्ति (न्), अन्तर्वर्त्ती &c.

To INTERJECT, *v. a.* मध्ये क्षिप् (c. 6. क्षिपति, क्षेप्तुं) or प्रक्षिप्, अन्तःक्षिप्.

INTERJECTION, *s.* (Throwing between) मध्यप्रक्षेपः -पणं, मध्यक्षेपः -पणं, अन्तःक्षेपणं.—(Exclamation) उद्गारः.

To INTERLACE, *v. a.* व्यामिश्र् (c. 10. -मिश्रयति -यितुं), अन्यद् अन्येन मिश्र्.

To INTERLARD, *v. a.* मध्ये निविश् (c. 10. -वेशयति -यितुं), अन्तर् निविश्.—(Mix, diversify) विमिश्र् (c. 10. -मिश्रयति -यितुं), सम्मिश्र्, सम्मिश्रीकृ, विचित्रीकृ.

To INTERLEAVE, *v. a.* (Insert a leaf) पत्रं निविश् (c. 10. -वेशयति -यितुं), पत्रनिवेशनं कृ.—(Insert a blank leaf between two other leaves) पुस्तकपत्रद्वयमध्ये शून्यपत्रं निविश्.

To INTERLINE, *v. a.* अक्षरपंक्तिद्वयमध्ये लिख् (c. 6. लिखति, लेखितुं) or अभिलिख्.

INTERLINEAR, INTERLINEARY, *a.* अक्षरपंक्तिद्वयमध्ये लिखितः -ता -तं.

INTERLOCUTION, *s.* संवादः, संलापः, सम्भाषा -षणं, द्वयोः संवादः, उत्तरप्रत्युत्तरं, उक्तिप्रत्युक्ती *f.* du., परस्परालापः, सङ्कथा, सम्प्रवदनं, कथोपकथनं.

INTERLOCUTOR, *s.* संवादी *m.* (न्), सांवादिकः, संवादकारी *m.* (न्),

सम्भाषकः, उत्तरप्रत्युत्तरकृत् *m.*, उक्तिप्रत्युक्तिकृत् *m.*, कथोपकथकः.—(An actor who in the intervals of the scenes explains the progress of the story) विष्कम्भः -म्भकः.

INTERLOCUTORY, *a.* संवादरूपः -पा -पं, सांवादिकः -की -कं, संवादात्मकः -त्मा -त्मं, संलापीयः -या -यं, उत्तरप्रत्युत्तररूपः -पा -पं.

To INTERLOPE, *v. n.* अधर्म्मतः पराधिकारं प्रविश् (c. 6. -विशति -वेष्टुं) or आविश् or अन्तर्गम् (c. 1. -गच्छति -गन्तुं) or अन्तरागम्, स्वाधिकारम् अतिक्रम्य पराधिकारप्रवेशं कृ.

INTERLOPER, *s.* पराधिकारप्रवेशकः -प्रवेष्टा *m.* (ष्टृ), पराधिकारान्तर्गामी *m.* (न्), पराधिकारमध्यवर्त्ती *m.* (न्), अनधिकारी *m.* (न्).

INTERLUDE, *s.* अङ्कद्वयान्तर्गतं कौतुकं, विलासिका.

INTERLUNAR, INTERLUNARY, *a.* अमावास्याकालिकः -की -कं, अमासम्बन्धी -न्धिनी -न्धि (न्).

INTERMARRIAGE, *s.* परस्परविवाहः, अन्योन्यविवाहः, विवाहव्यवहारः, परस्परदारपरिग्रहः, परस्परकन्याव्यवहारः, परिवर्त्तनविवाहः, प्रत्युद्वाहः; 'confusion of castes through intermarriage,' सङ्करः, साङ्कर्य्यं.

To INTERMARRY, *v. n.* परस्परं विवह् (c. 1. -वहति -वोढुं) or उद्वह्, परस्परविवाहं कृ, परस्परविवाहव्यवहारं कृ, परस्परदारपरिग्रहं कृ, परस्परकन्याव्यवहारं कृ, परस्परदारपरिणयनं कृ.

To INTERMEDDLE, *v. a.* परकार्य्याणि चर्च् (c. 1. चर्चति -र्चितुं), परव्यापारचर्चां कृ, परव्यापारान् प्रविश् (c. 6. -विशति -वेष्टुं), परव्यापारप्रवेशं कृ, परकार्य्याणि निरूप् (c. 10. -रूपयति -यितुं), परकार्य्यनिरूपणं कृ, पराधिकारचर्चां कृ, परनियोगचर्चां कृ, परकार्य्येषु व्यापृ in pass. (-प्रियते), परव्यापारान्तर्गमनं कृ.

INTERMEDDLER, *s.* परकार्य्यचर्चकः, परव्यापारप्रवेशकः, पराधिकारचर्चकः, परकार्य्यनिरूपकः, परकार्य्यव्यापारी *m.* (न्), परव्यापारान्तर्गामी *m.* (न्).

INTERMEDIATE, INTERMEDIAL, *a.* मध्यः -ध्या -ध्यं, मध्यमः -मा -मं, मध्यस्थितः -ता -तं, मध्यवर्त्ती -र्त्तिनी -र्त्ति (न्), मध्यगः -गा -गं, अन्तरालस्थः -स्था -स्थं, अन्तरालस्थितः -ता -तं, उभयमध्यस्थितः -ता -तं, अन्तर्गतः -ता -तं, अन्तरितः -ता -तं, व्यवधायकः -का -कं, व्यवहितः -ता -तं, विचालः -ला -लं, अन्तराल in comp.; 'intermediate space,' अन्तरं, अभ्यन्तरं, अन्तरालं; 'intermediate time,' कालान्तरं, अन्तरं; 'intermediate point of the compass,' अपदिशं, विदिक् *f.* (श्), उपदिक् *f.*; 'in an intermediate direction,' मध्यदिशि.

INTERMEDIATELY, *adv.* मध्यदिशि, मध्यमदिशि, मध्ये, सान्तरालं, अन्तरेण.

INTERMENT, *s.* भूमिखननं, निखननं, भूमिसमर्पणं, भूमौ खननं.

INTERMINABLE, *a.* अनन्तः -न्ता -न्तं -न्तकः -का -कं, निरवधिः -धिः -धि, अत्यन्तः -न्ता -न्तं, अपर्य्यन्तः -न्ता -न्तं, असीमः -मा -मं, निस्सीमः -मा -मं, अमितः -ता -तं, अपरिमितः -ता -तं, अविरतः -ता -तं, अनवरतः -ता -तं, असमापनीयः -या -यं.

INTERMINABLENESS, *s.* निरवधिता, अनन्तता, आनन्त्यं. सीमाहीनता.

INTERMINABLY, *adv.* अविरतं, अनारतं, अनवरतं, अनन्तं, अत्यन्तं, निरन्तरं.

To INTERMINGLE, *v. a.* सम्मिश्र् (c. 10. -मिश्रयति -यितुं), सम्मिश्रीकृ, व्यामिश्र्, विमिश्र्, संकॄ (c. 6. -किरति -करितुं -रीतुं), सङ्कीर्णीकृ, सङ्करीकृ, सङ्कुलीकृ, संसृज् (c. 6. -सृजति -स्रष्टुं).

To INTERMINGLE, *v. n.* सम्मिश्रीभू, व्यामिश्रीभू, सम्मिल् (c. 6. -मिलति -मेलितुं).

INTERMINGLED, *p. p.* व्यामिश्रः -श्रा -श्रं, सम्मिश्रः -श्रा -श्रं, सम्मिश्रीकृतः -ता -तं, व्यामिश्रीभूतः -ता -तं, मिश्रितः -ता -तं, सङ्कीर्णः -र्णा -र्णं, संसृष्टः -ष्टा -ष्टं, सम्पृक्तः -क्ता -क्तं, करम्बः -म्बा -म्बं -म्बितः -ता -तं, विभिन्नः -न्ना -न्नं.

INTERMISSION, *s.* विरतिः *f.*, विरामः, अवरतिः *f.*, उपरतिः *f.*, निवृत्तिः *f.*, विनिवृत्तिः *f.*, निर्वृत्तिः *f.*, निवर्त्तनं, निर्वर्त्तनं, छेदः, विच्छेदः, उपशमः, अपशमः, क्षयः; 'without intermission,' अविरतं, अनवरतं, निरन्तरं.

To INTERMIT, *v. a.* (Cause to cease) निवृत् (c. 10. -वर्त्तयति -यितुं), निर्वृत्, विरम् (c. 10. -रमयति -यितुं), उपरम्, शम् (c. 10. शमयति -यितुं), विछिद् (c. 7. -छिनत्ति -छेत्तुं).

To INTERMIT, *v. n.* विरम् (c. 1. -रमति -रन्तुं), उपरम् निवृत् (c. 1. -वर्त्तते -र्त्तितुं), निर्वृत्, विनिवृत्, शम् (c. 4. शाम्यति, शमितुं), अपया (c. 2. -याति -तुं), विगम् (c. 1. -गच्छति -गन्तुं), विछिद् in pass. (-छिद्यते), प्रत्यूह् (c. 1. -ऊहते -हितुं).

INTERMITTED, *p. p.* विरतः -ता -तं, उपरतः -ता -तं, निवृत्तः -त्ता -त्तं, शान्तः -न्ता -न्तं, शमितः -ता -तं, प्रशान्तः -न्ता -न्तं, विगतः -ता -तं, विच्छिन्नः -न्ना -न्नं.

INTERMITTENT, INTERMISSIVE, *a.* विरमन् -मन्ती -मत् (त्), सविरामः -मा -मं, सविच्छेदः -दा -दं.—(As a fever) विषमः -मा -मं, अन्तरितः -ता -तं; 'intermittent fever,' विषमज्वरः; 'occurring on alternate days,' एकान्तरः -रा -रं.

INTERMITTINGLY, *adv.* सविच्छेदं, सच्छेदं, विषमं, सविरामं, वैषम्येण.

To INTERMIX, *v. a.* सम्मिश्र् (c. 10. -मिश्रयति -यितुं), व्यामिश्र्, विमिश्र्, मिश्र्, सम्मिश्रीकृ, मिश्रीकृ. *See* INTERMINGLE.

INTERMIXED, *p. p.* मिश्रीभूतः -ता -तं, सम्मिश्रीकृतः -ता -तं, व्यामिश्रः -श्रा -श्रं, मिश्रितः -ता -तं, सङ्कुलितः -ता -तं, मुक्तः -क्ता -क्तं. *See* INTERMINGLED.

INTERMIXTURE, *s.* मिश्रणं, व्यामिश्रणं, सम्मिश्रणं, मिश्रीकरणं, सम्मिश्रीकरणं, व्यतिकरः, संसर्गः, सङ्कलनं, सम्पर्कः, सन्निपातः, साङ्कर्य्यं, सङ्करः, सङ्करीकरणं, योगः, संयोगः, मिलनं, सम्मिलनं.

INTERMONTANE, *a.* पर्व्वतमध्यस्थितः -ता -तं, गिरिमध्यस्थः -स्था -स्थं.

INTERMUNDANE, *a.* भुवनमध्यस्थितः -ता -तं, जगन्मध्यवर्त्ती -र्त्तिनी -र्त्ति (न्).

INTERMURAL, *a.* प्राकारान्तर्वर्त्ती -र्त्तिनी -र्त्ति (न्), प्राचीरान्तर्वर्त्ती &c.

INTERMUTATION, *s.* परिवर्त्तनं, परस्परपरिवर्त्तनं, विनिमयः, व्यतिहारः.

INTERNAL, *a.* अन्तरस्थः -स्था -स्थं, अन्तर्भूतः -ता -तं, अन्तर्वर्त्ती -र्त्तिनी -र्त्ति (न्), अन्तर्भवः -वा -वं, अन्तर्गतः -ता -तं, आन्तरः -री -रं, आभ्यन्तरः -री -रं, अभ्यन्तरस्थः -स्था -स्थं, आन्तरिकः -की -कं, अन्तरतमः -मा -मत्, गर्भस्थः -स्था -स्थं, अन्तःस्थः -स्था -स्थं, अन्तरङ्गः -ङ्गा -ङ्गं, अभ्यन्तर in comp., अन्तर् in comp.; 'internal feelings,' अन्तरात्मा *m.* (न्), अन्तःकरणं, अन्तःशरीरं, अन्तःप्रकृतिः *f.*; 'internal consciousness,' अन्तःसंज्ञा; 'internal heat,' अन्तर्दाहः, अन्तर्ज्वलनं; 'internal nature,' अन्तर्भावः; 'internal store,' अन्तःसारः.

INTERNALLY, *adv.* (Inwardly) अन्तर्, अन्तरे, अभ्यन्तरे, मध्ये; 'internally bad,' अन्तर्दुष्टः -ष्टा -ष्टं.—(Mentally) मनसा, बुद्ध्या, अन्तःकरणेन.

INTERNATIONAL, *a.* देशानां परस्परव्यवहारसम्बन्धी -न्धिनी -न्धि or परस्परसंसर्गसम्बन्धी &c.

INTERNODE, *s.* (In botany) ग्रन्थिद्वयमध्यं, पर्व्वद्वयमध्यं.

INTERNUNCIO, *s.* उभयपक्षदूतः, उभयपक्षवार्त्ताहरः.

To INTERPOLATE, *v. a.* छलेन or कपटेन निविश् (c. 10. वेशयति -यितुं) or क्षिप् (c. 6. क्षिपति, क्षेप्तुं) or निक्षिप् or अन्तःक्षिप्, मिथ्या अभिलिख् (c. 6. -लिखति -लेखितुं), मिथ्या क्लृप् (c. 10. कल्पयति -यितुं), कृत्रिमलेख्यं कृ.

INTERPOLATED, *p. p.* छलेन निवेशितः -ता -तं or क्षिप्तः -प्ता -प्तं or अन्तःक्षिप्तः -प्ता -प्तं, मिथ्याभिलिखितः -ता -तं, कपटेन कल्पितः -ता -तं, मिथ्याकल्पितः -ता -तं.

INTERPOLATION, *s.* छलेन निवेशनं or क्षेपणं or अन्तःक्षेपणं, कपटेन or

मिथ्या अभिलिखनं or कल्पनं, मिथ्याकल्पनं.—(Matter interpolated) छलेन निवेशितं वाक्यं or लेख्यं, मिथ्याभिलिखितं, मिथ्याकल्पितं.

INTERPOLATOR, *s.* छलेन निवेशनकारी *m.* (न्) or क्षेपणकर्त्ता *m.* (र्त्तृ).

To INTERPOSE, *v. a.* अन्तर्धा (c. 3. -दधाति -धत्ते -धातुं), व्यवधा, मध्ये स्था in caus. (स्थापयति -यितुं), अन्तः स्था, अन्तर्गतं -तां कृ, अन्तर्गम् (c. 10. -गमयति -यितुं), व्यवहितं -तां कृ, अन्तरितं -तां कृ.—(Introduce) मध्ये प्रविश् (c. 10. -वेशयति -यितुं) or निविश्.

To INTERPOSE, *v. n.* मध्ये स्था (c. 1. तिष्ठति, स्थातुं) or वृत् (c. 1. वर्त्तते -र्त्तितुं), अन्तर्गम् (c. 1. -गच्छति -गन्तुं), अन्तरि (c. 2. -एति -तुं), मध्यवर्त्ती -र्त्तिनी -र्त्ति भू.—(Intrude) मध्ये प्रविश् (c. 6. -विशति -वेष्टुं).

INTERPOSED, *p. p.* व्यवहितः -ता -तं, अन्तर्गतः -ता -तं, अन्तरितः -ता -तं, मध्ये स्थापितः -ता -तं or प्रवेशितः -ता -तं, प्रत्याकलितः -ता -तं.

INTERPOSER, *s.* मध्यवर्त्ती *m.* (न्), मध्यस्थः -स्थायी *m.* (न्), अन्तर्गामी *m.*

INTERPOSITION, *s.* मध्यस्थता, मध्यवर्त्तित्वं, माध्यस्थ्यं, अन्तरायः, अन्तर्गमनं, अन्तरागमनं, व्यवधानं, व्यवहितत्वं, अन्तर्गतकृत्यं, अन्तर्गतयत्नः, व्यवधायकत्वं, अनुसरणं.

To INTERPRET, *v. a.* व्याख्या (c. 2. -ख्याति -तुं), अर्थं व्याख्या or विवृ (c. 5. -वृणोति -वरितुं -रीतुं) or प्रकाश् (c. 10. -काशयति -यितुं), अर्थं बुध् (c. 10. बोधयति -यितुं) or प्रबुध् or व्यक्तीकृ or स्पष्टीकृ or व्याकृ or निरूप् (c. 10. -रूपयति -यितुं), व्याहृ (c. 1. -हरति -हर्त्तुं), विब्रू (c. 2. -ब्रवीति), व्याचक्ष् (c. 2. -चष्टे), परिशुध् (c. 10. -शोधयति -यितुं), प्रवच् (c. 2. -वक्ति -क्तुं), अर्थं कृ, विवरणं कृ.—(Translate) भाषान्तरीकृ.

INTERPRETABLE, *a.* व्याख्येयः -या -यं, विवरणीयः -या -यं, व्याख्यायोग्यः -ग्या -ग्यं.

INTERPRETATION, *s.* व्याख्या -ख्यानं, विवरणं, विवृतिः *f.*, व्याकरणं, व्याकृतिः *f.*, स्पष्टीकरणं, निरूपणं, वाचिकं, अर्थकरणं, अर्थबोधनं, अर्थबोधकं वाक्यं; 'of dreams,' स्वप्नविचारः, शाकुनिकं; 'of a sloka,' श्लोकलापनं.—(Meaning given, commentary) अर्थः, व्याख्या, टीका, भाष्यं; 'doubtful interpretation,' सन्दिग्धार्थः; 'far-fetched interpretation,' क्लिष्टार्थः.—(Translation) भाषान्तरं.

INTERPRETATIVE, *a.* वाचकः -का -कं, व्याख्याकारी -रिणी -रि (न्), विवरणकारी &c., अर्थबोधकः -का -कं, अर्थज्ञापकः -का -कं, प्रकाशकः -का -कं.

INTERPRETED, *p. p.* व्याख्यातः -ता -तं, विवृतः -ता -तं, व्याकृतः -ता -तं, प्रकाशितः -ता -तं, स्पष्टीकृतः -ता -तं, निरूपितः -ता -तं, व्याहृतः -ता -तं, वर्णितः -ता -तं, कृतविवरणः -णा -णं.—(Translated) भाषान्तरीकृतः -ता -तं.

INTERPRETER, *s.* व्याख्याता *m.* (तृ), व्याख्याकारी *m.* (न्), विवरणकर्त्ता *m.* (र्त्तृ), अर्थबोधकः, अर्थशोधकः, अर्थप्रकाशकः, अर्थप्रवक्ता *m.* (क्तृ), अर्थविज्ञापकः, वाचकः, फलवक्ता *m.*; 'of dreams,' स्वप्नविचारी *m.* (न्), स्वप्नप्रकाशकः.—(Translator, one who speaks two languages) द्विभाषावादी *m.* (न्), भाषान्तरवक्ता *m.*, द्विभाषी *m.* (न्), भाषाद्वयवक्ता *m.*—(Commentator) भाष्यकारः, भाष्यकरः.

INTERREGNUM, *s.* अनायकत्वं, अराजकत्वं, अराजकं, अनायकं, राजद्वयमध्यगत अराजककालः or अनायककालः.

To INTERROGATE, *v. a.* प्रच्छ् (c. 6. पृच्छति, प्रष्टुं), अनुप्रच्छ्, परिप्रच्छ्, समनुप्रच्छ्, अभिप्रच्छ्, प्रश्नं कृ, पृच्छनं कृ, अनुयुज् (c. 7. -युनक्ति -युङ्क्ते -योक्तुं), प्रश्नेन परीक्ष् (c. 1. -ईक्षते -क्षितुं), प्रश्नोत्तरक्रमेण परीक्ष्, ज्ञा in des. (जिज्ञासति -ते -सितुं).

INTERROGATED, *p. p.* पृष्टः -ष्टा -ष्टं, अभिपृष्टः -ष्टा -ष्टं, अनुयुक्तः -क्ता -क्तं.

INTERROGATION, *s.* प्रश्नः, पृच्छा -च्छनं, प्रच्छनं -ना, अनुयोगः, पर्य्यनुयोगः, जिज्ञासा, कथङ्कथिकता; 'note of interrogation,' प्रश्नचिह्नं, प्रश्नसूचकचिह्नं.

INTERROGATIVE, *a.* पृच्छकः -का -कं, प्रश्नकारकः -का -कं, प्रश्नरूपः -पा -पं, प्रश्नार्थकः -का -कं, प्रश्नात्मकः -का -कं, प्रश्नसूचकः -का -कं.

INTERROGATIVE, *s.* (Word used in asking questions) प्रश्नार्थकसर्व्वनाम *n.* (न्). Interrogative words are such as किं, किमु, किंस्वित्.

INTERROGATIVELY, *adv.* प्रश्नरूपेण, प्रश्नक्रमेण, अनुयोगरूपेण, प्रश्नतस्, अनुयोगतस्.

INTERROGATOR, *s.* प्रष्टा *m.* (ष्टृ), पृच्छकः, प्रच्छकः, प्रश्नकर्त्ता *m.* (र्त्तृ), अनुयोक्ता *m.* (क्तृ), जिज्ञासुः *m.*, कथङ्कथिकः, कथङ्कथितः.

INTERROGATORY, *s.* (A question) प्रश्नः, अनुयोगः, पृच्छा -च्छनं.

INTERROGATORY, *a.* *See* INTERROGATIVE, *a.*

To INTERRUPT, *v. a.* भञ्ज् (c. 7. भनक्ति, भंक्तुं), विच्छिद् (c. 7. -छिनत्ति -छेत्तुं), छिद्, खण्ड् (c. 10. खण्डयति -यितुं), भिद् (c. 7. भिनत्ति, भेत्तुं), लुप् (c. 6. लुम्पति, लोप्तुं, c. 10. लोपयति -यितुं), विलुप्, बाध् (c. 1. बाधते -धितुं), विहन् (c. 2. -हन्ति -न्तुं), व्याहन्, प्रतिहन्, निवृ (c. 10. -वारयति -यितुं), प्रतिबन्ध् (c. 9. -बध्नाति -बन्द्धुं), विघ्न (nom. विघ्नयति -यितुं), भङ्गं कृ, विच्छेदं कृ, खण्डनं कृ; 'he will interrupt my meditation by his complaints,' परिदेवनैः समाधिं मे भंक्ष्यति.

INTERRUPTED, *p. p.* विच्छिन्नः -न्ना -न्नं, भग्नः -ग्ना -ग्नं, खण्डितः -ता -तं, सविच्छेदः -दा -दं, सच्छेदः -दा -दं, सभङ्गः -ङ्गा -ङ्गं, लुप्तः -प्ता -प्तं, बाधितः -ता -तं, व्याहतः -ता -तं, प्रतिहतः -ता -तं, विघ्नितः -ता -तं.

INTERRUPTEDLY, *adv.* सविच्छेदं, सच्छेदं, सभङ्गं, विच्छिन्नं, खण्डतस्.

INTERRUPTER, *s.* विच्छेदकारी *m.* (न्), भङ्गकारी *m.*, भंक्ता *m.* (क्तृ), खण्डनकृत्, व्याघातकृत्, विघ्नकर्त्ता *m.* (र्त्तृ), बाधकः.

INTERRUPTION, *s.* भङ्गः, विच्छेदः, छेदः, खण्डनं, अन्तरायः, व्याघातः, विघ्नः, बाधः -धा, प्रतिहतिः *f.*, रोधः, प्रतिरोधः, निवारणं, स्तम्भः, प्रतिबन्धः.

To INTERSECT, *v. a.* and *n.* परस्परं छिद् (c. 7. छिनत्ति, छेत्तुं) or परिच्छिद् or विच्छिद्, परस्परच्छेदं कृ, परिच्छेदं कृ.

INTERSECTED, *p. p.* परिच्छिन्नः -न्ना -न्नं, परस्परच्छिन्नः -न्ना -न्नं, विच्छिन्नः -न्ना -न्नं.

INTERSECTION, *s.* परिच्छेदः, विच्छेदः, छेदः, परस्परच्छेदः -दनं, परस्परविच्छेदः.

To INTERSPERSE, *v. a.* अन्यद्रव्यमध्ये इतस्ततः प्रक्षिप् (c. 6. -क्षिपति -क्षेप्तुं) or कृ (c. 6. किरति, करितुं -रीतुं) or विकृ or अवकृ or सङ्कृ, अन्यद्रव्यैः सह मिश्र् (c. 10. मिश्रयति -यितुं) or सम्मिश्र् or व्यामिश्र्, प्रतिमध्यावकिरणं कृ.

INTERSPERSED, *p. p.* मिश्रितः -ता -तं, व्यामिश्रः -श्रा -श्रं, सम्मिश्रः -श्रा -श्रं, अन्यद्रव्यमध्ये इतस्ततः प्रक्षिप्तः -प्ता -प्तं or कीर्णः -र्णा -र्णं or अवकीर्णः -र्णा -र्णं, संसृष्टः -ष्टा -ष्टं, करम्बितः -ता -तं, अनुविद्धः -द्धा -द्धं.

INTERSPERSION, *s.* मिश्रणं, व्यामिश्रणं, सम्मिश्रणं, अन्यद्रव्यमध्ये इतस्ततो विकिरणं or अवकिरणं or प्रक्षेपणं, प्रतिमध्यावकिरणं, अन्यद्रव्यैः सह संसर्गः.

INTERSTELLAR, *a.* तारामण्डलान्तर्गतः -ता -तं, तारामण्डलान्तःस्थितः -ता -तं, तारागणान्तर्वर्त्ती -र्त्तिनी -र्त्ति (न्), तारामण्डलमध्यवर्त्ती &c.

INTERSTICE, *s.* छिद्रं, विच्छेदः, अवच्छेदः, छेदः, सन्धिः *m.*, अन्तरं, अन्तरालः, रन्ध्रं, विवरं, अवकाशः; 'without interstices,' निरन्तरः -रा -रं, निरन्तरालः -ला -लं, अनन्तरः -रा -रं, निश्छिद्रः -द्रा -द्रं, नीरन्ध्रः -न्ध्रा -न्ध्रं, निर्विवरः -रा -रं, निविडः -डा -डं; 'having interstices,' सान्तरः -रा -रं, सान्तरालः -ला -लं, सच्छिद्रः -द्रा -द्रं.

INTERSTITIAL, *a.* सान्तरः -रा -रं, सान्तरालः -ला -लं, अन्तरीयः -या -यं.

INTERTEXTURE, *s.* ग्रन्थनं, परस्परग्रन्थनं, परस्परविरचना, परस्परव्यूतिः *f.*

To INTERTWINE, INTERTWIST, *s.* ग्रन्थ् (c. 9. ग्रथ्नाति, c. 1. ग्रन्थति -न्थितुं), परस्परं ग्रन्थ्, पुट् (c. 10. पुटयति -यितुं), लष् (c. 10. लषयति -यितुं), उल्लष्, परस्परं कुच् (c. 1. कुचति -चितुं, c. 10. कुचयति -यितुं)

or आकुच् or व्यावृत् (c. 10. -वर्त्तयति -यितुं).

INTERVAL, *s.* (Intermediate space) अन्तरं, अभ्यन्तरं, अभ्यन्तरस्थानं, अन्तरालः, अवकाशः, मध्यः, मध्यस्थानं, व्यवधानं, व्यवायः, सन्धिः *m.* —(Interval of time) कालान्तरं, अभ्यन्तरकालः, मध्यकालः, अवकाशः, अन्तरावसरः, अवधिः *m.*—(Pause, remission) विरामः, विच्छेदः, विरतिः *f.*, निवृत्तिः *f.*, सन्धिः *m.*, उपशमः, शान्तिः *f.*; 'without interval,' अनन्तरः -रा -रं, निरन्तरः -रा -रं, निरन्तरालः -ला -लं; 'at intervals,' काले काले, वारं वारं, शनैस्; 'interval between the equinoxes,' अयनकालः.

To INTERVENE, *v. n.* मध्ये गम् (c. 1. गच्छति, गन्तुं) or आगम् or आया (c. 2. -याति -तुं), अन्तर्गम्, अन्तरागम्, अन्तर्या, अन्तराया, मध्ये वृत् (c. 1. वर्त्तते -र्त्तितुं), अन्तर्वृत्, मध्ये स्था (c. 1. तिष्ठति, स्थातुं) or उपस्था, अन्तरि (c. 2. -एति -तुं, c. 1. -अयति), मध्ये चर् (c. 1. चरति -रितुं), व्यवधा in pass. (-धीयते), व्यवहितः -ता -तं भू, अन्तर्गतः -ता -तं भू, अन्तरितः -ता -तं भू.

INTERVENIENT, INTERVENING, *a.* or *part.* मध्यवर्त्ती -र्त्तिनी -र्त्ति (न्), व्यवहितः -ता -तं, अन्तर्गतः -ता -तं, अन्तरागतः -ता -तं, व्यवधायकः -का -कं, अन्तरितः -ता -तं, मध्यगः -गा -गं, मध्यमः -मा -मं, अन्तर्धायकः -का -कं, मध्यचारी -रिणी -रि (न्), मध्यस्थः -स्था -स्थं -स्थायी -यिनी -यि (न्), विचालः -ला -लं; 'intervening space,' अभ्यन्तरं, अन्तरं.

INTERVENTION, *s.* अन्तर्गमनं, अन्तरागमनं, व्यवधानं, मध्यवर्त्तनं, मध्यवर्त्तित्वं, मध्यस्थता, माध्यस्थ्यं, अन्तरायः, व्यवहितत्वं, व्यवधायकत्वं, योगः; 'by the intervention of another,' अन्यं नियुज्य.

INTERVIEW, *s.* अन्योन्यदर्शनं, परस्परदर्शनं, अन्योन्यदृष्टिः *f.*, दर्शनं, सन्दर्शनं, समागमः, सङ्गमः, समास्या, परस्परालापः.

To INTERWEAVE, *v. a.* परस्परं ग्रन्थ् (c. 9. ग्रथ्नाति, c. 1. ग्रन्थति -न्थितुं) or रच् (c. 10. रचयति -यितुं) or उत्तन्च्, परस्परं विरच् (c. 10. -रचयति -यितुं) or संयुज् (c. 7. -युनक्ति -योक्तुं, c. 10. -योजयति -यितुं), परस्परसंयोगं कृ, परस्पराश्लेषं कृ, परस्परसंसर्गं कृ.—(Intermingle) सम्मिश्र् (c. 10. -मिश्रयति -यितुं), व्यामिश्र्, विमिश्र्, सम्मिश्रीकृ.

INTERWOVEN, *p. p.* ग्रथितः -ता -तं, उद्ग्रथितः -ता -तं, रचितः -ता -तं, अनुविद्धः -द्धा -द्धं, परस्पराश्लिष्टः -ष्टा -ष्टं, परस्परसंयुक्तः -क्ता -क्तं, व्यामिश्रः -श्रा -श्रं, सम्मिश्रः -श्रा -श्रं, सम्मिश्रीभूतः -ता -तं, करम्बितः -ता -तं.

INTESTABLE, *a.* मृतपत्रकरणाक्षमः -मा -मं, मृत्युपत्रानधिकारी -रिणी -रि (न्), मृतलेखकरणाशक्तः -क्ता -क्तं.

INTESTACY, *s.* अकृतमृतपत्रता, अकृतमृत्युलेखत्वं, मृत्युपत्रम् अकृत्वा or अलिखित्वा मरणं.

INTESTATE, *a.* अकृतमृत्युपत्रः -त्रा -त्रं, अकृतमृतलेखः -खा -खं, मृत्युपत्रम् अकृत्वा or अलिखित्वा मृतः -ता -तं.

INTESTINAL, *a.* आन्त्रिकः -की -कं, औदर्यः -र्या -र्यं, धमनीलः -ला -लं, अन्त्रसम्बन्धी -न्धिनी -न्धि (न्), नाडिसम्बन्धी &c.

INTESTINE, *s.* (Bowel) अन्त्रं, नाडिः -डी *f.*, अन्त्रनाडी, नाली -लिः *f.*, पुरीतत् *m. n.*, धमनी -निः *f.*, शिरा, सिरा, कोष्ठः, उदरं, जठरः -रं, मलाशयः, पुरीषाशयः.

INTESTINE, *a.* (Internal) अन्तर्वर्त्ती -र्त्तिनी -र्त्ति (न्), अन्तर्भवः -वा -वं, आन्तरः -री -रं, आन्तरिकः -की -कं, आभ्यन्तरः -री -रं, अबाह्यः -ह्या -ह्यं.—(Domestic, not foreign) स्वदेशीयः -या -यं, देशिकः -की -कं, अविदेशजः -जा -जं, अविदेशीयः -या -यं, देशीयः -या -यं, स्वदेशान्तर्गतः -ता -तं; 'intestine broils,' गृहकलहः, गृहभेदः.

To INTHRAL, *v. a.* दासीकृ, वशीकृ, करदीकृ. *See* ENSLAVE.

INTHRALMENT, *s.* दास्यं, दासत्वं, दासभावः, परवशत्वं, बन्धनं.

To INTHRONE, *v. a.* सिंहासने उपविश् (c. 10. -वेशयति -यितुं). *See* ENTHRONE.

INTIMACY, *s.* परिचयः, सुपरिचयः, सौहृदं, दृढसौहृदं, संसर्गः, सुसंसर्गः, दृढसंसर्गः, संसर्गित्वं, परस्परपरिज्ञानं, परिज्ञानं, संसक्तिः *f.*, आसङ्गः, संस्तवः, दृढसंयोगः, अतिसौहृदं, अतिसौहार्द्दं, अतिमित्रता, अतिप्रणयः, अतिमैत्र्यं, अतिसख्यं, संघट्टनं.

INTIMATE, *a.* (Inward) अन्तरस्थः -स्था -स्थं, अन्तर्भवः -वा -वं, अन्तर्गतः -ता -तं, अन्तर्भूतः -ता -तं, आन्तरः -री -रं, आभ्यन्तरः -री -रं, अन्तरतमः -मा -मत्, अन्तरङ्गः -ङ्गा -ङ्गं.—(Close) गाढः -ढा -ढं, दृढः -ढा -ढं, सुदृढः -ढा -ढं.—(Near) सन्निकृष्टः -ष्टा -ष्टं, निकटः -टा -टं, सन्निहितः -ता -तं.—(Close in friendship) दृढसौहृदः -दा -दं, परिचितः -ता -तं, सुपरिचितः -ता -तं, सुहृत्तमः -मा -मं, संसर्गी -र्गिणी -र्गि (न्), सुसंसर्गी &c., संसक्तः -क्ता -क्तं, सुसंसक्तः -क्ता -क्तं, संस्तुतः -ता -तं, परस्परज्ञः -ज्ञा -ज्ञं.

INTIMATE, *s.* (A friend) सुपरिचितः, दृढसुहृद् *m.*, दृढमित्रं, सुसंसर्गी *m.* (न्), सुहृत्तमः, प्रियसुहृद्, प्रियवयस्यः.

To INTIMATE, *v. a.* सूच् (c. 10. सूचयति -यितुं), संसूच्, अनुसूच्, उद्दिश् (c. 6. -दिशति -देष्टुं), समुद्दिश्, सूचनां कृ, इङ्गितं कृ, सङ्केतं कृ, आकूतं कृ, उपन्यस् (c. 4. -अस्यति -असितुं), प्रतिपद् (c. 10. -पादयति -यितुं).

INTIMATED, *p. p.* सूचितः -ता -तं, अनुसूचितः -ता -तं, उद्दिष्टः -ष्टा -ष्टं.

INTIMATELY, *adv.* (Closely) दृढं, सुदृढं, गाढं.—(With close friendship) दृढसौहृदेन, सुपरिचितं, सुपरिचितवत्, दृढमित्रवत्, सुहृत्तमं, सुसंसर्गेण, दृढसंसर्गेण; 'intimately connected,' दृढसम्बन्धी -न्धिनी -न्धि (न्), दृढसंसर्गी -र्गिणी -र्गि (न्).

INTIMATION, *s.* सूचना -नं, सूचितं, उद्देशः -शनं, सन्देशः, समुद्देशः -शनं, इङ्गितं, सङ्केतः, उपन्यासः, आकारः, व्यंग्यः, व्यंग्योक्तिः *f.*, वक्रोक्तिः *f.*, वक्रवाक्यं, आकूतं, परिकरः.

To INTIMIDATE, *v. a.* त्रस् (c. 10. त्रासयति -यितुं), संत्रस्, वित्रस्, भी in caus. (भाययति -यितुं or भीषयति -यितुं), भयहेतुं दर्शयित्वा निवृत् (c. 10. -वर्त्तयति -यितुं) or निवृ (c. 10. -वारयति -यितुं), सभयं -यां -यं कृ.—(Dishearten) धैर्य्यभङ्गं कृ, उत्साहभङ्गं कृ.—(Threaten) भर्त्स् (c. 10. भर्त्सयति -यितुं).

INTIMIDATED, *p. p.* त्रासितः -ता -तं, भीषितः -ता -तं, जातशङ्कः -ङ्का -ङ्कं.

INTIMIDATION, *s.* त्रासकरणं, भीषणं, भीषा, भयकरणं, भयदर्शनं, भयप्रदर्शनं, भर्त्सनं, भर्त्सनकरणं, धैर्य्यभङ्गः.

INTO, *prep.* मध्ये, अन्तर्, अन्तरे, अभ्यन्तरे, अन्तरेण; 'into the forest,' अरण्यमध्ये. When 'into' follows verbs of motion it may be expressed by the accus. c.; as, 'come into the house,' गृहम् आयाहि; 'the river runs into the ocean,' नदी समुद्रं विशति. When it follows verbs denoting examination or inspection it may also be expressed by the acc. c.; as, 'he looks into the letter,' पत्रं निरूपयति. When it follows verbs denoting insertion or inclusion it may be expressed by the loc. c.; as, 'he inserts the wedge into the wood,' कीलं काष्ठे निवेशयति. When it follows verbs denoting mixture it may be expressed by the instrum. c., or by सह with the instrum. c.; as, 'he puts the wine into the water,' मद्यं जलेन सह मिश्रयति. When 'into' denotes the passing of a thing from one state to another it may be expressed by the affixed सात्; as, 'converted into water,' जलसात्कृतः -ता -तं, or by changing the final of the noun to ई; as, 'reduced into one mass,' पिण्डीभूतः -ता -तं. When 'into' is used for 'in' it may usually be expressed by the loc. c.; as, 'into the ear,' कर्णे. This last expression is also rendered by उपकर्णं.

INTOLERABLE, *a.* असह्यः -ह्या -ह्यं, असहनीयः -या -यं, न सहनीयः -या -यं, दुःसहः -हा -हं, निःसहः -हा -हं, दुर्विषहः -हा -हं, अक्षमणीयः -या -यं, न क्षमाप्यः -प्या -प्यं, अक्षमणीयः -या -यं, दुरासदः -दा -दं, सहनाशक्यः -क्या -क्यं, दुस्सहः -हा -हं.

INTOLERABLENESS, *s.* असह्यता, असहनीयता, दुःसहत्वं, दौःसह्यं, निःसहत्वं.

INTOLERABLY, *adv.* असहनीयं, यथा सोढुं न शक्यते तथाप्रकारेण.

INTOLERANCE, *s.* असहनं, असहनशीलता, असहिष्णुता -त्वं, अक्षमा, अक्षमता, अक्षान्तिः *f.*, अमर्षः, विमर्षः, असहत्वं, निःसहत्वं, अनुत्साहः, अतितिक्षा, क्षमाभावः.—(Of other's opinions) परमतासहनं, अन्यमतासहनं, परमतासहिष्णुता, परमतातितिक्षा.

INTOLERANT, *a.* असहनः -ना -नं, असहः -हा -हं, असहमानः -ना -नं, असहनशीलः -ला -लं, असहिष्णुः -ष्णुः -ष्णु, अक्षमः -मा -मं -मी -मिणी -मि (न्), अक्षमिता -त्री -तृ (तृ), अमर्षणः -णा -णं, विमर्षी -र्षिणी -र्षि (न्), कृतामर्षः -र्षा -र्षं, विमर्षी -र्षिणी -र्षि (न्), अतितिक्षुः -क्षुः -क्षु. —(Of other's opinions) परमतासहः -हा -हं, अन्यमतासहः -हा -हं, परमतासहिष्णुः -ष्णुः -ष्णु, परमतातितिक्षुः -क्षुः -क्षु, परमतासूयकः -का -कं.

To INTOMB, *v. a.* समाधौ निखन् (c. 1. -खनति -नितुं) or स्था in caus. (स्थापयति -यितुं) or समृ in caus. (-अर्पयति -यितुं) or निधा (c. 3. -दधाति -धातुं) or निक्षिप् (c. 6. -क्षिपति -क्षेप्तुं), समाधिस्थं -स्थां -स्थं कृ.

INTONATION, *s.* (Modulation of voice) स्वरभेदः, स्वरः, लयः; 'deep intonation,' गम्भीरस्वरः, गभीरस्वरः.

To INTONE, *v. a.* गम्भीरस्वरेण वद् (c. 1. वदति -दितुं) or वच् (c. 2. वक्ति -क्तुं), गम्भीरस्वरम् उदीर् (c. 10. -ईरयति -यितुं) or उदाहृ (c. 1. -हरति -हर्तुं).

INTORSION, *s.* आकुञ्चनं, अवकुञ्चनं, कुञ्चनं, आवर्त्तः -र्त्तनं, व्यावर्त्तनं.

To INTORT, *v. a.* आकुञ्च् (c. 1. -कुञ्चति -ञ्चितुं, c. 10. कुञ्चयति -यितुं), अवकुञ्च्, कुञ्च्, व्यावृत् (c. 10. -वर्त्तयति -यितुं), आवृत्.

To INTOXICATE, *v. a.* मद् (c. 10. मादयति, मदयति -यितुं), मत्तीकृ, उन्मत्तीकृ, मादं or उन्मादं जन् (c. 10. जनयति -यितुं) or उन्मद् (c. 10. -मादयति -यितुं).

INTOXICATED, *p. p.* मत्तः -त्ता -त्तं, उन्मत्तः -त्ता -त्तं, मदोन्मत्तः -त्ता -त्तं, उन्मदः -दा -दं, मदान्वितः -ता -तं, शौण्डः -ण्डा -ण्डं, क्षीवः -वा -वं, परिक्षीवः -वा -वं, प्रक्षीवितः -ता -तं, मदोद्धतः -ता -तं, मदयित्नुः -त्नुः -त्नु, सुमदः -दा -दं, उत्कटः -टा -टं; 'intoxicated with passion,' काममोहितः -ता -तं.

INTOXICATING, *a.* मादकः -का -कं, उन्मादकः -का -कं, मादजनकः -का -कं.

INTOXICATION, *s.* मादः, उन्मादः, मदः, मत्तत्वं -ता, उन्मत्तता, प्रामाद्यं, मद्योन्मत्तत्वं, क्षीवता, क्षैव्यं, शौण्डत्वं, परिक्षीवता, उत्कटः, विह्वलता, मद्यपानजन्यो ऽवस्थाविशेषः.

INTRACTABLE, *a.* अवश्यः -श्या -श्यं, दुःशासनः -ना -नं, दुःशास्यः -स्या -स्यं, अविनेयः -या -यं, अविधेयः -या -यं, दुर्निग्रहः -हा -हं, दुर्दमः -मा -मं, दुर्दान्तः -न्ता -न्तं, दुराधर्षः -र्षा -र्षं, दुर्धर्षः -र्षा -र्षं, अनायत्तः -त्ता -त्तं, अनिवार्यः -र्या -र्यं, अनिवारः -रा -रं, दुःसाध्यः -ध्या -ध्यं, दुरासदः -दा -दं, प्रतीपः -पा -पं, विप्रतीपः -पा -पं, उच्छृङ्खलः -ला -लं.

INTRACTABLENESS, *s.* अवश्यता, दुःशास्यता, अविनेयता, दुर्दान्तत्वं, दुर्धर्षता अनायत्तत्वं, दुःसाध्यता, प्रतीपता.

INTRACTABLY, *adv.* अवश्यं, अविनेयं, अविधेयं, प्रतीपवत्, विप्रतीपवत्.

INTRANSIENT, *a.* अक्षणिकः -की -कं, अभङ्गुरः -रा -रं, चिरस्थायी -यिनी -यि (न्).

INTRANSITIVE, *a.* (In grammar) अकर्म्मकः -का -कं.

INTRANSMUTABLE, *a.* अविकार्यः -र्या -र्यं, अवस्थान्तराक्षमः -मा -मं.

To INTRENCH, *v. a.* परिखादिना परिवेष्ट् (c. 10. -वेष्टयति -यितुं) or परिवृ (c. 5. -वृणोति -वरितुं -रीतुं), दुर्गपरितः परिखां कृ or खन् (c. 1. खनति -नितुं), परिखाविशिष्टं -ष्टां -ष्टं कृ, परिखाश्रितं -तां -तं कृ.—(Encroach) आक्रम् (c. 1. -क्रामति -क्रमितुं), अभिक्रम्.

INTRENCHED, *p. p.* परिखापरिवेष्टितः -ता -तं, परिखापरिवृतः -ता -तं, परिखावृतः -ता -तं, परिक्षिप्तः -प्ता -प्तं, निवृतः -ता -तं.

INTRENCHMENT, *s.* परिखा, परिकूटं, परिक्रिया, गुप्तिः *f.*, दुर्गपरिगतं परिखाप्राचीरादि.

INTREPID, *a.* निर्भयः -या -यं, अभयः -या -यं, अभीतः -ता -तं, विभीतः -ता -तं, विगतभयः -या -यं, विशङ्कः -ङ्का -ङ्कं, निःशङ्कः -ङ्का -ङ्कं, अभीरुः -रुः -रु, वीरः -रा -रं, प्रवीरः -रा -रं, शूरः -रा -रं, साहसशीलः -ला -लं, साहसिकः -की -कं.

INTREPIDITY, *s.* निर्भयत्वं, अभीतिः *f.*, अभीतता, वीर्य्यं, शौर्य्यं, वीरत्वं प्रवीरत्वं, शूरत्वं -ता, विक्रमः, सुविक्रमः, पौरुषं, साहसं.

INTREPIDLY, *adv.* सवीर्य्यं, महावीर्य्येण, वीरवत्, शूरवत्, शौर्य्येण, सशौर्य्यं, सविक्रमं, सपराक्रमं, निर्भयं, अभीतवत्, साहसपूर्व्वं.

INTRICACY, *s.* असरलता, असारल्यं, क्लिष्टता, दुःशोधनीयता, दुःशोध्यता, कठिनता, काठिन्यं, समस्तता, व्यस्तता, सङ्कुलता, वक्रत्वं, कुटिलत्वं, कौटिल्यं, विषमता, वैषम्यं, आकुञ्चितत्वं.

INTRICATE, *a.* असरलः -ला -लं, क्लिष्टः -ष्टा -ष्टं, दुःशोधनीयः -या -यं, दुःसंशोधनीयः -या -यं, दुःशोध्यः -ध्या -ध्यं, अपरिशोध्यः -ध्या -ध्यं, कठिनः -ना -नं, समस्तः -स्ता -स्तं, व्यस्तः -स्ता -स्तं, मिश्रितः -ता -तं, नानाप्रकारः -रा -रं, सङ्कुलः -ला -लं, वक्रः -क्रा -क्रं, कुटिलः -ला -लं, कुञ्चितः -ता -तं, आकुञ्चितः -ता -तं, विषमः -मा -मं.—(Obscure) दुर्ज्ञेयः -या -यं, अस्पष्टार्थः -र्था -र्थं, नानार्थः &c., गूढः -ढा -ढं.

INTRICATELY, *adv.* असरलं, दुःशोधनीयं, कठिनं, काठिन्येन, सङ्कुलं, कुटिलं.

INTRICATENESS, *s.* *See* INTRICACY.

INTRIGUE, *s.* वैदग्ध्यप्रयोगः, विदग्धयोगः, कपटप्रयोगः, विदग्धकल्पना, कुयुक्तिः *f.*, कुप्रयुक्तिः *f.*, कुकल्पना, विदग्धमन्त्रणा, विदग्धपरामर्शः, विदग्धनीतिः *f.*, वैदग्ध्यं, विदग्धता, कपटप्रबन्धः, सङ्कल्पः.—(Amour) कामचरितं.

To INTRIGUE, *v. n.* वैदग्ध्यप्रयोगं कृ, कपटप्रयोगं कृ, कुप्रयोगं कृ, विदग्धकल्पनां कृ, कपटप्रबन्धं कृ, वैदग्ध्यं कृ.

INTRIGUER, *s.* विदग्धनायकः, विदग्धप्रयोजकः, विदग्धजनः.

INTRINSIC, INTRINSICAL, *a.* (Internal) अन्तरस्थः -स्था -स्थं, अन्तर्भूतः -ता -तं, आन्तरिकः -की -कं, आभ्यन्तरः -री -रं.—(Genuine, real) वास्तवः -वी -वं -विकः -की -कं, प्रकृतः -ता -तं, सत्यः -त्या -त्यं, यथार्थः -र्था -र्थं, सारः -रा -रं, अकृत्रिमः -मा -मं.—(Essential) स्वाभाविकः -की -कं, प्राकृतिकः -की -कं, सांसिद्धिकः -की -कं.

INTRINSICALLY, *adv.* स्वभावतस्, स्वभावेन, प्रकृतितस्, वस्तुतस्, जातितस्, सारतस्, तत्त्वतस्, भावतस्.

To INTRODUCE, *v. a.* (To the presence of) प्रविश् (c. 10. -वेशयति -यितुं), दर्शनं कृ in caus. (कारयति -यितुं), प्रवेशनं कृ.—(Bring into use) प्रवृत् (c. 10. -वर्त्तयति -यितुं), प्रचल् (c. 10. -चालयति -यितुं), प्रचलीकृ, प्रचर् (c. 10. -चारयति -यितुं), स्था in caus. (स्थापयति -यितुं), प्रतिष्ठा.—(Cause to enter) प्रविश् or निविश् or आविश् or समाविश् in caus.—(Conduct, bring) आनी (c. 1. -नयति -नेतुं), उपानी,

आवह् (c. 1. -वहति -वोढुं), आगम् (c. 10. -गमयति -यितुं), गम्.—(Begin) आरभ् (c. 1. -रभते -रब्धुं), प्रवृत् (c. 1. -वर्त्तते -र्त्तितुं).

INTRODUCED, *p.p.* (To the presence of) प्रवेशितः -ता -तं.—(Brought into use) प्रवर्त्तितः -ता -तं, प्रचालितः -ता -तं, परिचालितः -ता -तं, प्रचलितः -ता -तं, प्रचलीकृतः -ता -तं, प्रचारितः -ता -तं.—(Brought in) आनीतः -ता -तं.—(Made to enter) निवेशितः -ता -तं, प्रवेशितः -ता -तं, प्रविष्टः -ष्टा -ष्टं, निविष्टः -ष्टा -ष्टं.—(In legal process) प्रत्याकलितः -ता -तं.

INTRODUCER, *s.* प्रवेशकः, निवेशकः.—(One who brings into use) प्रवर्त्तकः, प्रथमस्थापकः, प्रतिष्ठापकः, आरम्भकः.

INTRODUCTION, *s.* (Ushering into the presence of) प्रवेशनं, प्रवेशकरणं.—(Making persons known to each other) अन्योन्यपरिचयकरणं; 'letter of introduction,' अन्योन्यपरिचयप्रार्थनार्थं पत्रं.—(Bringing in) आनयनं, उपनयनं, आवहनं.—(Bringing into use) प्रवर्त्तनं, स्थापनं, प्रतिष्ठापनं, प्रचारः.—(Insertion, causing to enter) निवेशनं, प्रवेशनं, आवेशनं, समावेशनं, प्रसङ्गः.—(Preface) प्रस्तावना -नं, प्रस्तावः, आभाषः, आरम्भः, उपोद्घातः, उपन्यासः, प्रकरणं.—(Exordium) वाक्यारम्भः, वाङ्मुखं, परिभाषा, आभाषः, प्रारम्भः, वन्दना.

INTRODUCTORY, INTRODUCTIVE, *a.* प्रावेशिकः -की -कं, प्रवेशकः -का -कं.—(Preliminary) आरम्भकः -का -कं, प्रारम्भकः -का -कं, प्राथमिकः -की -कं.—(Prefatory) पारिभाषिकः -की -कं, प्रस्तावनारूपः -पा -पं, उपोद्घातरूपः -पा -पं.

INTROGRESSION, *s.* प्रवेशः -शनं, निवेशः -शनं, अन्तर्गमनं, अन्तरागमनं.

INTROMISSION, *s.* प्रवेशनं, प्रवेशकरणं, निवेशनं, अन्तःक्षेपणं.

To INTROMIT, *v. a.* प्रविश् (c. 10. -वेशयति -यितुं), प्रवेशद्वारं भू, प्रवेशसाधनं भू.

INTROSPECTION, *s.* अन्तरालोकनं, अन्तरवलोकनं, अन्तर्दर्शनं, अन्तर्दृष्टिः *f.*

INTROSPECTIVE, *a.* अन्तर्दर्शी -र्शिनी -र्शि (न्), अन्तर्दृष्टिः -ष्टिः -ष्टि.

To INTROVERT, *v. a.* अन्तर्मुखं -खां -खीं -खं कृ, अन्तर्मुखीकृ.

To INTRUDE, *v. n.* अन्यायतः or अनधिकारपूर्व्वं प्रविश् (c. 6. -विशति -वेष्टुं), अनाहूतः प्रविश् or आविश् or प्रसृप् (c. 1. -सर्पति -सप्तुं) or आगम् (c. 1. -गच्छति, गन्तुं), धर्षेण प्रविश् or आक्रम् (c. 1. -क्रामति -क्रमितुं) or अभिक्रम्, धर्ष् (c. 1. धर्षति -र्षितुं), धर्षां कृ.

INTRUDER, *s.* अनाहूतप्रवेशकः, अन्यायतः or अनधिकारपूर्व्वं प्रवेशकः or प्रसर्पकः, अनाहूतागन्ता *m.* (न्तृ), आगन्तुकः, अनधिकारी, धर्षकः, धर्षाकारी *m.* (न्).

INTRUSION, *s.* अनधिकारपूर्व्वः प्रवेशः, अनधिकारपूर्व्वं प्रवेशनं, अनाहूतप्रवेशनं, अनाहूतागमनं.

INTRUSIVE, *a.* पराधिकारचर्चकः -का -कं, धर्षाशीलः -ला -लं, धृष्टः -ष्टा -ष्टं, धर्षी -र्षिणी -र्षि (न्), प्रगल्भः -ल्भा -ल्भं.

To INTRUST, *v. a.* (Commit) ऋ in caus. (-अर्पयति -यितुं), सम्, निक्षिप् (c. 6. -क्षिपति -क्षेप्तुं), विनिक्षिप्, न्यस् (c. 4. -अस्यति -असितुं), उपन्यस्, न्यासीकृ, नियुज् (c. 7. -युनक्ति -योक्तुं, c. 10. -योजयति -यितुं), प्रतिपद् (c. 10. -पादयति -यितुं), परिदा (c. 3. -ददाति -दातुं), प्रणिधा.—(Place trust in) विश्वस् (c. 2. -श्वसिति -तुं), विश्वासं कृ, प्रत्ययं कृ.

INTRUSTED, *p.p.* अर्पितः -ता -तं, समर्पितः -ता -तं, निक्षिप्तः -प्ता -प्तं, न्यस्तः -स्ता -स्तं, न्यासीकृतः -ता -तं, नियोजितः -ता -तं, प्रतिपादितः -ता -तं, प्रणिहितः -ता -तं.

INTUITION, *s.* सहजज्ञानं, साहजिकज्ञानं, अन्तर्ज्ञानं, तात्कालिकज्ञानं, प्रमाणनिरपेक्षज्ञानं, अप्रामाणिकज्ञानं, विचारनिरपेक्षज्ञानं, सहजोपलब्धज्ञानं, अविचारपूर्व्वं ज्ञानं, अयत्नज्ञानं.

INTUITIVE, *a.* (Seen without arguments) अन्तर्ज्ञानोपलब्धः -ब्धा -ब्धं, सहजज्ञानोपलब्धः &c., अन्तर्ज्ञानोपलभ्यः -भ्या -भ्यं, प्रमाणनिरपेक्षज्ञेयः -या -यं, सहजज्ञेयः -या -यं, अविचारपूर्व्वम् उपलभ्यः -भ्या -भ्यं, अविचार्य्य ज्ञेयः -या -यं.—(Seeing without arguments) अन्तर्ज्ञानी -निनी -नि (न्), सहजज्ञः -ज्ञा -ज्ञं, प्रमाणनिरपेक्षज्ञः -ज्ञा -ज्ञं.

INTUITIVELY, *adv.* सहजज्ञानात्, अन्तर्ज्ञानेन, तात्कालिकज्ञानात्, प्रमाणनिरपेक्षं, विचारनिरपेक्षं, अविचारपूर्व्वं.

INTUMESCENCE, INTURGESCENCE, *s.* शोथः, स्फीतिः *f.*, स्फीतता -त्वं, शोफः, श्वयथुः *m.*, आध्मानं.

To INTWINE, INTWIST, *v. a.* ग्रन्थ् (c. 9. ग्रथ्नाति, c. 1. ग्रन्थति -न्थितुं), गुफ् (c. 6. गुफति -फितुं), गुम्फ् (c. 6. गुम्फति -म्फितुं), रच् (c. 10. रचयति -यितुं), विरच्.

INUENDO, *s.* *See* INNUENDO.

To INUMBRATE, *v. a.* छायां कृ, छायया छद् (c. 10. छादयति -यितुं), प्रच्छद्.

INUNCTION, *s.* अभ्यञ्जनं, अञ्जनं, अभ्यङ्गः, प्रदेहः, आलेपनं, विलेपनं.

To INUNDATE, *v. a.* जलेन प्लु (c. 10. प्लावयति -यितुं) or आप्लु or परिप्लु or सम्प्लु, जलप्लुतं -तां कृ, जलप्लावितं -तां कृ, जलव्याप्तं -प्तां कृ, जलप्लावनं कृ, जलप्रलयं कृ; 'is inundated,' प्लाव्यते.

INUNDATED, *p.p.* जलप्लावितः -ता -तं, आप्लावितः -ता -तं, जलप्लुतः -ता -तं, आप्लुतः -ता -तं, जलव्याप्तः -प्ता -प्तं, परिप्लुतः -ता -तं, जलमयः -यी -यं, उत्तरङ्गः -ङ्गा -ङ्गं.

INUNDATION, *s.* जलप्लावः -वनं, आप्लावः -वनं, जलाप्लावनं, जलप्रलयः, तोयविप्लवः, जलविप्लवः, सलिलोपप्लवः, जलोच्छ्वासः, जलवेगः, जलपरिप्लवः, परिप्लवः, जलौघः, ओघः, जलवृद्धिः *f.*, परीवाहः, परिवाहः, विदारः, स्रोतस् *n.*, वन्या.

INURBANITY, *s.* अविनयः, अविनीतता, अशिष्टता, असभ्यता, अदाक्षिण्यं.

To INURE, *v. a.* अभ्यस् (c. 4. -अस्यति -असितुं), अभ्यासं कृ, अभ्यस्तं -स्तां -स्तं कृ, शिक्ष् (c. 10. शिक्षयति -यितुं), नित्याभ्यासं कृ.—(Harden by constant practice) नित्याभ्यासेन कठिनीकृ or कठोरीकृ.

INURED, *p.p.* अभ्यस्तः -स्ता -स्तं, कृताभ्यासः -सा -सं, शिक्षितः -ता -तं, नित्याभ्यासेन कठिनीभूतः -ता -तं; 'inured to fatigue,' जितश्रमः -मा -मं.

INUREMENT, *s.* अभ्यासः, नित्याभ्यासः, निरन्तराभ्यासः, व्यवहारः, शिक्षा.

To INURN, *v. a.* समाधौ निधा (c. 3. -दधाति -धातुं) or निक्षिप् (c. 6. -क्षिपति -क्षेप्तुं).

INUSTION, *s.* दाहः, दाहनं, दहनं, तप्तलोहेन दाहनं.

INUTILITY, *s.* व्यर्थता, वैयर्थ्यं, विफलता, वैफल्यं, निरर्थकत्वं, अनर्थकत्वं, अनुपयोगः -गिता, निरुपयोगः -गिता, अयोग्यता -त्वं.

INUTTERABLE, *a.* अवाच्यः -च्या -च्यं, अवचनीयः -या -यं, अनिर्वचनीयः -या -यं, अनुच्चारणीयः -या -यं, अनुच्चार्य्यः -र्य्या -र्य्यं, अकथ्यः -थ्या -थ्यं.

To INVADE, *v. a.* आक्रम् (c. 1. -क्रामति -क्रमितुं), अभिक्रम्, अधिक्रम्, उपक्रम्, उपाक्रम्, अवस्कन्द् (c. 1. -स्कन्दति -स्कन्तुं), आस्कन्द्, समास्कन्द्, समवस्कन्द्, आसद् (c. 10. -सादयति -यितुं), समासद्, अभिद्रु (c. 1. -द्रवति -द्रोतुं), उपद्रु, समाद्रु, अभिप्रया (c. 2. -याति -तुं), अभिसृ (c. 1. -सरति -सर्त्तुं), अवस्कन्दं कृ, उपद्रवं कृ, उपप्लवं कृ, अभिनिर्य्याणं कृ, अभियोगं कृ; 'invade a country,' देशम् आक्रम्, देशाक्रमणं कृ, लोप्त्रार्थं or द्रोहकरणार्थं देशं प्रविश् (c. 6. -विशति -वेष्टुं).

INVADED, *p.p.* आक्रान्तः -न्ता -न्तं, उपद्रुतः -ता -तं, कृतावस्कन्दः -न्दा -न्दं, अवस्कन्दितः -ता -तं, उपप्लुतः -ता -तं, कृतोपद्रवः -वा -वं.

INVADER, *s.* आक्रामकः, देशाक्रामकः, आक्रमणकारी *m.* (न्), अवस्कन्दकृत् *m.*

IN VAIN, *adv.* वृथा, मुधा. *See* VAINLY.

INVALESCENSE, *s.* स्वास्थ्यं, स्वस्थता, आरोग्यं, शरीरकुशलं.

INVALID, *a.* (Of no force) निर्बलः -ला -लं, बलहीनः -ना -नं, शक्तिहीनः -ना -नं, अनिष्पन्नः -न्ना -न्नं, व्यर्थः -र्था -र्थं, मोघः -घा -घं, निष्फलः -ला -लं, विफलः -ला -लं, अप्रमाणः -णा -णं, निष्प्रमाणः -णा -णं, निष्प्रभावः -वा -वं, प्रभावहीनः -ना -नं, निस्तेजाः -जाः -जः (स्), लुप्तः -प्ता -प्तं, लघुः -घुः -घु, लघुप्रमाणः -णा -णं.

INVALID, *s.* (A sick or infirm person) रोगी *m.* -गिणी *f.*, रोगवान् *m.* -वती *f.*, रोगार्त्तः -र्त्ता, सरोगः -गा, अस्वस्थशरीरः -रा, अस्वस्थः -स्था, जन्मरोगी *m.* -गिणी, मरी *m.* -रिणी.

To INVALIDATE, *v. a.* अधरीकृ, मोघीकृ, व्यर्थीकृ, निष्फलीकृ, निष्फल (nom. निष्फलयति -यितुं), लुप् (c. 6. लुम्पति, लोप्तुं, c. 10. लोपयति -यितुं), मुधा कृ, वृथा कृ, मुधा विधा (c. 3. -दधाति -धातुं), निर्बलीकृ, निष्प्रभावीकृ, लघूकृ.

INVALIDATED, *p. p.* अधरीकृतः -ता -तं, अनिष्पन्नः -न्ना -न्नं, निर्बलीकृतः -ता -तं.

INVALIDITY, *s.* निर्बलता, बलहीनता, अनिष्पत्तिः *f.*, अनिष्पन्नता, व्यर्थता, मोघता, निष्फलता, विफलता, निष्प्रभावत्वं, प्रभावहीनता, शक्तिहीनता, दुर्बलता, दौर्बल्यं, अप्रामाण्यं, लघुत्वं, लाघवं.

INVALUABLE, *a.* अनर्घ्यः -र्घ्या -र्घ्यं, अमूल्यः -ल्या -ल्यं, अनर्घः -र्घा -र्घं, मूल्यातीतः -ता -तं, मूल्यातिगः -गा -गं, अतिमूल्यः -ल्या -ल्यं, अनुत्तमः -मा -मं, अत्युत्कृष्टः -ष्टा -ष्टं, बहुमूल्यकः -का -कं.

INVALUABLENESS, *s.* अनर्घ्यता -त्वं, अमूल्यता -त्वं, अनर्घत्वं, अत्युत्कृष्टत्वं.

INVARIABLE, *a.* अविकार्य्यः -र्य्या -र्य्यं, निर्विकारः -रा -रं, अविकारः -रा -रं, अविक्रियः -या -यं, नित्यः -त्या -त्यं, नैत्यिकः -की -कं, स्थिरः -रा -रं, सुस्थिरः -रा -रं, नियतः -ता -तं, अचलः -ला -लं, अचञ्चलः -ला -लं, अविकल्पः -ल्पा -ल्पं, निर्विकल्पः -ल्पा -ल्पं, व्यवस्थितः -ता -तं, धृतिमान् -मती -मत् (त्), अपरिवर्त्तनीयः -या -यं.

INVARIABLENESS, *s.* अविकार्य्यता -त्वं, निर्विकारत्वं, अविकारत्वं, नित्यता, नैत्यिकत्वं, स्थिरता, सुस्थैर्य्यं, सुस्थिरता.

INVARIABLY, *adv.* नित्यं, नित्यदा, सर्व्वदा, सततं, नियतं, निर्विकारं, सुस्थिरं.

INVASION, *s.* आक्रमणं, आक्रमः, अभिक्रमः -मणं, अधिक्रमः -मणं, आक्रान्तिः *f.*, अवस्कन्दः, अभिमर्द्दः, उपद्रवः, उपप्लवः, अभिनिर्याणं, प्रयाणं, अभियोगः, दिग्विजयक्रमः; 'of a country,' देशाक्रमणं.

INVASIVE, *a.* आक्रामकः -का -कं, अभिक्रामकः &c., उपद्रवी -विणी -वि (न्).

INVECTIVE, *s.* क्षेपः, अवक्षेपः, आक्षेपः, निन्दोक्तिः *f.*, निन्दावाक्यं, निन्दा, भर्त्सनवाक्यं, भर्त्सना, निर्भर्त्सनं -ना, अपवादः, परीवादः, परिभाषणं, दुर्वाक्यं, वाक्पारुष्यं, धिक्पारुष्यं, धिक्क्रिया, दुरुक्तं, तिरस्कारवाक्यं, तिरस्कारः, कुत्सावाक्यं, गर्हा, कटुवाक्यं, प्रतिकूलार्थं वचः.

INVECTIVE, *a.* निन्दकः -का -कं, निन्दामयः -यी -यं, निन्दाकरः -री -रं, निन्दात्मकः -का -कं, कुत्सावादी -दिनी -दि (न्), अपवादी &c., अपवादकः -का -कं.

To INVEIGH, *v. a.* अवक्षिप् (c. 6. -क्षिपति -क्षेप्तुं), अधिक्षिप्, परिक्षिप्, आक्षिप्, क्षिप्, निन्द् (c. 1. निन्दति -न्दितुं), प्रणिन्द्, विनिन्द्, अपवद् (c. 1. -वदति -ते -दितुं), परिवद्, भर्त्स् (c. 10. भर्त्सयति -यितुं), निर्भर्त्स्, अवभर्त्स्, अवगुर् (c. 6. -गुरते -रितुं), अभिशप् (c. 1. -शपति -शप्तुं), परिशप्, गर्ह् (c. 1. गर्हते -र्हितुं, c. 10. गर्हयति -ते -यितुं), विगर्ह्, परिगर्ह्, तिरस्कृ, धिक्कृ, दुर्वाक्यं वद्, निन्दावाक्यं वद्, उपालभ् (c. 1. -लभते -लब्धुं).

To INVEIGLE, *v. a.* प्रलुभ् (c. 10. -लोभयति -यितुं), परिलुभ्, लुभ्, लल् (c. 10. लालयति -यितुं), मधुरवचोभिः or चाटूक्त्या or चाटुकारेण प्रलुभ् or लल् or सान्त्व् (c. 10. सान्त्वयति -यितुं) or आकृष् (c. 1. -कर्षति, c. 6. -कृषति -क्रष्टुं) or प्रलभ् (c. 1. -लभते -लब्धुं) or मुह् (c. 10. मोहयति -यितुं), लालनं कृ, वञ्च् (c. 10. वञ्चयति -यितुं).

INVEIGLED, *p. p.* लालितः -ता -तं, प्रलोभितः -ता -तं, चाटुकारेणाकृष्टः -ष्टा -ष्टं.

INVEIGLER, *s.* प्रलोभकः, विलोभकः, लाली *m.* (न्), लालनकारी *m.* (न्), आकर्षकः, मोही *m.* (न्), विमोही *m.*, मोहकः, लोभदर्शकः, प्रलम्भकारी *m.*

INVEIGLING, INVEIGLEMENT, *s.* प्रलोभनं, विलोभनं, आकर्षणं, आकृष्टिः *f.*, लालनं, मोहनं, विमोहनं, लोभदर्शनं, वञ्चनं -ना, प्रवञ्चना, प्रतारणा, प्रलम्भः.

To INVENT, *v. a.* कॢप् (c. 10. कल्पयति -यितुं), परिकॢप्, रच् (c. 10. रचयति -यितुं), विरच्, सृज् (c. 6. सृजति, स्रष्टुं), विधा (c. 3. -दधाति -धातुं), घट् (c. 10. घटयति -यितुं), निर्मा (c. 2. -माति, c. 3. -मिमीते -मातुं), विनिर्मा, परिकल्पनां कृ.—(In the mind) मनसा कॢप् or परिकॢप् or सृज्, स्वमनसा कॢप्.—(Devise a plan) उपायं प्रचिन्त् (c. 10. -चिन्तयति -यितुं) or परिचिन्त्.—(Fabricate falsely) मिथ्या कॢप् or सृज्.—(Find out) निरूप् (c. 10. -रूपयति -यितुं).

INVENTED, *p. p.* कल्पितः -ता -तं, परिकल्पितः -ता -तं, कॢप्तः -प्ता -प्तं, मनःकल्पितः -ता -तं, मनःसृष्टः -ष्टा -ष्टं, रचितः -ता -तं, विरचितः -ता -तं, घटितः -ता -तं, निर्मितः -ता -तं.—(Devised) प्रचिन्तितः -ता -तं, घटितः -ता -तं.—(Fabricated, factitious) मिथ्याकल्पितः -ता -तं, काल्पनिकः -की -कं, कृत्रिमः -मा -मं, कृतकः -का -कं.—(Found out) निरूपितः -ता -तं.

INVENTION, *s.* (The act) कल्पना -नं, परिकल्पना -नं, कॢप्तिः *f.*, रचना, विरचना, सृष्टिः *f.*, निर्माणं, घटनं, निरूपणं.—(Power of invention, ingenuity) कल्पनाशक्तिः *f.*, कल्पना, युक्तिः *f.*, सुयुक्तिः *f.*, उपायज्ञानं, उपायज्ञत्वं.—(That which is invented) कल्पितं, परिकल्पितं, कल्पना, कॢप्तिः *f.*—(Fabrication, fiction) मिथ्याकल्पना, मिथ्याकल्पितं, मनःकल्पितं, मनःसृष्टिः *f.*; 'invention of one's own brain,' स्वकपोलकल्पितं.

INVENTIVE, *a.* कल्पकः -का -कं, उपायज्ञः -ज्ञा -ज्ञं, उपायी -यिनी -यि (न्), युक्तिमान् -मती -मत् (त्), चतुरः -रा -रं, कुशलः -ला -लं, उपायकुशलः -ला -लं, सुप्रयोगवान् &c.

INVENTIVENESS, *s.* उपायज्ञत्वं, युक्तिः *f.*, युक्तिमत्त्वं, सुयुक्तिः *f.*

INVENTOR, *s.* कल्पकः, परिकल्पकः, कल्पयिता *m.* (तृ), स्रष्टा *m.* (ष्टृ), निर्माता *m.* (तृ), विधायी *m.* (न्), विधाता *m.* (तृ), रचकः, विरचकः, निरूपकः, निरूपयिता *m.* (तृ).

INVENTORY, *s.* गृहोपस्करपरिसंख्या, गृहभाण्डपरिगणना, अस्थावरद्रव्यसंख्यापत्रं, अस्थावरवस्तुगणनापत्रं, गृहवस्तुपरिसंख्या, गृहसामग्र्यपरिगणना.

To INVENTORY, *v. a.* गृहोपस्करादि परिसंख्या (c. 2. -ख्याति -तुं) or परिगण् (c. 10. -गणयति -यितुं).

INVENTRESS, *s.* कल्पिका, परिकल्पिका, कल्पयित्री, निरूपयित्री.

INVERSE, *a.* व्यत्यस्तः -स्ता -स्तं, विपरीतः -ता -तं, विपर्य्यस्तः -स्ता -स्तं, पर्य्यस्तः -स्ता -स्तं, व्यस्तः -स्ता -स्तं, विलोमः -मा -मं, प्रतिलोमः -मा -मं, व्यतिक्रान्तः -न्ता -न्तं, प्रतिकूलः -ला -लं, प्रतीपः -पा -पं, विप्रतीपः -पा -पं, प्रसव्यः -व्या -व्यं, अपसव्यः -व्या -व्यं; 'Rule of three inverse,' विलोमत्रैराशिकं, व्यस्तत्रैराशिकं; 'in inverse ratio,' विपर्य्ययेण.

INVERSELY, *adv.* विपर्य्ययेण, व्यत्यासेन, व्युत्क्रमेण, विपरीतं, पर्य्यासेन.

INVERSION, *s.* विपर्य्ययः, विपर्य्यायः, व्यत्यासः, विपर्य्यासः, पर्य्यासः, व्युत्क्रमः, व्यतिक्रमः, विपरीतता, वैपरीत्यं, प्रतिकूलता, प्रातिकूल्यं, विलोमता, प्रतिलोमता, प्रातिलोम्यं, व्यत्ययः, व्यत्यस्तता, व्यस्तता, विप्रतीपता, प्रतीपता, प्रपञ्चः, प्रसव्यत्वं; 'rule of inversion in arithmetic,' विलोमक्रिया, व्यस्तविधिः *m.*

To INVERT, *v. a.* विपर्यस् (c. 4. -अस्यति -असितुं), पर्यस्, व्यत्यस्, विप-

रीतीकृ, वैपरीत्यं कृ, विपर्य्ययं कृ, व्यत्यस्तं -स्तां कृ, विपर्य्यस्तं -स्तां कृ, प्रतिकूलीकृ, विलोमीकृ.—(Turn upside down) अधोमुखीकृ, अधोमुखं -खां कृ, अधःकृ, अधरोत्तरीकृ, अर्द्धाधरीकृ, अपवृत् (c. 10. -वर्त्तयति -यितुं), परिवृत्; 'invert the glass in water,' पात्रम् अधोमुखं जले स्थापय.

Inverted, *p. p.* विपर्य्यस्तः -स्ता -स्तं, व्यत्यस्तः -स्ता -स्तं, पर्य्यस्तः -स्ता -स्तं, व्यस्तः -स्ता -स्तं, विपरीतः -ता -तं, व्यतिक्रान्तः -न्ता -न्तं, व्युत्क्रान्तः -न्ता -न्तं, विलोमः -मा -मं, प्रतिलोमः -मा -मं, प्रतिकूलः -ला -लं, प्रसव्यः -व्या -व्यं, प्रतिसव्यः -व्या -व्यं.—(Turned upside down) अधोमुखीकृतः -ता -तं, अधोमुखः -खा -खं, अधःकृतः -ता -तं, अधरोत्तरः -रा -रं, अपवृत्तः -त्ता -त्तं.

To invest, *v. a.* (Dress, clothe) वेष्ट् (c. 1. वेष्टते -ष्टितुं), परिवेष्ट्, प्रवेष्ट्, आच्छद् (c. 10. -च्छादयति -यितुं), प्रवृ (c. 5. -वृणोति -वरितुं -रीतुं), संव्ये (c. 1. -व्ययति -व्यातुं), परिव्ये, परिधा in caus. (-धापयति -यितुं), वस् (c. 10. वासयति -यितुं), विवस्.—(Invest with office) अधिकारे नियुज् (c. 7. -युनक्ति -युंक्ते, c. 10. योजयति -यितुं), अधिकारं प्रविश् (c. 10. -वेशयति -यितुं), अधिकारयुक्तं -क्तां कृ, अभिषिच् (c. 6. -षिञ्चति -षेक्तुं), संस्कारपूर्व्वम् अधिकारप्रवेशं कृ.—(Adorn) अलङ्कृ, भूष् (c. 10. भूषयति -यितुं), विभूष्.—(Indue, place in possession) युक्तं -क्तां कृ, सम्पन्नं -न्नां कृ, विशिष्टं -ष्टां कृ, उपेतं -तां कृ, अन्वितं -तां कृ, नियुज्, युज्.—(Inclose, besiege) परिवेष्ट्, उद्वेष्ट्, समन्तात् रुध् (c. 7. रुणद्धि, रोद्धुं) or उपरुध् or अवरुध्.—(Invest money) क्षेत्रगृहादि क्रीत्वा धनं प्रयुज्, धनप्रयोगं कृ.

Invested, *p. p.* (Clothed) वेष्टितः -ता -तं, आच्छादितः -ता -तं, परिच्छन्नः -न्ना -न्नं, परिहितः -ता -तं, संवीतः -ता -तं, आश्लिष्टः -ष्टा -ष्टं.—(With office) अधिकारे नियुक्तः -क्ता -क्तं, पदयुक्तः -क्ता -क्तं, पदविशिष्टः -ष्टा -ष्टं.—(Indued, placed in possession) युक्तः -क्ता -क्तं. *See* To Invest.—(Closed, besieged) परिवेष्टितः -ता -तं, उद्वेष्टितः -ता -तं, रुद्धः -द्धा -द्धं, समन्तादुपरुद्धः -द्धा -द्धं, पर्य्यवष्टब्धः -ब्धा -ब्धं, बाधितः -ता -तं.—(As money) प्रयुक्तः -क्ता -क्तं.

Investigable, *a.* निरूपणीयः -या -यं, निरूप्यः -प्या -प्यं, विचारणीयः -या -यं, विचार्य्यः -र्य्या -र्य्यं, अनुसन्धेयः -या -यं, निर्णेयः -या -यं, विचारयोग्यः -ग्या -ग्यं.

To investigate, *v. a.* निरूप् (c. 10. -रूपयति -यितुं), अनुसन्धा (c. 3. -दधाति -धातुं), परीक्ष् (c. 1. -ईक्षते -क्षितुं), समीक्ष्, अवेक्ष्, निरीक्ष्, विचर् (c. 10. -चारयति -यितुं), ज्ञा in des. (जिज्ञासते -सितुं), अन्विष् (c. 4. -इष्यति -एषितुं), अन्वेष् (c. 1. -एषते -षितुं), आलोच् (c. 10. -लोचयति -यितुं), आलोक् (c. 10. -लोकयति -यितुं), अनुयुज् (c. 7. -युनक्ति -युंक्ते -योक्तुं), विमृश् (c. 6. -मृशति -म्रष्टुं), निर्णी (c. 1. -णयति -णेतुं), निश्चि (c. 5. -चिनोति -चेतुं), विनिश्चि, विभू (c. 10. -भावयति -यितुं), चर्च् (c. 1. चर्चति -र्चितुं), मार्ग् (c. 10. मार्गयति -यितुं), मन् in des. (मीमांसते -सितुं), अभिनिध्यै (c. 1. -ध्यायति -ध्यातुं), विवेचनां कृ.

Investigated, *p. p.* निरूपितः -ता -तं, परीक्षितः -ता -तं, निरीक्षितः -ता -तं, अवेक्षितः -ता -तं, विचारितः -ता -तं, जिज्ञासितः -ता -तं, अन्वेषितः -ता -तं, अन्विष्टः -ष्टा -ष्टं, निर्णीतः -ता -तं, आलोचितः -ता -तं, चर्चितः -ता -तं.

Investigating, *part.* निरूपयन् -यन्ती -यत् (त्), परीक्षकः -का -कं, अन्वेषी -षिणी -षि (न्), अनुसन्धानी -निनी -नि (न्), अनुसन्धायी &c., विचारी &c.

Investigation, *s.* निरूपणं, अनुसन्धानं, परीक्षा -क्षणं, विचारः -रणं -णा, जिज्ञासा, अन्वेषणं -णा, निरीक्षणं, अवेक्षा -क्षणं, समीक्षणं, संवीक्षणं, प्रसमीक्षा, निर्णयः, निश्चयः, अनुयोगः, विवेचना, विवेकः, चर्चा, विमर्शः, निरूपणत्वं, परीष्टिः *f.*; 'under investigation,' निरूप्यमाणः -णा -णं, विचार्य्यमाणः -णा -णं, निरूप्यमाणः -णा -णं.

Investigator, *s.* परीक्षकः, विचारकः, निरूपयिता *m.* (तृ), अनुसन्धायी *m.* (न्), अन्वेष्टा *m.* (ष्टृ), अन्वेषी *m.* (न्), निर्णेता *m.* (तृ), चर्चाकारी *m.* (न्).

Investiture, *s.* (Investing with any office) प्रतिष्ठापनं, प्रतिष्ठा, अभिषेकः, अभिषेचनं, अधिकारप्रवेशकरणं, पदस्थापनं -ना.—(With the sacrificial cord, or yajnopavīta) उपनयः -यनं, आनयः -यनं, मौञ्जीबन्धनं, पवित्रारोपणं.

Investment, *s.* (Clothes) परिधानं, आच्छादनं, वस्त्रं.—(Besieging, surrounding) अवरोधः -धनं, प्रतिरोधः, रोधः, वेष्टनं, परिवेष्टनं -ष्टः, उद्वेष्टः, पर्य्यवष्टम्भनं.—(Laying out money) धनप्रयोगः.

Inveteracy, *s.* बद्धमूलता, निर्बन्धः, अभिनिवेशः, दृढता, स्थिरता, अभिनिविष्टता, चिरकालिकत्वं, बहुकालिकत्वं.

Inveterate, *a.* बद्धमूलः -ला -लं, दृढमूलः -ला -लं, दृढः -ढा -ढं, स्थिरः -रा -रं, निर्बद्धः -द्धा -द्धं, चिरस्थायी -यिनी -यि (न्), बहुकालिकः -की -कं, चिरकालिकः -की -कं, चिरकालीनः -ना -नं, अभिनिविष्टः -ष्टा -ष्टं; 'inveterate hatred,' बद्धवैरं, अच्युतवैरं; 'an inveterate fool,' प्रतिनिविष्टमूर्खः.

Inveterateness, *s.* *See* Inveteracy.

Invidious, *a.* (Envious) मत्सरी -रिणी -रि (न्), समत्सरः -रा -रं, ईर्ष्यी -र्ष्यिणी -र्ष्यि (न्), ईर्ष्यालुः -लुः -लु.—(Likely to provoke envy or ill-will) ईर्ष्याकरः -रा -रं, ईर्ष्याजनकः -का -कं, असूयाजनकः -का -कं, असूयोत्पादकः -का -कं, मात्सर्य्यजनकः -का -कं, मत्सरावहः -हा -हं, द्वेषजनकः -का -कं, द्वेष्यः -ष्या -ष्यं, द्वेषणीयः -या -यं, कुत्सितः -ता -तं, अप्रीतिजनकः -का -कं.

Invidiously, *adv.* (Enviously) समत्सरं, समात्सर्य्यं, सासूयं, सेर्ष्यं.—(In a manner so as to provoke hatred) यथा द्वेषः or असूया जायते तथा, यथा मात्सर्य्यम् उत्पद्यते तथा.

Invidiousness, *s.* द्वेषजनकत्वं, असूयाजनकत्वं, ईर्ष्याजनकत्वं.

To invigorate, *v. a.* बलं वृध् (c. 10. वर्धयति -यितुं), तेजो वृध् or कृ or दा, वीर्य्यं or सत्त्वं वृध् or दा, अग्निं or रुचिं दा or वृध्, सबलं -लां कृ, सबलीकृ, सवीर्य्यं -र्य्यां कृ, पुष् (c. 10. पोषयति -यितुं), पुष्टिं कृ or दा or वृध्, आप्यै (c. 10. -प्याययति -यितुं), समाप्यै, दीप् (c. 10. दीपयति -यितुं).

Invigorated, *p. p.* वर्धितबलः -ला -लं, वर्धिततेजाः -जाः -जः (स्), वृद्धसत्त्वः -त्त्वा -त्त्वं, तेजितः -ता -तं, पुष्टः -ष्टा -ष्टं, दीपितः -ता -तं, प्रदीप्तः -प्ता -प्तं, आप्यायितः -ता -तं.

Invigorating, *a.* बलवर्धकः -का -कं, बलवर्धी -र्धिनी -र्धि (न्), तेजस्करः -रा -रं, तेजोवर्धकः -का -कं, पुष्टिदः -दा -दं, पुष्टिकारकः -का -कं, पौष्टिकः -की -कं, वीर्य्यदः -दा -दं, सत्त्ववर्धकः &c., दीपकः -का -कं.

Invigoration, *s.* (The act) बलवर्धनं, तेजोवर्धनं, सत्त्ववर्धनं, पुष्टिकरणं.—(State) बलवृद्धिः *f.*, तेजोवृद्धिः *f.*

Invincible, *a.* अजेयः -या -यं, अजय्यः -य्या -य्यं, दुर्जयः -या -यं, दुर्जेयः -या -यं, अदम्यः -म्या -म्यं, अदमनीयः -या -यं, अपराजेयः -या -यं, अपराजेतव्यः -व्या -व्यं, अपराजितः -ता -तं, अपराभाव्यः -व्या -व्यं, अप्रधृष्यः -ष्या -ष्यं, सर्व्वजित् *m. f. n.*

Invincibleness, *s.* अजेयता -त्वं, दुर्जेयता, अपराजेयत्वं, अदम्यता.

Invincibly, *adv.* अजेयं, अपराजेयं, अदमनीयं, यथा जेतुं न शक्यते.

Inviolable, *a.* (Not to be broken) अलंघ्यः -घ्या -घ्यं, अलंघनीयः -या -यं, अभेद्यः -द्या -द्यं, अनतिक्रमणीयः -या -यं, अनतिक्रम्यः -म्या

-र्व्यं, अभक्तः -क्ता -क्तं, भक्तायोग्यः -ग्या -ग्यं.—(Not to be treated irreverently, not to be hurt) अलंघनीयः -या -यं, अनुल्लंघनीयः -या -यं, अबाध्यः -ध्या -ध्यं, अबाधनीयः -या -यं, अनपकार्य्यः -र्य्या -र्य्यं, धिक्कारानर्हः -र्हा -र्हं.—(Not to be put to death) अवध्यः -ध्या -ध्यं, अघ्नः -घ्ना -घ्नं. These last are used in reference to an ambassador or herald.

INVIOLABLENESS, INVIOLABILITY, *s.* अलंघ्यता -त्वं, अलंघनीयता -त्वं, अभेद्यता, अनतिक्रमणीयता, अबाध्यत्वं.—(Of an ambassador or herald) अवध्यता -त्वं, अवध्यभावः.

INVIOLABLY, *adv.* अलंघनीयं, अभक्तेन, यथा न भिद्यते तथाप्रकारेण.

INVIOLATE, *a.* अलंघितः -ता -तं, अभग्नः -ग्ना -ग्नं, अक्षतः -ता -तं, अखण्डः -ण्डा -ण्डं, अभक्तः -क्ता -क्तं, अभेदितः -ता -तं, अभिन्नः -न्ना -न्नं, अबाधितः -ता -तं.

INVIOUS, *a.* दुर्गमः -मा -मं, अगम्यः -म्या -म्यं, अगमनीयः -या -यं, दुरत्ययः -या -यं, गहनः -ना -नं, सम्बाधः -धा -धं, गत्वूनः -ना -नं.

To INVISCATE, *v. a.* चूर्णादिना श्यानद्रव्येण लिप् (c. 6. लिम्पति, लेप्तुं).

INVISIBILITY, INVISIBLENESS, *s.* अदृश्यता -त्वं, अलक्ष्यता -त्वं, परोक्षता, अलोकनीयत्वं, दृष्ट्यगोचरता, अप्रत्यक्षता, दुर्दृश्यता, दुर्दर्शत्वं, दुर्लक्ष्यता -त्वं, अदर्शनं, परोक्षं, अलोकनं, अन्तर्द्धा -र्द्धानं -र्द्धिः *m.*, अन्तर्हितत्वं, अविषयः.

INVISIBLE, *a.* अदृश्यः -श्या -श्यं, अदर्शनीयः -या -यं, अलक्ष्यः -क्ष्या -क्ष्यं, अप्रत्यक्षः -क्षा -क्षं, दृष्ट्यगोचरः -रा -रं, दृगगोचरः -रा -रं, अलोकनीयः -या -यं, अप्रेक्षणीयः -या -यं, परोक्षः -क्षा -क्षं, दुर्दृश्यः -श्या -श्यं, दुर्दर्शः -र्शा -र्शं, दुर्लक्ष्यः -क्ष्या -क्ष्यं, दुर्लक्षः -क्षा -क्षं, असमक्षः -क्षी -क्षं, दृष्ट्यविषयः -या -यं, चक्षुरग्राह्यः -ह्या -ह्यं, दर्शनातीतः -ता -तं, दर्शनपथातीतः -ता -तं, अनालोक्यः -क्या -क्यं, अदृष्टरूपः -पा -पं, अन्तर्हितः -ता -तं, तिरोहितः -ता -तं, अन्तरितः -ता -तं, प्रकाशेतरः -रा -रं, अरूपः -पा -पं, अचाक्षुषः -षी -षं, असाक्षात् indec.; 'to become invisible,' अन्तर्धा in pass. (-धीयते), तिरोधा.

INVISIBLY, *adv.* अदर्शनीयं, अप्रत्यक्षं -क्षेण -क्षतस्, परोक्षं -क्षेण, असाक्षात्, अप्रकाशं, अप्रादुस्, असमक्षं, अदृष्टरूपेण, दुर्दर्शं, दृष्ट्यगोचरेण; 'moving invisibly,' अलक्ष्यगतिः -तिः -ति.

INVITATION, *s.* निमन्त्रणं, आमन्त्रणं, आह्वानं, आह्वयः, आहूतिः *f.*, आवाहनं, आकारणं, केतनं, सङ्केतः; 'invitation to dinner,' भोजनार्थं निमन्त्रणं.

INVITATORY, *a.* निमन्त्रयिता -त्री -तृ (तृ), आमन्त्रयिता &c., आह्वानार्थकः -का -कं.

To INVITE, *v. a.* निमन्त्र् (c. 10. -मन्त्रयति -यितुं), आमन्त्र्, उपनिमन्त्र्, सन्निमन्त्र्, आह्वे (c. 1. -ह्वयति -ह्वातुं), समाह्वे, उपह्वे, केत् (c. 10. केतयति -यितुं), सङ्केत्, अभ्यर्थ् (c. 10. -अर्थयते -ति -यितुं), आकृ (c. 10. -कारयति -यितुं), आवह् (c. 10. -वाहयति -यितुं), सङ्केतं कृ; 'invite to dine,' भोजनार्थं or भोजनाय निमन्त्र्.—(Allure) आकृष् (c. 1. -कर्षति -क्रष्टुं), प्रलुभ् (c. 10. -लोभयति -यितुं).

INVITED, *p. p.* निमन्त्रितः -ता -तं, आमन्त्रितः -ता -तं, आहूतः -ता -तं, केतितः -ता -तं, अभ्यर्थितः -ता -तं, आवाहितः -ता -तं, आकारितः -ता -तं; 'invited to dine,' भोजनार्थं निमन्त्रितः -ता -तं; 'the persons invited,' निमन्त्रणीयजनाः *m. pl.*, निमन्त्रिताः *m. pl.*—(Allured) आकृष्टः -ष्टा -ष्टं, प्रलोभितः -ता -तं.

INVITING, *a.* (Alluring) आकर्षकः -का -कं, आकर्षी -र्षिणी -र्षि (न्).

To INVOCATE, *v. a.* *See* *To* INVOKE.

INVOCATION, *s.* आह्वानं, आह्वयः, आहूतिः *f.*, प्रह्वायः, अभिमन्त्रणं, आमन्त्रणं, अनुकर्षणं, उपहवः, नामग्रहणं, नामस्मरणं, नामोच्चारणं, आवाहनं.

INVOICE, *s.* बीजकं, वाणिज्यभाण्डानां समर्पितद्रव्यपरिसंख्यापत्रं.

To INVOKE, *v. a.* ह्वे (c. 1. ह्वयति -ह्वातुं), आह्वे, उपह्वे, प्रह्वे, विह्वे, अभिमन्त्र् (c. 10. -मन्त्रयति -यितुं), आमन्त्र्, आवद् (c. 1. -वदति -दितुं), अभिवद्, आवच् (c. 2. -वक्ति -क्तुं), अभिवच्, प्रार्थ् (c. 10. प्रार्थयति -यितुं), अनुकृष् (c. 1. -कर्षति -क्रष्टुं), आह्वानं कृ.—(Call on by name) सम्बोधनं कृ, नाम ग्रह् (c. 9. गृह्णाति, ग्रहीतुं) or स्मृ (c. 1. स्मरति, स्मर्तुं), नामग्रहणं कृ, आवाहनं कृ.—(Invoke blessings) आशास् (c. 2. -शास्ते -शासितुं).

INVOKED, *p. p.* आहूतः -ता -तं, आमन्त्रितः -ता -तं, आवाहितः -ता -तं.

INVOLUNTARILY, *adv.* अनिच्छातस्, अकामतस्, अनिकामतस्, अनिच्छापूर्व्वं, अकामपूर्व्वं, अमतिपूर्व्वं, अबुद्धिपूर्व्वं, अबोधपूर्व्वं, असन्तोषेण, असन्तोषपूर्व्वं, अज्ञानतस्, अज्ञानपूर्व्वं, निष्कामं.

INVOLUNTARY, *a.* अनैच्छिकः -की -कं, अनिच्छापूर्व्वः -र्व्वा -र्व्वं, अकामिकः -का -कं, अनभिकामिकः -का -कं, अकाम्यः -म्या -म्यं, अबुद्धिपूर्व्वः -र्व्वा -र्व्वं, असन्तोषपूर्व्वः -र्व्वा -र्व्वं, अज्ञानपूर्व्वः -र्व्वा -र्व्वं, अमतिपूर्व्वः -र्व्वा -र्व्वं, अस्वेच्छागतः -ता -तं, अवशः -शा -शं, अनिच्छाधीनः -ना -नं, इच्छावाह्यः -ह्या -ह्यं.—(Not having will, unwilling) अकामः -मा -मं, निष्कामः -मा -मं, अनिच्छुः -च्छुः -च्छु.

INVOLUTION, *s.* (Act of involving or enveloping) आवेष्टनं, परिवेष्टनं, वेष्टनं, आवरणं, आच्छादनं.—(State of being entangled) आश्लिष्टता, अन्योन्यसंश्लेषः, अन्योन्यसंलग्नता, ग्रन्थिलत्वं, जटिलत्वं, सङ्कीर्णता, व्यतिकरः.

To INVOLVE, *v. a.* (Envelop) आवेष्ट् (c. 1. -वेष्टते -ष्टितुं, c. 10. -वेष्टयति -यितुं), परिवेष्ट्, संवेष्ट्, आच्छद् (c. 10. -च्छादयति -यितुं), आवृ (c. 5. -वृणोति -वरितुं -रीतुं), परिवृ; 'is involved,' आव्रियते.—(Implicate, connect, join) सम्बन्ध् (c. 9. -बध्नाति -बन्द्धुं), अनुबन्ध्, बन्ध्, संश्लिष् (c. 10. -श्लेषयति -यितुं), आश्लिष्, परिश्लिष्, संयुज् (c. 7. -युनक्ति -योक्तुं, c. 10. -योजयति -यितुं), संसृज् (c. 6. -सृजति -स्रष्टुं); 'he is involved in many crimes,' बहुपापैः सम्बध्यते or लिप्यते.—(Comprise) परिग्रह् (c. 9. -गृह्णाति -ग्रहीतुं), अन्तर्गण् (c. 10. -गणयति -यितुं), परिसमाप् (c. 5. -आप्नोति -आप्तुं).

INVOLVED, *p. p.* (Enveloped) आवेष्टितः -ता -तं, परिवेष्टितः -ता -तं, वेष्टितः -ता -तं, आवृतः -ता -तं, आच्छादितः -ता -तं, आच्छन्नः -न्ना -न्नं, समाच्छन्नः -न्ना -न्नं, व्याप्तः -प्ता -प्तं.—(Comprised, included) अन्तर्गतः -ता -तं, अन्तर्गणितः -ता -तं, परिगृहीतः -ता -तं, समाविष्टः -ष्टा -ष्टं, आकलितः -ता -तं, सहितः -ता -तं, प्रतिष्ठितः -ता -तं, अवान्तरः -रा -रं, गर्भः -र्भा -र्भं in comp.—(Implicated, connected) सम्बद्धः -द्धा -द्धं, अनुबद्धः -द्धा -द्धं, निबद्धः -द्धा -द्धं, बद्धः -द्धा -द्धं, संसृष्टः -ष्टा -ष्टं, संश्लिष्टः -ष्टा -ष्टं, संसक्तः -क्ता -क्तं, अनुषक्तः -क्ता -क्तं, संयुक्तः -क्ता -क्तं, ग्रस्तः -स्ता -स्तं, लिप्तः -प्ता -प्तं; 'involved in crime,' पापसम्बद्धः -द्धा -द्धं, पापलिप्तः -प्ता -प्तं; 'in calamity,' विपद्ग्रस्तः -स्ता -स्तं; 'in debt,' ऋणग्रस्तः -स्ता -स्तं.—(Implied) ध्वनितः -ता -तं, फलितः -ता -तं; 'involved meaning,' फलितार्थः, ध्वनितार्थः.—(Confused, not clear) अस्पष्टः -ष्टा -ष्टं, अव्यक्तः -क्ता -क्तं, अभिन्नः -न्ना -न्नं.

INVULNERABLE, *a.* अभेद्यदेहः -हा -हं, अवेध्यदेहः -हा -हं, अच्छेद्यदेहः -हा -हं, अप्रहार्य्यदेहः, -हा -हं, अनाघातनीयः -या -यं, असम्भाव्यक्षतः -ता -तं, अशक्यक्षतः -ता -तं, क्षताक्षमः -मा -मं, आघाताक्षमः -मा -मं, वज्रदेहः -हा -हं, वज्रशरीरः -रा -रं.

INVULNERABLENESS, *s.* अभेद्यता, अवेध्यता, अच्छेद्यता, अघातनीयत्वं.

INWARD, *a.* अन्तरस्थः -स्था -स्थं, अन्तःस्थः -स्था -स्थं, आन्तरः -री -रं -रिकः -की -कं, अन्तर्भूतः -ता -तं, अन्तर्वर्त्ती -र्त्तिनी -र्त्ति (न्), अन्तर्भवः -वा -वं, अन्तर्गतः -ता -तं, अभ्यन्तरः -रा -रं, आभ्यन्तरः -री -रं, अन्तरतमः

-मा -मत्, अन्तरङ्गः -ङ्गा -ङ्गं. Often expressed by अन्तर् in comp.; as, 'inward heat,' अन्तर्दाहः; 'inward spirit,' अन्तरात्मा m. (न्), अन्तःकरणं, अन्तःप्रकृतिः f.; 'inward consciousness,' अन्तःसंज्ञा; 'inward purity,' अन्तःशौचं; 'inward discipline,' अन्तर्यमनं, अन्तःकरणसंयमः, दमः; 'inward meditation,' अन्तर्भावना.

INWARDLY, adv. अन्तर्, अन्तरे -रेण, अभ्यन्तरेण; 'inwardly bad,' अन्तर्दुष्टः -ष्टा -ष्टं.—(In the heart, secretly) अन्तःकरणेन, मनसा, निभृतं, सुनिभृतं.

INWARDS, s. pl. अन्त्राणि n. pl., अन्तर्नाड्यः f. pl., उदरं.

To INWEAVE, v. a. ग्रन्थ् (c. 9. ग्रथ्नाति, c. 1. ग्रन्थति -न्थितुं). See To INTERWEAVE.

To INWRAP, v. a. आवेष्ट् (c. 1. -वेष्टते -ष्टितुं, c. 10. -वेष्टयति -यितुं), परिवेष्ट्, आच्छद् (c. 10. -छादयति -यितुं), अवगुण्ठ् (c. 10. -गुण्ठयति -यितुं).

To INWREATHE, v. a. मालया परिवेष्ट् (c. 1. -वेष्टते -ष्टितुं), मालायुक्तं -क्तां कृ.

INWROUGHT, p. p. खचितः -ता -तं, जडितः -ता -तं, जुरितः -ता -तं.

IOTA, s. लवलेशः, लेशः, बिन्दुः m., बिन्दुमात्रं, तिलमात्रं.

IRASCIBLE, a. शीघ्रकोपी -पिनी -पि (न्), शीघ्रक्रोधी -धिनी -धि (न्), सुलभकोपः -पा -पं, क्रोधशीलः -ला -लं, कोपी -पिनी -पि (न्), क्रोधी &c., क्रोधिष्ठः -ष्ठा -ष्ठं, कोपिष्ठः -ष्ठा -ष्ठं, चण्डः -ण्डा -ण्डं, चण्डस्वभावः -वा -वं, पित्तवेगी -गिनी -गि (न्), पित्तस्वभावः -वा -वं, सन्तापी -पिनी -पि (न्).

IRASCIBLENESS, s. शीघ्रकोपित्वं, क्रोधशीलता, स्वभावचण्डता, पित्तस्वभावः, क्रोधस्वभावः, पित्तप्रकृतिः f.

IRATE, a. क्रुद्धः -द्धा -द्धं, कुपितः -ता -तं, क्रोधी -धिनी -धि (न्).

IRE, s. क्रोधः, कोपः, अमर्षः, रोषः, मन्युः m., संरम्भः, सन्तापः.

IREFUL, a. क्रोधी -धिनी -धि (न्), कोपी -पिनी -पि (न्), क्रुद्धः -द्धा -द्धं, सकोपः -पा -पं, समन्युः -न्युः -न्यु, संरम्भी -म्भिणी -म्भि (न्).

IREFULLY, adv. सकोपं, सक्रोधं, सरोषं, सामर्षं, कोपेन, क्रोधेन.

IRIS, s. (Rainbow) इन्द्रायुधं, इन्द्रधनुस् n.—(Of the eye) नेत्रतारकामण्डलं, कनीनिकामण्डलं, कनीनिकापरिधिः m., तारामण्डलं, उपतारा.—(Plant) गोलोमी, श्वेतदूर्व्वा, भूतकेशः.

To IRK, v. a. आयस् (c. 10. -यासयति -यितुं), दुःख् (c. 10. दुःखयति -यितुं), खिद् (c. 10. खेदयति -यितुं), पीड् (c. 10. पीडयति -यि°), बाध् (c. 1. बाधते -धितुं).

IRKSOME, a. खेदजनकः -का -कं, क्लेशकरः -री -रं, क्लेशदः -दा -दं, दुःखदः -दा -दं, दुःखकरः -री -रं, आयासहेतुकः -का -कं, कष्टकरः -री -रं, कष्टः -ष्टा -ष्टं, श्रमजनकः -का -कं, गुरुः -र्व्वी -रु.

IRKSOMENESS, s. खेदजनकत्वं, क्लेशजनकत्वं, क्लेशकत्वं, कष्टत्वं, गुरुता.

IRON, s. लोहं -हः, अयस् n., आयसं, लौहं -हः, कृष्णायसं, कालायसं, कृष्णं, कालं, तीक्ष्णं, शस्त्रकं, पिण्डं, अश्मसारः, गिरिजं, गिरिसारः, शिलाजं, शिलात्मजं, निशितं, कान्तं, दृढं, मलीमसः; 'green sulphate of iron,' धातुशेखरः, पुष्पकासीशः, नयनौषधं, कासीसं, काशीशं, हंसलोमशं; 'red sulphate of iron,' धातुकासीशः; 'pyritic iron-ore,' स्वर्णमाक्षिकं, विट्माक्षिकं, सुवर्णमुखी; 'iron-filings,' लोहचूर्णं; 'rust of iron,' मण्डूरं, सिंहानं, अयोमलं. See RUST; 'sulphuret of iron,' पांशुकासीसं, ताप्यं, धातुमाक्षिकं; 'tipped with iron,' अयोमुखः -खा -खं, अयोग्रः -ग्रा -ग्रं, लोहाग्रः -ग्रा -ग्रं; 'wrought iron,' कुशी.—(Smoothing iron) वस्त्रादिश्लक्ष्णीकरणार्थं लोहयन्त्रं.—(Fetter) लौहबन्धः -न्धं -न्धनं.

IRON, a. (Made of iron) लौहः -ही -हं, लोहमयः -यी -यं, लोहलः -ला -लं, आयसः -सी -सं, अयोमयः -यी -यं, अयस्मयः -यी -यं, लोहात्मकः -का -कं, लोह in comp.; as, 'an iron arrow,' लोहनालः; 'iron-image,' लोहप्रतिमा; 'iron armour,' लोहवर्म्म n. (न्); 'iron pike,' लोहशङ्कुः m.; 'iron medicine,' लोहभस्म n. (न्); 'iron-toothed,' अयोदत् -दती -दत् (त्); 'having an iron constitution,' वज्रदेहः -हा -हं.

To IRON, v. a. (Smooth with an iron) लोहयन्त्रेण श्लक्ष्णीकृ.—(Fetter) शृङ्खलया बन्ध् (c. 9. बध्नाति, बन्द्धुं), शृङ्खल (nom. शृङ्खलयति -यितुं).

IRON-BAR, s. कुशी, लोहकुशी, लोहपिण्डः -ण्डं.

IRON-FILINGS, s. pl. लोहचूर्णं, लोहकिट्टं, लोहजं.

IRON-FISTED, a. वज्रमुष्टिः -ष्टिः -ष्टि, लोहमुष्टिः -ष्टिः -ष्टि.

IRON-FOUNDER, s. लोहकारः, अयस्कारः, व्योकारः,

IRON-FOUNDERY, s. लोहविलयनशाला, कुप्यशाला, सन्धानी.

IRON-HEARTED, a. अयोहृदयः -या -यं, वज्रहृदयः -या -यं, लोहहृदयः -या -यं.

IRON-MOLD, s. लोहचिह्नं, लोहाङ्कः, लोहकलङ्कः.

IRON-MONGER, s. लोहकारः, लोहद्रव्यविक्रेता m. (तृ) -विक्रयी m. (न्), लौहभाण्डविक्रयी m., पिठरकटाहादिभाण्डविक्रेता m.

IRON-MONGERY, s. लोहद्रव्याणि n. pl., लौहभाण्डानि n. pl., लोहमयद्रव्याणि, पिठरकटाहादीनि लोहनिर्म्मितभाण्डानि.

IRONICAL, a. मृषावादी -दिनी -दि (न्), विकत्थनः -ना -नं, साक्षेपः -पा -पं, सव्यञ्जनः -ना -नं, उपरोधी -धिनी -धि (न्), औपरोधिकः -की -कं, उपरोधात्मकः -का -कं, अवक्षेपकः -का -कं.

IRONICALLY, adv. सविकत्थनं, साक्षेपं, सव्यञ्जनं, विपरीतलक्षणापूर्व्वं, निह्नवेन, सनिह्नवं, सोल्लुण्ठनं, मृषावादेन, मृषा.

IRONY, s. (Speech expressing one thing and meaning another) व्याजोक्तिः f., व्यञ्जना, व्यंग्यः, आक्षेपः, अवक्षेपः, विपरीतलक्षणा, उपरोधः.—(Ironical praise) व्याजस्तुतिः f., निन्दास्तुतिः f., व्याजनिन्दा, विकत्था -त्थनं, सोत्प्रासः, सोल्लुण्ठः -ण्ठनं, मृषावादः, अन्यथास्तोत्रं.—(Dissimulation) निह्नवः, निह्नुतिः f., अपह्नवः, अपलापः, अवहित्था.

IRONY, a. (Made of iron) लौहिकः -की -कं, लोहमयः -यी -यं, अयोमयः &c.

IRRADIANCE, IRRADIANCY, s. दीप्तिः f., द्युतिः f., प्रभा, कान्तिः f., तेजस्.

To IRRADIATE, v. a. प्रकाश् (c. 10. -काशयति -यितुं), विकाश्, दीप् (c. 10. दीपयति -यितुं), विदीप्, प्रदीप्, उद्दीप्, द्युत् (c. 10. द्योतयति -यितुं), विद्युत्, प्रद्युत्, विराज् (c. 10. -राजयति -यितुं).

IRRADIATED, p. p. प्रकाशितः -ता -तं, विकाशितः -ता -तं, दीपितः -ता -तं, प्रदीपितः -ता -तं, राजितः -ता -तं, विराजितः -ता -तं, द्योतितः -ता -तं.

IRRADIATION, s. प्रकाशनं, विकाशनं, दीपनं, प्रदीपनं, उद्दीपनं, दीप्तिः f., प्रदीप्तिः f., द्योतनं, प्रद्योतनं, उद्द्योतः -तनं, द्युतिः f., उज्ज्वलनं, उज्ज्वलता, उद्भासः, प्रकाशता.

IRRATIONAL, a. (Void of reason) बुद्धिहीनः -ना -नं, बुद्धिरहितः -ता -तं, निर्बुद्धिः -द्धिः -द्धि, निर्बोधः -धा -धं, अबुद्धिमान् -मती -मत् (त्), ज्ञानहीनः -ना -नं, ज्ञानशक्तिरहितः -ता -तं, अज्ञानी -निनी -नि (न्), प्रज्ञाहीनः -ना -नं, अचेतनः -ना -नं, चैतन्यरहितः -ता -तं, अचित्तः -त्ता -त्तं, निश्चित्तः -त्ता -त्तं, चित्ताशून्यः -न्या -न्यं, पशुधर्म्मा -र्म्मा -र्म्म (न्), पशुस्वभावः -वा -वं, पशुसमानः -ना -नं.—(Contrary to reason, absurd) अन्याय्यः -य्या -य्यं, न्यायविरुद्धः -द्धा -द्धं, अन्यायी -यिनी -यि (न्), असम्बद्धः -द्धा -द्धं, असङ्गतः -ता -तं, अतर्कितः -ता -तं, अतार्किकः -की -कं, अयुक्तिकः -का -कं, अयुक्तिसिद्धः -द्धा -द्धं, युक्तिविरुद्धः -द्धा -द्धं, अयुक्तः -क्ता -क्तं, असमञ्जसः -सा -सं, अनर्थकः -का -कं.

IRRATIONALITY, s. बुद्धिहीनता, ज्ञानहीनता, निर्बुद्धित्वं, अन्याय्यता.

IRRATIONALLY, adv. न्यायविरोधेन, असङ्गतं, असम्बद्धं, अतर्कितं, पशुवत्.

IRRECLAIMABLE, a. दुष्कर्म्मनिवर्त्तयितव्यः -व्या -व्यं, कुकर्म्मोपरावर्त्तनीयः

-या -यं, अशक्यविप्रतीसार: -रा -रं, उपदेशवहिर्भूत: -ता -तं, अनुद्धार्य्य: -र्य्या -र्य्यं, अशोधनीय: -या -यं.

IRRECONCILABLE, *a.* (Not to be brought to amity) असन्धेय: -या -यं, असन्धातव्य: -व्या -व्यं, असमाधेय: -या -यं, अशमनीय: -या -यं, अशाम्य: -म्या -म्यं, अशक्यशम: -मा -मं.—(That cannot be made to agree, inconsistent) असङ्गत: -ता -तं, परस्परविरुद्ध: -द्धा -द्धं -विरोधी -धिनी -धि (न्), परस्परपराहत: -ता -तं, विसङ्गत: -ता -तं, असदृश: -शी -शं, असम्भावनीय: -या -यं, असम्भाव्य: -व्या -व्यं, अन्योन्यविपरीत: -ता -तं, असमञ्जस: -सा -सं.

IRRECONCILABLENESS, *s.* असङ्गति: *f.*, परस्परविरोध:, अन्योन्यविपरीतता.

IRRECOVERABLE, *a.* असमाहार्य्य: -र्य्या -र्य्यं, अपुन:प्राप्य: -प्या -प्यं, पुनरप्राप्य: -प्या -प्यं, अपुनर्लभ्य: -भ्या -भ्यं, पुनरलभ्य: -भ्या -भ्यं, अपुनरादेय: -या -यं, अनावाप्य: -प्या -प्यं, अनुद्धरणीय: -या -यं.

IRRECOVERABLY, *adv.* असमाहार्य्यं, अनुद्धरणीयं, यथा उद्धर्त्तुं न शक्यते तथा.

IRREFRAGABLE, *a.* अखण्डनीय: -या -यं, अखण्ड्य: -ण्ड्या -ण्ड्यं, अप्रत्याख्येय: -या -यं, अबाध्य: -ध्या -ध्यं, अविवदनीय: -या -यं, असन्दिग्ध: -ग्धा -ग्धं, सुनिश्चित: -ता -तं, दृढप्रमाण: -णा -णं, दृढप्रमाण: -णा -णं.

IRREFRAGABLENESS, *s.* अखण्डनीयता, अखण्ड्यता, अबाध्यत्वं.

IRREFRAGABLY, *adv.* अखण्डनीयं, यथा खण्डनं कर्त्तुं न शक्यते तथा.

IRREFUTABLE, *a.* अखण्डनीय: -या -यं, अखण्डितव्य: -व्या -व्यं, अशक्यखण्डन: -ना -नं, खण्डनाशक्य: -क्या -क्यं, अनिरसनीय: -या -यं.

IRREGULAR, *a.* विधिविरुद्ध: -द्धा -द्धं, विधिभञ्जक: -का -कं, विधिहीन: -ना -नं, अविधि: -धि: -धि, अवैध: -धी -धं, अवैधिक: -की -कं, विधिघ्न: -घ्नी -घ्नं, नियमविरुद्ध: -द्धा -द्धं, अयथाविधि: -धि: -धि, शास्त्रविरुद्ध: -द्धा -द्धं, उत्सूत्र: -त्रा -त्रं, विसूत्र: -त्रा -त्रं.—(Immethodical) अक्रमक: -का -कं -मिक: -का -कं, क्रमविरुद्ध: -द्धा -द्धं, क्रमहीन: -ना -नं, क्रमशून्य: -न्या -न्यं, क्रमरहित: -ता -तं, क्रमबाह्य: -ह्या -ह्यं, अव्यवस्थित: -ता -तं, असंस्थित: -ता -तं, अपर्य्याय: -या -यं, उच्छृङ्खल: -ला -लं.—(In conduct) व्यभिचारी -रिणी -रि (न्), अमर्य्याद: -दा -दं, उत्क्रान्तमर्य्याद: -दा -दं. धर्म्मविरोधी -धिनी -धि (न्), धर्म्मविरुद्ध: -द्धा -द्धं, विपथगामी -मिनी -मि (न्), अपथगामी &c., अपथवर्त्ती -र्त्तिनी -र्त्ति (न्), अन्यथाचारी &c., आचारवर्जित: -ता -तं, कुचरित: -ता -तं.—(In grammar, to be excepted) वर्ज्जनीय: -या -यं, निपातित: -ता -तं, निपातनीय: -या -यं.—(Uneven, unequal) विषम: -मा -मं, असम: -मा -मं; 'irregular fever,' विषमज्वर:.—(In shape) विरूप: -पा -पी -पं.

IRREGULARITY, *s.* अविधि: *m.*, अविधानं, अविधिता, विधिविरोध:, विधिभङ्ग:, अवैधत्वं, उत्सूत्रता, विसूत्रता, शास्त्रविरोध:, नियमविरोध:, अनियम:, अक्रम:, उत्क्रम:, व्यतिक्रम:, क्रमविरोध:, अव्यवस्था, अपरिपाटि: *f.*—(In conduct) व्यभिचार:, विपथगमनं, कुपथगमनं, अपथ:, कुपथ:, अधर्म्म: -र्म्मत्वं, अनाचार:.—(In grammar, exception) निपात: -तनं, वर्ज्जनं, निषेध:.—(Unevenness) विषमता, वैषम्यं, विषमं, असमता; 'irregularity in diet,' कुपथ्यं, अपथ्यं.

IRREGULARLY, *adv.* अविधितस्, अविधानतस्, अविधिवत्, विधिविरुद्धं, विधिविरोधेन, नियमविरुद्धं, अनियमतस्, अयथाविधि, अक्रमेण, क्रमविरुद्धं, विसूत्रं, अव्यवस्थितं, अयथाशास्त्रं.

IRRELATIVE, *a.* असम्बन्धी -न्धिनी -न्धि (न्), नि:सम्बन्ध: -न्धा -न्धं, सम्बन्धहीन: -ना -नं, असङ्ग: -ङ्गा -ङ्गं, नि:सङ्ग: -ङ्गा -ङ्गं, अविषयक: -का -कं, अनानुषङ्गिक: -की -कं.

IRRELEVANCY, *s.* अप्रासङ्गिकत्वं, अप्रस्तुतता, अप्रसङ्ग:, अविषयत्वं, निर्विषयता, अनन्वय:, अन्वयाभाव:, असम्बन्ध:, असम्पर्क:, असङ्गतत्वं, अप्रयुक्ति: *f.*

IRRELEVANT, *a.* अप्रासङ्गिक: -की -कं, अप्रस्तुत: -ता -तं, निर्विषय: -या

IRR

-यं, अनन्वित: -ता -तं, असम्बन्धी -न्धिनी -न्धि (न्), अप्रसक्त: -क्ता -क्तं, प्रसङ्गबाह्य: -ह्या -ह्यं, प्रस्तुतवहिर्भूत: -ता -तं, असङ्गत: -ता -तं, अप्रकृत: -ता -तं, अप्राकरणिक: -की -कं, असम्पर्कीय: -या -यं, अनुपपन्न: -न्ना -न्नं, अप्रयुक्त: -क्ता -क्तं, अयौक्तिक: -की -कं.

IRRELEVANTLY, *adv.* अप्रस्तुतं, निर्विषयं, प्रस्तुतवहिस्, असङ्गं, असम्बन्धेन, असङ्गतं, अप्रयुक्तं, असम्पर्केण, अप्रसक्तं.

IRRELIGION, *s.* अधर्म्म: -र्म्मत्वं, वैधर्म्यं, निर्धर्म्मत्वं, धर्म्मलोप:, धर्म्महीनता, अपूजा, अभक्ति: *f.*, भक्तिहीनता, अभक्तत्वं, देवनिन्दा, अपुण्यत्वं, दुष्टता, पापिष्ठत्वं, सपापत्वं, दुष्कृतं.

IRRELIGIOUS, *a.* अधर्म्मी -र्म्मिणी -र्म्मि (न्), अधार्म्मिक: -की -कं, निर्धर्म्म: -र्म्मा -र्म्मं, अधर्म्मिष्ठ: -ष्ठा -ष्ठं, धर्म्महीन: -ना -नं, त्यक्तधर्म्मा -र्म्मा -र्म्म (न्), अपूजक: -का -कं, अभक्त: -क्ता -क्तं, भक्तिहीन: -ना -नं, देवनिन्दक: -का -कं, दुष्ट: -ष्टा -ष्टं, अपुण्य: -ण्या -ण्यं, असाधु: -ध्वी -धु, पापी -पिनी -पि (न्).

IRRELIGIOUSLY, *adv.* अधर्म्मतस्, अधर्म्मेण, अधार्म्मिकवत्, अपुण्यवत्, पापिष्ठं.

IRREMEABLE, *a.* अपुनरागम्य: -म्या -म्यं, अप्रत्यागम्य: &c., अपरावर्त्ती -र्त्ती -र्त्ति.

IRREMEDIABLE, *a.* अप्रतिकार्य्य: -र्य्या -र्य्यं, अशक्यप्रतीकार: -रा -रं, अप्रतिकार: -रा -रं, अविद्यमानप्रतीकार: -रा -रं, निरुपाय: -या -यं, अनुपाय: -या -यं, निरुपायी -यिनी -यि (न्), उपायहीन: -ना -नं, उपायातीत: -ता -तं, अशक्योपाय: -या -यं, अचिकित्स्य: -त्स्या -त्स्यं, अचिकित्सनीय: -या -यं, चिकित्सितुम् अशक्य: -क्या -क्यं, असमाधेय: -या -यं, अप्रतिसमाधेय: -या -यं.

IRREMEDIABLENESS, *s.* निरुपायत्वं, अप्रतिकार्य्यत्वं, प्रतीकारहीनता, असमाधेयता.

IRREMEDIABLY, *adv.* निरुपायं, यथा प्रतिकर्त्तुं न शक्यते तथाप्रकारेण, यथा उपायो न विद्यते तथा.

IRREMISSIBLE, *a.* अक्षन्तव्य: -व्या -व्यं, अमोचनीय: -या -यं, क्षमानर्ह: -र्हा -र्हं.

IRREMOVABLE, *a.* अनपादेय: -या -यं, अनपहरणीय: -या -यं, अपरिहार्य्य: -र्य्या -र्य्यं, अनि:सारणीय: -या -यं, अनपनेतव्य: -व्या -व्यं, अचल: -ला -लं, स्थिर: -रा -रं.

IRREPARABLE, *a.* असाध्य: -ध्या -ध्यं, असाधनीय: -या -यं, असन्धेय: -या -यं, असमाधेय: -या -यं, अप्रतिसमाधेय: -या -यं, अप्रतिकार्य्य: -र्य्या -र्य्यं, अप्रतिकार: -रा -रं, अशक्यप्रतीकार: -रा -रं, अचिकित्सनीय: -या -यं, अनुद्धार्य्य: -र्य्या -र्य्यं, अनुद्धरणीय: -या -यं.

IRREPARABLENESS, *s.* असाध्यता, अप्रतिकार्य्यत्वं, असमाधेयता, अनुद्धार्य्यत्वं.

IRREPARABLY, *adv.* असाधनीयं, यथा प्रतिकारो न विद्यते तथा, अचिकित्सनीयं, अप्रतिसमाधेयं.

IRREPREHENSIBLE, *a.* अनिन्द्य: -न्द्या -न्द्यं, अनिन्दनीय: -या -यं, निर्दोष: -षा -षं, दोषशून्य: -न्या -न्यं, अगर्ह्य: -र्ह्या -र्ह्यं, अविगर्ह्य: -र्ह्या -र्ह्यं.

IRREPREHENSIBLENESS, *s.* अनिन्द्यता, अनिन्दनीयता, दोषशून्यता, निर्दोषत्वं.

IRREPREHENSIBLY, *adv.* अनिन्दनीयं, निरपराधं, अनपराधेन, दोषं विना.

IRREPRESSIBLE, *a.* अनिग्रहीतव्य: -व्या -व्यं, दुर्निग्रह: -हा -हं, अनियन्तव्य: -व्या -व्यं, अनिवार्य्य: -र्य्या -र्य्यं, असंहरणीय: -या -यं, अयन्त्रणीय: -या -यं.

IRREPROACHABLE, *a.* अनिन्द्य: -न्द्या -न्द्यं, अनिन्दनीय: -या -यं, अनिन्दित: -ता -तं, अगर्ह्य: -र्ह्या -र्ह्यं, अविगर्ह्य: &c., अविगर्हित: -ता -तं, अपरिवाद्य: -द्या -द्यं, अनपवाद्य: -द्या -द्यं, अनवद्य: -द्या -द्यं, निरवद्य: -द्या -द्यं, निर्दोष: -षा -षं, निरपराध: -धा -धं, अपरिभाषणीय: -या -यं, अकुत्सित: -ता -तं, अनवगीत: -ता -तं, निष्कलङ्क: -ङ्का -ङ्कं, अदूष्य: -ष्या -ष्यं, अवाच्य: -च्या -च्यं, निर्वाच्य: -च्या -च्यं, अवचनीय: -या -यं, अदुर्वृत्त: -त्ता -त्तं.

IRREPROACHABLENESS, *s.* अनिन्द्यता, अनिन्दनीयता, अगर्ह्यत्वं, अपरिवाद्यता.

IRREPROACHABLY, *adv.* अनिन्दनीयं, अनिन्दितं, अगर्हणीयं, अविगर्हितं.

IRRESISTIBLE, *a.* अप्रतिकार्य्य: -र्य्या -र्य्यं, अप्रतीकार्य्य: &c., अनिवार्य्य:

-र्य्यो -र्य्यं, अनिवारणीयः -या -यं, अनिवारः -रा -रं, दुर्निवारः -रा -रं, अवार्य्यः -र्य्या -र्य्यं, निवार्य्यः -र्य्या -र्य्यं, अनवग्रहः -हा -हं, दुर्निग्रहः -हा -हं, असंहार्य्यः -र्य्या -र्य्यं, दुर्धरः -रा -रं, निर्धारणीयः -या -यं, निर्धार्य्यः -र्य्या -र्य्यं, अबाध्यः -ध्या -ध्यं, अबाधनीयः -या -यं, अनतिक्रमणीयः -या -यं, अप्रतिहतः -ता -तं, अप्रतिद्वन्द्वः -न्द्वा -न्द्वं, सर्व्वदमनः -ना -नं.

IRRESISTIBLENESS, *s.* अप्रतिकार्य्यत्वं, अनिवार्य्यता, अनिवारणीयता, अवारणीयत्वं, दुर्निग्रहत्वं, अबाध्यत्वं.

IRRESISTIBLY, *adv.* अनिवारणीयं, अवारणीयं, अप्रतिकार्य्यं, दुर्निग्रहं, यथा निवारयितुं न शक्यते तथाप्रकारेण.

IRRESOLUTE, *a.* अस्थिरमतिः -तिः -ति, अस्थिरचित्तः -त्ता -त्तं, अस्थिरबुद्धिः -द्धिः -द्धि, अस्थिरमनस्कः -स्का -स्कं, चञ्चलबुद्धिः -द्धिः -द्धि, चञ्चलवृत्तिः -त्तिः -त्ति, चलचित्तः -त्ता -त्तं, विकल्पशीलः -ला -लं, विकल्पयन् -यन्ती -यत् (त्), संशयात्मा -त्मा -त्म (न्), सन्दिग्धमतिः -तिः -ति, संशयापन्नमानसः -सा -सं, चपलात्मकः -का -कं, अधीरः -रा -रं, अदृढमनस्कः -स्का -स्कं, अनवस्थितः -ता -तं, धैर्य्यहीनः -ना -नं, तरलः -ला -लं.

IRRESOLUTELY, *adv.* अस्थिरं, अधीरं, स्थैर्य्यपूर्व्वं, धैर्य्यपूर्व्वं, अधैर्य्येण, अस्थैर्य्येण, अस्थिरचेतसा, चञ्चलबुद्ध्या, विकल्पशीलत्वात्, चञ्चलं, चपलवत्.

IRRESOLUTION, *s.* अस्थैर्य्यं, अस्थिरता, अधैर्य्यं, अधीरता, चित्तास्थैर्य्यं, विकल्पशीलता, बुद्धिचाञ्चल्यं, चञ्चलबुद्धिः *f.*, अस्थिरबुद्धिः *f.*, चलचित्तता, चञ्चलत्वं, अदृढता, अधृतिः *f.*, अधारणा, चपलता, चापल्यं, अनवस्थितिः *f.*

IRRESPECTIVE, *a.* निरपेक्षः -क्षा -क्षं, अनपेक्षः -क्षा -क्षं, अपेक्षाहीनः -ना -नं, निर्व्यपेक्षः -क्षा -क्षं, अप्रतीक्षकः -का -कं.

IRRESPECTIVELY, *adv.* निरपेक्षं, अनपेक्षं, अनपेक्ष्य, अप्रतीक्ष्य, अनुद्दिश्य.

IRRESPONSIBILITY, *s.* अनुयोगानधीनता, अपृच्छाधीनता, प्रश्नायोग्यत्वं, अननुयोज्यता.

IRRESPONSIBLE, *a.* अननुयोगाधीनः -ना -नं, अनुयोगानधीनः -ना -नं, अपृच्छाधीनः -ना -नं, अप्रश्नयोग्यः -ग्या -ग्यं, पृच्छानर्हः -र्हा -र्हं, अननुयोज्यः -ज्या -ज्यं, अननुयोक्तव्यः -व्या -व्यं.

IRRESTRAINABLE, *a.* अनिवार्य्यः -र्य्या -र्य्यं, अनिग्रहीतव्यः -व्या -व्यं, दुर्निग्रहः -हा -हं, अनिवर्त्तयितव्यः -व्या -व्यं, अनिवर्त्तनीयः -या -यं.

IRRETRIEVABLE, *a.* अपुनःप्राप्यः -प्या -प्यं, पुनरप्राप्यः -प्या -प्यं, अपुनर्लभ्यः -भ्या -भ्यं, पुनरलभ्यः -भ्या -भ्यं, अनुद्धरणीयः -या -यं, अनुद्धार्य्यः -र्य्या -र्य्यं, असमाहार्य्यः -र्य्या -र्य्यं, अप्रतिसमाधेयः -या -यं.

IRRETRIEVABLENESS, *s.* अपुनःप्राप्यता, अनुद्धरणीयता, अप्रतिसमाधेयत्वं.

IRRETRIEVABLY, *adv.* अनुद्धरणीयं, यथा प्रतिसमाधातुं न शक्यते तथा.

IRREVERENCE, *s.* अपूजा, अपमानं, अवमानं, अनादरः, अवज्ञानं, अवज्ञा, असम्मानं, परिभवः, परिभूतिः *f.*, परिभावः, अवधीरणा, उपेक्षा, अमर्य्यादा.

IRREVERENT, *a.* अपूजकः -का -कं, अपमानी -निनी -नि (न्), अवमानी &c., अपमानकारी &c., अवज्ञाकारी &c., अनादरकारी &c., परिभावी -विनी -वि (न्), अनादरी -रिणी -रि (न्), अनादरबुद्धिः -द्धिः -द्धि.

IRREVERENTLY, *adv.* अपूजया, अपूजापूर्व्वं, सावमानं, सावज्ञानं, अनादरेण.

IRREVERSIBLE, *a.* अपरावर्त्यः -र्त्या -र्त्यं, अपरावर्त्तनीयः -या -यं, अनिवर्त्यः -र्त्या -र्त्यं, अनिवर्त्तनीयः -या -यं, परावर्त्तनाशक्यः -क्या -क्यं, परावर्त्तनार्हः -र्हा -र्हं, अलोप्यः -प्या -प्यं, अलोपनीयः -या -यं, अखण्डनीयः -या -यं, अखण्ड्यः -ण्ड्या -ण्ड्यं.

IRREVERSIBLENESS, *s.* अपरावर्त्यत्वं, अपरावर्त्तनीयता, अलोप्यता, अखण्ड्यत्वं.

IRREVERSIBLY, *adv.* अपरावर्त्तनीयं, यथा परावर्त्तितुं न शक्यते तथा.

IRREVOCABLE, *a.* अपरावर्त्यः -र्त्या -र्त्यं, अविकार्य्यः -र्य्या -र्य्यं, अनन्यथाकरणीयः -या -यं.

IRREVOCABLY, *adv.* अपरावर्त्तनीयं, अपरिवर्त्तनीयं, अनन्यथाकरणीयं.

To IRRIGATE, *v. a.* सिच् (c. 6. सिञ्चति, सेक्तुं), अभिषिच्, अवसिच्, जलेन प्लु (c. 10. प्लावयति -यितुं) or क्लिद् (c. 10. क्लेदयति -यितुं) or अभ्युक्ष् (c. 1. -उक्षति -क्षितुं) or प्रोक्ष्, अभिवृष् (c. 1. -वर्षति -र्षितुं), प्रणालिकासिञ्चनं कृ.

IRRIGATED, *p. p.* सिक्तः -क्ता -क्तं, जलसिक्तः &c., सलिलसिक्तः &c., जलप्लावितः -ता -तं, समुक्षितः -ता -तं.

IRRIGATION, *s.* सेकः, सेचनं, सिञ्चनं, निषेकः, अवसेकः, अवसेचनं, जलप्लावनं, क्लेदनं, अभ्युक्षणं, प्रोक्षणं, प्रणालिकासिञ्चनं.

IRRIGUOUS, *a.* जलसिक्तः -क्ता -क्तं, सिक्तः -क्ता -क्तं, जलाढ्यः -ढ्या -ढ्यं, अनूपः -पा -पं, बहूदकः -का -कं, सजलः -ला -लं, आर्द्रः -र्द्रा -र्द्रं, समुक्षः -क्षा -क्षं.

IRRISION, *s.* उपहासः, अवहासः, अपहासः, परिहासः, हास्यं, अवहेला.

IRRITABILITY, *s.* शीघ्रकोपित्वं, कोपशीलता, क्रोधशीलता, सुक्रोधनीयता, चण्डस्वभावः, उच्चण्डता, सुखोत्तापनीयत्वं.

IRRITABLE, *a.* (Easily made angry) शीघ्रकोपी -पिनी -पि (न्), सुलभकोपः -पा -पं, सुलभक्रोधः -धा -धं, शीघ्रक्रोधी &c., सुलभमन्युः -न्युः -न्यु, सुक्रोधनीयः -या -यं, सुप्रकोपणीयः -या -यं, कोपशीलः -ला -लं, क्रोधशीलः -ला -लं, सन्तापशीलः -ला -लं, कोपिष्ठः -ष्ठा -ष्ठं, क्रोधिष्ठः -ष्ठा -ष्ठं, चण्डस्वभावः -वा -वं, पित्तस्वभावः -वा -वं, पित्तवेगी -गिनी -गि (न्), उच्चण्डः -ण्डा -ण्डं, उष्णस्वभावः -वा -वं.—(Easily excited) शीघ्रोत्तेजनीयः -या -यं, सुखोत्तापनीयः -या -यं.

To IRRITATE, *v. a.* कुप् (c. 10. कोपयति -यितुं), प्रकुप्, सङ्कुप्, क्रुध् (c. 10. क्रोधयति -यितुं), कोपं जन् (c. 10. जनयति -यितुं), क्रोधं जन्.—(Excite) उत्तप् (c. 10. -तापयति -यितुं), सन्तप्, उत्तिज् (c. 10. -तेजयति -यितुं).

IRRITATED, *p. p.* प्रकोपितः -ता -तं, प्रकुपितः -ता -तं, कुपितः -ता -तं, जातकोपः -पा -पं, जातक्रोधः -धा -धं, जातामर्षः -र्षा -र्षं, उपजातक्रोधः -धा -धं, इद्धमन्युः -न्युः -न्यु.—(Excited) उत्तेजितः -ता -तं, समुत्तेजितः -ता -तं, उत्तापितः -ता -तं, उत्तप्तः -प्ता -प्तं.

IRRITATING, *part.* or *a.* कोपजनकः -का -कं, क्रोधजनकः -का -कं, उत्तापकः -का -कं, सन्तापकः -का -कं, चित्तोत्तापकारी -रिणी -रि (न्).

IRRITATION, *s.* (The act) प्रकोपः -पणं, क्रोधकरणं, कोपकरणं.—(State) कोपः, क्रोधः, अमर्षः, विमर्षः, मन्युः *m.*, क्रोधावेशः, क्रुद्धता, रागावेशः.—(Excitement) उत्तापः, उत्तप्तता, सन्तापः, सन्तप्तता, उत्तेजनं, समुत्तेजनं, दाहः; 'irritation of the throat,' कासः, खवथुः *m.*

IRRITATIVE, *a.* उत्तापकः -का -कं, सन्तापकः -का -कं, दाहजनकः -का -कं.

IRRUPTION, *s.* अवस्कन्दः -न्दनं, उपद्रवः, अभिद्रवः, उपप्लवः, विप्लवः, अभिक्रमः -मणं, आक्रमः, अभिमर्द्दः, अभिग्रहः, अवलुम्पनं; 'to make an irruption,' अवस्कन्द् (c. 1. -स्कन्दति -स्कन्तुं), समवस्कन्द्, आस्कन्द्, उपद्रु (c. 1. -द्रवति -द्रोतुं), अभिद्रु, समाद्रु, अभिधाव् (c. 1. -धावति -वितुं).

ISCHURETIC, *a.* मूत्रावरोधघ्नः -घ्नी -घ्नं, मूत्रावष्टम्भनाशकः -का -कं.

ISCHURY, *s.* मूत्रावरोधः, मूत्रावष्टम्भः, मूत्रकृच्छ्रं, विष्टम्भः, मूत्रानुबन्धः, विबन्धः, आनाहः.

ISINGLASS, *s.* अभ्रं -भ्रकं, मत्स्यान्त्रनिर्म्मितम् अतिसंलग्नभावं श्यानद्रव्यं.

ISLAND, *s.* द्वीपः -पं, अन्तरीपं, उपद्वीपं, पयोगडं; 'one of alluvial formation,' पुलिनं.

ISLAND, *a.* द्वीप्यः -प्या -प्यं, द्वैप्यः -प्या -प्यं, द्वैपः -पी -पं, द्वीपसम्बन्धी -न्धिनी -न्धि (न्), द्वीपस्थः -स्था -स्थं.

ISLANDER, *s.* द्वीपवासी *m.* (न्), द्वीपनिवासी *m.*, द्वीपी *m.* (न्), द्वीपस्थः, द्वीपवासः, द्वैपः, द्वीप्यः.

ISLE, *s.* द्वीपः -पं, अन्तरीपं. *See* ISLAND.

ISLET, *s.* क्षुद्रद्वीपः -पं, अल्पद्वीपः -पं, उपद्वीपः -पं.

ISOCHRONAL, ISOCHRONOUS, *a.* समकालिकः -की -कं, समसंख्यकालः -ला -लं.

To ISOLATE, *v. a.* वियुज् (c. 7. -युनक्ति -योक्तुं), विछिद् (c. 7. -छिनत्ति -छेत्तुं), अवछिद्, अन्यभेदं कृ, अन्यविभेदं कृ, अन्यवियोगं कृ, परविश्लेषं कृ, पृथक् स्था in caus. (स्थापयति -यितुं). *See To* INSULATE.

ISOLATED, *p. p.* असक्तः -क्ता -क्तं, निःसक्तः -क्ता -क्तं, गतसक्तः -क्ता -क्तं, वियुक्तः -क्ता -क्तं, विभिन्नः -न्ना -न्नं, परविभिन्नः -न्ना -न्नं, अन्यविश्लिष्टः -ष्टा -ष्टं, व्यासक्तः -क्ता -क्तं, अनन्यसंसक्तः -क्ता -क्तं, अन्यासक्तः -क्ता -क्तं, पृथक्स्थितः -ता -तं, स्वतन्त्रः -न्त्रा -न्त्रं. *See* INSULATED.

ISOLATION, *s.* असङ्गः, परवियोगः, परविभेदः, विच्छेदः, अवच्छेदः, व्यासङ्गः, विभिन्नता, पृथक्त्वं. *See* INSULATION.

ISOSCELES, *a.* समद्विभुजः -जा -जं, समद्विबाहुः -हुः -हु, समद्विपार्श्वः -र्श्वा -र्श्वं; 'isosceles triangle,' समद्विबाहुकत्रिभुजः, तुल्यद्विबाहुकत्रिभुजः द्विसमत्रिभुजः -जा; 'angles at the base of an isosceles triangle,' तुल्यद्विबाहुकत्रिभुजस्य भूलग्नकोणौ *m.* du.

ISSUE, *s.* (Egress) निःसरणं, निस्सरणं, निर्गमः, निर्गतिः *f.*, निर्याणं, निष्क्रमणं, विनिर्गमः, बहिर्गमनं, बहिस्सरणं, निःसारः -रणं, अपसारः, अपसरणं, प्रवहः.—(Event, consequence, last result) गतिः *f.*, उद्भूतं, अनुवृत्तं, संवृत्तं, उत्पन्नं, फलं, फलमुत्तरं, परिणामः, शेषः, अन्तः, सिद्धिः *f.*, प्रयुक्तिः *f.*, अन्वयः, निष्पन्नं; 'happy issue,' सद्गतिः *f.*, शुभगतिः *f.*, शुभफलं; 'expectation of a favourable issue,' शुभफलाकांक्षा.—(Progeny) प्रजा, अपत्यं, सन्तानं, सन्ततिः *f.*, अन्वयः, तन्तुः *m.*—(Flux) आमातिसारः, रक्तातिसारः, रक्तशुद्धिः *f.*—(Ulcer, fontanel) कृत्रिमव्रणः.

To ISSUE, *v. n.* (Flow out) प्रस्रु (c. 1. -स्रवति -स्रोतुं), निःस्रु, स्रु.—(Pass out, go out) निःसृ (c. 1. -सरति -सर्तुं), विनिःसृ, निर्गम् (c. 1. -गच्छति -गन्तुं), विनिर्गम्, निर्या (c. 2. -याति -तुं), विनिर्या, निष्क्रम् (c. 1. -क्रामति -क्रमितुं), विनिष्क्रम्, अभिनिष्क्रम्, निश्चर् (c. 1 -चरति -रितुं), विनिश्चर्, निरि (c. 2. -एति -तुं), बहिर्गम्.—(Proceed, arise) उत्पद् (c. 4. -पद्यते -पत्तुं), जन् (c. 4. जायते, जनितुं), प्रवृत् (c. 1. -वर्त्तते -र्त्तितुं), प्रभू.—(Close, end) निष्पद्, विगम्, समाप् in pass. (-आप्यते), निवृत्, अपया.

To ISSUE, *v. a.* (Send out) निःसृ (c. 10. -सारयति -यितुं), प्रचल् (c. 10. -चालयति -यितुं), प्रचर् (c. 10. -चारयति -यितुं), प्रचलीकृ.—(Make public) प्रकाश् (c. 10. -काशयति -यितुं), ख्या in caus. (ख्यापयति -यितुं), घुष् (c. 10. घोषयति -यितुं), विघुष्, प्रसिद्धीकृ.

ISSUED, *p. p.* निःसृतः -ता -तं, निर्गतः -ता -तं, प्रसृतः -ता -तं, उत्पन्नः -न्ना -न्नं.

ISSUELESS, *s.* असन्तानः -ना -नं, अनपत्यः -त्या -त्यं, अप्रजः -जा -जं, अप्रसूतः -ता -तं, निःसन्तानः -ना -नं, निरन्वयः -या -यं, निर्वंशः -शा -शं.

ISTHMUS, *s.* संयोगभूमिः *f.*, योगभूमिः *f.*, सम्बन्धभूमिः *f.*

IT, *pron.* तद्, एतद्, इदं. Sometimes 'it' is not expressed, but is inherent in the verb; as, 'it is well ascertained that the figure of the earth is globular,' पृथिवी गोलाकारा भवति इति सुनिश्चितं.

ITALIAN, *a.* इटालिदेशसम्बन्धी -न्धिनी -न्धि (न्), इटालिदेशजः -जा -जं, इटालिदेशीयः -या -यं, इटालिदेशस्थः -स्था -स्थं.

ITALICS, *s. pl.* इटालिकसंज्ञको मुद्राक्षरविशेषः.

ITCH, *s.* (The disease) कण्डूः *f.*, कण्डुः *f.*, खर्जूः *f.*, कच्छूः *f.*, कच्छुः *f.*, सुकण्डुः *f.*, सृकण्डुः *f.*, खसः, पाम *n.* -मा *f.* (न्), कण्डूतिः *f.*—(An itching) कण्डूतिः *f.*, कण्डूयनं, कण्डूया.—(Eager desire) अतिस्पृहा, अतिशयेच्छा, अत्यभिलाषः.

To ITCH, *v. n.* कण्डू (nom. कण्डूयति -ते), कण्डूयां कृ, कण्डूतिं कृ, स्पन्द् (c. 1. स्पन्दते -न्दितुं), स्फुर् (c. 6. स्फुरति -रितुं), कण्डूलः -ला -लं भू.

—(Desire eagerly) अतिशयेन इष् (c. 6. इच्छति, एषितुं) or अभिलष् (c. 1. -लषति -षितुं), गृध् (c. 4. गृध्यति, गर्धितुं).

ITCHY, *a.* कण्डूलः -ला -लं, कच्छुरः -रा -रं, कण्डुरोगी -गिणी -गि (न्), पामनः -ना -नं.

ITEM, *adv.* (Also) अपरच, अपिच, अपच, चैव, पुनरपि.

ITEM, *s.* (Article, separate particular) पदं, विषयः, प्रकरणं, अधिकरणं.

To ITERATE, *v. a.* (Utter again) पुनर् वद् (c. 1. वदति -दितुं), मुहुर् वद्, अनुवद्, पुनरुक्तिं कृ.—(Do again) पुनः कृ, मुहुः कृ, पुनःपुनः कृ.

ITERATION, *s.* पुनरुक्तिः *f.*, पौनरुक्त्यं, पुनर्वचनं, अनुवादः, मुहुर्भाषा.—(Doing again) पुनःकरणं, पनरावृत्तिः *f.*, द्विरावृत्तिः *f.*

ITERATIVE, *a.* पुनर्वादी -दिनी -दि (न्), पुनःकारी -रिणी -रि (न्).

ITINERANT, *a.* अटमानः -ना -नं, पर्यटनकारी -रिणी -रि (न्), अध्वगः -गा -गं -गामी -मिनी -मि (न्), भ्रमणकारी &c., परिभ्रमी -मिणी -मि (न्), अध्वनिचरः -रा -रं, यात्रिकः -की -कं, चक्राटः -टा -टं.

ITINERARY, *s.* मार्गवृत्तान्तपुस्तकं, मार्गक्रमणलेखः, प्रवासवृत्तान्तलेखः.

To ITINERATE, *v. n.* देशभ्रमणं कृ, देशपर्यटनं कृ, परिभ्रम् (c. 4. -भ्राम्यति -भ्रमितुं), पर्यट् (c. 1. -अटति -टितुं).

ITS, *pron.* तदीयः -या -यं, तस्य gen. c. (तद्), अस्य gen. c. (इदं).

ITSELF, *pron.* तद् एतद्, स्वयं.

IVORY, *s.* हस्तिदन्तः, करिदन्तः, गजदन्तः, दन्तिदन्तः -न्ती.

IVORY, *a.* दान्तः -न्ती -न्तं, हस्तिदन्ती -न्तिनी -न्ति (न्), हस्तिदन्तनिर्म्मितः -ता -तं, दन्तिदन्तमयः -यी -यं.

IVY, *s.* वृक्षगृहादिरोही लताविशेषः, तरुरुहा, तरुरोहिणी.

J.

To JABBER, *v. n.* जल्प् (c. 1. जल्पति -ल्पितुं), उपजल्प्, त्वरितं वद् (c. 1 वदति -दितुं), अव्यक्तं or अस्पष्टं वद्, वद् in freq. (वावद्यते), प्रलप् (c. 1. -लपति -पि॰), बटबट (nom. बटबटायते), अनर्थकवचनं कृ.

JABBERER, *s.* जल्पकः, जल्पाकः, जल्पी *m.* (न्), उपजल्पी *m.*, वाचालः, वाचाटः, वावदूकः, बहुभाषी *m.* (न्), अस्पष्टवक्ता *m.* (क्तृ).

JABBERING, *s.* जल्पः -ल्पनं, प्रजल्पः, जल्पितं, वावदूकता, प्रलापः, विप्रलापः, प्रलपितं, त्वरितवचनं, अस्पष्टवचनं, अव्यक्तवचनं, निरर्थकवचनं.

JACK, *s.* (Instrument for pulling off boots) पादुकानिष्कर्षणयन्त्रं.—(Instrument for turning a spit) यन्त्रं यद्द्वारेण पाकशूलः परिवर्त्तते.—(A fish) जलसूचिः *m.*—(Coat of mail) कवचः -चं, तनुत्रं.—(Horse, wooden frame) मञ्चः, वृषः, उपस्तम्भः, आधारः.—(Male of certain animals) expressed by पुं prefixed.—(Flag at the end of a bow-sprit) नौकाग्रबहिःप्रलम्बो ध्वजपटः.—(Bread-fruit tree) पनसः, पनसनालिका, कण्टकिफलः.

JACK-A-LANTERN, *s.* पिशाचदीपिका, भूतदीपिका, मिथ्यादीप्तिः *f.*

JACKAL, *s.* शृगालः, सृगालः, जम्बुकः, जम्बूकः, गोमायुः *m.*, वञ्चकः, क्रोष्टा *m.* (ष्टु), गोमी *m.* (न्), क्रम्पा *m.* (न्), भूरिमायः, घोररासनः, हूरवः, मृगधूर्त्तः *m.*, फेरः, फेरण्डः, फेरवः.—(Female) शृगाली, क्रोष्ट्री, शिवा.

JACKANAPES, *s.* वानरवृत्तिः *m.*, कपिस्वभावः, मर्कटशीलः, वानरचरित्रः.

JACKASS, *s.* गर्द्दभः, रासभः, खरः, धूसरः, चक्रीवान् *m.* (त्), बालेयः.

JACK-BOOTS, *s. pl.* चर्म्मनिर्म्मितं जङ्घोत्तरीयं or जङ्घात्राणं, बृहत्पादुका.

JACK-DAW, *s.* काकजातीयः पक्षिभेदः, काकविशेषः, काकः, वायसः.

JACKET, *s.* कञ्चुकः, कञ्चुलिका, निचोलः -लकः, चोलः -लकः, निचुलः, अङ्गिका, कूर्पासकः.

JACK-KETCH, *s.* घातुकपुरुषः, दण्डपाशिकः, मृतपाः *m.*, उद्बन्धकः.

JACK-PUDDING, *s.* भण्डः, भाण्डः, वैहासिकः, परिहासवेदी *m.* (न्), विदूषकः.

JACOBIN, *s.* हीनवर्णपक्षपाती *m.* (न्), राजद्रोही *m.* (न्), राजयुध्वा *m.* (न्).

JACOB'S-STAFF, *s.* (Pilgrim's staff) कार्पटिकदण्डः, कार्पटिकयष्टिः *m.f.* —(A staff concealing a weapon) कूटायुधं, कूटास्त्रं, अन्तर्गुप्तनिशितास्त्रो वहिःकाष्ठमयो दण्डः.

JADE, *s.* (Sorry horse) कदश्वः, अश्वतरः, अश्वकः.—(A name of reproach for a woman) बन्धकी, कुलटा, भ्रष्टा, पापीयसी. *See* JADISH.

To JADE, *v. a.* खिद् (c. 10. खेदयति -यितुं), आयस् (c. 10. -यासयति -यितुं), श्रम् (c. 10. श्रमयति -यितुं), क्लम् (c. 10. क्लमयति -यितुं), सद् (c. 10. सादयति -यितुं), अवसद्, क्लिश् (c. 9. क्लिश्नाति, क्लेशितुं), तप् (c. 10. तापयति -यितुं), कृष् (c. 10. कर्षयति -यितुं), कष्टं कृ.

To JADE, *v. n.* (Become weary) खिद् in pass. (खिद्यते), आयस् (c. 4. -यस्यति -यसितुं), श्रम् (c. 4. श्राम्यति, श्रमितुं), क्लम् (c. 4. क्लाम्यति, क्लमितुं), सद् (c. 1. सीदति, सत्तुं), अवसद्, कष्ट (nom. कष्टायते).

JADED, *p. p.* खिन्नः -न्ना -न्नं, खेदितः -ता -तं, श्रान्तः -न्ता -न्तं, परिश्रान्तः -न्ता -न्तं, श्रमार्त्तः -र्त्ता -र्त्तं, क्लिष्टः -ष्टा -ष्टं, ग्लानः -ना -नं.

JADISH, *a.* (Bad) दुष्टः -ष्टा -ष्टं, पापीयान् -यसी -यः (स्), कुत्सितः -ता -तं, कु or कद् or दुर् prefixed.—(Unchaste, applied to a woman) बन्धकी, असती, असाध्वी, व्यभिचारिणी, पुंश्चली, धृष्टा, धर्षिणी, अविनीता, कामगा.

JAG, JAGG, *s.* (Notch) छेदः, अवच्छेदः, विच्छेदः, भङ्गः, दन्तः, क्रकचदन्तरूपो भङ्गः or छेदः.

To JAGG, *v. a.* जर्ज्जरीकृ, क्रकचदन्तरूपेण छिद् (c. 7. छिनत्ति, छेत्तुं) or विच्छिद् or अवच्छिद्, छेदं कृ, अवच्छेदं कृ, क्रकचरूपेण भङ्गुरं -रां -रं कृ, or भङ्गुरीकृ or जर्ज्जरं -रां -रं कृ, जर्ज्जरीकं -कां -कं कृ.

JAGGED, *p. p. a.* जर्ज्जरः -रा -रं, जर्ज्जरीकः -का -कं, क्रकचदन्तरूपेण विच्छिन्नः -न्ना -न्नं or दन्तुरः -रा -रं or दन्ती -न्तिनी -न्ति (न्), अनुक्रकचः -चा -चं, क्रकचधाराकारः -रा -रं, भङ्गुरः -रा -रं, विषमधारः -रा -रं.

JAGGEDNESS, *s.* जर्ज्जरता, जर्ज्जरीकता, दन्तुरत्वं, भङ्गुरत्वं.

JAGGY, *a.* दन्तुरः -रा -रं, अनुक्रकचः -चा -चं. *See* JAGGED.

JAIL, *s.* कारा, कारागारं, कारागृहं, कारावेश्म *n.* (न्), बन्धनागारं, बन्धनालयः, बन्धनगृहं, बन्धनस्थानं, निरोधस्थानं, बन्दिशाला, गुप्तिः *f.*, चारः.

JAILER, *s.* कारारक्षकः, कारागृहाध्यक्षः, कारागाराधिपतिः *m.*, बन्धनालयरक्षकः, गुप्तिपालकः, बन्दिपालः.

JAKES, *s.* शौचकूपः, पायुक्षालनवेश्म *n.* (न्), अवस्करस्थानं.

JAM, *s.* मिष्टफलं, मिष्टान्नं, खाण्डवं, सन्धितफलं, सन्धितं.

To JAM, *v. a.* सम्पीड् (c. 10. -पीडयति -यितुं), सम्मृद् (c. 9. -मृद्नाति -मर्द्दितुं), सम्बाध् (c. 1. -बाधते -धितुं), सङ्कुलीकृ, सङ्कटीकृ.

JAMB, *s.* उपस्तम्भः, अवष्टम्भः -म्भनं, स्तम्भः, गृहस्तम्भः, आधारः.

JAMMED, *p. p.* सम्पीडितः -ता -तं, सम्मर्द्दितः -ता -तं, सम्बाधः -धा -धं, सङ्कुलः -ला -लं, सङ्कटः -टा -टं, चूर्णितः -ता -तं.

To JANGLE, *v. n.* वाग्युद्धं कृ, वाक्कलहं कृ, विवद् (c. 1. -वदते -दितुं), विप्रलापं कृ, व्यवक्रोशनं कृ, विरोधोक्तिं कृ, कलह (nom. कलहायते).

JANGLE, *s.* (Wrangling) वाग्युद्धं, वाक्कलहः, विप्रलापः, व्यवक्रोशनं.—(Discordant sound) झञ्झा -झनं.

JANGLER, *s.* वाक्कलहकारी *m.* (न्), वाग्युद्धप्रियः, व्यवक्रोशनप्रियः.

JANGLING, *s.* (Wrangling) वाक्कलहः, व्यवक्रोशनं, विवादः.—(Discordant sound) झञ्झा -झनं, क्वः, कर्कशस्वनः.

JANITOR, *s.* द्वारपालः, द्वाररक्षकः, द्वारस्थः, प्रतिहारः, प्रतीहारः.

JANTILY, *adv.* चपलं, चापल्येन, चपलशीलत्वात्, लघु, स्वभावलाघवात्.

JANTINESS, *s.* चापल्यं, चपलशीलता, लघुता, स्वभावलाघवं.

JANTY, *a.* चपलः -ला -लं, चपलशीलः -ला -लं, लघुस्वभावः -वा -वं.

JANUARY, *s.* पौषमाघं, पौषः, माघः, उत्तरपौषः, पूर्व्वमाघः, पुष्यः, तैषः, तिष्यः -ष्यकः, प्रथममासः.

JAPAN, *s.* जापान्नामा चित्रकुङ्कुमविशेषः.

To JAR, *v. n.* (Make a grating sound) कर्कशशब्दं कृ, झञ्झा (nom. झञ्झायते), परस्परघर्षणजं झञ्झाशब्दं कृ.—(Clash) सङ्घट्ट् (c. 1. -घट्टते -ट्टितुं), परस्परसमाघातं कृ, परस्परसङ्घट्टनं कृ.—(Quarrel) विवद् (c. 1. -वदते -दितुं), कलह (nom. कलहायते).

JAR, *s.* (Grating sound) कर्कशशब्दः, परस्परघर्षणजः कटुशब्दः, परस्परसङ्घट्टनजो झञ्झाशब्दः, झञ्झनं.—(Clash) सङ्घट्टः -ट्टनं, समाघातः, परस्परसमाघातः, परस्परविरोधः.—(An earthen vessel) घटः, कुम्भः, कलशः -शी -शं, मणिकं, अलिञ्जरः, आलुः *f.*, कर्करी, कुण्डी, मृत्तिकापात्रं, मृद्भाण्डं, मृण्मयपात्रं, उदपात्रं, जलपात्रं.—(Bottom of a jar) सूर्य्यग्रहः.—(A little open, half open, said of a door) ईषदुद्घाटितः -ता -तं, अर्द्धोद्घाटितः -ता -तं.

JARGON, *s.* अनर्थकभाषा, असम्बद्धभाषा, पिशाचभाषा, राक्षसी भाषा, मिश्रितभाषा.

JARRING, *part.* or *a.* परस्परपराहतः -ता -तं, परस्परविरोधी -धिनी -धि (न्), अन्योन्यविरुद्धः -द्धा -द्धं.—(Making a harsh sound) कर्कशशब्दकारी -रिणी -रि (न्).

JASMIN, *s.* कुन्दः -न्दं, जाती -तिः *f.*, स्फाटी -टा, जातीकुसुमं, मालती, यूथी, यूथिका, स्वर्णयूथी, मल्लिका, जीवनी, सुगन्धः, माधुरं, सुमनाः *f.* (स्), मकरन्दः, मुद्गरः; 'double jasmin,' शिशुगन्धा; 'relating to the jasmin,' कौन्दः -न्दी -न्दं; 'the jasmin creeper,' कौन्दी लता.

JASPER, *s.* सूर्य्यकान्तः, भास्वराख्यो मणिविशेषः.

JAUNDICE, *s.* पाण्डुः *m.*, पाण्डुरोगः, पाण्डुरः, पाण्डुकः, कामला -लः, कुम्भकामला, हलीमकं; 'incipient jaundice,' पाण्डुच्छाया.

JAUNDICED, *a.* (Having the jaundice) पाण्डुरोगी -गिणी -गि (न्), पाण्डुरोगग्रस्तः -स्ता -स्तं.—(Prejudiced) साचीकृतः -ता -तं, वक्रदृष्टिः -ष्टिः -ष्टि.

To JAUNT, *v. n.* परिभ्रमणं कृ, पर्य्यटनं कृ, विहारं कृ, विहारार्थम् इतस्ततः परिभ्रम् (c. 4. -भ्राम्यति -भ्रमितुं), विहृ (c. 1. -हरति -हर्त्तुं), विहारार्थं पर्य्यट् (c. 1. -अटति -टितुं).

JAUNT, *s.* विहारः, विहरणं, भ्रमणं, विहारार्थं परिभ्रमणं or पर्य्यटनं.

JAUNTINESS, *s.* *See* JANTINESS.

JAVELIN, *s.* शल्यं, शलाका, शङ्कुः *m.*, प्रासः, क्षिपणिः *m.*, शक्तिः *f.*, पाणिमुक्तं, करमुक्तं, मुक्तकं, मुक्तामुक्तं, शूलः -लं, अस्त्रं, दूरवेधी *m.* (न्), कासूतरी.

JAW, *s.* हनुः *m. f.*, हनूः *f.*; 'the lower jaw,' पीचं, कुञ्जः, चिबुकं, चिबुः *m.*; 'big-jawed,' महाहनुः -नुः -नु; 'locked jaw,' हनुग्रहः, हनुस्तम्भः; 'jaw-tooth,' दाढा, दंष्ट्रा.—(Mouth) मुखं, वक्त्रं; 'jaws of death,' मृत्युवक्त्रं.—(Scolding, abuse) आक्रोशः, क्रुष्टं, तर्ज्जनं, वाक्पारुष्यं, भर्त्सनं.

To JAW, *v. n.* (Scold) आक्रुश् (c. 1. -क्रोशति -क्रोष्टुं), तर्ज् (c. 10. तर्जयति -यितुं).

JAW-BONE, *s.* हन्वस्थि *n.*, चिबुकास्थि *n.*, पीचास्थि *n.*

JAWED, *a.* हनुमान् -मती -मत् (त्), हनूमान् &c., हनुविशिष्टः -ष्टा -ष्टं.

JAY, *s.* चाषः, चासः, मणिकण्ठः, नीलकण्ठः, किकिः *m.*, किकिदिविः *m.*, किकीदिवः, किकीदीविः *m.*, चालः.

JEALOUS, *a.* (Apprehensive of rivalship, uneasy at another's success) मत्सरी -रिणी -रि (न्), मत्सरः -रा -रं, समत्सरः -रा -रं,

परगुणमत्सरः -रा -रं, परोत्कर्षद्वेषी -षिणी -षि (न्), परोत्कर्षासहनः -ना -नं, परोत्कर्षासूयकः -का -कं, परोत्कर्षशङ्की -ङ्किनी -ङ्कि (न्), अन्यशुभाशङ्की -ङ्किनी -ङ्कि (न्), परप्रशंसासहनः -ना -नं, परशुभामर्षणः -णा -णं, ईर्षी -र्षिणी -र्षि (न्) सेर्ष्यः -र्ष्या -र्ष्यं, असूयकः -का -कं, साभ्यसूयः -या -यं, कृतेर्ष्यः -र्ष्या -र्ष्यं, स्पर्धी -र्धिनी -र्धि (न्), वक्रदृष्टिः -ष्टिः -ष्टि. —(Suspicious in love) प्रेमविपर्य्यासशङ्की &c., प्रेमसंशयी -यिनी -यि (न्), प्रेमशङ्की &c., प्रेमव्यत्ययाशङ्की, प्रीतिविपर्य्ययाशङ्की &c.; 'a husband of a wife,' परपुरुषाशङ्की, परपुरुषशङ्कितः, जारशङ्कितः; 'a wife of a husband,' परस्त्रीशङ्किता, परस्त्रीशङ्किनी.—(Suspiciously fearful) शङ्काशीलः -ला -लं, शङ्कास्वभावः -वा -वं.—(Careful for the honour of) अभिमानी -निनी -नि (न्), कृताभिमानः -ना -नं, कृतादरः -रा -रं, साभिमानः -ना -नं, आदृतः -ता -तं.

JEALOUSLY, *adv.* समत्सरं, मात्सर्य्येण, सेर्ष्यं, असूयया, सासूयं, साभ्यसूयं, परोत्कर्षासूयया, परोत्कर्षशङ्कया, प्रेमविपर्य्यासशङ्कया, शङ्काशीलवत्, वक्रदृष्ट्या, स्पर्धया.

JEALOUSY, JEALOUSNESS, *s.* मात्सर्य्यं, मत्सरः -रता, ईर्ष्या, असूया, स्पर्धा, परगुणमात्सर्य्यं, परोत्कर्षासहिष्णुता, परोत्कर्षद्वेषः, परोत्कर्षासूया, परोत्कर्षशङ्का, परप्रशंसासहनं, परशुभाशङ्का, अन्यशुभद्वेषः, सापत्न्यं, सापत्नभावः, दृष्टिवक्रता.—(Suspiciousness in love) प्रेमशङ्का, प्रीतिशङ्का, प्रेमसंशयः, प्रेमविपर्य्यासशङ्का, प्रेमव्यत्ययशङ्का, प्रीतिव्यत्यासशङ्का; 'of a husband respecting a wife,' परपुरुषशङ्का, व्यभिचारशङ्का, अन्यपुरुषाशङ्का, जारशङ्का; 'of a wife respecting a husband,' परस्त्रीशङ्का.—(Suspicious fear) शङ्का, शङ्काशीलता.—(Concern for the honour of) अभिमानचिन्ता.

To JEER, *v. a.* अवहस् (c. 1. -हसति -सितुं), अपहस्, अवहासभूमिं कृ, अपहासास्पदीकृ, अवक्षिप् (c. 6. -क्षिपति -क्षेप्तुं), अवज्ञा (c. 9. -जानाति -ज्ञातुं), तिरस्कृ, मुखरीकृ, गर्ह् (c. 1. गर्हते -र्हितुं), अवगर्ह्, भर्त्स् (c. 10. भर्त्सयते -ति -यितुं).

JEER, *s.* उपहासः, अवहासः, अपहासः, परिहासः, क्षेपः, अवक्षेपः, अवज्ञा, अवमानं, अवहेला, व्यञ्जनं -ना, व्यंग्यः.

JEERER, *s.* उपहासकः, परिहासकर्त्ता *m.* (र्तृ), क्षेपकः, अवक्षेपकः.

JEERINGLY, *adv.* उपहासेन, सोपहासं, परिहासेन, सावक्षेपं, हास्यपूर्व्वं.

JEJUNE, *a.* रूक्षः -क्षा -क्षं, रूक्षः -क्षा -क्षं, नीरसः -सा -सं, विरसः -सा -सं, रसहीनः -ना -नं, शुष्कः -ष्का -ष्कं, शून्यः -न्या -न्यं, निःसारः -रा -रं, निःसत्त्वः -त्त्वा -त्त्वं.

JEJUNENESS, *s.* रूक्षता, रौक्ष्यं, नीरसता, विरसता, रसाभावः, शुष्कता, शून्यता, सारहीनता, सत्त्वहीनता.

JELLY, *s.* (Of animal substance) मांसघननिष्क्वाथः, क्वथितमांसनिर्म्मितो घनीभूतः स्वच्छरसः, मांसस्य श्यानरसः or घनरसः.—(Of fruit) फलानां शर्करादिना सह निष्क्वथितानां घनरसः, फलपाकः.—(Glutinous substance) श्यानद्रव्यं, सान्द्रद्रव्यं.

JENNET, *s.* See GENET.

To JEOPARD, *v. a.* संशयस्थं -स्थां कृ, संशयितं -तां कृ, सन्देहस्थं -स्थां कृ, शङ्कास्थं -स्थां कृ, संशयापन्नं -न्नां कृ, सन्देहदोलस्थं -स्थां कृ, भयस्थं -स्थां कृ, शङ्कास्पदीकृ; 'one who jeopards his life,' संशयितजीवितः.

JEOPARDED, *p. p.* संशयितः -ता -तं, संशयक्रमितः -ता -तं, शङ्कास्पदीकृतः -ता -तं.

JEOPARDOUS, *a.* सांशयिकः -की -कं, सन्दिग्धः -ग्धा -ग्धं, भयाक्रान्तः -न्ता -न्तं.

JEOPARDY, *s.* (Hazard) संशयः, शङ्का, सन्देहः, भयं, विकल्पः, आतङ्कः, भयहेतुः *m.*; 'any thing exposed to jeopardy,' भयस्थानं, संशयस्थानं, शङ्कास्पदं; 'jeopardy of life,' जीवितसंशयः, प्राणसन्देहः, प्राणनाशसंशयः, प्राणबाधः; 'brought into jeopardy,' संशयितः -ता -तं; 'to be in jeopardy,' संशयस्थः -स्था -स्थं भू, शङ्कास्पदीभू.

To JERK, *v. a.* (Give a sharp or sudden twitch or push) लघुप्रहारं कृ, लघ्वाघातं कृ, आकस्मिकप्रहारं कृ, लघुप्रहारेण तड् (c. 10. ताडयति -यितुं) or आहन् (c. 2. -हन्ति -न्तुं).—(Throw with a sharp sudden motion, or by stopping the arm half way) लघुप्रहारेण or आकस्मिकप्रहारेण क्षिप् (c. 6. क्षिपति, क्षेप्तुं), बाहुवेगम् अर्द्धेन स्तम्भयित्वा क्षिप्, अकस्मात् क्षिप्.

JERK, *s.* लघुप्रहारः, लघ्वाघातः, आकस्मिकप्रहारः, लघुक्षेपः, आकस्मिकक्षेपः, लघुप्रहारेण क्षेपः, बाहुवेगस्तम्भनपूर्व्वः क्षेपः.

JERKIN, *s.* कञ्चुकः, कञ्चुलिका, चोलिका, कूर्पासकः, क्षुद्रनिचोलः.

JESSAMINE, *s.* See JASMIN.

JEST, *s.* हास्यं, परिहासः, परीहासः, हासिका, नर्म्म (न्), परिहासवाक्यं, परिहासोक्तिः *f.*, विनोदोक्तिः *f.*, विनोदभाषणं, क्ष्वेडः, लालिका, दद्दुरी, व्याहारः.—(Object of laughter) उपहासस्थानं, उपहासास्पदं, हास्यास्पदं, उपहासपात्रं, विनोदास्पदं.—(Fun) खेला, क्रीडा, कौतुकं, केलिः *m. f.*; 'in jest,' परिहासेन.

To JEST, *v. n.* हस् (c. 1. हसति -सितुं), विहस्, प्रहस्, सम्प्रहस् संविहस्, परिहासं कृ, विनोदं कृ, परिहासवाक्यं वद् (c. 1. वदति -दितुं), विनोदवाक्यं वद्, भण्ड् (c. 1. भण्डते -ण्डितुं), क्रीड् (c. 1. क्रीडति -ते -डितुं), प्रक्रीड्, विक्रीड्, परिक्रीड्, विलस् (c. 1. -लसति -सितुं), खेला (nom. खेलायति); 'speak in jest,' परिहासेन वद्.

JESTER, *s.* परिहासकारी *m.* (न्), परिहासवेदी *m.* (न्), हास्यकारी *m.*, विनोदकारी *m.*, विनोदभाषी *m.* (न्), वैहासिकः, विदूषकः.—(Buffoon) भण्डः, वैहासिकः, चाटुपटुः *m.*, चाटुवटुः *m.*, रवणः, नटः, क्रीडामृगः.—(Companion of a king) नर्म्मसचिवः, विदूषकः, नर्म्मदः, राजविनोदी *m.* (न्).

JESTING, *s.* परिहासकरणं, नर्म्मकरणं, नर्म्मद्युतिः *f.*, विनोदः, भण्डः.

JESTINGLY, *adv.* परिहासेन, हास्येन, परिहासमात्रेण, विनोदेन, विनोदार्थं.

JET, *s.* (Spouting of water) जलोत्क्षेपः, जलोत्सेकः.—(Black stone) कृष्णप्रस्तरः, कृष्णवर्णः प्रस्तरविशेषः.

JET-BLACK, *s.* घनकृष्णः -ष्णा -ष्णं, सुकृष्णः -ष्णा -ष्णं, अतिकृष्णः -ष्णा -ष्णं.

JETSAM, JETSON, JETTISON, *s.* नौव्यसनकाले नौकालघुकरणार्थं समुद्रमध्ये क्षिप्तद्रव्याणि.

JETTY, *s.* भूमिबहिर्गतः समुद्रस्थसेतुः, काष्ठस्तम्भनिर्म्मितः, क्षुद्रसेतुः.

JETTY, *a.* (Black as jet) कृष्णवर्णः -र्णा -र्णं, कृष्णप्रस्तरसवर्णः -र्णा -र्णं.

JEW, *s.* यिहुदीयः, यिहुदीयदेशजः, यिहुदीयदेशवासी *m.* (न्).

JEWEL, *s.* (Precious stone) मणिः *m. f.*, मणी, रत्नं, प्रस्तरः, मणिरत्नं, चारुशिला; 'jewel in a snake's head,' फणमणिः; 'necklace of jewels,' मणिमाला, रत्नावलिः *f.*; 'having jewels in the ears,' मणिकर्णः -र्णा -र्णं.—(A term of endearment) रत्नं; 'a jewel of a woman,' स्त्रीरत्नं.

JEWEL-HOUSE, JEWEL-OFFICE, *s.* मणिशाला, रत्नशाला, राजकीयरत्नागारं.

JEWEL-MINE, *s.* रत्नाकरः, रत्नखनिः *f.*, मणिभूमिः *f.*, रत्नभूमिः.

JEWELLED, *p. p.* or *a.* रत्नवान् -वती -वत् (त्), मणिमान् -मती -मत् (त्), मणिखचितः -ता -तं, रत्नमयः -यी -यं, मणिमयः -यी -यं, मणिशः -शा -शं.

JEWELLER, *s.* मणिकारः, रत्नकारः -रकः, रत्नजीवी *m.* (न्), वैकटिकः; 'jeweller's shop,' रत्नशाला.

JEWELRY, *s.* रत्नानि *n. pl.*, रत्नादि भूषणं or अलङ्कारः, कोशः, कोषः.

JEWESS, *s.* यिहुदीया, यिहुदीया स्त्री, यिहुदीयदेशजा.

JEWISH, *a.* यिहुदीयः -या -यं, यिहुदीयदेशसम्बन्धी -न्धिनी -न्धि (न्), यिहुदीयधर्म्मा -र्म्मा -र्म्म (न्).

JEW'S HARP, *s.* मुखवाद्यं, वक्रतालः -लं.

JIB, *s.* नौकाग्रस्थवसनं, अग्रस्थवसनं, नौकाग्रबहिःस्थं वातवसनं.

JIFFY, *s.* निमेषः, क्षणः, पलं; 'in a jiffy,' निमेषमात्रेण, एकपदे, सपदि.

JIG, *s.* लघुनृत्यं, लघुनर्त्तनं, लघुतालसहितो नृत्यविशेषः.

To JIG, *v. n.* पूर्व्वोक्तप्रकारेण नृत् (c. 4. नृत्यति, नर्त्तितुं), लघु नृत्.

JILT, *s.* प्रतारिका, वञ्चिका, विप्रलम्भिका, सङ्केतलंघिनी, सङ्केतितान्यगामिनी, चपला, चपलशीला, एकपुरुषम् आश्वासयित्वा अन्यं गच्छति or गृह्णाति या स्त्री, प्रेमसिद्ध्याशां जनयित्वा खण्डयति या स्त्री.

To JILT, *v. a.* or *n.* प्रेमविषये एकपुरुषम् आश्वासयित्वा अन्यं गम् (c. 1. गच्छति, गन्तुं) or ग्रह् (c. 9. गृह्णाति, ग्रहीतुं), प्रेमसिद्ध्याशां जनयित्वा खण्ड् (c. 10. खण्डयति -यितुं), सङ्केतं लंघ् (c. 10. लंघयति -यितुं), प्रेमविषये वञ्च् (c. 10. वञ्चयते -ति -यितुं) or प्रतॄ (c. 10. -तारयति -यितुं) or विप्रलभ् (c. 1. -लभते -लब्धुं).

JILTED, *p. p.* खण्डितः -ता -तं, खण्डितप्रेमसिद्ध्याशः -शा -शं.

To JINGLE, *v. n.* शिञ्ज् (c. 2. शिंक्ते, c. 1. शिञ्जते -ञ्जितुं), विशिञ्ज्, क्वण् (c. 1. क्वणति -णितुं), झणझण (nom. झणझणायते), किङ्किण (nom. किङ्किणायते), झम्झमनं कृ, विरु (c. 2. -रौति -रवितुं).

JINGLE, *s.* शिञ्जा -ञ्जः, शिञ्जितं, आशिञ्जितं, झम्झमनं, झम्झा, झनत्कारः, झङ्कारः, झं, क्वणनं, क्वणितं, किङ्किणिशब्दः, झणझणशब्दः.

JINGLING, *part.* or *a.* शिञ्जी -ञ्जिनी -ञ्जि (न्), झम्झमनकारी -रिणी -रि (न्), क्वणन् -णन्ती -णत् (त्), क्वणितः -ता -तं.

JOB, *s.* (Piece of work) कर्म्म *m.* (न्), कार्य्यं, कृत्यं, क्रिया, व्यापारः. —(Mean business) क्षुद्रकर्म्म *n.*, नीचकर्म्म *n.*, अधमक्रिया.—(Work done for private profit or ends) स्वार्थप्रयुक्तं कर्म्म, स्ववृद्ध्यर्थं कर्म्म, स्वार्थमात्रापेक्षकं कर्म्म, स्वार्थमात्रोद्देशकं कर्म्म or कार्य्यं, स्वार्थकर्म्म *n.*

To JOB, *v. n.* क्षुद्रकर्म्म कृ, नीचकर्म्म कृ, स्वार्थप्रयुक्तं कर्म्म कृ, स्वार्थमात्रमपेक्ष्य or स्वार्थमात्रमुद्दिश्य कार्य्यं कृ.—(Buy and sell as a broker) परार्थं क्रयविक्रयं कृ or पण् (c. 1. पणते -णितुं, पणायति -यितुं), पणायां कृ. —(Deal in, hire) प्रयुज् (c. 7. -युनक्ति -युंक्ते -योक्तुं), प्रयोगं कृ.

JOBBER, *s.* (One who does small jobs) क्षुद्रकर्म्मकारी *m.* (न्), नीचकर्म्मकृत्, तुच्छकर्म्मव्यवसायी *m.* (न्), अल्पकर्म्मव्यापारी *m.*—(Broker) परार्थं क्रयविक्रयकारी *m.* or क्रयविक्रयप्रयोजकः, घटकः.—(One who does a work for his own ends) स्वार्थप्रयुक्तकर्म्मव्यवसायी *m.*, स्वार्थप्रवर्त्तकः, स्ववृद्ध्यर्थं कार्य्यव्यापारी.—(Dealer) क्रयविक्रयिकः, पणिकः, विपणी *m.* (न्).

JOBBING, *s.* क्षुद्रकर्म्मव्यवसायः, नीचकर्म्मप्रवृत्तिः *f.*, स्वार्थप्रयुक्तकार्य्यप्रवृत्तिः *f.*, स्वार्थप्रवर्त्तनं, स्ववृद्धिप्रवर्त्तनं.

JOB-HORSE, *s.* पण्याश्वः, प्रयोज्यवाजी *m.* (न्), भाटकीयवाजी *m.*, अश्वकः.

JOCKEY, *s.* अश्वविद् *m.*, अश्वशिक्षकः, अश्वप्रेरकः, अश्वारूढः, अश्वशिक्षाजीवी *m.* (न्), अश्वोपजीवी *m.* (न्), अश्वज्ञः, हयज्ञः, अश्वविद्याविशारदः, हयविद्याविशारदः, अश्वकोविदः.

To JOCKEY, *v. a.* अश्वशिक्षकवत् प्रतॄ (c. 10. -तारयति -यितुं) or वञ्च् (c. 10. वञ्चयते -ति -यितुं) or प्रलभ् (c. 1. -लभते -लब्धुं).

JOCKEYISM, JOCKEYSHIP, *s.* अश्वविद्या, अश्वारोहणविद्या, अश्वशिक्षा.

JOCOSE, *a.* परिहासशीलः -ला -लं, परिहासकः -का -कं, प्रहासी -सिनी -सि (न्), रसिकः -का -कं, रसी -सिनी -सि (न्), सरसः -सा -सं, कौतुकी -किनी -कि (न्), सकौतुकः -का -कं, विनोदी -दिनी -दि (न्). *See* JOCULAR.

JOCOSELY, *adv.* परिहासेन, प्रहासेन, सरसं, सकौतुकं, रसिकवत्.

JOCOSENESS, *s.* परिहासशीलता, प्रहासः, रसिकत्वं, सरसता, कौतुकं.

JOCULAR, *a.* परिहासकः -का -कं, रसिकः -का -कं, विनोदी -दिनी -दि (न्), विनोदकारी -रिणी -रि (न्), हास्यकारी &c., विनोदात्मकः -का -कं, हास्यावहः -हा -हं. *See* JOCOSE.

JOCULARITY, *s.* परिहासकत्वं, प्रहसनं, प्रहसितं, हासिका, रसिकता, विनोदः, कौतुकं, उल्लसता, हर्षः, उल्लासः.

JOCULARLY, *adv.* परिहासेन, सकौतुकं, विनोदार्थं, हर्षेण, हृष्टवत्.

JOCUND, *a.* प्रमोदी -दिनी -दि (न्), उल्लसः -सा -सं, प्रहृष्टः -ष्टा -ष्टं, हृष्टहृदयः -या -यं, आनन्दी -न्दिनी -न्दि (न्), आनन्दवृत्तिः -त्तिः -त्ति.

JOCUNDITY, *s.* उल्लसता, प्रहर्षः, आनन्दः, मुदा, हृष्टचित्तत्वं.

JOCUNDLY, *adv.* हर्षेण, सहर्षं, प्रमोदेन, सानन्दं, उल्लासेन, हृष्टवत्.

To JOG, *v. a.* अरत्निना तड् (c. 10. ताडयति -यितुं) or चल् (c. 10. चालयति -यितुं), ईषत् तड् or चल्, इङ्गितं कृ.

To JOG, *v. n.* (Jog on slowly) शनैः शनैः or मन्दं मन्दं or क्रमे क्रमे चल् (c. 1. चलति -लितुं) or चर् (c. 1. चरति -रितुं) or सृ (c. 1. सरति, सर्त्तुं).

JOG, JOGGING, *s.* चालनं, ईषच्चालनं, ईषत्क्षोभः, ईषदाघातः, ईषत्प्रहारः, ईषत्ताडनं, इङ्गितं.

To JOGGLE, JOGGLING. *See* JOG, JOGGING.

To JOIN, *v. a.* युज् (c. 7. युनक्ति, युंक्ते, योक्तुं, c. 10. योजयति -यितुं), संयुज्, आयुज्, समायुज्, सन्धा (c. 3. -दधाति -धातुं), उपसन्धा, सम्बन्ध् (c. 9. -बध्नाति -बन्धुं), संश्लिष् (c. 10. -श्लेषयति -यितुं), श्लिष्, संहन् (c. 2. -हन्ति -न्तुं), सङ्क्रम् (c. 10. -गमयति -यितुं), संलग्नीकृ, एकीकृ, एकत्र कृ. —(Tie together) ग्रन्थ् (c. 9. ग्रथ्नाति, ग्रन्थितुं), योक्त्र (nom. योक्त्रयति -यितुं).

To JOIN, *v. n.* (Be in contact, unite) संयुज् in pass. (-युज्यते), समायुज्, सन्धा in pass. (-धीयते), संश्लिष् in pass. (-श्लिष्यते), संहन् in pass. (-हन्यते), सङ्गम् (c. 1. -गच्छति -गन्तुं), समे (समेति -तुं, rt. इ), संलग्नीभू, एकीभू, संसक्तीभू, एकत्र भू, सम्मिल् (c. 6. -मिलति -मेलितुं).

JOINED, *p. p.* युक्तः -क्ता -क्तं, संयुक्तः -क्ता -क्तं, संयोजितः -ता -तं, समायुक्तः -क्ता -क्तं, संयुतः -ता -तं, योजितः -ता -तं, समायुतः -ता -तं, युतः -ता -तं, संश्लिष्टः -ष्टा -ष्टं, श्लिष्टः -ष्टा -ष्टं, संहतः -ता -तं, अभिसंहतः -ता -तं, संसक्तः -क्ता -क्तं, समासक्तः -क्ता -क्तं, सम्बद्धः -द्धा -द्धं, बद्धः -द्धा -द्धं, लग्नः -ग्ना -ग्नं, संलग्नः -ग्ना -ग्नं, विलग्नः -ग्ना -ग्नं, संहितः -ता -तं, सन्धितः -ता -तं, उपाहितः -ता -तं, सङ्गतः -ता -तं, समितः -ता -तं, मिलितः -ता -तं, एकीकृतः -ता -तं, घटितः -ता -तं; 'with joined hands,' संश्लिष्टाभ्यां पाणिभ्यां, बद्धाञ्जलिः -लिः -लि, अवहिताञ्जलिः -लिः -लि, अभिगृहीतपाणिः -णिः -णि.

JOINER, *s.* सूत्रधारः, काष्ठतक्षकः, तक्षकः, तक्षा *m.* (न्), त्वष्टा *m.* (ष्टृ).

JOINERY, *s.* काष्ठतक्षणं, त्वष्टिः *f.*, तक्षणं, सूत्रधारकर्म्म *n.* (न्), तक्षकक्रिया.

JOINING, *s.* संयोगः, योगः, सन्धानं, सन्धिः *m.*, श्लेषः, संश्लेषः, संघातः, सङ्गः, सङ्क्रमः, समागमः, समासक्तिः *f.*, संसक्तिः.

JOINT, *s.* (Of the body) सन्धिः *m.*, ग्रन्थिः *m.*, अस्थिसन्धिः *m.*, अस्थिग्रन्थिः *m.*, परग्रन्थिः *m.*, पर्व्व *n.* (न्), अस्थिपर्व्व *n.*, मर्म्म *n.* (न्), काण्डः -ण्डं, जीवस्थानं, परुस् ind.; 'the knee-joint,' जानुसन्धिः *m.*, जङ्घोरुसन्धिः; 'the thigh-joint,' ऊरुपर्व्व *n.*; 'the thumb-joint,' अङ्गुष्ठपर्व्व *n.*; 'of the neck,' ग्रीवासन्धिः *m.*, सन्धिः; 'of the shoulder,' विरु *n.*; 'to put out of joint,' विसन्धीकृ.—(Knot of a plant) ग्रन्थिः *m.*, पर्व्व *n.* (न्).

JOINT, *a.* (Shared by two or more) संविभक्तः -क्ता -क्तं, अविभक्तः -क्ता -क्तं, अंशितः -ता -तं, साधारणः -णा -णी -णं, सामान्यः -न्या -न्यं, अनेकस्वामिकः -का -कं, usually expressed by सह in comp.; as, 'joint proprietor,' सहस्वामी *m.* (न्), सहाधिकारी *m.* (न्); 'joint possessor,' सहभोजी *m.* (न्); 'joint-heir,' समाधिकारी.—(United in the same office) एकाधिकारी *m.* (न्), एककार्य्यकारी *m.* (न्), सद्वितीयः -या -यं.—(Combined) सङ्घातवान् -वती -वत् (त्), सम्भूयकारी -रिणी -रि (न्).

To JOINT, *v. a.* (Form with joints) सन्धिविशिष्टं -ष्टां कृ, ग्रन्थियुक्तं -क्तां कृ.—(Divide in the joints) सन्धिभेदं कृ, सन्धिभङ्गं कृ.

JOINTED, *p. p.* or *a.* (Formed with joints) ग्रन्थिलः -ला -लं, ग्रन्थिमान् -मती -मत् (त्), सन्धिविशिष्टः -ष्टा -ष्टं, सन्धियुक्तः -क्ता -क्तं.—(Divided in the joints) भिन्नसन्धिः -न्धिः -न्धि, विसन्धितः-ता -तं.

JOINT-HEIR, *s.* समांशी *m.* (न्), समभागी *m.* (न्), समाधिकारी *m.* (न्), समांशहारी *m.* (न्), भागी *m.* (न्), संविभागी, भागहरः, समभागहारी *m.*, भागधेयः, सहाधिकारी *m.* *See* COHEIR.

JOINTLY, *adv.* संयोगतस्, योगतस्, सहितं, समं, सह, सम्भूय, एकचित्तीभूय, अपृथक्, युगपत्, सार्द्धं.

JOINTURE, *s.* विधवाधनं, स्त्रीधनं, स्त्रीवृत्तिः *f.*, भर्तृदत्तं, स्वामिदत्तं.

JOIST, *s.* गृहतलालम्बी दीर्घदारुः, हर्म्यतलोत्तम्भकं दीर्घकाष्ठं.

JOKE, *s.* परिहासः, हास्यं, हासिका, परिहासवाक्यं, परिहासोक्तिः *f.*, रसः, रसिकवाक्यं, नर्म्म *n.* (न्), विनोदः, विनोदोक्तिः *f.*, लालिका, क्ष्वेलः, टट्टरी, व्याहारः, प्रपञ्चः, कौतुकं; 'in joke,' परिहासेन; 'jokes to the bridegroom,' जामृलः.

To JOKE, *v. a.* हस् (c. 1. हसति -सितुं), प्रहस्, विहस्, संविहस्, व्यतिहस्, सम्प्रहस्, परिहस्, परिहासं कृ, हास्यं कृ, परिहासवाक्यं वद् (c. 1. वदति -दितुं), विनोदं कृ, विनोदवाक्यं वद्, भण्ड् (c. 1. भण्डते -ण्डितुं), विलस् (c. 1. -लसति -सितुं), खेला (nom. खेलायति), नर्म्म कृ; 'speak in joke,' परिहासेन वद्.

JOKER, *s.* परिहासवेदी *m.* (न्), परिहासकः, हास्यकारी *m.* (न्), विनोदभाषी *m.* (न्), वैहासिकः, विदूषकः, विलासी *m.* (न्).

JOLE, *s.* गण्डः-ण्डं, कपोलः, गण्डस्थलः-ली; 'cheek by jole,' गण्डागण्डि.

JOLLITY, JOLLINESS, *s.* उत्सवकरणं, उत्सवः, समुत्सवः, उल्लसता, उल्लासः, आनन्दः, आह्लादः, हर्षः, प्रहर्षः, प्रमोदः, प्रहसनं, प्रहासः, प्रहसितं, प्रहृष्टता, प्रफुल्लता, सानन्दता, आमोदः, मुदा.

JOLLY, *a.* उत्सवकारी -रिणी -रि (न्), सोत्सवः -वा -वं, हृष्टः -ष्टा -ष्टं, प्रहृष्टः -ष्टा -ष्टं, आनन्दी -न्दिनी -न्दि (न्), सानन्दः -न्दा -न्दं, हृष्टहृदयः -या -यं, हर्षणः -णा -णं, उल्लसः -सा -सं, उल्लसितः -ता -तं, उल्लासी -सिनी -सि (न्), प्रहासी -सिनी -सि (न्), प्रमोदी -दिनी -दि (न्), मुदितः -ता -तं, प्रफुल्लः -ल्ला -ल्लं, हासी &c., परिहासशीलः -ला -लं, विलासी -सिनी -सि (न्), कृतकौतुकः -का -कं, सुमनाः -नाः -नः (स्).

JOLLY-BOAT, *s.* वृहन्नौकासम्बन्धिनी क्षुद्रनौका.

To JOLT, *v. a.* क्षुभ् (c. 10. क्षोभयति -यितुं), क्षोभं कृ, विषमभूमिगमनप्रयुक्तं क्षोभं कृ, आकस्मिकक्षोभं कृ.

To JOLT, *v. n.* विषमभूमिगमनत्वात् क्षुभ् (c. 4. क्षुभ्यति, क्षोभितुं).

JOLT, *s.* क्षोभः, रथक्षोभः, विषमभूमिगमनप्रयुक्तः क्षोभः, आकस्मिकक्षोभः.

JOLTED, *p.p.* क्षुब्धः -ब्धा -ब्धं, विक्षुब्धः -ब्धा -ब्धं, क्षोभितः -ता -तं.

JOLTHEAD, *s.* स्थूलबुद्धिः *m.*, मन्दबुद्धिः *m.*, मूर्खः, बटुकः.

JONQUIL, *s.* उत्पलजातीयो नानावर्णः पुष्पभेदः.

To JOSTLE, *v. a.* जनसम्मर्द्दे स्कन्धेन ताडयित्वा क्षुभ् (c. 10. क्षोभयति -यितुं) or निरस् (c. 4. -अस्यति -असितुं) or निःसृ (c. 10. -सारयति -यितुं) or निराकृ or सबाध् (c. 1. -बाधते -धितुं).

JOSTLING, *s.* जनसम्मर्द्दे परस्परसंक्षोभः or परस्परसमाघातः, परस्परघर्षणं, परस्परसम्मर्द्दः, स्कन्धताडनं, प्रतिघातः.

JOT, *s.* लवः, लवमात्रं, कणमात्रं, बिन्दुमात्रं, लवलेशः, लेशः, अणुः *m.*, परमाणुः *m.*, कणिका, रजःकणः, तिलमात्रं.

To JOT, *v. a.* स्मरणार्थं किञ्चिद् लिख् (c. 6. लिखति, लेखितुं) or अभिलिख्.

JOTTING, *s.* स्मरणार्थं किञ्चिल्लिखनं, स्मरणार्थलिखितं.

JOURNAL, *a.* (Diary) दिनवृत्तपत्रं, दिनव्यवहारलेख्यं, आह्निकव्यवहारपुस्तकं, दिनचर्य्यालेखः, दैनिकवृत्तान्तपुस्तकं, दिनचरित्रलेखः, आह्निकपत्रकं, दैनिकपत्रकं, पञ्जिका, पञ्जिः -ञ्जी *f.*, पदभञ्जिका.—(Newspaper published daily) प्रतिदिनं प्रकाशीकृतं समाचारपत्रं, वार्त्तापत्रं, वाचिकपत्रं.

JOURNALIST, *s.* आह्निकपत्रलेखकः, दैनिकपत्रलिख् *m.* (ख्).—(Conductor of a newspaper) समाचारपत्रप्रकाशकः, वार्त्तापत्रलेखकः.

JOURNEY, *s.* अध्वा *m.* (न्), अध्वगमनं, मार्गः, मार्गगमनं, मार्गक्रमणं, यात्रा, यात्राकरणं, यानं, प्रयाणं, प्रस्थानं, प्रस्थितिः *f.*, व्रज्या, भ्रमणं, देशभ्रमणं, पर्यटनं, प्रवासः, प्रवासगमनं; 'a long journey,' दीर्घाध्वा *m.* -ध्व *n.* (न्); 'a day's journey,' एकाहगमः -मनं; 'to return from a journey,' प्रवासाद् आगम् (c. 1. -गच्छति -गन्तुं); 'a pleasant journey to you,' शिवास् ते पन्थानः सन्तु.

To JOURNEY, *v. n.* अध्वना or मार्गेण गम् (c. 1. गच्छति, गन्तुं) or या (c. 2. याति -तुं) or व्रज् (c. 1. व्रजति -जितुं) or चर् (c. 1. चरति -रितुं), मार्गगमनं कृ, अध्वगमनं कृ, यात्रां कृ, देशभ्रमणं कृ, देशाद्देशं भ्रम् (c. 4. भ्राम्यति, भ्रमितुं) or परिभ्रम् or पर्यट् (c. 1. अटति -टितुं).

JOURNEYER, *s.* अध्वगः -गामी *m.* (न्), अध्वनीनः, अध्वन्यः, यात्रिकः, यायी *m.* (न्), पथिकः, सारणिकः, पादविकः.

JOURNEYING, *s.* अध्वगमनं, मार्गगमनं, यात्राकरणं, देशभ्रमणं.

JOURNEYMAN, *s.* वेतनार्थं कर्म्मकारः or कर्म्मकरः or शिल्पकारः or शिल्पकर्म्मकरः, हस्तकर्म्मकारः, वैतनिकः, वेतनार्थी *m.* (न्), व्रातीनः.

JOURNEY-WORK, *s.* शिल्पकर्म्म *n.* (न्), हस्तकर्म्म *n.*, वैतनिककर्म्म *n.*, शिल्पं.

JOVE, *s.* (The god). *See* INDRA.

JOVIAL, *a.* उत्सवकारी -रिणी -रि (न्), नित्योत्सवी -विनी -वि (न्), सदोत्सवी &c., कृतोत्सवः -वा -वं, उल्लासी -सिनी -सि (न्), सदानन्दी -न्दिनी -न्दि (न्), प्रहृष्टः -ष्टा -ष्टं, परिहासशीलः -ला -लं, सदाप्रमोदी -दिनी -दि (न्), उत्सवप्रियः -या -यं.

JOVIALLY, *adv.* सोत्सवं, महोत्सवेन, सदानन्दपूर्व्वं, उत्सववत्, प्रहृष्टवत्.

JOVIALITY, JOVIALNESS, *s.* उत्सवकरणं, नित्योत्सवः, सदानन्दः, नित्यानन्दः, उल्लसता, नित्योल्लासः, हर्षः, प्रहर्षः, आह्लादः, प्रहसनं, हास्यं, प्रहासः, प्रहृष्टता.

JOWL, *s.* (Cheek) गण्डः, कपोलः. *See* JOLE.

JOWLER, *s.* मृगव्यकुक्कुरः, मृगव्यश्वा *m.* (न्), मृगदंशकः.

JOY, *s.* आनन्दः, हर्षः, आह्लादः, प्रह्लादः, प्रमोदः, आमोदः, नन्दः, ह्लादः -दनं, मोदः, मुदा, मुद् *f.*, तुष्टिः *f.*, हृष्टता, प्रहर्षः, प्रहृष्टता, मदः, प्रमदः, मादः, तुष्टिः *f.*, तोषः, परितोषः, सन्तोषः, सन्तुष्टिः *f.*, विलासः, उल्लासः, उल्लसता -त्वं, प्रफुल्लता, प्रीतिः *f.*, प्रीतता, सुखं, सौख्यं, चित्तप्रसन्नता, शर्म्म *n.* (न्), नन्दथुः *m.*, धन्यता, आनन्दथुः *m.*, उत्सवः, रभसः, उत्साहः.—(The cause of joy) नन्दनः -ना -नं, आनन्ददः -दा -दं; 'joy and sorrow,' हर्षोद्वेगं.

To JOY, *v. n.* नन्द् (c. 1. नन्दति -न्दितुं), आनन्द्, हृष् (c. 4. हृष्यति, हर्षितुं), ह्लाद् (c. 1. ह्लादते -दितुं), उल्लस् (c. 1. -लसति -सितुं), रम् (c. 4. रमते, रन्तुं), तुष् (c. 4. तुष्यति, तोष्टुं), मद् (c. 4. माद्यति, मदितुं).

To JOY, *v. a.* (Cause joy) नन्द् (c. 10. नन्दयति -यितुं), हृष् (c. 10. हर्षयति -यितुं), प्रहृष्.—(Give one joy, congratulate) अभिनन्द्, अभिवन्द् (c. 1. -वन्दते -न्दितुं), धन्यवादं कृ. *See To* CONGRATULATE.

JOYFUL, *a.* आनन्दी -न्दिनी -न्दि (न्), आनन्दितः -ता -तं, सानन्दः -न्दा

-न्दं, तुष्टः -ष्टा -ष्टं, प्रहृष्टः -ष्टा -ष्टं, हृष्टमानसः -सा -सं, हृष्टहृदयः -या -यं, प्रहर्षितः -ता -तं, हर्षितः -ता -तं, प्रहर्षणः -णा -णं, हर्षमाणः -णा -णं, हर्षणः -णा -णं, आह्लादी -दिनी -दि (न्), ह्लादी &c.. प्रह्लादितः -ता -तं, आह्लादितः -ता -तं, ह्लादितः -ता -तं, प्रमोदी -दिनी -दि (न्), प्रमुदितः -ता -तं, मुदितः -ता -तं, मुदान्वितः -ता -तं, हर्षान्वितः -ता -तं, प्रमुद् *m.f.n.*, प्रफुल्लः -ल्ला -ल्लं, हर्षयुक्तः -क्ता -क्तं, तुष्टः -ष्टा -ष्टं, परितुष्टः -ष्टा -ष्टं, उल्लसः -सा -सं, उल्लासी -सिनी -सि (न्), उल्लसितः -ता -तं, प्रीतः -ता -तं, प्रह्लन्नः -न्ना -न्नं, आनन्दमयः -यी -यं, हर्षाक्रान्तः -न्ता -न्तं, हर्षाविष्टः -ष्टा -ष्टं, सुखी -खिनी -खि (न्), मत्तः -त्ता -त्तं, विशोकः -का -कं.—(Causing joy) हर्षकः -का -कं, हर्षदः -दा -दं, हर्षावहः -हा -हं, आनन्ददः -दा -दं, आनन्दकरः -री -रं, मोदकः -का -कं, सुभगः -गा -गं.

JOYFULLY, *adv.* सानन्दं, सहर्षं, साह्लादं, हर्षेण, प्रहर्षेण, प्रह्लादेन, प्रमोदेन, सामोदं, उल्लासेन, सोल्लासं, आनन्दपूर्वं, हृष्टमनसा, हृष्टवत्, सन्तोषेण.

JOYFULNESS, *s.* सानन्दत्वं, हृष्टता, प्रहृष्टता, प्रफुल्लता, आनन्दः. *See* JOY.

JOYLESS, *a.* निरानन्दः -न्दा -न्दं, आनन्दहीनः -ना -नं, आनन्दशून्यः -न्या -न्यं, अहर्षः -र्षा -र्षं, अहृष्टः -ष्टा -ष्टं, अहर्षितः -ता -तं, हर्षहीनः -ना -नं, आह्लादहीनः -ना -नं, निराह्लादः -दा -दं, अनाह्लादी -दिनी -दि (न्), असुखी -खिनी -खि (न्), असुखः -खा -खं.—(Giving no joy) असुखदः -दा -दं, असुखावहः -हा -हं, अनानन्ददः -दा -दं, अहर्षदः -दा -दं.

JOYLESSNESS, *s.* निरानन्दत्वं, आनन्दहीनता, निराह्लादत्वं, हर्षशून्यता.

JOYOUS, *a.* आनन्दी -न्दिनी -न्दि (न्), सानन्दः -न्दा -न्दं, प्रहृष्टः -ष्टा -ष्टं, आनन्दवृत्तिः -त्तिः -त्ति, प्रसन्नचित्तः -त्ता -त्तं, उल्लासी -सिनी -सि (न्). *See* JOYFUL.

JOYOUSLY, *adv.* सानन्दं, सहर्षं, साह्लादं, हृष्टचेतसा, प्रसन्नमनसा.

JOYOUSNESS, *s.* हृष्टता, प्रहृष्टता, सानन्दत्वं, चित्तप्रसन्नता, प्रफुल्लता.

JUBILANT, *a.* जयशब्दकारी -रिणी -रि (न्), जयशब्दोच्चारी -रिणी -रि (न्), जयध्वनिकारी &c., जयप्रशंसाकारी &c., जयशब्दघोषी -षिणी -षि (न्).

JUBILEE, *s.* महोत्सवः, महोत्सवकालः, समुत्सवः, उत्सवः, उत्सवकालः:

JUCUNDITY, *s.* रम्यता, रमणीयता, प्रियता, नन्दकत्वं, कान्तत्वं.

JUDAIC, JUDAICAL, *a.* यिहुदीयः -या -यं, यिहुदीयव्यवहारः -रा -रं.

JUDGE, *s.* (Officer who hears and determines causes) धर्म्माध्यक्षः, धर्म्माधिकारी *m.* (न्), न्यायाधीशः, न्यायाधिपतिः *m.*, प्राड्विवाकः, विचारकर्त्ता *m.* (र्तृ), विचारकः, दण्डनायकः, व्यवहर्त्ता *m.* (र्तृ), अक्षदर्शकः, आक्षपाटिकः, स्थेयः, आधिकरणिकः, निर्णेता *m.* (तृ), निर्णयकारः.—(One who has skill to decide on the merits of any thing, a connoisseur) गुणग्राही *m.* (न्), गुणग्राहकः, गुणज्ञः, अभिज्ञः, विज्ञः, ज्ञानी *m.* (न्), परीक्षकः, तद्विद् *m.*, रसज्ञः, विवेकी *m.* (न्), विवेचकः, विवेकदृश्वा *m.* (न्), परिच्छेदकः.

To JUDGE, *v. n.* (Form an opinion, determine) विचर् (c. 10. -चारयति -यितुं), विचारं कृ, निर्णी (c. 1. -णयति -णेतुं), निर्णयं कृ, निश्चि (c. 5. -चिनोति -चेतुं), निश्चयं कृ, निर्धृ (c. 10. -धारयति -यितुं), अवधृ, निर्धारणं कृ.—(Weigh, consider, deliberate) मनसा विचर्, वितर्क् (c. 10. -तर्कयति -यितुं), वितर्कं कृ, विमृश् (c. 6. -मृशति -म्रष्टुं), विगण् (c. 10. -गणयति -यितुं), विक्लृप् (c. 10. -कल्पयति -यितुं), समर्थ (nom. समर्थयति -यितुं), समर्थनां कृ, मनसा विवेचनं कृ.—(Discriminate) विज्ञा (c. 9. -जानाति -नीते -ज्ञातुं), परिच्छिद् (c. 7. -छिनत्ति -छेत्तुं), विविच् (c. 7. -विनक्ति -वेक्तुं, c. 10. -वेचयति -यितुं), विभू (c. 10. -भावयति -यितुं), विचर्, विवेकं कृ, परिच्छेदं कृ.—(Examine) परीक्ष् (c. 1. -ईक्षते -क्षितुं), परीक्षां कृ.—(Determine causes judicially, pass sentence) विचर्, विचारं कृ, निर्णी, निर्णयं कृ, प्रणयनं कृ, व्यवहारदर्शनं कृ, तीर् (c. 10. तीरयति -यितुं), न्यायं कृ.

To JUDGE, *v. a.* (Examine, bring under investigation) परीक्ष् (c. 1. -ईक्षते -क्षितुं), अनुसन्धा (c. 3. -दधाति -धातुं), अनुयुज् (c. 7. -युनक्ति -युंक्ते -योक्तुं), परीक्षितं -तां कृ.—(Judicially) विचर् (c. 10. -चारयति -यितुं), निर्णी (c. 1. -णयति -णेतुं), तीर् (c. 10. तीरयति -यितुं), विचारणं कृ, निर्णयं कृ.—(Censure, impute fault) निन्द् (c. 1. निन्दति -न्दितुं), दोषीकृ, दोषारोपणं कृ, अपवद् (c. 1. -वदति -दितुं), दोषप्रसङ्गं कृ.—(Consider, reckon) तर्क् (c. 10. तर्कयति -यितुं), मन् (c. 4. मन्यते, मन्तुं).

JUDGESHIP, *s.* धर्म्माध्यक्षत्वं, न्यायाधीशत्वं, धर्म्माधिकारः -रिता.

JUDGMENT, *s.* (Discrimination) विवेकः, विवेचनं, परिच्छेदः, विचारः -रणं -णा, विज्ञानं, विभावनं, विवेकदृश्वत्वं, अवबोधः, विविक्तिः *f.*—(Exercise of judgment after deliberation) विचारः -रणं -णा, विवेचना, सम्प्रधारणा.—(Knowledge derived from the comparison of ideas) अनुभवः, अनुभूतिः, अनुमानं, अनुमितिः *f.*, तर्कः, परामर्शः, ज्ञानं.—(Notion, opinion) बुद्धिः *f.*, मतिः *f.*, मतं, सङ्कल्पः, बोधः; 'according to one's judgment,' यथाबुद्धि, यथामति.—(The faculty concerned in weighing the merits or advantages of any thing) गुणागुणविषयका बुद्धिः, हिताहितविषयका बुद्धिः or धीशक्तिः.—(Determination, decision) निर्णयः, निश्चयः, निश्चितं, विचारः, सङ्कल्पः, निर्धारणं, अवधारणं, निष्पत्तिः *f.*—(Judicial sentence) निर्णयपादः, निर्णयः, विचारः, दण्डाज्ञा, आधर्षणं, तीरणं, तीरितं.—(Divine ordinance) ईश्वरविधिः *m.*, ईश्वरविधानं, ईश्वरनियमः, ईश्वरशासनं.

JUDGMENT-DAY, *s.* विचारदिनं, विचारदिवसः, न्यायकरणदिवसः.

JUDGMENT-HALL, *s.* विचारसभा, धर्म्मसभा, न्यायसभा, विचारशाला.

JUDGMENT-SEAT, *s.* धर्म्मासनं, न्यायासनं, विचारासनं.

JUDICATORY, *s.* (Court of justice) धर्म्मसभा, विचारसभा, विचारस्थानं, न्यायसभा, व्यवहारमण्डपः, व्यवहारदर्शनशाला, राजद्वारं, धर्म्माधिकरणं, न्यायागारं, सदस् *n.*

JUDICATURE, *s.* (Power of administering justice) व्यवहारदर्शनाधिकारः, विचाराध्यक्षता, न्यायाधिकारः, न्यायकरणाधिकारः, धर्म्माधिकरणं, विचारकरणाधिकारः; 'simple judicature,' व्यवहारमातृका.—(Court of judicature) धर्म्मसभा. *See* JUDICATORY.

JUDICIAL, *a.* (Pertaining to the practice of courts of justice) व्यावहारिकः -की -कं, व्यवहारिकः -की -कं, व्यवहारी -रिणी -रि (न्), व्यवहारसम्बन्धी -न्धिनी -न्धि (न्), व्यवहारविषयः -या -यं; 'judicial proceedings or investigation,' व्यवहारः, व्यवहारदर्शनं, क्रिया, विचारः.—(Pertaining to the administration of justice) व्यवहारदर्शनसम्बन्धी &c., न्यायकरणसम्बन्धी &c.—(Proceeding from court of justice) व्यवहारदर्शनप्रयुक्तः -क्ता -क्तं, न्यायदर्शनप्रयुक्तः -क्ता -क्तं.—(Inflicted as a penalty) दण्डरूपः -पा -पं, शिक्षाहेतुकः -का -कं.

JUDICIALLY, *adv.* विचारानुसारेण, विचारानुक्रमेण, धर्म्मानुसारात्, व्यवहारानुक्रमेण, यथाव्यवहारं, विचारसभासकाशात्.

JUDICIARY, *a.* विचारकः -का -कं, व्यावहारिकः -की -कं, निर्णायकः -का -कं, व्यवहारदर्शनसम्बन्धी -न्धिनी -न्धि (न्), धर्म्मसभासम्बन्धी &c.

JUDICIOUS, *a.* (According to sound judgment) विवेकानुसारी -रिणी -रि (न्), सुयुक्तः -क्ता -क्तं, युक्तः -क्ता -क्तं, उपयुक्तः -क्ता -क्तं, यथोचितः -ता -तं, उचितः -ता -तं, समञ्जसः -सा -सं, न्याय्यः -य्या -य्यं, सङ्गतः -ता -तं, सविवेकः -का -कं.—(Acting with judgment, possessing judgment, said of persons) विवेकी -किनी -कि (न्), विवेकदृश्वा -श्वा -श्व (न्), बुद्धिमान् -मती -मत् (त्), मतिमान् &c., नीतिमान् &c., नीतिज्ञः -ज्ञा -ज्ञं, विज्ञः -ज्ञा -ज्ञं, प्राज्ञः -ज्ञा -ज्ञं, मनस्वी -स्विनी -स्वि (न्), विमृश्यकारी -रिणी -रि (न्), समीक्ष्यकारी &c., ज्ञानी -निनी -नि (न्), विशेषज्ञः -ज्ञा -ज्ञं, हिताहितदर्शी &c., सदसद्दर्शी &c., सुपरिच्छेदकः -का -कं, उचितज्ञः -ज्ञा -ज्ञं.

JUDICIOUSLY, *adv.* विवेकानुसारेण, सविवेकं, विज्ञवत्, प्राज्ञवत्, नीतिज्ञवत्, सपरिच्छेदं, विज्ञजनवत्, बुधवत्, युक्तं, यथोचितं, समञ्जसं, सम्यक्, सुष्ठु, सुविमृश्य, सुविचार्य्य.

JUDICIOUSNESS, *s.* युक्तता, उपयुक्तता, सविवेकत्वं, बुद्धिमत्त्वं, विज्ञता.

JUG, *s.* कुम्भः, मृत्कांश्यं, मृत्कांस्यं, कांस्यं, कंसः -सं, कंशः, मृद्भाण्डं, पुटग्रीवः, कलशः, कलसः, जलपात्रं, उदपात्रं.

To JUGGLE, *v. a.* (Play tricks by sleight of hand) मायां कृ, इन्द्रियमायां कृ, दृष्टिमायां कृ, इन्द्रियमोहं कृ, दृष्टिमोहं कृ, कुहकं कृ, इन्द्रियजालं कृ, हस्तलाघवं कृ, कुसृतिं कृ, दृष्टिबन्धनं कृ.—(Deceive by trick) मुह् (c. 10. मोहयति -यितुं), छल् (c. 10. छलयति -यितुं), वञ्च् (c. 10. वञ्चयते -ति -यितुं).

JUGGLE, *s.* माया, मोहः, कुहकः, छलं, कूटता, कूटः, वञ्चनं.

JUGGLER, *s.* मायी *m.* (न्), मायाकारः, मायाजीवी *m.* (न्), मायावी *m.* (न्), कुहककारः, कुहकजीवी *m.*, कुहकः, इन्द्रजालिकः, ऐन्द्रजालिकः, इन्द्रियमोही *m.* (न्), प्रतिहारः -रकः, प्रातिहारिकः -रकः, कौसृतिकः, योगी *m.* (न्), सम्प्रयोगी *m.*, अभिचारविद् *m.*, शौभिकः, आहितुण्डिकः; 'female juggler,' माया, मायिनी, मायाजीविनी, शाम्बरी.

JUGGLERY, JUGGLING, *s.* (Legerdemain) हस्तलाघवं, हस्तचापल्यं, माया, कुहकः, कुहकवृत्तिः *f.*, इन्द्रजालं, इन्द्रियमोहः, कुसृतिः *f.*, दृष्टिमोहः, दृष्टिबन्धः, अभिचारः, जालं, योगः, सम्प्रयोगः.—(Trickery) कूटता, छलं, वञ्चना.

JUGULAR, *a.* कण्ठ्यः -ण्ठ्या -ण्ठ्यं, कण्ठसम्बन्धी &c., कण्ठस्थः -स्था -स्थं, ग्रीवासम्बन्धीयः -या -यं.

JUICE, *s.* रसः, द्रवः, निर्यासः, सारः, सुधा, आसवः, नीरं, मज्जा, स्वेदः.—(From the elephant's temples) मदः, दानं, हस्तिमदः, गजकुसुमं; 'its issue from the forehead,' मदप्रयोगः.

JUICELESS, *a.* नीरसः -सा -सं, विरसः -सा -सं, अरसः -सा -सं, निरसः -सा -सं, रसहीनः -ना -नं, रसशून्यः -न्या -न्यं, असारः -रा -रं, निस्सारः -रा -रं, सारवर्जितः -ता -तं, शुष्कः -ष्का -ष्कं, पिञ्जरः -रा -रं.

JUICINESS, *s.* सरसता, रसवत्त्वं, रसिकत्वं, रसबाहुल्यं, बहुरसत्वं.

JUICY, *a.* सरसः -सा -सं, रसवान् -वती -वत् (त्), रसी -सिनी -सि (न्), रसिकः -का -कं, रसाढ्यः -ढ्या -ढ्यं, रस्यः -स्या -स्यं, बहुरसः -सा -सं, सारवान् &c., बहुसारः -रा -रं.

JUJUBE, *s.* (The tree) बदरः -री *f.* -रिः *m.*, बदरिका, वदरिका, राजबदरः, कर्कन्धूः *m. f.* -न्धुः, कोलिः -ली *f.*, कुकोलं, सौवीरं, कर्कशी -शिका, कुवलः; 'the fruit,' बदरं.

JULY, *s.* आषाढः -ढकः, श्रावणः -णिकः, उत्तराषाढः, पूर्व्वश्रावणः, आषाढश्रावणं, सप्तममासः.

To JUMBLE, *v. a.* सम्मिश्र् (c. 10. -मिश्रयति -यितुं), सम्मिश्रीकृ, व्यामिश्र्, मिश्र्, सङ्कॄ (c. 6. -किरति -करितुं -रीतुं), सङ्करीकृ, सङ्कीर्णीकृ, सङ्कुलीकृ, व्यस्तव्यस्तीकृ, संक्षिप् (c. 6. -क्षिपति -क्षेप्तुं), विक्षिप्.

To JUMBLE, *v. n.* (Be jumbled) सम्मिश्रीभू, सङ्कॄ in pass. (-कीर्य्यते), सङ्कीर्णीभू, सङ्करीभू, सङ्कुलीभू, सम्मिश्रितः -ता -तं भू.

JUMBLE, *s.* सम्मिश्रणं, मिश्रणं, सङ्करः, साङ्कर्य्यं, सङ्कीर्णत्वं, व्यस्तव्यस्तता, सङ्कुलता, सन्निपातः, संक्षोभः, व्यतिकरः, सङ्कलनं.

JUMBLED, *p. p.* सम्मिश्रितः -ता -तं, सम्मिश्रः -श्रा -श्रं, सम्मिश्रीकृतः -ता -तं, मिश्रितः -ता -तं, सङ्करीकृतः -ता -तं, सङ्कीर्णः -र्णा -र्णं, सङ्कुलः -ला -लं, व्यस्तव्यस्तः -स्ता -स्तं, सन्निपतितः -ता -तं, संक्षुब्धः -ब्धा -ब्धं.

JUMNÁ, *s.* (A river which rises in a mountain called Kalinda, in the Himalaya range, and, after a course of 378 miles, falls into the Ganges below Allahabad; she is daughter of the sun and sister of Yama) यमुना, कालिन्दी, कलिन्दकन्या, कलिन्दनन्दिनी, कलिन्दशैलजाता.—(As daughter of the sun) सूर्य्यजा, सूर्य्यतनया, सूर्य्यपुत्री, दैवाकरी.—(As sister of Yama) यमस्वसा *f.* (ृ), यमभगिनी.—(Of a dark blue colour) श्यामा.

To JUMP, *v. a.* प्लु (c. 1. प्लवते, प्लोतुं), वल्ग् (c. 1. वल्गति -ल्गितुं), आवल्ग्, स्कन्द् (c. 1. स्कन्दते, स्कन्तुं), झम्पं कृ; 'to jump over,' लङ्घ् (c. 10. लङ्घयति -यितुं), अभिलङ्घ्; 'to jump over a wall,' प्राकारलङ्घनं कृ; 'jump up,' उत्प्लु, समुत्प्लु, उत्पत् (c. 1. -पतति -तितुं), प्रोत्पत्, उत्सृप् (c. 1. -सर्पति -सर्प्तुं); 'jump down,' अवप्लु, अवस्कन्द्; 'to jump out from,' प्रस्कन्द्; 'to jump about,' नृत् (c. 4. नृत्यति, नर्त्तितुं); 'having jumped up,' उत्प्लुत्य.

JUMP, *s.* प्लवः, प्लवनं, प्लुतं, उत्प्लवनं, उत्प्लुतं, झम्पः -म्पा, वल्गितं, उच्छलः, उत्पतनं, उत्सर्पणं, अवस्कन्दः.

JUMPED, *p.p.* प्लुतः -ता -तं, उत्प्लुतः -ता -तं, वल्गितः -ता -तं, उत्पतितः -ता -तं.

JUMPER, *s.* प्लवकः, प्लवनकारी *m.* (न्), झम्पकारी *m.*, झम्पी *m.* (न्), उत्प्लवकः, उत्पतिता *m.* (ृ); 'going by jumps,' प्लवगः -गतिः *m.*

JUMPING, *s.* (Act of jumping) प्लवनं, उत्प्लवनं, उत्पतनं, उत्सर्पणं.

JUMPING, *part.* प्लवमानः -ना -नं, वल्गन् -ल्गन्ती -ल्गत् (त्), उत्पतिष्णुः -ष्णुः -ष्णु, उत्पतिता -त्री -तृ (ृ).

JUNCATE, *s.* किलाटपिष्टकः, दधिशर्कराादिमयो मोदकः, मिष्टान्नं.

JUNCOUS, *a.* दर्भविकीर्णः -र्णा -र्णं, नडकीयः -या -यं.

JUNCTION, *s.* योगः, संयोगः, संयोजनं, समायोगः, सम्प्रयोगः, युक्तिः *f.*, सन्धिः *m.*, सन्धानं, श्लेषः, संश्लेषः, सङ्गः -ङ्गमः -ङ्गतिः *f.* -तं, समागमः, संहतिः *f.*, संघातः, संसक्तिः *f.*, समासक्तिः *f.*, संसृष्टिः *f.*, संसर्गः, मेलनं, सम्पर्कः, सम्बन्धः, सक्तिः *f.*, आसक्तिः *f.*, प्रसक्तिः *f.*—(Point of union) सन्धिस्थानं.

JUNCTURE, *s.* (Point of time, crisis) लग्नं, सन्धिः *m.*, कालसन्धिः *m.*, सन्धिवेला, समयः, वेला, कालः, प्रसङ्गः, अवकाशः.—(Joint, articulation) सन्धिः *m.*, ग्रन्थिः *m.*—(Seam) सीवनं.

JUNE, *s.* ज्येष्ठः, आषाढः -ढकः, ज्यैष्ठः, ज्येष्ठामूलीयः, पूर्व्वाषाढः, उत्तरज्येष्ठः, ज्येष्ठाषाढकं.

JUNGLE, *s.* जङ्गलं, जाङ्गलं, प्रस्तारः, जङ्गलस्थानं, गुल्मावृतस्थानं.

JUNGLY, *a.* जाङ्गलः -ली -लं, जङ्गली -लिनी -लि (न्), प्रस्तारी &c.

JUNIOR, *a.* अवरः -रा -रं, अवरवयस्कः -स्का -स्कं, अवरवयाः -याः -यः (स्) अवरजः -जा -जं, अवरजातः -ता -तं, अनुजः -जा -जं, अनुजातः -ता -तं, अनुजन्मा -न्मा -न्म (न्), जघन्यजः -जा -जं, यवीयान् -यसी -यः (स्), कनीयान् -यसी -यः (स्), यविष्ठः -ष्ठा -ष्ठं, कनिष्ठः -ष्ठा -ष्ठं.

JUNIPER, *s.* शूर्पिपराख्यो वृक्षप्रभेदः.

JUNK, *s.* चीनदेशीयो वृहन्नौकाविशेषः, चीननौका.—(Pieces of old cable) जीर्णरज्जुखण्डाः *m. pl.*

JUNKET, *s.* निभृते कृतं परमान्नभोजनं or उत्तमान्नसम्भोजनं or सहभोजनं, छलेन कृतो महोत्सवः, निभृतोत्सवः.

To JUNKET, *v. n.* निभृतोत्सवं कृ, निभृते or छलेन सहभोजनं कृ or उत्सवं कृ.

JUNTA, JUNTO, *s.* (Council) सभा, समाजः, शिष्टसभा, महासभा.—(Cabal) गोपनीयकर्म्मसाधनार्थं कतिपयजनसंसर्गः, कुसंसर्गः.

Jupiter, *s.* (The planet) बृहस्पतिः *m.*, गुरुः *m.*, वाक्पतिः *m.*, ग्रहराजः. *See* Vrihaspati. (The god). *See* Indra.

Juridical, *a.* धर्म्मसभासम्बन्धी &c., विचारसभासम्बन्धी &c., न्यायसभासम्बन्धी &c., व्यावहारिकः -की -कं, व्यवहारिकः -की -कं.

Juridically, *adv.* विचारानुसारेण, व्यवहारानुसारेण, धर्म्मानुसारात्, यथाव्यवहारं, यथान्यायं.

Jurisconsult, *s.* स्मृतिशास्त्रज्ञः, धर्म्मशास्त्रज्ञः, व्यवहारपण्डितः, व्यवहारसचिवः, व्यवस्थाज्ञः, धर्म्मप्रवक्ता *m.* (क्तृ).

Jurisdiction, *s.* अधिकारः -रिता, विचारकरणाधिकारः, न्यायकरणाधिकारः, आधिपत्यं, प्रभुत्वं, व्यवहारदर्शनाधिकारः, धर्म्माधिकारः.

Jurisprudence, *s.* व्यवहारः, व्यवहारशास्त्रं, व्यवहारविधिः *m.*, व्यवहारज्ञानं, व्यवहारविद्या, धर्म्मशास्त्रं, स्मृतिशास्त्रं; 'a title or head of jurisprudence,' व्यवहारविषयः, व्यवहारमार्गः, व्यवहारस्थानं, व्यवहारपदं.

Jurisprudent, *a.* व्यवहारज्ञः -ज्ञा -ज्ञं, व्यवहारशास्त्रज्ञः &c., स्मृतिशास्त्रज्ञः &c., धर्म्मशास्त्रज्ञः &c., व्यवहारपण्डितः -ता -तं.

Jurist, *s.* धर्म्मशास्त्री *m.* (न्), धर्म्मज्ञः, व्यवहारवेत्ता *m.* (त्तृ), स्मृतिज्ञः.

Juror, *s.* शापितजनः, शापितपुरुषः, धर्म्मसभायां सुविचारार्थं शापितः प्रमाणपुरुषः or स्येयः or मध्यस्थः.

Jury, *s.* धर्म्मसभायां सुविचारार्थं शापितानां द्वादशप्रमाणपुरुषाणां गणः, शापितप्रमाणपुरुषपंक्तिः *f.*, स्येयगणः.

Juryman, *s.* सुविचारार्थं शापितः प्रमाणपुरुषः. *See* Juror.

Just, *a.* (Upright, honest, equitable) न्यायाचारः -रा -रं -री -रिणी -रि (न्), न्यायी -यिनी -यि (न्), न्यायवृत्तिः -त्तिः -त्ति, न्यायवर्त्ती -र्त्तिनी -र्त्ति (न्), न्यायकारी -रिणी -रि (न्), धार्म्मिकः -की -कं, धर्म्मकारी &c., न्यायशीलः -ला -लं, न्यायपरः -रा -रं, धर्म्मी -र्म्मिणी -र्म्मि (न्), शुचिः -चिः -चि, सात्त्विकः -की -कं, महासत्त्वः -त्त्वा -त्त्वं, सच्चरितः -ता -तं, साधुः -धुः -ध्वी -धु, साधुवृत्तिः -त्तिः -त्ति, ऋजुः -जुः -जु, विमलात्मा -त्मा -त्म (न्), मायाहीनः -ना -नं, नीतिमान् -मती -मत् (त्), निष्कपटः -टा -टं, निर्व्यलीकः -का -कं, अकूटव्यवहारः -रा -रं.—(According to equity) न्याय्यः -य्या -य्यं, यथान्यायः -या -यं, न्यायानुसारी -रिणी -रि (न्), यथानीतिः -तिः -ति, याथार्थिकः -की -कं, तात्त्विकः -की -कं, न्यायसिद्धः -द्धा -द्धं.—(Exact, correct, right, proper) यथार्थः -र्था -र्थं, याथार्थिकः -की -कं, समञ्जसः -सा -सं, अञ्जसः -सा -सं, शुद्धः -द्धा -द्धं, सत्यः -त्या -त्यं, तथ्यः -थ्या -थ्यं, सम्यङ् समीची सम्यक्, युक्तः -क्ता -क्तं, योग्यः -ग्या -ग्यं, यथायोग्यः -ग्या -ग्यं, उचितः -ता -तं, सङ्गतः -ता -तं.—(Impartial, fair) विपक्षपातः -ता -तं, समदर्शी -र्शिनी -र्शि (न्), समः -मा -मं, समानवृत्तिः -त्तिः -त्ति, धर्म्यः -र्म्या -र्म्यं.—(Full) अन्यूनः -ना -नं, अविकलः -ला -लं, सम्पूर्णः -र्णा -र्णं.

Just, *adv.* (Close, near to, in reference to place) निकटे, समीपं, उपान्ते, अन्तिके, अभितस्.—(Nearly in time, almost) प्रायस्, प्रायशस्, भूयिष्ठं, कल्पः; 'just dead,' मृतप्रायः, मृतकल्पः or expressed by the desid. adj. मुमूर्षुः; 'just going,' जिगमिषुः -षुः -षु; 'just finished,' समाप्तभूयिष्ठः -ष्ठा -ष्ठं.—(In the instant, just now) सद्यस्, मात्रं; 'just heated,' सद्यस्तप्तः -प्ता -प्तं; 'just born,' सद्योजातः -ता -तं, जातमात्रः -त्री -त्रं; 'just dead,' सद्योमृतः -ता -तं; 'just done,' सद्यःकृतः -ता -तं.—(Exactly) यथार्थं, युक्तं, सम्यक्, यथावत्, अञ्जसा, समञ्जसं, यथातथं, तावत्; 'just so far, just so much,' तावन्मात्रं, तदन्तं; 'just so,' युक्तं, युज्यते, एवमेव, तथैव; 'just the same, neither more nor less,' नाधिकं न च न्यूनं; 'just as,' यद्वत्, यत्प्रकारेण.—(Merely, barely) मात्रं, कष्टेन, कृच्छ्रेण. 'Just' is often used redundantly, in which case it is expressed by तावत्; as, 'just wait a moment,' तिष्ठ तावत् मुहूर्त्तं.

Just, *s.* (A tournement) सादिनां or अश्वारोहिणां क्रीडायुद्धं.

To just, *v. n.* पूर्व्वोक्तक्रीडायुद्धं कृ, पूर्व्वोक्तप्रकारेण परस्परसमाघातं कृ.

Justice, *s.* (The virtue which consists in giving what is due, integrity, honesty) धर्म्मः, न्यायः, नीतिः *f.*, नयः, धर्म्मन्यायः, न्यायशीलता, न्यायिता, न्यायाचारता, धार्म्मिकत्वं, ऋजुता, शुचिता, साधुता.—(Equity, agreeableness to right) न्याय्यत्वं -ता, न्यायता, युक्तिः *f.*, योग्यता, उपयुक्तता, यथायोग्यता, यथार्थता, याथार्थ्यं, सामञ्जस्यं, सम्यक्त्वं.—(Right application of justice, redress of wrong) न्यायः, दण्डः, दण्डयोगः.—(Impartiality) साम्यं, समता, सर्व्वसमता, अपक्षपातः.—(Merited punishment, retribution) उपयुक्तदण्डः, न्याय्यदण्डः, यथापराधदण्डः, यथापराधशासनं, योग्यशिक्षा, प्रतिक्रिया.—(One who administers justice) धर्म्माधिकारी *m.* (न्), धर्म्माध्यक्षः, न्यायाधिकारी *m.*, दण्डनायकः; 'administration of justice,' न्यायप्रणयनं, न्यायकरणं, न्यायदर्शनं, व्यवहारदर्शनं; 'court of justice,' धर्म्मसभा. *See* Judicatory.

Justiceship, *s.* धर्म्माध्यक्षता -त्वं, न्यायाधीशत्वं, धर्म्माधिकारः -रिता.

Justiciable, *a.* व्यवहार्य्यः -र्य्या -र्य्यं, व्यवहर्त्तव्यः -व्या -व्यं.

Justiciary, *s.* न्यायाध्यक्षः, न्यायदर्शी *m.* (न्), न्यायप्रणेता *m.* (तृ). *See* Judge.

Justifiable, *a.* निरसनीयदोषः -षा -षं, निराकरणीयदोषः -षा -षं, आरोपितदोषमोचनीयः -या -यं, शोधनीयदोषः -षा -षं, शोधनीयः -या -यं, परिशोधनीयः -या -यं, शोध्यः -ध्या -ध्यं, खण्डनीयदोषारोपः -पा -पं, अनारोपणीयदोषः -षा -षं, दोषनिरासशक्यः -क्या -क्यं, परिशुद्धिक्षमः -मा -मं, निवार्य्यदोषः -षा -षं, मार्जनीयदोषः -षा -षं, दोषमोचनीयः -या -यं, यथान्यायः -या -यं, रक्षणीयः -या -यं.

Justifiableness, *s.* शोधनीयत्वं, शोध्यता, परिशुद्धिक्षमता, दोषमोच्यता.

Justifiably, *adv.* परिशोधनीयं, यथा दोषो निरसितुं शक्यते तथा.

Justification, *s.* शुद्धिः *f.*, शोधनं, परिशुद्धिः *f.*, परिशोधनं, विशुद्धिः *f.*, दोषशुद्धिः *f.*, दोषशोधनं, दोषमार्जना -नं, दोषमोचनं, दोषमुक्तिः *f.*, निर्दोषीकरणं, आरोपितदोषमुक्तिः *f.*, आरोपितदोषशोधनं, आरोपितदोषमार्जना, दोषप्रतीकारः, दोषनिराकरणं, दोषनिवारणं, दोषनिरसनं.

Justificatory, *a.* शोधकः -का -कं, परिशोधकः -का -कं, शुद्धिकरः -रा -रं.

Justified, *p. p.* शोधितः -ता -तं, परिशोधितः -ता -तं, निर्दोषीकृतः -ता -तं, दोषमुक्तः -क्ता -क्तं, मुक्तदोषः -षा -षं, निवृत्तदोषः -षा -षं, निरस्तदोषः -षा -षं, निवारितदोषः -षा -षं.

Justifier, *s.* शोधकः, परिशोधकः, परिशुद्धिकरः, दोषमोचकः, निर्दोषीकर्त्ता *m.* (र्त्तृ), दोषनिवारकः, दोषप्रतिकारकः.

To justify, *v. a.* शुध् (c. 10. शोधयति -यितुं), परिशुध्, दोषात् परिशुध् or मुच् (c. 6. मुञ्चति, मोक्तुं), निर्दोषीकृ, निरपराधीकृ, निष्कलङ्कीकृ, आरोपितदोषाद् मुच्, आरोपितदोषं निराकृ or प्रतिकृ or निवृ (c. 10. -वारयति -यितुं), दोषशोधनं कृ, अपराधशोधनं कृ, दोषनिराकरणं कृ, दोषनिरसनं कृ.

To justle. *v. a.* and *n.* *See* *To* jostle.

Justly, *adv.* (Conformably to justice or propriety) यथान्यायं, न्यायानुसारेण, न्यायेन, न्यायतस्, न्यायवत्, धर्म्मतस्, धर्म्मेण, यथाधर्म्मं, युक्तं, उपयुक्तं, यथायोग्यं, सम्यक्, यथोचितं, समञ्जसं.—(According to truth) यथार्थं, याथार्थ्येन, सत्यं, यथातथ्यं, अवितथं, अर्थतस्, परमार्थतस्.—(Fairly, honestly) समं, साम्येन, सार्जवं, निर्व्याजं, निर्व्यलीकं, सारल्येन.—(Exactly, accurately, fitly) यथावत्,

यथातथं, अञ्जसा, समञ्जसं, यथार्हं -र्हतस्, यथार्थं, युक्तं, स्थाने.

JUSTNESS, *s.* (Exactness, accuracy) यथार्थता, याथार्थ्यं, सम्यक्त्वं, सामञ्जस्यं, समञ्जसं, याथातथ्यं, शुद्धता, युक्तता.—(Conformity to truth) सत्यता, यथार्थता, अवितथत्वं, तथ्यत्वं, युक्तता.—(Justice, equity) न्याय्यत्वं -ता, न्यायता, युक्तिः *f.*, युक्तत्वं, योग्यता, यथायोग्यता, याथार्थ्यं, सामञ्जस्यं, सम्यक्त्वं, शस्तत्वं.—(Impartiality) समता, साम्यं, सर्वसमता, अपक्षपातः.

To JUT, *v. n.* (Project) बहिःस्था (c. 1. -तिष्ठति -ष्ठातुं), बहिर्वृत् (c. 1. -वर्त्तते -र्त्तितुं), बहिर्भू, बहिर्लम्ब् (c. 1.-लम्बते -म्बितुं), बहिःप्रलम्ब्, अतिवृत्, अतिक्रम् (c. 4. -क्राम्यति -क्रमितुं).

JUT, *s.* बहिर्वर्त्तनं, बहिर्लम्बत्वं, प्रलम्बता, उदग्रता, आभोगः, प्रसरः.

JUTTING, *part.* प्रलम्बः -म्बा -म्बं, बहिर्लम्बः -म्बा -म्बं, उदग्रः -ग्रा -ग्रं.

JUVENILE, *a.* यौवनवान् -वती -वत् (त्), युवा युवतिः -ती or यूनी युव (न्), यौवनेयकः -की -कं, तरुणः -णा -णं, कौमारः -री -रं, अल्पवयस्कः -स्का -स्कं, अभिनववयस्कः -स्का -स्कं, प्रथमवयस्कः -स्का -स्कं, तरुणवयस्कः -स्का -स्कं, बालिशः -शा -शं, युवकालीनः -ना -नं.

JUVENILITY, *s.* यौवनं, यौवनावस्था, तारुण्यं, तारुण्यावस्था, कुमारभावः, कौमारं, सौकुमार्य्यं, बालत्वं, बाल्यं.

JUXTAPOSITION, *s.* संस्थितिः *f.*, उपस्थानं, संस्थानं, संस्थत्वं, समीपता, सन्निधिः *m.*, सान्निध्यं, संसर्गः, नैकट्यं, उपश्लेषः, उपन्यासः.

K.

KALE, *s.* शाकभेदः, शाकं, हरितकं, शूरणं, शिग्रुः *m.*

KALENDAR, *s.* *See* CALENDAR.

KÁMADEVA, *s.* (The god of love or Hindu Cupid, son of Vishnu or Krishna by Lakshmí, who is then called Máyá or Rukminí. According to another account he was first produced in the heart of Brahmá, and coming out in the form of a beautiful female, was looked upon by Brahmá with amorous emotions. He is usually represented as a handsome youth, sometimes riding on a parrot, and attended by nymphs, one of whom bears his banner, which consists of a fish on a red ground. Endeavouring to influence Śiva with the passion of love for his wife Párvatí, he discharged an arrow at him; but Śiva, enraged at the attempt, reduced him to ashes, or as some say, to a mere mental essence, by a beam of fire darted from his central eye. Afterwards the relenting god declared that he should be born again in the form of Pradyumna, son of Krishna by Máyá or Rukminí. The bow of Kámadeva is made of flowers, with a string formed of bees, and his five arrows are each tipped with the blossom of a flower which is devoted to, and supposed to preside over, a sense. He is lord of the Apsarasas. As god of desire he is called) कामः, कामदेवः, कमनः, रमः -मणः, रमतिः *m.*, रामिलः, शृङ्गारयोनिः *m.*, रागरज्जुः *m.*, रागवृन्तः, रागचूर्णः, रतनारीचः.—(The mind-agitator) मन्मथः.—(The maddener) मदनः.—(The inflamer) दर्पकः.—(The inflamer of Brahmá) कन्दर्पः.—(Born in the heart) मनसिजः, चित्तजन्मा *m.* (न्), मनोजन्मा *m.*, चित्तभूः *m.*, चेतोभूः, मनोभूः *m.*, मनोभवः, मनसिशयः, हृच्छयः, मनोयोनिः *m.*—(Born only in the heart, self-born) अनन्यजः, आत्मभूः *m.*, आत्मयोनिः *m.*—(The ideal one) स्मरः.—(The son of Lakshmí) लक्ष्मीपुत्रः, श्रीनन्दनः, श्रीजः.—(The son of Krishna) प्रद्युम्नः.—(The son of Lakshmí in the form of Máyá or Illusion) मायी *m.* (न्), मायासुतः.—(The bodiless one) अनङ्गः, अशरीरः.—(The fish-bannered one) मकरकेतुः *m.*, मीनकेतनः, मकरध्वजः, झषकेतनः.—(Having a bow made of flowers) पुष्पधनुः *m.*, पुष्पधन्वा *m.* (न्), पुष्पचापः, कुसुमकार्मुकः, पुष्पशरासनः.—(Having arrows of flowers) कुसुमायुधः, पुष्पशरः, पुष्पेषुः *m.*, पुष्पास्त्रः, कुसुमेषुः *m.*, प्रसूनेषुः *m.*, सुरभिबाणः.—(Having five arrows) पञ्चबाणः, पञ्चशरः, पञ्चेषुः *m.*—(Having a flower as a symbol) पुष्पकेतनः, पुष्पकेतुः *m.*—(The beautiful) सुन्दरः.—(The destroyer) मारः.—(The lord) ईश्वरः.—(The destroyer of the Daitya, Śambara) शम्बरसूदनः, शम्बरारिः *m.*—(The destroyer of devotional tranquillity) शमान्तकः.—(The water-born) इराजः.—(The husband of Rati) रतिरमणः, रतिपतिः *m.* Another name of this god is मुर्मुरः. The wife of Kámadeva is called Rati. *See* RATI. His son is called अनिरुद्धः, ऋष्याङ्कः, उषापतिः *m.*, उषेशः; 'his daughter,' तृषा; 'his son's wife,' प्रीतिजुषा and उषा; 'his fish,' जलरूपः.

KANDAHAR, *s.* (The country) गान्धारः.

KANGAROO, *s.* (The animal) काङ्गरूसंज्ञको विदेशीयजन्तुभेदः.

KANSA, *s.* (The uncle and enemy of Krishna) कंसः, उग्रसेनजः, उग्रसेनपुत्रः, उग्रसेनतनयः, उग्रसेनसुतः.

KÁRTIKEYA, *s.* (The god of war, or Hindu Mars, generated from the vivifying principle of Śiva cast into Agni, or Fire, who, unable to retain it, cast it into Gangá, or the Ganges. On the banks of this river was born the beautiful boy who was destined to lead the armies of the gods, and to be the destroyer of Táraka, a demon who, by his austerities, had alarmed both gods and men, and gained the dominion of the universe. When born, Kártikeya was nursed by six nymphs, called the Krittikás, or Pleiades, who each called him her son, and, offering her breast, the child assumed to himself six mouths, and received nurture from each. He is considered to be the brother of Ganeśa, who was the reputed eldest son of Śiva and Párvatí. He is represented riding on a peacock. (As having the six Krittikás for his foster-mothers, he is called) कार्त्तिकेयः, कृत्तिकासुतः, षाण्मातुरः, बाहुलेयः, विशाखः.—(As god of war he is called) स्कन्दः, महासेनः, सेनापतिः *m.*, सेनानीः *m.*—(As born in the fire) अग्निभूः *m.*, अग्निभुवः.—(The beautiful boy) कुमारः.—(Born on the Ganges) गङ्गापुत्रः, गङ्गासुतः.—(Brought up in thickets of grass) शरजन्मा *m.* (न्), शरजः.—(Son of Párvatí) पार्वतीनन्दनः, गौरीजः, गौरीपुत्रः.—(The six-faced) षडाननः, षण्मुखः.—(The twelve-eyed) द्वादशलोचनः, द्वादशाक्षः.—(The twelve-handed) द्वादशकरः.—(The conqueror of Táraka) तारकजित् *m.*, तारकारिः *m.*, तारकरिपुः *m.*, तारकहा *m.* (न्), तारकसूदनः.—(The destroyer of the demon Krauncha) क्रौञ्चदारणः, क्रौञ्चारातिः *m.*, क्रौञ्चारिः *m.*—(The mysterious one) गुहः.—(The spear-holder) शक्तिधरः, शक्तिग्रहः, शक्तिपाणिः *m.*, शक्तिभृत् *m.*—(Borne on the peacock) शिखिवाहनः, बर्हिणवाहनः. His wife is called सेना.

KASKAS, *s.* (Grass) मृणालं, अमृणालं.

To KAW, *v. n.* कै (c. 1. कायति, कातुं), ध्रांक्ष् (c. 1. ध्रांक्षति -क्षितुं) or ध्रांख् or ध्वांक्ष् or ध्मांक्ष् (c. 1. ध्मांक्षति -क्षितुं), काकवद् रु (c. 2. रौति, रवितुं).

KAW, *s.* काकरुतं, काकरावः, काकरवः, काकशब्दः, ध्मांक्षरुतं, का शब्दः.

To KECK, *v. n.* वम् (c. 1. वमति -मितुं), उद्वम्, उद्वमनं कृ, अर्द्धशोधनं कृ.

KEEL, *s.* नौकातलं, नौकातले दीर्घकाष्ठं, नौकाधोभागे दीर्घदारुः *m.*

KEEN, *a.* (Sharp, having a fine edge) तीक्ष्णः -क्ष्णा -क्ष्णं, तीक्ष्णधारः -रा -रं, शितः -ता -तं, निशितः -ता -तं, शितधारः -रा -रं, धाराधरः -रा -रं, तीक्ष्णधाराधरः -रा -रं, खरः -रा -रं, तीव्रः -व्रा -व्रं, तिग्मः -ग्मा -ग्मं, शातः -ता -तं, निशातः -ता -तं, तेजोवान् -वती -वत् (त्), तीक्ष्णाग्रः -ग्रा -ग्रं, प्रखरः -रा -रं.—(As hunger, cold, &c.) तीक्ष्णः -क्ष्णा -क्ष्णं, तीव्रः -व्रा -व्रं.—(Eager, vehement) तीक्ष्णकर्म्मा -र्म्मा -र्म्म (न्), तीक्ष्णस्वभावः -वा -वं, व्यग्रः -ग्रा -ग्रं, कुतूहली -लिनी -लि (न्), उत्सुकः -क्ता -क्तं, उत्साही &c., अत्यभिलाषी &c., उत्सुकः -का -कं.—(In mind) सूक्ष्मबुद्धिः -द्धिः -द्धि, तीक्ष्णबुद्धिः &c., कुशाग्रीयमतिः -तिः -ति, विदग्धः -ग्धा -ग्धं.—(Acrimonious) तिग्मः -ग्मा -ग्मं, अरुन्तुदः -दा -दं, कटुः -टुः -ट्वी -टु, उग्रः -ग्रा -ग्रं, दंशी -शिनी -शि (न्), दंशकः -का -कं; 'keen words,' वागसिः *f.*, वागिषुः *m.f.*

KEENLY, *adv.* तीक्ष्णं, तीव्रं, तैक्ष्ण्येन, सतैक्ष्ण्यं, तिग्मं, सतैग्म्यं, कटु, उग्रं, तीक्ष्णतया, उग्रतया, निष्ठुरं, खरं, प्राखर्य्येण, तेजसा.

KEENNESS, *s.* (Sharpness of edge) तीक्ष्णता, तैक्ष्ण्यं, धारातीक्ष्णता, धाराशितत्वं, निशितत्वं, तीव्रता, तीक्ष्णाग्रत्वं, तिग्मता.—(Eagerness, vehemence) तीक्ष्णता, स्वभावतीक्ष्णता, व्यग्रता, कौतूहलं, उत्सुकता, अत्यभिलाषः, उत्साहः, अनुरागः.—(Of mind) बुद्धिसूक्ष्मता -सौक्ष्म्यं, बुद्धितीक्ष्णता -तैक्ष्ण्यं, कुशाग्रीयमतित्वं, विदग्धता.—(Acrimony) तिग्मता, तैग्म्यं, कटुता, उग्रता, अरुन्तुदत्वं, प्राखर्य्यं, निष्ठुरता, नैष्ठुर्य्यं.

To KEEP, *v. a.* (Hold) धृ (c. 1. धरति, धर्त्तुं, c. 10. धारयति -यितुं), सन्धृ, धा (c. 3. धत्ते, धातुं), रक्ष् (c. 1. रक्षति -क्षितुं), संरक्ष्; 'to keep in the memory or heart,' हृदये कृ or धृ.—(Have in custody) रक्ष्, अभिरक्ष्, परिरक्ष्, संरक्ष्, पाल् (c. 10. पालयति -यितुं), गुप् (c. 1. गोपायति, गोप्तुं), रक्षणं कृ, रक्षां कृ, पालनं कृ.—(Preserve, guard) रक्ष्, प्रतिरक्ष्, पाल् or पा (c. 2. पाति -तुं), परिपाल्, अनुपाल्, प्रतिपाल्, सम्पाल्, अभिपाल्, उपपाल्, गुप् (c. 1. or c. 10. गोपयति -यितुं), अनुगुप्, अभिगुप्, प्रगुप्, त्रै (c. 1. त्रायते, त्रातुं), परित्रै, संत्रै, अव् (c. 1. अवति -वितुं), गुप्तिं कृ, गोपनं कृ.—(Detain) धृ, निरुध् (c. 7. -रुणद्धि -रोद्धुं), अवरुध्, रुध्, बन्ध् (c. 9. बध्नाति, बन्द्धुं), प्रतिबन्ध्.—(Restrain) निरुध्, वृ (c. 10. वारयति -यितुं), निवृ, निषिध् (c. 1. -षेधति -षेद्धुं), प्रतिषिध्.—(Tend, feed) पाल्, रक्ष्; 'keep cattle,' गोपालनं कृ, गोरक्षणं कृ, पाशुपाल्यं कृ.—(Practise, perform, observe) आचर् (c. 1. -चरति -रितुं), समाचर्, सेव् (c. 1. सेवते -वितुं), आस्था (c. 1. -तिष्ठति -स्थातुं), अनुष्ठा, समास्था, समुपास्था, विधा (c. 3. -दधाति -धातुं), भज् (c. 1. भजते, भक्तुं), आलम्ब् (c. 1. -लम्बते -म्बितुं), समालम्ब्, अवलम्ब्; 'keep silence,' मौनं भज् or सेव् or अवलम्ब्.—(Fulfil) साध् (c. 10. साधयति -यितुं); 'keep a promise,' प्रतिज्ञां शुध् (c. 10. शोधयति -यितुं), प्रतिज्ञां पाल्.—(Not to divulge) धृ (c. 10. धारयति), न प्रकाश् (c. 10. काशयति -यितुं); 'to keep a secret,' रहस्यं धृ or रक्ष् or गुप्, रहस्यगोपनं कृ.—(Maintain, board) भृ (c. 1. भरति, c. 3. बिभर्त्ति, भर्त्तुं), सम्भृ, भरणं कृ, भृतिं कृ or दा, पाल्, पुष् (c. 10. पोषयति -यितुं), पोषणं कृ, पालनं कृ.—(Entertain) सत्कृ.—(Have in pay) वेतनं दा.—(Keep back) निग्रह् (c. 9. -गृह्णाति -ग्रहीतुं), विनिग्रह्, सन्निग्रह्, संहृ (c. 1. -हरति -हर्त्तुं), उपसंहृ, विधृ, निवृ, उच्छिद् (c. 7. -छिनत्ति -छेत्तुं), उपसंहरणं कृ.—(Keep company with) सह चर्, सह वस् (c. 1. वसति, वस्तुं), संवस्.—(Keep in, conceal) गुह् (c. 1. गूहति -हितुं), निगुह्, छद् (c. 10. छादयति -यितुं), अन्तर्धा, अपवृ, संवृ, गोपनं कृ.—(Keep off) प्रतिवृ, निवृ, वृ, प्रतिहन् (c. 2. -हन्ति -न्तुं), प्रतिकृ, निरुध्, व्यपोह् (c. 1. -ऊहते -हितुं), अपसिध्, प्रतिषिध्.—(Keep under) वशीकृ, स्वाधीनीकृ, निग्रह्, प्रत्याहृ.—(Keep up, maintain) धृ, सन्धृ, भृ, सम्भृ, प्रवृत् (c. 10. -वर्त्तयति -यितुं), संस्था in caus. (-स्थापयति -यितुं), पाल्, प्रवर्त्तनं कृ.—(Keep out) निषिध्, निवृ.

To KEEP, *v. n.* (Remain, continue) स्था (c. 1. तिष्ठति -ते, स्थातुं), वृत् (c. 1. वर्त्तते -र्त्तितुं); 'to keep on doing any thing,' may be expressed by आस् (c. 2. आस्ते) with the pres. or indec. part. of another verb; as, 'he keeps following me,' मम पश्चाद् आगच्छन् आस्ते. *See* CONTINUE, *v. n.* (Last, endure) स्था, चिरस्थायी -यिनी -यि भू.—(Persevere) पर्य्यवस्था, निर्बन्धं कृ, आग्रहं कृ.—(Adhere, cohere) संसञ्ज् in pass. (-सज्यते -सज्जते), संश्लिष् in pass. (-श्लिष्यते), अनुबन्ध् in pass. (-बध्यते), संलग्नीभू, अनुलग्नीभू.—(Lodge) वस् (c. 1. वसति, वस्तुं), निवस्.—(Keep from) निवृत् (c. 1. -वर्त्तते -र्त्तितुं), परिहृ (c. 1. -हरति -हर्त्तुं), वृज् (c. 10. वर्जयति -यितुं), परिवृज्, विवृज्.—(Keep on) प्रवृत्, प्रारभ्, सम्पद् (c. 10. -पादयति -यितुं).

KEEP, *s.* (Custody, charge) रक्षा -क्षणं, पालनं, गुप्तिः *f.*, गोपनं.—(Condition) अवस्था, स्थितिः *f.*, भावः, वृत्तिः *f.*; 'in good keep,' सुस्थितः -ता -तं.—(Board, maintenance) भृतिः *f.*, ग्रासाच्छादनं, अन्नजलं, भोजनं.—(Stronghold) दुर्गं.—(Dungeon) कारा, कारागारं, निरोधस्थानं, बन्धनागारं, गुप्तिः *f.*

KEEPER, *s.* रक्षकः, रक्षी *m.* (न्), पालकः, पालः, पालयिता *m.* (तृ), रक्षिता *m.* (तृ), अध्यक्षः, पतिः *m.* पः in comp.; as, 'keeper of sheep or cattle,' पशुपालः, मेषपोषकः, गोरक्षकः, गोपालः, गोपः, गवीश्वरः; 'of a prison,' कारारक्षकः, कारागाराध्यक्षः, बन्दिपालः; 'of mad people,' उन्मत्तपालकः; 'of a park,' उद्यानपालः -लकः, उद्यानरक्षकः; 'of a gaming-house,' सभापतिः *m.*, सभिकः, द्यूतसभाधिकारी *m.* (न्).

KEEPERSHIP, *s.* रक्षकत्वं, पालकत्वं, अध्यक्षत्वं, अधिकारित्वं.

KEEPING, *s.* (Custody, guard) रक्षा -क्षणं, गुप्तिः *f.*, पालनं, गोपनं.—(Congruity, harmony) ऐक्यं, सङ्गतत्वं, साङ्गत्यं, सादृश्यं, अविरोधः, योग्यता, आनुरूप्यं.

KEEPSAKE, *s.* स्मरणार्थकदानं, स्मरणार्थं दत्तं द्रव्यं or वस्तु, स्मरणार्थं गृहीतं द्रव्यं, स्मृतिजनकदानं, स्मृतिदानं, प्रीतिदानं, प्रीतिदायं.

KEG, *s.* क्षुद्रभाण्डं, काष्ठभाण्डं, दीर्घगोलाकारं क्षुद्रभाजनं.

To KEN, *v. a.* (Descry) दूराद् आलोक् (c. 1. -लोकते, c. 10. -लोकयति -यितुं) or अवलोक् or दृश् (c. 1. पश्यति, द्रष्टुं) or प्रदृश्.—(Know) ज्ञा (c. 9. जानाति, ज्ञातुं).

KEN, *s.* (Reach of sight) चक्षुर्विषयः, नयनविषयः.—(Reach of understanding) बुद्धिविषयः; 'beyond the ken,' अविषयः -या -यं, बुद्ध्यतीतः -ता -तं.

KENNEL, *s.* (House for dogs) श्वशाला, कुक्कुरालयः, श्वगृहं, कुक्कुरागारं.—(Pack of hounds) श्वगणः, कुक्कुरगणः, मृगव्यकुक्कुरगणः.—(Water-course) प्रणाली, जलमार्गः, जलवाहनी.

To KENNEL, *v. n.* कुक्कुरालये वस् (c. 1. वसति, वस्तुं) or स्था (c. 1. तिष्ठति, स्थातुं), श्ववद् or शृगालवद् गर्त्ते वस् or स्था.

To KENNEL, *v. a.* कुक्कुरालये वस् (c. 10. वासयति -यितुं).

KEPT, *p. p.* धृतः -ता -तं, धारितः -ता -तं, रक्षितः -ता -तं, पालितः -ता -तं, गुप्तः -प्ता -प्तं, भृतः -ता -तं, पोषितः -ता -तं.

KERCHIEF, *s.* (Head-dress) मस्तकाभरणं, मुकुटं, किरीटः, शेखरः; 'handkerchief,' नक्तकः, वस्त्रं, मुखमार्जनी; 'neckkerchief,' कण्ठवेष्टनं, ग्रीवावेष्टनं, कण्ठवस्त्रं.

KERNEL, *s.* बीजं, गर्भः, फलबीजं, फलगर्भः, अष्ठिः *f.*, अष्ठीला -लिका.—(Central part of any thing) मध्यं, गर्भः, उदरं, हृदयं, अभ्यन्तरं.

KERNELLY, *a.* बीजी -जिनी -जि (न्). बीजवान् -वती -वत् (त्), बीजपूर्णः -र्णा -र्णं, बीजमयः -यी -यं, बीजाकारः -रा -रं.

KESTREL, *s.* श्येनजातीयः पक्षिभेदः, कपोतारिः *m.*

KETCH, *s.* द्विकूपकविशिष्टा नौका, कूपकद्वययुक्ता नौः.

KETTLE, *s.* स्थाली, उदस्थाली, पिठरः -रं, कटाहः, उखा, पिष्टपचनं, कन्दुः *m. f.*, चुल्लीपं.

KETTLE-DRUM, *s.* भेरी, मृदङ्गः, मुरजः, पटहः, दुन्दुभिः *m.*, मर्द्दलः, डिण्डिमः, आनकः, ढक्का.

KETTLE-DRUMMER, *s.* मार्द्दङ्गः -ङ्गिकः, मौरजिकः, भेरीताडकः, पटहताडकः.

KEY, *s.* उद्घाटनं, उद्घाटकः -कं, उद्घाटकयन्त्रं, कुञ्चिका, कूञ्चिका, ताली, तालिका, अङ्कुटः.—(Explanation) निर्वचनं, व्याख्या.—(Key-note) वादी *m.* (न्); 'change of key in music,' शुद्धान्तयुक् *f.* (ज्).

KEY-HOLE, *s.* उद्घाटनछिद्रं, कुञ्चिकाछिद्रं, उद्घाटनरन्ध्रं, कुञ्चिकारन्ध्रं.

KEY-STONE, *s.* बन्धनप्रस्तरः, सन्धानप्रस्तरः, संयोगप्रस्तरः, मध्यमप्रस्तरः, मध्यस्थप्रस्तरः.

KIBE, *s.* पादस्फोटः, पाददारी, विपादिका, स्फुटिः *f.*, अलसः.

To KICK, *v. a.* or *n.* पादेन तड् (c. 10. ताडयति -यितुं) or आहन् (c. 2. -हन्ति -न्तुं) or प्रहृ (c. 1. -हरति -हर्त्तुं), खुरेण or पार्ष्णिना तड् or आहन्, पादाघातं कृ, पादप्रहारं कृ, खुराघातं कृ, खुरक्षेपं कृ, खुरं क्षिप् (c. 6. क्षिपति -क्षेप्तुं) or प्रक्षिप्, पार्ष्णिं क्षिप्, पादं प्रक्षिप्.

KICK, *s.* पादाघातः, पादप्रहारः, पादाहतिः *f.*, पादाभिघातः, खुराघातः, खुराभिघातः, खुरक्षेपः, पार्ष्णिः *m.*, पार्ष्णिक्षेपः, पदाघातः.

KICKED, *p.p.* पादाहतः -ता -तं, खुराहतः -ता -तं, पदाहतः -ता -तं.

KICKER, *s.* पादाघातकृत् *m.*, पादप्रहारकर्त्ता *m.* (र्त्तृ), खुरक्षेपकः.

KICKING, *s.* पादाघातकरणं, पादप्रहरणं, खुरक्षेपणं, खुराघातः.

KID, *s.* (Young goat) छागशावकः, अजशावकः, छागवत्सः, छागशिशुः *m.*, अजपोतकः.—(Fagot) काष्ठभारः, काष्ठकूर्चः.

To KID, *v. n.* छागशावकं सु (c. 2. सूते, c. 4. सूयते, सोतुं) or प्रसु or जन् (c. 10. जनयति -यितुं) or उत्पद् (c. 10. -पादयति -यितुं).

KIDDER, *s.* धान्यादीनां पूर्व्वक्रेता *m.* (तृ) or पूर्व्वग्राहकः.

To KIDNAP, *v. a.* बालकस्तेयं कृ, मनुष्यस्तेयं कृ, बालकं हृ (c. 1. हरति, हर्त्तुं) or अपहृ or अभिहृ or चुर् (c. 10. चोरयति -यितुं), बालापहरणं कृ, मनुष्यापहरणं कृ.

KIDNAPPED, *p.p.* चौरहृतः -ता -तं, चौरापहृतः -ता -तं, बलादपहृतः -ता -तं.

KIDNAPPER, *s.* बालकस्तेयकृत् *m.*, मनुष्यस्तेयकृत्, बालापहारकः.

KIDNAPPING, *s.* बालकस्तेयं, मनुष्यस्तेयं, बालापहरणं, मनुष्यापहारः.

KIDNEY, *s.* वृक्कः -क्का -क्कं, बुक्कः, वूक्कः, बूक्का *m.* (न्), मूत्रपिण्डः.

KIDNEY-BEAN, *s.* मुद्गः, मुद्गपर्णी, मुकुष्टः -ष्टकः, माषः, माषपर्णी, शिम्बिकः, शिम्बिपर्णी -र्णिका, मकुष्ठकः, मकुष्ठकः; 'a field of kidney beans,' माष्यं, माषीणं.

KILDERKIN, *s.* दीर्घगोलाकारं काष्ठभाण्डं, मानविशेषः.

To KILL, *v. a.* हन् (c. 2. हन्ति -न्तुं), निहन्, अभिहन्, आहन्, अभ्याहन्, समाहन्, विनिहन्, विहन्, प्रहन्, प्रणिहन्, निप्रहन्; 'the two last require the gen. c. of the object; हन् in caus. (घातयति -यितुं), व्यापद् (c. 10. -पादयति -यितुं), मृ (c. 10. मारयति -यितुं), सूद् (c. 10. सूदयति -यितुं), निसूद्, अभिसूद्, विनिसूद्, सन्निसूद्, वध्,—(Defective, usually found in the 3d pret. अवधीत् and fut. वधिष्यति -ते), नश् (c. 10. नाशयति -यितुं), विनश्, प्रमी in caus. (-मापयति -यितुं), शद् (c. 10. शातयति -यितुं), शस् (c. 1. शसति -सितुं), विशस्, क्षण् (c. 8. क्षणोति -णितुं), परिक्षण्, विक्षण्, निपत् (c. 10. -पातयति -यितुं), विनिपत्, क्षि (c. 5. क्षिणोति, क्षेतुं or caus. क्षययति क्षपयति -यितुं), हिंस् (c. 7. हिनस्ति, c. 1. हिंसति -सितुं), तृह् (c. 6. तृहति, c. 7. तृणेढि, तर्हितुं), तुभ् (c. 9. तुभ्नाति, तोभितुं), तुप्, तुफ्, तुम्प्, तुम्फ्, उद्वस् (c. 10. -वासयति -यितुं), with gen. c., कृत् (c. 6. कृन्तति, कर्त्तितुं), निकृत्, निष्कृत्, वधं कृ, प्राणहत्यां कृ, प्राणघातं कृ, जीवहत्यां कृ, पञ्चत्वं गम् (c. 10. गमयति -यितुं), लोकान्तरं गम् or प्राप् (c. 10. -आपयति -यितुं).

KILLED, *p. p.* हतः -ता -तं, निहतः -ता -तं, विहतः -ता -तं, आहतः -ता -तं, अभिहतः -ता -तं, समाहतः -ता -तं, विनिहतः -ता -तं, व्यापादितः -ता -तं, व्यापन्नः -न्ना -न्नं, घातितः -ता -तं, मारितः -ता -तं, सूदितः -ता -तं, निषूदितः -ता -तं, नाशितः -ता -तं, विनाशितः -ता -तं, विशसितः -ता -तं, निपातितः -ता -तं, विनिपातितः -ता -तं, क्षतः -ता -तं, विक्षतः -ता -तं, हतप्राणः -णा -णं, हतजीवितः -ता -तं, नष्टजीवितः -ता -तं, नष्टप्राणः -णा -णं, हतचैतन्यः -न्या -न्यं; 'being killed,' हन्यमानः -ना -नं, निहन्यमानः -ना -नं; 'to be killed,' हननीयः -या -यं, घातव्यः -व्या -व्यं, व्यापादनीयः -या -यं, व्यापादयितव्यः -व्या -व्यं.

KILLER, *s.* हन्ता *m.* (न्तृ), निहन्ता *m.*, घातकः, घाती *m.* (न्), मारकः, वधकारी *m.* (न्), वधकः, प्राणहन्ता *m.*, जीवहन्ता *m.*, हत्याकृत्, प्राणहत्याकृत्, नाशकः, विनाशकः, विशसिता *m.* (तृ), अन्तकः in comp., सूदनः, घ्नः in comp.

KILLING, *s.* घातः -तनं, हननं, निहननं, व्यापादनं, मारणं, वधः, प्राणघातः -तनं, प्राणहत्या, प्रमापणं, सूदनं, निषूदनं, क्षणनं, नाशः, प्राणनाशः, शसनं, विशसनं, विदारणं -णा, विमर्द्दनं, मर्द्दनं, मथनं, प्रमथनं, प्रमयः, विशरः, विशारणं, निशारणं, निकारणं, निर्हिंसनं, निबर्हणं, निकृन्तनं, आलम्भः, हत्या in comp.

KILN, *s.* पाकपुटी, आपाकः, पचनं; 'brick-kiln,' इष्टकापचनस्थानं.

KIMBO, *s.* विभुग्नः -ग्ना -ग्नं, अवभुग्नः -ग्ना -ग्नं, कुटिलः -ला -लं, वक्रः -क्रा -क्रं; 'arms a-kimbo,' विभुग्नभुजौ *m.* du., बहिर्भुग्नभुजौ.

KIN, *s.* (Relationship) ज्ञातित्वं, ज्ञातिभावः, बन्धुता, बान्धवत्वं.—(Kindred) स्वकुलं, कुलं, ज्ञातयः *m. pl.*, स्वज्ञातयः, बान्धवाः *m. pl.*, सपिण्डाः *m. pl.*, सगोत्राः *m. pl.*, सम्बन्धिनः *m. pl.*, गोत्रं; 'of kin,' सगोत्रः -त्रा -त्रं, समानगोत्रः &c., स्वजातीयः -या -यं, सजातीयः -या -यं, गोत्रसम्बन्धी &c.; 'next of kin,' अनन्तरः -रा -रं, अनन्तरजातीयः -या -यं, अनन्तरजन्मा -न्मा -न्म (न्).

KIND, *a.* (Disposed to make others happy, benevolent) प्रियकरः -री -रं, प्रियङ्करः -री -रं, प्रियकारः -री -रं, प्रियकृत् *m. f. n.*, प्रियः -या -यं, प्रीतः -ता -तं, प्रीतिमान् -मती -मत् (त्), हितः -ता -तं, प्रियैषी -षिणी -षि (न्), हितैषी &c., हितवान् -वती -वत् (त्), सुहितः -ता -तं, हितकामः -मा -मं, हितकरः -री -रं, हितबुद्धिः -द्धिः -द्धि, उपकारशीलः -ला -लं, उपकारी -रिणी -रि (न्), उपकारपरः -रा -रं, परोपकारी &c., लोकोपकारी &c., उपकारबुद्धिः -द्धिः -द्धि, स्निग्धः -ग्धा -ग्धं, स्नेहशीलः -ला -लं, स्नेही -हिनी -हि (न्), हृदयालुः -लुः -लु.

सुहृदयः -या -यं, सुहृत्तमः -मा -मं, अनुकूलः -ला -लं, कृपालुः -लुः -लु, कृपाशीलः -ला -लं, अनुकम्पकः -का -कं, अनुकम्पी -म्पिनी -म्पि (न्), दयालुः -लुः -लु, करुणात्मा -त्मा -त्म (न्), दयावान् &c., लोकानुकम्पनः -ना -नं, अद्रोही -हिणी -हि (न्), परहितेच्छुः -च्छुः -च्छु, परकल्याणेच्छुः &c., सुशीलः -ला -लं, प्रसन्नः -न्ना -न्नं, अनुनयी -यिनी -यि (न्), अनुग्राही &c.; 'kind to servants,' भृत्यकामकृत्; 'kind to the poor,' दरिद्रोपकारी &c., दीनानुकम्पनः -ना -नं, दीनवत्सलः -ला -लं; 'kind offices,' उपकारः, उपचारः; 'kind act,' सुकृतं, सुकृतिः *f.*, प्रीतिकर्म्म *n.* (न्); 'kind words,' प्रीतिवचस् *n.*, प्रियभाषणं; 'speaking kind words,' प्रियवादी -दिनी -दि (न्), प्रियंवदः -दा -दं; 'kind present,' प्रीतिदानं.

KIND, *s.* (Genus, class) जातिः *f.*, गणः, वर्णः, वर्गः, सामान्यं.—(Sort) विशेषः, भेदः, प्रभेदः, प्रकारः, आकारः, जातिः *f.* -तं, रूपं, विधिः *m.*, विधानं, विधः in comp.; 'a kind of fish,' मत्स्यभेदः, मत्स्यविशेषः; 'of various kinds,' विविधः -धा -धं, नानाविधः -धा -धं, नानारूपः -पी -पं; 'of many kinds,' बहुविधः -धा -धं, बहुरूपः -पी -पं, अनेकाकारः -रा -रं, अनेकरूपः -पी -पं; 'of two kinds,' द्विविधः -धा -धं; 'of four kinds,' चतुर्विधः -धा -धं, चतुःप्रकारः -रा -रं; 'of all kinds,' सर्व्वप्रकारः -रा -रं; 'all kinds of food,' सर्व्वप्रकारमन्नं; 'of the same kind,' सविधः -धा -धं, सजातिः -तिः -ति, सजातीयः -या -यं, समानजातीयः -या -यं; 'of such a kind,' एवंविधः -धा -धं, तथाविधः -धा -धं, एवंरूपः -पा -पं.—(Manner, way) रीतिः *f.*, प्रकारः, विधानं, प्रभृतिः *f.*

KIND-HEARTED, *a.* सुहृदयः -या -यं, सुहृदयवान् -वती -वत् (त्), हृदयालुः -लुः -लु, हृदयी -यिनी -यि (न्), हृदयिकः -का -कं, चित्तवान् &c.

To KINDLE, *v. a.* ज्वल् (c. 10. ज्वलयति, ज्वालयति -यितुं), प्रज्वल्, संज्वल्, समिन्ध् (c. 7. -इन्द्धे -इन्धितुं), तप् (c. 10. तापयति -यितुं, c. 1. तपति, तप्तुं), सन्तप्, दीप् (c. 10. दीपयति -यितुं), प्रदीप्, आदीप्, सन्दीप्, उपदीप्, उद्दीप्, सन्धुक्ष् (c. 10. -धुक्षयति -यितुं), दह् (c. 1. दहति, दग्धुं), प्रदह्, परिदह्, सम्प्रदह्.—(Excite) उत्तप्, उत्तिज् (c. 10. तेजयति -यितुं), समुत्तिज्, उत्सह् (c. 10. -साहयति -यितुं), प्रोत्सह्.—(Provoke) प्रकुप् (c. 10. -कोपयति -यितुं).

To KINDLE, *v. n.* समिन्ध् in pass. (-इध्यते), समिद्धीभू, दह् (c. 4. दह्यति -ते, दग्धुं), दीप् (c. 4. दीप्यते, दीपितुं), सन्दीप्, प्रदीप्, ज्वल् (c. 1. ज्वलति -लितुं), प्रज्वल्, तप् (c. 1. तपति, तप्तुं or in pass. तप्यते), सन्धुक्ष् (c. 1. -धुक्षते -क्षितुं), अग्निदीप्तः -प्ता -प्तं भू.

KINDLED, *p. p.* समिद्धः -द्धा -द्धं, इद्धः -द्धा -द्धं, दीप्तः -प्ता -प्तं, प्रदीप्तः -प्ता -प्तं, दीपितः -ता -तं, उद्दीप्तः -प्ता -प्तं, ज्वलितः -ता -तं, प्रज्वालितः -ता -तं, तप्तः -प्ता -प्तं, सन्तप्तः -प्ता -प्तं, तापितः -ता -तं, सन्धुक्षितः -ता -तं, दग्धः -ग्धा -ग्धं, उत्तेजितः -ता -तं; 'one whose anger is kindled,' समिद्धकोपः -पा -पं, कोपज्वलितः -ता -तं.

KINDLINESS, *s.* मृदुता, सौम्यता -त्वं, स्निग्धता, कोमलता, प्रीतता, प्रीतिः *f.*

KINDLY, *a.* (Congenial) समशीलः -ला -लं, समानशीलः -ला -लं, समानभावः -वा -वं, अनुगुणः -णा -णं, अनुकूलः -ला -लं.—(Bland, gentle) सौम्यः -म्या -म्यं, मृदुः -दुः -द्वी -दु, स्निग्धः -ग्धा -ग्धं, कोमलः -ला -लं, प्रीतः -ता -तं, दयालुः -लुः -लु.

KINDLY, *adv.* प्रीत्या, प्रीतिपूर्व्वं, सुशीलवत्, सुशीलत्वात्, सुजनत्वात्, सानुनयं, सद्भावात्, कृपया, दयया, सदयं, प्रियं, हितं, स्नेहेन, सस्नेहं, सानुग्रहं, परहितेच्छया, उपकारशीलत्वात्, सानुकूल्यं; 'kindly affected,' सुरक्तः -क्ता -क्तं, अनुरक्तः -क्ता -क्तं, हितबुद्धिः -द्धिः -द्धि; 'speaking kindly,' प्रियवादी -दिनी -दि (न्).

KINDNESS, *s.* (Of disposition) प्रीतता, प्रीतिः *f.*, उपकारशीलता, स्निग्धता, स्नेहशीलता, स्नेहः, कृपालुता, दयालुता, प्रियता, दयाशीलता, कृपाशीलता, सुहितत्वं, हितत्वं, हितेच्छा, परहितेच्छा, हितकाम्या, सौजन्यं, सुजनत्वं, अनुग्रहः, प्रसादः, प्रसन्नता, उपकारबुद्धिः *f.*, परहितबुद्धिः *f.*, लोककृपा, सौहृद्यं, प्रेम *n.* (न्), अनुकूलता, आनुकूल्यं, अनुरोधः, मृदुशीलता, सौम्यत्वं.—(Act of kindness) उपकारः, उपकृतं -तिः *f.*, सुकृतं, सुकृतिः *f.*, प्रियं, परोपकारः, कृतोपकारः, हितं.

KINDRED, *s.* (Relationship) ज्ञातित्वं -ता, ज्ञातिभावः, सजातित्वं, बन्धुता, बान्धवत्वं, कुलसन्निधिः *m.*, सपिण्डता, एकपिण्डता, सगोत्रता, सम्बन्धित्वं, सगर्भत्वं.—(Relatives) ज्ञातयः *m.pl.*, बान्धवाः *m.pl.*, बन्धुजनः, बन्धुवर्गः, ज्ञातिवर्गः, बान्धवगणः, बान्धवजनः, स्वजनः -नाः *m. pl.*, सगोत्राः *m. pl.*, सकुल्याः *m. pl.*, स्वजातीयाः *m. pl.*, सजातीयाः, सम्बन्धिनः *m. pl.*, गोत्रं, बान्धवसमुदायः, गोत्रसमुदायः, गोत्रजाः *m. pl.*, कुलसन्निधिः *m.*

KINDRED, *a.* (Related) सजातीयः -या -यं, समानजातीयः -या -यं, सगोत्रः -त्रा -त्रं, समानगोत्रः -त्रा -त्रं, सकुल्यः -ल्या -ल्यं, समानवंशः -शा -शं, सवंशीयः -या -यं, सवर्णः -र्णा -र्णं, सम्बन्धी -न्धिनी -न्धि (न्), सम्बन्धीयः -या -यं.—(Congenial) समधर्म्मा -र्म्मा -र्म्म (न्), सधर्म्मा &c., समगुणः -णा -णं, तुल्यगुणः -णा -णं, समानभावः -वा -वं, तुल्यवृत्तिः -त्तिः -त्ति, अनुगुणः -णा -णं.

KINE, *s. pl.* गावः *m. pl.*, गोकुलं, गोवृन्दं, गोसमूहः.

KING, *s.* राजा *m.* (न्), नृपतिः *m.*, नृपः, नरपतिः *m.*, भूपतिः *m.*, भूपः, भूपालः, महीपतिः *m.*, पार्थिवः, पार्थः, पृथिवीपतिः *m.*, पृथिवीपालः, भूमिपः -पतिः *m.*, महीक्षित् *m.*, महीपः, महीपालः, क्षितिपः -पतिः *m.* -पालः, पृथिवीक्षित् *m.*, नरेश्वरः, नराधिपः, नरेशः, नरेन्द्रः, प्रजेश्वरः, प्रजापः -पतिः *m.*, जगतीपतिः *m.*, जगतीपालः, जगत्पतिः *m.*, अवनिपतिः *m.*, अवनिपालः, अवनीशः, अवनीश्वरः, क्षितीशः, क्षितीश्वरः, पृथिवीशकः, भूमिभृत् *m.*, क्षितिभृत् *m.*, भूभृत्, क्ष्माभृत्, क्ष्मापः, वसुधाधिपः, अधिपः, अधिपतिः *m.*, नायकाधिपः, महीभुक् *m.* (ज्), जगतीभुक् *m.*, क्ष्माभुक्, भूभुक् *m.*, भूमीन्द्रः, महीभर्त्ता *m.* (र्तृ), भर्त्ता *m.*, स्वामी *m.* (न्), प्रभुः *m.*, भगवान् *m.* (त्), छत्रपः -पतिः *m.*, राज्यभाक् *m.* (ज्), लोकपालः, लोकेशः, लोकेश्वरः, लोकनाथः, नरदेवः, राट् *m.* (ज्), इरावान् *m.* (त्), इन्द्रः in comp.; as, 'the king of beasts,' मृगेन्द्रः; 'the king of birds,' खगेन्द्रः; 'the king of men,' नरेन्द्रः; 'king of kings,' राजेन्द्रः, राजाधिराजः, राजराजः, राजाधिपः; 'supreme king,' अधिराजः, अधिराट् (ज्), महाराजः *m.* अधीश्वरः, सम्राट् (ज्), मण्डलेश्वरः, सर्व्वेश्वरः, राजसिंहः; 'a king's son,' राजपुत्रः, राजकुमारः, भर्तृदारकः; 'king's daughter,' राजपुत्री, राजकुमारी, राजकन्या; 'a line of kings,' राजावली -लिः *f.*, राजसन्ततिः *f.*; 'having no king,' अराजकः -का -कं, अनायकः -का -कं.

KING-CRAFT, *s.* राज्यनयनविद्या, राज्यकर्तृत्वं, राजत्वकरणं, राज्यचातुर्य्यं, राजनीतिः *f.*, राजनयः, राज्यरीतिः *f.*

KINGDOM, *s.* राज्यं, राजत्वं, ऐश्वर्य्यं, आधिपत्यं, स्वाम्यं, प्रभुत्वं, माहिनं.—(Country subject to a king) राष्ट्रं, राज्यं, विषयः.—(Government) राज्यं, राज्याधिकारः, राजाधिकारः, राज्यपालनं, राज्यनीतिः *f.* —(Population) प्रजा.—(Animal kingdom) जीवजातिः *f.*, प्राणिजातिः *f.*, जीवगणः.—(Vegetable kingdom) तृणजातिः *f.*, मूलजातिः, तृणगणः.—(Mineral kingdom) धातुजातिः *f.*, धातुगणः.

KINGFISHER, *s.* मत्स्यरङ्कः -ङ्कः, मत्स्यरङ्कः, मत्स्याशनः, सुचिपक्षः, छत्रकः, कुट्टकः.

KINGLESS, *a.* अराजकः -का -कं, राजहीनः -ना -नं, अनायकः -का -कं.

KINGLIKE, KINGLY, *a.* राजकीयः -या -यं, राजयोग्यः -ग्या -ग्यं, राजसदृशः -शी -शं, राजार्हः -र्हा -र्हं, नृपोचितः -ता -तं, राजोचितः -ता -तं, राजसन्निभः -भा -भं, राजसम्बन्धी -न्धिनी -न्धि (न्), राज in comp.; as, 'kingly policy,' राजनीतिः.

KING'S-EVIL, *s.* (A scrofulous disease) गण्डमाला.

KINGSHIP, *s.* राजता -त्वं, राज्यं, नृपत्वं, नरेन्द्रत्वं, भूपता -त्वं, महीपत्वं, नरैश्वर्य्यं, प्रभुत्वं, प्रजैश्वर्य्यं, प्राजापत्यं, आधिपत्यं, राजाधिकारः, राजपदं.

KINSFOLK, *s.* बान्धवाः *m. pl.*, बन्धुवर्गः, बन्धुजनः, बान्धववर्गः, स्वजनाः *m. pl.*, स्वजनः, ज्ञातिवर्गः, सजातीयाः *m. pl.*, सगोत्राः *m. pl.*

KINSMAN, *s.* बन्धुजनः, बन्धुः *m.*, बान्धवः, ज्ञातिः *m.*, स्वज्ञातिः *m.*, स्वजातीयः, सजातीयः, स्वबन्धुः *m.*, स्वजनः, स्वकुल्यः, सकुल्यः, स्ववंशीयः, सवंश्यः, वंश्यः, स्वकीयः, स्वकुटुम्बी *m.* (न्), कुटुम्बी *m.*, स्वः, कुलपुरुषः, गोत्रपुरुषः, सगोत्रः, गोत्रजः, गोत्रः, समानगोत्रः, गोत्रबन्धुः *m.*, सपिण्डः, सनाभिः *m.*, दायादः -दवः, समानोदकः, उदकदः, उदकदायी *m.* (न्); 'a number of kinsmen,' बन्धुगणः, बन्धुता; 'bewailing a kinsman,' बान्धवाक्रोशी *m.* (न्).

KINSWOMAN, *s.* बन्धुजनः, स्वजातीया, स्वकुल्या, गोत्रजा, गोत्रस्त्री.

KIRK, *s.* (Place of worship) भजनालयः, भजनमन्दिरं.—(Body of believers) भक्तसमूहः, भक्तगणः, भक्तवृन्दं. *See* CHURCH.

To KISS, *v. a.* चुम्ब् (c. 1. चुम्बति -म्बितुं, c. 10. चुम्बयति -यितुं), चुम्बनं कृ or दा, निंस् (c. 2. निंस्ते, निंसितुं), प्रणिंस्, परिणिंस्, निक्ष् (c. 1. निक्षति -क्षितुं), प्रणिक्ष्, मूर्ध्नि or मूर्धनि or शिरसि आघ्रा (c. 1. -जिघ्रति -घ्रातुं) or उपाघ्रा or उपघ्रा or समुपाघ्रा or समाघ्रा or अवघ्रा, अधरपानं कृ, अधररसं पा (c. 1. पिबति, पातुं).

KISS, *s.* चुम्बनं, चुम्बितं, परिणिंसा, निक्षणं, प्रणिक्षणं, निमित्रकं, अधरपानं, दशनोच्छिष्टः; 'giving a kiss,' चुम्बनदानं.

KISSED, *p. p.* चुम्बितः -ता -तं, प्रणिंसितः -ता -तं, परिणिंसितः -ता -तं, निक्षितः -ता -तं; 'to be kissed,' चुम्बनीयः -या -यं, प्रणिंसितव्यः -व्या -व्यं.

KISSER, *s.* चुम्बकः, चुम्बनदाता *m.* (तृ), परिणिंसकः.

KISSING, *part.* चुम्बन् -म्बन्ती -म्बत् (त्), चुम्बितवान् -वती -वत् (त्).

KIT, *s.* (A large bottle) महाकूपी.—(A small fiddle) क्षुद्रसारङ्गी.—(A soldier's baggage) सैनिकसामग्री -ग्र्यं, सैनिकपरिच्छदः.—(Complement of necessary utensils) उपकरणसामग्र्यं -ग्री, उपकरणसमुदायः, सोपकारद्रव्यसम्भारः, द्रव्यसम्भारः, सम्भारः.

KITCHEN, *s.* पाकशाला, पाकस्थानं, पाकगृहं, पाकागारं, महानसः -सं, रसवती, सूदशाला; 'superintendent of the kitchen,' पाकशालाध्यक्षः, पाकगृहाधिकारी *m.* (न्), सूदाध्यक्षः.

KITCHEN-GARDEN, *s.* शाकवाटिका, शाकवाटी, शाकशाकटं, शाकशाकिनं.

KITCHEN-MAID, *s.* पाककर्म्मकरी, पाकचेटी, महानसचेटी, पाचकसहकारिणी दासिका or दासी.

KITCHEN-WORK, *s.* पाककर्म्म *n.* (न्), पाककार्य्यं, पाकागारकर्म्म.

KITE, *s.* (The bird) चिल्लः, आतायी *m.* (न्), आतापी *m.* (न्), वियचारी *m.* (न्), खभ्रान्तिः *m.*, श्येनः.

KITLING, *s.* शावः -वकः, शिशुः *m.*, वत्सः, डिम्भः, डिम्भः.

KITTEN, *s.* मार्जारशावकः, विडालशिशुः *m.*, विडालशावकः, मार्जारवत्सः, क्षुद्रविडालः.

To KITTEN, *v. n.* मार्जारशावकं सु (c. 2. सूते, c. 4. सूयते, सोतुं) or प्रसु or जन् (c. 10. जनयति -यितुं) or प्रजन् (c. 4. -जायते -जनितुं).

To KLICK, *v. n.* *See To* CLICK.

To KNAB, *v. a.* दंश् (c. 1. दशति, दंष्टुं), दन्तैर् ग्रह् (c. 9. गृह्णाति, ग्रहीतुं), or धृ (c. 1. धरति, धर्त्तुं).

KNACK, *s.* (Toy) क्रीडनकं.—(Dexterity) दक्षता, हस्तदक्षता, हस्तकौशल्यं, हस्तलाघवं, युक्तिः *f.*, चातुर्य्यं, नैपुण्यं, निपुणता, प्रयोगः, सुप्रयोगः -गता, पटुता, पाटवं, व्यापारः, क्षिप्रता, व्यापारक्षिप्रता, अभ्यासः.

To KNACK, *v. n.* आकस्मिकक्कणितं कृ, आकस्मिकशब्दं कृ, स्फुत्कारं कृ.

KNACKER, *s.* जीर्णाश्वक्रेता *m.* (तृ), जीर्णाश्वविशसिता *m.* (तृ).

KNAG, *s.* (Knot in wood) ग्रन्थिः *m.*, काष्ठसन्धिः *m.*, पर्व्व *n.* (न्).

KNAGGY, *a.* ग्रन्थिलः -ला -लं, बहुग्रन्थिः -न्थिः -न्थि, पर्व्वविशिष्टः -ष्टा -ष्टं.

KNAP, *s.* (Protuberance) गण्डः, पिण्डः, गुल्मः, ग्रन्थिः *m.*, आभोगः.

To KNAP, *v. a.* (Bite) अकस्माद् दंश् (c. 1. दशति, दंष्टुं), आकस्मिकदंशनं कृ.—(Make a sharp sound) अकस्मात् क्कण् (c. 1. क्कणति -णितुं), आकस्मिकक्कणितं कृ.

KNAPSACK, *s.* पृष्ठेन भृतं सोपकारद्रव्यभाण्डं or सोपकारद्रव्याधारः, सैनिकेन यात्रामध्ये पृष्ठतो भृतं सोपकारद्रव्यभाजनं.

KNAR, *s.* (Knot in wood) ग्रन्थिः *m.*, पर्व्व *n.* (न्). *See* GNARLED.

KNAVE, *s.* धूर्त्तः, कितवः, वञ्चकः, प्रवञ्चकः, शठः, दुष्टजनः, तस्करः, पिशुनः, प्रतारकः, कूटकः, कूटकारः, दाम्भिकः, कुहकः, छिद्वरः, कपटी *m.* (न्), कपटिकः.

KNAVERY, *s.* धूर्त्तता, कैतवं, तस्करविद्या, शाठ्यं, शठता, कूटता, पैशुन्यं, वञ्चनं, वञ्चकत्वं, व्याजः, कापट्यं, छलं, कपटः, दुष्टता.

KNAVISH, *a.* धूर्त्तः -र्त्ता -र्त्तं, धूर्त्तस्वभावः -वा -वं, धूर्त्तशीलः -ला -लं, कितवशीलः -ला -लं, शठः -ठा -ठं, तस्करस्वभावः -वा -वं, कपटी -टिनी -टि (न्), कापटिकः -की -कं, कौटिकः -की -कं, वञ्चकः -का -कं, पिशुनः -ना -नं.

KNAVISHLY, *adv.* धूर्त्तवत्, कितववत्, सकैतवं, कैतवेन, तस्करवत्, शठवत्, शाठ्येन, सकपटं, सकापट्यं, सव्याजं, सकूटं, वञ्चकवत्, वञ्चनार्थं, छलेन.

KNAVISHNESS, *s.* धूर्त्तता, कैतवं, धूर्त्तशीलता, कितवशीलता, शठता.

To KNEAD, *v. a.* हस्ताभ्यां मृद् (c. 9. मृद्नाति, मर्द्दितुं, c. 10. मर्दयति -यितुं), अवमृद्, विमृद्, प्रमृद्, उपमृद्, अभिमृद्, सम्मृद्, कराभ्यां पिष् (c. 7. पिनष्टि, पेष्टुं) or चूर्ण् (c. 10. चूर्णयति -यितुं), प्रचूर्ण्, विचूर्ण्, सञ्चूर्ण्, चूर्णीकृ or घृष् (c. 1. घर्षति -र्षितुं), हस्ताभ्यां सम्पीड् (c. 10. -पीडयति -यितुं), हस्तसम्पीडनपूर्व्वं पिण्डीकृ.—(Knead the limbs) संवाह् (c. 1. -वाहति -हितुं, c. 10. -वाहयति -यितुं), कराभ्यां संवाह्, संवाहनं कृ.

KNEADED, *p. p.* हस्ताभ्यां मर्दितः -ता -तं or सम्मर्दितः -ता -तं or विमर्दितः -ता -तं or मृदितः -ता -तं or उपमर्दितः -ता -तं or अवमर्दितः -ता -तं, कराभ्यां पिष्टः -ष्टा -ष्टं or सम्पिष्टः -ष्टा -ष्टं or चूर्णितः -ता -तं or घर्षितः -ता -तं or सम्पीडितः -ता -तं or पिण्डीकृतः -ता -तं.—(As the limbs) संवाहितः -ता -तं, कृतसंवाहः -हा -हं; 'to be kneaded,' संवाह्यः -ह्या -ह्यं.

KNEADING, *s.* हस्ताभ्यां मर्दनं or विमर्दनं or अवमर्दः -र्दनं or उपमर्दः -र्दनं, कराभ्यां पेषणं or घर्षणं or सम्पीडनं.—(Of the limbs) संवाहः -हनं, संहननं.—(Kneading-trough) द्रोणिः -णी *f.*

KNEE, *s.* जानु *n.* -नुः *m.*, जानुसन्धिः *m.*, अष्ठीवान् *m.* -वत् *n.* (त्), ऊरुपर्व्व *n.* (न्), ऊरुसन्धिः *m.*, जङ्घोरुसन्धिः *m.*, जङ्घोरुपर्व्व *n.*, कुर्परः, कूर्परः, नलकीलः, पर्व्वकं, चक्रिका; 'he fell on his knees,' जानुभ्यां भूमिम् अगमत् or भूमौ पपात.

KNEE-DEEP, *a.* जानुदघ्नः -घ्नी -घ्नं, जानुद्वयसः -सी -सं, जानुमात्रः -त्री -त्रं.

To KNEEL, *v. n.* जानुनी भूमौ न्यस् (c. 4. -अस्यति -असितुं), जानुनी भूमौ कृ, जानुभ्यां स्था (c. 1. तिष्ठति, स्थातुं), जानुभ्यां भूमौ पत् (c. 1. पतति -तितुं), or निपत्, जानुनी नम् (c. 10. नमयति -यितुं).

KNEELING, *part.* or *a.* भूमिन्यस्तजानुः -नुः -नु, क्षितिन्यस्तजानुः -नुः -नु, नतजानुकः -की -कं.

KNEEPAN, *s.* जानुफलकं, कपोली, नलकिनी, अष्ठीवत् *n.*, जानुफलं.

KNEE-TRIBUTE, *s.* जानुपूजा, जानुभ्यां पूजा, जानुनतिपूर्व्वा सेवा or अर्चना.

KNELL, *s.* प्रेतनयनकाले घण्टाध्वनिः *m.* or घण्टाशब्दः.

KNICK KNACK. *s.* क्रीडनकं, क्रीडाद्रव्यं, क्रीडावस्तु *n.*, क्रीडाविषयः.

KNIFE, *s.* छुरिका, छुरी, कर्त्तरिका, क्षुरी, कृन्तनिका, कृन्तत्रं, शस्त्री, कृपाणी -णिका, असिपुत्रिका.

KNIFE-GRINDER, *s.* भ्रमाजीवी *m.* (न्), भ्रमासक्तः, भ्रमद्वारेण छुरिकातेजकः.

KNIGHT, *s.* सादी *m.* (न्), कुलीनसादी *m.*, अश्वसादी *m.*, अश्ववारः, कुलीनयोद्धा *m.* (द्धृ).

To KNIGHT, *v. a.* सादिपदे नियुज् (c. 7. -युनक्ति -योक्तुं), सादिख्यातिं दा, सादिपद्धतिं दा, कुलीनख्यातिं दा.

KNIGHTHOOD, *s.* सादिपदं, कुलीनसादिपदं, सादित्वं, सादिख्यातिः *f.*

To KNIT, *v.a.* दीर्घसूचिद्वारेण सूत्राणि ग्रन्थ् (c. 9. ग्रथ्नाति, c. 1. ग्रन्थति, ग्रन्थितुं), तन्तुग्रन्थनं कृ.—(Knit together, connect) संयुज् (c. 7. -युनक्ति -योक्तुं, c. 10. -योजयति -यितुं), सम्बन्ध् (c. 9. -बध्नाति -बन्द्धुं), संश्लिष् (c. 10.-श्लेषयति-यितुं), योक्त्र (nom. योक्त्रयति -यितुं), संलग्नीकृ. —(Knit the brows) भ्रुवौ संहन् (c. 2. -हन्ति -न्तुं), भ्रूसंहतिं कृ.

KNIT, *p. p.* ग्रथितः -ता -तं.—(Well-knit) संहतः -ता -तं, सुसंहतः -ता -तं, दृढसन्धिः -न्धिः -न्धि; 'having the brows knit,' संहतभ्रूः -भ्रूः -भ्रु.

KNITTING, *s.* दीर्घसूचिद्वारा तन्तुग्रन्थनं or सूत्रग्रन्थनं, सूत्रश्लेषः; 'knitting the brows,' भ्रूसंहतिः *f.*

KNITTING-NEEDLE, *s.* दीर्घसूचिः -ची *f.*, सूत्रग्रन्थनार्थं दीर्घसूचिः or दीर्घशलाका.

KNOB, *s.* पिण्डः -ण्डं, गण्डः -ण्डका, गुल्मः, ग्रन्थिः *m.* आभोगः.—(In wood) ग्रन्थिः *m.*, पर्व्व *n.* (न्).

KNOBBED, KNOBBY, *a.* पिण्डी -ण्डिनी -ण्डि (न्), पिण्डितः -ता -तं, सपिण्डः -ण्डा -ण्डं, गण्डी -ण्डिनी -ण्डि (न्), सगण्डः -ण्डा -ण्डं, ग्रन्थिलः -ला -लं.

To KNOCK, *v. a.* (Strike, hit) तड् (c. 10. ताडयति -यितुं), वितड्, तुद् (c. 6. तुदति -ते, तोत्तुं), आतुद्, वितुद्, प्रहृ (c. 1. -हरति -हर्त्तुं), हन् (c. 2. हन्ति -न्तुं), अभिहन्, निहन्, आहन्, विहन्, समाहन्, अभ्याहन्. —(Strike a door) द्वारं तड्.—(Knock down) पत् (c. 10. पातयति -यितुं), अवपत्, निपत्, भ्रंश् (c. 10. भ्रंशयति -यितुं), आघातेन or प्रहारेण भूमौ पत्.—(Knock out) आघातेन वहिष्कृ; 'to knock out the brains,' मस्तकं निष्पिष् (c. 7. -पिनष्टि -पेष्टुं), आघातेन मस्तिष्कं वहिष्कृ.—(Knock off) आघातेन पत्; 'do quickly,' सत्वरं सम्पद् (c. 10. -पादयति -यितुं), त्वरितं कृ.—(Knock up, fatigue) खिद् (c. 10. खेदयति -यितुं), अवसद् (c. 10. -सादयति -यितुं), आयासेन सत्त्वं or बलं हृ (c. 1. हरति, हर्त्तुं) or अपहृ.—(Knock on the head) मस्तकम् आहत्य or ताडयित्वा व्यापद् (c. 10. -पादयति -यितुं).

To KNOCK, *v. n.* (Strike) ताडनं कृ, आघातं कृ, अभिघातं कृ, प्रहारं कृ, 'to knock with a stick,' वेत्राघातं कृ, दण्डप्रहारं कृ, दण्डपातनं कृ; 'with the fist,' मुष्ट्याघातं कृ, मुष्टिप्रहारं कृ, बाहुप्रहरणं कृ, मुष्टिपातं कृ. —(Strike against, clash) अभिहन् (c. 2. -हन्ति -न्तुं), प्रतिहन्, प्रतिघातं कृ, सङ्घट्ट् (c. 1. -घट्टते -ट्टितुं), आपत् (c. 1. -पतति -तितुं), अभिपत्.—(Knock under, submit) उपगम् (c. 1. -गच्छति -गन्तुं), वशं गम्, वशीभू.—(Knock up) श्रम् (c. 4. श्राम्यति, श्रमितुं), खिद् (c. 4. खिद्यते, खेत्तुं), अत्यायासात् or अतिखेदात् गतसत्त्वः -त्त्वा -त्त्वं भू.

KNOCK, *s.* (Blow) आघातः, अभिघातः, घातः, प्रहारः, आहतिः *f.*, हतिः *f.*, ताडनं, घातः -तनं; 'a knock with a stick,' वेत्राघातः; 'a knock with the fist,' मुष्टिप्रहारः; 'a knock-down argument,' गलहस्तः.

KNOCKED, *p. p.* ताडितः -ता -तं, आहतः -ता -तं, अभिहतः -ता -तं, समाहतः -ता -तं, प्रहतः -ता -तं.—(Knocked down) निपातितः -ता -तं, पातितः -ता -तं, भ्रंशितः -ता -तं.

KNOCK-KNEED, *a.* संहतजानुः -नुः -नु, संहतजानुकः -का -कं, संज्ञुः -ज्ञुः -ज्ञु, संज्ञः -ज्ञा -ज्ञं.

KNOCKER, *s.* (One that knocks) ताडयिता *m.* (तृ), प्रहर्त्ता *m.* (र्त्तृ), ताडनकृत्.—(Of a door) द्वारताडनी, द्वारमुद्गरः, द्वारताडनयन्त्रं.

To KNOLL, *v. a.* or *n.* प्रेतनयनकाले घण्टाध्वनिं कृ or घण्टाशब्दं कृ.

KNOLL, *s.* क्षुद्रपर्व्वतः, ईषदुन्नतो भूभागः or भूमिभागः or मृत्तिकाचयः, वप्रः -प्री, वल्मीकं, नाकुः *m.*

KNOT, *s.* ग्रन्थिः *m.*, ग्रन्थिका, बन्धः -न्धनं, गण्डः; 'tying a knot,' ग्रन्थिबन्धनं.—(Joint in a plant) पर्व्व *n.* (न्), ग्रन्थिः *m.*, परुः *m.*, गण्डुः *f.*, बाकलकः.—(In wood) काष्ठग्रन्थिः *m.*, काष्ठसन्धिः *m.*, काण्डसन्धिः *m.*—(Articulation) सन्धिः *m.*—(Bond of union) सन्धिः *m.*, सम्बन्धः, संहतिः *f.*, संयोगः.—(Gang, crew) गणः, सङ्घः, समूहः, संसर्गः, निवहः, मण्डलं.—(Bunch, clump) पिण्डः -ण्डं, गुल्मः, गुच्छः -च्छकः, स्तवकः, काण्डः, स्तम्बः.—(Knotty point) ग्रन्थिः *m.*, गूढार्थः; 'one who removes knots,' ग्रन्थिहरः.

To KNOT, *v. a.* ग्रन्थिं कृ, ग्रन्थ् (c. 1. ग्रन्थति -न्थितुं), ग्रन्थिरूपेण संश्लिष् (c. 10. -श्लेषयति -यितुं).

To KNOT, *v. n.* ग्रन्थिरूपेण संश्लिष्टीभू, ग्रन्थिं बन्ध् (c. 9. बध्नाति, बन्द्धुं).

KNOTTINESS, *s.* ग्रन्थिलत्वं, सग्रन्थित्वं, ग्रन्थिपूर्णता, सपर्व्वत्वं, ग्रन्थिमत्त्वं.

KNOTTY, KNOTTED; *a.* ग्रन्थिलः -ला -लं, ग्रन्थिमान् -मती -मत् (त्), ग्रन्थी -न्थिनी -न्थि (न्), ग्रन्थिमयः -यी -यं, पर्व्वमयः -यी -यं, बहुग्रन्थिः -न्थिः -न्थि.—(Intricate, difficult) गूढार्थः -र्था -र्थं, दुर्ज्ञेयः -या -यं, दुर्गमः -मा -मं, दुःशोधनीयः -या -यं.

To KNOW, *v. a.* and *n.* ज्ञा (c. 9. जानाति -नीते, ज्ञातुं), परिज्ञा, संज्ञा, विज्ञा, विद् (c. 2. वेत्ति, वेदितुं), संविद्, बुध् (c. 1. बोधति -ते -धितुं, c. 4. बुध्यते, बोद्धुं), अवबुध्, सम्बुध्, अवगम् (c. 1. -गच्छति -गन्तुं), अवे (c. 2. अवैति -तुं, rt. इ), मन् (c. 4. मन्यते, मन्तुं); 'know thou,' अवेहि, जानीहि.—(Recognize) अभिज्ञा, प्रतिज्ञा, प्रत्यभिज्ञा, समभिज्ञा. —(Be familiar or acquainted with) परिचयं कृ, परिचितः -ता -तं भू or अस्.—(Understand, perceive) उपलभ् (c. 1. -लभते -लब्धुं), ग्रह् (c. 9. गृह्णाति, ग्रहीतुं), अर्थं ग्रह्.—(Carnally) प्रज्ञा, सङ्गम् (c. 1. -गच्छति -गन्तुं), भज् (c. 1. भजते, भक्तुं), स्त्रीसङ्गं कृ, स्त्रीसङ्ग्रहणं कृ.

KNOWABLE, *a.* ज्ञातव्यः -व्या -व्यं, ज्ञेयः -या -यं, विज्ञेयः -या -यं, ज्ञानीयः -या -यं, वेदनीयः -या -यं, वेद्यः -द्या -द्यं, अवगम्यः -म्या -म्यं, अवगन्तव्यः -व्या -व्यं.

KNOWER, *s.* ज्ञाता *m.* -त्री *f.* (तृ), ज्ञानी *m.* -निनी *f.* (न्), वेत्ता *m.* -त्री *f.* (त्तृ), वेदिता *m.* (तृ), वेदी *m.* -दिनी *f.* (न्), अभिज्ञः -ज्ञा, ज्ञः ज्ञा in comp.

KNOWING, *a.* (Shrewd) अभिज्ञः -ज्ञा -ज्ञं, विज्ञः -ज्ञा -ज्ञं, ज्ञानी -निनी -नि (न्), विदग्धः -ग्धा -ग्धं, तद्विद् *m.f. n.*, तज्ज्ञः -ज्ञा -ज्ञं, पक्वबुद्धिः -द्धिः -द्धि, विचक्षणः -णा -णं, नागरः -रा -रं, निपुणः -णा -णं, प्रवीणः -णा -णं.

KNOWINGLY, *adv.* ज्ञानतस्, ज्ञानात्, ज्ञानपूर्व्वं, मत्या, बुद्ध्या, मतिपूर्व्वं, बुद्धिपूर्व्वं, बोधपूर्व्वं.—(Cunningly) विज्ञवत्, विदग्धवत्.

KNOWLEDGE, *s.* (Certain perception, opposed to ignorance of) ज्ञानं, परिज्ञानं, विज्ञानं, अभिज्ञानं, बोधः -धनं, प्रबोधः, अवबोधः, उद्बोधः, प्रज्ञा, उपलब्धिः *f.*, वेदनं, संवेदः -दनं, अवगमः, प्रमा, प्रमितिः *f.*, समुदागमः, उपलम्भः, ज्ञप्तिः *f.*, प्रतीतिः *f.*, ज्ञातृत्वं, वेत्तृत्वं, विपश्यं.—(Learning, science) विद्या, ज्ञानं, विज्ञानं, विज्ञता, वैदुष्यं, पाण्डित्यं,

प्राज्ञत्वं, श्रुतिः *f.*, व्युत्पत्तिः *f.*—(Spiritual knowledge) आत्मविद्या, आत्मज्ञानं, परमार्थविद्या, परमार्थज्ञानं, परमार्थः, अध्यात्मविद्या, तत्त्वज्ञानं, ज्ञानविद्या, ज्ञानं, ब्रह्मज्ञानं, ब्रह्मविद्या; 'instruction in spiritual knowledge,' ब्रह्मदानं, ब्रह्मोपदेशः, ज्ञानोपदेशः, आत्मबोधः; 'versed in it,' ज्ञानवान् -वती -वत् (त्), ज्ञानपरः -रा -रं, ज्ञाननिष्ठः -ष्ठा -ष्ठं, —(Sacred and profane knowledge) ज्ञानविज्ञानं.—(Recognition) प्रत्यभिज्ञानं, प्रत्यभिज्ञा, अभिज्ञानं, संवित्तिः *f.*—(Acquaintance with persons) परिचयः, सौहृद्यं.—(Conversancy) परिज्ञानं, अभिज्ञता, विज्ञता, नैपुण्यं, प्रवीणता, पाटवं; 'acquiring knowledge,' विद्यागमः, विद्याप्राप्तिः *f.*, विद्यार्जनं, विद्यालाभः; 'giving knowledge,' विद्यादानं; 'eager after knowledge,' विद्यार्थी -र्थिनी -र्थि (न्), जिज्ञासुः -सुः -सु, ज्ञानेच्छुः -च्छुः -च्छु, ज्ञानेप्सुः -प्सुः -प्सु; 'thirst after knowledge,' जिज्ञासा, विद्यार्थः, ज्ञानेच्छा; 'attainable by knowledge,' ज्ञानगम्यः -म्या -म्यं; 'gained by knowledge,' विद्यार्जितः -ता -तं, विद्यालब्धः -ब्धा -ब्धं; 'according to one's knowledge,' यथाज्ञानं; 'without the knowledge of,' अगोचरेण; 'with the knowledge of,' गोचरेण; 'with my knowledge,' मम गोचरेण, मद्गोचरेण.

KNOWN, *p. p.* ज्ञातः -ता -तं, परिज्ञातः -ता -तं, अभिज्ञातः -ता -तं, विज्ञातः -ता -तं, विदितः -ता -तं, वित्तः -त्ता -त्तं, विन्नः -न्ना -न्नं, बुधितः -ता -तं, बुद्धः -द्धा -द्धं, अवगतः -ता -तं, मतः -ता -तं, उपलब्धः -ब्धा -ब्धं, गृहीतार्थः -र्था -र्थं; 'to make known,' ज्ञा in caus. (ज्ञापयति, ज्ञपयति -यितुं), विज्ञा, निविद् (c. 10. -वेदयति -यितुं), विद्, बुध् (c. 10. बोधयति -यितुं); 'made known,' ज्ञप्तः -प्ता -प्तं, विज्ञप्तः -प्ता -प्तं, ज्ञापितः -ता -तं, विज्ञापितः -ता -तं, वेदितः -ता -तं, निवेदितः -ता -तं; 'to be known,' ज्ञा in pass. (ज्ञायते), प्रती in pass. (-ईयते), परिचि in pass. (-चीयते); 'be it known,' विदितम् अस्तु, ज्ञातम् अस्तु.—(Celebrated) विश्रुतः -ता -तं, ख्यातः -ता -तं, विख्यातः -ता -तं, विज्ञातः-ता-तं, प्रसिद्धः-द्धा-द्धं, प्रतीतः-ता-तं; 'known quantity,' रूपं.

KNUCKLE, *s.* अङ्गुलिसन्धिः *m.*, अङ्गुलिग्रन्थिः *m.*, अङ्गुलिपर्व्व *n.* (न्), सन्धिः *m.*, पर्व्व *n.* (न्), ग्रन्थिः *m.*

To KNUCKLE, *v. n.* वशं गम् (c. 1. गच्छति, गन्तुं), वशीभू, उपगम्, अभ्युपगम्, नम्रीभू, पराधीनीभू.

KNUCKLED, *a.* सन्धियुक्तः -क्ता -क्तं, सन्धिविशिष्टः -ष्टा -ष्टं, ग्रन्थिलः -ला -लं.

KNURL, *s.* ग्रन्थिः *m.*, ग्रन्थिका, पिण्डः -ण्डं, गण्डः.

KNURLED, *a.* ग्रन्थिलः -ला -लं, ग्रन्थिमयः -यी -यं, बहुग्रन्थिः -न्थिः -न्थि.

KRISHNA, *s.* (The most celebrated form of Vishnu, or rather identified with Vishnu, as distinct from his ten Avatárs, or Incarnations. The following particulars of the history of this very popular deity, whose votaries are still so numerous in India, are given as an introduction to the enumeration of his various names. Vasudeva, a descendant of Yadu and Yayáti, had two wives, Rohiní and Devakí. The latter had eight sons, of whom the eighth was Krishna. Kansa, a demon, the sister of Devakí, and king of Mathurá, was informed by the gods that one of these sons would kill him. He therefore kept Vasudeva and his wife Devakí in confinement in his palace, and slew their first six children. The seventh son was Balaráma, who was saved by being abstracted from the womb of Devakí, and transferred to that of Rohiní. The eighth was Krishna, who was born with skin as black as the dark leaves of the lotus, and with a peculiar mark on his breast: he was born at midnight, and immediately taken up by Vasudeva, who, favoured by the gods, was able to elude the vigilance of the guards, and make his escape through the gates of Mathurá to the banks of the Yamuná river. Here Sesha, the many-headed serpent, spread his hoods above the heads of the father and child, and thus protecting them, Vasudeva was enabled to cross the stream, and finding a a cowherd named Nanda, whose wife Yaśodá had just been delivered of a child, he quietly substituted his own son in its place, and returned with the child of the cowherd to the bedside of Devakí. When Kansa found that the infant Krishna had escaped, he summoned certain demons, his servants, and gave orders that a search should be made for the child, and that all male children in whom were signs of unusual vigour, should be killed. At the same time he released Vasudeva and his wife, as no longer endangering his safety. The cowherd Nanda, with his wife Yaśodá, taking the infant Krishna, and accompanied by Rohiní and the infant Balaráma, went to reside at a village called Gokula, or Vraja, where they settled. Here the female demon Pútaná tried to destroy the young Krishna by offering him her breast to suck, but was killed by the child. Soon the child, with his playfellow Balaráma, began to be unruly; and one day his foster-mother passed the folds of a rope round his body and tied him to a large wooden bowl, but the strength of the young Krishna enabled him to drag the bowl against the trunks of two trees, which were uprooted by the shock. The family of Nanda now removed from Vraja to Vrindávana, and here Krishna and Balaráma grew up together, and, roaming about the woods, joined in the sports of the herdsmen's sons. One day Krishna came to the banks of the Yamuná, within which was the fearful pool of the serpent Káliya. Krishna jumped boldly in. A terrible combat ensued, in which the divine child was victorious, and commanded the snake-king to depart from the Yamuná to the ocean. About the same time Balaráma killed the demon Dhenuka, who sought to destroy the two boys, and soon afterwards killed the demon Pralamba, who had assumed the shape of a young cowherd, that he might mix in their sports. Not long after, the young Krishna, who delighted in playing tricks upon his elders, resolved to rouse the anger of the god Indra, who, according to some, was his elder brother. He persuaded Nanda to cease sacrificing to Indra, and to worship the mountain Govardhana, which sheltered the shepherds and their cattle. This they did, but the exasperated Indra would have destroyed them and their flocks with heavy rain, had not Krishna lifted up the mountain and sheltered them under it. Indra, foiled in his revenge, descended from heaven to praise Krishna, and made him lord over the cattle. Meanwhile Krishna had grown a beautiful youth, and soon began to sport with the Gopís, or shepherdesses, of whom seven or eight became his wives, and amongst them his favorite, Rádhá. In this character he is usually represented with flowing hair and with a flute in his hand, and has been compared to Apollo accompanied by the muses. In his pastimes with the shepherdesses he invented a kind of round dance, called Rása or Mandala nrityam, in which he and Rádhá being in the centre, the attendant Gopís danced round them. But the happiness of Krishna was interrupted by his tyrannical uncle Kansa, who sent formidable demons to destroy him; Arishta, in the form of a bull, Keśin, in the form of a horse, Kálanemi, and others. They were all killed by the young Krishna. Kansa then sent a messenger, named Akrúra, to entice Krishna and Balaráma to his city Mathurá, under pretext of being present at some games. They accepted the invitation and went. At the entrance of the town Krishna killed Kansa's washerman, who insulted him. Having clothed himself in the washerman's yellow clothes, he proceeded, and meeting a crooked woman carrying ointment, miraculously made her straight by a touch of his hand. At the games he killed the king's boxer, Chánúra, and afterwards Kansa himself, and placed Kansa's father, Ugrasena, upon the throne. He then became the pupil of Sándípani, and, to rescue his son, killed the demon Panchajana, and, taking the conch shell, formed of his bones, bore it as his horn. Still living in Mathurá, he was attacked by a prince named Kálayavana, who advanced with a large force against the Yadu tribe. Upon this Krishna built and fortified a city called Dwáraka, in the province of Guzerat, and thither transferred the inhabitants of Mathurá. One day Krishna went forth unarmed, and, being pursued by Kálayavana, took refuge in a cavern, where Muchukunda, king of men, was asleep. Kálayavana, entering the cavern, was reduced to ashes by an angry glance from the eye of Muchukunda. Krishna then returned to Dwáraka. Soon after he was accused of stealing a wonderful jewel called 'syamantaka,' in the possession of a man named Prasena. But the jewel was really lost by the death of Prasena in a forest, and was picked up by a lion, who, in his turn, was killed by the king of the bears, Jámbavat. The latter took the jewel to his cavern, where he was found by Krishna, and compelled to restore the gem. At the same time the bear gave him his daughter Jámbavatí in marriage. He next married Satyabhāmā, daughter of Satrájit, and afterward carried off Rukminí, daughter of Bhíshmaka. By the latter he had a son called Pradyumna, who is usually identified with Kámadeva, the god of love, and a daughter named Chárumatí, as well as many other children. Besides these wives he had more than sixteen thousand others, who bore him a numerous progeny of one hundred and eighty thousand sons. The other incidents of his life are thus briefly related. Indra came to Dwáraka, and reported to Krishna the tyranny of the demon Naraka. Krishna went to his city, and slew him and another demon named Mura, who assisted in the defence of the city. He afterwards ascended to the heaven of Indra, with his wife Satyabhámá, and, visiting the gardens of Swarga, was induced by his wife to carry off the Párijáta tree, or celebrated tree of Paradise. Sachí, the wife of Indra, excited her husband to its rescue, and a conflict ensued between the gods and Krishna, who defeated them, and carried the tree to Dwáraka. Soon after this, Ushá, the daughter of the Daitya Bána, became enamoured of Aniruddha, son of Pradyumna and grandson of Krishna, and induced her father to carry him off. Krishna, Balaráma, and Pradyumna, came to his rescue. Siva and Skanda aided Bána, but the former was disabled and the latter put to flight; and Krishna, encountering Bána, cut off all his arms. After this, Paundraka, one of the family of Vasudeva, assumed the insignia and title of Krishna, and was supported by the king of Benares. Krishna advanced against them, mounted on his vehicle Garuda, and having destroyed them, set fire to Benares by the radiance from his chakra or discus. Lastly, being recalled by the gods to heaven, he destroyed all his own family the Yádavas. Amongst them died Balaráma, out of whose mouth, as he expired, issued the great serpent, Ananta or Sesha, of which he was an incarnation. Krishna himself was killed by a chance shot from a hunter, and again became one with the Universal Spirit. From this summary of the history of Krishna his various names will become intelligible. Many of these names, as well as many of his attributes and peculiarities, are identical with those of Vishnu. *See* VISHNU. As being of a black or dark blue colour he is called) कृष्णः, नीलमाधवः.—(As descended from Yadu) यादवः, यदुनाथः, कुकुराधिनाथः.—(As son of Vasudeva) वासुदेवः, वसुदेवभूः *m.*—(Son of Devakí) देवकीनन्दनः, देवकीपुत्रः, देवकीसूनुः *m.*, दैवकीनन्दनः.—(As bearing the mark Srívatsa on his breast) श्रीवत्सभृत् *m.*, श्रीवत्सलाञ्छनः, श्रीवत्साङ्कः.—(As foster-son of Nanda) नन्दनन्दनः, नन्दकी *m.* (न्), नन्दात्मजः.—(As slayer of Pútaná) पूतनाहा *m.* (न्), पूतनारिः *m.*, पूतनासूदनः.—(As having a rope round his body) दामोदरः.—(As destroying a tree in the forest of Vrindávana) यमलार्जुनहा *m.*—(Conqueror of Káliya) कालियजित्.—(Younger brother of Indra) उपेन्द्रः, इन्द्रानुजः, इन्द्रावरजः.—(Upholder of Govardhana) गोवर्धनधरः.—(Chief of shepherds and Protector of cattle) गोविन्दः, गोपालः -लकः, गोपेन्द्रः, गोपेशः.—(The long-haired) केशवः,

केशी *m.* (न्), केशः, केशटः.—(Bearer of the flute) वंशीधरः, मुरलीधरः.—(Lord of the shepherdesses) गोपीनाथः.—(Beloved of Rádhá) राधाकान्तः, राधावल्लभः, राधानाथः.—(Destroyer of Arishta) अरिष्टसूदनः.—(Of Keśin) केशिहा *m.* (न्), केशिसूदनः.—(Of Kálanemi) कालनेमिहा *m.*, कालनेमिरिपुः *m.*, कालनेमिशत्रुः *m.*, कालनेम्यरिः *m.*—(Dressed in yellow clothes) पीताम्बरः.—(Conqueror of Chánúra) चानूरजित्.—(Killer of Kansa) कंसहा *m.*, कंसजित् *m.*, कंसारिः *m.*, कंसारातिः *m.*—(Lord of Mathurá) मथुरेशः.—(Bearer of the couch Pánchajanya) पाञ्चजन्यधरः.—(Conqueror of Kálayavana) कालयवनजित्.—(Lord of Dwáraka) द्वारकेशः, द्वारकनाथः.—(Husband of Jámbavatí) जाम्बवतीपतिः *m.*—(Conqueror of Naraka) नरकजित्, नरकान्तकः.—(Destroyer of Mura) मुरहा *m.*, मुरारिः *m.*, मुररिपुः *m.*—(Conqueror of Paundraka) पौण्ड्रकजित्.—(Bearing the discus) चक्रधरः, चक्री *m.* (न्), चक्रपाणिः *m.*, चक्रहस्तः, चक्रवान् *m.* (त्), चक्रभृत् *m.*—(Bearing the conch) शङ्खी *m.* (न्), शङ्खभृत् *m.*—(Blowing the conch) ध्मः.—(Bearing a chaplet or garland) वनमाली *m.* (न्), मालः.—(Bearing the jewel on his breast) कौस्तुभवक्षाः *m.*, कौस्तुभलक्षकः.—(Destroyer of the demon Madhu) माधवः, मधुजित्, मधुरिपुः *m.*, मधुभिद् *m.*, मधुमथनः.—(Having Garuda as his symbol) गरुडध्वजः, तार्क्ष्यध्वजः, तार्क्ष्यनायकः.—(Foe of barbarians) यवनारिः.—(Foe of the daityas) दैत्यारिः *m.*—(The undecaying one) अच्युतः, अनन्तः.—(Worshipped by men) जनार्द्दनः.—(Lord of the senses) हृषीकेशः. The following are other names of this deity, some of which will be explained under the head of Vishnu हरिः *m.*, नारायणः, वैकुण्ठः, स्वभूः *m.*, पुण्डरीकाक्षः, विष्टरश्रवाः *m.* (स्), शार्ङ्गी *m.* (न्), पद्मनाभः, वासुभद्रः, वासुः *m.*, त्रिविक्रमः, विष्वक्सेनः, चतुर्भुज, शौरिः *m.*, पुरुषोत्तमः, बलिध्वंसी *m.* (न्), विश्वम्भरः, विधुः *m.*, अधोक्षजः, कैटभजित् *m.*, राहुभेदी *m.* (न्), कुशुभः, उरुगायः. Krishna's mace or club is called कौमोदकी; 'his sword,' नन्दकः; 'his jewel,' कौस्तुभः, स्यमन्तकः; 'his discus,' सुदर्शनः, चक्रं; 'his conch,' पाञ्चजन्यः, शङ्खः; 'his garland,' वनमाला; 'his charioteer,' सात्यकिः *m.*, शैनेयः, दारुकः, युयुधानः; 'his heaven,' गोलोकः; 'a festival in his honour,' रासयात्रा; 'his paternal uncle and friend,' अक्रूरः; 'his grandfather,' शूरः; देवकः; 'his city,' द्वारकः -का, द्वारिका, द्वारवती, अब्धिनगरी. A modern reformer of the Vaishnava faith called चैतन्यः is considered in Bengal as an avatár of Vishnu. He is also called गौरचन्द्रः, गौराङ्गः.

KRORE, *s.* (Ten millions) कोटिः -टी.

KURÁN, *s.* यावनधर्म्मग्रन्थः, यावनधर्म्मपुस्तकं, यवनीयधर्म्मशास्त्रं.

KUVERA, *s.* (God of wealth, the Hindu Plutus, chief of the Yakshas and Guhyakas, into whose forms transmigrate the souls of those men who in this life are absorbed in the pursuit of riches. He is the son of Viśravas by Ilavilá and regent of the north. He is represented in external appearance as a mere man, but with a deformed body, having three legs and but eight teeth. Hence he is called) कुवेरः, मनुष्यधर्म्मा *m.* (न्), कुहः.—(As lord of wealth) धनपतिः *m.*, धनाधिपः, धनदः, धनकेलिः *m.*, धनाध्यक्षः, वित्तेशः, वसुः *m.*, अर्थपतिः *m.*, श्रीमान् *m.* (त्), श्रीदः.—(Chief of the Yakshas) यक्षराजः, यक्षराट् *m.* (ज्), यक्षेन्द्रः, यक्षेशः, पुण्यजनेश्वरः, राक्षसेन्द्रः, यक्षः.—(Son of Viśravas) वैश्रवणः.—(Son of Ilavilá) ऐलविलः, ऐलविलः, ऐडविलः, ऐडविडः.—(Regent of the north) उत्तराशापतिः *m.*—(Lord of the Kinnaras) किन्नरेशः, किन्नरेश्वरः, किम्पुरुषेश्वरः, मयुराजः.—(Descended from Pulasti or Pulastya) पौलस्त्यः.—(King of kings) राजराजः.—(King of men) मनुराट्.—(Borne by men) नरवाहनः.—(Friend of Siva) त्र्यम्बकसखः, ईशसखः -खा.—(Having a yellow mark in place of one of his eyes) एकपिङ्गः -ङ्गलः.—(Lord of Alaká) अलकाधिपः -पतिः *m.*—(Inhabiting Kailása) कैलासनिकेतनः, कैलासौकाः.—(Lord of the divine treasures) निधिनाथः, निधीशः.—(The very fleet) रयिष्ठः. Kuvera's vehicle or car is called पुष्पं -ष्पकं; 'his garden,' चैत्ररथं; 'his city,' अलका, वसुधारा, वसुभारा, वसुस्थली, यक्षराट्पुरी.—(The mountain on which his city is situated) कैलासः, कुवेराचलः, कुवेराद्रिः *m.*—(His wife) कौवेरी, चार्व्वी, यक्षी, चामुण्डा.—(His son) नलकूवरः, नलकूवरः, नलकूवेरः, मणिग्रीवः, मायुराजः.—(His attendants, who are shaped like men with the heads of horses) किन्नरः, किम्पुरुषः, तुरङ्गवदनः, तुरङ्गवक्त्रः, तुरङ्गाननः, तुरङ्गास्यः, अश्ववक्त्रः, अश्ववदनः, मयुः.—(His divine treasure) निधिः *m.*, निधानं, शेवधिः *m.*, सेवधिः. There are nine of these treasures or gems, viz. पद्मः, महापद्मः, शङ्खः, मकरः, कच्छपः, मुकुन्दः, नन्दः, नीलः, खर्व्वः.—(Relating to Kuvera) कौवेरः -री -रं.

L.

LABEL, *s.* पत्रं, सूचकपत्रं, अङ्कपत्रं, अङ्कपटः, योजकं.

To LABEL, *v. a.* सूचकपत्रम् आरुह् (c. 10. -रोपयति -यितुं) or अनुबन्ध् (c. 9. -बध्नाति -बन्धुं) or बन्ध्.

LABIAL, *a.* ओष्ठ्यः -ष्ठ्या -ष्ठ्यं, ओष्ठसम्बन्धी -न्धिनी -न्धि (न्); 'a labial letter,' ओष्ठ्यं.

LABIODENTAL, *a.* दन्तोष्ठ्यः -ष्ठ्या -ष्ठ्यं, दन्तौष्ठ्यः &c., दन्त्योष्ठ्यः &c.

LABOR, *s.* (Exertion) उत्साहः, उद्योगः, यत्नः, प्रयत्नः, व्यवसायः, अध्यवसायः, उद्यमः, आयासः, कर्म्म *n.* (न्), क्रिया, प्रवृत्तिः *f.*, व्यापारः, चेष्टा.—(Toil) आयासः, प्रयासः, क्लेशः, श्रमः, परिश्रमः, कष्टं, दुःखं, नित्यश्रमः, नित्यक्लेशः.—(Bodily or manual labor) कायक्लेशः, देहक्लेशः, शरीरायासः, शरीरक्लेशः, शरीरश्रमः, व्रातं.—(Unpaid labor) विष्टिः, आजूः *f.*—(Travail, childbirth) प्रसववेदना, प्रसूतिवेदना, गर्भवेदना, प्रसवयातना, प्रसवकालः, प्रसूतिकालः; 'acquired by one's own labor,' स्वकष्टार्जितः -ता -तं.

To LABOR, *v. n.* (Exert strength, make effort) यत् (c. 1. यतते -तितुं), प्रयत्, व्यवसो (c. 4. -स्यति -सातुं), उद्यम् (c. 1. -यच्छति -यन्तुं), चेष्ट् (c. 1. चेष्टते -ष्टितुं), विचेष्ट्, उद्योगं कृ, उत्साहं कृ, यत्नं कृ, व्यवसायं कृ, आयासं कृ.—(Toil) आयस् (c. 4. -यस्यति -यसितुं), आयासं कृ, श्रम् (c. 4. श्राम्यति, श्रमितुं), परिश्रम्, क्लिश् (c. 4. क्लिश्यते, क्लेशितुं), परिक्लिश्, शरीरायासं कृ, व्रातं कृ, शरीरायासेन कर्म्म कृ, कष्टं कृ.—(Be in distress) क्लिश्, व्यथ् (c. 1. व्यथते -थितुं), पीड् in pass. (पीड्यते), तप् in pass. (तप्यते), कृच्छ्र (nom. कृच्छ्रायते), खिद् in pass. (खिद्यते), परिखिद्.—(Be in travail) प्राप्तप्रसववेदना भू, प्राप्तगर्भवेदना भू, प्राप्तप्रसवकाला भू.—(Labor under) उपहन् in pass. (-हन्यते), पीड् in pass. (पीड्यते), उपहतः -ता -तं भू, पीडितः -ता -तं भू; 'to labor under a disease,' रोगपीडितः -ता -तं भू, रोगार्त्तः -र्त्ता -र्त्तं भू.

To LABOR, *v. a.* (Form with labor) महायत्नेन or बहुश्रमेण or आयासेन कृ or संस्कृ or परिष्कृ or साध् (c. 10. साधयति -यितुं) or सिद्धीकृ or क्लृप् (c. 10. कल्पयति -यितुं) or विधा (c. 3. -दधाति -धातुं), यत्नेन सेव् (c. 1. सेवते -वितुं) or उपसेव् or अनुष्ठा (c. 1. -तिष्ठति -ष्ठातुं) or आस्था.—(Till, cultivate) कृष् (c. 6. कृषति, क्रष्टुं).

LABORATORY, *s.* (Work-room) उद्योगशाला, उद्योगगृहं, शिल्पशाला.—(House for chemical experiments) रसायनकर्म्मगृहं, रसायनकर्म्मशाला, रससंस्कारशाला.

LABORED, *p. p.* or *a.* श्रमसिद्धः -द्धा -द्धं, आयाससिद्धः -द्धा -द्धं, यत्नसिद्धः -द्धा -द्धं, कष्टसिद्धः &c., यत्नपूर्व्वः -र्व्वा -र्व्वं, श्रमपूर्व्वः &c., आयासपूर्व्वः &c.

LABORER, *s.* (One engaged in any toilsome work) आयासी *m.* (न्), कृतायासः, श्रमी *m.* (न्), कृतश्रमः, उद्योगी *m.* (न्), कृतोद्योगः, व्यवसायी *m.* (न्), कर्म्मी *m.* (न्), कार्म्मः.—(A hired or day laborer) ग्रातीनः, कर्म्मकरः, कर्म्मकारः -रकः, कर्म्मकारी *m.* (न्), भृतकः, भृतः, भृतिभुक् *m.* (ज्), वैतनिकः, भरण्यभुक् *m.*, वेतनार्थी *m.* (न्), वेतनग्राही *m.* (न्), वर्त्तिकः.—(Cultivator of soil) कृषकः, कर्षकः, क्षेत्रिकः, क्षेत्री *m.* (न्), क्षेत्रकर्षकः, कीनाशः, कृषीवलः.

LABORING, *part.* or *a.* कृतश्रमः -मा -मं, कृतायासः -सा -सं, श्रमकारी -रिणी -रि (न्); 'a laboring man.' *See* LABORER. (Laboring under) उपहतः -ता -तं, पीडितः -ता -तं; 'laboring under a disease,' रोगपीडितः -ता -तं.

LABORIOUS, *a.* (Using labor, industrious) आयासी -सिनी -सि (न्), श्रमी -मिणी -मि (न्), परिश्रमी &c., कृतश्रमः -मा -मं, श्रमशीलः -ला -लं, बहुश्रमः -मा -मं, उद्योगी -गिनी -गि (न्), उद्योगशीलः -ला -लं, उत्साही -हिनी -हि (न्), कर्म्मशीलः -ला -लं, कर्म्मी -र्म्मिणी -र्म्मि (न्), कार्म्मः -र्म्मी -र्म्मं, कर्म्मोद्युक्तः -क्ता -क्तं, सयत्नः -त्ना -त्नं, यत्नशीलः -ला -लं, प्रयत्नवान् -वती -वत् (त्), व्यवसायी -यिनी -यि (न्), उद्यमी &c., सोत्साहः -हा -हं, कर्म्मपरायणः -णा -णं, श्रमसहः -हा -हं, आमिकः -की -कं, अनलसः -सा -सं, निरालस्यः -स्या -स्यं, प्रयासभाक् *m.f.n.* (ज्), सोद्योगः -गा -गं.—(Requiring labor) श्रमसाध्यः -ध्या -ध्यं, कष्टसाध्यः -ध्या -ध्यं, आयाससाध्यः &c., श्रमसिद्धः -द्धा -द्धं, दुःसाध्यः &c., कठिनः -ना -नं, दुःखेन or कृच्छ्रेण साध्यः -ध्या -ध्यं, दुःखसाध्यः &c., कष्टः -ष्टा -ष्टं.

LABORIOUSLY, *adv.* श्रमेण, बहुश्रमेण, सश्रमं, श्रमपूर्व्वं, आयासेन, प्रयासेन, सायासं, कष्टेन, कृच्छ्रेण, उद्यमेन, सोत्साहं, सोद्योगं, यत्नेन, यत्नतस्, सयत्नं.

LABORIOUSNESS, *s.* (Diligence) आयासशीलता, उद्योगशीलता, कर्म्मशीलता, उद्योगः, सोद्योगत्वं, यत्नः, सयत्नता, व्यवसायः, उद्यमः.—(Toilsomeness) श्रमसाध्यता, कष्टसाध्यता, आयाससाध्यता, दुःखसाध्यत्वं, सकष्टत्वं, काठि *f.*

LABYRINTH, *s.* गहनं, सुगहनस्थानं, दुस्तरस्थानं, सुदुस्तरस्थानं, भ्रमजनको बहुव्यत्यस्तमार्गः प्रदेशः, भ्रान्तिजनको बहुविपरीतमार्गः प्रदेशः or बहुवक्रमार्गो भूमिभागः, अशक्यनिर्गमः प्रदेशः.

LABYRINTHIAN, *a.* गहनः -ना -नं, सुगहनः -ना -नं, सुदुस्तरः -रा -रं.

LAC, *s.* (A resinous substance used as a red dye, produced mainly upon the Banyan-tree by the insect Coccus lacca, analogous to the cochineal insect. The following names apply either to the dye or the insect, लाक्षा, राक्षा, अलक्तः -क्तकं, लक्तकं, जतु *n.*, जतुकं, जतुरसः, यावः -वकः, कार्पटः, द्रुमकः, गराधिका, द्रुमव्याधिः *m.*, द्रुमामयः, कीटजा, कृमिः *m.*, सितिभः;

'made of lac,' लाक्षिकः -की -कं; 'liquified lac dye,' अलक्तरसः.—(The number). *See* LACK.

LACE, *s.* (Texture of interwoven threads) जालं, जालिका, जालकं, जालाभरणं, जालरूपं सूक्ष्मतन्तुनिर्म्मितं वस्त्राभरणं or वस्त्राञ्चलं.—(String, cord) सूत्रं, तन्तुः *m.*, गुणः.

To LACE, *v. a.* (Fasten with a string) सूत्रेण बन्ध् (c. 9. बध्नाति, बन्द्धुं) or संयुज् (c. 7. -युनक्ति -योक्तुं) or संश्लिष् (c. 10. -श्लेषयति -यितुं), सूत्रबद्धं -द्धा -द्धं कृ.—(Adorn with lace) जालाभरणैर् अलङ्कृ or भूष् (c. 10. भूषयति -यितुं).

LACEMAN, *s.* जालाभरणविक्रयी *m.* (न्), जालालङ्कारविक्रयी *m.*, जालविक्रेता *m.* (तृ).

LACERABLE, *a.* विदारणीयः -या -यं, विदार्य्यः -र्य्या -र्य्यं, दारणीयः -या -यं.

To LACERATE, *v. a.* दॄ (c. 9. दृणाति, दरितुं -रीतुं, c. 10. दारयति -यितुं), विदॄ, अवदॄ, विभिद् (c. 7. -भिनत्ति -भेत्तुं), निर्भिद्, व्यवछिद् (c. 7. -छिनत्ति -छेत्तुं), निकृत् (c. 6. -कृन्तति -कर्त्तितुं), विनिकृत्, विदल् (c. 10. -दलयति -यितुं), विदलीकृ, व्रश्च् (c. 6. वृश्चति, व्रश्चितुं), प्रव्रश्च्; 'to be lacerated,' विदॄ in pass. (-दीर्य्यते).

LACERATED, *p. p.* विदारितः -ता -तं, विदीर्णः -र्णा -र्णं, दारितः -ता -तं, दीर्णः -र्णा -र्णं, प्रविदारितः -ता -तं, विभिन्नः -न्ना -न्नं, भिन्नः -न्ना -न्नं, विदलितः -ता -तं, दलितः -ता -तं, पाटितः -ता -तं, विपाटितः -ता -तं, विदलीकृतः -ता -तं.

LACERATION, *s.* (The act of tearing) विदारः -रणं -णा, विदरः, दारणं, विदलीकरणं, प्रविदारणं, विभेदः, व्रश्चनं, पाटनं, विपाटनं.—(The rent made) छिद्रं, भेदः, विदलं.

LACHRYMAL, *a.* (Secreting tears) अश्रुजनकः -का -कं, अश्रूत्पादकः -का -कं, अश्रुवाहकः -का -कं.—(Pertaining to tears) अश्रुसम्बन्धी -न्धिनी -न्धि (न्).

LACHRYMATORY, *s.* अश्रुपात्रं, अश्रुभाजनं, नयनवाष्पाधारः, मरणकाले मृतजनमित्रैः पातितानाम् अश्रूणां काचादिनिर्म्मितपात्रं तच्च पूर्व्वकाले मृतशरीरेण सह भूमौ न्यस्यते.

LACHRYMOSE, *a.* अश्रुमयः -यी -यं, साश्रः -श्रा -श्रं, वाष्पाकुलः -ला -लं.

To LACK, *v. a.* or *n.* (Be destitute of) हीनः -ना -नं or विहीनः -ना -नं or परिहीणः -णा -णं or रहितः -ता -तं or विरहितः -ता -तं or वर्जितः -ता -तं or विवर्जितः -ता -तं or शून्यः -न्या -न्यं or अपेतः -ता -तं भू or अस्, हा in pass. (हीयते) or विहा with abl. or instr. c., वियुज् in pass. (-युज्यते) with instr. c., or expressed by अ or निर् prefixed; as, 'he lacks wisdom,' बुद्धिहीनः or बुद्धिरहितः or निर्बुद्धिर् अस्ति; 'he lacks means,' असाधनोऽस्ति.—(Not to have) न धा (c. 3. दधाति, धत्ते, धातुं), न धृ (c. 10. धारयति -यितुं), न विधा.—(Be wanting) न्यूनीभू, न्यूनः -ना -नं भू or अस्, न्यूनता भू or अस्, प्रयोजनम् अस्; 'what lack I yet?' मम किं न्यूनं or मम केन प्रयोजनं.

LACK, *s.* (Want, destitution) हीनता, रहितत्वं, शून्यता, अभावः, असम्भवः, विरहः, अविभवः, न्यूनता.—(Need) प्रयोजनं.—(One hundred thousand) लक्षं -क्षा, लक्ष्यं.

LACK-A-DAY, *exclam.* अहो, अहोबत, अहह, हन्त, आ, हा, कष्टं.

LACK-A-DAISICAL, *a.* ध्यानपरः -रा -रं, उद्विग्नमनाः -नाः -नः (स्), उन्मनाः &c., चिन्ताकुलः-ला-लं, विषादी-दिनी-दि (न्), उत्कण्ठितः-ता-तं.

LACKBRAIN, *s.* निर्बुद्धिः *m.*, अबुद्धिः *m.*, ज्ञानहीनः, मूर्खः, मूढः.

LACKER, *s.* (Kind of varnish) लाक्षादिनिर्म्मितः कुङ्कुमकविशेषः, लाक्षा.

To LACKER, *v. a.* पूर्व्वोक्तकुङ्कुमकेन लिप् (c. 6. लिम्पति, लेप्तुं).

LACKEY, *s.* पार्श्वानुचरः, परिचरः, किङ्करः, प्रेष्यः, भृत्यः, दासः.

To LACKEY, *v. a.* or *n.* उपचर् (c. 1. -चरति -रितुं), पार्श्वे परिचर्, पार्श्वानुचरो भू.

LACK-LUSTRE, *a.* निस्तेजाः -जाः -जः (स्), तेजोहीनः -ना -नं, निष्प्रभः -भा -भं, अप्रभः -भा -भं, मन्दच्छायः -या -यं, मन्दकान्तः -न्ता -न्तं, मलिनप्रभः -भा -भं.

LACONIC, LACONICAL, *a.* (Concise, expressed in few words) संक्षिप्तः -प्ता -प्तं, सांक्षेपिकः -की -कं, अविस्तीर्णः -र्णा -र्णं, अल्पशब्दकः -का -कं, परिमितशब्दः -ब्दा -ब्दं, परिमितवाक्यः -क्या -क्यं, परिमितोक्तिः -क्तिः -क्ति, संक्षिप्तोक्तिः -क्तिः -क्ति, मितशब्दकः -का -कं, अबहुशब्दः -ब्दा -ब्दं.—(Laconic speaker) परिमितभाषी -षिणी -षि (न्), मितभाषी &c., संक्षिप्तभाषी &c., संक्षिप्तवक्ता -क्त्री -क्तृ (क्तृ), अविस्तीर्णवक्ता &c., अल्पभाषी &c.

LACONICALLY, *adv.* संक्षेपतस्, संक्षेपेण, अविस्तरेण, अविस्तरशस्, परिमितोक्त्या, मितोक्त्या, समासतस्.

LACONISM, LACONICISM, *s.* संक्षिप्तोक्तिः *f.*, संक्षिप्तवाक्यं, अल्पशब्दकवाक्यं, मितशब्दकवाक्यं, परिमितवाक्यं, अविस्तीर्णवाक्यं, संक्षेपवाक्यं.

LACQUER, *s.* *See* LACKER.

LACSHMÍ, *s.* *See* LAKSHMÍ.

LACTARY, *a.* क्षीरी -रिणी -रि (न्), क्षीरविशिष्टः -ष्टा -ष्टं.

LACTARY, *s.* (Dairy) गोरसगृहं, गोदुग्धगृहं, गव्यगृहं, दधिस्थानं, क्षीरस्थानं.

LACTATION, *s.* (Act of giving milk) स्तन्यदानं, क्षीरदानं, पयोदानं.

LACTEAL, *a.* (Milky) क्षीरी -रिणी -रि (न्), दुग्धी -ग्धिनी -ग्धि (न्), क्षीरमयः -यी -यं, दुग्धवान् -वती -वत् (त्), पयस्यः -स्या -स्यं, पायसः -सी -सं, क्षीरसम्बन्धी &c.—(Conveying chyle) अन्नरसवाहकः -का -कं, अन्नरसचालकः -का -कं.

LACTEAL, *s.* (A vessel of the body) अन्नरसवाहिनी, रसायनी -नं.

LACTEOUS, *a.* क्षीरी -रिणी -रि (न्). *See* LACTEAL.

LACTESCENCE, *s.* दुग्धता, क्षीरोत्पादकत्वं, क्षीरजनकता, दुग्धवत्त्वं.

LACTESCENT, *a.* क्षीरोत्पादकः -का -कं, दुग्धजनकः -का -कं, क्षीरमयः -यी -यं.

LACTIFEROUS, *a.* क्षीरवाहकः -का -कं, क्षीरवाही -हिनी -हि (न्), दुग्धप्रवाहकः -का -कं, दुग्धचालकः -का -कं.

LACTOMETOR, *s.* क्षीरमापनयन्त्रं, क्षीरमापनी, दुग्धमापनी.

LAD, *s.* कुमारकः, माणवकः, कुमारः, वटुः *m.*, वटुकः, बालः -लकः, दारकः, शिशुः *m.*, किशोरः; 'a mere lad,' वटुमात्रं.

LADDER, *s.* सोपानं, सोपानपद्धतिः *f.*, अधिरोहिणी, निःश्रेणी, निःश्रयणी -यिणी, आरोहणं, शालारं, वन्दिः *f.*

To LADE, *v. a.* *See* *To* LOAD, *To* LADLE.

LADED, LADEN, *p. p.* or *a.* भारवान् -वती -वत् (त्), भारी -रिणी -रि (न्), भारयुक्तः -क्ता -क्तं, धुरीणः -णा -णं, धुरन्धरः -रा -रं, धुरीयः -या -यं, धुर्वहः -हा -हं, भारन्धरः -रा -रं, सभारः -रा -रं; 'heavily laden,' सुभरः -रा -रं, अतिभारी &c., अतिभारवान् &c.; 'laden with mud,' पङ्कभारकः -का -कं, पङ्कभारी &c.

LADING, *s.* (Of a ship) नौभारः, नौकाभारः, नौकास्थद्रव्यं, पोतस्थद्रव्यं.

LADLE, *s.* दर्वी, दर्विः *f.*, दर्विकः, दर्वी, दर्विः *f.*, दर्विका, दार्वी, कम्बिः *f.*, कम्बी, खजः, खजाकः -का, खजिका, पाणिका; 'wooden ladle,' तर्द्दूः *m. f.*, दारुहस्तकः; 'sacrificial ladle,' स्रुक् *f.* (च्), स्रुवः -वा, स्रुवं, स्रूः *f.*, चमसः.

To LADLE, *v. a.* दर्विकेण जलादि उत्तॄ (c. 10. -तारयति -यितुं) or पत् (c. 10. पातयति -यितुं).

LADLEFUL, *s.* दर्विपूरणं, कम्बिपूरणं, कम्बिपूरकं, कम्बिभरकं.

LADY, *s.*, आर्य्या, आर्य्यिका, आर्य्यका, भाविनी, भवती, कुलवधूः *f.*, कुलस्त्री, कुलाङ्गना, कुलनारी, कुलीना, कुलजा, आर्य्यस्त्री, सभ्यस्त्री, शिष्टस्त्री, सत्कुलीना, कुलपालिका, नायिका; 'O lady!' भवति voc. c.

LADY-BIRD, LADY-BUG, LADY-FLY, LADY-COW, *s.* इन्द्रगोपः, शक्रगोपः, इन्द्रकीटः, शक्रकीटः, ताम्रकृमिः *m.*, अग्निकः.

LADY-DAY, *s.* ख्रीष्टमातृविज्ञापनोद्देशकं वत्सरस्य पूर्व्वपादावसाने पर्व्व or वत्सरस्य तृतीयमासान्ते पर्व्व *n.* (न्).

LADY-LIKE, *a.* आर्य्यस्त्रीयोग्यः -ग्या -ग्यं, सभ्यस्त्रीयोग्यः &c., कुलस्त्र्युचितः -ता -तं, कुलस्त्रीसदृशः -शी -शं, आर्य्यवृत्तिः -त्तिः -त्ति, सभ्यः -भ्या -भ्यं, शिष्टः -ष्टा -ष्टं, सुविनीतः -ता -तं, सुन्दरः -री -रं; 'a lady-like woman,' शिष्टस्त्री, सुन्दरी, विनीता.

LADY-LOVE, *s.* प्रिया, कान्ता, कामिनी, रागिणी, प्रणयिनी, अनुरागवती.

LADYSHIP, *s.* (Her ladyship) भवती, अत्रभवती.

LADY'S-MAID, *s.* स्त्रीवस्त्रपरिकल्पिका, स्त्रीवस्त्रमाल्यादिपरिकल्पिका, स्त्रीप्रसाधका, स्त्रीपरिधानकृत् *m.*, अङ्गसंस्कर्त्री.

To LAG, *v. n.* मन्द् (nom. मन्दायते), विलम्ब् (c. 1. -लम्बते -म्बितुं), चिर (nom. चिरायति -ते), मन्दगत्या चल् (c. 1. चलति -लितुं), मन्दं चल् or चर् (c. 1. चरति -रितुं).

LAG, *s.* (Lowest class) अन्त्यजाः *m. pl.*, हीनजनाः *m. pl.*, पृथग्जनाः, खलाः.

LAGGER, *s.* विलम्बी *m.* (न्), विलम्बकारी *m.* (न्), मन्दगतिः *m.*, मन्दायमानः.

LAGGING, *part.* मन्दायमानः -ना -नं, चिरायमाणः -णा -णं, विलम्बी -म्बिनी &c.

LAGOON, LAGUNE, *s.* अनूपभूः *f.*, कच्छभूः *f.*, कच्छः, समुद्रीयकच्छः.

LAIC, LAICAL, *a.* गृहस्थी -स्थिनी -स्थि (न्), गार्हस्थिकः -की -कं, गृहस्थसम्बन्धी -न्धिनी -न्धि (न्), गृहस्थवर्गसम्बन्धी &c., पुरोहितवर्गभिन्नः -न्ना -न्नं, पौरोहित्यभिन्नः -न्ना -न्नं, सामान्यलोकसम्बन्धी &c., साधारणलोकसम्बन्धी &c., धर्म्मपदस्थभिन्नः -न्ना -न्नं.

LAID, *p. p.* न्यस्तः -स्ता -स्तं, विन्यस्तः -स्ता -स्तं, उपन्यस्तः -स्ता -स्तं, स्थापितः -ता -तं, निहितः -ता -तं, आहितः -ता -तं, उपनिहितः -ता -तं, उपहितः -ता -तं, प्रणिहितः -ता -तं, निवेशितः -ता -तं, निक्षिप्तः -प्ता -प्तं, प्रतिपादितः -ता -तं, अर्पितः -ता -तं, नियुक्तः -क्ता -क्तं, नियोजितः -ता -तं, रोपितः -ता -तं, आरोपितः -ता -तं; 'laid on the ground,' भूमौ निहितः -ता -तं or न्यस्तः -स्ता -स्तं.—(Laid aside) सन्न्यस्तः -स्ता -स्तं, निरस्तः -स्ता -स्तं, न्यस्तः -स्ता -स्तं, अस्तः -स्ता -स्तं, त्यक्तः -क्ता -क्तं.—(Laid out, as goods) प्रसारितः -ता -तं.—(Laid out, as ground) सुपर्य्याप्तः -प्ता -प्तं.—(Laid out, as money) प्रयुक्तः -क्ता -क्तं, उपयुक्तः -क्ता -क्तं.—(Laid hold of) गृहीतः -ता -तं, धृतः -ता -तं.—(Laid, as dust) संसिक्तः -क्ता -क्तं, सिक्तः -क्ता -क्तं, निहितः -ता -तं.

LAIN, *p. p.* उपविष्टः -ष्टा -ष्टं, पतितः -ता -तं, शयितः -ता -तं, संविष्टः -ष्टा -ष्टं.

LAIR, *s.* श्वापदस्थानं, श्वापदशयनं, श्वापदशयनस्थानं, श्वापदालयः, श्वापदायतनं, श्वापदनिलयः, अरण्यपशुशयनस्थानं, आरण्यपशोर् वासस्थानं or आश्रयः or आलयः.

LAITY, *s.* गृहस्थवर्गः, सामान्यलोकः, साधारणलोकः, सामान्यवर्गः, साधारणवर्गः, साधारणलोकवर्गः, पुरोहितभिन्नवर्गः, धर्म्मपदस्थभिन्नवर्गः, पौरोहित्यभिन्नवर्गः.

LAKE, *s.* सरस् *n.*, ह्रदः, जलाशयः, जलाधारः, सरोवरः -रं, सरसी, तडागः, वापी -पिः *f.*, कासारः, पुष्करिणी, खातं, पूरः.

LAKSHMÍ, *s.* (The goddess of fortune or prosperity, wife of the god Vishnu. She is said also to preside over beauty; and in this respect, as well as in the story of her birth, agrees in character with Venus. She was born, according to the usual account, from the ocean, when churned by the gods and Asuras; and emerged from the foam of the sea, seated on a full-blown lotus, and holding a lotus in her hand. Her countenance is represented as incomparably beautiful. As presiding over abundance she resembles Ceres. She is by some considered to be the daughter of Daksha, and by others of Bhrigu. Sometimes she is regarded as the wife of Dharma. As goddess of prosperity she is called) लक्ष्मीः *f.*, श्रीः *f.*—(As wife of Vishnu) विष्णुवल्लभा, हरिप्रिया, वैष्णवी.—(The ocean-born) जलधिजा, क्षीराब्धिजा, क्षीराब्धितनया.—(As seated on and holding the lotus, or as identified with this flower, which is the symbol of prosperity) पद्मा, कमला, पद्मालया, पद्मवासा, पद्महस्ता.—(As wife of Vishnu in the avatár of Krishna) रुक्मिणी.—(As mother of Kámadeva) माया.—(As wife of Náráyana) नारायणी.—(As wife of Vishnu in the avatár of Rámachandra) सीता.—(As mother of the world) लोकमाता *f.* (तृ), माता.—(As wife of Vishnu in the Varáha avatár) वाराही.—(The fickle one, a name applied to Lakshmí as goddess of fortune) चपला, चञ्चला, चला, लोला.—(As identified with a celebrated Apsaras) रम्भा. Other names of this goddess are, रमा, इन्दिरा, मा, नेत्री, हीरा, लज्जा.

LAMB, *s.* मेषशावकः, मेषशिशुः *m.*, मेषवत्सः, वर्करः, अविपोतकः.

To LAMB, *v. a.* मेषशावकं सु (c. 2. सूते, c. 4. सूयते, सोतुं) or प्रसु.

LAMBATIVE, *a.* लेह्यः -ह्या -ह्यं, अवलेह्यः -ह्या -ह्यं.

LAMBATIVE, *s.* (Medicine) लेहः, अवलेहः, लेह्यं, अवलेह्यं.

LAMBENT, *a.* इतस्ततश् चलमानः -ना -नं or चपलः -ला -लं.

LAMBKIN, *s.* क्षुद्रमेषशावकः, क्षुद्रमेषशिशुः *m.*, क्षुद्रवर्करः.

LAMBLIKE, *a.* मेषस्वभावः -वा -वं, मेषशावकवत् कोमलस्वभावः -वा -वं or मृदुस्वभावः -वा -वं or मृदुशीलः -ला -लं.

LAMB'S-WOOL, *s.* मेषशावकलोम *n.* (न्), मेषलोम *n.*, वर्करलोम *n.*

LAME, *a.* खञ्जः -ञ्जा -ञ्जं, पङ्गुः -ङ्गुः -ङ्गु, खोडः -डा -डं, खोलः -ला -लं, खोरः -रा -रं, गतिविकलः -ला -लं, पादविकलः -ला -लं, विकलगतिः -तिः -ति, विकलाङ्गः -ङ्गा -ङ्गं, व्यङ्गः -ङ्गा -ङ्गं, भूमिस्पृक् *m. f. n.* (श्).—(Imperfect) विकलः -ला -लं, हीनः -ना -नं, न्यूनः -ना -नं, सच्छिद्रः -द्रा -द्रं.

To LAME, *v. a.* खञ्जीकृ, पङ्गूकृ, पादविकलीकृ, विकलीकृ.

LAMELLAR, *a.* सूक्ष्मफलकविशिष्टः -ष्टा -ष्टं, शकली -लिनी -लि (न्).

LAMELY, *adv.* खञ्जवत्, पङ्गुवत्, विकलगत्या; 'going lamely,' विकलगतिः -तिः -ति.—(Imperfectly) विकलं, वैकल्येन, असम्यक्.

LAMENESS, *s.* खञ्जत्वं -ता, पङ्गुता -त्वं, खोडता, गतिवैकल्यं, विकलगतित्वं, पादवैकल्यं, अङ्गवैकल्यं.—(Imperfection) वैकल्यं, विकलता, हीनता, न्यूनता, सच्छिद्रत्वं, दुर्बलता.

To LAMENT, *v. n.* विलप् (c. 1. -लपति -पितुं), प्रलप्, लप्, क्रन्द् (c. 1. क्रन्दति -न्दितुं), आक्रन्द्, रुद् (c. 2. रोदिति -तुं), प्ररुद्, परिदेव् (c. 1. -देवते -वितुं), क्रुश् (c. 1. क्रोशति, क्रोष्टुं), विक्रुश्, परिक्रुश्, अभिक्रुश्, शुच् (c. 1. शोचति -चितुं), परिशुच्, उद्विज् (c. 6. -विजते -जितुं), व्यथ् (c. 1. व्यथते -थितुं), विलपनं कृ, शोकं कृ, शोचनं कृ; 'to lament exceedingly,' शुच् in freq. (शोशुच्यते), लप् in freq. (लालप्यते).

To LAMENT, *v. a.* शुच् (c. 1. शोचति -चितुं), अनुशुच्, परिदेव् (c. 1. -देवति -ते -वितुं), विलप् (c. 1. -लपति -पितुं), क्रन्द् (c. 1. क्रन्दति -न्दितुं), आक्रन्द्, रुद् (c. 2. रोदिति -तुं), अभिक्रुश् (c. 1. -क्रोशति -क्रोष्टुं), उत्कण्ठ् (c. 1. -कण्ठते -ण्ठितुं), all with acc. c.; as, 'they lament the dead,' गतासून् शोचन्ति; 'they lamented each other,' अन्योन्यम् अभिचुक्रुशुः.

LAMENTABLE, *a.* शोचनीयः -या -यं, शोच्यः -च्या -च्यं, शोचितव्यः -व्या -व्यं, शोकार्हः -र्हा -र्हं, शोचनार्हः -र्हा -र्हं, विलपनीयः -या -यं, क्रन्दनीयः -या -यं, शोकयोग्यः -ग्या -ग्यं, शोकविषयः -या -यं, शोकास्पदः -दा -दं.

LAMENTABLY, *adv.* शोचनीयं, शोचनीयप्रकारेण, यथा शोको जायते तथा.

LAMENTATION, LAMENT, *s.* शोकः, शोचनं, शुक् *f.* (च्), अनुशोचनं, क्रन्दनं, विलपनं, विलापः, परिदेवनं -ना, रोदनं, रुदितं, रुदनं, क्रन्दितं, आक्रन्दनं, विलपितं, प्रलापः, क्रुष्टं, विक्रुष्टं, उद्वेगः, मनस्तापः, हाहाकारः, मनोवेदना, परिवेदनं, परिवेदितं.

LAMENTED, *p. p.* शोचितः -ता -तं, अनुशोचितः -ता -तं, विलपितः -ता -तं, क्रन्दितः -ता -तं, रुदितः -ता -तं, क्रुष्टः -ष्टा -ष्टं, अभिक्रुष्टः -ष्टा -ष्टं, परिदेवितः -ता -तं.

LAMENTER, *s.* शोचकः, अनुशोचकः, परिदेवकः, परिदेवी *m.* (न्), विलपनकृत्.

LAMENTING, *part.* रुदन् -दती -दती -दत् (त्), परिदेवी -विनी -वि (न्), विलपन् -पन्ती -पत् (त्), शोचमानः -ना -नं, रुद्यमानः -ना -नं.

LAMINA, *s.* (Thin plate, scale) फलकः -कं, पत्रं, शल्कं, शकलं, कवचः.

LAMINATE, LAMINATED, *a.* फलकी -किनी -कि (न्), शकली &c., सपत्रः -त्रा -त्रं.

LAMINATION, *s.* (Drawing out into a thin plate) उत्कर्त्तनं.

LAMMAS-DAY, *s.* अष्टममासस्य प्रथमदिनोद्देशकं पर्व्व *n.* (न्).

LAMP, *s.* दीपः, प्रदीपः, दीपकः -पिका, वर्त्ती -र्त्तिः *f.*, शिखावान् *m.* (त्), शिखी *m.* (न्), कज्जलध्वजः, दशाकर्षः, दशेन्धनं, दोषास्यः, स्नेहाशः, स्नेहप्रियः; 'lamp in a doorway,' देहलीदीपः; 'row of lamps,' दीपमाला, दीपावलिः *f.*, दीपाली, दीपशृङ्खला; 'flame of a lamp,' दीपशिखा; 'wick of a lamp,' वर्त्ती -र्त्तिका, दीपकूपी; 'stand of a lamp,' दीपवृक्षः, दीपपादपः, दीपाधारः, शिखातरुः *m.*; 'smell of an extinguished lamp,' दीपनिर्वाणगन्धः; 'relating to a lamp,' दैपः -पी -पं.

LAMP-BLACK, *s.* दीपकिट्टं, कज्जलं, कज्ज्वलं, दीपकज्जलं, दीपशिखा, दीपध्वजः -जं, मषी.

LAMP-LIGHT, *s.* दीपद्युतिः *f.*, प्रदीपद्युतिः, दीपप्रकाशः, दीपप्रभा.

LAMP-LIGHTER, *s.* दीपतैलदः, तैलदायी *m.* (न्), दीपप्रकाशकः, दीपज्वलनकृत्.

LAMPOON, *s.* निन्दालेखः, निन्दार्थको लेखः, अवगीतं, निन्दागीतं, विदूषणलेखः, विदूषणार्थको लेखः, क्षेपः, आक्षेपः.

To LAMPOON, *v. a.* निन्दालेखद्वारेण आक्षिप् (c. 6. -क्षिपति -क्षेप्तुं) or अवगै (c. 1. -गायति -गातुं), निन्दालेखं कृ.

LAMPOONED, *p. p.* निन्दालेखेन अवगीतः -ता -तं or आक्षिप्तः -प्ता -प्तं.

LAMPREY, *s.* अन्धाहिजातीयो मत्स्यभेदः, कुञ्चिका, जलव्यालः.

LANATE, LANATED, *a.* लोमशः -शा -शं, लोमविशिष्टः -ष्टा -ष्टं.

LANCE, *s.* शक्तिः *f.*, तोमरः, कुन्तः -न्ती, शूलः -लं, प्रासः, शल्यं, कीलः, शलाका.—(Armed with a lance) शाक्तीकः. *See* LANCER.

To LANCE, *v. a.* शूलेन or शक्त्या व्यध् (c. 4. विध्यति, व्यद्धुं), शक्तिविद्धं -द्धां कृ, शक्तिभिन्नं -न्नां कृ, शूल (nom. शूलयति -यितुं), कील (c. 10. कीलयति -यितुं); 'with a lancet,' शलाकया or वृद्धिपत्रेण व्यध्.

LANCED, *p. p.* शलाकाविद्धः -द्धा -द्धं, वृद्धिपत्रविद्धः -द्धा -द्धं.

LANCEOLATE, *a.* शूलाकारः -रा -रं, शूलाकृतिः -तिः -ति, शक्तिरूपः -पा -पं.

LANCER, *s.* शाक्तीकः, शक्तिधरः, शक्तिग्रहः, शक्तिहेतिकः, शूली *m.* (न्), शूलधरः, प्रासिकः, कौन्तिकः, शलाकी *m.* (न्).

LANCET, *s.* शलाका, अर्द्धधारं, वृद्धिपत्रं, वेतसपत्रं.

To LANCH, *v. a.* अस् (c. 4. अस्यति, असितुं), प्रास्, क्षिप् (c. 6. क्षिपति, क्षेप्तुं), मुच् (c. 6. मुञ्चति, मोक्तुं), प्रमुच्, सृज् (c. 6. सृजति, स्रष्टुं), प्रहृ (c. 1. -हरति -हर्तुं), पत् (c. 10. पातयति -यितुं).

LANCHED, *p. p.* मुक्तः -क्ता -क्तं, प्रमुक्तः -क्ता -क्तं, क्षिप्तः -प्ता -प्तं.

To LANCINATE, *v. a.* विदॄ (c. 10. -दारयति -यितुं), निर्भिद् (c. 7. -भिनत्ति -भेत्तुं).

LANCINATION, *s.* विदारणं, प्रविदारणं, विभेदः, विपाटनं, व्रश्चनं.

LAND, *s.* (Country, region) देशः, प्रदेशः, विषयः, राष्ट्रं.—(As opposed to water) स्थलं -ली; 'land and water,' स्थलजलं, जलस्थलं; 'relating to dry land,' धन्व *n.* (न्), स्थलीयः -या -यं; 'produced on it,' स्थलजः -जा -जं; 'confusion of land and water through inundation,' जलस्थलभ्रमः; 'the way by land,' स्थलमार्गः; 'by land,' स्थलमार्गेण.—(Ground, soil, earth) भूमिः *f.*, भूः *f.*, क्षेत्रं, मृत् *f.*, मृत्तिका; 'arable land,' क्षेत्रभूमिः *f.*; 'ploughed land,' कृष्टं, कृष्टभूमिः *f.*, फालकृष्टं, सीताभूमिः; 'barren land,' मरुः *m.*, मरुस्थलं -ली, धन्वा *m.* (न्), भूर्तिः *f.*, ऊषः -षरः; 'marshy land,' कच्छभूः *f.*, अनूपभूमिः *f.*; 'waste land,' खिलः; 'fallow land,' अप्रहतभूमिः; 'table land,' सानुः *m.*, प्रस्थः, स्नुः *m.* —(Estate, lands) क्षेत्रं, भूमिः, स्थावरं; 'paternal lands,' पैतृकभूमिः; 'gift of lands,' भूमिदानं.

To LAND, *v. a.* उत्तॄ (c. 10. -तारयति -यितुं), नौकाया अवतॄ or अवरुह् in caus. (-रोपयति -यितुं), स्थलं or कूलम् उपस्था in caus. (-स्थापयति -यितुं), नावम् उपक्षिप् (c. 10. -क्षेपयति -यितुं), उत्कूल् (nom. उत्कूलयति -यितुं).

To LAND, *v. n.* उत्तॄ (c. 1. -तरति -रितुं -रीतुं), प्रत्युत्तॄ, नौकाया अवतॄ or उत्तॄ or अवरुह् (c. 1. -रोहति -रोढुं), स्थलम् उपस्था (c. 1. -तिष्ठति -स्थातुं).

LANDED, *p. p.* (Disembarked) उत्तीर्णः -र्णा -र्णं, अवतीर्णः -र्णा -र्णं, नौकोत्तीर्णः -र्णा -र्णं, नौकावरूढः -ढा -ढं, नौकातीतः -ता -तं, अतितीः -तीः -तु, उत्कूलितः -ता -तं.—(Having an estate in land) क्षेत्री *m.* (न्), क्षेत्रवान् *m.* (त्), क्षेत्रसम्पन्नः -न्ना -न्नं, भूमिसम्पन्नः -न्ना -न्नं, भूमिधनः -ना -नं; 'landed property,' भूमिः *f.*, क्षेत्रं, स्थावरं, स्थावरधनं; 'donation of landed property,' भूमिदानं.

LAND-ANIMAL, *s.* स्थलचरजन्तुः *m.*, भूमिचरजन्तुः *m.*, भूचरजन्तुः.

LAND-FIGHT, *s.* स्थलयुद्धं, स्थलविग्रहः, स्थलीययुद्धं.

LAND-FLOOD, *s.* जलाप्लावनं, आप्लावः, जलप्रलयः, जलविप्लवः.

LAND-FORCE, *s.* स्थलबलं, स्थलसैन्यं, सेना, स्थलयोधाः *m. pl.*

LAND-HOLDER, *s.* भूस्वामी *m.* (न्), क्षेत्रपतिः *m.*, भूमिपतिः, भूमीश्वरः, क्षेत्रस्वामी *m.* (न्), क्षेत्राधिकारी *m.* (न्).

LANDING, LANDING-PLACE, *s.* उत्तरणस्थानं, तरस्थानं, तरणस्थानं, तरः, घट्टः -ट्टी, उमः, गुल्मः, नौकावरोहणस्थानं.—(Act of landing, disembarkation) उत्तरणं, प्रत्युत्तरणं.

LANDLADY, *s.* (Woman who has tenants) भूस्वामिनी, क्षेत्रस्वामिनी. —(Mistress of an inn) उत्तरणगृहस्वामिनी, उत्तरणशालास्वामिनी, उपकारिकागृहाधिकारिणी, शौल्किकी.

LANDLOCKED, *a.* भूवेष्टितः -ता -तं, भूमिवेष्टितः -ता -तं, भूप्रतिबद्धः -द्धा -द्धं.

LANDLORD, *s.* (Owner of land) भूस्वामी *m.* (न्), क्षेत्रस्वामी *m.*, क्षेत्रपतिः *m.*, भूमीश्वरः.—(Owner of a house) गृहपतिः *m.*, गृहस्वामी *m.*, गृहेश्वरः.—(Master of an inn) उत्तरणगृहपतिः *m.*, उत्तरणगृहस्वामी *m.*, उपकारिकागृहाधिकारी *m.* (न्).

LANDMARK, *s.* स्थलसीमा *m.* (न्), भूमिसीमा, सीमा *m.* (न्), सीमा *f.*, सीमालिङ्गं, सीमाचिह्नं, स्थण्डिलं, चैत्यं, अञ्चलः.—(Of a field) क्षेत्रसीमाचिह्नं, क्षेत्रमर्यादाचिह्नं.—(An elevated mark on land to serve as a guide to seamen) समुद्रयायिनां पथदर्शनार्थम् उन्नतभूभागे स्थापितं चिह्नं.

LANDOWNER, *s.* भूस्वामी *m.* (न्), क्षेत्रस्वामी *m.*, क्षेत्रपतिः *m.*, भूमीश्वरः.

LANDSCAPE, *s.* (Portion of land which the eye can comprehend in a single view) दृष्टिपातान्तर्गतदेशः, नयनपथान्तर्गतदेशः, दृष्टिगतदेशः, दृष्टिगोचरदेशः, देशः, प्रदेशः, भूप्रदेशः.—(Picture) चित्रगतो भूमिप्रदेशः.

LANDSMAN, *s.* स्थलवासी *m.* (न्), स्थलवर्त्ती *m.* (न्), स्थलीयः, स्थलगः.

LAND-TAX, *s.* भूमिकरः, क्षेत्रकरः, भूकरः.

LAND-WAITER, *s.* शौल्कः, शौल्किकः, उत्तरणस्थाने करग्राही *m.* (न्) or शुल्कग्राही *m.*

LANE, *s.* सङ्कटपथः, सङ्कटमार्गः, सम्बाधपथः, सङ्कटवीथिः *f.*, सम्बाधवीथिः.

LANGUAGE, *s.* (Speech, ideas expressed in words) भाषा -षणं, भाषितं, उक्तिः *f.*, वचनं, वचस्, वाक्यं, उक्तं, वाक् *f.* (च्), वाणी, व्याहारः, निगदः, निगादः, लपितं, अभिलापः, वदन्तिः *f.*—(Word, expression) शब्दः, वाक्यं, वचनं, पदं; 'bad language,' दुरुक्तिः *f.* दुर्भाषणं, दुर्वचस् *n.*, दुर्वाक्यं, दुर्वचनं, दुरालापः; 'abusive language,' वाक्पारुष्यं, वाग्दोषः, परुषवचनं, परुषोक्तिः *f.*; 'low language,' खलोक्तिः *f.*—(A language) भाषा, उक्तिः *f.*; 'a foreign language,' भाषान्तरं, विदेशीयभाषा; 'a barbarous language,' म्लेच्छभाषा, म्लेच्छितं; 'the Sanskrit language,' संस्कृतभाषा, संस्कृतोक्तिः *f.*—(Diction, style of expression) वाग्व्यापारः, वाग्रीतिः *f.*, वाक्यरचना, वाग्विन्यासः, वाक्सरणिः *f.*

LANGUID, *a.* म्लानः -ना -नं, परिम्लानः -ना -नं, क्लान्तः -न्ता -न्तं, परिक्लान्तः -न्ता -न्तं, क्लान्तः -न्ता -न्तं, क्लान्तमनस्कः -स्का -स्कं, शिथिलः -ला -लं, शिथिलाङ्गः -ङ्गी -ङ्गं, शिथिलबलः -ला -लं, शिथिलवीर्य्यः -र्य्या -र्य्यं, क्षीणबलः -ला -लं, अवसन्नः -न्ना -न्नं, सन्नः -न्ना -न्नं, अवसादी -दिनी -दि (न्), विषादी &c., विषण्णः -ण्णा -ण्णं, विसस्तवीर्य्यः -र्य्या -र्य्यं, स्रंसी -सिनी -सि (न्), विश्लथः -था -थं, विश्लथाङ्गः -ङ्गी -ङ्गं, श्लथाङ्गः &c., अलसः -सा -सं, मन्दः -न्दा -न्दं, अनुत्सुकः -का -कं, निरुत्सुकः -का -कं.

LANGUIDLY, *adv.* अवसादेन, सविषादं, विषादेन, सावसादं, अवसन्नवत्, क्लान्तमनसा, अलसवत्, मन्दं, मान्द्येन, समान्द्यं.

LANGUIDNESS, *s.* ग्लानिः *f.*, म्लानिः *f.*, म्लानता, क्लान्तता, अवसन्नता, विषण्णता, अवसादः, शिथिलता -त्वं, बलशैथिल्यं, अङ्गशैथिल्यं, अलसता, आलस्यं, मान्द्यं.

To LANGUISH, *v. n.* अवसद् (c. 1. -सीदति -सत्तुं), विषद्, व्यवसद्, सद्, म्लै (c. 1. म्लायति, म्लातुं), परिम्लै, ग्लै (c. 1. ग्लायति, ग्लातुं), परिग्लै, क्लम् (c. 4. क्लाम्यति, क्लमितुं), परिक्लम्, विक्लम्, क्षि in pass. (क्षीयते), तम् (c. 4. ताम्यति, तमितुं), आतम्, प्रतम्, ध्वंस् (c. 1. ध्वंसते -सितुं), विध्वंस्, स्रंस् (c. 1. स्रंसते -सितुं), विस्रंस्, विशॄ in pass. (-शीर्य्यते), प्रली (c. 4. -लीयते -लेतुं), शद् (c. 1. शीयते, शत्तुं), गल् (c. 1. गलति -लितुं), शिथिलीभू, खिद् in pass. (खिद्यते), आयस् (c. 4. -यस्यति -यसितुं), विषण्णीभू, अवसन्नीभू.—(Pine with love) उत्कण्ठ् (c. 1. -कण्ठते -ण्ठितुं), उत्सुक (nom. उत्सुकायते), उत्सुकीभू.—(Look tenderly and softly) कामालसदृष्टिः -ष्टिः -ष्टि भू, कामार्द्रदृष्टिः -ष्टिः -ष्टि भू.

LANGUISHING, *part.* or *a.* (Drooping, fading) म्लायन् -यन्ती -यत् (त्), म्लायमानः -ना -नं, ग्लायन् &c., ग्लायमानः -ना -नं, क्षीयमाणः -णा -णं, विषादी -दिनी -दि (न्), अवसादितः -ता -तं, विशीर्य्यमाणः -णा -णं, खिद्यमानः -ना -नं.—(Pining with love) उत्कण्ठितः -ता

-नं, उत्सुकः -का -कं; 'having languishing looks,' अलसेक्षणा, कामालसेक्षणा, कामालसदृष्टिः *f.*, कामार्द्रदृष्टिः *f.*

LANGUISHINGLY, *adv.* अवसादेन, विषादेन, सविषादं, सावसादं.—(With languishing looks) कामालसदृष्ट्या, कामार्द्रदृष्ट्या.

LANGUISHMENT, *s.* विषण्णता, अवसन्नता, उत्कण्ठा, उत्कण्ठितत्वं, उत्सुकता, औत्सुक्यं.—(Softness of look) कामालसदृष्टित्वं, कामार्द्रदृष्टित्वं.

LANGOUR, *s.* ग्लानिः *f.*, ग्लानता -त्वं, ग्लानिः *f.*, ग्लानता, क्लानिः *f.*, क्लान्तता, अवसादः, विषादः, सादः, अवसन्नता, विषण्णता, शिथिलता, शैथिल्यं, अङ्गशैथिल्यं, अङ्गक्षयः, अङ्गविक्षयः, क्षीणता, मन्दता, मान्द्यं, खेदः, तन्द्रा -न्द्रिः *f.* -न्द्रिका, तन्द्री, प्रमीला, उदासीनता, आलस्यं, अलसता -त्वं, यत्नविमुखता, यत्नपराङ्मुखता, कार्य्यविमुखता, जडता, जाड्यं.

To LANIATE, *v. a.* विद् (c. 10. -दारयति -यितुं), खण्डं खण्डं कृ, खण्डशः कृ.

LANIFEROUS, LANIGEROUS, *a.* लोमजनकः -का -कं, लोमोत्पादकः -का -कं.

LANK, *a.* (Thin, meagre) कृशः -शा -शं, परिकृशः -शा -शं, कृशाङ्गः -ङ्गी -ङ्गं, कृशशरीरः -रा -रं, क्षीणशरीरः -रा -रं, क्षीणमांसः -सा -सं, शुष्कमांसः -सा -सं, शुष्काङ्गः -ङ्गी -ङ्गं, क्षामः -मा -मं, अविपुलः -ला -लं, अपुष्टः -ष्टा -ष्टं, अतुन्दः -न्दा -न्दं.—(Tall) दीर्घदेहः -हा -हं, दीर्घतनुः -नुः -नु.—(Loose, flaccid) शिथिलः -ला -लं, श्लथः -था -थं, असंहतः -ता -तं.

LANKNESS, *s.* (Meagreness) कृशता, कृशाङ्गत्वं, शरीरकृशता, कार्श्यं, शरीरक्षीणता, क्षामता -त्वं, अतुन्दता, अविपुलता, अपुष्टता.—(Tallness) शरीरदीर्घता, दीर्घदेहत्वं.—(Flaccidity) शैथिल्यं, शिथिलता.

LANKY, *a.* कृशदीर्घः -र्घा -र्घं, क्षीणदीर्घः -र्घा -र्घं, दीर्घक्षामः -मा -मं.

LANNER, LANNERET, *s.* श्येनजातीयः पक्षिभेदः.

LANTERN, *s.* दीपः, प्रदीपः, दीपिका, प्रच्छन्नदीपः, गूढदीपः, आवृतदीपिका, कोशस्थदीपः, आकाशदीपः, आकाशप्रदीपः.

LANTERN-JAWED, *a.* तनुवदनः -ना -नं, क्षीणवदनः -ना -नं, दीर्घवदनः -ना -नं.

LANUGINOUS, *a.* लोमशः -शा -शं, लोममयः -यी -यं, लोमवान् -वती -वत् (त्), मृदुलोमवान् &c., मृदुलोमा -मा -म (न्), स्निग्धपर्णः -र्णा -र्णं.

LANYARD, *s.* नाविकभाषायां बन्धनरज्जुः *m. f.* or क्षुद्रसूत्रं or गुणः.

LAP, *s.* (The end or skirt of a garment that hangs loose) वस्त्राञ्चलः -लं, वसनान्तः, वस्त्रान्तः, वसनदशा, वस्त्रदशा, वस्तिः *m.*, तरी.—(The part about the thighs or hips when a person sits down) अङ्कः, क्रोडं -डा, उत्सङ्गः, ऊरुदेशः, सक्थिप्रदेशः, जानुदेशः; 'to place on the lap,' अङ्के or क्रोडे or उत्सङ्गे or अंकोर् उपरि न्यस् (c. 4. -अस्यति -असितुं) or कृ, क्रोडीकृ, अङ्कीकृ.

To LAP, *v. a.* (Fold) पुटीकृ, व्यावृत् (c. 10. -वर्त्तयति -यितुं), विपरिवृत्, व्यावर्त्तनं कृ.—(Wrap, infold) वेष्ट् (c. 1. वेष्टते -ष्टितुं), आवेष्ट्, परिवेष्ट्, कोशेन परिवेष्ट्.—(Lick up) लिह् (c. 2. लेढि, लीढे, लेढुं), आलिह्, संलिह्, परिसंलिह्, जिह्वास्वादं कृ, जिह्वालेहनं कृ.

To LAP, *v. n.* (Be turned over) व्यावृत् (c. 1. -वर्त्तते -र्त्तितुं), विपरिवृत्.

LAP-DOG, *s.* अङ्ककुक्कुरः, अङ्के पालनीयः क्षुद्रकुक्कुरः, अङ्कपालनयोग्यः क्षुद्रकुक्कुरः, अङ्कपालितकुक्कुरः.

LAP-FUL, *s.* अङ्कपूरणं, क्रोडपूरणं, अङ्कपूरकं, अङ्कभरकं.

LAPIDARIOUS, *a.* प्रस्तरमयः -यी -यं, मणिमयः &c., शिलामयः &c.

LAPIDARY, *s.* मणिकारः, रत्नकारः, मणिपरिष्कारकः, रत्नपरिष्कारकः, प्रस्तरच्छिद् *m.*, रत्नोपजीवी *m.* (न्), रत्नविक्रयी *m.* (न्), मणिविक्रेता *m.* (तृ).

To LAPIDATE, *v. a.* प्रस्तरप्रक्षेपेण or प्रस्तराघातेन हन् (c. 2. हन्ति -न्तुं) or व्यापद् (c. 10. -पादयति -यितुं).

LAPIDATION, *s.* प्रस्तराघातेन or पाषाणप्रक्षेपेण हननं or व्यापादनं or मारणं.

LAPIDEOUS, *a.* पाषाणमयः -यी -यं, शिलेयः -यी -यं, आश्मिकः -की -कं.

LAPIDESCENCE, *s.* पाषाणभूयं, प्रस्तरभूयं, शिलाभूयं.

LAPIDIFICATION, *s.* पाषाणसात्करणं, प्रस्तरसात्करणं, पाषाणीकरणं.

LAPIS-LAZULI, *s.* वैदूर्य्यं, विदूरजं, नीलोपलः -लं, असितोपलः, असिताश्मा *m.* (न्), बालराजः, बालसूर्य्यं, बालवायजं, अभ्ररोहं, गल्वर्कः.

LAPLING, *s.* विषयसेवी *m.* (न्), विषयोपभोगासक्तः, आत्मम्भरिः *m.*

LAPPET, *s.* वस्त्राञ्चलः -लं, वसनान्तः, वसनाञ्चलः, वसनदशा, वस्तिः *m.*

LAPSE, *s.* (Flow, course) गतिः *f.*, प्रवाहः, प्रवृत्तिः *f.*; 'lapse of time,' कालगतिः *f.*—(Passing away) अत्ययः, अतिक्रमः, प्रतीतिः *f.*—(Falling) पातः, पतनं, च्युतिः *f.*, च्यवनं, भ्रंशः, प्रभ्रंशः, ध्वंसः.—(Error) भ्रमः, प्रमादः, स्खलनं, स्खलितं.

To LAPSE, *v. n.* (Pass slowly away) शनैः शनैः or क्रमे क्रमे अती (c. 2. अत्येति -तुं, rt. इ) or व्यती or अतिक्रम् (c. 4. -क्राम्यति, c. 1. -क्रामति -क्रमितुं) or अतिवृत् (c. 1. -वर्त्तते -र्त्तितुं) or प्रवृत् or वृत्.—(Pass on by degrees) क्रमेण गम् (c. 1. गच्छति, गन्तुं) or प्रगम् or या (c. 2. याति -तुं) or प्रया or सृप् (c. 1. सर्पति, सर्प्तुं) or प्रसृप्.—(Fall in moral conduct) भ्रंश् (c. 4. -भ्रश्यति, भ्रंशितुं), विभ्रंश्, च्यु (c. 1. च्यवते, च्योतुं), विच्यु, विचल् (c. 1. -चलति -लितुं), उत्क्रम्, व्युत्क्रम्.—(Slip, make a mistake) स्खल् (c. 1. स्खलति -लितुं), प्रस्खल्, भ्रम् (c. 4. भ्राम्यति, भ्रमितुं), प्रमादं कृ, दोषं कृ.—(Pass from one proprietor to another) सङ्क्रम्, उपसङ्क्रम्, अपवृत्.

LAPSED, *p. p.* (Fallen) भ्रष्टः -ष्टा -ष्टं, प्रभ्रष्टः -ष्टा -ष्टं, च्युतः -ता -तं, पतितः -ता -तं.—(Passed from one proprietor to another) सङ्क्रान्तः -न्ता -न्तं, उपसङ्क्रान्तः -न्ता -न्तं, सङ्क्रामितः -ता -तं, अपवृत्तः -त्ता -त्तं, परहस्तगतः -ता -तं; 'lost by time,' वेलाहीनः -ना -नं.

LAPSIDED, *a.* See LOPSIDED.

LAPSUS LINGUÆ, *s.* जिह्वादोषः, मुखदोषः, वाग्दोषः; 'a lapsus of the hand or pen,' हस्तदोषः.

LAPWING, *s.* (A bird) टिट्टिभः -भकः, टिटिभकः, कोयष्टिः *m.* -ष्टिकः, पङ्ककीरः, शिखरी *m.* (न्)

LAR, *s.* (A household deity) कुलदेवता, गृहदेवता.

LARBOARD, *s.* (Left hand side of a ship) नावो वामपार्श्वः or वामभागः.

LARCENY, *s.* स्तेयं, चौर्य्यं, चौरं, स्तैनं, स्तैन्यं, चौर्य्यकर्म्म *n.* (न्), तस्करता, तास्कर्य्यं, चौरिका, चुरा, परद्रव्यापहारः.

LARCH, *s.* देवदारुजातीयो वृक्षभेदः.

LARD, *s.* शूकरमेदस् *n.*, शूकरवसा, शूकरमांसस्नेहः, शूकरमांसस्नेहः.—(Bacon) शूकरमांसं, शूकरस्य शुष्कमांसं, वल्लूरं.

To LARD, *v. a.* शूकरमेदसा पृ (c. 10. पूरयति -यितुं), शूकरमांसस्नेहं मध्ये निविश् (c. 10. -वेशयति -यितुं) or अन्तर् निविश्.—(Fatten) प्यै in caus. (प्याययति -यितुं), आप्यै, पुष् in caus. (पोषयति -यितुं), पुष्टीकृ.—(Interlard, mix) विमिश्र् (c. 10. -मिश्रयति -यितुं), सम्मिश्र्, सम्मिश्रीकृ, मिश्र्.

LARDER, *s.* खाद्यमांसागारं, भक्ष्यमांसागारं, मांसरक्षणगृहं, भोज्यमांसशाला, भोजनागारं, खाद्यद्रव्यागारं.

LARES, *s.* कुलदेवताः *f. pl.*, गृहदेवताः *f. pl.*, गृह्या देवताः *f. pl.*

LARGE, *a.* (Big, bulky in size) बृहन् -हती -हत् (त्), विपुलः -ला -लं, विशालः -ला -लं, पृथुः -थुः -थ्वी -थु, पृथुलः -ला -लं, स्थूलः -ला -लं, बृहत्कायः -या -यं, महाकायः -या -यं, महान् -हती -हत् (त्), महा in comp., बृहत् in comp., उरुः -रुः -र्व्वी -रु, विकटः -टा -टं, विशङ्कटः -टा -टी -टं, गुरुः -र्व्वी -रु, परिवृढः -ढा -ढं, वृढः -ढा -ढं, वड्रः -ड्रा -ड्रं, मन्थरः -रा -रं, मन्दरः -रा -रं, वाष्कलः -ला -लं, भभुः -भुः -भु.—(Extensive, wide) विपुलः -ला -लं, विस्तीर्णः -र्णा -र्णं, विशालः -ला -लं, आयतः -ता -तं, लब्धः -ब्धा -ब्धं.—(Abundant, copious) प्रचुरः -रा -रं, विपुलः -ला -लं, पुष्कलः -ला -लं, बहुः -हुः -ह्वी -हु, बहुलः -ला -लं, भूरिः -रिः -रि, यथेष्टः -ष्टा -ष्टं.—(Fat) पीनः -ना -नं, पीवरः -रा -रं, पीवा -वा -व (न्), पुष्टः -ष्टा -ष्टं.—(Having a large body) बृहच्छरीरः -रा -रं, पृथुशरीरः -रा -रं, स्थूलशरीरः -रा -रं, विकटशरीरः -रा -रं, बृहत्कायः -या -यं, बृहदङ्गः -ङ्गा -ङ्गं, स्थूलकायः -या -यं; 'larger,' बृहत्तरः -रा -रं, उरुतरः -रा -रं, वरीयान् -यसी -यः (स्), महत्तरः -रा -रं, अधिकः -का -कं; 'largest,' वरिष्ठः -ष्ठा -ष्ठं, बृहत्तमः -मा -मं; 'at large, without restraint,' निर्यन्त्रितं, निर्यन्त्रणं, निर्विघ्नं, निरवरोधेन, अनिवारितं, स्वेच्छया; 'at large, diffusely,' विस्तरशस्, विस्तरेण, सुविस्तरं.

Large-headed, *a.* स्थूलशिराः -राः -रः (स्), बृहच्छिराः &c., बृहच्छीर्षः -र्षा -र्षं, स्थौलशीर्षः -र्षा -र्षं, बृहन्मस्तकः -का -कं, स्थूलमस्तकः -का -कं.

Large-limbed, *a.* बृहदङ्गः -ङ्गी -ङ्गं, स्थूलाङ्गः -ङ्गी -ङ्गं, पृथ्वङ्गः -ङ्गी -ङ्गं.

Largely, *adv.* प्रचुरं, प्राचुर्य्येण, विपुलं, बाहुल्येन, बहु, भूरि, पुष्कलं, वैपुल्येन, विस्तरशस्, विस्तरेण.

Largeness, *s.* बृहत्त्वं, विपुलता, वैपुल्यं, विशालता, स्थूलता, स्थौल्यं, पृथुता -त्वं, पार्थवं, महत्त्वं, उरुता, विकटत्वं, वैकट्यं, प्रथिमा *m.* (न्), परिप्रथिमा.—(Extent) विस्तीर्णता, विस्तारः, विस्तृतिः *f.*, आयतिः *f.* —(Amplitude, abundance) प्राचुर्य्यं, प्रचुरता -त्वं, बाहुल्यं, बहुत्वं, पुष्कलता.—(Fatness) पीनता, पीवरत्वं, पुष्टता.—(Largeness of body) शरीरबृहत्त्वं, शरीरपृथुता, स्थूलशरीरत्वं.

Largess, *s.* वितरणं, विसर्ज्जनं, विश्राणनं, प्रदानं, त्यागः, पारितोषिकं.

Largo, *s.* (Slow time in music) विलम्बितं, तत्त्वं, विलम्बितवृत्तिः *f.*

Lark, *s.* (The bird) भरद्वाजः, भारद्वाजः -जकः, भारयः, व्याघ्राटः, भरतपक्षी *m.* (न्).

Larum, *s.* (Noise giving notice of danger) आसन्नभयघोषणा, आसन्नभयसूचकघोषः.—(Alarm-bell) आसन्नभयसूचका घण्टा.

Larva, larve, *s.* कीटः, कीटडिम्भः, कृमिः *m.*, कोशस्थः.

Laryngotomy, *s.* कण्ठनालच्छेदः -दनं, कृकच्छेदनं.

Larynx, *s.* कण्ठनालः -ली, कण्ठनाडिः -डी, कृकः.

Lascar, *s.* नाविकः, पोतवाहः, निर्यामः, समुद्रयायी *m.* (न्).

Lascivious, *s.* कामुकः -का -कं, कामी -मिनी -मि (न्), रतार्थी -र्थिनी -र्थि (न्), सुरतार्थी &c., रतासक्तः -क्ता -क्तं, रतिकर्म्मासक्तः &c., कामासक्तः &c., व्यवायी -यिनी -यि (न्), कामलः -ला -लं, कामनः -ना -नं, कमनः -ना -नं, कामकेलिः -लिः -लि, भोगासक्तः -क्ता -क्तं, कामप्रवणः -णा -णं, तरलः -ला -लं, तारलः -ला -लं, अनुकः -का -कं, अभीकः -का -कं, स्त्रीव्यसनी *m.* (न्), स्त्रीलम्पटः, लम्पटः.—(Proceeding from lust) कामहेतुकः -का -कं, काममूलकः -का -कं, कामसूचकः -का -कं.

Lasciviously, *adv.* कामुकवत्, सकामं, लम्पटवत्, स्त्रीलम्पटवत्, कामासक्तत्वात्, रतासक्तवत्, तरलं, तरलवत्, कामपूर्व्वं, कामयुक्ता.

Lasciviousness, *s.* कामुकत्वं, सकामत्वं, कामासक्तिः *f.*, रतासक्तिः *f.*, रतार्थित्वं, लम्पटत्वं -ता, लाम्पट्यं, तरलता, तारल्यं, भोगासक्तिः *f.*, व्यवायः, व्यवायासक्तिः *f.*, वैयात्यं, हेला -लनं.

Lash, *s.* (Thong) कशा, कषा, प्रतिष्कषः -शः, चलिसङ्गः, चर्म्मबन्धः, चर्म्मरज्जुः *m.f.*, वरत्रा, नद्धी, वध्री, वद्ध्री, वार्द्धी -द्ध्री.—(Stroke with a whip) कशाघातः, कशाप्रहारः, कशाताडनं.—(Stroke of satire) वाग्गतिः *f.*

To lash, *v. a.* (Strike with a lash) कशया or चर्म्मरज्ज्वा तड् (c. 10. ताडयति -यितुं) or आहन् (c. 2. -हन्ति -न्तुं) or प्रहृ (c. 1. -हरति -हर्त्तुं), कश (nom. कशयति -यितुं), कशाघातं कृ.—(Beat, shake about) विधू (c. 5. -धूनोति -धवितुं), धू, विचल् (c. 10. -चालयति -यितुं); 'he lashes his tail,' पुच्छं धूनोति.—(Tie or bind with a rope) रज्जुना or रज्ज्वा बन्ध् (c. 9. बध्नाति, बन्द्धुं), रज्जुबद्धं -द्धां -द्धं कृ.—(Censure with severity) अरुन्तुदवाचा or तीक्ष्णवाक्यैः or तिग्मवाचा निन्द् (c. 1. निन्दति -न्दितुं).

To lash, *v. n.* कशाघातं कृ, कशाताडनं कृ.—(Lash out, run into excess) मर्य्यादाम् अतिक्रम् (c. 1. -क्रामति -क्रमितुं), उत्क्रम्, व्युत्क्रम्, अवधिम् अतिचर् (c. 1. -चरति -रितुं).

Lashed, *p. p.* कशाहतः -ता -तं, कशाताडितः -ता -तं; 'worthy of being lashed,' कश्यः -श्या -श्यं, कशार्हः -र्हा -र्हं.—(Made fast) रज्जुबद्धः -द्धा -द्धं.

Lass, *s.* तरुणी, कुमारी, कन्या, बाला -लिका, दारिका, पुत्री.

Lassitude, *s.* ग्लानिः *f.*, ग्लानता, अवसादः, सादः, अवसन्नता, विषादः, विषण्णता, तन्द्रा -न्द्री -न्द्रिका -न्द्रिः *f.*, खेदः, प्रमीला, अङ्गशैथिल्यं, अङ्गशिथिलता, मन्दता, मान्द्यं, क्लान्तिः *f.*, क्लान्तता, म्लानिः *f.*, श्रान्तिः *f.*, परिश्रान्तिः, श्रमः.

Lasso, *s.* पाशः, पाशरज्जुः *m.f.*, पाशबन्धः, वागुरा.

Last, *a.* (Final) अन्तिमः -मा -मं, अन्त्यः -न्त्या -न्त्यं, अन्त in comp., शेष in comp., अपरः -रा -रं, चरमः -मा -मं, अवरतमः -मा -मं.—(Hindmost) पश्चिमः -मा -मं, जघन्यः -न्या -न्यं, अवरः -रा -रं, पाश्चात्यः -त्या -त्यं, पश्चातीयः -या -यं.—(Next before the present) गतः -ता -तं, अतीतः -ता -तं, भूतः -ता -तं.—(Last but one) उपान्तः -न्ता -न्तं, उपान्तिकः -की -कं, उपान्त्यः -न्त्या -न्त्यं.—(Extreme) परमः -मा -मं, अत्यन्तः -न्ता -न्तं, आत्यन्तिकः -की -कं, उत्तमः -मा -मं.—(Lowest) अधमः -मा -मं, अवरः -रा -रं, अधरः -रा -रं, अपमः -मा -मं, अपकृष्टः -ष्टा -ष्टं; 'come last,' अपरागतः -ता -तं, चरमागतः -ता -तं; 'born last,' अवरजः -जा -जं, जघन्यजः -जा -जं; 'last state,' शेषावस्था, शेषदशा, परिणामः; 'last past,' शेषभागः; 'last part of the night,' शेषरात्रिः *f.*; 'last half,' अपरार्द्धं, पश्चार्द्धं; 'last night,' गतरात्रिः *f.*; 'last month,' गतमासः; 'last year,' गतवत्सरः, परुत्; 'belonging to last year,' परुत्नः -त्ना -त्नं; 'year before last,' परारि; 'belonging to the year before last,' परारित्नः -त्ना -त्नं; 'at last,' शेषे, अन्ते, शेषतस्, अवशेषे, अन्ततस्, अनन्तरं, चिरकालात्परं, दीर्घकालात्परं, चरमं; 'to the last,' शेषं यावत्.

Last, *adv.* अपरं, चरमं, अन्ततस्, अन्ते, शेषतस्, पश्चात्, अवरस्तात्, अपरस्तात्; 'come last,' अपरागतः -ता -तं, चरमागतः -ता -तं; 'born last,' अवरजः -जा -जं, जघन्यजः -जा -जं.

Last, *s.* (Of a shoe) काष्ठमयः पादुकासंस्कारः or पादुकाकारः.

To last, *v. n.* स्था (c. 1. तिष्ठति -ते, स्थातुं), संस्था, पर्यवस्था, स्थिरीभू, चिरस्थायी -यिनी -यि भू.

Lasting, *a.* स्थायी -यिनी -यि (न्), चिरस्थायी &c., दीर्घकालस्थायी &c., चिरकालस्थायी &c., चिरकालिकः -का -कं, स्थिरः -रा -रं, स्थावरः -रा -रं, संस्थः -स्था -स्थं, स्थितिमान् -मती -मत् (त्), अनपायी -यिनी -यि (न्), नित्यस्थायी &c., नित्यः -त्या -त्यं, ध्रुवः -वा -वं, शाश्वतः -ती -तं, अविनाशी-गिणी-गि (न्), अजरः -रा -रं, अक्षयः -या -यं, चिरन्तनः -नी -नं.

Lastingness, *s.* स्थायित्वं, चिरस्थायित्वं, स्थिरता, स्थितिः *f.*, संस्थितिः *f.*, स्थावरत्वं, नित्यता, अजरत्वं, अनपायः, ध्रुवता, ध्रौव्यं.

Lastly, *adv.* अन्ततस्, अन्ते, शेषतस्, शेषे, अवशेषे -षतस्, अवरस्तात्.

Last-mentioned, *a.* उत्तरोक्तः -क्ता -क्तं, अपरोक्तः -क्ता -क्तं, अवरोक्तः -क्ता -क्तं.

Latch, *s.* तालकं, तालः, तालयन्त्रं, अर्गलः -ला -ली, कीलः, कपाटबन्धनी, द्वारबन्धनी, द्वारयन्त्रं.

To latch, *v. a.* तालकादिना द्वारं बन्ध् (c. 9. बध्नाति, बन्द्धुं).

Latchet, *s.* पादुकाबन्धनं -नी, पादुकाबन्धः, पादुकायोक्त्रं.

Late, *a.* (After the usual time, tardy) कालातीतः -ता -तं, समयातीतः -ता -तं, अतीतकालः -ला -लं, कालातिक्रान्तः -न्ता -न्तं, अतिक्रान्तकालः -ला -लं, वेलातीतः -ता -तं, विलम्बागतः -ता -तं, विलम्बेनागतः -ता -तं, विलम्बितः -ता -तं, मन्दः -न्दा -न्दं, चिरकालीनः -ना -नं, चिरकालादागतः -ता -तं, अतिकालः -ला -लं.—(Far advanced towards the close) अवसन्नः -न्ना -न्नं, अवसितः -ता -तं, परिणतः -ता -तं; 'at a late hour of the day,' अवसन्ने दिवसे, अपराह्णे, पराह्णे; 'at a late hour of the night,' अवसन्नायां रात्रौ, अपररात्रौ, रात्रिमध्ये, शेषरात्रौ; 'at a late period of life,' परिणते वयसि.—(Ripening after the time) नियमितकालात् परं or उपयुक्तकालात् परं पक्वः -क्वा -क्वं or परिणतः -ता -तं.—(Recent) नूतनः -ना -नं, नवः -वा -वं, अभिनवः -वा -वं, अचिरः -रा -रं, आधुनिकः -की -कं, अधुनातनः -नी -नं, इदानीन्तनः -नी -नं, सद्यस्कः -स्का -स्कं, सद्यस्कालीनः -ना -नं, अर्व्वाचीनः -ना -नं, अप्राचीनः -ना -नं, प्रत्यग्रः -ग्रा -ग्रं, वर्त्तमानकालीनः -ना -नं, अव्यवहितदीर्घकालः -ला -लं.—(Past, gone) अतीतः -ता -तं, व्यतीतः -ता -तं, गतः -ता -तं, भूतः -ता -तं.—(Former) प्राक्तनः -नी -नं, पूर्व्वतनः -नी -नं, पौर्व्विकः -की -कं.

Late, *adv.* (After the usual time, after delay) विलम्बेन, विलम्बात्, चिरकाले -लात्, अतिकालं, अतिसमयं, अतीतकालं, मन्दं, विलम्बितं, चिरात् -रेण; 'come late,' विलम्बागतः -ता -तं, विलम्बेनागतः &c., चिरादागतः &c., चिरकालादागतः &c.; 'ripening late,' उपयुक्तकालात् परं पक्वः -क्वा -क्वं; 'late at night,' अवसन्नायां रात्रौ, रात्रिमध्ये, मध्यरात्रे, अपररात्रे, महानिशायां; 'late in the day,' अपराह्णे, पराह्णे, अवसन्ने दिवसे; 'late in life,' परिणते वयसि.—(Not long ago, recently) नूतनं, अव्यवहितदीर्घकाले, अव्यवहितपूर्व्वकाले; 'too late in the evening,' अतिसाये; 'too late in the day,' अतिपराह्णे; 'too late in life,' अतिपरिणतवयसि, सुपरिणतवयसि.

Lateen, *s.* लतीन्नामा त्रिभुजाकारो वातवसनविशेषः.

Lately, *adv.* अव्यवहितदीर्घकाले, अव्यवहितपूर्व्वकाले, नूतनं, अर्व्वाक्, अर्व्वाक्काले, नूतनकाले, सद्यस्काले, अधुनातनकाले, इदानीन्तनकाले, अधुना, अप्राक्काले, प्रत्यग्रं.

Lateness, *s.* कालातीतता, अतीतकालत्वं, कालातिक्रान्तता, अतिकालता, चिरकालीनता, कालातिक्रमः, परिणतिः *f.*, परिणामः.

Latent, *a.* गूढः -ढा -ढं, गुप्तः -प्ता -प्तं, निगूढः -ढा -ढं, छन्नः -न्ना -न्नं, प्रच्छन्नः -न्ना -न्नं, अदृष्टः -ष्टा -ष्टं, अदृश्यः -श्या -श्यं, गुह्यः -ह्या -ह्यं, निभृतः -ता -तं, रहस्यः -स्या -स्यं, अन्तर्हितः -ता -तं, अप्रत्यक्षः -क्षा -क्षं, अप्रकटः -टा -टं, अप्रकाशः -शा -शं; 'as a disease,' मज्जागतः -ता -तं, धातुस्थः -स्था -स्थं.

Later, *a.* उत्तरः -रा -रं, परः -रा -रं, अवरः -रा -रं, पाश्चात्यः -त्या -त्यं.

Lateral. *a.* पार्श्विकः -की -कं, पार्श्वीयः -या -यं, पार्श्वः -र्श्वा -र्श्वं, पार्श्वतीयः -या -यं, अनुपार्श्वः -र्श्वा -र्श्वं, पार्श्वस्थः -स्था -स्थं, पार्श्वसम्बन्धी -न्धिनी -न्धि (न्).

Laterally, *adv.* पार्श्वतस्, पार्श्वे, अनुपार्श्वं, पार्श्वभागे, पार्श्वदिशि.

Lath, *s.* सूक्ष्मफलकः -कं, सूक्ष्मकाष्ठं, सूक्ष्मदारुः *m.*, दीर्घकाष्ठं, दीर्घफलकः -कं, तनुफलकः -कं, काष्ठफलकः.

To lath, *v. a.* सूक्ष्मफलकैर् आवृ (c. 5. -वृणोति -वरितुं -रीतुं) or आस्तृ (c. 9. -स्तृणाति -स्तरितुं -रीतुं), फलक (nom. फलकयति -यितुं).

Lathe, *s.* भ्रमः, भ्रमिः *f.*, कुन्दः, चक्रं, चक्रभ्रमं, यन्त्रकः.

Lather, *s.* अञ्जनफेनः, अभ्यञ्जनफेनः, मार्जनतैलफेनः, मार्जनलेपफेनः.

To lather, *v. a.* अञ्जनफेनेन लिप् (c. 6. लिम्पति, लेप्तुं), फेनलिप्तं -प्तां कृ.

To lather, *v. n.* फेन (nom. फेनायते -यितुं), फेनलः -ला -लं भू.

Lathy, *a.* काष्ठफलकवत् तनुः -नुः -न्वी -नु, सूक्ष्मः -क्ष्मा -क्ष्मं.

Latifolious, *a.* पृथुपत्रः -त्रा -त्रं, पृथुपर्णी -र्णी -र्णि.

Latin, *s.* (The language) लातिनाख्या भाषा, लातिन्भाषा.

Latinism, *s.* लातिन्भाषानुसारिणी वाग्वृत्तिः, लातिन्भाषासम्प्रदायः.

Latinity, *s.* लातिन्भाषायाः शुद्धता or विशुद्धिः *f.*

Latitancy, *s.* गुप्तता, गूढता, गुप्तभावः, प्रच्छन्नता, अप्रकाशता.

Latitant, *a.* गुप्तः -प्ता -प्तं, गूढः -ढा -ढं, प्रच्छन्नः -न्ना -न्नं, निभृतः -ता -तं.

Latitude, *s.* (Terrestrial) अक्षः, पलः, विषुवद्वृत्तान्तरं, विषुवरेखान्तरं.—(Celestial) विक्षेपः, शरः; 'a degree of latitude,' अक्षभागः, अक्षांशः; 'opposite degrees of latitude,' अनुपातः; 'latitude of a planet,' पतनं; 'argument of latitude,' अक्षकर्णः; 'circle or parallel of latitude,' अक्षवृत्तं, अक्षांशवृत्तं, स्वदेशपरिधिः *m.*, स्वदेशमध्यपरिधिः *m.*; 'having no latitude,' निरक्षः -क्षा -क्षं.—(Breadth) पृथुता, प्रथिमा *m.* (न्), विस्तृतिः *f.*, प्रस्थः.—(Laxity) शैथिल्यं, शिथिलता -त्वं, अनिर्बन्धः, निर्बन्धहीनता, नियमातिक्रमः, नियमोपेक्षा, अधृतिः *f.*

Latitudinal, *a.* अनुप्रस्थः -स्था -स्थं, अन्वायतनः -ना -नं, अक्षीयः -या -यं.

Latitudinarian, *a.* शिथिलः -ला -लं, निर्बन्धहीनः -ना -नं, अधृतिमान् -मती -मत् (त्), शास्त्रशैथिल्यानुयायी -यिनी -यि (न्), नियमातिक्रमी -मिणी -मि (न्), नियमोपेक्षकः -का -कं, मतशैथिल्यावलम्बी -म्बिनी -म्बि (न्), शिथिलबुद्धिः -द्धिः -द्धि.

Latitudinarianism, *s.* मतशैथिल्यं, शैथिल्यं, शिथिलता -त्वं, शिथिलबुद्धित्वं, अनिर्बन्धः, निर्बन्धहीनता, नियमातिक्रमः, निर्बन्धोपेक्षा, अधृतिः *f.*

Latrant, *a.* भषकः -का -कं, रावी -विणी -वि (न्), हुङ्कारी &c.

Latrociny, *s.* स्तेयं, चौर्य्यं, स्तैन्यं. *See* Larceny.

Latten, *s.* कांस्यं, रीतिः *f.*, पित्तलं.—(Sheet tin) त्रपुपत्रं.

Latter, *a.* (Opposed to former) उत्तरः -रा -रं, अपरः -रा -रं, परः -रा -रं, अवरः -रा -रं, पश्चिमः -मा -मं, चरमः -मा -मं, जघन्यः -न्या -न्यं, पाश्चात्यः -त्या -त्यं, पश्चात्तीयः -या -यं, अन्तिमः -मा -मं, अन्त्यः -न्त्या -न्त्यं; 'the latter,' अपरं; 'former and latter,' पूर्व्वापरं.—(Last-mentioned) उत्तरोक्तः -क्ता -क्तं, अपरोक्तः -क्ता -क्तं.—(Modern) नूतनः -ना -नं, आधुनिकः -की -कं, अर्व्वाचीनः -ना -नं, अप्राचीनः -ना -नं; 'in the latter part of the day,' अपराह्णे, पराह्णे.

Latterly, *adv.* अव्यवहितपूर्व्वकाले, नूतनकाले, अर्व्वाक्, अर्व्वाक्काले, अर्व्वाचीनकाले, अधुनातनकाले, इदानीन्तनकाले.

Lattice, *s.* (Window) जालं -लिका, जालकः, गवाक्षजालं, वातायनं, झर्झरं, वधूशयनं.

Lattice-work, *s.* जालकर्म्म *n.* (न्), जालं, व्यत्यस्तरेखाविशिष्टं कर्म्म.

Laud, *s.* प्रशंसा, श्लाघा, स्तुतिः *f.*, स्तुतिवादः, वन्दना, यशोवर्णना, ईडा.

To laud, *v. a.* प्रशंस् (c. 1. -शंसति -सितुं), स्तु (c. 2. स्तौति, स्तोतुं), अभिष्टु, संस्तु, श्लाघ् (c. 1. श्लाघते -घितुं, c. 10. श्लाघयति -यितुं), कॄत् (c. 10. कीर्त्तयति -यितुं), वन्द् (c. 1. वन्दते -न्दितुं).

Laudable, *a.* श्लाघ्यः -घ्या -घ्यं, श्लाघनीयः -या -यं, प्रशंसनीयः -या -यं, प्रशस्यः -स्या -स्यं, प्रशस्तः -स्ता -स्तं, स्तुत्यः -त्या -त्यं, स्तोतव्यः -व्या -व्यं, स्तवनीयः -या -यं, वन्द्यः -न्द्या -न्द्यं, वन्दनीयः -या -यं, कीर्त्तनीयः -या -यं, वर्णनीयः -या -यं, ईड्यः -ड्या -ड्यं, गेयः -या -यं, उपलभ्यः -भ्या -भ्यं, प्रशंसार्हः -र्हा -र्हं, श्लाघार्हः &c., स्तवार्हः &c.

Laudableness, *s.* श्लाघ्यता, श्लाघनीयता, प्रशस्यत्वं, प्रशस्तता, वन्द्यता.

LAUDABLY, *adv.* श्लाघनीयं, प्रशस्यं, यथा प्रशंसाम् अर्हति तथा.

LAUDANUM, *s.* अफेनरसः, अहिफेनरसः, खसखसरसः.

LAUDATION, *s.* प्रशंसनं, श्लाघाकरणं, स्तुतिकरणं, कीर्त्तनं, गुणोत्कीर्त्तनं.

LAUDATORY, *a.* स्तुतिमयः -यी -यं, स्तुतिरूपः -पा -पं, श्लाघामयः -यी -यं, प्रशंसामयः -यी -यं, प्रशंसाकरः -री -रं, स्तुतिपाठकः -का -कं, स्तावकः -का -कं, गुणप्रकाशकः -का -कं, कीर्त्तिप्रकाशकः -का -कं, वन्दारुः -रुः -रु.

LAUDED, *p.p.* प्रशंसितः -ता -तं, स्तुतः -ता -तं, अभिष्टुतः -ता -तं, श्लाघितः -ता -तं.

LAUDER, *s.* प्रशंसकः, स्तोता *m.* (तृ), स्तुतिपाठकः, वन्दी *m.* (न्), वर्णकः.

To LAUGH, *v. n.* हस् (c. 1. हसति -सितुं), प्रहस्, विहस्, सम्प्रहस्, स्मि (c. 1. स्मयते, स्मेतुं), हासं कृ, हसनं कृ, हास्यं कृ, तक् (c. 1. तकति -कितुं), कक्ख् (c. 1. कक्खति -क्खितुं), कख् or कक्ख् (c. 1. कखति -खितुं), 'to laugh violently,' अतिहस्, अत्यन्तं हस्, अतिहासं कृ, अट्टहासं कृ, महाहासं कृ, आच्छुरितं कृ; 'to laugh in one's sleeve,' अन्तर्हासं कृ, उच्चघनं कृ; 'to laugh at,' अवहस्, अपहस्, उपहस्, उत्स्मि, अभिस्मि, अवहासभूमिं कृ, अपहासास्पदं कृ. *See To* DERIDE.

LAUGH, *s.* हासः, हसनं, हसितं, हास्यं, हसः, विहसितं, प्रहसितं, परिहासः, प्रहासः, उपहसितं, स्मितं, हः, हा, हं; 'a horse-laugh,' अट्टहासः, अट्टहसितं, आच्छुरितं -तकं, अवच्छुरितं, सोत्प्रासः; 'an inward laugh,' अन्तर्हासः, उच्चघनं.

LAUGHABLE, *a.* हास्यः -स्या -स्यं, उपहास्यः -स्या -स्यं, अवहास्यः -स्या -स्यं, परिहास्यः &c., हासकरः -री -रं, हास्यजनकः -का -कं, हस्योत्पादकः -का -कं, तक्यः -क्या -क्यं.

LAUGHABLENESS, *s.* हास्यता -त्वं, उपहास्यता, हासजनकत्वं.

LAUGHABLY, *adv.* उपहास्यप्रकारेण, यथा हासो जायते तथाप्रकारेण.

LAUGHER, *s.* हासकः, हासी *m.* (न्), उपहासकः, परिहासकः, हासकर्त्ता *m.* (र्त्तृ), हसनकृत्, प्रहसनकृत्.

LAUGHING, *a.* हास्यमुखः -खी -खं, हास्यवदनः -ना -नं, सुहसाननः -ना -नं, स्मेरमुखः -खी -खं, हास्यप्रियः -या -यं.

LAUGHINGLY, *adv.* सहासं, सहास्यं, सहसितं, सस्मितं, परिहासेन, विहस्य.

LAUGHING-STOCK, *s.* हास्यास्पदं, उपहासस्थानं, उपहासास्पदं, अपहासास्पदं, हास्यभूमिः *f.*, अवहासभूमिः *f.*, उपहासभूमिः, उपहासविषयः, अवहासविषयः.

LAUGHTER, *s.* हासः, हसनं, हसितं, हास्यं, प्रहसितं, विहसितं, उपहसितं, प्रहासः, परिहासः, हसः; 'loud or violent laughter,' प्रहासः, प्रहसनं, अतिहासः, अतिहसितं, महाहासः, अट्टहासः, आच्छुरितकं. *See* LAUGH.

To LAUNCH, *v. a.* (A ship) नावं मुच् (c. 6. मुञ्चति, मोक्तुं, c. 10. मोचयति -यितुं) or स्थलाद् मुक्ता जलं प्रविश् (c. 10. -वेशयति -यितुं), स्थलस्थनावं चल् (c. 10. चालयति -यितुं) or प्रचल् or वह् (c. 10. वाहयति -यितुं) or भास् (c. 10. भासयति -यितुं).

To LAUNCH, *v. n.* जलं प्रविश् (c. 6. -विशति -वेष्टुं), मुच् in pass. (मुच्यते).

LAUNCH, *s.* नौमुक्तिः *f.*, नौमोचनं, स्थलस्थनौकामुक्तिः *f.*, जलप्रवेशनं.

LAUNCHED, *p.p.* स्थलमुक्तः -क्ता -क्तं, जलप्रवेशितः -ता -तं, जलप्रविष्टः -ष्टा -ष्टं.

LAUNDER, LAUNDRESS, *s.* वस्त्ररजकी, वस्त्रधावकी, वस्त्रनिर्णेजकी.

LAUNDERER, *s.* रजकः, वस्त्ररजकः, वस्त्रधावकः, वस्त्रनिर्णेजकः.

LAUNDRY, *s.* वस्त्रधावनशाला, निर्णेकगृहं, वस्त्रमार्जनशाला.

LAUREATE, *a.* वक्ष्यमाणवृक्षपत्रशोभितः -ता -तं, लारेलाख्यवृक्षपत्रभूषितः -ता -तं, मानसूचकमालाभूषितः -ता -तं.

LAUREL, *s.* लारेलाख्यो वृक्षभेदः, श्यामवृक्षविशेषः.

LAURELLED, *s.* पूर्व्वोक्तवृक्षपत्रभूषितः -ता -तं, मालाभूषितः -ता -तं.

LAVA, *s.* ज्वालामुखीनिर्गतद्रवः, आग्नेयपर्व्वतनिर्गतद्रवः.

LAVATION, *s.* धावनं, प्रक्षालनं, स्नानं, मार्जनं, निर्णेकः, मलापकर्षणं.

LAVATORY, *s.* धावनस्थानं, धावनशाला, प्रक्षालनस्थानं, मार्जनशाला.

To LAVE, *v. a.* धाव् (c. 1. धावति -वितुं, c. 10. धावयति -यितुं), प्रधाव्, क्षल् (c. 10. क्षालयति -यितुं), प्रक्षल्, स्ना in caus. (स्नापयति, स्नपयति -यितुं).

To LAVE, *v. n.* स्ना (c. 2. स्नाति -तुं), जले निमस्ज् (c. 6. -मज्जति -मंक्तुं).

LAVEMENT, *s.* (Clyster) वस्तिः *m. f.*, नेत्रं. *See* CLYSTER.

LAVENDER, *s.* लावेन्दराख्यः सुगन्धीयौषधिभेदः or सुगन्धितृणभेदः.

LAVER, *s.* प्रक्षालनपात्रं, धावनपात्रं, जलाधारः, द्रोणी.

LAVISH, *a.* (Prodigal) अतिव्ययी -यिनी -यि (न्), अपव्ययी &c., व्ययशीलः -ला -लं, अपरिमितव्ययः -या -यं, मुक्तहस्तः -स्ता -स्तं, अपचेता -त्री -तृ (तृ), उत्सर्गी -र्गिणी -र्गि (न्), अतुलत्सर्गी &c., अतिदाता -त्री -तृ (तृ), अतित्यागी -गिनी -गि (न्), बहुप्रदः -दा -दं.—(Copious, unrestrained) अपरिमितः -ता -तं, अतिरिक्तः -क्ता -क्तं, अति prefixed; 'lavish expenditure,' अतिव्ययः, अपरिमितव्ययः.

To LAVISH, *v. a.* अपरिमितं or अपरिमाणेन व्यय् (c. 1. व्ययति, c. 10. व्यययति -यितुं, rt. इ) or व्ययीकृ, अपरिमितव्ययं कृ, अतिव्ययं कृ, मुक्तहस्तेन दा (c. 3. ददाति, दातुं) or विसृज् (c. 6. -सृजति -स्रष्टुं) or उत्सृज् or त्यज् (c. 1. त्यजति, त्यक्तुं) or अपचि (c. 5. -चिनोति -चेतुं) or वितृ (c. 1. -तरति -रितुं -रीतुं), विक्षिप् (c. 6. -क्षिपति -क्षेप्तुं).

LAVISHED, *p.p.* व्ययितः -ता -तं, विसर्ज्जितः -ता -तं, अपचितः -ता -तं, मुक्तहस्तेन दत्तः -त्ता -त्तं or प्रदत्तः -त्ता -त्तं, अतिबाहुल्येन विक्षिप्तः -ता -तं or वितीर्णः -र्णा -र्णं.

LAVISHER, *s.* अतिव्ययी *m.* (न्), अपरिमितव्ययी *m.*, अतुलत्सर्गी *m.* (न्), अतिदाता *m.* (तृ).

LAVISHLY, *adv.* अतिव्ययेन, अपरिमितव्ययेन, महाव्ययेन, अपरिमितं, अपरिमाणेन, मुक्तहस्तेन, अतुलत्सर्गेण, अकार्पण्येन, अबाहुल्येन.

LAVISHMENT, LAVISHNESS, *s.* अतिव्ययः, अपरिमितव्ययः, अपव्ययः, महान् व्ययः, अतुलत्सर्गः, अतिसर्जनं, अतित्यागः, अतिमोक्षणं, अतिदानं, मुक्तहस्तत्वं, बहुप्रदत्वं, अकार्पण्यं.

LAW, *s.* (Ordinance, decree, statute of a state) व्यवस्था, शासनं, विधिः *m.*, विधानं, नियमः, अनुशासनं, सूत्रं, निदर्शनं, नियोगः, राजाज्ञा, आदेशः, निदेशः, व्यवस्थापत्रं, शासनपत्रं, चोदना, उक्तवाक्यं.—(The rules by which judicature is regulated, jurisprudence) धर्म्मः, स्मृतिः *f.*, व्यवहारः, आचारः, व्यवहारविधिः *m.*, व्यवहारशास्त्रं, धर्म्मशास्त्रं, धर्म्मविधिः *m.*; 'a code of laws,' धर्म्मसंहिता, धर्म्मशास्त्रं, व्यवहारविधिः *m.*; 'a work on law,' स्मृतिशास्त्रं; 'criminal law,' दण्डविधिः *m.*, दण्डनीतिः *f.*; 'administration of the law,' धर्म्मप्रणयनं, धर्म्माधिकरणं; 'court of law,' धर्म्मसभा, 'matter cognizable by law,' व्यवहारविषयः, व्यवहारपदं; 'to go to law,' विवादं गम् (c. 1. गच्छति, गन्तुं), विवद् (c. 1. -वदते -दितुं), व्यवहृ (c. 1. -हरति -हर्तुं); 'knowledge of law,' धर्म्मज्ञानं; 'learned in the law,' धर्म्मज्ञः, स्मृतिशास्त्रज्ञः, व्यवहारपण्डितः; 'breaking a law,' व्यवस्थातिक्रमः, व्यवस्थालङ्घनं, व्यवस्थातिवर्त्तनं.—(Legal process) व्यवहारः, व्यवहारमार्गः.—(Rule of action) नियमः, विधिः *m.*, विधानं, मर्य्यादा, स्थितिः *f.*, कार्य्याकार्य्यनियमः, कर्त्तव्याकर्त्तव्यनियमः, विधिनिषेधनियमः.—(Principle, rule of science, &c.) नियमः, सूत्रं, विधिः *m.*, स्थितिः *f.*, तत्त्वं, उक्तवाक्यं, न्यायः, उत्सर्गः.—(Conformity to law, right) धर्म्मः, धर्म्मानुसारः, न्यायः, नीतिः *f.*—(The law of works, considered as a yoke of bondage) कर्म्ममार्गः, प्रवृत्तिमार्गः, कर्म्मबन्धः -न्धनं.

LAW-BREAKER, *s.* व्यवस्थातिक्रमी *m.* (न्), व्यवस्थातिवर्त्ती *m.* (न्), व्यवस्थालङ्घी *m.* (न्), व्यवस्थाभेदी *m.*, व्यवस्थालोपी *m.*

LAWFUL, *a.* (Conformable to law) धर्म्यः -र्म्या -र्म्यं, धर्म्मानुसारी -रिणी -रि (न्), धर्म्मानुयायी -यिनी -यि (न्), धर्म्मशास्त्रसम्मतः -ता -तं, स्मृतिशास्त्रसम्मतः &c., धर्म्मशास्त्रानुमतः &c., धर्म्मशास्त्रानुरूपः -पा -पं, व्यवस्थानुसारी &c., राज्यनियमसम्मतः &c., व्यवहारानुसारी &c., व्यावहारिकः -की -कं, स्मृतिशास्त्रानुसारी &c., स्मार्त्तः -र्त्ती -र्त्तं, शास्त्रीयः -या -यं, आचारिकः -की -कं, आचारी -रिणी -रि (न्), न्यायानुसारी &c., राज्यव्यवस्थानुयायी &c., सौत्रः -त्री -त्रं.—(Constituted by law) धर्म्मशास्त्रप्रोक्तः -क्ता -क्तं, स्मृतिशास्त्रप्रोक्तः &c., व्यवहारविधिप्रोक्तः &c., स्मृत्युक्तः &c., स्मृतिशास्त्रविहितः -ता -तं, शास्त्रोक्तः &c.—(Not forbidden) अनिषिद्धः -द्धा -द्धं, शास्त्रानिषिद्धः -द्धा -द्धं, धर्म्माविरोधी -धिनी -धि (न्).—(Rightful) न्यायी -यिनी -यि (न्), न्याय्यः -य्या -य्यं, यथान्यायः -या -यं; 'lawful wife,' धर्म्मपत्नी; 'by lawful means,' धर्म्मोपायेन; 'lawful and unlawful food,' भक्ष्याभक्ष्यं.

LAWFULLY, *adv.* धर्म्मेण, धर्म्मतस्, धर्म्मानुसारेण -रात्, धर्म्मशास्त्रानुसारेण, स्मृतिशास्त्रानुसारेण, व्यवहारविध्यनुसारेण, व्यवस्थानुरूपेण, राज्यनियमानुरूपेण, न्यायतस्, न्यायानुसारेण, यथान्यायं, न्याय्यं.

LAWFULNESS, *s.* धर्म्यत्वं, धर्म्मानुसारित्वं, धर्म्मानुसारः, धर्म्मशास्त्रानुसारिता, स्मृतिशास्त्रानुयायिता, धर्म्मशास्त्रानुकूल्यं, न्यायानुसारः -रिता, न्याय्यत्वं.

LAWGIVER, *s.* स्मृतिकारः, व्यवस्थाकारः -रकः, विधिस्थापकः, विधिकर्त्ता *m.* (र्त्तृ), व्यवस्थाकर्त्ता *m.*, विधिप्रवर्त्तकः, व्यवस्थापकः, शासिता *m.* (तृ), विचारयिता *m.* (तृ), प्रयोजकः, शास्त्रकर्त्ता *m.*, धर्म्मशास्त्ररचकः, विधिदाता *m.* (तृ), विधिदायकः, विधायी *m.* (न्), विधायकः.

LAWLESS, *a.* (Not subject to law, said of persons) दुराचारः -रा -रं, अनाचारी -रिणी -रि (न्), आचारभ्रष्टः -ष्टा -ष्टं, निराचारः -रा -रं, आचारहीनः -ना -नं, आचारवर्जितः -ता -तं, निर्म्मर्य्यादः -दा -दं, अमर्य्यादः -दा -दं, मर्य्यादातिवर्त्ती -र्त्तिनी -र्त्ति (न्), मर्य्यादातिचारी &c., मर्य्यादातिक्रमी &c., अतिक्रान्तमर्य्यादः -दा -दं, त्यक्तमर्य्यादः -दा -दं, त्यक्तधर्म्मा -र्म्मा -र्म्म (न्), धर्म्मभ्रष्टः -ष्टा -ष्टं, कामाचारी &c., यथेष्टाचारी &c., स्वेच्छाचारी &c., कामवृत्तः -त्ता -त्तं, स्वैरगतिः -तिः -ति, अशिष्टः -ष्टा -ष्टं, अवशः -शा -शं, अनियतः -ता -तं, उच्छृङ्खलः -ला -लं, शास्त्रातिवर्त्ती &c., व्यवस्थातिवर्त्ती &c., व्यवस्थातिक्रमी &c.—(Contrary to law) धर्म्मविरुद्धः -द्धा -द्धं, स्मृतिविरुद्धः &c., व्यवहारविरुद्धः &c., व्यवस्थाविरुद्धः &c., धर्म्मरोधी -धिनी -धि (न्), अधर्म्यः -र्म्या -र्म्यं, अस्मार्त्तः -र्त्ती -र्त्तं, अव्यवस्थितः -ता -तं. *See* ILLEGAL.

LAWLESSLY, *adv.* धर्म्मविरोधेन, स्मृतिविरोधेन, व्यवहारविरुद्धं, आचारविरोधेन, दुराचारवत्, धर्म्मभ्रष्टवत्, अशिष्टवत्, अवशं, उच्छृङ्खलं.

LAWLESSNESS, *s.* दुराचारत्वं, आचारभ्रष्टता, मर्य्यादातिवर्त्तनं, मर्य्यादातिक्रमः, अमर्य्यादा, अनाचारः, व्यभिचारः, व्यतिक्रमः, कामाचारित्वं, कामवृत्तता, नियमातिक्रमः, व्यवस्थातिक्रमः, नियमातिवर्त्तनं, व्यवस्थातिवर्त्तनं, उच्छृङ्खलत्वं.

LAWN, *s.* (Space of ground covered with grass) तृणावृतो भूमिभागः, सतृणस्थलं, शाड्वलस्थलं, हरितस्थलं, तृणावृतस्थलं.—(Fine linen) अंशुकं, दुकूलं.

LAW-SUIT, *s.* अर्थः, विवादः, व्यवहारः, कार्य्यं, अभ्रः, वादः, व्यवहरणं.

LAWYER, *s.* धर्म्मज्ञः, धर्म्मशास्त्रज्ञः, धर्म्मशास्त्रवेत्ता *m.* (तृ), स्मृतिशास्त्रज्ञः, व्यवहारपण्डितः, व्यवस्थापकः, व्यवस्थानिरूपकः, आचारज्ञः, व्यवहारसचिवः.

LAX, *a.* (Loose) शिथिलः -ला -लं, श्लथः -था -थं, प्रश्लथः -था -थं, विगलितः -ता -तं, स्रस्तः -स्ता -स्तं, अबद्धः -द्धा -द्धं.—(In morals) अनवस्थः -स्था -स्थं, दुराचारः -रा -रं, अनाचारी -रिणी -रि (न्), धर्म्मभ्रष्टः -ष्टा -ष्टं, कर्म्मभ्रष्टः &c., व्यभिचारी &c.—(In the bowels) मृदुकोष्ठः -ष्ठा -ष्ठं, अबद्धकोष्ठः -ष्ठा -ष्ठं.—(In discipline) अतीक्ष्णदण्डः -ण्डा -ण्डं, शिथिलदण्डः -ण्डा -ण्डं.

LAX, *s.* (Diarrhœa) सारणः, अतिसारः, प्रवाहिका, विरेकः.

LAXATIVE, *a.* मलावष्टम्भघ्नः -घ्नी -घ्नं, मलावरोधनाशकः -का -कं, सारकः -का -कं, कोष्ठविस्रंसनः -ना -नं, रेचकः -की -कं, विरेचकः -की -कं.

LAXATIVE, *s.* विस्रंसनं, रेचकः, मलसारकम् औषधीयद्रव्यं.

LAXITY, LAXNESS, *s.* (Looseness) शैथिल्यं, शिथिलता -त्वं, श्लथत्वं, प्रश्लथः, विस्रंसः, विस्रस्तता, अधृतिः *f.*, अबद्धता.—(In morals) अनवस्थितिः *f.*, अनवस्थता, व्यभिचारः, अनाचारः, आचारभ्रष्टता, मर्य्यादातिक्रमः, व्यतिक्रमः, इन्द्रियासंयमः.—(In discipline) दण्डातैक्ष्ण्यं, दण्डशैथिल्यं.—(Of the bowels) अतिसारः, सारणः, कोष्ठमृदुता.

To LAY, *v. a.* (Place, set) धा (c. 3. दधाति, धातुं), निधा, आधा, न्यस् (c. 4. -अस्यति -असितुं), स्था in caus. (स्थापयति -यितुं), निविश् (c. 10. -वेशयति -यितुं), आरुह् in caus. (-रोपयति -यितुं), ऋ in caus. (अर्पयति -यितुं), दा (c. 3. ददाति, दातुं), भृ (c. 1. भरति, भर्त्तुं), कृ; 'he lays the cup on the ground,' पात्रं भूमौ निदधाति or न्यस्यति; 'he lays the goat on his shoulders,' छागं स्कन्धे or स्कन्धेन करोति; 'lay your hand on my shoulder,' मत्स्कन्धे हस्तं देहि.—(Place in order) विन्यस्, विधा, संविधा, प्रतिविधा, विरच् (c. 10. -रचयति -यितुं), क्रमेण स्था.—(Beat down) पत् (c. 10. पातयति -यितुं), निपत्.—(Spread) आस्तृ (c. 9. -स्तृणाति, c. 5. -स्तृणोति -स्तरितुं -रीतुं), विस्तृ; 'to lay snares,' जालं विस्तृ; 'he lays sacred grass over the ground,' भूमिं कुशैर् आस्तृणाति.—(Spread on a surface) लिप् (c. 6. -लिम्पति, लेप्तुं) with acc. and instr. c.—(Still, quiet, calm) शम् (c. 10. शमयति -यितुं), प्रशम्, उपशम्, सान्त्व् or शान्त्व् (c. 10. सान्त्वयति -यितुं), अभिशान्त्व्, परिशान्त्व्.—(Lay a wager) पण् (c. 1. पणते -णितुं), विपण्, निक्षिप् (c. 6. -क्षिपति -क्षेप्तुं), पणं कृ, प्रतिज्ञां कृ.—(Lay eggs) अण्डानि सु (c. 2. सूते, c. 4. सूयते, सोतुं) or प्रसु.—(Lay the blame) कस्मिंश्चिद् दोषम् आरुह् or क्षिप्, दोषारोपणं कृ, दोषप्रसङ्गं कृ.—(Apply) आधा, न्यस्, संयुज् (c. 10. -योजयति -यितुं), ऋ in caus.—(Impose) न्यस्, निविश्, नियुज्, आरुह् in caus.—(Lay a command) आदेशं कृ, आज्ञां कृ, नियुज्.—(Lay an ambush) पराक्रमणार्थं सैन्यं निभृते स्था in caus.—(Lay a plot, scheme) कपटप्रबन्धं कृ, सङ्कल्पं कृ, उपायं प्रचिन्त् (c. 10. -चिन्तयति -यितुं) or घट् (c. 1. घटते -टितुं) or विधा or प्रयुज्.—(Lay siege) परिवेष्ट् (c. 1. -वेष्टते -ष्टितुं), रुध् (c. 7. रुणद्धि, रोद्धुं), अवरुध्, उपरुध्.—(Lay waste) उपद्रु (c. 1. -द्रवति -द्रोतुं), उपप्लु (c. 1. -प्लवते -प्लोतुं), बाध् (c. 1. बाधते -धितुं), प्रबाध्, परिबाध्, निर्दह् (c. 1. -दहति -दग्धुं), दह्, निर्जनीकृ.—(Lay aside) न्यस्, सन्न्यस्, त्यज् (c. 1. त्यजति, त्यक्तुं), परित्यज्, सन्त्यज्, हा (c. 3. जहाति, हातुं), अपहा, उत्सृज् (c. 6. -सृजति -स्रष्टुं), उज्झ् (c. 6. उज्झति -ज्झितुं), प्रोज्झ्, अपहृ (c. 1. -हरति -हर्त्तुं), अपमुच् (c. 6. -मुञ्चति -मोक्तुं); 'one who has laid aside his anger,' अस्तकोपः -पा -पं.—(Lay before) प्रसृ (c. 10. -सारयति -यितुं), निविद् (c. 10. -वेदयति -यितुं), उपन्यस्, ऋ in caus.—(Lay by) सन्न्यस्, परिरक्ष् (c. 1. -रक्षति -क्षितुं), रक्ष्, निधा, निधिं कृ; 'he lays by the food left by the crows,' काकेभ्यः शिष्टं मांसं रक्षति.—(Lay down, deposit) न्यस्, उपन्यस्, प्रतिन्यस्, निक्षिप्, निधा, अवधा, न्यासीकृ.—(Lay down, give up) त्यज्, परित्यज्, विमुच्, विहा.—(Lay down, put down, cause to lie down) निधा, शी (c. 10. शाययति -यितुं), उपविश्, निविश्.—(Lay one's self down) शी (c. 2. शेते, शयितुं), संविश् (c. 6. -विशति -वेष्टुं), शयनं कृ.—(Lay hold of) ग्रह् (c. 9. गृह्णाति, ग्रहीतुं), परिग्रह्,

सङ्ग्रह्, हस्तेन ग्रह्, धृ (c. 1. धरति, धर्त्तुं), हस्तेन भृ.—(Lay in) सङ्ग्रह्, सङ्ग्रहं कृ, सञ्चयं कृ, पर्य्याहारं कृ, सञ्चि (c. 5. -चिनोति -चेतुं); 'lay in a store of grain,' धान्यसङ्ग्रहं कृ.—(Lay on) पत् (c. 10. पातयति -यितुं), प्रयुज्, नियुज्, क्षिप् in caus.; 'lay on blows,' दण्डं पत्.—(Lay open) विवृ (c. 5. -वृणोति -वृणुते -वरितुं -रीतुं), अपवृ, प्रकाश् (c. 10. -काशयति -यितुं), विकाश्, प्रकटीकृ, व्यक्तीकृ.—(Lay out money, expend) व्यय् (c. 10. व्ययति -यितुं, rt. इ), व्ययीकृ, विनियुज् (c. 7. -युंक्ते -योक्तुं), उपयुज्.—(Lay out, display) प्रसृ (c. 10. -सारयति -यितुं), प्रकाश्, प्रकटीकृ.—(Lay out, dispose in order) विन्यस्, विरच्, सुपर्य्याप्तं -प्तां कृ, परिकॢप् (c. 10. -कल्पयति -यितुं), क्रमेण स्था.—(Lay one's self out) आत्मानं चेष्ट् (c. 1. चेष्टते -ष्टितुं), यत् (c. 1. यतते -तितुं), यत्नं कृ.—(Lay out, spread out) आस्तॄ, विस्तॄ.—(Lay to a ship) नौगतिरोधं कृ.—(Lay up) निधा (c. 3. or c. 10. -धापयति -यितुं). *See* Lay by, lay in. 'A king should lay up treasure,' राज्ञा निधिर् निधातव्यः.—(To be laid up) रोगोपहतत्वात् शयनाद् उत्थातुं or शयनगृहाद् निर्गन्तुम् अक्षमः -मा भू.—(Lay the dust) मार्गरेणुं सिच् (c. 6. सिञ्चति, सेक्तुं) or संसिच्.—(Lay down life) प्राणान् त्यज् or मुच् or न्यस्.

To lay, *v. n.* (Produce eggs) अण्डानि सू (c. 2. सूते, c. 4. सूयते, सोतुं) or प्रसू or जन् (c. 10. जनयति -यितुं) or प्रजन् (c. 4. -जायते -जनितुं) or उत्पद् (c. 10. -पादयति -यितुं).

Lay, *s.* (Stratum, layer) स्तरः, आस्तरणं, आस्तरः, फलकः -कं, पुटः.—(Song) गीतं, गानं, कविता, काव्यं.

Lay, *a.* (Not clerical) गृहस्थवर्गसम्बन्धी -न्धिनी -न्धि (न्), गृहस्थी -स्थिनी -स्थि (न्), गार्हस्थिकः -की -कं, पुरोहितवर्गभिन्नः -न्ना -न्नं, पौरोहित्यभिन्नः -न्ना -न्नं, धर्म्मपदस्थभिन्नः -न्ना -न्नं, धर्म्मपदस्थातिरिक्तः -क्ता -क्तं, सामान्यलोकसम्बन्धी &c., साधारणलोकसम्बन्धी &c., धर्म्माधिकार-दीक्षाहीनः -ना -नं, अजातधर्म्माधिकारदीक्षः -क्षा -क्षं.

Layer, *s.* (Stratum) आस्तरणं, आस्तरः, स्तरः, फलकः -कं, पार्थिवांशपुटः; 'layer of rock,' शिलाफलकं.—(Young twig, shoot) पल्लवः, किसलयः, प्ररोहः.

Lay-figure, *s.* चित्रकर्म्मणि प्रयुक्ता काष्ठनिर्म्मिता पुरुषाकारा मूर्त्तिः.

Lay-man, *s.* गृहस्थः, सामान्यलोकः, सामान्यजनः, साधारणलोकः, साधारणपदस्थः, सामान्यपदस्थः, दीक्षाहीनः, अदीक्षितः, अजातदीक्षः.

Lay-stall, *s.* पुरीषराशिः *m.*, शकृद्राशिः *m.*, अमेध्यराशिः, अवस्करचयः.

Lazar, *s.* कुष्ठी *m.* (न्), श्वित्री *m.* (न्), दुश्चर्म्मा *m.* (न्), त्वग्रोगी *m.* (न्), त्वग्रोगोपहतः, त्वग्व्याधिग्रस्तः, चर्म्मरोगोपहतः, चर्म्मरोगदूषितः.

Lazar-house, lazaretto, *s.* कुष्ठिशाला, त्वग्रोगदूषितशाला, त्वग्रोगिशाला, चर्म्मरोगिशाला, रोगप्रतीकारशाला, रोगसम्पर्कदूषितानां or रोगसंसर्गदूषितानां रक्षणशाला.

Lazar-like, lazarly, *a.* त्वग्रोगी -गिणी -गि (न्). *See* Lazar.

Lazaroni, *s.* अलसजनः, अलसलोकः, दरिद्रजनः, निर्व्यापारजनः.

Lazily, *adv.* अलसवत्, आलस्येन, सालस्यं, अलसं, मन्दं, मन्दं मन्दं, मन्दगत्या, समान्द्यं, अनुद्योगेन, जडवत्, सजाड्यं, शाड्येन.

Laziness, *s.* आलस्यं, अलसता -त्वं, मन्दता, मान्द्यं, अलसशीलता, आलस्यशीलता, अनुद्योगः -गिता, अनुद्योगशीलता, उद्योगद्वेषः, कार्य्यप्रद्वेषः, उत्साहप्रद्वेषः, उत्साहविमुखता, उद्योगवैमुख्यं, कर्म्मपराङ्मुखता, अव्यवसायः, कुण्ठता, अपटुता, जडता, जाड्यं, तन्द्रिका, तन्द्रालुता, क्लीबता, क्लैब्यं.

Lazuli, *s.* वैदूर्य्यं, विदूरजं. *See* Lapis lazuli.

Lazy, *a.* अलसः -सा -सं, आलस्यः -स्या -स्यं, आलस्यशीलः -ला -लं,

मन्दः -न्दा -न्दं, मन्थरः -रा -रं, मन्दरः -रा -रं, अनुद्योगशीलः -ला -लं, उद्योगद्वेषी -षिणी -षि (न्), उद्योगविमुखः -खा -खं, उद्योगपराङ्मुखः -खा -खं, उत्साहविमुखः &c., अकर्म्मशीलः -ला -लं, निरुद्योगः -गा -गं -गी -गिनी -गि (न्), अनुद्योगः &c., निरुत्साहः -हा -हं -ही -हिनी -हि (न्), व्यवसायविमुखः &c., अव्यवसायी &c., अव्यवसायशीलः &c., मनाक्करः -री -रं, कुण्ठः -ण्ठा -ण्ठं, जडः -डा -डं, शीतः -ता -तं, अपटुः -ट्वी -टु, क्लीबः -बा -बं, तन्द्रालुः -लुः -लु, मन्दगतिः -तिः -ति; 'a lazy fellow,' तुन्दपरिमृजः, तुन्दपरिमार्जः, शीतकः.

Lea, ley, *s.* यावसभूमिः *f.*, यवसीयभूमिः *f.*, यवसावृतो भूमिभागः.

Lead, *s.* (The metal) सीसं, सीसकं, सीसपत्रकं, नागं, वप्रं, योगेष्टं, वपुः *n.*, वपुस् *n.*, वङ्गं, कुवङ्गं, पिच्चटं, शिरावृत्तं, तमरं, जडं, चीनं, बहुमलं, यामुनेष्टकं, परिपिष्टकं, सिन्दूरकारणं, तारशुद्धिकरं; 'red-lead,' सिन्दूरं -रिका, नागसम्भवं, नागजं, नागरक्तं, नागगर्भः, शोणं, सौभाग्यं, रक्तचूर्णं, रक्तवालुकं, रक्तरेणुः *m.*, शृङ्गारं, शृङ्गारभूषणं; 'marked with red-lead,' सिन्दूरतिलकः -का -कं.—(Plummet) लम्बः -म्बकः, लम्बसीसकं.

To lead, *v. a.* (Conduct, guide) नी (c. 1. नयति, नेतुं), आनी, समानी, उपानी, गम् (c. 10. गमयति -यितुं), प्राप् (c. 10. -आपयति -यितुं), with two acc. c.—(Show the way) मार्गं or पथं दृश् (c. 10. दर्शयति -यितुं) or आदिश् (c. 10. -देशयति -यितुं) or निर्दिश्.—(Lead by the hand) हस्तेन नी.—(Direct) निर्दिश्, उपदिश्, उद्दिश्, आदिश्.—(Draw, entice, allure) आकृष् (c. 1. -कर्षति, c. 6. -कृषति -क्रष्टुं), सङ्कृष्, कृष्, प्रलुभ् (c. 10. -लोभयति -यितुं), परिलुभ्.—(Induce, influence) अनुनी, आनी, प्रवृत् (c. 10. -वर्त्तयति -यितुं), प्रेर् (c. 10. -ईरयति -यितुं), प्रोत्सह् (c. 10. -साहयति -यितुं), नियुज् (c. 10. -योजयति -यितुं), प्रयुज्.—(Pass time) कालं नी or वृत् (c. 10. वर्त्तयति -यितुं) or प्रवृत् or या in caus. (यापयति -यितुं) or गम् in caus.—(Lead forth, lead up) उन्नी, उत्कृष्, प्रकृष्, उद्गम् in caus.—(Lead back) प्रत्यानी, निवृत् in caus.

To lead, *v. n.* (Go before) अग्रे or अग्रतः सृ (c. 1. सरति, सर्त्तुं) or गम् (c. 1. गच्छति, गन्तुं), पुरः or पुरतो गम् or चर् (c. 1. चरति -रितुं), अग्रे स्था (c. 1. तिष्ठति, स्थातुं) or वृत् (c. 1. वर्त्तते -र्त्तितुं), मुख्यः -ख्या -ख्यं भू, मुख्यतो वृत् or स्था.—(Lead to, bring about) आवह् (c. 1. -वहति -वोढुं), उत्पद् (c. 10. -पादयति -यितुं).

Lead, *s.* (Precedence, guidance) पुरोगतिः *f.*, अग्रगतिः *f.*, अग्रगमनं, पुरोगमनं, अग्रसरणं, अग्रयानं, प्राग्गमनं, पुरःसरणं, पुरतोगमनं, नेतृत्वं, नायकत्वं, नयः -यनं, मुख्यत्वं -ता, प्रधत्वं; to take the lead.' *See* *To* lead, *v. n.*

Leaded, *p. p.* or *a.* सीसकयुक्तः -क्ता -क्तं, सीसकावृतः -ता -तं, सीसबद्धः -द्धा -द्धं.

Leaden, *a.* सैसकः -की -कं, सीसमयः -यी -यं, सीसनिर्म्मितः -ता -तं.

Leader, *s.* (Guide, conductor) नेता *m.* (तृ), नायकः, नेयः, विनेता *m.*, पथदर्शकः, मार्गदर्शकः, मार्गनिर्देष्टा *m.* (ष्टृ), पथनिर्देशकः, मार्गदेष्टा *m.*, मार्गोपदेशी *m.* (न्), उपदेष्टा *m.*, सञ्चारकः.—(Chief) मुख्यः, मुखरः, प्रमुखः, अधिपः, अधिष्ठाता *m.* (तृ), ईश्वरः, पतिः *m.*—(One who goes first) पुरोगः -गमः, पुरोगामी *m.* (न्), पुरोगतिः *m.*, अग्रगः, अग्रसरः, अग्रेसरः -रिकः, अग्रतःसरः, पुरःसरः, पुरस्सरः, अग्रगामी, प्रष्ठः, शिरोवर्त्ती *m.* (न्), शिरस्थः.—(Of an army) सेनाग्रगः, सेनानीः *m.*, सेनापतिः *m.*, सेनाधिपः, सेनाध्यक्षः, दण्डनायकः, योधमुख्यः, वाहिनीपतिः *m.*, चमूपतिः *m.*; 'an able leader in war,' सांयुगीनः.—(Of a religious order or sect) आचार्य्यः, गुरुः *m.*

LEADERSHIP, *s.* नेतृत्वं, नायकत्वं, मुख्यता -त्वं, अधिष्ठातृत्वं, प्रमुखता.

LEADING, *part.* or *a.* (Preceding) अग्रगः -गा -गं, अग्रगामी -मिनी -मि (न्), पुरोगामी &c., प्राग्गामी &c., अग्रसरः -रा -रं, अग्रेसरः -रा -रं, पुरःसरः -रा -रं, पुरोगः -गा -गं, पुरोगमः -मा -मं.—(Chief) मुख्यः -ख्या -ख्यं, प्रमुखः -खा -खं, अग्रः -ग्रा -ग्रं, अग्रियः -या -यं, अग्र्यः -ग्र्या -ग्र्यं, प्राग्र्यः -ग्र्या -ग्र्यं, प्रधान in comp., परमः -मा -मं, परः -रा -रं, उत्तमः -मा -मं.—(Leading to, conducive to) आवहः -हा -हं, सम्पादकः -का -कं; 'leading to happiness,' सुखावहः -हा -हं, सुखोदर्कः -र्का -र्कं; 'road leading to the city,' नगरगामी मार्गः; 'leading note,' वादी *m.* (न्).

LEADING, *s.* (Guidance) नयः -यनं, नायः, नीतिः *f.*, नेतृत्वं, प्रणयनं.

LEADING-STRINGS, *s.* बालकालम्बनसूत्रं -त्राणि *n. pl.*, बालकालम्बः -म्बनं.

LEAD-WORT, *s.* (A plant) पाठी *m.* (न्), चित्रकः, वह्निः *m.*, अग्निः *m.*, अनलः, पावकः, दहनः, कृशानुः *m.*

LEADY, *a.* सीसकवर्णः -र्णा -र्णं, वापुषः -षी -षं, सैसकः -की -कं.

LEAF, *s.* (Of a tree, &c.) पत्रं -त्रकं, पर्णं, दलं -लः, पलाशं, छदः -दनं, अंशुकं, रार्ण, वातार्य.—(Of a book, &c.) पत्रं -त्रकं, पत्रिका, फलकः, पुस्तकपत्रं.—(Of a door, table, &c.) कपाटः -टी -टं; 'the junction of two leaves,' कपाटसन्धिः *m.*—(Gold-leaf) सुवर्णपत्रं, अष्टापदपत्रं; 'fallen leaf of a tree,' प्रपर्णं; 'withered leaf,' शीर्णपर्णं; 'vein of a leaf,' पत्रशिरा, दलस्नसा; 'to strip off the leaves,' निष्पत्र (nom. निष्पत्रयति -यितुं), निष्पत्रीकृ.

To LEAF, *v. n.* सपत्रीभू, सपर्णीभू, स्फुटितपत्रः -त्रा -त्रंभू, प्ररूढपत्रः -त्रा -त्रंभू.

LEAFED, *a.* सपत्रः -त्रा -त्रं, सपर्णः -र्णा -र्णं, पत्रयुक्तः -क्ता -क्तं.

LEAFINESS, *s.* पत्रबाहुल्यं, बहुपर्णत्वं, पर्णबाहुल्यं, पत्रप्राचुर्यं, प्रचुरपत्रत्वं, सपर्णत्वं, सपत्रत्वं, सदलता.

LEAFLESS, *a.* निष्पत्रः -त्रा -त्रं, निष्पर्णः -र्णा -र्णं, अपत्रः -त्रा -त्रं, अपर्णः -र्णा -र्णं, अदलः -ला -लं, पत्रहीनः -ना -नं, पर्णशून्यः -न्या -न्यं, दलशून्यः -न्या -न्यं.

LEAFLESSNESS, *s.* निष्पत्रता, निष्पर्णता, अदलत्वं, पत्रहीनता, पर्णशून्यता.

LEAFLET, *s.* पत्रकं, क्षुद्रपत्रं, सूक्ष्मपत्रं, क्षुद्रपर्णं, सूक्ष्मपर्णं.

LEAF-STALK. *s.* पत्रमञ्जरी, पर्णमञ्जरी, पत्रनाली, पर्णनाली.

LEAFY, *a.* पर्णी -र्णिनी -र्णि (न्), पत्री -त्रिणी -त्रि (न्), पर्णसः -सा -सं, दलसः -सा -सं, बहुपत्रः -त्रा -त्रं, बहुपर्णः -र्णा -र्णं, प्रचुरपर्णः -र्णा -र्णं, सपत्रः -त्रा -त्रं, पर्णमयः -यी -यं, पर्णवान् -वती -वत् (त्); 'leafy hut,' पर्णोटजं.

LEAGUE, *s.* (Alliance, confederacy) सन्धिः *m.*, सन्धानं, साहित्यं, सहायता, सङ्घातः, सम्बन्धः, सङ्घट्टनं, संयोगः, ऐक्यं, संयोजनं, समाहारः, समाहरणं, प्रतीहारः, सङ्गमः, समागमः, संसृष्टिः *f.*, परस्परोपकारप्रतिज्ञा, सार्थं.—(The distance) क्रोशः, क्रोशयुगं, गव्यूतिः *f. m.*, गव्यूतं.

To LEAGUE, *v. n.* सन्धा (c. 3. -धत्ते -धातुं), सन्धिं कृ or विधा, सन्धानं कृ, साहित्यं कृ, सङ्घट्ट् (c. 1. -घट्टते -ट्टितुं), संयुज् in pass. (-युज्यते), संहन् in pass. (-हन्यते), संहतः -ता -तं भू, सहितः -ता -तं भू, सम्मिल् (c. 6. -मिलति -मेलितुं).

LEAGUED, *p. p.* or *a.* सन्धितः -ता -तं, कृतसन्धिः -न्धिः -न्धि, कृतसम्बन्धः -न्धा -न्धं, सङ्घातवान् -वती -वत् (त्), सहितः -ता -तं, सङ्गतः -ता -तं, संयुक्तः -क्ता -क्तं, कृतसंसर्गः -र्गा -र्गं, संयोजितः -ता -तं, संहतः -ता -तं, संसृष्टः -ष्टा -ष्टं, मिलितः -ता -तं, स्वीकृतः -ता -तं; 'having leagued,' सम्भूय, मिलित्वा.

LEAGUER, *s.* सङ्गी *m.* (न्), संसर्गी *m.* (न्), सम्बन्धी *m.* (न्), सहकारी *m.* (न्), सम्भूयकारी *m.*, परस्परोपकारी *m.*

LEA

LEAK, *s.* धारा, नौकातले छिद्रं or रन्ध्रं or सन्धिः *m.*, नौकापार्श्वे दारुभित्तिः *f.* or जलग्राहकछिद्रं or जलप्रवेशकछिद्रं.—(Oozing) धारा, स्रवः, द्रवः, स्यन्दः.

To LEAK, *v. n.* नौदारुछिद्रेण जलं प्रविश् (c. 10. -वेशयति -यितुं) or जलं ग्रह् (c. 9. गृह्णाति, ग्रहीतुं) or जलम् आदा (c. 3. -ददाति -दातुं), नौकापार्श्वे or नौकातले दारुरन्ध्रेण जलं प्रविश्.—(Ooze) री (c. 4. रीयते -रेतुं), क्षर् (c. 1. क्षरति -रितुं), स्यन्द् (c. 1. स्यन्दते -न्दितुं), स्रु (c. 1. स्रवति, स्रोतुं); 'water leaks from the jar,' जलं घटाद् रीयते.

LEAKAGE, *s.* यत्किञ्चिद् जलादि भाण्डछिद्रेण रीयते, द्रवः.

LEAKING, *s.* स्यन्दः -न्दनं, निस्यन्दः, द्रवः -वणं, क्षरणं, स्रावः, रयः, धारा.

LEAKY, *a.* सच्छिद्रः -द्रा -द्रं, छिद्री -द्रिणी -द्रि (न्), जर्जरीकः -का -कं, जर्जरः -रा -रं, सरन्ध्रः -न्ध्रा -न्ध्रं, दारुछिद्रेण जलग्राहकः -का -कं or जलादायी -यिनी -यि (न्).

To LEAN, *v. n.* (Incline, bend) नम् (c. 1. नमति, नन्तुं), अवनम्, आनम्, नम्रीभू.—(Bend out of the perpendicular) वहिर्लस् (c. 1. -लसते -सितुं), वहिःप्रलम्ब्, तिर्यक् प्रलम्ब्, वक्रीभू.—(Lean on, rest on) अवलम्ब्, समालम्ब्, अवलम्बनं कृ, संश्रि (c. 1. -श्रयति -ते -यितुं), समाश्रि, उपाश्रि, निली (c. 4. -लीयते -लेतुं); 'she leans on the arms of Rāma,' सा रामस्य बाहू संश्रयति or अवलम्बते.

LEAN, *a.* (Thin, meagre) कृशः -शा -शं, परिकृशः -शा -शं, कृशाङ्गः -ङ्गी -ङ्गं, क्षीणशरीरः -रा -रं, क्षीणमांसः -सा -सं, अमांसः -सा -सं, शुष्कमांसः -सा -सं, क्षीणः -णा -णं, अपुष्टः -ष्टा -ष्टं, विपुष्टः -ष्टा -ष्टं, तनुः -नुः -न्वी -नु, प्रतनुः &c., वितनुः &c., क्षामः -मा -मं, शीर्णः -र्णा -र्णं, शातः -ता -तं, शुष्काङ्गः -ङ्गी -ङ्गं.

LEAN, *s.* (That part of the flesh which consists of muscle without the fat) स्नायुः *m.*, वसा, मांसस्नायुः, मांसं, मेदोभिन्नः or वसाभिन्नो मांसभागः.

LEAN-FACED, *a.* कृशमुखः -खी -खं, क्षीणमुखः &c., क्षीणवदनः -ना -नं.

LEANING, *part.* or *a.* (Bending, deviating from the straight line) प्रणतः -ता -तं, आनतः -ता -तं, प्रवणः -णा -णं, वहिर्लसः -सा -सं, प्रलम्बः -म्बा -म्बं, नतः -ता -तं, वक्रः -क्रा -क्रं.—(Resting on) अवलम्बी -म्बिनी -म्बि (न्), अवलम्बनः -ना -नं, अवलम्बितः -ता -तं, संश्रितः -ता -तं, समाश्रितः -ता -तं, उपाश्रितः -ता -तं.

LEANNESS, *s.* कृशता -त्वं, कार्श्यं, परिकृशता, कृशाङ्गता, क्षामता, शरीरक्षीणता, मांसक्षीणता, क्षीणता, अमांसत्वं, अपुष्टता, विपुष्टता, तनुता -त्वं, तानवं, शरीरशोषणं, मांसशुष्कता, शुष्काङ्गता.

To LEAP, *v. n.* प्लु (c. 1. प्लवते, प्लोतुं), वल्ग् (c. 1. वल्गति -ल्गितुं), आवल्ग्, नृत् (c. 4. नृत्यति, नर्त्तितुं), झम्पं कृ, उत्फालं कृ, विस्फुल् (c. 6. -स्फुलति -लितुं); 'to leap up,' उत्प्लु, समुत्प्लु, उत्पत् (c. 1. -पतति -तितुं), प्रोत्पत्; 'to leap down,' अवप्लु; 'to leap over,' लङ्घ् (c. 10. लङ्घयति -यितुं), विलङ्घ्, उल्लङ्घ्, अभिलङ्घ्; 'to leap forth from,' प्रस्कन्द् (c. 1. -स्कन्दति -स्कन्तुं), प्रोत्पत्.

LEAP, *s.* प्लवः -वनं, प्लुतं, वल्गितं, झम्पः -म्पा, लङ्घनं, उत्प्लवनं, उत्प्लुतं, अवस्कन्दः, उत्फालः; 'going by leaps,' प्लुतगतिः -तिः -ति, प्लवगः -गा -गं.

LEAPED, *p. p.* प्लुतः -ता -तं, वल्गितः -ता -तं, लङ्घितः -ता -तं.

LEAPER, *s.* प्लवकः, प्लवः, प्लवनकारी *m.* (न्), झम्पी *m.* (न्), वल्गितकृत्.

LEAPING, *part.* प्लवमानः -ना -नं, प्लवः -वा -वं, वल्गन् -ल्गन्ती -ल्गत् (त्); 'leaping up,' उत्पतिष्णुः -ष्णुः -ष्णु, उत्प्लुत.

LEAPING, *s.* (The act) प्लवनं, प्लुतकरणं, झम्पकरणं; 'leaping up,' उत्प्लवनं, उत्पतनं; 'leaping down,' अवस्कन्दः; 'leaping over,' लङ्घनं, उल्लङ्घनं.

LEAP-YEAR, *s.* चतुर्थः संवत्सरो यस्मिन् अधिकदिवसो निवेश्यते, अधिकदिनवत्सरः, अधिकदिवसवर्षः.

To LEARN, *v. a.* (Acquire knowledge of any thing by study, &c.) शिक्ष् (c. 1. शिक्षते -क्षितुं), उपशिक्ष्, अधी (c. 2. अधीते, अध्येतुं, rt. इ), अधिगम् (c. 1. -गच्छति -गन्तुं), पठ् (c. 1. पठति -ठितुं), अभ्यस् (c. 4. -अस्यति -असितुं), अध्ययनेन or अभ्यासेन विद्यां ग्रह् (c. 9. गृह्णाति, ग्रहीतुं) or लभ् (c. 1. लभते, लब्धुं) or प्राप् (c. 5. -आप्नोति -आप्तुं) or अवाप्, अभ्यासं कृ, विद्याभ्यासं कृ, विद्यागमं कृ.—(Gain the knowledge of, become informed of) ज्ञा (c. 9. जानाति -नीते ज्ञातुं), परिज्ञा, अवगम्, उपलभ्, विज्ञः -ज्ञा -ज्ञं भू, गृहीतार्थः -र्था -र्थं भू; 'to learn by heart,' अभ्यस्.

To LEARN, *v. n.* शिक्षां कृ, अध्ययनं कृ, अधिगमं कृ, अभ्यासं कृ, विद्याभ्यासं कृ, विद्याप्राप्तिं कृ, विद्याग्रहणं कृ, विद्यालब्धिं कृ, विद्यागमं कृ.

LEARNED, LEARNT, *p. p.* शिक्षितः -ता -तं, अधीतः -ता -तं, अधिगतः -ता -तं, अभ्यस्तः -स्ता -स्तं, पठितः -ता -तं, अवगतः -ता -तं, उपलब्धः -ब्धा -ब्धं; 'learnt by heart,' अभ्यस्तः -स्ता -स्तं, कण्ठस्थः -स्था -स्थं; 'to be learnt,' शिक्षितव्यः -व्या -व्यं, अभ्यस्यः -स्या -स्यं, अभ्यसनीयः -या -यं.

LEARNED, *a.* (Versed in literature and science) विद्वान् -दुषी -द्वत् (स्), पण्डितः -ता -तं, ज्ञानी -निनी -नि (न्), विद्यावान् -वती -वत् (त्), विद्याविशिष्टः -ष्टा -ष्टं, विद्यासम्पन्नः -न्ना -न्नं, कृतविद्यः -द्या -द्यं, विद्यालङ्कृतः -ता -तं, सविद्यः -द्या -द्यं, लब्धविद्यः &c., वैद्यः -द्यी -द्यं, ज्ञानवान् &c., विपश्चित् *m. f. n.*, प्राज्ञः -ज्ञा -ज्ञं, प्रज्ञः -ज्ञा -ज्ञं, प्रज्ञावान् &c., व्युत्पन्नः -न्ना -न्नं, कृतधीः -धीः -धि, अधीयानः -ना -नं, अधीती -तिनी &c., बहुश्रुतः -ता -तं, कोविदः -दा -दं, मनीषी -षिणी -षि (न्), बुद्धिमान् &c., धीमान् &c., बुधः -धा -धं, धीरः -रा -रं, संख्यावान् &c., कविः -विः -वी -वि, सूरिः &c., सूरी -रिणी -रि (न्), कृती -तिनी -ति (न्), लब्धवर्णः -र्णा -र्णं, अक्षरसम्पन्नः -न्ना -न्नं, साक्षरः -रा -रं, सारस्वतः -ती -तं, अध्ययनसम्पन्नः &c., विद्यावृद्धः -द्धा -द्धं, सन् सती सत्, तत्त्वदर्शी -र्शिनी -र्शि (न्), दीर्घदर्शी &c., दूरदर्शी &c.; 'a learned man,' विद्वज्जनः, पण्डितः, बुधः, सर्व्वरसः; 'learned in the Vedas,' श्रोत्रियः, वेदवित्, वेदविद्वान् *m.* (स्), अनूचानः, छान्दसः.—(Conversant with, skilled in) अभिज्ञः -ज्ञा -ज्ञं, विज्ञः -ज्ञा -ज्ञं, विशारदः -दा -दं, विचक्षणः -णा -णं, निपुणः -णा -णं, कुशलः -ला -लं, प्रवीणः -णा -णं, चतुरः -रा -रं, वेत्ता -त्री -त्तृ (तृ), ज्ञः ज्ञा ज्ञं or विद् in comp.; as, 'learned in the law,' स्मृतिज्ञः &c., धर्म्मविद् *m. f. n.*, 'learned in music,' गान्धर्व्वतत्त्वज्ञः.

LEARNEDLY, *adv.* पण्डितवत्, सपाण्डित्यं, पाण्डित्येन, प्राज्ञवत्, विद्वज्जनवत्, सविद्यं, वैदुष्येण, सज्ञानं, ज्ञानपूर्व्वं.

LEARNER, *s.* शिष्यः, विद्यार्थी *m.* (न्), अध्येता *m.* (तृ), अध्यायी *m.* (न्), शिक्षिताक्षरः, विद्याभ्यासकर्त्ता *m.* (र्त्तृ), अभ्यासकृत्.

LEARNING, *s.* (Knowledge of literature, erudition) विद्या, पाण्डित्यं, ज्ञानं, विज्ञानं, वैदुष्यं, विद्वत्ता, ज्ञातृत्वं, व्युत्पत्तिः *f.*, प्राज्ञत्वं, पण्डितता -त्वं, वेत्तृत्वं, विद्यासम्पत्तिः *f.*, अक्षरसम्पत्तिः *f.*, साक्षरता, अध्ययनसम्पत्तिः *f.*—(Literature) विद्या, शास्त्रं, अक्षरं, साहित्यं.—(Sacred learning) श्रुतिः *f.*, श्रोत्रियत्वं.—(Act of learning, acquisition of learning) शिक्षा, अध्ययनं, अभ्यासः, विद्याभ्यासः, विद्याप्राप्तिः *f.*, विद्यालब्धिः *f.*, विद्यार्जनं, विद्यागमः; 'cultivation of learning,' विद्यानुसेवनं; 'patronising learning,' विद्यानुपालनं; 'to affect great learning,' पण्डित (nom. पण्डितायते).

LEASE, *s.* (Of lands, houses, &c.) पट्टः, पट्टोलिका, कूमकीला, विहितकालं यावद् नियमितमूल्यम् अपेक्ष्य क्षेत्रगृहादीनां परहस्तसमर्पणं.

To LEASE, *v. a.* पट्टं दा, पट्टोलिकां दा, पट्टेन क्षेत्रगृहादि परप्रयोजनीयं दा, पट्टोलिकापूर्व्वं नियमितमूल्यम् अपेक्ष्य क्षेत्रगृहादि परप्रयोजनीयं दा or विसृज् (c. 6. -सृजति -स्रष्टुं), आविहितकालाद् निरूपितमूल्यम् अपेक्ष्य क्षेत्रगृहादि परहस्ते सम् in caus. (-अर्पयति -यितुं).

LEASED, *p. p.* पट्टेन or पट्टलिखनपूर्व्वम् आविहितकालात् परहस्तसमर्पितः -ता -तं.

LEASEHOLD, *a.* पट्टेन or पट्टोलिकालिखनपूर्व्वम् अध्युषितः -ता -तं.

LEASH, *s.* (Leather thong) चर्म्मबन्धः -न्धनी, चर्म्मरज्जुः *m. f.*, बन्धनरज्जुः.—(Tierce, three) त्रयं, त्रिकं; 'a leash of hares,' शशकत्रयं.

To LEASH, *v. a.* चर्म्मरज्जुना or चर्म्मरज्ज्वा बन्ध् (c. 9. बध्नाति, बन्द्धुं).

LEASING, *s.* असत्यता, अनृतता, अलीकता, कापट्यं, मृषावादः. *See* FALSEHOOD.

LEAST, *a.* (Smallest) अल्पिष्ठः -ष्ठा -ष्ठं, कनिष्ठः -ष्ठा -ष्ठं, क्षुद्रतमः -मा -मं, क्षोदिष्ठः -ष्ठा -ष्ठं, कनीयान् -यसी -यः (स्), तनिष्ठः -ष्ठा -ष्ठं, तनीयान् &c., लघिष्ठः &c., स्तोकतमः -मा -मं, सूक्ष्मतमः -मा -मं, अतिक्षुद्रः -द्रा -द्रं, स्वल्पः -ल्पा -ल्पं, अवरः -रा -रं, अवरतमः -मा -मं, न्यूनः -ना -नं; 'least of all,' सर्व्वकनिष्ठः -ष्ठा -ष्ठं, सर्व्वकनीयान् &c., सर्व्वस्मात् क्षुद्रः -द्रा -द्रं; 'the least particle,' लेशः, लवः, कणः; 'not the least darkness is in that place,' तत्र अन्धकारस्य लेशो ऽपि नास्ति.

LEAST, *adv.* (In the least) मनाक्, किञ्चित्, अल्पिष्ठं, कनिष्ठं, लेशमपि, कियत्, सूक्ष्मं, स्तोकं; 'not in the least,' न मनाक्, न मनागपि, न किञ्चिदपि, न किमपि, न कियदपि, न सूक्ष्ममपि, न स्तोकमपि, न लेशमपि, अलेशं; 'three witnesses at least,' अवराः साक्षिणः; 'at least, at any rate,' तावत्.

LEATHER, *s.* चर्म्म *n.* (न्), दृतिः *m.*, पशुत्वक् *f.* (च्), पशुचर्म्म *n.*, कृत्तिः *f.*, अजिनं, वर्ध्रं, शिपिः *f.*; 'a leather thong,' चर्म्मबन्धः -न्धनं, वरत्रा, वर्ध्री; 'covered with leather,' चर्म्मावृतः -ता -तं, चर्म्मावनद्धः -द्धा -द्धं, चर्म्माच्छादितः -ता -तं.

LEATHER, *a.* चर्म्म in comp., चर्म्ममयः -यी -यं; 'a leather shoe,' चर्म्मपादुका; 'a leather band,' चर्म्मबन्धः. *See* LEATHERN.

To LEATHER, *v. a.* चर्म्मदण्डेन तड् (c. 10. ताडयति -यितुं) or प्रहृ (c. 1. -हरति -हर्त्तुं).

LEATHER-CUTTER, *s.* चर्म्मच्छिद् *m.*, चर्म्मच्छेदनकारी *m.* (न्), चर्म्मावकर्त्ती *m.*

LEATHER-DRESSER, *s.* चर्म्मकारः -रकः, चर्म्मकारी *m.* (न्), चर्म्मकृत्, चर्म्मारः.

LEATHERN, *a.* चार्म्मिकः -की -कं, चार्म्मः -र्म्मी -र्म्मं, चर्म्मी -र्म्मिणी -र्म्मि (न्), चर्म्ममयः -यी -यं, चर्म्मनिर्म्मितः -ता -तं, दार्त्तेयः -यी -यं, अजिनीयः -या -यं, पशुत्वङ्मयः -यी -यं, चर्म्म in comp.; 'a leathern bottle,' दृतिः *m.*

LEATHER-SELLER, *s.* चर्म्मविक्रेता *m.* (तृ), चर्म्मविक्रयी *m.* (न्), चर्म्मविक्रयोपजीवी *m.*

LEATHERY, *a.* चर्म्मवद् दुःखभेद्यः -द्या -द्यं, चर्म्मसगुणः -णा -णं.

LEAVE, *s.* (Permission) अनुज्ञा, अनुमतिः *f.*, अभ्यनुज्ञा, अनुज्ञानं, समनुज्ञानं, अनुमोदनं; 'leave to depart,' अनुज्ञा; 'to give leave,' अनुज्ञा (c. 9. -जानाति -ज्ञातुं), अनुमन् (c. 4. -मन्यते -मन्तुं), अनुज्ञां कृ or दा.—(Farewell) आमन्त्रणं, आप्रच्छनं; 'to bid farewell,' आमन्त्र् (c. 10. -मन्त्रयते -यितुं), अनुमन्त्र्, आप्रच्छ् (c. 6. -पृच्छते -ति -प्रष्टुं).

To LEAVE, *v. a.* (Abandon, forsake) त्यज् (c. 1. त्यजति, त्यक्तुं), परित्यज्, सन्त्यज्, हा (c. 3. जहाति, हातुं), अपहा, विहा, प्रहा, अपाहा, उत्सृज् (c. 6. -सृजति -स्रष्टुं), विसृज्, अतिसृज्, व्यपसृज्, रह् (c. 10. रहयति -यितुं), विरह्, उज्झ् (c. 6. उज्झति -झितुं), प्रोज्झ्, परिहृ (c. 1. -हरति -हर्त्तुं), वृज् (c. 10. -वर्जयति -यितुं), परिवृज्, विवृज्.—(Depart from)

अपगम् (c. 1. -गच्छति -गन्तुं), व्यपगम्, विगम्, अपया (c. 2. -याति -तुं), अपे (c. 2. अपैति -तुं), व्यपे, अपसृ (c. 1. -सरति -सर्त्तुं), प्रस्था (c. 1. -तिष्ठति -स्थातुं), विप्रस्था.—(Leave remaining, suffer to remain) शिष् (c. 10. शेषयति -यितुं), अवशिष्, परिशिष्, उच्छिष्, समवशिष्, उद्वृत् (c. 10. -वर्त्तयति -यितुं), शिष्टं -ष्टां कृ, अवशिष्टं -ष्टां कृ, अवशिष्टीकृ; 'to be left remaining,' शिष् in pass. (शिष्यते), अवशिष्.—(Commit, trust to) समृ in caus. (-अर्पयति -यितुं), निक्षिप् (c. 6. -क्षिपति -क्षेप्तुं), न्यस् (c. 4. -अस्यति -असितुं), न्यासीकृ.—(Bequeath) मृतुपत्रेण प्रदा or मृत्युलेखेन दा.—(Leave off, desist from) विरम् (c. 1. -रमति -रन्तुं), उपरम्, निवृत् (c. 1. -वर्त्तते -र्त्तितुं), विनिवृत् with abl. c., मुच् (c. 6. मुञ्चति, मोक्तुं), अवमुच्, अवसृज्, अपास् (c. 4. -अस्यति -असितुं), व्युदस्, त्यज्, परित्यज्; 'the peacock leaves off dancing,' परित्यक्तनर्त्तनो मयूरः; 'it leaves off raining,' निर्वर्षति.—(Leave out) वृज्, अपास्, हा, अपाहा.—(Leave behind, distance) दूरीकृ, दव (nom. दवयति -यितुं).

To LEAVE, *v. n.* (Cease, leave off) विरम् (c. 1. -रमति -रन्तुं), उपरम्, निवृत् (c. 1. -वर्त्तते -र्त्तितुं), निर्वृत्, विनिवृत्, विगम् (c. 1. -गच्छति -गन्तुं), अपया (c. 2. -याति -तुं), शम् (c. 4. शाम्यति, शमितुं), विच्छिद् in pass. (-छिद्यते).

LEAVED, *a.* (Having leaves) पत्री -त्रिणी -त्रि (न्), पर्णी -र्णिनी &c., सपत्रः -त्रा -त्रं, सपर्णः -र्णा -र्णं, सदलः -ला -लं; 'two-leaved,' द्विपर्णः -र्णा -र्णं.

LEAVEN, *s.* किण्वः -ण्वं, नग्नहूः *m.*, मण्डः -ण्डं, कारोत्तरः, कारोत्तमः, कादम्बरीबीजं.—(Any thing which works a change in the mass) विकारजनकं किञ्चिद् वस्तु.

To LEAVEN, *v. a.* किण्वनिवेशनपूर्व्वम् अम्लरसेकं or अम्लत्वापं जन् (c. 10. जनयति -यितुं), अम्लरसेककरणार्थं किण्वं निविश् (c. 10. -वेशयति -यितुं) or प्रविश्.—(Taint, imbue) दुष् (c. 10. दूषयति -यितुं), रञ्ज् (c. 10. रञ्जयति -यितुं).

LEAVINGS, *s. pl.* (Any thing left, remnants) शिष्टं, अवशिष्टं, उच्छिष्टं, परिशिष्टं, शेषः -षं, परिशेषः, अवशेषः, उच्छेषणं, शेषभागः, परभागः, शेषखण्डः -ण्डं, उद्वर्त्तः, जुष्टं, समुज्झितं.—(Of food) शेषान्नं, उच्छिष्टान्नं, भुक्तशेषः -षं, भुक्तावशेषः -षं, अन्नशेषः -षं, भुक्तसमुज्झितं, परभुक्तोज्झितं, भुक्तोच्छिष्टं, भक्षितशेषं, खादितं, फेल्लकः, फेला -लिः -ली *f.*; 'one who eats leavings,' शेषभुक् *m.* (ज्), शेषभोजी *m.* (न्), उच्छिष्टभोजनः; 'eating leavings,' शेषभोजनं, उच्छिष्टभोजनं.—(Offal) मलं, विमांसं.

LECHER, *s.* लम्पटः, स्त्रीलम्पटः, कामुकः, कामुकजनः, व्यवायी *m.* (न्), रतार्थी *m.* (न्), सुरतार्थी *m.* (न्), स्त्रीपरः.

To LECHER, *v. n.* लम्पटवद् आचर् (c. 1. -चरति -रितुं), रतार्थी भू, कामुको भू.

LECHEROUS, *a.* कामुकः -का -कं, कामी -मिनी -मि (न्), कामनः -ना -नं, रतार्थी -र्थिनी -र्थि (न्), सुरतार्थी &c., कामासक्तः -क्ता -क्तं, व्यवायी -यिनी -यि (न्), सम्भोगी -गिनी -गि (न्), सम्भोगासक्तः &c., सम्भोगार्थी &c., भोगासक्तः &c., व्यवायपरायणः -णा -णं, स्त्रीपरः, स्त्रीरतः, स्त्रीव्यासक्ती *m.* (न्), स्त्रीलम्पटः, स्त्रीव्यसनी *m.* (न्), तरलः -ला -लं, अभीकः -का -कं, वियातः -ता -तं.

LECHEROUSLY, *adv.* लम्पटवत्, कामुकवत्, सकामं, रतासक्तवत्, कामपूर्व्वं.

LECHEROUSNESS, LECHERY, *s.* कामुकत्वं, लम्पटत्वं -ता, लाम्पट्यं, रतार्थित्वं, रतासक्तिः *f.*, कामासक्तिः *f.*, सम्भोगासक्तिः *f.*, व्यवायः -यित्वं, स्त्रीव्यसनं, स्त्रीव्यासङ्गः, वैयात्यं, हेला -लनं.

LECTION, *s.* (Reading) पाठः, अध्ययनं.—(Variety in copies of a manuscript) पाठान्तरं, पाठभेदः, पाठः, द्विरूपपाठः.

LECTOR, *s.* पाठकः, पठिता *m.* (तृ), अध्येता *m.* (तृ), अध्यायी *m.* (न्).

LECTURE, *s.* पाठः, निपाठः, पाठनं, पठनं, अध्यायः, अध्ययः -यनं, अध्यापनं, वादः, व्याख्यानं.—(Reprimand) वाग्दण्डः, वाक्शासनं, भर्त्सनवाक्यं.

To LECTURE, *v. a.* पठ् (c. 10. पाठयति -यितुं), अधी in caus. (अध्यापयति -यितुं, rt. इ), उपदिश् (c. 6. -दिशति -देष्टुं), पाठं कृ, अध्यापनं कृ.—(Reprove) प्रत्यादिश्, निन्द् (c. 1. निन्दति -न्दितुं), वाग्दण्डं कृ, निन्दावाक्यं कृ.

To LECTURE, *v. n.* पठ् (c. 1. पठति -ठितुं), अधी (c. 2. अधीते, अध्येतुं, rt. इ), वाक्यं श्रु (c. 10. श्रावयति -यितुं), पाठं कृ, अध्ययनं कृ.

LECTURED, *p. p.* अध्यापितः -ता -तं, पाठितः -ता -तं.—(Reprimanded) प्रत्यादिष्टः -ष्टा -ष्टं, निन्दितः -ता -तं, उपालब्धः -ब्धा -ब्धं.

LECTURER, *s.* पाठकः, अध्यापकः, पठिता *m.* (तृ), अध्येता *m.* (तृ), अध्यायी *m.* (न्), पाठकारी *m.* (न्), शिक्षकः, उपदेशकः, व्याख्याता *m.* (तृ), प्रवक्ता *m.* (क्तृ), वक्ता, वादी *m.* (न्), वाचकः, मागरः; 'in theology,' धर्म्मप्रवक्ता *m.*, धर्म्मभाषकः.

LECTURE-ROOM, *s.* पाठशाला, पाठगृहं, अध्ययनशाला, अध्ययनगृहं.

LECTURESHIP, *s.* पाठकत्वं, अध्यापकत्वं, प्रवक्तृत्वं, वक्तृत्वं, शिक्षकत्वं.

LED, *p. p.* नीतः -ता -तं, आनीतः -ता -तं, समानीतः -ता -तं; 'being led,' नीयमानः -ना -नं.—(Guided) सञ्चारितः -ता -तं.—(As life, time) नीतः -ता -तं, गमितः -ता -तं, यापितः -ता -तं, प्रवृत्तः -त्ता -त्तं.—(Led on by, headed by) पुरःसरः -रा -रं, पुरस्सरः -रा -रं, पुरोगमः -मा -मं, मुखः -खा -खं in comp.; as, 'led on by Karna,' कर्णमुखः -खा -खं, कर्णपुरोगमः -मा -मं &c.; 'having led,' नीत्वा.

LEDGE, *s.* (Stratum, layer) फलकः -कं, स्तरः, आस्तरः -रणं.—(Ridge, projecting part) कटकः -कं, कूटं, दन्तः -न्तकः.—(Row) आलिः -ली.—(Ledge of a rock) शिला, शिलाफलकं.

LEDGER, *s.* महागणनापुस्तकं, बृहद्गणनापुस्तकं, वाणिज्यपुस्तकं.

LEE, *s.* (Sediment). *See* LEES. (Calm or sheltered place) निर्वातस्थानं, निर्वातदेशः.—(Side opposite to that on which the wind blows) वाताभिमुखदिशा, वायुप्रतिमुखदेशः; 'under the lee of the land,' तीरोपान्ते.

LEE-WARD, *a.* or *adv.* (In the same direction as the wind) वातानुकूलः -ला -लं, वातानुलोमः -मा -मं, अनुवातं.—(In an opposite direction to the wind) प्रतिवातं, वाताभिमुखदिशि, वाताभिमुखं, वायुप्रतिमुखदिशि.

LEECH, *s.* रक्तपा, रक्तपायिनी, रक्तपाता, जलौका, जलूका, जलौकाः *f.* (स्), जलुका, जलोका, जलिका, जलौकसः -सा -सं, जलायुका, जलालुका, जलायुका, जलालोका, जलोरगी, जलजन्तुका, जलसर्पिणी, जलाटनी, पटालुका, वार्य्योकाः *f.* (स्), वार्य्योकः, वारिक्रिमिः *m.*, वेधिनी, भ्रमणी, वारुक्ष्मी.—(Physician) वैद्यः, चिकित्सकः, रोगहृत् *m.*, रोगशामकः, भिषक् *m.* (ज्).

To LEECH, *v. a.* कित् in des. (चिकित्सति -त्सितुं), रोगशमनं कृ.

LEEK, *s.* कन्दः -न्दं, तीक्ष्णकन्दः, महाकन्दः, पलाण्डुः *m.*, सुकन्दकः, शाकः.

LEER, *s.* कटाक्षः, नेत्रकटाक्षः, अपाङ्गदर्शनं, कटाक्षवीक्षणं, कटाक्षापलोकनं, अपाङ्गप्रसरः, दृष्टिविक्षेपः, तिर्य्यक्प्रेक्षणं, साचिविलोकितं, काक्षः, वक्रेराटः, अक्रेराट् *m.*, विकूणनं, दृष्टिबाणः, कुञ्चितं.

To LEER, *v. n.* कटाक्षेण दृश् (c. 1. पश्यति, द्रष्टुं), अपाङ्गाद् दृश् or ईक्ष् (c. 1. ईक्षते -क्षितुं), कटाक्ष (nom. कटाक्षयति -यितुं), कटाक्षावेक्षणं कृ, कटाक्षवीक्षणं कृ, अपाङ्गदर्शनं कृ, दृष्टिविक्षेपं कृ, साचि or तिर्य्यग् विलोक् (c. 1. -लोकते, c. 10. -लोकयति -यितुं), कुञ्च् (c. 1.

-स्मयते -स्मेतुं).

LEERED UPON, *p. p.* कटाक्षितः -ता -तं, कटाक्षावेक्षितः -ता -तं, कटाक्षेण दृष्टः -ष्टा -ष्टं, साचिविलोकितः -ता -तं, कुस्मितः -ता -तं.

LEERING, *part.* or *a.* लोलापाङ्गः -ङ्गा -ङ्गं, अपाङ्गदर्शी -र्शिनी -र्शि (न्), कटाक्षावलोकी -किनी -कि (न्), साचिदृष्टिः -ष्टिः -ष्टि, तिर्य्यग्दृष्टिः &c., कुस्मेरः -रा -रं.

LEES, *s. pl.* मलं, उच्छिष्टं, शेषं, किट्टं, खलं, कल्कं, विनीयः.

LEFT, *p. p.* (Abandoned) त्यक्तः -क्ता -क्तं, परित्यक्तः -क्ता -क्तं, उत्सृष्टः -ष्टा -ष्टं, विसर्जितः -ता -तं, रहितः -ता -तं, विरहितः -ता -तं, हीनः -ना -नं, उज्झितः -ता -तं, समुज्झितः -ता -तं, प्रोज्झितः -ता -तं, विधुतः -ता -तं, वर्जितः -ता -तं, धूतः -ता -तं.—(Left remaining) शिष्टः -ष्टा -ष्टं, अवशिष्टः -ष्टा -ष्टं, अवशेषितः -ता -तं, शेषः -षा -षं, उच्छिष्टः -ष्टा -ष्टं, उद्वृत्तः -त्ता -त्तं, उद्वर्त्तः -र्त्ता -र्त्तं, उद्वेरितः -ता -तं, अतिरितः -ता -तं; 'to be left remaining,' शिष् in pass. (शिष्यते), अवशिष्.

LEFT, *a.* (Not right) वामः -मा -मं, सव्यः -व्या -व्यं, दक्षिणेतरः -रा -रं, प्रतिलोमः -मा -मं; 'the left,' सव्यं; 'left and right,' सव्यापसव्यं; 'the left hand,' वामहस्तः, वामपाणिः *m.*, सव्यं; 'the left arm,' वामबाहुः *m.*; 'the left shoulder,' वामस्कन्धः; 'the left side,' वामकुक्षिः *m.*, वामाङ्गं; 'that is on the left side,' वामस्थः -स्था -स्थं.

LEFT-HANDED, *a.* सव्यसाची -चिनी -चि (न्), वामहस्तसेवी -विनी -वि (न्), दक्षिणहस्तात् वामहस्तम् अधिकं व्यवहरति यः or या.

LEG, *s.* जङ्घा, प्रसृता, पादः, प्रेङ्खा, टङ्का, टङ्कः, अंह्रिः *m.*, अंघ्रिः *m.*, अधमाङ्गं; 'relating to the leg,' जाङ्घिकः -की -कं; 'enlargement of the leg,' श्लीपदं; 'having a swelled leg,' कुम्भपादः *m.*, कुम्भपदी *f.*; 'long-legged,' दीर्घजङ्घः -ङ्घा -ङ्घं, अर्द्धजानुः -नुः -नु, अर्द्धगुः -गुः -गु, अर्द्धेडः -डा -डं, दीर्घपादः -दा -दं, दीर्घपाद् *m. f. n.*

LEGACY, *s.* मृत्युलेखार्पितदानं, मृतपत्रार्पितदानं, मृत्युपत्रस्थदानं, मृतदानं, मृतलेखदानं, मृतपत्राङ्कितदानं, मुमूर्षुदानं, मुमूर्षुदत्तं, उत्तरदानं, मृतलेखस्थदानं, आसन्नमरणे दानं or प्रदानं.

LEGAL, *a.* (Conformable to law) धर्म्यः -र्म्या -र्म्यं, धर्म्मानुसारी -रिणी -रि (न्), स्मार्त्तः -र्त्ती -र्त्तं, व्यावहारिकः -की -कं, व्यवहारिकः &c., स्मृतिशास्त्रानुमतः -ता -तं, धर्म्मशास्त्रानुसारी &c., आचारिकः -की -कं, शास्त्रीयः -या -यं, राज्यव्यवस्थानुसारी &c., व्यवस्थानुरूपः -पा -पं, राज्यनियमानुसारी &c., न्यायानुसारी &c.—(Relating to law) स्मार्त्तः &c., व्यावहारिकः &c., व्यवहारसम्बन्धी &c., व्यवहारविषयः -या -यं, धर्म्म in comp., स्मृति in comp.—(Enjoined, permitted by law) स्मृत्युक्तः -क्ता -क्तं, शास्त्रोक्तः &c., स्मृतिशास्त्रविहितः -ता -तं, स्मृतिशास्त्रप्रोक्तः &c., राज्यनियमविहितः -ता -तं, व्यवहारविधिविहितः -ता -तं, धर्म्मानिषिद्धः -द्धा -द्धं, शास्त्रानिषिद्धः &c.—(According to the law of works, resting on works for salvation) कर्म्ममार्गी -र्गिणी -र्गि (न्), कर्म्ममार्गावलम्बी -म्बिनी -म्बि (न्), कर्म्ममार्गसेवी -विनी -वि (न्), कर्म्ममार्गाश्रयी -यिणी -यि (न्), कर्म्मशीलः -ला -लं; 'legal proceeding,' व्यवहारः; 'a written legal opinion,' पट्टोलिका; 'incorrect legal opinion,' अव्यवस्था. *See* LAW, LAWFUL.

LEGALIST, *s.* (One who relies on works for salvation) कर्म्ममार्गावलम्बी *m.* (न्), कर्म्मावलम्बी *m.*, कर्म्ममार्गाश्रयी *m.* *See* LEGAL.

LEGALITY, *s.* धर्म्यता, धर्म्मानुसारः -रित्वं, धर्म्मशास्त्रानुसारः -रिता, स्मृतिशास्त्रानुसारः -रिता, व्यवहारविध्यनुरूपता, राज्यव्यवस्थानुरूपता, व्यावहारिकत्वं. *See* LAWFULNESS.—(Reliance on works for salvation) कर्म्मावलम्बनं, कर्म्मनिष्ठा, कर्म्ममार्गसेवा, कर्म्ममार्गाश्रयणं.

To LEGALIZE, *v. a.* धर्म्यं -र्म्यां -र्म्यं कृ, शास्त्रसम्मतं -तां कृ, स्मृतिसम्मतं -तां कृ, धर्म्मसम्मतं -तां कृ, व्यवस्थागतं -तां कृ, विधिगतं -तां कृ, विहितं -तां कृ, विधिविहितं -तां कृ, अनुमन् (c. 4. -मन्यते -मन्तुं), अनुज्ञा (c. 9. -जानाति -नीते -ज्ञातुं), व्यवस्था in caus. (-स्थापयति -यितुं).

LEGALIZED, *p. p.* व्यवस्थागतः -ता -तं, विधिगतः -ता -तं, धर्म्मसम्मतः -ता -तं.

LEGALLY, *adv.* धर्म्मेण, धर्म्मतस्, धर्म्मानुसारेण -रात्, यथाधर्म्मं, न्यायतस्, न्यायानुसारेण, यथान्यायं, स्मृतिशास्त्रानुसारेण, धर्म्मशास्त्रानुसारेण. *See* LAWFULLY.

LEGATE, *s.* दूतः, राजदूतः, राजप्रतिनिधिः *m.*—(Pope's ambassador) रोमीयधर्म्माधिपतेर् दूतः or प्रतिनिधिः.

LEGATEE, *s.* मृतपत्रदानाधिकारी *m.* (न्), मृतलेखदानाधिकारी *m.*, मृतदानग्राही *m.*, मृतरिक्थभागी *m.*, मृतधनभागी *m.*, मृत्युपत्रस्थदानाधिकारी *m.*, उत्तराधिकारी *m.*, अंशभाक् *m.* (ज्).

LEGATION, *s.* दूत्यं, दौत्यं, दूतत्वं, दूतकर्म्म *n.* (न्), दूतक्रिया, दूतधर्म्मः.

LEGATOR, *s.* मृत्युलेखदानकारी *m.* (न्), मृत्युपत्रदानकारी, उत्तरदानकारी *m.*, मृत्युपत्रेण दानकारी *m.*, मृत्युकाले रिक्थप्रदाता *m.* (तृ).

LEGEND, *s.* पुरावृत्तकथा, पुराणकथा, प्राचीनकथा, पुरावृत्ताख्यानं, पुरावृत्तोपाख्यानं, पुरावृत्तं, लोककथा, जनकथा, कथा, आख्यानं, आख्यायिका, चरित्रं, चरितं, पुराणं, इतिहासः.—(Story of a saint or holy place) माहात्म्यं.

LEGENDARY, *a.* पुराणकथितः -ता -तं, पुराणोक्तः -क्ता -क्तं, पौराणिकः -की -कं, पुरावृत्तकथकः -का -कं, ऐतिहासिकः -की -कं, काथिकः -की -कं.

LEGENDARY, *s.* (Reciter of legends) पुरावृत्तकथिकः, पुराणकथकः, इतिहासवक्ता *m.* (क्तृ), ऐतिहासिकः.

LEGERDEMAIN, *s.* हस्तलाघवं, लघुहस्तत्वं, हस्तचापल्यं, इन्द्रजालः -लं, जालं, माया, कुहकः, कुहकवृत्तिः *f.*, कुसृतिः *f.*, इन्द्रियमोहः.

LEGGED, *a.* (In composition) जङ्घः -ङ्घा -ङ्घं, पादः -दा -दं, पदः -दा -दं, पाद् *m. f. n.*; 'long-legged,' दीर्घजङ्घः &c.; 'two-legged,' द्विपदः &c.

LEGGINGS, *s.* स्थूलवस्त्रमयं जङ्घात्राणं or जङ्घारक्षणं, जङ्घोत्तरीयं.

LEGIBILITY, *s.* पठनीयता, पाठ्यता, पठनयोग्यता, पठनशक्यता, सुवाच्यता, स्पष्टाक्षरत्वं, स्पष्टता, व्यक्तता.

LEGIBLE, *a.* पठनीयः -या -यं, पाठ्यः -ठ्या -ठ्यं, पठनयोग्यः -ग्या -ग्यं, पठनशक्यः -क्या -क्यं, सुवाच्यः -च्या -च्यं, स्पष्टाक्षरः -रा -रं, व्यक्ताक्षरः -रा -रं, सुस्पष्टः -ष्टा -ष्टं, अध्येतव्यः -व्या -व्यं, अध्ययनीयः -या -यं.

LEGIBLY, *adv.* स्पष्टाक्षरैः, सुस्पष्टाक्षरेण, सुस्पष्टं, सुव्यक्तं.

LEGION, *s.* (Body of soldiers) सैन्यदलं, सैन्यगुल्मः, सैन्यव्यूहः, सैन्यसमूहः, योधसमूहः.—(Host) चमूः *f.*, सेना, वाहिनी.—(A multitude, great number) वृन्दं, समवायः, निवहः, बाहुल्यं, चक्रं.

LEGIONARY, *a.* वाहिनीसम्बन्धी -न्धिनी -न्धि (न्), चाक्रिकः -की -कं.

To LEGISLATE, *v. a.* व्यवस्थां कृ or विधा (c. 3. -दधाति -धातुं), नियमान् or विधीन् स्था in caus. (स्थापयति -यितुं) or रच् (c. 10. रचयति -यितुं) or प्रकॢप् (c. 10. -कल्पयति -यितुं) or प्रशास् (c. 2. -शास्ति -शासितुं), व्यवस्था in caus.

LEGISLATION, *s.* व्यवस्थाकरणं, नियमस्थापना, विधिस्थापना, व्यवस्थारचना, -नं, व्यवस्थाप्रकल्पनं, विधिप्रकल्पनं, व्यवस्थाविधानं.

LEGISLATIVE, *a.* व्यवस्थाकारी -रिणी -रि (न्), व्यवस्थापकः -का -कं, नियमस्थापकः -का -कं, विधिस्थापकः -का -कं, नियमरचकः -का -कं, नियमविधायी -यिनी -यि (न्), व्यवस्थाविधायी, &c., स्मृतिकारी &c.

LEGISLATOR, *s.* व्यवस्थाकारः -रकः, व्यवस्थाविधायी *m.* (न्), विधिस्थापकः, नियमस्थापकः, व्यवस्थारचकः, व्यवस्थापकः, धर्म्मशास्त्ररचकः, शासिता *m.* (तृ), शास्ता *m.* (स्तृ), प्रयोजकः.

LEGISLATURE, *s.* विधिस्थापनाधिकारिणी सभा, व्यवस्थाकरणाधिकारिणी सभा, व्यवस्थाविधायिनी सभा, विधिस्थापकसभा, व्यवस्थारचकसभा.

LEGIST, *s.* *See* LAWYER.

LEGITIMACY, *s.* (Lawfulness of birth) औरसता -त्वं, उरस्यता -त्वं, धर्म्मजत्वं, धर्म्मपत्नीजत्वं, धर्म्मपत्नीजन्म *n.* (न्), औरसजन्म *n.*, दम्पतिजन्म *n.*, दम्पत्युद्भवः, सुजन्म *n.*, जात्यता -त्वं, वैधजन्म *n.*—(Genuineness) सत्यता, यथार्थता, अकृत्रिमता, अकल्पितत्वं, वास्तविकता.

LEGITIMATE, *a.* (Lawfully born) धर्म्मजः -जा -जं, औरसः -सी -सं, उरस्यः -स्या -स्यं, धर्म्मपत्नीजः -जा -जं, दम्पतिजातः -ता -तं, सुजन्मा -न्मा -न्म (न्), जात्यः -त्या -त्यं, औरसजातः -ता -तं, विवाहजातः &c., विधिजातः &c., धर्म्यः -र्म्या -र्म्यं; 'a legitimate wife,' धर्म्मपत्नी; 'a legitimate son,' औरसः, उरस्यः, औरस्यः; 'daughter,' औरसी, उरस्या.—(Genuine, just, right) सत्यः -त्या -त्यं, वास्तवः -वी -वं, यथार्थः -र्था -र्थं, यथान्यायः -या -यं, न्याय्यः -य्या -य्यं, यथायोग्यः -ग्या -ग्यं, युक्तः -क्ता -क्तं.

To LEGITIMATE, *v. a.* औरसीकृ, औरसत्वं दा, औरससमं -मां कृ, धर्म्यं -र्म्यां कृ.

LEGITIMATELY, *adv.* धर्म्मेण, धर्म्मानुसारेण, यथाधर्म्मं, न्यायतस्, न्यायानुसारेण, यथान्यायं, युक्तं, उपयुक्तं, सम्यक्, यथायोग्यं, यथोचितं, समञ्जसं.

LEGITIMATION, *s.* औरसीकरणं, औरससमीकरणं, औरसाधिकारदानं.

LEGUME, LEGUMEN, *s.* शमी, सिम्बा, बीजकोशः, बीजगुप्तिः *f.*, पुटः.—(Pulse) शमीधान्यं, द्विदलं, त्रिपुटः, धान्यवीरः, सतीलकः.

LEISURABLE, *a.* सावकाशः -शा -शं, निर्व्यापारः -रा -रं, व्यापारशून्यः -न्या -न्यं, निष्कर्म्मकः -का -कं, निष्क्रियः -या -यं, कर्म्मरहितः -ता -तं, कार्य्यशून्यः -न्या -न्यं.

LEISURE, *s.* अवकाशः, अवसरः, सावकाशता, विश्रामः, कार्य्यनिवृत्तिः *f.*, कार्य्यविच्छेदः, निर्वृतिः *f.*, विश्रान्तिः *f.*, विश्रमः, स्वाधीनकालः, क्षणः, वितानं, सन्धिः *m.*; 'at leisure,' सावकाशः -शा -शं, अवकाशप्राप्तः -प्ता -प्तं, प्राप्तावकाशः -शा -शं, प्राप्तावसरः -रा -रं, व्यापारशून्यः -न्या -न्यं, निर्व्यापारः -रा -रं, कार्य्यरहितः -ता -तं, निष्क्रियः -या -यं, निष्कर्म्मकः -का -कं, शून्यः -न्या -न्यं; 'want of leisure,' अनवकाशः, अनवसरः; 'having no leisure,' निरवकाशः -शा -शं, अनवकाशः -शा -शं, निरवसरः -रा -रं.

LEISURELY, *a.* (Done at leisure) सावकाशः -शा -शं, अत्वरितः -ता -तं, विलम्बितः -ता -तं, मन्दः -न्दा -न्दं, अक्षिप्रः -प्रा -प्रं, अशीघ्रः -घ्रा -घ्रं.

LEISURELY, *adv.* सावकाशं, अत्वरितं, अत्वरया, मन्दं, मन्दं मन्दं, विलम्बेन, विलम्बितं, शनैः, शनैः शनैः, अक्षिप्रं, अशीघ्रं.

LEMON, *s.* (The fruit) जम्बीरफलं, जम्भीरफलं.—(The tree) जम्बीरः, जम्भीरः, जम्भिरः, जम्भः -म्भकः -म्भलः -म्भरः -म्भी *m.* (न्), फलपूरः -रकः, बीजपूरः, अम्लकेशरः, केशराम्लः, दन्तशठः, पूर्णबीजः, बीजकः, बीजपूर्णः, मातुलुङ्गः -ङ्गकः, गिलः, रुचकः, इक्ष्वकः, बृहच्छिम्बः, छोलङ्गः.

LEMONADE, *s.* जम्बीररसः, शर्करादिमिश्रितं जम्बीररसमयं पानीयं.

LEMURES, *s. pl.*, रात्रिचराः *m. pl.*, वेतालाः *m. pl.*, पिशाचाः *m. pl.*, राक्षसाः *m. pl.*

To LEND, *v. a.* (Give to another for temporary use) निरूपितकालं यावत् किञ्चिद् द्रव्यं परप्रयोजनीयं दा (c. 3. ददाति, दातुं), आविहितकालात् प्रयोज्यं किञ्चिद् द्रव्यं परहस्ते समृ in caus. (-अर्पयति -यितुं) or ऋ or निक्षिप् (c. 6. -क्षिपति -क्षेप्तुं) or न्यस् (c. 4. -अस्यति -असितुं) or परस्मिन् समृ, निरूपितकाले प्रतिदातव्यं or प्रतिदेयं किञ्चिद् द्रव्यं दा or समृ, निरूपितकालपर्य्यन्तं द्रव्यप्रयोगं कृ.—(Give to be returned in kind, as money, a loaf of bread, &c.) ऋणं दा, ऋणं समृ or ऋ in caus., ऋणदानं कृ; 'to lend money,' धनप्रयोगं दा or कृ, परप्रयोज्यं धनं दा, आविहितकालात् प्रयोजनीयं धनं परस्मै दा or परस्मिन् समृ; 'to lend money at interest,' कुसीदं कृ, कौसीद्यं कृ, कलान्तिकां कृ; 'lend me three loaves of bread,' पूपत्रयं मह्यं ऋणं देहि.—(Grant, furnish, afford) दा, प्रदा, ऋ, समृ, परिकॢप् (c. 10. -कल्पयति -यितुं), उपस्था in caus. (-स्थापयति -यितुं); 'he lends an ear,' कर्णं ददाति, कर्णम् अर्पयति, कर्णार्पणं करोति; 'to lend assistance,' उपकृ, साहाय्यं कृ.

LENDER, *s.* ऋणदाता *m.* (तृ), ऋणदायी *m.* (न्), ऋणदः, ऋणसमर्पकः, निक्षेप्ता *m.* (प्तृ), न्यासकर्त्ता *m.* (र्तृ), प्रयोगदाता, उत्तमर्णः -र्णी *m.* (न्).

LENDING, *s.* ऋणदानं, ऋणसमर्पणं, ऋणार्पणं, निरूपितकालपर्य्यन्तं or आविहितकालात् परहस्ते द्रव्यसमर्पणं.

LENGTH, *s.* (Extent) दैर्घ्यं दीर्घत्वं -ता, द्राघिमा *m.* (न्), आयामः, आयतिः *f.*, प्रयामः, विस्तारः, विस्तृतिः *f.*, विस्तरः, विततिः *f.*, प्रततिः *f.*, सततिः *f.*, वितानः -नं -नकं, प्रपञ्चः, आरोहः, पाटः; 'length of the journey,' अध्वदीर्घत्वं.—(Measure) परिमाणं, प्रमाणं, मानं; 'the length of a rope,' रज्जुपरिमाणं; 'the length of the day and night,' अहोरात्रस्य परिमाणं.—(Extent of duration) कालदीर्घत्वं, कालदैर्घ्यं, दीर्घकालः, चिरकालः -लं; 'for a length of time,' चिरकालं, बहुकालं -लात्; 'length of life,' आयुर्दीर्घत्वं.—(Reach, range, limit) पर्य्यन्तं, मार्गः, अवधिः *m.*, अन्तः, प्रमाणं, मर्य्यादा; 'to such a length,' एतावत्पर्य्यन्तं; 'to a great length,' अतिमात्रं, अतिमर्य्यादं, अत्यन्तं.—(At length, at full length) विस्तरेण, सुविस्तरेण, सुविस्तरं, विस्तरशस्, सविस्तरं, सुविस्तीर्णं, असंक्षेपतस्, असंक्षिप्तं; 'spread out at full length,' विस्तीर्णः -र्णा -र्णं, विस्तृतः -ता -तं; 'to lie at full length,' दण्डवत् पत् (c. 1. पतति -तितुं), दण्डासनं कृ.—(At length, at last, after long delay) शेषे, अनन्तरं, तदनन्तरं, चिरकालात्परं, दीर्घकालात्परं, दीर्घकाले गते.

To LENGTHEN, *v. a.* दीर्घीकृ, द्राघ (nom. द्राघयति -यितुं), वितन् (c. 8. -तनोति -नितुं), प्रतन्, विततीकृ, प्रसृ (c. 10. -सारयति -यितुं), विसृ, आयम् (c. 1. -यच्छति -यन्तुं), प्रपञ्च् (c. 10. -पञ्चयति -यितुं), विस्तृ (c. 10. -स्तारयति -यितुं).

To LENGTHEN, *v. n.* द्राघ् (c. 1. द्राघते -घितुं), दीर्घीभू, आयम् (c. 1. -यच्छते -यन्तुं), आयतीभू, विततीभू, विस्तृ in pass. (-स्तीर्य्यते).

LENGTHENED, *p. p.* दीर्घीकृतः -ता -तं, आयतः -ता -तं, आयामितः -ता -तं, समायतः -ता -तं, व्यायतः -ता -तं, विततः -ता -तं, प्रविततः -ता -तं, आततः -ता -तं, विस्तृतः -ता -तं, विस्तीर्णः -र्णा -र्णं, विरूढः -ढा -ढं, प्रसृतः -ता -तं.

LENGTHWISE, *adv.* अन्वायततं, अन्वायामं, अन्वायति, आयामदिशि.

LENGTHY, *a.* दीर्घः -र्घा -र्घं, द्राघिमवान् -वती -वत् (त्), आयतिमान् &c., आयामवान् &c., विस्तीर्णः -र्णा -र्णं, दीर्घसूत्रः -त्रा -त्रं.

LENIENCY, *s.* क्षमा, मृदुता, म्रदिमा *m.* (न्), मार्दवं, सौम्यता, स्निग्धता, अनुग्रता, कोमलता, साम *n.* (न्), सामबुद्धिः *f.*, अतीक्ष्णता, अतैक्ष्ण्यं, अतीव्रता, दयानुग्रता, अनुग्रदण्डत्वं, अपरुषता, दया, दयार्द्रभावः, कृपा. *See* LENITY.

LENIENT, *a.* क्षमावान् -वती -वत् (त्), क्षमी -मिणी -मि (न्), मृदुः -दुः -द्वी -दु, सौम्यः -म्या -म्यं, स्निग्धः -ग्धा -ग्धं, कोमलः -ला -लं, अनुग्रः -ग्रा -ग्रं, सामबुद्धिः -द्धिः -द्धि, अतीक्ष्णः -क्ष्णा -क्ष्णं, अतीव्रः -व्रा -व्रं, अपरुषः -षा -षं, अनुग्रदण्डः -ण्डा -ण्डं, सदयः -या -यं, दयार्द्रः -र्द्रा -र्द्रं, दयालुः -लुः -लु, सामोपचारी -रिणी -रि (न्), कृपालुः -लुः -लु.—

(Assuasive) शमकः -का -कं, शमी -मिनी -मि (न्). *See* LENITIVE; 'a lenient measure,' सामोपचारः, सामोपायः.

LENIENTLY, *adv.* क्षमापूर्व्वं, क्षमया, अनुग्रं, अतीक्ष्णं, साम्ना, समार्द्दवं, सदयं, दयया, स्निग्धं, अपरुषं, कोमलं.

To LENIFY, *v. a.* शम् (c. 10. शमयति -यितुं), उपशम्, प्रशम्, सान्त्व् or शान्त्व् (c. 10. सान्त्वयति -यितुं), परिशान्त्व्.

LENITIVE, *a.* शमकः -का -कं, शान्तिकः -की -कं, शान्तिकरः -रा -रं, शान्तिदः -दा -दं, शान्तिकर्त्ता -र्त्री -र्तृ (र्तृ), स्नेही -हिनी -हि (न्), स्निग्धः -ग्धा -ग्धं, स्निग्धकारी &c., चिक्कणः -णा -णं.

LENITIVE, *s.* (A medicine that softens pain) वेदनाशामिकं, वेदनाशमकम् औषधं, क्लेशापहं, उपशमनं, प्रशमनं, शूलघ्नं, सामोपचारः.

LENITY, *s.* क्षमा, क्षमाशीलता, मृदुता, सौम्यता, सामोपचारबुद्धिः *f.*, अनुग्रता. —(Mildness of discipline) अनुग्रदण्डत्वं, अतीक्ष्णदण्डत्वं, अल्पदण्डः -ण्डनं, अल्पशिक्षा. *See* LENIENCY.

LENS, *s.* काचः; 'a convex lens,' मध्योन्नतकाचः; 'a double convex lens,' यवः; 'a concave lens,' मध्यनिम्नकाचः; 'a chrystal lens,' दीप्तोपलः, अर्कोश्मा *m.* (न्), सूर्य्याश्मा *m.*, सूर्य्यकान्तः.

LENT, *p. p.* (Given to another for temporary use) आविहितकालात् परहस्ते समर्पितः -ता -तं or अर्पितः -ता -तं or निक्षिप्तः -प्ता -प्तं or न्यस्तः -स्ता -स्तं, निरूपितकालं यावद् विसृष्टः -ष्टा -ष्टं, कालकृतः -ता -तं, प्रयुक्तः -क्ता -क्तं.

LENT, *s.* (Fast of forty days) चत्वारिंशद्दिनपर्य्यन्तो महोपवासः.

LENTEN, *a.* पूर्व्वोक्तमहोपवाससम्बन्धी -न्धिनी -न्धि (न्).

LENTICULAR, *a.* मसूरसरूपः -पा -पं, मसूरोपमः -मा -मं.

LENTIFORM, *a.* यवसरूपः -पा -पं, यवाकृतिः -तिः -ति, यवाकारः -रा -रं.

LENTIGINOUS, *a.* जतुली -लिनी -लि (न्), ददुणः -णा -णं.

LENTIGO, *s.* (Freckly eruption) जतुलोत्पत्तिः *f.*, तिलकोत्पत्तिः *f.*, ददुः *m.*

LENTIL, *s.* मसूरः, मसुरः, मङ्गल्यकः.

LENTOR, *s.* (Viscousness) सान्द्रता, श्यानता.—(Slowness) मन्दता.

LENTOUS, *a.* सान्द्रः -न्द्रा -न्द्रं, श्यानः -ना -नं, घनः -ना -नं.

LEO, *s.* (The sign of the zodiac) सिंहः, आरण्यराशिः *m.*

LEONINE, *a.* सैंहः -ही -हं, सैंहिकः -की -कं, सिंहधर्म्मा -र्म्मा -र्म्म (न्), सिंहस्वभावः -वा -वं, सिंहशीलः -ला -लं, सिंहसम्बन्धी -न्धिनी &c.

LEOPARD, *s.* चित्रकः, चित्रव्याघ्रः, तरक्षुः -क्षुकः, मृग्याघ्रः, पृदाकुः *m.*, पुण्डरीकः, मृगादनः.

LEPER, *s.* कुष्ठी *m.* -ष्ठिनी *f.*, श्वित्री *m.* -त्रिणी *f.* (न्), त्वग्रोगी *m.* -गिणी *f.* (न्), कुष्ठरोगी &c., दुष्टचर्म्मा *m.* (न्), दुश्चर्म्मा *m.*

LEPORINE, *a.* शशसम्बन्धी -न्धिनी -न्धि (न्), शशकीयः -या -यं.

LEPROSY, *s.* कुष्ठं, कुष्ठरोगः, श्वित्रं, श्वैत्रं, श्वेतं, श्वैत्यं, त्वग्रोगः, त्वग्दोषः, चर्म्मदूषिका, दुष्टचर्म्मत्वं, दुश्चर्म्मत्वं, सिध्मला, चित्रं, मण्डलकं, कोठः; 'black leprosy,' रक्तकुष्ठं, महारोगः, महाव्याधिः *m.*, व्याधिः; 'afflicted with it,' रक्तकुष्ठी *m.* (न्), महारोगी *m.* (न्); 'white leprosy,' श्वेतकुष्ठं; 'wasting leprosy,' गलत्कुष्ठं.

LEPROUS, *a.* कुष्ठी -ष्ठिनी -ष्ठि (न्), श्वित्री -त्रिणी -त्रि (न्), कुष्ठरोगी -गिणी -गि (न्), त्वग्रोगी &c., चर्म्मरोगी &c., दुष्टचर्म्मा -र्म्मा -र्म्म (न्), दुश्चर्म्मा &c., महारोगी &c., महाव्याधिग्रस्तः -स्ता -स्तं.

LESION, *s.* क्षतिः *f.*, परिक्षतिः *f.* -तं, अपकारः, द्रोहः, पीडा, बाधः.

LESS, *a.* न्यूनः -ना -नं, ऊनः -ना -नं, अल्पतरः -रा -रं, अल्पीयान् -यसी -यः (स्), अल्पः -ल्पा -ल्पं, क्षुद्रतरः -रा -रं, क्षोदीयान् &c., कनीयान् &c., स्तोकतरः -रा -रं, तनीयान् &c., सूक्ष्मतरः -रा -रं, अवरः -रा -रं with abl. c.; as, 'water is less heavy than quicksilver,' जलगुरुत्वं पारदगुरुत्वाद् अल्पं भवति; 'less or more,' न्यूनाधिकं, न्यूनातिरेकं. The privative affix 'less' is expressed by हीनः -ना -नं, रहितः -ता -तं, विरहितः &c., विहीनः &c., शून्यः &c., वर्जितः &c., अपेतः &c., व्यतिरिक्तः &c. affixed, or by अ, निर्, नि, वि, वीत, विगत prefixed; as, 'childless,' पुत्रहीनः -ना -नं, अपुत्रः -त्रा -त्रं, निष्पुत्रः &c.; 'penniless,' द्रव्यहीनः &c., निष्किञ्चनः &c.; 'senseless,' बुद्धिहीनः &c., निर्बुद्धिः &c.; 'worthless,' सारहीनः &c., निर्गुणः &c.; 'fearless,' वीतभयः &c., अभयः &c.

LESS, *adv.* न्यूनं, अल्पतरं, अल्पं, क्षुद्रतरं, स्तोकं, स्तोकतरं with abl. c. *See* LESS, *a.* 'How much less,' किमुत, किम्पुनर्.

LESS, *s.* न्यूनत्वं, ऊनता, अल्पत्वं -ता.—(An inferior) अवरजनः.

LESSEE, *s.* पट्टधारी *m.* (न्), पट्टोलिकाधारी *m.*, पट्टग्राही *m.*, पट्टादायी *m.*

To LESSEN, *v. a.* न्यूनीकृ, अल्पीकृ, ऊन् (c. 10. ऊनयति -यितुं), न्यून्, ह्रस् (c. 10. ह्रासयति -यितुं), कन् (c. 10. कनयति -यितुं), लघ (nom. लघयति -यितुं), लघूकृ.

To LESSEN, *v. n.* न्यूनीभू, ऊनीभू, अल्पीभू, ह्रस् (c. 1. ह्रसते -सितुं), क्षि in pass. (क्षीयते), अपचि in pass. (-चीयते); 'to lessen by a quarter,' पादशो न्यूनीभू.

LESSENED, *p. p.* न्यूनीभूतः -ता -तं, अल्पीभूतः -ता -तं, ह्रसितः -ता -तं.

LESSER, *a.* अल्पः -ल्पा -ल्पं, अल्पतरः -रा -रं, अल्पीयान् -यसी -यः (स्), क्षुद्रतरः -रा -रं, क्षुद्रः -द्रा -द्रं, अवरः -रा -रं.

LESSON, *s.* पाठः -ठनं, अध्यायः, अध्ययः -यनं, निपाठः, व्याख्यानं.—(Precept, matter inculcated) उपदेशः, शिक्षा, अध्यापनं, बोधनं, निर्देशः.—(Reprimand) वाग्दण्डः, वाक्शासनं.

To LESSON, *v. a.* उपदिश् (c. 6. -दिशति -देष्टुं), शिक्ष् (c. 10. शिक्षयति -यितुं), अधी in caus. (अध्यापयति -यितुं), शास् (c. 2. शास्ति, शासितुं), उपदेशं कृ.

LESSOR, *s.* पट्टदाता *m.* (तृ), पट्टोलिकादाता *m.*, पट्टदायी *m.* (न्).

LEST, *conj.* यदि, यदि न, चेत्, न चेत्, नो चेत्, यदि कदाचित्, यदाकदाचित्, कदाचित्. In using these particles to express the word 'lest' it will be necessary to vary the form of the sentence according to the particle employed, as in the following examples selected from modern Sanskrit. 'I fear lest your minds should be corrupted,' चेद् युष्माकं मनांसि दुष्येयुर् मनैषा भीतिर् जायते; 'beware lest he strike thee,' सावधानो भव चेत् त्वामपि ताडयति; or the particle may be omitted; as, 'beware lest any man deceive you,' सावधाना भवत को ऽपि युष्मान् न भ्रमयेत्: or other particles may be used in more classical Sanskrit, the construction of the sentence being changed accordingly; as, 'commit not evil lest thou obtain the same,' पापं मा कुरु पापे हि कृते त्वया तादृशं प्राप्तव्यं; 'he commanded to kill the captives lest they should escape,' बन्द्यः पलायिष्यन्ते इत्याशङ्कया or इति बुद्ध्या तान् हन्तुम् आदिदेश; 'justice is not to be killed, lest being killed, it destroy us,' धर्म्मो न हन्तव्यो मा नो धर्म्मो हतो वधीत्.

To LET, *v. a.* (Permit, allow) अनुज्ञा (c. 9. -जानाति -नीते -ज्ञातुं), अभ्यनुज्ञा, अनुमन् (c. 4. -मन्यते -मन्तुं), सह् (c. 1. सहते, सोढुं), विषह्, अनुज्ञां कृ or दा or sometimes expressible by the causal form; as, 'he lets perish,' नाशयति; 'he lets enter,' प्रवेशयति.—(Let out, lease out) विहितकालं यावद् निरूपितमूल्य-

मपेक्ष्य गृहक्षेत्रादि परप्रयोजनीयं दा or विसृज् (c. 6. -सृजति -स्रष्टुं), नियमितमूल्यमपेक्ष्य किञ्चिद् द्रव्यं परप्रयोजनीयं दा, आविहितकालाद् निरूपितमूल्यमपेक्ष्य गृहक्षेत्रादि परहस्ते सम् in caus. (-अर्पयति -यितुं) or ऋ, नियमितपारितोषिकमपेक्ष्य किञ्चिद् वस्तु परस्मिन् सम्.—(Hinder) निष् (c. 10. -वारयति -यितुं), रुध् (c. 7. रुणद्धि, रोद्धुं), प्रतिरुध्, निरुध्.—(Let alone) त्यज् (c. 1. त्यजति, त्यक्तुं), परित्यज्, विसृज् (c. 6. -सृजति -स्रष्टुं, c. 10. सर्जयति -यितुं), उत्सृज्.—(Let down) अवतॄ (c. 10. -तारयति -यितुं), अवरुह् in caus. (-रोपयति -यितुं), अवपत् (c. 10. -पातयति -यितुं), अवमुच् (c. 6. -मुञ्चति -मोक्तुं), अवसृज्.—(Let go, let loose) मुच्, अवमुच्, विमुच्, विसृज्, अवसृज्, शिथिलीकृ, शिथिल (nom. शिथिलयते -ति -यितुं), श्लथ् (c. 10. श्लथयति -यितुं) or श्रथ्, स्रंस् (c. 10. स्रंसयति -यितुं), विस्रंस्, विस्रस्तं -स्तां कृ; 'having let go the hold,' स्रस्तहस्तः -स्ता -स्तं, शिथिलितहस्तः -स्ता -स्तं.—(Let in) प्रविश् or निविश् or आविश् in caus.—(Let out) मुच्, विमुच्, निर्मुच्, मोक्ष् (c. 10. मोक्षयति -यितुं), विमोक्ष्, विसृज्.—(Let off, discharge) मुच्, प्रमुच्, सृज्, अस् (c. 4. अस्यति, असितुं), प्रास्, क्षिप् (c. 6. क्षिपति, क्षेप्तुं), प्रक्षिप्, ईर् (c. 10. ईरयति -यितुं); 'let off a gun,' लोहगुलिकां युद्धनाडेः प्रक्षिप् or निःसृ (c. 10. -सारयति -यितुं). *See* TO FIRE. (Let blood) रक्तं स्रु (c. 10. स्रावयति -यितुं). *See* TO BLEED, *v. a.* (Let slip) मुच्, विमुच्, विसृज्, शिथिलीकृ; 'I will not let slip the occasion,' अवकाशं न शिथिलयिष्ये. The sense of 'let' is often inherent in the imperative; as, 'let him go,' गच्छतु; 'let it be,' भवतु.

LET, *s.* (Hinderance) रोधः, व्याघातः, प्रत्यूहः, विघ्नः, अन्तरायः, बाधः.

LET LOOSE, *p. p.* मुक्तः -क्ता -क्तं, विमुक्तः -क्ता -क्तं, विमोचितः -ता -तं, विसृष्टः -ष्टा -ष्टं, शिथिलीकृतः -ता -तं, शिथिलितः -ता -तं, स्रस्तः -स्ता -स्तं, विस्रस्तः &c.

LETHAL, *a.* मारात्मकः -का -कं, प्राणनाशकः -का -कं, प्राणहरः -रा -रं, प्राणघातकः -का -कं, मृत्युजनकः -का -कं. *See* DEADLY.

LETHARGIC, *a.* निद्रालुः -लुः -लु, अतिनिद्रालुः &c., निद्रालसः -सा -सं, सुप्तबुद्धिः -द्धिः -द्धि, जडः -डा -डं, जडबुद्धिः &c., निद्राशीलः -ला -लं, स्वप्नशीलः -ला -लं, नैद्रः -द्री -द्रं, सुषुप्सुः -प्सुः -प्सु.

LETHARGICALLY, *adv.* निद्रालुवत्, निद्रालसवत्, जडवत्, सजाड्यं.

LETHARGICALNESS, LETHARGY, *s.* निद्रालुता, अतिनिद्रालुत्वं, निद्रालसता, निद्राशीलता, स्वप्नशीलता, जडता, जाड्यं, जडबुद्धित्वं, अलसता, आलस्यं, सुप्तबुद्धित्वं, शयालुता, तन्द्रा -न्द्रिः *f.*, प्रमीला.—(Deep sleep) घोरनिद्रा, गाढनिद्रा, सुनिद्रा, निर्भरनिद्रा.

LETHE, *s.* विस्मृतिः *f.*, अस्मृतिः *f.*, स्मृतिनाशः, स्मृतिहानिः *f.*

LETHEAN, *a.* विस्मृतिजनकः -का -कं, विस्मृतिकारकः -का -कं.

LETHIFEROUS, *a.* मृत्युजनकः -का -कं, निधनावहः -हा -हं. *See* DEADLY.

LETTER, *s.* (Of the alphabet, character) अक्षरं, वर्णः -र्णं, मातृका, अभिनिधानः, अर्णः, कारः; the latter word is only used in naming any letter; as, 'the letter a,' अकारः; the letter 'r,' is called रेफः.—(Printing letter or type) मुद्राक्षरं, अक्षरमुद्रा; 'compound letter,' संयुक्ताक्षरं, सन्ध्यक्षरं; 'letter by letter,' अक्षरशस्; 'beginning to learn the letters,' अक्षरारम्भः.—(Epistle) पत्रं, लेखः, लेख्यं, पत्रिका, पत्री, पत्रकं, लिखितं, सन्देशपत्रं, लिपिः *f.*; 'by letter,' पत्रद्वारा, पत्रद्वारेण; 'on sight of the letter,' पत्रदर्शनात्; 'a letter from an inferior to a superior,' निवेदनपत्रं, आवेदनपत्रं, विज्ञापनपत्रं; 'from a superior officer,' आज्ञापत्रं; 'a letter to a son, daughter, &c.,' आशीर्वादपत्रं.—(The literal meaning, verbal expression) शब्दार्थः, अक्षरार्थः, वाच्यार्थः, प्रथमार्थः, पदार्थः, वचनं, ग्रन्थार्थः; 'in the spirit and in the letter,' अर्थतो ग्रन्थतश्च, अर्थतो वचनतश्च.—(Letters, literature) अक्षरं, विद्या, शास्त्रं; 'a man of letters,' शिक्षिताक्षरः, साक्षरजनः, कृतविद्यः.—(Dead letter) निरर्थकविधिः *m.*

To LETTER, *v. a.* अक्षराङ्कितं -तां कृ, अक्षरमुद्रितं -तां कृ, अक्षरैर् अङ्क् (c. 10. अङ्कयति -यितुं) or मुद्र् (nom. मुद्रयति -यितुं) or मुद्रीकृ or चिह्न् (nom. चिह्नयति -यितुं), अक्षरचिह्नितं -तां कृ, अक्षरयुक्तं -क्तां कृ.

LETTER-CARRIER, *s.* पत्रवाहः -हकः, पत्रवाही *m.* (न्), लेखहारः -रकः, लेखहारी *m.* (न्), लेखनिकः.

LETTERED, *p. p.* (Stamped with letters) अक्षराङ्कितः -ता -तं, अक्षरमुद्रितः -ता -तं, अक्षरचिह्नितः -ता -तं, अक्षरयुक्तः -क्ता -क्तं; 'well-lettered,' शुद्धवर्णः -र्णा -र्णं, शुद्धाक्षरः -रा -रं. (Versed in literature) शिक्षिताक्षरः -रा -रं, साक्षरः -रा -रं, कृतविद्यः -द्या -द्यं, गृहीतविद्यः &c., कृतबुद्धिः -द्धिः -द्धि.

LETTER-PRESS, *s.* अक्षरमुद्रा, मुद्राक्षरं, मुद्रिताक्षरं, अक्षरं.

LETTER-WRITER, *s.* पत्रलेखकः, पत्रलिपिकारः, पत्रलिखनकृत्.

LETTUCE, *s.* शाकभेदः, हरितकं, शिग्रुः *m.*

LEUCOPHLEGMACY, *s.* कफोदरं, कफशोथः, जलोदरं, उदकोदरं, आध्मानं.

LEUCOPHLEGMATIC, *a.* कफोदरी-रिणी-रि(न्), कफशोथरोगी-गिणी-गि(न्).

LEVANT, *a.* पूर्व्वदेशीयः -या -यं, पूर्व्वदिश्यः -श्या -श्यं, पूर्व्वदिक्स्थः -स्था -स्थं, पूर्व्वदेशजः -जा -जं, पूर्व्वदेशसम्बन्धी -न्धिनी &c., सूर्य्योदयदेशसम्बन्धी &c.

LEVANT, *s.* पूर्व्वदेशः, प्राग्देशः, प्राचीनदेशः, सूर्य्योदयदेशः.

LEVEE, *s.* राजदर्शनं, राजसभा, सभा, दर्शनं, प्रातःसभा.

LEVEL, *a.* (Even, flat) समः -मा -मं, समानः -ना -नं, समस्थः -स्था -स्थं, सपाटः -टा -टं, समरेखः -खा -खं.—(Horizontal) क्षितिजसमसूत्रः -त्रा -त्रं.—(On the same plane or line with) समरेखः -खा -खं, समसूत्रः -त्रा -त्रं, समदेशस्थः -स्था -स्थं, समभूमिस्थः &c.; 'level ground,' समभूमिः *f.*, समस्थलं -ली, प्रस्थः, पाटः, आक्रिः *f.*; 'level surface,' समपृष्ठं, समतलं.

LEVEL, *s.* (Even surface) समं, समस्थलं -ली, समभूमिः *f.*, समतलं, समपृष्ठं, समदेशः, प्रस्थः, पाटः; 'liquids always find their own level,' द्रवपदार्थाः सदा समानपृष्ठा भवन्ति; 'the water in the tube rises to a level with the water in the vessel,' नलस्थजलं प्रांशुत्वेन पात्रस्थजलसमं भवति.—(State of equality, equal elevation) समता, समानता, साम्यं, तुल्यता, समसमानता.—(Line of direction in which a weapon is aimed) लक्ष्यं, लक्ष्यदेशः, लक्ष्यसूत्रं, सन्धानं, अभिसन्धानं.—(Instrument for finding the level) सूत्रं.—(Rule, plan) नियमः, सूत्रं.

To LEVEL, *v. a.* (Make even) समीकृ, समानीकृ, समं -मां -मं कृ.—(Reduce to an even surface) समस्थलीकृ, समपृष्ठीकृ, समतलीकृ.—(Aim) अभिसन्धा (c. 3. -दधाति -धातुं), प्रतिसन्धा, लक्षीकृ.—(Direct at) उद्दिश् (c. 6. -दिशति -देष्टुं), समुद्दिश्.

LEVELED, *p. p.* (Made even) समीकृतः -ता -तं, समानीकृतः -ता -तं.—(Reduced to an even surface) समस्थलीकृतः -ता -तं.—(Aimed) प्रतिसंहितः -ता -तं, अभिसंहितः -ता -तं, उद्दिष्टः -ष्टा -ष्टं.

LEVELER, *s.* समकारी *m.* (न्), समानकारी *m.*—(One who destroys distinctions) पदनाशकः, पदघातकः, भावविघातकः.

LEVELING, *s.* समीकरणं, समानीकरणं, समस्थलीकरणं, तुल्यीकरणं.

LEVELNESS, *s.* समता, साम्यं, समानता -त्वं, समभूमिस्थभावः, समस्थलस्थभावः, तुल्यता.

LEVER, *s.* उत्तोलनदण्डः -ण्डं, उत्तोलनदारु *m.*, उत्तोलनी, लोहदण्डः, उत्तोलनयन्त्रं; 'to raise with a lever,' लोहदण्डेन or दारुणा उत्तुल् (c. 10. -तोलयति -यितुं).

LEVERET, *s.* शशशावकः, शशवत्सः, शशशिशुः *m.*, बालशशकः.

LEVIATHAN, *s.* तिमिः *m.*, तिमिङ्गिलः, मीनरः, समुद्रारुः *m.*

To LEVIGATE, *v. a.* (Grind to a fine powder) चूर्ण् (c. 10. चूर्णयति -यितुं), चूर्णीकृ.—(Polish, make smooth) परिष्कृ, श्लक्ष्णीकृ, स्निग्धीकृ.

LEVIGATION, *s.* चूर्णीकरणं, पेषणं, क्षोदीकरणं, परिष्कारः, श्लक्ष्णीकरणं.

LEVITE, *s.* लीवैताख्यो यिहुदीयानां पुरोहितः or याजकः.

LEVITICAL, *a.* पौरोहितः -ती -तं, याजकीयः -या -यं, पूर्व्वक्रियाजकसम्बन्धी -न्धिनी -न्धि (न्), धर्म्मोपदेशविषयः -या -यं.

LEVITY, *s.* (Lightness) लघुता, लाघवं, लघिमा *m.* (न्), अगुरुता.—(Unsteadiness) चञ्चलत्वं, चाञ्चल्यं, चपलता, चापल्यं, चापलं, लोलता, लौल्यं, मनोलौल्यं, अस्थिरता, अस्थैर्य्यं, अनवस्थितिः *f.*, अधृतिः *f.*—(Want of seriousness) अगुरुता, गौरवहीनता.

To LEVY, *v. a.* (Raise troops) योद्धृमध्ये समारोप्य सैन्यान् समूहीकृ or व्यूहीकृ or समूह् (c. 1. -ऊहते -हितुं) or समाहृ (c. 1. -हरति -हर्त्तुं), सेनां or वरूथिनीं युज् (c. 10. योजयति -यितुं), सैन्यसमूहं कृ, सैन्यसमाहारं कृ, सैन्यपरिसंख्यां कृ, शस्त्राणि or अस्त्राणि ग्रह् in caus. (ग्राहयति -यितुं), युद्धकर्म्मणि प्रवृत् (c. 10. -वर्त्तयति -यितुं), सैन्यमध्ये अभिलिख् (c. 6. -लिखति -लेखितुं) or समारुह् in caus. (-रोपयति -यितुं) or आरुह्.—(Levy a tax) करं ग्रह् (c. 9. गृह्णाति, ग्रहीतुं) or आदा (c. 3. -ददाति -दातुं) or दा in caus. (दापयति -यितुं) or अवहृ (c. 10. -हारयति -यितुं), शुल्कग्रहणं कृ.—(Levy contributions) एकैकस्मात् किञ्चिद्धनग्रहणं or धनोत्तोलनं कृ.

LEVY, *s.* (Act of collecting troops) सैन्यसमाहारः, सैन्यसमाहरणं, सैन्याभिलेखनं, सैन्यव्यूहकरणं.—(Troops raised) सैन्यसमूहः, सैन्यसमुदायः.—(Of taxes) करग्रहणं, शुल्कग्रहणं.—(Of money) धनोत्तोलनं, एकैकस्मात् किञ्चिद्धनग्रहणं.

LEWD, *a.* कामुकः -का -कं, कामी -मिनी -मि (न्), रतार्थी -र्थिनी &c., सुरतार्थी &c., व्यवायी -यिनी &c., व्यवायपरः -रा -रं, कामासक्तः -क्ता -क्तं, सम्भोगार्थी &c., तरलः -ला -लं, स्त्रीलम्पटः, लम्पटः, स्त्रीव्यसनी *m.*—(Wicked) दुष्टः -ष्टा -ष्टं, दुराचारः -रा -रं, दुरात्मा -त्मा -त्म (न्), पापी -पिनी -पि (न्).

LEWDLY, *adv.* कामुकवत्, लम्पटवत्, कामुकं, सकामं, दुष्टवत्.

LEWDNESS, *s.* कामुकत्वं, लम्पटता, लाम्पट्यं, रतार्थित्वं, रतासक्तिः *f.*, सकामता, सम्भोगार्थित्वं, व्यवायः -यित्वं, वैयात्यं, वियातता, हेला, स्त्रीव्यसनं.—(Wickedness) दुष्टता, दुराचारता, अधमाचारता, कुसृतिः *f.*

LEXICOGRAPHER, *s.* कौशिकः, कोशकारः, कोशरचकः, अभिधानकर्त्ता *m.* (र्तृ).

LEXICOGRAPHICAL, *a.* कौशिकः -की -कं, कोषरचनासम्बन्धी -न्धिनी -न्धि (न्).

LEXICOGRAPHY, *s.* शब्दकोशरचना, शब्दकोशकरणं, कोषरचना.

LEXICON, *s.* कोषः, कोशः, शब्दकोषः, शब्दकोशः, शब्दसङ्ग्रहः, अभिधानं, शब्दग्रन्थः, शब्दजालं, निर्वचनं, निघण्टुः *m.*

LIABLE, *a.* (Subject to) अधीनः -ना -नं, योग्यः -ग्या -ग्यं, अर्हः -र्हा -र्हं, वशः -शा -शं, शीलः -ला -लं in comp.; 'liable to be punished,' दण्डयोग्यः &c.; 'liable to death,' मरणाधीनः -ना -नं; 'liable to disease,' रोगाधीनः -ना -नं; 'not liable,' अनधीनः -ना -नं.—(Responsible, amenable) आह्वानाधीनः -ना -नं, अभियोक्तव्यः -व्या -व्यं, अभियोज्यः -ज्या -ज्यं, अभियोक्त्राह्वानाधीनः -ना -नं, व्यवहार्य्यः -र्य्या -र्य्यं, व्यवहर्त्तव्यः -व्या -व्यं; 'liable for the debt,' उत्तमर्णाह्वानाधीनः -ना -नं, धनिकाह्वानाधीनः &c.; 'he is liable to pay,' दातुम् अर्हति. Sometimes 'liable' may be expressed by the affix. आलु; as, 'liable to fall,' पतयालुः -लुः -लु.

LIABLENESS, LIABILITY, *s.* अधीनता, योग्यता -त्वं, शीलता; 'liability to disease,' रोगाधीनता; 'liability to fall,' पतनशीलता, पतयालुता.—(Responsibility) आह्वानाधीनता, अभियोज्यता, अनुयोगाधीनता, व्यवहार्य्यता; 'for debt,' उत्तमर्णाह्वानाधीनता, धनिकाह्वानाधीनता.—(Debt) ऋणं.

LIAISON, *s.* सम्बन्धः, संयोगः, प्रेमबन्धः, प्रेमसम्बन्धः.

LIAR, *s.* असत्यवादी *m.* -दिनी *f.* (न्), मिथ्यावादी -दिनी, मृषावादी -दिनी, असत्यवक्ता *m.*, क्त्री *f.* (क्तृ), मिथ्याभाषी -षिणी (न्), अनृतभाषी &c., अनृतवादी &c., अनृतवाक् *m. f.* (च्), अनृतवदनशीलः, असत्यवदनशीलः, अनृती *m.* (न्), अतथ्यवादी &c., अलीकवाक् *m.*, द्विजिह्वः, अनेकजिह्वः, असत्यचूडामणिः *m.*

LIBATION, *s.* (The act) उदकतर्पणं, उदकदानं, उदकक्रिया, उदकनिषेकः, उदकपातनं, देवतोद्देशकः पेयनिषेकः or पानीयनिषेकः or मद्यनिषेकः or पेयत्यागः, पात्रस्थरसनिषेकः.—(The liquor poured out) तर्पणोदकं, तर्पणरसः, तर्पणद्रव्यं, निषिक्तरसं, पातितरसः; 'to make libations,' उदकादिदानेन or उदकादिनिषेकेण तृप् (c. 10. तर्पयति -यितुं), देवतामुद्दिश्य पात्रस्थरसं पत् (c. 10. पातयति -यितुं) or पात्रस्थमद्यं निषिच् (c. 6. -षिञ्चति -षेक्तुं) or अवसिच्.

LIBEL, *s.* अपवादपत्रं, अपवादलेखः, अपवादलेख्यं, परिवादलेख्यं, निन्दापत्रं, निन्दालेखः, अभिशापपत्रं, अमुकोद्देशकं पिशुनलेख्यं, कलङ्कसूचकपत्रं, अख्यातिसूचकपत्रं.

To LIBEL, *v. a.* अपवादपत्रेण निन्द् (c. 1. निन्दति -न्दितुं), निन्दापत्रेण अपवद् (c. 1. -वदति -दितुं) or परिवद् or कलङ्क् (nom. कलङ्कयति -यितुं) or कीर्त्तिकलङ्कं कृ, अमुकजनमुद्दिश्य अपवादपत्रं लिख् (c. 6. लिखति, लेखितुं) or निन्दापत्रं लिख्.

LIBELED, *p. p.* पत्रापवादितः -ता -तं, पत्रनिन्दितः -ता -तं, पत्राभिशस्तः -स्ता -स्तं, लेखनिन्दितः &c., पत्रकलङ्कितः -ता -तं.

LIBELER, *s.* पत्रापवादी *m.* (न्), पत्राभिशंसकः, अपवादपत्रलेखकः, निन्दापत्रलेखकः, कलङ्ककरः, अभ्यसूयकः.

LIBELLOUS, *a.* अपवादकः -का -कं, अभिशंसकः -का -कं, कलङ्ककरः -री -रं, अकीर्त्तिकरः -री -रं, अपयशस्करः -री -रं, गुणापवादकः -का -कं, निन्दकः -का -कं, पिशुनः -ना -नं, अभ्यसूयकः -का -कं.

LIBERAL, *a.* उदारः -रा -रं, दानशीलः -ला -लं, बहुदः -दा -दं, बहुप्रदः -दा -दं, अतिदाता -त्री -तृ (तृ), दायकः -का -कं, बहुदायकः -का -कं, दानरतः -ता -तं, त्यागशीलः -ला -लं, वदान्यः -न्या -न्यं, स्थूललक्ष्यः -क्ष्या -क्ष्यं, स्थूललक्षः -क्षा -क्षं, मुक्तहस्तः -स्ता -स्तं, बहुत्यागी -गिनी -गि (न्), दाश्वः -श्वा -श्वं, दाश्वन् -श्वती -श्वत् (त्), दारुः -र्वी -रु, व्ययशीलः -ला -लं, उदारहस्तः &c., उदात्तः -त्ता -त्तं, सुकलः -ला -लं, अकृपणः -णा -णं, परिनिर्विवप्सुः -प्सुः -प्सु.—(Liberal-minded) उदारचेताः -ताः -तः (स्), उदारधीः -धीः -धि, उदारचरितः -ता -तं, माहात्मिकः -की -कं, महात्मा -त्मा -त्म (न्), महामनाः -नाः -नः (स्), महानुभावः -वा -वं, महेच्छः -च्छा -च्छं, महाशयः -या -यं.—(Of good birth) महाकुलः -ला -लं, सत्कुलीनः -ना -नं.—(Exuberant) बहुलः -ला -लं, प्रचुरः -रा -रं, परिपूर्णः -र्णा -र्णं, उद्रिक्तः -क्ता -क्तं, अतिरिक्तः -क्ता -क्तं, पुष्कलः -ला -लं, विपुलः -ला -लं.—(Liberal arts) अलङ्कारकला, अलङ्कारविद्या, कला.

LIBERALITY, *s.* उदारता, औदार्य्यं, दानशीलता, त्यागशीलता, त्यागिता, त्यागः, दानं, अतिदानं, दातृत्वं -ता, अतिदातृत्वं, अतिसर्ज्जनं, बहुप्रदत्वं, वदान्यता, स्थूललक्ष्यता, व्ययशीलता, मुक्तहस्तत्वं, विलम्भः, अकार्पण्यं,

अकृपणता, परिनिर्विवक्षा.—(Nobleness of mind) माहात्म्यं, उदारचित्तत्वं; 'act of pious liberality,' पूर्त्तं.

LIBERALLY, *adv.* बाहुल्येन, अकार्पण्येन, अतित्यागेन, अतिदानेन, मुक्तहस्तेन, वदान्यवत्, उदारवत्, बहुशस्, अतिव्ययेन, स्थूललक्ष्यवत्.

To LIBERATE, *v. a.* मुच् (c. 6. मुञ्चति, मोक्तुं, c. 10. मोचयति -यितुं), विमुच्, निर्मुच्, मोक्ष् (c. 10. मोक्षयति -यितुं), विमोक्ष्, विसृज् (c. 6. -सृजति -स्रष्टुं, c. 10. -सर्जयति -यितुं), निस्तॄ (c. 10. -तारयति -यितुं), उद्धृ (c. 1. -हरति -हर्त्तुं), त्रै (c. 1. त्रायते, त्रातुं), परित्रै, मुक्तिं कृ, विमोचनं कृ.—(From confinement) बन्धनात् or बन्धनालयाद् मुच्.

LIBERATED, *p. p.* मुक्तः -क्ता -क्तं, मोचितः -ता -तं, विमोचितः -ता -तं, विमुक्तः -क्ता -क्तं, मोक्षितः -ता -तं, विसृष्टः -ष्टा -ष्टं, उद्धृतः -ता -तं, समुद्धृतः -ता -तं, त्रातः -ता -तं, त्राणः -णा -णं, बन्धनमुक्तः -क्ता -क्तं.

LIBERATION, *s.* मुक्तिः *f.*, विमुक्तिः *f.*, वैमुक्तं, मोचनं, विमोचनं, मोक्षः -क्षणं, विमोक्षः -क्षणं, परिमोक्षणं, त्राणं, परित्राणं, निस्तारः, निस्तरणं, उद्धारः, उद्धरणं, समुद्धरणं, विसर्जनं, विसृष्टिः *f.*, मुक्तिदानं.

LIBERATOR, *s.* मोचकः, विमोचकः, मोक्षकः, मुक्तिदाता *m.* (तृ), उद्धर्त्ता *m.* (र्तृ), समुद्धर्त्ता *m.*, निस्तारकः, निस्तारयिता *m.* (तृ), तारकः, रक्षकः.

LIBERTINE, *a.* व्यसनी -निनी -नि (न्), व्यसनीयः -या -यं, व्यभिचारी -रिणी -रि (न्), विषयासक्तः -क्ता -क्तं, विषयी -यिणी &c., विषयानुरागी -गिणी &c., कामासक्तः -क्ता -क्तं, भोगासक्तः -क्ता -क्तं, कामुकः -का -कं, तरलः -ला -लं, अनवस्थः -स्था -स्थं, अमर्य्यादः -दा -दं, निर्मर्य्यादः -दा -दं, दुराचारः -रा -रं, कामवृत्तः -त्ता -त्तं.

LIBERTINE, *s.* लम्पटः, स्त्रीलम्पटः, स्त्रीव्यसनी *m.* (न्), स्त्रीसेवी *m.* (न्), स्त्रीपरः, स्त्रीरतः, स्त्रीव्यासक्ती *m.* (न्), नागरः, नागरीटः, विटः.

LIBERTINISM, *s.* व्यसनिता -त्वं, व्यसनं, व्यभिचारः, व्यतिक्रमः, लम्पटता, लाम्पट्यं, अनवस्थितिः *f.*, अनवस्थता, विषयासक्तिः *f.*, विषयानुरागः, कामासक्तिः *f.*, भोगासक्तिः, कामुकत्वं, स्त्रीसेवा, स्त्रीप्रसङ्गः, स्त्रीव्यसनं, स्त्रीव्यासङ्गः, दुर्वृत्तता, दुराचारत्वं, अमर्य्यादा, इन्द्रियासंयमः, वनितोपभोगः, नारीप्रसङ्गः.

LIBERTY, *s.* (Freedom from restraint or servitude) स्वतन्त्रता, स्वातन्त्र्यं, स्वाधीनता, अनधीनता, स्वच्छन्दता, स्वाच्छन्द्यं, आत्माधीनता, अपराधीनता, स्ववशत्वं, अपरवशत्वं, अवशत्वं, विवशत्वं, अपारतन्त्र्यं, अनायत्तता, अपरायत्तता, स्वायत्तता, स्वेच्छाचारता, अदास्यं, अदासत्वं, अपरप्रेष्यत्वं, दास्याभावः, सेवाभावः, अयन्त्रणं, निर्यन्त्रणं, अयन्त्रितत्वं.—(Freedom of the will) स्वेच्छा, स्वच्छन्दता, स्वकामः, यदृच्छा.—(Ability to act) क्षमता, शक्तिः *f.*—(Freedom in general) मुक्तिः *f.*, विमुक्तिः *f.*, मोक्षः, विमोक्षः, परिमोक्षणं, मोचनं, विमोचनं, वैमुक्तं, बन्धनाभावः, बन्धनराहित्यं.—(Leave) अनुज्ञा, अनुमतिः *f.*, अभ्यनुज्ञा.—(Exemption from) मुक्तिः *f.*, विरहः, राहित्यं, शून्यता, अभावः, मोक्षः.—(Freedom from necessity) भवितव्यानधीनता, दैवानधीनता, कर्म्मावशता, दैवावशता.—(Breach of decorum) अविनयः, अमर्य्यादा, विनयातिक्रमः, मर्य्यादातिक्रमः, मर्य्यादातिवर्त्तनं, मर्य्यादातिचारः, विनयोल्लंघनं; 'to set at liberty,' मुच् (c. 6. मुञ्चति, मोक्तुं), विमुच्, मोक्ष् (c. 10. मोक्षयति -यितुं), विमोक्ष्, निस्तॄ (c. 10. -तारयति -यितुं); 'at liberty,' अनियतः -ता -तं, अयन्त्रितः -ता -तं, निर्यन्त्रितः -ता -तं, निरवग्रहः -हा -हं, क्षमः -मा -मं. *See* FREE.

LIBIDINOUS, *a.* कामुकः -का -कं, कामी -मिनी -मि (न्), कामनः -ना -नं, कामलः -ला -लं, कामात्मा -त्मा -त्म (न्), कमनः -ना -नं, कामकेलिः -लिः -लि, कमिता -त्री -तृ (तृ), रतार्थी -र्थिनी -र्थि (न्), सुरतार्थी &c., व्यवायी -यिनी -यि (न्), कामासक्तः -क्ता -क्तं, तरलः -ला -लं, सकामः -मा -मं, कामबुद्धिः -द्धिः -द्धि, कामप्रवणः -णा -णं, कामशीलः -ला -लं, कामवृत्तिः -त्तिः -त्ति, अभीकः -का -कं, अनुकः -का -कं. *See* LECHEROUS, LUSTFUL, LEWD, &c.

LIBIDINOUSLY. *adv.* सकामं, कामुकवत्, कामुकं, लम्पटवत्, तरलवत्.

LIBIDINOUSNESS, *s.* सकामता, कामुकता -त्वं, कामित्वं, कामात्मता, कामासक्तिः *f.*, रतासक्तिः *f.*, व्यवायित्वं, वैयात्यं, रतार्थित्वं, हेला -लनं.

LIBRA, *s.* (Sign of the zodiac) तुला, तुलाधारः, घटः.

LIBRARIAN, *s.* पुस्तकशालाध्यक्षः, पुस्तकशालाधिकारी *m.* (न्), पुस्तकाध्यक्षः, ग्रन्थाध्यक्षः, पुस्तकागाररक्षकः, पुस्तकागारपालकः.

LIBRARY, *s.* (Collection of books) पुस्तकसङ्ग्रहः, पुस्तकसमूहः, ग्रन्थसङ्ग्रहः.—(Edifice or room for holding it) पुस्तकशाला, पुस्तकालयः, पुस्तकागारं, पुस्तकाधारः, ग्रन्थगृहं, ग्रन्थसङ्ग्रहशाला, ग्रन्थकुटी.

To LIBRATE, *v. a.* तुल् (c. 10. तुलयति -यितुं), समतोलीकृ, तुल्यभारीकृ.

LIBRATION, *s.* तोलनं, समतोलीकरणं, भारतुल्यता, तुल्यबलता, तुल्यता.

LICE, *s. pl.* यूकाः *m. f. pl.*, केशकीटाः *m. pl.*, षट्पदाः *m. pl.*

LICENSE, *s.* (Leave, permission) अनुज्ञा, अनुमतिः *f.*, अनुज्ञानं, अभ्यनुज्ञा, समनुज्ञानं, क्षमता, आज्ञा; 'written license,' अनुज्ञापत्रं, आज्ञापत्रं.—(Excess of liberty) मर्य्यादातिक्रमः, व्यतिक्रमः, अनर्गलता, उत्क्रमः, विधिव्यतिक्रमः, विधिनियमातीतता.

To LICENSE, *v. a.* अनुज्ञापत्रेण अनुमन् (c. 4. -मन्यते -मन्तुं), अनुज्ञा (c. 9. -जानाति -नीते -ज्ञातुं), अनुज्ञां दा, अनुज्ञापत्रं दा, आज्ञापत्रं दा.

LICENSED, *p. p.* अनुज्ञातः -ता -तं, पत्रानुज्ञातः -ता -तं, गृहीतानुज्ञः -ज्ञा -ज्ञं, अभ्यनुज्ञातः -ता -तं, अनुमतः -ता -तं.

LICENSER, *s.* अनुज्ञादाता *m.* (तृ), अनुमतिदाता *m.*, अनुज्ञापत्रप्रकाशकः.

LICENTIATE, *s.* गृहीतानुज्ञः, सानुज्ञः, अधिकारयुक्तः, अधिकारी *m.* (न्).

LICENTIOUS, *a.* (Exceeding the limits of law or propriety) निर्मर्य्यादः -दा -दं, मर्य्यादातिवर्त्ती -र्त्तिनी -र्त्ति (न्), मर्य्यादातिक्रमी -मिणी &c., त्यक्तमर्य्यादः -दा -दं, अतिक्रान्तमर्य्यादः &c., उत्क्रान्तमर्य्यादः &c., अमर्य्यादः &c., व्यभिचारी -रिणी &c., दुराचारी &c., दुराचारः -रा -रं, अनाचारी &c., स्वेच्छाचारी &c., यथेष्टाचारी &c., कामाचारी &c., कामवृत्तः -त्ता -त्तं, उच्छृङ्खलः -ला -लं, अशिष्टः -ष्टा -ष्टं, अशिष्टाचारः &c., धर्म्मभ्रष्टः -ष्टा -ष्टं, त्यक्तधर्म्मा -र्म्मा -र्म्म (न्), अत्याचारी &c., अवद्धः -द्धा -द्धं, अनर्गलः -ला -लं.—(Profligate, dissolute) व्यसनी -निनी &c., व्यसनीयः -या -यं, व्यसनासक्तः -क्ता -क्तं, विषयासक्तः &c., विषयी -यिणी &c., विषयानुरागी -गिणी &c., भोगासक्तः &c., कामुकः -का -कं, अनवस्थः -स्था -स्थं, दुष्टः -ष्टा -ष्टं, पापीयान् -यसी -यः (स्), पापिष्ठः -ष्ठा -ष्ठं, दुर्वृत्तः -त्ता -त्तं, लम्पटः, स्त्रीलम्पटः, स्त्रीव्यसनी, व्यवायपरः -रा -रं.

LICENTIOUSLY, *adv.* अशिष्टवत्, उच्छृङ्खलं, व्यभिचारेण, लम्पटवत्, कामुकं, कामुकवत्, विषयानुरागात्, दुष्टवत्, पापिष्ठवत्.

LICENTIOUSNESS, *s.* व्यभिचारः, व्यतिक्रमः, मर्य्यादातिक्रमः, मर्य्यादातिवर्त्तनं, नियमातिक्रमः, अशिष्टता, उच्छृङ्खलत्वं, दुराचारत्वं, अनाचारः, अत्याचारः, आचारभ्रष्टता, दुर्वृत्तता, व्यसनिता, अनवस्थितिः *f.*, अनवस्थता, पापिष्ठत्वं, लम्पटता, लाम्पट्यं, कामुकत्वं, इन्द्रियासंयमः, स्त्रीप्रसङ्गः, स्त्रीसेवा, स्त्रीव्यसनं, भोगासक्तिः *f.*

LICHEN, *s.* शिलावल्का, शूकरी, शूकरी, शूकराक्रान्ता, वराहक्रान्ता.

To LICK, *v. a.* लिह् (c. 2. लेढि, लीढे, लेढुं), आलिह्, अवलिह्, परिलिह्, संलिह्, परिसंलिह्, जिह्वालेहनं कृ, अवलेहनं कृ.—(Lick up, devour) ग्रस् (c. 1. ग्रसते -सितुं), भक्ष् (c. 10. भक्षयति -यितुं), सम्भक्ष्, गॄ (c. 6. गिरति, गरितुं -रीतुं), निगॄ, संगॄ.—(Beat) तड् (c. 10. ताडयति -यितुं), प्रहृ (c. 1. -हरति -हर्त्तुं), वेत्राघातं कृ, दण्डाघातं कृ.

LICK, *s.* लेहः -हनं.—(A blow) आघातः, प्रहारः, ताडनं, दण्डाघातः.

LICKED, *p. p.* लीढः -ढा -ढं, आलीढः -ढा -ढं, अवलीढः -ढा -ढं.

LICKERISH, *a.* (Dainty) सुरसः -सा -सं, रसिकः -का -कं, स्वादुः -द्वी -दु, मिष्टः -ष्टा -ष्टं.—(Eager to taste) प्राशनोत्सुकः -का -कं, लेहनोत्सुकः &c., भोगोत्सुकः &c.

LICKERISHNESS, *s.* रसिकत्वं, सरसता, सौरस्यं, मिष्टता, स्वादुता, लालित्यं.

LICKING, *s.* (With the tongue) लेहः -हनं, अवलेहः -हनं, जिह्वालेहनं, जिह्वास्वादः.—(Beating) ताडनं, आघातः, दण्डः, दण्डप्रहारः, वेत्राघातः.

LICORICE, *s.* यष्टिमधु *n.* -धुका, मधुयष्टिका, मधुकं, मधूली, क्लीतकं, यष्टिकः, तिक्तपर्व्वी *f.* (न्).

LICTOR, *s.* पूर्व्वकाले काष्ठखण्डयुक्तपरशुधारी धर्म्माध्यक्षपरिचरः.

LID, *s.* पिधानं, शरावः, शरवः, मुद्गः, आच्छादनं, छादनं, आवरणं, पटलं, छदः -दनं, पुटः -टी -टं, वर्द्धमानकः, उदश्वनं, कूर्म्मपृष्ठकं, कपाटः, मार्त्तिकः; 'opening of a lid,' शरावोद्घट्टनं; 'a box having a lid,' सपिधानं भाजनं, समुद्गं करण्डकं, सम्पुटकः; 'lid of the eye,' नेत्रच्छदः, नयनच्छदः, अक्षिपुटः, नेत्रकपाटः.

LIE, *s.* (Falsehood) अनृतं, असत्यं, वितथं, अतथ्यं, अलीकं, अनृतवाक्यं, मृषावाक्यं, मृषोक्तिः *f.*, मृषोद्यं, मिथ्योक्तिः *f.*, मिथ्यावादः, मृषावादः, मिथ्याभाषणं, असत्यवादः, असत्यभाषणं, अनृतोक्तिः *f.*, मिथ्यावचनं, असत्यवचनं, मृषाभिधानं.

To LIE, *v. n.* (Utter a falsehood) असत्यं or अनृतं वद् (c. 1. वदति -दितुं), अनृतवाक्यं वद्, मृषा or मिथ्या वद्, मिथ्यावादं कृ, मृषावादं कृ, मृषाभिधानं कृ.

To LIE, *v. n.* (Down to rest, lie horizontally) शी (c. 2. शेते, शयितुं), शयनं कृ, संविश् (c. 6. -विशति -वेष्टुं), उपविश्, पत् (c. 1. पतति -तितुं); 'he lies on the ground,' भूमौ शेते; 'he lies on the bed,' खट्वायां शेते; 'to lie down upon,' अधिशी with acc. c.; as, 'he lies down upon the couch,' शय्याम् अधिशेते.—(Lean, rest upon) अवलम्ब् (c. 1. -लम्बते -म्बितुं), समालम्ब्, संश्रि (c. 1. -श्रयति -ते -यितुं), समाश्रि, उपाश्रि, निली (c. 4. -लीयते -लेतुं), अवलम्बनं कृ.—(Remain, be situated, be) वृत् (c. 1. वर्त्तते -र्त्तितुं), स्था (c. 1. तिष्ठति, स्थातुं), आस् (c. 2. आस्ते, आसितुं); 'to lie near,' समीपस्थः -स्था -स्थं भू or अस्; 'to lie towards the east,' पूर्व्वदिश्यः -श्या -श्यं भू or अस्.—(Lie by, rest) विश्रम् (c. 4. -श्राम्यति -श्रमितुं), कार्य्याद् निवृत् (c. 1. -वर्त्तते -र्त्तितुं), कार्य्यविच्छेदं कृ.—(Lie in the way) रुध् (c. 7. रुणद्धि, रोद्धुं), अन्तरायो भू.—(Lie hard upon) पीड् (c. 10. पीडयति -यितुं), अभिपीड्, निपीड्.—(Lie in wait) गुप्ते or निभृते स्था.—(Lie up, keep in the house) गृहावस्थितः -ता -तं भू.—(Lie to, as a ship) रुद्धगतिः -तिः -ति भू.—(Lie on, be a matter of obligation). *See* INCUMBENT. (Lie in, be in childbed) प्राप्तप्रसवकाला भू, प्राप्तप्रसवावस्था भू.—(Lie with, carnally) सङ्गम् (c. 1. -गच्छति -गन्तुं), अभिगम्, सम्भोगं कृ.

LIEF, *adv.* कामं, प्रकामं, सकामं, कामतस्, इच्छातस्, यथेप्सितं.

LIEGE, *a.* (Bound to be loyal) भक्तः -क्ता -क्तं, भक्तिबद्धः -द्धा -द्धं, सेवाबद्धः &c., प्रभुभक्तः &c., स्वामिभक्तः &c., ईश्वराधीनः -ना -नं, ईश्वरायत्तः -त्ता -त्तं, प्रभुवशः -शा -शं.

LIEGE, *s.* (Lord) स्वामी *m.* (न्), प्रभुः *m.*, ईश्वरः, पतिः *m.*

LIEGE-MAN, *s.* (Vassal) भक्तः, सेवाबद्धः, प्रभुसेवी *m.* (न्).

LIENTERIC, *a.* आमातिसारी -रिणी -रि (न्), आमातिसारसम्बन्धी &c.

LIENTERY, *s.* आमातिसारः, अतिसारः, सारणः, आमरक्तः.

LIEU, *s.* स्थानं, भूमिः *f.*, स्थलं; 'in lieu of,' स्थाने, भूमौ, प्रति with abl. c., विनिमयात् -येन.

LIEUTENANCY, *s.* प्रतिनिधित्वं, सेनायां प्रतिनिधेः or प्रतिपुरुषस्य पदं or अवस्था or अधिकारः.

LIEUTENANT, *s.* सैन्याधिपतिप्रतिनिधिः *m.*, सैन्याध्यक्षप्रतिनिधिः *m.*, प्रतिनिधिः *m.*, प्रतिपुरुषः, नियोगी *m.* (न्); 'lord-lieutenant,' राजप्रतिनिधिः *m.*

LIFE, *s.* (Existence) जीवनं, जीवितं, जीवः -वा, प्राणनं, प्राणः, प्राणपरिग्रहः, सत्त्वं, सत्ता, जन्म *n.* (न्), जीवातुः *m.*, जीवथः, जीवदशा, उक्थं.—(Vitality, principle of life) प्राणः -णाः *m. pl.*, जीवात्मा *m.* (न्), आत्मा *m.*, जीवः -वितं, जीवित्वं, चेतना, चैतन्यं, प्राणवायुः *m.*, प्राणात्मा *m.*, भूतात्मा *m.*, पञ्चप्राणाः *m. pl.*—(Possession of breath) असुधारणं, प्राणधारणं, प्राणपरिग्रहः.—(Drawing breath) श्वासप्रश्वासं, श्वासनिःश्वासं, निश्वसनप्रश्वसनं; 'endowed with life,' जीवी -विनी -वि (न्), जीवभूतः -ता -तं, सजीवः -वा -वं, प्राणी -णिनी &c., प्राणभृत् *m. f. n.*, सचेतनः -ना -नं; 'giving life,' प्राणदः -दा -दं, प्राणप्रदः -दा -दं, जीवदः -दा -दं; 'destroying life,' प्राणहरः -रा -रं, प्राणहारी -रिणी &c., जीवितहारी &c., प्राणान्तिकः -की -कं; 'the giving or saving of life,' प्राणदानं, जीवदानं; 'abandonment of life,' जीवोत्सर्गः, प्राणत्यागः, प्राणोत्सर्गः, जीवितत्यागः, प्राणपरित्यागः, देहत्यागः, देहन्यासः; 'fear of losing life,' जीवितसंशयः; 'peril of life,' प्राणबाधः; 'love of life,' जीविताशा, जिजीविषा, प्राणिणिषा; 'wishing for life,' जिजीविषुः -षुः -षु, प्राणिणिषुः -षुः -षु; 'dread of life, impatience of life,' जीवनत्रासः, जीवनद्वेषः, मुमूर्षा; 'impatient of life,' मुमूर्षुः -र्षुः -र्षु; 'deprived of life,' हतप्राणः -णा -णं, हतजीवितः -ता -तं, नष्टप्राणः -णा -णं, नष्टजीवितः -ता -तं; 'support or maintenance of life,' प्राणयात्रा, प्राणधारणं, प्राणरक्षणं; 'reckless of life,' जीवितव्ययी -यिनी &c., प्राणव्ययी &c.; 'recklessness of life,' जीवितव्ययः; 'the end or object of life,' जीवनहेतुः *m.*; 'means of life,' जीवनोपायः; 'a happy life,' सुजीवितं.—(Age, duration of life, term of life) आयुस् *n.*, आयुः -यु *m. n.*, वयस् *n.*, परमायुस्, जीवितकालः, जन्म *n.* (न्), जन्मकालः, आयुःपरिमाणं, जीवपरिमाणं, आयुर्मर्य्यादा, कालविशेषावच्छिन्नं जीवनं; 'advanced in life,' गतायूः -यूः -यु (स्), प्रवयाः -याः -यः (स्); 'conferring long life,' आयुष्यः -ष्या -ष्यं, आयुष्करः -रा -री -रं; 'end of life,' आयुःशेषः; 'for life, during life, all one's life,' यावज्जीवं, जीवनपर्य्यन्तं, आमरणात्, यावज्जन्म, जन्मपर्य्यन्तं, यावद्देहं; 'in all one's life,' जन्मतः प्रभृति, जन्मत आरभ्य, जन्मारभ्यः, जन्मावधि, आजन्मतः, जन्मतः; 'lasting all one's life,' यावज्जीविकः -का -कं, आमरणान्तिकः -का -कं.—(Life in the world, the present life) इहलोकवासः, इहलोकवर्त्तनं, भूलोकवासः, इहकालः, इहजन्म *n.* (न्), संसारः, संसरणं, संसृतिः *f.*, गुणत्रयाभ्यासः; 'active or secular life,' प्रवृत्तिः *f.*, प्रवृत्तिमार्गः, संसारमार्गः, लोकव्यवहारः, प्रवर्त्तनं; 'retired life,' निवृत्तिः *f.*, निवृत्तिमार्गः; 'engaging in public life,' लोकव्यवहारप्रवृत्तिः *f.*; 'in this life,' इह, इहकाले, इहलोके; 'the vicissitudes of life,' संसारचक्रं, कालचक्रं, कालावृत्तिः *f.*—(Conduct, manner of living) वृत्तिः *f.*, व्यवहारः, आचारः, आचरणं, रीतिः *f.*, स्थितिः *f.*, चेष्टितं, चर्य्या, प्रवृत्तिः *f.*, स्थितिः *f.*; 'virtuous life,' धर्म्माचरणं.—(Vivacity) तेजस् *n.*, रसः, रसिकत्वं, तीक्ष्णता, सत्त्वं, वीर्य्यं.—(Narrative of a life, memoir) चरित्रं, चरितं, चरित्ररचना, चरिताख्यानं, आख्यानं.—(State, condition) अवस्था, दशा, भावः, स्थितिः *f.*, वृत्तिः *f.*, गतिः *f.*; 'the two states of life,' अवस्थाद्वयं;

these are 'happiness,' सुखावस्था, सुखदशा and 'misery,' दुःखावस्था, दुःखदशा; 'the three states of life,' अवस्थात्रयं; these are 'waking state,' जाग्रदवस्था; 'dreaming state,' स्वप्नावस्था and 'state of sound sleep,' सुषुप्त्यवस्था.

LIFE-GIVING, *a.* जीवदः -दा -दं, जीवदायकः -का -कं, जीवदाता -त्री -तृ (तृ), तेजस्करः -री -रं, तेजोवर्धकः -का -कं, वीर्यदः -दा -दं.

LIFE-GUARD, *s.* राजशरीररक्षकः, राजदेहरक्षी *m.* (न्), राजपरिचरः, राजपरिधिस्थः.

LIFELESS, *a.* निर्जीवः -वा -वं, अजीवः -वा -वं, अप्राणी -णिनी -णि (न्), प्राणहीनः -ना -नं, गतप्राणः -णा -णं, नष्टप्राणः -णा -णं, निःप्राणः -णा -णं, प्राणरहितः -ता -तं, प्राणविरहितः -ता -तं, अचेतनः -ना -नं, विचेतनः -ना -नं, चैतन्यरहितः -ता -तं, असुः -सुः -सु, गतासुः -सुः -सु, अचेष्टः -ष्टा -ष्टं.—(Spiritless) निस्तेजाः -जाः -जः (स्), तेजोहीनः -ना -नं, विरसः -सा -सं, रसहीनः -ना -नं, निस्सत्त्वः -त्त्वा -त्त्वं, सत्त्वहीनः -ना -नं.

LIFETIME, *s.* जीवितकालः, आयुस् *n.*, वयस् *n.*, जन्मकालः, आयुष्यं; 'during life-time,' यावज्जीवं, जीवपर्य्यन्तं, जन्मपर्य्यन्तं.

To LIFT, *v. a.* (Raise) उत्तुल् (c. 10. -तोलयति -यितुं), उच्छ्रि (c. 1. उच्छ्रयति -यितुं, rt. श्रि), समुच्छ्रि, प्रोच्छ्रि, उन्नम् (c. 10. -नमयति -यितुं), उद्यम् (c. 1. -यच्छति -यन्तुं), उत्था in caus. (-थापयति -यितुं, rt. स्था), उत्क्षिप् (c. 6. -क्षिपति -क्षेप्तुं), समुत्क्षिप्, उद्धन् (c. 2. -हन्ति -न्तुं), उन्नी (c. 1. -नयति -नेतुं), उत्कृष् (c. 1. -कर्षति -क्रष्टुं), उद्धृ (c. 1. -हरति -हर्तुं), उद्वृह् (c. 6. -वृहति -वर्हितुं), उत्तोलनं कृ, ऊर्ध्वीकृ.—(Raise in rank) पदवृद्धिं कृ, उत्कृष्टपदे प्रतिपद् (c. 10. -पादयति -यितुं), संवृध् (c. 10. -वर्धयति -यितुं), प्रतिपत्तिं कृ or दा.—(Fill with pride or joy) दृप् (c. 10. दर्पयति -यितुं), उल्लस् (c. 10. -लासयति -यितुं), उन्नतं -तां कृ; 'to be lifted up with pride,' दृप् (c. 4. दृप्यति, दर्प्तुं), उन्नतीभू, उन्नतचित्तः -त्ता -त्तं भू.

LIFT, *s.* उत्तोलनं, उत्थापनं, उन्नमनं, उद्यामः, उन्नयनं, उच्छ्रयः, समुच्छ्रयः, उत्कर्षः.—(Help) साहाय्यं, उपकारः, उपकृतं.

LIFTED, *p. p.* उत्तोलितः -ता -तं, उत्थापितः -ता -तं, उच्छ्रितः -ता -तं, समुच्छ्रितः -ता -तं, उन्नतः -ता -तं, उद्यतः -ता -तं, उद्धृतः -ता -तं, समुद्धृतः -ता -तं, उद्धतः -ता -तं, उत्कर्षितः -ता -तं, उद्बर्हितः -ता -तं, उत्क्षिप्तः -प्ता -प्तं, उद्वाहितः -ता -तं; 'having the hands lifted up,' अभ्युच्छ्रितपाणिः -णिः -णि, उत्थितहस्तः -स्ता -स्तं; 'having his weapon lifted up,' उद्यतायुधः -धा -धं; 'having the arms lifted up,' ऊर्ध्वबाहुः -हुः -हु.

LIGAMENT, *s.* (Any thing that unites or ties) बन्धनं, बन्धः, योक्त्रं, सेतुः, सन्दानं, पाशः, निगडः, शृङ्खला -लं, चारः, प्रसितिः *f.*—(In anatomy) सन्धिबन्धनं, सन्धिबन्धः, ग्रन्थिबन्धनं, अस्थिबन्धनं.

LIGATURE, *s.* बन्धः -न्धनं, पट्टः, पट्टकः, आवेष्टनं, परिवेष्टनं, वेष्टनं, रज्जुः *m.f.*, कवलिका.

LIGHT, *s.* द्युतिः *f.*, दीप्तिः *f.*, तेजस्, ज्योतिस् *n.*, ज्योतिः *f.*, प्रभा, प्रकाशः, आभा, छविः *f.*, आलोकः, रुचिः *f.*, रुच् *f.* (च्), कान्तिः *f.*, छटा, निभा, भा, भास् *f.*, निभा, छाया, त्विषा, त्विट् *f.* (ष्), शोचिस् *n.*, शोभा, वर्चस् *n.*, महस् *n.*, द्योतः, दृशानं, मरीचिः *m.f.*, ज्वलिका; 'light of the moon or stars,' ज्योत्स्ना, कौमुदी, दीपिका; 'shining by its own light,' स्वप्रकाशः -शा -शं, स्वयंज्योतिः -तिः -ति; 'day-light,' सूर्य्यप्रकाशः, सूर्य्यरश्मिः *m.*, दिनालोकः.—(Any thing that gives light, candle) दीपः -पकः, प्रदीपः, दीपिका.—(Knowledge) ज्ञानं, बोधः, अवगमः, प्रकाशः.—(Public notice) प्रकाशः, प्रकाशता, प्राकट्यं, प्रसिद्धिः *f.*, लोकप्रसिद्धिः *f.*, लौकिकं, प्रख्यातिः *f.*

—(Light of a picture) प्रकाशितचित्रांशः, चित्रस्य प्रकाशितभागः, चित्रस्यं प्रकाशितस्थलं.—(Point of view) दृष्टिः *f.*, लक्ष्यं, दृष्टिसूत्रं, दृष्टिपातमार्गः, दृष्टिपातसूत्रं, लक्ष्यसूत्रं; 'to throw light upon,' प्रकाश् (c. 10. -काशयति -यितुं), विकाश्; 'throwing light upon,' प्रकाशकः -का -कं; 'to bring to light,' प्रकटीकृ, प्रकाशीकृ, स्पष्टीकृ, आविष्कृ, प्रादुष्कृ, विवृ (c. 5. -वृणोति -वरितुं -रीतुं); 'to come to light,' आविर्भू, प्रादुर्भू, प्रकाशीभू, प्रसिद्धिं गम् (c. 1. गच्छति, गन्तुं). In scientific treatises 'light' is called प्रकाशः.

LIGHT, *a.* (Having little weight) लघुः -घुः -घ्वी -घु, अगुरुः -रुः -र्वी -रु, अल्पभारः -रा -रं, लघुभारः -रा -रं, अल्पप्रमाणः -णा -णं, लघुप्रमाणः -णा -णं, गौरवहीनः -ना -नं, सुवहः -हा -हं, सुवाह्यः -ह्या -ह्यं, सुखवाह्यः -ह्या -ह्यं.—(Not oppressive, easy to be endured) लघुः -घ्वी -घु, सुसहः -हा -हं, सुसहनीयः -या -यं, अक्लेशकः -का -कं, अल्पक्लेशकरः -री -रं; 'very light,' लघिष्ठः -ष्ठा -ष्ठं.—(Easy) सुखः -खा -खं, सुकरः -रा -री -रं, निरायासः -सा -सं, सुगमः -मा -मं, अकष्टः -ष्टा -ष्टं, अकठिनः -ना -नं, अविषमः -मा -मं, सुसाध्यः -ध्या -ध्यं, लघुः &c.—(Easy of digestion) सुपाच्यः -च्या -च्यं, सुपचनीयः -या -यं, सुपचः -चा -चं, सुखपथ्यः -थ्या -थ्यं.—(Active, nimble) चपलः -ला -लं, लघुशरीरः -रा -रं, लघुगतिः -तिः -ति.—(Not dense) अस्थूलः -ला -लं, अघनः -ना -नं, शिथिलावयवः -वा -वं, विरलावयवः -वा -वं.—(Not steady, gay, airy) लघुचित्तः -त्ता -त्तं, लघुचेताः -ताः -तः (स्), लघुस्वभावः -वा -वं, चञ्चलः -ला -लं, चपलः -ला -लं, प्रकृतितरलः -ला -लं, अस्थिरः -रा -रं, लोलः -ला -लं, अनवस्थः -स्था -स्थं, गौरवहीनः -ना -नं, गाम्भीर्य्यहीनः -ना -नं.—(Trivial, inconsiderable) लघुः &c., लघुप्रभावः -वा -वं, अल्पप्रभावः &c., लघ्वर्थः -र्था -र्थं, अल्पार्थः -र्था -र्थं, तुच्छः -च्छा -च्छं, अगण्यः -ण्या -ण्यं, तृणप्रायः -या -यं.—(Light in color) पाण्डुः -ण्डुः -ण्डु, श्वेतः -ता -तं or expressed by ईषत्, आ prefixed; 'light red,' श्वेतरक्तः -क्ता -क्तं, ईषद्रक्तः -क्ता -क्तं; 'light blue,' आनीलः -ला -लं; 'light brown,' श्वेतपिङ्गः -ङ्गा -ङ्गं; 'light blue,' श्वेतनीलः -ला -लं.—(Bright, not dark) दीप्तिमान् -मती -मत् (त्), द्युतिमान् &c., प्रभावान् &c., दीप्रः -प्रा -प्रं, सप्रकाशः -शा -शं, प्रकाशमयः -यी -यं, तेजोमयः &c., तैजसः -सी -सं, प्रकाशयुक्तः -क्ता -क्तं, रुचिरः -रा -रं, शोभनः -ना -नं; 'the light half of the month when the moon increases,' शुक्लः, शुक्लपक्षः, शुद्धपक्षः.—(To make light of) लघूकृ, तुच्छीकृ, तृणाय मन् (c. 4. मन्यते, मन्तुं).

LIGHT, *adv.* लघु, लाघवेन, सलाघवं, अगुरु, लघु prefixed in comp.

To LIGHT, *v. a.* (Make light, illuminate) प्रकाश् (c. 10. -काशयति -यितुं), विकाश्, द्युत् (c. 10. द्योतयति -यितुं), प्रद्युत्, विद्युत्, दीप् (c. 10. दीपयति -यितुं), उद्दीप्, प्रदीप्, विदीप्, प्रकाशितं -तां कृ, द्योतितं -तां कृ, सप्रकाशं -शां कृ.—(Give light) प्रकाशं दा, प्रकाशनं कृ, द्योतनं कृ, तेजः कृ or दा.—(Kindle, set on fire) ज्वल् (c. 10. ज्वलयति, ज्वालयति -यितुं), प्रज्वल्, उज्ज्वल्, संज्वल्, समिन्ध् (c. 7. -इन्द्धे -इन्धितुं), सन्धुक्ष् (c. 10. -धुक्षयति -यितुं), तप् (c. 10. तापयति -यितुं), सन्तप्, दीप्, प्रदीप्, उद्दीप्, आदीप्.

To LIGHT, *v. n.* (Fall on) आपत् (c. 1. -पतति -तितुं), निपत्, आसद् (c. 10. -सादयति -यितुं), अकस्माद् आसद् or उपस्था (c. 1. -तिष्ठति -स्थातुं) or आगम् (c. 1. -गच्छति -गन्तुं) or उपागम्.—(Descend) अवरुह् (c. 1. -रोहति -रोढुं), अवतॄ (c. 1. -तरति -रितुं -रीतुं), अवया (c. 2. -याति -तुं), अधो गम्, अवपत्.—(Settle, rest upon) अध्यास् (c. 2. -आस्ते -आसितुं), निली (c. 4. -लीयते -लेतुं), निषद् (c. 1. -षी-

इति -मन्थुं), अधिवस् (c. 1. -वसति -वस्तुं), अवस्था, संस्था, सङ्गीनं कृ. —(Kindle) समिन्ध् in pass. (-इध्यते), ज्वल् (c. 1. ज्वलति -लितुं).

Light-armed, *a.* लघ्वायुधः -धा -धं, लघुशस्त्री -स्त्रिणी -स्त्रि (न्), लघ्वस्त्रधारी -रिणी -रि, लघुशस्त्रभृत् *m. f. n.*

Lighted, *p. p.* इद्धः -द्धा -द्धं, समिद्धः -द्धा -द्धं, ज्वलितः -ता -तं, सन्तप्तः -प्ता -प्तं, सन्धुक्षितः -ता -तं, प्रज्वालितः -ता -तं.—(Lighted up, illuminated) प्रकाशितः -ता -तं, विकाशितः -ता -तं, द्योतितः -ता -तं, प्रद्योतितः -ता -तं, उद्द्योतितः -ता -तं, उद्दीपितः -ता -तं, भासितः -ता -तं, विभासितः -ता -तं, उद्भासितः -ता -तं, उज्ज्वलितः -ता -तं.

To lighten, *v. n.* (Flash, as lightning) स्फुर् (c. 6. स्फुरति -रितुं), विद्युत् (c. 1. -द्योतते -तितुं), अकस्मात् प्रकाश् (c. 1. -काशते -शितुं) or ज्वल् (c. 1. ज्वलति -लितुं) or उज्ज्वल्, विद्युद्वत् कम्प् (c. 1. कम्पते -म्पितुं).

To lighten, *v. a.* (Make bright) प्रकाश् (c. 10. -काशयति -यितुं), विकाश्, द्युत् (c. 10. द्योतयति -यितुं), दीप् (c. 10. दीपयति -यितुं), विदीप्. —(Make less heavy) लघूकृ, लघ (nom. लघयति -यितुं), न्यूनभारं -रां -रं कृ, अल्पभारीकृ, भारन्यूनतां कृ.—(Alleviate) शम् (c. 10. शमयति -यितुं), प्रशम्, उपशम्, लघूकृ.

Lightened, *p. p.* (Made less heavy) लघूकृतः -ता -तं, न्यूनभारः -रा -रं, शमितः -ता -तं, प्रशमितः -ता -तं.

Lighter, *s.* (More light) लघुतरः -रा -रं, लघीयान् -यसी -यः (स्), न्यूनभारः -रा -रं.—(One that lights or kindles) प्रकाशकः, प्रकाशदः, दीपकः, उद्दीपकः, द्युतिदः, द्युतिकरः, अग्निदः.—(Large, flat-bottomed boat) तरालुः *m.*, तरान्धुः *m.*, तरणिः -णी *f.*, वहित्रं, उडुपः -पं.

Lighterman, *s.* नाविकः, पोतवाहः, तरिकः, पूर्वोक्तनौकाकर्णधारः.

Light-fingered, *a.* लघुहस्तः -स्ता -स्तं, चपलहस्तः &c., पाणिचपलः -ला -लं.

Light-footed, *a.* लघुपादः -दा -दं, लघुगतिः -तिः -ति, द्रुतगतिः -तिः -ति.

Light-headed, *a.* (Delirious) रोगोपहतज्ञानः -ना -नं, रोगोपहतत्वाद् भ्रान्तचित्तः -त्ता -त्तं or भ्रान्तबुद्धिः -द्धिः -द्धि or विक्षिप्तबुद्धिः -द्धिः -द्धि or क्षिप्तचित्तः &c., बुद्धिविभ्रमात् प्रलापकारी -रिणी &c.—(Thoughtless, volatile) चपलचित्तः &c., लघुचित्तः &c.

Light-headedness, *s.* चित्तविभ्रमः, ज्ञानभ्रान्तिः *f.*, बुद्धिभ्रान्तिः, बुद्धिविप्लवः.

Light-hearted, *a.* लघुचित्तः -त्ता -त्तं, लघुचेताः -ताः -तः (स्), हृष्टचित्तः &c., हृष्टहृदयः -या -यं, हृष्टमानसः -सी -सं, उल्लसः -सा -सं, आनन्दी -न्दिनी -न्दि (न्), सुमनस्कः -स्का -स्कं.

Light-house, *s.* दीपस्तम्भः, दीपगृहं, आकाशदीपः, समुद्रयायिनां पथदर्शनार्थम् उन्नतभूभागे निर्म्मितं दीपगृहं.

Lighting, *part.* प्रकाशयन् -यन्ती -यत् (त्), उद्भासयन् -यन्ती -यत् (त्), द्योतयमानः -ना -नं, उद्दीपकः -का -कं, प्रदीपकः -का -कं—(Resting on) निषण्णः -ण्णा -ण्णं, निलीयमानः -ना -नं, सन्निविशमानः -ना -नं.

Lightless, *a.* निष्प्रभः -भा -भं, अप्रकाशः -शा -शं, निरालोकः -का -कं.

Lightly, *adv.* (With little weight) लघु, लाघवेन, सलाघवं, अगुरु, अल्पभारेण, अल्पप्रमाणेन.—(Easily) सुखेन, अनायासेन, अकष्टेन, अक्लेशेन, अयत्नेन.—(Without reason) हेतुना विना, कारणेन विना. —(Nimbly) लघुगत्या, चपलं.—(With levity) लघुचेतसा, चञ्चलं, चञ्चलवत्, अस्थिरं; 'to think lightly of,' लघूकृ, तुच्छीकृ.

Lightness, *s.* (Want of weight) लघुता -त्वं, लाघवं, लघिमा *m.* (न्), अगुरुता, गौरवहीनता, भारलघुता, भारहीनता, अल्पभारत्वं, भाराभावः, सुवाह्यता, भाररहित्यं.—(Easiness) सुखत्वं, अनायासः, निरायासत्वं, सुकरत्वं, सुसाध्यता, लघुता, सुगमत्वं, अकष्टत्वं, अकाठिन्यं.—(State of being easy to be borne) लघुता, सुसह्यता, सुसहनीयता.—(Nimbleness) शरीरलघुता, लघुशरीरत्वं, लघुगतित्वं, द्रुतत्वं.—(Levity) चञ्चलत्वं, चाञ्चल्यं, चपलता, चापल्यं, लोलता, लौल्यं, अस्थिरता, अस्थैर्य्यं, अनवस्थितिः *f.*, अगुरुता, अगौरवं.—(Trivialness) लघुता, लाघवं, लघ्वर्थता, अल्पप्रभावत्वं, तुच्छता; 'lightness of hand,' हस्तलाघवं, हस्तचापल्यं.

Lightning, *s.* विद्युत् *f.*, तडित् *f.*, सौदामिनी, सौदाम्नी, सौदामनी, मेघज्योतिस् *n.*, मेघवह्निः *m.*, मेघदीपः, घनज्वाला, क्षणप्रभा, अचिरप्रभा, क्षणद्युतिः *f.*, ह्रादिनी, ह्रदिनी, शतह्रदा, शम्पा, सम्पा, चपला, चञ्चला, क्षणिका, आकालिकी, चला, ऐरावती, छटाभा, रोहिणी, अशुभा, अशुभा, वज्रस्फुलिङ्गः -ङ्गं, घनवल्लिका, धीपा, महोल्का, अग्निभीः *m.*, चटुला, रुक् *f.* (च), नीलाञ्जना; 'forked lightning,' विद्युल्लता, तडिल्लता, क्षौत्रं; 'flash of lightning,' विद्युत्प्रकाशः, विद्युत्स्फुरणं, सौदामिनीस्फुरणं, विद्युत्कम्पः, विद्युद्दाम *n.* (न्), विद्युज्ज्वाला; 'the falling of lightning,' विद्युत्पातः; 'struck by lightning,' उपहतः -ता -तं, विद्युत्पातोपहतः &c.; 'relating to lightning,' वैद्युतः -ती -तं.

Lights, *s. pl.* पुस्फुसः, पुप्फुसः, फुप्फुसः, रक्तफेनजः.

Lightsome, *a.* (Not dark, luminous) दीप्तिमान् -मती -मत् (त्), तेजोमयः -यी -यं, सप्रकाशः -शा -शं, प्रकाशमयः -यी -यं, सुप्रकाशः -शा -शं, तेजस्वी -स्विनी -स्वि (न्), प्रभावान् &c., सुप्रभः -भा -भं.—(Cheerful, gay) उल्लसः -सा -सं, हृष्टः -ष्टा -ष्टं, प्रहृष्टः -ष्टा -ष्टं, सानन्दः -न्दा -न्दं, आनन्दी -न्दिनी &c., आनन्ददः -दा -दं, हर्षदः -दा -दं.

Lightsomeness, *s.* (Brightness) सप्रकाशता, दीप्तिमत्त्वं, दीप्तता.—(Cheerfulness) उल्लसता, उल्लासः, सानन्दता, हृष्टता, प्रहर्षः

Light-spirited, *a.* लघुहृदयः -या -यं, हृष्टहृदयः -या -यं, हृष्टचित्तः -त्ता -त्तं.

Ligneous, *a.* काष्ठी -ष्ठिनी -ष्ठि (न्), काष्ठमयः -यी -यं, दारुमयः &c., दारवः -वी -वं, काष्ठरूपः -पा -पं, दारुरूपः -पा -पं, काष्ठघटितः -ता -तं.

Ligniferous, *a.* काष्ठदः -दा -दं, काष्ठदायकः -का -कं, काष्ठोत्पादकः -का -कं.

Ligniform, *a.* काष्ठरूपः -पा -पं, काष्ठाकारः -रा -रं, काष्ठाकृतिः -तिः -ति.

To lignify, *v. a.* काष्ठसात्कृ, दारुसात्कृ, काष्ठरूपीकृ, दारुरूपीकृ.

Like, *a.* (Resembling) सदृशः -शी -शं, सदृक्षः -क्षा -क्षं, सदृक् *m. f. n.* (श्), तुल्यः -ल्या -ल्यं, समः -मा -मं, समीपः -पा -पं, समानः -ना -नं, सन्निभः -भा -भं, अनुकारी -रिणी -रि (न्), निर्विशेषः -षा -षं, प्रातिभासिकः -की -कं. The following can only be used in comp. at the end of a word उपमः -मा -मं, निभः -भा -भं, प्रतिमः -मा -मं, उपमितः -ता -तं, प्रख्यः -ख्या -ख्यं, सङ्काशः -शा -शं, रूपः -पा -पं, विधः -धा -धं, नीकाशः -शा -शं, निकाशः -सा -सं, प्रतीकाशः &c., प्रतिकाशः &c., प्रतिकासः &c., प्रतीकासः &c., भूतः -ता -तं; 'like the moon,' चन्द्रनिभः -भा -भं, चन्द्रोपमः -मा -मं; 'like, but with a degree of inferiority,' कल्पः -ल्पा -ल्पं. The propositions स and अनु are often used indifferently with सम, समान, and तुल्य to express 'like'; as, 'of like form,' सरूपः -पा -पी -पं, अनुरूपः -पा -पं, समरूपः -पा -पं, तुल्यरूपः &c., तुल्याकृतिः -तिः -ति, तुल्याकारः -रा -रं; 'of like properties or qualities,' सगुणः -णा -णं, अनुगुणः -णा -णं, समगुणः -णा -णं, तुल्यगुणः &c., समानगुणः &c., सधर्म्मा -र्म्मा -र्म्म (न्), अनुधर्म्मा &c., समानधर्म्मा &c., समभावः -वी -वं; 'of like tribe, class, or kind,' सजातिः -तिः -ति, सजातीयः -या -यं, समानजातिः &c., समानजातीयः &c., सवर्णः -र्णा -र्णं, तुल्यवर्णः &c., सविधः -धा -धं, सवर्गः -र्गा -र्गं, सवर्गीणः -णा -णं, सवर्गीयः -या -यं; 'like this or that,' ईदृशः -शी -शं, ईदृक् *m. f. n.* (श्), ईदृक्षः -क्षा -क्षं, एतादृशः &c., एतादृक् &c., एतादृक्षः &c., तादृशः &c.,

तादृक् &c., तादृक्षः &c.; 'like what?' कीदृशः &c., कीदृक् &c., कीदृक्षः &c.; 'like which,' यादृशः &c., यादृक् &c., यादृक्षः &c.; 'like me,' मादृशः &c., मादृक् &c., मादृक्षः &c.; 'like thee,' त्वादृशः &c., त्वादृक् &c., त्वादृक्षः &c.; 'like your honor,' भवादृशः &c., भवादृक् &c., भवादृक्षः &c. 'To be like,' अनुकृ, सदृशः -शी -शं भू, तुल्यः -ल्या -ल्यं भू, सदृशीभू, तुल्यीभू. The following examples illustrate the use and construction of some of the above words. 'The son is very like the father,' पुत्रो बहुधा पितुर् अनुकरोति or पुत्रः पितृरूपो भवति; 'like another son,' पुत्रनिर्विशेषः -षा -षं; 'there never has been, nor ever will be, any one like him,' अनेन सदृशो न भूतो न भविष्यति; 'there is nobody like him,' तेन सदृशः कश्चिदपि नास्ति or न तस्य तुल्यः कश्चन or न कोपि तस्य समः; 'like the sun,' आदित्यसदृशः -शी -शं, आदित्येन तुल्यः &c.; 'a crime like that of Brahmanicide,' ब्रह्महत्यासमं पापं; 'like me,' मम समः or मम तुल्यः or मम अनुरूपः or मद्रूपः &c. or मद्विधः -धा -धं. —(Probable) सत्यसङ्काशः -शा -शं, सम्भाव्यः -व्या -व्यं.

LIKE, *s.* (Match, equal) तुल्यः -ल्या, तुल्यगुणः -णा, सदृशः -शी, तुल्यरूपः -पी, समानगुणः -णा, यमकः -का, युग्मकः -का; 'his like will never be again,' अनेन सदृशो न कदाचिद् भविष्यति.—(Likes and dislikes) प्रियाप्रियाणि *n. pl.*, प्रियाप्रियं.

LIKE, *adv.* (In the same manner) वत् affixed, इव, यथा, तथा, निर्विशेषं -षेण; 'like a dream,' स्वप्नवत्; 'like the moon,' चन्द्रवत्, चन्द्र इव, चन्द्रो यथा; 'cherished like another son,' पुत्रनिर्विशेषं पालितः; 'like king, like people,' यथा राजा तथा प्रजा; 'in like manner,' तथैव, तद्वत्, तथा, एवं, एवम्प्रकारेण, तथाविधेन, एवंविधेन, एवमेव; 'to act like,' अनुकृ.

To LIKE, *v. a.* (Approve of, be pleased with) रुच् (c. 1. रोचते -चितुं) used impersonally, रुच् (c. 10. रोचयति -यितुं), अनुरुच्, अभिरुच्, अभिमन् (c. 4. -मन्यते -मन्तुं), अनुमन्, सम्मन्, मन्, अभिनन्द् (c. 1. -नन्दति -ते -न्दितुं), प्रतिनन्द्, नन्द्, अनुमुद् (c. 1. -मोदते -दितुं), अनुरुध् (c. 4. -रुध्यते -ति -रोद्धुं), प्रशंस् (c. 1. शंसति -सितुं), प्री (c. 4. प्रीयते), जुष् (c. 6. जुषते, जोषितुं), तुष् (c. 4. तुष्यति, तोष्टुं), सन्तुष्, परितुष्, दय् (c. 1. दयते -यितुं), अनुरञ्ज् (c. 4. -रज्यते), स्निह् (c. 4. स्निह्यति, स्नेहितुं), प्रियः -या -यं भू or अस्, अभिमतः -ता -तं भू, इष्टः -ष्टा -ष्टं भू, प्रीतः -ता -तं भू, दयितः -ता -तं भू. OBS. Since some of the above verbs have a neuter sense, and some of these again are susceptible of an active sense if used in other forms, the construction of the sentence must vary accordingly; thus, 'I like that,' तद् मह्यं or मम रोचते or अहं तद् रोचयामि or तद् मया प्रशस्यते or अहं तद् अनुमन्ये or तद् मया अनुमतं or तद् मम अभिमतं; 'he does not like the gift,' दत्तं नाभिनन्दति or दत्तेन न तुष्यति; 'they like their king,' स्वराजानम् अनुरुध्यन्ते; 'he likes his brother's wife,' भ्रातुर् भार्य्यायाम् अनुरज्यते; 'women like everybody,' सर्व्वे स्त्रीणां प्रियाः.

To LIKE, *v. n.* रुच् (c. 1. रोचते -चितुं), इष् (c. 6. इच्छति, एषितुं), अभिलष् (c. 1. -लषति, c. 4. -लष्यति -षितुं); 'as you like,' यथा भवते रोचते, यथाकामं; 'doing what one likes,' कामकारी -रिणी -रि (न्), कामचारः -रा -रं; 'going where one likes,' कामगामी -मिनी &c.; 'eating what one likes,' कामभक्षः -क्षा -क्षं; 'taking what form one likes,' कामरूपः -पा -पं.

LIKED, *p. p.* अभिमतः -ता -तं, अनुमतः -ता -तं, यथाभिमतः -ता -तं, अनुमोदितः -ता -तं, प्रियः -या -यं, प्रीतः -ता -तं, इष्टः -ष्टा -ष्टं, मनोनीतः -ता -तं, दयितः -ता -तं, अनुरक्तः -क्ता -क्तं, मतः -ता -तं.

LIKELIHOOD, LIKELINESS, *s.* सम्भाव्यता -त्वं, सम्भावनीयता, योग्यता -त्वं, सम्भावना, सम्भवः, अभ्युपगम्यता, अभ्युपगमः, अनुमेयता -त्वं, सत्यसादृश्यं, सत्यसङ्काशत्वं -ता, आभासः.

LIKELY, *a.* सम्भाव्यः -व्या -व्यं, सम्भावनीयः -या -यं, सम्भावितः -ता -तं, योग्यः -ग्या -ग्यं, सत्यसङ्काशः -शा -शं, सत्यसन्निभः -भा -भं, सत्यसदृशः -शी -शं, अनुमेयः -या -यं, अभ्युपगम्यः -म्या -म्यं; 'it is likely,' युज्यते, उपपद्यते.

LIKELY, *adv.* सम्भावनीयं, यथायोग्यं, यथासम्भवं, प्रायस्, प्रायशस्.

LIKEMINDED, *a.* समानशीलः -ला -लं, समस्वभावः -वा -वं, समभावः -वा -वं.

To LIKEN, *v. a.* उपमा (c. 2. -माति, c. 3. -मिमीते -मातुं), सदृशीकृ, समीकृ, तुल्यीकृ, समानीकृ, समान (nom. समानयति -यितुं); 'to whom shall I liken him,' केन तम् उपमास्यामि.

LIKENED, *p. p.* उपमितः -ता -तं, उपमेतः -ता -तं, समीकृतः -ता -तं.

LIKENESS, *s.* (Resemblance) सादृश्यं, सदृशता -त्वं, सारूप्यं, सरूपता, समरूपता, अनुरूपता, आनुरूप्यं, समता, साम्यं, समानता, तुल्यता -त्वं, तुला, तौल्यं, औपम्यं, उपमा, उपमानं -नता, उपमितिः *f.*, प्रतिमानं -नता, प्रतिमता, आनुगुण्यं, अनुकारः, अनुहारः, सानुधर्म्यं, रूपसमता, स्वभावसमता.—(Form, appearance) आकृतिः *f.*, आकारः, रूपं, मूर्त्तिः *f.*, संस्कारः.—(A picture or image resembling a person or thing) उपमा, उपमितिः *f.*, उपमानं, प्रतिमा, प्रतिमानं, प्रतिरूपं -पकं, प्रतिकृतिः *f.*, प्रतिमूर्त्तिः *f.*, प्रतिकायः, प्रतिनिधिः *m.*, प्रतिच्छन्दः, प्रतियातना, प्रतिबिम्बं, चित्रं, आकृतिः *f.*; 'a speaking likeness,' आकृतिः संवादिनी.

LIKEWISE, *adv.* (In like manner) तथा, तथैव, तद्वत्, एवं, एवमेव.—(Moreover) अपिच, अपरञ्च, किञ्च, चैव, तथा, एवं.

LIKING, *s.* (Fondness for, delight in, pleasure) रुचिः *f.*, अभिरुचिः *f.*, सन्तोषः, तोषः, तुष्टिः *f.*, सन्तुष्टिः *f.*, परितोषः, अनुरागः, अनुरक्तिः *f.*, अभिमतता, अनुमतिः *f.*, अनुमोदनं, इच्छा, अभिलाषः, अभिलषितं, प्रियता, प्रीतिः *f.*, छन्दं, छन्दस् *n.*; 'that husband was not to her liking,' स भर्त्ता तस्याः सन्तोषाय नाभवत्; 'likings and dislikings,' प्रियाप्रियाणि.—(State of body) शरीरस्थितिः *f.*, देहस्थितिः *f.*, शरीरभावः.

LILAC, *s.* लैलकाख्यः पारसीकदेशीयो गुल्मप्रभेदः.

LILY, *s.* पद्मः -द्मं, पद्मिनी, उत्पलं, कमलं, कुमुदं, नलिनं, पङ्कजं, कुवलयं, इन्दीवरं, सौगन्धिकं, अब्जं, नीलाम्बुजन्म *n.* (न्), रक्तसन्ध्यकं, हल्लकं, कैरवं. These names properly apply to the water lily. *See* LOTUS.

LIMATION, *s.* लोहमार्जनेन घर्षणं or परिष्कारः or परिष्करणं, मार्जनं.

LIMATURE, *s.* (Filings) लोहचूर्णं, कृष्णचूर्णं, लोहजं, लोहकिट्टं.

LIMB, *s.* अङ्गं, अवयवः, गात्रं, अपघनः, प्रतीकः; 'limb by limb,' अवयवशस्, गात्रं गात्रं; 'over every limb,' सर्व्वाङ्गीणः -णा -णं, प्रत्यङ्गं; 'having large limbs,' बृहदङ्गः -ङ्गी -ङ्गं; 'kneading of the limbs,' गात्रसंवाहः -हनं, अङ्गमर्द्दनं.—(Edge, border) कोटिः *f.*, प्रान्तः, सीमा.

To LIMB, *v. a.* अङ्गात् अङ्गम् अवछिद् (c. 7. -छिनत्ति -छेत्तुं), अवयवशो निकृत् (c. 6. -कृन्तति -कर्त्तितुं), गात्राणि पृथक्कृ, व्यङ्गीकृ.

LIMBED, *a.* अङ्गी -ङ्गिनी -ङ्गि (न्), साङ्गः -ङ्गा -ङ्गं, अवयवी -विनी -वि (न्), सावयवः -वा -वं; 'large-limbed,' बृहदङ्गः -ङ्गी -ङ्गं, बृहदवयवः -वा -वं, महाङ्गः -ङ्गा -ङ्गं; 'slender-limbed,' कृशाङ्गः -ङ्गी -ङ्गं.

श्रीणाङ्गः &c., तन्वङ्गः &c.

Limber, *a.* (Flexible) मृदुः -दुः -द्वी -दु, शिथिलः -ला -लं, कोमलः -ला -लं, अदृढः -ढा -ढं, आनम्यः -म्या -म्यं, नम्यः -म्या -म्यं, आनम्यः -म्या -म्यं.

Limber, *s.* (Of a cannon) युद्धयन्त्रवाहनं, युद्धयन्त्रधुरा.

Limberness, *s.* शैथिल्यं, शिथिलता -त्वं, मृदुता, कोमलता, नम्यता.

Limbless, *a.* निरवयवः -वा -वं, अनङ्गः -ङ्गा -ङ्गं, निरङ्गः -ङ्गा -ङ्गं, अङ्गहीनः -ना -नं, अङ्गशून्यः -न्या -न्यं, अवयवहीनः -ना -नं.

Limbmeal, *adv.* अवयवशस्, गात्रं गात्रं, खण्डशस्, खण्डं खण्डं.

Limbo, *s.* (Hell) नरकः, निरयः.—(Prison) कारागारं, बन्धनागारं.

Lime, *s.* (Calcareous earth used for mortar) चूर्णं, कर्करः -रं, सुधा, क्षुरा, लेपः, विलेपः; 'nodule of lime,' चूर्णखण्डः, कर्करखण्डः, —(Bird-lime) पक्षिबन्धनलेपः, अतिश्यानद्रव्यं येन पक्षिणो बध्यन्ते, उदपेयविशेषः.—(Lime-tree, citrus acida) जम्बीरः, गुरुवक्षीरः, वक्रशोधी -धन: *m.*

To lime, *v. a.* पूर्व्वोक्तश्यानद्रव्येण लिप् (c. 6. लिम्पति, लेप्तुं) or विलिप्.

Lime-burner, *s.* चूर्णकारः, चूर्णकर्त्ता *m.* (र्तृ), चूर्णदाहकः, चूर्णदाहकृत्.

Lime-kiln, *s.* चूर्णदहनस्थानं, चूर्णपचनस्थानं, चूर्णपाकः.

Lime-stone, *s.* चूर्णखण्डः -ण्डं, कर्करखण्डः, कर्करं, चूर्णोपलः, कर्करोपलः.

Lime-water, *s.* चूर्णसंसृष्टं जलं, चूर्णजलं, कर्करजलं.

Limit, *s.* सीमा *f.*, सीमा *m.* (न्), परिसीमा *f. m.*, अवधिः *m.*, अन्तः -न्तं, पर्य्यन्तः -न्तं, सामन्तः, प्रान्तः, मर्य्यादा, परिच्छेदः, अवच्छेदः, वेला, नेमः, पर्य्याप्तिः *f.*, परिमाणं, परिमितिः *f.*, अवसानं, पर्यवसानं, परिसरः, शेषः, आघाटः, चक्रवाटः, पारः -रं; 'that forms a limit,' अवधिभूतः -ता -तं.

To limit, *v. a.* (Bound) प्रान्त (nom. प्रान्तयति -यितुं), सामन्त (nom. सामन्तयति -यितुं) or पर्य्यन्त, परिच्छिद् (c. 7. -छिनत्ति -छेत्तुं), अवछिद्, परिच्छेदं कृ, सावधिकं -कां कृ, सोपाधिकं -कां कृ, समर्य्यादं -दां कृ, ससीमं -मां कृ.—(Confine within certain bounds, circumscribe) परिमा (c. 2. -माति, c. 3. -मिमीते -मातुं), परिमितं -तां कृ, मितं -तां कृ, सपरिमाणं -णां कृ, संयम् (c. 1. -यच्छति -यन्तुं), नियम्, निग्रह् (c. 9. गृह्णाति -ग्रहीतुं), संहृ (c. 1. -हरति -हर्त्तुं), निबन्ध् (c. 9. -बध्नाति -बन्द्धुं), निरूप् (c. 10. -रूपयति -यितुं).

Limitable, *a.* परिमेयः -या -यं, परिच्छेदनीयः -या -यं, निरूपणीयः -या -यं.

Limitation, *s.* (The act of bounding) सीमाकरणं, मर्य्यादाकरणं, अवधिकरणं, पर्य्यन्तकरणं, परिच्छेदः -दनं, अवच्छेदः -दनं, परिमाणकरणं. —(A state of restriction) परिमितता -त्वं, सावधिकता, समर्य्यादत्वं, सोपाधिकत्वं, ससीमत्वं, अवधिता, अवधिः *m.*, पर्य्यन्त -न्तत्वं, अव्यापित्वं, निबन्धनं, बन्धः -न्धनं.

Limited, *p. p.* परिमितः -ता -तं, मितः -ता -तं, समर्य्यादः -दा -दं, सावधिकः -का -कं, सोपाधिकः -का -कं, ससीमः -मा -मं, सपरिमाणः -णा -णं, परिच्छिन्नः -न्ना -न्नं, नियतः -ता -तं, संयतः -ता -तं, निबद्धः -द्धा -द्धं, बद्धः -द्धा -द्धं, संहृतः -ता -तं, अव्याप्तः -प्ता -प्तं, अव्याप्यः -प्या -प्यं, अव्यापी -पिनी -पि (न्), सङ्कुचितः -ता -तं, सबाधः -धा -धं; 'of limited meaning,' मितार्थः -र्था -र्थं.

Limiter, *s.* मर्य्यादाकारी *m.* (न्), सीमाकर्त्ता *m.* (र्तृ), परिच्छेदकः, अवधिकृत्.

Limitless, *a.* अपरिमितः -ता -तं, अमितः -ता -तं, अनन्तः -न्ता -न्तं, निरवधिः -धिः -धि.

To limn, *v. a.* लिख् (c. 6. लिखति, लेखितुं), आलिख्, विलिख्, अभिलिख्, चित्रं लिख्, चित्र् (c. 10. चित्रयति -यितुं).

Limner, *s.* चित्रकरः, चित्रकारः, चित्रलिख् *m.* (ख्), चित्रकर्म्मविद् *m.*

Limous, *a.* पङ्किलः -ला -लं, पङ्की -ङ्किनी -ङ्कि (न्), सकर्दमः -मा -मं.

To limp, *v. n.* लङ्ग् (c. 1. लङ्गति -ङ्गितुं), खञ्ज् (c. 1. खञ्जति -ञ्जितुं), खोर् (c. 1. खोरति -रितुं), खोल् (c. 1. खोलति -लितुं), खोड् (c. 1. खोडति -डितुं), खोट् (c. 1. खोटति -टितुं), खुड्ड् (c. 1. खुड्डते -ड्डितुं), पङ्ग् (c. 1. पङ्गति -ङ्गितुं).

Limp, *s.* लङ्गः, खञ्जनं, लङ्गगतिः *f.*, खञ्जगतिः *f.*

Limp, *a.* मृदुः -दुः -द्वी -दु, शिथिलः -ला -लं, कोमलः -ला -लं.

Limper, *s.* लङ्गगतिः *m.*, लङ्गगामी *m.* (न्), खञ्जगतिः *m.*, खञ्जः.

Limpid, *a.* स्वच्छः -च्छा -च्छं, स्वच्छजलः -ला -लं, अच्छः -च्छा -च्छं, निर्म्मलः -ला -लं, विमलः -ला -लं, अमलः -ला -लं, निर्म्मलजलः -ला -लं, सुजलः -ला -लं.

Limpidness, limpidity, *s.* स्वच्छता, निर्म्मलता, विमलता, सुजलता, जलनैर्म्मल्यं.

Limping, *part.* or *a.* खञ्जः -ञ्जा -ञ्जं, पङ्गुः -ङ्गुः -ङ्गु, खोरः -रा -रं, खोलः -ला -लं, खोडः -डा -डं, लङ्गगतिः -तिः -ति, खञ्जगतिः &c., लङ्गगामी -मिनी -मि (न्), विकलगतिः &c.

Limpingly, *adv.* खञ्जवत्, पङ्गुवत्, सलङ्गं, लङ्गगत्या, खञ्जगत्या.

Limsy, limpsy, *a.* शिथिलः -ला -लं, मृदुः -दुः -दु, कोमलः -ला -लं.

Limy, *a.* चूर्णमयः -यी -यं, सचूर्णः -र्णा -र्णं, कर्करीयः -या -यं, प्रचुरचूर्णः -र्णा -र्णं, कर्करमयः -यी -यं.—(Viscous) सान्द्रः -न्द्रा -न्द्रं, श्यानः -ना -नं, चूर्णसगुणः -णा -णं, चूर्णोपमः -मा -मं.

Lin, *s.* (Flax) अतसी, उमा, क्षुमा, क्षौमी, क्षणं.

Linch-pin, *s.* अक्षाग्रकीलः -लकः, अक्षाग्रशङ्कुः *m.*, अक्षाग्रशलाका, अणिः *m.*, आणिः *m. f.*, उद्रथः.

Lincture, *s.* (Medicine) अवलेहः, अवलेह्यं, लेह्यं, अवलेह्यौषधं.

Line, *s.* रेखा, लेखा, सरणिः -णी, धारणी, राजिः -जिका *f.*, राजी, पंक्तिः *f.*, पद्धतिः *f.*, आलिः -ली *f.*, आवलिः -ली *f.*, पालिः -ली *f.*, ततिः *f.*, श्रेणिः -णी *m. f.*—(Ruled line) वर्त्तिः *f.*, रेखा, लेखा, अङ्कः. —(Row, range) पंक्तिः *f.*, श्रेणिः -णी, राजिः -जी *f.*, पद्धतिः *f.*, आवलिः -ली *f.*, माला, हारः; 'in a line,' पंक्तिक्रमेण; 'in the same line,' समरेखः -खा -खं, एकरेखः &c.—(Line of troops) दण्डः, पंक्तिः *f.*, व्यूहः, विन्यासः, सैन्यपंक्तिः *f.* बलविन्यासः; 'an array of troops in line,' दण्डव्यूहः; 'line of infantry,' पत्तिपंक्तिः *f.*, पत्तिश्रेणी.—(String, cord) सूत्रं, रज्जुः *m. f.*, गुणः, तन्तुः *m.*—(Cord extended to direct any operation) सूत्रं; 'by line and rule,' यथासूत्रं.—(Line of the face, &c.) मुखरेखा, वदनरेखा, रेखा; 'a lucky line,' आयुष्यरेखा, पद्मरेखा, स्वस्तिकः.—(Line of print, &c.) पंक्तिः *f.*—(Line of a stanza) पदं.—(Outline) पार्श्वरेखा, बहिर्लेखा.—(Contour) आकारः, आकृतिः *f.*, परिधिः *m.*—(Rampart, trench) प्राकारः, वप्रः, दुर्गवप्रः, परिखा, परिकूटं.—(Method, disposition) क्रमः, अनुक्रमः, पर्य्यायः, मार्गः, परम्परा, विन्यासः, परिपाटिः -टी *f.*—(Series) श्रेणी -णिः *m. f.*, पंक्तिः *f.*, परम्परा, पारम्पर्य्यं, आवलिः -ली *f.*, माला, आनुपूर्व्यं; 'in regular line,' क्रमशस्, अनुक्रमशस्, अनुपूर्व्वशस्, पारम्पर्य्येण.—(Line of a family) वंशावलिः *f.*, वंशपरम्परा, वंशपारम्पर्य्यं, कुलपरम्परा.—(Line of conduct) मार्गः, पथः, व्यवहारः, रीतिः *f.*, वृत्तिः *f.*; 'correct line of conduct,' सुमार्गः, सुपथः; 'incorrect line,' उन्मार्गः, विमार्गः, विपथः, कुपथः, कुसृतिः *f.*—(Line of study) अध्ययनमार्गः, अध्ययनक्रमः.—(Department) देशः, विषयः, अङ्गं.—(Direction, course) दिक् *f.* (श्), पथः, मार्गः; 'line of direction in mechanics,' गुरुत्वलम्बः; 'it goes in a different line,' भिन्नदिशं गच्छति.—(Fishing-line) वरशः, बडिशसूत्रं, मत्स्यग्रहणसूत्रं.—(Equator) विषुवच्चक्रं, विषुवमण्डलं, विषुवद्वृत्तं, विषुवद्वृत्तं, विषुवरेखा, नाडीवृत्तं, नाडीमण्डलं, भूगोलरेखा, भूपरिधिः *m.*, भूचक्रं, भूमध्यरेखा.—(To draw lines) लिख् (c. 6.

लिखति, लेखितुं), उल्लिख्, प्रोल्लिख्, रेखां कृ; 'to draw lines on the ground,' रेखादिना भूमिम् उल्लिख् or अङ्क् (c. 10. अङ्कयति -यितुं); 'act of drawing lines,' रेखाकरणं, प्रोल्लेखनं, उल्लेखनं; 'drawing lines,' उल्लिखन् -खन्ती -खत् (त्), प्रोल्लिखन् &c.

To LINE, *v. a.* (Cover on the inside) अन्तर् or अन्तर्भागे छद् (c. 10. छादयति -यितुं) or आछद्, अन्तश्छादनं कृ, अभ्यन्तरे छद्, अन्तःपटलं कृ, अन्तःपुटं कृ.—(Place in a line) पंक्तिक्रमेण स्था in caus. (स्थापयति -यितुं).

LINEAGE, *s.* अन्वयः, वंशः, सन्ततिः *f.*, सन्तानः, कुलं, अन्ववायः, गोत्रं, वंशविततिः *f.*, वंशपरम्परा, आवली -लिः *f.*, वंशावलिः, परम्परा, जातिः *f.*, जननं, अभिजनः; 'of royal lineage,' राजवंश्यः -श्या -श्यं; 'of high lineage,' महाकुलः -ला -लं.

LINEAL, *a.* (Compound of lines) रेखामयः -यी -यं, रेखारूपः -पा -पं, अङ्कितः -ता -तं.—(Derived from ancestors in a direct line) परम्परागतः -ता -तं, परम्परायातः -ता -तं, परम्पराप्राप्तः -प्ता -प्तं, क्रमागतः -ता -तं, क्रमायातः -ता -तं, क्रमप्राप्तः -प्ता -प्तं, वंशक्रमागतः -ता -तं, परम्परीणः -णा -णं, पारम्परिकः -की -कं; 'a lineal descendant,' सन्तानः, सन्ततिः *f.*; 'lineal descent,' क्रमागमः, वंशक्रमागमः, क्रमागतत्वं, अन्वयागमः.

LINEALLY, *adv.* क्रमागमेन, वंशक्रमेण, पारम्पर्य्येण, परम्परतस्; 'lineally descended,' वंशक्रमागतः -ता -तं, वंशक्रमायातः -ता -तं, अन्वयागतः -ता -तं, कुलक्रमायातः -ता -तं.

LINEAMENT, *s.* (Feature) रेखा, वदनरेखा, मुखरेखा, वदनाकृतिः *f.*, वदनाकारः, मुखावयवः, रूपचिह्नं, रूपलक्षणं, अङ्गचिह्नं, अङ्गलक्षणं.—(Outline) बहिर्लेखा, बाह्यरेखा, वस्तु *n.*, वस्तुमात्रं; 'of just lineaments,' सुरेखः -खा -खं.

LINEAR, *a.* पांक्तः -क्ती -क्तं, पांक्तेयः -यी -यं, पंक्तिरूपः -पा -पं, पंक्तिमयः -यी -यं, रेखामयः -यी -यं, रेखारूपः &c., रेखासम्बन्धी -न्धिनी -न्धि (न्).

LINED, *p. p.* अन्तर्भागे छादितः -ता -तं, अन्तराच्छादितः -ता -तं, अन्तरावृतः &c.

LINEN, *a.* (Made of flax or hemp) क्षौमः -मी -मं, क्षोमः -मी -मं, क्षौमकः -की -कं, शाणः -णी -णं, अतसीमयः -यी -यं, शणमयः &c.

LINEN, *s.* क्षौमवस्त्रं, क्षौमपटः, शाणवस्त्रं, शाणपटः, क्षौमी, क्षोमवस्त्रं, क्षोमपटः, क्षौमाम्बरं.

LINEN-DRAPER, *s.* क्षौमवस्त्रविक्रेता *m.* (तृ), क्षौमपटविक्रयी *m.* (न्), वस्त्रविक्रयोपजीवी *m.* (न्), वस्त्रक्रयविक्रयिकः, वस्त्रवाणिज्यकारी *m.* (न्).

LING, *s.* (Plant) जङ्गलरुहं तृणं, जङ्गलरोही तृणभेदः.

To LINGER, *v. n.* विलम्ब् (c. 1. -लम्बते -म्बितुं), मन्द् (nom. मन्दायते), चिर (nom. चिरयति, चिरायति), अवस्था (c. 1. -तिष्ठति -स्थातुं), कालं क्षिप् (c. 6. क्षिपति, क्षेप्तुं), विलम्बनं कृ, कालक्षेपं कृ.—(Hesitate) विक्लृप् (c. 1. -कल्पते -ल्पितुं, c. 10. -कल्पयति -यितुं), विचर् (c. 10. -चारयति -यितुं), विकल्पं कृ, विचारणं कृ.—(Remain long in any state) चिरेण or चिरं or चिरकालं or दीर्घकालं स्था or अवस्था or वृत् (c. 1. -वर्त्तते -र्त्तितुं), सुचिरं स्था; 'on a bed of sickness,' चिररोगी -गिणी भू.—(Proceed slowly) मन्दं मन्दं चल् (c. 1. चलति -लितुं) or चर् (c. 1. चरति -रितुं).

LINGERER, *s.* विलम्बी *m.* (न्), विलम्बकारी *m.*, मन्दगामी *m.* (न्), मन्दगतिः *m.*, चिरक्रियः, कालक्षेपकः, कालयापकः, दीर्घसूत्री *m.* (न्).

LINGERING, *part.* मन्दायमानः -ना -नं, मन्दयमानः -ना -नं, विलम्बी -म्बिनी -म्बि (न्), विलम्बितः -ता -तं, चिरायमाणः -णा -णं.—(Remaining long) चिरस्थः -स्था -स्थं, चिरस्थायी -यिनी -यि (न्), चिरस्थितः -ता -तं, चिरकालस्थः -स्था -स्थं, दीर्घकालीनः -ना -नं, चिरकालीनः -ना -नं.

LINGERINGLY, *adv.* विलम्बेन, विलम्बात्, सविलम्बं, मन्दं मन्दं, मन्दगत्या, कालक्षेपेण, सकालक्षेपं, दीर्घसूत्रवत्, दीर्घसूत्रतया.

LINGET, *s.* (Mass of metal) धातुपिण्डः, लोहपिण्डः.

LINGUADENTAL, *a.* जिह्वादन्त्यः -न्त्या -न्त्यं, जिह्वादान्तः -न्ती -न्तं.

LINGUAL, *a.* जिह्वासम्बन्धी -न्धिनी -न्धि (न्), जैह्विकः -की -कं, जिह्वा in comp.

LINGUIFORM, *a.* जिह्वारूपः -पा -पं, जिह्वाकारः -रा -रं, जिह्वाकृतिः -तिः -ति.

LINGUIST, *s.* भाषाज्ञः, बहुभाषाज्ञः, नानाभाषाज्ञः, अनेकभाषाज्ञः, बहुभाषावेत्ता *m.* (तृ), नानाभाषानिपुणः, शाब्दिकः, शब्दव्युत्पन्नः, बहुभाषावादी *m.* (न्), उच्चारणज्ञः.

LINIMENT, *s.* स्नेहनं, उपदेहः, लेपः, आलेपः, प्रलेपः, विलेपनं, अनुलेपनं, अभ्यङ्गः, अभ्यञ्जनं, मर्द्दनौषधं.

LINING, *s.* अन्तश्छादनं, अन्तराच्छादनं, अन्तर्वेष्टनं, अन्तःपटलं, अन्तःपुटः -टं, आस्तरः -रणं, अन्तरास्तरणं.

LINK, *s.* (Of a chain) शृङ्खलासन्धिः *m.*, शृङ्खलसन्धिः, शृङ्खलाग्रन्थिः *m.*—(A chain, any thing connecting) शृङ्खलः -ला, सन्धिः *m.*, बन्धनं, पाशः, संयोगः, सम्बन्धः.—(Part of a connected series) अन्वयः, समन्वयः, प्रबन्धः.—(Torch) उल्का, उल्मुकं, ज्वलनकाष्ठं, अग्निकाष्ठं.

To LINK, *v. a.* सन्धा (c. 3. -दधाति -धत्ते -धातुं), संयुज् (c. 7. -युनक्ति -योक्तुं, c. 10. -योजयति -यितुं), सम्बन्ध् (c. 9. -बध्नाति -बन्द्धुं), संश्लिष् (c. 10. -श्लेषयति -यितुं), योक्त्र (nom. योक्त्रयति -यितुं), ग्रन्थ् (c. 9. ग्रथ्नाति, ग्रन्थितुं), शृङ्खलारूपेण सन्धा.

LINK-BOY, *s.* उल्काभृत्, उल्काधारी *m.* (न्), ज्वलनकाष्ठभृत्.

LINKED, *p. p.* सन्धितः -ता -तं, संयुक्तः -क्ता -क्तं, सम्बद्धः -द्धा -द्धं, अनुसम्बद्धः &c., अनुबद्धः &c., अन्वितः -ता -तं, समन्वितः -ता -तं, सान्वयः -या -यं.

LINNET, *s.* लिखिताख्यो मधुररुतविशिष्टः क्षुद्रपक्षी.

LINSEED, *s.* अतसीबीजं, उमाबीजं, क्षुमाबीजं, अतसी, उमा, क्षुमा, मसीना, मसृणा, चणका, सुवर्चला, मालिका.

LINSEY-WOOLSEY, *a.* क्षौमोर्णः -र्णा -र्णं, क्षोमोर्णः &c., शाणोर्णः &c.

LINSTOCK, *s.* अग्निदयष्टिः *m.*, अग्निदकाष्ठं, अग्निदशलाका, अग्निदण्डः, ज्वलनदण्डः, ज्वलनकाष्ठं, शलाका.

LINT, *s.* विकेशिका, व्रणशोषणार्थं क्षौमवस्त्रखण्डः or क्षौमपटखण्डः or शाणवस्त्रखण्डः.

LINTEL, *s.* द्वारोपरिस्थकाष्ठं, द्वारोपरिस्थदारुः *m.*, द्वारोपरिस्थितं काष्ठं, द्वाराग्रकाष्ठं.

LION, *s.* सिंहः, केसरी *m.* (न्), केशरी *m.*, हरिः *m.*, मृगेन्द्रः, मृगराजः, मृगराट् *m.* (ज्), मृगपतिः *m.*, पशुराजः, पशुपतिः *m.*, वनराजः, मृगरिपुः *m.*, मृगारिः *m.*, गजारिः *m.*, कुञ्जरारातिः *m.*, द्विरदान्तकः, हस्तिकक्ष्यः, भीमनादः, भीमविक्रान्तः, भारिः *m.*, हरित् *m.*, हर्य्यक्षः, पञ्चास्यः, पञ्चमुखः, पञ्चाननः, पञ्चवक्त्रः, पञ्चशिखः, सटाङ्कः, जटिलः; 'a lion's mane,' केशरः, केसरः, सिंहकेशरः; 'lion's mouth,' सिंहमुखं, मृगेन्द्रमुखं; 'lion's roar,' सिंहनादः -दकः, सिंहध्वनिः *m.*; 'abounding with lions,' सिंहाढ्यः -ढ्या -ढ्यं; 'he plays the lion,' सिंहायते.—(Sign in the zodiac) सिंहः. *See* LEO.—(Object of curiosity) कौतुकं.

LIONESS, *s.* सिंही, केशरिणी, केसरिणी, मृगराज्ञी, वनराज्ञी.

LION-LIKE, LIONLY, *a.* सैंहः -ही -हं, सैंहिकः -की -कं, सिंहस्वभावः -वा -वं.

LIP, *s.* ओष्ठः, अधरः, दशनच्छदः, रदनच्छदः, रदच्छदः, दन्तच्छदः, दच्छदः, दशनवासस् *n.*, वाग्दलं, ओष्ठपल्लवं, अधरपुटं, ओष्ठपुटः -टं; 'the upper lip,' is properly ओष्ठः; 'the lower lip,' अधरः.—

(The lips) ओष्ठाधरौ *m.* du., ओष्ठौ *m.* du., अधरौ du., दन्तच्छदौ, रदनच्छदौ, दशनच्छदौ, दशनवाससी *n.* du.; 'red or cherry lip,' बिम्बोष्ठः or बिम्बौष्ठः, बिम्बाधरः; 'having red lips,' बिम्बोष्ठः -ष्ठा -ष्ठं or बिम्बौष्ठः; 'nectar of the lips,' अधरामृतं; 'drinking the nectar of the lips,' अधरपानं; 'to bite the lips,' ओष्ठं or अधरं or ओष्ठाधरौ दंश् (c. 1. दशति, दंष्टुं) or सन्दंश्, दन्तैर् ओष्ठं खाद् (c. 1. खादति -दितुं), अधरावलोपं कृ, ओष्ठदंशनं कृ; 'biting the lips,' सन्दष्टौष्ठः -ष्ठा -ष्ठं, दष्टदच्छदः -दा -दं, सन्दष्टौष्ठपुटः -टा -टं.—(Edge of a cup, &c.) पात्रकण्ठः, पात्रमुखं, पात्रधारः, पात्रकर्णः, पात्रपार्श्वः.

Lip-devotion, *s.* ओष्ठभक्तिः *f.*, अधरभक्तिः *f.*, ओष्ठपूजा, अधरपूजा.

Lipless, *a.* ओष्ठहीनः -ना -नं, अधरहीनः -ना -नं, निरोष्ठः -ष्ठा -ष्ठं.

Lipothymous, *a.* मूर्च्छितः -ता -तं, मूर्च्छालुः -लुः -लु, नष्टचेतनः -ना -नं.

Lipothymy, *s.* मूर्च्छा -र्च्छनं -ना, मोहः, सम्मोहः, प्रमोहः, प्रलयः, चेतनाहानिः *f.*, चैतन्यहानिः *f.*, चैतन्यनाशः.

Lipped, *a.* ओष्ठवान् -वती -वत् (त्), ओष्ठी -ष्ठिनी -ष्ठि (न्), ओष्ठ or अधर in comp.; as, 'red lipped,' बिम्बोष्ठः -ष्ठा -ष्ठं or बिम्बौष्ठः &c., बिम्बाधरः -रा -रं.

Lippitude, *s.* चुल्लत्वं, पिल्लत्वं, चिल्लत्वं, क्लिन्नाक्षता, नयनक्लिन्नता.

Lip-salve, *s.* ओष्ठलेपः, ओष्ठप्रलेपः, ओष्ठस्नेहनं, अधराभ्यञ्जनं.

Liquefaction, *s.* (The act) द्रावः -वणं, विद्रावः -वणं, द्रवीकरणं, विलयः -यनं, लयः -यनं, गलनं, गालनं, परिगलनं, विगलनं, क्षरणं, जलसात्करणं.—(The state) द्रवत्वं, द्रावितत्वं, विलीनता, गलितत्वं, द्रुतत्वं, विद्रुतता.

Liquefiable, liquable, *a.* द्राव्यः -व्या -व्यं, विद्राव्यः -व्या -व्यं, विलयनीयः -या -यं, गलनीयः -या -यं, द्रवणीयः -या -यं or द्रावणीयः सुविलयः -या -यं, विलयनशीलः -ला -लं, द्रावग्राही -हिणी -हि, द्रवग्राही -हिणी -हि, क्षरणीयः -या -यं, क्षरभावः -वा -वं, याव्यः -व्या -व्यं.

Liquefied, *p. p.* द्रुतः -ता -तं, विद्रुतः -ता -तं, द्रावितः -ता -तं, विद्रावितः -ता -तं, द्रवीकृतः -ता -तं, द्रवीभूतः -ता -तं, लीनः -ना -नं, विलीनः -ना -नं, निलीनः -ना -नं, गलितः -ता -तं, गालितः -ता -तं, परिगलितः -ता -तं, विगलितः -ता -तं.

To liquefy, *v. a.* विली in caus. (-लाययति -लापयति -यितुं), विद्रु (c. 10. -द्रावयति -यितुं), द्रु, द्रवीकृ, गल् (c. 10. गालयति -यितुं), विगल्, गलितीकृ, विलीनीकृ, जलसात्कृ, आर्द्रीकृ.

To liquefy, *v. n.* विली (c. 4. -लीयते -लेतुं), प्रविली, प्रली, द्रु (c. 1. द्रवति, द्रोतुं), विद्रु, गल् (c. 1. गलति -लितुं), विगल्, क्षर् (c. 1. क्षरति -रितुं), द्रवीभू, विलीनीभू, जलसाद्भू.

Liquid, *a.* द्रवः -वा -वं, द्रुतः -ता -तं, द्रवरूपः -पा -पं, सद्रवः -वा -वं, विद्रुतः -ता -तं, विलीनः -ना -नं, लीनः -ना -नं, गलितः -ता -तं, तरलः -ला -लं, विह्वलः -ला -लं, प्रवाही -हिणी -हि (न्), प्रवाहधर्म्मकः -का -कं, पयस्यः -स्या -स्यं.

Liquid, *s.* द्रवः, द्रवद्रव्यं, द्रवपदार्थः, द्रववस्तु *n.*, सद्रवपदार्थः, रसः, आर्द्रद्रव्यं, आर्द्रवस्तु *n.*, जलं, वारि *n.*, पयस् *n.*

To liquidate, *v. a.* शुध् (c. 10. शोधयति -यितुं), परिशुध्, मुच् (c. 6. मुञ्चति, मोक्तुं, c. 10. मोचयति -यितुं), विमुच्, मोक्ष् (c. 10. मोक्षयति -यितुं), विसृज् (c. 6. -सृजति -स्रष्टुं, c. 10. -सर्जयति -यितुं), निस्तॄ (c. 10. -तारयति -यितुं), अपनी (c. 1. -नयति -नेतुं), विनी, अपवृज् (c. 10. -वर्जयति -यितुं), अपाकृ, साध् (c. 10. साधयति -यितुं); 'settle a debt,' ऋणं शुध् or अपनी or विनी or अपाकृ or अपवृज् or साध्, ऋणशोधनं कृ, ऋणसिद्धिं कृ, ऋणमुक्तिं कृ.

Liquidated, *p. p.* शोधितः -ता -तं, परिशोधितः -ता -तं, परिशुद्धः -द्धा -द्धं, सिद्धः -द्धा -द्धं, साधितः -ता -तं, ऋणमुक्तः -क्ता -क्तं, ऋणमोचितः -ता -तं, अपाकृतः -ता -तं, विगणितः -ता -तं, निस्तारितः -ता -तं, उत्तीर्णः -र्णा -र्णं.

Liquidation, *s.* शोधनं, परिशोधनं, शुद्धिः *f.*, परिशुद्धिः *f.*, मुक्तिः *f.*, विमुक्तिः *f.*, मोक्षः -क्षणं, परिमोक्षणं, निस्तारः, उत्तरणं, अपाकरणं, सिद्धिः *f.*, साधनं, अपनयनं; 'of a debt,' ऋणशोधनं, ऋणसिद्धिः *f.*, ऋणापाकरणं, ऋणमुक्तिः *f.*, ऋणापनयनं, ऋणापनोदनं, विगणनं, निरादेशः.

Liquidity, liquidness, *s.* द्रवत्वं -ता, द्राव्यत्वं -ता, विद्रुतत्वं, विलीनता, गलितत्वं, द्रवभावः, रसता, प्रवाहधर्म्मः.

Liquor, *s.* (Fluid) द्रवः, द्रवद्रव्यं, द्रवपदार्थः, सद्रवपदार्थः, द्रववस्तु *n.*, रसः, जलं.—(Drink) पेयं, पानीयं, पेयद्रव्यं.—(Spirituous liquor) मद्यं, मदिरा, मदः, सुरा -री, वारुणी, शुण्डा, शीधुः *m.* -धु, सीधुः *m.*, हाला, आसवं, कल्यं -ल्या, कश्यं; 'drinker of spirituous liquor,' सुरापः -पी *f.*, मद्यपः -पी *f.*, शीधुपः -पी *f.*, शुण्डापायी *m.* -यिनी *f.*

Liquor-shop, *s.* मदिरागृहं, मद्यविक्रयस्थानं, शुण्डापानं.

Liquorice, *s.* मधुयष्टिका, यष्टिमधु *n.*, मधुकं, मधूली. *See* Licorice.

To lisp, *v. a.* or *n.* गद्गद् (nom. गद्गदति), गद्गदवाचा वद् (c. 1. वदति -दितुं), बालकवद् उच्चर् (c. 10. -चारयति -यितुं), भग्नदन्तैर् इव उच्चर्, भग्नदन्तोच्चारणं कृ, भग्नस्वरेण or भिन्नस्वरेण वद् or उच्चर्, अस्पष्टवाचा or अस्फुटवाचा उच्चर्, अस्पष्टोच्चारणं कृ, अस्फुटोच्चारणं कृ, जल्प् (c. 1. जल्पति -ल्पितुं).

Lisp, lisping, *s.* गद्गदः, गद्गदवाक् *f.* (च्), गद्गदपदं, गद्गदवाक्यं, भग्नदन्तोच्चारणं, भग्नस्वरोच्चारणं, भिन्नस्वरोच्चारणं, अस्फुटोच्चारणं, अस्पष्टोच्चारणं, बालकवद् उच्चारणं.

Lisped, *p. p.* भग्नदन्तोच्चारितः -ता -तं, अस्पष्टोच्चारितः -ता -तं.

Lisper, lisping, *a.* अस्फुटवाक् *m. f. n.* (च्), अस्पष्टवाक् *m. f. n.*, गद्गदवाक् *m. f. n.*, अस्फुटजल्पः -ल्पा -ल्पं, चित्रजल्पः &c., लोहलः -ला -लं, भग्नदन्तोच्चारणकृत्.

Lispingly, *adv.* अस्फुटवाचा, अस्पष्टवाचा, गद्गदवाचा, बालकवत्.

List, *s.* (Catalogue) आवलिः -ली *f.*, अनुक्रमणिका, परिसंख्या, परिसंख्यापत्रं, परिगणना, सूचिः -ची *f.*, सूचिपत्रं; 'a list of names,' नामावलिः -ली *f.*, नामावलिपत्रं, नामपरिसंख्यापत्रं; 'list of errata,' शुद्धिपत्रं.—(Strip of cloth) पट्टः -ट्टकः, पटखण्डः, वस्त्रखण्डः.—(Border or edge of cloth) वस्त्रधारः, वस्त्रप्रान्तः, वसनप्रान्तः, वस्त्रान्तः, वसनान्तः, वस्तिः *m.*, तरी, दशा.—(Ground enclosed as a field of combat) रङ्गभूमिः *f.*, रणभूमिः, रङ्गाङ्गनं, रङ्गः, युद्धभूमिः *f.*, युद्धक्षेत्रं, रणाजिरं, मल्लभूमिः *f.*, मल्लभूः *f.*—(Liking, desire) इच्छा, रुचिः *f.*, अभिरुचिः *f.*, स्पृहा.

To list, *v. a.* (Enroll) नामावलिपत्रे or नामपरिसंख्यापत्रे नामानि समारुह् in caus. (-रोपयति -यितुं) or आरुह् or अभिलिख् (c. 6. -लिखति -लेखितुं) or लिख्.—(Cover with strips of cloth) पट्टैः or पटखण्डैः छद् (c. 10. छादयति -यितुं) or आच्छद्, पट्टबन्धनं कृ.—(Sew together strips of cloth) पटखण्डान् संसिव् (c. 4. -सीव्यति, सेवितुं) or निसिव्.—(Hearken) आकर्ण् (c. 10. -कर्णयति -यितुं), कर्णं दा.

To list, *v. n.* (Desire, choose) इष् (c. 6. इच्छति, एषितुं), अभिलष् (c. 1. -लषति -षितुं), रुच् (c. 1. रोचते) used impersonally; 'doing as one lists,' कामचारी -रिणी -रि (न्), कामचारः -री -रं, 'going as one lists,' कामगामी -मिनी &c., कामगः -गा -गं; 'as one lists,' कामतस्, कामचारतस्. *See* Like.

To Listen, *v. n.* आकर्ण् (c. 10. -कर्णयति -यितुं), श्रु (c. 5. शृणोति,

श्रोतुं), आश्रु, उपश्रु, निशम् (c. 10. -शामयति -यितुं), कर्णं दा (c. 3. ददाति, दातुं), श्रवणं कृ.—(Heed, lend the mind) अवधा (c. 3. -धत्ते -धातुं), मनो धा, सावधानः -ना -नं भू, अवहितः -ता -तं भू or अस्, अवधानं कृ; 'listen,' शृणु, कर्णं देहि, अवधीयतां.—(Obey, follow admonition) श्रु in des. (शुश्रूषते -षितुं), अनुविधा in pass. (-धीयते), अनुवृत् (c. 1. -वर्त्तते -र्त्तितुं).

LISTENER, s. श्रोता m. -त्री f. (तृ), श्रवणकर्त्ता m. -र्त्री f. (र्त्तृ), निशमनकारी m. -रिणी f. (न्).

LISTLESS, a. अनुत्सुकः -का -कं, निरुत्सुकः -का -कं, अनिच्छुः -च्छुः -च्छु, अनिच्छुकः -का -कं, निरिच्छः -च्छा -च्छं, निःस्पृहः -हा -हं, निरीहः -हा -हं, उदासीनः -ना -नं, उदासी -सिनी -सि (न्), निरपेक्षः -क्षा -क्षं, विरक्तः -क्ता -क्तं, वीतरागः -गा -गं, विकौतुकः -का -कं, अनभिलाषः -षा -षं, अनवधानः -ना -नं, अनवहितः -ता -तं, निरुद्योगः -गा -गं, निरुद्यमः -मा -मं, अप्रयत्नः -त्ना -त्नं, अप्रयत्नशीलः -ला -लं, अनास्थः -स्था -स्थं, आस्थाहीनः -ना -नं, सुप्तबुद्धिः -द्धिः -द्धि, जडः -डा -डं, जडबुद्धिः &c., अव्यग्रः -ग्रा -ग्रं, निःसङ्गः -ङ्गा -ङ्गं, म्लानः -ना -नं, प्रमादी -दिनी &c. See LANGUID.

LISTLESSLY, adv. अनुत्सुकं, निरुत्सुकं, अनिच्छया, अनौत्सुक्येन, उदासीनवत्, अनभिलाषेण, अनवधानेन, अनवहितं, अनपेक्षया, जडवत्, अव्यग्रं. See LANGUIDLY.

LISTLESSNESS, s. अनुत्सुकता, अनौत्सुक्यं, निरुत्सुकता, अनिच्छा, अनीहा, निरीहता -त्वं, अस्पृहा, निःस्पृहता, अनभिलाषः, उदासीनता, औदास्यं, विरक्तिः f., विरक्तता, वैराग्यं, अननुरागः, अनपेक्षा, अनवेक्षा, अनुत्साहः, अनुद्योगः, अप्रयत्नः -त्नता, अनास्था, आस्थाहीनता, सुप्तबुद्धित्वं, जडता, जाड्यं, अव्यग्रता, मान्द्यं, ग्लानिः f. See LANGUOR.

LITANY, s. ख्रीष्टीयमतधारिभिर् व्यवहृतः प्रार्थनामार्गः, ख्रीष्टीयसमाजव्यवहारिता प्रार्थना.

LITERAL, a. (Not figurative) मूलार्थकः -का -कं, मुख्यार्थकः -का -कं, मुख्यः -ख्या -ख्यं, अरूपकः -का -कं, अव्यञ्जकः -का -कं, विवक्षितः -ता -तं, शक्यः -क्या -क्यं; 'literal occupation,' मुख्यत्वं, मुख्यार्थः, मूलार्थः, प्रकृतार्थः.—(Following the letter or exact words) मूलशब्दानुसारी -रिणी -रि (न्), मूलशब्दानुयायी -यिनी &c., मूलपदानुसारी &c., शब्दार्थानुसारी &c., अवयवार्थानुसारी &c., शब्दानुसारी &c., यथाशब्दः -ब्दा -ब्दं, शाब्दिकः -की -कं.—(Consisting of letters) अक्षरी -रिणी &c., अक्षरमयः -यी -यं.

LITERALITY, s. मुख्यत्वं -ता, मुख्यार्थत्वं, मूलार्थत्वं, मुख्यार्थः, मूलार्थः, प्रकृतार्थः, शब्दार्थः, अव्यञ्जनं -ना, अरूपकं.

LITERALLY, adv. (Not figuratively) मूलार्थानुसारेण, मुख्यार्थानुसारेण, मूलार्थतस्.—(Close to the letter or exact words) शब्दतस्, ग्रन्थतस्, यथाशब्दं, शब्दानुसारेण -रतस्, मूलशब्दानुसारेण, मूलपदानुसारात्, शब्दार्थतस्.—(Letter by letter) अक्षरशस्.

LITERARY, a. (Pertaining to literature) विद्यासम्बन्धी -न्धिनी -न्धि (न्), विद्याविषयः -या -यं, अक्षरसम्बन्धी &c., शास्त्रिकः -की -कं, शास्त्रीयः -या -यं, विद्याप्रकरणसम्बन्धी &c., साहित्यसम्बन्धी &c.—(Versed in literature, fond of it) विद्यावान् -वती -वत् (त्), शास्त्राभिज्ञः -ज्ञा -ज्ञं, विद्याप्रियः -या -यं, विद्यासेवी -विनी &c., विद्यानुसेवी &c., विद्यानुरागी -गिणी &c., विद्याव्यवसायी -यिनी &c., विद्यानुपाली -लिनी &c., विद्याविशिष्टः -ष्टा -ष्टं, विद्यासम्पन्नः -न्ना -न्नं.

LITERATE, a. पण्डितः -ता -तं, विद्यावान् -वती -वत् (त्), विद्यासम्पन्नः -न्ना -न्नं, व्युत्पन्नः -न्ना -न्नं, विद्वान् -दुषी -द्वत् (स्), विपश्चित् m. f. n., साक्षरः -रा -रं.

LITERATI, s. pl. पण्डितमण्डली -लं, पण्डितसमाजः, विद्वत्समाजः, पण्डितगणः, पण्डितवर्गः, पण्डितसमूहः, विद्वद्वृन्दं.

LITERATURE, s. (Learning) विद्या, शास्त्रं, शास्त्रविद्या, अक्षरं, साहित्यं, वाङ्मयं.—(Collective body of literary productions) शास्त्रसमुदायः, शास्त्रसमवायः, शास्त्रसमूहः, often expressible by शास्त्र in the sing. number; as, 'poetical literature,' काव्यशास्त्रं; 'branch of literature,' अङ्गं, उपशास्त्रं.

LITHE, a. शिथिलः -ला -लं, मृदुः -दुः -द्वी -दु, सुखनमनीयः -या -यं.

LITHENESS, s. शिथिलता, शैथिल्यं, सुनमनीयता, मृदुता, कोमलता.

To LITHOGRAPH, v. a. प्रस्तरोपरि or शिलोपरि लिख् (c. 6. लिखति, लेखितुं) or आलिख्, प्रस्तरं रेखादिना मुद्रीकृ or मुद्र (nom. मुद्रयति -यितुं) or अङ्क् (c. 10. अङ्कयति -यितुं).

LITHOGRAPH, s. प्रस्तरमुद्रा, शिलामुद्रा, पाषाणमुद्रा, प्रस्तरालेख्यं, पट्टः.

LITHOGRAPHER, s. प्रस्तरलेखकः, प्रस्तरलिक् m. (ख्), प्रस्तरमुद्राकृत्, शिलामुद्राकृत्, शिलालेखकः, प्रस्तरालेख्यकृत्.

LITHOGRAPHY, s. प्रस्तरलिखनविद्या, प्रस्तरमुद्राङ्कनविद्या, शिलालिखनविद्या, शिलामुद्राङ्कनं, पाषाणलिखनं.

LITHONTRIPTIC, LITHONTRYPTIC, LITHONTHRYPTIC, a. अश्मरीघ्नः -घ्नी -घ्नं, अश्मरीहरः -रा -रं, मूत्राश्मनाशकः -का -कं.

LITHOTOMY, s. मूत्राश्मोच्छेदः, वस्तिस्थशर्करोच्छेदः, उच्छेदनद्वारा मूत्राश्मनिष्कर्षणं, वस्तिच्छेदनं, मूत्राधारच्छेदः.

LITHOTRIPSY, s. अश्मरीघर्षणं, अश्मरीसङ्घर्षः, अश्मरीसम्मर्दः, अश्मरीसम्पेषः.

LITIGANT, a. विवादी -दिनी -दि (न्), विवदमानः -ना -नं, विवादार्थी -र्थिनी -र्थि (न्), व्यवहारी -रिणी &c., व्यावहारिकः -की -कं, व्यवहारिकः &c., कार्य्यवान् -वती -वत् (त्), कार्य्यी -र्य्यिणी &c., विवदन् -दन्ती -दत् (त्).

LITIGANT, s. व्यवहर्त्ता m. (र्त्तृ), विवादी m. (न्), विवादार्थी, वादी m., अर्थी m., कार्य्यवान् m. (त्), कार्य्यी m.

To LITIGATE, v. n. विवद् (c. 1. -वदते -दितुं), व्यवहृ (c. 1. -हरति -ते -हर्त्तुं), विवादं कृ, विवादार्थी -र्थिनी भू or अस्.

To LITIGATE, v. a. विवादास्पदीकृ, व्यवहारास्पदीकृ, वादग्रस्तं -स्तां कृ.

LITIGATED, p. p. विवादास्पदीकृतः -ता -तं, विवादास्पदीभूतः -ता -तं, विवादानुगतः -ता -तं, वादानुगतः -ता -तं, वादग्रस्तः -स्ता -स्तं, विवादग्रस्तः -स्ता -स्तं.

LITIGATION, s. विवादः, विवादकरणं, वादः, वादकरणं, व्यवहारः, व्यवहारकरणं, रिक्थं; 'under litigation,' विवादास्पदीभूतः -ता -तं, वादग्रस्तः -स्ता -स्तं. See LITIGATED.

LITIGIOUS, a. विवादी -दिनी -दि (न्), विवादशीलः -ला -लं, विवादप्रियः -या -यं, विवादार्थी -र्थिनी &c., वादप्रियः -या -यं, विवादप्रवणः -णा -णं, विवादबुद्धिः -द्धिः -द्धि, विवादासक्तः -क्ता -क्तं, विवादरतः -ता -तं.

LITIGIOUSNESS, s. विवादशीलता, विवादार्थित्वं, विवादासक्तिः f., विवादबुद्धिः f.

LITTER, s. (Bed borne on the shoulders) शिबिका, याप्ययानं, डयनं, डलकं, प्रवहणं, डुला, शिरस्का.—(Bed of straw) तृणशय्या, तृणशयनं, तृणसंस्तरः, तृणास्तरणं.—(Brood of young animals) शावकगणः, यः शावकगण एकवारे जायते, शावकसमूहः; 'of pigs,' शूकरशावकगणः.—(Shreds scattered about) इतस्ततो विकीर्णा वस्त्रखण्डाः.—(Confusion of things scattered about) द्रव्यविक्षिप्तता, द्रव्यविकीर्णता, द्रव्यव्यस्तता, द्रव्यसङ्करः, साङ्कर्य्यं, वस्तव्यस्तता.

To LITTER, v. a. (Bring forth a number of young ones) शावकगणं सु (c. 2. सूते, c. 4. सूयते, सोतुं) or प्रसु or जन् (c. 10. जनयति -यितुं) or प्रजन् (c. 4. -जायते -जनितुं) or उत्पद् (c. 10. -पादयति

-यितुं), प्रस्तरं कृ.—(Cover with straw) तृणावृतं -तां कृ, तृणास्तीर्णं -र्णां कृ, तृणास्तृतं -तां कृ, सतृणं -णां कृ, तृणास्तरणं कृ.—(Scatter about confusedly) इतस्ततो विकृ (c. 6. -किरति -करितुं -रीतुं) or व्याकृ or विक्षिप् (c. 6. -क्षिपति -क्षेप्तुं), अस्तव्यस्तीकृ.

LITTERED, *p. p.* (Covered with straw) तृणावृतः -ता -तं, तृणास्तीर्णः -र्णा -र्णं, तृणास्तृतः -ता -तं.—(Scattered about) इतस्ततो विकीर्णः -र्णा -र्णं or व्याकीर्णः -र्णा -र्णं, अस्तव्यस्तः -स्ता -स्तं, बहुधा विक्षिप्तः -प्ता -प्तं, बहुधास्तीर्णः -र्णा -र्णं.

LITTLE, *a.* (Small in size or extent, not great) अल्पः -ल्पा -ल्पं, क्षुद्रः -द्रा -द्रं, अल्पकः -का -कं, क्षुद्रकः -का -कं, अल्पपरिमाणः -णा -णं, क्षुद्रपरिमाणः -णा -णं, सूक्ष्मः -क्ष्मा -क्ष्मं, तनुः -नुः -नु, स्तोकः -का -कं, लघुः -घुः -घु, लघुपरिमाणः -णा -णं, ह्रस्वः -स्वा -स्वं, क्षुल्लकः -का -कं, श्लक्ष्णः -क्ष्णा -क्ष्णं, कृशः -शा -शं, दभ्रः -भ्रा -भ्रं, कणीकः -का -कं, अणुकः -का -कं, अणुः -ण्वी -णु, कणः, लेशः, लवः, मात्रा *f.*, त्रुटिः -टी *f.*—(Small in body) अल्पतनुः -नुः -नु, अल्पशरीरः -रा -रं, क्षुद्रतनुः &c., ह्रस्वशरीरः -रा -रं, स्तोककायः -या -यं, अल्पमूर्त्तिः -र्त्तिः -र्त्ति.—(Small in quantity, not much) अल्पः -ल्पा -ल्पं, अल्पमात्रः -त्रा -त्रं, स्तोकः -का -कं, अबहुः -हुः -ह्वी -हु, अबहुलः -ला -लं, अप्रचुरः -रा -रं, ईषत् in comp.—(Very little) अल्पल्पः -ल्पा -ल्पं, अल्पाल्पः -ल्पा -ल्पं, अल्पीयान् -यसी -यः (स्), अल्पिष्ठः -ष्ठा -ष्ठं, कनीयान् &c., अणीयान् &c., क्षोदीयान् &c., क्षोदिष्ठः &c.; 'not a little,' अनल्पः -ल्पा -ल्पं; 'little finger,' कनिष्ठाङ्गुलिः -ली *f.*; 'a little wealth,' अल्पधनं, अर्थलेशः; 'having little wealth,' अल्पधनः -ना -नं; 'of little merit,' ईषद्गुणः -णा -णं; 'a little hot,' ईषदुष्णः -ष्णा -ष्णं; 'a little animal,' क्षुद्रजन्तुः *m.*; 'of little weight,' अल्पप्रभावः -वा -वं, अल्पप्रमाणः -णा -णं; 'for a little while,' किञ्चित्कालं, कियत्कालं.

LITTLE, *s.* (Small quantity) अल्पभागः, अल्पांशः, किञ्चित्, अल्पं, स्तोकं, ईषत् ind., अल्पिका, अल्पमात्रं, मात्रा, किञ्चिद्भागः, किञ्चन, लवं, अबहुभागः, अबाहुल्यं, अप्राचुर्यं; 'little or much,' स्तोकं प्रचुरं वा; 'by little and little,' अल्पशस्, अल्पाल्पं, स्तोकशस्; 'desiring little,' अल्पाकांक्षी -क्षिणी -क्षि (न्); 'doing little,' ईषत्करः -री -रं.

LITTLE, *adv.* ईषत्, कियत्, स्तोकं, मनाक्, अल्पमात्रं, अबहु, अभृशं, अभूरि, तावत्; 'a little distance, a little way,' कियद्दूरं, ईषद्दूरं, नातिदूरं -रे, कियत्पर्य्यन्तं; 'a little less,' किञ्चिन्न्यूनः -ना -नं, ईषदूनः -ना -नं; 'little drunk,' ईषत्पानः -ना -नं, ईषत्पीतः -ता -तं; 'little-minded,' कृपणबुद्धिः -द्धिः -द्धि, कृपणधीः -धीः -धि.

LITTLENESS, *s.* अल्पता -त्वं, क्षुद्रता -त्वं, सूक्ष्मता, सौक्ष्म्यं, तनुता, स्तोकता, लघुता, लाघवं, लघिमा *m.* (न्), ह्रस्वता.—(Of body) अल्पशरीरता, शरीरह्रस्वता, शरीरक्षुद्रता.—(Meanness) कृपणता, कार्पण्यं, तुच्छत्वं, दीनता, कदर्य्यता, अपकृष्टता; 'of mind,' बुद्धिकार्पण्यं.

LITTORAL, *a.* तीरस्थः -स्था -स्थं, तटस्थः -स्था -स्थं, तीरसम्बन्धी -न्धिनी &c.

LITURGICAL, *a.* समाजप्रार्थनापद्धतिसम्बन्धी -न्धिनी -न्धि (न्), प्रार्थनपद्धतिविषयः -या -यं, प्रार्थनाविधिसम्बन्धी &c.

LITURGY, *s.* ख्रीष्टीयसमाजप्रार्थनापद्धतिः *f.*, प्रार्थनापद्धतिः, सामाजिकप्रार्थनापद्धतिः, सामाजिकभक्तिमार्गः, प्रार्थनामार्गः, ख्रीष्टीयप्रार्थनाविधिः *m.*

To LIVE, *v. n.* (Have the vital principle) जीव् (c. 1. जीवति -वितुं), प्राण् (c. 2. प्राणिति -तुं, rt. अन्), श्वस् (c. 2. श्वसिति -तुं), श्वासप्रश्वासं कृ.—(Exist, be in existence) वृत् (c. 1. वर्त्तते -र्त्तितुं), प्रवृत्, विद् in pass. (विद्यते), धृ in pass. (ध्रियते -ति); 'as long as you live,' यावद् धरिष्यसे, यावत्ते प्राणा धरिष्यन्ति, यावज्जीवं.—(Pass life or time) जीवनं or कालं वृत् (c. 10. वर्त्तयति -यितुं) or वह् (c. 10. वाहयति -यितुं) or निर्वह् or गम् (c. 10. गमयति -यितुं) or नी (c. 1. नयति, नेतुं), कालनिर्वाहं कृ, जीवननिर्वाहं कृ.—(Dwell, remain) वस् (c. 1. वसति, वस्तुं), निवस्, अधिवस्, स्था (c. 1. तिष्ठति, स्थातुं), अधिष्ठा, वृत्, आस् (c. 2. आस्ते -सितुं), वासं कृ.—(Subsist) उपजीव्, उपजीवनं कृ, निर्वह् (c. 1. -वहति -वोढुं), निर्वाहं कृ, शरीरयात्रां कृ, प्राणयात्रां कृ, प्राणधारणं कृ, उदरनिर्वाहं कृ.

LIVE, *a.* जीवी -विनी -वि (न्), जीवन् -वन्ती -वत् (त्). *See* LIVING, *part.*

LIVELIHOOD, *s.* जीविका, उपजीविका, उपजीवनं, उपजीव्यं, आजीवः -वनं, प्रजीवनं, जीवनं, जीवनोपायः, उपजीवनोपायः, वृत्तिः *f.*, वर्त्तनं, वार्त्ता, वृत्तिता, वृत्त्युपायः, जीवनवृत्तिः *f.*, जीवनसाधनं, जीवसाधनं, उपजीवनसाधनं, जीवनार्थः, शरीरयात्रा, प्राणयात्रा; 'bare livelihood,' ग्रासाच्छादनं, अन्नाच्छादनं, अशनाच्छादनं -ने *n. du.*, अन्नोदकं, दिननिर्वाहः, दिनचर्य्या; 'obtaining a livelihood,' जीविकाप्राप्तः -प्ता -प्तं.

LIVELINESS, *s.* तेजस् *n.*, तेजस्विता, तेजोवत्त्वं, उल्लसता, उल्लासः, प्रफुल्लता, प्रहृष्टता, प्रहर्षः, सानन्दता, सत्त्वं, तीव्रता, सजीवत्वं, लघुता, लाघवं, क्षिप्रत्वं; 'of countenance,' वदनप्रफुल्लता, मुखश्रीः *f.*

LIVELONG, *a.* दीर्घकालीनः -ना -नं, दीर्घकालिकः -की -कं, चिरकालीनः &c.

LIVELY, *a.* तेजोवान् -वती -वत् (त्), तेजस्वी -स्विनी -स्वि (न्), उल्लसः -सा -सं, उल्लासी -सिनी &c., प्रफुल्लः -ल्ला -ल्लं, प्रहृष्टः -ष्टा -ष्टं, आनन्दी -न्दिनी &c., सानन्दः -न्दा -न्दं, उल्लासवृत्तिः -त्तिः -त्ति, आनन्दवृत्तिः &c., सत्त्वपूर्णः -र्णा -र्णं, तीव्रः -व्रा -व्रं, तीक्ष्णः -क्ष्णा -क्ष्णं, बहुसत्त्वः -त्त्वा -त्त्वं, ससत्त्वः &c.—(In countenance) प्रफुल्लवदनः -ना -नं, हास्यमुखः -खी -खं, सुहसाननः -ना -नं, हास्यवदनः &c., प्रसन्नमुखः &c.—(Energetic) तीक्ष्णकर्म्मा -र्म्मा -र्म्म (न्), उद्योगशीलः -ला -लं, उत्साहशीलः -ला -लं.

LIVELY, LIVELILY, *adv.* तेजसा, तेजोपूर्व्वं, उल्लासेन, उल्लसवत्, प्रफुल्लवत्.

LIVER, *s.* (One who lives) जीवी *m.* (न्), उपजीवी *m.*, जीवकः. *See* LIVING, *part.* (The organ which secretes the bile) यकृत्, कालखण्डं, कालकं, कालिका, कालेयं, कालखञ्जनं, पित्ताशयः, पित्ताधारः; 'enlargement of the liver,' यकृद्गुल्मः.

LIVER-COLOR, *a.* यकृद्वर्णः -र्णा -र्णं, कालेयः -यी -यं, नीलरक्तः -क्ता -क्तं.

LIVERY, *s.* (Particular dress) वेषः, वेशः, कुलवेशः, कुलवेषः, कुलचिह्नं.—(Of a servant) सेवकवेषः, भृत्यवेशः, परिचारवेषः, कुलसेवकवेषः.—(Keeping a horse at a certain rate) निरूपितमूल्यमपेक्ष्य अश्वपोषणं or अश्वपालनं.

LIVERY-MAN, *s.* कुलवेशधारी *m.* (न्), कुलवेशभृत् *m.*—(Freeman) पौरवेशः, पौरलिङ्गी *m.* (न्), पौरलिङ्गधारी *m.* (न्).

LIVERY-STABLE, *s.* अश्वपोषणशाला, अश्वपालनशाला, अश्वशाला.

LIVE-STOCK, *s.* जीवधनं, जीवत् *n.*

LIVID, *a.* नीलः -ला -लं, नीलवर्णः -र्णा -र्णं, नीलकृष्णः -ष्णा -ष्णं, कृष्णवर्णः -र्णा -र्णं, सीसकवर्णः &c., कालः -ला -लं, कालिकः -की -कं.

LIVIDITY, LIVIDNESS, *s.* नीलता, नीलवर्णः, नीलिमा *m.* (न्), कृष्णता, कृष्णिमा *m.*, सीसकवर्णः.

LIVING, *part.* or *a.* (Having life) जीवी -विनी -वि (न्), जीवन् -वन्ती -वत् (त्), सजीवः -वा -वं, जीवितः -ता -तं, जीवभूतः -ता -तं, जीवन्तः -न्ती -न्तं, प्राणी -णिनी -णि (न्), प्राणन् -णन्ती -णत् (त्), प्राणभृत् *m. f. n.*, प्राणधारी -रिणी &c., प्राणमयः -यी -यं, सप्राणः -णा -णं, चेतनः -ना -नं, चेतनावान् -वती -वत् (त्), सचेष्टः -ष्टा -ष्टं, चेष्टितः -ता -तं; 'a living being,' जन्तुः *m.*, प्राणी *m.* (न्), प्राणभृत् *m.*,

जन्मी *m.*, शरीरी *m.*, देही *m.*, चेतनः, भूतं, सत्त्वं; 'living creatures,' प्राणिनः *m. pl.*, जीवन्तः *m. pl.*, चेतनाः *m. pl.*; 'the land of the living,' जीवलोकः.—(Existent) वर्त्तमानः -ना -नं, ध्रियमाणः -णा -णं, विद्यमानः -ना -नं, वर्त्तिष्णुः -ष्णुः -ष्णु, वर्त्ती -र्त्तिनी &c.—(Subsisting) उपजीवी -विनी &c., उपजीवकः -का -कं, आजीवी -विनी &c., आजीवः -वा -वं; 'living by agriculture,' कृष्युपजीवी &c.; 'living by learning,' विद्योपजीवी -विनी &c.; 'living by arms,' शस्त्रोपजीवी &c., शस्त्राजीवः -वा -वं; 'living virtuously,' सद्वर्त्ती -र्त्तिनी &c., सद्वृत्तिः -त्तिः -त्ति, सद्वृत्तः -त्ता -त्तं, सद्व्यवहारः -रा -रं; 'living wickedly,' असद्वृत्तिः &c., कुवृत्तिः &c., कुवर्त्ती -र्त्तिनी &c.; 'a living sacrifice,' जीवोपहारः; 'a living death,' जीवितमरणं.

LIVING, *s.* (The act) जीवनं, प्राणधारणं, वर्त्तनं, वृत्तिः *f.*, वासः, निवासः.—(Subsistence, means of subsistence) उपजीविका, जीविका, उपजीवनं, उपजीव्यं, आजीवः -वनं, जीवनोपायः, उपजीवनोपायः, वृत्त्युपायः, वृत्तिः, वर्त्तनं, जीवसाधनं, प्राणयात्रा, यात्रा, शरीरयात्रा, प्राणस्थितिः *f.*, निर्वाहः, जीवननिर्वाहः, प्राणनिर्वाहः, उदरनिर्वाहः; 'living by learning,' विद्योपजीवनं; 'living by husbandry,' कृष्युपजीवनं; 'having a living,' वृत्तिमान् -मती -मत् (त्); 'good living,' सुभोजनं, मिष्टभोजनं, परमान्नभोजनं, उत्तमान्नभोजनं, आप्यायनं; 'poor living,' कुभोजनं, कदन्नभोजनं.—(Benefice) धर्म्मदायः, धर्म्माध्यापकवृत्तिः *f.*, धर्म्मशिक्षकवृत्तिः.

LIXIVIAL, LIXIVIOUS, *a.* क्षाराम्बुसंसृष्टः -ष्टा -ष्टं, क्षारव्याप्तः -प्ता -प्तं, क्षारविशिष्टः -ष्टा -ष्टं, क्षाराक्तः -क्ता -क्तं, लवणाक्तः &c.

LIXIVIUM, *s.* क्षाराम्बु *n.*, क्षारजलं, क्षारसंसृष्टजलं, क्षारितजलं.

LIZARD, *s.* सरटः, सरटुः *m.*, सरट् *m.*, कृकलासः, कृकवाकुः *m.*, कृकुलासः, कृकलाशः, गोधा -धिका, प्रतिसूर्य्यः -र्य्यकः, पल्लिः -ल्लिका, लट्टिका, शरद्वः, बहुरूपः, अण्डजः, क्रकचपाद् *m.*, शुष्काङ्गी, वेदारः, विदारुः *m.*, साञ्जनः, साशयन्दकः, वृक्षशः; 'house-lizard,' गृहगोधा -धिका, गृहगोलिका, गृहालिका, मुसली, मुषली, मुशली, टट्टनी, ज्येष्ठा -ष्ठी.

Lo! *exclam.* पश्य, पश्यत, प्रेक्षस्व.

LOAD, *s.* भारः, धुरा, धूः *f.* (धुर्), स्थौरं, पर्य्याहारः; 'a heavy load,' सुभारः, अतिभारः, दुर्भारः, गुरुभारः.—(Encumbrance, any thing grievous) बाधा, पीडा, कष्टं; 'bearing a load,' भारवाहनः -ना -नं, भारवाही -हिनी -हि (न्), भारवाहिकः -की -कं, भारसहः -हा -हं, धुरन्धरः -रा -रं, धुर्वहः -हा -हं, भारहरः -रा -रं, भारहारिकः -की -कं; 'the act of bearing a load,' भारवहनं, भारोद्वहनं, भारोद्धरणं.

To LOAD, *v. a.* भारं न्यस् (c. 4. -अस्यति -असितुं) or निविश् (c. 10. -वेशयति -यितुं) or निधा (c. 3. -दधाति -धातुं) or आरुह् in caus. (-रोपयति -यितुं) or स्था in caus. (स्थापयति -यितुं), भारवन्तं -वतीं -वत् कृ, भाराक्रान्तं -न्तां -न्तं कृ, सभारं -रां कृ, भारेण पीड् (c. 10. पीडयति -यितुं), भारग्रस्तं -स्तां कृ.—(With powder) आग्नेयचूर्णं निविश्, चूर्णगर्भं -र्भां कृ, आग्नेयचूर्णेन पॄ (c. 10. पूरयति -यितुं).

LOADED, *p. p.* भारवान् -वती -वत् (त्), भारी -रिणी -रि (न्), सभारः -रा -रं, भाराक्रान्तः -न्ता -न्तं, भारग्रस्तः -स्ता -स्तं, अर्पितभारः -रा -रं, निवेशितभारः -रा -रं, आरोपितभारः -रा -रं, धुरीणः -णा -णं, गर्भः -र्भा -र्भं in comp.; 'loaded with powder,' चूर्णगर्भः -र्भा -र्भं, आग्नेयचूर्णपूरितः -ता -तं, दाह्यचूर्णपूर्णः -र्णा -र्णं; 'heavily loaded,' सुभरः -रा -रं, सुभारवान् &c., सुभारी &c., अतिभारी &c.

LOADER, *s.* भारकर्त्ता *m.* (र्त्तृ), भारदाता *m.* (तृ), भारारोपकः.

LOADING, *s.* (The act) भारार्पणं, भारारोपणं.—(Cargo) भारः.

LOADSTONE, *s.* लोहचुम्बकः, चुम्बकः, चुम्बकप्रस्तरः, चुम्बकमणिः *m.*, लोहकान्तः -न्तं, अयस्कान्तः, आकर्षः -र्षकः, आकर्षकप्रस्तरः, महालोहं, कृष्णलोहं, द्रावकः, भ्रामरः, वैक्रान्तं.

LOAF, *s.* अपूपः, पूपः, पिष्टकः, उत्स्वेदकः, ओकुलः, पोलिका, करम्भः -म्भकः.—(A mass) पिण्डः.

LOAM, *s.* चिक्कणमृत्तिका, स्निग्धमृत्तिका, पङ्कवालुकायुक्तो मृत्तिकाविशेषः, पङ्किलमृत्तिका, पङ्कः, चिकिलः.

LOAMY, *a.* चिक्कणः -णा -णं, चिक्कणमृत्तिकामयः -यी -यं.

LOAN, *s.* (Of money) ऋणं, ऋणदानं, धनप्रयोगः, प्रयोगः, कुसीदं, कलान्तिः *f.* -न्तिका, निरूपितकालपर्य्यन्तं धनप्रयोगः.—(Temporary use of any thing) निरूपितकालपर्य्यन्तं द्रव्यप्रयोजनं or द्रव्यप्रयोगः.—(Something to be given back) प्रतिदेयं.

LOATH, *a.* अनिच्छुः -च्छुः -च्छु, अनिच्छुकः -का -कं, अनिच्छन् -च्छन्ती -च्छत् (त्), विरक्तः -क्ता -क्तं, विमुखः -खा -खं, पराङ्मुखः -खा -खं, विमतः -ता -तं, असम्मतः -ता -तं, अकामः -मा -मं, निष्कामः -मा -मं, निस्पृहः -हा -हं.

To LOATHE, *v. a.* अत्यन्तं द्विष् (c. 2. द्वेष्टि -ष्टुं) or प्रद्विष्, अतिद्वेषं कृ, गर्ह् (c. 1. गर्हते -र्हितुं), बाध् in des. (बीभत्सते -त्सितुं), घृण् (c. 1. घृणते -णितुं), घृणां कृ, बीभत्सं कृ.

LOATHED, *p. p.* अतिद्विष्टः -ष्टा -ष्टं, गर्हितः -ता -तं, घृणितः -ता -तं.

LOATHFUL, *a.* अतिद्वेषी -षिणी -षि (न्), घृणाकारी -रिणी &c., बीभत्सकारी &c., बीभत्सः -त्सा -त्सं, बीभत्सजनकः -का -कं.

LOATHING, *s.* बीभत्सः -त्सं, घृणा, गर्हा -र्हणं, अतिद्वेषः -षणं, अत्यन्तद्वेषः, विकृतं, वैकृतं -त्यं, कुत्सा, विरक्तिः *f.*, निर्वेदः, न्यक्कारः.

LOATHINGLY, *adv.* सबीभत्सं, बीभत्सपूर्व्वं, अतिद्वेषेण, घृणापूर्व्वं, कुत्सापूर्व्वं.

LOATHSOME, *a.* बीभत्सजनकः -का -कं, घृणाजनकः -का -कं, घृणोत्पादकः -का -कं, अतिगर्हितः -ता -तं, गर्हितः -ता -तं, गर्हणीयः -या -यं, गर्ह्यः -र्ह्या -र्ह्यं, कुत्सितः -ता -तं, घृणार्हः -र्हा -र्हं, द्वेष्यः -ष्या -ष्यं, अतिद्वेषणीयः -या -यं, विरक्तिजनकः &c.

LOATHSOMELY, *adv.* गर्हितं, गर्हणीयं, अतिद्वेषणीयं, गर्ह्यप्रकारेण.

LOATHSOMENESS, *s.* गर्ह्यता, गर्हणीयता, कुत्सितत्वं, कौत्सित्यं, घृणाजनकत्वं, घृणार्हता, बीभत्सजनकता, द्वेष्यता.

LOB, LOB-COCK, *s.* स्थूलशरीरः, स्थूलकायः, स्थूलबुद्धिः *m.*, स्थूलजनः.

LOBBY, *s.* सभोपशाला, सभोपगृहं, उपशाला, बाह्यशाला, गमनागमनशाला.

LOBE, *s.* (Of the ear) कर्णलतिका, पालिका, कर्णपालिः *f.* -ली -लिका.—(Of the lungs) फुप्फुसभागः, फुप्फुसलतिका.—(Of the liver) यकृद्भागः, यकृदंशः.—(Part, division) अंशः, भागः.

LOBED, *a.* पालिकाविशिष्टः -ष्टा -ष्टं, भागी -गिनी -गि (न्).

LOBSTER, *s.* कर्कटजातीयो दीर्घनखविशिष्टो मत्स्यभेदः.

LOCAL, *a.* दैशिकः -की -कं, देश्यः -श्या -श्यं, देशी -शिनी -शि (न्), देशीयः -या -यं, स्थानिकः -की -कं, स्थानीयः -या -यं, ऐहस्थानिकः -की -कं, ऐहदेशिकः -की -कं, देश or स्थान in comp.; as, 'local usage,' देशव्यवहारः, देशाचारः; 'local law,' देशधर्म्मः.—(Relating to a place) देशसम्बन्धी -न्धिनी &c., स्थानसम्बन्धी -न्धिनी &c.—(Limited to a particular place) एकदेशिकः -का -कं, एकदेशीयः -या -यं, एकदेशी -शिनी &c., एकस्थानिकः -की -कं, विशेषदेशीयः -या -यं, विशेषस्थानिकः -की -कं.

LOCALITY, *s.* स्थानं, देशः, प्रदेशः, स्थलं, आस्पदं, स्थानता, देशता, देशसम्बन्धः, स्थानसम्बन्धः, स्थितिः *f.*

LOCALLY, *adv.* स्थानविषये, स्थानतस्, स्थानमुद्दिश्य, देशमुद्दिश्य, देशे.

To LOCATE, *v. a.* स्था in caus. (स्थापयति -यितुं), अवस्था, प्रतिष्ठा, विन्यस् (c. 4. -अस्यति -असितुं), निविश् (c. 10. -वेशयति -यितुं), रुह् in caus. (रोपयति -यितुं), स्थापनं कृ.

LOCATED, *p. p.* स्थापितः -ता -तं, प्रतिष्ठापितः -ता -तं, अवस्थितः -ता -तं, निवेशितः -ता -तं, विनिवेशितः -ता -तं, रोपितः -ता -तं.

LOCATION, *s.* (Act of placing) स्थापनं, प्रतिष्ठापनं, निवेशनं, रोपणं, विन्यासः.—(Situation) स्थानं, अवस्थानं, अवस्थितिः *f.*, प्रतिष्ठा, प्रतिष्ठानं, स्थितिः *f.*, आधिकारण्यं, आधिकरण्यं.—(In grammar) अधिकरणं, आधिकारण्यं.

LOCATIVE, *s.* (Case in grammar) अधिकरणं, सप्तमी विभक्तिः.

LOCH, *s.* *See* LAKE.

LOCK, *s.* (Instrument for fastening doors, &c.) तालयन्त्रं, तालकं, तालः, अर्गलं, विष्कम्भः, द्वारयन्त्रं, द्वारकीलः.—(Of a gun) चूर्णज्वलनयन्त्रं, अग्निदयन्त्रं, अग्निजनकयन्त्रं.—(Of hair) अलकः, केशपाशः -शी, जटा, शिरोरुहः, काकपक्षः; 'clotted lock of an ascetic,' जटा, सटा, शटा; 'lock left on the crown or sides of the head at tonsure,' चूडा, शिखा, शिखण्डः -ण्डकः, शिखण्डिका, शिखाण्डकः, काकपक्षः, केशपाशी.—(In a river or canal) जलस्तम्भनी, जलप्रतिबन्धकं, जलबन्धनी, जलबन्धनयन्त्रं, महायन्त्रं.—(Hug) आलिङ्गनं, गाढालिङ्गनं, अङ्कसङ्गः.

To LOCK, *v. a.* (Fasten with a lock) तालयन्त्रेण बन्ध् (c. 9. बध्नाति बन्द्धुं), कील् (c. 10. कीलयति -यितुं), तालकेन or अर्गलेन बन्ध्, तालबद्धं -द्धां कृ; 'lock a door,' द्वारं बन्ध् or रुध् (c. 7. रुणद्धि, रोद्धुं), द्वाररोधं कृ.—(Close) पिधा (c. 3. -दधाति -धातुं), अपिधा, बन्ध्.—(Confine) रुध्, निरुध्.—(Embrace closely) गाढम् आलिङ्ग् (c. 1. -लिङ्गति -ङ्गितुं), गाढालिङ्गनं कृ.

To LOCK, *v. n.* (Be fastened) तालकेन बन्ध् in pass. (बध्यते) or बद्धीभू.—(Unite by mutual embrace) परस्पराश्लेषेण or परस्परालिङ्गनेन संलग्नीभू or संबद्धीभू, परस्परं संश्लिष्टः -ष्टा -ष्टं भू.

LOCKED, *p. p.* (Fastened by a lock) तालयन्त्रेण बद्धः -द्धा -द्धं, तालकबद्धः -द्धा -द्धं, अर्गलबद्धः &c., कीलितः -ता -तं.—(Confined) रुद्धः -द्धा -द्धं, निरुद्धः -द्धा -द्धं.—(Closely embraced) गाढालिङ्गितः -ता -तं, गाढाश्लिष्टः -ष्टा -ष्टं.

LOCKED-JAW, LOCK-JAW, *s.* हनुस्तम्भः, हनुग्रहः.

LOCKER, *s.* तालकयुक्तं कोष्ठकं, कोष्ठः, सम्पुटः -टकः, भाजनं.

LOCKET, *s.* (Clasp, catch) कुडुपः.—(Ornament) स्मरणकेशाधारः.

LOCKSMITH, *s.* तालककारः, तालककृत् *m.*, तालयन्त्रकारी *m.* (न्).

LOCOMOTION, *s.* (Act of moving from place to place) स्थानान्तरगमनं, स्थलान्तरगमनं, स्थानात् स्थानं गमनं, गमनागमनं, इतस्ततो गमनं or चलनं, स्थानान्तरकरणं, स्थलान्तरकरणं, स्थानान्तरं, स्थलान्तरं, वीक्षा.—(Power of moving from place to place) स्थानान्तरगमनशक्तिः *f.*, चलनशक्तिः *f.*, गमनागमनशक्तिः *f.*

LOCOMOTIVE, *a.* जङ्गमः -मा -मं, चलः -ला -लं, चलनः -ना -नं, चलनशीलः -ला -लं, चलनधर्म्मकः -का -कं, चलनशक्तिकः -का -कं, चरः -रा -री -रं, चरिष्णुः -ष्णुः -ष्णु, सृत्वरः -रा -रं, गामुकः -का -कं, गतिमान् -मती -मत् (त्), गत्वरः -री -रं, गमनशक्तिविशिष्टः -ष्टा -ष्टं, पादुकः -का -कं.

LOCUM-TENENS, *s.* प्रतिनिधिः *m.*, प्रतिपुरुषः, प्रतिहस्तकः.

LOCUS, *s.* (In astronomy or geometry) निधिः *m.*

LOCUST, *s.* शलभः, शरभः, शकुन्तिका, शिरिः *m.*, पतङ्गः, शूककीटः.

LOCUTION, *s.* उक्तिः *f.*, वाक्यं, उक्तं, वाक् *f.* (च्), वाग्व्यापारः.

LODE, *s.* (Metallic vein) धातुरेखा, धातुपद्धतिः -ती *f.*

LODESTONE, *s.* *See* LOADSTONE.

LODH, *s.* (Tree, the bark of which is used in dyeing) लोधः, लोध्रः, पट्टिका, पट्टी, क्रमुकः, लाक्षाप्रसादनः, गालवः, शावरः, तिरीटः, तिल्वः, मार्ज्जनः.

To LODGE, *v. a.* (Furnish with a temporary habitation) वस् (c. 10. वासयति -यितुं), निवस्, वासस्थानं दा, आश्रयं दा, निरूपितकालपर्य्यन्तं वस्.—(Fix, set, place) स्था in caus. (स्थापयति -यितुं), न्यस् (c. 4. -अस्यति -असितुं), निधा (c. 3. -दधाति -धातुं), प्रणिधा, प्रतिनिधा, निविश् (c. 10. -वेशयति -यितुं), ऋ in caus. (अर्पयति -यितुं), रुह् in caus. (रोपयति -यितुं).

To LODGE, *v. n.* (Reside temporarily) वस् (c. 1. वसति, वस्तुं), निवस्, आवस्, प्रतिवस्, समावस्, सन्निवस्, आश्रि (c. 1. -श्रयति -ते -यितुं), वासं कृ, निवासं कृ, आश्रयं कृ, निरूपितकालपर्य्यन्तं वस्; 'having lodged,' उषित्वा, उष्ट्वा, उष्य; 'having lodged for a night,' रात्रिम् एकाम् उषित्वा.—(Rest, remain) स्था (c. 1. तिष्ठति, स्थातुं), वृत् (c. 1. वर्त्तते -र्त्तितुं), निली (c. 4. -लीयते -लेतुं), संली.—(Become fixed, adhere) अनुबन्ध् (c. 9. -बध्नाति -बन्द्धुं or pass. -बध्यते), लग् (c. 1. लगति -गितुं).

LODGE, *s.* उद्यानगृहं, उद्यानस्थगृहं, उपगृहं, उटजः, कुटीरः.

LODGED, *p. p.* वासितः -ता -तं, कृतावासः -सा -सं.—(Placed, fixed, deposited) स्थापितः -ता -तं, न्यस्तः -स्ता -स्तं, निहितः -ता -तं, प्रणिहितः -ता -तं, अर्पितः -ता -तं, निवेशितः -ता -तं, निविष्टः -ष्टा -ष्टं, निष्ठितः -ता -तं, निरूढः -ढा -ढं.

LODGER, *s.* (One who lies or boards in another's house at a settled rate) निरूपितमूल्येन परगृहे निवासी *m.* (न्) or भोजनशयनादिकर्त्ता *m.* (र्तृ), निरूपितकालपर्य्यन्तं परगृहे वासी *m.* or वासकृत् *m.*

LODGING, *s.* वासः, निवासः, वासस्थानं, आवासः, आवासस्थानं, वसतिः *f.*, निवसतिः *f.*, निवेशनं, निकेतः -तनं, आयतनं, निलयः -यनं, आलयः, अवस्थानं, आवसथः, आश्रयः, संश्रयः, कृतावासः, वेश्म *n.* (न्); 'he asked a lodging,' आवासं प्रार्थितवान्.

LODGMENT, *s.* (The act) स्थापनं, संस्थापनं -ना, निवेशनं, वासः -सनं.—(The state) स्थितिः *f.*, अवस्थितिः *f.*, संस्थितिः *f.*—(Encampment) निवेशनं, समावासः.

LOFT, *s.* उपरिकोष्ठः, उपरिस्थकोष्ठः, उपरिस्थः प्रकोष्ठः, अट्टः -ट्टालः.

LOFTILY, *adv.* (Haughtily) सदर्पं, सगर्व्वं, साटोपं, सावहेलं, सावलेपं, दर्पेण, गर्व्वेण, उद्धतं, औद्धत्येन.—(On high) उच्चैस्, उच्चकैस्, ऊर्द्ध्वं.

LOFTINESS, *s.* (Height) उच्चत्वं -ता, उन्नतिः *f.*, समुन्नतिः *f.*, उत्कर्षः, उत्कृष्टता, तुङ्गता, उत्तुङ्गता, उच्छ्रयः, समुच्छ्रयः, उच्छ्रितिः *f.*, उत्सेधः, समुत्सेधः, उन्नतता, ऊर्द्ध्वत्वं -ता, प्रोन्नता, प्रांशुता, औत्कर्ष्यं.—(Haughtiness) उद्धतिः *f.*, औद्धत्यं, चित्तसमुन्नतिः *f.*, चित्तोन्नतिः *f.*, साटोपत्वं, आटोपः, अभिमानं -निता, अवहेला, अवलेपः, अवलिप्तता, सावलेपत्वं, दर्पः, दृप्तता, गर्व्वः, शौटीर्य्यं, शौण्डीर्य्यं, प्रौढता, प्रगल्भता.

LOFTY, *a.* (High) उच्चः -च्चा -च्चं, अत्युच्चः &c., प्रांशुः -शुः -शु, तुङ्गः -ङ्गा -ङ्गं, उत्तुङ्गः -ङ्गा -ङ्गं, उन्नतः -ता -तं, समुन्नतः -ता -तं, उच्छ्रितः -ता -तं, समुच्छ्रितः -ता -तं, अभ्युच्छ्रितः -ता -तं, उच्चकः -का -कं, उदग्रः -ग्रा -ग्रं, ऊर्द्ध्वः -र्द्ध्वा -र्द्ध्वं, उत्कृष्टः -ष्टा -ष्टं, सोच्छ्रायः -या -यं, उन्नतः -ता -तं, उत्तालः -ला -लं, करालः -ला -लं, विलङ्घिताकाशः -शा -शं.—(Haughty) उद्धतः -ता -तं, समुद्धतः -ता -तं, गर्व्वोद्धतः -ता -तं, दर्पोद्धतः -ता -तं, दृप्तः -प्ता -प्तं, उन्नतचेताः -ताः -तः (स्), उच्चचेताः &c., उत्सिक्तः -क्ता -क्तं, गर्व्वी -र्व्विणी -र्व्वि (न्), गर्व्वितः -ता -तं, साटोपः -पा -पं, अवलिप्तः -प्ता

-ग्रं, सावहेलः -ला -लं, अर्द्धदृष्टिः -ष्टिः -ष्टि, मदोद्धतः -ता -तं, मदोदग्रः -ग्रा -ग्रं, शौटीरः -रा -रं, शौण्डीरः -रा -रं, प्रौढः -ढा -ढं.

Log, *s.* (Shapeless or bulky piece of wood) स्थूलकाष्ठं, स्थूलदारुः *m.*, काष्ठखण्डः -ण्डं, बृहत्काष्ठं, दारुखण्डः, बृहद्दारुखण्डः, काष्ठं.—(Machine for measuring the velocity of a ship) नौकागतिमापकयन्त्रं, परिमापककाष्ठं.

Log-book, *s.* नौकागतिविषयकं दैनिकविवरणपुस्तकं.

Logarithm, *s.* घातप्रमापकः, घातप्रमापकसंख्या, लाघवतमाख्यसंख्या, परिकर्म्म *n.* (न्).

Logarithmic, *a.* घातप्रमापकसम्बन्धी -न्धिनी -न्धि (न्).

Loggerhead, *s.* स्थूलबुद्धिः *m.*, स्थूलधीः *m.*, मूढः, मूर्खः, जडः, जडबुद्धिः *m.*, जडमतिः *m.*, बर्ब्बरः, बटुकः.

Loggerheaded, *a.* स्थूलबुद्धिः -द्धिः -द्धि, स्थूलधीः -धीः -धि, जडबुद्धिः.

Logic, *s.* तर्कः, तर्कविद्या, तर्कशास्त्रं, न्यायः, न्यायविद्या, न्यायशास्त्रं, विचारविद्या, व्यूहः, प्रोहः, अभ्यूहः, निरूहः, ऊहः, वैशेषिकं, आन्वीक्षिकी, अनुमानोक्तिः *f.*, ध्रुवः. The न्याय school was instituted by the sage Gautama, the branch of it called वैशेषिकं was founded by Kaṇáda. The following are some of the terms of logic; 'universal pervadence or extension,' व्याप्तिः *f.*, अभिव्याप्तिः; 'extreme extension or conclusion unwarranted by the premises,' अतिव्याप्तिः; 'individual or particular extension,' अव्याप्तिः *f.*, अव्याप्यवृत्तिः *f.*; sign of the existence of an inherent property,' व्याप्तिलक्षणं; 'subject of an inference,' व्याप्यं. Other terms are उपलप्रक्षेपः, उत्थाप्याकांक्षा, प्रवृत्तिनिमित्तं, वैयर्थ्यं, व्याप्यकोटिः *f.*, सिद्धसाधनदोषः.

Logical, *a.* (Pertaining to logic) तार्किकः -की -कं, न्यायी -यिनी -यि (न्), नैयायिकः -की -कं, तर्कसम्बन्धी -न्धिनी &c., तर्कविद्यासम्बन्धी &c., तर्कविद्याविषयः -या -यं, तर्कशास्त्रविषयः &c., प्रोहः -हा -हं, ऊही -हिनी &c., यौक्तिकः -की -कं; 'logical conclusion,' विनिगमः, निगमनं.—(According to the rules of logic) तर्कशास्त्रसिद्धः -द्धा -द्धं, न्यायशास्त्रसिद्धः &c., युक्तिसिद्धः &c., तर्कानुसारी -रिणी &c., न्यायानुसारी &c., न्यायशास्त्रानुसारी &c., तर्कशास्त्रसम्मतः -ता -तं, न्यायशास्त्रसम्मतः -ता -तं, तर्कशास्त्रानुयायी -यिनी &c.

Logically, *adv.* न्यायतस्, यथान्यायं, तर्कानुसारेण, न्यायानुसारेण, तर्कशास्त्रानुसारेण, तर्कशास्त्रानुरूपेण, न्यायशास्त्रवत्.

Logician, *s.* तर्की *m.* (न्), तार्किकः, नैयायिकः, न्यायविद् *m.*, तर्कशास्त्रज्ञः, न्यायशास्त्रज्ञः, न्यायशास्त्रपण्डितः, न्यायशास्त्रवेत्ता *m.* (तृ), तर्कशास्त्री *m.*, (न्), न्यायशास्त्री *m.*, सांवादिकः, ऊही *m.*; 'versed in the system of Gautama,' आक्षपादः, अक्षपादः; 'in that of Kaṇáda,' वैशेषिकः.

Logomachy, *s.* वाग्युद्धं, वाक्कलहः -हं.—(Dispute about words) शब्दवादः, शब्दविवादः, शब्दयुद्धं.

Logwood, *s.* (A kind of wood used in dyeing) पतङ्गः.

Loin, *s.* श्रोणिः -णी *f.*, कटिः -टी *f.*, कटिदेशः, श्रोणिदेशः, श्रोणिफलकं, श्रोणितटं, कटीतटं, कटितटं, नितम्बः, जघनं, ककुद्मती, कलत्रं, प्रोथः, कटः, कटिशीर्षकं; 'girding the loins,' कटिबन्धनं; 'having the loins girded,' बद्धकटिः -टिः -टि; 'the cavities of the loins,' कुकुन्दरे *n.* du., ककुन्दरे *n.* du., कटीरे *n.* du., कटीरः, कटः; 'girdle worn round the loins,' कटिसूत्रं, कटिशृङ्खला, श्रोणिबिम्बं; 'sprung from one's loins,' अङ्गजः -जा -जं, अङ्गजातः -ता -तं.

To **loiter**, *v. n.* विलम्ब् (c. 1. -लम्बते -म्बितुं), मन्द् (nom. मन्दायते), विलम्बनं कृ, विलम्बं कृ, कालं क्षिप् (c. 6. क्षिपति, क्षेप्तुं), कालक्षेपं कृ, अवस्था (c. 1. -तिष्ठति -स्थातुं), चिर (nom. चिरयति, चिरायति), चिरं or चिरकालं स्था or अवस्था, मन्दं मन्दं चल् (c. 1. चलति -लितुं) or चर् (c. 1. चरति -रितुं), विलम्बेन गम् (c. 1. गच्छति, गन्तुं).

Loiterer, *s.* विलम्बी *m.* (न्), विलम्बकारी *m.*, विलम्बगतिः *m.*, विलम्बगामी *m.* (न्), मन्दगामी *m.*, मन्दगतिः *m.*, कालक्षेपकः.

Loitering, *part.* मन्दायमानः -ना -नं, मन्दयमानः -ना -नं, विलम्बी -म्बिनी -म्बि (न्), विलम्बगामी -मिनी &c., चिरायमाणः -णा -णं.

Loitering, *s.* विलम्बनं, विलम्बगमनं, मन्दगमनं, कालक्षेपः.

To **loll**, *v. n.* (Recline lazily) आलस्येन शी (c. 2. शेते, शयितुं) or अवलम्ब् (c. 1. -लम्बते -म्बितुं) or संविश् (c. 6. -विशति -वेष्टुं), सुखेन शी or अवलम्ब्.—(Loll the tongue) जिह्वां लल् or लड् (c. 1. ललति, लडति, c. 10. लालयति, लडयति -यितुं), जिह्वाललनं कृ, जिह्वां बहिष्कृ; 'one who lolls the tongue,' ललजिह्वः -ह्वा -ह्वं.

Lolling, *s.* (Of the tongue) ललनं, जिह्वाललनं.—(Lolling and languishing as indicative of passion) लालित्यं, ललितं, लालनं.

Lone, **lonely**, *a.* (Solitary, unfrequented) निर्जनः -ना -नं, विजनः -ना -नं, विलोकः -की -कं, निर्मनुजः -जा -जं, निर्मनुष्यः -ष्या -ष्यं, एकान्तः -न्ता -न्तं, विविक्तः -क्ता -क्तं, निभृतः -ता -तं, जनानाकीर्णः -र्णा -र्णं, जनैरनाकीर्णः &c., निःशलाकः -का -कं, निश्शलाकः &c., न्यूनसञ्चारः -रा -रं, हीनसञ्चारः -रा -रं; 'a lonely place,' निर्जनस्थानं.—(Single, standing by itself) एकाकी -किनी -कि (न्), एकः -का -कं, असहायः -या -यं, असङ्गः -ङ्गा -ङ्गं, केवलः -ला -लं, केवली -लिनी &c.—(Fond of solitude) विविक्तप्रियः -या -यं, विविक्तसेवी -विनी &c., एकान्तप्रियः -या -यं, एकान्तसेवी &c.

Loneliness, *s.* (Solitude, retirement) निर्जनता, विजनता, विविक्तता, विविक्तं, निर्मनुष्यता, निभृतता, एकान्तत्वं, निःशलाकता, सञ्चारहीनता, सञ्चारन्यूनता, एकाकिता -त्वं, असहायता, असङ्गता.—(Love of retirement) विविक्तसेवा, विविक्तप्रीतिः *f.*, विविक्तरुचिः *f.*, एकान्तप्रीतिः *f.*

Lonesome, *a.* निर्जनः -ना -नं, विजनः -ना -नं, दारुणः -णा -णं, निरानन्दः -न्दा -न्दं; 'a lonesome road,' प्रान्तरं.

Lonesomeness, *s.* निर्जनता, विजनता, विविक्तता, निरानन्दता, दारुणता.

Long, *a.* (In time or space) दीर्घः -र्घा -र्घं, द्राघिमवान् -वती -वत् (त्), आयतः -ता -तं, आयामी -मिनी -मि (न्), आयामवान् -वती &c., व्यायतः -ता -तं, आयतिमान् -मती &c., लम्बः -म्बा -म्बं, चिर in comp., this last is restricted to time. (Long in extent or size) दीर्घपरिमाणः -णा -णं, दीर्घाकारः -रा -रं, दीर्घाकृतिः -तिः -ति, दीर्घतनुः -नुः -नु.—(Extended) आयतः -ता -तं, समायतः -ता -तं, आयामितः -ता -तं, विस्तीर्णः -र्णा -र्णं, विस्तृतः -ता -तं, प्रसृतः -ता -तं.—(Tedious, dilatory) दीर्घसूत्रः -त्रा -त्रं, चिरकारी -रिणी &c., चिरक्रियः -या -यं, विलम्बकारी &c., विलम्बी -म्बिनी &c., दीर्घसूत्री -त्रिणी &c., प्रलम्बः -म्बा -म्बं.—(Continuing for a long time) दीर्घकालीनः -ना -नं, चिरकालीनः -ना -नं, दीर्घकालिकः -की -कं, चिरकालिकः &c., चिरस्थः -स्था -स्थं, चिरस्थायी -यिनी &c., चिरस्थितः -ता -तं, चिरन्तनः -नी -नं, चिरत्नः -त्नी -त्नं, दीर्घकालस्थायी -यिनी &c., चिरकालस्थायी -यिनी &c.—(Long, in the sense of distant) दूरः -रा -रं, विदूरः -रा -रं; 'going a long way,' दूरगः -गा -गं; 'a long way off,' दूरस्थः -स्था -स्थं, दूरस्थायी -यिनी &c.—(Extended to any measure) expressed by परिमाणः -णा -णं or परिमितः -ता -तं or मितः -ता -तं in comp.; as, 'a line an inch long,' अङ्गुलपरिमाणा or अङ्गुलपरिमिता or

चतुरङ्गुलमिता रेखा; 'four fingers long,' चतुरङ्गुलः -ली -लं, चतुरङ्गुलपरिमितः -ता -तं.—(A long period) दीर्घकालः, चिरकालः, बहुकालः, अनेककालः, आयतायतिः *f.*; 'for a long time,' दीर्घकालं, चिरकालं, बहुकालं -लात्, अनेककालं, चिरं -रेण -रात् -राय, चिरदिवसं, चिररात्रं -त्राय, दीर्घरात्रं; 'long absent,' चिरगतः -ता -तं, चिरप्रवासी -सिनी &c.; 'long ill,' दीर्घरोगी -गिणी &c., दीर्घामयः -या -यं, चिररोगी &c.; 'long sought for,' चिरचेष्टितः -ता -तं; 'cherished for a long time,' चिरकालपालितः -ता -तं, चिरपालितः &c.; 'accumulated after a long time,' चिरकालोपार्जितः -ता -तं, चिरलब्धः -ब्धा -ब्धं; 'living long,' दीर्घजीवी -विनी &c., चिरजीवी &c.; 'a long life,' दीर्घजीवः; 'long since abandoned,' चिरोज्झितः -ता -तं, 'for a short time,' अल्पकालं, अल्पमात्रं, कियत्कालं, 'lasting for a short time,' क्षणस्थायी -यिनी &c., 'the long run,' आयतिः *f.*, 'long-haired,' दीर्घकेशः -शी -शं; 'long-leaved,' दीर्घपत्रः -त्रा -त्रं, दीर्घपर्णः -र्णा -र्णं; 'long-tongued,' दीर्घजिह्वः -ह्वा -ह्वं, दीर्घरसनः -ना -नं, 'having a long line of ancestors,' दीर्घवंशः -शा -शं, 'a long journey,' दीर्घवर्त्म *n.* (न्), दीर्घाध्व *n.* (न्), 'a long vowel,' दीर्घस्वरः, 'the long sound of vowels,' प्लवः, प्लुतः -तं, 'long syllable,' दीर्घाक्षरं, हारः.

LONG, *adv.* (To a great extent in space) दूरं, चिदरं, दूरतस्, दूरपर्यन्तं, दीर्घपर्यन्तं, दीर्घपरिमाणं -णेन.—(To a great extent in time, for a long period) दीर्घकालं, चिरकालं -लात्, बहुकालं -लात्, अनेककालं, चिरं -रेण -राय -रात् -रस्य -रे, चिरदिवसं, चिररात्रं -त्राय, दीर्घरात्रं -त्राय, बहुकालपर्यन्तं, दीर्घकालपर्यन्तं; 'very long,' सुचिरं -रेण -रात्; 'how long?' कियत्कालं, कियन्तं कालं, कियता कालेन, कियत्कालपर्यन्तं, कियत्कालं यावत्, कतिकालं; 'how long!' कियच्चिरं -रेण -रात्; 'ere long,' अचिरेण -रात्; 'long ago,' प्रागेव, प्राक्काले, पूर्व्वं, पूर्व्वकाले, अतीतदीर्घकाले, गतदीर्घकाले, व्यवहितपूर्व्वकाले; 'not long ago,' अव्यवहितपूर्व्वकाले; 'as long,' यत्कालं, यावत्कालं, यत्क्षणं; 'so long,' तत्कालं, तावत्कालं, तत्क्षणं.—(Through the whole extent or duration of) पर्य्यन्तं affixed, आ prefixed, यावत्; as, 'the whole year long,' वर्षपर्य्यन्तं, आवर्षान्तात्; 'whole life, as long as one lives,' यावज्जीवं, आमरणात्, मरणं यावत्; 'long-absent, long-ill, long-sought, &c.' *See* under LONG, *a.*

To LONG, *v. n.* (Desire eagerly) अत्यन्तम् अभिलष् (c. 1. -लषति, c. 4. -लष्यति -लषितुं) or वाञ्छ् (c. 1. वाञ्छति -ञ्छितुं) or अभिवाञ्छ् or कांक्ष् (c. 1. कांक्षति -क्षितुं) or आकांक्ष् or अभिकांक्ष् or अनुकांक्ष्, अतिशयेन स्पृह् (c. 10. स्पृहयति -यितुं) or इष् (c. 6. इच्छति, एषितुं) or आप् in des. (ईप्सति -प्सितुं) or अभ्याप् or पर्याप् or लभ् in des. (लिप्सते -प्सितुं) or अभिलभ् or अभिरुच् (c. 10. -रोचयति -यितुं) or कम् (c. 10. कामयते -यितुं) or ईह् (c. 1. ईहते -हितुं) or समीह्, लुभ् (c. 4. लुभ्यति, लोब्धुं), गृध् (c. 4. गृध्यति, गर्धितुं), भुज् in des. (बुभुक्षति -ते -क्षितुं), तृष् (c. 4. तृष्यति, तर्षितुं), आशंस् (c. 1. -शंसते -सितुं), आशास् (c. 2. -शास्ते, c. 1. -शासते -सितुं), अभिध्यानं कृ.—(As a pregnant woman) दोहदं कृ, दोहदवती भू, दौहृदिनी भू.

LONGANIMITY, *s.* सहनशीलता, चिरसहिष्णुता, क्षमा, क्षान्तिः *f.*

LONG-ARMED, *a.* दीर्घबाहुः -हुः -हु, दीर्घभुजः -जा -जं, लम्बहस्तः -स्ता -स्तं.

LONG-BELLIED, *a.* लम्बोदरः -रा -रं, लम्बजठरः -रा -रं, दीर्घोदरः -रा -रं.

LONG-BOAT, *s.* दीर्घनौका, बृहन्नौका, महानौका, उपनौका.

LONG-CONCEALED, *a.* चिरगुप्तः -प्ता -प्तं, चिरकालप्रच्छन्नः -न्ना -न्नं.

LONG-CONTINUED, *a.* चिरस्थितः -ता -तं, चिरकालस्थायी -यिनी -यि (न्).

LONG-EARED, *a.* लम्बकर्णः -र्णा -र्णं, दीर्घकर्णः -र्णा -र्णं, आयतकर्णः -र्णा -र्णं.

LONG-EYED, *a.* आयताक्षः -क्षी -क्षं, आयतनेत्रः -त्री -त्रं, दीर्घनयनः -नी -नं.

LONG-FACED, *a.* दीर्घमुखः -खी -खं, दीर्घवक्त्रः -क्त्रा -क्त्रं, दीर्घाननः -ना -नं.

LONG-FORGOTTEN, *a.* चिरविस्मृतः -ता -तं, चिरकालविस्मृतः -ता -तं.

LONG-HEADED, *a.* विदग्धमतिः -तिः -ति, उत्पन्नमतिः &c., निपुणमतिः &c., सूक्ष्मबुद्धिः -द्धिः -द्धि, दीर्घसन्धानी -निनी -नि (न्).

LONG-LASTING, *a.* चिरस्थायी -यिनी -यि (न्), चिरकालस्थायी &c., चिरस्थः -स्था -स्थं, चिरकालीनः -ना -नं, चिरकालिकः -की -कं, दीर्घकालिकः -की -कं.

LONG-LEGGED, *a.* दीर्घजङ्घः -ङ्घा -ङ्घं, दीर्घपादः -दा -दं, आयतजङ्घः &c., ऊर्द्ध्वजानुः -नुः -नु, ऊर्द्ध्वज्ञः -ज्ञा -ज्ञं, ऊर्द्ध्वज्ञुः -ज्ञुः -ज्ञु, दीर्घसक्थः -क्था -क्थं.

LONG-LIVED, *a.* दीर्घजीवी -विनी -वि (न्), चिरजीवी &c., चिरञ्जीवी &c., चिरजीवकः -का -कं, दीर्घायुः -युः -यु or दीर्घायूः -यूः -युः (स्), चिरायुः &c., दीर्घायुष्यः -ष्या -ष्यं, चिरायुष्यः &c., आयुषः -षी -षं, जीवथः -था -थं, जैवातृकः -का -कं, आयुष्मान् -ष्मती -ष्मत् (त्); this last is generally used in addressing a king or superior in the voc. c.; as, 'O long-lived one,' आयुष्मन्.

LONG-LOST, *a.* चिरगतः -ता -तं, चिरभ्रष्टः -ष्टा -ष्टं, चिरकालगतः -ता -तं.

LONG-NECKED, *a.* दीर्घग्रीवः -वा -वं, आयतग्रीवः &c., दीर्घकण्ठः -ण्ठा -ण्ठं.

LONG-PEPPER, *s.* पिप्पली -लिः *f.*, शौण्डी, कोला, उषणा, कृष्णा, उपकुल्या, मागधी, वैदेही, चपला, कणा, वशिरः, वसिरः, श्रेयसी, करिपिप्पली, कपिवल्ली, कोलवल्ली, चव्यं -व्या, चवी, चविका -कं.—(Its root) पिप्पलीमूलं, ग्रन्थिकं, चटिकाशिरस् *n.*

LONG-SIGHTED, *a.* दीर्घदर्शी -र्शिनी -र्शि (न्), दीर्घदृष्टिः -ष्टिः -ष्टि, दूरदर्शी &c., दूरदृष्टिः -ष्टिः -ष्टि.

LONG-SIGHTEDNESS, *s.* दीर्घदृष्टिः *f.*, दीर्घदर्शनं, दूरदृष्टिः *f.*, दूरदर्शनं.

LONG-SUFFERANCE, LONG-SUFFERING, *s.* सहनशीलता, सहिष्णुता, चिरसहिष्णुता -त्वं, चिरसहनं, बहुक्षमता, क्षमा, क्षान्तिः *f.*, सहनं, तितिक्षा, अपकारेऽपि चिरन्तस्याविकारः.

LONG-SUFFERING, *a.* सहनशीलः -ला -लं, सहिष्णुः -ष्णुः -ष्णु, चिरसहिष्णुः -ष्णुः -ष्णु, बहुक्षमः -मा -मं, बहुसहः -हा -हं, सर्व्वसहः -हा -हं, क्षमावान् -वती -वत् (त्), क्षान्तः -न्ता -न्तं, क्षमी -मिणी -मि (न्), तितिक्षुः -क्षुः -क्षु.

LONG-WINDED, *a.* दीर्घसूत्रः -त्रा -त्रं -त्री -त्रिणी -त्रि (न्), कष्टजनकः -का -कं.

LONGER, *a.* दीर्घतरः -रा -रं, द्राघीयान् -यसी -यः (स्); 'for a longer period,' दीर्घतरकालं, बहुतरकालं; 'why do you delay any longer?' किम् अतःपरं विलम्बसे.

LONGEST, *a.* दीर्घतमः -मा -मं, द्राघिष्ठः -ष्ठा -ष्ठं; 'for the longest period,' दीर्घतमकालं, सुदीर्घकालं.

LONGEVAL, LONGEVOUS, *s.* दीर्घजीवी -विनी -वि (न्), चिरजीवी &c. *See* LONG-LIVED.

LONGEVITY, *s.* दीर्घजीवः, चिरजीवित्वं, दीर्घजीवित्वं, चिरञ्जीवित्वं, दीर्घायुष्यं, चिरायुष्यं, चिरायुस् *n.*, दीर्घायुस् *n.*, आयुस् *n.*; 'conducive to longevity,' आयुष्यः -ष्या -ष्यं.

LONGIMANOUS, *a.* दीर्घहस्तः -स्ता -स्तं, दीर्घपाणिः -णिः -णि, लम्बहस्तः &c.

LONGIMETRY, *s.* दूरत्वमितिः *f.*, दूरत्वमापनं, दैर्घ्यमानं, दैर्घ्यमापनं.

LONGING, *s.* अत्यभिलाषः, अतिस्पृहा, अत्यन्तवाञ्छा, अतीच्छा, अतिशयेच्छा, अतिकांक्षा, अत्याकांक्षा, लालसा, उत्कण्ठा, कौतूहलं, औत्सुक्यं, कामः, तृष्णा, अतिलिप्सा, इच्छा, आशा, कांक्षा, अभिकांक्षा, नितान्तस्पृहा; 'longing of a pregnant woman,' दोहदं.

Longing, *part.* or *a.* (Eagerly desirous) अभिलाषी -षिणी -षि (न्), अभिकांक्षी -क्षिणी &c., आकांक्षन् -क्षन्ती -क्षत् (त्), अतीच्छः -च्छा -च्छं, अतिलिप्सुः -प्सुः -प्सु, कुतूहली -लिनी &c., उत्सुकः -का -कं, उत्कः -त्का -त्कं, उत्कण्ठितः -ता -तं, काम्यः -म्या -म्यं, लालसी -सिनी &c., स्पृहयालुः -लुः -लु; 'a longing woman,' दोहदवती, दौहृदिनी, दोहदान्विता.

Longitude, *s.* द्राघिमा *m.* (न्), भुवकः.—(Position to east or west) रेखान्तरं, रेखांशः; 'of a country,' देशान्तरं.—(Of the earth) रेखांशः, रेखापरिधिः *m.*, रेखागणः, रेखासमूहः.—(Of any point or object in the heavens) भोगः; 'of the sun,' रविभोगः; 'of a planet reckoned from the vernal equinoctial point,' सायनं.—(Meridian or circle of longitude) याम्योत्तरवृत्तं, रेखावृत्तं, रेखांशवृत्तं.

Longitudinal, *a.* अन्वायतनः -ना -नं, अनुदैर्घ्यः -र्घ्या -र्घ्यं, अनुद्राघिमा -मा -म (न्), आयतः -ता -तं, आयतनानुसारी -रिणी -रि (न्), अन्वायतिः -तिः -ति.

Loobily, *adv.* स्थूलजनवत्, असभ्यजनवत्, ग्राम्यजनवत्, वृषलवत्.

Looby, *s.* स्थूलजनः, ग्राम्यजनः, असभ्यजनः, स्थूलबुद्धिः *m.*, वृषलः.

To look, *v. a.* (Direct the eye, look at) दृश् (c. 1. पश्यति, द्रष्टुं) अनुदृश्, प्रतिदृश्, अभिदृश्, परिदृश्, सन्दृश्, ईक्ष् (c. 1. ईक्षते -क्षितुं), समीक्ष्, वीक्ष्, अभिवीक्ष्, प्रेक्ष्, अभिप्रेक्ष्, सम्प्रेक्ष्, अवेक्ष्, अन्वीक्ष्, निरीक्ष्, उदीक्ष्, आलोक् (c. 10. -लोकयति -यितुं, c. 1. -लोकते -कितुं), समालोक्, अवलोक्, विलोक्, आलोच् (c. 10. -लोचयति -यितुं), निरूप् (c. 10. -रूपयति -यितुं), निर्वर्ण् (c. 10. -वर्णयति -यितुं), लक्ष् (c. 10. लक्षयति -ते -यितुं), आलक्ष्, समालक्ष्, उपलक्ष्, संलक्ष्, दृष्टिं कृ, विलोकनं कृ, अवलोकनं कृ.—(Look about) समन्तात् or समन्ततस् or इतस्ततो दृश्.—(Look after, search for) अन्विष् (c. 4. -इष्यति -एषितुं), निरूप्, अवेक्ष्, परीक्ष्.—(Look after, take care of) पाल् (c. 10. पालयति -यितुं), रक्ष् (c. 1. रक्षति -क्षितुं), गुप् (c. 1. गोपायति, गोप्तुं), अवेक्ष्.—(Look at, consider) अवेक्ष्, समीक्ष्, आलोक्, आलोच्, आलक्ष्, निरूप्, मन् (c. 4. मन्यते, मन्तुं), अवेक्षां कृ.—(Look down) अवलोक्, अधो दृश्.—(Look down on, despise) अवमन्, उपेक्ष्, उपप्रेक्ष्.—(Look for, expect) प्रतीक्ष्, अपेक्ष्, व्यपेक्ष्, सम्प्रतीक्ष्, उदीक्ष्, निरीक्ष्, प्रतिपाल्, उद्दृश्.—(Look into) निरीक्ष्, परीक्ष्, निरूप्; 'look into affairs,' कार्य्यदर्शनं कृ, कार्य्येक्षणं कृ, कार्य्यावेक्षणं कृ.—(Look on, regard) अवेक्ष्, अपेक्ष्, प्रतीक्ष्, आलोक्, निरूप्, मन्, दृश्.—(Look on, be a spectator) प्रेक्ष्, दृश्, मिष् (c. 6. मिषति, मेषितुं), प्रेक्षकः -का -कं भू.—(Look over) परीक्ष्, अनुसन्धा (c. 3. -दधाति -धातुं), निरूप्.—(Look out, be on the watch) अवधा, सावधानः -ना -नं भू, सावहितः -ता -तं भू, अवधानं कृ.—(Look up) उदीक्ष्, उद्वीक्ष्, उद्दृश्, ऊर्द्ध्वं दृश्, उन्मुखीभू; 'to look up to heaven,' नभोदृष्टिः -ष्टिः -ष्टि भू.—(Look up to, esteem) सम्मन्, प्रतिमन्, मन्.—(Seem, appear) प्रतिभा (c. 2. -भाति -तुं), सम्प्रभा, आभा, निभा, दृश् in pass. (दृश्यते), लक्ष् in pass. (लक्ष्यते); 'to look well,' शुभ् (c. 1. शोभते -भितुं); 'he looks astonished,' विस्मित इव प्रतिभाति; 'look, look ye!' पश्य, पश्यत.

Look, *s.* दृष्टिः *f.*, दर्शनं, ईक्षणं, प्रेक्षणं -णा, प्रेक्षितं, वीक्षणं, वीक्षितं, आलोकनं, अवलोकनं, विलोकनं, दृष्टिपातः, दृष्टिनिपातः; 'a look of displeasure,' अदृष्टिः *f.*; 'side-look,' कटाक्षः, अर्द्धवीक्षणं, अर्द्धदृष्टिः *f.*, अपाङ्गदृष्टिः *f.*, अपाङ्गदर्शनं.—(Air, appearance) रूपं, आकारः, आकृतिः *f.*, दर्शनं, रीतिः *f.*, चर्य्या, प्रतिभा, आभा, छाया.—(Cast of countenance) वदनाकारः, मुखच्छाया, मुखं, वदनं.

Looked, *p. p.* दृष्टः -ष्टा -ष्टं, आलोकितः -ता -तं, ईक्षितः -ता -तं, दत्तदृष्टिः -ष्टिः -ष्टि; 'to be looked for,' अपेक्षणीयः -या -यं; 'having looked,' दृष्ट्वा, अवलोक्य, वीक्ष्य, निर्वर्ण्य, निरूप्य.

Looker, *s.* द्रष्टा *m.* (ष्टृ), दर्शी *m.* (न्), वीक्षकः, आलोचकः, विलोकनकृत्, अवलोकनकृत्.—(Looker on) प्रेक्षकः, प्रेक्षणिकः, प्रेक्षमाणः.

Looking, *part.* पश्यन् -श्यन्ती -श्यत् (त्), ईक्षमाणः -णा -णं, प्रेक्षमाणः -णा -णं, दर्शी -र्शिनी -र्शि (न्), दृष्टि in comp.; as, 'looking in all directions,' इतस्ततो दत्तदृष्टिः -ष्टिः -ष्टि; 'looking up,' ऊर्द्ध्वदृष्टिः -ष्टिः -ष्टि, उन्मुखः -खा -खं; 'looking up to heaven,' नभोदृष्टिः -ष्टिः -ष्टि.—(Looking well, good-looking) सुदर्शनः -ना -नं, शुभदर्शनः -ना -नं, सुदृश्यः -श्या -श्यं, दर्शनीयः -या -यं, दृश्यः -श्या -श्यं, शुभाननः -ना -नी -नं, सुरूपः -पी -पं.

Looking, *s.* (Act of directing the eye) दर्शनं, दृष्टिः *f.*, दृष्टिपातः, ईक्षणं, वीक्षणं, प्रेक्षणं -णा, प्रेक्षा, आलोकः -कनं, आलोचनं, विलोकनं, अवलोकनं, सन्दर्शनं, निरूपणं, निर्वर्णनं, निध्यानं.—(Search) अन्वेषणं, संवीक्षणं, अनुसन्धानं.—(Looking for) अपेक्षा, प्रतीक्षा, व्यपेक्षा.

Looking-glass, *s.* दर्पणः -णं, आदर्शः, दर्शनं, आत्मदर्शः, प्रतिबिम्बाशः, सम्मुखी *m.* (न्), मुकुरः, मकुरः, मकुरः, कर्करः, मण्डलकं; 'surface of a looking-glass,' आदर्शतलं.

Looking-glass maker, *s.* दर्पणकारः, दर्पणकृत्, दर्पणविक्रयी *m.* (न्).

Look-out, *s.* सुसमीक्षा, इतस्ततः समीक्षा, अवेक्षा, अवधानं, सावधानता.

Loom, *s.* वेमा *m.* -म *n.* (न्), वेमः, वायदण्डः, वापदण्डः, वाणदण्डः, सूत्रयन्त्रं, आवापनं, तन्त्रं, तन्त्रयन्त्रं, कुविः *m.*

To loom, *v. n.* समुद्रमध्ये सुदूरस्थितत्वाद् अस्पष्टाकारः -रा -रं or अतिस्थूलाकारः -रा -रं भू or विद् in pass. (विद्यते) or अस्पष्टरूपेण दृश् in pass. (दृश्यते).

Loon, *s.* कापुरुषः, दुर्जनः, धूर्त्तः, ठकः, कितवः, तुच्छजनः.

Loop, *s.* (A folding, noose) पाशः, शिक्यं -क्या, काचः, पुटः, व्यावर्त्तनं.—(Opening, aperture) छिद्रं, रन्ध्रं; 'suspended in a loop,' काचितः -ता -तं, शिक्यितः -ता -तं.

Loop-hole, *s.* (Small opening in a wall, &c.) गवाक्षः -क्षं, जालं, वातायनं, रन्ध्रं, छिद्रं, प्रच्छदं.—(Means of escape) निर्गमः, निर्गतिः *f.*, निर्गमोपायः, निर्गमद्वारं, पलायनं, अपक्रमः, उत्तरणं, मुक्तिः *f.*, मोक्षः.

To loose, loosen, *v. a.* (Relax) शिथिलीकृ, शिथिल (nom. शिथिलयति -ते -यितुं), श्लथ् (c. 10. श्लथयति -यितुं), श्रथ् (c. 1. श्रथति, c. 10. श्रथयति, श्राथयति -यितुं), श्रन्थ् (c. 9. श्रथ्नाति, श्रन्थितुं), श्लथीकृ, प्रश्लथीकृ, स्रंस् (c. 10. स्रंसयति -यितुं), विस्रंस्, विगल् (c. 10. -गलयति -यितुं), विस्रस्तीकृ.—(Set free) मुच् (c. 6. मुञ्चति, मोक्तुं, c. 10. मोचयति -यितुं), अवमुच्, प्रमुच्, विमुच्, प्रविमुच्, निर्मुच्, उन्मुच्; मोक्ष् (c. 10. मोक्षयति -यितुं), विमोक्ष्.—(Untie, unbind, unfasten) उद्ग्रन्थ् (c. 9. -ग्रथ्नाति, c. 1. -ग्रन्थति -न्थितुं), समुद्ग्रन्थ्, उन्मुच्, अवमुच्, वियुज् (c. 7. -युनक्ति -योक्तुं, c. 10. -योजयति -यितुं), विसन्धा (c. 3. -दधाति -धातुं), विसन्धीकृ, विपाश् (nom. -पाशयति -यितुं), उत्सूत्रीकृ.

To loose, loosen, *v. n.* (Become loose) शिथिलीभू, शिथिल (nom. शिथिलायते), श्लथ (nom. श्लथायते -ति), श्रथ (nom. श्रथायते), श्रन्थ् (c. 1. श्रन्थते -न्थितुं), श्लथीभू, स्रंस् (c. 1. स्रंसते -सितुं), स्रस्तीभू.—(Loose a ship) नौकां मुच् (c. 6. मुञ्चति, मोक्तुं) or चल् (c. 10. चालयति -यितुं).

Loose, *a.* (Not tight, lax) शिथिलः -ला -लं, श्लथः -था -थं, प्रश्लथः -था -थं, स्रस्तः -स्ता -स्तं, विस्रस्तः -स्ता -स्तं, विगलितः -ता -तं, चलितः

-ता -तं, अदृढः -ढा -ढं.—(Untied, unfastened) अबद्धः -द्धा -द्धं, मुक्तः -क्ता -क्तं, प्रमुक्तः &c., उद्ग्रन्थितः -ता -तं, उद्ग्रथितः -ता -तं, असन्धितः -ता -तं, विगलितः -ता -तं, बन्धनरहितः -ता -तं, बन्धनशून्यः -न्या -न्यं, अनिगृहीतः -ता -तं, उच्छ्वसितः -ता -तं, उद्दामः -मा -मं, उत्सूत्रः -त्रा -त्रं, उद्बद्धः -द्धा -द्धं.—(Free) मुक्तः -क्ता -क्तं, विमुक्तः -क्ता -क्तं.—(Not close or compact) विरलः -ला -लं, असंहतः -ता -तं, अदृढसन्धिः -न्धिः -न्धि, शिथिलसन्धिः &c.—(Not concise, rambling) असंक्षिप्तः -प्ता -प्तं, विस्तीर्णः -र्णा -र्णं.—(Indeterminate) अनियतः -ता -तं, अव्यवस्थितः -ता -तं, अनिर्णीतः -ता -तं, अपरिमितः -ता -तं, सन्दिग्धः -ग्धा -ग्धं.—(Unconnected) असम्बद्धः -द्धा -द्धं, निःसम्बन्धः -न्धा -न्धं, अबद्धः &c.—(Not rigid) अनियतः -ता -तं, अस्थिरः -रा -रं, अधीरः -रा -रं, अव्यवस्थितः -ता -तं.—(Dissolute) अनवस्थः -स्था -स्थं, व्यभिचारी -रिणी -रि (न्), दुराचारः -रा -रं, दुर्वृत्तः -त्ता -त्तं, अयशाः -शा -शं, व्यसनी -निनी &c.; 'loose conduct,' व्यभिचारः; 'a loose man,' लम्पटः; 'a loose woman,' पुंश्चली, बन्धकी, भ्रष्टा, व्यभिचारिणी. *See* LAX. (To let loose) मुच् (c. 6. मुञ्चति, मोक्तुं, c. 10. मोचयति -यितुं), विमुच्, निर्मुच्, मोक्ष् (c. 10. मोक्षयति -यितुं), विमोक्ष्, विसृज् (c. 6. -सृजति -स्रष्टुं, c. 10. सर्जयति -यितुं), बन्धनाद् मुच्. *See To* LOOSE. (To break loose) बन्धनानि भिद् (c. 7. भिनत्ति, भेत्तुं) or छिद् (c. 7. छिनत्ति, छेत्तुं), पलाय् (c. 1. पलायते -यितुं, rt. इ), मुक्तबन्धनः -ना -नं भू, बन्धनाद् भ्रंश् (c. 4. भ्रश्यति, भ्रंशितुं), परिभ्रंश्, विभ्रंश्; 'broken loose,' प्रभ्रष्टः -ष्टा -ष्टं, बन्धनात्भ्रष्टः &c., परिभ्रष्टः &c.

LOOSED, LOOSENED, *p. p.* शिथिलीकृतः -ता -तं, शिथिलितः -ता -तं, अन्थितः -ता -तं, स्रस्तः -स्ता -स्तं, विस्रस्तः &c., विगलितः -ता -तं, मुक्तः -क्ता -क्तं, विमुक्तः -क्ता -क्तं, मोचितः -ता -तं, विमोचितः -ता -तं, मोक्षितः -ता -तं, चीतः -ता -तं, मुक्तबन्धनः -ना -नं, बन्धनमुक्तः -क्ता -क्तं, छिन्नबन्धनः -ना -नं.

LOOSELY, *adv.* (Not firmly) शिथिलं, शैथिल्येन, सशैथिल्यं, अदृढं.—(Not closely) असंहतं, विरलं.—(Unconnectedly) असम्बद्धं, असम्बन्धेन.—(Not rigidly) अनियतं.—(Dissolutely) सव्यभिचारं, लम्पटवत्, दुर्वृत्तवत्.

LOOSENESS, *s.* (State of being loose or not tight) शिथिलता -त्वं, शैथिल्यं, श्लथता, प्रश्रथः, श्रन्थः, स्रंसः, विस्रंसः, स्रस्तता, विस्रस्तता, अदृढता, श्लथितिः.—(Looseness of texture) विरलता, वैरल्यं, असंहतत्वं.—(Of morals or conduct) व्यभिचारः, अनवस्थितिः *f.*, अनवस्थता, व्यसनिता, लम्पटता, लाम्पट्यं, दुर्वृत्तता. *See* LAXITY, (Of bowels) मृदुकोष्ठत्वं, कोष्ठमृदुता, रेकः, रेचना -नं.

LOOSENING, LOOSING, *s.* शिथिलीकरणं, मोचनं, विमोचनं, मोक्षणं, विमोक्षणं, श्रन्थनं, श्रथनं, मुक्तिः *f.*

To LOP, *v. a.* छिद् (c. 7. छिनत्ति, छेत्तुं), अवछिद्, अवकृत् (c. 6. -कृन्तति -कर्त्तितुं), निकृत्, लू (c. 9. लुनाति, लवितुं), लुप् (c. 6. लुम्पति, लोप्तुं).

LOPPED, *p.p.* अवच्छिन्नः -न्ना -न्नं, लूनः -ना -नं, लुप्तः -प्ता -प्तं, कर्त्तितः -ता -तं.

LOPPER, *s.* छेत्ता *m.* (त्तृ), अवच्छेत्ता *m.*, छेदकः, छिद् in comp., लोपनकृत्.

LOPSIDED, *a.* एकपार्श्वे पतनशीलः -ला -लं or पतयालुः -लुः -लु.

LOQUACIOUS, *a.* वावदूकः -का -कं, वाचालः -ला -लं, बहुभाषी -षिणी -षि (न्), बहुवादी -दिनी &c., वाग्मी -ग्मिनी &c., जल्पकः -का -कं, जल्पाकः -का -कं, गदयित्नुः -त्नुः -त्नु, वाचोयुक्तिपटुः -टुः -टु, मुखरः -रा -रं, वक्ता -क्त्री -क्तृ (क्तृ), अतिवक्ता &c.

LOQUACIOUSNESS, LOQUACITY, *s.* वावदूकता, वाचालता, बहुभाषित्वं, अतिभाषणं, अतिशयोक्तिः *f.*, अतिवादः, जल्पः -ल्पकता, जल्पितं, गदयित्नुता, वाग्मित्वं, बहालापः, बहुवादित्वं, मुखरता, मौखर्य्यं.

LORD, *s.* ईश्वरः, ईशः, पतिः *m.*, स्वामी *m.* (न्), प्रभुः *m.*, नाथः, राजा *m.* (न्), अधीशः, अधिपतिः *m.*, अधिपः, अधीश्वरः, भर्त्ता *m.* (र्त्तृ), भगवान् *m.* (त्), इन्द्र in comp.; 'supreme lord,' अधिराजः, सर्वेश्वरः, सर्वस्वामी *m.*, अधिनाथः; 'lord of men,' नरेश्वरः, नराधिपः, नरेशः, नृपतिः *m.*, नरपतिः, नरेन्द्रः; 'lord of earth,' भूपतिः *m.*, भूमिपतिः *m.*, महीपतिः *m.*, पृथिवीपतिः, क्षितिपतिः; 'lord of heaven,' स्वर्गपतिः *m.*, स्वर्गराजः, स्वर्गभर्त्ता *m.* (र्त्तृ), नाकनाथः; 'lord of beasts,' मृगेन्द्रः; 'my lord,' स्वामिन् voc. c. —(Husband) पतिः *m.*, भर्त्ता *m.*, स्वामी *m.*; 'lord of life,' जीवितेशः, प्राणेशः, प्राणनाथः, प्राणाधिनाथः.—(The Supreme Being) परमेश्वरः, परेश्वरः, ईश्वरः, भगवान्, प्रभुः *m.*; 'to be lord of,' ईश् (c. 2. ईष्टे, ईशितुं), प्रभू (c. 1. -भवति -वितुं).

To LORD, *v. n.* दर्पेण or धर्षेण or धर्षपूर्व्वम् आधिपत्यं कृ or ईश् (c. 2. ईष्टे, ईशितुं) or शास् (c. 2. शास्ति -सितुं).

LORDLINESS, *s.* (Imperiousness) धृष्टता, धर्षः, दर्पः, ऐश्वर्य्यदर्पः, अवलिप्तता, उत्सिक्तता, अवहेला, गर्व्वः, प्रगल्भता, प्रागल्भ्यं.

LORDLY, LORDLIKE, *a.* ईश्वरीयः -या -यं, ऐश्वरः -री -रं, ऐशः -शी -शं, ऐशिकः -की -कं, ईश्वरयोग्यः -ग्या -ग्यं, स्वामियोग्यः &c., प्रभुयोग्यः &c., राजकीयः -या -यं, ईश्वरार्हः -र्हा -र्हं, ईश्वरसदृशः -शी -शं, ईश्वरोचितः -ता -तं, ईश्वर in comp.; as, 'lordly nature,' ईश्वरभावः. —(Imperious) धृष्टः -ष्टा -ष्टं, धर्षी -र्षिणी -र्षि (न्), दृप्तः -प्ता -प्तं, गर्व्वितः -ता -तं, उद्धतः -ता -तं, अवलिप्तः -प्ता -प्तं, ऐश्वर्य्यदृप्तः &c.

LORDLY, *adv.* धर्षेण, ऐश्वर्य्यदर्पेण, ऐश्वर्य्यदृप्तवत्, सावहेलं, सधर्षं.

LORDSHIP, *s.* ऐश्वर्य्यं, ईशत्वं, आधिपत्यं, अधिपतित्वं, प्रभुत्वं, स्वामित्वं, पतित्वं, स्वाम्यं, राजत्वं, राज्यं, अधिकारः, अधिकारित्वं.—(Title) भवान् *m.* (त्), अत्रभवान्, तत्रभवान्, भगवान्, स्वामी *m.* (न्), प्रभुः.

LORD'S SUPPER, *s.* ख्रीष्टमृत्युस्मरणार्थकं भोजनं, ख्रीष्टस्मरणोद्देशकं भोजनं.

LORE, *s.* पाण्डित्यं, विद्या, ज्ञानं, व्युत्पत्तिः *f.*, वैदुष्यं, विज्ञता.

LORN, *a.* निःशरणः -णा -णं, अशरणः -णा -णं. *See* FORLORN, *a.*

LORY, *s.* शुकः, कीरः, रक्तपर्णः शुकजातीयः पक्षिभेदः.

To LOSE, *v. a.* (Be separated or parted from a thing) हा in pass. (हीयते), प्रहा, विप्रहा, परिहा, विहा with instr. or sometimes with abl. c., भ्रंश् (c. 4. भ्रश्यति, भ्रंशितुं), परिभ्रंश्, विभ्रंश्, प्रभ्रंश् with abl. c., च्यु (c. 1. च्यवते, च्योतुं), प्रच्यु, विच्यु with abl. c., वियुज् in pass. (-युज्यते) with instr. c., अपवृत् (c. 1. -वर्त्तते -र्त्तितुं) with abl. of the person; 'he loses his life,' प्राणैः or प्राणेभ्यो हीयते; 'he loses his kingdom,' राज्याद् भ्रश्यति or च्यवते, तस्माद् राज्यम् अपवर्त्तते; 'he loses his friends,' सुहृज्जनैर् वियुज्यते.— (Let go, drop) हा (c. 3. जहाति, हातुं, or caus. हापयति -यितुं), विहा, अपहा, त्यज् (c. 1. त्यजति, त्यक्तुं), परित्यज्, हृ (c. 10. हारयति -यितुं), अपहृ; 'he lost his life,' प्राणान् जहौ; 'he loses his son,' पुत्रं जहाति; 'he loses his money,' धनं हारयति.—(Ruin, destroy, waste) नश् (c. 10. नाशयति -यितुं), विनश्, प्रणश्, क्षि (c. 5. क्षिणोति, क्षेतुं, c. 10. क्षययति, क्षपयति -यितुं), ध्वंस् (c. 10. ध्वंसयति -यितुं), विध्वंस्, प्रध्वंस्, क्षयीकृ, अपचि (c. 5. -चिनोति -चेतुं), क्षिप् (c. 6. क्षिपति, क्षेप्तुं); 'he loses his wealth,' अर्थं नाशयति; 'he loses his time,' कालं क्षिपति, कालक्षेपं or कालहरणं करोति. —(Forfeit) दण्ड् in pass. (दण्ड्यते), भ्रंश् or च्यु with abl. c., वञ्च् in pass. (वञ्च्यते) with instr. c.; 'he loses his office,' स्वाधिकाराद् भ्रश्यति; 'he loses his reward,' फलाद् भ्रश्यति or

फलेन वध्यते.—(Not to win, be defeated) पराजितः -ता -तं भू, जि in pass. (जीयते), पराजि; 'he loses the battle,' रणे जीयते.—(Lose the game) अक्षवत्यां जि or पराजि in pass., द्यूतक्रीडायां जि in pass., विदिव् (c. 4. -दीव्यति -देवितुं), पराजितः -ता -तं भू.—(Lose the way) पथात् or मार्गात् or पथो भ्रंश् or प्रभ्रंश् or च्यु or विच्यु or विचल् (c. 1. -चलति -लितुं), पथभ्रष्टः -ष्टा -ष्टं भू, वर्त्मवर्जितः -ता -तं भू.—(Lose one's wits) मुह् (c. 4. मुह्यति, मोहितुं), बुद्धिं हा, बुद्धिहीनः -ना -नं भू.—(Lose one's consciousness, lose one's self) चेतनां or चैतन्यं हा, नष्टचेतनः -ना -नं भू, मुर्छ् (c. 1. मूर्छति -र्छितुं), भ्रम् (c. 4. भ्राम्यति, भ्रमितुं), भ्रान्तबुद्धिः -द्धिः -द्धि भू.

To LOSE, *v. n.* (Be defeated) जि in pass. (जीयते), पराजि, पराजितः -ता -तं भू.—(Decline, fail) क्षि in pass. (क्षीयते), परिक्षि, परिहा in pass. (-हीयते), ध्वंस् (c. 1. ध्वंसते -सितुं).

LOSER, *s.* क्षतिप्रापकः, हानिप्रापकः, अपायप्रापकः, अनुभूतक्षयः, प्राप्तापायः, प्राप्तक्षयः, लब्धापायः, लब्धहानिः *m.*, अपायप्राप्तः, पराजितः.

LOSS, *s.* क्षयः, हानिः *f.*, अपायः, क्षतिः *f.*, अपचयः, नाशः, अपचितिः *f.*, उपक्षयः, परिक्षयः, संक्षयः, क्षिया, व्ययः, ध्वंसः, प्रध्वंसः, परिध्वंसः, भ्रंशः, अपहारः, हारः, हरणं, अत्ययः, च्युतिः *f.*, त्यागः, परित्यागः, विनाशः, प्रणाशः, भेषः, अलाभः, वियोगः, व्यसनं, दूषणं, प्रहीणः.—(Ruin, destruction) नाशः, विनाशः, क्षयः.—(Defeat) पराजयः, पराभवः, अपजयः, बलव्यसनं, भङ्गः.—(Profit and loss) लाभालाभौ *m.* du., लाभालाभं.—(Loss of caste) जातिभ्रंशः.—(Loss of time) कालक्षेपः, कालहरणं, कालव्ययः; 'without loss of time,' अकालक्षेपं.—(To be at a loss) मुह् (c. 4. मुह्यति, मोहितुं); 'at a loss,' भ्रान्तबुद्धिः -द्धिः -द्धि, मोहितः -ता -तं, विमूढः -ढा -ढं; 'at a loss how to act,' इतिकर्त्तव्यतामूढः -ढा -ढं.

LOST, *p. p.* or *a.* नष्टः -ष्टा -ष्टं, प्रणष्टः -ष्टा -ष्टं, विनष्टः -ष्टा -ष्टं, हारितः -ता -तं, भ्रष्टः -ष्टा -ष्टं, विभ्रष्टः -ष्टा -ष्टं, च्युतः -ता -तं, परिच्युतः -ता -तं, गतः -ता -तं, विगतः -ता -तं, वीतः -ता -तं, क्षीणः -णा -णं, परिक्षीणः -णा -णं, अपचितः -ता -तं, अन्तरितः -ता -तं, लुप्तः -प्ता -प्तं, विलुप्तः -प्ता -प्तं, हीनः -ना -नं, प्रहीणः -णा -णं, त्यक्तः -क्ता -क्तं, ध्वंसितः -ता -तं, ध्वस्तः -स्ता -स्तं; 'one who has lost his kingdom,' राज्यभ्रष्टः, भ्रष्टराज्यः, राज्यच्युतः, राज्यात्प्रभ्रष्टः; 'one who has lost his office,' च्युताधिकारः; 'one who has lost his wealth,' गतविभवः -वा -वं, नष्टार्थः -र्था -र्थं, अर्थहीनः -ना -नं; 'one who has lost desire,' विगतस्पृहः -हा -हं, वीतकामः -मा -मं; 'one who has lost life,' त्यक्तजीवनः -ना -नं, प्रहीणजीवितः; 'one who has lost the road,' पथभ्रष्टः -ष्टा -ष्टं, मार्गप्रभ्रष्टः -ष्टा -ष्टं, वर्त्मवर्जितः -ता -तं, त्यक्तमार्गः -र्गा -र्गं; 'one who has lost an eye,' एकाक्षिविकलः -ला -लं; 'one who has lost every thing,' हृतसर्व्वस्वः -स्वा -स्वं, परिच्युतः -ता -तं, परिक्षीणः -णा -णं; 'lost to shame,' लज्जाहीनः -ना -नं, त्यक्तलज्जः -ज्जा -ज्जं, निरस्तलज्जः &c., लज्जोज्झितः -ता -तं, निर्लज्जः -ज्जा -ज्जं; 'lost in thought,' ध्याननिष्ठः -ष्ठा -ष्ठं, चिन्ताकुलः -ला -लं, चिन्तापरः -रा -रं; 'relating to any thing lost,' नाष्टिकः -की -कं; 'it is lost,' हार्य्यते, अपचीयते.—(Bewildered) मोहितः -ता -तं, विमूढः -ढा -ढं, भ्रान्तबुद्धिः -द्धिः -द्धि, भ्रमयुक्तः -क्ता -क्तं.

LOT, *s.* (Destiny, state assigned by fate) भाग्यं, भागधेयं, दैवदशा, दैवस्थितिः *f.*, दैवयोगः, दैवं, दैविकं, दैवगतिः *f.*, भवितव्यता, भोगः, भोग्यं, भोक्तृत्वं.—(Share, portion) अंशः, भागः, विभागः, भाज्यं, भाजितं, वण्टः.—(Die used in determining a person's portion) गुटिका, शकुनः; 'to cast lots,' गुटिकाः पत् (c. 10. पातयति -यितुं); 'casting lots,' गुटिकापातः, पाटः -टकः.

LOTH, *a.* अनिच्छुः -च्छुः -च्छु. *See* LOATH.

LOTION, *s.* औषधीयजलं, धावनौषधं, प्रक्षालनौषधं, धावनं -नी.

LOTTERY, *s.* गुटिकापातः, पाटकः, गुटिकापातपूर्व्वो विभागकल्पना.

LOTUS, LOTOS, *s.* (Flower) पद्मः -द्मं, कमलं, उत्पलं, कुमुदं, कुमुद् *n.*, नलिनं, कुवलयं, अरविन्दं, महोत्पलं, पङ्कजं, पङ्केरुहं, सरसिजं, सरसीरुहं, सरोजं, सरोरुहं, जलेजातं, अम्भोजं, वार्य्युद्भवं, अम्बुजं, अम्भोरुहं, पुण्डरीकं, मृणाली *m.* (न्), शतपत्रं, सहस्रपत्रं, कुशेशयं, इन्दिरालयं, तामरसं, पुष्करं, सारसं, रमाप्रियं, विसप्रसूनं, कुवलं, कुवं, कुटपं, पुटकं, श्रीपर्णः, श्रीकरं, श्यामहं. Other varieties, red, white, and blue, are हल्लकं, रक्तसन्ध्यकं, रक्तसरोरुहं, रक्तकमलं, रक्तोत्पलं, कोकनदं, सिताम्भोजं, कल्हारं, सौगन्धिकं, इन्दीवरं, इन्दीवारं, कैरवं, नीलाम्बुजन्म *n.* (न्), नीलोत्पलं, नीलकमलं, सूर्य्यकमलं, स्थलकमलं, स्थलपद्मं.—(The plant as distinguished from the flower) पद्मिनी, कमलिनी, नलिनी, कुमुदिनी; 'stalk of a lotus,' नालः -ला -ली -लं, पद्मनालं, नाडिः -डी *f.*, पद्मिनी, कुमुद्वती, नलिनी, पद्मतन्तुः *m.*; 'fibres or film attached to the stalk,' मृणालः -लं, विसं, विशं, विषं, नलिनीरुहः; 'root,' शालूकं, शालुकं, शिफाकन्दः -न्दं, करहाटः; 'seed,' कमलाक्षः, पद्माक्षः, पद्मबीजं; 'seed-vessel or pericarp,' बीजकोशः, कर्णिका, वर्णिकारः, वराटकः; 'filament,' केशरः, केसरः, किञ्जल्कः, किञ्जलः, किञ्जं; 'petal,' पद्मच्छदः, कमलच्छदः, पद्मान्तरः; 'new leaf,' संवर्त्तिः *f.*, संवर्त्तिका, नवदलं, नवपत्रं; 'abounding with lotuses,' कुमुद्वान् -द्वती -द्वत् (त्), कुमुदिकः -की -कं; 'place abounding with lotuses,' कुमुदिनी, कुमुद्वती, कुमुदाकरः, कुमुदवनं, कुमुदावासः, कुमुदवती, पद्मिनी, पद्माकरः, पद्मिनीखण्डं, पद्मखण्डं, कमलिनी, कमलाकरः, नलिनी, कुवलयिनी, अरविन्दिनी, पुष्करिणी; 'an assemblage or quantity of lotus flowers,' पद्मिनी, नलिनी, विसिनी, मृणालिनी, कमलिनी, उत्पलिनी, कुमुद्वती, पुटकिनी, पद्मखण्डं, षण्डः -ण्डं, शण्डं; 'lotus-like,' उत्पलाभः -भा -भं; 'lotus-shaped,' पद्माकारः -रा -रं; 'lotus-eyed,' उत्पलचक्षूः -क्षूः -क्षुः (स्); 'smelling like the lotus,' पद्मगन्धः -न्धा -न्धं, उत्पलगन्धिः -न्धिः -न्धि.

LOUD, *a.* महास्वनः -ना -नं, महाध्वनिकः -का -कं, उच्चः -च्चा -च्चं, उच्चैःस्वरकः -का -कं, महास्वरकः -का -कं, महाध्वनिकरः -री -रं, महाशब्दकः -का -कं, महाशब्दी -ब्दिनी -ब्दि (न्), महाशब्दकारः -रा -रं, अतिशब्दनः -ना -नं, अतिशब्दवान् -वती -वत् (त्), महास्वनवान् &c., स्वनवान् &c., शब्दनः -ना -नं, महानादी -दिनी -दि (न्), तुमुलः -ला -लं, तुमुलकारी -रिणी &c., उत्तालः -ला -लं.—(Clamorous) घोषणः -णा -णं, घोषकरः -री -रं, बहुघोषः -षा -षं, महाघोषः -षा -षं; 'a loud sound or noise,' उच्चैःस्वरः, उच्चस्वरः, महाशब्दः, महास्वनः, महाघोषः, उच्चैर्घुष्टं, प्रणादः; 'loud speaking,' उच्चभाषणं; 'louder,' उच्चैस्तरः -रा -रं; 'loudest,' उच्चैस्तमः -मा -मं.

LOUD, LOUDLY, *adv.* उच्चैस्, उच्चकैस्, प्रोच्चैस्, उच्चैस्तमाम्, उच्चैःस्वरेण, उच्चशब्देन, महास्वरेण, महाशब्देन, अतिशब्देन, महाशब्दपूर्व्वं, स्वनवत्, उच्चैःकारं; 'speaking loud,' उच्चभाषी -षिणी -षि (न्); 'crying loud,' उच्चरावी -विणी &c.

LOUDNESS, *s.* उच्चता -त्वं, महाशब्दकारित्वं, महाशब्दकत्वं, शब्दमहत्त्वं, महाशब्दः, उच्चस्वरः, महाध्वनिः *m.*, उत्तालता.

LOUD-VOICED, *a.* उच्चस्वरः -रा -रं, उच्चस्वरवान् -वती -वत् (त्).

To LOUNGE, *v. a.* आलस्यं कृ, अलसीभू, आलस्यात् कालं क्षिप् (c. 6. क्षिपति, क्षेप्तुं) or कालक्षेपं कृ or कालहरणं कृ or कालव्ययं कृ, उदास् (c. 2. -आस्ते -आसितुं), निर्व्यापारत्वात् सुखेन शी (c. 2. शेते, शयितुं).

Lounger, *s.* अलसजनः, आलस्यकारी *m.* (न्), मुखनिरीक्षकः, लालाटिकः, कालक्षेपकः, अव्यापारी *m.* (न्), कार्य्यपुटः, उदासीनः, निर्व्यापारत्वात् सुखशायी *m.* (न्); 'woman with a lounging gait,' मत्तेभगमना.

Louse, *s.* यूकः -का, केशकीटः, केशटः, षट्पदः -दी, आपालिः *m.*, रोमविध्वंशः, वारकीरः; 'egg of a louse,' लिक्षा.

To louse, *v. a.* निर्यूकीकृ, यूक (nom. यूकयति -यितुं), यूकवर्जितं -तां कृ.

Lousiness, *s.* सयूकत्वं -ता, बहुयूकता, यूकपूर्णता, यूकबाहुल्यं.

Lousy, *a.* युकालः -ला -लं, सयूकः -का -कं, बहुयूकः -का -कं, यूकपूर्णः -र्णा -र्णं, यूकसेवितः -ता -तं, यूकोपद्रुतः -ता -तं, यूकी -किनी -कि (न्).

Lout, *s.* ग्राम्यजनः, वृषलः, स्थूलजनः, स्थूलबुद्धिः *m.*, मूढजनः.

Loutish, *a.* स्थूलबुद्धिः -द्धिः -द्धि, स्थूलस्वभावः -वा -वं, ग्राम्यबुद्धिः &c., स्थूलः -ला -लं, ग्राम्यः -म्या -म्यं, ग्रामिकः -की -कं, अशिष्टः -ष्टा -ष्टं, असभ्यः -भ्या -भ्यं.

Loutishly, *adv.* स्थूलजनवत्, ग्राम्यजनवत्, वृषलवत्, बुद्धिस्थौल्यात्.

Loutishness, *s.* स्थूलता -त्वं, स्थौल्यं, बुद्धिस्थूलता, ग्राम्यता, अशिष्टता.

Louver, *s.* धूमरन्ध्रं, धूमनिर्गमः, धूमायनं, वातायनं, छिद्रं.

Lovable, *a.* स्नेहार्हः -र्हा -र्हं, प्रियगुणकः -का -कं, प्रियगुणविशिष्टः -ष्टा -ष्टं, स्नेहोत्पादकशीलः -ला -लं, प्रीत्युत्पादकशीलः -ला -लं, प्रियः -या -यं.

Lovage, *s.* अजमोदा, यवानी -निका, यमानी -मिका, इन्दुलेखा, भूतीकं.

To love, *v. a.* (Have affection for) प्रेम कृ, प्री (c. 4. प्रीयते, प्रेतुं), स्नेहं कृ, प्रीतिं कृ, स्निह् (c. 4. स्निह्यति, स्नेहितुं), कम् (c. 10. कामयते -ति -यितुं), दय् (c. 1. दयते -यितुं), अनुरञ्ज् (c. 4. -रज्यते), अनुरागं कृ, अनुरक्तः -क्ता -क्तं भू, अनुरागवान् -वती भू, अनुरुध् (c. 4. -रुध्यते -रोद्धुं), भज् (c. 1. भजते, भक्तुं); 'he loves God,' ईश्वरे प्रेम करोति, ईश्वरभक्तिं करोति; 'they love him,' तस्मिन् प्रीयन्ते; 'he loves his brother more than me,' मत्तो ऽधिकं भ्रातरि प्रीयते or स्नेहं करोति; 'I love my son,' पुत्रेण सह मम महान् स्नेहः; 'she loves him,' तस्मिन् अनुरागवती भवति; 'he loves his wife,' भार्य्यायाम् अनुरज्यते or अनुरक्तो ऽस्ति; 'they love the king,' राजानम् अनुरुध्यन्ते; 'women love everybody,' सर्व्वे स्त्रीणां प्रियाः.

To love, *v. n.* (Delight in) आनन्द् (c. 1. -नन्दति -न्दितुं), अभिनन्द्, हृष् (c. 4. हृष्यति, हर्षितुं), प्री (c. 4. प्रीयते, प्रेतुं), तुष् (c. 4. तुष्यति, तोष्टुं), रुच् (c. 1. रोचते -चितुं).

Love, *s.* (Fondness, affection) प्रीतिः *f.*, प्रेम *n.* (न्), स्नेहः, अनुरागः, अनुरक्तिः *f.*, प्रणयः, वात्सल्यं, वत्सलता, रागः, हार्द्दं, प्रश्रयः, अनुरोधः, रुचिः *f.*, अभिरुचिः *f.*, सन्तोषः, प्रेमभावः, प्रीतिभावः, स्नेहभावः; 'love for God,' ईश्वरभक्तिः *f.*; 'undivided love,' अनन्यभक्तिः.—(Love of the sexes, passion) प्रेम *n.*, स्त्रीपुरुषप्रेम, शृङ्गारः, शृङ्गारभावः, कामः, कामिता, मदनः, मन्मथः, रागः, अनुरागः, रतिः *f.*, रसः, वश्चिनं, कैशिकः, उज्ज्वलः, शुचिः *m.*—(Cupid) कामः, मन्मथः, मदनः, कन्दर्पः, स्मरः, मनसिजः, मनसिशयः, चित्तभूः *m.*, चेतोभूः, चित्तजन्मा *m.* (न्), सङ्कल्पजः, अनङ्गः, शमान्तकः, भराभीरुः *m.* *See* Kámadeva. 'In love, under the influence of love,' कामार्त्तः -र्त्ता -र्त्तं, कामातुरः -रा -रं, मदनावस्थः -स्था -स्थं, मदनवशः -शा -शं, जातमन्मथः -था -थं, जातकामः -मा -मं, स्मराकुलः -ला -लं, कामासक्तः -क्ता -क्तं, काममोहितः -ता -तं, कामबद्धः -द्धा -द्धं, शृङ्गारी -रिणी -रि (न्), शृङ्गारितः -ता -तं; 'to fall in love with, be in love with,' अनुरागवान् -वती भू with loc. or gen. of the person, जातानुरागः -गा भू, मोहितः -ता -तं भू; 'to make love,' विवाहार्थं प्रेम कृ, विवाहहेतुकस्नेहं कृ, विवाहार्थं चित्ताराधनं कृ.—(Delight in) रुचिः *f.*, अभिरुचिः *f.*, अनुरागः, प्रीतिः, आसक्तिः *f.*; 'love of life,' जीविताशा.—(Airs or gestures of love) हावः, भावः, ललितं, विलासः, विभ्रमः.

Love-broker, *s.* घटकः, प्रेमघटकः, मदनदूतः -ती *f.*, दूतिका *f.*

Loved, *p. p.* प्रीतः -ता -तं, दयितः -ता -तं, स्निग्धः -ग्धा -ग्धं, प्रियः -या -यं, हृद्यः -द्या -द्यं, हृदयप्रियः -या -यं, इष्टः -ष्टा -ष्टं, मनीषितः -ता -तं, सुभगः -गा -गं.

Love-knot, *s.* प्रेमग्रन्थिः *m.*, प्रीतिग्रन्थिः *m.*, शृङ्गारग्रन्थिः *m.*

Love-letter, *s.* मदनलेखः, अनङ्गलेखः, मन्मथलेखः, शृङ्गारपत्रं, प्रेमपत्रं, अनङ्गपत्रं, प्रीतिपत्रं.

Loveliness, *s.* कान्तता, कान्तिः *f.*, सौन्दर्य्यं, सुन्दरता, अतिसौन्दर्य्यं, लावण्यं, रूपलावण्यं, चारुता, सौम्यता, लालित्यं, वामता, मुग्धता, कमनीयता, अभिरामता, दीप्तिः *f.*, शोभा, रमणीयता, मनोहरत्वं -ता, रम्यता, सुभगता, सश्रीकता.

Lovely, *a.* कान्तः -न्ता -न्तं, सुन्दरः -रा -री -रं, अतिसुन्दरः &c., लावण्यवान् -वती -वत् (त्), सुरूपः -पी -पं, सुरूपवान् &c., चारुः -र्वी -रु, चारुमान् -मती &c., ललितः -ता -तं, सौम्यः -म्या -म्यं, मुग्धः -ग्धा -ग्धं, वामः -मा -मं, मनोरमः -मा -मं, मनोहरः -रा -रं, रम्यः -म्या -म्यं, रमणीयः -या -यं, कमनीयः -या -यं, सुभगः -गा -गं, मनोज्ञः -ज्ञा -ज्ञं, अभिरामः -मा -मं.

Lovely-faced, *a.* मुग्धाननः -ना -नं, चारुमुखः -खी -खं, सुमुखः &c.

Love-match, *s.* प्रीतिविवाहः, प्रेमविवाहः, प्रीतिसम्बन्धः, प्रेमसम्बन्धः.

Love-quarrel, *s.* प्रीतिकलहः, प्रेमकलहः, प्रणयकोपः.

Lover, *s.* प्रणयी *m.* (न्), प्रियः, कान्तः, नायकः, रमणः, रमकः, रमः, दयितः, वल्लभः, कामी *m.* (न्), हृदयेशः, प्राणेशः, जीवितेशः, प्राणपतिः *m.*, प्रियतमः, बन्धुः *m.*, इष्टः; 'lover of knowledge,' विद्यानुरागी *m.* (न्), ज्ञानेप्सुः *m.*

Love-shaft, *s.* मदनशरः, स्मरशरः, कामशरः, कन्दर्पबाणः, मदनेषुः *m.* The god of love is fabled by the Hindús as having five arrows, each tipped with the blossom of a flower. *See* Kámadeva.

Love-sick, *a.* कामरोगी -गिणी -गि (न्), मदनरोगी &c., कामातुरः -रा -रं, कामार्त्तः -र्त्ता -र्त्तं, कामपीडितः -ता -तं, मदनपीडितः &c., कामविह्वलः -ला -लं.

Love-song, *s.* मदनगीतं, प्रेमगीतं, शृङ्गारगीतं, शृङ्गारगानं.

Love-tale, *s.* कामकथा, शृङ्गारकथा, मदनकथा प्रेमकथा, शृङ्गाराख्यानं, प्रेमव्याख्यानं.

Love-token, *s.* प्रीतिलक्षणं, प्रेमलक्षणं, प्रीतिदानं, प्रेमस्मारकं.

Love-trick, *s.* प्रेमक्रीडा, अनङ्गक्रीडा, हावः, भावः, ललितं, विलासः.

Loving, *a.* प्रणयी -यिनी -यि (न्), प्रणयवान् -वती -वत् (त्), कामी -मिनी &c., स्नेही -हिनी &c., अनुरक्तः -क्ता -क्तं, अनुरागवान् -वती &c., प्रकामः -मा -मं, प्रीतिमान् -मती &c., वत्सलः -ला -लं, प्रीतियुक्तः -क्ता -क्तं.—(Delighting in, attached to) अनुरागी -गिणी &c., आनन्दी -न्दिनी &c., प्रमोदी -दिनी &c., मोदी &c., प्रियः -या -यं, आसक्तः -क्ता -क्तं, सेवी -विनी &c., रतः -ता -तं, निरतः -ता -तं.

Loving-kindness, *s.* कृपा, दया, कारुण्यं, वात्सल्यं, करुणार्द्रता, अनुकम्पा, प्रसादः, अनुग्रहः, स्नेहः, हितेच्छा.

Lovingly, *adv.* सप्रणयं, प्रणयेन, सानुरागं, स्नेहेन, सस्नेहं, प्रीतिपूर्व्वं, प्रीत्या, वात्सल्येन, सवात्सल्यं.

Low, *a.* (Not high) नीचः -चा -चं, नीचकः -का -कं, नीचस्थः -स्था -स्थं, निम्नः -म्ना -म्नं, अधरः -रा -रं, अनुच्चः -च्चा -च्चं, अतुङ्गः -ङ्गा -ङ्गं,

अधःस्थः -स्था -स्थं, अधस्तनः -नी -नं; 'low ground,' निम्नभूमिः *f.*—(Short, low in stature) ह्रस्वः -स्वा -स्वं, नीचः -चा -चं, न्यक्, नीची, न्यक् (च्), ह्रस्वतनुः -नुः -नु, अल्पतनुः -नुः -नु.—(Not loud) नीचस्वरः -रा -रं, नीचशब्दकः -का -कं, नीचः -चा -चं, नीचकः -का -कं.—(Deep or grave in sound) मन्द्रः -न्द्रा -न्द्रं, मन्द्रः -न्द्रा -न्द्रं, आमन्द्रः -न्द्रा -न्द्रं, मन्थरः -रा -रं, धीरः -रा -रं, गम्भीरः -रा -रं, गभीरः -रा -रं.—(Mean, inferior, base) अधमः -मा -मं, अवरः -रा -रं, नीचः -चा -चं, नीचकः -का -कं, हीनः -ना -नं, निकृष्टः -ष्टा -ष्टं, अपकृष्टः -ष्टा -ष्टं, अवमः -मा -मं, जघन्यः -न्या -न्यं, जघन्यवृत्तिः -त्तिः -त्ति, प्रतिकृष्टः -ष्टा -ष्टं, खलः -ला -लं, क्षुद्रः -द्रा -द्रं, दुष्टः -ष्टा -ष्टं, दुर्वृत्तः -त्ता -त्तं, पार्थिवः -ली -लं, प्राकृतः -ती -तं, न्यड्, नीची, न्यक् (च्), कृपणः -णा -णं, अर्वा -र्वती -र्वत् (त्), चरमः -मा -मं, अणकः -का -कं, अनकः -का -कं, आणकः -का -कं, इतरः -रा -रं, अनार्यः -र्या -र्यं, रेफः -फा -फं, रेपः -पा -पं, रेफाः -फाः -फः (स्), रेपाः &c., याप्यः -प्या -प्यं, खेटः -टा -टं, अवद्यः -द्या -द्यं, क्षुद्रः -द्रा -द्रं, क्षुद्रकः -का -कं, कुपूयः -या -यं, गर्ह्यः -र्ह्या -र्ह्यं, अश्लीलः -ला -लं; 'a low man,' प्राकृतजनः, निहीनजनः, पृथग्जनः, इतरजनः, अपसदः, दुर्वृत्तः, अधमाचारः, दुराचारः, पामरः, पाल्लः, विवर्णः; 'low language,' अश्लीलं, खलोक्तिः *f.*, अश्लीलाक्षेपः.—(Of low rank or birth) हीनजातिः -तिः -ति, न्यग्जातिः -तिः -ति, नीचजातिः -तिः -ति, अन्त्यजातीयः -या -यं, हीनजन्मा -न्मा -न्म (न्), दुष्कुलीनः -ना -नं, अकुलीनः -ना -नं, नीचकुलजातः -ता -तं, हीनकुलः -ला -लं.—(Depressed, dejected) विषण्णः -ण्णा -ण्णं, विषादी -दिनी &c., अवसन्नः -न्ना -न्नं, दीनमनस्कः -स्का -स्कं, विमनाः -नाः -नः (स्), दुर्मनाः &c., विमनस्कः -स्का -स्कं, म्लानः -ना -नं, खिन्नः -न्ना -न्नं, उद्विग्नः -ग्ना -ग्नं, म्लानः -ना -नं.—(Moderate) परिमितः -ता -तं, अल्पः -ल्पा -ल्पं, स्वल्पः -ल्पा -ल्पं.—(In price) अल्पमूल्यः -ल्या -ल्यं.—(Not rich, not nourishing, as diet) निस्सारः -रा -रं, कर्शकः -का -कं, कृशकारी -रिणी &c., अपोषकः -का -कं, अपौष्टिकः -की -कं.

Low, *adv.* नीचैस्, नीचकैस्, नीचे, अधस्, अनुच्चं, नीच in comp.; as, 'going low,' नीचगः -गा -गं.—(In a low tone) नीचस्वरेण.

To low, *v. n.* (As cattle) हम्भारवं कृ, हम्भ (nom. हम्भायते), रम्भ् (c. 1. रम्भते -म्भितुं), रेभ् (c. 1. रेभते -भितुं), गज् (c. 1. गजति -जितुं), नद् (c. 1. नदति -दितुं), नर्द् (c. 1. नर्दति -र्दितुं), गर्ज् (c. 1. गर्जति -र्जितुं).

Low-born, *a.* हीनजातिः -तिः -ति, न्यग्जातिः &c., नीचकुलजातः -ता -तं, हीनकुलप्रसूतः -ता -तं, अनुच्चकुलजातः -ता -तं, हीनजन्मा -न्मा -न्म (न्), अन्त्यजातीयः -या -यं, अधमवंशोद्भवः -वा -वं, अवरवर्णजः -जा -जं, अधमवंशीयः -या -यं, अधमजातीयः -या -यं, अवरजः -जा -जं.

Lower, *a.* (Less high) अधरः -रा -रं, अधरस्थः -स्था -स्थं, अधःस्थः -स्था -स्थं, अधोभवः -वा -वं, अधस्तनः -नी -नं, नीचस्थः -स्था -स्थं, अधमः -मा -मं, अवाङ् -वाची -वाक् (च्), अवाचीनः -ना -नं, अवमः -मा -मं, जघन्यः -न्या -न्यं, अपकृष्टः -ष्टा -ष्टं, अधस् in comp.; as, 'the lower part,' अधोभागः; 'lower part of the body,' अधःकायः; 'the lower region,' अधोलोकः, अधोभुवनं, अपाची; 'lower garment,' अधोंशुकं, अधरीयं, उपसंव्यानं, परिधानं; 'the lower line,' अधःस्थपंक्तिः *f.*, अधरपंक्तिः; 'the lower classes,' अन्त्यजातीयाः *m. pl.*, अधमजातीयाः *m. pl.*, हीनजातीयाः *m. pl.*, अवरवर्णाः *m. pl.*

To lower, *v. a.* (Cause to descend, let down) अधःकृ, अधःपत् (c. 10. -पातयति -यितुं), अवपत्, अवतॄ (c. 10. -तारयति -यितुं), नीचीकृ.—(Abase, humble) अपकृष् (c. 1. -कर्षति -क्रष्टुं), नम् (c. 10. नमयति -यितुं), अवनम्, नम्रीकृ, भंश् (c. 10. भंशयति -यितुं), दर्पं or गर्वं भञ्ज् (c. 7. भनक्ति, भंक्तुं), गौरवं हृ (c. 1. हरति, हर्तुं), तिरोभू (c. 10. -भावयति -यितुं), पत्.—(Diminish) न्यूनीकृ, अल्पीकृ, ऊन् (c. 10. ऊनयति -यितुं), न्यून्, ऊन् (nom. ऊनयति -यितुं), ह्रस् (c. 10. ह्रासयति -यितुं), लघु (nom. लघयति -यितुं).

To lower, *v. n.* (Grow less, sink) न्यूनीभू, पत् (c. 1. पतति -तितुं), नम्रीभू.

To lower, *v. n.* (Be dark and gloomy, be clouded) मेघावृतः -ता -तं भू, मेघाच्छन्नः -न्ना -न्नं भू, मेघ (nom. मेघायते), अभ्र (nom. अभ्रायते), तमोवृतः -ता -तं भू, मलिनीभू, कलुषीभू.—(Frown, look black) भ्रूभङ्गं कृ, भ्रूसङ्कोचनं कृ, मलिनमुखः -खी -खं भू.

Lower, *s.* (Gloominess, cloudiness) साभ्रता, मेघाच्छन्नता, मेघतिमिरं, तमोवृतत्वं, मेघसंहतिः *f.*, दुर्दिनं.—(Of countenance) मुखमालिन्यं, मलिनमुखत्वं.

Lowered, *p. p.* (Let down) पातितः -ता -तं, अवपातितः -ता -तं, अधःकृतः -ता -तं.—(Humbled) भग्नदर्पः -र्पा -र्पं, भग्नगर्वः -र्वा -र्वं, गतगौरवः -वा -वं, हृतगौरवः -वा -वं, भग्नगौरवः -वा -वं.—(Diminished) न्यूनीकृतः -ता -तं, अल्पीकृतः -ता -तं, ह्रसितः -ता -तं.

Lowering, *a.* (Gloomy, cloudy) मेघाच्छन्नः -न्ना -न्नं, तमोवृतः -ता -तं, दुर्दिनग्रस्तः -स्ता -स्तं, मलिनः -ना -नं, अप्रियः -या -यं, मलिनमुखः -खी -खं.

Lowermost, lowest, *a.* अवरः -रा -रं, अधरः -रा -रं, अवरतमः -मा -मं, अधरतमः -मा -मं, अधमः -मा -मं, नीचः -चा -चं, नीचतमः -मा -मं, अतिनीचः -चा -चं, अधःस्थः -स्था -स्थं, अधरस्थः -स्था -स्थं, अवरस्थः -स्था -स्थं; 'at the lowest price,' अवरमूल्यमपेक्ष्य, न्यूनमूल्यमपेक्ष्य.

Lowing, *s.* (Of cattle) हम्भा, हम्भारवः, रम्भः, रम्भितं, रेभणं, गोनादः, गोरावः.

Lowing, *part.* हम्भारवविरावी -विणी -वि (न्), हम्भायमानः -ना -नं.

Lowland, *s.* निम्नभूमिः *f.*, निम्नभूः *f.*, निम्नदेशः, नीचभूमिः, नीचप्रदेशः.

Lowlander, *s.* निम्नदेशवासी *m.* (न्), नीचदेशस्थः, निम्नदेशीयः.

Lowlily, *adv.* नम्रचेतसा, नम्रं, विनयं, अदर्पेण, निरभिमानेन, नम्रशीलत्वात्, सविनयं, सनिर्वेदं, गर्वं विना, गर्वत्यागपूर्वं.

Lowliness, *s.* नम्रता, बुद्धिनम्रता, विनम्रता, विनयः, विनतिः *f.*, नम्रशीलता, गर्वहीनता, दर्पशून्यता, दम्भहीनता, निरभिमानं, अनभिमानं, अनहङ्कारः, अगर्वः, दीनता, निर्वेदः, दैन्यं, आनतिः *f.*, सन्नतिः *f.*, अपकर्षः, अपकृष्टता, नम्रवृत्तिः *f.*

Lowly, *a.* नम्रः -म्रा -म्रं, नम्रबुद्धिः -द्धिः -द्धि, नम्रशीलः -ला -लं, नम्रवृत्तिः -त्तिः -त्ति, नम्रमनाः -नाः -नः (स्), नम्रमनस्कः -स्का -स्कं, विनतचेताः -ताः -तः (स्), विनतः -ता -तं, विनयी -यिनी -यि (न्), सविनयः -या -यं, निरभिमानः -ना -नं, अनभिमानी -निनी &c., अनहङ्कारः -रा -रं -री -रिणी &c., निरहङ्कारः -रा -रं, निरहम्मानी -निनी &c., अभिमानहीनः -ना -नं, अगर्वः -र्वा -र्वं, वीतगर्वः -र्वा -र्वं, गर्वरहितः -ता -तं, वीतदम्भः -म्भा -म्भं, दर्पहीनः &c., निर्विण्णः -ण्णा -ण्णं, अनुद्धतः -ता -तं, अपकृष्टः -ष्टा -ष्टं, अप्रगल्भः -ल्भा -ल्भं, अप्रौढः -ढा -ढं, नीचः -चा -चं.

Lowly, *adv.* सविनयं, अनुद्धतं, सापकर्षं, नम्रवत्. *See* Lowlily.

Low-minded, *a.* दुष्टचेताः -ताः -तः (स्), खलात्मा -त्मा -त्म (न्), दुरात्मा &c.

Lowness, *s.* नीचता, निम्नता, अनुच्चता, अनुन्नता; 'lowness of ground,' भूमिनिम्नता.—(Meanness) नीचता, अधमता, अपकृष्टता, निकृष्टता, अपकर्षः, जघन्यता, हीनता, खलता, क्षुद्रता, दुष्टता, कृपणता, कार्पण्यं, दुर्वृत्तता, अनार्यता, अनुत्कर्षः.—(Of spirits) विषादः, विषण्णता, अवसादः, अवसन्नता, उद्वेगः, निर्विण्णता, क्लान्तिः *f.*, ग्लानिः *f.*, म्लानिः, दीनता, वैमनस्यं, विमनस्कता, दौर्मनस्यं, दुर्मनस्कता.—(Of sound) नीचता, मन्दता, मन्द्रता, गम्भीरता, गाम्भीर्यं.—(Of price) मूल्यन्यूनता, अल्पमूल्यत्वं.

Low-priced, *a.* अल्पमूल्यः -ल्या -ल्यं, न्यूनमूल्यः &c., सुमूल्यः &c.

Low-spirited, *a.* विषादी -दिनी -दि (न्), विषण्णः -ण्णा -ण्णं, अवसन्नः -न्ना -न्नं, उद्विग्नमनाः -नाः -नः (स्), दुर्मनाः &c., क्षाममनाः &c., अनन्यमनाः &c., दीनमनाः &c., विमनाः &c., दुर्मनस्कः -स्का -स्कं, विमनस्कः &c. उद्विग्नमनस्कः &c., हीनचेतनः -ना -नं, उदासवृत्तिः -त्तिः -त्ति.

Loyal, *a.* भक्तः -क्ता -क्तं, दृढभक्तिः -क्तिः -क्ति, भक्तिमान् -मती -मत् (त्), भक्तियुक्तः -क्ता -क्तं, सानुरागः -गा -गं, अनुरक्तः -क्ता -क्तं; 'to a sovereign or superior,' राजभक्तः &c., प्रभुभक्तः &c., राजानुरक्तः &c., राजसेवी -विनी &c., राजभक्तिनिष्ठः -ष्ठा -ष्ठं, स्वामिभक्तः &c., राजाज्ञावर्त्ती -र्त्तिनी &c., राजासक्तः -क्ता -क्तं, प्रजाधर्म्मनिष्ठः -ष्ठा -ष्ठं, प्रजाधर्म्मपरायणः -णा -णं, प्रजाधर्म्मतत्परः -रा -रं.—(As a wife) पतिव्रता, साध्वी, सती, सुचरित्रा, एकपत्नी, स्वीया.—(As a husband) स्वदारनिरतः, स्वदारैकतानः, अनन्यनारीसामान्यः, अनुकूलः.

Loyalist, *s.* *See* Loyal.

Loyally, *adv.* दृढभक्त्या, राजभक्त्या, राजभक्तवत्, राजभक्तिपूर्व्वं, सानुरागं, राजानुरक्तवत्, स्वराजनिष्ठापूर्व्वं.

Loyalty, *s.* भक्तिः *f.*, राजभक्तिः *f.*, प्रभुभक्तिः, स्वामिभक्तिः, राजभक्तता, दृढा भक्तिः, राजानुरागः, राजानुरक्तिः *f.*, स्वराजासक्तिः *f.*, स्वराजनिष्ठा, प्रजाधर्म्मनिष्ठा, प्रजाधर्म्मतात्पर्य्यं; 'test of loyalty,' उपधा.—(In a wife) पातिव्रत्यं, साध्वीत्वं, सतीत्वं.—(In a husband) स्वदारनिरतिः *f.*, स्वदारनिष्ठा, अनुकूलता.

Lozenge, *s.* (A quadrangular figure having two acute and two obtuse angles) चतुष्कोणविशेषो यस्य त्रिकोणाव् अन्तर्लग्नौ त्रिकोणौ बहिर्लग्नौ.—(Sweetmeat) पदकं, मोदकं, लड्डुकं.

Lubber, *s.* स्थूलजनः, स्थूलबुद्धिः *m.*, स्थूलधीः *m.*, अलसजनः, स्थूलशरीरः; 'land-lubber,' स्थलवासी *m.* (न्), स्थलचरः.

Lubberly, *a.* स्थूलः -ला -लं, स्थूलस्वभावः -वा -वं, अदक्षः -क्षा -क्षं.—(Relating to dry land) स्थलीयः -या -यं.

Lubberly, *adv.* सस्थौल्यं, स्थूलजनवत्, अदक्षं, अदक्षवत्.

Lubric, *a.* चिक्कणः -णा -णं, स्निग्धः -ग्धा -ग्धं, मेदुरः -रा -रं.

To lubricate, *v. a.* अभ्यञ्ज् (c. 7. -अनक्ति -अंक्तुं), स्नेहेन अञ्ज्, स्नेहाक्तं -क्तं कृ, स्निग्धीकृ, चिक्कणीकृ, स्नक्ष्ण (nom. स्नक्ष्णयति -यितुं).

Lubricated, *p. p.* अभ्यक्तः -क्ता -क्तं, स्नेहाक्तः -क्ता -क्तं, व्याघारितः -ता -तं.

Lubrication, *s.* अभ्यञ्जनं, स्नेहाभ्यञ्जनं, स्निग्धीकरणं, चिक्कणीकरणं.

Lubricity, *s.* स्निग्धता, स्नैग्ध्यं, स्नेहः -हनं, चिक्कणता, मेदुरता.

Lubricous, *a.* स्निग्धः -ग्धा -ग्धं, स्नेही -हिनी -हि (न्), चिक्कणः -णा -णं, पिच्छिलः -ला -लं, मेदुरः -रा -रं.

Lucent, *a.* द्योती -तिनी -ति (न्), प्रकाशमानः -ना -नं, द्योतमानः &c.

Lucid, *a.* (Bright) दीप्तिमान् -मती -मत् (त्), तेजोमयः -यी -यं, तैजसः -सी -सं, उज्ज्वलः -ला -लं, तेजस्वी -स्विनी -स्वि (न्), कान्तिमान् &c., शोभनः -ना -नं, सुप्रभः -भा -भं.—(Pellucid) स्वच्छः -च्छा -च्छं, निर्मलः -ला -लं, विमलः -ला -लं, अमलः -ला -लं, विशदः -दा -दं, प्रसन्नः -न्ना -न्नं, शुद्धः -द्धा -द्धं.—(Perspicuous) स्पष्टः -ष्टा -ष्टं, स्पष्टार्थः -र्था -र्थं, प्रसन्नः -न्ना -न्नं, व्यक्तः -क्ता -क्तं, भिन्नार्थः -र्था -र्थं.

Lucidly, *adv.* स्पष्टं, सुस्पष्टं, व्यक्तं, सुव्यक्तं, स्पष्टार्थं, भिन्नार्थं, विशदं.

Lucidness, *s.* (Brightness) दीप्तिः *f.*, कान्तिः *f.*, तेजस् *n.*, उज्ज्वलता, छविः *f.*, द्युतिः *f.*, दीप्तिमत्त्वं.—(Clearness) स्पष्टता, सुस्पष्टता, व्यक्तता, प्रसादः, स्पष्टार्थत्वं, वैशद्यं, स्वच्छता.

Lucifer, *s.* (Planet Venus) शुक्रः, उशनाः *m.* (स्), भार्गवः.

Lucifer-match, *s.* शलाका, ज्वलनशलाका, अग्निदशलाका, ज्वलत्तृणं, ज्वलनतृणं, अग्निदतृणं, अग्निदं.

Luciferous, lucific, *a.* अग्निदः -दा -दं, प्रकाशजनकः -का -कं, प्रकाशकः -का -कं, दीप्तिकरः -रा -रं, प्रकाशोत्पादकः -का -कं.

Luciform, *a.* तेजोगुणकः -का -कं, प्रकाशगुणकः -का -कं, तेजोमयः -यी -यं.

Luck, *s.* दैवं, भाग्यं, भागः, भागधेयं, दैवयोगः, दैवगतिः *f.*, दैवदशा, दैविकं; दिष्टं, अदृष्टं, नियतिः *f.*, विधिः *m.*, कालनियोगः, भवितव्यता, रिष्टं, सत्कृतिः *f.*; 'good luck,' सौभाग्यं, सुभाग्यं, कुशलं -लता, कौशल्यं, शुभं, कल्याणं, भद्रं, मङ्गलं, माङ्गल्यं, पुण्योदयः, शर्म्म *n.* (न्), सन्नतिः *f.*, सम्पत्तिः *f.*, सम्पद् *f.*, श्रयः, श्रीः *f.*, लक्ष्मीः *f.*; 'bad luck,' दौर्भाग्यं, दुर्भाग्यं, दुर्दैवं, विपत्तिः *f.*, दुर्गतिः *f.*, अशुभं, अमङ्गलं; 'good luck to you,' दिष्ट्या, दिष्ट्या वर्धसे; 'good and ill luck,' शुभाशुभं, भद्राभद्रं, मङ्गलामङ्गलं.

Luckily, *adv.* सौभाग्येन -ग्यात्, सुभाग्येन -ग्यात्, दैववशात्, भाग्यवशात्, कल्याणात्, कौशल्यात्, माङ्गल्येन, शुभदैवात्, दिष्ट्या, श्रिया, सुभगं.

Luckiness, *s.* सौभाग्यं, सुभाग्यवत्त्वं, धन्यता, कल्याणता, माङ्गल्यं, पुण्यवत्त्वं, कौशल्यं, मङ्गलं.

Luckless, *a.* दुर्भाग्यः -ग्या -ग्यं, मन्दभाग्यः &c., मन्दभागी -गिनी -गि (न्), अभाग्यः -ग्या -ग्यं, अभागी -गिनी &c., भाग्यहीनः -ना -नं, हीनभाग्यः -ग्या -ग्यं, दुर्भगः -गा -गं, निर्दैवः -वा -वं, दैवहीनः -ना -नं, अधन्यः -न्या -न्यं, विपन्नः -न्ना -न्नं.

Lucklessly, *adv.* दुर्भाग्येन -ग्यात्, दुर्दैवात्, दौर्भाग्यवशात्, दुर्दैववशात्.

Lucky, *a.* सौभाग्यवान् -वती -वत् (त्), भाग्यवान् &c., धन्यः -न्या -न्यं, मङ्गलः -ला -लं, कल्याणः -णा -णं -णी -णिनी -णि (न्), शर्म्मवान् &c., पुण्यवान् &c., श्रीमान् &c., कुशलः -ला -लं, शुभः -भा -भं, भद्रः -द्रा -द्रं, सुभद्रः -द्रा -द्रं, शुभंयुः -युः -यु, श्रयवान् &c., सुभगः -गा -गं, शिवः -वा -वं, श्रीयुक्तः -क्ता -क्तं, लक्ष्मीवान् &c., भाग्यशाली -लिनी &c., सभाग्यः -ग्या -ग्यं; 'lucky moment,' शुभलग्नः, लग्नवेला.

Lucrative, *a.* लाभकरः -रा -रं, लाभदः -दा -दं, लाभकृत् *m.f.n.*, लाभदायकः -का -कं, सफलः -ला -लं, फलदः -दा -दं, अर्थदः -दा -दं, अर्थकरः -री -रं, लाभजनकः -का -कं, फलोत्पादकः -का -कं, फलावहः -हा -हं, हितावहः -हा -हं.

Lucratively, *adv.* सफलं, साफल्येन, सलाभं, लाभपूर्व्वं, सार्थं.

Lucrativeness, *s.* साफल्यं, सफलता -त्वं, सलाभत्वं, सार्थता, फलदता.

Lucre, *s.* लाभः, अर्थः, वृद्धिः *f.*, धनलाभः, प्राप्तिः *f.*, फलं, धनोपार्ज्जनं, अर्थलब्धिः *f.*, अर्ज्जनं, योगक्षेमः, लभ्यं, लभ्यांशः, प्राप्तव्यांशः, आयः, फलोदयः.

To lucubrate, *v. n.* निशाध्ययनं कृ, रात्र्यध्ययनं कृ, निशाभ्यासं कृ, रात्रौ or निशि विद्याभ्यासं कृ or विद्यासेवां कृ.

Lucubration, *s.* (Nocturnal study) निशाध्ययनं, रात्र्यध्ययनं, निशाभ्यासः.—(That which is composed by night) निशाभ्यासेन रचितो ग्रन्थः.

Luculent, *a.* प्रसन्नः -न्ना -न्नं, विशदः -दा -दं, स्वच्छः -च्छा -च्छं, स्पष्टः -ष्टा -ष्टं, निर्मलः -ला -लं, सुप्रभः -भा -भं, तेजोमयः -यी -यं.

Ludicrous, *a.* हास्यजनकः -का -कं, हास्यकरः -रा -रं, हास्यः -स्या -स्यं, अवहास्यः &c., उपहास्यः &c., हास्योत्पादकः -का -कं, हासोत्पादकः -का -कं, हासकरः -रा -रं, परिहासकरः -रा -रं, असङ्गतः -ता -तं, कौतुकजनकः -का -कं.

Ludicrously, *adv.* असङ्गतं, हास्यप्रकारेण, यथा हासो जायते तथा.

Ludicrousness, *s.* हास्यता, हास्यजनकता, उपहास्यता, हास्योत्पादकत्वं, असङ्गतत्वं, कौतुकजनकत्वं, अवहास्यत्वं.

Lues venerea, *s.* उपदंशः; 'afflicted with it,' उपदंशी -शिनी (न्).

To luff, *v. a.* प्रतिवातं नौकां परिवृत् (c. 10. -वर्त्तयति -यितुं).

To lug, *v. a.* (Drag with force) बलेन कृष् (c. 1. कर्षति, c. 6.

कृषति, क्रष्टुं, कर्ष्टुं), बलात् or प्रसभम् आकृष् or अपकृष् or हृ (c. 1. हरति, हर्त्तुं) or अपहृ.

LUGGAGE, *s.* परिच्छदः, पथिकपरिच्छदः, यात्रिकसामग्री, सामग्र्यं, यात्रिकभाण्डानि *n. pl.*, वस्त्रभाण्डानि *n. pl.*, वस्त्रपात्राणि *n. pl.*

LUGGER, *s.* त्रिकूपकविशिष्टा दीर्घवातवसना क्षुद्रनौका.

LUGUBRIOUS, *a.* शोकसूचकः -का -कं, शोकात्मकः -का -कं, शोकमयः -यी -यं, दुःखबोधकः -का -कं, कारुण्यिकः -की -कं, खेदसूचकः -का -कं, शोकी -किनी -कि (न्).

LUKEWARM, *a.* ईषदुष्णः -ष्णा -ष्णं, कवोष्णः -ष्णा -ष्णं, मन्दोष्णः &c., कदुष्णः &c., कोष्णः &c., अनुष्णः &c., ईषत्तप्तः -प्ता -प्तं.—(Not zealous) मन्दोत्साहः -हा -हं, मन्दोद्योगः -गा -गं, निरुत्सुकः -का -कं, अतीक्ष्णः-क्ष्णा-क्ष्णं, अव्यग्रः -ग्रा -ग्रं, ईषदुत्सुकः-का -कं, उदासीनः-ना-नं.

LUKEWARMLY, *a.* ईषदुष्णं, ईषत्तापेन, कवोष्णं, अनुत्तापेन, मन्दोद्योगेन.

LUKEWARMNESS, *s.* कवोष्णता, मन्दोष्णता, कोष्णता -त्वं, ईषदुष्णता, कदुष्णत्वं, अनुष्णत्वं, ईषत्तापः, ईषत्तप्तता.—(Want of zeal) मन्दोत्साहः, मन्दोद्योगः, ईषदुत्सुकता, ईषदुत्तापः, अनौत्सुक्यं, अतीक्ष्णता, उदासीनता.

To LULL, *v. a.* (Compose to sleep) स्वप् (c. 10. स्वापयति -यितुं), संस्वप्, सम्प्रस्वप्.—(Quiet, soothe) शम् (c. 10. शमयति -यितुं), प्रशम्, उपशम्, सान्त्व् or शान्त्व् (c. 10. सान्त्वयति -यितुं), अभिशान्त्व्, परिशान्त्व्, उपसान्त्व्, लल् (c. 10. लालयति -यितुं), प्रसद् (c. 10. -सादयति -यितुं), प्रसन्नीकृ.

To LULL, *v. n.* (Subside, become calm) शम् (c. 4. शाम्यति, शमितुं), प्रशम्, उपशम्, निवृत् (c. 1. -वर्त्तते -र्त्तितुं), विरम् (c. 1. -रमति -रन्तुं), विगम् (c. 1. -गच्छति -गन्तुं), प्रसद् (c. 1. -सीदति -सत्तुं), सम्प्रसद्, विश्रम् (c. 4. -श्राम्यति -श्रमितुं), निर्वा (c. 2. -वाति -तुं), निर्वातीभू, विगतवातीभू, निर्वेगीभू, निवृत्तवायुः -युः -यु भू.

LULL, *s.* (Temporary quiet after storm) शान्तिः *f.*, वायुशान्तिः, निवृत्तिः *f.*, वायुनिवृत्तिः *f.*, निर्वातः, विरामः, विरतिः *f.*, वायुविरामः, विश्रामः, निर्वृतिः *f.*, शमः, उपशमः, विच्छेदः, वायुशमः, वातविच्छेदः, वायुस्थैर्य्यं.

LULLABY, *s.* बालकस्वापकरणार्थकं गीतं, बालस्वापकगीतं, लालनगीतं, शान्तिकगीतं, बालसान्त्वनगीतं, शिशुशमकगीतं.

LULLED, *p. p.* (Put to sleep) स्वापितः -ता -तं.—(Quieted) शमितः -ता -तं, शान्तः -न्ता -न्तं, उपशान्तः -न्ता -न्तं, प्रसादितः -ता -तं, उपगूढः -ढा -ढं.

LULLER, *s.* शमकः, शान्तिकरः, शान्तिदः, सान्त्वनकृत्, लाली *m.* (न्).

LUMBAGO, *s.* गृध्रसी, ग्रध्रसी, कटिवातः, श्रोणिवातः, कटिवेदना.

LUMBAL, LUMBAR, *a.* कटिसम्बन्धी -न्धिनी -न्धि (न्), श्रोणिसम्बन्धी &c.

LUMBER, *s.* निरर्थकद्रव्यं, अनर्थकद्रव्यं, बाधकद्रव्यं, क्लेशकद्रव्यं, बाधकं, भारः, अतिभारः.

To LUMBER, *v. a.* निरर्थकद्रव्यैः पृ (c. 10. पूरयति -यितुं), निरर्थकद्रव्याणि इतस्ततो विकृ (c. 6. -किरति -करितुं -रीतुं) or विक्षिप् (c. 6. -क्षिपति -क्षेप्तुं).

LUMBER-ROOM, *s.* निरर्थकद्रव्यकोष्ठः, बाधकद्रव्यकोष्ठकं.

LUMINARY, *s.* ज्योतिस् *n.*, ज्योतिष्मान् *m.* (त्), भास्वान् *m.* (त्), प्रतिभावान् *m.* (त्), खद्योतनः, भास्करः, प्रभाकरः, खोल्कः, गगणेचरः, खेचरः, खचरः, प्रकाशकपदार्थः, प्रकाशयुक्तपदार्थः, तेजोराशिः *m.*

LUMINOUS, *a.* तेजोमयः -यी -यं, दीप्तिमान् -मती -मत् (त्), प्रदीप्तिमान् &c., प्रभावान् &c., भास्वान् &c., भानुमान् &c., प्रकाशयुक्तः -क्ता -क्तं, विशदः -दा -दं.—(Shining by its own light) स्वप्रकाशः -शा -शं; 'the sun is a luminous body,' सूर्य्यः स्वप्रकाशः.

LUMINOUSLY, *adv.* तेजसा, दीप्त्या, प्रभया, स्वप्रकाशेन, विशदं.

LUMP, *s.* पिण्डः -ण्डं, स्थूलं, घनः, स्थूलभागः, स्थूलांशः, गण्डः, गण्डका, शर्करा, घनौघः.—(Collection, heap) राशिः *m.*, ओघः, सङ्घः, पूगः, स्तोमः, पुञ्जः, वृन्दं, समूहः, सञ्चयः, सञ्चयः, स्तूपः, उत्करः.—(Gross) साकल्यं, समुदायः, समासः; 'a lump of flesh,' मांसपिण्डः, लोथकः; 'of earth,' मृत्पिण्डः; 'having lumps in the neck,' गण्डमाली -लिनी -लि (न्); 'in the lump,' साकल्येन.

To LUMP, *v. a.* पिण्डीकृ, पिण्ड् (c. 1. पिण्डते, c. 10. पिण्डयति -यितुं), एकपिण्डीकृ, राशीकृ, एकराशीकृ, ओघीकृ, एकौघीकृ, घनीकृ, स्थूलीकृ, वृन्दीकृ, पुञ्जीकृ, पूगीकृ, एकत्रीकृ.

LUMPED, *p. p.* पिण्डीकृतः -ता -तं, पिण्डीभूतः -ता -तं, पिण्डितः -ता -तं.

LUMPISH, *a.* स्थूलः -ला -लं, स्थूलस्वभावः -वा -वं, स्थूलबुद्धिः -द्धिः -द्धि.

LUMPISHLY, *adv.* स्थूलवत्, स्थौल्येन, सस्थौल्यं, स्थूलजनवत्, बुद्धिस्थौल्यात्.

LUMPISHNESS, *s.* स्थूलता, स्थौल्यं, स्वभावस्थूलता, बुद्धिस्थौल्यं.

LUMPY, *a.* पिण्डी -ण्डिनी -ण्डि (न्), पिण्डितः -ता -तं, सपिण्डः -ण्डा -ण्डं, पिण्डलः -ला -लं, पिण्डीभूतः -ता -तं, पिण्डमयः -यी -यं, पिण्डपूर्णः -र्णा -र्णं.

LUNACY, *s.* उन्मत्तता, उन्मादः, उन्मादवायुः *m.*, बुद्धिभ्रमः, मतिभ्रमः, बुद्धिभ्रंशः, चित्तविभ्रमः, चित्तविप्लवः, बुद्धिविक्षेपः, बुद्धिक्षिप्तता, मदः, प्रमादः, अपस्मारः.

LUNAR, LUNARY, *a.* चान्द्रः -न्द्री -न्द्रं, चान्द्रिकः -की -कं, चान्द्रमसः -सी -सं, चन्द्रसम्बन्धी -न्धिनी -न्धि (न्), सौम्यः -म्या -म्यं, सौमिकः -की -कं, ऐन्दवः -वी -वं; 'lunar month,' चान्द्रमासः; 'lunar asterism or mansion,' नक्षत्रं, दाक्षायिणी; 'the twenty-seven lunar asterisms collectively,' दाक्षायिण्यः *f. pl.*, नक्षत्रचक्रं; 'lunar day,' तिथिः *m.f.* Of these lunar days there are fourteen for the waxing, and fourteen for the waning moon; the first lunar day is called प्रतिपद् *f.*, पक्षतिः -ती *f.*; the day of new moon is called अमावसी, अमावस्या, अमा; 'the day of full moon,' पूर्णिमा, पौर्णिमा, पौर्णमासी, पूर्णेन्दुः *m.* The eleventh तिथि of each शुक्लपक्षः or waxing, and कृष्णपक्षः or waning moon, is regarded as sacred to Vishnu; and the following are the names given by Major Candy for the two एकादशी of each month: चैत्रः, 1. कामदा, 2. पापमोचनी; वैशाखः, 1. मोहिनी, 2. वरूथिनी; ज्येष्ठः, 1. निर्जला, 2. अपरा; आषाढः, 1. शयनी, 2. योगिनी; श्रावणः, 1. पुत्रदा, 2. कामिका; भाद्रः, 1. परिवर्त्तिनी, 2. अजा; आश्विनः, 1. पाशाङ्कुशा, 2. इन्दिरा; कार्त्तिकः, 1. बोधिनी, 2. रमा; मार्गशीर्षः, 1. मोक्षदा, 2. सफलदा; पौषः, 1. प्रजावर्धिनी, 2. सफला; माघः, 1. जयदा, 2. षट्तिला; फाल्गुनः, 1. आमलकी, 2. विजया. The एकादशी of the शुक्लपक्षः of the months आषाढः and कार्त्तिकः are both particularly sacred. On the first, or शयनैकादशी, Vishnu goes to sleep, and on the second awakes. (Difference of solar and lunar days) क्षयतिथिः *f.*; 'inauspicious lunar day,' घाततिथिः *f.*, दग्धतिथिः *f.*; 'observance of the fasts and rites of the several lunar days,' तिथिपालनं; 'lunar eclipse,' चन्द्रग्रहणं; 'lunar measurement,' चान्द्रमानं; 'the lunar dynasty,' सोमवंशः.—(Resembling the moon). *See* LUNIFORM.

LUNATED, *a.* अर्द्धचन्द्राकारः -रा -रं, अर्द्धचन्द्राकृतिः -तिः -ति.

LUNATIC, *a.* उन्मत्तः -त्ता -त्तं, उन्मादी -दिनी -दि (न्), उन्मादवान् -वती -वत् (त्), सोन्मादः -दा -दं, उन्मदः -दा -दं, विक्षिप्तः -प्ता -प्तं, विक्षिप्तबुद्धिः -द्धिः -द्धि, विक्षिप्तमनाः -नाः -नः (स्), हतबुद्धिः &c., भ्रष्टबुद्धिः &c., बुद्धिभ्रष्टः -ष्टा -ष्टं, नष्टेन्द्रियः -या -यं, वातुलः -ला -लं, अपस्मारी -रिणी &c.

LUNATION, *s.* चन्द्रपरिवर्त्तनं, चन्द्रावृत्तिः *f.*, चन्द्रपरिवृत्तिः *f.*

LUNCH, LUNCHEON, *s.* उपाहारः, अल्पाहारः, लघ्वाहारः, लघुभोजनं, अल्पभोजनं, अर्द्धभोजनं, अर्द्धाहारः, अर्द्धाशनं, अर्द्धशनं, ग्रासः, ग्रासपरिमिताहारः.

LUNE, *s.* (In geometry) चन्द्रखण्डं.—(Leash). *See* the word.

LUNGS, *s.* फुप्फुसः, पुप्फुसः, पुस्फुसः, फुस्फुसः, रक्तफेनजः.

LUNIFORM, *a.* चन्द्राकारः -रा -रं, चन्द्राकृतिः -तिः -ति, चन्द्ररूपः -पा -पं.

LUPINE, *s.* द्विदलं, कलायः, शमीधान्यं, त्रिपुटः, सतीलकः.

LURCH, *s.* अकस्मात् एकपार्श्वे नौकापरिवर्त्तनं or नौकापरिवृत्तिः *f.*—(To leave a person in the lurch) दुर्दशायस्तं कञ्चिज्जनं त्यज् (c. 1. त्यजति, त्यक्तुं) or परित्यज्.

To LURCH, *v. n.* (Roll suddenly on one side) नाविकभाषायाम् ऊर्म्मिप्रलोठनाद् एकपार्श्वे अकस्माद् परिवृत् (c. 1. -वर्त्तते -र्त्तितुं).

LURCHER, *s.* (Poacher) कौटिकः, कौटिलिकः, कूटोपायेन वनपक्षिग्राहकः.—(Dog) कौटिकश्वा *m.* (न्), कौटिककुक्कुरः.

LURE, *s.* (For hawks) श्येनामिषं.—(Any thing which entices, allurement) प्रलोभनं, विलोभनं, आकर्षणं, आकृष्टिः *f.*, आमिषं, लोभः, आमिषदर्शनं.

To LURE, *v. n.* (Call hawks by holding out a bait) आमिषदर्शनेन श्येनादीन् आकृष् (c. 1. -कर्षति -क्रष्टुं), आमिषं दर्शयित्वा श्येनान् आह्वे (c. 1. -ह्वयति -ह्वातुं) or श्येनाह्वानं कृ.—(Allure) प्रलुभ् (c. 10. -लोभयति -यितुं), लुभ्, आकृष्, मुह् (c. 10. मोहयति -यितुं), लल् (c. 10. लालयति -यितुं).

LURED, *p. p.* आकृष्टः -ष्टा -ष्टं, प्रलोभितः -ता -तं, लालितः -ता -तं.

LURID, *a.* मलिनमुखः -खा -खी -खं, मलिनप्रभः -भा -भं, मलिनः -ना -नं, मलिनतेजाः -जाः -जः (स्), तमोवृतः -ता -तं, उग्रदर्शनः -ना -नं, घोररूपः -पा -पं, दुर्द्दिनग्रस्तः -स्ता -स्तं.

To LURK, *v. n.* निभृते or निभृतं or सुनिभृतं or प्रच्छन्नं स्था (c. 1. तिष्ठति, स्थातुं) or वृत् (c. 1. वर्त्तते -र्त्तितुं), गुप्तः -प्ता -प्तं वृत् or भू, गुप् in pass. (गुप्यते).

LURKER, *s.* निभृतवर्त्ती *m.* (न्), प्रच्छन्नस्थायी *m.* (न्), निभृते स्थायी *m.*

LURKING-PLACE, *s.* गुप्तिः *f.*, गुप्तिस्थानं, गोपनस्थानं, निभृतस्थानं, गूढस्थानं.

LUSCIOUS, *a.* अतिमधुरः -रा -रं, अतिमिष्टः -ष्टा -ष्टं, अतिस्वादुः -दुः -द्वी -दु, स्वादिष्टः -ष्टा -ष्टं, सुमधुरः -रा -रं, सुस्वादुः &c., मधुमयः -यी -यं, मधुमान् -मती -मत् (त्), अतितृप्तिजनकः -का -कं, अतितुष्टिजनकः-का-कं.

LUSCIOUSLY, *adv.* अतिमधुरं, अतिमिष्टं, अतिमाधुर्य्येण, सुमधुरं.

LUSCIOUSNESS, *s.* अतिमाधुर्य्यं, सुमाधुर्य्यं, अतिमधुरता, अतिमिष्टता, अतिस्वादुता, माधुर्य्यं, तृप्तिजनकत्वं.

LUSORY, *a.* विनोदी -दिनी -दि (न्), सविनोदः -दा -दं, लीलायितः -ता -तं, सलीलः -ला -लं, लीलाखेलः -ला -लं, सकौतुकः -का -कं, क्रीडा in comp.

LUST *s.* (Carnal desire) कामः, कामिता, कामुकत्वं, कामना, कामाग्निः *m.*, कामानलः, रतार्थित्वं, मैथुनार्थित्वं, मैथुनेच्छा, मदनः, मदनेच्छा, रताभिलाषः, रमणेच्छा, विषयाभिलाषः.—(Eager desire) लालसा, अत्यभिलाषः, अतिस्पृहा, अतिशयेच्छा, अतीच्छा, लोभः, अतिलोभः, वाञ्छा, आकांक्षा, कांक्षा, लिप्सा, तृष्णा, अतिलिप्सा.—(Depraved affections) दुष्टवासना, दुर्वासना, कुवासना, असद्वासना; 'inflamed with lust,' कामाग्निदीप्तः -प्ता -प्तं.

To LUST, *v. n.* (Have carnal desire) कामार्त्तः -र्त्ता -र्त्तं भू, कामुकः -का -कं भू, रतार्थी -र्थिनी -र्थि भू, मैथुनार्थी &c. भू, मैथुनाभिलाषी -षिणी -षि भू, मैथुनम् अभिलष् (c 1. -लषति -षितुं), कम् (c. 10. कामयते -यितुं), अभिकम्, विषयाभिलाषी भू; 'to lust after a woman,' कामतः स्त्रीसङ्गम् अभिलष्.—(Desire eagerly) अत्यन्तम् अभिलष् or इष् (c. 6. इच्छति, एषितुं) or वाञ्छ् (c. 1. वाञ्छति -ञ्छितुं) or अभिवाञ्छ्, अतिशयेन स्पृह् (c. 10. स्पृहयति -यितुं) or कांक्ष् (c. 1. कांक्षति -क्षितुं) or आकांक्ष् or अभिकांक्ष् or लभ् in des. (लिप्सते -प्सितुं), लुभ् (c. 4. लुभ्यति, लोब्धुं).

LUSTFUL, *a.* कामुकः -का -कं, कामी -मिनी -मि (न्), कामवृत्तिः -त्तिः -त्ति, कामप्रवणः -णा -णं, कामासक्तः -क्ता -क्तं, सकामः -मा -मं, कामनः -ना -नं, कमनः -ना -नं, कमः -मा -मं, कमिता -त्री -तृ (तृ), कामयिता &c., रतार्थी -र्थिनी &c., मैथुनार्थी &c., सुरतार्थी &c., मैथुनाभिलाषी -षिणी &c., सम्भोगाभिलाषी &c., रताभिलाषी &c., मैथुनेच्छुः -च्छुः -च्छु, व्यवायी -यिनी &c., अनुकः -का -कं, अभीकः -का -कं, अभिकः -का -कं, लाषुकः -का -कं, अभिलाषुकः -का -कं, व्यवायपरायणः -णा -णं, लम्पटः, स्त्रीलम्पटः, स्त्रीव्यसनी *m.* (न्), स्त्रीसङ्गाभिलाषी &c., स्त्रीसम्भोगाभिलाषी, स्त्रीरतः, स्त्रीपरः.—(Under the influence of lust) कामार्त्तः -र्त्ता -र्त्तं, कामातुरः -रा -रं, कामान्धः -न्धा -न्धं, कामान्वितः -ता -तं, कामाविष्टः -ष्टा -ष्टं, कामग्रस्तः -स्ता -स्तं, कामाधीनः -ना -नं, कामयुक्तः -क्ता -क्तं, कामाक्रान्तः -न्ता -न्तं, कामपीडितः -ता -तं, जातकामः -मा -मं, कामोपहतः -ता -तं.

LUSTFULLY, *adv.* सकामं, कामुकवत्, कामपूर्व्वं, कामतस्, लम्पटवत्.

LUSTFULNESS, *s.* कामुकत्वं -ता, कामिता, सकामता, रतार्थित्वं, मैथुनार्थित्वं.

LUSTILY, *adv.* बलवत्, महाबलेन, सवीर्य्यं, ससत्त्वं, वीर्य्येण, मांसलवत्, हृष्टपुष्टवत्, तेजसा, पौरुषेण, सपौरुषं.

LUSTINESS, *s.* बलवत्त्वं, सबलता, मांसलता, दृढाङ्गता, शरीरदृढता, ससत्त्वता, वीर्य्यवत्त्वं, वीर्य्यं, सत्त्वं, अंशलता, पृथुशरीरता, वज्रदेहत्वं, व्यूढोरस्कत्वं, शरीरपृथुता, हृष्टपुष्टता.

LUSTRAL, *a.* शुद्धिकरः -री -रं, शुचिकरः -री -रं, शोधकः -का -कं, पावकः -का -कं, पावनः -ना -नं; 'lustral water,' शान्त्युदं -दकं, पावनोदकं, पावनं; 'vessel containing it,' शान्त्युदकुम्भः.

To LUSTRATE, *v. a.* शुध् (c. 10. शोधयति -यितुं), परिशुध्, विशुध्, पू (c. 9. पुनाति, पवितुं), परिपू, विपू, पवित्रीकृ, शोधनं कृ.

LUSTRATION, *s.* शुद्धिकरणं, शोधनं, शुचिकरणं, शुद्धिः *f.*, पावनं, पवित्रीकरणं, मलापकर्षणं; 'lustration of arms, a ceremony performed by a king before taking the field,' लोहाभिहारः, लोहाभिसारः, नीराजनं -ना.

LUSTRE, *s.* तेजस् *n.*, द्युतिः *f.*, प्रभा, शोभा, रुचिः *f.*, ओजस् *n.*, ओजस्विता, प्रतापः, बृहद्द्युतिः *f.*, उज्ज्वलता, उद्योतः, छविः *f.*, कान्तिः *f.*, दीप्तिः *f.*, रुच् *f.* (च्), भास् *f.*, प्रकाशः -शनं, राढा; 'of metal or a gem,' ओजस् *n.*, तेजस् *n.*

LUSTROUS, *a.* तेजस्वी -स्विनी -स्वि (न्), सुप्रभः -भा -भं, कान्तिमान् -मती -मत् (त्), द्युतिमान् &c., दीप्तिमान् &c., ओजस्वी &c., प्रतापी -पिनी &c., प्रतापवान् &c., शोभनः -ना -नं, प्रभावान् &c., उज्ज्वलः -ला -लं.

LUSTRUM, *s.* युगं, वर्षपञ्चकं, वत्सरपञ्चकं, अब्दपञ्चकं.

LUSTY, *a.* मांसलः -ला -लं, दृढाङ्गः -ङ्गा -ङ्गं, दृढशरीरः -रा -रं, पृथुशरीरः -रा -रं, बलवान् -वती -वत् (त्), महाबलः -ला -लं, महाबाहुः -हुः -हु, अंशलः -ला -लं, अंसलः -ला -लं, वज्रदेहः -हा -हं, व्यूढोरस्कः -स्का -स्कं, महाकायः -या -यं, स्थूलशरीरः -रा -रं, मेदस्वी -स्विनी -स्वि (न्), वीर्य्यवान् -वती &c., सवीर्य्यः -र्य्या -र्य्यं, ससत्त्वः -त्त्वा -त्त्वं, हृष्टपुष्टः -ष्टा -ष्टं, बृहदङ्गः -ङ्गा -ङ्गं, बृहच्छरीरः &c.

LUTANIST, *s.* वैणिकः, वीणावादः -दकः, वीणापाणिः *m.*

LUTANOUS, *a.* (Living in mud) पङ्कस्थः -स्था -स्थं, कर्द्दमस्थः -स्था -स्थं,

पङ्कवासी -सिनी &c., पङ्कजः -जा -जं.—(Pertaining to it) पङ्किलः -ला -लं, पङ्की -ङ्किनी &c., कार्द्दमः -मी -मं.—(Of the colour of mud) पङ्कवर्णः -र्णा -र्णं.

LUTE, s. वीणा, वल्लकी, विपञ्ची -ञ्चिका, तन्त्री m. (न्), हुड्डी, मद्दुर्गः, सारङ्गी, शारङ्गी, पिनाकी; 'with seven strings,' परिवादिनी; 'the wire of a lute,' तन्त्री, तन्त्रं; 'the neck,' वीणादण्डः, प्रवालः; 'a piece of wood under the neck called the belly,' ककुभः, प्रसेवकः; 'the tie,' उपनाहः, वीणानुबन्धः, निबन्धनं; 'the whole body of the lute, comprising the gourd, neck, and belly,' कोलम्बकः; 'the quill or bow,' कोणः, परिवादः, शारिका, रणः.

To LUTE, *v. a.* पङ्केन लिप् (c. 6. लिम्पति, लेप्तुं), पङ्कलेपेन संलग्नीकृ.

LUTER, LUTIST, *a.* वीणावादः -दकः. *See* LUTANIST.

LUTE-STRING, s. वीणातन्त्रं, तन्त्री, वीणातारः -रा.

LUTULENT, *a.* पङ्किलः -ला -लं, पङ्की -ङ्किनी -ङ्कि (न्), कार्द्दमः -मी -मं.

To LUXATE, *v. a.* विसन्धीकृ, सन्धित्रोटनं कृ, अस्थिसन्धिं or अस्थिग्रन्थिं त्रुट् (c. 10. त्रोटयते -यितुं) or विसन्धा (c. 3. -दधाति -धातुं) or भञ्ज् (c. 7. भनक्ति, भंक्तुं), सन्धिभङ्गं कृ, सन्धिविश्लेषं कृ, सन्धिच्युतिं कृ.

LUXATED, *p. p.* विसन्धितः -ता -तं, त्रुटितसन्धिः -न्धिः -न्धि, च्युतसन्धिः &c., सन्धिच्युतः -ता -तं, सन्धिविश्लिष्टः -ष्टा -ष्टं, स्थानभ्रष्टः -ष्टा -ष्टं.

LUXATION, s. सन्धित्रोटनं, सन्धिविश्लेषः, सन्धिच्युतिः *f.*, विसन्धीकरणं.

LUXURIANCE, LUXURIANCY, s. अतिवृद्धिः *f.*, अधिकवृद्धिः *f.*, अतिवर्धनं, अत्यन्तवर्धनं, नितान्तवृद्धिः *f.*, वृद्धिबाहुल्यं, समृद्धिः *f.*, सामृद्ध्यं, वृद्ध्याधिक्यं, अतिस्फीतिः *f.*, अतिस्फातिः *f.*, उद्रेकः, उत्सेकः, आप्यायनं.

LUXURIANT, *a.* अतिवर्धिष्णुः -ष्णुः -ष्णु, अतिवर्धमानः -ना -नं, अतिवर्धितः -ता -तं, अतिवर्धी -र्धिनी -र्धि (न्), अतिवर्धनः -नी -नं, अतिस्फीतः -ता -तं, अतिपीनः -ना -नं, अतिसमृद्धः -द्धा -द्धं, अतिपुष्कलः -ला -लं, अतिबहुलः -ला -लं, अतिप्रचुरः -रा -रं, उत्सिक्तः -क्ता -क्तं, उद्रिक्तः -क्ता -क्तं, अतिरिक्तः -क्ता -क्तं.

LUXURIANTLY, *adv.* अतिवृद्ध्या, अतिवृद्धिपूर्व्वं, बाहुल्येन, अतिबहुलं, अतिबहुशस्, अतिप्रचुरं, अतिप्राचुर्य्येण, अतिपुष्कलं, अतिरिक्तं, उद्रेकेण.

To LUXURIATE, *v. n.* (Grow exuberantly) अत्यन्तं वृध् (c. 1. वर्धते -र्धितुं) or ऋध् (c. 5. ऋध्नोति, c. 4. ऋध्यति, अर्धितुं) or समृध् or प्यै (c. 1. प्यायते, प्यातुं) or आप्यै or स्फाय् (c. 1. स्फायते -यितुं), अतिबहुलीभू, अतिप्रचुरीभू, अतिवृद्धिम् इ (c. 2. एति -तुं), अतिस्फीतिम् इ. —(Live or feed luxuriously) अतिविलासेन or अतिसुखेन or सुखोपभोगेन वृत् (c. 1. वर्त्तते -र्त्तितुं) or चर् (c. 1. चरति -रितुं) or विहृ (c. 1. -हरति -हर्त्तुं) or भ्रम् (c. 4. भ्राम्यति, भ्रमितुं).

LUXURIOUS, *a.* (Contributing to luxury, furnished with luxuries) सुखभोगवान् -वती -वत् (त्), सुखभोगकरः -रा -रं, सुखभोगावहः -हा -हं, अतिसुखावहः -हा -हं, अतिसुखी -खिनी -खि (न्), सुखभोगसाधकः -का -कं, सुखभोगमयः -यी -यं, अतिसुखमयः &c., सुखोपभोगदः -दा -दं, सविलासः -सा -सं, विलासी -सिनी &c., विलासमयः &c., विलासयुक्तः -क्ता -क्तं, विलाससुखमयः &c. —(Indulging in luxury) विलासी -सिनी &c., विलासासक्तः -क्ता -क्तं, भोगासक्तः -क्ता -क्तं, सुखभोगासक्तः &c., सुखभोगपरायणः -णा -णं, विषयासक्तः -क्ता -क्तं, विषयोपभोगव्यग्रः -ग्रा -ग्रं, वैषयिकः -की -कं, देहम्भरः -रा -रं, आत्मम्भरिः -रिः -रि, विषयोपसेवी -विनी &c., सुखसेवी &c.

LUXURIOUSLY, *adv.* विलासेन, सुखेन, अतिसुखेन, अतिविलासपूर्व्वं, सविलासं, सुखोपभोगेन, सुखोपभोगपूर्व्वं, सुखासक्तवत्, परमसुखोपभोगेन.

LUXURIOUSNESS, s. विलासित्वं -ता, सविलासत्वं, सुखोपभोगः, सुखभोगः, अतिसुखिता, सुखासक्तिः *f.*, सुखभोगासक्तिः *f.*, भोगासक्तिः *f.*, विषयभोगासक्तिः *f.*, विषयभोगः, विषयसेवा, विषयोपसेवा, सुखसेवा, सुखास्वादः.

LUXURY, s. विलासः, विलासित्वं -ता. *See* LUXURIOUSNESS. (That which gratifies the senses or appetite) सुखं, सुखसाधनं, भोगः, भोगसाधनं, सौख्यं, सुखसाहित्यं, विषयसुखं, विषयसुखसाहित्यं, आमिषं, आमिषं.—(Dainty) स्वाद्वन्नं, परमान्नं, विशिष्टान्नं, उत्तमान्नं, मिष्टान्नं, भोजनविशेषः, विशिष्टभोजनं, विशिष्टामिषं.

LYE, s. क्षारोदकं, क्षारजलं, क्षारितजलं, क्षारसंसृष्टं जलं.

LYING, *part.* (Reclining) शायी -यिनी -यि (न्), शयः -या -यं, शयानः -ना -नं, शयितः -ता -तं, पतन् -तन्ती -तत् (त्), पतितः -ता -तं, संविष्टः -ष्टा -ष्टं, उपविष्टः -ष्टा -ष्टं; 'lying on a bed,' शयने संविष्टः -ष्टा -ष्टं; 'lying prostrate,' अपमूर्द्धशयः -या -यं, क्षिप्तदेहः -हा -हं; 'lying with the face upwards,' उत्तानशयः -या -यं.—(Act of lying) शयनं, पतनं, संवेशः.—(Lying in) प्रसवकालः, प्रसवावस्था, सूतिकालः, प्रसूतिकालः; 'lying-in chamber,' सूतिकागृहं, सूतिगृहं, सूतिकाभवनं, सूतिगृहं, सूतीगृहं, अरिष्टशय्या, अरिष्टं, गर्भः, अपवरकः.

LYING, s. (Telling falsehood) मृषावादः, मिथ्यावादः, मिथ्याभाषणं, मिथ्याकथनं, असत्यभाषणं, मृषाभाषिता -षणं, मृषाभिधानं, मिथ्योक्तिः *f.*, असत्योक्तिः *f.*, अनृतवादः.

LYING, *part.* or *a.* (Addicted to falsehood) मिथ्यावादी -दिनी -दि (न्), मृषावादी &c., असत्यवादी &c., अनृतवादी &c., असत्यभाषी -षिणी &c., अनृतभाषी &c., अनृतवाक् *m. f. n.* (च्), असत्यः -त्या -त्यं, निःसत्यः -त्या -त्यं.

LYMPH, s. मेदस् *n.*, वसा, चर्म्माम्भस् *n.*, त्वगम्भस् *n.*, त्वगुदकं, चर्म्मोदकं, चर्म्मसारः, त्वक्सारः, असृक्करः, उदकधातुः *m.*

LYMPHATE, LYMPHATED, *a.* उन्मत्तः -त्ता -त्तं, वातुलः -ला -लं.

LYMPHATIC, s. मेदोवहं, मेदोवाहिनी, चर्म्माम्भोवाहिनी, त्वक्सारवाहिनी, शरीरान्तर्गतजलवाहिनी.

LYNX, s. वनबिडालः, वनमार्जारः, सूक्ष्मदृष्टिः क्षुद्रव्याघ्रविशेषः.

LYRE, s. वल्लकी, वीणा, विपञ्ची -ञ्चिका, तन्त्री. *See* LUTE.

LYRIC, LYRICAL, *a.* वैणिकः -की -कं, वीणावादनसहितः -ता -तं.

LYRIST, s. वल्लकीवादकः, वल्लकीपाणिः *m.*, वैणिकः.

LYTHRUM, s. (A plant) अग्निज्वाला, सुभिक्षा, धातकी, धातुपुष्पिका.

M

MACAROON, s. बादामनिर्म्मितो मिष्टपिष्टकविशेषः.

MACAW, MACAO, s. शुकः, कीरः, वक्रचञ्चुः *m.*, वक्रतुण्डः.

MACE, s. (Club, ensign of authority) वेत्रं, गदा, यष्टिः *m. f.*, यष्टिकः, दण्डः -ण्डं, मुषलः, मुसलः, लगुडः, लगुरः, मुद्गरः, वार्तद्धिः *m.*—(The spice) जातीकोशं, जातिकोशं, जातीकोषं, जातिकोषं, जातिः -ती *f.*, जातिफलं, जातीफलं, फलं, जातीपत्री, जातिपत्रं, जातिपुष्पं, गुडत्वचं, राजभोग्यं.

MACE-BEARER, s. वेत्रधरः, वेत्रधारी *m.* (न्), वेत्री *m.* (न्), वेत्रपाणिः *m.*, गदाधरः, गदी *m.* (न्), गदापाणिः *m.*, गदाहस्तः, दण्डधरः, दण्डी *m.* (न्), दण्डहस्तः, लगुडहस्तः, दण्डधारी *m.*, दण्डिकः, दण्डभृत् *m.*, यष्टिग्रहः, याष्टीकः.

To MACERATE, *v. a.* (Make lean, waste) कृश (nom. कृशयति -यितुं), कृशीकृ, परिकृशीकृ, क्षि in caus. (क्षपयति -यितुं), क्षीणं -णां -णं कृ, क्षीणीकृ, ग्लै in caus. (ग्लपयति -यितुं), मांसक्षयं कृ.—(Steep) जलसेकेन or जलप्लावनेन कोमलीकृ, चिरकालं जलेन समाप्लु (c. 10. -प्लावयति -यितुं) or जलसमाप्लुतं -तां कृ or जलसिक्तं -क्तां कृ or आर्द्रीकृ; 'macerate indigo,' नीलसन्धानं कृ, नीलपाचनं कृ.

MACERATED, *p.p.* (Made lean) कृशीकृतः -ता -तं, परिकृशः -शा -शं, क्षीणः -णा -णं. —(Steeped) जलसेकेन कोमलीकृतः -ता -तं or मृदूकृतः -ता -तं.

MACERATION, *s.* (Making thin, mortification) कृशीकरणं, क्षीणकरणं, कर्शनं, क्लेशकरणं, क्लेशदानं, मांसक्षयः, मांसशोषणं, शरीरपाकः, शरीरशोषः, कायक्लेशः, क्लेशः, कायकृच्छ्रं.—(Steeping) जलसेकेन कोमलीकरणं, आर्द्रीकरणं; 'of indigo,' नीलसन्धानं, नीलपाचनं.

To MACHINATE, *v. a.* परिकॢप् (c. 10. -कल्पयति -यितुं), उपायं कॢप् or घट् (c. 1. घटते -टितुं) or विधा (c. 3. -दधाति -धातुं) or अनुसन्धा or संविधा, मन्त्र् (c. 10. मन्त्रयति -यितुं), सम्प्रधृ (c. 10. -धारयति -यितुं), कल्पनां कृ, परिकल्पनां कृ, अनुसन्धानं कृ.—(Plot) द्रुह् (c. 4. द्रुह्यति, द्रोग्धुं), कपटप्रबन्धं कृ, कपटप्रबन्धेन द्रोहं कृ.

MACHINATION, *s.* कल्पना, परिकल्पना -नं, कॢप्तिः *f.*, मन्त्रणा, कुकल्पना, कुमन्त्रणा, कुयुक्तिः *f.*, कुप्रयुक्तिः *f.*, कुसृष्टिः *f.*, कुसङ्कल्पः, कपटप्रयोगः, कपटप्रबन्धः, घटनं -ना, कुघटना, विधानं, संविधानं, अनुसन्धानं, दुष्टकार्य्यसाधनार्थम् उपायचिन्तनं, द्रोहचिन्तनं; 'against the king,' राजद्रोहः, राजशरीराभिद्रोहः.

MACHINATOR, *s.* परिकल्पकः, परिकल्पनाकृत् *m.*, कुमन्त्रणाकृत्, कुकल्पनाकारी *m.* (न्), घटकः, उपायचिन्तकः, द्रोहचिन्तकः.

MACHINE, *s.* यन्त्रं, उपकरणं, विलालः, साधनं, साधनयन्त्रं.

MACHINERY, (Collective mechanism) यन्त्रसाहित्यं, यन्त्रशक्तिसाहित्यं, यान्त्रं, यान्त्रिकं, यन्त्रत्वं.—(Machines in general) यन्त्रसामग्र्यं, यन्त्रसमूहः, यन्त्रसमुदायः, यान्त्रं, यन्त्रविद्या.

MACHINIST, *s.* यन्त्रकारः -रकः, यन्त्रकृत् *m.*, यन्त्रनिर्म्माणशिल्पज्ञः. यन्त्रविद्यानिपुणः, यन्त्रविद्, कलाज्ञः.

MACILENCY, *s.* कृशता, कार्श्यं, कृशाङ्गता, क्षीणता, क्षामता, मांसक्षीणता.

MACILENT, *a.* कृशः -शा -शं, क्षीणः -णा -णं, क्षीणमांसः -सा -सं.

MACROCOSM, *s.* जगत्सर्वं, जगत्कृत्स्नं, विश्वजगत् *n.*, विश्वं, त्रिभुवनं.

MACROLOGY, *s.* दीर्घसूत्रता, अतिविस्तीर्णवाक्यं, अतिविस्तरः.

MACTATION, *s.* उपहारार्थं घातनं or निहननं or प्रमापणं, विशसनं.

MACULA, *s.* कलङ्कः, लाञ्छनं, चिह्नं, विन्दुः *m.*, कलुषं, अङ्कः.

To MACULATE, *v. a.* कलङ्क (nom. कलङ्कयति -यितुं), मलिन (nom. मलिनयति -यितुं), कलुष (nom. कलुषयति -यितुं), चिह्न (nom. चिह्नयति -यितुं), लाञ्छ् (c. 1. लाञ्छति -ञ्छितुं).

MACULATE, MACULATED, *a.* कलङ्कितः -ता -तं, कलङ्की -ङ्किनी -ङ्कि (न्), कलुषितः -ता -तं, लाञ्छितः -ता -तं, चिह्नितः -ता -तं.

MAD, *a.* उन्मत्तः -त्ता -त्तं, उन्मादः -दा -दं, उन्मादवान् -वती -वत् (त्), उन्मादी -दिनी -दि (न्), सोन्मादः -दा -दं, उन्मदः -दा -दं, उन्मदिष्णुः -ष्णुः -ष्णु, मत्तः -त्ता -त्तं, वातुलः -ला -लं, वातूलः -ला -लं, प्रमदः -दा -दं, सून्मदः -दा -दं, सून्मादः -दा -दं, हतबुद्धिः -द्धिः -द्धि, नष्टबुद्धिः &c., विक्षिप्तबुद्धिः &c., भ्रष्टबुद्धिः &c., बुद्धिभ्रष्टः -ष्टा -ष्टं, हतज्ञानः -ना -नं, विप्लुतचित्तः -त्ता -त्तं, भ्रान्तचित्तः -त्ता -त्तं, विक्षिप्तमतिः -तिः -ति, विक्षिप्तः -प्ता -प्तं, मूढचेताः -ताः -तः (स्), नष्टेन्द्रियः -या -यं.—(Proceeding from madness) उन्मादप्रयुक्तः -क्ता -क्तं, उन्मादसूचकः -का -कं, बुद्धिभ्रंशसूचकः -का -कं.—(Furious) मदोत्कटः -टा -टं, मदोदग्रः -ग्रा -ग्रं, कोपाकुलः -ला -लं, संरब्धः -ब्धा -ब्धं; 'a mad dog,' अलर्कः, अलकः; 'a mad fellow,' प्रमदजनः; 'to go mad,' उन्मद् (c. 4. -माद्यति -मदितुं), उन्मत्तीभू; 'drive mad,' उन्मद् (c. 10. -मादयति -यितुं).

MADAM, *s.* आर्य्या, आर्य्यिका, आर्य्यका, भवती, भाविनी.—(As a complimentary title) आर्य्ये voc. c., भवति voc. c.

MAD-BRAIN, MAD-BRAINED, *a.* विक्षिप्तबुद्धिः -द्धिः -द्धि, विप्लुतबुद्धिः &c.

MAD-CAP, *s.* प्रमदजनः, उन्मत्तजनः, साहसिकः, साहसकर्म्मी *m.* (न्).

To MADDEN, *v. a.* उन्मद् (c. 10. -मादयति -यितुं), मद्, उन्मत्तीकृ, मत्तीकृ.

To MADDEN, *v. n.* उन्मद् (c. 4. -माद्यति -मदितुं), उन्मत्तीभू, मत्तीभू, मद्.

MADDENED, *p. p.* उन्मादितः -ता -तं, उन्मत्तीकृतः -ता -तं, संरब्धः -ब्धा -ब्धं.

MADDENING, *a.* उन्मादकः -का -कं, उन्मादजनकः -का -कं, उन्मादन -ना -नं.

MADDER, *s.* (The plant) मञ्जिष्ठा, विकसा, जिङ्गया, मण्डूकपर्णी, ताम्रवल्ली, योजनवल्ली, योजनपर्णी, भण्डीरी, भण्डिरी, भण्डी, जिङ्गी, समङ्गा, कालमेषिका, चित्राङ्गी, कालमषिका.

MADE, *p. p.* कृतः -ता -तं, निर्म्मितः -ता -तं, कल्पितः -ता -तं, प्रकल्पितः -ता -तं, रचितः -ता -तं, विरचितः -ता -तं, घटितः -ता -तं, विहितः -ता -तं; 'made of,' मयः -यी -यं, निर्म्मितः -ता -तं, घटितः -ता -तं in comp.; as, 'made of wood,' काष्ठमयः -यी -यं, काष्ठघटितः -ता -तं, काष्ठनिर्म्मितः -ता -तं; 'made known,' निवेदितः -ता -तं, आवेदितः -ता -तं, सूचितः -ता -तं, आख्यातः -ता -तं, ज्ञापितः -ता -तं, विज्ञापितः -ता -तं; 'made ready,' सज्जीकृतः -ता -तं; 'made favorable,' प्रसादीकृतः -ता -तं; 'made up, as the mind,' स्थिरीकृतः -ता -तं, स्थिरः -रा -रं; 'made up, reconciled,' सन्धितः -ता -तं, शान्तविवादः -दा -दं; 'made up, settled,' सिद्धः -द्धा -द्धं, साधितः -ता -तं, निष्पन्नः -न्ना -न्नं; 'made over,' सङ्क्रामितः -ता -तं, सञ्चारितः -ता -तं, प्रतिपादितः -ता -तं; 'made light of,' लघूकृतः -ता -तं; 'made good,' साधितः -ता -तं; 'made to do any thing,' expressed by the caus. pass. part.; as, 'made to pay,' दापितः -ता -तं; 'made to go,' गमितः -ता -तं; 'made to know,' ज्ञापितः -ता -तं; 'one who has made an agreement,' कृतसङ्केतः -ता -तं.

MADEFACTION, *s.* आर्द्रीकरणं, क्लेदनं, संक्लेदनं, समुन्दनं, क्लिन्नीकरणं.

To MADEFY, *v.a.* आर्द्रीकृ, क्लिद् (c. 10. क्लेदयति -यितुं), संक्लिद्, परिक्लिद्.

MADHOUSE, *s.* उन्मत्तालयः, उन्मत्तपालनगृहं, उन्मत्तस्थानं.

MADLY, *adv.* उन्मत्तवत्, सोन्मादं, मत्तवत्, वातुलवत्, चित्तविभ्रमात्, चित्तविप्लवात्, उन्मादेन, प्रामाद्यात्, प्रमदजनवत्.

MADMAN, *s.* उन्मत्तजनः, मत्तजनः, प्रमदजनः, उन्मादकः, वातुलः.

MADNESS, *s.* उन्मत्तता, उन्मादः, सोन्मादता, मत्तता, वातुलता, विक्षिप्तता, बुद्धिविक्षिप्तता, बुद्धिविक्षेपः, बुद्धिभ्रमः, मतिभ्रमः, चित्तविभ्रमः, चित्तविप्लवः, बुद्धिनाशः, बुद्धिभ्रंशः, मतिभ्रंशः, मदः, प्रमदता, प्रामाद्यं, उन्मादवायुः *m.*

MÆNORRHAGIA, *s.* (A disease) योन्यर्शस् *n.*, प्रदरः, प्रदरामयः.

MAGAZINE, *s.* (Storehouse) भाण्डागारं, भाण्डगृहं, कोषागारं.—(Of arms, ammunition, &c.) युद्धद्रव्यागारं, शस्त्रागारं, अस्त्रागारं, युद्धभाण्डागारं, आयुधागारं.—(A miscellany published periodically) काले काले प्रकाशितो नानाविषयसङ्ग्रहः or नानावस्तुविषयको ग्रन्थः.

MAGGOT, *s.* कीटः, कृमिः *m.*, अलिः *m.*, कीटाण्डजं.

MAGGOTY, *s.* कीटपूर्णः -र्णा -र्णं, कृमिपूर्णः -र्णा -र्णं, कृमिमयः -यी -यं.

MAGI, MAGIANS, *s. pl.* पूर्व्वदेशीयपण्डिताः *m. pl.*, प्राग्देशीयविज्ञजनाः.

MAGIC, *s.* अभिचारः, अभिचारविद्या, माया, मायाविद्या, योगः, सम्प्रयोगः, यज्ञक्रिया, मूलकर्म्म *n.* (न्), चित्रकर्म्म *n.*, जालं, जालकर्म्म *n.*, इन्द्रजालं, अभिमन्त्रणं, कार्म्मणं, कार्म्मणत्वं, पिशाचविद्या, कुविद्या, मोहः, कुहकः, कुसृतिः *f.*, संवदनं -ना, मन्त्रः, मन्त्रमोहनं.

MAGIC, MAGICAL, *a.* आभिचारिकः -की -कं, अभिचारिकः -की -कं, अभिचारी -रिणी -रि (न्), मायामयः -यी -यं, मायी -यिनी -यि (न्), मायावी -विनी &c., मायिकः -की -कं, ऐन्द्रजालिकः -की -कं, मोही -हिनी &c., कौसृतिकः -की -कं.

MAGICALLY, *adv.* अभिचारेण, अभिचारविद्यानुसारात्, मायया, सेन्द्रजालं.

MAGICIAN, *s.* अभिचारविद् *m.*, अभिचारविद्याज्ञः, मायाकारः, मायाकृत् *m.*, मायी *m.* (न्), मायिकः, मायावी *m.* (न्), मायाजीवी *m.* (न्), पिशाचविद्याज्ञः, अभिचारी *m.* (न्), चित्रकर्म्मविद् *m.*, मूलकर्म्मविद् *m.*, इन्द्रजालिकः, ऐन्द्रजालिकः, इन्द्रियमोही *m.* (न्), कुहकः, कुहककारः, कुहकजीवी *m.*, योगी *m.* (न्), योगेश्वरः, सम्प्रयोगी *m.*, कौसृतिकः, सिद्धः, चित्रकर्म्मी *m.* (न्).

MAGISTERIAL, *a.* (Pertaining to a magistrate or magistracy) धर्म्माधिकारसम्बन्धी -न्धिनी &c., धर्म्माध्यक्षसम्बन्धी &c., दण्डनीतिसम्बन्धी &c., आधिकारिकः -की -कं, वैनयिकः -की -कं.—(Pertaining to a master) प्रभुसम्बन्धी &c., स्वामिसम्बन्धी &c., प्रभुत्वविशिष्टः -ष्टा -ष्टं, आधिकारिकः -की -कं.—(Imperious) आज्ञापकः -का -कं, आदेशकः -का -कं, धृष्टः -ष्टा -ष्टं, शासनरूपः -पा -पं.

MAGISTERIALLY, *adv.* धर्म्माध्यक्षवत्, दण्डनायकवत्, अधिकारेण, शासनरूपेण.

MAGISTRACY, *s.* (Office of a magistrate) धर्म्माधिकारः -रित्वं, धर्म्माधिकरणं, धर्म्माधिपत्यं, धर्म्माध्यक्षता, न्यायाधिकारः, न्यायाधीशता.—(Body of magistrates) धर्म्माधिकारिणः *m. pl*, धर्म्माधिकारिगणः, धर्म्माध्यक्षगणः, धर्म्माध्यक्षसमूहः, न्यायाधीशगणः, न्यायाधीशमण्डलं.

MAGISTRATE, *s.* धर्म्माध्यक्षः, धर्म्माधिकारी *m.* (न्), न्यायाध्यक्षः, न्यायाधीशः, न्यायाधिपतिः *m.*, दण्डनायकः, प्राड्विवाकः, दण्डप्रणेता *m.* (तृ), नीतिशास्ता *m.* (स्तृ), विचारकर्त्ता *m.* (र्त्तृ), अक्षदर्शकः, आक्षपाटिकः.

MAGNANIMITY, *s.* माहात्म्यं, महात्मता -त्वं, माहात्मिकता, मनोमहत्त्वं, मतिमहत्त्वं, मनोमहिमा *m.* (न्), औदार्य्यं, उदारता, चित्तोदारता, उदारचित्तता, महेच्छा, महानुभावः, महाशयत्वं, मनःप्रौढता, महापुरुषत्वं, शौर्य्यं, वीरत्वं, प्रभावः, महिमा *m.*

MAGNANIMOUS, *a.* महात्मा -त्मा -त्म (न्), महामनाः -नाः -नः (स्), महामनस्कः -स्का -स्कं, माहात्मिकः -की -कं, महामतिः -तिः -ति, उदारचेताः -ताः -तः (स्), उदारमतिः -तिः -ति, उदारः -रा -रं, महानुभावः -वा -वं, महाशयः -या -यं, महेच्छः -च्छा -च्छं, उन्नतमनाः &c., शूरः -रा -रं.—(Proceeding from magnanimity) माहात्म्यपूर्ब्बः -र्ब्बा -र्ब्बं, औदार्य्यपुरःसरः -रा -रं, माहात्म्ययोग्यः -ग्या -ग्यं.

MAGNANIMOUSLY, *adv.* औदार्य्येण, उदारवत्, माहात्म्येन, समाहात्म्यं, मनोमहत्त्वात्, मनोमहिम्ना, महानुभावात्, उदारचित्तत्वात्, महेच्छया, शूरवत्, महाशयवत्, उदारचेतसा.

MAGNATE, *s.* उत्कृष्टपदस्थः, उच्चपदस्थः, महाकुलीनः, राजन्यः.

MAGNESIA, *s.* अम्लपित्तनाशकं शुक्लचूर्णं or चूर्णाकारं मृत्तिकाभस्म *n.* (न्).

MAGNET, *s.* लोहचुम्बकः, लोहकान्तः -न्तं, अयस्कान्तः, चुम्बकः, चुम्बकप्रस्तरः, चुम्बकमणिः *m.*, अयस्कान्तमणिः *m.*, अयस्कान्तमणिशलाका, आकर्षः -र्षकः, आकर्षकमणिः *m.*, वैक्रान्तं, लौहाकर्षकप्रस्तरः.

MAGNETIC, MAGNETICAL, *a.* आकर्षिकः -का -कं, आकर्षकः &c., आकर्षणगुणः -णा -णं, आकर्षणधर्म्मकः -का -कं, लोहचुम्बनशीलः -ला -लं, लोहचुम्बनधर्म्मकः -का -कं, लोहचुम्बकसम्बन्धी -न्धिनी -न्धि (न्), लोहचुम्बकविषयः -या -यं; 'magnetic attraction,' आकर्षः.

MAGNETICALLY, *adv.* आकर्षणशक्तिद्वारेण, आकर्षणपूर्ब्बं, लोहचुम्बनशक्त्या.

MAGNETISM, *s.* आकर्षणशक्तिः *f.*, लोहचुम्बनशक्तिः *f.*, लोहचुम्बनधर्म्मः, लोहचुम्बकगुणः, अयस्कान्तगुणः, अयस्कान्तमणिधर्म्मः.

To MAGNETIZE, *v. a.* आकर्षणशक्तिं or लोहचुम्बनशक्तिं दा (c. 3. ददाति, दातुं).

MAGNIFIC, MAGNIFICAL, *a.* महाप्रतापः -पा -पं. *See* MAGNIFICENT.

MAGNIFICENCE, *s.* प्रतापः, महाप्रतापः, महान् प्रतापः, अतिप्रतापः, सुप्रतापः, तेजस् *n.*, अतितेजस् *n.*, महातेजस् *n.*, विभूतिः *f.*, वैभवं, विभवः, ऐश्वर्य्यं, अतिशोभा, अतिकान्तिः *f.*, महादीप्तिः *f.*, महती शोभा, बृहद्दीप्तिः *f.*, अतिप्रभा, ओजस्विता, उज्ज्वलता, श्रीः *f.*, महिमा *m.* (न्), महत्त्वं.

MAGNIFICENT, *a.* महाप्रतापः -पा -पं, प्रतापवान् -वती -वत् (त्), महातेजाः -जाः -जः (स्), प्रतापी -पिनी -पि (न्), अतिप्रतापी &c., तेजस्वी -स्विनी &c., अतितैजसः -सी -सं, शोभनः -ना -नं, अतिशोभनः -ना -नं, सुप्रभः -भा -भं, अतिकान्तिमान् -मती &c., ओजस्वी -स्विनी &c., उज्ज्वलः -ला -लं, महाप्रभः -भा -भं, देदीप्यमानः -ना -नं, विभूतिमान् -मती &c.

MAGNIFICENTLY, *adv.* महाप्रतापेन, सुप्रतापेन, अतिप्रतापेन, अतितेजसा, महातेजसा, सप्रतापं, विभूत्या, अतिशोभापूर्ब्बं, ऐश्वर्य्येण.

MAGNIFIED, *p. p.* अधिकीकृतः -ता -तं, विपुलीकृतः -ता -तं, वर्धितः -ता -तं, उपचितः -ता -तं, विशालीकृतः -ता -तं, करालीकृतः -ता -तं, करालितः -ता -तं, अत्युक्तिपूर्ब्बं वर्णितः -ता -तं, बहुलीकृतः -ता -तं, कीर्त्तितः -ता -तं.

MAGNIFIER, *s.* वर्धकः, वृद्धिकर्त्ता *m.* (र्त्तृ), वर्धनकृत् *m.*, आधिक्यकृत्.—(Optical instrument) विपुलदर्शककाचः.

To MAGNIFY, *v. a.* (Make great or greater) अधिकीकृ, विपुलीकृ, विशालीकृ, वृध् (c. 10. वर्धयति -यितुं), महत्तरं -रां कृ, विपुलतरं -रां कृ, आधिक्यं कृ.—(Amplify) अत्युक्त्या or अतिशयोक्त्या वृध् or विस्तृ (c. 10. -स्तारयति -यितुं), वाग्विस्तारेण वृध् or अधिकीकृ, अतिशयोक्तिं कृ, अत्युक्तिं कृ.—(Extol) अतिशयेन कृत् (c. 10. कीर्त्तयति -यितुं) or वर्ण् (c. 10. वर्णयति -यितुं), अतिवर्णनं कृ.

MAGNIFYING, *part.* or *a.* वर्धी -र्धिनी -र्धि (न्), वर्धकः -का -कं, अधिककारी -रिणी &c., विपुलकारी &c., विपुलदर्शकः -का -कं.—(Glass) विपुलदर्शककाचखण्डः -ण्डं.

MAGNILOQUENCE, *s.* अत्युक्तिः *f.*, अतिशयोक्तिः *f.*, अतिभाषणं, प्रगल्भभाषणं, प्रौढभाषणं, चित्रोक्तिः *f.*, गर्व्वितवाक्यं, गर्व्वोक्तिः *f.*, शब्दमात्रं.

MAGNILOQUENT, *a.* प्रौढभाषी -षिणी -षि (न्), प्रगल्भभाषी &c., चित्रभाषी &c., गर्व्वितवाक्यकारी -रिणी &c.

MAGNITUDE, *s.* (Size, extent) परिमाणं, परिमितिः *f.*, प्रमाणं, मानं, आकारपरिमाणं, आकृतिपरिमाणं, रूपपरिमाणं, आकारमानं, महत्त्वपरिमाणं, मात्रं; 'of the magnitude of an egg,' अण्डपरिमाणः -णा -णं; 'of the same magnitude,' सममात्रः -त्री -त्रं, समपरिमाणः -णा -णं.—(Bulk) भारमानं, भारपरिमाणं.—(Greatness) महत्त्वं, बृहत्त्वं, स्थूलता, स्थौल्यं, विपुलता, वैपुल्यं, विशालता, पृथुता -त्वं, प्रथिमा *m.* (न्), महिमा *m.* (न्), उरुता -त्वं, विकटता, वैकट्यं, विस्तीर्णता.

MAGPIE, *s.* चाषः, किकिः *m.*, किकिदिविः *m.*, किकीदिवः, किकीदीविः *m.*

MAHOGANY, *s.* नन्दिकः, तुन्नः, तुणिः *m.*

MAHOMMEDAN, *a.* यावनः -नी -नं, यवनदेशीयः -या -यं. *See* MOHAMMEDAN.

MAHRATTA, *s.* (Country) महाराष्ट्रं.—(Dialect) महाराष्ट्री.

MAID, MAIDEN, *s.* कन्या, कुमारी, तरुणी, युवती, बालिका, बाला, कन्यिका, कन्यका, कुमारिका, गौरी, गौरिका, धीदा, रोहिणी, नग्निका, कनी. Some of these words refer to particular ages; as, 'a maid of eight,' गौरी -रिका; 'of nine,' कन्या, रोहिणी; 'of ten,' लग्निका, नग्निका; 'of from ten to twelve,' कुमारी -रिका; 'of from sixteen to thirty,' तरुणी; 'of the age of puberty,' मध्या, मध्यमा, मुग्धा.—(Unmarried woman, virgin) अनूढा, अविवाहिता, अपरिणीता, निवरा, अपरा, अदत्ता, अप्रत्ता, अक्षता, अक्षतयोनिः *f.*, अविद्धयोनिः *f.*, पुरुषास्पृष्टा.—(Female servant) दासी -सिका, चेटी, परिचारिका, सहचारिणी, कर्म्मकरी, सैरन्ध्री, सैरिन्ध्री.

MAIDEN, *a.* (Pertaining to a maid) कौमारः -री -रं, कुमारिकासम्बन्धी -न्धिनी -न्धि (न्), कन्यासम्बन्धी &c., कुमारिकाविषयः -या -यं, कन्याविषयः -या -यं.—(Consisting of maids) कन्यामयः -यी -यं, कुमा-

रीमयः -यी -यं.—(Fresh, unused) नवः -वा -वं, अभिनवः -वा -वं, अपूर्व्वः -र्व्वा -र्व्वं, अकृतोपभोगः -गा -गं, अज्ञातोपभोगः -गा -गं, अक्षतः -ता -तं, अखण्डः -ण्डा -ण्डं.

MAIDENHEAD, MAIDENHOOD, *s.* कौमारं, कौमार्य्यं, कुमारीत्वं, कन्यात्वं, तरुणीत्वं, तारुण्यं, कुमारीभावः, कुमारीदशा, कुमारिकाभावः.—(Freshness) नवत्वं -ता, अक्षतत्वं, अखण्डता.

MAIDENLIKE, MAIDENLY, *a.* कुमारीयोग्यः -ग्या -ग्यं, कुमारीसदृशः -शी -शं, कन्यायोग्यः -ग्या -ग्यं, कुमारिकोचितः -ता -तं, कन्योचितः -ता -तं, कुमारिकानुरूपः -पा -पं, कुमारीतुल्यः -ल्या -ल्यं.

MAID-SERVANT, *s.* दासी -सिका, चेटी, प्रेष्या, कर्म्मकरी, प्रेष्यवधूः *f.*, प्रतीहारी, परिचारिका, सेवकी.

MAIL, *s.* (Armour) कवचः -चं, सन्नाहः, वर्म्म *n.* (न्), लोहवर्म्म *n.*, अयोवर्म्म *n.*, कञ्चुकः, तनुत्रं, तनुत्राणं, सज्जा, युद्धसज्जा, दंशनं, दंसनं, उरश्छदः, कङ्कटकः, कङ्कटः, जागरः, जगरः, कायवलनं, उरस्त्राणं, वक्षस्त्राणं, आयसी, वाणवारः, वारवाणः -णं.—(Post) पत्रवाहनं, लेख्यवाहनं, राजनियोगिभृतः पत्रकोषः, राजधावकभृतो लेख्यकोषः.

MAILED, *p. p.* वर्म्मितः -ता -तं, संवर्म्मितः -ता -तं, सन्नद्धः -द्धा -द्धं, दंशितः -ता -तं, परिदंशितः -ता -तं, कवची -चिनी -चि (न्), सकवचः -चा -चं, कृतसन्नाहः -हा -हं, सज्जः -ज्जा -ज्जं, सज्जितः -ता -तं, सज्जीकृतः -ता -तं, कञ्चुकी -किनी &c., व्यूढकङ्कटः -टा -टं, ऊढकङ्कटः -टा -टं.

To MAIM, *v. a.* विकल (nom. विकलयति -यितुं), विकलीकृ, विकलाङ्गीकृ, व्यङ्गीकृ, न्यूनाङ्गीकृ, हीनाङ्गीकृ, अङ्गं छिद् (c. 7. छिनत्ति, छेत्तुं) or लू (c. 9. लुनाति, लवितुं) or व्रश्च् (c. 6. वृश्चति, व्रश्चितुं) or खण्ड् (c. 10. खण्डयति -यितुं).

MAIM, *s.* अङ्गवैकल्यं, वैकल्यं, विकलीकरणं, व्यङ्गीकरणं, अङ्गच्छेदः.

MAIMED, *p. p.* विकलाङ्गः -ङ्गा -ङ्गं, विकलीकृतः -ता -तं, विकलः -ला -लं, छिन्नाङ्गः &c., हीनाङ्गः &c., लूनाङ्गः &c., खण्डिताङ्गः &c., व्यङ्गः &c., अपाङ्गः &c., अङ्गविकलः -ला -लं, अङ्गहीनः -ना -नं, विहस्तीकृतः -ता -तं, क्षतविक्षतः -ता -तं.

MAIMING, *s.* विकलीकरणं, व्यङ्गीकरणं, अङ्गच्छेदनं, अङ्गखण्डनं.

MAIN, *a.* (Principal) मुख्यः -ख्या -ख्यं, प्रमुखः -खा -खं, प्रधानः -ना -नं, परमः -मा -मं, परः -रा -रं, अग्रः -ग्रा -ग्रं, अग्र्यः -ग्र्या -ग्र्यं, श्रेष्ठः -ष्ठा -ष्ठं, उत्तमः -मा -मं, प्रवरः -रा -रं, विशिष्टः -ष्टा -ष्टं, मूलिकः -की -कं.—(Most important) गुरुतमः -मा -मं, गरिष्ठः -ष्ठा -ष्ठं, परमः -मा -मं; 'main evil,' प्रधानदूषणं, गुरुदूषणं; 'main matter,' गुरुकार्य्यं, गुरुकं; 'main entrance,' सिंहद्वारं; 'main stock,' मूलद्रव्यं.

MAIN, *s.* (The bulk, gross) प्रधानभागः, प्रधानांशः, अधिकभागः, मुख्यभागः, मुख्यांशः, बहुतरभागः, स्थूलांशः, बाहुल्यं, साकल्यं, समुदायः, सामग्र्यं; 'in the main,' बाहुल्येन, बहुशस्, साकल्येन, सामान्यतस्, भूयिष्ठं.—(Force, strength) बलं, शक्तिः *f.*; 'with might and main,' सर्व्वबलेन, सकलबलेन, प्रसभं, प्रसह्य.—(The ocean) समुद्रः, महासागरः, महोदधिः *m.*, महार्णवः.—(Continent) महाद्वीपः, प्रधानद्वीपः.—(At cock-fighting) समाह्वयः, साह्वयः, प्राणिद्यूतं.

MAIN-LAND, *s.* महाद्वीपः, मुख्यभूमिः *f.*, मध्यभूमिः, मूलभूमिः, मध्यस्थलं, स्थलं -ली, भूखण्डः, पृथिवीखण्डः, द्वीपः, प्रधानद्वीपः, अविच्छिन्नभूमिः.

MAINLY, *adv.* मुख्यशस्, मुख्यतस्, प्रधानतस्, प्राधान्यतस्, प्राधान्येन, विशेषतस्, विशेषेण, बाहुल्येन, बहुशस्, भूयिष्ठं, बहुतरं, सामान्यतस्, साकल्येन, परमं.

MAIN-MAST, *s.* महाकूपकः, महागुणवृक्षकः, प्रधानकूपकः, मध्यकूपकः.

MAINPRIZE, *s.* दर्शनप्रातिभाव्यपूर्व्वकम् आसिद्धजनमोक्षणं.

MAINSAIL, *s.* महाकूपकसम्बन्धि वातवसनं, महाकूपकवसनं.

To MAINTAIN, *v. a.* (Hold) धृ (c. 1. धरति, धर्त्तुं, c. 10. धारयति -यितुं), सन्धृ.—(Support) भृ (c. 1. भरति, c. 3. बिभर्त्ति, भर्त्तुं), सम्भृ, आलम्ब् (c. 1. -लम्बते, c. 10. -लम्बयति -यितुं), अवलम्ब्, समवलम्ब्, उत्तम्भ् (c. 10. -तम्भयति -यितुं, rt. स्तम्भ्), संस्तम्भ्, विष्टम्भ्, सङ्ग्रह् (c. 9. -गृह्णाति -ग्रहीतुं), वृध् (c. 10. वर्धयति -यितुं), संवृध्, भरणं कृ.—(Keep) पाल् (c. 10. पालयति -यितुं), अनुपाल्, रक्ष् (c. 1. रक्षति -क्षितुं), संरक्ष्, पालनं कृ, रक्षणं कृ, संरक्षणं कृ.—(Support with food) भृ, सम्भृ, भरणं कृ, भृतिं दा, पुष् (c. 10. पोषयति -यितुं), पोषणं कृ, अन्नवस्त्रं दा, अन्नाच्छादनं दा, योगक्षेमं कृ; 'maintain a family,' कुलालम्बनं कृ; 'maintain one's self,' निर्व्वाहं कृ, उदरनिर्व्वाहं कृ.—(Vindicate, make good) प्रतिपद् (c. 10. -पादयति -यितुं), प्रतिपादनं कृ, व्यवस्था in caus. (-स्थापयति -यितुं), व्यवस्थापनं कृ, अनुपाल्, अनुपालनं कृ, प्रतिपालनं कृ, समर्थनं कृ, पक्षपातं कृ.—(Affirm) निश्चयेन वद् (c. 1. वदति -दितुं), दार्ढ्येन वद्.

MAINTAINABLE, *a.* भरणीयः -या -यं, भर्त्तव्यः -व्या -व्यं, भार्य्यः -र्य्या -र्य्यं, सम्भार्य्यः -र्य्या -र्य्यं, भरण्यः -ण्या -ण्यं, धर्त्तव्यः -व्या -व्यं, धार्य्यः -र्य्या -र्य्यं, धरणीयः -या -यं, पालनीयः -या -यं, रक्षणीयः -या -यं, पोषणीयः -या -यं, वर्धनीयः -या -यं, पोष्यः -ष्या -ष्यं.

MAINTAINED, *p. p.* भृतः -ता -तं, सम्भृतः -ता -तं, धृतः -ता -तं, धारितः -ता -तं, आलम्बितः -ता -तं, पालितः -ता -तं, पोषितः -ता -तं, पुष्टः -ष्टा -ष्टं, रक्षितः -ता -तं, वर्धितः -ता -तं, भर्त्रिमः -मा -मं; 'being maintained,' धार्य्यमाणः -णा -णं.

MAINTAINER, *s.* भर्त्ता *m.* (र्त्तृ), भरः, भरणकृत् *m.*, धर्त्ता *m.* (र्त्तृ), धरः, पालकः, पोषकः, पोष्टा *m.* (ष्टृ), भृतिदाता *m.* (तृ), प्रतिपालकः, रक्षिता *m.* (तृ), आलम्बी *m.* (न्); 'of a family,' कुलालम्बी *m.*

MAINTENANCE, *s.* (Support) भृतिः *f.*, भरणं, सम्भृतिः *f.*, धारणं, भृतिः *f.*, भृत्या, पालनं, पोषणं, परिपालनं, प्रतिपालनं, रक्षणं, संरक्षणं, वर्धनं, संवर्धनं.—(Means of support, subsistence) जीवनोपायः, वृत्त्युपायः, उपजीवनं, जीविका, उपजीविका, वृत्तिः *f.*, वर्त्तनं, निर्व्वाहः, उदरनिर्व्वाहः, प्राणधारणं, प्राणयात्रा, शरीरधारणं, शरीरयात्रा, योगक्षेमः.—(Food and clothing) अन्नवस्त्रं, अन्नाच्छादनं, ग्रासाच्छादनं, अन्नवस्त्रं, कशिपूः *m.* du.—(Defence, vindication) रक्षणं, प्रतिपादनं, व्यवस्थापनं, स्थापनं -ना.

MAIN TOP, *s.* महाकूपकाग्रं, प्रधानकूपकाग्रं, मध्यकूपकाग्रं.

MAIZE, *s.* शस्यं, स्तम्बकरिः *m.*, शस्यविशेषः.

MAJESTIC, MAJESTICAL, *a.* राजश्रीयुक्तः -क्ता -क्तं, राजश्रीमान् -मती -मत् (त्), राजयोग्यः -ग्या -ग्यं, राजसदृशः -शी -शं, राजतुल्यः -ल्या -ल्यं, राजतेजोमयः -यी -यं, राजतेजोरूपः -पा -पं, राजतेजोवान् -वती &c., प्रतापवान् -वती &c., राजप्रतापी -पिनी &c., राजप्रतापयुक्तः &c., गौरवयुक्तः &c., ऐश्वरः -री -रं, ऐश्वर्य्यवान् -वती &c., राजैश्वर्य्यवान् &c., महामहिमा -मा -म (न्), ऐशिकः -की -कं, सम्राजीयः -या -यं, राजकीयः -या -यं, विभूतिमान् &c., प्रभाववान् &c., प्रभावी -विणी &c., राजप्रभावी &c., प्रभविष्णुः -ष्णुः -ष्णु, माहात्मिकः -की -कं.

MAJESTICALLY, *adv.* राजतेजसा, राजप्रतापेन, सप्रतापं, सप्रभावं, राजैश्वर्य्येण, महामहिम्ना, विभूत्या, राजप्रभावेण, राजयोग्यं, राजसदृशं, राजवत्, राजवैभवेन, सगौरवं.

MAJESTY, *s.* राजश्रीः *f.*, राजतेजस् *n.*, राजप्रतापः, तेजस् *n.*, प्रतापः, प्रभावः, राजप्रभावः, ऐश्वर्य्यं, राजैश्वर्य्यं, महिमा *m.* (न्), राजमहिमा, महामहिमा, राजसायुज्यं, विभूतिः *f.*, राजविभूतिः *f.*, वैभवं, विभवः, राजविभवः, राजप्रभवः, भूतिः *f.*, माहात्म्यं, राजत्वं, राज्यं, प्रभुता, राजगौरवं; 'your majesty,' देव voc. c., श्रीमद्देव voc. c., आयुष्मन् voc. c., राजन् voc. c.; 'he speaks ill of your majesty,'

देवपादान् अधिक्षिपति; 'his majesty,' भर्त्ता m. (र्त्तृ), प्रभुः m., भगवान् m. (त्), स्वामी m. (न्), महाराजः, भवान् m. (त्), अत्रभवान् m., तत्रभवान् m., प्रभविष्णुः m.; 'her majesty,' अत्रभवती, तत्रभवती, देवी; 'requisites of majesty,' प्रकृतिः f.

MAJOR, a. (Greater in number) अधिकः -का -कं, अधिकतरः -रा -रं, अधिकसंख्यः -ख्या -ख्यं, अधिकपरिमाणः -णा -णं, भूयान् -यसी -यः (स्), भूयिष्ठः -ष्ठा -ष्ठं, बहुतरः -रा -रं.—(Greater in dignity) मुख्यः -ख्या -ख्यं, प्रधानः -ना -नं, प्रमुखः -खा -खं, श्रेयान् -यसी &c., श्रेष्ठः -ष्ठा -ष्ठं, गुरुः -र्व्वी -रु, गरीयान् -यसी &c.—(Major premiss) गुर्व्ववयवः, पूर्व्वपक्षः.

MAJOR, s. (Person of full age) प्राप्तव्यवहारः, व्यवहारप्राप्तः, जातव्यवहारः, लब्धव्यवहारः, व्यवहारज्ञः, व्यवहारयोग्यः, व्यवहारक्षमः, व्यवहारार्हः, व्यवहाराधिकारी m. (न्), त्यक्तशैशवः.—(Military officer) सैन्यदलाध्यक्षः, गुल्मपतिः m., सैन्याधिपतिः m.

MAJOR-DOMO, s. गृहाधिकृतः, गृहकार्य्याधीशः, गृहकर्म्माध्यक्षः, कार्य्याधीशः.

MAJORITY, s. (Greater number) अङ्काधिक्यं, अङ्काधिकत्वं, अङ्काधिकसंख्या, अङ्काधिकपक्षः, अधिकपक्षः, अधिकसंख्या, अधिकभागः, बहुतरभागः, बहुतरपक्षः, परार्द्धं, भूयिष्ठं.—(State of being greater) आधिक्यं, अधिकत्वं -ता.—(Full age) व्यवहारः, व्यवहारप्राप्तिः f., व्यवहारक्षमता, व्यवहारज्ञत्वं, व्यवहार्य्यवयस् n., व्यवहार्य्यता, व्यवहार्य्यावस्था, प्राप्तव्यवहारत्वं, जातव्यवहारत्वं, व्यवहारयोग्यता, शैशवत्यागः; 'one who has attained his majority,' प्राप्तव्यवहारः. *See* MAJOR.

To MAKE, v. a. (Form, create) कृ (c. 8. करोति, कुरुते, कर्त्तुं), सङ्कृ, अभिकृ, निर्म्मा (c. 2. -माति, c. 3. -मिमीते, c. 4. -मायते -मातुं), विनिर्म्मा, कॢप् (c. 10. कल्पयति -यितुं), संकॢप्, विधा (c. 3. -दधाति -धातुं), रच् (c. 10. रचयति -यितुं), विरच्, घट् (c. 10. घटयति -यितुं), उत्पद् (c. 10. -पादयति -यितुं), जन् (c. 10. जनयति -यितुं), सञ्जन्.—(Do, perform) कृ, सङ्कृ, विधा, अनुष्ठा (c. 1. -तिष्ठति -ष्ठातुं), आचर् (c. 1. -चरति -रितुं), समाचर्.—(Constitute, compose) निर्म्मा, कॢप्, घट्, संस्था in caus. (-स्थापयति -यितुं) or expressed by निर्म्मितः -ता -तं, मयः -यी -यं, घटितः -ता -तं, रूपः -पा -पं, आत्मकः -का -कं, सम्भृतः -ता -तं in comp. *See* CONSTITUTED, consisting of, made of.—(Effect) साध् (c. 10. साधयति -यितुं), उत्पद् (c. 10. -पादयति -यितुं), निष्पद्, सम्पद्, जन् (c. 10. जनयति -यितुं), कल् (c. 10. कलयति -यितुं), निर्म्मा, कृ.—(Produce) उत्पद्, जन्, सञ्जन्.—(Cause to be) कृ, or expressed by the caus. form; as, 'good fortune makes a man proud,' श्रीः पुरुषं दर्पयति.—(Compel, force) expressed by the causal form usually in conjunction with बलात् or बलेन. *See To* FORCE. 'He is made to perform that action' कार्य्यते तत् कर्म्म.—(Gain) प्राप् (c. 5. -आप्नोति -आप्तुं), लभ् (c. 1. लभते, लब्धुं), उत्पद्.—(Adjust, arrange) रच्, विरच्, विन्यस् (c. 4. -अस्यति -असितुं), परिकॢप्; 'to make a bed,' शय्यां विन्यस्.—(Make amends) निष्कृतिं दा, निस्तारं कृ, पारितोषिकं दा, प्रतिफलं दा, क्षतिपूरणं कृ.—(Make account of) मन् (c. 10. मानयति -यितुं), सम्मन्, अपेक्ष् (c. 1. -ईक्षते -क्षितुं), प्रतीक्ष्.—(Make away) व्यापद् (c. 10. -पादयति -यितुं), हन् (c. 2. हन्ति -न्तुं, c. 10. घातयति -यितुं), वधं कृ.—(Make good, fulfil) निष्पद्, सम्पद्, सम्पॄ (c. 10. -पूरयति -यितुं), सिद्धीकृ, साध्.—(Make good a loss) क्षतिपूरणं कृ, प्रत्युपकृ, अपाकृ, निष्कृ, प्रतिकृ, निष्कृतिं दा, प्रतिदा.—(Make known) ज्ञा in caus. (ज्ञापयति -यितुं), निविद् (c. 10. -वेदयति -यितुं), सूच् (c. 10. सूचयति -यितुं). *See* KNOWN. (Make light of) लघूकृ, तुच्छीकृ.—(Make love) विवाहार्थं प्रेम कृ.—(Make merry) उत्सवं कृ.—(Make much of) बहु मन्.—(Make over) परस्मै or परस्मिन् सम् in caus. (-अर्पयति -यितुं), द्रव्याधिकारित्वं पराधीनं कृ or परवशं कृ or परस्वत्वे प्रतिपद् (c. 10. -पादयति -यितुं), परसमर्पणं कृ.—(Make out) निरूप् (c. 10. -रूपयति -यितुं), उपलभ्, अवगम् (c. 1. -गच्छति -गन्तुं), ग्रह् (c. 9. गृह्णाति, ग्रहीतुं), विज्ञा (c. 9. -जानाति -ज्ञातुं), ज्ञा.—(Make out, prove) प्रमाणीकृ, साध्, सूच्.—(Make up, collect) समानी (c. 1. -नयति -नेतुं), सम्भृ (c. 1. -भरति -भर्त्तुं), समादा, एकीकृ, एकत्रीकृ, समूहीकृ.—(Make up, reconcile) सन्धा, समाधा, विवादं शम् (c. 10. शमयति -यितुं), विवादसान्त्वनं कृ.—(Make up, settle) साध्, सिद्धीकृ, निर्णी.—(Make up one's mind) निश्चयं कृ, निर्णयं कृ, दृढसङ्कल्पं कृ.—(Make water) मूत्रं कृ, मूत्रोत्सर्गं कृ, मूत्रत्यागं कृ.

To MAKE, v. n. (Move towards) अभिया (c. 2. -याति -तुं), प्रतिया, आया, प्रत्याया, उपया; प्रतिगम् (c. 1. -गच्छति -गन्तुं), अभिगम्, अभ्यागम्, उपसृप् (c. 1. -सर्पति -सर्प्तुं), आक्रम् (c. 1. -क्रामति -क्रमितुं) उपक्रम्, अभिक्रम्, अभिसृ (c. 1. -सरति -सर्त्तुं), प्रतिसृ.—(Contribute, conduce) आवह् (c. 1. -वहति -वोढुं), आनी (c. 1. -नयति -नेतुं), सम्पद् (c. 10. -पादयति -यितुं); 'to make for one's advantage,' आत्महिताय भू, आत्मविवृद्धये भू.—(Make as if) प्रतिभा (c. 2. -भाति -तुं), आभा.—(Make off) पलाय् (c. 1. पलायते -यितुं, rt. इ), विपलाय्, अपधाव् (c. 1. -धावति -वितुं), अपक्रम्, अपसृप्, अपया, अपसृ, अपगम्, चल् (c. 1. चलति -लितुं), अपचल्.—(Make up, be reconciled) सन्धा (c. 3. -धत्ते -धातुं), शान्तविवादः -दा -दं भू.

MAKE, s. आकारः, आकृतिः f., संस्कारः, रूपं, संस्थानं, विग्रहः, मूर्त्तिः f., वपुस् n., निर्म्माणं, निर्म्मितिः f., व्यूहनं.

MAKE-BATE, s. कलहकारी m. (न्), द्वन्द्वकारी m. (न्), कलिकारकः, भेदकरः.

MAKE-PEACE, s. सन्धाता m. (तृ), सन्धानकर्त्ता m. (र्त्तृ), सन्धिकृत् m.

MAKER, s. कर्त्ता m. (र्त्तृ), कारः -रकः, कारी m. (न्), कृत् m., कारुः m., निर्म्माता m. (तृ), निर्म्माणकृत् m., निर्म्माणकर्त्ता, विधाता m. (तृ), विधायी m. (न्), कल्पकः, परिकल्पकः, रचकः, घटकः, उत्पादकः.—(Creator) स्रष्टा m. (ष्टृ), विधाता m., धाता m. सृज् m. (ज्), सृष्टिकर्त्ता m., जनकः, जनिता m. (तृ), जनयिता m.—(Of the world) जगत्कर्त्ता m., जगत्स्रष्टा m. (ष्टृ), विश्वसृक् m., विश्वविधायी m., विश्वकृत् m., लोककृत् m.

MAKING, s. करणं, निर्म्माणं, निर्म्मितिः f., कल्पनं -ना, विधानं, रचनं -ना, घटनं -ना, जननं, उत्पादनं, सृष्टिः f., सर्ज्जनं.

MAL, as a prefix is expressed by अ, दुर्, वि, कु, अप, कत्, असत्.

MALABAR, s. (The country) मलयः, मलयदेशः, केरलः.

MAL-ADMINISTRATION, s. असम्यक्पालनं, दुर्णीतिः f., दुर्णयः, दुःशासनं, कुनीतिः f., अनीतिः f., दुर्णीतं, दुर्निर्वाहः.

MALADY, s. रोगः, व्याधिः m., आमयः, विकारः, विकृतिः f., पीडा, दुःखं, रुक् f., (ज्), रुजा, गदः, तापः, उपतापः, अस्वास्थ्यं, अस्वस्थता, बाधा, क्लेशः, आर्त्तिः f., कष्टं.

MALAPERT, a. अविनीतः -ता -तं, दुर्विनीतः -ता -तं, अविनयः -या -यं, धृष्टः -ष्टा -ष्टं, धर्षितः -ता -तं, प्रगल्भः -ल्भा -ल्भं, प्रतिभानवान् -वती -वत् (त्).

MALAPERTLY, adv. दुर्विनीतवत्, अविनयेन, दुर्विनयात्, धृष्टवत्, प्रगल्भं.

MALAPERTNESS, s. अविनयः, दुर्विनयः, अविनीतता, दुर्विनीतता, धृष्टता, प्रगल्भता, प्रागल्भ्यं, प्रतिभा -भानं, दुर्वृत्तता.

MALAPROPOS, adv. अस्थाने, अकाले, अयोग्यं, असमयेन, अनवसरेण, अप्रसक्तवत्, अप्रसङ्गेन, अप्रस्तुतं, अप्रासङ्गिकः -की -कं.

MALARIA, s. पूतिवातः, दुर्वायुः m., दुर्वातः, रोगजनकः कुवायुः m., पूतिबाष्पः, मारकबाष्पः, दूषकबाष्पः.

MALCONTENT, MALCONTENTED, *a.* (Discontented) असन्तुष्टः -ष्टा -ष्टं, अतुष्टः -ष्टा -ष्टं.—(With the government) राज्यमार्गासन्तुष्टः -ष्टा -ष्टं, राज्यनीतिवितुष्टः -ष्टा -ष्टं, राज्यवितुष्टः &c.

MALE, *s.* पुमान् *m.* (पुंस् or पुमस्), पुरुषः, पूरुषः, नरः, ना *m.* (नृ), मानुषः, मनुष्यः, मानवः, मनुजः, पुंव्यक्तिः *m.*, पुम्प्राणी *m.*, पञ्चजनः; 'duties of the male,' पुन्धर्म्मः, नृधर्म्मः; 'male and female,' स्त्रीपुरुषौ *m.* du., मिथुनं, युग्मं, द्वन्द्वं.—(In botany) पुरुषः.— —(Screw) नरः.

MALE, *a.* पुं in comp., पुरुष in comp., पौरुषेयः -यी -यं, पुरुषजातीयः -या -यं, पुंजातीयः -या -यं, पुरुषजातिसम्बन्धी -न्धिनी -न्धि (न्), नर in comp.; 'male species,' पुंजातिः *f.*, पुरुषजातिः *f.*; 'male offspring,' पुमपत्यं, पुंसन्तानं, पुमन्वयः, अन्वयः; 'the male organ,' पुंलिङ्गं, पुंश्चिह्नं; 'a male tiger,' पुंव्याघ्रः; 'male attire,' पुरुषवेशः, नरवेशः, नृवेशः.

MALEDICTED, *a.* शप्तः -प्ता -प्तं, अभिशप्तः -प्ता -प्तं, आक्रुष्टः -ष्टा -ष्टं.

MALEDICTION, *s.* शापः, अभिशापः, शपः -पनं, शपथः, परिशापः, आक्रोशः -शनं, अवक्रोशः, उपक्रोशः, भर्त्सनं, अभिषङ्गः, दुर्वाक्यं, अमङ्गलवचनं, अकल्याणवचनं, अमङ्गलेच्छा, मौखर्य्यं.

MALEDICTORY, *a.* अभिशापकः -का -कं, आक्रोशकः -की -कं, रुशन् -शन्ती -शत् (त्), अनिष्टप्रार्थकः -का -कं, अमङ्गलाशंसकः -का -कं, दुर्वाक्यमयः -यी -यं.

MALEFACTOR, *s.* अपराधी *m.* (न्), पापी *m.* (न्), पातकी *m.* (न्), महापातकी *m.*, कुकर्म्मा *m.* (न्), पापकर्म्मा *m.*, दुष्कृती *m.* (न्), पापकारी *m.* (न्), कुकर्म्मकारी *m.*, दुष्कर्म्मा *m.*, दुष्कृतकर्म्मा *m.*, अन्यायी *m.* (न्), एनस्वी *m.* (न्), दोषी *m.*, कृतापराधः, कृतागाः *m.* (स्), कृष्णकर्म्मा *m.*, असत्कर्म्मा *m.*

MALEVOLENCE, *s.* दुष्टभावः, भावदुष्टता, दुष्टबुद्धिः *f.*, द्रोहबुद्धिः *f.*, दुर्बुद्धिः *f.*, द्वेषबुद्धिः *f.*, द्वेषभावः, दुष्टचित्तत्वं, कुभावः, कुबुद्धिः *f.*, द्रोहचिन्तनं, द्रोहः, असूया, अभ्यसूया, दौरात्म्यं, अहितत्वं, अप्रीतिः *f.*, मात्सर्य्यं, पापदर्शनं, अहितेच्छा, अहितेप्सा, अहितैषा, अपकारेच्छा, अनिष्टेच्छा, पुरोभागिता.

MALEVOLENT, *a.* दुष्टबुद्धिः -द्धिः -द्धि, दुष्टभावः -वा -वं, द्रोहबुद्धिः &c., द्वेषबुद्धिः &c., कुबुद्धिः &c., दुर्बुद्धिः &c., कुभावः -वा -वं, अहितबुद्धिः &c., सासूयः -या -यं, साभ्यसूयः -या -यं, मत्सरः -रा -रं -री -रिणी -रि (न्), दुरात्मा -त्मा -त्म (न्), दुष्टात्मा &c., दुष्टचेताः -ताः -तः (स्), दुष्टमतिः -तिः -ति, पापदर्शी -र्शिनी -र्शि (न्), दोषैकदृक् (श्), द्रोहचिन्तकः -का -कं, अनिष्टचिन्तकः &c., अपकारार्थी -र्थिनी &c., अनिष्टार्थी &c., अहितकामः -मा -मं, अहितेच्छुः -च्छुः -च्छु, अहितैषी -षिणी &c., अहितः -ता -तं, दुष्टशीलः -ला -लं, हिंसाशीलः &c., अपकारशीलः &c., दुःशीलः &c. दुर्हृदयः -या -यं, विषहृदयः -या -यं, पुरोभागी -गिनी &c.

MALEVOLENTLY, *adv.* दुष्टभावेन -वात्, दुष्टबुद्धित्वात्, द्रोहबुद्ध्या, अहितबुद्ध्या, मात्सर्य्येण, मत्सरवत्, सासूयं, साभ्यसूयं, दुष्टचेतसा, अहितेच्छया, दुष्टशीलत्वात्.

MALICE, *s.* दुष्टभावः, द्रोहः, द्रोहबुद्धिः *f.*, द्रोहचिन्ता -न्तनं, द्वेषभावः, द्वेषः, दीर्घद्वेषः, असूया, अभ्यसूया, ईर्ष्या, मात्सर्य्यं, मत्सरता, हिंसाबुद्धिः *f.*, हिंसाशीलता, नृशंस्यं, नृशंसता, दंशः, दौर्जन्यं, दुष्टशीलता, दुःशीलता, अपकारेच्छा, अहितेच्छा, अनिष्टेच्छा, मानसहिंसा, दौरात्म्यं, दुरात्मता, हिंसा, परिहिंसा, खलता; 'malice prepense,' द्रोहचिन्तनं, व्यापादः; 'secret malice,' मानसद्वेषः, मानसद्रोहः; 'bearing malice,' दीर्घद्वेषी -षिणी -षि (न्).

MALICIOUS, *a.* द्रोहबुद्धिः -द्धिः -द्धि, द्रोही -हिणी -हि (न्), दुष्टभावः -वा -वं, मत्सरः -रा -रं, मत्सरी -रिणी &c., नृशंसः -सा -सं, हिंसाशीलः -ला -लं, हिंसात्मकः -का -कं, हिंसालुः -लुः -लु, द्रोहशीलः &c., परिहिंसाशीलः &c., हिंसारुचिः -चिः -चि, द्वेषी -षिणी &c., अतिद्वेषी &c., अतिद्वेषकः -का -कं, अतिद्वेष्टा -ष्ट्री -ष्टृ (ष्टृ), कुबुद्धिः &c., कुमेधाः -धाः -धः (स्), दंशी -शिनी &c., साभ्यसूयः -या -यं, सासूयः &c., दुर्जनः -ना -नं, खलः -ला -लं, पिशुनः -ना -नं, भैरवः -वा -वं. *See* MALEVOLENT. (Proceeding from malice) द्वेषमूलकः -का -कं, मात्सर्य्यहेतुकः -का -कं, द्रोहमूलः -ला -लं, दौर्जन्यहेतुकः -का -कं.

MALICIOUSLY, *adv.* द्रोहबुद्ध्या, द्रोहशीलत्वात्, दुष्टभावेन, अपकारेच्छया, सद्वेषं, द्रोहचिन्तापूर्व्वं, समात्सर्य्यं; 'maliciously intentioned,' द्रोहबुद्धिः -द्धिः -द्धि.

MALICIOUSNESS, *s.* द्रोहबुद्धित्वं, हिंसाशीलता, कौटिल्यं. *See* MALICE.

MALIGN, *a.* अतिदुष्टः -ष्टा -ष्टं, विषपूर्णः -र्णा -र्णं. *See* MALIGNANT.

To **MALIGN,** *v. a.* अपवद् (c. 1. -वदति -दितुं), परिवद्, अभिशंस् (c. 1. -शंसति -सितुं), कलङ्क (nom. कलङ्कयति -यितुं), असूय (nom. असूयति -यितुं), मुखरीकृ.

MALIGNANT, *a.* (Malicious) द्रोहबुद्धिः -द्धिः -द्धि, दुष्टबुद्धिः &c., दुर्बुद्धिः &c., दुष्टमतिः -तिः -ति, दुर्मतिः &c., दुराशयः -या -यं, अहितः -ता -तं, नृशंसः -सा -सं, विषहृदयः -या -यं. *See* MALICIOUS, MALEVOLENT. (Virulent, acrimonious) उग्रः -ग्रा -ग्रं, अत्युग्रः &c., अतिकटुः -टुः -टु, अरुन्तुदः -दा -दं, अतितिग्मः -ग्मा -ग्मं, अतिदुष्टः -ष्टा -ष्टं, बहुविषः -षा -षं, विषालुः -लुः -लु, विषपूर्णः -र्णा -र्णं; 'a malignant ulcer,' दुष्टव्रणः.—(Dangerous to life, difficult to be cured) मारात्मकः -का -कं, प्राणनाशकः -का -कं, शरीरनाशकः -का -कं, साङ्घातिकः -की -कं, दुश्चिकित्स्यः -त्स्या -त्स्यं, दुश्चिकित्सः -त्सा -त्सं, दुःसाध्यः -ध्या -ध्यं, दुःशमनीयः -या -यं, सान्निपातिकः -की -कं, काल in comp.; 'malignant fever,' कालज्वरः, सन्निपातज्वरः, मारकः, मरकः.—(Unpropitious in astrology) अनिष्टः -ष्टा -ष्टं, अनिष्टसूचकः -का -कं, अमङ्गलः -ला -लं, अकल्याणः -णा -णं.

MALIGNANTLY, *adv.* सद्रोहं, अतिदुष्टं, अत्युग्रं, अतितिग्मं, दुष्टभावात्, सविषं.

MALIGNED, *p. p.* मिथ्याभिशस्तः -स्ता -स्तं, मिथ्याभियुक्तः -क्ता -क्तं, कलङ्कितः &c.

MALIGNER, *s.* अपवादी *m.* (न्), अभिशस्तकः, असूयकः, गुणघाती *m.*

MALIGNITY, MALIGNANCY, *s.* (Maliciousness) दुष्टबुद्धित्वं, बुद्धिदुष्टता, भावदुष्टता, दुर्बुद्धित्वं, द्रोहः, द्रोहबुद्धित्वं, अतिदुष्टता, द्वेषः, अतिद्वेषः, दुर्मतिः *f.* -तित्वं, पैशुन्यं. *See* MALICE, MALICIOUSNESS. (Virulence) उग्रता, अत्युग्रता, अतिकटुता, अतितिग्मता, अतिदुष्टता, सविषत्वं, विषपूर्णता, बहुविषत्वं.—(Destructive tendency) मारात्मकत्वं -ता, अतिनाशकता, साङ्घातिकता, दुश्चिकित्स्यता.

MALKIN, *s.* (Mop) मार्जनी, सम्मार्जनी.—(Drab) नीचस्त्री, अशुद्धा.

MALL, *s.* (Heavy hammer) बृहन्मुद्गरः, काष्ठमुद्गरः, घनः.—(Public walk) जनाकीर्णमार्गः, लोकाकीर्णमार्गः, लोकमार्गः, लोकपथः, सर्व्वसामान्यपथः.

MALLEABILITY, *s.* आघातवर्धनीयता, ताडनवर्धनीयता, मुद्गराघातवर्धनीयत्वं, घनवर्धनीयत्वं, घनवर्धिष्णुता, उद्वर्त्तनक्षमता, उद्वर्त्तनीयता.

MALLEABLE, *a.* आघातवर्धनीयः -या -यं, ताडनवर्धनीयः -या -यं, मुद्गराघातवर्धनीयः -या -यं, उद्वर्त्तनक्षमः -मा -मं, घनवर्धनीयः -या -यं, घनवर्धिष्णुः -ष्णुः -ष्णु.

To **MALLEATE,** *v. a.* मुद्गराघातेन उद्वर्त्तनं कृ or उद्वृत् (c. 10. -वर्त्तयति -यितुं).

MALLEATION, *s.* मुद्गराघातवर्धनं, घनवर्धनं, ताडनवर्धनं, उद्वर्त्तनं.

MALLET, *s.* मुद्गरः, काष्ठमुद्गरः, घनः, काष्ठघनः, द्रुघणः.

MAL-PRACTICE, *s.* कुचर्य्या, कुचरितं, कुचेष्टितं, दुश्चरितं, दुश्चेष्टितं, दुराचारः.

MALT, *s.* चिरकालेन जलस्थितं यवबीजं, ईषत्स्फुटत् or ईषत्फुल्लवत् यवबीजं,

यवपानीयवीजं.

MALT-DRINK, MALT-LIQUOR, *s.* यवसुरा, यवरसः, यवजं, यवपानीयं.

MALT-HOUSE, *s.* यवपाचनगृहं, यवसन्धानस्थानं, यववीजगृहं.

To MALTREAT, *v. a.* अपकृ, अपकारं कृ, शत्रुवद् आचर् (c. 1. -चरति -रितुं).

MALTREATED, *p. p.* अपकृतः -ता -तं, कृतापकारः -रा -रं, दुराचरितः -ता -तं.

MALTREATMENT, *s.* अपकारः, अपक्रिया, अपकृतिः *f.*, निकारः, पीडा.

MALVERSATION, *s.* दुराचरितं, अनुचिताचारः, धूर्त्तता, शाठ्यं, खलता, कुसृतिः *f.*

MÁLWA, *s.* (Province) मालवः, दाशेरकः; 'the people of Málwa,' मालवाः *m. pl.*, मालव्याः *m. pl.*, मालवी *f. sing.*

MAM, MAMMA, *s.* मा, माता *f.* (तृ), अम्बा, अम्बिका, अम्बालिका.

MAMMALIA, *s. pl.* सस्तनाः *m. pl.*, स्तनविशिष्टो जन्तुगणः, सस्तनजातिः *f.*

MAMMARY, *a.* स्तनसम्बन्धी -न्धिनी -न्धि (न्), कुचसम्बन्धी &c.

MAMMET, *s.* पुत्तली -लिका, पुत्रिका, पाञ्चाली -लिका, पाञ्चलिका.

MAMMIFER, MAMMIFEROUS, *a.* सस्तनः -ना -नं, स्तनवान् -वती -वत् (त्).

MAMMIFORM, *a.* स्तनाकारः -रा -रं, स्तनाकृतिः -तिः -ति, कुचाकारः -रा -रं.

MAMMILLARY, *a.* स्तनसम्बन्धी -न्धिनी -न्धि (न्), स्तनाकारः -रा -रं.

MAMMON, *s.* धनं, धनेश्वरः, लक्ष्मीः *f.*; 'serving mammon,' धनसेवनं, लक्ष्मीपूजनं, धनसम्पादनं, अर्थसेवा, अर्थपरता.

MAMMOTH, *s.* मेम्मथ्संज्ञकः प्राचीनकालिको हस्ती.

MAN, *s.* (A male of the human race) पुरुषः, नरः, मनुष्यः, मानुषः, मानवः, मनुजः, जनः, पुमान् *m.* (पुंस् or पुमस्), मर्त्यः, पूरुषः, मनुः *m.*, पञ्चजनः, मनुभूः *m.*, पुंव्यक्तिः *m.*, वीरः, मालः, वृषसानः, वृषसानुः *m.*, चर्षणिः *m.*, भूस्पृक् *m.* (श्); 'an eminent man,' पुरुषसिंहः, पुरुषव्याघ्रः, पुरुषर्षभः, पुरुषशार्दूलः, पुरुषपुङ्गवः, पुरुषोत्तमः, पुरुषचन्द्रः, पुरुषपुण्डरीकः, नरसिंहः, नृसिंहः; 'a low man,' पुरुषाधमः; 'a man of truth,' सत्यवीरः.—(Mankind) मनुष्यजातिः *f.*, पुरुषजातिः *f.*, मानुष्यं, पुरुषाः *m. pl.*, मानुषाः *m. pl.*, मानवाः *m. pl.*, नराः *m. pl.*, लोकः, मनुष्यलोकः, मनुभूः *m.*; 'the fear of man,' पुरुषभीतिः *f.*, जनभीतिः *f.*; 'the measure or stature of a man,' पौरुषं, पुरुषपरिमाणं.—(Person) जनः, व्यक्तिः *f.*—(Male servant) सेवकः, प्रेष्यः, किङ्करः, दासजनः.—(Man at chess, &c.) नरः, सारः, शारः, शारिः *m.*, सारिः -री -रिका, खतुपुत्रकः, नयः.—(Adult) प्रौढवयस्कः, मानुष्यप्राप्तः.

To MAN, *v. a.* मनुष्ययुक्तं -क्तां कृ, समनुष्यं -ष्यां कृ, सैन्यान् प्रविश् (c. 10. -वेशयति -यितुं) or निविश्, पुरुषप्रवेशनात् सज्जीकृ.

MANACLE, *s.* हस्तबन्धनं, करबन्धनं, हस्तपाशः, पाणिबन्धः.

To MANACLE, *v. a.* हस्तौ पाशेन बन्ध् (c. 9. बध्नाति, बन्द्धुं), पाणिबन्धनं कृ, करसंयमनं कृ, करयन्त्रणं कृ.

MANACLED, *p. p.* बद्धहस्तः -स्ता -स्तं, संयमितकरः -रा -रं, यन्त्रितकरः &c.

To MANAGE, *v. a.* (Conduct, carry on) प्रणी (c. 1. -णयति -णेतुं), सम्प्रणी, विधा (c. 3. -दधाति -धातुं), वह् (c. 10. वाहयति -यितुं), निर्वह्, आचर् (c. 1. -चरति -रितुं), घट् (c. 1. घटते -टितुं), प्रवृत् (c. 10. -वर्त्तयति -यितुं), वृत्, कृ.—(Direct, control) शास् (c. 2. शास्ति -सितुं), नियन्त्, वशीकृ, अनुशास्, समनुशास्, नियम् (c. 1. -यच्छति -यन्तुं), विनियम्, सन्नियम्, यन्त् (c. 10. यन्त्रयति -यितुं).—(Train) विनी, शिक्ष् (c. 10. शिक्षयति -यितुं), अनुशिक्ष्; 'let it be managed,' विधीयतां.

To MANAGE, *v. n.* निर्वाहं कृ, प्रणयनं कृ, उपायप्रयोगं कृ, प्रयोगं कृ.

MANAGEABLE, *a.* विनेयः -या -यं, प्रणेयः -या -यं, विधेयः -या -यं, सुविधेयः -या -यं, गृह्यकः -का -कं, वश्यः -श्या -श्यं, सुकरः -रा -रं, आयत्तः -त्ता -त्तं, शासनीयः -या -यं, विनीतः -ता -तं.

MANAGED, *p. p.* प्रणीतः -ता -तं, विहितः -ता -तं, निर्वाहितः -ता -तं, निर्वहितः -ता -तं, वाहितः -ता -तं, घटितः -ता -तं, प्रवर्त्तितः -ता -तं, वर्त्तितः -ता -तं, आचरितः -ता -तं, नियतः -ता -तं, विनियतः -ता -तं, प्रयुक्तः -क्ता -क्तं; 'well managed,' सुघटितः -ता -तं, सुप्रयुक्तः -क्ता -क्तं, सुनीतः -ता -तं; 'badly managed,' दुर्घटितः -ता -तं, असम्यक् चेष्टितः -ता -तं.

MANAGEMENT, *s.* (Conduct, carrying on) प्रणयनं, सम्प्रणयनं, नीतिः *f.*, नयः, प्रणीतिः *f.*, नायः, नेतृत्वं, निर्वाहः, निर्वहणं, निर्वाहणं, व्यवहर्त्तृत्वं, आचरणं, सम्पादनं, विधानं, घटनं -ना, प्रयोगः, प्रवर्त्तनं, प्रवृत्तिः *f.*, करणं; 'of affairs,' कर्म्मनिर्वाहः.—(Control) अधिकारः, प्रभुत्वं, अधिष्ठातृत्वं, शासनं, अनुशासनं, विनियमः.—(Contrivance) उपायः, प्रयोगः, उपायप्रयोगः, युक्तिः *f.*, युक्तिप्रयुक्तिः *f.*, उपायज्ञता; 'good management,' सुनयः, सुनीतिः *f.*; 'bad management,' दुर्णयः, दुर्णीतिः; 'management of a drama,' स्थापना.

MANAGER, *s.* नायकः, नेता *m.* (तृ), प्रणेता *m.*, सम्प्रणेता *m.*, निर्वाहकः, वाहकः, सम्पादकः, व्यवहर्त्ता *m.* (र्त्तृ), घटकः, अधिष्ठाता *m.* (तृ), प्रवर्त्तकः, प्रयोजकः, चालकः, अधिकारी *m.* (न्), अधिकृतः, कर्त्ता *m.* (र्त्तृ), कारकः; 'manager of affairs,' कर्म्मनिर्वाहकः, कार्य्याध्यक्षः, कार्य्यद्रष्टा (ष्टृ), कार्य्यावेक्षिता *m.* (तृ), कर्म्माधिकारी *m.*; 'manager of the treasury,' कोषाध्यक्षः, धनाधिकारी *m.*, अर्थाधिकारी.—(Stage manager) सूत्रधारः -री *m.* (न्), मारिषः, स्थापकः, सूचकः.—(Expert in the use of means) उपायज्ञः, युक्तिमान् *m.* (त्), विदग्धः.—(Economical) परिमितव्ययी *m.* (न्), परिमिताचारी *m.*

MANAGING, *a.* उपायज्ञः -ज्ञा -ज्ञं, उपायकुशलः -ला -लं, विदग्धः -ग्धा -ग्धं.

To MANCIPATE, *v. a.* दासीकृ, वशीकृ, करदीकृ, बन्ध् (c. 9. बध्नाति, बन्द्धुं).

MANCIPATION, *s.* दास्यं, दासत्वं, दासीकरणं, वशीकरणं, परप्रेष्यत्वं, बन्धनं.

MANCIPLE, *s.* भोजनाधिकारी *m.* (न्), भोजनादिपरिकल्पकः.

MANDATE, *s.* आज्ञा, आदेशः, निदेशः, निर्देशः, नियोगः, शासनं, शास्तिः *f.*, नियमः, चोदना -नं, विधिः *m.*, विधानं; 'written,' आज्ञापत्रं, शासनपत्रं, पट्टं.

MANDATORY, *a.* आदेशकः -का -कं, आदेशी -शिनी -शि (न्), निर्देशकः -का -कं, आज्ञापकः -का -कं, आज्ञासूचकः -का -कं, आज्ञाबोधकः -का -कं, शासकः -का -कं.

MANDIBLE, *s.* हनुः *m. f.*—(Lower jaw) पीचं, कुञ्जः, चिबुकं.

MANDRAKE, *s.* (A plant) लक्ष्मणा, पुत्रदात्री, पुत्रदा, दूदाफलं.

To MANDUCATE, *v. a.* चर्व् (c. 1. चर्वति -र्वितुं, c. 10. चर्वयति -यितुं), चर्वणं कृ.

MANDUCATION, *s.* चर्वणं -णा, दन्तपेषणं, रोमन्थः, भक्षणं, भोजनं.

MANE, *s.* (Of a horse, &c.) केशरः, केसरः.—(Of a lion) सिंहकेशरः, सटा.

MAN-EATER, *s.* पुरुषादः, मनुष्यादः, मानवादः, मनुष्यभोजी *m.* (न्), नरभोजी *m.*, मनुष्यभक्षी *m.*, नरभुक् *m.* (ज्), नराशी *m.*, नृचक्षः, नृमांसखादकः, मनुष्यमांसभुक् *m.*

MANED, *a.* केशरी -रिणी -रि (न्), केसरी &c., सकेशरः -रा -रं.

MANEGE, *s.* (Art of training horses) अश्वशिक्षणविद्या, अश्वदमनविद्या.—(School for training horses) अश्वशिक्षाशाला.

MANES, *s. pl.* (Deceased ancestors) पितरः *m. pl.*, पितृलोकः, पितृपितामहादि *n.*—(Ghost) प्रेतलोकः, प्रेतः, प्रेतनरः, परेतः, पितृवनेचरः.—(Eater of the funeral oblation) पिण्डादः, पिण्डाशी *m.* (न्), पिण्डाशः, पिण्डभाक् *m.* (ज्), पिण्डी *m.* (न्), श्राद्धभुक् *m.* (ज्), श्राद्धी *m.* (न्), श्राद्धिकः; 'collective class of manes or deceased ancestors,' पितृगणः, पितृवर्गः, पितृसामान्यं, certain of these classes are सोमसद्, अग्निष्वात्ताः, सोमपाः, आज्यपाः, अर्य्यमा *m.* (न्),

सुकाली *m.* (न्), हविष्मत्, कव्यवाहनः, कव्यवालः, वारिषद्, अग्निदग्धः, अनग्निदग्धः, सोमः; 'business of offering oblations to the manes,' पितृकर्म्म *n.* (न्), पितृक्रिया, पितृव्रतं, पितृकार्य्यं, श्राद्धकर्म्म *n.*, श्राद्धक्रिया, पितृयज्ञः, पितृमेधः; 'oblation to the manes,' श्राद्धं, पिण्डः -ण्डी, कव्यं, various forms of these oblations are पार्वणश्राद्धं, एकोद्दिष्टश्राद्धं, नित्यश्राद्धं, नैमित्तिकश्राद्धं, काम्यश्राद्धं, आह्निकश्राद्धं, वृद्धिश्राद्धं, सपिण्डनश्राद्धं, उदकुम्भश्राद्धं, नान्दीश्राद्धं, नान्दीमुखं, प्रीतिश्राद्धं, हिरण्यश्राद्धं, आमश्राद्धं, पाथेयश्राद्धं, तिलतर्पणं; 'the offering of a cake,' पिण्डदानं, पिण्डनिर्वपणं; 'of water,' उदकदानं, उदकक्रिया; 'gifts in honor of the manes,' पितृदानं -नकं, पितृतर्पणं; 'one who makes the oblation,' पिण्डदः, श्राद्धदः, श्राद्धकरः, श्राद्धकृत् *m.*; 'day sacred to the manes,' पितृतिथिः *m. f.*, पितृदिवसः; 'heaven of the manes,' पितृलोकः, पितृपदं, पितृस्थानं. Oblations to the manes are made by the relations of the deceased soon after his death, and are repeated once, or, according to some, twice in every year, *i. e.* on the anniversary of the death, and on the same lunar day of the waning half of the month Bhádra. The latter are called महालयः. These obsequial rites are supposed to be necessary to secure the residence of the souls of the deceased in a world appropriated to the manes.

MANEUVER, MANŒUVRE, *s.* उपायः, उपायप्रयोगः, युक्तिः *f.*, सुयुक्तिः *f.*, प्रयुक्तिः, युक्तिप्रयुक्तयः *f. pl.*, माया, व्यपदेशः, कैतवप्रयोगः, विदग्धप्रयोगः, छलं, उपसरः.—(Military manœuvre) युद्धछलं, युद्धव्यपदेशः; 'evolutions of troops,' सैन्यविन्यासः, सैन्यव्यूहः, योग्या.

To MANEUVER, *v. n.* उपायप्रयोगं कृ, कैतवप्रयोगं कृ, विदग्धप्रयोगं कृ, व्यपदेशं कृ, छलं कृ; 'to distribute troops,' छलार्थं सैन्यान् विन्यस् (c. 4. -अस्यति -सितुं) or व्यूह् (c. 1. -ऊहते -हितुं).

MANFUL, *a.* पौरुषः -षी -षं, पौरुषेयः -यी -यं, पुरुषयोग्यः -ग्या -ग्यं, वीरयोग्यः &c., शूरयोग्यः &c., महावीर्य्यः -र्य्या -र्य्यं, साहसिकः -की -कं.

MANFULLY, *adv.* पुरुषवत्, पौरुषेण, सपौरुषं, सवीर्य्यं, वीरवत्, सविक्रमं, शूरवत्, महावीर्य्येण, सपराक्रमं, निर्भयं.

MANFULNESS, *s.* पौरुषं, पुरुषता -त्वं, वीर्य्यं, सुवीर्य्यं, विक्रमः, साहसं.

MANGE, *s.* खर्ज्जूः *f.*, कच्छूः *f.*, कण्डूः *f.*, पाम *n.* (न्), सिध्म *n.* (न्), त्वक्पुष्पं, त्वग्रोगः, दुश्चर्म्मत्वं, चर्म्मदुष्टता.

MANGER, *s.* गवादनी, अश्वादनी, गवादनपात्रं, तृणपात्रं, भोजनपात्रं.

MANGINESS, *s.* कच्छुरता -त्वं, सिध्मलत्वं, सिध्मवत्त्वं, दुश्चर्म्मत्वं.

To MANGLE, *v. a.* (Lacerate) व्यवछिद् (c. 7. -छिनत्ति -छेत्तुं), व्रश्च् (c. 6. वृश्चति, व्रश्चितुं), प्रव्रश्च्, विदृ (c. 10. -दारयति -यितुं), बहुलखण्डशः खण्ड् (c. 10. खण्डयति -यितुं) or छिद्, बहुलखण्डशः कृ, खण्डं खण्डं कृ, बहुलखण्डीकृ, विनिकृत् (c. 6. -कृन्तति -कर्त्तितुं), छिन्नभिन्नीकृ, क्षतविक्षतीकृ.—(Smooth linen) वस्त्रमार्ज्जनयन्त्रेण वस्त्रं मृज् (c. 2. मार्ष्टि -र्ष्टुं) or प्रमृज् or स्निग्धीकृ or श्लक्ष्णीकृ or श्लक्ष्ण (nom. श्लक्ष्णयति -यितुं).

MANGLE, *s.* (For clothes) वस्त्रमार्ज्जनार्थं चक्रयन्त्रं, वस्त्रमार्ज्जनचक्रं.

MANGLED, *p. p.* (Lacerated) क्षतविक्षतः -ता -तं, छिन्नभिन्नः -न्ना -न्नं, व्यवछिन्नः -न्ना -न्नं, विशसितः -ता -तं, विनिकृत्तः -त्ता -त्तं.—(As linen) मृष्टः -ष्टा -ष्टं, मार्ज्जितः -ता -तं.

MANGO, *s.* (Tree) आम्रः, चूतः -तकः, रसालः, सहारः, माकन्दः, मधुदूतः, वसन्तदूतः, कामवल्लभः, मदिरासखः, कामशरः, कामाङ्गः, गन्धबन्धुः *m.*, शरेष्टः, नालितदः, पिकबन्धुः *m.*, पिकवल्लभः, कोकिलावासः, पलालदोहदः, कोषी *m.* (न्); 'its fruit,' आम्रफलं, चूतफलं, फलश्रेष्ठः; 'a fragrant sort of mango tree,' सहकारः, मकरन्दः; 'juice of the mango,' आम्ररसः; 'inspissated juice,' आम्रावर्त्तः; 'piece of dried mango,' आम्रपेशी; 'tuft of mango,' आम्रपल्लवः; 'mango-grove,' आम्रवनं, मकरन्दवनं; 'made of mango,' आम्रमयः -यी -यं.

MANGO-FISH, *s.* तपस्वी *m.* (न्), तपःकरः, तपस्यामत्स्यः.

MANGY, *a.* कच्छुरः -रा -रं, सिध्मलः -ला -लं, सिध्मवान् -वती -वत् (त्), पामनः -ना -नं, दुश्चर्म्मा -र्म्मा -र्म्म (न्), त्वग्रोगी -गिणी -गि (न्).

MAN-HATER, *s.* पुरुषद्वेषी *m.* -षिणी *f.*, मनुष्यद्वेषी &c., मनुष्यद्वेष्टा *m.* (ष्टृ), मनुष्यवैरी *m.* (न्), मनुष्यशत्रुः *m.*, मनुष्यद्रोही *m.*

MANHOOD, *s.* पौरुषं, पुरुषता -त्वं, पौरुषता, मनुष्यत्वं, मानुष्यं, पुरुषभावः, पुरुषदशा, मानुषत्वं -ता, मानव्यं, पुरुषधर्म्मः.—(Virility) पुंस्त्वं, पुंस्ता, पुम्भावः, पुरुषत्वं, पौरुषत्वं, पौरुषं, ओजस् *n.*, तेजस् *n.*, ऊर्ज्जः.—(Not boyhood) यौवनं, तारुण्यं, प्रौढता, प्रौढिः *f.*, व्यवहारावस्था.—(Courage) पौरुषं, वीर्य्यं, शूरता.

MANIA, *s.* उन्मादः, उन्मत्तता, मदः, मत्तता, बुद्धिभ्रमः, चित्तविभ्रमः.

MANIAC, *a.* उन्मत्तः -त्ता -त्तं, उन्मादवान् -वती -वत् (त्). *See* MAD.

MANIAC, *s.* उन्मत्तजनः, मत्तजनः, प्रमदजनः, भ्रान्तबुद्धिः *m.*, नष्टबुद्धिः.

MANIFEST, *a.* स्पष्टः -ष्टा -ष्टं, सुस्पष्टः -ष्टा -ष्टं, व्यक्तः -क्ता -क्तं, अभिव्यक्तः -क्ता -क्तं, सुव्यक्तः -क्ता -क्तं, प्रव्यक्तः &c., प्रत्यक्षः -क्षा -क्षं, स्फुटः -टा -टं, प्रस्फुटः -टा -टं, प्रकाशः -शा -शं, सुप्रकाशः -शा -शं, प्रकाशितः -ता -तं, साविष्कारः -रा -रं, प्रकटः -टी -टं, प्रकटीभूतः -ता -तं, प्रकटितः -ता -तं, आविर्भूतः -ता -तं, प्रादुर्भूतः -ता -तं, प्रत्यक्षभूतः -ता -तं, प्रसिद्धः -द्धा -द्धं, उद्भूतः -ता -तं; 'becoming manifest,' पुरःस्फुरन् -रन्ती -रत् (त्); 'to become manifest,' प्रादुर्भू, आविर्भू, प्रादुरस्, स्पष्टीभू, प्रत्यक्षीभू, व्यक्तीभू, प्रकाश् (c. 1. -काशते -शितुं), प्रकाशीभू; 'to make manifest, made manifest.' *See To* MANIFEST, MANIFESTED.

To MANIFEST, *v. a.* (Show plainly) व्यक्तीकृ, आविष्कृ, प्रादुष्कृ, प्रत्यक्षीकृ, स्पष्टीकृ, प्रकटीकृ, प्रकट (nom. प्रकटयति -यितुं), प्रकाश् (c. 10. -काशयति -यितुं), विकाश्, व्यञ्ज् (c. 7. -अनक्ति -अंक्तुं, c. 10. -अञ्जयति -यितुं), स्फुटीकृ.—(Exhibit) सूच् (c. 10. सूचयति -यितुं), दृश् (c. 10. दर्शयति -यितुं).

MANIFESTATION, *s.* (Act) आविष्करणं, आविष्कारः, प्रादुष्करणं, व्यक्तीकरणं, प्रत्यक्षीकरणं, स्पष्टीकरणं, प्रकटीकरणं, प्रकाशनं, प्रकाशकरणं, व्यञ्जनं, विकाशनं, स्पष्टकरणं.—(State) व्यक्तिः *f.*, अभिव्यक्तिः *f.*, व्यक्तता -त्वं, प्रकाशः -शता, प्रादुर्भावः, आविर्भावः, आविर्भवनं, प्रत्यक्षता, स्पष्टता, प्राकट्यं, प्रकटत्वं, स्फुटता, आविर्भूतता, प्रादुर्भूतता, उद्भूतता, उद्भवः, प्रसिद्धिः *f.*, अवभासः.

MANIFESTED, *p. p.* (Made apparent, become evident) प्रादुष्कृतः -ता -तं, आविष्कृतः -ता -तं, व्यक्तीकृतः -ता -तं, प्रत्यक्षीकृतः -ता -तं, स्पष्टीकृतः -ता -तं, प्रकटीकृतः -ता -तं, प्रकटितः -ता -तं, प्रत्यक्षभूतः -ता -तं, आविर्भूतः -ता -तं, प्रादुर्भूतः -ता -तं, प्रकाशितः -ता -तं, व्यञ्जितः -ता -तं, विकाशितः -ता -तं, स्फुटितः -ता -तं, प्रस्फुटितः -ता -तं, अभिव्यज्यमानः -ना -नं.—(Exhibited) सूचितः -ता -तं.

MANIFESTER, *s.* प्रकाशकः, विकाशकः, प्रत्यक्षकर्त्ता *m.* (र्त्तृ), अभिव्यञ्जकः.

MANIFESTLY, *adv.* व्यक्तं, सुव्यक्तं, स्पष्टं, सुस्पष्टं, प्रत्यक्षतस्, प्रत्यक्षेण, प्रकाशं, स्फुटं, साक्षात्, प्रादुस्, आविस्, साविष्कारं, प्रकटं, प्राकट्येन.

MANIFESTNESS, *s.* व्यक्तता, प्रत्यक्षता, प्रादुर्भावः, आविर्भावः, स्पष्टता, प्रकाशता, प्राकट्यं, स्फुटता, आविर्भूतता.

MANIFESTO, *s.* ज्ञापनपत्रं, ख्यापनपत्रं, घोषणापत्रं, प्रकाशनपत्रं, प्रसिद्धिपत्रं.

MANIFOLD, *a.* बहुविधः -धा -धं, बहुगुणः -णा -णं, अनेकविधः -धा -धं, बहुप्रकारः -रा -रं, नानाविधः -धा -धं, विविधः -धा -धं, बहुरूपः -पा -पं, नानारूपः -पी -पं, अनेकरूपः -पा -पं, बहुलः -ला -लं, अनेकः -का -कं.

MANIFOLDLY, *adv.* बहुधा, अनेकधा, बहुविधेन, नानाविधेन, बाहुल्येन.

MANIFOLDNESS, *s.* बहुरूपत्वं, बहुलता, बाहुल्यं, अनेकता, अनैक्यं.

MANIKIN, *s.* माणवकः, माणवः, मानवकः, मनुष्यकः, क्षुद्रपुरुषः.

MANIPLE, *s.* (Handful) मुष्टिः *m.f.*, हस्तपूरणं.—(Small band) क्षुद्रगुल्मः.

To MANIPULATE, *v. a.* हस्ताभ्यां कृ, हस्तव्यापारपूर्व्वं कृ, हस्तकर्म्मद्वारा कृ. —(Move the hands) हस्तादि सञ्चल् (c. 10. -चालयति -यितुं), हस्तसञ्चालनं कृ.

MANIPULATION, *s.* हस्तकर्म्म *n.* (न्), हस्तव्यापारः.—(Movement of the hands, &c.) हस्तादिसञ्चालनं, अङ्गसञ्चालनं, हस्तादिविक्षेपः.

MANKIND, *s.* मनुष्यजातिः *f.*, पुरुषजातिः *f.*, नरजातिः *f.*, मानवजातिः *f.*, मनुष्याः *m. pl.*, मानुषाः *m. pl.*, मानवाः *m. pl.*, पुरुषाः *m. pl.*, नराः *m. pl.*, मर्त्याः *m. pl.*, जनाः *m. pl.*, मनुजाः *m. pl.*, जनपदाः *m. pl.*, मनुष्यगणः, लोकः, जीवलोकः -कं, जगती, मनुभूः *m.*

MANLINESS, *s.* पौरुषं, पुरुषता -त्वं, पौरुषता, वीर्य्यं, सुवीर्य्यं, वीरता, शूरता, शौर्य्यं, विक्रमः, पराक्रमः, साहसं, पुंस्त्वं, मनुष्यत्वं.

MANLY, *a.* पौरुषः -षी -षं, पौरुषेयः -यी -यं, पुरुषयोग्यः -ग्या -ग्यं, नारः -री -रं, नरयोग्यः &c., वीरः -रा -रं, शूरः -रा -रं, प्रवीरः -रा -रं, वीरयोग्यः &c., महावीर्य्यः -र्य्या -र्य्यं, पुरुष or नर in comp.; 'manly act,' पुरुषकारः; 'manly office,' पुरुषाधिकारः; 'manly duty,' नरधर्म्मः.

MANNA, *s.* (Of the bamboo) वंशरोचना, वंशलोचना, कर्म्मरी. The Hebrew word may be rendered by मान्ना.

MANNER, *s.* (Form, fashion, way) प्रकारः, रीतिः *f.*, विधः, विधिः *m.*, रूपं, विधानं, वृत्तिः *f.*, आकारः, आकृतिः *f.*; 'in this manner,' अनेन प्रकारेण, अनया रीत्या, अनयत्या; 'in such a manner,' एवंविधं -धेन, तथाविधं -धेन, एवंरूपेण, एवम्प्रकारेण, इत्यादिविधानेन; 'in the manner before mentioned,' पूर्व्वोक्तप्रकारेण, पूर्व्वोक्तरीत्या. —(Kind) प्रकारः, विधः, भेदः, प्रभेदः, विशेषः; 'all manner of food,' सर्व्वप्रकारम् अन्नं.—(Method, mode of doing) रीतिः *f.*, मार्गः, क्रमः, पर्य्यायः, पद्धतिः *f.*, परिपाटी, क्रिया, वृत्तान्तः, वृत्तिः *f.*, चर्य्या.—(Custom, habitual practice) आचारः, आचरणं, व्यवहारः, व्यवहृतिः *f.*, प्रचारः, समाचारः, चर्य्या, रीतिः *f.*, नियमः, नित्यकृत्यं, अभ्यासः, धारा, अनुसारः, स्थितिः *f.*, चरितं, सम्प्रदायः, व्यापारः, शीलः, आवृत्तिः *f.*, मार्गः, पथः; 'manners and customs of a country,' देशाचारः, देशव्यवहारः, देशरीतिः *f.*, देशसम्प्रदायः; 'good manners,' सदाचारः, शिष्टाचारः, शिष्टसम्प्रदायः, मर्य्यादा, सुनीतिः *f.*, विनयः, सुशीलता; 'bad manners,' दुराचारः, दुर्णीतिः *f.*, अनीतिः *f.*, अविनयः, कुरीतिः *f.*, अमर्य्यादा, कुचर्य्या, दुःशीलता; 'violation of good manners,' मर्य्यादातिक्रमः, विनयभङ्गः, सदाचारलंघनं.—(Mien, air) आकारः, वदनाकारः, रूपं, गतिः *f.*, वदनं.—(Peculiar way) विशेषरीतिः *f.*—(Style) वृत्तिः *f.*—(In like manner) तथैव, तथा, एवं, एवमेव, तथाहि, तद्वत्.

MANNERED, *a.* (Having good manners) सुशीलः -ला -लं, विनीतः -ता -तं, शिष्टाचारी -रिणी -रि (न्); 'ill-mannered,' दुःशीलः -ला -लं, वामशीलः -ला -लं, कुशीलः -ला -लं, दुर्मर्य्यादः -दा -दं, अविनयः -या -यं, प्रणष्टविनयः &c., अशिष्टः -ष्टा -ष्टं.

MANNERISM, *s.* एकरीतिसेवनं, एकरसासक्तिः *f.*, अनन्यरससेवनं, एकरसत्वं.

MANNERLINESS, *s.* शिष्टता, सभ्यता, सुशीलता, विनयः, शिष्टाचारत्वं, सौजन्यं.

MANNERLY, *a.* शिष्टः -ष्टा -ष्टं, सभ्यः -भ्या -भ्यं, विनीतः -ता -तं, विनयवान् -वती -वत् (त्), सुशीलः -ला -लं, शिष्टाचारी -रिणी -रि (न्), सदाचारी &c., सुव्यवहारी &c., सुजनः -ना -नं.

MANNERLY, *adv.* सभ्यवत्, सुशीलवत्, सविनयं, शिष्टाचारानुसारेण, सौजन्यात्.

MANNERS, *s. pl.* सदाचारः, शिष्टाचारः, मर्य्यादा, विनयः, सुनीतिः *f.*, शिष्टता, सभ्यता, सभ्याचारः, सुशीलता. *See* MANNER.

MANNISH, *a.* पुरुषस्वभावः -वा -वं, पुरुषवृत्तिः -त्तिः -त्ति, पुरुषधर्म्मकः -का -कं, पुम्प्रकृतिः -तिः -ति, पुरुषाकारः -रा -रं, पुरुषोपमः -मा -मं, पुरुषयोग्यः -ग्या -ग्यं.

MANŒUVRE, *s.* *See* MANEUVER.

MAN-OF-WAR, *s.* बृहत्परिमाणा युद्धनौका or युद्धनौः *f.*

MANOR, *s.* ग्रामेश्वराधीना भूमिः, ग्रामेश्वरभूमिः *f.*; 'Lord of the manor,' ग्रामेश्वरः, ग्रामणीः *m.*, देशमुखः.

MANORIAL, *a.* ग्रामेश्वरभूमिसम्बन्धी -न्धिनी -न्धि (न्).

MANSE, *s.* धर्म्माध्यापकगृहं, धर्म्मोपदेशकवेश्म *n.* (न्).

MANSION, *s.* हर्म्यं, भवनं, मन्दिरं, धाम *n.* (न्), सदनं, सौधं, शाला, सद्म *n.* (न्), गृहं, गेहं, वेश्म *n.* (न्), निवेशनं, निकेतनं, आयतनं, वासस्थानं, निवासस्थानं, आलयः, निलयः, निवसतिः *f.*—(Lunar mansion) नक्षत्रं, विधुप्रिया, चन्द्रप्रिया, दक्षजा, चन्द्रदाराः *pl.* The last of these words is applied to the twenty-seven lunar mansions collectively, as in mythology they are supposed to be so many nymphs, daughters of Daksha, and wedded to the moon. The following are the names of the twenty-seven *nakshatras* in order: 1. अश्विनी, 2. भरणी, 3. कृत्तिका, 4. रोहिणी, 5. मृगशिरस् *n.*, 6. आर्द्रा, 7. पुनर्वसुः *m.*, 8. पुष्यः -ष्या, 9. आश्लेषा, 10. मघा, 11. पूर्व्वफाल्गुनी, 12. उत्तरफाल्गुनी, 13. हस्तः, 14. चित्रा, 15. स्वातिः -ती *f.*, 16. विशाखा, 17. अनुराधा, 18. ज्येष्ठा, 19. मूलः -लं, 20. पूर्व्वाषाढा, 21. उत्तराषाढा, 22. श्रवणः -णा, 23. धनिष्ठा, 24. शतभिषा, 25. पूर्व्वभाद्रपदा, 26. उत्तरभाद्रपदा, 27. रेवती. Some add a twenty-eighth, अभिजित्. Astrologers divide the twenty-seven lunar mansions into three classes of nine each, called देवगणः, राक्षसगणः, मनुष्यगणः.

MANSLAUGHTER, *s.* (Killing of a man) मनुष्यमारणं, मनुष्यहत्या, मनुष्यघातः, मनुष्यवधः.—(In law) असमीक्ष्यघातः, असमीक्ष्यवधः, असमीक्ष्यहत्या, अहेतुकृतहत्या.

MANSLAYER, *s.* मनुष्यमारकः, मनुष्यघातकः, नृहन्ता *m.* (न्), मनुष्यहन्ता *m.*, नृघातकः, मनुष्यवधकः.

MAN-STEALER, *s.* मनुष्यापहारकः, मनुष्यचोरः, मनुष्यस्तेयकृत् *m.*

MAN-STEALING, *s.* मनुष्यापहारः, मनुष्यहरणं, मनुष्यापहरणं, मनुष्यस्तेयं, मनुष्यचौर्य्यं.

MANSUETE, *a.* गृह्यः -ह्या -ह्यं, वश्यः -श्या -श्यं, दमितः -ता -तं, दान्तः -न्ता -न्तं.

MANSUETUDE, *s.* गृह्यता, वश्यता, विनेयता, विधेयता, दान्तता, शान्तता.

MANTELET, *s.* स्त्रीलोकभृतः क्षुद्रप्रावारः.—(In war) पारश्वधावरणं, पारश्वधवारणं, सैन्यावरणं.

MANTLE, *s.* प्रावारः -रकः, प्रावृतं -ता -तः, उत्तरीयं, आवारः, आवरणं, पिधानं, संव्यानं, नीशारः, जवनिका, प्रच्छदपटः, गात्रीयवस्त्रं, निवीतः -ता -तं, निवृतः -ता -तं.

To MANTLE, *v. a.* (Cloak) प्रावृ (c. 5. -वृणोति -वरितुं -रीतुं), आवृ, छद् (c. 10. छादयति -यितुं), आच्छद्, प्रच्छद्.

To MANTLE, *v. n.* (Expand, spread) विस्तृ in pass. (-स्तीर्य्यते), प्रवृध् (c. 1. -वर्धते -र्द्धितुं), प्रसृप् (c. 1. -सर्पति -सृप्तुं), विसृप्.—(Rise, rush upwards) उद्गम् (c. 1. -गच्छति -गन्तुं), उत्सृप्, उद्गतः -ता -तं भू.—(Gather froth) फेन (nom. फेनायते), उत्सेचनं कृ, उत्सेकं कृ, फेनावृतः -ता -तं भू.

Mantua, s. स्त्रीवस्त्रं, स्त्रीकटीवस्त्रं, स्त्रीवसनं, स्त्रीपरिधानं.

Mantua-maker, s. स्त्रीवस्त्रकर्त्री f. (र्तृ), स्त्रीवसनकृत्, स्त्रीपरिधानकृत्.

Manual, a. (Pertaining to the hand) हस्त्यः -स्त्या -स्त्यं, हस्तसम्बन्धी -न्धिनी -न्धि (न्), हस्त in comp.—(Performed by the hand) हस्तकृतः -ता -तं, हस्तसाध्यः -ध्या -ध्यं, हस्तसाधनीयः -या -यं; 'manual operation,' हस्तकर्म्म n. (न्), हस्तक्रिया, हस्तव्यापारः; 'manual labor,' व्रातं, शिल्पकर्म्म; 'manual art,' शिल्पं; 'knowledge of it,' शिल्पविद्या; 'relating to it,' शिल्पिकः -की -कं; 'manual skill or dexterity,' हस्तकौशल्यं, हस्तकौशलं, हस्तलाघवं, हस्तचापल्यं; 'sign manual,' हस्ताक्षरं, स्वहस्ताक्षरं, स्वाक्षरं.

Manual, s. (Small book for carrying in the hand) पद्धतिः -तीf., सारग्रन्थः, सारसङ्ग्रहः, सारसंक्षेपः, संक्षिप्तग्रन्थः, संहिता; 'of laws,' धर्म्मसंहिता.

Manufactory, s. शिल्पशाला -लं, शिल्पिशाला -लं, यन्त्रगृहं, आवेशनं, प्रावेशनं, अन्वासनं.

Manufactural, a. शिल्पिकः -की -कं, शिल्पकर्म्मसम्बन्धी -न्धिनी -न्धि (न्).

Manufacture, s. (The act) निर्म्माणं, निर्म्मितिः f., कल्पनं -ना, रचनं -ना, विरचना, घटनं, सन्निवेशः, पर्य्यायः, शिल्पकर्म्म n. (न्), शिल्पेन or शिल्पकर्म्मणा निर्म्माणं or करणं.—(The article) शिल्पिकद्रव्यं, शिल्पनिर्म्मितद्रव्यं, शिल्पिकवस्तु n.

To manufacture, v. a. शिल्पेन or शिल्पकर्म्मणा निर्मा (c. 2. -माति -तुं, c. 3. -मिमीते caus. मापयति -यितुं) or विनिर्मा or क्लृप् (c. 10. कल्पयति -यितुं) or कृ (c. 8. करोति, कर्त्तुं, c. 10. कारयति -यितुं) or संस्कृ or रच् (c. 10. रचयति -यितुं) or विरच् or घट् (c. 1. घटते -टितुं).

Manufactured, p. p. शिल्पनिर्म्मितः -ता -तं, शिल्पकृतः -ता -तं, शिल्पकल्पितः -ता -तं, निर्म्मितः -ता -तं, शिल्पिकः -की -कं, कार्म्मिकः -की -कं.

Manufacturer, s. शिल्पी m. (न्), शिल्पिकः, शिल्पकारः.

Manumission, s. दास्यमुक्तिः f., दास्यमोचनं, दास्यमोक्षः -क्षणं, दासमोक्षः &c.

To manumit, v. a. दास्याद् विमुच् (c. 6. -मुञ्चति -मोक्तुं) or मुच् or मोक्ष् (c. 10. मोक्षयति -यितुं) or विमोक्ष्, विसृज् (c. 6. -सृजति -स्रष्टुं, c. 10. -सर्जयति -यितुं).

Manumitted, p. p. दास्यमुक्तः -क्ता -क्तं, दास्यमोक्षितः -ता -तं, मुक्तदास्यः -स्या -स्यं, दास्यविमोचितः -ता -तं, अभुजिष्यः -ष्या -ष्यं.

To manure, v. a. भूमिं पुरीषादिना लिप् (c. 6. लिम्पति, लेप्तुं), उर्व्वराकरणार्थं गोमयादिसम्मिश्रद्रव्यं भूमौ प्रक्षिप् (c. 6. -क्षिपति -क्षेप्तुं) or क्षिप् or धा (c. 3. दधाति, धातुं), भूमिलेपनेन or पांशुप्रक्षेपेण उर्व्वरात्वं जन् (c. 10. जनयति -यितुं) or बहुशस्योत्पादकत्वं जन्, आलवालं स्था in caus. (स्थापयति -यितुं).

Manure, s. भूमिलेपः -पनं, पांशुः m., पांसुः m., सारः, पुरीषादि n., पुरीषादिसम्मिश्रद्रव्यं, गोमयादिसम्मिश्रद्रव्यं, शस्योत्पादकद्रव्यं.

Manuscript, s. हस्तलेखः -खनं, हस्तलिखितं, हस्तलेख्यं, लेख्यं, लिखितं, पुस्तकं -की, पुस्तं -स्ती.

Manuscript, a. हस्तलिखितः -ता -तं, लेख्यकृतः -ता -तं, लिखितः -ता -तं.

Many, a. बहुः -हुः -ह्वी -हु, बहुलः -ला -लं, अनेकः -का -कं, प्रचुरः -रा -रं, भूरिः -रिः -रि, बहुसंख्यकः -का -कं, भूयान् -यसी -यः (स्), भूयिष्ठः -ष्ठा -ष्ठं, नैकः -का -कं, अनल्पः -ल्पा -ल्पं, पुष्कलः -ला -लं, विपुलः -ला -लं, प्राज्यः -ज्या -ज्यं, प्रभूतः -ता -तं, पुरुः -रुः -रु, पुरुहः -हा -हं, पुरुहुः -हुः -हु, अदभ्रः -भ्रा -भ्रं, बहुतिथः -था -थं, स्फिरः -रा -रं, नाना in comp.; 'as many as,' यावान् -वती -वत् (त्) or यावत् indec., यावत्संख्यकः -का -कं, यत्संख्यकः -का -कं, यतयः यतीनि or यति indec.; 'so many,' तावान् -वती -वत् (त्) or तावत् indec., तावत्संख्यकः -का -कं, तत्संख्यकः -का -कं, ततयः m. f. ततीनि n. or तति indec.; 'how many?' कियान् -यती -यत् (त्) or कियत् indec., कतिः -तिः -ति or plur. कतयः, कतीनि; 'of how many sorts?' कतिविधः -धा -धं; 'in many places,' बहुत्र, अनेकत्र; 'in many ways,' बहुधा, अनेकधा; 'in how many ways?' कतिधा; 'many times,' बहुशस्, अनेकशस्, बहुवारं, बहुकृत्वस्, मुहुर् मुहुः, भूयस्, पुनः पुनर्.

Many, s. (A multitude) समूहः, समवायः, समुदायः, समाजः, संघातः, ओघः, निवहः, वृन्दं; 'the interests of the many,' समूहकार्य्यं.

Many-colored, a. नानावर्णः -र्णा -र्णं, नानारङ्गः -ङ्गा -ङ्गं, बहुवर्णः -र्णा -र्णं, चित्रविचित्रः -त्रा -त्रं, बहुरङ्गी -ङ्गिणी -ङ्गि (न्).

Many-cornered, a. बहुकोणः -णा -णं, अनेककोणविशिष्टः -ष्टा -ष्टं.

Many-fibered, a. बहुतन्त्री -न्त्रिणी -न्त्रि (न्), बहुसूत्री -त्रिणी &c.

Many-flowered, a. बहुपुष्पः -ष्पा -ष्पं, प्रचुरकुसुमः -मा -मं.

Many-headed, a. बहुशिराः -राः -रः (स्), बहुशिरस्कः -स्का -स्कं, बहुमस्तकः -का -कं, अनेकमस्तकः -का -कं, बहुमूर्द्धा -र्द्धा -र्द्ध (न्).

Many-leaved, a. बहुपर्णः -र्णा -र्णं, बहुपत्रः -त्रा -त्रं, प्रचुरपर्णः &c.

Many-legged, a. बहुपादः -दा -दं, बहुपाद् m. f. n., बहुजङ्घः -ङ्घा -ङ्घं.

Many-streamed, a. बहुप्रवाहः -हा -हं, बहुस्रोताः -ताः -तः (स्).

Many-stringed, a. बहुसूत्री -त्रिणी -त्रि (न्), बहुतन्त्रिकः -का -कं.

Many-tongued, a. बहुजिह्वः -ह्वा -ह्वं, अनेकजिह्वः -ह्वा -ह्वं.

Map, s. देशालेख्यपत्रं, भूपृष्ठालेख्यपत्रं, देशालेख्यं, देशसमुद्राद्यालेख्यं, भूगोलस्य देशसमुद्रनगराद्यालेख्यं, देशचित्रं, भूपृष्ठभङ्गिप्रदर्शनपत्रं, भूपृष्ठदेशालेख्यं.

To map, v. a. भूपृष्ठदेशान् लिख् (c. 6. लिखति, लेखितुं) or आलिख् or चित्र् (c. 10. चित्रयति -यितुं), देशालेख्यं कृ, भूपृष्ठालेख्यं कृ.

To mar, v. a. दुष् (c. 10. दूषयति -यितुं), नश् (c. 10. नाशयति -यितुं), हन् (c. 2. हन्ति -न्तुं), व्याहन्, विहन्, क्षतिं कृ.

Marasmus, s. क्षयः, क्षयरोगः, क्षयथुः m., यक्ष्मा m. (न्), राजयक्ष्मा m., शोषः.

To maraud, v. n. युद्धसमये गोधान्यादिग्रहणार्थम् इतस्ततो भ्रम् (c. 4. भ्राम्यति, भ्रमितुं) or परिभ्रम्, लोप्त्रार्थं परिभ्रम् or उपद्रवं कृ or विप्लवं कृ or उपद्रु (c. 1. -द्रवति -द्रोतुं).

Marauder, s. लोप्त्रार्थं परिभ्रमणकारी m. (न्), उपद्रवी m. (न्), विप्लवकारी m., उपद्रवकारी m., उपप्लवकृत्, लुण्टाकः.

Marauding, s. युद्धकाले गोधान्याद्यपहरणार्थम् इतस्ततः परिभ्रमणं, विप्लवः, उपप्लवः, उपद्रवः, विप्लवकरणं.

Marble, s. मार्वेलाख्यो नानावर्णः प्रस्तरः, रुचिरप्रस्तरः, चारुप्रस्तरः, पाषाणः, ग्रावा m. (न्), शिला, उपलः.

Marble, a. (Made of marble) पूर्व्वोक्तप्रस्तरमयः -यी -यं, पाषाणनिर्म्मितः -ता -तं.—(Variegated) प्रस्तररेखानुकारेण चित्रितः -ता -तं.

Marble-hearted, a. पाषाणहृदयः -या -यं, वज्रहृदयः &c., वज्रचित्तः -त्ता -त्तं.

Marcasite, s. आवर्त्तः, सुवर्णमाक्षिकं, सुवर्णमुखी.

Marcescent, a. विशीर्य्यमाणः -णा -णं, क्षीयमाणः -णा -णं, म्लायमानः -ना -नं.

March, s. (The month) फाल्गुनः -निकः, चैत्रः -त्रिकः, फाल्गुनोत्तरार्द्धं, चैत्रपूर्व्वार्द्धं, पूर्व्वचैत्रः, उत्तरफाल्गुनः, तपस्यः, मधुः m., तृतीयमासः.—(Movement of soldiers, &c.) गमनं, यानं, यात्रा, सैनिकगमनं, सैनिकयात्रा, गमः, गतिः f., सैनिकगतिः f., व्रज्या, सरणं, संसरणं.—(Marching onwards, progression) प्रयाणं, प्रस्थानं, प्रस्थितिः f., प्रगमनं,

अपगमनं.—(Marching against) अभिषेणनं, अभिनिर्याणं; 'setting out on a march,' यात्राकरणं; 'toilsome march,' दुर्गसञ्चारः, दुर्गसञ्चारः, सञ्चारः.

To MARCH, *v. n.* यात्रां कृ, गमनं कृ, सैनिकवद् गमनं कृ or प्रगम् (c. 1. -गच्छति -गन्तुं) or प्रया (c. 2. -याति -तुं) or प्रस्था (c. 1. -तिष्ठति -ते -स्थातुं) or व्रज् (c. 1. व्रजति -जितुं) or चर् (c. 1. चरति -रितुं) or चल् (c. 1. चलति -लितुं) or प्रचल्; 'to march against,' अभिनिर्या (c. 2. -याति -तुं), अभिप्रया, प्रतिव्रज्, अभिप्रस्था, प्रत्यभिप्रस्था, अभिगम्, प्रतिगम्; 'one who marches slow,' मन्दगामी *m.* (न्), मन्थरः; 'fast,' अतिजवः, जंघालः, जंघिलः.

To MARCH, *v. a.* अभिषेणय (nom. अभिषेणयति -यितुं), सेनां प्रस्था in caus. (-स्थापयति -यितुं) or चल् (c. 10. चलयति -यितुं) or प्रतिगम् (c. 10. -गमयति -यितुं), यात्रां कृ (c. 10. कारयति -यितुं).

MARCHES, *s. pl.* (Confines) देशसीमा, देशसमन्ताः *m. pl.*, देशप्रान्ताः *m. pl.*

MARE, *s.* अश्वा, अश्विनी, वाजिनी, तुरगी, तुरङ्गी, तुरङ्गिणी, वडवा, वडवा, घोटिका, अर्वती, वामी, प्रसूः *f.*, प्रसूका.

MARGARITE, *s.* (Pearl) मुक्ता, मुक्तिका, मौक्तिकं, शुक्तिबीजं, शुक्तिजं.

MARGIN, *s.* प्रान्तः, अन्तः -न्तं, सीमा, उपान्तं, पर्य्यन्तं, कच्छः, धारः -रा, तटं, समन्तः, उत्सङ्गः, कोटिः *f.*, परिसरः; 'of a river,' तीरं, कूलं, तटं, कच्छः, कच्छान्तः; 'on the margin,' प्रान्ततस्.—(Of a book) समासः, पुस्तकप्रान्तः.

MARGINAL, *a.* प्रान्तस्थः -स्था -स्थं, समासस्थः &c., समासलिखितः -ता -तं.

MARGINALLY, *adv.* (Along the margin) प्रान्ततस्, प्रान्ते, अनुप्रान्तं.

MARINE, *a.* सामुद्रः -द्री -द्रं, समुद्रीयः -या -यं, समुद्रियः -या -यं, सामुद्रिकः -की -कं, समुद्रसम्बन्धी -न्धिनी -न्धि (न्), समुद्रविषयः -या -यं, सैन्धवः -वी -वं, सिन्धुकः -का -कं, समुद्रजः -जा -जं, समुद्रोद्भवः -वा -वं, जलधिसम्भवः -वा -वं, सागरसम्बन्धी &c.; 'marine engagement,' नौयुद्धं.

MARINE, *s.* (A soldier that serves on board a ship) नौयोद्धा *m.* (द्धृ), नौसैन्यः, नाविकसैन्यः, समुद्रीयसैनिकः.—(Navy) युद्धनौसमूहः.—(Naval affairs) नाविकविषयः, नाविककर्म्म *n.* (न्), नाविकप्रकरणं, जलयानविषयः, जलयानप्रकरणं.

MARINER, *s.* नाविकः, नाविकजनः, समुद्रयायी *m.* (न्), समुद्रगः, समुद्रगामी *m.*, पोतवाहः, निर्यामः, जलपथोपजीवी *m.* (न्), उदधिक्रा: *m.* (म्), समुद्रीयजनः.

MARITAL, *a.* भर्तृसम्बन्धी -न्धिनी -न्धि (न्), पतिसम्बन्धी &c., भर्तृविषयः -या -यं, पतिविषयः &c., स्वामिविषयः &c.

MARITIME, *a.* (Relating to the sea) सामुद्रः -द्री -द्रं, समुद्रियः -या -यं, समुद्र in comp. *See* MARINE, *a.* (Naval) नाविकः -की -कं, नाव्यः -व्या -व्यं, नौ in comp.—(Bordering on the sea) समुद्रतटस्थः -स्था -स्थं, समुद्रतीरस्थः -स्था -स्थं.

MARJORAM, *s.* तुलसी, मरुवकः, समीरणः, प्रस्थपुष्पः, फणिज्झकः, पर्णासः, जम्भीरः, कठिञ्जरः, कुठेरकः, अर्ज्जकः.

MARK, *s.* (Sign, token by which a thing is known) चिह्नं, लक्षणं, लाञ्छनं, लिङ्गं, अङ्कः -ङ्कं, अभिज्ञानं, व्यञ्जनं, व्यञ्जकः -कं, लक्ष्यं, लक्ष्म *n.* (न्), लक्ष्मणं, ललामं.—(Spot) कलङ्कः, अङ्कः, चिह्नं, बिन्दुः *m.*, विप्रुट् (ष्), विप्रुद्, गण्डः.—(Mark on the body) सामुद्रं, सामुद्रचिह्नं, सामुद्रिकलक्षणं, तिलः -लकः, तिलकालकः; 'an interpreter of marks on the body,' सामुद्रिकः; 'an auspicious mark,' सुलक्षणं, सुचिह्नं; 'having auspicious marks,' सुलक्षणी -णिनी -णि (न्), सुलक्षणिकः -का -कं; 'having thirty-two auspicious marks,' द्वात्रिंशल्लक्षणोपेतः -ता -तं; 'an inauspicious mark,' कुलक्षणं, अपलक्षणं, दुर्लक्षणं, दुश्चिह्नं; 'having inauspicious marks,' कुलक्षणी -णिनी &c., कुलक्षणः -णा -णं.—(Butt for shooting at) लक्ष्यं, बाणलक्ष्यं, लक्षं, वेध्यं, व्यध्यः, शरव्यं, दृष्टिगुणः, प्रतिकायः; 'hitting the mark,' लक्ष्यभेदः; 'to hit the mark,' लक्ष्यं भिद् (c. 7. भिनत्ति, भेत्तुं) or व्यध् (c. 4. विध्यति, व्यद्धुं), लक्ष्यवेधनं कृ.—(Line) रेखा, लेखा.

To MARK, *v. a.* (Stamp, impress with a mark) चिह्न (nom. चिह्नयति -यितुं), अङ्क् (c. 10. अङ्कयति -यितुं), लक्ष् (c. 10. लक्षयति -यितुं), मुद्र (nom. मुद्रयति -यितुं), लाञ्छ् (c. 1. लाञ्छति -ञ्छितुं), अङ्कं कृ, चिह्नं कृ, लक्षणं कृ, लक्षीकृ.—(Stain) कलङ्क (nom. कलङ्कयति -यितुं), मलिन (nom. मलिनयति -यितुं), कलङ्कीकृ, लाञ्छ्.—(Draw a line) लिख् (c. 6. लिखति, लेखितुं), आलिख्, रेखां कृ.—(Notice, observe) लक्ष्, आलक्ष्, उपलक्ष्, अवेक्ष् (c. 1. -ईक्षते -क्षितुं), निरीक्ष्, वीक्ष्, समीक्ष्, प्रेक्ष्.—(Mark out, define) परिच्छिद् (c. 7. -च्छिनत्ति -च्छेत्तुं), परिच्छेदं कृ, निर्दिश् (c. 6. -दिशति -देष्टुं), लक्ष्, लक्षीकृ.—(Mark out, trace the outline) बाह्यरेखां लिख् or अङ्क् or कृ, बहिर्लेखां कृ.

To MARK, *v. n.* (Note, take notice) आलोच् (c. 10. -लोचयति -यितुं), आलक्ष् (c. 10. -लक्षयति -यितुं), निरूप् (c. 10. -रूपयति -यितुं), समीक्ष् (c. 1. -ईक्षते -क्षितुं), समीक्षां कृ, बुध् (c. 4. बुध्यते, बोद्धुं), विमृश् (c. 6. -मृशति -म्रष्टुं), परामर्शं कृ, विवेचनं कृ.

MARKED, *p. p.* चिह्नितः -ता -तं, अङ्कितः -ता -तं, लक्षितः -ता -तं, उपलक्षितः -ता -तं, लाञ्छितः -ता -तं, कृतलक्षणः -णा -णं, कृताङ्कः -ङ्का -ङ्कं, कृतलाञ्छनः -ना -नं, मुद्रितः -ता -तं, मुद्राङ्कितः -ता -तं.—(Defined) परिच्छिन्नः -न्ना -न्नं, निर्दिष्टः -ष्टा -ष्टं, लक्षितः -ता -तं.

MARKER, *s.* चिह्नकर्त्ता *m.* (र्त्तृ), अङ्कनकृत् *m.*, अङ्कयिता *m.* (तृ), लक्षयिता *m.*

MARKET, *s.* पण्यवीथी -थिका, पण्यशाला, विक्रयशाला, विक्रयस्थानं, क्रयविक्रयस्थानं, पण्यस्थानं, आपणः, हट्टः, विपणिः *m.* -णी *f.*, निगमः, चघट्टः, क्रयारोहः, पुरतटी, निषद्या, निर्वेटं, पण्याजिरः *m.*, पण्याजीर्णवर्त्तं; 'a free market,' अचक्रमं.—(Sale) विक्रयः, विपणः.

To MARKET, *v. n.* क्रयविक्रयं कृ, पण् (c. 1. पणते -णितुं, पणायति -यितुं), पणायां कृ.

MARKET-DAY, *s.* क्रयविक्रयदिवसः, हट्टदिवसः, हट्टवारः.

MARKET-PLACE, *s.* चत्वरं, चतुष्पथं, क्रयविक्रयचत्वरं, पणायाचत्वरं, पणाया, पण्यायास्थानं, विपणिः -णी *m. f.* *See* MARKET.

MARKET-RATE, MARKET-PRICE, *s.* आपणिकः, पण्यभावः, पण्यमूल्यं, अर्घबलाबलं.

MARKET-TOWN, *s.* ग्राममुखः, मुख्यग्रामः, नगरमुखः, मुख्यनगरं -री, कर्व्वटः -टं.

MARKETABLE, *a.* विक्रेयः -या -यं, विक्रयणीयः -या -यं, पण्यः -ण्या -ण्यं, पणितव्यः -व्या -व्यं, पण्यार्हः -र्हा -र्हं, क्रेयः -या -यं, क्रयविक्रययोग्यः -ग्या -ग्यं.

MARKING, *s.* अङ्कनं, मुद्राङ्कनं, चिह्नाङ्कनं, चिह्नकरणं, अङ्ककरणं, लिखनं.

MARKING-INK, *s.* दहनमसिः *f.*, दहनमसिका, दहनरसः, वस्त्राङ्कनमसिः.

MARKING-NUT, *s.* दहनं, निर्दहनं, भल्लिका, भल्लातः -तकी, भल्ली.

MARKSMAN, *s.* लक्ष्यवेधी *m.* (न्), लक्ष्यभेदी *m.*, लक्ष्यलक्षः, सुसन्धानी *m.* (न्), सुप्रयोगबाणः, सुप्रयोगविशिखः, शराभ्यासकुशलः, धनुर्विद्, आयुधविद्.

MARL, *s.* मालीख्यो मृत्तिकाविशेषः, चिक्कणमृत्तिका, पांशुः *m.*

To MARL, *v. a.* पूर्व्वोक्तमृत्तिकया लिप् (c. 6. लिम्पति, लेप्तुं).

MARMALADE, *s.* मिष्टफलं, मिष्टान्नं, शर्करादिसंसृष्टा नारङ्गत्वक् *f.* (च्).

MARMOREAN, *a.* श्वेतप्रस्तरमयः -यी -यं, पाषाणनिर्म्मितः -ता -तं.

MARMOSET, *s.* सूक्ष्मवानरः, सूक्ष्ममर्कटः, क्षुद्रप्लवङ्गः.

MAROON, *a.* (Dark red) घनरक्तः -क्ता -क्तं, घनारुणः -णा -णं, कपिशः -शा -शं.

MARPLOT, *s.* कार्य्यविघातकः, कार्य्यविनाशकः, कार्य्यबाधकः.

MARQUEE, *s.* पटमण्डपः, पटवासः, बृहत्पटवेश्म *n.* (न्), वस्त्रगृहं.

MARQUESS, *s.* उपाग्रणीः *m.*, उपनायकः, उपाधिपः, कुलीनपदमध्याद् द्वितीयपदस्थः, द्वितीयकुलीनपदभाक् *m.* (ज्).

MARQUISATE, *s.* पूर्व्वोक्तकुलीनजनस्य अधिकारः, उपाधिपत्यं.

MARRED, *p. p.* दूषितः -ता -तं, विहतः -ता -तं, व्याहतः -ता -तं, नाशितः -ता -तं, विनाशितः -ता -तं, क्षतः -ता -तं, विक्षतः -ता -तं.

MARRER, *s.* दूषकः, दूषयिता *m.* (तृ), नाशकः, विनाशकः, विघातकः.

MARRIAGE, *s.* विवाहः, उद्वाहः -हनं, उद्वहनं, परिणयः -यनं, पाणिग्रहः -हणं, पाणिग्राहः, पाणिपीडनं, हस्तेकरणं, दारपरिग्रहः, दारसङ्ग्रहः, दारक्रिया, दारकर्म्म *n.* (न्), दाराधिगमनं, उपयमः, उपयामः, लग्नकार्य्यं, मैथुनं, वाधुक्यं, निवेशः; 'marriage-rite,' विवाहविधिः *m.*, विवाहक्रिया, विवाहसंस्कारः; 'giving in marriage,' दारिकादानं, दारिकाप्रदानं; 'marriage-contract,' वाङ्निश्चयः; 'marriage-settlement,' शुल्कः -ल्कं; 'auspicious season for marriage,' लग्नतिथिः *f.*, लग्नमुहूर्त्तः -र्त्तं; 'marriage-string, or ring hung round the neck of the bride, who wears it till she becomes a widow, when it is broken,' मङ्गलसूत्रं, माङ्गल्यतन्तुः *m.*, सौभाग्यतन्तुः *m.*, कौतुकं; 'marriage gifts,' यौतकं, वैवाहिकं, पारिणाय्यं, हरणं, सुदायः -यं; 'marriage festival,' विवाहोत्सवः, विवाहमहोत्सवः; 'ablution at marriage,' मङ्गलस्नानं; 'compliments at marriage,' जम्बूलः, जम्बूलमालिका; 'second marriage,' द्वितीयविवाहः, द्वितीयसम्बन्धः. The following are different forms of marriage, explained in Manu, chap. iii. verses 27 et seq.: आसुरविवाहः, आर्षविवाहः, गान्धर्व्वविवाहः, दैवविवाहः, पैशाचविवाहः, प्राजापत्यविवाहः, ब्राह्मविवाहः, राक्षसविवाहः, प्रीतिविवाहः. The स्वयंवरः is a form of marriage in which a girl chooses her own husband.

MARRIAGEABLE, *a.* विवाह्यः -ह्या -ह्यं, उद्वाह्यः &c., वोढव्यः -व्या -व्यं, विवाहयोग्यः -ग्या -ग्यं, विवाहोचितः -ता -तं, विवाहोपयुक्तः -क्ता -क्तं, विवाहकालप्राप्तः -प्ता -प्तं, विवाहवयस्कः -स्का -स्कं, परिणेयः -या -यं; 'as a girl,' दृष्टरजाः *f.* (स्), सञ्जातार्त्तवा, आगतार्त्तवा, ऋतुयुक्ता, ऋतुमती, मध्यमा, मध्या, पतीयन्ती.

MARRIED, *p. p.* विवाहितः -ता -तं, उद्वाहितः -ता -तं, ऊढः -ढा -ढं, उपोढः -ढा -ढं, समूढः -ढा -ढं, कृतविवाहः -हा -हं, जातविवाहः -हा -हं, कृतोद्वाहः -हा -हं, कृतदारपरिग्रहः -हा -हं, परिणीतः -ता -तं, कृतोपयमः -मा -मं, जातोपयमः -मा -मं, निर्विष्टः -ष्टा -ष्टं, प्रत्तः -त्ता -त्तं; 'a married man,' सभार्य्यः, सपत्नीकः, स्त्रीमान् *m.* (त्), कृतदारः, सदारः, कृतदारपरिग्रहः, कुटुम्बी *m.* (न्), सकुटुम्बः, भार्य्योढः; 'a married woman,' सभर्तृका, सपतिका, पतिवत्नी, सधवा, सुवासिनी; 'newly married woman,' नववधूः *f.*, नववरिका; 'twice-married woman,' पुनर्भूः *f.*, दिधिषूः *f.*, दिधीषूः *f.*, दिधिषुः *f.*; 'one who is married before his elder brother,' परिवेत्ता *m.* (त्तृ).

MARROW, *s.* मज्जा, वपा, वसा, मेदस् *n.*, मेदः, मज्जा *m.* (न्), मज्जनं, सारः, अस्थिसारः, देहसारः, बीजं, स्निग्धा, वपाकृत् *m.*, अस्थिकृत्, अस्थिजं, अस्थिजः, हड्डुजं, शुक्रकरः, तेजस् *n.*, मधुरं, जीवनं, मणिच्छिद्रा. —(Pith, essence) सारः, गर्भः, सारता, श्रेष्ठांशः.

MARROW-BONE, *s.* मज्जापूर्णम् अस्थि, मेदोयुक्तम् अस्थि.

MARROWLESS, *a.* मज्जाहीनः -ना -नं, मेदोहीनः -ना -नं, वपाशून्यः -न्या -न्यं, गतसारः -रा -रं, असारः -रा -रं, निःसारः -रा -रं.

MARROWY, *a.* मज्जावान् -वती -वत् (त्), सारवान् &c., मेदस्वी -स्विनी -स्वि (न्).

To MARRY, *v. a.* (Unite a man and woman in wedlock) विवाहसंस्कारेण स्त्रीपुरुषौ संयुज् (c. 7. -युनक्ति -योक्तुं, c. 10. -योजयति -यितुं) or सम्बन्ध् (c. 9. -बध्नाति -बन्द्धुं) or विवाहसंयुक्तौ कृ, विवाहसंस्कारं कृ. —(Take for wife) विवह् (c. 1. -वहति -ते -वोढुं), उद्वह्, समुद्वह्, उदावह्, परिणी (c. 1. -णयति -णेतुं), उपयम् (c. 1. -यच्छते -ति -यमते -यन्तुं), पाणिं ग्रह् (c. 9. गृह्णाति, ग्रहीतुं), कन्यां परिग्रह् or प्रतिग्रह् or सङ्ग्रह्, दारपरिग्रहं कृ, दारसङ्ग्रहं कृ, दाराधिगमनं कृ, कन्यापरिणयं कृ, भार्य्यां विद् (c. 6. विन्दते -ति, वेत्तुं) or अनुविद्; 'he should marry a wife,' कन्यां विवहेत् or उपयच्छेत, कन्यायाः पाणिं गृह्णातु. —(Take for husband) पतिं विद् or वृ (c. 5. वृणोति, वरितुं -रीतुं), भर्त्रा संयुज् in pass. (-युज्यते), पतिवरणं कृ, भर्तृवरणं कृ. —(Dispose of in marriage) विवाहार्थं कन्यां दा or प्रदा.

To MARRY, *v. n.* भर्त्रा or भार्य्यया संयुज् in pass. (-युज्यते) or युज्, विवाहं कृ, उद्वाहं कृ, परिणयं कृ, पाणिग्रहणं कृ, दारपरिग्रहं कृ, उपयमं कृ.

MARS, *s.* (The planet, fabled as the son of the earth) मङ्गलः, मङ्गलग्रहः, भौमः, अङ्गारकः, कुजः, भूमिजः, भूसुतः, महीसुतः, क्षितिसुतः, आवनेयः, धरात्मजः, धरासुतः, धरापुत्रः, नवदीधितिः *m.*, आषाढभवः, शिवघर्म्मजः, गगणोल्मुकः, खोल्मुकः, लोहितः -तकः, लोहिताङ्गः, रक्ताङ्गः, रुधिरः, आरः, वक्रः, ऋणान्तकः, चरः, क्रूरः. (In mythology, the god of war). *See* KÁRTIKEYA.

MARSH, *s.* कच्छः, कच्छभूः *f.*, कच्छभूमिः *f.*, अनूपभूः *f.*, अनूपभूमिः *f.*, सजलभूमिः *f.*, जलाढ्यभूः *f.*, आर्द्रभूमिः *f.*, पङ्कः.

To MARSHAL, *v. a.* विन्यस् (c. 4. -अस्यति -असितुं), व्यूह् (c. 1. -ऊहते -हितुं), विरच् (c. 10. -रचयति -यितुं), रच्, क्रमेण स्था in caus. (स्थापयति -यितुं), व्यवस्था, विधा (c. 3. -दधाति -धातुं), संविधा, प्रतिविधा.

MARSHAL, MARSHALLER, *s.* विधाता *m.* (तृ), संविधाता *m.*, व्यवस्थापकः, विरचकः, व्यूहरचकः, विन्यासकृत् *m.*

MARSHY, *a.* अनूपः -पा -पं, आनूपः -पी -पं, कच्छः -च्छा -च्छं, जलाढ्यः -ढ्या -ढ्यं, जलप्रचुरः -रा -रं, जलमयः -यी -यं, सजलः -ला -लं, जलप्रायः -या -यं, आप्यः -प्या -प्यं, आर्द्रः -र्द्रा -र्द्रं.

MART, *s.* विक्रयस्थानं, क्रयविक्रयस्थानं, पण्यस्थानं, आपणः, विपणिः *m.* -णी *f.*, निगमः, निषद्या, पण्यवीथी -थिका, अवट्टः.

MARTIAL, *a.* (Relating to war) युद्धसम्बन्धी -न्धिनी -न्धि (न्), रणसम्बन्धी &c., युद्धविषयः -या -यं, रणविषयकः -का -कं, साङ्ग्रामिकः -की -कं, सामरिकः -की -कं, साम्परायिकः -की -कं. —(Suited to war) रणयोग्यः -ग्या -ग्यं, युद्धोपयुक्तः -क्ता -क्तं, रणोपयोगी -गिनी &c. —(Given to war) रणप्रियः -या -यं, रणासक्तः -क्ता -क्तं, रणवीरः -रा -रं, रणकामी -मिनी &c.; 'martial music,' रणवाद्यं.

MARTINET, *a.* उग्रदण्डः, उग्रशासनः, तीक्ष्णदण्डः, दण्डबुद्धिः *m.*, उद्यतदण्डः, तीक्ष्णशासनः, निष्ठुरबुद्धिः *m.*, निष्ठुरः.

MARTINGAL, MARTINGALE, *s.* तलिका, तलसारकः, अधोबन्धनं.

MARTYR, *s.* साक्षी *m.* (न्), स्वधर्म्मार्थं प्राणत्यागी *m.* (न्) or देहत्यागी *m.* or जीवितत्यागी *m.*, स्वमतार्थं त्यक्तप्राणः or अर्पितप्राणः, स्वधर्म्मप्रमाणार्थं न्यस्तप्राणः or न्यस्तदेहः or न्यस्तजीवितः or जीवोत्सर्गी *m.* or साक्षी *m.*

To MARTYR, *v. a.* स्वधर्म्मार्थं हन् (c. 2. हन्ति -न्तुं or caus. घातयति -यितुं).

MARTYRDOM, *s.* स्वधर्म्मार्थं प्राणत्यागः or जीवितत्यागः, स्वमतार्थं जीवोत्सर्गः or प्राणोत्सर्गः, स्वधर्म्मप्रमाणार्थं देहन्यासः or प्राणन्यासः or प्राणार्पणं.

MARTYRED, *p. p.* स्वधर्म्मार्थं, हतः -ता -तं or व्यापादितः -ता -तं, स्वधर्म्मप्रमाणार्थं हतजीवितः -ता -तं or नष्टप्राणः -णा -णं.

Martyrology, *s.* साक्षिचरित्रशास्त्रं, सधर्म्मार्थं प्राणत्यागिनां चरित्रविवरणं or चरित्रलिखनं.

Marvel, *s.* कौतुकं, अद्भुतं, अद्भुतवस्तु *n.*, आश्चर्य्यवस्तु *n.*, आश्चर्य्यं, चमत्कारः, चित्रवस्तु *n.*, चित्रं, विस्मयजनकवस्तु, उत्पातः, उपसर्गः.

To marvel, *v. n.* विस्मितः -ता -तं भू, विस्मयान्वितः -ता -तं भू, सविस्मयः -या -यं भू, विस्मि (c. 1. -स्मयते -स्मेतुं) with instr. loc. or acc. c., साश्चर्य्यः -र्य्या -र्य्यं भू, चमत्कृतः -ता -तं भू, आश्चर्य्यं ज्ञा (c. 9. जानाति, ज्ञातुं) or मन् (c. 4. मन्यते, मन्तुं).

Marvellous, *a.* आश्चर्य्यः -र्य्या -र्य्यं, अद्भुतः -ता -तं, विस्मयजनकः -का -कं, विस्मयोत्पादकः -का -कं, आश्चर्य्यकरः -रा -रं, आश्चर्य्यकारकः -का -कं, आश्चर्य्यजनकः -का -कं, चमत्कारजनकः -का -कं, चित्रः -त्रा -त्रं, विचित्रः -त्रा -त्रं, ताप्तः -ता -तं; 'a marvellous tale,' चित्रोक्तिः *f.*; 'a marvellous action,' अद्भुतकर्म्म *n.* (न्), आश्चर्य्यकर्म्म.

Marvellously, *adv.* अद्भुतं, अद्भुतप्रकारेण, विचित्रं, आश्चर्य्यप्रकारेण, यथा विस्मयो जायते तथा.

Marvellousness, *s.* अद्भुतता -त्वं, आश्चर्य्यत्वं, विचित्रता, साश्चर्य्यत्वं, वैचित्र्यं, विस्मयजनकता, अपूर्व्वत्वं.

Marwar, *s.* (The province) मरुः *m.*, मरुभूः *f.*—(The inhabitants) मरवः *m. pl.*, मरुभुवः *m. pl.*

Masculine, *a.* पौरुषः -षी -षं, पौरुषेयः -यी -यं, पुरुषजातीयः -या -यं, पुंजातीयः -या -यं, पुं in comp., पुरुष in comp., अक्लीवः -वा -वं.—(Having the qualities of a man, resembling a man) पुरुषस्वभावः -वा -वं, पुरुषवृत्तिः -त्तिः -त्ति, पुरुषशीलः -ला -लं, पुरुषधर्म्मकः -का -कं, पुरुषप्रकृतिः -तिः -ति, पुम्प्रकृतिः -तिः -ति; 'the masculine gender,' पुंलिङ्गं, पुमान् *m.* (पुंस्), पुरुषः; 'a masculine woman,' वृषभी.

Masculinely, *adv.* पुरुषवत्, नरवत्, सपौरुषं, पौरुषेण, पुंवत्.

Masculineness, *s.* पुंस्त्वं, पुरुषत्वं -ता, पौरुषं, पौरुषता, पुरुषशीलता, पुरुषस्वभावः, पुरुषप्रकृतिः *f.*

Mash, *s.* उदपेषः -षणं, उदकपेषः, सम्पेषः -षणं, नानाद्रव्यसम्पेषः, नानाद्रव्यमिश्रणं, जलमिश्रितं नानासम्पिष्टद्रव्यं, नानासम्मिश्रद्रव्यपिण्डः.

To mash, *v. a.* सम्पिष् (c. 7. -पिनष्टि -पेष्टुं), सम्मृद् (c. 9. -मृद्नाति -मर्द्दितुं), सम्पेषणं कृ, सम्मर्द्दनं कृ, चूर्ण् (c. 10. चूर्णयति -यितुं), सञ्चूर्ण्, क्षुद् (c. 7. क्षुणत्ति, क्षोत्तुं), सम्पेषणपूर्व्वं पिण्डीकृ.

Mashed, *p. p.* सम्पिष्टः -ष्टा -ष्टं, सम्मर्द्दितः -ता -तं, सञ्चूर्णितः -ता -तं, क्षुण्णः -ण्णा -ण्णं, सम्पेषणानन्तरं पिण्डीभूतः -ता -तं.

Mask, *s.* (Cover for the face) कृत्रिममुखं, छद्ममुखं, छद्मास्यं, कपटमुखं, उपमुखं.—(Pretext, subterfuge) छद्म *n.* (न्), कपटः -टं, व्यपदेशः, अपदेशः, व्याजः, छलं, कूटं.—(Masquerade) छद्मवेशः, कपटवेशः, कृत्रिमवेशः, छद्मवेशधारणं, विडम्बनं.

To mask, *v. a.* (Disguise with a mask) कृत्रिममुखेन छद् (c. 10. छादयति -यितुं) or गुह् (c. 1. गूहति -हितुं), मुखगोपनं कृ.—(Conceal) छद्, आच्छद्, गुप् (c. 1. गोपायति, गोप्तुं), गोपनं कृ, अपवृ (c. 10. -वारयति -यितुं).

To mask, *v. n.* विडम्बनं कृ, छद्मवेशी -शिनी -शि भू, कपटवेशी &c. भू.

Masked, *p. p.* (Having the face covered) गुप्तमुखः -खी -खं, छद्ममुखी -खिनी -खि (न्), कृत्रिममुखी &c.—(Disguised) छद्मवेशी -शिनी &c., कपटवेशी &c., छद्मवेशधारी -रिणी &c., कपटवेशः -शा -शं, छद्मवेशः &c., कपटरूपी -पिणी &c., विडम्बितवेशी &c., अलक्षितः -ता -तं.—(Concealed) गुप्तः -प्ता -प्तं, गोपितः -ता -तं, आच्छादितः -ता -तं.

Masker, *s.* छद्मवेशी *m.* (न्), कपटवेशी *m.*, छद्मवेशभृत्, छद्मरूपी *m.*, विडम्बितवेशः, कृत्रिमवेशधारी *m.*, विडम्बनकृत्.

Mason, *s.* लेपकः, लेपी *m.* (न्), लेपकरः, गृहनिर्म्माता *m.* (तृ), सुधाजीवी *m.* (न्), लेपजीवी *m.*, प्रलेपकः, प्रस्तरन्यासकृत्, इष्टकान्यासजीवी *m.*

Masonry, *s.* लेपकर्म्म *n.* (न्), इष्टकान्यासकर्म्म *n.*, सुधाकर्म्म *n.*, गृहनिर्म्माणं, गृहकरणं, गृहनिर्म्माणे प्रस्तरन्यासः or प्रस्तरादिविन्यासः.—(Brickwork, any thing made of stone, brick, &c.) इष्टकाकर्म्म *n.*, प्रस्तरकर्म्म *n.*, प्रस्तरनिर्म्मितं प्राकारादि.

Masquerade, *s.* छद्मवेशधारणं, वेशधारणं, छद्मवेशक्रीडा, छद्मवेशसमारम्भः, छद्मवेशः, कपटवेशिनां यात्रा, विडम्बनं, विडम्बनक्रीडा.

To masquerade, *v. n.* छद्मवेशी -शिनी -शि भू, कपटवेशी &c. भू, छद्मवेशं धृ (c. 10. धारयति -यितुं), विडम्ब् (c. 10. -डम्बयति -यितुं), विडम्बनं कृ.

Masquerader, *s.* छद्मवेशी *m.* (न्), वेशधारी *m.*, विडम्बनकर्त्ता *m.* (र्तृ). *See* Masker.

Mass, *s.* (Lump) पिण्डः -ण्डं, घनः, ओघः, घनौघः, स्थूलं, गण्डः -ण्डका; 'a mass of iron,' लोहपिण्डः.—(Heap) राशिः *m.*, सञ्चयः, निचयः, प्रचयः, समुच्चयः, चयः, चितिः *f.*, चायः, निकरः, उत्करः, ओघः, पुञ्जः, पूगः, स्तूपः, स्तोमः.—(Collection) समूहः, सङ्घः, सङ्घातः, संहतिः *f.*, समुदायः, वृन्दं, संहारः, समाहारः, समयः, निवहः; 'in masses,' सङ्घशस्.—(Gross, bulk) साकल्यं, सामग्र्यं, समुदायः; 'in the mass,' साकल्येन.

Massacre, *s.* महामारणं, महाघातः, महावधः, निषूदनं, विशसनं, निहननं, संहारः, विमर्द्दनं, निकृन्तनं, प्रमापणं, निशारणं.

To massacre, *v. a.* अतिनैष्ठुर्य्येण हन् (c. 2. हन्ति -न्तुं, c. 10. घातयति -यितुं) or निहन् or मृ (c. 10. मारयति -यितुं) or सूद् (c. 10. सूदयति -यितुं) or निसूद् or विनिसूद् or विशस् (c. 1. -शसति -सितुं) or निकृत् (c. 6. -कृन्तति -कर्त्तितुं).

Massacred, *p. p.* अतिनैष्ठुर्य्येण हतः -ता -तं or विनिहतः -ता -तं or घातितः -ता -तं or निषूदितः -ता -तं or विशसितः -ता -तं.

Massiveness, massiness, *s.* स्थूलता -त्वं, स्थौल्यं, स्थूलाकारता, वृहत्त्वं, गुरुत्वं -ता, सभारता -त्वं, भारिता -त्वं, भारवत्त्वं, पिण्डाकारता, महत्त्वं, स्थानता.

Massive, massy, *a.* स्थूलः -ला -लं, स्थूलाकारः -रा -रं, स्थूलरूपः -पा -पं, भारी -रिणी -रि (न्), भारवान् -वती -वत् (त्), सभारः -रा -रं, गुरुः -र्व्वी -रु, पिण्डितः -ता -तं, पिण्डाकारः -रा -रं, वृहन् -हती -हत् (त्), वृहत्परिमाणः -णा -णं, स्थूलपरिमाणः -णा -णं, स्थानः -ना -नं.

Mast, *s.* (Of a ship) कूपकः, कूपः, गुणवृक्षकः, गुणवृक्षः, नौकूपकः.

Mast-head, *s.* गुणवृक्षकाग्रं, गुणवृक्षाग्रं, कूपकाग्रं.

Master, *s.* (One who rules or has servants under him) स्वामी *m.* (न्), प्रभुः *m.*, पतिः *m.*, ईश्वरः, ईशः, नाथः, अधिपतिः *m.*, अधिपः, अधिभूः *m.*, ईशिता *m.* (तृ), नायकः, भर्त्ता *m.* (र्तृ), आर्य्यः, भरण्डः, भरण्युः *m.*, सेव्यः; 'master of a family,' कुलपतिः *m.*, कुटुम्बी *m.* (न्), कौटुम्बिकः; 'serving two masters,' उभयवेतनः -ना -नं, उभयस्वामिकः -का -कं; 'one's own master,' स्वाधीनः -ना -नं, स्वतन्त्रः -न्त्रा -न्त्रं.—(Owner) अधिकारी *m.* (न्), स्वामी *m.*, ईश्वरः, पतिः *m.*, प्रभुः *m.*, परिवृढः.—(Superintendent, director) अध्यक्षः, अधिष्ठाता *m.* (तृ), अधिकृतः, अधिकारी *m.*, अधिपतिः *m.*, अधिपः, अधीशः, नायकः, नेता *m.* (तृ); 'master of the horse,' अश्वाध्यक्षः; 'master of the house,' गृहपतिः, भवनपतिः; 'master of the mint,' टङ्कपतिः *m.*, रूप्याध्यक्षः; 'master of the sports,' केलिसचिवः, नर्म्मसचिवः.—(Chief, head) नायकः, पतिः *m.*, अधिपतिः *m.*, अधिष्ठाता *m.* (तृ), अग्रगः, अग्रणीः *m.*, मुखरः, श्रेष्ठः, मुख्य or प्रधान in comp.—(Teacher, director of a school) अध्यापकः,

शिक्षकः, शिक्षागुरुः *m.*, गुरुः *m.*, आचार्य्यः, शिक्षादाता *m.* (तृ), विद्यादाता *m.*, विद्यागुरुः *m.*, आर्य्यः, उपाध्यायः, उपदेशकः, शिक्षाकरः.—(Well skilled in) निपुणः, कुशलः, सम्पन्नः, व्युत्पन्नः, पण्डितः, कृती *m.* (न्), पारगतः.—(Of a ship) नौकाधिपतिः *m.*, नौपतिः *m.*

To MASTER, *v. a.* (Subdue) वशीकृ, स्ववशीकृ, स्वाधीनीकृ, जि (c. 1. जयति -ते, जेतुं), विजि, दम् (c. 10. दमयति -यितुं), आयत्तीकृ, पराभू, अभिभू, प्रभू.—(Make one's self master of a subject) वशीकृ, पारं गम् (c. 1. गच्छति, गन्तुं), सर्व्वतत्त्वानि ज्ञा (c. 9. जानाति, ज्ञातुं); 'you must master the Sanskrit language,' भवद्भिः संस्कृतव्याख्यानि वशीकर्त्तव्यानि.

MASTER-BUILDER, *s.* प्रधानस्थपतिः *m.*, मुख्यस्थपतिः *m.*

MASTERED, *p. p.* वशीकृतः -ता -तं, स्ववशीभूतः -ता -तं, स्वहस्तगतः -ता -तं.

MASTER-KEY, *s.* प्रधानोद्घाटकयन्त्रं, अग्रकुञ्चिका, मुख्योद्घाटनं.

MASTERLY, *a.* अत्युत्तमः -मा -मं, अत्युत्कृष्टः -ष्टा -ष्टं, अनुपमः -मा -मं, अनुपमेयः -या -यं, निरुपमः -मा -मं, सर्व्वोत्तमः -मा -मं, सर्व्वोत्कृष्टः -ष्टा -ष्टं, सर्व्वजित् *m.f.n.*, सर्व्वश्रेष्ठः -ष्ठा -ष्ठं, असामान्यः -न्या -न्यं, अतुलनीयः -या -यं, सुनिपुणः -णा -णं, अतिकुशलः -ला -लं.

MASTERLY, *adv.* परमयुक्त्या, सुनिपुणवत्, अतिकुशलवत्, अत्युत्तमं, अत्युत्कृष्टं.

MASTERPIECE, *s.* अत्युत्तमकर्म्म *n.* (न्), अनुपमकर्म्म *n.*, अत्युत्कृष्टकर्म्म, उत्तमकर्म्म *n.*, परमकर्म्म *n.*, प्रधानकर्म्म *n.*, सर्व्वोत्कृष्टकर्म्म *n.*

MASTERSHIP, *s.* प्रभुत्वं -ता, स्वाम्यं, स्वामित्वं, आधिपत्यं, ऐश्वर्य्यं, अधिकारित्वं, भर्त्तृत्वं, प्रधानत्वं, प्राधान्यं, श्रेष्ठता, श्रैष्ठ्यं.

MASTER-STROKE, *s.* उत्तमकर्म्म *n.* (न्), परमकर्म्म *n.*, अत्युत्तमक्रिया.

MASTERY, *s.* (Dominion) ऐश्वर्य्यं, आधिपत्यं, प्रभुत्वं, ईशत्वं, स्वामित्वं, स्वाम्यं, अधिकारः, भर्त्तृता.—(Ownership) स्वाम्यं, अधिकारित्वं -ता, प्रभुता, स्वत्वं.—(Pre-eminence) श्रेष्ठत्वं, श्रैष्ठ्यं, प्रधानत्वं, प्राधान्यं, उत्कर्षः, उत्कृष्टता, मुख्यता, प्रकृष्टता, प्रभुत्वं, आधिक्यं, परमपदं.—(Victory) विजयः.—(Great skill) अतिकौशल्यं, अतिनैपुण्यं, अतिपाटवं, परमयुक्तिः *f.*, परमोत्कर्षः; 'to have the mastery,' प्रभू, अभिभू.

MASTICABLE, *a.* चर्व्यः -र्व्या -र्व्यं, चर्वणीयः -या -यं, चर्वितव्यः -व्या -व्यं.

To MASTICATE, *v. a.* चर्व् (c. 1. चर्वति -र्वितुं, c. 10. चर्वयति -यितुं), चर्वणं कृ, दन्तैः पिष् (c. 7. पिनष्टि, पेष्टुं), विदंश् (c. 1. -दशति -दंष्टुं).

MASTICATED, *p. p.* चर्वितः -ता -तं, कृतचर्वणः -णा -णं, दन्तपिष्टः -ष्टा -ष्टं.

MASTICATION, *s.* चर्वणं, चर्वणक्रिया, चर्वणकर्म्म *n.* (न्), दन्तपेषणं, पेषणं.

MASTICATORY, *a.* चर्वणसाधकः -का -कं, चर्वणोपयोगी -गिनी -गि (न्).

MASTICATORY, *s.* (Substance to be chewed) चर्वणौषधं, चर्व्यद्रव्यं, चर्व्यं.

MASTICH, MASTIC, *s.* मास्तिचाख्यो वृक्षनिर्यासः.—(Cement) लेपविशेषः.

MASTIFF, *s.* वृहत्कुक्कुरः, अतिसाहसशीलः कुक्कुरभेदः.

MASTLESS, *a.* कूपकहीनः -ना -नं, अकूपकः -का -कं, हृतकूपकः -का -कं.

MAT, *s.* कटः, किलिञ्जकः, पादपाशी, आस्तरणं, तृणपूली, तलाची, वटरः, वानं, चचा.

To MAT, *v. a.* (Lay with mats) कटैर् आस्तृ (c. 9. -स्तृणाति -स्तरितुं -रीतुं), कटान् विस्तृ, कटास्तरणं कृ.—(Interweave, entangle) संश्लिष् (c. 10. -श्लेषयति -यितुं), आश्लिष्, ग्रन्थ् (c. 9. ग्रथ्नाति, c. 1. ग्रन्थति -न्थितुं); 'to mat the hair,' जटिलीकृ.

MATCH, *s.* (One who is equal to another in strength) तुल्यबलः -ला, तुल्यशक्तिः *m.f.*, समानबलः -ला, तुल्यविक्रमः -मा; 'to be a match for,' अलङ्कृ.—(One that tallies with another) यमः -मा -मं, यमकः -का -कं, यमलः -ला -लं, युग्मकः, समः -मा, समानः -ना, समकक्षः -क्षा, समानकक्षः -क्षा, समतोलः -ला.—(Union by marriage) विवाहसम्बन्धः, सम्बन्धः, विवाहः, प्रेमसम्बन्धः; 'scheming to effect a match,' विवाहघटनं -ना, सन्दर्भः.—(Contest) युद्धं, कलहः, कलिः *m.*; 'a match of cocks, &c.,' प्राणिद्यूतं, समाह्वयः, आह्वयः; 'boxing match,' मल्लयात्रा, माल्लवी, मल्लयुद्धं.—(For lighting fires) शलाका, ज्वलनशलाका, ज्वलशलाका, ज्वलतृणं, ज्वलनतृणं, अरणिः -णी *m. f.*

To MATCH, *v. a.* (Equal, make equal) समीकृ, समानीकृ, सदृशीकृ, समान (nom. समानयति -यितुं), उपमा (c. 2. -माति -तुं), प्रतिमा, तुल् (c. 10. तुलयति -यितुं), तुल्यीकृ.—(Show an equal) समं or तुल्यं or युग्मकं दृश् (c. 10. दर्शयति -यितुं) or निर्दिश् (c. 6. -दिशति -देष्टुं), प्रतिमां or उपमां or उपमानं or प्रतिरूपं दृश्.—(Oppose as equal in contest) प्रतियुध् in caus. (-योधयति -यितुं), तुल्यबलं or तुल्यविक्रमं कञ्चित् पुरस्कृ.—(Adapt) युज् (c. 10. योजयति -यितुं), समायुज्.—(Give in marriage) विवाहार्थं दा or प्रदा.

To MATCH, *v. n.* (Correspond, tally) युज् in pass. (युज्यते), उपयुज्, तुल्यः -ल्या -ल्यं भू, तुल्यीभू, समीभू, समानीभू, सदृशीभू, अनुरूपः -पा -पं भू or अस्, प्रतिरूपीभू, उपमितः -ता -तं भू.—(Be united in marriage) विवाहसम्बन्धं कृ, प्रेमसम्बन्धं कृ.—(Be a match for) अलङ्कृ, अलम्भू, अलन्तमः -मा -मं भू.

MATCHED, *p. p.* (Equalled, evenly matched) तुल्यः -ल्या -ल्यं, तुल्यीभूतः -ता -तं, तुल्यबलः -ला -लं, तुल्यशक्तिः -क्तिः -क्ति, तुल्यविक्रमः -मा -मं, समतोलः -ला -लं, समानतोलः -ला -लं, समानकक्षः -क्षा -क्षं, सप्रतिमः -मा -मं, सप्रतिरूपः -पा -पं, उपमितः -ता -तं.—(Married) कृतविवाहः -हा -हं, कृतोपयमः -मा -मं.

MATCHLESS, *a.* अतुल्यः -ल्या -ल्यं, अनुपमः -मा -मं, निरुपमः -मा -मं, अप्रतिमः -मा -मं, अतुलनीयः -या -यं, अतुलः -ला -लं, निस्तुलः -ला -लं, अनुपमेयः -या -यं, अप्रतिमेयः -या -यं, अप्रतिरूपः -पा -पं, अगम्यरूपः -पा -पं, अद्वितीयः -या -यं, असदृशः -शी -शं, सर्व्वोत्तमः -मा -मं, सर्व्वश्रेष्ठः -ष्ठा -ष्ठं, सर्व्वजित् *m. f. n.*, विषमः -मा -मं, अपूर्व्वः -र्व्वा -र्व्वं.

MATCHLESSLY, *adv.* अतुल्यं, अनुपमेयं, अप्रतिमेयं, निरुपमं, सर्व्वश्रेष्ठं.

MATCHLESSNESS, *s.* अतुल्यता, अनुपमेयता, अप्रतिमेयता, अनुपमता, अनौपम्यं.

MATCHLOCK, *s.* अन्तरग्निबलेन लोहगुलिकाप्रक्षेपणी सुषिरनाडी.

MATCH-MAKER, *s.* (Maker of matches for burning) शलाकाकारी *m.* (न्), ज्वलशलाकाकृत् *m.*—(Contriver of marriages) घटकः, विवाहघटकः, प्रेमघटकः, प्रेमविषये मध्यस्थः.

MATE, *s.* (Companion, associate) सहायः, सहचरः -री *f.*, सहवर्त्ती *m.* -र्त्तिनी *f.*, सहवासी *m.* -सिनी, सखा *m.* -खी *f.*, सहभावी *m.* -विनी *f.*, सङ्गी *m.* -ङ्गिनी *f.*, मित्रं.—(Husband) भर्त्ता *m.* (र्त्तृ), स्वामी *m.* (न्), पतिः *m.*—(Wife) स्त्री, वधूः *f.*, पत्नी, भार्य्या, जाया, वल्लभा, प्रिया, दयिता, प्रियतमा.—(The male or female of animals which associate for propagation) सहचरः *m.* -री *f.* In poetry the above words for husband and wife are used in this sense: 'the elephant's mate,' करिणी *f.*, हस्तिनी *f.*—(An assistant) सहकारी *m.* -रिणी *f.* (न्), सहायः; 'in a ship,' नौपतिसहायः.

To MATE, *v. a.* *See* *To* MATCH, *v. a.*

MATER-FAMILIAS, *s.* कुटुम्बिनी *f.*, गृहिणी, गेहिनी, स्वामिनी, कौटुम्बिकी.

MATERIAL, *a.* (Consisting of matter, not spiritual) भौतिकः -की -कं, आधिभौतिकः -की -कं, भूतात्मकः -का -कं, भूतमयः -यी -यं, पाञ्चभौतिकः -की -कं, पञ्चभूतात्मकः -का -कं, अनात्मीयः -या -यं, अनात्मिकः -की -कं, अपारमार्थिकः -की -कं, मूर्त्तिमान् -मती -मत् (त्), मूर्त्तः -र्त्ता -र्त्तं, द्रव्यमयः -यी -यं, विषयात्मकः -का -कं, प्राकृतिकः -की -कं,

प्राकृतः -ती -तं, घनः -ना -नं; 'the material world,' भूतसृष्टिः *f.*, भूतसर्गः, भूतसंसारः; 'material universe,' ब्रह्माण्डः -ण्डं; 'material body,' स्थूलशरीरं.—(Substantial) वास्तविकः -की -कं, वास्तवः -वी -वं, सारवान् -वती &c., मूर्त्तिमान् &c., घनः -ना -नं.—(Important) गुरुः -र्वी -रु, गुर्वर्थः -र्था -र्थं, गुरुप्रभावः -वा -वं, परमार्थः -र्था -र्थं, अलघुः -घुः -घु, मुख्यः -ख्या -ख्यं, आवश्यकः -की -कं, प्रधान in comp.; 'material cause,' उपादानं, उपादानकारणं, समवायिकारणं.

MATERIAL, *s.* साधनं, उपकरणं, द्रव्यं, साधनद्रव्यं, पदार्थः, वस्तु *n.*, मूर्त्तिः *f.*, सारः, घनः, मात्रा; 'materials, collectively,' साधनं -नानि *n. pl.*, सामग्र्यं -ग्री, द्रव्यसामग्र्यं, सम्भारः, द्रव्यसम्भारः, उपकरणसम्भारः, सज्जा, परिच्छदः; 'writing-materials,' लेखसाधनं, लिपिसज्जा; 'the material of cloth,' वस्त्रयोनिः *f.*

MATERIALISM, *s.* देहात्मवादः, अनात्मवादः, अनात्ममतं, लोकायतं, चार्वाकमतं.

MATERIALIST, *s.* देहात्मवादी *m.* (न्), अनात्मवादी *m.*, लौकायतिकः, लोकायतिकः, विषयी *m.* (न्), विषयायी *m.* (न्), चार्वाकमतावलम्बी *m.* (न्), चार्वाकमतधारी *m.*

MATERIALITY, *s.* भौतिकत्वं, आधिभौतिकत्वं, मूर्त्तिमत्त्वं, अनात्मिकत्वं.

MATERIALLY, *adv.* वस्तुतस्, अर्थतस्, सारतस्, प्रकृतितस्, पदार्थतस्, तत्त्वतस्, अवश्यं, विशेषतस्.

MATERIALNESS, *s.* *See* MATERIALITY. (Importance) गौरवं, गुरुत्वं.

MATERNAL, *a.* मातृकः -की -कं, मातृसम्बन्धी -न्धिनी -न्धि (न्), मातृयोग्यः -ग्या -ग्यं, मातृधर्म्मकः -का -कं; 'maternal affection,' अपत्यस्नेहः, वात्सल्यं; 'maternal duty,' मातृधर्म्मः.

MATERNITY, *s.* मातृत्वं -ता, मातृभावः, मातृकत्वं, मातृधर्म्मः, जननीत्वं.

MATHEMATIC, MATHEMATICAL, *a.* (Relating to mathematics) गणितसम्बन्धी -न्धिनी -न्धि (न्), गणितविषयः -या -यं, गणितविद्यासम्बन्धी &c., संख्यापरिमाणविद्यासम्बन्धी &c., रेखावीजादिगणितविषयः -या -यं.—(According to the principles of mathematics) गणितशास्त्रानुसारी -रिणी &c., गणितानुरूपः -पा -पं, गणितविद्यानुसारी &c.

MATHEMATICALLY, *adv.* गणितविद्यानुसारेण, गणितानुरूपेण, गणितशास्त्रवत्.

MATHEMATICIAN, *s.* गणितविद्याज्ञः, संख्यापरिमाणविद्याज्ञः, रेखावीजादिगणितविद् *m.*, गणितशास्त्रज्ञः, क्षेत्रपरिमापकविद्यावान् *m.* (त्), गणनाविद्याज्ञः, गणितज्ञः.

MATHEMATICS, *s. pl.* गणितं, गणितविद्या, संख्यापरिमाणविद्या, गणनाविद्या, रेखावीजादिगणितं, रेखावीजादिगणितविद्या, पाटीवीजादिगणितविद्या, रेखादिगणितं, वीजादिगणितं, गणितशास्त्रं, वीजादिगणितशास्त्रं, क्षेत्रादिपरिमाणविद्या, मानविद्या.

MATIN, *a.* (Relating to the morning) प्रातःकालिकः -की -कं, प्रातःकालीनः -ना -नं, औषिकः -की -कं, प्रगेतनः -नी -नं, वैयुष्टः -ष्टी -ष्टं.

MATINS, *s. pl.* प्रातःकृत्यं, प्रातर्भजनं, प्रातःस्मरणं, प्रातःपूजा.

MATRICE, *s.* (Womb) गर्भाशयः, योनिः *m.f.*, गर्भकोशः, जरायुः *m.*—(Of a type) मुद्राक्षरसंस्कारः, मुद्राक्षरगर्भः, मुद्राक्षराकारः.

MATRICIDE, *s.* (The act) मातृहत्या, मातृवधः, मातृघातः, जननीवधः.—(The killer) मातृहन्ता *m.* (न्), मातृहा *m.* (न्), मातृघातुकः, मातृघातकः, मातृघाती *m.* (न्), मातृघ्नः.

To MATRICULATE, *v. a.* संस्कारपूर्व्वं or नामाभिलिखनपूर्व्वं विद्यालयं प्रविश् (c. 10. -वेशयति -यितुं).

MATRICULATED, *p. p.* संस्कारपूर्व्वं विद्यालयप्रवेशितः -ता -तं.

MATRICULATION, *s.* संस्कारपूर्व्वं or नामाभिलेखनपूर्व्वं विद्यालयप्रवेशनं.

MATRIMONIAL, *a.* वैवाहिकः -की -कं, उद्वाहिकः -का -कं, औद्वाहिकः -की -कं, उद्वाही -हिनी -हि (न्), विवाही &c., विवाहसम्बन्धी -न्धिनी &c., पाणिग्रहणिकः -की -कं.

MATRIMONIALLY, *adv.* विवाहनियमानुसारेण, विवाहरीत्यनुरूपेण, विवाहविधिवत्.

MATRIMONY, *s.* विवाहः, उद्वाहः, परिणयः, पाणिग्रहः -हणं, पाणिग्राहः, उपयमः, उपयामः, विवाहावस्था, विवाहितावस्था.

MATRIX, *s.* गर्भाशयः, गर्भकोशः, योनिः *m.f.* *See* MATRICE.

MATRON, *s.* कुटुम्बिनी, गृहिणी, गेहिनी, कौटुम्बिकी, जननी, मध्यमवयस्का, पुत्रवती, प्रजावती, पुत्रिणी, सुतिनी, पतिपुत्रवती, प्रौढा, प्रौढस्त्री, वीरा, पुरन्ध्री -न्ध्रिः *f.*, त्रयी, विजाता.

MATRONLY, *a.* कुटुम्बिनीयोग्यः -ग्या -ग्यं, पुरन्ध्रियोग्यः &c., गृहिणीयोग्यः &c., पुत्रिणीयोग्यः &c., गम्भीरा, धीरा, मध्यमवयस्का.

MATTED, *p. p.* or *a.* (Laid with mats) कटी -टिनी -टि (न्), कटास्तीर्णः -र्णा -र्णं; 'matted hair,' जटा, सटा, जटिः, जुटकं, जूटः; 'having matted hair,' जटी -टिनी &c., जटिलः -ला -लं, जटावान् -वती -वत् (त्).

MATTER, *s.* (Body, substance, not spirit, that which is visible) मूर्त्तिः *f.*, वस्तु *n.*, द्रव्यं, अनात्मद्रव्यं, अनात्मा, अनात्मीयवस्तु *n.*, अनात्मिकवस्तु *n.*, भूतात्मकवस्तु *n.*, पाञ्चभौतिकवस्तु *n.*, मूर्त्तिमद्वस्तु *n.*, साकारवस्तु *n.*, घनवस्तु *n.*, घनद्रव्यं, घनः, दृश्यस्पृश्यवस्तु *n.*, सारः, विषयः, शरीरं.—(Cause of the material world or substratum of the universe) प्रकृतिः *f.*, प्रधानं, माया.—(Material cause, materials, that of which any thing is composed) साधनं, साधनवस्तु *n.*, साधनभूतवस्तु, प्रकृतिः *f.*, सारः, उपकरणं, कारणं, उपादानं, उपादानकारणं.—(Thing) द्रव्यं, वस्तु *n.*, अर्थः, पदार्थः.—(Subject) विषयः, प्रकरणं, वस्तु *n.*, अर्थः, पदं, प्रस्तावः, प्रसङ्गः, सारः, वृत्तान्तः, विधिः *m.*, आस्पदं; 'matter in hand,' प्रस्तुतं; 'an important matter,' परमार्थः, गुर्वर्थः; 'an unimportant matter,' लघ्वर्थः, लघुविषयः, अल्पविषयः, स्वल्पविषयः; 'matter of dispute,' विवादास्पदं, विवादविषयः, वादविषयः; 'what is the matter?' को वृत्तान्तः.—(Cause) प्रयोजनं, हेतुः *m.*, प्रयोगः, कारणं.—(Import, consequence) अर्थः, गौरवं, गुरुत्वं, प्रभावः; 'of no matter,' अनर्थकः -का -कं, निरर्थकः -का -कं, निष्प्रभावः -वा -वं, अगुरुः -र्वी -रु.—(Business, affair) कर्म्म *n.* (न्), कार्य्यं, विषयः, व्यापारः, अर्थः, प्रयोगः.—(Pus, purulent matter) पूयं, पूयरक्तं, पूयशोणितं, दूष्यं, मलजं, क्षतजं, प्रसितं, अवक्लेदः.

To MATTER, *v. n.* (Be of importance) expressed by अर्थ in comp. or प्रभाव in comp.; as, 'it matters not,' निरर्थकं or अनर्थकं भवति; 'to matter but little,' लघ्वर्थः -र्था -र्थं or अल्पार्थः -र्था -र्थं or लघुप्रभावः -वा -वं भू; 'to matter greatly,' गुर्वर्थः -र्था -र्थं or गुरुप्रभावः -वा -वं भू, प्रभू.—(Form purulent matter) पूय् (c. 1. पूयते -यितुं), सपूयः -या -यं भू, पूयपूर्णः -र्णा -र्णं भू, पूयगर्भः -र्भा -र्भं भू.

MATTERY, *a.* (Purulent) पूययुक्तः -क्ता -क्तं, सपूयः -या -यं, पूयपूर्णः -र्णा -र्णं, पूयगर्भः -र्भा -र्भं, पूयस्रावी -विणी -वि (न्), पूयविशिष्टः -ष्टा -ष्टं.

MATTOCK, *s.* खनित्रं, खात्रं, शैलभित्तिः *f.*, पाषाणदारणः, टङ्कः, खनहननी.

MATTRESS, *s.* तूलिका, तूला -ली, आस्तरणं, चोरपट्टी, तूलादिनिर्म्मितम् आस्तरणं, आस्तरः, प्रस्तरः, संस्तरः, स्तरिमा *m.* (न्), शयनीयं.

To MATURATE, *v. a.* पच् (c. 1. पचति, पक्तुं, c. 10. पाचयति -यितुं), पाकं कृ or जन् (c. 10. जनयति -यितुं), सपूयं -यां कृ.

To MATURATE, *v. n.* पक्वः -क्वा -क्वं भू, परिपक्वीभू, पूयपूर्णः -र्णा -र्णं भू,

सपूयः -या -यं भू, पूयगर्भः -र्भा -र्भं भू, पूय् (c. 1. पूयते -यितुं).

MATURATION, *s.* पाकः, परिपाकः, विपाकः, पचनं, पक्वता, परिपक्वता, पाचा -चिका, पचा, पूयत्वं, सपूयत्वं, पूयपूर्णता, पूयसंस्रावः, पूयस्रावः.

MATURATIVE, *a.* पाकलः -ला -लं, पाचलः -ला -लं, पाचनः -ना -नं, पचिष्णुः -ष्णुः -ष्णु, उत्पचिष्णुः &c., पक्तृः &c., पाककरः -रा -रं, पाकजनकः -का -कं, पूयजनकः -का -कं.

MATURE, *a.* पक्वः -क्वा -क्वं, सुपक्वः &c., परिपक्वः &c., पक्त्रिमः -मा -मं, विपक्त्रिमः -मा -मं, पाकिमः -मा -मं, पक्वतापन्नः -न्ना -न्नं, पक्वदशाप्राप्तः -प्ता -प्तं, पक्वदशापन्नः -न्ना -न्नं, परिणतः -ता -तं, पाकोन्मुखः -खा -खं, फलोन्मुखः -खा -खं; 'ready to drop,' विनाशोन्मुखः -खा -खं.—(Brought to perfection, complete) सम्पन्नः -न्ना -न्नं, सिद्धः -द्धा -द्धं, सम्पूर्णः -र्णा -र्णं, प्रौढः -ढा -ढं; 'mature deliberation,' सुसमीक्षा -क्षणं, सुविचारः -रणा.

To MATURE, *v. a.* पच् (c. 1. पचति, पक्तुं, c. 10. पाचयति -यितुं), पक्वं -क्वां कृ, पक्वीकृ, परिपक्वं -क्वां कृ, परिपक्वीकृ, पाकं कृ or जन् (c. 10. जनयति -यितुं), पक्वतां or परिपाकं कृ or जन्, परिणामं कृ or जन्, सिद्धं -द्धां कृ, सिद्धीकृ, साध् (c. 10. साधयति -यितुं), सम्पन्नं -न्नां कृ, सम्पद् (c. 10. -पादयति -यितुं).

To MATURE, *v. n.* पक्वः -क्वा -क्वं भू, परिपक्वः -क्वा -क्वं भू, पच् in pass. (पच्यते), परिपच्, पक्वतां or पक्वदशां or परिणामं या (c. 2. याति -तुं) or इ (c. 2. एति -तुं) or गम् (c. 1. गच्छति, गन्तुं), परिणतः -ता -तं भू, पाकोन्मुखः -खा -खं भू, सिद्धः -द्धा -द्धं भू, सम्पन्नः -न्ना -न्नं भू.

MATURED, *p. p.* पक्वः -क्वा -क्वं, परिपक्वः -क्वा -क्वं, परिणतः -ता -तं, पक्वतापन्नः -न्ना -न्नं, सिद्धः -द्धा -द्धं, प्रौढः -ढा -ढं, सम्पन्नः -न्ना -न्नं, सम्पूर्णः -र्णा -र्णं.

MATURELY, *adv.* सपाकं, सपरिणामं, परिपक्वं, सम्पन्नं, सम्पूर्णं.—(With full deliberation) सुसमीक्ष्य, सुविमृश्य, सुविचार्य्य.

MATURESCENT, *a.* पाकोन्मुखः -खा -खं, आपक्वः -क्वा -क्वं, परिणामोन्मुखः &c., पचतिकल्पः -ल्पा -ल्पं, पचतिदेशीयः -या -यं, पचतिदेश्यः -श्या -श्यं.

MATURITY, MATURENESS, *s.* पाकः, परिपाकः, पक्वता, पक्तिः *f.*, परिपक्वता, विपाकः, सुपक्वता, सुपक्तिः, परिणतिः *f.*, परिणामः, परिणतता -त्वं, पक्वभावः, पक्वदशा, पक्वावस्था, परिणतावस्था, पचा, पाचा -चिका, प्रौढिः *f.*, प्रौढता, सिद्धता, सिद्धिः *f.*, सम्पन्नता, सम्पूर्णता.

MATUTINAL, MATUTINE, *a.* प्रातःकालीनः -ना -नं, प्रातःकालिकः -की -कं, औषिकः -की -कं, औषसः -सी -सं, उषस्यः -स्या -स्यं, प्रगेतनः -नी -नं, वैयुष्टः -ष्टी -ष्टं, प्राबोधिकः -की -कं, औदयिकः -की -कं, प्रातःकालसम्बन्धी -न्धिनी -न्धि (न्).

MAUDLIN, *a.* ईषन्मत्तः -त्ता -त्तं, मत्तकल्पः -ल्पा -ल्पं, मत्तदेशीयः -या -यं.

MAUL, *s.* वृहन्मुद्गरः, काष्ठमुद्गरः, स्थूलमुद्गरः, घनः.

To MAUL, *v. a.* स्थूलवेत्रेण तड् (c. 10. ताडयति -यितुं) or आहन् (c. 2. -हन्ति -न्तुं) or प्रहृ (c. 1. -हरति -हर्तुं), वेत्राघातं कृ, वेत्राघातेन क्षतविक्षतीकृ.

MAULED, *p. p.* वेत्रादिप्रहारेण परिक्षतः -ता -तं or अतिक्षुण्णः -ण्णा -ण्णं.

MAUSOLEAN, *a.* चिताचूडकसम्बन्धी -न्धिनी -न्धि (न्), चैत्यसम्बन्धी &c.

MAUSOLEUM, *s.* चिताचूडकं, चैत्यं, चित्यं, चैत्यः, समाधिः *m.*

MAUVAISE-HONTE, *s.* सभाभीतिः *f.*, सभाकम्पः, जनभीतिः, लोकभीतिः, जनलज्जा.

MAW, *s.* पशूनां जठरः or उदरं.—(Of fowls) उपजठरः.

MAWKISH, *a.* विरसः -सा -सं, नीरसः -सा -सं, अरसिकः -का -कं.

MAWKISHLY, *adv.* विरसं, वैरस्येन, सवैरस्यं, रसं विना, अरसिकं.

MAWKISHNESS, *s.* विरसता -त्वं, वैरस्यं, अरसता, अरसिकत्वं, फल्गुता.

MAXILLAR, MAXILLARY, *a.* हनुसम्बन्धी -न्धिनी -न्धि (न्) हनु in comp.

MAXIM, *s.* सूत्रं, वचनं, वाक्यं, तत्त्वं, विधिः *m.*, विधानं, नियमः, स्थितिः *f.* आदेशः, निदेशः, निर्देशः, कल्पः, न्यायः, नीतिः *f.*, क्रमः, चोदना, निगमः, सिद्धान्तः, मतं.

MAXIMUM, *s.* उत्तमसंख्या, परमसंख्या, अधिकसंख्या, उत्तमपरिमाणं.

MAY, *s.* (The month) वैशाखोत्तरार्द्धं, ज्येष्ठपूर्वार्द्धं, वैशाखः, माधवः, राधः, ज्यैष्ठः, शुक्रः, पञ्चममासः.

MAY, *v. auxil.* (Be possible) सम्भू, शक् in pass. (शक्यते), शक्यः -क्या -क्यं भू or expressed by the potential.—(Have liberty, be allowed) expressed by the potential; as, 'he may do that,' स तत् कुर्य्यात्. *See also* PERMITTED, ALLOWED, &c. (May be) स्यात्.

MAY-DAY, *s.* पूर्व्वोक्तपञ्चममासस्य प्रथमदिवसः.

MAY-POLE, *s.* क्रीडादण्डविशेषो यत्परितो मण्डलनृत्यं क्रियते.

MAYOR, *s.* नगराध्यक्षः, पुराध्यक्षः, नगराधिकारी *m.* (न्).

MAYORALTY, *s.* नगराध्यक्षता -त्वं, पुराध्यक्षता, नगराधिकारः -रिता, नगराध्यक्षपदं, नगराध्यक्षाधिकारः.

MAYORESS, *s.* नगराधिकारिणी, नगराध्यक्षस्त्री, नगराध्यक्षपत्नी.

MAZE, *s.* (Labyrinth) गहनं, सुगहनस्थानं, दुर्निर्गमस्थानं, अशक्यनिर्गमः प्रदेशः, भ्रमजनकः प्रदेशः, दुर्गतिः *f.*—(Intricacy, perplexity) वक्रता, कौटिल्यं, विषमता, वैषम्यं, क्लिष्टता, काठिन्यं, दुःशोध्यता, व्यस्तता.

MAZY, *a.* गहनः -ना -नं, सुगहनः -ना -नं, दुर्निर्गमः -मा -मं, वक्रः -क्रा -क्रं, अतिवक्रः -क्रा -क्रं, भ्रमजनकः -का -कं, भ्रान्तिजनकः -का -कं, दुःशोध्यः -ध्या -ध्यं.

ME, *pron.* acc. c. मां; 'by me,' मया; 'to me,' मह्यं; 'of me,' मम.

MEACOCK, *s.* गेहेशूरः, गेहेनर्दी *m.* (न्), कापुरुषः, स्त्रीविधेयः.

MEAD, *s.* मधु *n.*, मधुपानीयं, मधुनीरं, मधुपयस् *n.*

MEAD, MEADOW, *s.* क्षेत्रं, केदारः, यवसस्थानं, शाद्वलस्थानं, गोचरः, गोप्रचारः; 'meadow-grass,' यवसः, क्षेत्रियं; 'relating to a meadow,' कैदारः -री -रं, क्षेत्रिकः -की -कं.

MEADOWY, *a.* यवसमयः -यी -यं, यवसीयः -या -यं, शाद्वलः -ला -लं.

MEAGER, MEAGRE, *a.* कृशः -शा -शं, परिकृशः -शा -शं, कृशाङ्गः -ङ्गी -ङ्गं, क्षीणः -णा -णं, क्षीणशरीरः -रा -रं, क्षीणमांसः -सा -सं, शुष्कमांसः -सा -सं, शुष्काङ्गः &c., क्षामः -मा -मं, क्षामशरीरः &c., अपुष्टः -ष्टा -ष्टं, विपुष्टः -ष्टा -ष्टं, तनुः -नुः -न्वी -नु, वितनुः &c., प्रतनुः &c., शातः -ता -तं.—(Barren as soil) रूक्षः -क्षा -क्षं, वन्ध्यः -न्ध्या -न्ध्यं; 'a barren soil,' मरुस्थलं -ली.—(As style) विरसः -सा -सं, फल्गुः -ल्गुः -ल्गु.

MEAGERLY, *adv.* परिकृशं, सकार्श्यं, कार्श्येन, क्षीणतया, रूक्षं.

MEAGERNESS, MEAGRENESS, *s.* कृशता -त्वं, कार्श्यं, परिकृशता, कृशाङ्गता, क्षीणता, क्षामता, शरीरक्षीणता, मांसक्षीणता, शुष्कता, मांसशुष्कता, अपुष्टता, विपुष्टता, अमांसत्वं -ता, तनुता, शुष्काङ्गता, मांसहीनता, रूक्षता.

MEAL, *s.* (Flour) शक्तुः *m.*, क्षोदः, पिष्टं, चूर्णं, गोधूमचूर्णं, गोधूमक्षोदः, अपूप्यः, क्षोदितं, गुण्डिकः -का, समीदः; 'barley-meal,' यवक्षोदः.—(Repast) आहारः, भोजनं, भक्षणं, भक्षिका, अशनं, प्राशनं, अभ्याहारः, अन्नं; 'good meal,' सुभोजनं, इष्टाभोजनं; 'poor meal,' कुभोजनं; 'light meal,' लघ्वाहारः, अल्पाहारः, फलाहारः; 'morning meal,' प्रातर्भोजनं, प्रातरशनं, प्रातराशः; 'meal at noon,' माध्याह्निकं; 'at night, रात्रिभोजनं; 'meal supplied by another,' पराह्नं; 'row or party at a meal,' पंक्तिः *f.*; 'to make a meal,' आहारं कृ, भोजनं कृ; 'one who has made a meal,' कृताहारः -रा -रं, कृतभोजनः -ना -नं; 'making one's meals at irregular hours,' विषमभोजनं; 'meal-time,' भोजनकालः, अन्नकालः.

Mealiness, *s.* सचूर्णता -त्वं, क्षोदितत्वं, कोमलता, शक्तुपूर्णता, मृदुता.

Mealman, *s.* शक्तुविक्रयी *m.* (न्), चूर्णविक्रेता *m.* (तृ), क्षोदविक्रयोपजीवी *m.*

Mealy, *a.* चूर्णमयः -यी -यं, क्षोदमयः -यी -यं, सचूर्णः -र्णा -र्णं, शक्तुपूर्णः -र्णा -र्णं, कोमलः -ला -लं, मृदुलः -ला -लं, मसृणः -णा -णं.

Mealy-mouthed, *a.* मृदुभाषी -षिणी -षि (न्), कोमलमुखः -खी -खं, मृदुमुखः &c.

Mean, *a.* (Base, low-minded) नीचः -चा -चं, दीनः -ना -नं, कृपणः -णा -णं, अपकृष्टः -ष्टा -ष्टं, निकृष्टः -ष्टा -ष्टं, कुत्सितः -ता -तं, क्षुद्रः -द्रा -द्रं, तुच्छः -च्छा -च्छं, हीनः -ना -नं, कदर्य्यः -र्य्या -र्य्यं, अनार्य्यः &c., जघन्यः -न्या -न्यं, खलः -ला -लं, दुष्टः -ष्टा -ष्टं, अधमः -मा -मं, प्राकृतः -ती -तं, पामरः -री -रं, अधमवृत्तिः -त्तिः -त्ति, जघन्यवृत्तिः &c., दीनवृत्तिः &c., पामरवृत्तिः &c., हीनवृत्तिः &c., कृपणबुद्धिः -द्धिः -द्धि, कु or का prefixed, as, 'a mean man,' कुपुरुषः, कापुरुषः.—(Low in rank or birth,' हीनजातिः -तिः -ति, अधमजातिः &c., अधमजातीयः -या -यं, अन्त्यजातीयः -या -यं, जघन्यजातिः &c., नीचजातिः &c., अकुलीनः -ना -नं, अकुलः -ला -लं, दुष्कुलीनः -ना -नं, अधमवर्णजातः -ता -तं.—(Contemptible, worthless,) गर्ह्यः -र्ह्या -र्ह्यं, गर्हितः -ता -तं, कुत्सितः -ता -तं, तुच्छः -च्छा -च्छं, निर्गुणः -णा -णं, तृणप्रायः -या -यं, क्षुल्लकः -का -कं, लघुः -घुः -घ्वी -घु, लघुप्रभावः -वा -वं.—(Middle, moderate in size) मध्यः -ध्या -ध्यं, मध्यमः -मा -मं, मध्यपरिमाणः -णा -णं, मध्यमप्रमाणः -णा -णं, न स्थूलो न सूक्ष्मः &c.—(Intermediate, intervening) मध्यः &c., मध्यमः &c., मध्यस्थः -स्था -स्थं, मध्यस्थितः -ता -तं, मध्यवर्त्ती -र्त्तिनी -र्त्ति (न्), अन्तर्गतः -ता -तं, व्यवहितः -ता -तं; 'in the mean time,' अनन्तरं -रे, तदनन्तरं, अत्रान्तरे, इतोमध्ये.—(In geometry or mathematics) मध्यः &c., मध्यमः &c., समः -मा -मं; 'mean anomaly,' मध्यकेन्द्रं; 'mean motion of a planet,' मध्यमगतिः *f.*

Mean, *s.* (Middle place, middle rate, medium) मध्यता -त्वं, समता, साम्यं, मध्यमपरिमाणं, सामान्यपरिमाणं, समपरिमाणं, सामान्यपक्षः, समपक्षः.—(Intervening time) मध्यकालः, अभ्यन्तरकालः, अन्तरकालः, कालान्तरं, कालाभ्यन्तरं, अन्तरं, अन्तर्गतकालः, मध्यान्तरं, मध्यावसरः, मध्यावधिः *m.*, अवधिः *m.*—(In geometry, &c.) समं, मध्यं.—(Instrument, means or medium through which any thing is done) साधनं, उपायः, कारणं, उपकरणं, करणं, द्वारं, द्वार् *f.*, अभ्युपायः, हेतुः *m.*, विधानं, कर्म्मसाधनं, कार्य्यसाधकं, कार्य्यसाधनं, सम्भवः, अङ्गं, उपचारः, योगः, गतिः *f.*, उपपत्तिः *f.*, साहाय्यं, साधनसामग्री -ग्र्यं, सामग्री, साहित्यं; 'by means of,' उपायेन, द्वारेण, द्वारा, हेतुना, हेतोः, कारणेन; 'by means of a lever,' उत्तोलनदण्डोपायेन or उत्तोलनदण्डद्वारेण -द्वारा; 'by lawful means,' धर्म्मोपायेन, धर्म्मोपायैः or expressed by the indecl. part.; as, 'by means of numerous experiments,' अनेकवारं परीक्ष्य; 'means of subsistence,' जीवनोपायः, जीवनहेतुः *m.*, उपजीविका -विका, उपजीवनं; 'by all means, in all ways,' सर्व्वथा, सर्व्वथैव, सर्व्वप्रकारेण; 'by all means, certainly,' अवश्यं, अवश्यमेव; 'by any means,' कथमपि, कथञ्चन, कथञ्चित्, यथाकथञ्चित्, कथं कथमपि; 'by no means,' न कथञ्चन, न कथञ्चित्.—(Means, resources, income) विभवः, द्रव्यं, धनं, अर्थः, आयः, आगमः, धनागमः, सम्भवः, शक्तिः *f.*, बलं, सामर्थ्यं; 'according to one's means,' यथाविभवं, यथासम्भवं, यथाशक्ति, यथासामर्थ्यं; 'having small means,' अल्पधनः -ना -नं, अल्पविभवः -वा -वं.

To mean, *v. a.* (Intend) अभिप्रे (c. 2. अभिप्रैति -तुं, rt. इ), अभिप्रायं कृ, उद्दिश् (c. 6. -दिशति -देष्टुं), मनसा उद्दिश्, अभिसन्धा (c. 3. -दधाति -धातुं), इष् (c. 6. इच्छति, एषितुं), उपलक्ष् (c. 10. -लक्षयति -यितुं) or expressed by the des. form of a verb; as, 'to mean to do,' कृ in des. (चिकीर्षति -र्षितुं); 'to mean to go,' गम् in des. (जिगमिषति -षितुं); 'to mean to say,' वच् in des. (विवक्षति -क्षितुं), or by काम with the infin.; as, 'what do you mean to say?' किं वक्तुकामो ऽसि; 'what do you mean to do?' किं कर्त्तुकामो ऽसि; 'where do you mean to go?' कुत्र गन्तुकामो ऽसि.—(Signify, indicate) सूच् (c. 10. सूचयति -यितुं), उद्दिश्, निर्दिश्, बुध् (c. 10. बोधयति -यितुं), उद्बुध्.

To mean, *v. n.* (Have meaning) अर्थवान् -वती -वद् भू, सार्थः -र्था -र्थं भू, वच् in des. (विवक्षति -क्षितुं), अर्थं सूच् (c. 10. सूचयति -यितुं) or expressed by अर्थ *i.e.* signification, meaning) in comp.; as, 'a speech that means to convey censure,' निन्दार्थो वादः.

Meander, *s.* वक्रता, वक्रगतिः *f.*, वक्रिमा *m.* (न्), जिह्मता, जैह्म्यं, जिह्मगतिः *f.*, कुटिलता, कौटिल्यं, कुटिलगतिः *f.*, तिर्य्यक्त्वं, तिर्य्यग्गतिः *f.*, असमानगतिः, विसर्पणं, सर्पः -र्पणं, सर्पगतिः *f.*; 'of a river's bank,' रोधोवक्रता.

To meander, *v. n.* विसृप् (c. 1. -सर्पति -सर्प्तुं), विसर्पणं कृ, वक्रं or जिह्मं गम् (c. 1. गच्छति, गन्तुं), कुटिलं or तिर्य्यग् या (c. 2. याति -तुं), सर्पवद् या.

Meandering, *part.* or *a.* वक्रः -क्रा -क्रं, वक्रिमः -मा -मं, वक्रगतिः -तिः -ति, वक्रगामी -मिनी -मि (न्), जिह्मः -ह्मा -ह्मं, जिह्मगतिः &c., जिह्मगामी &c., कुटिलः -ला -लं, कुटिलगतिः &c., कुटिलगामी &c., तिर्य्यङ् तिरश्ची तिर्य्यक् (क्), तिर्य्यग्गतिः &c., तिर्य्यग्गामी &c., विसर्पी -र्पिणी &c., सर्पगतिः &c., वक्रतीरः -रा -रं, वक्ररोधाः -धाः -धः (स्), असमानगतिः &c., विषमगतिः &c.

Meaning, *s.* (Intention) अभिप्रायः, अभिप्रेतं, आशयः, उद्देशः, आकांक्षा, अर्थः, तात्पर्य्यं, आकूतं, इच्छा, छन्दः, छन्दस् *n.*, सङ्कल्पः, बुद्धिः *f.*, मतिः *f.*, मतं, इङ्गितं, उपलक्षितं, हृदयं, भावः.—(What is intended to be said) विवक्षितं, विवक्षा.—(Sense, signification) अर्थः, अभिप्रायः, विवक्षितं, विवक्षा, आकांक्षा, छन्दस् *n.*, विषयः; 'meaning or force of a word,' पदार्थः, भावार्थः, शक्तिः *f.*, विग्रहः; 'original meaning,' मुख्यार्थः, मुख्यत्वं, मूलार्थः; 'literal meaning,' अवयवार्थः, पदार्थः; 'metaphorical meaning,' गौणार्थः, गौणत्वं; 'latent or hidden meaning,' मर्म्म *n.* (न्), अन्तर्गर्भः; 'deep in meaning,' गूढार्थः -र्था -र्थं, निगूढार्थः -र्था -र्थं, गुर्व्वर्थगह्वरः -रा -रं; 'having little meaning,' अल्पार्थः -र्था -र्थं, अल्पविषयः -या -यं.

Meaning, *part.* or *a.* अभिप्रेत्य, उद्दिश्य, अभिसन्धाय.—(Significant) अर्थवान् -वती -वत् (त्), सार्थः -र्था -र्थं, पूर्णार्थः -र्था -र्थं, अर्थान्वितः -ता -तं, साकूतः -ता -तं, उद्बोधकः -का -कं, वाचकः -का -कं.

Meaningless, *a.* अर्थहीनः -ना -नं, निरर्थकः -का -कं, अनर्थकः -का -कं.

Meaningly, *adv.* सार्थं, साकूतं, अर्थवत्, पूर्णार्थतस्, गुर्व्वर्थतस्.

Meanly, *adv.* (Poorly, in a low way) कृपणं, कार्पण्येन, सकार्पण्यं, कुत्सितं, दीनं, सदैन्यं, अपकृष्टं, निकृष्टं, कृपणवत्, निकृष्टवत्, खलवत्, अधमवत्, अधमप्रकारेण, जघन्यवत्, तुच्छवत्, कदर्य्यवत्, अनार्य्यवत्; 'meanly born,' हीनजातिः -तिः -ति, अधमजातिः &c.—(Moderately) परिमितं, अभृशं.—(Contemptuously) सावमानं, अनादरेण, सलाघवं, लाघवेन, लघु.

Meanness, *s.* (Baseness, lowness) कृपणता -त्वं, कार्पण्यं, दीनता -त्वं,

MEA

दैन्यं, अपकृष्टता, निकृष्टता, नीचता, क्षुद्रता, अधमता, हीनता, तुच्छता, कदर्य्यता, अनार्य्यता, जघन्यता, खलता, दुष्टता, पामरता, अधमवृत्तिता, हीनवृत्तित्वं, मनोहीनता, बुद्धिकार्पण्यं, कृपणबुद्धित्वं, अनुदारता; 'of birth,' हीनजातित्वं, अधमजातित्वं, अकुलीनता, दुष्कुलीनता.—(Contemptibleness) गर्ह्यता, तुच्छत्वं, लघुता, लाघवं, कुत्सितत्वं, निर्गुणता.

MEAN-SPIRITED, *a.* कृपणबुद्धिः -द्धिः -द्धि, कृपणमतिः &c., दीनबुद्धिः &c.

MEANS, *s. pl.* (Resources) विभवः.—(Instrument) साधनं, उपायः. *See* MEAN, *s.*

MEANT, *p.p.* अभिप्रेतः -ता -तं, उद्दिष्टः -ष्टा -ष्टं, विवक्षितः -ता -तं.

MEANWHILE, *adv.* अनन्तरं -रे, तदनन्तरं, अत्रान्तरे, इतोमध्ये, अतोमध्ये, मध्यकाले, अभ्यन्तरकाले, यावत्.

MEASLED, *a.* वक्ष्यमाणरोगग्रस्तः -स्ता -स्तं, गोवरोपहतः -ता -तं.

MEASLES, *s. pl.* रक्तस्फोटोत्पत्तिलक्षितो रोगविशेषः. The Mahratti words गोवर, and शुभा, may perhaps be used.

MEASURABLE, *a.* मेयः -या -यं, प्रमेयः -या -यं, परिमेयः -या -यं, मापनीयः -या -यं, माप्यः -प्या -प्यं, मातव्यः -व्या -व्यं, परिमाणयोग्यः -ग्या -ग्यं.

MEASURE, *s.* मानं, प्रमाणं, परिमाणं, मात्रं, योतुः *m.*, यौतवं, पौतवं, द्रुवयं, पाय्यं; 'of short measure,' अल्पप्रमाणः -णा -णं; 'measure of capacity,' प्रतीमाणं, प्रस्थः; 'of weight,' तुलामानं; 'of length,' अङ्गुलिमानं; 'of time,' कालपरिमाणं. The following are some of the measures of capacity: मुष्टिः *m.* = a handful, कुञ्चिः *f.* = 8 handfuls, कुडवः = 12 handfuls, प्रस्थः = 48 handfuls or 4 kudavas, आढकः = 4 prasthas, द्रोणः = 4 ádhakas, खारी = 16 dronas, कुम्भः = 20 dronas, वाहः = 10 kumbhas, निकुञ्चकः = $\frac{1}{4}$ of a kudava, गोष्पदं = the measure of a cow's foot. The following are measures of weight: रक्तिका or रतिः = $2\frac{1}{4}$ grains, गुञ्जा = $2\frac{3}{16}$ grains, or $\frac{1}{8}$ of a másha, काकिणी = $\frac{1}{4}$ of a másha, माषः = 17 grains, पलं = 2 máshas, धरणः -णं = 10 palas, कर्षः or अक्षः = 16 máshas or 280 grains troy, तोलः = 210 grains, तुला = 100 palas or 145 ounces troy, भारः = 2000 palas, आचितं = 10 bháras. The following are measures of length: यवः = 1 barley-corn, अङ्गुलः = 8 barley-corns, प्रादेशः = 10 angulas or the span of the thumb and forefinger, वितस्तिः *f.* or गोकर्णः = 12 angulas or the span of the thumb and little finger, रत्निः -त्नी *m.f.* = 18 angulas or a cubit measured from the elbow to the end of the closed fist, अरत्निः *m.* = 21 angulas or a cubit measured from the elbow to the tip of the little finger, हस्तः = 24 angulas or a cubit measured from the elbow to the tip of the middle finger, गजः = 2 cubits or between 2 and 3 feet, व्यामः = a fathom or $3\frac{1}{2}$ hastas or the space between the tips of the fingers of either hand when the arms are extended, काकिणी = $\frac{1}{4}$ of a danda, दण्डः = a pole or 4 cubits, निवर्त्तनं = 200 square cubits or 20 rods, गोचर्म्म *n.* = a hide of land 300 feet long by 10 broad, क्रोशः = a kos or 4000 cubits, गव्यूतिः *m. f.* or गव्यूतं = 2 kos or 2000 dandas or 8000 cubits, योजनं = 4 kos. The following are measures of time, निमेषः or निमिषः = a twinkling of the eye, काष्ठा = 18 twinklings, कला = 30 kashthás or 8 seconds, क्षणः = 30 kalás or 4 minutes, दण्डः or घटिका = 6 kshanas or the 60th part of a day or 24 minutes, मुहूर्त्तः -र्त्तं = 12 kshanas or the 30th part of a day or 48 minutes, अहोरात्रः = a day or 30 muhúrtas, पक्षः = 15 days, पलं, विपलं, and त्रुटिः are short measures of time, equal to about a minute.—(Rule, standard by which any thing is measured) परिमाणं, प्रमाणं.—(Proportion) मानं, परिमाणं, प्रमाणं, मितिः *f.*, परिमितिः, तारतम्यं; 'according to measure,' प्रमाणतस्.—(Portion allotted) भागः, विभागः, अंशः.—(Degree) प्रमाणं, परिमाणं, पर्य्यन्तं, मात्रं; 'in some measure,' किञ्चित्, अल्पमात्रं, ईषत्.—(Limit) पर्य्यन्तं, अन्तः -न्तं, मर्य्यादा, सीमा; 'beyond measure,' अतिमात्रं, अतिमर्य्यादं, नितान्तं, अतिशयेन, अतीव, अति prefixed.—(Moderation) परिमितिः *f.*, परिमितता; 'in measure,' परिमितं.—(Quantity, measure of a vowel, &c.) मात्रा.—(Musical time) तालः, मात्रा; 'in musical measure,' स्वरबद्धः -द्धा -द्धं.—(Metre, measure of verse) छन्दः, छन्दस्, वृत्तं, वर्णवृत्तं, वेदः, पद्यं; 'false measure,' छन्दोभङ्गः.—(Means to an end, step) उपायः, उपचारः, साधनं, अभ्युपायः, योगः, प्रयोगः, युक्तिः *f.*, विधानं, क्रिया, कर्म्म *n.* (न्), कार्य्यं, कारणं, करणं; 'mild measures,' सामोपचारः, सौम्योपचारः, सामोपायः; the four measures of war are 'causing dissension,' भेदः; 'force of arms,' दण्डः; 'bribery,' दानं; 'conciliation,' साम *n.* (न्); 'to take measures,' उपायप्रयोगं कृ.—(Common measure in arithmetic, &c.) अपवर्त्तः; 'having no common measure,' निरपवर्त्तः -र्त्ता -र्त्तं.

To MEASURE, *v. a.* मा (c. 2. माति, c. 3. मिमीते, c. 4. मायते, मातुं, c. 10. मापयति -यितुं), प्रमा, परिमा, तुल् (c. 10. तुलयति -यितुं), तूल् (c. 10. तूलयति -यितुं), मापनं कृ, परिमाणं कृ.—(Ascertain the degree or extent) मानं or परिमाणं निरूप् (c. 10. -रूपयति -यितुं) or ज्ञा (c. 9. जानाति, ज्ञातुं) or परीक्ष् (c. 1. -ईक्षते -क्षितुं), परिमाणनिरूपणं कृ.—(Compute) गण् (c. 10. गणयति -यितुं), विगण्, प्रगण्.—(Make a comparison of measurement) उपमा.—(Allot) विभज् (c. 1. -भजति -भक्तुं) or परिक्लृप् (c. 10. -कल्पयति -यितुं).

To MEASURE, *v. n.* (Be of a certain extent or size) expressed by परिमाण or परिमित or मित in comp.; as, 'a line which measures eight inches,' अष्टाङ्गुलपरिमिता रेखा; 'to measure an inch,' अङ्गुलपरिमितः -ता -तं भू, अङ्गुलमितः -ता -तं भू, अङ्गुलपरिमाणः -णा -णं भू.

MEASURED, *p. p.* मितः -ता -तं, प्रमितः -ता -तं, परिमितः -ता -तं, सम्मितः -ता -तं, उन्मितः -ता -तं, मापितः -ता -तं.—(Uniform) समानः -ना -नं, समः -मा -मं, धीरः -रा -रं.—(In music) तालबद्धः -द्धा -द्धं.—(Limited) मितः -ता -तं, परिमितः -ता -तं, निबद्धः -द्धा -द्धं, नियतः -ता -तं.

MEASURELESS, *a.* अमेयः -या -यं, अपरिमेयः -या -यं, अप्रमेयः -या -यं, अमितः -ता -तं, अपरिमितः -ता -तं, अपरिमाणः -णा -णं.

MEASUREMENT, *s.* मापनं, परिमाणं, मितिः *f.*, परिमितिः *f.*, प्रमितिः *f.*, प्रमाणं, मानं, मानपरीक्षा, परिमाणपरीक्षा, माननिरूपणं, मापकरणं; 'rough measurement,' स्थूलमानं; 'exact measurement,' सूक्ष्ममानं.

MEASURER, *s.* मापकः, परिमापकः, मापनकर्त्ता *m.* (र्त्तृ), मापनकृत्, माननिरूपकः, परिमाणनिरूपकः, परिमाणपरीक्षकः.

MEASURING, *s.* मापनं; 'measuring-line,' प्रमाणसूत्रं; 'rod,' प्रमाणदण्डः.

MEAT, *s.* (Flesh) मांसं, खाद्यमांसं, मांसाहारः, आमिषं, आमिषाहारः; 'butcher's meat,' सौनं, शौनं, सौनिकं, शौनिकं.—(Food) अन्नं, भोजनं, आहारः, खाद्यं, भक्ष्यद्रव्यं, खाद्यद्रव्यं; 'meat and drink,'

अन्नोदकं, अन्नजलं, अन्नपानं; 'seller of meat,' मांसिकः, सौनिकः, शौनिकः, कौटिकः, वैतंसिकः.

MEAT-OFFERING, s. नैवेद्यं, अन्ननिवेदनं, अन्नोपहारः, अन्नोपहरणं.

MECHANIC, MECHANICAL, a. (Pertaining to machines) यान्त्रः -न्त्री -न्त्रं, यान्त्रिकः -की -कं, यन्त्री -न्त्रिणी -न्त्रि (न्), यन्त्रीयः -या -यं, यन्त्रसम्बन्धी -न्धिनी &c., यन्त्रविषयः -या -यं, शिल्पिकः -की -कं, शिल्पी -ल्पिनी &c., यन्त्रविद्यासम्बन्धी &c., शिल्पविद्यासम्बन्धी &c.—(Constructed or performed by the rules of mechanics) यन्त्रविद्यानुसारी -रिणी &c., यन्त्रशास्त्रानुरूपः -पा -पं, शिल्पशास्त्रानुसारी &c., यन्त्रशास्त्रसिद्धः -द्धा -द्धं, शिल्पविद्याकृतः -ता -तं, यन्त्रविद्यासिद्धः &c., शिल्पविद्यानिर्मितः -ता -तं, यौक्तिकः -की -कं; 'mechanical art,' शिल्पं, कला.—(Skilful in mechanical art) यन्त्रविद्यानिपुणः, शिल्पविद्याज्ञः, शिल्पकर्म्मकुशलः.—(Employed in mechanical pursuits) शिल्पी m. (न्), शिल्पकर्म्मकारी m., शिल्पजीवी m., शिल्पोपजीवी m. (न्), शिल्पिकः.—(Moving like a machine) यन्त्रगतिकः -का -कं, यन्त्रगतिः -तिः -ति, यन्त्रप्रायः -या -यं, यन्त्रतुल्यः -ल्या -ल्यं.

MECHANIC, s. (Artisan) शिल्पी m. (न्), शिल्पकारः, शिल्पकर्म्मकारः, शिल्पिकः, शिल्पोपजीवी m. (न्), शिल्पकर्म्मोपजीवी m., कर्म्मकारः, कर्म्मारः, कारुः m. -रुकः.

MECHANICALLY, adv. यन्त्रविद्यानुसारेण, शिल्पविद्यानुसारेण, यन्त्रशास्त्रानुरूपेण, शिल्पिकं, शिल्पवत्.—(By the mere laws of motion) यन्त्रगतिमात्रौपम्यात्, यन्त्रतुल्यगत्या, अबुद्धिपूर्व्वं, अमतिपूर्व्वं.

MECHANICIAN, s. यन्त्रविद्याज्ञः, शिल्पशास्त्रज्ञः, यन्त्रविद्यानिपुणः.

MECHANICS, s. यन्त्रविद्या, शिल्पविद्या, यन्त्रशास्त्रं, शिल्पशास्त्रं, शिल्पिशास्त्रं, यान्त्रं, गतिविद्या, यन्त्रगतिविद्या, यन्त्रनिर्बन्धः.

MECHANISM, s. (Construction of a machine) यन्त्ररचना, यन्त्रविधानं, कला, युक्तिः f. See MACHINERY. (Action of a machine) यन्त्रचेष्टा, यन्त्रगतिः f, यन्त्रक्रिया, यन्त्रव्यापारः; 'a piece of mechanism,' कारुजः.

MECHANIST, s. यन्त्रनिर्म्माता m. (तृ), यन्त्रकर्त्ता m., यन्त्रविद्यानिपुणः.

MECONIUM, s. (Of poppies) खसखसरसः, खसखसनिर्यासः, खसखसस्रावः.—(First fæces of infants) सद्योजातबालकानां प्रथमोच्चारः.

MEDAL, s. मुद्रा, प्रतिमामुद्रा, कीर्त्तिमुद्रा, कीर्त्तिदमुद्रा, मानसूचकमुद्रा, निदर्शनमुद्रा.

MEDALIST, s. (Person skilled in medals) मुद्राविद्याज्ञः, मुद्राविद् m., मुद्रापरीक्षकः.—(One who has gained a medal) कीर्त्तिमुद्राधारी m. (न्), कीर्त्तिमुद्रावान् m. (त्).

MEDALLION, s. प्राचीनकालिकमुद्रा, प्राचीनमुद्रा, महामुद्रा.

To MEDDLE, v. n. (Interfere or intrude officiously) परकार्य्याणि चर्च् (c. 1. चर्चति -र्चितुं), परव्यापारचर्चां कृ, परनियोगचर्चां कृ, पराधिकारचर्चां कृ, अनुपचारेण or अनधिकारपूर्व्वं परकार्य्याणि निरूप् (c. 10. -रूपयति -यितुं) or परकार्य्यनिरूपणं कृ or परकार्य्येषु व्यापृ in pass. (-ध्रियते) or व्यापृतः -ता -तं भू, पराधिकारं प्रविश् (c. 6. -विशति -वेष्टुं), परकार्य्यप्रवेशं कृ, परव्यापारप्रवेशं कृ, चर्चां कृ.—(Have to do with) व्यापृ in pass., व्यापृतः -ता -तं भू.—(Handle) स्पृश् (c. 6. स्पृशति, स्प्रष्टुं).

MEDDLER, s. परकार्य्यचर्चकः, पराधिकारचर्चकः, पराधिकारप्रवेशकः, परकार्य्यनिरूपकः, परचेष्टानिरूपकः, परकार्य्यव्यापारी m. (न्), पराधिकारव्यापारी m., परव्यापारानुगामी m.

MEDDLESOME, a. पराधिकारचर्चाशीलः -ला -लं, परचेष्टानिरूपणशीलः &c.

MEDDLING, a. परकार्य्यचर्चकः -का -कं, परकार्य्यनिरूपकः -का -कं, पराधिकारप्रवेशकः -का -कं, पराधिकारव्यापारी -रिणी -रि (न्).

MEDDLING, s. पराधिकारचर्चा, अनधिकारचर्चा, पराधिकारप्रवेशः, परकार्य्यप्रवेशः, परव्यापारचर्चा, पराधिकारव्यापारः, परनियोगव्यापारः, परकार्य्यनिरूपणं, परचेष्टानिरूपणं, चर्चा.

To MEDIATE, v. n. मध्यस्थः -स्था -स्थं भू or अस्, मध्यवर्त्ती -र्त्तिनी -र्त्ति भू, माध्यस्थ्यं कृ, मध्ये वृत् (c. 1. वर्त्तते -र्त्तितुं) or स्था (c. 1. तिष्ठति, स्थातुं), मध्ये गम् (c. 1. गच्छति, गन्तुं), अन्तर्गम्.

To MEDIATE, v. a. माध्यस्थ्येन सन्धिं कृ or सन्धा (c. 3. -दधाति -धातुं).

MEDIATE, a. मध्यस्थः -स्था -स्थं -स्थायी -यिनी यि (न्), मध्यवर्त्ती -र्त्तिनी &c., मध्यः -ध्या -ध्यं, मध्यमः -मा -मं, अन्तर्गतः -ता -तं, अन्तर्वर्त्ती &c.

MEDIATELY, adv. अन्यद्वारेण, अन्यद्वारा, परद्वारेण, माध्यस्थ्येन, माध्यस्थेन, उपकरणद्वारेण, अनुरूपेण.

MEDIATION, s. माध्यस्थ्यं, माध्यस्थं, मध्यस्थत्वं -ता, मध्यवर्त्तित्वं, मध्यवर्त्तनं, मध्यस्थितिः f., अन्तर्गमनं, अन्तरागमनं, अनुरूपं.

MEDIATOR, s. मध्यस्थः, मध्यवर्त्ती m. (न्), मध्यस्थायी m., माध्यस्थः, मध्यस्थितः, चरपुरुषः.

MEDIATORIAL, a. मध्यस्थसम्बन्धी -न्धिनी -न्धि (न्), मध्यस्थविषयः -या -यं, माध्यस्थिकः -की -कं.

MEDIATORSHIP, s. मध्यस्थता -त्वं, माध्यस्थ्यं, मध्यस्थपदं, मध्यस्थाधिकारः, मध्यस्थकर्म्म n. (न्).

MEDICABLE, a. औषधोपचारसाध्यः -ध्या -ध्यं, वैद्योपचारसाध्यः &c., भेषजप्रयोगसाध्यः &c., औषधोपायसाध्यः &c., उपक्रमसाध्यः &c., वैद्योपक्रमसाध्यः &c., उपक्रमणीयः -या -यं, चिकित्स्यः -त्स्या -त्स्यं.

MEDICAL, a. वैद्यः -द्यी -द्यं, वैद्यकः -की -कं, वैद्यक्रियासम्बन्धी -न्धिनी न्धि (न्), वैद्यकसम्बन्धी &c., वैद्यकविषयः -या -यं, चिकित्सासम्बन्धी &c., औषधीयः -या -यं, औषधोपचारसम्बन्धी &c., भेषजप्रयोगसम्बन्धी &c., आयुर्वेदसम्बन्धी &c., आयुर्वेदी -दिनी &c., आयुर्वेदमयः -यी -यं, वैद्यशास्त्रीयः -या -यं; 'medical science,' वैद्यकशास्त्रं, वैद्यशास्त्रं, आयुर्वेदः -दं; 'medical treatment,' वैद्योपचारः, औषधोपचारः, भेषजोपचारः, औषधप्रयोगः, भेषजप्रयोगः; 'medical man,' वैद्यः, चिकित्सकः, चिकित्साजीवी m. आयुर्वेदी.

MEDICALLY, adv. वैद्यकशास्त्रानुसारेण, वैद्यकधर्म्मानुसारेण, वैद्यशास्त्रमुद्दिश्य, वैद्योपचारमुद्दिश्य, उपचारोद्देशेन.

MEDICAMENT, s. औषधं, भेषजं, भैषजं, भैषज्यं, अगदः, औषधीयद्रव्यं, भेषजद्रव्यं, द्रव्यं, आयुर्द्रव्यं, आयुः m., जारी, जाली, जीवनः, तालिका.

MEDICASTER. s. मिथ्याचिकित्सकः, दुश्चिकित्सकः, छद्मवैद्यः, अशास्त्रवैद्यः.

To MEDICATE, v. a. (Impregnate with medicinal substances) औषधीकृ, औषधादिना मिश्र् (c. 10. मिश्रयति -यितुं) or संसृज् (c. 6. -सृजति -स्रष्टुं) or संस्कृ, औषधसंस्कृतं -तां कृ, औषधगुणकं -कां कृ, औषधगुणविशिष्टं -ष्टां कृ.—(Dose with drugs) औषधं दा, भेषजं दा, भिषज् (nom. भिषज्यति).

MEDICATED, p. p. औषधसंस्कृतः -ता -तं, औषधीयद्रव्यसंसृष्टः -ष्टा -ष्टं, औषधादिमिश्रितः -ता -तं.

MEDICATION, s. औषधसंस्कारः, औषधसंस्करणं, औषधीकरणं, औषधीयद्रव्यसंसर्गः, औषधीयद्रव्यमिश्रणं.

MEDICINAL, a. (Having healing properties) औषधीयः -या -यं, भैषजः -जी -जं, भेषजीयः -या -यं, औषधोपयोगी -गिनी -गि (न्), रोगान्तकः -का -कं, रोगशमकः -का -कं, रोगहरः -रा -रं, रोगहारी -रिणी &c., रोगघ्नः -घ्नी -घ्नं.—(Pertaining to medicine) औषधसम्बन्धी &c., भेषजसम्बन्धी &c.

MEDICINE, *s.* (Substance having the property of mitigating disease) औषधं, भेषजं, भैषजं, भैषज्यं, अगदः, औषधीयद्रव्यं, जायुः *m.*, रोगिवल्लभः; 'administering medicine,' औषधोपचारः, भेषजोपचारः, औषधप्रयोगः, भेषजप्रयोगः; 'mild medicines,' सामोपचारः, साम्योपचारः.—(The practice of medicine) वैद्योपचारः, चिकित्सा, उपचारः, उपचर्य्या, उपचार्य्यः, वैद्यक्रिया, उपक्रमः, वैद्योपक्रमः, रुक्प्रतिक्रिया, परानसा.—(Science of medicine) वैद्यकं, आयुर्वेदः -दं; 'a treatise on medicine,' वैद्यकशास्त्रं, वैद्यशास्त्रं; 'a compounder of medicines,' योगविद् *m.*

MEDIEVAL, *a.* मध्यकालीनः -ना -नं, मध्यकालिकः -का -कं.

MEDIOCRE, MEDIOCRAL, *a.* मध्यमः -मा -मं, मध्यः -ध्या -ध्यं, मध्यमगुणः -णा -णं, मध्यमभावः -वा -वं, साधारणगुणः -णा -णं, अवरगुणः -णा -णं, अप्रधानगुणः -णा -णं, विगुणः -णा -णं, प्राकृतः -ती -तं.

MEDIOCRITY, *s.* मध्यमता, मध्यता, मध्यमभावः, मध्यमावस्था, मध्यमदशा, साधारण्यं, साधारणभावः, साधारणदशा, सामान्यता, मध्यममानं, मध्यमपक्षः.—(Moderation) परिमितता.

To MEDITATE, *v. n.* ध्यै (c. 1. ध्यायति, ध्यातुं), अनुध्यै, अभिध्यै, सन्ध्यै, प्रध्यै, चिन्त् (c. 10. चिन्तयति -यितुं), सञ्चिन्त्, विचिन्त्, भू (c. 10. भावयति -यितुं), सम्भू, विमृश् (c. 6. -मृशति -म्रष्टुं), मनसा विचर् (c. 10. -चारयति -यितुं), समाधा (c. 3. -धत्ते -धातुं), वितर्क् (c.10. -तर्कयति -यितुं), ध्यानं कृ, अभिध्यानं कृ, अन्तर्ध्यानं कृ, चिन्तां कृ, चिन्तापरः -रा -रं भू, ध्यानपरः -रा -रं भू, विचारणं कृ, विवेचनं कृ.—(Intend) मनः कृ, बुद्धिं कृ, मतिं कृ. *See To* INTEND.

To MEDITATE, *v. a.* प्रचिन्त् (c. 10. -चिन्तयति -यितुं), परिचिन्त्, चिन्त्, मन्त्र् (c. 10. मन्त्रयति -यितुं), परिक्लृप् (c. 10. -कल्पयति -यितुं), क्लृप्, मनसा परिक्लृप् or कल्पनां कृ; 'to meditate a plan,' उपायचिन्तां कृ, उपायकल्पनां कृ; 'to meditate doing,' कृ in des. (चिकीर्षति -र्षितुं). *See To* INTEND.

MEDITATED, *p. p.* ध्यातः -ता -तं, चिन्तितः -ता -तं, प्रचिन्तितः -ता -तं, भावितः -ता -तं, मनोगुप्तः -प्ता -प्तं, कल्पितः -ता -तं, परिकल्पितः -ता -तं, घटितः -ता -तं; 'being meditated upon,' ध्यायमानः -ना -नं, अभिध्यायमानः -ना -नं; 'to be meditated upon,' ध्येयः -या -यं, ध्यानीयः -या -यं, ध्यातव्यः -व्या -व्यं.

MEDITATION, *s.* ध्यानं, अभिध्यानं, आध्यानं, अन्तर्ध्यानं, समाधिः *m.*, समाधानं, चिन्ता, चिन्तनं, भावना, सम्भावनं -ना, ध्यानपरता, विचारणं -णा, विमर्शः, मनोगुप्तं, आत्मैकाग्रता, ध्याम *n.* (न्); 'religious and abstract meditation,' योगः, ध्यानयोगः, अन्तर्ध्यानं, समाधिः *m.*, समाधियोगः, समाधानं; 'considered as one of the five sacraments,' अयुतः; 'absorbed in meditation,' ध्याननिष्ठः -ष्ठा -ष्ठं, ध्यानस्थः -स्था -स्थं, ध्यानपरः -रा -रं, समाधिस्थः -स्था -स्थं, समाधिनिष्ठः &c., अधिरूढसमाधियोगः -गा -गं; 'posture suited to religious meditation,' ब्रह्मासनं.

MEDITATIVE, *a.* ध्यानशीलः -ला -लं, चिन्ताशीलः -ला -लं, ध्यानपरः -रा -रं, ध्यानतत्परः -रा -रं, चिन्तापरः -रा -रं, चिन्तापरायणः -णा -णं, चिन्तावान् -वती -वत् (त्), समाधिमान् -मती &c., ध्यानी -निनी -नि (न्), भावितात्मा -त्मा -त्म (न्), सचिन्तः -न्ता -न्तं, ध्यायन् -यन्ती -यत् (त्), ध्यानयुक्तः -क्ता -क्तं.

MEDITERRANEAN, MEDITERRANEOUS, *a.* (Inclosed with land) भूवेष्टितः -ता -तं, भूमिवेष्टितः -ता -तं, भूमध्यस्थः -स्था -स्थं, भूवलयितः -ता -तं, भूवलयाङ्कितः -ता -तं.—(Remote from the sea, inland) समुद्रदूरस्थः -स्था -स्थं, मध्यदेशीयः -या -यं, मध्यदेशस्थः -स्था -स्थं, समुद्रासमीपः -पा -पं.

MEDIUM, *s.* (Means, instrument) साधनं, द्वारं, द्वार् *f.*, अङ्गं, हेतुः *m.*, कारणं, करणं, निमित्तं -त्तकं, निमित्तकारणं, योगः, कर्म्मसाधनं.—(Channel, vehicle) मार्गः, पथः, वाहनं, द्वारं, अङ्गं; 'through the medium of the ear,' श्रवणमार्गेण, श्रुतिमार्गेण, श्रवणद्वारेण, श्रवणद्वारा; 'the medium by which medicine is administered,' भेषजाङ्गं; 'air is the medium of sound,' वायुः शब्दवाहनं or शब्दवाहकः.—(Instrumentality) कारणत्वं -ता, कारकत्वं, हेतुता, निमित्तत्वं, साधकत्वं, कर्तृत्वं, कर्तृकत्वं.—(Middle place, mean) मध्यता -त्वं, समता, साम्यं, मध्यमपक्षः, सामान्यपक्षः.

MEDLEY, *s.* सङ्करः, नानाद्रव्यसाङ्कर्य्यं, सन्निपातः, द्रव्यसङ्कुलं, नानाद्रव्यसन्निपातः, सङ्कीर्णद्रव्यसमूहः, प्रकीर्णद्रव्यसमूहः, प्रकीर्णकं, सङ्कीर्णकं, सम्मिश्रद्रव्यसन्निपातः, नानासम्मिश्रद्रव्यसमूहः, नानाद्रव्यसम्मिश्रणं.

MEDLEY, *a.* सान्निपातिकः -की -कं, सन्निपतितः -ता -तं, सङ्कीर्णः -र्णा -र्णं, प्रकीर्णः -र्णा -र्णं, सम्मिश्रः -श्रा -श्रं, अस्तव्यस्तः -स्ता -स्तं, क्षिप्तविक्षिप्तः -प्ता -प्तं, सङ्करीकृतः -ता -तं, नानाजातीयः -या -यं, सङ्करजातीयः -या -यं.

MEDULLAR, MEDULLARY, *a.* मज्जासम्बन्धी -न्धिनी -न्धि (न्), मेदोसम्बन्धी &c., मज्जामयः -यी -यं, अस्थिसारसम्बन्धी &c., मेदस्वी &c.

MEED, *s.* (Recompense) फलं, प्रतिफलं, प्रतिकृतिः *f.*, प्रतिक्रिया, पारितोषिकं.

MEEK, *a.* विनीतः -ता -तं, विनयी -यिनी -यि (न्), सौम्यः -म्या -म्यं, सौम्यवृत्तिः -त्तिः -त्ति, नम्रबुद्धिः -द्धिः -द्धि, नम्रवृत्तिः -त्तिः -त्ति, नम्रशीलः -ला -लं, नम्रचेताः -ताः -तः (स्), निर्विशेषः -षा -षं, निर्विशेषचेताः &c., मृदुस्वभावः -वा -वं, सविनयः -या -यं, सहनशीलः -ला -लं, विनतः -ता -तं, गर्व्वहीनः -ना -नं, दर्पहीनः -ना -नं, अगर्व्वः -र्व्वा -र्व्वं, निरहङ्कारः -रा -रं, दीनचेताः &c., अनुद्धतः -ता -तं, अनभिमानी -निनी &c., अनहङ्कारी &c., वश्यात्मा -त्मा -त्म (न्), वश्यः -श्या -श्यं, सुवश्यः &c.

MEEK-EYED, *a.* मृदुनेत्रः -त्रा -त्रं, मृदुलोचनः -ना -नं, सौम्यनेत्रः &c.

MEEKLY, *adv.* सविनयं, विनीतवत्, विनयात्, नम्रचेतसा, निर्विशेषचेतसा, नम्रं, विनम्रं, मृदुस्वभावेन, अगर्व्वेण, अनभिमानेन, अनहङ्कारेण, सनिर्वेदं, अनुद्धतं, सदैन्यं.

MEEKNESS, *s.* विनयः, विनीतता, विनीतिः *f.* सौम्यता, नम्रता, निर्विशेषता, स्वभावमृदुता, बुद्धिनम्रता, नम्रशीलता, वश्यता, सुवश्यता, दीनता, दैन्यं, अगर्व्वः, गर्व्वहीनता, दर्पहीनता, अनभिमानं -नता, अनौद्धत्यं, माधुर्य्यं, शान्तिः *f.*, विनतिः, सहनशीलता.

MEET, *a.* (Proper, fit) युक्तः -क्ता -क्तं, उचितः -ता -तं, उपयुक्तः -क्ता -क्तं, योग्यः -ग्या -ग्यं, समञ्जसः -सा -सं, उपपन्नः -न्ना -न्नं, सङ्गतः -ता -तं.

To MEET, *v. a.* and *n.* (Come together, encounter) समागम् (c. 1. -गच्छति -गन्तुं), सङ्गम्, उपागम्, मिल् (c. 6. मिलति, मेलितुं), सम्मिल्, समे (c. 2. समेति -तुं, rt. इ), आसद् (c. 10. -सादयति -यितुं), समासद्, प्रतिमुखं or अभिमुखं गम् or या (c. 2. याति -तुं), अभिया, उपाया, सम्मुखीभू.—(Go to meet) प्रतिगम्, प्रत्युद्गम्, अभिगम्, प्रत्युद्या, अभिया, प्रत्याया, प्रतिव्रज् (c. 1. व्रजति -जितुं), प्रतिवृत् (c. 1. -वर्त्तते -र्त्तितुं), अभिवृत्, प्रत्युद्गमं कृ; 'gone to meet,' प्रत्युद्गतः -ता -तं.—(Rise to meet) प्रत्युत्था (c. 1. -तिष्ठति -त्थातुं, rt. स्था); 'risen to meet,' प्रत्युत्थितः -ता -तं; 'rising to meet,' प्रत्युत्थानं.—(Assemble) समागम्, सङ्गम्, मिल्, सम्मिल्, एकत्र मिल्, एकत्र गम् or आगम्, समे समभ्ये, समावृत्, समूहीभू.—(Encounter in a hostile manner) संयुध् (c. 4. -युध्यते -योद्धुं), युद्धं कृ, युद्धाय समुपागम्, समाघातं कृ, युद्धारम्भं कृ, रणाभियोगं.—(Meet with, find) आसद्, अधिगम्, प्राप् (c. 5. -आप्नोति -आप्तुं), सम्प्राप्, समाप्, अवाप्, आप्, लभ् (c. 1. लभते

लभ्यं), विद् (c. 6. विन्दति, वेदितुं), अभिविद्; 'hard to meet with,' दुरासदः -दा -दं, दुरधिगमः -मा -मं, दुरधिगम्यः -म्या -म्यं, दुष्प्रापः -पा -पं, दुष्प्राप्यः -प्या -प्यं, दुर्लभः -भा -भं.—(In age) उपगम्, उपागम्, गम्, आप्, प्राप्, इ, अनुभू; 'they met with their death,' विनाशम् उपगताः.—(Meet as waters) सङ्गम्, सम्प्लु (c. 1. -प्लवते -प्लोतुं), सम्भेदं कृ.

MEETING, s. (Coming together) सङ्गमः, समागमः, सङ्गः, सङ्गतिः f., सङ्गतं, मिलनं, मेलनं, सम्मिलनं, सम्मेलनं, मेलकः, संयोगः, योगः, एकत्र मिलनं, एकत्र गमनं.—(Assembly, convention) सभा, समाजः, मेला, मेलः, मेलकः, संसद् f., सदस् n., परिषद्, समज्या, मनुष्यसभा, गोष्ठी, समितिः f., आस्थानं -नी, लोकसंघः, जनसमागमः, जनमेला, मण्डलं, जनसमवायः, जनसमुदायः, जनसमूहः; 'dismissal of a meeting,' सभाविसर्जनं; 'person present at a meeting,' सभासद् m., सभास्तारः, सभ्यः, सदस्यः.—(Confluence) सम्भेदः, सङ्गमः, सङ्गः.

MEETING-HOUSE, s. मनुष्यसभा, सभा, सभागृहं, सभास्थानं, सभामन्दिरं, समागमगृहं, समागमस्थानं.

MEETLY, adv. यथायोग्यं, यथोचितं, युक्तं, उपयुक्तं, उचितं, यथार्हं.

MEETNESS, s. योग्यता, युक्तता, उपयुक्तता, उचितत्वं, औचित्यं.

MEGALOSAURUS, s. महामकरः, वृहन्मकरः.

MEGRIM, s. शिरोवेदना, शिरःपीडा, अर्द्धशिरःपीडा, अर्द्धमस्तकशूलः.

MEIOSIS, s. (Figure of rhetoric) न्यूनालङ्कारः, न्यूनीकरणालङ्कारः.

MELANAGOGUE, s. कृष्णपित्तघ्नं, कृष्णपित्तनाशकम् औषधं.

MELANCHOLIC, s. सदाविषादी m. (न्), नित्यविषादी m., कुपितवायुग्रस्तः.

MELANCHOLILY, adv. सविषादं, अवसादेन, सोद्वेगं, सावसादं, उद्विग्नवत्.

MELANCHOLY, a. (Depressed in spirits) विषण्णः -ण्णा -ण्णं, अवसन्नः -न्ना -न्नं, विषादी -दिनी -दि (न्), उद्विग्नः -ग्ना -ग्नं, उद्विग्नमनाः -नाः -नः (स्), विमनाः &c., दुर्मनाः &c., अन्तर्मनाः &c., उन्मनाः &c., क्लान्तमनाः &c., दीनमनाः &c., दीनमनस्कः -स्का -स्कं, विमनस्कः &c., दीनचेतनः -ना -नं, म्लानः -ना -नं, क्षामः -मा -मं, ग्लानः -ना -नं, खिन्नः -न्ना -न्नं, खेदयुक्तः -क्ता -क्तं, खेदी -दिनी &c., उदासीनः -ना -नं, चिन्तापरः -रा -रं, चिन्ताकुलः -ला -लं.—(Habitually depressed) सदाविषादी -दिनी &c., नित्यविषादी &c., सदाखेदी &c., नित्यविषण्णः &c., नित्यावसन्नः &c., सदावसन्नः &c., विषण्णवृत्तिः -त्तिः -त्ति, खेदवृत्तिः &c.—(Mournful, expressing or causing sorrow) विषादसूचकः -का -कं, खेदसूचकः -का -कं, विषादात्मकः -का -कं, खेदात्मकः -का -कं, शोकसूचकः -का -कं, शोकजनकः -का -कं, खेदजनकः -का -कं, दुःखकरः -रा -रं; 'to be melancholy,' विषद् (c. 1. -षीदति -षत्तुं), अवसद्, विषण्णीभू, खिद् in pass. (खिद्यते), ग्लै (c. 1. ग्लायति, ग्लातुं), उद्विग्नीभू, दुर्मनस् (nom. दुर्मनायते), उन्मनस्.

MELANCHOLY, s. विषादः, विषण्णता, अवसादः, अवसन्नता, खेदः, खिन्नता, उद्वेगः, उद्विग्नता, ग्लानिः f., म्लानिः f., क्षामिः f., निर्विण्णता, निर्वेदः, दीनता, दैन्यं, उदासीनता, औदासीन्यं, उत्कण्ठा, चिन्तोद्विग्नता, चिन्ता, विषादवृत्तिः f., विषण्णवृत्तित्वं, विमनस्कता, वैमनस्यं.

MELÉE, s. (Confused fight) रणसङ्कुलं, युद्धसङ्कुलं, सङ्कुलयुद्धं.

MELILOT, s. त्रिपर्णभेदः, त्रिपत्रविशिष्ट ओषधिप्रभेदः.

To MELIORATE, v. a. भद्रतरं -रां कृ, भद्रतरीकृ. *See To* IMPROVE.

MELIORATION, s. वृद्धिः f., वर्धनं, श्रेयस्त्वं, भद्रतरभावः. *See* IMPROVEMENT.

MELLIFEROUS, a. मधुप्रदः -दा -दं, मधुजनकः -का -कं, मधूत्पादकः &c.

MELLIFICATION, s. मधुकरणं, मधूत्पादनं, मधूत्पत्तिः f., मधुकारित्वं.

MELLIFLUENCE, s. मधुस्रावः, मधुप्रवाहः, अमृतस्रावः, सुधाप्रवाहः.

MELLIFLUOUS, MELLIFLUENT, a. मधुस्रावी -विणी -वि (न्), अमृतस्रावी &c., मधुरः -रा -रं, मधुमयः -यी -यं.—(As applied to speech) मधुराक्षरः -रा -रं, मधुरवाक्यः -क्या -क्यं.

MELLIFLUOUSNESS, s. मधुरता -त्वं, माधुर्य्यं, स्वादुता, वाक्यमाधुर्य्यं.

MELLOW, a. पक्वः -क्वा -क्वं, परिपक्वः -क्वा -क्वं, पक्वमृदुः -द्वी -दु, मृदुपक्वः -क्वा -क्वं, पक्त्रिमः -मा -मं, विपक्त्रिमः -मा -मं.—(Soft) मृदुः -दुः -द्वी -दु, कोमलः -ला -लं, मृदुलः -ला -लं, स्निग्धः -ग्धा -ग्धं, ललितः -ता -तं, सुखस्पर्शः -र्शा -र्शं.—(To the ear) मृदुशब्दः -ब्दा -ब्दं, कोमलशब्दः &c., मृदुनादः -दा -दं, मञ्जुलः -ला -लं, मञ्जुस्वनः -ना -नं.

To MELLOW, v. a. पच् (c. 1. पचति, पक्तुं, c. 10. पाचयति -यितुं), पक्वं -क्वां कृ, मृदुपक्वं -क्वां कृ, परिपक्वं -क्वां कृ, परिपक्वीकृ, मृदूकृ, कोमलीकृ.

To MELLOW, v. n. पक्वः -क्वा -क्वं भू, परिपक्वः -क्वा -क्वं भू, पक्वीभू, पक्वतां or पक्वदशां या (c. 2. याति -तुं) or इ (c. 2. एति -तुं), मृदुपक्वः -क्वा -क्वं भू, मृदूभू, कोमलीभू.

MELLOWED, p. p. पाकेन मृदूकृतः -ता -तं or कोमलीकृतः -ता -तं.

MELLOWNESS, s. पक्वता, परिपक्वता, मृदुता, पक्वमृदुता, कोमलता, मार्दवं, म्रदिमा m. (न्), पाकः, परिपाकः, पक्तिः f., पक्वदशा, पक्वभावः.—(Of sound) शब्दमृदुता, नादमार्दवं.

MELODIOUS, a. मधुरः -रा -रं, सुश्राव्यः -व्या -व्यं, सुस्वरः -रा -रं, सुस्रवः -वा -वं, सुचारुस्वनः -ना -नं, मञ्जुस्वनः -ना -नं, श्रोत्रसुखः -खा -खं, श्रोत्राभिरामः -मा -मं, श्रुतिसुखः -खा -खं, मधुरस्वरः -रा -रं, मधुराक्षरः -रा -रं, मधुकः -का -कं, सुशब्दः -ब्दा -ब्दं, मञ्जुलः -ला -लं.

MELODIOUSLY, adv. मधुरं, सुस्वरं, मधुरस्वरेण, सुचारुस्वरेण, माधुर्य्येण.

MELODIOUSNESS, s. मधुरता, माधुर्य्यं, सुश्राव्यता, सुस्वरता, स्वरमधुरता, स्वरमाधुर्य्यं, श्रोत्राभिरामता.

MELODY, s. सुस्वरः, सुस्वरानुपूर्व्यं, सुस्वरानुपूर्वी, सुस्वरानुक्रमः, स्वरमाधुर्य्यं, स्वरानुक्रममाधुर्य्यं, माधुर्य्यं, मधुरता, सुश्राव्यता, कलता -त्वं, तालः, तालैक्यं, प्रतितालः.

MELON, s. (Water-melon) तरबुजं, लतापनसः, सेटुः m., कालिङ्गं, कालिन्दकं, गोडुम्बः.

To MELT, v. a. विली in caus. (-लाययति -लापयति -यितुं), विद्रु (c. 10. -द्रावयति -यितुं), द्रवीकृ, गल् (c. 10. गालयति -यितुं), विद्रावणं कृ, गालनं कृ, विद्रुतीकृ, विलीनीकृ, आर्द्रीकृ, सार्द्रीकृ.—(Soften to love or tenderness) करुणार्द्रीकृ, दयार्द्रीकृ, भावार्द्रीकृ, सार्द्रीकृ, आर्द्रीकृ, वत्सल (nom. वत्सलयति -यितुं), वत्सलीकृ.

To MELT, v. n. विली (c. 4. -लीयते -लेतुं), प्रविली, प्रली, द्रु (c. 1. द्रवति, द्रोतुं), विद्रु, गल् (c. 1. गलति -लितुं), विगल्, क्षर् (c. 1. क्षरति -रितुं), द्रवीभू, आर्द्रीभू, सार्द्रीभू, विलीनीभू, विद्रुतीभू.—(Be softened to love or tenderness) दयार्द्रीभू, करुणार्द्रीभू, आर्द्रहृदयः -या -यं भू, क्लिन्नहृदयः -या -यं भू, सार्द्रीभू, वत्सल (nom. वत्सलायते), वत्सलीभू.

MELTED, p. p. द्रुतः -ता -तं, द्रावितः -ता -तं, विद्रुतः -ता -तं, विद्रावितः -ता -तं, द्रवीभूतः -ता -तं, लीनः -ना -नं, विलीनः -ना -नं, निलीनः ना -नं, गलितः -ता -तं, गालितः -ता -तं, क्षरितः -ता -तं, परिगलितः -ता -तं, द्रवीकृतः -ता -तं, द्रवमाणः -णा -णं, अवदीर्णः -र्णा -र्णं, आर्द्रीकृतः -ता -तं, सार्द्रीकृतः -ता -तं.—(Softened to tenderness) करुणार्द्रीकृतः-ता-तं, दयार्द्रीभूतः-ता-तं, क्लिन्नहृदयीकृतः-ता-तं, वत्सलीकृतः-ता-तं.

MELTER, s. द्रावकः, विद्रावकः, द्रावकरः, विलयनकृत्, द्रवकर्त्ता m. (र्तृ).

MELTING, s. द्रावः -वणं, विद्राव -वणं, विलयः -यनं, द्रवत्वं, गलनं, गालनं, गलितत्वं, द्रवीकरणं, क्षरणं, विलीनता, आर्द्रीकरणं, सार्द्रीकरणं.

MELTING, *part.* or a. द्रवमाणः -णा -णं, गलन् -लन्ती -लत् (त्), क्षरन् &c., गाली -लिनी -लि (न्), वात्सल्यजनकः -का -कं.

MEMBER, *s.* (Limb of the body) अङ्गं, अवयवः, शरीराङ्गं, शरीरावयवः, गात्रं, पक्षः, प्रतीकः, अपघनः; 'a minor member of the body,' प्रत्यङ्गं; 'having members,' अङ्गी -ङ्गिनी -ङ्गि, अवयवी &c., साङ्गः -ङ्गा -ङ्गं.—(Of a discourse, &c.) अङ्गं, प्रकरणं, खण्डः -ण्डं, देशः, पदं, परिच्छेदः, विच्छेदः.—(Part, division) अङ्गं, भागः, विभागः, अंशः, अवयवः; 'member by member,' अवयवशस्; 'forming a member,' अङ्गभूतः -ता -तं.—(Of a community or association) गणाभ्यन्तरः, संसर्गाभ्यन्तरः.—(Of an assembly) सभासद्, सभ्यः, सभास्थः, सभास्तारः, सभाभ्यन्तरः, सामाजिकः, सदस्यः.—(Individual) व्यक्तिः *f.*, एकजनः.—(Of a compound word) पदं; 'first member of a compound,' उपपदं; 'last member,' उत्तरपदं.

MEMBERED, *a.* अङ्गी -ङ्गिनी -ङ्गि (न्), साङ्गः -ङ्गा -ङ्गं, अवयवी &c.

MEMBRANE, *s.* त्वक् *f.* (च्), आवरणत्वक् *f.*, आवरकत्वक् *f.*, तनुत्वक् *f.*, अन्तस्त्वक् *f.*, चर्म्म *n.* (न्), अन्तश्चर्म्म *n.*, किल्लिका, किल्ली, आवरणं.

MEMBRANEOUS, MEMBRANOUS, *a.* तनुत्वङ्मयः -यी -यं, आवरणत्वङ्मयः -यी -यं, तनुत्वगावृतः -ता -तं.

MEMBRUM VIRILE, *s.* शिश्नः, पुंलिङ्गं, पुंश्चिह्नं, पुरुषाङ्गं, नराङ्गं, लिङ्गं, ध्वजः, इन्द्रियं, जघन्यं, चर्म्मदण्डः -ण्डं.

MEMENTO, *s.* स्मरणार्थकवस्तु *n.*, स्मृतिजनकचिह्नं, स्मरणं.

MEMOIR, *s.* वृत्तान्तः, वृत्तान्तरचना, वृत्तान्तोपाख्यानं, वृत्तान्तलिखनं, चरित्रं, चरित्ररचना, चरित्रोपाख्यानं, चरित्रलिखनं, इतिहासः.

MEMORABLE, *a.* स्मरणीयः -या -यं, स्मरणयोग्यः -ग्या -ग्यं, स्मरणार्हः -र्हा -र्हं, स्मर्त्तव्यः -व्या -व्यं, स्मरणोपयुक्तः -क्ता -क्तं, चिरस्मरणीयः &c., अविस्मरणीयः &c.

MEMORANDUM, *s.* स्मरणं, स्मरणपत्रं, स्मारकपत्रं, स्मरणार्थकचिह्नं, पत्रकं.

MEMORATIVE, MEMORIAL, *a.* स्मारकः -का -कं, स्मार्त्तः -र्त्ती -र्त्तं, स्मृतिजनकः -का -कं, स्मरणार्थकः -का -कं, स्मृतिकरः -रा -रं.

MEMORIAL, *s.* स्मरणार्थकविषयः, स्मरणार्थकवस्तु *n.*, स्मारकविषयः, स्मारकवस्तु, स्मरणार्थकचिह्नं, स्मार्त्तविषयः, स्मार्त्तवस्तु *n.*, स्मरणं.—(Petition) निवेदनपत्रं, विज्ञापनपत्रं, प्रार्थनपत्रं.

MEMORIALIST, *s.* निवेदनकर्त्ता *m.* (र्तृ), विज्ञापनकृत् *m.*, प्रार्थकः, प्रार्थयिता *m.*, अर्थी *m.* (न्), प्रार्थनपत्रलेखकः.

To MEMORIALIZE, *v.a.* निवेदनपत्रेण प्रार्थ् (c. 10. -अर्थयति -यितुं), निवेदनपत्रं लिख् (c. 6. लिखति, लेखितुं), निवेदनं कृ.

MEMORY, *s.* स्मरणं, स्मृतिः *f.*, संस्मृतिः *f.*, संस्मरणं, अनुस्मृतिः *f.*, अविस्मृतिः *f.*, संस्कारः, स्मरणशक्तिः *f.*, धारणा -णं; 'retentiveness of memory,' धारणा, धारणाशक्तिः *f.*; 'having a good or retentive memory,' स्मृतिमान् -मती -मत् (त्), स्मरणशीलः -ला -लं, दृढस्मरणशीलः -ला -लं, अधिगतार्थस्मरणशीलः -ला -लं, अधिगतार्थाविस्मरणशीलः -ला -लं; 'to commit to memory,' हृदये कृ, मनसि कृ, अभ्यस् (c. 4. -अस्यति -असितुं), कण्ठे कृ; 'committed to memory,' कण्ठस्थः -स्था -स्थं, हृदयस्थः -स्था -स्थं, हृत्स्थः &c., अभ्यस्तः -स्ता -स्तं; 'within memory,' स्मार्त्तः -र्त्ती -र्त्तं.—(Time to which memory may extend) स्मार्त्तकालः, स्मरणकालः, स्मृतिकालः.

MEN, *s. pl.* पुरुषाः *m. pl.*, नराः *m. pl.*, मनुष्याः *m. pl.*, मानुषाः *m. pl.*

To MENACE, *v. a.* भर्त्स् (c. 10. भर्त्सयति -ते -यितुं), अवभर्त्स्, निर्भर्त्स्, अभिभर्त्स्, अभिनिर्भर्त्स्, परिभर्त्स्, तर्ज् (c. 10. तर्जयति -यितुं), अभितर्ज्, समार्ज्, अवगुर् (c. 6. -गुरते -रितुं), भर्त्सनं कृ, तर्जनं कृ, भयप्रदर्शनं कृ.

MENACE, *s.* भर्त्सनं -ना, निर्भर्त्सनं -ना, तर्जनं, भयप्रदर्शनं, भयदर्शनं, परोदितं, अपकारगीः *f.* (र्).

MENACED, *p. p.* भर्त्सितः -ता -तं, अभिभर्त्सितः -ता -तं, तर्जितः -ता -तं.

MENACER, *s.* भर्त्सनकारी *m.* (न्), निर्भर्त्सनकृत् *m.*, भयप्रदर्शकः.

MENAGERY, MENAGERIE, *s.* पशुपक्षिसङ्ग्रहः, पश्वादिसङ्ग्रहः, विदेशीयजन्तुपालिका, विदेशीयपशुशाला, विदेशीयपशुपालनस्थानं, नानाजातीयपशुसङ्ग्रहः, भिन्नजातीयजन्तुसङ्ग्रहः, विहंसः, वीतंसः.

MENAGOGUE, *s.* ऋतुवर्धकम् or ऋतुप्रवाहकम् or ऋतुजनकम् औषधं, मुक्तार्त्तवौषधं.

To MEND, *v. a.* (Repair) सन्धा (c. 3. -दधाति -धत्ते -धातुं), समाधा, प्रतिसमाधा, प्रतिकृ, प्रतिसंस्कृ, पूर्ववत् कृ, साध् (c. 10. साधयति -यितुं), उद्धृ (c. 1. -हरति -हर्त्तुं), जीर्णोद्धारं कृ, जीर्णोद्धरणं कृ, सुस्थं -स्थां कृ, स्वस्थं -स्थां कृ, सन्धानं कृ, प्रतिसमाधानं कृ.—(Correct) शुध् (c. 10. शोधयति -यितुं), परिशुध्, विशुध्, संशुध्.—(Help) उपकृ.—(Improve) वृध् (c. 10. वर्धयति -यितुं), संवृध्, अधिकीकृ.

To MEND, *v. n.* (Grow better) भद्रतरः -रा -रं भू, भद्रतरीभू, अधिकीभू, वृध् (c. 1. वर्धते -र्धितुं), वृद्धिं गम् (c. 1. गच्छति, गन्तुं) or इ (c. 2. एति -तुं), श्रेयान् -यसी -यो भू, सुस्थः -स्था -स्थं भू, स्वस्थः -स्था -स्थं भू.

MENDABLE, *a.* सन्धेयः -या -यं, समाधेयः -या -यं, प्रतिसमाधेयः -या -यं, साध्यः -ध्या -ध्यं, उद्धार्य्यः -र्य्या -र्य्यं, उद्धरणीयः -या -यं, प्रतिकार्य्यः -र्य्या -र्य्यं.

MENDACIOUS, *a.* असत्यवादी -दिनी -दि (न्), मिथ्यावादी &c., असत्यभाषी -षिणी, अनृतभाषी &c. *See* LYING, LIAR.

MENDACITY, *s.* असत्यभाषणं, मिथ्यावादः, अनृतभाषणं, मृषावादः.

MENDED, *p. p.* समाहितः -ता -तं, प्रतिसमाहितः -ता -तं, सन्धितः -ता -तं, साधितः -ता -तं, उद्धृतः -ता -तं, जीर्णोद्धृतः -ता -तं, प्रतिकृतः -ता -तं.

MENDER, *s.* सन्धानकर्त्ता *m.* (र्तृ), सन्धानकृत् *m.*, सन्धाता *m.* (तृ), प्रतिसमाधाता *m.*, साधकः, उद्धर्त्ता *m.* (र्तृ), जीर्णोद्धर्त्ता.

MENDICANCY, *s.* भिक्षुकता, भिक्षोपजीविता, भैक्ष्यं, भैक्षजीविका.

MENDICANT, *s.* (Beggar) भिक्षार्थी *m.* (न्), भिक्षुकः -की *f.*, भिक्षुः *m.*, भिक्षाकः -की, भिक्षोपजीवी *m.* (न्), भैक्षजीवी *m.*, भिक्षाशी *m.* (न्), भिक्षाहारः, भैक्षभुक् *m.* (ज्), भैक्षाशी *m.*, भिक्षाचरः, भिक्षणशीलः, वनीयकः, याचकः, याचनकः. *See* BEGGAR. (Religious mendicant) भिक्षुः *m.*, परिव्राजकः -जिका, परिव्राजः, परिव्राट् *m.* (ज्), प्रव्रजितः, पाराशरी *m.* (न्), पराशरी *m.*, योगी *m.* (न्), सन्न्यासी *m.* (न्), यती *m.* (न्). Other kinds of religious mendicants are दण्डी *m.* (न्), त्रिदण्डी *m.* (न्), वैरागी *m.* (न्), भैरवयोगी *m.*, दिगम्बरः, मस्करी *m.* (न्), अघोरपन्थाः *m.* (न्), कर्मन्दी *m.* (न्).

MENDICITY, *s.* भिक्षुकता -त्वं, भैक्ष्यं, भैक्षोपजीवनं, भैक्षजीविका, भैक्षचर्य्या, भैक्षचरणं, भिक्षाशितं, भिक्षाटनं, भिक्षावृत्तिः *f.*, भिक्षुकवृत्तिः *f.*, भिक्षा, प्रव्रज्या, परिव्रज्या -ज्यं, व्रज्या, याचनावृत्तिः *f.*, याचकवृत्तिः *f.*, याञ्चा, याचना, पैङ्गिन्यं.

MENDING, *s.* सन्धानं, सन्धानकरणं, समाधानं, प्रतिसमाधानं, साधनं, उद्धारः, उद्धरणं, जीर्णोद्धारः, जीर्णोद्धरणं, सुस्थकरणं, प्रतिकरणं.

MENIAL, *a.* गृहदाससम्बन्धी -न्धिनी -न्धि (न्), प्रेष्यसम्बन्धी &c., अपकृष्टः -ष्टा -ष्टं, वार्षलः -ली -लं, व्रातीनः -ना -नं; 'menial offices,' प्रेष्यकर्म्म *n.* (न्), भृत्यकर्म्म *n.*; 'menial service,' प्रेष्यभावः, दास्ययोगः.

MENIAL, *s.* गृहदासः -सी *f.*, प्रेष्यः -ष्या, भृत्यः, चेटः -टी *f.*, सेवकः -की, अपकृष्टः, अपकृष्टकर्म्मकरः, किङ्करः; 'menials,' परिजनः, परिचरः, दासवर्गः.

MENISCUS, *s.* अर्द्धचन्द्राकारः, अर्द्धचन्द्राकृतिः *f.*

MENOLOGY, *s.* (Register of months) मासविवरणं, मासपञ्जिका.

MEN-PLEASER, *s.* लोकरञ्जकः, जनरञ्जकः, जनानुसारी *m.* (न्), लोकानुसारी.

MENSAL, *a.* भोजनपात्रसम्बन्धी -न्धिनी -न्धि (न्), भोजनाधारसम्बन्धी &c.

MENSES, *s. pl.* ऋतुः *m.*, आर्त्तवं, पुष्पं, कुसुमं, रजस् *n.*, योनिरञ्जनं, स्त्री-

धर्म्मः, कला, मलं, योनिमलं; 'first appearance of the menses,' ऋतुदर्शनं, रजोदर्शनं; 'ceremonies on the event,' ऋतुशान्तिः *f.*, ऋतूत्सवः; 'suppression of them,' रजोबन्धः.

Menstrual, *a.* (Monthly) मासिकः -की -कं, मास्यः -स्या -स्यं, मासीयः -या -यं, मासीनः -ना -नं, प्रातिमासिकः -की -कं, मासानुमासिकः -की -कं.

To menstruate, *v. n.* ऋतुमती भू, पुष्पवती भू, रजस्वला भू.

Menstruation, *s.* ऋतुप्रवाहः, ऋतुस्रावः; 'woman in this state.' *See* the next.

Menstruous, *a.* (Woman) ऋतुमती, पुष्पवती, रजस्वला, मलिनी, स्त्रीधर्म्मिणी, उदक्या, आत्रेयी -यिका, अविः -वी, वृषली, अस्पर्शा, सरजाः, चाण्डाली, ब्रह्मघातिनी, रजकी, शूद्री.—(Relating to the menses) आर्त्तवः -वी -वं, ऋतुसम्बन्धी -न्धिनी -न्धि (न्), ऋतु in comp.

Menstruum, *s.* (Solvent) द्रावकरसः, द्रावणं, विद्रावकरसः, विद्रावणं. —(Medium for mixing medicines) योगवाही *m.* (न्).

Mensurability, *s.* मेयता, प्रमेयता, परिमेयता, मापनीयत्वं.

Mensurable, *a.* मेयः -या -यं, प्रमेयः -या -यं, परिमेयः -या -यं, मापनीयः -या -यं, माप्यः -प्या -प्यं, मापनक्षमः -मा -मं.

Mensural, *a.* मानसम्बन्धी &c., मानविषयः -या -यं, परिमाणविषयः &c.

To mensurate, *v. a.* मा (c. 2. माति -तुं, c. 10. मापयति -यितुं). *See To* measure.

Mensuration, *s.* मापनं, परिमाणं, प्रमाणं, मानं, मितिः *f.*, मापकरणं.

Mental, *a.* मानसः -सी -सं, मानसिकः -की -कं, मनस्कः -स्का -स्कं, मनसिजः -जा -जं, मनोजः -जा -जं, मनोगतः -ता -तं, मनोभवः -वा -वं, मनःस्थः -स्था -स्थं, बुद्धिस्थः &c., चित्तभवः -वा -वं, चित्तगतः -ता -तं, चित्तजः -जा -जं, मनोमयः -यी -यं, मनःकल्पितः -ता -तं, बुद्धिकल्पितः -ता -तं, मनःसम्बन्धी -न्धिनी &c.; 'mental suffering,' मनस्तापः, मनःपीडा; 'mental abstraction,' योगः, समाध्यानं, चित्तवृत्तिनिरोधः.

Mentally, *adv.* मनसा, बुद्ध्या, चिन्तया, बुद्धिमात्रेण; 'mentally blind,' अन्धधीः -धीः -धि, अन्धबुद्धिः -द्धिः -द्धि, अन्धीकृतात्मा -त्मा -त्म (न्).

Mention, *s.* अभिधानं, अभिधा, आख्यानं, कथनं, उपादानं, ग्रहणं, नामग्रहणं, नामनिर्देशः, निवेदनं, कीर्त्तनं, सङ्कीर्त्तनं, उच्चारणं, उद्देशः, उल्लेखः -खनं, श्रुतिः *f.*; 'no mention whatever,' न गन्धलेशः; 'to make mention.' *See* the next.

To mention, *v. a.* ख्या (c. 2. ख्याति -तुं), आख्या, कथ् (c. 10. कथयति -यितुं), सङ्कथ्, निविद् (c. 10. -वेदयति -यितुं), अभिधा (c. 3. -दधाति -धातुं), कृत् (c. 10. कीर्त्तयति -यितुं), अनुकृत्, उच्चर् (c. 10. -चारयति -यितुं), निर्दिश् (c. 6. -दिशति -देष्टुं), उद्दिश्, उद्देशं कृ, अभिधानं कृ. —(By name) नाम ग्रह् (c. 9. गृह्णाति, ग्रहीतुं), नामग्रहणं कृ, नामनिर्देशं कृ; 'it will be mentioned,' वक्ष्यते.

Mentioned, *p. p.* उक्तः -क्ता -क्तं, प्रोक्तः -क्ता -क्तं, कथितः -ता -तं, आख्यातः -ता -तं, अभिहितः -ता -तं, निवेदितः -ता -तं, कीर्त्तितः -ता -तं, स्मृतः -ता -तं; 'by name,' नामाभिहितः -ता -तं; 'before mentioned,' पूर्व्वोक्तः -क्ता -क्तं, पूर्व्वोदितः -ता -तं; 'about to be mentioned,' वक्ष्यमाणः -णा -णं.

Mentor, *s.* उपदेष्टा *m.* (ष्टृ), उपदेशकः, मन्ता *m.* (न्तृ), अभिमन्ता *m.*

Mephitic, mephitical, *a.* पूतिगन्धी -न्धिनी -न्धि (न्), पूतिगन्धः -न्धा -न्धं, पूतिगन्धात्मकः -का -कं, दुर्गन्धी &c., दूषकगन्धी &c., पूतिगन्धमयः -यी -यं, दुर्गन्धमयः -यी -यं, पूतिविषः -षा -षं, विषात्मकः -का -कं.

Meracious, *a.* तेजोमयः -यी -यं, सत्त्वपूर्णः -र्णा -र्णं, रसिकः -का -कं.

Mercantile, *a.* वाणिजिकः -की -कं, वाणिजः -जी -जं, वाणिज्यसम्बन्धी -न्धिनी -न्धि (न्), वणिक्पथसम्बन्धी &c., वणिक्सम्बन्धी &c., व्यवहारसम्बन्धी &c., आपणिकः -का -कं, पण्यायासम्बन्धी &c., नैगमः -मी -मं.

Mercature, *s.* क्रयविक्रयः, वाणिज्यं, पणायाः, वणिक्पथं.

Mercenarily, *adv.* लाभलोभात्, लाभापेक्षया, स्वार्थापेक्षया, लाभदृष्ट्या, लाभबुद्ध्या, फललोभात्, वेतनार्थं, फलार्थं, अर्थेतस्, भृतकवत्, सकामं.

Mercenariness, *s.* लाभलोभः, फललोभः, लाभदृष्टिः *f.*, वेतनार्थित्वं, लाभबुद्धिः *f.*, फलाशा, धनलोभः, धनलुब्धता, स्वार्थापेक्षा, सकामता, सकामबुद्धिः *f.*, वेतनापेक्षा.

Mercenary, *a.* (Hired, hireling) भृतकः -का -कं, वैतनिकः -की -कं, वेतनार्थी -र्थिनी -र्थि (न्), वस्निकः -का -कं, भृतिभुक् *m. f. n.* (ज्), भरण्यभुक् *m. f. n.*, भृत्यः -त्या -त्यं, वेतनभृत् *m. f. n.*—(Actuated by hope of gain, greedy of gain) लाभलोभी -भिनी &c., लाभार्थी -र्थिनी &c., लाभदृष्टिः -ष्टिः -ष्टि, लाभबुद्धिः -द्धिः -द्धि, धनलोभी &c., धनलुब्धः -ब्धा -ब्धं, धनार्थी &c., फलदर्शी -र्शिनी &c., स्वार्थः -र्था -र्थं, स्वार्थदर्शी &c., स्वार्थापेक्षकः -का -कं, सकामः -मा -मं, कामात्मा -त्मा -त्म (न्); 'from mercenary motives,' अर्थेतस्, स्वार्थेतस्, लाभलोभात्, फललोभात्.

Mercenary, *s.* (A hireling) भृतकः, भृतिभुक् *m.* (ज्), भरण्यभुक् *m.*, वैतनिकः, वस्निकः, वेतनार्थी *m.* (न्), वेतनभुक् *m.*, भृत्यः; 'soldier,' भृतकसैन्यः.

Mercer, *s.* कौशाम्बरविक्रयी *m.* (न्), कौशेयवणिक् *m.* (ज्), कौशिकवणिक्, दुकूलविक्रेता *m.* (तृ), कौशिकवस्त्रव्यवसायी *m.* (न्).

Mercery, *s.* कौशाम्बरं, कौशिकवस्त्रादि *n.*, कौशिकवस्त्रादिव्यवसायः.

Merchandise, *s.* (Goods) पण्यं, पण्यद्रव्यं, पण्यद्रव्याणि *n. pl.*, पण्यानि *n. pl.*, विक्रेयद्रव्याणि, विट्पण्यं, भाण्डकं, पण्यभाण्डकं, पण्यभाण्डानि *n. pl.*, वाणिज्यभाण्डानि, वाणिज्यद्रव्यं, वाणिज्यपण्यं, पणः, पणासः. —(Trade) वाणिज्यं -ज्या, वणिक्पथं, क्रयविक्रयः, पणाया, व्यापारः, व्यवहारः, व्यवसायः.

To merchandise, *v. n.* वाणिज्यं कृ, क्रयविक्रयं कृ, व्यापारं कृ.

Merchant, *s.* वणिक् *m.* (ज्), वाणिजः -जिकः, वाणिज्यजनः, महाजनः, सार्थवाहः, सार्थिकः, क्रयविक्रयिकः, आपणिकः, पणिकः, व्यवसायी *m.* (न्), व्यापारी *m.*, व्यवहारी *m.*, व्यवसायकः, वाणिज्योपजीवी *m.* (न्), श्रेष्ठी *m.* (न्), साधुः *m.*, साधुजनः, नैगमः; 'voyaging merchant,' पोतवणिक्, सांयात्रिकः; 'man of the mercantile or third class,' वैश्यः, विट् *m.* (श्); 'company of merchants,' सार्थः, निगमः.

Merchantable, *a.* पण्यः -ण्या -ण्यं, विक्रेयः -या -यं, पण्यार्हः -र्हा -र्हं.

Merchant-man, *s.* (Ship employed in trade) वाणिज्यनौः *f.*, वाणिज्यनौका.

Merciful, *a.* दयालुः -लुः -लु, दयावान् -वती -वत् (त्), कृपालुः -लुः -लु, कृपावान् &c., दयाशीलः -ला -लं, कृपाशीलः -ला -लं, सदयः -या -यं, सकरुणः -णा -णं, करुणाशीलः -ला -लं, कारुणिकः -की -कं, सानुकम्पः -म्पा -म्पं, अनुकम्पी -म्पिनी -म्पि (न्), सानुक्रोशः -शा -शं, हृदयालुः -लुः -लु, दयामयः -यी -यं, कृपामयः &c., करुणामयः &c., दयाबुद्धिः -द्धिः -द्धि, दयादृष्टिः -ष्टिः -ष्टि, क्षमाशीलः -ला -लं, क्षमावान् &c., अनुकम्पाशीलः -ला -लं, घृणी -णिनी &c., करुणार्द्रः -र्द्रा -र्द्रं, वत्सलः -ला -लं, कृपाकरः -रा -रं, दयायुक्तः -क्ता -क्तं.

Mercifully, *adv.* सदयं, सकारुण्यं, सानुकम्पं, कृपया, दयया, सानुक्रोशं, दयापूर्व्वं, कृपापूर्व्वं, दयाबुद्ध्या, कारुण्येन -ण्यात्, क्षमापूर्व्वं, वात्सल्यात्.

Mercifulness, *s.* दयालुता, कृपालुता, कारुण्यं, दयाशीलता, कृपाशीलता, सदयत्वं, सानुकम्पता, सानुक्रोशता, क्षमाशीलता, दया, कृपा, अनुकम्पा, करुणा, घृणा, वात्सल्यं.

Merciless, *a.* निर्दयः -या -यं, अदयः -या -यं, निष्कृपः -पा -पं, निर्घृणः

-णा -णं, निष्करुणः -णा -णं, अकरुणः -णा -णं, दयाहीनः -ना -नं, दयारहितः -ता -तं, दयाशून्यः -न्या -न्यं, कृपाहीनः -ना -नं, वीतघृणः -णा -णं, निठुरः -रा -रं.

MERCILESSLY, *adv.* निर्दयं, निष्कृपं, निष्करुणं, निठुरं, अतिनैठुर्य्येण.

MERCURIAL, *a.* (Containing mercury or quicksilver) पारदमयः -यी -यं, पारदात्मकः -का -कं, सपारदः -दा -दं.—(Volatile, sprightly) चञ्चलः -ला -लं, चपलः -ला -लं, चञ्चलबुद्धिः -द्धिः -द्धि, प्रकृतितरलः -ला -लं, तरलप्रकृतिः -तिः -ति, क्षणिकबुद्धिः &c., अस्थिरः -रा -रं.

MERCURY, *s.* (The planet, fabled as the son of Soma, or the moon, by Rohiní) सौम्यः, सोमभूः *m.*, बुधः, रौहिणेयः, रोधनः, बोधनः, राजपुत्रः, तुङ्गः, हकाङ्गः, श्यामाङ्गः, हकदेहः, प्रहर्षणः, पञ्चार्चिस् *m.*, अविष्ठाः.—(Quicksilver) पारदः, पार -रतः, रसः, रसधातुः *m.*, सिद्धधातुः, दिव्यरसः, चपलः, दारदः. *See* QUICKSILVER. (A preparation of mercury used in medicine) घनसारः, चन्द्रोदयः, चतुर्मुखः; 'Calx or oxid of mercury,' रसभस्म *n.* (न्), पारदभस्म *n.*; 'white sublimate or muriate of mercury,' रसकर्पूरः; 'sulphuret of mercury,' कज्जली.—(Interpreter or preceptor of the gods) बृहस्पतिः *m.*

MERCY, *s.* (Disposition to forgive, clemency) दया, कृपा, दयाशीलता, कृपाशीलता, क्षमाशीलता, दयालुता, कृपालुता, दयाबुद्धिः *f.*, क्षमाबुद्धिः *f.*—(Compassion) अनुकम्पा, कारुण्यं, करुणा, घृणा, अनुक्रोशः, कृपा, दया.—(Grace, favor) अनुग्रहः, प्रसादः, प्रसन्नता, अनुरोधः.—(Pardon) क्षमा, पापमार्जनं, पापशुद्धिः *f.*, निष्कृतिः *f.*; 'ocean or fountain of mercy,' दयासागरः, दयासमुद्रः, दयानिधिः *m.*, करुणाकरः; 'vessel or recipient of mercy,' दयापात्रं, कृपापात्रं, दयाभाजनं, अनुकम्पनीयः -या, अनुग्राह्यः -ह्या; 'to shew or have mercy,' दयां कृ, अनुकम्प् (c. 1. -कम्पते -म्पितुं), दय् (c. 1. दयते -यितुं), क्षम् (c. 1. क्षमते -मितुं, क्षन्तुं); 'mercy!' त्राहि, त्रायस्व, क्षमस्व, क्षम्यतां.

MERCY-SEAT, *s.* करुणासनं, ईश्वरासनं, परमेश्वरासनं, ईश्वरप्रसादासनं.

MERE, *a.* (Only, pure) मात्र in comp., मात्रकः -का -कं, केवलः -ला -ली -लं, केवली -लिनी -लि (न्), शुद्धः -द्धा -द्धं; 'a mere man,' मनुष्यमात्रः; 'mere touch,' स्पर्शमात्रं; 'mere words,' वाङ्मात्रं; 'by mere talk,' वाक्यमात्रेण; 'a mere grammarian,' केवलवैयाकरणः; 'a mere logician,' केवलनैयायिकः.

MERE, *s.* (A lake) सरस् *n.*, ह्रदः, सरोवरः, पयोराशिः *m.*—(Boundary) सीमा, परिसीमा, अन्तः, समन्तः, पर्य्यन्तं.

MERELY, *adv.* मात्रं, मात्रेण -त्रात्, केवलं, कुट्टारं, खलु; 'by merely inspecting,' निरीक्षणमात्रेण; 'from caste merely,' जातिमात्रात्.

MERETRICIOUS, *a.* (Relating to harlots) वेश्यासम्बन्धी -न्धिनी -न्धि (न्), वाराङ्गनीयः -या -यं, पण्याङ्गनीयः -या -यं.—(Having a false show, gaudy) कृत्रिमशोभावान् -वती -वत् (त्), कृत्रिमशोभामयः -यी -यं, मिथ्याशोभनः -ना -नं, कृत्रिमालङ्कारमयः -यी -यं, मिथ्यालङ्कारवान् &c., मिथ्यारागी -गिणी &c.

MERETRICIOUSLY, *adv.* वेश्यारूपेण, कृत्रिमशोभापूर्व्वं, मिथ्याशोभापूर्व्वं.

To MERGE, *v. a.* (Immerge) मज्ज् (c. 10. मज्जयति -यितुं), निमज्ज्, मग्नं -ग्नां कृ, अवगाह् (c. 10. -गाहयति -यितुं), गाह्.—(Cause to be swallowed up or lost) ग्रस्तं -स्तां कृ, विलीनं -नां कृ, निपीतं -तां कृ, नश् (c. 10. नाशयति -यितुं), नष्टं -ष्टां कृ.

To MERGE, *v. n.* मज्ज् (c. 6. मज्जति -ज्जितुं, मंक्तुं), अवगाह् (c. 1. -गाहते -हितुं -गाढुं), ग्रस्तः -स्ता -स्तं भू, निपीतः -ता -तं भू, नश् (c. 4. नश्यति -शितुं), मग्नः -ग्ना -ग्नं भू, विली (c. 4. -लीयते -लेतुं).

MERGED, *p. p.* मग्नः -ग्ना -ग्नं, निमग्नः -ग्ना -ग्नं, अवगाढः -ढा -ढं, लीनः -ना -नं, विलीनः -ना -नं, निलीनः -ना -नं, लुप्तः -प्ता -प्तं.

MERIDIAN, *s.* (Midday, noon) मध्याह्नः, मध्याह्नकालः, मध्यन्दिनं, दिनमध्यं.—(Meridian of the place in geography and astronomy) याम्योत्तरवृत्तं, समध्यं; 'meridians of right ascension,' क्रान्तिसूत्राणि *n. pl.*; 'distance from the first meridian,' रेखान्तरं, देशान्तरं; 'distance between the meridians,' स्पष्टपरिधिः *m.*—(Height, highest point) उच्चता, उच्चपदं, अग्रं, मध्यं.

MERIDIAN, *a.* (Relating to midday) माध्याह्निकः -की -कं, माध्यन्दिनः -नी -नं, मध्याह्नकालीनः -ना -नं.—(Pertaining to the meridian line) याम्योत्तरवृत्तसम्बन्धी -न्धिनी -न्धि (न्), समध्यसम्बन्धी &c.—(Highest) उच्चतमः -मा -मं, उत्तमः -मा -मं.

MERIDIONAL, *a.* दक्षिणदिक्स्थः -स्था -स्थं, दक्षिणमुखः -खा -खं, दक्षिणाभिमुखः &c., दाक्षिणिकः -की -कं, दक्षिणदेशीयः -या -यं.

MERIT, *s.* (Desert) गुणः, योग्यता, उपयोगः, उपयुक्तता, पात्रता.—(Excellence, great merit) गुणोत्कर्षः, गुणप्रकर्षः, गुणवैशेष्यं, गुणिता, गुणपूगं, सगुणता, गुणौघं, गुणवत्ता, गुणता, गुणमहत्त्व *n.*, उत्कर्षः, उत्कृष्टता, श्रेष्ठता, शस्यं, प्रशस्यं, सारता -त्वं; 'appreciating merit,' गुणग्रहणं; 'one who does so,' गुणग्राही *m.* (न्), गुणग्राहकः, गुणज्ञः.—(Merits, good or bad) गुणागुणं, गुणदोषौ *m.* du., गुणदोषं, सारासारं, पुण्यापुण्यं, धर्म्माधर्म्मं; 'testing one's merits,' गुणागुणपरीक्षा, गुणदोषपरीक्षणं.—(Merit acquired through works, according to the Hindu notion) पुण्यं, श्रेयस् *n.*, सुकृतं, धर्म्मः, वृषः, तपस् *n.*, नियमः, पुण्यसामग्री, सञ्चितं; 'acquisition of merit,' पुण्यार्जनं, पुण्यसम्पादनं, श्रेयःसम्पादनं; 'acquired by merit,' पुण्यार्जितः -ता -तं, पुण्यविभितः -ता -तं; 'reward of merits,' पुण्यफलं; 'good fortune, as the result of merits,' पुण्योदयः; 'merit acquired in some former birth,' पूर्व्वपुण्यं; 'mightiness of merit,' पुण्यप्रतापः; 'person of great merit,' पुण्यनिधिः *m.*, श्रेयोनिधिः *m.*, पुण्यसागरः, पुण्यराशिः *m.*, पुण्यात्मा *m.* (न्), पुण्यजनः; 'a work giving an account of the merits of any holy place or object,' माहात्म्यं.

To MERIT, *v. a.* अर्ह् (c. 1. अर्हति -ते -र्हितुं), अर्हः -र्हा -र्हं or उपयुक्तः -क्ता -क्तं or योग्यः -ग्या -ग्यं or उचितः -ता -तं भू or अस्; 'he merits a kingdom,' राज्यम् अर्हति; 'he merits punishment,' दण्डार्हो भवति or अस्ति; 'to merit confidence,' विश्वासपात्रं भू. *See* *To* DESERVE.

MERITED, *p. p.* उपयुक्तः -क्ता -क्तं, योग्यः -ग्या -ग्यं, अर्हितः -ता -तं.

MERITORIOUS, *a.* (Deserving a reward) वेतनार्हः -र्हा -र्हं, दक्षिणार्हः &c., प्रतिफलार्हः &c.—(Deserving of honor) श्लाघ्यः -घ्या -घ्यं, श्लाघनीयः -या -यं, प्रशंसनीयः -या -यं, शंस्यः -स्या -स्यं, प्रशस्तः -स्ता -स्तं, श्लाघार्हः -र्हा -र्हं, प्रशंसार्हः &c.—(Having great merit) गुणवान् -वती -वत् (त्), गुणसम्पन्नः -न्ना -न्नं, गुणी -णिनी -णि (न्), गुणान्वितः -ता -तं, श्रेष्ठः -ष्ठा -ष्ठं, उत्तमगुणविशिष्टः -ष्टा -ष्टं.—(Having great religious merit) पुण्यवान् -वती &c., पुण्यशाली -लिनी &c., पुण्यरूपः -पा -पं, पुण्यात्मकः -का -कं, कृतपुण्यपुञ्जः -ञ्जा -ञ्जं; 'meritorious act,' पुण्यकं, व्रतः -तं, नियमः, तपस् *n.*

MERITORIOUSLY, *adv.* यथा वेतनम् or प्रतिफलम् अर्हति तथा, श्लाघनीयं.

MERITORIOUSNESS, *s.* योग्यता, उपयुक्तता, वेतनार्हता, वेतनयोग्यता, उपयोगिता, पात्रता, गुणिता, गुणसम्पन्नता, श्लाघ्यता, पुण्यता, पुण्यवत्त्वं.

MERLIN, s. (Kind of hawk) श्येनभेदः, कपोतारिः m.

MERMAID, s. मत्स्यकन्या, मत्स्यकुमारी -रिका, कविकल्पितः कन्योर्द्धकायो मत्स्याधःकायो जन्तुविशेषः, समुद्रीयस्त्री.

MERRILY, adv. सहर्षं, सानन्दं, उल्लासेन, उल्लसितं, सहासं, सहास्यं, सहसितं, परिहासेन, हृष्टमनसा, सकौतुकं, प्रफुल्लमनसा, उल्लसवत्, हृष्टवत्, प्रमोदेन.

MERRIMENT, s. उल्लसता, उल्लासः, हर्षः, प्रहर्षः, आनन्दः, सानन्दता, प्रफुल्लता, हास्यं, प्रहसनं, हासिका, परिहासः, परीहासः, आह्लादः, मुदा, प्रमोदः, कौतुकं, प्रहृष्टता, हृष्टता, क्रीडा, क्रीडाकौतुकं, विलासः, लीला, खेला, हास्यविनोदः, उत्सवः, चर्भटी.

MERRINESS, s. हृष्टता, प्रहृष्टता, उल्लसता, उल्लासिता, हास्यमुखता, हास्यवृत्तिः f., सानन्दता, प्रफुल्लता, सदानन्दिता.

MERRY, a. हृष्टः -ष्टा -ष्टं, हृष्टहृदयः -या -यं, प्रहृष्टः -ष्टा -ष्टं, प्रहृष्टचित्तः -त्ता -त्तं, उल्लसः -सा -सं, उल्लासी -सिनी -सि (न्), उल्लासवृत्तिः -त्तिः -त्ति, परिहासशीलः -ला -लं, हास्यवृत्तिः -त्तिः -त्ति, हास्यमुखः -खी -खं, हास्यवदनः -ना -नं, सुहृष्टाननः -ना -नं, आनन्दी -न्दिनी &c., आनन्दवृत्तिः -त्तिः -त्ति, हासी -सिनी &c., प्रमोदी -दिनी &c., मुदान्वितः -ता -तं, मुदितः -ता -तं, विलासी &c., विनोदी &c., सुमनाः -नाः -नः (स्), कौतुकी &c., उपजातकौतुकः -का -कं.—(Causing mirth) हास्यजनकः -का -कं, हास्योत्पादकः -का -कं, विनोदकः -का -कं; 'to make merry,' उत्सवं कृ; 'to be merry,' उल्लस् (c. 1. -लसति -सितुं), सुमन (nom. सुमनायते), कौतुकं कृ.

MERRY-ANDREW, s. भण्डः, वैहासिकः, विदूषकः, परिहासवेदी m. (न्).

MERRY-MAKING, s. उत्सवः, उत्सवकरणं, महोत्सवः, विलासकरणं.

MERSION, s. मज्जनं, प्रमज्जनं, निमज्जनं, विगाहः -हनं, अवगाहनं.

MERU, s. (The sacred mountain, in the centre of the seven continents, at the extremity of the world's axis, where the gods reside, corresponding to Mount Olympus of the Greeks) मेरुः m., सुमेरुः m., सुरालयः, देवालयः, हेमाद्रिः m., रत्नसानुः m.

MESENTERIC, a. अन्त्रपेशीसम्बन्धी -न्धिनी &c., मध्यान्त्रिकः -की -कं.

MESENTERY, s. अन्त्रपेशी, अन्त्रावरणत्वक् f. (च्), मध्यान्त्रावरणत्वक् f., मध्यान्त्रबन्धनत्वक् f.; 'enlargement of the mesentery,' प्लीहा m. (न्).

MESH, s. (Interstice of a net) जालान्तरं, जालच्छिद्रं, जालरन्ध्रं.

To MESH, v. a. जाले or पाशे पत् (c. 10. पातयति -यितुं), जाले पातयित्वा बन्ध् (c. 9. बध्नाति, बन्द्धुं), जालबद्धं -द्धां कृ.

MESHY, a. जालरूपः -पा -पं, जालाकारः -रा -रं, जालमयः -यी -यं, जालवन्निर्मितः -ता -तं जालवद् बहुच्छिद्रमयः -यी -यं.

MESLIN, s. (Mixture of grain) मिश्रधान्यं, धान्यमिश्रणं, मिश्रान्नं.

MESS, s. (Dish or quantity of food) अन्नभागः, अन्नपात्रं, चरुः, सिद्धान्नं, यत् खाद्यद्रव्यम् एकपुरुषस्य परिवेष्यते.—(Food prepared for a number of persons in common) गणान्नं.—(Set of persons who eat together) पंक्तिः f., सहभोजिपंक्तिः f., सहभोजनपंक्तिः f., गणान्नपंक्तिः f., अग्निपंक्तिः f., सहभोजिगणः, सहभोजिनः m. pl., पंक्तिभोजिनः m. pl., गणान्नचक्रं, गणाचक्रं; 'not admissible into the same mess,' अपांक्तेयः -या -यं, अपांक्तः -क्ता -क्तं, अपांक्त्यः -क्त्या -क्त्यं.—(Medley, litter) सङ्करः, नानाद्रव्यसाङ्कर्यं, नानाद्रव्यसन्निपातः, नानाद्रव्यसम्मिश्रणं, सङ्कीर्णकं, सङ्कुलकं.—(Plight) दुर्दशा, दुर्गतिः f., कर्दमः; 'in a mess,' दुर्दशाग्रस्तः -स्ता -स्तं.

To MESS, v. n. (Eat in company) पंक्तिभोजनं कृ, एकपंक्तिभोजनं कृ, सहभोजनं कृ, एकत्र भोजनं कृ or आहारं कृ.

To MESS, v. a. (Make into a mess) सङ्करीकृ, सम्मिश्रीकृ.

MESSAGE, s. सन्देशः, सन्दिष्टं, वार्त्ता, दूत्यं, दौत्यं, वृत्तान्तः, वाचिकं, निदेशः, निर्दिष्टं, वचनोपन्यासः, आदेशः, समाचारः, आज्ञा, शासनं, शास्तिः f., वक्तव्यं, वचनं, प्रैषः; 'sending on a message,' प्रतिशासनं.

MESSED, p. p. सङ्करीकृतः -ता -तं, सम्मिश्रितः -ता -तं, सन्निपतितः -ता -तं.

MESSENGER, s. दूतः, सन्देशहरः, वार्त्ताहरः, वार्त्तायनः, वाचिकहरः, आख्यायकः, सञ्चगः, प्रयोज्यः, सञ्चारकः, चारः, धावकः, समाचारदायकः, कार्य्यङ्करः, निसृष्टार्थः; 'female messenger,' दूती -तिः -तिका, सञ्चारिका.

MESSIAH, s. (The Anointed) अभिषिक्तः, अभिषिक्तत्राता m. (तृ).

MESSMATE, s. पंक्तिभोजी m. (न्), एकपंक्तिः m., समपंक्तिः, सहभोजी m.

MESSUAGE, s. वासगेहं -हः, वासगृहं, गृहवाटिका, वास्तुवाटी.

MET, p. p. समागतः -ता -तं, सङ्गतः -ता -तं, समुपागतः -ता -तं, मिलितः -ता -तं, अभिमुख्यागतः -ता -तं, सम्मुखागतः -ता -तं, अभियातः -ता -तं.—(Met as a guest) प्रत्युद्गतः -ता -तं, प्रत्युद्यातः -ता -तं.—(Met with) आसादितः -ता -तं, समासादितः -ता -तं, प्राप्तः -प्ता -प्तं, अधिगतः -ता -तं; 'hard to be met with,' दुर्लभः -भा -भं. *See To* MEET. 'Easy to be met with,' सुलभः &c.

METACARPAL, a. करभसम्बन्धी -न्धिनी -न्धि (न्), पीलुसम्बन्धी &c.

METACARPUS, s. करभः, पीलुः m., करभास्थि n., प्रपाणिः m., प्रहस्तः.

METACHRONISM, s. न्यूनकालनिरूपणं, न्यूननिरूपितकालः.

METAL, s. धातुः m., लोहः, तैजसं, सुवर्णरूप्यादि n.; 'base metal,' कुप्यं; 'factitious metal,' कृत्रिमधातुः m.; 'fused,' रसधातुः m., रसः; 'inferior,' उपधातुः m.; 'melting metals together,' आवर्त्तनं; 'the metals collectively,' धातुजातं, अष्टधातु n. The eight metals are, 'gold,' सुवर्णं; 'silver,' रूप्यं; 'copper,' ताम्रं; 'brass,' पित्तलं; 'bell-metal, or a kind of pewter,' कांस्यं; 'tin,' त्रपु; 'lead,' सीसकं; 'iron,' लोहः. Some make 'steel,' तीक्ष्णायसं, one of the eight metals, instead of कांस्यं.

METALLIC, METALLICAL, a. (Pertaining to metals) धातुसम्बन्धी -न्धिनी -न्धि (न्), लोहसम्बन्धी &c.—(Consisting of metal) धातुमयः -यी -यं, लोहमयः -यी -यं, लौहः -ही -हं, धातुरूपः -पा -पं, धातुनिर्मितः -ता -तं, सिद्धरसः -सा -सं, तैजसः -सी -सं, धातुगुणकः -का -कं, धातु or लोह in comp.

METALLIFEROUS, a. धातूत्पादकः -का -कं, धातुजनकः -का -कं.

METALLIST, s. धातुपरीक्षकः, धातुज्ञः, धातुविद् m., धातुकर्म्मकारी m. (न्).

METALLOGRAPHY, s. धातुवर्णनं, धातुविवरणं, धातुविवरणविद्या.

METALLURGIST, s. धातुकर्म्मकारी m. (न्), धातुशोधकः, धातुशोधनकृत् m.

METALLURGY, s. धातुशोधनं, धातुशोधनविद्या, धातुकर्म्म n. (न्).

To METAMORPHOSE, v. a. रूपपरिणामं कृ, परिणतरूपं -पां कृ, शरीरपरिणामं कृ, आकारपरिणामं कृ, रूपान्तरं कृ, देहान्तरं कृ, रूपविकारं कृ, रूपभेदं कृ.

METAMORPHOSED, p. p. परिणतरूपः -पा -पं, परिणतशरीरः -रा -रं, परिणताकारः -रा -रं, परिणताकृतिः -तिः -ति, रूपान्तरीकृतः -ता -तं, विकृताकारः -रा -रं, परिणतः -ता -तं, विकृतः -ता -तं, भिन्नरूपः -पा -पं.

METAMORPHOSIS, s. रूपपरिणामः, रूपान्तरं, देहान्तरं, आकारपरिणामः, रूपविकारः, रूपभेदः, शरीरविकारः, परिणामः, विकारः, विकृतिः f.

METAPHOR, s. रूपकं, व्यञ्जनं -ना, व्यञ्जकः, लक्षणा, उपलक्षणं, ध्वनिः m., समासोक्तिः f., आरोपः, उपमा, उपमितिः f., दृष्टान्तः, उत्प्रेक्षा, निदर्शनं, जहल्लक्षणा, जहत्स्वार्था, रूपकालङ्कारः, उपचारः, उपक्षेपः.

METAPHORIC, METAPHORICAL, a. लाक्षणिकः -की -कं, उपलक्षितः -ता -तं, सरूपकः -का -कं, सव्यञ्जकः -का -कं, व्यञ्जकः -का -कं, आरोपितः

-ता -तं, ध्वनितः -ता -तं, गौणः -णी -णं, औपचारिकः -की -कं; 'metaphorical sense,' गौणार्थः.

METAPHORICALLY, *adv.* सरूपकं, सध्वनं, रूपकपूर्व्वं, रूपकक्रमेण, उपलक्षणपूर्व्वं, उपलक्षणतस्, लाक्षणिकं, ध्वनितं.

METAPHRASE, *s.* यथाशब्दं भाषान्तरं, यथाशब्दभाषान्तरं.

METAPHRAST, *s.* यथाशब्दभाषान्तरकर्त्ता *m.* (र्त्तृ).

METAPHYSIC, METAPHYSICAL, *a.* आन्वीक्षिकः -की -कं, आन्वीक्षिकीसम्बन्धी -न्धिनी -न्धि (न्), मानसधर्म्मविषयः -या -यं, आत्मविषयः -या -यं, आन्वीक्षिकीविषयः -या -यं, आत्मज्ञानसम्बन्धी &c., अध्यात्मविद्यासम्बन्धी &c., मानसः -सी -सं, आध्यात्मिकः -की -कं, नैयायिकः -का -कं.

METAPHYSICALLY, *adv.* मानसधर्म्मानुसारेण, आत्मविद्यानुरूपेण.

METAPHYSICIAN, *s.* आन्वीक्षिकीज्ञः, मानसधर्म्मज्ञः, मानसविद्याज्ञः, अध्यात्मविद्याज्ञः, नैयायिकः, अर्थतत्त्ववेत्ता *m.* (त्तृ).

METAPHYSICS, *s.* आन्वीक्षिकी, आन्वीक्षिकी विद्या, मानसधर्म्मविषयका विद्या, मानसधर्म्माः, आत्मविषयकं ज्ञानं, आत्मधर्म्मविषयका विद्या, अमूर्त्तविषयज्ञानं, आत्मविद्या, अध्यात्मविद्या, मानसविद्या, आत्मतत्त्वविद्या, आत्मतत्त्वशास्त्रं, अर्थतत्त्वशास्त्रं, अर्थतत्त्वविद्या, आत्मतत्त्वविचारः.

METASTASIS, *s.* रोगस्थानान्तरं, रोगस्थलान्तरं.

METATARSAL, *a.* प्रपदीनः -ना -नं, प्रपदीयः -या -यं, प्रपदसम्बन्धी &c.

METATARSUS, *s.* प्रपदं, पादस्य मध्यभागः.

METATHESIS, *s.* अक्षरविपर्य्ययः, वर्णव्यत्ययः, अक्षरपरिवर्त्तनं.

To METE, *v. a.* मा (c. 2. माति -तुं, c. 10. मापयति -यितुं), परिमा, मापनं कृ.

METED, *p. p.* मितः -ता -तं, सम्मितः -ता -तं, परिमितः &c., निर्म्मितः &c.

METEMPSYCHOSIS, *s.* प्राणिनां पुनर्जन्म *n.* (न्), अन्यजन्म *n.*, जन्मान्तरं, जन्मजन्मान्तरं, देहान्तरप्राप्तिः *f.*, शरीरान्तरप्राप्तिः *f.*, रूपान्तरग्रहणं, अन्यशरीरग्रहणं.

METEOR, *s.* उल्का, सोल्का -ल्कः, अग्न्युत्पातः, केतुतारा, शिखावज्ज्योतिस् *n.*, अग्निरेखाकारि गगणात्पतज्ज्योतिस्, उपाहितः, उपग्रहः, उत्पातः, दिव्योत्पातः.

METEORIC, *a.* (Pertaining to meteors) उल्कासम्बन्धी &c., उल्काविषयः -या -यं.—(Proceeding from) उल्कोत्पन्नः -न्ना -न्नं, उल्कोद्भवः -वा -वं, उल्काजः -जा -जं.

METEOROLOGIC, METEOROLOGICAL, *a.* विद्युदुल्कादिविषयकः -का -कं, आकाशोद्भववस्तुसम्बन्धी &c., दिव्युद्भवविषयसम्बन्धी &c., आकाशीयः -या -यं.

METEOROLOGY, *s.* विद्युदुल्कादिविद्या, आकाशोद्भववस्तुविद्या, अन्तरीक्षविषयविद्या, आकाशविद्या, अन्तरीक्षविद्या, सामान्यवायुविषयका विद्या, वायुचक्रशास्त्रं.

METEOROUS, *a.* उल्कागुणकः -का -कं, उल्काधर्म्मकः -का -कं.

METER, *s.* मापकः, परिमापकः, मापनकर्त्ता *m.* (र्त्तृ), माननिरूपकः.

METHEGLIN, *s.* (Kind of mead) मधु *n.*, मधुपानीयं, मधुनीरं.

METHINKS, *v. impers.* मन्ये, इति मन्ये, इति तर्कयामि.

METHOD, *s.* (Regular arrangement) क्रमः, अनुक्रमः, पर्य्यायः, व्यवस्था, व्यवस्थापनं, क्रमेण स्थापनं, आनुपूर्व्वं -र्व्यं, आनुपूर्व्वी, परिपाटिः -टी *f.*, पारिपाट्यं, परम्परा, पारम्पर्य्यं, विन्यासः, व्यूहनं, व्यूढिः *f.*, प्रतिविधानं, विधानं, संविधानं, रचना, विरचनं -ना, आवृत् *f.*—(Way, mode, process) रीतिः *f.*, मार्गः, विधिः *m.*, विधानं, विधः, प्रकारः, क्रमः, नियमः, सूत्रं, वृत्तिः *f.*, रूपं, युक्तिः *f.*, पद्धतिः *f.*, न्यायः, मर्य्यादा, वृत्तान्तः, कॢप्तिः *f.*, क्रिया, धारा; 'in this method,' अनेन विधानेन, अनेन प्रकारेण, अनया रीत्या, अनयर्त्या. *See* MANNER.

METHODICAL, *a.* (Said of persons) नियमशीलः -ला -लं, क्रमशीलः -ला -लं, यथाक्रमकारी -रिणी -रि (न्), क्रमानुगतः -ता -तं, क्रमानुकारी &c., क्रमकः -का -कं, क्रमिकः &c.—(Of things) क्रमिकः -का -कं, क्रमकः -का -कं, यथाक्रमः -मा -मं, सक्रमः -मा -मं, यथानुक्रमः -मा -मं, क्रमानुसारी &c., व्यवस्थितः -ता -तं, सूत्रितः -ता -तं, यथापर्य्यायः -या -यं, आनुपूर्व्वः -र्व्वी -र्व्वं, अनुक्रान्तः -न्ता -न्तं; 'methodical proceeding,' अनुक्रमः -मणं.

MET

METHODICALLY, *adv.* यथाक्रमं, अनुक्रमेण, यथानुक्रमं, सक्रमं, क्रमतस्, क्रमशस्, क्रमेण, क्रमात्, पर्य्यायेण, यथापर्य्यायं, यथानियमं, यथामार्गं, अनुपूर्व्वशस्, यथासूत्रं, विधितस्; 'done methodically,' अनुक्रान्तः -न्ता -न्तं.

METHODICALNESS, *s.* क्रमशीलता, क्रमिकत्वं, व्यवस्थितिः *f.*, सक्रमता.

METHODISM, *s.* नियमनिष्ठा, नियमासक्तिः *f.*, कर्म्मनिष्ठा.

METHODIST, *s.* नियमनिष्ठः, नियमासक्तः, नियमी *m.* (न्), कर्म्मनिष्ठः.

METHODISTICAL, *a.* नियमनिष्ठाशीलः -ला -लं, नियमनिष्ठासम्बन्धी &c.

To METHODIZE, *v. a.* व्यवस्था in caus. (-स्थापयति -यितुं), व्यवस्थापनं कृ, क्रमेण or यथाक्रमं स्था, विरच् (c. 10. -रचयति -यितुं), विधा (c. 3. -दधाति -धातुं), संविधा, प्रतिविधा, विन्यस् (c. 4. -अस्यति -असितुं) व्यूह् (c. 1. -ऊहते -हितुं).

METHODIZED, *p. p.* व्यवस्थितः -ता -तं, व्यवस्थापितः -ता -तं, विन्यस्तः -स्ता -स्तं, प्रतिविहितः -ता -तं, अनुक्रान्तः -न्ता -न्तं, परिपाटीकृतः -ता -तं.

METONYMICAL, *a.* अजहल्लाक्षणिकः -की -कं, अजहत्स्वार्थलाक्षणिकः -की -कं.

METONYMY, *s.* अजहत्स्वार्था, अजहल्लक्षणा, भक्तिः *f.*

METRE, *s.* छन्दस् *n.*, छन्दः, वृत्तं, वर्णवृत्तं, गणवृत्तं, मात्रछन्दस्, पद्यं, वक्त्रं, वेदः; 'violation of metre,' छन्दोभङ्गः. The following are certain forms of metre explained in Wilson's Dictionary: 1. अनुष्टुप् *f.* (भ्) or श्लोकः, of which varieties are चित्रपदा, माणवकः, विद्युन्माला, प्रमाणिका, 2. त्रिष्टुप् *f.*, varieties इन्द्रवज्रा, उपेन्द्रवज्रा, उपजातिः *f.*, रथोद्धता, 3. जगती, varieties वंशस्थविलं, द्रुतविलम्बितं, भुजङ्गप्रयातं, 4. अतिजगती, varieties मञ्जुभाषिणी, प्रहर्षिणी, पुष्पिताग्रा, 5. शक्वरी or शक्करी, varieties वसन्ततिलकः, अपराजिता, वासन्ती, लोला, नान्दीमुखं, 6. अतिशक्वरी or अतिशक्करी, varieties मालिनी or मानिनी, चित्रा, तूणकं, लीलाखेलः, 7. अष्टी, varieties चकिता, पञ्चचामरं, मदनललितं, वाणिनी *f.*, प्रवरललितं, 8. अत्यष्टी, varieties शिखरिणी, मन्दाक्रान्ता, हरिणी, भाराक्रान्ता, पृथ्वीभरः, 9. धृतिः *f.* varieties नाराचः, नन्दनं, शार्दूलललितः, कुसुमितलता, चित्रलेखा, 10. अतिधृतिः *f.* of which varieties are शार्दूलविक्रीडितः, मेघविस्फूर्जितं, सुरसा, फुल्लदाम *n.* (न्), 11. कृतिः *f.*, varieties सुवदना, गीतिका, शोभा, 12. प्रकृतिः, varieties स्रग्धरा, सरसी, 13. आकृतिः *f.*, varieties हंसी, मदिरा, 14. विकृतिः *f.*, 15. संकृतिः *f.*, 16. अतिकृतिः *f.*, variety क्रौञ्चपदा, 17. उत्कृतिः *f.*, variety भुजङ्गविजृम्भितं, 18. दण्डकः, varieties जीमूतः, लीला, शङ्खः, व्यालः, प्रचितं, 19. प्रतिष्ठा, varieties कन्या, सती, 20. सुप्रतिष्ठा, varieties पंक्तिः *f.*, प्रिया, 21. मध्या or मध्यमा, varieties नारी, मृगी, 22. उक्था, 23. अत्युक्था, 24. बृहती, varieties भुजङ्गशिशुः *m.*, भुजङ्गसङ्गता, मणिमध्यं, 25. पंक्तिः *f.*, varieties रुक्मवती, मनोरमा, त्वरितगतिः *f.*, 26. उष्णिक् *f.* (ह्), varieties मधुमती, कुमारललिता, 27. गायत्री, varieties तनुमध्या, शशिवदना, this and the preceding are found only in the Vedas. There is another class of metres regulated, not by the number of syllables, but by the number of syllabic instants or short syllables, each long syllable being supposed to contain two short. They are called, 1. आर्य्या, varieties पथ्या, विपुला, चपला, मुखचपला, जघनचपला, गीतिः *f.*, उपगीतिः *f.*, उद्गीतिः *f.*, आर्य्यागीतिः *f.*,

2. वैतालीयः, varieties औपच्छन्दसिकः, दोहडिका.

METRICAL, *a.* छान्दसः -सी -सं, छन्दोयुक्तः -क्ता -क्तं, छन्दोवान् -वती -वत् (त्), छन्दोबद्धः -द्धा -द्धं, छन्दोरूपः -पा -पं, छन्दोविशिष्टः -ष्टा -ष्टं, पद्यरूपः -पा -पं, पद्यात्मकः -का -कं, स्वरबद्धः &c., तालबद्धः &c.

METRONOME, *s.* तालमापकयन्त्रं, तालमापनी.

METROPOLIS, *s.* राजधानं -नी -नकं -निका, राजनगरी, मुख्यनगरी, पुरोत्तमः, कर्व्वटः.

METROPOLITAN, *a.* राजधानसम्बन्धी -न्धिनी -न्धि (न्), राजधानीयः -या -यं. —(Archbishop) प्रधानधर्म्माध्यक्षः, मुख्यधर्म्माध्यक्षः, धर्म्माध्यक्षाधिपतिः *m.*

METTLE, *s.* वीर्य्यं, साहसं, सत्त्वं, तेजस् *n.*, प्रभावः, प्रहर्षः, पौरुषं, ओजस्, ऊर्जः, मदः, मादः, मत्तता.

METTLED, METTLESOME, *a.* महासत्त्वः -त्त्वा -त्त्वं, महातेजाः -जाः -जः (स्), तेजोवान् -वती -वत् (त्), ओजस्वी -स्विनी -स्वि (न्), साहसिकः -की -कं, वीर्य्यवान् &c., मदोद्धतः -ता -तं, ऊर्जस्वी &c., मत्तः -त्ता -त्तं, मादवान् &c., प्रचण्डः -ण्डा -ण्डं.

METTLESOMENESS, *s.* मत्तता, मदोद्धतिः *f.*, प्रचण्डता, महासत्त्वता.

MEUM ET TUUM, *s.* स्वपरभेदः, आत्मपरभेदः, स्वपरविचारः.

MEW, *s.* (Cage) पञ्जरं, पिञ्जरं, वीतंसः.—(Sea-fowl) जलकुक्कुटः -टी. —(Cry of a cat) मेनादः, मार्जारनादः.

To MEW, *v. a.* (Shut up) पञ्जरे or कारागारे निरुध् (c. 7. -रुणद्धि -रोद्धुं) or अवरुध् or बन्ध् (c. 9. बध्नाति, बन्द्धुं).—(Molt, shed the feathers) पक्षान् or पर्णान् पत् (c. 10. पातयति -यितुं) or मुच् (c. 6. मुञ्चति, मोक्तुं) or निर्मुच्, पक्षनिर्मोकं कृ.—(Cry as a cat) मेनादं कृ, मार्जारवद् रु (c. 2. रौति, रवितुं).

To MEWL, *v. n.* शिशुवत् or बालकवत् क्रन्द् (c. 1. क्रन्दति -न्दितुं) or रुद् (c. 2. रोदिति -तुं), शिशुवत् क्रन्दनं कृ or रुदितं कृ or चीत्कारं कृ.

MEWS, *s. pl.* अश्वगोष्ठं, अश्वशाला, राजाश्वस्थानं.

MIASM, MIASMA, *s.* वायुदूषकः पूतिगन्धः or कुत्सितगन्धः, रोगजनकः कुवायुः or पूतिवातः, पूतिवाष्पः, मारकवाष्पः, दूषकवाष्पः.

MICA, *s.* अभ्रं, अभ्रकं, स्वच्छपत्रं, निर्म्मलं.

MICHAELMAS, *s.* वत्सरस्य तृतीयपादावसाने पर्व्व *n.* (न्), शरत्कालीनपर्व्व *n.*

MICROCOSM, *s.* सूक्ष्मजगत् *n.*, सूक्ष्मलोकः, सूक्ष्मसंसारः, क्षुद्रजगत्.

MICROSCOPE, *s.* सूक्ष्मदर्शकयन्त्रं, सूक्ष्मनिरीक्षणयन्त्रं, सूक्ष्मनिरीक्षणकाचः, सूक्ष्मद्रव्यदर्शनार्थं काचयन्त्रं.

MICROSCOPIC, *a.* पूर्व्वोक्तयन्त्रद्वारेण दृष्टः -ष्टा -ष्टं or उपलब्धः -ब्धा -ब्धं.

MICTURITION, *s.* मिमिक्षा, मेहनेच्छा, मूत्रत्यागेच्छा, मूत्रोत्सर्गेच्छा.

MID, *a.* मध्यः -ध्या -ध्यं, मध्यमः -मा -मं, मध्यस्थः -स्था -स्थं. *See* MIDDLE.

MID-AGE, *s.* मध्यवयस् *n.*, मध्यमवयस् *n.*, आयुर्मध्यं.

MID-COURSE, *s.* अर्द्धमार्गः, अर्द्धपथः, मार्गार्द्धं, मार्गमध्यं.

MID-DAY, *s.* मध्याह्नः, दिनमध्यं, दिवामध्यं, मध्यन्दिनं, उद्दिनं; 'at mid-day,' दिनमध्ये, मध्याह्ने.

MID-DAY, *a.* माध्याह्निकः -की -कं, माध्यन्दिनः -नी -नं; 'mid-day rites,' माध्याह्निकी क्रिया; 'mid-day meal,' मध्याह्नभोजनं.

MIDDLE, *a.* मध्यः -ध्या -ध्यं, मध्यमः -मा -मं, मध्यमीयः -या -यं, मध्यस्थः -स्था -स्थं, मध्यस्थितः -ता -तं, मध्यवर्त्ती -र्त्तिनी -र्त्ति (न्), माध्यः -ध्या -ध्यं, माध्यमः -मी -मं, गर्भस्थः &c., गर्भस्थितः -ता -तं; 'middle state,' मध्यस्थता, माध्यस्थ्यं; 'the middle classes,' मध्यमवर्णाः *m. pl.*, मध्यवर्णजाः *m. pl.*, मध्यमजातीयाः *m. pl.*

MIDDLE, *s.* मध्यं, मध्यभागः, मध्यदेशः, मध्यस्थानं, मध्यस्थलं, मध्यमप्रदेशः, अभ्यन्तरं, अन्तरं, गर्भः, हृदयं; 'the middle of the arm,' दोर्मध्यं; 'of the night,' रात्रिमध्यं; 'of a house,' गृहाभ्यन्तरं; 'of a bow,' लस्तकः; 'going in the middle,' मध्यगः -गा -गं, मध्यचारी -रिणी -रि (न्); 'in the middle,' मध्ये, मध्यतस्; 'in the middle of the night,' रात्रिमध्ये, महानिशायां; 'in the middle of the Ganges,' मध्येगङ्गं.

MIDDLE-AGED, *a.* मध्यमवयस्कः -स्का -स्कं, मध्यवयस्कः &c., अर्द्धवयस्कः &c., गतयौवनः -ना -नं, अतिक्रान्तयौवनः -ना -नं, अर्द्धवृद्धः -द्धा -द्धं; 'a middle-aged widow,' कात्यायनी.

MIDDLE-EARTH, *s.* मध्यलोकः, मध्यमलोकः, मध्यभुवनं, पृथिवी.

MIDDLE-FINGER, *s.* मध्यमा, मध्या, कर्णिका, ज्येष्ठः.

MIDDLE-MAN, *s.* मध्यस्थजनः, मध्यवर्त्ती *m.* (न्), मध्यस्थितः.

MIDDLEMOST, *a.* मध्यमः -मा -मं, मध्यमीयः -या -यं, मध्यस्थः -स्था -स्थं.

MIDDLE-SIZED, *a.* मध्यमपरिमाणः -णा -णं, न स्थूलो न सूक्ष्मः &c.

MIDDLING, *a.* मध्यमः -मा -मं, मध्यः -ध्या -ध्यं, मध्यमीयः -या -यं, माध्यः -ध्यी -ध्यं, माध्यमः -मी -मं.—(Of middle rank) मध्यमवर्णजः -जा -जं, मध्यमपदस्थः -स्था -स्थं.—(Of middle size) मध्यमपरिमाणः -णा -णं, न स्थूलो न सूक्ष्मः &c., मध्यमः -मा -मं.—(Of middle quality) विगुणः -णा -णं, मध्यमगुणः -णा -णं, सामान्यगुणः &c., सामान्यः -न्या -न्यं, साधारणः -णी -णं.

MIDGE, *s.* सूक्ष्ममशकः, सूक्ष्ममसकः, सूक्ष्ममक्षिका, दंशकः, सूचिवदनः.

MID-HEAVEN, *s.* खमध्यं, गगणमध्यं, अन्तरीक्षमध्यं, दशमलग्नं.

MIDLAND, *a.* मध्यदेशीयः -या -यं, माध्यदेशः -शी -शं, मध्यदेशस्थः -स्था -स्थं, मध्यदेशवर्त्ती -र्त्तिनी -र्त्ति (न्), समुद्रदूरस्थः -स्था -स्थं.

MIDLEG, *s.* जङ्घामध्यं, जङ्घाया मध्यदेशः.

MIDMOST, *a.* मध्यमः -मा -मं. *See* MIDDLEMOST.

MIDNIGHT, *s.* रात्रिमध्यं, मध्यरात्रः, अर्द्धरात्रः, अर्द्धनिशा, महारात्रः, महानिशा, निशीथः, सर्व्वावसरः, निःसम्पातः, निसम्पातः; 'at midnight,' रात्रिमध्ये.

MIDRIFF, *s.* शरीरमध्यं, उदरवक्षःस्थलमध्ये शरीरभागः.

MIDSEA, *s.* समुद्रमध्यं, सागरमध्यं, मध्यसमुद्रः.

MIDSHIPMAN, *s.* नाविककर्म्माभ्यासकृत् *m.*, नाविकशिष्यः.

MIDST, *s.* or *adv.* मध्यं, मध्ये, अन्तरं -रे; 'in the midst,' मध्ये; 'from the midst,' मध्यात्; 'to be in the midst of troubles,' दुःखग्रस्तः -स्ता -स्तं भू, दुःखसागरमग्नः -ग्ना -ग्नं भू. Sometimes मध्ये is put first in a compound; as, 'in the midst of the sea,' मध्येसमुद्रं, मध्येऽर्णवं,

MIDSTREAM, *s.* प्रवाहमध्यं, सरिन्मध्यं; 'in midstream,' सरिन्मध्ये.

MIDSUMMER, *s.* ग्रीष्मकालमध्यं, निदाघकालमध्यं, उष्णकालमध्यं.

MIDWAY, *s.* अर्द्धमार्गः, अर्द्धपथः, मार्गमध्यं, पथमध्यं, मार्गार्द्धं.

MIDWAY, *adv.* अर्द्धमार्गे, अर्द्धपथे, मार्गमध्ये, पथमध्ये, वर्त्ममध्ये.

MIDWIFE, *s.* साधिका, प्रसवकारिणी, प्रसवकारयित्री, अपत्यदा, गर्भिण्यवेक्षित्री, धात्री; 'man-midwife,' प्रसवकारी *m.* (न्), प्रसववैद्यः, सूतिवैद्यः, गर्भमोचकवैद्यः.

MIDWIFERY, *s.* प्रसवकर्म्म *n.* (न्), प्रसवकार्य्यं, प्रसवकरणं, प्रसवकारणं, सूतिकर्म्म *n.*, सूतिकरणं, गर्भिण्यवेक्षणं, गर्भमोचनविद्या, बालतन्त्रं, कुमारभृत्या.

MIDWINTER, *s.* शीतकालमध्यं, शिशिरमध्यं, मध्यशिशिरं, हेमन्तमध्यं.

MIEN, *s.* आकारः, वदनाकारः, चर्य्या, गतिः *f.*, रूपं, रीतिः *f.*, चरितं, व्यवहारः, चलनं, वृत्तिः *f.*, चारः, आचारः, आकृतिः *f.*

MIGHT, *s.* बलं, शक्तिः *f.*, सामर्थ्यं, विक्रमः, पराक्रमः, प्रभावः, ऐश्वर्य्यं, प्रतापः, ऊर्जः, अतिशक्तिः *f.*, तेजस्, वीर्य्यं, शौर्य्यं, प्राबल्यं; 'with all one's might,' यथाशक्ति, यथासामर्थ्यं, यथाबलं.

MIGHTILY, *adv.* बलेन, सबलं, ऐश्वर्य्येण, सविक्रमं, सपराक्रमं, प्रभावेण,

प्रतापेन, सवीर्य्यं, वीर्य्येण, प्रबलं, बलवत्.—(Greatly) भृशं, अत्यन्तं, अतिमात्रं.

MIGHTINESS, *s.* प्रबलता, प्राबल्यं, सामर्थ्यं, ऐश्वर्य्यं, सबलत्वं, अतिशक्तिता, प्रतापः, प्रभावः, वीर्य्यं, सारता, सप्रतापता, बलीयस्त्वं.

MIGHTY, *a.* प्रबलः -ला -लं, महाबलः -ला -लं, बलवान् -वती -वत् (त्), बली -लिनी -लि (न्), शक्तिमान् -मती &c., अतिशक्तिमान् &c., बलीयान् -यसी -यः (स्), बलिष्ठः -ष्ठा -ष्ठं, महाविक्रमः -मा -मं, उरुविक्रमः &c., गाढविक्रमः &c., महाशक्तिः -क्तिः -क्ति, ऊर्जितः -ता -तं, ऊर्जस्वी -स्विनी &c., विक्रान्तः -न्ता -न्तं, पराक्रान्तः &c., पराक्रमी &c., विक्रमी &c.—(Great, majestic) महान् -हती -हत् (त्), ऐश्वर्य्यवान् &c., प्रतापी &c., प्रतापवान् &c., महातेजाः -जाः -जः (स्), प्रभावी &c., विभूतिमान् &c., तेजोवान् &c., महौजाः &c., महोदारः -रा -रं; 'mighty lord,' परमेश्वरः, महेश्वरः.

To MIGRATE *v. n.* उत्क्रम् (c. 1. -क्रामति -क्रमितुं), देशाद् देशं भ्रम् (c. 4. भ्राम्यति, भ्रमितुं), एकदेशं त्यक्त्वा देशान्तरं गम् (c. 1. गच्छति, गन्तुं) or देशान्तरम् अधिवस्, देशान्तरं or स्थानान्तरं गत्वा वस्, देशभ्रमणं कृ, दिग्भ्रमणं कृ, देशाटनं कृ, विदेशगमनं कृ, देशपरिवर्त्तनं कृ.

MIGRATION *s.* उत्क्रमः, उत्क्रमणं, देशान्तरगमनं, स्थानान्तरगमनं, देशभ्रमणं, दिग्भ्रमणं, देशपरिवर्त्तनं, देशाटनं, विदेशगमनं.

MIGRATORY, *a.* देशभ्रमणशीलः -ला -लं, परिभ्रमणशीलः -ला -लं, पर्य्यटनशीलः -ला -लं, देशपरिवर्त्तनशीलः -ला -लं.

MILCH-COW, *s.* धेनुः *f.*, दोग्ध्री, धेनुका, गोधेनुः *f.*, स्त्रीगवी, पयस्विनी, क्षीरिणी, दुग्धवती, पीनोध्नी, पीवरस्तनी, पीतदुग्धा, नवसूतिका; 'a herd,' धैनुकं.

MILD, *a.* (Soft, not harsh) मृदुः -द्वी -दु, मृदुलः -ला -लं, कोमलः -ला -लं, सौम्यः -म्या -म्यं, स्निग्धः -ग्धा -ग्धं, शान्तः -न्ता -न्तं, अनुग्रः -ग्रा -ग्रं, अपरुषः -षा -षं, अप्रखरः -रा -रं, अकर्कशः -शा -शं, अतीक्ष्णः -क्ष्णा -क्ष्णं, मसृणः -णा -णं, सुकुमारः -रा -रं, अचण्डः -ण्डा -ण्डं, अखरः -रा -रं.—(Tender or gentle in temper) मृदुस्वभावः -वा -वं, मृदुभावः -वा -वं, कोमलस्वभावः &c., सौम्यवृत्तिः -त्तिः -त्ति, कोमलान्तःकरणः -णा -णं, दयार्द्रभावः -वा -वं, दयालुः -लुः -लु, दयावान् -वती -वत् (त्), सदयः -या -यं, सात्त्विकः -का -कं, सात्त्विकप्रकृतिः -तिः -ति, निर्गर्वः -र्वा -र्वं.—(Lenient) क्षमावान् &c., सामबुद्धिः -द्धिः -द्धि, अतीक्ष्णः -क्ष्णा -क्ष्णं, अतीव्रः -व्रा -व्रं, अनिष्ठुरः -रा -रं, अनुग्रदण्डः -ण्डा -ण्डं, सामोपचारी -रिणी &c., सामोपायी &c.; 'mild remedy,' सौम्योपचारः, सामोपचारः, बालोपचारः; 'mild means,' सामोपायः; 'by mild means,' सामोपायेन, साम्ना; 'mild air,' मृदुवातः, मृदुवायुः *m.*; 'mild speech,' सान्त्ववादः.

MILDEW, *s.* वृक्षदूषणं, तरुदूषणं, कलङ्कः, शुक्लकलङ्कः, श्वेतकलङ्कः, दूषणवस्तु *n.*, क्लेदमलं.

To MILDEW, *v. a.* शुक्लकलङ्केन दुष् (c. 10. दूषयति -यितुं), क्लेदमलेन दुष् or कलङ्क् (nom. कलङ्कयति -यितुं) or लिप् (c. 6. लिम्पति, लेप्तुं).

MILDEWED, *p. p.* शुक्लकलङ्कदूषितः -ता -तं, कलङ्कितः -ता -तं.

MILDLY, *adv.* मृदु, मृदुलं, कोमलं, सौम्यवत्, अनुग्रं, अपरुषं, अकर्कशं, साम्ना, सामोपायेन, मार्दवेन, समार्दवं, अतीक्ष्णं, अतीव्रं, अचण्डं, अप्रखरं, मन्दं.

MILDNESS, *s.* (Softness, not harshness) मृदुता -त्वं, मार्दवं, म्रदिमा *m.* (न्), सौम्यता, कोमलता, स्निग्धता, अनुग्रता, अपरुषता, अकार्कश्यं, शान्तता, शान्तिः *f.*—(Of temper) स्वभावमृदुता, प्रकृतिमृदुता, सौम्यवृत्तिता, कोमलस्वभावः, सात्त्विकप्रकृतिः *f.*, दयालुता.—(Leniency) मृदुता, क्षमा, सौम्यता, साम *n.* (न्), सामबुद्धिः *f.*, अतीक्ष्णता, अतैक्ष्ण्यं, अतीव्रता, दण्डानुग्रता, अनुग्रता, अनुग्रदण्डत्वं, कृपा.

MILE, *s.* The measure called क्रोशः, or kos, is about two English miles. One English mile will therefore be expressed by अर्द्धक्रोशः; 'three miles,' सार्द्धक्रोशः; 'four miles,' क्रोशद्वयं; 'five miles,' सार्द्धद्विक्रोशं; 'six miles,' क्रोशत्रयं.

MILE-STONE, *s.* अर्द्धक्रोशमापकप्रस्तरः, क्रोशमापनपाषाणः.

MILITANT, *a.* युद्धोद्युक्तः -क्ता -क्तं, युद्धोद्यतः -ता -तं, युद्धप्रवृत्तः -त्ता -त्तं, युद्धारूढः -ढा -ढं, युध्यमानः -ना -नं, युद्धकारी -रिणी -रि (न्), सङ्ग्रामोद्युक्तः &c.

MILITARY, *a.* (Pertaining to soldiers or arms) युद्धसम्बन्धी -न्धिनी &c., युद्धविषयकः -का -कं, साङ्ग्रामिकः -की -कं, सामरिकः -की -कं, सैनिकः -की -कं, आयुधिकः -की -कं, क्षात्रः -त्री -त्रं, साम्परायिकः -की -कं; 'military duty,' क्षत्रधर्म्मः, क्षात्रधर्म्मः; 'following it,' क्षत्रधर्म्मानुगः -गा -गं; 'military profession,' शस्त्रवृत्तिः *f.*, शस्त्रास्त्रभृत्त्वं.—(Engaged in the profession of arms) युद्धप्रवृत्तः -त्ता -त्तं, योधी -धिनी -धि (न्), शस्त्रजीवी &c., शस्त्राजीवी &c., शस्त्रोपजीवी &c., आयुधजीवी &c., शस्त्रास्त्रभृत्, शस्त्रभृत्.—(Man of the military class) क्षत्रियः, क्षत्रः, क्षत्री *m.* (न्), राजन्यः, विराट् *m.* (ज्), बाहुजः, मूर्द्धाभिषिक्तः; 'a woman of this class,' क्षत्रिया -यी -याणी; 'the duty of this class,' क्षत्रियधर्म्मः; 'the military class,' क्षत्रियजातिः *f.*

MILITARY, *s.* (The body of soldiers) सैनिकवर्गः, सैन्यवर्गः, सैनिकजातिः *f.*, क्षत्रं, क्षत्रियजातिः *f.*, क्षत्रवर्गः.

To MILITATE, *v. n.* विरुध् (c. 7. -रुणद्धि -रोद्धुं), प्रतिरुध्, विरुद्धः -द्धा -द्धं भू, प्रतिकूल (nom. प्रतिकूलयति -यितुं), विपरीतः -ता -तं भू.

MILITIA, *s.* देशरक्षकाः *m. pl.*, देशरक्षिणः *m. pl.*, नैमित्तिकसैन्याः *m. pl.*

MILK, *s.* दुग्धं, क्षीरं, पयस् *n.*, स्तन्यं, गोदुग्धं, गोरसः -सं, धेनुकादुग्धं, गव्यं, गव्यपयस् *n.*, अवदोहः, दोहः, ऊधस्यं, ऊधन्यं, दोहजं, दोहापनयः, पायसं, पीयूषं, पेयं, सोमजं; 'made from milk,' पयस्यः -स्या -स्यं; 'the skim of milk,' दुग्धफेनं; 'yielding much milk,' बहुदुग्धा, दोहीयान् -यसी -यः (स्); 'milk diet,' दुग्धाहारः; 'coagulated milk,' दधि *n.*, क्षीरजं; 'inspissated milk,' क्षीरविकृतिः *f.*; 'drinking milk,' क्षीरपः -पा -पं, क्षीरपायी -यिनी &c.; 'giving milk,' क्षीरदः -दा -दं; 'to give milk,' दुह् (c. 4. दुह्यते), क्षीरं दा.

To MILK, *v. a.* दुह् (c. 2. दोग्धि, दुग्धे, दोग्धुं), निर्दुह्, दोहनं कृ, दुग्धं सु (c. 10. स्रावयति -यितुं), गोस्तनं पीडयित्वा दुग्धं सु or मोक्ष् (c. 10. मोक्षयति -यितुं) or मुच् (c. 10. मोचयति -यितुं), दुग्धमोक्षणं कृ.

MILKED, *p. p.* दुग्धः -ग्धा -ग्धं, निर्दुग्धः -ग्धा -ग्धं, कृतदोहनः -ना -नं; 'a cow easily milked,' सुखदोह्या, सुखसन्दोह्या, सुव्रता.

MILKER, *s.* दोग्धा *m.* (ग्धृ), दोहकः, दोही *m.* (न्), धुक् *m.* (दुह्).

MILKINESS, *s.* दुग्धता, दुग्धवत्ता, दुग्धिता, क्षीरिता, पायसता, पयस्यत्वं, सक्षीरता, सदुग्धता, दुग्धसादृश्यं, दुग्धसगुणता.

MILK-LIVERED, *a.* भीरुहृदयः -या -यं, क्लीवहृदयः &c., कातरः -रा -रं.

MILK-MAID, *s.* गोदोग्ध्री, गोदोहिनी, गोपी, गोपिनी, गोपिका, आभीरी.

MILK-MAN, *s.* गोधुक् *m.* (-दुह्), दोग्धा *m.* (ग्धृ), दुग्धविक्रेता *m.* (तृ), क्षीरविक्रयी *m.* (न्), गोपः, आभीरः.

MILK-PAIL, MILK-PAN, *s.* दोहनं -नी, गोदोहनी, दुग्धभाण्डं, क्षीरभाण्डं, दुग्धपात्रं, दुग्धभाजनं, दोहनपात्रं, दधिभाण्डं, निपानं, दोहः, पारी.

MILK-PORRIDGE, MILK-POTTAGE, *s.* क्षैरेयी.

MILK-SOP, *s.* क्लीवहृदयः, मृदुहृदयः, कोमलहृदयः, कापुरुषः.

MILK-WHITE, *a.* दुग्धसवर्णः -र्णा -र्णं, क्षीरवच्छुक्लः -क्ला -क्लं, क्षीरवर्णः &c.

MILKWOMAN, *s.* दुग्धविक्रेत्री, दोहिनी, गोपिनी, गोपा, आभीरी, महाशूद्री.

Milky, *a.* दुग्धी -ग्धिनी -ग्धि (न्), क्षीरी -रिणी &c., पायसः -सी -सं, पयस्यः -स्या -स्यं, पयस्वी -स्विनी &c., दुग्धमयः -यी -यं, क्षैरेयः -यी -यं.—(Resembling milk) दुग्धसगुणः -णा -णं, क्षीरोपमः -मा -मं, दुग्धसदृशः -शी -शं.—(Yielding milk) क्षीरदः -दा -दं, बहुदुग्धः -ग्धा -ग्धं, दुग्धप्रदः -दा -दं.

Milky-way, *s.* मन्दाकिनी, आकाशगङ्गा, स्वर्गङ्गा, स्वर्नदी, सुरनदी, आकाशनदी, देवनदी, वियद्गङ्गा, नागवीथी, हरिताली.

Mill, *s.* पेषणं, पेषणी -णिः *f.*, पेषणयन्त्रं, पेषणचक्रं, चक्रं.

To mill, *v. a.* पिष् (c. 7. पिनष्टि, पेष्टुं), चूर्ण् (c. 10. चूर्णयति -यितुं), चूर्णीकृ.—(Beat with the fist) मुष्ट्या तड् (c. 10. ताडयति -यितुं) or प्रहृ (c. 1. -हरति -हर्त्तुं).

Millenarian, millenarial, *a.* सहस्रवर्षीयः -या -यं, सहस्रवर्षीणः -णा -णं, सहस्रवात्सरी -रिणी -रि (न्), सहस्रवार्षिकः -की -कं, सहस्राब्दिकः -की -कं, सहस्री -स्रिणी &c., साहस्रः -स्री -स्रं.

Millenium, millenary, *s.* सहस्रवर्षं, सहस्रवत्सरं, वर्षसहस्रकं, वर्षसाहस्रं, दशशतवर्षं, सहस्रवर्षपर्य्यन्तं साक्षाद्भूतं ख्रीष्टराज्यं.

Milleped, *s.* सहस्रपाद् *m.*, सहस्रपादविशिष्टः कीटभेदः.

Miller, *s.* शस्यपेषकः, धान्यपेषणजीवी *m.* (न्), पेषणोपजीवी *m.*

Millesimal, *a.* (Thousandth) सहस्रतमः -मी -मं.—(Consisting of a thousand parts) सहस्रांशरूपः -पा -पं, सहस्रांशात्मकः -का -कं.

Millet, *s.* (Panicum, a sort of grain) अणुः *m.*, प्रियङ्गुः *m.*; 'field of it,' अणव्यं.

Milliary, *a.* अर्द्धक्रोशमापकः -का -कं, क्रोशमापनः -नी -नं.

Milliner, *s.* स्त्रीपरिच्छदकारिणी, स्त्रीपरिच्छदविक्रेत्री, स्त्रीवस्त्रव्यापारिणी, स्त्रीवस्त्रकरणोपजीविनी, स्त्रीवस्त्रकृत् *f.*

Millinery, *s.* स्त्रीपरिच्छदः, स्त्रीवस्त्रसामग्र्यं, स्त्रीवस्त्रशिरस्कादि *n.*, स्त्रीसज्जा, स्त्रीलोकभृतं यत्किञ्चिद् वस्त्रादि.

Million, *s.* नियुतः -तं, प्रयुतः -तं, दशलक्षं; 'ten million,' कोटिः *f.*; 'one hundred million,' अर्बुदः; 'one thousand million,' महार्बुदः, महाशङ्कः; 'ten thousand million,' पद्मं; 'one hundred thousand million,' महापद्मं *m.*; 'million million,' खर्व्वं, खर्वं, निखर्वं; 'ten million million,' महाखर्वं. According to Wilson's Dictionary, खर्वं is equivalent to ten million million, according to the Mahrattí Dictionary to ten thousand million, and निखर्वं to a hundred thousand million: नियुतः is also used for one hundred thousand, and there seems to be much uncertainty in the use of some others of the above Sanskrit terms. The word कोटिः is used generally for a large number, and hence the expression 'by millions' कोटिशस्.

Millionaire, *s.* कोटीश्वरः, लक्षाधीशः, दशलक्षसम्पन्नः.

Millionary, *a.* नियुतसम्बन्धी -न्धिनी &c., नियुतीयः -या -यं.

Millionth, *a.* नियुततमः -मी -मं, प्रयुततमः -मी -मं.

Mill-stone, *s.* पेषणप्रस्तरः, पेषणपाषाणः, पेषणी -णिः *f.*, पेषणं, शिलापट्टः, शिलापुत्रः.

Milt, *s.* (Spleen) प्लीहा *m.* (न्), गुल्मः.—(Roe) मीनाण्डं, मत्स्याण्डं.

Milter, *s.* पुंमत्स्यः, पुंजातीयो मत्स्यः or मीनः.

Mime, *s.* (Actor, buffoon) नटः, नर्त्तकः, नाटकः, कुशीलवः, चारणः, रङ्गाजीवः, मायाजीवः, भण्डः, विदूषकः, वैहासिकः.

Mimic, mimical, *a.* उपहासबुद्ध्या परगतिचेष्टिताद्यनुकारी -रिणी -रि (न्) or अनुकरणशीलः -ला -लं, अनुकारी &c., अनुकरणस्वभावः -वा -वं, विडम्बनकारी &c.—(Consisting of imitation) अनुकरणरूपः -पा -पं, अनुकरणात्मकः -का -कं, विडम्बनरूपः -पा -पं; 'mimic art,' नाटकविधिः *m.*

Mimic, *s.* (Buffoon) भण्डः, भाण्डः, वैहासिकः, परिहासवेदी *m.* (न्), विदूषकः.—(Imitator) अनुकारी *m.* (न्), अनुकर्त्ता *m.* (र्तृ).

To mimic, mimick, *v. a.* उपहासबुद्ध्या परस्य गतिभाषितचेष्टितादि अनुकृ (c. 8. -करोति -कुरुते -कर्त्तुं), हास्योत्पादनार्थं परचेष्टितानुकरणं कृ or विडम्बनं कृ.

Mimicked, *p. p.* उपहासबुद्ध्या or हास्योत्पादनार्थम् अनुकृतः -ता -तं.

Mimicker, *s.* अनुकर्त्ता *m.* (र्तृ), अनुकारी *m.* (न्), विडम्बनकृत् *m.*

Mimicry, *s.* उपहासबुद्ध्या गतिभाषितचेष्टिताद्यनुकारः, हास्योत्पादनार्थं चेष्टितानुकरणं, अनुकारः, अनुकरणं, अनुकृतिः *f.*, अनुक्रिया, अनुकर्म्म *n.* (न्), विडम्बनं -ना, व्याजः; 'of a cry or sound,' रुतव्याजः.

Mimosa, *s.* (Kind of sensitive plant) गण्डकारी, गण्डकाली, समङ्गा, नमस्कारी, खदिरी, रक्तपर्णी, सुवहा, लज्जालुः *m.*, महाभीता, लज्जकारिका, स्पर्शलज्जा, राखा, युक्तरसा; 'fetid mimosa,' अरिमेदः, विट्खदिरः; 'mimosa albida,' शमी, शमीरः, सक्तुफला, शिवा.

Minacious, minatory, *a.* भर्त्सनकारी -रिणी -रि (न्), निर्भर्त्सनकृत् *m.f.n.*, भर्त्सनार्थकः -का -कं, भर्त्सनमयः -यी -यं, भयप्रदर्शकः -का -कं, भयसूचकः -का -कं.

Minaret, *s.* शिखरं, शृङ्गं, प्रासादशिखरं, भवनशिखरं, प्रासादशृङ्गं.

To mince, *v. a.* (Cut into small pieces) खण्डं खण्डं कृ, खण्डशः कृ or छिद् (c. 7. छिनत्ति, छेत्तुं), सूक्ष्मखण्डशः कृ or व्यवछिद्, बहुखण्डशः खण्ड् (c. 10. खण्डयति -यितुं), शकलीकृ, खण्डीकृ.—(Cut off in speaking) अवछिद्, भिन्नस्वरेण वद् (c. 1. वदति -दितुं).

To mince, *v. n.* (Walk with short steps or with affected delicacy) भिन्नगत्या or सलालित्यं or सलौल्यं चल् (c. 1. चलति -लितुं), ललितगत्या or विलक्षितगत्या चर् (c. 1. चरति -रितुं), सवैलक्ष्यं चर्.—(Speak affectedly) भिन्नस्वरेण वद् (c. 1. वदति -दितुं), ललितस्वरेण वद्, विलक्षितस्वरेण वद्, सवैलक्ष्यं वद्.

Minced, *p. p.* व्यवछिन्नः -न्ना -न्नं, सूक्ष्मखण्डीकृतः -ता -तं, सूक्ष्मशकलीकृतः -ता -तं, छिन्नभिन्नः -न्ना -न्नं, छिन्नविछिन्नः -न्ना -न्नं, खण्डितः -ता -तं.

Mince-meat, minced meat, *s.* छिन्नमांसं, खण्डमांसं, खण्डीकृतमांसं, व्यवछिन्नमांसं, व्यञ्जनादिना सह सिद्धं छिन्नमांसं.

Mince-pie, minced pie, *s.* छिन्नमांसव्यञ्जनादिगर्भः शष्कुलीविशेषः.

Mincingly, *adv.* खण्डशस्, लवशस्, भिन्नगत्या, भिन्नस्वरेण, सवैलक्ष्यं.

Mind, *s.* (The understanding, intellect) मनस् *n.*, मानसं, मतिः *f.*, बुद्धिः *f.*, धीः *f.*, चित्तं, चेतस् *n.*, मेधा, प्रज्ञा, आत्मा *m.* (न्), चेतना, बोधः, बोधशक्तिः *f.*, चित् *f.*, चिच्छक्तिः *f.*, ज्ञानशक्तिः *f.*, उपलब्धिः *f.*, शेमुषी, तुरगः, निगुः *m.*, अङ्गं; 'application of mind,' मनोयोगः, मनोनिवेशः, मनःप्रवेशः; 'to give the mind,' निविष्टचित्तः -त्ता -त्तं भू, आसक्तचित्तः -त्ता -त्तं भू, मनो निविश् (c. 10. -वेशयति -यितुं); 'exercise of mind,' मनोव्यापारः; 'out of one's mind,' अव्यवस्थितबुद्धिः -द्धिः -द्धि; 'fixed in the mind,' चित्तीकृतः -ता -तं; 'of inferior mind,' अपकृष्टचेतनः -ना -नं.—(Heart or seat of the affections) हृदयं, हृद् *n.*, चित्तं, चेतस्, अन्तःकरणं, अन्तरात्मा *m.* (न्), अन्तःप्रकृतिः *f.*, मनस्, अन्तर्भावः, भावः, अन्तरं, अभ्यन्तरं; 'working of the mind, emotion,' चित्तवृत्तिः *f.*, विकारः, मनोविकारः, मनोविकृतिः *f.*; 'control of the mind,' मनोदण्डः, मनोनिग्रहः; 'peace of mind,' मनःशान्तिः *f.*—(Opinion, thoughts) मतिः *f.*, बुद्धिः *f.*, मतं, मनोगतं, मनस् *n.*, मनोभावः, हृद्गतं; 'of one mind,' एकचित्तः -त्ता -त्तं; 'to be of one mind,' एकचित्तीभू. 'change of mind,' बुद्धिभेदः.—(Inclination, will, desire) मनोरथः, इच्छा, आकांक्षा, अभिलाषः, वासना, बुद्धिः *f.*, मतिः *f.*, कामः, अभिमतं, ईप्सितं, अभीप्सितं, इष्टं; 'according to one's mind,' यथाभिमतं, यथेष्टं, यथेप्सितं, मनोनुकूलः -ला -लं, 'having a mind to see,' द्रष्टुमनाः -नाः -नः (स्), 'having a mind to go,' गन्तुमनाः &c.—(Design, intention) बुद्धिः *f.*, मतिः *f.*, मनस् *n.*, अभिप्रायः, अभिप्रेतं, चिकीर्षितं, सङ्कल्पः, उद्देशः. To have a mind मतिं कृ. —(Memory, remembrance) स्मरणं, स्मृतिः *f.*, अनुस्मृतिः *f.*, संस्मृतिः *f.*, अनुचिन्ता, अनुबोधः, ध्यानं, आध्यानं; 'to call to mind,' स्मृ (c. 1. स्मरति, स्मर्त्तुं), अनुस्मृ, संस्मृ, अनुचिन्त् (c. 10. -चिन्तयति -यितुं), समनुचिन्त्, अनुबुध् (c. 4. -बुध्यते -बोद्धुं), 'to put in mind,' स्मृ (c. 10. स्मारयति -यितुं), बुध् (c. 10. बोधयति -यितुं), उद्बुध्; 'flashing across one's mind,' स्फुरणं.

To MIND, *v. a.* (Attend to, heed) अवधा (c. 3. -धत्ते -धातुं), मनो धा, अवधानं कृ, सावधानः -ना -नं भू, अवहितः -ता -तं भू or अस्; 'mind!' सावधानो भव.—(Regard) मन् (c. 4. मन्यते, मन्तुं), अनुमन्, मननं कृ, अपेक्ष् (c. 1. -ईक्षते -क्षितुं), अवेक्ष्, प्रतीक्ष्, बुध् (c. 1. बोधति, c. 4. बुध्यते, बोद्धुं), आबुध्, आलोक् (c. 10. लोकयति -यितुं), आलोच् (c. 10. -लोचयति -यितुं), अवेक्षणं कृ.—(Obey) सेव् (c. 1. सेवते -वितुं), श्रु in des. (शुश्रूषते -षितुं), अनुष्ठा (c. 1. -तिष्ठति -ष्ठातुं), अनुवृत् (c. 1. -वर्त्तते -र्त्तितुं), अनुविधा in pass. (-धीयते), अनुवर्त्तनं कृ.—(Take care of, look after) रक्ष् (c. 1. रक्षति -क्षितुं), पाल् (c. 10. पालयति -यितुं), अनुसन्धा; 'mind a family,' तन्त्र् (c. 10. तन्त्रयति -यितुं).

MINDED, *a.* (Disposed) प्रवृत्तः -त्ता -त्तं, प्रवणः -णा -णं, मनाः -नाः -नः or मनस्कः -स्का -स्कं in comp.; as, 'minded to go,' गमनमनाः &c., गन्तुमनाः &c., गमनमनस्कः &c. *See* INCLINED. (In composition) मनाः &c., मनस्कः &c., मतिः &c., बुद्धिः &c.; as, 'high-minded,' महामनाः &c., महामनस्कः &c., महामतिः -तिः -ति &c.

MINDFUL, *a.* (Attentive, heedful) सावधानः -ना -नं, अवहितः -ता -तं, कृतावधानः -ना -नं, अवहितचेताः -ताः -तः (स्), जागरः -रा -रं. —(Regarding with care) मन्यमानः -ना -नं, अनुमन्यमानः -ना -नं, अपेक्षकः -का -कं, अवेक्षकः -का -कं.—(Bearing in mind) स्मरन् -रन्ती -रत् (त्), स्मृतिमान् -मती -मत् (त्), अनुचिन्तयन् -यन्ती -यत् (त्); 'to be mindful,' स्मृ (c. 1. स्मरति, स्मर्त्तुं).

MINDFULLY, *adv.* सावधानं, अवहितं, अवहितचेतसा, स्मृतिपूर्व्वं, अवेक्षया.

MINDFULNESS, *s.* अवधानं, सावधानता, अवहितता, अवेक्षा -क्षणं, अपेक्षा.

MINDLESS, *a.* (Heedless) अनवधानः -ना -नं, अनवहितः -ता -तं, प्रमत्तः -त्ता -त्तं, निरपेक्षः -क्षा -क्षं.—(Forgetful) नष्टस्मृतिः -तिः -ति, अपस्मृतिः -तिः -ति.—(Stupid) निर्बुद्धिः -द्धिः -द्धि, बुद्धिहीनः -ना -नं.

MINE, *pron. a.* मदीयः -या -यं, अस्मदीयः -या -यं, मम gen. c. (अस्मद्), मामकीनः -ना -नं, आत्मीयः -या -यं, मत् in comp.; as, 'mine own master,' मत्प्रभुः *m.*

MINE, *s.* (Excavation in the earth for any metals, &c.) आकरः, खनिः -नी *f.*, खानिः -नी *m. f.*, खन्याकरः, गञ्जः -ञ्जा -ञ्जं, कुल्या, योनिः *m. f.*—(For gold, &c.) कनकस्थली, कनकस्थानं, काञ्चनकन्दरः, सुवर्णादिधातूत्पत्तिस्थानं, सुवर्णाद्युत्पत्तिस्थानं.—(For precious stones) खनिः -नी *f.*, मणिभूमिः *f.*, रत्नोत्पत्तिस्थानं, मणिस्थली, कुट्टिमः -मं, गञ्जः -ञ्जा -ञ्जं.—(For military purposes) सन्धिः *m.*, सुरुङ्गा, खानिकं, कुल्या, रन्ध्रं.—(Metaphorically) as, 'a mine of good qualities,' गुणाकरः, गुणनिधिः *m.*, गुणास्पदं.

To MINE, *v. a.* and *n.* (Excavate) खन् (c. 1. खनति -नितुं), आखन्, निखन्.—(Form a hole or subterraneous passage) सुरुङ्गां कृ, विवरं कृ, रन्ध्रं कृ, गूढरन्ध्रं कृ गूढमार्गं कृ or उत्खन्, गूढकुल्यां कृ, गूढकूपं कृ.—(Undermine) अधस्तात् खन् or गूढखातं कृ.

MINER, *s.* (Excavator) खनकः, खनिता *m.* (तृ), आकरिकः, खातकः, खनन् *m.* (त्), खनिकरः.—(Military) सुरुङ्गाखनकः, सुरुङ्गाकृत् *m.*, सौरुङ्गिकः.

MINERAL, *s.* धातुः *m.*, उपधातुः *m.*, खनिजवस्तु *n.*, आकरजवस्तु *n.*, खनिजं शिलाजं, आकरोद्भवद्रव्यं, आकरीयद्रव्यं.

MINERAL, *a.* (Pertaining to minerals) धातु in comp.; as, 'the mineral kingdom,' धातुजातिः *f.*, धातुजातं.—(Produced in a mine) खनिजः -जा -जं, आकरजः -जा -जं, आकरोद्भवः -वा -वं, आकरी -रिणी -रि (न्), आकरीयः -या -यं, शिलाजः -जा -जं.—(Consisting of minerals) धातुमयः -यी -यं, धातुरूपः -पा -पं, धातुमयः -यी -यं, शिलामयः &c., अश्ममयः &c., दार्षदः -दी -दं.—(Impregnated with minerals) धातुसंसृष्टः -ष्टा -ष्टं, धातुसंसर्गी -र्गिणी &c., धातुगुणकः -का -कं, धातुगुणोपेतः -ता -तं, धातुधर्म्मकः -का -कं.

MINERALOGIST, *s.* धातुविद्याज्ञः, खनिजवस्तुपरीक्षकः, आकरीयद्रव्यनिरूपकः, धातुवेत्ता *m.* (तृ), धातुगुणवादी *m.* (न्), कारन्धमी *m.* (न्).

MINERALOGY, *s.* धातुविद्या, धातुनिरूपणविद्या, धातुपरिज्ञानं, खनिजवस्तुपरिज्ञानं, आकरीयवस्तुपरीक्षा, धातुगुणविषयका विद्या, धातुगुणविचारः, पार्थिवांशविषयकं ज्ञानं.

To MINGLE, *v. a.* मिश्र् (c. 10. मिश्रयति -यितुं), सम्मिश्र्, विमिश्र्, मिश्रीकृ, सम्मिश्रीकृ, एकीकृ, संयुज् (c. 7. -युनक्ति -योक्तुं, c. 10. योजयति -यितुं), संसृज् (c. 6. -सृजति -स्रष्टुं), संसर्गं कृ, सङ्कॄ (c. 6. -किरति -करितुं -रीतुं), सम्पृच् (c. 7. -पृणक्ति -पर्च्चितुं), एकत्र कृ, व्यतिकरं कृ.

To MINGLE, *v. n.* मिश्रीभू, सम्मिश्रीभू, मिल् (c. 6. मिलति, मेलितुं), सम्मिल्, सङ्कॄ in pass. (-कीर्य्यते), संसृज् in pass. (-सृज्यते), संसृष्टीभू.

MINGLED, *p. p.* मिश्रितः -ता -तं, सम्मिश्रः -श्रा -श्रं, मिश्रः -श्रा -श्रं, मिश्रीकृतः -ता -तं, संसृष्टः -ष्टा -ष्टं, मिलितः -ता -तं, सङ्कीर्णः -र्णा -र्णं, सम्पृक्तः -क्ता -क्तं, व्यामिश्रः -श्रा -श्रं.

MINGLEMENT, *s.* मिश्रणं, सम्मिश्रणं, सम्पर्कः, संसर्गः, संयोगः, मिलनं.

MINIATURE, *s.* सूक्ष्माकारचित्रं, लघ्वाकारचित्रं, सूक्ष्मचित्रं.

MINIATURE, *a.* सूक्ष्मपरिमाणः -णा -णं, सूक्ष्माकारः -रा -रं.

MINIKIN, *a.* अतिसूक्ष्मः -क्ष्मा -क्ष्मं, अत्यल्पः -ल्पा -ल्पं, अणुकः -का -कं.

MINIM, *a.* (Note in music) दीर्घस्वरः.—(Dwarf) ह्रस्वमूर्त्तिः.

MINIMUM, *s.* कनिष्ठसंख्या, अवरसंख्या, अल्पिष्ठपरिमाणं, अल्पिष्ठांशः.

MINIMUS, *s.* अल्पिष्ठमूर्त्तिः *m.*, कनिष्ठः, ह्रस्वतममूर्त्तिः *m.*

MINING, *s.* खननं, खनिखननं, आकरखननं, खानिखननं, आखननं.

MINION, *s.* वल्लभः, राजवल्लभः, नृपवल्लभः, राजलाली *m.* (न्).

MINISTER, *s.* (Agent, official) कर्म्मकरः, कार्य्यसाधकः, कार्य्यनिर्वाहकः, नियोगी *m.* (न्), नियुक्तः, अधिकारी *m.* (न्), आधिकारिकः, अधिकारवान् *m.* (त्), आयुक्तः, कार्य्यप्रवर्त्तकः.—(Of the king or of the government) मन्त्री *m.* (न्), अमात्यः, आमात्यः, सचिवः, राजमन्त्री *m.*, राजसचिवः, राजामात्यः, महामात्रः, प्रकृतिः *f.*, प्रकृतिपुरुषः, प्रधानः, धुर्वहः, राज्यधुर्वहः, धुरीयः, धुर्य्यः, धुरीणः, धुरन्धरः, राज्यधुरन्धरः, राजकार्य्यभारी *m.* (न्), राजधर्म्मवित् *m.*, राजकर्म्मकरः, राजभृत्यः, मन्त्रकृत् *m.*, चारेक्षणः; 'prime minister,' प्रधानमन्त्री *m.*, मुख्यमन्त्री *m.*, महामन्त्री *m.*, प्रधानामात्यः, मुख्यामात्यः, पट्टाधिकारी *m.*; 'the minister of counsel,' धीसचिवः; 'the minister of action,' कर्म्मसचिवः; 'the minister of the king's amusements,'

नर्म्मसचिवः.—(Of religion) उपाध्यायः, आचार्य्यः, पुरोहितः, धर्म्माध्यापकः.—(At a foreign court) राजदूतः, राजप्रतिनिधिः *m.*, राजप्रस्थापितः.

To MINISTER, *v. a.* or *n.* (Supply necessary things) सोपकारद्रव्याणि परिकॢप् (c. 10. -कल्पयति -यितुं) or उपकॢप् or उपस्था in caus. (-स्थापयति -यितुं) or उपपद् (c. 10. -पादयति -यितुं) or सम्भृ (c. 1. -भरति -भर्तुं) or पुरस्कृ or प्रस्तुतीकृ.—(Serve, attend on) उपचर् (c. 1. -चरति -रितुं), उपाचर्, परिचर्, उपास् (c. 2. -आस्ते -आसितुं), पर्युपास्, समुपास्, सेव् (c. 1. सेवते -ति -वितुं, c. 10. सेवयति -यितुं), उपसेव्, उपस्था (c. 1. -तिष्ठति -स्थातुं), श्रु in des. (शुश्रूषते -षितुं), परिविष् (c. 10. -वेषयति -यितुं), उपचारं कृ, उपासनां कृ.—(Sacerdotally) उपाध्यायधर्म्मं कृ, उपाध्यायवृत्तिम् अनुष्ठा.

MINISTERED, *p. p.* (Supplied) उपकॢप्तः -प्ता -प्तं, उपस्थापितः -ता -तं. —(Served) उपासितः -ता -तं, कृतोपचारः -रा -रं.

MINISTERIAL, *a.* (Attendant upon) उपकारकः -का -कं, उपकारी रिणी -रि (न्), अनुवर्त्ती -र्त्तिनी &c., वशवर्त्ती &c., वशानुगः -गा -गं, उपासकः -का -कं, उपचारपरः -रा -रं, उपचारकृत्, सेवकः -का -कं. —(Official executive pertaining to an agent) आधिकारिकः -की -कं, नियोगसम्बन्धी &c., कार्य्यसाधकः -का -कं, कार्य्यनिर्वाहकः -का -कं, कार्य्यप्रवर्त्तकः -का -कं, कार्य्यसाधनसम्बन्धी &c.—(Pertaining to a minister of state) मन्त्राधिकारसम्बन्धी &c., मन्त्रधर्म्मकः -का -कं, मन्त्रकर्म्मसम्बन्धी &c.—(Sacerdotal) उपाध्यायधर्म्मसम्बन्धी &c.. उपाध्यायधर्म्मकः -का -कं.

MINISTERIALLY, *adv.* मन्त्राधिकारेण, अधिकारतस्, अमात्यवत्, मन्त्रिवत्.

MINISTERSHIP, *s.* *See* MINISTRY.

MINISTRATION, *s.* (Service) उपचारः, उपचारकरणं, उपासनं -ना, पर्युपासनं, सेवा -वनं, उपसेवा -वनं, परिचर्य्या, उपकारः, शुश्रूषा.—(Office of a minister) मन्त्राधिकारः, मन्त्रकर्म्म *n.* (न्), मन्त्रकरणं. (Sacerdotal) उपाध्यायाधिकारः, उपाध्यायकर्म्म *n.* (न्), उपाध्यायवृत्तिः *f.*

MINISTRY, *s.* (Office of minister) मन्त्रित्वं, साचिव्यं, मन्त्राधिकारः -रिता, अमात्यत्वं, अधिकारः -रिता -त्वं; 'office of a prime minister,' मुख्यमन्त्रित्वं, प्रधानमन्त्रित्वं, पट्टाधिकारः.—(Office of an agent) नियोगिता -त्वं, नियोगः, नियोगिपदं, अधिकारः.—(Agency, instrumentality) कारणत्वं, कारकत्वं -ता, साधकत्वं, कर्तृत्वं -ता, कर्तृकत्वं, प्रयोजकत्वं.—(Office of a minister of religion) उपाध्यायत्वं, उपाध्यायपदं, पौरोहित्यं.—(Body of ministers of state) मन्त्रिसमाजः, मन्त्रिगणः, मन्त्रिसमूहः, मन्त्रिणः *m. pl.*, अमात्यगणः, सचिवसमाजः, अमात्याः *m. pl.*, राजधुर्वहाः *m. pl.*—(Service). *See* MINISTRATION.

MINIUM, *s.* सिन्दूरं -रिका, नागगर्भं, नागरक्तं, रक्तचूर्णं, रक्तवालुकं. *See* LEAD.

MINOR, *a.* (Less) अवरः -रा -रं, अल्पतरः -रा -रं, अल्पीयान् -यसी -यः (स्), कनीयान् &c., लघीयान् &c., न्यूनः -ना -नं.—(Secondary) अप्रधानः -ना -नं, अमुख्यः -ख्या -ख्यं, गौणः -णी -णं; 'minor' in these senses is very commonly expressed by the preposition उप; as, 'a minor member of the body,' उपाङ्गं, प्रत्यङ्गं; 'a minor veda,' उपवेदः; 'minor science,' उपविद्या; 'a minor offence,' उपपातकं; 'minor offender,' उपपातकी *m.* (न्); 'minor planet,' उपग्रहः; 'minor deity,' उपदेवता; 'minor duty,' उपधर्म्मः; 'minor disease,' क्षुद्ररोगः.—(Inconsiderable) लघुः -घुः -घु, स्वल्पः -ल्पा -ल्पं, क्षुद्रः -द्रा -द्रं.

MINOR, *s.* (Person under age) अप्राप्तव्यवहारः, अप्राप्तव्यवहारकालः, अजातव्यवहारः, व्यवहारायोग्यः, बालः, शिशुः *m.*, अप्राप्तषोडशवर्षः, किशोरः, अज्ञातव्यवहारः, अप्राप्तकालः.—(Premise, in logic) उत्तरपक्षः, लघ्ववयवः.

MINORITY, *s.* (State of being under age) बाल्यं, बालदशा, बालावस्था, बालत्वं, बाल्यभावः, बाल्यकालः, शैशवं, शिशुभावः, शिशुकालः, अप्राप्तव्यवहारत्वं, अप्राप्तव्यवहारदशा.—(Smaller number, lessness) न्यूनपक्षः, अल्पपक्षः, अवरपक्षः, न्यूनता -त्वं, न्यूनभावः; 'in the minority,' न्यूनपक्षपाती *m.* (न्), न्यूनपक्षग्राही *m.* (न्), न्यूनपक्षाश्रितः.

MINOTAUR, *s.* नरवृषभः, नरवृषः, नृवृषभः, कविकल्पितोऽर्द्धेन पुरुषोऽर्द्धेन वृषभो जन्तुविशेषः.

MINSTREL, *s.* मागधः, मगधः, वैतालिकः, वादित्रगायकः, गीतवादनकुशलः, सङ्गीतविद्, सङ्गीतकुशलः, गायकः, वन्दी *m.* (न्), मधुकः, भाण्डिकः; 'celestial,' गन्धर्वः.

MINSTRELSY, *s.* मागधवृत्तिः *f.*, गन्धर्ववृत्तिः *f.*, गीतवादनं, गीतवादनकर्म्म *n.* (न्), गान्धर्वं, सङ्गीतव्यापारः, सङ्गीतं, सङ्गीतिः *f.*

MINT, *s.* (Place where money is coined) टङ्कशाला, टङ्ककशाला, मुद्राङ्किता, मुद्राङ्कनशाला, अवाकरः; 'master of it,' टङ्कपतिः *m.*, टङ्ककपतिः, रूप्याध्यक्षः, नैष्किकः.—(Plant) पोदिना, पुदिना.

To MINT, *v. a.* मुद्राङ्कनं कृ, मुद्रादि अङ्क् (c. 10. अङ्कयति -यितुं), मुद्रीकृ, मुद्र (nom. मुद्रयति -यितुं).

MINTAGE, *s.* मुद्राङ्कनं, अङ्कनं.—(That which is coined) मुद्रा, मुद्रितरूप्यं, मुद्राङ्कितरूप्यं.

MINTER, *s.* मुद्राङ्ककः, टङ्काङ्कयिता *m.* (तृ), मुद्राकारः -रकः.

MINT-MASTER, *s.* टङ्कपतिः *m.*, टङ्ककपतिः *m.*, रूप्याध्यक्षः, नैष्किकः.

MINUET, *s.* (Kind of dance) पदगतिः *f.*, मन्दनृत्यविशेषः.

MINUS, *s.* (Less) न्यूनः -ना -नं, ऊनः -ना -नं; 'minus something,' किञ्चिन्न्यूनः -ना -नं; 'minus a hand,' हस्तन्यूनः -ना -नं.—(In algebra) ऋणं, क्षयः; 'a thousand minus one,' एकहान्या सहस्रं.

MINUTE, *a.* (Very small) सूक्ष्मः -क्ष्मा -क्ष्मं, अतिसूक्ष्मः -क्ष्मा -क्ष्मं, अत्यल्पः -ल्पा -ल्पं, अल्पिष्ठः -ष्ठा -ष्ठं, अणुकः -का -कं, आणुकः -की -कं, कणीकः -का -कं, अणीयान् -यसी -यः (स्), अणुः -ण्वी -णु, अल्पकः -का -कं, क्षुद्रः -द्रा -द्रं, श्लक्ष्णः -क्ष्णा -क्ष्णं, अल्पाल्पः -ल्पा -ल्पं, क्षोदिष्ठः -ष्ठा -ष्ठं, तनुः -नुः -न्वी -नु, प्रतनुः -नुः -नु, क्षीणः -णा -णं, तनीयान् -यसी &c., तनिष्ठः -ष्ठा -ष्ठं, क्षौद्रक्यः -की -क्यं, कृशः -शा -शं.—(Attending to small things) सूक्ष्मदृष्टिः -ष्टिः -ष्टि, सूक्ष्मदर्शी -र्शिनी &c.; 'minute description,' प्रत्यवयववर्णना.

MINUTE, *s.* (Sixtieth part of an hour) षष्टिप्राणपादाः *m. pl.*, क्षणपादः, क्षणचतुर्थांशः, सार्द्धद्विपलं; 'half a minute,' त्रिंशत्प्राणपादाः. According to the Hindu reckoning a दण्डः or hour contains 24 minutes, and a पलं is equal to the 60th part of a दण्डः, therefore $2\frac{1}{2}$ palas are equal to a minute. A क्षणः is equal to 30 कला or 4 minutes. When, however, the word minute is used generally for a small portion of time it may be expressed by क्षणः, पलं, विपलं, त्रुटिः *f.*, निमिषः, निमेषः; as, 'a minute's delay,' क्षणक्षेपः; 'for a minute,' क्षणं -णात् -णेन; 'in a minute,' निमेषमात्रेण; 'a minute afterwards,' क्षणान्तरं -रे.—(In geometry, the sixtieth part of a degree) कला.—(Note, memorandum) स्मरणलेखः, स्मरणार्थलिखितं, लेखः, लिखितं, स्मरणचिह्नं.

To MINUTE, *v. a.* स्मरणार्थं किञ्चिद् लिख् (c. 6. लिखति, लेखितुं), अभिलिख्.

MINUTELY, *adv.* सूक्ष्मं, सौक्ष्म्येण, ससौक्ष्म्यं, सूक्ष्मत्वेन, सूक्ष्मतया, अतिसूक्ष्मतया, लवशस्, कणशस्.

MINUTENESS, *s.* (Extreme smallness) अतिसूक्ष्मता, सूक्ष्मता -त्वं, सौक्ष्म्यं, अतिसौक्ष्म्यं, अत्यल्पता, अल्पिष्ठता, क्षुद्रता, क्षोदिमा *m.* (न्), अणिमा *m.* (न्), तनुता, अतितनुता, अतितानवं, तनिष्ठता, क्षीणता. —(Attention to small things) सूक्ष्मदृष्टित्वं, सूक्ष्मदर्शनं, सूक्ष्मदर्शित्वं.

MINUTIÆ, *s. pl.* सूक्ष्मावयवाः *m. pl.*, सूक्ष्मांशाः *m. pl.*, सूक्ष्मविषयाः.

MINX, *s.* अविनीता, दुर्विनीता, धृष्टा, प्रगल्भा, बन्धकी, निर्लज्जा.

MIRACLE, *s.* आश्चर्य्यकर्म्म *n.* (न्), अद्भुतकर्म्म *n.*, अतिमानुषकर्म्म *n.*, अमानुषकर्म्म, अमानुषीयकर्म्म *n.*, जनातिगकर्म्म *n.*, अद्भुतक्रिया, चमत्कारः, अद्भुतं, देवकर्म्म *n.*, दिव्यकर्म्म *n.*, निसर्गातिगकर्म्म *n.*, प्रकृत्यतीतकर्म्म *n.*, दिव्यशक्तिसाधितकर्म्म *n.*, विभूतिसाधितकर्म्म *n.*

MIRACULOUS, *a.* आश्चर्य्यः -र्य्या -र्य्यं, अद्भुतः -ता -तं, अतिमानुषः -षा -षं, जनातिगः -गा -गं, पुरुषातिगः -गा -गं, अतिमर्त्यः -र्त्या -र्त्यं, अपौरुषेयः -यी -यं, अमानुषशक्तिसाध्यः -ध्या -ध्यं, अपुरुषशक्तिसाधितः -ता -तं, दिव्यशक्तिसाधितः -ता -तं, विभूतिसाधितः -ता -तं, निसर्गातिगः -गा -गं, प्रकृत्यतिगः -गा -गं.—(Having miraculous powers) अद्भुतशक्तिमान् -मती -मत् (त्), अतिमानुषशक्तिकः -का -कं, अद्भुतकारी -रिणी -रि (न्), अमानुषकर्म्मकारी &c., अलौकिकशक्तिः -क्तिः -क्ति.

MIRACULOUSLY, *adv.* अतिमानुषशक्तिपूर्व्वं, आश्चर्य्यशक्त्या, अद्भुतशक्त्या, अमानुषशक्त्या, दिव्यशक्त्या, जनातिगशक्त्या, अलौकिकशक्त्या.

MIRAGE, *s.* मृगतृष्णा -ष्णिका, मृगतृषा, मृगतृट् *f.* (ष्), मृगजलं, मरीचिका.

MIRE, *s.* पङ्कः, कर्दमः, जम्बालः -लं, मलकल्कः, कलुषं, मलं.

To MIRE, *v. a.* पङ्केन दुष् (c. 10. दूषयति -यितुं), पङ्कस्थं -स्थां कृ.

MIRINESS, *s.* सपङ्कता, पङ्किलत्वं, सकर्दमता, कलुषत्वं, कालुष्यं.

MIRROR, *s.* दर्पणः -णं, आदर्शः, मुकुरः, मकुरः, मकुरः, आत्मदर्शः, मण्डलकं, प्रतिबिम्बातः, सम्मुखी *m.* (न्), दर्शनं, अदर्शः, कर्करः; 'the surface of a mirror,' आदर्शतलं; 'mirror-like,' आदर्शतलोपमः -मा -मं. —(Exemplar) आदर्शः, प्रतिमा.

To MIRROR, *v. a.* दर्पणे बिम्ब (nom. बिम्बयति -यितुं), प्रतिबिम्ब.

MIRRORED, *p. p.* बिम्बितः -ता -तं, प्रतिबिम्बितः -ता -तं, दर्पणगतः -ता -तं.

MIRTH, *s.* हास्यं, हासः, प्रहसनं, परिहासः, परीहासः, हासिका, उल्लासः, उल्लसता, मुदा, कौतुकं, हर्षः, प्रहर्षः, हास्यक्रीडा, हास्यविनोदः, मुदितं, प्रमोदः, मुद् *f.*, विश्रम्भणं.

MIRTHFUL, *a.* हासी -सिनी -सि (न्), हास्यवृत्तिः -त्तिः -त्ति, हास्यमुखः -खी -खं, सुहसाननः -ना -नं, उल्लासी -सिनी &c., उल्लसः -सा -सं, उल्लासितः -ता -तं, मुदान्वितः -ता -तं, प्रमोदी -दिनी &c., मुदितः -ता -तं, हृष्टचित्तः -त्ता -त्तं, कौतुकी -किनी &c., आनन्दी &c.

MIRTHFULLY, *adv.* सहासं, सहास्यं, सहसितं, परिहासेन, उल्लासेन.

MIRY, *a.* पङ्किलः -ला -लं, पङ्की -ङ्किनी -ङ्कि (न्), पङ्कमयः -यी -यं, पङ्कक्लिन्नः -न्ना -न्नं, सपङ्कः -ङ्का -ङ्कं, सकर्दमः -मा -मं, कार्दमः -मी -मं, कर्दमितः -ता -तं, सजम्बालः -ला -लं, कलुषः -षा -षं, पङ्कदूषितः -ता -तं; 'a miry road,' पङ्कवर्त्म *n.* (न्).

MISACCEPTATION, *s.* विपरीतग्रहणं, अन्यथाग्रहणं, विपरीतार्थग्रहणं.

MISADVENTURE, *s.* अनिष्टापातः, अनिष्टं, विपद् *f.*, विपत्तिः *f.*, आपद् *f.*, दुर्गतिः.

MISADVENTURED, *a.* दुर्गतः -ता -तं, दुर्भाग्यः -ग्या -ग्यं, दुर्दशाग्रस्तः &c.

MIS-ADVISED, *a.* कुमन्त्रितः -ता -तं, कूपदिष्टः -ष्टा -ष्टं, कुपरामृष्टः -ष्टा -ष्टं.

MIS-AFFECTED, *a.* अहितः -ता -तं, विरक्तः -क्ता -क्तं, अननुरक्तः &c.

To MIS-ALLEDGE, *v. a.* अन्यथा वद् (c. 1. वदति -दितुं), मिथ्या वद्.

MIS-ALLEGATION, *s.* अन्यथाकथनं, अन्यथावादः, मिथ्यावादः, मिथ्याकथनं.

MISANTHROPE, MISANTHROPIST, *s.* पुरुषद्वेषी *m.* (न्), पुरुषद्वेष्टा *m.* (तृ), जनद्वेषी &c., लोकद्वेषी, पुरुषशत्रुः *m.*, जनशत्रुः, जनवैरी *m.* (न्), विश्वशत्रुः *m.*, विश्वद्रोही *m.* (न्), सर्व्वाभिसन्धकः, सर्व्वाभिसन्धी *m.* (न्).

MISANTHROPIC, MISANTHROPICAL, *a.* पुरुषद्वेषी -षिणी -षि (न्), जनद्वेषी &c., सर्व्वद्वेषी &c., विश्वद्वेषी &c., जनवैरी -रिणी &c., अपरिचयी -यिणी &c., अपरिचयशीलः -ला -लं, अपरिचेयः -या -यं.

MISANTHROPY, *s.* पुरुषद्वेषः, जनद्वेषः, सर्व्वलोकद्वेषः, जनवैरिता, जनशत्रुता, सर्व्वलोकशत्रुता, लोकवैरक्यं, अपरिचयशीलता, जनद्रोहः, मनुष्यत्रासः, जनापकारबुद्धिः *f.*

MISAPPLICATION, *s.* कुप्रयोगः, असत्प्रयोगः, अन्यथाप्रयोगः.—(Of money) असद्व्ययः, कुव्ययः, अन्यथाव्ययः.

To MISAPPLY, *v. a.* कुप्रयोगं कृ, कुविनियोगं कृ, अन्यथा or मिथ्या प्रयुज् (c. 7. -युनक्ति -युंक्ते, c. 10. -योजयति -यितुं) or विनियुज्.

To MISAPPREHEND, *v. a.* अन्यथा ग्रह् (c. 9. गृह्णाति, ग्रहीतुं) or बुध् (c. 1. बोधति -धितुं) or अवगम् (c. 1. -गच्छति -गन्तुं), विपरीतार्थं ग्रह्, विपरीतम् उपलभ् (c. 1. -लभते -लब्धुं), विपरीतार्थग्रहणं कृ.

MISAPPREHENSION, *s.* अन्यथाग्रहणं, विपरीतग्रहणं, अन्यथाबोधः, विपरीतबोधः, अन्यथार्थबोधः, अर्थविपर्यासकरणं, विपरीतार्थग्रहणं, विपरीतार्थबोधः, भ्रमः, मिथ्यामतिः *f.*

To MISBECOME, *v. a.* न युज् in pass. (युज्यते), न उपपद् (c. 4. -पद्यते).

MISBECOMING, *a.* अयोग्यः -ग्या -ग्यं, अयुक्तः -क्ता -क्तं, अनुचितः -ता -तं.

MISBEGOT, MISBEGOTTEN, *a.* विजातः -ता -तं, विजनितः &c., कुजातः &c.

To MISBEHAVE, *v. n.* अयुक्तं or असम्यक् चर् (c. 1. चरति -रितुं) or आचर् or वृत् (c. 1. वर्त्तते -र्त्तितुं), दुराचारः -रा -रं भू, दुराचारं कृ, व्यभिचारं कृ, मर्य्यादातिक्रमं कृ, दुर्वृत्तः -त्ता -त्तं भू.

MISBEHAVED, *a.* दुर्विनीतः -ता -तं, अविनीतः -ता -तं, दुश्चरितः -ता -तं, दुश्चेष्टितः -ता -तं, दुर्वृत्तः -त्ता -त्तं, कुशीलः -ला -लं, समुद्धतः -ता -तं. *See* ILL-BRED.

MISBEHAVIOUR, *s.* दुर्विनीतता, अविनयः, कुनीतिः *f.*, दुश्चेष्टितं, कुचेष्टितं, दुर्वृत्तिः *f.*, कुनीतिः *f.*, कुचरितं, कुचर्य्या, व्यभिचारः, दुराचारः, मर्य्यादातिक्रमः.

MISBELIEF, *s.* अन्यथाश्रद्धा, कुप्रत्ययः, कुश्रद्धा, मिथ्याविश्वासः.

To MISCALCULATE, *v. a.* अन्यथा or मिथ्या or असम्यग् गण् (c. 10. गणयति -यितुं) or विगण् or संख्या (c. 2. -ख्याति -तुं), मिथ्यागणनं कृ.

MISCALCULATED, *p. p.* मिथ्यागणितः -ता -तं, अन्यथागणितः &c., असम्यग्गणितः &c.

MISCALCULATION, *s.* मिथ्यागणना -नं, असम्यग्गणना, अन्यथागणना, दुर्गणना, कुगणना, कुपरिसंख्या.

To MISCALL, *v. a.* मिथ्याभिधानं कृ or दा, मिथ्या or अन्यथा आख्या (c. 2. -ख्याति -तुं) or अभिधा (c. 3. -दधाति -धातुं), मिथ्यानाम कृ.

MISCALLED, *p. p.* मिथ्याभिहितः -ता -तं, मिथ्याख्यातः -ता -तं.

MISCARRIAGE, *s.* (Failure) असिद्धिः *f.*, विपत्तिः *f.*, कार्य्यविपत्तिः *f.*, असम्पत्तिः *f.*, अनुपपत्तिः *f.*, अप्रतिपत्तिः *f.*, भङ्गः, अकरणिः *f.*, असन्नतिः *f.*, दुर्गतिः *f.*, वैफल्यं, असत्फलं, अशुभफलं, अशुभगतिः *f.*—(Ill-conduct) कुनीतिः *f.*, अनीतिः *f.*, अविनयः, दुर्वृत्तिः *f.*, कुचर्य्या, दुराचरणं, कुचेष्टितं. —(Bringing forth before the time) गर्भस्रावः, गर्भपातः, गर्भपतनं, गर्भस्रवः, गर्भप्रस्रवणं, गर्भच्युतिः *f.*, गर्भविस्रंसनं, गर्भस्यन्दनं, अप्राप्तकालगर्भनिःसरणं, पिण्डपतनं, स्रवः, स्रावः. When it takes place before the fourth month it is called गर्भस्रावः, after that गर्भपातः; 'to cause miscarriage,' गर्भं पत् (c. 10. पातयति -यितुं), or च्यु (c. 10. च्यावयति -यितुं) or स्रु (c. 10. स्रावयति -यितुं); 'causing it,' गर्भपाती -तिनी &c., गर्भपातकः -का -कं, गर्भस्रावी &c.

To MISCARRY, *v. n.* (Not to succeed) न सिध् (c. 4. सिध्यति, सेद्धुं),

न सम्पद् (c. 4. -पद्यते -पत्तुं), न उपपद्, प्रतिहन् in pass. (-हन्यते), विफलीभू, निष्फलीभू, वृथाभू, मोघीभू, भग्नः -ग्ना -ग्नं भू, सिद्धिं न प्राप् (c. 5. -आप्नोति -आप्तुं), असिद्धः -द्धा -द्धं भू.—(Bring forth before the time) स्रवद्गर्भा भू, पतद्गर्भा भू, अप्राप्तकाले च्युतगर्भा or निःसृतगर्भा भू or गर्भच्युता भू.

MISCELLANEOUS, *a.* नानाजातीयः -या -यं, अनेकजातीयः -या -यं, नानाप्रकारः -रा -रं, भिन्नजातीयः &c., विजातीयः &c., नानाविधः -धा -धं, अनेकविधः -धा -धं, प्रकीर्णः -र्णा -र्णं, सङ्कीर्णः -र्णा -र्णं, सान्निपातिकः -की -कं, नानाविषयकः -का -कं, विविधः -धा -धं, अवर्गीयः -या -यं, सम्पर्की -र्किणी -र्कि (न्), प्रकीर्णजातिः -तिः -ति.

MISCELLANEOUSLY, *adv.* प्रकीर्णं, सङ्कीर्णं, नानाविधं, नानाप्रकारैः, सन्निपाततस्.

MISCELLANEOUSNESS, *s.* प्रकीर्णता, सङ्कीर्णता, जातिप्रकीर्णता, नानाजातित्वं.

MISCELLANY, *s.* नानाद्रव्यसङ्ग्रहः, नानाविषयसङ्ग्रहः, नानावस्तुसमूहः, नानाद्रव्यसन्निपातः, सम्मिश्रद्रव्यसमूहः, प्रकीर्णद्रव्यसङ्ग्रहः, सङ्कीर्णवस्तुसमूहः, प्रकीर्णकं, सन्निपातः.—(Book, pamphlet) नानाविषयग्रन्थः, प्रकीर्णग्रन्थः, प्रकीर्णकं, प्रकीर्णं.

MISCHANCE, *s.* विपद् *f.*, विपत्तिः *f.*, आपद् *f.*, दुर्दैवं, दुर्गतिः *f.*, अपायः.

MISCHIEF, *s.* (Injury, harm) हिंसा, अपकारः, अपकृतं -तिः *f.*, अपक्रिया, अपायः, द्रोहः, अभिद्रोहः, घातः, अर्दना, दूषणं, अनिष्टं, अरिष्टं, खलता, खलीकारः.—(Damage) क्षतिः *f.*, क्षतं, परिक्षतिः *f.*, परिक्षतं, अपायः, नाशः, हानिः *f.*, अपकृतं, अपचयः, अपचितिः *f.*, ध्वंसः, बाधः, दुःखं, दोषः, व्यसनं, कष्टं; 'loving mischief,' अपकारप्रियः -या -यं, कदनप्रियः -या -यं.

MISCHIEF-MAKER, *s.* उपजापकः, कर्णेजपः, भेदकरः, भेदजनकः, सुहृद्भेदकरः, मित्रभेदकः, भेदकः, वैरकरः, कलिकारकः, पिशुनः, दुर्जनः, खलः.

MISCHIEF-MAKING, *s.* उपजापः, कर्णेजापः, सुहृद्भेदनं, मित्रभेदनं, वैरकरणं, पैशुन्यं, दौर्जन्यं, खलता, कलिकरणं.

MISCHIEVOUS, *a.* (Injurious) हिंस्रः -स्रा -स्रं, हिंसकः -का -कं, हिंसात्मकः -का -कं, हिंसालुः -लुः -लु, अपकारी -रिणी -रि (न्), अपकारकः -का -कं, आपकरः -री -रं, हिंसाशीलः -ला -लं, परहिंसाशीलः -ला -लं, हिंसारतः -ता -तं, क्षतिकरः -रा -रं, अनिष्टकरः -री -रं, नृशंसः -सा -सं, नृशंसवृत्तः -त्ता -त्तं, द्रोही -हिणी &c., घातुकः -का -कं, उपघातकः -का -कं, बाधकः -का -कं, अहितकारी &c., शार्वरः -री -रं, भीवरः -री -रं.—(Inclined to do harm) अपकारबुद्धिः -द्धिः -द्धि, क्षतिकरणशीलः -ला -लं, हिंसारुचिः -चिः -चि, बाधनशीलः &c., अपायशीलः &c., दूषणशीलः &c., दुष्टबुद्धिः &c., पापः -पा -पं.—(Noxious) शारुकः -का -कं, शरारुः -रुः -रु, दूषकः -का -कं, सबाधः -धा -धं, अहितः -ता -तं.—(Full of mischievous pranks) छान्दसः -सी -सं, कुचेष्टाप्रियः -या -यं, कुचेष्टितः -ता -तं, दुश्चेष्टितः -ता -तं, कितवः -वा -वं, व्यसनी -निनी &c., दुर्गुणी &c.; 'mischievous tricks,' कुचेष्टा, कुचेष्टितं, छन्दस् *n.*; 'mischievous person,' लोककण्टकः, पंक्तिदूषकः.

MISCHIEVOUSLY, *adv.* हिंसया, सापकारं, अपकारेण, सापायं, क्षतिपूर्वं, सक्षतं, अपकारबुद्ध्या, अपकारशीलत्वात्, दुष्टबुद्ध्या, सबाधं.

MISCHIEVOUSNESS, *s.* हिंस्रता, हिंसाशीलता, परहिंसाशीलता, हिंसारुचिता, हिंसालुता, क्षतिकारिता, अपकारशीलता, अपकारः, अपकृतिः *f.*, अपकारिता, बाधकत्वं, द्रोहबुद्धित्वं, दूषकता, कैतवं, कैतवप्रयोगः.

MISCIBLE, *a.* मिश्रणीयः -या -यं, मिश्रणयोग्यः -ग्या -ग्यं, मिश्रणार्हः -र्हा -र्हं, योजनीयः -या -यं, याव्यः -व्या -व्यं.

MISCOMPUTATION, *s.* मिथ्यागणना, असम्यग्गणनं, अन्यथागणनं, कुगणना.

To MISCONCEIVE, *v. a.* or *n.* अन्यथा or मिथ्या बुध् (c. 1. बोधति -धितुं) or ग्रह् (c. 9. गृह्णाति, ग्रहीतुं) or उपलभ् (c. 1. -लभते -लब्धुं) or अवगम् (c. 1. -गच्छति -गन्तुं), अन्यथार्थं ग्रह्, विपरीतार्थं ग्रह्, विपरीतबोधनं कृ, विपरीतार्थग्रहणं कृ, अर्थविपर्य्यासं कृ.

MISCONCEPTION, *s.* अन्यथाग्रहणं, मिथ्याग्रहणं, मिथ्यामतिः *f.*, मिथ्याबुद्धिः *f.*, विपरीतग्रहः -हणं, अन्यथाबोधः, अन्यथार्थबोधः, विपरीतबोधः, विपरीतार्थबोधः, विपरीतार्थग्रहणं, भ्रमः, भ्रान्तिः *f.*, अर्थविपर्य्यासः.

MISCONDUCT, *s.* (Ill-behaviour) दुश्चरितं, दुश्चेष्टितं, कुचेष्टितं, कुचरितं, अविनयः, अविनीतता, कुचर्य्या, कुचरितं, कुचेष्टितं, दुर्णीतं, दुर्णीतिः *f.*, दुर्णयः, दुराचारः, दुराचरणं, असदाचारः, असदाचरणं, कदाचारः, कुव्यवहारः, असद्व्यवहारः, कुकर्म्म *n.* (न्), कुकृतं, व्यभिचारः, अन्यथाचारः, अन्यथाचरणं, अपचारः, कुशीलता, अमर्य्यादा, मर्य्यादातिक्रमः.—(Ill-management) दुर्णयः -यनं, दुर्निर्वाहः, असन्निर्वाहः.

To MISCONDUCT, *v. a.* (Conduct badly) अन्यथा or अयुक्तं or दुष्टु or असम्यग् निर्वह् (c. 10. -वाहयति -यितुं) or प्रणी (c. 1. -णयति -णेतुं) or सम्प्रणी or प्रवृत् (c. 10.-वर्त्तयति -यितुं), दुर्निर्वाहं कृ, असन्निर्वाहं कृ, दुर्णयनं कृ.—(Misconduct one's self) अयुक्तं or असम्यक् चर् (c. 1. चरति -रितुं) or आचर् or वृत् (c. 1. वर्त्तते -र्त्तितुं), व्यभिचारं कृ, मर्य्यादातिक्रमं कृ.

MISCONDUCTED, *a.* दुर्विनीतः -ता -तं, दुश्चरितः -ता -तं. *See* MISBEHAVED.

MISCONJECTURE, *s.* मिथ्यानुमानं, अन्यथानुमानं, मिथ्यावितर्कः.

To MISCONJECTURE, *v. n.* मिथ्या or अन्यथा अनुमा (c. 2. -माति -तुं) or तर्क् (c. 10. तर्कयति -यितुं) or वितर्क्, मिथ्यानुमानं कृ.

MISCONSTRUCTION, *s.* अन्यथाग्रहणं, मिथ्याग्रहणं, विपरीतबोधनं, मिथ्याबोधनं, अयथार्थबोधनं, अन्यथाबोधनं, विपरीतग्रहणं, विपरीतार्थबोधः, अन्यथार्थबोधः, विपरीतार्थकरणं, अन्यथार्थकरणं, मिथ्यार्थव्याख्या.

To MISCONSTRUE, *v. a.* अन्यथा or मिथ्या अर्थं बुध् (c. 1. बोधति -धितुं) or ग्रह् (c. 9. गृह्णाति, ग्रहीतुं) or उपलभ् (c. 1. -लभते -लब्धुं), मिथ्या अर्थं व्याख्या (c. 2. -ख्याति -तुं), विपरीतार्थं ग्रह्, विपरीतबोधनं कृ, विपरीतार्थग्रहणं कृ.

MISCREANT, *a.* (Infidel) नास्तिकः.—(Vile wretch) पापीयान् *m.* (स्), पापिष्ठः, पापः, दुर्जनः, दुरात्मा *m.* (न्), दुर्वृत्तः, जाल्मः, खलः, नराधमः; 'daring miscreant,' साहसिकः.

MISDEED, *s.* कुकर्म्म *n.* (न्), दुष्कृतं, दुष्कर्म्म *n.*, अपकर्म्म *n.*, दुष्कृतिः *f.*, कुकृत्यं, अकर्म्म *n.*, कुक्रिया, पापकर्म्म *n.*, दुश्चरितं, कुचरितं, कुचेष्टितं, अपचारः.

To MISDEMEAN. *See To* MISCONDUCT, MISBEHAVE.

MISDEMEANOR, *s.* *See* MISCONDUCT. (Minor offence) उपपातकं.

To MISDIRECT, *v. a.* (Put in the wrong road) विमार्गं or विपरीतमार्गं दृश् (c. 10. दर्शयति -यितुं), विपथं प्रदृश्, अन्यथा मार्गं दृश् or उद्दिश् (c. 6. -दिशति -देष्टुं), विपरीतपथं प्रदिश्, विमार्गप्रदर्शनं कृ.—(A letter) अन्यथा पत्रसंज्ञां लिख् (c. 6. लिखति, लेखितुं) or कृ.

MISDIRECTION, *s.* विमार्गप्रदर्शनं, विपरीतमार्गदर्शनं, मिथ्योद्देशः.

MISDOER, *s.* कुकर्म्मकारी *m.* (न्), कुकर्म्मी *m.* (न्), पापकारी *m.* (न्), पापकर्त्ता *m.* (र्तृ), पापकरः, पापकृत् *m.*, पापकर्म्मी *m.*, असत्कर्म्मी *m.*, अन्यायकारी *m.*, अन्यथाचारी *m.*, मन्दचरितः.

MISDOING, *s.* दुष्कृतं, कुकर्म्म *n.* (न्), पापं, अपराधः. *See* MISDEED.

To MISEMPLOY, *v. a.* कुप्रयोगं कृ, कुविनियोगं कृ, असत्प्रयोगं कृ, अन्यथा or असम्यक् प्रयुज् (c. 7. -युनक्ति -योक्तुं, c. 10. -योजयति -यितुं) or विनियुज्.

MISEMPLOYED, *p.p.* कुप्रयुक्तः -क्ता -क्तं, कुविनियुक्तः &c., असम्यक्प्रयुक्तः &c.

MISEMPLOYMENT, *s.* कुप्रयोगः, कुविनियोगः, असत्प्रयोगः, असम्यक्प्रयोगः,

अन्यथाप्रयोगः, असदुपयोगः, कुव्यापारः, कुव्ययः, असद्व्ययः.

Miser, *s.* कृपणः, दृढमुष्टिः *m.*, गाढमुष्टिः, दानशत्रुः *m.*, दानविमुखः, दानपराङ्मुखः, अदानशीलः, अत्यागशीलः, स्वल्पव्ययी *m.* (न्), स्वल्पदाता *m.* (तृ), अदाता *m.*, मितम्पचः, किम्पचः, कदर्य्यः, मत्सरी *m.* (न्), व्ययशङ्कितः, व्ययपराङ्मुखः, अर्थपरः, धनलाभपरः.

Miserable, *a.* (Very unhappy) अतिदुःखी -खिनी -खि (न्), गाढदुःखान्वितः -ता -तं, अतिदुःखितः -ता -तं, अतिक्लेशी -शिनी &c., अतिक्लेशितः &c., अतिदुःखार्त्तः -र्त्ता -र्त्तं, अतिशोकार्त्तः -र्त्ता -र्त्तं, निरानन्दः -न्दा -न्दं, अतिदीनः -ना -नं, अनिर्वृतः -ता -तं, अनिर्वेशः -शा -शं; ‘making one’s self miserable,’ आत्मद्रोही &c.—(Very poor or mean) अतिकृपणः -णा -णं, कृपणः -णा -णं, कुत्सितः -ता -तं, तुच्छः -च्छा -च्छं, गर्ह्यः -र्ह्या -र्ह्यं, गर्हितः -ता -तं.—(Unfortunate) आपद्ग्रस्तः -स्ता -स्तं, विपद्ग्रस्तः &c., विपन्नः -न्ना -न्नं, आपन्नः -न्ना -न्नं, दुःखापन्नः &c., दुर्दशाग्रस्तः &c., मन्दभाग्यः -ग्या -ग्यं, दुर्भाग्यः &c., दैवोपहतः -ता -तं, आपत्प्राप्तः -प्ता -प्तं; ‘miserable wretch,’ तपस्वी *m.* (न्).

Miserableness, *s.* अतिदुःखिता, अतिदीनता, कृपणता, अतिकार्पण्यं.

Miserably, *adv.* कृपणं, अतिकृपणं, अतिकार्पण्येन, अतिदुःखितवत्.

Miserly, *a.* कृपणः -णा -णं, कदर्य्यः -र्य्या -र्य्यं, दानविमुखः -खा -खं, दानपराङ्मुखः &c., दृढमुष्टिः -ष्टिः -ष्टि, गाढमुष्टिः -ष्टिः -ष्टि, अदानशीलः -ला -लं, स्वल्पव्ययी -यिनी -यि (न्), व्ययपराङ्मुखः -खा -खं, व्ययशङ्कितः -ता -तं, मितम्पचः -चा -चं, किम्पचः -चा -चं, किम्पचानः -ना -नं, अत्यागशीलः -ला -लं, अदाता -त्री -तृ (तृ), अनुदारः -रा -रं, मत्सरी -रिणी &c., अर्थपरः -रा -रं, धनलाभपरः -रा -रं, क्षुद्रः -द्रा -द्रं, कीकटः -टी -टं.

Misery, *s.* (Great unhappiness, distress) अतिदुःखं, अतिशयदुःखं, दुःखं, क्लेशः, अतिक्लेशः, अतिशयक्लेशः, दुःखावस्था, दुःखदुःखं, गाढदुःखं, शोकः, गाढशोकः, दैन्यं, दीनता, अतिदीनता, विडम्बनं -ना, अनिर्वृतिः *f.* —(Extreme pain) अतिबाधा, अतिव्यथा, अतिशयतापः, परितापः, सन्तापः, अतिकृच्छ्रं, अतिवेदना.—(Calamity) दुःखं, व्यसनं, विपत्तिः *f.*, आपद् *f.*, विपद् *f.*, दुर्गतिः *f.*, दुर्दशा, दौर्गत्यं, दुरवस्था, अपायः, अनिष्टं, अरिष्टं, निर्वृतिः *f.*, व्यतिकरः.

Misfortune, *s.* (Ill-fortune) दुर्दैवं, दुर्भाग्यं, दौर्भाग्यं, कुभाग्यं, दुर्गतिः *f.*, दौर्गत्यं, अशुभं, अकुशलं, अभद्रं, अमङ्गलं, दुरदृष्टं, दुर्जातं, अश्रीकं, अनयः, अनर्थः, आलक्ष्म्यं, निर्वृतिः *f.*—(Calamity, disaster) आपद् *f.*, विपद्, विपत्तिः *f.*, व्यापद् *f.*, व्यसनं, अनिष्टं, अनिष्टपातः, अनिष्टापातः, अपायः, दुर्घटना, उत्पातः, अनयः, दुःखं, कष्टं, दुर्दशा, दुरवस्था.—(Misfortune personified) अलक्ष्मीः *f.*, अवलक्ष्मीः *f.*, महामाया; ‘fallen into misfortune,’ आपद्गतः -ता -तं, विपद्गतः -ता -तं, आपत्प्राप्तः -प्ता -प्तं, आपद्ग्रस्तः -स्ता -स्तं, अनयगतः -ता -तं.

To Misgive, *v. a.* (Used in English with heart and the reciprocal pronoun, and expressed in Sanskrit by) शङ्क् (c. 1. शङ्कते -ङ्कितुं), आशङ्क्, विशङ्क्, उद्विज् (c. 6. -विजते -जितुं), वेप् (c. 1. वेपते -पितुं), प्रवेप्, न विश्वस् (c. 2. -श्वसिति -तुं), न प्रती (c. 2. प्रत्येति -तुं rt. इ), सन्देहं कृ, संशयं कृ, विकॢप् (c. 1. -कल्पते -ल्पितुं, c. 10. -कल्पयति -यितुं); ‘my heart misgives me,’ वेपते मे हृदयं, उद्विजते मे हृदयं.

Misgiving, *s.* शङ्का, आशङ्का, सन्देहः, संशयः, विकल्पः, विकल्पितं, अविश्वासः, अप्रत्ययः, अप्रतीतिः *f.*; ‘having misgivings,’ साशङ्कः -ङ्का -ङ्कं, आशङ्कान्वितः -ता -तं, शङ्काशीलः -ला -लं.

Misgotten, *a.* अन्यायोपार्जितः -ता -तं, अन्यायार्जितः &c., वृजिनार्जितः &c.

To Misgovern, *v. a.* असम्यक् पाल् (c. 10. पालयति -यितुं) or शास् (c. 2. शास्ति -सितुं), असम्यक्पालनं कृ, कुशासनं कृ, असम्यक्शासनं कृ, असत्पालनं कृ.

Misgoverned, *p. p.* असम्यक्पालितः -ता -तं, कुशासितः -ता -तं.

Misgovernment, misgovernance, *s.* असम्यक्पालनं, असम्यक्शासनं, कुशासनं, कुशास्तिः *f.*, असत्पालनं, अन्यथाशासनं.

To Misguide, *v. a.* विमार्गेण or उन्मार्गेण or कुमार्गेण नी (c. 1. नयति, नेतुं), विमार्गं दृश् (c. 10. दर्शयति -यितुं) or उद्दिश् (c. 6. -दिशति -देष्टुं), अन्यथा नी.

Misguided, *a.* असम्यगुपदिष्टः -ष्टा -ष्टं, कुमन्त्रितः -ता -तं, कुशिक्षितः -ता -तं, दुर्विनीतः &c., सत्पथभ्रष्टः -ष्टा -ष्टं, सन्मार्गभ्रष्टः &c., मार्गप्रभ्रष्टः &c.

Mishap, *s.* विपद् *f.*, आपद् *f.*, विपत्तिः *f.*, दुर्गतिः *f.*, दौर्गत्यं, अनिष्टपातः, अनिष्टापातः, दुर्घटना, व्यसनं, दुर्जातं. *See* Misfortune.

To Misinfer, *v. a.* मिथ्या or अन्यथा अनुमा (c. 2. -माति -तुं), मिथ्यानुमानं कृ.

To Misinform, *v. a.* अयथार्थं or अन्यथा in caus. (ज्ञापयति, ज्ञपयति -यितुं), मिथ्या or मृषा बुध् (c. 10. बोधयति -यितुं), असम्यग् अर्थं ख्या (c. 2. ख्याति -तुं) or आख्या.

Misinformed, *p. p.* मिथ्याज्ञप्तः -प्ता -प्तं, मिथ्याबोधितः &c., अयथार्थज्ञप्तः &c.

To Misinterpret, *v. a.* अयथार्थं or अन्यथा व्याख्या (c. 2. -ख्याति -तुं), अन्यथार्थं व्याख्या.—(Understand in a wrong sense) अन्यथा or मिथ्या अर्थं बुध् (c. 1. बोधति -धितुं) or ग्रह् (c. 9. गृह्णाति, ग्रहीतुं), विपरीतार्थं ग्रह्, विपरीतार्थबोधनं कृ.

Misinterpretation, *s.* अयथार्थव्याख्यानं, अन्यथार्थव्याख्यानं, अयथार्थबोधः, मिथ्याबोधनं, विपरीतबोधनं, अन्यथाग्रहणं.

Misinterpreted, *p. p.* अन्यथाव्याख्यातः -ता -तं, अन्यथाबोधितः -ता -तं.

To Misjudge, *v. a.* अन्यथा or मिथ्या विचर् (c. 10. -चारयति -यितुं) or विभावनं कृ.

Misjudgement, *s.* मिथ्याविचारः, अन्यथाविचारः, कुविवेचना, कुनिष्पत्तिः *f.*

Mislaid, *p. p.* स्थानभ्रष्टः -ष्टा -ष्टं, स्थानप्रभ्रष्टः -ष्टा -ष्टं, अस्थानवर्त्ती -र्त्तिनी -र्त्ति (न्), अस्थानः -ना -नं, नष्टः -ष्टा -ष्टं; ‘a thing mislaid,’ नष्टः, नष्टा.

To Mislay, *v. a.* अस्थानीकृ, विस्थानीकृ, अपस्थानीकृ, अस्थाने कृ or धा (c. 3. दधाति, धातुं), अस्थाने धृ (c. 1. धरति, धर्त्तुं), नश् (c. 10. नाशयति -यितुं).

To Mislead, *v. a.* विमार्गेण or उन्मार्गेण नी (c. 1. नयति, नेतुं), विमार्गं or विपथं दृश् (c. 10. दर्शयति -यितुं) or उद्दिश् (c. 6. दिशति -देष्टुं) or प्रदिश्, अन्यथा or अयथार्थम् उपदिश् or निर्दिश् or आदिश् or शिक्ष् (c. 10. शिक्षयति -यितुं), कुशिक्षां कृ, कुनिर्देशं कृ, भ्रम् (c. 10. भ्रमयति -यितुं), भ्रान्तिं जन् (c. 10. जनयति -यितुं), विमार्गनयनं कृ, विमार्गप्रदर्शनं कृ.

Misled, *p. p.* भ्रान्तः -न्ता -न्तं, विमार्गगामी -मिनी -मि (न्), उन्मार्गगामी &c. सत्पथभ्रष्टः -ष्टा -ष्टं, सन्मार्गभ्रष्टः &c., उत्पथगामी &c., कुमार्गप्रवृत्तः -त्ता -त्तं, कुशिक्षितः -ता -तं, दुर्विनीतः -ता -तं.

To Mislike, *v. a.* *See* *To* dislike.

To Mismanage, *v. a.* अन्यथा or अयुक्तं or असम्यग् निर्वह् (c. 10. -वाहयति -यितुं) or प्रणी (c. 1. -णयति -णेतुं) or सम्प्रणी or प्रवृत् (c. 10. -वर्त्तयति -यितुं) दुर्निर्वाहं कृ, असन्निर्वाहं कृ, दुर्णयनं कृ, दुर्णीतिं कृ, असन्नयनं कृ, दुराचरणं कृ.

Mismanaged, *p. p.* दुर्णीतः -ता -तं, असम्यङ्नीतः -ता -तं, दुर्निर्वाहितः -ता -तं, कुनिर्वाहितः -ता -तं, कुप्रणीतः -ता -तं, कुप्रवर्त्तितः -ता -तं, दुर्घटितः -ता -तं, दुराचरितः -ता -तं.

Mismanagement, *s.* दुर्णयः -यनं, दुर्णीतिः *f.*, कुनीतिः *f.*, कुनयनं, कुनि-

वोढः, दुर्निर्वाहः, दुर्निर्वहणं, दुर्णीतं, असन्निर्वाहः, कुप्रणयनं, कुप्रवर्त्तनं, दुराचरणं, अन्यथाचरणं, दुर्वृत्तत्वं, असत्क्रिया.

To MISNAME, *v. a.* मिथ्यानाम कृ or दा, अन्यथानाम कृ. *See* MISCALL.

MISNOMER, *s.* मिथ्यानाम *n.* (न्), मिथ्याभिधानं, अन्यथानाम *n.*, अयोग्यनाम *n.*, असङ्गतनाम *n.*, अनुपयुक्तनाम *n.*, अनुपयुक्तसंज्ञा.

MISOGAMIST, *s.* विवाहद्वेषी *m.* -षिणी *f.*, उद्वाहद्वेषी &c., विवाहनिन्दकः.

MISOGAMY, *s.* विवाहद्वेषः, उद्वाहद्वेषः, विवाहनिन्दा, उद्वाहशत्रुता.

MISOGYNIST, *s.* स्त्रीद्वेषी *m.* (न्), स्त्रीद्वेष्टा *m.* (ष्टृ), स्त्रीनिन्दकः.

MISOGYNY, *s.* स्त्रीद्वेषः, स्त्रीनिन्दा, स्त्रीवैरं, स्त्रीशत्रुता.

To MISPLACE, *v. a.* अस्थानीकृ, विस्थानीकृ, अस्थाने कृ or धा (c. 3. दधाति, धातुं) or विधा, अनुपयुक्तपदे स्था in caus. (स्थापयति -यितुं), अन्यथा स्था, असम्यक् स्था or निधा (c. 3. -दधाति -धातुं) or प्रयुज् (c. 7. -युनक्ति -योक्तुं, c. 10. -योजयति -यितुं).

MISPLACED, *p. p.* अस्थानः -ना -नं, अस्थानीकृतः -ता -तं, अस्थाने निहितः -ता -तं or विहितः -ता -तं, अनुपयुक्तपदे स्थापितः -ता -तं.

MISPRINT, *s.* अशुद्धं, अशुद्धिः *f.*, अशोधनं, अशुद्धमुद्रा, पुस्तकमुद्राङ्कने दोषः, मुद्राङ्कनदोषः.

To MISPRINT, *v. a.* अशुद्धमुद्रां कृ, अशुद्धमुद्राङ्कनं कृ, मुद्राङ्कनदोषं कृ, अशुद्धमुद्रया अङ्क् (c. 10. अङ्कयति -यितुं), अशुद्धमुद्रीकृ.

MISPRINTED, *p. p.* अशुद्धमुद्राङ्कितः -ता -तं, अशुद्धमुद्रीकृतः -ता -तं.

MISPRISION, *s.* अपराधगोपनं.—(Of treason) राजाभिद्रोहगोपनं.

To MISPRONOUNCE, *v. a.* अशुद्धोच्चारणं कृ, अशुद्धम् उच्चर् (c. 10. -चारयति -यितुं).

MISPRONUNCIATION, *s.* अशुद्धोच्चारणं, असदुच्चारणं, अन्यथोच्चारणं.

MISPROPORTIONED, *a.* विषमप्रमाणः -णा -णं, असमप्रमाणकः -का -कं.

MISQUOTATION, *s.* मिथ्यावतरणं, अन्यथावतरणं, अयथार्थोद्धारः.

To MISQUOTE, *v. a.* अन्यथा or अयथार्थम् अवतॄ (c. 10. -तारयति -यितुं), अयथार्थतो वाक्यम् उद्धृ (c. 1. -हरति -हर्त्तुं), अयथार्थवाक्यम् उपन्यस् (c. 4. -अस्यति -असितुं).

MISREPORT *s.* मिथ्याकथनं, मिथ्यानिवेदनं, अन्यथानिवेदनं, अयथार्थाख्यानं, मिथ्याख्यापनं, मृषाकथा.

To MISREPORT, *v. a.* मिथ्या or अन्यथा कथ् (c. 10. कथयति -यितुं) or निविद् (c. 10. -वेदयति -यितुं), अयथार्थम् आख्या (c. 2. -ख्याति -तुं, caus. ख्यापयति -यितुं).

To MISREPRESENT, *v. a.* मिथ्या or अन्यथा or मृषा कथ् (c. 10. कथयति -यितुं) or आविद् (c. 10. -वेदयति -यितुं) or निविद्, अयथार्थतः ख्या (c. 2. -ख्याति -तुं, caus. ख्यापयति -यितुं), असम्यक् ख्या, असत्यं वर्ण् (c. 10. वर्णयति -यितुं) or विवृ (c. 5. -वृणोति -वरितुं -रीतुं), अर्थं साचीकृ or वक्रीकृ.

MISREPRESENTATION, *s.* मिथ्याकथनं, अन्यथाकथनं, अन्यथाख्यापनं, अन्यथानिवेदनं, मिथ्यानिवेदनं, अयथार्थख्यापनं, मिथ्यावादः, मृषावादः, अन्यथाविवरणं, मिथ्यावर्णनं, असत्यवर्णना, साचीकरणं, साचीकृतं, अर्थवक्रीकरणं.

MISRULE, *s.* असम्यक्पालनं, असम्यक्शासनं, कुशासनं, कुशास्तिः *f.*, असत्पालनं, दुःशासनं, दुर्णीतिः *f.*

To MISS, *v. a.* (Fail of reaching, not to hit) लक्ष्यम् अभिसन्धाय अपराध् (c. 4. -राध्यति, c. 5. -राध्नोति -राद्धुं) or अपराधं कृ or भ्रान्तिं कृ, भ्रमं कृ; 'one who misses the mark in archery,' अपराद्धपृषत्कः, लक्ष्यच्युतसायकः.—(Fail of finding, miss the way) भ्रम् (c. 4. भ्राम्यति, भ्रमितुं), मार्गात् or पथात् प्रभ्रंश् (c. 4. -भ्रश्यति -भ्रंशितुं) or भ्रंश्, मार्गाद् विचल् (c. 1. -चलति -लितुं), मार्गभ्रंशं कृ.—(Fail of obtaining) न प्राप् (c. 5. -आप्नोति -आप्तुं), न लभ् (c. 1. लभते, लब्धुं), न आसद् (c. 10. -सादयति -यितुं), अपराध्.—(Discover to be wanting or lost) नष्टं or स्थानभ्रष्टं किञ्चिद् ज्ञा (c. 9. जानाति ज्ञातुं), नष्टं मन् (c. 4. मन्यते, मन्तुं), नाशं or अभावं or अदर्शनं ज्ञा.—(Feel the want of, regret the absence of) उत्कण्ठ् (c. 1. -कण्ठते -ठितुं), उत्सुक (nom. उत्सुकायते), उन्मनस् (nom. उन्मनायते), उत्कण्ठां कृ, उत्कलिकां कृ.—(Omit) हा (c. 3. जहाति, हातुं), अपाहा, अपहा, विहा, त्यज् (c. 1. त्यजति, त्यक्तुं), अपास् (c. 4. -अस्यति -असितुं), विसृज् (c. 6. -सृजति -स्रष्टुं), वृज् (c. 10. वर्जयति -यितुं), परिवृज्.—(Lose) हा in pass. (हीयते) with instr. or abl. c., भ्रंश् with abl. c. *See To* LOSE.

To MISS, *v. n.* अपराध् (c. 4. -राध्यति -ते -राद्धुं), भ्रम् (c. 4. भ्राम्यति, भ्रमितुं), अपराद्धः -द्धा -द्धं भू, अपराधं कृ, भ्रमं कृ.—(Not to succeed, miscarry) न सिध् (c. 4. सिध्यति, सेद्धुं), न सम्पद् (c. 4. -पद्यते -पत्तुं), सिद्धिं न प्राप् (c. 5. -आप्नोति -आप्तुं) or गम् (c. 1. गच्छति, गन्तुं), असिद्धः -द्धा -द्धं भू.

MISS, *s.* (Error) भ्रमः, भ्रान्तिः *f.*, अपराधः, भ्रंशः, दोषः, भ्रेषः, उत्क्रमः; 'a miss is as good as a mile,' अन्तरं महदन्तरं.—(Loss, want) नाशः, हानिः *f.*, अभावः, असम्भवः, अविषयः, अदर्शनं, विरहः.—(Young girl) कुलकन्या, कुलीनकन्या, कुलकुमारी.

MISSED, *p. p.* अपराद्धः -द्धा -द्धं, कृतापराधः -धा -धं, भ्रान्तः -न्ता -न्तं.

To MIS-SEND, *v. a.* अन्यथा or वृथा प्रेर् (c. 10. प्रेरयति -यितुं) or प्रेष् (c. 10. प्रेषयति -यितुं).

MIS-SHAPED, MIS-SHAPEN, *a.* विरूपः -पा -पी -पं, अपरूपः &c., कुरूपः &c., अरूपः &c., विकृताकारः -रा -रं, विकृताङ्गः -ङ्गी -ङ्गं, विकृताकृतिः -तिः -ति, व्यङ्गः -ङ्गी -ङ्गं, व्याकारः &c.

MISSILE, *a.* क्षेपणीयः -या -यं, हस्तक्षेपणीयः &c., हस्तक्षेप्यः -प्या -प्यं, पाणिमोचनीयः -या -यं, क्षिपस्नुः -स्नुः -स्नु, दूरात् क्षेपणीयः &c., दूरवेधी -धिनी -धि (न्).

MISSILE, *s.* (Weapon) अस्त्रं, क्षिपणिः *m.*, करमुक्तं, पाणिमुक्तं, मुक्तकं, क्षेप्यायुधं.—(Circular one) चक्रं.

MISSING, *part.* or *a.* (Regretting the absence of) उत्कण्ठितः -ता -तं, उत्सुकः -का -कं, उन्मनाः -नाः -नः (स्), उत्कलितः -ता -तं.—(Lost, stray, absent from its place) नष्टः -ष्टा -ष्टं, भ्रष्टः -ष्टा -ष्टं, स्थानभ्रष्टः &c., प्रभ्रष्टः &c., स्थानप्रभ्रष्टः &c., स्थानच्युतः -ता -तं, प्रच्युतः &c., तिरोहितः -ता -तं, अदृष्टः -ष्टा -ष्टं.

MISSION, *s.* (Sending, commission) प्रेरणं, प्रेषणं, नियोजनं, प्रयोजनं; 'sending on a message,' प्रतिशासनं.—(Body of persons sent) प्रेरितसमूहः, प्रेरितजनसमूहः, प्रेरितगणः, नियुक्तजनसमूहः; 'for religious purposes,' धर्म्मप्रचारणार्थं प्रेरितजनाः *m. pl.*—(State of being sent) प्रेरितत्वं, प्रेषितत्वं, दूतत्वं, दौत्यं.

MISSIONARY, *s.* धर्म्मसन्देशहरः, धर्म्मसंवादकथकः, धर्म्मप्रचारणार्थं प्रेरितः, ख्रीष्टधर्म्मघोषणार्थं प्रेरितः.

MISSIVE, *a.* (Sent) प्रेरितः -ता -तं, प्रेषितः -ता -तं.—(Thrown) क्षिप्तः -प्ता -प्तं, अस्तः -स्ता -स्तं, मुक्तः -क्ता -क्तं; 'weapon,' क्षिपणिः *m.*, पाणिमुक्तं.—(Messenger) सन्देशहरः, वार्त्ताहरः, सञ्चारकः.—(Message) सन्देशः, दूत्यं, दौत्यं.

To MIS-SPEAK, *v. a.* or *n.* मिथ्या or अन्यथा वद् (c. 1. वदति -दितुं), अयथार्थं वद्.

To MIS-SPELL, *v. a.* अक्षरव्यत्ययं कृ, अक्षरव्यत्यासं कृ, अक्षरविपर्य्यासं कृ.

MIS-SPELLING, *s.* अक्षरव्यत्ययः, अक्षरव्यत्यासः, अक्षरविपर्य्यासः, अयथाक्षरं.

To mis-spend, *v. a.* अपात्रे or अस्थाने व्यय् (c. 1. व्ययति, c. 10. व्ययति -यितुं, rt. इ) or व्ययं कृ or विनियुज् (c. 7. -युंक्ते -योक्तुं), कुव्ययं कृ, असद्व्ययं कृ, अन्यथाव्ययं कृ, अपात्रव्ययं कृ, कुविनियोगं कृ, अयुक्तव्ययं कृ, दुर्व्ययं कृ.

Mis-spent, *p. p.* दुर्व्ययितः -ता -तं, कुव्ययितः -ता -तं, अन्यथाव्ययितः &c., अपव्ययितः &c., कुविनियुक्तः -क्ता -क्तं, अपचितः -ता -तं.

To mis-state, *v. a.* मिथ्या or अन्यथा कथ् (c. 10. कथयति -यितुं) or ज्ञा (c. 10. ज्ञापयति, ज्ञपयति -यितुं) or विज्ञा or आविद् (c. 10. -वेदयति -यितुं), अयथार्थतः ख्या (c. 2. ख्याति -तुं) or विवृ (c. 5. -वृणोति -वरितुं -रीतुं), अर्थं साचीकृ or वक्रीकृ.

Mis-stated, *p. p.* मिथ्याकथितः -ता -तं, मिथ्याख्यातः -ता -तं, साचीकृतः -ता -तं.

Mis-statement, *s.* मिथ्याकथनं, मिथ्यावादः, मिथ्योक्तिः *f.*, अन्यथाकथनं, अन्यथानिवेदनं, मिथ्याविज्ञप्तिः *f.*, अयथार्थविज्ञापनं, मिथ्याविवरणं, साचीकरणं, साचीकृतं.

Mist, *s.* धूमिका, धूपिका, धूलिका, शीकरः, तुषारः, खवाष्पः, मृगतृष्णा -ष्णिका -तृषा, मृगतृट् *f.* (ष्), कुज्झटिका, कुज्झटिः *f.* -टी -टिका, हिमझटिः *f.*, कुहेडिका, कुहेडी, कुहेलिका, कुहेली, कूहा, मेघधूमः, रुभेटिः *f.*, धूममहिषी.

To mistake, *v. a.* (Take wrong, misunderstand) मिथ्या or अन्यथा ग्रह् (c. 9. गृह्णाति, ग्रहीतुं), विपरीतं ग्रह् or उपलभ् (c. 1. -लभते -लब्धुं), विपरीतार्थं ग्रह्, अन्यथा or मिथ्या बुध् (c. 1. बोधति -धितुं), मिथ्या ज्ञा (c. 9. जानाति, ज्ञातुं) or मन् (c. 4. मन्यते, मन्तुं).

To mistake, *v. n.* (Err, make a mistake) भ्रम् (c. 4. भ्राम्यति, भ्रमितुं), विभ्रम्, भ्रमं कृ, भ्रान्तिं कृ, अपराध् (c. 4. -राध्यति, c. 5. -राध्नोति -राद्धुं), अपराधं कृ, प्रमद् (c. 4. -माद्यति -मदितुं), प्रमादं कृ, दोषं कृ, मुह् (c. 4. मुह्यति, मोहितुं), मिथ्यामतिं कृ.

Mistake, *s.* भ्रमः, भ्रान्तिः *f.*, मतिभ्रमः, मतिभ्रान्तिः *f.*, मिथ्यामतिः *f.*, मिथ्याबुद्धिः *f.*, विभ्रमः, मतिविभ्रमः, अपराधः, प्रमादः, दोषः, मोहः, व्यामोहः, परिभ्रमः, भ्रामः, विकल्पः, अनवधानता, विवर्त्तः, विचिकित्सा.

Mistaken, *p. p.* (In error) भ्रान्तः -न्ता -न्तं, भ्रान्तिमान् -मती -मत् (त्), अपराद्धः -द्धा -द्धं, सापराधः -धा -धं, प्रमादी -दिनी -दि (न्), प्रमादवान् &c., सन्दिग्धः -ग्धा -ग्धं.—(Erroneous) अयथार्थः -र्था -र्थं, अशुद्धः -द्धा -द्धं, मिथ्या or मृषा in comp.; 'a mistaken opinion,' मिथ्यामतिः *f.*

Mister, *s.* (Title of gentlemen) आर्य्यः or expressed by श्री prefixed.

Mis-timed, *a.* अकालिकः -की -कं. *See* Ill-timed.

Mistiness, *s.* सशीकरता, सतुषारता, तुषारव्याप्तिः *f.*, शीकरव्याप्तता.

Mistion, *s.* मिश्रणं, सम्मिश्रणं, संसर्गः, सम्पर्क्कः, योगः.

To mistle, *v. n.* शीकर (nom. शीकरायते), शीक् (c. 1. शीकते -कितुं).

Mistletoe, *s.* वृक्षरुहा, तरुरुहा, तरुभुक् *f.* (ज्), वृक्षादनी, वृक्षाश्रया.

To mistranslate, *v. a.* अयथार्थभाषान्तरं कृ, अन्यथा भाषान्तरं कृ.

Mistranslation, *s.* अयथार्थभाषान्तरं, मिथ्याभाषान्तरं.

Mistress, *s.* (Opposed to servant, a woman who governs) स्वामिनी, सेव्या, अधिष्ठात्री, ईश्वरी, शासित्री, शास्त्री, अध्यक्षा, कर्त्री.—(Of a family or house) गृहिणी, गेहिनी, गृहस्वामिनी, कुटुम्बिनी, कौटुम्बिकी.—(Proprietress) स्वामिनी, ईश्वरी, अधिकारिणी.—(Female teacher) अध्यापिका, उपदेशिनी, उपदेशिका, उपदेष्ट्री, शिक्षिका, आचार्य्या.—(Woman beloved, sweetheart) प्रिया, प्रियतमा, वल्लभा, कान्ता, दयिता, कामिनी, नायिका, वनिता, प्रमदा; 'an offended mistress,' मानिनी.—(Concubine) उपपत्नी, उपपत्नी, भोग्या स्त्री, भुजिष्या, दासी, अवरुद्धा.—(Well-skilled) कुशला, निपुणा, वेत्त्री.

Mistrust, *s.* अविश्वासः, अप्रत्ययः, अप्रतीतिः *f.*, शङ्का, आशङ्का, सन्देहः, निह्नवः, विश्वासाभावः.

To mistrust, *v. a.* शङ्क् (c. 1. शङ्कते -ङ्कितुं), आशङ्क्, अभिशङ्क्, परिशङ्क्, न विश्वस् (c. 2. -श्वसिति -तुं), न प्रती (c. 2. प्रत्येति -तुं).

Mistrustful, *a.* अविश्वासी -सिनी -सि (न्), अप्रत्ययी -यिनी &c., शङ्की -ङ्किनी &c., शङ्कान्वितः -ता -तं, साशङ्कः -ङ्का -ङ्कं, शङ्काशीलः -ला -लं, आशङ्की &c., शङ्कितः -ता -तं, आशङ्कितः -ता -तं, सन्देही &c., संशयी &c.

Mistrustfully, *adv.* अविश्वासेन, शङ्कया, सशङ्कं, साशङ्कं, शङ्कापूर्व्वं.

Mistrustfulness, *s.* अविश्वासित्वं, अप्रतीतिः *f.*, सशङ्कत्वं, आशङ्का.

Misty, *a.* सशीकरः -रा -रं, सतुषारः -रा -रं, शीकरीयः -या -यं, शीकरौघः -घा -घं, शीकरव्याप्तः -प्ता -प्तं, तुषारव्याप्तः -प्ता -प्तं, तुषारमयः -यी -यं, सधूमिकः -का -कं, धूमिकावृतः -ता -तं, शीकरावृतः -ता -तं.

To misunderstand, *v. a.* अन्यथा ग्रह् (c. 9. गृह्णाति -ग्रहीतुं) or बुध् (c. 1. बोधति -धितुं), मिथ्या or मृषा or विपरीतम् अर्थं ग्रह् or उपलभ् (c. 1. -लभते -लब्धुं) or अवगम् (c. 1. -गच्छति -गन्तुं), विपरीतार्थं ग्रह्, अयथार्थतो ज्ञा (c. 9. जानाति, ज्ञातुं) or विज्ञा, अर्थविपर्य्यासं कृ.

Misunderstanding, *s.* (Mistake of the meaning) मिथ्याग्रहणं, अन्यथाग्रहणं, विपरीतग्रहणं, अन्यथार्थग्रहणं, विपरीतार्थग्रहणं, अन्यथाबोधः, मिथ्याबोधः, मिथ्यामतिः *f.*, मिथ्योपलब्धिः *f.*, विपरीतबुद्धिः *f.*, अयथार्थबोधः, अयथार्थग्रहणं, भ्रमः, भ्रान्तिः *f.*, मतिभ्रमः.—(Disagreement) वैमत्यं, विमतिः *f.*, मतिभेदः, असम्मतिः *f.*, विसंवादः, द्वैधं, विप्रयोगः, वैमनस्यं, मतिविपर्य्ययः.

Misunderstood, *p. p.* मिथ्यावगतः -ता -तं, मिथ्योपलब्धः -ब्धा -ब्धं, मिथ्यामतः -ता -तं.

Misusage, misuse, *s.* कुव्यवहारः, दुर्व्यवहारः, कुप्रयोगः, मिथ्याप्रयोगः, असत्प्रयोगः, असम्यक्प्रयोगः, अन्यथाप्रयोगः, असदुपयोगः, कुव्यापारः, असदुपभोगः, कुविनियोगः, असद्विनियोगः, असाधुविनियोगः, व्यर्थीकरणं, असदभ्यासः, अयुक्तव्यवहारः.

To misuse, *v. a.* अन्यथा or मिथ्या or वृथा or असम्यक् प्रयुज् (c. 7. -युंक्ते -योक्तुं, c. 10. -योजयति -यितुं) or उपयुज् or विनियुज्, कुप्रयोगं कृ, असत्प्रयोगं कृ, अयुक्तं व्यवहृ (c. 10. -हारयति -यितुं), कुव्यवहारं कृ, दुर्व्यवहारं कृ, अनुचितम् अभ्यस् (c. 4. -अस्यति -असितुं), कुव्यापारं कृ, व्यर्थीकृ, कदर्थीकृ, वृथाकृ.

Misused, *p. p.* कुप्रयुक्तः -क्ता -क्तं, कुविनियुक्तः &c., असम्यगुपयोजितः -ता -तं, कुव्यवहृतः -ता -तं, कुव्यवहारितः -ता -तं, मिथ्याप्रयुक्तः &c., कदर्थीकृतः &c.

Mite, *s.* (Small piece of money) कपर्द्दकः, कपर्द्दिका, काकिणी, काकिनी, वराटकः, धनलवः, धनलेशः.—(Particle of any thing) कणः, कणिका, लवः, लेशः.

Miter, *s.* धर्म्माधिपतिकिरीटः, महाधर्म्माध्यक्षमुकुटं.

Mithridate, *s.* विषभञ्जनं, विषनाशनं, विषघ्नं, विषापहारकं.

Mitigable, *a.* शमनीयः -या -यं, प्रशमनीयः -या -यं, शाम्यः -म्या -म्यं.

Mitigant, *a.* शमकः -का -कं, प्रशमनः -ना -नं, शान्तिकः -की -कं, शान्तिदः -दा -दं, शान्तिकरः -रा -रं, उपशायी -यिनी -यि (न्).

To mitigate, *v. a.* शम् (c. 10. शमयति -यितुं), प्रशम्, उपशम्, शान्तिं दा, सान्त्व् or शान्त्व् (c. 10. सान्त्वयति -यितुं), उपसान्त्व्, परिशान्त्व्, अभिशान्त्व्.—(Alleviate pain) दुःखं हृ (c. 1. हरति, हर्त्तुं) or शम्.—(Lighten) लघ (nom. लघयति -यितुं), लघूकृ, मृदूकृ.—(Diminish) न्यूनीकृ, अल्पीकृ, ऊन (nom. ऊनयति -यितुं).

MITIGATED, *p. p.* शान्तः -न्ता -न्तं, शमितः -ता -तं, प्रशमितः &c., उपशान्तः &c., मृदूकृतः -ता -तं, लघूकृतः -ता -तं; 'to be mitigated,' शम् (c. 4. शाम्यति, शमितुं).

MITIGATION, *s.* शान्तिः *f.*, शमनं, प्रशमनं, उपशान्तिः, प्रशान्तिः *f.*, उपशमनं, शमः, उपशमः, मृदूकरणं, लघूकरणं, लाघवं, न्यूनीकरणं, न्यूनता, सान्त्वनं -ना; 'of a curse,' उद्धारः.

MITIGATIVE, MITIGATOR. *See* MITIGANT.

MITRE. *See* MITER, *s.*

To MIX, *v. a.* मिश्र् (c. 10. मिश्रयति -यितुं), सम्मिश्र्, व्यामिश्र्, विमिश्र्, मिश्रीकृ, सम्मिश्रीकृ, संयुज् (c. 7. -युनक्ति -योक्तुं -योजयति -यितुं), संसृज् (c. 6. -सृजति -स्रष्टुं), सम्पृच् (c. 7. -पृणक्ति -पर्चितुं), सकॄ (c. 6. -किरति -करितुं -रीतुं), एकीकृ, एकत्र कृ, संसर्गं कृ, संसृष्टं -ष्टां कृ, व्यतिकरं कृ, सम्मेलनं कृ.—(Mix confusedly) सङ्करीकृ, सङ्कुलीकृ, सङ्कीर्णीकृ, सङ्कॄ; 'mix ingredients,' योगं कृ, संस्कारं कृ, प्रक्षेपं कृ.

To MIX, *v. n.* मिश्रीभू, सम्मिश्रीभू, व्यामिश्रीभू, मिल् (c. 6. मिलति, मेलितुं), सम्मिल्, सङ्कॄ in pass. (-कीर्य्यते), संयुज् in pass., (-युज्यते), संसृज् in pass. (-सृज्यते), संसृष्टीभू, एकीभू, संयोगं इ (c. 2. एति -तुं), सम्पर्कम् इ, संसर्गम् इ, सङ्करीभू.

MIXABLE, *a.* मिश्रणीयः -या -यं, योजनीयः -या -यं, याव्यः -व्या -व्यं.

MIXED, *p.p.* मिश्रितः -ता -तं, सम्मिश्रितः -ता -तं, मिश्रः -श्रा -श्रं, सम्मिश्रः &c., मिश्रीकृतः -ता -तं, व्यामिश्रः -श्रा -श्रं, संयुक्तः -क्ता -क्तं, संयुतः -ता -तं, संसृष्टः -ष्टा -ष्टं, सङ्कीर्णः -र्णा -र्णं, सम्पृक्तः -क्ता -क्तं, मिलितः -ता -तं, सम्मिलितः &c., सङ्कुलितः &c., संवलितः &c., सन्निपतितः &c., समवेतः &c., सङ्करीकृतः &c., एकीकृतः &c., भावितः &c., करम्बितः &c., सम्बद्धः -द्धा -द्धं, सम्पर्की -र्किणी -र्कि (न्), संसर्गी &c., कुशितः -ता -तं; 'mixed with water,' जलमिश्रितः &c., जलसंसृष्टः &c.

MIXEN, *s.* पुरीषादिराशिः *m.*; 'mixen-grown,' विड्भवः -वा -वं.

MIXER, *s.* मिश्रकः, सम्मिश्रकः, मिश्रणकृत्, संयोगकारी *m.* (न्).

MIXTURE, MIXTION, MIXING, *s.* (Act) मिश्रणं, सम्मिश्रणं, मिश्रीकरणं, संयोगः, संयोजनं, सम्मेलनं, संसर्गः, सम्पर्कः, सङ्कलनं, सङ्किरणं, एकीकरणं, सङ्करीकरणं.—(State) मिश्रता, सम्मिश्रता, मिश्रीभावः, संसृष्टता, संसर्गः, संयुक्तता, संयोगः, सम्पर्कः, सङ्कीर्णता, साङ्कर्य्यं.—(Mixed mass) सन्निपातः, नानाद्रव्यसमूहः, सम्मिश्रद्रव्यसमूहः, नानावस्तुसमुदायः, समूहः, सङ्कः, सङ्करः; 'mixture with water,' जलसंसर्गः.

MIZZEN, *s.* (Sail) पश्चिमकूपकसम्बन्धि वातवसनं.

MIZZEN-MAST, *s.* पश्चिमकूपकः, नौपश्चाद्भागस्थः कूपकः.

MIZZLE, *s.* शीकरः, सीकरः, तुषारः. *See To* MISTLE, DRIZZLE.

MNEMONIC, *a.* स्मृतिसहायः -या -यं, स्मृतिप्रवर्त्तकः -का -कं, स्मृत्युपकारकः &c.

MNEMONICS, *s.* स्मरणविद्या, स्मृत्युपकरणविद्या, स्मरणशास्त्रं.

To MOAN, *v. n.* वेदनोपहतत्वाद् दीर्घनादं कृ or दीर्घरावं कृ, विलप् (c. 1. -लपति -पितुं), प्रलप्, लप्, परिदेव् (c. 1. -देवते -वितुं), क्रन्द् (c. 1. क्रन्दति -न्दितुं), आक्रन्द्, रुद् (c. 2. रोदिति -तुं), प्ररुद्, क्रुश् (c. 1. क्रोशति, क्रोष्टुं), स्तन् (c. 1. स्तनति -नितुं), विस्तन्, दीर्घं निःश्वस् or निश्वस् (c. 2. -श्वसिति -तुं), दीर्घं रु (c. 2. रौति, रवितुं), दीर्घचित्कारं कृ, दीर्घनिश्वासं कृ, गम्भीरनादं कृ, गम्भीरनिश्वासं कृ, आर्त्तनादं कृ, आर्त्तरावं कृ, हाहाशब्दं कृ, हाहाकारं कृ, वाश् (c. 1. वाशते, c. 4. वाश्यते -शितुं).

MOAN, *s.* आर्त्तनादः, आर्त्तरावः, दुःखार्त्तस्य दीर्घनादः or दीर्घरावः or दीर्घचित्कारः or गम्भीरनादः, दीर्घनिश्वासः, दीर्घनिःश्वासः, विलपितं, विलपनं, विलापः, परिदेवनं -ना, परिदेवितं, स्तनितं, क्रन्दितं, क्रुष्टं, हाहाकारः.

MOANFUL, *a.* विलापकारी -रिणी -रि (न्), परिदेवी -विनी &c., परिदेवनकारी &c., दीर्घनिश्वासी &c., हाहाकारी &c.

MOANFULLY, *adv.* विलापेन, सविलपितं, सपरिदेवनं, दीर्घनिश्वासपूर्व्वं.

MOANING, *s.* विलपनं, परिदेवनं, आर्त्तनादः, दीर्घनिश्वसितं, स्तननं.

MOAT, *s.* परिखा, खातं, खेयं, खातकं, खातभूः *f.*, खातभूमिः *f.*, प्रतिकूपः, उपकुल्या, कुल्या, खल्लः.

MOATED, *a.* परिखावेष्टितः -ता -तं, परिखावृतः &c., परिखान्वितः &c.

MOB, *s.* अधमजनसमूहः, नीचजनसम्मर्दः, प्राकृतजनसम्मर्दः, बहुजनसमूहः, बहुजनमेलकः, जनसम्मर्दः, लोकसङ्घः, जनसङ्कुलं, जनौघः, जनता, अव्यवस्थितसभा.

To MOB, *v. a.* बहुजनाकीर्णे स्थाने वपुषा संपृच् (c. 1. -घर्षति -र्षितुं) or सम्मृद् (c. 9. मृद्नाति -मर्दितुं) or सम्बाध् (c. 1. -बाधते -धितुं).

MOBBISH, *a.* लौकिकः -की -कं, सामान्यलोकयोग्यः -ग्या -ग्यं.

MOBILE, MOBILITY, *s.* (Mob, common people) सामान्यलोकः, साधारणलोकः, प्राकृतलोकः, असभ्यलोकः, अन्यलोकः, अधमलोकः, पृथग्जनाः *m. pl.*

MOBILITY, *s.* (Aptitude to motion) गमनयोग्यता, गतियोग्यता, गमनशीलता, चरिष्णुता, जङ्गमता, अस्थिरता, चाञ्चल्यं.

To MOCK, *v. a.* (Deride) अवहस् (c. 1. -हसति -सितुं), अपहस्, उपहस्, प्रहस्, विहस्, अवहासभूमिं कृ, अपहासास्पदं कृ, अवक्षिप् (c. 6. -क्षिपति -क्षेप्तुं), गर्ह् (c. 1. गर्हते -र्हितुं), अवगर्ह्, अवगुर् (c. 6. -गुरते -रितुं), आधर् (c. 10. -धारयति -यितुं), अवज्ञा (c. 9. -जानाति -ज्ञातुं), अवमन् (c. 4. -मन्यते -मन्तुं), भर्त्स् (c. 10. भर्त्सयते -यितुं), तिरस्कृ, मुखरीकृ, विकत्थ् (c. 1. -कत्थते -त्थितुं), परिभू, अवज्ञां कृ, तुच्छीकृ.—(Mimic) उपहासबुद्ध्या परचेष्टितानुकरणं कृ or विडम्बनं कृ.—(Deceive) वञ्च् (c. 10. वञ्चयते -यितुं), प्रतॄ (c. 10. -तारयति -यितुं), प्रलभ् (c. 1. -लभते -लब्धुं), प्रलुभ् (c. 10. -लोभयति -यितुं), मुह् (c. 10. मोहयति -यितुं).

MOCK, *s.* उपहासः, अवहासः, परिहासः, हास्यं, अवक्षेपः, अवज्ञा.

MOCKED, *p. p.* (Mimicked in derision) उपहासबुद्ध्यानुकृतः -ता -तं. —(Derided) उपहसितः -ता -तं, अवहसितः &c., अवक्षिप्तः -प्ता -प्तं, गर्हितः -ता -तं, विगर्हितः &c., तिरस्कृतः -ता -तं, अवज्ञातः &c., मुखरीकृतः &c., कृतोपहासः -सा -सं.—(Deceived) वञ्चितः -ता -तं, प्रलब्धः -ब्धा -ब्धं, मोहितः &c.

MOCKER, *s.* उपहासकः, अवहासकः, परिहासकर्त्ता *m.* (र्तृ), क्षेपकः, अवक्षेपकः, अवज्ञाकारी *m.* (न्), अवमानी *m.*, वञ्चकः.

MOCKERY, MOCKING, *s.* (Derision) उपहासः, अवहासः, अपहासः, परिहासः, परीहासः, हास्यं, तिरस्कारः, अवज्ञा, अवक्षेपः, अवमानं, अपमानं, अवहेला -लनं, अवलेपः, परिभवः, मुखरीकरणं, मौखर्य्यं, अवमानसूचको हासः.—(Subject of derision) उपहासास्पदं, उपहासभूमिः *f.*, अवहासस्थानं, उपहासविषयः, तिरस्कारविषयः, हास्यस्थानं, परिभवास्पदं, परिभवपदं, तिरस्कारपदं.—(Counterfeit appearance, deception, imitation) छद्म *n.* (न्), व्याजः, कपटः -टं, कूटं, वञ्चनं -ना, विडम्बनं.—(Vain effort) वृथायत्नः, वृथाप्रयत्नः, वृथोद्यमः, वृथोद्योगः, अनर्थकचेष्टा, निष्फलचेष्टा.

MOCKINGLY, *adv.* उपहासेन, सोपहासं, सावहासं, सतिरस्कारं, सावक्षेपं.

MODAL, *a.* रूपसम्बन्धी -न्धिनी -न्धि (न्), रूपविषयः -या -यं.

MODE, *s.* (Method, manner) रीतिः *f.*, मार्गः, विधिः *m.*, विधानं, प्रकारः, नियमः, वृत्तिः *f.*, स्थितिः *f.*, क्रमः, संविधानं, पर्य्यायः, मर्य्यादा, धारा, विध: in comp.; 'mode of living,' वृत्तिः *f.*; 'in this mode,' अनेन विधानेन, एवंविधं -धेन, अनेन प्रकारेण; 'mode of speaking,' वाग्व्यापारः, वाग्वृत्तिः *f.*—(Form) रूपं, आकारः, आकृतिः *f.*,

संस्कारः.—(Custom) आचारः, व्यवहारः, प्रचारः, रीतिः f., नियमः, अभ्यासः, स्थितिः f., आवृत्तिः f., सम्प्रदायः.—(Fashionable custom) सभ्यलोकव्यवहारः, सभ्यरीतिः f., शिष्टव्यवहारः, शिष्टमार्गः, सभ्यसम्प्रदायः, लोकाचारः.—(In metaphysics) विशेषवस्तुरूपं, विशेषद्रव्यरूपं, विशेषद्रव्यप्रकारः.—(In grammar) वाच्यं.—(In music) रागः m., रागिणी f., वर्णः. The musical modes are personified as either male or female. The male are called Rágas; the female are Ráginís, and are considered to be the wives of the Rágas. The following are some of the names for the male: भैरवः, मालवः, सारङ्गः, हिन्दोलः, वसन्तः, वसन्तदूतः, पञ्चमः, दीपकः, मेघः, नटः, नटनारायणः, कल्याणः, कामबोधः, बोटकः, विभासः. The following are some of the Ráginís, or female personifications: दीपिका, नटी, बोटकी, देशकारी, गौडी, जङ्गला, धनेश्वरी, भैरवी, रामकरी or रामकेली or रामकली, सैन्धवी, पूर्वी, भूपाली, मधुमाधवी.

Model, s. (Pattern, representation) प्रतिमा -मानं, प्रतिरूपं, प्रतिकृतिः, आदर्शः, उपमा -मानं, प्रतिमूर्त्तिः f., संस्कारः.—(Pattern, exemplar) आदर्शः, प्रतिमा, उपमा.—(Pattern for imitation) प्रमाणं, प्रमा, प्रमाता m. (तृ); 'model of propriety,' न्यायाधारः.—(Mould) संस्कारः, आकारः, संस्थानं, संधानः.

To model, v. a. or n. संस्कारं कृ, संस्कृ, प्रतिमां कृ, प्रतिरूपं कृ, आदर्शं कृ.—(Shape, form) रूप् (c. 10. रूपयति -यितुं), सरूपं -पां -पं कृ.

Modeler, s. उपमाता m. (तृ), उपमानकृत् m., प्रतिमानकर्त्ता m. (र्त्तृ).

Moderate, a. (Observing reasonable bounds, applied to persons) परिमिताचारी -रिणी -रि (न्), समवृत्तिः -त्तिः -त्ति, नियतवृत्तिः &c., मर्य्यादानतिक्रमी -मिणी &c., अनतिक्रान्तमर्य्यादः -दा -दं.—(Moderate in desires) अल्पाकांक्षी -क्षिणी &c., अल्पाभिलाषी &c., अलुब्धः -ब्धा -ब्धं, अलोभी &c., अल्पसन्तोषी &c., अल्पसन्तुष्टः -ष्टा -ष्टं, भोगाप्रसक्तः -क्ता -क्तं, अप्रसक्तः &c., अल्पभोगी &c., स्वल्पभोगी &c.—(Not extreme, not excessive) परिमितः -ता -तं, मितः -ता -तं, सपरिमाणः -णा -णं, समः -मा -मं, समर्य्यादः -दा -दं, नियतः -ता -तं, संयतः -ता -तं, सावधिकः -का -कं, अल्पः -ल्पा -ल्पं, स्वल्पः &c.—(In eating) मिताशनः -ना -नं, परिमिताहारः -रा -रं, स्वल्पाहारः -रा -रं, —(Middling in size) मध्यमः -मा -मं, मध्यः -ध्या -ध्यं, मध्यमपरिमाणः -णा -णं, न स्थूलो न सूक्ष्मः &c.

To moderate, v. a. (Temper) शम् (c. 10. शमयति -यितुं), उपशम्, प्रशम्.—(Lessen) न्यूनीकृ, अल्पीकृ, लघ् (c. 10. लघयति -यितुं), लघूकृ.—(Restrain from excess) नियम् (c. 1. -यच्छति -यन्तुं), विनियम्, संयम्, यम्, निग्रह् (c. 9. -गृह्णाति -ग्रहीतुं), संहृ (c. 1. -हरति -हर्त्तुं), प्रत्याहृ.

To moderate, v. n. (Abate, become less severe) शम् (c. 4. शाम्यति, शमितुं), प्रशम्, उपशम्, विगम् (c. 1. -गच्छति -गन्तुं), विरम् (c. 1. -रमति -रन्तुं), उपरम्, न्यूनीभू, ऊनीभू, अल्पीभू.

Moderated, p. p. (Tempered) शमितः -ता -तं, प्रशमितः -ता -तं.—(Lessened) न्यूनीकृतः -ता -तं, न्यूनीभूतः -ता -तं.—(Restrained) यतः -ता -तं, नियतः -ता -तं, निगृहीतः -ता -तं.—(Allayed) शान्तः -न्ता -न्तं, उपशान्तः &c.

Moderately, adv. परिमितं, नियतं, समर्य्यादं, समं, सपरिमाणं, अल्पं, स्वल्पं, अभृशं, यावन्मात्रं; 'moderately warm,' ईषदुष्णः -ष्णा -ष्णं, कोष्णः &c., मन्दोष्णः &c.; 'moderately ripe,' आपक्वः -क्वा -क्वं; 'moderately distant,' नातिदूरः -रा -रं.

Moderation, s. (Refraining from excess) परिमिताचारत्वं, नियतवृत्तित्वं, समवृत्तिता, समता, परिमितता, मितता, क्षमा, यमः, संयमः, निग्रहः, दमः, अनतिक्रमः, मर्य्यादानतिक्रमः.—(In desires) अल्पाकांक्षा, अल्पाभिलाषः, अलोभः, अलुब्धता, अल्पसन्तुष्टता, अप्रसक्तिः f., अप्रसक्तता, भोगाप्रसक्तिः f.—(Equanimity) क्षमा, शान्तिः f., समचित्तत्वं, समानवृत्तिः f., समभावः.

Moderator, s. (Restrainer) नियन्ता m. (न्तृ), विनियन्ता m., यन्ता m.—(At disputations) वादमध्यस्थः, वादसभाध्यक्षः, मध्यस्थः.

Modern, a. इदानीन्तनः -नी -नं, अधुनातनः -नी -नं, आधुनिकः -की -कं, वर्त्तमानकालीनः -ना -नं, नूतनकालीनः &c., नूतनः -ना -नं, नवः -वा -वं, सद्यस्कालीनः -ना -नं, नव्यः -व्या -व्यं, नवीनः -ना -नं, नूत्नः -त्ना -त्नं, अर्वाचीनः -ना -नं, अप्राचीनः -ना -नं, अपुराणः -णा -णं, अपुरातनः -नी -नं.

Modernness, s. नूतनता, नवता, नव्यता, अधुनातनत्वं, सद्यस्कालीनता, वर्त्तमानकालीनता, अप्राचीनता, अपुराणता.

Moderns, s. pl. सद्यस्कालीनलोकः, नूतनकालीनलोकः, अधुनातनाः m. pl.

Modest, a. (Not bold, restrained by a sense of shame or propriety) विनीतः -ता -तं, विनयी -यिनी -यि (न्), लज्जाशीलः -ला -लं, लज्जावान् -वती -वत् (त्), लज्जान्वितः -ता -तं, सलज्जः -ज्जा -ज्जं, व्रीडान्वितः -ता -तं, सव्रीडः -डा -डं, व्रीडितः -ता -तं, ह्रीमान् -मती &c., त्रपावान् &c., त्रपायुक्तः -क्ता -क्तं, त्रपान्वितः &c., त्रपितः -ता -तं, सत्रपः -पा -पं, सविनयः -या -यं, विनयभाक् m. f. n. (ज्), अप्रगल्भः -ल्भा -ल्भं, अधृष्टः -ष्टा -ष्टं, शालीनः -ना -नं, ह्रीणः -णा -णं, संह्रीणः &c., ह्रीतः -ता -तं, ह्रीकुः -कुः -कु.—(Unassuming, humble, not proud) निर्गर्वः -र्वा -र्वं, अगर्वः &c., निर्गर्वी &c., अगर्वी &c., गर्वहीनः -ना -नं, निरहङ्कारः -रा -रं, अनहङ्कारी &c., निरभिमानः -ना -नं, अनभिमानी &c., अनुद्धतः -ता -तं, अकत्थनः -ना -नं, अविकत्थनः &c., विनम्रः -म्रा -म्रं, नम्रशीलः -ला -लं, विनतः -ता -तं, निभृतः -ता -तं, प्रसृतः -ता -तं, वश्यात्मा -त्मा -त्म (न्), वशी -शिनी &c.—(Chaste, not loose) अव्यभिचारी -रिणी &c., यतेन्द्रियः -या -यं, सद्वृत्तः -त्ता -त्तं, अलम्पटः; 'a modest wife,' साध्वी, सती, पतिव्रता.—(Moderate) परिमितः -ता -तं, मितः &c.; 'modest speech,' विनयवाक् f. (च्).

Modestly, adv. सविनयं, विनयेन, विनयपूर्वं, विनीतवत्, सलज्जं, सव्रीडं, सत्रपं, लज्जया, लज्जापूर्वं, अगर्वेण, अनभिमानेन, अनुद्धतं, विनम्रं.

Modesty, s. विनयः, विनीतता, लज्जा, ह्रीः f., व्रीडा, त्रपा, ह्रणिया, ह्रीका, लज्जाशीलता, सलज्जत्वं, सत्रपता, शालीनता, अप्रगल्भता, अप्रागल्भ्यं, अधृष्टता, अधार्ष्ट्यं, मर्य्यादा, मन्दाक्षं, मन्दास्यं; 'false modesty,' मिथ्याविनयः.—(Humility) नम्रता, विनम्रता, नम्रशीलता, विनतिः f., अगर्व्वः, गर्व्वहीनता, अनभिमानं, दर्पहीनता, अनुद्धतिः f., अनौद्धत्यं, वश्यता.—(Chastity) अव्यभिचारः, सद्वृत्तता; 'in a wife,' साध्वीत्वं, सतीत्वं, पातिव्रत्यं.—(Moderation) परिमितता.

Modicum, s. अल्पांशः, अल्पभागः, अल्पमात्रं, अत्यल्पांशः, किञ्चित्, किञ्चन, किञ्चिद्भागः, अल्पिका, लेशः.

Modifiable, a. रूपविकारशक्यः -क्या -क्यं, रूपान्तरशक्यः &c., विकार्य्यः -र्य्या -र्य्यं, परिणामशक्यः &c., परिणामान्तरशक्यः &c., परिवर्त्तनीयः -या -यं, विवर्त्तनीयः &c.

Modification, s. (The act) रूपान्तरकरणं, परिणामान्तरकरणं, रूपपरिवर्त्तनं, विवर्त्त -र्त्तनं.—(Particular or different form) रूपभेदः, रूपप्रभेदः, रूपविशेषः, रूपान्तरं.—(Diversity, variety) भेदः, प्रभेदः, विभेदः, विशेषः.—(Altered state) विकारः, विकृतिः f., परिणामः, रूपान्तरं, विपरिणामः.

Modified, p. p. (Changed in form) विकारितः -ता -तं, विकृतः -ता

-तं, विकृतरूपः -पा -पं, परिणतरूपः &c., विपरिणामी -मिनी -मि (न्), विकृताकारः -रा -रं.—(Tempered, qualified) शमितः -ता -तं, नियमितः -ता -तं.

To MODIFY, *v. a.* (Change the form) रूपान्तरं कृ, रूपान्तरीकृ, रूपविकारं कृ, रूपपरिवर्त्तनं कृ, रूपभेदं कृ, रूपविभेदं कृ, विकृ, विकारं कृ, रूपं विकृ, अन्यरूपं -पां कृ, भिन्नरूपं -पां कृ, रूपपरिणामं कृ, परिणामान्तरं कृ रूपं परिवृत् (c. 10. -वर्त्तयति -यितुं) or विवृत्, रूपविवर्त्तनं कृ.—(Moderate) शम् (c. 10. शमयति -यितुं), उपशम्, प्रशम्.

MODISH, *a.* सभ्यव्यवहारानुसारी -रिणी -रि (न्), शिष्टरीत्यनुसारी &c., सभ्यमार्गानुयायी -यिनी &c., शिष्टमार्गानुरूपः -पा -पं, सभ्यसम्प्रदायानुसारी &c.

MODISHLY, *adv.* सभ्यव्यवहारानुसारेण, शिष्टरीत्यनुसारेण, सभ्यमार्गानुरूपेण.

To MODULATE, *v. a.* कल् (c. 10. कलयति -यितुं), स्वरलयं कृ, कलतां कृ, स्वरानुक्रमं कृ, स्वरानुपूर्व्यं कृ.—(Inflect or vary sound) स्वरभेदं कृ, स्वरविभेदं कृ, स्वरभङ्गं कृ, स्वरविभङ्गं कृ, स्वरपरिवर्त्तनं कृ.

MODULATION, *s.* कलता, लयः, स्वरलयः, कलनं, स्वरभेदः, स्वरविभेदः, स्वरभङ्गः, स्वरविभङ्गः, स्वरानुक्रमः.—(Transition from one key to another) शुद्धान्तयुक् *f.* (ज्), स्वरपरिवर्त्तनं.—(Melody) सुस्वरानुक्रमः, स्वरमाधुर्य्यं, माधुर्य्यं, सुश्राव्यस्वरः, तालः.

MODULATOR, *s.* स्वरभेदकारी *m.* (न्), स्वरविभेदकः, लयकारी *m.*

MODULE, *s.* *See* MODEL.

MOHAMMEDAN, *a.* यावनः -नी -नं, यवनदेशीयः -या -यं, यवनधर्म्मसम्बन्धी -न्धिनी -न्धि (न्), यवनधर्म्मावलम्बी -म्बिनी &c.

MOIETY, *s.* अर्द्धं -र्द्धः, अर्द्धभागः, अर्द्धांशः; 'of an estate,' रिक्थार्द्धं.

To MOIL, *v. a.* (Make dirty) मलिन (nom. मलिनयति -यितुं), मलिनीकृ, मलेन दुष् (c. 10. दूषयति -यितुं) or लिप् (c. 6. लिम्पति, लेप्तुं).

To MOIL, *v. n.* (Toil) अतिदेहक्लेशेन आयस् (c. 4. -यस्यति -यसितुं) or श्रम् (c. 4. श्राम्यति, श्रमितुं), अतिशरीरायासं कृ, कष्टं कृ.

MOIST, *a.* आर्द्रः -र्द्रा -र्द्रं, सार्द्रः -र्द्रा -र्द्रं, ईषदार्द्रः, &c., जलार्द्रः &c., क्लिन्नः -न्ना -न्नं, ईषत्क्लिन्नः &c., सिक्तः -क्ता -क्तं, ईषत्सिक्तः &c., उन्नः -न्ना -न्नं, समुन्नः &c., सरसः -सा -सं, सद्रवः -वा -वं, रसयुक्तः -क्ता -क्तं, तिमितः -ता -तं, स्तिमितः -ता -तं, वोदः -दा -दं; 'to be moist,' क्लिद् (c. 4. क्लिद्यति), तिम् or स्तिम् (c. 4. तिम्यति or तीम्यति).

To MOISTEN, *v. a.* क्लिद् (c. 10. क्लेदयति -यितुं), परिक्लिद्, ईषत् क्लिद्, आर्द्रीकृ, ईषदार्द्रीकृ, सिच् (c. 6. सिञ्चति, सेक्तुं), ईषत् सिच्, जलेन सिच्, उक्ष् (c. 1. उक्षति -क्षितुं), समुक्ष्, उन्द् (c. 7. उनत्ति, उन्दितुं).

MOISTENED, *p. p.* क्लिन्नः -न्ना -न्नं, क्लेदितः -ता -तं, परिक्लिन्नः &c., परिक्लेदितः -ता -तं, आर्द्रीकृतः -ता -तं, सिक्तः -क्ता -क्तं, जलसिक्तः &c., उक्षितः -ता -तं, समुक्षितः -ता -तं, उन्नः -न्ना -न्नं, समुन्नः &c., उन्नः -न्ना -न्नं, तिमितः -ता -तं, स्तिमितः -ता -तं.

MOISTENER, MOISTENING, *s.* or *part.* क्लेदकः -का -कं, क्लेदनः -ना -नं.

MOISTENING, *s.* क्लेदनं, सेचनं, जलसेचनं, उक्षणं, उन्दनं, समुन्दनं.

MOISTNESS, *s.* आर्द्रता, सार्द्रता, ईषदार्द्रता, जलार्द्रता, क्लिन्नता, ईषत्क्लिन्नता, सिक्तता, जलसिक्तता, उन्नता, सरसत्वं.

MOISTURE, *s.* क्लेदः -दं, संक्लेदः, क्लिन्नता, आर्द्रता, तेमः, स्तेमः, तेमनं, पिच्छिलं, रसः, स्नेहः, उन्दनं, समुन्दनं; 'of the lips,' अधररसः, अधरमधु *n.*, अधरामृतं, मुखसुरं.

MOLAR, *a.* (Tooth) दाढा, चर्वणदन्तः, महादन्तः, दंष्ट्रा.

MOLASSES, *s.* इक्षुसारः, इक्षुरसक्वाथः, मधुधूलिः *f.*, क्षारः, शर्कराक्षारः, रसिका, मधुरं, गुडः -डकं, रसजः, द्रवजः, सितादिः *m.*, फाणिः *f.*

MOLE, *s.* (Spot on the body) तिलः -लकः, तिलकालकः, किणः, सामुद्रं, कालकः, जटुलः.—(Mound) वप्रः -प्रं, पिण्डलः, पिण्डनः, सेतुः *m.*, चयः.—(The animal) छुछुन्दः, छुच्छुन्दरी, गर्त्ताश्रयः, विलवासी जन्तुभेदः.

MOLECULE, *s.* अणुः *m.*, परमाणुः, कणः, कणिका, लवः, काकिणिका.

MOLECULISM, *s.* अणिमा *m.* (न्), अणुत्वं.

MOLE-EYED, *a.* सूक्ष्मनयनः -ना -नं, सूक्ष्मदृष्टिः -ष्टिः -ष्टि.

MOLE-HILL, *s.* कृमिशैलः, भूस्रवा *m.* (स्), वल्मीकः -कं, कूलकः, वम्रीकूटं, मृत्तिकाकूटं, वामलूरं, स्यमीकः.

To MOLEST, *v. a.* आयस् (c. 10. -यासयति -यितुं), बाध् (c. 1. बाधते -धितुं), परिबाध्, प्रबाध्, अभिबाध्, उपरुध् (c. 7. -रुणद्धि -रोद्धुं), रुध्, तप् (c. 10. तापयति -यितुं), सन्तप्, पीड् (c. 10. पीडयति -यितुं), उपपीड्, अभिपीड्, क्लिश् (c. 9. क्लिश्नाति, क्लेशितुं), व्यथ् (c. 10. व्यथयति -यितुं), अर्द् (c. 10. अर्दयति -यितुं).

MOLESTATION, *s.* क्लेशः, बाधः -धा, बाधनं, उपरोधः, पीडा, व्यथा, दुःखं, आयासः, प्रयासः, उपद्रवः, उपप्लवः; 'free from molestation,' निरुपद्रवः -वा -वं.

MOLESTED, *a.* बाधितः -ता -तं, पीडितः -ता -तं, क्लिष्टः -ष्टा -ष्टं, क्लेशितः -ता -तं, परिक्लिष्टः -ष्टा -ष्टं, उपरुद्धः -द्धा -द्धं, व्यथितः -ता -तं, उपद्रुतः -ता -तं.

MOLLIENT, *a.* मृदुकारी -रिणी -रि (न्), स्निग्धकारी &c. *See* EMOLLIENT.

MOLLIFICATION, *s.* मृदूकरणं, स्निग्धीकरणं, शमनं, प्रशमनं, उपशमनं.

MOLLIFIED, *p. p.* मृदूकृतः -ता -तं, शमितः -ता -तं, उपशान्तः -न्ता -न्तं.

To MOLLIFY, *v. a.* मृदूकृ, स्निग्धीकृ, कोमलीकृ, शम् (c. 10. शमयति -यितुं), प्रशम्, उपशम्, सान्त्व् or शान्त्व् (c. 10. सान्त्वयति -यितुं), उपसान्त्व्, अभिशान्त्व्.

MOLLUSCA, *s. pl.* कोमलशरीरविशिष्टा प्राणिजातिः.

To MOLT, *v. a.* *See* *To* MOULT.

MOLTEN, *a.* विलीनः -ना -नं, द्रुतधातुमयः -यी -यं, विलीनधातुमयः &c.

MOMENT, *s.* (Minute portion of time) क्षणः, विपलं, पलं, त्रुटिः *f.*, निमेषः, निमिषः, मात्रा; 'the present moment,' आपातः; 'for the present moment,' आपाततस्; 'in a moment,' क्षणात् क्षणेन, निमेषमात्रेण, क्षणमात्रेण, क्षणान्तरे, एकपदे, एकविपले; 'for a moment,' क्षणं -णेन, क्षणमात्रं, निमेषमात्रं, मुहूर्त्तं; 'at that moment,' तत्क्षणात् -णे, तत्काले, तदानीमेव; 'every moment,' प्रतिक्षणं, अनुक्षणं, क्षणे क्षणे; 'the next moment,' क्षणान्तरं; 'auspicious moment,' लग्नं. *See* INSTANT. (Importance) गुरुता -त्वं, गौरवं, प्रभावः, भारः.

MOMENTARILY, *adv.* क्षणे -णं -णात्, तत्क्षणे, प्रतिक्षणं, सद्यस्, झपदि, क्षणमात्रं, निमेषमात्रं.

MOMENTARY, *a.* क्षणिकः -का -की -कं, क्षणी -णिनी -णि (न्), क्षणभूतः -ता -तं, क्षणमात्रस्थायी -यिनी &c., क्षणस्थायी &c., अत्यल्पकालस्थायी &c., अल्पकालीनः -ना -नं, अत्यल्पकालीनः -ना -नं, अचिरः -रा -रं, अचिरस्थायी &c., साद्यस्कः -स्की -स्कं, नैमिषः -षी -षं, नैमिषिकः -की -कं, तात्क्षणिकः -की -कं, तात्कालिकः -की -कं, क्षण in comp.; as, 'a momentary obstacle,' क्षणविघ्नः; 'a momentary flash,' क्षणप्रभा.

MOMENTOUS, *a.* गुरुः -र्वी -रु, गुर्वर्थः -र्था -र्थं, बह्वर्थः &c., महार्थः &c. गुरुप्रभावः -वा -वं, अलघुः -घुः -घु; 'a momentous affair,' गुरुकार्य्यं. *See* IMPORTANT.

MOMENTOUSNESS, *a.* गुरुता -त्वं, गौरवं, गुर्वर्थता, प्रभावः, अलघुता.

MOMENTUM, *s.* वेगः, आवेगः, संवेगः, आपातः, गतिवेगः.

MONACHAL, *a.* मठवाससम्बन्धी -न्धिनी -न्धि (न्). *See* MONASTIC.

MONACHISM, *s.* मठवासः, मठाध्यासनं, वनवासः, वानप्रस्थता, अरण्यवासः, वैखानसवृत्तिः *f.*, संसारत्यागः, उदासीनता.

MONAD, MONADE, *s.* तन्मात्रं, मात्रं, अणुमात्रं, अभेद्यवस्तु *n.*, अच्छेद्यवस्तु *n.*, अदृश्यवस्तु *n.*, अखण्डनीयवस्तु.

MONARCH, *a.* राजा *m.* (न्), नृपतिः *m.*, भूपतिः *m.*, नृपः, पार्थिवः, भूपः, नरपतिः *m.*, महीपतिः *m.*, अधिपः, अधिपतिः *m.*, महाराजः, अधिराजः, ईश्वरः, अधीश्वरः; 'universal monarch,' सम्राट् *m.* (ज्), मण्डलेश्वरः, चक्रवर्त्ती *m.* (न्). *See* KING.

MONARCHAL, MONARCHIC, MONARCHICAL, *a.* (Relating or suited to a monarch) राजकीयः -या -यं, राजयोग्यः -ग्या -ग्यं, राजोचितः -ता -तं, आधिराजिकः -की -कं, राज in comp.—(Vested in a single ruler) एकराजाधीनः -ना -नं, एकराजायत्तः -त्ता -त्तं, सम्राडधीनः -ना -नं, एकराजकः -का -कं, एकप्रभुकः -का -कं.

MONARCHY, *s.* एकराजशासनं, एकराजाधिपत्यं, एकाधिपत्यं, एकराजकत्वं, एकभर्तृकत्वं, एकस्वामित्वं, राजत्वं, राज्यं, नृपत्वं, नरेन्द्रत्वं.

MONASTERY, *s.* मठः, आश्रमः, वानप्रस्थाश्रमः, मुनिवासः, मुनिवासस्थानं, धर्म्मशाला, पुण्यस्थानं, पुण्यालयः, पुण्यवनं.

MONASTIC, MONASTICAL, *a.* मठवाससम्बन्धी -न्धिनी -न्धि (न्), आश्रमसम्बन्धी &c., आश्रमी -मिणी &c., आश्रमिकः -की -कं, मुनिसम्बन्धी &c.

MONDAY, *s.* सोमवारः, चन्द्रवारः, इन्दुवारः, सोमवासरः.

MONETARY, *a.* मुद्रासम्बन्धी -न्धिनी -न्धि (न्), मौद्रिकः -की -कं.

MONEY, *s.* (Coin) मुद्रा, दीनारः, नाणकं, टङ्कः, टङ्ककः, निष्कः -ष्कं, कार्षापणं.—(Riches, wealth) धनं, अर्थः, वित्तं, द्रव्यं, विभवः, वैभवं, सम्पत्तिः *f.*, रिक्थं, धनसम्पत्तिः *f.*, धनबाहुल्यं, धनसमृद्धिः *f.*, धनवैपुल्यं, 'love of money,' धनलोभः, अर्थलोभः, धनाशा; 'making money,' धनार्जनं, द्रव्यार्जनं.

MONEY-BAG, *s.* कोषः, कोशः, धनकोषः, मुद्राकोषः.

MONEY-BOX, *s.* मुद्राभाण्डं, मुद्रापात्रं, धनभाण्डं, दीनारभाण्डं.

MONEY-CHANGER, *s.* मुद्रापरिवर्त्तकः, हुण्डिकापत्रसुवर्णरूप्यादिपरिवर्त्तकः, धनव्यापारी *m.* (न्), मुद्राव्यापारी.

MONEYED, *a.* धनवान् -वती -वत् (त्), धनी -निनी -नि (न्), धनिकः -का -कं, सधनः -ना -नं, धनाढ्यः -ढ्या -ढ्यं, महाधनः -ना -नं, द्रव्यवान् &c., वित्तवान् &c.

MONEY-LENDER, *s.* कुसीदिकः, कुसीदः -दा -दं, कौसीदिकः, कुसीदजीवी *m.* (न्), वार्धुषिकः, वृद्धिजीवी *m.*, निमिद्धवृद्ध्युपजीवी *m.* (न्), कलोपजीवी *m.*, ऋणदाता *m.* (तृ), धनिकः, धनप्रयोगी *m.* (न्).

MONEY-LESS, *a.* धनहीनः -ना -नं, अधनः -ना -नं, निर्धनः -ना -नं, द्रव्यहीनः -ना -नं, अर्थहीनः &c., वित्तहीनः &c., क्षीणधनः &c., गतार्थः -र्था -र्थं.

MONGER, *s.* व्यापारी *m.* (न्), व्यवसायी *m.* (न्), क्रयविक्रयिकः, विक्रेता *m.* (तृ), वणिक् *m.* (ज्).

MONGREL, *a.* सङ्कीर्णजातीयः -या -यं, सङ्करजातीयः -या -यं, सङ्करजातः -ता -तं, सङ्करजः -जा -जं, विजातीयः -या -यं, सङ्कीर्णः -र्णा -र्णं.

MONITION, *s.* उपदेशः, प्रत्यादेशः, प्रबोधः -धनं, मन्त्रणं, बोधः -धनं.

MONITOR, *s.* (Warner, admonisher) मन्ता *m.* (तृ), अभिमन्ता *m.*, मन्त्री *m.* (न्), बोधकः, प्रबोधकः, उपदेशकः, प्रत्यादेशकः, शिक्षकः.—(In a school) उपशिक्षकः, उपगुरुः *m.*

MONITORIAL, *s.* उपशिक्षकसम्बन्धी -न्धिनी &c., उपशिक्षासम्बन्धी &c.

MONITORY, MONITIVE, *a.* उपदेशकः -का -कं, उपदेशात्मकः -का -कं, उपदेशरूपः -पा -पं, शिक्षकः -का -कं, उद्बोधकः -का -कं, प्रबोधकः &c.

MONK, *s.* मठवासी *m.* (न्), मुनिः *m.*, सन्न्यासी *m.* (न्), योगी *m.* (न्), यती *m.* (न्), तपस्वी *m.* (न्), वैखानसः, उदासीनः, वैरागी *m.* (न्), वैरागिकः, वैराग्याश्रमी *m.*, वानप्रस्थः, संसारत्यागी *m.*, लोकत्यागी *m.*, सर्व्वसङ्गपरित्यागी *m.*

MONKEY, *s.* वानरः, कपिः *m.*, प्लवगः, प्लवङ्गः -ङ्गमः, मर्कटः, शाखामृगः, वृक्षचरः, कम्पी *m.* (न्), कम्पाकः, कम्पारुः *m.*, वनौकाः *m.* (स्), वलिमुखः, वलीमुखः, कलिप्रियः, कीशः, हनुमान् *m.* (त्), रामदूतः; 'Female monkey,' वानरी *f.*, मर्कटी; 'monkey-like,' कापेयः -यी -यं; 'monkey-tricks,' वानरचेष्टा, मर्कटचेष्टा.—(Iron weight) लोहभारः.

MONKISH, *a.* मुनिसम्बन्धी -न्धिनी &c., मुनिसदृशः -शी -शं.

MONOCHORD, *s.* एकतन्त्री *m.* (न्), एकतारी *m.* (न्), एकतन्त्रीवाद्यं.

MONOCULAR, MONOCULOUS, *a.* एकाक्षः -क्षा -क्षं, एकलोचनः -ना -नं, एकनेत्रः -त्रा -त्रं, काणः -णा -णं, एकाक्षिविकलः -ला -लं.

MONOGAMIST, *s.* एकपत्नीकः, एकभार्य्यकः, सकृद्विवाही *m.* (न्), अपुनर्विवाही *m.*, एकस्त्रीकः.

MONOGAMY, *s.* एकपत्नीव्रतं, एकभार्य्याव्रतं, एकस्त्रीविवाहः, सकृद्विवाहः, अपुनर्विवाहः.

MONOGRAM, *s.* परस्परसंयुक्तं नामाद्याक्षरं.

MONOLOGUE, *s.* आत्मभाषणं, आत्मगतभाषणं, स्वगतभाषणं, स्वसमीपभाषणं.

MONOMACHY, *s.* द्वन्द्वयुद्धं, द्वन्द्वं, द्वन्द्वायोधनं, नियुद्धं.

MONOMANIA, *s.* एकविषयोन्मादः, एकविषयविक्षेपः, एकविषयभ्रान्तिः *f.*

MONOMANIAC, *s.* एकविषयोन्मत्तः, एकविषयविक्षिप्तः, एकविषयभ्रान्तः.

MONOPETALOUS, *a.* एकदलकः -का -कं, एकदलविशिष्टः -ष्टा -ष्टं.

MONOPOLIST, MONOPOLIZER, *s.* (One who purchases the whole of a commodity) पूर्व्वक्रेता *m.* (तृ), पूर्व्वक्रयी *m.* (न्), सर्व्वभाण्डक्रेता, एकव्यवसायी *m.*—(One who takes the whole) पूर्व्वग्राहकः, सर्व्वग्राहकः.

To MONOPOLIZE, *v. a.* (Purchase the whole of a commodity with the view of selling at higher prices) अधिकमूल्यविक्रयबुद्ध्या सर्व्वभाण्डं पूर्व्वं क्री (c. 9. क्रीणाति -णीते, क्रेतुं) or सर्व्वपण्यद्रव्याणि पूर्व्वं क्री or सर्व्वद्रव्याणां पूर्व्वक्रयं कृ.—(Take or obtain the whole) सर्व्वं ग्रह् (c. 9. गृह्णाति, ग्रहीतुं) or आप् (c. 5. -आप्नोति -आप्तुं), साकल्यं ग्रह् or पूर्व्वं ग्रह्.—(Have the sole right of dealing) एकव्यवसायं कृ, एकव्यापारं कृ, क्रयविक्रयाधिकारम् एकतो or असामान्येन धृ (c. 10. धारयति -यितुं).

MONOPOLIZED, *p. p.* पूर्व्वगृहीतः -ता -तं, पूर्व्वक्रीतः -ता -तं, पूर्व्वप्राप्तः &c.

MONOPOLY, *s.* एकव्यवसायः, एकव्यापारः, एकव्यवहारः, एकपण्यता, एकवाणिज्यं, असामान्यव्यवहारः, एकप्रयोगः, असामान्यप्रयोगः, क्रयविक्रययोर् एकाधिकारः.

MONOSYLLABIC, *a.* एकाक्षरः -रा -रं, एकाक्षरी -रिणी -रि (न्).

MONOSYLLABLE, *s.* एकाक्षरं, एकाक्षरशब्दः, एकाक्षरविशिष्टः शब्दः.

MONOTHEISM, *s.* अद्वैतं, अद्वैतवादः, केवलेश्वरवादः, केवलेश्वरमतं.

MONOTHEIST, *s.* अद्वैतवादी *m.* (न्), अद्वयवादी *m.*, केवलेश्वरवादी *m.*

MONOTONOUS, *a.* (Having but one tone) एकस्वरः -रा -रं, एकतानः -ना -नं, एकस्वनः -ना -नं, समस्वरः -रा -रं, समानस्वरः -रा -रं, अनन्यस्वरः -रा -रं.—(Always the same, tediously uniform) एकरूपः -पा -पं, एकप्रकारः -रा -रं, समरूपः -पा -पं, समानरूपः -पा -पं, समसमानः -ना -नं, एकसारः -रा -रं, निर्विकारः -रा -रं, निर्विक्रियः -या -यं, अविशेषः -षा -षं, एकरङ्गी -ङ्गिणी &c.

MONOTONOUSLY, *adv.* एकस्वरेण, समस्वरेण, एकरूपेण, समरूपेण, समसमानं, निर्विकारं, अविकारेण.

MONOTONY, *s.* (Sameness of tone) एकस्वरः, स्वरैक्यं, स्वराभेदः, स्वरसमता, स्वरसमानता, समानस्वरत्वं, स्वरभेदाभावः.—(Dull uniformity)

एकरूपता, समरूपता, समसमानता, समानरूपता, एकव्यापारत्वं, समव्यापारत्वं, व्यापाराभेदः, विकाराभावः, विशेषाभावः.

MONSOON, *s.* (Rainy season) वृष्टिकालः, मेघागमः, मेघकालः, मेघसमयः, घनसमयः, पर्जन्यकालः, जलदागमः, प्रावृट्कालः.

MONSTER, *s.* (Something unnatural) अद्भुतं, अद्भुतविषयः, अद्भुतवस्तु *n.*, अपूर्व्वविषयः, महोद्भुतं.—(Something deformed) अपरूपवस्तु *n.*, विरूपविषयः, अपरूपं, अपरूपता, वैरूप्यं.—(A being enormously large or very frightful) राक्षसशरीरः, भीमशरीरः, विकटाकारः, विकटरूपः, घोररूपी *m.* (न्), सुवृहत्परिमाणः.—(Horribly wicked person) राक्षसः, रावणः, घोरकर्म्मी *m.* (न्).

MONSTROSITY, *s.* *See* MONSTER.

MONSTROUS, *a.* (Unnatural, extraordinary, out of the course of nature) अद्भुतः -ता -तं, महोद्भुतः -ता -तं, अपूर्व्वः -र्व्वा -र्व्वं, विलक्षणः -णा -णं, विलक्षः -क्षा -क्षं, सृष्टिमार्गबहिर्गतः -ता -तं, सृष्टिरीतिबाह्यः -ह्या -ह्यं, सृष्टिक्रमबाह्यः &c.—(Deformed) अपरूपः -पा -पं, विरूपः -पा -पं.—(Enormously large) राक्षसशरीरः -रा -रं, अतिवृहच्छरीरः -रा -रं, विकटशरीरः &c., अतिमहान् -हती -हत् (त्), सुमहान् &c., अतिवृहन् -हती &c., सुवृहत्परिमाणः -णा -णं.—(Frightful) घोररूपी -पिणी &c., घोराकृतिः -तिः -ति, विकटाकारः -रा -रं, भीमदर्शनः -ना -नं, रौद्रदर्शनः &c., करालरूपः -पा -पं.—(Atrocious) दारुणः -णा -णं, अघोरः -रा -रं, विकटः -टा -टं.

MONSTROUSLY, *adv.* अद्भुतं, विकटं, दारुणं, भृशं, अतिशयं -येन, अतीव.

MONSTROUSNESS, *s.* अद्भुतता, अघोरता, घोरता, दारुणता, विकटता.

MONTH, *s.* मासः, मास् *m.*, पक्षद्वयं, पक्षयुगं, नाक्षत्रं, यव्यः, वर्षांशः, वर्षाङ्कः. The following are the twelve Hindu months, 1. चैत्रः, corresponding to the last half of March and the first half of April, 2. वैशाखः, April, May, 3. ज्येष्ठः, May, June, 4. आषाढः, June, July, 5. श्रावणः, July, August, 6. भाद्रः or भाद्रपदः, August, September, 7. आश्विनः or आश्वयुजः, September, October, 8. कार्त्तिकः, October, November, 9. मार्गशीर्षः, November, December, 10. पौषः, December, January, 11. माघः, January, February, 12. फाल्गुनः, February, March.—(Lunar month) चान्द्रमासः; 'half of a lunar month,' पक्षः; 'light or first half of the month,' शुक्लपक्षः, शुद्धपक्षः, सितपक्षः, पूर्व्वपक्षः, प्रथमपक्षः, देवपक्षः; 'dark or second half of the month,' कृष्णपक्षः, तमिस्रः, तमिस्रपक्षः, उत्तरपक्षः, अपरपक्षः, बहुलः; 'last day of the half-month,' पक्षान्तः, पक्षावसरः.—(Solar month) सौरमासः, सौरः; 'a month old,' मासजातः -ता -तं, मासीनः -ना -नं.

MONTHLY, *a.* मासिकः -की -कं, मासीनः -ना -नं, मास्यः -स्या -स्यं, प्रातिमासिकः -की -कं, मासानुमासिकः -का -कं; 'half-monthly,' आर्द्धमासिकः -की -कं, पाक्षिकः -की -कं; 'monthly allowance,' मासिकं.

MONTHLY, *adv.* प्रतिमासं, मासे मासे, मासि मासि, अनुमासं.

MONUMENT, *s.* (Memorial) स्मरणार्थकचिह्नं.—(Tomb, monument to the dead) चित्यं, चैत्यं, चितापूडकं, चैत्यः, स्तूपः, समाधिः *m.*

MONUMENTAL, *a.* (Memorial) स्मरणार्थकः -का -कं.—(Belonging to a tomb) चैत्यसम्बन्धी -न्धिनी -न्धि (न्).

MOOD, *s.* (Temper of mind) वृत्तिः *f.*, चित्तवृत्तिः *f.*, मनोवृत्तिः *f.*, भावः, मनोभावः, प्रकृतिः *f.*, मनःस्थितिः *f.*, मनोवस्था; 'cheerful mood,' आनन्दवृत्तिः *f.*, हास्यवृत्तिः *f.*—(In grammar) वाच्यं, अर्थः.—(In logic) प्रकारः, रूपं.

MOODINESS, *s.* उदासीनता, क्रोधशीलता, विषण्णता, कार्कश्यं, वक्रता.

MOODY, *a.* क्रोधवशात् उदासीनः -ना -नं or उदासवृत्तिः -त्तिः -त्ति or विषण्णः -ण्णा -ण्णं, क्रोधशीलः -ला -लं, उत्कण्ठितः -ता -तं, दीनमनाः -नाः -नः (स्), उद्विग्नमनाः &c., खिन्नोद्विग्नः -ग्ना -ग्नं, कर्कशभावः -वा -वं, वक्रभावः &c., रुष्टः -ष्टा -ष्टं.

MOON, *s.* चन्द्रः -न्द्रकः, चन्द्रमाः *m.* (स्), सोमः -मा *m.* (न्), इन्दुः *m.*, विधुः *m.*—(Marked like a hare or rabbit) शशी *m.* (न्), शशाङ्कः, शशधरः, शशभृत् *m.*, शशबिन्दुः *m.*, शशलाञ्छनः.—(Marking the night) रजनीकरः, निशाकरः, क्षपाकरः, निशाकेतुः *m.*—(Lord of the night) निशापतिः *m.*, क्षपानाथः, यामिनीपतिः *m.*, निशीथिनीनाथः, रजनीनाथः.—(Gem of the night) रात्रिमणिः *m.*, निशामणिः.—(Lord of the constellations) नक्षत्रनाथः, नक्षत्रपः, ऋक्षेशः, उडुपः, उडुपतिः, उडुराट् *m.* (ज्), दाक्षायणीपतिः *m.*, ताराधिपतिः *m.*, भपतिः *m.*—(The repository and producer of nectar or ambrosia, which is supposed to be distilled in its rays) अमृतसूः *m.*, अमृतदीधितिः *m.*, अमृताधारः, अमृतसुत् *m.*, सुधानिधिः *m.*, सुधाधारः, सुधाभृतिः *m.*, सुधासूतिः *m.*, सुधांशुः, सुधाकरः, सुधाङ्कः, पीयूषरुचिः *m.*, पीयूषमहाः *m.* (स्), पीयूषनिधिः *m.*—(Having cool rays or radiance) शीतांशुः *m.*, शीतमयूखः, शीतमरीचिः *m.*, शीतभानुः *m.*, हिमांशुः *m.*, हिमकरः, हिमरश्मिः *m.*, हिमद्युतिः *m.*, शीतरुक् *m.* (च्), शीतगुः *m.*, हिमप्रथः, प्रालेयांशुः *m.*, तुहिनांशुः *m.*—(Having white rays or pale radiance) शुभ्रांशुः *m.*, सितांशुः, सितरश्मिः *m.*, सितदीधितिः *m.*, श्वेतधामा *m.* (न्), श्वेतरोचिः *m.* (स्), शुचिरोचिः *m.* (स्), छायाभृत् *m.*—(Marked like a deer) मृगाङ्कः, मृगविप्रुः *m.*, हरिणाङ्कः, हरिणकलङ्कः, मृगलाञ्छनः, मृगधरः, छायामृगधरः.—(Containing many digits) कलानिधिः *m.*, कलापूर्णः, कलावान् *m.* (त्), कलाभृत् *m.*, कलापतिः *m.*—(Forming the crest of Śiva) शिवशेखरः, हरशेखरः, हरचूडामणिः *m.*—(Brother of Lakshmí, as having been reproduced with that goddess from the ocean when it was churned by the gods and asuras) लक्ष्मीसहजः, श्रीसहोदरः.—(Husband of Rohiṇí) रोहिणीपतिः *m.*, रोहिणीशः, रोहिणीवल्लभः.—(The butter of the ocean, or produced by the churning of the ocean) अब्धिनवनीतकः.—(Friend, companion or lord of the lotuses, many of these flowers opening their petals in the night and closing them in the day) कुमुदबान्धवः, कुमुदबन्धुः *m.*, कुमुदपतिः, कुमुदेशः, कुमुदप्रियः, कुमुदिनीपतिः *m.*, कुमुदिनीनायकः, अब्जः.—(Lord of plants or herbs) ओषधीनाथः, ओषधीपतिः *m.*, ओषधीशः.—(Drawn by white horses) श्वेतवाजी *m.* (न्), श्वेतवाहनः.—(Drawn by ten horses) दशवाजी *m.*—(Dispeller of darkness) तमोहरः, तमोनुद् *m.*, तमोनुदः, तमोघ्नः, तमोपहः, तिमिररिपुः *m.*—(Regulating the days of the month) तिथिप्रणीः *m.*, पर्व्वधिः *m.* (Garlanded with stars) तारापीडः.—(King of kings) राजराजः.—(Broken-bodied, having been cut in two by the trident of Śiva, as a punishment for having violated the wife of Vrihaspati) भग्नात्मा *m.*—(Lord of Brahmans) द्विजपतिः *m.*, द्विजराजः.—(Lord of the moonlight) कौमुदीपतिः *m.* Other names for the moon of less obvious derivation are जैवातृकः, ग्लौः, वैरवी *m.* (न्), कलापिनी, हरिः *m.*, मास् *m.*, चन्दः; 'the autumnal moon,' शरच्चन्द्रः; 'orb or disk of the moon,' चन्द्रबिम्बः, चन्द्रमण्डलं, चन्द्रगोलः -लं; 'day of the moon,' तिथिः.

See LUNAR ; 'digit of the moon,' चन्द्रकला, चन्द्ररेखा, इन्दुरेखा, चन्द्रलेखा ; 'full moon,' पूर्णचन्द्रः, पूर्णिमा, पूर्णेन्दुः. *See* FULL MOON ; 'new moon,' नवशशी *m.* (न्), नवचन्द्रः, अमा, अमावसी, अमावासी, अमावस्या, अमावास्या, अमामसी, प्रतिपच्चन्द्रः, दर्शः, सूर्य्येन्दुसङ्गमः, कुहूः *f.*, तिथिक्षयः, नष्टेन्दुकला ; 'moon of the first quarter,' बालचन्द्रः ; 'day of new moon,' मासान्तः ; 'full or new moon, or the last day of a lunar fortnight,' पञ्चदशी, पक्षान्तः ; 'the first day of the moon's increase or wane, or of a lunar fortnight,' प्रतिपद् *f.* ; 'fortnight of the waxing moon,' शुक्लपक्षः, सितपक्षः, शुद्धपक्षः ; 'fortnight of the waning moon,' कृष्णपक्षः, तमिस्रपक्षः, उत्तरपक्षः ; 'the full or change of the moon, or the junction of the 15th and 1st of a half-month,' पर्व्वसन्धिः *m.*, प्रतिपत्पञ्चदश्योरन्तरं ; 'moon a little gibbous, or one digit less than full,' अनुमतिः *f.*, कलाहीनः ; 'moon a little horned,' सिनीवाली ; 'half moon,' चन्द्रार्द्धं ; 'a false moon,' चन्द्राभासः ; 'having a face like the moon,' चन्द्रमुखी *f.*, शशिवदना ; 'rise of the moon,' चन्द्रोदयः ; 'spot's on the moon's disk,' लाञ्छनं, कलङ्कः ; 'the wife of the moon,' रोहिणी, चन्द्रकान्ता.

MOON-BEAM, *s.* चन्द्रपादः, शशिपादः, चन्द्रकिरणः, चन्द्ररश्मिः *m.*, शशिकिरणः, शशिकरः, शशिमयूखः, अंशुः *m.*, सोमांशुः *m.*, चन्द्रांशुः *m.*, चन्द्रिका, चन्द्रमरीचिः *m.*, पूर्णानकं.

MOONLESS, *a.* चन्द्रहीनः -ना -नं, शशिहीनः &c., नष्टचन्द्रः -न्द्रा -न्द्रं.

MOONLIGHT, *s.* चन्द्रप्रभा, शशिप्रभा, चन्द्रप्रकाशः, चन्द्रिका, चन्द्रिमा, ज्योत्स्ना, चन्द्रज्योतिस् *n.*, चन्द्रातपः, चन्द्रगोलिका, कौमुदी, चन्द्रशाला, दीपिका, चान्द्री, मालती, तुहिनं, अमृततरङ्गिणी, कैरवी, हरिचन्दनं, मुदी, चन्द्रकः.

MOONLIGHT, *a.* ज्यौत्स्नः -त्स्नी -त्स्नं, ज्योत्स्नायुक्तः -क्ता -क्तं ; 'a moonlight night,' ज्योत्स्नी, ज्यौत्स्नी -त्स्निका.

MOON-PLANT, *s.* चन्द्रवल्लरी, सोमवल्लरी -रिः *f.*, सोमवल्लिका, सोमलता, सोमः, वयस्था, वयःस्था, ब्रह्मी, ब्राह्मी, मत्स्याक्षी.

MOONSHINE, *s.* चन्द्रप्रभा, चन्द्रद्युतिः *f.*, चन्द्रदीप्तिः. *See* MOONLIGHT.

MOON-STONE, MOON-GEM, *s.* चन्द्रकान्तः, चन्द्रमणिः *m.*, सोमकान्तः, चन्द्रोपलः, चन्द्रिकाद्रावः.

MOONSTRUCK, *a.* विक्षिप्तबुद्धिः -द्धिः -द्धि, विलुप्तबुद्धिः &c., हतबुद्धिः &c.

MOONY, *a.* अर्द्धचन्द्रध्वजाङ्कितः -ता -तं, अर्द्धचन्द्रध्वजविशिष्टः -ष्टा -ष्टं.

MOOR, *s.* जङ्गलभूमिः *f.*, खिलभूमिः *f.*, अनुपभूः *f.*, कच्छः, कच्छभूः.

To MOOR, *v. a.* रज्जुना or रश्मा नौकां बन्ध् (c. 9. बध्नाति, बन्द्धुं).

MOORED, *p. p.* रज्जुना or गुणेन बद्धः -द्धा -द्धं, रज्जुबद्धः &c.

MOOR-LAND, *s.* अनूपभूमिः *f.*, कच्छभूमिः *f.*, खिलभूः *f.* *See* MOOR.

MOORY, *a.* अनूपः -पा -पं, आनूपः -पी -पं, कच्छः -च्छा -च्छं, खिलः -ला -लं.

MOOSE, *s.* (Kind of deer) शम्बरः, सम्बरः.

To MOOT, *v. a.* (Discuss) विचर् (c. 10. -चारयति -यितुं), वितर्क् (c. 10. -तर्कयति -यितुं), विवद् (c. 1. -वदति -ते -दितुं), विवादास्पदीकृ, विचारास्पदीकृ, वितर्कास्पदीकृ.—(Bring forward) उपन्यस् (c. 4. -अस्यति -असितुं).

MOOT, MOOT-CASE, MOOT-POINT, *s.* विचारविषयः, विचारपदं, विचारास्पदं, विचारस्थलं, विवादास्पदं, विवादविषयः, सन्दिग्धविषयः, अनिष्पन्नविषयः, असिद्धान्तः.

MOOTED, *p. p.* विचारितः -ता -तं, वादग्रस्तः -स्ता -स्तं, विचारास्पदीकृतः &c.

MOP, *s.* मार्ज्जनी, सम्मार्ज्जनी, शोधनी, विमार्गः, परिष्कारकः.

To MOP, *v. a.* मृज् (c. 2. मार्ष्टि -र्ष्टुं), सम्मृज्, शुध् (c. 10. शोधयति -यितुं).

To MOPE, *v. n.* विषद् (c. 1. -षीदति -षत्तुं), अवसद्, उदास् (c. 2. -आस्ते -आसितुं), विषण्णीभू, उद्विग्नीभू, दुर्मनस् (nom. दुर्मनायते), उन्मनस्, ग्लै (c. 1. ग्लायति, ग्लातुं).

MOPING, MOPISH, *a.* विषण्णः -ण्णा -ण्णं, अवसन्नः -न्ना -न्नं, उदासीनः -ना -नं, उदासी -सिनी -सि (न्), दुर्मनाः -नाः -नः (स्), उद्विग्नमनाः &c., उन्मनाः &c.

MOPPET, MOPSEY, *s.* पटपुत्रिका, वस्त्रपुत्रिका, वस्त्रखण्डमयी पुत्तलिका.

MORAL, *a.* (Virtuous) सदाचारः -रा -रं, सदाचारी -रिणी -रि (न्), धार्म्मिकः -की -कं, धर्म्माचारी &c., धर्म्मचारी &c., साधुः -धुः -ध्वी -धु, साधुवृत्तः -त्ता -त्तं, सुचरितः -ता -तं, सच्चरितः -ता -तं, साध्वाचारः -रा -रं, धर्म्यः -र्म्या -र्म्यं, धर्म्मी &c., सुधर्म्मा -र्म्मा -र्म्म (न्), धर्म्मभृत् *m.f.n.*, न्यायाचारः &c., वृत्तवान् -वती -वत् (त्), अव्यसनी &c., पुण्यः -ण्या -ण्यं, सात्त्विकः -की -कं, नीतिमान् &c.—(Relating to the practice of men, or to actions good or evil) लोकव्यवहारसम्बन्धी &c., लोकाचारविषयकः -का -कं, सदसदाचारसम्बन्धी &c., सदसद्व्यवहारविषयः -या -यं, विधिनिषेधान्वितः -ता -तं.—(Subject to moral laws, bound by precepts and prohibitions) विधिनिषेधाधीनः -ना -नं, विधिनिषेधायत्तः -त्ता -त्तं, विधिनिषेधवान् &c., नियमाधीनः &c.—(Supported by reason or probability, founded on experience) अनुमानसिद्धः -द्धा -द्धं, युक्तिसिद्धः &c., आनुमानिकः -की -कं, यौक्तिकः -की -कं, अनुभूतिसिद्धः &c., युक्तिभाव्यः -व्या -व्यं, अनुमानमूलः -ला -लं ; 'moral philosophy,' नीतिशास्त्रं, नीतिविद्या, व्यवहारशास्त्रं, नीतिः *f.*

MORAL, *s.* (Moral doctrine taught by a fiction) तात्पर्य्यं, तात्पर्य्यार्थः, अभिप्रायः, भावार्थः, तात्त्विकं, ध्वनितार्थः, गर्भः.

MORALIST, *s.* (Teacher of moral duties) नीतिशास्त्रोपदेशकः, नीत्युपदेष्टा *m.* (ष्टृ), नीतिशिक्षकः, धर्म्मोपदेशी *m.* (न्), नीतिविवेचकः, सदसद्विवेचकः, नीतिशास्त्रज्ञः, नीतिविद्याज्ञः, कर्त्तव्याकर्त्तव्योपदेशकः.—(Mere moral person) नीतिमार्गावलम्बी *m.*, केवलनीतिमार्गाश्रयी.

MORALITY, *s.* (System of moral duties) नीतिः *f.*, नीतिविद्या, नीतिशास्त्रं, व्यवहारशास्त्रं, नयः, नयविद्या, नयशास्त्रं, अर्थशास्त्रं, विनयविद्या, शीलविद्या, सदसद्विचारः, सदसद्विवेकः, कर्त्तव्याकर्त्तव्यविचारः, कर्त्तव्याकर्त्तव्यविवेकः ; 'as invented by Vrihaspati,' बार्हस्पत्यं.—(Practice of moral duties, virtue) धर्म्मानुष्ठानं, धर्म्माचरणं, धर्म्माचारता, धर्म्मः, धर्म्मत्वं, सदाचारत्वं, सच्चरितं, सुचरितं, साधुशीलता, पुण्यता, पुण्यशीलत्वं, साधुवृत्तं.—(Conformity to the principles of rectitude) धर्म्मानुसारित्वं, न्यायानुसारः, न्यायः, धर्म्यता, धर्म्मत्वं.

To MORALIZE, *v. a.* (Apply to the purposes of moral instruction) हितोपदेशास्पदीकृ, धर्म्मोपदेशास्पदीकृ, नीतिशिक्षास्पदीकृ.

To MORALIZE, *v. n.* (Make moral reflections) हितोपदेशं कृ, धर्म्मोपदेशं कृ, नीत्युपदेशं कृ, हितोपदेशं लिख् (c. 6. लिखति, लेखितुं).

MORALIZER, *s.* हितोपदेशकः, धर्म्मोपदेष्टा *m.* (ष्टृ), नीतिशिक्षकः.

MORALLY, *adv.* (According to the rules of morality) नीतिशास्त्रतस्, नीतिशास्त्रवत्, नीतितस्.—(Virtuously) धर्म्मेण, धर्म्मतस्, न्यायतस्.—(According to reason or the usual course of things) अनुमानेन, युक्त्या, अनुमानतस्, युक्तितस्, यथासम्भवं.

MORALS, *s.* (System of morality) नीतिः *f.*, नीतिशास्त्रं, नीतिविद्या. *See* MORALITY. (Conduct) आचारः, आचरणं, आचरितं, चरितं, व्यवहारः, वृत्तिः *f.*, प्रवृत्तिः *f.*, वृत्तं, रीतिः *f.* ; 'good morals,' विनयः, सदाचारः, सच्चरितं, सुचरितं, साधुचरितं, शीलः, सुशीलः.

MORASS, *s.* कच्छः, कच्छभूः *f.*, अनूपः, अनूपभूः *f.*, जलाढ्यभूमिः *f.*, पङ्किलभूः *f.*, आप्यभूः *f.*

MORBID, *a.* अस्वस्थः -स्था -स्थं, असुस्थः &c., रोगी -गिणी -गि (न्), रोगवान् -वती -वत् (त्), सरोगः -गा -गं, विकारी &c., विकृतः -ता -तं, व्याधितः -ता -तं.

MORBIDNESS, *s.* अस्वस्थता, अस्वास्थ्यं, असुस्थता, सरोगता, रोगित्वं.

MORBIFIC, MORBIFICAL, *a.* रोगजनकः -का -कं, रोगकरः -रा -रं, अस्वास्थ्यजनकः &c., व्याधिकरः -रा -रं, अनारोग्यकरः &c., रोगदः -दा -दं.

MORBOSE, *a.* रोगजनितः -ता -तं, रोगजः -जा -जं, असुस्थः -स्था -स्थं.

MORDACIOUS, *a.* दंशकः -का -कं, दंशनकारी -रिणी -रि (न्).

MORDACITY, *s.* दंशकता, दंशनशीलता, दंशनं, दंशनगुणः.

MORDICANT, *a.* खादकः -का -कं, अरुष्करः -री -रं, दंशकः &c.

MORE, *a.* अधिकः -का -कं, अधिकतरः -रा -रं, अधिकसंख्यकः -का -कं, भूयान् -यसी -यः (स्), भूयिष्ठः -ष्ठा -ष्ठं, उत्तरः -रा -रं, अतिरेकी -किणी -कि (न्), अतिरिक्तः -क्ता -क्तं, परः -रा -रं, परतरः -रा -रं; often expressed by the comparative affixes तर and ईयस्; as, 'more in number,' बहुतरः -रा -रं, भंहीयान् &c.; 'more or less,' न्यूनाधिकः -का -कं, न्यूनातिरेकः -का -कं; 'more than a thousand,' परःसहस्रः -स्रा -स्रं; 'more than a hundred,' परं शतं.

MORE, *s.* आधिक्यं, अधिकता, आतिरेक्यं, अतिरिक्तता, उद्रेकः, आतिशय्यं; 'more or less,' न्यूनाधिक्यं, न्यूनातिरेक्यं, न्यूनातिरिक्तं; 'neither more nor less,' अन्यूनानतिरिक्तं; 'no more,' कृतं, अलं with inst. c.; as, 'no more of this ceremony!' कृतम् आदरेण, अलम् आदरेण; 'what more need I say?' किम् अन्यत्, किम् बहुना.

MORE, *adv.* अधिकं, अधिकतरं, भूयस्, भूयिष्ठं, अतिरिक्तं, परं; or often expressed by the comparative affixes तर and ईयस्; as, 'more heavy,' गुरुतरः -रा -रं, गरीयान् -यसी -यः (स्); 'more and more,' उत्तरोत्तरं, अधिकाधिकं; 'how much more?' किम्पुनर्, किमुत, सुतरां.—(Any more, again) पुनर्, भूयस्.

MOREOVER, *s.* अपिच, अपरच, अपरं, परं, परच, परन्तु, अपरन्तु, अन्यच, किच, अधिकन्तु, अधिकं, पुनश्च, अपितु, अपि, अथ.

MORIBUND, *a.* मुमूर्षुः -र्षुः -र्षु, मृतकल्पः -ल्पा -ल्पं, मृतप्रायः -या -यं.

MORINGA, *s.* *See* MORUNGA.

MORION, *s.* शिरस्त्रं, शिरस्त्राणं, शिरस्कं, मस्तकरक्षणी, शीर्षकं.

MORN, MORNING, *s.* प्रभातं, प्रातःकालः, प्रातःसमयः, प्रभातकालः, प्रत्यूषकालः, प्रत्यूषः, प्रत्यूषस् *n.*, प्रत्युषः, प्रत्युषस् *n.*, उषः, उषस् *n.*, उषाकालः, विभातं -तकं, भातः, व्युष्टं, अरुणः, अरुणोदयः, कल्यं, काल्यं, अहर्मुखं, दिवसमुखं, दिनारम्भः, दिनादिः *m.*, निशावसानं, निशान्तः -न्तं, क्षपान्तः, रात्रिविगमः, प्राबोधिकः, वासरसङ्गः.—(As opposed to afternoon) पूर्व्वाह्णः or पूर्व्वाह्लः, प्राह्णः, पूर्व्वाह्णकालः, प्राह्णकालः; 'in the morning,' प्रातर्, प्रभाते, प्रातःकाले, प्रभातकाले, प्रत्यूषे, उषा, प्रगे, प्राह्णे, पूर्व्वाह्णे, निशान्ते, पूर्व्वेद्युस्; 'to be chanted in the morning,' प्रातर्गेयः -या -यं; 'early in the morning,' सुप्रातर्, अतिप्रभाते, अतिप्रगे; 'to-morrow morning,' श्वः प्रभाते; 'good morning,' सुप्रभातं; 'morning, noon, and evening,' त्रिकालं.

MORNING, *a.* प्रातर् in comp., प्रातःकालीनः -ना -नं, प्रातःकालिकः -की -कं, प्रभातीयः -या -यं, प्राभातिकः -की -कं, प्रगेतनः -नी -नं, प्राह्णेतनः -नी -नं, पूर्व्वाह्णेतनः -नी -नं, उषस्यः -स्या -स्यं, औषिकः -की -कं, औषसः -सी -सं, वैयुष्टः -ष्टी -ष्टं; 'morning duties,' प्रातःकृत्यं; 'morning ablution,' प्रातःस्नानं; 'morning meal,' प्रातराशः, प्रातर्भोजनं.

MORNING-GOWN, *s.* प्रातःकाले भृतो लघुप्रावारः, प्रातर्वसनं, प्रातर्वस्त्रं.

MORNING-STAR, *s.* प्रभातसूचकतारा, प्रभाततारा, शुक्रः.

MORNING-TWILIGHT, *s.* प्रातःसन्ध्या, प्राक्सन्ध्या, पूर्व्वसन्ध्या, प्रभातसन्ध्या.

MOROSE, *a.* कर्कशस्वभावः -वा -वं, कटुस्वभावः -वा -वं, कर्कशभावः -वा -वं, कर्कशशीलः -ला -लं, वक्रभावः -वा -वं, सदावक्रः -क्रा -क्रं, रूक्षस्वभावः -वा -वं, नैकृतिकः -की -कं, प्रतीपः -पा -पं, उदासीनः -ना -नं, उदासवृत्तिः -त्तिः -त्ति, अरुन्तुदः -दा -दं, दुःशीलः -ला -लं, वामशीलः &c.

MOROSELY, *adv.* कर्कशस्वभावात्, कटुस्वभावात्, कर्कशं, कार्कश्येन, वक्रभावेन, सदावक्रवत्, दुःशीलत्वात्, रूक्षस्वभावात्.

MOROSENESS, *s.* कार्कश्यं, कर्कशता, कर्कशशीलता, कटुता, कटुशीलता, दुःशीलता, दौःशील्यं, वक्रता, वक्रशीलता, स्वभाववक्रता, स्वभावकार्कश्यं, स्वभावकटुता, उदासीनता, उदासवृत्तित्वं, प्रतीपता, वामशीलता, निकृतिः *f.*, शुक्तता.

MORROW, *s.* (The day next after the present) परदिवसः, परदिनं, श्वस्तनदिवसः, आगामिदिवसः, कल्यं; 'to-morrow, on the morrow,' श्वस्, परेद्युस्, परदिने, परदिवसे, परेद्यवि, कल्लि, कल्ये, अन्येद्युस्.—(The next day subsequent to any day) उत्तरदिवसः, उत्तरदिनं, उत्तरेद्युस्; 'the day after to-morrow,' परश्वस्; 'to-morrow morning,' श्वः प्रभाते.

MORSEL, *s.* (Mouthful, small piece of food) ग्रासः, पिण्डः, कवलः; 'a morsel as big as an egg,' अण्डपरिमाणो ग्रासः.—(Piece, bit) खण्डः -ण्डकः, क्षुद्रभागः, लवः, शकलः, भित्तं, भिन्नं, भित्तिः *f.*; 'a dainty morsel,' सुग्रासः.

MORSURE, *s.* दंशनं, विदंशनं, दंशः, दंशकरणं.

MORTAL, *a.* (Subject to death) मरणाधीनः -ना -नं, मर्त्यः -र्त्या -र्त्यं, मर्त्तव्यः -व्या -व्यं, नाशाधीनः -ना -नं, कालाधीनः -ना -नं, मृत्यधीनः -ना -नं, मरणधर्म्मकः -का -कं, मृत्युधर्म्मकः -का -कं, मृत्युवशः -शा -शं, मरणवशः &c., अमवान् -वती -वत् (त्), अनित्यः -त्या -त्यं.—(Deadly) प्राणघातकः -का -कं, प्राणहरः -रा -रं, प्राणान्तिकः -की -कं, प्राणान्तकः &c., जीवान्तकः &c., प्राणहारी -रिणी -रि (न्), प्राणनाशकः -का -कं, मारात्मकः -का -कं, मृत्युजनकः -का -कं, मर्म्मभेदी -दिनी &c., मर्म्मान्तिकः &c., अन्तकरः -रा -रं.—(Belonging to man, human) मानुषः -षी -षं -षिकः -की -कं, मनुष्यजातीयः -या -यं, मनुष्यधर्म्मकः -का -कं, पौरुषेयः -यी -यं; 'mortal state,' मानुषदशा.

MORTAL, *s.* (A human being) मर्त्यः, मनुष्यः, मानुषः, मानवः, प्राणी *m.* (न्), प्राणभृत् *m.*, जन्मी *m.* (न्), जन्मवान् *m.*, शरीरी *m.*, देही *m.*, देहभृत् *m.*, तनुभृत् *m.*, चेतनः, मृत्युपात्रं, मरणपात्रं.

MORTALITY, *s.* (Subjection to death) मरणाधीनता, मर्त्यता, मृत्युवशता, नाशाधीनता, मृत्युधर्म्मः, मरणधर्म्मः, अनित्यता.—(Human nature) मनुष्यता -त्वं, मानुष्यं, मानुषत्वं -ता, पुरुषता.—(Death, death of great numbers) मृत्युः *m.*, मरणं, अत्ययः, नाशः, बहुनाशः, बहुजननाशः.

MORTALLY, *adv.* प्राणनाशेन, प्राणघातेन, सनाशं, सप्राणघातं, सप्राणनाशं; 'mortally wounded,' भिन्नमर्म्मा -र्म्मा -र्म्म (न्).

MORTAR, *s.* (Vessel in which substances are pounded) उलूखलं, उडूखलः -लं, उदूखलं; 'pestle and mortar,' उलूखलमुषले; 'pounded in a mortar,' उलूखलिकः -की -कं.—(Cement) सुधा, लेपः, विलेपः, चूर्णलेपः, कर्करलेपः, उदपेषः; 'very hard,' वज्रलेपः.

MORTGAGE, *s.* आधिः *m.*, स्थावराधिः *m.*, क्षेत्राधिः, स्थावरधनाधिः *m.*, आधानं, आधमनं, क्षेत्रन्यासः, स्थावरधनन्यासः, भूमिन्यासः, उपन्यासः, स्थावरबन्धकः, बन्धकः, उपनिधिः *m.*, भूमिनिक्षेपः.

To MORTGAGE, *v. a.* आधीकृ, क्षेत्रादि स्थावरधनं न्यस् (c. 4. -अस्यति

-चसितुं) or निक्षिप् (c. 6. -क्षिपति-क्षेप्तुं), न्यासं दा, बन्धकं दा, न्यासीकृ.

MORTGAGED, *p. p.* आधीकृतः -ता -तं, न्यासीकृतः -ता -तं, न्यस्तः -स्ता -स्तं, उपन्यस्तः &c.; 'to be mortgaged,' आधेयः -या -यं.

MORTGAGEE, *s.* आधिधारी *m.* (न्), न्यासधारी *m.* (न्), आधिग्राही *m.* (न्), बन्धकग्राही *m.*, बन्धकधारी *m.*, आधिग्राहकः.

MORTGAGER, *s.* आधिदाता *m.* (तृ), बन्धकदाता *m.*, आधीकर्त्ता *m.* (र्तृ).

MORTIFEROUS, *a.* मृत्युजनकः -का -कं, मरणावहः -हा -हं, प्राणघातकः &c.

MORTIFICATION, *s.* (In surgery, local extinction of life) मांसनाशः, मांसातिपाकः, मांसपाकः, चेतनानाशः, जीवितनाशः, मांसकोथः, मांसविद्रधिः *m.*, मांसपूतिः *f.*—(Subjugation of the passions and appetites) दमः, दान्तिः *f.*, दमनं, संयमः -मनं, इन्द्रियदमः, इन्द्रियजयः, इन्द्रियपराजयः, इन्द्रियसंयमः, जितेन्द्रियत्वं, इन्द्रियवशीकरणं, कामावसायः, वीतकामत्वं, विषयपराङ्मुखता.—(By penance, &c.) तपस्, तपश्चर्य्या, तपस्या, कृच्छ्रं, कायक्लेशः, वैराग्यं.—(Humiliation, vexation) अभिभवः, अभिभूतिः *f.*, मानभङ्गः, मानखण्डनं, अभिमानखण्डनं, मानहानिः *f.*, तेजोभङ्गः, दर्पभङ्गः, अपकर्षः -र्षणं, व्यथा, दुःखं, क्लेशः, विडम्बना.—(Disappointment) आशाभङ्गः, मनोभङ्गः, आशानाशः, इच्छानाशः, इच्छाविनाशः, इच्छाक्षयः, उत्साहभङ्गः.

MORTIFIED, *p. p.* (In surgery) नष्टमांसः -सा -सं, नष्टचेतनः -ना -नं, कोथवान् -वती -वत् (त्), अतिपक्वः -क्वा -क्वं.—(Subdued) दान्तः -न्ता -न्तं, दमितः -ता -तं, संयमितः -ता -तं, वशीकृतः -ता -तं, जितः -ता -तं; 'one whose passions are mortified,' जितेन्द्रियः, यतेन्द्रियः, संयतेन्द्रियः, वीतकामः, वीतरागः, वीतस्पृहः, विरक्तः, वैरागी *m.* (न्), जितकामः, जितकामक्रोधादिः *m.*—(Humiliated, vexed) अभिभूतः -ता -तं, पराभूतः -ता -तं, खण्डितः -ता -तं, भग्नमानः -ना -नं, क्लिष्टः -ष्टा -ष्टं, सव्यथः -था -थं, उद्विग्नः -ग्ना -ग्नं, विडम्बितः -ता -तं.

To MORTIFY, *v. a.* (Destroy the vitality of) जीवितं or चैतन्यं नश् (c. 10. नाशयति -यितुं), चेतनानाशं कृ, चैतन्यनाशं कृ.—(Subdue) दम् (c. 10. दमयति -यितुं), वशीकृ, जि (c. 1. जयति, जेतुं), पराजि; 'one's passions,' इन्द्रियाणि दम्, इन्द्रियदमनं कृ; 'the body,' शरीरक्लेशं कृ.—(Humble) अभिभू, अपकृष् (c. 1. -कर्षति -क्रष्टुं), मानं भञ्ज् (c. 7. भनक्ति, भंक्तुं) or खण्ड् (c. 10. खण्डयति -यितुं), अभिमानखण्डनं कृ, मानविध्वंसं कृ.—(Vex) क्लिश् (c. 9. क्लिश्नाति, क्लेशितुं), व्यथ् (c. 10. व्यथयति -यितुं), तप् (c. 10. तापयति -यितुं).

To MORTIFY, *v. n.* (Lose vitality, as flesh) नष्टचैतन्यः -न्या -न्यं भू, नष्टजीवितः -ता -तं भू, नष्टमांसः -सा -सं भू, मांसैकदेशे पूतीभू, कोथीभू.—(Practise austerities) तप् (c. 4. तप्यते), तपस् तप्, तपस् (nom. तपस्यति), तपश्चर्य्यां कृ, वैराग्याचरणं कृ, शरीरक्लेशं कृ, ब्रह्मचर्य्यं कृ.

MORTIFYING, *a.* मानभञ्जकः -का -कं, दर्पभञ्जकः &c., व्यथाकरः -रा -रं.

MORTISE, *s.* काष्ठछिद्रं, काष्ठसन्धिः *m.*, काष्ठग्रहणी, काष्ठधरणी, दारुछिद्रं, दारुसीवनं, काष्ठसीवनं, काष्ठरन्ध्रं.

To MORTISE, *v. a.* अन्यकाष्ठधरणार्थम् एककाष्ठाग्रं छिद् (c. 7. छिनत्ति, छेत्तुं), काष्ठद्वयसन्धानं कृ, काष्ठद्वयं सन्धा (c. 3. -दधाति -धातुं).

MORTMAIN, *s.* अन्यादेयभोगः, परादेयभोगः, अदेयभोगः.

MORUNGA, *s.* (Plant) शोभाञ्जनः, शोभनकः, शौभाञ्जनः, सोभाञ्जनः, शिग्रुः *m.*, तीक्ष्णगन्धः -न्धकः, अक्षीवः, आक्षीवः, काक्षीवः, मोचकः; 'its root,' शिग्रुमूलं; 'seed,' शिग्रुजं, शिग्रुवीजं.

MOSAIC, *a.* नानावर्णप्रस्तरखचितः -ता -तं, नानाविधप्रस्तरच्छुरितः -ता -तं, नानावर्णद्रव्यप्रविहितः &c.; 'mosaic work,' चित्रकर्म्म *n.* (न्).

MOSQUE, *s.* यावनधर्म्ममण्डपः, यावनधर्म्ममन्दिरं, यावनप्रासादः.

MOSS, *s.* शिलावल्का, शैवलः, शैवालः, शेवलः, शेवालः, शेपालः, शैवं, कावारं, मूकरी, शूकरी, शूकराक्रान्ता, वराहक्रान्ता.

MOSS-GROWN, *a.* शैवलावृतः -ता -तं, शैवलाच्छादितः -ता -तं, रूढशैवलः &c.

MOSSY, *a.* शैवालमयः -यी -यं, सशैवालः -ला -लं, शैवालयुक्तः -क्ता -क्तं, शैवालितः -ता -तं, शेवालविशिष्टः -ष्टा -ष्टं, शैवली -लिनी -लि (न्).

MOST, *a.* भूयिष्ठः -ष्ठा -ष्ठं, अधिकतमः -मा -मं, अधिकतरः -रा -रं, अधिकः -का -कं, अधिकसंख्यकः -का -कं, परमः -मा -मं, उत्तमः -मा -मं; 'the most part,' भूयान् -यसी -यः (स्), भूयिष्ठः &c., बहुतरः -रा -रं, बहुतमः -मा -मं; 'for the most part,' भूयिष्ठं, प्रायस्, प्रायशस्, बाहुल्येन, बहुशस्.

MOST, *adv.* भूयिष्ठं, अधिकं, अधिकतरं, अधिकतमं, भूयस्, परमं; often expressed by the superlative affixes तम and इष्ठ, as, 'most excellent,' श्रेष्ठतमः -मा -मं, श्रेष्ठः -ष्ठा -ष्ठं; 'most heavy,' गुरुतमः -मा -मं, गरिष्ठः &c., or by अति or सु or अत्यन्त or अतिशय prefixed; as, 'most powerful,' अतिबलवान् &c.

MOST, *s.* अधिकभागः, भूयिष्ठभागः, परभागः, परमभागः, बहुतरभागः, बहुतमभागः, अधिकपक्षः, उत्तमभागः, उत्तमपक्षः, अधिकांशः.

MOSTLY, *adv.* भूयिष्ठं, प्रायस्, प्रायशस्, प्रायेण, बहुशस्, बाहुल्येन, बहुधा, भूयस्, सामान्यतस्, बहुतरं, साधारण्येन.

MOTE, *s.* अणुः *m.*, अणुरेणुः *m.*, त्रसरेणुः *m. f.*, रिक्षा, लिक्षा, कणः, कणिका, पारिमाण्डल्यं, अणुरेणुजालं, जालसूर्य्यमरीचिस्थं रजस्, जालकान्तरप्रविष्टादित्यरश्मिस्थितं यद्रजस्, ध्वंसी *m.* (न्), समागमः.

MOTH, *s.* पतङ्गः, पतङ्गमः, पतङ्गिका, शलभः, शरभः, कीटः; 'moth-like,' शालभः -भी -भं.

MOTH-EATEN, *a.* कीटभक्षितः -ता -तं, कीटखादितः -ता -तं.

MOTHER, *s.* माता *f.* (तृ), जननी, जनयित्री, जनिका, प्रजनिका, प्रजायिनी, प्रसविनी, प्रसवित्री, प्रसवकर्त्री, प्रसूः *f.*, सूः *f.*, अम्बा, अम्बिका, अम्बालिका, जनी, प्रसवस्थली, धात्री, मा, उत्पादिका; 'mother of a son or of offspring,' पुत्रिणी, पुत्रवती, सुतिनी, सुतवती, प्रजावती, अपत्यवती; 'of one child,' एकोदरा; 'of seven children,' सुतवस्करा; 'who has recently had a child,' प्रसूतिका, सूतिका, प्रसूता; 'step-mother,' विमाता *f.* (तृ), सपत्नी माता; 'mother-in-law,' श्वश्रूः *f.*; 'mother and father,' मातापितरौ *m.* du., मातरपितरौ; 'mother of a hero,' वीरप्रसविनी; 'mother's house,' मातृगृहं; 'mother's family,' मातृकुलं; 'born of a different mother,' भिन्नोदरः -रा -रं, अन्योदरः &c., असोदरः &c.

MOTHER, *a.* (Native) स्वाभाविकः -की -कं, साहजिकः -की -कं, सहजः -जा -जं, जन्म or जाति in comp.; as, 'mother-tongue,' जन्मभाषा, जातिभाषा; 'mother-country,' जन्मभूमिः *f.*

MOTHER-IN-LAW, *s.* श्वश्रूः *f.*, गुरुपत्नी; 'mother and father in law,' श्वश्रूश्वशुरौ *m.* du.

MOTHER-OF-PEARL, *s.* शुक्तिवधूः *f.*, शुक्तिपुटं, मुक्तास्फोटः, मुक्तागारं.

MOTHERHOOD, *s.* मातृत्वं -ता, जननीत्वं, मातृभावः, पुत्रिणीत्वं, सुतिनीत्वं.

MOTHERLESS, *a.* अमातृकः -का -कं, मातृहीनः -ना -नं, मृतमातृकः &c., मातृरहितः -ता -तं, गतमातृकः -का -कं, हीनमातृकः &c.

MOTHERLY, *a.* मातृसन्निभः -भा -भं, मातृसदृशः -शी -शं, मातृकल्पः -ल्पा -ल्पं, मातृतुल्यः -ल्या -ल्यं, मातृकः -का -कं, मातृ in comp.

MOTHERLY, *adv.* मातृवत्, मातृरूपेण, मातृभावेन, मातृधर्म्मानुसारेण.

MOTION, *s.* गतिः *f.*, गमनं, चलनं, चारः, चरणं, सञ्चरणं, सरणं, चोपनं, खेलितं, खेलिका; 'swift motion,' त्वरितगतिः *f.*; 'slow motion,' मन्दगतिः *f.*, मन्दगमनं; 'backward motion,' विपरीतगतिः *f.*—(Animal action) चेष्टा, चेष्टितं.—(Gesture) इङ्गितं, इङ्गः, अङ्ग-

विक्षेपः, चाञ्चल्यचेष्टा.—(Agitation) क्षोभः, अन्तःक्षोभः, वेगः.—(Impulse, feeling) वेगः, मनोवेगः, मनोवृत्तिः f., मनोविकारः, रागः, चित्तरागः, चित्तक्षोभः, भावः, वासना, वृत्तिः f., कल्पना, रसः.—(Proposition made) कर्त्तव्योपन्यासः, उपन्यासः, कर्त्तव्यसूचकवाक्यं, वाक्यं.—(Stool) रेकः, रेचनं -ना, उच्चारः, उच्चरितं; 'to put in motion,' चल् (c. 10. चालयति -यितुं).

To MOTION, *v. a.* इङ्गितं कृ, सङ्केतं कृ, अङ्गविक्षेपं कृ, अङ्गसञ्चालनं कृ.

MOTIONLESS, *a.* अचलः -ला -लं, निश्चलः -ला -लं, निश्चेष्टः -ष्टा -ष्टं, अचेष्टः &c., निश्चेष्टः &c., गतिहीनः -ना -नं, गतिशून्यः -न्या -न्यं, निष्कम्पः -म्पा -म्पं, अस्पन्दः -न्दा -न्दं, निष्पन्दः &c., स्थिरः -रा -रं, स्तब्धः -ब्धा -ब्धं, अगतिकः -का -कं, स्तब्धः -ब्धा -ब्धं.

MOTIVE, *a.* (Causing motion, &c.) चालकः -का -कं, प्रवर्त्तकः -का -कं, सञ्चारकः -का -कं, प्रयोजकः -का -कं, व्यापारी -रिणी -रि (न्), हेतुकः -का -कं, कारणिकः -की -कं.

MOTIVE, *s.* (That which incites to action, cause) प्रयोजनं, हेतुः *m.*, कारणं, निमित्तं -त्तकं, प्रवृत्तिनिमित्तं, प्रवर्त्तकं, प्रयोजकं, प्रयोगः, उत्तेजनं, उत्तेजकं, निदानं, निबन्धनं, कार्य्यं; 'without motive,' अकस्मात्, निष्प्रयोजनं, असति प्रयोजने, अकारणात्, हेतुना विना; 'relation between the motive and the effect,' प्रयोज्यप्रयोजकभावः.

MOTLEY, *a.* चित्रविचित्रः -त्रा -त्रं, नानाविधः -धा -धं, नानाप्रकारः -रा -रं, नानावर्णः -र्णा -र्णं, नानारूपः -पा -पं, भिन्नरूपः -पा -पं, नानारङ्गी -ङ्गिणी -ङ्गि (न्), बहुरङ्गी &c., विविधः &c.

MOTOR, MOTORY, *a.* चालकः -का -कं, सञ्चारकः -का -कं, सारकः &c.

MOTTLED, *a.* चित्रितः -ता -तं, चित्रः -त्रा -त्रं, कर्व्वुरितः -ता -तं.

MOTTO, *s.* वाक्यं, वचनं, लेखः, श्लोकः, कविता, विज्ञापनलेखः, मुद्रालेखः.

MOULD, *s.* (Earth, soil) मृत्तिका, मृद् *f.*, मृदा, पांशुः *m.*, भूमिः *f.*, स्थलं; 'black mould,' नीलमृत्तिका.—(Concretion formed from damp) कलङ्कः, शुक्लकलङ्कः, क्लेदजकलङ्कः, क्लेदजमलं.—(Cast) संस्कारः, आकारः, आकृतिः *f.*, मूर्त्तिः *f.*, संस्थानं, संयानः, रूपं.

To MOULD, *v. a.* (Cause to contract mould) सकलङ्कं -ङ्कां कृ, कलङ्केन दुष् (c. 10. दूषयति -यितुं), कलङ्क (nom. कलङ्कयति -यितुं), क्लेदजमलेन दुष्.—(Fashion, form) संस्कृ, क्लृप् (c. 10. कल्पयति -यितुं), रूप् (c. 10. रूपयति -यितुं), सरूपं -पां कृ, रच् (c. 10. रचयति -यितुं), संस्कारं कृ.

To MOULD, *v. n.* (Contract mould) सकलङ्कः -ङ्का -ङ्कं भू, क्लेदव्याप्तत्वात् शुक्लकलङ्कं or शुक्लमलं बन्ध् (c. 9. बध्नाति, बन्द्धुं), कलङ्कावृतः -ता -तं भू.

MOULDED, *p. p.* कल्पितः -ता -तं, संस्कृतः -ता -तं.—(Kneaded) मर्द्दितः &c.

To MOULDER, *v. n.* चूर्णीभू, क्षि in pass. (क्षीयते), विशॄ in pass. (-शीर्य्यते), विशीर्णीभू, जॄ (c. 4. जीर्य्यति), शनैः शनैः क्षि or नश् (c. 4. नश्यति), अल्पाल्पशः क्षीणीभू or न्यूनीभू.

MOULDERING, *part.* शनैः शनैः क्षीयमाणः -णा -णं, अल्पाल्पं विशीर्य्यमाणः &c.

MOULDINESS, MOLDINESS, *s.* सकलङ्कता, समलता, मलिनता, कलङ्कवत्त्वं.

MOULDING, MOLDING, *s.* संस्कारः.—(Projecture of a wall) भित्तिशीर्षं -र्षकं.

MOULDY, *a.* सकलङ्कः -ङ्का -ङ्कं, समलः -ला -लं, मलिनः -ना -नं, कलङ्कावृतः -ता -तं, कलङ्कमयः -यी -यं, कलङ्कवान् -वती -वत् (त्), मलावृतः &c., शुक्लकलङ्कावृतः &c.

To MOULT, MOLT, *v. n.* (Shed the feathers) पक्षान् or वार्षिकपक्षान् पत् (c. 10. पातयति -यितुं) or मुच् (c. 6. मुञ्चति, मोक्तुं, c. 10. मोचयति -यितुं) or निर्मुच्, वार्षिकपक्षपातं कृ, पक्षनिर्मोकं कृ, पक्षगलनं कृ, पक्षपरिवर्त्तनं कृ.

MOULTED, *p. p.* गलितपक्षः -क्षा -क्षं, मुक्तपक्षः &c., पतितपर्णः -र्णा -र्णं.

MOULTING, *s.* पक्षपातः, पक्षपतनं, वार्षिकपक्षपतनं, पक्षनिर्मोकः, पक्षगलनं, वार्षिकपक्षगलनं, वार्षिकपक्षपरिवर्त्तनं.

MOUND, *s.* (Bank, rampart) वप्रः -प्रं, चयः, सेतुः *m.*, पिण्डनः, पिण्डलः, प्राकारः, धूलिकुट्टिमं, धूलिकेदारः.—(Elevation, hillock, heap of earth) मृत्तिकाचयः, उन्नतभूभागः, क्षुद्रपर्व्वतः, नाकुः *m.*, वामलूरः.

To MOUNT, *v. n.* (Rise on high) ऊर्द्ध्वं गम् (c. 1. गच्छति, गन्तुं), उपरि गम्, उच्चैर् गम्, ऊर्द्ध्वगमनं कृ, उपरिगमनं कृ.—(Mount on horseback) अश्वम् आरुह् (c. 1. -रोहति -रोढुं) or अधिरुह् or अध्यारुह् or समारुह् or अभिरुह् or अधिक्रम् (c. 1. -क्रामति -क्रमितुं), अश्वारोहणं कृ; 'to mount along side,' अन्वारुह्, समन्वारुह्.

To MOUNT, *v. a.* (Raise on high) ऊर्द्ध्वीकृ, उच्चीकृ, ऊर्द्ध्वं गम् (c. 10. गमयति -यितुं), उच्चैः कृ.—(Climb, ascend, as a hill or a horse) आरुह् (c. 1. -रोहति -रोढुं), अधिरुह्, अध्यारुह्, समारुह्, अभिरुह्, अधिक्रम् (c. 1. -क्रामति -क्रमितुं), अवस्कन्द् (c. 1. -स्कन्दति -स्कन्तुं), आरोहणं कृ.—(Place upon) आरुह् in caus. (-रोपयति -यितुं), समारुह्.

MOUNTAIN, *s.* पर्व्वतः, गिरिः *m.*, शैलः, अद्रिः *m.*, महीधरः, भूधरः, वसुधाधरः, धरणीधरः, धराधरः, महीध्रः, जगतीधरः, भूभृत् *m.*, भूध्रः, क्ष्माभृत् *m.*, क्षितिधरः, उर्व्वीधरः, कुध्रः, धरः, धरणीकीलकः, शिखरी *m.* (न्), पृथुशेखरः, तुङ्गशेखरः, सानुमान् *m.* (त्), ककुद्मान् *m.* (त्), ककुद्मी *m.* (न्), नगः, शिलोच्चयः, गोत्रः, अहार्य्यः, ग्रावा *m.* (न्), वलाहकः, पृथुनितम्बः; 'crest or peak of a mountain,' शिखरं, गिरिशिखरं, पर्व्वतशृङ्गं, पर्व्वताग्रं, पर्व्वतमस्तकः, ककुद् *f.*; 'brow of a mountain,' गिरिमूर्द्धा *m.* (न्); 'side or ridge,' कटकः, नितम्बः; 'mountain with three peaks,' त्रिकूटः, त्रिककुद् *m.*; 'Western mountain, behind which the sun sets,' अस्तः, चरमाचलः, चरमाद्रिः *m.*, चरमक्ष्माभृत् *m.*, पश्चिमपर्व्वतः; 'Eastern mountain, over which the sun rises,' उदयः, उदयपर्व्वतः, उदयगिरिः *m.*, उदयशैलः, उदयाचलः, उदयाद्रिः *m.*, पूर्व्वपर्व्वतः; 'hill near a mountain,' पादः, प्रत्यन्तपर्व्वतः; 'land at the foot of a mountain,' उपत्यका; 'on the top,' अधित्यका; 'range of mountains,' कुलपर्व्वतः, कुलाचलः, कुलगिरिः *m.*, कुलशैलः. There are seven principal ranges of mountains given, viz. महेन्द्रः, मलयः, सह्यः, शुक्तिमान्, ऋक्षः, विन्ध्यः, पारिपात्रः -त्रकः or पारियात्रः -त्रकः. Other names of celebrated mountains or mountain ranges are हिमवान्, हिमालयः, हिमाद्रिः *m.*, हेमकूटः, चक्रकूटः, माल्यवान् *m.* (त्), निषधः, मैनाकः also called हिरण्यनाभः and हिमवत्सुतः, गन्धमादनः, चित्रकूटः, क्रौञ्चः or क्रोञ्चः.

MOUNTAIN, *a.* पार्व्वतः -ती -तं, पर्व्वतीयः -या -यं, पार्व्वतीयः -या -यं, गैरः -री -रं, गैरिकः -की -कं, गैरेयः -यी -यं, शैलः -ली -लं, पार्व्वतेयः -यी -यं, पर्व्वत or गिरि in comp.; as, 'mountain torrent,' गिरिनदी.

MOUNTAINEER, *s.* पर्व्वतवासी *m.* (न्), गिरिवासी *m.*, पर्व्वतीयजनः, पार्व्वतीयः, गिरिजः, शैलजनः, गिरिभूः *m.*, शैलाटः.

MOUNTAINOUS, *a.* पार्व्वतीयः -या -यं, पार्व्वतेयः -यी -यं, पर्व्वतीयः -या -यं, सपर्व्वतः -ता -तं, पर्व्वतमयः -यी -यं, सशैलः -ला -लं, समहीधरः -रा -रं.

MOUNTEBANK, *s.* छद्मवैद्यः, मिथ्यावैद्यः, कितवः, धूर्त्तः, कापटिकः.

MOUNTED, *p. p.* आरूढः -ढा -ढं, आरोपितः -ता -तं, रोपितः -ता -तं, समारोपितः -ता -तं, समारूढः &c., अधिरूढः &c., रूढः &c.; 'on horseback,' अश्वारूढः, अश्वारोही *m.* (न्), हयारूढः, तुरगारूढः.

MOUNTING, *s.* (Rising) ऊर्द्ध्वगमनं, उपरिगमनं.—(Ascending, getting on horseback) आरोहः -हणं, अधिरोहणं, समारोहः -हणं.—

(Placing on horseback) आरोपणं, समारोपणं, आरूढीकरणं.

To MOURN, *v. n.* शुच् (c. 1. शोचति -चितुं), अनुशुच्, परिशुच्, शोकं कृ, शोकार्त्तः -र्त्ता -र्त्तं भू, शोचनं कृ, खिद् (c. 4. खिद्यते, खेत्तुं), परिखिद्, दुःख (nom. दुःखायते, दुःखीयते), विलप् (c. 1. -लपति -पितुं), प्रलप्, लप्, उद्विज् (c. 6. -विजते -जितुं), व्यथ् (c. 1. व्यथते -थितुं), प्रव्यथ्, सम्प्रव्यथ्, तप् in pass. (तप्यते), परितप्, सन्तप्, रुद् (c. 2. रोदिति -तुं), परिदेव् (c. 1. -देवते -वितुं), दु (c. 4. दूयते); 'mourn exceedingly,' शुच् in freq. (शोशुच्यते).

To MOURN, *v. a.* (Grieve for) अनुशुच् (c. 1. -शोचति -चितुं), परिदेव् (c. 1. -देवति -ते -वितुं), विलप् (c. 1. -लपति -पितुं), क्रन्द् (c. 1. क्रन्दति -न्दितुं), आक्रन्द्, रुद् (c. 2. रोदिति -तुं), अभिक्रुश् (c. 1. -क्रोशति -क्रोष्टुं).

MOURNED, *p. p.* शोचितः -ता -तं, अनुशोचितः &c., विलपितः -ता -तं.

MOURNER, *s.* शोचकः, अनुशोचकः, शोकी *m.* (न्), खेदी *m.* (न्), परिदेवी *m.* (न्), परिदेवकः, विलपनकृत् *m.*, विलापी *m.*, शोककर्त्ता *m.* (र्त्तृ), अनुतापी *m.*, खिद्यमानः.—(One who wears a funeral dress) अमङ्गलवेषी *m.* (न्).

MOURNFUL, *a.* (Expressing sorrow) शोकसूचकः -का -कं, खेदसूचकः &c., शोकबोधकः -का -कं, शोकार्थकः -का -कं.—(Sorrowful, said of persons) शोकी -किनी -कि (न्), शोकार्त्तः -र्त्ता -र्त्तं, शोकान्वितः -ता -तं, सशोकः -का -कं, खेदी &c., खेदयुक्तः -क्ता -क्तं, खिन्नः -न्ना -न्नं, उद्विग्नः -ग्ना -ग्नं, उद्विग्नमनाः -नाः -नः (स्), विषादी &c., दुःखी &c., दुःखान्वितः -ता -तं, दुर्मनाः &c., विमनाः &c., समन्युः -न्युः -न्यु.—(Causing sorrow, lamentable) शोकजनकः &c., शोकदः -दा -दं, शोचनीयः -या -यं, शोच्यः -च्या -च्यं, शोचितव्यः -व्या -व्यं, शोकावहः -हा -हं, दुःखावहः &c., खेदजनकः -का -कं, शोकार्हः -र्हा -र्हं, शोचनार्हः &c.

MOURNFULLY, *adv.* सशोकं, सखेदं, सदुःखं, सोद्वेगं, शोकेन, शोकपूर्व्वं.

MOURNFULNESS, *s.* शोकः, सशोकता, दुःखं, दुःखिता, उद्वेगः, उद्विग्नता, खेदः, शोच्यता, शोचनीयता, शोकजनकता.

MOURNING, *s.* (Sorrow, lamentation) शोकः, शोचनं, अनुशोचनं, खेदः, विलपनं, विलापः, परिदेवनं -ना, रोदनं, रुदनं, क्रन्दनं, आक्रन्दनं, दुःखं.—(Dress worn by mourners) अमङ्गलवेषः, अशुभवेषः, अमङ्गलकालीनवेषः, अशुभकालीनवेषः, शोकसूचकवेषः. According to the Hindu notion defilement is contracted by the death of a relation; hence the following terms, expressive of a season of mourning, imply a season of impurity; as, अशौचं, आशौचं, कालाशौचं, अघाहः; 'one in such a state,' आशौची -चिनी -चि (न्).

MOUSE, *s.* मूषिकः -का, मूषकः, आखुः *m.*, इन्दुरः, इन्दूरुः *m.*, गिरिः *f.*, गिरिका, दीना, बिलेशयः, वज्रदन्तः, धान्यारिः *m.*, चिक्का.

MOUSE-TRAP, *s.* मूषिकग्रहणार्थं कूटयन्त्रं, मूषिकोन्माथः, मूषिकपञ्जरः.

MOUTH, *s.* मुखं, वदनं, आस्यं, वक्त्रं, आननं, लपनं, तुण्डं -ण्डः, तुण्डिः -ण्डी *m. f.*, ज्मन् indec.; 'the corner of the mouth,' सृक्कन् *n.*, सृक्कं, सृक्वन् *n.*, सृक्वं, सृक्कि *n.*, सृक्वि *n.*, सृक्विन् *n.*, सृक्किन्, सृक्किणी *f.*, सृक्विणी; 'the two corners,' सृक्कणी *n.* du., ओष्ठप्रान्तौ *m.* du.; 'dryness of the mouth,' मुखशोषः; 'washing the mouth,' मुखमार्ज्जनं, मुखप्रक्षालनं; 'rincing the mouth,' आचमनं; 'to open the mouth', मुखं व्यादा; 'to stop the mouth,' वाक्स्तम्भं कृ; 'from the mouth,' मुखतस्; 'relating to the mouth,' मुखतीयः -या -यं.—(Aperture, orifice) मुखं, छिद्रं, द्वारं, प्रमुखं.—(Mouth of a river) सम्भेदः, सङ्गमः, सिन्धुसङ्गमः.

To MOUTH, *v. a.* and *n.* (Speak with a big pompous voice) उच्चैःस्वरेण or गर्व्वितस्वरेण वद् (c. 1. वदति -दितुं), उद्धतस्वरेण वद्.—(Chew, devour) चर्व्व् (c. 1. चर्व्वति -र्व्वितुं, c. 10. चर्व्वयति -यितुं), ग्रस् (c. 1. ग्रसति -सितुं), भक्ष् (c. 10. भक्षयति -यितुं).

MOUTHFUL, *s.* ग्रासः, पिण्डः, मुखपूरणं, कवलः, कवकः, गण्डूषः -षा, गडोलः, गण्डोलः, गुडेरः -रकः, सिनः; 'three mouthfuls of water,' जलगण्डूषत्रयं.

MOUTHLESS, *a.* मुखहीनः -ना -नं, मुखरहितः -ता -तं, निर्मुखः -खा -खं.

MOUTHPIECE, *s.* मुखनाली, पुटः, जिह्वाली; 'of a flute,' दर्दुरपुटः.—(One who speaks for others) मुखं.

MOVABLE, *a.* चरः -रा -रं, चरिष्णुः -ष्णुः -ष्णु, चलः -ला -लं, चलनः -ना -नं, चलिष्णुः &c., जङ्गमः -मा -मं, गमनशीलः -ला -लं, गमनयोग्यः -ग्या -ग्यं, गमनशक्यः -क्या -क्यं, अस्थावरः -रा -रं, त्रसः -सा -सं, जगन् -गती -गत् (त्), इङ्गः -ङ्गा -ङ्गं, चलनक्षमः -मा -मं; 'movable and immovable,' चराचरः -रा -रं, चलाचलः -ला -लं.

MOVABLENESS, *s.* चरिष्णुता, चलिष्णुता, गमनशीलता, चलनयोग्यता, गतिशीलत्वं, अस्थावरता, चरभावः, चलभावः, गमनशक्तिः *f.*

MOVABLES, *s. pl.* अस्थावराणि *n. pl.*, अस्थावरद्रव्यं -व्याणि *n. pl.*, चरद्रव्याणि, चलद्रव्याणि, जङ्गमद्रव्याणि, अस्थावरधनं.

To MOVE, *v. a.* (Put in motion, cause to change place) चल् (c. 10. चालयति -यितुं), विचल्, सञ्चल्, सृ (c. 10. सारयति -यितुं), चर् (c. 10. चारयति -यितुं), सञ्चर्, स्थानान्तरं गम् (c. 10. गमयति -यितुं), स्थानान्तरीकृ.—(Impel) प्रेर् (c. 10. -ईरयति -यितुं), नुद् (c. 6. नुदति, नोत्तुं), प्रणुद्, चुद् (c. 10. चोदयति -यितुं), प्रचुद्, सञ्चुद्.—(Draw) कृष् (c. 1. कर्षति, c. 6. कृषति -ते, क्रष्टुं), समाकृष्.—(Incite to action, influence) प्रवृत् (c. 10. -वर्त्तयति -यितुं), प्रयुज् (c. 10. -योजयति -यितुं), प्रोत्सह् (c. 10. -साहयति -यितुं), उत्सह्, चेष्ट् (c. 10. चेष्टयति -यितुं), प्ररुच् (c. 10. -रोचयति -यितुं), प्रेर्.—(Excite tenderness, pity, &c.) कारुण्यं जन् (c. 10. जनयति -यितुं), कारुण्यं or दयाम् उत्पद् (c. 10. -पादयति -यितुं), हृदयं व्यध् (c. 4. विध्यति, व्यद्धुं), हृदयं स्पृश् (c. 6. स्पृशति, स्प्रष्टुं), हृदयम् आर्द्रीकृ.—(Affect) उपहन् (c. 2. -हन्ति -न्तुं); 'with grief,' शोकोपहतं -तां कृ.—(Agitate) क्षुभ् (c. 10. क्षोभयति -यितुं), विक्षुभ्, आक्षुभ्.—(Make a proposal) उपन्यस् (c. 4. -अस्यति -असितुं), कर्त्तव्योपन्यासं कृ, कर्त्तव्योपस्थापनं कृ, कर्त्तव्योद्भावनं कृ.—(Move away, move off) अपसृ, अपानुद्, अपनुद्, व्यपनुद्.—(Move a piece at chess) शारिं परिणी (c. 1. -णयति -णेतुं) or समन्तात् नी, शारिपरिणायं कृ.

To MOVE, *v. n.* चल् (c. 1. चलति -लितुं), सृ (c. 1. सरति, सर्त्तुं), प्रसृ, चर् (c. 1. चरति -रितुं), गम् (c. 1. गच्छति, गन्तुं), या (c. 2. याति -तुं), इ (c. 2. एति -तुं), इङ्ग् (c. 1. इङ्गति -ङ्गितुं), चुप् (c. 1. चोपति -पितुं), अंह् (c. 1. अंहते -हितुं), गतिविशिष्टः -ष्टा -ष्टं भू.—(Change place) स्थानान्तरं गम्, स्थलान्तरं गम् or या.—(Change residence) गृहान्तरं गम्, वासान्तरं गम्.—(Have vital action) चेष्ट् (c. 1. चेष्टते -ष्टितुं), आत्मानं चेष्ट्, चेष्टां कृ.—(Begin a march) प्रस्थानं कृ, प्रस्था (c. 1. -तिष्ठति -स्थातुं); 'move on,' प्रसृ, प्रगम्, प्रया, चल्; 'move off,' अपसृ, अपया, अपक्रम् (c. 1. -क्रामति, क्रमितुं), अपगम्; 'move about,' इतस्ततः सृ or चल्, परिसृ.

MOVE, *s.* चलनं, सरणं, गमनं, चेष्टा, इङ्गितं, स्थानान्तरं, स्थानान्तरगमनं.—(At chess, &c.) परिणायः, परीणायः, शारिनयनं, खेला -लनं.

MOVED, *p. p.* चालितः -ता -तं, चलितः -ता -तं, चारितः -ता -तं, सञ्चारितः -ता -तं, सारितः -ता -तं, प्रचलितः -ता -तं, स्थानान्तरगतः -ता -तं, स्थानान्तरप्राप्तः -प्ता -प्तं, स्थलान्तरापन्नः -न्ना -न्नं.—(Impelled) प्रेरितः

-ता -तं, प्रचोदितः -ता -तं, प्रणुन्नः -न्ना -न्नं, प्रचोदितः -ता -तं.—(Drawn) कृष्टः -ष्टा -ष्टं, कर्षितः -ता -तं.—(Incited) प्रवर्त्तितः -ता -तं, प्रयोजितः -ता -तं, नियोजितः -ता -तं, प्रोत्साहितः &c., प्रवृत्तः -त्ता -त्तं.—(Excited to pity) जातकारुण्यः -ण्या -ण्यं, जातदयः -या -यं, दयास्पृष्टहृदयः -या -यं.—(Affected) स्पृष्टः -ष्टा -ष्टं, उपहतः -ता -तं.—(Agitated) क्षुब्धः -ब्धा -ब्धं, क्षोभितः -ता -तं.

Movement, *s.* चलनं, सरणं, चारः, चरणं, सञ्चरणं, गतिः *f.*, गमनं, गमः, चोपनं, चेष्टा, चेष्टितं, इङ्गितं, स्थानान्तरं, स्थलान्तरं, स्थानान्तरगमनं, स्थानभेदः.—(Agitation) क्षोभः, कम्पः.—(In music) ग्रामः, तालः, मूर्च्छना.

Mover, *s.* (That which gives motion) चालकः, सारकः, सञ्चारकः.—(That which moves) चरः, चलः, चलनः.—(Proposer) उपन्यासकृत्, कर्त्तव्योपन्यासकृत्, कर्त्तव्योपस्थापकः.—(One who impels to action) प्रवर्त्तयिता *m.* (तृ), प्रवर्त्तकः, प्रयोजकः, प्रेरकः.

Moving, *a.* (Exciting the affections) करुणाजनकः -का -कं, कारुण्योत्पादकः &c., दयाजनकः &c., करुणात्मकः &c., हृदयवेधकः &c., हृदयङ्गमः -मा -मं, हृदयस्पृक् (श्), मर्म्मस्पृक्, हृदयभेदी -दिनी -दि (न्), चित्तवेधकः &c., चित्तद्रावकः &c., भावार्द्रकारी &c., चित्तार्द्रकारी &c.

Moving, *part.* चलन् -लन्ती -लत् (त्), सरन् &c., चरन् &c., चलः -ला -लं, चरः -रा -रं, सरः -रा -रं, सरणः -णा -णं, चलनः -ना -नं, जङ्गमः -मा -मं, कम्पनः -ना -नं, गतिमान् -मती -मत् (त्), गामी -मिनी &c., चारी &c., सारी &c., यायी &c., सर्पी &c., गत्वरः -रा -रं, सृत्वरः -रा -रं; 'moving in the air,' आकाशगामी &c.

Movingly, *adv.* यथा हृदयं स्पृश्यते तथा, यथा करुणा जायते तथा, यथा कारुण्यम् उत्पद्यते तथा.

Mow, *s.* (Of hay or grain) तृणराशिः *m.*, धान्यराशिः *m.*, धान्यचितिः *f.*, धान्यचयः, धान्यसञ्चयः, तृणोत्करः, धान्योत्करः.

To mow, *v. a.* दात्रेण or लवित्रेण छिद् (c. 7. छिनत्ति, छेत्तुं) or अवछिद् or लू (c. 9. लुनाति, लवितुं) or कृत् (c. 6. कृन्तति, कर्त्तितुं) or अवकृत्, दो or दा (c. 4. द्यति, c. 2. दाति -तुं).

Mowed, mown, *p. p.* दात्रच्छिन्नः -न्ना -न्नं, दात्रलूनः -ना -नं, लवित्रच्छिन्नः &c., कर्त्तितः -ता -तं, अवकर्त्तितः &c., छिन्नः &c., लूनः &c.

Mower, *s.* तृणच्छेदकः, तृणच्छिद्, तृणलवकः, तृणलविता *m.* (तृ), निदाता *m.*

Mowing, *s.* तृणच्छेदः -दनं, तृणलवनं, तृणकर्त्तनं, तृणलावः.

Much, *a.* बहुः -हुः -ह्वी -हु, बहुलः -ला -लं, प्रचुरः -रा -रं, विपुलः -ला -लं, बहुसंख्यकः -का -कं, भूरिः -रिः -रि, भृशः -शा -शं, सुभृशः &c., गाढः -ढा -ढं, प्रगाढः &c., बाढः &c., उद्गाढः &c., निर्भरः -रा -रं, भरः, अत्यन्तः -न्ता -न्तं, अत्यर्थः -र्था -र्थं, अतिरिक्तः -क्ता -क्तं, अतिमात्रः -त्रा -त्रं, नितान्तः -न्ता -न्तं, प्राज्यः -ज्या -ज्यं, पुष्कलः -ला -लं, भूयान् -यसी -यः (स्), भूयिष्ठः -ष्ठा -ष्ठं, प्रभूतः -ता -तं, उत्कटः -टा -टं, पुरुः -रुः -रु, पुरुहः -हा -हं, पुरुहुः -हुः -हु, अदभ्रः -भ्रा -भ्रं, स्फिरः -रा -रं, अतिवेलः -ला -लं, अति or अतिशय or सु prefixed; as, 'much pain,' अतिव्यथा, अतिशयवेदना; 'much time,' बहुकालः, दीर्घकालः; 'as much,' यावान् -वती -वत् (त्), यतिः -तिः -ति; 'so much,' तावान् &c., एतावान् &c., इयान् -यती &c., ततिः -तिः -ति; 'so much time,' तावत्कालं; 'how much?' कियान् &c., कियत्प्रमाणः -णा -णं, कतिः -तिः -ति, कतिथः -था -थं, कतिपयथः &c.; 'how much time?' कियत्कालं, कियन्तं कालं.

Much, *adv.* बहु, भृशं, भूरि, गाढं, निर्भरं, अत्यन्तं, अतिशयं -येन, अत्यर्थं, नितान्तं, प्रगाढं, उद्गाढं, अतिमात्रं, एकान्ततस्, तीव्रं, अतितरां, सुतरां, महा in comp., सुमहत्, बलवत्, अति or अतिशय or सु prefixed; 'as much,' यावत्; 'so much,' तावत्, एतावत्, तावन्मात्रं, इयत्; 'how much?' कियत्, कति; 'how much more?' किमुत, किम्पुनर्, सुतरां.

Much, *s.* बहुत्वं, बाहुल्यं, प्राचुर्य्यं, भूयस् *n.*, बहुभागः; 'much of what we know about the heavens is founded on calculation,' आकाशीयज्ञानभूयो गणितेन जायते; 'to make much of,' बहु मन् (c. 4. मन्यते, मन्तुं).

Muchness, *s.* बहुत्वं -ता, बाहुल्यं, प्राचुर्य्यं, प्राज्यता, प्रचुरता -त्वं, विपुलता.

Mucilage, *s.* मेदस् *n.*, वसा, वपा, अस्थिस्नेहः, अस्थिमेदस् *n.*, कफः, श्लेष्मा *m.* (न्), श्लेष्मकः, चिक्कणवस्तु *n.*, मेदुरवस्तु, स्निग्धवस्तु.

Mucilaginous, *a.* चिक्कणः -णा -णं, चिक्किणः -णा -णं, मेदुरः -रा -रं, श्लेष्मणः -णा -णं, कफमयः -यी -यं, कफगुणकः -का -कं, मेदस्वी -स्विनी -स्वि (न्), स्निग्धः -ग्धा -ग्धं, श्लेष्मलः -ला -लं.

Muck, *s.* (Dung) पुरीषं, गोमयं, अमेध्यं.—(Dirt) मलं, अमेध्यं, पङ्कः, कुपङ्कः, कर्दमः, कल्कं, जम्बालः -लं, कलुषं; 'To run a muck,' उन्मत्तवद् अभिधाव्य यान् काँश्चित् सम्मुखीभूतजनान् अभिहन् (c. 2. -हन्ति -न्तुं).

To muck, *v. a.* अमेध्येन or मलेन लिप् (c. 6. लिम्पति, लेप्तुं), पङ्केन लिप्.

Muck-heap, muck-hill, *s.* अमेध्यराशिः *m.*, मलराशिः *m.*, मलसञ्चयः.

Muck-sweat, *s.* भृशस्वेदः, अतिस्वेदः, निर्भरस्वेदः, अत्यन्तस्वेदः.

Muck-worm, *s.* अमेध्यकीटः, मलजः कीटः, पङ्कजः कृमिः.

Mucky, *a.* समलः -ला -लं, मलवान् -वती -वत् (त्), मलिनः -ना -नं, मलमयः -यी -यं, पङ्की -ङ्किनी -ङ्कि (न्), मलपङ्की &c., पङ्किलः -ला -लं, अमेध्यः -ध्या -ध्यं, कलुषी &c., सकर्दमः -मा -मं.

Mucous, muculent, *a.* (Slimy, like mucus) चिक्कणः -णा -णं, चिक्किणः -णा -णं, मेदुरः -रा -रं, श्लेष्मगुणकः -का -कं, कफगुणः -णा -णं, श्लेष्मगुणः -णा -णं, श्लेष्मलः -ला -लं, श्लेष्मणः -णा -णं, श्लैष्मिकः -की -कं.—(Secreting mucus) कफोत्पादकः -का -कं, श्लेष्मोत्पादकः &c., मलोत्पादकः &c., कफादिमलोत्पादकः &c., श्लेष्मजनकः -का -कं, श्लेष्मकरः -रा -रं, कफकरः &c.

Mucousness, *s.* श्लेष्मत्वं, सश्लेष्मत्वं, सकफत्वं, चिक्कणता, मेदुरता.

Mucus, *s.* (Viscid substance secreted by a mucous membrane) श्लेष्मा *m.* (न्), श्लेष्मादिमलं, कफादिमलं, मलं, इन्द्रियमलं; 'of the nose,' सिंहानं, सिंहाणं, सिङ्घाणं -णकं, शिङ्घाणकं, नासामलं, नासिकामलं; 'of the throat,' कफः, श्लेष्मा *m.* (न्), क्लेदनः, क्लेदकः; 'of the urethra, &c.,' पुष्पिका; 'of the bowels,' आमः.

Mud, *s.* पङ्कः, कर्दमः, जम्बालः -लं, जलकल्कः, निषद्वरः, चिकिलः, शादः, परिखा, दलाढ्यः, चुलुकः, विजपिलं, द्रापः; 'soft mud,' पङ्ककर्वटः; 'free from mud,' निष्पङ्कः -ङ्का -ङ्कं.

Muddiness, *s.* पङ्कता, सपङ्कता, पङ्किलत्वं, सकर्दमता, सजम्बालता, कलुषता, कालुष्यं, समलता, मालिन्यं, मलवत्त्वं, आविलत्वं.

To muddle, *v. a.* कलुष (nom. कलुषयति -यितुं), मलिन (nom. मलिनयति -यितुं), आविल (nom. आविलयति -यितुं), दुष् (c. 10. दूषयति -यितुं), कलुषीकृ, समलीकृ, मलिनीकृ, आविलीकृ.—(Intoxicate slightly) ईषदुन्मत्तीकृ, ईषन्मूढीकृ.

Muddled, *p. p.* कलुषितः -ता -तं, मलिनितः -ता -तं, दूषितः -ता -तं.

Muddy, *a.* पङ्किलः -ला -लं, पङ्की -ङ्किनी -ङ्कि (न्), सपङ्कः -ङ्का -ङ्कं, पङ्कमयः -यी -यं, बहुपङ्कः -ङ्का -ङ्कं, प्रचुरपङ्कः &c., सकर्दमः -मा -मं, कार्दमः -मी -मं, सजम्बालः -ला -लं, मलपङ्की &c., पङ्कधारकः -का -कं.—(Turbid, foul) कलुषः -षा -षं -षी -षिणी -षि (न्), आविलः -ला -लं, मलिनः -ना -नं, समलः -ला -लं, मलवान् -वती &c., मलीमसः -सा -सं, मलदूषितः -ता -तं.

MUDDY-HEADED, MUDDLE-HEADED, *a.* स्थूलबुद्धिः -द्धिः -द्धि, जडबुद्धिः &c.

MUD-WALL, *s.* पङ्कभित्तिः *f.*, पङ्कनिर्म्मितः प्राकारः.

MUFF, *s.* शीतकाले स्त्रीलोकभृतं लोममयं हस्ताच्छादनं or हस्तावरणं or हस्तत्राणं.

MUFFIN, *s.* शिथिलपिष्टकविशेषो यो नवनीताक्तो भूत्वा खाद्यते.

To MUFFLE, *v. a.* मुखग्रीवादि वस्त्रेण बन्ध् (c. 9. बध्नाति, बन्द्धुं) or आवृ (c. 5. -वृणोति -वरितुं -रीतुं) or आच्छद् (c. 10. -च्छादयति -यितुं) or अवरुध् (c. 7. -रुणद्धि -रोद्धुं) or परिवेष्ट् (c. 1. -वेष्टते -ष्टितुं, c. 10. -वेष्टयति -यितुं) or आवेष्ट्.

MUFFLED, *p. p.* वस्त्रबद्धः -द्धा -द्धं, वस्त्रपरिवेष्टितः -ता -तं, वस्त्रावरुद्धः &c., वस्त्राच्छादितः -ता -तं, वस्त्रावृतः -ता -तं, आच्छन्नः -न्ना -न्नं, समाच्छन्नः &c.

MUFFLER, *s.* मुखाच्छादनं, मुखावरणं, मुखाच्छादनवस्त्रं, मुखावगुण्ठनं.

MUG, *s.* पानपात्रं, पानभाजनं, कांस्यं, कंसः -सं, कंशः, कांश्यं, मृत्कांस्यं, जलपात्रं, जलभाजनं, जलाधारः.

MUGGY, MUGGISH, *a.* उष्णाक्लिन्नः -न्ना -न्नं, आर्द्रग्रीष्मः -ष्मा -ष्मं, आर्द्रनिर्वातः -ता -तं, क्लिन्ननिर्वातः -ता -तं.

MULBERRY, *s.* तूदः, पूषः, क्रमुकः, ब्रह्मदारुः *m.*, पाहातः, टङ्कानकः.

MULCT, *s.* दण्डः, धनदण्डः, अर्थदण्डः, पणः, साहसं, दण्डलेशः.

To MULCT, *v. a.* दण्ड् (c. 10. दण्डयति -यितुं), धनं दा in caus. (दापयति -यितुं), साध् (c. 10. साधयति -यितुं), दण्डं प्रणी (c. 1. -णयति -णेतुं).

MULE, *s.* अश्वतरः -री, वेशरः, वेसरः, वेगसरः, खेसरः, प्रखरः, अतिभारगः, मयः, निषुष्वः.

MULETEER, MULE-DRIVER, *s.* अश्वतरपालः -लकः, अश्वतरप्रेरकः, अश्वतरप्रणोदकः, वेशरपः, वेशरपालः.

MULIEBRITY, *s.* स्त्रीता -त्वं, नारीत्वं, स्त्रीभावः, नारीभावः, स्त्रैणं.

MULISH, *a.* अश्वतरस्वभावः -वा -वं, अश्वतरवत् प्रतीपः -पा -पं.

To MULL, *v. a.* व्यञ्जनादिना वास् (c. 10. वासयति -यितुं), वासितं -तां कृ.

MULLER, *s.* शिलापट्टः, शिलापुत्रः -त्रकः, शिला, पेषणं -णिः -णी *f.*, पेषाकः, पेषणशिला, गृहकच्छपः, क्षोदः.

MULLIGRUBS, *s.* अन्त्रशूलं, अन्त्रवेदना, उदरव्यथा, परिणामशूलः -लं.

MULLION, *s.* वातायने or वातायनमध्ये व्यवधायकप्रस्तरः.

MULTANGULAR, *a.* बहुकोणः -णा -णं, बह्वस्रः -स्रा -स्रं, अनेककोणः &c.

MULTIFARIOUS, *a.* बहुविधः -धा -धं, अनेकविधः &c., विविधः &c., पृथग्विधः &c., नानाविधः &c., व्याविधः &c., बहुप्रकारः -रा -रं, अनेकप्रकारः &c., नानारूपः -पा -पं, बहुरूपः &c., भिन्नरूपः &c.

MULTIFORM, *a.* बहुरूपः -पा -पी -पं, नानारूपः &c., अनेकरूपः &c., अनेकाकारः -रा -रं, नानाकारः &c., बहुप्रकारः &c., बहुविधः -धा -धं, नानाप्रकारः &c., नानाकृतिः -तिः -ति.

MULTIFORMITY, *s.* रूपबाहुल्यं, आकारबाहुल्यं, बहुरूपता, नानारूपता, अनेकरूपता, अनेकाकारता, बहुविधता.

MULTILATERAL, *a.* बहुपार्श्वः -र्श्वा -र्श्वं, अनेकपार्श्वः -र्श्वा -र्श्वं.

MULTILINEAL, *a.* बहुरेखः -खा -खं, बहुपंक्तिः -क्तिः -क्ति.

MULTINOMINAL, *a.* बहुनामकः -का -कं, बहुसंज्ञकः -का -कं.

MULTIPAROUS, *a.* बहुप्रसवः -वा -वं, बहुप्रजः -जा -जं.

MULTIPLE, *s.* (In Arithmetic or Algebra) गुणाकारः.

MULTIPLIABLE, MULTIPLICABLE, *a.* गुणनीयः -या -यं, गुण्यः -ण्या -ण्यं, गुणनशक्यः -क्या -क्यं, हननीयः -या -यं, घातव्यः -व्या -व्यं, वध्यः -ध्या -ध्यं, गुणनक्षमः &c.

MULTIPLICAND, *s.* गुणनीयं, गुण्यं, गुण्याङ्कः, हननीयं, वध्याङ्कः, पूरणीयं, पूरणीयाङ्कः.

MULTIPLICATION, *s.* (In Arithmetic, &c.) गुणनं, हननं, घातः, वधः, पूरणं, गुणत्वं -ता, अङ्कपूरणं, हतं, अभ्यासः, अङ्कवृद्धिः *f.*, संख्यावृद्धिः *f.*, प्रत्युत्पन्नं, गुणाकारः -रं. The Hindus have different methods of multiplication; as, 'cross multiplication,' वज्राभ्यासः, वज्रवधः, वज्रघातः; 'duodecimal multiplication,' गोमूत्रिका; 'multiplication by a figure divided into squares,' कपाटसन्धिः *m.*; 'multiplication according to the places,' स्थानगुणनं; 'by sub-multiples of the multiplier,' विभागगुणनं; 'by dividing the multiplier into parts, and taking the sums of the products of the multiplier,' खण्डगुणनं; 'by the whole multiplier at once,' स्वरूपगुणनं.—(Act of increasing) बहुलीकरणं, प्रचुरीकरणं, वर्धनं, वृद्धिः *f.*

MULTIPLICATIVE, *a.* गुणकः -का -कं, गुणकारः -री -रं, गुणनकारी &c.

MULTIPLICITY, *s.* बाहुल्यं, बहुत्वं -ता, बहुलत्वं -ता, अनेकत्वं -ता, आनैक्यं, प्रचुरत्वं, प्राचुर्य्यं, प्रभूतत्वं; 'multiplicity of meanings,' अर्थबाहुल्यं, बह्वर्थत्वं, अनेकार्थत्वं; 'of occupations,' उद्योगबाहुल्यं; 'of objects,' विषयबाहुल्यं.

MULTIPLIED, *p. p.* or *a.* (In Arithmetic) गुणितः -ता -तं, गुणीकृतः -ता -तं, हतः -ता -तं, पूरितः -ता -तं, आहतः -ता -तं, प्रत्युत्पन्नः -न्ना -न्नं, गुण in comp.; 'a thousand multiplied by seventy-one,' एकसप्ततिगुणितं सहस्रं; 'multiplied by two,' द्विगुणः -णा -णं, द्विगुणितः -ता -तं, द्विगुणीकृतः -ता -तं, द्विगुणीभूतः -ता -तं; 'a number multiplied by itself, स्वगुणा संख्या; 'is multiplied,' हन्यते. —(Increased) बहुलीकृतः -ता -तं, प्रचुरीकृतः &c., बहुलीभूतः &c., वर्धितः -ता -तं, वर्धितसंख्यः -ख्या -ख्यं.

MULTIPLIER, MULTIPLICATOR, *s.* गुणकः, पूरकः, अङ्कपूरकः, गुणकाङ्कः, गुणः, प्रवृत्तिः *f.*

To MULTIPLY, *v. a.* (In Arithmetic, &c.) गुण् (c. 10. गुणयति -यितुं), हन् (c. 2. हन्ति -न्तुं, caus. घातयति -यितुं), पृ (c. 10. पूरयति -यितुं), गुणनं कृ, घातं कृ, हननं कृ, अङ्कपूरणं कृ.—(Increase in number) बहुलीकृ, प्रचुरीकृ, वृध् (c. 10. वर्धयति -यितुं), संख्यावृद्धिं कृ.

To MULTIPLY, *v. n.* (Grow, increase in number) बहुलीभू, प्रचुरीभू, बहुतरीभू, अधिकतरीभू, वृध् (c. 1. वर्धते -र्धितुं), पुष्कलीभू, वर्धितसंख्यः -ख्या -ख्यं भू, अधिकसंख्यः &c. भू, भृश (nom. भृशायते).

MULTIPOTENT, *a.* बहुकार्य्यशक्तिकः -का -कं, बहुकार्य्यसमर्थः -र्था -र्थं.

MULTIPRESENCE, *s.* बहुस्थानविद्यमानता, बहुस्थलविद्यमानता.

MULTISONOUS, *a.* बहुस्वनः -ना -नं, बहुध्वनिः -निः -नि, बहुनादः -दा -दं.

MULTITUDE *s.* (A collection, number) समूहः, गणः, सङ्घः, संहतिः *f.*, सङ्घातः, ओघः, समुदायः, समवायः, वृन्दं, निवहः, सञ्चयः, चयः, सञ्चयः, समुच्चयः, सन्दूहः, समाजः, समजः, मण्डलं -ली, स्तोमः, निकायः, वारः, विसरः, आकरः, व्यूहः, जातं, कदम्बं -म्बकः -कं, कदम्बदः, वर्गः, पेटकं, पूगः, पुञ्जः, सङ्गः, सन्दोहः, सङ्कुलः, व्रजः, सार्थः, कुलं, ग्रामः in comp.; 'in multitudes,' सङ्घशस्.—(Crowd, throng) बहुजनसमूहः, बहुजनसम्मर्दः, बहुजनसङ्घः, लोकसङ्घः, जनसमूहः, जननिवहः, लोकनिवहः, जनौघः, जनसमागमः, बहुजनमेलकः, जनता, मानुष्यकं.—(State of being many) बहुत्वं, बाहुल्यं, अनेकत्वं, आनैक्यं; 'multitude of villages,' ग्रामता.

MULTITUDINOUS, *a.* बहुलः -ला -लं, बहुः -हुः -ह्वी -हु, बहुसंख्यकः -का -कं, अनेकः -का -कं, अनेकसंख्यकः -का -कं, पुष्कलः -ला -लं, समवायी -यिनी -यि (न्).

MULTIVIOUS, *a.* बहुमार्गः -र्गा -र्गं, बहुपथः -था -थं, प्रचुरमार्गः &c.

Multocular, *a.* बहुनेत्रः -त्रा -त्रं, बहुनयनः -ना -नं, बहुलोचनः -ना -नं.

Mum, *a.* (Silent) निःशब्दः -ब्दा -ब्दं, तूष्णीकः -का -कं, अनालापः -पा -पं.

Mum, *interj.* शान्तं, शब्दं मा कुरु, तूष्णीम्भव, निःशब्दो भव, हूम्, नीचैस्.

To **mumble**, *v. a.* and *n.* अस्पष्टवाचा or अस्पष्टस्वरेण वद् (c. 1. वदति -दितुं), अस्पष्टोच्चारणेन or अव्यक्तोच्चारणेन वद्, अव्यक्तगिरा वद्, अस्पष्टं वद्, अव्यक्तं वद् or उच्चर् (c. 10. -चारयति -यितुं), नीचस्वरेण वद्, उपांशु वद्, जप् (c. 1. जपति -पितुं), प्रजप्.

Mumbled, *p. p.* अस्पष्टवाचा or नीचस्वरेण उच्चारितः -ता -तं.

Mumblingly, *adv.* अस्पष्टवाचा, अव्यक्तवाचा, अस्पष्टस्वरेण, नीचस्वरेण.

Mummer, *s.* विडम्बनकृत् *m.*, छद्मवेशी *m.* (न्), दम्भवृत्तिः *m.*

Mummery, *s.* विडम्बनं -ना, छद्म *n.* (न्), छद्मवेशः, दम्भः, मिथ्याधर्म्मः, धर्म्मोपधा, कपटधर्म्मः, भाण्डं, भण्डता.

Mummy, *s.* सुगन्धिद्रव्यरक्षितशवः, सिक्थादिरक्षितशवः, तिक्तौषधव्यञ्जनादिरक्षितं मृतशरीरं.

To **mump**, *v. a.* चर्व् (c. 1. चर्वति -र्वितुं, c. 10. चर्वयति -यितुं), दंश् (c. 1. दशति, दंष्टुं).

Mumps, *s.* लालापिण्डशोथः, लालाशयशोथः, गण्डमाला, कर्णमूलं.—(Sullenness) अन्तःक्रोधः, अन्तःकोपः.

To **munch**, *v. a.* and *n.* चर्व् (c. 1. चर्वति -र्वितुं, c. 10. चर्वयति -यितुं), शनैः सन्दंश् (c. 1. -दशति -दंष्टुं) or विदंश् or दंश्, शनैः खाद् (c. 1. खादति -दितुं) or संखाद्.

Mundane, *a.* लौकिकः -की -कं, ऐहलौकिकः -की -कं, सांसारिकः -की -कं, लौक्यः -क्या -क्यं, संसारी -रिणी -रि (न्), ऐहिकः -की -कं, इहलोकसम्बन्धी &c.; 'mundane egg,' ब्रह्माण्डं, हेमाण्डं, हिरण्यगर्भः.

Mundanity, *s.* लौकिकता -त्वं, ऐहलौकिकता, सांसारिकत्वं.

Mundivagant, *a.* भुवनचरः -रा -रं, लोकाटकः -का -कं, पृथिवीपर्य्यटकः &c.

Mungoose, *s.* नकुलः, सर्पहः, बभ्रुः *m.*, मूषिकादनः.

Mungrel, *s.* *See* Mongrel.

Municipal, *a.* नगरीयः -या -यं, नागरेयकः -की -कं, नगराधिकारसम्बन्धी &c., नगरसमाजसम्बन्धी -न्धिनी -न्धि (न्), नगरीयसमाजविषयः -या -यं, दैशिकः -की -कं, देशीयः -या -यं, नगर in comp.

Municipality, *s.* ग्रामसङ्घः, नगरसङ्घः, देशविभागः, मण्डलं, चक्रं, राष्ट्रं.

Munificence, *s.* स्थूललक्ष्यता -त्वं, अतिदानं, अतिदातृत्वं, बहुप्रदत्वं, अतिदानशीलता, अतित्यागशीलता, अतित्यागः, अतित्यागिता, वदान्यता, उदारता, औदार्य्यं, अतिसर्ज्जनं, दानवीरता, दानशूरता, दानशौर्य्यं, दानशौण्डता, मुक्तहस्तता.

Munificent, *a.* स्थूललक्ष्यः -क्ष्या -क्ष्यं, स्थूललक्षः -क्षा -क्षं, बहुप्रदः -दा -दं, अतिदाता -त्री -तृ (तृ), अतिदायकः -का -कं, बहुदायकः &c., वदान्यः -न्या -न्यं, अतिदानशीलः -ला -लं, अतित्यागशीलः &c., बहुत्यागी -गिनी &c., उदारः -रा -रं, दानवीरः -रा -रं, दानशूरः &c., दानशौण्डः -ण्डा -ण्डं.

Munificently, *adv.* स्थूललक्ष्यवत्, अतिदानेन, वदान्यवत्, सौदार्य्यं.

Muniment, *s.* दुर्गं, कोटिः *f.*, कोटः, कूटः, परिकूटं, गुप्तिः *f.*, रक्षास्थानं.

Munition, *s.* युद्धसामग्री -ग्र्यं, युद्धोपकरणं, युद्धसज्जा, युद्धसाहित्यं.

Mural, *a.* भित्तिसम्बन्धी -न्धिनी &c., प्राकारसम्बन्धी &c., प्राकारीयः -या -यं.

Murder, *s.* हत्या, वधः, घातः, घातनं, मारणं, हननं, निहननं, प्रमापणं, अपघातः, व्यापादनं, जीवहत्या, प्राणहत्या, सूदनं, निषूदनं, हिंसा, द्वेषपूर्व्वको मनुष्यवधः, द्वेषपूर्व्वा नृहत्या.

To **murder**, *v. a.* द्वेषपूर्व्वं हन् (c. 2. हन्ति -न्तुं, c. 10. घातयति -यितुं) or व्यापद् (c. 10. -पादयति -यितुं) or मृ (c. 10. मारयति -यितुं), द्वेषबुद्ध्या हन् or निहन् or वध्, this last is defective and not usually found, excepting in the 3d pret. and fut., द्वेषपूर्व्वं वधं कृ or मनुष्यवधं कृ, प्राणहत्यां कृ, जीवहत्यां कृ, जीवनाशं कृ.—(Destroy) नश् (c. 10. नाशयति -यितुं), विनश्.

Murdered, *p. p.* द्वेषपूर्व्वं हतः -ता -तं or निहतः -ता -तं or व्यापादितः &c. or घातितः &c., द्वेषबुद्ध्या मारितः -ता -तं or हतप्राणः &c.

Murderer, *s.* द्वेषपूर्व्वं or द्वेषबुद्ध्या हन्ता *m.* (न्तृ) or निहन्ता *m.* or घातकः or घाती *m.* (न्) or वधकः, वधकारी *m.*, वधोद्यतः, मारकः, प्राणहन्ता *m.*, जीवहन्ता *m.*, हत्याकृत्, प्राणहत्याकृत्, आततायी *m.* (न्), नरघाती *m.*, घ्नः in comp., हा *m.* (न्) in comp.; 'of a brother,' भ्रातृहा *m.*, भ्रातृघ्नः, भ्रातृघातकः &c.; 'of one asleep,' सुप्तघातकः.

Murderous, *a.* (Committing murder) घातकः -का -कं, घातुकः -का -कं, घाती -तिनी -ति (न्), वधकारी &c., प्राणघातकः &c., व्यापादकः -का -कं, प्राणान्तकः &c., जीवान्तकः &c., प्राणनाशकः &c.—(Premeditating murder, intending it) वधैषी -षिणी &c., वधोद्यतः -ता -तं, जिघांसुः -सुः -सु, वधाभिसन्धिः -न्धिः -न्धि, हिंसाबुद्धिः -द्धिः -द्धि, सन्नद्धः -द्धा -द्धं.—(Consisting in murder) मारात्मकः -का -कं, आत्ययिकः -की -कं.

Muriate, *s.* (Of mercury) रसकर्प्पूरः, रसपुष्पं.

Murk, *s.* अन्धकारः, तमस् *n.*, तिमिरं, तमिस्रं, मेघतिमिरं, साभ्रता.

Murky, *a.* सान्धकारः -रा -रं, सतिमिरः -रा -रं, तमस्वी -स्विनी -स्वि (न्), तमोमयः -यी -यं, तमोवृतः -ता -तं, मेघाच्छन्नः -न्ना -न्नं, साभ्रः -भ्रा -भ्रं, मलिनः -ना -नं.

Murmur, *s.* (Low sound) कलकलः, कलः, कलरवः, कलरुतं, कलस्वरः -रं, मन्दरुतं, मन्दरावः, रुतं, रावः, गुञ्जितं, गुञ्जनं, मर्म्मरः, मणितं, स्तनितं, झङ्कारः, रणत्कारः, रणरणशब्दः, गर्ज्जनं, गर्ज्जितं, मन्द्रशब्दः, गम्भीरशब्दः, मन्द्रध्वनिः *m.*, गम्भीरध्वनिः *m.*, आमन्द्रशब्दः, नीचशब्दः; 'murmur of applause,' प्रणादः, प्रणदनं.—(Suppressed sound of complaint) अन्तर्विलापः, अन्तर्विलपितं, गूढविलापः, गूढपरिदेवनं -ना, अन्तःपरिदेवना, असन्तोषसूचकशब्दः, असन्तोषार्थकशब्दः.

To **murmur**, *v. n.* (Make a low sound) कलकलशब्दं कृ, गुञ्ज् (c. 1. गुञ्जति -ञ्जितुं), गर्ज् (c. 1. गर्ज्जति -र्ज्जितुं), गर्ज्जनं कृ, गम्भीरं or मन्द्रशब्देन रु (c. 2. रौति, रवितुं) or विरु or अभिरु or स्तन् (c. 1. स्तनति -नितुं), गम्भीरस्तनितं कृ, गम्भीरशब्दं कृ, नीचशब्दं कृ, मन्द्रशब्दं कृ, आमन्द्रशब्दं कृ, घुर् (c. 6. घुरति -रितुं), रणरणशब्दं कृ.—(Mutter) जप् (c. 1. जपति -पितुं), प्रजप्, नीचस्वरेण वद् (c. 1. वदति -दितुं), नीचैर् वद्, उपांशु वद्.—(Make a sound of complaint) असन्तोषाद् विलप् (c. 1. -लपति -पितुं) or परिदेव् (c. 1. -देवते -वितुं), असन्तोषसूचकशब्दं कृ, असन्तोषार्थकशब्दं कृ, विवद् (c. 1. -वदते -दितुं).

Murmurer, *s.* असन्तुष्टत्वात् सदापरिदेवी *m.* (न्) or सदाविलापी *m.*, असन्तुष्टजनः, विवादी *m.* (न्).

Murmuring, *s.* (Low sound) गर्ज्जनं, परिगर्ज्जनं. *See* Murmur.

Murmuring, *part.* (Making a low sound) गुञ्जन् -ञ्जन्ती -ञ्जत् (त्), कलकलशब्दकारी -रिणी -रि (न्), मन्द्रशब्दकारी &c.

Murrain, *s.* गवादिजन्तुमारी, गवादिमारकः, मारी, महामारी.

Muscle, *s.* स्नायुः *m.*, वसा, पेशी, शिरा, मांसपेशी, मांसशिरा, मांसरज्जुः *m. f.*, वस्नसा, वहीरुः *m.*, सन्धिबन्धनं, ग्रन्थिबन्धनं; 'trapezium muscle,' मन्या, मन्याका.—(Shell-fish) शम्बुः, शम्बुकः, शम्बूकः.

Muscular, **musculous**, *a.* (Pertaining to a muscle) स्नायुसम्बन्धी -न्धिनी &c.; 'muscular action,' चालनं.—(Brawny, strong) मांसलः -ला -लं, स्नायुमान् -मती -मत् (त्), दृढाङ्गः -ङ्गी -ङ्गं, बलवान् &c.

Muse, *s.* विद्यादेवी, काव्यदेवता, वाग्देवता, विद्याधिष्ठात्री, काव्याधिष्ठात्री, सरस्वती.—(Deep thought) ध्यानं, चिन्ता.

To MUSE, *v. n.* चिन्त् (c. 10. चिन्तयति -यितुं), ध्यै (c. 1. ध्यायति, ध्यातुं), सन्ध्यै, विमृश् (c. 6. -मृशति -मर्ष्टुं), विचर् (c. 10. -चारयति -यितुं), मन् (c. 4. मन्यते, मन्तुं), चिन्तां कृ, ध्याननिष्ठः -ष्ठा -ष्ठं भू, चिन्तापरः -रा -रं भू.

MUSEFUL, *a.* ध्याननिष्ठः -ष्ठा -ष्ठं, ध्यानपरः -रा -रं, चिन्तापरः &c.

MUSEUM, *s.* कौतुकागारं, कौतुकालयः, कौतुकसङ्ग्रहालयः, कौतुकसङ्ग्रहस्थानं, दुर्लभद्रव्यागारं, दुर्लभवस्तुसङ्ग्रहस्थानं, आश्चर्य्यपदार्थालयः.

MUSHROOM, *s.* छत्रं -त्रा, छत्राकं, छत्रकः, छत्रिका, अतिछत्रः -त्रकः, उच्छिलीन्ध्रं -न्ध्रकं, शिलीन्ध्रं -न्ध्रकं, पालघ्नः, अर्थ्येक्षं, भक्षिपत्रं, दिलीरः.

MUSIC, *s.* (The art or science) गन्धर्ववेविद्या or गन्धर्वविद्या, सुस्वरविद्या, गन्धर्ववेदः, सङ्गीतविद्या, वादनविद्या, वाद्यविद्या, सुस्वरशास्त्रं, सङ्गीतशास्त्रं, सङ्गीतव्यापारः, विज्ञानं.—(Harmony, melody) सुस्वरः, सुस्वरसङ्गः, सुस्वरता, वाद्यघोषः, कलता -त्वं, तौर्य्यं, तालः; 'vocal and instrumental music,' सङ्गीतं -तिः *f.*, गीतवादनं; 'music with singing and dancing,' तौर्य्यत्रिकं; 'set to music,' स्वरबद्धः -द्धा -द्धं; 'fond of music,' सुस्वरानन्दी -न्दिनी &c., नादलुब्धः -ब्धा -ब्धं; 'music-room,' सङ्गीतशाला. For the seven notes of music *See* GAMUT.

MUSICAL, *a.* (Belonging to music) गन्धर्वविद्यासम्बन्धी -न्धिनी -न्धि (न्), सङ्गीतविद्यासम्बन्धी &c., सुस्वरविद्यासम्बन्धी &c., सुस्वरविषयः -या -यं, सुस्वरशास्त्रसम्बन्धी &c., सौवरः -री -रं, गानीयः -या -यं.—(Harmonious, melodious) सुस्वरः -रा -रं, सुश्राव्यः -व्या -व्यं, सुस्वरयुक्तः -क्ता -क्तं.—(Fond of music) सुस्वरप्रियः -या -यं, सुस्वरानन्दी &c., वाद्यप्रियः &c., वादनशीलः -ला -लं, नादप्रियः &c., नादलुब्धः -ब्धा -ब्धं, नादासक्तः -क्ता -क्तं, वादनासक्तः &c., वाद्यश्रवणासक्तः &c.; 'musical instrument,' वादित्रं, वाद्यं, तूर्य्यं, तालितं, आतोद्यं, भाण्डं; 'playing on musical instruments,' वाद्यवादनं, भाण्डवादनं; 'musical glasses,' जलतरङ्गः.

MUSICALLY, *adv.* सुस्वरं -रेण, सुस्वरपूर्व्वं, सुस्वरविद्यानुसारेण.

MUSICIAN, *s.* (One that plays on an instrument) वादकः, वाद्यवादकः, वादित्रवादकः, भाण्डवादकः, वादनकर्त्ता *m.* (र्त्तृ), भाण्डिकः.—(Singer) गायकः, गाथिकः, गायकः, गाता *m.* (तृ), गाथाकारः.—(One skilled in music) वादनकुशलः, वादित्रकुशलः, सुस्वरविद्याज्ञः, सङ्गीतविद्यातत्त्वज्ञः, गान्धर्वतत्त्वज्ञः; 'celestial musician,' गन्धर्वः, names for some of these are तुम्बुरुः *m.*, विश्वावसुः, चित्ररथः; the last is their chief. *See* GANDHARBA.

MUSING, *part.* or *a.* ध्यायन् -यन्ती -यत् (त्), चिन्तयन् &c. *See* MUSEFUL.

MUSK, *s.* कस्तूरी -रिका, कस्तुरिका, कस्तूरिकाण्डजः, मृगनाभिः *m.*, मृगमदः, मृगनाभिजं -जा, मृगाण्डजा, अण्डजा, नाभिः -भी *f.*, मदः, दर्पः, मदाह्वः, मदारः, गन्धधूलिः *f.*, गन्धचेलिका, योजनगन्धा, गन्धशेखरः, वातामोदा, मार्गः, ललिता; 'musk-bag,' अण्डं, मृगाण्डं, कस्तूरमल्लिका.

MUSK-DEER, *s.* कस्तूरीमृगः, गन्धमृगः, मृगपालिका, गन्धवाहः.

MUSKET, *s.* आग्नेयनाडिः -डी, गुलिकाप्रक्षेपणी, गुटिकाप्रक्षेपणी, गुलिकाप्रक्षेपणी सुषिरनाली; 'musket-ball,' गुलिका, गुटिका, गुलिः *f.*

MUSK-RAT, *s.* गन्धमूषिकः -का, गन्धाखुः *m.*, गन्धनकुलः, गन्धशुण्डिनी, गन्धाशुण्डिनी, गन्धसूची, गन्धसुखी, चिक्कः, पुंवृषः.

MUSKY, *a.* कस्तूरीगन्धयुक्तः -क्ता -क्तं, कस्तूरीवासितः -ता -तं, कस्तूरीगन्धवान् -वती -वत् (त्), मृगमदसगन्धः -न्धा -न्धं, सुगन्धिः -न्धिः -न्धि.

MUSLIN, *s.* अंशुकं, सूक्ष्मांशुकं, दुकूलं, सूक्ष्मदुकूलं, सूक्ष्मवस्त्रं.

MUSQUITO, MUSKETO, *s.* मशकः, मशः, मसकः, सूक्ष्ममशकः, सूक्ष्ममक्षिका, भम्भरालिका, सूचिवदनः, रणरणः, कटुकीटः, रात्रिजागरदः, प्राचिका; 'musquito-curtain,' मशहरी, चतुष्की.

MUSSULMAN, *s.* यवनः, यावनः, यावनदेशीयः, यावनमतधारी *m.* (न्), यावनधर्म्मावलम्बी *m.* (न्).

MUST, *v. n.* (Be necessitated). Expressed by the fut. pass. part.; as, 'anger must be restrained,' क्रोधो नियन्तव्यः; 'I must go, or it is to be gone by me,' मया गन्तव्यं; 'I must do that,' तन् मया कर्त्तव्यं or करणीयं or कार्य्यं. The adverb अवश्यं may be added; as, तन् मया अवश्यं कर्त्तव्यं. Sometimes the verb अर्ह् (c. 1. अर्हति -र्हितुं) has the sense of 'must;' as, 'he must not receive that,' न तत् प्राप्तुम् अर्हति.

MUST *s.* (Wine just pressed from the grape) नवमद्यं, नूतनमद्यं.

To MUST, *v. n.* (Grow mouldy and sour) अम्लीभू, दुर्गन्धीभू, विरसीभू.

MUSTACHE, MUSTACHIO, MUSTACHES, *s. pl.* गुम्फः, ओष्ठलोम *n.* (न्), ओष्ठलोमानि *n. pl.*, ओष्ठजं लोम *n.* or रोम, ओष्ठजलोम *n.*, श्मश्रु *n.*, पक्ष्म *n.* (न्), पक्ष्माणि *n. pl.*

MUSTARD, *s.* (Plant) सर्षपः, राजसर्षपः, सरिषपः, कटुकः, कटुस्नेहः, कदम्बकः -कं, कदम्बदः, विघटः, तन्तुभः; 'black mustard,' कृष्णिका, राजिका, आसुरी, क्षवः, क्षुधाभिजननः, क्षुताभिजननः; 'white mustard,' सिद्धार्थः -र्थकः; 'mustard-seed,' सर्षपबीजं, तन्तुभः, तन्तुकः; 'oil expressed from it,' सर्षपतैलं; 'used for seasoning,' उपस्करः; 'made of mustard,' सार्षपः -पी -पं.

MUSTARD-POT, *s.* सर्षपपात्रं, सर्षपतैलपात्रं, सर्षपभाजनं, सर्षपाधारः.

To MUSTER, *v. a.* समानी (c. 1. -नयति -नेतुं), समूहीकृ, एकत्र कृ, एकत्र सङ्गम् (c. 10. -गमयति -यितुं) or समागम्, एकीकृ, समूह् (c. 1. -ऊहते -हितुं), समाहृ (c. 1. -हरति -हर्त्तुं), समाह्वे (c. 1. -ह्वयति -ह्वातुं), सङ्ग्रह् (c. 9. -गृह्णाति -ग्रहीतुं), सङ्ग्रहं कृ.—(Assemble or call over soldiers) सैन्यान् संख्या (c. 2. -ख्याति -तुं) or परिसंख्या or सम्परिख्या or परिगण् (c. 10. -गणयति -यितुं), सैन्यनामानि पृथक् पृथक् ख्या, सैन्यान् एकत्र समानी.

To MUSTER, *v. n.* सङ्गम् (c. 1. -गच्छति -गन्तुं), समागम्, एकत्र आगम्, समे (समैति -तुं, rt. इ), सम्मिल् (c. 6. -मिलति -मेलितुं), एकत्र मिल्, समावृत् (c. 1. -वर्त्तते -र्त्तितुं), समूहीभू.

MUSTER-ROLL, *s.* सैन्यपरिसंख्या -ख्यानं, सैन्यपरिगणना, सैन्यनामावलिः *f.*, संख्या.

MUSTINESS, *s.* विरसता, वैरस्यं, पर्य्युषितत्वं, पूतिगन्धता, दुर्गन्धता.

MUSTY, *a.* विरसः -सा -सं, पर्य्युषितः -ता -तं, पूतिगन्धिकः -का -कं.

MUTABILITY, MUTABLENESS, *s.* अस्थिरता, अस्थैर्य्यं, अस्थायित्वं, अधीरता, अधृतिः *f.*, स्थैर्य्याभावः, विकारशीलता, परिणामशीलता.—(Fickleness) चञ्चलत्वं, चाञ्चल्यं, चपलता, चापल्यं, चलचित्तता, लोलता, अनवस्थितिः *f.*

MUTABLE *a.* अस्थिरः -रा -रं, अस्थायी -यिनी -यि (न्), अधीरः -रा -रं, अनवस्थः -स्था -स्थं, अनवस्थितः -ता -तं, परिणामशीलः -ला -लं, विकारशीलः &c., परिणामस्वभावः -वा -वं, अनियतः -ता -तं.—(Fickle) चञ्चलः -ला -लं, चपलः -ला -लं, चलचित्तः -त्ता -त्तं, लोलः -ला -लं, चञ्चलवृत्तिः -त्तिः -त्ति, चपलवृत्तिः &c., क्षणिकबुद्धिः -द्धिः -द्धि.

MUTATION, *s.* विकारः, विकृतिः *f.*, विक्रिया, परिणामः, विपरिणामः, परिवर्त्तः -र्त्तनं, अन्यथाभावः, अवस्थान्तरं, अवस्थाभेदः, स्थितिभेदः.

MUTE, *a.* मूकः -का -कं, जडवाक् *m.f.n.* (च्), जडः -डा -डं, वाक्शून्यः -न्या -न्यं, वाग्रहितः -ता -तं, वाक्शक्तिहीनः -ना -नं, वाणीहीनः -ना -नं, वाणीरहितः -ता -तं, निःशब्दः -ब्दा -ब्दं, निश्शब्दः &c., नादशून्यः &c., मुद्रितमुखः -खा -खं, निर्वचनः -ना -नं, अवाक् (च्), अनुस्वरः -रा -रं, निरुत्तरः -रा -रं.

MUTE, *s.* (Person who cannot speak) मूकजनः.—(In grammar) स्वरसहितोच्चार्यव्यञ्जनं.—(Dung of birds) पक्षिपुरीषं, पक्षिभिर् उत्सरितं मलं, गूथः.

To MUTE, *v.n.* पक्षिवत् पुरीषम् उत्सृज् (c.6. -सृजति -स्रष्टुं), पुरीषोत्सर्गं कृ.

MUTELY, *adv.* मूकवत्, जडवत्, मूकं, निःशब्दं, निरुत्तरं, तूष्णीं.

MUTENESS, *s.* मूकता, मौक्यं, वाक्शून्यता, वाग्राहित्यं, जडता, वाग्जाड्यं, वाक्स्तम्भः, वाग्रोधः, वागभावः, निःशब्दता, अवाक्त्वं, अभाषणं, मौनं, मौनभावः.

To MUTILATE, *v. a.* व्यवछिद् (c. 7. -छिनत्ति -छेत्तुं), अङ्गच्छेदनं कृ, प्रवृश्च् (c. 6. वृश्चति, व्रश्चितुं), प्रव्रश्च्, बहुखण्डशः कृ or छिद्, बहुखण्डीकृ, खण्डं खण्डं कृ, खण्ड् (c. 10. खण्डयति -यितुं), विनिकृत् (c. 6. -कृन्तति -कर्त्तितुं), क्षतविक्षतीकृ, छिन्नभिन्नीकृ, विकलीकृ, विकलाङ्गीकृ, व्यङ्गीकृ, विशस् (c. 1. -शसति -सितुं), अङ्गवैकल्यं कृ.

MUTILATED, *p. p.* छिन्नभिन्नः -न्ना -न्नं, क्षतविक्षतः -ता -तं, व्यवच्छिन्नः &c., व्यवच्छिन्नाङ्गः -ङ्गा -ङ्गं, लूनाङ्गः &c., छिन्नाङ्गः &c., विकलाङ्गः &c., विकलीकृतः -ता -तं, खण्डितः -ता -तं, खण्डिताङ्गः &c., खण्डितविग्रहः -हा -हं, न्यूनाङ्गः &c., हीनाङ्गः &c., अङ्गहीनः -ना -नं, अपाङ्गः &c., विकलेन्द्रियः -या -यं, नष्टेन्द्रियः &c.

MUTILATION, *s.* (The act) व्यवच्छेदः -दनं, अङ्गच्छेदः -दनं, विकलीकरणं, व्यङ्गीकरणं, अङ्गकर्त्तनं, विनिकर्त्तनं, प्रव्रश्चनं, खण्डनं, विशसनं.—(State) विकलता, वैकल्यं, अङ्गवैकल्यं, अङ्गहीनता, न्यूनाङ्गता, हीनाङ्गता, अपाङ्गता, लूनाङ्गता, खण्डितत्वं, खण्डिताङ्गता.

MUTINEER, *s.* आज्ञालङ्घी *m.* (न्), शासनलङ्घी *m.*, आज्ञाविरोधी *m.*, कलहकारी *m.*, सेनाक्षोभकारी *m.*, सेनायां प्रकोपकारी.

MUTINOUS, *a.* आज्ञालङ्घी -ङ्घिनी -ङ्घि (न्), शासनाविधायी &c., अवशवर्त्ती &c., कलहकारी &c., क्षोभकारी &c., प्रकोपकारी &c., प्रतीपः -पा -पं, विप्रतीपः -पा -पं, अवशः -शा -शं, दुःशासनः -ना -नं, दुःशास्यः -स्या -स्यं, अविधेयः -या -यं, अनायत्तः -त्ता -त्तं.

MUTINY, *s.* सेनाप्रकोपः, सैन्यप्रकोपः, सेनाकोपः, प्रकोपः, कोपः, सेनाक्षोभः, सैन्यक्षोभः, शासनलङ्घनं, आज्ञालङ्घनं, कलहः, सैन्यकलहः, सैन्यवैराग्यं, सैन्यविरक्तिः *f.*, शासनव्युत्थानं, आज्ञाव्युत्थानं.

To MUTINY, *v. n.* कलह (nom. कलहायते), कलहं कृ, सेनापतिशासनं लङ्घ् (c. 10. लङ्घयति -यितुं), प्रतीप (nom. प्रतीपायते), व्युत्था (c. 1. -तिष्ठति-थातुं, rt. स्था), कोपं कृ, प्रकोपं कृ, क्षोभं कृ, अवशीभू, अनायत्तीभू.

To MUTTER, *v. a.* and *n.* (Utter words with a low indistinct voice) अस्पष्टं वद् (c. 1. वदति -दितुं), अस्पष्टवाचा वद्, अस्पष्टस्वरेण वद्, अस्पष्टोच्चारणेन वद्, अव्यक्तं वद्, or उच्चर् (c. 10. -चारयति -यितुं), नीचवाचा or नीचस्वरेण वद्, नीचैर् वद्, जप् (c. 1. जपति -पितुं), प्रजप्; this last verb is applied especially to the muttering of prayers, though it may be used in other senses; as, 'to mutter into the ear,' कर्णे जप्, कर्णम् उपजप्.—(Sound with a low rumbling voice) गर्ज् (c. 1. गर्जति -र्जितुं), स्तन् (c. 1. स्तनति -नितुं), गम्भीरशब्दं कृ.

MUTTER, MUTTERING, *s.* (Uttering with a low voice) अस्पष्टोच्चारणं, अव्यक्तोच्चारणं, नीचभाषणं, नीचवाक्यं, नीचस्वरेण भाषणं, उपांशु वादः.—(Low rumbling sound) गर्जनं, गर्जितं, आमन्द्रशब्दः, गम्भीरशब्दः; 'of clouds,' मेघनिर्घोषः.—(Inaudible repetition of prayers, &c.) जपः, जापः, जपनं, स्वाध्यायः, जाप्यं, जपजाप्यं, उपांशुः *m.*

MUTTERED, *p. p.* उपांशु or अस्पष्टं or नीचवाचा उच्चारितः -ता -तं, जपितः &c.; 'to be muttered,' जप्यः -प्या -प्यं, जाप्यः &c., जपनीयः -या -यं; 'having muttered,' जपित्वा.

MUTTERER, *s.* अस्पष्टवादी *m.* (न्), नीचवादी *m.*, नीचभाषी *m.*, उपांशुवादी, जापकः, जपनकृत् *m.*; 'a devotee who mutters,' जपकः.

MUTTERINGLY, *adv.* अस्पष्टवाचा, नीचवाचा, उपांशु, नीचैस्.

MUTTON, *s.* औरभ्रं, औरभ्रमांसं, मेषमांसं, उरभ्रमांसं, अविमांसं.

MUTTON-CHOP, *s.* औरभ्रमांसखण्डः, मेषमांसखण्डः -ण्डं.

MUTUAL, *a.* परस्परः -रा -रं, अन्योन्यः -न्या -न्यं, इतरेतरः -रा -रं, व्यतिकरः -रा -रं, मिथः in comp.; 'mutual quarrel,' अन्योन्यकलहः; 'assistance,' परस्परोपकारः; 'assent,' परस्परानुमतिः *f.*; 'connexion,' अन्योन्यसम्बन्धः, मिथःसम्बन्धः, व्यतिषङ्गः; 'aversion,' अन्योन्यभेदः; 'dependence,' अन्योन्याश्रयः; 'enjoyment,' व्यतिकरसुखं; 'attraction,' अन्योन्याकर्षकत्वं. The idea of 'mutual' is often expressed by some of the prepositions वि, आ, अव, अति, प्रति, प्र in combination, or by an adverbial compound formed by doubling a word; as, 'mutual reproach or abuse,' व्यवक्रोशः, व्यावक्रोशी, व्यावभाषी; 'laughter,' व्यवहासः, व्यावहासी; 'striking,' दण्डादण्डि, प्रतिघातः, प्रतिहननं, व्यतिहारः; 'injury,' विप्रतिकारः, विप्रकारः, प्रतिकारः, विप्रकृतिः *f.*, प्रत्यपकारः; 'assistance,' प्रत्युपकारः; 'connexion,' विप्रतिपत्तिः *f.*; 'salutation,' प्रतिपूजनं, प्रत्यभिवादः; 'accusation,' प्रत्यभियोगः; 'recognition,' प्रत्यभिज्ञानं.

MUTUALITY, *s.* परस्परयोगः, अन्योन्ययोगः, इतरेतरयोगः, परस्परता, अन्योन्यत्वं, परस्परभावः, अन्योन्यभावः, व्यतिकरः, व्यतिहारः, व्यतीहारः, अन्योन्यसम्बन्धः, अन्योन्याश्रयः, व्यतिषङ्गः.

MUTUALLY, *adv.* परस्परं -रां, अन्योन्यं, इतरेतरं, मिथस्, अन्योन्यस्य, परस्पर &c. in comp., उभय in comp., 'mutually assisting,' परस्परोपकारी &c.; 'mutually agreed,' परस्परानुमतः -ता -तं, उभयानुमतः &c.; 'connected,' मिथःसक्तः -क्ता -क्तं, व्यतिषक्तः -क्ता -क्तं, व्यतिषङ्गवान् -वती &c.; 'taken,' अन्योन्यापहृतः -ता -तं.

MUZZLE, *s.* (Mouth, entrance) मुखं, छिद्रं, प्रवेशः, प्रवेशद्वारं, निःसरणं.—(Fastening for the mouth) मुखबन्धनं -नी, मुखरोधनी.

To MUZZLE, *v. a.* मुखं बन्ध् (c. 9. बध्नाति, बन्द्धुं) or रुध् (c. 7. रुणद्धि, रोद्धुं).

MUZZLED, *p. p.* बद्धमुखः -खा -खं, रुद्धमुखः -खा -खं, निरुद्धमुखः &c.

MY, *pron. a.* मम gen. c. (अस्मत्), मदीयः -या -यं, मामकीनः -ना -नं, अस्मदीयः -या -यं, मत् or अस्मत् in comp.; 'my master,' मम प्रभुः or मत्प्रभुः or अस्मत्प्रभुः; 'my daughter,' मम सुता or मत्सुता.

MYOGRAPHY, MYOLOGY, *s.* स्नायुवर्णना, स्नायुविवरणं, पेशीवर्णनं.

MYOPE, *s.* गजदृष्टिः *m. f.*, गजनेत्रः -त्रा, अल्पदृक् *m. f.*, अदीर्घदृष्टिः.

MYOPY, *s.* गजदृष्टित्वं, अदीर्घदृष्टित्वं, अदूरदर्शित्वं.

MYRIAD, *s.* दशसहस्रं, अयुतं; 'by myriads,' दशसहस्रशस्.

MYRMIDON, *s.* परिचरः, परिधिस्थः, भर्त्सनकारी सैनिकः or अनुचरः.

MYROBALAN, *s.* (Emblic myrobalan, plant or fruit) आमलकः -की -कं, तिष्यफला, अमृता, वयस्था, वयःस्था, कायस्था.—(Beleric) विभीतकः -की -कं, अक्षः -क्षकः, तुषः, तुसः, कर्षफलः, भूतवासः, कलिद्रुमः.—(Yellow) अभया, व्यथा, पथ्या, वयस्था, वयःस्था, कायस्था, पूतना, अमृता, हरीतकी, हैमवती, चेतकी, श्रेयसी, शिवा.—(The three myrobalans) त्रिफला.

MYRRH, *s.* गन्धरसः, रसगन्धः, सुरसं, महागन्धं, जातीरसं, गान्धारं, बोलः, प्राणः, पिण्डः, गोपः -पकः, गोसः, पिण्डगोसः, गोपरसः, गोलः -लकः, रसः, शशः, गोसशशः.

MYSELF, *pron.* सोऽहम्, आत्म *n.* (न्); 'I will kill myself,' आत्मानं हनिष्यामि.

MYSTERIOUS, *a.* गूढः -ढा -ढं, अतिगूढः &c., निगूढः &c., गूढार्थः -र्था -र्थं, निगूढार्थः &c., गुप्तः -प्ता -प्तं, अतिगुप्तः &c., गुप्तार्थः &c., गहनः -ना -नं, सुगहनः -ना -नं, गुह्यः -ह्या -ह्यं, गोप्यः -प्या -प्यं, गोपनीयः -या -यं, रहस्यः -स्या -स्यं, सुरहस्यः &c., दुर्ज्ञेयः -या -यं, दुर्बोधः -धा -धं, बोधागम्यः -म्या -म्यं, अव्यक्तः -क्ता -क्तं, अस्पष्टः -ष्टा -ष्टं; 'profoundly mysterious,' परमगहनः -ना -नं; 'mysterious in his ways,' अव्यक्तवर्त्मा -र्त्मा -र्त्म (न्).

MYSTERIOUSLY, *adv.* गूढं, अतिगूढं, परमगहनं, अव्यक्तं, सुरहस्यं.

MYSTERIOUSNESS, *s.* गूढता, अतिगूढता, निगूढता, गूढार्थता, निगूढार्थता, गुह्यता, गोप्यता, दुर्ज्ञेयता, रहस्यता, अव्यक्तता.

MYSTERY, *s.* गूढं, निगूढं, रहस्यं, गुह्यं, गूढतत्त्वं, निगूढतत्त्वं, गूढार्थः, निगूढार्थः, गहनवस्तु *n.*, मर्म्म *n.* (न्), गोप्यं, गोपनीयं, निगूढविषयः.

MYSTIC, MYSTICAL, *a.* गूढार्थः -र्था -र्थं, गुप्तार्थः &c., गुह्यः -ह्या -ह्यं. *See* MYSTERIOUSNESS. (Involving some secret meaning). गूढार्थगर्भः -र्भा -र्भं, गूढाभिप्रायः -या -यं, सङ्केतगर्भः &c., लाक्षणिकः -की -कं; 'mystic verse,' मन्त्रः; 'mystic letter,' बीजाक्षरं.

MYSTICALLY, *adv.* गूढार्थतस्, निगूढार्थतस्, सगूढार्थं, गुप्तार्थतस्.

MYSTICALNESS, MYSTICISM, *s.* गूढता, गूढार्थता, गुप्तार्थत्वं, गहनत्वं, रहस्यता.

MYSTIFIED, *p. p.* मोहितः -ता -तं, विमोहितः -ता -तं, सगूढार्थः -र्था -र्थं.

To MYSTIFY, *v. a.* गूढीकृ, गहनीकृ, सगूढार्थं -र्थां कृ, गूढतत्त्वानि कथयित्वा परबुद्धिं मुह् (c. 10. मोहयति -यितुं) or विमुह्.

MYTH, *s.* पुरावृत्तकथा, पुरावृत्तोपाख्यानं, पुराणकथा, पुराणोक्तोपाख्यानं, पुराणोक्तेतिहासः, पुरावृत्ताख्यानं, प्राचीनकथा, पुरावृत्तं, पुराणं, कूटार्थकथा.

MYTHIC, MYTHICAL, *a.* पुरावृत्तकथासम्बन्धी -न्धिनी &c., पौराणिकः -की -कं, पुराणकथितः -ता -तं, पुराणोक्तः -क्ता -क्तं, पुराकल्पितः -ता -तं, कूटार्थः -र्था -र्थं.

MYTHOLOGICAL, *a.* पुराणकथासम्बन्धी &c., पुरावृत्तसम्बन्धी &c., देवतादिकथाविषयः -या -यं, ऐतिहासिकः -की -कं, देवतोपाख्यानविषयः &c. *See* MYTHIC.

MYTHOLOGIST, *s.* पुरावृत्तकथकः, पुराणवित् *m.*, देवतोपाख्यानरचकः.

MYTHOLOGY, *s.* पुरावृत्तशास्त्रं, पुराणशास्त्रं, पुराणेतिहासः, इतिहासः, पुराणकथाविद्या, देवतादिकथाविषया विद्या, देवतोपाख्यानविषया विद्या, देवताख्यानं.

N.

To NAB, *v. a.* अकस्माद् ग्रह् (c. 9. गृह्णाति, ग्रहीतुं) or धृ (c. 1. धरति, धर्त्तुं).

NACRE, NACKER, NAKER, *s.* शुक्तिपुटं, मुक्तास्फोटः.

NADIR, *s.* अधःस्वस्तिकं, अधोबिन्दुः *m.*, अधरः, ब्रह्माण्डाधोभागः.

NAG, *s.* अश्वकः, अश्वः, घोटकः. *See* HORSE. (Paramour) जारः.

NÁGA, *s.* (A demigod, having a human face with a serpent's shape. These fabulous beings are said to have sprung from Kadrú, the wife of Kaśyapa, and to have been created in order to people Pátála, or the infernal regions.) नागः, काद्रवेयः, कद्रुपुत्रः, कद्रुसुतः. The chief of these beings is called शेषः, अनन्तः, वासुकिः *m.*, सर्पराजः. The following are some of the other principal Nágas: तक्षकः, पद्मः, महापद्मः, शङ्खः.

NAIAD, *s.* जलदेवता, अप्सराः *f.* (स्), अप्सरा, नदीदेवता, उदकवती.

NAIL, *s.* (Of the finger) नखः, नखरः -रा -रं, कररुहः, करजः, पाणिजः, पाणिरुहः, पाणिरुट् *m.* (ह्), करकण्टकः, अङ्गुलीसम्भूतः, पुनर्भवः, पुनर्नवः, भुजाकण्टः, कामाङ्कुशः; 'a pared nail,' खण्डकः. —(Of iron, &c.) लोहकीलः -लकः, लौहकीलः -लकः, लोहशङ्कुः *m.*, कीलः -लकः, शङ्कुः *m.*

To NAIL, *v. a.* (Fasten with nails) कील् (c. 10. कीलयति -यितुं), कीलैर् बन्ध् (c. 9. बध्नाति, बन्द्धुं) or व्यध् (c. 4. विध्यति, व्यद्धुं), कीलबद्धं -द्धां कृ, कीलविद्धं -द्धां कृ, शङ्कुबद्धं -द्धां कृ.

NAILED, *p. p.* कीलितः -ता -तं, कीलबद्धः -द्धा -द्धं, शङ्कुप्रतिबद्धः &c.

NAIVE, *a.* सरलमतिः -तिः -ति, विमलार्थकः -का -कं, निर्व्याजः -जा -जं, दक्षिणः-णा -णं, मायाहीनः -ना -नं, वैलक्ष्यहीनः &c., निर्व्यलीकः -का -कं.

NAIVELY, *adv.* सारल्येन, निर्व्याजं, अमायया, दाक्षिण्येन, अविलक्षितं.

NAIVETE, *s.* सारल्यं, सरलता, मायाहीनता, अमाया, अव्याजः, अवैलक्ष्यं, दाक्षिण्यं, निर्व्यलीकता, शुद्धमतित्वं, भावशुद्धता.

NAKED, *a.* (Having no clothes) नग्नः -ग्ना -ग्नं, नग्नकः -का -कं, विवस्त्रः -स्त्रा -स्त्रं, निर्वस्त्रः &c., अवस्त्रः &c., वस्त्रहीनः -ना -नं, वस्त्ररहितः -ता -तं, वस्त्रशून्यः -न्या -न्यं, अवासाः -साः -सः (स्), विवासाः &c., विवासः -सा -सं, दिग्वासाः &c., दिगम्बरः -रा -रं, अंशुकः -का -कं, विकोशः -शा -शं, विवसनः -ना -नं, वसनहीनः -ना -नं, आच्छादनहीनः -ना -नं, अपरिच्छन्नः -न्ना -न्नं, अपरिच्छदः -दा -दं, परिच्छदहीनः -ना -नं, वेशहीनः -ना -नं, अवधूतवेशः -शा -शं, गगणपरिधानः -ना -नं, अपरिधानः &c., कोशः -शा -शं, काकरूकः -का -कं.—(Open, uncovered, exposed) विवृतः -ता -तं, अनावृतः -ता -तं, अपवृतः -ता -तं, अनाच्छादितः -ता -तं.—(Unarmed) असन्नः -न्ना -न्नं, असज्जितः -ता -तं, असन्नद्धः -द्धा -द्धं.—(Unadorned) अभूषितः -ता -तं. —(Bare, mere) केवलः -ला -लं, मात्रकः -का -कं, मात्रं, शून्यः -न्या -न्यं, शुद्धः -द्धा -द्धं; 'it is not seen by the naked eye,' नेत्रमात्रेण or केवलनेत्रेण न दृश्यते; 'a naked woman,' नग्ना, नग्निका, कोटरी, कोटवी.

NAKEDLY, *adv.* (Without covering) वस्त्रेण विना, आच्छादनं विना, अपरिच्छन्नं, नग्नवत्.—(Barely) केवलं, मात्रेण, शून्यं.

NAKEDNESS, *s.* नग्नता -त्वं, विवस्त्रत्वं, वस्त्रहीनता, वस्त्रशून्यता, वस्त्ररहित्यं, वसनहीनता, वेशहीनता, आच्छादनहीनता, अपरिच्छदं, नग्नभावः, नग्नावस्था.—(Bareness, openness) शून्यता, शुद्धता, विवृतत्वं, अनावृतत्वं.

NAME, *s.* नाम *n.* (न्), नामधेयं -यः, संज्ञा, अभिधानं, अभिधा, अभिधेयं, आख्या, अभिख्या, आह्वा, आह्वयः, आह्वानं, आह्वायः, उपाधिः *m.*, अभिवचनं, लक्षणं, व्यपदेशः; 'bad name,' दुर्नाम *n.* (न्); 'family name,' कुलनाम *n.*, उपनाम, पद्धतिः -ती *f.*; 'name given at birth,' जन्मनाम *n.*; 'from the constellation,' नक्षत्रनाम *n.*; 'addressing by name,' नामग्रहः -हणं, सम्बोधनं; 'to address by name,' नाम ग्रह् (c. 9. गृह्णाति, ग्रहीतुं), नाम्ना अभिवद् (c. 1. -वदति -दितुं) or अभिवच् (c. 2. -वक्ति -क्तुं), सम्बोधनं कृ; 'giving a name,' नामकरणं; 'bearing the name of,' नामधारी -रिणी &c.; 'calling to mind the name of,' नामस्मरणं; 'forgetting the name,' नामविस्मृतिः *f.*; 'uttering the name of,' नामोच्चारणं; 'abusing by name,' नामापराधः; 'list of names,' नामावलिः *f.*; 'by name,' नाम्ना, नामतस्, नाम, नामधेयतस्; 'in my name,' मद्वचनात्, मम नाम्ना; 'what is his name?' किन्नामधेयः सः; 'affix to the name of Brahmans,' शर्म्मा *m.* (न्), as विष्णुशर्म्मा.—(Reputation) प्रतिष्ठा, मर्य्यादा, कीर्त्तिः *f.*, ख्यातिः *f.*; 'one who has established a name,' लब्धप्रतिष्ठः -ष्ठा -ष्ठं; 'good name,' सुकीर्त्तिः *f.*, सत्कीर्त्तिः *f.*, सुख्यातिः *f.*; 'bad name,' कुकीर्त्तिः *f.*, दुष्कीर्त्तिः *f.*, अपकीर्त्तिः *f.*, अकीर्त्तिः, कुख्यातिः *f.*, अख्यातिः *f.*

अमर्य्यादा, कुप्रतिष्ठा.—(Celebrity, renown) यशस् n., विश्रुतिः f., ख्यातिः f., विख्यातिः f., प्रख्यातिः f., परिख्यातिः, कीर्त्तिः f., प्रसिद्धिः f.

To NAME, v. a. अभिधा (c. 3. -दधाति -धातुं), आख्या (c. 2. -ख्याति -तुं), कृत् (c. 10. कीर्त्तयति -यितुं), प्रकृत्, संकृत्, परिकृत्, अनुकृत्, उदाहृ (c. 1. -हरति -हर्त्तुं), प्रचक्ष् (c. 2. -चष्टे), नाम कृ or दा, संज्ञां कृ; 'they named him Ráma,' तस्य नाम राम इति चक्रुः.—(Mention by name) नाम ग्रह् (c. 9. गृह्णाति, ग्रहीतुं), नामग्रहणं कृ, नाम्ना अभिवद् (c. 1. -वदति -दितुं), नामोदाहरणं कृ, सम्बुध् (c. 10. -बोधयति -यितुं), सम्बोधनं कृ, नामनिर्देशं कृ, नामोच्चारणं कृ, नामस्मरणं कृ.

NAMED, p. p. अभिहितः -ता -तं, आख्यातः -ता -तं, प्रोक्तः -क्ता -क्तं, संज्ञितः -ता -तं, उदाहृतः -ता -तं, प्रत्युदाहृतः -ता -तं, कीर्त्तितः -ता -तं, परिकीर्त्तितः -ता -तं, व्यपदिष्टः -ष्टा -ष्टं, स्मृतः -ता -तं, नामाभिहितः -ता -तं; the following may be used in composition: नामकः -का -कं, नामा -म्नी -म, अभिधानः -ना -नं, अभिधः -धा -धं, आख्यः -ख्या -ख्यं, आह्वः -ह्वा -ह्वं, आह्वयः -या -यं, नामधेयः -या -यं, संज्ञः -ज्ञा -ज्ञं; as, 'a king named Suvarna,' सुवर्णाख्यो राजा; 'in a city named Kánchanapur,' काञ्चनपुरनाम्नि नगरे; 'a prince named Súdraka,' शूद्रकनामा नृपतिः; 'named Vibhíshana,' विभीषणाभिधः or विभीषणाभिधानः; 'a woman named Chandrá,' चन्द्रानाम्नी स्त्री. Sometimes the adverb नाम is used as सुवर्णो नाम राजा, चन्द्रा नाम स्त्री.—(Having a name) संज्ञावान् -वती -वत् (त्), प्राप्तनामा -मा -म (न्), लब्धनामा &c., प्राप्ताभिधानः -ना -नं, नामधारी -रिणी -रि (न्), नामधारकः -का -कं; 'is named,' अभिधीयते, ख्यायते, आख्यायते.

NAMELESS, a. अनामकः -का -कं, नामहीनः -ना -नं, नामरहितः -ता -तं, अनभिधानः -ना -नं, अनामा -मा -म्नी -म (न्), अप्रसिद्धः -द्धा -द्धं.

NAMELY, adv. नाम, नामतस्, यथा, अर्थतस्, अर्थात्, यथाक्रमं.

NAMESAKE, s. समनामकः, समनामधारी m. (न्), एकनामकः.

NAMING, s. (Giving a name) नामकरणं, नामस्थापनं.—(Mentioning by name) नामग्रहः -हणं, नामनिर्देशः, नामोच्चारणं.

NAP, s. (Short sleep) अल्पनिद्रा, अदीर्घनिद्रा, अदीर्घस्वप्नः, वामकुक्षिः f.—(Down) लोम n. (न्), रोम n. (न्).

To NAP, v. n. अल्पनिद्रां कृ, अदीर्घनिद्रां कृ, अल्पकालमात्रं स्वप् (c. 2. स्वपिति -तुं), अदीर्घकालं स्वप्.

NAPE, s. (Of the neck) मन्या, मन्याका, कन्धरः -रा, ग्रीवा, घाटः -टी -टिका, कृकाटिका, कलम्बिका, सीमा m. (न्), पश्चाद्ग्रीवा शिरा.

NAPKIN, s. मुखमार्जनी, वदनमार्जनी, चरकं, नक्तकः.

NAPLESS, a. लोमहीनः -ना -नं, निर्लोमा -मा -म (न्), अविद्यमानलोमा &c.

NAPPY, a. लोमशः -शा -शं, बहुलोमा -मा -म (न्), लोममयः -यी -यं.—(Frothy) फेनलः -ला -लं, फेनिलः -ला -लं.

NARBADÁ, s. (River, which rises in the Vindhyá mountain called Amrakúta, and runs westward about 750 miles into the gulf of Cambay below Baroche) नर्म्मदा, रेवा, सोमसुता, सोमोद्भवा, मेखलकन्यका, मेकलकन्यका, मेकलाद्रिजा, मेखला, पूर्व्वगङ्गा.

NARCOTIC, a. स्वप्नकारी -रिणी -रि (न्), स्वप्नकृत् m. f. n., निद्राकारी &c., निद्राकृत् m. f. n., निद्राजनकः -का -कं, उपशायी -यिनी &c., उपशमनकारी &c.

NARCOTIC, s. निद्राजनकम् औषधं, उपशमनं, ग्राही m. (न्), उपविषं.

NARD, s. जटिला, जटावती, जटामांसी, जटाला. See SPIKENARD.

To NARRATE, v. a. कथ् (c. 10. कथयति -यितुं), सङ्कथ्, आख्या (c. 2. -ख्याति -तुं), समाख्या, ख्या in caus. (ख्यापयति -यितुं), निविद् (c. 10. -वेदयति -यितुं), आविद्, वर्ण् (c. 10. वर्णयति -यितुं), उपवर्ण्, अनुवर्ण्, संवर्ण्, शंस् (c. 1. शंसति -सितुं), श्रु (c. 10. श्रावयति -यितुं), आश्रु, संश्रु, निगद् (c. 1. -गदति -दितुं), अभिधा (c. 3. -दधाति -धातुं), विवृ (c. 5. -वृणोति -वरितुं -रीतुं), कृत् (c. 10. कीर्त्तयति -यितुं), अनुकृत्, व्याहृ (c. 1. -हरति -हर्त्तुं), उदाहृ, आचक्ष् (c. 2. -चष्टे), समाचक्ष्, विचक्ष्, परिचक्ष्, प्रचक्ष्, निरूप् (c. 10. -रूपयति -यितुं), वद् (c. 1. वदति -दितुं), विवरणं कृ, कथां कृ.

NARRATED, p. p. कथितः -ता -तं, आख्यातः -ता -तं, समाख्यातः -ता -तं.

NARRATION, s. (Act of telling) कथनं, आख्यानं, उपकथनं, उपाख्यानं, ख्यापनं, वर्णनं -ना, शंसनं, प्रशंसनं, विवरणं, अनुकीर्त्तनं, व्याहरणं, निरूपणं; 'of a story,' कथोपकथनं, कथोपाख्यानं.—(A story) कथा. See the next.

NARRATIVE, s. कथा, उपाख्यानं, उपकथा, परिकथा, आख्यानं, आख्यायिका, कथानुबन्धः, कथाप्रबन्धः, प्रबन्धः, वृत्तान्तः, वार्त्ता, चरित्रं, गोष्ठी, इतिहासः.

NARRATIVE, a. काथिकः -की -कं, विवरणकारी -रिणी &c., कथनः -ना -नं.

NARRATOR, s. कथकः, काथिकः, उपकथकः, आख्यायकः, कथनकृत् m.

NARROW, a. (Not broad, contracted, confined) अविस्तीर्णः -र्णा -र्णं, अविस्तृतः -ता -तं, सङ्कटः -टा -टं, सम्बाध in comp., निरन्तरालः -ला -लं, सङ्कुचितः -ता -तं, सङ्कोचितः -ता -तं, संवृतः -ता -तं, निरुद्धः -द्धा -द्धं, संरुद्धः &c., संहतः -ता -तं, संवृतः -ता -तं, अविपुलः -ला -लं, तनुः -नुः -न्वी -नु, अपृथुः &c.—(Confined in space) अल्पावकाशः -शा -शं, अल्पपरिमाणः -णा -णं, अविततः -ता -तं, अनायतः &c., निरायतः &c.—(Limited) मितः -ता -तं, परिमितः -ता -तं, नियतः -ता -तं, संयतः -ता -तं.—(Of narrow views) अल्पदृष्टिः -ष्टिः -ष्टि, कृपणबुद्धिः &c. See NARROW-MINDED. (Stingy) कृपणः -णा -णं, अव्ययशीलः -ला -लं, अनुदारः -रा -रं, स्वल्पव्ययी -यिनी &c.—(Close, accurate) सूक्ष्मः -क्ष्मा -क्ष्मं, अतिसूक्ष्मः &c.—(Small) अल्पः -ल्पा -ल्पं, स्वल्पः &c.

To NARROW, v. a. सङ्कुच् (c. 1. -कोचति -चितुं), सम्बाध् (c. 1. -बाधते -धितुं), संवृ (c. 5. -वृणोति -वरितुं -रीतुं), कुच् (c. 1. कुचति -चितुं, c. 10. कुचयति -यितुं), संहृ (c. 1. -हरति -हर्त्तुं), सङ्कटीकृ.—(Limit) परिमा (c. 2. -माति -तुं), संयम् (c. 1. -यच्छति -यन्तुं).

To NARROW, v. n. सङ्कुच् in pass. (-कुच्यते), सङ्कुचितः -ता -तं भू, सङ्कोचम् इ (c. 2. एति -तुं), सङ्कटीभू, सम्बाधीभू.

NARROWED, p. p. सङ्कुचितः -ता -तं, सङ्कोचितः -ता -तं, संवृतः -ता -तं, आकुञ्चितः -ता -तं, संहतः -ता -तं, संवृतः &c., संरुद्धः -द्धा -द्धं.

NARROWLY, adv. (With little breadth) अविस्तीर्णं, अविस्तृतं, सङ्कटं, सम्बाधं.—(Closely) सूक्ष्मं, अतिसूक्ष्मं, अभिनिवेशेन, स्ववहितं.—(Nearly, all but) ईषदूनं, अल्पोनं, कृच्छ्रेण, कष्टेन.

NARROW-MINDED, a. कृपणबुद्धिः -द्धिः -द्धि, कृपणधीः -धीः -धि, कृपणचेताः -ताः -तः (स्), मितमतिः -तिः -ति, मितबुद्धिः &c., अनुदारशीलः -ला -लं.

NARROWNESS, s. सम्बाधता, सङ्कटत्वं, अविस्तीर्णता, अविपुलता, अविस्तृतिः f., साङ्कट्यं, अल्पविस्तारः, अल्पविस्तृतिः f., सङ्कुचितत्वं, सङ्कोचः, अपृथुता, तनुता -त्वं, तानवं.—(Of extent) अल्पपरिमाणं, मितता, परिमितता, अल्पावकाशः, अवितृतिः f.—(Poverty) कार्पण्यं, दीनता.—(Illiberality) कृपणता, दैन्यं, अनुदारता.—(Of mind) बुद्धिकार्पण्यं, कृपणबुद्धित्वं, बुद्धिदीनता.—(Closeness) सूक्ष्मता, अतिसूक्ष्मता.

NASAL, a. नस्यः -स्या -स्यं, नास्यः -स्या -स्यं, नासिकासम्बन्धी -न्धिनी &c., नासिक्यः -क्या -क्यं.—(In grammar) अनुनासिकः -का -कं,

सानुनासिकः -का -कं, सानुस्वारः -रा -रं; 'the nasal dot,' अनुस्वारः, अनुनासिकचिह्नं.

NASAL, *a.* (Letter) अनुनासिकं, सानुनासिकं, अनुनासिकवर्णः.

NASTILY, *adv.* कुत्सितं, अशुद्धं, मलिनं, समलं, समालिन्यं, गर्हितं.

NASTINESS, *s.* मालिन्यं, मलिनता, समलता, मलं, अमेध्यता, कुत्सितत्वं, कौत्सित्यं, अशुद्धता, अपवित्रता, गर्ह्यता, गर्हितत्वं, बीभत्सजनकता.

NASTY, *a.* मलिनः -ना -नं, समलः -ला -लं, मलवान् -वती -वत् (त्), अशुद्धः -द्धा -द्धं, अमेध्यः -ध्या -ध्यं, कुत्सितः -ता -तं, गर्ह्यः -र्ह्या -र्ह्यं, गर्हितः -ता -तं, बीभत्सजनकः -का -कं, अपवित्रः -त्रा -त्रं; 'nasty conversation,' कुत्सितवाक्यं.

NATAL, *a.* जन्मसम्बन्धी -न्धिनी &c., जन्मविषयः -या -यं, जन्म in comp.; as, 'natal day,' जन्मदिवसः; 'natal country,' जन्मभूमिः *f.*

NATATION, *s.* (Swimming) तरणं, सन्तरणं, प्लवः -वनं.

NATION, *s.* जातिः *f.*, लोकः, जनपदः, प्रजा, वर्णः, जनता, देशः, विषयः, राष्ट्रं, देशजनः, देशलोकः, देशवासिनः *m. pl.*, राष्ट्रनिवासिनः, विशेषदेशजनता.

NATIONAL, *a.* (Pertaining to a nation) दैशिकः -की -कं, देशीयः -या -यं, देश्यः -श्या -श्यं, देशी -शिनी -शि (न्), जातीयः &c., राष्ट्रीयः &c., राष्ट्रिकः -की -कं, राष्ट्रियः -या -यं, देश in comp.; 'national custom,' देशव्यवहारः, देशाचारः; 'national law,' देशधर्म्मः, जनपदधर्म्मः; 'national calamity,' राष्ट्रं, उत्पातः.—(Proud of one's own country) स्वदेशाभिमानी -निनी -नि (न्), स्वलोकाभिमानी &c., स्वराष्ट्राभिमानी &c.; 'national pride,' देशाभिमानं.—(General) सामान्यः -न्या -न्यं, सर्व्वसामान्यः &c., साधारणः -णी -णं, सर्व्वजनीयः -या -यं.

NATIONALITY, *s.* स्वदेशाभिमानिता, स्वलोकाभिमानं, स्वराष्ट्राभिमानं.

NATIONALLY, *adv.* जातितस्, लोकतस्, देशधर्म्मानुसारेण, सामान्यतस्.

NATIVE, *a.* (Produced by nature, not artificial) सहजः -जा -जं, स्वाभाविकः -की -कं, स्वभावसिद्धः -द्धा -द्धं, स्वभावजः -जा -जं, प्रकृतिस्थः -स्था -स्थं, प्राकृतः -ती -तं, स्वयङ्कृतः -ता -तं, अकृत्रिमः -मा -मं, सांसिद्धिकः -की -कं; 'native salt,' स्वयङ्कृतम् ऊषरलवणं. *See* NATURAL. (Indigenous, not foreign) देशजः -जा -जं, देशोद्भवः -वा -वं, देशोत्पन्नः -न्ना -न्नं, स्वदेशजः &c., देशीयः -या -यं, दैशिकः -की -कं.—(Conferred by birth) जन्मप्राप्तः -प्ता -प्तं, जन्मसिद्धः -द्धा -द्धं, जन्मार्जितः -ता -तं.—(Natal) जन्म in comp., स्व in comp.; 'native country,' जन्मभूमिः *f.*, जन्मदेशः, जन्मवसुधा, स्वभूमिः *f.*, स्वराष्ट्रं, स्वविषयः, स्वदेशः, मूलायातनं, अभिजनः; 'native place,' जन्मस्थानं.

NATIVE, *s.* देशजः, देशोद्भवः, देशजातः, देशीयलोकः, देशीयजनः, देशलोकः, देशजनः, देशवासी *m.* (न्), राष्ट्रीयलोकः.

NATIVITY, *s.* जन्म *n.* (न्), जातिः *f.*, उत्पत्तिः *f.*, उद्भवः, सम्भवः, जनिमा *m.* (न्); 'astrological calculation of nativity,' जातकं; 'astrological record of it,' जन्मपत्रं -त्रिका; 'month of one's nativity,' जन्ममासः; 'name given at it,' जन्मनाम *n.* (न्), नक्षत्रनाम; 'star of one's nativity,' जन्मनक्षत्रं; 'sign,' जन्मराशिः *m.*, जन्मलग्नं.

NATRON, *s.* सर्ज्जिः *f.*, सर्ज्जिका, सर्ज्जिकाक्षारः, सृमिकाक्षारः, क्षारः, कापोतः, सौवर्च्चलः, सुमिका, सुखवर्चकः.

NATTY, *a.* विनीतः -ता -तं, परिमृष्टपरिच्छदः -दा -दं.

NATURAL, *a.* (Pertaining to nature, effected by nature, innate, not acquired) स्वाभाविकः -की -कं, प्राकृतिकः -की -कं, नैसर्गिकः -की -कं, सांसिद्धिकः -की -कं, स्वभावसिद्धः -द्धा -द्धं, प्रकृतिसिद्धः &c., सहजः -जा -जं, साहजिकः -की -कं, सहजातः -ता -तं, अन्तर्जातः -ता -तं, निजः -जा -जं, स्वजः &c., अन्तर्जः &c., स्वभावजः &c., निसर्गजः &c., अन्तर्भवः -वा -वं, स्वयङ्कृतः -ता -तं, स्वः -स्वा -स्वं, प्रकृतिस्थः -स्था -स्थं, सात्त्विकः -की -कं, भाविकः -की -कं, प्राकृतः -ती -तं, औत्सर्गिकः -की -कं, अन्तरुत्पन्नः -न्ना -न्नं, औत्पत्तिकः -की -कं; 'natural friend,' सहजमित्रं, प्राकृतमित्रं; 'natural enemy,' सहजारिः *m.*—(According to nature) भावानुगः -गा -गं, स्वभावानुगः &c., भावानुलोमः -मा -मं, स्वभावयोग्यः -ग्या -ग्यं, स्वभावानुसारी -रिणी &c., अनुलोमः -मा -मं, प्रकृत्यनुलोमः &c.—(According to the natural course, regular, proper) यथायोग्यः -ग्या -ग्यं, योग्यः &c., यथाक्रमः -मा -मं, यथामार्गः -र्गा -र्गं, यथायुक्तः -क्ता -क्तं, यथान्यायः -या -यं.—(Not artificial) अकृत्रिमः -मा -मं, अकृतकः -का -कं, अयत्नकृतः -ता -तं, अप्रतिविधानः -ना -नं, देवनिर्म्मितः -ता -तं; 'natural cave,' देवखातं.—(Not forced, easy, unaffected) अक्लिष्टः -ष्टा -ष्टं, अप्रतियत्नकृतः -ता -तं, सुलभः -भा -भं, अविलक्षितः -ता -तं, वैलक्ष्यहीनः -ना -नं.—(According to reality, true) यथार्थः -र्था -र्थं, सत्यः -त्या -त्यं, अकृत्रिमः -मा -मं, सरलः -ला -लं, प्रकृतः -ता -तं.—(Illegitimate) अनौरसः -सी, उपपत्नीजातः -ता, जारजः -जा, अविधिजातः -ता, विजातः -ता.—(Coming at the right time) यथाकालः -ला -लं, कालिकः -की -कं, कालोपयुक्तः -क्ता -क्तं, कालभूतः -ता -तं, अनपघाती -तिनी &c.; 'natural death,' सुमरणं.—(In Astronomy) सावनः -नी -नं; 'natural day,' सावनदिनं, अहोरात्रं; 'natural form,' स्वरूपं; 'natural temperament,' जन्मस्वभावः, जन्मप्रकृतिः *f.*, स्वभावः; 'natural history,' स्थावरजङ्गमविद्या स्थावरजङ्गमशास्त्रं, जडाजडविद्या; 'natural philosophy,' पदार्थविज्ञानं, पदार्थमात्रशास्त्रं.

NATURAL, *s.* (Idiot) यथाजातः, जडः, मूढः, न्यूनबुद्धिः *m.*

NATURALIST, *s.* स्थावरजङ्गमविद्याज्ञः, स्थावरजङ्गमविज्ञानी *m.* (न्), पदार्थविज्ञानी *m.*, पदार्थमात्रशास्त्रज्ञः.

NATURALIZATION, *s.* देशजाधिकारदानं, दैशिकाधिकारप्रतिपादनं.

To NATURALIZE, *v. a.* देशजाधिकारं दा, देशीयं -यां कृ, दैशिकं -कां कृ.—(Render familiar) अभ्यस् (c. 4. -अस्यति -असितुं), अभ्यासेन सुगमं -मां कृ.

NATURALLY, *adv.* (According to nature) स्वभावतस्, स्वभावेन -वात्, प्रकृतितस्, प्रकृत्या, भावतस्, स्वभावानुसारेण, जातितस्, जन्मतस्, गुणतस्.—(Regularly, according to the proper course) यथाक्रमं, यथायोग्यं, यथामार्गं.—(Not affectedly) यथार्थं, अवैलक्ष्येण.—(Not forcedly) अक्लिष्टं, अयत्नपूर्व्वं, सहजगत्या, सहजशक्त्या.—(Spontaneously) स्वतस्, स्वयं; 'done naturally,' स्वयङ्कृतः -ता -तं; 'very naturally,' स्वभावेनैव.

NATURALNESS, *s.* स्वाभाविकत्वं, प्राकृतत्वं, सहजत्वं, अकृत्रिमता.—(Conformity to reality) यथार्थता, याथातथ्यं, सत्यता, अवैलक्ष्यं, सरलता, सारल्यं.

NATURE, *s.* (The goddess who is the material cause of the world and all created things. According to the Hindú mythology this goddess is unreal, and identified with Máyá or Illusion, and sometimes with the Śakti or personified energy, or wife of a deity. She is in an especial manner the prototype of the female sex. Hence the following names for her) प्रकृतिः *f.*, माया, महामाया, आदिमाया, मायादेवी, प्रधानं, शक्तिः *f.*, आदिशक्तिः *f.*, लिङ्गं, अविद्या, दुर्गा, लक्ष्मीः *f.*; 'the illusion practised by nature,' मायाजालं; 'sleight of nature,' मायालाघवं.—(Essence, essential properties which constitute a thing) भावः, स्वभावः, प्रकृतिः *f.*,

प्रकृतिभावः, निसर्गः, सर्गः, सृष्टिः *f.*, संसिद्धिः *f.*, रूपं, स्वरूपं, धर्म्मः, स्वधर्म्मः, सत्त्वं, वस्तु *n.*, वस्तुस्वभावः, निसर्गभावः, आत्मा, जातिस्वभावः, समीक्षा, तत्त्वं, गुणः; the three 'gunas' or properties of nature are, 1. 'existence or truth,' सत्त्वं; 2. 'foulness or passion,' रजस् *n.*; 3. 'darkness,' तमस् *n.*—(Natural disposition or temper of mind) स्वभावः, प्रकृतिः *f.*, शीलः -लता, सहजः -जं, सहजभावः, सहजशीलः; 'good-nature,' सद्भावः, सुशीलः, साधुशीलत्वं.—(Natural form) स्वरूपं, सहजरूपं, प्रकृतिः *f.*, निसर्गः.—(Established, regular course of things) मार्गः, रीतिः *f.*, क्रमः, प्रकृतिमार्गः, सृष्टेरीतिः *f.*, सृष्टिक्रमः.—(System of created things) सृष्टिः *f.*, सर्गः, जगत् *n.*, विश्वजगत् *n.*, भूमण्डलं, ब्रह्मसृष्टिः, विश्वं.—(Natural feelings, affections or qualities) स्वभावगुणाः *m. pl.*, प्रकृतिगुणाः *m. pl.*, स्वभावधर्म्मः, प्रकृतिधर्म्मः, प्रकृतिभावः.—(Constitution, vital power of a body) जीवनशक्तिः *f.*, शक्तिः *f.*, जीवित्वशक्तिः *f.*, ओजस् *n.*, प्राणाः *m. pl.*, प्राणबलं, देहस्वभावः, शरीरस्थितिः *f.*—(Sort, kind) प्रकारः, जातिः *f.*, रूपं, रीतिः *f.*—(Law of action) विधिः *m.*, विधानं, नियमः, स्थितिः *f.*, धर्म्मः; 'by nature,' स्वभावेन, जात्या, जन्मतस्. *See* NATURALLY. 'Blind by nature,' जन्मान्धः -न्धा -न्धं, जात्यन्धः &c., गर्भान्धः &c.; 'offices of nature,' देहधर्म्मः, शरीरधर्म्मः; 'relieving nature,' मलविसर्गः, मलोत्सर्गः, मलमूत्रविसर्जनं.

NATURED, *a.* (Used in composition) expressed by स्वभावः -वा -वं, शीलः -ला -लं, प्रकृतिः -तिः -ति; as, 'good-natured,' सुशीलः -ला -लं; 'ill-natured,' दुष्प्रकृतिः -तिः -ति.

NAUFRAGE, *s.* (Shipwreck) नौभङ्गः, नौभेदः, नौकाभङ्गः.

NAUGHT, *s.* न किञ्चित्, न किञ्चन, न किमपि, अवस्तु.—(In arithmetic) शून्यं, खः; 'to set at naught,' अवज्ञा (c. 9. -जानाति -ज्ञातुं), लघूकृ. *See To* CONTEMN.

NAUGHT, *adv.* न किञ्चित्, न किञ्चिदपि, न किमपि.

NAUGHT, *a.* निर्गुणः -णा -णं, असारः -रा -रं, विगुणः -णा -णं.

NAUGHTILY, *adv.* प्रतीपं, प्रतीपवत्, दुष्टं, दुष्टभावेन, प्रतीपशीलत्वात्.

NAUGHTINESS, *s.* प्रतीपता, विप्रतीपता, अवश्यता, दुष्टता, दुर्वृत्तता.

NAUGHTY, *a.* प्रतीपः -पा -पं, विप्रतीपः -पा -पं, अवश्यः -श्या -श्यं, अविनेयः -या -यं, मन्दचरित्रः -त्रा -त्रं, दुश्चरित्रः &c., दुष्टः -ष्टा -ष्टं, दुर्वृत्तः -त्ता -त्तं.

NAULAGE, *s.* तरमूल्यं, तरपण्यं, तारिकं, तार्य्यं, आतरः, आतारः.

NAUMACHY, *s.* नौयुद्धं, नौकायुद्धं, नाविकयुद्धं, नौयुद्धकौतुकं.

NAUSEA, *s.* (Sickness) वमनेच्छा, विवमिषा, उत्क्लेशः, उत्क्लेदः.—(Loathing, disgust) बीभत्सः -त्सं, विकृतं, वैकृतं, वैकृत्यं, विकारः, कुत्सा, विरक्तिः *f.*, निर्वेदः.

To NAUSEATE, *v. n.* (Be inclined to vomit) वम् in des. (विवमिषति -षितुं), वमनेच्छुः -च्छुः -च्छु भू, विवमिषुः -षुः -षु भू.

To NAUSEATE, *v. a.* बाध् in des. (बीभत्सते -त्सितुं), घृण् (c. 1. घृणते -णितुं).

NAUSEATED, *p. p.* बीभत्सेन परित्यक्तः -क्ता -क्तं.

NAUSEOUS, *a.* (Causing sickness) वमनोत्पादकः -का -कं, वमनेच्छाजनकः -का -कं.—(Disgusting) बीभत्सजनकः -का -कं, घृणाजनकः &c., कुत्साजनकः &c., कुत्सितः -ता -तं, विरसः -सा -सं, गर्हितः -ता -तं.

NAUSEOUSNESS, *s.* बीभत्सजनकता, कुत्सितत्वं, विरसता, वैरस्यं.

NAUTIC, NAUTICAL, *a.* नौचालनविद्यासम्बन्धी -न्धिनी -न्धि (न्), नौकाचालनविषयः -या -यं, नाविकः -की -कं; 'nautical person,' नाविकः, नौकाजीवी *m.* (न्).

NAVAL, *a.* (Pertaining to ships) नाविकः -की -कं, नाव्यः -व्या -व्यं, नौकासम्बन्धी -न्धिनी &c., नौकाविषयः -या -यं.—(Consisting of ships) नौकामयः -यी -यं, नौकात्मकः -का -कं, नौकारूपः -पा -पं.

NAVE, *s.* (Of a wheel) नाभिः -भी *f.*, चक्रनाभिः *f.*, पिण्डिः -ण्डी *f.*, पिण्डिका.—(Of a church) पूजाशालाया मध्यभागः.

NAVEL, *s.* नाभिः -भी *f. m.*, तुण्डिः -ण्डी *f. m.*, तुण्डिका, तुन्दिः -न्दी *f.*, तुन्दिका, नालः, उदरावर्त्तः, मध्यवृत्तं, मणिपूरः, अमरा, अमला, भर्म्म, नाभिकमलं; 'hollow or pit of the navel,' नाभ्यावर्त्तः, तुन्दकूपी -पिका; 'region of the navel,' नाभिचक्रं; 'having a prominent navel,' तुन्दी -न्दिनी &c., तुन्दिकः -का -कं, तुन्दितः -ता -तं, तुन्दिलः -ला -लं, तुन्दिभः -भा -भं, तुन्दिकरः -रा -रं, तुन्दवान् -वती &c., तुण्डिलः &c., तुण्डिभः &c., गोण्डः -ण्डा -ण्डं.

NAVEL-STRING, *s.* नाभिनालः, नालः; 'cutting of it,' नाभिच्छेदनं, नालच्छेदः.

NAVIGABLE, *a.* नौतार्य्यः -र्य्या -र्य्यं, नाव्यः -व्या -व्यं, नौकागम्यः -म्या -म्यं, नौगम्यः &c., नौगमनार्हः -र्हा -र्हं.

NAVIGABLENESS, NAVIGABILITY, *s.* नौतार्य्यता, नौगम्यता, नाव्यता -त्वं.

To NAVIGATE, *v. a.* and *n.* नौकया or नावा तॄ (c. 1. तरति -रितुं -रीतुं) or अतित्तॄ or सन्तॄ or प्लु (c. 1. प्लवते, प्लोतुं) or गम् (c. 1. गच्छति, गन्तुं) or गमनागमनं कृ, समुद्रतरणं कृ, नौकापर्यटनं कृ, नौभ्रमणं कृ, नौकायात्रां कृ.—(Direct a ship) नौकां वह् (c. 10. वाहयति -यितुं) or चल् (c. 10. चालयति -यितुं) or आनी (c. 1. -नयति -नेतुं).

NAVIGATION, *s.* (Act of passing on the water in ships) नौकया or नावा तरणं or सन्तरणं or गमनं or गमनागमनं or पर्यटनं or भ्रमणं or यात्रा, समुद्रतरणं, समुद्रगमनं, नौगमनं, नौकायात्रा, नौगमनागमनं, नौभ्रमणं, नौपर्यटनं.—(Directing ships) नौकाचालनं, नौचालनं, नौकानयनं, नौकावाहनं.—(The art or science) नाविकविद्या, नौचालनविद्या, नौकानयनविद्या, नौवाहनविद्या.

NAVIGATOR, *s.* (One who sails) नाविकः, महानाविकः, समुद्रगामी *m.* (न्), समुद्रयायी *m.*, समुद्रतरः.—(One who directs a ship) नौचालकः, नौकावाहकः, पोतवाहकः, नौकानेता *m.* (तृ), नौकानयनकृत् *m.*

NAVY, *s.* युद्धनौसमूहः, युद्धनौकासमूहः, बृहन्नौकासमूहः, नौसमूहः.

NAY, *adv.* न, नो, नहि.—(Nay more) पुनर्, किम्पुनर्, अधिकन्तु, स्यं, किम् बहुना.—(Not only) न केवलं.

NEAP, *a.* (Low) नीचः -चा -चं, निम्नः -म्ना -म्नं; 'neap tide,' निम्नवेला, नीचवेला.

NEAR, *a.* (Not far distant) समीपः -पा -पं, निकटः -टा -टं, समीपस्थः -स्था -स्थं, निकटस्थः -स्था -स्थं, समीपवर्त्ती -र्त्तिनी -र्त्ति (न्), निकटवर्त्ती &c., समीपस्थायी &c., आसन्नः -न्ना -न्नं, सन्निकृष्टः -ष्टा -ष्टं, सन्निहितः -ता -तं, प्रत्यासन्नः -न्ना -न्नं, उपान्तः -न्ता -न्तं, अन्तिकः -का -कं, उपस्थः -स्था -स्थं, उपस्थायी &c., अभ्यासः -सा -सं, अभ्याशः -शा -शं, अभ्यर्णः -र्णा -र्णं, उपनतः -ता -तं, आरातीयः -या -यं, अभ्यग्रः -ग्रा -ग्रं, उपकण्ठः -ण्ठा -ण्ठं, सङ्काशः -शा -शं, सकाशः &c., सनीडः -डा -डं, सविधः -धा -धं, सवेशः -शा -शं, सवेधः -धा -धं, समर्य्यादः -दा -दं, अदूरः -रा -रं, अदूरस्थः &c., अविदूरः -रा -रं, संसक्तः -क्ता -क्तं, अव्यवहितः -ता -तं, अपदान्तरः -रा -रं, अपटान्तरः -रा -रं; 'nearer,' आसन्नतरः -रा -रं, नेदीयान् -यसी -यः (स्); 'nearest or very near,' आसन्नतमः -मा -मं, नेदिष्ठः -ष्ठा -ष्ठं, अन्तिकतमः -मा -मं, अन्तिमः -मा -मं.—(Closely connected) दृढसम्बद्धः -द्धा -द्धं, दृढसंसक्तः -क्ता -क्तं.—(Closely concerning or affecting one's interest) स्वार्थसम्बन्धी -न्धिनी &c., निकटसम्बन्धी &c., अन्तरङ्गः -ङ्गा -ङ्गं.—(Intimate) परिचितः -ता -तं, दृढसौहृदः -दा -दं.—(Stingy) कृपणः -णा -णं,

स्वल्पव्ययी -यिनी &c.—(Not rambling) अविस्तीर्णः -र्णा -र्णं; 'near at one's side,' पार्श्वस्थः &c.

NEAR, *adv.* समीपं -पतस्, निकटे, अन्तिकं, उपान्ते, अभितस्, आरात्, आसन्ने, सन्निकृष्टं, निकषा, अदूरे -रात् -रतस्, अविदूरं -रे -रात् -रतस्, सन्निधौ, सकाशं, also expressed by the prep. उप, *see* the next; 'near at one's side,' पार्श्वे -र्श्वतस्; 'situated near,' समीपस्थः -स्था -स्थं; 'going near,' समीपगः -गा -गं.—(Almost, within a little) प्रायस् -यशस्, भूयिष्ठं; 'a woman who is near her delivery,' आसन्नप्रसवा; 'one who is near his death,' आसन्नमृत्युः &c. *See* NEARLY.

NEAR, *prep.* उप, आ, अभि, प्रति; as, 'to go near,' उपगम् (c. 1. -गच्छति -गन्तुं) or उपागम् or अभिगम् or प्रतिगम्; 'brought near,' उपनीतः -ता -तं; 'near a mountain,' उपगिरि, उपगिरं; 'near the ear,' उपकर्णं; 'near the fire,' उपाग्नि; 'near the throat,' उपकण्ठं; 'near evening,' उपसन्ध्यं.

To NEAR, *v. a.* नेद् (nom. नेदयति -यितुं); 'come nearer to,' उपगम् (c. 1. -गच्छति -गन्तुं), उपागम्, अभिगम्. *See To* APPROACH.

NEARLY, *adv.* (At no distance) समीपं -पतस्, अदूरे -रं -रात् -रतस्. *See* NEAR, *adv.* (Closely) दृढं, गाढं; 'nearly connected,' दृढसम्बद्धः -द्धा -द्धं, गाढसम्बद्धः &c.—(Almost, within a little) प्रायस्, प्रायशस्, भूयिष्ठं, मनाक्, कल्पं, ईषदूनं, अल्पोनं; 'nearly finished,' समाप्तभूयिष्ठः -ष्ठा -ष्ठं; 'nearly dead,' मृतप्रायः -या -यं, मृतकल्पः -ल्पा -ल्पं, आसन्नमृत्युः -त्युः -त्यु, मुमूर्षुः -र्षुः -र्षु; 'the earth is nearly a sphere,' पृथिवी गोलप्राया; 'nearly cooked,' पचतिकल्पः &c.; 'nearly four, उपचतुराः *m. pl.*

NEARNESS, *s.* (Closeness) समीपता, सामीप्यं, नैकट्यं, निकटता, समीपवर्त्तित्वं, निकटवर्त्तित्वं, आसन्नता, सन्निकृष्टता, सान्निध्यं, सन्निधिः *m.*, सन्निधानं, सन्निकर्षः -र्षणं, सन्निधं, प्रत्यासत्तिः *f.*, प्रत्यासन्नता, आनन्तर्य्यं, अनन्तरं, उपस्थानं, अभ्यासत्वं.—(Closeness of connexion) दृढसम्बन्धः, दृढसंसक्तिः *f.*, दृढसंसर्गः, सुसंसर्गः.—(Intimacy) परिचयः, सुपरिचयः.—(Stinginess) कृपणता, कार्पण्यं, स्वल्पव्ययः.

NEAT, *a.* (Trim) विनीतः -ता -तं, परिमृष्टपरिच्छदः -दा -दं, सुरेखः -खा -खं, आकारशुद्धः -द्धा -द्धं.—(Clean) शुद्धः -द्धा -द्धं, श्लक्ष्णः -क्ष्णा -क्ष्णं, परिष्कृतः -ता -तं.

NEAT, *s.* (Cattle of the bovine genus) गवादिजन्तुः *m.*, गवादिपशुः *m.*

NEAT-HERD, *s.* गोपः, गोपालः, गोरक्षकः, गोचारकः, आभीरः.

NEATLY, *adv.* विनीतं, विनीतवत्, सपरिष्कारं, शुद्धं, श्लक्ष्णं, परिपाट्या, सुपरिपाट्या, परिष्कारपूर्व्वं.

NEATNESS, *s.* विनीतता -त्वं, शुद्धता, परिष्कारः, आकारशुद्धता, आकारशुद्धिः *f.*, परिमृष्टता, परिष्कृतता, शुद्धता, श्लक्ष्णता, परिपाटिः -टी, पारिपाट्यं.

NEBULA, *s.* (Opacity or film in the eye) शुक्लं, शुक्लपटलं.

NEBULOUS, *a.* मेघाच्छन्नः -न्ना -न्नं, मेघव्याप्तः -प्ता -प्तं, मेघाकीर्णः -र्णा -र्णं, बहुमेघः -घा -घं, साभ्रः -भ्रा -भ्रं, अभ्रियः -या -यं.

NECESSARIAN, *s.* दैववादी *m.* (न्), दैष्टिकः, दैवचिन्तकः, दैवैकवादी *m.*, अदृष्टवादी *m.*, दैवपरः.

NECESSARIES, *s. pl.* प्रतिदिनप्रयोजनीयद्रव्याणि *n. pl.*, प्रतिदिनप्रयोज्यद्रव्यसम्भारः, द्रव्यसम्भारः, उपकरणसम्भारः, उपकरणसामग्री; 'necessaries of life,' अन्नपानीयं, अन्नोदकं, अन्नवस्त्रं, अन्नाच्छादनं, कशिपु *m. du.*

NECESSARILY, *adv.* अवश्यं, अवशं, विवशं, अवश्यकं, अवश्यमेव, दैववशात्, दैववशतस्, कर्म्मवशतस्, कार्य्यवशात्, कार्य्यतस्, अनन्यगत्या, नूनं.

NECESSARY, *a.* (That must be, that cannot be otherwise) अवश्यकः -का -कं, आवश्यकः -की -कं, अवशः -शा -शं, अवश्यः -श्या -श्यं, विवशः -शा -शं, भवितव्यः -व्या -व्यं, भाव्यः -व्या -व्यं, अनन्यथासम्भवः -वा -वं, अनन्यथासाध्यः -ध्या -ध्यं, अनन्यथासिद्धः -द्धा -द्धं, अनन्योपायः -या -यं, अनन्यगतिकः -का -कं, अनिवार्य्यः -र्य्या -र्य्यं, नियतः -ता -तं.—(Requisite, needful, wanted) आकांक्षितः -ता -तं, अपेक्षितः -ता -तं, अवश्यकः -का -कं, अवश्यप्रापणीयः -या -यं, सर्व्वथा प्राप्यः -प्या -प्यं, अवश्योपयोगी -गिनी -गि (न्), अवश्यप्राप्तः -प्ता -प्तं, प्रयोजनीयः -या -यं.—(Indispensable, necessary to be done) आवश्यकः -की -कं, अवश्यकर्त्तव्यः -व्या -व्यं, अवश्यकरणीयः -या -यं, अवश्यभवितव्यः -व्या -व्यं, सर्व्वथा भवितव्यः &c. or भाव्यः -व्या -व्यं, अपरिहरणीयः -या -यं, अपरिहार्य्यः -र्य्या -र्य्यं; 'necessary act,' अवश्यकर्त्तव्यं.—(Acting from necessity) विधिवशः -शा -शं, विधिवशकारी &c., दैववशकारी &c., दैवाधीनः -ना -नं; 'the necessary consequence of acts,' कर्म्मवशः, कार्य्यवशः; 'it is necessary' may be expressed by the fut. pass. part., or by अर्हे. *See* MUST.

NECESSARY, *s.* (Privy) शौचकूपः, पायुक्षालनवेश्म *n.* (न्), अवस्करः कर्दमाटकः.—(A necessary thing). *See* NECESSARIES.

To NECESSITATE, *v. a.* (Make necessary) अवश्यकं -कां कृ, विवशं -शां कृ, विवशीकृ.—(Oblige, compel) अवश्यं कृ (c. 10. कारयति -यितुं) or प्रवृत् (c. 10. -वर्त्तयति -यितुं) or expressed by the causal form of any verb. *See* CONSTRAIN, COMPEL.

NECESSITATED, *p. p.* आवश्यकः -की -कं, विवशीकृतः -ता -तं. *See* CONSTRAINED.

NECESSITOUS, *a.* दरिद्रः -द्रा -द्रं, निर्धनः -ना -नं, दीनः -ना -नं, दुर्गतः -ता -तं.

NECESSITY, *s.* (Necessariness) अवश्यकता -त्वं, आवश्यकता, आवश्यकं, आवश्यं, अवश्यता -त्वं, विवशता, वैवश्यं, भवितव्यता, भाव्यता, अनन्यथासम्भवः, अनन्यगतिकत्वं, नियतिः *f.*, नियतत्वं -ता.—(Need, state of being requisite) प्रयोजनं, प्रयोगः, प्रयुक्तिः *f.*, उपयोगः, प्रयोजनीयता, आकांक्षा, अपेक्षा, सर्व्वथा प्रापणीयता.—(Occasion, cause) प्रयोजनं, हेतुः *m.*, निमित्तं, कार्य्यं; 'without any necessity,' प्रयोजनं विना, हेतुना विना; 'what necessity for this investigation?' एतया चर्चया किं प्रयोजनं.—(Indispensableness) कर्त्तव्यता, कार्य्यता, अवश्यकर्त्तव्यता, भवितव्यता, भाव्यता, कार्य्यवशः.—(Fate, fatality) दैवं, विधिः *m.*, दैवाधीनता, दैववशत्वं, दैवायत्तता, अदृष्टाधीनता, भवितव्यता, नियतिः *f.*—(Indigence) दरिद्रता, दारिद्र्यं, दीनता, दुर्गतिः *f.*

NECK, *s.* ग्रीवा, कन्धरा -रः, शिरोधिः *m. f.*, शिरोधरा, गलः, कण्ठः -ण्ठा -ण्ठी -ण्ठं, मस्तकमूलकं; 'back of the neck,' अवटुः *m. f.*, घाटा -टी -टः -टिका, कृकाटिका, कलम्बिका, सीमा *m.* (न्), पश्चाद्ग्रीवा; 'head and neck,' शिरोग्रीवं; 'of a pitcher, or any vessel,' कण्ठः; 'of the bladder,' वस्तिशिरस् *n.*; 'of a lute,' वीणादण्डः; 'of a horse,' निगालः; 'bending back the neck,' उत्कन्धरं; 'belonging to the neck,' ग्रैवः -वी -वं, ग्रैवेयः -यी -यं.

NECK-CLOTH, NECKERCHIEF, *s.* कण्ठवस्त्रं, ग्रीवावस्त्रं, ग्रीवावेष्टनं, ग्रीवावरणं, गलवस्त्रं, गलावेष्टनं, ग्रीवाबन्धनी, ग्रीवाभरणं, ग्रैवेयकं.

NECKED, *a.* ग्रीवः -वा -वं, कण्ठः -ण्ठा -ण्ठं in comp.; as, 'handsome-necked,' सुग्रीवः -वा -वं; 'long-necked,' दीर्घग्रीवः &c., दीर्घकण्ठः &c.

NECKLACE, *s.* माला -लिका, हारः, कण्ठमाला, सूत्रं, उरःसूत्रं -त्रिका, ग्रैवं -वेयं -यकं, कण्ठभूषा, कण्ठलता, लम्बनं, प्रालम्बिका, मलयः, तरलः.

ललन्तिका; 'of jewels,' मणिमाला, रत्नावली -लिः *f.*, मणिसरं; 'of pearls,' मुक्तावली -लिः *f.*, मुक्ताकलापः, मुक्ताप्रलम्बः, मुक्तालता; 'of gold,' हेमसूत्रकं, कनकसूत्रं; 'of beads,' अक्षमाला; 'of one string or row,' कण्ठिका; 'of a hundred strings,' देवच्छन्दः, शतयष्टिकः; 'of thirty-two strings,' गुच्छः; 'of thirty-four,' गुच्छार्द्धः.

NECROLOGY, *s.* मृतव्यक्तिविवरणं, मृतजनवृत्तान्तः, मृतजनपरिसंख्या.

NECROMANCER, *s.* श्मशानमन्त्रजापकः, प्रेतसिद्धिकर्त्ता *m.* (र्तृ). *See* MAGICIAN.

NECROMANCY, *s.* श्मशानमन्त्रजपनं, प्रेतसिद्धिः *f.*, भूतविद्या, भौतिकविद्या, पिशाचविद्या, कुविद्या. *See* MAGIC, *s.*

NECTAR, *s.* अमृतं, सुधा, सुधारसः, अमृतरसः, पीयूषं, पेयूषं, देवपेयं, लेह्यं, सोमः, पेयं, भक्तजा, कव्यं, तः; 'of flowers,' मधु *n.*, पुष्पमधु, पुष्परसः, पुष्पनिर्यासः, पुष्पसारः, पुष्पभवः, मकरन्दः, मरन्दः, नलदा.

NECTAREAN, NECTAREOUS, NECTARINE, *a.* अमृतमयः -यी -यं, सुधामयः &c., अमृततुल्यः -ल्या -ल्यं, अमृतोपमः -मा -मं, अमृतप्रायः -या -यं.

NEED, *s.* (Want, occasion for something) प्रयोजनं, प्रयोगः, प्रयुक्तिः *f.*, उपयोगः -गिता, कार्य्यं, कारणं, निमित्तं, हेतुः *m.*, आकांक्षा, अपेक्षा; 'there is need of me,' मया प्रयोजनं; 'there is need of a straw,' तृणेन कार्य्यं; 'what need is there of sorrow?' शोकेन किं प्रयोजनं, शोकस्य कः क्रमः or expressed by किं alone, as किं शोकेन; 'according to need,' प्रयोजनवत्, अर्थवत्, यथाप्रयोजनं, यथाकार्य्यं, यथासम्भवं.—(Indigence, distress, difficulty) दारिद्र्यं, दरिद्रता, दीनता, निर्धनता, दुर्गतिः *f.*, दुःखं, अनुपपत्तिः *f.*, सङ्कटं, कष्टं, संकष्टं, कृच्छ्रं, क्लेशः, बाधः.

To NEED, *v. a.* and *n.* (Require) आकांक्ष् (c. 1. -कांक्षति -क्षितुं), आकांक्ष्, अभिकांक्ष्, अपेक्ष् (c. 1. -ईक्षते -क्षितुं), प्रार्थ् (c. 10. -अर्थयति -यितुं), अर्ह् (c. 1. अर्हति -र्हितुं), often expressed by प्रयोजनं, उपयोगः or कार्य्यं; as, 'the healthy need not a physician,' निरामयाणां चिकित्सकेन प्रयोजनं नास्ति; 'he needs me,' तस्य मया प्रयोजनं. *See* also *To* LACK, *v. a.* (Be necessary). *See* MUST.

NEEDED, *p. p.* आकांक्षितः -ता -तं, अपेक्षितः -ता -तं, प्रयोजनीयः -या -यं.

NEEDFUL, *a.* आकांक्षणीयः -या -यं, प्रयोजनीयः -या -यं, प्रयोजनार्हः -र्हा -र्हं, अवश्यकः -का -कं, आवश्यकः -की -कं, अवश्यप्रापणीयः -या -यं, अवश्योपयोगी -गिनी -गि (न्), अपेक्षणीयः -या -यं, प्रार्थनीयः &c., आकांक्षितः -ता -तं, अपेक्षितः -ता -तं; 'needful to be done,' अवश्यकर्त्तव्यः -व्या -व्यं, अवश्यकार्य्यः -र्य्या -र्य्यं, अवश्यकरणीयः -या -यं; 'the one thing needful,' परमार्थः, परमप्रयोजनीयं.

NEEDINESS, *s.* दरिद्रता, दारिद्र्यं, निर्धनता, अधनता, दीनता, दैन्यं.

NEEDLE, *s.* सूचिः -ची *f.* -चिनी -चिका, सेवनी, कूर्चिका; 'eye of a needle,' सूचिरन्ध्रं, सूचिछिद्रं; 'point of one,' सूच्यग्रं.—(Magnetic needle) लोहकामः, अयस्कान्तमणिः *m.*, अयस्कान्तमणिशलाका.

NEEDLE-CASE, *s.* सूचिभाजनं, सूचिपात्रं, सूच्याधारः.

NEEDLE-MAKER, *s.* सूचिकारः -रकः, सूचिकरणोपजीवी *m.* (न्).

NEEDLE-WOMAN, *s.* सूचिका -की, सूचीशिल्पोपजीविनी.

NEEDLE-WORK, *s.* सूचिता, सूचिकर्म्म *n.* (न्), सूचिशिल्पकर्म्म, सूत्रकर्म्म.

NEEDLESS, *a.* निष्प्रयोजनः -ना -नं, निष्कारणः -णा -णं, अकारणः &c., अप्रयोजकः -का -कं, अप्रयोजनकः &c., अकारणकः &c., अहेतुकः &c., निरर्थकः &c., अनर्थकः &c., व्यर्थः -र्था -र्थं, किमर्थः -र्था -र्थं.

NEEDLESSLY, *adv.* प्रयोजनं विना, निष्प्रयोजनं, अकारणं, निष्कारणं, कारणं विना, हेतुना विना, हेतुं विना, अहेतुकं, निरर्थकं, व्यर्थं.

NEEDLESSNESS, *s.* अहेतुता -त्वं, अकारणत्वं, अकारणं, अप्रयोजकत्वं, अप्रयोजनं, निष्कारणत्वं, प्रयोजनाभावः, कारणाभावः.

NEEDS, *adv.* (Used with must) अवश्यं, अवश्यमेव. *See* MUST.

NEEDY, *a.* दरिद्रः -द्रा -द्रं, निर्धनः -ना -नं, अधनः -ना -नं, दीनः -ना -नं, दुर्गतः -ता -तं, अर्थहीनः -ना -नं, वित्तहीनः &c., अर्थी -र्थिनी -र्थि (न्).

NEFARIOUS, *a.* अतिदुष्टः -ष्टा -ष्टं, पापिष्ठः -ष्ठा -ष्ठं, अतिपापिष्ठः &c., अतिपापी -पिनी -पि (न्), दारुणः -णा -णं, घोरः -रा -रं, अघोरः -रा -रं, गर्ह्यः -र्ह्या -र्ह्यं, दुष्टतमः -मा -मं, अतिपातकी &c., महापातकी &c., अतिपापात्मा -त्मा -त्म (न्).

NEFARIOUSLY, *adv.* अतिदुष्टं, पापिष्ठं, दारुणं, घोरं, अघोरं, गर्हितं.

NEFARIOUSNESS, *s.* अतिदुष्टता, पापिष्ठता, दारुणता, घोरता, अतिगर्हितता.

NEGATION, *s.* निह्नवः, अपह्नवः, निह्नुतिः *f.*, अपह्नुतिः *f.*, अपलापः, प्रत्याख्यानं, अपवादः, अस्वीकारः, निषेधः, प्रत्यादेशः.—(In logic) अभावः according to one division it is of two kinds, 'universal negation,' संसर्गाभावः; 'relative or mutual negation,' अन्योन्याभावः; according to another division it is of four kinds, viz. 'extinction,' प्रध्वंसाभावः; 'antecedent non-existence,' प्रागभावः; 'reciprocal negation,' अन्योन्याभावः; 'simple non-existence,' अत्यन्ताभावः.

NEGATIVE, *a.* (Implying denial) अपलापी -पिनी -पि (न्), निह्नवसूचकः -का -कं, निह्नवार्थकः -का -कं, अपवादकः -का -कं, अस्वीकारसूचकः &c., निषेधसूचकः &c., निषेधार्थकः -का -कं.—(Implying absence, privative) अभावसूचकः -का -कं, अभावरूपः -पा -पं, अभावात्मकः -का -कं, अभावदर्शकः -का -कं, अकरणरूपः -पा -पं, अकरणात्मकः -का -कं, अननुष्ठानरूपः -पा -पं.—(Stopping by non-consent) निषेधद्वारा प्रतिबन्धकः -का -कं.

NEGATIVE, *s.* (Word) अस्वीकारसूचकशब्दः, निषेधसूचकशब्दः, अपलापसूचकशब्दः, निषेधार्थकशब्दः, अस्वीकारशब्दः.—(Proposition by which something is denied) अभावसूचकपक्षः, अभावसूचकवाक्यं, निषेधसूचकपक्षः, नास्तिपक्षः, अभावपक्षः.—(Right of preventing) निषेधाधिकारः, निषेधशक्तिः *f.*, प्रतिबन्धसामर्थ्यं.

To NEGATIVE, *v. a.* निषिध् (c. 1. -षेधति -षेद्धुं), प्रतिषिध्, निषेधद्वारा प्रतिबन्ध् (c. 9. -बध्नाति -बन्द्धुं), अपलप् (c. 1. -लपति -पितुं), निरस् (c. 4. -अस्यति -असितुं), निह्नु (c. 2. -ह्नुते -ह्नोतुं), अपह्नु, निषेधं कृ.—(Disprove). *See* the word.

NEGATIVED, *p. p.* निषिद्धः -द्धा -द्धं, निषेधितः -ता -तं, निरस्तः -स्ता -स्तं.

NEGATIVELY, *adv.* अस्वीकारेण, सनिषेधं, सापलापं, सापवादं, अभावरूपेण.

To NEGLECT, *v. a.* (Omit) त्यज् (c. 1. त्यजति, त्यक्तुं), परित्यज्, अतिचर् (c. 1. -चरति -रितुं), लङ्घ् (c. 10. लङ्घयति -यितुं), विलङ्घ्, उल्लङ्घ्, अतिक्रम् (c. 1. -क्रामति -क्रमितुं), व्यतिक्रम्, अतिवृत् (c. 1. -वर्त्तते -र्त्तितुं), हा (c. 3. जहाति, हातुं), अपहा, अपास् (c. 4. -अस्यति -असितुं), उत्सृज् (c. 6. -सृजति -स्रष्टुं), अतिसृज्, व्यपसृज्.—(Be careless about) प्रमद् (c. 4. -माद्यति -मदितुं), न अवधा (c. 3. -धत्ते -धातुं), अनवधानं कृ, प्रमादात् परित्यज्; 'he neglects his duty,' स्वधर्म्मात् प्रमाद्यति.—(Not to perform) न अनुष्ठा (c. 1. -तिष्ठति -ष्ठातुं), अननुष्ठानं कृ, न कृ.—(Forget to perform) विस्मृ (c. 1. -स्मरति -ते -स्मर्त्तुं), न स्मृ, अपस्मृ, विस्मरणात् परित्यज्.—(Disregard) उपेक्ष् (c. 1. -ईक्षते -क्षितुं), समुपेक्ष्, उपप्रेक्ष्, न सेव् (c. 1. सेवते -वितुं), असेवनं कृ.—(Slight) अवज्ञा (c. 9. -जानाति -ज्ञातुं), अवमन् (c. 4. -मन्यते -मन्तुं), अवधीर् (c. 10. -धीरयति -यितुं), अवगण् (c. 10. -गणयति -यितुं), अनादरं कृ,

खलीकृ; 'he neglects to honor the honorable,' पूज्यपूजाव्यतिक्रमं करोति.

NEGLECT, *s.* (Omission, forbearing to do any thing) त्यागः, परित्यागः, अननुष्ठानं, उपात्ययः, अतिपातः, पर्य्ययः, अनभ्यासः, अवक्रिया, लोपः, परिलोपः, अपासनं, उत्सर्जनं, अतिसर्जनं, अतिक्रमः, व्यतिक्रमः, अतिवर्त्तनं, लङ्घनं, विलङ्घनं, अतिचारः.—(Carelessness, inattention) प्रमादः, प्रमाद्यं, प्रमत्तता, अनवधानं.—(Forgetfulness) विस्मृतिः *f.*, विस्मरणं.—(Disregard) उपेक्षा, अनपेक्षा, अनवेक्षा, निरपेक्षा, उत्प्रेक्षा, उद्भावनं, अदर्शनं.—(Slighting) अवज्ञा, अवमानं, अनादरः, अमाननं, अवधीरणं, अवपालनं.

NEGLECTED, *p. p.* त्यक्तः -क्ता -क्तं, परित्यक्तः &c., लङ्घितः -ता -तं, उल्लङ्घितः -ता -तं, अतिक्रान्तः -न्ता -न्तं, अतीतः -ता -तं, अपासितः -ता -तं, उत्सृष्टः -ष्टा -ष्टं, विसर्जितः -ता -तं, अननुष्ठितः -ता -तं, असेवितः -ता -तं, उपेक्षितः -ता -तं, समुपेक्षितः -ता -तं, अनपेक्षितः -ता -तं, अवज्ञातः -ता -तं, अवधीरितः -ता -तं, अवमानितः -ता -तं, अवमतः -ता -तं, अवगणितः -ता -तं, अवपालितः &c., उद्भावितः &c., अरक्षितः, &c., अवसन्नः -न्ना -न्नं, खलीभूतः &c.

NEGLECTFUL, *a.* (Heedless, inattentive) अनवधानः -ना -नं, अनवहितः -ता -तं, असावधानः -ना -नं, प्रमादी -दिनी -दि (न्), प्रमादवान् -वती -वत् (त्), प्रमत्तः -त्ता -त्तं.—(Disregardful) उपेक्षकः -का -कं, निरपेक्षः -क्षा -क्षं, निर्व्यपेक्षः &c., मन्दादरः -रा -रं, अनादरकारी &c.

NEGLECTFULLY, *adv.* अनवधानेन, अनवहितं, प्रमादेन, सप्रमादं, निरपेक्षं, अनपेक्षया, उपेक्षया, अनपेक्ष्य, मन्दादरं, अवमानेन.

NEGLIGENCE, *s.* अनवधानं -नता, प्रमादः, प्रमाद्यं, प्रमत्तता, अनवहितत्वं, उपेक्षा, अनपेक्षा, अनवेक्षा, असमीक्षा, अव्यवसायः, बालिश्यं. *See* NEGLECT.

NEGLIGENT, *a.* अनवधानः -ना -नं, प्रमत्तः -त्ता -त्तं, प्रमादी -दिनी -दि (न्), प्रमादवान् -वती -वत् (त्), अनवहितः -ता -तं, असावधानः -ना -नं, उपेक्षकः -का -कं, निरपेक्षः -क्षा -क्षं, अव्यवसायी &c., मन्दादरः -रा -रं.

NEGLIGENTLY, *adv.* प्रमादात्, प्रमादेन, प्रमादतस्, प्रमादतस्, अनवधानात्, अनवधानेन, अवधानं विना, प्रमत्तवत्, असमीक्ष्य. *See* NEGLECTFULLY.

NEGOTIABLE, *a.* पणितव्यः -व्या -व्यं, पणायितव्यः &c., व्यवहर्त्तव्यः &c., व्यवहार्य्यः -र्य्या -र्य्यं, व्यवहारयोग्यः -ग्या -ग्यं, व्यवसाययोग्यः &c.

To NEGOTIATE, *v. a.* पण् (c. 1. पणते -णितुं, पणायति, c. 10. पणयति -यितुं), पणायां कृ, व्यवहृ (c. 1. -हरति -हर्त्तुं), व्यवसायं कृ.

NEGOTIATED, *p. p.* पणितः -ता -तं, पणायितः -ता -तं, व्यवहारितः -ता -तं.

NEGOTIATION, *s.* पणाया, पणनं, व्यवहारः, व्यवसायः, घटना, प्रपञ्चनं.—(Pacification) साम *n.* (न्), सन्धिकरणं, शमनं.

NEGOTIATOR, *s.* पणायाकृत्, पणिकः, आपणिकः, व्यवसायी *m.* (न्), व्यवहर्त्ता *m.* (र्त्तृ), व्यवहारी *m.* (न्), कर्म्मकारी *m.*—(Pacificator) सामवित् *m.*, सन्धिवित् *m.*, सन्धिविचक्षणः, सन्धिकुशलः, स्थेयः.

NEGRO, *s.* श्यामदेहः, श्यामशरीरः, श्यामाङ्गः, कृष्णदेहः, कृष्णाङ्गः.

To NEIGH, *v. n.* हेष् (c. 1. हेषते -षितुं) or ह्रेष्, हेष् (c. 1. हेषते -षितुं), रेष् (c. 1. रेषते -षितुं), अश्ववद् रु (c. 2. रौति, रवितुं) or नद् (c. 1. नदति -दितुं) or नादं कृ or चित्कारं कृ.

NEIGH, *s.* हेषा, ह्रेषा, ह्रेषितं, रेषणं, रेषितं, ह्रेषा, अश्वनादः.

NEIGHBOR, *s.* प्रतिवासी *m.* (न्), निकटवासी *m.*, निकटवर्त्ती *m.* (न्), समीपवासी *m.*, निकटस्थः, समीपस्थः, समीपस्थायी *m.*, प्रतिवेशवासी *m.*, प्रतिवेशी *m.*, प्रतिवेशिकः, सामन्तवासी *m.*, समीपदेशनिवासी जनः, समीपगृहवासी *m.*, सामन्तः, अधिवासः, संस्थः, संस्थितः; 'a next-door neighbor,' निरन्तरगृहवासी *m.*, प्रातिवेश्यः; 'next but one,' अनुवेश्यः; 'one should love one's neighbor as one's self,' आत्मौपम्येन परस्मिन् दयां कुर्य्यात्.

NEIGHBOR, *a.* प्रतिवासी -सिनी -सि (न्). *See* NEIGHBORING.

To NEIGHBOR, *v. a.* निकटे or समीपे स्था (c. 1. तिष्ठति, स्थातुं) or वृत् (c. 1. वर्त्तते -र्त्तितुं) or वस् (c. 1. वसति, वस्तुं), स्पृश् (c. 6. स्पृशति, स्प्रष्टुं).

NEIGHBORHOOD, *s.* (Vicinity, adjoining district) सामन्तदेशः, सामन्तं, समीपदेशः, समीपस्थानं, प्रतिवेशः, सन्निवेशः, अधिवासः, अन्तिकं, उपान्तं, निकषेणः.—(State of being near, proximity) समीपता, सामीप्यं, निकटता, नैकट्यं, सन्निधानं, सान्निध्यं, सन्निधिः *m.*, सन्निधं, सन्निकर्षः, सन्निकृष्टता, आसन्नता, अन्तिकता, अन्तिकं, उपान्तं -न्त्यं, प्रत्यासन्नता, प्रत्यासत्तिः *f.*, सामन्तत्वं, निकटवर्त्तित्वं, समीपवर्त्तित्वं, संस्थानं, उपस्थानं, अभ्यासत्वं; 'in the neighborhood of the house,' गृहसन्निधाने, गृहोपान्ते.—(Inhabitants of the neighborhood) समीपवासिनः *m. pl.*, निकटवासिनः *m. pl.*, सामन्तवासिनः *m. pl.*, प्रतिवासिनः *m. pl.*, समीपलोकाः *m. pl.*, तत्रत्यलोकाः *m. pl.*

NEIGHBORING, *a.* निकटवर्त्ती -र्त्तिनी -र्त्ति (न्), समीपवर्त्ती &c., निकटस्थः -स्था -स्थं, समीपस्थः &c., समीपस्थायी &c., समीपवासी &c., सामन्तवासी &c., प्रतिवासी &c., सामन्तस्थः &c., सामन्तः -न्ती -न्तं, समीपः -पा -पं, आसन्नः -न्ना -न्नं, निकटः -टा -टं, अन्तिकः -का -कं, उपान्तः -न्ता -न्तं, उपान्तिकः -की -कं, सन्निहितः -ता -तं, अभ्यासः -सा -सं, अभ्याशः -शा -शं, अदूरस्थः &c., अदूरीस्थः &c.; 'neighboring district,' 'neighboring people.' *See* NEIGHBORHOOD.

NEIGHBORLINESS, *s.* सामन्तव्यवहारयोग्यता, संस्थव्यवहारयोग्यता, सामन्तजनाचारानुसरणं, उपकारशीलता, मित्रत्वं, हितता.

NEIGHBORLY, *a.* सामन्तव्यवहारयोग्यः -ग्या -ग्यं, संस्थव्यवहारयोग्यः &c., प्रतिवासयोग्यः &c., सामन्ताचारानुसारी -रिणी &c., उपकारशीलः -ला -लं, सुहितः -ता -तं.

NEIGHING, *s.* हेषा, ह्रेषा, ह्रेषितं, ह्रेषा, रेषणं -षितं, ह्रेषितस्वनः, अश्वशब्दः, अश्वनादः, अश्वनिस्वनः.

NEITHER, *pron.* (Not either, not the one or the other) expressed by अन्यतरः -रा -रं or एकतरः -रा -रं or उभौ, or simply by the dual in conjunction with the negative न; as, 'neither of them can break the bow,' धनुर् भंक्तुम् एकतरो न शक्नोति or उभौ न शक्तः or simply न शक्तः.

NEITHER, *conj.* expressed by the negative न or न च, or by the prohibitive मा. Sometimes in conjunction with वा; as, 'he took neither food nor clothes for his journey,' यात्रार्थं भक्ष्यं वस्त्रं वा न जग्राह; 'take neither food nor clothes,' भक्ष्यं वस्त्रं वा मा गृहाण; 'do not eat the fruit neither touch it,' फलं मा खादत मा स्पृशत; 'he did not touch, neither did he smell,' नास्पृशद् न चाजिघ्रत्.

NEM. CON. सर्व्वसम्मत्या, सर्व्वानुमत्या, सर्व्वस्वीकारेण.

NEOGAMIST, *s.* नवोढः -ढा, नववधूः *f.*, नवभार्य्या *f.*, नवपतिः *m.*

NEOLOGIC, NEOLOGICAL, *a.* (Pertaining to neology) नूतनन्यायसम्बन्धी -न्धिनी &c., नूतनमतसम्बन्धी &c.—(Employing new words, &c.) *See* the next.

NEOLOGIST, *s.* नूतनशब्दसेवी *m.* (न्), नूतनन्यायाश्रयी *m.*, नूतनमताश्रयी *m.*, नूतनन्यायसेवी *m.*

NEOLOGY, *s.* नूतनन्यायः, नूतनमतं, नूतनविद्या.—(Employment of new words, &c.) नूतनशब्दसेवनं, नूतनमताश्रयणं.

NEOPHYTE, *s.* नवछात्रः, नवशिष्यः, प्राथमकल्पिकः, नूतनशिष्यः.

NEOTERIC, *a.* नूतनः -ना -नं, नवः -वा -वं, नवीनः -ना -नं, इदानीन्तनः -नी -नं, आधुनिकः -की -कं, अर्वाचीनः -ना -नं.

NEPAL, *s.* (The country) नेपालः.—(Belonging to it, or produced in it) नैपालिकः -की -कं, नैपालः -ली -लं.

NEPENTHE, *s.* दुःखशमनं, दुःखहारकम् औषधं, उपशमनं.

NEPHEW, *s.* (Brother's son) भ्रातृजः, भ्रात्रीयः, भ्रातृपुत्रः, भ्रातृसुतः, भ्रातृव्यः.—(Sister's son) भागिनेयः, स्वस्रीयः, भगिनीपुत्रः, स्वसृपुत्रः, भगिनीसुतः, स्वसृसुतः.

NEPHRITIC, NEPHRITICAL, *a.* (Relating to the kidneys) मूत्रपिण्डसम्बन्धी -न्धिनी &c., वृक्कसम्बन्धी &c.—(Relieving disease of the kidneys) मूत्रपिण्डरोगहारी -रिणी &c., मूत्ररोगनाशकः -का -कं, वृक्करोगघ्नः -घ्नी -घ्नं.

NEPOTISM, *s.* (Fondness for nephews) भ्रातृव्यभागिनेयस्नेहः.—(Undue attachment for relations) पुत्रपौत्रादिपक्षपातः, कुलपक्षता, अपत्यातिस्नेहः, सन्तानातिस्नेहः, बान्धवातिस्नेहः.

NEREID, *s.* (Sea-nymph) समुद्रीयदेवी, सामुद्रदेवी, जलदेवी.

NERVE, *s.* (Organ of sensation, connected with the marrow of the brain and spine) मज्जातन्तुः *m.*, ज्ञानतन्तुः, ज्ञानवाहिनी, चैतन्यवाहिनी, चैतन्यतन्तुः *m.*, शिरा, सिरा.—(Sinew, tendon) स्नायुः *m.*, वसा, शिरा, सिरा, धमनिः -नी *f.*, नाडिः -डी *f.*, वहीरुः *m.*, रसालसा, सन्धिबन्धनं.—(Strength of body) शरीरदृढता, शरीरदार्ढ्यं, गात्रदार्ढ्यं, शरीरबलं, तेजस् *n.*, वीर्य्यं, ओजस् *n.*, ऊर्जः.—(Strength of mind) धैर्य्यं, धीरता -त्वं, धृतिः *f.*, मनःस्थैर्य्यं, बुद्धिवैभवं.

To NERVE, *v. a.* बलं or धैर्य्यं दा or वृध् (c. 10. वर्धयति -यितुं), सबलीकृ.

NERVELESS, *a.* निर्बलः -ला -लं, दुर्बलः -ला -लं, बलहीनः -ना -नं.

NERVOUS, *a.* (Pertaining to the nerves) मज्जातन्तुसम्बन्धी -न्धिनी &c., मज्जातन्तुस्थः -स्था -स्थं, मज्जातन्तुगतः -ता -तं.—(Having the nerves affected, easily agitated) मज्जातन्तुरोगी -गिणी &c., मज्जातन्तुविकारी &c., शिरारोगी &c., धैर्य्यहीनः -ना -नं, कम्पशीलः -ला -लं, वेपनशीलः &c.—(Vigorous) वीर्य्यवान् -वती -वत् (त्), तेजोवान् &c., ओजस्वी &c., ऊर्जस्वान् &c., ऊर्जस्वलः -ला -लं, धीरः -रा -रं, दृढः -ढा -ढं, सुदृढः &c.

NERVOUSLY, *adv.* (With vigor) सवीर्य्यं, सधैर्य्यं, सबलं, धैर्य्येण.—(With weakness) धैर्य्येण विना, धैर्य्यं विना, सकम्पं, सवेपनं, कम्पशीलत्वात्.

NERVOUSNESS, *s.* (Vigor) वीर्य्यं, धैर्य्यं, धीरता -त्वं, तेजस् *n.*, ओजस् *n.*, दार्ढ्यं, दृढता, सुदृढता, ऊर्जः.—(Affection or weakness of the nerves, agitation) मज्जातन्तुरोगः, मज्जातन्तुविकारः -रिता, धैर्य्यहीनता, अधृतिः *f.*, कम्पशीलता, वेपनशीलता.

NESCIENCE, *s.* अज्ञानं -नता, ज्ञानाभावः, ज्ञानहीनता, अबोधः, अज्ञता.

NESS. This termination, denoting state or quality, is expressed in Sanskrit by the affixes ता, त्वं, and यं, the last usually requiring Vriddhi of the first syllable of the noun; as, from 'idle,' अलस; 'idleness,' अलसता, अलसत्वं, आलस्यं.

NEST, *s.* (Of birds) नीडः -डं, कुलायः, पक्षिस्थानं, पक्षिगृहं, खगस्थानं, जालकं, अङ्कुरकः.—(Any abode, receptacle) गृहं, स्थानं, निधिः *m.*, निधानं, आश्रयः, आलयः; 'sitting in a nest,' कुलायनिलायः.

To NESTLE, *v. n.* पक्षिवत् स्वनीडम् आश्रि (c. 1. -श्रयति -यितुं) or समाश्रि or संश्रि, सुखेन or सुखम् आश्रि, यथासुखम् आश्रि or शी (c. 2. शेते, शयितुं) or अधिशी or संविश् (c. 6. -विशति -वेष्टुं) or उपविश् or निली (c. 4. -लीयते -लेतुं).

To NESTLE, *v. a.* (Cherish) पाल् (c. 10. पालयति -यितुं), पुष् (c. 10. पोषयति -यितुं).

NESTLING, *s.* कुलायस्थः or नीडस्थः पक्षिशावकः, कुलायस्थायी *m.* (न्).

NESTOR, *s.* (Sage old man) वृहस्पतिः *m.*

NET, *s.* जालं, जालकं, आनायः, पाशः, पाशबन्धः -न्धं, वागुरा, उन्माथः, कूटः, कूटयन्त्रं, वीतंसः, वितंसः, पक्षिबन्धनं, बन्धनं -नी; 'for deer,' मृगबन्धिनी -नं, पाशिली; 'for fish,' मत्स्यधानी, मत्स्यजालं, मत्स्यग्रहणी, मत्स्यग्रहणार्थं जालं, कुपिनी, पञ्जराखेटः; 'maker of nets,' जालकारकः.

NET, *a.* (Clear, free from deductions) अशेषः -षा -षं, निरवशेषः &c., अभग्नः -ग्ना -ग्नं, अखण्डः -ण्डा -ण्डं, अन्यूनः -ना -नं, निरुद्धारः -रा -रं, शुद्धः -द्धा -द्धं.

To NET, *v. a.* (Make clear gain) अन्यूनं फलं लभ् (c. 1. लभते, लब्धुं).

NETHER, *a.* अधरः -रा -रं, अवरः -रा -रं, अधरस्थः -स्था -स्थं, अधःस्थः &c., अधोभवः -वा -वं, अधस्तनः -नी -नं, नीचस्थः &c., अधमः -मा -मं, अवमः &c., जघन्यः -न्या -न्यं; 'nether part,' अधोभागः; 'nether world,' अधोलोकः; 'nether garment,' अधोंशुकं, अन्तरीयं; 'nether sky,' नभस्तलं.

NETHERMOST, *a.* अवरः -रा -रं, अवरतमः -मा -मं, अधरतमः &c., नीचतमः &c.

NETTING, NET-WORK, *s.* जालं -लकं, जालकर्म्म *n.* (न्), जालप्राया.

NETTLE, *s.* (A plant) पीतपर्णी.

To NETTLE, *v. a.* प्रकुप् (c. 10. -कोपयति -यितुं), व्यथ् (c. 10. व्यथयति -यितुं), सन्तप् (c. 10. -तापयति -यितुं), कोपं जन् (c. 10. जनयति -यितुं).

NETTLED, *p. p.* ईषत्कुपितः -ता -तं, ईषत्सन्तप्तः -प्ता -प्तं, व्यथितः -ता -तं.

NEURALGIA, *s.* मज्जातन्तुवेदना, मज्जातन्तुव्यथा, शिरावेदना.

NEUROLOGY, *s.* मज्जातन्तुवर्णनं -ना, मज्जातन्तुविद्या, शिरावर्णनं.

NEUROTOMY, *s.* मज्जातन्तुछेदः -दनं, शिराव्यवच्छेदविद्या.

NEUTER, NEUTRAL, *a.* (Not adhering to either party, indifferent) अपक्षपाती -तिनी -ति (न्), विपक्षपातः -ता -तं, उभयपक्षसमानः -ना -नं, उभयपक्षसमः -मा -मं, उभयसामान्यः -न्या -न्यं, उभयसाधारणः -णी -णं, उभयपक्षभिन्नः -न्ना -न्नं, उदासीनः -ना -नं, उदासी &c., तटस्थः -स्था -स्थं, मध्यस्थः &c., समदर्शी &c., समदृष्टिः -ष्टिः -ष्टि, समबुद्धिः -द्धिः -द्धि, समभावः -वा -वं, समः -मा -मं.—(Neuter gender) क्लीबः -बं, नपुंसकः -कं, नपुंसकलिङ्गं, तृतीयप्रकृतिः *f.*, तृतीयाप्रकृतिः.

NEUTRALITY, *s.* माध्यस्थं -स्थ्यं, मध्यस्थता -त्वं, ताटस्थ्यं, तटस्थता -त्वं, उभयपक्षसमता, अपक्षपातः -तिता, विपक्षपातत्वं, उदासीनता, औदासीन्यं, औदास्यं, उभयसमता, उभयसाम्यं, उभयसामान्यं, उभयसाधारण्यं, समदृष्टिः *f.*, समता, साम्यं, समानता.

NEUTRALIZATION, *s.* (Act of destroying the peculiar properties of a body) विशेषगुणनाशः -शनं, विशेषधर्म्मनाशः -शनं, गुणविनाशनं, विशेषगुणप्रतीकारः.—(Act of reducing to a state of neutrality) उदासीनीकरणं, समीकरणं, उभयसमीकरणं.—(Rendering inefficient) निर्बलीकरणं, दुर्बलीकरणं.

To NEUTRALIZE, *v. a.* (Destroy the peculiar properties of) विशेषगुणान् नश् (c. 10. नाशयति -यितुं), विशेषगुणनाशनं कृ, विशेषधर्म्मनाशं कृ.—(Render neutral) उदासीनीकरणं, उभयसमीकरणं.—(Render inefficient) निर्बलीकृ, दुर्बलीकृ, बलं नश्.

NEUTRALIZED, *p. p.* नष्टगुणः -णा -णं, नष्टबलः -ला -लं, नष्टशक्तिः -क्तिः -क्ति.

NEUTRALIZER, *s.* विशेषगुणनाशकः, बलनाशकः, शक्तिनाशकः, गुणघ्नः.

NEUTRALLY, *adv.* उदासीनवत्, औदासीन्यपूर्व्वं, उभयसाम्येन, समदृष्ट्या.

NEVER, *adv.* न कदाचित्, न कदापि, न कदाचन, न कर्हिचित्, न जातु, न जातुचित्, sometimes expressed by न; as, 'there never has been and never will be any one like him,' अनेन सदृशः कश्चिन् न भूतो न भविष्यति.

NEVERTHELESS, *conj.* तथापि, पुनर्, परन्तु, परं, किन्तु, अपितु, किञ्च.

NEW, *a.* नवः -वा -वं, नवीनः -ना -नं, नूतनः -ना -नं, नूत्नः -त्ना -त्नं, नव्यः -व्या -व्यं, अभिनवः -वा -वं, प्रतिनवः -वा -वं, प्रत्यग्रः -ग्रा -ग्रं, तरुणः -णा -णं.—(Modern, not ancient) आधुनिकः -की -कं, इदानीन्तनः -नी -नं, अधुनातनः -नी -नं, सद्यस्कालीनः -ना -नं, अप्राचीनः -ना -नं, अपुरातनः -नी -नं.—(Never occurring before) अभूतपूर्व्वः -र्व्वा -र्व्वं, अदृष्टपूर्व्वः &c., अश्रुतपूर्व्वः &c., अपूर्व्वः &c., अयथापूर्व्वः &c. —(Not habituated, not familiar) अनभ्यस्तः -स्ता -स्तं, अपरिचितः -ता -तं.—(Not before used) अप्रयुक्तः -क्ता -क्तं, अनुपभुक्तः &c.; 'new moon., *See* MOON.

NEW-BORN, *a.* सद्योजातः -ता -तं, जातमात्रः -त्री -त्रं, नवोत्पन्नः -न्ना -न्नं.

NEW-COMER, *s.* आगन्तुकः, आगन्तु *m.*, नवागतः, नवाभ्यागतः.

NEW-FANGLED, *a.* नवकल्पितः -ता -तं, नवसृष्टः -ष्टा -ष्टं, नूतनः -ना -नं.

NEWLY, *adv.* नवं, नूतनं, नवीनं, अभिनवं, प्रतिनवं, प्रत्यग्रं, सद्यस्.

NEWNESS, *s.* नवता -त्वं, नवीनता, नूतनता -त्वं, नव्यता, नाव्यं, अभिनवता, प्रतिनवता, प्रत्यग्रता.—(State of not being known before) अपूर्व्वता -त्वं, अभूतपूर्व्वता.

NEWS, *s.* वार्त्ता, वृत्तान्तः, समाचारः, सन्देशः, सन्दिष्टं, संवादः, वृत्तं, वर्त्तमानं, प्रवृत्तिः *f.*, किंवदन्ती, उदन्तः -न्तकः, लोकवादः, लोकप्रवादः, जनवादः, जनश्रुतिः *f.*, वाचिकं, सूचना; 'What's the news?' का वार्त्ता; 'good news,' सुवार्त्ता, शुभवार्त्ता, शुभवृत्तान्तः; 'bad news,' दुर्वार्त्ता, अनिष्टवार्त्ता, अशुभवार्त्ता.

NEWSMONGER, *s.* वार्त्तायनः, वार्त्तावृत्तिः *m.*, समाचारवृत्तिः *m.*, वार्त्ताव्यवसायी *m.* (न्), वार्त्तावहनव्यापारी *m.*, वार्त्तिकः, कुशीलवः, समाचारव्यवसायी.

NEWSPAPER, *s.* समाचारपत्रं, वार्त्तापत्रं, वाचिकपत्रं, संवादपत्रं.

NEWS-VENDER, *s.* समाचारपत्रविक्रेता *m.* (तृ), वार्त्तापत्रविक्रयी *m.*

NEWT, *s.* तृणगोधा -धिका, सूक्ष्मगोधा -धिका, क्षुद्रगोधा.

NEW-TESTAMENT, *s.* नवीननियमः, नूतननियमः, नवनियमः.

NEW-YEAR'S DAY, *s.* वर्षप्रतिपद् *f.*, वत्सरप्रतिपद्, संवत्सरप्रतिपद्.

NEXT, *a.* (In time, &c.) अनन्तरः -रा -रं, निरन्तरः -रा -रं.—(Next in place, having nothing intervening) अव्यवधानः -ना -नं, अव्यवहितः -ता -तं, अनन्तरालः -ला -लं, निरन्तरालः -ला -लं, अपदान्तरः -रा -रं, सन्निहितः -ता -तं, पार्श्वस्थः -स्था -स्थं, अन्तिकः -का -कं, अन्तिमः -मा -मं. Next in time may also be expressed by परः -रा -रं or अपरं; as, 'the next day,' परदिवसः, पराहः; 'the next world,' परलोकः -कं, लोकान्तरं; 'in the next world,' परत्र, प्रेत्य, अमुत्र; 'relating to the next world,' पारत्रिकः -की -कं, अमुत्रत्यः -त्या -त्यं, आमुष्मिकः -की -कं; 'the next moment,' क्षणान्तरं; 'next born,' अनन्तरजः -जा -जं; 'next of kin,' अनन्तरः -रा -रं; 'next but one,' एकान्तरः -रा -रं; 'next but two,' द्व्यन्तरः -रा -रं, द्व्येकान्तरः -रा -रं.

NEXT, *adv.* अनन्तरं, तदनन्तरं, प्रत्यनन्तरं, परं -रेण, परतस्, परस्तात्, ततः परं, अतः परं, अत ऊर्द्ध्वं; 'next day,' परदिवसे, परेद्युस्; 'next moment,' क्षणान्तरे.

NIB, *s.* (Bill, beak) चञ्चुः *f.*, तुण्डः -ण्डिः *m.*, मुखः.—(Point) अग्रं, अणिः *m.*, अग्रभागः; 'of a pen,' कलमाग्रं.

NIBBED, *a.* अणिमान् -मती -मत् (त्), अग्रवान् -वती &c., साग्रः -ग्रा -ग्रं.

To NIBBLE, *v. a.* and *n.* अल्पाल्पशः or अल्पाल्पं चर्व् (c. 1. चर्वति -र्वितुं, c. 10. चर्वयति -यितुं) or दंश् (c. 1. दशति, दंष्टुं) or विदंश् or सन्दंश्, सम्मुखदन्तैर् अल्पाल्पं खाद् (c. 1. खादति -दितुं) or छिद् (c. 7. छिनत्ति, छेत्तुं), क्रमशः खाद् or भक्ष् (c. 10. भक्षयति -यितुं) or चर्वणं कृ.—(Carp at) दोषं or छिद्रम् अन्विष् (c. 4. -इष्यति -एषितुं) or ग्रह् (c. 9. गृह्णाति, ग्रहीतुं), छिद्रान्वेषं कृ, असूय (nom. असूयति).

NIBBLED, *p. p.* अल्पाल्पशः खादितः -ता -तं or चर्वितः -ता -तं or दष्टः -ष्टा -ष्टं, सम्मुखदन्तैर् जग्धः -ग्धा -ग्धं or छिन्नः -न्ना -न्नं or लूनः -ना -नं.

NICE, *a.* (Delicious, pleasant to the taste) स्वादुः -दुः -द्वी -दु, सुरसः -सा -सं, मिष्टः -ष्टा -ष्टं, सुखास्वादः -दा -दं, रुचिरः -रा -रं, रुचिकः -का -कं, रुच्यः -च्या -च्यं, रुचिकरः -रा -रं.—(Exact, accurate) सूक्ष्मः -क्ष्मा -क्ष्मं, अञ्जसः -सा -सं, समञ्जसः -सा -सं, सम्यङ् -मीची -म्यक् (क्), शुद्धः -द्धा -द्धं.—(Judging with exactness or minuteness) सूक्ष्मदृष्टिः -ष्टिः -ष्टि, सूक्ष्मदर्शी -र्शिनी -र्शि (न्), कुशाग्रदृष्टिः &c., कुशाग्रीयमतिः -तिः -ति, कुशाग्रीयबुद्धिः -द्धिः -द्धि, कुशाग्रबुद्धिः &c.—(Over-exact) अतिसूक्ष्मः &c., अतिसूक्ष्मदृष्टिः -ष्टिः -ष्टि.—(Delicate, soft) कोमलः -ला -लं, पेलवः -वा -वं, मृदुः -द्वी -दु, सुकुमारः -रा -री -रं. —(Not coarse, fine) अस्थूलः -ला -लं, सूक्ष्मः &c., विरलः &c. —(Pleasing, agreeable) रुचिरः -रा -रं, सुभगः -गा -गं, रम्यः -म्या -म्यं, मनोरमः -मा -मं, सुन्दरः -रा -री -रं.

NICELY, *adv.* (Exactly, accurately) सूक्ष्मं, सौक्ष्म्येण, ससौक्ष्म्यं, सूक्ष्मरूपेण, सूक्ष्मत्वेन, अञ्जसा, समञ्जसं, सम्यक्.—(Well, in a good manner) सु prefixed, सुष्ठु; 'nicely done,' सुकृतः -ता -तं.

NICENESS, NICETY, *s.* (Delicacy, deliciousness) स्वादुता, सुरसत्वं, सौरस्यं, मिष्टता.—(Pleasantness) रुचिरता, रुच्यता, रम्यता, रमणीयता.—(Exactness) सूक्ष्मता -त्वं, सौक्ष्म्यं, सामञ्जस्यं, सम्यक्त्वं, शुद्धता. —(Over-exactness or scrupulousness) अतिसूक्ष्मता, अतिसौक्ष्म्यं. —(Delicacy of perception or judgment) सूक्ष्मदृष्टिः *f.* -ष्टित्वं, सूक्ष्ममतित्वं, कुशाग्रीयमतित्वं, कुशाग्रबुद्धित्वं.—(Delicacy of management) युक्तिः *f.*, सुयुक्तिः *f.*, लाघवं, सुनीतिः *f.*

NICHE, *s.* प्रतिमास्थानं, प्रतिमाधारः, प्रतिमानिकेतः -तनं.

NICK, *s.* (Of time) कालसन्धिः *m.*, कालयोगः, शुभकालः, शुभयोगः, सुयोगः, शुभलग्नं, शुभक्षणः, युक्तसमयः, उपयुक्तसमयः, उपयुक्तकालः, उचितसमयः, अणिः *m.*—(Notch) छेदः, अवच्छेदः.

To NICK, *v. a.* (Touch at the right time) शुभलग्ने स्पृश् (c. 6. स्पृशति, स्प्रष्टुं) or आसद् (c. 10. -सादयति -यितुं), सुयुक्तिं कृ.—(Make a notch) अवच्छेदं कृ.

NICKNAME, *s.* उपाधिः *m.*, उपाधिनाम *n.* (न्), निन्दानाम *n.*, निन्दासूचकं नाम, तिरस्कारसूचकनाम, अपमानार्थकं नाम.

To NICKNAME, *v. a.* उपाधिं दा, उपाधिनाम कृ, तिरस्कारार्थं नाम दा.

To NICTATE, *v. n.* निमिष् (c. 6. -मिषति -मेषितुं), पक्षिवद् निमेषं कृ.

NICTATION, *s.* निमेषः, निमीलनं, पक्षिनिमेषः, पक्षिवद् निमेषः.

NICTITATING MEMBRANE, *s.* पक्षिणां चक्षुरावरणं, पक्षिनेत्रपटलं.

NIDIFICATION, *s.* नीडकरणं, नीडरचनं, कुलायरचना.

NIECE, *s.* (Brother's daughter) भ्रात्रीया, भ्रातृजा, भ्रातृपुत्री, भ्रातृसुता, भ्रातृकन्या.—(Sister's daughter) स्वस्रीया, भागिनेयी, स्वसृपुत्री, भगिनीसुता, भगिनीकन्या, स्वसृजा.

NIGGARD, *s.* कृपणजनः, अदाता *m.* (तृ), कदर्य्यजनः, गाढमुष्टिः *m.*

NIGGARD, NIGGARDLY, *a.* दृढमुष्टिः -ष्टिः -ष्टि, गाढमुष्टिः &c., कृपणः -णा -णं, व्ययशङ्की -ङ्किनी -ङ्कि (न्), व्ययशङ्कितः -ता -तं, अल्पव्ययी &c.,

स्वल्पव्ययी &c., कदर्य्यः -र्य्या -र्य्यं, मत्सरः -रा -रं, तनुत्यागः -गा -गं, त्यागपराङ्मुखः -खा -खं, दानपराङ्मुखः &c., क्षुद्रः -द्रा -द्रं, अर्थपरः -रा -रं. *See* MISER, MISERLY.

NIGGARDLINESS, NIGGARDNESS, *s.* कृपणता, कार्पण्यं, कदर्य्यता -त्वं, व्ययशङ्का, स्वल्पव्ययः, दृढमुष्टित्वं, मात्सर्य्यं, दानपराङ्मुखता.

NIGGARDLY *adv.* सकार्पण्यं, कृपणवत्, स्वल्पव्ययेन, व्ययशङ्कया.

NIGH, NIGHLY, NIGHNESS. *See* NEAR, NEARLY, NEARNESS.

NIGHT, *s.* रात्रिः *f.*, निशा, रजनी, क्षणदा, क्षपा, शर्वरी, निट् *f.* (श), त्रियामा, यामिनी, यामवती, नक्तं indecl. निशीथिनी, तमस्विनी, विभावरी, तमी -मा -मिः *f.*, निरातपा, निशीथ्या, निशीथः, शमनी, वासुरा, वाशुरा, श्यामा, शताक्षी, शत्वरी, शर्य्या, यामिः -मी -मिका *f.*, यामीरा, याम्या, दोषा; 'a dark night,' तमिस्रा, तामसी; 'a moonlight night,' ज्योत्स्नी; 'by night, in the night,' रात्रौ, निशायां, निशि, नक्तं, दोषा; 'a number of nights,' निशागणः, गणरात्रं, निशावृन्दं; 'coming on of night,' रात्रियोगः; 'end of night,' निशान्तः -न्तं, अपररात्रः, रात्रिविगमः; 'beginning of night,' निशादिः *f.*; 'every night,' प्रतिरात्रं, प्रतिनिशं, रात्रौ रात्रौ; 'day and night,' अहोरात्रं, अहर्निशं; 'night and day,' रात्रिन्दिवं, रात्र्यहनी *n. du.*; 'a night and two days,' पक्षिणी; 'a period of five nights,' रात्रकं; 'sitting up at night,' रात्रिजागरः -रणं; 'resting at night,' निशोपशायः; 'night attack,' सौप्तिकवधः, सौप्तिकं; 'last night,' गतरात्रिः *f.*

NIGHT-BLINDNESS, *s.* निशान्धता; 'affected with it,' निशान्धः -न्धा -न्धं, रात्र्यन्धः &c.

NIGHT-CAP, *s.* रात्रौ भृतं शिरोवेष्टनं or शिरोवस्त्रं, रात्रिशिरस्कं.

NIGHT-DEW, *s.* रात्रिजलं, निशाजलं, रजनीजलं, नैशाम्बु *n.*, निशापुष्पं.

NIGHT-CLOTHES, NIGHT-DRESS, *s.* रात्रिवस्त्रं, रात्रिवसनं, रात्रिवेशः.

NIGHT-FALL, *s.* रजनीमुखं, निशादिः *f.*, रात्र्यारम्भः, रात्रियोगः, सन्ध्याकालः, दिनावसानं, प्रदोषः, प्रदोषकालः.

NIGHT-GOWN, *s.* रात्रिवस्त्रं, रात्रिवसनं, रात्रिवेशः, रात्रौ भृतं वस्त्रं.

NIGHT-HAG, *s.* रात्रिचरी, रात्रिचरा -री, निशाचरा -री, रात्र्यटा.

NIGHTINGALE, *s.* वसन्तदूतः, मदनदूतः, कोकिलः, गातुः *m.*

NIGHTLY, *a.* नैशः -शी -शं, प्रादोषिकः -की -कं, रात्रिकृतः -ता -तं, रात्रिजः -जा -जं, शार्वरः -री -रं, प्रातिरात्रिकः -की -कं.

NIGHTLY, *adv.* (By night) रात्रौ, नक्तं, निशायां, निशि, दोषा.—(Every night) प्रतिरात्रं, प्रतिनिशं, रात्रौ रात्रौ, निशि निशि.

NIGHT-MAN, *s.* मलपूः *m.*, मलपूः *m.*, पुरीषवाहकः, पुरीषापकर्षी *m.*

NIGHTMARE, *s.* कुस्वप्नः, दुःस्वप्नः, अजीर्णप्रयुक्तस्वप्नः, स्वप्नकल्पितो हृदयदेशोपरिस्थो भारः, स्वप्नकल्पिता मिथ्यावासना or अपच्छाया.

NIGHTSHADE, *s.* (Prickly) कण्टकारी -रिका, निदिग्धिका, वृहती, धावनिका, दुःस्पर्शा, स्पृशी, व्याघ्री, कुली, प्रचोदिनी, क्षुद्रा, राष्ट्रिका.

NIGHT-WALKING, NIGHT-WANDERING, *a.* निशाचरः -रा -री -रं, रात्रिचरः &c., रात्रिञ्चरः &c., रजनीचरः &c., निशाचारी -रिणी -रि (न्), नक्तचारी &c., नक्तञ्चरः &c.

NIGHT-WATCH, *s.* यामः, प्रहरः, रात्रियामः, रात्रिप्रहरः.

NIHILITY, *s.* अभावः, अवस्तुत्वं, नास्तित्वं, असत्ता -त्त्वं, शून्यता -त्वं.

NIMBLE, *a.* लघुः -घुः -घ्वी -घु, लघुगतिः -तिः -ति, द्रुतगतिः &c., त्वरितगतिः &c., लघुशरीरः -रा -रं, लघुदेहः -हा -हं, चपलाङ्गः -ङ्गा -ङ्गं, अङ्गचपलः -ला -लं, चपलदेहः -हा -हं, चपलगतिः &c., क्षिप्रगतिः &c., क्षिप्रकारी -रिणी -रि (न्), आशुकारी &c., तीक्ष्णकर्म्मा -र्म्मा -र्म्म (न्), चपलः -ला -लं, चञ्चलः -ला -लं.

NIMBLE-FOOTED, *a.* लघुपादः -दा -दं, चपलपादः &c., पादचपलः -ला -लं.

NIMBLE-HANDED, *a.* लघुहस्तः -स्ता -स्तं, चपलपाणिः -णिः -णि, पाणिचपलः &c.

NIMBLENESS, *s.* लघुता, लाघवं, शरीरलाघवं, लघुगतित्वं, द्रुतगतित्वं, अङ्गचापल्यं, देहचापल्यं, चापल्यं, द्रुतता, क्षिप्रता, शीघ्रता, चञ्चलता, चाञ्चल्यं.

NIMBLE-WITTED, *a.* चपलबुद्धिः -द्धिः -द्धि, क्षिप्रबुद्धिः &c., शीघ्रबुद्धिः &c.

NIMBLY, *adv.* सलाघवं, लाघवेन, लघु, लघुगत्या, द्रुतं, द्रुतगत्या, त्वरितं, त्वरितगत्या, चापल्येन, चपलं, चपलगत्या, अङ्गचापल्येन, क्षिप्रं, शीघ्रं.

NINE, *a.* नव *m.f.n. pl.* (न्), नवसंख्यकः -का -कं.

NINE-FOLD, *a.* नवगुणः -णा -णं, नवविधः -धा -धं, नवधा indecl.

NINETEEN, *a.* नवदश *m.f.n. pl.* (न्), ऊनविंशतिः *f. sing.*, एकोनविंशतिः *f. sing.*, नवदशसंख्यकः -का -कं.

NINETEENTH, *a.* नवदशः -शी -शं, एकोनविंशः -शी -शं, ऊनविंशः &c., ऊनविंशतितमः -मी -मं, एकोनविंशतितमः &c.

NINETIETH, *a.* नवतः -ती -तं, नवतितमः -मी -मं.

NINETY, *a.* नवतिः *f. sing.*, नवतिसंख्यकः -का -कं; 'ninety-one,' एकनवतिः *f.*; 'ninety-two,' द्वानवतिः *f.*; 'ninety-three,' त्रयोनवतिः; 'ninety-four,' चतुर्णवतिः; 'ninety-five,' पञ्चनवतिः; 'ninety-six,' षण्णवतिः; 'ninety-seven,' सप्तनवतिः; 'ninety-eight,' अष्टानवतिः *f.*; 'ninety-nine,' ऊनशतं, एकोनशतं; 'above ninety years old,' दशमी *m.* (न्), दशमीस्थः, दशमीकृतः.

NINETY-FOLD, *a.* नवतिगुणः -णा -णं, नवतिविधः -धा -धं, नवतिधा indecl.

NINNY, NINNY-HAMMER, *s.* अल्पबुद्धिः *m.*, अल्पधीः *m.*, मूर्खः, निर्बुद्धिः.

NINTH, *a.* नवमः -मी -मं, नावमिकः -की -कं.

NINTHLY, *adv.* नवमतस्, नवतस्, नवमस्थाने, नवमपदे.

To NIP, *v. a.* (Cut or pinch off with the ends of the fingers) अङ्गुल्यग्रैः or अङ्गुलिनखैर् अवछिद् (c. 7. -छिनत्ति -छेत्तुं) or अवकृत् (c. 6. -कृन्तति -कर्त्तितुं) or निकृत् or छिद् or पीड्.—(Bite off) दंश् (c. 1. दशति, दंष्टुं), विदंश्, सन्दंश्, अवदंश्.—(Pinch in general) पीड् (c. 10. पीडयति -यितुं), मथ् (c. 1. मथति, c. 9. मथ्नाति -थितुं), आर्त्तं -र्त्तां -र्त्तं कृ, आर्त्तीकृ; as, 'to pinch with cold,' शीतेन पीड्, शीतार्त्तीकृ, हिमार्त्तीकृ.—(Blast, destroy) नश् (c. 10. नाशयति -यितुं), दुष् (c. 10. दूषयति -यितुं), मृ (c. 10. मारयति -यितुं), विशॄ (c. 10. -शारयति -यितुं), म्लानीकृ.

NIP, NIPPING, *s.* नखैर् अवच्छेदः or अवकृन्तनं or निकृन्तनं or कृन्तनं, हिमार्त्तीकरणं, शीतार्त्तीकरणं, हिमनाशः.

NIPPED, *p. p.* (With cold) हिमपीडितः -ता -तं, हिमार्त्तः -र्त्ता -र्त्तं, शीतार्त्तः &c., हिमदूषितः -ता -तं, हिमनाशितः &c.—(In general) पीडितः -ता -तं, मथितः &c.

NIPPERS, *s. pl.* सन्दंशः -शकं -शका, कङ्कमुखं.

NIPPLE, *s.* स्तनाग्रं, स्तनमुखं -खः, स्तनशिखा, कुचाग्रं, चूचुकः -कं, स्तनवृन्तः -न्तं, पिप्पलकं, नभ्मेडः, वृन्तं; 'the nipples,' पुरश्छदौ *m. du.*

NIT, *s.* लिक्षा, निक्षा, रिक्षा, दिक्षः, यूकाण्डं.

NITRE, *s.* यवक्षारः, यवजः, तर्ष्यः, पाक्यः, तीक्ष्णः, तीक्ष्णरसः, यवलासः, यवाग्रजः.

NITROGEN, *s.* expressed in modern treatises by the word रूचककारः.

NITROUS, NITRY, *a.* यवक्षारीयः -या -यं, यवक्षारमयः -यी -यं, यवक्षारगुणकः -का -कं, यवक्षारोत्पादकः -का -कं.

NITTY, *a.* बहुलिक्षः -क्षा -क्षं, लिक्षापूर्णः -र्णा -र्णं, प्रचुरलिक्षः &c.

NIVEOUS, *a.* हिम्यः -म्या -म्यं, तुषारमयः -यी -यं, हिममयः &c.

NO, *adv.* न, नो, नहि; 'or no,' न वा.

No, *a.* (None) usually expressible by न; as, 'no one,' न कश्चित् *m.*, न काचित् *f.*, न कोऽपि *m.*, न कापि *f.*, न कश्चन *m.*, न काचन *f.*; 'no thing,' न किञ्चित्, न किमपि, न किञ्चन; 'no other,' नान्यः -न्या -न्यत्; 'no where,' न क्वचित्, न क्वापि, न कुत्रचित्, न कुत्रापि; 'no more, not again,' न पुनर्; 'no great distance,' नातिदूरं. When 'no' is privative, it is expressed by निर्, अ, वि &c. prefixed, or by हीन, शून्य, वर्जित, रहित &c. affixed; as, 'having no fruit,' निष्फलः -ला -लं, अफलः &c., विफलः &c., फलहीनः -ना -नं, &c.

Nobility, *s.* (Antiquity of family, elevation of rank) महाकुलता, कुलीनता, महाकुलीनता, सत्कुलीनता, अभिजातता, आभिजात्यं, आभिजनं, कुलोत्कर्षः, कुलोत्कृष्टता, औत्कर्ष्यं, कौलीनं, सद्वंशता, वंशोत्कर्षः.—(Elevation or greatness of mind) माहात्म्यं, महात्मता -त्वं, महिमा *m.* (न्), महत्त्वं, उदारता, औदार्य्यं, चित्तोदारता, महेच्छा, महानुभावः.—(Distinction, eminence) उत्कर्षः, उत्कृष्टता, औत्कर्ष्यं, वैशिष्ट्यं, विशिष्टता, प्रधानता -त्वं, समुन्नतिः *f.*, प्रकर्षः, शिष्टता, श्रेष्ठत्वं, सेव्यता, सुख्यातिः *f.*—(Magnificence) प्रतापः, तेजस् *n.*, श्रीः *f.*—(The nobility, noblemen collectively) कुलीनलोकः, कुलीनजनसमूहः, कुलीनजनाः *m. pl.*, शिष्टजनाः *m. pl.*, कुलीनसमूहः, राजन्यकं.

Noble, *a.* (Of ancient family, or elevated rank) कुलीनः -ना -नं, महाकुलीनः -ना -नं, महाकुलः -ला -लं, सत्कुलीनः -ना -नं, सद्वंशः -शा -शं, अभिजनवान् -वती -वत् (त्), अभिजातः -ता -तं, उत्कृष्टः -ष्टा -ष्टं, उत्कृष्टकुलजातः -ता -तं, महाकुलजः -जा -जं, महाकुलप्रसूतः -ता -तं, सत्कुलजातः -ता -तं, विशुद्धकुलभवः, वंशविशुद्धः -द्धा -द्धं, सद्वंशजातः -ता -तं, प्रधानवंशोद्भवः -वा -वं, महावंशीयः -या -यं, उत्तमवंशजातः -ता -तं, कुलश्रेष्ठी -ष्ठिनी -ष्ठि (न्), श्रेष्ठकुलोद्भूतः -ता -तं, कुलोद्भतः -ता -तं, कुलिकः -का -कं, कौलेयः -यी -यं, प्रतिपत्तिमान् &c.—(Great in mind) उदारः -रा -रं, उदारमनाः -नाः -नः (स्), उदारमतिः -तिः -ति, उदारधीः -धीः -धि, महात्मा -त्मा -त्म (न्), महामनाः &c., महामनस्कः -स्का -स्कं, माहात्मिकः -की -कं, महामतिः -तिः -ति, महानुभावः -वा -वं, महेच्छः -च्छा -च्छं, महाशयः -या -यं, उन्नतमनाः &c.—(Distinguished, eminent, excellent) उत्कृष्टः -ष्टा -ष्टं, श्रेष्ठः -ष्ठा -ष्ठं, अत्युत्कृष्टः &c., शिष्टः -ष्टा -ष्टं, विशिष्टः &c., उत्तमः -मा -मं, प्रमुखः -खा -खं, उन्नतः -ता -तं, समुन्नतः -ता -तं, प्रशस्तः -स्ता -स्तं, महान् -हती -हत् (त्), महाभागः -गा -गं, महाभागधेयः -या -यं, सेव्यः -व्या -व्यं.—(Illustrious) ख्यातः -ता -तं, विख्यातः -ता -तं, यशस्वी &c., महायशाः &c., श्रीमान् &c., सुप्रतिष्ठः -ष्ठा -ष्ठं, कीर्त्तिमान् &c.—(Magnificent) महाप्रतापः -पा -पं, महातेजाः &c., विभूतिमान् &c., श्रीमान् &c. 'Noble' may sometimes be expressed by ऋषभः or पुङ्गवः or व्याघ्रः or सिंहः or शार्दूलः or इन्द्रः in comp.; as, 'a noble or eminent man,' पुरुषर्षभः, पुरुषव्याघ्रः, नरपुङ्गवः, नरेन्द्रः &c.; 'a noble elephant,' गजेन्द्रः; 'noble nature,' सत्त्वं; 'noble on both sides,' मातृतः पितृतश्चाभिजनवान् &c.

Noble, nobleman, *s.* कुलीनजनः, कुलीनलोकः, शिष्टजनः, शिष्टलोकः, कुलीनपदस्थः, उच्चपदस्थः, उत्कृष्टपदस्थः, कुलश्रेष्ठी *m.* (न्), सत्कुलीनः, अभिजनवान् *m.* (त्), राजन्यः.

Noble-minded, *a.* उदारमनाः -नाः -नः (स्), उदारधीः -धीः -धि, उदारमनस्कः -स्का -स्कं, उदारचेताः &c., महात्मा -त्मा -त्म (न्), सम्भावितात्मा &c., महेच्छः -च्छा -च्छं.

Nobleness, *s.* महत्त्वं, महिमा *m.* (न्), उत्कर्षः, उत्कृष्टता, श्रेष्ठता, प्रधानता, उदारता, औदार्य्यं, उन्नतिः *f.*, समुन्नतिः. *See* Nobility.

Noblesse, *s.* कौलीन्यं, कौलीनं, कुलीनलोकः, कुलीनसमूहः, कुलीनसभा.

Nobly, *adv.* (With nobleness of birth) कुलीनं, कुलीनवत्, साभिजात्यं; 'nobly-born,' महाकुलप्रसूतः -ता -तं, सत्कुलजातः -ता -तं. *See* Noble, *a.* (With greatness of mind) सौदार्य्यं, औदार्य्येण, उदारवत्, समाहात्म्यं, माहात्म्येन, मनोमहत्त्वात्, महिम्ना, उदारचित्तत्वात्, उदारचेतसा, महेच्छया.—(Magnificently) महाप्रतापेन, महातेजसा, अतितेजसा, सप्रतापं, ऐश्वर्य्येण.

Nobody, *s.* न कश्चित् *m.*, न काचित् *f.*, न कोऽपि *m.*, न कापि *f.*, न कश्चन *m.*, न काचन *f.*

Nocent, *a.* हिंस्रः -स्रा -स्रं, हिंसालुः -लुः -लु, अपकारकः -का -कं.

Noctambulation, *s.* निद्राभ्रमणं, निद्रापरिभ्रमणं, निद्राचारः.

Noctambulist, *s.* निद्राचारी *m.* (न्), निद्राभ्रमणकृत्. *See* Night-walking.

Noctivagant, *a.* निशाचरः -रा -री -रं, नक्तचारी -रिणी &c. *See* Night-walking.

Nocturnal, *a.* नैशः -शी -शं, रात्रिकालिकः -की -कं, रात्रिसम्बन्धी -न्धिनी &c., रात्रिकालसम्बन्धी &c., दोषातनः -नी -नं, प्रादोषिकः -की -कं, शार्व्वरः -री -रं, रात्रीयः -या -यं, निशासम्बन्धीयः -या -यं.

To **nod**, *v. a.* or *n.*, (Incline the head) शिरः or मस्तकं नम् (c. 1. नमति, नन्तुं, c. 10. नमयति -यितुं) or प्रणम् or अभिनम् or विनम् or आनम्.—(Make a sign by a motion of the head) मस्तकसङ्केतं कृ, शिरःसङ्केतं कृ, शिरसा सङ्केतं कृ or संज्ञां कृ or इङ्गितं कृ, शिरश् चल् (c. 10. चालयति -यितुं).

Nod, *s.* (Inclination of the head) शिरःप्रणामः, मस्तकप्रणामः, शिरःप्रणतिः *f.*—(Sign made by a movement of the head) मस्तकसङ्केतः, शिरःसङ्केतः, शिरसा सङ्केतः or संज्ञा or इङ्गितं, मस्तकसन्देशः, शिरश्चालनं.

Nodated, *a.* ग्रन्थिमान् -मती -मत् (त्), ग्रन्थिलः -ला -लं.

Noddle, *s.* मस्तकः -कं, शिरस् *n.*, शीर्षकं, मुण्डकं.

Noddy, *s.* अल्पबुद्धिः *m.*, अल्पधीः *m.*, मूर्खः, निर्बुद्धिः *m.*

Node, *s.* (In surgery) अस्थिगुल्मः, अध्यस्थि *n.*—(In astronomy) पातः, उपग्रहः; 'ascending node,' राहुः *m.*, स्वर्भानुः *m.*, विधुन्तुदः, सैंहिकेयः, तमस् *n.*; 'descending,' केतुः *m.*

Nodose, *a.* ग्रन्थिलः -ला -लं, ग्रन्थी -न्थिनी -न्थि (न्), बहुग्रन्थिः -न्थिः -न्थि.

Nodosity, *s.* ग्रन्थिलत्वं, ग्रन्थिमत्त्वं, सग्रन्थित्वं, सपर्व्वत्वं, ग्रन्थिपूर्णता.

Nodule, *s.* शर्करा, पिण्डः -ण्डं, घनः, लोष्टः -ष्टं -ष्टुः *m.*

Noise, *s.* शब्दः, महाशब्दः, अतिशब्दः, ध्वनिः *m.*, महाध्वनिः *m.*, स्वनः, महास्वनः, निःस्वनः, घोषः -षणं -णा, महाघोषः, नादः, महानादः, स्वरः, महास्वरः, उच्चैःस्वरः, उच्चस्वरः, प्रघोषकः, प्रस्वानः, निर्घोषः, निनादः, रणत्कारः, क्वणः, संह्रादः, निह्रादः, रणः, रणत्कारः, रावः, उद्रावः, कोलाहलः, रासः, रावणं, तुमुलं, ध्वनः, वणः, उत्क्रोशः.—(Public talk) जनवादः, जनप्रवादः, जनरवः, जनश्रुतिः *f.*

To **noise**, *v. a.* (Spread by report) घुष् (c. 10. घोषयति -यितुं), विघुष्, प्रकाश् (c. 10. -काशयति -यितुं), विकाश्, ख्या in caus. (ख्यापयति -यितुं), आख्या, विख्या, प्रचर् (c. 10. -चारयति -यितुं), प्रकटीकृ.

Noised abroad, *p. p.* घोषितः -ता -तं, विघोषितः -ता -तं, प्रचारितः -ता -तं, प्रकाशितः -ता -तं, प्रकटितः &c., प्रकटीकृतः &c., आख्यातः &c.

Noiseful, *a.* शब्दकारी -रिणी &c., ध्वनयन् -यन्ती -यत् (त्). *See* Noisy.

Noiseless, *a.* निःशब्दः -ब्दा -ब्दं, निश्शब्दः &c., अशब्दः &c., अघोषः -षा -षं, नीरवः -वा -वं, अरवः -वा -वं, शब्दहीनः -ना -नं.

Noiselessly, *adv.* शब्देन विना, अशब्देन, निःशब्दं, निश्शब्दं.

Noisily, *adv.* महाशब्देन, अतिशब्देन, महास्वरेण, उच्चैःस्वरेण.

NOISINESS, *s.* महाशब्दकत्वं, महाशब्दः, महाशब्दकारित्वं, महाध्वनिः *m.* -निता, महानादः -दता, शब्दकारिता, शब्दवत्त्वं, सशब्दता, शब्दनत्वं.

NOISOME, *a.* (Noxious, destructive) मारकः -का -कं, मारात्मकः &c., प्राणनाशकः &c., मृत्युजनकः &c., क्षयकरः -रा -रं, विनाशकः &c., प्राणहरः -रा -रं, नृशंसः -सा -सं, शरारुः -रुः -रु, शारुकः -का -कं, घातुकः -का -कं, बाधकः &c., अनिष्टजनकः &c., अहितकारी -रिणी &c.—(Offensive to the smell) दुर्गन्धः -न्धा -न्धं, दुर्गन्धी -न्धिनी -न्धि (न्), पूतिगन्धिकः -का -कं, कुत्सितः -ता -तं.

NOISOMENESS, *s.* दुर्गन्धता -त्वं, दौर्गन्धिः *m.*, पूतिगन्धता, कुत्सितगन्धः, उग्रगन्धता, पूतिः *f.*, कुत्सितत्वं, कौत्सित्यं.

NOISY, *a.* शब्दकारः -री -रं, महाशब्दकारः -री -रं, महाशब्दकः -का -कं, महाशब्दी -ब्दिनी -ब्दि (न्), महास्वनः -ना -नं, महाध्वनिकः -का -कं, महाध्वनिकरः -री -रं, महानादी &c., महानादः -दा -दं, महास्वरकः -का -कं, अतिशब्दनः -ना -नं, अतिशब्दवान् -वती -वत् (त्), तुमुलकारी &c., तुमुलः -ला -लं, कोलाहलकारी &c. कोलाहलकृत् *m.f.n.*, घोररवः -वा -वं, मुखरः -रा -रं.—(Clamorous) घोषणः -णा -णं, घोषकरः -री -रं, महाघोषः -षा -षं, बहुघोषः -षा -षं.—(Sounding) शब्दनः -ना -नं, नादी &c., स्वनवान् &c., संह्रादी &c., स्वनन् -नन्ती -नत् (त्), ध्वनयन् &c.

NOMAD, NOMADIC, *a.* पशुचारानुसारवासी -सिनी &c., पशुचारणानुजीवी.

NOMENCLATOR, *s.* नामस्थापकः, नामबोधकः, नामख्यापकः.

NOMENCLATURE, *s.* शब्दसङ्ग्रहः, शब्दमालं, शब्दमाला, निघण्टुः *m.*

NOMINAL, *a.* (Pertaining to a name) नामसम्बन्धी -न्धिनी &c., नामविषयः -या -यं.—(Relating to words) शाब्दः -ब्दी -ब्दं, शाब्दिकः -की -कं, वाचनिकः -की -कं, आभिधानीयकः -की -कं.—(Existing in name only) नामधारी -रिणी &c., नाममात्रधारी &c., नामभृत् *m.f.n.*, शब्दः -ब्दी -ब्दं, शाब्दिकः &c.—(Nominal verb). The grammatical symbol is लिङ्.

NOMINALLY, *adv.* नामतस्, नाम्ना, नाममात्रेण, शब्दतस्, शब्दमात्रेण.

To NOMINATE, *v. a.* (Give a name) नाम कृ or दा, संज्ञां कृ or दा.—(Designate by name) नाम निर्दिश् (c. 6. -दिशति -देष्टुं) or प्रदिश्.—(Appoint by name to an office) नाम निर्दिश्य नियुज् (c. 7. -युनक्ति -योक्तुं, c. 10. -योजयति -यितुं) or परिक्लृप् (c. 10. -कल्पयति -यितुं) or प्रक्लृप्.

NOMINATED, *p.p.* नामनिर्देशानन्तरं नियुक्तः -क्ता -क्तं or नियोजितः -ता -तं.

NOMINATION, *s.* (Act) नामनिर्देशानन्तरं नियोगः or नियोजनं.—(Power of nominating or appointing) नियोजनाधिकारः.

NOMINATIVE, *s.* (Case in grammar) कर्त्ता *m.* (र्त्तृ), कर्त्तृकारकः, कर्त्तृवाचकः, प्रथमा, प्रथमा विभक्तिः.

NOMINATOR, *s.* नियोजकः, नामनिर्देशपूर्व्वं नियोजयिता *m.* (तृ), निर्देशकः.

NOMINEE, *s.* नियोजितः, नियुक्तः, अधिकृतः.

NON. A prefix expressed in Sanskrit by अ or अन्.

NON-ACCEPTANCE, *s.* अपरिग्रहः, अग्रहणं, अप्रतिग्रहः, अस्वीकारः.

NONAGE, *s.* बाल्यं, बालदशा, व्यवहारायोग्यता, अप्राप्तव्यवहारत्वं.

NONAGENARIAN, *a.* दशमी *m.* (न्), दशमीस्थः, दशमीङ्गतः.

NON-APPEARANCE, *s.* अदर्शनं, अनुपस्थानं, अनुपस्थितिः *f.*, अविद्यमानता.

NON-ARRIVAL, *s.* अनागमः -मनं, अनभिगमनं, अनुपस्थानं.

NON-ATTAINMENT, *s.* अप्राप्तिः *f.*, अलाभः, अलब्धिः *f.*, अनवाप्तिः *f.*

NON-ATTENDANCE, *s.* अदर्शनं, दर्शनाभावः, अनुपस्थानं. *See* NON-APPEARANCE.

NON-ATTENTION, *s.* अनवधानं -नता, अनवहितत्वं, अलक्ष्यं.

NONCE, *s.* प्रयोजनं, अवसरः, वारः, समयः, उपयोगः.

NONCHALANCE, *s.* निरुत्सुकता, उदासीनता, जडता, अनपेक्षा, अनास्था.

NONCHALANT, *a.* निरुत्सुकः -का -कं, उदासीनः -ना -नं, अनपेक्षः -क्षा -क्षं, निरपेक्षः &c., जडः -डा -डं, अनभिलाषः -षा -षं, निःस्पृहः -हा -हं.

NON-COMMENCEMENT, *s.* अनारम्भः, अनारब्धिः *f.*, अनुपक्रमः.

NON-COMMISSIONED, *a.* अनधिकारवान् -वती -वत् (त्), अपदयुक्तः -क्ता -क्तं.

NON-COMPLIANCE, *s.* अननुरोधः -धनं, अस्वीकारः, अननुवृत्तिः *f.*

NON-CONDUCTOR, NON-CONDUCTING, *a.* अवाहकः -का -कं, अप्रापकः -का -कं, अनायकः -का -कं, अनेता -त्री -तृ (तृ).

NON-CONFORMIST, *s.* अननुरोधी *m.* (न्), अननुवर्त्ती *m.*, अननुसारी *m.*, अननुयायी *m.*, अननुकूलः.—(Dissenter from the established church) देशस्थापितधर्म्मविरोधी *m.* (न्), साधारणधर्म्मविरोधी *m.*, देशस्थापितधर्म्मविसम्मतः, मतान्तरावलम्बी *m.*, मतान्तरग्राही *m.*, मतान्तरधारी *m.*

NON-CONFORMITY, *s.* अननुरोधः -धनं, अननुवर्त्तनं, अननुसरणं, अस्वीकारः.—(Dissent) देशस्थापितधर्म्मविरोधः, देशस्थापितधर्म्मासम्मतिः *f.*, मतान्तरावलम्बनं, मतान्तरं.

NON-CONTACT, *s.* अस्पर्शः, असम्पर्कः, अस्पृष्टिः *f.*, असंसर्गः.

NON-DELIVERY, *s.* असमर्पणं, अप्रतिपादनं, अप्रदानं, असम्प्रदानं.

NONDESCRIPT, *a.* अवर्णितः -ता -तं, अवर्णनीयः -या -यं, अलक्षणः -णा -णं.

NONE, *a.* न कश्चित् *m.*, न काचित् *f.*, न किञ्चित् *n.*, न कोऽपि, न कापि *f.*, न किमपि *n.*, न कश्चन *m.*, न काचन *f.*, न किञ्चन *n.*, often expressed by न with another word; as, 'none other,' नान्यः -न्या -न्यत्.—(Not the least portion, not any, none at all) न किञ्चिदपि, न किमपि, न कियदपि, न सूक्ष्ममपि, न स्तोकमपि, न लेशमपि, न मनागपि, अलेशं, अलेशमपि, अलवलेशं.

NON-ELECT, *a.* अवृतः -ता -तं, अवृक्तः -क्ता -क्तं, अनुद्धृतः -ता -तं.

NON-ENJOYMENT, *s.* अभोगः, असम्भोगः, अनुपभोगः, अभुक्तिः *f.*

NONENTITY, *s.* (Non-existence) अभावः, असम्भवः, अभवः, असद्भावः, असत्त्वं, असत्ता, नास्तित्वं, नास्ति ind., अजीवः, अजीवित्वं, अजीवनिः *f.*, अवस्तुता -त्वं, अवर्त्तमानता, अवृत्तिता, अविद्यमानता, शून्यता.—(A nonentity) अपदार्थः, असत्पदार्थः, अलीकपदार्थः, अवस्तु *n.*, असद्वस्तु *n.*, असम्भवं, शून्यं.

NONES, *s. pl.* रोमीयपञ्जिकायां मासस्य पञ्चमो or सप्तमो दिवसः.

NONESSENTIAL, *a.* अनावश्यकः -की -कं, अवश्यकर्त्तव्यः -व्या -व्यं, कार्य्याकार्य्यः -र्य्या -र्य्यं, कृताकृतः -ता -तं, अनान्तरीयकः -का -कं.

NON-EXISTENCE, *s.* अभावः, असम्भवः, असद्भावः, नास्तित्वं. *See* NONENTITY.

NON-EXISTENT, *a.* अवर्त्तमानः -ना -नं, अविद्यमानः -ना -नं, असन् -सती -सत् (त्), असम्भवः -वा -वं, असम्भूतः -ता -तं, अभूतः -ता -तं, निःसत्त्वः -त्त्वा -त्त्वं, अध्रियमाणः -णा -णं.

NON-OBSERVANCE, *s.* अपालनं, अप्रतिपालनं, अरक्षणं, असेवनं.

NON-PAREIL, *a.* अनुपमः -मा -मं, अप्रतिमः &c., अद्वितीयः -या -यं.

NON-PERFORMANCE, *s.* अननुष्ठानं, अविधानं, अकरणं, अकर्म्म *n.* (न्).

NON-PLUS, *s.* अनुपायः, अगतिः *f.* -तित्वं, निरुपायत्वं, गतिहीनता, निरुत्तरत्वं, अनुत्तरत्वं, मोहः, व्यस्तता, कुण्ठता.

To NON-PLUS, *v. a.* निरुत्तरीकृ, अनुत्तरीकृ, निरुपायीकृ, गतिहीनं -नां कृ, मुह् (c. 10. मोहयति -यितुं), व्याकुलीकृ.

NON-PLUSED, *p. p.* निरुपायः -या -यं, गतिहीनः -ना -नं, उपायहीनः, निरुत्तरः -रा -रं, अनुत्तरः &c., हतोत्तरः &c., कुण्ठितः -ता -तं.

NON-RESIDENCE, *s.* अवसतिः *f.*, अवासः, अनिवसनं, अनिवासः, अनवस्थितिः *f.*

NON-RESIDENT, *a.* अवासी -सिनी -सि (न्), स्वस्थानावासी &c., अनवस्थितः &c.

NON-RESISTANCE, *s.* अप्रतीकारः, अप्रतिक्रिया, अप्रतिरोधः, अनिवारणं.

NON-RESUMPTION, *s.* अपुनरादानं, अपुनर्हरणं, अनपकर्म्म *n.* (न्).

NONSENSE, *s.* अनर्थकं, आनर्थक्यं, अनर्थकवाक्यं, अनर्थकभाषणं, निरर्थकवाक्यं, अबद्धं, असम्बद्धं, अबर्थ्यं, असम्बद्धवाक्यं, अनिबद्धवाक्यं, असम्बद्धकथा, वृथाकथा, मृषार्थकं, अयाथार्थ्यं, जल्पितं, प्रलपितं, प्रलापः, अनर्थः, अर्थहीनवचनं; 'talking nonsense,' असम्बद्धप्रलापी -पिनी -पि (न्), अनिबद्धप्रलापी &c., अनर्थकवक्ता -क्त्री -क्तृ (क्तृ), जल्पकः -का -कं, जल्पाकः -का -कं, वाचालः -ला -लं, वाचाटः -टा -टं, बहुगर्ह्यवाक् *m.f.n.*

NONSENSICAL, *a.* अनर्थकः -का -कं, निरर्थकः -का -कं, अनर्थः -र्था -र्थं, अर्थहीनः -ना -नं, अर्थशून्यः -न्या -न्यं, अर्थरहितः -ता -तं, मृषार्थकः &c., वृथार्थकः &c., असम्बद्धः -द्धा -द्धं, असम्बद्धार्थः -र्था -र्थं, अबद्धः &c., अनिबद्धः &c., असङ्गतः -ता -तं, अयथार्थः -र्था -र्थं, अयुक्तिकः -का -कं, अभिधेयरहितः -ता -तं.

NONSENSICALLY, *adv.* निरर्थकं, सानर्थक्यं, असम्बद्धं, वृथा, मृषा.

NONSENSICALNESS, *s.* अनर्थकता, निरर्थकता, आनर्थक्यं, अर्थहीनता, अर्थाभावः, असङ्गतता, असम्बद्धता, अयाथार्थ्यं, अयुक्तिः *f.*

NON-SOLUTION, *s.* अलापनं, अव्याख्या -ख्यानं, अपरिशोधनं, अलापनिका.

NON-SUITED, *p.p.* अवसन्नः -न्ना -न्नं, अवसादितः -ता -तं, हीनः -ना -नं, अर्थाद्धीनः -ना -नं, हीनवादः -दा -दं, नष्टवादः -दा -दं, हतवादः; 'to be non-suited,' अर्थाद् हा in pass. (हीयते), अवसद् (c. 1. -सीदति -सत्तुं), नष्टवादः -दा -दं भू.

NON-SUPERINTENDENCE, *s.* अनधिष्ठानं, अनधिष्ठितिः *f.*, अनधिष्ठातृत्वं, अनधिकारः.

NOODLE, *s.* अल्पबुद्धिः *m.*, अल्पधीः *m.*, मूर्खः, जडधीः *m.*

NOOK, *s.* कोणः, अस्रः, आरं, विविक्तस्थानं, गुप्तस्थानं.

NOON, NOON-DAY, NOON-TIDE, *s.* मध्याह्नः, मध्याह्नकालः, दिनमध्यं, दिवसमध्यं, दिवामध्यं, मध्यन्दिनं, उद्दिनं.

NOON, NOON-DAY, *a.* माध्याह्निकः -की -कं, माध्यन्दिनः -नी -नं.

NOOSE, *s.* पाशः, पाशबन्धः -न्धं -न्धनं, वागुरा, उन्माथः, कूटपाशः; 'for the neck,' गलपाशः; 'number of nooses,' पाश्या.

To NOOSE, *v. a.* पाश (nom. पाशयति -यितुं), पाशीकृ, पाशेन बन्ध् (c. 9. बध्नाति, बन्द्धुं), पाशे or उन्माथे पत् (c. 10. पातयति -यितुं).

NOOSED, *p.p.* पाशितः -ता -तं, पाशीकृतः &c., पाशबद्धः -द्धा -द्धं.

NOR. *adv.* न, न च, sometimes expressed by the prohibitive मा, or sometimes simply by वा in conjunction with a negative. *See* NEITHER, *conj.*

NORMAL, *a.* (Regular) वैधिकः -की -कं, यथाविधिः -धिः -धि, यथाक्रमः -मा -मं.—(Relating to rudiments, teaching rudiments) मूलविद्यासम्बन्धी -न्धिनी &c., विद्योपक्रमसम्बन्धी &c., विद्यारम्भोपदेशकः -का -कं, मूलविद्याशिक्षकः -का -कं.

NORTH, *s.* उत्तरा, उत्तरदिक् *f.* (श्), उत्तरदिशा, उत्तराशा, उदीची, कौवेरी, सौम्या. Kuvera, according to the Hindús, is the Regent of the North.

NORTH, *a.* उत्तरः -रा -रं, उत्तरस्थः -स्था -स्थं, उदीचीनः -ना -नं, उदङ् -दीची -दक् (च्), कौवेरः -री -रं; 'north-road,' उत्तरापथः; 'north-country,' उदीच्यः.

NORTH-EAST, *s.* प्रागुत्तरा, प्रागुदीची, पूर्व्वोत्तरं -रा, ऐशानी, अपराजिता; 'north-eastwards,' प्रागुत्तरेण, पूर्व्वोत्तरेण; 'north-east of the city,' प्रागुत्तरेण नगरात्.

NORTH-EAST, NORTH-EASTERLY, NORTH-EASTERN, *a.* प्रागुत्तरः -रा -रं, पूर्व्वोत्तरः -रा -रं, प्रागुदङ् -दीची -दक् (च्), प्रागुदीचीनः -ना -नं, प्रागुत्तरस्थः -स्था -स्थं, पूर्व्वोत्तरस्थः &c.

NORTHERLY, NORTHERN, *a.* उत्तरदिश्यः -श्या -श्यं, उत्तरः -रा -रं, उदीचीनः -ना -नं, उत्तरसम्बन्धी -न्धिनी -न्धि (न्); 'in a northerly direction,' उत्तरदिशि.

NORTH-POLE, NORTH-STAR, *s.* ध्रुवः, मेरुः *m.*, औत्तानपादिः *m.*

NORTHWARD, *a.* उत्तरदिश्यः -श्या -श्यं, उत्तरदिक्स्थः -स्था -स्थं, उदङ्मुखः -खी -खं, उत्तरस्थः -स्था -स्थं.

NORTHWARDS, *adv.* उत्तरेण -रात्, उत्तरतस्, उत्तरदिशि, उत्तरत्र.

NORTH-WEST. *s.* वायवी, वायुकोणः, वायुदिशा.

NORTH-WEST, NORTH-WESTERLY, NORTH-WESTERN, *a.* वायुकोणस्थः -स्था -स्थं, वायुदिक्स्थः &c., वायवः -वी -वं, वायवीसम्बन्धी -न्धिनी -न्धि (न्).

NORTH-WIND, *s.* उत्तरवायुः *m.*, उत्तरदिग्वायुः *m.*, उत्तरदिक्पवनः.

NOSE, *s.* नासा -सिका, नसा, नस्या, घ्राणं, घोणा, गन्धवहा, गन्धवाहः, गन्धज्ञा, गन्धनाली, प्रतिः *f.*, नाः *f.* (स्), नस्तः, नासिक्यं, नासिक्यकं, सिङ्घिनी, विकूणिका, तनुभस्त्रा, नक्रं, नकुटं, नर्कुटकं; 'aquiline nose,' शुकनासिका; 'having a sharp nose,' खरणसः -सा -सं, खरणाः -णाः -णः (स्); 'having a nose like a hoof,' खुरणसः -सा -सं, खुरणाः -णाः -णः (स्); 'having a flat nose,' नतनासिकः -का -कं, अवटीटः -टा -टं, अवनाटः -टा -टं, अवभ्रटः -टा -टं; 'having a prominent nose,' प्रलम्बघोणः -णा -णं; 'having a large nose,' उग्रनासिकः -का -कं; 'tip of the nose,' नासिकाग्रं, नासाग्रं; 'mucus of the nose,' नासिकामलं; 'running at the nose,' नासिकास्रावः, नासापरिस्रावः; 'thickening of the membrane of the nose,' नासानाहः; 'dryness of the nose,' नासाशोषः; 'breathing through the nose,' नासिकन्धमः -मा -मं; 'drinking through the nose,' नासिकन्धयः -यी -यं; 'led by the nose, as cattle, &c.' नस्तितः, नस्तोतः, नस्योतः.

NOSE-BRIDLE, *s.* (Rein passed through the nose of an ox) नास्यं, नासिकारज्जुः *m.f.*

NOSE-CUT, *a.* छिन्ननासः -सा -सं, छिन्ननासिकः -का -कं, छिन्ननाः -नाः -नः (स्).

NOSED, *a.* (Having a nose). *See* under NOSE.

NOSEGAY, *s.* कुसुमस्तवकः, पुष्पस्तवकः, पुष्पगुच्छः -च्छकः, गुच्छः -च्छकः, गुत्सः -त्सकः, गुच्छः, गुलुच्छः, समाली, कुटी, प्रकरः.

NOSELESS, *a* अनासिकः -का -कं, विनासिकः -का -कं, विनसः -सा -सं, गतनासिकः -का -कं, निर्नासिकः &c., नासिकाहीनः -ना -नं, नासिकाशून्यः -न्या -न्यं, विखः -खा -खं, विखुः -खुः -खु, विख्यः -ख्या -ख्यं, विख्रः &c., विखुः &c., विग्रः -ग्रा -ग्रं.

NOSOLOGY, *s.* रोगनिदानशास्त्रं, निदानविद्या, रोगवर्गीकरणविद्या.

NOSOPOETIC, *a.* रोगकरः -रा -रं, व्याधिजनकः -का -कं, रोगोत्पादकः &c.

NOSTRIL, *s.* नासारन्ध्रं, नासिकारन्ध्रं, नासाग्ररन्ध्रं, नासाविवरं, नासिकाच्छिद्रं, नासापुटं, नासाबिलं; 'air breathed through the nostrils,' स्वरः.

NOSTRUM, *s.* गूढौषधं, गुप्तौषधं, अप्रकाशितौषधं, मिथ्यौषधं.

NOT, *adv.* In absolute negation, denial, or refusal, 'not' is rendered by न, नो, ना, नहि. When prohibitive, by मा, मास्म, or sometimes by अलं or कृतं with instr. c. When privative, it is expressed by अ, अन्, निर्, वि prefixed; as, 'there is not,' नास्ति; 'he will not go,' न गमिष्यति; 'do not go,' मा गच्छ; 'do not grieve,' अलं शोकेन; 'not regardful,' अनपेक्षः -क्षा -क्षं, निरपेक्षः &c.; 'not at all,' अलेशं, न किञ्चिदपि; 'not so,' नैवं. In prohibitive phrases मा

may be used with the 3d pret., the augment being cut off; as, 'do not grieve' मा꞉शोचीः; 'do not fear,' मा꞉भैषीः. The interrogative 'is not?' is rendered by ननु.

NOTABLE, *a.* (Memorable) स्मरणीयः -या -यं, स्मरणार्हः -र्हा -र्हं.—(Remarkable, distinguished, notorious) विशिष्टः -ष्टा -ष्टं, विशेष in comp., प्रसिद्धः -द्धा -द्धं, लोकप्रसिद्धः &c., ख्यातः -ता -तं, लोकख्यातः &c., उत्कृष्टः -ष्टा -ष्टं.

NOTABLENESS, *s.* स्मरणीयता, प्रसिद्धता, लोकप्रसिद्धता, विशिष्टता.

NOTABLY, *adv.* प्रसिद्धं, लोकप्रसिद्धं, स्मरणीयं, विशिष्टप्रकारेण.

NOTARY, *s.* कायस्थः, लेखकः, लिपिकारः, लिपिजीवी *m.* (न्), लेख्यपत्रप्रमाता *m.* (तृ), पत्रप्रमाणजीवी.

NOTATION, *s.* अङ्कनं, अङ्ककरणं, चिह्नकरणं.—(In music) प्रस्तरः.

NOTCH, *s.* छेदः, अवच्छेदः, विच्छेदः, छिद्रं; 'of a bow,' अटनी -निः *f.*

To NOTCH, *v. a.* छिद् (c. 7. छिनत्ति, छेत्तुं), अवछिद्, छेदं कृ, अवच्छेदं कृ.

NOTCHED, *p. p.* अवच्छिन्नः -न्ना -न्नं, छिन्नः &c., सच्छेदः -दा -दं, सावच्छेदः &c.

NOTE, *s.* (Mark, token) चिह्नं, लक्षणं, अङ्कः -ङ्कं, लाञ्छनं, अभिज्ञानं, लक्ष्यं, कलङ्कः.—(Mark made as a memorandum) स्मरणार्थकचिह्नं, स्मरणचिह्नं, स्मरणं.—(Annotation, comment) टीका, भाष्यं, व्याख्या, टिप्पनी, वार्त्तिकं; 'with notes,' सटीकः -का -कं.—(Sound in music) स्वरः, मातृका, मूर्छना, कलः, क्वणः, विरिब्धः, विरावः; 'a false note,' अपस्वरः, विस्वरः, अपक्वणः; 'a high note,' तारः; 'a cracked note,' काकस्वरः; 'key note,' वादी *m.* (न्). The notes in music are निषादः or निषदः or निषधः, ऋषभः, गान्धारः, षड्जः, मध्यमः, पञ्चमः, धैवतः, घर्घरः.—(Note of birds) रुतं, वाशितं, वाशनं.—(Notice, heed) अवेक्षा -क्षणं, अपेक्षा, मनोयोगः, लक्षं -क्ष्यं.—(Reputation) कीर्त्तिः *f.*, ख्यातिः *f.*, प्रतिष्ठा, यशस् *n.*, गौरवं; 'of little note,' अल्पकीर्त्तिः -र्त्तिः -र्त्ति, अल्पिष्ठकीर्त्तिः &c. *See* NOTED. (Short letter) पत्रकं, पत्रं, लेखः, लेख्यं.—(Note of hand) पत्रलेख्यं.

To NOTE, *v. a.* (Observe) लक्ष् (c. 10. लक्षयति -यितुं), आलक्ष्, उपलक्ष्, अवेक्ष् (c. 1. -ईक्षते -क्षितुं), अपेक्ष्, अवेक्षां कृ, आलोक् (c. 10. -लोकयति -यितुं), निरूप् (c. 10. -रूपयति -यितुं), आलोच् (c. 10. -लोचयति -यितुं), आलोचनं कृ.—(Set down in writing, make a note of) अङ्क् (c. 10. अङ्कयति -यितुं), चिह्न् (c. 10. चिह्नयति -यितुं), स्मरणार्थकचिह्नं कृ, स्मरणपुस्तके or लेख्यपत्रे समारुह् in caus. (-रोपयति -यितुं) or आरुह्, अभिलिख् (c. 6. -लिखति -लेखितुं).

NOTE-BOOK, *s.* स्मरणपुस्तकं, स्मारकपुस्तकं, अङ्कनपुस्तकं.

NOTED, *p. p.* or *a.* (Observed) लक्षितः -ता -तं, आलक्षितः &c., उपलक्षितः &c., अवेक्षितः &c.—(Set down in writing) लेख्यारूढः -ढा -ढं, लेख्यारोपितः -ता -तं, स्मरणपुस्तकारोपितः &c.—(Celebrated) प्रसिद्धः -द्धा -द्धं, ख्यातः -ता -तं, विख्यातः &c. प्रथितः -ता -तं, विश्रुतः -ता -तं, लब्धशब्दः -ब्दा -ब्दं, लब्धप्रतिष्ठः -ष्ठा -ष्ठं.

NOTHING, *s.* (Not any thing) न किञ्चित्, न किमपि, न किञ्चन.—(Not any thing at all) न किञ्चिदपि, अलेशमपि, न कियदपि, न सूक्ष्ममपि, न स्तोकमपि.—(Non-existence, nonentity) अभावः, नास्तित्वं, नास्ति indec. असत्त्वं, अवस्तु *n.*, अवस्तुता, शून्यता -त्वं, शून्यं, असम्भवः, अविद्यमानता.—(Trifle, thing of no value) अल्पविषयः, स्वल्पविषयः, सुलघुविषयः, अल्पार्थविषयः; 'good for nothing,' व्यर्थः -र्था -र्थं, निरर्थकः -का -कं, किमर्थः -र्था -र्थं, अकिञ्चित्करः -रा -रं.

NOTHING, *adv.* न किञ्चित्, न किमपि, न किञ्चिदपि, न किञ्चन, अलेशमपि, अलेशम्, न कियदपि, न मनागपि, न मनाक्, असूक्ष्ममपि, अस्तोकमपि.

NOTHINGNESS, *s.* शून्यता, शून्यं, अवस्तुत्वं, नास्तित्वं, अभावः. *See* NONENTITY.

NOTICE, *s.* (Observation by the eye or other senses) अवलोकनं, आलोकनं, आलोचनं -ना, निरीक्षा, अवेक्षा -क्षणं, निरूपणं, दर्शनं, सन्दर्शनं, दृष्टिः *f.*, लक्षं.—(Regard, heed) अवेक्षा -क्षणं, अपेक्षा, प्रतीक्षा, अवधानं, मनोयोगः, विचारः.—(Intelligence, intimation) सन्देशः, निवेदनं, सूचना -नं, विज्ञप्तिः *f.*, उद्देशः, समुद्देशः -शनं, संवादः, बोधनं, बोधः.—(Mention) अभिधानं, कथनं, ग्रहणं, निर्देशः, उद्देशः.—(Proclamation) घोषः -षणं -णा, विघोषणं -णा, ख्यापनं; 'written notice,' घोषणपत्रं, निवेदनपत्रं, विज्ञापनपत्रं, सूचनपत्रं, बोधनपत्रं, प्रसिद्धिपत्रं.—(Respectful treatment) आदरः, सत्कारः, सत्क्रिया, मानं, सम्मानं, सम्भावना, पूजा, प्रतीतिः *f.*

To NOTICE, *v. a.* (Observe) लक्ष् (c. 10. लक्षयति -यितुं), आलक्ष्, समालक्ष्, संलक्ष्, आलोक् (c. 10. -लोकयति -यितुं), अवलोक्, आलोच् (c. 10. -लोचयति -यितुं), निरूप् (c. 10. -रूपयति -यितुं), अवेक्ष् (c. 1. -ईक्षते -क्षितुं), अपेक्ष्, निरीक्ष्, अवेक्षां कृ.—(Heed) अवधा (c. 3. -धत्ते -धातुं), मनो धा, सावधानः -ना -नं भू, अवेक्ष्, अपेक्ष्.—(Mention) अभिधा (c. 3. -दधाति -धातुं), निर्दिश् (c. 6. -दिशति -देष्टुं), उद्दिश्, कथ् (c. 10. कथयति -यितुं), निर्देशं कृ, उद्देशं कृ.—(Treat with attention or honor) सत्कृ, सम्मन् (c. 10. -मानयति -यितुं), सम्भू (c. 10. -भावयति -यितुं), आदृ (c. 6. -द्रियते -दर्त्तुं), आदरं कृ.

NOTICEABLE, *a.* लक्ष्यः -क्ष्या -क्ष्यं, लक्षणीयः -या -यं, आलक्ष्यः &c., अवेक्षणीयः &c., प्रतीक्षणीयः &c., प्रतीक्षणार्हः -र्हा -र्हं, निरूपणार्हः &c.

NOTICED, *p. p.* आलक्षितः -ता -तं, अवेक्षितः -ता -तं, उद्दिष्टः -ष्टा -ष्टं.

NOTIFICATION, *s.* घोषणं -णा, विघोषणं -णा, विज्ञापनं -ना, विज्ञप्तिः *f.*, ज्ञप्तिः *f.*, ज्ञापनं, ख्यापनं, निवेदनं, आवेदनं, बोधनं, सूचनं -ना.—(Written notice). *See* under NOTICE.

NOTIFIED, *p. p.* विज्ञप्तः -प्ता -प्तं, विज्ञापितः -ता -तं, ज्ञप्तः &c., ज्ञापितः -ता -तं, निवेदितः &c., घोषितः &c., विघोषितः &c., प्रख्यातः &c., सूचितः &c.

To NOTIFY, *v. a.* ज्ञा in caus. (ज्ञापयति, ज्ञपयति -यितुं), विज्ञा, निविद् (c. 10. -वेदयति -यितुं), आविद्, बुध् (c. 10. बोधयति -यितुं), प्रख्या (c. 2. -ख्याति -तुं, caus. ख्यापयति -यितुं), ख्या, सूच् (c. 10. सूचयति -यितुं), घुष् (c. 10. घोषयति -यितुं), विघुष्, आघुष्, कृत् (c. 10. कीर्त्तयति -यितुं), प्रकाश् (c. 10. -काशयति -यितुं).

NOTION, *s.* बुद्धिः *f.*, मतिः *f.*, मनःकल्पना, बुद्धिकल्पना, कल्पना, बुद्धिकल्पितं, सङ्कल्पः, मनोगतं, मनसिजं, वासना, भावना, सम्भावना, बोधः, भासः, आभासः, प्रतिभासः; 'under the notion,' बुद्ध्या.—(Sentiment, opinion) मतं, मतिः *f.*, बुद्धिः *f.*

NOTIONAL, *a.* मनोगतः -ता -तं, मनसिजः -जा -जं, मनोजः &c., मनोभवः -वा -वं, काल्पनिकः -की -कं, मनःकल्पितः -ता -तं, सङ्कल्पजः -जा -जं, मनःसृष्टः -ष्टा -ष्टं.

NOTORIETY, NOTORIOUSNESS, *s.* प्रसिद्धिः *f.*, लोकप्रसिद्धिः *f.*, लोकप्रसिद्धता, प्रसिद्धत्वं, प्रकाशता, प्रकाशः, ख्यातिः *f.*, विख्यातिः *f.*, प्रख्यातिः *f.*, विश्रुतिः *f.*, लोकविश्रुतिः, प्राकट्यं, लौकिकता -त्वं, रूढिः *f.*, प्रथा, सम्प्रथा, प्रथितिः *f.*, सम्प्रतीतिः *f.*—(In a bad sense) वाच्यता, कुकीर्त्तिः *f.*, कुख्यातिः *f.*, कुप्रतिष्ठा, कुप्रसिद्धिः *f.*

NOTORIOUS, *a.* प्रसिद्धः -द्धा -द्धं, लोकप्रसिद्धः &c., लोकविश्रुतः -ता -तं, लोकप्रथितः -ता -तं, लोकविदितः &c., लोकसिद्धः &c., लौकिकः -की -कं, सार्वलौकिकः &c., ख्यातः -ता -तं, विख्यातः &c., प्रथितः &c., विश्रुतः &c., विज्ञातः &c., रूढः -ढा -ढं, प्रकटः -टी -टं, प्रकटितः -ता -तं.—(In a bad sense) ख्यातगर्हणः -णा -णं, वाच्यः -च्या -च्यं, कुकी-

त्रिमान् -मती -मत् (त्), कुख्यातः -ता -तं, कुख्यातिमान् &c., कुप्रसिद्धः &c.; 'a notorious offender,' महापातकी m. (न्).

NOTORIOUSLY, *adv.* प्रसिद्धं, लोकप्रसिद्धं, प्रकाशं, प्रकटं, ख्यातगर्हणं.

NOTUS, *s.* (South wind) दक्षिणवायुः, दक्षिणदिग्वायुः m.

NOTWITHSTANDING, *conj.* तथापि, परन्तु, परं, किन्तु, अथापि, तत्रापि, तदपि.

NOUGHT. *See* NAUGHT, NOTHING.

NOUN, *s.* नाम n. (न्), विशेष्यं, संज्ञा, सत्त्वं, द्रव्यवाचकः, पदार्थवाचकः, आख्या, शब्दः, सङ्केतशब्दः; 'noun of action,' कारकः, क्रिया; 'of agency,' कर्तृवाच्यं; 'animate,' प्राणिवाचकः; 'abstract,' भाववाचकः; 'collective,' समूहवाचकः; 'communicative,' अपादानवाच्यं; 'denominative,' क्रियावाचकः; 'ending in a vowel,' अजन्तः; 'gentile,' जातिवाचकः; 'inanimate,' अप्राणिवाचकः; 'instrumental,' कारणवाच्यं; 'inflected, or of any case,' कारकं; 'passive,' कर्म्मवाचकः, कर्म्मणिवाच्यशब्दः, सम्प्रदानवाच्यं; 'possessive,' अधिकरणवाच्यं; 'proper,' नामवाचकः; 'simple,' भाववाच्यं, लिङ्गं; 'verbal,' क्रियावाचकः.

To NOURISH, *v. a.* पुष् (c. 10. पोषयति -यितुं, c. 1. पोषति -षितुं, c. 9. पुष्णाति), परिपुष्, पाल् (c. 10. पालयति -यितुं), प्रतिपाल्, भृ (c. 1. भरति, c. 3. बिभर्त्ति, भर्त्तुं), सम्भृ, अन्नेन सन्तुष् (c. 10. -तोषयति -यितुं) or तुष् or सन्तृप् (c. 10. -तर्पयति -यितुं) or तृप् or संवृध् (c. 10. -वर्धयति -यितुं) or वृंह् (c. 10. वृंहयति -यितुं) or आप्यै (c. 10. -प्याययति -यितुं) or जीव् (c. 10. जीवयति -यितुं), पोषणं कृ, पालनं कृ, पालनपोषणं कृ.

NOURISHABLE, *a.* पोषणीयः -या -यं, पोष्यः -ष्या -ष्यं, पालनीयः -या -यं, वृंहणीयः -या -यं, भरणीयः -या -यं, भरण्यः -ण्या -ण्यं, भार्य्यः &c., सम्भार्य्यः &c.

NOURISHED, *p. p.* पुष्टः -ष्टा -ष्टं, पोषितः -ता -तं, पुषितः &c., पालितः &c., प्रतिपालितः &c., भृतः -ता -तं, सम्भृतः &c., भरितः &c., वृंहितः &c.

NOURISHER, *s.* पोष्टा m. (ष्टृ), पोषयिता m. (तृ), पालयिता m., प्रतिपालयिता m., पालकः, भर्त्ता m. (र्त्तृ), पालनकर्त्ता m., अन्नदाता m., वृंहकः, अन्नदः.

NOURISHING, *a.* पोषकः -का -कं, पालकः -का -कं, प्रतिपालकः &c., पौष्टिकः -की -कं, पुष्टिदः -दा -दं, वृंहणः -णा -णी -णं, धातुपोषकः &c.

NOURISHMENT, *s.* (Act of nourishing) पोषः -षणं, पालनं, प्रतिपालनं, भरणं, भरिमा m. (न्), भृतिः f., सम्भृतिः f., आप्यायनं, वृंहणं, पुष्टिदानं, अन्नदानं.—(Food, aliment) आहारः, भोजनं, भक्ष्यं, खाद्यं, अन्नं, आहार्य्यं, अभ्याहार्य्यं, अभ्यवहारः, अभ्यवहार्य्यं, शरीरयात्रा, देहयात्रा, जीवनं -नकः, पौष्टिकं, भृतिः f., सम्भृतिः f., सम्भारः.

NOVEL, *a.* नवः -वा -वं, अभिनवः -वा -वं, नवीनः -ना -नं, नूतनः -ना -नं, नूत्नः -त्ना -त्नं, नव्यः -व्या -व्यं, प्रत्ययः -या -यं, अपूर्व्वः -र्व्वा -र्व्वं, अभूतपूर्व्वः &c., अदृष्टपूर्व्वः &c., अश्रुतपूर्व्वः &c., अप्राचीनः -ना -नं, अद्भुतः -ता -तं, अलौकिकः -की -कं, विलक्षणः -णा -णं.

NOVEL, *s.* (Fictitious tale) कल्पितकथा, परिकथा, उपकथा, कथा, उपाख्यानं, आख्यानं, कूटार्थकथा, कूटार्थोपाख्यानं, मिथ्याकथा, प्रबन्धकल्पना.

NOVELTY, *s.* नवता, नवीनता, नूतनता -त्वं, नव्यता, नाव्यं, अभिनवता, प्रत्ययता, अपूर्व्वता -त्वं, अद्भुतत्वं, अलौकिकत्वं, विलक्षणता, वैलक्षण्यं.—(A novelty) नववस्तु n., नूतनवस्तु n., कौतुकं, आश्चर्य्यवस्तु.

NOVEMBER, *s.* मार्गशीर्षपूर्व्वार्द्धं, कार्त्तिकोत्तरार्द्धं, मार्गशीर्षः, मार्गशिरः, मार्गः, अग्रहायणः, आग्रहायणः, आग्रहायणिकः, सहाः m. (स्), कार्त्तिकः, कार्त्तिकिकः, बाहुलः, ऊर्जः.

NOVENNIAL, *a.* नववर्षीयः -या -यं, नववर्षीणः -णा -णं, नववार्षिकः -की -कं.

NOVERCAL, *a.* वैमात्रिकः -की -कं, वैमात्रीयः -या -यं, विमातृयोग्यः -ग्या -ग्यं.

NOVICE, *s.* नवशिष्यः, नवच्छात्रः, नूतनशिष्यः, नवीनशिष्यः, प्राथमकल्पिकः, शैक्षः, क्रियाकारः, नवाभ्यासी m. (न्), नवीनाभ्यासी m., नूतनाभ्यासी, विद्यारम्भकः.

NOVITIATE, *s.* (State) नवशिष्यत्वं, नवच्छात्रता -त्वं, नवच्छात्रदशा, नवाभ्यासित्वं, नूतनाभ्यासित्वं.—(Period of being a novice) नवाभ्यासकालः, नवीनाभ्यासित्वकालः, विद्यारम्भकालः.

NOW, *adv.* (At the present time) इदानीम्, अधुना, सम्प्रति, साम्प्रतं, अद्य, एतर्हि, इहसमये, वर्त्तमानकाले, तत्काले, अद्यत्काले, साम्प्रतकाले, अधुनातनकाले, प्रस्तुतकाले; 'now and then,' कदाचित्, कदापि, कदाचन, कर्हिचित्, जातु, काले काले, वारं वारं, अनुकालं; 'till now,' अद्यापि, अद्यावधि; 'from now,' अद्यारभ्य, अद्यप्रभृति, इतःपरं; 'just now,' अव्यवहितदीर्घकाले, नूतनकाले; 'it was but now,' नन्विदानीम्.—(As an inceptive or connective particle) अथ. अथो.—(After this) ततस्, अतस्.

NOW-A-DAYS, *adv.* साम्प्रतकाले, अधुनातनकाले, वर्त्तमानकाले, अद्य.

NO WAY, NO WAYS, NO WISE, *adv.* न कथञ्चन, न कथञ्चित्, न कथमपि, न सर्व्वथा, न सर्व्वथैव.

NOWHERE, *adv.* न क्वापि, न कुत्रापि, न क्वचित्, न कुत्रचित्.

NOXIOUS, *a.* हिंस्रः -स्रा -स्रं, हिंसकः -का -कं, हिंसालुः -लुः -लु, हिंसात्मकः -का -कं, अपकारी -रिणी -रि (न्), अपकारकः -का -कं, अनिष्टकारी &c., अहितकारी &c., नृशंसः -सा -सं, शरारुः -रुः -रु, शारुकः -का -कं, दंशेरः -रा -रं, घातुकः -का -कं, उपघातकः &c., नंशुकः &c., अपायजनकः &c., दुष्टः -ष्टा -ष्टं, दूषकः -का -कं, बाधकः -का -कं, कुत्सितः -ता -तं.

NOXIOUSNESS, *s.* हिंस्रता, अपकारकत्वं, दूषकता, दुष्टता, घातुकत्वं.

NOZZLE, *s.* नासाग्रं, नासिकाग्रं, मस्तः, प्रोथः -थं, पोत्रं, मुखं, अग्रं; 'nozzled as an ox,' नस्तितः.

NUBILE, *a.* विवाह्यः -ह्या -ह्यं, विवाहयोग्यः -ग्या -ग्यं, उद्वाह्यः &c.

NUBILOUS, *a.* साभ्रः -भ्रा -भ्रं, अभ्रियः -या -यं, समेघः -घा -घं, मेघाकीर्णः -र्णा -र्णं, मेघाच्छन्नः -न्ना -न्नं, मेघाच्छादितः -ता -तं. *See* CLOUDY.

NUCLEUS, *s.* समुच्चयास्पदं, सञ्चयास्पदं, हृदयं, गर्भः, बीजं.

NUDATION, *s.* नग्नीकरणं, विवस्त्रीकरणं, निर्वस्त्रीकरणं.

NUDE, *a.* नग्नः -ग्ना -ग्नं, विवस्त्रः -स्त्रा -स्त्रं, निर्वस्त्रः &c. *See* NAKED.

To NUDGE, *v. a.* चल् (c. 10. चालयति -यितुं), अरत्निना तड् (c. 10. ताडयति -यितुं).

NUDITY, *s.* नग्नता -त्वं, विवस्त्रत्वं, वस्त्रशून्यता, अपरिच्छदः. *See* NAKEDNESS.

NUGACITY, *s.* अनर्थकत्वं -ता, मोघता, निष्फलता, लाघवं, लघुता.

NUGATORY, *a.* (Vain) निरर्थकः -का -कं, अनर्थकः -का -कं, तृणप्रायः -या -यं, व्यर्थः -र्था -र्थं.—(Of no force) मोघः -घा -घं, निष्फलः -ला -लं, विफलः &c., फलहीनः -ना -नं, अनिष्पन्नः -न्ना -न्नं, निर्बलः -ला -लं, प्रभावहीनः &c., निष्प्रभावः &c., लुप्तः -प्ता -प्तं, निष्प्रमाणः &c.

NUISANCE, *s.* कष्टं, बाधा, बाधकः, पीडा, व्यथा, विडम्बना, कण्टकः -कं, उत्पातः; 'public nuisance,' लोककण्टकः; 'domestic,' गृहोत्पातः.

NULL, *a.* मोघः -घा -घं, व्यर्थः -र्था -र्थं, अनिष्पन्नः -न्ना -न्नं, लुप्तः -प्ता -प्तं, निरर्थकः -का -कं, अनर्थकः -का -कं, निष्फलः -ला -लं, विफलः -ला -लं, निष्प्रभावः -वा -वं, निर्बलः -ला -लं, निर्जीवः -वा -वं, वृथा indec. मुधा indec.

To NULLIFY, *v. a.* मोघीकृ, व्यर्थीकृ, अपरीकृ, निष्फलीकृ, निष्फल (nom. निष्फलयति -यितुं), विफलीकृ, लुप् (c. 6. लुम्पति, लोप्तुं, c. 10. लोप-

यति -यितुं), खण्ड् (c. 10. खण्डयति -यितुं), निर्बलीकृ, निष्प्रभावीकृ, मुधा कृ, वृथा कृ.

NULLITY, s. (Want of force) मोघता, व्यर्थता, निरर्थकता, अनर्थकता, आनर्थक्यं, अनिष्पन्नता, लुप्तता, निष्फलता.—(Nonentity) अभावः, नास्तित्वं, अवस्तु n., शून्यता.

NUMB, a. सुप्तः -प्ता -प्तं, सुप्तत्वक् m.f.n. (च्), जडः -डा -डं, स्तब्धः -ब्धा -ब्धं, स्तब्धचेष्टः -ष्टा -ष्टं, स्तम्भितचेष्टः &c., कुण्ठः -ण्ठा -ण्ठं, गतिशक्तिहीनः -ना -नं, स्पन्दनरहितः -ता -तं, स्तम्भितचेतनः -ना -नं, अचेतनः -ना -नं, चैतन्यरहितः &c.; 'with cold,' शीताकुलः -ला -लं.

To NUMB, v. a. जडीकृ, स्तब्धीकृ, चैतन्यं स्तम्भ् (c. 10. स्तम्भयति -यितुं, c. 5. स्तभ्नोति, स्तम्भितुं), चैतन्यस्तम्भं कृ, चेतनास्तम्भनं कृ, चैतन्यं हृ (c. 1. हरति, हर्तुं), त्वक्सुप्तिं कृ, शीताकुलीकृ.

NUMBED, p. p. सुप्तः -प्ता -प्तं, जडीकृतः -ता -तं. *See* NUMB, a.

NUMBER, s. संख्या.—(Assemblage of two or more units) राशिः m., संख्या; 'even number,' समसंख्या; 'odd,' विषमसंख्या; 'whole number,' अभिन्नं; 'five in number,' पञ्चसंख्यः -ख्या -ख्यं, पञ्चसंख्यकः -का -कं.—(Amount) संख्या, गणना, परिगणना, समुदायः, परिमाणं.—(Multitude, collection) गणः, समूहः, समवायः, सङ्घः, सङ्घातः, सञ्चयः, वृन्दं, सङ्ग्रहः, स्तोमः, राशिः m., पुञ्जः, पूगः; 'a number of young women,' तरुणीगणः; 'a number of men,' पुरुषसमूहः, पुरुषसमवायः.—(A great number, many) बाहुल्यं, बहुत्वं, बहुः -हुः -ह्वी -हु, बहुलः -ला -लं, बहुसंख्यकः -का -कं, अनेकः &c., प्रचुरः -रा -रं; 'in great number,' बहुशस्, अनेकशस्.—(Figure, arithmetical sign) अङ्कः, संख्या.—(Science of numbers) अङ्कविद्या, गणनाविद्या, गणितं, व्यक्तं; 'table of numbers,' अङ्कपत्रं, अङ्कजालं, सारणी.—(Verse) पद्यं, छन्दस् n., कविता, पद्यरचना.—(In grammar) वचनं; 'singular number,' एकवचनं; 'dual,' द्विवचनं; 'plural,' बहुवचनं, अनेकवचनं.

To NUMBER, v. a. (Count) संख्या (c. 2. -ख्याति -तुं), परिसंख्या, सम्परिख्या, गण् (c. 10. गणयति -यितुं), विगण्, प्रगण्, अङ्क् (c. 10. अङ्कयति -यितुं), कल् (c. 10. कलयति -यितुं), गणनां कृ, गणीकृ.—(Affix a number) अङ्क्, अङ्कं स्था in caus. (स्थापयति -यितुं) or लिख् (c. 6. लिखति, लेखितुं).

NUMBERED, p. p. संख्यातः -ता -तं, गणितः -ता -तं, अङ्कितः &c., कलितः &c., गणीभूतः -ता -तं, गणीकृतः -ता -तं, परिगणितः &c.

NUMBERER, s. संख्याकृत् m., गणकः, अङ्कगणकः, गणनाकारी m. (न्).

NUMBERING, s. गणनं -ना, परिगणनं -ना, संख्यानं, संख्याकरणं, गणितं.

NUMBERLESS, a. असंख्येयः -या -यं, असंख्यः -ख्या -ख्यं, अगणनीयः -या -यं, अगण्यः -ण्या -ण्यं, असंख्यातः -ता -तं, गणनातीतः -ता -तं, कोट्यवधिः -धिः -धि.

NUMBLES, s. pl. (Entrails of a deer) मृगान्त्रं, मृगान्त्राणि n. pl.

NUMBNESS, s. त्वक्सुप्तिः f., त्वक्स्वापः, सुप्तिः f., स्वापः, जडता, जाड्यं, चैतन्यस्तम्भः, चेतनास्तम्भः, चैतन्यस्तब्धता, चैतन्यराहित्यं, गतिशक्तिहीनता, कुण्ठता, भिर्द्धं.

NUMERABLE, a. संख्येयः -या -यं, गणनीयः -या -यं, गण्यः -ण्या -ण्यं, गणेयः -या -यं, गणितव्यः -व्या -व्यं, परिगणनीयः -या -यं.

NUMERAL, a. (Pertaining to or consisting of numbers) सांख्यः -ख्यी -ख्यं, संख्यात्मकः -का -कं, संख्याविषयः -या -यं, संख्यासम्बन्धी -न्धिनी &c., संख्यावाचकः &c., गणनासम्बन्धी &c., अङ्की -ङ्किनी &c., अङ्कात्मकः &c.

NUMERAL, s. (Figure) अङ्कः, संख्या, संख्याचिह्नं, गणनाचिह्नं.

NUMERALLY, adv. संख्यानुसारात् -रेण, यथासंख्यं, संख्यावत्.

NUMERARY, a. अमुकसंख्यासम्बन्धी -न्धिनी &c., अमुकसंख्यः -ख्या -ख्यं.

NUMERATION, s. संख्यानं, संख्यता, गणना, परिगणना, संख्यापरिमाणं.

NUMERATOR, s. (Of a fraction) अंशः, लवः, भोगः, हारः, हारकः; 'numerator and denominator together,' राशिः m.

NUMERICAL, a. सांख्यः -ख्यी -ख्यं, यथासंख्यः -ख्या -ख्यं, संख्यापेक्षकः -का -कं, संख्योद्देशकः -का -कं, संख्यासम्बन्धी &c. *See* NUMERAL, a.

NUMERICALLY, adv. यथासंख्यं, संख्यामपेक्ष्य, संख्यामुद्दिश्य, यथागणनं, गणनां कृत्वा, संख्यां कृत्वा or गणयित्वा.

NUMEROUS, a. बहुः -हुः -ह्वी -हु, बहुलः -ला -लं, बहुसंख्यकः -का -कं, बहुसंख्यः -ख्या -ख्यं, महासंख्यः &c., अनेकः -का -कं, प्रचुरः -रा -रं, भूरिः -रिः -रि, भूयिष्ठः -ष्ठा -ष्ठं, भूयान् -यसी -यः (स्), नैकः -का -कं, पुष्कलः -ला -लं, प्राज्यः -ज्या -ज्यं, विपुलः -ला -लं.

NUMEROUSLY, adv. बहुशस्, अनेकशस्, बाहुल्येन, सङ्घशस्.

NUMEROUSNESS, s. बहुत्वं, बाहुल्यं, अनेकत्वं -ता, अनैक्यं, बहुसंख्यत्वं.

NUMISMATIC, a. मुद्राविषयः -या -यं, नाणकविषयकः &c., मुद्रासम्बन्धी &c.

NUMISMATICS, s. मुद्राविद्या, नाणकविद्या, मुद्राविषयका विद्या.

NUMSKULL, s. स्थूलबुद्धिः m., स्थूलधीः m., अल्पबुद्धिः, जडधीः.

NUN, s. मठनिवासिनी, मठवासिनी, संसारत्यागिनी, लोकत्यागिनी, सङ्गपरित्यागिनी, सन्न्यासिनी, तपस्विनी, वैरागिणी, तपोनिष्ठा, तपस्यासक्ता, धर्म्मभगिनी, ब्रह्मचारिणी, योगिनी.

NUNCIO, s. रोमीयधर्म्माध्यक्षसकाशाद् दूतः, महाधर्म्माध्यक्षदूतः.

NUNCUPATIVE, NUNCUPATORY, a. साक्षात् कथितः -ता -तं, अलिखितः &c.

NUNNERY, s. धर्म्मभगिनीमठः, तपस्विनीमठः, ब्रह्मचारिणीमठः.

NUPTIAL, a. वैवाहिकः -की -कं, उद्वाहिकः -का -कं, औद्वाहिकः -की -कं, पाणिग्रहणिकः -की -कं, विवाहीयः -या -यं, विवाही -हिनी -हि (न्), उद्वाही &c., विवाहसम्बन्धी &c., विवाह in comp.; 'nuptial feast,' विवाहमहोत्सवः; 'nuptial gift,' यौतकं, औद्वाहिकं, पारिणाय्यं, हरणं, सुदायः -यं.

NUPTIALS, s. pl. विवाहः, उद्वाहः, परिणयनं, विवाहविधिः m., विवाहक्रिया, विवाहसंस्कारः, पाणिग्रहणं.

NURSE, s. धात्री, धात्रेयी -यिका, अङ्कपाली, उपमाता f. (तृ), मातृका, प्रतिपालिका, पालयित्री, धन्या, वपुः f.—(In sickness) उपचारकर्त्री, उपचारिका, रुग्णपरिचारिका, रोगार्त्तपालिका, रोगसेविका.—(Fosterer, cherisher) पालकः, प्रतिपालकः, पालयिता m. (तृ), पोषकः, पोष्टा m. (ष्टृ).

To NURSE, v. a. (Foster, take care of a child, &c.) पाल् (c. 10. पालयति -यितुं), प्रतिपाल्, अङ्के पाल्, क्रोडे पाल्, पुष् (c. 1. पोषति, c. 9. पुष्णाति, c. 10. पोषयति -यितुं) or परिपुष्, क्रोडीकृ, अङ्कीकृ.—(Attend upon a sick person) रोगिणम् उपचर् (c. 1. -चरति -रितुं) or परिचर् or पाल् or प्रतिपाल् or सेव् (c. 1. सेवते -वितुं) or उपसेव्.—(Suckle) दुग्धं or स्तन्यं or स्तनं दा (c. 3. ददाति, दातुं) or पा in caus. (पाययति -यितुं) or धे in caus. (धापयति -यितुं), स्तनदानेन or स्तन्यदानेन पुष् or पाल्.—(Nourish, cherish) भृ (c. 1. भरति, c. 3. बिभर्त्ति, भर्त्तुं), सम्भृ, पाल्.

NURSED, p. p. पालितः -ता -तं, अङ्के पालितः -ता -तं or प्रतिपालितः &c., पोषितः -ता -तं, पुष्टः -ष्टा -ष्टं, भरितः -ता -तं.—(In sickness, &c.) उपचरितः -ता -तं.

NURSERY, s. बालस्थानं, बालगृहं, बालकस्थानं, पालनस्थानं, पोषणस्थानं.

NURSERY-MAN, s. पुष्पाजीवी m. (न्), पुष्पशाकोत्पत्तिजीवी m. (न्).

NURSING, s. पालनं, अङ्केपालनं, अङ्कपालिका, प्रतिपालनं, पोषणं, भरणं, चुलुम्पः, लालनं, क्रोडीकरणं.—(In sickness, &c.) उपचारः.

NURSLING, *s.* स्तनन्धयः -या, स्तनपः -पा -पाः *m.*, स्तनपायी *m.* (न्), बालः.

NURTURE, *s.* (Nourishment, food) आहारः, भक्ष्यं, शरीरयात्रा, भृतिः *f.*, सम्भृतिः *f.*, पौष्टिकं.—(Education, bringing up) शिक्षा, उपदेशः, अभ्यासः, पुष्टिः *f.*, पोषः -षणं, पालनं, प्रतिपालनं, भरिमा *m.* (न्).

To NURTURE, *v. a.* (Nourish) पुष् (c. 10. पोषयति -यितुं), परिपुष्, पाल् (c. 10. पालयति -यितुं), प्रतिपाल्, भृ (c. 1. भरति, c. 3. बिभर्त्ति, भर्त्तुं), पालनं कृ, पोषणं कृ.—(Educate) शिक्ष् (c. 10. शिक्षयति -यितुं), विनी (c. 1. -नयति -नेतुं).

To NUSTLE, *v. a.* अङ्के पाल् (c. 10. पालयति -यितुं), अङ्कीकृ, क्रोडीकृ.

NUT, *s.* स्वाद्वबीजगर्भम् अण्डाकृति दृढफलं or घनफलबीजं.

NUTANT, *a.* प्रणतशिराः -राः -रः (स्), अवनतशिराः &c., नतशिराः &c.

NUT-BROWN, *a.* पूर्व्वोक्तफलवत् श्यावः -वा -वं or श्यामः -मा -मं.

NUT-CRACKERS, *s. pl.* सन्दंशः, सन्दंशकं, सन्दंशका.

NUTMEG, *s.* जातिकोशं, जातिफलं, जातिः -ती *f.*, जातीकोशं, जातीकोषं, जातीफलं, समुद्रान्तं, पुन्नागः, द्विधात्मकं, लवं, तृस्वं. *See* MACE.

NUTRIMENT, *s.* (Food) आहारः, भोजनं, पौष्टिकं. *See* NOURISHMENT.

NUTRITION, *s.* (Act) पोषणं, पुष्टिः *f.*, पोषः, आप्यायनं. *See* NOURISHMENT.

NUTRITIOUS, NUTRITIVE, *a.* पौष्टिकः -की -कं, पुष्टिदः -दा -दं, पोषकः -का -कं, धातुपोषकः &c., धातुवर्धकः -का -कं, पुष्टिकरः -री -रं, पुष्टिकारकः -का -कं, पुष्टिजनकः &c., धातुभृत् *m. f. n.*, बलवर्धकः &c., बलवर्धनः -ना -नं, बृंहणः -णा -णी -णं.

NUTSHELL, *s.* बीजकवचः -चं, बीजकञ्चुकः, बीजपुटः.

NUX-VOMICA, *s.* (Poisonous fruit) वरघरा.

NYCTALOPS, *s.* रात्रिदृष्टिः *m. f.*, निशादृष्टिः *m. f.*, रात्रिदृक् *m.* (श्).

NYCTALOPY, NYCTALOPIA, *s.* रात्रिदृष्टिः *f.*, निशादृष्टिः *f.*

NYMPH, *s.* अप्सराः *f.* (स्), अप्सरा, जलवनदेवता, जलदेवता, वनदेवता, जलदेवी, वनदेवी, जलवनदेवी, नदीदेवता, यक्षिणी, विद्याधरी.—(Beautiful woman, lass) सुन्दरी, मुग्धा, प्रमदा, तन्वङ्गी, कन्या.

NYMPH-LIKE, *a.* अप्सरायोग्यः -ग्या -ग्यं, अप्सरस्तुल्यः -ल्या -ल्यं.

NYMPHOMANIA, *s.* (A disease) अतिचरणा.

O.

O! *exclam.* (Vocative) भोः, भोस्, भो, भोभो, हे.—(To inferiors) रे, अरे, अरेरे, है, अहो.—(Expressive of surprise, grief, anger, &c.) आ, आः, हा, अहह, अहहा, हन्त, अहो, अहोवत्.

OAF, *s.* स्थूलबुद्धिः *m.*, स्थूलजनः, मन्दबुद्धिः, जडबुद्धिः, मूर्खः, मूढः, बर्बरः.

OAFISH, *a.* स्थूलस्वभावः -वा -वं, मन्दस्वभावः &c., अबुद्धिः -द्धिः -द्धि.

OAK, *s.* सिन्दूरः, सिन्दूरवृक्षः, वनवृक्षभेदः, वन्यपादपभेदः, वनराजिः.

OAKEN, *s.* सिन्दूरकाष्ठमयः -यी -यं, सिन्दूरवृक्षनिर्म्मितः -ता -तं.

OAKUM, *s.* जीर्णरज्जुखण्डः, शणखण्डः, खण्डितरज्जुः *m. f.*, शणसूत्रकं.

OAR, *s.* क्षेपणिः -णी *f.*, क्षिपणिः -णी, क्षपणी, नौकादण्डः, नौदण्डः, अरित्रं, आरित्रं, तरण्डः, तरिरथः.

OARED, *a.* दण्डवान् -वती -वत् (त्), दण्डी -ण्डिनी -ण्डि (न्); 'four-oared,' चतुर्दण्डवान् &c., चतुर्दण्डी &c.

OARSMAN, *s.* नौकादण्डधरः -धारी *m.* (न्), नौदण्डचालकः.

OASIS, *s.* मरुभूमिमध्यगतं शाड्वलस्थलं, मरुमध्यस्थं शाद्वलस्थानं.

OAT, *s.* ओट्संज्ञकः शस्यभेदः or धान्यभेदः.

OATEN, *a.* पूर्व्वोक्तशस्यमयः -यी -यं, पूर्व्वोक्तधान्यचूर्णमयः &c.

OATH, *s.* शपथः, शापः, शपः -पनं, अभिशापः, परिशापः, दिव्यं, सत्यं, समयः, प्रत्ययः, अभीषङ्गः, अभिषङ्गः, परिग्रहः, क्रिया; 'to take an oath,' शप् (c. 1. शपति -ते, c. 4. शप्यति -ते, शप्तुं), अभिशप्, शपथं कृ, शपथं शप्; 'he took an oath,' शपथं शेपे; 'to administer an oath,' शप् (c. 10. शापयति -यितुं); 'made to take an oath,' शापितः -ता -तं; 'with an oath,' सशपथं, शपथपूर्व्वं, शपथपुरःसरं.

OATH-BREAKING, *s.* शपथभङ्गः, दिव्यभङ्गः, मिथ्याशपथः, मिथ्यादिव्यं.

OAT-MEAL, *s.* ओट्संज्ञकशस्यचूर्णं, पूर्व्वोक्तधान्यक्षोदः.

OBDURACY, *s.* स्तब्धचित्तता, चित्तस्तब्धता, स्तब्धता, कठिनचित्तत्वं, चित्तकाठिन्यं, कठिनता, दृढता, दार्ढ्यं, अननुतापशीलता, अनुतापविमुखता, आग्रहः, आग्रहशीलता, पापाग्रहः, पापात्यागः.

OBDURATE, *a.* स्तब्धचित्तः -त्ता -त्तं, कठिनचित्तः &c., दृढचित्तः &c., अननुतापशीलः -ला -लं, अनुतापविमुखः -खा -खं, अनुतापपराङ्मुखः -खा -खं, दुराग्रही -हिणी -हि (न्), पापाग्रही &c., पापात्यागी &c.

OBDURATELY, *adv.* स्तब्धचित्तत्वात्, कठिनचित्तत्वात्, सकाठिन्यं.

OBEDIENCE, *s.* आज्ञानुवर्त्तनं, आज्ञानुसरणं, आज्ञाकरणं, आज्ञापालनं, आज्ञानुवृत्तिः *f.*, आज्ञानुकूलता, आज्ञानुकूल्यं, आज्ञाग्राहित्वं, आज्ञाधारणं, आज्ञाधीनता, आज्ञानुरोधः, आज्ञासेवनं, आदेशकरणं, निदेशकरणं, आज्ञापरता, आज्ञानुविधायिता, वशता, वश्यता, शुश्रूषा -षणं, अनुवर्त्तनं, अनुवृत्तिः *f.*, अनुकूलता, आनुकूल्यं, वशवर्त्तनं, मान्यता, आज्ञामाननं, वशीभूतता.

OBEDIENT, *a.* आज्ञानुवर्त्ती -र्त्तिनी -र्त्ति (न्), आज्ञापालकः -का -कं, आज्ञाधीनः -ना -नं, आज्ञानुयायी &c., आज्ञानुसारी &c., आज्ञाकरः -री -रं, आज्ञाकारी &c., आदेशकारी &c., निदेशकारी &c., आदेशकरः &c., वचनकरः &c., वचस्करः &c., आज्ञासेवी &c., आज्ञापरः -रा -रं, अनुशासनपरः &c., वशः -शा -शं, वश्यः -श्या -श्यं, वशवर्त्ती &c., वशानुगः -गा -गं, शुश्रूषुः -षुः -षु, आज्ञावहः -हा -हं, आज्ञावाहकः -का -कं, आज्ञासम्पादकः &c., आज्ञासम्पादी &c., आज्ञाधारी &c., अनुवर्त्ती &c., अनुविधायी &c., विधायी &c., अनुकूलः -ला -लं, सेवी &c., आज्ञाग्राही &c., वचनग्राही &c., निदेशग्राही &c., आश्रवः -वा -वं, अधीनः -ना -नं; 'obedient to a parent,' पितृवाक्परः -रा -रं, पितृवचनकरः -रा -रं, पितृवशः -शा -शं, पितृवशानुगः &c.

OBEDIENTLY, *adv.* शुश्रूषया, सानुवर्त्तनं, आज्ञानुवर्त्तनपूर्व्वं, सानुकूल्यं, आज्ञानुसारेण -रतस्, आज्ञानुवर्त्तनेन, यथादिष्टं, यथादेशं, यथाज्ञं, यथानुज्ञं.

OBEISANCE, *s.* नमस्कारः, प्रणामः, प्रणतिः *f.*, प्रणिपातः, प्रणिपतनं, नमस् indecl., नमस्या, सन्नतिः *f.*, नतिः *f.*, नमनं, विनयः, विनीतिः *f.*, उपसङ्ग्रहः; 'from inferiors to superiors,' अञ्जलिः *m.*, अञ्जलिकर्म्म *n.* (न्), अञ्जलिबन्धनं, वन्दनं; 'from a Brahman,' आशीर्वादः; 'from an inferior to a religious preceptor, Guru, &c.,' अभिवादनं, अभिवन्दनं; 'from Hindús of inferior caste,' दण्डवत्; 'to an idol, &c.,' वन्दनं.—(Profound obeisance with all the members of the body) साष्टाङ्गप्रणामः, साष्टाङ्गनमस्कारः, अष्टाङ्गपातः, अष्टाङ्गप्रणामः; 'to make obeisance,' नमस्कृ, प्रणम् (c. 1. -णमति -णन्तुं), शिरसा प्रणम्, कायं प्रणम्, प्रणिपत् (c. 1. -पतति -तितुं), साष्टाङ्गपातं प्रणिपत्; 'having made obeisance,' प्रणम्य.

OBELISK, *s.* सूच्याकारः स्तम्भः, दीर्घप्रस्तरमयः स्तम्भविशेषः.

OBERRATION, *s.* भ्रमणं -णा, परिभ्रमणं, पर्य्यटनं, इतस्ततो भ्रमणं.

OBESE, *a.* मेदस्वी -स्विनी -स्वि (न्), पीनः -ना -नं, पीवरः -रा -रं, स्थूलः -ला -लं, स्थूलकायः -या -यं, मांसलः ला -लं.

OBESENESS, OBESITY, *s.* मेदस्विता, मेदोवृद्धिः *f.*, स्थूलता, पीनता.

To OBEY, *v. a.* आज्ञाम् or वचनम् अनुवृत् (c. 1. -वर्त्तते -र्त्तितुं), यथादिष्टम् अनुष्ठा (c. 1. -तिष्ठति -ष्ठातुं), यथाज्ञप्तं विधा (c. 3. -दधाति -धातुं) or कृ, श्रु in des. (शुश्रूषते -षितुं), अनुविधा in pass. (-धीयते), अनुरुध् in pass. (-रुध्यते), सेव् (c. 1. सेवते -वितुं), उपसेव्, आज्ञां or

वचनं प्रतीष् (c. 6. -इच्छति -एषितुं) or सम्प्रतीष्, उपचर् (c. 1. -चरति -रितुं), उपाचर्, उपास् (c. 2. -आस्ते -आसितुं), पर्य्युपास्, समुपास्, अभ्युपे (c. 2. अभ्युपैति -तुं, rt. इ), मन् (c. 10. मानयति -यितुं), आज्ञां पाल् (c. 10. पालयति -यितुं) or ग्रह् (c. 9. गृह्णाति, ग्रहीतुं) or प्रतिग्रह् अनुकूल (nom. अनुकूलयति -यितुं), उपजीव् (c. 1. -जीवति -वितुं), आज्ञानुवर्त्तनं कृ.—(Submit to the control of another) परवशीभू, परवशं गम् (c. 1. गच्छति, गन्तुं).

OBEYED, *p.p.* शुश्रूषितः -ता -तं, यथादिष्टम् अनुष्ठितः -ता -तं or विहितः -ता -तं, मानितः -ता -तं, पर्य्युपासितः -ता -तं, सेवितः -ता -तं.

To OBFUSCATE, *v. a.* मलिनीकृ, तिमिर (nom. तिमिरयति -यितुं), तिमिरीकृ, कलुषीकृ, मलिन (nom. मलिनयति -यितुं).

OBFUSCATED, *p.p.* मलिनीकृतः -ता -तं, तिमिरीकृतः &c., कलुषीकृतः &c.

OBFUSCATION, *s.* कलुषीकरणं, मलिनीकरणं, निष्प्रभता, सान्धकारता.

OBIT, *s.* मृतक्रिया, मृतकर्म्म *n.* (न्), अन्त्यकर्म्म *n.* *See* OBSEQUIES.

OBITUARY, *s.* (List of the dead) मृतसंख्यापत्रं, मृतपरिसंख्या, मृतनामावलिपत्रं.—(Account of the dead) मृतवर्णनं -ना, मृतचरित्रं, मृतविवरणं.

OBJECT, *s.* (That about which any power or faculty is employed, or by which something is presented to the mind) विषयः, अर्थः, इन्द्रियार्थः, गोचरः, पात्रं, भाजनं, भूमिः *f.*, आस्पदं, स्थानं. The first four of these words refer properly to objects of sense, of which five are given, viz. 'form,' रूपं; 'sound,' शब्दः; 'odour,' गन्धः; 'flavor,' रसः; 'touch,' स्पर्शः. The other words are used elegantly in composition, thus, 'an object of confidence,' विश्वासपात्रं, विश्वासभूमिः *f.*, विश्वासास्पदं, विश्वासस्थानं; 'of affection,' स्नेहभूमिः *f.*, प्रीतिपात्रं; 'of favor,' प्रसादभूमिः *f.*; 'of compassion,' कृपापात्रं, दयाभाजनं; 'of disgrace,' अभिभवास्पदं; 'of blame,' निन्दापात्रं, निन्दाविषयः; 'of praise,' स्तुतिभाजनं; 'of honor,' मानभाजनं; 'of charity or liberality,' दानपात्रं; 'of dispute or litigation,' व्यवहारविषयः, व्यवहारस्थानं; 'of taxation,' शुल्कस्थानं; 'deserving object of charity, &c.,' सुपात्रं, पात्रं; 'undeserving,' कुपात्रं, अपात्रं; 'visible object,' चक्षुर्विषयः.—(Purpose, end, that to which the mind is directed) अभिप्रायः, आशयः, अभिप्रेतं, अर्थः, विषयः, उद्देशः, तात्पर्य्यं, कार्य्यं, कार्य्यवस्तु *n.*, प्रयोजनं, प्रयोगः, अभिसन्धिः *m.*, प्रार्थितं, इष्टं, पदार्थः, लक्ष्यं, लक्ष्यं, हेतुः *m.*, निमित्तं, अग्रभूमिः; 'accomplishment of one's object,' स्वार्थसिद्धिः *f.*, कार्य्यसिद्धिः *f.*, इष्टसिद्धिः *f.*, कृतार्थता, चरितार्थता, इष्टापत्तिः *f.*, आशाप्राप्तिः *f.*; 'one who has accomplished his object,' कृतार्थः -र्था -र्थं, चरितार्थः &c., प्राप्तार्थः &c., कृतकृत्यः -त्या -त्यं, आशाप्राप्तः -प्ता -प्तं; 'I have gained my object,' कृतार्थोऽस्मि, चरितार्थोऽस्मि; 'one's own private object or end,' स्वार्थः, स्वहितं, स्वसाधनं; 'highest object,' परमार्थः; 'important object,' गुर्वर्थः; 'the four objects of human pursuit collectively,' चतुर्वर्गः, चतुर्भद्रं; these are 'virtue,' धर्म्मः; 'wealth,' अर्थः; 'love,' कामः; 'final beatitude,' मोक्षः; 'the three objects without the last,' त्रिवर्गः, त्रिगणं; 'with what object,' किमर्थं, किमुद्दिश्य.—(In grammar) कर्म्म *n.* (न्), कर्म्मपदं.

To OBJECT, *v. a.* or *n.* बाध् (c. 1. बाधते -धितुं), बाधार्थं हेतुं वद् (c. 1. वदति -दितुं), विरुद्धहेतुं वद्, बाधां कृ, बाधार्थं वचनं वद्, विरुद्धवचनं वद्, अपवद्, विसंवद्, विपरीतं वद्, अपरीकृ, वितर्क् (c. 1. -तर्कते -र्कितुं), पर्य्युदस् (c. 4. -अस्यति -असितुं), निरस्, विरोधार्थं वचनं वद्, विरुध् (c. 7. -रुणद्धि -रोद्धुं), प्रतिरुध्, न सम्मन् (c. 4. -मन्यते -मन्तुं), न अनुमन्, न प्रतिग्रह् (c. 9. -गृह्णाति -ग्रहीतुं), न अनुमुद् (c. 1. -मोदते -दितुं), न स्वीकृ, अस्वीकारं कृ, असम्मतिं कृ, असम्मतः -ता -तं भू, अननुमोदनं कृ, उद्ग्राहं कृ, परवाक्यं खण्ड् (c. 10. खण्डयति -यितुं), व्याघातं कृ, आपत्तिं कृ.

OBJECTED TO, *p.p.* पर्य्युदस्तः -स्ता -स्तं, अपवादितः -ता -तं, अस्वीकृतः -ता -तं.

OBJECTION, *s.* बाधा -धः -धकं, विरुद्धहेतुः *m.*, बाधार्थकहेतुः *m.*, विरोधार्थकहेतुः *m.*, विरुद्धवचनं, उद्ग्राहः, कक्षा, अपवादः, शङ्का, आशङ्का, अपवादः, विपरीतवचनं, वाक्यखण्डनं, वाक्यविरोधः, व्याघातः, प्रतिबन्धः, आपत्तिः *f.*, विप्रतिपत्तिः *f.*, प्रत्यवायः, वितर्का, आक्षेपः, पर्य्युदासः; 'making an objection,' विरुद्धहेतुवादः, कक्षावादः; 'settling an objection,' समाधिः *m.*, समाधानं.

OBJECTIONABLE, *a.* बाध्यः -ध्या -ध्यं, बाधनीयः -या -यं, सबाधः -धा -धं, परिहरणीयः -या -यं, परिहार्य्यः -र्य्या -र्य्यं, वर्जनीयः -या -यं, वर्ज्यः -र्ज्या -र्ज्यं, अपवाद्यः -द्या -द्यं, सदोषः -षा -षं, प्रतिषेधार्हः -र्हा -र्हं, निषेधार्हः &c., शङ्कनीयः -या -यं, आशङ्कनीयः &c., प्रतिबन्धार्हः &c.; 'objectionable person or thing,' परिहारः.

OBJECTIONABLENESS, *s.* बाध्यता, सबाधत्वं, बाधः, सदोषता.

OBJECTIVE, *a.* (Pertaining to the object) स्वाधारस्थितः -ता -तं, स्वाधारनिष्ठः -ष्ठा -ष्ठं, विषयाश्रितः -ता -तं, विषयनिष्ठः &c., पदार्थाश्रितः -ता -तं, विषयसम्बन्धी -न्धिनी &c., पात्रनिष्ठः &c., पात्रसम्बन्धी &c.—(In grammar) कर्म्मपदविषयः -या -यं.

OBJECTOR, *s.* बाधकः, विरुद्धहेतुवादी *m.* (न्), कक्षावादी, अपवादकः.

To OBJURGATE, *v. a.* निन्द् (c. 1. निन्दति -न्दितुं), उपालभ् (c. 1. -लभते -लब्धुं), आक्रुश् (c. 1. -क्रोशति -क्रोष्टुं), समाक्रुश्, भर्त्स् (c. 10. भर्त्सयते -ति -यितुं), क्षिप् (c. 6. क्षिपति, क्षेप्तुं), अवक्षिप्, आक्षिप्, अधिक्षिप्, धिक्कृ.

OBJURGATION, *s.* निन्दा, उपालम्भः, तिरस्कारः, भर्त्सनवाक्यं, निर्भर्त्सनं, क्षेपः, अवक्षेपः, धिक्कारः, परीवादः.

OBJURGATORY, *a.* निन्दकः -का -कं, निन्दार्थकः -का -कं, तिरस्कारार्थकः &c.

OBLATION, *s.* (Offering to the gods, &c.) बलिः *m.*, उपहारः, देवोपहारः, उपहरणं, हुतं, हव्यं, होमः, हुतहोमं, आहुतिः *f.*, आहवः -वनं, हवनं, उपायनं, देवोपायनं, कव्यं, निर्वपणं, अवदानं, सत्रं, चरुः *m.*, प्रयागः, इष्टिः *f.*, वैतानं, वितानः -नं, सवः, पात्रीरः, कुशपाय्यः.—(Of eatable articles, &c.) नैवेद्यं, निवेदनं.—(Of curds) पृषदाज्यं.—(Of rice-milk and sugar) परमान्नं, पायसः.—(A respectful oblation of rice, &c. with water) अर्घ्यं, अर्घः; 'the presentation of it,' अर्घदानं.—(Oblation to all the deities) वैश्वदेवं, वैश्वदेवकर्म्म *n.*—(To the manes) कव्यं. *See* MANES. (To the gods and manes) हव्यकव्यं; 'dressed oblation,' हव्यपाकः; 'grand and extraordinary oblation,' महाबलिः *m.*, महानैवेद्यं; 'proper for an oblation,' हव्यः -व्या -व्यं; 'to make an oblation to fire,' अनले होमं कृ.

OBLECTATION, *s.* आनन्दः, आह्लादः, हर्षः, प्रमोदः, मदः.

To OBLIGATE, *v. a.* बन्ध् (c. 9. बध्नाति, बन्द्धुं), निबन्ध्, बद्धं -द्धां -द्धं कृ, नियमेन बन्ध्, नियमपूर्व्वं or प्रतिज्ञापूर्व्वं, बन्ध्.

OBLIGATION, *s.* (Binding power, as of a vow, promise, debt, &c., incumbency) अवश्यकता -त्वं, आवश्यकता, अवश्यकर्त्तव्यता -त्वं, अवश्यकार्य्यता, कर्त्तव्यता, विधेयता, अवश्यम्भावः, आवश्यं, भारः, ऋणं; 'under the obligation of a debt,' ऋणी -णिनी -णि (न्); 'free from obligation,' अनृणी &c., अवतीर्णर्णः -र्णा -र्णं, उत्तीर्णः

&c., ऋणमुक्तः -क्ता -क्तं; 'religious obligation,' व्रतं, यमः, नियमः, विषयः; 'under a religious obligation,' व्रती &c., व्रतस्थः -स्था -स्थं; 'observing or taking on one's self a religious obligation,' व्रताचरणं, व्रतसङ्ग्रहः; 'violating it,' व्रतलोपः -पनं.—(Engagement, compact) नियमः, समयः, प्रतिज्ञा -ज्ञानं, संविद् *f.*, संस्कारः, उपगमः, अभ्युपगमः, अभ्युपायः, सन्धा, सन्धानं, सन्धिः *m.*, संश्रवः.—(Bound state) बद्धता, निबद्धता.—(Favor, any act by which a person becomes bound to another) उपकारः, अनुग्रहः, उपकृतं, सुकृतं, हितं, प्रियं, उपचारः, कृतोपकारः; 'to lay under an obligation,' उपकृ, उपकारेण बद्धं -द्धां कृ, उपकारबद्धं -द्धां कृ.

OBLIGATORY, *a.* अवश्यकः -का -कं, आवश्यकः -की -कं, अवश्यकर्त्तव्यः -व्या -व्यं, अवश्यः -श्या -श्यं, अवश्यकार्य्यः -र्य्या -र्य्यं, अवश्यमन्तव्यः -व्या -व्यं, अवश्यमाननीयः -या -यं, अवश्यपालनीयः -या -यं.

To OBLIGE, *v. a.* (Constrain, compel). Expressed by the causal form usually in conjunction with बलात् or बलेन or बलात्कारेण; as, 'to oblige a man to do any thing,' बलेन पुरुषं किञ्चित् कृ in caus. (कारयति -यितुं) or प्रवृत् in caus. (-वर्त्तयति -यितुं); 'to oblige to pay,' दा in caus. (दापयति -यितुं); 'to oblige to go,' बलेन गम् (c. 10. गमयति -यितुं); 'he obliged me to take the book,' शास्त्रं मां ग्राहयामास. The root अर्ह् is sometimes used in this sense. *See To* COMPEL. (Bind) बन्ध् (c. 9. बध्नाति, बन्द्धुं), निबन्ध्.—(By a compact or agreement) नियमेन or नियमपूर्व्वं or प्रतिज्ञापूर्व्वं बन्ध्.—(By a favor or kindness) उपकारेण बन्ध् or बद्धं -द्धां कृ, उपकारबद्धं -द्धां कृ.—(Favor, do a favor to) अनुग्रह् (c. 9. -गृह्णाति -ग्रहीतुं), अनुग्रहं कृ, अनुरुध् (c. 4. -रुध्यति -ते -रोद्धुं), उपकृ, उपकारं कृ, साहाय्यं कृ, हितं कृ, प्रियं कृ; 'to be obliged.' *See* the next.

OBLIGED, *p. p.* (Compelled) expressed by the pass. part. of the causal form. *See* COMPELLED, CONSTRAINED. (Bound) बद्धः -द्धा -द्धं; 'by a favor,' उपकारबद्धः &c.—(Favored, indebted) अनुगृहीतः -ता -तं, उपकृतः -ता -तं; 'I am obliged to you for your advice,' अनुगृहीतोऽस्मि or अनुगृहीतोऽहं तवोपदेशेन.

OBLIGING, *a.* (Having the disposition to do favors) उपकारशीलः -ला -लं, उपकारी -रिणी -रि (न्), परोपकारी &c., उपकारबुद्धिः -द्धिः -द्धि, अनुग्राही &c., अनुरोधी &c., अनुकूलः -ला -लं, प्रियङ्करः -रा -रं, सुशीलः -ला -लं.

OBLIGINGLY, *adv.* उपकारशीलत्वात्, उपकारबुद्ध्या, सानुग्रहं, अनुग्रहेण, अनुरोधेन, सानुकूल्यं, प्रीत्या, सुशीलवत्, सुशीलत्वात्.

OBLIGINGNESS, *s.* उपकारशीलता, परोपकारशीलता, परोपकारिता, अनुग्रहः, अनुग्रहशीलता, अनुरोधः, अनुकूलता, आनुकूल्यं, सुशीलता.

OBLIQUE, *a.* (Not direct) वक्रः -क्रा -क्रं, वक्रिमः -मा -मं, कुटिलः -ला -लं, जिह्मः -ह्मा -ह्मं, विजिह्मः &c., तिर्य्यङ् -रश्ची -र्य्यक् (च्), असरलः -ला -लं, अनृजुः -जुः -जु, वक्री -क्रिणी -क्रि (न्), विषमः -मा -मं.—(As language, &c.) वक्रः -क्रा -क्रं, अस्पष्टः -ष्टा -ष्टं, उपरोधी &c.; 'oblique speech,' वक्रोक्तिः *f.*, वक्रभणितं.—(In grammar) कारकविभक्तिकः -का -कं; 'oblique case,' कारकं, कारकविभक्तिः *f.*, कारकं.—(Oblique vision) वक्रदृष्टिः *f.*; 'having it,' वक्रदृष्टिः -ष्टिः -ष्टि, तिर्य्यग्दृष्टिः &c.

OBLIQUELY, *adv.* वक्रं, कुटिलं, तिर्य्यक्, तिरस्, जिह्मं, विजिह्मं, असरलं.

OBLIQUENESS, OBLIQUITY, *s.* वक्रता, कुटिलता, कौटिल्यं, जिह्मता, तिर्य्यक्त्वं, असरलता, असारल्यं, अनृजुता -त्वं, विषमता; 'of vision,' वक्रदृष्टिः *f.*, दृष्टिवक्रता, वक्रदृष्टित्वं, तिर्य्यग्दृष्टित्वं.—(Deviation from moral rectitude) विमार्गगमनं, विपथगमनं, उत्पथगमनं, कुपथगमनं, सत्पथभ्रंशः, सत्पथत्यागः, असदाचारः, व्यभिचारः.

To OBLITERATE, *v. a.* अपमृज् (c. 2. -मार्ष्टि -र्ष्टुं), व्यामृज्, प्रमृज्, अवमृज्, व्यामृश् (c. 6. -मृशति -म्रष्टुं), अवमृश्, व्यामर्षं कृ, अवमर्षणं कृ, उच्छिद् (c. 7. -छिनत्ति -छेत्तुं), लुप् (c. 6. लुम्पति, लोप्तुं), लोपं कृ, विनश् (c. 10. -नाशयति -यितुं), उन्मूल् (c. 10. -मूलयति -यितुं); 'is obliterated from the memory,' विस्मार्य्यते.

OBLITERATED, *p. p.* अपमृष्टः -ष्टा -ष्टं, व्यामृष्टः &c., उन्मृष्टः &c., उच्छिन्नः -न्ना -न्नं, लुप्तः -प्ता -प्तं, वितीर्णः -र्णा -र्णं.

OBLITERATION, *s.* मार्ज्जना, अपमार्ज्जना, व्यामर्षः, अवमर्षणं, लोपः.

OBLIVION, *s.* विस्मृतिः *f.*, विस्मरणं, अस्मृतिः *f.*, अस्मरणं, स्मृतिनाशः, स्मृतिहानिः *f.*, व्यामोहः.—(Remission of offences) दोषविस्मरणं, सकलापराधमोचनं.

OBLIVIOUS, *a.* (Causing forgetfulness) विस्मारकः -का -कं, विस्मृतिजनकः -का -कं, विस्मृतिकारकः &c.—(Forgetful) विस्मरणशीलः -ला -लं.

OBLIVIOUSNESS, *s.* विस्मरणशीलता, विस्मृतिः *f.* *See* FORGETFULNESS.

OBLONG, *a.* आयतः -ता -तं, आयतिमान् -मती -मत् (त्), दीर्घचतुरस्रः -स्रा -स्रं, दीर्घचतुरस्राकारः -रा -रं, दीर्घाकारः &c.

OBLONG, *a.* (The figure) आयतः -तं, दीर्घचतुरस्रः -स्रं.

OBLOQUY, *s.* निन्दा, परीवादः, परिभाषणं, अपवादः, निन्दोक्तिः *f.*, परुषोक्तिः *f.*, दुर्वाक्यं, दुरुक्तं, वाच्यता, तिरस्कारः.

OBMUTESCENCE, *s.* मौनं, अभाषणं, वाक्स्तम्भः, वाग्रोधः, गतवाक्त्वं.

OBNOXIOUS, *a.* (Liable, subject) योग्यः -ग्या -ग्यं, अधीनः -ना -नं, वशः -शा -शं, अर्हः -र्हा -र्हं, उपयुक्तः -क्ता -क्तं, पात्र in comp., आस्पद in comp., विषय in comp., अधिकारी -रिणी &c.; 'obnoxious to punishment,' दण्डयोग्यः &c., दण्ड्यः -ण्ड्या -ण्ड्यं, दण्डनीयः -या -यं, दण्डार्हः -र्हा -र्हं; 'to disease,' रोगाधीनः -ना -नं, रोगपात्रं, रोगास्पदं; 'to death,' मरणाधीनः &c., मरणपात्रं; 'to blame,' निन्दाविषयः -या -यं.—(Odious, offensive) द्वेष्यः -ष्या -ष्यं, द्वेषणीयः -या -यं, द्वेषी &c., अप्रियः -या -यं, विप्रियः &c., अनिष्टः -ष्टा -ष्टं, असन्तोषकरः -रा -रं, अप्रीतिकरः &c.

OBNOXIOUSLY, *adv.* द्वेषणीयं, अप्रियं, विप्रियं, व्यलीकं, विरुद्धं.

OBNOXIOUSNESS, *s.* (Liability) योग्यता, अधीनता, वशता.—(Odiousness) द्वेष्यता, द्वेषणीयता, अप्रियता, अनिष्टता.

OBSCENE, *a.* अवाच्यः -च्या -च्यं, गर्ह्यः -र्ह्या -र्ह्यं, गर्हितः -ता -तं, अशुद्धः -द्धा -द्धं, अवचनीयः -या -यं, अनक्षरः -रा -रं, अपवित्रः -त्रा -त्रं, कुत्सितः -ता -तं, बीभत्सः -त्सा -त्सं, दुरुक्तः -क्ता -क्तं, कुत्साव्यः -व्या -व्यं; 'obscene word,' अपशब्दः, दुर्वचनं.—(Ill-omened) अशुभः -भा -भं, अमङ्गलः -ला -लं, अभद्रः -द्रा -द्रं, अमङ्गलसूचकः -का -कं.

OBSCENELY, *adv.* अवाच्यं, गर्हितं, गर्हणीयं, अशुद्धं, कुत्सितं.

OBSCENENESS, OBSCENITY, *s.* अवाच्यता, गर्ह्यता, अशुद्धता -त्वं, कुत्सितत्वं, बीभत्सता; 'of language,' दुर्वचनं, दुर्वाक्यं, दुर्भाषणं, दुरुक्तिः *f.*, अपशब्दः.

OBSCURATION, *s.* (Act) कलुषीकरणं, तिमिरीकरणं, मलिनीकरणं, प्रकाशहरणं, कान्तिहरणं.—(State) निष्प्रभता, सान्धकारता, तेजःक्षयः, तेजोहानिः *f.*, प्रभाक्षयः, प्रकाशक्षयः.—(Of a planet) अस्तः -स्तं.

OBSCURE, *a.* (Dark, dim) निष्प्रभः -भा -भं, निःप्रभः &c., अप्रभः &c., मलिनः -ना -नं, मलिनप्रभः &c., निस्तेजाः -जाः -जः (स्), तेजोहीनः -ना -नं, अप्रकाशः -शा -शं, सान्धकारः -रा -रं, सतिमिरः -रा -रं, तमस्वी -स्विनी -स्वि (न्), दुर्दर्शः -र्शा -र्शं.—(Not easily understood, not clear) गूढः -ढा -ढं, गूढार्थः -र्था -र्थं, गूढार्थकः -का -कं, निगूढः

-ढा -ढं, दुर्ज्ञेयः -या -यं, दुर्गमः -मा -मं, दुर्बोधः -धा -धं, बोधागम्यः -म्या -म्यं, व्याख्यागम्यः &c., अव्याख्येयः -या -यं, अस्पष्टः -ष्टा -ष्टं, अव्यक्तः -क्ता -क्तं, अस्फुटः -टा -टं, गहनार्थः &c., कठिनः -ना -नं.—(Not noted) अप्रसिद्धः -द्धा -द्धं, अख्यातः -ता -तं, अविख्यातः &c., अल्पप्रतिष्ठः -ष्ठा -ष्ठं, अल्पकीर्त्तिः -र्त्तिः -र्त्ति.

To OBSCURE, *v. a.* (Darken) निष्प्रभीकृ, तिमिरीकृ, मलिनीकृ, तिमिर (nom. तिमिरयति -यितुं), मलिन (nom. मलिनयति -यितुं), प्रच्छद् (c. 10. -च्छादयति -यितुं), कलुषीकृ, तेजो हृ (c. 1. हरति, हर्त्तुं), प्रकाशं हृ, कान्तिं हृ, प्रभां हृ, प्रकाशक्षयं कृ.—(With clouds) मेघावृतं -तां कृ, मेघाच्छन्नं -न्नां कृ.—(Make difficult to be understood) गूढीकृ, निगूढीकृ, दुर्ज्ञेयं -यां कृ, दुर्गमीकृ, अस्पष्टीकृ.

OBSCURED, *p. p.* तमोवृतः -ता -तं, नष्टप्रभः -भा -भं, मलिनप्रभः &c., हतप्रभः &c., क्षीणप्रभः &c., नष्टप्रकाशः -शा -शं, हतप्रकाशः &c., तमोभूतः -ता -तं, कलुषीकृतः -ता -तं, नष्टतेजाः -जाः -जः (स्), नष्टतेजस्कः -स्का -स्कं, हततेजाः &c., नष्टकान्तिः -न्तिः -न्ति, क्षीणकान्तिः &c., विगततेजाः &c., मलिनितः -ता -तं, मलिनः -ना -नं, क्षततेजाः &c., क्षतप्रभः &c., क्षतकान्तिः &c., क्षतौजाः &c., हतौजाः &c., हतज्योतीः -तीः -तिः (स्), अरोकः -का -कं.

OBSCURELY, *adv.* (Darkly) सान्धकारं, निष्प्रभं, सतिमिरं, अप्रकाशं.—(Not clearly) अस्पष्टं, अव्यक्तं, गूढं, निगूढं, दुर्ज्ञेयं.

OBSCURITY, OBSCURENESS, *s.* (Darkness) निष्प्रभता, सान्धकारता, तिमिरं, तमिस्रं, तमस् *n.*, अन्धकारः, तेजोहीनता, तेजोहानिः *f.*, अप्रकाशत्वं, अल्पप्रकाशः, प्रभाहीनता, प्रभाहानिः *f.*, अवतमसं.—(Darkness of meaning) गूढार्थता, गूढता, निगूढता, दुर्ज्ञेयता, दुर्बोधता, अस्पष्टता, अव्यक्तता -त्वं, गहनता, दुर्गमता, बोधागम्यता, व्याख्यागम्यता, अव्याख्या -ख्यानं.—(State of being unknown to fame) अप्रसिद्धिः *f.*, अप्रसिद्धता, अख्यातिः *f.*, अविख्यातिः *f.*, अल्पप्रतिष्ठा, अल्पकीर्त्तिः *f.*, कीर्त्तिन्यूनता, कीर्त्त्यभावः.

To OBSECRATE, *v. a.* निर्बन्धेन प्रार्थ् (c. 10. -अर्थयति -ते -यितुं), विनयेन प्रार्थ्.

OBSECRATION, *s.* निर्बन्धपूर्व्वं प्रार्थनं or प्रार्थना, विनयेन प्रार्थनं.

OBSEQUIAL, *a.* और्द्ध्वदेहिकः -की -कं, आमतकर्म्मिकः -की -कं, उत्तरक्रियासम्बन्धी -न्धिनी -न्धि (न्), अन्त्येष्टिसम्बन्धी &c., अन्त्येष्टियोग्यः -ग्या -ग्यं.

OBSEQUIES, *s. pl.* उत्तरक्रिया, उत्तरकर्म्म *n.* (न्), उत्तरकार्य्यं, प्रेतक्रिया, प्रेतकर्म्म *n.*, प्रेतकृत्यं, प्रेतकार्य्यं, प्रेतसंस्कारः, अन्त्यकर्म्म *n.*, अन्त्यक्रिया, अन्तकर्म्म *n.*, अन्त्येष्टिः *f.*, अन्त्येष्टिक्रिया, शवकर्म्म *n.*, मृतकर्म्म *n.*, मृतक्रिया, मृतकार्य्यं, मृतसंस्कारः, अतीतसंस्कारः, और्द्ध्वदेहिकं -कं, मृतसत्क्रिया, अन्तसत्क्रिया, मृतकं, श्राद्धं, श्राद्धादिकर्म्म *n.*, पारलौकिकं, अशुभकर्म्म *n.*, अशुभकार्य्यं. The श्राद्धं consists of obsequial oblations to the manes of deceased ancestors. *See* MANES; 'monthly obsequies,' अन्वाहार्य्यं -र्य्यकं, अनुहार्य्यः, मासिकं.

OBSEQUIOUS, *a.* अत्यनुकूलः -ला -लं, अत्यनुरोधी -धिनी -धि (न्) वशवर्त्ती &c., छन्दोनुवर्त्ती &c., छन्दोनुरोधी &c., अनुवर्त्ती &c., अनुविधायी &c., वशंवदः -दा -दं, वशानुगः -गा -गं, विनतः -ता -तं, नम्रः -म्रा -म्रं, आज्ञाकारी &c.

OBSEQUIOUSLY, *adv.* अत्यनुकूलं, अत्यनुरोधेन, छन्दोनुरोधपूर्व्वं.

OBSEQUIOUSNESS, *s.* अत्यनुकूलता, अत्यानुकूल्यं, अत्यनुरोधः -धनं, छन्दोनुरोधः, छन्दोनुवृत्तिः *f.*, छन्दोनुवर्त्तनं, छन्दोनुवृत्तं.

OBSERVABLE, *a.* दृश्यः -श्या -श्यं, दर्शनीयः -या -यं, दृष्टिगोचरः -रा -रं, लक्ष्यः -क्ष्या -क्ष्यं, आलोकनीयः -या -यं, प्रेक्ष्यः -क्ष्या -क्ष्यं, प्रेक्षणीयः -या -यं.—(That may be practised) व्यवहार्य्यः -र्य्या -र्य्यं, व्यवहर्त्तव्यः -व्या -व्यं.

OBSERVANCE, *s.* (Act of keeping or performing) पालनं, रक्षणं, सेवनं, निषेवनं, धारणं, आचरणं, अनुष्ठानं.—(Practising) आचरणं, अनुष्ठानं, करणं, विधानं, अभ्यासः, निषेवनं.—(Following) अनुसारः, अनुसरणं.—(Custom, practice) व्यवहारः, आचारः, चर्य्या, चरितं, रीतिः *f.*—(Religious observance) व्रतं, नियमः, यमः, नियामः, विधिः *m.*, विधानं.—(Respect) आदरः, सत्कारः, मानं.

OBSERVANT, *a.* (Taking notice) निरीक्षकः -का -कं, प्रेक्षकः -का -कं.—(Keeping, practising, following) पालकः -का -कं, निषेवकः -का -कं, अनुष्ठायी -यिनी -यि (न्), धारी &c., अनुसारी &c., आस्थितः -ता -तं, निष्ठितः -ता -तं, आश्रितः -ता -तं.—(Of orders) आज्ञापालकः.—(Of benefits received) कृतवेदी &c., कृतज्ञः -ज्ञा -ज्ञं.

OBSERVATION, *s.* (Act of looking at or taking notice) निरीक्षणं, निरीक्षा, अवेक्षणं, अवेक्षा, अवलोकनं, आलोकनं, आलोचनं, निरूपणं, सन्दर्शनं, दृष्टिः *f.*, लक्ष्यं, लक्षं.—(Result of taking notice) लिखितं, चर्चा. *See* NOTE, NOTICE; 'in one's observation,' प्रत्यक्षे -क्षतस्.

OBSERVATORY, *s.* ताराकूटं, ग्रहनक्षत्रादिदर्शनस्थानं.

To OBSERVE, *v. a.* and *n.* (See, look at) दृश् (c. 1. पश्यति, द्रष्टुं), अनुदृश्, प्रतिदृश्, अभिदृश्, परिदृश्, प्रदृश्, सम्प्रदृश्, सन्दृश्, लक्ष् (c. 10. लक्षयति -यितुं), आलक्ष्, समालक्ष्, संलक्ष्, उपलक्ष्, समुपलक्ष्, ईक्ष् (c. 1. ईक्षते -क्षितुं), समीक्ष्, वीक्ष्, प्रेक्ष्, निरीक्ष्, अवेक्ष्, प्रत्यवेक्ष्, अभिप्रेक्ष्, सम्प्रेक्ष्, उदीक्ष्, आलोक् (c. 10. -लोकयति -यितुं, c. 1. -लोकते -कितुं), समालोक्, अवलोक्, विलोक्, आलोच् (c. 10. -लोचयति -यितुं), निरूप् (c. 10. -रूपयति -यितुं), विलोकनं कृ, अवलोकनं कृ.—(With the intellect) उपलभ् (c. 1. -लभते -लब्धुं), विज्ञा (c. 9. -जानाति -नीते -ज्ञातुं), विभू (c. 10. -भावयति -यितुं), विभावनं कृ, अनुभू.—(Keep, perform, practise) पाल् (c. 10. पालयति -यितुं), प्रतिपाल्, परिपाल्, अनुपाल्, सम्पाल्, अभिपाल्, रक्ष् (c. 1. रक्षति -क्षितुं), अभिरक्ष्, परिरक्ष्, संरक्ष्, आचर् (c. 1. -चरति -रितुं), समाचर्, अनुष्ठा (c. 1. -तिष्ठति -ष्ठातुं), आस्था, समास्था, समुपास्था, विधा (c. 3. -दधाति -धातुं), सेव् (c. 1. सेवते -वितुं), निषेव्, उपसेव्, समासेव्; 'observe propriety,' विनयं रक्ष्.—(Utter, make a remark) वाक्यं वद् (c. 1. वदति -दितुं) or प्रवद्, चर्चां कृ.—(Adhere to) आश्रि (c. 1. -श्रयति -यितुं), अवलम्ब् (c. 1. -लम्बते -म्बितुं), उपास् (c. 2. -आस्ते -आसितुं).

OBSERVED, *p. p.* (Noticed by the eye) दृष्टः -ष्टा -ष्टं, ईक्षितः -ता -तं, निरीक्षितः -ता -तं, प्रेक्षितः -ता -तं, आलोकितः -ता -तं, आलोचितः -ता -तं, निरूपितः -ता -तं.—(Kept, performed) पालितः -ता -तं, आचरितः &c., अनुष्ठितः &c., सेवितः &c., निषेवितः &c., अनुसृतः &c.

OBSERVER, *s.* (Looker on) प्रेक्षकः, वीक्षकः, प्रेक्षणिकः, द्रष्टा *m.* (ष्टृ), दर्शी *m.* (न्), आलोचकः. *See* OBSERVANT.

OBSERVINGLY, *adv.* सुनिरूपणपूर्व्वं, चर्चया, मनोयोगेन, सावधानं.

OBSOLETE, *a.* अव्यवहारितः -ता -तं, निरूढः -ढा -ढं, नैरूढः -ढी -ढं, कालान्तरितः -ता -तं, गतकालिकः -का -कं, लुप्तः -प्ता -प्तं, अप्रचलः -ला -लं, अप्रचलितः -ता -तं, अचलितः -ता -तं, अप्रचरितः -ता -तं, अव्यवहार्य्यः -र्य्या -र्य्यं, अनुपस्थितः -ता -तं, अनुपलब्धः -ब्धा -ब्धं, विकटः -टा -टं.

OBSOLETENESS, *s.* अव्यवहार्य्यता, अव्यवहारितत्वं, लुप्तता, अप्रचलितत्वं, अप्रचारः, लोपः, अनुपस्थितिः *f.*, अनुपलब्धिः *f.*

OBSTACLE, *s.* विघ्नः, अन्तरायः, व्याघातः, प्रत्यूहः, प्रतिबन्धः -न्धकं, रोधः -धनं, अवरोधः, उपरोधः, विरोधः, संरोधः, निरोधः, स्तम्भः -म्भनं, प्रतिष्टम्भः, विष्टम्भः, विघातः -तं, विष्कम्भः, बाधा -धः -धकः, व्यवधानं, विष्कम्भः; 'removal of obstacles,' विघ्नसिद्धिः *f.*, विघातसिद्धिः *f.*,

विघ्ननाशः -शनं, विघ्नहरणं; 'causing obstacles,' विघ्नकरः -रा -रं, विघ्नकारी -रिणी -रि (न्).

OBSTETRIC, *a.* प्रसवकर्म्मसम्बन्धी -न्धिनी &c., सूतिकर्म्मसम्बन्धी &c., गर्भमोचनसम्बन्धी &c., गर्भमोचनविषयकः -का -कं, सावकः -विका -कं.

OBSTETRICS, *s.* प्रसवकर्म्म *n.* (न्), प्रसवकार्य्यं, गर्भमोचनविद्या.

OBSTINACY, OBSTINATENESS, *s.* स्तब्धता, स्तब्धिः *f.*, स्तब्धमतित्वं, धैर्य्यं, धीरता -त्वं, निर्बन्धः, दृढता, दार्ढ्यं, कठिनता, काठिन्यं, धृतिः *f.*, जडता, जाड्यं, अवश्यता, अविनेयता, स्वैरिता, स्वैरता, प्रतीपता, दुष्टता, आग्रहः, दुराग्रहः, दुर्मदः, अभिनिवेशः, निर्बन्धशीलता, हठः; 'in adhering to belief,' श्रद्धाजाड्यं.

OBSTINATE, *a.* स्तब्धः -ब्धा -ब्धं, निर्बन्धशीलः -ला -लं, स्तब्धमतिः -तिः -ति, धीरः -रा -रं, दृढः -ढा -ढं, कठिनः -ना -नं, जडः -डा -डं, अवश्यः -श्या -श्यं, अविनेयः -या -यं, दुराग्रही -हिणी -हि (न्), आग्रही &c., स्वैरी &c., स्वैरः -रा -रं, प्रतीपः -पा -पं, दुष्टः -ष्टा -ष्टं.—(Difficult of cure) कृच्छ्रसाध्यः -ध्या -ध्यं, दुःखसाध्यः &c., दुःसाध्यः &c.. दुरुपचारः -रा -रं,

OBSTINATELY, *adv.* निर्बन्धेन, सनिर्बन्धं, धैर्य्येण, सधैर्य्यं, सदार्ढ्यं, सजाड्यं, सकाठिन्यं, दुराग्रहेण, प्रतीपवत्, स्वैरवत्, दुष्टवत्.

OBSTIPATION, *s.* मलावरोधः, मलावष्टम्भः, मलस्तम्भः, मलस्तब्धिः *f.*

OBSTREPEROUS, *a.* (Vociferous) उच्चैःस्वरकारी -रिणी -रि (न्), तुमुलकारी &c., बहुघोषः -षा -षं, कोलाहलकारी &c.—(Perverse) प्रतीपः -पा -पं.

OBSTREPEROUSLY, *adv.* उच्चैःस्वरेण, बहुघोषेण, कोलाहलेन, सकोलाहलं.

OBSTREPEROUSNESS, *s.* घोषणत्वं, बहुघोषत्वं, तुमुलकारित्वं, प्रतीपता.

To OBSTRUCT, *v. a.* रुध् (c. 7. रुणद्धि, रोद्धुं), प्रतिरुध्, निरुध्, उपरुध्, विरुध्, संरुध्, स्तम्भ् (c. 10. स्तम्भयति -यितुं, c. 9. स्तभ्नाति, स्तम्भितुं), विष्टम्भ्, प्रतिबन्ध् (c. 9. -बध्नाति -बन्द्धुं), बाध् (c. 1. बाधते -धितुं), विहन् (c. 2. -हन्ति -न्तुं), व्याहन्, प्रतिहन्, विघ्न (nom. विघ्नयति -यितुं), वृ (c. 10. वारयति -यितुं), निवृ, विनिवृ, आवृ, समावृ, प्रतिवृ, प्रतिषिध् (c. 1. -षेधति -षेद्धुं), रोधं कृ, अवरोधं कृ, गतिरोधं कृ, प्रतिबन्धं कृ, निराकृ.

OBSTRUCTED, *p. p.* रुद्धः -द्धा -द्धं, प्रतिरुद्धः &c., विरुद्धः &c., निरुद्धः &c., उपरुद्धः &c., स्तम्भितः -ता -तं, स्तब्धः -ब्धा -ब्धं, विष्टब्धः &c., प्रतिबद्धः &c., विहतः -ता -तं, प्रतिहतः -ता -तं, पराहतः -ता -तं, बाधितः -ता -तं, विघ्नितः -ता -तं, वारितः -ता -तं, निवारितः -ता -तं, अन्तरितः -ता -तं, सार्गलः -ला -लं.

OBSTRUCTER, *s.* विघ्नकारी *m.* (न्), रोधकः, अवरोधकः, प्रतिबन्धकः, बाधकः.

OBSTRUCTION, (Act) रोधः -धनं, स्तम्भनं, प्रतिबन्धनं, विघ्नकरणं, वारणं, आवरणं.—(Impediment) विघ्नः, रोधः, प्रतिरोधः, उपरोधः, संरोधः, निरोधः, प्रतिबन्धः, स्तम्भः, विष्टम्भः, प्रतिष्टम्भः, हेतुः. *See* OBSTACLE, HINDERANCE. (In any organ of the body) नाहः, आनाहः, अवरोधः, निबन्धः.

OBSTRUCTIVE, OBSTRUCTING, OBSTRUENT, *a.* विघ्नकारी -रिणी &c., विघ्नकरः -री -रं, प्रतिरोधी &c., विरोधी &c., रोधकः -का -कं, अवरोधकः &c., प्रतिरोधकः &c., विघाती &c., व्याघातकः -का -कं, विष्टम्भी &c., औपरोधिकः -की -कं, वारकः -का -कं, निवारकः &c., निराकरिष्णुः -ष्णुः -ष्णु, क्षिप्नुः -प्नुः -प्नु, व्याघातजनकः -का -कं, बाधकः -का -कं, प्रतिबाधकः -का -कं, विघ्नजनकः &c., प्रतिबन्धकारी &c., प्रतिबन्धकः &c.

To OBTAIN, *v. a.* आप् (c. 5. आप्नोति, आप्तुं), प्राप्, सम्प्राप्, अवाप्, समवाप्, समाप्, लभ् (c. 1. लभते, लब्धुं), उपलभ्, अर्ज् (c. 10. अर्जयति -यितुं, c. 1. अर्जति -र्जितुं), उपार्ज्, आसद् (c. 10. -सादयति -यितुं), समासद्, अधिगम् (c. 1. -गच्छति -गन्तुं), गम्, सम्पद् (c. 10. -पादयति -यितुं), प्रतिपद् (c. 4. -पद्यते -त्ति -पत्तुं), आपद्, अभिपद्, समापद्, इ (c. 2. एति -तुं), अभी, ऋ (c. 1. ऋच्छति, अर्त्तुं), विद् (c. 6. विन्दति, वेत्तुं, वेदितुं), अभिविद्, प्रतिविद्, आविश् (c. 6. -विशति -वेष्टुं), समाविश्, अश् (c. 5. अश्नुते, अशितुं), समश्, उपाश्, स्पृश् (c. 6. स्पृशति, स्प्रष्टुं).

To OBTAIN, *v. n.* (Be in use, be established) प्रचलीभू, प्रचलितः -ता -तं भू, प्रचर् (c. 1. -चरति -रितुं), प्रचल् (c. 1. -चलति -लितुं), प्रवृत् (c. 1. -वर्त्तते -र्त्तितुं), स्थापितः -ता -तं भू, प्रसिद्धीभू, प्रबलीभू, प्रभू, संस्था (c. 1. -तिष्ठति -स्थातुं).

OBTAINABLE, *a.* प्राप्यः -प्या -प्यं, प्रापणीयः -या -यं, प्राप्तव्यः -व्या -व्यं, लभ्यः -भ्या -भ्यं, उपलभ्यः &c., आसादनीयः -या -यं, आसाद्यः -द्या -द्यं, समासाद्यः &c., अधिगम्यः -म्या -म्यं, अधिगमनीयः -या -यं, अधिगन्तव्यः -व्या -व्यं; 'easily obtainable,' सुलभः -भा -भं, सुप्राप्यः -प्या -प्यं, सुसाध्यः -ध्या -ध्यं; 'difficultly,' दुर्लभः &c., दुःप्राप्यः &c., दुष्प्राप्यः &c., दुःखलभ्यः &c., दुष्प्रापः -पा -पं, दुरापः -पा -पं; 'with exertion,' यत्नलभ्यः &c.

OBTAINED, *p. p.* प्राप्तः -प्ता -प्तं, आप्तः &c., अवाप्तः &c., लब्धः -ब्धा -ब्धं, उपलब्धः &c., अर्जितः -ता -तं, उपार्जितः -ता -तं, आसादितः -ता -तं, समासादितः -ता -तं, अधिगतः -ता -तं, आपन्नः -न्ना -न्नं, विन्नः -न्ना -न्नं, भावितः -ता -तं, भूतः -ता -तं, लब्धिमः -मा -मं, सम्पन्नः &c., सम्पादितः -ता -तं, अभिरम्भितः -ता -तं.

OBTAINER, *s.* प्रापकः, लब्धा *m.* (ब्धृ), उपार्जकः, सम्पादकः.

OBTAINMENT, *s.* प्राप्तिः *f.*, सम्प्राप्तिः *f.*, आप्तिः *f.*, प्रापणं, आपत्तिः *f.*, लब्धिः *f.*, लाभः, आसादनं, समासादनं, अर्जनं, उपार्जनं, प्रतिपत्तिः *f.*, सम्पादनं, अधिगमः.

To OBTEST, *v. a.* विनयेन प्रार्थ् (c. 10. प्रार्थयति -यितुं) or याच् (c. 1. याचति -चितुं).

OBTESTATION, *s.* अञ्जलिकर्म्मपूर्व्वं प्रार्थनं, विनयेन प्रार्थनं, अभ्यर्थना.

To OBTRUDE, *v. a.* धर्षेण or बलेन or परानिच्छया प्रविश् (c. 10. -वेशयति -यितुं) or प्रसृ (c. 10. -सारयति -यितुं) or अनधिकारपूर्व्वं प्रविश्.—(Urge upon another with unreasonable importunity) अतिनिर्बन्धेन अनिच्छन्तं जनं किञ्चिद् ग्रह् (c. 10. ग्राहयति -यितुं), अतिनिर्बन्धपूर्व्वम् उपस्था in caus. (-स्थापयति -यितुं) or उपहृ (c. 1. -हरति -हर्त्तुं) or प्रदा.

To OBTRUDE, *v. n.* धर्षेण or बलेन or परानिच्छया प्रविश् (c. 6. -विशति -वेष्टुं), अनाहूतः प्रविश् or आविश् or आगम् (c. 1. -गच्छति -गन्तुं) or आक्रम् (c. 1. -क्रामति -क्रमितुं) or अभिक्रम्.

OBTRUDED, *p. p.* धर्षेण or परानिच्छया प्रवेशितः -ता -तं or प्रसारितः &c.

OBTRUSION, *s.* धर्षेण or परानिच्छया प्रवेशः -शनं, अनधिकारपूर्व्वं प्रवेशनं, अनाहूतप्रवेशनं, अनाहूतागमनं.

OBTRUSIVE, *a.* परानिच्छया प्रवेशकः -का -कं, धृष्टः -ष्टा -ष्टं.

To OBTUND, *v. a.* घनीकृ, अतीक्ष्णीकृ, अतीव्रीकृ, स्थूलीकृ, जडीकृ, तेजो हृ (c. 1. हरति, हर्त्तुं), विरुग्णीकृ, तेजोहीनं -नां कृ.

OBTUSE, *a.* (Blunt, not acute) अतीक्ष्णः -क्ष्णा -क्ष्णं, अतीव्रः -व्रा -व्रं, अनग्रः -ग्रा -ग्रं, निरग्रः &c., अप्रखरः -रा -रं, धाराहीनः -ना -नं, तेजोहीनः &c., घनः -ना -नं, स्थूलः -ला -लं, निस्तेजाः -जाः -जः (स्); 'obtuse angle,' बहिर्लम्बकोणः.—(Dull, stupid) जडः -डा -डं, मन्दः -न्दा -न्दं, स्थूलः -ला -लं, मूढः -ढा -ढं, मन्दबुद्धिः -द्धिः -द्धि, स्थूलधीः -धीः -धि, मन्दमतिः -तिः -ति, जडमतिः &c., अविदग्धः -ग्धा -ग्धं.

OBTUSE-ANGLED, OBTUSE-ANGULAR, *a.* बहिर्लम्बः -म्बा -म्बं, बहिर्लम्बकोणः -णा -णं.

OBTUSELY, *adv.* अतीक्ष्णं, अतीव्रं, अप्रखरं, स्थूलवत्, जाड्येन, सजाड्यं, जडवत्.

OBTUSENESS, *s.* (Bluntness) अतीक्ष्णता, अतीव्रता, निरग्रता, धाराहीनता, तेजोहीनता, घनता, स्थूलता.—(Of intellect) जडता, जाड्यं, स्थूलता, स्थूलबुद्धित्वं, मूढता, मन्दता, मन्दमतित्वं, बुद्धिमान्द्यं, अविदग्धता.

To OBUMBRATE, *v. a.* प्रच्छद् (c. 10. -छादयति -यितुं), तिमिर (nom. तिमिरयति -यितुं), तिमिरीकृ, छायां कृ. *See To* OBSCURE.

To OBVIATE, *v. a.* वृ (c. 10. वारयति -यितुं), निवृ, विनिवृ, प्रतिवृ, आवृ, रुध् (c. 7. रुणद्धि, रोद्धुं), निरुध्, विरुध्, अवरुध्, प्रतिरुध्, उपरुध्, निवृत् (c. 10. -वर्त्तयति -यितुं), विच्छिद् (c. 7. -छिनत्ति -छेत्तुं), परिच्छिद्, बाध् (c. 1. बाधते -धितुं), प्रतिबन्ध् (c. 9. -बध्नाति -बन्द्धुं), विहन् (c. 2. -हन्ति -न्तुं), व्याहन्, निरस् (c. 4. -अस्यति -असितुं), परिहृ (c. 1. -हरति -हर्त्तुं).

OBVIATED, *p. p.* वारितः -ता -तं, निवारितः -ता -तं, रुद्धः -द्धा -द्धं, अवरुद्धः &c., बाधितः -ता -तं, परिहृतः &c., अपहृतः &c., निवृत्तः -त्ता -त्तं.

OBVIOUS, *a.* स्पष्टः -ष्टा -ष्टं, स्पष्टार्थः -र्था -र्थं, व्यक्तः -क्ता -क्तं, सुव्यक्तः &c., सुस्पष्टः &c., प्रव्यक्तः &c., अभिव्यक्तः &c., भिन्नार्थः &c., प्रकाशः -शा -शं, सुप्रकाशः &c., सुग्राह्यः -ह्या -ह्यं, स्फुटः -टा -टं, सुज्ञेयः -या -यं, सुगमः -मा -मं, सुगोचरः -रा -रं.—(To the eye) दृष्टिगोचरः -रा -रं, नयनगोचरः &c., दृष्टः -ष्टा -ष्टं, सुदर्शी -र्शी -र्शि, सुलक्ष्यः &c., समक्षः -क्षी -क्षं, प्रत्यक्षः -क्षा -क्षं; 'obvious danger,' दृष्टं.

OBVIOUSLY, *adv.* स्पष्टं, सुस्पष्टं, स्पष्टार्थतस्, व्यक्तं, सुव्यक्तं, प्रकाशं, सुप्रकाशं, प्रत्यक्षतस् -क्षेण, साक्षात्, स्फुटं, प्रादुस्.

OBVIOUSNESS, *s.* स्पष्टता, सुस्पष्टता, व्यक्तता, सुव्यक्तता -त्वं, स्पष्टार्थता -त्वं, सुग्राह्यता, सुज्ञेयता, सुगमता, प्रत्यक्षता, प्रकाशता, सुप्रकाशता, स्फुटता, सुगोचरता, सुलक्ष्यता.

OCCASION, *s.* (Opportunity, favorable season) अवसरः, अवकाशः, समयः, प्रस्तावः, प्रसङ्गः, प्रसरः, कालः, कालयोगः, कार्य्यकालः, वारः, सन्धिः *m.*, कालसन्धिः *m.*, सन्धिवेला, वेला, स्थानं; 'according to the occasion,' यथावसरं, यथावकाशं, यथाप्रसङ्गं, प्रसङ्गवशात्; 'suitable to the occasion,' प्रस्तावसदृशः -शी -शं, प्रास्ताविकः -की -कं, प्रस्तावयोग्यः -ग्या -ग्यं; 'on this particular occasion,' इह समये.—(Incident, event) वृत्तं, भूतं, सम्भवः, सङ्गतं, सङ्गतिः *f.*, समुपागतं, समुपस्थितं, घटना -नं; 'as occasion may be,' यथासम्भवं.—(Need) प्रयोजनं, प्रयोगः, प्रयुक्तिः *f.*, उपयोगः -गिता, कार्य्यं, कारणं; 'there is no occasion for me,' मया न प्रयोजनं; 'there is occasion for a straw,' तृणेन प्रयोजनं or कार्य्यं.—(Accidental cause) प्रयोजनं, हेतुः *m.*, कारणं, निमित्तं, उपाधिः *m.*

To OCCASION, *v. a.* उत्पद् (c. 10. -पादयति -यितुं), समुत्पद्, उपपद्, सम्पद्, जन् (c. 10. जनयति -यितुं), सञ्जन्, साध् (c. 10. साधयति -यितुं), भू (c. 10. भावयति -यितुं), उद्भू, कृ, निमित्त (nom. निमित्तायते), कारणीभू, निमित्तीभू.

OCCASIONAL, *a.* (Occurring at times, but not regular) कादाचित्कः -त्की -त्कं, अनित्यः -त्या -त्यं, विरलागतः -ता -तं, विरलः -ला -लं, अनुकालः -ला -लं, क्वाचित्कः -त्की -त्कं, कार्हिचित्कः &c., अनियतः -ता -तं, आगन्तुकः -का -कं, अनियतकारणकः -का -कं.—(Produced or occurring on some special occasion) नैमित्तिकः -की -कं, प्रासङ्गिकः -की -कं, प्रास्ताविकः -की -कं, सामयिकः &c., प्रसङ्गप्राप्तः -प्ता -प्तं, प्रसङ्गोत्पन्नः -न्ना -न्नं, प्रसङ्गागतः -ता -तं, प्रसङ्गोपस्थितः -ता -तं, प्रसङ्गकारणकः -का -कं.

OCCASIONALLY, *adv.* (From time to time) कदाचित्, कदापि, कदाचन, कर्हिचित्, काले काले, वारं वारं, जातु, अनुकालं, अनुवेलं.—(According to the exigence) यथाप्रसङ्गं, यथावसरं, प्रसङ्गानुसारेण, प्रसङ्गानुरूपेण, प्रसङ्गवशात्.

OCCASIONED, *p. p.* उत्पादितः -ता -तं, उत्पन्नः -न्ना -न्नं, जनितः -ता -तं, जातः -ता -तं, प्रयुक्तः -क्ता -क्तं, प्रयोजितः -ता -तं, उद्भवः -वा -वं, प्रभवः -वा -वं, प्रवृत्तः -त्ता -त्तं, उदितः -ता -तं, समुदितः -ता -तं, निमित्तकः -का -कं, हेतुकः -का -कं, कर्त्तृकः -का -कं; 'misery occasioned by crime,' पापप्रयुक्तं दुःखं, पापनिमित्तकं दुःखं; 'fever occasioned by fasting,' उपवासप्रयुक्तो ज्वरः.

OCCIDENT, *s.* पश्चिमदिक् *m.* (श्), पश्चिमदिशा, पश्चिमा, प्रतीची.

OCCIDENTAL, *a.* पश्चिमः -मा -मं, प्रतीचीनः -ना -नं, प्रत्यङ् -तीची -त्यक् (च्).

OCCIPUT, *s.* मस्तकपृष्ठं, शिरःपृष्ठं, मस्तकस्य पश्चाद्भागः.

OCCULT, *a.* गूढः -ढा -ढं, गूढार्थः -र्था -र्थं, गूढार्थकः -का -कं, निगूढः -ढा -ढं, गुप्तः -प्ता -प्तं, गुह्यः -ह्या -ह्यं, निभृतः -ता -तं, दुर्ज्ञेयः -या -यं, अज्ञातः -ता -तं, अविदितः -ता -तं, अप्रसिद्धः -द्धा -द्धं, अगम्यः -म्या -म्यं, दुर्गम्यः &c.

OCCULTATION, *s.* (In astronomy) समागमः.

OCCULTNESS, *s.* गूढता, गुप्तता, निगूढता, गुह्यता, दुर्ज्ञेयता, अप्रसिद्धिः *f.*

OCCUPANCY, *s.* अधिकारः, अधिकृतिः *f.*, आधिकारत्वं, भोगः, परिभोगः, भुक्तिः *f.*, आवेशः -शनं, समावेशः, आक्रमणं.

OCCUPANT, *s.* अधिकारी *m.* (न्), भोक्ता *m.* (क्तृ), परिभोक्ता *m.*, भोगी *m.*, (न्), परिभोगी *m.*, शाली *m.* (न्), भोगकारी *m.* (न्).

OCCUPATION, *s.* (Act of taking possession) परिग्रहः -हणं, आवेशनं, समावेशनं, आक्रमणं, अधिकारकरणं, भोगकरणं, अधिवासः -सनं, अधिष्ठानं.—(Possession). *See* OCCUPANCY. (Employment, business) व्यापारः, कार्य्यं, कर्म्म *n.* (न्), व्यवसायः, व्यवहारः, उद्योगः, उद्यमः, प्रवृत्तिः *f.*, प्रवर्त्तनं, वृत्तिः *f.*, कार्य्योद्योगः, कर्म्मोद्योगः, चरितं, व्यवस्था; 'daily or settled occupation,' नित्यकर्म्म *n.*, नित्यकृत्यं.—(Something to be done) कर्त्तव्यं, कार्य्यं, करणीयं, कृत्यं; 'customary morning occupations,' उचितानि प्रभातकरणीयानि.—(Vocation, trade, profession) वृत्तिः *f.*, वर्त्तनं, जीवनवृत्तिः *f.*, जीविका, उपजीविका, उपजीवनं, जीवनोपायः, आजीवनार्थं.—(Office, appointed duty) नियोगः, नियुक्तिः *f.*, स्वकर्म्म *n.*, स्वधर्म्मः, प्रकरणं; 'approved occupation,' अवदानं, अपदानं.

OCCUPIED, *p. p.* (Possessed, tenanted) भुक्तः -क्ता -क्तं, परिभुक्तः &c., आविष्टः -ष्टा -ष्टं, समाविष्टः &c., अध्युषितः -ता -तं, अध्यासितः -ता -तं, अधिष्ठितः -ता -तं, आश्रितः -ता -तं, अधिगतः -ता -तं.—(Employed, engaged) व्यापृतः -ता -तं, व्यापारी -रिणी -रि (न्), व्यवसायी &c., प्रवृत्तः -त्ता -त्तं, सव्यापारः -रा -रं, कर्म्मनिष्ठः -ष्ठा -ष्ठं, कर्म्मरतः -ता -तं, कर्म्मी &c., कर्म्मोद्युक्तः -क्ता -क्तं, कार्य्यवान् -वती -वत् (त्), क्रियावान् &c.; 'in reading,' अध्ययनरतः &c. *See* ENGAGED; 'to be occupied,' व्यापृ in pass. (-प्रियते) with loc. c., वृत् (c. 1. वर्त्तते -र्त्तितुं) with loc. c.; 'he is occupied in the affairs of others,' परकार्य्येषु व्याप्रियते; 'in penance,' तपसि व्याप्रियते.

OCCUPIER, *s.* *See* OCCUPANT, *s.*

To OCCUPY, *v. a.* (Take possession) आविश् (c. 6. -विशति -वेष्टुं), प्रथमभोगं कृ, आक्रम् (c. 1. -क्रामति -क्रमितुं), समाक्रम्.—(Possess, hold) धृ (c. 10. धारयति -यितुं), भुज् (c. 7. भुनक्ति, भुंक्ते, भोक्तुं), उपभुज्, परिभुज्, धा (c. 3. धत्ते, धातुं), शील् (c. 10. शीलयति -यितुं), भोगं कृ, परिभोगं कृ.—(Take up, pervade) व्याप् (c. 5. -आप्नोति -आप्तुं), पॄ (c. 10. पूरयति -यितुं), अतिक्रम्.—(Tenant) अध्यास् (c. 2. -आस्ते -आसितुं), समध्यास्, अधिवस् (c. 1. -वसति -वस्तुं), अध्यावस्, आश्रि (c. 1. -श्रयति -ते -यितुं), अधिष्ठा (c. 1. -तिष्ठति -ष्ठातुं), वासं कृ.—

(Employ) व्याप् (c. 10. -पारयति -यितुं), प्रवृत् (c. 10. -वर्त्तयति -यितुं), प्रयुज् (c. 7. -युंक्ते -योक्तुं, c. 10. -योजयति -यितुं), उपयुज्, कार्य्ये नियुज्.—(Occupy one's self) व्याप् in pass. (-प्रियते), व्यापृतः -ता -तं भू or अस्; 'do not occupy yourself with the affairs of others,' मा परकार्य्येषु व्यापृतो भूः.

To OCCUPY, *v. n.* व्यापारं कृ, व्यवसायं कृ, व्यवहारं कृ, वाणिज्यं कृ.

To OCCUR, *v. n.* (Meet, come to) उपस्था (c. 1. -तिष्ठति -स्थातुं), समुपस्था, आगम् (c. 1. -गच्छति -गन्तुं), उपागम्, समुपागम्.—(Arise, be found) उत्पद् (c. 4. -पद्यते -पत्तुं), विद् in pass. (विद्यते), जन् in pass. (जायते), वृत् (c. 1. वर्त्तते -र्त्तितुं), संवृत्.—(Take place, happen) घट् (c. 1. घटते -टितुं), सम्पद्, समापद्, उपपद्, उपस्था, उपस्थितः -ता -तं भू, आपत् (c. 1. -पतति -तितुं), निपत्, सम्भू, भू.—(Suggest itself to the mind) स्फुर् (c. 6. स्फुरति -रितुं).

OCCURRED, *p. p.* उपस्थितः -ता -तं, समुपस्थितः &c., उपागतः -ता -तं, समुपागतः &c., आगतः -ता -तं, उत्पन्नः -न्ना -न्नं, समुत्पन्नः &c., वृत्तः -त्ता -त्तं, संवृत्तः &c., घटितः -ता -तं, सम्भूतः &c.

OCCURRENCE, *s.* वृत्तं, उत्पन्नं, समुत्पन्नं, उत्पत्तिः *f.*, समुत्पत्तिः *f.*, उपागतं, उपागमः, समुपागतं, उपस्थितं, समुपस्थितं, सङ्गतं, सङ्गतिः *f.*, सम्भवः, भूतं, सम्भूतं, घटना -नं, समुच्चयः, उपस्थानं, उपस्थितिः *f.*; 'of rare occurrence,' चिरलागतः -ता -तं, दुर्लभः -भा -भं, चिरचेष्टितः -ता -तं, चिरलब्धः -ब्धा -ब्धं.

OCEAN, *s.* समुद्रः, अर्णवः, महार्णवः, सागरः, महासागरः, जलनिधिः *m.*, उदधिः *m.*, महोदधिः *m.*, पयोनिधिः *m.*, जलधिः *m.*, अब्धिः *m.*, अम्बुधिः *m.*, तोयनिधिः *m.*, तोयधिः *m.*, पाथोधिः *m.*, वारिधिः *m.*, वारिनिधिः *m.*, वारान्निधिः *m.*, वार्द्धिः *m.*, अपान्निधिः *m.*, कीलालधिः *m.*, सलिलनिधिः *m.*, पयोधिः *m.*, पयोधाः *m.* (स्), अम्भोधिः *m.*, अम्भोनिधिः *m.*, नीरधिः *m.*, नीरनिधिः *m.*, अम्बुराशिः *m.*, अम्भोराशिः *m.*, वारिराशिः *m.*, नदीपतिः *m.*, सरित्पतिः *m.*, अपान्नाथः, सिन्धुनाथः, जलपतिः *m.*, यादःपतिः *m.*, यादसाम्पतिः *m.*, सिन्धुः *m.*, उदन्वान् *m.* (त्), सरस्वान् *m.* (त्), रत्नाकरः, पारावारः, पारापारः, दूरपारः, अकूपारः, द्वीपवान् *m.* (त्), महाकच्छः, धरणीप्लवः, तरीषः, तिमिः *m.*, पेनः, दभः, मीरः, तीर्थराजः; 'the southern ocean,' दक्षिणार्णवः; 'ocean-bound,' सागरान्तः -न्ता -न्तं, समुद्रमेखलः -ला -लं, समुद्रवलयः -या -यं, समुद्ररसनः -ना -नं, अर्णवमेखलः &c.; 'ocean-king,' जलनिधिनाथः; 'ocean of trouble,' दुःखसागरः; 'of business,' कार्य्याब्धिः *m.*; 'of misery,' व्यसनार्णवः. Seven oceans are fabled to exist by the Hindús, viz. 'the ocean of salt,' लवणोदः; 'of syrup or sugar-cane juice,' इक्षुरसोदः; 'of spirituous liquor,' सुरोदः; 'of ghee or clarified butter,' घृतोदः; 'of milk,' क्षीरोदः; 'of curds,' दध्युदः; 'of pure water,' शुद्धोदः; 'churning of the ocean,' समुद्रमन्थनं. The mountain मन्दरः is fabled to have been used by the Suras and Asuras in the churning of the ocean after the deluge, for the recovery or production of fourteen sacred things. These were, 1. 'the goddess Lakshmí,' लक्ष्मीः, 2. 'the jewel of Krishna,' कौस्तुभः, 3. 'the tree of paradise,' पारिजातः, 4. 'spirituous liquor personified as a nymph,' सुरा -री, 5. 'the physician of the gods,' धन्वन्तरिः *m.*, 6. 'the moon,' चन्द्रः, 7. 'the cow of plenty,' कामधेनुः *f.*, कामदुघा, कामधुक् *f.* (-दुह्), 8. 'the elephant of Indra,' ऐरावतः, 9. 'the horse of Indra,' उच्चैःश्रवाः *m.* (स्), 10. 'nymph of Indra's heaven,' अप्सराः *f.* (स्), अप्सरा, 11. 'a deadly poison,' विषं, हलाहलः -लं, हालहालं, हालहलं, कालकूटः -टं, 12. 'nectar or ambrosia,' अमृतं, 13. 'Indra's bow,' इन्द्रधनुस्, 14. 'conch,' शङ्खः. The mountain Mandara is also called इन्द्रकीलः.

OCEAN, OCEANIC, *a.* सामुद्रः -द्री -द्रं, सामुद्रिकः -की -कं, समुद्रीयः -या -यं, समुद्रियः -या -यं, सैन्धवः -वी -वं, समुद्रसम्बन्धी -न्धिनी &c., महासागरसम्बन्धी &c.

OCHER, OCHRE, *s.* रक्तोपलं, सुवर्णं, सुवर्णगैरिकं.

OCHLOCRACY, *s.* अधमवर्णाधिपत्यं, अधमवर्णप्रभुत्वं, अधमलोकप्रभुत्वं.

OCTAGON, *s.* अष्टकोणः -णं, अष्टास्रं, अष्टभुजः, अष्टकोणाकृतिः *f.*

OCTAGONAL, OCTANGULAR, *a.* अष्टकोणः -णा -णं, अष्टास्रयः -या -यं, अष्टास्रः -स्रा -स्रं, अष्टभुजः -जा -जं, अष्टभुजविशिष्टः -ष्टा -ष्टं.

OCTAVE, *s.* अष्टकं, अष्टमी; 'division of an octave,' श्रुतिः *f.*

OCTAVO, *a.* अष्टपत्रकः -का -कं, अष्टफलकः -का -कं, अष्टकः -का -कं.

OCTENNIAL, *a.* (Happening every eight years) प्रत्यष्टाब्दिकः -की -कं, अष्टवर्षिकः -की -कं, अष्टवर्षीणः -णा -णं.—(Lasting eight years) अष्टवर्षस्थायी -यिनी -यि (न्), वर्षाष्टकस्थायी.

OCTOBER, *s.* आश्विनोत्तरार्द्धं, कार्त्तिकपूर्वार्द्धं, आश्विनः, इषः, आश्वयुजः, कार्त्तिकः, बाहुलः, ऊर्जः, कार्त्तिकिकः.

OCTOGENARIAN, OCTOGENARY, *a.* अशीतिकः -का -कं, अशीतिवयस्कः -स्का -स्कं.

OCTOPETALOUS, *a.* अष्टदलः -ला -लं, अष्टदलयुक्तः -क्ता -क्तं.

OCTUPLE, *a.* अष्टगुणः -णा -णं, अष्टविधः -धा -धं, अष्टकः -का -कं.

OCULAR, *a.* चाक्षुषः -षी -षं, प्रत्यक्षः -क्षा -क्षं, नेत्रसम्बन्धी -न्धिनी -न्धि (न्), चक्षुःसम्बन्धी &c.; 'ocular demonstration or proof,' प्रत्यक्षप्रमाणं, चक्षुःप्रमाणं, चाक्षुषप्रमाणं, चाक्षुषज्ञानं, प्रत्यक्षं.

OCULARLY, *adv.* चक्षुषा, चाक्षुषप्रमाणेन, प्रत्यक्षेण, प्रत्यक्षप्रमाणेन.

OCULIST, *s.* चक्षुर्वैद्यः, नेत्रवैद्यः, नयनवैद्यः, चक्षूरोगचिकित्सकः.

ODD, *a.* (Not even) विषमः -मा -मं, असमः -मा -मं, अयुग्मः -ग्मा -ग्मं, अयुगः -गा -गं, अयुगलः -ला -लं, अयुक् *m. f. n.* (ज्).—(Remaining over a specified number) विवक्षितसंख्यातिरिक्तः -क्ता -क्तं.—(Strange, singular) विलक्षणः -णा -णं, असङ्गतः -ता -तं, अपरूपः -पा -पं, अद्भुतः -ता -तं, अपूर्व्वः -र्व्वा -र्व्वं, चित्रः -त्रा -त्रं, विचित्रः &c. (Uncommon) असामान्यः -न्या -न्यं, असाधारणः -णी -णं; 'game of odd and even,' मुष्टिद्यूतं.

ODDITY, ODDNESS, *s.* (State of being not even) विषमता, वैषम्यं, असमता, असाम्यं, विषमभावः, असमभावः, अयुग्मता.—(Strangeness) वैलक्षण्यं, विलक्षणता, विलक्षणभावः, असङ्गतत्वं, असङ्गतिः *f.*, अपरूपता, अद्भुतता -त्वं, अपूर्व्वता.—(Odd thing) कौतुकं.

ODDLY, *adv.* (Unevenly) विषमं, असमं, वैषम्येन.—(Strangely) असङ्गतं, विलक्षणं, सवैलक्षण्यं, अद्भुतं, विचित्रं, चित्रं, अपूर्व्वं.

ODDS, *s.* (Inequality, difference) न्यूनाधिकं, न्यूनाधिकभावः, वैषम्यं, विषमता, तारतम्यं.—(Superiority) आधिक्यं, श्रेष्ठता, विशिष्टता, वैशिष्ट्यं.

ODE, *s.* गीतं, गेयं, गानं, स्तोत्रं, काव्यं, कविता.

ODIOUS, *a.* (Hateful) द्वेष्यः -ष्या -ष्यं, द्वेषार्हः -र्हा -र्हं, विद्वेषणीयः -या -यं, विद्वेष्यः &c., गर्ह्यः -र्ह्या -र्ह्यं, गर्हितः -ता -तं, कुत्सितः -ता -तं, द्वेषयोग्यः -ग्या -ग्यं, कुत्सितः -ता -तं, कुत्सनीयः -या -यं, द्वेषपात्रं, द्वेषभाजनं, द्वेषास्पदं, द्वेषविषयः, घृण्यः -ण्या -ण्यं, अप्रियः -या -यं.—(In a high degree) अतिद्वेष्यः &c., अतिगर्हितः -ता -तं, अत्यप्रियः -या -यं.—(Causing hatred, invidious) द्वेषजनकः -का -कं, द्वेषोत्पादकः &c., द्वेषावहः -हा -हं, द्वेषकारकः &c., असूयाजनकः &c.

ODIOUSLY, *adv.* द्वेषणीयं, विद्वेषणीयं, गर्हणीयं, गर्हितं, कुत्सितं.

ODIOUSNESS, *s.* द्वेष्यता, द्वेषणीयता, विद्वेष्यता, गर्ह्यता, द्वेषार्हत्वं.

ODIUM, *s.* (Hatred) द्वेषः, विद्वेषः, प्रद्वेषः, द्वेष्यता, विद्विष्टता, जनविद्वेषः, गर्हा, घृणा.—(Invidiousness) द्वेषजनकता, असूयाजनकता -त्वं.

ODONTALGY, *s.* दन्तशूलः, दन्तवेदना, दन्तव्यथा, दन्तपीडा.

ODORATE, *a.* उग्रगन्धः -न्धा -न्धं -न्धी -न्धिनी -न्धि (न्), तीक्ष्णगन्धः &c.

ODORIFEROUS, ODOROUS, *a.* गन्धवान् -वती -वत् (त्), गन्धी -न्धिनी -न्धि (न्), सगन्धः -न्धा -न्धं, गन्धवहः -हा -हं, सुगन्धः -न्धा -न्धं, सौगन्धिकः -की -कं, सुगन्धिकः -का -कं, सुवासिकः -का -कं, सवासः -सा -सं, सामोदः -दा -दं, आमोदी &c., सुरभिः -भिः -भि, सुगन्धिः &c., परिमलयुक्तः -क्ता -क्तं, परिमलविशिष्टः -ष्टा -ष्टं, परिमली &c., सपरिमलः -ला -लं.

ODORIFEROUSLY, *adv.* सगन्धं, सुगन्धेन, सामोदं, सवासं, सपरिमलं, सुरभि.

ODORIFEROUSNESS, *s.* सगन्धता, सुगन्धता, सौगन्ध्यं, सामोदत्वं, सपरिमलत्वं.

ODOUR, *s.* गन्धः, वासः; 'fragrant odour,' सुगन्धः, सुगन्धिः *m.*, सौगन्ध्यं. सुवासः, सौरभ्यं, आमोदः, मोदः, वासः, परिमलः; 'bad odour,' दुर्गन्धः, दौर्गन्धिः *m.*, दौर्गन्ध्यं, कुत्सितगन्धः; 'bad odour, disfavor,' अरुचिः *f.*, अदृष्टिः *f.*, कुदृष्टिः *f.*

ŒCONOMICAL, ŒCONOMY. *See* ECONOMICAL, ECONOMY.

ŒCUMENICAL, *a.* सार्व्वलौकिकः -की -कं, विश्वलौकिकः &c., सर्व्वसाधारणः -णी -णं.

ŒSOPHAGUS, *s.* अन्नवाहिस्रोतस् *n.*, अन्नमार्गः, अन्नपथः.

OF, *prep.* expressed generally by the genitive case; as, 'of me,' मम; 'of him,' तस्य; 'of that man,' तस्य पुरुषस्य. It is frequently expressed by the crude form of a noun in the first member of a compound; as, 'best of all,' सर्व्वश्रेष्ठः -ष्ठा -ष्ठं; 'lord of men,' नरपतिः *m.*; 'made of wood,' काष्ठनिर्म्मितः -ता -तं. When it denotes 'out of,' 'from amongst,' it is expressed by मध्यात् or मध्ये, affixed to the gen. c., or crude form; as, 'of all men,' सर्व्वपुरुषमध्यात् or सर्व्वपुरुषाणां मध्यात् or मध्ये. It may sometimes be rendered by the abl. c., in phrases where 'from' may be substituted in English; as, 'of a child, or from childhood,' बाल्यात्; 'of a race of kings, or descended from a race of kings,' राजकुलात् प्रसूतः or राजकुलप्रसूतः. It may even be rendered by the instr. c., in phrases where 'by' may be substituted in English; as, 'hospitably entertained of the king,' *i.e.* 'by the king,' राज्ञा सत्कृतः. Where 'of' denotes 'property,' 'possession,' 'connexion with,' 'belonging to,' &c., it may either be expressed by the use of such words as सम्बन्धी -न्धिनी &c., विषयः -या -यं, विषयकः &c., or by the gen. case, as in some of the foregoing examples. Very frequently an adjective compound involves some of these senses of the preposition; as, 'a bird of a red color,' रक्तवर्णः पक्षी; 'a man of great valor,' महावीर्य्यः पुरुषः; 'a woman of great wealth,' महाधना स्त्री. For the other senses of this preposition, *see* 'by,' 'from,' 'out,' 'among.' 'Of late,' अर्व्वाक्, अर्व्वाक्काले, नूतनकाले; 'of old,' पुरा, पुरस्तात्, पूर्व्वं, प्राक्काले; 'son of a grandson,' प्रपौत्रः; 'pupil of a pupil,' प्रशिष्यः,

OFF, *adv.* or *prep.* (Denoting distance) दूरे -रे -रतस्, विदूरतस्, अन्तरं -रेण; 'be off, get off,' दूरम् अपसर or अपैहि; 'far off,' दूरस्थः -स्था -स्थं, दूरस्थायी -यिनी -यि (न्); 'a good distance off,' अतिदूरस्थः &c., अतिदूरं; 'one off,' एकान्तरः -रा -रं, अेकान्तरः -रा -रं.—(Denoting separation) expressed by अप, अव, वि, नि, उत्; as, 'to cut off,' अवच्छिद्, अवकृत्, निकृत्, उच्छिद्; 'to take off,' अवमुच्, विमुच्, अपनी, अवतॄ, उच्छद्, उत्कृष्; 'to cast off,' अपास्; 'to break off,' अवभञ्ज्, अवभिद्; 'to get off, alight from,' अवतॄ, अवरुह्, अवपत्.—(Denoting departure, abatement, remission) expressed by अप, वि, अव, नि, उप; as, 'to go off,' अपगम्, अपया, विगम्; 'to leave off,' विरम्, उपरम्, निवृत्, विनिवृत्, विगम्, विच्छिद्, अवमुच्; 'go off, explode,' विभिद्, भिद्; 'creep off, slink off,' अपसृप्, व्यपसृप्.—(Away, from) अप, अव.—(Off hand) अचिन्तापूर्व्वः -र्व्वा -र्व्वं, आकस्मिकः -की -कं, प्रस्तुतः -ता -तं, प्रत्युत्पन्नः -न्ना -न्नं.—(Badly off) दुःस्थः -स्था -स्थं, दुःस्थितः -ता -तं, दुर्गतः -ता -तं, अनुपपन्नः -न्ना -न्नं, आपन्नः &c.—(Well off) सुस्थः &c., सुस्थितः -ता -तं, सुखी -खिनी -खि (न्), सम्पन्नः -न्ना -न्नं.

OFF, *a.* (Distant) दूरस्थः -स्था -स्थं, दूरस्थितः -ता -तं, दूरस्थायी -यिनी -यि (न्), दूरवर्त्ती -र्त्तिनी &c.

OFF, *interj.* दूरमपसर, दूरमपैहि, दूरमपेहि, अपगच्छ.

OFFAL, *s.* उच्छिष्टमांसं, उच्छिष्टं, उच्छिष्टांशं, विमांसं, मांसावशिष्टं, मांसोच्छिष्टं, भुक्तावशिष्टं, अवशिष्टमांसं, मांसावशेषः -षं, मांससमुज्झितं, शेषांशं, शेषमांसं, मलं.

OFFENCE, *s.* (Displeasure, anger) कोपः, क्रोधः, रोषः, मन्युः *m.*, अमर्षः, अतुष्टिः *f.*, असन्तोषः, अप्रीतिः *f.*; 'easily taking offence,' सुलभकोपः -पा -पं, सुलभमन्युः -न्युः -न्यु, शीघ्रकोपी -पिनी &c.—(Affront) विप्रियं, अपमानं, अवज्ञा, विध्वंसः.—(Crime, transgression) अपराधः, पातकं, पापं, दोषः, आगस् *n.*, अघं, दुरितं, मन्तुः *m.*, अन्यायः, दुष्कृतं, दुष्कर्म्म *n.* (न्), कुकर्म्म *n.*, कुक्रिया, दुष्कृतिः *f.*, दूषणं, —(Cause of stumbling, impediment) स्खलनं, बाधा, विघ्नः, प्रत्यूहः, व्याघातः, अन्तरायः, रोधः.

OFFENCELESS, *a.* निरपराधः -धा -धं, निर्दोषः -षा -षं. *See* INNOCENT.

To OFFEND, *v. a.* (Make angry) कुप् (c. 10. कोपयति -यितुं), प्रकुप्, सङ्कुप्, क्रुध् (c. 10. क्रोधयति -यितुं), रुष् (c. 10. रोषयति -यितुं), कोपं जन् (c. 10. जनयति -यितुं), क्रोधं or रोषं जन्.—(Displease, affront any one) कस्यापि विप्रियं or अप्रियं or व्यलीकं or अनार्य्यं कृ, कस्मिन्नपि or कस्यापि अपराध् (c. 4. -राध्यति, c. 5. -राध्नोति -राद्धुं), कस्यापि अतुष्टिं or अप्रसादं जन्.—(Pain, wound, distress) पीड् (c. 10. पीडयति -यितुं), व्यथ् (c. 10. व्यथयति -यितुं), सन्तप् (c. 10. -तापयति -यितुं), व्यथां कृ, क्लेशं दा.—(Transgress, violate) अपराध्, अतिक्रम् (c. 1. -क्रामति -क्रमितुं), व्यतिक्रम्, लङ्घ् (c. 10. लङ्घयति -यितुं), उल्लङ्घ्, विलङ्घ्, अतिवृत् (c. 1. -वर्त्तते -र्त्तितुं), लुप् (c. 10. लोपयति -यितुं), अतिचर् (c. 1. -चरति -रितुं), लङ्घनं कृ.—(Cause to stumble, impede) स्खल् (c. 10. स्खलयति -यितुं), प्रस्खल्, बाध् (c. 1. बाधते -धितुं), रुध् (c. 7. रुणद्धि, रोद्धुं), अन्तरायं जन्.

To OFFEND, *v. n.* (Commit a crime or sin) अपराधं कृ, पापं कृ, पातकं कृ, अन्यायं कृ, अपराध् (c. 4. -राध्यति, c. 5. -राध्नोति -राद्धुं), अपराधी -धिनी -धि भू.—(Cause anger) कोपं जन् (c. 10. जनयति -यितुं) or उत्पद् (c. 10. -पादयति -यितुं), रोषं जन्.—(Offend against, transgress) अतिक्रम् (c. 1. -क्रामति -क्रमितुं), व्यतिक्रम्, लङ्घ् (c. 10. लङ्घयति -यितुं), उल्लङ्घ्, विलङ्घ्, अतिचर् (c. 7. -चरति -रितुं), अभिचर्, भञ्ज् (c. 7. भनक्ति, भंक्तुं), भिद् (c. 7. भिनत्ति, भेत्तुं).

OFFENDED, *p. p.* (Displeased, made angry) कुपितः -ता -तं, प्रकु-

पितः -ता -तं, रुषितः -ता -तं, रुष्टः -ष्टा -ष्टं, प्रकोपितः -ता -तं, क्रुद्धः -द्धा -द्धं, संक्रुद्धः &c., जातामर्षः -र्षा -र्षं, जातरोषः -षा -षं, कृतमन्युः -न्युः -न्यु, आगतमन्युः &c., उपजातकोपः -पा -पं, विरुद्धः &c., असन्तुष्टः -ष्टा -ष्टं.—(Caused to stumble, impeded) जातस्खलनः -ना -नं, बाधितः -ता -तं, व्याहतः -ता -तं, जातान्तरायः -या -यं.—(To be offended or made angry) कुप् (c. 4. कुप्यति, कोपितुं), प्रकुप्, क्रुध् (c. 4. क्रुध्यति, क्रोद्धुं), रुष् (c. 4. रुष्यति, रोषितुं).

OFFENDER, *s.* अपराधी *m.* (न्), पापकारी *m.* (न्), पापी *m.* (न्), दोषी *m.*, सापराधः, कृतापराधः, अपराद्धः, पातकी *m.*, दुष्कृती *m.*, कुकर्म्मी *m.* (न्), कुकर्म्मकारी *m.*, सदोषः, दोषयुक्तः, दोषवान् *m.* (त्), अपराधकृत् *m.*, अपराधकारी *m.*, अन्यायी *m.*, अन्यायकृत् *m.*, अन्यायकर्त्ता *m.* (र्तृ), कृतान्यायः, एनस्वी *m.*, जातदोषः; 'grievous offender,' महापातकी *m.*, महापातककारी *m.*

OFFENSIVE, *a.* (Causing anger) कोपजनकः -का -कं, क्रोधजनकः &c., कोपोत्पादकः &c.—(Displeasing, disagreeable) अप्रियः -या -यं, विप्रियः -या -यं, विरुद्धः -द्धा -द्धं, अतुष्टिकरः -री -रं, अप्रीतिकरः &c., व्यलीकः -का -कं, अरुचिरः -रा -रं, अरुचिजनकः &c., अरम्यः -म्या -म्यं, असुखदः -दा -दं, असभ्यः -भ्या -भ्यं; 'to the ear,' कर्णकटुः -टुः -टु, कुश्राव्यः -व्या -व्यं, विस्वरः -रा -रं; 'to the taste,' विरसः -सा -सं.—(Disgusting) बीभत्सकरः -री -रं, बीभत्सजनकः -का -कं, घृणोत्पादकः -का -कं, कुत्सितः -ता -तं, गर्ह्यः -र्ह्या -र्ह्यं; 'offensive smell,' कुत्सितगन्धः, दुर्गन्धः, पूतिगन्धः.—(Injurious) अपकारकः -का -कं, अपकारी -रिणी &c., आपकरः -री -रं, अहितकरः &c., अनिष्टकरः &c., घातुकः -का -कं, उपघातकः &c.; 'as a weapon,' मारकः -का -कं, परघातोपयोगी &c.—(Assailant, opposed to defensive) आक्रामकः -का -कं, आक्रमकः &c., पराक्रामकः &c., पराक्रमणकः &c., आघातकः &c., अभिघाती &c.; 'offensive and defensive alliance,' परस्परोपकारः.

OFFENSIVELY, *adv.* अप्रियं, विप्रियं, विरुद्धं, व्यलीकं, सापकारं, अपकारेण.

OFFENSIVENESS, *s.* (Quality of causing anger) क्रोधजनकता, कोपजनकता, क्रोधोत्पादकत्वं.—(Unpleasantness) अप्रियता, विप्रियता, विरुद्धता, व्यलीकता -त्वं, अरुचिरता, कुत्सितत्वं.—(Injuriousness) अपकारकता -त्वं, घातुकता, उपघातकत्वं, आक्रामकत्वं.

To OFFER, *v. a.* (Present for acceptance) उपहृ (c. 1. -हरति -हर्त्तुं), समुपहृ, आहृ, उपाहृ, अभ्याहृ, उपहारीकृ, उपस्था in caus. (-स्थापयति -यितुं), उपनी (c. 1. -नयति -नेतुं), प्रदा (c. 3. -ददाति -दातुं), अभिदा, सम्प्रदा, उपदा, प्रयम् (c. 1. -यच्छति -दातुं), सम्प्रयम्, प्रतिपद् (c. 10. -पादयति -यितुं), ऋ in caus. (अर्पयति -यितुं), सम्, निविद् (c. 10. -वेदयति -यितुं), उपढौक (nom. उपढौकयति -यितुं), ग्रह् (c. 10. ग्राहयति -यितुं), प्रतिग्रह्, निक्षिप् (c. 6. -क्षिपति -क्षेप्तुं), लभ् in caus. (लम्भयति -यितुं), स्पृश् (c. 10. स्पर्शयति -यितुं), उपहरणं कृ.—(Propose, make a proposal) उपन्यस् (c. 4. -अस्यति -असितुं), अभिधा (c. 3. -दधाति -धातुं), निर्दिश् (c. 6. -दिशति -देष्टुं), प्रदिश्, आदिश्, उपन्यासं कृ, प्रतिज्ञां कृ.—(Exhibit) दृश् (c. 10. दर्शयति -यितुं), प्रदृश्, प्रसृ (c. 10. -सारयति -यितुं), प्रत्यक्षीकृ.—(Present, as a sacrifice or oblation) उपहृ, उपहारीकृ, निविद्, निवेदनं कृ, निर्वप् (c. 1. -वपति -वप्तुं), निर्वपणं कृ, उत्सर्गं कृ, उत्सृज् (c. 6. -सृजति -स्रष्टुं), बलिं कृ, बलिदानं कृ, उपायनं कृ, अर्पणं कृ, समर्पणं कृ.—(Offer a burnt offering) होमं कृ, हु (c. 3. जुहोति, होतुं), हव्यं कृ, हवनं कृ, आहवनं कृ.—(Offer a price) अमुकमूल्यं दित्सामीति or दातुमिच्छामीति वद् (c. 1. वदति -दितुं) or अभिधा, मूल्यम् अभिधा.—(Offer violence) बलात्कारं कृ.

To OFFER, *v. n.* (Present itself, be at hand) उपस्था (c. 1. -तिष्ठति -स्थातुं), उपस्थितः -ता -तं भू, प्रस्तुतः -ता -तं भू, दृश् in pass. (दृश्यते), लक्ष् in pass. (लक्ष्यते), प्रादुर्भू, आविर्भू.—(Declare a willingness) expressed by the desid. form, or by the future or present tense in conjunction with the root वद्; as, 'he offers to go,' जिगमिषामि or गमिष्यामि or गच्छामि इति वद् (c. 1. वदति -दितुं) or प्रवद्.—(Make an attempt) उद्यमं कृ, उद्योगं कृ, उद्यतः &c. भू, उद्युक्तः &c. भू or अस्.

OFFER, *s.* (Proposal) उपन्यासः, प्रतिज्ञा, निवेदनं, निर्देशः, प्रदेशनं, वाक्यं, अभिधानं.—(Of a price) मूल्यदित्सा, अमुकमूल्यं दित्सामीति वादः or स्थापनं.—(Attempt) उद्यमः, उद्योगः, प्रवृत्तिः *f.*, उपक्रमः.

OFFERED, *p.p.* (Presented for acceptance) उपहृतः -ता -तं, समुपहृतः -ता -तं, उपनीतः &c., उपस्थापितः &c., प्रदत्तः -त्ता -त्तं, प्रत्तः &c., अर्पितः &c., समर्पितः &c., प्रतिपादितः &c., उपनिहितः &c.—(As an oblation) उपहृतः &c., उपहारीकृतः &c., निर्वापितः &c., निवेदितः &c., उत्सृष्टः -ष्टा -ष्टं, अर्पितः &c.—(As a burnt-offering) हुतः -ता -तं, आहुतः &c.—(Proposed) उपन्यस्तः -स्ता -स्तं, अभिहितः &c., निर्दिष्टः &c., आदिष्टः &c.—(Exhibited, presented) प्रसारितः &c., दर्शितः -ता -तं.

OFFERER, *s.* उपहर्त्ता *m.* (र्तृ), उपनेता *m.* (तृ), निवेदकः, अर्पकः, समर्पकः.—(Of oblations) बलिकरः, बलिदाता *m.* (तृ), बलिकर्त्ता *m.*, होता *m.* (तृ), हवनकृत्.

OFFERING, *s.* (The act) उपहरणं, उपनयनं, निवेदनं, अर्पणं, समर्पणं, अभिवाह्यं.—(Act of offering oblations) बलिदानं, बलिकरणं, बलिकर्म्म *n.* (न्), उत्सर्गकरणं, निर्वपणं, निर्वापणं, हवनं, आहवनं.—(Oblation) बलिः *m.*, उपहारः, उत्सर्गः, देवोपहारः, नैवेद्यं. *See* OBLATION. (Burnt offering) होमः, हुतं, हव्यं, हुतहोमं, आहुतिः *f.*, अवदानं; 'of sesamum,' तिलहोमं.—(Respectful or complimentary offering) अर्घ्यं, अर्घः, उपढौकनं, उपायनं, उपदा, प्राभृतं. *See* OBLATION.

OFFICE, *s.* (Post, charge, trust) अधिकारः, पदं, पदवी, अधिकारपदं, नियोगः, स्थानं, आस्पदं; 'invested with office, in office,' अधिकारप्राप्तः -प्ता -प्तं, प्राप्ताधिकारः -रा -रं, अधिकारापन्नः -न्ना -न्नं, अधिकृतः -ता -तं, अधिकारस्थः -स्था -स्थं, अधिकारारूढः -ढा -ढं, पदारूढः &c., अधिकारस्थितः -ता -तं; 'resignation of office,' अधिकारत्यागः, अधिकारोत्सर्गः; 'dismissed from office,' अधिकारच्युतः -ता -तं, अधिकारभ्रष्टः -ष्टा -ष्टं, अधिकारभ्रंशितः -ता -तं, पदच्युतः &c., पदभ्रष्टः &c., च्युताधिकारः -रा -रं; 'hereditary office,' स्थिराधिकारः; 'temporary,' चलाधिकारः.—(Function, particular business or duty) कर्म्म *n.* (न्), कार्य्यं, कृत्यं, क्रिया, व्यापारः, व्यवसायः, वृत्तिः *f.*, प्रवृत्तिः *f.*, व्यवहारः, धर्म्मः, गुणः, विषयः, व्रतं.—(Act of kindness, good office) उपकारः, उपकृतिः *f.*, उपक्रिया, उपकृतं, सुकृतं, सुकृतिः *f.*—(Ill office) अपकारः, अपकृतिः *f.*, अपक्रिया.—(Formulary) पद्धतिः *f.*, विधिसङ्ग्रहः, विधानसङ्ग्रहः, विधानमाला.—(Place for transacting business) लेख्यस्थानं, लेख्यगृहं, उद्योगस्थानं, व्यापारस्थानं, उद्योगागारं, कर्म्मस्थानं, ग्रन्थकुटी.—(Outhouses) उपगृहाणि *n. pl.*, महानसादि *n.*

OFFICER, *s.* (Person appointed to perform any duty) नियोगी *m.* (न्), नियुक्तः, अधिकारी *m.* (न्), अधिकारवान् *m.* (त्), आधिकारिकः, कर्म्मकरः, कार्य्यसाधकः, कार्य्यप्रवर्त्तकः, भृत्यः, आयुक्तः.—(Of the king or government) राजभृत्यः, राजनियोगी *m.*, राजकर्म्मकरः,

राजमन्त्री *m.* (न्), प्रकृतिः *f.*, प्रकृतिपुरुषः, राजपुरुषः, पुरुषः.—(Of justice) धर्म्माधिकारी *m.*, धर्म्माध्यक्षः, न्यायाधिपतिः *m.*, राजपुरुषः.—(In the army) सेनायाम् अधिकारी *m.* or अधिकारवान् *m.* (त्) or पदवान् *m.* or पदभाक् *m.* (ज्) or अधिकारस्थः, सैनिकाध्यक्षः, सैनिकाधिकृतः, सैनिकाधिपतिः *m.*—(In the navy) नाविकाध्यक्षः, नाविकाधिकृतः.—(Superintendent) अध्यक्षः.

OFFICIAL, *a.* (Pertaining to an office) आधिकारिकः -की -कं, अधिकारसम्बन्धी -न्धिनी &c., पदसम्बन्धी &c., अधिकारविषयः -या -यं.—(Derived from or communicated by authority) अधिकारप्रयुक्तः -क्ता -क्तं, आधिकारिकः &c.

OFFICIAL, *s.* आधिकारिकः, अधिकारी *m.* (न्), नियोगी *m.*, राजपुरुषः, पुरुषः, राजभृत्यः, कर्म्मकरः, भृत्यः.

OFFICIALLY, *adv.* अधिकारेण, अधिकारतस्, अधिकारप्रयुक्तं, अधिकारपूर्व्वं, अधिकारानुसारात् -रेण.

To OFFICIATE, *v. n.* अधिकारिकर्म्म कृ, नियोगिकर्म्म कृ, आधिकारिककार्य्यं कृ or निर्वह् (c. 10. -वाहयति -यितुं) or अनुष्ठा (c. 1. -तिष्ठति -ष्ठातुं), कर्म्म कृ or विधा (c. 3. -दधाति -धातुं).

OFFICIOUS, *a.* (Obliging) उपकारी -रिणी -रि (न्), उपकारशीलः -ला -लं.—(Over-obliging) अत्युपकारी &c., अत्युपचारी &c., अत्युपचारः -रा -रं.—(Meddlesome) परकार्य्यचर्चकः -का -कं, पराधिकारप्रवेशकः &c., अनधिकारचर्चाशीलः &c.

OFFICIOUSLY, *adv.* अत्युपचारेण, अत्युपकारशीलत्वात्, अनधिकारचर्चया.

OFFICIOUSNESS, *s.* अत्युपचारशीलता, अत्युपकारशीलता, परकार्य्यचर्चा, अनधिकारचर्चा, पराधिकारचर्चा, परकार्य्यप्रवेशः, पराधिकारप्रवेशः, परव्यापारचर्चा.

OFFING, *s.* तीरदूरस्थः or तीरदूरवर्त्ती समुद्रभागः.

OFFSCOURING, *s.* मलं, अवस्करः, अवकरः, अपस्करः, उच्छिष्टं, कल्कं.

OFFSET, *s.* प्ररोहः, अङ्कुरः, पल्लवः, किसलयः.

OFFSPRING, *s.* सन्तानं -नः, सन्ततिः *f.*, अपत्यं, प्रजा, प्रजोत्पत्तिः *f.*, सूतिः *f.*, प्रसूतिः *f.*, प्रसवः, तन्तुः *m.*, सूनुः *m.*, सवः, प्रवरं, डिम्भः, तोकं, शावकः, वंशः, कुलं; 'male offspring,' पुत्रसन्तानं -नः, पुत्रसन्ततिः *f.*, पुंसन्तानं, पुंसन्ततिः *f.*, पुमपत्यं, पुत्रपौत्रादिवंशः; 'female offspring,' कन्यासन्तानं, कन्यासन्ततिः *f.*, स्त्रीसन्तानं, स्त्रीसन्ततिः *f.*, स्त्र्यपत्यं; 'tender offspring,' बालापत्यं; 'having offspring,' प्रजावान् -वती -वत् (त्), सप्रजः -जा -जं, सापत्यः -त्या -त्यं, अपत्यवान् &c., सन्ततिमान् &c., ससन्तानः -ना -नं; 'having male offspring,' पुत्री *m.* (न्); 'want of offspring,' अनपत्यता.

To OFFUSCATE, OFFUSCATION. *See* OBFUSCATE, OBFUSCATION.

OFT, OFTEN, OFTENTIMES, OFTTIMES, *adv.* बहुशस्, अनेकशस्, असकृत्, बहुवारं, अनेकवारं, अनेकदा, बहुकृत्वस्, बहुवेलं, अनेककृत्वस्, पुनः पुनर्, वारं वारं, भूयस्, मुहुस्, मुहुर्मुहुस्, अभीक्ष्णं; 'how often?' कतिकृत्वस्, कतिवारं; 'as often as,' यावत्, यतिवारं; 'so often,' तावत्, ततिवारं.

OGLE, *s.* कटाक्षः, कटाक्षावेक्षणं, कटाक्षदर्शनं, अपाङ्गदर्शनं, अपाङ्गवीक्षणं, भ्रूक्षेपः, भ्रूविलासः, भ्रूविकारः.

To OGLE, *v. n.* कटाक्षेण दृश् (c. 1. पश्यति, द्रष्टुं), कटाक्षदर्शनं कृ, कटाक्षेण वीक्ष् (c. 1. -ईक्षते -क्षितुं) or अवेक्ष्, कटाक्षावेक्षणं कृ, अपाङ्गवीक्षणं कृ, भ्रूक्षेपं कृ, भ्रूविलासं कृ.

OGLING, *s.* कटाक्षावेक्षणं, अपाङ्गदर्शनं, भ्रूक्षेपालापः.

OGLIO, *s.* *See* OLIO.

OGRE, *s.* राक्षसः, दैत्यः, दानवः, उग्रशरीरः, क्रव्याद् *m.*, पुरुषादः.

OH, *interj.* अहो, अहोवत्, हा, हन्त, आ, आस्, अहह. *See* O.

OIL, *s.* तैलं, स्नेहः, तिलस्नेहः, तिलरसः, तिलतैलं, तेलं, अभ्यञ्जनं; 'a small quantity of oil,' तैलकं; 'dressed or cooked with oil,' स्नेहपक्वः -क्वा -क्वं.

To OIL, *v. a.* तैलेन or स्नेहेन लिप् (c. 6. लिम्पति, लेप्तुं) or अञ्ज् (c. 7. अनक्ति, अंक्तुं, c. 10. अञ्जयति -यितुं) or दिह् (c. 2. देग्धि -ग्धुं), तैलाक्तं -क्तां कृ, तैलाभ्यक्तं -क्तां कृ, तैलाक्तीकृ, स्निग्धीकृ.

OIL-BOTTLE, *s.* कुतूः *f.*; 'small one,' कुतुपः.

OIL-CAKE, *s.* तैलकिट्टं, पिण्डं, तैलपिण्डकः, पिण्याकः.

OIL-CLOTH, *s.* तैलपटः, तैलाक्तम् आस्तरणवस्त्रं.

OILED, *p. p.* तैलाक्तः -क्ता -क्तं, तैलाभ्यक्तः &c., स्नेहाक्तः &c., स्नेहाभ्यक्तः &c., तैललिप्तः -प्ता -प्तं, अभ्यक्तः &c.

OILINESS, *s.* सतैलता, स्निग्धता, स्नैग्ध्यं, तैलाक्तत्वं, सस्नेहता, तैलवत्त्वं, स्नेहः, चिक्कणता -त्वं, तैलप्राचुर्य्यं.

OIL-MAN, *s.* तैलकारः, तैलिकः, तैली *m.* (न्), तैलकः, चाक्रिकः, स्नेहकारः, तिलादिबीजानां पेष्टा *m.* (ष्टृ).

OIL-MILL, OIL-PRESS, *s.* तैलिकयन्त्रं, तैलिकचक्रं, तिलपेषणचक्रं, तिलादिबीजपेषणार्थं चक्रं, तैलिशाला.

OIL-SHOP, *s.* तैलविक्रयस्थानं, तैलविक्रयगृहं.

OILY, *a.* सतैलः -ला -लं, तैली -लिनी -लि (न्), तैलमयः -यी -यं, तैलयुक्तः -क्ता -क्तं, तैलवान् -वती -वत् (त्), स्नेही &c., स्नेहवान् &c., सस्नेहः -हा -हं, स्निग्धः -ग्धा -ग्धं, चिक्कणः -णा -णं, तैलाक्तः &c., तैलाभ्यक्तः &c.

OINTMENT, *s.* लेपः -पनं, विलेपनं, प्रलेपः, अनुलेपनं, अभ्यञ्जनं, अञ्जनं, स्नेहः, उपदेहः, मर्दनद्रव्यं.

OLD, *a.* (Advanced in years or life) वृद्धः -द्धा -द्धं, जीर्णः -र्णा -र्णं, स्थविरः -रा -रं, वयोवृद्धः &c., गतायुः -युः -युः (स्), गतवयस्कः -स्का -स्कं, वयोगतः -ता -तं, जरी -रिणी -रि (न्), जरणः -णा -णं, जरठः -ठा -ठं, जरातुरः -रा -रं, जरापरिणतः -ता -तं, जरद्धः -द्धा -द्धं, जरन् -रती -रत् (त्), जीर्णवान् -वती -वत् (त्), वयस्थः &c., प्रवयाः -याः -यः (स्), वयोधिकः -का -कं, अतीतवयाः &c., उत्तरवयाः &c., उत्तरवयस्कः &c., अतिवयस्कः &c., वर्षीयान् -यसी -यः (स्), वर्षिष्ठः -ष्ठा -ष्ठं, ज्यायान् &c., पुराणः -णा -णं, जीनः -ना -नं, अर्णः -र्णा -र्णं; 'to grow old,' जॄ (c. 4. जीर्य्यति, जरितुं -रीतुं), परिजॄ, वृद्धीभू; 'an old man,' जरी *m.* (न्), जरन् *m.* (त्), पलितः; 'an assembly of old men,' वृद्धसंघः, वार्द्धकं; 'old woman,' जरती, पलिता, पलिक्नी.—(Ancient) पुराणः -णा -णी -णं, प्राचीनः -ना -नं, पुरातनः -नी -नं, प्राक्तनः -नी -नं, प्रतनः -नी -नं, प्रत्नः -त्ना -त्नं, पौराणः -णी -णं, प्राक्कालीनः -ना -नं, पूर्व्वकालीनः &c., प्राक्कालिकः -की -कं, पूर्व्वकालिकः &c., पुरावृत्तः -त्ता -त्तं.—(Of long continuance) चिरकालिकः &c., चिरकालीनः &c., चिरन्तनः -नी -नं, चिरः -रा -रं, चिरस्थायी &c., चिरकालस्थायी &c., बहुकालिकः &c., बहुकालस्थायी &c.; 'an old friend,' चिरमित्रं, कालमित्रं; 'an old servant,' चिरसेवकः, चिरभृत्यः, मूलभृत्यः; 'old retainer,' चिराश्रितः.—(Decayed or worn out by time) जीर्णः -र्णा -र्णं, जर्जरः -रा -रं, जर्जरीकः -का -कं, अर्णः -र्णा -र्णं; 'old cloth,' जीर्णवस्त्रं, पटच्चरं; 'an old bambu,' जर्जरवंशः.—(Of any duration whatever) expressed by वर्ष, वर्षीण, वर्षीय, आयुस् &c. in comp.; as, 'two years old,' द्विवर्षीणः -णा -णं, द्विवर्षः -र्षा -र्षं; 'a son twenty years old,' विंशतिवर्षीयः पुत्रः; 'a three years old heifer,' त्रिवर्षिका; 'more than ninety years old,' दशमी -मिनी -मि (न्), दशमीकृतः -ता -तं, दशमीस्थः -स्था -स्थं; 'a hundred years old,' शतायुः

-यूः -युः (स्); 'how old?' किंवयीयाः -या -यं, किंवयीयः &c.; 'how old are you?' किंवयीयोऽसि.—(Former) पूर्व्वः -र्व्वा -र्व्वं, पूर्व्वतनः -नी -नं; 'of old.' पुरा, पूर्व्वं.

Old-age, *s.* वृद्धता -त्वं, वार्धक्यं, वार्धकं, वृद्धावस्था, वृद्धभावः, वार्धक्यावस्था, जरा, जीर्णत्वं -ता, जीर्णिः *f.*, ज्यानिः *f.*, जीर्णावस्था, स्थाविरं, स्थविरत्वं; 'bowed down with old age,' जरापरिणतः -ता -तं; 'reverence for old age,' वृद्धसेवा.

Old-clothes, *s. pl.* जीर्णवस्त्रं -स्त्राणि *n. pl.*, जर्जरवस्त्रं -स्त्राणि.

Olden, *a.* पुराणः -णा -णी -णं, प्राचीनः -ना -नं, पुरातनः &c. *See* Old.

Older, *a.* ज्यायान् -यसी -यः (स्), अधिकवयाः &c. *See* Elder.

Oldest, *a.* ज्येष्ठः -ष्ठा -ष्ठं, वयोज्येष्ठः &c., वर्षिष्ठः &c., श्रेष्ठः &c.

Old-fashioned, *a.* पुराणरीत्यनुसारी -रिणी -रि (न्), प्राचीनव्यवहारानुरूपः -पा -पं, प्राक्तनमतानुयायी &c.

Oldish, *a.* ईषद्वृद्धः -द्धा -द्धं, ईषज्जीर्णः -र्णा -र्णं, ईषत्पुराणः &c.

Oldness, *s.* (Old age). *See* the word. (Antiquity, state of being of long standing) पुराणता -त्वं, प्राचीनता -त्वं, प्राक्तनता, पुरातनत्वं, प्रत्नता, प्राक्कालिकत्वं, प्राक्कालीनता, चिरकालीनता, चिरता. —(As of clothes, &c.) जीर्णता, जर्जरता.

Oleaginous, *a.* स्निग्धः -ग्धा -ग्धं, स्नेही -हिनी -हि (न्), चिक्कणः -णा -णं, मेदुरः -रा -रं, स्नेहवान् &c. *See* Oily.

Oleaginousness, *s.* स्निग्धता, स्नैग्ध्यं, चिक्कणता, मेदुरता. *See* Oiliness.

Oleander, *s.* प्रतिहासः, प्रतीहासः, शतप्रासः, चण्डातः, हयमारकः, करवीरः, अश्वमारः, कृकरः, तुरङ्गारिः *m.*

Oleraceous, *a.* शाकसम्बन्धी -न्धिनी -न्धि (न्), शाकविषयकः -का -कं.

Olfactory, *a.* घ्राणेन्द्रियसम्बन्धी -न्धिनी &c., घ्राणेन्द्रियविषयकः -का -कं, घ्राणसम्बन्धी &c., घ्राणबोधकः -का -कं, नस्यः -स्या -स्यं.

Olibanum, *s.* (The perfume) कुन्दुः *f.*, कुन्दुरः -रुः *m. f.*, कुन्दुरुकः, रसालं, खोटीरसः, कूर्म्मधूपः.—(The tree) रसालः, कुन्दुरुकः -की, खोटी.

Oligarchal, oligarchical, *a.* अल्पजनाधिपत्यसम्बन्धी -न्धिनी &c., कतिचिज्जनप्रभुत्वविषयः -या -यं, अल्पजनस्वामिकः -का -कं, कतिपयस्वामिकः &c.

Oligarchy, *s.* अल्पजनाधिपत्यं, अल्पजनप्रभुत्वं, कतिपयजनप्रभुत्वं, कतिचिज्जनाधिपत्यं, कतिपयाधिपत्यं, कतिपयजनपालितं राज्यं, कुलीनाधिपत्यं.

Olio, *s.* प्रकीर्णकं, नानाद्रव्यसन्निपातः, प्रकीर्णद्रव्यसमूहः.

Olive, *s.* (Tree) जितवृक्षः.—(Berry) जितफलं.

Omelet, *s.* अण्डशाकादिनिर्म्मितः पिष्टकविशेषः, अण्डपिष्टकः.

Omen, *s.* पूर्व्वलक्षणं, पूर्व्वचिह्नं, पूर्व्वलिङ्गं, शुभाशुभलक्षणं, मङ्गलामङ्गललक्षणं, भाविसूचकचिह्नं, भविष्यत्सूचकचिह्नं, शकुनं -नः, चिह्नं, लक्षणं, अजन्यं, निमित्तं, उत्पातः, पूर्व्वरूपं, भविष्यद्बोधकचिह्नं; 'good omen,' सुचिह्नं, सुलक्षणं; 'bad omen,' दुर्लक्षणं, दुश्चिह्नं, अपचिह्नं, अपलक्षणं, अपशकुनं -नः, दुःशकुनं -नः, अनिष्टसूचकचिह्नं, अशुभलक्षणं, अशुभचिह्नं, अमङ्गलचिह्नं, उपलिङ्गं; 'interpretation of omens,' शाकुनिकं.

Omened, *a.* (Ill-omened) अनिष्टसूचकः &c. *See* Ill-omened.

Omentum, *s.* मेदोधरा, अन्त्रवेष्टनं, अन्त्रावरणं, अन्त्राच्छादकं.

Ominous, *a.* (Pertaining to omens) शाकुनिकः -की -कं, शाकुनः -नी -नं, शकुनसम्बन्धी -न्धिनी &c., शुभाशुभसूचकः -का -कं, भाविसूचकः &c., भविष्यत्सूचकः &c., भविष्यद्बोधकः &c.—(Foreboding evil) अनिष्टसूचकः &c., अशुभसूचकः &c., अमङ्गलसूचकः &c., अभद्रसूचकः &c., अनिष्टावेदी &c., अनिष्टशंसी &c., अशुभशंसी &c., दुर्लक्षणी &c.—(Foreboding good) शुभशंसी &c., शुभसूचकः &c., मङ्गलसूचकः &c.

Ominously, *adv.* अशुभसूचनापूर्व्वं, दुर्लक्षणेन, अशुभलक्षणपूर्व्वं.

Ominousness, *s.* अनिष्टसूचकत्वं, अशुभसूचकता, शाकुनिकत्वं.

Omission, *s.* त्यागः, परित्यागः, वर्जनं, अपासनं, लङ्घनं, अन्तरं, लोपः, परिलोपः, उपात्ययः, विसंयोगः, उत्सर्गः, विसर्गः, भ्रमः, भ्रान्तिः *f.*; 'failure to do something,' अननुष्ठानं, अकरणं, अपक्रिया, अकरणिः *f.*, अनाचरणं, अविधानं; 'without omission,' निरन्तरं, नैरन्तर्य्येण; 'making omission,' औत्सर्गिकः -की -कं.

To omit, *v. a.* परित्यज् (c. 1. -त्यजति -त्यक्तुं), त्यज्, हा (c. 3. जहाति, हातुं, caus. हापयति -यितुं), अपहा, विहा, अपाहा, वृज् (c. 10. वर्जयति -यितुं), परिवृज्, विवृज्, अपास् (c. 4. -अस्यति -असितुं), व्युदस्, अतिक्रम् (c. 1. -क्रामति -क्रमितुं), व्युत्क्रम्, उत्सृज् (c. 6. -सृजति -स्रष्टुं), विसृज्, लङ्घ् (c. 10. लङ्घयति -यितुं).—(Not to perform) न अनुष्ठा (c. 1. -तिष्ठति -ष्ठातुं), न कृ, न विधा (c. 3. -दधाति -धातुं); 'omitting this, including that,' एतद् वर्जयित्वा तत्सहितः.

Omitted, *p. p.* परित्यक्तः -क्ता -क्तं, त्यक्तः -क्ता -क्तं, वर्जितः -ता -तं, अपास्तः -स्ता -स्तं, अपासितः -ता -तं, विसर्जितः -ता -तं, विसृष्टः -ष्टा -ष्टं, अन्तरितः -ता -तं, अननुष्ठितः -ता -तं, अकृतः -ता -तं.

Omnifarious, *a.* सर्व्वविधः -धा -धं, सर्व्वप्रकारः -रा -रं, सर्व्वरूपः -पा -पं.

Omnigenous, *a.* सर्व्वविधः -धा -धं, सर्व्वजातीयः -या -यं.

Omnipotence, omnipotency, *s.* सर्व्वशक्तित्वं, अनन्तशक्तित्वं, अमितशक्तित्वं, सर्व्वशक्तता, अपारशक्तिः *f.*, अनन्तसामर्थ्यं, सर्व्वकार्य्यशक्तिः *f.*, सर्व्वसामर्थ्यं.

Omnipotent, *a.* सर्व्वशक्तिमान् -मती -मत् (त्), सर्व्वशक्तिकः -का -कं, अनन्तशक्तिः -क्तिः -क्ति, दुरन्तशक्तिः &c., अमितशक्तिः -क्तिः -क्ति, अपारशक्तिकः &c., सर्व्वसमर्थः -र्था -र्थं.

Omnipresence, *s.* व्याप्तिः *f.*, सर्व्वत्र व्याप्तिः *f.*, सर्व्वव्याप्तिः *f.*, विश्वव्याप्तिः *f.*, विश्वव्यापकत्वं, सर्व्वव्यापित्वं, विश्वव्यापिता, अभिव्याप्तिः *f.*, सर्व्वगत्वं, त्रैलोक्यविस्तारः, सर्व्वत्र विस्तारः, सर्व्वत्रविद्यमानता.

Omnipresent, *a.* सर्व्वव्यापी -पिनी -पि (न्), सर्व्वव्यापकः -का -कं, विश्वव्यापी &c., विश्वव्यापकः -का -कं, सर्व्वत्रगः -गा -गं, सर्व्वत्रगामी &c., सर्व्वगतः -ता -तं, सर्व्वात्मकः -का -कं, त्रैलोक्यविस्तीर्णः -र्णा -र्णं, सर्व्वत्र विस्तीर्णः &c. or विद्यमानः -ना -नं, विश्वरूपः -पा -पं, सर्व्वभूतभूतान्तरः -रा -रं.

Omniscience, *s.* सर्व्वज्ञत्वं -ता, सर्व्वज्ञानं, सर्व्वविषयज्ञानं, अनन्तज्ञानं, अपारज्ञानं, सर्व्वज्ञातृत्वं.

Omniscient, *a.* सर्व्वज्ञः -ज्ञा -ज्ञं, सर्व्ववित् *m. f. n.*, सर्व्ववेदी -दिनी -दि (न्), सर्व्वज्ञाता -त्री -तृ (तृ), कृत्स्नज्ञः &c., कृत्स्नविद् *m. f. n.*, अनन्तज्ञानी &c., सर्व्वदर्शी &c., सर्व्वसाक्षी -क्षिणी -क्षि (न्), त्रिकालज्ञः &c., त्रिकालविद् *m. f. n.*, त्रिकालदर्शी &c.

Omnivagant, omnivagous, *a.* सर्व्वगः -गा -गं, सर्व्वत्रगः &c., सर्व्वत्रगामी -मिनी &c., सर्व्वत्रभ्रमकः -का -कं, सर्व्वत्रविहारी &c.

Omnivorous, *a.* सर्व्वभक्षः -क्षा -क्षं, सर्व्वभक्षकः -का -कं, सर्व्वान्नभक्षकः &c., सर्व्वभोजी -जिनी -जि (न्), सर्व्वाशी &c., सर्व्वखादकः -का -कं, स्वेच्छाहारः -रा -रं, सर्व्वान्नीनः -ना -नं.

Omphalic, *a.* नाभ्यः -भ्या -भ्यं, नाभिसम्बन्धी -न्धिनी -न्धि (न्).

Omphalocele, *s.* नाभिवर्धनं, नाभिगोलकः, नाभिगुडकः, नाभिकण्टकः.

Omphalotomy, *s.* नाभिच्छेदः -दनं, नाभिनालीच्छेदनं.

On, *prep.* अधि, नि prefixed, उपरि affixed.—(Denoting contact with the upper part of a thing) expressed by the loc. c., or by उपरि affixed to the crude form or gen. c.; as, 'on the table,' फलके or फलकोपरि or फलकस्योपरि; rain falls on the ground,' भूमौ पतति वृष्टिः; 'having placed the wood on his shoulder,' काष्ठं स्कन्धे कृत्वा; 'placed on the fire,' अग्निस्थः

-श -र्श. The instr. c. is elegantly used for the loc. in similar phrases; as, 'he carries the wood on his shoulder,' काष्ठं स्कन्धेन वहति; 'to go on foot,' पादाभ्यां गम्; 'conduct me home on a horse,' अश्वेन मां वसतिं नय.—(At, or near) expressed by loc. c., or by निकटे, समीपे, उपान्ते &c. affixed, or by उप prefixed; as, 'on the shore,' तीरे, तीरनिकटे, तीरोपान्ते, उपतीरं; 'on the throat,' उपकण्ठं.—(At the time of) expressed by the loc. c., as, 'on Monday,' सोमवारे; 'on their arrival,' तेषु आगतेषु; 'on the corn being cut,' शस्ये लूने सति, or even by the abl. c., as, 'on seeing him,' तद्दर्शनात्, or by the indecl. part., as, 'on seeing that,' तद् दृष्ट्वा; 'on hearing that,' तच्छ्रुत्वा.—(Toward or for) प्रति affixed, or expressed by gen. or loc. c; as, 'have pity on me,' मां प्रति or मम or मयि दयां कुरु.—(Dependence on) expressed by acc. c., after such verbs as अवलम्ब्, आश्रि &c.; as, 'he relies on me,' माम् अवलम्बते.—(Concerning, relating to) विषयः -या -यं, विषयकः -का -कं, सम्बन्धी -न्धिनी &c.; as, 'a treatise on mathematics,' गणितविषयकं शास्त्रं.—(Performing on an instrument) expressed by acc. c. after वद् in caus.; as, 'he plays on a lute,' वीणां वादयति. The affixes तस्, त्र and दा, often express the sense of 'on'; as, 'on both sides,' उभयतस्, उभयत्र, उभयपार्श्वतस्; 'on all sides,' सर्व्वतस्, समन्ततस्, अभितस्, समन्तात्, सर्व्वत्र; 'on the one hand,' एकतस्; 'on all occasions,' सर्व्वदा; 'on one occasion,' एकदा; 'on another occasion,' अन्यदा. The following are other examples of instr., and other cases used adverbially to express this prep.; 'on the north-east of the city,' प्रागुत्तरेण नगरात्; 'on this account,' अनेन हेतुना; 'on account of, or in consequence of anger,' कोपात्. *See* ACCOUNT; 'on the other side,' अन्यपार्श्वेन, अन्येन पार्श्वेन; 'immediately on hearing this,' तच्छ्रवणमात्रात्; 'on a sudden,' अकस्मात्, सहसा; 'on high,' उच्चैस्, उच्चकैस्, उर्द्ध, ऊर्द्ध्वं, ऊर्द्धं; 'set on foot,' आरब्धः -ब्धा -ब्धं, उद्यतः -ता -तं, प्रचलीकृतः &c.

ON, *adv.* (Forward, in progression) अग्रे, अग्रं, अग्रतस् or expressed by प्र prefixed; as, 'going on,' अग्रे गमनं, प्रगमनं.—(Continuance) expressed by the verb आस् in combination with the pres. or indecl. part. of another verb. *See* KEEP, CONTINUE. (Upon the body, as clothes, &c.). *See To* PUT ON.

ONCE, *adv.* (One time) सकृत्, एकवारं -रे, एककृत्वस्, एककाले, एकसमये.—(On a certain time) एकदा, कदाचित्.—(Formerly) पूर्व्वं, पुरा. *See* the word. (At once, at the same time) समकाले, एककाले, एकवारे, एकदा.—(All at once) युगपत्, यौगपद्येन, एकपदे -दे.—(All at once in a body) सङ्घशस्.—(All at once, suddenly) अकस्मात्.—(At once, immediately) सद्यस्, तत्काले, तत्क्षणे.—(Once more) पुनरपि.

ON-DIT, *adv.* किंवदन्ती, जनप्रवादः, जनवादः, लोकप्रवादः.

ONE, *a.* (Single in number) एकः -का -कं; 'one man,' एकपुरुषः.—(Indefinitely) 'some one,' 'any one,' कश्चित् &c., कश्चन &c., कोऽपि &c. *See* SOME. (Mutuality) 'one another,' परस्परः -रा -रं, इतरेतरः &c., अन्योन्यः -न्या -न्यं; 'things that are equal to the same, are equal to one another,' यावन्तः पदार्थाः प्रत्येकम् एकेन केनचित् समास् ते सर्व्वे मिथः समानाः; 'one after another,' अनुपूर्व्वशस्, क्रमशस्, क्रमे क्रमे.—(Same, like) एकः -का -कं, समः -मा -मं, तुल्यः -ल्या -ल्यं; 'at one time,' एककाले, एकपदे; 'of one color,' एकवर्णः -र्णा -र्णं, समवर्णः &c.; 'having one object,' एकार्थः -र्था -र्थं, एकाग्रः -ग्रा -ग्रं; 'having one occupation,' एकवृत्तिः &c.; 'in one place,' एकस्थाने, एकत्र; 'collected in one place,' एकस्थः &c., एकीभूतः -ता -तं.—(One only, but one) अनन्यः -न्या -न्यं; 'having one only refuge,' अनन्यगतिः &c.; 'having the mind fixed on one object,' अनन्यमनस्कः &c., अनन्यभावः &c.—(One by one) एकैकं, एकैकशस्, एकशस्, प्रत्येकं, पृथक्, पृथक् पृथक्.—(One day) एकदा, कदाचित्; 'in one way,' एकधा; 'on the one hand,' एकतस्; 'one of many,' एकतमः -मा -मं; 'one of two,' एकतरः -रा -रं; 'one of these,' तेषाम् एकः, तत्रैकः; 'one year old heifer,' एकाब्दा; 'one year old calf,' एकवत्सरो वत्सः.

ONE, *s.* (Such a one, such and such a person) अमुकः, अमुकजनः.—(A man, a person) जनः, व्यक्तिः *f.*, मनुष्यः; 'one's self,' आत्मा *m.* (न्), स्वयं indecl.; 'by resemblance to one's self,' आत्मौपम्येन; 'done by one's self,' स्वयङ्कृतः -ता -तं; 'one's own,' स्व, आत्म in comp.; 'like one's own body,' स्वशरीरवत्; आत्मशरीरवत्; 'one's own house,' आत्मगृहं, स्वगृहं. *See* OWN.

ONE-EYED, *a.* एकाक्षः -क्षा -क्षं, एकदृक् *m.f.n.* (श्), एकाक्षिविकलः -ला -लं, एकनेत्रः -त्रा -त्रं, एकचक्षूः -क्षूः -क्षुः (स्), काणः -णा -णं, काणेयः -यी -यं, काणेरः -री -रं.

ONE-HANDED, *a.* एककरः -रा -रं, एकहस्तः -स्ता -स्तं, एकपाणिः -णिः -णि.

ONEIROCRITIC, ONEIROCRITICAL, *a.* स्वप्नविचारी *m.* (न्), स्वप्नप्रकाशकः, स्वप्नार्थज्ञापकः, स्वप्नार्थबोधकः.

ONEIROMANCY, *s.* स्वप्नविचारः, स्वप्नप्रकाशनं, स्वप्नार्थज्ञापनं, स्वप्नार्थबोधनं, स्वप्नपरीक्षा, स्वप्नादिलक्षणाद् भविष्यत्सूचनं or शुभाशुभकथनं.

ONENESS, *s.* एकता -त्वं, ऐक्यं, एकीभावः, ऐक्यभावः, अद्वैतं, अभेदः.—(Doctrine of oneness in theology). *See* UNITY.

To ONERATE, *v. a.* सभारं -रीं कृ, भारवन्तं -वतीं -वत् कृ. *See To* LOAD.

ONEROUS, *a.* दुर्भरः -रा -रं, दुःसहः -हा -हं, दुर्वहः -हा -हं, भारी -रिणी -रि (न्), भारवान् -वती -वत् (त्), सभारः -रा -रं, कष्टकरः -रा -रं, पीडाकरः &c., गुरुः -रुः -रु.

ONION, *s.* पलाण्डुः *m.*, सुकन्दकः, मुकन्दकः, मुकुन्दकः, दुर्द्रुमः, दुद्रुमः, लताकः, गृञ्जनः, मुखगन्धकः, मुखदूषणः, तीक्ष्णकन्दः, महाकन्दः, नीचभोज्यः.

ONLY, *a.* (Single, one alone) एकः -का -कं, केवलः -ला -ली -लं, केवली -लिनी -लि (न्), कैवल्यः -ल्या -ल्यं, मात्रः in comp. मात्रकः -का -कं, अद्वितीयः -या -यं; 'an only son,' एकपुत्रः, एकसूनुः *m.*—(This and no other) अनन्यः -न्या -न्यं, नान्यः -न्या -न्यत्; 'having one only refuge,' अनन्यगतिः -तिः -ति; 'his only business is reading the Vedas,' वेदाध्ययनात् तस्य कार्य्यं नान्यत्.

ONLY, *adv.* केवलं, मात्रं -त्रेण -त्रात्, कुद्धारं, एकान्ततस्, एव; 'by calculation only,' गणितमात्रेण, केवलगणितेन, गणितेनैव; 'touch only,' स्पर्शमात्रं; 'from touch only,' स्पर्शमात्रात्.

ONOMANCY, *s.* नामाक्षरलक्षणाद् भविष्यत्सूचनं or शुभाशुभकथनं.

ONOMATOPŒIA, *s.* (In rhetoric) अनुकरणं, अनुकरणशब्दः, शब्दानुकरणं.

ONSET, *s.* आक्रमः -मणं, अभिक्रमः -मणं, अधिक्रमः -मणं, अभियोगः, अभिग्रहः, अवस्कन्दः -न्दनं, अभ्याघातः; 'emulative onset,' अहम्पूर्व्विका.

ONTOLOGIST, *s.* सत्त्वविज्ञः, सत्त्वमात्रविचारी *m.* (न्), भूतमात्रविचारी *m.*

ONTOLOGY, *s.* सत्त्वविद्या, सत्त्वमात्रविचारः, भूतमात्रविचारः.

ONWARD, ONWARDS, *adv.* अग्रे, अग्रतस्, पुरस्, पुरतस्, पुरस्तात्, अभितस्, अभिमुखं -खे, प्रतिमुखं -खे, अग्रभागं प्रति, उत्तरेण, ऊर्द्ध्वं, or expressed by प्र; as, 'proceeding onwards,' अग्रे गमनं, अग्रगमनं, प्रगमनं, प्रस्थानं.—(A little further) किञ्चिदन्तरं -रेण, किञ्चिदपरतस्.

ONWARD, *a.* (Advanced, in advance) अग्रः -ग्रा -ग्रं, अग्रिमः -मा -मं, अग्रगामी -मिनी -मि (न्), अग्रगः -गा -गं, अग्रतःसरः -रा -रं, अग्रसरः -रा -रं, प्रगतः -ता -तं.—(Increased) वर्धितः -ता -तं, प्रवृद्धः -द्धा -द्धं, प्ररूढः -ढा -ढं.

ONYX, *s.* (Precious stone) गोमेदकः -कं, शिवधातुः *m.*

To OOZE, *v. n.* शनैः शनैः स्रु (c. 1. स्रवति, स्रोतुं) or स्यन्द् (c. 1. स्यन्दते -न्दितुं) or प्रस्यन्द् or क्षर् (c. 1. क्षरति -रितुं) or री (c. 4. रीयते, रेतुं) or गल् (c. 1. गलति -लितुं), क्रमे क्रमे or विन्दुक्रमेण क्षरणं कृ.

OOZE, *s.* (Moist mud) सद्रवपङ्कः, चिक्कणपङ्कः, क्षरत्पङ्कः.—(Exudation) स्यन्दनं, स्रवः, विन्दुस्रावः, स्रवद्रसः, स्वेदः, द्रवः, धारा.

OOZING, *s.* शनैः शनैः स्रवणं or स्यन्दनं or क्षरणं or गलनं.

OOZING, *part.* शनैः शनैः स्यन्दी -न्दिनी -न्दि (न्) or स्यन्दमानः -ना -नं or निस्यन्दमानः -ना -नं or स्रवः -वा -वं or क्षरन् -रन्ती -रत् (त्) or स्रवन् &c. or रीणः -णा -णं.

OOZY, *a.* सद्रवपङ्कमयः -यी -यं, क्षरत्पङ्कमयः &c., सद्रवः -वा -वं.

OPACITY, OPAQUENESS, *s.* (The quality of being impervious to light) प्रकाशाभेद्यता, प्रभाभेद्यता, किरणाभेद्यता, अस्वच्छता, प्रकाशप्रतिबन्धकत्वं, प्रकाशरोधकत्वं, दृष्टिरोधकता.—(Obscurity) निष्प्रभता, अप्रकाशता, कलुषत्वं, प्रभाहीनता, सान्धकारता, अप्रसन्नता.—(Disease in the eyes) शुक्लं.

OPAQUE, OPACOUS, *a.* (Impervious to light) प्रकाशाभेद्यः -द्या -द्यं, प्रभाभेद्यः &c., किरणाभेद्यः &c., प्रकाशप्रतिबन्धकः -का -कं, प्रकाशरोधकः -का -कं, किरणरोधकः &c.—(Not shining by its own light) परप्रकाशः -शा -शं.—(Obscure, not transparent) अस्वच्छः -च्छा -च्छं, निष्प्रभः -भा -भं, अप्रकाशः -शा -शं, प्रकाशहीनः -ना -नं, सान्धकारः -रा -रं, कलुषः -षा -षं.

OPAL, *s.* शिवधातुः *m.*, पाण्डुमृत्तिका, वज्राभः, क्षीरस्फटिकः, गोमेदसन्निभः.

To OPEN, *v. a.* (Unclose) विवृ (c. 5. -वृणोति -णुते -वरितुं -रीतुं), अपावृ, अपवृ, उद्घट् (c. 10. -घाटयति -यितुं), व्यादा (c. 3. -ददाति -दातुं); 'he opens the door,' द्वारं विवृणोति or उद्घाटयति.—(Unbar) निरर्गलीकृ.—(Open the mouth) मुखं व्यादा.—(Open the eyes) लोचने or चक्षुषी उन्मील् (c. 10. -मीलयति -यितुं) or प्रोन्मील्, उन्मिष् (c. 6. -मिषति -मेषितुं) or उत्पल् (c. 10. -पालयति -यितुं), नयने विवृ.—(Open a book) पुस्तकं मुच् (c. 6. मुञ्चति, मोक्तुं) or विस्तृ, पुस्तकमोचनं कृ.—(Open a letter) उन्मुद्रीकृ, विमुद्रीकृ.—(Expand) विस्तृ (c. 10. -स्तारयति -यितुं), विकाश् (c. 10. -काशयति -यितुं), विकस् (c. 10. -कासयति -यितुं), विवृ, व्यादा.—(Lay open, make manifest) व्यञ्ज् (c. 7. -अनक्ति -अङ्क्तुं, c. 10. -अञ्जयति -यितुं), विकाश्, प्रकाश्, प्रकटीकृ, व्यक्तीकृ.—(Split, break, cut open) भिद् (c. 7. भिनत्ति, भेत्तुं), विभिद्, निर्भिद्, छिद् (c. 7. छिनत्ति, छेत्तुं), विच्छिद्.—(Expound) व्याख्या (c. 2. -ख्याति -तुं), व्याकृ, प्रकाश्, स्पष्टीकृ, व्यक्तीकृ, विवृ, विवरणं कृ.—(Clear) शुध् (c. 10. शोधयति -यितुं), विशुध्.—(Begin) आरभ् (c. 1. -रभते -रब्धुं), उपक्रम् (c. 1. -क्रमते -मितुं).

To OPEN, *v. n.* (Unclose itself) विवृतः -ता -तं भू, अपावृतः -ता -तं भू.—(Expand) विस्तृ in pass. (-स्तीर्य्यते), विवृ in caus. pass. (-वार्य्यते), विजृम्भ् (c. 1. -जृम्भते -म्भितुं), विततीभू.—(As flowers) विकस् (c. 1. -कसति -सितुं), प्रविकस्, स्फुट् (c. 6. स्फुटति -टितुं), फुल्ल् (c. 1. फुल्लति -ल्लितुं), विकसितः -ता -तं भू, विमुद्रीभू.—(Crack, open in chinks) स्फुट्, विदल् (c. 1. -दलति -लितुं), विदृ in pass. (-दीर्य्यते), भिद् in pass. (भिद्यते), विभिद्.—(Begin) आरभ् (c. 1. -रभते -रब्धुं), समारभ्, प्रवृत् (c. 1. -वर्त्तते -र्त्तितुं).

OPEN, *a.* (Unclosed) विवृतः -ता -तं, अनावृतः -ता -तं, अपावृतः -ता -तं, असंवृतः -ता -तं, उद्घाटितः -ता -तं, व्यात्तः -त्ता -त्तं, अपरावृतः &c.—(As the mouth) व्यात्तः -त्ता -त्तं, विवृतः &c.—(As the eyes) उन्मीलितः -ता -तं, उन्मिषितः -ता -तं, विवृतः &c.—(As a book) मुक्तः -क्ता -क्तं.—(Expanded) विततः -ता -तं, विस्तृतः -ता -तं, विस्तीर्णः -र्णा -र्णं, विकाशितः -ता -तं, विजृम्भितः -ता -तं, उज्जृम्भितः -ता -तं, उज्जृम्भः -म्भा -म्भं, जृम्भितः -ता -तं, जृम्भः -म्भा -म्भं, अपेतः -ता -तं.—(Unsealed, as a letter, &c.) उन्मुद्रः -द्रा -द्रं, विमुद्रः -द्रा -द्रं, उन्मुद्रीकृतः -ता -तं.—(Not stopped, without obstruction) अनर्गलः -ला -लं, निरर्गलः &c., असम्बाधः -धा -धं, अरुद्धः -द्धा -द्धं, अपिहितः -ता -तं, प्रतिबन्धरहितः -ता -तं, अव्यवधानः -ना -नं.—(Free, clear, unimpeded) मुक्तः -क्ता -क्तं, विमुक्तः &c., मोचितः -ता -तं, शुद्धः -द्धा -द्धं, विशुद्धः &c., अबद्धः -द्धा -द्धं, निर्यन्त्रणः -णा -णं, उच्छृङ्खलः -ला -लं, विशृङ्खलः -ला -लं, निर्विघ्नः -घ्ना -घ्नं, निरवरोधः -धा -धं.—(Plain, evident) व्यक्तः -क्ता -क्तं, प्रव्यक्तः &c., अभिव्यक्तः &c., स्पष्टः -ष्टा -ष्टं, विस्पष्टः &c.—(Public) प्रकाशः -शा -शं, सुप्रकाशः &c., प्रकटः -टा -टं.—(Not close, roomy) विरलः -ला -लं.—(Not covered with trees, as a country) निर्वनः -ना -नं, निर्वृक्षः -क्षा -क्षं, वृक्षशून्यः -न्या -न्यं.—(Ingenuous, candid) निष्कपटः -टा -टं, निर्व्याजः -जा -जं, निर्व्यलीकः -का -कं, विमलः -ला -लं, विमलात्मा -त्मा -त्म (न्), सरलः -ला -लं, शुद्धमतिः -तिः -ति, सरलमतिः &c., मायाहीनः -ना -नं, अवक्रः -क्रा -क्रं, अगूढभावः -वा -वं, उदारः -रा -रं; 'having an open countenance,' उदारलक्षणः -णा -णं.—(Unsheltered) अनाश्रयः -या -यं, निराश्रयः &c.—(Not hidden) अगूढः -ढा -ढं, अगुप्तः -प्ता -प्तं; 'to lay open,' प्रकाश् (c. 10. -काशयति -यितुं), प्रकाशीकृ. *See To* OPEN; 'an open space,' विविक्तता; 'open to the weather,' अभ्रावकाशिकः -की -कं; 'open to all comers,' मुक्तद्वारः -रा -रं; 'open at one end,' एकमुखः -खा -खं; 'an open vowel,' उदात्तः; 'open day,' प्रकाशं; 'having gone out into the open air,' प्रकाशं निर्गत्य; 'open state of the organs of speech,' विवारः, विवृतता -त्वं.

OPENED, *p. p.* (Unclosed) उद्घाटितः -ता -तं, उद्घट्टितः -ता -तं, अपावृतः -ता -तं. *See* OPEN. (Unbarred) निरर्गलीकृतः -ता -तं.—(Unsealed) उन्मुद्रीकृतः -ता -तं, विमुद्रीकृतः &c.—(Uncovered) अनावृतः -ता -तं, अनाच्छादितः -ता -तं, अपवृतः -ता -तं.—(Split) स्फुटितः -ता -तं, दलितः -ता -तं, विदलितः &c., भिन्नः -न्ना -न्नं.—(As flowers) विकसितः -ता -तं, फुल्लः -ल्ला -ल्लं, स्फुटः -टा -टं, विमुद्रः -द्रा -द्रं.—(Made plain) व्यक्तीकृतः -ता -तं, प्रकाशितः -ता -तं, स्पष्टीकृतः &c., व्याख्यातः &c.—(Cleared) शोधितः -ता -तं.

OPENER, *s.* उद्घाटकः, उद्घाटनकृत्, विवरणकृत्, विकाशकः.

OPEN-EYED, *a.* विवृताक्षः -क्षी -क्षं, उत्फुल्लनयनः -ना -नं, सचेतनः &c.

OPEN-HANDED, *a.* मुक्तहस्तः -स्ता -स्तं, उदारहस्तः &c., उदारः -रा -रं.

OPEN-HEARTED, *a.* सरलमतिः -तिः -ति, शुद्धमतिः &c., अगूढभावः -वा -वं.

OPEN-HEARTEDNESS, *s.* सरलमतित्वं, शुद्धमतित्वं, उदारता, मायाहीनता.

OPENING, *s.* (Act of opening) उद्घाटनं, उद्घट्टनं, व्यादानं, विवृतिः *f.*, विवरणं.—(Aperture) छिद्रं, रन्ध्रं, द्वारं, मुखं.—(Beginning, commencement) आरम्भः, प्रारम्भः, उपक्रमः, उपोद्घातः.

OPENING, *a.* or *part.* (Commencing, first in order) आरम्भकः -का -कं, प्रारम्भकः &c., प्रथमः -मा -मं, आद्यः -द्या -द्यं.—(Expanding, as a flower) विकाशी -शिनी -शि (न्), विकासी &c., विकशन् -शन्ती -शत् (त्), विकसन् &c., प्रविकशन् &c., स्फुटन् &c.

OPENLY, *adv.* प्रकाशं, प्रकटं, प्राकट्येन, व्यक्तं, सुव्यक्तं, स्फुटं.

OPEN-MOUTHED, *a.* विवृतास्यः -स्या -स्यं, व्यात्तवक्त्रः -क्त्रा -क्त्रं, मुक्तकण्ठः -ण्ठा -ण्ठं, प्रमुक्तकण्ठः &c., गुहामुखः -खी -खं.

OPENNESS, *s.* (Freedom from covering or obstruction) विवृतत्वं, विवृतिः *f.*, अनावृतत्वं, अनावृतिः *f.*, व्यात्तता, मुक्तता -त्वं, अरुद्धता, निर्विघ्नता.—(Plainness, clearness) व्यक्तत्वं -ता, प्रव्यक्तता, स्पष्टता, शुद्धता, शुद्धिः *f.*, वैमल्यं, निर्म्मलता.—(Freedom from disguise) निर्व्याजता, अव्याजः, व्याजहीनता, कपटहीनता, निष्कपटत्वं, निष्कापट्यं.—(Frankness) सारल्यं, सरलता, अकापट्यं, अमाया, मायाहीनता, अवक्रता, दाक्षिण्यं, निर्व्यलीकता, भावागूढता, भावशुद्धता, शुद्धमतित्वं, अजिह्मता, उदारता.—(Publicity) प्रकाशता, प्रकाशः, प्राकट्यं, प्रसिद्धिः *f.*, प्रसिद्धता, अगूढता, अगुप्तता.—(Roominess, freedom from closeness) विरलता, वैरल्यं.—(Want of shelter) निराश्रयता, अनाश्रयता, आश्रयहीनत्वं, अभावकाशिकत्वं.—(Of a country) निर्वेनत्वं.

OPERA, *s.* सङ्गीतं, तौर्य्यत्रिकं, नाट्यं, सङ्गीतविशिष्टो नाटकः.

To OPERATE, *v. n.* (Act, exert action) कृ, चेष्ट् (c. 1. चेष्टते -ष्टितुं), विचेष्ट्, कर्म्म कृ, चेष्टां कृ, प्रवृत् (c. 10. -वर्त्तयति -यितुं), कर्त्तृकः -का -कं भू.—(Effect, produce effect) उत्पद् (c. 10. -पादयति -यितुं), समुत्पद्, उपपद्, सम्पद्, फलम् उत्पद्, जन् (c. 10. जनयति -यितुं), सञ्जन्, साध् (c. 10. साधयति -यितुं), कार्य्यं साध्, प्रबलीभू, प्रभू.—(In surgery) शस्त्रक्रियां कृ, शस्त्रोपायं कृ, शस्त्रोपचारं कृ.

OPERATION, *s.* (Agency) कर्त्तृत्वं, कर्त्तृकत्वं, कारणत्वं, कारत्वं, हेतुता, प्रवर्त्तकत्वं, प्रयोजकत्वं.—(Action) क्रिया, कृतिः *f.*, कर्म्म *n.* (न्), चेष्टा, व्यापारः, विधानं, प्रवृत्तिः *f.*, प्रवर्त्तनं.—(Act, deed) कर्म्म *n.*, कार्य्यं, कृत्यं, चेष्टितं, विचेष्टितं; 'mental operation,' मनोव्यापारः; 'arithmetical,' परिकर्म्म *n.*, कर्म्म *n.*; 'secret in operation,' निगूढकार्य्यः -र्य्या -र्य्यं; 'speedy in operation,' आशुकारी -रिणी -रि (न्); 'slow,' मन्दकारी &c.—(In surgery) शस्त्रोपचारः, शस्त्रोपचारः, शस्त्रक्रिया, शस्त्रकृत्यं, शस्त्रोपायः, शस्त्रकर्म्म *n.*, उपचारः.

OPERATIVE, *a.* (Exerting agency) कर्म्मकारी -रिणी -रि (न्), कर्म्मकारः -रा -रं, क्रियाकारी &c., कारकः -का -कं, कर्त्तृकः -का -कं, कारयिकः -की -कं, हेतुकः -का -कं, प्रवर्त्तकः -का -कं, प्रयोजकः -का -कं.—(Producing effect, efficacious) कार्य्यसाधकः -का -कं, कार्य्यसम्पादकः &c., फलोत्पादकः &c., सिद्धिकरः -री -रं, गुणकारी &c., गुणावहः -हा -हं, प्रबलः -ला -लं, प्रभविष्णुः -ष्णुः -ष्णु.

OPERATIVE, *s.* कर्म्मकारः, शिल्पकारः, कारुकः, कारुः *m.*, शिल्पकर्म्मकारी *m.*

OPERATOR, *s.* कर्त्ता *m.* (र्त्तृ), कारकः, कर्त्तृकः, कार्य्यकर्त्ता *m.*, प्रवर्त्तकः.—(In surgery) शस्त्रोपचारकृत् *m.*, उपचारकारी *m.* (न्), उपचारकर्त्ता *m.*

OPEROSE, *a.* श्रमसाध्यः -ध्या -ध्यं, कष्टसाध्यः &c., श्रमी -मिणी &c.

OPHIOLOGY, *s.* सर्पविद्या, भुजङ्गविद्या, सर्पादिविषयका विद्या.

OPHIOMANCY, *s.* सर्पादिलक्षणात् भविष्यत्सूचना or भविष्यदनुमानं.

OPHIOPHAGOUS, *a.* सर्पभक्षकः -का -कं, सर्पभोजी -जिनी -जि (न्).

OPHTHALMIA, OPHTHALMY, *s.* अभिमन्थः, अधिमन्थः, रक्ताधिमन्थः, रक्ताभिमन्थः, अर्बुदः -दं, पिञ्जटः, चक्षूरोगः, नेत्ररोगः, नेत्रामयः, अक्षिरोगः, लोचनामयः.

OPHTHALMIC, *a.* चाक्षुषः -षी -षं, नेत्रसम्बन्धी -न्धिनी &c., नेत्रविषयः &c.

OPIATE, *s.* स्वप्नकारकम् or निद्राकारकम् औषधं, उपशमनं.

OPIATE, *a.* स्वप्नकृत् *m. f. n.*, निद्राकारी -रिणी -रि (न्), निद्राजनकः -का -कं, स्वापनः -ना -नं, उपशमनकारी &c., उपशायी &c., उपशमकृत्.

To OPINE, *v. n.* मन् (c. 4. मन्यते, मन्तुं), तर्क् (c. 10. तर्कयति -यितुं). *See To* THINK.

OPINIATED, OPINIATIVE, *a.* स्वमताभिमानी -निनी -नि (न्), मताभिमानी &c., स्वमताग्रही &c., मताग्रही &c., स्वमतवादी &c., मतवादी &c., दुराग्रही &c.

OPINIATIVENESS, *s.* स्वमताभिमानं -निता, स्वमताग्रहः, मताभिमानं, दुराग्रहः, स्वमतवाद्यं.

OPINION, *s.* मतं, मतिः *f.*, बुद्धिः *f.*, सम्मतं, तर्कः, विचारः, अनुमानं, बोधः, भासः, छन्दः; 'a different opinion,' विकल्पः, परमतं; 'difference of opinion,' मतिभेदः, मतभेदः, विप्रतिपत्तिः *f.*; 'opposed in opinion,' विप्रतिपन्नः -न्ना -न्नं; 'public opinion,' लोकमतं, जनमतं; 'regard for it,' लोकलज्जा, जनलज्जा; 'atheistical opinion,' नास्तिकमतं; 'legal opinion,' सूत्रं.—(Estimation) मानं, सम्मानं.

OPINIONATED, OPINIONATIVE. *See* OPINIATED, &c.

OPIUM, *s.* अफेनं, अहिफेनं, खसखसरसः, उपविषं.

OPPIDAN, *a.* नागरिकः -की -कं, नागरः -री -रं, पौरः -री -रं.

OPPILATED, *p. p.* सम्बाधः -धा -धं, सङ्कीर्णः -र्णा -र्णं, सङ्कुलः -ला -लं.

OPPONENT, *a.* विरोधी -धिनी -धि (न्), प्रतिरोधी &c., विरुद्धः -द्धा -द्धं, वैरी -रिणी &c., प्रतियोगी &c., प्रतिकूलः -ला -लं, विपक्षः -क्षा -क्षं, प्रतिपक्षः &c., विपरीतः -ता -तं, विमुखः -खा -खं, पराङ्मुखः &c., विमतः -ता -तं, प्रतीपकः &c.

OPPONENT, *s.* प्रतिरोधी *m.* (न्), विरोधी *m.*, वैरी *m.*, शत्रुः *m.*, अरिः *m.*, प्रतियोगी *m.*, प्रतिरोद्धा *m.* (द्धृ), प्रतिरोधकः, प्रतिबन्धकः, प्रतियोद्धा *m.* (द्धृ), प्रतिपक्षः, अभियाती *m.* (न्), विजिगीषुः *m.*—(In controversy) विवादी *m.* (न्), पूर्व्ववादी *m.*, अग्रवादी *m.*, प्रतिवादी *m.*, उत्तरवादी *m.*, पूर्व्वपक्षी *m.*, प्रतिपक्षी *m.*, वादी *m.*

OPPORTUNE, *a.* समयोपयुक्तः -क्ता -क्तं, समयोचितः -ता -तं, समयानुकूलः -ला -लं, सामयिकः -की -कं, कालिकः &c., कालसदृशः -शी -शं, कालयोग्यः -ग्या -ग्यं, प्रस्तावसदृशः &c., प्रास्ताविकः -की -कं, प्राप्तावसरः -रा -रं, प्राप्तकालः -ला -लं, प्राप्तसमयः -या -यं, प्रसङ्गोपयुक्तः &c., काकतालीयः -या -यं.

OPPORTUNELY, *adv.* यथावसरं, काले, स्थाने, समयानुसारेण, समयोपयुक्तं, प्रसङ्गानुसारात्, प्रस्तावसदृशं, यथावकाशं, यथासमयं, यथाप्रसङ्गं, कालयोग्यं, यथायोग्यं, वेलायां.

OPPORTUNENESS, *s.* समयोपयुक्तता, कालयोग्यता, समयौचित्यं, प्रसङ्गयोग्यता, प्रसङ्गानुकूल्यं, कालिकत्वं.

OPPORTUNITY, *s.* अवसरः, प्रसङ्गः, समयः, प्रस्तावः, अवकाशः, कालः, कार्य्यकालः, कालयोगः, सन्धिः *m.*, कालसन्धिः *m.*, वेला, योगः, सुयोगः, स्थानं, वारः, प्रक्रमः; 'according to opportunity,' यथावसरं, यथाप्रसङ्गं, यथावकाशं; 'to lose one's opportunity,' कालं हृ (c. 1. हरति, हर्त्तुं) or हा (c. 3. जहाति, हातुं); 'to await it,' अवसरं प्रतिपाल् (c. 10. -पालयति -यितुं); 'one who has found an opportunity,' लब्धावकाशः -शा -शं.—(Means) साधनं, उपायः, सम्पादनं.

To OPPOSE, *v. a.* and *n.* (Act against, resist) प्रतिकृ, विप्रतिकृ, विप्रकृ, प्रतिरुध् (c. 7. -रुणद्धि -रोद्धुं), विरुध्, संरुध्, विरुद्धीभू, प्रतिकूल (nom. प्रतिकूलयति -यितुं), प्रतिकूलीभू, पर्य्यवस्था (c. 1. -तिष्ठति -स्थातुं),

प्रतिसमास् (c. 2. -आस्ते -आसितुं), प्रतीप (nom. प्रतीपायते), प्रतिहन् (c. 2. -हन्ति -न्तुं), विपरीतः -ता -तं भू or अस्.—(Put in opposition, set one against the other) विरुद्धं -द्धां कृ, विरुद्धीकृ, परस्परं विरुध्, प्रतिकूलीकृ, विरोधिनं -नीं कृ.—(Hinder) निवृ (c. 10. -वारयति -यितुं), विघ्न (nom. विघ्नयति -यितुं), बाध् (c. 1. बाधते -धितुं), प्रतिबन्ध् (c. 9. -बध्नाति -बन्धुं), विहन्, प्रतिहन्, व्याहन्, रुध्.—(Check) निग्रह् (c. 9. -गृह्णाति -ग्रहीतुं).

OPPOSED, *p. p.* विरुद्धः -द्धा -द्धं, प्रतिरुद्धः &c., पर्य्यवस्थितः -ता -तं, विपरीतः -ता -तं, प्रतिकूलः -ला -लं, प्रातिकूलिकः -की -कं, विरोधी -धिनी -धि (न्), विप्रतिकृतः -ता -तं, विप्रकृतः &c., विप्रतिपन्नः -न्ना -न्नं, प्रतियातः -ता -तं.—(Hindered, checked) वारितः -ता -तं, निवारितः -ता -तं, बाधितः -ता -तं, विहतः &c., प्रतिहतः &c., रुद्धः &c., विघ्नितः &c.; when 'opposed' signifies 'the opposite of,' इतर may be used; as, 'opposed to movable,' जङ्गमेतरः -रा -रं.

OPPOSER, *s.* विरोधी *m.* (न्), प्रतिरोधी *m.*, पर्यवस्थाता *m.* (तृ), प्रतियोगी *m.* (न्), विरोधकः, प्रातिकूलिकः, प्रतिहन्तकः. *See* OPPONENT.

OPPOSITE, *a.* (Situated in front, facing) अभिमुखः -खा -खी -खं, अभिमुखगतः -ता -तं, अभिमुखस्थः -स्था -स्थं, सम्मुखः -खा -खं, सम्मुखस्थः -स्था -स्थं, अभिसम्मुखः -खा -खं, सम्मुखीनः -ना -नं, प्रतिमुखः -खा -खं.—(Adverse, contrary) विपरीतः -ता -तं, प्रतिकूलः -ला -लं, विरुद्धः -द्धा -द्धं, विरोधी -धिनी -धि (न्), प्रतिरोधी &c., विपर्य्यस्तः -स्ता -स्तं, अपसव्यः -व्या -व्यं, प्रसव्यः &c., अपसव्यकः &c., प्रतिपक्षः -क्षा -क्षं, विपक्षः &c, अवकटः -टा -टं.—(Further, on the other side) परः -रा -रं, अपरः -रा -रं; 'the opposite bank,' पारं, परतीरं, तीरान्तरं.—(Reverse of) व्यत्यस्तः -स्ता -स्तं, इतर in comp.; as, 'the opposite of movable,' जङ्गमेतरः -रा -रं; 'of white,' सितेतरः &c.; 'of left,' वामेतरः &c.; 'of innate,' सहजेतरः &c.—(Opposite side of the argument) उत्तरपक्षः, परपक्षः, प्रतिपक्षः.

OPPOSITE, *s.* विपर्य्ययः, विपर्य्यायः, व्यत्ययः, व्यत्यासः, विपर्य्यासः, विपरीतं.

OPPOSITELY, *adv.* (In front) अभिमुखं, सम्मुखं, प्रतिमुखं, सम्मुखीनं.—(Adversely) विपरीतं, वैपरीत्येन, प्रतिकूलं, विरुद्धं, विरोधेन, विपर्य्ययेण, प्रातिकूल्येन.

OPPOSITION, *s.* विरोधः -धनं, प्रतिरोधः -धनं, प्रतिकारः, विप्रतिकारः, प्रतिक्रिया, प्रत्यवस्थानं, पर्य्यवस्था -स्थानं, प्रतियोगः -गिता, विप्रतिपत्तिः *f.*, प्रतिबन्धकता, प्रतिबन्धिता, प्रतियत्नः.—(State of being opposed) विरुद्धता, विपरीतता, वैपरीत्यं, प्रतिकूलता, प्रतिपक्षता, प्रातिकूल्यं.—(Contrariety) विपर्य्ययः, विपर्य्यायः, पर्य्ययः, विपर्य्यासः, वैपरीत्यं, व्यत्ययः, व्यत्यासः, निकारः.—(Impediment) व्याघातः, विघ्नः, बाधः -धा, प्रतिबन्धः, अवरोधः, उपरोधः, निरोधः, रोधः.—(Collective body of opposers) विरोधिजनसमूहः, प्रतियोगिपक्षः, विरोधकपक्षः.—(Hostile feeling) विरुद्धभावः, द्वेषभावः; 'opposition of interests,' विप्रतिपत्तिः *f.*; 'in opposition to what was before said,' पूर्व्वोक्तप्रतिपक्षे.

To OPPRESS, *v. a.* पीड् (c. 10. पीडयति -यितुं), अभिपीड्, उपपीड्, निपीड्, उपनिपीड्, बाध् (c. 1. बाधते -धितुं), प्रबाध्, परिबाध्, अभिबाध्, द्रुह् (c. 4. द्रुह्यति, द्रोहितुं, द्रोग्धुं), अभिद्रुह्, कृष् (c. 10. कर्षयति -यितुं), अभिद्रोहं कृ, अर्द् (c. 10. अर्दयति -यितुं), विडम्ब् (c. 10. -डम्बयति -यितुं), अपकृ, अपकारं कृ, मर्दनं कृ, उपमर्दनं कृ, प्रधृष् (c. 10. -धर्षयति -यितुं), उपद्रवं कृ, उपप्लवं कृ, नैष्ठुर्य्यं कृ, क्रौर्य्यं कृ, क्रूरवत् कृ, अभिभू, बलात्कारं कृ.

OPPRESSED, *p. p.* पीडितः -ता -तं, बाधितः -ता -तं, अतिदुःखः -खा -खं, अभिद्रुह्यमाणः -णा -णं, उपद्रुतः -ता -तं, विडम्बितः -ता -तं, अभिभूतः -ता -तं, अपकृतः -ता -तं, आकुलितः -ता -तं.

OPPRESSION, *s.* (The act) पीडनं, प्रजापीडनं, अभिद्रोहः, द्रोहः -हणं, उपद्रवः, उपद्रवकरणं, उपमर्दः -र्दनं, विमर्दः -र्दनं, बाधः -धनं, कर्षणं, परिप्लवः, उपप्लवः, उपप्लवकरणं, अपकारः, अपकर्म्म *n.* (न्), अपक्रिया, बलात्कारः, निष्ठुरता, नैष्ठुर्य्यं, क्रूरता, क्रौर्य्यं, दौरात्म्यं, उत्पातः, विडम्बनं -ना, हठः, अन्यायकरणं.—(State) पीडा, बाधा, पीडितत्वं.—(Weight) भारः.

OPPRESSIVE, *a.* (Cruelly severe, or tyrannical) बाधकः -का -कं, पीडाकरः -रा -रं, पीडकः -का -कं, उपद्रवकारी -रिणी -रि (न्), उपद्रवी &c., उपमर्दकः -का -कं, अपकारकः &c., सबाधः -धा -धं, निष्ठुरः -रा -रं, क्रूरः -रा -रं, निर्दयः -या -यं, दुर्वृत्तः -त्ता -त्तं, क्लेशदायकः -का -कं, क्लेशदः -दा -दं, अन्यायकारी &c.—(Heavy) भारी -रिणी &c.

OPPRESSIVENESS, *s.* बाधकत्वं -ता, सबाधता, क्लेशकता, नैष्ठुर्य्यं, क्रौर्य्यं.

OPPRESSOR, *s.* प्रजापीडकः, उपद्रवकर्त्ता *m.* (र्तृ), उपद्रवी *m.* (न्), क्रूरचरितः, निष्ठुरः, निर्दयः, अत्याचारः, दुरात्मा *m.* (न्), दुर्जनः, दुर्वृत्तः, दस्युः *m.*

OPPROBRIOUS, *a.* निन्दकः -का -कं, निन्दार्थकः &c., निन्दारूपः -पा -पं, निन्दात्मकः &c., गर्हात्मकः &c., गर्हार्थकः &c., अपवादकः &c., मुखरः -रा -रं, दुर्मुखः -खा -खं, परुषः -षा -षं, गर्ह्यः -र्ह्या -र्ह्यं.

OPPROBRIOUSLY, *adv.* निन्दापूर्व्वं, सापवादं, सतिरस्कारं, गर्हणीयं.

OPPROBRIOUSNESS, *s.* निन्दकत्वं, अपवादकता, अभिवादः, पौरुष्यं, मौखर्य्यं.

OPPROBRIUM, *s.* निन्दा, अपवादः, घृणा, गर्हा -र्हणं, कुत्सा, तिरस्कारः, अवज्ञा -ज्ञानं, परिभवः, अपमानं, वाच्यता, वचनीयता, धिक्क्रिया, कुख्यातिः *f.*

To OPPUGN, *v. a.* प्रतिकृ, विप्रतिकृ, प्रतिरुध्, विरुध् &c. *See To* OPPOSE.

OPPUGNANCY, *s.* विरोधः, प्रतिरोधः, प्रातिकूल्यं, वैपरीत्यं, प्रतियोगिता.

OPPUGNED, OPPUGNER. *See* OPPOSED, OPPOSER, OPPONENT.

OPTATIVE, *a.* इच्छासूचकः -का -कं, इच्छाबोधकः &c., अभिलाषबोधकः &c., अभिलाषज्ञापकः &c. The grammatical symbol is सन्नन्तः.

OPTIC, OPTICAL, *a.* (Pertaining to vision) चाक्षुषः -षी -षं, दृष्टिविषयकः -का -कं, दृष्टिसम्बन्धी -न्धिनी &c.—(Pertaining to optics) दृक्शास्त्रसम्बन्धी &c., दृक्शास्त्रविषयकः &c.

OPTIC, *s.* (Organ of sight) दृगिन्द्रियं, चक्षुरिन्द्रियं, दर्शनसाधनं.

OPTICIAN, *s.* (Maker of optic instruments) चाक्षुषयन्त्रकारकः -कर्त्ता *m.* (र्तृ), दृष्टिसाधकयन्त्रकारः, दृष्टियन्त्रविक्रेता *m.* (तृ), चाक्षुषयन्त्रविक्रयी *m.*—(Skilled in optics) दृक्शास्त्रज्ञः, चाक्षुषज्ञानी *m.* (न्).

OPTICS, *s. pl.* दृग्विद्या, चाक्षुषविद्या, दृष्टिविद्या, दृक्शास्त्रं, दृष्टिविषया विद्या, चाक्षुषं ज्ञानं, दर्शनानुशासनं.

OPTIMACY, *s.* कुलीनवर्गः, कुलीनलोकः, कौलीन्यं, कुलीनता -त्वं.

OPTIMISM, *s.* उत्तमता -त्वं, अत्युत्तमता -त्वं, सत्तमता -त्वं.

OPTION, *s.* (Power of choosing) विकल्पः -ल्पकः, अनुकल्पः, कल्पः, विभाषा, इच्छा, वरणाधिकारः.—(Wish) इच्छा, अभिलाषः, कामः, मनस्कामः, रुचिः *f.*, अभिरुचिः, ईप्सितं, अभीप्सितं.

OPTIONAL, *a.* वैकल्पिकः -की -कं, विकल्पकः &c., सविकल्पकः -का -कं, आनुकल्पिकः -की -कं, विकल्पितः -ता -तं, सविकल्पः -ल्पा -ल्पं, ऐच्छिकः -की -कं, काम्यः -म्या -म्यं, अभिकामिकः &c., यथाकामः -मा -मं, विभाषितः -ता -तं; 'an optional matter,' विकल्पविषयः, विभाषाविषयः.

OPTIONALLY, *adv.* सविकल्पं -ल्पकं, सानुकल्पं, विकल्पेन, विकल्पपूर्व्वं.

OPULENCE, *s.* धनाढ्यता, धनबाहुल्यं, धनसम्पत्तिः *f.*, सम्पत्तिः *f.*, धनैश्वर्य्यं, ऐश्वर्य्यं, महाधनत्वं, धनसमृद्धिः *f.*, लक्ष्मीः *f.*, श्रीः *f.*, लक्ष्मीवत्त्वं.

OPULENT, *a.* श्रीमान् -मती -मत् (त्), धनाढ्यः -ढ्या -ढ्यं, महाधनः -ना -नं, बहुधनः -ना -नं, अतिधनी -निनी -नि (न्), धनी &c., अतिधनवान् &c., धनवान् &c., बहुवित्तवान् &c., बहुद्रव्यवान् &c., वसुमान् &c., अर्थवान् &c., सम्पत्तिमान् &c., लक्ष्मीवान् &c., समृद्धः -द्धा -द्धं, सम्पन्नः -न्ना -न्नं, धनेश्वरः, लक्ष्मीशः, सुराः *m. f.* (रै), आढ्यः &c., वर्धिष्णुः -ष्णुः -ष्णु, इभ्यः -भ्या -भ्यं.

OPULENTLY, *adv.* धनबाहुल्येन, धनाढ्यवत्, महाधनवत्, सम्पत्तिपूर्व्वं.

OR, *conj.* वा placed after a word, वापि, अथवा, यद्वा; 'friend or foe,' मित्रं वा शत्रुर् वा.—(Or else) अथवा, किंवा, अन्यथा, इतरथा, आहोस्वित्.

ORACLE, *s.* (Answer of a god to an inquiry made) शकुनं -नः, प्रश्नः, प्रसादः; 'through a voice,' देववाणी, आकाशवाणी.—(The deity who gives the answer) प्रश्नदेवता, प्रसाददेवता, प्रश्नदेवः, शकुनदेवः.—(The place where the answer is given) प्रश्नस्थानं, शकुनस्थानं, प्रसादस्थानं.—(A person whose opinion is of great authority) प्रमाणं, आप्तः.—(A wise or authoritative sentence) आप्तवचनं, आप्तोक्तिः *f.*

ORACULAR, ORACULOUS, *a.* शाकुनिकः -की -कं, शाकुनः -नी -नं, शकुनदः -दा -दं.—(Like an oracle) देववाणीतुल्यः -ल्या -ल्यं, देववाणीसदृशः -शी -शं.—(Authoritative) प्रामाणिकः -की -कं, आप्तः -प्ता -प्तं.—(Obscure) गूढार्थः -र्था -र्थं.

ORACULARLY, *adv.* देववाणीपूर्व्वं, देववाणीसादृश्येन, सशकुनं.

ORAL, *a.* (Spoken by the mouth, not written) मुखतीयः -या -यं, उक्तः -क्ता -क्तं, अलिखितः -ता -तं, मुखकथितः -ता -तं, श्रुतः -ता -तं.

ORALLY, *adv.* मुखतस्, मुखात् -खेन, अलिखितं, मुखद्वारा.

ORANGE, *s.* (Tree) नारङ्गः, नागरङ्गः, नार्य्यङ्गः, सुरङ्गः, त्वग्गन्धः, दन्तशठः, ऐरावतः, किर्म्मीरः, योलकी *m.* (न्), लतातरुः *m.*, नादेयः, भूमिजम्बुका, राजफणिज्झकः.—(The fruit) नारङ्गफलं, नागरङ्गफलं, पिच्छिलः.

ORANGE-COLORED, *a.* नारङ्गवर्णः -र्णा -र्णं, कौसुम्भः -म्भी -म्भं, पिच्छिलवर्णः &c.

ORANGE-PEEL, *s.* पिच्छिलत्वक् *m.* (च्), नारङ्गफलत्वक् *m.* (च्).

ORANGERY, *s.* नारङ्गवृक्षवाटिका, नारङ्गतरुवाटिका.

ORATION, *s.* वाक्प्रबन्धः, वाक्यप्रबन्धः, वाक्यं, प्रवचनं, सालङ्कारवाक्यं, सालङ्कारभाषणं, सोपपत्तिकवाक्यं, अलङ्कारमयं वाक्यं.

ORATOR, *s.* (Public declaimer) सभावक्ता *m.* (क्तृ), सभाप्रवक्ता *m.*, सभावादी *m.* (न्), सभापण्डितः, वक्ता *m.*, प्रवक्ता *m.*, वादी *m.*, प्रवचनकर्त्ता *m.*—(Eloquent speaker) वाक्पटुः *m.*, प्रवचनपटुः *m.*, सुवक्ता *m.*, सद्वक्ता *m.*, वागीशः, वागीश्वरः, वाक्पण्डितः, वाग्विद् *m.*, वाग्विदग्धः, सभापण्डितः, वाग्विशारदः, वाक्यद्वारेण विस्मयजनकः.

ORATORICAL, *a.* वागलङ्कारमयः -यी -यं, वाङ्मयः -यी -यं, वाक्चातुर्य्यमयः &c., सालङ्कारवाक्यमयः &c., सभावक्तृत्वसम्बन्धी &c., सभापाण्डित्यसम्बन्धी &c., सभापाण्डित्यविषयः -या -यं, प्रवचनसम्बन्धी &c.

ORATORIO, *s.* तालबद्धं धर्म्मकीर्त्तनं, धर्म्मकीर्त्तनविषया सुस्वररचना or सुस्वरसङ्गः.

ORATORY, *s.* (Art of public speaking) सभावक्तृत्वं, सभाप्रवचनविद्या, सभाप्रवचनं, सभाप्रवचनपाण्डित्यं, सभापाण्डित्यं.—(Art of speaking eloquently) वाक्पटुता, प्रवचनपटुता, सुवक्तृत्वं, सद्वक्तृता, वक्तृत्वशक्तिः *f.*, वाक्शक्तिः *f.*, वाक्चातुर्य्यं, शब्दचातुर्य्यं, वाचाशक्तिः *f.*, वाचोयुक्तिः *f.*, शब्दपाण्डित्यं, सुप्रलापः.—(Place for prayer) प्रार्थनागारं, प्रार्थनस्थानं.

ORB, *s.* मण्डलं, गोलः -लं, गोलकः, वर्त्तुलं, विम्बः -म्बं, बिम्बकं, परिमण्डलं, चक्रं, चक्रवालं, वृत्तं, वलयः -यं; 'circular array,' चक्रव्यूहः.

ORBATE, *a.* विहीनः -ना -नं, हीनः -ना -नं, मातृपितृहीनः &c.

ORBED, ORBICULAR, ORBICULATE, *a.* मण्डलाकारः -रा -रं, मण्डलाकृतिः -तिः -ति, गोलाकारः &c., मण्डली -लिनी -लि (न्), बिम्बी &c., वर्त्तुलः -ला -लं, वर्त्तुलाकारः &c., चक्राकारः &c., चाक्रिकः -की -कं, चक्री &c., चाक्रेयः -यी -यं.

ORBICULARLY, *adv.* मण्डलाकारेण, गोलाकारेण, वर्त्तुलरूपेण, चक्रवत्.

ORBICULARNESS, *s.* मण्डलाकारता, गोलाकारता, मण्डलता, वर्त्तुलता.

ORBIT, *s.* (Of a planet) कक्षा -क्षः, ग्रहपथः, ग्रहमार्गः, मण्डलं; 'apex of an orbit,' उच्चः; 'apsis,' मन्दोच्चः.

ORCHARD, *s.* वृक्षवाटिका, फलवृक्षवाटी, तरुवाटिका, वाटिका, वाटः -टी -टं, उपवनं, वृक्षोद्यानं, फलवृक्षोद्यानं.

ORCHESTRA, *s.* (Place for musicians) वादित्रस्थानं, वाद्यभाण्डस्थानं, वादित्रस्थलं, भाण्डवादकस्थानं.—(Body of musicians) भाण्डवादकगणः, वादित्रसमुदायः, वाद्यभाण्डं, वादकसमूहः.

ORCHESTRAL, *a.* वाद्यभाण्डसम्बन्धी &c., वादकगणसम्बन्धी &c.

To ORDAIN, *v. a.* (Institute) विधा (c. 3. -दधाति -धातुं), अभिधा, क्लृप् (c. 10. कल्पयति -यितुं), प्रक्लृप्, परिक्लृप्, स्था in caus. (स्थापयति -यितुं), प्रतिष्ठा, संस्था, व्यवस्था, प्रचुद् (c. 10. -चोदयति -यितुं), आदिश् (c. 6. -दिशति -देष्टुं), सन्दिश्, निर्दिश्.—(Appoint) नियुज् (c. 7. -युनक्ति -युंक्ते -योक्तुं, c. 10. -योजयति -यितुं), अधिकृ, प्रकृ, समादिश्, व्यादिश्.—(To any office) अधिकारे or पदे नियुज् or अभिषिच् (c. 6. -षिञ्चति -षेक्तुं), नियोजनं कृ, अधिकृतं -तां कृ.—(Invest with sacerdotal functions) धर्म्माधिकारे or धर्म्मपदे नियुज्, धर्म्माधिकारयुक्तं कृ, धर्म्मपदनियुक्तं कृ, दीक्ष् (c. 1. दीक्षते -क्षितुं), दीक्षां कृ, दीक्षाकर्म्मपूर्व्वं धर्म्माधिकारं प्रविश् (c. 10. -वेशयति -यितुं), धर्म्मपददीक्षितं कृ.

ORDAINED, *p. p.* (Instituted, established) विहितः -ता -तं, कल्पितः -ता -तं, प्रकल्पितः &c., स्थापितः &c., प्रतिष्ठापितः, व्यवस्थापितः &c., व्यवस्थितः &c., चोदितः &c., प्रचोदितः &c., निर्दिष्टः -ष्टा -ष्टं, नियमितः &c., नियतः &c.—(Appointed) नियुक्तः -क्ता -क्तं, नियोजितः -ता -तं, अधिकृतः -ता -तं, योजितः -ता -तं.—(To any office) अधिकारे or पदे नियुक्तः &c., अधिकारयुक्तः &c., अभिषिक्तः &c.—(To sacerdotal functions) धर्म्माधिकारे नियुक्तः &c., धर्म्मपदनियुक्तः, धर्म्माधिकारयुक्तः, धर्म्मपददीक्षितः, दीक्षितः.

ORDAINER, *s.* प्रकल्पकः, विधाता *m.* (तृ), विधायी *m.* (न्), विधायकः, स्थापकः, प्रचोदकः, नियोजकः, योजकः.

ORDEAL, *s.* परीक्षा, धर्म्माधर्म्मपरीक्षा, दिव्यं, सत्यं, प्रमाणं, कोषः -षं, कोशः, शापः, शपथः, शपनं, प्रत्ययः, क्रिया; 'fiery ordeal,' अग्निपरीक्षा, तप्तदिव्यं; 'ordeal of the balance,' तुलापरीक्षा, तुलाकोशः; 'purification by ordeal,' कोषशुद्धिः *f.*; 'the act of undergoing an ordeal,' दिव्यग्रहणं, दिव्यकरणं, कोषग्रहणं; 'that undergoes one,' दिव्यकारी -रिणी -रि (न्), कोषग्राही &c.; 'to undergo one,' कोषं or सत्यं or दिव्यं कृ; 'proved by ordeal,' शापितः -ता -तं.

ORDER, *s.* (Regular disposition, arrangement) क्रमः, अनुक्रमः, पर्य्यायः, आनुपूर्व्यं, आनुपूर्वी, परिपाटी -टिः *f.*, पारिपाट्यं, विन्यासः, व्यूहनं, व्यूढिः *f.*, आवृत् *f.*, पारम्पर्य्यं, परम्परा, व्यवस्था, व्यवस्थापनं, क्रमेण स्थापनं, प्रतिविधानं, संविधानं, विरचनं -ना; 'inverted order,' व्यतिक्रमः, व्युत्क्रमः; 'natural order of words,' अन्वयः.—(Established mode of proceeding) क्रमः, मार्गः, रीतिः *f.*, नियमः, पद्धतिः *f.*; 'direct order,' आनुलोम्यं; 'in direct order,' अनुलोमः -मा -मं; 'inverse order,' प्रातिलोम्यं; 'in inverse order,' प्रतिलोमः -मा -मं, विलोमः &c.—(Command) आज्ञा,

आदेशः, निदेशः, निर्देशः, शासनं, शिष्टिः *f.*, शास्तिः *f.*, नियोगः, प्रेरणा, अववादः, प्रयुक्तिः *f.*—(Precept, rule) नियमः, चोदनं -ना, विधिः *m.*, विधानं, वचनं; 'written order,' आज्ञापत्रं, शासनपत्रं; 'general order,' सामान्यशासनं, साधारणाज्ञा.—(Class, grade) गणः, वर्गः, वर्णः, जातिः *f.*; 'the lower orders,' अवरवर्णाः *m. pl.*, अधमवर्णाः, प्राकृतवर्गः, अन्त्यवर्गः, अन्त्यजातीयाः *m. pl.*, अधमजातीयाः *m. pl.*; 'the middle or common order,' सामान्यवर्गः, सामान्यपक्षः, साधारणपक्षः.—(Religious order) आश्रमः. There are four Áśramas, corresponding to the four stages of the Brahman's life. Every Brahman who has passed through these four stages is supposed to have passed through the four orders in succession. When, in the first, he is called ब्रह्मचारी *m.*; in the 2d, गृहस्थः; in the 3d, वानप्रस्थः or वैखानसः or यती; in the 4th, भिक्षुः *m.*, सन्न्यासी *m.* The first order, or that of the religious student, is also called लिङ्गं. Other terms, expressive of religious orders, are परायणं, मार्गः, सम्प्रदायः, पन्थाः *m.* (पथिन्); 'head of a religious order,' आश्रमगुरुः *m.*—(In good order, in proper state) सुस्थः -स्था -स्थं, सुस्थितः -ता -तं, सुरक्षितः -ता -तं.—(In order, properly arranged) सुविन्यस्तः -स्ता -स्तं, सुरचितः -ता -तं, सुव्यवस्थितः -ता -तं, क्रमेण स्थापितः -ता -तं; 'in regular order,' यथाक्रमं, क्रमेण -मात्, क्रमशस्, अनुपूर्व्वशस्, अनुक्रमशस्, सुपरिपाट्या.—(In order to, for the purpose) अर्थं or अर्थे affixed; as, 'in order to read,' अध्ययनार्थं, or expressed by the dat. c.; as, 'in order to find a fourth quantity,' चतुर्थराशेर् अवगमाय.—(Out of order) अव्यवस्थितः -ता -तं, अनवस्थितः &c., भग्नक्रमः -मा -मं, असुस्थः -स्था -स्थं, अस्वस्थः &c.

To ORDER, *v. a.* (Dispose, arrange) विधा (c. 3. -दधाति -धातुं), संविधा, विरच् (c. 10. -रचयति -यितुं), विन्यस् (c. 4. -अस्यति -असितुं), परिक्लृप् (c. 10. -कल्पयति -यितुं), व्यूह् (c. 1. -ऊहते -हितुं), क्रमेण स्था in caus. (स्थापयति -यितुं), व्यवस्था.—(Command) आज्ञा in caus. (-ज्ञापयति -यितुं), समाज्ञा, आदिश् (c. 6. -दिशति -देष्टुं), समादिश्, सन्दिश्, व्यादिश्, प्रतिसन्दिश्, प्रक्लृप्, क्लृप्, चुद् (c. 10. चोदयति -यितुं), अभिचुद्, प्रेर् (c. 10. -ईरयति -यितुं), शास् (c. 2. शास्ति, शासितुं), आशास्, अनुशास्.—(Manage) विधा, प्रणी (c. 1. -णयति -णेतुं), सम्प्रणी, निर्वह् (c. 10. -वाहयति -यितुं).

ORDERED, *p. p.* (Disposed, arranged) व्यवस्थापितः -ता -तं, व्यवस्थितः -ता -तं, विरचितः -ता -तं, रचितः -ता -तं, विन्यस्तः -स्ता -स्तं, विहितः -ता -तं, प्रतिविहितः -ता -तं.—(Commanded) आज्ञापितः -ता -तं, आज्ञप्तः -प्ता -प्तं, आदिष्टः -ष्टा -ष्टं, समादिष्टः &c., निर्दिष्टः &c., चोदितः -ता -तं, प्रचोदितः &c., प्रेरितः -ता -तं.—(Managed) प्रणीतः -ता -तं, निर्वाहितः -ता -तं.

ORDERER, *s.* आज्ञापकः, आज्ञापयिता *m.* (तृ), आज्ञाकर्त्ता *m.* (र्तृ), आदेष्टा *m.* (ष्टृ), आदेशी *m.* (न्), निदेष्टा *m.*, प्रकल्पकः.

ORDERLESS, *a.* क्रमहीनः -ना -नं, क्रमरहितः -ता -तं, क्रमशून्यः -न्या -न्यं, अक्रमः -मा -मं, अव्यवस्थितः -ता -तं, अनवस्थितः &c.

ORDERLINESS, *s.* सक्रमत्वं, क्रमिकता, यथाक्रमता, यथानुक्रमता, अनुक्रमः -मणं, व्यवस्थितिः *f.*, व्यवस्थितत्वं, व्यवस्था. *See* METHODICALNESS.

ORDERLY, *a.* क्रमिकः -का -कं, क्रमकः -का -कं, यथाक्रमः -मा -मं, यथानुक्रमः &c., सक्रमः &c., क्रमानुगतः -ता -तं, व्यवस्थितः -ता -तं, यथापर्य्यायः -या -यं, क्रमानुसारी -रिणी -रि (न्), अनुक्रान्तः -न्ता -न्तं, आनुपूर्व्वः -र्व्वा -र्व्वं, आन्वयिकः &c. *See* METHODICAL.

ORDERLY, *adv.* यथाक्रमं, यथानुक्रमं, अनुक्रमं -मेण, सक्रमं, यथापर्य्यायं.

ORDINAL, *a.* क्रमसूचकः -का -कं, क्रमवाचकः &c., क्रमिकः -का -कं.

ORDINAL, *s.* (Number) क्रमिकसंख्या, क्रमवाचकसंख्या.—(Book containing services of the church) पद्धतिः *f.*, नियमसङ्ग्रहः, विधिसङ्ग्रहः.

ORDINANCE, *s.* (Rule, established law) नियमः, विधिः *m.*, विधानं, व्यवस्था, शासनं, निदर्शनं, चोदना, नियोगः, सूत्रं, अनुशासनं, निदेशः, आदेशः, निरूपणं.—(Of religion) विधिः *m.*, धर्म्मविधिः, विधानं, शास्त्रविधानं, संस्कारः, मर्य्यादा, शास्त्रमर्य्यादा, कर्म्म *n.* (न्), क्रिया, नित्यकर्म्म *n.*, अनुष्ठानं, दैवकर्म्म *n.*, कल्पः, संविधानं; 'subsidiary ordinance,' प्रतिविधानं, प्रतिविधिः *m.*

ORDINARILY, *adv.* प्रायस्, प्रायशस्, प्रायेण, सामान्यतस्, साधारण्येन, बहुशस्, बाहुल्येन, भूयस्, भूयिष्ठं.

ORDINARY, *a.* (Common, usual) प्रायिकः -की -कं, सामान्यः -न्या -न्यं, साधारणः -णा -णी -णं, प्रसिद्धः -द्धा -द्धं, लोकप्रसिद्धः &c.—(Customary) व्यवहारिकः -की -कं, व्यावहारिकः &c., आचारिकः -की -कं, यथाव्यवहारः -रा -रं, नैयमिकः -की -कं, यथारीतिः -तिः -ति, नित्यः -त्या -त्यं, नैत्यकः -की -कं, नैत्यिकः &c., यथापद्धतिः -तिः -ति.—(Vulgar, middling, inferior) प्राकृतः -ता -तं, लौकिकः -की -कं, मध्यमः -मा -मं, अवरः -रा -रं.

ORDINARY, *s.* (Bishop) धर्म्माध्यक्षः.—(Place for eating in common) साधारणभोजनशाला, सामान्यभोजनस्थानं; 'in ordinary,' नित्यः -त्या -त्यं, प्रायिकः -की -कं, साधारणः -णी -णं.

ORDINATE, *a.* क्रमिकः -का -कं, यथाक्रमः -मा -मं, यथानुक्रमः &c.

ORDINATION, *s.* (Institution) विधानं, व्यवस्थापनं, स्थापनं -ना, कल्पनं, प्रकल्पनं, चोदना.—(Appointment) नियोगः, नियोजनं, नियुक्तिः *f.*—(To sacerdotal functions) धर्म्माधिकारनियोजनं, धर्म्माधिकारदीक्षा, धर्म्मपदनियोगः, दीक्षा.

ORDNANCE, *s.* आग्नेययन्त्रसमूहः, युद्धयन्त्रसमूहः, युद्धास्त्रसामग्री.

ORDURE, *s.* पुरीषं, विष्ठा, विशा, विट् *f.* (ष्), शकृत् *n.*, अमेध्यं, उच्चारः, उच्चरितं, मलं, शरीरमलं, अवस्करः, अपस्करः, कल्कं, गूथः -थं, दूष्यं, हन्नं, पूतिकं, शमलं; 'to void it,' पुरीषोत्सर्गं कृ, पुरीषम् उत्सृज् (c. 6. -सृजति -स्रष्टुं) or उच्चर् (c. 1. -चरति -रितुं).

ORE, *s.* धातुः *m.*, असंस्कृतधातुः *m.*, अशोधितधातुः *m.*, अपरिष्कृतधातुः *m.*, आकरीयधातुः *m.*, खनिजधातुः *m.*

ORGAN, *s.* (Instrument of action) साधनं, कर्म्मसाधनं, करणं, उपकरणं, कारणं.—(Organ of action) कर्म्मेन्द्रियं. Of these, five are given: 1. 'the larynx or voice,' वाक् *f.* (च्); 2. 'the hand,' पाणिः *m.*; 3. 'the foot,' पादः; 4. 'the organ of excretion,' पायुः *m.*; 5. 'of generation,' उपस्थः.—(Organ of sense or perception) इन्द्रियं, ज्ञानेन्द्रियं, ज्ञानसाधनं, विषयि *n.* (न्), हृषीकं. Of these, five are reckoned: 1. 'the eye,' चक्षुस्; 2. 'the ear,' श्रोत्रं; 3. 'the nose,' घ्राणं; 4. 'the tongue,' जिह्वा; 5. 'the skin,' त्वक् *f.* (च्). The word इन्द्रियं may be affixed to any of these; as, 'the organ of sight,' चक्षुरिन्द्रियं &c.; for the corresponding विषय or 'objects of sense,' *see* OBJECT.—(Internal organ, or organ of the intellect) अन्तरिन्द्रियं, धीन्द्रियं. Of these, four are enumerated: 1. 'the mind, or organ of thought,' मनस्; 2. 'apprehension,' बुद्धिः *f.*; 3. 'individuality, or sense of self,' अहङ्कारः; 4. 'feeling,' चित्तं. In opposition to the 'internal organs,' the organs of perception and action are sometimes called 'external organs,' बहिरिन्द्रियाणि. The organs collectively, इन्द्रियग्रामः, इन्द्रियवर्गः.—(Instrument, or means of communication) द्वारं, साधनं.—(Musical instrument) वंशी, सुषिरवंशपूर्व्वाद्यं.

ORGANIC, ORGANICAL, *a.* (Pertaining to the organs) ऐन्द्रियिकः -की -कं, इन्द्रियसम्बन्धी -न्धिनी &c.—(Consisting of, or containing organs) इन्द्रियमयः -यी -यं, कर्म्मसाधनमयः &c.—(Produced by the organs) इन्द्रियोत्पन्नः -न्ना -न्नं, इन्द्रियजनितः -ता -तं.—(Possessing organs) इन्द्रियवान् -वती -वत् (त्), इन्द्रियसम्पन्नः -न्ना -न्नं, इन्द्रियविशिष्टः -ष्टा -ष्टं, जीवितसाधनविशिष्टः &c., प्राणितसाधनसम्पन्नः &c., करणसम्पन्नः &c., सकरणः -णा -णं.—(Instrumental) कारणिकः -की -कं.

ORGANICALLY, *adv.* इन्द्रियव्यूहेन, इन्द्रियव्यूहपूर्व्वं, इन्द्रियतस्.

ORGANIST, *s.* वंशीवादकः, पूर्व्वोक्तसुषिरवाद्यवादकः.

ORGANIZATION, *s.* (Formation with organs) इन्द्रियकरणं, इन्द्रियव्यूहनं, इन्द्रियविन्यासः, इन्द्रियविशिष्टता, सेन्द्रियता.—(Arrangement of the parts or divisions of a body) भागविन्यासः, भागव्यूहनं, भागव्यूढिः *f.*, भागविरचना, भागसंविधानं, भागप्रतिविधानं, भागव्यवस्थापनं.—(Structure) व्यूहः -हनं, व्यूढिः *f.*, संव्यूहः -हनं, विधानं, संविधानं, विन्यासः, संस्थापनं, संस्थितिः *f.*, निर्म्माणं, निर्म्मितिः *f.*, सृष्टिः *f.*, घटनं.

To ORGANIZE, *v. a.* (Form with organs or suitable parts) इन्द्रियवन्तं -वतीं -वत् कृ, इन्द्रियसम्पन्नं -न्नां कृ, इन्द्रियुक्तं -क्तां कृ, सेन्द्रियं -यां कृ, साङ्गं -ङ्गां कृ, सावयवं -वां कृ, अवयवसम्पन्नं -न्नां कृ, साङ्गोपाङ्गं -ङ्गां कृ, अङ्गोपाङ्गसम्पन्नं -न्नां कृ.—(Form, construct) क्लृप् (c. 10. कल्पयति -यितुं), रच् (c. 10. रचयति -यितुं), विरच्, विधा (c. 3. -दधाति -धातुं), संस्था in caus. (-स्थापयति -यितुं), निर्म्मा (c. 2. -माति, c. 3. -मिमीते -मातुं), घट् (c. 10. घटयति -यितुं), पिश् (c. 6. पिंशति, पेशितुं), रचनां कृ, विरचनां कृ.—(Dispose or distribute into suitable parts) व्यूह् (c. 1. -ऊहते -हितुं), विन्यस् (c. 4. -अस्यति -असितुं), विधा, संविधा.

ORGANIZED, *p. p.* व्यूढः -ढा -ढं, विन्यस्तः -स्ता -स्तं, विहितः -ता -तं, प्रतिविहितः &c., व्यवस्थापितः &c., संस्थापितः -ता -तं, रचितः -ता -तं, विरचितः -ता -तं, कल्पितः -ता -तं, परिकल्पितः &c., सृष्टः -ष्टा -ष्टं, घटितः -ता -तं, परिपाटीकृतः -ता -तं, संव्यूढः -ढा -ढं.

ORGASM, *s.* उत्तापः, उत्तेजनं, उत्तेजितत्वं, उन्मदः, उद्धतिः *f.*, आवेशः, आविष्टता, क्षोभः, वेगः, व्याक्षोभः, क्षुब्धता, सन्तापः.

ORGIES, *s. pl.* नैशोत्सवः, नैशिकोत्सवः, रात्र्युत्सवः, मद्यपानपूर्व्वम् निशि सेवितम् उत्सवादि, समद्यपानं रात्रौ कृतम् उत्सवादि.

ORICHALCH, *s.* पित्तलं, पीतलोहं, पीतलं -लकं, रीतिः *f.*, कांस्यं.

ORIENT, *a.* (Rising) उदयी -यिनी -यि (न्), उदयमानः -ना -नं.—(Eastern). See ORIENTAL.

ORIENT, *s.* (The east) पूर्व्वदिक् *f.* (श्), प्राची, सूर्य्योदयदेशः.

ORIENTAL, *a.* पूर्व्वदेशीयः -या -यं, पूर्व्वदिश्यः -श्या -श्यं, प्राच्यः -च्या -च्यं, प्राचीनः -ना -नं, पूर्व्वः -र्व्वा -र्व्वं, पूर्व्वीयः -या -यं, पूर्व्वजः -जा -जं, पूर्व्वदेशस्थः -स्था -स्थं.

ORIENTAL, *s.* पूर्व्वदेशवासी *m.* (न्), पूर्व्वदेशस्थः, प्राचीनदेशवासी.

ORIENTALIST, *s.* पूर्व्वदेशीयभाषाज्ञः, प्राग्देशीयभाषापण्डितः.

ORIFICE, *s.* मुखं, छिद्रं, द्वारं, सुषिरं, शुषिरं, रन्ध्रं, विवरं, बिलं; 'of a pipe,' दर्दुरपुटः; 'of the ear,' वृकधः.

ORIGIN, *s.* (First existence, beginning) मूलं, आरम्भः, मूलारम्भः, प्रारम्भः, उद्भवः, उत्पत्तिः *f.*, प्रथमोद्भवः, प्रथमोत्पत्तिः *f.*, उद्गमः, सम्भवः, प्रभवः, जन्म *n.* (न्), जातिः *f.*, आगमः, उपक्रमः.—(Source, fountain) आदिः *m.*, योनिः *m.f.*, मूलं, बीजं, हेतुः *m.*, कारणं, आदिकारणं, गर्भः, निबन्धनं, निदानं, उत्पत्तिस्थानं, उद्गमस्थानं.—(Original instigator) प्रयोजकः, प्रवर्त्तकः; 'of low origin,' दुर्योनिः -निः -नि, हीनयोनिः &c., हीनजातिः -तिः -ति, हीनजन्मा -न्मा -न्म (न्); 'of noble origin,' मौलः -ली -लं, उत्कृष्टजातिः &c., उत्तमवंशजातः -ता -तं; 'prosperity has its origin in the king,' राजमूला सम्पत्तिः.

ORIGINAL, *s.* (Origin). See the preceding. (First copy, archetype) आदर्शः, प्रत्युपमानं, प्रत्युपमा, मूलं, मूलपत्रं.—(Text) मूलं, मूलग्रन्थः.

ORIGINAL, *a.* (Primitive, first in order) मौलः -ली -लं, मौलिकः -की -कं, मूलिकः -का -कं, प्रथमः -मा -मं, प्राथमिकः -की -कं, आद्यः -द्या -द्यं, आदिमः -मा -मं आदि in comp., पूर्व्वः -र्व्वा -र्व्वं.—(Not made or done before, or by another) अपूर्व्वः -र्व्वा -र्व्वं, अपूर्व्वकर्त्तृकः -का -कं, अपूर्व्वसिद्धः -द्धा -द्धं, अपूर्व्वरचितः -ता -तं, अपूर्व्वप्रतिमः -मा -मं, स्वयङ्कृतः &c., स्वयङ्कल्पितः &c., स्वतःकल्पितः &c.—(Having the power to originate new thoughts) अपूर्व्वकल्पकः -का -कं, स्वयङ्कल्पकः &c., स्वतःकल्पकः &c., अपूर्व्वयोजकः &c., अनुयोगी &c.

ORIGINALITY, *s.* (Power of originating new thoughts) अपूर्व्वकल्पनाशक्तिः *f.*, अपूर्व्वकल्पकत्वं.—(State of being original) अपूर्व्वता, अपूर्व्वसिद्धता, अपूर्व्वरचितत्वं, मौलता.

ORIGINALLY, *adv.* आदौ, आदितस्, उत्पत्तितस्, मूलतस्, जातितस्, प्रथमं, प्रथमतस्, आरम्भे, प्रारम्भे, आरम्भतस्.

To ORIGINATE, *v. a.* प्रथमम् उत्पद् (c. 10. -पादयति -यितुं) or जन् (c. 10. जनयति -यितुं) or उद्भू (c. 10. -भावयति -यितुं) or सृज् (c. 6. सृजति, स्रष्टुं) or क्लृप् (c. 10. कल्पयति -यितुं), प्रथमोत्पादनं कृ, प्रथमोत्पत्तिं कृ, प्रथमोद्भवं कृ, आरभ् (c. 1. -रभते -रब्धुं), समारभ्, प्रारभ्, आरम्भं कृ, प्रारम्भं कृ, प्रवृत् (c. 10. -वर्त्तयति -यितुं), उपक्रम् (c. 1. -क्रमते -मितुं).

To ORIGINATE, *v. n.* उत्पद् (c. 4. -पद्यते -पत्तुं), व्युत्पद्, समुत्पद्, जन् (c. 4. जायते, जनितुं), प्रजन्, प्रभू (c. 1. -भवति -वितुं), उद्भू, सम्भू, प्रसृ (c. 1. -सरति -सर्त्तुं), निःसृ, विनिःसृ, उद्गम् (c. 1. -गच्छति -गन्तुं), निर्गम्, प्रवृत् (c. 1. -वर्त्तते -र्त्तितुं), उत्था (c. 1. -तिष्ठति -थातुं, rt. स्था), उपस्था.

ORIGINATED, *p. p.* उत्पन्नः -न्ना -न्नं, प्रथमोत्पन्नः &c., उत्पादितः -ता -तं, जातः -ता -तं, प्रवृत्तः -त्ता -त्तं, प्रवर्त्तितः -ता -तं, प्रथमकल्पितः &c., निःसृतः -ता -तं, विनिःसृतः &c.

ORIGINATION, *s.* प्रथमोत्पादनं, प्रथमोत्पत्तिः *f.*, प्रथमोद्भावनं, प्रथमोद्भवः, आरम्भः, प्रारम्भः, आरब्धिः *f.*

ORIGINATOR, *s.* प्रथमोत्पादकः, प्रथमोद्भावकः, मूलोत्पादकः, प्रवर्त्तकः, प्रयोजकः, प्रथमकल्पकः, आरम्भकः.

ORION, *s.* (Constellation) मृगशिरस् *n.*, मृगशीर्षं, आग्रहायणी.

ORISON, *s.* प्रार्थना, स्तवः, स्तुतिः *f.*, वाचिकप्रार्थना.

ORISSA, *s.* (The country) उत्कलः, उत्कलदेशः.

ORNAMENT, *s.* (Embellishment) अलङ्कारः, अलङ्करणं, अलङ्क्रिया, भूषणं, विभूषणं, भरणं, आभरणं, शोभा -भनं, भूषा, विभूषा, मण्डनं, परिष्कारः, संस्कारः, परिकर्म्म *n.* (न्), प्रतिकर्म्म, प्रसाधनं, रञ्जनं, कल्पना, सज्जा, रङ्गः, नेपथ्यं.—(That which ornaments, an ornament) अलङ्कारः, भूषणं, आभरणं, भरणं, कङ्कणः -णं, कलापः, अङ्गदं; 'ornament of language,' अलङ्कारः, शब्दालङ्कारः; of sense,' अर्थालङ्कारः; 'for the feet or ankles,' नूपुरः -रं, पादाङ्गदं.

To ORNAMENT, *v. a.* अलङ्कृ, समलङ्कृ, भूष् (c. 10. भूषयति -यितुं), विभूष्,

शुभ् (c. 10. शोभयति -यितुं), उपशुभ्, मण्ड् (c. 10. मण्डयति -यितुं), परिकर्म्म (nom. -कर्म्मयति -यितुं), रञ्ज् (c. 10. रञ्जयति -यितुं).

ORNAMENTAL, *a.* अलङ्कारकः -का -कं, अलङ्करिष्णुः -ष्णुः -ष्णु, शोभाकरः -रा -रं, शोभाकारकः -का -कं, शोभावहः -हा -हं, शोभकः -का -कं, शोभादायकः -का -कं, शोभाप्रदः -दा -दं, भूषकः -का -कं, विभूषकः -का -कं, भूषाकरः -रा -रं.

ORNAMENTALLY, *adv.* अलङ्करणार्थं, विभूषणार्थं, शोभाकरणार्थं.

ORNAMENTED, *p. p.* अलङ्कृतः -ता -तं, भूषितः -ता -तं, विभूषितः -ता -तं, शोभितः -ता -तं, उपशोभितः -ता -तं, मण्डितः -ता -तं, कृतालङ्कारः -रा -रं, सालङ्कारः &c., प्रसाधितः -ता -तं, विरचितः &c.

ORNATE, *a.* *See* the last. (As style) पुष्पितः -ता -तं, अलङ्कृतः -ता -तं, सालङ्कारः -रा -रं, अलङ्कारमयः -यी -यं.

ORNATELY, *adv.* सालङ्कारं, अलङ्कारेण, शोभापूर्व्वं.

ORNITHOLOGIST, *s.* पक्षिविद्याज्ञः, पक्षिविषयकविद्याज्ञः.

ORNITHOLOGY, *s.* पक्षिविद्या, पक्षिविषयका विद्या, शाकुनविद्या.

ORPHAN, *s.* or *a.* (Bereaved of both parents) मातृपितृहीनः -ना -नं, मातापितृहीनः &c., पितामातृहीनः &c., मातृपितृविहीनः &c., मातापितृभ्यां विहीनः &c., मातृपितृरहितः &c.—(Bereaved of father) पितृहीनः -ना -नं, पितृविहीनः &c., पित्रा विहीनः, मृतपितृकः -का -कं, गतपितृकः &c., अपितृकः &c., अनाथः -था -थं, निर्नाथः &c., क्षेमवृद्धः, कुमण्डः.—(Of mother) मातृहीनः -ना -नं, अमातृकः -का -कं, मातृरहितः -ता -तं, मृतमातृकः -का -कं, गतमातृकः &c., हीनमातृकः &c.

ORPHANAGE, ORPHANISM, *s.* मातृपितृहीनता, निर्नाथता, अनाथत्वं.

ORPIMENT, *s.* (Yellow) हरितालं -लकं, पीतकं, पिञ्जरं, तालं, आलं, अलं.—(Red) रक्तधातुः *m.*

ORRERY, *s.* ग्रहगतिसूचकयन्त्रं, ग्रहादिगतिदर्शकयन्त्रं.

ORRIS, *s.* (Root) श्वेतवचा, वचा, हैमवती, उग्रगन्धा, उग्रा, शतपर्व्विका, षड्ग्रन्था, सुपर्णा, गोलोमी, काङ्क्षा, गानिनी.

ORT, *s.* *See* ORTS.

ORTHODOX, *a.* सत्पथगामी -मिनी -मि (न्), सत्पथवर्त्ती &c., सत्पथावलम्बी &c., सन्मार्गगामी &c., सत्यधर्म्मा -र्म्मा -र्म्म (न्), सत्यधर्म्मावलम्बी &c., दक्षिणमार्गी &c., दक्षिणमार्गानुयायी &c., दक्षिणाचारी &c., यथाशास्त्रः -स्त्रा -स्त्रं, शास्त्रीयः -या -यं, शास्त्रसम्मतः -ता -तं, सत्यमतः -ता -तं, सत्यमतधारी &c., सत्पथानुसारी &c., सत्यधर्म्मानुसारी &c., सच्छास्त्रानुसारी &c.

ORTHODOXY, *s.* सत्पथः, सन्मार्गः, दक्षिणमार्गः, सद्धर्म्मः, सच्छास्त्रं, सत्पथानुसरणं, सन्मार्गानुयायित्वं, सत्पथावलम्बनं, सत्यमतधारणं, यथार्थमतधारणं, यथाशास्त्रता -त्वं.

ORTHOEPIST, *s.* शुद्धोच्चारणविद्याज्ञः, शुद्धोच्चारणविद्.

ORTHOEPY, *s.* शुद्धोच्चारः -रणं, शुद्धोच्चारणविद्या.

ORTHOGON, *s.* समकोणाकृतिः *f.*, समचतुरस्रं, समचतुष्कोणः, दीर्घचतुरस्रं.

ORTHOGONAL, *a.* समकोणाकृतिः -तिः -ति, समासाकृतिः &c., समकोणः &c.

ORTHOGRAPHIC, ORTHOGRAPHICAL, *a.* शुद्धाक्षरविन्याससम्बन्धी -न्धिनी -न्धि (न्), शुद्धाक्षरविन्यासविषयकः -का -कं, वर्णविन्याससम्बन्धी &c.

ORTHOGRAPHICALLY, *adv.* शुद्धाक्षरविन्यासपूर्व्वं, शुद्धाक्षरविन्यासानुसारेण.

ORTHOGRAPHY, *s.* शुद्धाक्षरविन्यासः, शुद्धवर्णविन्यासः, शुद्धवर्णलिखनं, वर्णविन्यासविद्या, अक्षरविन्यासविद्या, सन्धिः *m.*

ORTS, *s. pl.* उच्छिष्टं, अवशिष्टं, शिष्टं, शेषं, भुक्तोच्छिष्टं, भुक्तावशेषं, भक्षितशेषं, भुक्तसमुज्झितं, परभुक्तोज्झितं, उच्छिष्टान्नं, शेषान्नं, अन्नशेषं, भुक्तशेषं, आदिष्टं, मेलकः, मेला -लिः -ली.

To OSCILLATE, *v. n.* दोल (nom. दोलायते -यितुं), आन्दोल्, प्रेङ्खोल (nom. प्रेङ्खोलायते), प्रेङ्ख् (c. 1. प्रेङ्खति -ते -ङ्खितुं, rt. इङ्ख्), स्पन्द् (c. 1. स्पन्दते -न्दितुं), विस्पन्द्, परिस्पन्द्, इतस्ततो विचल् (c. 1. -चलति -लितुं) or चल् or क्षुभ् (c. 4. क्षुभ्यति -ते, क्षोभितुं) or विक्षुभ् or विस्फुर् (c. 6. -स्फुरति -रितुं) or कम्प् (c. 1. कम्पते -म्पितुं) or विकम्प्.

OSCILLATION, *s.* आन्दोलनं, प्रेङ्खोलनं, प्रेङ्खणं, स्पन्दनं, विस्पन्दनं, इतस्ततो विचलनं or विस्फुरणं or कम्पनं or विकम्पनं or विक्षोभः or गतागतं.

OSCILLATING, OSCILLATORY, *a.* दोलायमानः -ना -नं, आन्दोलायमानः -ना -नं, आन्दोलितः -ता -तं, प्रेङ्खन् -ङ्खन्ती -ङ्खत् (त्), प्रेङ्खमाणः -णा -णं, प्रेङ्खोलितः -ता -तं, स्पन्दमानः -ना -नं, विस्पन्दमानः -ना -नं, कम्पमानः -ना -नं, स्फुरन् &c., विस्फुरन् &c., स्फुरितः -ता -तं, विस्फुरितः &c.

OSCITANCY, OSCITATION, *s.* जृम्भः -म्भणं -म्भा, विजृम्भणं, जृम्भिका.

OSCITANT, *a.* जृम्भमाणः -णा -णं, विजृम्भमाणः &c., जृम्भः -म्भा -म्भं, जृम्भी -म्भिणी -म्भि (न्), जृम्भावान् -वती -वत् (त्).

To OSCITATE, *v. n.* जृम्भ् (c. 1. जृम्भते -म्भितुं), विजृम्भ्, जृम्भणं कृ.

OSIER, *s.* विदलं, वेतसः, वेत्रं, वेणुः *m.* These words may be used, but there is no proper Sanskrit equivalent.

OSPRAY, *s.* कुररः -री, उत्क्रोशः, समुत्क्रोशः, पंक्तिचरः, खरः.

OSSEOUS, *a.* अस्थिमयः -यी -यं, अस्थिवान् -वती -वत् (त्), अस्थिमान् &c., अस्थिगुणकः -का -कं, अस्थिसगुणः -णा -णं.

OSSICLE, *s.* अस्थिकं, हड्डकं, सूक्ष्मास्थि *n.*, क्षुद्रास्थि *n.*

OSSIFIC, *a.* अस्थिकरः -रा -रं, अस्थिकारकः -का -कं, अस्थिजनकः &c.

OSSIFICATION, *s.* अस्थिता -त्वं, अस्थिभावः, अस्थिपरिणामः, अस्थिभूयं.

OSSIFIED, *p. p.* अस्थिभूतः -ता -तं, अस्थिसात्कृतः -ता -तं.

To OSSIFY, *v. a.* अस्थिसात्कृ, अस्थिसमभावं -वां कृ, अस्थिवत् कृ.

To OSSIFY, *v. n.* अस्थिसाद्भू, अस्थिसमभावः -वा -वं भू, अस्थिवद् भू.

OSSIVOROUS, *a.* अस्थिखादकः -का -कं, अस्थिभक्षकः &c., अस्थिभोजी -जिनी &c.

OSSUARY, *s.* अस्थिस्थानं, अस्थिसञ्चयस्थानं, अस्थ्यागारं.

OSTENSIBLE, *a.* व्यक्तः -क्ता -क्तं, स्पष्टः -ष्टा -ष्टं, व्यक्तोदितः -ता -तं, व्यक्तकथितः -ता -तं, प्रकाशः -शा -शं, प्रत्यक्षः -क्षा -क्षं, प्रत्यक्षदर्शितः -ता -तं, प्रत्यक्षप्रकाशितः &c., प्रसिद्धः -द्धा -द्धं, प्रादुर्भूतः &c., आविर्भूतः &c., आविष्कृतः &c., प्रकटः -टा -टं, बाह्यः -ह्या -ह्यं, बहिर्भूतः -ता -तं, अगूढः -ढा -ढं.

OSTENSIBLY, *adv.* प्रत्यक्षतस्, प्रकाशं, व्यक्तं, स्पष्टं, प्रादुस्, आविस्, बहिस्, बाह्यतस्, प्रकटं, प्रसिद्धं, अगूढं.

OSTENTATION, *s.* दम्भः, आडम्बरः -रं, दम्भार्थं स्वगुणप्रकाशनं, आत्मश्लाघा, दर्पः, विकत्था, प्रतिष्ठा, स्तोभः.

OSTENTATIOUS, *s.* दम्भी -म्भिनी -म्भि (न्), दाम्भिकः -की -कं, सदम्भः -म्भा -म्भं, दम्भशीलः -ला -लं, आडम्बरी -रिणी &c., आडम्बरशीलः &c., दम्भार्थं स्वगुणप्रकाशकः &c., आत्मश्लाघी &c.

OSTENTATIOUSLY, *adv.* दम्भार्थं, सदम्भं, साडम्बरं, दम्भपूर्व्वं, दम्भं कृत्वा, लोकदर्शनार्थं, दाम्भिकवत्, आत्मश्लाघापूर्व्वं.

OSTEOCOPE, *s.* अस्थिवेदना, अस्थिव्यथा, अस्थिशूलः -लं.

OSTEOLOGY, *s.* अस्थिविद्या, अस्थिविवरणं -णा, अस्थिवर्णनं -ना.

OSTIARY, *s.* नदीमुखं, समुद्रसम्भेदः, समुद्रसङ्गमः, समुद्रसङ्गः.

OSTLER, *s.* अश्वपालः -लकः, अश्वरक्षकः, सादी *m.* (न्), अश्वसेवकः, हड्डिकः, हड्डकः. *See* OSTLER, GROOM.

OSTRACISM, *s.* *See* BANISHMENT, EXPULSION.

OSTRICH, *s.* The word उष्ट्रमृगः may be used.

OTHER, *a.* अन्यः -न्या -न्यत्, इतरः -रा -रं, परः -रा -रं, अपरः -रा -रं, अन्यदीयः -या -यं, अन्यतरः -रा -रत्, परकीयः -या -यं, व्यतिरिक्तः -क्ता -क्तं अन्तरं in comp.; 'other's wealth,' परधनं, अन्यधनं; 'other kings,' राजानमराणि n. pl.; 'the other world,' परलोकः -कं, अपरलोकः; 'the other day,' अन्यदिवसे, अन्यस्मिन् दिवसे, अन्येद्युस्; 'on the other side,' अपरतस्; 'on the other hand,' परतस्, अन्यच, परपक्षे.—(Different) भिन्नः -न्ना -न्नं, विभिन्नः &c., अपरः -रा -रं, अन्यः -न्या -न्यत्, इतरः -रा -रं, त्वः -त्वा -त्वं; 'other than this,' एतद्भिन्नः &c.; 'he has no other business than reading the Vedas,' वेदाध्ययनात् तस्य कार्य्यं नान्यत्.—(Each other) परस्परः -रा -रं, अन्योन्यः -न्या -न्यं, इतरेतरः -रा -रं.—(Rest) शिष्टः -ष्टा -ष्टं, अवशिष्टः &c.; 'the others,' शिष्टजनाः m. pl., अपरे m. pl.

OTHERWHERE, adv. अन्यत्र, इतरत्र, अपरत्र, परत्र, स्थानान्तरे.

OTHERWISE, adv. (In a different manner) अन्यथा, इतरथा, परतस्.—(In other ways) अन्यथा, अन्यप्रकारैः, अन्यविधेन.—(Or else) अथवा, अन्यथा, किंवा, नो चेत्, न चेत्, अनेन; 'but not otherwise,' न त्वन्यथा.

OTTAR, OTTO, s. (Of rose) जवापुष्पनिर्य्यासः, कोषुपुष्पनिर्य्यूहः.

OTTER, s. (The animal) उद्रः, जलमार्जारः, जलनकुलः, पानीयनकुलः, नीरजः, नीराखुः m.

OUGHT, v. irreg. (Be bound, be obliged, be necessary) expressed by the fut. pass. part.; as, 'you ought to marry the damsel,' त्वया कन्या वोढव्या; 'we ought to restrain anger,' अस्माभिः कोपः नियन्तव्यः; 'I ought not to do that,' मया तत् न कर्त्तव्यं or करणीयं or कार्य्यं, or sometimes by the potential mood; as, 'he ought to treat his son like a friend,' पुत्रं मित्रवद् आचरेत्, or by the use of the verb अर्ह्; as, 'he ought to give,' दातुम् अर्हति; 'to act as one ought,' यथोचितं or यथायोग्यं or यथार्हं कृ.

OUNCE, s. (Weight) पलं, अर्द्धटङ्कः, टङ्कार्द्धं.—(Animal) द्वीपी m. (न्).

OUR, a. अस्माकं gen. c. pl. (अस्मत्), अस्मदीयः -या -यं अस्मद् prefixed; as, 'our country,' अस्माकं देशः or अस्मदीयदेशः or अस्मद्देशः; 'our own' is expressed by आत्म in comp.; as, 'our own country,' आत्मदेशः.

OURANG-OUTANG, s. मनुष्यशरीरः कपिभेदः.

OURSELVES, pron. reciprocal, expressed by आत्मा m. (न्) or by आत्म in comp. or by स्वयं in comp.; 'we will kill ourselves,' वयम् आत्मनो हनिष्यामः; 'done by ourselves,' आत्मकृतः -ता -तं; 'we ourselves,' ते वयं.

To OUST v. a. निःसृ (c. 10. -सारयति -यितुं), वहिष्कृ, वहिःकृ, निराकृ, अपास् (c. 4. -अस्यति -असितुं), निरस्, स्थानाद् भ्रंश् (c. 10. भ्रंशयति -यितुं), निष्कस् (c. 10. -कासयति -यितुं).

OUSTED, p. p. निःसारितः -ता -तं, वहिष्कृतः -ता -तं, स्थानभ्रष्टः -ष्टा -ष्टं.

OUT, adv. (Without, not in) वहिस्, निर्, वि, विनिर्, अप prefixed, governing the abl. c.; 'to go out,' वहिर्गम्, निर्गम्, विनिर्गम्, अपगम्; 'to draw out,' निष्कृष्; 'to be out,' वहिर्भू; 'having gone out into the open air,' प्रकाशे निर्गत.—(Denoting disclosure or discovery) expressed by the prep. वि, अप, प्र, परि, नि, निर्, अव &c., in combination with various roots; as, 'to give out,' प्रकाश्, विकाश्, निविद्, विघुष्; 'to find out,' परिज्ञा, अभिज्ञा, निकृप्, उपलभ्, निर्णी; 'to be out, be disclosed,' विवृतः -ता -तं भू, प्रकाशितः -ता -तं भू; 'the secret is out,' रहस्यं भिन्नं or विभिन्नं or प्रकाशितं.—(Denoting extinction) expressed by निर्, with the root वा; as, 'to put out,' निर्वा in caus.; 'to go out,' निर्वा, निर्वाणः -णा -णं भू.—(In a state of exhaustion or being empty) क्षीणः -णा -णं, परिक्षीणः -णा -णं, शून्यः -न्या -न्यं, गतः -ता -तं, विगतः -ता -तं.—(Out of employment) क्षीणवृत्तिः -त्तिः -त्ति, निर्व्यापारः -रा -रं, अव्यापारी -रिणी &c., व्यापारशून्यः -न्या -न्यं.—(Out of office) अधिकारभ्रष्टः -ष्टा -ष्टं, भ्रष्टाधिकारः -रा -रं, च्युताधिकारः &c.—(To the end) अवसानपर्य्यन्तं, अन्तं or शेषं यावत्, आन्तम्; 'hear me out,' मद्वचनम् अवसानपर्य्यन्तं शृणु.—(Loudly) उच्चैस्, उच्चैःस्वरेण, मुक्तकण्ठं; 'to speak out,' उच्चैःस्वरेण वद्.—(Openly) प्रकाशं, व्यक्तं, प्रकटं.—(In error) अपराद्धः -द्धा -द्धं, भ्रान्तः -न्ता -न्तं, सापराधः -धा -धं.—(Deficient) न्यूनः -ना -नं, क्षीणः -णा -णं.—(Out of, in the sense of from) usually expressed by the abl. c. alone, or in combination with a root and some of the prep. वहिस्, निर्, विनिर्, अप &c. See FROM. (Out of, in the sense of beyond) expressed by अति prefixed; as, 'out of one's power,' अतिशक्ति; 'out of the power of man,' अतिमानुषः -षी -षं; 'to pass out of one's sight,' चक्षुर्विषयम् अतिक्रम्; or by the fut. pass. part.; as, 'out of one's power,' अशक्यः -क्या -क्यं, असाध्यः -ध्या -ध्यं, असाधनीयः -या -यं; 'out of one's reach,' अपारणीयः -या -यं, अपार्य्यः -र्य्या -र्य्यं, अप्राप्यः -प्या -प्यं, अविषयः -या -यं, विषयातिक्रान्तः -न्ता -न्तं; or by अगोचर in comp.; as, 'out of hearing,' कर्णागोचरः -रा -रं.—(Out of, denoting exclusion, cessation, deviation from, omission, absence, dereliction, &c.) variously expressed by अ, निर्, वि, अप, गत, विगत, अतीत, त्यक्त, विरुद्ध &c.; as, 'out of use,' अव्यवहारितः -ता -तं; 'out of tune,' विस्वरः -रा -रं, अस्वरः &c.; 'out of fashion,' लोकव्यवहारविरुद्धः -द्धा -द्धं; 'out of time,' गतकालिकः -का -कं; 'out of season,' अपूर्वकालः -ला -लं, अकालिकः &c.; 'out of the road,' मुक्तमार्गः -र्गा -र्गं, पथभ्रष्टः &c.; 'out of one's mind,' बुद्धिभ्रष्टः &c., हतबुद्धिः &c., नष्टबुद्धिः &c.; 'out of order,' विधिविरुद्धः &c., विधिभिन्नः -न्ना -न्नं, अयथाविधिः &c., विसूत्रः -त्रा -त्रं; 'out of place,' अस्थानः -ना -नं; 'out of health,' अस्वस्थः -स्था -स्थं; 'out of hope,' निराशः -शा -शं; 'out of patience,' अक्षमः -मा -मं.—(Out of, denoting in consequence of) expressed by the abl. c., as, 'out of anger,' कोपात्; 'out of unsteadiness of mind,' अस्थिरचित्ततात्.—(Out of hand) सद्यस्, तत्काले, तत्क्षणे. See IMMEDIATELY.

OUT, interj. (Out upon you, out upon it) अपेहि, दूरमपसर, अपेहि, अपसर, धिक्, छी.

To OUT-ACT, v. n. अतिचर् (c. 1. -चरति -रितुं), कर्म्मणा or कार्य्येण अतिक्रम् (c. 1. -क्रामति -क्रमितुं), अधिकं कृ.

To OUT-BALANCE, v. a. See To OUTWEIGH.

To OUTBID, v. a. अधिकमूल्यं दित्सामीति or दातुमिच्छामीति वद् (c. 1. वदति -दितुं).

OUTBIDDER, s. अधिकमूल्यदित्सुः m., अधिकमूल्यं दित्सामीति वादी m. (न्).

To OUTBRAVE, v. a. अधिकं भर्त्स् (c. 10. भर्त्सयति -ते -यितुं), अधिकभर्त्सनेन पराभू.

OUTBREAK, s. उद्भेदः, प्रोद्भेदः, स्फोटः -टनं, सवेगो निर्गमः.

OUTCAST, a. or s. (Expelled from society or one's own class or caste) जातिभ्रष्टः -ष्टा -ष्टं, जातिवहिष्कृतः -ता -तं, जातिच्युतः -ता

-र्तं, जातिहीनः -ना -नं, हीनजातिः -तिः -ति, जातिपतितः -ता -तं, वर्णभ्रष्टः &c., वर्णहीनः &c., हीनवर्णो -र्णा -र्णं, वर्णापेतः -ता -तं, पंक्तिबाह्यः &c., अपांक्तः -क्ती -क्तं, अपांक्तेयः -या -यं, पंक्तिदूषकः -का -कं, पतितः -ता -तं, लोकबाह्यः &c., प्रस्कन्नः -न्ना -न्नं, व्रात्यः -त्या, जुङ्गितः -ता.—(Of a degraded or low caste or class) चाण्डालः -ली, चण्डालः -ली, अपसदः, विवर्णः -र्णा -र्णं, नीचः -चा -चं, निहीनः -ना -नं, नीचजातिः -तिः -ति, न्यग्जातिः &c., अन्त्यजातीयः -या -यं, अधमजातीयः &c., अधमवर्णः &c., अधमाचारः -रा -रं, दुराचारः &c., दुर्वृत्तः -त्ता -त्तं, आचारहीनः &c., आचारवर्जितः -ता -तं, पृथग्जनः, पामरः, जाल्मः.

OUTBURST, *s.* उद्भेदः, प्रोद्भेदः. *See* OUTBREAK, ERUPTION.

OUTCRY, *s.* (Clamor, loud cry) कोलाहलः, उत्क्रोशः, उत्क्रुष्टं, उच्चैःस्वरः, उच्चैर्घुष्टं, संहूतिः *f.*, बहुभिः कृता संहूतिः, चित्कारः, चीत्कारः, कलकलः, तुमुलं; 'popular outcry,' लोकापवादः, जनापवादः, लोकरवः, जनरवः, जनरावः.—(Cry of pain) आर्त्तनादः.

To OUTDO, *v. a.* अतिक्रम् (c. 1. -क्रामति -क्रमितुं), अतिचर् (c. 1. -चरति -रितुं), अतिशी (c. 2. -शेते -शयितुं), अतिरिच् in pass. (-रिच्यते), अभिभू. *See To* SURPASS.

OUT-DOOR, *a.* द्वारबहिःस्थः -स्था -स्थं, द्वारबहिर्भूतः -ता -तं.

OUTER, OUTERMOST, *a.* बहिःस्थः -स्था -स्थं, बाह्यः -ह्या -ह्यं, बहिर्भूतः -ता -तं, बहिर्भवः -वा -वं, बहिर्वर्त्ती -र्त्तिनी -र्त्ति (न्), बाहीकः -का -कं, बहिर्भागस्थः &c., बहिस् in comp.; as, 'outer part,' बहिर्भागः; 'outer door,' बहिर्द्वारं. *See* OUTMOST.

OUTFIT, *s.* (Equipment for a voyage, &c.) सज्जा, सम्भारः, सोपकारद्रव्यसम्भारः, सम्भृतिः *f.*, सामग्री -ग्र्यं, उपकरणसामग्री, परिच्छदः, परिच्छदसामग्री, सन्नाहः.—(Of a ship) नौकासज्जा.

To OUTGO, *v. a.* अतिगम् (c. 1. -गच्छति -गन्तुं), अती (c. 2. अत्येति -तुं, rt. इ), अतिचर् (c. 1. -चरति -रितुं), अतिक्रम (c. 1. -क्रामति -क्रमितुं).

OUTGOING, *s.* (Expenditure) व्ययः, अपव्ययः, अपचयः, उपक्षयः, विनियोगः, अपहारः; 'incomings and outgoings,' आयव्ययौ *m.* du.

To OUTGROW, *v. a.* अतिवृध् (c. 1. -वर्धते -र्धितुं), अधिकं वृध्, अतिशयवृद्धिं कृ, अधिकवृद्धिं कृ, अधिकवर्धनं कृ.

OUT-HOUSE, *s.* बाह्यगृहं, बहिर्गृहं, बहिःस्थगृहं, उपगृहं.

OUTLANDISH, *a.* (Foreign) विदेशीयः -या -यं, वैदेशिकः -की -कं, अन्यदेशीयः &c., विदेशजः -जा -जं, दूरदेशीयः -या -यं, परदेशीयः &c., दूरदेशवासी -सिनी -सि (न्), दूरवासी &c.—(Rustic, barbarous) ग्रामीयः &c., ग्राम्यः -म्या -म्यं, असभ्यः -भ्या -भ्यं, अशिष्टः -ष्टा -ष्टं, असंस्कृतः -ता -तं.

OUTLAW, *s.* व्यवहारबाह्यः, न्यायरक्षणबहिःस्थः, राजरक्षणबाह्यः, धर्म्मबहिःस्थः, पाषण्डः.

To OUTLAW, *v. a.* धर्म्मद्वाराद् बहिष्कृ, धर्म्माद् बहिष्कृ, न्यायद्वाराद् बहिष्कृ, व्यवहारबाह्यं -ह्यां कृ, धर्म्मबाह्यं -ह्यां कृ.

OUTLAWED, *p. p.* धर्म्मद्वारबहिष्कृतः -ता -तं, न्यायरक्षणबहिष्कृतः -ता -तं, व्यवहारबहिर्भूतः -ता -तं, राजरक्षणबहिर्भूतः &c.

OUTLAWRY, *s.* न्यायरक्षणबहिष्करणं, व्यवहारबहिष्करणं, राजरक्षणबहिष्करणं, धर्म्मबहिष्करणं, धर्म्मद्वारबहिष्करणं.

OUTLAY, *s.* व्ययः, अपव्ययः, धनव्ययः, अपचयः, उत्सर्गः, धनोत्सर्गः, धनत्यागः, क्षयः, उपक्षयः. *See* EXPENDITURE.

OUTLET, *s.* द्वारं, निर्गमद्वारं, मुखं, निर्गममार्गः, निर्गमपथः, निर्गमः; 'having a hundred outlets,' शतमुखः -खा -खं.

OUTLINE, *s.* (Exterior line) बाह्यरेखा, बहिर्लेखा.—(Slight sketch of a figure or subject) पाण्डुलेख्यं, पाण्डुरेखा, पाण्डुलेख्यमात्रं, आलेख्यं, लम्बालेख्यं, वस्तुमात्रं, वस्तु *n.*, आकारः.—(Of a picture) चित्रारम्भः.

To OUTLINE, *v. a.* बाह्यरेखामात्रं लिख् (c. 6. लिखति, लेखितुं), पाण्डुलेख्यं कृ, पाण्डुरेखाम् अङ्क् (c. 10. अङ्कयति -यितुं).

To OUTLIVE, *v. a.* अतिजीव् (c. 1. -जीवति -वितुं), अधिककालं जीव्, दीर्घतरकालं जीव्, धृ (c. 6. ध्रियते, धर्त्तुं), ध्रियमाणः -णा -णं भू.

OUTLYING, *a.* बहिःस्थः -स्था -स्थं, बहिर्वर्त्ती -र्त्तिनी -र्त्ति (न्).

To OUTMARCH, *v. a.* अतिया (c. 2. -याति -तुं), अतिव्रज् (c. 1. व्रजति -जितुं), अतिगम् (c. 1. -गच्छति -गन्तुं), शीघ्रतरयात्रां कृ, अग्रे या or यात्रां कृ.

OUTMOST, *a.* अतिबहिःस्थः -स्था -स्थं, अतिबाह्यः -ह्या -ह्यं, मध्यातिदूरस्थः &c. *See* OUTER.

To OUTNUMBER, *v. a.* अधिकसंख्यकः -का -कं भू or अस्, बहुतरसंख्यः -ख्या -ख्यं भू, अधिकीभू, बहुतरीभू.

OUTPOST, *s.* उपरक्षणं, बहिःस्थं सैन्यस्थानं or सैनिकस्थानं.

To OUTPOUR, *v. a.* उत्सिच् (c. 6. -सिञ्चति -सेक्तुं), उत्सृज् (c. 6. -सृजति -स्रष्टुं).

OUTPOURING, *s.* उत्सेकः, उत्सेचनं, अवसेचनं, उत्सर्गः, मोक्षणं.

To OUTRAGE, *v. a.* अभिद्रुह् (c. 4. -द्रुह्यति -द्रोहितुं -द्रोग्धुं), द्रुह्, धृष् (c. 10. धर्षयति -यितुं), प्रधृष्, उपद्रवं कृ, उपमर्दनं कृ, साहसं कृ, प्रमथ् (c. 1. -मथति -थितुं, c. 10. -माथयति -यितुं), प्रमाथं कृ, पारुष्यं कृ, उपघातं कृ, बलात्कारं कृ, न्यक्कृ, अवलेपं कृ, अत्याहितं कृ, दुष् (c. 10. दूषयति -यितुं).

OUTRAGE, *s.* साहसं, महासाहसं, अतिसाहसं, अभिद्रोहः, द्रोहः, प्रमाथः, धर्षः -र्षणं, उपमर्दः, अत्याहितं, उपद्रवः, उपघातः, बलात्कारः, अवलेपः, न्यक्कारः, न्यक्करणं, उद्रेकः, उत्सेकः, अत्ययः, अत्याचारः, उत्पातः, अतिक्रमः, मर्य्यादातिक्रमः, अन्यायः.

OUTRAGED, *p. p.* धर्षितः -ता -तं, प्रधर्षितः -ता -तं, अभिद्रुग्धः -ग्धा -ग्धं, प्रमाथितः -ता -तं, कृतसाहसः -सा -सं, उपमर्दितः -ता -तं, कृतोपद्रवः -वा -वं, न्यक्कृतः -ता -तं, अत्ययितः &c.

OUTRAGEOUS, *a.* अतिसाहसिकः -की -कं, अतिसाहसी -सिनी -सि (न्), अतिसाहसकर्म्मा -र्म्मा -र्म्म (न्), उग्रः -ग्रा -ग्रं, अत्युग्रः &c., उच्चण्डः -ण्डा -ण्डं, अत्याचारी &c., प्रमाथी &c., राक्षसी &c., राक्षसकर्म्मा &c., राक्षसः -सी -सं, राक्षसयोग्यः -ग्या -ग्यं, दारुणः -णा -णं, घोरः -रा -रं, अतिदुष्टः -ष्टा -ष्टं, अतिदुराचारः &c.

OUTRAGEOUSLY, *adv.* अतिसाहसपूर्व्वं, अतिसाहसं कृत्वा, अत्युग्रं, उपद्रवपूर्व्वं, सोपद्रवं, दारुणं, अतिदारुणं, घोरं, अतिदुष्टं, अत्याचारपूर्व्वं.

OUTRAGEOUSNESS, *s.* अतिसाहसिकत्वं, अत्युग्रता, दारुणता, घोरता, अतिदुष्टता -त्वं, राक्षसयोग्यता, उत्सिक्तता.

OUTRÉ, *a.* अतिमर्य्यादः -दा -दं, लोकव्यवहारविरुद्धः -द्धा -द्धं.

To OUTREACH, *v. a.* अतिगम् (c. 1. -गच्छति -गन्तुं), अतिक्रम् (c. 1. -क्रामति -क्रमितुं).

OUTRIDER, *s.* अश्वारूढः परिचरः or अनुचरः or परिधिस्थः.

OUTRIGHT, *adv.* (At once) सद्यस्, तत्काले, तत्क्षणे, सपदि, सम्प्रति, झटिति, अविलम्बितं.—(Completely) सु or अति prefixed, सर्व्वतस्, सम्यक्, अखिलेन, आमूलं, साद्यन्तं.—(Plainly) सुव्यक्तं, सुस्पष्टं, अवक्रं.

To OUTROOT, *v. a.* उन्मूल् (c. 10. -मूलयति -यितुं), समुन्मूल्, उच्छिद् (c. 7. -छिनत्ति -छेत्तुं), उत्पट् (c. 10. -पाटयति -यितुं). *See To* ERADICATE.

To OUTRUN, *v. a.* अतिधाव् (c. 1. -धावति -वितुं), पश्चात् त्यक्त्वा पूर्व्वं or अग्रे धाव् or पूर्व्वम् उपस्था (c. 1. -तिष्ठति -स्थातुं).

OUTSET, *s.* आरम्भः, प्रारम्भः, प्रथमारम्भः, आगमः, उपक्रमः, प्रक्रमः, आदिः *m.*, उपोद्घातः; 'at the very outset,' प्रथमारम्भे, आदौ, आदावेव, प्रथमदर्शनात्; 'the outset and termination,' आगमनिर्गमौ *m.* du., आद्यन्तं.

To OUTSHINE, *v. a.* अतिरुच् (c. 1. -रोचते -ति -चितुं), अधिकं प्रकाश् (c. 1. -काशते -शितुं) or शुभ् (c. 1. शोभते -भितुं), अधिकप्रभां दा, अधिकशोभां दा, अधिकतेजो दा, अधिकप्रकाशं दा; 'the sun outshines the moon,' सूर्य्यश् चन्द्रम् अतिरोचति तेजसा.

OUTSIDE, *s.* (The exterior) बहिर्भागः, बाह्यभागः, उपरिस्थभागः; 'on the outside,' बहिर्भागे, बहिस्.—(Outer side of an enclosure, &c.) बहिःप्रदेशः, बहिर्देशः.—(The utmost limit) परमावधिः *m.*, उत्तमावधिः *m.*

OUTSIDE, *adv.* (On the outside of) बहिस्, बहिर्भागे, अन्तरं -रेण; 'outside the fort,' दुर्गाद् अन्तरं or अन्तरेण.

OUTSIDE, *a.* बहिस् in comp., बाह्यः -ह्या -ह्यं, बहिःस्थः -स्था -स्थं.

OUTSKIRT, *s.* उपान्तः -न्तं, पर्य्यन्तः -न्तं, समन्तः, अन्तः -न्तं, प्रान्तः, सीमा, सीमाप्रदेशः, उत्सङ्गः, परिसरः, धारः; 'of a town,' नगरोपान्तं, नगरप्रान्तः, नगरपरिसरः; 'of a village,' ग्रामान्तः, उपशल्यं, उपशल्यं; 'of a wood,' वनान्तः, वनधारः.

To OUTSPREAD, *v. a.* विस्तृ (c. 10. -स्तारयति -यितुं), विसृ (c. 10. -सारयति -यितुं), प्रसृ, विततीकृ.

OUTSPREAD, *p.p.* विततः -ता -तं, प्रविततः &c., विस्तारितः -ता -तं, विस्तीर्णः -र्णा -र्णं, विस्तृतः -ता -तं, प्रसारितः &c., विसारितः &c.

OUTSTANDING, *a.* अशोधितः -ता -तं, असिद्धः -द्धा -द्धं, असाधितः -ता -तं.

To OUTSTARE, *v. a.* अधिकप्रागल्भ्येन निरीक्ष्य लज्जां गम् (c. 10. गमयति -यितुं), प्रगल्भवदनम् अधिकप्रागल्भ्येन निरीक्ष् (c. 1. -ईक्षते -क्षितुं).

To OUTSTRETCH, *v.a.* प्रसृ (c. 10. -सारयति -यितुं), प्रग्रह् (c. 9. -गृह्णाति -ग्रहीतुं).

OUTSRETCHED, *p.p.* प्रसारितः -ता -तं, प्रसृतः -ता -तं, उच्छ्रितः &c., अभ्युच्छ्रितः &c.; 'with outstretched neck,' उद्ग्रीवः -वा -वं; 'arm,' उद्बाहुः -हुः -हु, अभ्युच्छ्रितबाहुः &c.

To OUTSTRIP, *v. a.* अतिक्रम् (c. 1. -क्रामति -क्रमितुं), अतिचर् (c. 1. -चरति -रितुं), अतिगम् (c. 1. -गच्छति -गन्तुं), अती (c. 2. अत्येति -तुं, rt. इ), लङ्घ् (c.10. लङ्घयति-यितुं); 'outstripping the wind,' अत्यनिलः-ला-लं.

OUTSTRIPPED, *p.p.* अतिक्रान्तः -न्ता -न्तं, अतीतः -ता -तं, अन्तरितः -ता -तं.

To OUTVIE, *v. a.* अतिक्रम् (c. 1. -क्रामति -क्रमितुं), अभिभू, परिभू, अतिभू.

OUTWARD, *a.* (External) बाह्यः -ह्या -ह्यं, बहिःस्थः -स्था -स्थं, बहिःस्थितः -ता -तं, बाह्लीकः -का -कं, बहिर्भवः -वा -वं, बहिर्भूतः -ता -तं, बहिर्वर्त्ती -र्त्तिनी -र्त्ति (न्), बहिस् in comp.—(Visible) दृश्यः -श्या -श्यं, दृष्टः -ष्टा -ष्टं, आविर्भूतः -ता -तं.—(Not real) अवास्तवः -वी -वं.—(Tending out) बहिर्दिश्यः -श्या -श्यं.

OUTWARD, OUTWARDS, *adv.* बहिर्भागं प्रति, बहिस्, बहिर्दिशि, बहिर्देशं प्रति.

OUTWARDLY, *adv.* बाह्यतस्, बहिस्, बहिरङ्गे, बहिरङ्गतस्, बहिर्भागे, बहिर्भागतस्.—(Not really) अवस्तुतस्.

To OUTWEIGH, *v. a.* अधिकभारी -रिणी -रि भू or अस्, अतिभारी &c. भू, गुरुतरभारी &c. भू, गुरुतरः -रा -रं भू, भारेण वृध् (c. 1. वर्धते -र्धितुं).

To OUTWIT, *v. a.* अतिसन्धा (c. 3. -दधाति -धातुं), भ्रम् (c. 10. -तारयति-यितुं).

OUTWORK, *s.* दुर्गबहिःस्थितं प्राकारप्राचीरादि, बाह्यपरिक्रिया.

OVAL, *a.* अण्डाकारः -रा -रं, अण्डाकृतिः -तिः -ति, अण्डस्वरूपः -पा -पं.

OVAL, *s.* अण्डाकारः, अण्डाकृतिः *f.*, कक्षः, अधिककलितिं.

OVARIOUS, *a.* अण्डमयः -यी -यं, अण्डयुक्तः -क्ता -क्तं, अण्डरूपः -पा -पं.

OVARY, *s.* अण्डाशयः, अण्डाधारः, डिम्बाशयः, डिम्बकोषः.

OVATE, OVATED, *a.* अण्डाकृतिः -तिः -ति, अण्डाकारः -रा -रं.

OVEN, *s.* चुल्ली -ल्लिः *f.*, कन्दुः *m.f.*, आपाकः, उखा; 'baked in an oven,' कन्दुपक्वः -क्वा -क्वं, कान्दवः -वी -वं.

OVER, *prep.* (Above in place, position, rank, or value) अधि, उपरि, ऊर्द्ध्व prefixed; as, 'placed over,' अधिकृतः -ता -तं, अधिरोपितः -ता -तं; 'standing over,' अधिष्ठितः -ता -तं, अधिष्ठाता *m.* (तृ), ऊर्द्ध्वस्थितः &c.; 'situated over,' उपरिस्थः -स्था -स्थं; 'heaped over,' उपरिचितः -ता -तं; 'a tooth growing over another,' अधिदन्तः. When उपरि is not compounded with another word it governs the gen. c.; as, 'over all,' उपरि सर्व्वेषां. Sometimes उपरि is repeated; as, उपर्य्युपरि सर्व्वेषां.—(From side to side, across) expressed by various prepositions, such as अति, अधि, उत्, सम्, अभि, वि &c.; as, 'to cross over,' अतितॄ, उत्तॄ, समुत्तॄ, सन्तॄ, अतिक्रम्, समतिक्रम्, व्यतिक्रम्, संक्रम्, अती; 'to leap over,' उल्लङ्घ्, विलङ्घ्, अभिलङ्घ्, उत्प्लु. Sometimes expressed by पारं in comp.; as, 'to cross over a river,' नदीपारं गम्; 'crossing over,' पारगः -गा -गं.—(Denoting superiority) expressed by प्र, अधि, उत्, वि, ऊर्द्ध्व &c. prefixed; as in the following words signifying pre-eminence, or 'advantage over,' प्रधानता, प्रमुखता, अधिकत्वं, आधिक्यं, उत्कर्षः, उन्नतिः *f.*, विशिष्टता, ऊर्द्ध्वस्थितिः *f.*—(Upon the whole surface or through the whole extent) expressed by परि, वि prefixed; as, 'to wander over the earth,' पृथिवीं परिभ्रम् or पर्य्यट् or विभ्रम्.—(Over against) अभि, अभितस्, प्रति, अभिमुखं -खेन, सम्मुखं -खेन, प्रतिमुखं -खेन.

OVER, *adv.* (On the opposite side) पारे -रं; 'the boat is over the river,' पारगता नौका.—(From one to another by passing) expressed by the prepositions प्रति, नि, सम् &c., in combination with roots; as, 'to deliver over,' प्रतिपद्, निक्षिप्, संक्रम्.—(Above the top, running over). *See* OVERFLOWING. (More than the proper quantity, over and above) अधिकं, अधिकतरं, अतिरिक्तं, परं, भूयस्.—(Beyond) अति prefixed.—(Remaining, left over) उद्वृत्तः -त्ता -त्तं, उद्वृत्तः -त्ता -त्तं, शिष्टः -ष्टा -ष्टं, उच्छिष्टः &c., अवशिष्टः &c., अन्तरं, अन्तरितः -ता -तं; 'a part over,' कलान्तरं; 'that which is over,' उद्वृत्तं, शिष्टं, अवशिष्टं, or expressed by परि; as, 'one over,' एकावशिष्टं, एकपरि.—(Throughout) अधि prefixed, आद्यन्तं, आद्यन्तं; 'to read over,' अधिगम्, अधी, or expressed by पार; as, 'one who reads over the Vedas,' वेदपारगः; 'to get over, complete,' पार (nom. पारयति -यितुं), तीर (nom. तीरयति -यितुं), पारं गम्.—(Too much, excessively) अति or अतिशय or एकान्त prefixed, अतिशयेन, अधिकं, अतीव, एकान्ततस्.—(Over again) पुनर्; 'over and over again,' पुनःपुनर्, मुहुर्मुहुस्, वारं वारं.—(To be over). *See* *To* CEASE, *v. n.*—(To give over). *See* *To* GIVE, *v. a.*—(To turn over). *See* OVERTURN. For other senses of 'over,' *see* the verbs, &c., which follow.—(Past) वृत्तः -त्ता -त्तं, भूतः -ता -तं, अतीतः -ता -तं, गतः -ता -तं, अतिक्रान्तः -न्ता -न्तं, व्यतीतः -ता -तं.

To OVERABOUND, *v. n.* अतिरिक्तः -क्ता -क्तं भू, अतिबहुलीभू.

To OVERACT, *v. a.* अतिशयेन कृ, अधिकं कृ, अत्याचर् (c. 1. -चरति -रितुं).

To OVERAWE, *v. a.* सम्भ्रमेण उपहन् (c. 2. -हन्ति -न्तुं), त्रासयित्वा निग्रह् (c. 9. -गृह्णाति -ग्रहीतुं) or निषिध् (c. 1. -षेधति -षेद्धुं), अतिशयेन त्रस् (c. 10. त्रासयति -यितुं), आकुलीकृ, व्याकुलीकृ.

OVERAWED, *a.* सम्भ्रमोपहतः -ता -तं, सम्भ्रमाकुलितः -ता -तं.

To OVERBALANCE, *v. a.* *See* *To* OUTWEIGH.

OVERBALANCE, *s.* अधिकभारः, अतिभारः, अधिकतरभारः, सुभारः.

To OVERBEAR, *v. a.* (Bear down) निपत् (c. 10. -पातयति -यितुं), दम् (c. 10. दमयति -यितुं), प्रदम्, वशीकृ, धृष् (c. 10. धर्षयति -यितुं).

OVERBEARING, *a.* धृष्टः -ष्टा -ष्टं, धर्षितः -ता -तं, प्रधृष्टः &c., प्रधर्षितः -ता -तं, धर्षी -र्षिणी -र्षि (न्), उद्धतः -ता -तं, अवलिप्तः -प्ता -प्तं, धृष्णुः -ष्णुः -ष्णु; 'to be overbearing,' धृष् (c. 5. धृष्णोति, धर्षितुं).

OVERBOARD, *adv.* नौकावहिस्, नौकोपरिष्टात्, नौपृष्ठतस्, नौपार्श्वात्, नौपार्श्वतस्, नौकातस्, समुद्रमध्ये, मध्येसमुद्रं, मध्येऽर्णवं.

To OVERBURDEN, *v. a.* अतिभारं न्यस् (c. 4. -अस्यति -असितुं), अतिभारेण पीड् (c. 10. पीडयति -यितुं), अतिभारयुक्तं -क्तां कृ.

OVERBURDENED, *p.p.* अतिभारी -रिणी -रि (न्), अतिभारवान् -वती -वत् (त्), अतिभाराक्रान्तः -न्ता -न्तं, अतिभारयुक्तः -क्ता -क्तं.

To OVERCAST, *v. a.* मेघावृतं -तां कृ, मेघाच्छन्नं -न्नां कृ, मेघैः प्रच्छद् (c. 10. -छादयति-यितुं) or आच्छद्, कलुषीकृ, तिमिरीकृ, साभ्रं -भ्रां कृ, समेघं -घां कृ.

OVERCAST, *a.* मेघावृतः -ता -तं, मेघाच्छन्नः -न्ना -न्नं, मेघाच्छादितः -ता -तं, तमोवृतः -ता -तं, घनोपरुद्धः -द्धा -द्धं, घनारुद्धः &c., घनावरुद्धः &c.

OVERCAUTIOUS, *a.* अत्यवहितः -ता -तं, एकान्तावहितः &c., स्ववहितः &c.

To OVERCHARGE, *v. a.* (In an account) अतिमूल्यं or अधिकमूल्यं प्रार्थ् (c. 10. -अर्थयते -ति -यितुं). *See To* OVERBURDEN, OVERLOAD.

OVERCHARGE, *s.* (Asking too much) अतिमूल्यप्रार्थनं, अधिकमूल्यप्रार्थनं.

To OVERCLOUD, *v. a.* मेघावृतं -तां कृ. *See To* OVERCAST, *v. a.*

To OVERCOME, *v. a.* (Subdue) जि (c. 1. जयति -ते, जेतुं), पराजि, निर्जि, विजि, सञ्जि, अभिभू, प्रभू, पराभू, वशीकृ, दम् (c. 10. दमयति -यितुं), प्रदम्, धृष् (c. 10. धर्षयति -यितुं), प्रधृष्, हन् (c. 2. हन्ति -न्तुं), पर्यामृश् (c. 6. -मृशति -म्रष्टुं), अलङ्कृ.—(Surmount, get the better of) अतिक्रम् (c. 1. -क्रामति -क्रमितुं), अधिक्रम्, अधिरुह् (c. 1. -रोहति -रोढुं), अध्यारुह्, आरुह्, अती (c. 2. अत्येति -तुं, rt. इ), व्यती, अतिशी (c. 2. -शेते -शयितुं), तॄ (c. 1. तरति -रितुं -रीतुं), पार् (c. 10. पारयति -यितुं), अभिभू.—(Exhaust, distress) सद् (c. 10. सादयति -यितुं), अवसद्, खिद् (c. 10. खेदयति -यितुं), व्याकुल् (c. 10. -कुलयति -यितुं).

OVERCOME, *p. p.* (Subdued) जितः -ता -तं, पराजितः -ता -तं, विजितः -ता -तं, अभिभूतः -ता -तं, पराभूतः &c., वशीकृतः &c., वशीभूतः &c., दमितः -ता -तं, दान्तः -न्ता -न्तं.—(Distressed, agitated) आक्रान्तः -न्ता -न्तं, आर्त्तः -र्त्ता -र्त्तं, आतुरः -रा -रं, ग्रस्तः -स्ता -स्तं, आकुलः -ला -लं, व्याकुलः -ला -लं, परिगतः -ता -तं; 'with hunger,' क्षुधाक्रान्तः &c., क्षुधार्त्तः -र्त्ता -र्त्तं, क्षुधातुरः -रा -रं; 'with sorrow,' शोकार्त्तः &c., शोकाकुलः -ला -लं; 'with shame,' ह्रीणितः -ता -तं, लज्जापरिगतः -ता -तं.

OVER-COMPASSIONATE, *a.* एकान्तकरुणः -णा -णं, अतिकारुणिकः -की -कं.

OVER-CONFIDENT, *s.* अतिविश्वासी -सिनी -सि (न्), एकान्तविश्वासी &c.

To OVERDO, *v. a.* अतिशयेन कृ, अधिकं कृ.—(Cook too much) अतिशयेन पच् (c. 1. पचति, पक्तुं), अतिपाकं कृ, अतिपक्वं -क्वां कृ.

OVERDONE, *p. p.* (Cooked too much) अतिपक्वः -क्वा -क्वं.—(Too much wearied) अतिश्रान्तः -न्ता -न्तं, अतिश्रमार्त्तः -र्त्ता -र्त्तं.

To OVER-EAT, *v. a.* अतिभोजनं कृ, अत्यशनं कृ, अतिसौहित्यं कृ.

To OVER-ESTIMATE, *v. a.* अधिकं or अतिशयेन मन् (c. 4. मन्यते, मन्तुं).

OVER-EXCITEMENT, *s.* अत्युत्तापः, अत्युद्योगः, अत्युत्कम्पः.

OVER-FATIGUE, *s.* अतिश्रान्तिः *f.*, अतिश्रमः, अतिक्लेशः, अतिशयखेदः.

To OVER-FLOW, *v. n.* (Run over the brim) उत्सेचनं कृ, उत्सेकं कृ, अतिपूर्णः -र्णा -र्णं भू, अत्यन्तपूर्णः -र्णा -र्णं भू, परिपूर्णः &c. भू, परिपूर्णीभू, जलोत्सेकं कृ, जलोत्सेचनं कृ, जलाप्लावनं कृ, उपचितः -ता -तं भू, उपचितजलः -ला -लं भू, समाप्लुतः -ता -तं भू, सम्प्लुतजलः -ला -लं भू, स्फाय् (c. 1. स्फायते -यितुं), स्फीतः -ता -तं भू, स्फीतजलः -ला -लं भू.—(Be exuberant) अतिबहुलीभू, अतिप्रचुरीभू, अतिरिक्तः -क्ता -क्तं भू, उद्रिक्तः &c. भू, पुष्कलीभू, वृध् (c. 1. वर्धते -र्धितुं), प्रवृद्धः -द्धा -द्धं भू; 'overflows with tears,' बाष्पायते; 'their eyes overflowed with tears,' तेषां नेत्राणि समाप्लुतानि वारिणा.

To OVERFLOW, *v. a.* जलेन प्लु (c. 10. प्लावयति -यितुं) or आप्लु or परिप्लु or संप्लु, जलप्लुतं -तां कृ, जलप्लावितं -तां कृ, जलाप्लावितं -तां कृ, जलव्याप्तं -प्तां कृ, जलाप्लावनं कृ, जलप्लावनं कृ.

OVERFLOW, *s.* उत्सेकः, उत्सेचनं, जलप्लावः -वनं, जलाप्लावनं, जलपरिप्लवः, जलोच्छ्वासः, जलोत्सेकः, जलवृद्धिः *f.*, जलौघः, जलप्रवृद्धिः *f.*, जलागमः.

OVERFLOWED, *p.p.* जलप्लावितः -ता -तं, जलाप्लावितः &c., आप्लावितः &c., जलप्लुतः -ता -तं, जलपरिप्लुतः &c., आप्लुतः &c., परिप्लुतः &c., जलव्याप्तः -प्ता -प्तं, व्याप्तः &c.; 'is overflowed,' प्लाव्यते.

OVERFLOWING, *part.* or *a.* (So full as to run over) उत्सेचनकारी -रिणी -रि (न्), उत्सिच्यमानः -ना -नं, उत्सिक्तः -क्ता -क्तं, अतिपूर्णः -र्णा -र्णं, अत्यन्तपूर्णः &c., परिपूर्णः &c., पर्याकुलः -ला -लं; 'with water,' सम्प्लुतोदकः -का -कं, सम्प्लुतजलः -ला -लं, जलोत्सिच्यमानः &c.—(Exuberant) अतिबहुलः -ला -लं, बहुलः &c., पुष्कलः -ला -लं, प्रचुरः -रा -रं, उद्रिक्तः -क्ता -क्तं, अतिरिक्तः &c., उपचितः -ता -तं; 'eyes overflowing with tears,' अश्रुसमाप्लुतानि नेत्राणि; 'having overflowing eyes,' अश्रुप्लुताक्षः -क्षी -क्षं; 'overflowing its bounds,' उद्वेलः -ला -लं.

OVERFLOWING, *s.* उत्सेकः, उत्सेचनं, जलाप्लावनं, जलोत्सेकः, प्रवृद्धिः *f.*, वृद्धिः, अतिरिक्तता, उद्रिक्तता, परिपूर्णता, अतिपूर्णता, उपचयः, आतिशय्यं, आधिक्यं, अतिबाहुल्यं; 'of a river beyond its banks,' विदारः. *See* OVERFLOW. 'To fill to overflowing,' प्लु (c. 10. प्लावयति -यितुं), परिप्लु.

To OVERGROW, *v. a.* or *n.* अतिवृध् (c. 1. -वर्धते -र्धितुं), अधिकं वृध्, अत्यन्तं or अतिमात्रं वृध् or रुह् (c. 1. रोहति, रोढुं) or प्ररुह्.

OVERGROWN, *p.p.* or *a.* अतिवर्धितः -ता -तं, कालप्ररूढः -ढा -ढं, अतिरूढः &c.

OVERGROWTH, *s.* अतिवृद्धिः *f.*, अतिवर्धनं, अधिकवृद्धिः, कालप्ररूढिः *f.*

To OVERHANG, *v. n.* बहिर्लम्ब् (c. 1. -लम्बते -म्बितुं), प्रलम्ब्, अवलम्ब्, बहिःप्रलम्ब्, बहिःस्था (c. 1. -तिष्ठति -स्थातुं).

OVERHASTY, *a.* अतिसाहसी -सिनी -सि (न्), एकान्तसाहसी &c.

To OVERHAUL, *v. a.* इतस्ततः समाकृष्य परीक्ष् (c. 1. -ईक्षते -क्षितुं) or निरूप् (c. 10. -रूपयति -यितुं), पुनःपुनः परिवर्त्य परीक्ष्, पुनः परीक्ष्.

OVERHEAD, *adv.* मस्तकोपरि, शीर्षोपरि, उपरिष्टात्, उपरिस्थाने, अर्द्धस्थाने, ऊर्द्ध्वं, ऊर्द्ध्वं, उच्चं, विहायसा.

To OVERHEAR, *v. a.* प्रच्छन्नं स्थित्वा द्वयोः संलापं श्रु (c. 5. शृणोति, श्रोतुं) or उपश्रु or आकर्ण् (c. 10. -कर्णयति -यितुं), अकस्मात् आकर्ण्.

OVERHEARD, *p.p.* आकर्णितः -ता -तं, अकस्मात् आकर्णितः &c., श्रुतः -ता -तं.

To OVERJOY, *v. a.* अत्यन्तम् आनन्द् (c. 10. -नन्दयति -यितुं) or प्रहृष् (c. 10. -हर्षयति -यितुं), अतिशयेन प्रहृष्.

OVERJOY, *s.* अत्यानन्दः, परमानन्दः, परमहर्षः, परमाह्लादः.

OVERJOYED, *p. p.* परमहृष्टः -ष्टा -ष्टं, परमसंहृष्टः &c., परमानन्दितः -ता -तं, परमाह्लादितः -ता -तं, हर्षाकुलः -ला -लं, हर्षविह्वलः -ला -लं, रोमाञ्चितः -ता -तं, हर्षरोमाञ्चितः -ता -तं, पुलकितः -ता -तं, हर्षपुलकितः -ता -तं, उल्लासितः -ता -तं, उल्लसितः -ता -तं, उल्लासी -सिनी -सि (न्), परमप्रीतः -ता -तं, हृष्टचित्तः -त्ता -त्तं, प्रहृष्टः &c., प्रहृष्टमनाः -नाः -नः

(न्), अतिहर्षयुक्तः -क्ता -क्तं, अतितुष्टः &c.; 'to be overjoyed,' परमम् आनन्द् (c. 1. -नन्दति -न्दितुं), परमानन्दं कृ.

OVERLAID, *p. p.* आच्छन्नः -न्ना -न्नं, पिहितः -ता -तं, पिनद्धः -द्धा -द्धं; 'with gold,' सुवर्णपत्रपिनद्धः -द्धा -द्धं.

OVERLARGE, *a.* अतिबृहन् -हती -हत् (त्), अतिमहान् -हती &c., अतिस्थूलः -ला -लं, अतिविपुलः &c., एकान्तस्थूलः &c., अतिरिक्तः -क्ता -क्तं.

To OVERLAY, *v. a.* (An infant) शय्यास्तरणभारेण पीडयित्वा शिशुप्राणघातं कृ.—(Cover, spread over) छद् (c. 10. छादयति -यितुं), आछद्, पिधा (c. 3. -दधाति -धातुं), अपिधा.—(Oppress with too great a weight) अतिभारेण पीड् (c. 10. पीडयति -यितुं).

To OVERLEAP, *v. a.* लङ्घ् (c. 10. लङ्घयति -यितुं), उल्लङ्घ्, विलङ्घ्, लङ्घनं कृ, उत्प्लु (c. 1. -प्लवते -प्लोतुं).

OVERLENIENT, *a.* अतिमृदुः -दुः -द्वी -दु, एकान्तमृदुः &c.

To OVERLOAD, *v. a.* अतिभारं न्यस् (c. 4. -अस्यति -असितुं) or आरुह् in caus. (-रोपयति -यितुं), अतिभाराक्रान्तं -न्तां कृ, अत्यन्तं or अतिशयेन पृ (c. 10. पूरयति -यितुं), अतिपूर्णं -र्णां कृ.

OVERLOADED, *p. p.* अतिभाराक्रान्तः -न्ता -न्तं, अतिभारार्त्तः -र्त्ता -र्त्तं, अतिभारी -रिणी -रि (न्), अतिपूर्णः -र्णा -र्णं, अतिपूरितः &c. *See* OVERBURDENED.

OVERLOADING, *s.* अतिभारन्यासः, अतिभारारोपणं, आक्रमः -मणं.

To OVERLOOK, *v. a.* (View from a high place) उन्नतस्थानाद् अवलोक् (c. 10. -लोकयति -यितुं, c. 1. -लोकते -कितुं) or निरीक्ष् (c. 1. -ईक्षते -क्षितुं) or अवेक्ष् or अभिवीक्ष्.—(Superintend, preside over) अधिष्ठा (c. 1. -तिष्ठति -ष्ठातुं), कार्य्यावेक्षणं कृ, कार्य्यदर्शनं कृ, कार्य्येक्षणं कृ, कार्य्याणि अवेक्ष्, अध्यक्षः -क्षा -क्षं भू.—(Let pass, excuse) उपेक्ष्, अवसृज् (c. 6. -सृजति -स्रष्टुं), मुच् (c. 6. मुञ्चति, मोक्तुं), क्षम् (c. 1. क्षमते -ति, क्षन्तुं), दोषाच्छादनं कृ, दोषक्षालनं कृ, उपेक्षां कृ, उपेक्षणं कृ.

OVERLOOKED, *p. p.* (Viewed from above) उन्नतस्थानाद् or उन्नतप्रदेशाद् अवलोकितः -ता -तं.—(Superintended) अधिष्ठितः -ता -तं, अवेक्षितः -ता -तं.—(Passed over, excused) उपेक्षितः -ता -तं, अवसृष्टः -ष्टा -ष्टं.

OVERLOOKER, *s.* अवेक्षिता *m.* (तृ), अध्यक्षः, उपद्रष्टा *m.* (ष्टृ), कार्य्यद्रष्टा.

OVERMUCH, *a.* अति or अतिशय prefixed, अधिकः -का -कं, अत्यन्तः -न्ता -न्तं, एकान्तः -न्ता -न्तं, अतिमात्रः -त्रा -त्रं, अतिमर्य्यादः -दा -दं, अतिरिक्तः -क्ता -क्तं.

OVERMUCH, *s.* अतिबाहुल्यं, आधिक्यं, अधिकता, अतिरिक्तता, एकान्तत्वं.

OVERMUCH, *adv.* अति prefixed, अतिशयेन, अत्यन्तं, अतिमर्य्यादं, एकान्ततस्.

OVER-OFFICIOUS, *a.* अत्युपचारी -रिणी -रि (न्), अत्युपकारी &c., अत्युपचारः &c.

To OVERPASS, *v. a.* अतिक्रम् (c. 1. -क्रामति -क्रमितुं), अतिचर् (c. 1. -चरति -रितुं).

OVERPAST, *p. p.* अतिक्रान्तः -न्ता -न्तं, अतीतः -ता -तं, गतः -ता -तं.

To OVERPAY, *v. a.* अतिमूल्यं or अधिकमूल्यं दा (c. 3. ददाति, दातुं).

OVERPLUS, *s.* उद्वर्त्तः, उद्वृत्तं, अवशिष्टं, उच्छिष्टं, शिष्टं, परभागः.

To OVERPOWER, *v. a.* अभिभू, पराभू, पराजि (c. 1. -जयते -जेतुं), निर्जि, दम् (c. 10. दमयति -यितुं), प्रदम्, आक्रम् (c. 1. -क्रामति -क्रमितुं), पराक्रम्, वशीकृ. *See To* OVERCOME.

OVERPOWERED, *p. p.* पराजितः -ता -तं, आक्रान्तः -न्ता -न्तं. *See* OVERCOME.

To OVERRATE, OVERPRIZE, *v. a.* अधिकं or अतिशयेन मन् (c. 4. मन्यते, मन्तुं, c. 10. मानयति -यितुं), अधिकमूल्यं or अतिमूल्यं कृ.

OVE

To OVERREACH, *v. a.* अतिसन्धा (c. 3. -दधाति -धातुं), अभिसन्धा, प्रलभ् (c. 1. -लभते -लब्धुं), विप्रलभ्, प्रतॄ (c. 10. -तारयति -यितुं).

OVERREACHED, *p. p.* अतिसंहितः -ता -तं, प्रलब्धः -ब्धा -ब्धं, प्रतारितः -ता -तं.

OVERREACHING, *s.* अतिसन्धानं, अतिसन्धिः *m.*, प्रलम्भः, प्रतारणं -णा.

OVERRIPE, *a.* अतिपक्कः -क्का -क्कं, कालप्ररूढः -ढा -ढं, विनाशोन्मुखः &c.

To OVERRULE, *v. a.* अधिकृ, प्रभू, अधिष्ठा (c. 1. -तिष्ठति -ष्ठातुं), विनियम् (c. 1. -यच्छति -यन्तुं), नियम्, सन्नियम्, संयम्, यम्, शास् (c. 2. शास्ति, शासितुं), अनुशास्, अधिकारं कृ.

OVERRULER, *s.* अधिकारी *m.* (न्), अधिष्ठाता *m.* (तृ), प्रभुः *m.*, अनुशास्ता.

To OVERRUN, *v. a.* आक्रम् (c. 1. -क्रामति -क्रमितुं), अधिक्रम्, उपद्रु (c. 1. -द्रवति -द्रोतुं), उपद्रवं कृ, उपप्लवं कृ.

OVERRUN, *p. p.* आक्रान्तः -न्ता -न्तं, आक्रमितः -ता -तं, उपद्रुतः -ता -तं, उपप्लुतः &c., आकीर्णः -र्णा -र्णं, आस्तीर्णः &c., व्याप्तः -प्ता -प्तं.

To OVERSEE, *v. a.* उपदृश् (c. 1. -पश्यति -द्रष्टुं), अवेक्ष् (c. 1. -ईक्षते -क्षितुं), कार्य्यावेक्षणं कृ, कार्य्यदर्शनं कृ, कार्य्येक्षणं कृ, अधिष्ठा (c. 1. -तिष्ठति -ष्ठातुं).

OVERSEER, *s.* अध्यक्षः, उपद्रष्टा *m.* (ष्टृ), अवेक्षिता *m.* (तृ), कार्य्यावेक्षिता *m.*, अधिष्ठाता *m.*, अधिकर्म्मिकः, कार्य्यद्रष्टा *m.*, कार्य्याधीशः, अधिकारी *m.* (न्), अधिकृतः; 'of a village,' स्थायुकः.

To OVERSET, *v. a.* पर्यस् (c. 4. -अस्यति -असितुं), परिवृत् (c. 10. -वर्त्तयति -यितुं), आक्षिप् (c. 10. -क्षेपयति -यितुं), निपत् (c. 10. -पातयति -यितुं), अधः कृ.

To OVERSET, *v. n.* परिवृत् (c. 1. -वर्त्तते -र्त्तितुं). *See To* UPSET.

To OVERSHADOW, *v. a.* छायया छद् (c. 10. छादयति -यितुं) or प्रच्छद्, छायां कृ, छायावृतं -तां कृ, वितानीकृ.

OVERSHADOWED, *p. p.* छायावृतः -ता -तं, छायाच्छादितः &c., छायाच्छन्नः -न्ना -न्नं.

To OVERSHOOT, *v. a.* लक्ष्यम् अतिक्रम् (c. 1. -क्रामति -क्रमितुं) or लङ्घ् (c. 10. लङ्घयति -यितुं) or उल्लङ्घ्, लक्ष्यातिक्रमं कृ, लक्ष्योल्लङ्घनं कृ, लक्ष्यातिक्षेपं कृ.

OVERSIGHT, *s.* (Error) दृष्टिदोषः, भ्रमः, भ्रान्तिः *f.*, प्रमादः.

To OVERSLEEP, *v. a.* अतिशयेन or अतिदीर्घं or सुदीर्घं स्वप् (c. 2. स्वपिति, स्वप्तुं), अतिनिद्रां कृ, अतिस्वापं कृ.

To OVERSPREAD, *v. a.* आक्रम् (c. 1. -क्रामति -क्रमितुं), आछद् (c. 10. -छादयति -यितुं), आवृ (c. 5. -वृणोति -वरितुं -रीतुं), समावृ, अवतन् (c. 5. -तनोति -नितुं), वितन्, वितानीकृ, अवकॄ (c. 6. -किरति -करितुं -रीतुं), समवकॄ, आकॄ, पृ (c. 10. पूरयति -यितुं).

OVERSPREAD, *p. p.* आक्रान्तः -न्ता -न्तं, समाक्रान्तः &c., आच्छादितः -ता -तं, आच्छन्नः -न्ना -न्नं, प्रच्छादितः &c., आवृतः -ता -तं, आकीर्णः -र्णा -र्णं, आस्तीर्णः &c., व्याप्तः -प्ता -प्तं, संवीतः &c., परिवीतः &c., पूरितः &c., गाहितः &c., श्रितः &c., वितानीकृतः &c., पूर्णः -र्णा -र्णं.

To OVERSTATE, *v. a.* अतिशयेन or वागाधिक्येन वद् (c. 1. वदति -दितुं), अत्युक्तिं कृ, अतिशयोक्तिं कृ.

To OVERSTEP, *v. a.* अतिक्रम् (c. 1. -क्रामति -क्रमितुं), लङ्घ् (c. 10. लङ्घयति -यितुं), उल्लङ्घ्, विलङ्घ्, अभिलङ्घ्.

OVERSTOCK, *s.* अतिसञ्चयः, अधिकसञ्चयः, अतिसम्भारः, अतिसङ्ग्रहः.

To OVERSTOCK, *v. a.* अतिशयेन सम्भृ (c. 1. -भरति -भर्त्तुं) or उपक्लृप् (c. 10. -कल्पयति -यितुं) or पृ (c. 10. पूरयति -यितुं), अतिसम्भारं कृ, अतिसञ्चयं कृ, अधिकसम्भारं कृ, अतिपूर्त्तिं कृ, अधिकपूर्त्तिं कृ.

OVERSTOCKED, *p. p.* अतिसम्भृतः -ता -तं, अतिपूरितः -ता -तं, अतिपूर्णः -र्णा -र्णं.

To OVERSTRAIN, *v. n.* अतियत्नं कृ, अतिप्रयत्नं कृ, अतिशयेन यत् (c. 1. यतते -तितुं).

Overt, *a.* प्रकाशः -शा -शं, स्पष्टः -ष्टा -ष्टं, व्यक्तः -क्ता -क्तं, विस्पष्टः -ष्टा -ष्टं, अभिव्यक्तः &c., विवृतः -ता -तं, प्रकटः -टा -टं, अगूढः -ढा -ढं, आविर्भूतः &c., प्रत्यक्षः -क्षा -क्षं.

To **overtake**, *v. a.* ग्रह् (c. 9. गृह्णाति, ग्रहीतुं), प्राप् (c. 5. -आप्नोति -आप्तुं), सम्प्राप्, धृ (c. 1. धरति, धर्त्तुं), ग्रस् (c. 1. ग्रसते -सितुं), आक्रम् (c. 1. -क्रामति -क्रमितुं), पश्चाद्धावन् or पश्चाद् अनुधाव्य आक्रम् or आक्रमणं कृ.—(Come upon unexpectedly) अकस्माद् आसद् (c. 10. -सादयति -यितुं) or प्राप्.

Overtaken, *p. p.* प्राप्तः -प्ता -प्तं, सम्प्राप्तः -प्ता -प्तं, ग्रस्तः -स्ता -स्तं, धृतः -ता -तं, गृहीतः -ता -तं, आक्रान्तः -न्ता -न्तं, आक्रमितः -ता -तं.—(Come upon suddenly) अकस्मात् आसादितः -ता -तं.

To **overtask**, **overtax**, *v. a.* अतिभारं न्यस् (c. 4. -अस्यति -असितुं) or ऋ in caus. (अर्पयति -यितुं), अधिकभारं न्यस्.

To **overthrow**, *v. a.* (Defeat) पराजि (c. 1. -जयते -जेतुं), विजि, निर्जि, जि, पराहन् (c. 2. -हन्ति -न्तुं), अभिभू, पराभू, परास् (c. 4. -अस्यति -असितुं), दम् (c. 10. दमयति -यितुं), प्रदम्, पर्य्यामृश् (c. 6. -मृशति -म्रष्टुं), वशीकृ.—(Turn upside down, upset, subvert) पर्य्यस्, पराक्षिप् (c. 6. -क्षिपति -क्षेप्तुं), आक्षिप् (c. 10. क्षेपयति -यितुं), परिवृत् (c. 10. -वर्त्तयति -यितुं), संक्षुभ् (c. 10. -क्षोभयति -यितुं), पत् (c. 10. पातयति -यितुं), निपत्.—(Destroy, &c.). *See* **Overturn**.

Overthrow, *s.* (Defeat) पराजयः, अपजयः, जयः, पराभवः, अभिभवः, अभिभूतिः *f.*, परिभवः.—(Ruin, destruction) नाशः, विनाशः, प्रणाशः, क्षयः, ध्वंसः, विध्वंसः, प्रध्वंसः, उच्छेदः, समुच्छेदः, सादः -दनं घातः, विघातः, भङ्गः, भेदः, व्यसनं; 'of an army,' बलव्यसनं.—(Upsetting, subverting) पर्य्यासः, पर्य्यसनं, परिवर्त्तनं, पातनं, निपातनं.

Overthrown, *p. p.* पराजितः -ता -तं, जितः &c., पराभूतः &c., अभिभूतः &c., पराहतः &c., परास्तः -स्ता -स्तं, उपास्तः &c., नष्टः -ष्टा -ष्टं, नाशितः -ता -तं, विनाशितः &c., हतः &c., भग्नः -ग्ना -ग्नं, पातितः -ता -तं, निपातितः &c., ध्वंसितः &c., जातव्यसनः -ना -नं.

Overtly, *adv.* प्रकाशं, स्पष्टं, विस्पष्टं, व्यक्तं, प्रकटं, आविस्, प्रादुस्, अगूढं, प्रत्यक्षं -क्षेण -क्षतस्.

Overture, *s.* (Opening) विवृतिः *f.*, विवरणं, प्रकाशः -शनं.—(Proposal) उपन्यासः, निवेदनं, प्रसङ्गः, अभिधानं; 'secret overture,' उपजापः -जापः.—(Musical or dramatic prelude) पूर्व्वरङ्गः, प्रस्तावना, प्रकरणं, उपोद्घातः, नान्दी; 'player or speaker of it,' नान्दीवादी, नान्दीकरः.

To **overturn**. *v. a.* परावृत् (c. 10. -वर्त्तयति -यितुं), परिवृत्, अपवृत्, पर्य्यस् (c. 4. -अस्यति -असितुं), पराक्षिप् (c. 6. -क्षिपति -क्षेप्तुं), आक्षिप् (c. 10. -क्षेपयति -यितुं), पत् (c. 10. पातयति -यितुं), निपत्, उत्सद् (c. 10. सादयति -यितुं), संक्षुभ् (c. 10. -क्षोभयति -यितुं), अधोमुखीकृ, अधरोत्तरीकृ, अधः कृ, न्युब्जीकृ.—(Destroy, &c.) नश् (c. 10. नाशयति -यितुं), विनश्, प्रणश्, ध्वंस् (c. 10. ध्वंसयति -यितुं), विध्वंस्, प्रध्वंस्, उच्छिद् (c. 7. -छिनत्ति -छेत्तुं), हन् (c. 2. हन्ति -न्तुं, c. 10. घातयति -यितुं), सद्.

Overturn, *s.* पर्य्यासः, पर्य्यसनं, परिवर्त्तनं, परावर्त्तनं, पातनं, निपातनं, उत्सादनं, क्षोभः, संक्षोभः, ध्वंसः, ध्वंसनं, प्रध्वंसः. *See* **Overthrow**.

Overturned, *p. p.* पर्य्यस्तः -स्ता -स्तं, पराक्षिप्तः -प्ता -प्तं, परावर्त्तितः -ता -तं, परिवर्त्तितः &c., परावृत्तः -त्ता -त्तं, अपवृत्तः &c., पातितः &c., निपातितः &c., उत्सादितः &c., संक्षोभितः &c., अधःकृतः &c., ध्वंसितः &c. *See* **Overthrown**.

Overturning, *s.* परावर्त्तनं, परिवर्त्तनं, पर्य्यसनं, उत्सादनं. *See* **Overturn**.

To **overvalue**, *v. a.* अधिकं or अतिशयेन मन् (c. 4. मन्यते, मन्तुं, c. 10. मानयति -यितुं), अधिकमूल्यं or अतिमूल्यं कृ or स्था in caus. (स्थापयति -यितुं).

Overweening, *a.* अत्यभिमानी -निनी -नि (न्), अतिमानी &c., अत्यहङ्कारी &c., अत्यहंयुः -युः -यु, आत्मश्लाघी &c.

Overweeningly, *adv.* अत्यभिमानेन, अत्यहङ्कारेण, अत्यभिमानपूर्व्वं.

Overweight, *s.* अतिभारः, अधिकभारः, भाराधिक्यं, अतिशयभारः.

To **overwhelm**, *v. a.* (Crush, beat down) अवमृद् (c. 9. -मृद्नाति -मर्दितुं), प्रमृद्, आमृद्, अवपत् (c. 10. -पातयति -यितुं), निपत्, पुष् (c. 10. पोषयति -यितुं), निष्पिष् (c. 7. -पिनष्टि -पेष्टुं), सम्पिष्, विनिष्पिष्.—(Overspread) आछद् (c. 10. छादयति -यितुं), समाछद्, आवृ (c. 5. -वृणोति -वरितुं -रीतुं), समावृ, आक्रम् (c. 1. क्रामति -क्रमितुं), अवकॄ (c. 6. -किरति -करितुं -रीतुं), समवकॄ, अवाकॄ; 'he overwhelms them with arrows,' तान् अवाकिरति शरैः.—(Immerge, submerge) मज्ज् (c. 10. मज्जयति -यितुं), निमज्ज्, अवगाह् (c. 10. -गाहयति -यितुं), समाप्लु (c. 10. -प्लावयति -यितुं, c. 1. -प्लवते), समभिप्लु, अभिप्लु, परिप्लु, अभिपरिप्लु, उपप्लु, विप्लु, समाप्लुतं -तां कृ, परिप्लुतं -तां कृ, समभिप्लुतं &c. कृ, मग्नं -ग्नां कृ.

Overwhelmed, *p. p.* मर्दितः -ता -तं, अवमर्दितः &c., अवपातितः &c., सम्पिष्टः -ष्टा -ष्टं, आछन्नः -न्ना -न्नं, आच्छादितः -ता -तं, आवृतः -ता -तं, आक्रान्तः -न्ता -न्तं, समाक्रान्तः &c., आकीर्णः -र्णा -र्णं, मग्नः -ग्ना -ग्नं, निमग्नः &c., प्रमग्नः &c., गाहितः &c., अभिप्लुतः &c., अभिपरिप्लुतः &c., समभिप्लुतः &c., उपप्लुतः &c., परिप्लुतः &c., समाप्लुतः &c., सम्प्लुतः &c., उपद्रुतः &c., ग्रस्तः -स्ता -स्तं, परिगतः &c., आकुलः -ला -लं; 'with care,' चिन्तामग्नः &c., चिन्ताकुलः &c.; 'with shame,' ह्रीपरिगतः &c.

Overwhelming, *part.* or *a.* अवमर्दी -र्दिनी -र्दि (न्), उपप्लवी &c., विप्लवकारी &c., उपप्लवकारकः -का -कं.

Overwise, *a.* अतिप्राज्ञः -ज्ञा -ज्ञं, अतिज्ञानी -निनी -नि (न्), एकान्तप्राज्ञः &c., अतिपण्डितः -ता -तं, पण्डितम्मन्यः -न्या -न्यं.

To **overwork**, *v. a.* अतिशयेन or एकान्ततः or अधिकम् आयस् (c. 10. -यासयति -यितुं), अत्यायासं or अतिक्लेशं कृ or दा.

Overwork, *s.* अत्यायासः, अतिक्लेशः, एकान्तक्लेशः, अतिश्रमः.

Overworked, *p. p.* अत्यायासितः -ता -तं, अतिक्लेशितः &c., अतिक्लिष्टः -ष्टा -ष्टं.

Overwrought, *a.* अतिसंस्कृतः -ता -तं, अतिपरिष्कृतः &c., अतिसिद्धः -द्धा -द्धं.

Overzealous, *a.* अत्युत्सुकः -का -कं, अत्यासक्तः -क्ता -क्तं, अतिव्यग्रः -ग्रा -ग्रं, अत्युद्यमः -मा -मं, अतिचण्डः -ण्डा -ण्डं, अत्युत्कण्ठितः &c.

Oviform, *a.* अण्डाकारः -रा -रं, अण्डाकृतिः -तिः -ति, अण्डरूपः -पा -पं.

Oviparous, *a.* अण्डजः -जा -जं, अण्डजनकः -का -कं, अण्डप्रजः -जा -जं, अण्डप्रसूः -सूः -सु, अण्डोत्पादकः -का -कं, द्विजः -जा -जं, द्विजन्मा -न्मा -न्म (न्), द्विजातिः -तिः -ति, अयोनिजः &c.; 'any oviparous animal,' द्विजः, द्विजातिः &c.

To **owe**, *v. a.* (Owe money) धृ (c. 10. धारयति -यितुं) with acc. and dat.; as, 'he owes a hundred pieces of money to Devadatta,' देवदत्ताय शतं मुद्रा धारयति; 'he repaid me the money which he owed me,' धारयन् मह्यं वसूनि प्रत्यपद्यत.—(Be indebted) ऋणी -णिनी -णि भू, ऋणवान् -वती -वद् भू, ऋणबद्धः -द्धा -द्धं भू, ऋणं कृ.—(Be obliged) अनुगृहीतः -ता -तं भू; 'I owe you many thanks for your advice,' अनुगृहीतोऽस्मि तवोपदेशेन. The sense of 'owe' may be expressed by the fut. pass.

part.; as, 'I owe him money,' मया तस्मै धनं प्रतिदेयं or प्रतिदातव्यं, or by changing the construction of the sentence thus, 'I owe my deliverance to you,' भवान् मम रक्षाकारणम् इति ज्ञातव्यं. *See* the next word.

OWING, *part.* (Due) देयः -या -यं, प्रतिदेयः -या -यं, दातव्यः -व्या -व्यं, प्रतिदातव्यः &c., दानीयः -या -यं, शोधनीयः -या -यं.—(Following as effect and cause) प्रयुक्तः -क्ता -क्तं, जनितः -ता -तं, उत्पादितः &c., उद्भवः -वा -वं, प्रभवः &c., कारणभूतः -ता -तं; 'my deliverance is owing to you,' भवान् मम रक्षाकारणं or मम रक्षणं भवत्प्रयुक्तं.—(Imputable) आरोपणीयः -या -यं, अध्यारोपणीयः -या -यं, सम्बन्धनीयः &c.

OWL, *s.* उलूकः, उल्लूकः, पेचकः, कौशिकः, वायसारातिः *m.*, दिवान्धः, दिवाभीतः, निशाटः, निशाचरः, नक्तञ्चरः, निशादर्शी *m.* (न्), नक्तचारी *m.* (न्), रजनीचरः, काकभीरुः *m.*, कायरुकः, घूकः, वक्रनासिकः, रक्तनासिकः.

OWL-LIGHT, *s.* ईषत्प्रकाशः, मन्दप्रकाशः, मन्दप्रभा, निशादिः *m.*

OWN, *a.* स्वः स्वा स्वं, आत्म in comp., स्व in comp., स्वकीयः -या -यं, आत्मीयः -या -यं, स्वीयः -या -यं, स्वकः -का -कं, निजः -जा -जं, नैजः -जी -जं प्रातिस्विकः -की -कं, आत्मसम्बन्धी -न्धिनी -न्धि (न्), आत्माधीनः -ना -नं, आत्मभूतः -ता -तं; 'my own,' मदीयः -या -यं; 'thy own,' त्वदीयः -या -यं; 'our own,' अस्मदीयः -या -यं; 'of one's own self or own accord,' स्वयं.—(Belonging to no other) अनन्यसम्बन्धी &c., अनन्यस्वामिकः -का -कं, अनन्याधीनः -ना -नं, अनन्यवर्त्ती &c. Compounds with स्व and आत्म, are most frequent to express 'own,' as applicable to the first, second, or third person; thus, 'one's own act,' स्वकर्म्म *n.* (न्), आत्मकर्म्म, स्वयङ्कृतं; 'one's own son,' स्वपुत्रः, आत्मजः, स्वजः; 'own nature,' स्वभावः; 'own fancy,' स्वच्छन्दस् *n.*; 'own duty,' स्वधर्म्मः; 'own country,' स्वदेशः; 'own caste or tribe,' स्वजातिः *f.*; 'own family,' स्वकुलं; 'own advantage,' स्वार्थः, आत्महितं; 'for one's own sake,' आत्मार्थे -र्थं; 'one's own wife,' स्वकीया, स्वीया, स्वभार्य्या; 'to make one's own,' आत्मसात्कृ.

To OWN, *v. a.* (Have the legal right to) अधिकारी -रिणी -रि भू or अस्, स्वामी &c. भू, ईश्वरः -रा -री -रं भू; 'to own land,' क्षेत्राधिकारी &c. भू, क्षेत्रस्वामी &c. भू; or expressed by the use of अस् or भू with the gen. c., or with मदीयः -या -यं, आत्मीयः -या -यं, स्वकीयः -या -यं, आत्माधीनः -ना -नं, स्वाधीनः &c.; as, 'I own that land,' तत् क्षेत्रं मदीयम् अस्ति or आत्माधीनं or मम भवति; 'the king owns this money,' एतद् धनं राजाधीनम् अस्ति. *See To* BELONG. (Acknowledge to belong to one's self, claim to one's self) स्वीकृ, आत्मसात्कृ, स्वीयमिति वद् (c. 1. वदति -दितुं), ममेति वद्, स्वत्वम् अभिमन्, स्वत्वं ज्ञा (c. 10. ज्ञापयति -यितुं, c. 9. जानाति) or अभिज्ञा or बुध् (c. 10. बोधयति -यितुं), स्वकीयं -यां कृ, आत्मीयं -यां कृ.—(Confess, acknowledge) स्वीकृ, अङ्गीकृ, उरीकृ, अनुग्रह् (c. 9. -गृह्णाति -ग्रहीतुं), ग्रह्, अभिमन् (c. 4. -मन्यते -मन्तुं), अभिज्ञा (c. 9. -जानाति -ज्ञातुं), प्रतिज्ञा, प्रत्यभिज्ञा, समभिज्ञा, अनुभाष् (c. 1. -भाषते -षितुं), स्वीकारं कृ.

OWNED, *p. p.* (Confessed, acknowledged) स्वीकृतः -ता -तं, अङ्गीकृतः &c., अभिज्ञातः -ता -तं, प्रतिज्ञातः &c.—(The legal right vested in) स्वत्वविशिष्टः -ष्टा -ष्टं; 'owned by me,' मत्स्वत्वविशिष्ट &c.

OWNER, *s.* अधिकारी *m.* -रिणी *f.* (न्), स्वामी *m.* -मिनी *f.* (न्), ईश्वरः -रा -री, पतिः *m.*, प्रभुः *m.*, अधिभूः *m.*, अधिपः, ईशिता *m.* (तृ), नेता *m.* (तृ), नायकः, परिवृढः, भरण्डः; 'of cattle,' गवीश्वरः; 'of land,' क्षेत्राधिकारी *m.*

OWNERSHIP, *s.* स्वाम्यं, स्वामित्वं, स्वत्वं, अधिकारः -रिता -त्वं, प्रभुत्वं -ता, ऐश्वर्य्यं, नायकत्वं.

OWNING, *s.* (Confession) स्वीकारः, स्वीकरणं, अङ्गीकारः, अङ्गीकरणं.

OX, *s.* (Male of the bovine genus) गौः *m.* (गो), वृषभः, वृषः, ऋषभः, बलीवर्द्दः, उक्षा *m.* (न्), वहतः -तिः -तुः *m.*, ककुद्मान् *m.* (त्), अनड्वान् *m.* (डुह्), शक्करः, शाक्करः, भाक्तः, विसनः; 'stupid as an ox,' गोमूढः; 'relating to an ox,' औक्षः -क्षी -क्षं.—(Draft ox) शकटः.

OXEN, *pl.* गावः *m. pl.*; 'herd of oxen,' गोकुलं, गोवृन्दं, औक्षकं, गोसमूहः, पशुगणः, गव्या, गोत्रा, पाशवं, उक्ष्णां संहतिः *f.*, गवां व्रजः; 'yoke of oxen,' गोयुगं, गोगोयुगं; 'property in oxen,' गोधनं; 'carriage drawn by oxen,' गोयानं.

OX-FLY, *s.* गोमक्षिका, गोमक्षकः.

OXYD, OXIDE, *s.* रीतिः *f.*; 'of iron,' क्षारं; 'of mercury,' रसभस्म *n.* (न्).

To OXYDATE, OXYDIZE, *v. a.* क्षारणं कृ, साधनं कृ, भस्मीकृ, आतञ्चनं कृ, प्रतीवापं कृ; 'oxydized iron,' क्षारं.

OXYDATION, *s.* क्षारणं, साधनं, आतञ्चनं, प्रतीवापः, भस्मीकरणं.

OXYGEN, *s.* The word used in modern treatises is अम्लकरः.

OYEZ, OYES, शृणुत शृणुत आर्य्याः.

OYSTER, *s.* शुक्तिः *f.*, शुक्तिका, तोयशुक्तिका, पटोलकः, पुटिका, मुक्तास्फोटः, मुक्तागारं, मुक्ताप्रसूः *f.*; 'oyster-shell,' शुक्तिपुटं, शुक्तिपेशी.

OYSTER-WOMAN, OYSTER-WENCH, *s.* शुक्तिविक्रयिणी, शुक्तिविक्रेत्री.

P.

PABULAR, PABULOUS, *a.* पौष्टिकः -की -कं, पोषकः -का -कं, पुष्टिकरः &c.

PABULUM, *s.* भोजनं, आहारः, भोज्यं, भक्ष्यं, पौष्टिकं. *See* FOOD.

PACE, *s.* (A step) पदपातः, पादपातः, पदक्रमः, पदन्यासः, पादन्यासः, पदविक्षेपः, पादविक्षेपः, पदनिक्षेपः, पदक्रमः, पदं, क्रमः.—(Gait) गतिः, गमनं, चारः, चरणं, चलनं, अयनं.—(Of horses) धारः -रा, चारः, चारकः पदविक्षेपः, अयनं; 'a horse with a good pace,' सुखायनः, सुखचारः. A horse's paces are, 'walk,' आस्कन्दितं; 'trot,' धौरितकं; 'sidling,' रेचितं; 'gallop,' वल्गितं; 'vaulting,' प्लुतं.—(Of an elephant) गजक्रमः.—(Degree of celerity) क्रमः, पदक्रमः, गतिवेगः; 'a quick pace,' द्रुतपदं; 'at a good pace,' त्वरितपदक्रमं; 'going at a quick pace,' द्रुतगामी -मिनी -मि (न्), द्रुतक्रमः -मा -मं, अविलम्बितक्रमः &c.

To PACE, *v. n.* क्रम् (c. 1. क्रामति, c. 4. क्राम्यति, क्रमितुं), क्रमे क्रमे चल् (c. 1. चलति -लितुं) or व्रज् (c. 1. व्रजति -जितुं) or चर् (c. 1. चरति -रितुं) or गम् (c. 1. गच्छति, गन्तुं) or पदन्यासं कृ; 'to pace up and down,' इतस्ततः क्रम् or चल् or भ्रम् (c. 4. भ्राम्यति, भ्रमितुं), परिक्रमं कृ; 'pacing to and fro,' चङ्क्रम्यमाणः -णा -णं.

To PACE, *v. a.* पदन्यासेन मा (c. 2. माति -तुं, c. 10. मापयति -यितुं).

PACED, *a.* (Having a particular gait) गति in comp., गतिक in comp.; as, 'slow-paced,' मन्दगतिः -तिः -ति, मन्दगतिकः -का -कं.

PACIFIC, PACIFICATORY, *a.* शमकः -का -कं, शान्तिकः -की -कं, शमी -मिनी -मि (न्), शमकारी &c., शमकारकः -का -कं, उपशमकः &c., प्रशमकः &c., शान्तिकरः -रा -रं, शान्त्यात्मकः &c., सामोपचारकः &c., सामोपायकः &c.

PACIFICATION, *s.* शमनं, प्रशमनं, उपशमनं, शान्तिः *f.*, उपशान्तिः *f.*, प्रशान्तिः *f.*, शान्तिकरणं, सान्त्वनं -ना, साम *n.* (न्), सामोपचारः,

सामोपायः, सामोपायप्रयोगः, कलहशान्तिः f., विग्रहशान्तिः, क्रोधशान्तिः, क्रोधहरणं.—(Making peace) सन्धिकरणं, ऐक्यकरणं.—(Peace made) सन्धिः m.

Pacificator, pacifier, s. सन्धिकर्त्ता m. (र्त्तृ), शमकः. *See* Pacific.

Pacified, p. p. शान्तः -न्ता -न्तं, शमितः -ता -तं, उपशान्तः &c., प्रशान्तः &c., कृतशान्तिः -न्तिः -न्ति, शान्तक्रोधः -धा -धं, गतक्रोधः &c.; 'to be pacified,' शम् (c. 4. शाम्यति, शमितुं), प्रसद् (c. 1. -सीदति -सत्तुं), तुष् (c. 4. तुष्यति, तोष्टुं).

To pacify, v. a. शम् (c. 10. शमयति -यितुं), प्रशम्, उपशम्, सान्त्व् or शान्त्व् (c. 10. सान्त्वयति -यितुं), उपसान्त्व्, अभिशान्त्व्, परिशान्त्व्, प्रसद् (c. 10. -सादयति -यितुं), अभिप्रसद्, साम् (c. 10. सामयति -यितुं), तुष् (c. 10. तोषयति -यितुं), सन्तुष्, परितुष्, सम्परितुष्.

Pack, s. (Bundle, bale) भाण्डकं, भाण्डं, भारः, कूर्च्चः, पोटलिका, पोट्टली, गुच्छः -च्छकः, वासनं, वरण्डः -ण्डकः.—(Of hounds or dogs) श्वगणः, कुक्कुरगणः, श्वसंघः, कुक्कुरसमूहः, शुनीरः; 'one who keeps a pack of hounds,' श्वगणिकः.—(Number of persons) गणः, जनसमूहः, संघः, मण्डलं, सङ्घः.—(Heap) राशिः m., समूहः, सञ्चयः, वृन्दं, समवायः.

To pack, v. a. (Bundle up, press together) पुट् (c. 10. पुटयति -यितुं), पुटीकृ, सम्पुटीकृ, वासनीकृ, भाण्डीकृ, कूर्च्चीकृ, कूर्च्चं कृ, गुच्छीकृ, पोटलिकां कृ, कोशीकृ.—(In a box) भाण्डे निविश् (c. 10. -वेशयति -यितुं) or निधा (c. 3. -दधाति -धातुं), कोशे or कोषे निविश् or निधा.—(Put together or unite with fraudulent design) कुकर्म्मसम्पादनार्थं संयुज् (c. 10. -योजयति -यितुं) or सङ्क्रम् (c. 10. -गमयति -यितुं) or एकीकृ.—(A jury or assembly of any kind) स्वार्थसम्पादनार्थं स्वपक्षपातिनो धर्म्मसभां प्रविश् or स्वपक्षपातिनः सभ्यपदे or सभासदधिकारे नियुज्.—(Pack off, dismiss) प्रस्था in caus. (-स्थापयति -यितुं), अपसृ (c. 10. -सारयति -यितुं).

To pack, v. n. (Be pressed together, or bundled together) पुटीभू, सम्पुटीभू, वासनीभू.—(Be placed in a box) भाण्डस्थः -स्था -स्थं भू, कोषस्थः &c. भू.—(Depart in haste) त्वरितम् अपगम् (c. 1. -गच्छति -गन्तुं).

Package, s. भाण्डकं, भाण्डं, वासनं, वरण्डः -ण्डकः, कूर्च्चः, पोटलिका.

Pack-cloth, s. वासनं, वासनपटः, वेष्टनं, वेष्टनपटः.

Packed, p. p. (Bound together in a bundle) पुटीकृतः -ता -तं, सम्पुटीकृतः &c., कूर्च्चीकृतः &c.—(In a box) भाण्डस्थः -स्था -स्थं, वासनस्थः &c., भाण्डीकृतः &c., वासनीकृतः &c.

Packet, s. (Small package) कूर्च्चः, पोटलिका, पोट्टली, समुद्गका.—(Ship employed in carrying despatches) पत्रवाहिनी नौः, राजपत्रवाहका नौः, लेखहारिणी नौका, वेगवती नौका; 'steam-packet,' वाष्पीयनौः f.

Pack-horse, s. स्थूरी m. (न्), स्थौरी m., स्थूरी m., स्थोरी m., पृष्ठ्यः.

Pack-saddle, s. पर्य्याणं, पर्य्ययणं, पल्यनं, पल्याणं.

Pack-thread, s. शणसूत्रं, सणसूत्रं, सनसूत्रं, शणतन्तुः f., पवित्रकं.

Pact, paction, s. समयः, नियमः, संविद् f., उपगमः, सङ्केतः.

Pactional, pactitious, a. सामयिकः -की -कं, साङ्केतिकः -की -कं.

Pactolus, s. (A fabulous river) जम्बुः m., जम्बुनदी.

Pad, s. (An easy paced horse) सुखायनः, सुखचारः.—(Foot-pad) मार्गविलुम्पः, पादविलुम्पः, परिपन्थी m. (न्), पारिपन्थिकः.—(Bolster, cushion) उपधानं -नीयं, विष्टरः, विस्तरः, बालिशं, आस्तरणं, उपबर्हः, अजिनं, पट्टः, पटः.—(Hair or other soft substance) लोमादि मृदुवस्तु n.

To pad, v. a. (Stuff or furnish with hair or other soft substance) लोमादिमृदुवस्तुना आस्तृ (c. 5. -स्तृणोति -स्तरितुं -रीतुं), मृदुलोमादिना पॄ (c. 10. पूरयति -यितुं) or युज् (c. 10. योजयति -यितुं) or समायुज्.

To pad, v. n. (Travel slowly) क्रमे क्रमे or शनैः शनैर् व्रज् (c. 1. व्रजति -जितुं).

Padded, p. p. or a. मृदुलोमादिपूरितः -ता -तं, मृदुवस्तुपूरितः -ता -तं.

Padding, s. मृदुलोमादि n., लोमादिमृदुवस्तु n., पूरणं, भरणं.

To paddle, v. n. (Beat the water with an oar) नौकादण्डेन जलं क्षिप् (c. 6. क्षिपति, क्षेप्तुं) or तड् (c. 10. ताडयति -यितुं), जलक्षेपणं कृ.—(Play in the water) जले क्रीड् (c. 1. क्रीडति -डितुं), जलक्रीडां कृ.—(Finger) अङ्गुलिचेष्टं कृ, अङ्गुलिव्यापारं कृ.

To paddle, v. a. (Propel by a paddle) नौकादण्डेन चल् (c. 10. चालयति -यितुं).

Paddle, s. (Oar) नौकादण्डः, क्षेपणिः -णी f., क्षिपणिः -णी f., अरित्रं, नौचालनी. *See* Oar.—(Blade of the oar) क्षेपणिफलकं.

Paddle-box, s. क्षेपणिकोशः, क्षेपणिकोषः, क्षेपण्याधारः.

Paddle-wheel, s. क्षेपणिचक्रं, नौचालनचक्रं, नौचालनी.

Paddock, s. वाटी, वाटिका, वाटः -टं, विवीतः, प्राचीरपरिवृतं क्षेत्रं.

Padlock, s. तालकं, तालः -ला, तालयन्त्रं, प्रतिताली, द्वारकीलः.—(Clasp) कुडुपः.

To padlock, v. a. तालकेन बन्ध् (c. 9. बध्नाति, बन्धुं), तालबद्धं -द्धां कृ.

Pæan, pean, s. जयगानं, जयशब्दः, जयध्वनिः m., जयगीतं.

Pagan, s. देवतार्च्चकः, देवतापूजकः, प्रतिमापूजकः, मूर्त्तिपूजकः, देवतासेवी m. (न्), असद्धर्म्मसेवी m. (न्), असद्धर्मावलम्बी m. *See* Idolater.

Pagan, a. प्रतिमापूजकसम्बन्धी -न्धिनी -न्धि (न्), मूर्त्तिपूजकसम्बन्धी.

Paganism, s. प्रतिमापूजा, मूर्त्तिपूजा, देवतार्च्चा, देवतार्च्चनं -ना, मूर्त्तिसेवा -वनं, असद्धर्म्मावलम्बनं. *See* Idolatry, Heathenism.

Page, s. (Of a book) पृष्ठं, फलकः -कं, पत्रं, पत्रिका.—(Boy attendant) पार्श्वानुचरः, पार्श्वपरिचरः, बालसेवकः, बालानुचरः.

To page, v. a. पृष्ठाङ्कनं कृ, पत्राङ्कनं कृ, पृष्ठसंख्याङ्कनं कृ.

Pageant, s. (Statue in show, &c.) शोभामूर्त्तिः f., शोभाप्रतिमा.—(Show, spectacle) कौतुकं, चमत्कारः, चमत्कृतिः f., चमत्करणं, आडम्बरं, प्रेक्षा, प्रेक्षणं, शोभा, यात्रा.

Pageant, a. कौतुकी -किनी -कि (न्), आडम्बरी &c., चमत्कारकः -का -कं, शोभनः -ना -नं, अतिशोभनः &c., यात्रिकः -की -कं.

Pageantry, s. कौतुकं, चमत्कारः, आडम्बरं, शोभा. *See* Pageant, s.

Paginal, a. पृष्ठ्यः -ष्ठ्या -ष्ठ्यं, पुस्तकपत्रसम्बन्धी &c.

Pagoda, s. देवतामन्दिरं, देवताभवनं, देवतायतनं, देवमन्दिरं.

Paid, p. p. शोधितः -ता -तं, परिशोधितः &c., परिशुद्धः -द्धा -द्धं, अपाकृतः -ता -तं, सिद्धः -द्धा -द्धं, साधितः -ता -तं, विगणितः -ता -तं, निस्तारितः -ता -तं, निरादिष्टः -ष्टा -ष्टं, गृहीतवेतनः -ना -नं.

Pail, s. पात्रं, भाजनं, काष्ठपात्रं, जलपात्रं, जलभाजनं; 'for milk,' दोहनं -नी, गोदोहनी, दुग्धभाण्डं. *See* Milk-pail.

Pain, s. दुःखं, पीडा, वेदना -नं, व्यथा, आर्त्तिः f., तापः, सन्तापः, परितापः, बाधा, विबाधा, आबाधा, यातना, कृच्छ्रं, कष्टं, क्लेशः, खेदः, उद्वेगः, यन्त्रणं, दुष्खं, दुःखितं, असुखं, तोदः -दनं, रायणं, विधानकं, विराधानं, प्रसूतिजं, आमनस्यं, आमानस्यं, अमानस्यं, आभीलं; 'bodily pain as opposed to mental,' शरीरपीडा, वेदना, कृच्छ्रं, व्याधिः m.; 'pain in the head,' शिरोवेदना, शिरःपीडा, शिरोर्त्तिः f.; 'in the teeth,' दन्तवेदना; 'sharp pain,' शूलः -लं, तीव्रवेदना; 'creeping or flying pain,' वेगः; 'rheumatic pains in the bones,' अस्थिशूलः -लं; 'in the loins,' कटिवेदना; 'pains of hell,'

यातना, कारणा, याम्ययातना; 'of labor,' प्रसववेदना, गर्भवेदना, प्रसवव्यथा; 'of death,' प्राणान्तवेदना; 'suffering pain,' दुःखभागी -गिनी -गि (न्), दुःखभोगी &c., दुःखी &c.; 'accession of pain,' दुःखसंयोगः; 'causing pain,' पीडाकरः -रा -रं, दुःखकरः &c.; 'act of causing pain,' पीडाकरणं, पीडनं; 'freed from pain,' दुःखातीतः -ता -तं.—(Mental pain, disquietude) मनोदुःखं, मनःपीडा, मनस्तापः, मनोव्यथा, मानसी व्यथा, चित्तवेदना, चित्तोद्वेगः, आधिः m.—(Pains, toil, effort) यत्नः, प्रयत्नः, कष्टं, आयासः, प्रयासः, उद्योगः, उत्साहः, व्यवसायः, चेष्टा, उद्यमः, श्रमः, परिश्रमः, क्लेशः, आस्था; 'to take pains,' यत् (c. 1. यतते -तितुं), प्रयत्, व्यवसो (c. 4. -स्यति -सातुं), उद्यम् (c. 1. -यच्छति -यन्तुं), चेष्ट् (c. 1. चेष्टते -ष्टितुं), विचेष्ट्, घट् (c. 1. घटते -टितुं), उद्योगं कृ, यत्नं कृ, उत्साहं कृ.—(Penalty) दण्डः, साहसं, शिष्टिः f., शिक्षा.

To PAIN, *v. a.* पीड् (c. 10. पीडयति -यितुं), आपीड्, उपपीड्, दुःख् (c. 10. दुःखयति -यितुं), व्यथ् (c. 10. व्यथयति -यितुं), तप् (c. 10. तापयति -यितुं), सन्तप्, परितप्, उपतप्, बाध् (c. 1. बाधते -धितुं), उद्विज् (c. 10. -वेजयति -यितुं), क्लिश् (c. 9. क्लिश्नाति, क्लेशितुं, क्लेष्टुं), अर्द् (c. 10. अर्दयति -यितुं), दुःखं कृ or दा, पीडां कृ, व्यथां कृ.

PAINED, *p. p.* पीडितः -ता -तं, दुःखितः -ता -तं, व्यथितः &c., आर्त्तः -र्त्ता -र्त्तं in comp., दुःखार्त्तः &c., दुःखी -खिनी खि (न्), दुःखान्वितः -ता -तं, दुःखोपेतः &c., बाधितः -ता -तं, तापितः &c., सन्तापितः &c., तप्तः -प्ता -प्तं, सन्तप्तः &c., उद्वेजितः &c., क्लेशितः &c., क्लिष्टः &c., आतुरः -रा -रं, अर्दितः &c., अभ्यर्दितः &c., अनुभूतवेदनः -ना -नं, कृच्छ्रगतः &c., क्लेशी &c., कष्टी &c., कष्टः -ष्टा -ष्टं, आधिमान् -मती -मत् (त्), दूनः -ना -नं, सव्यथः -था -थं, सवेदनः -ना -नं; 'being pained,' पीड्यमानः -ना -नं, तप्यमानः &c., आतप्यमानः &c., क्लिश्यमानः &c., धूपायितः -ता -तं; 'to be pained,' पीड् in pass. (पीड्यते), दुःख (nom. दुःखायते, दुःखीयति), दुःखार्त्तीभू, व्यथ् (c. 1. व्यथते -थितुं), प्रव्यथ्, तप् in pass. (तप्यते), परितप्, सन्तप्, क्लिश् (c. 4. क्लिश्यते).

PAINFUL, *a.* (Causing pain) पीडाकरः -रा -रं, दुःखकरः -रा -रं, पीडाकारकः -का -कं, पीडाजनकः -का -कं, दुःखजनकः &c., दुःखदः -दा -दं, दुःखप्रदः -दा -दं, दुःखावहः -हा -हं, वेदनाकारकः -का -कं, वेदनाजनकः &c., व्यथाकरः &c., व्यथकः -का -कं, कष्टकरः &c., कष्टकारकः &c., कष्टावहः -हा -हं, क्लेशकरः &c., क्लेशदः &c., क्लेशावहः -हा -हं, क्लेशकः -का -कं, बाधकः -का -कं, उद्वेजकः -का -कं, सन्तापकः -का -कं, दूदः -दा -दं.—(Full of pain) दुःखमयः -यी -यं, दुःखी -खिनी -खि (न्), क्लेशी &c., सबाधः -धा -धं, सव्यथः -था -थं, सवेदनः -ना -नं.—(Requiring labor or toil) कष्टसाध्यः -ध्या -ध्यं, श्रमसाध्यः &c., दुःसाध्यः &c., दुष्करः -रा -रं, कठिनः -ना -नं.

PAINFULLY, *adv.* (With pain) सव्यथं, सवेदनं, सबाधं, सदुःखं, सक्लेशं, सोद्वेगं, सकष्टं, दुःखपूर्व्वं.—(With toil) श्रमेण, सश्रमं, आयासेन, सायासं, कृच्छ्रेण, सकृच्छ्रं.

PAINFULNESS, *s.* दुःखकारकत्वं, पीडाजनकत्वं, कष्टकारकत्वं, दुःखिता, सदुःखत्वं, दुःखं, सक्लेशत्वं, सोद्वेगता, कष्टं, सकष्टत्वं, सकष्टता.

PAINLESS, *a.* दुःखहीनः -ना -नं, दुःखरहितः -ता -तं, व्यथाहीनः -ना -नं, दुःखशून्यः -न्या -न्यं, निर्दुःखी -खिनी -खि (न्), निर्व्यथः -था -थं.

PAINS, *s. pl.* यत्नः, प्रयत्नः, उद्योगः, कष्टं. *See* PAIN.

PAINSTAKER, *s.* उद्योगी *m.* (न्), उत्साही *m.*, उद्यमी *m.*, व्यवसायी.

PAINSTAKING, *a.* कृतप्रयत्नः -त्ना -त्नं, कृतयत्नः &c., प्रयत्नवान् -वती -वत् (त्), यत्नशीलः -ला -लं, प्रयत्नशीलः -ला -लं, उद्योगशीलः &c., उद्यमशीलः &c., उद्योगी -गिनी -गि (न्), व्यवसायी &c., कृतश्रमः -मा -मं, प्रसितः -ता -तं. *See* INDUSTRIOUS.

To PAINT, *v. a.* (Draw in colors) चित्र् (c. 10. चित्रयति -यितुं), लिख् (c. 6. लिखति, लेखितुं), आलिख्, अभिलिख्.—(Cover or besmear with color) रञ्ज् (c. 10. रञ्जयति -यितुं), वर्ण् (c. 10. वर्णयति -यितुं), लिप् (c. 6. लिम्पति, लेप्तुं), रङ्गेण लिप्, रञ्जनं कृ.—(Describe) वर्ण्, अनुवर्ण्, उपवर्ण्, संवर्ण्, वर्णनं कृ, विलिख्.

PAINT, *s.* रङ्गः, वर्णकः -का, चित्रं, लेपः, विलेपः, रञ्जनलेपः, रञ्जनं.

PAINTED, *p. p.* चित्रितः -ता -तं, चित्रगतः -ता -तं, चित्रार्पितः -ता -तं, आलिखितः &c., अभिलिखितः &c., आलेख्यगतः &c., आलेख्यसमर्पितः &c., वर्णितः -ता -तं, वर्णगतः &c., रञ्जितः &c., चित्रः -त्रा -त्रं; 'painted on the surface,' चित्रतलः -ला -लं.

PAINTER, *s.* चित्रकरः, चित्रकारः, चित्रलेखकः, चित्रलिख् (ख्), चित्रकृत् *m.*, चित्रकः, चित्रकर्म्मविद् *m.*, रङ्गाजीवः -वी *m.* (न्), रञ्जकः, वर्णी *m.* (न्), वर्णधारकः, वर्णाटः, लेखकः, आलेखकः, आलेख्यकृत् *m.*, पटकारः, तौलिकः, तौलिकिकः; 'painter's brush,' तूलिः *f.*, तूलिका, ईषिका, वर्त्तिका.

PAINTING, *s.* (The act) चित्रलिखनं, चित्रलेखनं, चित्रलिपिः *f.*, लिपिः *f.*, आलेखनं, लेखनं, लिखनं, चित्रकरणं, रञ्जनं, वर्णनं.—(The art or business) चित्रकर्म्म *n.* (न्), चित्रविद्या, चित्रक्रिया.—(A painting or picture) चित्रलेखा, चित्रं, आलेख्यं, चित्रलिखितं, चित्रगतं.—(Painting the body) पत्रलेखा, पत्राङ्गुलिः *f.*, पत्रावली -लिः *f.*, वर्णः,

PAIR, *s.* मिथुनं, द्वयं, द्वन्द्वं, युगं, युग्मं, युगलं, यमलं, यामलं, यमः, यमकं, युतकं; 'a pair of doves,' पारावतमिथुनं; 'a pair of oxen,' गोमिथुनं, गोयुगं; 'a pair of birds,' पक्षिणोर् मिथुनं, पक्षिमिथुनं, पक्षिद्वयं; 'a married pair,' दम्पती *m.* du., भार्य्यापती *m.* du., स्त्रीपुरुषौ. The word द्वन्द्वः is used to denote that form of grammatical combination which unites two or more words of similar or opposite signification; thus, 'hand and foot,' पाणिपादं; 'affection and hatred,' रागद्वेषौ *m.* du.

To PAIR, *v. n.* (Suit, fit) युज् in pass. (युज्यते), संयुज्, उपयुज्.—(Be joined in pairs) स्त्रीपुरुषवत् or दम्पतिवत् सङ्गम् (c. 1. -गच्छति -गन्तुं) or संयुज्, मैथुनार्थं सङ्गम्, मैथुनं कृ.

To PAIR, *v. a.* संयुज् (c. 7. -युनक्ति -योक्तुं, c. 10. -योजयति -यितुं), युज्, संयोगं कृ, मिथुनसंयोगं कृ, मैथुनार्थं संयुज्.

PALACE, *s.* राजगृहं, राजमन्दिरं, नृपगृहं, नृपमन्दिरं, राजवेश्म *n.* (न्), नृपवेश्म *n.*, राजधाम *n.* (न्), नृपधाम *n.*, राजभवनं, राजसदनं, राजप्रासादः, राजहर्म्यं, राजवसतिः *f.*, नृपतिवसतिः *f.*, राजशाला, राजधानी, प्रासादः, हर्म्यं, मन्दिरं -रा, भवनं, सौधं, अट्टालः -लिका, विमानं, शाला, विशिर्षं, विच्छर्दकः, माडिः *m.*, उपकार्य्या, उपकारी -रिका; 'palace-court,' राजसभा; 'palace-yard,' राजाङ्गनं.

PALÆSTRA, *s.* मल्लभूः *f.*, मल्लभूमिः *f.*, मल्लराट् *m.* (ज्), मल्लयात्रा.

PALANKEEN, PALANQUIN, *s.* शिबिका, डयनं, डलकं, याप्ययानं, नरयानं, प्रवहणं, इत्या, शिरस्का.

PALATABLE, *a.* रुचिकरः -री -रं, रुच्यः -च्या -च्यं, आस्वाद्यः -द्या -द्यं, स्वादुः -द्वी -दु, सुरसः -सा -सं, सरसः -सा -सं, रसिकः -का -की -कं, मुखप्रियः -या -यं.

PALATABLENESS, *s.* रुच्यता -त्वं, आस्वाद्यता, स्वादुता, सरसता, रसिकत्वं.

PALATAL, PALATIAL, PALATIC, *a.* (Pertaining to the palate) तालव्यः -व्या -व्यं, तालुसम्बन्धी &c.; 'a palatal letter,' तालव्यं.

PALATE, *s.* तालु *n.*, तालुका, काकुदं -दः; 'soft palate,' शुण्डिका,

शूना, सूना, अलिजिह्वा, अधोजिह्विका. *See* UVULA.

PALATIAL, *a.* राजप्रासादीयः -या -यं, प्रासादीयः &c., राजगृहयोग्यः -ग्या -ग्यं. राजमन्दिरयोग्यः &c.

PALAVER, *s.* चाटूक्तिः *f.*, चाटुकारः, सान्त्वोक्तिः *f.*, मधुरवाक्यं, मिथ्योक्तिः.

To PALAVER, *v. a.* चाटूक्त्या सान्त्व् (c. 10. सान्त्वयति -यितुं), मिथ्या सान्त्व्.

PALE, *a.* पाण्डुः -ण्डुः -ण्डु, पाण्डुरः -रा -रं, पाण्डरः -रा -रं, विपाण्डुरः &c., विवर्णः -र्णा -र्णं, गतवर्णः &c., नीरक्तः -क्ता -क्तं, रागहीनः -ना -नं; 'pale in color,' पाण्डुवर्णः &c.; 'having a pale face,' विवर्णवदनः -ना -नं.—(Dim, not bright) मन्दप्रभः -भा -भं, हततेजाः -जाः -जः (स्), मन्दच्छायः -या -यं, निस्तेजाः &c., हतकान्तिः -न्तिः -न्ति, न्यूनकान्तिः &c., न्यूनप्रभः &c., मलिनप्रभः &c., म्लानतेजाः &c., म्लानकान्तिः &c.—(Light in color) expressed by ईषत्, आ, श्वेत; as, 'pale red,' ईषद्रक्तः -क्ता -क्तं, आरक्तः &c., श्वेतरक्तः &c.; 'pale blue,' आनीलः -ला -लं, श्वेतनीलः &c.

PALE, *s.* (Stake) शङ्कुः *m.*, कीलः, स्थाणुः *m.*, शल्यं, शूलं.—(Inclosure, limit) आवरणं, वृतिः *f.*, वेष्टनं, आवेष्टनं, अवरोधकं, वारणं, वरणः, वलयः.

To PALE, *v. a.* शङ्कुवलयेन परिवृ (c. 5. -वृणोति -वरितुं -रीतुं) or परिवेष्ट् (c. 1. -वेष्टते -ष्टितुं) or अवरुध् (c. 7. -रुणद्धि -रोद्धुं).

PALE-EYED, *a.* पाण्डुनेत्रः -त्रा -त्रं, पाण्डुनयनः &c., न्यूनप्रभाक्षः &c.

PALE-FACED, *a.* विवर्णवदनः -ना -नं, पाण्डुमुखः -खी -खं, म्लानवदनः &c.

PALENESS, *s.* पाण्डुता -त्वं, पाण्डुरता -त्वं, पाण्डुवर्णः, पाण्डुरागः, विवर्णता, वैवर्ण्यं, मुखवैवर्ण्यं, नीरक्तता, रागहीनता.—(Dimness) प्रभाहानिः *f.*, तेजोहानिः *f.*, न्यूनप्रभा, न्यूनकान्तिः *f.*

PALETTE, *s.* *See* PALLET.

PALFREY, *s.* स्त्रीलोकारोहणयोग्यः क्षुद्रघोटकः.

PALINDROME, *s.* अनुलोमविलोमश्लोकः, मुरजबन्धः.

PALING, *s.* शङ्कुपंक्तिः *f.*, आवरणं, आवारः, वारणं -णी, कटञ्जनं.

PALISADE, *s.* दुर्गपरिगता स्तम्भपंक्तिः or शङ्कुपंक्तिः शङ्कुवलयः, यष्टिवलयः, स्तम्भवलयः, दुर्गावरोधका स्तम्भपंक्तिः, दुर्गावरोधकं.

PALISH, *a.* ईषत्पाण्डुः -ण्डुः -ण्डु, आपाण्डुः &c., आपाण्डुरः -रा -रं.

PALL, *s.* (Mantle of state) राजप्रावारः, राजकीयप्रावारः.—(Cloak) प्रावारः, प्रच्छदपटः, आच्छादनपटः.—(For a dead body) शवाच्छादनं.

To PALL, *v. n.* विरसीभू, विरसः -सा -सं भू, अरुचिरः -रा -रं भू.

To PALL, *v. a.* विरसीकृ, अरुचिं or बीभत्सं जन् (c. 10. जनयति -यितुं).

PALLADIUM, *s.* पुरदेवता, नगरदेवता.—(Defence) रक्षा -क्षणं.

PALLET, *s.* (Board for mixing colors) वर्णपत्रं -त्रः, रङ्गपत्रं.—(Small bed) खट्वा, क्षुद्रखट्वा, तल्पः, क्षुद्रतल्पः.

To PALLIATE, *v. a.* (As a fault, crime, &c.) दोषं or पापं शम् (c. 10. शमयति -यितुं) or उपशम् or छद् (c. 10. छादयति -यितुं) or आच्छद् or मृज् (c. 2. मार्ष्टि -र्ष्टुं), पापशमनं कृ, दोषमार्जनं कृ, दोषक्षालनं कृ, पापापनोदनं कृ, पापाच्छादनं कृ, न्यूनीकृ.

PALLIATED, *p. p.* शमितः -ता -तं, आच्छादितः -ता -तं, न्यूनीकृतः &c.

PALLIATION, *s.* (Of a fault or crime) पापशमनं, पापशान्तिः *f.*, दोषाच्छादनं, पापशान्तिः *f.*, पापमार्जना, दोषक्षालनं, दोषप्रक्षालनं, पापापनोदनं, पापापनुत्तिः *f.*, दोषन्यूनीकरणं, उपशमः, उपशमनं, लघूकरणं, उपशान्तिः *f.*

PALLIATIVE, *a.* (Extenuating) पापशमनः -ना -नं, दोषशमकः -का -कं, दोषाच्छादकः &c.—(Mitigant) शान्तिकः -की -कं. *See* MITIGANT.

PALLIATIVE, *s.* (That which extenuates) पापशमनं, दोषशमनं, शान्तिकं.—(That which mitigates pain) वेदनाशान्तिकं, वेदनाशमकम् औषधं, क्लेशापहं, शूलघ्नं, उपशमनं.

PALLID, *a.* पाण्डुः -ण्डुः -ण्डु, पाण्डुवर्णः -र्णा -र्णं, पाण्डुरः -रा -रं, विपाण्डुरः -रा -रं, विवर्णः -र्णा -र्णं &c. *See* PALE.

PALLOR, *s.* पाण्डुता -त्वं, पाण्डुरता -त्वं, विवर्णता. *See* PALENESS.

PALM, *s.* (Of the hand) तलः -लं, हस्ततलः -लं, करतलः -लं, तालः -लिका, प्रतलः, प्रहस्तः, प्रपाणिः *m.*, चपेटः, चर्पटः, चपटः, कर्परीकं, चलशुयः, गोकालः; 'the palms joined,' संहतलः, सिंहतलः, संहततलः; 'the hollowed palm,' प्रसृतः, प्रसृतिः *f.*, चुलुकः; 'the hollowed palms joined,' अञ्जलिः *m.*; 'having the palms hollowed and placed one above the other in sign of reverence,' कृताञ्जलिः -लिः -लि, कृताञ्जलिपुटः -टा -टं, बद्धाञ्जलिः &c.—(Tree) तालः, तृणद्रुमः, दीर्घतरुः *m.*, दीर्घद्रुः *m.*, गुच्छपत्रः, लेख्यपत्रकः, द्रुमश्रेष्ठः, द्रुमेश्वरः, दुरारोहः; 'date-palm,' खर्जूरः -री -खर्जूरवृक्षः; 'cocoa-nut palm,' नारिकेलः &c. *See* COCOA-NUT. 'Palm-leaf,' तालपत्रं, तालपर्णं; 'fibres,' तालजटा, तालप्रलम्बं; 'spirituous juice of the palm,' ताली, तालकी.

To PALM, *v. a.* (Conceal in the palm) करतले गुप्, करतलगुप्तं -प्तां कृ, हस्ततलस्थं -स्थां कृ.—(Impose by fraud) छल् (c. 10. छलयति -यितुं), छलेन प्रचलीकृ, वञ्च् (c. 10. वञ्चयते -ति -यितुं), प्रतृ &c.

PALMA-CHRISTI, *s.* (Castor-oil tree) एरण्डः -ण्डकः, उरुबूकः, उरुवुकः, रुवूकः, रुवुकः, रुबुकः, रुवुः *m.*, रुचकः, व्याडम्बकः, व्याडम्बनः, व्याडम्बरः, व्याघ्रपुच्छः, गन्धर्वहस्तकः, चञ्चुः *m.*, मण्डः, आमण्डः, आमण्डः, वर्धमानः, पञ्चाङ्गुलः.

PALMATE, PALMATED, *a.* हस्ततलाकारः -रा -रं, करतलाकृतिः -तिः -ति.

PALMER, *s.* तालपत्रभृत् कार्पटिकविशेषः or यात्रिकविशेषः.

PALMER-WORM, *s.* लोमावृतः कीटविशेषः or कृमिप्रभेदः.

PALMIFIED, *a.* जालपादः -दा -दं, जालपाद् *m. f. n.*, जालाकारपादः &c.

PALMISTER, *a.* हस्तरेखादिनिरीक्षणाद् दैवकथकः or शुभाशुभदर्शकः, करतलरेखानिरीक्षणेन भविष्यत्सूचकः, सामुद्रिकः, सामुद्रविद् *m.*, हस्तरेखाविद्.

PALMISTRY, *s.* हस्तरेखादिनिरीक्षणाद् दैवकथनं or शुभाशुभदर्शनं, करतलरेखादिनिरीक्षणेन भविष्यत्सूचनं, हस्तरेखाविद्या, हस्तसामुद्रिकं, सामुद्रविद्या.

PALMY, *a.* (Bearing or abounding with palms) तालवान् -वती -वत् (त्), तालावृतः -ता -तं, तालसङ्कीर्णः -र्णा -र्णं.—(Flourishing) समृद्धः -द्धा -द्धं, वर्धिष्णुः -ष्णुः -ष्णु, श्रीमान् -मती &c., अधिकर्द्धिः -र्द्धिः -र्द्धि.

PALMYRA, *s.* (Tree) तृणद्रुमः, तृणराजः, आसवद्रुः *m.*, महोन्नतः. *See* PALM.

PALPABILITY, PALPABLENESS, *s.* स्पृश्यता, स्पर्शनीयता, स्पर्शेन्द्रियग्राह्यता, स्पर्शगोचरता.—(Clearness) व्यक्तता, प्रत्यक्षता.

PALPABLE, *a.* (Perceptible by the touch) स्पृश्यः -श्या -श्यं, स्पर्शनीयः -या -यं, स्पर्शेन्द्रियग्राह्यः -ह्या -ह्यं, स्पर्शगोचरः -रा -रं, स्पर्शवेद्यः -द्या -द्यं, स्पर्शज्ञेयः -या -यं, त्वगिन्द्रियज्ञेयः &c., सूचीभेद्यः -द्या -द्यं.—(Gross, thick) स्थूलः -ला -लं, घनः -ना -नं; 'palpable darkness,' घनान्धकारः.—(Plain, clear) व्यक्तः -क्ता -क्तं, स्पष्टः -ष्टा -ष्टं, प्रत्यक्षः -क्षा -क्षं, सुग्राह्यः &c.

PALPABLY, *adv.* व्यक्तं, सुव्यक्तं, स्पष्टं, सुस्पष्टं, प्रत्यक्षतस्, प्रत्यक्षेण, स्फुटं, प्रादुस्.

To PALPITATE, *v. n.* स्पन्द् (c. 1. स्पन्दते -न्दितुं), प्रतिस्पन्द्, परिस्पन्द्, कम्प् (c. 1. कम्पते -म्पितुं), विकम्प्, वेप् (c. 1. वेपते -पितुं), स्फुर् (c. 6. स्फुरति -रितुं), क्षुभ् (c. 4. क्षुभ्यति, क्षोभितुं), उच्छ्वस् (c. 2. -श्वसिति -तुं, rt. श्वस्), पिट् (c. 1. पेठति -ठितुं); 'my heart palpitates,' वेपते मे हृदयं.

PALPITATING, *part.* स्पन्दमानः -ना -नं, वेपमानः -ना -नं, कम्पमानः -ना -नं, स्फुरितः -ता -तं, उच्छ्वासी -सिनी -सि (न्).

PALPITATION, *s.* स्पन्दनं, प्रतिस्पन्दनं, वेपनं, वेपथुः *m.*, कम्पः -म्पनं,

स्फुरणं, क्षोभः; 'of the heart,' हृदयवेपनं, हृदयकम्पः, हृत्कम्पः.

Palsical, palsied, *a.* पक्षाघाती -तिनी -ति (न्), पक्षवायुग्रस्तः -स्ता -स्तं, कम्पवायुग्रस्तः &c., अर्द्धाङ्गवायुग्रस्तः &c.

Palsy, *s.* (Paralysis) स्तम्भः, संस्तम्भः, विष्टम्भः, अवष्टम्भः, स्तापः, सुप्तिः *f.* —(Hemiplegia) पक्षाघातः, पक्षवायुः *m.*, अर्द्धाङ्गवायुः *m.*, अर्द्धाङ्गं, भङ्गः.—(Shaking palsy) कम्पवायुः *m.*, कम्पवातः.

To palsy, *v. a.* स्तम्भं or स्वापं जन् (c. 10. जनयति -यितुं), स्तब्धीकृ, जडीकृ.

Paltriness, *s.* तुच्छता, लघुता, लाघवं, असारता, कुत्सितत्वं, क्षुद्रता.

Paltry, *a.* तुच्छः -च्छा -च्छं, लघुः -घुः -घ्वी -घु, क्षुद्रः -द्रा -द्रं, कुत्सितः -ता -तं, असारः -रा -रं, सारहीनः -ना -नं, तृणप्रायः -या -यं, लघुप्रभावः -वा -वं, क्षुल्लकः -का -कं, अपकृष्टः -ष्टा -ष्टं, अधमः -मा -मं, or expressed by कु prefixed; as, 'a paltry action,' कुकर्म्म *n.* (न्).

To pamper, *v. a.* परमान्नेन तृप् (c. 10. तर्पयति -यितुं) or सन्तृप् or पॄ (c. 10. पूरयति -यितुं) or परिपॄ or भृ (c. 3. बिभर्त्ति, c. 1. भरति, भर्त्तुं) or संवृध् (c. 10. -वर्धयति -यितुं) or पुष् (c. 10. पोषयति -यितुं) or आप्यै (c. 10. -प्याययति -यितुं), अत्यन्तं पुष् or आप्यै.

Pampered, *p. p.* अतिपुष्टः -ष्टा -ष्टं, सुपुष्टः &c., अतिपोषितः -ता -तं, सुपोषितः &c., सुष्टपुष्टः &c., परमान्नपोषितः &c., परमान्नभृतः &c.

Pampering, *s.* अतिपोषणं, परमान्नपोषणं, परमान्नसंवर्धनं, भरणं, अतिभरणं, परमान्नभृतिः *f.*, आप्यायनं, सुपोषणं.

Pamphlet, *s.* पत्रिका, पुस्तकं -की, क्षुद्रपुस्तकं, लघुपुस्तकं.

Pan, *s.* पात्रं, भाजनं, भाण्डं, आधारः, कटाहः, पिठरः, स्थाली, कन्दुः -न्दूः *m.f.*, खेदनी -निका; 'frying pan,' अम्बरीषं, भ्राष्ट्रः, भृज्जरीषं.

Panacea, *s.* सर्व्वरोगशमकभेषजं, सर्व्वरोगघ्नभेषजं, सर्व्वरोगप्रतीकारकम् औषधं, सर्व्वौषधिचूर्णं, त्रैलोक्यचिन्तामणिः *m.*

Pan-cake. *s.* कन्दुपक्वपिष्टकः, अम्बरीषपक्वपिष्टकः, भृष्टपिष्टकः.

Pancratic, pancratical, *a.* मल्लयुद्धकुशलः -ला -लं, मल्लयुद्धनिपुणः -णा -णं.

Pancratium, *s.* मल्लयुद्धं, मल्लक्रीडा, बाहुयुद्धं, बाहुप्रहरणं.

Pandect, *s.* विद्यासङ्ग्रहः.—(Of laws) संहिता, स्मृतिशास्त्रसंहिता.

Pandemic, *a.* सार्व्वलौकिकः -की -कं, सर्व्वव्यापकः -का -कं, सर्व्वजनव्यापकः &c., सार्व्वजनिकः -की -कं, सर्व्वजनीनः -ना -नं, विश्वजनीनः -ना -नं, सर्व्वसाधारणः -णी -णं.

Pandemonium, *s.* पिशाचसभं, सर्व्वपिशाचसभा, सर्व्वभूतसभा.

Pander, *s.* विटः, कुट्टनी *m.* (न्), रतताली *m.* (न्), सञ्चारकः, दूतः, वेश्याचार्य्यः, कौट्टिन्यकर्त्ता *m.* (र्तृ), सन्धानकर्त्ता *m.*, लाम्पट्यप्रयोजकः.

To pander, *v. a.* or *n.* परकामान् सम्पद् (c. 10. -पादयति -यितुं) or प्रयुज् (c. 10. -योजयति -यितुं), कौट्टिन्यं कृ, लाम्पट्यं प्रयुज्.

Pandering, panderism, *s.* कौट्टिन्यं, विटकर्म्म *n.* (न्), लाम्पट्यप्रयोजकत्वं.

Pandiculation, *s.* जृम्भणं, विजृम्भणं, हाफिका. *See* Yawning.

Pandit, *s.* (Learned Brahman) पण्डितः. *See* Pundit.

Pane, *s.* (Of glass) काचशिला, काचमयसमानशिला.

Panegyric, *s.* स्तुतिवादः, स्तुतिवाक्यं, प्रशंसावादः, स्तुतिपाठः, वन्दिपाठः, स्तुतिः *f.*, गुणस्तुतिः *f.*, गुणोत्कीर्त्तनं, गुणगानं, स्तोत्रं, श्लाघा, वन्दना, वर्णना. *See* Encomium.

Panegyrical, *a.* स्तुतिमयः -यी -यं, प्रशंसकः -का -कं, प्रशंसाकरः -रा -रं, गुणवर्णकः -का -कं, गुणश्लाघी -घिनी -घि (न्). *See* Laudatory.

Panegyrist, *s.* स्तुतिपाठकः, वन्दी *m.* (न्), वन्दिजनः, स्तोता *m.* (तृ), वर्णकः.

Panel, *s.* (Of a door) कपाटः -टी -टं, द्वारकपाटः, कवाटः -टा -टं, द्वारशाखा.—(Whole body of the jury) शापितप्रमाणपुरुषगणः, स्थेयगणः.

Pang, *s.* व्यथा, यातना, वेदना, शूलः -लं, अतिवेदना, अतिव्यथा; 'of childbirth,' गर्भवेदना, प्रसववेदना.

Panic, *s.* (Sudden fright) आकस्मिकभयं, आकस्मिकत्रासः, अकस्मात्-भयं, निष्कारणभयं, विद्रवः, विप्लवः, त्रासः; 'general panic in a country,' पालः; 'struck with panic,' भयविप्लुतः -ता -तं; 'as an army,' पिच्छः -च्छा -च्छं, पिच्छलः -ला -लं, समुत्पिञ्जः &c., समुत्पिञ्जलः &c.—(Sort of seed or grain) अणुः *m.*, प्रियङ्गुः -ङ्गूः *f.*, कङ्गुः -ङ्गूः *f.*, कङ्गुनी; 'field of it,' अणव्यं.

Pánini, *s.* (The grammarian) पाणिनिः *m.*, पाणिनः, दाक्षीपुत्रः, दाक्षेयः, सालातुरीयः, शालातुरीयः; 'connected with him,' पाणिनीयः -या -यं.

Panjáb, *s.* (The country) पञ्चनदः, वाहीकः; 'the Chenáb river,' चन्द्रभागा.

Pannel, *s.* (Kind of saddle) पर्य्याणं.—(Of a door). *See* Panel.

Pannier, *s.* (Basket) करण्डः, डलकं, डल्लकं, कण्डोलः, पेटकः.

Panoplied, *a.* संवर्म्मितः -ता -तं, कवचसंवृतः -ता -तं, कृतसन्नाहः -हा -हं.

Panoply, *s.* सर्व्वाङ्गकवचः -चं, सर्व्वशरीरवर्म्म *n.* (न्), सर्व्वगात्रत्राणी.

Panorama, *s.* चतुर्दिग्दर्शकचित्रं, सर्व्वदिग्दर्शकचित्रं.

To pant, *v. n.* (Palpitate) स्पन्द्, परिस्पन्द्, कम्प्, विकम्प्, वेप्, उच्छ्वस्.—(Have the breast heave with difficult respiration) कृच्छ्रेण श्वस् (c. 2. श्वसिति -तुं), कृच्छ्रेण श्वासप्रश्वासं कृ, उद्धन्तं कृ, उद्धम् (c. 1. -धमति -ध्मातुं), प्राणकृच्छ्रोपहतः -ता -तं भू.—(Long for) अभिलष्, आकाङ्क्ष्, अभिवाञ्छ् &c.

Pant, *s.* स्पन्दनं, प्रतिस्पन्दनं, कम्पः -म्पनं, वेपनं, उद्धमः.

Pantaloon, *s.* (Kind of trowsers) अङ्घ्रिपिलकञ्चुकविशेषः, जङ्घाच्छादनयोग्यम् अङ्घ्रिपिलवस्त्रं, जङ्घापरिधानं.—(Buffoon) भण्डः, विदूषकः.

Pantheism, *s.* जगदीश्वरमतं, जगदीश्वरवादः, अद्वैतमतं, अद्वैतवादः, अभेदमतं, अभेदवादः, विराट्स्वरूपमतं.

Pantheist, *s.* जगदीश्वरवादी *m.* (न्), जगदीश्वरमतावलम्बी *m.*, जगदीश्वरमताश्रयी *m.*, अद्वैतवादी *m.*, अभेदवादी *m.*, अद्वैतमतावलम्बी *m.*

Pantheistic, pantheistical, *a.* जगदीश्वरमतसम्बन्धी -न्धिनी &c., जगदीश्वरमतविषयकः -का -कं, अद्वैतमतसम्बन्धी &c., अद्वैतमतविषयकः &c.

Pantheon, *s.* सर्व्वदेवतामन्दिरं, सर्व्वदेवालयं, सर्व्वदेवतायतनं, सर्व्वदेवभवनं.

Panther, *s.* द्वीपी *m.* (न्), अतिक्रूरशीलो वनमार्जारभेदः or क्षुद्रव्याघ्रभेदः.

Panting, *s.* उच्छ्वासः, दुःश्वासः, श्वासकृच्छ्रं, प्राणकृच्छ्रं, उद्धमः, स्पन्दनं.

Panting, *part.* उच्छ्वसन् -सती &c., कृच्छ्रेण श्वसन् &c., स्पन्दमानः -ना -नं, कम्पमानः &c. *See* Gasping, Heaving.

Pantomime, *s.* (One that represents by dumb show) मुग्धाभिनयी *m.* (न्), मुग्धाभिनेता *m.* (तृ), मुग्धनर्त्तकः, मुग्धनाटकः, केवलाभिनयी *m.* (न्), हस्तपादादिसञ्चालनमात्रेण अभिनयी *m.* or अभिनेता *m.*, रङ्गावतारी *m.*—(Representation by dumb show) मुग्धनाट्यं, मुग्धनृत्यं, मुग्धाभिनयः, हस्तपादादिसञ्चालनं, हस्तपादादिसञ्चालनाभिनयः, लास्यं, ताण्डवं.

Pantomime, pantomimic, *a.* मुग्धनाट्यसम्बन्धी &c., मुग्धाभिनयविषयकः &c.

Pantry, *s.* कोष्ठः -ष्ठकं, खाद्यद्रव्यागारः -रं, खाद्यकोष्ठकं, कुटिः -टी *m.f.*

Pap, *s.* (Nipple) स्तनाग्रं, स्तनमुखः -खं, कुचाग्रं.—(Breast) स्तनः, कुचः, कुचातटं; 'the paps,' स्तनौ *m.* du.—(Soft food for infants) बालकपोषणयोग्यं मृद्वन्नं, मृद्वाहारः, मृदुखाद्यं, बालकाहारः.

Papa, *s.* पिता *m.* (तृ), तातः &c. *See* Father.

Papal, *a.* रोमीयधर्म्माधिपतिसम्बन्धी -न्धिनी &c., रोमीयधर्म्माध्यक्षसम्बन्धी.

Papaverous, *a.* खस्खसगुणोपेतः -ता -तं, खस्खसतुल्यगुणः -णा -णं.

Paper, *s.* (The substance) कार्पासं, कार्पासिकपत्रं.—(For writing) पत्रं, लिखनपत्रं, लेखनपत्रं, लेख्यपत्रं.—(Written sheet) पत्रं, पत्रकं,

पत्रिका, लेखः.—(Document, deed) पत्रं -त्री, लेख्यं, लेख्यपत्रं, साधनपत्रं, लेख्यप्रसङ्गः.

PAPER, *a.* (Made of paper) कार्पासिकः -की -कं, कार्पासः -सी -सं.

To PAPER, *v. a.* चित्रकार्पासेन or कार्पासिकपत्रेण छद् (c. 10. छादयति -यितुं) or आछद् or आस्तॄ (c. 5. -स्तृणोति -स्तरितुं, -रीतुं).

PAPER-MAKER, *s.* कार्पासकृत्, कार्पासकारः, कार्पासिकपत्रकृत्.

PAPESCENT, *a.* मज्जामयः -यी -यं, समज्जः -ज्जा -ज्जं.

PAPILIO, *s.* चित्रपतङ्गः, पतङ्गः. *See* BUTTERFLY.

PAPILLARY, PAPILLOUS, *a.* स्तनाग्रसदृशः -शी -शं, कुचाग्रोपमः -मा -मं.

PAPIST, *s.* रोमीयधर्म्मावलम्बी *m.* (न्), रोमीयधर्म्मनिष्ठितः, रोमीयधर्म्मस्थः. रोमीयमतधारी *m.* (न्).

PAPPY, *a.* मज्जामयः -यी -यं, मज्जावान् -वती -वत् (त्), मज्जागुणकः -का -कं, समज्जः -ज्जा -ज्जं, मृदुः -द्वी -दु, आर्द्रमृदुः &c., कोमलः -ला -लं.

PAPULÆ, *s. pl.* दद्रुः *m.*, खर्ज्जूः *f.*, वरटी, वरण्डकः, रक्तस्फोटः.

PAPULOSE, PAPULOUS, *a.* दद्रुणः -णा -णं, सस्फोटः -टा -टं.

PAR, *s.* (State of equality) समता, साम्यं, समभावः, समानता, तुल्यता, साम्यता; 'that is at par,' समानकक्षः -क्षा -क्षं, समकक्षः &c.; 'that is above par,' अधिकोत्तरः -रा -रं.

PARABLE, *s.* दृष्टान्तः, दृष्टान्तरूपकथा, उत्प्रेक्षा, उपमा, समासोक्तिः *f.*, समासोक्तिरूपकथा, निदर्शनं, उदाहरणं, हितोपदेशः.

PARABOLA, *s.* (A conic section) समकलच्छिन्नं.

PARABOLIC, PARABOLICAL, *a.* (Allegorical, expressed by parable) दृष्टान्तरूपः -पा -पं, दृष्टान्तोक्तः -क्ता -क्तं, दार्ष्टान्तिकः -की -कं.—(Having the form of a parabola) समकलच्छिन्नाकारः -रा -रं.

PARABOLICALLY, *adv.* दृष्टान्तरूपेण, दृष्टान्ततस्, दृष्टान्तपूर्व्वं.

PARACENTRIC, PARACENTRICAL, *a.* मण्डलत्यागी -गिनी -गि (न्).

PARADE, *s.* (Ostentation) कौतुकं, दम्भः, आडम्बरं. *See* the word.—(Place for military exercise) खलूरिका, प्रेक्षणं.—(Military exercise) अस्त्रशिक्षा, योग्या, युद्धाभ्यासः, शस्त्राभ्यासः, सैन्यव्यायामः.—(Procession) यात्रा, सैन्ययात्रा.

To PARADE, *v. a.* (Exhibit ostentatiously) दम्भार्थं or कौतुकार्थं or प्रेक्षार्थं दृश् (c. 10. दर्शयति -यितुं) or प्रदृश् or प्रकाश्.—(Marshal soldiers) सैन्यान् अस्त्रशिक्षार्थं or युद्धाभ्यासार्थं व्यूह् or विन्यस्.

To PARADE, *v. n.* (Go about in military procession) प्रेक्षार्थं or अस्त्रशिक्षार्थं यात्रां कृ.

PARADIGM, *s.* (Example) प्रतिमा, प्रतिरूपं, उपमा.—(In grammar) निदर्शनार्थप्रदर्शितविभक्तिः *f.*, निदर्शनार्थप्रदर्शितक्रियारूपं.

PARADISE, *s.* स्वर्गः, आनन्दलोकः, आनन्दभुवनं, नन्दनं, सुखलोकः, सुखभुवनं, सुखाधारः, सुखदं, सुखधाम *n.* (न्), अमर्त्यभुवनं, स्वर्लोकः, त्रिदिवः -वं, दिवं, द्यौः *f.* (दिव्), द्यौ *f.* (द्यो), नाकः, अपरलोकः, ताविषः, ऋभुक्षः, वैकुण्ठं; the last word refers properly to the paradise of Vishnu, that of Indra is स्वर्गः.

PARADISIACAL, *a.* स्वर्गीयः -या -यं, स्वर्ग्यः -र्ग्या -र्ग्यं, स्वर्गयोग्यः -ग्या -ग्यं, आनन्दलोकसम्बन्धी -न्धिनी &c., स्वर्गसम्बन्धी &c.

PARADOX, *s.* लोकविरुद्धाभासः, असत्याभासः, अयुक्ताभासः, लोकविरुद्धमतं.

PARADOXICAL, *a.* (Said of opinions) लोकमतविरुद्धः -द्धा -द्धं, अयुक्ताभासरूपः -पा -पं.—(Of persons) लोकविरुद्धाभासवादी *m.* (न्), लोकविरुद्धाभाससेवी *m.* (न्), लोकविरुद्धमतावलम्बी *m.*, अयुक्ताभासवादी *m.*

PARAGON, *s.* (Model) प्रतिमा, प्रमाणं, प्रमाता *m.* (तृ), उपमा, प्रतिरूपं, उत्तमप्रमाणं.—(An unequalled object) अनुपमवस्तु *n.*, निरुपमवस्तु *n.*, अद्वितीयवस्तु *n.*, अप्रतिरूपवस्तु.

PARAGRAPH, *s.* परिच्छेदः, विच्छेदः, खण्डः, लेखपरिच्छेदः, लेखखण्डः, वाक्यपरिच्छेदः, वाक्यखण्डः, वाक्यं.

PARALIPOMENA, *s.* शेषग्रन्थः, उपग्रन्थः, परिशिष्टं, उत्तरखण्डः.

PARALLAX, *s.* (In astronomy) शीघ्रः, लम्बनं, स्थानभेदः.

PARALLEL, *a.* (In geometry) एकदिङ्मुखसमान्तरः -रा -रं, एकदिग्गतसमान्तरः -रा -रं, समान्तरः -रा -रं, सरलसमान्तरः -रा -रं; 'two parallel lines,' एकदिग्गतसमान्तररेखाद्वयं, सरलसमान्तररेखाद्वयं, सरलरेखाद्वयं.—(Like, similar) समः -मा -मं, समानः -ना,-नं, तुल्यः -ल्या -ल्यं, सदृशः -शी -शं, अनुरूपः -पा -पं, समभावः -वा -वं, समरूपः -पा -पं.

PARALLEL, *s.* (A line equidistant from another) समान्तररेखा; 'of latitude,' स्पष्टपरिधिः *m.*, अक्षवृत्तं, अक्षांशवृत्तं.—(Likeness, conformity) सादृश्यं, सदृशता, सारूप्यं, अनुरूपता, आनुरूप्यं, समरूपता, समता, साम्यं, समानता.—(Comparison) उपमा, औपम्यं.

To PARALLEL, *v. a.* (Make parallel) समान्तरीकृ, समान्तरं -रां कृ.—(Compare) उपमा, तुल्, साधारणीकृ, समीकृ.—(Correspond, be equal to) समीभू, सदृशीभू, अनुरूपः -पा -पम् अस् or भू.

PARALLELISM, *s.* समान्तरता -त्वं, समान्तरभावः.—(Resemblance) सादृश्यं, सदृशता, अनुरूपता, आनुरूप्यं, समता, तुल्यता.

PARALLELOGRAM, *s.* दीर्घचतुरस्रं, दीर्घचतुर्भुजः, आयतचतुरस्रं, दीर्घचतुष्कोणः, समद्विभुजः, समसमद्विभुजः.

PARALLELOGRAMIC, PARALLELOGRAMICAL, *a.* दीर्घचतुरस्रः -स्रा -स्रं, समद्विभुजः -जा -जं.

PARALLELOPIPED, *s.* (In geometry) समखातः.

PARALOGISM, PARALOGY, *s.* आभासः, सिद्धान्ताभासः, हेत्वाभासः, पक्षाभासः, मिथ्याहेतुः *m.*, अयुक्तिः *f.*

PARALYSIS, *s.* स्तम्भः, अवष्टम्भः, विष्टम्भः, संस्तम्भः, सुप्तिः *f.*, त्वक्सुप्तिः *f.*, स्वापः, जाड्यं; 'of the thigh,' ऊरुस्तम्भः.—(Paralytic stroke) पक्षाघातः, पक्षवायुः *m.*, अर्द्धाङ्गवायुः *m.*, अर्द्धाङ्गं, भङ्गः.

PARALYTIC, PARALYTICAL, *a.* (Affected with paralysis) पक्षाघाती -तिनी -ति (न्), पक्षाघातरोगी &c., पक्षवायुग्रस्तः -स्ता -स्तं, अर्द्धाङ्गरोगी &c., सुप्तत्वक् *m. f. n.* (च्).

To PARALYZE, *v, a.* स्तम्भं जन् (c. 10. जनयति -यितुं), स्तम्भीकृ, स्तम्भ् (c. 5. स्तभ्नोति, c. 9. स्तभ्नाति, c. 10. स्तम्भयति -यितुं), विष्टम्भ्, जडीकृ, जाड्यं कृ, स्वापं जन्.

PARALYZED, *p. p.* स्तम्भितः -ता -तं, स्तम्भीकृतः -ता -तं, जडीकृतः -ता -तं, स्तब्धः -ब्धा -ब्धं, विष्टब्धः &c., अवष्टब्धः &c., निस्तब्धः &c., स्तम्भितः -ता -तं. *See* NUMB, *a.*

PARAMOUNT, *a.* परमः -मा -मं, सर्व्वश्रेष्ठः -ष्ठा -ष्ठं, श्रेष्ठः &c., अधिकः -का -कं, सर्व्वाधिकः &c., प्रमुखः -खा -खं, प्रधान in comp.; 'possessing paramount dominion,' साम्राज्यिकः -की -कं, सार्व्वभौमः -मी -मं; 'paramount sovereign,' सम्राट् *m.* (ज्), सर्व्वेश्वरः, सर्व्वेशः, सर्व्वस्वामी *m.* (न्); 'sway of a lord paramount,' साम्राज्यं.

PARAMOUR, *s.* (Gallant) जारः, उपपतिः *m.*, पापपतिः *m.*, रमणः, विटः, चेटकः.—(Mistress) उपस्त्री, उपपत्नी, जारिणी.

PARAPET, *s.* वक्षःपर्य्यन्तः प्राकारः, भित्तिः *f.*, परिसरः.

PARAPHERNALIA, *s. pl.* (Articles which a wife brings with her) स्त्रीधनं, यौतकं, औद्वाहिकं, पारिणाय्यं.—(Appendages, trappings) परिच्छदः, सामग्र्यं, पारिणाह्यं, उपकरणं, व्यञ्जनं.

PARAPHRASE, *s.* टीका, सविस्तरव्याख्या, सविस्तरभाषान्तरं सविस्तरार्थकथनं, सविस्तरविवरणं, मूलशब्दविस्तारः, भाष्यं, टिप्पनी.

To PARAPHRASE, *v. a.* विस्तरशस् or विस्तरेण or मूलशब्दविस्तारेण व्याख्या (c. 2. -ख्याति -तुं) or भाषान्तरीकृ or मूलार्थविवरणं कृ or मूलशब्दव्याख्यां कृ, मूलशब्दविस्तारं कृ, मूलशब्दाधिक्यं कृ.

PARAPHRASED, *p. p.* मूलशब्दविस्तारेण व्याख्यातः -ता -तं or विवृतः -ता -तं.

PARAPHRAST, *s.* मूलशब्दविस्तारेण व्याख्याता *m.* (तृ), टीकालेखकः.

PARAPHRASTIC, PARAPHRASTICAL, *a.* अधिकशब्दकः -का -कं, मूलाधिकशब्दकः &c., मूलशब्दविस्ताररूपः -पा -पं, विस्ताररूपः -पा -पं.

PARAPHRASTICALLY, *adv.* मूलशब्दविस्तारेण, मूलशब्दाधिक्यपूर्वं.

PARAQUET, PARAQUITO, *s.* क्षुद्रशुकः, अल्पशरीरः कीरभेदः.

PARASITE, *s.* (One who dines with others or sponges on his neighbor) परान्नः, परान्नभोजी *m.* (न्), परान्नभक्षी *m.*, परान्नपुष्टः, परान्नरुचिः *m.*, परपाकरुचिः *m.*, परपिण्डादः, पात्रेसमितः, पीठकेलिः *m.*, पीठमर्द्दः.—(In botany, a plant which attaches itself to others) वृक्षरुहा, तरुरुहा, तरुरोहिणी, तरुभुक् *m.* (ज्), वृक्षादनी, पराश्रया, वन्दा, वन्दाका, वन्दका, जीवन्तिका, आकाशवल्ली, खवल्ली, उपदी.

PARASITIC, PARASITICAL, *a.* (As a plant) वृक्षरुहः -हा -हं, तरुरुहः &c., तरुरोही -हिणी -हि (न्), तरुभुक् *m. f. n.* (ज्), पराश्रयः -या -यं.—(Sponging on others) पराश्रयी &c., परान्नपुष्टः -ष्टा -ष्टं.

PARASOL, *s.* आतपत्रं, आतपवारणं, छत्रं, उष्णवारणः -णं, अनघा; 'royal one,' नृपछत्रं, नृपलक्ष्म *n.* (न्).

To PARBOIL, *v. a.* ईषत् क्वथ्, अर्द्धेन क्वथ्, ईषत् स्थाल्यां पच् or श्रा.

PARBOILED, *p. p.* अर्द्धक्वथितः -ता -तं, ईषत्क्वथितः &c., अर्द्धश्राणः -णा -णं.

PARCEL, *s.* (Small bundle) पोटलिका, पोट्टली, कूर्चः, पीटिका.—(Portion, part) भागः, विभागः, अंशः, वण्टः -ण्टकः, उद्धारः, भाजितं, खण्डः.—(Quantity) राशिः *m.*, सञ्चयः, निचयः, चयः, सङ्घः, समूहः.—(Number of persons) गणः, समूहः, वृन्दं, मण्डलं.

To PARCEL, *v. a.* विभज् (c. 1. -भजति -ते -भक्तुं), प्रविभज्, विभागशः or अंशांशि कॢप् (c. 10. कल्पयति -यितुं) or विन्यस् (c. 4. -अस्यति -असितुं), वण्ट् (c. 10. वण्टयति -यितुं).

PARCENARY, *s.* समांशिता, समाधिकारिता, अविभक्तदायभोगः.

PARCENER, *s.* समांशी *m.* (न्), समभागी *m.*, समाधिकारी *m.*, अंशकः.

To PARCH, *v. a.* तप् (c. 1. तपति, तप्तुं, c. 10. तापयति -यितुं), सन्तप्, दह् (c. 1. दहति, दग्धुं), परिदह्, भ्रस्ज् (c. 6. भृज्जति -ते, भष्टुं, भर्ष्टुं), भृज् (c. 1. भर्जते -र्जितुं).

PARCHED, *p. p.* तप्तः -प्ता -प्तं, उपतप्तः &c., अभितप्तः &c., तापितः -ता -तं, दग्धः -ग्धा -ग्धं, भृष्टः -ष्टा -ष्टं, भ्रष्टः &c., भर्जितः -ता -तं, निर्जलः -ला -लं, शोषितजलः &c.; 'having the throat parched with thirst,' पिपासाक्षामकण्ठः -ण्ठा -ण्ठं.

PARCHMENT, *s.* चर्म्मपटः, चर्म्मपत्रं -त्रकं, झिल्ली, झिल्लिका, लेखनचर्म्म *n.* (न्), लिखनचर्म्म *n.*, चर्म्म *n.*

To PARDON, *v. a.* क्षम् (c. 1. क्षमते -ति, क्षन्तुं), संक्षम्, मुच् (c. 6. मुञ्चति, मोक्तुं), विमुच्, अवसृज्, मृष्, भुज्, अनुज्ञा, सह्, निर्यत्, क्षमां कृ, अपराधक्षमां कृ, अपराधमोचनं कृ, पापमुक्तिं कृ; 'deign to pardon my offence,' अपराधं मे क्षन्तुम् अर्हसि. *See To* FORGIVE.

PARDON, *s.* क्षमा, क्षान्तिः *f.*, मोचनं, विमोचनं, पापमोचनं, अपराधमुक्तिः *f.*, अपराधमोचनं, दोषमुक्तिः *f.*, अपराधक्षमा, अपराधमार्जना -नं, पापमार्जना, निष्कृतिः *f.*, दया, कृपा; 'to beg pardon,' क्षम् (c. 10. क्षमयति -यितुं), क्षमां प्रार्थ्, क्षमस्व or क्षम्यताम् इति वद्.

PARDONABLE, *a.* क्षन्तव्यः -व्या -व्यं, क्षमणीयः -या -यं, क्षमार्हः -र्हा -र्हं, क्षमायोग्यः -ग्या -ग्यं, क्षमोचितः -ता -तं, सहव्यः -व्या -व्यं, सहनीयः -या -यं, उपेक्षणीयः -या -यं.

PARDONABLY, *adv.* यथाक्षन्तव्यं, यथाक्षमणीयं, यथासहव्यं, क्षमणीयं.

PARDONED, *p. p.* क्षान्तः -न्ता -न्तं, दोषमुक्तः -क्ता -क्तं, दण्डमुक्तः &c., शासनमुक्तः &c., मुक्तदण्डः -ण्डा -ण्डं, मुक्तदोषः -षा -षं, मुक्तशासनः -ना -नं, मुक्तापराधः -धा -धं, दण्डमोचितः -ता -तं.

To PARE, *v. a.* (Clip, chip, cut off) तक्ष् (c. 1. तक्षति -क्षितुं), त्वक्ष् (c. 1. त्वक्षति -क्षितुं), तनूकृ, छिद्, अवछिद्, अवकृत्, कृत्, लू, खण्ड्, खण्डीकृ, विदलीकृ, कॢप्; 'to pare the nails,' नखखण्डनं कृ, नखच्छेदनं कृ, नखकल्पनं कृ.—(Peel, skin) त्वच (nom. त्वचयति -यितुं), निस्त्वचीकृ, त्वक्परिपुटनं कृ, निस्तुषीकृ.

PARED, *p. p.* तष्टः -ष्टा -ष्टं, त्वष्टः &c., तनूकृतः -ता -तं, कॢप्तः -प्ता -प्तं, छिन्नः -न्ना -न्नं, अवछिन्नः &c., खण्डितः -ता -तं, उत्क्षिप्तितः -ता -तं, 'pared nails,' खण्डकः; 'having pared nails,' कॢप्तनखः -खा -खं.

PAREGORIC, *a.* दुःखशमकः -का -कं, उपशमकः &c., शान्तिदः -दा -दं.

PARENT, *s.* (He or she that produces) जननः *m.* -नी *f.*, जनकः *m.*, जनिका *f.*, जनयिता *m.* -त्री *f.* (तृ), जन्मदः, धाता *m.* (तृ), सम्भूः *m.*, जः, पिता *m.*, माता *f.* *See* FATHER, MOTHER. 'Parents,' मातापितरौ *m. du.*, मातरपितरौ *m. du.*, तातजनयित्र्यौ *f. du.*, जनकजनन्यौ *f. du.*; 'parent of all,' विश्वधाता *m.*—(Cause, source) कारणं, हेतुः *m.*, उत्पादकः, जन्महेतुः *m.*, प्रभवः.

PARENTAGE, *s.* जन्म *n.* (न्), जातिः *f.*, वंशः, कुलं, उत्पत्तिः *f.*; 'of royal parentage,' राजवंश्यः -श्या -श्यं, नृपात्मजः -जा -जं, राजबीजी &c.; 'of honorable parentage,' महाकुलः -ला -लं.

PARENTAL, *a.* (Pertaining to parents) मातापितृसम्बन्धी -न्धिनी &c., जननसम्बन्धी &c., पैतृकः -की -कं.—(Becoming parents) मातापितृयोग्यः -ग्या -ग्यं, मातापितृसन्निभः -भा -भं; 'parental affection,' अपत्यस्नेहः, पुत्रस्नेहः, सुतस्नेहः, वात्सल्यं, वत्सलता.

PARENTHESIS, *s.* निवेशितवाक्यं, प्रक्षिप्तवाक्यं, अप्रधानवाक्यं, प्रासङ्गिकवाक्यं, उपवाक्यं, प्रक्षिप्ताप्रधानवाक्यं, अनन्वितवाक्यं.

PARENTHETIC, PARENTHETICAL, *a.* प्रासङ्गिकः -की -कं, अनन्वितः -ता -तं, अप्रधान in comp., मूलवाक्यानन्वितः &c.

PARENTHETICALLY, *adv.* प्रसङ्गतस्, प्रसङ्गक्रमेण, मूलवाक्यानन्वितं.

PARENTLESS, *a.* मातापितृहीनः -ना -नं, मातापितृरहितः -ता -तं.

PARER, *s.* तष्टा *m.* (ष्टृ), त्वष्टा *m.*; 'nail-parer,' नखच्छेदनी.

PARHELION, *s.* सूर्य्याभासः, मिथ्यासूर्य्यः, कृत्रिमसूर्य्यः.

PARING, *s.* (The act) तक्षणं, त्वक्षणं.—(That which is pared off) तष्टं, तक्षितं, विदलं, शकलं, खण्डः, भित्तं.

PARISH, *s.* पुरोहिताधीनः प्रदेशः or ग्रामः, धर्म्माध्यापकाधीनो देशः or ग्रामः, पौरोहित्यदेशः, पौरोहित्यभूमिः *f.*; 'parish-priest,' ग्रामयाजकः, ग्रामपुरोहितः.

PARISHIONER, *s.* ग्रामवासी *m.* (न्), ग्रामस्थः, ग्रामेवासी *m.*, ग्रामिकः, ग्रामीयः, पुरोहिताधीनदेशस्थः.

PARITY, *s.* समता, साम्यं, समानता, तुल्यता -त्वं, तौल्यं, साम्यता, समभावः, कक्षा; 'parity of reason,' न्यायसाम्यं, न्यायसमता, समानन्यायत्वं, तुल्यन्यायत्वं; 'by parity of reason,' न्यायसाम्यात्.

PARK, *s.* उद्यानं, राजोद्यानं, क्रीडावनं, क्रीडावाटिका, आक्रीडः -डं, प्रमदवनं, साधारणवनं, साधारणोद्यानं, कृत्रिमवनं, मृगयास्थानं, मृगयालयं, मृगयाभूमिः *f.*; 'open space in a town,' सन्निवेशः, निकर्षणं.

PARKER, PARK-KEEPER, *s.* उद्यानपालः -लकः, उद्यानरक्षकः.

PARLANCE, *s.* सम्भाषणं, संवादः, संलापः, आलापः, कथोपकथनं.

To PARLEY, *v. n.* (Confer) सम्भाष्, संवद्, संलप्; 'with an enemy,' युद्धमध्ये शत्रुणा सह सम्भाष्, सन्धिप्रसङ्गं कृ.

Parley, *s.* सम्भाषा -षणं, संलापः, वादः, संवादः; 'in war,' युद्धमध्ये शत्रुणा सह सम्भाषा, सन्धिसम्भाषणं, सन्धिप्रसङ्गः.

Parliament, *s.* विचारसभा, सम्मन्त्रणसभा, वादशाला, संवादशाला, मन्त्रशाला, महासभा, शिष्टसभा, प्रजाप्रतिनिधिसभा.

Parlor, *s.* आलापशाला, संलापशाला, कथोपकथनशाला, उपवेशनशाला.

Parochial, *a.* पुरोहिताधीनदेशसम्बन्धी -न्धिनी &c., पौरोहित्यदेशसम्बन्धी &c., ग्रामिकः -की -कं, ग्रामीयः -या -यं, ग्राम्यः -म्या -म्यं.

Parody, *s.* विनोदार्थानुकरणकविता, हास्यकरणार्थम् अनुकरणकाव्यं.

To parody, *v. a.* विनोदार्थं or हास्यकरणार्थं शब्दपरिवर्त्तनं कृ.

Parole, parol, *s.* वचनं, प्रतिज्ञा, अङ्गीकारः, स्वीकारः, उरीकारः.

Paronomasia, paronomasy, *s.* श्लेषः, श्लेषवाक्यं, द्व्यर्थवाक्यं.

Paronychia, *a.* नखम्पचः, कुनिः *m.*, चिप्पं, नखरोगः.

Parotis, *s.* (The parotid gland) लालाशयः, लालाधारः.

Paroxysm, *s.* आवेशः, अवतारः -तरणं, आक्रमः -मणं, वेगः; 'of anger,' क्रोधावेशः; 'of lust,' कामावेशः. *See* Fit, *s.*

Parricidal, parricidious, *a.* (Pertaining to parricide) पितृहत्यासम्बन्धी &c., पितृवधविषयकः -का -कं, पितृहत्यारूपः -पा -पं, पितृवधात्मकः -का -कं.—(Committing parricide) पितृघ्नः -घ्नी -घ्नं, पितृघातकः &c.

Parricide, *s.* (One who murders his father) पितृहा *m.* (न्), पितृहन्ता *m.* (न्), पितृघ्नः, पितृघाती *m.* (न्), पितृघातकः, पितृघातुकः,—(Murder of a father) पितृहत्या, पितृवधः, पितृघातः, पितृहिंसा.

Parrot, *s.* शुकः, कीरः, वक्रचञ्चुः *m.*, वक्रतुण्डः, रक्ततुण्डः, चिमिः *m.*, चिरिः *m.*, रक्तपादः, कुमारः, किङ्किरातः, फलाशनः, फलादनः, दाडिमप्रियः, मेधावी *m.* (न्); 'a flock of parrots,' शौकं.

To parry, निवृ (c. 10. -वारयति -यितुं), वृ, प्रतिहन् (c. 2. -हन्ति -न्तुं), प्रतिषिध् (c. 1. -षेधति -षेद्धुं), प्रतिघातं कृ, वारणं कृ.

To parse, *v. a.* पदभञ्जनं कृ, पदच्छेदं कृ, लिङ्गनिर्देशं कृ, शब्दान्वयनिरूपणं कृ.

Parsee, *s.* (Persian) पारसीकः, पारसिकः.

Parsimonious, *a.* अल्पव्ययी -यिनी -यि (न्), व्ययशङ्कितः -ता -तं, व्ययपराङ्मुखः -खा -खं, परिमितव्ययी &c., मितव्ययी &c., कृपणः -णा -णं, अर्थपरः &c. *See* Miserly.

Parsimoniously, *adv.* अल्पव्ययेन, अल्पव्ययपूर्व्वं, सकार्पण्यं, कृपणवत्.

Parsimoniousness, parsimony, *s.* अल्पव्ययः, स्वल्पव्ययः, कार्पण्यं, कृपणता -त्वं, व्ययशङ्का, व्ययपराङ्मुखता, परिमितव्ययः, मितव्ययः, दृढमुष्टित्वं.

Parsing, *s.* पदभञ्जनं, पदच्छेदः, शब्दान्वयनिरूपणं, लिङ्गनिर्देशः.

Parsley, *s.* (Apium involucratum) अजमोदा.

Parson, *s.* ग्रामपुरोहितः, ग्रामयाजकः, ग्रामधर्म्माध्यक्षः, ग्रामगुरुः *m.*, ग्रामाचार्य्यः, धर्म्माध्यापकः, उपाध्यायः.

Parsonage, *s.* धर्म्माध्यापकगृहं, ग्रामपुरोहिताध्युषितं गृहादि.

Part, *s.* (Portion, piece) भागः, अंशः, खण्डः -ण्डकः, विभागः, शकलः -लं, भित्तं, भिन्नं, भित्तिः *f.*, लवः, दलं, विदलं, अर्द्धः.—(A portion or division considered by itself, but not really separated) देशः, प्रदेशः, उद्देशः, एकदेशः, भागः, अङ्गं, अवयवः; 'part of a wood,' वनैकदेशः, वनोद्देशः.—(Component part, member) अङ्गं, अवयवः; 'inward part,' अन्तरङ्गं.—(Particular division) प्रकरणं, विषयः, अङ्गं; 'minor part,' प्रत्यङ्गं.—(Share, portion allotted) विभागः, भागः, अंशः, उद्धारः, भाजितं, भाज्यं, वण्टः -ण्टकः.—(Interest, concern in) सम्बन्धः, अभिसम्बन्धः.—(Side, party) पक्षः; 'to take one's part,' पक्षं ग्रह् or उद्ग्रह्, पक्षोद्ग्राही or पक्षपाती &c. भू.—(Particular business or duty) कर्म्म *n.* (न्), कार्य्यं, धर्म्मः, स्वकर्म्म *n.*, स्वधर्म्मः, वृत्तिः *f.*, प्रवृत्तिः *f.*, गुणः.—(Character in a drama) भूमिका, वृत्तिः *f.*; 'act the part of a dear friend towards the rival wives,' कुरु प्रियसखीवृत्तिं सपत्नीजने.—(Parts, qualities) गुणाः *m. pl.*, बुद्धिः *f.*—(Parts, region) देशः, प्रदेशः, उद्देशः; 'for the most part,' प्रायस्, प्रायशस्, प्रायेण, भूयस्, भूयिष्ठं, बाहुल्येन, बहुशस्, बहुतरं; 'by parts, in parts,' अंशतस्, भागतस्, भागशस्, अवयवशस्; 'in part, partly,' अंशतस्, भागतस्, किञ्चित्, ईषत्; 'in two parts,' द्विधा; 'in four parts,' चतुर्धा; 'in many parts,' बहुधा; 'in how many parts?' कतिधा; 'in good part,' सानुग्रहं, प्रसन्नं, हितं, प्रियं, अनुकूलं.

To part, *v. a.* (Disunite, divide, separate) वियुज्, विच्छिद्, भिद्, विभिद्, विच्छिद्, विविच्, पृथक्कृ, शकलीकृ.—(Distribute, divide into shares) विभज्, प्रविभज्, संविभज्, पृथक् पृथग् विभज्, अंश् (c. 10. अंशयति -यितुं), व्यंस् (c. 10. -अंसयति -यितुं), वण्ट्, परिक्लृप्.—(Part the hair) सीमन्त (nom. सीमन्तयति -यितुं).

To part, *v. n.* (Be separated or divided) वियुज् in pass. (-युज्यते), विभिद् in pass. (-भिद्यते), भिद्, विच्छिद् (c. 4. (-छिद्यति -छेत्तुं), विच्छिद् in pass., विगम् (c. 1. -गच्छति -गन्तुं), वियुक्तः -क्ता -क्तं भू.—(Open in two, cleave open) स्फुट् (c. 1. स्फोटति, c. 6. स्फुटति -टितुं), दल् (c. 1. दलति -लितुं), विदल्, विदलीभू, विदलितः -ता -तं भू.—(Depart) अपगम्, व्यपगम्, अपया, व्यपया.—(Bid farewell) आमन्त्र्, अनुमन्त्र्.—(Part with) त्यज् (c. 1. त्यजति, त्यक्तुं), परित्यज्. *See* Resign.

To partake, *v. n.* अंशं or भागं ग्रह् (c. 9. गृह्णाति, ग्रहीतुं) or हृ (c. 1. हरति, हर्त्तुं), भागी -गिनी -गि भू, भज् (c. 1. भजते, भक्तुं), संविभज्, अंशं भुज् (c. 7. भुनक्ति, भुंक्ते, भोक्तुं); 'in common with another,' अन्येन सह भुज् or भज्.

Partaker, *s.* भागी *m.* -गिनी *f.* (न्), अंशी *m.* -शिनी *f.* (न्), संविभागी &c., भागहारी *m.* (न्), भागहरः, भागग्राही *m.*, अंशहारी *m.*, अंशहरः, अंशग्राही *m.*, अंशकः, अंशभोगी *m.*, सहभोगी *m.*, सहभागी *m.*, भाक् *m.* (ज्) in comp., भुक् *m.* (ज्) in comp.

Parted, *p. p.* (Separated) वियुक्तः -क्ता -क्तं, विच्छिन्नः -न्ना -न्नं, विभक्तः &c., विविक्तः &c., विगतः -ता -तं; 'as the hair,' सीमन्त्यमानः -ना -नं.

Parterre, *s.* पुष्पवाटी -टिका, कुसुमाकरः, पुष्पाकरः, उद्यानं.

Partial, *a.* (Inclined to favor one side) पक्षपाती -तिनी -ति (न्), पक्षस्नेही &c., स्वपक्षस्नेही &c., पक्षानुरागी &c., पक्षोद्ग्राही &c., सपक्षपातः -ता -तं, पक्षपातकृतस्नेहः -हा -हं, स्वपक्षकृतस्नेहः &c., सङ्गी &c., सङ्गवान् -वती -वत् (त्), सङ्गयुक्तः -क्ता -क्तं, पाक्षिकः -की -कं,—(Not fair) असमः -मा -मं, असमदर्शी &c., असमदृष्टिः -ष्टिः -ष्टि, असमानवृत्तिः -त्तिः -त्ति.—(Not general or total) असार्वत्रिकः -की -कं, अपूर्णः -र्णा -र्णं, असम्पूर्णः &c., असकलः -ला -लं, असमग्रः -ग्रा -ग्रं, अव्यापी &c., अव्यापकः -का -कं, अव्याप्तः -प्ता -प्तं, असाधारणः -णा -णी -णं, असर्व्वव्यापी &c., एकाङ्गी &c., एकदेशी &c., एकपक्षी &c., खण्डितः -ता -तं, खण्ड in comp.; 'partial deluge,' खण्डप्रलयः; 'partial shower,' खण्डवृष्टिः *f.*; 'partial eclipse,' खण्डग्रासः.

Partiality, *s.* (Inclination to favor one side) पक्षपातः -तिता, पक्षस्नेहः, स्वपक्षस्नेहः, पक्षोद्ग्राहः -हित्वं, सङ्गः, स्नेहः, असमता, असमदृष्टिः *f.*, असमबुद्धिः *f.*, पक्षता, पक्षानुरागः.—(Fondness for) स्नेहः, रुचिः *f.*, अभिरुचिः *f.*, अनुरागः, अनुरक्तिः *f.*, प्रणयः, प्रेम *n.* (न्).

PARTIALLY, *adv.* (With undue bias to one side) सपक्षपातं, सपक्षस्नेहं, पक्षपातपूर्व्वं, सङ्गपूर्व्वं, असमं, असमदृष्ट्या.—(Not generally or totally) असर्व्वतस्, असर्व्वेण, सखण्डतस्, खण्डशस्, अंशतस्, असकलं, असाकल्येन, अकृत्स्नशस्, असमग्रं, भागतस्, एकदेशेन, एकभागेन, एकाङ्गतस्, अपूर्णं, असम्पूर्णं, खण्ड or खण्डित in comp.; as, 'partially learned,' खण्डविद्यः -द्या -द्यं or खण्डितविद्यः.

PARTIBLE, *a.* विभाज्यः -ज्या -ज्यं, अंशनीयः -या -यं, अंश्यः -श्या -श्यं, अंशयितव्यः -व्या -व्यं, वण्टनीयः -या -यं, पृथक्करणीयः &c.

PARTICIPANT, *a.* भागी -गिनी -गि (न्), संविभागी &c., अंशी &c., समांशी &c., अंशग्राही -हिणी &c., भाक् *m.f.n.* (ज्). *See* PARTAKER.

To PARTICIPATE, *v. n.* भज्, संविभज्, भागं or अंशं ग्रह् or हृ. *See To* PARTAKE.

PARTICIPATION, *s.* अंशग्रहणं, भागग्रहणं, अंशहरणं, भागहरणं, भजनं, संविभागः -गित्वं, संविभजनं, अंशभोगः, अंशप्राप्तिः *f.*, अंशप्रापणं, सहभोगः, सहभुक्तिः *f.*

PARTICIPIAL, *a.* सकालकृदन्तरूपः -पा -पं, कृदन्तधर्म्मकः -का -कं.

PARTICIPLE, *s.* सकालकृदन्तः, कालबोधककृदन्तः, कृदन्तः.

PARTICLE, *s.* कणः, कणिका, कणिकः, लवः, लेशः, अणुः *m.*, परमाणुः *m.*, कला, काकिणिका, सूक्ष्मः, सूक्ष्माणुः, तिलः, अंशुः *m.*, अंशः, क्षुद्रांशः, सूक्ष्मांशः, तूलं, रेणुः *m.*; 'very minute particle,' अणुरेणुः *m.f.*, अतिसूक्ष्माणुः *m.*, सूक्ष्ममृत्तिका.—(In grammar) अव्ययः -यं, अव्ययशब्दः, निपातः; 'declinable particle,' अर्द्धाव्ययं.

PARTICULAR, *a.* (Noting something peculiar or distinctive) विशेष in comp., विशिष्टः -ष्टा -ष्टं, विशेषकः -का -कं, सविशेषः -षा -षं, विशेषवान् -वती -वत् (त्), विशेषणः -णा -णं, अवच्छेदकः -का -कं, विच्छेदकः &c., परिच्छेदकः &c.; 'particular mark,' विशेषलक्षणं; 'particular duty,' विशेषधर्म्मः; 'particular condition,' दशाविशेषः; 'at particular times,' विशेषकाले, कालविशेषे.—(Distinct individual) विशिष्टः &c., विशेष in comp., व्यक्तः -क्ता -क्तं, व्यक्तिकः -का -कं, पृथग्व्यक्तिकः &c., पृथगात्मकः &c., उद्दिष्टः -ष्टा -ष्टं, उद्देशकः -का -कं, भिन्नः -न्ना -न्नं, विविक्तः &c.; 'particular person,' अमुकजनः, अमुकव्यक्तिः *f.*—(Not general) असाधारणः -णा -णी -णं, असामान्यः -न्या -न्यं, अव्यापी -पिनी -पि (न्), अव्यापकः -का -कं, अव्याप्यः -प्या -प्यं.—(Not common) अप्राकृतः -ता -तं, अलौकिकः -की -कं, अप्रसिद्धः -द्धा -द्धं.—(Special, more than ordinary) विशेष in comp., विशेषकः &c., अधिकोत्तरः -रा -रं, लोकोत्तरः &c.; 'particular rule,' विशेषविधिः *m.*; 'particular occasion,' समयविशेषः.—(Odd, singular) विलक्षणः -णा -णं, अपूर्व्वः -र्व्वा -र्व्वं, अलौकिकः -की -कं.—(Minute, attentive to particulars, strict) सूक्ष्मदर्शी -र्शिनी &c., सूक्ष्मदृष्टिः -ष्टिः -ष्टि, सूक्ष्मः -क्ष्मा -क्ष्मं.

PARTICULAR, *s.* विशेषः, अवच्छेदः, व्यवच्छेदः, विच्छेदः.—(Single or distinct point) अर्थः, विषयः, प्रकरणं, विशेषः; 'the particulars of a story,' वृत्तान्तः; 'he told all the particulars,' सर्व्ववृत्तान्तम् अकथयत्; 'in particular,' विशेषतस्.

PARTICULARITY, *s.* (Distinct notice of particulars) एकैकशो निर्देशः or समुद्देशः or उद्देशः, विशेषकथनं, सर्व्ववृत्तान्तकथनं, विशेषनिर्देशः, व्यवच्छेदः.—(Individuality) व्यक्तता, अव्याप्तिः *f.*, अव्यापकत्वं, असाधारणता.—(Distinctness) भिन्नता, व्यक्तिः *f.*, पार्थक्यं, विशिष्टता.—(Detail) विवरणं, विस्तारः.

PARTICULARIZATION, *s.* विशेषवर्णनं -ना, विशेषनिर्देशः, विशेषकथनं, सर्व्ववृत्तान्तकथनं, समुद्देशः, व्यवच्छेदः, परिसंख्या -ख्यानं.

To PARTICULARIZE, *v. a.* एकैकशो निर्दिश् (c. 6. -दिशति -देष्टुं) or उद्दिश् or समुद्दिश् or कथ् (c. 10. कथयति -यितुं) or वर्ण् (c. 10. वर्णयति -यितुं), विशेषवर्णनं कृ, विशेषनिर्देशं कृ, विशेषकथनं कृ, विशेष (nom. विशेषयति -यितुं), विशिष् (c. 7. -शिनष्टि -शेष्टुं).

PARTICULARIZED, *p. p.* एकैकशो निर्दिष्टः -ष्टा -ष्टं or समुद्दिष्टः &c. or उद्दिष्टः &c. or कथितः -ता -तं, विशेषितः &c., व्यवच्छिन्नः -न्ना -न्नं.

PARTICULARLY, *adv.* (In an especial manner) विशेषतस्, विशेषेण, सविशेषं, मुख्यशस्, प्रधानतस्.—(Distinctly, severally) व्यक्तं, विविक्तं, पृथक्, अवयवशस्.—(Minutely) अतिसूक्ष्मत्वेन.

PARTING, *s.* (Separation) वियोगः, विप्रयोगः, विगमः, विरहः, विश्लेषः, प्रविश्लेषः, विप्रलम्भः, भेदः, विभेदः, विभागः, प्रविभागः, पृथग्भावः, पृथक्त्वं, अपगमः.—(Of the hair) सीमन्तः.

PARTING, *a.* (Given at parting) प्रस्थानिकः -की -कं, प्रास्थानिकः -की -कं, प्रस्थान or प्रयाण in comp.; as, 'a parting embrace,' प्रस्थानालिङ्गनं.

PARTISAN, *s.* पक्षपाती *m.* (न्), सपक्षः, एकपक्षः, पक्षकः, पक्षधारी *m.*, पक्षधरः, पक्षावलम्बी *m.* (न्), पक्षः, पार्श्वकः, पार्श्विकः, सहोत्थायी *m.* (न्), अर्थी *m.*, आनुग्राहकः, सङ्गी *m.*, अनुषङ्गी *m.* (न्).

PARTISANSHIP, *s.* पक्षपातिता, पक्षपातः, पक्षधारणं -रिता, पक्षावलम्बनं.

PARTITION, *s.* (Separation) परिच्छित्तिः *f.*, परिच्छेदः. *See* PARTING, *s.*—(Division of shares) विभागः, विभागकल्पनं -ना, भागकरणं, भागः, अंशनं, उद्धारः, उद्धारविभागः, वण्टनं.—(That by which separation is made, a wall, &c.) भित्तिः *f.*, भित्तिका, व्यवधानं, व्यवधा, सन्धिः *m.*

To PARTITION, *v. a.* (Divide) विभिद्, भिद्, विच्छिद्, परिच्छिद्, छिद्, विभज्, पृथक्कृ.—(Distribute into shares) विभज्, प्रविभज्, संविभज्, अंश्, अंश्, अंशांशि दा or क्लृप् or परिक्लृप्, वण्ट्, वण्टनं कृ.

PARTITIONED, *p. p.* विभक्तः -क्ता -क्तं, प्रविभक्तः &c., संविभक्तः &c., अंशितः -ता -तं, परिकल्पितः &c., उद्धृतः &c., कृतवण्टनः -ना -नं.

PARTLY, *adv.* अंशतस्, भागतस्, किञ्चित्, ईषत्, कियत्, कियत्पर्य्यन्तं, अल्पं, अल्पमात्रं.

PARTNER, *s.* सहायः, सहकारी *m.* (न्), सङ्गी *m.* (न्), सम्भूयकारी *m.*, अंशी *m.*, समांशी *m.*, संसर्गी *m.*, अंशग्राही *m.*, अंशभोगी *m.*, सहभोगी *m.*, सहभागी *m.*, सहवर्त्ती *m.*, भागी *m.*, प्रतियोगी *m.*, प्रसङ्गी *m.*, अनुषङ्गी *m.*, सक्तुः *m.* (स्), पक्षकः.—(Partner of joys and sorrows, as a husband or wife) समदुःखसुखः -खा. *See* HUSBAND, WIFE, MATE, &c.

PARTNERSHIP, *s.* समांशिता -त्वं, सहायता, सम्भूयकारिता -त्वं, सम्भूयसमुत्थानं, संसर्गिता -त्वं, प्रतियोगिता, सहकारिता.

PARTRIDGE, *s.* तित्तिरः, तित्तिरिः *m.*, चकोरः -रकः, कृकणः, क्रकणः, क्रकरः, कपिञ्जलः, टिट्टिभः; 'flock of partridges,' तैत्तिरं.

PARTURIENT, *a.* आसन्नप्रसवा, आसन्नप्रसववेदना, प्रसवोन्मुखा, उपस्थितप्रसवकाला, आसन्नप्रसवकाला.

PARTURITION, *s.* प्रसवः, प्रसूतिः *f.*, सूतिः *f.*, सूः *f.*, सूता, जननं, उत्पादनं.

PARTY, *s.* (Side, cause) पक्षः, मतं; 'one's own party,' आत्मपक्षः, स्वपक्षः; 'belonging to one's own party,' स्वपक्षावलम्बी *m.*, स्वपक्षपाती, आत्मपक्षधारी *m.* (न्); 'one of the opposite party,' विपक्षः, प्रतिपक्षः; 'attachment to a party,' पक्षपातः. *See* PARTIALITY, PARTISANSHIP.—(Number of persons associated in opposition to others) पक्षः, सपक्षिकाः *m. pl.*, सपक्षिणां गणः

or संसर्गः or समूहः or सङ्घातः or सङ्गः, शाखा.—(One of two litigants) वादी *m.* (न्), अर्थी *m.*—(Set of people) गणः, पंक्तिः *f.*, समूहः, सङ्घः, सङ्घातः, मण्डलं, दलं; 'a party of men,' पुरुषगणः, जनसमूहः; 'of soldiers,' सैन्यदलं; 'of rogues,' धूर्त्तमण्डलं.—(Assembly) सभा, पंक्तिः *f.*, समाजः, रासेरसः.—(Convivial party) सहभोजनं, सम्भोजनं, सहपानं, सम्प्रीतिः *f.*, उत्सवतालं.—(Person particularized) विवक्षितजनः, व्यक्तिः *f.*, मनुष्यः, जनः, विवक्षितमनुष्यः.—(One concerned or interested) सम्बन्धी *m.* (न्), भागी *m.*, अंशी *m.*

PARTY, *a.* पक्ष in comp., पाक्षिकः -की -कं, पाक्षः -क्षी -क्षं.

PARTY-COLORED, *a.* नानावर्णः -र्णा -र्णं, नानारङ्गः -ङ्गा -ङ्गं, चित्रविचित्रः -त्रा -त्रं, विचित्रवर्णः &c., विचित्ररङ्गः &c.

PARTYISM, *s.* पक्षपातिता. *See* PARTISANSHIP, PARTIALITY.

PARTY-MAN, *s.* पक्षपाती *m.* (न्), पक्षकः, पाक्षिकः. *See* PARTISAN.

PARTY-WALL, *s.* भित्तिः *f.*, भित्तिका, कुड्यं -ड्यकं. *See* PARTITION.

PÁRVATÍ, *s.* (The goddess Durgá, the wife of Śiva and mother of Kártikeya and Ganeśa, called Párvatí in her capacity of daughter of Himála, the sovereign of the snowy mountains. She has many names, some of which will be found under the head of Bhavání and Durgá. They are here all collected together) पार्व्वती, हैमवती, हिमवत्सुता, हिमशैलजा, हिमजा, देवी, महादेवी, उमा, दुर्गा, काली, चण्डी, चण्डिका, कालिका, भवानी, गौरी, मङ्गलागौरी, सर्व्वमङ्गला, भैरवी, भद्रकाली, रुद्राणी, शर्व्वाणी, ईश्वरी, शिवा, मृडानी, अम्बा, अम्बिका, जगदम्बा, जगन्माता *f.* (तृ), दक्षजा, श्यामा, भगवती, ज्येष्ठागौरी, महामाया, शाकम्भरी, कात्यायनी, अपर्णा, शाम्भवी, शावरी षष्ठी.

PARVENU, *s.* (An upstart) आगन्तुकः, आगन्तुः *m.*

PASQUINADE, *s.* निन्दालेखः, निन्दार्थकलेखः, उपहासककविता.

To PASS, *v. n.* (Move, go) गम्, या, चल्, चर्, सृ, इ &c.—(Be spent, go on, as time, &c.) वृत् (c. 1. वर्त्तते -र्त्तितुं), प्रवृत्, गम्—(Gain currency) प्रचलीभू, प्रचलितः -ता -तं भू, प्रचल्, प्रचर्.(Be enacted) सिध् (c. 4. सिध्यति, सेद्धुं), सिद्धीभू, निष्पन्नीभू, व्यवस्थापितः -ता -तं भू.—(Be approved) सम्मतः -ता -तं भू.—(Occur, come to pass) उपस्था, समुपस्था, उपपद्, सम्पद्, उपपन्नः -न्ना -न्नं भू, आपत्, सम्भू, संवृत्, संवृत्तः -त्ता -त्तं भू, आगम्, उपागम्, घट्.—(Be transferred) संक्रम् (c. 1. -क्रामति -क्रमितुं), उपसंक्रम्.—(Pass away, disappear, fade away) नश्, प्रणश्, क्षि, प्रली, विली, प्रविली, तिरोगम्, तिरोभू, क्षर्.—(Pass away, as time, &c.) अतिक्रम्, अतिवृत्, अती, व्यती, समती, गम्; 'six months passed away,' षण्मासम् अत्यवर्त्तत; 'six seasons passed away,' ऋतूनां षट् समत्ययुः; 'let not the moment pass away,' नातिवर्त्तेत क्षणं.—(Pass by) अतिक्रम्, अती, अतिगम्, अतिचर्, अतिया, समतिया.—(Pass on) प्रया, प्रगम्, प्रवृत्, प्रसृ, गम्, या; 'jokes pass,' प्रवर्त्तन्ते हासाः.—(Pass over, cross) तॄ, अतितॄ, निस्तॄ, अतिक्रम्, अती.—(Let pass, omit) त्यज्, परित्यज्, उत्सृज्, विसृज्, उपेक्ष्; 'let it pass,' यातु; 'that which passes in the mind,' मनोगतं, अन्तर्गतं मनः.

To PASS, *v. a.* (Go over, through, beyond, cross or pass over) तॄ (c. 1. तरति -रितुं -रीतुं), अतितॄ, सन्तॄ, निस्तॄ, उत्तॄ, समुत्तॄ, अतिक्रम्, व्यतिक्रम्, अती, व्यती, अतिगम्, पारं गम् (c. 1. गच्छति, गन्तुं); 'to pass a river,' नदीपारं गम्.—(Spend time, &c.) गम् (c. 10. गमयति -यितुं), परिगम्, वृत् (c. 10. वर्त्तयति -यितुं), नी (c. 1. नयति, नेतुं), वह् (c. 10. वाहयति -यितुं), विहृ (c. 1. -हरति -ते -हर्त्तुं), विवस् (c. 1. -वसति -वस्तुं); 'eight years were passed,' अष्टौ समाः परिगमिताः; 'he passes his days,' दिवसानि गमयति; 'he passed the night,' निशां निनाय; 'passing the night there,' तत्र रात्रिं उष्य.—(Cause to move) चल् (c. 10. चालयति -यितुं), सञ्चल्, सञ्चर् (c. 10. -चारयति -यितुं), स्थानान्तरीकृ.—(Transfer) संक्रम् (c. 10 -क्रामयति -यितुं), उपसंक्रम्.—(Enact) सिद्धं -द्धां कृ, सिद्धीकृ, निष्पन्नं -न्नां कृ, निष्पद् (c. 10. -पादयति -यितुं), व्यवस्था in caus. (-स्थापयति -यितुं), स्था, व्यवस्थां कृ.—(Pass sentence) निर्णयं कृ, प्रणयनं कृ.—(Pass by) अतिक्रम्, व्यतिक्रम्, समतिक्रम्, अतिवृत्, अतिचर्, अतिगम्, अतिया, समतिया, अती, व्यती, अत्यभिसृ.—(Pass by, neglect) त्यज्, परित्यज्, हा, अपहा, अपास्, उत्सृज्, अतिसृज्, लङ्घ्, उल्लङ्घ्.—(Pass off). *See To* PALM.—(Pass over, overlook) उपेक्ष्, समुपेक्ष्, क्षम् &c. *See* OVERLOOK.—(Pass through the bowels, &c.) *See To* EVACUATE.

PASS, *s.* (Narrow passage, defile) सङ्कटपथः, सङ्कटमार्गः, दुर्गमार्गः, सङ्कटं, सञ्चरः, सञ्चारः, दुर्गं, घर्घरः.—(Fissure between hills) दरी -रा, विदरः, रन्ध्रं.—(Passport) अभिज्ञानपत्रं, अभयपत्रं.—(Thrust in fencing) प्रहारः, यष्टिप्रसारणं.—(State, distressed state) दशा, अवस्था, गतिः *f.*, दुर्दशा, दुर्गतिः *f.*, कष्टं.

PASSABLE, *a.* (That may be crossed or travelled over) तार्य्यः -र्य्या -र्य्यं, तरणीयः -या -यं, गम्यः -म्या -म्यं, गमनीयः -या -यं, गमनयोग्यः -ग्या -ग्यं, सुगमः -मा -मं, उल्लंघ्यः -घ्या -घ्यं.—(Tolerable) विगुणः -णा -णं, सहनीयः -या -यं, सह्यः -ह्या -ह्यं.—(Current) प्रचलः -ला -लं.

PASSABLY, *adv.* विगुणं, सहनीयं, यावत्तावत्. *See* TOLERABLY.

PASSAGE, *s.* (Act of passing) गमनं, तरणं, उत्तरणं, चलनं, गतिः *f.*, तरः; 'to and fro,' गमनागमनं, गतागतं, यातायातं.—(Passing through or beyond) सङ्क्रमः -मणं, सङ्क्रान्तिः *f.*, सञ्चारः, क्रान्तिः *f.*, अतिक्रमः -मणं, पारगमनं, उल्लंघनं.—(Time of passing) गमनकालः, सङ्क्रमकालः, पारगमनकालः.—(Road, way) पथः, मार्गः, द्वारं.—(Difficult passage) संक्रमः -मं, संक्रामः, सञ्चारः, सञ्चरः, दुर्गमार्गः, दुर्गपथः, दुर्गं.—(Liberty to pass) गमनशक्तिः *f.*, गमनाधिकारः.—(Of a book) स्थलं, देशः, एकदेशः, वचनं; 'a passage of scripture,' वेदस्य एकदेशः.—(Occurrence) वृत्तं, भूतं.

PASSAGE-MONEY, *s.* आतारः, आतरः, तरमूल्यं, तरपण्यं, तारिकं, तार्य्यं.

PASSED, *p. p.* (Gone by) अतिक्रान्तः -न्ता -न्तं, अतीतः -ता -तं, व्यतीतः &c., सम्प्रवृत्तः -त्ता -त्तं.—(Crossed, gone through or over) तीर्णः -र्णा -र्णं, उत्तीर्णः &c., संक्रान्तः -न्ता -न्तं, पारगतः -ता -तं; 'hard to be passed,' दुस्तरः -रा -रं, दुरत्ययः -या -यं, दुर्गमः -मा -मं.—(Passed over) लंघितः -ता -तं, उल्लंघितः &c.—(Spent, as time) गमितः -ता -तं, नीतः -ता -तं.—(As fæces, &c.) हन्नः -न्ना -न्नं, गूनः -ना -नं, उच्चरितः -ता -तं, उत्सारितः &c.—(Ended, gone). *See* PAST.

PASSENGER, *s.* (Traveller) पथिकः, यात्रिकः, यायी *m.* (न्), गामी *m.*, गमी *m.*, मार्गस्थः, पथस्थः, पादविकः, सारणिकः.—(One who crosses) तरी *m.*, तरः, तरिता *m.* (तृ), तत्तरीकः, उत्तरणकृत् *m.*—(In a vessel) नौयायी *m.*, नौगामी *m.*, नौकान्तर्वर्त्ती *m*, नौकारूढः, औडुपिकः.

PASSER. *s.* तरी *m.* (न्), तरः, तरिता *m.* (तृ), तत्तरीकः, गामी *m.*

PASSIBILITY, *s.* सुखदुःखक्षमता, सुखदुःखवेदनक्षमता, सुखदुःखयोग्यता, सुखदुःखसहत्वं, सुखदुःखवेदित्वं.

PASSIBLE, *a.* सुखदुःखक्षमः -मा -मं, सुखदुःखवेदनक्षमः -मा -मं, सुखदुःखयोग्यः -ग्या -ग्यं, सुखदुःखवेदी -दिनी -दि (न्).

PASSING, *s.* (The act) तरणं, उत्तरणं, गमनं, चलनं. *See* PASSAGE. (Passing by) अत्ययः, अतिक्रमः.

PASSING, *part.* तरन् -रन्ती -रत् (त्), गामी -मिनी -मि (न्), यायी &c. —(Surpassing) अतिगः -गा -गं, अतिक्रामकः -का -कं.

PASSING, *a.* (Eminent) उत्तमः -मा -मं, परमः -मा -मं, श्रेष्ठः -ष्ठा -ष्ठं.

PASSING, *adv.* अत्यन्तं, अतिशयेन, अतिमात्रं, अति or अतिशय in comp.

PASSION, *s.* (Feeling or affection of the mind) मनोभावः, भावः, मनोविकारः, मनोविकृतिः *f.*, विकारः, विकृतिः *f.*, मनोवृत्तिः *f.*, वृत्तिः *f.*, रागः, मनोरागः, रसः, मनोधर्म्मः; 'passion of love,' कामविकारः, कामविकृतिः *f.*; 'of anger,' क्रोधविकारः; 'of lust,' लोभविकारः. The word इन्द्रियाणि *n. pl.* may sometimes be used generally to express 'the passions'; as, 'restraint of the passions,' इन्द्रियनिग्रहः, इन्द्रियदमनं, कामक्रोधलोभादिदमनं; 'having the passions subdued,' जितेन्द्रियः -या -यं; 'void of passions,' वीतरागः -गा -गं, विरक्तः -क्ता -क्तं, विरागी &c.; 'absence of passion,' वैराग्यं, विरागः, विरक्तिः, रागहीनता; 'having passions,' रागी &c., अनुरागी &c.; 'the class of six passions, viz. desire, wrath, avarice, bewilderment, pride, and envy,' षड्वर्गः.—(Anger, warmth of temper, rage) क्रोधः, कोपः, प्रकोपः, रोषः, अमर्षः, संरम्भः, प्रतिरम्भः, उत्तापः, उग्रता -त्वं, चण्डता, तिग्मता, उष्मः, रुष्यं, भामः, कौशिकः; 'fit of passion,' क्रोधावेशः; 'in a passion,' क्रुद्धः -द्धा -द्धं, क्रोधी &c., जातक्रोधः -धा -धं, जातामर्षः -र्षा -र्षं.—(Mental agitation or excitement) मनःक्षोभः, चित्तक्षोभः, चित्तवेगः, मनस्तापः, मनोव्याकुलता, उत्तापः, व्याक्षोभः.—(Love, lust) कामः, कामिता, कामुकत्वं, मदः, मदनः, स्मरः, अनुरागः, स्मरमोहः, कौशिकः.—(Eager desire) लालसा, लोभः, उत्कण्ठा, उत्सुकता, औत्सुक्यं.—(Suffering) दुःखभोगः, दुःखं, व्यथा, पीडा, क्लेशः, श्रमः.—(As opposed to action) सहनं, सहत्वं, ग्रहणं, कर्म्माश्रयत्वं, कर्म्मपात्रता.—(The quality or property of passion) रजस् *n.*

PASSIONATE, *a.* (Easily moved to anger) शीघ्रकोपी -पिनी -पि (न्), शीघ्रक्रोधी &c., सुलभकोपः -पा -पं, क्रोधी &c., क्रोधनः -ना -नं, कोपी &c., कोपनः -ना -नं, क्रोधशीलः -ला -लं, कोपशीलः &c., अमर्षी &c., संरम्भी &c., अमर्षणः -णा -णं, रोषणः -णा -णं, रोषशीलः &c., संरम्भशीलः &c., कोपिष्ठः -ष्ठा -ष्ठं, क्रोधिष्ठः &c., चित्तवेगी &c., भामी &c., चित्तस्वभावः -वा -वं; 'very passionate,' अत्यन्तकोपनः -ना -नं.—(Highly excitable, warm, ardent) सन्तापशीलः -ला -लं, उत्तापशीलः &c., चण्डः -ण्डा -ण्डं, उच्चण्डः &c., चण्डवान् -वती -वत् (त्), उष्णः -ष्णा -ष्णं, उग्रः -ग्रा -ग्रं, रौद्रः -द्री -द्रं, तिग्मः -ग्मा -ग्मं, तीक्ष्णः -क्ष्णा -क्ष्णं.—(Full of strong feeling) रागी &c., रागवान् &c., रागान्वितः -ता -तं, सरागः -गा -गं, संरक्तः -क्ता -क्तं, सानुरागः &c., अनुरागी &c., रागिष्ठः &c., अनुरक्तः &c., सरसः -सा -सं, रसी &c., रसिकः &c., उत्कण्ठितः -ता -तं.—(Having the quality or property of passion) रजोगुणी &c.; 'a passionate woman,' कोपना, भामिनी.

PASSIONATELY, *adv.* (With strong feeling) सरागं, रागेण, रागपूर्व्वं, सानुरागं, सरसं.—(Ardently) अतिकौतूहलेन, तीक्ष्णं, सतैक्ष्ण्यं, चण्डं, प्रचण्डं, उच्चण्डं, उत्कण्ठापूर्व्वं.—(With anger) सक्रोधं, सक्रोधं, सरोषं, सामर्षं, संरम्भपूर्व्वं.

PASSIONATENESS, *s.* शीघ्रकोपिता, कोपशीलता, क्रोधशीलता, क्रोधवशता, क्रोधाधीनता, चित्तस्वभावः.—(Strong feeling) सानुरागता, सरागता, अनुरागः.

PASSIONLESS, *a.* वीतरागः -गा -गं, रागहीनः -ना -नं, शान्तरागः &c., विरागी -गिणी -गि (न्), विरक्तः -क्ता -क्तं, अननुरागी &c.

PASSIVE, *a.* (Suffering without resistance) सहनः -ना -नं, सहः -हा -हं, सहिष्णुः -ष्णुः -ष्णु, सहनधर्म्मकः -का -कं, सहनवृत्तिः -त्तिः -त्ति, सहनशीलः -ला -लं, सहनधर्म्मा -र्म्मा -र्म्म (न्), तितिक्षुः -क्षुः -क्षु, अनिवारकः -का -कं, अप्रतीकारकः &c.—(Opposed to active, not an actor) निश्चेष्टः -ष्टा -ष्टं, निष्क्रियः -या -यं, अप्रवर्त्तकः -का -कं, क्रियाशून्यः -न्या -न्यं, कर्म्मपात्रं, कर्म्माधारः, कर्म्माश्रयः.—(In grammar, the passive voice) कर्म्मणिवाच्यं, कर्म्मणि आत्मनेपदं; 'reflective passive,' कर्म्मणिकर्त्तृवाच्यं; 'impersonal passive,' भाववाच्यं. The grammatical symbol for the passive is यभावः.

PASSIVENESS, PASSIVITY, *s.* सहनत्वं, सहिष्णुता, सहनशीलता, सहनधर्म्मः, सहनवृत्तिः *f.*—(Opposed to activity) निश्चेष्टता -त्वं, निष्क्रियता, कर्म्मपात्रता, कर्म्माश्रयता.

PASSPORT, *s.* अभयपत्रं, अभयवाच् *f.* (च्), अभिज्ञानपत्रं, अभिज्ञानमुद्रा, अभिज्ञानं, मुद्रा.

PAST, *p. p.* or *a.* (Gone by, not present) गतः -ता -तं, भूतः -ता -तं, अतीतः -ता -तं, व्यतीतः &c., समतीतः &c., व्यपेतः &c., वृत्तः -त्ता -त्तं, संवृत्तः &c., अतिक्रान्तः -न्ता -न्तं, निभृतः -ता -तं, परोक्षः -क्षा -क्षं, प्रतीतः -ता -तं. *See* PASSED. (Former, relating to the past) पूर्व्वः -र्व्वा -र्व्वं, पौर्व्वः -र्व्वी -र्व्वं, पौर्व्विकः -की -कं, पूर्व्वतनः -नी -नं, प्राक्तनः -नी -नं; 'in past times,' पुरा, पूर्व्वं, परोक्षे.—(Ended, accomplished) वृत्तः -त्ता -त्तं, निर्वृत्तः &c., समाप्तः -प्ता -प्तं.—(Past tense) अद्यतनभूतः -तं, परोक्षभूतं, अतीतकालः.

PAST, *s.* (Past time) गतकालः, भूतकालः, अतीतकालः, प्राक्कालं, पूर्व्वकालं, परोक्षं; 'knowing past and future,' परावरदृक् *m.f.n.* (श्).

PAST, *adv.* (Beyond) अति prefixed; as, 'past mortal strength,' अतिमानुषशक्तिः. Expressed also by अ or निर् prefixed, or by the use of the passive participle अतीत, हीन, त्यक्त, नष्ट, अतिक्रान्त &c. in comp.; as, 'past cure,' असाध्यः -ध्या -ध्यं, निरुपचारः -रा -रं, औषधिपथातिगः -गा -गं; 'past the range of sight,' चक्षुर्विषयातिक्रान्तः -न्ता -न्तं; 'past work,' अतीतव्यवहारः -रा -रं; 'past remedy,' उपायातीतः -ता -तं; 'past age,' वयोतीतः &c.; 'past all sense of shame,' निर्लज्जः -ज्जा -ज्जं, लज्जाहीनः -ना -नं, नष्टलज्जः &c., त्यक्तलज्जः &c.

PASTE, *s.* उदपेषं, उदकपेषं, जलपेषं, उदकचूर्णं, गोधूमसम्भवं.

To PASTE, *v. a.* उदपेषेण बन्ध् (c. 9. बध्नाति, बन्धुं) or सम्बन्ध्, उदपेषेण लिप् (c. 6. लिम्पति, लेप्तुं).

PASTEBOARD, *s.* स्थूलकार्पासं, घनपत्रं, दृढकार्पासं, स्थूलपत्रं.

PASTERN, *s.* अश्वखुरसन्धिः *m.*, अश्वस्य खुरोपरिस्थः पादभागः.

PASTIME, *s.* विनोदः, क्रीडा, विहारः, खेला -लनं, विलासः, कौतुकं, क्रीडाकौतुकं, केलिः -ली *m.f.*, लीला, देवनं, परीहासः, नर्म्मन् *n.* (न्), कूर्द्दनं, रासेरसः; 'juvenile,' बालक्रीडा, बाललीला, बालचरितं.

PASTOR, *s.* (Shepherd) मेषपालः -लकः, मेषपोषकः.—(Religious instructor) धर्म्मोपदेशकः, धर्म्माध्यापकः, आचार्य्यः, गुरुः *m.*, उपाध्यायः.

PASTORAL, *a.* (Pertaining to shepherds) मेषपालसम्बन्धी &c.,

मेषपालविषयः -या -यं.—(Pertaining to a minister of religion) धर्म्मोपदेशकसम्बन्धी &c., धर्म्माध्यापकसम्बन्धी &c., धर्म्मोपदेशविषयः -या -यं.

PASTORAL, *s.* (Poem) मेषपालनादिविषयकं काव्यं, गोमेषादिविषयं गीतं.

PASTRY, *s.* पिष्टकं, पिष्टिकं, पिष्टान्नं, मिष्टान्नं, आपूपिकं, शाष्कुलिकं.

PASTRY-COOK, *s.* पिष्टककारी *m.* -रिणी *f.* (न्), पिष्टान्नकृत् *m.*, मिष्टान्नकृत्, पिष्टकविक्रयी *m.* -यिणी *f.* (न्), आपूपिकः -की.

PASTURAGE, *s.* (Grazing ground) गोचरः, गोप्रचारः, गोमेषादिचारणस्थानं, गोचारणक्षेत्रं, गोचारणभूमिः.—(Meadow grass) यवसः, यावसः, क्षेत्रियं, पाशवपालनं, पशव्यं, घासः, तृणं, गवादनं.

PASTURE, *s.* (Grass for cattle) गवादनं, गोभक्षणं, यवसः, पशव्यं, पशुभोजनं, पशुखाद्यं, घासः, तृणं.—(Ground covered with grass for grazing) यावसभूमिः *f.*, यवसीयभूमिः *f.*, गोचारणभूमिः *f.*, पशुचारणभूः *f.*, शाड्वलभूः *f.*, शाद्वलभूमिः. *See* PASTURAGE.

To PASTURE, *v. a.* (Graze) चर् (c. 10. चारयति -यितुं), तृणं भुज् or खाद् or दा.

To PASTURE, *v. n.* (Graze) चर् (c. 1. चरति -रितुं), तृणं, तृणं खाद् &c.

PASTY, *a.* औदपेषिकः -की -कं, उदपेषगुणकः -का -कं.

PASTY, *s.* (Pie made of paste) पिष्टकः -कं, पिष्टिकं, शष्कुली.

PAT, *a.* युक्तः -क्ता -क्तं, योग्यः -ग्या -ग्यं, सङ्गतः -ता -तं. *See* FIT.

PAT, *adv.* युक्तं, यथायोग्यं, सम्यक्, अञ्जसा, समञ्जसं. *See* FITLY.

PAT, *s.* (Light blow) लघुप्रहारः, लघ्वाघातः, चपेटः, चपेटाघातः.—(Flattish lump) ईषच्चिपिटपिण्डः; 'of butter,' नवनीतपिण्डः.

To PAT, *v. a.* चपेटेन प्रहृ or आहन्, लघुप्रहारं कृ, लघु प्रहृ.—(A horse, &c.) स्फल् (c. 10. स्फालयति -यितुं), आस्फल्, स्फालनं कृ.

PATCH, *s.* (Piece of cloth) वस्त्रखण्डः, पटखण्डः; 'patched garment,' कर्पटः, कन्था; 'weaving one,' कन्थाधारणं, कर्पटधारणं; 'a beggar who wears one,' कर्पटधारी *m.* (न्), कन्थाधारी *m.*, कर्पटी *m.*, कर्पटिकः.—(Piece of any thing) खण्डः -ण्डं, शकलः -लं.

To PATCH, *v. a.* वस्त्रखण्डं निषिव् (c. 4. -षीव्यति -षेवितुं) or निविश् (c. 10. -वेशयति -यितुं), जीर्णवस्त्राणि समाधा (c. 3. -दधाति -धत्ते -धातुं) or सन्धा, कन्था (nom. कन्थायति), कर्पट (nom. कर्पटायति).

PATCHED, *p. p.* or *a.* खण्डी -ण्डिनी -ण्डि (न्), खण्डमयः -यी -यं, खण्डयुक्तः -क्ता -क्तं, खण्डरूपः -पा -पं; 'patched garments.' *See* PATCH, *s.*

PATCHER, *s.* वस्त्रखण्डसन्धाता *m.* (तृ), जीर्णवस्त्रसमाधाता *m.*

PATCH-WORK, *s.* खण्डकर्म्म *n.* (न्), कन्थाकरणं, कर्पटकरणं.

PATE, *s.* मस्तकाग्रं, मस्तकः -कं, मुण्डः -ण्डं -ण्डकं. *See* HEAD, *s.*

PATENT, *a.* (Plain) स्पष्टः -ष्टा -ष्टं, विस्पष्टः &c., व्यक्तः -क्ता -क्तं, प्रव्यक्तः &c., प्रत्यक्षः -क्षा -क्षं, प्रकाशः -शा -शं, सुगमः -मा -मं.

PATENT, *s.* विशेषाधिकारपत्रं -त्रिका, प्रकाशपत्रं, प्रकाशलेख्यं.

PATENTEE, *s.* प्रकाशपत्रधारी *m.* (न्), अधिकारपत्रधारी *m.* (न्).

PATER-FAMILIAS, *s.* कुटुम्बी *m.* (न्), कौटुम्बिकः, कुलपतिः *m.*, कुलोद्वहः.

PATERNAL, *a.* पैतृकः -की -कं, पैत्रिकः &c., पितृकः -का -कं, पैत्रः -त्री -त्रं, पित्र्यः -त्र्या -त्र्यं, पितृ in comp.; 'paternal mansion,' पितृमन्दिरं; 'paternal aunt,' पितृष्वसा *f.* (सृ); 'paternal affection,' पुत्रस्नेहः, सुतस्नेहः, वात्सल्यं.—(Like a father) पितृतुल्यः -ल्या -ल्यं, पितृसदृशः -शी -शं, पितृसन्निभः -भा -भं, पितृसमः -मा -मं.—(Derived from a father) पितृप्राप्तः -प्ता -प्तं, पित्रागतः -ता -तं, पितृक्रमायातः -ता -तं; 'paternal estate,' पैतृकभूमिः *f.*

PATERNALLY, *adv.* पितृवत्, तातवत्, जनकवत्, पितृरूपेण.

PATERNITY, *s.* पितृत्वं -ता, जनकता -त्वं, पितृभावः, पैतृकत्वं, पितृधर्म्मः.

PATH, *s.* पथः, पन्थाः *m.* (पथिन्), मार्गः, पद्धतिः -ती *f.*, पदविः -वी *f.*, सरणिः -णी *f.*, सृतिः *f.*, वर्त्म *n.* (न्), वर्त्मनिः *f.*, वर्त्तनिः -नी *f.*, अध्वा *m.* (न्), अयनं, पद्या, एकपदी; 'of the planets,' कक्षः -क्षा; 'the right path,' सत्पथः, सन्मार्गः; 'the wrong path,' उत्पथः, कुपथः, उन्मार्गः, विमार्गः; 'going on the wrong path,' उन्मार्गगामी &c.; 'to seduce from the right path,' उत्पथं नी (c. 1. नयति, नेतुं).

PATHETIC, PATHETICAL, *a.* करुणारसमयः -यी -यं, करुणारसात्मकः -का -कं, रसिकः -का -कं, करुणाजनकः -का -कं, करुणोत्पादकः -का -कं, कारुणिकः -की -कं, करुणात्मकः -का -कं, हृदयङ्गमः -मा -मं, हृदयवेधकः &c., हृदयाविद् *m. f. n.* (ध्), मनोद्रावकः &c., चित्तमोहकः &c., चित्तमोहजनकः &c. *See* MOVING, *a.*

PATHETICALLY, *adv.* सरसं, करुणारसपूर्व्वं, सकारुण्यं, करुणं, यथा करुणा जायते or यथा हृदयं स्पृश्यते तथाप्रकारेण.

PATHIC, *s.* (Catamite) विटः, वेश्याचार्य्यः, नारकुः; 'keeper of pathics,' विटपः.

PATHLESS, *a.* अपथः -था -थं, निष्पथः -था -थं, अमार्गः -र्गा -र्गं, अगम्यः -म्या -म्यं.

PATHOLOGIC, PATHOLOGICAL, *a.* निदानविषयकः -का -कं, रोगनिदानसम्बन्धी &c.

PATHOLOGY, *s.* निदानविद्या, रोगनिदानविद्या, निदानशास्त्रं, रोगलक्षणविद्या, रोगलक्षणशास्त्रं, रोगनिरूपणविद्या.

PATHOS, *s.* करुणारसः, कारुण्यरसः, रसः, रागः, करुणा, कारुण्यं, रसिकता -त्वं, चित्तद्रावकत्वं, करुणाजनकता.

PATHWAY, *s.* पथः, मार्गः, पदविः -वी *f.*, वर्त्म *n.* (न्), गमनागमनपथः.

PATIENCE, *s.* क्षमा, क्षान्तिः *f.*, सहिष्णुता -त्वं, सहनं, सहनशीलता, सहनशक्तिः *f.*, सहत्वं, तितिक्षा, धैर्य्यं, धृतिः *f.*, धीरता, दमः, दमथः, दमथुः *m.*, मर्षः -र्षणं, उत्साहः, साहनं.

PATIENT, *a.* सहिष्णुः -ष्णुः -ष्णु, सहनः -ना -नं, सहनशीलः -ला -लं, क्षमावान् -वती -वत् (त्), सहः -हा -हं, क्षमः -मा -मं, तितिक्षुः -क्षुः -क्षु, क्षमी -मिणी -मि (न्), क्षमायुक्तः -क्ता -क्तं, क्षान्तिमान् -मती -मत् (त्), क्षन्ता -न्त्री -न्तृ (तृ), क्षमिता &c., क्षमाशीलः -ला -लं, तितिक्षाशीलः &c., धीरः -रा -रं, धैर्य्यवान् &c., धृतिमान् &c., मर्षी &c., मर्षणः -णा -णं, मर्षितः -ता -तं, मर्षितवान् &c., क्षान्तः -न्ता -न्तं, सासहिः -हिः -हि, सहमानः -ना -नं, दान्तः -न्ता -न्तं. The words सह and क्षम are especially used in comp.; as, 'patient of labor,' क्लेशसहः -हा -हं; 'of austerities,' तपःसहः, तपःक्षमः &c.; 'very patient,' बहुक्षमः -मा -मं, बहुसहः &c., विश्वसहः &c.; 'to be patient of,' सह् (c. 1. सहते, सोढुं), क्षम् (c. 1. क्षमते, क्षन्तुं), तिज् in des. (तितिक्षते -क्षितुं), मृष् (c. 4. मृष्यति, मर्षितुं).

PATIENT *s.* (As apposed to agent) कर्म्मपात्रं, कर्म्माधारः, कर्म्माश्रयः.—(Sick person) रोगी *m.* -गिणी *f.* (न्), आतुरः -रा, रोगार्त्तः -र्त्ता, सरोगः -गा.

PATIENTLY, *adv.* क्षमापूर्व्वं, तितिक्षापूर्व्वं, तितिक्षया, सधैर्य्यं, समर्षं, तितिक्षितं.

PATLY, *adv.* युक्तं, यथायोग्यं, सङ्गतं. *See* PAT, *adv.*

PATRIARCH, *s.* आदिपुरुषः, मूलपुरुषः, वृद्धपिता *m.* (तृ), गोत्रपतिः *m.*, प्रजापतिः *m.*, गोत्रस्वामी *m.* (न्), वंशपतिः *m.*, गोत्रजनकः.—(Venerable person) वृद्धजनः, गुरुजनः.

PATRIARCHAL, *a.* आदिपुरुषसम्बन्धी -न्धिनी &c., मूलपुरुषसम्बन्धी &c.

PATRICIAN, *a.* कुलीनः -ना -नं, महाकुलीनः &c., सत्कुलीनः &c., सद्वंशः -शा -शं, सद्वंशीयः -या -यं, अप्राकृतः -ता -तं, असामान्यः &c., अभिजातः &c. *See* NOBLE.

PATRICIAN, *s.* कुलीनजनः, कुलीनपुरुषः, शिष्टजनः, अभिजनवान् *m.* (त्).

PATRIMONIAL, *a.* (Inherited from a father, &c.) पैतृकः -की -कं, पितृप्राप्तः -प्ता -प्तं, पित्रागतः -ता -तं, पितृक्रमायातः &c., दायप्राप्तः &c., दायलब्धः -ब्धा -ब्धं, दायोपागतः &c.—(Relating to a patrimony) पैतृकरिक्थसम्बन्धी &c., दायसम्बन्धी &c.

PATRIMONY, *s.* पैतृकरिक्थं, पैतृकं रिक्थं or ऋक्थं, गोत्ररिक्थं, पैतृकधनं, ऋक्थभागः, गोत्रधनं, दायः, पैतृकं, औद्धारकं, क्रमागतरिक्थं, पित्रागतरिक्थं, पित्रागतधनं; 'confiscation of it,' वृत्तिच्छेदः; 'title deed of it,' रिक्थपत्रं.

PATRIOT, *s.* स्वदेशाभिमानी *m.* (न्), स्वदेशानुरागी *m.* (न्), जन्मभूम्यनुरागी *m.*, जन्मभूमिवत्सलः, स्वदेशभक्तः, स्वदेशहितैषी *m.*

PATRIOTIC, *a.* स्वदेशाभिमानी -निनी -नि (न्), स्वदेशानुरागी -गिणी &c., स्वदेशानुरक्तः -क्ता -क्तं, जन्मभूम्यनुरक्तः &c., जन्मभूमिवत्सलः -ला -लं, स्वदेशभक्तः -क्ता -क्तं, स्वदेशासक्तः &c., स्वदेशहितैषी -षिणी &c., स्वदेशहितकारी &c., स्वदेशपालकः -का -कं.

PATRIOTISM, *s.* स्वदेशाभिमानं, स्वदेशानुरागः, स्वदेशानुरक्तिः *f.*, देशाभिमानं, देशानुरागः, जन्मभूम्यनुरागः, जन्मभूमिवात्सल्यं, स्वदेशभक्तिः *f.*, स्वदेशासक्तिः *f.*, स्वदेशप्रीतिः *f.*, स्वदेशप्रतिपालनं, स्वदेशहितैषा.

PATROL, *s.* (Walking round by a guard in the night) रक्षकेण रात्रौ परिक्रमणं or परिभ्रमणं.—(The guard who goes the round) रात्रिपरिचरः, रात्रिचरः, रात्रिरक्षकः, रक्षकः, आरक्षकः, रक्षी *m.* (न्).

To PATROL, *v. n.* रक्षकवद् रात्रौ परिक्रम् (c. 1. -क्रामति, c. 4. -क्राम्यति -क्रमितुं) or परिभ्रम् (c. 4. -भ्राम्यति -भ्रमितुं).

PATRON, *s.* (One who supports and protects) पालकः, प्रतिपालकः, अनुपालकः, उपकारकः, उपकारी *m.* (न्), संवर्धकः, अनुग्राही *m.*, पक्षधारी *m.*, पोषकः, रक्षकः, आश्रयः, आश्रयभूतः, शरणं, शरणभूतः, आश्रयस्थानं, नाथः, पुरस्कारी *m.*, पुरस्कर्त्ता *m.* (र्तृ), उपकर्त्ता *m.*, साहाय्यकारी *m.*, सहायः, पिच्छदः.—(Appreciator of merit) गुणग्राही *m.* (न्), गुणग्राहकः, गुणज्ञः, गुणदर्शी *m.*; 'patron of learning,' विद्यानुपालकः.

PATRONAGE, *s.* पालनं, अनुपालनं, प्रतिपालनं, उपकारः, आश्रयः, संश्रयः, अनुग्रहः, उपग्रहः, सङ्ग्रहः, आग्रहः, आधारः, अवष्टम्भः, वर्धनं, संवर्धनं, अवलम्बः -म्बनं, शरण्यता, पुरस्कारः, रक्षा -क्षणं, अभिरक्षा, पोषणं, पालनपोषणं, साहाय्यं, सहायत्वं, साहित्यं, प्रतिपालकता.—(Appreciation of merit) गुणग्रहणं, गुणज्ञानं.

PATRONAL, *a.* पालकः -का -कं, उपकारकः &c., संवर्धकः &c., रक्षकः &c.

PATRONESS, *s.* प्रतिपालिका, उपकारिणी, अभिरक्षिका, रक्षाकारिणी.

To PATRONIZE, *v. a.* प्रतिपाल् (c. 10. -पालयति -यितुं), अनुपाल्, अनुग्रह् (c. 9. -गृह्णाति -ग्रहीतुं), उपग्रह्, संवृध् (c. 10. -वर्धयति -यितुं), अभिरक्ष् (c. 1. -रक्षति -क्षितुं), उपकृ, साहाय्यं कृ; 'to patronize learning,' विद्यानुपालनं कृ.

PATRONIZED, *p. p.* प्रतिपालितः -ता -तं, अनुपालितः &c., संवर्धितः &c., अवलम्बितः &c., अभिरक्षितः &c., अनुगृहीतः &c.

PATRONLESS, *a.* निराश्रयः -या -यं, अनाश्रयः &c., अशरणः -णा -णं, निरवलम्बः -म्बा -म्बं, निःसहायः -या -यं, निराधारः -रा -रं.

PATRONYMIC, *s.* अपत्यवाचकः, अपत्यवाचकनाम *n.* (न्), पैतृकनाम *n.*, पितृप्राप्तनाम *n.*, पित्रागतनाम *n.*, गोत्रनाम *n.*, उपाधिः *m.*

PATTEN, *s.* काष्ठपादुका, स्त्रीजनव्यवहारिता काष्ठमयपादुका.

To PATTER, *v. n.* पटपट (nom. पटपटायते -ति), पटपटशब्दं कृ.

PATTER, PATTERING, *s.* पटपटशब्दः; 'of rain,' धाराध्वनिः *m.*

PATTERN, *s.* (Model, exemplar) उपमा -मानं, प्रतिमा -मानं, आदर्शः, निदर्शनं, प्रतिरूपं, प्रतिकृतिः *f.*, प्रतिमूर्त्तिः *f.*, संस्कारः, प्रमाणं, प्रतिछन्दक *m.* (श्); 'of propriety,' न्यायाधारः.—(Specimen) आदर्शः, निदर्शनं.—(Figure) आकारः, संस्कारः, रूपं.

PAUCITY, *s.* अल्पता, स्वल्पता, स्वाल्पं, संख्याल्पता, अबहुत्वं, स्तोकता.

PAUNCH, *s.* (Belly) उदरं, जठरं, तुन्दं -न्दि *n.*, कुक्षिः *m.*, पिचिण्डः; 'having one,' उदरी -रिणी &c., तुन्दी &c., पिचिण्डिलः -ला -लं.—(Protuberant belly) लम्बोदरं.

To PAUNCH, *v. a.* निरुदरीकृ, निरन्त्रीकृ, उदरादि बहिष्कृ.

PAUPER, *s.* (Poor person who lives on alms) भिक्षोपजीवी *m.* -विनी *f.*, भैक्षजीवी *m.* (न्), भिक्षाजीवी *m.* &c., भिक्षुः *m.*, भिक्षुकः *m.* -की *f.*, अन्यदत्तोपजीवी *m.* &c., दरिद्रः, निर्ग्रन्थः, छिद्रः.—(In law) साकाङ्क्षः.

PAUPERISM, *s.* भिक्षोपजीवनं, भैक्षोपजीवनं, भैक्षजीविका, भिक्षोपजीविका, अन्यदत्तोपजीविका, भिक्षावृत्तिः *f.*, भिक्षुकवृत्तिः *f.*

PAUSE, *s.* (Temporary stop) विरामः, विरतिः *f.*, अवरतिः *f.*, उपरतिः *f.*, उपरमः, निवृत्तिः *f.*, विश्रामः, विच्छेदः, उपशमः, शमः, शान्तिः *f.*, अपशमः, अवसायः, अवसानं, आश्वासः, खण्डः, यतिः *f.*, यामः, सन्धिः *m.*—(Interval) अन्तरं, कालान्तरं, अवकाशः, व्यवधानं, सन्धिः *m.*—(Suspense) कर्म्मान्तरं, भावसन्धिः *m.*—(In poetry or music) यतिः *f.*, अवसानं.

To PAUSE, *v. n.* विरम् (c. 1. -रमति -रन्तुं), उपरम्, निवृत् (c. 1. -वर्त्तते -र्त्तितुं), विनिवृत्, निर्वृत्, विश्रम् (c. 4. -श्राम्यति -श्रमितुं), विच्छिद् in pass. (-छिद्यते), शम् c. 4. शाम्यति, शमितुं), विरामं कृ, अवसानं कृ.

To PAVE, *v. a.* प्रस्तरैः or इष्टकाभिर् आस्तॄ (c. 9. -स्तृणाति -स्तरितुं).

PAVED, *p. p.* प्रस्तरास्तीर्णः -र्णा -र्णं, पाषाणास्तीर्णः &c., इष्टकास्तीर्णः &c.

PAVEMENT, *s.* परिस्तरः, पाषाणास्तरः, प्रस्तरास्तरणं, शिलास्तरः, शिलाफलकं, इष्टकाफलकं, इष्टकास्तरः -रणं.

PAVER, PAVIER, *s.* प्रस्तरास्तरणकृत् *m.*, परिस्तरकृत् *m.*, शिलाफलकास्तरिता *m.* (तृ), इष्टकास्तरिता *m.*

PAVILION, *s.* मण्डपः -पं, पटमण्डपः, हर्म्यं, मन्दिरं, वातायनं.

PAW, *s.* (Foot of a beast) पशुपादः, पशुपदं.—(Hand) हस्तः, करः.

To PAW, *v. a.* or *n.* (As a horse) खुराभिघातं कृ, खुरप्रसारणं कृ.—(Handle) हस्तेन स्पृश् or परिस्पृश् or परामृश् or आलभ् or समालभ्.

PAWN, *s.* (Pledge) न्यासः, उपन्यासः, निक्षेपः, आधिः *m.*, बन्धकः -कं, उपनिधिः *m.*, उपनिधानं, उपनिक्षेपः, आधानं, अन्वाधिः *m.*, पणः, परिपणनं, आधीकरणं, प्रतिदेयं.—(At chess) नरः, शारः -रिः *m.*

To PAWN, *v. a.* आधीकृ, न्यासीकृ, न्यस् (c. 4. -अस्यति -असितुं), उपन्यस्, निक्षिप् (c. 6. -क्षिपति -क्षेप्तुं), पण् (c. 1. पणते -णितुं), परिपण्, परिपणनं कृ, न्यासं कृ, बन्धकं कृ or दा; 'having pawned,' आधीकृत्य.

PAWNBROKER, *s.* बन्धकव्यापारी *m.* (न्), निक्षेपव्यापारी *m.*, निक्षेपव्यवसायी *m.*

PAWNED, *p. p.* न्यस्तः -स्ता -स्तं, उपन्यस्तः &c., न्यासीकृतः -ता -तं, आधीकृतः &c., निक्षिप्तः -प्ता -प्तं, पणितः -ता -तं, परिपणितः &c.

To PAY, *v. a.* (Discharge a debt) ऋणं शुध् or अपनी or विनी or अपाकृ or अपवृज् or साध् or तॄ, ऋणशोधनं कृ, ऋणसिद्धिं कृ, ऋणमुक्तिं कृ.—(Liquidate) शुध्, परिशुध्, संशुध् विनी, अपनी.—(Fulfil, perform) सम्पद्, निष्पद्, सम्पॄ, पॄ, साध्.—(Give, render) दा, कृ.—(Give pay to) वेतनं दा, वर्त्तनं दा.—(Pay the price of any thing bought) मूल्यं दा.—(Pay for, atone for) निस्तॄ (c. 10. -तारयति -यितुं), उद्धृ, निष्कृ, निष्कृतिं दा or कृ, प्रायश्चित्तं कृ.

—(Pay off, discharge) वेतनं दत्त्वा विसृज् or मुच्.—(Pay off, retaliate) प्रतिकृ.

PAY, s. वेतनं, मूल्यं, वर्त्तनं, भृतिः f., भृत्या, भाटिः f., भाटकः -कं; 'monthly pay,' मासिकं; 'yearly pay,' वार्षिकं.

PAYABLE, a. देयः -या -यं, शोध्यः -ध्या -ध्यं, शोधनीयः -या -यं, संशोध्यः &c., परिशोधनीयः -या -यं, दातव्यः -व्या -व्यं, दानीयः -या -यं, दानयोग्यः -ग्या -ग्यं, दानोचितः -ता -तं.

PAY-DAY, s. वेतनदानदिवसः, वर्त्तनदानदिवसः, शोधनदिनं, परिशोधनदिवसः, भृतिदानदिवसः.

PAYER, s. दाता m. (तृ), शोधयिता m., शोधकः, परिशोधकः.

PAY-MASTER, s. वेतनदाता m. (तृ), वर्त्तनदाता m., भृतिदाता m., वेतनाध्यक्षः.

PAYMENT, s. शोधनं, परिशोधनं, संशोधनं, शुद्धिः f., परिशुद्धिः f., दानं, साधनं, सिद्धिः f., अपकरणं, अपाकरणं, अपनयनं, निस्तारः, निस्तरणं, उत्तरणं; 'of a debt,' ऋणशोधनं, ऋणसिद्धिः f., ऋणापाकरणं, ऋणापनयनं, ऋणमुक्तिः f., ऋणापनोदनं, विगणनं, निरादेशः, आनृण्यं; 'of wages, &c.,' वेतनदानं, वर्त्तनदानं, भृतिदानं; 'non-payment,' अनपक्रिया, अनपकरणं, अनपाकरणं, अनपाकर्म्म n. (न्), अनपकर्म्म n.

PEA, s. कलायः, सतीनः -नकः, सतीलः -ला -लकः, सितीलकः, सातीलकः, सातिलकः, खण्डिकः, हरेणुः m., वर्त्तुलः.

PEACE, s. (Freedom from war) सन्धिः m., सन्धानं, अयुद्धं, युद्धाभावः, अविग्रहः, विग्रहाभावः, असङ्ग्रामः, निर्द्वन्द्वं; 'peace and war,' सन्धिविग्रहौ m. du.; 'to make peace,' सन्धिं कृ, सन्धा (c. 3. -दधाति -धत्ते -धातुं); 'made peace with,' सन्हितः -ता -तं; 'wishing to make peace,' सन्धित्सुः -त्सुः -त्सु.—(State of rest or quiet) निर्वृतिः f., शान्तिः f., विश्रामः, विश्रान्तिः f., शमः, उपशमः, प्रशान्तिः f., निवृत्तिः f., सुखं, सौख्यं, स्वस्थता, स्वास्थ्यं, समाधानं, निरुद्वेगः; 'peace of mind,' मनःशान्तिः f.; 'internal peace,' अन्तःसुखं.—(Harmony) ऐक्यं, सन्धिः m., सख्यं, मैत्र्यं, सङ्गः, अविरोधः, विरोधाभावः.—(Freedom from commotion or riot) निरुपद्रवता, उपद्रवाभावः, निरुपप्लवता -त्वं, उपप्लवाभावः, निष्कण्टकत्वं, कण्टकाभावः, स्वस्थता, स्वास्थ्यं.—(Silence) मौनं, मौन्यं, अभाषणं, तूष्णीम्भावः; 'to hold one's peace,' तूष्णीम्भू, मौनीभू, वाचं यम् or नियम्, निःशब्दीभू; 'peace,' तूष्णीम्भव, मौनीभव, नियच्छ वाचं, शान्तं.—(Peace be with thee) स्वस्ति.

PEACEABLE, a. (Free from war, tumult, &c.) युद्धहीनः -ना -नं, सङ्ग्रामहीनः &c., विग्रहहीनः &c., निर्द्वन्द्वः -न्द्वा -न्द्वं, निरुपद्रवः -वा -वं, निरुपप्लवः &c., निरुपसर्गः -र्गा -र्गं, उपद्रवहीनः &c., निष्कण्टकः -का -कं.—(Quiet, calm) शान्तः -न्ता -न्तं, प्रशान्तः &c., अक्षुब्धः -ब्धा -ब्धं, प्रसन्नः -न्ना -न्नं, स्वस्थः -स्था -स्थं, अव्याकुलः -ला -लं, निराकुलः &c.; 'in mind,' शान्तात्मा -त्मा -त्म (न्), प्रशान्तात्मा &c., शान्तचेताः -ताः -तः (स्).—(Fond of peace, not wishing to fight) सन्धिप्रियः -या -यं, शान्तिप्रियः &c., युद्धविमुखः -खा -खं, युद्धपराङ्मुखः &c., युयुत्सारहितः -ता -तं, सन्धित्सुः -त्सुः -त्सु, अयुयुत्सुः &c., कलहपराङ्मुखः &c., कलहविमुखः &c., अकलहकारी &c.

PEACEABLENESS, s. (Freedom from war) युद्धाभावः, युद्धहीनता, उपद्रवाभावः, निरुपद्रवता. See PEACE. (Quietness) शान्तता, शान्तिः f., प्रशान्तिः f., स्वास्थ्यं, स्वस्थता.—(Aversion to fight) युद्धविमुखता, युद्धद्वेषः, कलहद्वेषः, सन्धित्सा, अयुयुत्सा.

PEACEABLY, adv. (Without war, &c.) युद्धव्यतिरेकेण, युद्धं विना, निरुपद्रवं.—(Quietly) शान्तं, शान्त्या, प्रशान्तं, शान्तिपूर्व्वं.—(With pacific measures) सामोपायैः, सामोपायेन, साम्ना.

PEACE-BREAKER, s. सन्धिभेदकः, सन्धिभञ्जकः, सन्धिविघातकः.

PEACEFUL, PEACEFULNESS, PEACEFULLY. See PEACEABLE, &c.

PEACE-MAKER, s. सन्धिकर्त्ता m. (र्तृ), सन्धानकर्त्ता m., सन्धिविद् m.

PEACE-MAKING, s. सन्धिकरणं, सन्धानकरणं, सन्धानं.

PEACE-OFFERING, s. शान्तिहोमः, शान्तिनैवेद्यं, शान्तिकबलिः m.

PEACOCK, s. मयूरः, बर्हिणः, बर्ही m. (न्), शिखी m. (न्), शिखावलः, शिखण्डी m. (न्), शिखाधारः -धरः, कलापी m., नीलकण्ठः, श्यामकण्ठः, शुक्लापाङ्गः, सितापाङ्गः, भुजङ्गभुक् m. (ज्), भुजङ्गभोजी m., भुजङ्गहा m. (न्), भुजगाभोजी m., भुजगदारणः, भुजगान्तकः, भुजगाशनः, सर्पाशनः, केकी m. (न्), नर्त्तकः, नर्त्तनप्रियः, मेघानन्दी m., मेघसुहृद् m., मेघनादानुलासी m. (न्), वर्षामदः, चित्रमेखलः, चित्रपिच्छकः, कुमारवाही m. (न्), रामसारसः, कान्तपक्षी m., शुक्रभुक् m. (ज्), शापठिकः, दार्व्वाघाटः; 'flock of peacocks,' सायूरं; 'peacock's tail,' बर्हः -र्हं, शिखण्डः -ण्डी m., पिच्छं, कलापः, शिखिपुच्छं; 'his crest,' शिखा, चूडा, शेखरं, शिखिशेखरं, शिखिशिखा; 'his train,' बर्हभारः; 'eye in his tail,' चन्द्रकः, मेचकः, गुच्छः; 'his cry,' केका, मयूरनादः, मयूरशब्दः.

PEAHEN, s. मयूरी, बर्हिणी, शिखिनी, शिखण्डिनी, कलापिनी, नर्त्तकी, केकिनी, कुमारवाहिनी.

PEAK, s. (Of a mountain, &c.) शिखरं, शृङ्गं, कूटः, ककुद् f., ककुदः -दं, चूडा, पर्व्वताग्रं, शैलाग्रं, अद्रिशृङ्गं, दशनः, वातरायणः, टङ्कः; 'three peaks,' शृङ्गाटकं; 'having three peaks,' त्रिकूटः -टा -टं, त्रिककुद् m. f. n.—(Point or end of any thing) अग्रं, शिखरं.

PEAKED, a. शिखरी -रिणी -रि (न्), शृङ्गी -ङ्गिणी -ङ्गि &c., शृङ्गवान् -वती -वत् (त्), कूटवान् &c., सकूटः -टा -टं, ककुद्मान् &c., ककुद्मी &c., शेखरितः -ता -तं.—(Having a sharp point) तीक्ष्णाग्रः -ग्रा -ग्रं, सूच्यग्रः &c.

PEAL, s. (Of bells) घण्टाध्वनिः m., घण्टाशब्दः.—(Loud sound) महाध्वनिः m., उच्चध्वनिः m., महाशब्दः, उच्चशब्दः.

To PEAL, v. n. उच्चशब्देन ध्वन् (c. 1. ध्वनति -नितुं) or स्वन् (c. 1. स्वनति -नितुं) or क्वण् (c. 1. क्वणति -णितुं), महाध्वनिं कृ, उच्चध्वनिं कृ, महाशब्दं कृ, उच्चशब्दं कृ.

PEAR, s. (The Indian prickly pear) थिदरं, विषसारकं.

PEARL, s. मुक्ता, मौक्तिकं -का, शुक्तिजं, शौक्तेयं, शुक्तिवीजं, मुक्तं, मुक्ताफलं, मुक्तिका, तौतिकं, मञ्जरं -री -रिः f., हेमवलं; 'mother of pearl,' शुक्तिवधूः f., मौक्तिकप्रसवा, मुक्ताप्रसूः f., मुक्तास्फोटः; 'pearl-necklace,' मुक्तावलिः -ली f., मुक्ताहारः, मौक्तिकहारः, मौक्तिकाहारः, मुक्तालता, मुक्ताकलापः, मुक्ताप्रलम्बः, मणिसरं; 'pearl in the head of an elephant,' गजमुक्ता.

PEARLED, a. मुक्तालङ्कृतः -ता -तं, मुक्ताखचितः &c., मुक्तापिनद्धः -द्धा -द्धं.

PEARL-OYSTER, s. शुक्तिः f., शुक्तिका, मौक्तिकशुक्तिः f., मुक्तागारं, मुक्ताप्रसूः f., मौक्तिकप्रसवा, मुक्तास्फोटः, तौतिकं; 'its shell,' शुक्तिपुटं, शुक्तिपेशी.

PEARLY, a. मौक्तिकः -की -कं, मुक्तामयः -यी -यं, मुक्ताप्रचुरः -रा -रं, मुक्तापूर्णः -र्णा -र्णं.—(Resembling pearls) मुक्तोपमः -मा -मं, मुक्तातुल्यः -ल्या -ल्यं, मुक्ताशुभ्रः -भ्रा -भ्रं, मुक्ताधवलः -ला -लं, मुक्तागौरः -रा -री -रं.

PEASANT, s. ग्रामवासी m. (न्), ग्राम्यजनः, ग्रामी m. (न्), ग्रामीयः, क्षेत्रिकः, क्षैत्रिकः, क्षेत्री m. (न्), क्षेत्राजीवः, क्षैत्रिकः, कृषकः, कर्षकः, कृषिकः, कृषिजीवी m., कृषीवलः, कार्षकः, गोपः, गोपालः, गोरक्षः -क्षकः, जानपदः, कुटुम्बी m., पशुपालकः.

PEASANTRY, s. ग्राम्यलोकः, क्षेत्रजनता, क्षेत्रिकजनसमूहः.

PEASE, s. कलायः, सतीलः -लकः, सतीनः -नकः &c. See PEA.

PEA-SHELL, PEAS-COD, *s.* कलायपुटं, कलायपेशी, शमि: -मी *f.*

PEAS-PORRIDGE, PEAS-SOUP, *s.* जूषं, यूष: -षं, जुष्कक:.

PEBBLE, PEBBLE-STONE, *s.* शर्करा, चूर्णखण्ड:, कर्करखण्ड:, उपल:, कर्करोपल:, क्षुद्रप्रस्तर:, सूक्ष्मप्रस्तर:, शिला, क्षुद्रशिला; 'pebble sacred to Vishnú,' सालग्राम:, शालग्राम:.

PEBBLY, PEBBLED, *a.* शर्करावान् -वती -वत् (त्), शर्करिल: -ला -लं, शार्करीय: -यी -यं, शार्करिक: -की -कं, सशर्कर: -रा -रं, चूर्णखण्डपूर्ण: -र्णा -र्णं.

PECCABILITY, *s.* पापाधीनता, पापक्षमता, पापवशता, पापसम्भव:.

PECCABLE, *a.* पापाधीन: -ना -नं, पापक्षम: -मा -मं, पापवश: -शा -शं, शक्यपाप: &c., सम्भाव्यपाप: &c., पापसम्भवधर्म्मा -र्म्मा -र्म्म (न्), पापायत्त: -त्ता -त्तं.

PECCADILLO, *s.* अल्पदोष:, अल्पापराध:, क्षुद्रापराध:.

PECCANCY, *s.* दोष:, सदोषत्वं, विकार:, विकृति: *f.*

PECCANT, *a.* (Criminal) अपराधी -धिनी -धि (न्), दोषी -षिणी &c., सापराध: -धा -धं, सदोष: -षा -षं.—(Vibrated) दोषयुक्त: -क्ता -क्तं, दूषित: -ता -तं, विकृत: -ता -तं; 'peccant state of the humors,' दोष:.

PECCAVI, *s.* दोषस्वीकार:, अपराधस्वीकार:, दोषाङ्गीकार:; 'to cry peccavi,' अपराद्धोऽहम् इति दोषं स्वीकृ.

PECK, *s.* आढकपाद:, द्रोणपाद:. *See* MEASURE.

To PECK, *v. a.* (Strike with the beak) चंचा प्रतुद् (c. 6. -तुदति -तोत्तुं) or आतुद् or तुद्, चंचा लिख् (c. 6. लिखति, लेखितुं) or प्रलिख् or अभिहन् (c. 2. -हन्ति -न्तुं) or आहन् or अभ्याहन्.—(Pick up grain, &c., with the beak) धान्यादि चंचा ग्रह् (c. 9. गृह्णाति, ग्रहीतुं) or आदा (c. 3. -ददाति -दत्ते -दातुं) or अवलिह (c. 2. -लेढि -ढुं) or खाद् (c. 1. खादति -दितुं).

PECKED, *p. p.* प्रतुन्न: -न्ना -न्नं, चञ्चुप्रतुन्न: &c., चञ्चुलिखित: -ता -तं, चञ्चुहत: -ता -तं, मुखोपहत: &c.—(Picked up or eaten with the beak) चंचा गृहीत: -ता -तं or खादित: &c. or जग्ध: -ग्धा -ग्धं or अवलीढ: -ढा -ढं.

PECKER, *s.* (Bird that pecks) प्रतुद:.

PECTORAL, *a.* (Relating to the breast) उर:सम्बन्धी &c., उरस्य: -स्या -स्यं, वक्ष:सम्बन्धी &c.—(Relieving the lungs) कासघ्न: -घ्नी -घ्नं, कासशमक: -का -कं, कफनाशक: &c., श्लेष्मघ्न: -घ्नी -घ्नं.

PECTORAL, *s.* कासघ्नं, कासशमकं, कफघ्नं, श्लेष्मघ्नं.

To PECULATE, *v. n.* ग्रस् (c. 1. ग्रसते -सितुं), निक्षिप्तद्रव्यं छलेन or निह्नवेन स्वीयं कृ or स्वीकृ, परद्रव्यं छलेन स्वकीयं कृत्वा हृ (c. 1. हरति, हर्तुं) or अपहृ or मुष् (c. 9. मुष्णाति, मोषितुं), मोषणं कृ, मूषणं कृ.

PECULATION, *s.* ग्रसनं, छलेन निक्षिप्तद्रव्यहरणं or न्यस्तद्रव्यापहार:, मोषणं, मूषणं, स्तेयकरणं.

PECULATOR, *s.* मोषक:, मूषणकृत्, स्तेयकृत्, निक्षिप्तद्रव्यहारी *m.* (न्), चाट:.

PECULIAR, *a.* (Appropriate, exclusively own) स्व in comp., स्वीय: -या -यं, स्वकीय: -या -यं, आत्म in comp., आत्मीय: -या -यं, आत्मकीय: -या -यं, स्वक: -का -कं, निज in comp., निज: -जा -जं, आत्मभूत: -ता -तं, अव्यापक: -का -कं, अव्यापी -पिनी -पि (न्), अव्याप्य: -प्या -प्यं, अनन्यसम्बन्धी &c., असाधारण: -णा -णी -णं, असामान्य: -न्या -न्यं, अनन्यवर्त्ती, तन्मात्रवर्त्ती &c., तन्मात्राधीन: -ना -नं, यथास्व: -स्वा -स्वं; 'peculiar duty,' स्वधर्म्म:.—(Particular) विशेष in comp., विशेषक: -का -कं, विशेषण: -णा -णं, विशिष्ट: -ष्टा -ष्टं, सविशेष: -षा -षं, विशेषवान् -वती -वत् (त्), अवच्छेदक: -का -कं, विच्छेदक: &c., परिच्छेदक: &c., असाधारण: -णा -णी -णं, असामान्य: -न्या -न्यं; 'peculiar mark,' विशेषलक्षणं; 'peculiar condition,' दशाविशेष:.—(Natural, inherent) स्वाभाविक: -की -कं, स्वभावज: -जा -जं, निज: &c., सहज: &c.

PECULIAR, *s.* (Exclusive possessions) निजधनं, स्वधनं, आत्मधनं, निजस्वं, स्वस्वं, असाधारणधनं, असामान्यधनं, अनन्यस्वामिकधनं.

PECULIARITY, *s.* विशेष:, विशेषणं, विशेषकं -कं, विशेषधर्म्म:, विशेषगुण:, विशेषलक्षणं, स्वधर्म्म:, स्वगुण:, स्वलक्षणं, स्वभाव:, विशेषभाव:, धर्म्म:, गुण:, लक्षणं, उपाधि: *m.*, असाधारण्यं, असाधारणता, अनन्यवर्त्तित्वं.

PECULIARLY, *adv.* विशेषतस्, सविशेषं, विशेषेण, असाधारणतस्, असामान्यतस्, स्वतस्, यथास्वं.

PECUNIARY, *a.* (Pertaining to money) धन in comp., धनिक: -का -कं, धनसम्बन्धी &c., आर्थिक: -की -कं, अर्थसम्बन्धी &c., द्रव्य in comp., द्रव्यसम्बन्धी &c., धनविषय: -या -यं.—(Consisting of money) धनरूप: -पा -पं, द्रव्यरूप: &c.

PEDAGOGUE, *s.* बालकाध्यापक:, अर्भकाध्यापक:, बालशिक्षक:, बालपाठक:, शिशुपाठक:, बालोपदेशक:.

PEDAL, *a.* पादिक: -की -कं, पादी -दिनी -दि (न्), पदिक: &c., पादसम्बन्धी &c., पादविषयक: -का -कं.

PEDAL, *s.* पादसञ्चारितं वाद्योपकरणं.

PEDANT, *s.* पण्डितम्मन्य:, पण्डितमानी *m.* (न्), पाण्डित्याभिमानी *m.*, विद्याभिमानी *m.*, विद्यागर्व्वित:, पाण्डित्यगर्व्वी *m.*, विद्यासमुद्धत:, विद्यादाम्भिक:.

PEDANTIC, PEDANTICAL, *a.* पाण्डित्यदर्शक: -का -कं, पाण्डित्यदर्शी -र्शिनी -र्शि (न्), समुद्धत: -ता -तं.

PEDANTICALLY, *adv.* पण्डितम्मन्यवत्, विद्यागर्व्वितवत्, विद्याभिमानेन.

PEDANTRY, *s.* पण्डितम्मन्यता, पाण्डित्याभिमानं, विद्याभिमानं, दम्भार्थं पाण्डित्यदर्शनं or विद्यादर्शनं.

To PEDDLE, *v. a.* (Be occupied in trifles) तुच्छविषयेषु or लघुविषयेषु व्यापृ in pass.—(Travel about on foot and retail goods) पादभ्रमणं कृत्वा तुच्छवाणिज्यं कृ or क्षुद्रवाणिज्यं कृ.

PEDDLER, *s.* क्षुद्रभाण्डविक्रयार्थं पादभ्रमणकृत् *m.*, तुच्छद्रव्यविक्रेता *m.* (तृ), तुच्छवाणिज्यकारी *m.* (न्).

PEDDLERY, *s.* तुच्छभाण्डकं, तुच्छभाण्डानि *n. pl.*, तुच्छपण्यानि *n. pl.*

PEDESTAL, *s.* स्तम्भतल: -लं, स्तम्भपदं, स्तम्भपाद:, स्तम्भाधोभाग:, पादनिकेत:, फलक: -कं, मञ्च:.

PEDESTRIAN, *a.* (Going on foot) पादचारी -रिणी -रि (न्), पादगामी -मिनी &c., पादग: -गा -गं, पदग: -गा -गं, पादव्राजक: -का -कं, पद्ग: -द्गा -द्गं, पत्कापी -पिणी -पि (न्), चरणगामी &c.—(Performed on foot) पाद in comp. पादिक: -की -कं, पदिक: &c.

PEDESTRIAN, *s.* पदग:, पदिक:, पद्ग:, पदाति: *m.*, पदातिक:, पादातिक:, पादात:, पत्ति: *m.*, पादगामी *m.* (न्), पादचारी *m.* (न्).

PEDESTRIANISM, *s.* पादचार:, पादगमनं, पदगमनं, पादव्रजनं.

PEDICLE, *s.* मञ्जरि: -री *f.*, वल्लरि: -री *f.*, वल्लिका.—(Foot-stalk) वृन्तं, पुष्पबन्धनं, प्रसवबन्धनं.

PEDICULAR, PEDICULOUS, *a.* यूकाल: -ला -लं. *See* LOUSY.

PEDIGREE, *s.* (Lineage) वंशावलि: -ली *f.*, वंशपरम्परा, वंशविततिः *f.*, वंश:, अन्वय:, सन्तति: *f.*, सन्तान:, कुलं.—(List of a line of ancestors) वंशावलिपत्रं, वंशपरिसंख्यापत्रं, पितृपितामहादिपरिसंख्या.—(Account of ancestors) वंशचरितं, वंशानुचरितं.

PEDILUVIUM, PEDILUVY, *s.* पादक्षालनं, पादप्रक्षालनं, पादधावनं.

PEDLER, PEDLERY, *s.* *See* PEDDLER, PEDDLERY.

PEDOBAPTISM, *s.* शिशुमज्जनं, बालकमज्जनं, शैशवकाले मलसंस्कारेण

कृीडीयधर्म्मप्रवेशनं or कृीडीयानां मध्ये प्रवेशनं.

Pedobaptist, *s.* शिशुमज्जनमतावलम्बी *m.*, बालकमज्जनमतधारी *m.*

Pedometer, *s.* पादन्यासमापकयन्त्रं, पदक्रमपरिमापकयन्त्रं.

Peduncle, *s.* वृन्तं, मञ्जरिः -री *f.*, प्रसवबन्धनं, पुष्पबन्धनं.

To peel, *v. a.* त्वच (nom. त्वचयति -यितुं), निस्त्वचीकृ, त्वक्परिपुटनं कृ, त्वचं निष्कृष् (c. 1. -कर्षति -क्रष्टुं) or निर्हृ (c. 1. -हरति -हर्तुं), वल्क (nom. वल्कयति -यितुं), वल्कं or वल्कलं निर्हृ, निर्वल्कलीकृ, त्वक्ष् (c. 1. त्वक्षति -क्षितुं), निस्तुषीकृ, निस्तुष (nom. निस्तुषयति -यितुं), निश्चर्म्म (nom. निश्चर्म्मयति -यितुं).

To peel, *v. n.* निस्त्वचीभू, निस्तुषीभू, निर्वल्कलीभू, शकलीभू.

Peel, *s.* त्वक् *f.* (च्), त्वचा -चं, वल्कलं, वल्कं, वल्कुतं, चर्म्म *n.* (न्), शल्कं -स्कलं, शल्कं, छल्लिः -ल्ली *f.*; 'having much peel,' त्वचीयान् -यसी -यः (स्), त्वचिष्ठः -ष्ठा -ष्ठं.

Peeled, *p. p.* निस्त्वचः -चा -चं, निस्त्वचीकृतः -ता -तं, निस्त्वक् *m. f. n.* (च्), हृतत्वक् *m. f. n.*, परिपुटितः -ता -तं, निस्तुषः -षा -षं, निस्तुषितः -ता -तं.

Peeling, *s.* त्वक्परिपुटनं, परिपुटनं, निस्त्वचीकरणं, त्वक्षणं.

To peep, *v. n.* (Look narrowly or slyly) सूक्ष्मं निरूप् (c. 10. -रूपयति -यितुं) or निरीक्ष् or निर्वर्ण्, प्रच्छन्नस्थानात् सूक्ष्मनिरूपणं कृ, प्रच्छन्नछिद्रात् सूक्ष्मं निरीक्ष्.—(Come forth from concealment, appear gradually) प्रच्छन्नस्थानात् or गूढस्थानात् शनैः शनैर् निर्गम् or प्रतिभा (c. 2. -भाति -तुं) or निर्भा or प्रादुर्भू or प्रभू or प्रकाश् or आविर्भू or दृश् in pass., or लक्ष् in pass.

Peep, *s.* (Curious or sly look) सूक्ष्मनिरूपणं, सूक्ष्मवीक्षणं, सूक्ष्मवीक्षितं, सूक्ष्मदृष्टिः *f.*, प्रच्छन्नस्थानात् सूक्ष्मनिरीक्षा -क्षणं.—(First appearance) पूर्व्वदर्शनं, पूर्व्वप्रकाशनं, पूर्व्वप्रतिभा; 'of day,' प्रभातं, पूर्व्वप्रभा.

Peep-hole, peeping-hole, *s.* छिद्रं, प्रच्छन्नछिद्रं, निरूपणयोग्यं प्रच्छन्नछिद्रं.

Peeping, *s.* प्रच्छन्नस्थानात् सूक्ष्मनिरीक्षणं, प्रच्छन्नछिद्रात् सूक्ष्मवीक्षणं.

Peer, *s.* (One of the same rank) समपदस्थः, समानपदस्थः, तुल्यपदस्थः.—(Fellow, associate) वयस्यः, सचिवः, सहायः.—(Nobleman) कुलीनजनः, शिष्टजनः &c.

To peer, *v. n.* (Appear). *See* the word. (Look narrowly). *See To* peep.

Peerage, *s.* (Rank of a peer) कुलीनपदं, कुलीनपदविः *f.*, शिष्टपदं.—(Body of peers) कुलीनलोकः, कुलीनजनसमूहः, कुलीनजनाः *m. pl.*, शिष्टजनाः *m. pl.*, कौलीन्यं, राजन्यकं.

Peerer, *s.* सूक्ष्मनिरूपकः, सूक्ष्मनिरीक्षकः, वानरदृष्टिः *m.*

Peeress, *s.* कुलीना, कुलीनस्त्री, शिष्टस्त्री, कुलीनपदस्था.

Peerless, *a.* अनुपमः -मा -मं, निरुपमः &c., अप्रतिमः &c., अप्रतिरूपः -पा -पं, अतुलः -ला -लं, अतुल्यः -ल्या -ल्यं, अतुलनीयः -या -यं, अद्वितीयः -या -यं, असहायः -या -यं, सर्व्वोत्तमः -मा -मं, सर्व्वोत्कृष्टः -ष्टा -ष्टं.

Peevish, *a.* प्रतीपः -पा -पं, कर्कशः -शा -शं, वक्रः -क्रा -क्रं, कर्कशस्वभावः -वा -वं, कर्कशशीलः -ला -लं, वक्रभावः &c., वक्रशीलः &c., सदावक्रः &c., रूक्षशीलः &c., दुष्प्रकृतिः -तिः -ति.

Peevishly, *adv.* प्रतीपवत्, कर्कशवत्, सकार्कश्यं, वक्रभावेन.

Peevishness, *s.* कर्कशता, कार्कश्यं, कर्कशशीलता, वक्रशीलता, वक्रभावः, वक्रस्वभावः, स्वभाववक्रता, प्रकृतिवक्रता, स्वभावरूक्षता.

Peg, *s.* कीलः -लकः, शङ्कुः *m.*, नागदन्तः -न्तकः; 'of a lute,' कूणिका.

To peg, *v. a.* कील (nom. कीलयति -यितुं), कीलकेन बन्ध् (c. 9. बध्नाति, बन्द्धुं).

Pegasus, *s.* (In astronomy) प्रोष्ठपदा, भाद्रपदा.

Pegged, *p. p.* कीलितः -ता -तं, कीलबद्धः -द्धा -द्धं, कीलकबद्धः &c.

Pelf, *s.* अन्यायार्जितद्रव्यं, वृजिनार्जितद्रव्यं, अन्यायोपार्जितधनं.

Pellet, *s.* गुटिका, गुलिका, गुलिः -ली *f.*, गुडिका.

Pellicle, *s.* तनुत्वक् *f.* (च्), सूक्ष्मत्वक् *f.*, तनुचर्म्म *n.* (न्), सूक्ष्मचर्म्म *n.*, पटलं, पुटः -टं, सूक्ष्मपटलं.

Pell-mell, *s.* सङ्कुलं, सङ्कीर्णं, साङ्कर्य्येण, अक्रमेण, क्रमेण विना.

Pellucid, *a.* स्वच्छः -च्छा -च्छं, निर्म्मलः -ला -लं, विमलः &c., अमलः &c., विशदः -दा -दं, प्रसन्नः -न्ना -न्नं, अच्छः &c., शुद्धः -द्धा -द्धं, स्फटिकप्रभः -भा -भं, किरणभेद्यः -द्या -द्यं, दृष्ट्यरोधकः -का -कं, अदृष्टिरोधकः &c.

Pellucidity, pellucidness, *s.* स्वच्छता, निर्म्मलता, नैर्म्मल्यं, विमलता, वैमल्यं, विशदता, वैशद्यं, अच्छता, प्रसादः, प्रसन्नता, किरणभेद्यता, दृष्ट्यरोधकता.

Pelt, *s.* (Hide) पशुचर्म्म *n.* (न्), पशुलोम *n.* (न्), दृतिः *f.*, अजिनं, कृत्तिः *f.*—(Blow, throw) प्रहारः, आघातः, क्षेपः -पणं.

To pelt, *v. a.* तड् (c. 10. ताडयति -यितुं), प्रहृ (c. 1. -हरति -हर्तुं), हन् (c. 2. हन्ति -न्तुं), अभिहन्, आहन्, अभ्याहन्; 'with stones,' प्रस्तरैः प्रहृ, प्रस्तराघातं कृ, प्रस्तरान् क्षिप् (c. 6. क्षिपति, क्षेप्तुं) or पत् (c. 10. पातयति -यितुं).

To pelt, *v. n.* (Rain hard) धारासारेण or धारासम्पातेन वृष्, उपलान् इव वृष् or पत्, तीव्रं वृष्, बलवद् वृष्.

Pelt-monger, *s.* पशुचर्म्मविक्रयी *m.* (न्), पशुलोमव्यापारी *m.*

Pelvis, *s.* (In anatomy) वस्तिदेशः, वस्तिप्रदेशः.

Pen, *s.* (Instrument for writing) लेखनी, आलेखनी, कलमः, तूलिः *f.* -लिका, अक्षरतूलिका, वर्णिका, वर्णाङ्का, अक्षरकरणः, मसिपथः.—(Inclosure, coop) अवरोधः -धकं, व्रजः; 'for cattle,' गोव्रजः.

To pen, *v. a.* (Write, commit to paper) लिख् (c. 6. लिखति, लेखितुं), लेख्यारूढं -ढां कृ.—(Shut up in a pen) व्रजे निरुध् or अवरुध्, व्रजं प्रविश् (c. 10. -वेशयति -यितुं).

Penal, *a.* (Pertaining to punishment) दण्डसम्बन्धी -न्धिनी &c. दण्डविषयकः -का -कं, ताडनसम्बन्धी &c., शासनसम्बन्धी &c., दाण्डः -ण्डी -ण्डं, दाण्डिकः -की -कं, वैनयिकः -की -कं.—(Subject to it) दण्डनीयः -या -यं, दाण्ड्यः -ण्ड्या -ण्ड्यं, दण्डयोग्यः -ग्या -ग्यं, दण्डार्हः -र्हा -र्हं.

Penalty, *s.* दण्डः, शासनं, अनुशासनं, शिष्टिः *f.*—(Pecuniary) दण्डः, धनदण्डः, अर्थदण्डः, साहसं; 'to exact penalty,' दा in caus. (दापयति -यितुं).

Penance, *s.* तपस् *n.*, तपस्या, प्रायश्चित्तं, कृच्छ्रं -च्छ्रः, तपश्चर्य्या, कायक्लेशः, देहक्लेशः, देहदण्डः, कायतपनं, यमः, पावनं, व्रतं, प्रगाढं; 'general penance for all sins,' सर्व्वप्रायश्चित्तं; 'mortal or extreme penance,' देहान्तप्रायश्चित्तं. The different kinds of penance as described in Manu, Book XI. v. 211, &c., are: प्राजापत्यं, सान्तपनं, अतिकृच्छ्रं, तप्तकृच्छ्रं, पराकः, चान्द्रायणं; 'of these the last or 'lunar penance,' चान्द्रायणव्रतं, चान्द्रायणविधानं is the most celebrated; it consists in diminishing the food by one mouthful each day during the fortnight of the moon's wane, and increasing it in the same proportion during the other fortnight, eating fifteen mouthfuls on the day of the opposition, and fasting entirely on the day of conjunction. 'To perform penance,' तपस् तप् in pass. (तप्यते), सन्तप्, तपस् (nom. तपस्यति), तपस् or व्रतं चर् (c. 1. चरति -रितुं), or आचर् or अनुष्ठा or आस्था, प्रायश्चित्त (nom. प्रायश्चित्तीयते).

Penates, *s.* कुलदेवताः *f. pl.*, गृहदेवताः *f. pl.*, गृह्या देवताः *f. pl.*, आराध्यदेवताः *f. pl.*; 'worship of them,' कुलदेवकार्य्यं.

PEN

PENCHANT, s. अभिरुचिः f., रुचिः f., अनुरक्तिः f., अनुरागः, अभिलाषः.

PENCIL, s. लेखनी, आलेखनी, ईषिका, तूलिका, चित्रवर्त्तिका, लेख्यचूर्णिका, वर्त्तिका, कूर्चिका.

To PENCIL, v. a. लिख् (c. 6. लिखति, लेखितुं), आलिख्, ईषिकया लिख् or अङ्क् (c. 10. अङ्कयति -यितुं).

PENDANT, s. प्रलम्बः -म्बकः -कं, लोलकः.—(Ear-ring) कुण्डलं.

PENDENT, a. लम्बः -म्बा -म्बं, प्रलम्बः &c., लम्बमानः -ना -नं, प्रलम्बमानः &c., विलम्बमानः &c., अवलम्बितः -ता -तं, प्रलम्बितः &c., आलम्बितः &c., लम्बितः &c., अवलम्बी -म्बिनी -म्बि (न्), विलम्बी &c., आलम्बी &c., प्रलम्बी &c., लम्बी &c.; 'pendent branch,' अवरोहः.

PENDING, a. अनिर्णीतः -ता -तं, अजातनिर्णयः -या -यं, अनिश्चितः -ता -तं, अजातनिश्चयः -या -यं, असिद्धः -द्धा -द्धं, अनिष्पन्नः -न्ना -न्नं, अनिर्धारितः &c., अजातनिर्धारः -रा -रं, अतीरितः -ता -तं, विलम्बितः -ता -तं.

PENDULOSITY, PENDULOUSNESS, s. लम्बता -त्वं, प्रलम्बता -त्वं, विलम्बः.

PENDULOUS, a. लम्बः -म्बा -म्बं, प्रलम्बः &c., लोलः -ला -लं, लोलमानः -ना -नं, आन्दोलितः -ता -तं, स्रंसी -सिनी -सि (न्). *See* PENDENT.

PENDULUM, s. लोला, लोलकः, आन्दोलकसूत्रं.

PENETRABILITY, s. वेध्यता, वेधनीयता, भेद्यता, प्रवेश्यता, व्याप्यता.

PENETRABLE, a. वेध्यः -ध्या -ध्यं, वेधनीयः -या -यं, व्याध्यः -ध्या -ध्यं, भेद्यः -द्या -द्यं, भेदनीयः -या -यं, प्रवेशनीयः -या -यं, प्रवेश्यः -श्या -श्यं, प्रवेष्टव्यः -व्या -व्यं, वेधनार्हः -र्हा -र्हं, भेदार्हः &c., भेदयोग्यः -ग्या -ग्यं, भेदशक्यः -क्या -क्यं, वेधनशक्यः &c.—(That may be pervaded) व्याप्यः -प्या -प्यं.

PENETRANT, a. वेधकः -का -कं, प्रवेशकः &c. *See* PENETRATIVE.

To PENETRATE, v. a. or n. व्यध् (c. 4. विध्यति, व्यद्धुं), परिव्यध्, प्रविश् (c. 6. -विशति -वेष्टुं), निविश्, आविश्, विश्, भिद् (c. 7. भिनत्ति, भेत्तुं), निर्भिद्, छिद्र् (c. 10. छिद्रयति -यितुं), छिद् (c. 7. छिनत्ति, छेत्तुं), गाह् (c. 1. गाहते -हितुं, गाढुं), निखन् (c. 1. -खनति -ते -नितुं), वेधनं कृ, प्रवेशं कृ.—(Pervade) व्याप्.—(Read the meaning) अर्थभेदं कृ, मर्म्मभेदं कृ, अर्थबोधं कृ, अर्थं गम् or बुध्.

PENETRATED, p. p. विद्धः -द्धा -द्धं, वेधितः -ता -तं, भिन्नः -न्ना -न्नं, प्रविष्टः -ष्टा -ष्टं, छिद्रितः &c., व्याप्तः -प्ता -प्तं.

PENETRATION, s. (Act of piercing or entering) वेधनं, वेधः, प्रवेशः -शनं, निवेशः -शनं, आवेशः -शनं, वेशः -शनं, भेदः -दनं.—(Pervading) व्यापनं, व्याप्तिः f.—(Penetrating the meaning) अर्थभेदः, अर्थबोधः, मर्म्मभेदः.—(Acuteness, shrewdness) बुद्धिसूक्ष्मता, सूक्ष्मबुद्धित्वं, सूक्ष्मबुद्धिः f., तीक्ष्णबुद्धित्वं, बुद्धितीक्ष्णता, सूक्ष्मदृष्टिः f., दूरदृष्टिः f., कुशाग्रमतित्वं, कुशाग्रबुद्धित्वं, कुशाग्रीयबुद्धिः f., विदग्धता, वैदग्ध्यं; 'a man of penetration,' सूक्ष्मबुद्धिः m., मर्म्मज्ञः, मर्म्मवेदी m. (न्), मर्म्मिकः, मार्म्मिकः, मर्म्मविद् m.

PENETRATIVE, PENETRATING, a. (Entering, piercing) वेधकः -का -कं, वेधी -धिनी -धि (न्), भेदकः &c., भेदी &c., प्रवेशकः -का -कं, आवेशिकः -की -कं, वेशकः -का -कं, भेदकारी &c., प्रवेशकारी &c.; 'penetrating deep,' गम्भीरवेधः -धा -धं.—(Pervading) व्यापी &c., व्यापकः -का -कं.—(Acute, discerning) सूक्ष्मबुद्धिः -द्धिः -द्धि, तीक्ष्णबुद्धिः &c., तीक्ष्णमतिः -तिः -ति, कुशाग्रबुद्धिः &c., कुशाग्रीयमतिः &c., प्रखरबुद्धिः &c., अर्थभेदी &c., विषयवेधकः &c., मर्म्मभेदी &c., मर्म्मवेदी &c., मर्म्मिकः &c., सूक्ष्मदर्शी &c., दूरदर्शी &c., सूक्ष्मदृष्टिः -ष्टिः -ष्टि, दूरदृष्टिः &c., अव्यक्तमार्गविद् m. f. n.

PENINSULA, s. द्वीपप्रायः -यं, द्वीपकल्पः, द्वीपः, प्रायो जलवेष्टितभूमिः f.; 'of India,' दक्षकः.

PENINSULAR, a. द्वीपकल्पसम्बन्धी &c., द्वीपकल्पस्थः -स्था -स्थं, द्वीपकल्परूपः -पा -पं, द्वीपकल्पाकारः -रा -रं, प्रायो or प्रायशो जलवेष्टितः -ता -तं.

PENIS, s. शिश्नः, पुंलिङ्गं, पुंचिह्नं, लिङ्गं, ध्वजः, उपस्थः, जघन्यं, नराङ्गं, पुरुषाङ्गं, चर्म्मदण्डः -ण्डं; 'its glans,' मणिः m. f., लिङ्गाग्रं, शिश्नाग्रं.

PENITENCE, PENITENCY. s. पश्चात्तापः, अनुतापः, अनुशोकः, अनुशोचनं, पश्चात्तापबुद्धिः f., अनुतापबुद्धिः f., अनुशयः, सन्तापः, विसूरितं, खेदः, पापखेदः, पापसन्तापः, दुष्कृतखेदः, पापशोकः, दुष्कृतखेदः, काप्यकारः.

PENITENT, a. पश्चात्तापी -पिनी -पि (न्), अनुतापी &c., कृतपश्चात्तापः -पा -पं, जातपश्चात्तापः &c., सञ्जातपश्चात्तापः &c., जातानुतापः &c., पश्चात्तापयुक्तः -क्ता -क्तं, पश्चात्तापबुद्धिः -द्धिः -द्धि, अनुतापबुद्धिः &c., अनुशोचकः -का -कं, अनुशयी &c., काप्यकरः -रा -रं.

PENITENTIAL, a. पश्चात्तापसूचकः -का -कं, पश्चात्तापबोधकः -का -कं, पश्चात्तापवाचकः -का -कं, पश्चात्तापरूपः -पा -पं, पश्चात्तापार्थकः &c., अनुतापार्थकः &c., पश्चात्तापजनितः -ता -तं, अनुतापजनितः &c.

PENITENTIALLY, adv. सपश्चात्तापं, सानुतापं, पश्चात्तापबुद्ध्या.

PENITENTIARY, s. (House of correction or penance) प्रायश्चित्तशाला, प्रायश्चित्तगृहं, प्रायश्चित्तस्थानं, कारागारं.—(Prescriber of penance) प्रायश्चित्तविधायकः, प्रायश्चित्तनिर्देशकः.

PENITENTLY, adv. सपश्चात्तापं, पश्चात्तापेन, पापखेदपूर्व्वं, सखेदं.

PENKNIFE, s. कलमच्छेदनी, कलमकर्त्तनी, कलमकृन्तत्रं.

PENMAN, s. लेखनपटुः, लिखनकुशलः, लेखननिपुणः, लेखकः, लिपिज्ञः, लिखनज्ञः, लिपिकरः.

PENMANSHIP, s. (Art of writing) लिखनविद्या, लेखनविद्या, लिपिविद्या, लिपिः f.—(Good writing) सुलिपिः f., सल्लिपिः f., सुलिखनं.

PENNANT, PENNON, s. पताका, सूक्ष्मपताका, केतुवसनं, ध्वजः.

PENNATE, PENNATED, a. सपक्षः -क्षा -क्षं, पक्षी -क्षिणी -क्षि (न्), पक्षयुक्तः -क्ता -क्तं, पक्षवान् -वती -वत् (त्), पक्षविशिष्टः -ष्टा -ष्टं.

PENNILESS, a. निर्धनः -ना -नं, अधनः -ना -नं, धनहीनः -ना -नं, द्रव्यहीनः &c., निष्काञ्चनः -ना -नं, निष्किञ्चनः -ना -नं, अकाञ्चनः &c.

PENNY, s. ताम्रमुद्रा, क्षुद्रमुद्रा, मुद्रापादः.

PENSILE, a. लम्बः -म्बा -म्बं, लम्बमानः -ना -नं. *See* PENDENT, a.

PENSION, s. वृत्तिः f., वार्षिकवृत्तिः f., वार्षिकं, जीर्णसेवकवृत्तिः f., जीर्णभृत्यवृत्तिः f., जीर्णसेवकवेतनं, कर्म्मनिवृत्तवेतनं, कर्म्मनिवृत्तमूल्यं, सेवानिवृत्तवेतनं, भूतसेवामूल्यं, वृत्तसेवापेक्षकवेतनं.

To PENSION, v. a. वृत्तिं दा, वार्षिकवृत्तिं दा, जीर्णसेवकस्य वृत्तसेवामपेक्ष्य वार्षिकवेतनं दा or वार्षिकमूल्यं दा.

PENSIONER, s. वृत्तिभोगी m. (न्), वार्षिकवृत्तिभोगी m., वृत्तिधारी m., वेतनग्राही कर्म्मनिवृत्तसेवकः.—(Dependant) आश्रितः, अनुजीवी m. उपजीवी m. (न्).

PENSIVE, a. ध्यानपरः -रा -रं, चिन्तापरः &c., ध्यानस्थः -स्था -स्थं, ध्यायन् -यन्ती -यत् (त्), सचिन्तः -न्ता -न्तं, चिन्ताक्रान्तः -न्ता -न्तं, सखेदध्यानस्थः &c., सखेदचिन्तकः &c., उदासीनः -ना -नं, उदासः -सा -सं, उन्मनस्कः -स्का -स्कं, भावनायुक्तः -क्ता -क्तं, समाधिस्थः &c.

PENSIVELY, adv. सचिन्तं, ध्यानपूर्व्वं, सध्यानं, सखेदचिन्तापूर्व्वं.

PENSIVENESS, s. ध्यानपरता, चिन्तापरता, सखेदचिन्ता, सखेदध्यानं, औदास्यं, उदासीनता, औदासीन्यं, उन्मनस्कता, विषादः, विमनस्ता.

PENT, p. p. or a. (Pent up) संरुद्धः -द्धा -द्धं, सबाधः -धा -धं, रुद्धः &c.

PENTACHORD, s. पञ्चतारावाद्यं, पञ्चतन्त्रिवाद्यं, पञ्चतन्त्रीकवाद्यं.

PENTAGON, s. पञ्चकोणः -णं, पञ्चभुजः, पञ्चास्रं -स्री, पञ्चकोणा मूर्त्तिः.

PENTAGONAL, a. पञ्चकोणः -णा -णं, पञ्चभुजः -जा -जं, पञ्चास्रः -स्रा -स्रं, पञ्चकोणाकृतिः -तिः -ति, पञ्चकोणाकारः -रा -रं.

Pentameter, *s.* पञ्चपादी *m.* (न्), पञ्चपदी *m.* (न्).

Pentangular, *a.* पञ्चकोणः -णा -णं, पञ्चास्रः -स्रा -स्री -स्रं.

Pentapetalous, *a.* पञ्चदलः -ला -लं, पञ्चदलविशिष्टः -ष्टा -ष्टं.

Pentarchy, *s.* पञ्चजनराज्यं, पञ्चजनप्रभुत्वं.

Pent-house, *s.* वहिर्गृहं, वहिःस्थगृहं, वहिःस्थितगृहं, वाह्यगृहं, उपगृहं.

Penultima, *s.* उपधा, उपान्त्यः, उपान्त्याक्षरं.

Penultimate, *a.* उपान्त्यः -न्त्या -न्त्यं, उपान्तिकः -की -कं, अन्त्योपसन्नः -न्ना -न्नं.

Penumbra, *s.* अपूर्णच्छाया, खण्डच्छाया, छायाकल्पः.

Penurious, *a.* कृपणः -णा -णं, व्ययशङ्की -ङ्किनी -ङ्कि (न्), व्ययशङ्कितः -ता -तं, गाढमुष्टिः -ष्टिः -ष्टि, दृढमुष्टिः &c., बद्धमुष्टिः &c. *See* Niggardly, Miserly.

Penuriously, *adv.* सकार्पण्यं, कृपणवत्, व्ययशङ्कया, स्वल्पव्ययेन, कार्पण्येन.

Penuriousness, *s.* कृपणता, कार्पण्यं, व्ययशङ्का, दृढमुष्टित्वं. *See* Niggardness.

Penury, *s.* दरिद्रता, दारिद्र्यं, दारिद्रं, निर्धनता, अधनता, निष्किञ्चनत्वं, कार्पण्यं, कृपणता -त्वं, दीनता, दैन्यं, दुर्गतिः *f.*, निःस्वता.

Peon, *s.* (Foot-soldier) पदातिः *m.* -तिकः, पादातिः *m.* -तिकः, पत्तिः *m.*

People, *s.* (Body of persons who compose a nation, &c.) जनता, देशजनाः *m. pl.*, देशलोकः, देशवासिनः *m. pl.*, प्रजा, प्रजाः *f. pl.*, लोकः, जनपदः, विशेषदेशलोकः, विशेषदेशजनता, देशमनुष्याः *m. pl.* —(Commonalty) प्रजा, लोकः, जनः, जनपदः, जगती; 'courting the people,' लोकरञ्जनं, जनरञ्जनं; 'fear of the people,' लोकलज्जा, जनलज्जा.—(Common people) अवरलोकः, अवरवर्णाः *m. pl.*, अन्त्यवर्णाः *m. pl.*, अन्त्यजातीयाः *m. pl.*, अधमलोकः, हीनलोकः, पृथग्जनाः *m. pl.*, सामान्यलोकः, प्राकृतलोकः, साधारणलोकः.—(Folk) लोकः, जनः, मनुष्यः, जनपदः, मनुष्यजातिः *f.*, नृजातिः *f.*, जगती.—(Particular class) वर्गः, वर्णः, गणः, जनः, लोकः; 'country people,' ग्रामीयलोकः; 'people of the brahminical class,' ब्राह्मणवर्गः; 'of the servile class,' शूद्रवर्गः, शूद्रवर्णः, शूद्रलोकः.—(Servants, attendants) सेवकजनः, सेवकवर्गः, परिजनः, परिवारः.

To people, *v. a.* सजनीकृ, सजनं -नां कृ, समनुष्यीकृ, समनुष्यं -ष्यां कृ, जनपूर्णं -र्णां कृ, वस् (c. 10. वासयति -यितुं).

Peopled, *p. p.* सजनीकृतः -ता -तं, जनविशिष्टः -ष्टा -ष्टं, वासितः -ता -तं.

Pepper, *s.* (Black) मरीचं, मरिचं, कोलं -लकं, कृष्णं, कालमरीचं, उषणं, ऊषणं, वेल्लजं, धर्म्मपत्तनं, त्रिकटुः *m.* -टु *n.*, वल्लीजं, शिरोवृत्तं, शाकाङ्गं, आपनं, क्षुत्करी, क्षुताभिजननः, क्षुधाभिजननः.—(White pepper) धवलं.—(Long pepper) पिप्पली -लिः *f.* *See* the word; 'the plant,' पिप्पलवृक्षः.

To pepper, *v. a.* मरीच (nom. मरीचयति -यितुं), समरीचीकृ, मरीचाक्तं -क्तां कृ.—(Sprinkle, pelt) कॄ, अवकॄ, अवाकॄ, प्रहृ.

Pepper-box, *s.* मरीचपात्रं, मरिचपात्रं, मरीचाधारः.

Pepper-corn, *s.* मरीचबीजं, मरीचफलं, मरिचबीजं.

Peppered, *p. p.* मरीचितः -ता -तं, मारिचिकः -की -कं, समरीचः -चा -चं.

Peptic, *a.* पाचकः -का -कं, पाचनः -ना -नं, अग्निवर्धकः -का -कं, अग्निदः -दा -दं, वह्निकरः -रा -रं, अग्निदीपकः -का -कं, आग्नेयः -यी -यं.

Peracute, *a.* अतितीक्ष्णः -क्ष्णा -क्ष्णं, अतितीव्रः -व्रा -व्रं, अतिप्रखरः -रा -रं.

Peradventure, *adv.* किंस्वित्, अपिनाम, दैवात्, दैववशात्, अदृष्टवशात्, कदापि, कदाचित्, नाम.

To peragrate, *v. a.* (Wander over) भ्रम्, परिभ्रम्, परिक्रम्, संक्रम्, पर्यट्, परिगम्, अनुगम्, अनुचर्, गाह्, अवगाह्.

Peragration, *s.* परिभ्रमणं, परिक्रमः, पर्यटनं, संक्रमणं, संक्रान्तिः *f.*

To perambulate, *v. a.* परिक्रम् (c. 1. -क्रामति -क्रमितुं), परिभ्रम् (c. 4. -भ्राम्यति -भ्रमितुं), भ्रम्, पर्यट् (c. 1. -अटति -टितुं), इतस्ततश् चर् (c. 1. चरति -रितुं), विचर्, परिसृ (c. 1. -सरति -सर्त्तुं), क्रम् in freq. (चंक्रम्यते).

Perambulation, *s.* परिक्रमः -मणं, परिभ्रमणं, पर्यटनं, परिसारः, परीसारः, परिसर्य्या.

Per-annum, *s.* प्रतिवर्षं, प्रतिवत्सरं, वर्षे वर्षे, वत्सरे वत्सरे.

Perceivable, perceivableness, &c. *See* Perceptible, &c.

To perceive, *v. a.* (Receive impressions through the senses or bodily organs) इन्द्रियैर् ग्रह् (c. 9. गृह्णाति, ग्रहीतुं) or ज्ञा (c. 9. जानाति, ज्ञातुं) or विज्ञा or आज्ञा or विद् (c. 10. वेदयति -ते -यितुं) or अनुभू.—(See) दृश्, अनुदृश्, परिदृश्, सम्प्रदृश्, प्रतिदृश्, लक्ष्, संलक्ष्, आलक्ष्, उपलक्ष्, ईक्ष्, समीक्ष्, वीक्ष् प्रेक्ष्, आलोक्, आलोच्.—(Know) ज्ञा, परिज्ञा, विज्ञा, बुध् अवबुध्, विद् संविद्, अवगम्.—(Apprehend, understand, observe) उपलभ्, अवगम्, अवबुध्, ऊह्, अवे, विभू, अनुभू, सूच्.—(Be affected by) अनुभू, विद्, उपहतः -ता -तं भू.

Perceived, *p. p.* अनुभूतः -ता -तं, ज्ञातः -ता -तं, विदितः &c., दृष्टः -ष्टा -ष्टं, लक्षितः &c., उपलब्धः -ब्धा -ब्धं, अवगतः -ता -तं, विज्ञप्तः -प्ता -प्तं; 'by the senses,' इन्द्रियारूढः -ढा -ढं, इन्द्रियगोचरः -रा -रं; 'by the ear,' कर्णगोचरः &c.

Perceiver, *s.* विषयग्राहकः, विषयग्राही *m.* (न्), अनुभावी *m.*, लक्षकः.

Per-cent, per-centage. The sense of these words may be expressed by उत्तरः -रा -रं; as, 'one per-cent,' एकोत्तरं; 'five per-cent,' पञ्चोत्तरं. *See also* Interest. A 'percentage' or commission is शुल्कः -ल्कं.

Perceptibility, *s.* इन्द्रियगोचरता, इन्द्रियगम्यता, वेद्यता, वेदनीयता, उपलभ्यता, विभाव्यता, प्रत्यक्षता, दृष्टिगोचरता.

Perceptible, *a.* वेदनीयः -या -यं, वेद्यः -द्या -द्यं, उपलभ्यः -भ्या -भ्यं, विभाव्यः -व्या -व्यं, ज्ञेयः -या -यं, प्रत्यक्षः -क्षा -क्षं, व्यक्तः -क्ता -क्तं, उद्भूतः -ता -तं, चातुरः -री -रं, गोचर or विषय or ग्राह्य &c. in comp.; as, 'by the eye,' दृष्टिगोचरः -रा -रं, दृष्टिविषयः -या -यं, दृष्टिगम्यः -म्या -म्यं, दृष्टिग्राह्यः -ह्या -ह्यं, चक्षुर्ग्राह्यः -ह्या -ह्यं; 'by the ear,' कर्णगोचरः -रा -रं, कर्णविषयः &c.; 'by the senses,' इन्द्रियगोचरः &c., इन्द्रियविषयः &c., इन्द्रियग्राह्यः &c., ऐन्द्रियिकः -की -कं.

Perceptibly, *adv.* प्रत्यक्षतस्, प्रत्यक्षेण, व्यक्तं, यथा उपलभ्येत तथा.

Perception, *s.* (Act of perceiving) बोधः, वेदनं, संवेदः -दनं, उपलब्धिः *f.*, उपलम्भः, अनुबोधः, अनुभवः, अनुभूतिः *f.*, अवगमः, विषयवेदनं, विभावनं, भावनं, ज्ञानं, परिज्ञानं, विज्ञानं, अभिज्ञानं, इन्द्रियज्ञानं, इन्द्रियबुद्धिः *f.*, विषयग्रहः -हणं, इन्द्रियग्रहः, रूपादिबोधः, व्यक्तिः *f.*, संस्पर्शः.—(Faculty of perceiving) विषयग्रहणशक्तिः *f.*, विषयवेदनशक्तिः *f.*, विषयग्राहकत्वं, विषयग्रहणक्षमता, चैतन्यं, चित्शक्तिः *f.*

Perceptive, *a.* ग्राहकः -का -कं, ग्राही -हिणी -हि (न्). *See* Percipient.

Perch, *s.* वासयष्टिः *m. f.*, सण्डीनयष्टिः *m. f.*, सण्डीनस्थानं, सण्डीनकाष्ठं, सण्डीनदण्डः, अध्यासयष्टिः *m. f.*, पक्षिवासदण्डः, यष्टिः *m. f.*, दण्डः.

To perch, *v. n.* सण्डीनं कृ, सण्डी (c. 1. -डयते, c. 4. -डीयते -डयितुं), वासयष्टिम् अध्यास् (c. 2. -आस्ते -आसितुं) or निली (c. 4. -लीयते -लेतुं) or निषद् (c. 1. -षीदति -सत्तुं); 'on a branch,' विटपम् अध्यास्.

Perchance, *s.* अपिनाम, किंस्वित्, कदाचित्, कदापि, स्यात्, दैवात्, दैववशात्, किल, यदाकदाचित्.

Perched, *p. p.* निलीयमानः -ना -नं, निषण्णः -ण्णा -ण्णं, सन्निविष्टमानः -ना -नं.

Percipience, *s.* *See* Perception.

PERCIPIENT, *a.* विषयग्राहकः -का -कं, विषयग्राही -हिणी -हि (न्) विषयग्रहणशक्तिकः -का -कं, विषयग्रहणसमर्थः -र्था -र्थं, ग्रहणक्षमः -मा -मं, विषयवेदनक्षमः &c., अनुभावी &c., चेतनः -ना -नं, सचेतनः &c

To PERCOLATE, *v. n.* (Flow in drops) लवशः or बिन्दुक्रमेण स्रु or स्यन्द् or क्षर् or री or गल् or च्युत्.

To PERCOLATE, *v. a.* (Filter) जलं शुध् or बिन्दुक्रमेण स्रु in caus.

PERCOLATION, *s.* लवशः स्यन्दनं or क्षरणं or स्रवः, उत्पवनं.

PERCOLATOR, *s.* उत्पवनयन्त्रं, जलशोधकः, जलोत्पवनकृत्.

PERCUSSION, *s.* समाघातः, आघातः, प्रतिघातः, संघट्टः -ट्टनं, प्रहारः.

PERDITION, *s.* नाशः, विनाशः, प्रणाशः, क्षयः, उच्छेदः.—(Eternal) अधोगतिः *f.*, दुर्गतिः *f.*, अधोगमनं, अधःपातः, अधःपतनं, नरकपातः.

To PEREGRINATE, *v. n.* (Roam about) भ्रम्, परिभ्रम्, अट्, पर्यट्, परिभ्रमणं कृ, देशभ्रमणं कृ, देशाटनं कृ, देशाद् देशं गम्.

PEREGRINATION, *s.* भ्रमणं, परिभ्रमणं, देशभ्रमणं, देशाटनं, नानादेशभ्रमणं, अटनं, पर्यटनं, विदेशगमनं, परदेशगमनं, व्रज्या, प्रव्रज्या, प्रवासः, विदेशवासः, सम्प्रपदं.

PEREGRINATOR, *s.* देशभ्रमणकारी *m.* (न्), विदेशगामी *m.*, परिभ्रमणकृत्.

PEREGRINE, *a.* विदेशीयः -या -यं, विदेशी -शिनी &c. वैदेशिकः -की -कं.

PEREMPTORILY, *adv.* स्पष्टं, सुस्पष्टं, व्यक्तं, सुव्यक्तं, स्पष्टार्थतस्, भिन्नार्थतस्, सुनिश्चितं, सुनिश्चयेन, सुनिश्चयपूर्व्वं, सुनियतं, दार्ढ्येन, दृढनिश्चयपूर्व्वं, अवश्यमेव.

PEREMPTORINESS, *s.* दृढनिश्चयः, सुनिश्चयः, दृढता, दार्ढ्यं, अव्यक्तता, सुस्पष्टता, सुव्यक्तता, सुनियतत्वं, दृढनिर्णयः, सुनिर्णीतत्वं.

PEREMPTORY, *a.* (Express, positive) स्पष्टः -ष्टा -ष्टं, सुस्पष्टः &c., व्यक्तः -क्ता -क्तं, सुव्यक्तः &c., अव्यक्तः -क्ता -क्तं, स्पष्टार्थः -र्था -र्थं, भिन्नार्थः &c., आवश्यकः -का -कं.—(Determinate, final) निश्चितः -ता -तं, निर्णीतः &c., सुनिश्चितः &c., नियतः &c., सुनियतः &c., सिद्धः -द्धा -द्धं.—(Said of persons) सकृद्वादी -दिनी -दि (न्), अपुनर्वादी &c., दार्ढ्येन वादी &c., दृढमतिः -तिः -ति, स्थिरमतिः -तिः -ति.

PERENNIAL, *a.* (Lasting through the year) वर्षस्थायी -यिनी -यि (न्), संवत्सरस्थायी &c., वर्षावधिकः -का -कं.—(Perpetual, never failing) नित्यः -त्या -त्यं, नित्यस्थायी &c., अनन्तः -न्ता -न्तं, निरन्तरः -रा -रं, सततस्थायी &c., अविनाशी &c., अविसर्गी &c., अविरतः -ता -तं.—(In botany, lasting more than two years) वर्षद्वयाधिकस्थायी &c., द्विवर्षाधिकजीवी &c.

PERERRATION, *s.* परिभ्रमणं, पर्यटनं, नानादेशभ्रमणं, विहरणं.

PERFECT, *a.* सिद्धः -द्धा -द्धं, संसिद्धः &c., सम्पूर्णः -र्णा -र्णं, सम्पन्नः -न्ना -न्नं, समाप्तः -प्ता -प्तं, पर्याप्तः &c., परिपूर्णः &c., पूर्णः &c., निष्पन्नः -न्ना -न्नं, परिणतः &c.—(Entire, having no defect) समग्रः -ग्रा -ग्रं, सकलः -ला -लं, समस्तः -स्ता -स्तं, अविकलः -ला -लं, अखण्डः -ण्डा -ण्डं, अक्षतः -ता -तं, अन्यूनः -ना -नं, अशेषः -षा -षं, अदोषः -षा -षं, निर्दोषः &c., दोषहीनः -ना -नं, साङ्गः -ङ्गा -ङ्गं, अव्यङ्गः &c. —(Consummate) परमः -मा -मं, उत्कृष्टः -ष्टा -ष्टं, प्रकृष्टः &c., उत्तमः -मा -मं.—(Completely skilled) सम्पन्नः -न्ना -न्नं, व्युत्पन्नः &c., पारङ्गतः -ता -तं, पारगतः &c., निपुणः -णा -णं, अभिज्ञः -ज्ञा -ज्ञं, कुशलः -ला -लं, प्रवीणः -णा -णं, अतिप्रवीणः &c., पक्वः -क्वा -क्वं, परिपक्वः &c.—(In grammar) परोक्षभूतः -ता -तं, भूतः &c.; 'tense,' परोक्षभूतं.

To PERFECT, *v. a.* साध् (c. 10. साधयति -यितुं), संसाध्, समाप् (c. 10. -आपयति -यितुं), सम्पॄ (c. 10. -पूरयति -यितुं), संस्कृ, पुरस्कृ, सम्पद्, निष्पद्, निर्वृत्, निर्वृत्, तीर्, पार्. *See To* FINISH, COMPLETE.

(Make proficient) सम्पन्नं -न्नां कृ, व्युत्पन्नं -न्नां कृ, सम्पन्नीकृ.

PERFECTED, *p. p.* सिद्धः -द्धा -द्धं, संसिद्धः &c., सम्पन्नः -न्ना -न्नं, निष्पन्नः &c., राद्धः -द्धा -द्धं, पुरस्कृतः -ता -तं, संस्कृतः &c., प्रौढः -ढा -ढं. *See* COMPLETED, FINISHED.

PERFECTER, *s.* साधकः, सिद्धिकर्त्ता *m.* (र्तृ), सम्पादकः, निष्पादकः.

PERFECTION, PERFECTNESS, *s.* (State of being perfect) सिद्धिः *f.*, संसिद्धिः *f.*, सिद्धता, सम्पन्नता, सम्पत्तिः *f.*, सम्पूर्णता, परिपूर्णता, पूर्णता, निष्पत्तिः *f.*, निष्पन्नता, समाप्तिः *f.*, राद्धिः *f.*, राद्धता, पर्याप्तिः *f.*, प्रौढिः *f.*, समग्रता, अविकलता, अखण्डता, अन्यूनता, निर्दोषत्वं, दोषहीनता, पूर्त्तिः *f.*, परिपूर्त्तिः *f.*, सम्पद् *f.*—(Complete skilfulness) सम्पन्नता, व्युत्पन्नता, अतिप्रवीणता, परिपक्वता, नैपुण्यं.—(Highest state of excellence) उत्कृष्टता, सर्व्वोत्कृष्टता, सर्व्वोत्कर्षः, सर्व्वसिद्धिः *f.*, सर्व्वसिद्धता, सर्व्वोत्तमता, सर्व्वगुणोत्कर्षः, सर्व्वसम्पन्नता, उत्तमता, सर्व्वपूर्णता. —(Maturity) पाकः, परिपाकः, पक्वता, परिपक्वता, विपाकः, परिणामः, परिणतिः *f.*—(A perfection or excellent quality) गुणः, परमगुणः, उत्तमगुणः, सद्गुणः.

PERFECTIVE, *a.* साधकः -का -कं, सिद्धिकारी -रिणी &c., सम्पादकः -का -कं, निष्पादकः &c., समापकः &c., सम्पूर्णकारी &c.

PERFECTLY, *adv.* साकल्येन, समग्रं, सर्व्वतस्, सर्व्वशस्, कृत्स्नशस्, अखिलेन, सम्पूर्णं, पर्याप्तं, अविकलं, अन्यूनं, अखण्डतस्, अशेषतस्, अशेषेण, सम्यक्.

PERFECTNESS, *s.* *See* PERFECTION.

PERFIDIOUS, *a.* विश्वासघाती -तिनी -ति (न्), विश्रम्भघाती &c., विश्वासघातकः -का -कं, विश्वासभञ्जकः &c., विश्वासभेदी &c., वञ्चकः -का -कं, कुटिलाचारः -रा -रं, मिथ्याचारः &c., छिद्रसेवी &c., भग्नभक्तिः -क्तिः -क्ति, क्षीणभक्तिः &c., मिथ्याप्रतिज्ञः -ज्ञा -ज्ञं, भग्नप्रतिज्ञः &c., असत्यसन्धः -न्धा -न्धं.

PERFIDIOUSLY, *adv.* विश्वासघातपूर्व्वं, सविश्वासभङ्गं, प्रतिज्ञाभङ्गपूर्व्वं, विश्रम्भघातकवत्, वञ्चकवत्, धूर्त्तवत्, कितववत्, मिथ्या.

PERFIDIOUSNESS, *s.* विश्वासघातकत्वं, विश्रम्भघातित्वं, वञ्चकता.

PERFIDY, *s.* विश्वासघातः, विश्वासभङ्गः, विश्वासभेदः, विश्रम्भघातः, विसंवादः, छिद्रसेवा, शत्रुसेवा, वञ्चकता, वञ्चनं -ना, कैतवं, कापट्यं, भक्तिभङ्गः, प्रतिज्ञाभङ्गः.

To PERFORATE, *v. a.* (Bore, pierce) व्यध्, छिद्र्, निर्भिद्, निखन्, शुषिरीकृ.

PERFORATED, *p. p.* विद्धः -द्धा -द्धं, वेधितः -ता -तं, छिद्रितः -ता -तं, भिन्नः -न्ना -न्नं, जर्जरः -रा -रं, जर्जरीकृतः -ता -तं, रन्ध्रितः &c., सरन्ध्रः -न्ध्रा -न्ध्रं, शुषिरः -रा -रं.

PERFORATION, *s.* (The act) वेधः -धनं, व्यधः -धनं, छिद्रकरणं, निर्भेदनं, भेदनं, शुषिरीकरणं, जर्जरीकरणं, सूचिः -ची *f.*, सूचनं -ना.—(Hole bored) छिद्रं, रन्ध्रं, विवरं, शुषिरं, शुषिः -षी *f.*, विद्रं.—(State of being perforated) विद्धता, शुषिरता,

PERFORATOR, *s.* वेधकः, वेधी *m.* (न्), आविधः, वेधनिका, भेदकः.

PERFORCE, *adv.* बलात्, बलेन, बलात्कारेण, सबलं, प्रसभं, प्रसह्य, अभिप्रसह्य, बलवत्, बलापकर्षं.

To PERFORM, *v. a.* (Do, execute) कृ, सङ्कृ, अभिकृ, विधा, अनुष्ठा, आस्था, समास्था, निर्वह्, आचर्, समाचर्, चर्, प्रवृत् in caus., निर्वृत्, निवृत्, वृत्, साध्, संसाध्, प्रयुज्, प्रणी.—(Fulfil, make good) पॄ, सम्पॄ, सम्पद्, निष्पद्, साध्, सिद्धीकृ; 'a promise,' प्रतिज्ञां शुध् or अपवृज् or तॄ.—(Act a part). *See To* ACT.

PERFORMABLE, *a.* विधातव्यः -व्या -व्यं, विधेयः -या -यं, अनुष्ठातव्यः &c., अनुष्ठेयः &c., साध्यः -ध्या -ध्यं, साधनीयः &c., करणीयः -या -यं, सम्पादनीयः &c., सम्पाद्यः -द्या -द्यं, निर्वोढव्यः -व्या -व्यं, आचरणीयः &c.

PERFORMANCE, *s.* (Execution) करणं, विधानं, अनुष्ठानं, आचरणं, निर्वहणं, निर्वाहः, साधनं, सम्पादनं, निष्पादनं, निष्पत्तिः *f.*, निर्वर्त्तनं, प्रवर्त्तनं, चर्य्या.—(Act, action) क्रिया, कर्म्म *n.* (न्), कृतिः *f.*, कृत्या, प्रवृत्तिः *f.*, चेष्टा, विचेष्टितं, व्यापारः.—(Theatrical) अभिनयः, नटनं, नाट्यं, नर्त्तनं, नटचर्य्या, नाटः -टनं, नाटकः.

PERFORMED, *p. p.* कृतः -ता -तं, अनुष्ठितः &c., आचरितः &c., विहितः &c., निर्वाहितः &c., निष्पादितः &c., सम्पादितः &c., साधितः &c., सिद्धीकृतः &c.; 'one who has performed his duty,' कृतकृत्यः.

PERFORMER, *s.* कर्त्ता *m.* (र्तृ), कारकः, अनुष्ठाता *m.* (तृ), विधायी *m.* (न्), अनुष्ठायी *m.*, साधकः, सम्पादकः, निर्वाहकः, प्रवर्त्तकः, प्रणेता *m.* (तृ), प्रयोजकः.—(Actor) नटः, अभिनेता *m.* (तृ), अभिनयी *m.* (न्), अभिनयकारी *m.*—(Musical) वाद्यवादकः, भाण्डवादकः, वादकः.

PERFUME, *s.* (Scent) सुगन्धः, सुगन्धिः *m.*, सुवासः, आमोदः, परिमलः, सुरभिः *m.*, सौरभ्यं, सौरभं, गन्धः, इष्टगन्धः, वासः, मोदः, घ्राणतर्पणः.—(Substance that emits scent) गन्धः, सुगन्धिद्रव्यं, सुरभिद्रव्यं, सामोदद्रव्यं, सुवासिकद्रव्यं, परिमलद्रव्यं, धूपः, जवादिः *m.*—(For the person) विलेपः -पनं, अनुलेपः -पनं, गात्रानुलेपनी, वर्णकं, अभ्यञ्जनं, वर्त्तिः -र्त्ती; 'perfumed paste,' यक्षकर्द्दमः.—(Compounded perfume) कृत्रिमधूपकः, वृकधूपः, वकधूपः.

To PERFUME, *v. a.* सुरभीकृ, वास् (c. 10. वासयति -यितुं), अनुवास्, अधिवास्, धूपेन वास्, धूप् (c. 10. धूपयति -यितुं, c. 1. धूपायति), परिधूप्, अवधूप्, सुगन्धीकृ, सामोदीकृ, आमोद (nom. आमोदयति -यितुं), परिमल (nom. परिमलयति -यितुं), सपरिमलीकृ, अनुवासनं कृ, सवासीकृ.

PERFUMED, *p. p.* वासितः -ता -तं, अधिवासितः -ता -तं, अनुवासितः &c., सुवासितः &c., सवासः -सा -सं, वाशितः &c., सुरभितः &c., आमोदितः &c., परिमलितः &c., सुगन्धितः &c., धूपितः &c., धूपायितः &c., परिधूपितः &c., भावितः &c., चर्चितः &c.

PERFUMER, *s.* गन्धविक्रयी *m.* (न्), गन्धविक्रेता *m.* (तृ), गन्धवणिक् *m.* (ज्), गन्धोपजीवी *m.*, गन्धविक्रयोपजीवी *m.*, गन्धाजीवः, गान्धिकः, सुगन्धिद्रव्यव्यवसायी *m.*

PERFUMERY, *s.* पूर्व्वोक्तवणिग्विक्रीता सुगन्धिद्रव्यसामग्री or गन्धादिद्रव्यसामग्री, गन्धद्रव्यं, गन्धादिद्रव्यं, सुगन्धिद्रव्यादि *n.*, सुरभिद्रव्यं.

PERFUMING, *s.* (The act) वासनं, सुगन्धिद्रव्यवासनं, अनुवासनं.—(Perfuming the person) चर्चा, चर्चिका, चार्च्चिक्यं, अनुलेपनं, विलेपनं, अभ्यञ्जनं, स्थासकः, अङ्गरागः.

PERFUNCTORILY, *adv.* ईषदपेक्षया, अनवधानेन, ईषदवधानेन, ईषद्यत्नपूर्व्वं.

PERFUNCTORINESS, *s.* ईषदपेक्षा, ईषदवधानं, ईषत्प्रयत्नत्वं, ईषदुद्योगः.

PERFUNCTORY, *a.* ईषदवहितः -ता -तं, ईषद्यत्नकृतः &c., ईषदवधानकृतः &c.

PERHAPS, *adv.* अपिनाम, किंस्वित्, स्यात्, कदापि, कदाचित्, किल, अपि, नाम, दैवात्, दैववशात्, नुवा, नूनं, प्रायेण, यदाकदाचित्, यथाकदाचित्; 'if perhaps,' यदि कदाचित्, यदि कदापि; 'or perhaps,' अपिवा, स्याद्वा, यद्वा.

PERIAPT, *s.* (Amulet) कवचः -चं, संवदनं.

PERICARDIUM, *s.* हृदाशयः, हृदयाशयः, हृत्कोशः, हृदयकोशः.

PERICARP, *s.* वीजकोशः, वीजगुप्तिः *f.*, वीजमातृका, कर्णिका, कर्णिकारः.

PERICRANIUM, *s.* (Membrane investing the skull) कपालावरणत्वक् *f.* (च्), कपालावरकत्वक् *f.*, कपालावरकान्तस्त्वक् *f.*, कपालावरणं.—(Skull) कपालः -लं.

PERIERGY, *s.* अत्युद्योगः, अतियत्नः, अत्युत्साहः, अत्याचारः.

PERIGEE, PERIGEUM, *s.* नीचं, नीचस्थानं.

PERIL, *s.* भयं, भयहेतुः *m.*, संशयः, सन्देहः, संशयहेतुः *m.*, शङ्का, विकल्पः. *See* DANGER.—(Peril of life) जीवितसंशयः, प्राणसंशयः, प्राणसङ्कटं, प्राणसन्देहः. *See* JEOPARDY.

To PERIL, *v. a.* संशयस्थं -स्थां कृ, सन्देहस्थं -स्थां कृ, भयस्थं -स्थां कृ, शङ्कास्पदीकृ, भयस्थानीकृ. *See To* ENDANGER, HAZARD.

PERILED, *p. p.* संशयितः -ता -तं, शङ्कास्पदीकृतः -ता -तं.

PERILOUS, *a.* भयहेतुकः -का -कं, संशयहेतुकः &c., सन्दिग्धः -ग्धा -ग्धं, भयानकः -का -कं, भयङ्करः -री -रं, सभयः -या -यं, ससंशयः -या -यं, सशङ्कः -ङ्का -ङ्कं, दुस्तरः -रा -रं; 'a perilous business,' प्राणान्तव्यवहारः. *See* DANGEROUS, HAZARDOUS.

PERILOUSLY, *adv.* सभयं, ससंशयं, ससन्देहं, सशङ्कं, सन्दिग्धं, शङ्कापूर्व्वं, भयानकं, शङ्कया. *See* DANGEROUSLY.

PERILOUSNESS, *s.* सभयता -त्वं, सशङ्कत्वं, सन्दिग्धता, भयानकत्वं, भयं.

PERINEUM, PERINÆUM, *s.* (In anatomy) विटपः, महावीर्य्यं.

PERIOD, *s.* (Revolution of time) कालचक्रं, कालपरिणामः, कालपर्य्यायः, कालावृत्तिः *f.*, कालावर्त्तः, कालपरिवृत्तिः *f.*, वर्षचक्रं, संवत्सरचक्रं, कालमानं, वर्षगणः.—(Term or specified portion of time) कालावधिः *m.*, अवधिः *m.*, कालमर्य्यादा, कालान्तरं, अन्तरं, नेमः, नियतकालः, निरूपितकालः; 'period of five years,' वर्षपञ्चकं, वत्सरपञ्चत्वं, युगं; 'of four years,' वर्षचतुष्टयं.—(End, conclusion) अन्तः -न्तं, अवसानं, शेषः, निर्वृत्तिः *f.*—(Indefinite portion of any continued state) अवस्था, दशा, कालांशः, कालभागः, कालावयवः, कालविभक्तिः *f.*; 'period of life,' वयस् *n.*; 'first period of life,' प्रथमवयस्; 'middle period,' मध्यमवयस्; 'last period,' अन्त्यवयस्; 'one who is in the middle period,' मध्यमवयाः -याः -यः (स्), मध्यमवयस्कः -स्का -स्कं; 'the four periods of life,' अवस्थाचतुष्टयं.—(Complete sentence) पूर्णवाक्यं, कण्डिका.—(Mark of the end of a complete sentence) पूर्णवाक्यचिह्नं.—(Astronomical period) योगः, गणः. The period called मन्वन्तरं, is equal to 71 ages of the gods, or 306,720,000 years of mortals, and with its सन्धिः or period of universal deluge, to 308,448,000 years. Fourteen 'Manwantaras' constitute a कल्पः, or the grand period of creation and destruction, consisting of 4,320,000,000 years.

PERIODIC, PERIODICAL, *a.* (Happening by revolution, regularly recurring) नियतकालिकः -की -कं, नियमितकालिकः &c., निरूपितकालिकः &c., नित्यः -त्या -त्यं, नैमित्तिकः -की -कं, नित्यनैमित्तिकः &c., सामयिकः -की -कं.—(Pertaining to a revolution, performed in one) चाक्रिकः -की -कं, परिवर्त्तनात्मकः -का -कं, परिवर्त्तनसम्बन्धी -न्धिनी &c., परिवर्त्तनविशिष्टः -ष्टा -ष्टं, कालावृत्तिविशिष्टः &c.

PERIODICALLY, *adv.* काले काले, कालक्रमेण, नियतशस्, नित्यदा, नित्यं, नित्यकाले, नियतकालानुसारेण, नियतकाले, नियतं, निरूपितसमये, नियतसमये, समयतस्,

PERIODICALNESS, PERIODICITY, *s.* कालनियतत्वं, नियतकालिकत्वं, नित्यता.

PERIOSTEUM, *s.* (In anatomy) अस्थित्वक् *f.* (च्), अस्थित्वचा, अस्थ्यावरणत्वक् *f.*, अस्थ्यावरणचर्म्म *n.* (न्).

PERIPHERY, *s.* परिधिः *m.*, परिणाहः, परीणाहः. *See* CIRCUMFERENCE.—(Of a wheel) प्रधिः *m.*, प्रधिमण्डलं, नेमिः -मी *f.*, चक्रपरिधिः *m.*

PERIPHRASE, PERIPHRASIS, *s.* वाक्प्रपञ्चः, वाग्विस्तारः, वाक्यबाहुल्यं.

To PERIPHRASE, *v. a.* वाग्बाहुल्येन or वाक्यबाहुल्येन or वाग्विस्तारेण व्याख्या (c. 2. -ख्याति -तुं), वाग्विस्तारं कृ, वाक्प्रपञ्चं कृ.

PERIPHRASTIC, PERIPHRASTICAL, *a.* बहुवाक्यः -क्या -क्यं, विस्तीर्णवाक्यः

&c., वाक्यविस्तारकः -का -कं, वाग्विस्तारकः &c., वक्रः -क्रा -क्रं.

PERIPHRASTICALLY, *adv.* वाग्बाहुल्येन, वाक्यबाहुल्येन, वाग्विस्तारेण.

PERIPNEUMONY, *s.* फुप्फुसदाहः, फुस्फुसदाहः, फुप्फुसतापः, वक्षोज्वाला

To PERISH, *v. n.* (Die, be destroyed) मृ, सम्मृ, नश्, प्रणश्, विनश्, क्षि in pass., प्रक्षि, संक्षि, ध्वंस्, विध्वंस्, प्रली, प्रविली, प्रमी, विपद्, व्यापद्, नाशं गम् or प्राप्, विनाशम् उपगम्, नष्टः -ष्टा -ष्टं भू.—(Be lost eternally) नरकं गम्, नरके पत्, अधः पत्, अधो गम्.—(Ready to perish) विनाशोन्मुखः -खा -खं.

PERISHABLE, *a.* नश्वरः -रा -रं, विनश्वरः -रा -रं, नाशाधीनः -ना -नं, नाशवशः -शा -शं, मरणाधीनः &c., नाशधर्म्मकः -का -कं, मरणधर्म्मकः &c., नाशशीलः -ला -लं, क्षयिष्णुः -ष्णुः -ष्णु, क्षयी -यिणी -यि (न्), ध्वंसी &c., विध्वंसी &c., अस्थायी &c., नाशवान् -वती -वत् (त्), क्षयवान् &c., भङ्गुरः -रा -रं, क्षणभङ्गुरः &c., क्षणिकः -का -कं.

PERISHING, *part.* or *a.* नश्यन् -श्यन्ती -श्यत् (त्) क्षीयमाणः -णा -णं, म्रियमाणः &c., नाशी -शिनी -शि (न्), विनाशी &c., विध्वंसी &c.

PERISTALTIC, *a.* कृमिसदृशः -शी -शं, कृमिगतिसदृशः &c., सर्पगतिसदृशः &c.; 'peristaltic motion,' सर्पगतिः *f.*, कृमिगतिः *f.*

PERISTYLE, *s.* हर्म्यपरिगता स्तम्भपंक्तिः or स्तम्भश्रेणी.

PERITONEUM, *s.* अन्त्रवेष्टनं, अन्त्रावरणत्वक् *f.* (च्), अन्त्रावरकत्वक्, उदरवेष्टनत्वक् *f.*, उदरान्तस्त्वक् *f.*, उदरवेष्टनं.

To PERJURE, *v. a.* (One's self) मिथ्याशपथं कृ or शप्, मिथ्या शप् (c. 1. शपति -ते, c. 4. शप्यति, शप्तुं), मृषा शप्, असत्यशपथं कृ, कूटशपथं कृ, मिथ्यादिव्यं कृ, कूटसाक्ष्यं कृ, कौटसाक्ष्यं कृ, मिथ्यासाक्ष्यं कृ, अतथ्यसाक्ष्यं कृ.

PERJURED, *p. p.* मिथ्याशपकः -का -कं, मिथ्याशापकारी -रिणी -रि (न्), कूटशपथकारी &c., कूटसाक्षी &c., क्रियाभ्रष्टः -ष्टा -ष्टं, क्रियानष्टः &c.

PERJURER, *s.* कूटशपथकारी *m.* (न्), कूटसाक्षी *m.* *See* PERJURED.

PERJURY, *s.* मिथ्याशपनं, कूटशपनं, कूटसाक्ष्यं, कौटसाक्ष्यं, मिथ्यासाक्ष्यं, मिथ्याशपथः, कूटदिव्यं, असत्यशपथः.

PERMANENCE, PERMANENCY, *s.* स्थिरता, स्थैर्य्यं, स्थायित्वं, संस्थितिः *f.*, व्यवस्थितिः *f.*, अवस्थितिः *f.*, स्थितिः *f.*, ध्रुवता, ध्रौव्यं, धृतिः *f.*, स्थावरता -त्वं, स्थाणुता, स्थितिमत्त्वं, नित्यता, नित्यस्थायित्वं, अक्षयता, चिरस्थायित्वं, अनपायः.

PERMANENT, *a.* स्थिरः -रा -रं, स्थायी -यिनी -यि (न्), संस्थः -स्था -स्थं, स्थावरः -रा -रं, स्थितिमान् -मती -मत् (त्), स्थेयान् -यसी -यः (स्), ध्रुवः -वा -वं, अक्षयः -या -यं, अच्युतः -ता -तं, नित्यस्थायी &c., नित्यः -त्या -त्यं. *See* LASTING, ENDURING.

PERMANENTLY, *adv.* स्थिरं, स्थैर्य्येण, नित्यं, ध्रुवं, सध्रौव्यं, नित्यशस्, नित्यकालं, सर्व्वकालं, शाश्वतं.

PERMEABILITY, *s.* व्याप्यता -त्वं, प्रवेशनीयता, भेदनगम्यता, प्रवेश्यता.

PERMEABLE, *a.* व्याप्यः -प्या -प्यं, प्रवेश्यः -श्या -श्यं, प्रवेशनीयः -या -यं, भेदनीयः -या -यं, भेदनगम्यः -म्या -म्यं, भेदनयोग्यः -ग्या -ग्यं.

PERMEANT, *a.* व्यापी -पिनी -पि (न्), व्यापकः -का -कं.

To PERMEATE, *v. a.* (Pervade, penetrate) व्याप्, अभिव्याप्, प्रविश्, व्यध्, भिद्, गाह्, विगाह्, व्यञ्ज्, अतिक्रम्, व्यतिक्रम्, समतिक्रम्, समञ्ज्.

PERMEATION, *s.* व्याप्तिः *f.*, अभिव्याप्तिः *f.*, व्यापनं, प्रवेशः -शनं, वेधनं, भेदनं, विगाहः -हनं.

PERMISSIBLE, *a.* अनुज्ञेयः -या -यं, समनुज्ञेयः &c., अभ्यनुज्ञेयः &c., अनुज्ञातव्यः -व्या -व्यं, अनुज्ञार्हः -र्हा -र्हं, अभ्यनुज्ञार्हः &c., अनुज्ञायोग्यः -ग्या -ग्यं, धर्म्यः -म्या -म्यं.

PERMISSION, *s.* अनुज्ञा -ज्ञानं, समनुज्ञानं, अभ्यनुज्ञा -ज्ञानं, अनुमतिः *f.*, अनुमतं, अनुमोदनं, आज्ञा, क्षमता, शक्तिः *f.*, सामर्थ्यं.

PERMISSIVE, *a.* अनुज्ञादायकः -का -कं, अनुज्ञादः -दा -दं, अनुज्ञाप्रदः &c.

To PERMIT, *v. a.* अनुज्ञा (c. 9. -जानाति -नीते -ज्ञातुं), अभ्यनुज्ञा, समनुज्ञा, अनुमन् (c. 4. -मन्यते -मन्तुं), अनुमुद् (c. 1. -मोदते -दितुं), अभ्यनुमुद्, अनुज्ञां दा, अनुमतिं दा, आज्ञां दा, उपेक्ष् (c. 1. -ईक्षते -क्षितुं), इष् (c. 6. इच्छति, एषितुं). Sometimes the sense of 'permit' is expressed by the causal form; as, 'he permits to perish,' नाशयति; 'he permits to take,' हारयति.

PERMIT, *s.* अनुज्ञापत्रं, आज्ञापत्रं, अनुज्ञा, क्षमतापत्रं, अनुमतिः *f.*

PERMITTED, *p. p.* अनुज्ञातः -ता -तं, अभ्यनुज्ञातः &c., समनुज्ञातः &c., अनुमतः &c., अनुमोदितः &c., दत्तानुज्ञः -ज्ञा -ज्ञं, गृहीतानुज्ञः &c., अनिषिद्धः -द्धा -द्धं, अविरुद्धः &c., उपेक्षितः &c., अवर्जितः &c.

PERMUTATION, *s.* विनिमयः, परिवर्त्तनं, परिवृत्तिः *f.*, व्यतिहारः, निमयः.

PERNICIOUS, *a.* घातुकः -का -कं, घाती -तिनी -ति (न्), घातकः &c., विघातकः &c., उपघातकः &c., विनाशकः &c., अपकारकः &c., अपकारी -रिणी &c., हिंसकः &c., हिंस्रः -स्रा -स्रं, आत्ययिकः -की -कं, अपायकारी &c., अहितकारी &c., दुष्टः -ष्टा -ष्टं, दूषकः -का -कं. *See* INJURIOUS.

PERNICIOUSLY, *adv.* सापकारं, सापायं, सनाशं, सद्रोहं, अहितं, हिंस्रं.

PERNICIOUSNESS, *s.* घातुकत्वं, अपकारकत्वं, विनाशकत्वं, दूषकता.

PERORATION, *s.* वाक्योपसंहारः, कथोपसंहारः, भाषणोपसंहारः.

To PERPEND, *v. a.* मनसा विगण् (c. 10. -गणयति -यितुं) or विचर् (c. 10. -चारयति -यितुं).

PERPENDICULAR, *a.* लम्बरूपः -पा -पं, अधोलम्बरूपः &c., लम्बकरूपः &c. —(Falling at right angles) समकोणपाती -तिनी -ति (न्), समकोणगामी &c.—(Vertical) ऋजुः -जुः -जु, अजिह्मः -ह्मा -ह्मं, सूत्री &c., सरलोर्द्ध्वाधःस्थितः -ता -तं.

PERPENDICULAR, *s.* लम्बः -म्बं, लम्बकः, अधोलम्बः, आलम्बः, अवलम्बः, वलम्बः; 'of a triangle,' कोटिः *f.*

PERPENDICULARLY, *adv.* लम्बरूपेण, अधोलम्बरूपेण, लम्बदिशि; 'the sun's rays fall there perpendicularly,' तत्र रविकिरणा लम्बरूपाः पतन्ति.

To PERPETRATE, *v. a.* (Do, commit) कृ, विधा, समाचर्, आचर्.

PERPETRATED, *p. p.* कृतः -ता -तं, समाचरितः -ता -तं, विहितः -ता -तं.

PERPETRATION, *s.* करणं, आचरणं, समाचरणं, विधानं, सम्पादनं.

PERPETUAL, *a.* नित्यः -त्या -त्यं, निरन्तरः -रा -रं, शाश्वतः -ती -तं, सततः -ता -तं, सन्ततः &c., नैत्यिकः -की -कं, अविरतः -ता -तं, नियतः &c., अनवरतः &c., अनारतः &c., अनन्तः -न्ता -न्तं, सर्व्वकालीनः -ना -नं, सर्व्वकालस्थायी &c., नित्यस्थायी &c., चिरस्थायी &c., सार्व्वकालिकः -की -कं, सनातनः -नी -नं, अभीक्ष्णः -क्ष्णा -क्ष्णं; 'perpetual motion,' सततगतिः *f.*

PERPETUALLY, *adv.* नित्यं, नित्यशस्, नित्यदा, सततं, निरन्तरं, अविरतं, शाश्वतं, शश्वत्, अभीक्ष्णं, अनुक्षणं, अनिशं, सना. *See* CONTINUALLY, CONSTANTLY.

To PERPETUATE, *v. a.* शाश्वतीकृ, निरन्तरीकृ, सततीकृ, स्थिरीकृ, नित्यीकृ, नित्यस्थं -स्थां कृ, नित्यस्थायिनं -यिनीं -यि कृ.

PERPETUATED, *p.p.* शाश्वतीकृतः -ता -तं, सततीकृतः &c., स्थिरीकृतः &c.

PERPETUATION, *s.* शाश्वतीकरणं, सततीकरणं, स्थिरीकरणं.

PERPETUITY, *s.* नित्यता -त्वं, नैत्यं, नैत्यिकत्वं, नैरन्तर्य्यं, आनन्त्यं, नित्यस्थायित्वं, नित्यकालस्थायिता -त्वं, नित्यस्थितिः *f.*, अविरामः, अविरतिः *f.*, निरन्तरस्थितिः *f.*, निरन्तरस्थायित्वं, स्थिरता, स्थैर्य्यं, स्थिरस्थितिः *f.*,

संस्थितिः f., अव्यवस्थितिः f., अक्षयस्थितिः f., अनवरतत्वं, अविरतत्वं, सन्ततिः f., अविच्छेदः, सन्ततत्वं, आनन्त्यं, चिरस्थायिता.

To perplex, *v. a.* (Complicate, embarrass) सङ्कुलीकृ, आकुलीकृ, व्याकुलीकृ, समाकुलीकृ, सङ्करीकृ, सङ्कीर्णीकृ, व्याकुल (nom. व्याकुलयति -यितुं) or आकुल, बाध्, क्लिश्, क्लिष्टीकृ, रुध्, क्लेशं कृ or दा, शल्यं कृ.—(Bewilder, confound) मुह्, व्यामुह्, विमुह्, परिमुह्, सम्मुह्, व्याकुलीकृ, आकुलीकृ, विभ्रम्, सम्भ्रम्, भ्रम्, मोहं कृ or जन्, सम्भ्रमं जन्, चित्तभ्रान्तिं कृ, चित्तवैकल्यं कृ, व्यस्तचित्तं -त्तां कृ, व्यस्ततां जन्.

Perplexed, *p. p.* व्याकुलः -ला -लं, व्याकुलीकृतः -ता -तं, आकुलः -ला -लं, आकुलितः &c., व्याकुलितः &c., व्याकुलचित्तः -त्ता -त्तं, व्यस्तः -स्ता -स्तं, व्यस्तचित्तः -त्ता -त्तं, भ्रान्तहृदयः -यी -यं, सम्भ्रान्तः -न्ता -न्तं, विक्षिप्तचित्तः &c., विमोहितः &c., मोहितः &c., व्यग्रः -ग्रा -ग्रं, सन्दिग्धमनस्कः -स्का -स्कं, विमनस्कः &c., विमनाः -नाः -नः (स्), उद्विग्नमनाः &c., दुर्मनाः &c., मूढः -ढा -ढं, विमूढः &c., मुग्धः -ग्धा -ग्धं, विमुग्धः &c., कातरः -रा -रं, विहस्तः -स्ता -स्तं, व्यग्रः -ग्रा -ग्रं, अधीरः -रा -रं, विप्रतिपन्नः -न्ना -न्नं.

Perplexing, *part.* or *a.* भ्रान्तिजनकः -का -कं, मोहजनकः &c., मोहकः -का -कं, मोहनः -ना -नी -नं, भ्रान्तिकरः -रा -रं, मोहकरः &c., भ्रामकः -का -कं, विमोहनः -ना -नी -नं, विमोहकः &c., भ्रमजनकः &c., बाधकः &c.

Perplexity, perplexedness, *s.* व्याकुलता -त्वं, आकुलता -त्वं, व्यस्तता, व्यग्रता, व्यस्तचित्तत्वं, चित्तव्यस्तता, चित्तभ्रान्तिः f., कातरता -त्वं, चित्तवैकल्यं, विप्लवः, चित्तविभ्रमः, विक्षिप्तता, मोहः, व्यामोहः, सम्भ्रमः, सन्देहः, विप्रतिपत्तिः f.

Perquisite, *s.* शुल्कः -ल्कं, अवान्तरलाभः, अधिकलाभः, अतिरिक्तलाभः, आगन्तुकलाभः, वेतनाधिकलाभः.

Perquisition, *s.* परीक्षा -क्षणं, अतिपरीक्षा, अन्वेषणा, पर्येषणा.

To persecute, *v. a.* बाध् (c. 1. बाधते -धितुं), प्रबाध्, परिबाध्, प्रतिबाध्, बाधार्थम् or द्रोहार्थम् अनुसृ (c. 1. -सरति -सर्त्तुं, c. 10. -सारयति -यितुं), द्वेषपूर्व्वम् अनुसृ, द्रुह् (c. 4. द्रुह्यति, द्रोहितुं), क्लिश् (c. 9. क्लिश्नाति, क्लेशितुं), क्लेशं or द्रोहं कृ, अभिद्रोहं कृ, उपद्रवं कृ.

Persecuted, *p. p.* बाधितः -ता -तं, द्वेषपूर्व्वम् or बाधार्थम् अनुसृतः &c., अभिद्रुग्धः -ग्धा -ग्धं, अभिद्रुह्यमाणः -णा -णं, उपद्रुतः &c.

Persecution, *s.* बाधः -धा -धनं, बाधार्थं or द्रोहार्थम् अनुसरणं, द्रोहः -हणं, अभिद्रोहः -हणं, क्लेशकरणं, उपद्रवकरणं, उपद्रवः, क्लेशः, दुःखं.

Persecutor, *s.* बाधकः, प्रतिबाधकः, अभिद्रोही m. (न्), क्लेशकरः.

Perseverance, *s.* अभिनिवेशः, अभिनिविष्टता, व्यवस्थितिः f., व्यवसायः, अध्यवसायः, दीर्घव्यवसायः, अतिव्यवसायः, दीर्घप्रयत्नः -त्नत्वं, उद्योगः, उत्साहः, दीर्घोद्योगः, दीर्घोत्साहः, निर्बन्धः, अतिनिर्बन्धः, पर्य्यवस्थितिः f., आग्रहः, प्रसक्तिः f., प्रारब्धसम्पादनं, उद्यमः, दीर्घोद्यमः, अनवरतप्रयत्नः, निरन्तरचेष्टा, धृतिः f., धैर्य्यं, स्थिरता, स्थैर्य्यं, स्थितिः f., संस्थितिः f., प्रवृत्तिः f., अभियुक्तता, प्रयत्नः, अधिवासः, गुरणं, निर्व्यूढं; 'in religious austerities,' चर्य्या.

To persevere, *v. n.* पर्य्यवस्था (c. 1. -तिष्ठति -स्थातुं), अभिनिवेशेन or दीर्घोत्साहेन प्रारब्धानि सम्पद् (c. 10. -पादयति -यितुं), अभिनिवेशं कृ, निर्बन्धं कृ, दीर्घव्यवसायं कृ, दीर्घप्रयत्नं कृ, अनवरतप्रयत्नं कृ, अतिव्यवसायं कृ, निरन्तरचेष्टां कृ, आग्रहं कृ, अभिनिविष्टः -ष्टा -ष्टं भू.

Persevering, *a.* अभिनिवेशशीलः -ला -लं, अभिनिविष्टः -ष्टा -ष्टं, व्यवसायी -यिनी -यि (न्), अध्यवसायी &c., दीर्घप्रयत्नी &c., दीर्घप्रयत्नवान् -वती -वत् (त्), दीर्घोद्योगी &c., दीर्घोत्साही &c., दीर्घोद्यमी &c., महोत्साही &c., महोद्यमी &c., उद्यमी &c., उत्साही &c., उद्योगी &c., उत्साहवान् &c., आग्रही &c., आग्रहशीलः &c., प्रसक्तः -क्ता -क्तं, निर्बन्धशीलः &c., दृढकारी &c., प्रारब्धसम्पादकः -का -कं, अध्यवसाययुक्तः -क्ता -क्तं, उद्युक्तः &c., कृतश्रमः -मा -मं, प्रसितः -ता -तं, व्यवस्थितः &c., स्थितिमान् &c., प्रवर्त्तमानः &c., महोत्साहः -हा -हं, महोद्यमः -मा -मं.

Perseveringly, *adv.* अभिनिवेशेन, दीर्घप्रयत्नपूर्व्वं, दीर्घप्रयत्नतस्, अध्यवसायं, दीर्घोत्साहेन, साग्रहं, सनिर्बन्धं, प्रसक्तं, सोद्योगं, सोत्साहं.

Persia, *s.* (The country) पारसीकः, पारसिकः.

Persian, *a.* पारसिकः -की -कं, पारसीकः &c., पारसीकदेशीयः -या -यं; 'the language,' पारसिकभाषा.

To persist, *v. n.* अतिनिर्बन्धेन पर्य्यवस्था, अतिनिर्बन्धं कृ. *See* To persevere.

Persistence, persistency, *s.* निर्बन्धः, अतिनिर्बन्धः, आग्रहः, अभिनिवेशः, व्यवस्थितिः f., पर्य्यवस्थितिः f. *See* Perseverance.

Person, *s.* (Individual) जनः, व्यक्तिः f., एकजनः, पुरुषः, मनुष्यः; 'a female person,' स्त्रीजनः, अङ्गनाजनः.—(Body) अङ्गं, शरीरं, देहः, मूर्त्तिः f., कायः, गात्रं, वपुस् n., तनुः f., विग्रहः, अहङ्कारास्पदं; 'embellishment of the person,' अङ्गसंस्कारः, शरीरसंस्कारः; 'rubbing the person,' अङ्गमर्द्दनं; 'attendance on the person,' शरीरशुश्रूषा.—(Form, exterior appearance) रूपं, आकारः, आकृतिः f., मूर्त्तिः f.—(Character in a drama) भूमिका, रूपं, वेषः.—(Person in grammar) पुरुषः; 'first person,' उत्तमपुरुषः, प्रथमपुरुषः, अस्मद्वाच्यं, प्रथमा; 'second,' द्वितीयपुरुषः, मध्यमपुरुषः, युष्मद्वाच्यं; 'third,' तृतीयपुरुषः, उत्तरपुरुषः, नामवाच्यं. Native grammarians consider the third person as प्रथमपुरुषः.—(In person, in one's own person) साक्षात्, प्रत्यक्षं -क्षतस् -क्षेण, स्वतस्.

Personable, *a.* सुरूपः -पी -पं, सुरूपी -पिणी -पि (न्), रूपवान् -वती -वत् (त्), सुगात्रः -त्री -त्रं, स्वङ्गः -ङ्गी -ङ्गं, वराङ्गः &c., चारुदर्शनः -ना -नं, आकारशुद्धः -द्धा -द्धं.

Personage, *s.* जनः, व्यक्तिः f., पुरुषः, मनुष्यः. *See* Person.—(Eminent person) श्रेष्ठजनः, शिष्टजनः, महाजनः.

Personal, *a.* (Belonging to persons, not things) पौरुषेयः -यी -यं, पौरुषः -षी -षं, पुरुषवाचकः -का -कं, व्यक्तिवाचकः &c., पुरुष in comp.; 'a personal pronoun,' पुरुषवाचकसर्व्वनाम *n.*—(Peculiar or proper to individuals) आत्म or स्व in comp., निज in comp., विशेषव्यक्तिसम्बन्धी &c.; 'personal advantage,' आत्महितं, स्वहितं; 'personal experience,' स्वानुभवः.—(Belonging to the body or exterior person) शारीरिकः -की -कं, दैहिकः &c., आङ्गिकः -की -कं, शरीर in comp., अङ्ग in comp., रूपसम्बन्धी &c.; 'personal union,' शरीरयोगः; 'personal attendance,' शरीरशुश्रूषा; 'personal cleanliness,' अङ्गसंस्कारः, शरीरसंस्कारः; 'personal contact,' अङ्गसङ्गः; 'personal relation,' अङ्गाङ्गिभावः.—(Reflecting on an individual) विशेषजनोद्देशकः -का -कं, विशेषव्यक्त्युद्देशक &c., विशेषव्यक्तिस्पृक् m. f. n. (श्), विशेषोद्देशक &c., विशेषसंस्पर्शक &c., विशेषस्पर्शकः &c., विशेषव्यक्तिनिर्देशकः &c.—(Done in person) स्वयङ्कृतः -ता -तं, स्वकृतः -ता -तं, साक्षात्कृतः &c.; 'personal connexion,' साक्षात्सम्बन्धः.—(In law) अस्थावरः -रा -रं, जङ्गमः -मा -मं; 'personal property,' अस्थावरं, अस्थावरधनं.

Personality, *s.* (Individuality) व्यक्तिता -त्वं, व्यक्तिः f., पृथक्त्वं, पृथगात्मिका, स्वत्वं.—(Reflection on an individual) विशेषजनोद्देशकता, विशेषव्यक्त्युद्देशकत्वं, विशेषव्यक्तिप्रयोगः, विशेषव्यक्तिसंस्पर्शः, विशेषनिर्देशः, विशेषसंस्पर्शिता.—(A personal remark) विशेषोद्देशकवाक्यं, व्यक्तिनिर्देशकभाषणं, विशेषस्पर्शकवाक्यं.

PERSONALLY, *adv.* (In one's own person, by bodily presence) साक्षात्, प्रत्यक्षतस्, स्वशरीरतस्, स्वाङ्गतस्, स्वयं, स्वतस्, अङ्गतस्, शरीरतस्.—(Individually) व्यक्तितस्, विशेषतस्, पृथक्.

To **PERSONATE**, *v. a.* अभिनी (c. 1. -नयति -नेतुं), नट् (c. 10. नाटयति -यितुं), रूप् (c. 10. रूपयति -यितुं), अभिनयं कृ.—(Pretend to be, feign) छद्म कृ, कूटं कृ, ध्वजीकृ, वेशं or वेषं धृ (c. 10. धारयति -यितुं) or भृ (c. 3. बिभर्त्ति, भर्त्तुं), छद्मवेशं धृ; 'he personates a king,' राजवेशं धारयति; 'personating a king,' राजवेशधारी *m.* (न्), राजवेशभृत् *m.* Sometimes expressible by a nominal verb; as, राजायते, राजायमानः.

PERSONATION, *s.* अभिनयः -यनं, छद्मवेशधारणं, वेशधारणं, तदात्म्यधारणं, तदात्म्यग्रहणं.

PERSONATOR, *s.* अभिनेता *m.* (तृ), अभिनयी *m.* (न्), वेशधारी *m.*, वेशभृत्, छद्मवेशी *m.*, छद्मवेशधारी *m.*

PERSONIFICATION, *s.* चेतनधर्म्मारोपः -पणं, चेतनगुणारोपः -पणं, मनुष्यगुणारोपः -पणं, पुरुषभावारोपः, चेतनत्वारोपः -पणं, चेतनधर्म्मोत्प्रेक्षा, आरोपगर्भितोत्प्रेक्षा. The sense of this word is sometimes expressed by साक्षात्; as, 'a personification of justice,' साक्षाद्धर्म्मः, साक्षाद्भूतधर्म्मः; 'of death,' साक्षात्कृतान्तः; 'of time,' कालमूर्त्तिः *f.*

PERSONIFIED, *p. p.* साक्षाद्भूतः -ता -तं, मूर्त्तिमान् -मती -मत् (त्), साक्षात् or मूर्त्ति in comp. *See* the last word.

To **PERSONIFY**, *v. a.* चेतनगुणान् or चेतनभावं or चेतनधर्म्मं or चेतनत्वम् आरुह् in caus. (-रोपयति -यितुं).

PERSPECTIVE, *s.* (In drawing) यथास्थानदृष्टिचित्रलेखनविद्या, यथादर्शनचित्रलेखनं.

PERSPICACIOUS, *a.* (Quick-sighted) तीक्ष्णदृष्टिः -ष्टिः -ष्टि, तीव्रदृष्टिः &c., सूक्ष्मदृष्टिः &c., शीघ्रदृष्टिः &c., दृक्कुशलः -ला -लं.—(Discerning acutely) तीक्ष्णबुद्धिः -द्धिः -द्धि, सूक्ष्मबुद्धिः &c., कुशाग्रबुद्धिः &c., कुशाग्रीयमतिः &c.

PERSPICACIOUSNESS, **PERSPICACITY**, *s.* तीक्ष्णदृष्टित्वं, दृष्टितीक्ष्णता, दृष्टिसूक्ष्मता, दृष्टिपाटवं, दृक्कौशलं, तीक्ष्णबुद्धित्वं, बुद्धिसूक्ष्मता.

PERSPICUITY, *s.* स्पष्टता, स्पष्टार्थता, व्यक्तता, सुव्यक्तता, वैशद्यं, सुज्ञेयता, सुबोधता, प्रसादः, प्रसत्तिः *f.*, निर्म्मलता.

PERSPICUOUS, *a.* स्पष्टः -ष्टा -ष्टं, स्पष्टार्थः -र्था -र्थं, सुस्पष्टः &c., व्यक्तः -क्ता -क्तं, सुव्यक्तः &c., व्यक्तार्थः &c., विशदः -दा -दं, विशदार्थः &c., सुज्ञेयः -या -यं, सुबोधः -धा -धं, निर्म्मलः -ला -लं, प्रसन्नः -न्ना -न्नं.

PERSPICUOUSLY, *adv.* स्पष्टं, सुस्पष्टं, व्यक्तं, व्यक्तार्थतस्, विशदं.

PERSPIRATION, *s.* (The act) स्वेदनं, स्वेदस्रावः, स्वेदस्रवणं, घर्म्मस्रावः, घर्म्मस्रवणं, घर्म्मस्रुतिः *f.*, स्वेदजलस्रावः, स्वेदबिन्दुस्रावः.—(Matter perspired) स्वेदः -दनं, घर्म्मः, स्वेदजलं, स्वेदबिन्दुः *m.*, स्वेदाम्बु *n.*, घर्म्माम्बु *n.*, स्वेदोदकं, घर्म्मोदकं, घर्म्मबिन्दुः *m.*, घर्म्मपयस् *n.*, स्वेदपयस् *n.*, स्वेदविप्रुट् *f.* (ष्), तनुरसः, देहरसः, स्वेदजलं, क्लेदः -दं, खिन्नः, स्रवणं, प्रस्रवणः -णं; 'violent perspiration,' प्रस्वेदः; 'in a perspiration,' सस्वेदः -दा -दं, सघर्म्मः -र्म्मा -र्म्मं, प्रखिन्नः -न्ना -न्नं, प्रस्वेदितः -ता -तं, प्रस्वेदितवान् -वती -वत् (त्); 'in a violent perspiration,' भृशस्विद्.

To **PERSPIRE**, *v. n.* स्विद् (c. 4. स्विद्यति, स्वेत्तुं), प्रस्विद्, स्वेदं सु (c. 10. स्रावयति -यितुं), स्वेदबिन्दून् सु, स्वेदस्रावं कृ, घर्म्मस्रावं कृ, स्वेदस्रवणं कृ, सस्वेदः -दा -दं भू, स्वेदोत्सर्गं कृ.

To **PERSPIRE**, *v. a.* (Excrete through the pores) रोमकूपद्वारा or रोमरन्ध्रद्वारा विसृज् or उत्सृज् or निःसृ in caus. or निरस् or सु in caus.

PERSPIRING, *part.* स्वेदितः -ता -तं, प्रस्वेदितः -ता -तं, प्रखिन्नः -न्ना -न्नं, प्रस्वेदितवान् -वती -वत् (त्), स्रवत्स्वेदः -दा -दं, स्रवत्स्वेदबिन्दुः -न्दुः -न्दु, स्रवत्स्वेदजलः -ला -लं, स्वेदस्रावी -विणी -वि (न्), घर्म्मस्रावी &c., सस्वेदः -दा -दं, सघर्म्मः -र्म्मा -र्म्मं, घर्म्मितः -ता -तं; 'perspiring violently,' भृशस्विद् *m. f. n.*

PERSUADABLE, *a.* अनुनेयः -या -यं, अनुनेतव्यः -व्या -व्यं, परिभाषणीयः -या -यं, प्रबोधनीयः -या -यं, प्ररोचनीयः &c., प्रोत्साहनीयः &c.

To **PERSUADE**, *v. a.* (Influence by good arguments, to engage in any action) सुहेतुवादेन कस्मिंश्चित् कर्म्मणि प्रवृत् (c. 10. -वर्त्तयति -यितुं) or नियुज् (c. 10. -योजयति -यितुं) or प्रयुज्, अनुनी (c. 1. -नयति -नेतुं), प्रोत्सह् (c. 10. -साहयति -यितुं), उत्सह्, समुत्सह्, प्ररुच् (c. 10. -रोचयति -यितुं), आकृष् (c. 1. -कर्षति -क्रष्टुं), परिभाष् (c. 1. -भाषते -षितुं), प्रबोधं or मन्त्रणां दा; 'why do you persuade me to commit such an action?' किम् एवंविधे कर्म्मणि मां नियोजयसि or प्रवर्त्तयसि. Sometimes the causal form may express this sense of 'persuade;' as, 'he persuades to return,' निवर्त्तयति.—(Convince, induce to believe) शङ्कानिवृत्तिं कृ, सन्देहनिवृत्तिं कृ, संशयविच्छेदं कृ, सन्देहभञ्जनं कृ, विश्वासं or प्रत्ययं or निश्चयं or दृढनिश्चयं or दृढविश्वासं जन्, संशयं or सन्देहं छिद् (c. 7. छिनत्ति, छेत्तुं) or नश् (c. 10. नाशयति -यितुं).

PERSUADED, *p. p.* प्रयोजितः -ता -तं, नियोजितः &c., अनुनीतः &c., प्रोत्साहितः &c.—(Convinced) जातनिश्चयः -या -यं, जातविश्वासः, जातदृढनिश्चयः &c., जातप्रत्ययः &c., छिन्नसंशयः &c.; 'I am persuaded,' मम दृढनिश्चयो भवति.

PERSUADER, *s.* प्रयोजकः, प्रवर्त्तकः, नियोजकः, प्रोत्साहकः.

PERSUASION, *s.* (Act of influencing by good arguments to engage in any action) सुहेतुवादेन कस्मिंश्चित् कर्म्मणि प्रवर्त्तनं or प्रयोजनं or नियोजनं, प्रोत्साहः -हनं, प्ररोचना, परिभाषणं, अनुनयः, अनुनयनं, प्रबोधः.—(Act of convincing) निश्चयकरणं, विश्वासकरणं, प्रत्ययकरणं, सन्देहच्छेदः, संशयच्छेदः, शङ्कानिवृत्तिः *f.*, सन्देहनिवृत्तिः.—(Conviction, state of being convinced) दृढनिश्चयः, दृढविश्वासः, दृढप्रत्ययः.—(Religious opinion or creed) मतं, मतिः *f.*, मार्गः, पन्थाः (पथिन्), सम्प्रदायः.

PERSUASIVE, **PERSUASORY**, *a.* अनुनयी -यिनी -यि (न्), सानुनयः -या -यं, प्रवर्त्तकः -का -कं, प्रयोजकः &c., प्रोत्साहकः &c., प्ररोचकः &c., वशकरः -रा -रं, वशकारकः &c., सभावशकरः &c., प्रवृत्तिजनकः &c.—(Convincing) निश्चयजनकः -का -कं, दृढविश्वासजनकः &c., प्रत्ययकारी &c., संशयच्छेदकः &c., सन्देहच्छेदकः &c.

PERSUASIVELY, *adv.* सानुनयं, अनुनयपूर्व्वं, यथा निश्चयो जायते तथा.

PERT, *a.* (Brisk, lively) चपलः -ला -लं, लघुः -घुः -घ्वी -घु.—(Saucy) उत्तरदायकः -की -कं, उत्तरदायी -यिनी -यि (न्), अविनीतः -ता -तं, अविनयः -या -यं, धृष्टः -ष्टा -ष्टं.

To **PERTAIN**, *v. n.* सम्बन्ध् in pass. (-बध्यते), सम्बन्धी -न्धिनी -न्धि भू or अस्, सम्पर्क्की &c. भू. *See To* BELONG, *To* RELATE.

PERTEREBRATION, *s.* वेधनं, वेधः, शुषिरीकरणं, छिद्रकरणं, सुषिरता.

PERTINACIOUS, *a.* निर्बन्धशीलः -ला -लं, अभिनिवेशशीलः &c., आग्रही -हिणी -हि (न्), दुराग्रही &c., धीरः -रा -रं, दृढः -ढा -ढं, जडः -डा -डं, स्थिरप्रतिज्ञः -ज्ञा -ज्ञं, दृढप्रतिज्ञः &c.

PERTINACIOUSLY, *adv.* सनिर्बन्धं, अतिनिर्बन्धेन, साभिनिवेशं, साग्रहं.

PERTINACITY, PERTINACIOUSNESS, *s.* निर्बन्धः, निर्बन्धशीलता, अभिनिवेशः, अभिनिविष्टता, आग्रहः, दुराग्रहः, धीरता, धैर्य्यं, दृढता, दार्ढ्यं, जडता; 'in adhering to belief,' श्रद्धाजाड्यं.

PERTINENCE, PERTINENCY, *s.* प्रासङ्गिकत्वं, प्रसङ्गसङ्गतिः *f.*, प्रसङ्गयोग्यता, प्रसङ्गानुसारः, सार्थकत्वं, अर्थवत्त्वं, याथार्थ्यं, यथार्थता, योग्यता, यथायोग्यता, युक्तता, उपयुक्तता -त्वं, उपयोगिता, प्रस्तुतयोग्यता, प्रस्तुतसङ्गतिः *f.*

PERTINENT, *a.* प्रासङ्गिकः -की -कं, प्रसङ्गानुसारी -रिणी -रि (न्), प्रसङ्गसङ्गतः -ता -तं, प्रसङ्गसदृशः -शी -शं, प्रसङ्गयोग्यः -ग्या -ग्यं, सार्थकः -का -कं, अर्थवान् -वती -वत् (त्), योग्यः -ग्या -ग्यं, यथायोग्यः &c., यथार्थः -र्था -र्थं, उपयुक्तः -क्ता -क्तं, युक्तः &c., उपयोगी &c., यथायुक्तः &c., उपपन्नः -न्ना -न्नं, प्रस्तुतयोग्यः &c., प्रस्तुतसङ्गतः &c., प्रस्तुतः &c.; 'is pertinent,' उपपद्यते, युज्यते.

PERTINENTLY, *adv.* प्रसङ्गानुसारेण, प्रसङ्गसदृशं, प्रसङ्गयोग्यं, यथाप्रसङ्गं, यथायोग्यं, प्रसङ्गतस्, युक्तं, यथायुक्तं, योग्यं, प्रस्तुतयोग्यं, सङ्गतं, उपपन्नं, सार्थकं.

PERTLY, *adv.* अविनयेन, अविनीतं, चपलं, चापल्येन, धृष्टवत्.

PERTNESS, *s.* (Briskness) चपलता, चापल्यं, लघुता.—(Sauciness) अविनयः, अविनीतता, धृष्टता, धार्ष्ट्यं, उत्तरदायकता.

To PERTURB, PERTURBATE, *v. a.* (Disturb, disquiet) क्षुभ्, विक्षुभ्, बाध्, आकुलीकृ, व्याकुलीकृ, मुह्, व्यामुह्, कातरीकृ, व्यग्रीकृ, उपहन्.—(Disorder) व्यस्, अव्यवस्थीकृ, सङ्कुलीकृ, संक्षुभ्.

PERTURBATION, *s.* क्षोभः, चित्तक्षोभः, व्याक्षोभः, मनःक्षोभः, आकुलता, व्याकुलता, आकुलचित्तता, व्यस्तता, व्यग्रता, कातरत्वं, पारिप्लवत्वं, पारिप्लाव्यं, वैक्लव्यं, उद्वेगः, मोहः, औत्सुक्यं, व्यामोहः.

PERTURBATOR, PERTURBER, *s.* क्षोभकः, क्षोभकारी *m.* (न्), बाधकः, मोहकः.

PERTURBED, *p. p.* क्षुब्धः -ब्धा -ब्धं, क्षोभितः -ता -तं, आकुलः -ला -लं, व्याकुलः &c., आकुलचित्तः -त्ता -त्तं, आकुलितः -ता -तं, व्याकुलितः &c., व्यस्तः -स्ता -स्तं, व्यग्रः -ग्रा -ग्रं, पारिप्लवः -वी -वं, कातरः -रा -रं, उपहतः &c.

PERUSAL, *s.* अध्ययनं, अधीतिः *f.*, पठनं, पाठः, पारायणं. *See* READING.

To PERUSE, *v. a.* अधी, समधी, पठ्, अधिगम्. *See To* READ.

PERUSED, *p. p.* अधीतः -ता -तं, पठितः &c., आगमितः &c. *See* READ.

To PERVADE, *v. a.* व्याप् (c. 5. -व्याप्नोति -व्याप्तुं), अभिव्याप्, व्यश् (c. 5. -अश्नुते -अशितुं), सर्व्वत्र विस्तृ in pass. (-स्तीर्य्यते), सर्व्वत्र गम् or प्रविश् (c. 6. -विशति -वेष्टुं) or आक्रम् (c. 1. -क्रामति -क्रमितुं) or व्यतिक्रम् or समाक्रम्, गाह् (c. 1. गाहते -हितुं), विगाह्, समक्ष् (c. 1. -अक्षति -ते -क्षितुं).

PERVADED, *p. p.* व्याप्तः -प्ता -प्तं, अभिव्याप्तः &c., प्रवेशितः -ता -तं, आक्रान्तः -न्ता -न्तं, समाक्रान्तः &c., व्यस्तः -स्ता -स्तं, भावितः &c., परिवीतः &c.

PERVADING, PERVASIVE, *a.* व्यापकः -का -कं, व्यापी -पिनी -पि (न्), अभिव्यापकः &c., व्याप्तिमान् -मती -मत् (त्), व्यश्नुवानः -ना -नं, समश्नुवानः &c., विस्तीर्णः -र्णा -र्णं; 'pervading all things,' सर्व्वव्यापी &c., सर्व्वगः -गा -गं, सर्व्वत्रगः -गा -गं, सर्व्वत्रगामी &c.; 'the whole body,' सर्व्वाङ्गीणः -णा -णं; 'the world,' जगद्व्यापी &c.

PERVASIBLE, *a.* व्याप्यः -प्या -प्यं, अभिव्याप्यः &c., व्यापनीयः -या -यं, प्रवेशनीयः -या -यं, प्रवेश्यः -श्या -श्यं.

PERVASION, *s.* (Act of pervading) व्याप्तिः *f.*, व्यापनं, व्यापकत्वं, अभिव्याप्तिः *f.*, अभिव्यापनं, प्रवेशनं, सम्मूर्च्छनं, आक्रमणं, विगाहः -हनं, सर्व्वत्र विस्तारः.

PERVERSE, *a.* (Petulant, obstinate) प्रतीपः -पा -पं, विप्रतीपः &c., प्रतीपकारी -रिणी -रि (न्), विपरीतकारी &c., विपरीतः -ता -तं, प्रतिकूलः -ला -लं, विलोमः -मी -मं, कुटिलशीलः -ला -लं, वक्रशीलः &c., कुटिलबुद्धिः -द्धिः -द्धि, दुर्बुद्धिः &c., वक्रस्वभावः -वा -वं, निकृतः -ता -तं, उच्छृङ्खलः -ला -लं, शठः -ठा -ठं.—(Distorted) कुटिलः -ला -लं, अनृजुः -जुः -जु, वक्रः -क्रा -क्रं, विकृतः &c.

PERVERSELY, *adv.* प्रतीपं, विप्रतीपं, प्रतिकूलं, विपरीतं, वैपरीत्येन, प्रातिकूल्येन, वामत्वेन, कुटिलं, कुटिलशीलत्वात्, वक्रशीलत्वात्.

PERVERSENESS, PERVERSITY, *s.* प्रतीपता -त्वं, विप्रतीपता -त्वं, विपरीतता, वैपरीत्यं, प्रतिकूलता, प्रातिकूल्यं, कुटिलत्वं, कौटिल्यं, कुटिलशीलता, वक्रता, वक्रशीलता -त्वं, विपर्य्ययः, विपर्य्यासः, वामत्वं, विलोमत्वं, विलोमक्रिया, विपरीतगतिः *f.*, विक्रिया, दुष्टता, दौरात्म्यं.

PERVERSION, *s.* विक्रिया, विकृतिः *f.*, विकारः, अन्यथाकरणं, विपरिणामः, साचीकरणं, विपरीतकरणं, वक्रीकरणं, विरूपकरणं, विलोमकरणं, विलोमक्रिया, विपर्य्यासकरणं, साचीकृतं, असङ्गिनियोगः.

To PERVERT, *v. a.* विकृ, साचीकृ, वक्रीकृ, कुटिलीकृ, अन्यथाकृ, विरूप् (c. 10. -रूपयति -यितुं), विरूपीकृ, विलोमीकृ, विपरीतीकृ, वैपरीत्यं कृ, विपरिणामं कृ, विपर्य्ययं कृ, असङ्गिनियोगं कृ, भ्रंश् (c. 10. भ्रंशयति -यितुं), भ्रष्टीकृ.

PERVERTED, *p. p.* विकृतः -ता -तं, साचीकृतः &c., वक्रीकृतः &c., विरूपीकृतः &c., अन्यथाकृतः &c., विपरिणतः &c., भ्रंशितः &c., भ्रष्टः -ष्टा -ष्टं.

PERVERTER, PERVERTING, *s.* or *a.* विकारी -रिणी -रि (न्), विकारजनकः -का -कं, विपरिणामजनकः &c., विपरिणामी &c., विरूपकारी &c., विपर्य्यासकारी &c., विलोमकारी &c.; 'perverting the mind,' चित्तविकारी &c.

PERVESTIGATION, *s.* अतिपरीक्षा -क्षणं, अत्यन्वेषणं -णा, अतिनिरूपणं.

PERVICACIOUS, *a.* अतिप्रतीपः -पा -पं. *See* PERVERSE, OBSTINATE.

PERVIOUS, *a.* व्याप्यः -प्या -प्यं, व्यापनीयः -या -यं, प्रवेश्यः -श्या -श्यं, प्रवेशनीयः -या -यं, भेद्यः -द्या -द्यं, भेदनीयः -या -यं, प्रवेशयोग्यः -ग्या -ग्यं, अरोधकः -का -कं.

PERVIOUSNESS, *s.* व्याप्यता -त्वं, प्रवेश्यता -त्वं, भेद्यता, भेदनीयता.

PEST, *s.* (Pestilence) मारी -रिः *f.*, मारः -रकः, मरकः, महामारी, महाव्याधिः *m.*, तीक्ष्णं.—(Any noxious or hateful thing) कण्टकः, दूषकः, शल्यं, घातकः; 'of society,' लोककण्टकः, पंक्तिदूषकः.

To PESTER, *v. a.* (Harass) बाध्, पीड्, अभिपीड्, तप्, व्यथ्, क्लिश्.

PESTERED, *p. p.* बाधितः -ता -तं, पीडितः &c., आयासितः &c., क्लिशितः &c.

PESTERER, *s.* बाधकः, क्लेशकः, कष्टकरः, आयासकरः, पीडकः.

PEST-HOUSE, *s.* सांक्रामिकरोगग्रस्तालयः -यं, मारिग्रस्तालयः -यं.

PESTIFEROUS, *a.* मारकजनकः -का -कं, मारकोत्पादकः &c., मारकः -का -कं, मारात्मकः &c., प्राणनाशकः &c., विनाशकः &c., साङ्घातिकः &c.

PESTILENCE, *s.* मारी -रिः *f.*, मारः -रकः, मरकः, महामारी, महाव्याधिः *m.*, व्याधिः *m.*, तीक्ष्णं, प्रतीवापः, आतचनं, कृत्या.

PESTILENT, PESTILENTIAL, *a.* (Producing the plague). *See* PESTIFEROUS.—(Noxious, pernicious) घातुकः -का -कं, घातकः &c., उपघातकः &c., अपकारकः &c., अपकारी &c., मारकः -का -कं, विनाशकः &c., दूषकः &c., बाधकः &c.

PESTLE, *s.* मुसलं -लः, मुषलं -लः, गोकीलः, गोकिलः, अयोग्रं, मुद्गरः, मुसं; 'pestle and mortar,' उलूखलमुषले; 'to be pounded with a pestle,' मुसल्यः -ल्या -ल्यं.

PET, *s.* (Fit of peevishness) ईषत्कोपावेशः, ईषत्कोपः, ईषत्क्रोधः, ईषद्विरागः, ईषद्वैरस्यं.—(A fondling) प्रेमपात्रं, प्रेमास्पदं, प्रीतिपात्रं, अनुरागपात्रं, क्रीडामृगः, सदानुगतः.

To PET, *v. a.* (Fondle) लल् (c. 10. लालयति -यितुं), अङ्के पाल्, प्रेम कृ.

PETAL, *s.* दलं, पुष्पदलं, पुष्पपत्रिका, पुष्पपत्रं.

Petaled, petalous, *a.* सदलः-ला-लं, दलवान् -वती-वत् (त्), दलसः &c.

Petit, *a.* अल्पः -ल्पा -ल्पं, क्षुद्रः -द्रा -द्रं. *See* Petty, Little, &c.

Petition, *s.* प्रार्थना -नं, अभ्यर्थना, अर्थः, याच्ञा, निवेदनं, विज्ञापनं-ना. —(Written) निवेदनपत्रं, विज्ञापनपत्रं, प्रार्थनपत्रं.

To petition, *v. a.* (Beg, request) प्रार्थ्, अभ्यर्थ्, अर्थ्, याच्, निवेदनपत्रेण प्रार्थ्, निविद् (c. 10. -वेदयति -यितुं), विज्ञा in caus. (-ज्ञापयति -यितुं).

Petitioner, *s.* प्रार्थकः, प्रार्थयिता *m.* (तृ), अर्थी *m.*, याचकः, निवेदयिता *m.* (तृ), निवेदनकृत् *m.*, विज्ञापनकृत्, कार्पटः, अभ्यर्थयमानः.

Petrescent, *a.* आरब्धपाषाणपरिणामः -मा -मं.

Petrifaction, *s.* (Process of conversion into stone) पाषाणीकरणं, प्रस्तरीकरणं, दृषत्करणं, पाषाणपरिणामः, प्रस्तरपरिणामः, पाषाणसात्करणं, पाषाणभूयं.—(Thing petrified) पाषाणीभूतवस्तु *n.*, दृषद्भूतवस्तु *n.*, कृत्रिमपाषाणः.

Petrified, *p. p.* or *a.* पाषाणीभूतः -ता -तं, पाषाणीकृतः &c., प्रस्तरीभूतः &c., पाषाणसात्कृतः &c., पाषाणत्वापन्नः -न्ना -न्नं, प्राप्तपाषाणत्वः -त्वा -त्वं.—(Fixed in amazement) काष्ठवत् स्तब्धः -ब्धा -ब्धं, गतप्राणः -णा -णं.

To petrify, *v. a.* पाषाणीकृ, प्रस्तरीकृ, पाषाणसात्कृ, पाषाणपरिणामं कृ, पाषाणत्वं प्राप् (c. 10. -आपयति -यितुं).—(Make callous) कठिनीकृ, निष्ठुरीकृ, पाषाणसमभावं -वां कृ.—(Fix with amazement, &c.) काष्ठवत् or प्रेतवत् स्तब्धीकृ.

To petrify, *v. n.* पाषाणीभू, प्रस्तरीभू, पाषाणत्वं प्राप् (c. 5. -आप्नोति -आप्तुं).

Petroleum, *s.* शिलातैलं, शिलारसः, शैलनिर्यासः, भूमितैलं.

Petticoat *s.* शाटकः, शाटी, स्त्रीशाटकः, चण्डातकः -कं, अर्द्धोरुकं, चोटी, नीवी, चलनकं, कौशेयं, पटवासः, पटमयं, स्त्रीकटिवस्त्रं, स्त्रीजनभृतम् अधोवसनं or अधोवस्त्रं or अर्धोंशुकं or अन्तर्वासस् *n.* or अन्तरीयं or उपसंव्यानं or परिधानं; 'under petticoat government,' स्त्रीवशवर्त्ती *m.* (न्), स्त्रीजितः.

Pettifogger, *s.* जघन्यवृत्तिः *m.*, अधमवृत्तिः *m.*, कुत्सितप्रतिनिधिः *m.*, कुत्सितव्यापारी *m.* (न्), क्षुद्रविवादव्यापारी *m.*

Pettiness, *s.* अल्पता, क्षुद्रता -त्वं, लघुता, लाघवं, तुच्छता.

Pettish, *a.* वक्रभावः -वा -वं, कर्कशभावः &c., प्रतीपः -पा -पं, कर्कशः -शा -शं, नैकृतिकः-की-कं, ईषत्कोपी-पिनी-पि (न्), ईषत्क्रिरुक्षः -क्षा -क्षं.

Pettishly, *adv.* सकार्कश्यं, कर्कशं, ईषत्कोपेन, वक्रशीलत्वात्.

Pettishness, *s.* कार्कश्यं, कर्कशता, कर्कशशीलता, प्रतीपता, प्रतीपशीलता, वक्रशीलता, ईषत्कोपावेशः, ईषत्कोपिता, ईषद्वैरक्ष्यं.

Petty, *a.* अल्पः -ल्पा -ल्पं, क्षुद्रः -द्रा -द्रं, लघुः -घुः -घु, क्षुल्लकः -का -कं, उप prefixed, कल्प or देशीय in comp.; as, 'a petty crime,' उपपातकं; 'a petty prince,' राजदेशीयः, राजकल्पः.

Petulance, petulancy, *s.* प्रतीपता, वामशीलता, दुःशीलता, धृष्टता, अविनयः, अविनीतत्वं, प्रगल्भता, प्रागल्भ्यं, चापल्यं, तिग्मता.

Petulant, *a.* प्रतीपः -पा -पं, वामशीलः -ला -लं, दुःशीलः &c., अविनीतः -ता -तं, प्रगल्भः -ल्भा -ल्भं, धृष्टः -ष्टा -ष्टं.

Petulantly, *adv.* प्रतीपं, प्रगल्भं, सप्रागल्भ्यं, अविनीतवत्, धृष्टवत्.

Pewter, *s.* कांस्यं -स्यकं, कांसीयं, कंसः -सं, पीतलोहं.

Pewterer, *s.* कांस्यकारः -रकः, कंसकारः -रकः, कांस्यवणिक् *m.* (ज्).

Phalanx, *s.* भोगव्यूहः, घनव्यूहः, गाढव्यूहः.

Phallus, *s.* (Emblem of Śiva) लिङ्गं. According to the Mahratti Dictionary there are 12; viz. 1. महाकालेश्वरः, 2. सोमनाथः, 3. केदारेश्वरः, 4. विश्वेश्वरः, 5. ओङ्कारेश्वरः, 6. त्र्यम्बकेश्वरः, 7. घृष्णेश्वरः, 8. नागनाथः, 9. वैद्यनाथः, 10. भीमाशङ्करः, 11. मल्लिकार्जुनः, 12. रामेश्वरः.

Phantasm, phantasma, *s.* आभासः, भासः, छाया, अवच्छाया, वासना, माया, मनोरथसृष्टिः *f.*, कल्पनासृष्टिः *f.*

Phantasy, *s.* वासना, कल्पना, भासः, आभासः. *See* Fancy.

Phantom, *s.* वेतालः, भूतः -तं, प्रेतः, प्रेतनरः, रात्रिचरः, रात्रिचरः, निशाचरः, निशाटः.—(Fancied vision). *See* Phantasm.

Pharisaic, pharisaical, *a.* साधुम्मन्यः -न्या -न्यं, दाम्भिकवृत्तिः -त्तिः -त्ति, कुहकवृत्तिः &c., दाम्भिकः -की -कं, धर्म्मध्वजी -जिनी -जि (न्), धर्म्मोपधः -धा -धं, कपटधर्म्मी -र्म्मिणी -र्म्मि (न्), कुहकधर्म्मी &c.

Pharisaicalness, pharisaism, *s.* साधुम्मन्यता, दाम्भिकवृत्तिः *f.*, कुहकवृत्तिः *f.*, कुहना, कपटधर्म्मः, दम्भः, दाम्भिकत्वं, धर्म्मोपधा.

Pharisee, *s.* धर्म्मध्वजी *m.* (न्), कपटव्रती *m.*, दम्भी *m.* *See* Hypocrite.

Pharmaceutic, pharmaceutical, *a.* औषधसंस्कारसम्बन्धी &c., अगदसंस्कारविद्यासम्बन्धी &c.

Pharmacopœia, *s.* औषधसंस्कारविषयको ग्रन्थः, औषधसंस्कारशास्त्रं.

Pharmacopolist, *s.* औषधविक्रेता *m.* (तृ), भेषजविक्रेता *m.*, अगदविक्रयी *m.* (न्).

Pharmacy, *s.* औषधसंस्कारः, भेषजसंस्कारः, अगदसंस्कारः, औषधक्रिया, औषधसंस्कारविद्या, औषधकरणविद्या, अगदसंस्कारविद्या, चिकित्सा.

Pharos, *s.* दीपस्तम्भः, दीपगृहं, दीपागारं, आकाशदीपः.

Phase, phasis, *s.* दर्शनं, सन्दर्शनं, दर्शनभेदः, दर्शनप्रकारः.

Pheasant, *s.* जीवञ्जीवः, जीवजीवः, जिवाजिवः, चीरनः, कृकणः.

Phenix, *s.* स्वभस्मजपक्षी *m.* (न्), कविकल्पितः स्वभस्मोत्पद्यमानः पक्षिविशेषः.—(Singularly eminent person) अद्वितीयः. *See* Paragon.

Phenomenon, *s.* (Any thing visible, an appearance of any kind) दृग्विषयः, दृष्टिविषयः, दृग्गोचरो विषयः, दृष्टिगोचरो विषयः, दर्शनं.—(Remarkable or unusual appearance) अद्भुतदर्शनं, अद्भुतविषयः, अद्भुतं, उत्पातः, उपद्रवः.

Phial, *s.* क्षुद्रकूपी, काचकूपी, काचपात्रं, अल्पपरिमाणा काचकूपी.

Philanthropic, philanthropical, *a.* जनप्रियः -या -यं, लोकप्रियः &c., नरप्रियः &c., जनवत्सलः -ला -लं, जनहितैषी -षिणी -षि (न्), जनहितेच्छुः -च्छुः -च्छु, जनहितेप्सुः -प्सुः -प्सु, जनोपकारशीलः -ला -लं, जनोपकारी &c., लोकोपकारी &c., परोपकारशीलः &c., सर्व्वोपकारी &c., विश्वोपकारी &c., सर्व्वहितैषी &c., जगदुपकारी &c., विश्वमित्रः -त्रा -त्रं, जगन्मित्रः &c., जगद्वत्सलः -ला -लं, जगत्सुहृद् *m. f. n.*

Philanthropist, *s.* जनहितैषी *m.* (न्). *See* Philanthropic.

Philanthropy, *s.* जनप्रियता, लोकप्रियता, नरप्रियता, जनप्रीतिः *f.*, जनहितैषा, जनहितेच्छा, जनहितेप्सा, सर्व्वजनप्रीतिः *f.*, सर्व्वजनहितैषा, सर्व्वप्राणिप्रियता, सर्व्वभूतदया, जनोपकारशीलता, सर्व्वोपकारशीलता, विश्वप्रीतिः *f.*, जगत्सौहृदं.

Philippic, *s.* भर्त्सनार्थकवाक्यं, भर्त्सनात्मकवाक्यं, भर्त्सनवाक्यं, भर्त्सनारूपभाषणं, भर्त्सनारूपवाक्प्रबन्धः.

Philologer, philologist, *s.* शब्दशास्त्रज्ञः, शब्दविद्याज्ञः, शाब्दिकः, शब्दशास्त्री *m.* (न्), शब्दशास्त्रवेत्ता *m.* (तृ), शब्दशास्त्रविद्, वैयाकरणः, व्युत्पत्तिज्ञः.

Philological, *a.* शाब्दिकः -की -कं, शब्दशास्त्रीयः -या -यं, शब्दशास्त्रसम्बन्धी, शब्दव्युत्पत्तिविषयः -या -यं, शब्दोत्पत्तिविषयकः -का -कं.

Philology, *s.* शब्दविद्या, शब्दशास्त्रं, शब्दव्युत्पत्तिविद्या, शब्दोत्पत्तिविद्या, शब्दशासनविद्या.

PHILOMATH, *s.* विद्यानुरागी *m.* (न्), विद्याप्रियः, विद्यानुसेवी *m.*, विद्यावल्लभः, विद्याभक्तः, जिज्ञासुः *m.*

PHILOMATHY, *s.* विद्यानुरागः, विद्यानुसेवनं, विद्याभक्तता, जिज्ञासा.

PHILOPROGENITIVENESS, *s.* अपत्यस्नेहः, पुत्रस्नेहः, प्रजास्नेहः.

PHILOSOPHER, *s.* ज्ञानी *m.* (न्), महाज्ञानी *m.*, ज्ञानवान् *m.* (त्), विद्वान् *m.* (स्), पण्डितः, पण्डितबुद्धिः *m.*, विद्यावान् *m.* (त्), ज्ञाननिष्ठः, ज्ञानविज्ञाननिष्ठः, प्राज्ञः, प्रज्ञावान् *m.*, तत्त्वविद् *m.*, तत्त्वज्ञः, तत्त्वज्ञानी *m.*, तत्त्वविचारकः, तात्त्विकः, पदार्थविज्ञानी *m.*, पदार्थपरिज्ञानी *m.*, तार्किकः, नैयायिकः, भट्टः, दमनः.

PHILOSOPHER'S-STONE, *s.* स्पर्शमणिः *m.*, स्पर्शप्रस्तरः, रसेन्द्रः; 'the gold proceeding from its touch,' स्पर्शमणिप्रभवं.—(Possession securing every thing desired, fabled by the Hindús either as a tree, or cow, or gem) कल्पद्रुमः, कल्पवृक्षः, कल्पतरुः *m.*, कल्पलता, कामधेनुः *f.*, कामदुघा, कामधुक् *f.*, कामदः, चिन्तामणिः *m.*

PHILOSOPHIC, PHILOSOPHICAL, *a.* (Pertaining to philosophy) तत्त्वज्ञानविषयकः -का -कं, तत्त्वज्ञानसम्बन्धी &c., ज्ञानविज्ञानसम्बन्धी &c., ज्ञानसम्बन्धी &c., विद्यासम्बन्धी &c., तर्कादिविद्यासम्बन्धी &c., न्यायादिविद्याविषयः -या -यं.—(Skilled in philosophy) तत्त्वज्ञाननिष्ठः -ष्ठा -ष्ठं, ज्ञाननिष्ठः &c., ज्ञानपरः -रा -रं, विद्यापरः -रा -रं, ज्ञानविज्ञाननिष्ठः &c., तत्त्वविचारनिष्ठः &c., तत्त्वविचारपरः &c.

PHILOSOPHICALLY, *adv.* तत्त्वशास्त्रानुसारेण, न्यायशास्त्रानुसारात्, तत्त्वज्ञानतस्, ज्ञानतस्, ज्ञानविज्ञानतस्, तत्त्वतस्.

To PHILOSOPHIZE, *v. n.* तत्त्वान्वीक्षणं कृ, तत्त्वविचारं कृ, तत्त्वजिज्ञासां कृ, तत्त्वनिरूपणं कृ, तत्त्वनिर्णयं कृ, ज्ञानविज्ञानविचारं कृ.

PHILOSOPHY, *s.* तत्त्वज्ञानं, तत्त्वविज्ञानं, तत्त्वविद्या, ज्ञानं, विज्ञानं, ज्ञानविज्ञानं, तत्त्वशास्त्रं, ज्ञानशास्त्रं, पाण्डित्यं.—(Moral philosophy) नीतिः *f.*, नीतिविद्या, नीतिशास्त्रं.—(Logical) तर्कविद्या, तर्कशास्त्रं, तर्कः, न्यायः, न्यायशास्त्रं, न्यायविद्या, विचारविद्या, आन्वीक्षिकी.—(Natural) पदार्थविज्ञानं, पदार्थविद्या, पदार्थशास्त्रं.—(Stoicism) औदास्यं, उदासीनता.

PHILTER, *s.* वशीकरणार्थं पेयौषधं, वशीकरणौषधं, अभिचारौषधं, संवदनौषधं, संवदनं, वशक्रिया.

PHIZ, *s.* मुखं, वदनं, आननं, आस्यं, वक्त्रं, श्रीमुखं.

PHLEBOTOMIST, *s.* सिरावेधकः, शिरावेधकः, रक्तस्रावकः, रक्तस्रावी, शिराछेदकः, शिरामोक्षकः, शिराच्छिद् *m.*, शिराविद् *m.* (ध्), रक्तमोचकः.

PHLEBOTOMY, *s.* शिरावेधनं, सिरावेधनं, शिरावेधः, शिरावेधनविद्या, शिराछेदः -दनं, शिरामोक्षः -क्षणं, रक्तमोक्षणं, रक्तमोचनं, रक्तस्रावणं, असृक्स्रावः.

PHLEGM, *s.* कफः, श्लेष्मा *m.* (न्), श्लेष्मकः, क्लेदनः, क्लेदकः, शिङ्घाणकः, सिङ्घाणकः, सङ्घातः, लवनः, खटः, बलाशः, बलहा *m.* (न्), निद्रासञ्जननं.—(Dulness, coldness) जडता, जाड्यं, मन्दता, मान्द्यं.—(Removing phlegm) श्लेष्मघ्नः -घ्नी -घ्नं, कफनाशनः -ना -नं.

PHLEGMAGOGUE, *s.* श्लेष्मघ्नं, श्लेष्महः, कफनाशनं, कफसारकम् औषधं.

PHLEGMATIC, *a.* (Relating to phlegm) कफसम्बन्धी &c., श्लेष्मसम्बन्धी &c.—(Abounding in it, having it) श्लेष्मलः -ला -लं, श्लेष्मणः -णा -णं, श्लेष्मवान् -वती -वत् (त्), कफी -फिनी -फि (न्), कफेलूः -लूः -लु, कफमयः -यी -यं, कफप्रचुरः -रा -रं, बहुकफः -फा -फं.—(Generating or exciting it) कफकरः -री -रं, कफवर्धकः -का -कं, कफवर्धनः -नी -नं, कफजनकः &c., कफोत्पादकः &c., श्लैष्मिकः -की -कं, श्लेष्मजनकः &c.—(Proceeding from it) श्लेष्मजः -जा -जं.—(Dull, apathetic) जडः -डा -डं, जडप्रकृतिः -तिः -ति, जडस्वभावः -वा -वं, शीतप्रकृतिः &c., शीतः -ता -तं, मन्दः -न्दा -न्दं.

PHLEME, *s.* पशुसिरावेधनी, पशुरक्तमोक्षणयन्त्रं. *See* FLEAM.

PHŒNIX, *s.* कविकल्पितः स्वभस्मजन्मपक्षी *m.* (न्). *See* PHENIX.

PHONETIC, *a.* शाब्दिकः -की -कं, शाब्दः -ब्दी -ब्दं, यथाशब्दः -ब्दा -ब्दं, यथास्वरः -रा -रं, ध्वनिसम्बन्धी &c., स्वरसम्बन्धी &c., ध्वनिविषयकः -का -कं.

PHONETICS, PHONICS, *s.* ध्वनिविद्या, ध्वनिशास्त्रं, स्वरविद्या.

PHONOCAMPTIC, *a.* ध्वनिपरिवर्तकः -का -कं, ध्वनिपरिवर्तनकारी -रिणी &c.

PHOSPHOR, PHOSPHORUS, *s.* (In chemistry) प्रकाशदः.—(Morning star) प्रातर्नक्षत्रं, प्रातरुदितनक्षत्रं, शुक्रः.

PHRASE, *s.* (Short sentence) वाक्यं, वाक् *f.* (च्), उक्तिः *f.*, उक्तं, वचनं.—(Particular mode of speech) विशेषवाक्यं, वाक्यविशेषः, वाक्यप्रकारः, वाक्यभेदः, वाग्व्यापारः, वाग्रीतिः *f.*, वाग्व्यवहारः, वाग्धारा, भाषणसम्प्रदायः, भाषणपर्यायः, भाषणप्रकारः.

PHRASEOLOGY, *s.* वाग्व्यापारः, वाग्रीतिः *f.*, वाक्यरीतिः *f.*, वाग्व्यवहारः, वाग्वृत्तिः *f.*, वाक्यपर्यायः, भाषणपर्यायः, वाक्यरचना, शब्दरचना, उक्तिपर्यायः, उक्तिव्यापारः, उक्तिः *f.*; 'dramatic phraseology,' नाट्योक्तिः *f.*

PHRENETIC, *a.* उन्मत्तः -त्ता -त्तं, सोन्मादः -दा -दं. *See* FRANTIC.

PHRENITIS, PHRENSY, *s.* (In medicine) सन्निपातज्वरः.—(Madness) उन्मादः, सम्मादः, उन्मादवायुः *m.*

PHRENOLOGY, *s.* कपाललक्षणविद्या, कपालविद्या, कपालसामुद्रिकं.

PHTHISIC, *s.* (Dyspnœa) श्वासावरोधः, श्वासकृच्छ्रं, दुःश्वासः.

PHTHISICAL, *a.* क्षयरोगी -गिणी -गि (न्), क्षयी -यिणी -यि (न्), श्वासावरोधविशिष्टः -ष्टा -ष्टं, श्वासकृच्छ्रविशिष्टः &c., दुःश्वासी &c.

PHTHISIS, *s.* क्षयः, क्षयरोगः, क्षयथुः *m.*, कफक्षयः, यक्ष्मा *m.* (न्), जक्ष्मा *m.*, यक्ष्मरोगः, राजयक्ष्मा *m.*, रोगराजः. *See* CONSUMPTION.

PHYLACTERY, *s.* रक्षणी, कवचः -चं, रक्षणलिपिः *f.*

PHYSIC, *s.* (Art of healing diseases) चिकित्सा -त्सनं, वैद्यकं, वैद्यकर्म्म *n.* (न्), वैद्यक्रिया, वैद्योपचारः, उपचारः, उपचार्य्यः, उपचर्य्या, औषधोपचारः, औषधप्रयोगः, भेषजप्रयोगः, रुक्प्रतिक्रिया.—(Medicine) औषधं, भेषजं, भैषजं -ज्यं, अगदः.

To PHYSIC, *v. a.* औषधं दा, भेषजं दा, कित् in des. (चिकित्सति -त्सितुं), भिषज् (nom. भिषज्यति), उपचर् (c. 1. -चरति -रितुं), औषधप्रयोगं कृ, औषधोपचारं कृ, उपचारं कृ.

PHYSICAL, *a.* (Pertaining to natural or material things as opposed to moral) साकारपदार्थसम्बन्धी &c., साकारवस्तुसम्बन्धी &c., साकारपदार्थरूपः -पा -पं, साकारद्रव्यरूपः &c., स्थूलपदार्थसम्बन्धी &c., स्थूलपदार्थरूपः &c., सिद्धपदार्थसम्बन्धी &c., साकारः -रा -रं, स्थूलः -ला -लं, जडः -डा -डं; 'physical force,' आक्रबलं, साकारद्रव्यबलं, जडबलं; 'physical substance,' साकारवस्तु *n.*, साकारद्रव्यं, स्थूलवस्तु *n.*, स्थूलपदार्थः, अनात्मीयद्रव्यं. *See* MATERIAL.—(Medicinal). *See* the word.

PHYSICALLY, *adv.* स्वभावतस्, स्वभावेन -वात्, भावतस्, प्रकृतितस्, प्रकृत्या, जन्मतस्, जातितस्. *See* NATURALLY.

PHYSICIAN, *s.* चिकित्सकः, वैद्यः, भिषक् *m.* (ज्), चिकित्साजीवी *m.* (न्), भिषग्वृत्त्युपजीवी *m.*, रोगज्ञानकः, रोगहृत् *m.*, रोगहारी *m.*, रोगहा *m.* (न्), अगदङ्कारः, आयुर्वेदी *m.*, आयुर्वेददृक् *m.* (श्), दोषज्ञः, प्राणाचार्य्यः. The physician of the gods is धन्वन्तरिः or काशिराजः. The twin sons of अश्विनी, called अश्विनौ, आश्विनेयौ, अश्विनीकुमारौ, अश्विनीपुत्रौ, अश्विनीसुतौ, are also physicians of heaven.

Hence some of the following names for an eminent physician: धन्वन्तरिः *m.*, अश्विनीकुमारः, अश्विनीपुत्रः, राजवैद्यः, शतमारी *m.* (न्).

PHYSICKED, *p. p.* चिकित्सितः -ता -तं, कृतोपचारः -रा -रं.

PHYSICS, *s. pl.* साकारपदार्थविज्ञानं, स्थूलपदार्थविज्ञानं, साकारपदार्थविद्या, साकारपदार्थशास्त्रं, पदार्थविज्ञानं, सिद्धपदार्थविज्ञानं.

PHYSIOGNOMIST, *s.* मुखलक्षणज्ञः, मुखलक्षणविद् *m.*, मुखसामुद्रिकः.

PHYSIOGNOMY, *s.* (Art of discerning the character from the features) मुखलक्षणनिरूपणविद्या, मुखलक्षणनिरूपणात् स्वभावपरिच्छेदः. —(Countenance) मुखं, वदनं, आननं, आस्यं, वक्त्रं.

PHYSIOLOGIC, PHYSIOLOGICAL, *a.* प्राणिधर्म्मगुणविद्यासम्बन्धी &c., प्राणिधर्म्मगुणविद्याविषयकः -का -कं.

PHYSIOLOGIST, *s.* प्राणिधर्म्मगुणविद्याज्ञः, प्राणिधर्म्मगुणवेत्ता *m.* (तृ).

PHYSIOLOGY, *s.* प्राणिधर्म्मगुणविद्या, प्राणिधर्म्मगुणज्ञानं, प्राणिधर्म्मगुणशास्त्रं, जन्तुगुणधर्म्मविद्या, द्रव्यतत्त्वज्ञानं.

PIACULAR, PIACULOUS, *a.* प्रायश्चित्तकारी-रिणी-रि(न्), अयनाशकः-का-कं.

PIA-MATER, *s.* मस्तिष्कावरणत्वक् *f.* (च्), मस्तिष्कावरणं.

PIANO, *s.* (In music) मन्दं.—(A kind of instrument) तन्त्रीकवाद्यविशेषः.

PIAZZA, *s.* स्तम्भपंक्तिप्रान्तितो मण्डपपथः or मण्डपस्य छन्नपथः.

PICAROON, *s.* समुद्रयायी दस्युविशेषः or अपहारकविशेषः.

To PICK, *v. a.* (Gather by plucking) अङ्गुलिभिर् ग्रह् (c. 9. गृह्णाति, ग्रहीतुं) or आदा (c. 3. -ददाति -दत्ते -दातुं) or चि (c. 5. चिनोति, चेतुं) or अवचि or लू or छिद्; 'he picks a branch from the tree,' वृक्षपल्लवम् आदत्ते.—(Clean with the teeth or claws) दन्तैः or नखैः or अङ्गुलिभिः शुध् or मृज् or परिष्कृ.—(Pick a bone) अस्थिमांसम् दन्तैर् उत्कृष् (c. 1. -कर्षति -क्रष्टुं) or निष्कृष् or चर्व् (c. 1. चर्वति -र्वितुं), अस्थिपरिष्कारं कृ, अस्थिशोधनं कृ.—(Cull, select) उद्धृ (c. 1. -हरति -हर्त्तुं), समुद्धृ, उद्ग्रह्, वृ, उद्धृ, चूर्णिं कृ.—(Separate with the fingers) अङ्गुलिभिः पृथक्कृ or खण्डीकृ.—(Pick off) प्रत्येकं or एकैकशो हृ or उद्धृ, पृथक् पृथग् उद्धृ.—(Pick out, select) उद्धृ, समुद्धृ.—(Pick out, pluck out) उत्पट् (c. 10. -पाटयति -यितुं), उल्लुप् (c. 1. -लुपति -पितुं), उद्धृ, समुद्धृ, उत्कृष्, उद्धरणं कृ.—(Pick up) उद्धृ, समुद्धृ, आदा, ग्रह्, उद्ग्रह्, प्रतिग्रह्, उत्था in caus. (-थापयति -यितुं, rt. स्था), समुत्था.—(Pick the ear) कर्णशोधनं कृ, कर्णनिर्घर्षणं कृ.—(Pick the nose) नासाशोधनं कृ, नासानिर्घर्षणं कृ.—(Pick the teeth) दन्तशोधनं कृ, दन्तनिर्घर्षणं कृ.—(Pick the pocket) कोषस्थद्रव्यं छलेन अपहृ or हृ, कोषं छित्त्वा तत्रस्थद्रव्यम् अपहृ.—(Pick holes) छिद्रान्वेषणं कृ.

To PICK, *v. n.* (Eat by morsels) अल्पाल्पशः or अल्पखण्डशः खाद्.

PICK, *s.* (Axe) पाषाणदारणः. *See* the next.—(Choice) उद्धारः, उद्धरणं, उद्धरणाधिकारः, वरणाधिकारः, विकल्पः -ल्पकः.

PICK-AXE, *s.* पाषाणदारणः, पाषाणभेदनी, टङ्कः, शैलभित्तिः *f.*, शिलाकुट्टकः, खनित्रं.

PICKED, *p. p.* उद्धृतः -ता -तं, उद्गृहीतः &c., वृतः &c., परिगणितः &c.

PICKET, *s.* सेनायाः पुरतः स्थापितं रक्षकदलं, सञ्चनं, उपरक्षणं, सेनारक्षः. —(Stake) शङ्कुः *m.*, शल्यं.

PICKING, *s.* (Plucking, selecting) ग्रहणं, अङ्गुलिभिर् ग्रहणं, उद्ग्रहणं, उद्धारः, उद्धरणं.—(Stealing) अपहारः, अपहरणं, क्षुद्रद्रव्यहरणं.—(Extra gain) अधिकलाभः, अधिकप्राप्तिः *f.*, अवान्तरलाभः.

PICKLE, *s.* (Vegetable, &c., pickled) सन्धितं, सन्धानं, लवणशाकः, सन्धितशाकः, लवणितशाकः.—(Brine) लवणोदं, लवणं.—(State of difficulty) दुर्दशा, दुर्गतिः *f.*, दुरवस्था.

To PICKLE, *v. a.* सन्धा (c. 3. -दधाति -धातुं), सन्धितं -तां कृ, लवणीकृ, लवण (nom. लवणयति -यितुं), सलवणीकृ, उपस्कृ.

PICKLED, *p. p.* सन्धितः -ता -तं, लवणितः-ता-तं, लवणीकृतः &c., उपस्कृतः &c.

PICK-POCKET, *s.* कोषच्छेदकः, कोषस्थद्रव्यापहारकः, ग्रन्थिच्छेदकः, चिल्लाभः.

PIC-NIC, *s.* वनभोजनं, अरण्यभोजनं, गणभोजनं.

PICTORIAL, *a.* (Pertaining to pictures) चित्रसम्बन्धी &c., चित्रलेखासम्बन्धी &c.—(Illustrated by pictures) सचित्रः -त्रा -त्रं, चित्रयुक्तः -क्ता -क्तं, चित्रलिखितः -ता -तं.

PICTURE, *s.* चित्रं, चित्रलेखा, चित्रलिखितं, आलेख्यं, प्रतिमा -मानं, चित्रफलकः, प्रतिकृतिः *f.*, प्रतिरूपं, प्रतिच्छाया, प्रतिच्छन्दकं, प्रतिबिम्बं, बिम्बः -म्बं, कर्बुरीकः, प्रतिनिधिः *m.*, प्रतियातना; 'represented in a picture,' आलिखितः -ता -तं; 'immoveable as in a picture,' आलिखित इव निश्चलः.

To PICTURE, *v. a.* (Paint a resemblance) चित्र् (c. 10. चित्रयति -यितुं), आलिख् (c. 6. -लिखति -लेखितुं), लिख्, चित्रं लिख्, वर्ण् (c. 10. वर्णयति -यितुं), बिम्ब (nom. बिम्बयति -यितुं), प्रतिबिम्ब, प्रतिमानं कृ, आलेख्यं कृ.—(Figure to one's self mentally) मनसा क्लृप् or संक्लृप् or भू (c. 10. भावयति -यितुं) or विभू.

PICTURED, *p. p.* or *a.* चित्रगतः -ता -तं, चित्रसंस्थः -स्था -स्थं, आलिखितः -ता -तं, चित्रलिखितः &c., आलेख्यसमर्पितः &c., चित्रसमर्पितः &c., बिम्बितः &c., प्रतिबिम्बितः &c., बिम्बागतः &c.—(In the mind) मनसा कल्पितः -ता -तं.

PICTURE-FRAME, *s.* चित्रावरणकाष्ठं, चित्रपरिगतकाष्ठं, चित्रावरणं.

PICTURE-GALLERY, *s.* चित्रशाला, चित्ररक्षणशाला, आलेख्यशाला.

PICTURE-MAKER, *s.* चित्रकरः, चित्रकारः, चित्रकृत् *m.*, चित्रकर्म्मी *m.* (न्).

PICTURESQUE, *s.* (Like a picture) चित्रसदृशः -शी -शं, चित्रोपमः -मा -मं, चित्रलेखातुल्यः -ल्या -ल्यं.—(Diversified with hill, dale, wood, &c.) आकुलः -ली -लं, सङ्कुलः -ला -लं, पर्व्वतवननदीमिश्रितः &c., पर्व्वतनदीवनादिमिश्रितः &c.

To PIDDLE, *v. n.* (Deal in trifles). *See To* PEDDLE.—(Make water, as a child) बालकवद् मूत्रं कृ or मूत्रोत्सर्गं कृ, मूत्र् (c. 10. मूत्रयति -यितुं).

PIE, *s.* शष्कुली; 'number of pies,' शाष्कुलिकं.

PIEBALD, *a.* नानावर्णः -र्णा -र्णं, नानारङ्गः -ङ्गा -ङ्गं, शबलः -ला -लं, कर्बुरः -रा -रं, चित्राङ्गः -ङ्गी -ङ्गं, चित्रविचित्रः -त्रा -त्रं; 'piebald horse,' हलाहः -हा, हालाहः -हा.

PIECE, *s.* (Fragment, part separated from the whole) खण्डः -ण्डं -खण्डकः, लवः, अंशः, भागः, शकलः -लं, भिन्नं, भित्तं, भित्तिः *f.*, दलं, विदलं; 'in pieces,' खण्डशस्, खण्डं खण्डं, लवशस्, भागशस्; 'to break in pieces,' खण्डशः कृ, खण्डं खण्डं कृ, लवशः कृ, विदलीकृ, शकलीकृ, लवशः खण्ड् (c. 10. खण्डयति -यितुं); 'in many pieces,' बहुखण्डशः कृ, बहुलवशः कृ; 'in a hundred pieces,' शतखण्डशः कृ; 'to fall to pieces,' विदल् (c. 1. -दलति -लितुं), विदलीभू; 'broken in a hundred pieces,' शतचूर्णः -र्णा -र्णं.—(Part of any thing) भागः, अंशः, विभागः, खण्डः -ण्डकः, अङ्गं; 'piece of wood,' काष्ठखण्डः; 'piece of cloth,' वस्त्रखण्डः.—(Separate composition or performance) रचना, प्रबन्धः, बन्धः or expressed by the word itself; as, 'a piece of poetry,' काव्यरचना, काव्यबन्धः, काव्यप्रबन्धः, कविता; 'piece of work,' कर्म्म *n.* (न्), कर्म्मप्रबन्धः.—(Piece of money) मुद्रा; 'gold piece,'

सुवर्णमुद्रा.—(Piece of water) सलिलराशिः m., जलराशिः m., पयश्चयः, जलगुल्मः, जलाधारः, वारिधारः -रं.—(Piece at chess, &c.) शारः -रिः m. -रिका, सारिः m. -री f. -रिका, सारः, खेलनी, नरः, नयः, शतुरूत्रकः.—(A piece to each) प्रत्येकं, एकैकशस्, पृथक् पृथक्.—(Of a piece, of the same sort) एकप्रकारः -रा -रं.—(Of a piece with) सदृशः -शी -शं, अनुरूपः -पा -पं.—(Of a piece, without juncture) अखण्डः -ण्डा -ण्डं.

To PIECE, *v. a.* सन्धा (c. 3. -दधाति -धत्ते -धातुं), समाधा, संयुज् (c. 7. -युनक्ति -युंक्ते -योक्तुं), अधिकखण्डं निविश् (c. 10. -वेशयति -यितुं). *See To* PATCH.

PIECED, *p. p.* सन्धितः -ता -तं, कृतसन्धिः -न्धिः -न्धि, सखण्डः -ण्डा -ण्डं.

PIECELESS, *a.* अखण्डः -ण्डा -ण्डं, खण्डहीनः -ना -नं, खण्डरहितः -ता -तं.

PIECEMEAL, *adv.* खण्डशस्, खण्डं खण्डं, खण्डशः खण्डशः, लवशस्, अंशतस्, भागशस्, विभागशस्, भागतस्, अंशांशि, पृथक्.

PIECEMEAL, *a.* खण्डी -ण्डिनी -ण्डि (न्), भागी &c., अंशी &c.

PIED, *a.* नानावर्णः -र्णा -र्णं, शबलः -ला -लं, चित्रितः -ता -तं, चित्राङ्गः -ङ्गी -ङ्गं, कर्बुरितः &c., चित्रविचित्रः -त्रा -त्रं.

PIER, *s.* (Mole, projecting into the sea) समुद्रीयसेतुः m., सेतुः m., सेतुबन्धः.—(Support of a bridge, &c.) स्तम्भः, उपस्तम्भः, स्थूणा.

To PIERCE, *v. a.* (Penetrate, enter) व्यध् (c. 4. विध्यति, व्यद्धुं), प्रतिव्यध्, परिव्यध्, प्रविश्, निविश्, छिद्र्, भिद्, निर्भिद्, छिद्, निखन्, वेधनं कृ, व्यधनं कृ, रन्ध्रं कृ, शुषिरीकृ.

To PIERCE, *v. n.* (Enter) प्रविश्, निविश्, आविश्, विश्, प्रवेशं कृ.

PIERCED, *p. p.* विद्धः -द्धा -द्धं, वेधितः -ता -तं, अपविद्धः &c., छिद्रितः -ता -तं, भिन्नः -न्ना -न्नं, निर्भिन्नः &c., छिन्नः &c.; 'pierced through the heart,' भिन्नहृदयः -या -यं; 'having the ears pierced,' विद्धकर्णः -र्णा -र्णं, छिद्रकर्णः &c.; 'pierced by an arrow,' शरविद्धः &c., बाणनिकृत्तः -त्ता -त्तं.

PIERCER, *s.* वेधकः, वेधी m. (न्), भेदकः, छेदकः, वेधनकृत्.—(Instrument) वेधनिका, वेधनी.

PIERCING, *s.* वेधः -धनं, व्यधः -धनं, भेदनं, निर्भेदः, छेदः -दनं, सूचिः f., सूचनं -ना, सूचा; 'in the wrong direction,' अपवेधः.

PIERCING, *part.* or *a.* वेधकः -का -कं, वेधी -धिनी -धि (न्), भेदकः -का -कं, भेदी &c., सूची &c., सूचकः -का -कं, छेदकः &c., छेदी &c., प्रवेशकः -का -कं, भिद् or छिद् in comp.; 'piercing the heart,' हृदयभिद् *m. f. n.*, हृदयभेदी &c.

PIERCINGNESS, *s.* वेधकत्वं, भेदकत्वं, वेधिता, प्रवेशकत्वं.

PIETISM, *s.* धर्म्माभिमानं, भक्त्यभिमानं, साधुम्मन्यता.

PIETIST, *s.* धर्म्माभिमानी m. (न्), भक्त्यभिमानी m., साधुम्मन्यः.

PIETY, *s.* ईश्वरभक्तिः f., परमेश्वरभक्तिः f., देवभक्तिः f., भगवद्भक्तिः f., धर्म्मः -र्म्मत्वं, धर्म्मनिष्ठा, धर्म्मासक्तिः f., धर्म्मशीलता, धर्म्मपरता, धर्म्मनिबन्धः, धर्म्मपरायणबुद्धिः f., धर्म्मसेवा, ईश्वरसेवा, ईश्वरनिष्ठा, भक्तिः f., भक्तता -त्वं, भक्तिपरायणबुद्धिः f., पुण्यता, ईश्वरपूजा, परमेश्वरपूजा, देवपूजा, पूजा, पवित्रता -त्वं, शुचिता -त्वं, ब्रह्मण्यता, सौजन्यं; 'eminent in piety,' धर्म्मप्रधानः -ना -नं; 'path of piety,' भक्तिमार्गः.—(Reverence of parents, &c.) मातापितृभक्तिः f. -भक्तता, मातापितृसेवा, पुत्रधर्म्मः, अपत्यधर्म्मः.

PIG, *s.* शूकरशावकः, सूकरशावकः, शूकरः, सूकरः, ग्राम्यशूकरः, ग्राम्यः, गृहशूकरः, गृहसूकरः, पङ्कक्रीडः, बहुप्रजः, विट्चरः. *See* HOG.—(Of metal) कुशी, लोहपिण्डः -ण्डं, असंस्कृतलोहपिण्डः.

To PIG, *v. a.* शूकरशावकान् सु (c. 2. सूते, c. 4. सूयते, सोतुं) or प्रसु or जन्.

PIG-IRON, *s.* असंस्कृतलोहः, अशोधितलोहः, आकरीयलोहः.

PIGEON, *s.* कपोतः, पारावतः, पारवतः, पारापतः, कलरवः, कपोतिका, गृहनाशनः, धूम्रलोचनः, कोकदेवः, अग्रगामी m. (न्), रक्तदृक् m. (श्), मिश्रीकण्ठः; 'domestic pigeon,' गृहकपोतः, गृहकपोतः; 'wood-pigeon,' हारितः, हारीतः.

PIGEON-HEARTED, *a.* हरिणहृदयः -या -यं, भीरुहृदयः &c., चकितहृदयः &c.

PIGEON-HOLE, *s.* कपोतविवरं, कपोतबिलं, कपोतरन्ध्रं.

PIGEON-HOUSE, PIGEON-COT, *s.* कपोतपालिका, कपोतपाली, कपोतगृहं, कपोतालयः -यं, कपोतागारः -रं, पारावतालयः, विटङ्कः.

PIGGERY, *s.* शूकरालयः -यं, शूकरगृहं, शूकरपालिका, शूकरावरणं.

PIGGISH, *a.* सौकरः -री -रं, सूकरोपमः -मा -मं, शूकरसदृशः -शी -शं.

PIG-HEADED, *a.* स्थूलमस्तकः -का -कं, स्थूलशिराः -राः -रः (स्), स्थूलः &c.

PIGMENT, *s.* वर्णकः -का, वर्णः, रङ्गः. *See* PAINT.

PIGMY, *s.* वामनः, वामनमूर्त्तिः m., खर्वः, ह्रस्वमूर्त्तिः m.

PIGMY, PIGMEAN, *a.* वामनशरीरः -रा -रं, अल्पमूर्त्तिः -र्त्तिः -र्त्ति, अल्पतनुः -नुः -नु.

PIG-STY, *s.* शूकरालयः -यं, शूकरगृहं, शूकरस्थानं, शूकरागारं.

PIG-TAIL, *s.* अवटुजः, शूकरपुच्छाकारेण रचितः पश्चाद्ग्रीवाकेशः, पुच्छवत् पृष्ठतो लम्बमानः केशपाशः.

PIKE, *s.* (Weapon) शूलः -लं, प्रासः, शल्यं, शक्तिः f., कीलः, शङ्कुः m., कुन्तः -न्ती, सर्मिका, कोटिः f., परिघः; 'for driving an elephant,' तोत्रं, वैणुकं.—(The fish) जलसूचिः m.

PIKEMAN, *s.* शूली m. (न्), शूलधरः, शूलधारी m. (न्), शूलपाणिः m., शक्तिग्रहः, शक्तिधरः, शाक्तीकः, कौन्तिकः, प्रासिकः.

PIKE-STAFF, *s.* शूलदण्डः -ण्डं, प्रासदण्डः, शक्तिदण्डः, कुन्तदण्डः.

PILASTER, *s.* चतुष्कोणस्तम्भः, चतुष्कोणाकृतिर् अर्द्धस्तम्भः.

PILE, *s.* (Heap) राशिः m., चयः, सञ्चयः, निचयः, चितिः f., उत्करः, प्रकरः, निकरः, पुञ्जः, ओघः, स्तूपः, स्तोमः, समवायः, समूहः, वायः.—(Funeral pile) चितिः f., चिता, चित्या, स्तूपः, कूपकः, काष्ठमठी, मुः m.—(Stake for support) स्थूणा, स्थाणुः m., स्तम्भः, उपस्तम्भः, शङ्कुः m., कीलः.—(Edifice) हर्म्यं, महामन्दिरं, महागृहं, महाभावनं, बृहन्मन्दिरं, बृहद्धर्म्यं.—(Disease). *See* PILES.

To PILE, *v. a.* (Heap) राशीकृ, आचि, समाचि, सञ्चि, समाक्षिप् &c.

PILED, *p. p.* राशीकृतः -ता -तं, राशीभूतः &c., चितः &c., उपरिचितः &c. *See* HEAPED.

PILES, *s. pl.* (Disease) अर्शस् *n.*, अर्शः, अर्शोरोगः, गुदरोगः, गुदाङ्कुरः, गुदकीलः, मूलव्याधिः m., अर्सस् *n.*; 'having them,' अर्शी -र्शिनी -र्शि (न्), अर्शोरोगी -गिणी &c., अर्शोरोगयुतः -ता -तं; 'destroying them,' अर्शोघ्नः -घ्नी -घ्नं.

To PILFER, *v. a.* and *n.* मुष् (c. 9. मुष्णाति, मोषितुं), परिमुष्, प्रमुष्, अल्पाल्पं चुर् (c. 10. चोरयति -यितुं) or अपहृ (c. 1. -हरति -हर्त्तुं).

PILFERED, *p. p.* अल्पाल्पशो मूषितः -ता -तं or अपहृतः -ता -तं.

PILFERER, *s.* मोषकः, मूषकः, मूषिकः, आमोषी m. (न्), मोषी m., मुमुषिषुः m., अल्पचौर्य्यकृत्, अल्पस्तेयकृत् m., धनहरी m. (न्), धनहारी m., चौरः, पार्श्विकः.

PILFERING, *s.* मूषणं, मोषा -षणं, मुषिः f., मुष्टं, अल्पचौर्य्यं, अल्पस्तेयं.

PIL-GARLIC, PILLED-GARLIC, *s.* तपस्वी m. (न्), हताशः, गलितकेशः.

PILGRIM, *s.* यात्रिकः, तीर्थयात्रिकः, तीर्थसेवी m. -विनी f. (न्), कार्पटिकः, यात्राकारी m. (न्), यात्राकृत्, उदासीनः, सार्थिकः, पथिकः; 'a company of pilgrims,' यात्रा, सार्थः, यात्रिकसंघः.

PILGRIMAGE, *s.* यात्रा, तीर्थयात्रा, यात्राप्रसङ्गः, तीर्थगमनं, तीर्थाटनं, तीर्थसेवा -वनं; 'setting out on a pilgrimage,' यात्राकरणं; 'place of pilgrimage,' तीर्थः -र्थं, पुण्यतीर्थं, वरदानं, गोपीर्थं, समवतारः, प्रायणः; 'the great place of pilgrimage, or Benares,' तीर्थराजी; 'pilgrimage to it,' महायात्रा; 'to the Ganges,' गङ्गायात्रा; 'ceremonies to be observed at a place of pilgrimage,' तीर्थविधिः *m.*; 'favors granted by the idol at a place of pilgrimage, consisting of flowers, ashes, holy water, &c.,' तीर्थप्रसादः.

PILL, *s.* गुली, गुलिका, गुटिका, वटः -टी, वटिका; 'magical pill, by putting which in the mouth a person has the power of ascending to heaven,' विद्या.

To PILLAGE, PILL, *v. a.* लुण्ठ् (c. 1. लुण्ठति -ण्ठितुं), रुण्ठ्, लुण्ट्, रुण्ट्, लुण्ड्, धनद्रव्यादि हृ (c. 1. हरति, हर्त्तुं), अपहृ, अभिहृ, लुण्ठनं कृ, लुण्टनं कृ, विलुप् (c. 6. -लुम्पति -लोप्तुं), लुप्, कल् (c. 10. कालयति -यितुं), प्रकल्.

PILLAGE, *s.* लुण्ठनं, लुण्ठा, लुण्टनं, लुण्टा, अपहारः, हरणं, लोप्त्रं, लोत्रं, लोतः -तं, लुप्तं, अभिग्रहः, धनापहारः.

PILLAGER, *s.* अपहारकः, अपहारी *m.* (न्), हारकः, लुण्टाकः, लुण्टनकृत्.

PILLAR, *s.* स्तम्भः, अवष्टम्भः -म्भनं, उपस्तम्भः -म्भनं, स्थूणा, सूर्म्मिः *f.* -र्म्मी, शूर्म्मिः *f.* -र्म्मी, यूपः -पं, यष्टिः *m. f.*; 'of a house,' गृहस्तम्भः, गृहस्थूणा, गृहमेधीयान् *m.* (स्); 'main pillar of a house,' मूलस्तम्भः.

PILLORY, *s.* हडिः *m.*, अपराधिनो हस्तमस्तकादिबन्धनार्थं काष्ठयन्त्रं.

PILLOW, *s.* उपधानं -नीयं, उपबर्हः, बालिशं, उच्छीर्षकं, उपस्तम्भः, गण्डुः *m. f.*, चातुरः, गल्लचातुरी, मसुरालिकः; 'a round pillow,' चक्रगण्डुः.

PILLOW-CASE, *s.* उपधानावेष्टनं, उपधानाच्छादनं, बालिशवेष्टनं, बालिशकोशः, उपधानकोशः.

PILLOWED, *p. p.* or *a.* उपहितः -ता -तं, आलम्बितः &c., उपधानालम्बितः &c.

PILOSE, PILOUS, *a.* लोमशः -शा -शं, रोमशः &c., बहुलोमा -मा -म (न्).

PILOSITY, *s.* लोमशत्वं, रोमशत्वं, लोमप्राचुर्य्यं, लोमबाहुल्यं.

PILOT, *s.* कर्णधारः, कर्णधारी *m.* (न्), कर्णग्राहः, कर्णिकः, कर्णी *m.*, नाविकः, समुद्रमार्गप्रदर्शकः, समुद्रपथदर्शकः, नौकावाहकः.—(Guide) मार्गदर्शकः.

To PILOT, *v. a.* कर्णेन or कर्णिकवद् नावम् आनी (c. 1. -नयति -नेतुं) or वह् (c. 10. वाहयति -यितुं), नौमार्गं दृश् (c. 10. दर्शयति -यितुं), नौपथं दृश्, नौकानयनं कृ, नौकावाहनं कृ, नौमार्गदर्शनं कृ.

PILOTAGE, *s.* कर्णधारवेतनं, कर्णग्राहवेतनं, कर्णिकवेतनं, कर्णिकमूल्यं.

PIMP, *s.* विटः, कुट्टाशी *m.* (न्), रतताली *m.* (न्), सुरतताली *m.*, सञ्चारकः, रतोपकारी *m.*, रतप्रवर्त्तकः, रतसम्पादकः, सुरतप्रवर्त्तकः.

To PIMP, *v. n.* विटवृत्तिं कृ or अनुष्ठा (c. 1. -तिष्ठति -ष्ठातुं), रतोपकारी भू.

PIMPLE, *s.* रक्तस्फोटः -टकः, क्षुद्रस्फोटः, सूक्ष्मस्फोटः, रक्तपिडकः, तनुव्रणः, सूक्ष्मव्रणः, क्षुद्रव्रणः, गण्डः, रक्तगण्डः, सूक्ष्मगण्डः, अवगण्डः, वरण्डः -ण्डकः, कच्छपिका, रक्तवरटी, रक्तवटी, पिडकः -का, नरङ्गः, मुखगण्डः, इरावेल्लिका.

PIMPLED, PIMPLY, *a.* सस्फोटः -टा -टं, रक्तस्फोटपूर्णः -र्णा -र्णं, तनुव्रणवान् -वती -वत् (त्), रक्तवटीपूर्णः &c., व्रणी -णिनी -णि (न्), दद्रुणः -णा -णं, दद्रूणः &c.

PIN, *s.* कीलः -लकः, शलाका, सूक्ष्मकीलकः, शङ्कुः *m.*, शल्यं.—(Peg, bolt) कीलः -लकः, शङ्कुः *m.*, अर्गलं, अपलं, अपलः, वर्कुटः.—(Of a carriage, axle) अक्षाग्रकीलः -लकः, अक्षाग्रशङ्कुः *m.*, अक्षाग्रशलाका, अणिः *m.*—(Trifle, pin's head) वालाग्रं.

To PIN, *v. a.* कील् (c. 10. कीलयति -यितुं), कीलकेन बन्ध् (c. 9. बध्नाति, बन्द्धुं).

PINAFORE, *s.* अग्रमलग्रवस्त्रं, बालकैर् भृतं वक्षस्स्थलछादनयोग्यम् उत्तरीयवस्त्रं, मलनिवारणयोग्यम् उत्तरवस्त्रं.

PINCERS, *s. pl.* सन्दंशः -शकं, सन्दंशिका, कङ्कमुखं.

To PINCH, *v. a.* (With the fingers) अङ्गुलिभिः or अङ्गुल्यग्रैः or अग्राङ्गुलिभिः पीड् (c. 10. पीडयति -यितुं) or सम्पीड्, अङ्गुलिसङ्कोचेन पीड् or सम्पीड्, कूर्चं कृ, सम्पीडनं कृ.—(Gripe) सङ्ग्रह्, मुष्टिना सङ्ग्रह्, मुष्टिसङ्ग्राहेण पीड्, सङ्ग्राहं कृ.—(Straiten, distress) पीड्, बाध् (c. 1. बाधते -धितुं), सम्बाध्, सङ्कुच् (c. 1. -कोचति -चितुं), संहृ (c. 1. -हरति -हर्त्तुं), सङ्कटीकृ, क्लिश् (c. 9. क्लिश्नाति, क्लेशितुं), मथ् (c. 1. मथति -थितुं), संघट्ट् (c. 1. -घट्टते -ट्टितुं), आर्त्तीकृ, आर्त्तं -र्त्तां कृ.—(Pinch with cold) शीतेन पीड्, शीतार्त्तीकृ.

PINCH, *s.* कूर्चः -र्चं, अङ्गुल्यग्रैः पीडनं or सम्पीडनं or पीडा, सङ्ग्राहः, सङ्ग्रहणं, ग्रहः, अङ्गुलिसङ्कोचः -चनं.—(Of snuff) नस्यकूर्चः -र्चं, नस्यचूर्णकूर्चः -र्चं.—(Strait, distress) बाधा -धनं, सम्बाधनं, सङ्कटं, कष्टं.

PINCHED, *p. p.* पीडितः -ता -तं, सम्पीडितः &c., अङ्गुलिसङ्कोचपीडितः &c., अङ्गुलिपीडितः &c., अग्राङ्गुलिपीडितः &c., बाधितः -ता -तं, सम्बाधितः &c., सङ्कुचितः &c., मथितः &c., घट्टितः &c., क्लिष्टः -ष्टा -ष्टं, क्लेशितः -ता -तं, आर्त्त in comp.; 'with cold,' हिमार्त्तः -र्त्ता -र्त्तं, हिमपीडितः &c.

PINCH-FIST, *s.* दृढमुष्टिः *m.*, गाढमुष्टिः *m.*, बद्धमुष्टिः *m.*, अमुक्तहस्तः.

PINCUSHION, *s.* सूक्ष्मकीलकाधारः, सूक्ष्मशलाकाधारः, स्त्रीकीलकाधारः.

PINE, *s.* (The tree) सरलः, शरलः, देवदारुः -रु *m. n.*, पीतदारुः *m.*, दारु *n.* -रुकं, मर्म्मरः; 'juice of the pine,' सरलद्रवः -द्रवं.

To PINE, *v. n.* (Languish) ग्लै (c. 1. ग्लायति, ग्लातुं), परिग्लै, म्लै, परिम्लै, अवसद्, विषद्, व्यवसद्, सद्, तम्, आतम्, प्रतम्, क्षि in pass., खिद् in pass., म्ली, विषण्णीभू.—(Languish, with desire for) उत्कण्ठ्, उत्सुक.

PINE-APPLE, *s.* अननसः or अननासः may be used.

PINING, *s.* ग्लानिः *f.*, ग्लानता, अवसादः, विषादः, उत्कण्ठा.

PINING, *part.* ग्लायमानः -ना -नं, ग्लायन् -यन्ती -यत् (त्), म्लायमानः &c., क्षीयमानः &c., खिद्यमानः &c., विषादी -दिनी -दि (न्), अवसादितः -ता -तं, ग्लानः -ना -नं, क्षीणः -णा -णं.—(With desire) उत्कण्ठितः -ता -तं, उत्सुकः -का -कं, पर्य्युत्सुकः &c., उत्कः -त्का -त्कं.

PINION, *s.* (Wing) पक्षः.—(Joint of a wing) पक्षसन्धिः *m.*—(Fetters for the arms) बाहुबन्धः -न्धनं, बाहुपाशः.

To PINION, *v. a.* (Bind the wings) पक्षौ बन्ध् (c. 9. बध्नाति, बन्द्धुं), पक्षबन्धनं कृ.—(The arms) बाहू बन्ध्, बाहुबन्धनं कृ.

PINIONED, *p. p.* बद्धबाहुः -हुः -हु, बाहुबद्धः -द्धा -द्धं, बाहुबन्धनः -ना -नं, बद्धपक्षः -क्षा -क्षं, पक्षबद्धः &c.

PINK, *s.* (The color) पाटलः, पाटलवर्णः, पाटलरक्तः, श्वेतरक्तः.—(Pinnacle of perfection) अग्रं, शिखरं, सीमा.

PINK, *a.* (Of a pink color) पाटलः -ला -लं, पाटलवर्णः -र्णा -र्णं श्वेतरक्तः -क्ता -क्तं.

To PINK, *v. a.* व्यध् (c. 4. विध्यति, व्यद्धुं), छिद्र् (c. 10. छिद्रयति -यितुं), त्वक्छेदं कृ, त्वग्भेदं कृ, शुषिरीकृ.

PINK-EYED, *a.* गभनेत्रः -त्रा -त्री -त्रं, गननयनः -ना -नं, सूक्ष्मनयनः &c.

PIN-MAKER, *s.* शलाकाकारः, सूक्ष्मशलाकाकृत्, कीलककर्त्ता *m.* (र्तृ).

PIN-MONEY, *s.* स्त्रीधनं, स्त्रियाः स्ववस्त्राभ्यञ्जनादिक्रयणार्थं भर्त्तृदत्तं वार्षिकधनं.

PINNACE, *s.* क्षुद्रनौका, लघुनौका, अष्टदण्डचालिता नौका.

PINNACLE, *s.* शिखरं, गृहशिखरं, शृङ्गं, अग्रं, प्रासादशृङ्गं, प्रासादाग्रं, कलसः, वडभिः *f.*, शिखा, पृष्ठं, तल्पः, लासकः.

PINNED, *p. p.* कीलितः -ता -तं, कीलायितः &c., कीलकबद्धः -द्धा -द्धं.

PINT, *s.* अर्द्धकुडवः, द्रवद्रव्याणां परिमाणविशेषः.

PIONEER, *s.* पारम्पथः -थिकः, आटविकः, स्थाणुच्छेदकः, स्थाणुच्छिद् *m.*, स्तम्भच्छेदकः, स्तम्भापकर्षी *m.* (न्), मार्गशोधकः, सैन्यपथशोधकः.

To PIONEER, *s.* स्थाणुस्तम्भादिच्छेदेन सैन्यमार्गं शुध् (c. 10. शोधयति -यितुं), सैन्यमार्गशोधनार्थं स्थाणुस्तम्भादि छिद् (c. 7. छिनत्ति, छेत्तुं) or अपनी (c. 1. -नयति -नेतुं).

PIOUS, *a.* धार्म्मिकः -की -कं, धर्म्मशीलः -ला -लं, धर्म्मी -र्म्मिणी -र्म्मि (न्), धर्म्मात्मा -त्मा -त्म (न्), भक्तिमान् -मती -मत् (त्), ईश्वरभक्तिमान् &c., ईश्वरभक्तः -क्ता -क्तं, ईश्वरपूजकः -का -कं, पूजाशीलः &c., पूजकः -का -कं, पुण्यशीलः &c., पुण्यात्मा &c., भजनशीलः &c., ईश्वरसेवी &c., शुचिः -चिः -चि, शुचिव्रतः -ता -तं, व्रती &c., धर्म्मचारी &c., धर्म्मिष्ठः -ष्ठा -ष्ठं, ईश्वरमनस्कः -स्का -स्कं, पूजामनस्कः &c., ईश्वरपरायणः -णा -णं, देवपूजकः &c., देवभक्तिनिष्ठः &c., भक्तिनिष्ठः &c., धर्म्मनिष्ठः &c., भक्तिप्रवणः &c., धर्म्मप्रवणः &c., भक्तिपरायणः &c., धर्म्मनिबन्धी &c., परमार्थपरायणः &c., परमार्थी &c.; 'for pious purposes,' धर्म्मार्थं.—(Proceeding from piety) धर्म्मप्रयुक्तः -क्ता -क्तं, धर्म्ममूलकः -का -कं, भक्तिमूलकः &c., ईश्वरभक्तिमूलः -ला -लं.

PIOUSLY, *adv.* धार्म्मिकवत्, धर्म्मशीलत्वात्, ईश्वरभक्त्या, भक्त्या, पुण्यशीलत्वात्, पुण्यं, भक्तियुक्त्या, पूजाशीलत्वात्, देवपूजकवत्.

PIP, *s.* (Of fruit) बीजं, बीजकं.—(Spot) बिन्दुः *m.*, चिह्नं, अङ्कः.

To PIP, *v. n.* पक्षिशावकवत् कूज् (c. 1. कूजति -जितुं), कूजितं कृ.

PIPE, *s.* (Musical instrument) वंशः -शी, वेणुः *m.*, सानेयी -यिका, सानिका, मुरली, ध्वनिनाला, विवरनालिका, दर्दुरः, सुषिरं, नन्दः.—(Tube) नालः -लिः *f.* -ली -लं, नाडिः -डी *f.*, प्रणालिका, प्रणालः -ली, सुषिः *f.*—(Iron pipe) लोहनालः.—(Water pipe) सारणी -णिः *f.*, प्रणालः -ली -लिका.

To PIPE, *v. n.* (Play on a pipe) वंशीं or वेणुं ध्मा (c. 1. धमति, ध्मातुं) or प्रध्मा or वद् (c. 10. वादयति -यितुं) or प्रवद्.—(Cry) उच्चस्वरेण क्रुश् or क्रन्द् or रुद्.

PIPER, *s.* वेणुध्मः, वेणुवादः -दकः, वंशवादकः, वांशिकः, वंशीधरः.

PIPKIN, *s.* क्षुद्रभाण्डं, क्षुद्रपिठरः, क्षुद्रस्थाली.

PIQUANCY, *s.* उग्रता, कटुता, तिग्मता, तीव्रता, तीक्ष्णता, रसिकता, सरसत्वं.

PIQUANT, *a.* (Pungent) उग्रः -ग्रा -ग्रं, कटुः -टुः -टु, तिग्मः -ग्मा -ग्मं, तीक्ष्णः -क्ष्णा -क्ष्णं, खरः -रा -रं, प्रखरः -रा -रं, उष्णः -ष्णा -ष्णं, चण्डः -ण्डा -ण्डं.—(Seasoned, having flavor) सुसंस्कृतः -ता -तं, मिष्टः -ष्टा -ष्टं, सरसः -सा -सं, रसिकः -की -कं.

PIQUANTLY, *adv.* तीक्ष्णं, उग्रं, तिग्मं, प्रखरं, कटु, सरसं.

PIQUE, *s.* ईषत्कोपः, ईषद्वैरक्तं, ईषद्विरक्तिः *f.*, ईषद्रोषः, ईषद्वितुष्टिः.

To PIQUE, *v. a.* (Offend slightly) ईषत् कुप् (c. 10. कोपयति -यितुं) or प्रकुप् or रुष् (c. 10. रोषयति -यितुं), ईषत्कोपं or ईषद्वैरक्तं जन्.—(Stimulate, excite) उत्तप्, उत्तिज्, प्ररुच्, प्रवृत्, उत्सह्, प्रोत्सह्.—(Pique one's self) आत्मानं श्लाघ् (c. 1. श्लाघते -घितुं), अभिमन् (c. 4. -मन्यते -मन्तुं), विकत्थ् (c. 1. -कत्थते -त्थितुं); 'to pique one's self on one's learning,' पण्डितम्मन्यः -न्या -न्यं भू or अस्; 'on one's good looks,' दर्शनीयमानी &c. भू.

PIQUED, *p. p.* ईषत्कुपितः -ता -तं, ईषद्रुषितः &c., ईषद्विरक्तः -क्ता -क्तं.

PIQUET, *s.* सेनारक्षः -क्षकः, उपरक्षणं. *See* PICKET.

PIRACY, *s.* समुद्रीयचौर्य्यं, समुद्रीयलुण्ठनं, समुद्रीयापहारः, समुद्रीयापहरणं, समुद्रीयसाहसं, समुद्रीयस्तेयं, समुद्रीयदस्युत्वं.—(Of printed books, &c.) मुद्रितवागपहारः, ग्रन्थलिखितापहारः, वागपहरणं, मुद्रितशब्दचौर्य्यं.

PIRATE, *s.* समुद्रयायी दस्युः *m.*, समुद्रीयदस्युः *m.*, समुद्रगामी साहसिकः or अपहारकः or अपहारी, समुद्रीयसाहसिकः, समुद्रीयचौरः, समुद्रीयलुण्टाकः.—(Ship) साहसिकनौः *f.*, साहसिकनौका.—(Of printed books, &c.) मुद्रितवागपहारकः, ग्रन्थलिखितापहारी *m.* (न्), वागपहारकः, शब्दचोरः, मुद्रितशब्दचौरः, पुस्तकापहारी *m.*

To PIRATE, *v. a.* or *n.* अपहृ (c. 1. -हरति -हर्त्तुं), अभिहृ, लुण्ट् (c. 1. लुण्टति -ण्टितुं).

PIRATED, *p. p.* अपहृतः -ता -तं, अनधिकारपूर्व्वं हृतः -ता -तं.

PIRATICAL, *a.* साहसिकः -की -कं, साहसी -सिनी -सि (न्), अपहारकः -का -कं, साहसार्थकः -का -कं, अपहारार्थकः &c., साहसैकरसिकः -का -कं.

PISCATION, *s.* मत्स्यबन्धनं, मत्स्यग्रहणं, मत्स्यधरणं, मत्स्यघातनं.

PISCATORIAL, PISCATORY, *a.* मात्सिकः -की -कं, मात्स्यिकः &c., मात्स्यः -त्स्यी -त्स्यं, मीनरः -रा -रं, मत्स्यसम्बन्धी &c., मत्स्यविषयकः -का -कं, मत्स्यग्रहणसम्बन्धी &c.

PISCES, *s.* (Sign of the Zodiac) मीनः, मीनराशिः *m.*, मीनलग्नं, मत्स्यः.

PISCINAL, *a.* मीनालयसम्बन्धी &c., मत्स्यालयसम्बन्धी &c.

PISCIVOROUS, *a.* मत्स्याशी -शिनी -शि (न्), मत्स्याशनः -ना -नं, मत्स्यादः -दा -दं, मत्स्यभुक् *m. f. n.* (ज्), मत्स्यभोजी &c., मत्स्याहारी &c.

PISMIRE, *s.* (Emmet) पिपीलिका, पुत्तिका.

To PISS, *v. a.* मूत्र् (c. 10. मूत्रयति -यितुं), अवमूत्र्, मिह् (c. 1. मेहति, मेढुं), मूत्रं कृ, मूत्रोत्सर्गं कृ, मूत्रत्यागं कृ, प्रस्रावं कृ, मूत्रप्रस्रावं कृ, मूत्रप्रस्रवणं कृ.

PISS, *s.* मूत्रं, मेहः, प्रस्रावः, वस्तिमलं. *See* URINE, *s.*

PISTIL, *s.* स्त्रैणकेसरः, स्त्रीकेसरः, गर्भकेसरः, पुष्पगर्भतन्तुः *m.*

PISTOL, *s.* गुलिकाप्रक्षेपणी हस्तनाडिः -डी, सूक्ष्मगुलिप्रक्षेपणी.

PISTON, *s.* यन्त्रस्तम्भः, यन्त्रनालस्तम्भः, नालस्तम्भः, यन्त्राङ्गं.

PIT, *s.* (Cavity, hole) गर्त्तः, विवरं, विलं, अवटः -टिः *m.*, कुहरं, कूपः, गुहा, कुण्डं, सन्धिका.—(Of the stomach) मणिपूरं, मुखपुटं, उदरमूलं, जठरमूलं.—(Of the arm) कक्षः, खण्डिकः, बाहुमूलं, भुजकोटरः, दोर्मूलं.—(Of a theatre) अङ्गनं, रङ्गाङ्गणं.

To PIT, *v. a.* (With little hollows) सूक्ष्मकूपकैर् अङ्क् (c. 10. अङ्कयति -यितुं) or चिह्न् (c. 10. चिह्नयति -यितुं), सूक्ष्मकूपाङ्कितं -तां कृ.—(Set in competition) प्रतियोधनाय or परस्परयोधनाय एकत्र स्था in caus. (स्थापयति -यितुं), प्रतियुध् in caus.

PITAPAT, *s.* or *adv.* पटपटा, पटपटाशब्दः, कटकटा.

PITCH, *s.* (Resinous substance used for calking boats, &c.) क्षितिसारकः, तिन्दुः *m.*, तिन्दुकी, अग्निवल्लभः, वह्निवल्लभः, यक्षधूपः, सर्ज्जरसः, तीक्ष्णतैलं, रालः, अरालः.—(Mineral pitch). *See* BITUMEN.—(Point of elevation) अग्रं, शिखरं, सीमा, पदं; 'highest pitch,' उत्तमाग्रं, उत्तमपदं, उत्तमता.—(Degree) परिमाणं, पर्य्यन्तं, क्रमः; 'to such a pitch,' एतावत्पर्य्यन्तं, एतावत्.—(Of a hill) उत्सङ्गः, कटकः.—(Of a note or voice) स्वरः.

To PITCH, *v. a.* (Cast, throw) क्षिप्, प्रक्षिप्, अस्, प्रास्, पत् in caus.—(Fix a tent, camp, &c.) शिबिरं निविश् (c. 10. -वेशयति -यितुं) or स्था in caus. (स्थापयति -यितुं) or रुह् in caus. (रोपयति -यितुं) or समावस् in caus.—(A note or the voice) स्वर् (c. 10. स्वरयति -यितुं), स्वरस्थितिं कृ.—(Smear with pitch) तिन्दुना लिप् or अञ्ज्, तिन्दुलिप्तं -प्तां कृ, अरालाक्तं -क्तां कृ.

To PITCH, *v. n.* (Light, settle) अध्यास्, निली, निषद्, अवस्था, संस्था, अवरुह्, अवपत्, आपत्, निपत्, अवतॄ, उत्तॄ, अधो गम्.—(Encamp) निविश्, उपविश्, शिबिरे वस् or समावस् or अध्यास्.—(Fall headlong) अधोमुखः पत्, अधोमुखेन पत्, अवाङ्मुखेन पत्, अवाक् पत्.—(Pitch upon). *See To* CHOOSE.

PITCHED, *p. p.* (Fixed, set) स्थापितः -ता -तं, रोपितः &c., निवेशितः &c.

—(Thrown) क्षिप्तः -प्ता -प्तं, अस्तः -स्ता -स्तं.—(As a note) स्वरितः -ता -तं.

PITCHER, *s.* कुम्भः, कलशः -शी -शं, घटः, कुटः -टी -टिका, उदकपात्रं, उदपात्रं, जलपात्रं, उदकभाण्डं, मृत्पात्रं, मृद्भाण्डं -ण्डकं, मृत्कांस्यं, मृद्भाजनं, मृन्मयपात्रं, जलभाजनं, मृत्स्नाभाण्डकं, आलुः *f.*, आलूः *m.*, पुटग्रीवः, मणिकं, कर्करी, अलिञ्जरः, गलन्तिका; 'half of a broken pitcher,' कपालः -लं; 'bottom of a pitcher,' सूर्य्यग्रहः.

PITCH-FORK, *s.* शूलः -लं, त्रिशिखशूलं, त्र्यग्रशूलः.

PITCHY, *a.* (Covered with pitch) जरालाक्तः -क्ता -क्तं, तिन्दुलिप्तः -प्ता -प्तं, तीक्ष्णतैलमयः -यी -यं.—(Resembling it) जरालगुणकः -का -कं, तिन्दुगुणकः &c., तीक्ष्णतैलोपमः -मा -मं.—(Dark as pitch) अतिकृष्णः -ष्णा -ष्णं, अतिश्यामः -मा -मं, अतितामसः -सी -सं.

PIT-COAL, *s.* खनिजाङ्गारः, आकरजाङ्गारः, आकरोद्भवाङ्गारः.

PITEOUS, *a.* (Deserving or exciting pity) करुणोत्पादकः -का -कं, दयाजनकः &c., अनुकम्पाजनकः &c., अनुकम्प्यः -म्प्या -म्प्यं, अनुकम्पनीयः -या -यं, करुणारसोत्पादकः &c., करुणायोग्यः -ग्या -ग्यं, दयायोग्यः &c., करुणः -णा -णं, कारुणिकः -की -कं; 'piteous accents,' करुणस्वरः, करुणशब्दः.—(Wretched) दीनः -ना -नं, कृपणः -णा -णं, दुःखान्वितः -ता -तं.—(Compassionate). *See* PITIFUL.

PITEOUSLY, *adv.* करुणं, यथा दया or करुणा जायते or उत्पद्यते तथाप्रकारेण, अनुकम्पनीयं, सकरुणं.

PITEOUSNESS, *s.* करुणोत्पादकत्वं, दयाजनकत्वं, अनुकम्प्यता, करुणायोग्यता, दयायोग्यता, कारुण्यं, दीनता.

PIT-FALL, *s.* गूढकूपः, अन्धकूपः, छन्नकूपः, गूढगर्त्तः.

PITH, *s.* (Of plants, &c.) सारः, मज्जा, गर्भः, साररसः.—(Essence) सारः -रता, सारांशः, वस्तु *n.*, सारवस्तु *n.*, मूलवस्तु *n.*, रसः, साररसः, तत्त्वं, मूलं, पदार्थः, तत्त्वं, तत्त्वार्थः, निर्य्यासः, निकरः, गर्भः, मज्जः.—(Essential extract) निर्यासः, रसः, मज्जः -ज्जं.—(Energy, spirit, vigor) सत्त्वं, सारः, सारता, वीर्य्यं, तेजस् *n.*, प्रभावः, शक्तिः *f.*, बलं.

PITHILY, *adv.* सारतस्, सारेण, ससत्त्वं, सत्त्वतस्, सवीर्य्यं, वीर्य्यतस्.

PITHINESS, *s.* सारता -त्वं, सारवत्त्वं, सारपूर्णता, ससारत्वं, सत्त्वपूर्णता, ससत्त्वता, सत्त्ववत्त्वं, सत्त्वं, मज्जावत्त्वं, वीर्य्यं, वीर्य्यवत्त्वं.

PITHLESS, *a.* असारः -रा -रं, निःसारः &c., निस्सारः &c., सारहीनः -ना -नं, गतसारः -रा -रं, सत्त्वहीनः &c., निःसत्त्वः -त्त्वा -त्त्वं, वीर्य्यहीनः &c., सारवर्जितः -ता -तं, फल्गुः -ल्गुः -ल्गु, विरसः -सा -सं, निरसः &c., रसहीनः &c., वितानः -ना -नं, सारभङ्गः -ङ्गा -ङ्गं.

PITHY, *a.* (Having pith) सारवान् -वती -वत् (त्), ससारः -रा -रं, सारपूर्णः -र्णा -र्णं, सारमयः -यी -यं, ससत्त्वः -त्त्वा -त्त्वं, मज्जावान् &c., मज्जामयः &c., सगर्भः -र्भा -र्भं, सरसः -सा -सं, रसिकः -का -कं, रसवान् &c.—(Forcible, energetic) ससत्त्वः -त्त्वा -त्त्वं, सत्त्ववान् &c., वीर्य्यवान् &c., सप्रभावः -वा -वं, तेजोवान् &c.

PITIABLE, *a.* अनुकम्प्यः -म्प्या -म्प्यं, अनुकम्पनीयः -या -यं, दयायोग्यः -ग्या -ग्यं, करुणायोग्यः &c., घृणायोग्यः &c., अनुकम्पायोग्यः &c., दयाविषयः, दयापात्रं, दयाभाजनं.—(Wretched) दीनः -ना -नं, कृपणः -णा -णं, अतिदुःखी -खिनी -खि (न्), अतिदुःखान्वितः -ता -तं.

PITIABLENESS, *s.* अनुकम्प्यता, अनुकम्पनीयता -त्वं, दयायोग्यता.

PITIABLY, *adv.* करुणं, अनुकम्पनीयं. *See* PITEOUSLY.

PITIED, *p. p.* अनुकम्पितः -ता -तं, घृणितः -ता -तं, दयितः -ता -तं.

PITIFUL, *a.* (Compassionate) कारुणिकः -की -कं, करुणः -णा -णं, सकरुणः -णा -णं, करुणाशीलः -ला -लं, दयालुः -लुः -लु, दयावान् -वती -वत् (त्), सदयः -या -यं, दयायुक्तः -क्ता -क्तं, दयामयः -यी -यं, दयाविशिष्टः -ष्टा -ष्टं, दयान्वितः -ता -तं, दयापूर्णः -र्णा -र्णं, दयाढ्यः -ढ्या -ढ्यं, दयासम्पन्नः -न्ना -न्नं, दयार्द्रः -र्द्रा -र्द्रं, दयार्द्रचित्तः -त्ता -त्तं, दयार्द्रमनस्कः -स्का -स्कं, दयारूपः -पा -पं, करुणामयः &c., कृपामयः &c., कृपावान् &c., कृपालुः &c., सानुकम्पः -म्पा -म्पं, घृणावान् &c., घृणी &c., घृणाशीलः &c., हृदयालुः &c., हृदयवान् &c. The following are phrases for a pitiful person: दयासागरः, दयानिधिः *m.*, दयाकरः, करुणासागरः, करुणानिधिः *m.*, अनाथनाथः, अनाथबन्धुः *m.*, दीननाथः, दीनबन्धुः *m.*, दीनवत्सलः.—(Exciting pity) *See* PITEOUS.—(Miserable, wretched) दीनः -ना -नं, कृपणः -णा -णं, तुच्छः -च्छा -च्छं, क्षुल्लकः -का -कं.

PITIFULLY, *adv.* सदयं, सानुकम्पं, सकारुण्यं, सकरुणं, करुणं, दयापूर्वं, दयापुरःसरं. *See* PITEOUSLY.

PITIFULNESS, *s.* दयालुता -त्वं, कारुण्यं, सकरुणता, दयार्द्रता, करुणार्द्रता, सानुकम्पता, कृपालुता, दया, कृपा.

PITILESS, *a.* निर्दयः -या -यं, अदयः -या -यं, दयाहीनः -ना -नं, दयारहितः -ता -तं, निष्करुणः -णा -णं, अकरुणः -णा -णं, निष्कृपः -पा -पं, कृपाहीनः -ना -नं, निर्घृणः -णा -णं, वीतघृणः &c., निठुरः -रा -रं, क्रूरः -रा -रं.

PITILESSLY, *adv.* निर्दयं, निष्करुणं, निष्कृपं, निर्घृणं, निठुरं, क्रूरं.

PITILESSNESS, *s.* निर्दयत्वं, दयाहीनता, दयाशून्यता, निष्करुणत्वं, क्रूरता.

PITTANCE, *s.* (Small quantity allowed) अल्पांशः, अल्पाल्पांशः, अल्पभागः, अल्पवेतनं, परिमितवेतनं, अल्पमूल्यं.—(Allowance of food, &c., barely sufficient for the day) दिननिर्वाहः, दिनचर्य्या, ग्रासाच्छादनं, अन्नाच्छादनं.

PITTED, *p. p.* (With small hollows) सूक्ष्मकूपाङ्कितः -ता -तं, लघुकूपकचिह्नितः -ता -तं.—(For combat) परस्परयोधनार्थं or परस्परजयार्थम् एकत्र स्थापितः -ता -तं or एकत्रीकृतः &c., विजिगीषार्थम् एकत्रीकृतः &c.

To PITTER-PATTER, *v. n.* पटपटा (nom. पटपटायते), पटपटाशब्दं कृ.

PITUITARY, *a.* कफोत्पादकः -का -कं, कफकरः -री -रं, श्लेष्मजनकः &c.

PITUITOUS, *a.* कफमयः -यी -यं, श्लेष्मलः -ला -लं, कफगुणकः -का -कं.

PITY, *s.* दया, करुणा, अनुकम्पा, कृपा, घृणा, कारुण्यं, करुणारसः, अनुक्रोशः, माया, करुणः, अनुग्रहः; 'full of pity,' दयायुक्तः -क्ता -क्तं. *See* PITIFUL.—(Ground of pity, cause of grief) दयाहेतुः *m.*, दुःखहेतुः *m.*, दुःखकारणं.

To PITY, *v. a.* अनुकम्प् (c. 1. -कम्पते -म्पितुं), समनुकम्प् with acc. c., दयां कृ, अनुकम्पां कृ, करुणां कृ, कृपां कृ, दय् (c. 1. दयते -यितुं), with gen. c., करुण (nom. करुणायते), कृपा (nom. कृपायते), अनुकृपा.

PIVOT, *s.* परिवर्त्तनकीलः -लकः, विवर्त्तनकीलः -लकः.

PIZZLE, *s.* चर्म्मदण्डः -ण्डं, वायुदण्डः, पशूनां मूत्रशुक्रादिमार्गः.

PLACABILITY, PLACABLENESS, *s.* शाम्यता -त्वं, सान्त्वनीयता -त्वं, आराध्यता, आराधनीयता, सुखाराध्यता, सान्त्वनशक्यता.

PLACABLE, *a.* शाम्यः -म्या -म्यं, सान्त्वनीयः -या -यं, आराध्यः -ध्या -ध्यं, सुखाराध्यः &c., आराधनीयः -या -यं, शमनीयः &c., सुखशाम्यः &c., सान्त्वनशक्यः -क्या -क्यं, सान्त्वनयोग्यः -ग्या -ग्यं, तोषणीयः -या -यं, सन्तोषणीयः &c., प्रसाद्यः -द्या -द्यं.

PLACARD, *s.* लोकसेवितस्थाने स्थापितं प्रकटनपत्रं or घोषणपत्रं or विघोषणपत्रं or विज्ञापनपत्रं or बोधनपत्रं.

To PLACARD, *v. a.* लोकसेवितस्थाने प्रकटनपत्राणि or घोषणपत्राणि स्था in caus. (स्थापयति -यितुं).

PLACE, *s.* (Particular portion of space) स्थानं, स्थलं -ली, देशः, प्रदेशः, भूः *f.*, भूमिः *f.*, निलयः -यं, धिष्ण्यं; 'in one place,' एकत्र; 'in many places,' बहुत्र; 'in both places,' उभयत्र; 'from various places,' नानादिग्देशात् -शेभ्यः.—(Situation) स्थानं, अवस्थानं, पदं, आस्पदं, पदविः -वी *f.*, भूमिः *f.*, स्थितिः *f.*; 'place of residence,' वासस्थानं, निवासस्थानं, वसतिः *f.*, निवसतिः *f.*—(Rank) पदं, आस्पदं, पदविः *f.*; 'highest place,' उत्तमपदं, परमपदं.—(Passage of a book) स्थलं, देशः, एकदेशः.—(Proper place of) स्थानं, शाला; 'place for dancing,' नृत्यस्थानं, नृत्यशाला; 'in its proper place,' स्थाने, स्वस्थाने; 'out of place,' अस्थाने, अपदे.—(Office, post) पदं, पदविः -वी *f.*, अधिकारः, अधिकारपदं, स्थानं, स्थलं, आस्पदं, नियोगः; 'out of place, dismissed from place,' पदच्युतः -ता -तं, स्थानभ्रष्टः -ष्टा -ष्टं, पदभ्रष्टः &c., अधिकारभ्रष्टः &c., च्युताधिकारः -रा -रं, स्थलच्युतः &c.; 'having no place,' अपदः -दा -दी -दं, अस्थानः -ना -नं.—(Room, stead) स्थानं, स्थलं, भूमिः *f.*; 'in the place of,' स्थाने, स्थले, भूमौ; 'she stands in the place of a friend,' सखीभूमौ वर्त्तते; 'in the place of a parent,' पितृस्थाने.—(Ground, cause) आस्पदं, स्थानं, हेतुः *m.*, कारणं; 'place for doubt,' शङ्कास्पदं; 'for fear,' भयस्थानं, भयहेतुः *m.*—(Room, space) अवकाशः, अवसरः, प्रसरः.—(Degree in order of proceeding) क्रमः, पदं or expressed by adverbial affixes; as, 'in the first place,' प्रथमतस्, पूर्व्वतस्, प्रथमं, प्रथमपदे; 'in the second place,' द्वितीयतस्, द्वितीयपदे; 'in the third place,' तृतीयतस्, तृतीयपदे; 'in the fourth place,' चतुर्थतस्, तुरीयतस्, चतुर्थपदे; 'in the last place,' अन्ततस्; 'in the next place,' पुनर्, पुनश्च, परं, परञ्च, अपरं, अपरञ्च.—(To give place) स्थानं or पदं त्यज् (c. 1. त्यजति, त्यक्तुं), अपसृ (c. 1. -सरति -सर्त्तुं), पन्थानं or मार्गं त्यज्.—(To take place). *See To* HAPPEN.

To PLACE, *v. a.* (Put, set) स्था in caus. (स्थापयति -यितुं), न्यस् (c. 4. -अस्यति -असितुं), विन्यस्, धा (c. 3. दधाति, धातुं), निधा, आधा, समाधा, निविश् (c. 10. -वेशयति -यितुं), विनिविश्, रुह् in caus. (रोपयति -यितुं) आरुह्, धृ (c. 1. धरति, धर्त्तुं), दा (c. 3. ददाति, दातुं), कृ (c. 8. करोति, कर्त्तुं), with acc. of the thing placed, and loc. or instr. or gen. of the thing on which it is placed; as, 'he places his hand in the serpent's mouth,' हस्तं सर्पमुखे न्यस्यति; 'let not the burden be placed on such as me,' न मद्विधे न्यस्यतां भारः; 'having placed the goat on his shoulder,' स्कन्धे or स्कन्धेन छागं कृत्वा; 'he places his hand on my shoulder,' मत्स्कन्धे हस्तं ददाति; 'having placed his knee on my shoulder,' मत्स्कन्धस्य जानु दत्त्वा; 'having placed the end of a straw in water,' तृणाग्रं जलाग्नः कृत्वा; 'to place near,' सन्निधा, उपन्यस्; 'to place over,' अधिकृ, अधिष्ठा.—(Establish, fix) प्रतिष्ठा, अवस्था, संस्था, विधा.—(In any office, &c.) पदे or अधिकारे नियुज् (c. 10. -योजयति -यितुं) or विनियुज्.—(Place out, invest) निक्षिप् (c. 6. -क्षिपति -क्षेप्तुं), प्रयोगं कृ.

PLACED, *p. p.* स्थापितः -ता -तं, न्यस्तः -स्ता -स्तं, विन्यस्तः &c., निवेशितः -ता -तं, विनिवेशितः &c., आहितः &c., विहितः &c., उपहितः &c., प्रणिहितः &c., रोपितः &c., निक्षिप्तः -प्ता -प्तं; 'placed near,' उपन्यस्तः -स्ता -स्तं, सन्निहितः -ता -तं; 'placed over,' अधिकृतः -ता -तं, अधिष्ठितः -ता -तं; 'placed upon or on,' रोपितः -ता -तं, आरूढः -ढा -ढं, स्थः -स्था -स्थं in comp.; 'placed on the fire,' अग्निष्ठः -ष्ठा -ष्ठं; 'on the arm,' दोःस्थः -स्था -स्थं; 'on a dish,' पात्रस्थः &c.; 'placed in any office or post,' पदनियुक्तः -क्ता -क्तं, पदारूढः -ढा -ढं, अधिकारारूढः &c., अधिकारस्थः &c., अधिकारस्थितः -ता -तं, स्थानारूढः &c.

PLACENTA, *s.* गर्भपरिस्रवः, गर्भवेष्टनं, गर्भपरिवेष्टनं.

PLACER, *s.* स्थापकः, स्थापयिता *m.* (तृ), रोपकः, विधायी *m.* (न्).

PLACID, *a.* शान्तः -न्ता -न्तं, प्रशान्तः -न्ता -न्तं, उपशान्तः &c., शान्तमनस्कः -स्का -स्कं, शान्तचित्तः -त्ता -त्तं, शान्तात्मा -त्मा -त्म (न्), उपशान्तात्मा &c., उपशमशीलः -ला -लं, प्रसन्नचेताः -ताः -तः (स्), प्रसन्नः -न्ना -न्नं, प्रसादचित्तः &c., सुप्रसादः -दा -दं, निराकुलचित्तः &c., सुसमाहितः &c., अचपलशीलः -ला -लं, जितक्रोधः -धा -धं, जितरोषः -षा -षं, अक्रोधः -धा -धं, विनीतः -ता -तं, सौम्यः -म्या -म्यं, सम्भ्रमहीनः -ना -नं, सुमनस्कः &c., अन्तर्वेगहीनः -ना -नं; 'in countenance,' सुप्रसन्नमुखः -खा -खी- खं, प्रसादमुखः &c.

PLACIDLY, *adv.* शान्त्या, शान्तं, चित्तशान्त्या, चित्तप्रसादेन, प्रसन्नचेतसा, सुप्रसादेन, सप्रसादं, शान्तचेतसा, प्रशान्तचेतसा, निराकुलचेतसा, निराकुलं.

PLACIDNESS, PLACIDITY, *s.* शान्तता, प्रशान्तता, शान्तिः *f.*, प्रशान्तिः *f.*, उपशान्तिः *f.*, उपशान्तता, शमः, उपशमः, चित्तशान्तिः *f.*, शान्तचित्तत्वं, प्रसादः, प्रसन्नता, सुप्रसादः, चित्तप्रसादः, निराकुलता, अव्याकुलता, सौम्यता, अक्रोधः, असम्भ्रमः, सौमनस्यं.

PLAGIARISM, *s.* शब्दचौर्य्यं, काव्यचौर्य्यं, ग्रन्थचौर्य्यं, वागपहारः, हरणं, पुस्तकचौर्य्यं, पुस्तकापहारः -हरणं.

PLAGIARIST, PLAGIARY, *s.* (Literary thief) शब्दचोरः, काव्यचोरः, काव्यचोरः, वागपहारी *m.* (न्), वागपहारकः, पुस्तकापहारी *m.*, अननुज्ञाध्यायी *m.*, कुम्भिलः, चन्द्रगुप्तः *m.*

PLAGUE, *s.* मारी -रिः *f.*, मारकः, मारः, मरकः, महामारी, महाव्याधिः *m.*, तीक्ष्णं, प्रतीवापः.—(Great calamity) उत्पातः, विनिपातः, विनिहितः, अरिष्टं, अरिष्टापातः, अनर्थः, अनर्थापातः, उपप्लवः, उपद्रवः.—(Pest) कण्टकः, दूषकः, शल्यं.

To PLAGUE, *v. a.* (Infest with pestilence) मारीग्रस्तं -स्तां कृ, मारीपीडितं -तां कृ, मारकग्रस्तं -स्तां कृ.—(Harass) बाध्, परिबाध्, प्रबाध्, अभिबाध्, पीड्, अभिपीड्, तप्, व्यथ्, क्लिश्, दुःख्.

PLAGUING, PLAGUY, *a.* बाधकः -का -कं, क्लेशकः -का -कं, क्लेशकरः -रा -रं, क्लेशदः -दा -दं, दुःखकरः &c., पीडकः -का -कं, तापकः -का -कं.

PLAIN, *a.* (Even, level) समः -मा -मं, समानः -ना -नं, सपाटः -टा -टं, श्लक्ष्णः -क्ष्णा -क्ष्णं, अरूक्षः -क्षा -क्षं.—(Neat) विनीतः -ता -तं, आकारशुद्धः -द्धा -द्धं.—(Void of ornament) अभूषितः -ता -तं, अनलङ्कृतः &c., अनलङ्कारः -रा -रं, निरलङ्कारः &c., अलङ्कारहीनः -ना -नं, निर्भूषणः -णा -णं, भूषणहीनः -ना -नं.—(Artless, simple) निर्व्याजः -जा -जं, निष्कपटः -टा -टं, कपटहीनः -ना -नं, अमायिकः -की -कं, अमायः -या -यं, मायाहीनः -ना -नं, सरलः -ला -लं, दक्षिणः -णा -णं, छलहीनः -ना -नं.—(Open, frank, honest) अवक्रः -क्रा -क्रं, अजिह्मः -ह्मा -ह्मं, निर्व्यलीकः -का -कं, निर्व्याजः -जा -जं, विमलः -ला -लं, सरलः -ला -लं, सरलमतिः -तिः -ति, सरलबुद्धिः -द्धिः -द्धि, शुद्धः -द्धा -द्धं, शुद्धमतिः -तिः -ति, श्लक्ष्णः -क्ष्णा -क्ष्णं, सात्त्विकः -की -कं.—(Mere, bare) केवलः -ला -लं, शुद्धः -द्धा -द्धं, मात्रकः -का -कं, मात्र in comp.—(Clear, intelligible) स्पष्टः -ष्टा -ष्टं, विस्पष्टः &c., स्पष्टार्थः -र्था -र्थं, सुस्पष्टः &c., व्यक्तः -क्ता -क्तं, अभिव्यक्तः &c., सुव्यक्तः &c., स्फुटार्थः &c., सुबोधः -धा -धं, सुगम्यः -म्या -म्यं, सुगमः -मा -मं, सुगः -गा -गं, सुग्राह्यः -ह्या -ह्यं, भिन्नार्थः -र्था -र्थं, अगूढः -ढा -ढं, अगूढार्थः -र्था -र्थं, विशदः -दा -दं, विमलः -ला -लं.—(Evident, manifest) प्रत्यक्षः -क्षा -क्षं, स्फुटः -टा -टं, प्रस्फुटः &c., प्रकाशः -शा -शं, सुप्रकाशः &c., प्रकटः -टी -टं, स्पष्टः -ष्टा -ष्टं, व्यक्तः -क्ता -क्तं, समक्षः -क्षी -क्षं, सुदृश्यः -श्या -श्यं, साविष्कारः -रा -रं, प्रसिद्धः -द्धा -द्धं, पुरःस्फुरन् -रन्ती -रत् (त्), उल्बणः -णा -णं.—(Not figurative) अव्यञ्जनः -ना -नं, निर्व्यञ्जनः

&c., अव्यञ्जनहीनः -ना -नं.—(Not seasoned) अव्यञ्जनः -ना -नं, व्यञ्जनशून्यः -न्या -न्यं, असंस्कृतः -ता -तं, अनुपस्कृतः &c., उपस्करहीनः -ना -नं.—(Not beautiful, not handsome) असुन्दरः -रा -री -रं, कुरूपः -पा -पं, कुरूपी -पिणी -पि (न्), साधारणरूपः &c., मध्यमरूपः &c., कुदृश्यः -श्या -श्यं.—(Fair, unobstructed) समः -मा -मं, असबाधः -धा -धं, निर्विघ्नः -घ्ना -घ्नं, अरुद्धः -द्धा -द्धं, निरवरोधः -धा -धं.

PLAIN, *s.* (Level land) समभूमिः *f.*, समभूभागः, समभूः *f.*, समस्थलं -ली, समस्थानं, सपाटभूः *f.*, पाटः, समं, आजिः *f.*

PLAIN, *adv.* व्यक्तं, सुव्यक्तं, स्पष्टं, अगूढं. *See* PLAINLY.

To PLAIN, *v. a.* समीकृ, समस्थलीकृ, सपाटीकृ, समतलीकृ.

PLAIN-DEALING, *a.* न्यायाचारी -रिणी -रि (न्), सरलाचारी &c., सरलकर्म्मा -र्म्मा -र्म्म (न्), शुद्धाचारी &c., समाचारी &c., शुचिकर्म्मा &c., ऋजुः -जुः -जु, ऋजुकर्म्मा &c., निर्व्याजकर्म्मा &c., निर्व्याजाचारी &c.

PLAIN-DEALING, *s.* ऋजुता, आर्जवं, निर्व्याजाचारः, निष्कपटाचारः, सारल्यं.

PLAINLY, *adv.* (Clearly, intelligibly) स्पष्टं, सुस्पष्टं, स्पष्टार्थं -र्थतस्, व्यक्तं, सुव्यक्तं, भिन्नार्थं -र्थतस्, अगूढं, अगूढार्थतस्; 'too plainly,' अतिव्यक्तं,सुव्यक्तं.—(Evidently, manifestly) प्रत्यक्षतस्-क्षेण, प्रकाशं, सुप्रकाशं, स्पष्टं, व्यक्तं, स्फुटं, प्रकटं, साविष्कारं, साक्षात्, प्रादुस्, आविस्.—(Without disguise or cunning) निर्व्याजं, अव्याजेन, व्याजेन विना, कपटं विना, अमायया, मायां विना, कपटव्यतिरेकेण, सरलं, सारल्येन, सदाक्षिण्यं, छलेन विना.—(Neatly, without ornament) विनीतं, विनीतवत्, सपरिष्कारं, अलङ्कारं विना, भूषणं विना; 'plainly dressed,' विनीतवेशः -शा -शं.—(Frankly, honestly) अवक्रं, आर्जवं, निर्व्यलीकं, निर्व्याजं, निष्कपटं, न्यायतस्, सरलवत्, शुचिवत्, समं.

PLAINNESS, *s.* (Levelness) समता, साम्यं, समानता, श्लक्ष्णता.—(Neatness) विनीतता -त्वं, विनयः, आकारशुद्धता; 'of dress,' वेशविनीतत्वं.—(Want of ornament) अभूषितत्वं, अनलङ्कृतत्वं, अलङ्कारहीनता भूषणहीनता, भूषणाभावः, अलङ्काराभावः.—(Artlessness, simplicity) अव्याजः, अकापट्यं, अमाया, व्याजहीनता, कपटाभावः, निर्व्याजत्वं, कपटहीनता, सरलता, सारल्यं, दाक्षिण्यं, आनौद्धत्यं.—(Frankness, honesty) सारल्यं, अवक्रता, ऋजुता, आर्जवं, शुचिता, अकपटः, न्यायिता, निर्व्यलीकता, विमलता, शुद्धता -त्वं.—(Clearness) व्यक्तता -त्वं, सुव्यक्तत्वं, स्पष्टता, सुस्पष्टत्वं, व्यक्तिः *f.*, अभिव्यक्तिः *f.*, सुबोधता, सुगम्यता, भिन्नार्थत्वं, अगूढता -त्वं, विशदता, वैशद्यं, प्रत्यक्षता, स्फुटता -त्वं, प्रकाशता, प्राकट्यं, प्रसिद्धता, सुदृश्यता.—(Ugliness) कुरूपता, असौन्दर्यं.

PLAIN-SPOKEN, *a.* स्पष्टवाक् *m.f.n.* (च्), स्पष्टवक्ता -क्त्री -क्तृ (क्तृ), व्यक्तवाक् &c.

PLAINT, *s.* (Complaint) विलापः, विलपनं, विलापेन स्वार्थनिवेदनं.—(In law) पूर्व्वपक्षपादः, भाषापादः -दं, पूर्व्ववादः, अभियोगः.

PLAINTIFF, *s.* वादी *m.* (न्), पूर्व्ववादी *m.*, अग्रवादी *m.*, पूर्व्ववादकः, परिवादी *m.*, परिवादकः, क्रियावादी *m.*, कारणवादी *m.*, अर्थी *m.* (न्), विवादार्थी *m.*, अभियोगी *m.* (न्), अभियोक्ता *m.* (क्तृ), कार्य्यी *m.* (न्), पूर्व्वावेदकः, व्यवहर्त्ता *m.* (र्तृ); 'plaintiff and defendant,' अर्थिप्रत्यर्थिनौ *m. du.*

PLAINTIVE, *a.* (Complaining) विलापी -पिनी -पि (न्), परिदेवी &c., परिदेवकः -का -कं, विलपनकारी &c.—(Expressing sorrow) शोकसूचकः -का -कं, खेदसूचकः &c., दुःखबोधकः &c., शोकार्थकः -का -कं.

PLAINTIVELY, *adv.* विलापेन, सविलपनं, सपरिदेवनं, करुणं.

PLAIT, *s.* (Fold) ऊर्म्मिः *m.f.*, ऊर्म्मी -र्म्मिका, व्यावर्त्तनं, तरङ्गः, पुटः, चूडः.—(Braid) वेणिः -णी, प्रवेणिः, कबरः -री, धम्मिल्लः, केशग्रन्थिः *m.*

To PLAIT, *v. a.* (Braid, fold) ग्रन्थ्, वेणीकृ, वेणीरूपेण ग्रन्थ् or रच्, व्यापृत्, पुटीकृ, वे.

PLAN, *s.* (Scheme, project) उपायः, कल्पना, सङ्कल्पः, निश्चितं, कल्पितं, अनुसन्धानं, प्रयोगः, प्रयुक्तिः *f.*, युक्तिः *f.*, व्यवसायः, अपदेशः, व्यपदेशः, अभिप्रायः, उद्देशः, बुद्धिः *f.*, मन्त्रणा, चिन्ता; 'a good plan,' सुयुक्तिः *f.*, सुकल्पना.—(Draught, representation on paper) सूत्रं, सूत्रपातः, आलेख्यं, वस्तु *n.*, वस्तुमात्रं.—(Mode of construction) कल्पना, कॢप्तिः *f.*, कला.

To PLAN, *v. a.* (Devise) मनसा कॢप् or परिकॢप्, उपायं कॢप्, मन्त्र्, प्रचिन्त्, परिचिन्त्, अनुसन्धा, घट्, व्यवसो, आलोच्.—(Form a draught) सूत्रपातं कृ, आलिख् (c. 6. -लिखति -लेखितुं), आलेख्यं कृ.

To PLANCH, PLANCHED. *See To* PLANK, PLANKED.

PLANE, *a.* (Level) समः -मा -मं, समानः -ना -नं, समतलः -ला -लं.

PLANE, *s.* (In geometry, a level, surface) समं, समतलं, समपृष्ठं, पाटः, तलं; 'a plane figure,' क्षेत्रं.—(The tool) तक्षणी, त्वक्षणी, तक्षणयन्त्रं.

To PLANE, *v. a.* (Make smooth) समीकृ, श्लक्ष्णीकृ.—(Pare with a carpenter's plane) तक्ष् (c. 1. तक्षति-क्षितुं), त्वक्ष् (c. 1. त्वक्षति-क्षितुं).

PLANED, *p. p.* तष्टः -ष्टा -ष्टं, तक्षणयन्त्रेण श्लक्ष्णीकृतः &c.

PLANET, *s.* ग्रहः, भ्रमन् ग्रहः, तारा, तारका -कं, ज्योतिस् *n.*, ज्योतिषी, ज्योतिष्कः, खेचरः, खगः, गगणेचरः, गगणाध्वगः, विहगः, खोल्कः, नक्षत्रं, ऋक्षः, द्युषद् *m.*, द्युसद् *m.*, भं; 'minor planet,' उपग्रहः; 'the planets collectively,' ग्रहगणः, ज्योतिर्गणः, ग्रहमण्डलं, भ्रमन्तो ग्रहाः *m. pl.*; 'the nine planets,' नवग्रहाः *m. pl.* These, according to the Hindús, are 1. the sun, सूर्य्यः; 2. the moon, चन्द्रः; 3. Mercury, बुधः; 4. Venus, शुक्रः; 5. Mars, मङ्गलः; 6. Jupiter, गुरुः *m.*; 7. Saturn, शनिः *m.*; 8. the ascending node, राहुः *m.*; 9. the descending node, केतुः *m.* The two last are considered to be minor planets. The other names of the planets will be found under each separate head of Mercury, &c.—(Auspicious planet) शुभग्रहः, सुग्रहः, सौम्यग्रहः; of these there are four, viz. Mercury, Venus, Jupiter, and the Moon.—(Inauspicious planet) कुग्रहः, अशुभग्रहः, पापग्रहः; of these there are five, viz. Mars, Saturn, the Sun, and the two nodes. 'Planet at its apex,' तुङ्गी *m.* (न्); 'motion of the planets,' ग्रहचारः; 'motion in their orbits,' गतिः *f.*; 'passage of a planet,' सङ्क्रमः, सङ्क्रान्तिः *f.*; 'conjunction,' सङ्गमः; 'aspect,' ग्रहदशा; 'influence,' ग्रहयोगः, ग्रहावेशः; 'unpropitious influence,' ग्रहपीडा, ग्रहबाधा; 'propitious influence,' ग्रहानुकूल्यं, ग्रहबलं; 'worship of the planets,' ग्रहपूजा; 'propitiation of them,' ग्रहशान्तिः *f.*, ग्रहसाधनं; 'sacrifice in propitiation of them,' ग्रहयागः, ग्रहयज्ञः, ग्रहमखः; 'presents made to Bráhmans for propitiating them,' ग्रहदानं; 'incantations to render them propitious,' ग्रहजपः; 'ascertainment of their aspect,' ग्रहसाधनं; 'calculations or tables for determining their position,' ग्रहसारणी; 'diagram representing their aspect,' ग्रहकुण्डली; 'meeting of the seven planets under one sign,' सप्तग्रहसङ्गमः.

PLANETARY, *a.* ग्रह in comp., ग्रहसम्बन्धी &c., ग्रहविषयकः -का -कं, नाक्षत्रिकः -की -कं, नाक्षत्रः -त्री -त्रं, तारकी -किणी -कि (न्); 'planetary influence,' ग्रहावेशः; 'planetary conjunction,' ग्रहसङ्गमः.

PLANET-STRUCK, *a.* ग्रहपीडितः -ता -तं, ग्रहोपहतः &c., ग्रहाविष्टः -ष्टा -ष्टं.

PLANING, *s.* तक्षणं, त्वक्षणं, सरलीकरणं, समीकरणं.

PLANK, *s.* फलकः -कं, काष्ठफलकः -कं, दारुफलकः, दीर्घकाष्ठं, दीर्घदारुः *m.*, सूक्ष्मदारुः *m.*, काष्ठं, किलिञ्चः, कटः.

To PLANK, *v. a.* फलकैः or दीर्घकाष्ठैः or काष्ठफलकैर् आस्तॄ (c. 9. -स्तृणाति -स्तरितुं -रीतुं), फलक (nom. फलकयति -यितुं), सफलकीकृ.

PLANKED, *p. p.* फलकास्तीर्णः -र्णा -र्णं, फलकी -किनी -कि (न्), सफलकः &c.

PLANNED, *p. p.* कल्पितः -ता -तं, परिकल्पितः &c., मनसा कल्पितः &c., मन्त्रितः &c., प्रचिन्तितः &c., घटितः &c., विहितः &c.

PLANNING, *s.* उपायकल्पना, उपायपरिकल्पना, अनुसन्धानं, घटनं.

PLANT, *s.* उद्भिद् *m. f. n.*, ओषधिः -धी *f.*, औषधिः -धी *f.*, उद्भिज्जं, उद्भिदं, पल्लवः -वं, अङ्कुरः, प्ररोहः, रोहः, शाकः; 'gramineous,' तृणं.

To PLANT, *v. a.* (Put in the ground for growth) रुह् in caus. (रोपयति -यितुं), निरुह्, निखन् (c. 1. -खनति -नितुं), रोपणं कृ.—(Fix, set, place) स्था in caus., प्रतिष्ठा, न्यस्, विन्यस्, धा, निधा, निविश्, रुह् or आरुह् in caus.; 'to plant the foot,' पादं न्यस्.—(Plant a colony) वस् in caus. (वासयति -यितुं).

PLANTAIN, *s.* (Tree) कदली -लः, कदलकः, रम्भा, तृणसारा, गुच्छफला, ततपत्री, मोचा, मोचकः, अंशुमत्फला, काष्ठीला, वारणबुषा, वारणवुसा, वारणवल्लभा, वारबुषा; 'the fruit,' कदलीफलं, मोचं, मोचाटः, रम्भा; 'wild plantain tree,' काष्ठकदली; 'mixture of sugar and milk with plantains and spices,' शिखरिणी.

PLANTATION, *s.* (Act of planting) रोपणं, आरोपणं, आरोपः.—(Place planted) वृक्षवाटिका, वृक्षवाटी, वाटः -टी -टिका, कृत्रिमवनं, उपवनं, वनं, कर्म्मान्तः, शाकटं or शाकिनं in comp.; as, 'a plantation of sugar canes,' इक्षुशाकटं, इक्षुशाकिनं.

PLANTED, *p. p.* रोपितः -ता -तं, आरोपितः &c., निखातः -ता -तं, न्यस्तः -स्ता -स्तं, विन्यस्तः &c., स्थापितः -ता -तं.

PLANTER, *s.* रोपयिता *m.* (तृ), आरोपयिता *m.*, रोपकः, आरोपकः, रोपणकृत् *m.*, आरोपणकृत्; 'of trees,' वृक्षरोपयिता *m.*, वृक्षरोपकः.—(Owner of a plantation) वाटिकापतिः *m.*, वाटिकेश्वरः.

PLASH, *s.* वर्त्मोदकः, क्षुद्रजलौघः, क्षुद्रजलगुल्मः, पङ्कगुल्मः.

To PLASH, *v. n.* जले or पङ्के क्रीड् (c. 1. क्रीडति -डितुं).

PLASHY, *a.* अनूपः -पा -पं, जलाढ्यः -ढ्या -ढ्यं, जलपङ्कमयः -यी -यं.

PLASTER, *s.* (For covering a wall, &c.) लेपः, विलेपः, चूर्णलेपः, कर्करलेपः, सुधा, उद्पेषः.—(For a wound) उपनाहः, उपदेहः, अनुलेपनं.

To PLASTER, *v. a.* लिप् (c. 6. लिम्पति, लेप्तुं), अनुलिप्, आलिप्, विलिप्, प्रलिप्, उपलिप्, दिह् (c. 2. देग्धि -ग्धुं), लेपनं कृ, अनुलेपनं कृ, विलेपनं कृ, प्रलेपनं कृ, उपनाहनं कृ.

PLASTERED, *p. p.* लिप्तः -प्ता -प्तं, अनुलिप्तः &c., उपलिप्तः &c., आलिप्तः &c., प्रलिप्तः &c., दिग्धः -ग्धा -ग्धं, निदिग्धः &c., उपचितः &c.; 'with cement,' सुधालिप्तः &c., सुधाधवलितः &c., सुधामयः -यी -यं.

PLASTERER, *s.* लेपकः, प्रलेपकः, विलेपकः, लेपकरः, विलेपनकृत् *m.*, सुधाजीवी *m.* (न्).

PLASTERING, *s.* लेपनं, विलेपनं, अनुलेपनं, उपलेपः -पनं, लिपिः *f.*, पुस्तं.

PLASTIC, *a.* रूपकारी -रिणी -रि (न्), रूपकरः -रा -रं, आकारदः -दा -दं, आकारकरः -रा -रं, मूर्त्तिदः &c., कल्पकः -का -कं, कल्पनक्षमः -मा -मं.

To PLAT, *v. a.* (Weave) ग्रन्थ्, उद्ग्रन्थ्, वे, स्तम्भ्, उत्तम्भ्, गुम्फ्.

PLAT, *s.* (Of ground). *See* PLOT.

PLATE, *s.* (Vessel from which food is eaten) पात्रं, भोजनपात्रं, शरावः, भाजनं, भाण्डं.—(Wrought silver, &c.) कोशः, कोषः, सुवर्णरूप्यादिमयभाण्डानि *n. pl.*—(Flat piece of metal) पत्रं, फलकः -कं; 'gold plate,' सुवर्णपत्रं; 'copper-plate,' ताम्रपत्रं.—(Plate of metal for engraving or inscription) पट्टः -ट्टं, पत्रं, फलकं; 'copper-plate,' ताम्रपट्टं, ताम्रफलकं; 'a plate of copper on which a grant or edict is inscribed,' शासनपत्रं, पट्टः.

To PLATE, *v. a.* रूप्यपत्रपिनद्धं -द्धां कृ, राजतीकृ, राजतान्वितं -तां कृ.

PLATED, *p. p.* or *a.* राजतान्वितः -ता -तं, रसितः -ता -तं, राजतपत्रपिनद्धः -द्धा -द्धं, रूप्यप्रतिबद्धः -द्धा -द्धं, रूप्यपत्रोपेतः -ता -तं.

PLATFORM, *s.* मञ्चः, मञ्चकः, शिबिका, कशीवंशः, इन्दुकोषः; 'for any particular ceremony,' मङ्गलमण्डपः.—(Plan). *See* the word.

PLATINUM, *s.* No Sanskrit equivalent. प्लाटिनं may be used.

PLATOON, *s.* (Particular array of soldiers) पत्तिः *m.*

PLATTER, *s.* शरावः, पात्रं, भाजनं, भोजनपात्रं, बृहत्पात्रं.

PLAUDIT, *s.* प्रशंसा, प्रवादः, जयशब्दः, धन्यवादः, प्रशंसाशब्दः.

PLAUSIBILITY, *s.* सत्याभासः -सत्वं, प्रमाणाभासः -सत्वं, सत्यसङ्काशता -त्वं, सत्यसादृश्यं, सत्यसन्निभता.

PLAUSIBLE, *a.* सत्यसङ्काशः -शा -शं, सत्यसन्निभः -भा -भं, सत्यसदृशः -शी -शं, सत्याभासरूपः -पा -पं, सत्याभासात्मकः -का -कं, प्रमाणाभासरूपः &c., सव्याजः -जा -जं, ग्राह्यः -ह्या -ह्यं, ग्रहणीयः -या -यं, वाह्यतो दर्शनीयः -या -यं or सुदृश्यः -श्या -श्यं or रमणीयः -या -यं.—(Using plausible arguments) आभासवादी -दिनी -दि (न्).

PLAUSIBLY, *adv.* सत्याभासपूर्वं, प्रमाणाभासपूर्वं, प्रमाणाभासेन, सत्यसादृश्येन, सत्यसदृशं, सत्यसन्निभं, सव्याजं.

To PLAY, *v. n.* (Frolic, sport) क्रीड् (c. 1. क्रीडति -ते -डितुं), आक्रीड्, विक्रीड्, संक्रीड्, परिक्रीड्, अनुक्रीड्, दिव् (c. 4. दीव्यति -ते, देवितुं), खेला (nom. खेलायति), रम् (c. 1. रमते, रन्तुं), विहृ (c. 1. -हरति -हर्त्तुं), विलस् (c. 1. -लसति -सितुं), तेव् (c. 1. तेवते -वितुं), लल् (c. 1. ललति -लितुं), कुर्द् or कूर्द् (c. 1. कूर्दते -र्दितुं), क्रीडां कृ, खेलां कृ.—(Play as a child) कुमार् (c. 10. कुमारयति -यितुं) or कुमाल्, कुड् (c. 6. कुडति -डितुं), कुमारवत् क्रीड्.—(Play at dice or any game) दिव्, प्रदिव्, प्रतिदिव्, अक्षैः or अक्षान् दिव्, अक्षैः क्रीड्, ग्लह् (c. 1. ग्लहते -हितुं), अक्षादिक्रीडां कृ, द्यूतक्रीडां कृ, अक्षद्यूतं कृ.—(On a musical instrument) वद् (c. 10. वादयति -यितुं), संवद्, वादित्रं वद्.—(Act in any character) अभिनयं कृ, नट्, often expressed by a nominal verb; as, 'he plays the king,' राजायते; 'he plays the lion,' सिंहायते; 'he plays the fool,' मूर्खायते.—(Move about, wanton) इतस्ततश् चल् (c. 1. चलति -लितुं) or सृ (c. 1. सरति, सर्त्तुं), विलस्.—(Operate, be in action or motion) चेष्ट् (c. 1. चेष्टते -ष्टितुं), विचेष्ट्, वृत् (c. 1. वर्त्तते -र्त्तितुं), प्रवृत्, चल्.

To PLAY, *v. a.* (Put in action or motion) प्रवृत् (c. 10. -वर्त्तयति -यितुं), चल् (c. 10. चालयति -यितुं), सञ्चल्, सृ (c. 10. सारयति -यितुं), चर् (c. 10. चारयति -यितुं), सञ्चर्.—(A musical instrument) वादित्रं or तूर्य्यं वद् (c. 10. वादयति -यितुं) or संवद् or मुर्च्छ् (c. 10. मूर्च्छयति -यितुं); 'a finger instrument,' मृ or चल्.—(Represent dramatically) अभिनी (c. 1. -नयति -नेतुं), नट् (c. 10. नाटयति -यितुं), रूप् (c. 10. रूपयति -यितुं), अभिनयं कृ.—(Perform, act, do) कृ, विधा (c. 3. -दधाति -धातुं), अनुष्ठा (c. 1. -तिष्ठति -ष्ठातुं), आस्था.

PLAY, *s.* क्रीडा -डनं, खेला -लनं, केलिः *m. f.*, देवनं, विलासः, विलसनं -सितं, लीला, विनोदः, परिहासः, परीहासः, विहारः, क्रीडाकौतुकं, कौतुकं, नर्म्म *n.* (न्), कूर्दनं, कुर्दनं, तेवनं, खेलितं; 'play of fancy,'

बुद्धिविलासः; 'in play,' परिहासेन, लीलया, विलासेन; 'play of children,' बालक्रीडा, बाललीला; 'game of play,' रासः, रासेरसः.—(Playing at dice, &c.) अक्षादिक्रीडा, अक्षक्रीडा, द्यूतक्रीडा, अक्षद्यूतं, द्यूतं, पणपूर्व्विका क्रीडा, देवनं.—(Action, operation) चेष्टा, चेष्टितं, प्रवृत्तिः *f.*, प्रवर्त्तनं, क्रिया, व्यवसायः, व्यापारः.—(Motion) चलनं, चरणं, सञ्चलनं, चरणं, सञ्चरणं, चारः, सरणं, खेलितं, खेलिका, खेल्या.—(Room for free motion) अवकाशः, प्रसरः, अवसरः, चेष्टापर्य्याप्तस्थलं-स्थानं.—(Drama, dramatic composition) नाटकं, प्रकरणं, रूपं -पकं.—(Dramatic show) प्रेक्षणं, प्रेक्षा, कौतुकं.

PLAY-DAY, *s.* क्रीडादिवसः, क्रीडनदिनं, विश्रामदिवसः, अनध्यायदिवसः, अनध्यायतिथिः *m. f.*, अस्वाध्यायतिथिः *m. f.*

PLAYED, *p. p.* क्रीडितः -ता -तं.—(As an instrument) वादितः -ता -तं, प्रवादितः &c.—(Set in motion) चालितः -ता -तं, सञ्चालितः &c., सारितः &c., सञ्चारितः &c.—(Acted) अभिनीतः -ता -तं.—(Performed) कृतः -ता -तं, अनुष्ठितः &c.

PLAYER, *s.* (One who sports) क्रीडकः, क्रीडाकारी *m.* (न्), देवकः, देवी *m.*, खेलाकारी *m.*—(Actor) नटः, कुशीलवः, रङ्गाजीवः, रङ्गजीवकः, अभिनेता *m.* (तृ), रङ्गावतारकः, नर्त्तकः; 'manager of a company of players,' सूत्रधारः, मारिषः.—(At dice, &c.) द्यूतक्रीडकः, अक्षक्रीडकः, अक्षदेवी *m.* (न्), अक्षधूर्त्तः, अक्षधूः *m.*, देवी *m.*—(On an instrument of music) वाद्यवादकः, भाण्डवादकः.

PLAY-FELLOW, PLAY-MATE, *s.* सहक्रीडकः, सहदेवी *m.* (न्), सहदेवकः.

PLAYFUL, *a.* क्रीडावान् -वती -वत् (त्), क्रीडाशीलः -ला -लं, लीलाशीलः -ला -लं, क्रीडापरः -रा -रं, लीलापरः -रा -रं, लीलाखेलः -ला -लं, विलासी -सिनी -सि (न्), क्रीडासक्तः -क्ता -क्तं, विनोदी &c., सलीलः -ला -लं, लीलावान् &c., केलिकः -का -कं, केलिपरः &c., खेलापरः -रा -रं, कलाकेलिः -लिः -लि, कौतुकी &c., कृतकौतुकः -का -कं, अभिलुलितः -ता -तं, चपलः -ला -लं, क्रीडापरायणः -णा -णं, क्रीडकः -का -कं; 'playful anger,' क्रीडाकोपः.

PLAYFULLY, *adv.* विलासेन, सकौतुकं, लीलया, परिहासेन, क्रीडापूर्व्वं.

PLAYFULNESS, *s.* क्रीडाशीलता, सलीलत्वं, सविलासत्वं, चपलता, क्रीडासक्तिः *f.*, क्रीडापरता, लीलापरता, लीलासक्तता.

PLAY-GROUND, *s.* क्रीडास्थानं, केलिस्थानं, क्रीडारामः, देवनं, निष्कुटः.

PLAY-HOUSE, *s.* नाटकशाला, रङ्गशाला, नाटकमन्दिरं, नृत्यशाला, रङ्गः.

PLAY-THING, *s.* क्रीडनकं, क्रीडाद्रव्यं, खेलनी, क्रीडावस्तु *n.*, क्रीडामृगः.

PLEA, *s.* (Excuse) छद्म *n.* (न्), उत्तरं, व्यपदेशः, अपदेशः, उपदेशः, निमित्तं, कारणं.—(In law) उत्तरं, उत्तरवादः, उत्तरपादः; 'special plea,' कारणोत्तरं, प्राङ्न्यायः; 'false plea,' अपार्थकरणं; 'raising a plea,' छलीकरणं.

To PLEAD, *v. n.* उत्तरं वद् (c. 1. वदति -दितुं), उत्तरं कृ or दा, निमित्तं वद्, व्यपदेशं कृ, व्यपदिश् (c. 6. -दिशति -देष्टुं), अपदेशं कृ.—(Supplicate earnestly) विनयेन प्रार्थ् (c. 10. -अर्थयति -यितुं), विनयेन स्वार्थं निविद् (c. 10. -वेदयति -यितुं).

To PLEAD, *v. a.* (Adduce in proof) प्रमाणीकरणार्थम् उपन्यस् (c. 4. -अस्यति -असितुं), हेतुम् or निमित्तम् उपन्यस् हेतूपन्यासं कृ, निमित्तोपन्यासं कृ.—(Alledge in excuse) व्यपदेशार्थं वद् (c. 1. वदति -दितुं) or उपन्यस्, अपदेशार्थं वद्.—(Plead the cause of another) परार्थं वद्, परार्थम् उत्तरं वद्.

PLEADABLE, *a.* व्यपदेशार्थं or प्रमाणीकरणार्थम् उपन्यसनीयः -या -यं or उपन्यास्यः -स्या -स्यं.

PLEADED, *p. p.* व्यपदेशार्थं or प्रमाणीकरणार्थम् उपन्यस्तः -स्ता -स्तं.

PLEADER, *s.* उत्तरवादी *m.* (न्), हेतुवादी *m.*, निमित्तवादी *m.*—(For another) परार्थं वादी *m.* or उत्तरवादी *m.*

PLEADING, *s.* उत्तरवादः, हेतुवादः, निमित्तवादः, व्यपदेशकरणं, छलकरणं, प्रमाणीकरणार्थं or व्यपदेशार्थं हेतूपन्यासः or निमित्तोपन्यासः.

PLEASANT, *a.* रम्यः -म्या -म्यं, रमणीयः -या -यं, प्रियः -या -यं, सुप्रियः -या -यं, मनःप्रियः &c., मनोरमः -मा -मं, रामः -मा -मं, अभिरामः -मा -मं, मनोभिरामः -मा -मं, मनोज्ञः -ज्ञा -ज्ञं, सुभगः -गा -गं, अभिमतः -ता -तं, यथाभिमतः -ता -तं, सुखः -खा -खं, सुखदः -दा -दं, सुखावहः -हा -हं, सुखप्रदः -दा -दं, सुखकरः -रा -रं, सुखदायकः -का -कं, यथासुखः -खा -खं, काम्यः -म्या -म्यं, कमनीयः -या -यं, कान्तः -न्ता -न्तं, नन्दकः -का -कं, आनन्ददः -दा -दं, आनन्दकरः &c., हर्षकः &c., हर्षणः -णा -णं, हर्षकरः &c., हर्षावहः -हा -हं, मोदकः -का -कं, मधुरः -रा -रं, रुचिकरः &c., रुचिरः -रा -रं, रुच्यः -च्या -च्यं, प्रशस्तः -स्ता -स्तं, तुष्टिकरः &c., हृदयङ्गमः -मा -मं, हृद्यः -द्या -द्यं, सुरभिः -भिः -भि, मनोरञ्जकः &c., मनोरञ्जनः &c., चोक्षः -क्षा -क्षं, चौक्षः -क्षी -क्षं.

PLEASANTLY, *adv.* सुखेन, सुखं, यथासुखं, सुखरूपेण, रम्यं, रमनीयं, मनोरमं, सुभगं, यथाभिमतं, प्रियं, सुप्रियं, मधुरं, रुचिरं.

PLEASANTNESS, *s.* रम्यता, रमणीयता, अभिरामता, प्रियता, सुप्रियता, काम्यत्वं, कामता, अभिमतत्वं, सुखत्वं, सौख्यं, सुखदायकत्वं.

PLEASANTRY, *s.* विनोदः, विनोदवाक्यं, विनोदोक्तिः *f.*, नर्म्मोक्तिः *f.*, नर्म्मभाषणं, परिहासः, परीहासः, हासिका.

To PLEASE, *v. a.* (Gratify) सुख् (c. 10. सुखयति -यितुं), सन्तुष् (c. 10. -तोषयति -यितुं), परितुष्, प्री (c. 9. प्रीणाति, c. 10. प्रीणयति -यितुं), तृप्, प्रमुद्, रम्, ह्लाद्, आह्लाद्, हृष्, विनुद् (c. 10. -नोदयति -यितुं), अनुरञ्ज् (c. 10. -रञ्जयति -यितुं), आराध् (c. 10. -राधयति -यितुं), सभाज्, सुखं कृ or दा, प्रीतिं कृ or दा; 'anxious to please,' अनुग्रहकातरः -रा -रं.—(Approve itself to) रुच् (c. 1. रोचते -चितुं) with dat. or gen. of the person, शुभ् (c. 1. शोभते -भितुं), अभिमतः -ता -तं भू, अनुमतः -ता -तं भू, प्रियः -या -यं भू; 'that pleases me,' तन् मह्यं or मम रोचते, तन् मया or मम अनुमतं or अभिमतं. *See To* LIKE.

To PLEASE, *v. n.* (Choose) रुच् (c. 1. रोचते -चितुं, c. 10. रोचयति -यितुं), इष् (c. 6. इच्छति, एषितुं); 'as you like,' यथा भवते रोचते, यथाकामं. *See To* LIKE, *v. n.*—(Condescend, as a word of ceremony) कृपां or दयां कृ. Usually expressed by the 2d or 3d person of the rt. अर्ह्, or by the use of तावत्, or some other particle; as, 'Be pleased to speak to me,' मां वक्तुम् अर्हसि or अर्हति भवान्; 'please to go,' गच्छ तावत्.

PLEASED, *p. p.* प्रीतः -ता -तं, प्रीतात्मा -त्मा -त्म (न्), तुष्टः -ष्टा -ष्टं, सन्तुष्टः &c., परितुष्टः &c., हृष्टः &c., हृष्टचित्तः -त्ता -त्तं, प्रसन्नः -न्ना -न्नं, प्रसादितः -ता -तं, मोदितः &c., मुदितः &c., आह्लादितः &c., प्रह्लादितः &c., आनन्दितः &c., अभिरुचितः &c., तृप्तः -प्ता -प्तं, रममाणः -णा -णं, प्रतीतः -ता -तं; 'in mind,' प्रीतमनाः -नाः -नः (स्).

PLEASING, *a.* रम्यः -म्या -म्यं, मनोरमः -मा -मं, रमणीयः -या -यं, सुभगः -गा -गं, नन्दकः -का -कं, मोदकः &c., कमनीयः -या -यं, रुचिरः -रा -रं, रोचिष्णुः -ष्णुः -ष्णु, वन्दकः -का -कं, मञ्जुलः -ला -लं, मनोज्ञः -ज्ञा -ज्ञं, मनोनुकूलः -ला -लं, मनआपः -पा -पं, मनोरञ्जकः &c. *See* PLEASANT, *a.*—(To the eye) चक्षुष्यः -ष्या -ष्यं, सुदृश्यः -श्या -श्यं, चारुरूपः -पा -पी -पं, दृश्यः &c. *See* BEAUTIFUL.—(To the ear) सुश्रवः -वा -वं, श्रोत्रसुखः -खा -खं, श्रुतिसुखः &c., श्रोत्राभिरामः -मा -मं, सुचारुस्वनः -ना -नं, मञ्जुस्वनः &c., सुश्राव्यः -व्या -व्यं; 'pleasing language,' चाटुः -टु *m. n.*, चाटूक्तिः *f.*

PLEASINGLY, *adv.* सुभगं, रमणीयं, रम्यं, मनोरमं, सुख or चारु or मधु in comp.; as, 'singing pleasingly,' चारुस्वनः -ना -नं, सुखस्वनः &c., मधुस्वनः &c.

PLEASURABLE, *a.* रम्यः -म्या -म्यं, रमणीयः -या -यं, सौख्यीयः -या -यं, सुखावहः -हा -हं, भोगवान् -वती -वत् (त्). *See* PLEASANT.

PLEASURE, *s.* (Gratification, enjoyment) प्रीतिः *f.*, सुखं, सौख्यं, आनन्दः, तुष्टिः *f.*, सन्तोषः, परितोषः, तोषः, हर्षः, मोदः, आमोदः, प्रमोदः, आह्लादः, प्रह्लादः, रतिः *f.*, उल्लासः, अभिरुचिः *f.*, नन्दः, ह्लादः, मुदा, मुद् *f.*, विलासः, कुतूहलं, कौतुकं, शर्म्म *n.* (न्), उत्साहः; 'intense pleasure,' परमानन्दः, अत्यानन्दः, रोमहर्षः -र्षणं, पुलकः, रोमाञ्चः; 'in pleasure and pain,' सुखदुःखयोः loc. du.—(Liking, friendship for) रुचिः *f.*, अभिरुचिः *f.*, इच्छा, अभिमतता, अनुरक्तिः *f.*, अभिलाषः, अभिलषितं, छन्दं, छन्दस् *n.*; 'one's own pleasure,' स्वेच्छा; 'at one's pleasure,' स्वेच्छया, स्वेच्छातस्, कामतस्, यथाकामं, कामं, अनुकामं.—(Sensual pleasure) विषयभोगः, विषयकामः, विषयसुखं, विषयानुरागः, कामः, भोगः.—(Sexual pleasure) रतिः *f.*, सुरतं, रतं, भोगः, भोगविलासः.—(Cause of pleasure) सुखहेतुः *m.*, सुखकारणं; 'goddess of pleasure,' रक्तदेवता.

PLEASURE-BOAT, *s.* क्रीडानौका, केलिनौका, विलासनौका.

PLEASURE-GROUND, *s.* उद्यानं, क्रीडोद्यानं, आरामः, क्रीडारामः, क्रीडावनं, विलासवनं, क्रीडाकाननं, विलासकाननं, केलिकाननं, केलिवनं, प्रमदवनं, विलोद्यानं, तेवनं.

PLEASURE-HOUSE, *s.* केलिगृहं, क्रीडागृहं, विलासगृहं, विलासमन्दिरं.

PLEASURIST, *s.* भोगासक्तः, विषयासक्तः, विषयसेवी *m.* (न्), केलिनागरः, केलिपरः, विषयी *m.* (न्), वैषयिकः, भोगपरायणः.

PLEBEIAN, *a.* प्राकृतः -ती -तं, दुष्कुलीनः -ना -नं, अकुलीनः -ना -नं, लौकिकः -की -कं, साधारणः -णा -णी -णं, सामान्यः -न्या -न्यं, अवरवर्णः -र्णा -र्णं, अधमवर्णः &c., अन्त्यवर्णः &c., अधमजातीयः -या -यं, अन्त्यजातीयः -या -यं, पामरः -री -रं.

PLEBEIAN, *s.* प्राकृतजनः, पृथग्जनः, निहीनजनः, इतरजनः, अकुलीनजनः, वृषलः, अपसदः, नीचजनः, पामरजनः.

PLECTRUM, *s.* कोणः, शारिका, परिवादः, रणः.

PLEDGE, *s.* (Any thing deposited as a security) न्यासः, निक्षेपः, आधिः *m.*, आधानं, उपन्यासः, बन्धकः, उपनिधिः *m.*, उपनिक्षेपः, उपनिधानं, औपनिधिकं, अन्वाधिः *m.*, पणः, परिपणनं, आधमनं, आधीकरणं; 'counter-pledge,' प्रतिपाणं.—(Any thing deposited as security for the repayment of something borrowed) गृहीतस्य द्रव्यस्योपरि विश्वासार्थम् अधमर्णेनोत्तमर्णे न्यस्त आधिः; 'act of depositing a pledge,' आधीकरणं.—(Hostage) बन्धकः, शरीरबन्धकः.—(Token) अभिज्ञानं.

To PLEDGE, *v. a.* आधीकृ, न्यस् (c. 4. -अस्यति -असितुं), प्रतिन्यस्, उपन्यस्, निक्षिप् (c. 6. -क्षिपति -क्षेप्तुं), उपनिक्षिप्, निधा (c. 3. -दधाति -धातुं), आधा, पण् (c. 1. पणते -णितुं), परिपण्, न्यासीकृ.—(Pledge one's self, pledge one's word) प्रतिज्ञा (c. 9. -जानीते -ज्ञातुं), प्रतिज्ञां कृ, प्रतिज्ञाबद्धः -द्धा -द्धं भू, वचनबद्धः -द्धा -द्धं भू, अङ्गीकृ, उरीकृ.

PLEDGED, *p.p.* आधीकृतः -ता -तं, न्यस्तः -स्ता -स्तं, उपन्यस्तः &c., निक्षिप्तः -प्ता -प्तं, परिपणितः -ता -तं, न्यासीकृतः -ता -तं.—(Promised) प्रतिज्ञातः -ता -तं, अङ्गीकृतः &c., अभ्युपेतः &c.; 'that has pledged his word,' कृतप्रतिज्ञः -ज्ञा -ज्ञं, प्रतिज्ञाबद्धः -द्धा -द्धं, वचनबद्धः &c., दत्तप्रतिज्ञः &c., दत्तवचनः &c.

PLEDGET, *s.* (In surgery) विकेशिका, पट्टः -ट्टकः, आवेष्टनं, कवलिका.

PLEIADS, PLEIADES, *s. pl.* कृत्तिका, बहुलाः *f. pl.*

PLENARY, *a.* सम्पूर्णः -र्णा -र्णं, परिपूर्णः &c., निःशेषः -षा -षं.

PLENILUNAR, PLENILUNARY, *a.* पूर्णचन्द्रसम्बन्धी &c., पूर्णेन्दुसम्बन्धी &c.

PLENIPOTENCE, *s.* पूर्णसामर्थ्यं, सामर्थ्यपूर्णता, पूर्णशक्तित्वं, शक्तिपूर्णता.

PLENIPOTENT, *a.* पूर्णशक्तिः -क्तिः -क्ति, पूर्णशक्तिमान् -मती -मत् (त्).

PLENIPOTENTIARY, *s.* पूर्णशक्तियुक्तः, पूर्णशक्तिविशिष्टः, पूर्णशक्तिकः.

PLENIST, *s.* पूर्णतावादी *m.* (न्), पूर्णत्ववादी *m.*

PLENITUDE, *s.* पूर्णता, सम्पूर्णता -त्वं, परिपूर्णता -त्वं, पूर्त्तिः *f.*, आपूर्त्तिः *f.*, पुष्कलता, विपुलता, समृद्धिः *f.*, सामृद्ध्यं, प्राचुर्य्यं, उत्सेकः.

PLENTEOUS, PLENTIFUL, *a.* बहुलः -ला -लं, बहुः -हुः -ह्वी -हु, प्रचुरः -रा -रं, पुष्कलः -ला -लं, विपुलः -ला -लं, समृद्धः -द्धा -द्धं, परिपूर्णः -र्णा -र्णं, भूरिः -रिः -रि, अतिरिक्तः -क्ता -क्तं, उद्रिक्तः &c., उत्सिक्तः &c., उपचितः &c.

PLENTEOUSLY, PLENTIFULLY, *adv.* बाहुल्येन, बहुशस्, प्राचुर्य्येण, प्रचुरं, पुष्कलं, विपुलं, वैपुल्येन, भूरिशस्, भूरि, बहु, अनेकशस्, अतिरिक्तं, उद्रेकेण.

PLENTEOUSNESS, PLENTIFULNESS, *s.* बाहुल्यं, प्राचुर्य्यं, पुष्कलत्वं. *See* next.

PLENTY, *s.* बाहुल्यं, बहुत्वं -ता, प्राचुर्य्यं, प्रचुरता -त्वं, वैपुल्यं, विपुलता, पुष्कलता, समृद्धिः *f.*, सामृद्ध्यं, वृद्धिः *f.*, समृद्धता, प्रभूतता, उद्रेकः, अतिरेकः, उत्सेकः, अतिरिक्तता, उत्सिक्तता, स्फीतिः *f.*, स्फातिः *f.*; 'time of plenty or abundance of corn, &c.,' सुभिक्षं, धान्यसमृद्धिः *f.*; 'cow of plenty,' कामदा, कामदुघा, कामधुक् *f.* (ह्). *See* PHILOSOPHER'S STONE.

PLEONASM, *s.* शब्दातिशयः, शब्दबाहुल्यं, शब्दाधिक्यं, स्वार्थं, मात्रं.

PLEONASTIC, *a.* स्वार्थः -र्था -र्थं, अतिरिक्तः -क्ता -क्तं, अतिरिक्तशब्दः -ब्दा -ब्दं.

PLEONASTICALLY, *adv.* शब्दबाहुल्येन, शब्दाधिक्येन, स्वार्थतस्.

PLETHORA, *s.* रक्तपित्तं -त्तः, पित्तरक्तं, असृक्पित्तं, रक्तातिशय्यं, रक्ताधिक्यं, अतिपुष्टिः *f.*

PLETHORIC, *a.* रक्तपित्तरोगी -गिणी -गि (न्), अतिपुष्टिशीलः -ला -लं, अतिपुष्टः -ष्टा -ष्टं, अतिशयपुष्टः -ष्टा -ष्टं.

PLEURISY, *s.* (Disease of the chest) उरोग्रहः, वक्षोग्रहः.

PLEURITIC, *a.* उरोग्रहरोगी -गिणी -गि (न्), उरोग्रही &c., वक्षोग्रही &c.

PLIABILITY, PLIANCY, *s.* सुनम्यता, सुनमनीयत्वं, नमनशीलता, आनम्यता, आयम्यता, मृदुता, मार्दवं, कोमलता, शिथिलता, शैथिल्यं, अदृढता.

PLIANT, PLIABLE, *a.* सुनम्यः -म्या -म्यं, सुखनम्यः &c., सुनमनीयः -या -यं, नमनशीलः -ला -लं, आनम्यः &c., नम्यः &c., नमनीयः &c., आयम्यः &c., मृदुः -दुः -द्वी -दु, कोमलः -ला -लं, शिथिलः -ला -लं, अदृढः -ढा -ढं.

To PLIGHT, *v. a.* *See* *To* PLEDGE.

PLIGHT, *s.* (Condition) अवस्था, दशा, स्थितिः *f.*, भावः, वृत्तिः *f.*, गतिः *f.*; 'bad plight,' दुर्दशा, दुःस्थितिः *f.*, दुर्गतिः *f.*; 'in bad plight,' दुर्दशाग्रस्तः -स्ता -स्तं, दुःस्थः -स्था -स्थं.—(Gage). *See* PLEDGE.

PLIGHTED, *p. p.* परिपणितः -ता -तं, न्यस्तः -स्ता -स्तं, उपन्यस्तः &c., प्रतिज्ञातः -ता -तं, कृतप्रतिज्ञः -ज्ञा -ज्ञं; 'in marriage,' प्रतिज्ञाविवाहितः &c., वाग्दत्तः -त्ता -त्तं.

PLINTH, *s.* प्राकारमूलं, भित्तिमूलं, प्राकारतलं, स्तम्भमूलं, स्तम्भतलं.

To PLOD, *v. n.* मन्दं मन्दं निरन्तरायासेन or अविरतक्लेशेन श्रम् (c. 4. श्राम्यति, श्रमितुं) or अविरतश्रमेण आयस् (c. 4. -यस्यति -यसितुं), अतिमान्द्येन नित्यश्रमं कृ or नित्यायासं कृ or नित्यकष्टं कृ or नित्यक्लेशं कृ or नित्यप्रवृत्तिं कृ.

PLODDER, *s.* अतिमान्द्येन निरन्तरायासी *m.* (न्) or अविरतायासी *m.* or निरन्तरश्रमी or नित्यश्रमी *m.* (न्) or नित्योद्योगी *m.* (न्) or नित्य-

व्यवसायी, आयासाध्ययनी m. (न्), श्रमाभ्यायी m., आयासव्यासक्ती m., आयासगामी m., पिपीलिकाधर्म्मी m. (न्).

PLODDING, s. अतिमान्द्यपूर्व्वो निरन्तरायासः or अविरतायासः, अतिमान्द्येन नित्यश्रमः or नित्योद्योगः or नित्यव्यवसायः, आयासाध्ययनं, श्रमाध्ययनं, पिपीलिकाधर्म्मः.

PLODDING, a. अतिमान्द्यपूर्व्वं निरन्तरायासी -सिनी -सि (न्) or नित्यश्रमी &c.

PLOT, s. (Complicated scheme, deep-laid stratagem) कपटप्रबन्धः, छलप्रबन्धः, कापट्यप्रबन्धः, उपायप्रबन्धः, कूटप्रबन्धः, कल्पना, उपायकल्पना, सङ्कल्पः, उपायप्रयोगः, प्रयोगः, युक्तिः f., अपदेशः, व्यपदेशः, मन्त्रणा, उपायः.—(Scheme of mischief) कुसङ्कल्पः, कुकल्पना, कुमन्त्रणा, कुकर्म्मसम्पादनार्थं or द्रोहसम्पादनार्थं कपटप्रबन्धः.—(Of a drama, &c.) वस्तु n.; 'secondary plot,' प्रतिमुखं; 'good plot,' सुवस्तु; 'a play with a plot composed by Kálidása,' कालिदासग्रथितवस्तुनाटकः.—(Of ground) स्थलं -ली -ला, भूमिभागः, भूभागः, भूप्रदेशः, भूमिप्रदेशः, भूमिः f., वसुधा.

To PLOT, v. a. or n. (Form a scheme) मनसा उपायप्रबन्धं कृप् (c. 10. कल्पयति -यितुं) or प्रचिन्त् (c. 10. -चिन्तयति -यितुं) or अनुसन्धा (c. 3. -दधाति -धातुं), मन्त्र् (c. 10. मन्त्रयते -यितुं), सम्मन्त्र्, उपायकल्पनां कृ, कपटप्रबन्धं कृ, उपायप्रबन्धं कृ, सङ्कल्पं कृ.—(Form a scheme of mischief) कुसङ्कल्पं कृ, कुकर्म्मसम्पादनार्थं कपटप्रबन्धं कृ or उपायकल्पनां कृ, द्रोहकरणार्थं कुमन्त्रणां कृ or सम्मन्त्रणां कृ.—(Plot against) द्रुह् (c. 4. द्रुह्यति, द्रोग्धुं), अभिद्रुह्, द्रोहं चिन्त् or प्रचिन्त्, कपटप्रबन्धेन द्रोहं कृ.

PLOTTER, s. कपटप्रबन्धकारी m. (न्), उपायकल्पकः, उपायचिन्तकः, द्रोहचिन्तकः, कुमन्त्रणाकृत्, कुकल्पनाकृत् m., कुसङ्कल्पकारी m. (न्).

PLOUGH, s. हलं, लाङ्गलं, गोदारणं, सीरः, शीरः, हालः, गोकीलः, गोकिलः, कृन्तत्रं, कर्षणी, आकर्षणी, राधरङ्कुः, कुन्तलः; 'body of a plough,' फालः, फलं, निरीशं, निरीषं, कूटकं; 'the share,' *see* PLOUGHSHARE; 'the pole or shaft,' ईषा, ईशा, लाङ्गलदण्डः; 'the yoke,' युगं, कुशः; 'pin of it,' युगकीलकः; 'tie of it,' योक्त्रं, योत्रं, आबन्धः; 'handle of a plough,' ईषादण्डः, ईशादण्डः; 'relating or belonging to a plough,' हालिकः -की -कं, लाङ्गलिकः &c., सैरिकः -की -कं; 'to hold, drive or follow the plough,' लाङ्गलं or हलं ग्रह् (c. 9. गृह्णाति, ग्रहीतुं) or भृ or धृ or वह् (c. 10. वाहयति -यितुं) or चल् (c. 10. चालयति -यितुं).

To PLOUGH, v. a. हलेन or लाङ्गलेन कृष् (c. 1. कर्षति, क्रष्टुं) or कर्षणं कृ, लाङ्गलेन भूमिं दृ (c. 10. दारयति -यितुं) or भिद् (c. 7. भिनत्ति, भेत्तुं), हल् (c. 1. हलति -लितुं, c. 10. हलयति -यितुं), हलहतिं कृ, लाङ्गलहतिं कृ, हलहतं -तां कृ, हलकृष्टं -ष्टां कृ.

To PLOUGH, v. n. (Drive a plough) लाङ्गलं or हलं वह् (c. 10. वाहयति -यितुं) or चल् (c. 10. चालयति -यितुं).

PLOUGHABLE, a. कर्षणीयः -या -यं, कृषियोग्यः -ग्या -ग्यं, सीत्यः -त्या -त्यं, हल्यः -ल्या -ल्यं, हलहतियोग्यः &c.

PLOUGH-BOY, s. बालकृषकः, बालकर्षकः, बालहालिकः.

PLOUGHED, p.p. कृष्टः -ष्टा -ष्टं, कर्षितः -ता -तं, हलकृष्टः &c., फालकृष्टः &c., फालकर्षितः &c., सीत्यः -त्या -त्यं, शीत्यः &c., हल्यः -ल्या -ल्यं; 'twice-ploughed,' द्विगुणाकृतः -ता -तं, द्वितीयाकृतः &c., द्विहल्यः &c., द्विसीत्यः -त्या -त्यं, शम्बाकृतः -ता -तं, सम्बाकृतः &c.; 'thrice-ploughed,' त्रिसीत्यः &c., त्रिगुणाकृतः &c., तृतीयाकृतः &c., त्रिहल्यः &c.; 'ploughed by two ploughs,' हलद्वयेन कृष्टः &c. or वाहितः; 'a ploughed field,' फालकृष्टक्षेत्रं, फालकृष्टं, हल्यक्षेत्रं; 'land ploughed after sowing,' बीजाकृतः -ता -तं, उप्तकृष्टः -ष्टा -ष्टं.

PLOUGHER, s. कृषकः, कर्षकः, कर्षी m. (न्), हालिकः, सैरिकः.

PLOUGH-GEAR, s. हलोपकरणं, लाङ्गलोपकरणं, लाङ्गलसामग्री, हलसज्जा.

PLOUGH-HANDLE, s. ईषादण्डः, ईशादण्डः, ईषायष्टिः m. f.

PLOUGHING, s. कर्षणं, कृषिः f., कार्षिः f., उत्कर्षणं, प्रकर्षणं, सङ्कर्षणं, लाङ्गलकर्षणं, भूमिकर्षणं, क्षेत्रकर्षणं, भूमिदारणं, हलहतिः f., हलभृतिः f., लाङ्गलग्रहणं, उत्कषणं.

PLOUGH-LAND, s. हल्यक्षेत्रं, हल्यभूमिः f., फालकृष्टं, हल्यं, सीत्यं, शीत्यं, हालिकं, हालिकक्षेत्रं, लाङ्गलिकं. *See* PLOUGHED.

PLOUGH-MAN, s. हालिकः, लाङ्गलिकः, लाङ्गली m. (न्), लाङ्गलग्रहः, हलधरः, लाङ्गलधरः, हलभृत् m., लाङ्गलभृत् m., हलवाहकः, कृषिकः, कृषकः, कर्षकः, कृषिजीवी m. (न्), कर्षी m. (न्), कार्षकः -र्षिकः, कृषीवलः, क्षेत्रकर्षकः, भूमिकर्षकः, सैरिकः, शैरिकः.

PLOUGH-SHARE, s. फालः, कृषिकः -का, कृषकः, फलं, जित्या, कुशी, कूटकं.

PLOUGH-TAIL, s. लाङ्गलपृष्ठं, लाङ्गलस्य पश्चाद्भागः or पश्चिमभागः.

To PLUCK, v. a. (Pull off, out or from) उत्कृष् (c. 1. -कर्षति -क्रष्टुं), निष्कृष्, कृष्, उद्धृ (c. 1. -हरति -हर्त्तुं), निर्हृ, हृ, उत्पट् (c. 10. -पाटयति -यितुं), उत्पाटनं कृ.—(As the hair) लुञ्च् (c. 1. लुञ्चति -ञ्चितुं), उल्लुञ्च्, अवलुञ्च्, केशान् उत्पट्, केशोत्पाटनं कृ, केशोल्लुञ्चनं कृ.—(As feathers, &c.) पक्षान् or पर्णान् उत्पट् or निष्कृष् or निर्हृ or हृ, पक्षोत्पाटनं कृ, निष्पक्षीकृ, निष्पर्णीकृ, निष्पत्रीकृ.—(Gather by plucking) अङ्गुलिभिर् ग्रह् (c. 9. गृह्णाति, ग्रहीतुं) or आदा (c. 3. -ददाति -दत्ते -दातुं) or चि or अवचि or लू or छिद्.—(Pluck up) उत्पट्, उद्धृ, समुद्धृ, उन्मूल् (c. 10. -मूलयति -यितुं), समुन्मूल्, उच्छिद्, उत्खन्.

PLUCK, s. (Of an animal) पशोर् हृद्यकृदादि n.—(Mettle, courage) वीर्य्यं, सत्त्वं, साहसं, पौरुषं.

PLUCKED, p.p. हृतपर्णः -र्णा -र्णं, उद्धृतपर्णः &c., हृतलोमा -मा -म (न्).

PLUCKER, s. उत्पाटयिता m. (तृ), उत्पाटी m. (न्), उद्धर्त्ता m. (र्तृ).

PLUCKING, s. उत्पाटः -टनं, उत्कर्षणं, निष्कर्षणं, उद्धरणं.—(As of hair) उल्लुञ्चनं, अवलुञ्चनं.—(Gathering) चयः -यनं, अवचयः, ग्रहणं.

PLUG, s. रोधनी, निरोधनी, स्तम्भनी, पिधानं.

To PLUG, v. a. रुध् (c. 7. रुणद्धि, रोद्धुं), निरुध्, स्तम्भ् (c. 10. स्तम्भयति -यितुं), पिधा (c. 3. -दधाति -धातुं).

PLUM, s. (Fruit) आम्रफलभेदः.—(Sum of one hundred thousand) लक्षं -क्षा, लक्ष्यं; 'one who is worth a plum,' लक्षाधीशः.

PLUMAGE, s. पक्षः, पर्णः, पक्षिपर्णाः m. pl., पक्षिपत्राणि n. pl., पतत्रं, पिच्छं, गरुत् m.; 'of a peacock,' गुच्छः -च्छकः, वृषं; 'having good or beautiful plumage,' सुपर्णः -र्णा -र्णं, सुपर्णी -र्णिनी -र्णि (न्), सुपक्षवान् -वती -वत् (त्), चारुपर्णः &c., चारुपर्णी &c.

PLUMB, s. लम्बः -म्बकः, लम्बसीसकं, ससीसकसूत्रं. *See* PLUMMET.

PLUMB, a. लम्बः -म्बा -म्बं, लम्बरूपः -पा -पं, ऋजुः -जुः -जु.

To PLUMB, v. a. (Adjust with a line) सूत्र् (c. 10. सूत्रयति -यितुं), सूत्रेण समायुज् (c. 10. -योजयति -यितुं) or युज्.—(Sound depth) सूत्रेण वेधपरिमापणं कृ or गाम्भीर्य्यपरिमापणं कृ.

PLUMBEAN, PLUMBEOUS, a. सीसमयः -यी -यं, सीसगुणकः -का -कं, सैसकः &c.

PLUMBER, s. सीसकारः -रकः, सीसकर्त्ता m. (र्तृ), सीसकव्यापारी m.

PLUMB-LINE, s. लम्बसीसकं, लम्बसूत्रं. *See* PLUMB, s.

PLUM-CAKE, s. चित्रापूपः, चित्रपिष्टकः, शुष्कफलपूरितापूपः.

PLUME, s. (Feather) पक्षः, पर्णः, पिच्छं.—(Feather worn as ornament, crest) शेखरः, चूडा, शिखा, किरीटः, मुकुटं, मौलिः m. f.

To PLUME, *v. a.* (Adjust feathers) पक्षान् or पर्णान् रच् (c. 10. रचयति -यितुं) or विरच्.—(Strip of feathers) पक्षान् or पर्णान् उत्कृष् or निष्कृष् or हृ or उत्पट्, निष्पक्षीकृ. *See To* PLUCK.—(Pride one's self) अभिमन् (c. 4. -मन्यते -मन्तुं), आत्मानं श्लाघ् (c. 1. श्लाघते -घितुं); 'to plume one's self on one's learning,' पण्डितम्मन्यः -न्या -न्यं भू or अस्.

PLUMELESS, *a.* पक्षहीनः -ना -नं, चूडाहीनः &c., अपक्षः -क्षा -क्षं.

PLUMIGEROUS, *a.* पक्षवान् -वती -वत् (त्), पक्षी -क्षिणी -क्षि (न्), सपक्षः -क्षा -क्षं.

PLUMIPED, *a.* सपक्षपादः -दा -दं, सपर्णपादः &c., सपक्षचरणः &c.

PLUMMET, *s.* लम्बः -म्बकः, लम्बसीसकं, ससीसकसूत्रं, सीसालम्बितसूत्रं, सीसलग्नसूत्रं, सूत्रलग्नसीसकं, लम्बसूत्रं, लम्बकसूत्रं.

PLUMOSE, PLUMOUS, *s.* सपक्षः -क्षा -क्षं, सपिच्छः -च्छा -च्छं, पक्षवान् -वती -वत् (त्), पिच्छिलः -ला -लं. *See* FEATHERED.

PLUMP, *a.* पीवरः -रा -रं, पीनः -ना -नं, घनः -ना -नं, घनमांसः -सा -सं, उन्नतमांसः &c., उन्नतः -ता -तं, पुष्टः -ष्टा -ष्टं, परिपुष्टः &c., मांसपुष्टः &c., स्थूलमांसः &c., सुललितः -ता -तं, सुललितमांसः &c., आप्यानः -ना -नं, स्थूलः -ला -लं, उच्छूनः -ना -नं, तुन्दी -न्दिनी -न्दि (न्), तुन्दिकः -का -कं, स्फीतः -ता -तं, स्फातः &c., पुष्टः -ष्टा -ष्टं.

PLUMP, *adv.* अकस्मात्, आकस्मिकशब्देन, आस्फोटनशब्देन.

To PLUMP, *v. a.* आप्यै (c. 10. -प्याययति -यितुं), स्थूलीकृ, पीवरीकृ, स्थूलय् (c. 10. स्थूलयति -यितुं), श्वि (c. 10. श्वाययति -यितुं), उच्छूनीकृ, शूनीकृ.

To PLUMP, *v. n.* अकस्मात् or आकस्मिकशब्देन or आस्फोटनशब्देन पत् (c. 1. पतति -तितुं), अतिभारेण पत्.

PLUMPLY, *adv.* सुव्यक्तं, सुस्पष्टं, अतिव्यक्तं, व्यक्तार्थतस्, अवक्रं.

PLUMPNESS, *s.* घनता, स्थूलता -त्वं, पीवरत्वं, पीनत्वं, पुष्टता, सुपुष्टता, पुष्टिः *f.*, सुपुष्टिः *f.*, स्फीतिः *f.*, स्फीतता -त्वं, स्फातिः *f.*, पुष्टता, आप्यानं, उन्नतिः *f.*

PLUM-PUDDING, *s.* चित्रापूपः, चित्रपोलिका, मोदकादिपूरितपोलिका.

PLUMY, *a.* सपक्षः -क्षा -क्षं, पक्षविशिष्टः -ष्टा -ष्टं. *See* FEATHERED.

PLUNDER, *s.* लोप्त्रं, लोत्रं, लुम्नं, लोतः -तं, लुण्ठनं, लुण्ठा, लुण्टनं, लुण्टा, हरणं, अपहारः, अभिग्रहः, धनापहारः -हरणं, नष्टाप्तिसूत्रं, होढं.

To PLUNDER, *v. a.* धनद्रव्यादि हृ (c. 1. हरति, हर्त्तुं) or अपहृ or अभिहृ, लुण्ठ् (c. 1. लुण्ठति -ण्ठितुं) or लुण्ट् or लुण्ड् or रुण्ठ् or रुण्ट्, चुर् (c. 10. चोरयति -यितुं), विलुप् (c. 6. -लुम्पति -लोप्तुं), लुप्, कल् (c. 10. कालयति -यितुं), प्रकल्, साहसेन or साहसपूर्व्वम् अपहृ.

PLUNDERED, *p. p.* हृतधनः -ना -नं, हृतद्रव्यः -व्या -व्यं, हृतस्वः -स्वा -स्वं, अपहृतस्वः &c., लुण्ठितः -ता -तं, साहसेन or साहसपूर्व्वम् अपहृतः -ता -तं, लुप्तः -प्ता -प्तं, होढः -ढा -ढं.

PLUNDERER, *s.* अपहारकः, अपहारी *m.* (न्), हारकः, हारी *m.*, अपहर्त्ता *m.* (र्तृ), लुण्टाकः, लुण्ठनकृत् *m.*, साहसेन or साहसपूर्व्वम् अपहारी *m.*, साहसिकः.

PLUNDERING, *s.* अपहारः, अपहरणं, हरणं, धनापहारः, लुण्ठनं, लुण्टनं.

To PLUNGE, *v. a.* (Immerse) मस्ज् (c. 10. मज्जयति -यितुं), निमस्ज्, प्लु (c. 10. प्लावयति -यितुं), आप्लु, अवगाह् (c. 10. -गाहयति -यितुं), जलं प्रविश् in caus., जले निविश्, स्ना in caus.

To PLUNGE, *v. n.* (Dive) मस्ज् (c. 6. मज्जति -ज्जितुं, मंक्तुं), निमस्ज्, अवगाह् (c. 1. -गाहते -हितुं -गाढुं), व्यवगाह्, विगाह्, आप्लु (c. 1. -प्लवते -प्लोतुं), जलमध्ये प्रविश्, जलान्तः प्रविश्, जलं प्रविश्, जलान्तः-प्रवेशं कृ, जलान्तःप्लवनं कृ, स्ना.

PLUNGE, PLUNGING, *s.* मज्जनं, निमज्जनं, प्रमज्जनं, प्लवनं, आप्लवः, आप्लावः -वनं, अवगाहनं, विगाहः -हनं, गाहनं, जलप्रवेशः, जलान्तःप्लवनं, जलान्तःप्रवेशः, निमज्जनं; 'of an elephant,' निर्वाणं.

PLUNGED, *p. p.* मग्नः -ग्ना -ग्नं, निमग्नः &c., मज्जितः -ता -तं, निमज्जितः &c., प्रमग्नः &c., गाहितः -ता -तं, अवगाहितः &c., अवगाढः -ढा -ढं, विगाढः &c., आप्लुतः -ता -तं, निवेशितः &c., अभिनिवेशितः &c., निविष्टः -ष्टा -ष्टं, अभिनिविष्टः &c., लीनः -ना -नं, निर्वाणः -णा -णं; 'in a sea of sorrow,' शोकसागरमग्नः &c., शोकसागरावगाढः -ढा -ढं. *See* IMMERSED.

PLUNGEON, *s.* (The Diver bird) प्लवः, प्लावी *m.* (न्).

PLUNGER, *s.* गाहिता *m.* (तृ), अवगाहिता *m.*, मंक्ता *m.* (क्तृ), निर्मंक्ता *m.*

PLURAL, *a.* अनेकः -का -कं, बहुः -हुः -ह्वी -हु, बहुलः -ला -लं.—(Plural number, in grammar) अनेकवचनं, बहुवचनं.

PLURALITY, *s.* अनेकत्वं -ता, अनैक्यं, बहुत्वं -ता, बाहुल्यं, अनेकसंख्यत्वं; 'of gods,' देवबहुत्वं; 'of wives,' सापत्न्यं.

PLUS, *s.* (In Algebra) धनं, स्वं.

PLUSH, *s.* स्थूलदुकूलं, घनदुकूलं, घनलोमवद् दुकूलं.

PLUTO, *s.* (God of the infernal regions) यमः. *See* YAMA.

PLUTUS, *s.* (God of wealth) कुवेरः, धनपतिः *m.* *See* KUVERA.

PLUVIAL, PLUVIOUS, *a.* वृष्टिमान् -मती -मत् (त्), वर्षुकः -का -कं, वर्षिकः -की -कं, वार्षिकः &c., वृष्टिमयः -यी -यं, प्रचुरवृष्टिः -ष्टिः -ष्टि, बहुवृष्टिः &c.

PLUVIAMETER, *s.* वृष्टिमापनयन्त्रं, वृष्टिमापकः, वृष्टिमापनी.

To PLY, *v. a.* (Lay on) ऋ in caus. (अर्पयति -यितुं), प्रयुज् (c. 10. -योजयति -यितुं), न्यस्, आधा, धा, पत् in caus.; 'to ply with repeated blows,' पुनः पुनः पत्, मुहुर्मुहुः पत् or दण्डपातनं कृ.—(Employ diligently) यत्नतः or निर्बन्धेन प्रयुज् or उपयुज् or प्रवृत्.—(Keep in motion) प्रयत्नतस् or अविरतं चल् (c. 10. चालयति -यितुं), or सञ्चल्.—(Urge, press perseveringly) निर्बन्धेन प्रत्युपस्था (c. 1. -तिष्ठति -स्थातुं) or उपस्था or आक्रम् (c. 1. -क्रामति -क्रमितुं); 'with entreaties,' अतिनिर्बन्धेन प्रार्थ् or अभ्यर्थ् or प्रार्थनं कृ.

To PLY, *v. n.* (Be steadily employed) अनालस्येन or अतन्द्रितस् or अविरतं व्याप in pass. (-प्रियते) or व्यापृतः -ता -तं भू or निविष्टः -ष्टा -ष्टं भू or प्रवृत् or यत्, अविरतयत्नं कृ.

PLY, *s.* (Fold) ऊर्म्मिः *m.f.*, ऊर्म्मी -र्म्मिका, व्यावर्त्तनं, तरङ्गः, पुटः.

PNEUMATIC, PNEUMATICAL, *a.* (Consisting of air) वायुमयः -यी -यं. वायुरूपः -पा -पं.—(Pertaining to air) वायवः -वी -वं, वायुसम्बन्धी -न्धिनी -न्धि (न्), वायुविषयकः -का -कं, वायु in comp.—(Moved or played by air) वायु in comp., वायुसञ्चारितः -ता -तं, वायुवादितः -ता -तं; 'pneumatic instrument,' वायुयन्त्रं, वायुवाद्यं.

PNEUMATICS, *s. pl.* वायुविद्या, वायुधर्म्मविद्या, वायुगुणविद्या, वायुशास्त्रं, वायुगुणविषयका विद्या.

PNEUMONIA, *s.* (Inflammation of the lungs) फुप्फुसदाहः.

PNEUMONIC, *a.* फुप्फुससम्बन्धी &c., फुप्फुसविषयकः -का -कं.

To POACH, *v. a.* (Boil eggs slightly) अण्डानि तप्तजलान्तः कृत्वा ईषत् पच् (c. 1. पचति, पक्तुं) or श्रप् or अर्द्धसिद्धानि कृ.—(Steal or pocket game) वनपक्ष्यादि or जङ्गलपश्वादि चुर् or गूढकोषान्तः कृत्वा अपहृ. *See* the next.

To POACH, *v. n.* कूटयन्त्रेण वनपक्षिणो ग्रह् (c. 9. गृह्णाति, ग्रहीतुं), कूटोपायेन जङ्गलपश्वादि ग्रह् or चुर् (c. 10. चोरयति -यितुं) or अपहृ (c. 1. -हरति -हर्त्तुं), जाङ्गलजन्तुचौर्य्यं कृ, वन्यजन्तुहरणं कृ, वन्यजन्तुस्तेयं कृ, मृगयाचौर्य्यं कृ.

POACHER, *s.* कौटिकः, कौटकिकः, कौटिलिकः, कूटयत्नेन वनपक्षिग्राहकः, कूटोपायेन वन्यजन्तुहारी *m.* (न्) or जाङ्गलपशुपहारकः, जाङ्गलचौरः, मृगयाचौरः, वनचौरः, मृगयाचोरः, वैतंसिकः.

POACHING, *s.* कूटयत्नेन वनपक्षिग्रहणं, कूटोपायेन जाङ्गलपक्षिग्रहणं or जाङ्गलजन्तुहरणं, मृगयाचौर्य्यं, जाङ्गलचौर्य्यं, वन्यजन्तुचौर्य्यं, वन्यजन्तुस्तेयं, वनचौर्य्यं, वनस्तेयं.

POCK, *s.* रक्तवरटी, रक्तवटी, वटी, वरटी, रक्तस्फोटः, सूक्ष्मस्फोटः -टकः, स्फोटः -टकः, विस्फोटः, सिध्मं, सिध्म *n.* (न्), गुटिका.

POCKET, *s.* वस्त्रान्तःस्थकोषः, वस्त्रस्थकोषः, वस्त्रान्तरस्थकोषः, कोषः, कोशः, आधारः.

To POCKET, *v. a.* कोषान्तः कृ, कोषे or कोशे निविश् (c. 10. -वेशयति -यितुं) or निधा (c. 3. -दधाति -धातुं), वस्त्रान्तर्गतं -तां कृ, कोषान्तः स्था in caus. (स्थापयति -यितुं), कोषस्थं -स्थां कृ.—(Put up with) सह् (c. 1. सहते, सोढुं), क्षम् (c. 1. क्षमते, क्षन्तुं).

POCKET-BOOK, *s.* कोषस्थपुस्तकं, कोषगतपुस्तकं, कोषपुस्तकं.

POCKETED, *p. p.* कोषान्तःकृतः -ता -तं, कोषान्तः स्थापितः -ता -तं, कोषनिवेशितः &c., कोषगतः -ता -तं, कोषान्तर्गतः &c., कोषान्तर्हितः &c., कोषगुप्तः -प्ता -प्तं.

POCKET-HANDKERCHIEF, *s.* नासामार्जनी, नासिकामार्जनी, मुखमार्जनी, नक्तकः, चरकं.

POCKET-HOLE, *s.* कोषछिद्रं, कोशछिद्रं, वस्त्रान्तःस्थकोषछिद्रं.

POCKET-MONEY, *s.* क्षुद्रद्रव्यक्रयणार्थं वारे वारे दत्तं धनं.

POCKY, *a.* रक्तवरटीपूर्णः -र्णा -र्णं, रक्तस्फोटविशिष्टः -ष्टा -ष्टं.

POD, *s.* बीजकोशः, बीजगुप्तिः *f.*, सिम्बा -म्बिः -म्बी *f.*, शिम्बा म्बिः -म्बी *f.*, शिम्बिका, शमिः *f.*, शमी, पुटः; 'grain in pods,' शमीधान्यं.

PODAGRICAL, *a.* वातकी -किनी -कि (न्), वातरोगी -गिणी &c., वातिकः -की -कं, वातुलः -ला -लं, सन्धिवायुरोगी &c., सन्धिवायुग्रस्तः -स्ता -स्तं.

PODDED, *a.* सिम्बियुक्तः -क्ता -क्तं, शिम्बीयुक्तः &c., शमियुक्तः &c.

POEM, *s.* काव्यं, कविता, कवनं, काव्यबन्धः; 'interspersed with prose,' चम्पूकाव्यं.

POESY, *s.* (Art of composing poems) कविता, काव्यविद्या, काव्यरचनविद्या, काव्यलेखनविद्या, काव्यरचना, श्लोकरचना, कविताशक्तिः *f.*, कविकर्म्म *n.* (न्), रसविद्या, रसज्ञता.—(Metrical composition) कविता, काव्यं, अक्षरनावृत्तिः *f.* *See* POETRY.

POET, *s.* कविः *m.*, काव्यरचकः, कविताराचकः, पद्यरचकः, काव्यकर्त्ता *m.* (र्तृ), कविताकर्त्ता *m.*, रसज्ञः, वप्ता *m.* (प्तृ), भविनः, वागीशः; 'a quasi poet,' कविकल्पः; 'a ready poet,' शीघ्रकविः *m.*

POETASTER, *s.* कुकविः *m.*, कविकल्पः, कविदेशीयः, कविदेश्यः.

POETESS, *s.* काव्यकर्त्री, कविताकर्त्री, काव्यरचका.

POETIC, POETICAL, *a.* (Relating to poetry, suitable to it) कवितासम्बन्धी -न्धिनी &c., कविताविषयः -या -यं, काव्यरचनयोग्यः -ग्या -ग्यं, काव्ययोग्यः &c.—(Possessing the beauties of poetry) रसिकः -का -कं, सरसः -सा -सं, रसी -सिनी &c., रसवान् -वती -वत् (त्), काव्यरसवान् &c., कविता or काव्य in comp.; as, 'poetical genius,' कविताशक्तिः *f.*—(Expressed in poetry or measure) श्लोकबद्धः -द्धा -द्धं, पद्यरूपः -पा -पं, श्लोकरूपः &c., काव्यरूपः -पा -पं. कवितारूपः &c., कवितामयः -यी -यं, श्लोकमयः &c., छन्दोरूपः &c., छन्दोबद्धः &c.

POETICALLY, *adv.* कवितायोग्यं, कवितारूपेण, पद्यरूपेण, कवितापूर्व्वं, छन्दोनुसारेण, काव्यरसपूर्व्वं, सरसं.

POETICS, *s.* काव्यशास्त्रं, कविताशास्त्रं, रसशास्त्रं, पद्यशास्त्रं,

To POETIZE, *v. n.* काव्यं रच् (c. 10. रचयति -यितुं), काव्यरचनां कृ, कवितां कृ.

POET-LAUREATE, *s.* बन्दी *m.* (न्), वन्दारुः *m.*, राजवन्दी *m.*, राजस्तुतिपाठकः.

POETRY, *s.* (Metrical composition, verse) कविता -त्वं, काव्यं, कवनं, पद्यं.—(Art or practice of composing in verse) कविता -त्वं, काव्यरचना, श्लोकरचना, काव्यविद्या, काव्यरचनविद्या, कविकर्म्म *n.* (न्), कविताविद्या, रसविद्या, रसज्ञता.—(Poetical works) काव्यशास्त्रं, पद्यशास्त्रं, साहित्यं.

POIGNANCY, *s.* तीक्ष्णता, तीव्रता, तिग्मता, उग्रता -त्वं, कटुता, मार्म्मिकत्वं.

POIGNANT, *a.* तीक्ष्णः -क्ष्णा -क्ष्णं, तीव्रः -व्रा -व्रं, तिग्मः -ग्मा -ग्मं, उग्रः -ग्रा -ग्रं, कटुः -टुः -टु, बहुन्तुदः -दा -दं, मर्म्मस्पृक् *m.f.n.* (श्), मर्म्मभेदी -दिनी -दि (न्), मार्म्मिकः -की -कं.

POINT, *s.* (Sharp end) अग्रं, शिखा, शिखरं, अणिः *m.*, आणिः *m.*, अंशुः *m.*, अग्रांशुः *m.*, मुखं, कण्टकः, शलाका; 'of a needle,' सूच्यग्रं, कण्टकः; 'of the foot,' पादाग्रं, प्रपदं.—(Of a blade, &c.) धारा -रं, कोटिः *f.*, अश्रिः *f.*, पालिः -ली *f.* -लिका, अणिः *m.*, शिखरं, अग्रं; 'a sharp point,' तीक्ष्णाग्रं.—(Of land, head-land) भूमिनासिका, उदग्रभूमिः *f.*, उदग्रस्थलं, भूशलाका.—(Sting, wit of an epigram, &c.) दंशः, उपदंशः, मर्म्म *n.* (न्), रसः, रहस्यं.—(Of space or time) अणुः *m.*, परमाणुः *m.*, सन्धिः *m.*—(Of the compass) दिक् *f.* (श्), दिशा, ककुभ् *f.*, काष्ठा, आशा, हरित् *f.*, दिग्विभागः; 'intermediate point,' विदिक् *f.*, प्रदिक् *f.*, अपदिशं.—(Dot) बिन्दुः *m.*, शून्यं, विप्रुट् *f.* (ष्), अङ्कः, चिह्नं.—(Mark in punctuation) चिह्नं, विश्रामचिह्नं, विरामचिह्नं.—(Particular subject, case under discussion) विषयः, अर्थः, पदं, स्थलं, आस्पदं, प्रकरणं, प्रसङ्गः, प्रस्तावः; 'being to the point,' प्रासङ्गिकः -की -कं, प्रास्ताविकः &c.; 'on this point at least,' अत्र तावत्.—(Aim, object) लक्ष्यं, लक्ष्यं, अर्थः, आशयः, उद्देशः, अभिप्रायः.—(Characteristic mark, as of a horse, &c.) लक्षणं, विशेषणं, गुणः.—(Degree, pitch) पर्य्यन्तं, अन्तः -न्तं, परिमाणं, पदं, आस्पदं, पर्य्यायः, क्रमः; 'highest point,' उत्तमपदं, परमपदं, परमास्पदं; 'to such a point,' एतावत्पर्य्यन्तं, एतावत्; 'to what point?' किम्पर्य्यन्तं, कियत्पर्य्यन्तं; 'to that point,' तदन्तं, तत्पर्य्यन्तं.—(Critical moment) सन्धिः *m.*, कालसन्धिः *m.*, समयः; 'on the point of, at the point of,' उद्यतः -ता -तं, उद्युक्तः -क्ता -क्तं, उन्मुखः -खा -खं, or expressed by the desiderative or other forms of adjective, thus, 'on the point of dying, at the point of death,' मरणोन्मुखः -खा -खं, मुमूर्षुः -र्षुः -र्षु, आसन्नमृत्युः -त्युः -त्यु, आसन्नमरणः -णा -णं, मृतप्रायः -या -यं, मृतकल्पः -ल्पा -ल्पं, अन्त्यावस्थः -स्था -स्थं; 'on the point of going,' गमनोद्यतः -ता -तं, गन्तुमुद्यतः &c., गमनोन्मुखः &c., जिगमिषुः -षुः -षु, गन्तुकामः -मा -मं; 'on the point of bringing forth,' प्रसवोन्मुखी, आसन्नप्रसवा, आसन्नप्रसवकाला; 'he is on the point of rising,' उत्थातुमुद्यतोऽस्ति, उत्थातुम् इच्छति.—(Point of view) दृष्टिः *f.*—(Punctilio, nicety) सूक्ष्मता, सौक्ष्म्यं.

To POINT, *v. a.* (Sharpen to a point) तीक्ष्णाग्रीकृ, तीक्ष्णीकृ, तीक्ष्णधारीकृ, शिताग्रीकृ, निशो (c. 4. -श्यति -शातुं), तिज् (c. 10. तेजयति -यितुं), साग्रीकृ.—(Direct towards, aim at) लक्ष्यीकृ, उद्दिश्, समुद्दिश्, निर्दिश्, अभिसन्धा, लक्ष्; 'pointing to,' उद्दिश्य.—(Punctuate) विश्रामचिह्नानि or विरामचिह्नानि अङ्क् (c. 10. अङ्कयति -यितुं) or कृ.—(Point out, show by the finger, &c.) प्रदिश्

(c. 6. -दिशति -देष्टुं), निर्दिश्, उद्दिश्, विनिर्दिश्, सन्दिश्, आदिश्, अङ्गुल्या निर्दिश् or प्रदिश् or दृश् (c. 10. दर्शयति -यितुं) or प्रदृश् or सूच् (c. 10. सूचयति -यितुं) or संसूच्; 'point out the way,' मार्गम् आदेशय.

To POINT, *v. n.* (With the finger) अङ्गुलिनिर्देशं कृ, अङ्गुल्या निर्दिश् or प्रदिश्. *See* the last.—(Have direction or aim) उद्दिश्, उद्देशकः -का -कं भू, उद्देशं कृ, लक्षीकृ or expressed by दिश्य or मुख or अग्र in comp.; as, 'to point towards the south,' दक्षिणदिश्यः -श्या -श्यं भू, दक्षिणमुखः &c. भू, दक्षिणाग्रः &c. भू.

POINT-BLANK, *a.* or *adv.* समसूत्रः -त्रा -त्रं, एकसूत्रः &c., समरेखः -खा -खं, क्षितिसैकसूत्रः &c., समसूत्रेण, एकसूत्रेण.

POINTED, *p. p.* or *a.* (Have a sharp end) तीक्ष्णाग्रः -ग्रा -ग्रं, शिताग्रः &c., साग्रः &c., तीक्ष्णशिखः -खा -खं, शातशिखः &c., अंशुमान् -मती -मत् (त्), तीक्ष्णांशुमान् &c., शिखावलः -ला -लं, शिखाधरः -रा -रं, शितः -ता -तं, निशितः &c., शैक्ष्यः -क्ष्या -क्ष्यं.—(Epigrammatical, keen, witty) रसिकः -का -कं, सरसः -सा -सं, रसवान् &c., मार्म्मिकः -की -कं, मर्म्मस्पृक् *m. f. n.* (श्), अरुन्तुदः -दा -दं, दंशकः -का -कं; 'pointed words,' वागसिः *f.*—(Pointed out) निर्दिष्टः -ष्टा -ष्टं, उद्दिष्टः &c., प्रदिष्टः &c., सूचितः -ता -तं, अङ्गुलिनिर्दिष्टः &c.

POINTEDLY, *adv.* अमुकममुद्दिश्य, उद्दिश्य, उद्देशपूर्व्वं, समर्म्मभेदं.

POINTEDNESS, *s.* रसिकता -त्वं, सरसता, दंशकता -त्वं, मार्म्मिकत्वं.

POINTER, *s.* निर्देशकः, देशकः, प्रदेशकः, निर्देष्टा *m.* (ष्टृ), निदेष्टा *m.*, निर्देशी *m.* (न्), प्रदेशी *m.*, देशी *m.*, दर्शकः, प्रदर्शकः, सूचकः.—(Dog) वनपक्षिनिर्देशको मृगयाकुक्कुरः, वन्यपक्षिनिर्देशने शिक्षितो मृगयाश्वा *m.* (न्).

POINTING, *s.* निर्देशः -शनं, अङ्गुलिनिर्देशः, निदेशः, सूचनं, अङ्गुलिप्रदर्शनं.

POINTLESS, *a.* (Having no point or edge) निरग्रः -ग्रा -ग्रं, अग्रहीनः -ना -नं, धाराहीनः &c., अतीक्ष्णः -क्ष्णा -क्ष्णं.—(Destitute of wit) विरसः-सा -सं, अरसिकः -का -कं, रसहीनः &c., मृदुः -दुः -दु.

POISE, *s.* (Weight) भारः, तुला, तोलः.—(Balance, equilibrium) भारतुल्यता, भारसमता, भारसाम्यं, समतौल्यं, समतोलः, तुल्यता, तुलासाम्यं.

To POISE, *v. a.* समभारीकृ, तुल्यभारीकृ, समतोलीकृ, समीकृ, तुल्यीकृ, तुल् (c. 10 .तुलयति -यितुं).

POISON, *s.* विषं, गरं-रः, गरलं, गरदं, भूगरं, जीवनाघातं, अङ्कुलं, जाङ्गुलं, हलाहलं -लः, हालाहलं, हालहालं, हालहलं, हलहलं, हाहलं -लः, कालकूटं -टः, वत्सनाभः, काकोलं -लः, सौराष्ट्रिकं, सोराष्ट्रिकं, दारदः, प्रदीपनः, ब्रह्मपुत्रः, शौक्लिकेयः, वत्सनाभः, धूलकं, निदः, क्ष्वेडः; 'administering poison,' विषप्रयोगः, विषविधानं, विषदानं; 'taking poison,' विषभक्षणं; 'worthy of death by poison,' विष्यः -ष्या -ष्यं; 'yielding poison,' विषदः -दा -दं; 'removing or curing poison,' विषघ्नः -घ्नी -घ्नं, विषनाशी -शिनी -शि (न्), विषघाती &c., विषहरः -री -रं, विषापहः -हा -हं, गरघ्नः &c.; 'art of curing poisons,' विषविद्या, विषनाशनविद्या; 'curer of poisons,' विषवैद्यः, विषभिषक् *m.* (ज्), जाङ्गुलिकः, जाङ्गुलिः *m.*, गारुडिकः; 'charm against poison,' गारुडः -डं.

To POISON, *v. a.* (Infect with poison) विषाक्तं -क्तां कृ, विषयुक्तं -क्तां कृ, विषेण दुष् (c. 10. दूषयति -यितुं), विषदिग्धं -ग्धां कृ.—(Administer poison, kill by it) विषं दा, विषप्रयोगं कृ, विषेण हन् or मृ in caus., विषदानेन हन्.—(Poison one's self, take or eat poison) विषं भुज् or भक्ष् or खाद्, विषेण or विषप्रयोगेण आत्मानं हन्.—(Corrupt, taint) दुष्, सन्दुष्, लिप्, नश् in caus.

POISONED, *p. p.* or *a.* (Infected with poison) विषाक्तः -क्ता -क्तं, विषदिग्धः -ग्धा -ग्धं, विषलिप्तः -प्ता -प्तं, विषदूषितः -ता -तं; 'a poisoned arrow,' दिग्धः, लिप्तकः.—(Killed by poison) विषमारितः -ता -तं, विषनाशितः &c.

POISONER, *s.* विषदः, विषदायी *m.* (न्), गरदः, गरदायी *m.*, तीक्ष्णरसदायी.

POISONING, *s.* विषप्रयोगः, विषदानं, विषविधानं, विषेण मारणं.

POISONOUS, *a.* विषालुः -लुः -लु, गरली -लिनी -लि (न्), विषमयः -यी -यं, सविषः -षा -षं, विषधरः -रा -रं, विषगुणकः -का -कं, विषधर्म्मकः -का -कं, विषदः -दा -दं, सगरः -रा -रं, तीक्ष्णविषः -षा -षं, विषपूर्णः -र्णा -र्णं, विषयुक्तः -क्ता -क्तं, दूषकः -का -कं, विष in comp.; as, 'poisonous snake,' विषभुजङ्गः.

POISONOUSLY, *adv.* सविषं, सगरं, सगरलं, सदूषणं, दूषकप्रकारेण.

POISONOUSNESS, *s.* विषालुता, सविषत्वं, सगरत्वं, विषपूर्णता, दूषकत्वं.

POITREL, *s.* उरस्त्राणं, वक्षस्त्राणं, उरश्छदः, वक्षस्त्रं.

To POKE, *v. a.* (Thrush, push against, stick) तड् (c. 10. ताडयति -यितुं), दण्डादि प्रसारयित्वा तड् or आहन् (c. 2. -हन्ति -न्तुं) or अभ्याहन् or प्रहृ (c. 1. -हरति -हर्तुं), प्रसृ (c. 10. -सारयति -यितुं), प्रविश् (c. 10. -वेशयति -यितुं), ताडनं कृ, आघातं कृ, प्रहारं कृ.—(Search for, grope for, with a long instrument) दण्डादि प्रसारयित्वा परामृश् (c. 6. -मृशति- म्रष्टुं) or अन्विष् (c. 4. -इष्यति -एषितुं).

To POKE, *v. n.* (Grope) तमः प्रविश्य परामृश् or परिमृश्, अन्धकारे दण्डादि प्रसारयित्वा अन्विष् or निरूप्.—(Dawdle, trifle) विलम्बेन किञ्चित् कृ, विलम्ब्. *See To* PEDDLE.

POKE, *s.* ताडनं, आघातः, प्रहारः, अभिघातः, आहतिः *f.*, दण्डप्रसारणं.

POKER, *s.* शलाका, लोहशलाका, अङ्गारचालनशलाका, अङ्गारचालकः, अङ्गारचालकदण्डः, अङ्गारोत्थापकः.

POLAR, *a.* ध्रुवसम्बन्धी -न्धिनी -न्धि (न्), मेरुसम्बन्धी &c., ध्रुवविषयकः -का -कं, ध्रुवस्थः -स्था -स्थं, केन्द्रस्थः &c., ध्रुवनिकटस्थः &c.; 'polar star,' ध्रुवः, औत्तानपादिः *m.*, उत्तानपादजः, नक्षत्रनेमिः *m.*, ध्रुतिकरः, ज्योतीरथः; 'polar circle,' कदम्बभ्रमवृत्तं; 'polar distance,' ध्रुवज्याचापांशः.

POLARITY, *s.* ध्रुवाभिसरणशीलता, ध्रुवाभिगमनशीलता, ध्रुवाभिजिगमिषा, ध्रुवाभिमुखशीलता, ध्रुवाभिमुखता, केन्द्राभिमुखता.

POLARY, *a.* ध्रुवाभिसरणशीलः -ला -लं, ध्रुवाभिगमनशीलः &c., ध्रुवाभिजिगमिषुः -षुः -षु, ध्रुवाभिगामी -मिनी -मि (न्), ध्रुवाभिसारी &c., ध्रुवाभिमुखशीलः &c.

POLE, *s.* (Long piece of wood) दण्डः -ण्डं, यष्टिः *m. f.*, दीर्घकाष्ठं, काष्ठं; 'for carrying burdens,' भारयष्टिः *m. f.*, विहङ्गिका; 'raised on a pole,' उद्दण्डः -ण्डा -ण्डं.—(Of a carriage) धूः *f.* (धुर्), धुरा, धूर्वी, कूबरः, युगन्धरः, यानमुखं.—(Of a plough) ईषा, ईशा, हलदण्डः, लाङ्गलदण्डः.—(The measure) दण्डः.—(In astronomy) ध्रुवः, मेरुः *m.*, केन्द्रं; 'north pole,' उत्तरध्रुवः, ध्रुवः, मेरुः *m.*, उत्तराग्रं; 'south pole,' दक्षिणध्रुवः, कुमेरुः *m.*, दक्षिणाग्रं; 'elevation of the pole,' ध्रुवोन्नतिः *f.*; 'pole of the ecliptic,' कदम्बः.

POLE-AXE, *s.* परशुः *m.*, कुठारः, दीर्घयष्टिलग्नपरशुः *m.*, दीर्घदण्डः.

POLE-CAT, *s.* पूतिशारिजा, लोमशमार्जारः, गन्धमार्जारः, गन्धोतुः *m.*, पूतिका, शाहकः, मृगचैटकः, कस्तूरीमृगः, गात्रसङ्कोची *m.* (न्), खट्टाशः -शी.

POLEMIC, POLEMICAL, *a.* विवादी -दिनी -दि (न्), विवादात्मकः -का -कं, वादानुवादात्मकः -का -कं, वादानुवादार्थकः -का -कं, वादानुवादी &c.,

वादप्रतिवादी &c., विसंवादी &c., विप्रतिपत्तिकः -का -कं.

POLEMIC, POLEMICAL, *s.* वादानुवादशीलः, वादानुवादप्रियः, वादानुवादकुशलः, विवादप्रियः, विवादकुशलः, वादरतः, वादानुवादकारी *m.* (न्), वादविवादकर्त्ता *m.* (र्तृ).

POLEMICS, *s.* धर्म्मविषयो वादानुवादः or विवादः or विसंवादः.

POLE-STAR, *s.* (Fabled as the son of Uttánapáda, and grandson of the first Manu) ध्रुवः, औत्तानपादिः *m.*, उत्तानपादजः. *See* POLAR, *a.*

POLICE, *s.* (Government of a city or town) नगरव्यवस्था, नगरव्यवस्थितिः *f.*, नगरानुशासनं, नगरकार्य्यानुशासनं.—(Internal regulation of a kingdom) राष्ट्रानुशासनं, देशानुशासनं, देशकार्य्यानुशासनं, राष्ट्रव्यवस्था, देशव्यवस्था, राष्ट्रव्यवस्थितिः *f.*—(Body of police-officers) नगररक्षिणः *m.pl.*, नगररक्षकाः *m.pl.*, नगररक्षिपुरुषाः *m.pl.*, नगरपालाः *m.pl.*, नगरपालकाः *m. pl.*, नगररक्षिगणः, नगरपालगणः, नगरपालवर्गः; 'rural police,' ग्रामरक्षिणः *m. pl.*, ग्रामरक्षकाः *m. pl.*, ग्रामपालाः; 'highway police,' मार्गपालाः -लकाः, मार्गरक्षकाः *m. pl.*

POLICE-MAGISTRATE, *s.* दण्डनायकः, दण्डप्रणेता *m.* (तृ), दण्डाधिकारी *m.* (न्).

POLICE-MAN, POLICE-OFFICER, *s.* नगररक्षी *m.* (न्), नगररक्षकः, नगररक्षिपुरुषः, नगरपालः -लकः, आरक्षकः, राजपुरुषः.

POLICY, *s.* (Art or manner of governing or managing public affairs) नीतिः *f.*, नीतिविद्या, नयः, नयनं, नयप्रयोगः, राजनीतिः *f.*, राजनयः, राज्यशासनरीतिः *f.*, राज्यनयनं, राज्यनयनरीतिः *f.*, राज्यनिर्वाहरीतिः *f.*, राज्यव्यवहारमार्गः, राज्यानुशासनमार्गः; 'good policy,' सुनीतिः *f.* सुनयः; 'bad policy,' दुर्नीतिः *f.*, दुर्नीतं, दुर्नयः, दुर्नीतिः &c.—(Prudence or skill in the management of public affairs) नीतिकौशल्यं, नीतिकुशलता, नीतिचातुर्य्यं, राज्यनयनयुक्तिः *f.*, राज्यकरणयुक्तिः *f.*, राज्यशासनयुक्तिः *f.*, राज्यचातुर्य्यं, राज्यकौशल्यं, नीतिज्ञता.—(In the management of affairs generally, prudence) व्यवहारयुक्तिः *f.*, व्यवहारचातुर्य्यं, व्यवहारदक्षता, व्यवहारकौशल्यं, कर्म्मनिर्वाहयुक्तिः *f.*; 'good policy,' सुयुक्तिः *f.*; 'prudential policy,' समीक्ष्यकारित्वं, सुविमृश्यकारित्वं, समीक्षापुरःसरं उपायप्रयोगः.

To POLISH, *v. a.* (Make smooth and glossy) तिज् (c. 10. तेजयति -यितुं), परिष्कृ, निष्टप् (c. 10. निष्टापयति -यितुं, rt. तप्), कान्तिं दा, स्निग्धीकृ, श्लक्ष्णीकृ, मृज् (c. 2. मार्ष्टि -र्ष्टुं), प्रमृज्.—(Refine, make polite) परिष्कृ, संस्कृ, शिष्टीकृ, सभ्यं -भ्यां कृ, सभ्यतां or शिष्टतां जन् (c. 10. जनयति -यितुं) or दा.

POLISH, *s.* (Glossiness) कान्तिः *f.*, शोभा, स्निग्धता, चैक्कण्यं, श्लक्ष्णता.—(Finish) परिष्कारः, परिष्कृतिः *f.*, संस्कारः, संस्कृतिः *f.*—(Refinement) शिष्टता, परिष्कारः, सभ्यता, सभाचातुर्य्यं, सुजनता, सौजन्यं, शिष्टाचारसम्पन्नता, सभ्याचारसम्पन्नता.

POLISHED, *p. p.* (Made glossy) परिष्कृतः -ता -तं, तेजितः -ता -तं, निष्टप्तः -प्ता -प्तं, स्निग्धीकृतः &c., श्लक्ष्णीकृतः &c., मृष्टः -ष्टा -ष्टं, प्रमृष्टः &c., निर्धौतः -ता -तं, निशातः -ता -तं, उज्ज्वलितः -ता -तं—(Refined) परिष्कृतः -ता -तं, संस्कृतः &c., शिष्टः -ष्टा -ष्टं, सभ्यः -भ्या -भ्यं, शिष्टाचारसम्पन्नः -न्ना -न्नं, सभ्याचारसम्पन्नः &c., अग्राम्यः -म्या -म्यं.

POLISHER, *s.* परिष्कर्त्ता *m.* (र्तृ), परिष्कारकः, तेजकः, कान्तिदः, कान्तिदायकः, निर्णेजकः, मार्जकः, सम्मार्जकः.

POLISHING, *s.* परिष्कारः, परिष्कृतिः *f.*, संस्कारः, तेजनं, श्लक्ष्णीकरणं.

POLITE, *a.* (Refined in manners) शिष्टः -ष्टा -ष्टं, सभ्यः -भ्या -भ्यं, शिष्टाचारी -रिणी -रि (न्), सभ्याचारी &c., सभ्यशीलः -ला -लं, शिष्टाचारसम्पन्नः -न्ना -न्नं, सभ्याचारसम्पन्नः &c., सुजनः -ना -नं, विनीतः -ता -तं, विनयवान् -वती -वत् (त्), सविनयः -या -यं, अग्राम्यः -म्या -म्यं.—(Courteous, obliging) सुशीलः -ला -लं, आदरशीलः &c., वन्दारुः -रुः -रु, दक्षिणः -णा -णं, अनुनयी &c., सानुनयः -या -यं, अनुरोधी &c., अनुकूलः -ला -लं, प्रियंवदः -दा -दं, अभिवादकः -का -कं, शक्रुः -क्रुः -क्रु, सत्कारी &c.

POLITELY, *adv.* सभ्यवत्, शिष्टवत्, विनीतवत्, सविनयं, सानुनयं, सुशीलवत्, सदाक्षिण्यं, सभ्याचारानुसारेण, शिष्टाचारानुसारात्.

POLITENESS, *s.* (Refinement of manners) शिष्टता, सभ्यता, सभ्यशीलता, शिष्टाचारित्वं, सभ्याचारित्वं, विनीतता -त्वं, विनयः, सुजनता, सौजन्यं, अग्राम्यता.—(Courteousness) सुशीलता, आदरशीलता, दाक्षिण्यं, अनुनयः, आनन्दनं, अनुरोधः, अनुकूलता.—(Polite behaviour) शिष्टाचारः, शिष्टाचरणं, सभ्याचारः, सभ्याचरणं.

POLITIC, *a.* (Skilful in managing public affairs) नीतिकुशलः -ला -लं, नीतिज्ञः -ज्ञा -ज्ञं, नीतिविद्याज्ञः -ज्ञा -ज्ञं, नीतिविशारदः -दा -दं, नीतिदक्षः -क्षा -क्षं, नीतिमान् -मती -मत् (त्), नीतिविद् *m. f. n.*, नयविद्, नीतिचतुरः -रा -रं.—(Skilful in the management of affairs generally) व्यवहारकुशलः -ला -लं, व्यवहारदक्षः -क्षा -क्षं, कर्म्मनिर्वाहकुशलः -ला -लं, कुशलः -ला -लं, विचक्षणः -णा -णं, निपुणः -णा -णं.—(Wise, well devised, adapted to its end) सुनीतः -ता -तं, सुयुक्तः -क्ता -क्तं, सुप्रयुक्तः &c., सुघटितः &c., सम्यङ्नीतः &c., यौक्तिकः -की -कं, सुसमीक्ष्य or सुविमृश्य or सुसमीक्षापूर्व्वं कृतः -ता -तं, अर्थसम्पादकः -का -कं, अर्थसाधकः -का -कं, कार्य्यसाधकः &c., अर्थकरः -रा -री -रं, हितः -ता -तं.

POLITICAL, *a.* नीतिसम्बन्धी -न्धिनी &c., नीतिविद्यासम्बन्धी &c., राजनीतिसम्बन्धी &c., राज्यनयनसम्बन्धी &c., राज्यव्यवहारसम्बन्धी &c., नीतिविषयकः -का -कं, राजनीतिविषयः -या -यं, राजकीयः -या -यं, नीति or देश or राष्ट्र or राज्य in comp.; as, 'political lore,' नीतिविद्या, नीतिशास्त्रं; 'political rights,' देशाधिकारः, पौरजनाधिकारः.

POLITICAL ECONOMY, *s.* नीतिविद्या, देशपोषणविद्या, देशपालनविद्या, राष्ट्रपालनविद्या, राष्ट्रपोषणविद्या, राज्यव्यवस्थाविद्या, राज्यनिर्वाहविद्या, राज्यकर्म्मनयः -यनं.

POLITICALLY, *adv.* नीतिमपेक्ष्य, नीतिविद्यामपेक्ष्य, राज्यव्यवस्थामपेक्ष्य.

POLITICIAN, *s.* नीतिज्ञः, नीतिकुशलः, नीतिविद् *m.*, नीतिवेदी *m.* (न्), नीतिविशारदः, नीतिविद्याज्ञः, राजनीतिकुशलः, राजनीतिविशारदः, नयविशारदः.

POLITICS, *s.* (Science of government) नीतिः *f.*, नीतिविद्या, नयः, राजनीतिः *f.*, राजनीतिविद्या, नीतिशास्त्रं, राजनीतिशास्त्रं, राज्यनयनविद्या, राज्यशासनविद्या.—(Political or public affairs) राज्यविषयाः *n. pl.*, राज्यकर्म्माणि *n. pl.*, राज्यकार्य्याणि *n. pl.*, देशव्यवहारः, राष्ट्रव्यवहारः.

POLITY, *s.* (System of government) राज्यनीतिः *f.*, राज्यरीतिः *f.*, राज्यनीतिरूपं, राज्यव्यवस्था, राज्यस्थितिः *f.*, राज्यनियमः, राज्यविधिः *m.*, राज्यप्रवृत्तिः *f.*, राज्यकरणनियमः, नीतिः *f.*, दण्डनीतिः *f.*

POLL, *s.* (Head) मुण्डः -ण्डं -ण्डकं, शिरस् *n.*, शीर्षं, मस्तकः -कं.—(Entry of the names of electors) नामाभिलेखनं, नामलिखनं, नामलेखनं, नामारोपणं, नामसमारोपणं.—(List of names) नामावलिः -ली *f.*, नामपरिसंख्या.

To POLL, *v. a.* (Cut off the hair) केशान् छिद् or लू or वप्.—(Enter names of electors, &c., in a list) नामावलिपत्रे or नामपरिसंख्यापत्रे नामानि समारुह् in caus. or आरुह् or अभिलिख् or लिख्,

POLLARD, *s.* छिन्नाग्रवृक्षः, छिन्नाग्रद्रुमः, लूनाग्रवृक्षः, लूनाग्रतरुः *m.*

POLLED, *p. p.* (Lopped) छिन्नः -न्ना -न्नं, लूनः -ना -नं.—(Registered as the names of voters) नामावलिपत्रारोपितः -ता -तं, अभिलिखितः -ता -तं.

POLLEN, *s.* (Of a flower) परागः, रजस् *n.*, पुष्परजस् *n.*, पुष्परेणुः *m.*, पांशुः *m.*; 'laden with pollen,' परागवान् -वती -वत् (त्), परागी -गिणी -गि (न्).

To POLLUTE, *v. a.* दुष् (c. 10. दूषयति -यितुं), सन्दुष्, प्रतिदुष्, मलिनीकृ, मलिन (nom. मलिनयति -यितुं), कलुषीकृ, कलुष (nom. कलुषयति -यितुं), लिप् (c. 6. लिम्पति, लेप्तुं), अनुलिप्, दिह् (c. 2. देग्धि -ग्धुं), मलेन दुष् or लिप् or अञ्ज् (c. 7. अनक्ति, अंक्तुं), कलङ्क (nom. कलङ्कयति -यितुं), समलीकृ, अमेध्येन लिप्, अमेध्यीकृ, मलीमसीकृ, अपवित्रीकृ.—(Taint with guilt) दुष्, भ्रंश् (c. 10. भ्रंशयति -यितुं), भ्रष्टीकृ, भ्रष्टं -ष्टां कृ.—(A virgin) कन्यां दुष् or धृष् (c. 10. धर्षयति -यितुं).

POLLUTED, *p. p.* दूषितः -ता -तं, दुष्टः -ष्टा -ष्टं, मलदूषितः &c., मलिनितः -ता -तं, मललिप्तः -प्ता -प्तं, लिप्तः &c., अमेध्यलिप्तः &c., अमेध्याक्तः -क्ता -क्तं, कलुषितः -ता -तं, कलुषीकृतः &c., मलीमसः -सा -सं, समलः -ला -लं, मलवान् -वती -वत् (त्), कलङ्कितः -ता -तं.—(As a virgin) दूषिता, भ्रष्टा, धर्षिता.

POLLUTER, *s.* दूषकः, दूषणः, कलुषकारी *m.* (न्), मलावहः, अशौचकृत्.

POLLUTION, *s.* (The act) दूषणं, मलदूषणं, मललेपनं, मलिनीकरणं, कलुषीकरणं, अमेध्यदूषणं, अमेध्यलेपः, अपवित्रीकरणं.—(The state) मलिनत्वं, मालिन्यं, समलता -त्वं, अमेध्यता -त्वं, मलदूषितत्वं, अमेध्यलिप्तता, अमेध्याक्तत्वं, अशुचित्वं, अशौचं -चत्वं, अपवित्रता -त्वं, दुष्टता -त्वं.—(Nocturnal) स्वप्नदोषः, स्वप्नावस्था, स्वप्नमध्ये शुक्रपातः.

POLTROON, *s.* कापुरुषः, कुपुरुषः, क्लीबः, कातरः, हतकः, कृपणः, भीरुजनः, निर्वीर्य्यः, धैर्य्यहीनः, शौर्य्यहीनः, अधीरः.

POLTROONERY, *s.* क्लीबता, कापुरुषत्वं, अपौरुषं, कातरता, भीरुता.

POLYANDROUS, POLYANDRIST, *s.* बहुभर्तृका, बहुपतिका, अनेकभर्तृका.

POLYANDRY, *s.* बहुभर्तृत्वं, बहुभर्तृधारणं, अनेकपतिधारणं.

POLYCHORD, *a.* बहुतन्त्री -न्त्रिणी -न्त्रि (न्), बहुतन्तुः -न्तुः -न्तु, अनेकतन्त्री &c.

POLYGAMIST, *s.* (Practiser of polygamy) बहुभार्य्यः, अनेकभार्य्यः, बहुपत्नीकः, दारी *m.* (न्), अनेकस्त्रीकः.—(Defender of it) बहुपत्नीवादी *m.* (न्).

POLYGAMY, *s.* बहुपत्नीत्वं, बहुभार्य्यत्वं -ता, अनेकभार्य्यता, सापत्न्यं.

POLYGENOUS, *a.* बहुविधः -धा -धं, अनेकविधः &c., बहुप्रकारः -रा -रं.

POLYGLOT, *a.* बहुभाषः -षा -षं, अनेकभाषः -षा -षं.

POLYGLOT, *s.* बहुभाषग्रन्थः, अनेकभाषग्रन्थः, बहुभाषपुस्तकं.

POLYGON, *s.* बहुकोणः -णं, बहुभुजः, बह्वस्रं -स्री, अनेकास्रं -स्री, बहुकोणाकृतिः *f.*, बह्वस्राकृतिः *f.*, बहुकोणा मूर्त्तिः.

POLYGONAL, POLYGONOUS, *a.* बहुकोणः -णा -णं, बहुभुजः -जा -जं, बह्वस्रः -स्रा -स्रं, अनेकास्रः -स्रा -स्रं.

POLYMATHY, *s.* बहुविद्याज्ञानं, अनेकविद्याज्ञानं, बहुशास्त्रज्ञानं.

POLYPETALOUS, *a.* बहुदलः -ला -लं, अनेकदलः &c., बहुदली -लिनी &c.

POLYPHAGOUS, *a.* बहुभक्षः -क्षा -क्षं, बहुखादकः -का -कं, बह्वाशी -शिनी &c.

POLYPHONOUS, *a.* बहुस्वरः -रा -रं, बहुस्वनः -ना -नं, बहुध्वनिः -निः -नि.

POLYPUS, *s.* बहुपादः, बहुपाद् *m.*, अनेकपाद्, बहुमूलः, अनेकमूलः,

POLYSPERMOUS, *a.* बहुवीजः -जा -जं, प्रचुरवीजः &c., अनेकवीजः &c.

POLYSYLLABIC, *a.* बह्वक्षरः -रा -रं, अनेकाक्षरः &c., बह्वक्षरी -रिणी -रि (न्).

POLYSYLLABIC, *s.* बह्वक्षरं, बह्वक्षरशब्दः, अनेकाक्षरशब्दः.

POLYTHEISM, *s.* बहुदेवमतं, बहुदेववादः, अनेकदेवमतं, अनेकवादः.

POLYTHEIST, *s.* बहुदेवमतावलम्बी *m.* (न्), अनेकदेववादी *m.*, अनेकवादी *m.*

POMANDER, *s.* भावितं, वासितं, वासितचूर्णं, सुगन्धिचूर्णं.

POMATUM, POMADE, *s.* विलेपनं, सुगन्धिलेपः, गात्रानुलेपनी, यक्षकर्दमः.

POMEGRANATE, *s.* (The tree) दाडिमः -मी, दाडिम्बः, दालिमः, डालिमः, करकः, रक्तवीजः, शुकवल्लभः, फलषाडवः, मणिवीजः, मधुवीजः, लाम्लः, कुचफलः, सुनीलः, पिण्डीरः, नीरसः.—(Its fruit) दाडिमं, दालिमं, दाडिमफलं.

POMMEL, *s.* (Knob) पिण्डः, गण्डः, गुल्मः, आभोगः.—(Of a saddle) पर्य्याणपिण्डः, पर्य्याणबहिःस्थपिण्डः, पर्य्याणगुल्मः.

To POMMEL, *v. a.* तड् (c. 10. ताडयति -यितुं), चपाघातं कृ, दण्डाघातं कृ.

POMP, *s.* (Procession) यात्रा, यात्राप्रसङ्गः.—(Show) आडम्बरं, ऐश्वर्य्यं, शोभा, प्रतापः, अतिप्रतापः, अतिशोभा, दम्भार्थं शोभा or तेजस् *n.*, चमत्कारः, कौतुकं. *See* PARADE, PAGEANTRY.

POMPOUS, *a.* (Displaying pomp, showy) महाप्रतापः -पा -पं, अतिप्रतापी -पिनी -पि (न्), अतिशोभनः -ना -नं, आडम्बरी &c., कौतुकी &c.—(Ostentatious) दाम्भिकः -की -कं, दम्भी &c., दम्भार्थकः -का -कं, साटोपः -पा -पं, अतिगर्व्वितः -ता -तं, दर्पाध्मातः &c., गर्व्वितः &c., गर्व्वितवाक्यः -क्या -क्यं, विकत्थनः -ना -नं.

POMPOUSLY, *adv.* (Magnificently) अतिप्रतापेन, अतिशोभापूर्व्वं, साडम्बरं.—(Ostentatiously) दम्भार्थं, सदम्भं, दम्भपूर्व्वं, सगर्व्वं, गर्व्वितप्रकारेण, लोकदर्शनार्थं, विकत्थनपूर्व्वं, साटोपं.

POMPOUSNESS, *s.* (Magnificence) ऐश्वर्य्यं, सप्रतापत्वं. *See* POMP.—(Ostentatiousness) दम्भः, दाम्भिकत्वं, साटोपत्वं, गर्व्वितत्वं, विकत्था, दर्पाध्मातता.

POND, *s.* तडागः, जलाशयः, जलाधारः, सरस् *n.*, ह्रदः, खातं, सरोवरः -रं, क्रीडासरोवरः, वापी -पिः *f.*, कासारः, पुष्करिणी, सरसी, पद्माकरः, मीनगोधिका; 'a natural pond,' अखातं, देवखातकं; 'an oblong pond,' दीर्घिका.

To PONDER, *v. a.* and *n.* मनसा विचर् (c. 10. -चारयति -यितुं) or विगण् (c. 10. -गणयति -यितुं), चिन्त् (c. 10. चिन्तयति -यितुं), विचिन्त्, सञ्चिन्त्, ध्यै (c. 1. ध्यायति, ध्यातुं), अनुध्यै, अभिध्यै, सन्ध्यै, भू (c. 10. भावयति -यितुं), विभू, सम्भू, विमृश् (c. 6. मृशति -म्रष्टुं), परिमृश्, वितर्क् (c. 10. -तर्कयति -यितुं), अनुतर्क्.

PONDERABLE, *a.* (That may be weighed) तुलायोग्यः -ग्या -ग्यं, तुलनीयः -या -यं.—(To be pondered) चिन्त्यः -न्त्या -न्त्यं, चिन्तनीयः -या -यं.

PONDERATION, *s.* (Act of weighing) तुलाधारणं.—(Act of pondering) सुविचारणं -णा, सुचिन्तनं, विगणनं -ना, सम्भावना.

PONDERED, *p. p.* चिन्तितः -ता -तं, सुविचारितः &c., विगणितः &c., सुचिन्तितः &c.

PONDEROSITY *s.* भारित्वं, सभारत्वं, अतिभारित्वं, गुरुता, अतिगुरुता -त्वं. गरिमा *m.* (न्), भारवत्त्वं.

PONDEROUS, *a.* भारी -रिणी -रि (न्), अतिभारी &c., सभारः -रा -रं, भारवान् -वती -वत् (त्), गुरुः -र्वी -रु, अतिगुरुः &c.

PONDEROUSLY, *adv.* अतिभारेण, सुभारेण, सभारं, सगौरवं, अतिगुरु.

PONIARD, *a.* खड्गारः, कृपाणी, शङ्कुः *m.*, छुरिका, असिपुत्रिका, कर्त्तरी.

To PONIARD, *v. a.* खड्गारेण व्यध् (c. 4. विध्यति, व्यद्धुं), छुर् (c. 6. छुरति -रितुं).

PONTAGE, *s.* सेतुकरः, सेतुशुल्कः -ल्कं, सेतुदेयं.

PONTIFF, *s.* प्रधानधर्म्माध्यक्षः, प्रधानधर्म्माधिकारी *m.* (न्), मुख्यधर्म्माध्यक्षः, महाधर्म्माध्यक्षः, महाधर्म्माधिकारी *m.* (न्), प्रधानयाजकः, मुख्यपुरोहितः, महायाजकः.

PONTIFICAL, *a.* प्रधानधर्म्माध्यक्षसम्बन्धी -न्धिनी &c., प्रधानयाजकीयः -या -यं.

Pontificate, *s.* प्रधानधर्म्माध्यक्षस्य पदं or अधिकारः, धर्म्माध्यक्षता -त्वं.

Pontoon, *s.* सेतुबन्धने प्रयुक्तस् तरालुः or तरान्धुः; 'bridge,' तरालुबद्धसेतुः.

Pony, *s.* क्षुद्रघोटकः, क्षुद्राश्वः, क्षुद्रशरीरी घोटकः or अश्वः.

Pool, *s.* तडागः, जलाशयः, जलाधारः, पल्वलं, कुण्डं, सरस् *n.*, ह्रदः, कासारः, पुष्करिणी, निपानं, परिवापः, कूपं.

Poop, *s.* नावः पश्चिमभागः or पश्चाद्भागः, नौपृष्ठं, नौकापृष्ठं.

Poor, *a.* (Destitute of money or property) दरिद्रः -द्रा -द्रं, निर्धनः -ना -नं, अधनः -ना -नं, धनहीनः &c., अल्पधनः &c., निर्धनकः -का -कं, क्षीणधनः -ना -नं, धनशून्यः -न्या -न्यं, दीनः -ना -नं, अर्थहीनः &c., वित्तहीनः &c., द्रव्यहीनः &c., द्रव्यशून्यः &c., विभवहीनः &c., अल्पद्रव्यः -व्या -व्यं, निःस्वः -स्वा -स्वं, गतार्थः -र्था -र्थं, दुर्गतः -ता -तं, अनर्थः -र्था -र्थं, निष्किञ्चनः -ना -नं, निःकाञ्चनः &c., अकाञ्चनः &c., निष्किञ्चनः &c., दारिद्र्यग्रस्तः -स्ता -स्तं, दरिद्रितः -ता -तं, दरिद्रायकः -का -कं, दरिद्रिता -त्री -तृ (तृ), कृपणः -णा -णं, अधन्यः -न्या -न्यं, दुराढ्यः -ढ्या -ढ्यं, किंवान् -वती -वत् (त्); 'to be poor,' दरिद्रा (c. 2. दरिद्राति -द्रितुं), दरिद्रीभू.—(Paltry, mean, inferior) तुच्छः -च्छा -च्छं, कृपणः -णा -णं, कुत्सितः -ता -तं, गर्हितः &c., निर्गुणः -णा -णं, विगुणः &c., क्षुद्रकः -का -कं, अधमः -मा -मं, जघन्यः -न्या -न्यं, खलः -ला -लं, तृणप्रायः -या -यं, अनुत्तमः -मा -मं, or expressed by दुर्, कु, अल्प, पाश, देशीय in comp.; as 'a poor poet,' कुकविः *m.*, कविकल्पः &c.; 'a poor grammarian,' कुवैयाकरणः, वैयाकरणपाशः; 'poor fare,' कदन्नं.—(Wretched, pitiable) दीनः -ना -नं, कृपणः -णा -णं, दुर्बलः -ला -लं, अनुकम्प्यः -म्प्या -म्प्यं, दुःखी -खिनी &c., दुःखान्वितः &c., वराकः -की -कं; 'poor wretch,' तपस्वी *m.* (न्), कृपणजनः.—(As soil) रूक्षः -क्षा -क्षं, ईरिणः -णा -णं.—(Word of endearment) प्रियः -या, दयितः -ता, वत्सः -त्सा.

Poor-house, poor-asylum, *s.* धर्म्मशाला, दरिद्रशाला, दरिद्रालयः -यं, दरिद्राश्रयः, दरिद्रगृहं.

Poorly, *a.* (Somewhat indisposed) अस्वस्थः -स्था -स्थं, ईषदस्वस्थः &c., ईषद्रोगी -गिणी -गि (न्), असुस्थः -स्था -स्थं, ईषद्रोगार्त्तः -र्त्ता -र्त्तं.

Poorly, *adv.* (Without wealth, in indigence) दारिद्र्येण, सदारिद्र्यं, दरिद्रवत्, निर्धनवत्, कृपणं, दीनं, सदैन्यं, धनेन विना.—(With little success) असिद्धिपूर्व्वं, असिद्ध्या, सिद्धिं विना, फलं विना, निष्फलं.

Poorness, *s.* (Want of money or property) दरिद्रता, दारिद्र्यं, दारिद्र्यं, निर्धनता -त्वं, अधनता, धनहीनता, धनशून्यता, दीनता, दैन्यं, अर्थहीनता, वित्तहीनता. *See* Poverty.—(Meanness, paltriness) तुच्छता, कृपणता, कार्पण्यं, निर्गुणता, खलता.—(Barrenness, unproductiveness) रूक्षता, शुष्कता -त्वं, निष्फलता, विफलता -त्वं, अफलदत्वं, अफलोत्पादकता.

Poor-spirited, *a.* कृपणबुद्धिः -द्धिः -द्धि, दीनबुद्धिः &c., दीनमनस्कः -स्का -स्कं.

Pop, *s.* (Sharp, sudden sound) स्फुत्कारः, स्फुत् indecl., आकस्मिकशब्दः, पट्शब्दः, क्ष्वेडितं, आकस्मिकध्वनिः *m.*. अकस्माच्छब्दितं.

To **pop**, *v. n.* (Enter suddenly) अकस्मात् प्रविश् (c. 6. -विशति -वेष्टुं) or निविश्, आकस्मिकध्वनिपूर्व्वं प्रविश्, आकस्मिकप्रवेशं कृ.—(Pop out) अकस्मात् or आकस्मिकध्वनिपूर्व्वं निर्गम् (c. 1. -गच्छति -गन्तुं) or निर्गतः -ता -तं भू; 'in and out,' गमनागमनं कृ.—(Make a sudden sound) स्फुत् शब्दं कृ, आकस्मिकध्वनिं कृ, अकस्मात् क्ष्वण् (c. 1. क्ष्वणति -णितुं) or ध्वन्, पट् शब्दं कृ.

To **pop**, *v. a.* (Cause to enter suddenly) अकस्मात् प्रविश् (c. 10. -वेशयति -यितुं) or निविश्, आकस्मिकध्वनिपूर्व्वं प्रविश्.—(Cause to issue suddenly, pop out) अकस्मात् निर्गम् (c. 10. -गमयति -यितुं) or निःसृ (c. 10. -सारयति -यितुं).

Pop, *adv.* स्फुत्कारेण, स्फुत् शब्देन, अकस्मात्, आकस्मिकध्वनिपूर्व्वं.

Pope, *s.* रोमीयधर्म्माध्यक्षः, रोमीयधर्म्माधिपतिः *m.*, महाधर्म्माध्यक्षः.

Popinjay, *s.* शुकः, कीरः. *See* Parrot.

Popish, *a.* रोमीयधर्म्माध्यक्षसम्बन्धी &c., रोमीयधर्म्मसम्बन्धी &c.

Poplar, *s.* दीर्घवृक्षः, दीर्घतरुः *m.*, दीर्घपादपः, दीर्घद्रुमः.

Poppy, *s.* खस्खसः; 'its juice,' खस्खसरसः; 'seed,' लिक्षा, लिक्ष्या.

Populace, *s.* लोकः, प्रजा, सामान्यलोकः -काः *m. pl.*, साधारणलोकः -काः *m. pl.*, प्राकृतलोकः, प्राकृतजनाः *m. pl.*, अवरजनाः, अवरलोकाः *m. pl.*, अवरवर्णाः *m. pl.*

Popular, *a.* (Pertaining to the common people) लौकिकः -की -कं, साधारणलोकसम्बन्धी &c., सामान्यलोकसम्बन्धी &c., लोक or जन in comp.; 'courting popular favor,' लोकरञ्जनं, जनरञ्जनं, लोकानुरञ्जनं.—(Prevailing among the people, general) लौकिकः -की -कं, सार्व्वलौकिकः &c., लोकसिद्धः -द्धा -द्धं, लोकप्रसिद्धः &c., लोकरूढः -ढा -ढं, रूढः &c., लोकसम्मतः -ता -तं, लोकमतः &c., लोक or जन in comp.; 'popular usage or custom,' लोकव्यवहारः, जनव्यवहारः, लोकाचारः, जनाचारः, लौकिकाचारः, लोकमर्य्यादा, जनमर्य्यादा, जनरीतिः *f.*, लौकिकरीतिः *f.*, लोकरीतिः *f.*, लोकप्रवाहः; 'popular rumour or report,' लोकप्रवादः, जनप्रवादः, लोकवादः, जनवादः, लोकवार्त्ता, जनवार्त्ता, जनश्रुतिः *f.*, जनरवः, लोकवदन्ती, जनवदन्ती; 'popular story,' लोककथा, जनकथा; 'popular accusation,' जनापवादः; 'odium,' जनविद्वेषः; 'tumult,' प्रकृतिक्षोभः; 'apprehension or acceptation,' लोकग्रहः; 'conforming to popular opinion,' लोकानुसरणं, लौकिकानुसरणं, गतानुगमनं; 'one who does so,' लोकानुसारी *m.* (न्), गतानुगतिकः.—(Suitable to common people) सामान्यलोकयोग्यः -ग्या -ग्यं, सामान्यलोकोपयोगी -गिनी -गि (न्), सर्व्वलोकयोग्यः &c., साधारणः -णी -णं.—(Pleasing to the people, enjoying the favor of people) लोकप्रियः -या -यं, सर्व्वलोकप्रियः &c., जनप्रियः &c., लोकानुकूलः -ला -लं, लोकग्राह्यः -ह्या -ह्यं, सर्व्वप्रियः &c., सकलप्रियः &c.

Popularity, *s.* लोकप्रीतिः *f.*, जनप्रीतिः *f.*, लोकप्रियता, सर्व्वलोकप्रीतिः *f.*, लोकानुकूल्यं, लोकानुकूलता, जनानुकूल्यं, जनानुकूलता, जनप्रियता, सर्व्वप्रियता, लोकानुरागः, जनानुरागः, लोकरञ्जनं, लोकसम्मानं, लोकग्राह्यता; 'desire of it,' लोकरञ्जनेच्छा, लोकानुरञ्जनैषा.

Popularly, *adv.* लोकतस्, लोकयोग्यं, लौकिकप्रकारेण, लोकरञ्जनार्थं.

To **populate**, *v. a.* (People) सजनीकृ, सजनं -नां कृ, जनविशिष्ट -ष्टां कृ, वस् in caus.

To **populate**, *v. n.* प्रजोत्पत्तिं कृ, प्रजोत्पादनं कृ, प्रजावृद्धिं कृ or जन्, प्रजन् (c. 4. -जायते -जनितुं), प्रजाम् उत्पद् (c. 10. -पादयति -यितुं).

Population, *s.* प्रजा, प्रजासंख्या, जनसंख्या, लोकसंख्या, जनाः *m. pl.*, जनता, देशजनता, देशजनाः *m. pl.*, देशप्रजा, लोकः, देशलोकः.

Populous, *a.* बहुप्रजः -जा -जं, बहुजनः -ना -नं, प्रचुरजनः &c., प्रचुरपुरुषः -षा -षं, प्रचुरप्रजः &c., जनसम्बाधः -धा -धं, प्रजाबहुलः -ला -लं, जनपदायुतः -ता -तं, वासितः -ता -तं.

Populousness, *s.* बहुप्रजत्वं, प्रजाप्राचुर्य्यं, प्रजाबाहुल्यं, बहुजनत्वं, जनबाहुल्यं, लोकबाहुल्यं, पुरुषप्राचुर्य्यं, पुरुषबाहुल्यं.

Porcelain, *s.* कौलालकं, मृन्मयभाजनानि *n. pl.*, मृद्भाजनानि *n. pl.*, मार्त्तिकं.

Porch, *s.* देहली -लिः *f.*, द्वारमण्डपः -पं, वातायनं, द्वारप्रकोष्ठकं, निष्काशः; 'side seat of a portico,' मृगासनं; 'portico before a temple,' सभामण्डपः -पं.

PORCUPINE, *s.* शल्यकण्ठः, शल्यः -ल्यकः, शलाका, शल्लकी *m.* (न्), श्वाविद् *m.* (ध्), कण्टकागारः, सेधा; 'his quills,' शललं -ली, शलः -लं.

PORE, *s.* (Of the skin) रोमकूपः, तनुकूपः, रोमरन्ध्रं, लोमरन्ध्रं, लोमकूपः, स्वेदद्वारं, स्वेदमार्गः.—(Small spiracle) सूक्ष्मरन्ध्रं.

To **PORE**, *v. n.* (Read books with fixed application) बद्धदृष्ट्या or स्थिरदृष्ट्या or अनिमिषनयनाभ्यां or अनन्यदृष्ट्या ग्रन्थान् अधी (c. 2. अधीते, अध्येतुं, rt. इ), अत्यभिनिवेशेन or अभिनिविष्टचेतसा or अनन्यमनसा ग्रन्थाध्ययनं कृ, अनन्यदृष्टिर् अध्ययनं कृ.

PORK, *s.* शूकरमांसं, सूकरमांसं, वराहमांसं, वाराहं, शौकरं.

PORKER, *s.* शूकरः, वराहः, पचनयोग्यः शूकरशावकः, क्षुद्रशूकरः.

POROUS, *a.* (Having interstices in the skin) रोमकूपयुक्तः -क्ता -क्तं, रोमकूपविशिष्टः -ष्टा -ष्टं, रोमकूपमयः -यी -यं, सरोमकूपः -पा -पं.—(Having minute spiracles) सूक्ष्मरन्ध्रयुक्तः -क्ता -क्तं, सूक्ष्मरन्ध्रपूर्णः -र्णा -र्णं, सूक्ष्मरन्ध्रविशिष्टः -ष्टा -ष्टं, सरन्ध्रः -न्ध्रा -न्ध्रं.—(Having interstices for exudation) विरलावयवकः -का -कं, शिथिलावयवकः &c., द्रावकावयवकः &c., स्वेदमार्गविशिष्टः -ष्टा -ष्टं.

POROUSNESS, POROSITY, *s.* सरोमकूपत्वं, रोमकूपपूर्णता, सूक्ष्मरन्ध्रपूर्णता, बहुरन्ध्रपूर्णता, सूक्ष्मरन्ध्रबाहुल्यं, सरन्ध्रता, विरलावयवत्वं, शिथिलावयवत्वं, द्रावकावयवत्वं.

PORPOISE, *s.* शिशुकः, शिशुमारः, उलुपी *m.* (न्), चुलुकी *m.* (न्), अम्बुकूर्म्मः, अम्बुकीशः, सीरकः, वारिकिटिः *m.*, जलशूकरः, वारिशूकरः, समुद्रीयशूकरः.

PORRIDGE, *s.* यूषं, यूषः -षं, जुष्कलः, मन्थः, चूर्णधान्यमन्थः.

PORRINGER, *s.* यूषपात्रं, यूषपात्रं, पात्रं, भाजनं, भाण्डं.

PORT, *s.* (Harbour, haven) नौकाश्रयः, नौकाश्रयः, आश्रयः, आश्रयस्थानं, उत्तरणस्थानं, खातं, उत्तरणखातं, नौकोत्तरणयोग्यं खातं, नौबन्धनखातं, नौबन्धनयोग्यं खातं, नौरक्षणस्थानं; 'reaches the desired port,' इष्टस्थानं or इष्टदेशं गच्छति.—(Gate) द्वारं.

PORTABILITY, *s.* वाह्यता, सुवाह्यता, सुवहनीयता, हस्तवाह्यत्वं, लघुता.

PORTABLE, *a.* सुवाह्यः -ह्या -ह्यं, वाह्यः &c., वहनीयः -या -यं, सुवहनीयः &c., सुखवाह्यः &c., अनायासवाह्यः &c., सुखवहनीयः &c., हस्तवाह्यः &c., सहजवाह्यः &c., लघुः -घुः -घ्वी -घु.

PORTAL, *s.* द्वारं, द्वार् *f.*, उपद्वारं, प्रतीहारः, प्रवेशद्वारं, मुखं.

PORTCULLIS, *s.* नगरद्वारोपरिस्थो जालकपाटः तेन च शत्रोरागमनकाले पातितेन द्वारवर्त्म रुध्यते, द्वारवर्त्मरोधनयन्त्रं.

To **PORTEND**, *v. a.* अग्रे सूच् (c. 10. सूचयति -यितुं), पूर्व्वं or पूर्व्वं दृश् (c. 10. दर्शयति -यितुं) or प्रदृश्, अनिष्टं सूच् or आविद् (c. 10. वेदयति -यितुं), पूर्व्वचिह्नं or पूर्व्वलक्षणं दा, पूर्व्वलक्षणेन भविष्यत् सूच् or अनिष्टसूचनं कृ or भाविव्यसनसूचनं कृ, भाविक्षयं or उत्पातं or विनिपातं शंस् (c. 1. शंसति -सितुं), कुलक्षणं दा.

PORTENT, *s.* (Omen) पूर्व्वलक्षणं, पूर्व्वचिह्नं, पूर्व्वलिङ्गं, शकुनं, भाविसूचकचिह्नं, भविष्यत्सूचकचिह्नं.—(Omen of ill, prodigy) उत्पातः, उपसर्गः, विनिपातः, व्यतीपातः, अद्भुतं, अरिष्टं, दुर्लक्षणं, अवलक्षणं, दुश्चिह्नं, अपचिह्नं, अपशकुनं, उपप्लवः, उपलिङ्गं, उपद्रवः, अत्याहितं, उपाकृतं, अजन्यं, विनिहतः, अशुभलक्षणं, अनिष्टसूचकचिह्नं, भाविव्यसनसूचकं or भाविक्षयसूचकं चिह्नं, कुलक्षणं; 'ceremonies to avert portents,' अद्भुतशान्तिः *f.*

PORTENTOUS, *a.* उत्पातशंसी -सिनी -सि (न्), विनिपातशंसी &c., औत्पातिकः -की -कं, औपसर्गिकः -की -कं, अनिष्टशंसी &c., अनिष्टसूचकः -का -कं, अनिष्टावेदी &c., अशुभशंसी &c., अशुभसूचकः &c., भविष्यसूचकः &c., अभद्रसूचकः &c., अद्भुतशंसी &c., अद्भुतसूचकः &c., अद्भुतः -ता -तं, अत्याहित &c., शाकुनः -नी -नं, शाकुनिकः -की -कं.

PORTENTOUSLY, *adv.* सोत्पातं, अद्भुतं, उत्पातपूर्व्वं, दुर्लक्षणेन, कुलक्षणेन.

PORTER, *s.* (Gate-keeper) द्वारपालः, द्वारी *m.* (न्), द्वाररक्षकः, द्वाःस्थः, द्वारस्थः, द्वाराध्यक्षः, दौवारिकः, द्वारिकः, प्रतिहारः, प्रतीहारः -री *f.*, द्वाःस्थितः, द्वाःस्थितदर्शकः, दर्शकः.—(Carrier of burdens) भारवाहः -हकः, भारवाही *m.* (न्), भारवाहिकः, भारिकः, भारी *m.* (न्), भारहरः, भारहारी *m.*, भारहारकः, वोढा *m.* (ढृ).

PORTERAGE, *s.* (Cost of carriage) वहनमूल्यं, वाहनमूल्यं, भारवाहनमूल्यं.—(Business of a porter) भारवाहनं, भारिककर्म्म *n.* (न्).

PORTFOLIO, *s.* पत्राधारः, पृथुपत्राधारः, महापत्राधारः, बृहत्पत्राधारः.

PORTHOLE, *s.* नौपार्श्वच्छिद्रं, नौपार्श्वमुखं, नौपार्श्ववातायनं.

PORTICO, *s.* वरण्डः, द्वारप्रकोष्ठकं, बहिर्द्वारप्रकोष्ठकं, द्वारमण्डपः -पं, देहली -लिः *f.*, निष्काशः, वरण्डकः, वातायनं, पिण्डः, द्वारपिण्डः.

PORTION, *s.* (Part) अंशः, भागः, विभागः, खण्डः -ण्डकः, अवयवः, अर्द्धं, भिन्नं, छेदः, भित्तं, शकलः -लं.—(Portion allotted, share) विभागः, अंशः, भागः, भाजितं, भाज्यं, वण्टः -ण्टकः, उद्धारः.—(Share of an estate) ऋक्थांशः, ऋक्थभागः, रिक्थभागः, पैतृकरिक्थभागः, दायः, उद्धारः, औद्धारिकं.—(Wife's fortune) स्त्रीधनं, यौतकं, यौतुकं, युतकं, शुल्कं, औद्वाहिकं, अध्यावाहनिकं, कन्याधनं, परिबर्हं.

To **PORTION**, *v. a.* (Parcel out) विभज् (c. 1. -भजति -ते -भक्तुं), प्रविभज्, वण्ट् (c. 10. वण्टयति -यितुं), विभागशः or अंशांशि क्लृप् or परिक्लृप् or विन्यस्, अंश्, व्यंस्.—(Endow) यौतकं or शुल्कं or वृत्तिं दा, प्रतिष्ठां कृ, प्रतिष्ठा.

PORTIONABLE, *a.* विभाज्यः -ज्या -ज्यं, भाज्यः &c., वण्टनीयः &c., औद्धारिकः &c.

PORTIONED, *p. p.* (Divided out) विभक्तः -क्ता -क्तं, प्रविभक्तः &c., संविभक्तः &c., अंशितः -ता -तं, परिकल्पितः &c.—(Endowed) प्रतिष्ठितः -ता -तं, गृहीतशुल्कः -ल्का -ल्कं, गृहीतयौतकः &c.

PORTIONING, *s.* विभागः, विभाजनं, प्रविभागः, विभागकरणं, भाजनं, अंशनं, उद्धारविभागः, विभागकल्पना, वण्टनं.

PORTIONLESS, *a.* अनंशः -शा -शं, अंशहीनः -ना -नं, शुल्कहीनः -ना -नं.

PORTLINESS, *s.* उदरविस्तारः, कायविस्तारः, शरीरगौरवं, शरीरस्थूलता, स्थूलशरीरत्वं, स्थूलकायत्वं, शरीरबृहत्त्वं.

PORTLY, *a.* (Dignified in mien) गौरवशाली -लिनी -लि (न्), साटोपगामी &c., गौरवगतिः -तिः -ति, गौरववृत्तिः &c.—(Bulky, corpulent) विस्तीर्णोदरः -रा -रं, विस्तीर्णकायः -या -यं, पृथूदरः -रा -रं, स्थूलकायः &c., बृहत्कायः &c., स्थूलशरीरः &c.

PORTMANTEAU, *s.* चर्म्ममयं वस्त्रपात्रं or वस्त्रभाजनं, वस्त्राधारः.

PORTRAIT, *s.* प्रतिमा, प्रतिमानं, उपमा, उपमानं, उपमितिः *f.*, प्रतिमूर्त्तिः *f.*, प्रतिकृतिः *f.*, चित्रलेखा, आलेख्यं, चित्राकृतिः *f.*, चित्रं, प्रतिच्छन्दः -न्दकं, प्रतिच्छाया, जीवितव्यक्तिप्रतिमा.

PORTRAIT-PAINTER, *s.* उपमाता *m.* (तृ), चित्रलेखकः, चित्रकारः, चित्रकरः, चित्रलिख् *m.* (ख्), आलेख्यकृत् *m.*, उपमानकृत् *m.*, प्रतिमानकृत् *m.*

PORTRAIT-PAINTING, *s.* चित्रलिखनं, चित्रलेखनं, उपमानकरणं, रूपकरणं.

To **PORTRAY**, *v. a.* (Paint) आलिख्, विलिख्, लिख्, चित्र्, वर्ण्, उपवर्ण्.—(Describe) वर्ण्, अनुवर्ण्, उपवर्ण्, निरूप्.

PORTRAYED, *p. p.* वर्णितः -ता -तं, आलिखितः &c., चित्रितः &c., चित्रगतः &c.

PORTRESS, PORTERESS, *a.* दौवारिकी, द्वारपालिका, प्रतीहारी, द्वाररक्षकी.

To **POSE**, *v. a.* निरुत्तरीकृ, वाग्रोधं कृ, उत्तररोधं कृ, वाक्यरोधं कृ, प्रतिवाक्यरोधं कृ, वाक्यखण्डनं कृ, उपमर्दं कृ, बाध् (c. 1. बाधते -धितुं), मुह् (c. 10. मोहयति -यितुं), विमुह्, शल्यं कृ.

POSED, *p. p.* निरुत्तरः -रा -रं, निरुत्तरीकृतः -ता -तं, बाधितः -ता -तं,

मोहितः -ता -तं, विमोहितः &c., कुण्ठितः &c., इतिकर्त्तव्यतामूढः -ढा -ढं.

POSER, *s.* उपमर्दकः, बाधकः, वाग्रोधकः, मोहकः, विमोहकः.

POSITION, *s.* (Situation) स्थानं, स्थितिः *f.*, अवस्थितिः *f.*, संस्थानं, पदं, आस्पदं, पदविः -वी *f.*—(Attitude) अङ्गस्थितिः *f.*, शरीरस्थितिः *f.*, आकारः; 'of the feet,' पदन्यासः, पादविन्यासः.—(Principle laid down, proposition advanced) पक्षः, प्रतिज्ञा, फक्किका, प्रमेयं, प्रतिज्ञेयं, प्रतिज्ञातं, भाषा, हेतुः *m.*, पूर्व्वपक्षः, उपन्यासः, अर्थः; 'false position,' हेत्वाभासः, पक्षाभासः, आभासः, मिथ्याहेतुः *m.*—(State, circumstances) अवस्था, स्थितिः *f.*, दशा, संस्थितिः *f.*, भावः, वृत्तिः *f.*, गतिः *f.*

POSITIVE, *a.* (Explicit, express, direct) स्पष्टः -ष्टा -ष्टं, स्पष्टार्थः -र्था -र्थं, व्यक्तः -क्ता -क्तं, सुव्यक्तः &c., सुस्पष्टः &c., अवक्रः -क्रा -क्रं, अवक्रार्थः -र्था -र्थं, असन्दिग्धार्थः &c., अगूढः -ढा -ढं, अगर्भितः -ता -तं, प्रत्यक्षः -क्षा -क्षं.—(Peremptory, definite) नियतः -ता -तं, अवश्यकः -का -कं, आवश्यकः -की -कं, सुनियतः -ता -तं, निश्चितः &c., सुनिश्चितः &c., निर्णीतः &c., अवैकल्पिकः -की -कं, अविकल्पकः -का -कं, —(Absolute, real, existing in fact) वास्तवः -वी -वं, वास्तविकः -की -कं, तथ्यः -थ्या -थ्यं, सत्यः -त्या -त्यं, यथार्थः -र्था -र्थं, सन् सती सत् (त्), विद्यमानः -ना -नं, भूतः -ता -तं, तात्त्विकः -की -कं; 'positive charge,' तत्त्वाभियोगः.—(Settled by arbitrary appointment, not inbred) नियोगसिद्धः -द्धा -द्धं, नियोगप्रयुक्तः -क्ता -क्तं, नियोगहेतुकः -का -कं, अभावसिद्धः &c., अस्वाभाविकः -की -कं, अनैसर्गिकः -की -कं, असहजः -जा -जं, बहिर्जातः -ता -तं.—(Confident, sure) दृढनिश्चयः -या -यं, कृतनिश्चयः &c., जातनिश्चयः &c., निश्चितमनाः -नाः -नः (स्), निश्चितमनस्कः -स्का -स्कं, निश्चयी -यिनी -यि (न्), बद्धनिश्चयः -या -यं, दृढमतिः -तिः -ति, निःसंशयः -या -यं, निःसन्देहः -हा -हं.—(Confident in assertion) दार्ढ्येन स्वमतवादी &c., or स्वमताग्रही &c., मताग्रही &c., स्वमताभिमानी &c., मताभिमानी &c., दृढोक्तिः -क्तिः -क्ति, उक्तनिर्वाही &c., प्रोक्तनिर्वाही &c.

POSITIVELY, *adv.* (Expressly) स्पष्टं, सुस्पष्टं, व्यक्तं, सुव्यक्तं, स्पष्टार्थतस्, अवक्रं, असन्दिग्धं.—(Peremptorily, definitely) नियतं, सुनियतं, अवश्यं, अवश्यमेव, निश्चितं, सुनिश्चितं, विकल्पेन विना.—(Absolutely, really) वस्तुतस्, तत्त्वतस्, यथार्थतस्, तथ्यं, सत्यं, सत्यमेव.—(Confidently, surely) निश्चयेन, दृढनिश्चयेन, दृढनिश्चयपूर्व्वं, सुनिश्चयेन, सुनिश्चयपूर्व्वं, दार्ढ्येन, दृढं, सुदृढं.—(Dogmatically) स्वमताग्रहेण, मताग्रहेण, मताभिमानेन, दृढोक्त्या.

POSITIVENESS, *s.* (Reality of existence) वास्तविकत्वं, तथ्यता, यथार्थत्वं, सत्ता, सत्त्वं, विद्यमानता, सत्यता -त्वं.—(Peremptoriness) दृढनिश्चयः -यत्वं, सुनिश्चयत्वं, दृढता, सुदृढता, दार्ढ्यं, अवक्रता, सुस्पष्टता, नियतत्वं, सुनियतत्वं, दृढनिर्णयः, सुनिर्णीतत्वं.—(Dogmaticalness) स्वमताग्रहः, मताग्रहः, मताभिमानं, दृढोक्तिः *f.*

To POSSESS, *v. a.* (Have, hold) धृ (c. 10. धारयति -यितुं, c. 1. धरति, धर्त्तुं), धा (c. 3. दधाति, धत्ते, धातुं), आधा, विधा, भृ (c. 3. बिभर्त्ति, भर्त्तुं), दध् (c. 1. दधते -धितुं), शील् (c. 10. शीलयति -यितुं), भुज्, आप्, प्राप्.—(Hold in use, enjoy, occupy) भुज् (c. 7. भुनक्ति, भुंक्ते, भोक्तुं), उपभुज्, परिभुज्, अनुभुज्, अधिभुज्, भोगं कृ, परिभोगं कृ, अधिष्ठा, अध्यास्.—(Gain, obtain information of) आप् (c. 5. आप्नोति, आप्तुं), प्राप्, अवाप्, लभ्, उपलभ्, आसद्, अधिगम्, आविश्, समाविश्, आक्रम्, अध्याक्रम्.—(Have power over) अधिकृ, प्रभू, अधिष्ठा, वशीकृ.—(Engross, take up, as a thought, passion, &c.) आविश्, व्याप्, ग्रस्, आक्रम्.—(As an evil spirit, &c.) आविश्, समाविश्.—(Give possession, make possessed of) अधिकारं दा, अधिकृ, युज् in caus. *See* POSSESSED OF.

POSSESSED, *p. p.* (Held, occupied, enjoyed) धृतः -ता -तं, धारितः &c., आविष्टः -ष्टा -ष्टं, समाविष्टः &c., आक्रान्तः -न्ता -न्तं, भुक्तः -क्ता -क्तं, परिभुक्तः &c., हस्तगतः -ता -तं, ग्रस्तः -स्ता -स्तं, आस्वादितः &c., अधिष्ठितः &c., अध्यासितः &c., आश्रितः &c., अधीनः -ना -नं.—(Gained) आप्तः -प्ता -प्तं, प्राप्तः &c., लब्धः -ब्धा -ब्धं, आसादितः -ता -तं, अधिगतः &c.—(Engrossed, affected by) आविष्टः &c., समाविष्टः &c., आक्रान्तः -न्ता -न्तं, ग्रस्तः -स्ता -स्तं, उपहतः &c.; as, 'by love,' कामाविष्टः &c.; 'by avarice,' लोभाविष्टः &c.—(Possessed of, endowed with) युक्तः -क्ता -क्तं, अन्वितः -ता -तं, उपेतः -ता -तं, समन्वितः -ता -तं, उपपन्नः -न्ना -न्नं, सम्पन्नः &c., संयुतः -ता -तं, अनपेतः -ता -तं, विशिष्टः -ष्टा -ष्टं, शीलितः &c., सनाथः -था -थं or expressed by the affixes वत्, मत्, and इन्; as, 'possessed of wealth,' धनवान् -वती -वत् (त्), धनी -निनी -नि (न्), धनयुक्तः &c., धनान्वितः &c.; 'possessed of prosperity,' श्रीमान् &c.; 'possessed of learning,' विद्यावान् &c., विद्यासम्पन्नः &c.; 'of a father,' पितृमान्. *See* POSSESSING.—(By evil spirits) भूताविष्टः &c., भूतसमाविष्टः &c., पिशाचाविष्टः &c., भूतग्रस्तः &c., भूतसञ्चारितः &c., भूतार्त्तः -र्त्ता -र्त्तं, प्रेतवाहितः &c., भूतोपहतः &c.

POSSESSING, *part.* धारी -रिणी -रि (न्), धारयन् -यन्ती -यत् (त्), दधत् -धती -धत् (त्), दधानः -ना -नं, दधः -धा -धं, शाली &c. *See* POSSESSED OF.

POSSESSION, *s.* (Having, holding) धारणं, धरणं.—(Occupancy, ownership) अधिकारः, अधिकृतिः *f.*, आधिकारण्यं, अधिकारिता -त्वं, भोगः, भुक्तिः, परिभोगः, आवेशः, समावेशः; 'taking possession,' आवेशनं, समावेशनं, आक्रमणं, आक्रान्तिः *f.*, अध्याक्रमणं; 'to take possession of,' आविश् (c. 6. -विशति -वेष्टुं), समाविश्, आक्रम् (c. 1. -क्रामति -क्रमितुं), अध्याक्रम्; 'to put in possession,' नियुज् (c. 7. -युनक्ति -युंक्ते, c. 10. -योजयति -यितुं), युज्, अधिकृ, अधिकारं दा; 'come into one's possession,' हस्तगतः -ता -तं, स्वाधीनभूतः -ता -तं, स्वाधीनः -ना -नं.—(State of being possessed of or by) आविष्टता, आवेशः, आक्रान्तता, सम्पन्नता, युक्तता, शालिता, विशिष्टता.—(By evil spirits) भूतावेशः, पिशाचावेशः, आवेशः, समावेशः, भूतसञ्चारः, पिशाचसञ्चारः, भूतग्रस्तता, भूतोपहतत्वं, भूतबाधा, पिशाचबाधा, भूताक्रान्तिः *f.*, भूतक्रान्तिः *f.*, ग्रहामयः, भूतपीडा, पिशाचपीडा, उपद्रवः, उपसर्गः.—(Thing possessed of, property) स्वं, स्वाधीनद्रव्यं, स्वाधीनवस्तु *n.*, द्रव्यं, वस्तु *n.*—(Goods, possessions) द्रव्यं -व्याणि *n. pl.*, वस्तु -स्तूनि *n. pl.*, वित्तं, विभवः, अर्थः, धनं, द्रविणं, वसु *n.*, रिक्थं, स्वापतेयं, पृक्तं, क्षेत्रादि *n.*, भूमिः *f.*

POSSESSIVE, *a.* (In grammar) सम्बन्धवाचकः -का -कं, अधिकरणवाचकः &c.; 'possessive case,' सम्बन्धः, षष्ठी, षष्ठी विभक्तिः.

POSSESSOR, *s.* धारी *m.* -रिणी *f.* (न्), धारयन् *m.* -यन्ती *f.* (त्), धारयः -या, अधिकारी *m.* -रिणी *f.* (न्), भोक्ता *m.* (तृ), परिभोक्ता *m.*, भोगी *m.* (न्), परिभोगी *m.*, उपभोक्ता *m.*, शाली *m.* (न्), स्वामी *m.* -मिनी *f.*

POSSIBILITY, *s.* सम्भवः, सम्भावनं -ना, सम्भाव्यता, सम्भावनीयता, शक्यता, साध्यता, करणीयता, सम्भूतिः *f.*

POSSIBLE, *a.* शक्यः -क्या -क्यं, सम्भाव्यः -व्या -व्यं, सम्भावनीयः -या -यं, सम्भावितः -ता -तं, घटनशक्यः &c.; 'possible to be done,' करणीयः -या -यं, साध्यः -ध्या -ध्यं, साधनीयः -या -यं, कर्त्तुं शक्यः &c., उपपाद्यः -द्या -द्यं, सम्पाद्यः &c., सम्पादनीयः -या -यं; 'as much as possible,' यथाशक्ति, यथाशक्यं; 'to be possible,' शक् in pass. (शक्यते), सम्भू; 'it is not possible,' न सम्भवति. The root शक् gives a passive sense to the infin.; as, 'it is not possible to be done,' कर्तुं न शक्यते.

Possibly, *adv.* (By any power). This sense must be rendered by शक्यं, or the root शक् thus, 'all that can possibly be known,' यत् सर्वं ज्ञातुं शक्यते or शक्यं.—(Any how, by any means) कथञ्चित्, यथाकथञ्चित्, कथञ्चन, यथाकथञ्चन.—(Perhaps) किंस्वित्, अपिनाम, किल, स्यात्, कदापि, कदाचित्, नाम.

Post, *s.* (Piece of timber set upright, pillar) स्तम्भः, स्थाणुः *m.*, स्थूणा, अवष्टम्भः, अपस्तम्भः, उपस्तम्भः, दारुः *m.*; 'of a house,' गृहस्तम्भः, गृहदारुः *m.*; 'for securing an elephant,' आलानं, बन्धस्तम्भः.—(Office) अधिकारः, पदं, पदवी -विः *f.*, नियोगः; 'post under government,' अधिकारपदं; 'an honorable post,' श्लाघ्यपदं.—(Station, position) स्थानं, पदं, पदविः -वी *f.*, आस्पदं, स्थितिः *f.*, अवस्थितिः *f.*—(Military station) गुल्मस्थानं, सैन्यस्थानं.—(Post of danger in battle) वीराशंसनं, भयप्रदा युद्धभूमिः.—(For carrying letters) पत्रवाहनं, राजपत्रवाहनं, राजपत्रवाही *m.* (न्), लेखवाहनं, राजलेख्यवाहनं -हकः, राजनियोगिभिर् भृतः पत्रकोषः, राजधावकभृतो लेख्यकोषः, राजपत्रवाहकः, राजलेखहारी *m.*

To post, *v. n.* (Travel with post horses or with speed) जवेन गम् (c. 1. गच्छति, गन्तुं), जववाहनेन गम्, जवतुरगैः or जवाश्वैः or जवघोटकैर् गम् or व्रज् (c. 1. व्रजति -जितुं).

To post, *v. a.* (Station) स्था in caus. (स्थापयति -यितुं), अवस्था, प्रतिष्ठा, नियुज् (c. 7. -युनक्ति -युंक्ते, c. 10. -योजयति -यितुं), विनियुज्.—(Fix to a post) स्तम्भे बन्ध्, स्तम्भबद्धं -द्धां कृ.—(Expose to public reproach) नामादि प्रकाशयित्वा परिभवास्पदं कृ or अवमानास्पदं कृ or तिरस्कारास्पदीकृ.—(Place in the post-office) पत्रस्थाने or लेख्यस्थाने निविश् in caus.

Postage, *s.* पत्रवाहनमूल्यं, लेख्यवाहनमूल्यं, वाहनमूल्यं.

Post-boy, *s.* जवाश्वपः, जवाश्वपालः, जवाश्वारोही *m.* (न्), जवाश्वप्रेरकः.

Post-chaise, *s.* जववाहनं, जवनरथः, पत्रवाहनं, जवाश्वयुक्तं वाहनं.

To post-date, *v. a.* पश्चात् or परस्तात् कालं लिख् (c. 6. लिखति, लेखितुं).

Post-diluvial, post-diluvian, *a.* प्रलयोत्तरकालीनः -ना -नं, प्रलयानन्तरः -रा -रं.

Poster, *s.* जवी *m.* (न्), प्रजवी *m.*, जवनः, जवः, जवाश्वः, जवनाश्वः.

Posterior, *a.* पश्चात्कालीनः -ना -नं, पश्चात्कालिकः -की -कं, उत्तरकालीनः -ना -नं, पाश्चात्यः -त्या -त्यं, उत्तरः -रा -रं, अपरः -रा -रं, अवरः &c., परः &c., अवरकालिकः -की -कं, अपरकालिकः -की -कं.

Posteriority, *s.* पश्चात्कालीनता, पश्चात्कालिकत्वं, अपरता -त्वं, अवरता -त्वं, परता, उत्तरता -त्वं, अपरकालिकत्वं, अवरकालिकत्वं.

Posteriorly, *adv.* पश्चात्, अपरतस्, उत्तरतस्, परतस्, अवरतस्, परस्तात्, परं, अपरं, उत्तरं.

Posteriors, *s.* नितम्बः, गुदप्रदेशः, गुददेशः, परिणायः, वटिकं, पश्चाद्देशः, पश्चाद्भागः.

Posterity, *s.* (Descendants, offspring) सन्तानं -नः, सन्ततिः *f.*, अपत्यं, वंशः, कुलसन्ततिः *f.*, कुलं.—(Succeeding generations in a general sense) पुत्रपौत्राः *m. pl.*, पुत्रपौत्रादि *n.*, पुत्रपौत्रादिसन्तानं.

Postern, *s.* पक्षद्वारं, प्रच्छन्नद्वारं, पक्षकः, क्षुद्रद्वारं, उपद्वारं, खडक्किका.

Post-haste, *adv.* जवेन, सजवं, सवेगं, जवाश्ववत्, जवनाश्ववत्.

Post-horse, *s.* जवाश्वः, जवनाश्वः, जवतुरगः, जवघोटकः.

Posthumous, *a.* (Born after the death of the father) पितृमरणोत्तरजः -जा -जं, जनकमृत्युत्तरजः &c., पितृमरणोत्तरकः -का -कं.—(Published after the death of the author) कर्तृमृत्युत्तरकः -का -कं, कर्तृमरणोत्तरकः -का -कं, कर्तृगतयुत्तरकः &c.

Postillion, *s.* जवाश्वारोही *m.* (न्), रथवाहकः, सारथिः *m.*, सूतः.

Postman, *s.* पत्रवाहकः, पत्रवाहः, पत्रवाही *m.* (न्), लेख्यवाहकः, लेखवाहकः, लेखहारः -रकः, लेखहारी *m.*, लेखमिकः.

Postmaster, *s.* पत्रवाहकाध्यक्षः, लेखहारकाध्यक्षः, पत्रवाहनादिकर्म्माध्यक्षः, पत्रप्रेरणादिकर्म्माधिकारी *m.* (न्).

Postmeridian, *a.* आपराह्णिकः -की -कं, अपराह्णकालिकः -की -कं, पराह्णकालिकः -की -कं.

Postmortem, *a.* मरणोत्तरः -रा -रं, मृत्युत्तरः &c., मरणानन्तरः -रा -रं.

Postnate, *a.* उत्तरः -रा -रं, उत्तरजः -जा -जं, अवरजः &c., परः -रा रं.

Post-office, *s.* पत्रस्थानं, लेखस्थानं, लेख्यस्थानं, पत्रगृहं, पत्रागारं, लेख्यागारं, लेखगृहं, लेख्यकुटी, लेख्यगृहं.

To postpone, *v. a.* आकालान्तरात् or परकालं यावत् त्यज् (c. 1. त्यजति, त्यक्तुं) or परित्यज्, उत्तरकालं यावद् विसृज् (c. 6. -सृजति -स्रष्टुं) or अवसृज् or या in caus. (यापयति -यितुं), विलम्ब् (c. 1. -लम्बते -म्बितुं, c. 10. -लम्बयति -यितुं), विलम्बनं कृ, शिथिल (nom. शिथिलयति -यितुं).

Postponed, *p. p.* आकालान्तरात् or परकालं यावत् त्यक्तः -क्ता -क्तं or परित्यक्तः &c. or विसर्जितः -ता -तं or विसृष्टः -ष्टा -ष्टं or यापितः -ता -तं, विलम्बितः -ता -तं, शिथिलितः &c.

Postponement, *s.* आकालान्तरात् or परकालं यावत् त्यागः or परित्यागः or विसर्जनं or यापनं, कालयापः -पनं, विलम्बः -म्बनं.

Postscript, *s.* पश्चाल्लेखः, पश्चाल्लिखितं, पश्चाल्लिपिः *f.*, अनुलिखितं.

Postulate, *s.* अनुमानमूलं, स्वीकृतपक्षः, देश्यं, सिद्धवद् गृहीतपदं.

Posture, *s.* अङ्गस्थितिः *f.*, अङ्गसंस्थितिः *f.*, अङ्गविन्यासः, शरीरस्थितिः *f.*, शरीरविन्यासः, शरीरसंस्था, स्थितिः *f.*, भूमिः *f.*, भूमिका.—(A posture in religious meditation as practised by devotees, &c.) आसनं, ध्यानयोगासनं. Eighty-four kinds of these postures are enumerated, of which some are the following: पद्मासनं, भद्रासनं, भद्रासनं, कूर्म्मासनं, मयूरासनं, प्रेतासनं, कुक्कुटासनं, गोमुखासनं, गोरक्षासनं, वीरासनं, दक्षासनं, वासनं, मुद्रा.—(Position, condition) स्थितिः *f.*, अवस्था, संस्थितिः *f.*, दशा.

Posture-master, *s.* अङ्गविन्यासशिक्षकः, शरीरविन्यासशिक्षकः, अङ्गविक्षेपशिक्षकः, अङ्गविन्यासदेशिकः.

Posy, *s.* (Motto on a ring, &c.) अङ्गुरीयकलेखः, मुद्रास्थवाक्यं.—(Nosegay) पुष्पगुच्छः -च्छकः, पुष्पस्तबकः.

Pot, *s.* (For culinary or domestic purposes) भाण्डं, पात्रं, भाजनं, स्थाली -लं, पिठरः -रं, उखा, पिष्टपचनं, वासनं, पाडिनी, कुण्डं, उखाः 'interior of a pot,' स्थालीबिलं.—(Water pot) घटः, कुम्भः -म्भी, कुम्भी, कलशः, कलसः -सी, उदकपात्रं, उदकुम्भः, कमण्डलुः *m.*, निपः, अलुः; 'iron pot,' अयस्कुम्भः; 'boiled in a pot,' स्थालीपक्वः -क्वा -क्वं; 'fit to be boiled in a pot,' स्थालीबिलीयः -या -यं, स्थालीबिल्यः -ल्या -ल्यं.

To pot, *v. a.* भाण्डे निविश् in caus. or निधा or रक्ष्, भाण्डीकृ, उपस्कृ.

Potable, *a.* पेयः -या -यं, पानीयः &c., पानयोग्यः -ग्या -ग्यं, पानार्हः -र्हा -र्हं.

Potash, *s.* क्षारः, यवक्षारः, सर्ज्जिकाक्षारः, सर्ज्जिः *f.*, सर्ज्जिका.

Potation, *s.* पानं, पानोत्सवः, सम्पीतिः *f.*, सपीतिः *f.*, पानसमारम्भः.

Potato, *s.* आलुः *m.*, आलुकं.—(Sweet potato) मध्वालुकं, मधुमूलं, सलकालुः -लुकं, लकद्रणी.

Pot-bellied, *a.* लम्बोदरः -रा -रं, लम्बजठरः -रा -रं, बृहत्कुक्षिः -क्षिः -क्षि, बृहन्नाभिः -भिः -भि, तुन्दी -न्दिनी -न्दि (न्), तुन्दिकः -का -कं, तुन्दिलः -ला -लं, तुन्दितः -ता -तं, तुन्दिभः -भा -भं, तुन्दिकरः -रा -रं, तुन्दवान् -वती -वत् (त्), तुन्दिलः -ला -लं, तुन्दिभः &c., पिचिण्डिलः -ला -लं, पिचिण्डवान् &c.

Pot-belly, *s.* लम्बोदरं, लम्बजठरं, बृहत्कुक्षिः *m.*, पिचिण्डः.

Pot-boy, *s.* यवसुरादिविक्रयगृहे भाण्डवाहकः or भाण्डवाही *m.*

Pot-companion, *s.* सहपायी *m.* (न्), पानसहायः, पानसुहृद् *m.*

Potency, *s.* प्रभावः -वत्वं, प्राबल्यं, बलं, शक्तिः *f.*, वीर्य्यं, तेजस् *n.*, सत्त्वं, प्रतापः, ओजस् *n.*, पराक्रमः, प्रभविष्णुता.

Potent, *a.* प्रबलः -ला -लं, महाबलः &c., महाबलवान् -वती -वत् (त्), सप्रभावः -वा -वं, शक्तिमान् &c., महाशक्तिमान् &c., प्रभविष्णुः -ष्णुः -ष्णु, प्रतापी -पिनी -पि (न्), तेजोवान् &c., महौजाः -जाः -जः (स्), सतेजाः &c., बलाढ्यः -ढ्या -ढ्यं, प्रतापवान् &c., वीर्य्यवान् &c., पराक्रमी &c., महोदारः -रा -रं.

Potentate, *s.* अधिपतिः *m.*, महीपतिः *m.*, नरेश्वरः, नरपतिः *m.* *See* King.

Potential, *a.* (Existing in possibility) सम्भाव्यः -व्या -व्यं, सम्भावनीयः -या -यं, भाविसम्भाव्यः &c.—(Potential mood) सम्भावनं, विधिलिङ्.

Potentiality, *s.* सम्भाव्यता -त्वं, सम्भावनीयता -त्वं, सम्भावनं -ना.

Potently, *adv.* प्रबलं, सबलं, प्राबल्येन, सप्रभावं, सप्रतापं, महाबलेन.

Pother, *s.* क्षोभः, तुमुलं, व्यग्रता, व्यस्तता, वैक्लव्यं, सम्भ्रमः, बाधा.

Potherb, *s.* शाकः -कं, हरितकं, शिग्रुः *m.*, सिग्रुः *m.*; 'its stalk,' कडङ्गः, कलम्बः. The following are various sorts of pot-herbs: विशल्या, अग्निशिखा, अनन्ता, फलिनी, शक्रपुष्पी, सूक्ष्मगन्धा, सुगन्धा, छगलान्त्री, छगलांघ्री, आवेगी, वृद्धदारकः, जुङ्गः -ङ्गा, चितुलं, सुनिषण्णकं, शूरणं.

Pothouse, *s.* शुण्डागृहं, शुण्डापानं, शुण्डा, यवसुरागृहं, पानगोष्ठिका.

Potion, *s.* पेयौषधं, पानीयौषधं, औषधीयपेयं, औषधं.

Potsherd, *s.* भिन्नभाण्डं, भिन्नपात्रं, भग्नभाण्डं, भग्नभाण्डशकलं, कपालिका, शर्क्करा, भग्नमृण्मयभाजनशकलं.

Pottage, *s.* सूपं, यूषः -षं, शुष्ककः, शृतमांसपेयं.

Potter, *s.* कुम्भकारः -रकः, कुलालः, घटीकारः, घटकारः -रकः, घटिन्धमः, मृत्करः, चक्रजीवकः, चक्री *m.* (न्), भटः; 'potter's wheel,' कुलालचक्रं.

Pottery, *s.* (Place where earthen vessels are made) कुम्भशाला, घटशाला, घटनिर्म्माणस्थानं.—(Earthenware) कौलालकं, मृण्मयं, मृण्मयभाण्डानि *n. pl.*, मार्त्तिकं, कुलालकर्म्म *n.* (न्).

Pottle, *s.* क्षुद्रपरिमाणो मद्यधारणयोग्यः दीर्घकरङ्कः.

Potulent, *a.* ईषन्मत्तः -त्ता -त्तं.—(Fit to drink) पानयोग्यः -ग्या -ग्यं.

Pouch, *s.* (Bag) कोषः, कोशः, पेशी.—(Of an animal) पेशिः -शी *f.* —(Of a bird, &c.) पूर्व्वजठरः, उपजठरः, पूर्व्वोदरं.—(A protuberant belly) लम्बोदरं, लम्बजठरः.

To pouch, *v. a.* कोषे निविश् (c. 10. -वेशयति -यितुं), कोषस्थं -स्थां कृ.

Pouched, *p. p.* (Pocketed) कोषनिवेशितः -ता -तं, कोषस्थः -स्था -स्थं. —(Having a pouch) पेशीविशिष्टः -ष्टा -ष्टं, कोषविशिष्टः &c.

Poulterer, *s.* खाद्यपक्षिविक्रेता *m.* (तृ), खाद्यपक्षिविक्रयी *m.* (न्), गृह्यपक्षिविक्रेता *m.* (तृ), ग्राम्यपक्षिविक्रयी, कुक्कुटादिविक्रेता *m.*, वैतंसिकः, शौनिकः.

Poultice, *s.* उत्कारिका, लेपः, प्रलेपः, उपनाहः, पाकजनकपिष्टप्रलेपः.

To poultice, *v. a.* उपनाहेन or उत्कारिकया लिप् (c. 6. लिम्पति, लेप्तुं).

Poultry, *s.* गृह्यपक्षिणः *m. pl.*, ग्राम्यपक्षिणः *m. pl.*, कुक्कुटादिग्राम्यपक्षिणः *m. pl.*, कुक्कुटादिखाद्यपक्षिणः *m. pl.*

Poultry-yard, *s.* ग्राम्यपक्षिपोषणयोग्या वाटिका, कुक्कुटादिस्थानं.

Pounce, *s.* (Powder to prevent ink from spreading) मसीशोषणचूर्णं, मसिशोषकचूर्णं.—(Talon, claw) नखः, नखरः.

To pounce, *v. n.* (Fall upon suddenly and seize) अकस्मात् पतित्वा नखैर् ग्रह् (c. 9. गृह्णाति, ग्रहीतुं) or धृ (c. 1. धरति, धर्त्तुं), ग्रहणार्थम् अकस्माद् आपत् (c. 1. -पतति -तितुं) or आक्रम् (c. 1. -क्रामति -क्रमितुं).

Pounce-box, pouncet-box, *s.* शोषकचूर्णाधारः, शोषणचूर्णपात्रं.

Pound, *s.* (Weight or measure) प्रस्थः.—(Fence for stray cattle, &c.) यूथभ्रष्टपशुरोधकं, यूथभ्रष्टपशुवारणी -णं, भ्रष्टपशुरक्षणस्थानं, भ्रष्टपशुरोधनस्थानं, अवरोधः -धकं, अवरोधस्थानं.—(Gold coin) स्वर्णमुद्रा.

To pound, *v. a.* (Confine in a pound) यूथभ्रष्टपश्वादि अवरोधस्थाने निरुध् (c. 7. -रुणद्धि -रोद्धुं) or रक्ष्.—(Comminute) पिष् (c. 7. पिनष्टि, पेष्टुं), निष्पिष्, सम्पिष्, विनिष्पिष्, प्रतिपिष्, उत्पिष्, चूर्ण्, प्रचूर्ण्, विचूर्ण्, सञ्चूर्ण्, चूर्णीकृ, मृद्, अवमृद्, विमृद्, प्रमृद्, अभिमृद्, सम्मृद्, क्षुद् (c. 7. क्षुणत्ति, क्षोत्तुं), प्रक्षुद्, संक्षुद्, क्षोदीकृ, पुथ् (c. 10. पोथयति -यितुं), विपुथ्, मथ् or मन्थ् (c. 1. मथति, मन्थति, c. 9. मथ्नाति, मथितुं), कुट्ट् (c. 10. कुट्टयति -यितुं), प्रकुट्ट्, गुण्ड् (c. 10. गुण्डयति -यितुं), खण्डशः कृ, खण्डीकृ.—(Beat) तड्, वितड्, तुद्, आतुद्.

Poundage, *s.* (Fee, due) शुल्कः -ल्कं, देयं, करः, राजग्राह्यं.

Pounded, *p. p.* (Comminuted) चूर्णितः -ता -तं, सञ्चूर्णितः &c., चूर्णीकृतः &c., चूर्णीभूतः &c., पिष्टः -ष्टा -ष्टं, सम्पिष्टः &c., निष्पिष्टः &c., मर्दितः -ता -तं, क्षोदितः &c., क्षुण्णः -ण्णा -ण्णं, क्षोदीकृतः &c., खण्डितः &c., गुण्डितः &c., गुण्ठितः &c., रूषितः -ता -तं; 'finely pounded,' क्षोदिष्टः -ष्टा -ष्टं; 'pounded coarsely,' अवचूर्णितः -ता -तं, अपध्वस्तः -स्ता -स्तं, अवध्वस्तः &c.

Pounder, *s.* पेष्टा *m.* (ष्टृ), सम्पेष्टा *m.*, पेषकः, पेषणिः -णी *f.*, पेषकः, मर्द्दनकृत्, कुट्टनकृत्.—(Pestle) मुसलं, मुषलं -लः, मुद्गरः.

Pounding, *s.* चूर्णनं, सञ्चूर्णनं, चूर्णीकरणं, पेषणं, सम्पेषणं, मर्द्दनं, विमर्द्दनं, सम्मर्द्दः, खण्डनं, क्षोदीकरणं, मथनं, मन्थनं, कुट्टनं, अवहननं.

To pour, *v. a.* (Cause to flow in a stream) स्रु (c. 10. स्रावयति -यितुं), प्रस्रु, सिच् (c. 6. सिञ्चति, सेक्तुं), निषिच्, अवसिच्.—(Pour out) पत् (c. 10. पातयति -यितुं), उत्सिच्, अवतॄ (c. 10. -तारयति -यितुं), प्रस्रु, उत्सृज्, प्रमुच्, स्कन्द्.—(Emit) उत्सृज् (c. 6. -सृजति -स्रष्टुं), विसृज्, मुच्, मुच्, प्रमुच्, स्कन्द्, निरस्, निःसृ in caus., उत्क्षिप्, क्षिप्, उद्, उदीर्, उद्गम्.—(Scatter or pour forth in profusion) कॄ (c. 6. किरति, करितुं -रीतुं), प्रकॄ, विकॄ, बहुशः क्षिप्, वृष् (c. 1. वर्षति -र्षितुं), प्रवृष्; 'the clouds poured forth blood,' मेघाः शोणितं ववृषुः; 'he poured forth arrows,' शरान् ववर्ष.

To pour, *v. n.* (Flow in a stream) स्रु (c. 1. स्रवति, स्रोतुं), प्रस्रु, बहुशः or बाहुल्येन स्रु or प्रस्रु or परिस्रु, स्यन्द्, प्रस्यन्द्, क्षर्, री, गल्, च्युत् or श्च्युत्, जलं or तोयं स्रु, जलं प्रवह्.—(As rain) वृष् (c. 1. वर्षति -र्षितुं), प्रवृष्, अभिवृष्, अभिप्रवृष्, अत्यन्तं or अतिशयेन वृष्.—(Issue forth) निःस्रु, प्रस्रु, निःसृ, विनिःसृ, निर्गम्.—(Rush in a crowd) बहुशो निपत् or प्रपत्.

Poured, *p. p.* स्रावितः -ता -तं, प्रस्रावितः &c., सिक्तः -क्ता -क्तं, अवसिक्तः &c., उत्सिक्तः &c., पातितः -ता -तं, स्कन्दितः -ता -तं, उत्सृष्टः -ष्टा -ष्टं.

Pourer, *s.* सेक्ता *m.* (क्तृ), सेचकः, निषेक्ता *m.*, स्रावकः, स्रावयिता *m.* (तृ).

Pouring, *s.* सेचनं सेकः, निषेकः, निषेचनं, स्रावणं, प्रस्रावणं, स्रवः -वणं' श्चोतः, इश्च्योतः, प्राधारः.

Pouring, *part.* बहुशः सुतः -ता -तं or प्रसुतः &c., स्रवन् -यन्ती -वत् (त्) or स्यन्दी -न्दिनी -न्दि (न्), वर्षन् &c., अतिवर्षन् &c., बहुवर्षकारी &c., बहुजलस्रावी &c.

To pout, *v.n.* अन्तःक्रोधाद् ओष्ठौ प्रसृ (c. 10. -सारयति -यितुं), ओष्ठप्रसारणं कृ, ओष्ठौ or ओष्ठाधरौ प्रसार्य्य अन्तःकोपं दृश् (c. 10. दर्शयति -यितुं) or सूच्, अन्तःकोपात् प्रसारितोष्ठः -ष्ठा or प्रसारितौष्ठः,-ष्ठा स्था (c. 1. तिष्ठति, स्थातुं) or वृत्, अन्तःक्रोधेन ओष्ठौ प्रसार्य्य उदासीनः -ना स्था or वृत्.—(Be prominent) उन्नतः -ता -तं भू, उन्नतीभू, प्ररूढः -ढा -ढं भू.

Pout, *s.* (Fish) स्थूलशिरस्कः समुद्रीयमत्स्यभेदः.—(Fit of sullenness) अन्तःक्रोधावेशः, अन्तःकोपावेशः, वैरक्त्यावेशः.

Pouting, *s.* अन्तःक्रोधात् or अन्तःकोपाद् ओष्ठप्रसारणं, अन्तःकोपसूचनार्थम् ओष्ठाधरप्रसारणं, अन्तःकोपजा उदासीनता.

Poverty, *s.* दरिद्रता, दारिद्र्यं, दारिद्रं, निर्धनता -त्वं, धनहीनता, अल्पधनता, अधनता -त्वं, दरिद्रदशा, दरिद्रावस्था, धनाभावः, अर्थहीनता, अर्थाभावः, द्रव्यहीनता, द्रव्याभावः, निर्द्रव्यता, दीनता, दैन्यं, निष्किञ्चनत्वं -ता, निष्काञ्चनत्वं, अनिर्वृतिः *f.*, दुर्गतिः *f.*; 'reduced to poverty,' गतधनः -ना -नं, विगतधनः &c., गतविभवः -वा -वं, नष्टधनः &c., नष्टार्थः -र्था -र्थं, धनच्युतः -ता -तं, गतार्थः &c., विगतश्रीकः -का -कं, गतश्रीकः &c., दरिद्रितः -ता -तं.

Poverty-stricken, *a.* दारिद्र्यग्रस्तः -स्ता -स्तं, दारिद्र्योपहतः -ता -तं.

Powder, *s.* चूर्णं, पिष्टं, क्षोदः, क्षोदितं, पिष्टातः, पटवासः -सकः, रेणुः *m.*, पांशुः *m.*, वासयोगः, गुण्डकः -ण्डिकः -का.—(Gunpowder) आग्नेयचूर्णं, शीघ्रदाह्यचूर्णं; 'to reduce to powder,' चूर्णीकृ, क्षोदीकृ, रेणुशः कृ.

To powder, *v. a.* (Pulverize) चूर्ण् (c. 10. चूर्णयति -यितुं), चूर्णीकृ, क्षोदीकृ, पिष् (c. 7. पिनष्टि, पेष्टुं), निष्पिष्, क्षुद् (c. 7. क्षुणत्ति, क्षोत्तुं), गुण्ड्, कुट्ट्, रेणुशः कृ.—(Cover with powder) चूर्णावृतं -तां कृ, चूर्णाकीर्णं -र्णां कृ, सचूर्णीकृ.

Powder-box, *s.* चूर्णाधारः, चूर्णपात्रं, केशचूर्णाधारः.

Powdered, *p. p.* चूर्णितः -ता -तं, चूर्णीकृतः &c., सञ्चूर्णितः &c., पिष्टः -ष्टा -ष्टं, क्षोदितः -ता -तं, क्षोदीकृतः &c., गुण्डितः &c.; 'finely powdered,' क्षोदिष्ठः -ष्ठा -ष्ठं; 'coarsely,' अवचूर्णितः &c.

Powder-magazine, *s.* आग्नेयचूर्णागारं, दाह्यचूर्णागारं.

Powdery, *a.* (Friable) सुचूर्णनीयः -या -यं, चूर्णयोग्यः -ग्या -ग्यं.—(Made of powder, resembling it) चूर्णी -र्णिनी -र्णि (न्), चूर्णमयः -यी -यं, चूर्णवान् -वती -वत् (त्), क्षोदवान् &c., सचूर्णः -र्णा -र्णं, सक्षोदः -दा -दं, पांशुलः -ला -लं.

Power, *s.* (Force, strength) शक्तिः *f.*, बलं, सामर्थ्यं, समर्थता, वीर्य्यं, ऊर्जः, प्रभावः, पराक्रमः, प्राणः, सहः -हं, सहस् *n.*, द्रविणं.—(Ability, faculty) शक्तिः *f.*, आशक्तिः *f.*, शक्तता, बलं, सामर्थ्यं, क्षमता, कर्तृत्वं, विभवः; 'according to one's power, to the utmost of one's power,' यथाशक्ति, यथाबलं, यथासामर्थ्यं, यावच्छक्यं, शक्तितस्; 'power of utterance,' वाक्शक्तिः *f.*, वाग्विभवः.—(Power of the mind) मनःशक्तिः *f.*, धीशक्तिः *f.*—(Energy, might) वीर्य्यं, तेजस्, प्रतापः, पराक्रमः, विक्रमः, ऊर्जः, शौर्य्यं, सारता, स्थाम *n.* (न्), शुष्म *n.* (न्), शुष्मं.—(Momentum) वेगः, आपातः, तरस् *n.*—(Efficacy, influence) प्रभावः, प्रभवः, प्राबल्यं, प्रभुता, प्रभविष्णुता, प्राभवत्यं, अधिकारः, शक्तिः *f.*, बलं, गौरवं, भारः, प्रतापः, वशं.—(Command, subjection, authority) वशं, अधिकारः -रित्वं, आधिपत्यं, ऐश्वर्य्यं, प्रभुत्वं -ता, ईशत्वं, अधीनत्वं; 'to bring under one's power,' वशीकृ, आत्मवशीकृ, आत्मवशं नी, आत्माधीनं -नां कृ, स्वाधीनं -नां कृ, स्ववशीकृ, आत्मायत्तं -त्तां कृ; 'in the power or under the power of,' वशः -शा -शं, अधीनः -ना -नं, आयत्तः -त्ता -त्तं in comp.; as, 'in the power of the king,' राजवशः -शा -शं, राजाधीनः -ना -नं.—(Possession, occupancy) अधिकारः, आधिकारत्वं, हस्तः; 'fallen into one's power,' हस्तगतः -ता -तं.—(Legal authority) अधिकारः.—(Superhuman power) विभूतिः, भूतिः *f.*, प्रभावः.—(Sovereign, one invested with power) अधिपतिः *m.*, अधिकारी *m.* (न्), प्रभुः *m.*, अधीशः.—(Force, army) बलं, सैन्यं, सेना, सैन्यभारः.—(In algebra and arithmetic) कुट्टकः, घातः; 'to have power over,' प्रभू (c. 1. -भवति -वितुं), ईश् (c. 2. ईष्टे, ईशितुं).

Powerful, *a.* (Having great strength or force) बलवान् -वती -वत् (त्), बली -लिनी -लि (न्), प्रबलः -ला -लं, सबलः -ला -लं, महाबलः &c., शक्तिमान् &c., महाशक्तिः -क्तिः -क्ति, शक्तः -क्ता -क्तं, बलिष्ठः -ष्ठा -ष्ठं, बलाढ्यः -ढ्या -ढ्यं, समर्थः -र्था -र्थं, क्षमः -मा -मं, ऊर्जस्वलः -ला -लं, ऊर्जस्वी &c., ऊर्जस्वान् -स्वती &c., ऊर्जितः -ता -तं, बलोर्जितः &c., प्रभावी &c., सप्रभावः -वा -वं, प्रभविष्णुः -ष्णुः -ष्णु, बलवत्तमः -मा -मं, कुण्डीरः -रा -रं.—(Mighty, puissant, potent) महाविक्रमः -मा -मं, उरुविक्रमः &c., पराक्रान्तः -न्ता -न्तं, पराक्रमी &c., विक्रमी &c., ऐश्वर्य्यवान् &c., प्रतापवान् &c., प्रतापी &c., वीर्य्यवान् &c., महान् -हती -हत् (त्), महातेजाः -जाः -जः (स्), महौजाः &c., विभूतिमान् &c., महोदारः -रा -रं.—(Efficacious) सप्रभावः -वा -वं, प्रभविष्णुः -ष्णुः -ष्णु, सतेजाः &c., तेजस्वी &c., अमोघः -घा -घं, क्षमः -मा -मं.—(Forcible to persuade) सुनिश्चायकः -का -कं, सुनिश्चयजनकः -का -कं, प्रबलः &c., सबलः &c., सुदृढः -ढा -ढं.

Powerfully, *adv.* बलवत्, सबलं, प्रबलं, प्राबल्येन, महाबलेन, सप्रभावं, प्रभावेण, महाशक्त्या, महाशक्तिपूर्व्वं.

Powerfulness, *s.* सबलता, महाबलता, प्रबलता, प्राबल्यं, बलवत्त्वं, शक्तता, शक्तिमत्त्वं, सप्रभावत्वं, वीर्य्यवत्त्वं.

Powerless, *a.* निर्बलः -ला -लं, अबलः &c., बलहीनः -ना -नं, शक्तिहीनः &c., अशक्तः -क्ता -क्तं, असमर्थः -र्था -र्थं, निःशक्तिः &c., शक्तिशून्यः -न्या -न्यं, निष्पराक्रमः -मा -मं, निष्प्रभावः -वा -वं, सामर्थ्यहीनः &c., वीर्य्यहीनः &c., विवशः -शा -शं, अवशः &c.

Powerlessness, *s.* अशक्तिः *f.*, निर्बलता, बलहीनता, असामर्थ्यं, शक्तिहीनता, शक्तिशून्यता, बलाभावः, प्रभावाभावः, निष्प्रभावत्वं.

Pox, *s.* (Small pox) रक्तवटी, रक्तवरटी, विस्फोटः, रक्तस्फोटः, शीतला. *See* the word.—(Cow pox) गोस्तनशीतला.—(Venereal disease) उपदंशः, वृषणकच्छूः *f.*; 'afflicted with it,' उपदंशी -शिनी &c.

Practicability, practicableness, *s.* साध्यता -त्वं, करणीयता, सुसाध्यता, शक्यता -त्वं, करणशक्यता, सम्भाव्यता -त्वं, सुगमत्वं.

Practicable, *a.* साध्यः -ध्या -ध्यं, करणीयः -या -यं, करणशक्यः -क्या -क्यं, शक्यः &c., कर्तुं शक्यः &c., कृत्यः -त्या -त्यं, सम्भाव्यः -व्या -व्यं, सम्भावनीयः -या -यं, उपपाद्यः -द्या -द्यं, सुकरः -रा -रं, सुगमः -मा -मं, सुसाध्यः &c., सुखसाध्यः &c., अदुष्करः -रा -रं.

Practical, *a.* (Pertaining to practice or action) आभ्यासिकः -की -कं, अभ्याससम्बन्धी -न्धिनी -न्धि (न्), क्रियासम्बन्धी &c., कार्म्मिकः -की -कं, कार्य्यिकः &c.—(Capable of practice) अभ्यासी &c., व्यवसायी &c., अभ्यासात्मकः -का -कं, क्रियावान् -वती -वत् (त्), अभ्यासक्षमः -मा -मं.—(That may be used in practice) व्यवहार्य्यः

-ग्यी -ग्यि, व्यवहारयोग्यः -ग्या -ग्यं, अभ्यासयोग्यः &c., व्यवहारोचितः -ता -तं, व्यवहारोपयोगी &c.—(Derived from practice) अभ्याससिद्धः -द्धा -द्धं, क्रियासिद्धः &c., अभ्यासजनितः -ता -तं, अभ्यासप्राप्तः -प्ता -प्तं.—(Having practical knowledge) कर्म्मदृष्टः -ष्टा -ष्टं, कर्म्मज्ञः -ज्ञा -ज्ञं, दृष्टकर्म्मा -र्म्मा -र्म्म (न्), कर्म्मज्ञानी &c., बहुदृष्टः -ष्टा -ष्टं, व्यवहारज्ञः -ज्ञा -ज्ञं, व्यवहारवृद्धः -द्धा -द्धं.

PRACTICALLY, *adv.* अभ्यासतस्, अभ्यासेन, कर्म्मतस्, कार्य्यतस्, व्यवहारतस्, व्यवसायतस्, अभ्यासपूर्व्वं, व्यवहारमपेक्ष्य.

PRACTICE, *s.* (Frequent or habitual doing) अभ्यासः, अभ्यसनं, निरन्तराभ्यासः, नित्याभ्यासः, नित्यकृत्यं, नित्यकर्म्म *n.* (न्), निरन्तरकर्म्म *n.*, नित्यक्रिया, निरन्तरप्रवृत्तिः *f.*, नित्यवृत्तिः *f.*, नित्यप्रवृत्तिः *f.*, नित्यचर्य्या, आवर्त्तनं, आवृत्तिः *f.*, वृत्तिः.—(Actual doing or performance) करणं, आचरणं, विधानं, अनुष्ठानं, अनुष्ठा, क्रिया, कृतिः *f.*, प्रवृत्तिः *f.*, निर्वर्त्तनं, प्रवर्त्तनं, चर्य्या, चरितं, वृत्तं, व्यापारः, व्यवसायः.—(Course of procedure, custom) आचारः, व्यवहारः, व्यवहृतिः *f.*, समाचारः, प्रचारः, रीतिः *f.*, सम्प्रदायः, मार्गः, क्रियामार्गः, कर्म्मविधिः *m.*, क्रमः, पद्धतिः *f.*, नियमः, अनुसारः; 'according to usual practice,' यथाव्यवहारं, यथारीति; 'ancient practice,' वृद्धाचारः, वृद्धपरम्परा; 'noble practice,' शिष्टाचारः; 'family practice,' कुलाचारः, कुलधर्म्मः; 'local,' देशाचारः, देशरीतिः *f.*; 'popular or general practice,' लोकाचारः, लोकरीतिः *f.*, जनव्यवहारः; 'good practice,' सदाचारः; 'following good practices,' सदाचारी -रिणी -रि (न्), सद्वृत्तिः -त्तिः -त्ति, सद्वृत्तः -त्ता -त्तं; 'bad practice,' दुराचारः, असदाचारः, दुर्वृत्तिः *f.*; 'following bad practices,' दुराचारः -रा -रं, दुराचारी &c., कदाचारः &c., असदाचारी &c., दुर्वृत्तः -त्ता -त्तं, दुर्वृत्तिः -त्तिः -त्ति, जघन्यवृत्तिः &c.—(Exercise of a profession) सेवनं, निषेवणं, अनुसेवनं, आचरणं, करणं, अनुष्ठानं.—(Of medicine) उपचारः, वैद्योपचारः, उपचर्य्या, उपचार्य्यः, उपक्रमः, वैद्योपक्रमः, औषधप्रयोगः, वैद्यक्रिया, चिकित्सा, रुक्प्रतिक्रिया.—(Of arms) शस्त्राभ्यासः, शस्त्रभृत्त्वं.—(Of the law courts) व्यवहारः, व्यवहारविधिः *m.*

To PRACTISE, *v. a.* (Do habitually) अभ्यस् (c. 4. -अस्यति -असितुं), नित्यम् अभ्यस् or कृ, निरन्तरम् अभ्यस् or कृ, नित्याभ्यासं कृ, निरन्तराभ्यासं कृ.—(Do, perform) आचर् (c. 1. -चरति -रितुं), समाचर्, चर्, अनुष्ठा (c. 1. -तिष्ठति -ष्ठातुं), आस्था, समास्था, विधा (c. 3. -दधाति -धत्ते -धातुं), कृ, संकृ, अभिकृ, प्रवृत् in caus., वृत्.—(Use, employ) प्रयुज्, उपयुज्, व्यवहृ, सेव्, निषेव्, अनुसेव्, आश्रि.—(Exercise a profession or business) आचर्, कृ, सेव्, निषेव्, अनुसेव्, आसेव्, समासेव्, उपसेव्, अभ्युपसेव्, उपास्; 'he practises the law,' व्यवहारं सेवते or निषेवते, व्यवहारसेवनं करोति, व्यवहारं करोति; 'he practises gambling,' द्यूतं सेवते.—(Practise medicine) वैद्योपचारं कृ, उपचारं कृ, औषधप्रयोगं कृ, चिकित्सां कृ, कित् in desid.—(Practise arms) शस्त्राभ्यासं कृ.

To PRACTISE, *v. n.* अभ्यासं कृ, नित्याभ्यासं कृ, अभ्यस्. *See* the last.—(Use artifices) छलं कृ, व्यपदेशं कृ, छद्म कृ, कपटं कृ, कपटप्रयोगं कृ, छलप्रयोगं कृ, कैतवप्रयोगं कृ.

PRACTISED, *p. p.* (Habitually done or performed) अभ्यस्तः -स्ता -स्तं, आचरितः -ता -तं, चरितः -ता -तं, अनुष्ठितः &c., सेवितः -ता -तं, निषेवितः &c., व्यवहृतः -ता -तं, व्यवहारितः &c., कृतः -ता -तं.—(Having had much practice) बहुदृष्टः -ष्टा -ष्टं, दृष्टकर्म्मा -र्म्मा -र्म्म (न्), कर्म्मज्ञः -ज्ञा -ज्ञं, कृतकर्म्मा -र्म्मा -र्म्म (न्), व्यवहारज्ञः -ज्ञा -ज्ञं, ज्ञानवृद्धः -द्धा -द्धं, पक्वबुद्धिः -द्धिः -द्धि, पक्वः -क्वा -क्वं, कोविदः -दा -दं, परिज्ञाता -त्री -तृ (तृ), व्युत्पन्नः -न्ना -न्नं.

PRACTISING, *part.* अभ्यासी -सिनी -सि (न्), कृताभ्यासः -सा -सं, आचरन् -रन्ती -रत् (त्), आस्थितः -ता -तं, आश्रितः &c., प्रवर्त्तमानः -ना -नं, सेवी &c., सेवमानः -ना -नं, निषेवमाणः -णा -णं, व्यवसायी &c., शाली &c., आस्थाय indec.

PRACTITIONER, *s.* (One who exercises any profession or businsss) व्यवसायी *m.* (न्), व्यापारी *m.*, सेवी *m.*, वृत्ति or प्रवृत्ति or वृत्तिक in comp.—(Medical) वैद्यः, वैद्यवृत्तिः *m.*, वैद्यवृत्तिकः, चिकित्सकः, उपचारकः, उपचारकृत् *m.*, औषधप्रयोगी *m.*—(Lawyer) व्यवहारज्ञः, व्यवहारविद् *m.*, दृष्टव्यवहारः, आचारज्ञः, व्यवहारदर्शी *m.*

PRAGMATIC, PRAGMATICAL, *a.* परकार्य्यचर्चकः -का -कं, अनधिकारचर्चकः &c., पराधिकारचर्चकः &c., पराधिकारव्यापारी -रिणी -रि (न्), परव्यापारचर्चकः &c.

PRAGMATICALLY, *adv.* अनधिकारचर्चया, पराधिकारचर्चया, परव्यापारचर्चया.

PRAGMATICALNESS, *s.* परकार्य्यचर्चा, परव्यापारचर्चा, अनधिकारचर्चा.

PRAIRIE, *s.* दीर्घतृणावृतः सुविस्तीर्णः समभूभागः.

PRAISE, *s.* प्रशंसा, स्तुतिः *f.*, स्तवः, श्लाघा, शंसा, प्रशंसनं, संस्तवः, स्तवनं, कीर्त्तनं, अनुकीर्त्तनं, स्तोत्रं, स्तोतृत्वं, ईडा, नुतिः *f.*, नवः, नव्यः, वर्णनं -ना, वन्दना, चाटूक्तिः *f.*, सामीची, व्यावृत्तिः *f.*; 'ground of praise,' स्तुतिहेतुः *m.*, स्तुतिकारणं.

To PRAISE, *v. a.* प्रशंस् (c. 1. -शंसति -सितुं), अभिप्रशंस्, स्तु (c. 2. स्तौति, स्तोतुं), संस्तु, अभिष्टु, विष्टु, परिसंस्तु, श्लाघ् (c. 1. श्लाघते -घितुं, c. 10. श्लाघयति -यितुं), कृत् (c. 10. कीर्त्तयति -यितुं), अनुकृत्, ईड् (c. 2. ईट्टे -डितुं), प्रसमीड्, वर्ण् (c. 10. वर्णयति -यितुं), वन्द् (c. 1. वन्दते -न्दितुं), विख्या (c. 2. -ख्याति -ते -तुं), प्रख्या, प्रथ् (c. 10. प्रथयति -यितुं), नु or नू (c. 2. नौति, c. 6. नुवति, नवितुं, नुवितुं), अभिनु, अभिप्रणु, प्रणु, पण् (c. 1. पणायति -यितुं, पणितुं) or पन्, अर्च् (c. 6. अर्चति, अर्चितुं), ईल् (c. 1. ईलते -लितुं).

PRAISED, *p. p.* प्रशंसितः -ता -तं, स्तुतः -ता -तं, संस्तुतः &c., अभिष्टुतः &c., प्रस्तुतः &c., प्रशस्तः -स्ता -स्तं, शस्तः &c., शंसितः &c., श्लाघितः -ता -तं, कीर्त्तितः &c., अनुकीर्त्तितः &c., ईडितः -ता -तं, प्रसमीडितः &c., वर्णितः &c., विख्यातः &c., नुतः -ता -तं, नूतः &c., प्रणुतः &c., पणायितः -ता -तं, पनायितः &c., पणितः &c., पनितः &c., ईलितः &c., गीर्णः -र्णा -र्णं, अपिगीर्णः &c.

PRAISER, *s.* प्रशंसकः, स्तोता *m.* (तृ), प्रशंसिता *m.* (तृ), शंसिता *m.*, शंस्ता *m.* (स्तृ), स्तावकः, प्रशंसाकृत् *m.*, वर्णकः, स्तुतिपाठकः, वन्दी *m.* (न्), स्तुतिकारकः, स्तवनकृत् *m.*

PRAISEWORTHINESS, *s.* श्लाघ्यता, श्लाघनीयता, प्रशंसनीयता, स्तुतियोग्यता.

PRAISEWORTHY, *a.* श्लाघ्यः -घ्या -घ्यं, श्लाघनीयः -या -यं, प्रशंसनीयः -या -यं, प्रशंसितव्यः -व्या -व्यं, प्रशंस्यः -स्या -स्यं, शंस्यः &c., प्रशस्यः &c., शस्यः &c., स्तुत्यः -त्या -त्यं, स्तोतव्यः -व्या -व्यं, स्तुतियोग्यः -ग्या -ग्यं, ईड्यः -ड्या -ड्यं, पाय्यः -य्या -य्यं. *See* LAUDABLE.—(Praiseworthy person) स्तुतिपात्रं, प्रशंसापात्रं, श्लाघापात्रं, श्लाघाभाजनं.

To PRANCE, *v. n.* अश्ववत् प्लु (c. 1. प्लवते, प्लोतुं) or नृत् (c. 4. नृत्यति, नर्त्तितुं) or वल्ग् (c. 1. वल्गति -ल्गितुं) or प्लुतगत्या चल् (c. 1. चलति -लितुं).

PRANCING, *s.* अश्वप्लुतं, प्लुतगतिः *f.*, प्लुतं, प्लवः, वल्गितगतिः *f.*, वल्गितं.

PRANCING, *part.* or *a.* प्लुतगतिः -तिः -ति, प्लवगतिः &c., वल्गितगतिः &c.

PRANK, *s.* कुचेष्टा, चेष्टा, मर्कटचेष्टा, वानरचेष्टा, मर्कटक्रीडा, वानरक्रीडा, क्रीडा, चापलं, खेला, लीला, छन्दस् *n.*, छन्दः, कुछन्दस्, लहरी.

To PRANK, *v. a.* दम्भार्थं or लोकदर्शनार्थं भूष् or अलङ्कृ.

PRANKISH, *a.* कुचेष्टः -ष्टा -ष्टं, वानरचेष्टः -ष्टा -ष्टं, मर्कटचेष्टः &c., वान-

रचेष्टाकारी -रिणी -रि (न्), वानरशीलः -ला -लं, क्रीडाशीलः &c., छन्दी &c., चपलः -ला -लं.

To PRATE, *v. n.* जल्प् (c. 1. जल्पति -ल्पितुं), उपजल्प्, प्रलप् (c. 1. -लपति -पितुं), अनर्थकं or वृथा भाष् (c. 1. भाषते -षितुं) or वद् (c. 1. वदति -दितुं), बहु भाष् or वद्, अतिशयेन or अत्यन्तं भाष्, अनर्थकवचनं कृ, बालस्यवचनं कृ, वृथाकथां कृ.

PRATER, *s.* जल्पकः, जल्पाकः, जल्पी *m.* (न्), उपजल्पी *m.*, वाचालः, वाचाटः, वावदूकः, बहुभाषी *m.* (न्), बहुवादी *m.*

PRATING, *s.* जल्पः -ल्पनं, प्रजल्पः, जल्पितं, प्रलापः, प्रलपितं, निरर्थकभाषणं, वृथाभाषणं, अनर्थकवचनं, बहुभाषणं.

PRATIQUE, *s.* संसर्गानुज्ञा, गमनागमनानुज्ञा, सम्पर्कानुज्ञा.

To PRATTLE, *v. n.* बालवद् जल्प् or भाष्, चटचट (nom. चटचटायते). *See* *To* PRATE.

PRATTLE, PRATTLING, *s.* जल्पितं, जल्पः, प्रलापः, प्रलपितं, बालप्रलापः, बालालापः, बालभाषणं, बालवचनं, बालशब्दः, कलभाषणं. *See* PRATING.

PRATTLER, *s.* बालवद् जल्पी or जल्पकः, बालालापी *m.* (न्), बालभाषी *m.*

PRAVITY, *s.* भ्रष्टता, भ्रंशः, दुष्टता, विप्रदुष्टता, भेषः, विक्रिया.

PRAWN, *s.* वृहच्छल्कः, इचाकः, गङ्गाटेयः, अग्निमत्स्यः.

To PRAY, *v. n.* प्रार्थ् (c. 10. -अर्थयते -यितुं), प्रार्थनां कृ, प्रार्थनं कृ, कृताञ्जलिः or अञ्जलिं कृत्वा प्रार्थ्.—(To God) ईश्वरप्रार्थनां कृ, देवप्रार्थनां कृ, भगवत्प्रार्थनां कृ, ईश्वरपूजां कृ.—(Invoke by prayer) आशास् (c. 2. -शास्ते, c. 1. -शासते -सितुं).—(Pray in a low voice) जप् (c. 1. जपति -पितुं), प्रजप्, जपनं कृ.

To PRAY, *v. a.* (Entreat, implore) प्रार्थ्, अभ्यर्थ्, सम्प्रार्थ्, अर्थ्, कृताञ्जलिः प्रार्थ् or याच् or अभियाच् or संयाच् or सम्प्रयाच्, विनयेन स्वार्थं निविद्, विनी, याच्ञां कृ.

PRAYED, *p.p.* प्रार्थितः -ता -तं, अभ्यर्थितः &c., याचितः &c., अभियाचितः &c.

PRAYER, *s.* प्रार्थना, प्रार्थनं, अभ्यर्थना, अर्थः, याचना, याच्ञा, विनयेन स्वार्थनिवेदनं; 'to God,' ईश्वरप्रार्थना, देवप्रार्थना, भगवत्प्रार्थना, ईश्वरपूजा; 'inaudible repetition of prayers,' जपः, जपनं, जपयज्ञः; 'engaged in repeating prayers,' जपपरायणः -णा -णं; 'granting prayers,' वरदः -दा -दं.

PRAYER-BOOK, *s.* प्रार्थनापद्धतिः -ती *f.*, प्रार्थनासंहिता, प्रार्थनाग्रन्थः.

PRAYERFUL, *a.* प्रार्थनापरः -रा -रं, प्रार्थनाशीलः -ला -लं, जपपरायणः -णा -णं, जपनशीलः &c., भजनशीलः &c., ईश्वरपूजाशीलः &c., ईश्वरभावनः -ना -नं, प्रार्थनानिष्ठः -ष्ठा -ष्ठं, भजनपरायणः -णा -णं.

To PREACH, *v. n.* धर्म्मं प्रवच् (c. 2. -वक्ति -क्तुं) or प्रचर् (c. 10. -चारयति -यितुं) or उपदिश् (c. 6. -दिशति -देष्टुं), धर्म्मोपदेशं कृ, धर्म्मप्रवचनं कृ, धर्म्मप्रचारणं कृ, धर्म्मकथनं कृ, धर्म्मोपदेशभाषणं कृ, धर्म्मोपदेशविषयवाक्यं कृ.

To PREACH, *v. a.* (Proclaim, publish) प्रचर् (c. 10. -चारयति -यितुं), उच्चर्, विघुष् (c. 10. घोषयति -यितुं), घुष्, उद्घुष्, प्रख्या (c. 2. -ख्याति -तुं or caus. -ख्यापयति -यितुं), आख्या, ख्या, कथ्, प्रवच्, प्रवद्, कृत्, प्रकृत्, प्रकटीकृ.—(Deliver, pronounce) वद्, प्रवद्, वच्, उच्चर्, उदाहृ, उदीर्.

PREACHER, *s.* (Of religion) प्रवक्ता *m.* (कृ), धर्म्मप्रवक्ता *m.*, प्रचारकः, धर्म्मप्रचारकः, उपदेशकः, धर्म्मोपदेशकः, उपदेशी *m.* (न्), धर्म्मोपदेशी *m.*, कथकः, धर्म्मकथकः.—(Proclaimer) घोषकः, विघोषकः, ख्यापकः, घोषणाकृत्.

PREACHING, *s.* धर्म्मोपदेशः, उपदेशः, धर्म्मप्रचारणं, प्रचारणं, धर्म्मप्रवचनं, प्रवचनं, उच्चारणं, घोषणं -णा, विघोषणा, ख्यापनं.

PREAMBLE, *s.* प्रस्तावना, उपोद्घातः, आभाषः, आरम्भः, उपन्यासः, प्रकरणं.

PREBEND, PREBENDARY, *s.* *See* CANON, CANONRY, *s.*

PRECARIOUS, *a.* (Uncertain, doubtful) अनिश्चितः -ता -तं, सन्दिग्धः -ग्धा -ग्धं, सन्देहस्थः -स्था -स्थं, संशयस्थः &c., सांशयिकः -की -कं, शङ्कान्वितः -ता -तं, शङ्कनीयः -या -यं, सशङ्कः -ङ्का -ङ्कं, शङ्कामयः -यी -यं, वैकल्पिकः -की -कं, अस्थिरः -रा -रं, अध्रुवः -वा -वं, अनैष्ठिकः -की -कं, स्थितिसंशयी &c., स्थितिशङ्की &c.—(Depending on the will of another) अन्याधीनः -ना -नं, पराधीनः &c., परायत्तः -त्ता -त्तं, अस्वाधीनः &c., अस्वायत्तः &c.

PRECARIOUSLY, *adv.* अनिश्चितं, सन्दिग्धं, सशङ्कं,ससंशयं, अस्थिरं.

PRECARIOUSNESS, *s.* अनिश्चितत्वं, अनैश्चित्यं, सन्दिग्धता, सशङ्कता -त्वं, शङ्कनीयता -त्वं, अस्थैर्य्यं, अस्थिरता -त्वं, अन्याधीनता, पराधीनता, अस्वाधीनता, स्थितिसंशयः, स्थितिशङ्का.

PRECATIVE, PRECATORY, *a.* प्रार्थकः -का -कं, प्रार्थनात्मकः &c., प्रार्थनारूपः -पा -पं, प्रार्थनाकारी -रिणी -रि (न्), याचकः -का -कं.—(Precative tense) प्रवर्त्तना.

PRECAUTION, *s.* पूर्व्वोपायः, अग्रोपायः, निवारणोपायः, अनिष्टनिवारणोपायः, अनिष्टवारणोपायः, निषेधनोपायः, प्रतिषेधोपायः, आपद्वारणोपायः, अपायनिवारणोपायः, पूर्व्वावधानं -नता, अग्रावधानं, पूर्व्वसमीक्षा, पूर्व्वचिन्ता; 'to take precautions,' पूर्व्वावधानं कृ.

PRECAUTIONARY, *a.* पूर्व्वोपायसाधकः -का -कं, पूर्व्वोपायरूपः -पा -पं, पूर्व्वोपायैर् अनिष्टनिवारकः -का -कं or अनिष्टप्रतिषेधकः &c., पूर्व्वोपायेन अनिष्टवारकः &c.

To PRECEDE, *v. a.* अग्रे or अग्रतो गम् (c. 1. गच्छति, गन्तुं) or सृ (c. 1. सरति, सर्त्तुं), पुरस् or पुरतो गम् or सृ or चर् (c. 1. चरति -रितुं) or या (c. 2. याति -तुं), अग्रे वृत् (c. 1. वर्त्तते -र्त्तितुं), पुरतो वृत्, मुख्यः -ख्या -ख्यं भू, मुख्यतो वृत्.—(In rank) अग्रपदस्थः -स्था -स्थं भू, अग्रमानार्हः -र्हा -र्हं भू, अग्रमानम् अर्ह् (c. 1. अर्हति -र्हितुं), अग्रपदे वृत् or स्था.

PRECEDED, *p. p.* पुरोगतः -ता -तं, अग्रगतः -ता -तं, पुरःसरः -रा -रं in comp., पुरोगमः -मा -मं in comp., पूर्व्वकः -का -कं in comp.

PRECEDENCE, PRECEDENCY, *s.* (Going before) पुरोगतिः *f.*, पुरोगमनं, अग्रगतिः *f.*, अग्रगमनं, अग्रसरणं, अग्रतःसरणं, अग्रेसरणं, अग्रवर्त्तनं, अग्रवर्त्तित्वं.—(In rank) अग्रपदं, अग्रपदवर्त्तनं, श्रेष्ठपदं, श्रेष्ठपदवर्त्तनं, अग्रमानं, अग्रमान्यता, अग्रगण्यता, अग्रपूजा, अग्रपूज्यता, अग्रमानार्हता -त्वं, अधिकपदं, अधिकमानार्हता, श्रेष्ठता, प्राग्भावः, ज्यैष्ठ्यं, मुख्यता, प्रधानता, प्राधान्यं, प्रथमता, प्राथम्यं, आदित्वं, उत्कर्षः.

PRECEDENT, *s.* (Previous example) पूर्व्वप्रतिमा, पूर्व्वदृष्टान्तः, पूर्व्वनिदर्शनं, पूर्व्वोदाहरणं, प्रतिमा, प्रमाणं; 'an unheard of precedent,' अपूर्व्वप्रतिमा.

PRECEDENT, PRECEDING, *a.* or *part.* अग्रगः -गा -गं, अग्रगामी -मिनी -मि (न्), अग्रसरः -रा -रं, अग्रेसरः &c., अग्रतःसरः &c., पुरोगः -गा -गं, पुरोगमः -मा -मं, पुरोगामी &c., पुरःसरः -रा -रं, प्राग्गामी &c., पुरःसरः &c., पुरस्सरः &c., पूर्व्वसरः &c., पुरोगतः -ता -तं, पुरोगतिः -तिः -ति, पूर्व्वः -र्व्वा -र्व्वं, पूर्व्वकः -का -कं, प्राक्तनः -नी -नं.

PRECEDENTED, *a.* दृष्टपूर्व्वः -र्व्वा -र्व्वं, भूतपूर्व्वः &c., दृष्टप्रतिमः -मा -मं, सपूर्व्वप्रतिमः &c., दृष्टोदाहरणः -णा -णं, दृष्टसादृश्यः -श्या -श्यं.

PRECEDENTLY, *adv.* पूर्व्वं, पूर्व्वतस्, अग्रे, अग्रतस्, पूर्व्वे, पुरस्, पुरतस्.

PRECENTOR, *s.* अग्रगायकः, अग्रगाता *m.* (तृ), पूर्व्वगाता, पूर्व्वगायकः.

PRECEPT, *s.* विधिः *m.*, विधानं, नियमः, कल्पः, निदेशः, निर्देशः, सूत्रं, शासनं, अनुशासनं, आदेशः, चोदना, प्रचोदनं, आज्ञा, नियोगः, निगमः, क्रमः,

स्थितिः f., व्यवस्था, स्मरणं, उपदेशः; 'secondary precept,' अनुकल्पः.

PRECEPTIVE, a. वैधिकः -की -कं, वैधः -धी -धं, विधिरूपः -पा -पं, विधिमयः -यी -यं, विधायकः -का -कं, विधिप्रदर्शकः -का -कं, विधिप्रकाशकः &c., नैयमिकः -की -कं, अनुशासकः -का -कं, आदेशकः &c., उपदेशकः &c., काल्पः -ल्पी -ल्पं, सौत्रः -त्री -त्रं.

PRECEPTOR, s. उपदेशकः, उपदेशी m. (न्), उपदेष्टा m. (ष्टृ), शिक्षकः, शिक्षाकरः, अध्यापकः, बालाध्यापकः, शासिता m. (तृ), अनुशासिता m., शिक्षादाता m.; 'spiritual preceptor,' आचार्य्यः, उपाध्यायः, गुरुः m., पाठकः; 'family preceptor,' कुलगुरुः m., कुलाचार्य्यः.

PRECEPTRESS, s. उपदेशिका, उपदेशिनी, शिक्षिका, अध्यापिका, उपदेष्ट्री.

PRECESSION, s. (Going before) पुरोगतिः f., अग्रगतिः f.—(Of the equinoctial points) अयनचलनं, विषुवायनं, अयनांशः.

PRECINCT, s. (Limit) सीमा, परिसीमा, अवधिः m., मर्य्यादा, समन्तः, पर्य्यन्तः, परिसरः, परिच्छेदः, अवच्छेदः.—(Vicinity) उपान्तं, उपान्त्यं, अन्तिकं, परिसरः, सामन्तं, सामन्तदेशः.

PRECIOUS, a. महार्घः -र्घा -र्घं, महामूल्यः -ल्या -ल्यं, बहुमूल्यः &c., बहुमूल्यकः -का -कं, महार्हः -र्हा -र्हं, उत्कृष्टः -ष्टा -ष्टं, अत्युत्कृष्टः &c., अनर्घ्यः -र्घ्या -र्घ्यं, अनर्घः -र्घा -र्घं, अर्घ्यः &c., अमूल्यः &c., गुरुः -र्व्वी -रु, गुर्व्वर्थः &c., बहुमतः -ता -तं, महाधनः -ना -नं, प्रेयाः -याः -यः (स्); 'precious stone,' रत्नं, मणिः m.; 'precious metals,' सुवर्णादि n., हेमादि; 'more precious,' गरीयान् -यसी -यः (स्); 'most precious,' गरिष्ठः -ष्ठा -ष्ठं.

PRECIOUSNESS, s. महार्घता -त्वं, महामूल्यता -त्वं, बहुमूल्यता -त्वं, बहुमूल्यं, उत्कृष्टता, अत्युत्कृष्टता, बहुमतिः f., अनर्घ्यता -त्वं, गुरुता.

PRECIPICE, s. प्रपातः, अतटः -टं, पातुकः, पातुकभूमिः f., प्रवणभूमिः f., भृगुः m., तटः, दरद् f., विषमं, विषमभूमिः f., कटकः -कं; 'casting one's self down a precipice,' भृगुपातः -तनं.

PRECIPITANCE, PRECIPITANCY, s. साहसं, क्षिप्रकारित्वं, अविमृश्यकारित्वं, असमीक्ष्यकारित्वं, गमकारित्वं, विषमसाहसं.

PRECIPITATE, PRECIPITANT, a. (Rashly, impetuous) साहसी -सिनी -सि (न्), साहसिकः -की -कं, क्षिप्रकारी -रिणी &c., गमकारी &c., अविमृश्यकारी &c., असमीक्ष्यकारी &c., अतिक्षिप्रः -प्रा -प्रं, जाल्मः -ल्मा -ल्मं, जातविभ्रमः -मा -मं.—(Headlong) अधोमुखः -खी -खं, अवाङ्मुखः &c. See the word.

To PRECIPITATE, v. a. अधः or अवाक् क्षिप् (c. 6. क्षिपति, क्षेप्तुं), अधः or अवाक् पत् (c. 10. पातयति -यितुं) or निपत् or प्रपत् or अवपत् or अवनी in caus. (-नाययति -यितुं).

PRECIPITATED, p. p. अधःक्षिप्तः -प्ता -प्तं, अधःपातितः -ता -तं, अवपातितः &c., अवाक्क्षिप्तः &c., अवाक्पातितः &c., अवाङ् निपात्यमानः -ना -नं, पात्यमानः -ना -नं.

PRECIPITATELY, adv. सहसा, अनवेक्षया, साहसेन, ससाहसं, साहसिकवत्, जाल्मवत्, असमीक्ष्य, अविमृश्य, क्षिप्रं, अतिक्षिप्रं, द्रुतपदं.—(Headlong) अवाक्, अधोमुखेन, अवाङ्मुखेन.

PRECIPITATION, s. (Rash impetuosity) अतिक्षिप्रता, अतिक्षिप्रकारित्वं, क्षिप्रकारिता, गमकारित्वं, अविमृश्यकारित्वं, असमीक्ष्यकारित्वं, साहसं, दुःसाहसं, साहसिकत्वं, जाल्मता.—(Act of throwing headlong) अधःपातनं, अधःक्षेपः -पणं, अवाक्क्षेपणं, अवाक्पातनं, अवपातनं, अवनायः -यनं.

PRECIPITOUS, a. (Steep) पातुकः -का -कं, प्रवणः -णा -णं, दुरवरोहः -हा -हं, दुरारोहः -हा -हं.—(Headlong, rash). See the word.

PRECIPITOUSNESS, s. पातुकत्वं -ता, प्रवणता -त्वं, दुरवरोहत्वं, दुरारोहत्वं.

PRECISE, a. (Exact, nice, definite) सूक्ष्मः -क्ष्मा -क्ष्मं, समञ्जसः -सा -सं, सम्यक् -मीची -म्यक् (च्), नियतः -ता -तं, निश्चितः -ता -तं, सुनिश्चितः &c., निर्दिष्टः -ष्टा -ष्टं, सुनिर्दिष्टः &c., वस्तुनिर्देशकः -का -कं, नामनिर्देशकः &c., नामनिर्देशात्मकः &c., यथार्थः -र्था -र्थं, केवलः -ला -लं.—(Distinct) व्यक्तः -क्ता -क्तं, सुव्यक्तः &c., स्फुटः -टा -टं, भिन्नार्थः -र्था -र्थं; 'precise measurement,' सूक्ष्ममानं; 'precise area,' स्फुटफलं.—(Punctilious) सूक्ष्मनियमनिष्ठः -ष्ठा -ष्ठं, सूक्ष्मोपचारनिष्ठः &c., सूक्ष्मादरनिष्ठः &c., सूक्ष्मादरशीलः -ला -लं, अत्याचारी &c.—(Keeping to stipulated agreement) सामयिकः -की -कं, समयपालकः -का -कं, नैयमिकः -की -कं.

PRECISELY, adv. नियतं, सम्यक्, समञ्जसं, अञ्जसा, सुनिर्दिष्टं, सूक्ष्मं, सूक्ष्मत्वेन, सूक्ष्मतया, यथार्थं, यथार्थतस्, व्यक्तं, सुव्यक्तं, भिन्नार्थतस्; 'precisely so,' एवमेव, तथैव.

PRECISENESS, PRECISION, s. (Exactness) सूक्ष्मता -त्वं, सौक्ष्म्यं, सम्यक्त्वं, सामञ्जस्यं, नियतत्वं, निर्देशः, निर्दिष्टता -त्वं, सुनिश्चितत्वं, नामनिर्देशः, वस्तुनिर्देशः, यथार्थता, याथार्थ्यं.—(Distinctness) व्यक्तता, भिन्नता, स्फुटता.—(Punctiliousness) सूक्ष्मनियमपरता, सूक्ष्मनियमनिष्ठा, सूक्ष्मोपचारनिष्ठा, सूक्ष्मोपचारशीलता.

To PRECLUDE, v. a. प्रतिबन्ध् (c. 9. -बध्नाति -बन्द्धुं), निरुध् (c. 7. -रुणद्धि -रोद्धुं), अवरुध्, रुध्, निषिध् (c. 1. -षेधति -षेद्धुं), प्रतिषिध्, वृ (c. 10. वारयति -यितुं), निवृ, बाध् (c. 1. बाधते -धितुं), सार्गलीकृ.

PRECLUDED, p. p. प्रतिबद्धः -द्धा -द्धं, रुद्धः -द्धा -द्धं, निरुद्धः &c., अवरुद्धः &c., निषिद्धः -द्धा -द्धं, वारितः -ता -तं, निवारितः -ता -तं, भोगवारितः &c., बाधितः &c., सार्गलः -ला -लं.

PRECLUSION, s. प्रतिबन्धः -न्धनं, रोधः -धनं, निरोधः -धनं, निषेधः, प्रतिषेधः, वारणं, निवारणं, भोगप्रतिबन्धः, भोगवारणं.

PRECLUSIVE, a. प्रतिबन्धकः -का -कं, रोधकः -का -कं, निरोधकः -का -कं, निषेधकः &c., निवारकः &c., बाधकः -का -कं.

PRECOCIOUS, a. (Ripe before the proper time) अपूर्णकालपक्वः -क्वा -क्वं, कालपूर्व्वपक्वः &c., कालपूर्व्वफली -लिनी -लि (न्), कालपूर्व्वफलितः -ता -तं.—(Applied to persons) प्रौढबुद्धिः -द्धिः -द्धि, प्रौढः -ढा -ढं, बालप्रौढः &c., बालपक्वः -क्वा -क्वं.

PRECOCIOUSNESS, PRECOCITY, s. अपूर्णकालपक्वता, प्रौढिः f., बुद्धिप्रौढता, प्रौढबुद्धित्वं, बालप्रौढिः f., बालपक्वता.

To PRECOGITATE, v. a. अग्रे or पूर्व्वं चिन्त् or विचर् or विमृश् or विवेचनां कृ.

PRECOGITATION, s. अग्रचिन्ता, पूर्व्वचिन्ता, अग्रविचारणं, अग्रविवेचना.

PRECOGNITION, s. अग्रज्ञानं, पूर्व्वज्ञानं, अग्रविज्ञानं, अग्रबोधः -धनं.

To PRECONCEIVE, v. a. अग्रे or पूर्व्वं मन् or बुध् or मनसा क्लृप् in caus.

PRECONCEIVED, p. p. अग्रकल्पितः -ता -तं, पूर्व्वकल्पितः &c., अग्रोपलब्धः -ब्धा -ब्धं.

PRECONCEPTION, s. अग्रकल्पना, पूर्व्वकल्पना, अग्रबुद्धिः f., अग्रमतिः f., पूर्व्वबोधः, पूर्व्वज्ञानं, अग्रवासना, अग्रोपलब्धिः f., पूर्व्वतर्कः.

To PRECONCERT, v. a. पूर्व्वसङ्केतेन घट् or सञ्चिन्त् or साध् or परिक्लृप्.

PRECONCERTED, p. p. पूर्व्वसङ्केतघटितः -ता -तं, पूर्व्वसङ्केतपरिकल्पितः &c., पूर्व्वसङ्केतसिद्धः -द्धा -द्धं, पूर्व्वघटितः &c., अग्रघटितः &c., साङ्केतिकः -की -कं.

PRECONCERTION, s. अग्रघटनं, पूर्व्वघटनं, पूर्व्वसङ्केतघटनं, पूर्व्वसङ्केतपरिकल्पना.

PRECURSOR, s. प्राग्गामी m. (न्), अग्रगामी m., पूर्व्वगः, अग्रगः, अग्रसरः, पुरोगामी m., प्राग्भावी m., प्राग्वर्त्ती m., अग्रवर्त्ती.—(Sign which precedes) पूर्व्वचिह्नं, पूर्व्वलक्षणं, अग्रलक्षणं, पूर्व्वलिङ्गं.

PRECURSORY, a. पूर्व्वसूचकः -का -कं, अग्रसूचकः &c., पूर्व्वगः -गा -गं, अग्रगः &c., अग्रसरः -रा -रं, पुरःसरः &c., अग्रवर्त्ती -र्त्तिनी -र्त्ति (न्), प्राग्भावी &c.

PREDATORY, *a.* लुण्ठनकारी -रिणी -रि (न्), अपहारकः -का -कं, अपहारार्थकः -का -कं, लुण्टाकः -का -कं, उपद्रवी &c., उपद्रवार्थकः &c.

PREDECESSOR, *s.* पूर्व्वाधिकारी *m.* (न्), पूर्व्वगः, अग्रगः, पूर्व्वभोगी *m.* (न्).

PREDESTINARIAN, *s.* दैष्टिकः, दैववादी *m.* (न्), अदृष्टवादी *m.* (न्), अदृष्टमतावलम्बी *m.*, दैवचिन्तकः, दैवपरः, दैवाधीनः, दैवायत्तः, दैवपरायणः, प्रारब्धवादी *m.*

To PREDESTINATE, PREDESTINE, *v. a.* अग्रे or पूर्व्वं निरूप् (c. 10. -रूपयति -यितुं) or प्रकॢप् or निर्दिश् or नियुज् or प्रयुज् or विधा.

PREDESTINATED, PREDESTINED, *p. p.* अग्रनिरूपितः -ता -तं, पूर्व्वनिरूपितः &c., अग्रप्रकल्पितः &c., पूर्व्वनिर्दिष्टः -ष्टा -ष्टं, दैष्टिकः -की -कं, अवश्यम्भावी -विनी -वि (न्), भावी &c., अवश्यम्भवितव्यः -व्या -व्यं, दैवाधीनः -ना -नं, दैवपरः -रा -रं, अदृष्टाधीनः &c.

PREDESTINATION *s.* अग्रनिरूपणं, पूर्व्वनिरूपणं, पूर्व्वयोजनं -ना, पूर्व्वनियोजनं, पूर्व्वनिर्देशः, अग्रप्रकल्पनं -ना.—(The doctrine) दैष्टिकता -त्वं, दैववादः, अदृष्टवादः, दैवमतं, अदृष्टमतं, प्रारब्धवादः, दैवचिन्ता.—(State of being predestined) दैवाधीनता, दैवायत्तता -त्वं, अदृष्टाधीनता, दैवपरता, अवश्यम्भवितव्यता.

PREDETERMINATION, *s.* अग्रनिश्चयः, पूर्व्वनिश्चयः, पूर्व्वसङ्कल्पः, पूर्व्वनिर्णयः.

To PREDETERMINE, *v. a.* अग्रे or पूर्व्वं निश्चि or निर्णी, पूर्व्वनिश्चयं कृ, पूर्व्वसङ्कल्पं कृ.

PREDETERMINED, PREDETERMINATE, *v. a.* पूर्व्वनिश्चितः -ता -तं, अग्रनिश्चितः &c., अग्रनिर्णीतः &c., पूर्व्वनिर्णीतः &c., पूर्व्वसङ्कल्पितः -ता -तं, पूर्व्वनिर्दिष्टः -ष्टा -ष्टं.

PREDIAL, *a.* क्षैत्रिकः -की -कं, क्षेत्र in comp.; 'predial slave,' क्षेत्रदासः.

PREDICABILITY, *s.* वाच्यता, कथनीयता, कथ्यता, वक्तुं शक्यता, वाह्यता.

PREDICABLE, *a.* वाच्यः -च्या -च्यं, कथनीयः -या -यं, वक्तुं शक्यः -क्या -क्यं, वाह्यः -ह्या -ह्यं.

PREDICAMENT, *s.* (In logic) पदार्थः, समानाधिकरणं, समानपदं, समानवर्गः, प्रकृतिः *f.*—(Condition, plight) दशा, अवस्था, स्थितिः *f.*, गतिः *f.*, दुर्दशा.

To PREDICATE, *v. a.* वद् (c. 1. वदति -दितुं), कथ् (c. 10. कथयति -यितुं), वच् (c. 2. वक्ति -क्तुं), उपदिश् (c. 6. -दिशति -देष्टुं), अभिधा (c. 3. -दधाति -धातुं), अवच्छेदं कृ, विशेषणं कृ, विशिष् (c. 10. -शेषयति -यितुं).

PREDICATE, *s.* वाच्यं, पदवाच्यं, विशेषणं, विशेषकं, लक्षणं, वाक्यं, पदाभिधेयं, पदशक्यं, अवच्छेदः -दकः; 'relation between the predicate and the subject,' वाच्यवाचकभावः, विशेषणविशेष्यभावः; 'subject of a predicate,' विशेष्यं, अनुवाद्यं.

PREDICATED, *p. p.* कथितः -ता -तं, विशेषितः -ता -तं, अवच्छिन्नः -न्ना -न्नं, विहितः -ता -तं; 'is predicated,' उच्यते, कथ्यते, उपदिश्यते.

PREDICATION, *s.* कथनं, विशेषणं, अवच्छेदनं, पदाभिधानं, विधानं.

To PREDICT, *v. a.* (Foretell) अग्रे or अग्रतः or पूर्व्वं कथ् (c. 10. कथयति -यितुं) or वद् (c. 1. वदति -दितुं) or प्रवद् or वच्, प्राक्सम्भवात् कथ्, भविष्यद् वद् or कथ्, भावि कथ्, भाविकथनं कृ, भविष्यत्कथनं कृ, भविष्यत् or अनागतं प्रदृश् in caus. or अग्रे दृश्, प्रव्याहृ (c. 1. -हरति -ते -हर्त्तुं).

PREDICTED, *p. p.* अग्रकथितः -ता -तं, पूर्व्वकथितः &c., प्राक् सम्भवात् कथितः &c. or उक्तः -क्ता -क्तं or प्रदर्शितः &c.

PREDICTION, *s.* भाविकथनं, भविष्यत्कथनं, अनागतकथनं, अग्रकथनं, पूर्व्वकथनं, प्राक्सम्भवात् कथनं, प्रदर्शनं, अनागतप्रदर्शनं, भविष्यद्बोधनं, भविष्यद्वाक्यं, उद्बोधनं.

PREDICTIVE, *a.* पूर्व्वकथकः -का -कं, अग्रकथकः &c., प्रदर्शकः &c., उद्बोधकः &c.

PREDICTOR, *s.* भाविकथकः, भविष्यत्कथकः, भविष्यद्वक्ता *m.* (कृ), अग्रवादी *m.* (न्), पूर्व्ववादी *m.*, प्रदर्शकः, अनागतदर्शकः, भाविवक्ता *m.*, भाविदर्शकः, दैवज्ञः, नैमित्तिकः.

PREDILECTION, *s.* पूर्व्वानुरागः, पूर्व्वानुरक्तिः *f.*, पूर्व्वप्रीतिः *f.*, पूर्व्वस्नेहः, पूर्व्वरुचिः *f.*, पूर्व्वच्छन्दस् *n.*, प्रावण्यं.

To PREDISPOSE, *v. a.* अग्रे or पूर्व्वं प्रवृत् in caus. or प्रयुज् or नियुज् or प्रोत्सह् in caus., प्रवणीकृ, प्रवणं -णां कृ, उन्मुखीकृ, उन्मुखं -खां कृ; 'to predispose to disease,' रोगसुग्राह्यं कृ, रोगयोग्यं -ग्यां कृ, रोगपात्रं कृ, रोगास्पदं कृ; 'to anger,' क्रोधप्रवणं -णां कृ.

PREDISPOSED, *p. p.* प्रवणः -णा -णं, अग्रप्रवर्त्तितः -ता -तं, उन्मुख in comp.

PREDISPOSITION, *s.* प्रावण्यं, प्रवणता, मनःप्रावण्यं, प्रवाहः, प्रवृत्तिः *f.*, उन्मुखता; 'to disease,' रोगसुग्राह्यता, रोगयोग्यता, रोगसुभेद्यता, रोगसुग्राह्यदशा.

PREDOMINANCE, PREDOMINANCY, *s.* प्राबल्यं, प्रबलता, प्राधान्यं, प्रधानता, प्रभावः, प्रभुता, प्रभूतता -त्वं, प्राभवं, आधिक्यं, अधिकत्वं, अतिरेकः, अतिरिक्तता.

PREDOMINANT, *a.* प्रबलः -ला -लं, प्रभविष्णुः -ष्णुः -ष्णु, प्रभूतः -ता -तं, प्रभवः -वा -वं, प्रधानः -ना -नं, अधिकः -का -कं, अतिरिक्तः -क्ता -क्तं, अतिरेकी -किणी -कि (न्), अतिशयी &c., सातिशयः -या -यं.

PREDOMINANTLY, *adv.* प्रबलं, प्राबल्येन, प्रधानतस्, प्रभावतस्, अतिरिक्तं.

To PREDOMINATE, *v. n.* प्रभू, अतिरिच् in pass. (-रिच्यते), उद्रिच्, व्यतिरिच्, प्रबलः -ला -लं भू, प्रबलीभू, अधिकः -का -कं भू, अधिकीभू.

PRE-EMINENCE, *s.* श्रेष्ठत्वं -ता, श्रैष्ठ्यं, सर्व्वश्रेष्ठता, उत्कर्षः, उत्कृष्टता, सर्व्वोत्कृष्टता, औत्कर्ष्यं, प्रकर्षः, प्रकृष्टता -त्वं, प्रमुखता -त्वं, मुख्यता, प्रधानता, सर्व्वप्रधानता, प्राधान्यं, विशिष्टता, वैशिष्ट्यं, ज्येष्ठता, प्रभुता -त्वं, उन्नतिः *f.*, समुन्नतिः *f.*, आधिक्यं, अधिकत्वं, शिष्टता, वैशेष्यं, गुणवैशेष्यं, पुरोगतिः *f.*, अग्रगण्यता, उत्तमता, सर्व्वोत्तमता.

PRE-EMINENT, *a.* श्रेष्ठः -ष्ठा -ष्ठं, सर्व्वश्रेष्ठः &c., सर्व्वोत्तमः -मा -मं, उत्कृष्टः -ष्टा -ष्टं, उत्तमः -मा -मं, सर्व्वोत्कृष्टः &c., प्रधानः -ना -नं, सर्व्वप्रधानः &c., प्रधानोत्तमः -मा -मं, प्रमुखः -खा -खं, विशिष्टः &c., शिष्टः &c., मुख्यः -ख्या -ख्यं, अग्रियः -या -यं, अग्र्यः -ग्र्या -ग्र्यं, अग्रगण्यः -ण्या -ण्यं, अग्रणीः -णीः -णि, परमः -मा -मं, परः -रा -रं, ज्येष्ठः -ष्ठा -ष्ठं, सर्व्वज्येष्ठः &c., वृन्दारकः -का -कं, सातिशयः -या -यं or expressed by इन्द्रः, व्याघ्रः, सिंहः, शार्दूलः, ऋषभः, पुङ्गवः, नागः, चन्द्रः, कुञ्जरः, मुख्यः, प्रकाण्डः in comp. *See* EXCELLENT.

PRE-EMINENTLY, *adv.* परमं, प्रधानतस्, प्राधान्यतस्, सर्व्वप्रधानतस्, मुख्यशस्, सर्व्वश्रेष्ठं, सातिशयं, अतिशयेन, अधिकं, अत्यन्तं.

PRE-EMPTION, *s.* पूर्व्वक्रयः -यणं, अग्रक्रयः, पूर्व्वक्रयाधिकारः, अग्रक्रयाधिकारः; 'claimed by right of pre-emption,' प्रख्यातः -ता -तं.

To PRE-ENGAGE, *v. a.* पूर्व्वनियमेन or पूर्व्वसङ्केतेन बन्ध् or बद्धं -द्धां कृ, पूर्व्वं प्रतिज्ञा, पूर्व्वनियमं कृ, पूर्व्वसङ्केतं कृ, पूर्व्वप्रतिज्ञां कृ.

PRE-ENGAGED, *p. p.* पूर्व्वनियमबद्धः -द्धा -द्धं, पूर्व्वसङ्केतबद्धः &c., पूर्व्वनियमितः -ता -तं, पूर्व्वप्रतिज्ञातः &c., पूर्व्वसङ्केतितः &c.

PRE-ENGAGEMENT, *s.* पूर्व्वनियमः, पूर्व्वसङ्केतः, पूर्व्वप्रतिज्ञा, पूर्व्वसमयः.

PRE-EXAMINATION, *s.* पूर्व्वनिरूपणं, अग्रनिरूपणं, पूर्व्वविचारणं, पूर्व्वपरीक्षा.

To PRE-EXIST, *v. n.* अग्रे or अग्रतः or पूर्व्वं भू or वृत् or विद् or जीव्.

PRE-EXISTENCE, *s.* प्राग्भावः, पूर्व्वभावः, पूर्व्वभवः, पूर्व्वभूतिः *f.*, पूर्व्वजन्म *n.* (न्), पूर्व्वसत्त्वं, पूर्व्ववृत्तिः *f.*, प्राग्वृत्तिः *f.*, पूर्व्वदेहः, पूर्व्वजीवनं, पूर्व्वसत्ता, पूर्व्ववर्त्तनं.

PRE-EXISTENT, *a.* पूर्व्वभवः -वा -वं, पूर्व्वभूतः -ता -तं, पूर्व्वजीवी -विनी -वि (न्), पूर्व्ववर्त्ती &c., पूर्व्वदेहवान् -वती -वत् (त्).

PREFACE, *s.* प्रस्तावना -नं, प्रस्तावः, आभाषः, परिभाषा, उपोद्घातः, उपन्यासः, वाङ्मुखं, प्रकरणं, प्रारम्भः, प्रारम्भोक्तिः *f.*, आरम्भोक्तिः *f.*, उपक्रमोक्तिः *f.*, सूची.

To PREFACE, *v. a.* प्रस्तावनां कृ or लिख् (c. 6. लिखति, लेखितुं), प्रस्तु (c. 2. -स्तौति -स्तुते, c. 10. -स्तावयति -यितुं), प्रब्रू (c. 2. -ब्रवीति -वक्तुं), अग्रतः or पूर्व्वतो ब्रू or वद् or वच् or भाष्, वाक्यारम्भं कृ, परिभाषां कृ, सप्रस्तावनं -नां कृ.

PREFATORY, *a.* पारिभाषिकः -की -कं, प्रस्तावनारूपः -पा -पं, आभाषिकः &c., उपोद्घातरूपः -पा -पं, आरम्भकः &c.

PREFECT, *s.* पुराध्यक्षः, पुराधिपतिः *m.*, नगराध्यक्षः, नगराधिष्ठाता *m.* (तृ), अधिष्ठाता *m.*, अधिपतिः *m.*, नगराधिकारी *m.*

PREFECTURE, *s.* पुराध्यक्षता, नगराध्यक्षता, अध्यक्षता, अधिष्ठातृत्वं.

To PREFER, *v. a.* (Esteem more, value more, have greater liking for) अधिकं मन् (c. 4. मन्यते, मन्तुं, c. 10. मानयति -यितुं) or प्रशंस् (c. 1. -शंसति -सितुं), अधिकं रुच् (c. 10. रोचयति -यितुं, c. 1. रोचते -चितुं) or अनुरुच् or अभिरुच् or इष् with abl., अधिकानुरागं कृ, अधिकानुरक्तः -क्ता -क्तं भू, अधिकाभिमतः -ता -तं भू. The construction of the sentence will vary as the Sanskrit verb may have an active or neuter sense; thus, 'I prefer this to that,' एतत् तस्मात् मह्यम् अधिकं रोचते, एतत् तस्माद् अधिकं रोचयामि or इच्छामि or प्रशंसामि, or मया अधिकं प्रशस्यते or मया अधिकम् अनुमतं or मम अधिकम् अभिमतं. The adverb वरं or the root शिष् with वि may be used to express the sense of 'prefer'; thus, 'I prefer death to poverty,' वरं मृत्युर् न च दारिद्र्यं (*i. e.* 'better death and not poverty'); 'I prefer death to dishonour,' अपमानात् प्राणत्यागो विशिष्यते.—(Choose before) पूर्व्वं वृ (c. 5. वृणोति -णुते, c. 9. वृणाति -णीते, c. 1. वरति -रितुं, c. 10. वरयति -यितुं), पूर्व्वं or अग्रे ग्रह् (c. 9. गृह्णाति, ग्रहीतुं) or वावृत्, पुरोधा (c. 3. -दधाति -धातुं); 'I prefer retirement to all pleasures,' अपक्रमणं सर्व्वकामैः or सर्व्वकामेभ्यो वृणे.—(Exalt, promote to an office, &c.) पदं वृध् (c. 10. वर्धयति -यितुं) or संवृध्, श्रेष्ठपदे or उत्कृष्टपदे नियुज् or प्रतिपद्, पदवृद्धिं कृ, प्रतिपत्तिं दा, पुरस्कृ.—(Present, offer) सॄ in caus., निविद् in caus., उपहृ, निवेदनं कृ, समर्पणं कृ.

PREFERABLE, *a.* (Worthy to be chsoen before, more desirable or excellent) वरं indec., वरीयान् -यसी -यः (स्), वरिष्ठः -ष्ठा -ष्ठं, वरणीयः -या -यं, पूर्व्ववरणीयः &c., अधिकवरणीयः &c., पूर्व्वग्राह्यः -ह्या -ह्यं, प्रथमग्राह्यः &c., अग्रग्राह्यः &c., श्रेयान् &c., श्रेष्ठः &c., गरीयान् &c., अधिकं प्रार्थनीयः -या -यं. The adverb वरं is usually followed by न च or न पुनर्; as, 'death is preferable to poverty,' वरं मृत्युर् न च दारिद्र्यं; 'death is preferable to intercourse with the base,' वरं प्राणत्यागो न पुनर् अधमानाम् उपगमः. *See* examples under *To* PREFER.

PREFERABLENESS, *s.* वरता -त्वं, पूर्व्वग्राह्यता, प्रथमग्राह्यता, श्रेष्ठता, श्रैष्ठ्यं, श्रेयस्त्वं, वरीयस्त्वं, गरीयस्त्वं.

PREFERABLY, *adv.* वरं, वरीयस्, श्रेयस्, गरीयस्, वरिष्ठं, श्रेष्ठं.

PREFERENCE, *s.* अधिकरुचिः *f.*, अधिकाभिरुचिः *f.*, पूर्व्वरुचिः *f.*, अग्ररुचिः *f.*, अधिकानुरागः, पूर्व्वानुरागः, अधिकमानं, अभिप्रेतं, वरता -त्वं, वरणं, वृतिः *f.*

PREFERMENT, *s.* (Advancement to a higher office) पदवृद्धिः *f.*, पदवर्धनं, स्थानवृद्धिः *f.*, प्रतिपत्तिः *f.*, वर्धनं, संवर्धनं -ना, प्रवर्धनं.—(Act of presenting) निवेदनं, समर्पणं.

PREFERRED, *p. p.* (Chosen before others) पूर्व्वगृहीतः -ता -तं, वृतः -ता -तं, पूर्व्ववृतः &c., मनोनीतः -ता -तं, पुरोहितः -ता -तं—(Advanced in rank) संवर्धितः -ता -तं, श्रेष्ठपदनियुक्तः -क्ता -क्तं, पुरस्कृतः &c.

PREFIGURATION, *s.* प्रतिरूपद्वारेण पूर्व्वप्रदर्शनं or पूर्व्वसूचनं, दृष्टान्तद्वारा प्राक्प्रदर्शनं, प्रतिरूपकद्वारेण अग्रप्रदर्शनं, सादृश्येन पूर्व्वदर्शनं, पूर्व्वलक्षणदर्शनं, पूर्व्वलक्षणकरणं.

PREFIGURATIVE, *a.* उद्बोधकः -का -कं, पूर्व्वप्रदर्शकः &c., पूर्व्वलाक्षणिकः -की -कं, लाक्षणिकः &c., बोधकः -का -कं, पूर्व्वसूचकः &c.

To PREFIGURE, *v. a.* प्रतिरूपद्वारेण पूर्व्वं प्रदृश् (c. 10. -दर्शयति -यितुं) or पूर्व्वतो दृश् or अग्रे प्रदृश्, दृष्टान्तद्वारा पूर्व्वं प्रदृश् or सूच् (c. 10. सूचयति -यितुं), प्रतिरूपकं दा or कृ, प्रतिबिम्बं दा, पूर्व्वलक्षणं दा or दृश्.

PREFIGURED, *p. p.* प्रतिरूपकद्वारा पूर्व्वप्रदर्शितः -ता -तं or पूर्व्वसूचितः &c.

To PREFIX, *v. a.* (Put or place before) पुरस्कृ, पुरतस्कृ, अग्रतस्कृ, पुरोधा (c. 3. -दधाति -धातुं), अग्रे or पुरतः स्था in caus.—(In writing) अग्रे or अग्रतः or पुरतः or मुखे लिख्.—(Settle beforehand) अग्रे or पूर्व्वं निश्चि or निर्णी or निरूप् or प्रक्लृप् or नियुज्.

PREFIX, *s.* (In grammar, particle prefixed) उपसर्गः.

PREFIXED, *p.p.* (Put before) पुरस्कृतः -ता -तं, पुरतस्कृतः &c., पुरःकृतः &c., पुरोहितः &c., अग्रे स्थापितः &c.—(Settled before) पूर्व्वनिश्चितः -ता -तं, पूर्व्वनिरूपितः -ता -तं.

PREGNANCY, *s.* गर्भधारणं, गर्भिणीत्वं, गर्भिणीभावः, गर्भग्रहणं, सगर्भता, धृतगर्भता, पूर्णगर्भता, सञ्जातगर्भता, गर्भपोषणं, ससत्त्वता, आपन्नसत्त्वता, सगर्भावस्था, अन्तरापत्यता, गर्भः.

PREGNANT, *a.* (Being with young) गर्भिणी, गर्भवती, सगर्भा, धृतगर्भा, गर्भधारिणी, गृहीतगर्भा, पूर्णगर्भा, आपन्नगर्भा, सञ्जातगर्भा, प्ररूढगर्भा, ससत्त्वा, आपन्नसत्त्वा, अन्तर्वत्नी, उदरिणी, गुर्व्विणी, अन्तरापत्या, द्विहृदया; 'a pregnant woman longing for any thing,' दोहदवती, श्रद्धालुः *f.*; 'number of pregnant women,' गार्भिणं -ण्यं.—(Full of, abounding with) पूर्णः -र्णा -र्णं, सम्पूर्णः &c., गर्भः -र्भा -र्भं in comp., सङ्कुलः -ला -लं, आढ्यः -ढ्या -ढ्यं.—(Fruitful) सफलः -ला -लं, अवन्ध्यः -न्ध्या -न्ध्यं.

PREGUSTATION, *s.* पूर्व्वस्वादनं, पूर्व्वास्वादनं, अग्रास्वादनं, पूर्व्वप्राशनं.

To PREJUDGE, PREJUDICATE, *v. a.* अग्रे or पूर्व्वं विचर् (c. 10. -चारयति -यितुं) or निर्णी (c. 1. -णयति -णेतुं) or निश्चि, पूर्व्वविचारं कृ, पूर्व्वविचारणं कृ, पूर्व्वनिर्णयं कृ, पूर्व्वनिश्चयं कृ, वृत्तान्तम् अनिरूप्य or अविचार्य्य निर्णयं कृ, अविचारपूर्व्वं निर्णयं कृ or निष्पत्तिं कृ, वृत्तान्तनिर्णयम् अकृत्वा निष्पत्तिं कृ, वृत्तान्तनिरूपणम् अकृत्वा निर्णयं कृ.

PREJUDGED, *p.p.* पूर्व्वविचारितः -ता -तं, पूर्व्वनिर्णीतः &c., पूर्व्वनिष्पन्नः -न्ना -न्नं.

PREJUDGMENT, *s.* पूर्व्वनिर्णयः, पूर्व्वविचारः -रणं, पूर्व्वनिष्पत्तिः *f.*, पूर्व्वनिश्चयः.

PREJUDICE, *s.* (Decision or opinion formed without due examination) अविचारपूर्व्वो निर्णयः, अनिरूपणपूर्व्वो निश्चयः, अपरीक्षापूर्व्वा बुद्धिः *f.*, अविचारपूर्व्विका मतिः *f.*, अविचारबुद्धिः *f.*, अविचारमतिः *f.*, अविचारितनिश्चयः, अविचारितनिर्णयः.—(Bias) दुराग्रहः, सङ्गः, मनोवक्रता, बुद्धिवक्रता, वक्रमतं, साचीकृतं, वक्रीकृतं, वक्रीभावः, आग्रहः, ग्रहः; 'free from prejudice,' मुक्तसङ्गः -ङ्गा -ङ्गं.—(Partiality for) पक्षपातः.—(Damage, detriment) क्षतिः *f.*, हानिः *f.*, अपचयः, अपायः, अपकारः, नाशः, हिंसा, क्षयः, बाधः, दूषणं, ध्वंसः.

To PREJUDICE, *v. a.* (Bias) साचीकृ, वक्रीकृ, बुद्धिवक्रतां कृ or जन्, दुराग्रहं कृ, दुराकर्षणं कृ, आकृष्, आवृज् (c. 10. -वर्जयति -यितुं), दुरावर्जनं कृ, चित्ताकर्षणं कृ, चित्तावर्जनं कृ.—(Injure, damage)

PRE

क्षतिं कृ, अपकृ, हिंस्, क्षण्, दुष्, क्षि, नश्, बाध्.

PREJUDICED, *p. p.* (Biased) साचीकृतः -ता -तं, वक्रीकृतः &c., सङ्गी -ङ्गिनी -ङ्गि (न्), सङ्गयुक्तः -क्ता -क्तं, साचीकृतबुद्धिः -द्धिः -द्धि, वक्रीकृतबुद्धिः &c., साचीकृतमतिः -तिः -ति.—(Damaged) अपकृतः -ता -तं, प्राप्तहानिः -निः -नि.

PREJUDICIAL, *a.* अहितः -ता -तं, अपकारकः -का -कं, क्षतिजनकः &c., अहितकरः -रा -रं, हानिजनकः &c., हिंसकः &c., घातुकः &c. *See* INJURIOUS.

PREJUDICIALLY, *adv.* अहितं, सापकारं, सापायं, हिंसया, सक्षतं.

PREKNOWLEDGE, *s.* पूर्व्वज्ञानं, अग्रज्ञानं, पूर्व्वबोधः, अग्रबोधः.

PRELACY, PRELATE. *See* EPISCOPACY, BISHOP, &c.

PRELECTION, *s.* पाठः -ठनं, पठनं, अध्यायः. *See* LECTURE.

PRELECTOR, *s.* पाठकः, पाठकारी *m.* (न्). *See* LECTURER.

PRELIBATION, *s.* पूर्व्वभोगः, पूर्व्वभुक्तिः *f.*, पूर्व्वानुभवः, आदिभोगः. *See* FORETASTE.

PRELIMINARY, *a.* प्राथमिकः -की -कं, आरम्भकः -का -कं, प्रारम्भकः &c., पूर्व्वः -र्व्वा -र्व्वं, पौर्व्विकः -की -कं, प्रथमः -मा -मं, पूर्व्वकर्त्तव्यः -व्या -व्यं, पूर्व्वकरणीयः -या -यं, अग्रकर्त्तव्यः &c., अग्रकरणीयः -या -यं, आद्यः -द्या -द्यं, आदि in comp., आदिकः -का -कं, आदिस्थः -स्था -स्थं, आरम्भस्थः &c., उपक्रमस्थः &c.—(Prefatory) पारिभाषिकः -की -कं, प्रस्तावनारूपः -पा -पं.

PRELIMINARY, *s.* पूर्व्वविषयः, पूर्व्वाङ्गं, पूर्व्वकर्म्म *n.* (न्), आद्याङ्गं, पूर्व्वोपायः, आरम्भकर्म्म *n.*, प्रारम्भकर्म्म *n.*, उपकरणं.—(Preliminary remarks) परिभाषा, आभाषः. *See* PREFACE.

PRELUDE, *s.* (In music) पूर्व्वरङ्गः, पूर्व्ववादनं, आरम्भवाद्यं.—(Dramatic) प्रस्तावना -नं, प्रस्तावः, आमुखं.—(Something introductory) आरम्भः, प्रारम्भः, उपक्रमः, प्रकरणं.—(Forerunner, something indicatory) पूर्व्वलक्षणं, पूर्व्वसूचकं, पूर्व्वचिह्नं, पूर्व्वरूपं.

To PRELUDE, *v. a.* प्रस्तु (c. 2. -स्तौति -स्तुते, c. 10. स्तावयति -यितुं), प्रस्तावनां कृ, पूर्व्वरङ्गं कृ, आरभ् (c. 1. -रभते -रब्धुं), समारभ्, उपक्रम् (c. 1. -क्रमते -मितुं), प्रक्रम्, प्रकृ, सम्प्रकृ.

PRELUDER, *s.* प्रस्तावनाकृत्, पूर्व्वरङ्गकारी *m.* (न्), पूर्व्ववादकः, आरम्भकः.

PRELUSIVE, PRELUSORY, *a.* आरम्भकः -का -कं, पूर्व्वसूचकः -का -कं.

PREMATURE, *a.* कालपूर्व्वपक्वः -क्वा -क्वं, प्राक्पूर्णकालात्पक्वः &c., अपूर्णकालः -ला -लं, अपूर्णकालिकः -का -कं, असम्पूर्णकालः &c., पूर्णकालपूर्व्वजः -जा -जं, अपूर्णकालजः -जा -जं, अकालपक्वः -क्वा -क्वं, अपक्वः &c., अपूर्णकालोत्पन्नः -न्ना -न्नं, अकालजः &c., अकालोत्पन्नः &c., अकालभवः -वा -वं, अकालिकः -की -कं, अप्राप्तकालः -ला -लं, असामयिकः -की -कं.—(Not waiting for the proper time) अकालसहः -हा -हं. *See* PRECIPITATE.

PREMATURELY, *adv.* प्राक्पूर्णकालात्, पूर्णकालात्पूर्व्वं, अपूर्णकाले, असम्पूर्णकाले, अकाले, असमये; 'prematurely born,' अपूर्णकालजः -जा -जं, अपूर्णकालोत्पन्नः -न्ना -न्नं, पूर्णकालपूर्व्वजातः -ता -तं; 'prematurely grey-haired,' युवपलितः -ता -तं; 'prematurely old,' युवजरन् -रती -रत् (त्), युवाजरन् &c.; 'prematurely bald,' युवखलतिः -तिः -ती -ति.

PREMATURENESS, PREMATURITY, *s.* कालपूर्व्वपक्वता, अपूर्णकालत्वं, अपूर्णकालिकत्वं -ता, अकालपक्वता, अकालोत्पत्तिः *f.*, अपूर्णकालोत्पत्तिः *f.*, अकालजत्वं, अकालिकत्वं.

To PREMEDITATE, *v. a.* पूर्व्वं or अग्रे चिन्त् or मनसा कृप्, पूर्व्वकल्पनां कृ.

To PREMEDITATE, *v. n.* पूर्व्वं or अग्रे चिन्त् or ध्यै or विचर् or विमृश् or विगण्, पूर्व्वचिन्तां कृ, पूर्व्वविवेचनां कृ, पूर्व्वोपायं चिन्त्, पूर्व्वविचारणां कृ.

PREMEDITATED, *p. p.* or *a.* पूर्व्वकल्पितः -ता -तं, पूर्व्वचिन्तितः &c., पूर्व्वघटितः &c., बुद्धिपूर्व्वः -र्व्वा -र्व्वं, मतिपूर्व्वः &c., बुद्धिकृतः -ता -तं, पूर्व्वसङ्कल्पितः -ता -तं, साङ्कल्पिकः -की -कं, सङ्कल्पकृतः &c., पूर्व्वरचितः &c., पूर्व्वयोजितः &c.

PREMEDITATION, *s.* पूर्व्वकल्पना, पूर्व्वसङ्कल्पः, पूर्व्वपरिकल्पना, पूर्व्वघटना, पूर्व्वरचना, पूर्व्वयोजना, पूर्व्वानुसन्धानं, पूर्व्वचिन्ता -न्तनं, पूर्व्वविचारणा, पूर्व्वविवेचना.

PREMICES, *s. pl.* (First-fruits) नवान्नं, प्रथमफलं. *See* the word.

PREMIER, *a.* मुख्यः -ख्या -ख्यं, प्रमुखः -खा -खं, प्रधानः -ना -नं.

PREMIER, *s.* (Prime-minister) मुख्यमन्त्री *m.* (न्), प्रधानमन्त्री *m.*, प्रधानामात्यः, महामन्त्री *m.*, प्रधानसचिवः, मुख्यप्रधानः.

PREMIERSHIP, *s.* मुख्यमन्त्रिता -त्वं, प्रधानमन्त्रिता -त्वं.

To PREMISE, *v. a.* उपन्यस् (c. 4. -अस्यति -असितुं), पूर्व्वं or अग्रे or वाङ्मुखे कथ् (c. 10. कथयति -यितुं) or ब्रू (c. 2, ब्रवीति, वक्तुं) or वद् (c. 1. वदति -दितुं) प्रस्तावपूर्व्वं कथ् or व्याख्या (c. 2. -ख्याति -तुं), पूर्व्वव्याख्यां कृ, पूर्व्वकथनं कृ, प्राक्कथनं कृ, प्रस्तावपूर्व्वकथनं कृ, उपक्रम् (c. 1. -क्रमते -मितुं), प्रक्रम्, प्रस्तु (c. 2. -स्तौति -स्तुते, c. 10. -स्तावयति -यितुं).

PREMISE, *s.* (In logic) पक्षः, अवयवः, प्रतिज्ञा, उपन्यासः, साधनं; 'major premise,' गुर्व्ववयवः, गुरुपक्षः, पूर्व्वपक्षः, आद्यपक्षः, हेत्वादिपक्षः; 'minor premise,' लघ्ववयवः, उत्तरपक्षः.

PREMISED, *p. p.* उपन्यस्तः -स्ता -स्तं, पूर्व्वकथितः -ता -तं, प्रस्तावपूर्व्वकथितः &c., प्रस्तावपूर्व्वसूचितः &c., प्रस्तुतः -ता -तं, प्रक्रान्तः -न्ता -न्तं; 'having premised,' उपन्यस्य, प्रतिपाद्य.

PREMISES, *s. pl.* (In logic). *See* PREMISE.—(In law, house with its adjuncts) गृहवाटिकादि *n.*, गृहक्षेत्रादि *n.*, गृहादि *n.*

PREMIUM, *s.* पारितोषिकं, मूल्यं, फलं, लभ्यं, लाभः, अधिकमूल्यं, अतिरिक्तमूल्यं, मूल्यातिरिक्तपारितोषिकं.

To PREMONISH, *v. a.* (Forewarn) अग्रे or पूर्व्वं बुध् in caus. or प्रबुध् or प्रत्यादिश् or उपदिश् or ज्ञा in caus., पूर्व्वं सूच् (c. 10. सूचयति -यितुं), पूर्व्वसूचनं कृ, पूर्व्वलक्षणं दा, पूर्व्वरूपं दा.

PREMONISHED, *p.p.* पूर्व्वबोधितः -ता -तं, पूर्व्वोपदिष्टः -ष्टा -ष्टं, पूर्व्वसूचितः &c.

PREMONITION, PREMONISHMENT, *s.* पूर्व्वबोधः -धनं, पूर्व्वप्रबोधः, पूर्व्वसूचना -नं, पूर्व्वलक्षणं, पूर्व्वरूपं.

PREMONITORY, *a.* पूर्व्वसूचकः -का -कं, पूर्व्वबोधकः -का -कं, उद्बोधकः &c., पूर्व्वसूचनकारी -रिणी -रि (न्), पूर्व्वलक्षणदः -दा -दं, पूर्व्वलाक्षणिकः -की -कं, पूर्व्वज्ञापकः &c.

PRENOMEN, *s.* व्यक्तिनाम *n.* (न्), उपाधिः *m.*

PRENTICE, *s.* अन्तेवासी *m.* (न्), छात्रः, सङ्केतपत्रबद्धशिष्यः, शिष्यः.

PRENTICESHIP, *s.* अन्तेवासित्वं, अन्तवासित्वं, अन्तेवासिभावः, अन्तेवासित्वकालः.

PRE-OCCUPATION, PRE-OCCUPANCY, *s.* पूर्व्वभोगः, पूर्व्वभुक्तिः *f.*, पूर्व्वधारणं, पूर्व्वग्रहणं.

PRE-OCCUPIED, *p.p.* पूर्व्वगृहीतः -ता -तं, पूर्व्वाविष्टः -ष्टा -ष्टं, पूर्व्वभुक्तः -क्ता -क्तं.

To PRE-OCCUPY, *v. a.* पूर्व्वं or अग्रे धृ or ग्रह् or भुज्, पूर्व्वधारणं कृ.

To PRE-ORDAIN, *v. a.* अग्रे or पूर्व्वं विधा or कॢप् or प्रकॢप् or निर्दिश् or स्था in caus., पूर्व्वविधानं कृ, पूर्व्वविधिं कृ, पूर्व्वस्थापनां कृ.

PREPARATION, *s.* (Act of getting ready, providing or fitting for any purpose) सज्जनं -ना, सज्जीकरणं, सज्जकर्म्म *n.* (न्), साधनं, सिद्धीकरणं, आयोजनं, उपकल्पनं -ना, परिकल्पनं -ना, कल्पनं -ना,

पुरस्करणं, पुरस्कारः, संस्कारः, संस्करणं, रचनं -ना, विरचनं -ना, उपाकर्म्म *n.* (न्), सम्भारः, सम्भृतिः *f.*, सन्धानं, समवधानं, प्रतिविधानं, उद्योगः, प्रस्तुतीकरणं.—(State of preparation) सिद्धिः *f.*, सिद्धता -त्वं.—(Previous or preparative measure) उपायः, साधनोपायः, अभ्युपायः, साधनं.—(That which is prepared or compounded, a compound) योगः, रसायनं; 'a preparation of mercury,' रसगर्भं, रसपुष्पं.—(Of medicine or food) संस्कारः, पाकः, पचनं.—(Prepared food) पक्वान्नं, सिद्धान्नं.

PREPARATIVE, PREPARATORY, *a.* सिद्धिजनकः -का -कं, सिद्धिकारकः -का -कं, सिद्धताजनकः -का -कं, साधकः -का -कं, उपक्रमसाधकः &c., आरम्भसाधकः &c., सिद्धिसाधकः &c., उपक्रमसहायः -या -यं, आरम्भोपकारी -रिणी -रि (न्), उपक्रमोपकारी &c., उपकल्पकः &c., परिकल्पकः &c., आयोजनकारी &c., उपक्रमप्रवर्त्तकः &c., प्रस्तुतकारी &c., योग्यताजनकः &c., आरम्भकारी &c.

PREPARATIVE, *s.* उपक्रमसाधनं, आरम्भसाधनं, सिद्धिसाधनं, सिद्धिजनकविषयः, सिद्धिजनककर्म्म *n.* (न्), परिकर्म्म *n.*, सिद्धताजनकविषयः.

PREPARATIVELY, *adv.* आयोजनपूर्व्वं, उपक्रमसाधनार्थं, आरम्भसाधनार्थं.

To PREPARE, *v. a.* (Make ready, fit for any purpose) सज्जीकृ, उपक्लृप् (c. 10. -कल्पयति -यितुं, c. 1. -कल्पते -ल्पितुं), परिक्लृप्, प्रक्लृप्, क्लृप्, युज् (c. 10. योजयति -यितुं), आयुज्, समायुज्, सिद्धीकृ, प्रस्तुतीकृ, उपस्कृ, संस्कृ, पुरस्कृ, रच् (c. 10. रचयति -यितुं), विरच्, सम्भृ (c. 1. -भरति -भर्त्तुं), सज्ज् (c. 1. सज्जति -ज्जितुं), साध् (c. 10. साधयति -यितुं), प्रतिविधा (c. 3. -दधाति -धातुं), विधा, विनिर्म्मा (c. 2. -माति -तुं), योग्यं -ग्यां कृ, उपयुक्तं -क्तां कृ, कार्य्यक्षमं -मां कृ, कार्य्योपयुक्तं -क्तां कृ.—(Provide with all necessary articles) सोपकारद्रव्यैः समायुज्, उपयुक्तद्रव्याणि परिक्लृप् or उपक्लृप् or सम्यक्लृप् or उपस्था in caus. (-स्थापयति -यितुं) or उपपद् (c. 10. -पादयति -यितुं) or विधा, सोपकारद्रव्ययुक्तं -क्तां कृ, उपयुक्तद्रव्यसाधनं कृ.—(Dress) रच्, विरच्, प्रसाध्, विन्यस्.—(Prepare food) अन्नं संस्कृ or सिद्धीकृ or पच् or सन्धा.

To PREPARE, *v. n.* (Make all things ready) उपयुक्तद्रव्याणि परिक्लृप् or उपक्लृप्, सोपकारद्रव्यसम्भारं कृ, द्रव्यसम्भारं कृ, उपकरणसम्भारं कृ, सज्जनं कृ, संस्कारं कृ.—(Make one's self ready, be ready) उद्यतः -ता -तं भू, समुद्यतः -ता -तं भू, अभ्युद्यतः -ता -तं भू, उद्युक्तः -क्ता -क्तं भू, प्रस्तुतः -ता -तं भू; 'he prepared to kill the child,' स बालं हन्तुम् उद्यतः.

PREPARED, *p. p.* or *a.* सज्जीकृतः -ता -तं, सज्जितः -ता -तं, सज्जः -ज्जा -ज्जं, प्रस्तुतः -ता -तं, उपकल्पितः &c., परिकल्पितः &c., कल्पितः &c., उपक्लृप्तः -प्ता -प्तं, प्रक्लृप्तः &c., सम्भृतः -ता -तं, सिद्धः -द्धा -द्धं, सम्प्रस्तुतः -ता -तं, पुरस्कृतः -ता -तं, उद्यतः -ता -तं, समुद्यतः &c., अभ्युद्यतः &c., उद्युक्तः -क्ता -क्तं, आयुक्तः &c., संस्कृतः &c., संस्कारितः &c., संहितः &c., सोपकारद्रव्ययुक्तः &c., उपपादितः -ता -तं, परिनिर्म्मितः &c.; 'to be prepared,' उद्यतः -ता -तं भू or अस्, उद्युक्तः &c. भू, सज्जीभू.

PREPAREDNESS, *s.* सिद्धता -त्वं, सिद्धिः *f.*, प्रस्तुतत्वं, उद्यतत्वं, उद्युक्तत्वं.

PREPARER, *s.* उपकल्पकः, परिकल्पकः, आयोजनकर्त्ता *m.* (र्त्तृ), सिद्धिकर्त्ता *m.*, साधकः, रचकः, विरचकः, संस्कर्त्ता *m.* (र्त्तृ).

PRE-PAYMENT, *s.* पूर्व्वशोधनं, पूर्व्वशुद्धिः *f.*, पूर्व्वसिद्धिः *f.*, पूर्व्वदानं.

PREPENSE, PREPENSED, *a.* *See* PREMEDITATED.—(Malice prepense) द्रोहचिन्ता -न्तनं, आपादः -दनं; 'with malice prepense,' द्रोहचिन्तापूर्व्वं, बुद्धिपूर्व्वं, मतिपूर्व्वं, कामतस्; 'without malice prepense,' अबुद्धिपूर्व्वकं, अमतिपूर्व्वकं, अकामात् -मतस्.

PREPONDERANCE, *s.* (Superiority of weight) भाराधिक्यं, भारातिरिक्तता, भारातिरेक्यं, अधिकभारः, अतिरिक्तभारः, गुरुतरभारः.—(Superiority of power or force) अधिकप्रभावः, प्रभावाधिक्यं, प्रधानता, प्राधान्यं, प्रभविष्णुता, प्रभावः, प्राबल्यं, प्रबलता, गौरवं, अधिकशक्तिः *f.*, बलाधिक्यं.

PREPONDERANT, *a.* अधिकभारी -रिणी -रि (न्), अतिरिक्तभारी &c., अतिभारी &c.

To PREPONDERATE, *v. n.* अधिकभारी -रिणी -रि भू or अस्, अतिरिक्तभारी &c. भू, अतिभारी &c. भू, गुरुतरभारी &c. भू, गुरुतरः -रा -रं भू, भारेण अतिरिच् in pass. (-रिच्यते) or वृध् (c. 1. वर्धते -र्धितुं), गौरवेण अतिरिच् or वृध्, प्रभावेण अतिरिच्, अधिकः -का -कं भू, अधिकप्रभावः &c. भू or अस्, अधिकशक्तिः -क्तिः -क्ति भू.

PREPOSITION, *s.* (In grammar) उपसर्गः, शब्दयोगी अव्ययशब्दः.

PREPOSITIONAL, PREPOSITIVE, *a.* औपसर्गिकः -की -कं, उपसर्गसम्बन्धी -न्धिनी &c.

To PREPOSSESS, *v. a.* (Pre-occupy). *See* the word.—(Bias in favor of) चित्ताकर्षणं, चित्तावर्जनं कृ, चित्तम् आकृष् or आवृज्.—(Bias against). *See To* PREJUDICE.

PREPOSSESSED, *p. p.* आकृष्टचित्तः -त्ता -त्तं, आकर्षितचित्तः &c., पूर्व्वाकर्षितः -ता -तं, प्रथमदर्शनादपि or दर्शनमात्राद् आकृष्टचित्तः &c., दृष्टमात्राद् एव आकृष्टचित्तः &c., सङ्गी -ङ्गिनी -ङ्गि (न्), ससङ्गः -ङ्गा -ङ्गं.

PREPOSSESSING, *a.* दर्शनमात्रात् or अवलोकनक्षणात् or प्रथमदर्शनात् चित्ताकर्षकः -का -कं, दृष्टमात्रचित्ताकर्षकः &c., चित्तापहारी -रिणी -रि (न्).

PREPOSSESSION, *s.* (Pre-occupation). *See* the word.—(Previous impression). *See* PRECONCEPTION.—(Inclination in favor of) चित्ताकर्षणं, सङ्गः, ग्रहः, आग्रहः, पक्षपातः.

PREPOSTEROUS, *a.* (Inverted in order) विपरीतः -ता -तं, विपरीतक्रमः -मा -मं, विपर्य्यस्तः &c. *See* INVERTED.—(Absurd) असङ्गतः -ता -तं, अयुक्तः -क्ता -क्तं, अनर्थकः -का -कं, युक्तिविरुद्धः -द्धा -द्धं, असम्बद्धः -द्धा -द्धं, अयुक्तिकः -का -कं, न्यायविरुद्धः &c., असमञ्जसः -सा -सं, अयथोचितः -ता -तं.

PREPOSTEROUSLY, *adv.* असङ्गतं, अयुक्तं, अयुक्तिपूर्व्वं, युक्तिविरुद्धं, विपरीतक्रमेण.

PREPOSTEROUSNESS, *s.* असङ्गतत्वं, अयुक्तता -त्वं, युक्तिविरुद्धता, अयुक्तिः *f.*, अनर्थकता, असम्बद्धता -त्वं, न्यायविरुद्धता, असामञ्जस्यं, वैपरीत्यं, क्रमविपर्य्यासः, विपरीतता.

PREPOTENCY, *s.* प्रभावाधिक्यं, बलाधिक्यं, प्रबलता. *See* PREDOMINANCE.

PREPUCE, *s.* लिङ्गाग्रत्वक् *f.* (च्), शिश्नाग्रत्वक् *f.*, लिङ्गाग्रचर्म्म *n.* (न्), अग्रत्वक् *f.*; 'frenum of the prepuce,' सेवनं, सीवनी.

PREREQUISITE, *a.* पूर्व्वाकाङ्क्षितः -ता -तं, पूर्व्वापेक्षितः &c., पूर्व्वावश्यकः -का -कं.

PREREQUISITE, *s.* पूर्व्वावश्यकविषयः, पूर्व्वाकाङ्क्षितविषयः, पूर्व्वावश्यकवस्तु *n.*

PREROGATIVE, *s.* विशेषाधिकारः, असाधारणाधिकारः, अद्वितीयाधिकारः, असामान्याधिकारः, विशेषशक्तिः *f.*, असाधारणशक्तिः *f.*, अद्वितीयक्षमता, विशेषसत्ता.

PRESAGE, *s.* पूर्व्वलक्षणं, पूर्व्वलिङ्गं, पूर्व्वचिह्नं, पूर्व्वसूचना, भविष्यत्सूचना.

To PRESAGE, *v. a.* पूर्व्वं or अग्रे सूच् (c. 10. सूचयति -यितुं), पूर्व्वलक्षणं दा or कृ, पूर्व्वचिह्नं दा, पूर्व्वसूचनं कृ, अग्रसूचनं कृ.

PRESCIENCE, *s.* पूर्व्वज्ञानं, अग्रज्ञानं, अग्रनिरूपणं, भविष्यज्ज्ञानं, भाविज्ञानं, भविष्यज्ञानं, भविष्यद्दर्शनं, प्रवेक्षणं. *See* FOREKNOWLEDGE.

PRESCIENT, *a.* भविष्यज्ज्ञानी -निनी -नि (न्), भाविज्ञानी &c., भविष्यद्दर्शी &c., भविष्यज्ज्ञानी &c., भविष्यद्दर्शी &c., प्रवेक्षन् -क्षन्ती -क्षत् (त्), प्रपश्यन् &c., अनागतदर्शी &c.

To PRESCRIBE, *v. a.* (Direct) निर्दिश् (c. 6. -दिशति -देष्टुं), आदिश्,

प्रदिश्, विनिर्दिश्, कृप्, प्रकृप्, विधा, संविधा, आज्ञा in caus., चुद्, प्रचुद्, शास्, प्रशास्, अनुशास्, सूच्, आज्ञां कृ, नियमं कृ, विधिं कृ.—(Direct medically) उपचारं कृ, औषधं विधा or निर्दिश्.

To PRESCRIBE, *v. n.* (Direct remedies) उपचारं कृ, औषधोपचारं कृ, औषधविधानं कृ, औषधविधिं कृ, औषधप्रयोगं कृ, भेषजप्रयोगं कृ, औषधनिर्देशं कृ.

PRESCRIBED, *p. p.* निर्दिष्टः -ष्टा -ष्टं, निदिष्टः -ष्टा -ष्टं, विहितः -ता -तं, नियमितः &c., चोदितः &c., प्रचोदितः &c., विधियुक्तः -क्ता -क्तं, विधिप्रोक्तः &c., उदितः -ता -तं, वैधिकः -की -कं, वैधः -धी -धं, वाचनिकः -की -कं, उद्दिष्टः -ष्टा -ष्टं, विधीयमानः -ना -नं.

PRESCRIBER, *s.* निर्देष्टा *m.* (ष्टृ), निर्देशकः, आदेष्टा *m.*, विधायी *m.* (न्), अनुशासकः.

PRESCRIPT, *s.* निर्देशः, आदेशः, विधिः *m.*, विधानं, आज्ञा. *See* COMMAND.

PRESCRIPTION, *s.* (Direction) निर्देशः, आदेशः, निदेशः, विधानं, विधिः *m.*, चोदनं -ना, प्रचोदनं, नियमः, शासनं, शास्तिः *f.*, अनुशासनं, प्रेरणा, वचनं.—(Recipe, prescribed medicine) उपचारलेखः, उपचारपत्रं, चिकित्सालेखः, चिकित्सापत्रं, औषधविधिः *m.*, औषधविधानं, उपचारविधिः *m.*—(Immemorial use) अनादिपरम्परा, चिरकालभोगः, चिरकालव्यवहारः, चिरकालीनव्यवहारः, चिरकालपरम्परा, प्राचीनव्यवहारः, प्राचीनभोगः, आचारः.

PRESCRIPTIVE, *a.* (Consisting in or acquired by immemorial use) अनादिपरम्पराप्राप्तः -प्ता -प्तं, अनादिपरम्परायातः -ता -तं, चिरकालभुक्तः -क्ता -क्तं, चिरकालव्यवहृतः -ता -तं, चिरकालव्यवहारितः &c., चिरकालभोगाश्रयी -यिणी -यि (न्), चिरव्यवहारसिद्धः -द्धा -द्धं, आचारिकः -की -कं, व्यवहारिकः &c.

PRESENCE, *s.* (As opposed to absence) प्रत्यक्षता, समक्षता, आभिमुख्यं, अभिमुखता -त्वं, सन्निधानं, सान्निध्यं, सन्निधिः *m.*, पारिमुख्यं, सम्मुखता -त्वं, विद्यमानता -त्वं, वर्त्तमानता, अन्तिकं -कता -त्वं, अपरोक्षता, उपस्थानं, उपस्थितिः *f.*; 'in my presence,' मत्सन्निधाने; 'in presence of,' प्रत्यक्षे -क्षतस्, समक्षं -क्षे, साक्षात्, अग्रे, सम्मुखं -खे, प्रतिमुखं, अभितस्; 'into the presence of,' सकाशं, समीपं, अन्तिकं, साक्षात्; 'they took him into the presence of the magistrate,' धर्म्माधिकारिसमीपं तम् आनीतवन्तः; 'into the presence of her husband,' भर्त्तुः सकाशं or समीपं; 'into my presence,' मत्सकाशं, ममान्तिकं.—(Mien, personal appearance) आकारः, आकृतिः *f.*, रूपं, शरीररूपं, शरीराकारः, शरीरसंस्थानं.—(Presence of mind) चित्ताभ्रान्तिः *f.*, अव्यग्रचित्तत्वं, अव्यग्रता, अभ्रान्तचित्तत्वं, स्वस्थचित्तत्वं, स्थिरचित्तता -त्वं, असम्भ्रमः, अव्यस्तता, अव्याकुलता, सावधानता, चित्तसत्त्वं, सत्त्वं, अस्तब्धता; 'having presence of mind,' अव्यग्रचित्तः -त्ता -त्तं, तत्कालधीः -धीः -धि. *See* PRESENT.

PRESENCE-CHAMBER, *s.* दर्शनशाला, दर्शनगृहं, राजदर्शनशाला.

PRESENT, *a.* (Not absent) प्रत्यक्षः -क्षा -क्षं, विद्यमानः -ना -नं, वर्त्तमानः -ना -नं, अभिमुखः -खा -खी -खं, पारिमुखिकः -की -कं, उपस्थायी -यिनी -यि (न्), उपस्थितः -ता -तं, सन्निहितः -ता -तं, अपरोक्षः -क्षा -क्षं, सम्मुखः -खा -खं, सम्मुखीनः -ना -नं, सन्निधिस्थः -स्था -स्थं, अभिमुखस्थः &c., अन्तिकः -का -कं, समीपः -पा -पं; 'to be present,' उपस्था, वृत्, समास्.—(Now in view or under consideration) प्रस्तुतः -ता -तं, विद्यमानः -ना -नं, उपस्थितः -ता -तं, प्रकृतः -ता -तं; 'present matter,' प्रस्तुतविषयः.—(Now existing, not past or future) वर्त्तमानः -ना -नं, तात्कालिकः -की -कं, तत्क्षणिकः -का -की -कं, सद्यस्कालीनः -ना -नं, सद्यस्कः -स्का -स्कं, वर्त्तमानकालीनः -ना -नं, अधुनातनः -नी -नं, इदानीन्तनः -नी -नं, आधुनिकः -की -कं, साम्प्रतिकः -की -कं, प्रस्तुतकालीनः -ना -नं, अद्यतनः -नी -नं, ऐहिकः -की -कं, ऐहकालिकः &c., अनपेतः -ता -तं; 'present time,' वर्त्तमानकालः, तत्कालः, तत्क्षणः -णं, सद्यस्कालः, तदात्वं, इहकालः, साम्प्रतकालः, इहसमयः, अस्ति indec. भवन्तिः *m.*; 'at the present time,' वर्त्तमानकाले, तत्काले, तत्क्षणे, सद्यस्काले, इहकाले, इहसमये, इदानीं, अधुना, इह, अधुनातनकाले, सम्प्रति, साम्प्रतं, साम्प्रतकाले, एतर्हि, अद्य, प्रस्तुतकाले; 'for the present,' प्रस्तुतकालं, साम्प्रतकालं, इहकालं, साम्प्रतं.—(Present tense) वर्त्तमानं, विद्यमानं; 'the grammatical symbol is लट्.—(Having presence of mind) सावधानः -ना -नं, अभ्रान्तचित्तः -त्ता -त्तं, स्थिरचित्तः &c., अव्यग्रचित्तः &c., स्वस्थचित्तः &c., समाहितचित्तः &c., समाहितमनाः -नाः -नः (स्), सुसमाहितः -ता -तं, अव्याकुलचित्तः &c., तत्कालधीः -धीः -धि, अवहितः -ता -तं.

PRESENT, *s.* (Gift) दानं, प्रदानं, सम्प्रदानं, दत्तं, उपदा, उपदानकं, उपायनं, दक्षिणा, उपहारः -रकं, उपग्राह्यं, उपढौकनं, प्रीतिदानं, प्रदेशनं, प्रादेशनं, पारितोषिकं, प्राभृतं, वितरणं &c. *See* GIFT.—(The time being, the present) वर्त्तमानकालः, तत्कालः, तत्क्षणः, सद्यस्कालः, तदात्वं, साम्प्रतकालः, अधुनातनकालः, इदानीन्तनकालः, प्रस्तुतकालः, आयातः, भवन्तिः *m.*, अस्ति indec., प्रमुखं; 'present and future,' दृष्टादृष्टं.

To PRESENT, *v. a.* (Introduce to the presence of another) प्रविश् (c. 10. -वेशयति -यितुं), दर्शनं कृ in caus., दृश् in caus., पुरस्कृ, प्रवेशनं कृ, परसमीपं or परसकाशम् आनी.—(Present one's self or itself) आत्मानं दृश् in caus. (दर्शयति -यितुं), उपस्था (c. 1. -तिष्ठति -स्थातुं), प्रविश् (c. 6. -विशति -वेष्टुं), दर्शनं दा, प्रवेशं कृ, उपस्थितः -ता -तं भू, आविर्भू, प्रादुर्भू, दृश् in pass., लक्ष् in pass.—(Exhibit) दृश् in caus., प्रदृश्, प्रत्यक्षीकृ, प्रकटीकृ, प्रादुष्कृ, आविष्कृ, व्यक्तीकृ, सूच्, प्रकाश्, प्रसृ in caus.—(Offer, present for acceptance) आहृ, उपाहृ, अभ्याहृ, उपहृ, समुपहृ, उपहारीकृ, प्रदा, अभिदा, सम्प्रदा, उपदा, दा, प्रयम्, ग्रह् in caus., प्रतिग्रह्, प्रतिपद् in caus., उपपद्, ऋ in caus., समृ, निविद् in caus., निक्षिप्, उपढौक्, ढौक्, उपस्था in caus., उपनिधा, उपहरणं कृ.—(Present an oblation) उपहृ, उपहारीकृ, निविद्, निवेदनं कृ, निर्वप्, निर्वपणं कृ, उत्सृज्, उत्सर्गं कृ, बलिदानं कृ, उपायनं कृ.—(Give) दा, प्रदा, उपदा, उपायनं कृ.—(Lay before) उपन्यस्, निविद्, ऋ in caus., समृ.

PRESENTABLE, *a.* (That may be introduced) प्रवेशनीयः -या -यं.—(That may be exhibited) दर्शनीयः -या -यं.—(That may be offered) देयः -या -यं, प्रदेयः -या -यं, उपहार्य्यः -र्य्या -र्य्यं, निवेदनीयः -या -यं.—(Admissible into society) सभ्यः -भ्या -भ्यं, सभायोग्यः -ग्या -ग्यं, पांक्तेयः -या -यं, पांक्त्यः -क्त्या -क्त्यं; 'not presentable,' असभ्यः &c., अपांक्तेयः &c., अपांक्तः &c., अपांक्त्यः &c.

PRESENTATION, *s.* उपहरणं, प्रतिपादनं, प्रतिपत्तिः *f.*, अर्पणं, समर्पणं, निवेदनं, प्रदानं, अभिवाद्यं.—(Of an oblation) बलिदानं, निर्वपणं, निर्वापणं, निर्वापः, उत्सर्गकरणं.—(To a benefice) धर्म्माध्यापकवृत्तिप्रतिपादनं, धर्म्मवृत्तिनियोजनाधिकारः.—(Bad presentation of the child at birth) मूढगर्भः.

PRESENTED, *p. p.* (Introduced to the presence of another) प्रवेशितः -ता -तं, पुरस्कृतः &c., परसमीपं or परसकाशं or परसाक्षाद् आनीतः -ता -तं.—(Exhibited) दर्शितः -ता -तं, प्रदर्शितः &c., प्रत्यक्षीकृतः &c., प्रसारितः &c.—(Presented for acceptance) उपहृतः

-ता -तं, समुपहृतः &c., प्रदत्तः -त्ता -त्तं, प्रत्तः &c., अर्पितः -ता -तं, समर्पितः &c., प्रतिपादितः &c., उपपादितः &c., उपनीतः &c., उपनिहितः &c., उपस्थापितः &c., ढौकितः &c., उपढौकितः &c.—(As an oblation, &c.) उपहृतः &c., उपहारीकृतः &c., निवेदितः &c., निवेदितः &c., उत्सृष्टः -ष्टा -ष्टं, अर्पितः &c.—(Given) दत्तः -त्ता -त्तं, प्रदत्तः &c., नीतः &c., निहितः &c., निक्षिप्तः -प्ता -प्तं, वितारितः -ता -तं, वितीर्णः -र्णा -र्णं.—(Laid before) उपन्यस्तः -स्ता -स्तं, समर्पितः -ता -तं.

Presentiment, *s.* पूर्व्वबोधः, अग्रबोधः, पूर्व्ववासना, पूर्व्ववेदनं, अग्रवेदनं, पूर्व्वभावना, पूर्व्वकल्पना.

Presently, *adv.* (At present) तत्काले, तत्क्षणे, सद्यस्काले. *See* under Present, *a.*—(Soon, in a short time) अनन्तरं, अचिरेण, अचिरात्, क्षणान्तरे, नचिरेण, नचिरात्, शीघ्रं, सत्वरं, आशु, झटिति, सपदि, द्राक्.—(Immediately) अनन्तरं.

Preservable, *a.* रक्षणीयः -या -यं, संरक्षणीयः &c., रक्ष्यः -क्ष्या -क्ष्यं, संरक्ष्यः &c., रक्षितव्यः -व्या -व्यं, गोपनीयः -या -यं, गोप्यः -प्या -प्यं, पालनीयः -या -यं, अवनीयः -या -यं.

Preservation, *s.* रक्षणं, रक्षा, परिरक्षणं, अभिरक्षा -क्षणं, संरक्षा -क्षणं, संरक्षः, गुप्तिः *f.*, त्राणं, परित्राणं, पालनं, प्रतिपालनं, परिपालनं, गोपनं, संगोपनं, अवनं, तारणं, पोषणं, स्थितिः *f.*

Preservative, *a.* रक्षकः -का -कं, संरक्षकः &c., रक्षी -क्षिणी -क्षि (न्), रक्षणकारी -रिणी -रि (न्), पालकः -का -कं, गोपकः -का -कं, गोपिलः -ला -लं, पौष्टिकः -की -कं, रक्षिता -त्री -तृ (तृ), तारकः -का -कं, रक्षणसाधकः -का -कं.

Preservative, *s.* रक्षणं, रक्षणसाधनं, रक्षणोपायः, त्राणं in comp., त्राणसाधनं, त्रं in comp., गुप्तिसाधनं, पात्रं.

To **preserve**, *v. a.* (Save from injury) रक्ष् (c. 1. रक्षति -क्षितुं), अभिरक्ष्, परिरक्ष्, संरक्ष्, प्रतिरक्ष्, त्रै (c. 1. त्रायते, त्रातुं), परित्रै, संत्रै, पाल् (c. 10. पालयति -यितुं), परिपाल्, अभिपाल्, प्रतिपाल्, अनुपाल्, सम्पाल्, उपपाल्, पा (c. 2. पाति -तुं), परिपा, गुप् (c. 1. गोपायति, गोप्तुं, c. 10. गोपयति -यितुं), अभिगुप्, अनुगुप्, प्रगुप्, तॄ in caus. (तारयति -यितुं), अव् (c. 1. अवति -वितुं), धृ (c. 10. धारयति -यितुं), पर्य्याप् in des. (परीप्सति -ते -प्सितुं), परिप्राप् in des., रक्षणं कृ, रक्षां कृ, पालनं कृ, गुप्तिं कृ, गोपनं कृ, अवनं कृ.—(Maintain) धृ, सन्धृ, भृ, सम्भृ, भरणं कृ, पुष् (c. 10. पोषयति -यितुं), पोषणं कृ.—(Conserve, pickle) सन्धा, उपस्कृ, मिष्टीकृ.

Preserve, *s.* (Fruit preserved in sugar) मिष्टफलं, सन्धितफलं, सन्धितं.—(Place for the shelter of game) वीतंसः, वितंसः, जङ्गलपक्ष्यादिरक्षणस्थानं.

Preserved, *p. p.* रक्षितः -ता -तं, संरक्षितः &c., अभिरक्षितः &c., त्राणः -णा -णं, त्रातः -ता -तं, गुप्तः -प्ता -प्तं, गोपितः -ता -तं, संगोपितः &c., पालितः -ता -तं, प्रतिपालितः &c., परिपालितः &c., गोपायितः -ता -तं, तारितः &c., अवितः -ता -तं, धारितः &c., भृतः &c., पोषितः -ता -तं.—(Pickled) सन्धितः -ता -तं, उपस्कृतः &c.

Preserver, *s.* रक्षकः, रक्षी *m.* (न्), त्राता *m.* (तृ), पालकः, पालः, पालयिता *m.* (तृ), रक्षिता *m.* (तृ), संरक्षकः, गोप्ता *m.* (तृ), गोपकः, संगोपकः, गोपः, गोपी *m.* (न्), गुप्तकः, गोपिलः, गोपायकः, तारकः, रक्षणकारी *m.*, रक्षणकर्त्ता *m.* (र्तृ), पालनकारी *m.*, पालनकृत् *m.*, पः in comp., गुप्तिकर्त्ता *m.* (र्तृ), स्थितिकर्त्ता *m.*

To **preside**, *v. a.* अधिष्ठा (c. 1. -तिष्ठति -ते -ष्ठातुं), समधिष्ठा, अध्यास् (c. 2. -आस्ते -आसितुं), अधीश् (c. 2. -ईष्टे -ईशितुं), अध्यक्षः -क्षा -क्षं भू or अस्, अधिकृतः -ता -तं भू, अधिकारी -रिणी -रि भू, अधिभू, प्रभू, अधिपतिर् भू or अस्.—(Exercise superintendence, watch over) अवेक्ष् (c. 1. -ईक्षते -क्षितुं), कार्य्यावेक्षणं कृ, कार्य्येक्षणं कृ, कार्य्यदर्शनं कृ, कार्य्याधीशो भू; 'the deity who presides over learning,' विद्याधिष्ठात्री देवता.

Presided over, *p. p.* अधिष्ठितः -ता -तं, समधिष्ठितः &c., अध्यासितः &c., प्रभूतः &c.

Presidency, *s.* (Superintendence) अध्यक्षता -त्वं, अधिकारः, अधीकारः, अधिष्ठितिः *f.*, अधिष्ठानं, अध्यासः. *See* the word.—(Office of a president) अधिष्ठातृत्वं -ता, अध्यक्षता, अध्यक्षपदं, अधिकारित्वं, अधीशता, आधिपत्यं, प्रभुता, उपद्रष्टृत्वं.—(Country under the jurisdiction of a president) अध्यक्षाधीनः प्रदेशः or देशः or विषयः, मण्डलं.

President, *s.* अध्यक्षः, अधिष्ठाता *m.* (तृ), अध्यासीनः, अधिकारी *m.* (न्), अधिकृतः, अधीशः, अधिपतिः *m.*, अधिपः, पतिः *m.*, प्रभुः *m.*, अधीश्वरः, कर्म्माध्यक्षः, श्रेष्ठी *m.* (न्), नायकः, प्रामाणिकः, उपद्रष्टा *m.*, मुख्यः, उदास्थितः; 'of an assembly,' सभापतिः *m.*, सभाध्यक्षः, सभानायकः, गोष्ठीपतिः *m.*

Presidentship, *s.* अध्यक्षता -त्वं, अधिष्ठातृत्वं, आधिपत्यं. *See* Presidency.

Presiding, *part.* or *a.* अध्यासीनः -ना -नं, अध्यक्षः -क्षा -क्षं, अधिष्ठाता -त्री -तृ (तृ); 'presiding deity,' अधिष्ठात्री देवता; 'the deity presiding over learning,' विद्याधिष्ठात्री देवता.

To **press**, *v. a.* (Squeeze, compress) पीड् (c. 10. पीडयति -यितुं), सम्पीड्, निपीड्, अभिनिपीड्, आपीड्, संकुच्, संहृ, प्रतिसंहृ, घट्ट्, संघट्ट्, संवृ, संहन्.—(Urge, drive) प्रेर्, कृष्, आकृष्, समाकृष्, प्रणुद्.—(Urge, importune) अतिनिर्बन्धेन प्रार्थ् or अभ्यर्थ् or याच्, आग्रहेण प्रार्थ्, वारं वारं प्रार्थ्, पुनः पुनः प्रार्थ्, अतिप्रार्थनेन परम् उद्विज् or आयस् or आक्रम् or उपस्था.—(Inculcate urgently) अतिनिर्बन्धेन or मुहुर्मुहुर् उपदिश् or शिक्ष्.—(Force, constrain) बलेन or बलात्कारेण or बलात् कृ in caus. or प्रवृत् in caus., or expressed generally by the causal form.—(Distress, straiten) बाध् (c. 1. बाधते -धितुं), प्रबाध्, परिबाध्, अधिबाध्, पीड्, उपपीड्, अभिपीड्, क्लिश्, व्यथ्, तप्, सन्तप्, उद्विज् in caus., क्लेशं कृ or दा.—(Impress seamen) बलात्कारेण पुरुषान् धृत्वा नाविकादिकर्म्मणि व्यापृ in caus.

To **press**, *v. n.* (Go forward with force or effort) यत्नतस् or महायत्नेन or सोद्योगं or सोत्साहं प्रया or प्रगम् or अग्रे गम् or अग्रे सृ.—(Bear on, encroach upon) आक्रम्, अभिक्रम्, अध्याक्रम्, उपस्था (c. 1. -तिष्ठति -स्थातुं), समुपस्था, प्रत्युपस्था.—(Crowd, press upon) बाध् (c. 1. बाधते -धितुं), प्रबाध्.

Press, *s.* (Instrument for pressing) चक्रयन्त्रं, चक्रं, पीडनयन्त्रं, पेषणयन्त्रं; 'oil-press,' घरट्टः, तैलिकयन्त्रं, तैलिकचक्रं.—(For printing) मुद्राङ्कनयन्त्रं, मुद्राङ्कनचक्रं.—(Printed publications in general) मुद्रितपुस्तकगणः, मुद्राङ्कितपुस्तकसमूहः.—(Crowd, throng) जनसम्मर्दः, जनसङ्कुलं, लोकसंघः, लोकसम्मर्दः.—(Urgency, urgent pressure) बाधा -धः -धनं, निर्बन्धः, पीडा, भारः.

Pressed, *p. p.* (Squeezed) पीडितः -ता -तं, निपीडितः &c., सम्पीडितः &c., घट्टितः &c., संघट्टितः &c.—(Urged) प्रेरितः -ता -तं.—(Importuned) अतिनिर्बन्धेन प्रार्थितः -ता -तं.—(Distressed, straitened) बाधितः -ता -तं, पीडितः &c., क्लेशितः &c.

Presser, *s.* पीडकः, पीडयिता *m.* (तृ), बाधकः, प्रबाधकः.

PRESSING, *a.* अतिप्रार्थकः -का -कं, निर्बन्धेन प्रार्थकः &c., अतियाचकः &c., निर्बन्धशीलः -ला -लं, बाधकः &c.

PRESSINGLY, *adv.* निर्बन्धेन, सनिर्बन्धं, आग्रहेण, साग्रहं, सबाधं.

PRESSURE, *s.* पीडा, पीडनं, निपीडनं.—(Force) शक्तिः *f.*, बलं, वेगः, भारः, प्रभावः.—(Impulse) प्रेरणा, प्रवर्त्तनं, प्रणोदः, प्ररोचनं, प्रोत्साहः.—(Distress) बाधः -धा -धनं, क्लेशः, पीडा, आकुलता.

PRESTIGE, *s.* मायाशक्तिः *f.*, माया, मोहनशक्तिः *f.*, आकर्षणशक्तिः, इन्द्रियजालं, इन्द्रजालं, वचनशक्तिः *f.*, प्रतारणशक्तिः *f.*

PRESTIGIOUS, *a.* मायाकरः -रा -रं, मायावी -विनी -वि (न्), मायामयः -यी -यं, मायी &c., ऐन्द्रजालिकः -की -कं, मोही &c.

PRESTO, *adv.* द्रुतं, आशु, शीघ्रं, क्षिप्रं, त्वरितं, सत्वरं, अविलम्बितं.

To PRESUME, *v. a.* अविचार्य्य or अविचारपूर्व्वं or अनिर्णयपूर्व्वं or अनिश्चित्य or अनिश्चयपूर्व्वम् अनुमा (c. 2. -माति -तुं, c. 3. -मिमीते) or तर्क् (c. 10. तर्कयति -यितुं) or अनुतर्क् or अवगम् or ऊह् or अनुमानं कृ.

To PRESUME, *v. n.* (Venture without leave, be bold or arrogant) धृष् (c. 5. धृष्णोति, धर्षितुं), प्रधृष्, धृष्टत्वात् or प्रगल्भत्वात् किञ्चिद् अननुज्ञातः कृ, धृष्टत्वात् or प्रगल्भशीलत्वाद् अननुज्ञापूर्व्वं or अनधिकारपूर्व्वं किञ्चित् कृ, धर्षेण आक्रम् (c. 1. -क्रामति -क्रमितुं) or अतिक्रम्, मर्य्यादातिक्रमं कृ, प्रगल्भवद् आचर् (c. 1. -चरति -रितुं), धृष्टवत् or धार्ष्ट्यपूर्व्वं किञ्चित् कृ, प्रगल्भ् (c. 1. -गल्भते -ल्भितुं), दृप् (c. 4. दृप्यति -ते).

PRESUMPTION, *s.* (Supposition without direct proof) अनुमानं, अनुमितिः *f.*, अनुमा, अनुमेयत्वं, अनिर्णयपूर्व्वम् or अनिश्चयपूर्व्वम् or असिद्धान्तपूर्व्वम् अनुमानं, अनिर्णयपूर्व्वा कल्पना, तर्कः, अनुमानग्रहणं.—(Strong probability) सम्भावना, सम्भावनीयता -त्वं, सम्भवः, सत्यसङ्काशता -त्वं.—(Arrogance) धृष्टता, धार्ष्ट्यं, धर्षः, प्रगल्भता, प्रागल्भ्यं, दर्पः, अभिमानं, अत्यभिमानं, निर्लज्जत्वं, अहङ्कारः, अवलेपः, स्मयः, प्रगल्भत्वाद् मर्य्यादातिक्रमः or अत्याचारः -रित्वं.

PRESUMPTIVE, *a.* आनुमानिकः -की -कं, अनुमानसिद्धः -द्धा -द्धं, सम्भावितः -ता -तं, सम्भाव्यः -व्या -व्यं, सम्भावनीयः -या -यं, अनुमानावलम्बी -म्बिनी -म्बि (न्); 'presumptive proof or evidence,' अनुमानं, आनुमानिकप्रमाणं, अनुमाननिर्णयः, अर्थापत्तिः *f.*; 'heir-presumptive,' सम्भावितस्थानाधिकारी *m.* (न्), सप्रतिबन्धस्थानाधिकारी *m.*, सलोपस्थानाधिकारी *m.*, उत्तराधिकारी *m.*

PRESUMPTUOUS, *a.* (Arrogant) धृष्टः -ष्टा -ष्टं, धृष्णुः -ष्णुः -ष्णु, प्रगल्भः -ल्भा -ल्भं, प्रधृष्टः &c., प्रधर्षितः -ता -तं, दृप्तः -प्ता -प्तं, अवलिप्तः -प्ता -प्तं, अभिमानी -निनी -नि (न्), अत्यभिमानी &c., साहसिकः -की -कं, धृष्णक् *m.f.n.* (ज्), निर्लज्जः -ज्जा -ज्जं.—(Founded on presumption) अभिमानमूलः -ला -लं.

PRESUMPTUOUSLY, *adv.* सधर्षं, सधार्ष्ट्यं, धृष्टं, प्रधर्षितं, धृष्टवत्, सप्रागल्भ्यं, प्रागल्भ्येन, प्रगल्भं, प्रगल्भवत्, साभिमानं, अभिमानपुरःसरं.

PRESUMPTUOUSNESS, *s.* धार्ष्ट्यं, धृष्णुत्वं, धृष्टता, प्रगल्भता, प्रागल्भ्यं, प्रधृष्टता, दृप्तता, अवलिप्तता, अभिमानं, अत्यभिमानं, अभिमानिता, साहसिकत्वं.

To PRESUPPOSE, *v. a.* पूर्व्वं or अग्रे क्लृप् or भू in caus., or सूच् (c. 10. सूचयति -यितुं), पूर्व्वसूचनं कृ, पूर्व्वकल्पनां कृ, पूर्व्वग्रहणं कृ, पूर्व्वभावनां कृ.

PRESUPPOSED, *p. p.* पूर्व्वकल्पितः -ता -तं, पूर्व्वभावितः &c., पूर्व्वगृहीतः &c.

PRESUPPOSITION, *s.* पूर्व्वकल्पना, पूर्व्वभावना, पूर्व्वग्रहणं, पूर्व्वमतं.

PRETENCE, *s.* (Pretext, feint) छद्म *n.* (न्), अपदेशः, व्यपदेशः, छलं, व्याजः, उपधा, कूटः -टं, कपटः, कैतवं, अलीकरणं, मिषं.—(False plea) मिथ्याहेतुः *m.*, मिथ्यानिमित्तं, हेतुः *m.*, निमित्तं; 'under pretence of studying the Shastras,' शास्त्राध्ययनहेतुना.—(Claim) अधिकारः, अभिमानं, अभियोगः; 'false claim' मिथ्याभिमानं, मिथ्याभियोगः.

To PRETEND, *v. a.* or *n.* (Sham, feign) छद्म कृ, कूटं कृ, व्याजं कृ, छलं कृ, कपटं कृ, अलीकं कृ, छल् (c. 10. छलयति -यितुं), वेशं धृ (c. 10. धारयति -यितुं) or भृ, छद्मवेशं धृ. Often expressed by the root दृश् in caus., or by मिथ्या in comp.; as, 'he pretends to be asleep,' आत्मानं प्रसुप्तम् इव or प्रसुप्तवद् दर्शयति, मिथ्यासुप्तो or मिथ्याप्रसुप्तो भवति; 'he pretends to be dead,' आत्मानं मृतवत् सन्दर्शयति; 'to pretend to be just,' साधुवेशं धृ, आर्य्यवेशं धृ, धर्म्मध्वजी -जिनी -जि भू, आर्य्यरूपः -पा -पं भू.—(Allege a false plea) मिथ्याहेतुं वद्, मिथ्यानिमित्तं वद्, मिथ्या वद्.—(Lay claim, pretend to) अभिमन् (c. 4. -मन्यते -मन्तुं), मिथ्या अभिमन्, मिथ्याभिमानं कृ, मिथ्या ग्रह्, अनधिकारपूर्व्वं ग्रह्, अभिप्रेतः -ता -तं भू; 'to pretend to learning,' विद्याभिमानं कृ, विद्याभिप्रेतः -ता -तं भू, विद्याभिमानी -निनी -नि भू. *See* PRETENDER, *s.*

PRETENDED, *p.p.* छाद्मिकः -की -कं, कौटिकः -की -कं, कौटः -टी -टं, सव्याजः -जा -जं, सच्छलः -ला -लं, अलीकृतः -ता -तं, ध्वजी &c. in comp., छद्म or कपट or कूट or मिथ्या in comp.; as, 'a pretended ascetic,' तापसध्वजी *m.* (न्), छद्मतापसः, कूटतापसः; 'pretended services,' मिथ्योपचारः; 'pretended reason,' मिथ्याहेतुः *m.*, मिथ्यानिमित्तं.

PRETENDEDLY, *adv.* मिथ्या, सकपटं, सव्याजं, सकूटं, छलेन, छद्म or कपट in comp.; as, 'pretendedly asleep,' मिथ्याप्रसुप्तः -प्ता -प्तं; 'pretendedly religious,' कपटधर्म्मी &c.

PRETENDER, *s.* छाद्मिकः, सव्याजः, वेशधारी *m.* (न्), अभिमानी *m.* (न्), अभियोक्ता *m.* (क्तृ), अभियोगी *m.* (न्), ध्वजी *m.*, मन्य or मिथ्या in comp.; as, 'a pretender to learning,' विद्याभिमानी *m.*, विद्याभिप्रेतः, मिथ्यापण्डितः, पण्डितम्मन्यः, विद्याध्वजी *m.* (न्); 'pretender to virtue or religion,' कपटधर्म्मी *m.*, धर्म्मध्वजी *m.*, सव्याजधर्म्मी *m.*, धर्म्माभिमानी *m.*, साधुम्मन्यः आर्य्यवेशधारी *m.*, धार्म्मिकवेशधारी *m.*; 'to the sovereignty,' राज्याभियोगी *m.* (न्), राज्यस्वत्ववादी *m.*, राज्यलिप्सुः *m.*

PRETENSION, *s.* अभिमानं, अधिकारः, स्वत्ववादः, स्वाधिकारवादः, स्वामित्ववादः, स्वार्थवादः, अभियोगः; 'pretension to learning,' विद्याभिमानं; 'false pretension,' मिथ्याभिमानं, मिथ्याभियोगः.—(Desire of obtaining honor, power, fame, &c.) यशोलिप्सा, यशोलोभः, प्रभावाकांक्षा, प्रभावलिप्सा, प्रभुत्वलिप्सा, महत्त्वलिप्सा, महत्त्वाकांक्षा, प्रतिष्ठालिप्सा, जिगीषा; 'pretension to the sovereignty,' राज्यलिप्सा, राज्यस्वत्ववादः, राज्याभियोगः.

PRETER-IMPERFECT, *a.* (In grammar) अपूर्णभूतः -ता -तं.

PRETERIT, *a.* (In grammar) भूतः -ता -तं, परोक्षः -क्षा -क्षं; 'tense,' भूतं, परोक्षं, परोक्षभूतं.

PRETERITION, *s.* अतिक्रमः -मणं, अत्ययः, व्यतिक्रमः, अतिचारः, अतिचरणं.

PRETERMISSION, *s.* त्यागः, परित्यागः, अपासनं, उपात्ययः, लंघनं.

To PRETERMIT, *v. a.* (Omit) परित्यज्, त्यज्, अपास्, अतिक्रम्, व्युत्क्रम्.

PRETERMITTED, *p. p.* परित्यक्तः -क्ता -क्तं, अपासितः -ता -तं, अन्तरितः &c.

PRETERNATURAL, *a.* प्रकृतिक्रमबाह्यः -ह्या -ह्यं, प्रकृतिक्रमवहिर्भूतः -ता -तं, निसर्गक्रमबाह्यः &c., प्रकृतिनियमबाह्यः &c., निसर्गनियमबाह्यः &c., प्रकृतिक्रमातीतः -ता -तं, प्रकृतिमार्गातीतः &c., प्रकृतिमार्गबाह्यः &c., अतिप्रकृतिः -तिः -ति, अप्राकृतः -ता -तं, विलक्षणः -णा -णं, अद्भुतः -ता -तं, आश्चर्य्यः -र्य्या -र्य्यं.

PRETERNATURALLY, *adv.* प्रकृतिमार्गवहिस्, प्रकृतिक्रमवहिस्, अद्भुतं, वैलक्षण्येन.

PRETERPERFECT, *a.* (In grammar) पूर्णभूतः -ता -तं, परोक्षभूतः &c.

PRETERPLUPERFECT, *a.* (In grammar) प्राक्पूर्णभूतः -ता -तं.

PRETEXT, *s.* छद्म *n.* (न्), अपदेशः, व्यपदेशः, उपधा, व्याजः, छलं, उपदेशः, निमित्तं, छद्मीकरणं, मिथ्याहेतुः *m.*, मिथ्यानिमित्तं, संवरणं.

PRETTILY, *adv.* चारु, सुन्दरं, सौन्दर्य्येण, मञ्जु, चारु or मञ्जु in comp.; 'singing prettily,' मञ्जुस्वनः -ना -नं; 'smiling prettily,' चारुहासी -सिनी -सि (न्).

PRETTINESS, *s.* चारुता -त्वं, सौन्दर्य्यं, सुरूपता, चारुरूपता, सुदृश्यता, दर्शनीयता, वामता -त्वं, विनीतता -त्वं, मञ्जुता -त्वं, रूपलावण्यं.

PRETTY, *a.* चारुः -र्वी -रु, चारुदर्शनः -ना -नं, सुन्दरः -रा -री -रं, चारुमान् -मती -मत् (त्), सुदृश्यः -श्या -श्यं, सुरूपः -पी -पं, रूपवान् -वती -वत् (त्), चारुरूपः &c., सुरूपी -पिणी -पि (न्), सुरेखः -खा -खं, दर्शनीयः -या -यं, विनीतः -ता -तं, आकारशुद्धः -द्धा -द्धं, वामः -मा -मं, मञ्जुः -ञ्जुः -ञ्जु, मञ्जुलः -ला -लं; 'having a pretty face,' चारुवदनः -ना -नी -नं, सुमुखः -खा -खी -खं; 'having pretty eyes,' चारुलोचनः -ना -नी -नं, सुनयनः -ना -नी -नं; 'having pretty teeth,' सुदन्तः -न्ता -न्तं, चारुदन्तः &c.

PRETTY, *adv.* (Moderately, in some degree) ईषत्, कियत्, अल्पं, अल्पमात्रं, स्तोकं, अभृशं, परिमितं, आ prefixed, कल्प or देश्य or देशीय affixed; 'pretty warm,' ईषदुष्णः -ष्णा -ष्णं, मन्दोष्णः &c., 'pretty ripe,' आपक्वः -क्वा -क्वं; 'pretty clever,' पटुकल्पः -ल्पा -ल्पं, पटुदेश्यः -श्या -श्यं, पटुदेशीयः -या -यं.—(Pretty nearly) प्रायस्, प्रायशस्, भूयिष्ठं, ईषदूनं, अल्पोनं; 'pretty nearly finished,' समाप्तभूयिष्ठः -ष्ठा -ष्ठं; 'pretty nearly dead,' मृतप्रायः -या -यं.

To PREVAIL, *v. n.* (Overcome) प्रभू, अभिभू, पराभू, जि, पराजि, विजि, निर्जि, अतिक्रम्, अधिक्रम्, अतिशी.—(Be predominant, efficacious) अतिरिच् in pass. (-रिच्यते), व्यतिरिच्, उद्रिच्, प्रभू, प्रबलीभू, प्रबलः -ला -लं भू, प्रोथ् (c. 1. प्रोथति -थितुं), सबलः -ला -लं भू, क्षमः -मा -मं भू, बलवत्तमः -मा -मं भू.—(Be in force) प्रभू, प्रबलीभू, प्रचलः -ला -लं भू, प्रचरितः -ता -तं भू, प्रचलीभू, सिद्धः -द्धा -द्धं भू, प्रसिद्धः -द्धा -द्धं भू, सिद्धीभू, प्रसिद्धीभू, निष्पन्नः -न्ना -न्नं भू.—(Succeed) सिध् (c. 4. सिध्यति -ते), सिद्धीभू.—(Persuade, induce) अनुनी, आकृष्, प्रोत्सह्, उत्सह्, प्रवृत् in caus., नियुज् in caus., प्रयुज् or expressed by the causal form. *See To* PERSUADE, &c.

PREVAILING, *part.* or *a.* (Predominant) प्रबलः -ला -लं, प्रभूतः -ता -तं, प्रसिद्धः -द्धा -द्धं, अतिरिक्तः -क्ता -क्तं, अतिरेकी -किणी &c., अधिकः -का -कं, प्रधानः -ना -नं भू, प्रचलः -ला -लं.—(Efficacious) प्रभावी &c., सप्रभावः -वा -वं, प्रभविष्णुः -ष्णुः -ष्णु, साधकः -का -धिका -कं, सफलः -ला -लं.—(General) साधारणः -णा -णी -णं, प्रसिद्धः -द्धा -द्धं, सर्व्वत्र प्रचलः -ला -लं or प्रचलितः -ता -तं. *See* PREVALENT.

PREVALENCE, PREVALENCY, *s.* प्रचारः, प्रचलत्वं, प्रसिद्धिः *f.*, प्रसिद्धता, प्रभावः, प्राबल्यं, प्रचरणं, प्रचलनं, प्रचलितत्वं, सर्व्वत्र व्याप्तिः *f.* or अभिव्याप्तिः *f.* or विस्तारः, व्यापकता -त्वं, प्रभूतता -त्वं, प्रबलता, प्रभविष्णुता, प्रवृत्तिः *f.*, प्रधानता, प्राधान्यं, प्राभवं, अतिरेकः, अतिरिक्तता, आधिक्यं, साधारणता, साधारण्यं, सर्व्वसाधारणव्यवहारः.

PREVALENT, *a.* प्रबलः -ला -लं, प्रचलितः -ता -तं, प्रचरितः -ता -तं, प्रसिद्धः -द्धा -द्धं, प्रभूतः -ता -तं, प्रबलः -ला -लं, प्रभविष्णुः -ष्णुः -ष्णु, प्रवृत्तः -त्ता -त्तं, व्यापकः -का -कं, साधारणः -णा -णी -णं; 'universally prevalent,' सर्व्वत्र प्रचलः &c. or प्रसिद्धः &c.

PREVALENTLY, *adv.* प्रसिद्धं, प्रबलं, प्राबल्येन, अतिरिक्तं, सप्रभावं.

To PREVARICATE, *v. n.* अर्थवैकल्यं कृ, वक्रोक्त्या सत्यवैकल्यं कृ or यथार्थवैकल्यं कृ, वक्रोक्तिं कृ, वक्रं वद् (c. 1. वदति -दितुं), वाक्छलं कृ, निह्नु (c. 2. -ह्नुते -ह्नोतुं), अपदिश् (c. 6. -दिशति -देष्टुं), व्यपदिश्, अपदेशं कृ, व्यपदेशं कृ, निह्नवेन वद्, अपदेशेन वद्, निह्नवोत्तरं कृ, हीनवादं कृ, अन्यवादं कृ, अपलापं कृ.

PREVARICATING, *a.* हीनवादी -दिनी -दि (न्), अन्यवादी &c., निह्नववादी &c., वक्रवादी &c., वक्रोक्तिवादी &c., व्यपदेशवादी &c.

PREVARICATION, *s.* वक्रोक्तिः *f.*, हीनवादः, वाक्छलं, अर्थवैकल्यं, यथार्थवैकल्यं, सत्यवैकल्यं, अन्यवादः, अन्यवचनं, हीनवचनं, निह्नुतिः *f.*, निह्नवोत्तरं, अपलापः, अपदेशः, व्यपदेशः, व्यपदेशवादः, छद्मवादः, उत्तराभासः.

PREVARICATOR, *s.* हीनवादी &c., निह्नववादी &c., अन्यवादी. *See* PREVARICATING.

PREVENIENT, *a.* अग्रगः -गा -गं, अग्रवर्त्ती -र्त्तिनी -र्त्ति (न्), अग्रगामी &c., पूर्व्वसरः -रा -रं, अग्रसरः &c. *See* PRECEDENT, *a.*

To PREVENT, *v. a.* (Hinder) निवृ (c. 10. -वारयति -यितुं), विनिवृ, प्रतिवृ, आवृ, वृ, रुध्, प्रतिरुध्, निरुध्, संरुध्, अवरुध्, उपरुध्, प्रतिषिध्, निषिध्, बाध्, प्रतिबन्ध्, विहन्, व्याहन्, प्रतिहन्, स्तम्भ्, विष्टम्भ्, निवृत् (c. 10. -वर्त्तयति -यितुं), प्रत्याख्या (c. 2. -ख्याति -तुं), विघ्न, रोधं कृ, अवरोधं कृ, प्रतिबन्धं कृ, प्रतिकृ.—(Go before) अग्रे गम् or सृ, अग्रे या or वृत्. *See To* PRECEDE.

PREVENTABLE, *a.* निवारणीयः -या -यं, निवार्य्यः -र्य्या -र्य्यं, वारणीयः &c.

PREVENTED, *p. p.* निवारितः -ता -तं, वारितः &c., रुद्धः -द्धा -द्धं, निरुद्धः &c., विरुद्धः &c., अवरुद्धः &c., उपरुद्धः &c., प्रतिषिद्धः -द्धा -द्धं, निषिद्धः &c., बाधितः -ता -तं, प्रतिबद्धः -द्धा -द्धं, विहतः -ता -तं, व्याहतः &c., प्रतिहतः &c., विघ्नितः &c., स्तम्भितः &c., निवर्त्तितः &c., साप्रतिनिवृत्तः -त्ता -त्तं; 'prevented from seeing by the smoke,' धूमोपरुद्धदृष्टिः -ष्टिः -ष्टि.

PREVENTION, *s.* निवारणं, वारणं, निवारः, रोधः -धनं, अवरोधनं, निरोधः, प्रतिरोधः, उपरोधः, संरोधः, प्रतिबन्धः -न्धनं, प्रतिषेधः -धनं, निषेधः, विघातः, व्याघातः, प्रतीकारः. *See* HINDERANCE.—(Going before) अग्रगमनं, पुरोगमनं.

PREVENTIVE, *a.* वारकः -का -कं, निवारकः &c., बाधकः &c., प्रतिषेधकः &c., प्रतिबाधकः &c., रोधकः &c., प्रतिरोधकः &c., व्याघातकः &c.

PREVENTIVE, *s.* वारणं, निवारणं, बाधकः, प्रतिबन्धकं, निवारकं.

PREVIOUS, *a.* पूर्व्वः -र्व्वा -र्व्वी -र्व्वं, पौर्व्विकः -की -कं, पूर्व्वकः &c., पूर्व्वगतः -ता -तं, पूर्व्वभूतः -ता -तं, पूर्व्ववृत्तः -त्ता -त्तं, पूर्व्वसिद्धः -द्धा -द्धं, पूर्व्वजातः &c., भूतपूर्व्वः -र्व्वा -र्व्वं, पूर्व्वतनः -नी -नं, वृत्तपूर्व्वः &c., जातपूर्व्वः &c., प्रागागतः -ता -तं, प्राग्भूतः &c., प्राग्भवः -वा -वं, अग्रः -ग्रा -ग्रं, अग्रभूतः -ता -तं, प्रथमः -मा -मं, प्राक् in comp.; 'previous possession,' पूर्व्वभुक्तिः *f.*; 'previous existence,' प्राग्भावः.

PREVIOUSLY, *adv.* पूर्व्वं, पूर्व्वकं, पूर्व्वतस्, अग्रे, अग्रतस्, पुरस्, पुरस्तात्, प्राक्, प्रथमतस्; 'done previously,' पूर्व्वकृतः -ता -तं.

PREVIOUSNESS, *s.* पूर्व्वत्वं -ता, अग्रत्वं -ता, प्रथमता -त्वं, प्राथम्यं, आदित्वं.

PREVISION, *s.* पूर्व्वदृष्टिः *f.*, अग्रदृष्टिः *f.*, प्रदर्शनं, अग्रनिरूपणं.

PREY, *s.* (That which is seized to be devoured) आमिषं, मांसं, भक्ष्यं, भक्षणीयं, खाद्यं, भोज्यं.—(Booty) लोप्त्रं, लोत्रं, लोतं, लुप्तं, लुण्टा. *See* PLUNDER.—(Beast of prey) हिंस्रपशुः *m.*, पशुभक्षकः, पशूपजीवी *m.* (न्), आमिषाशी *m.*, आमिषभुक् *m.* (ज्), आमिषप्रियः, मांसाशी *m.*, मांसखादकपशुः *m.*, दशेरः, प्रसहः -हनः.—(Bird of prey) प्रतुदः, विष्किरः, नखविष्किरः, बलिभुक् *m.* (ज्), बलिप्रियः.

To PREY, *v. a.* (Seize and devour) आमिषं धृत्वा or हत्वा भक्ष् or खाद् or ग्रस्.—(Corrode) क्रमशः क्षि in caus. or नश् in caus. —(Prey upon) लुण्ट् or लुस्ट्. *See To* PLUNDER.

PRIAPISM, *s.* ध्वजोच्छ्रायः, ध्वजोच्छ्रयः, शिश्नोच्छ्रयः, लिङ्गोच्छ्रायः.

PRICE, *s.* (Value set or paid) मूल्यं, अर्घः, अवक्रयः, पणः, भाटकः, पण्यं, पणता; 'high price,' बहुमूल्यं, महामूल्यं, दुर्मूल्यं, महार्घः, महार्घ्यं; 'low price,' अल्पमूल्यं, सुमूल्यं; 'what is the price?' कियता मूल्येन विक्रीयते; 'I will not give such a price,' एतावन् मूल्यं न दिास्यामि.—(Reward, recompense) फलं, वेतनं.

PRICED, *a.* (High-priced) महामूल्यः -ल्या -ल्यं, दुर्मूल्यः &c., बहुमूल्यः &c., महार्घः -र्घा -र्घं, महार्घ्यः -र्घ्या -र्घ्यं.—(Low-priced) अल्पमूल्यः &c., अल्पार्घः -र्घा -र्घं, सुमूल्यः &c.

PRICELESS, *a.* अनर्घ्यः -र्घ्या -र्घ्यं, अनर्घः -र्घा -र्घं, अमूल्यः -ल्या -ल्यं.

To PRICK, *v. a.* (Puncture) व्यध् (c. 4. विध्यति, व्यद्धुं), तुद् (c. 6. तुदति, तोत्तुं), वितुद्, छिद्र् (c. 10. छिद्रयति -यितुं), भिद् (c. 7. भिनत्ति, भेत्तुं), निर्भिद्; 'with a thorn or sharp-pointed substance,' कण्टकेन or शल्येन व्यध् or वितुद्; 'with a needle,' सूच्या व्यध् or भिद्.—(Pain by puncture, sting) व्यथ् (c. 10. व्यथयति -यितुं), पीड्, तप्, सन्तप्, मर्म्म व्यध्.—(Goad) प्रतोदेन तुद् or वितुद्.—(Incite) प्रेर्, प्रचुद्, प्रणुद्, उत्तिज्, प्रोत्सह्.—(Erect the ears) कर्णौ स्तब्धीकृ or उन्नम् or उच्छ्रि or उन्नी or उच्चीकृ; 'an animal that pricks its ears,' स्तब्धकर्णः -र्णा -र्णं, स्तब्धश्रोत्रः -त्रा -त्रं.—(Designate by a puncture) सूच्या अङ्क् or चिह्न्.

PRICK, *s.* (Puncture) वेधः -धनं, तोदः, सूचिः -ची *f.*, सूचनं -ना, व्यधः -धनं, उत्तुण्डितं.—(Instrument for pricking) तोदनं, प्रतोदः, तोत्रं, सूचिः -ची -चिनी -चिका, शल्यं, कण्टकः.—(Sharp pain) तोदः, शूलः -लं, व्यथा, यातना, तीक्ष्णव्यथा.

PRICKED, *p. p.* विद्धः -द्धा -द्धं, वेधितः -ता -तं, तोदितः -ता -तं, तुन्नः -न्ना -न्नं, छिद्रितः -ता -तं, भिन्नः -न्ना -न्नं, सशल्यः -ल्या -ल्यं, शल्यविद्धः &c., कण्टकविद्धः &c., सूचिभिन्नः &c.; 'at heart,' विद्धमर्म्मा -र्म्मा -र्म्म (न्), भिन्नमर्म्मा &c., विद्धहृदयः -या -यं.—(Pained) व्यथितः -ता -तं, अनुभूततीक्ष्णव्यथः -था -थं.

PRICKER, *s.* (Instrument for pricking) तोदनं, तोत्रं, प्रतोदः, सूचिः -ची *f.*, सूचिका, शल्यं.—(One who pricks) वेधकः.

PRICKING, *s.* (Act of piercing with a sharp point) वेधः -धनं, व्यधः -धनं, शल्यवेधनं, कण्टकवेधनं, तोदः -दनं, प्रतोदः -दनं, सूचिः -ची *f.*, सूचनं -ना.—(Sensation of sharp pain) तोदः, शूलः -लं, तीक्ष्णव्यथा.

PRICKLE, *s.* कण्टकः -कं, शूकः -कं, सूचिः -ची *f.*, त्वक्कण्टकः.

PRICKLINESS, *s.* कण्टकितत्वं, सकण्टकत्वं, सशूकत्वं, बहुकण्टकत्वं.

PRICKLY, *a.* कण्टकितः -ता -तं, कण्टकी -किनी -कि (न्), सकण्टकः -का -कं, बहुकण्टकः -का -कं, प्रचुरकण्टकः &c., शूकी &c., शूकवान् -वती -वत् (त्), सशूकः -का -कं, बहुशूकः &c.

PRICKLY-PEAR, *s.* विदरं, विषसारकं.

PRIDE, *s.* गर्व्वः, दर्पः, अहङ्कारः, अहङ्कृतिः *f.*, अभिमानं -नता, अभिमानिता, मानं, मानिता, उद्धतिः *f.*, औद्धत्यं, चित्तसमुन्नतिः *f.*, चित्तोन्नतिः *f.*, मदः, मादः, दृप्तता, अवलेपः, अवहेला -लनं, अहम्मानं, अहम्मतिः *f.*, ममता, दम्भः, मन्युः *m.*, आत्माभिमानं, उन्मादः, आटोपः, साटोपत्वं, प्रतिभानं, प्रौढता, धर्षः, प्रगल्भता, उन्माथः, शौटीर्य्यं, शौण्डीरता, आवेशः, उत्सेकः, उत्सिक्तता; 'pride of caste,' जात्यभिमानं; 'of riches,' धनदर्पः; 'of strength,' बलदर्पः, बलावलेपः.—(Generous or proper pride) अभिमानं, गुणाभिमानं, स्वगुणाभिमानं.

To PRIDE, *v. a.* (One's self) आत्मानं श्लाघ् (c. 1. श्लाघते -घितुं), कत्थ् (c. 1. कत्थते -त्थितुं), विकत्थ्, both with instr. c. of the thing on which one prides one's self; आत्मानं मन् (c. 4. मन्यते, मन्तुं), अभिमन् with two acc., अभिमानं कृ; 'he prides himself on his learning,' आत्मानं विद्यया श्लाघते, आत्मानं पण्डितं मन्यते, विद्याभिमानं करोति; 'one who prides himself on his learning,' पण्डितम्मन्यः; 'she prides herself on her beauty,' आत्मानं सौन्दर्य्येण श्लाघते, आत्मानं सुन्दरीं मन्यते; 'one who does so,' सुन्दरीम्मन्या, रूपगर्विता.

PRIER, *s.* परकार्य्यनिरूपकः, परचेष्टानिरूपकः, परकार्य्यचर्चकः.

PRIEST, *s.* (Member of the Brahminical caste) ब्राह्मणः, विप्रः, द्विजः, द्विजातिः *m.*, द्विजन्मा *m.* (न्), देवलः, भूदेवः; 'who is learned in the Vedas,' श्रोत्रियः, वेदविद् *m.*, वेदविद्वान् *m.* (स्), मन्त्रविद् *m.*, मन्त्रज्ञः.—(Sacrificing or officiating priest) याजकः, याज्ञिकः, याजी *m.* (न्), यज्ञकृत् *m.*, होता *m.* (तृ), हविर्याजी *m.*, प्रवर्ग्यः.—(Family or domestic priest) पुरोहितः, पुरोधाः *m.* (स्), ऋत्विक् *m.* (ज्), कुलविप्रः, कुलाचार्य्यः.—(Spiritual preceptor, officiator in sacred offices) आचार्य्यः, उपाध्यायः, गुरुः *m.*, पुरोहितः, धर्म्माध्यापकः, धर्म्मशिक्षकः, धर्म्मोपदेशकः. *See* CLERGYMAN.

PRIESTCRAFT, *s.* पुरोहितछलं, उपाध्यायछलं, उपाध्यायकैतवं, उपाध्यायकपटः -टं, आचार्य्यकापट्यं, धर्म्माध्यापककैतवं.

PRIESTESS, *s.* याजिनी, याज्ञिका, होत्री, उपाध्याया, धर्म्मोपदेशिनी.

PRIESTHOOD, *s.* (Office or character of a priest) पौरोहित्यं, पुरोहितत्वं, आर्त्विज्यं, उपाध्यायपदं, धर्म्माध्यापकपदं, ब्राह्मण्यं, ब्राह्मणता -त्वं.—(The order of priests) पुरोहितवर्गः, पुरोहितगणः, उपाध्यायवर्गः, याज्ञिकवर्गः, धर्म्माध्यापकवर्गः, धर्म्माध्यापकगणः, याजकसमूहः, उपाध्यायसमूहः, पौरोहित्यं.

PRIESTLY, *a.* पौरोहितः -ती -तं, पौरोहितिकः -की -कं, पुरोहितयोग्यः -ग्या -ग्यं, पुरोहितसम्बन्धी &c., याजकीयः -या -यं, याज्ञिकसम्बन्धी &c., उपाध्यायसम्बन्धी &c., पौरोहित्यसम्बन्धी &c., धर्म्माध्यापकसम्बन्धी &c.

PRIEST-RIDDEN, *a.* पुरोहिताधीनः -ना -नं, उपाध्यायाधीनः &c., पुरोहितवशः &c.

PRIG, *s.* दाम्भिकः, दम्भी *m.* (न्), रूपगर्वितः, दर्शनीयमानी *m.* (न्).

PRIGGISH, *a.* दाम्भिकः -की -कं, आत्माभिमानी -निनी -नि (न्).

PRIM, *s.* अतिविनीतः -ता -तं, स्वकामविनीतः &c., अतिसूक्ष्मः -क्ष्मा -क्ष्मं, सूक्ष्मनियमनिष्ठः -ष्ठा -ष्ठं, सूक्ष्मादरशीलः -ला -लं, अत्यादरशीलः &c., अत्याचारी &c.

PRIMACY, *s.* प्रधानधर्म्माध्यक्षपदं, मुख्यधर्म्माध्यक्षपदवी.

PRIMARILY, *adv.* प्रथमतस्, प्राथम्येन, पूर्व्वं, पूर्व्वतस्, मुख्यशस्, मुख्यतस्, आदितस्, प्रधानतस्, प्राधान्येन.

PRIMARINESS, *s.* प्रथमता, प्राथम्यं, मुख्यता, प्रधानता, प्राधान्यं.

PRIMARY, *a.* (First) प्रथमः -मा -मं, प्राथमिकः -की -कं, आद्यः -द्या -द्यं, आदिमः -मा -मं, आदि in comp., पूर्व्वः -र्व्वा -र्व्वं, पौर्व्विकः -की -कं. —(Original) मौलः -ली -लं, मौलिकः -की -कं, मूलिकः -का -कं, आद्यः -द्या -द्यं; 'primary cause,' निदानं, आदिकारणं, आदिबीजं, आद्यबीजं. *See* PRIMITIVE.—(First in dignity, chief) प्रधानः -ना -नं, मुख्यः -ख्या -ख्यं, प्रमुखः -खा -खं, अग्र्यः -ग्र्या -ग्र्यं, अग्रियः -या -यं, अग्र्यः -ग्र्या -ग्र्यं.—(Elementary) आरम्भकः -का -कं, प्रारम्भकः.

PRIMATE, *s.* प्रधानधर्म्माध्यक्षः, मुख्यधर्म्माध्यक्षः, प्रधानोपाध्यायः, मुख्योपाध्यायः, प्रधानधर्म्माधिपतिः *m.*, मुख्यधर्म्माधिपतिः *m.*

PRIME, *a.* (First) प्रथमः -मा -मं, प्राथमिकः &c. *See* PRIMARY.—(First in rank, chief) मुख्यः -ख्या -ख्यं, प्रधानः -ना -नं, प्रमुखः -खा -खं, अग्रः -ग्रा -ग्रं, उत्तमः -मा -मं; 'prime minister,' मुख्यमन्त्री *m.* (न्), प्रधानमन्त्री *m.*, महामन्त्री *m.*, प्रधानामात्यः, मुख्यामात्यः; 'office of prime minister,' मुख्यमन्त्रिता.—(First in excellence) उत्कृष्टः -ष्टा -ष्टं, श्रेष्ठः -ष्ठा -ष्ठं, शिष्टः -ष्टा -ष्टं, उत्तमः -मा -मं, वरः -रा -रं, सर्वोत्कृष्टः &c., सर्वश्रेष्ठः &c.—(Full, blooming) प्रौढः -ढा -ढं.

PRIME, *s.* (Dawn) उदयः, दिनारम्भः, दिवसमुखं, दिनादिः *m.*—(Beginning) आरम्भः, आदिः *m.*—(Best state, heyday, height) प्रौढिः *f.*, प्रौढता, अक्षतता -त्वं, उत्तमता -त्वं, उत्तमावस्था, उत्तमदशा, सिद्धिः *f.*; 'the prime of youth,' यौवनप्रौढिः *f.*, प्रौढयौवनं, अक्षतयौवनं, नवयौवनं, यौवनश्रीः *f.*, 'in the prime of youth,' प्रौढयौवनः-ना-नं, अक्षतयौवनः &c.—(Best part) उत्तमभागः, उत्तमांशः.

To PRIME, *v. a.* आग्नेययन्त्रोपरि ज्वलनचूर्णं धा (c. 3. दधाति, धातुं).

PRIMELY, *adv.* प्रथमतस्, प्रधानतस्.—(Excellently) उत्तमं, श्रेष्ठं, सुष्ठु.

PRIMENESS, *s.* श्रेष्ठता, उत्कृष्टता, उत्तमता, उत्कर्षः, सारत्वं.

PRIMER, *s.* बालकशिक्षार्थं प्रथमपुस्तकं or आरम्भपुस्तकं, व्याकरणारम्भः.

PRIMEVAL, PRIMEVOUS, *a.* प्राक्तनः -नी -नं, सनातनः -नी -नं, आद्यः -द्या -द्यं, आद्यकालीनः -ना -नं, मौलः -ली -लं, मौलिकः -की -कं, प्राक्तनकालीनः -ना -नं, प्राक्कालीनः &c.

PRIMITIVE, *a.* (Pertaining to the beginning, original) प्रथमकालिकः -की -कं, आद्यकालिकः &c., प्राथमिकः -की -कं, प्रथमः -मा -मं. *See* the last.—(Not derived, primary) मूलिकः -का -कं, मौलिकः -की -कं, मौलः -ली -लं, अव्युत्पन्नः -न्ना -न्नं.—(Following ancient forms) प्राक्कालीनरीतिनिष्ठः -ष्ठा -ष्ठं, वृद्धाचारसेवी &c., प्राक्तनव्यवहारसेवी -विनी -वि (न्), प्राक्तनरीतिसेवी &c., प्राक्तनमार्गानुयायी &c., प्राक्तनमार्गानुसारी &c., आद्यकालानुसारी &c.

PRIMITIVELY, *adv.* (Originally) आदौ, आदितस्, मूलतस्, प्रथमतस्, आरम्भतस्, आरम्भे.—(According to primitive custom) प्राक्तनव्यवहारानुसारेण, प्राक्तनरीत्यनुसारेण, आद्यकालानुसारतस्, आद्यकालानुरूपेण, वृद्धाचारतस्.

PRIMITIVENESS, *s.* (State of being original) मौलत्वं -ता, मौलिकत्वं, प्राथमिकत्वं, प्राथम्यं, प्रथमता, आद्यत्वं, आदित्वं.—(Conformity) प्राक्तनव्यवहारसेवनं, प्राक्कालीनरीत्यनुसारः, प्राक्तनमार्गानुयायिता, वृद्धाचारसेवनं.

PRIMNESS, *s.* अतिविनीतता -त्वं, सूक्ष्मनियमनिष्ठा, सूक्ष्मादरशीलता, अतिसूक्ष्मता, अतिसौक्ष्म्यं, अत्यादरसेवनं, अत्याचारसेवनं.

PRIMOGENIAL, *a.* प्रथमजातः -ता -तं, प्रथमजः -जा -जं, आदिजातः &c.

PRIMOGENITURE, *s.* ज्येष्ठता -त्वं, ज्यैष्ठ्यं, पूर्व्वजत्वं, पूर्व्वजातत्वं, अग्रजत्वं, अग्रजातत्वं, वयोज्येष्ठता, ज्येष्ठवयस्कता, आदिजत्वं, आदिजातत्वं.

PRIMORDIAL, *a.* प्राक्कालीनः -ना -नं, प्राक्कालिकः -की -कं, प्राक्तनकालिकः &c., प्राक्तनः -नी -नं, आद्यः -द्या -द्यं, आदिकालिकः &c., मौलिकः -की -कं, मौलः -ली -लं.

PRIMROSE, *s.* वसन्तकुसुमः or वसन्तपुष्प ओषधिभेदः.

PRINCE, *s.* (Sovereign) राजा *m.* (न्), नृपतिः *m.*, भूपतिः *m.*, पार्थिवः, महीपतिः *m.*, छत्रपः, छत्रपतिः *m.*, पः in comp. *See* KING.—(Sovereign of a certain territory or province) देशपतिः *m.*, राष्ट्रपतिः *m.*, मण्डलपतिः.—(Son of a king) राजपुत्रः, राजसुतः, राजतनयः, राजकुमारः, नृपात्मजः, नृपसुतः, नृपपुत्रः, नृपनन्दनः, युवराजः, कुमारः.—(In theatrical language) भर्तृदारकः.

PRINCEDOM, *s.* (Kingdom) राज्यं, राजत्वं. *See* the word.—(Rank or condition of a king's son) यौवराज्यं, युवराजत्वं.

PRINCELINESS, *s.* राजतेजस् *n.*, राजश्रीः *f.*, राजैश्वर्यं. *See* MAJESTY.

PRINCELY, PRINCELIKE, *a.* (Resembling a prince, royal) राजसदृशः -शी -शं, नृपसदृशः &c., राजसन्निभः -भा -भं, नृपोपमः -मा -मं, राजजातीयः -या -यं, नृपजातीयः &c., राजकीयः -या -यं, प्रतापवान् -वती -वत् (त्), प्रतापशाली -लिनी -लि (न्), वैभवशाली &c., ऐश्वर्य्यवान् &c. *See* MAJESTIC.—(Having the rank of a prince) राजजातीयः -या -यं, नृपजातीयः &c., राजकुलजः -जा -जं, राजकुलप्रसूतः -ता -तं, राजवंश्यः -श्या -श्यं.—(Becoming a prince) राजयोग्यः -ग्या -ग्यं, राजार्हः -र्हा -र्हं, नृपोचितः -ता -तं, राजोचितः &c., राजोपयुक्तः -क्ता -क्तं, राजकीयः &c.

PRINCE'S-METAL, *s.* (Compound of copper and zinc) कांस्यं -स्यकं, कंसः -सं.

PRINCESS, *s.* (Female sovereign) राज्ञी, महिषी. *See* QUEEN.—(Daughter of a king) राजपुत्री -त्रिका, राजकुमारी, राजकन्या, राजसुता, नृपसुता, नृपात्मजा, राजतनया, नृपनन्दिनी, कुमारी, युवराजपत्नी.—(In theatrical language) भर्तृदारिका.

PRINCIPAL, *a.* मुख्यः -ख्या -ख्यं, परमः -मा -मं, प्रधानः -ना -नं, प्रमुखः -खा -खं, अग्रः -ग्रा -ग्रं, अग्र्यः -ग्र्या -ग्र्यं, प्राग्र्यः &c., वरः -रा -रं, प्रवरः &c., वरेण्यः -ण्या -ण्यं, वर्य्यः -र्य्या -र्य्यं, उत्तमः -मा -मं, पुरोगमः -मा -मं, श्रेष्ठः -ष्ठा -ष्ठं, विशिष्टः -ष्टा -ष्टं, उत्कृष्टः &c., शिष्टः &c., प्रथमः -मा -मं, अग्रगण्यः -ण्या -ण्यं, विशेष्यः -ष्या -ष्यं, मूलिकः -की -कं, मौलिकः &c., सिंह in comp. *See* CHIEF, EMINENT, EXCELLENT; 'principal door,' सिंहद्वारं; 'principal queen,' पट्टमहिषी, पट्टदेवी; 'principal minister.' *See* PRIME, *a.*

PRINCIPAL, *s.* (Chief, head) मुख्यः, मुखरः, पतिः *m.*, अधिपतिः *m.*, अध्यक्षः, नायकः. *See* LEADER, PRESIDENT; 'principal of a convent,' आश्रमगुरुः *m.*; 'of a college,' विद्यालयपतिः *m.*, विद्यालयाधिपतिः *m.*, विद्यालयाध्यक्षः.—(Capital) मूलधनं, मूलं, धनमूलं, मूलद्रव्यं, नीविः -वी *f.*, परिपणं, परिणतं, कायः, प्रयोज्यं; 'of a debt,' सामकं.—(Principal perpetrator) प्रवर्त्तकः.

PRINCIPALITY, *s.* (Territory of a prince) राष्ट्रं, देशः, मण्डलं, राज्यं, माण्डलिकराष्ट्रं, माण्डलिकराज्यं, माण्डलिकदेशः, माण्डलिकविषयः.

PRINCIPALLY, *adv.* प्रधानतस्, प्राधान्यतस्, मुख्यशस्, मुख्यतस्, विशेषतस्, विशेषेण, अधिकन्तु.

PRINCIPALNESS, *s.* प्राधान्यं, प्रधानत्वं, मुख्यता -त्वं, श्रेष्ठता, उत्कृष्टता.

PRINCIPLE, *s.* (Cause, source, origin) कारणं, हेतुः *m.*, आदिकारणं, आदिः *m.*, बीजं, मूलं, प्रयोजनं, आदिकारणं, आदिहेतुः *m.*—(Element, constituent part) मूलवस्तु *n.*, तत्त्वं, मूलं, मूलतत्त्वं, अङ्गं, अवयवः, मूलद्रव्यं, मूलावयवः, मूलाङ्गं, वस्तु *n.*, धातुः *m.*, सारः, साधनं, बीजं, मात्रं, तन्मात्रं.—(Fundamental or elementary truth) तत्त्वं, मूलतत्त्वं, सूत्रं, मूलसूत्रं, प्रथमसूत्रं, बीजं, परिभाषा, आरम्भः.—(Rule, general truth) नियमः, सूत्रं, विधिः *m.*, स्थितिः *f.*, न्यायः, उक्तवाक्यं, वचनं, उत्सर्गः.—(Settled law or property) धर्म्मः, गुणः, भावः, क्रमः, स्वभावः, व्यवस्था.—(Settled process) रीतिः *f.*, क्रमः, मार्गः, विधानं, मर्य्यादा, धारा.—(Ground, foundation) हेतुः *m.*, प्रमाणं, प्रामाण्यं, उपपत्तिः *f.*, उपपादनं, मूलं, आधारः, आश्रयः, उपष्टम्भः.

PRINCIPLED, *a.* (High-principled, well-principled) धर्म्मनिष्ठः -ष्ठा -ष्ठं, धर्म्मतत्त्वनिष्ठः &c., पुण्यनियमनिष्ठः &c., सुनियमनिष्ठः &c., सुनियमनिष्ठितः -ता -तं, उदारः -रा -रं, उदारशीलः -ला -लं.

To PRINT, *v. a.* मुद्र (nom. मुद्रयति -यितुं), मुद्रीकृ, मुद्रितं -तां कृ, मुद्राङ्कितं -तां कृ, मुद्राक्षरीकृ, अङ्क् (c. 10. अङ्कयति -यितुं), मुद्राक्षरैर् अङ्क्, समुद्रीकृ. *See To* IMPRINT, IMPRESS.

PRINT, *s.* (Mark made by impression) मुद्रा, मुद्रिका, अङ्कः, चिह्नं. —(Instrument for impressing) मुद्रा, मुद्राङ्कनयन्त्रं.—(Impression of types or the type itself) मुद्राक्षरचिह्नं, मुद्राक्षरं.—(State of being printed) मुद्रितत्वं, मुद्राङ्कितत्वं; 'in print,' मुद्रितः -ता -तं; 'out of print,' समुद्रितः &c.—(Print of a foot) पादचिह्नं, पदाङ्कः, पादमुद्रा, पदं, पदवी.

PRINTED, *p. p.* मुद्रितः -ता -तं, मुद्राङ्कितः &c., मुद्रीकृतः &c., मुद्राक्षरैरङ्कितः -ता -तं, मुद्राक्षराङ्कितः &c., अङ्कितः &c., कृतमुद्रः -द्रा -द्रं, कृताङ्कः -ङ्का -ङ्कं, समुद्रः &c.; 'printed book,' मुद्रितपुस्तकं.

PRINTER, *s.* मुद्राकरः, मुद्राकारी *m.* (न्), मुद्राकृत्, मुद्रकः, मुद्राङ्कनकृत्.

PRINTING, *s.* मुद्राङ्कनं, मुद्राकरणं, मुद्रीकरणं, अङ्कनं, मुद्राक्षरप्रयोगः.

PRINTING-HOUSE, *s.* मुद्राङ्कनशाला, मुद्रायन्त्रालयः -यं, यन्त्रालयः.

PRINTING-INK, *s.* मुद्राङ्कनमसिः -सी, मुद्राङ्कनमसिका, अङ्कनमसी.

PRINTING-PRESS, *s.* मुद्राङ्कनयन्त्रं, मुद्रायन्त्रं, मुद्राङ्कनचक्रं.

PRIOR, *a.* पूर्व्वः -र्व्वा -र्व्वं, पूर्व्वकः -का -कं, पौर्व्विकः -की -कं, पौरस्त्यः -स्त्या -स्त्यं, अग्रः -ग्रा -ग्रं, प्राक् in comp., प्राक्तनः -नी -नं, आद्यः -द्या -द्यं, आदिमः -मा -मं, आदि in comp., प्रथमः -मा -मं; 'prior possession,' पूर्व्वभुक्तिः *f.*; 'prior existence,' प्राग्भावः; 'prior and subsequent,' पूर्व्वापरः -रा -रं, परापरः -रा -रं, परावरः -रा -रं, परावरीणः -णा -णं.

PRIOR, *s.* (Superior of a convent) आश्रमगुरुः *m.*, मठाधिपतिः *m.*, मठाध्यक्षः, आश्रमाध्यक्षः, मठाधिकारी *m.* (न्).

PRIORITY, *s.* पूर्व्वता -त्वं, अग्रता -त्वं, प्रथमता -त्वं, प्राथम्यं, आद्यता, आदित्वं.—(In rank) अग्रपदं, श्रेष्ठपदं, प्राधान्यं, प्रधानता, अग्रमान्यता, अग्रगण्यता, अग्रपूज्यता, अग्रमानं, अग्रपूजा.

PRIORY, *s.* मठः, आश्रमः, आवसथः, वीहारः, धर्म्मशाला.

PRISM, *s.* त्रिपार्श्वकाचः, चतुर्भुजाकृतिः पार्श्वत्रयविशिष्टः काचखण्डः.

PRISMATIC, *a.* (Pertaining to a prism) त्रिपार्श्वकाचसम्बन्धी &c.—(Resembling one) त्रिपार्श्वकाचाकारः -रा -रं.—(Distributed or formed by one) त्रिपार्श्वकाचविकीर्णः -र्णा -र्णं, त्रिपार्श्वकाचकल्पितः -ता -तं.

PRISON, *s.* कारागारं, कारागृहं, कारा, कारावेश्म *n.* (न्), बन्धनागारं, बन्धनालयः, बन्धनगृहं, बन्धनस्थानं, निरोधस्थानं, निरोधगृहं, निरोधशाला, वन्दिशाला, वन्दिवेश्म *n.*, गुप्तिः *f.*, चारः.

To PRISON, *v. a.* *See To* IMPRISON.

PRISONER, *s.* वन्दिः *f.*, वन्दी *f.*, कारास्थः, कारागारस्थः, कारागुप्तः, प्रग्रहः, उपग्रहः, ग्रहणः, कवरकी *f.*, करमरी *m.* (न्), वारिः *f.*, गोरुतः *m.*—(One taken in war) युद्धधृतः, युद्धगृहीतः, शत्रुधृतः, शत्रुगृहीतः, युद्धदासः.

PRISTINE, *a.* प्राक्तनः -नी -नं, पुरातनः &c., प्राक्कालीनः -ना -नं, प्राक्कालिकः -की -कं, आद्यकालिकः &c., पूर्व्वकालीनः &c., पूर्व्वकालिकः &c., पुराणः -णा -णी -णं, प्राचीनः -ना -नं.

PRIVACY, *s.* (State of retirement or secrecy) विविक्तता -त्वं, विविक्तभावः, विविक्तवासः, एकान्तता, एकान्तभावः, एकान्तवासः, रहस् *n.*, रहः, रहोभावः, रहीभावः, रहोवासः, रहस्यत्वं, निभृतत्वं, गुप्तता, छन्नता, प्रच्छन्नता, निर्जनता, विजनता.—(Place of seclusion, retreat) विविक्तस्थानं, रहःस्थानं, रहःस्थलं, एकान्तस्थानं, निर्जनस्थानं, विजनस्थानं, निर्जनदेशः.

PRIVATE, *a.* (Separate, unconnected with others) विविक्तः -क्ता -क्तं, विभिन्नः -न्ना -न्नं, पृथक्स्थितः -ता -तं, पृथगात्मकः -का -कं, असाधारणः -णा -णी -णं, असामान्यः -न्या -न्यं.—(Peculiar to one's self) स्व in comp., आत्म in comp., स्वकीयः -या -यं, स्वीयः &c. *See* PECULIAR; 'private conclusion,' स्वानुमितिः *f.*; 'private advantage,' आत्महितं; 'private property,' स्वस्वं, स्वधनं, आत्मधनं, निजस्वं, असाधारणधनं, अनन्यस्वामिकधनं.—(Sequestered, secluded, retired) विविक्तः -क्ता -क्तं, विजनः -ना -नं, निर्जनः &c., एकान्तः -न्ता -न्तं, निभृतः -ता -तं, निःशलाकः -का -कं.—(Secret, not open) रहस्यः -स्या -स्यं, गूढः -ढा -ढं, गुप्तः -प्ता -प्तं, गुह्यः -ह्या -ह्यं, छन्नः -न्ना -न्नं, प्रच्छन्नः &c., अव्यक्तः -क्ता -क्तं, अप्रकाशः -शा -शं, अप्रकटः -टा -टं, अस्पष्टः -ष्टा -ष्टं, अन्तर् in comp.; 'very private,' सुगुप्तः &c., सुगूढः &c.; 'private intelligence,' गूढभाषितं, गूढवार्त्ता; 'private road,' गूढमार्गः; 'private door,' अन्तर्द्वारं, गूढद्वारं, प्रच्छन्नं, पक्षद्वारं; 'private apartments,' अन्तर्गृहं, अन्तःपुरं, अवरोधनं, उपरोधकं, अन्तर्भवनं, कक्षान्तरं, निष्कुटः, दर्भटः; 'private room,' अन्तःशाला -लिका, अन्तःकोष्ठकं, उपरोधकं; 'private part,' गुह्यं, रहस् *n.*, उपस्थः, अधोङ्गं.—(Not in public office or employment) अनधिकारी -रिणी -रि (न्), अनधिकारस्थः -स्था -स्थं, अनधिकारस्थितः -ता -तं; 'a private person,' पृथग्जनः, पृथग्लोकः, पृथग्जानपदः, अनधिकारस्थव्यक्तिः *f.*—(Not official) अनाधिकारिकः -की -कं.—(In private). *See* PRIVATELY.

PRIVATE, *s.* (Common soldier) सैनिकः, सैन्यः, पृथक्सैन्यः.

PRIVATEER, *s.* गृहीतानुज्ञापत्रेण पृथग्जनेन सज्जीकृता साहसिकनौः.

PRIVATELY, *adv.* रहसि, रहस्, रहस्यं, निभृतं -ते, विविक्तं -क्ततस्, एकान्ततस्, एकान्तं, विजने, गूढं, गूढतस्, गुप्तं, उपांशु, प्रच्छन्नं -न्ने, अप्रकाशं, अप्रकटं, मिथस्; 'going privately,' गूढचारी -रिणी &c., गुप्तगतिः -तिः -ति.

PRIVATENESS, *s.* विविक्तता -त्वं. *See* PRIVACY.

PRIVATION, *s.* (Deprivation, absence of) अभावः, विरहः, रहितत्वं, राहित्यं, हानिः *f.*, असम्भवः, अविषयः, अप्राप्तिः *f.*, वियोगः, अपचयः, नाशः, क्षतिः *f.*, क्षयः, हरणं, लोपः.—(Absence of food or things necessary to comfort) अन्नवस्त्राभावः, आहारविरहः, आहाराभावः, अन्नवस्त्रहानिः *f.*, ग्रासाच्छादनराहित्यं, अन्नोदकाभावः, अन्नोदकलोपः, सुखसाधनाभावः, सुखसाधनलोपः.

PRIVATIVE, *a.* (Causing privation) हानिकरः -रा -रं, हानिकारकः -का -कं, लोपकरः &c., क्षयकरः &c., नाशकरः &c.—(Consisting in the absence of something) अभावसूचकः -का -कं, अभावरूपः -पा -पं, अभावात्मकः -का -कं, अभावदर्शकः &c.

PRIVATIVE, *s.* (Word) अभावशब्दः, अभावसूचकशब्दः.—(Prefix, in grammar) नपदं, नञ्पदं. Privative prefixes are such as अ, अन्, निर्, वि.

PRIVATIVELY, *adv.* अभावरूपेण, सनिषेधं, निषेधरूपेण, अभावतस्.

PRIVILEGE, *s.* अधिकारः, विशेषाधिकारः, असाधारणाधिकारः, असामान्याधिकारः, स्वाधिकारः, स्वत्वं.

To PRIVILEGE, *v. a.* अधिकारं दा, विशेषाधिकारं दा, अधिकारवन्तं -वतीं -वत् कृ, साधिकारं -रां कृ, विशेषाधिकारयुक्तं -क्तां कृ.

PRIVILEGED, *p. p.* or *a.* अधिकारवान् -वती -वत् (त्), साधिकारः -रा -रं, विशेषाधिकारवान् &c., विशेषाधिकारयुक्तः -क्ता -क्तं, अधिकारविशिष्टः -ष्टा -ष्टं.—(Exempt from tax) अकरः -रा -रं.

PRIVILY, *adv.* रहसि, गुप्तं, निभृतं, सुनिभृतं, *See* PRIVATELY.

PRIVITY, *s.* (Joint knowledge with another) सहज्ञानं, सहबोधः, सहवेदनं, समवेदनं, समज्ञानं, समवेतृत्वं.—(Private part) गुह्यं, गुह्याङ्गं, गूढाङ्गं, गुप्ताङ्गं, गोप्याङ्गं, गुह्येन्द्रियं, गुप्तेन्द्रियं, गुह्यस्थानं, गुप्तस्थानं, गुह्यस्थलं, रहस् *n.*, कौलीनं, उपस्थः -स्थं, अधोङ्गं; 'of a man,' शिश्नः, ध्वजः, *see* MEMBRUM VIRILE; 'of a woman,' *see* PUDENDUM.

PRIVY, *a.* (Private). *See* the word. (Admitted to the participation of knowledge) सहज्ञानी -निनी -नि (न्), समज्ञानी &c., सहज्ञाता *m.* (तृ), सहवेत्ता *m.* (तृ), सहवेदी *m.*, समवेत्ता *m.*—(Privy council) गूढसभा, प्रधानमन्त्रिणां गूढसभा, धीसचिवानां सभा, शिष्टसभा.

PRIVY, *s.* शौचकूपः, पायुक्षालनवेश्म *n.* (न्), कर्दमाटकः, अवस्करः.

PRIVY-COUNSELLOR, *s.* गूढसभाभ्यन्तरः, गूढसभासद्, गूढसभास्थः.

PRIZE, *s.* (That which is taken in war) युद्धजितद्रव्यं, युद्धसम्पादितद्रव्यं, युद्धोपार्जितद्रव्यं, युद्धजितधनं.—(That which is gained as the reward of success or victory) जयफलं, सिद्धिफलं, जयलब्धफलं, जयलाभः, जयलब्धवस्तु *n.*, पणजितद्रव्यं, जयपारितोषिकं, स्पर्द्धाफलं.—(That which is offered as the reward of contest) स्पर्द्धाजेयं, पणजेयं, पणः.—(Reward) फलं, प्रतिफलं, पारितोषिकं.—(Valuable acquisition) रत्नं, निधिः *m.*

To PRIZE, *v. a.* (Estimate) मन् (c. 4. मन्यते, मन्तुं, c. 10. मानयति -यितुं), सम्मन्, प्रतिमन्, मूल्यं or अर्घं निरूप् or निर्णी or संख्या.—(Value highly) बहु मन्, बहु सम्मन्, अतिशयेन सम्मन्, बहुमतिं कृ.

PRIZED, *p. p.* बहुमतः -ता -तं, बहुसम्मानितः &c., इष्टः -ष्टा -ष्टं, प्रतिष्ठितः -ता -तं; 'by mankind,' जनेष्टः -ष्टा -ष्टं.

PRIZE-FIGHTER, *s.* मल्लयोद्धा *m.* (द्धृ), मल्लयोधी *m.* (न्), मल्लः, झल्लः.

PRIZE-FIGHTING, *s.* मल्लयुद्धं, झल्लयुद्धं, मुष्टियुद्धं, बाहुयुद्धं.

PRO, (Forward, forth) प्र, अग्रे.—(For). In the phrase 'pro and con,' pro may be expressed by विधिपक्षः, कर्त्तव्यपक्षः, and con by निषेधपक्षः, अकर्त्तव्यपक्षः, अभावपक्षः.

PROBABILITY, *s.* सम्भावना, सम्भवः, सम्भाव्यता -त्वं, सम्भावनीयता -त्वं, अनुमेयता -त्वं, प्रमेयता, अभ्युपगमः, अभ्युपगम्यता, सम्भावनायोग्यता, भवनयोग्यता, योग्यता -त्वं, सत्यसङ्काशता.

PROBABLE, *a.* सम्भाव्यः -व्या -व्यं, सम्भावनीयः -या -यं, सम्भावितः -ता -तं, सम्भावनार्हः -र्हा -र्हं, सत्यसङ्काशः -शा -शं, अनुमेयः -या -यं, अभ्युपगम्यः -म्या -म्यं, अभ्युपगतः -ता -तं, प्रमेयः -या -यं, सम्भावनायोग्यः -ग्या -ग्यं, भवनयोग्यः &c.; 'this is probable,' इदम् उपपद्यते or सम्भवति or युज्यते.

PROBABLY, *adv.* सम्भावनीयं, यथासम्भवं, यथायोग्यं, प्रायस्, प्रायशस्, स्यात्, किल, नाम.

PROBATE, *s.* (Of a will) मृतपत्रप्रमाणं, मृतलेखप्रमाणं.

PROBATION, *s.* (Trial) परीक्षा -क्षणं, उपधा, कषिः *f.*—(Proof) प्रमाणं, प्रामाण्यं, निर्णयः. *See* PROOF.

PROBATIONARY, PROBATIONAL, *a.* परीक्षकः -का -कं, परीक्षाकारी -रिणी -रि (न्), परीक्ष्यमाणः -णा -णं, परीक्षा in comp., उपधा in comp.

PROBATIONER, *s.* परीक्ष्यमाणः, परीक्षारूढः, परीक्षाविषयः, परीक्षापात्रं, प्राथमकल्पिकः, नूतनशिष्यः, नवीनशिष्यः.

PROBATOR, *s.* परीक्षकः, विचारकः, अनुसन्धाता *m.* (तृ), परीक्षाकृत्.

PROBATORY, *a.* परीक्षकः -का -कं. *See* PROBATIONARY, *a.*

PROBE, *s.* शलाका, एषणी, वारा, वारं, क्षतशोधनी, जाम्बवौष्ठं.

To PROBE, *v. a.* शलाकाद्वारेण क्षतशोधनं कृ or उन्मन्थनं कृ or क्षतान्वेषणं कृ, क्षतान्तः शलाकां प्रविश् (c. 10. -वेशयति -यितुं) or निविश्.—(Search to the bottom, scrutinise) मर्म्मान्वेषणं कृ, सूक्ष्मपरीक्षां कृ, सूक्ष्मजिज्ञासां कृ, मर्म्मनिरीक्षणं कृ.

PROBING, *s.* शलाकाद्वारेण क्षतशोधनं, क्षतपरीक्षा, उन्मन्थनं, मर्म्मान्वेषणं.

PROBITY, *s.* सारल्यं, साधुता, ऋजुता, उपधाशुचित्वं. *See* INTEGRITY.

PROBLEM, *s.* (In logic, questionable proposition) विकल्पविषयः, विवादविषयः, प्रश्नः, वादः.—(In geometry) कृत्यं, कृतिसापेक्षसिद्धान्तः.—(In general) प्रश्नः, जिज्ञासा.

PROBLEMATICAL, *a.* वैकल्पिकः -की -कं, सविकल्पः -ल्पा -ल्पं, सन्दिग्धः -ग्धा -ग्धं, संशयस्थः -स्था -स्थं,ससंशयः -या -यं, अनिश्चितः -ता -तं, अनिर्णीतः &c.

PROBLEMATICALLY, *adv.* सविकल्पं, ससंशयं, सन्दिग्धं, संशयपूर्व्वं.

PROBOSCIS, *s.* (Of an elephant, &c.) शुण्डा, हस्तः, करः.

PROCEDURE, *s.* (Proceeding, measure taken) क्रिया, व्यवहारः, व्यापारः, चरितं, कृतिः *f.*, कर्म्म *n.* (न्), अनुष्ठानं, आचरणं, आचरितं, आचारः, वृत्तिः *f.*, वृत्तं, उपायः, साधनं, उपचारः, विधानं.—(Mode of proceeding) रीतिः *f.*, मार्गः, विधिः *m.*, क्रियाविधिः *m.*, क्रियाप्रसङ्गः, पर्य्यायः, क्रमः, मर्य्यादा, सम्प्रदायः.—(Legal) व्यवहारः, व्यवहारमार्गः, व्यवहारविधिः *m.*

To PROCEED, *v. n.* (Go forward) प्रगम् (c. 1. -गच्छति -गन्तुं), अग्रे गम्, पुरो गम् प्रया, अग्रे या, अग्रतो या, प्रसृ, अग्रे सृ, प्रसृप्, प्रवृत्, चल्, प्रचल्, प्रचर्, प्रविचर्, प्रस्था, क्रम्, प्रे (c. 2. प्रैति -तुं, rt. इ); 'the work proceeds,' कर्म्म प्रवर्त्तते; 'let the game proceed,' द्यूतं प्रवर्त्ततां.—(Proceed from one topic to another) पुनर् वद् (c. 1. वदति -दितुं), क्रमेण वद्, वचनप्रसङ्गं कृ, वचनप्रबन्धं कृ.—(Issue, arise from) उत्पद् (c. 4. -पद्यते -पत्तुं), समुत्पद्, जन् (c. 4. जायते, जनितुं), प्रभू, निःसृ, प्रवृत्, उच्चर्, उदि; 'his uneasiness proceeds from no other cause,' अस्य बाधा न अन्यनिमित्ता भवति.—(Proceed in an undertaking, carry on measures) प्रवृत्, प्रारब्धं प्रवृत् (c. 10. -वर्त्तयति -यितुं) or सम्पद् (c. 10. -पादयति -यितुं) or निष्पद् or निर्वह् (c. 10. -वाहयति -यितुं), प्रारब्धसम्पादनं कृ.—(Enter upon a business, begin) प्रवृत्, प्रवृत्तिं कृ, प्रक्रम्, उपक्रम्, आरभ्.—(Proceed against at law) अभियुज्.

PROCEEDING, *part.* (Issuing from) उत्पन्नः -न्ना -न्नं, समुत्पन्नः &c., जातः -ता -तं, सञ्जातः &c., निःसृतः -ता -तं, विनिःसृतः &c., प्रवृत्तः -त्ता -त्तं, प्रभवः -वा -वं, उद्भवः &c. in comp., उत्थितः -ता -तं; 'sound proceeding from the throat,' कण्ठोत्थितः स्वरः.

PRROCEEDING, *s.* क्रिया, कर्म्म *n.* (न्), व्यवहारः, चरितं, चरित्रं, चेष्टितं, चेष्टा, व्यापारः, आचरणं, आचरितं, वृत्तिः *f.*, प्रवृत्तिः *f.*, वृत्तं, अनुष्ठानं, आचारः, चर्य्या, विधानं.—(Course of proceeding) रीतिः *f.*, मार्गः, पर्य्यायः, क्रियाविधिः *m.*, क्रियाप्रसङ्गः, क्रमः, गतिः *f.* *See* PROCEDURE.

PROCEEDS, *s.* उत्पन्नं, समुत्पन्नं, उत्पन्नधनं, समुत्पन्नधनं.

PROCELEUSMATICUS, *s.* (Metrical foot) द्वयः.

PROCESS, *s.* (Proceeding on, progressive course) प्रगमनं, अग्रगमनं, प्रयाणं, प्रक्रमः, प्रवृत्तिः *f.*, प्रसरः, गतिः *f.*—(Gradual course) क्रमः -मणं, क्रमे क्रमे गमनं, क्रमशो गमनं or गतिः *f.*, क्रमिकगतिः *f.*—(Of time) कालगतिः *f.*, कालपर्य्यायः, कालावृत्तिः *f.*, कालान्तरं; 'in process of time,' कालान्तरे, दिनेषु गच्छत्सु.—(Regular course or order) क्रमः, अनुक्रमः, रीतिः *f.*, मार्गः, पर्य्यायः, प्रसङ्गः, नियमः, व्यवस्था, पद्धतिः *f.*, परिपाटी, परिपाटिः *f.*, विधिः *m.*, धारा, गतिः *f.*, वृत्तिः *f.*, प्रबन्धः.—(Course of proceeding) क्रियाप्रसङ्गः, क्रिया-

विधिः m., क्रियाप्रबन्धः.—(Legal) व्यवहारः, व्यवहारमार्गः, व्यवहरणं, कार्य्यं, अर्थः.

PROCESSION, s. (Issuing) निर्गमः, निर्गतिः f., निःसरणं, निस्सरणं, विनिर्गमः, निष्क्रमणं, प्रवृत्तिः f., उत्पत्तिः f., अपसरणं.—(Proceeding on) प्रगमनं, गमनं, प्रयाणं, प्रस्थानं, गतिः f., चलनं.—(Train of persons moving) यात्रा, यात्राप्रसङ्गः, दण्डयात्रा, जनयात्रा, लोकयात्रा, लोकश्रेणी, गतिः f.

PROCESSIONAL, PROCESSIONARY, a. यात्रिकः -की -कं, यात्रासम्बन्धी &c., दण्डयात्रासम्बन्धी &c., यात्रारूपः-पा-पं, दण्डयात्रारूपः &c., दण्डयात्रिकः &c.

To PROCLAIM, v. a. ख्या in caus. (ख्यापयति -यितुं), प्रख्या, आख्या, घुष् (c. 10. घोषयति -यितुं), विघुष्, आघुष्, उद्घुष्, कॄत् (c. 10. कीर्त्तयति -यितुं), प्रकॄत्, परिकॄत्, अनुकॄत्, उत्कॄत्, प्रकाश् (c. 10. -काशयति -यितुं), उच्चर् (c. 10. -चारयति -यितुं), प्रचर्, प्रकटीकृ, व्यक्तीकृ.—(Cry out) उत्क्रुश्, प्रकाशं घुष्, उच्चैःस्वरेण घुष्.—(Outlaw) घोषणापूर्व्वं बहिष्कृ.

PROCLAIMED, p. p. घोषितः -ता -तं, विघोषितः &c., आघोषितः &c., उद्घोषितः &c., घुष्टः -ष्टा -ष्टं, अवघुष्टः &c., विघुष्टः &c., प्रख्यातः -ता -तं, ख्यापितः &c., उत्कीर्त्तितः &c., प्रकीर्त्तितः &c., उच्चारितः &c., प्रकाशितः &c., प्रकटीकृतः &c.

PROCLAIMER, s. घोषकः, विघोषकः, घोषणकारी m. (न्), ख्यापकः.

PROCLAMATION, s. घोषणा -णं, विघोषणं -णा, घोषः, ख्यापनं, प्रकाशनं, उत्कीर्त्तनं, प्रकीर्त्तनं, अनुकीर्त्तनं, प्रचारणं, उच्चारणं, राजाज्ञापत्रेण प्रकाशनं; 'written,' घोषणापत्रं, विघोषणपत्रं, राजाज्ञापत्रं, आज्ञापत्रं; 'food given by proclamation,' घुष्टान्नं.

PROCLIVITY, s. प्रावण्यं, प्रवणता, प्रवृत्तिः f., प्रवाहः, शीलता.

PROCLIVOUS, a. प्रवणः -णा -णं, प्रवृत्तः -त्ता -त्तं. See INCLINED, PRONE.

To PROCRASTINATE, v. a. विलम्ब् (c. 1. -लम्बते -म्बितुं), आकालान्तरात् त्यज् (c. 1. त्यजति, त्यक्तुं) or या in caus. (यापयति -यितुं), परकालं यावत् त्यज्.

To PROCRASTINATE, v. n. विलम्ब् (c. 1. -लम्बते -म्बितुं), आलस्यात् कालं या in caus. (यापयति -यितुं) or क्षिप् (c. 6. क्षिपति, क्षेप्तुं), चिर (nom. चिरयति, चिरायति -ते -यितुं), मन्द (nom. मन्दायते), आकालान्तरात् or कालान्तरं यावत् कार्य्यत्यागं कृ or कार्य्योपेक्षां कृ, मन्दकार्य्यः -र्य्या -र्य्यं भू or अस्.

PROCRASTINATION, s. विलम्बः -म्बनं, कालयापः -पनं, कालक्षेपः -पणं, आकालान्तरात् कार्य्यत्यागः, कालान्तरं यावत् कार्य्योपेक्षा, मान्द्यं, मन्दता, दीर्घसूत्रता.

PROCRASTINATOR, s. विलम्बी m. (न्), कालयापकः, कालक्षेपकः, आकालान्तरात् कार्य्यत्यागी m., कालान्तरं or परकालं यावत् कार्य्योपेक्षकः, मन्दकर्म्मी m. (न्), मन्दकार्य्यः, दीर्घसूत्री m. (न्), दीर्घसूत्रः.

To PROCREATE, v. a. (Generate) जन्, सञ्जन्, प्रजन्, प्रसू or प्रसु (c. 1. -सवति, c. 2. -सूते, c. 4. -सूयते -सोतुं), सम्प्रसु, सु, उत्पद्.

PROCREATED, p. p. जनितः -ता -तं, उत्पादितः -ता -तं, प्रसूतः -ता -तं.

PROCREATION, s. जननं, प्रजननं, उत्पादनं, प्रसूतिः f., प्रसवः, उत्पत्तिः f., उत्पन्नत्वं, प्रजोत्पादनं, प्रजोत्पत्तिः f.

PROCREATIVE, a. जनकः -का -कं, उत्पादकः -का -कं, सावकः -विका -कं, प्रजोत्पादकः &c., प्रजननशक्तिकः -का -कं, प्रजननशक्तियुक्तः -क्ता -क्तं.

PROCREATIVENESS, s. प्रजननशक्तिः f., जननशक्तिः, उत्पादनशक्तिः, पुंस्त्वं.

PROCREATOR, s. जनकः, जनयिता m. (तृ), जननः, जनिता m., उत्पादकः.

PROCTOR, s. (Attorney, agent) प्रतिनिधिः m., परकार्य्यसम्पादकः.

PROCUMBENT, a. शयानः -ना -नं, पतितः -ता -तं, क्षिप्तदेहः -हा -हं.

PROCURABLE, a. प्राप्तव्यः -व्या -व्यं, प्रापणीयः -या -यं, प्राप्यः -प्या -प्यं, लभ्यः -भ्या -भ्यं, उपलभ्यः &c., आसादनीयः -या -यं, अधिगम्यः -म्या -म्यं; 'procurable with exertion,' यत्नलभ्यः &c.; 'without exertion,' अयत्नलभ्यः &c. See OBTAINABLE.

To PROCURE, v. a. (Obtain) आप् (c. 5. आप्नोति, आप्तुं), प्राप्, अवाप्, सम्प्राप्, लभ् (c. 1. लभते, लब्धुं), उपलभ्, अर्ज्, उपार्ज्, आसद्, समासद्, अधिगम्, विद् (c. 6. विन्दति, वेदितुं, वेत्तुं), अभिविद्, प्रतिविद्, उपकॢप् (c. 10. -कल्पयति -यितुं), प्रतिपद्, आपद्, आविश्.—(Bring about, effect) सम्पद् (c. 10. -पादयति -यितुं), उपपद्, उत्पद्, साध्, घट्, प्रवृत् in caus.

PROCURED, p. p. प्राप्तः -प्ता -प्तं, लब्धः -ब्धा -ब्धं, उपलब्धः &c., अर्जितः -ता -तं, उपार्जितः &c. See OBTAINED; 'is procured,' लभ्यते, उत्पद्यते.

PROCUREMENT, s. प्राप्तिः f., प्रापणं, लब्धिः f., लाभः, उपार्जनं, सम्पादनं.—(Panderism) कौट्टिन्यं.

PROCURER, s. प्रापकः, उपार्जकः, लब्धा m. (ब्धृ), सम्पादकः, प्रवर्त्तकः, प्रयोजकः.—(Pimp) रतसम्पादकः, रतप्रवर्त्तकः. See PIMP, PANDER.

PROCURESS, s. कुट्टिनी, कुट्टनी, दूती, दूतिका, सञ्चारिका, कुटी, चुन्दी, वेश्याचार्य्या, शम्भली, सम्भली, रतताली f., सुरतताली, रतोपकारिणी, रतसम्पादिका, कौट्टिन्यकर्त्री, लाम्पट्यप्रयोजिका.

PRODIGAL, a. अतिव्ययी -यिनी -यि (न्), बहुव्ययी &c., अपरिमितव्ययी &c., अपरिमितव्ययः -या -यं, अपव्ययी &c., अतिव्ययशीलः -ला -लं, व्ययशीलः &c., अपचेता -त्री -तृ (तृ), उत्सर्गी -र्गिणी &c., अत्युत्सर्गी &c., अतित्यागी &c., अतिदाता -त्री -तृ (तृ), बहुदः -दा -दं, बहुप्रदः &c., महाव्ययकारी &c., अतिमोक्षणशीलः &c., मुक्तहस्तः -स्ता -स्तं, धनोत्सर्गी &c., अर्थोत्सर्गी &c., धनत्यागी &c.

PRODIGAL, s. अतिव्ययी m. (न्), बहुव्ययी m. See the last.

PRODIGALITY, s. अतिव्ययः, बहुव्ययः, अपव्ययः, महान् व्ययः, महाव्ययः, अपरिमितव्ययः, अतित्यागः, अत्युत्सर्गः, अतिमोक्षणं, अतिसर्जनं, अर्थोत्सर्गः, धनोत्सर्गः, धनत्यागः, अर्थत्यागः, बहुप्रदत्वं, बहुदत्वं, मुक्तहस्तत्वं.

PRODIGALLY, adv. अतिव्ययेन, बहुव्ययेन, महाव्ययेन, अपरिमितव्ययेन, अत्युत्सर्गेण, अतित्यागपूर्व्वं, महाव्ययपूर्व्वं, सापव्ययं, मुक्तहस्तेन.

PRODIGIOUS, a. (Very great, huge) अतिमहान् -हती -हत् (त्), अतिवृहन् -हती &c., अद्भुतशरीरः -रा -रं, अद्भुतकायः -या -यं, अद्भुतपरिमाणः -णा -णं, वृहत्परिमाणः &c., विकटशरीरः &c., राक्षसशरीरः &c.—(Wonderful) अद्भुतः -ता -तं, महाद्भुतः -ता -तं, अद्भुततमः -मा -मं, आश्चर्य्यः -र्य्या -र्य्यं, सुचित्रः -त्रा -त्रं, विलक्षणः -णा -णं, अपूर्व्वः -र्व्वा -र्व्वं, सृष्टिमार्गबाह्यः -ह्या -ह्यं, प्रकृतिक्रमबाह्यः &c.

PRODIGIOUSLY, adv. अद्भुतं, महाद्भुतं, आश्चर्य्यं, अतिशयेन, अत्यन्तं.

PRODIGIOUSNESS, s. अद्भुतत्वं -ता, अतिमहत्त्वं, अतिवृहत्त्वं.

PRODIGY, s. अद्भुतं, उत्पातः, उपसर्गः, महाद्भुतं, अद्भुतविषयः, अद्भुतवस्तु n., अपूर्व्वविषयः, अपूर्व्ववस्तु n., महदाश्चर्य्यं.

PRODITION, s. विश्वासघातः, विश्वासभङ्गः, शत्रुहस्तार्पणं, शत्रुसमर्पणं.

To PRODUCE, v. a. (Bring forward, offer to view or notice) प्रणी (c. 1. -णयति -णेतुं), अभिप्रणी, आनी, उपनी, अग्रे नी, अग्रे आनी, दृश् (c. 10. दर्शयति -यितुं), प्रदृश्, प्रसृ (c. 10. -सारयति -यितुं), प्रत्यक्षीकृ, प्रादुष्कृ, आविष्कृ, पुरस्कृ, अग्रे स्था in caus.—(Bring forth, generate) उत्पद् (c. 10. -पादयति -यितुं), जन् (c. 10. जनयति -यितुं), संजन्, प्रजन् (c. 10. or c. 4. -जायते -जनितुं), उपजन्, प्रसु, सु.—(Effect, bring into existence) उत्पद्, समुत्पद्, उपपद्, सम्पद्, जन्, संजन्, कृ, साध्, संसाध्, भू in caus., उद्भू, सृज् (c. 6. सृजति, स्रष्टुं), तन्, सिद्धीकृ.—(Make) कृ, कॢप्, विधा, घट्.—(Yield) दा, प्रदा.

PRODUCE, *s.* (That which is produced or yielded) उत्पन्नं, निष्पन्नं, फलं, लाभः, उत्पत्तिः *f.*, उद्भूतं, प्रसवः, प्रसूतिः *f.*; 'of agriculture,' कृषिफलं, क्षेत्रफलं; 'of a tree,' वृक्षफलं, वृक्षोत्पन्नं; 'of labour,' कर्म्मफलं.

PRODUCED, *p. p.* (Brought into view) उपनीतः -ता -तं, प्रणीतः &c., अग्रे आनीतः &c., दर्शितः &c., प्रदर्शितः &c., प्रसारितः &c., प्रादुष्कृतः &c.—(Brought into life or being) उत्पन्नः -न्ना -न्नं, उत्पादितः -ता -तं, समुत्पादितः &c., जातः -ता -तं, जनितः &c., उपजातः &c., सञ्जातः &c., प्रसूतः &c., प्ररूढः -ढा -ढं, प्रभवः -वा -वं, उद्भवः &c., उद्भूतः -ता -तं, उत्थितः -ता -तं; 'produced in water,' जलोद्भवः -वा -वं.—(Effected, resulting from) उत्पादितः &c., सम्पादितः &c., निष्पादितः &c., निष्पन्नः &c., जनितः &c., जातः &c., जन्यः -न्या -न्यं, प्रयुक्तः -क्ता -क्तं, प्रवृत्तः -त्ता -त्तं, हेतुकः -का -कं, कर्म्मकः &c.; 'misery produced by crime,' पापप्रयुक्तं दुःखं; 'fever produced by fasting,' उपवासजन्यो ज्वरः.

PRODUCER, PRODUCING, *s.* or *part.* उत्पादकः -का -कं, जनकः -का -कं, साधकः -धिका -कं, प्रसवन् -वन्ती -वत् (त्), प्रसवी -विनी -वि (न्), प्रदः -दा -दं, दायी -यिनी &c., दः -दा -दं in comp., आवहः -हा -हं, कारी &c., करः -रा -रं, निष्पादकः &c.; 'producing fruit,' फलदः -दा -दं, फलप्रदः &c., फलदायी &c., फलोत्पादकः &c., फलनिष्पादकः &c.; 'producing pain,' दुःखकरः -रा -रं, दुःखकारी &c., दुःखजनकः &c., दुःखावहः -हा -हं; 'a lake producing lotuses,' पद्मोत्पादकसरस्, अम्भोजप्रसवि सरस्.

PRODUCIBLE, *a.* जन्यः -न्या -न्यं, उत्पादनीयः -या -यं, जननीयः &c.

PRODUCT, *s.* (That which is produced, &c.) उत्पन्नं, निष्पन्नं, फलं. *See* PRODUCE.—(Effect, result) फलं, परिणामः, प्रयुक्तिः *f.*, उत्तरं, सिद्धिः *f.*, फलोदयः.—(In arithmetic) घातः, वधः, गुणाकारः, फलिताङ्कः, फलं, उत्पन्नं, प्रत्युत्पन्नं.

PRODUCTION, *s.* (Act or process of producing, generation) उत्पादनं, उत्पत्तिः *f.*, जननं, प्रजननं, जन्म *n.* (न्), जनिः -नी *f.*, उद्भवः, सम्भवः, प्रभवः, सम्भूतिः *f.*, प्रसूतिः *f.*, प्रसवः, जनुस् *n.*, रूढिः *f.*, प्ररूढिः *f.*—(Act of effecting or forming) निष्पादनं, निष्पत्तिः *f.*, सम्पादनं, उपपत्तिः *f.*, उद्भावनं, करणं, निर्म्माणं, निर्म्मितिः *f.*, कल्पनं -ना, सर्ज्जनं, सृष्टिः *f.*, घटनं, विधानं; 'law of reciprocal production and reproduction,' बीजाङ्कुरन्यायः.—(Thing produced) उत्पन्नं, समुत्पन्नं, फलं. *See* PRODUCE.—(Of art, manufacture, &c.) निर्म्मितवस्तु *n.*, निर्म्मितद्रव्यं, निर्म्मितपदार्थः, शिल्पनिर्म्मितद्रव्यं, शिल्पिकवस्तु *n.*, वस्तु *n.*

PRODUCTIVE, *a.* (Fruitful) फलदः -दा -दं, फलप्रदः -दा -दं, फलदायी -यिनी -यि (न्), फलदायकः -का -कं, फलोत्पादकः -का -कं, फलवान् -वती -वत् (त्), बहुफलः -ला -लं, सफलः &c., अवन्ध्यः -न्ध्या -न्ध्यं, बहुप्रसवः -वा -वं, साधकः &c. *See* FRUITFUL, PRODUCING.—(Causing, effective of) उत्पादकः -का -कं, जनकः &c., कारकः &c., करः -रा -री -रं, कारी -रिणी &c., निष्पादकः &c., सम्पादकः &c., प्रतिपादकः &c., साधकः -का -कं, आवहः -हा -हं; 'productive of wealth,' अर्थोत्पादकः &c., अर्थावहः -हा -हं; 'of satisfaction,' तृप्तिजनकः -का -कं.—(Lucrative) लाभदः -दा -दं, लाभकरः -रा -रं, फलावहः &c.

PRODUCTIVENESS, *s.* साफल्यं, सफलता, फलदत्वं, फलवत्त्वं, फलोत्पादकत्वं, फलजनकता, बहुफलत्वं, बहुप्रसवत्वं.

PROEM, *s.* वाङ्मुखं, आरम्भवाक्यं, परिभाषा, आभाषः. *See* PREFACE.

PROFANATION, *s.* अतिक्रमः -मणं, व्यतिक्रमः -मणं, समतिक्रमः, दूषणं, लोपः -पनं, अपवित्रीकरणं, भ्रष्टीकरणं, भ्रष्टकरणं.

PROFANE, *a.* (Irreverent, impious) धर्म्मनिन्दकः -का -कं, धर्म्मद्वेषी -षिणी -षि (न्), देवनिन्दकः &c., ईश्वरनिन्दकः &c., धर्म्मोपवादकः &c., धर्म्मनिन्दात्मकः &c., धर्म्मनिन्दारूपः -पा -पं.—(Not pure) अपुण्यः -ण्या -ण्यं, अपवित्रः -त्रा -त्रं, अशुद्धः -द्धा -द्धं, भ्रष्टः -ष्टा -ष्टं.—(Not sacred, not consecrated) अप्रतिष्ठितः -ता -तं, अप्रणीतः -ता -तं, असंस्कृतः &c., प्रतिष्ठाहीनः -ना -नं, संस्कारहीनः &c., व्रात्यः -त्या -त्यं.—(Secular) लौकिकः -की -कं, व्यावहारिकः -की -कं, सांसारिकः &c., प्रापञ्चिकः &c., धर्म्मप्रकरणव्यतिरिक्तः -क्ता -क्तं.

To PROFANE, *v. a.* (Violate) अतिक्रम् (c. 1. -क्रामति -क्रमितुं), व्यतिक्रम्, समतिक्रम्, लुप्, लंघ्.—(Pollute, render impure) अपवित्रीकृ, भ्रष्टीकृ, अशुद्धीकृ, दुष् (c. 10. दूषयति -यितुं), दुष्टीकृ.—(Dishonour) अवमन्, अपमन्, अवज्ञा, अवधीर्, लघूकृ, अपमानं कृ, अनादरं कृ, निन्दां कृ.

PROFANED, *p. p.* दूषितः -ता -तं, अतिक्रान्तः -न्ता -न्तं, भ्रष्टीकृतः &c., अवमानितः &c., अपमानितः &c., अनादृतः &c., कृतावज्ञः -ज्ञा -ज्ञं, अवधीरितः &c.

PROFANELY, *adv.* धर्म्मनिन्दया, धर्म्मनिन्दापूर्व्वं, देवनिन्दाबुद्ध्या, धर्म्मनिन्दकवत्, सधर्म्मनिन्दनं, अपुण्यवत्, धर्म्मद्वेषकवत्.

PROFANENESS, PROFANITY, *s.* धर्म्मनिन्दा -न्दनं, देवनिन्दा -न्दनं, ईश्वरनिन्दा, धर्म्मापवादः, धर्म्मलोपः, धर्म्मातिक्रमः, ईश्वरावमानं, ईश्वरावज्ञा, धर्म्मावज्ञा.

PROFANER, *s.* धर्म्मनिन्दकः, धर्म्मापवादकः, धर्म्मपरिभाषकः, धर्म्मपरिभाषी *m.* (न्), ईश्वरनिन्दकः, दूषकः, अपमानकः, अवज्ञाता *m.* (तृ).

To PROFESS, *v. a.* (Avow, declare openly) प्रतिज्ञा (c. 9. -जानाति -नीते -ज्ञातुं), अङ्गीकृ, स्वीकृ, उरीकृ, ऊरीकृ, अनुभाष्, प्रकाशं ख्या in caus., प्रकाशं or व्यक्तं वद्, प्रतिज्ञापूर्व्वं वद् or कथ्, अङ्गीकारपूर्व्वं वद्, प्रतिज्ञां कृ, प्रकाश्.—(Make a show of, profess one's self) छद्म कृ, वेशं धृ, आत्मानं दृश्. *See To* PRETEND.—(Profess an art, business, &c.) वृत्तिं कृ, प्रवृत्तिं कृ, व्यवसायं कृ, व्यापारं कृ; 'to profess the science of medicine,' चिकित्साप्रवृत्तिं कृ, चिकित्सावृत्तिं कृ, चिकित्साव्यवसायं कृ, चिकित्सां कृ.

PROFESSED, PROFEST, *a.* सप्रतिज्ञातः -ता -तं, प्रतिज्ञापूर्व्वः -र्व्वा -र्व्वं, प्रतिज्ञापुरःसरः -रा -रं, स्वीकृतः &c., अङ्गीकृतः &c., प्रकाशः -शा -शं, प्रकाशोदितः &c., व्यक्तोदितः &c., प्रकाशकथितः &c., प्रकाशितः -ता -तं, ख्यापितः &c.; 'professed religion,' स्वीकृतधर्म्मः.

PROFESSEDLY, *adv.* प्रतिज्ञापूर्व्वं, सप्रतिज्ञं, साङ्गीकारं, स्वीकारपूर्व्वं.

PROFESSION, *s.* (Avowal, open declaration) अङ्गीकारः, स्वीकारः, उरीकारः, ऊरीकारः, ख्यापनं, प्रकाशख्यापनं, प्रतिज्ञा, प्रकाशप्रतिज्ञा, प्रकाशवचनं, प्रकाशवादः, प्रकाशकथनं, प्रकाशकीर्त्तनं, स्वमतप्रकाशनं, प्रकाशनं, साक्ष्यं; 'empty profession,' निरर्थकप्रतिज्ञा; 'of religion,' धर्म्मस्वीकारः. *See* PRETENDER.—(Calling, business) वृत्तिः *f.*, व्यापारः, व्यवसायः, वर्त्तनं, प्रवृत्तिः *f.*, वृत्तं, वृत्तिता, जीविका, उपजीविका, जीवनवृत्तिः *f.*, जीवनोपायः, उपजीवनं, आजीवः, आजीवनार्थं, उद्योगः, वार्त्ता, व्यवहारः; 'military,' शस्त्रवृत्तिः *f.*, शस्त्राजीवः; 'medical,' चिकित्सावृत्तिः *f.*

PROFESSIONAL, *a.* (Pertaining to a profession) वृत्तिसम्बन्धी -न्धिनी &c., वृत्तिविषयकः -का -कं.—(Engaged in a profession) वृत्तिमान् -मती -मत् (त्), व्यापारी -रिणी -रि (न्), व्यवसायी &c.

PROFESSIONALLY, *adv.* वृत्तितस्, व्यापारतस्, व्यवहारतस्, व्यापारेण.

Professor, *s.* (One who makes open declaration) ख्यापकः, प्रकाशख्यापकः, व्यक्तख्यापकः, प्रतिज्ञाता *m.* (तृ), प्रतिज्ञाकारी *m.* (न्), अङ्गीकर्त्ता *m.* (र्तृ), स्वीकर्त्ता *m.*, स्वीकारकृत्; 'of the Christian religion,' ख्रीष्टीयधर्म्मस्वीकर्त्ता -र्त्री -र्तृ (र्तृ), ख्रीष्टीयमतस्वीकारी *m.* (न्), ख्रीष्टीयधर्म्मध्वजी *m.* (न्), ख्रीष्टीयवेशधारी *m.*, ख्रीष्टीयधर्म्मा *m.* (न्), ख्रीष्टीयमतावलम्बी *m.*—(Public teacher) प्रकाशपाठकः, प्रकाशाध्यापकः, प्रकाशोपदेशकः, विद्यालये छात्रपाठकः or पाठकः.

Professorship, *s.* प्रकाशपाठकपदं, विद्यालये पाठकस्य पदं.

Proffer, *To* **proffer**. *See* Offer, *To* offer, &c.

Proficiency, proficience, *s.* व्युत्पत्तिः *f.*, व्युत्पन्नता, सम्पन्नता, प्रवीणता, प्रावीण्यं, नैपुण्यं, निपुणता, निवेशः, प्रवेशः, सन्निवेशः, अभिनिवेशः, निविष्टता, अभिज्ञता, परत्वं.

Proficient, *a.* व्युत्पन्नः -न्ना -न्नं, सम्पन्नः &c., प्रवीणः -णा -णं, निपुणः &c., निविष्टः -ष्टा -ष्टं, अभिनिविष्टः &c., सन्निविष्टः &c., अभिज्ञः -ज्ञा -ज्ञं, विचक्षणः -णा -णं, विज्ञः &c., वैज्ञानिकः -की -कं, पटुः -टुः -टु, निष्णातः -ता -तं, कृतागमः -मा -मं.

Profile, *s.* अर्द्धमुखं, अर्द्धाननं, अर्द्धमुखाकारः, अर्द्धमुखालेख्यं, मुखपार्श्वः, मुखपार्श्वालेख्यं.

Profit, *s.* लाभः, लब्धिः *f.*, प्राप्तिः *f.*, फलं, फलोदयः, लभ्यं, लभ्यांशः, आयः, उदयः, उत्पन्नं, पणाया, पण्यफलत्वं, वृद्धिः *f.*, विवृद्धिः *f.*, प्रतिपत्तिः *f.*, योगक्षेमः, प्रयोगः, कलान्तरं, उपस्वत्वं, अर्जनं, उपार्जनं; 'profit and loss,' लाभालाभौ; 'non-enjoyment of profit,' फलाभोगः; 'with profit,' सलाभः -भा -भं, सफलः -ला -लं, सोदयः -या -यं.—(Benefit, advantage) हितं, लाभः, अर्थः.

To **profit**, *v. a.* (Cause benefit or advantage) हितं कृ, लाभं or फलं कृ or दा, अर्थं कृ, उपकृ, उपकारं कृ, हितावहः -हा -हं भू, हिताय भू, उपयोगी -गिनी -गि भू.—(Profit one's self). *See* the next.

To **profit**, *v. n.* (Gain advantage) फलं or हितं प्राप् or लभ्, लाभं प्राप्, उपकारं प्राप्.—(Improve, grow, better or wiser) वृध् (c. 1. वर्धते -र्धितुं), वृद्धिं गम्, भद्रतरः -रा -रं भू, श्रेयान् -यसी -यो भू, आगमं कृ, ज्ञानं प्राप् or लभ्, ज्ञानागमं कृ, विद्यागमं कृ, विद्याप्राप्तिं कृ.—(Be of use or advantage) हिताय भू, फलाय भू, हितावहः -हा -हं भू, उपयोगी -गिनी -गि भू, उपकृ.

Profitable, *a.* (Gainful, lucrative) लाभकरः -रा -रं, लाभदः -दा -दं, फलदः -दा -दं, सफलः -ला -लं, फलदायकः -का -कं, फलजनकः &c., लाभजनकः &c., फलावहः -हा -हं, लाभावहः &c., लाभोत्पादकः &c., फली -लिनी -लि (न्), प्राप्तिजनकः &c.—(Useful, advantageous) हितकरः -रा -रं, हितकारकः -का -कं, हितजनकः &c., हितावहः -हा -हं, हितः -ता -तं, अर्थकरः &c., अर्थकारकः &c., अर्थवान् -वती -वत् (त्), अर्थदः -दा -दं, अर्थप्रदः &c., सार्थकः -का -कं, सोपकारः -रा -रं, उपकारी &c., उपकारकः &c., उपयोगी &c., उपयुक्तः -क्ता -क्तं, हितप्रदः &c., हितदायकः &c., अफल्गुः -ल्गुः -ल्गु.

Profitableness, *s.* साफल्यं, सफलता -त्वं, फलजनकता, लाभजनकता, हितकारकत्वं, अर्थकारकत्वं, हितजनकता, सार्थकत्वं, सलाभत्वं, फलदत्वं, उपकारकता, उपकारित्वं, उपयोगिता, अफल्गुता.

Profitably, *adv.* सफलं, साफल्येन, सलाभं, सार्थं, सोपकारं, सहितं, हिताय, फलाय, यथा हितं or फलं प्राप्यते तथा, अवृथा, अमुधा.

Profited, *p. p.* उपकृतः -ता -तं, कृतलाभः -भा -भं, प्राप्तफलः -ला -लं, प्राप्तोपकारः -रा -रं, कृतागमः -मा -मं, वर्धितः -ता -तं.

Profitless, *a.* निष्फलः -ला -लं, अफलः &c., फलहीनः -ना -नं, लाभहीनः &c., निर्लाभः -भा -भं, अहितः -ता -तं, व्यर्थः -र्था -र्थं, निरर्थकः -का -कं, असार्थकः &c., अनुपयोगी &c., अनामिषः -षा -षं, निरायः -या -यं.

Profligacy, *s.* व्यसनिता, दुष्टता, दुर्वृत्तिः *f.*, दुर्वृत्तता, भ्रष्टता, नष्टता, भ्रष्टाचारत्वं, दुष्टाचारता, भोगासक्तिः *f.*, विषयासक्तता, अनवस्थितिः *f.*, लम्पटत्वं, लाम्पट्यं, अशिष्टाचारत्वं, धूर्त्तता, कुपथं.

Profligate, *a.* व्यसनी -निनी -नि (न्), दुर्व्यसनी &c., व्यसनीयः -या -यं, दुष्टाचारः -रा -रं, दुर्वृत्तः -त्ता -त्तं, दुश्चरित्रः -त्रा -त्रं, दुष्टः -ष्टा -ष्टं, पापीयान् -यसी -यः (स्), दुराचारी &c., भ्रष्टाचारी &c., भ्रष्टः -ष्टा -ष्टं, अशिष्टाचारः -रा -रं, भोगासक्तः -क्ता -क्तं, विषयासक्तः &c., निकृतः -ता -तं, असम्यक्कारी &c., धूर्त्तः -र्त्ता -र्त्तं.

Profligate, *s.* व्यसनी *m.* (न्), व्यसनीयः, लम्पटः, कामुकः. *See* the last.

Profligately, *adv.* सव्यसनं, लम्पटवत्, दुष्टवत्, धूर्त्तवत्, सलाम्पट्यं.

Profound, *a.* (Deep) गम्भीरः -रा -रं, गभीरः -रा -रं, अगाधः -धा -धं, गाढः -ढा -ढं, अवगाढः &c., गहनः -ना -नं, निम्नः -म्ना -म्नं, घनः -ना -नं.—(Abstruse, not obvious) गूढार्थः -र्था -र्थं, निगूढार्थः &c., निगूढः -ढा -ढं, गूढः &c., गम्भीरार्थः -र्था -र्थं, गहनः -ना -नं, गहनार्थः &c., सुगहनः &c., परमगहनः &c., दुर्ज्ञेयः -या -यं, बोधागम्यः -म्या -म्यं.—(One who has penetrated deeply into any science, &c.) अभिनिविष्टः -ष्टा -ष्टं, निविष्टः &c., व्युत्पन्नः -न्ना -न्नं, पारगः -गा -गं, पारगतः -ता -तं, निष्णातः -ता -तं, गम्भीरार्थावधारणक्षमः -मा -मं, गूढार्थोपलब्धिक्षमः &c., गूढतत्त्वज्ञः -ज्ञा -ज्ञं, गूढार्थज्ञः -ज्ञा -ज्ञं, गम्भीरार्थज्ञः &c., निगूढार्थविद्, पारदर्शी -र्शिनी &c.—(Excessive) गाढः -ढा -ढं, अत्यन्तः -न्ता -न्तं, घनः -ना -नं, अति or सु prefixed; 'profound sorrow,' गाढशोकः; 'profound sleep,' सुषुप्तिः *f.*, अघोरनिद्रा; 'profound secret,' सुरहस्यं, सुगोपनीयं; 'profound secrecy,' गाढसंवृतिः *f.*, घनसंवृतिः *f.*, सुगुप्तिः *f.*

Profoundly, *adv.* गम्भीरं, गाढं, प्रगाढं, अत्यन्तं, निर्भरं, भृशं, अभिनिविष्टं, अभिनिवेशेन, अति or सु prefixed; 'profoundly skilled,' सुनिपुणः -णा -णं, अतिनिपुणः &c.; 'profoundly wise' विद्याभिनिविष्टः -ष्टा -ष्टं, विद्यापारदृक् *m.* (श्), सुपण्डितः &c. *See* Deeply.

Profoundness, profundity, *s.* (Depth) गम्भीरता, गभीरता, गाम्भीर्यं, अगाधता, गाढता, घनता, निम्नता.—(Of meaning) गूढता, निगूढता, गूढार्थता -त्वं.—(Of knowledge) अभिनिवेशः, निवेशः, व्युत्पन्नता, व्युत्पत्तिः *f.*, गूढार्थज्ञता.

Profuse, *a.* (Lavish) अतिव्ययी -यिनी -यि (न्), मुक्तहस्तः -स्ता -स्तं. *See* Prodigal, Lavish.—(Extravagant, exceeding bounds) अपरिमितः -ता -तं, अत्यन्तः -न्ता -न्तं, अतिरिक्तः -क्ता -क्तं, अति prefixed; 'profuse expenditure,' अतिव्ययः, अपरिमितव्ययः.—(Exuberant, copious) समृद्धः -द्धा -द्धं, अतिबहुलः -ला -लं, अतिरिक्तः -क्ता -क्तं, अधिकः -का -कं, उद्रिक्तः &c., अतिशय in comp., भृश in comp., अति or सु prefixed; 'profuse perspiration,' अतिस्वेदः, भृशस्वेदः.

Profusely, *adv.* (Lavishly) अतिव्ययेन, अपरिमितं. *See* the word.—(Copiously) बाहुल्येन, अतिबहुलं, प्राचुर्येण, अतिप्रचुरं, अतिरिक्तं, भूरि, भूरिशस्, अत्यन्तं, भृशं, अति prefixed; 'perspiring profusely,' अतिस्विद् *m. f. n.*, भृशस्विद्.

Profuseness, *s.* (Lavishness) अतिव्ययः, मुक्तहस्तत्वं -ता. *See* Lavishness, Prodigality.—(Great abundance). *See* the next.

Profusion, *s.* समृद्धिः *f.*, सामृद्ध्यं, अतिबाहुल्यं, बाहुल्यं, अतिबहुत्वं, अति-

प्राचुर्य्यं, अतिप्रचुरत्वं, विपुलता, वैपुल्यं, अतिवैपुल्यं, पुष्कलता, उद्रेकः, अतिरिक्तता, अतिरेकः, वृद्धिः *f.*, उत्सेकः.

Prog, *s.* अन्नं, खाद्यं, भोजनं, भक्ष्यं.—(Got by begging) भिक्षान्नं.

Progenitor, *s.* पूर्व्वजः, पितामहः, कुलपुरुषः, पूर्व्वपुरुषः, पूर्व्वजनकः, पूर्व्वजनिता *m.* (तृ), पूर्व्वजननः, अग्रजननः, जनयिता *m.* (तृ), प्रजननः, प्रजनः, जन्मदः, बीजप्रदः, बीजी *m.* (न्), यन्ता *m.* (न्तृ).

Progeny, *s.* सन्तानं -नः, सन्ततिः *f.*, अपत्यं, प्रजा. *See* Offspring.

Prognosis, *s.* (In medicine) परिभाषा, परिभाषणं.

Prognostic, *s.* पूर्व्वलक्षणं, पूर्व्वचिह्नं, पूर्व्वरूपं, पूर्व्वलिङ्गं, पूर्व्वसूचकचिह्नं, लक्षणं, चिह्नं, निमित्तं, जन्यं, शकुनं -नः, भाविसूचकचिह्नं, भविष्यसूचकचिह्नं, अनिष्टसूचकचिह्नं, भविष्यद्बोधकचिह्नं.

Prognostic, *a.* पूर्व्वसूचकः -का -कं, अग्रसूचकः &c., भविष्यसूचकः &c., भविष्यत्सूचकः &c., भाविसूचकः &c., उद्बोधकः &c., भविष्यद्बोधकः &c.

To prognosticate, *v. a.* पूर्व्वं or अग्रे सूच् (c. 10. सूचयति -यितुं), पूर्व्वं or अग्रतो दृश् (c. 10. दर्शयति -यितुं) or प्रदृश् or भविष्यत् सूच्, पूर्व्वलक्षणेन भविष्यत् सूच् or दृश्, पूर्व्वलक्षणं दा, पूर्व्वचिह्नं दा.—(Foretell from signs) पूर्व्वलक्षणदर्शनाद् भविष्यद् वद् or ज्ञा or अनागतं ज्ञा in caus. or अनुमा.

Prognostication, *s.* पूर्व्वसूचनं -ना, अग्रसूचनं, पूर्व्वलक्षणेन भविष्यत्सूचनं or भाविसूचनं or पूर्व्वलक्षणदर्शनाद् भविष्यज्ज्ञानं or अनागतज्ञानं or भविष्यदनुमानं.

Prognosticator, *s.* पूर्व्वसूचकः, अग्रसूचकः, पूर्व्वलक्षणेन भविष्यत्सूचकः or भाविसूचकः or भाविदर्शकः or अनागतदर्शकः, पूर्व्वलक्षणज्ञः, पूर्व्वचिह्नज्ञः.

Programme, *s.* पूर्व्वलेख्यं, पूर्व्वलेखः, पूर्व्वलिखितं, परिसंख्यापत्रं, वस्तुपरिसंख्या, परिगणनापत्रं, सूचिपत्रं.

Progress, *s.* (Moving or proceeding on) गमनं, प्रगमनं, गतिः *f.*, प्रयाणं, अग्रगमनं, अग्रसरणं, अग्रगतिः *f.*, प्रसरणं, प्रसरः, यात्रा, प्रक्रमः, क्रमः -मणं, क्रान्तिः *f.*, अनुक्रमणं, प्रस्थानं, प्रवाहः, चारः, अयनं in comp.; 'difficult progress,' संक्रमः, संक्रामः, सञ्चारः, सञ्चरः, दुर्गसञ्चरः.—(Increase) वृद्धिः *f.*, प्रवृद्धिः *f.*, वर्धनं, क्रमशो वृद्धिः *f.*, प्ररूढिः *f.*, उत्क्रमः.—(Improvement) वृद्धिः *f.*, प्राप्तिः *f.*, आगमः, संवृद्धिः *f.*—(In learning) विद्यागमः, विद्याप्राप्तिः *f.*, वृद्धिः *f.*, अभ्यासः, निवेशः.

To progress, *v. n.* (Proceed) प्रगम्, अग्रे गम्, प्रया, अग्रे या, प्रसृ, अग्रे सृ, प्रवृत्, प्रस्था, क्रम्.—(Improve) वृध्, प्रवृध्, वृद्धिं गम् or प्राप्, आगमं कृ.

Progression, *s.* (Moving forward). *See* Progress.—(Arithmetical) श्रेढी, अनुपातः, चयः.—(Geometrical) गुणोत्तरं, चयः; 'common difference in progression,' उत्तरं; 'last term in progression,' अन्त्यपदं, अन्त्यधनं.

Progressive, *a.* क्रमकः -का -कं, क्रमिकः -का -कं, आनुक्रमिकः &c., क्रममाणः -णा -णं, प्रक्रममाणः &c., क्रमशो वर्धमानः -ना -नं, उत्तरोत्तरं or अधिकाधिकं वर्धमानः &c., प्रसरः -रा -रं, उत्तरोत्तरः -रा -रं, अधिकाधिकः -का -कं, वर्धिष्णुः -ष्णुः -ष्णु.

Progressively, *adv.* क्रमशस्, क्रमतस्, क्रमे क्रमे, उत्तरोत्तरं, अधिकाधिकं.

Progressiveness, *s.* क्रमकगतिः *f.*, अनुक्रमणं, क्रमशो वृद्धिः *f.*, क्रमकता.

To prohibit, *v. a.* (Forbid, interdict, hinder) निषिध् (c. 1. -षेधति -षेद्धुं), प्रतिषिध्, प्रत्याख्या, अन्तःख्या, वृ in caus., निवृ, निरुध्, प्रतिरुध्, अवरुध्, उपरुध्, बाध्, प्रतिबन्ध्, निषेधं कृ, प्रतिषेधं कृ, वारणं कृ, निवारणं कृ; 'is prohibited,' निवार्य्यते. *See To* forbid.

Prohibited, *p. p.* निषिद्धः -द्धा -द्धं, प्रतिषिद्धः &c., वारितः -ता -तं, निवारितः &c., प्रत्याख्यातः &c., अन्तःख्यातः &c., बाधितः &c.

Prohibition, *s.* निषेधः, प्रतिषेधः -धनं, वारणं, निवारणं, प्रत्याख्यानं, प्रतिषेधोक्तिः *f.*, निषेधोक्तिः *f.*, अन्तःख्यानं, बाधः -धा -धनं, रोधः, निरोधः, पर्य्युदासः, आसेधः, वज्रः; 'written prohibition,' निवारणपत्रं, निषेधपत्रं.

Prohibitor, *s.* प्रतिषेद्धा *m.* (द्धृ), प्रतिषेधकः, निषेद्धा *m.*, निवारकः.

Prohibitory, *a.* निषेधकः -का -कं, प्रतिषेधकः -का -कं, वारकः &c., निवारकः &c., माङ्शब्दिकः -की -कं, निषेधार्थकः &c., निषेधकरः -रा -रं.

Project, *s.* कल्पना, सङ्कल्पः, कल्पितं, परिकल्पना, परिकल्पितं, युक्तिः *f.*, प्रयुक्तिः, प्रयोगः, उपायः, उपायकल्पना, अनुसन्धानं, व्यवसायः, अभिप्रायः, आशयः, उद्देशः.

To project, *v. a.* (Cast forward) प्रक्षिप् (c. 6. -क्षिपति -क्षेप्तुं), क्षिप्, अस्, प्रास्, प्रमुच्, पत् in caus.—(In the mind) मनसा क्लृप् (c. 10. कल्पयति -यितुं) or परिक्लृप्, उपायं क्लृप् or अनुसन्धा, अग्रे or पूर्व्वं चिन्त् or प्रचिन्त् or परिचिन्त्, अग्रे निरूप्, घट्, व्यवसो, आलोच्, अग्रकल्पनां कृ. *See To* plain, contrive.

To project, *v. n.* (Jut out, be prominent) बहिःस्था (c. 1. -तिष्ठति -स्थातुं), बहिर्वृत्, बहिर्भू, बहिर्लम्ब्, बहिःप्रलम्ब्, प्रसृ (c. 1. -सरति -सर्त्तुं), प्रसरः -रा -रं भू, अतिवृत्, अतिक्रम्, उदग्रः -ग्रा -ग्रं भू, प्ररूढः -ढा -ढं भू, प्ररुह् (c. 1. -रोहति -रोढुं), उन्नतः -ता -तं भू or अस्; 'projecting beyond,' अतिक्रम्य, क्रान्त्वा.

Projected, *p. p.* (Cast forward) प्रक्षिप्तः -प्ता -प्तं, क्षिप्तः &c., पातितः -ता -तं.—(Planned) मनसा कल्पितः &c. or परिकल्पितः &c., घटितः &c.

Projectile, *a.* दूरवेधी -धिनी -धि (न्); 'weapon,' दूरवेधि शस्त्रं, अस्त्रं.

Projecting, *part.* (Jutting out) बहिःस्थः -स्था -स्थं, बहिर्वर्त्ती -र्त्तिनी &c., बहिर्लम्बः -म्बा -म्बं, प्रलम्बः &c., बहिःप्रलम्बः &c., उदग्रः -ग्रा -ग्रं, प्रसरः -रा -रं, अतिक्रमी &c., अतिवर्त्ती &c., उन्नतः -ता -तं, प्ररूढः -ढा -ढं, सुरूढः &c.; 'having a projecting nose,' प्रलम्बघोणः -णा -णं, उन्नसः -सा -सं; 'having projecting teeth,' उदग्रदन् -दती -दत् (त्), उद्धुरः -रा -रं, करालः -ला -लं, करालदन्तः -न्ता -न्तं, दंष्ट्री &c., दंष्ट्राकरालवदनः -ना -नं; 'having a projecting breast,' स्तनाभोगविशिष्टः -ष्टा -ष्टं.

Projection, *s.* (Jutting out) बहिर्वर्त्तित्वं, बहिर्लम्बत्वं, प्रलम्बता, उदग्रता, आभोगः, प्रसरः -रणं.—(Part jutting out) बहिर्लम्बभागः, बहिःस्थभागः, उदग्रभागः, उन्नतभागः, प्ररूढभागः, आभोगः, प्रसरः, निर्यूहः, दन्तकः.—(In astronomy) भङ्गिः *f.*, छेद्यकं; 'projection of an eclipse,' परिलेखः.—(The act of scheming) उपायकल्पना. *See* Project.

Projector, *s.* उपायकल्पकः, परिकल्पकः, उपायचिन्तकः, अग्रचिन्तकः.

Prolapse, prolapsus, *s.* (As of an intestine) भ्रंशः; 'prolapsus ani,' गुदभ्रंशः; 'uteri,' गर्भाशयभ्रंशः, योन्यर्शस् *n.*

To prolapse, *v. n.* भ्रंश् (c. 4. भ्रश्यति, c. 1. भ्रंशते -शितुं), प्रभ्रंश्, परिभ्रंश्.

Prolated, *p. p.* दीर्घोच्चारितः -ता -तं.—(Vowel) प्लुतः -तं.

Prolation, *s.* (Drawling utterance) दीर्घोच्चारणं, द्राविडप्राणायामः.

Prolegomena, *s.* परिभाषा, आभाषः, आरम्भोक्तिः *f.*, आरम्भवाक्यं, पूर्व्ववाक्यं.

Prolepsis, *s.* पूर्व्वग्रहणं, अग्रग्रहणं, अप्राप्तकालग्रहणं, पूर्व्वादानं.

Prolific, *a.* बहुप्रजः -जा -जं, बहुप्रसवः -वा -वं, बहुप्रजावान् -वती -वत् (त्), प्रजावान् &c., प्रसवशीलः -ला -लं, प्रचुरप्रजः &c., बहुपत्यः -त्या -त्यं, बहुसुती -तिनी -ति (न्), सुती &c., प्रजनिष्णुः -ष्णुः -ष्णु, बहुजन्यः -न्या -न्यं, गर्भधारणशीलः -ला -लं, बहुसन्तानः -ना -नं.—(Productive) बहुफलदः -दा -दं, बहुफलः -ला -लं, बहुफलोत्पादकः -का -कं. *See* the word.

Prolix, *a.* दीर्घसूत्रः -त्रा -त्रं, दीर्घसूत्री -त्रिणी -त्रि (न्), अतिविस्तीर्णः

-र्णा -र्णं, अतिविस्तृतः -ता -तं, अतिदीर्घः -र्घा -र्घं, प्रपञ्चितः -ता -तं, अत्यायतः -ता -तं, अतिक्रान्तः -न्ता -न्तं, विस्तीर्णः &c., आयतः &c.

PROLIXITY, PROLIXNESS, *s.* दीर्घसूत्रता -त्वं, अतिविस्तीर्णता, अतिविस्तरः, अतिदीर्घता, अतिप्रपञ्चः, विस्तीर्णता, विस्तारः, विस्तरः, वाक्यविस्तारः, वाग्विस्तरः, प्रपञ्चः -ञ्चनं, अतिप्रसङ्गः, अतिबाहुल्यं.

PROLIXLY, *adv.* अतिविस्तरेण, सुविस्तरेण, वाग्विस्तारेण, विस्तरशस्.

PROLOGUE, *s.* प्रस्तावना -नं, नान्दी, प्रवेशकः, पूर्व्वरङ्गः, आमुखं, प्रकरणं, आरम्भः, आरम्भवाक्यं; 'speaker of it,' नान्दीवादी *m.* (न्), नान्दीकरः.

To PROLONG, PROLONGATE, *v. a.* (Lengthen) दीर्घीकृ, द्राघ (nom. द्राघयति -यितुं), वितन्, प्रतन्, विततीकृ, विस्तृ, विस्तीर्णीकृ, प्रपञ्च्, आयम्, आयतीकृ, विसृ, प्रसृ.

PROLONGATION, *s.* दीर्घीकरणं, द्राघिमा *m.* (न्), विस्तारः, विस्तरः, विस्तृतिः *f.*, विततिः *f.*, विततीकरणं, आयतिः *f.*, आयतीकरणं, प्रपञ्चः -ञ्चनं.

PROLONGED, *p. p.* दीर्घीकृतः -ता -तं, आयतीकृतः &c., विततीकृतः &c., विस्तृतः &c., आयामितः &c.; 'prolonged note,' लयः.

PROLUSION, *s.* पूर्व्वरङ्गः, पूर्व्वपरीक्षा. *See* PRELUDE.

PROMENADE, *s.* (Walk for amusement) विहारः, विहरणं, परिक्रमः. —(Place for walking) विहारस्थानं, विहरणस्थानं.

To PROMENADE, *v. n.* विहृ (c. 1. -हरति -ते -हर्तुं), विहारं कृ, परिक्रमं कृ.

PROMINENCE, PROMINENCY, *s.* (A standing out) उन्नतिः *f.*, समुन्नतिः *f.*, उदग्रता, प्रलम्बता, उत्तुङ्गता, सुरूढता, प्ररूढता, आभोगः; 'of the breast,' स्तनाभोगः. —(Conspicuousness) प्रधानता, प्राधान्यं, प्रमुखत्वं, विशिष्टता, वैशिष्ट्यं, उत्कृष्टता, उत्कर्षः, समुन्नतिः *f.*, श्रेष्ठता, परमपदं, मुख्यस्थानं, मुख्यता.

PROMINENT, *a.* (Standing out) उन्नतः -ता -तं, समुन्नतः &c., उदग्रः -ग्रा -ग्रं, उत्तुङ्गः -ङ्गा -ङ्गं, सुरूढः -ढा -ढं, प्रलम्बः -म्बा -म्बं, आभोगवान् -वती -वत् (त्), साभोगः -गा -गं, उद् or उत् prefixed; 'having prominent teeth,' उन्मुरः -रा -रं, उदग्रदन् &c. *See* PROJECTING; 'having a prominent nose,' उन्नसः -सा -सं, प्रलम्बघोणः -णा -णं; 'having prominent breasts,' स्तनाभोगः -गा -गं, स्तनाभोगविशिष्टः -ष्टा -ष्टं, उन्नतस्तनः &c.—(Conspicuous) सुदृश्यः -श्या -श्यं, सुदर्शनीयः -या -यं, सुव्यक्तः -क्ता -क्तं, सुप्रकाशः -शा -शं, प्रथमदृग्विषयः -या -यं, प्रथमदृग्गोचरः -रा -रं.—(Eminent, principle) प्रमुखः -खा -खं, मुख्यः -ख्या -ख्यं, प्रधानः -ना -नं, उत्कृष्टः -ष्टा -ष्टं, प्रकृष्टः &c., विशिष्टः -ष्टा -ष्टं, परमः -मा -मं.

PROMINENTLY, *adv.* उन्नतं, सुव्यक्तं, सुप्रकाशं, प्रधानतस्, प्राधान्यतस्.

PROMISCUOUS *a.* प्रकीर्णः -र्णा -र्णं, सङ्कीर्णः &c., सङ्कुलः -ला -लं, सान्निपातिकः -की -कं, अविविक्तः -क्ता -क्तं, निर्विशेषः -षा -षं, अपरिच्छिन्नः -न्ना -न्नं, अपरिच्छेदः -दा -दं, अभेदः -दा -दं, मिश्रितः -ता -तं, क्रमविचारहीनः -ना -नं, भेदविचारहीनः &c., अवर्गीयः -या -यं; 'promiscuous intercourse,' सङ्करः, साङ्कर्य्यं.

PROMISCUOUSLY, *adv.* अविविक्तं, अविशेषेण, निर्विशेषं -षेण, अविशेषतस्, अभेदेन, सङ्कीर्णं, प्रकीर्णं, अक्रमेण, अपरिच्छेदेन; 'going about promiscuously,' सङ्कीर्णचारी -रिणी &c.

PROMISCUOUSNESS, *s.* सङ्कीर्णता, प्रकीर्णता, सङ्कुलत्वं, अविविक्तता, निर्विशेषत्वं, परिच्छेदहीनता, भेदहीनता, क्रमविचारहीनता, भेदविचारराहित्यं, अवर्गीयता.

PROMISE, *s.* प्रतिज्ञा, प्रतिज्ञानं, प्रतिज्ञातं, वचनं, अभ्युपायः, अङ्गीकारः, स्वीकारः, उरीकारः, ऊरीकारः, उररीकारः, संश्रवः, प्रतिश्रवः, उपश्रुतिः *f.*, संविद् *f.*, नियमः, प्रत्ययः, उपगमः, अभ्युपगमः, परिपणनं; 'hollow or empty promise,' निरर्थकप्रतिज्ञा, असत्यप्रतिज्ञा, रिक्तभाषणं, रिक्तवचनं, शब्दपाण्डित्यं; 'to keep or fulfil a promise,' प्रतिज्ञां पाल् or शुध् or तॄ or अपवृज् or सत्याकृ or सत्यीकृ, उक्तं निर्वह् (c. 10. -वाहयति -यितुं), वचनोद्धारं कृ; 'one who keeps a promise,' कृतप्रतिज्ञः -ज्ञा -ज्ञं, सत्यसन्धः -न्धा -न्धं; 'to break a promise,' प्रतिज्ञाभङ्गं कृ, वचनभङ्गं कृ, संविद्व्यतिक्रमं कृ, प्रतिज्ञाव्यतिक्रमं कृ, प्रतिज्ञालंघनं कृ, विसंवद् (c. 1. -वदति -दितुं), विसंवादं कृ, विप्रलम्भं कृ, प्रतिज्ञासन्न्यासं कृ; 'slow in performing a promise,' प्रतिज्ञामन्थरः -रा -रं; 'to confirm a promise by touching water,' उदकस्पर्शं कृ; 'a sure, unfailing promise,' सत्यप्रतिज्ञा, सत्यवचनं, भीष्मप्रतिज्ञा, रामप्रतिज्ञा, रामवचनं.

To PROMISE, *v. a.* and *n.* प्रतिज्ञा (c. 9. -जानीते -ज्ञातुं), सम्प्रतिज्ञा with dat. or gen. of the person and acc. of the thing; प्रतिज्ञां कृ, अङ्गीकृ, उरीकृ, ऊरीकृ, उररीकृ, प्रतिश्रु (c. 5. -शृणोति -श्रोतुं), संश्रु, उपश्रु, उपगम् (c. 1. -गच्छति -गन्तुं), उपगमं कृ, अभ्युपे (c. 2. अभ्युपैति -तुं, rt. इ), पणं कृ, परिपणनं कृ, संगॄ (c. 6. -गिरते -गरितुं -रीतुं) पण् (c. 1. पणते -णितुं), परिपण्, वाग्दानं कृ; 'I promise this to thee,' तुभ्यम् इदं ददानि or दास्यामि इति प्रतिज्ञापूर्व्वं वद्; 'he promises a cow to the Brahmin,' विप्राय गां प्रतिशृणोति; 'to promise marriage,' विवाहप्रतिज्ञां कृ, वाग्दानं कृ, वाचादानं कृ, वाग्निश्चयं कृ.

PROMISE-BREACH, *s.* प्रतिज्ञाभङ्गः, वचनभङ्गः, प्रतिज्ञाव्यतिक्रमः.

PROMISE-BREAKER, *s.* प्रतिज्ञाभञ्जकः, प्रतिज्ञालंघी *m.* (न्), प्रतिज्ञाव्यतिक्रमी *m.*, वचनघाती *m.*, संविद्व्यतिक्रमी *m.*, संविद्व्यतिक्रमकारी *m.*, विसंवादी *m.*

PROMISED, *p. p.* प्रतिज्ञातः -ता -तं, कृतप्रतिज्ञः -ज्ञा -ज्ञं, अङ्गीकृतः -ता -तं, उरीकृतः &c., ऊरीकृतः &c., उररीकृतः &c., प्रतिश्रुतः -ता -तं, संश्रुतः &c., उपश्रुतः &c., आश्रुतः &c., स्वीकृतः &c., उपगतः &c., अभ्युपगतः &c., अभ्युपेतः &c., परिपणितः &c., संविदितः &c., सन्दिष्टः -ष्टा -ष्टं, वाग्दत्तः -त्ता -त्तं, वाचादत्तः &c., वचनदत्तः &c., सङ्कीर्णः -र्णा -र्णं, समाहितः -ता -तं.

PROMISE-KEEPER, *s.* प्रतिज्ञापालकः, सत्यप्रतिज्ञः, सत्यसन्धः, कृतप्रतिज्ञः, वचननिर्वाहकः, उक्तिनिर्वाहकः.

PROMISER, *s.* प्रतिज्ञाकारी *m.* (न्), प्रतिज्ञाकृत् *m.*, प्रतिज्ञाता *m.* (तृ).

PROMISING, *part.* or *a.* आशाजनकः -का -कं, आशाजननः -ना -नं, आशाकारी &c.

PROMISSORY, *a.* सप्रतिज्ञः -ज्ञा -ज्ञं, प्रतिज्ञायुक्तः -क्ता -क्तं, प्रतिज्ञाविशिष्टः &c.

PROMONTORY, *s.* भूनासिका, भूमिनासिका, भूशलाका, अन्तरीपः -पं, समुद्रमध्ये महाद्वीपबहिःस्थो भूमिभागः, महाद्वीपनासिका, उदग्रभूमिः *f.*, उदग्रभूः *f.*, समुद्रविच्छिन्नभूमिः *f.*, स्थूलोच्चयः.

To PROMOTE, *v. a.* (Further) उपकृ, पुरस्कृ, साहाय्यं कृ, उपकारं कृ, प्रवृत् (c. 10. -वर्त्तयति -यितुं), प्रयुज् (c. 10. -योजयति -यितुं), सिद्धिसाधनं कृ.—(Excite, incite) उत्तिज्, समुत्तिज्, उद्युज्, प्रणुद्, प्रचुद्, प्रत्रुष्, प्रवृत्.—(Exalt, prefer) पदं वृध् (c. 10. वर्धयति -यितुं) or संवृध् or प्रवृध्, श्रेष्ठपदे or उत्कृष्टपदे नियुज् or प्रतिपद्, पदवृद्धिं कृ, पदवर्धनं कृ, प्रतिपत्तिं दा, पुरस्कृ.

PROMOTED, *p. p.* (Furthered) प्रवर्त्तितः -ता -तं, उपकृतः -ता -तं, कृतोपकारः -रा -रं, कृतसाहाय्यः -य्या -य्यं.—(Exalted, preferred) संवर्धितः -ता -तं, प्रवर्धितः &c., श्रेष्ठपदनियुक्तः -क्ता -क्तं.

PROMOTER, *s.* प्रवर्त्तकः, प्रयोजकः, प्रयोजककर्त्ता *m.* (र्तृ), उत्तेजकः.

PROMOTION, *s.* (Furtherance) उपकारः, सहायता, साहाय्यं, प्रवर्त्तनं, पुरस्कारः, संवर्धनं -ना.—(Preferment, exaltation) पदवृद्धिः *f.*, पदवर्धनं, संवर्धना -नं, प्रवर्धनं, वर्धनं, प्रतिपत्तिः *f.*, श्रेष्ठपदनियोजनं, श्रेष्ठपदप्राप्तिः *f.*

PROMOTIVE, *a.* संवर्धक: -का -कं, वर्धक: &c., प्रवर्त्तक: -का -कं, साधक: &c., सिद्धिसाधक: &c., संवर्धनकारी -रिणी -रि (न्).

PROMPT, *a.* उद्युक्त: -क्ता -क्तं, उद्यत: -ता -तं, अविलम्ब: -म्बा -म्बं, अविलम्बी -म्बिनी -म्बि (न्), अविलम्बित: -ता -तं, प्रत्युत्पन्न: -न्ना -न्नं, प्रत्युत्पन्नमति: -ति: -ति, आशुकारी -रिणी &c., सुप्रस्तुत: -ता -तं, प्रस्तुत: -ता -तं, उद्योगी &c., उद्यमी &c., प्रतिभानवान् -वती -वत् (त्), प्रतिभावान् &c., सप्रतिभ: -भा -भं, प्रगल्भ: -ल्भा -ल्भं, पटु: -टु: -ट्वी -टु, अदीर्घसूत्र: -त्रा -त्रं, अविचार: -रा -रं, क्षिप्र: -प्रा -प्रं, सत्वर: -रा -रं.

To PROMPT, *v. a.* (Incite) उद्युज् (c. 10. -योजयति -यितुं), प्रयुज्, नियुज्, प्रेर्, प्रवृत्, प्रोत्सह्, उत्सह्, प्ररुच्, प्रणुद्, प्रणुद्, उत्तिज्, प्रवर्त्तनं कृ, प्रोत्साहनं कृ.—(Suggest something forgotten) विस्मृतबोधनं कृ, विस्मृतसूचनं कृ, उत्तरसाधनं कृ, सूचनां कृ.

PROMPTED, *p. p.* प्रेरित: -ता -तं, प्रोत्साहित: &c., प्रवर्त्तित: &c., नियोजित: &c., प्रयोजित: &c., उद्युक्त: -क्ता -क्तं, उत्तेजित: -ता -तं, सूचित: &c.

PROMPTER, *s.* (Inciter) प्रेरक:, प्रवर्त्तक:, प्रोत्साहक:, प्रयोजक:.—(One who suggests something forgotten) विस्मृतबोधक:, विस्मृतसूचक:, अपस्मृतसूचक:, उत्तरसाधक:, सूचनाकारी *m.* (न्), सूचक:.—(At a theatre) सूचक:, सूत्रधार:.

PROMPTING, *s.* (Act of inciting) प्रेरणं, प्रवर्त्तनं, प्रोत्साहनं, प्ररोचनं, उत्तेजनं.—(Suggesting something forgotten) विस्मृतसूचनं -ना, अपस्मृतसूचनं, सूचना.

PROMPTITUDE, PROMPTNESS, *s.* अविलम्ब:, प्रत्युत्पन्नता, उद्यम:, उद्युक्तता, उद्योग:, क्षिप्रता -त्वं, सत्वरता, पटुता, प्रस्तुतता, सुप्रस्तुतता, आशुकारित्वं, प्रतिभा, अविचार:.

PROMPTLY, *adv.* अविलम्बेन, अविलम्बितं, सद्यस्, सत्वरं, क्षिप्रं, आशु, अचिरेण, अचिरात्, अविचारेण, सोद्योगं, सोद्यमं, सप्रतिभं.

To PROMULGATE, *v. a.* (Publish, proclaim) प्रकाश्, विकाश्, ख्या in caus., प्रख्या, प्रचर् in caus., प्रकटीकृ, कृत्, उत्कृत्, प्रकृत्, घुष् &c.

PROMULGATED, *p. p.* प्रकाशित: -ता -तं, प्रकीर्त्तित: &c., उत्कीर्त्तित: &c., प्रचारित: &c., प्रकटीकृत: &c., प्रकाशम् अभिहित: -ता -तं. *See* PUBLISHED, PROCLAIMED.

PROMULGATION, *s.* प्रकाशनं, प्रचारणं, प्रकीर्त्तनं, उत्कीर्त्तनं, विघोषणं.

PROMULGATOR, *s.* प्रकाशक:, प्रचारक:, ख्यापक:, विघोषक:, घोषक:.

PRONE, *a.* (Bending forward, not erect, looking down) प्रणत: -ता -तं, नत: &c., नम्र: -म्रा -म्रं, प्रणतशिरस्क: -स्का -स्कं, अधोमुख: -खा -खी -खं, अधोवदन: -ना -नं.—(Lying with the face downwards) अधोमुख: &c., अधोवदन: &c., अधोमुखशय: -या -यं.—(Inclined, disposed) प्रवण: -णा -णं, उन्मुख: -खा -खं, प्रवर्त्तित: -ता -तं, शील in comp. *See* INCLINED.—(Disposed to fall) पातुक: -का -कं, पतयालु: -लु: -लु.

PRONENESS, *s.* (State of bending downwards) प्रणतत्वं -ता, नम्रता, अधोमुखता.—(Inclination, disposition) प्रवणता, प्रावण्यं, मन:-प्रावण्यं, उन्मुखता, प्रवृत्ति: *f.*, प्रवाह:, शीलता; 'proneness to fall,' पातुकता -त्वं, पतयालुता, पतनशीलता.

PRONG, *s.* शूल: -लं, शिखा, अग्रं, कण्टक:; 'having two prongs,' द्विशिख: -खा -खं, द्व्यग्र: -ग्रा -ग्रं; 'having three prongs,' त्रिशिख: &c., त्र्यग्र: &c.

PRONOMINAL, *a.* सर्व्वनामसम्बन्धी -न्धिनी -न्धि (न्), सर्व्वनामविषयक: -का -कं.

PRONOUN, *s.* (In grammar) सर्व्वनाम *n.* (न्), सामान्यसंज्ञा.

To PRONOUNCE, *v. a.* (Utter articulately) उच्चर् (c. 10. -चारयति -यितुं), उदाहृ (c. 1. -हरति -हर्त्तुं), व्याहृ, समुदाहृ, गद् (c. 1. गदति -दितुं), उदीर्, समुदीर्.—(Speak) वद् (c. 1. वदति -दितुं), प्रवद्, वच्, प्रवच्, गद्, निगद्.—(Affirm confidently) निश्चयपूर्व्वं वद्, दृढनिश्चयेन वद्, निर्णयपूर्व्वं वद्.—(Declare) प्रख्या, कृत्, प्रकृत्.—(Pronounce sentence) निर्णयं कृ, निर्णयपादं कृ.

PRONOUNCEABLE, *a.* उच्चारणीय: -या -यं, उच्चार्य्य: -र्य्या -र्य्यं, उदाहरणीय: &c.; 'easily pronounceable,' सुखोच्चार्य्य: &c., सुखोद्य: -द्या -द्यं.

PRONOUNCED, *p. p.* (Uttered) उच्चारित: -ता -तं, उदाहृत: &c., समुदाहृत: &c., व्याहृत: &c., अभिव्याहृत: &c., उदीरित: &c., समुदीरित: &c.; 'pronounced imperfectly,' ग्रस्त: -स्ता -स्तं, लुप्तवर्णपद: -दा -दं.—(Spoken) उक्त: -क्ता -क्तं, गदित: -ता -तं, निगदित: &c.—(Declared) ख्यापित: -ता -तं, कीर्त्तित: &c., प्रकीर्त्तित: &c.

PRONUNCIATION, *s.* उच्चारणं, उच्चार:, उल्लेख:, उल्लेखनं, उदाहरणं, उदाहार:, व्याहार:, व्याहरणं, उदीरणं; 'of letters,' वर्णोच्चार: -रणं, वर्णोदाहार:, अक्षरव्याहार:; 'easy of pronunciation,' सुखोच्चार्य्य: -र्य्या -र्य्यं, सुखोद्य: -द्या -द्यं; 'difficult,' दु:खोच्चार्य्य: &c., दुरुदाहर: -रा -रं, दुर्वच: -चा -चं; 'science of pronunciation,' शिक्षा.

PROOF, *s.* (Evidence, demonstration) प्रमाणं, प्रामाण्यं, साधनं, उपपादनं, उपपत्ति: *f.*, प्रतिपत्ति: *f.*, प्रतिपादनं, सिद्धि: *f.*, सिद्धान्त:, निर्देश:, निर्णय:, निर्णेतृत्वं, प्रमाता *m.* (तृ), प्रमातृत्वं, क्रियानिर्देश:; 'written proof,' लेख्यप्रमाणं, साधनपत्रं; 'ocular,' प्रत्यक्षप्रमाणं; 'production of proof,' साधननिर्देश:; 'having proof,' सप्रमाण: -णा -णं; 'absence of proof,' अप्रामाण्यं, प्रमाणाभाव:; 'according to proof,' प्रमाणतस्, प्रामाण्यतस्; 'party on whom rests the onus of proof,' साध्यवान् *m.* (त्); 'admitted as proof,' प्रमाणीभूत: -ता -तं.—(In arithmetic) उपपत्ति: *f.*; 'by algebra,' अव्यक्तक्रियया उपपत्ति:.—(Evident or sure sign) लक्षणं, सनिश्चयलक्षणं.—(Trial, test) परीक्षा, उपधा, प्रतीति: *f.*, कष्टि: *f.*; 'to put to the proof,' परीक्ष् (c. 1. -ईक्षते -क्षितुं). *See* *To* PROVE; 'this may be put to the proof,' एतत्प्रतीतिर् उत्पाद्या.—(Rough impression, first impression) स्थूलमुद्रा, प्रथममुद्रा, पूर्व्वमुद्रा.—(Imprenetrability) अभेद्यता, अभेदनीयता, अतिदृढता, सुदृढता, अविकार्य्यता; 'proof against,' अभेद्य: -द्या -द्यं, अविकार्य्य: -र्य्या -र्य्यं, अहार्य्य: &c., अबाध्य: &c.; 'proof against temptation,' अलोभनीय: -या -यं, अप्रलोभनीय: &c.

PROOFLESS, *a.* निष्प्रमाण: -णा -णं, अप्रमाण: &c., प्रमाणरहित: -ता -तं.

To PROP, *v. a.* (Support) आलम्ब् (c. 1. -लम्बते -म्बितुं, c. 10. -लम्बयति -यितुं), अवलम्ब्, समवलम्ब्, उपस्तम्भ्, विष्टम्भ्, संस्तम्भ्, धृ in caus., सन्धृ, अभिधृ.

PROP, *s.* आधार:, उपस्तम्भ:, अवष्टम्भ:, अवलम्बनं, आलम्ब: -म्बनं, धारणं, उपघ्न:, आश्रय:, उपलम्भ:; 'as a tree of a creeper,' लताश्रय:.

To PROPAGATE, *v. a.* (Multiply the kind by successive production) उत्पत्तिपारम्पर्य्येण or परम्परप्रसवेन जातिं वृध् (c. 10. वर्धयति -यितुं), आनुक्रमिकप्रसवेन सन्तानं or वंशं वृध्, क्रमिकजननेन प्रजावृद्धिं कृ or सन्तानवृद्धिं कृ.—(Generate successively) पारम्पर्य्येण उत्पद् (c. 10. -पादयति -यितुं), क्रमे क्रमे जन् (c. 10. जनयति -यितुं) or प्रजन् or सु or प्रसु.—(Increase, extend) वृध् (c. 10. वर्धयति -यितुं), प्रवृध्, परिवृध्, बहुतरीकृ, अधिकतरीकृ, विस्तृ in caus., वितन्, सन्तन्, प्रसृ in caus., विसृ, प्रथ्.—(Disseminate doctrines, &c.) प्रचर् (c. 10. -चारयति -यितुं), प्रचरीकृ, प्रचलीकृ.

To PROPAGATE, *v. n.* (Have young) शावकान् प्रसू (c. 2. -सूते, c. 4. -सूयते -सोतुं) or जन् (c. 10. जनयति -यितुं) or उत्पद् (c. 4. -पाद-

यति -यितुं), प्रसवं कृ, प्रसूतिं कृ.

PROPAGATED, *p. p.* परम्परप्रसवेन or आनुक्रमिकप्रसवेन वर्धितः -ता -तं or वर्धितजातिः -तिः -ति or वर्धितवंशः -शा -शं or वर्धितप्रजः -जा -जं, क्रमे क्रमे or अनुक्रमं or पारम्पर्य्येण प्रसूतः -ता -तं or जातः -ता -तं or उत्पन्नः &c. or उत्पादितः -ता -तं.—(Increased, extended) वर्धितः- ता -तं, प्रवृद्धः -द्धा -द्धं, सन्ततः -ता -तं, प्रसारितः &c., विस्तीर्णः -र्णा-र्णं, प्रथितः&c.—(Disseminated) प्रचारितः-ता-तं, प्रचलीकृतः&c.

PROPAGATION, *s.* (Multiplication of the kind by successive production) उत्पत्तिपारम्पर्य्येण प्रजावृद्धिः *f.*, परम्परप्रसवेन सन्तानवृद्धिः *f.*, आनुक्रमिकप्रसवेन जातिवर्धनं.—(Successive generation) पारम्पर्य्योत्पत्तिः *f.*, उत्पत्तिपारम्पर्य्यं, परम्परोत्पत्तिः *f.*, परम्परप्रसूतिः *f.*, प्रसूतिपारम्पर्य्यं, क्रमिकोत्पत्तिः *f.*, अनुक्रमोत्पत्तिः *f.*, प्रत्युत्पत्तिः *f.*—(Extension, spreading) वर्धनं, प्रवर्धनं, विस्तारः, प्रसारणं, विततिः *f.*, सन्ततिः *f.*, प्रथनं.—(Dissemination) प्रचारणं, प्रचलीकरणं, व्यापनं, व्याप्तिः *f.*

PROPAGATOR, *s.* क्रमिकोत्पादकः, उत्पत्तिपारम्पर्य्येण प्रजावर्धकः or वंशवर्धकः or सन्तानवर्धकः, प्रचारकः, विस्तारकः.

To PROPEL, *v. a.* प्रेर् (c. 10. प्रेरयति -यितुं), प्रणुद् (c. 6. -णुदति -णोत्तुं), चल् (c. 10. चालयति -यितुं), सञ्चल्, सृ (c. 10. सारयति -यितुं), सञ्चर् (c. 10. -चारयति -यितुं), कृष् (c. 1. कर्षति, क्रष्टुं), समाकृष्.

PROPELLED, *p. p.* प्रेरितः -ता -तं, प्रणोदितः -ता -तं, प्रणुन्नः -न्ना -न्नं, चालितः -ता -तं, सञ्चालितः &c., सञ्चारितः &c., सारितः &c.

PROPENSE, *a.* प्रवणः -णा -णं, उन्मुखः -खा -खं. *See* PRONE.

PROPENSION, PROPENSITY, *s.* प्रवणता -त्वं, प्रावण्यं, मनःप्रावण्यं, चित्तप्रावण्यं, उन्मुखता, प्रवृत्तिः *f.*, प्रवाहः, शीलता -त्वं in comp., आलुता affixed; 'propensity to fall,' पतनशीलता, पतयालुता, पतनोन्मुखता; 'good propensity,' सुशीलता, साधुशीलत्वं; 'having good propensities,' सुशीलः -ला -लं; 'evil propensity,' दुर्व्यसनं, व्यसनं, दुःशीलता, दुर्गुणः; 'having evil propensities,' दुर्व्यसनी -निनी -नि (न्), दुःशीलः -ला -लं.

PROPER, *a.* (Peculiar) स्व in comp., स्वकीयः -या -यं, स्वीयः -या -यं, स्वकः -का -कं, आत्म in comp., आत्मीयः -या -यं, आत्मकीयः &c., निज in comp., निजः -जा -जं, अव्यापी -पिनी &c., असाधारणः -णा -णी -णं; 'proper nature,' आत्मभावः, स्वभावः; 'proper duty,' स्वधर्म्मः.—(Fit, suitable) योग्यः -ग्या -ग्यं, यथायोग्यः &c., युक्तः -क्ता -क्तं, उपयुक्तः &c., उपयोगी -गिनी &c., उचितः -ता -तं, यथोचितः &c., समुचितः &c., औपयिकः -की -कं, समञ्जसः -सा -सं, सङ्गतः -ता -तं, सङ्गतार्थः -र्था -र्थं, उपपन्नः -न्ना -न्नं, पर्य्याप्तः -प्ता -प्तं, न्याय्यः -य्या -य्यं, अर्हः -र्हा -र्हं, यथार्हः &c., पथ्यः -थ्या -थ्यं, अभिनीतः -ता -तं, प्रशस्तः -स्ता -स्तं, क्षमः -मा -मं. Sometimes expressible by the fut. pass. part.; as, 'proper to be done,' कर्त्तव्यः -व्या -व्यं, करणीयः -या -यं, कार्य्यः -र्य्या -र्य्यं; 'a proper course,' कर्त्तव्यता; 'proper to be eaten,' खाद्यः -द्या -द्यं; 'proper for diet,' पथ्यः &c.; 'eating what is proper,' पथ्याशी &c.; 'to be proper,' युज् in pass. (युज्यते), अर्ह् (c. 1. अर्हति -र्हितुं), उपपद् in pass. (-पद्यते). *See* OUGHT.—(Proper noun) नामवाचकः.

PROPERLY, *adv.* यथायोग्यं, यथोचितं, युक्तं, योग्यं, उचितं, यथायुक्तं, यथार्हं -र्हतस्, सम्यक्, उपयुक्तं, योगतस्, यथार्थं, यथायथं, यथातथं, समञ्जसं, न्यायतस्, धर्म्मतस्, साम्प्रतं, स्थाने.—(Strictly) तत्त्वतस्, वस्तुतस्.

PROPERTY, *s.* (Quality, inherent or natural characteristic) गुणः, धर्म्मः, स्वभावः, स्वधर्म्मः, विशेषः -षणं, विशेषलक्षणं, लक्षणं, सहजगुणः, सहजभावः, प्रकृतिभावः, प्रकृतिगुणः, रूपं, स्वरूपं, वस्तु *n.*, वस्तुस्वभावः, वस्तुशक्तिः *f.*, निसर्गभावः, व्यवच्छेदः -दकः; 'specific property,' जातिस्वभावः, जातित्वं; 'properties, a collection of them,' गुणसमूहः, गुणजातं; 'the three properties of nature,' गुणत्रयं; *see* NATURE; 'possession of properties,' गुणवत्ता -त्वं, गुणता, गुणिता; 'possessed of them,' गुणान्वितः -ता -तं, गुणवान् &c.; 'a general or common property' साधारणगुणः साधारणधर्म्मः; 'latent property,' मर्म्म *n.* (न्), गूढधर्म्मः; 'some properties belong to all numbers,' कतिचिद् धर्म्माः सर्व्वसंख्याविषयका भवन्ति.—(Right of possessing) स्वत्वं, अधिकारः, अधिकारित्वं -ता, स्वाम्यं, स्वामित्वं, प्रभुत्वं.—(Thing owned, own possession) स्वं, स्वधनं, स्ववित्तं, स्वद्रव्यं, आत्मधनं.—(Possessions in general, money, estates, &c.) धनं, वित्तं, वसु *n.*, विभवः, द्रव्यं, द्रविणं, अर्थः, रिक्थं, ऋक्थं, दायः, राः *m.* (रै), भूतिः *f.*, आर्थ्यमाणत्वं, योगक्षेमः; 'fixed property,' स्थावरं, स्थावरधनं, निबन्धः; 'moveable property,' अस्थावरं, अस्थावरधनं; 'landed property,' भूमिधनं, भूमिः *f.*, क्षेत्रं, पांशुः *m.*, स्थावरं; 'property in cattle,' गोधनं, गोवृन्दं; 'public or common property,' गणद्रव्यं, गणधनं; 'possessing property,' धनी -निनी &c., धनवान् &c., रिक्थी &c.; 'accession of property,' धनागमः; 'accumulation of it,' धनसम्पत्तिः *f.*, धनोपचयः; 'heir to it,' धनाधिकारी *m.* (न्), ऋक्थभागी *m.*, रिक्थहारी *m.*, धनहारी *m.*, धनहरः, धनग्राहः; 'receiving or inheriting it,' ऋक्थग्रहणं, धनग्रहणं, धनादानं; 'division of it,' ऋक्थभागः, दायभागः, दायविभागः; 'forfeiture of it,' दायापवर्त्तनं; 'acquisition of it,' धनार्जनं.

PROPHECY, *s.* (Act of prediction) भविष्यत्कथनं, भविष्यकथनं, भाविकथनं, भाविविषयकथनं, भविष्यत्प्रदर्शनं, भविष्यद्दर्शनं, प्रदर्शनं, भाविविषयप्रदर्शनं, भाविप्रदर्शनं, भविष्यत्सूचनं, भाविनिरूपणं, अग्रनिरूपणं, सिद्धादेशः. *See* PREDICTION.—(The prediction itself, or matter predicted) भविष्यद्वाक्यं, भविष्यद्वचनं, भविष्यवादः, भविष्यद्वाक् *f.* (च्), भविष्यार्थः, भविष्यत् *n.*, भवितव्यं.

PROPHESIED, *p. p.* प्रदर्शितः -ता -तं, पूर्व्वकथितः &c., प्राक्सम्भवाद्दर्शितः &c.

To PROPHESY, *v. a.* भविष्यत् कथ् (c. 10. कथयति -यितुं) or प्रदृश् (c. 10. -दर्शयति -यितुं) or दृश्, भविष्यत् सूच्, भाविकथनं कृ, भाविविषयं प्रदृश् or कथ्, भाविविषयं or भविष्यार्थं पूर्व्वं दृश् or अग्रे सूच् or निरूप्, भाविप्रदर्शनं कृ, अनागतं दृश् or ज्ञा in caus. *See To* PREDICT, FORETELL.

PROPHET, *s.* भविष्यद्वक्ता *m.* (क्तृ), भविष्यद्वादी *m.* (न्), भाविवक्ता *m.*, भविष्यत्कथकः, भाविकथकः, प्रदर्शकः, भविष्यत्प्रदर्शकः, भाविप्रदर्शकः, भाविदर्शकः, भविष्यद्दर्शकः, भाविसूचकः, भविष्यत्सूचकः, अनागतदर्शकः, अनागतवक्ता *m.*, अग्रनिरूपकः, पूर्व्वनिरूपकः, भाविनिरूपकः, अनागतज्ञापकः, भाविज्ञापकः, पुराविद् *m.*, दूरदर्शी *m.* (न्), भाविदर्शी *m.*, दैवज्ञः.

PROPHETESS, *s.* भविष्यद्वक्त्री, भविष्यद्वादिनी, अनागतदर्शिनी, दैवज्ञा.

PROPHETIC, PROPHETICAL, *a.* भविष्यत्सूचकः -का -कं, भाविसूचकः &c., भविष्यद्दर्शकः &c., भाविदर्शकः &c., भाविप्रदर्शकः &c., प्रदर्शकः &c., भविष्यत्कथनविषयः -या -यं, भाविकथनसम्बन्धी &c., आर्षः -र्षी -र्षं.

PROPHETICALLY, *adv.* भविष्यत्कथनपूर्व्वं, भाविसूचनपूर्व्वं, भाविकथनक्रमेण.

PROPHYLACTIC, PROPHYLACTICAL, *a.* रोगनिवारकः -का -कं, रोगवारकः &c.

PROPINQUITY, *s.* समीपता, सामीप्यं, सन्निधिः *m.*, सन्निधानं, सन्निकर्षः, प्रत्यासत्तिः *f.*, प्रत्यासन्नता, आसन्नता; 'close propinquity,' आनन्तर्य्यं, अनन्तरं. *See* NEARNESS.

PROPITIABLE, *a.* आराधनीयः -या -यं, आराध्यः -ध्या -ध्यं, प्रसादनीयः &c.

To PROPITIATE, *v. a.* आराध् (c. 10. -राधयति -यितुं), अभिराध्, प्रसद् (c. 10. -सादयति -यितुं), सम्प्रसद्, अभिप्रसद्, अनुरञ्ज् (c. 10. -रञ्जयति -यितुं), सान्त्व् (c. 10. सान्त्वयति -यितुं), शम् (c. 10. शमयति -यितुं), प्रसाध् (c. 10. -साधयति -यितुं), तुष् (c. 10. तोषयति -यितुं), सन्तुष्, परितुष्, सम्परितुष्, अनुनी (c. 1. -नयति -नेतुं), अभिप्रणी, प्रसन्नीकृ.

PROPITIATED, *p. p.* आराधितः -ता -तं, प्रसादितः &c., प्रसन्नः -न्ना -न्नं, अनुरञ्जितः &c., अभिराद्धः -द्धा -द्धं, शमितः -ता -तं, शान्तः -न्ता -न्तं, प्रशमितः &c., अनुनीतः &c., अभिप्रणीतः &c.

PROPITIATION, *s.* आराधनं -ना, प्रसादनं, सान्त्वनं -ना, सान्त्वः -न्त्वं, शान्त्वः -न्त्वं, शान्त्वनं, अनुरञ्जनं, शमनं, शान्तिः *f.*, प्रशान्तिः *f.*, उपशान्तिः *f.*, शान्तिकर्म्म *n.* (न्), प्रशमनं, उपशमनं, अनुनयः, अभिप्रणयः, सन्तोषणं, साम *n.* (न्); 'for sin,' प्रायश्चित्तं.

PROPITIATOR, *s.* आराधकः, शान्तिकर्त्ता *m.* (र्तृ), सान्त्वनकृत्, अनुरञ्जकः.

PROPITIATORY, *a.* शान्तिकः -की -कं, शमकः -का -कं, शान्तिकरः -रा -रं, सान्त्वकरः &c., शमकारकः -का -कं, उपशमकः &c., आराधकः &c., प्रसन्नकारकः &c.; 'propitiatory ceremonies,' शान्तिकं, शान्तिकपौष्टिकं; 'course of such ceremonies,' अनुष्ठानं; 'water used at them,' शान्त्युदं -दकं.

PROPITIOUS, *a.* (Favorable) प्रसन्नः -न्ना -न्नं, सुप्रसन्नः &c., अनुकूलः -ला -लं, सुमनस्कः -स्का -स्कं, अनुग्राही -हिणी -हि (न्), आनुग्राहकः -की -कं, हितकामः -मा -मं, हितबुद्धिः -द्धिः -द्धि, सुहितः -ता -तं, उपकारशीलः -ला -लं, अभिमुखः -खा -खं.—(As a god granting boons) वरदः -दा -दं, वरप्रदः -दा -दं.—(Auspicious) शुभः -भा -भं, कल्याणः -णी -णं, शुभङ्करः -रा -रं, शुभदः -दा -दं, माङ्गलिकः -की -कं, मङ्गल्यः -ल्या -ल्यं, मङ्गलकरः &c., क्षेमकरः &c., क्षेमङ्करः &c., भद्रङ्करः &c., स्वस्तिङ्करः &c., क्षेमकारः -री -रं, शर्म्मदः -दा -दं, शङ्करः &c., शर्म्मवान् -वती -वत् (त्), इष्टः -ष्टा -ष्टं, अभीष्टः &c.

PROPITIOUSLY, *adv.* प्रसन्नं, प्रसादेन, सप्रसादं, अनुकूलं, सानुकूल्यं, सानुग्रहं, कल्याणं, समाङ्गल्यं, क्षेमेण. *See* AUSPICIOUSLY.

PROPITIOUSNESS, *s.* प्रसन्नता, प्रसादः, अनुकूलता, आनुकूल्यं, सुप्रसन्नता, अभिमुखता, आभिमुख्यं, माङ्गल्यं, मङ्गलता, कल्याणं -णता, शुभता.

PROPONENT, *s.* पूर्व्ववादी *m.* (न्), अग्रवादी *m.*, पूर्व्वपक्षी *m.*, प्रतिज्ञावादी *m.*

PROPORTION, *s.* (Comparative relation or adaptation of one thing to another) प्रमाणं, परिमाणं, सम्मितिः *f.*, प्रमितिः *f.*, परस्परप्रमाणं, परस्परानुगुण्यं, अनुगुणता, आनुगुण्यं, परस्परानुरूप्यं, परस्परानुरूपता, परस्परसादृश्यं, अन्योन्यसादृश्यं, अन्योन्यसमता, परस्परानुषङ्गः, मिथःसादृश्यं, परस्परसम्बन्धः, अन्योन्यसम्बन्धः, मिथःसम्बन्धः, परस्परान्वयः, व्यतिषङ्गः. *See* PROPORTIONATENESS; 'in proportion to,' अनुगुणः -णा -णं, अनुरूपः -पा -पं, अनुसारी -रिणी &c., सदृशः -शी -शं, समः -मा -मं, सादृश्येन, यथाप्रमाणं, प्रमाणतस्, अनुरूपेण, अनुसारेण, सदृशं, or expressed by अनु or यथा prefixed or तस् affixed; as, 'in proportion to one's strength,' यथाशक्ति, शक्तितस्, आत्मशक्तिसादृश्येन, स्वशक्तितस्, आत्मशक्तिसमं.—(Relation in general) अन्वयः, समन्वयः, अनुषङ्गः, सम्बन्धः, सम्पर्कः.—(In arithmetic) अनुपातः; 'the four numbers are in proportion,' चतस्रः संख्या अनुपातस्थाः सन्ति; 'dependence of larger numbers on smaller in a progressive series,' तारतम्यं.—(Symmetry, adaptation) सम्मितिः *f.*, सम्मितता, सन्धानं, अनुसन्धानं, संयोगः, सन्वयः; 'of parts or form,' अङ्गसंयोगः, अङ्गसन्धानं, अवयवसंयोगः, आकारशुद्धता, आकारशुद्धिः *f.*; 'of just proportions,' आकारशुद्धः -द्धा -द्धं.—(Just share) अंशः, भागः, विभागः, उद्धारः.

To PROPORTION, PROPORTIONATE, *v. a.* परस्परं or अन्योन्यं सदृशीकृ or अनुरूपीकृ or अनुगुणीकृ or समीकृ, परस्परानुगुण्यं कृ, परस्परानुरूप्यं कृ, परस्परसादृश्यं कृ, मिथःसादृश्यं कृ, सम्मितं -तां कृ, प्रमाणं कृ, समप्रमाणीकृ. *See To* ADJUST.

PROPORTIONATE, PROPORTIONABLE, PROPORTIONAL, *a.* समप्रमाणः -णा -णं, समपरिमाणः -णा -णं, समप्रमाणकः -का -कं, सम्मितः -ता -तं, प्रमितः -ता -तं, परिमितः -ता -तं, अनुगुणः -णा -णं, सदृशः -शी -शं, समः -मा -मं, तुल्यः -ल्या -ल्यं, अनुरूपः -पा -पं, अनुसारी &c., आनुषङ्गिकः -की -कं, अनुषङ्गिकः &c., अनुषङ्गी &c., परस्परानुगुणः &c., परस्परानुरूपः -पा -पं, परस्परसदृशः &c., परस्परानुषङ्गिकः -की -कं, समतोलः -ला -लं; 'proportionate to one's strength,' आत्मशक्तिसदृशः &c., आत्मशक्तिसमः &c.

PROPORTIONATENESS, PROPORTIONABLENESS, *s.* प्रमाणसमता, परिमाणसमता, समप्रमाणकता, सम्मितिः *f.*, अनुगुणता, आनुगुण्यं, सदृशता, सादृश्यं, समता, तुल्यता, अनुरूपता, आनुरूप्यं, परस्परानुगुण्यं. *See* PROPORTION.

PROPORTIONABLY, *adv.* अनुरूपतस्, अनुरूपं, अनुसारेण -रतस्, सादृश्येन, सदृशं, प्रमाणतस्, यथाप्रमाणं, यथापरिमाणं, प्रमाणानुसारात् -रेण, यथांशतस्, विभागशस्; 'to one's strength,' *see* under PROPORTION.

PROPORTIONED, *p. p.* यथाप्रमाणं परिकल्पितः -ता -तं, प्रमाणानुसारात् कल्पितः &c. or विहितः &c. *See* PROPORTIONATE.

PROPOSAL, *s.* उपन्यासः, कर्त्तव्योपन्यासः, प्रतिज्ञा, प्रतिज्ञातं, कर्त्तव्यसूचना -नं, कर्त्तव्यप्रतिज्ञा, कर्त्तव्यनिर्देशः, अभिधानं, अभिहितं, उक्तं, वाक्यं.—(Of marriage), *see* the next.

To PROPOSE, *v. a.* उपन्यस् (c. 4. -अस्यति -असितुं), उपन्यासं कृ, उपन्यासीकृ, कर्त्तव्योपन्यासं कृ, कर्त्तव्यसूचनं कृ, प्रतिज्ञा (c. 9. -जानाति -नीते -ज्ञातुं), प्रतिज्ञां कृ, कर्त्तव्यप्रतिज्ञां कृ, निविद् (c. 10. -वेदयति -यितुं), निवेदनं कृ, अभिधा (c. 3. -दधाति -धातुं), कर्त्तव्यं or यथाकर्त्तव्यं निर्दिश् (c. 6. -दिशति -देष्टुं) or सूच् (c. 10. सूचयति -यितुं), कर्त्तव्यनिर्देशं कृ.—(Intend), *see* the word.—(Make an offer of marriage) विवाहप्रतिज्ञां कृ, प्रेमनिवेदनं कृ.

PROPOSED, *p. p.* उपन्यस्तः -स्ता -स्तं, उपन्यासीकृतः -ता -तं, प्रतिज्ञातः &c., निवेदितः -ता -तं, निर्दिष्टः -ष्टा -ष्टं, अभिहितः &c.

PROPOSITION, *s.* उपन्यासः, प्रतिज्ञा, प्रतिज्ञातं, वाक्यं, उक्तं, वचनं.—(In logic, geometry, &c.) प्रतिज्ञा, प्रतिज्ञेयं, फक्किका, प्रमेयं, पूर्व्वपक्षः, प्रतिज्ञातार्थः; 'abandonment of the original proposition,' प्रतिज्ञासंन्यासः, प्रतिज्ञाहानिः *f.*; 'denial of a proposition,' प्रतिज्ञाविरोधः; 'completing it,' आकांक्षापूरणं; 'subsequent proposition,' प्रतिज्ञान्तरं.

To PROPOUND, *v. a.* (Propose) उपन्यस्, प्रतिज्ञा, निर्दिश्, अभिधा, सूच् (c. 10. सूचयति -यितुं), निविद्, प्रतिपद् (c. 10. -पादयति -यितुं).

PROPOUNDED, *p. p.* उपन्यस्तः -स्ता -स्तं, प्रतिज्ञातः -ता -तं, निर्दिष्टः -ष्टा -ष्टं.

PROPRIETARY, *a.* स्वामिसम्बन्धी -न्धिनी -न्धि (न्), स्वाम्यधीनः -ना -नं; 'proprietary right,' स्वत्वं, अधिकारः -रिता, स्वामित्वं, स्वाम्यं, प्रभुत्वं -ता.

PROPRIETOR, *s.* स्वामी *m.* (न्), अधिकारी *m.* (न्), प्रभुः *m.*, पतिः *m.*, ईश्वरः, स्वत्ववान् *m.* (त्), अधिकारवान् *m.*, स्वत्वाधिकारी *m.*; 'without title,' अनपसरः.

PROPRIETORSHIP, *s.* स्वामित्वं, स्वाम्यं, स्वत्वं, अधिकारिता -त्वं, प्रभुत्वं.

PROPRIETRESS, *s.* स्वामिनी *f.*, अधिकारिणी *f.*, स्वत्वाधिकारिणी *f.*

PROPRIETY, *s.* यथायोग्यता, युक्तता, योग्यता, यथायुक्तता, युक्तिः *f.*, उपयुक्तता, उपयोगिता -त्वं, उचितत्वं, औचित्यं, यथोचितत्वं, उपपत्तिः *f.*, सामञ्जस्यं, समञ्जसं, सम्भावना, न्यायः -यता, सङ्गतत्वं, साङ्गत्यं, याथार्थ्यं, यथार्हता, याथातथ्यं, अभेषः, पर्य्याप्तिः, पात्रं -त्रता; 'of conduct,' मर्य्यादा, मर्य्यादानतिक्रमः, विनयः, विनीतता, सुचर्य्या, सुचरितं, स्थितिः *f.*, संस्था, अनतिक्रमः, अव्यभिचारः, कर्त्तव्यता, इतिकर्त्तव्यता; 'pattern of propriety,' न्यायाधारः.

PROROGATION, *s.* चिरकालपर्य्यन्तं महासभाविसर्जनं or कार्य्यनिवृत्तिः *f.* or कार्य्यत्यागः.—(Prolongation) दीर्घीकरणं.

To PROROGUE, *v. a.* (Adjourn to a distant period) चिरकालपर्य्यन्तं महासभां विसृज् (c. 6. -सृजति -स्रष्टुं, c. 10. -सर्जयति -यितुं) or कार्य्यनिवृत्तिं कृ or कार्य्यत्यागं कृ.—(Prolong) द्राघ (nom. द्राघयति -यितुं), दीर्घीकृ, दीर्घकालस्थं -स्थां कृ, चिरकालस्थं -स्थां कृ.

PROROGUED, *p. p.* चिरकालपर्य्यन्तं विसर्जितः -ता -तं or विसृष्टः -ष्टा -ष्टं.

PROSAIC, *a.* गद्यरूपः -पा -पं, गद्यमयः -यी -यं, गद्यात्मकः -का -कं, छन्दोहीनः -ना -नं, छन्दोरहितः -ता -तं.—(Dull) विरसः -सा -सं, अरसिकः -का -कं, फल्गुः -ल्गुः -ल्गु, रसहीनः -ना -नं, तेजोहीनः &c., लवणहीनः &c.

To PROSCRIBE, *v. a.* (Doom to destruction) घोषणापूर्व्वं वधदण्डार्हं ख्या in caus. (ख्यापयति -यितुं), प्रकाशलेखेन वधार्हं ज्ञा in caus., or वधदण्डार्हं निर्दिश् or वध्यं निर्दिश् or घातव्यं निर्दिश्, अमुकजनो वध्यो ऽस्ति इति सूचनार्थं प्रकटनपत्रे नाम लिख् (c. 6. लिखति, लेखितुं) or अभिलिख्, मृत्युपात्रं निर्दिश्.—(Denounce and expel) प्रकटनपत्रेण बहिष्कृ or निरस् or प्रत्यादिश्.—(Interdict) प्रकाशनपत्रेण निषिध् or प्रतिषिध्, प्रकटनलेखेन निवृ or बाध्.

PROSCRIBED, *p. p.* वध्यनामावलिपत्राभिलिखितः -ता -तं, वधदण्डार्हः -र्हा -र्हं, प्रकाशपत्रेण निषिद्धः -द्धा -द्धं or प्रतिषिद्धः &c. or निवारितः -ता -तं.

PROSCRIPTION, *s.* प्रकाशनपत्रेण वध्यजननिर्देशः or वध्यनामावलिनिर्देशः, घोषणापूर्व्वं वधदण्डार्हख्यापनं, प्रकटनपत्रेण वधार्हज्ञापनं.

PROSE, *s.* गद्यं, हारकः, छन्दोरहितवाक्यं; 'prose and verse,' गद्यपद्यं; 'alternate prose and verse,' चम्पूः *m.*

To PROSE, *v. n.* दीर्घोच्चारणेन विरसवाक्यानि or विरसकथाः वद् (c. 1. वदति -दितुं), दीर्घसूत्रतया or दीर्घसूत्रवद् विरसकथोपाख्यानं कृ.

To PROSECUTE, *v. a.* (Pursue, follow up, carry on continuously) अनवरतम् अनुष्ठा (c. 1. -तिष्ठति -ष्ठातुं), अविरतम् अनुसेव् (c. 1. -सेवते -वितुं) or उपसेव् or सेव्, नित्यं प्रवृत् (c. 1. -वर्त्तते -र्त्तितुं), अविरतप्रवृत्तिं कृ, निर्वह् (c. 10. -वाहयति -यितुं); 'to prosecute one's efforts,' अविरतयत्नं कृ, अनवरतप्रयत्नं कृ, नित्योत्साहं कृ; 'one's undertakings,' प्रारब्धानि सम्पद् (c. 10. -पादयति -यितुं); 'one's studies,' नित्याध्ययनं कृ, अविरताध्ययनं कृ, विद्यानुसेवनं कृ.—(In law) अभियुज् (c. 7. -युनक्ति -योक्तुं), अभियोगं कृ, अभिशंस् (c. 1. -शंसति -सितुं), अभिशंसनं कृ, व्यवहाराभियोगं कृ, व्यवहाराभिशंसनं कृ.

PROSECUTED, *p. p.* (Carried on continuously) अविरतम् अनुष्ठितः -ता -तं or अनुसेवितः &c. or सेवितः &c., निर्वाहितः &c.—(In law) अभियुक्तः -क्ता -क्तं, अभिशस्तः -स्ता -स्तं, व्यवहाराभियुक्तः -क्ता -क्तं, व्यवहाराभिशस्तः -स्ता -स्तं.

PROSECUTION, *s.* (Carrying on continuously) अविरतानुष्ठानं, नित्यानुष्ठानं, नित्यानुसेवनं, नित्यसेवनं, नित्यप्रवृत्तिः *f.*, अविरतप्रवृत्तिः *f.*, नित्यप्रवर्त्तनं, निर्वाहनं; 'of efforts,' अविरतयत्नकरणं, नित्योद्योगः; 'of study,' नित्याध्ययनं, अविरताध्ययनं, विद्यानुसेवनं, विद्यानुपालनं, प्रवृत्तिः *f.*—(In law) अभियोगः, अभिशंसनं, व्यवहाराभियोगः, व्यवहाराभिशंसनं, अभियुक्तता.

PROSECUTOR, *s.* (One who carries on continuously) अविरतानुष्ठायी *m.* (न्), अविरतानुसेवी *m.*, निर्वाहकः.—(In law) अभियोगी *m.* (न्), अभियोक्ता *m.* (तृ), अभिशंसकः, व्यवहाराभियोगकृत्, व्यवहाराभिशंसनकृत् *m.*, अभियोगकारी *m.* (न्), विवादार्थी *m.*, अर्थी *m.*

PROSELYTE, *s.* धर्म्मपरिवर्त्तकः, धर्म्मान्तरग्राही *m.* (न्), मतान्तरग्राही *m.*, धर्म्मान्तरावलम्बी *m.*, स्वधर्म्मग्राही *m.*, स्वधर्म्मावलम्बी *m.*, अन्यधर्म्मग्राही *m.*, अन्यधर्म्मावलम्बी *m.*, स्वधर्म्मी *m.*, धर्म्मान्तरप्राप्तः, परधर्म्माश्रितः, स्वधर्म्मत्यागी *m.*, स्वधर्म्मत्यागपूर्व्वं धर्म्मान्तरग्राही *m.*; 'to Judaism,' यिहुदीयधर्म्मग्राही *m.*; 'to Christianity,' ख्रीष्टीयधर्म्मग्राही *m.*, ख्रीष्टीयमतग्राही *m.*

To PROSELYTE, PROSELYTIZE, *v. a.* धर्म्मान्तरं or स्वधर्म्मं ग्रह् in caus., मतान्तरं or स्वमतं ग्रह्, धर्म्मपरिवर्त्तकं कृ; 'to Judaism,' यिहुदीयमतं ग्रह् in caus.

PROSELYTISM, *s.* धर्म्मपरिवर्त्तनं, धर्म्मान्तरग्रहणं, धर्म्मान्तरप्रापणं.

PROSER, *s.* दीर्घोच्चारणेन विरसकथाख्यायकः, दीर्घसूत्री *m.* (न्).

PROSING, *s.* दीर्घोच्चारणेन विरसकथोपाख्यानं, दीर्घसूत्रता -त्वं.

PROSODIAL, PROSODICAL, *a.* छान्दसः -सी -सं, छन्दःशास्त्रसम्बन्धी &c., छन्दःशास्त्रविषयकः -का -कं, छन्दोविषयकः &c., छन्दःसम्बन्धी &c.

PROSODIAN, *s.* छन्दःशास्त्रज्ञः, छन्दःशास्त्रविद् *m.*, छन्दःशास्त्रव्युत्पन्नः.

PROSODY, *s.* छन्दस् *n.*, छन्दःशास्त्रं, छन्दोविद्या, छन्दोज्ञानं.

PROSOPOPŒIA, *s.* *See* PERSONIFICATION.

PROSPECT, *s.* (View) दृष्टिः *f.*, दर्शनं, दृष्टिपातः, दृक्पातः.—(View of future events, expectation) भाविदर्शनं, भविष्यद्दर्शनं, भाविघटनादर्शनं, अनागतदर्शनं, मानसिकदृष्टिः *f.*, अपेक्षा, उदीक्षणं, आशा, प्रत्याशा.—(That which is presented to the view) दृक्पातविषयः, दृष्टिपातविषयः, दृष्टिगतदेशः, दृक्पातान्तर्गतदेशः, दृष्टिपातगतप्रदेशः, दृष्टिगोचरदेशः, दृग्गोचरप्रदेशः.

PROSPECTIVE, *a.* भाविकालापेक्षकः -का -कं, उत्तरकालापेक्षकः &c., भाविकालसापेक्षः -क्षा -क्षं, भविष्यदपेक्षकः &c., आगामिकालसापेक्षः &c., भाविस्पृक् *m.f.n.* (श्).

PROSPECTIVELY, *adv.* भाविकालापेक्षया, उत्तरकालापेक्षया, भविष्यदपेक्षया, भाविकालसापेक्षं, आगामिकालसापेक्षं, भाविकालमपेक्ष्य, उत्तरकालमपेक्ष्य.

PROSPECTIVENESS, *s.* भाविकालापेक्षा, उत्तरकालापेक्षा -क्षकता -त्वं.

PROSPECTUS, *s.* कर्त्तव्यसूचनपत्रं, कर्त्तव्यार्थसूचनपत्रं, कर्त्तव्यार्थबोधनपत्रं.

To PROSPER, *v. a.* (Render successful, favor) सफलीकृ, सिद्धिं or सिद्धतां कृ or नी (c. 1. नयति, नेतुं) or साध् (c. 10. साधयति -यितुं), सिद्धीकृ, सिद्धिमन्तं -मतीं -मत् कृ, वृध् (c. 10. वर्धयति -यितुं), संवृध्, ऋध् (c. 10. ऋधयति -यितुं), समृद्धीकृ, उपकृ, अनुग्रह्, उपग्रह्, प्रतिपाल्, अनुपाल्.

To PROSPER, *v. n.* (Thrive) ऋध् (c. 4. ऋध्यति, c. 5. ऋध्नोति, अर्धितुं), समृध्, समृद्धीभू, समृद्धः -द्धा -द्धं भू, वृध् (c. 1. वर्धते -र्धितुं), संवृध्, विवृध्, एध् (c. 1. एधते -धितुं), समेध्, सम्पत्तिं गम्, समृद्धिम् इ or गम्, सश्रीकः -का -कं भू, श्रीमान् -मती &c. भू or अस्.—(Be successful) सिध् (c. 4. सिध्यति, सेद्धुं), सिद्धिं गम् or इ, कृतार्थीभू, प्राप्तार्थीभू, सिद्धार्थीभू, सम्पद् (c. 4. -पद्यते -पत्तुं), सम्पदं or सम्पत्तिं गम्, सफलीभू, सफलः -ला -लं भू.

PROSPERITY, *s.* समृद्धिः *f.*, सामृद्ध्यं, ऋद्धिः *f.*, सम्पत्तिः *f.*, सम्पद् *f.*, सुसम्पद् *f.*, वृद्धिः *f.*, संवृद्धिः *f.*, उदयः, पुण्योदयः, अभ्युदयः, श्रीः *f.*, लक्ष्मीः *f.*, सौभाग्यं, भाग्यं, भूतिः *f.*, क्षेमः -मं, एधा, कुशलं -लता, कौशल्यं, शर्म्म *n.*

(न्), कल्याणं, मङ्गलं, माङ्गल्यं, भद्रं, शुभं, शिवं, भूतिः *f.*, रिष्टं, उपचयः; 'season of prosperity,' समृद्धिसमयः, समृद्धिकालः, उदयकालः.—(Success) सिद्धिः *f.*, साध्यसिद्धिः *f.*, अर्थसिद्धिः *f.*, कृतार्थता, सफलता, साफल्यं; 'national,' योगक्षेमः.

PROSPEROUS, *a.* (Thriving) समृद्धः -द्धा -द्धं, वर्धमानः -ना -नं, वर्धिष्णुः -ष्णुः -ष्णु, श्रीमान् -मती -मत् (त्), लक्ष्मीवान् &c., क्षेमवान् &c., वृद्धिमान् &c., समृद्धिमान् &c., उदयी -यिनी -यि (न्), शर्म्मवान् &c., विपद्रहितः -ता -तं, निरापद् *m. f. n.*, सुस्थः -स्था -स्थं, ऋध्यमानः -ना -नं, समेधमानः &c., श्रीलः -ला -लं, सश्रीकः -का -कं, लक्ष्मणः -णा -णं, श्रीयुक्तः -क्ता -क्तं, अधिकर्द्धिः -र्द्धिः -र्द्धि.—(Successful) सफलः -ला -लं, सिद्धिमान् &c., सिद्धः -द्धा -द्धं, सिद्धार्थः -र्था -र्थं, कृतार्थः &c.—(Fortunate, favorable, auspicious) कल्याणः -णा -णं, कल्याणी &c., मङ्गलः -ला -लं, माङ्गलिकः -की -कं, शुभः -भा -भं, शिवः -वा -वं, शुभान्वितः -ता -तं, सौभाग्यवान् &c., भाग्यवान् &c., धन्यः -न्या -न्यं, कुशलः -ला -लं, क्षेमः -मा -मं, क्षेम्यः -म्या -म्यं, भद्रः -द्रा -द्रं, प्रसन्नः -न्ना -न्नं, शङ्करः -रा -रं, शिवङ्करः &c., श्रीकरः &c.

PROSPEROUSLY, *adv.* समृद्ध्या, सम्पदा, सुसम्पदा, श्रिया, सक्षेमं, सौभाग्येन, कौशल्येन, सकल्याणं, कल्याणं, कुशलं, शुभं, अभ्युदयेन, सफलं, अवृथा.

PROSPICIENCE, *s.* प्रदर्शनं. *See* FORESIGHT.

PROSTITUTE, *s.* वेश्या, गणिका, पण्यस्त्री, वारस्त्री, साधारणस्त्री, वाराङ्गना, भोग्या, पण्याङ्गना, सामान्या स्त्री, बन्धुरा. *See* HARLOT.

To PROSTITUTE, *v. a.* गर्ह्यकर्म्मार्थं or कुत्सितकर्म्मार्थं प्रयुज् (c. 7. -युनक्ति -युंक्ते -योक्तुं) or उपयुज् or विनियुज्, गर्ह्यकर्म्मणि or कुत्सितकर्म्मणि नियुज्, पण्यं -ण्यां कृ, साधारणीकृ, सर्व्वोपभोग्यं -ग्यां कृ.

PROSTITUTION, *s.* वेश्यात्वं, वेश्यावृत्तिः *f.*, पौंश्चल्यं, वारसेवा, भगवृत्तिः *f.*, भगव्यापारः, भगजीविका, वेश्याजीविका. *See* HARLOTRY.—(Devoting to infamous purposes) गर्ह्यकर्म्मार्थं प्रयोगः, कुत्सितकर्म्मार्थं विनियोगः, गर्ह्यकर्म्मणि or कुत्सितकर्म्मणि नियोजनं, पण्यकरणं, सर्व्वोपभोग्यकरणं; 'wages of prostitution,' पण्यस्त्रिया भृतिः *f.* or भाटकं, वेशः.

PROSTRATE, *a.* (Lying at length) अवमूर्द्धशयः -या -यं, क्षिप्तदेहः -हा -हं, भूमिशायी -यिनी -यि (न्), भूनिकृतः -ता -तं, अवनिकृतः &c.—(In supplication, adoration, &c.) साष्टाङ्गपतितः -ता -तं, साष्टाङ्गप्रणतः &c., साष्टाङ्गनमस्कारं प्रणिपतितः &c., शरणागतः -ता -तं, चरणपतितः -ता -तं, पादपतितः &c., दण्डवत् पतितः &c., पादप्रणतः &c., प्रणिपतितः &c., प्रपतितः &c., उपनतः &c., प्रणतः &c., नतः &c.

To PROSTRATE, *v. a.* (Throw down) पत् (c. 10. पातयति -यितुं), निपत्, अधःपत्, ध्वंस् (c. 10. ध्वंसयति -यितुं), प्रध्वंस्, नश् (c. 10. नाशयति -यितुं), विनश्, प्रणश्, अधरोत्तरीकृ, भूमिं गम् in caus.—(One's self in reverence, &c.) प्रणिपत् (c. 1. -पतति -तितुं), साष्टाङ्गं or साष्टाङ्गपातं प्रणिपत् or पत्, प्रणिपतनं कृ, प्रणम् (c. 1. -णमति -णन्तुं), कायं प्रणम्, साष्टाङ्गप्रणामं कृ, साष्टाङ्गनमस्कारं कृ, अष्टाङ्गपातं कृ, अष्टाङ्गप्रणामं कृ, प्रणिपातं कृ, पादप्रणामं कृ, चरणप्रणामं कृ, दण्डवत् पत् or भू or पतनं कृ, चरणपतनं कृ, पादपतनं कृ, दण्डवत् प्रणामं कृ.—(The strength) सर्व्वशक्तिं हृ (c. 1. हरति, हर्त्तुं), शक्तिपातं कृ, शक्तिनाशं कृ, क्षीणशक्तिं कृ.

PROSTRATED, *p. p.* पातितः -ता -तं, निपातितः &c., अधःपातितः &c., दण्डवत् पातितः &c., प्रणिपातितः &c., प्रणिपतितः &c., भूमिं गमितः &c.—(As strength) हृतशक्तिः -क्तिः -क्ति, नष्टशक्तिः &c., क्षीणशक्तिः &c., गतशक्तिः &c., हृतौजाः -जाः -जः (स्), गतौजाः &c., नष्टौजाः &c.

PROSTRATION, *s.* (Of the body in reverence, &c.) प्रणिपातः, प्रणिपतनं, अष्टाङ्गपातः, अष्टाङ्गप्रणिपातः, साष्टाङ्गप्रणामः, साष्टाङ्गपातः, साष्टाङ्गनमस्कारः, दण्डवत् पतनं or पातः, दण्डवत् प्रणामः, चरणपतनं, पादपतनं, पादप्रणामः, देहपातनं, शरीरपातनं, प्रपतनं.—(Of strength) शक्तिपातः, शक्तिहानिः *f.*, सत्त्वहानिः *f.*, शक्तिक्षयः, विश्रंसः -सा, ग्लानिः *f.*—(Of spirits) अवसादः, अवसन्नता, विषादः, विषण्णता, ग्लानिः *f.*

PROSY, *s.* विरसः -सा -सं, अरसिकः -का -कं, फल्गुः -ल्गुः -ल्गु. *See* PROSER.

To PROTECT, *v. a.* (Guard) रक्ष् (c. 1. रक्षति -क्षितुं), अभिरक्ष्, परिरक्ष्, संरक्ष्, प्रतिरक्ष्, गुप् (c. 1. गोपायति, c. 10. गोपयति -यितुं), अनुगुप्, निर्गुप्, अभिगुप्, प्रगुप्, संगुप्, अभिसंगुप्, पाल्, परिपाल्, अनुपाल्, प्रतिपाल्, अभिपाल्, सम्पाल्, उपपाल्, पा, परिपा, त्रै, परित्रै, संत्रै, तृ in caus., अव्, पुष्, गुप्तिं कृ, गोपनं कृ, संगोपनं कृ, रक्षणं कृ, संरक्षणं कृ, पालनं कृ, परिपालनं कृ, पोषणं कृ.

PROTECTED, *p. p.* रक्षितः -ता -तं, संरक्षितः &c., अभिरक्षितः &c., परिरक्षितः &c., सुरक्षितः &c., गुप्तः -प्ता -प्तं, गोपितः -ता -तं, गोपायितः &c., सङ्गोपितः &c., पालितः &c., उपपालितः &c., अनुपालितः &c., प्रतिपालितः &c., त्रातः &c., त्राणः -णा -णं, अवितः -ता -तं, तारितः &c., अभ्युपपन्नः -न्ना -न्नं, आश्रितः &c., समाश्रितः &c.

PROTECTION, *s.* (The act) रक्षा, रक्षणं, संरक्षणं, अभिरक्षा -क्षणं, परिरक्षणं, प्रतिरक्षणं, गुप्तिः *f.*, गोपनं, सङ्गोपनं, पालनं, परिपालनं, प्रतिपालनं, अनुपालनं, अभिपालनं, त्राणं, परित्राणं, अवनं, क्षेमकरणं, क्षेमः, अभ्युपपत्तिः *f.*—(That which protects or shelters) आश्रयः, संश्रयः, समाश्रयः, श्रयणं, आश्रयणं, शरणं, शरण्यता, शरण्यं; 'to seek the protection of, go for protection,' आश्रि (c. 1. -श्रयति -यितुं), संश्रि, समाश्रि, शरणार्थं गम्.—(Favor, countenance) प्रसादः, अनुग्रहः, सङ्ग्रहः, अनुपालनं, आश्रयः.—(Writing that protects) अभयपत्रं.

PROTECTIVE, *a.* रक्षकः -का -कं, संरक्षकः &c., पालकः -का -कं, प्रतिपालकः &c., गोपकः &c., रक्षाकारी -रिणी -रि (न्), पौष्टिकः -की -कं.

PROTECTOR, *s.* रक्षकः, रक्षी *m.* (न्), रक्षिता *m.* (तृ), गोप्ता *m.* (प्तृ), गोपकः, गोपायकः, गोपी *m.* (न्), गोपः, संरक्षकः, पालकः, प्रतिपालकः, पालयिता *m.* (तृ), पालः, पः in comp., त्राता *m.* (तृ), भयत्राता *m.*, शरणं, शरण्यं, आश्रयः, आश्रयभूतः, शरणभूतः, आश्रयदाता *m.* (तृ).

PROTECTRESS, *s.* रक्षका, रक्षिणी, रक्षित्री, पालका, पालयित्री, रक्षाकारिणी, गोपिनी, गोपिका, गोपी, त्रायन्ती, आश्रयदात्री.

PROTEGÉ, *s.* आश्रितः, संश्रितः, रक्षणीयः, पालनीयः, पोष्यः, शरणागतः.

To PROTEND, *v. a.* प्रसृ (c. 10. -सारयति -यितुं), प्रसारणं कृ. *See* *To* EXTEND.

To PROTEST, *v. n.* (Declare solemnly) दृढनिश्चयपूर्व्वं or दृढप्रतिज्ञापूर्व्वं वद्, दृढोक्त्या वद्, दार्ढ्येन वद्, दृढं वद्, दृढोक्तिपूर्व्वं ख्या or आख्या or प्रख्या, दृढोक्तिं कृ.—(Make a solemn declaration expressive of dissent or opposition) अस्वीकारसूचकं दृढवाक्यं वद् or दृढवादं कृ or दृढनिषेधं कृ, असम्मतिसूचकां दृढोक्तिं कृ, विरोधसूचकां दृढप्रतिज्ञां कृ, दृढोक्तिपूर्व्वम् अस्वीकारं ख्या in caus. or ज्ञा in caus., दृढनिश्चयपूर्व्वं or दृढप्रतिज्ञापूर्व्वम् असम्मतिं ज्ञा in caus. or प्रकाश् (c. 10. -काशयति -यितुं), दृढोक्तिपूर्व्वं निषेधं कृ, दृढवाक्यपूर्व्वं न सम्मन्ये or न स्वीकरोमि इति वद्, दृढोक्तिपूर्व्वं मतान्तरं ख्या or प्रकाश्, दृढप्रतिज्ञापूर्व्वं न सम्मन् or विपरीतं मन् or अन्यथा मन्.—(In writing) असम्मतिलेखं प्रकाश्, अस्वीकारपत्रं प्रकाश्.

PROTEST, *s.* अस्वीकारसूचकं दृढनिषेधवाक्यं, असम्मतिसूचकं दृढविरोधवाक्यं, अस्वीकारवादः, दृढोक्तिपूर्व्वो निषेधः, दृढप्रतिज्ञापूर्व्वो निषेधः, दृढनि-

श्चयपूर्व्वम् अस्वीकारप्रकाशनं, दृढप्रतिज्ञापूर्व्वम् असम्मतिप्रकाशनं, दृढोक्तिपूर्व्वं मतान्तरख्यापनं or असम्मतिख्यापनं or विपरीतमतख्यापनं, दृढनिश्चयपूर्व्वम् अस्वीकारवाक्यं or असम्मतिवाक्यं or अनङ्गीकारवाक्यं.—(In writing) दृढनिषेधसूचकं or दृढविरोधार्थकम्, अस्वीकारपत्रं or असम्मतिपत्रं or अनङ्गीकारपत्रं.

PROTESTANT, *s.* असम्मतः, अस्वीकारवादी *m.* (न्), अस्वीकर्त्ता *m.* (र्तृ), रोमीयमतविरोधी *m.* (न्), रोमीयमतविरुद्धः, रोमीयधर्म्मासम्मतः.

PROTESTATION, *s.* (Solemn declaration) दृढोक्तिः *f.*, दृढवाक्यं, दृढवादः, दृढप्रतिज्ञापूर्व्वो वादः, दृढभाषणं, दृढप्रतिज्ञापूर्व्वं भाषणं. *See* PROTEST.

PROTEUS, *s.* (Taking any shape at will) कामरूपी *m.* (न्), कामरूपः, छद्मरूपी *m.*, छद्मरूपः, टुः *m.*

PROTOTYPE, *s.* मूलरूपं, मूलप्रतिमा, मूलमूर्त्तिः *f.*, आदर्शः, मूलादर्शः, मूलं, प्रतिरूपं, प्रतिकृतिः *f.*, प्रत्युपमा -मानं, प्रतिमूर्त्तिः *f.*

To PROTRACT, *v. a.* (Lengthen) दीर्घीकृ, द्राघ (nom. द्राघयति -यितुं). *See To* PROLONG, LENGTHEN.—(Delay) विलम्ब्. *See* the word.

PROTRACTED, *p. p.* दीर्घः -र्घा -र्घं, द्राघिमवान् -वती -वत् (त्), विलम्बितः -ता -तं, चिरायितः &c., चिरस्थः -स्था -स्थं, चिरस्थितः -ता -तं; 'sound,' प्लुतः -तं.

PROTRACTION, *s.* दीर्घीकरणं, द्राघिमा *m.* (न्), दीर्घता, विलम्बः -म्बनं.

To PROTRUDE, *v. a.* (Thrust forward) प्रसृ (c. 10. -सारयति -यितुं), बहिःसृ, बहिर् निःसृ, बहिर् गम् (c. 10. गमयति -यितुं), प्रसारणं कृ.

To PROTRUDE, *v. n.* बहिः सृ (c. 1. सरति, सर्त्तुं), प्रसृ, बहिर् निःसृ, बहिर् गम् (c. 1. गच्छति, गन्तुं), बहिर् भू, बहिःस्था, बहिर् वृत्, अतिवृत्, अतिक्रम्, उद्भिद् in pass. (-भिद्यते), प्रोद्भिद्, उद्भेदं कृ, प्रलम्ब्, बहिर् लम्ब्. *See To* PROJECT, *v. n.*

PROTRUDED, *p. p.* बहिर्गतः -ता -तं बहिःसृतः &c., बहिर्भूतः -ता -तं, बहिःस्थितः &c., बहिर्वेल्लितः &c., निःसारितः &c., बहिःसारितः &c., बहिर् निःसारितः &c., प्रसृतः &c., प्रसारितः &c., उद्भिन्नः -न्ना -न्नं, प्रोद्भिन्नः &c.

PROTRUDING, *part.* बहिःस्थः -स्था -स्थं, बहिर्वेल्ली -ल्लिनी -ल्लि (न्), बहिर्गतः -ता -तं, बहिर्लम्बः &c. *See* PROJECTING.

PROTRUSION, *s.* बहिर्वेल्लनं, बहिःसरणं, उद्भेदः, प्रोद्भेदः. *See* PROJECTION.

PROTUBERANCE, *s.* (Tumour, prominence) स्फोटः, विस्फोटः, गुल्मः, गण्डः -ण्डका, शोथः, आभोगः, उन्नतिः *f.*, प्रलम्बता. *See* PROJECTION.

PROTUBERANT, *a.* उन्नतः -ता -तं, प्रलम्बः -म्बा -म्बं, बहिर्लम्बः &c., गुल्मी -ल्मिनी -ल्मि (न्), आभोगी &c., बृहद्विवेशः -शा -शं. *See* PROJECTING.

To PROTUBERATE, *v. n.* उन्नतः -ता -तं भू, प्रलम्ब्, बहिर्लम्ब्. *See To* PROJECT, *v. n.*

PROUD, *a.* गर्व्वितः -ता -तं, गर्व्वी -र्व्विणी -र्व्वि (न्), सगर्व्वः -र्व्वा -र्व्वं, गर्व्वरः -रा -रं, गर्व्ववान् -वती -वत् (त्), गर्व्वितचित्तः -त्ता -त्तं, दृप्तः -प्ता -प्तं, सदर्पः -र्पा -र्पं, दर्पवान् &c., दृप्रः -प्रा -प्रं, दर्पी &c., मानी &c., मानवान् &c., अभिमानी &c., अभिमानवान् &c., साभिमानः -ना -नं, अहङ्कारी &c., अहङ्कारवान् &c., अहंयुः -युः -यु, साहङ्कारः -रा -रं, अहम्मानी &c., प्रगल्भः -ल्भा -ल्भं, उद्धतः -ता -तं, उद्धतचित्तः -त्ता -त्तं, उद्धतमनाः -नाः -नः (स्), समुद्धतः &c., प्रौढः -ढा -ढं, उन्नद्धः -द्धा -द्धं, उन्नद्धचेताः &c., समुन्नद्धः &c., साटोपः -पा -पं, आटोपी &c., उत्सिक्तः -क्ता -क्तं, उन्नतशिरस्कः -स्का -स्कं, उन्नतमनस्कः &c., समुन्नतचित्तः &c., ऊर्द्धदृष्टिः -ष्टिः -ष्टि, अवलिप्तः -प्ता -प्तं, दर्पध्मातः &c., सावहेलः -ला -लं, प्रधृष्टः -ष्टा -ष्टं; 'proud of one's beauty,' रूपगर्व्वितः -ता -तं, रूपाभिमानी &c.; 'of one's birth,' कुलाभिमानी &c.; 'of one's learning,' पाण्डित्याभिमानी &c., पण्डितम्मन्यः -न्या -न्यं; 'of the body,' देहमानी &c.; 'to be proud,' गर्व्व् (c. 1. गर्व्वति -र्व्वितुं, c. 10. गर्व्वयते -यितुं), गर्व्वितः &c. भू, सगर्व्वीभू, दृप् (c. 4. दृप्यति, दर्प्तुं, द्रप्तुं), मन् (c. 4. मानयते -यितुं), प्रगल्भ् (c. 1. -गल्भते -ल्भितुं); 'to render proud,' दृप् (c. 10. दर्पयति -यितुं), गर्व्वितं -तां कृ.

PROUDLY, *adv.* सगर्व्वं, सदर्पं, समानं, साभिमानं, साहङ्कारं, साटोपं, सोन्मादं, गर्व्वितं, उन्नतचेतसा, सावहेलं, सावलेपं, गर्व्वितवत्, दृप्तवत्, प्रगल्भवत्.

PROVABLE, *a.* प्रमेयः -या -यं, साधनीयः &c., साध्यः -ध्या -ध्यं, उपपादनीयः &c., उपपाद्यः -द्या -द्यं, प्रतिपाद्यः &c., प्रतिपादनीयः &c., समर्थनीयः &c., सूच्यः -च्या -च्यं.

To PROVE, *v. a.* (Establish as truth) साध् (c. 10. साधयति -यितुं), सिद्धीकृ, प्रमाण (nom. प्रमाणयति -यितुं), प्रमाणीकृ, सप्रमाणं -णां कृ, उपपद् (c. 10. -पादयति -यितुं), प्रतिपद्, विभू (c. 10. -भावयति -यितुं), भू, निर्णी (c. 1. -णयति -णेतुं), सत्याकृ, सत्यीकृ; 'by testimony or other evidence,' साक्षिणा or साक्ष्येण or प्रमाणेन साध् or भू or उपपद्.—(Evince, demonstrate) सूच् (c. 10. सूचयति -यितुं), दृश् (c. 10. दर्शयति -यितुं), अभिदृश्, अनुदृश्, निर्दिश् (c. 6. -दिशति -देष्टुं), विनिर्दिश्, प्रदिश्, निर्णी, समर्प् (c. 10. -अर्पयति -यितुं), प्रकाश्.—(Try, ascertain, bring to the test) परीक्ष् (c. 1. -ईक्षते -क्षितुं), परीक्षां कृ, निरूप्, ज्ञा in des., निर्णी, निश्चि, अनुभू, प्रतीतिं कृ.—(Experience) अनुभू, अनुभवं कृ, अनुभूतिं कृ.

To PROVE, *v. n.* (Be found, turn out) सम्भू (c. 1. -भवति -वितुं), सम्पद् (c. 4. -पद्यते -पत्तुं), उत्पद्, उपपद्, विद् in pass. (विद्यते), सिध् (c. 4. सिध्यति -ते), आपत् (c. 1. -पतति -तितुं), संवृत्, वृत्.—(Be ascertained or shown to be true) निर्णी in pass. (-णीयते), निश्चि in pass. (-चीयते), सूच् in pass. (सूच्यते), अनुभू in pass. (-भूयते), विभू, प्रमाणीभू, प्रती in pass. (-ईयते).

PROVED, *p. p.* (Established as true) सिद्धः -द्धा -द्धं, साधितः -ता -तं, उपपादितः &c., उपपन्नः -न्ना -न्नं, प्रमाणितः -ता -तं, प्रमाणीकृतः &c., भावितः &c., विभावितः &c., प्रतिपादितः &c., प्रमितः -ता -तं.—(Evinced, demonstrated) सूचितः -ता -तं, दर्शितः &c., निर्दिष्टः -ष्टा -ष्टं, निर्णीतः -ता -तं, समर्पितः &c.—(Tested, ascertained) परीक्षितः -ता -तं, निरूपितः -ता -तं, निश्चितः &c., निर्णीतः &c., अनुभूतः &c., प्रतीतः -ता -तं; 'thing to be proved,' साध्यं, प्रमेयं; 'proved by evidence,' साक्षिभावितः &c., साक्ष्यसिद्धः &c.

PROVENDER, *s.* पाथेयं, यात्रिकं, शम्बलं, सम्बलः -लं, खाद्यद्रव्यं, भक्ष्यद्रव्यं, पश्वादिखाद्यद्रव्यं, शुष्कतृणादि *n.*, शुष्कघासादि, माषादि, शस्यादि.

PROVER, *s.* उपपादकः, सिद्धिकर्त्ता *m.* (र्तृ), साधकः, प्रमाता *m.* (तृ), प्रतिपादकः, उपपत्तिकारी *m.* (न्), प्रतिपत्तिकारकः, निर्णेता *m.*, विभावकः.

PROVERB, *s.* लोकवाक्यं, लोकोक्तिः *f.*, प्राचीनवाक्यं, पुराणवाक्यं, लोकप्रचलितवाक्यं, वाक्यं, वचनं, वाक् *f.* (च्), सूत्रं, प्राचीनसूत्रं, पुराणसूत्रं, उपमानं, उपदेशवाक्यं, उपदेशसूत्रं, न्यायः, न्यायवाक्यं.

PROVERBIAL, *a.* (Mentioned in a proverb) प्राचीनसूत्रप्रोक्तः -क्ता -क्तं, पुराणसूत्रप्रोक्तः &c., लोकप्रोक्तः &c., लोकोक्तः &c.—(Comprised in a proverb, current as one) प्राचीनसूत्ररूपः -पा -पं, पुराणसूत्ररूपः &c., लोकप्रसिद्धः -द्धा -द्धं, लोकप्रचलितः -ता -तं, लोकप्रचलः -ला -लं, न्यायरूपः &c., न्यायप्रसिद्धः &c.

PROVERBIALLY, *adv.* लोकप्रसिद्धं, जनप्रसिद्धं, प्राचीनसूत्रानुसारेण.

To PROVIDE, *v. a.* (Procure or prepare beforehand) अग्रे or पूर्व्वं कॢप् (c. 10. कल्पयति -यितुं) or उपकॢप् or परिकॢप् or सम्प्रकॢप् or

सोपकारद्रव्याणि क्लृप् or विधा or उपस्था in caus. or उपपद् in caus. or सम्भृ or पुरस्कृ or प्रस्तुतीकृ or निर्मा, अग्रे द्रव्यपरिकल्पनं कृ or द्रव्यसम्भारं कृ or उपकरणसम्भारं कृ or द्रव्यसामग्र्यं परिक्लृप्. *See* To PREPARE.—(Make a previous stipulation) पूर्व्वनियमं कृ, पूर्व्वपणं कृ, पूर्व्वसन्धिं कृ, पूर्व्वसङ्केतं कृ, पूर्व्वप्रतिज्ञां कृ.—(Provide against or for) expressed by some of the above roots in conjunction with अर्थं or अर्थे in comp.; 'to provide necessaries against a time of want,' आपदर्थं द्रव्याणि सम्भृ or आपदर्थं द्रव्यसम्भारं कृ; 'to provide thick clothing against the cold,' शीतनिवारणार्थं स्थूलवस्त्राणि क्लृप्; 'to provide for another,' परार्थं प्रयोजनीयद्रव्याणि परिक्लृप् or परं प्रयोजनीयद्रव्ययुक्तं कृ; 'to provide for another comfortably,' परस्वास्थ्यं कृ or जन्, परसुस्थतां कृ, परं सुस्थं कृ; 'to provide for, take measures against,' पूर्व्वोपायं कृ, अग्रे उपायं कृ, पूर्व्वोपायं प्रयुज्, उपायप्रयोगं कृ.

PROVIDED, *p. p.* (Furnished or prepared beforehand) अग्रे परिकल्पितः -ता -तं or परिक्लृप्तः -प्ता -प्तं or उपक्लृप्तः -प्ता -प्तं or सम्प्रक्लृप्तः &c. or कल्पितः -ता -तं, पूर्व्वं सम्भृतः -ता -तं or युक्तः -क्ता -क्तं or समायुक्तः &c. or संयुक्तः &c. or अन्वितः -ता -तं or समन्वितः &c. or उपेतः &c. or संहितः &c. or निर्म्मितः -ता -तं; 'provided for,' प्रयोजनीयद्रव्ययुक्तः -क्ता -क्तं, सर्व्वसोपकारद्रव्ययुक्तः &c., जातस्वास्थ्यः -स्थ्या -स्थ्यं, अन्नवस्त्रयुक्तः &c.—(Stipulated previously) पूर्व्वनियमितः -ता -तं, पूर्व्वपणितः &c., पूर्व्वसङ्केतितः &c.; 'provided that, with this condition,' पूर्व्वनियमे कृते, पूर्व्वसङ्केते कृते, एतेन सन्धिना.

PROVIDENCE, *s.* (Fore-sight, fore-thought) पूर्व्वदृष्टिः *f.*, अग्रदृष्टिः *f.*, दूरदृष्टिः *f.*, दूरदर्शनं, दीर्घदृष्टिः *f.*, दीर्घदर्शनं, पूर्व्वचिन्ता, अग्रचिन्ता, पूर्व्वविवेचनं, पूर्व्वविचारः -रणं -णा, अग्रविचारः, भविष्यद्दर्शनं, भविष्यच्चिन्ता, भाविचिन्ता, भाविकालावलोकनं, पूर्व्वविमर्शः, प्रसमीक्षा.—(The providence of God) ईश्वरानुसन्धानं, ईश्वरविधिः *m.*, ईश्वरविधानं.—(Divine Providence himself) विधाता *m.* (तृ), धाता *m.*, अनागतविधाता *m.*, भविष्यद्विधाता *m.*, विधिः *m.*, ईश्वरः, परमेश्वरः.

PROVIDENT, *a.* दीर्घदर्शी -र्शिनी -र्शि (न्), दूरदर्शी &c., दीर्घदृष्टिः -ष्टिः -ष्टि, दूरदृष्टिः &c., परिणामदर्शी &c., अग्रदर्शी &c., भविष्यद्दर्शी &c., अनागतदर्शी &c., भविष्यच्चिन्तकः -का -कं, भाविचिन्तकः &c., पूर्व्वविचारी &c., पूर्व्वविवेकी &c., अन्तरज्ञः -ज्ञा -ज्ञं.

PROVIDENTIAL, *a.* ईश्वरकृतः -ता -तं, ईश्वरविहितः &c., ईश्वरानुसन्धानप्रयुक्तः -क्ता -क्तं, ईश्वरविधानप्रयुक्तः &c., विधातृकृतः -ता -तं, विधातृसिद्धः -द्धा -द्धं, ईश्वरसिद्धः &c.

PROVIDENTIALLY, *adv.* ईश्वरविधानेन, ईश्वरविधिना, ईश्वरानुसन्धानात्, दिष्ट्या.

PROVIDENTLY, *adv.* दीर्घदृष्ट्या, अग्रदर्शनात्, परिणामदर्शनात्, भविष्यद्दर्शनात्, चिन्तापूर्व्वं, विवेचनापूर्व्वं, पूर्व्वविचारेण, पूर्व्वविचारं कृत्वा, पूर्व्वविवेचनं कृत्वा, प्रसमीक्ष्य, प्रविमृश्य.

PROVIDER, *s.* परिकल्पकः, उपकल्पकः. *See* PROCURER, &c.

PROVINCE, *s.* (Division of a kingdom) मण्डलं, चक्रं, देशः, प्रदेशः, विषयः, राष्ट्रं, निर्गः, ग्रामजातं; 'governor of a province,' मण्डलेश्वरः, मण्डलपतिः *m.*, मण्डलाध्यक्षः, मण्डलाधिपतिः *m.*, माण्डलिकः.—(Peculiar office or business) स्वधर्म्मः, स्वकर्म्म *n.* (न्), कर्म्म *n.*, कार्य्यं, अधिकारः, प्रकरणं, क्रिया, नियोगः, निबन्धनं; 'woman's province,' स्त्रीधर्म्मः, स्त्रीनिबन्धनं.—(Department of science, &c.) प्रकरणं, देशः, अङ्गं, विषयः.

PROVINCIAL, *a.* दैशिकः -की -कं, देशीयः -या -यं, प्रदेशीयः &c., देश्यः -श्या -श्यं, देशी -शिनी -शि (न्), माण्डलिकः -की -कं, मण्डलसम्बन्धी &c., राष्ट्रिकः -की -कं, राष्ट्रीयः -या -यं, देश in comp., ग्रामीयः -या -यं, ग्राम्यः -म्या -म्यं, जानपदः -दी -दं.

PROVINCIAL, *s.* देशस्थः, देशजः, देशवासी *m.* (न्), ग्रामस्थः, ग्राम्यजनः.

PROVINCIALISM, *s.* देशभाषा, प्रदेशिकभाषा, ग्रामीयभाषा, ग्रामिकभाषा.

PROVISION, *s.* (Act of providing) उपकल्पनं, परिकल्पनं, कल्पनं, सम्भारः, विधानं, उपस्थापनं, उपपादनं, प्रस्तुतीकरणं.—(Measures taken beforehand) पूर्व्वोपायः, अग्रोपायः, उपायः, पूर्व्वकल्पना, पूर्व्वविधानं; *see* PREPARATION.—(Store or stock collected) सम्भारः, संग्रहः, सञ्चयः, सञ्चितं, सामग्री -ग्र्यं, साहित्यं; 'provision of victuals,' अन्नसम्भारः, अन्नसंग्रहः, खाद्यद्रव्यसामग्री; 'of materials,' द्रव्यसामग्री, उपकरणसामग्री, उपकरणसम्भारः.—(Victuals, provisions) अन्नं, भोजनं, भोज्यं, भक्ष्यं, आहारः, खाद्यद्रव्यं, भक्ष्यद्रव्यं, पाथेयं, यात्रिकं, निर्वाहः, शम्बलं, सम्बलः -लं; 'furnished with provisions,' खाद्यद्रव्ययुक्तः -क्ता -क्तं, पाथेयवान् -वती -वत् (त्).—(Previous stipulation) पूर्व्वनियमः, पूर्व्वसन्धिः *m.*, पूर्व्वसङ्केतः, पूर्व्वप्रतिज्ञा, पूर्व्वपणः, पूर्व्वसमयः. *See* PROVISO.

To PROVISION, *v. a.* (Furnish with provisions) खाद्यद्रव्ययुक्तं -क्तां कृ, खाद्यद्रव्याणि सम्भृ or उपक्लृप्, खाद्यद्रव्यसम्भारं कृ, अन्नसम्भारं कृ, खाद्यद्रव्यसम्भृतं -तां कृ.

PROVISIONAL, *a.* आपाततः स्थापितः -ता -तं, आपाततो नियोजितः -ता -तं, सामयिकः -की -कं, प्रासङ्गिकः &c., समयोपयोगी -गिनी -गि (न्), समयानुरूपः -पा -पं, अल्पकालीनः -ना -नं.

PROVISIONALLY, *adv.* आपाततस्, यथासमयं, यथाप्रयोजनं, अल्पकालमात्रं.

PROVISIONARY, PROVISORY, *a.* *See* PROVISIONAL.

PROVISO, *s.* उपनियमः, प्रकरणं, नियमप्रकरणं, सङ्केतः, उपसङ्केतः, प्रतिबन्धः, अनुबन्धः, नियमानुबन्धः, नियमपत्रानुबन्धः, नियमपत्राङ्गं, नियमपत्रखण्डः, नियमपत्रावयवः, नियमैकदेशः; 'to annex one,' अर्थान्तरोपन्यासं कृ.

PROVISORY, *a.* (Conditional) साङ्केतिकः -की -कं, सप्रतिबन्धः -न्धा -न्धं.

PROVOCATION, *s.* (Act of exciting anger) प्रकोपः -पणं, क्रोधकरणं, कोपकरणं, क्रोधोत्पादनं, कोपोत्पादनं, क्रोधोद्दीपनं, क्रोधोत्तेजनं.—(Cause of anger) कोपकारणं, क्रोधकारणं, कोपहेतुः *m.*—(Act of exciting) उत्तेजनं, उद्दीपनं, उद्बोधनं, प्रवर्त्तनं.

PROVOCATIVE, *a.* उद्दीपकः -का -कं, अग्निवर्धकः &c., क्षुधाजनकः &c.

PROVOCATIVE, *s.* अग्निवर्धनं, रोचकः -कं, रुचकं, प्ररोचनं, रञ्जिका.

To PROVOKE, *v. a.* (Excite to anger) प्रकुप् (c. 10. -कोपयति -यितुं), कुप्, क्षुभ् (c. 10. क्षोभयति -यितुं), कोपं or क्रोधं जन् or उत्तिज् or उद्दीप् or उत्पद् (c. 10. -पादयति -यितुं), कोपोत्पादनं कृ, क्रोधोत्तेजनं कृ, क्रोधोद्दीपनं कृ.—(Excite) उद्दीप् (c. 10. -दीपयति -यितुं), उत्तिज् (c. 10. -तेजयति -यितुं), उत्तप् in caus., प्रवृत् in caus., प्ररुच् in caus.—(Challenge) आह्वे, समाह्वे, उपाह्वे.

PROVOKED, *p. p.* प्रकोपितः -ता -तं, प्रकुपितः &c., कुपितः &c., कोपितः &c., उपजातकोपः -पा -पं, जातकोपः &c., इद्धमन्युः -न्युः -न्यु, इद्धक्रोधः -धा -धं, उद्दीप्तमन्युः &c., कोपदीप्तः -प्ता -प्तं, उपजातमन्युः &c., उत्तेजितः -ता -तं, उद्दीपितः &c., उत्तापितः &c., उत्तप्तः -प्ता -प्तं, सन्तप्तः &c., सन्तापितः &c.

PROVOKING, *part.* or *a.* प्रकोपजनकः -का -कं, कोपजनकः &c., क्रोधजनकः &c., प्रकोपकः -का -कं, क्रोधोत्पादकः &c., क्रोधोद्दीपकः &c., कोपोद्दीपकः &c., क्रोधोत्तेजकः &c., उत्तेजकः &c., उद्दीपकः &c., उद्बोधकः &c.

PROVOKINGLY, *adv.* यथा कोपो जायते तथा, यथा क्रोध उद्दीप्यते तथा.

PROVOST, *s.* अध्यक्षः, अधीशः, अधिकारी *m.* (न्), अधिपतिः, श्रेष्ठी *m.*

PROW, *s.* नौकाग्रं, नौकाग्रभागः, नौपूर्व्वभागः, नौकोदग्रभागः.

PROWESS, *s.* पराक्रमः, विक्रमः, सुविक्रमः, शौर्य्यं, वीर्य्यं, सुवीर्य्यं, रणशौर्य्यं, रणोत्साहः, पौरुषं, कृतपौरुषं, अतिशक्तिता, शनौजस् *n.*, प्रौढिः *f.*, कर्म्मोदारं; 'personal prowess,' बाहुवीर्य्यं; 'gained by one's own prowess,' स्वहस्तार्जितः -ता -तं, स्वभुजोपार्जितः &c.; 'man of great prowess,' सुपराक्रमी *m.* (न्), सुविक्रमी *m.*, पराक्रान्तः, अतिशक्तिमान् *m.* (त्); 'to show prowess,' पराक्रम् (c. 1. -क्रामति -क्रमति -मितुं), विक्रम्.

To PROWL, *v. n.* मांसार्थं or आमिषार्थं भ्रम् (c. 4. भ्राम्यति, भ्रमितुं) or परिभ्रम्, मांसान्वेषणार्थं भ्रम् or पर्य्यट् (c. 1. -अटति -टितुं).

PROWLER, *s.* मांसार्थं भ्रमणकारी *m.* (न्) or परिभ्रमणकारी *m.*, परिभ्रमी *m.*

PROWLING, *s.* मांसार्थं or मांसान्वेषणार्थं भ्रमणं or परिभ्रमणं or पर्य्यटनं.

PROXIMATE, *a.* समीपः -पा -पं, निकटः -टा -टं, समीपस्थः -स्था -स्थं, निरन्तरः -रा -रं, सन्निहितः -ता -तं, निरन्तरालः -ला -लं, उपस्थः -स्था -स्थं, उपस्थायी -यिनी -यि (न्), आसन्नः -न्ना -न्नं, अन्तिकः -का -कं, उपश्लिष्टः -ष्टा -ष्टं, संसक्तः -क्ता -क्तं, सन्निकृष्टः -ष्टा -ष्टं, समीपगः &c. *See* NEAR, NEXT; 'proximate cause,' उपादानकारणं, उपादानं.

PROXIMATELY, *adv.* समीपतस्, सन्निहितं, सन्निकृष्टं, निरन्तरालं, अनन्तरालं.

PROXIMITY, *s.* समीपता, सामीप्यं, सन्निकर्षः, सन्निकृष्टता, सन्निधिः *m.*, सान्निध्यं, सन्निधानं, सन्निधं, अन्तिकं -कता, उपस्थानं, उपस्थितिः *f.*, नैकट्यं, प्रत्यासत्तिः *f.*, प्रत्यासन्नता, संसक्तिः *f.*, संसर्गः, उपश्लेषः, आनन्तर्य्यं, तादस्थ्यं. *See* NEARNESS.

PROXY, *s.* (Agency of another who acts as substitute) प्रतिनिधित्वं -ता.—(Person who acts) प्रतिनिधिः *m.*, प्रतिपुरुषः, प्रतिहस्तः -स्तकः; 'by proxy,' प्रतिनिधिद्वारा, प्रतिनिधिद्वारेण; 'one who signs a paper by proxy,' लेखनिकः.

PRUDE, *s.* मिथ्याविनीता, अत्यन्तविनयनिष्ठा, विनयाभिमानिनी, अतिविनीतात्मन्या, सूक्ष्मविनयनिष्ठा, सूक्ष्माचारनिष्ठा, अत्याचारिणी, अत्याचारसेविनी, सुव्रीडितात्मन्या, अतिविनयसेविनी, अत्यन्तविनीता.

PRUDENCE, *s.* पूर्व्वविचारः -रणा, परिणामदृष्टिः *f.*, पूर्व्वसमीक्षा, प्रसमीक्षा, समीक्षा -क्षणं, समीक्ष्यकारिता -त्वं, विमृश्यकारिता, परिणामदर्शनं, दीर्घदृष्टिः, सदसद्दर्शनं, सदसद्विवेकः, विनयः, विनीतता, नीतिः *f.*, नीतिज्ञता, प्राज्ञता, प्रज्ञता, विज्ञता, विवेकः, मनस्विता, विचारशीलता, पूर्व्वापरविचारः, मतिमत्त्वं, बुद्धिः *f.*, मनीषा, हिताहितविवेकः, पूर्व्वचिन्ता, चिन्ता, कार्य्यचिन्ता, परिवेदना, सावधानता, पूर्व्वदृष्टिः *f.*, अग्रदृष्टिः *f.*, विमर्शः, विवेचना, पूर्व्वविवेचना.

PRUDENT, *a.* परिणामदर्शी -र्शिनी -र्शि (न्), पूर्व्वविचारशीलः -ला -लं, दीर्घदर्शी &c., दीर्घदृष्टिः -ष्टिः -ष्टि, समीक्ष्यकारी -रिणी &c., विमृश्यकारी &c., समीक्षाकारी &c., प्राज्ञः -ज्ञा -ज्ञं, प्रज्ञः &c., विज्ञः &c., मनस्वी -स्विनी &c., मतिमान् -मती -मत् (त्), बुद्धिमान् &c., प्रज्ञावान् &c., मनीषी -षिणी &c., परिवेदी -दिनी &c., परिवेदकः -का -कं, बुधः -धा -धं, सुबोधः -धा -धं, विनीतः &c., विनयवान् &c., नीतिमान् &c., नीतिज्ञः -ज्ञा -ज्ञं, पूर्व्वापरविचारी &c., विचारशीलः -ला -लं, सदसद्दर्शी &c., सदसद्विवेकी &c., दूरदर्शी &c., हिताहितविवेकी &c., पूर्व्वचिन्तकः -का -कं, पूर्व्वचिन्ताशीलः &c., कार्य्यचिन्तकः &c., धीरः -रा -रं, सावधानः -ना -नं, कृतावधानः -ना -नं, कृतधीः -धीः -धि, प्रयतः -ता -तं.

PRUDENTIAL, *a.* पूर्व्वविचारप्रयुक्तः -क्ता -क्तं, पूर्व्वसमीक्षाप्रयुक्तः &c., प्रसमीक्षाप्रयुक्तः &c., सविचारः -रा -रं, सविवेकः -का -कं.

PRUDENTLY, *adv.* सविचारं, समीक्षापूर्व्वं, प्रसमीक्ष्य, सुसमीक्ष्य, सुविमृश्य, परिणामदर्शनात्, परिणामदृष्ट्या, पूर्व्वविचारेण, सावधानं, सपरिवेदनं, प्राज्ञवत्, विज्ञवत्.

PRUDERY, *s.* मिथ्याविनयः, मिथ्यालज्जा, एकान्तविनयः, सूक्ष्मविनयनिष्ठा, सूक्ष्माचारनिष्ठा, अत्याचारनिष्ठा, विनयाभिमानं, अतिसूक्ष्मशीलता, अतिसूक्ष्मता, अतिविनीतता.

PRUDISH, *a.* मिथ्याविनीतः -ता -तं, एकान्तविनीतः &c., अत्यन्तविनीतः &c., अतिसूक्ष्मः -क्ष्मा -क्ष्मं, विनयाभिमानी -निनी &c. *See* PRUDE, *s.* PRECISE, *a.*

To PRUNE, *v. a.* क्षुद्रपल्लवान् or निरर्थकविटपान् अवछिद् (c. 7. -छिनत्ति -छेत्तुं) or अवकृत् (c. 6. -कृन्तति -कर्त्तितुं) or लू (c. 9. लुनाति लवितुं) or लुप् (c. 6. लुम्पति, लोप्तुं).

PRUNED, *p. p.* छिन्नपल्लवः -वा -वं, छिन्नविटपः -पा -पं, लूनविटपः &c.

PRUNER, *s.* विटपछिद् *m.*, पल्लवछिद् *m.*, निरर्थकविटपछेत्ता *m.* (तृ).

PRUNING, *s.* पल्लवावच्छेदः, विटपावच्छेदः, निरर्थकविटपावकर्त्तनं.

PRUNING-HOOK, PRUNING-KNIFE, *s.* पल्लवच्छेदनी, विटपच्छेदनी, पल्लवकर्त्तनी.

PRURIENCE, PRURIENCY, *s.* कण्डूतिः *f.*, कण्डूः *f.*, कण्डुः *f.*, कण्डूया, कण्डूयनं.—(Longing desire for any thing) अतिस्पृहा, अत्यन्तस्पृहा, अतिशयेच्छा, अत्यभिलाषः.

PRURIENT, *a.* कण्डूलः -ला -लं, कण्डूतिमान् -मती -मत् (त्), सकण्डूतिः -तिः -ति.

PRURIGO, *s.* कण्डूः *f.*, कण्डुः *f.*, खर्जूः *f.*, कच्छूः *f.*, कच्छुः *f.*, सुकण्डुः *f.*

To PRY, *v. a.* सूक्ष्मं निरूप् (c. 10. -रूपयति -यितुं), सूक्ष्मं निरीक्ष् (c. 1. -ईक्षते -क्षितुं) or दृश् (c. 1. पश्यति, द्रष्टुं), सूक्ष्मदर्शनं कृ, सूक्ष्मम् अन्विष् (c. 4. -इष्यति -एषितुं) or अनुसन्धा (c. 3. -दधाति -धातुं), सूक्ष्मान्वेषणं कृ, सूक्ष्मानुसन्धानं कृ, सूक्ष्मं चर्च् (c. 1. चर्चति -र्चितुं), सूक्ष्मचर्चां कृ, चर्चां कृ, अनधिकारचर्चां कृ, मर्म्मान्वेषणं कृ, सूक्ष्मगवेषणं कृ, मर्म्मगवेषणं कृ.

PRYING, *s.* सूक्ष्मनिरूपणं, सूक्ष्मनिरीक्षणं, सूक्ष्मदर्शनं, सूक्ष्मदृष्टिः *f.*, सूक्ष्मान्वेषणं, सूक्ष्मानुसन्धानं, सूक्ष्मचर्चा, अनधिकारचर्चा, चर्चा, मर्म्मान्वेषणं.

PSALM, *s.* गीतं, स्तुतिगीतं, गानं, स्तुतिगानं, स्तोत्रं, सङ्कीर्त्तं, सङ्गीतं, ईश्वरस्तुतिगीतं, भक्तिगीतं, भक्तिगानं, धर्म्मगीतं.

PSALMIST, *s.* गीतरचकः, स्तुतिगीतरचकः, स्तोत्ररचकः, गीतकारः, गीतकविः *m.*

PSALMODY, *s.* स्तुतिगानं, स्तोत्रगानं, स्तोत्रगीतिः *f.*, ईश्वरस्तुतिगानं.

PSALMOGRAPHY, *s.* गीतरचनं, स्तुतिगीतरचनं, स्तोत्ररचनं, गीतकरणं.

PSALTER, *s.* गीतपुस्तकं, गीतसंहिता, गीतसंग्रहः, स्तोत्रपुस्तकं, खिलं.

PSEUDO. A prefix expressed in Sanskrit by मिथ्या, मृषा, कृत्रिम, कु &c. prefixed, or कल्प, देशीय &c. affixed; as, 'a pseudo-poet,' मिथ्याकविः *m.*, कुकविः, कविकल्पः, कविदेशीयः; pseudology,' मिथ्यावादः, मृषावादः; 'pseudo-morphous,' कृत्रिमरूपः -पा -पं; 'pseudonymous,' कृत्रिमनामा &c.

PSHAW, *exclam.* धिक्, धै, अये, अरे, रे, किल, हुम्, अपेहि.

PSYCHOLOGICAL, *a.* आत्मतत्त्वविषयः -या -यं, अध्यात्मविषयकः -का -कं.

PSYCHOLOGY, *s.* आत्मतत्त्वविद्या, अध्यात्मविद्या, अध्यात्मशास्त्रं.

PUBERTY, PUBESCENCE, *s.* यौवनं, यौवनावस्था, तारुण्यं, तारुण्यावस्था, तरुणत्वं, युवत्वं, यौवनकालः, प्रौढता, प्रौढिः *f.*, प्रौढदशा; 'attained to puberty,' प्राप्तयौवनः -ना -नं, प्राप्तयौवनकालः -ला -लं; 'not attained to it,' अप्राप्तयौवनः &c.

PUBESCENT, *a.* प्राप्तयौवनः -ना -नं, अङ्कुरितयौवनः &c., प्राप्ततारुण्यः -ण्या -ण्यं.

PUBLIC, *a.* (Pertaining to the community) सर्व्वसम्बन्धी -न्धिनी -न्धि (न्), सर्व्वलोकसम्बन्धी &c., प्रजासम्बन्धी &c., लोक in comp., प्रजा in comp. (General, common to many,) साधारणः -णा -णी -णं, सामान्यः -न्या -न्यं, सर्व्वसाधारणः &c., सर्व्वसामान्यः &c., सार्व्वलौकिकः -की -कं, लौकिकः &c., सार्व्वजनिकः -की -कं, सर्व्वजनीनः -ना -नं, सर्व्वजनीयः -या -यं, विश्वजनीनः &c., विश्वजनीयः -या -यं, सर्व्वः -र्व्वा -र्व्वं, सार्व्वः -र्व्वी -र्व्वं, सर्व्वीयः -या -यं, लोक or जन in comp., (Commonly known or current) प्रसिद्धः -द्धा, लोकप्रसिद्धः &c., सर्व्वप्रसिद्धः &c., जनप्रसिद्धः &c., सर्व्वजनप्रसिद्धः &c., सर्व्वलोकप्रसिद्धः &c., जगत्प्रसिद्धः &c., देशप्रसिद्धः &c., लोकविश्रुतः -ता -तं, सर्व्वत्र प्रचलः -ला -लं or प्रचलितः -ता -तं, लोक or जन in comp., *see* POPULAR.—(Open to all) प्रकाशः -शा -शं, सर्व्वप्रकाशः &c., सर्व्वलोकप्रकाशः &c., प्रकटः -टा -टं, सर्व्वप्रकटः &c., लोकप्रकाशः &c., अविविक्तः -क्ता -क्तं; 'public sale,' प्रकाशविक्रयः प्रकाशक्रयः; 'public benefit,' लोकोपकारः; 'public business,' लोकव्यवहारः व्यवहारः; 'public odium,' जनविद्वेषः; 'public property,' गणद्रव्यं; 'public feeling,' लोकचित्तं, प्रकृतिचित्तं.

PUBLIC, *s.* लोकः, सर्व्वलोकः, सर्व्वजनाः *m. pl.*, प्रजा, प्रजालोकः; 'for the benefit of the public,' प्रजार्थं, लोकार्थं, लोकोपकारार्थं; 'in public,' प्रकाशं, प्रकाशतस्, प्रकटं, प्राकट्येन, सर्व्वप्रकाशं, लोकसाक्षात्, लोकसम्मुखं; 'in public and in private,' प्रकाशं विविक्ते च, प्रकाशम् एकान्तत्र; 'regard for the public or public opinion,' लोकलज्जा, जनलज्जा.

PUBLICAN, *s.* (Collector of tribute or toll) करग्रहः, करग्राही *m.* (न्), करसंग्राही *m.*, शुल्कग्राही *m.*—(Retailer of beer and spirits) शौण्डिकः, शुण्डी *m.* (न्), यवसुरादिविक्रयी *m.* (न्) शुण्डादिविक्रेता *m.* (तृ) सुराविक्रयी *m.*

PUBLICATION, *s.* (The act) प्रकाशनं, प्रकटनं, प्रकटीकरणं, प्रसिद्धीकरणं, प्रकाशीकरणं.—(A published book) प्रकाशितपुस्तकं, प्रसिद्धपुस्तकं.

PUBLIC-HOUSE, *s.* शुण्डास्थानं, मद्यस्थानं, पानगोष्ठिका, शुण्डापानं, शुण्डा, मदिरागृहं, मदिराशाला, आपानं, यवसुरादिविक्रयस्थानं, शुण्डादिविक्रयस्थानं, सुराविक्रयस्थानं.

PUBLICITY, *s.* प्रकाशता, लोकप्रकाशता, लोकप्रकाशः, जनप्रकाशः, प्रकाशः, प्राकट्यं, लोकप्राकट्यं, प्रसिद्धिः *f.*, लोकप्रसिद्धिः *f.*, प्रसिद्धता, लोकप्रसिद्धता -त्वं, लोकविश्रुतिः *f.*, विश्रुतिः, जनप्रसिद्धिः *f.*, प्रख्यातिः *f.*, विख्यातिः *f.*, ख्यातिः *f.*, लौकिकता -त्वं, स्फुटता, व्यक्तता, स्पष्टता.

PUBLICLY, *adv.* (Openly, before the world) प्रकाशं, प्रकाशतस्, प्रकटं, प्राकट्येन, लोकप्रकाशं, सर्व्वप्रकाशं, प्रसिद्धं, अविविक्तं; 'publicly and privately,' *see* PUBLIC, *s.*—(Without concealment) व्यक्तं, सुव्यक्तं, स्पष्टं, स्फुटं, साक्षात्, प्रादुस्, आविस्, आविष्कारं, अगूढं.

PUBLIC-SPIRITED, PUBLIC-MINDED, *a.* लोकोपकारशीलः -ला -लं, लोकोपकारबुद्धिः -द्धिः -द्धि, लोकार्थबुद्धिः &c., जनार्थबुद्धिः &c., लोकार्थी -र्थिनी -र्थि (न्), जनार्थी &c., लोकहितेच्छुः -च्छुः -च्छु, लोकहितः -ता -तं, सर्व्वजनहितैषी &c., साधारणमङ्गलेच्छुः &c.

PUBLIC-SPIRITEDNESS, *s.* लोकोपकारशीलता, लोकोपकारबुद्धिः *f.*, लोकहितेच्छा.

To PUBLISH, *v. a.* (Make generally known) प्रकाश् (c. 10. -काशयति -यितुं), विकाश्, प्रकटीकृ, प्रकट (nom. प्रकटयति -यितुं), प्रसिद्धीकृ, ख्या in caus. (ख्यापयति -यितुं), प्रख्या, विख्या, आख्या, घुष् (c. 10. घोषयति -यितुं), विघुष्, आघुष्, प्रचर् (c. 10. -चारयति -यितुं), विज्ञा in caus. (-ज्ञापयति -ज्ञपयति -यितुं), बुध् (c. 10. बोधयति -यितुं), प्रथ् (c. 10. प्रथयति -यितुं), निविद् (c. 10. -वेदयति -यितुं), विद्, आविष्कृ, प्रादुष्कृ.—(Publish a book) पुस्तकं प्रकाश् or प्रसिद्धीकृ.—(Put into circulation) प्रचलीकृ, प्रचल् (c. 10. -चलयति -यितुं), प्रचर्.

PUBLISHED, *p.p.* प्रकाशितः -ता -तं, प्रकटीकृतः -ता -तं, प्रकटितः -ता -तं, प्रसिद्धीकृतः &c., ख्यापितः -ता -तं, घोषितः &c., विघोषितः &c., आघोषितः &c., विज्ञापितः &c., प्रख्यातः -ता -तं, प्रचलीकृतः &c., प्रचारितः &c., आविष्कृतः &c., प्रादुष्कृतः &c., प्रथितः &c.

PUBLISHER, *s.* प्रकाशकः, प्रकाशयिता *m.* (तृ), ख्यापकः, विज्ञापकः, प्रसिद्धकर्त्ता *m.* (र्तृ), आविष्कर्त्ता *m.*, प्रादुष्कर्त्ता *m.*

To PUCKER, *v. a.* संकुच् (c. 1. -कोचति -चितुं), कुच् (c. 1. कुचति -चितुं), आकुच्, संहृ (c. 1. -हरति -हर्तुं), पुटीकृ, सम्पुटीकृ, सङ्कोचं कृ.

PUCKER, PUCKERING, *s.* पुटः, पुटीकरणं, सङ्कोचः -चनं, कुचनं, आकुचनं.

PUDDER, *s.* तुमुलं, कोलाहलः, सम्भ्रमः, विप्लवः, व्यग्रता, व्यस्तता.

PUDDING, *s.* पोलिका, पोलिका; 'plum-pudding,' *see* the word.

PUDDLE, *s.* पल्वलकः, पङ्कजलौघः, कर्दमजलौघः, सपङ्कजलौघः, पङ्कजलगुल्मः, मलिनजलौघः, समलजलौघः, पङ्कगुल्मः.

To PUDDLE, *v. a.* समलीकृ, पङ्किलीकृ, कलुषीकृ, आविलीकृ. *See* MUDDLE.

PUDENCY, PUDICITY, *s.*, *see* MODESTY.

PUDENDUM, PUDENDA, *s.* (Of a woman) भगं, योनिः *f.*, अधोङ्गं, अधोपरं, अधोवशः, अधस्, अधस्तात्, उपस्थः, गुह्याङ्गं, रतिकुहरं, रतिमन्दिरं, रतिगृहं. *See* PRIVITY.

PUERILE, *a.* बालिशः -शा -शं, बालेयः -या -यं, बालकीयः -या -यं, बालयोग्यः -ग्या -ग्यं, शिशुयोग्यः &c., बालधर्म्मकः -का -कं, बालबुद्धिः -द्धिः -द्धि.

PUERILITY, *s.* बालिश्यं, बालेयत्वं -ता, बालकीयता, बालयोग्यता.

PUERPERAL, *a.* प्रासूतिकः -की -कं, प्रसवसम्बन्धी -न्धिनी -न्धि (न्).

PUERPEROUS, *a.* बालप्रसविनी, बालप्रसवन्ती, प्रसूतिका, सूतिका.

PUFF, *s.* (Breath from the mouth) श्वासः, श्वसितं, मुखमरुतः, वदनमरुतः.—(A puff or sudden whiff) फूत्कृतं, फुत्कारः, फूत्कृतं, फूत्कारः फूत् indec.—(Blast, gust) ध्मानं, आध्मानं, ध्मातं, वातः, वातक्रमः, वात्या, निर्घातः, प्रभञ्जनः.—(Kind of cake) पिष्टकं, आपूपिकं.—(Tumid commendation) अतिशयप्रशंसा, अत्युक्तिरूपा प्रशंसा, अधिकप्रशंसा, अतिशयोक्तिः *f.*

To PUFF, *v. n.* (Breathe) श्वस् (c. 2. श्वसिति -तुं), श्वासं कृ, प्रश्वासं कृ.—(Pant) कृच्छ्रेण श्वस्, कृच्छ्रेण श्वासप्रश्वासं कृ, उद्ध्मा (c. 1. -धमति -ध्मातुं), उद्धमं कृ, प्राणकृच्छ्रोपहतः -ता -तं भू.—(Blow) ध्मा, प्रध्मा.—(Eject air from the mouth suddenly) अकस्माद् वदनमरुतं or मुखमरुतं निरस् (c. 4. -अस्यति -असितुं) or निःसृ in caus.—(Blow upon with a puffing noise) फुत्कृ, फूत्कृ, फुत्कारं कृ, फूत्कारं कृ, फुत्कारेण or फूत्शब्देन प्रश्वस्.—(Swell or be inflated with air) ध्मा in pass. (ध्मायते), आध्मा, वातेन पृ in pass. (पूर्य्यते).

To PUFF, *v. a.* (Inflate, dilate with air) ध्मा (c. 1. धमति, ध्मा͂), आध्मा, समाध्मा, प्रध्मा, उपध्मा, वातेन पृ (c. 10. पूरयति -यितुं), श्वासेन पृ, वायुपूरितं -तां कृ.—(Blow away) अपध्मा, विध्मा.—(Puff up with pride, &c.) दर्पाध्मातं -तां कृ, गर्वाध्मातं -तां कृ, उद्धतीकृ, उन्मत्तीकृ.—(Praise with exaggeration) अत्युक्त्या or अतिशयोक्त्या प्रशंस्, अतिशयप्रशंसां कृ.

PUFFED, *p.p.* (Inflated) ध्मातः -ता -तं, आध्मातः &c., समाध्मातः &c., प्रध्मातः &c., वातपूरितः -ता -तं, वायुपूर्णः -र्णा -र्णं, श्वासपूरितः &c.—(Puffed up with pride, &c.) दर्पाध्मातः -ता -तं, गर्वाध्मातः &c., उद्धतः &c., दर्पोद्धतः &c., मदोद्धतः &c.

PUFFY, *a.* आध्मातः -ता -तं, वातमयः -यी -यं, शब्दमात्रः -त्रा -त्रं.

PUG-DOG, *s.* मर्कटमुखः क्षुद्रकुक्कुरभेदः.

PUG-FACED, *a.* वानरमुखः -खी -खं, मर्कटवदनः -ना -नं, कपिमुखः &c.

PUG-NOSE, *s.* चिपिटः, चिपिटकः, चिपुटः, चिक्किनः, अवभ्रटः.

PUGILISM, *s.* मुष्टियुद्धं, मुष्टियोधनं, मुष्टिपातः, मल्लयुद्धं, मुष्टीमुष्टि, बाहुयुद्धं.

PUGILIST, *s.* मुष्टियोद्धा *m.* (द्धृ), मुष्टियोधः, मुष्टियोधी *m.* (न्), बाहुयोधी *m.*

PUGILISTIC, *a.* मुष्टियुद्धसम्बन्धी -न्धिनी -न्धि (न्), बाहुयुद्धसम्बन्धी &c.

PUGNACIOUS, *a.* युयुत्सुः -त्सुः -त्सु, कलहप्रियः -या -यं, युद्धप्रियः &c., रणप्रियः &c., युद्धेच्छुः -च्छुः -च्छु, युद्धकारी -रिणी -रि (न्), कलहकारी &c., रणकामी -मिनी &c., युद्धकामी &c.

PUGNACITY, *s.* युयुत्सा, युद्धेच्छा, युद्धप्रियता, कलहप्रियता, कलहेच्छा.

PUISNE, *a.* अवरः -रा -रं, अवरपदस्थः -स्था -स्थं, अवरजः -जा -जं.

PUISSANCE, *s.* पराक्रमः, विक्रमः, प्रभावः, ऐश्वर्य्यं, तेजस् *n.*, प्राबल्यं.

PUISSANT, *a.* पराक्रमी -मिणी -मि (न्), विक्रमी &c., पराक्रान्तः -न्ता -न्तं, विक्रान्तः &c., महाबलः -ला -लं, बलवान् -वती -वत् (त्), महाशक्तिः -क्तिः -क्ति, महाविक्रमः -मा -मं.

To PUKE, *v. n.* वम् (c. 1. वमति -मितुं), वमनं कृ, छर्द् (c. 10. छर्दयति -यितुं).

PUKE, *s.* वान्तिकारकम् औषधं, वान्तिकृत्, छर्दनकृत्.

PUKING, *s.* वान्तिः *f.*, वमनं, छर्दनं; *part.*, वमी -मिनी -मि (न्).

PULCHRITUDE, *s.* See BEAUTY.

To PULE, *v. n.* (Like a child) बालकवद् रु (c. 2. रौति, रवितुं), शिशुवद् रुद् (c. 2. रोदिति -तुं); 'like a chicken,' पक्षिशावकवत् कूज् (c. 1. कूजति -जितुं).

To PULL, *v. a.* or *n.* (Draw, drag) कृष् (c. 1. कर्षति, c. 6. कृषति -ते, क्रष्टुं, कर्ष्टुं), आकृष्, समाकृष्, परिकृष्, प्रतिकृष्, संकृष्, कर्षणं कृ.—(Pull forcibly) हृ (c. 1. हरति, हर्त्तुं), हरणं कृ.—(Pluck, gather by plucking) ग्रह् (c. 9. गृह्णाति, ग्रहीतुं), आदा (c. 3. -ददाति -दत्ते -दातुं), अङ्गुलिभिर् ग्रह् or आदा or चि or अवचि; 'to pull the hair,' केशग्रहं कृ, केशग्रहणं कृ, केशान् ग्रह्.—(Pull down) अपकृष्, अवकृष्, व्यपकृष्, पत् in caus., अधःपत्.—(Pull off) अपकृष्, अवकृष्, व्यपकृष्, उत्कृष्, अपहृ, व्यपहृ, अपनी, अवतॄ in caus. (-तारयति -यितुं); 'he pulls off his clothes,' वस्त्रम् अवतारयति.—(Pull out) उत्कृष्, निष्कृष्, उद्धृ, निर्हृ, उत्पट् (c. 10. -पाटयति -यितुं), उत्खन् (c. 1. -खनति -नितुं), निर्णी in caus., उत्पाटनं कृ; 'the hair,' लुञ्च् (c. 1. लुञ्चति -ञ्चितुं), उल्लुञ्च्, अवलुञ्च्, विलुञ्च्, उत्पट्, केशोल्लुञ्चनं कृ, केशोत्पाटनं कृ.—(Pull towards) आकृष्, समाकृष्, प्रतिकृष्.—(Pull in pieces, pull in two) विदॄ (c. 10. -दारयति -यितुं), अवदॄ, विभिद्, विदलीकृ, खण्डशः कृ, खण्डं खण्डं कृ.—(Pull up) उत्पट्, उद्धृ, समुद्धृ, उच्छिद्, उत्खन्; 'by the roots,' उन्मूल् (c. 10. -मूलयति -यितुं), समुन्मूल्, समूलं or आमूलम् उद्धृ.

PULL, *s.* कर्षणं, कृष्टिः *f.*, कर्षः, आकर्षः -र्षणं, आकृष्टिः *f.*, संकर्षणं, विकर्षणं.

PULLED, *p. p.* कर्षितः -ता -तं, कृष्टः -ष्टा -ष्टं, आकर्षितः &c., आकृष्टः &c., अवकृष्टः &c., विकर्षितः &c., विकृष्टः &c., हृतः -ता -तं, गृहीतः -ता -तं; 'pulled by the hair,' केशगृहीतः &c., केशेषु गृहीतः; &c.; 'pulled off, as clothes, &c.,' अवतारितः -ता -तं; pulled out,' उत्कृष्टः -ष्टा -ष्टं, निष्कर्षितः &c., उद्धृतः &c., उत्पाटितः &c.; 'as the hair,' उल्लुञ्चितः &c.; 'pulled up,' उन्मूलितः -ता -तं, उत्पाटितः &c., उत्खातः &c., व्यपरोपितः &c.

PULLET, *s.* कुक्कुटीशावकः, कुक्कुटशावकः, पक्षिशावकः, पक्षिणीशावकः.

PULLEY, *s.* काष्ठान्तर्गतं क्षुद्रचक्रं, काष्ठान्तःस्थं सूक्ष्मचक्रं तच्च रज्जुसंयुक्तं भूत्वा कीलकोपरि परिवर्त्तते, कीलकोपरि परिवर्त्तमानं क्षुद्रचक्रं.

PULLING, *s.* कर्षणं, कृष्टिः *f.*, आकर्षणं, आकृष्टिः *f.*, संकर्षणं, विकर्षः -र्षणं, उत्कर्षः, हरणं, ग्रहणं, अङ्गुलिग्रहणं; 'pulling the hair,' केशग्रहः -हणं; 'mutual pulling of the hair,' केशाकेशि indec.; 'pulling up the hair,' केशलुञ्चनं, केशोल्लुञ्चनं.

To PULLULATE, *v. n.* (Germinate) स्फुट्, फुल्ल्, अङ्कुर्, विकस्.

PULLULATION, *s.* स्फुटनं, फुल्लतिः *f.*, फुल्लिः *f.*, उद्भेदः, विकसनं.

PULMONARY, PULMONIC, *a.* फुप्फुससम्बन्धी -न्धिनी -न्धि (न्), फुप्फुसनिष्ठः -ष्ठा -ष्ठं, फुप्फुसस्थः -स्था -स्थं, फुप्फुसीयः -या -यं.

PULP, *s.* मज्जा, मज्जा *m.* (न्), मज्जनं, सारः, गर्भः.—(Of fruit) फलसारः, फलगर्भः, फलस्य कोमलभागः or मृदुभागः.

PULPINESS, *s.* समज्जता, मज्जावत्त्वं, मज्जागुणकत्वं, कोमलता, मृदुता.

PULPIT, *s.* उपदेशासनं, उपदेशपीठं, धर्म्मोपदेशपीठं, पीठं, पुरोहितासनं, धर्म्मोपदेशकासनं, धर्म्माध्यापकासनं, धर्म्माध्यापकपीठं.

PULPOUS, PULPY, *a.* मज्जागुणकः -का -कं, मज्जोपमः -मा -मं, मज्जामयः -यी -यं, समज्जः -ज्जा -ज्जं, मांसलः -ला -लं, मांसगुणकः -का -कं, कोमलः -ला -लं, आर्द्रमृदुः -द्वी -दु, मृदुः &c.

To PULSATE, *v. n.* (Palpitate) स्पन्द्, स्फुर्, कम्प्, वेप्.

PULSATION, *s.* स्पन्दनं, प्रतिस्पन्दनं, स्पन्दितं, कम्पः -म्पनं, स्फुरणं, विष्पन्दः, चलत्वं; 'of the heart,' हृदयस्पन्दनं, हृत्कम्पः; 'of an artery,' नाडिस्फुरणं, नाड्याघातः.

PULSE, *s.* (Of the blood or an artery) नाडिः -डी *f.*, नालि -लिः *f.*, नाडीस्फुरणं, नालीस्फुरणं, नाडीस्पन्दनं, नाड्याघातः; 'feeling the pulse,' नाडीपरीक्षा; 'to feel the pulse,' नाडीपरीक्षां कृ.—(Leguminous plant) कलायः, सतीनः -नकः, सतीलः -ला -लकः, सितीलकः, सातीलकः, सातिलकः, द्विदलं, त्रिपुटः, खण्डिकः, हरेणुः *m.*, शमीधान्यं, वनसङ्कटः, धान्यवीरः, मुद्गः, वर्त्तुलः; 'pulse ground and fried,' वडा, वटकः,

PULVERABLE, *a.* क्षोदनीयः -या -यं, चूर्णनीयः &c., चूर्णीकरणयोग्यः &c.

PULVERIZATION, *s.* चूर्णीकरणं, क्षोदीकरणं, चूर्णनं, सञ्चूर्णनं, क्षोदनं.

To PULVERIZE, *v. a.* चूर्ण् (c. 10. चूर्णयति -यितुं), संचूर्ण्, प्रचूर्ण्, विचूर्ण्, चूर्णीकृ, क्षुद् (c. 7. क्षुणत्ति, क्षोत्तुं), प्रक्षुद्, संक्षुद्, क्षोदीकृ, पिष्, गुण्ड् &c. See *To* POUND, POWDER.

PULVERIZED, *p. p.* चूर्णितः -ता -तं, चूर्णीकृतः -ता -तं, संचूर्णितः &c., चूर्णीभूतः -ता -तं, क्षोदितः -ता -तं, क्षोदीकृतः &c., पिष्टः -ष्टा -ष्टं, गुण्डितः -ता -तं, गुण्डितः -ता -तं.

PULVERULENT, *a.* चूर्णमयः -यी -यं, पांशुलः -ला -लं. See POWDERY.

PUMMEL, *s.* (Of a saddle) वङ्का.

PUMP, *s.* जलोत्तोलनयन्त्रं, जलोत्तोलननाडिः -डी *f.*, जलोत्क्षेपणयन्त्रं, जलोत्क्षेपकयन्त्रं, जलोत्क्षेपकनाडी, जलोत्तोलनी, जलोत्क्षेपणी, जलनाडी, जलनाली; 'place where water is distributed,' प्रपा.

To PUMP, *v. a.* or *n.* नाडीद्वारेण जलम् उत्तुल् (c. 10. -तोलयति -यितुं) or उत्क्षिप् (c. 6. -क्षिपति -क्षेप्तुं) or जलोत्तोलनं कृ or जलोत्क्षेपणं कृ, जलनाडीं सञ्चल् (c. 10. -चालयति -यितुं), जलोत्तोलनयन्त्रं सञ्चल्.—(Interrogate artfully) सव्याजं प्रच्छ् or अनुप्रच्छ् or परिप्रच्छ्, प्रश्नेन परीक्ष् or अनुसन्धा.

PUMPKIN, *s.* कुष्माण्डः -ण्डा -ण्डी, कुष्माण्डकः, कूष्माण्डः -ण्डी -ण्डकः, अलाबूः *f.*, अलाबुः *f.*, आलाबुः *f.*, तुम्बी, कर्कारुः *m.*

PUN, *s.* श्लेषः, श्लेषोक्तिः *f.*, श्लेषवाक्यं, श्लेषालङ्कारः, द्व्यर्थवाक्यं, अर्थापत्तिः *f.*

To PUN, *v. n.* श्लेषोक्तिं कृ, श्लेषवाक्यं वद् (c. 1. वदति -दितुं)

PUNCH, *s.* (Instrument for perforating) वेधनी, वेधनिका.—(Thrust, blow) आघातः, अभिघातः, प्रहारः; 'with the elbow,' कोलः

-ला, कीलाघातः, अरत्निप्रहारः.—(Kind of drink) शर्करादिमिश्रितं मद्यजम्बीरादिरसमयं पानीयं.—(In a puppet show) पुत्तलिकाक्रीडायां वैहासिकः or विदूषकः.

To Punch. *v. a.* (Pierce with a punch) पृष्ठीकयन्त्रेण व्यध्.—(With the elbow) अरत्निना तड् (c. 10. ताडयति -यितुं) or आहन् (c. 2. -हन्ति -न्तुं) or प्रहृ (c. 1. -हरति -हर्तुं), अरत्निं प्रसार्य्य तड्, कीलाघातं कृ.

Puncheon, *s.* (Instrument), *see* Punch.—(A measure), *see* Cask.

Punchy, *a.* ह्रस्वस्थूलः -ला -लं स्थूलह्रस्वः -स्वा -स्वं, घनह्रस्वः &c.

Punctilio, *s.* सूक्ष्मविषयः, सूक्ष्मविधिः *m.*, सूक्ष्मनियमः, सूक्ष्मता, अतिसूक्ष्मता, सौक्ष्म्यं, अतिसौक्ष्म्यं, शिष्टाचारसौक्ष्म्यं, सभ्याचारसूक्ष्मता.

Punctilious, *a.* अतिसूक्ष्मदृष्टिः -ष्टिः -ष्टि, अतिसूक्ष्मदर्शी -र्शिनी -र्शि (न्), अतिसूक्ष्मः -क्ष्मा -क्ष्मं, सूक्ष्मोपचारदर्शी, सूक्ष्माचारनिष्ठः -ष्ठा -ष्ठं, अतिसूक्ष्माचारी &c., सूक्ष्मनियमनिष्ठः &c., सूक्ष्मोपचारनिष्ठः &c., सूक्ष्मोपचारशीलः -ला -लं, सूक्ष्मादरनिष्ठः &c., सूक्ष्मनियमी &c., नियमनिष्ठः &c., सभ्याचारी &c.

Punctiliousness, *s.* अतिसूक्ष्मदर्शनं, अतिसूक्ष्मदृष्टिः *f.*, सूक्ष्मोपचारनिष्ठा, सूक्ष्मनियमनिष्ठा, सूक्ष्मादरनिष्ठा, सूक्ष्मसत्कारनिष्ठा, सूक्ष्मादरशीलता, सभ्याचारः.

Punctual, *a.* समयपालकः -का -कं, समयरक्षकः -का -कं, समयनिष्ठः -ष्ठा -ष्ठं, समयसेवी -विनी -वि (न्), कालरक्षकः -का -कं, कालनिष्ठः -ष्ठा -ष्ठं, कालपालकः -का -कं, कालसेवी &c., सामयिकः -की -कं, सङ्केतपालकः -का -कं, सङ्केतनिष्ठः &c., नियमपालकः &c., नियमनिष्ठः &c., वचननिष्ठः &c., प्रतिज्ञानिष्ठः &c., प्रतिज्ञापालकः &c., दृढनियमी &c.

Punctuality, punctualness, *s.* समयपालनं, समयनिष्ठा, समयसेवनं, कालनिष्ठा, कालसेवनं, कालपालनं, समयरक्षणं, कालरक्षणं, सङ्केतपालनं, सङ्केतनिष्ठा, नियमनिष्ठा, नियमपालनं, वचननिष्ठा, प्रतिज्ञानिष्ठा.

Punctually, *adv.* यथासमयं, समयतस्, यथाकालं, कालतस्, नियमतस्, यथानियमं, यथासङ्केतं, समयनिष्ठापूर्व्वं, कालनिष्ठापूर्व्वं.

To punctuate, *v. a.* विरामचिह्नैर् अङ्क् (c. 10. अङ्कयति -यितुं) विरामचिह्नानि लिख् (c. 6. लिखति, लेखितुं) or कृ, विरामचिह्नाङ्कनं कृ, विरामचिह्नाङ्कितं -तां कृ.

Punctuated, *p. p.* विरामचिह्नाङ्कितः -ता -तं, अवसानचिह्नाङ्कितः -ता -तं.

Punctuation, *s.* विरामचिह्नाङ्कनं, अवसानचिह्नाङ्कनं, विरामचिह्नलिखनं.

To puncture, *v. a.* सूक्ष्मकीलकाग्रेण व्यध् (c. 4. विध्यति, व्यद्धुं). *See To* prick.

Puncture, *s* वेधः -धनं, सूक्ष्मकीलकवेधः, व्यधः -धनं. *See* Prick.

Punctured, *p.p.* वेधितः -ता -तं, कीलकवेधितः &c., कीलकविद्धः -द्धा -द्धं.

Pundit, *s.* पण्डितः, विद्वान् *m.* (स्), प्राज्ञः, बहुश्रुतः, अधीयानः, श्रोत्रियः, वेदविद् *m.*, वेदविद्वान् *m.*, अनूचानः. *See* Learned.

Pungency, *s.* कटुता -त्वं, उग्रता -त्वं, तीव्रता, तिग्मता -त्वं, खरता, प्रखरता, प्राखर्य्यं, तैग्म्यं, तीक्ष्णता, तैक्ष्ण्यं, अरुन्तुदत्वं, चण्डता -त्वं, उष्णता -त्वं, चौषणं, चोषणः, दाहः, विदाहः.

Pungent, *a.* कटुः -टुः -ट्वी -टु, उग्रः -ग्रा -ग्रं, तीव्रः -व्रा -व्रं, तिग्मः -ग्मा ग्मं, तीक्ष्णः -क्ष्णा -क्ष्णं, खरः -रा -रं, प्रखरः रा -रं, अरुन्तुदः दा -दं, चण्डः -ण्डा -ण्डं, उष्णः -ष्णा -ष्णं, तिक्तः -क्ता -क्तं, विदाही -हिनी -हि (न्), दाही &c.

Puniness, *s.* अल्पता, क्षुद्रता -त्वं, शरीरक्षुद्रता, अल्पशरीरता, तनुता.

To punish, *v. a.* दण्ड् (c. 10. दण्डयति -यितुं), शास् (c. 2. शास्ति, -सितुं, c. 10. शासयति -यितुं), अनुशास्, तड् (c. 10. ताडयति -यितुं), निग्रह् (c. 9. -गृह्णाति -ग्रहीतुं), दम् (c. 10. दमयति -यितुं) वियत् (c. 10. -यातयति -यितुं) बन्ध् (c. 9. बध्नाति बन्द्धुं), दण्डं प्रणी. *See To* inflict.—(Pain) पीड्, व्यथ्, तप्, सन्तप्.

Punishable, *a.* दण्डनीयः -या -यं, दण्ड्यः -ण्ड्या -ण्ड्यं, दण्डार्हः -र्हा -र्हं, दण्डनार्हः &c., ताडनीयः -या -यं, ताड्यः -ड्या -ड्यं, शासनीयः -या -यं, शास्यः -स्या -स्यं, शासनार्हः -र्हा -र्हं, दमनीयः -या -यं, दण्डयोग्यः -ग्या -ग्यं, शिक्षणीयः &c., शिक्ष्यः -क्ष्या -क्ष्यं, शिक्षार्हः &c., विनेयः -या -यं.

Punished, *p. p.* दण्डितः -ता -तं, शासितः -ता -तं, शिष्टः -ष्टा -ष्टं, ताडितः -ता -तं, निगृहीतः &c., पीडितः &c., विनीतः &c., शिक्षितः &c.

Punisher, *s.* दण्डयिता *m.* (तृ), शासिता *m.*, शास्ता *m.*, शासकः, ताडयिता *m.*, ताडकः, दण्डप्रणेता *m.*, शिक्षकः.

Punishment, *s.* दण्डः, दण्डनं, शासनं, अनुशासनं, शास्तिः *f.*, शिष्टिः *f.*, ताडनं, साहसं, दमः, दमनं, दमथः -थं, दमथुः *m.*, निग्रहः, शिक्षणं; 'corporal punishment,' शरीरदण्डः -ण्डनं, शारीरदण्डः, शारीरिकदण्डः, शारीरः, देहदण्डः -ण्डनं; 'just punishment,' सम्यग्दण्डनं; 'infliction of punishment,' दण्डयोगः, दण्डप्रयोगः, दण्डप्रणयनं, *see* Infliction; 'capital punishment,' वधदण्डः, प्राणदण्डः, प्राणान्तदण्डः, जीवान्तदण्डः, देहान्तदण्डः, उत्तमसाहसं; 'severity of punishment,' दण्डपारुष्यं; 'repeated punishment,' त्रिवारदण्डः; 'fear of punishment,' दण्डभीतिः *f.*, दण्डभयं; 'through fear of it,' दण्डभयात्.

Punitive, punitory, *a.* दाण्डः -ण्डी -ण्डं, दाण्डिकः -की -कं, दण्डसम्बन्धी -न्धिनी &c., साहसिकः -की -कं, दण्डविषयकः -का -कं, दण्ड in comp.

Punjáb, *s.* (The country) पञ्चनदः. *See* Panjáb.

Punka, *s.* तालवृन्तः -न्तं, पवित्रं, मरुदान्दोलः.

Punster, *s.* सश्लेषवक्ता *m.* (क्तृ), सश्लेषवादी *m.* (न्).

Punt, *s.* तरालुः *m.*, तरान्धुः *m.*, तरण्डः -ण्डं, वहित्रं.

Puny, *a.* क्षुद्रः -द्रा -द्रं, अल्पः -ल्पा -ल्पं, क्षुद्रशरीरः -रा -रं.

Pup, *s.* कुक्कुरशिशुः *m.*, कुक्कुरशावकः, शिशुः *m.*, डिम्भः.

To pup, *v. n.* कुक्कुरशावकान् सु or प्रसु or जन्, कुक्कुरशिशून् सु.

Pupil, *s.* (Scholar) शिष्यः, विद्यार्थी *m.* (न्), छात्रः, अन्तेवासी *m.* (न्), अन्तेवासिजनः, अध्यायी *m.*, अध्येता *m.* (तृ), प्राचार्य्यः, बालः, शिशुः *m.*, माणवकः, मृडङ्कुणः, प्रवालः.—(Of the eye) तारा, तारका, अक्षितारा -रका, तारः -रकं, कनीनिका, दृष्टिः *f.*, लोचकः, ज्योतिस् *n.*, नयना.

Pupilage, *s.* शिष्यत्वं, शिष्यावस्था, शिष्यदशा, विद्यार्थित्वं -ता, अन्तेवासित्वं, बालत्वं, शिशुत्वं -ता, शैशवं.

Pupilary, *a.* शैष्यः -ष्यी -ष्यं, शिष्यसम्बन्धी &c., शैशवः -वी -वं.

Puppet, *s.* पुत्रिका, दारुपुत्रिका, पाञ्चालिका, पाञ्चलिका, पाञ्चाली, पुत्तली -लिका, शालाङ्गी, शालभञ्जी -ञ्जिका, दारुस्त्री, दारुगर्भा, कुरुण्टी, अञ्जलिकारिका, यात्रा.

Puppet-show, *s.* पुत्तलिकाक्रीडा, पुत्रिकाक्रीडा, पाञ्चालिकाक्रीडा.

Puppy, *s.* कुक्कुरशावकः, कुक्कुरशिशुः *m.*, शिशुः *m.*, डिम्भः.—(Conceited person) दर्शनीयमानी *m.* (न्), आत्माभिमानी *m.*, मानी *m.*, रूपगर्वितः, दाम्भिकः.

To pur, *v. n.* मार्जारवत् सन्तोषसूचकं रणरणशब्दं कृ or रणत्कारं कृ.

Purána, *s.* (Sacred and mythological poem, derived from the same religious system as the Rámáyana and Mahábhárata, or from the mytho-heroic style of Hindú belief; being a departure from the purer system of the Vedas. They are eighteen in number, and each one is supposed to treat of five topics, viz. 1. the creation, 2. the destruction and renovation of worlds, 3. the genealogy of gods and heroes, 4. the reign of the Manus, 5. the transactions of their descendants. From this five-fold division, and from the antiquity of the stories narrated, come the general names पुराणं, पञ्चलक्षणं. The specific titles are as follows: 1. ब्रह्मपुराणं or ब्राह्मपुराणं, 2. पद्मपुराणं, 3. विष्णुपुराणं, 4. शिवपुराणं, 5. भागवतपुराणं or भगवत्पुराणं, 6. नारदपुराणं, 7. मार्कण्डपुराणं, मार्कण्डेयपुराणं, 8. अग्निपुराणं, 9. भविष्यपुराणं, 10. ब्रह्मवैवर्त्तपुराणं, 11. लिङ्गपुराणं, 12. वराहपुराणं, 13. स्कन्दपुराणं, 14. वामनपुराणं, 15. कूर्म्मपुराणं, 16. मत्स्यपुराणं, 17. गारुडपुराणं, 18. ब्रह्माण्डपुराणं. Sometimes a Purána called the वायुपुराणं or वायवीयपुराणं is substituted for the शिवपुराणं, and another called the नरसिंहपुराणं for the ब्रह्माण्डपुराणं. These eighteen mythological works are the repository of the modern and popular religious creed of the Hindús. They are amplifications of the two great heroic and historical poems or Itihása, called Rámáyana and Mahábhárata, giving a more connected and definite explanation of the mythical fictions and historical traditions contained in those works. They are consequently remarkable for attributing paramount importance to the two divinities, Śiva and Vishnu, who, under one form or other, are almost the sole objects that are made to claim homage. Each separate Purána cannot, therefore, be taken as a guide to Hindú belief as a whole, but rather to some separate branch of it, in which the worship of either one of these deities in particular incarnations is encouraged in preference to that of the other. The most celebrated of them all is the fifth in the above list, or Bhágavata Purána, designed for the glorification of Bhagavat or Vishnu, in the form of Krishna. This exercises a more direct and powerful influence on the opinions of the natives of India than any other. The third, or Vishnu Purána, translated by Professor Wilson, is also a work of great celebrity, and conforms most closely to the definition of Panchalakshanam, *i. e.* treating of five specified topics. There are also eighteen Upapuránas, or similar poems of inferior sanctity and different appellations, viz.: 1. सनत्कुमारं, 2. नारसिंहं, 3. नारदीयं, 4. शिवं, 5. दुर्वाससं, 6. कापिलं, 7. मानवं, 8. औशनसं, 9. वरुणं, 10. कालिका, 11. शाम्बं, 12. नन्दिकेश्वरं, 13. सौरं, 14. पाराशरं, 15. आदित्यं, 16. माहेश्वरं, 17. भागवतं, 18. वशिष्ठं. The collector and arranger of the Puránas, as well as of the more ancient Vedas, was a sage named Krishna कृष्णः, or Dwaipáyana द्वैपायनः, or Krishnadwaipáyana कृष्णद्वैपायनः. The surname of Vyása व्यासः or 'Arranger' (from the root अस् with वि, meaning to 'dispose' or 'set in order'), was given to him, and is now used to denote any expounder of the Vedas or Puránas. His seat is called व्यासासनं, व्यासपीठं.

PURÁNIC, *a.* पौराणिकः -की -कं, पौराणः -णी -णं, पुराणविषयकः &c.

PURBLIND, *a.* अल्पदृष्टदृक् *m. f. n.* (श्), अव्यक्तदृक् *m. f. n.*, हतदृष्टिः -ष्टिः -ष्टि, अदीर्घदृष्टिः &c., ईषदन्धः -न्धा -न्धं.

PURCHASABLE, *a.* क्रेयः -या -यं, क्रेतव्यः -व्या -व्यं, क्रय्यः -य्या -य्यं.

To PURCHASE, *v. a.* क्री (c. 9. क्रीणाति -णीते, क्रेतुं), उपक्री, संक्री, मूल्यं दत्त्वा लभ् or प्राप्, पण् (c. 1. पणते -णितुं), पणीकृ.

PURCHASE, *s.* (The act of buying) क्रयः, क्रयणं, संक्रयणं, उपक्रयः, क्रीणनं.—(Thing purchased) क्रीतवस्तु *n.*, क्रीतद्रव्यं.—(Hold, force) ग्रहणं, ग्राहः, संग्राहः, संग्रहणं, ग्रहः, आग्रहः, धृतिः *f.*, ग्रहणशक्तिः *f.*, शक्तिः *f.*

PURCHASED, *p. p.* क्रीतः -ता -तं, क्रयक्रीतः &c., संक्रीतः &c., उपक्रीतः &c.

PURCHASE-MONEY, *s.* क्रयमूल्यं, क्रयणमूल्यं, मूल्यं, अर्घः.

PURCHASER, *s.* क्रयी *m.* (न्), क्रेता *m.* (तृ), क्रायकः, क्रयिकः, क्रयकर्त्ता *m.*

PURE, *a.* (Clean, free from dirt) निर्मलः -ला -लं, विमलः -ला -लं, अमलः &c., अमली -लिनी -लि (न्), मलहीनः -ना -नं, शुद्धः -द्धा -द्धं, विशुद्धः &c., पवित्रः -त्रा -त्रं, स्वच्छः -च्छा -च्छं, अच्छः &c., शुचिः -चिः -चि.—(Free from sin or guilt, morally pure) शुद्धः -द्धा -द्धं, शुचिः -चिः -चि, पुण्यः -ण्या -ण्यं, अनघः -घा -घं, निष्कलङ्कः -ङ्का -ङ्कं, निष्पापः -पा -पं, अदृष्टपापः &c., अपापः &c., पापहीनः -ना -नं, अकृतपापः &c., अज्ञातपापः &c., अकल्मषः -षा -षं, धूतकल्मषः &c., अलिप्तः -प्ता -प्तं, साधुः -ध्वी -धु, अदृष्टदोषः -षा -षं, सात्त्विकः -की -कं, प्राञ्जलः -ला -लं.—(Ceremonially clean) पवित्रः -त्रा -त्रं, पूतः -ता -तं, पावनः -ना -नं, पवनः -ना -नं, शुचिः -चिः -चि, शौचवान् -वती -वत् (त्), शौचोपेतः -ता -तं, मेध्यः -ध्या -ध्यं.—(Unadulterated, incorrupted) अदूषितः -ता -तं, अदुष्टः -ष्टा -ष्टं, शुद्धः -द्धा -द्धं, अविकारितः -ता -तं, अभ्रष्टः -ष्टा -ष्टं, असंसृष्टः -ष्टा -ष्टं.—(Mere, simple) केवलः -ला -लं, केवली &c., मात्रकः -का -कं, मात्र in comp., शुद्धः &c.—(Free from corrupt words, as speech) अपभ्रंशहीनः -ना -नं, अपशब्दरहितः -ता -तं, अपशब्दशून्यः -न्या -न्यं, शुद्धः -द्धा -द्धं, अपप्रयोगहीनः -ना -नं.—(Chaste, ignorant of carnal intercourse) अज्ञातव्यवायः -या -यं, अज्ञातमैथुनः -ना -नं; 'as a woman,' पुरुषास्पृष्टा.—(Of pure descent or blood) मौलः -ली -लं.—(Pure in heart or mind) शुद्धमतिः -तिः -ति, शुद्धात्मा -त्मा -त्म (न्), शुद्धहृदयः &c., *see* PURE-MINDED; 'to be pure,' शुध् (c. 4. शुध्यति -ते, शोद्धुं), शुद्धीभू, शुचि (nom. शुचीयते), पवित्रीभू.

PURELY, *adv.* (Cleanly) निर्मलं, विमलं, शुद्धं, पवित्रं, शुचि.—(Merely) मात्रं, केवलं. *See* MERELY.

PURE-MINDED, *a.* शुद्धमतिः -तिः -ति, शुद्धात्मा -त्मा -त्म (न्), विमलात्मा &c., अमलात्मा &c., निर्मलान्तःकरणः -णा -णं, शुद्धहृदयः -या -यं, प्रयतात्मा &c.

PURENESS, *s.* निर्मलता, शुचिता, शुद्धता -त्वं, शुद्धिः *f.* *See* PURITY.

PURGATION, *s.* रेचनं, विरेचनं, रेकः, विरेकः, शोधनं, शुद्धिः *f.*

PURGATIVE, *a.* रेचकः -की -कं, विरेचकः &c., शोधकः -का -कं, उदरशोधकः &c., अधोभागहरः -रा -रं, अतिसारी -रिणी -रि (न्), सारकः -का -कं, अतिसारकः &c.

PURGATIVE, *s.* (Medicine) रेचकं, रेचनं, विरेचनं, विरेकः, अधोभागहरं, उदरशोधनं, अधोभागशोधकं, सारकं, सारकौषधं.

PURGATORY, *a.* शोधकः -का -कं, पावनः -ना -नं, पावकः -का -कं, पापशोधनः -ना -नं, पापनाशकः &c., पापनाशनः -ना -नं, पापघ्नः -घ्नी -घ्नं, अघनाशनः &c., अघमर्षणः -णी -णं.

PURGATORY, *s.* पापशोधनस्थानं, अघशोधनस्थानं, यातनास्थानं; 'pain of purgatory.' यातना, भैरवी यातना.

To PURGE, *v. a.* (The bowels, &c.) विरिच् (c. 7. -रिणक्ति -रिंक्ते -रेक्तुं),

रिच्, उदरं or अधोभागं शुध् (c. 10. शोधयति -यितुं), उदरशोधनं कृ, मलं सृ in caus. (सारयति -यितुं), मलशोधनं कृ, मलशुद्धिं कृ.—(Cleanse from guilt) पापात् शुध् or परिशुध् or विशुध्, पापशोधनं कृ, अघशोधनं कृ.—(Cleanse in general) पू, परिपू, शुध्, मलापकर्षणं कृ.

PURGE, *s.* रेचनं, विरेचनं, रेचकं, विरेकः, उदरशोधनं, अधोभागहरं.

PURGED, *p. p.* (As the bowels) रेचितः -ता -तं, विरेचितः &c., रिक्तः -क्ता -क्तं, विरिक्तः &c., शोधितः -ता -तं, सारितः &c.—(Cleared) शोधितः &c., पूतः &c., पावितः &c.

PURGING, *s.* (Of the bowels) रेचना -नं, रेकः, विरेकः, सारणः, अतिसारः. *See* DIARRHŒA, DYSENTERY.

PURIFICATION, *s.* शोधनं, संशोधनं, विशोधनं, परिशोधनं, शोधः, परिशोधः, शुद्धिः *f.*, संशुद्धिः *f.*, विशुद्धिः *f.*, पावनं, पवित्रीकरणं, मार्जनं, परिमार्जनं, निर्मलीकरणं, विमलीकरणं, मलापकर्षणं, मलापनयनं, मलहरणं, शुचीकरणं, क्षालनं, प्रक्षालनं, निर्णेकः, स्वच्छीकरणं.—(State) शुद्धिः *f.*, संशुद्धिः, शुद्धता -त्वं, विशुद्धता, शोधितत्वं, शौचं, शुचिता, पवित्रता, पूतत्वं, पावितत्वं, पूतिः *f.*, निर्मलता; 'of a new house,' शल्योद्धारः, वास्तुसंशमनं.

PURIFICATIVE, PURIFICATORY, *a.* पावकः -का -कं, पावनः -ना -नं, पावी -विनी -वि (न्), पावमानः -ना -नं, शोधकः -का -कं, शोधनः -ना -नं, संशोधकः &c., विशोधकः &c., शुद्धिकरः -रा -री -रं, मलापकर्षकः -का -कं.

PURIFIED, *p. p.* पावितः -ता -तं, पूतः &c., परिपूतः &c., शोधितः -ता -तं, शुद्धः -द्धा -द्धं, संशोधितः &c., संशुद्धः &c., विशुद्धः &c., पवित्रः -त्रा -त्रं, पवित्रितः &c., पवित्रीकृतः -ता -तं, कृतशौचः -चा -चं, मार्जितः &c., प्रक्षालितः &c., निर्णिक्तः -क्ता -क्तं, धौतः -ता -तं, अवदातः &c.; 'from sin' पापशोधितः -ता -तं, पापपूतः -ता -तं, अघनिष्कृतः -ता -तं; 'by austerity,' प्रयतः -ता -तं; 'to be purified,' शुध् (c. 4. शुध्यति -ते, शोद्धुं), पू in pass. (पूयते), पवित्रीभू, शुद्धीभू.

To PURIFY, *v. a.* पू (c. 9. पुनाति -नीते, पवितुं, c. 10. पावयति -यितुं), परिपू, विपू, शुध् (c. 10. शोधयति -यितुं), विशुध्, परिशुध्, संशुध्, शुद्धीकृ, पवित्रीकृ, पवित्र (nom. पवित्रयति -यितुं), निर्मलीकृ, विमलीकृ, मृज् (c. 1. मार्जति, c. 2. मार्ष्टि -ष्टुं), सम्मृज्, निर्णिज् (c. 3. -णेनेक्ति -णेक्तुं), धाव् (c. 10. धावयति -यितुं), शुचीकृ, मलं हृ (c. 1. हरति, हर्तुं) or अपनी (c. 1. -नयति -नेतुं), मलापकर्षणं कृ, परिष्कृ, प्रक्षल्.

PURIFYING, *part.* or *a.* पुनानः -ना -नं, पावमानः -ना -नं, पवमानः &c., पावनः -ना -नं, पावकः -का -कं. *See* PURIFICATIVE.

PURITAN, *s.* पवित्रमतावलम्बी *m.* (न्), पवित्रमतधारी *m.* (न्).

PURITY, *s.* (Freedom from dirt, defilement &c.) निर्मलता -त्वं, नैर्मल्यं, निर्माल्यं, विमलता, वैमल्यं, मलहीनता, मलराहित्यं, शुद्धता -त्वं, शुद्धिः *f.*, विशुद्धिः *f.*, पवित्रता, पूतता, पूतिः *f.*, शुचिता, शौचं, मेध्यता, अलिप्तता.—(Clearness, transparency) प्रसादः, प्रसन्नता, प्रसत्तिः, *f.*, स्वच्छता, वैशद्यं, विशदत्वं.—(Freedom from guilt, moral purity) शुचिता -त्वं, शुद्धता, शुद्धिः *f.*, अनघता, पापहीनता, अघहीनता, निष्पापत्वं, पुण्यता, साधुता, निष्कलङ्कता.—(Purity of mind) चित्तशुद्धिः *f.*, मतिशुद्धता, विमलचित्तत्वं, शुद्धमतित्वं.—(Chastity in a woman) सतीत्वं, पुरुषास्पृष्टता, साध्वीत्वं.—(Of language) शुद्धिः अपशब्दहीनता.

To PURL, *v. n.* नदीप्रकारेण रणरणशब्दं कृ or सुभगस्तनितं कृ.

PURLIEU, *s.* समन्तः, सामन्तदेशः, पर्य्यन्तदेशः, उपान्तदेशः, सामन्तं, परिसरः.

To PURLOIN, *v. a.* चुर्, हृ, अपहृ, मुष्, परिमुष्. *See To* PILFER.

PURLOINED, *p. p.* अपहृतः -ता -तं, मुषितः -ता -तं, चौरहृतः -ता -तं.

PURLOINER, *s.* अपहर्त्ता *m.* (र्तृ), परिमोषी *m.* (न्), स्तेयकृत्. *See* PILFERER.

PURPLE, *a.* धूम्रः -म्रा -म्रं, धूम्रवर्णः -र्णा -र्णं, धूमलः -ला -लं, कृष्णलोहितः -ता -तं, नीललोहितः &c., धूमाभः -भा -भं, बालसन्ध्याभः &c., धूम्ररुच् *m. f. n.* (च्).

PURPLE, *s.* धूम्रवर्णः, धूम्रः, धूमलः, धूमलवर्णः, रक्तः.

To PURPLE, *v. a.* धूम्रीकृ, लोहितीकृ, धूम्रवर्णेन रञ्ज् (c. 10. रञ्जयति -यितुं).

PURPLISH, *a.* ईषद्धूम्रः -म्रा -म्रं, आधूम्रः &c., आधूमलः ला -लं.

PURPORT, *s.* अर्थः, अभिप्रायः तात्पर्य्यं, आशयः, अभिप्रेतं, उद्देशः, भावार्थः, भावः, विवक्षितं, विवक्षा, अन्वयः, छन्दः. *See* MEANING.

To PURPORT, *v. a.* or *n.* अभिप्रे, उद्दिश्, वच् in des., अर्थवान् &c. भू or अस्. *See To* MEAN.

PURPOSE, *s.* अभिप्रायः, अभिप्रेतं, चिकीर्षितं, चिकीर्षा, आशयः, सङ्कल्पः, मनःसङ्कल्पः, उद्देशः, अर्थः, तात्पर्य्यं, इच्छा, आकांक्षा, कार्य्यं, बुद्धिः *f.*, कल्पना, परिकल्पना, आकूतं, मनोनिरूपणं, चिन्ता, प्रयोजनं, उपयोगः, *See* INTENTION; 'fixed purpose,' निश्चयः, निश्चितं; 'of unfailing purpose,' सत्यसङ्कल्पः -ल्पा -ल्पं; 'declared purpose,' ईरिताकूतं, 'one who does not effect his purpose,' अकृतार्थः -र्था -र्थं, असिद्धार्थः &c., अचरितार्थः &c., वृथार्थः &c., अकृतकृत्यः -त्या -त्यं; 'one who effects it,' कृतार्थः &c.; 'for the purpose of,' अर्थं or अर्थे or हेतोः affixed, कृते, निमित्ते; 'for the purpose of religion, or for religious purposes,' धर्म्मार्थं; 'to no purpose,' वृथा, मुधा, व्यर्थः -र्था -र्थं; 'for what purpose,' किमर्थं, किमुद्दिश्य; 'on purpose,' बुद्धिपूर्व्वं, बुद्ध्या. *See* PURPOSELY.

To PURPOSE, *v. a.* अभिप्रे, अभिप्रायं कृ, कृ in des., उद्दिश्, मनसा उद्दिश्, अभिसन्धा, इष्, परिक्लृप्, सङ्कल्पं कृ, बुद्धिं कृ. *See To* INTEND.

PURPOSED, *p. p.* अभिप्रेतः -ता -तं, चिकीर्षितः &c., उद्दिष्टः -ष्टा -ष्टं.

PURPOSELY, *adv.* बुद्धिपूर्व्वं -र्व्वकं, बुद्धिपुरःसरं, मतिपूर्व्वं, साभिप्रायं, अभिप्रायपूर्व्वं, बुद्ध्या, कामतस्, इच्छातस्. *See* INTENTIONALLY.

PURSE, *s.* कोषः धनकोषः, मुद्राकोषः, कटिबन्धः, ग्रन्थिः *m.*, कौलिकं.

To PURSE, *v. a.* (Put in a purse) कोषे निविश्; in caus.—(Contract) संकुच्, संहृ, संकृ, आकुच्.

PURSE-CUTTING, *s.* ग्रन्थिभेदः, ग्रन्थिभेदनं, ग्रन्थिच्छेदः, कोषच्छेदः.

PURSE-PRIDE, *s.* धनगर्वः, धनदर्पः, धनाभिमानं, अर्थगर्वः, द्रव्याभिमानं.

PURSE-PROUD, *a.* धनगर्वितः -ता -तं, द्रव्यगर्वितः &c., धनाभिमानी -निनी &c.

PURSER, *s.* युद्धनावि कोषाधिकारी *m.* (न्), or धनभोजनादिपरिकल्पकः.

PURSUANCE, *s.* अनुसरणं, अनुसारः, अनुवर्त्तनं, अनुगमनं 'in pursuance of,' अनुसारेण, अनुसारतस्, अनुरूपेण.

PURSUANT, *a.* अनुसारी -रिणी -रि (न्), अनुरूपः -पा -पं, अनुवर्त्ती &c.

PURSUANTLY, *adv.* अनुसारेण -रात्, अनुसारतस्, अनुरूपेण.

To PURSUE, *v. a.* (Follow) अनुसृ (c. 1. -सरति -सर्त्तुं), अनुगम् (c. 1. -गच्छति -गन्तुं) अनुया (c. 2. -याति -तुं), अनुवृत्, अनुव्रज्, अनुक्रम्.—(Chase) अनुधाव्, (c. 1. -धावति -वितुं), पश्चाद् धाव्, अनुसृ, पश्चाद् वृत्.—(Prosecute, practise), अनुष्ठा (c. 1. -तिष्ठति -ष्ठातुं) आस्था, आचर् (c. 1. -चरति -रितुं), समाचर्, सेव्, निषेव्, अनुसेव्. *See* PROSECUTE.—(Carry on) निर्वह् in caus., प्रवृत् in caus., प्रणी, सम्प्रणी, विधा.—(Endeavour to obtain) आप् in des. (ईप्सति -प्सितुं), अभ्याप in des., प्राप् in des., लभ् in des. (लिप्सते -प्सितुं) अभिलभ्.—Imitate) अनुकृ, अनुगम्.

PURSUED, *p. p.* (Followed) अनुसृतः -ता -तं, अनुगतः &c., अनुयातः

&c., अनुगम्यमानः -ना -नं, अन्वीयमानः &c.—(Chased) अनुधावितः -ता -तं.—(Prosecuted, practised) अनुष्ठितः -ता -तं, आचरितः &c., सेवितः -ता -तं, निषेवितः &c.

PURSUER, *s.* अनुगामी *m.* (न्), अनुयायी *m.*, अनुसारी *m.*, अनुधावकः.

PURSUIT, *s.* (Following) अनुसरणं, अनुवर्त्तनं, अनुगमनं, अनुव्रजनं.—(Running after, chasing) अनुधावनं, अभिधावनं, पश्चाद् धावनं, अनुसरणं, अनुसारः, अन्वेषणं, मार्गणं, मृगणं.—(Prosecution, carrying on with a view to obtain) अनुष्ठानं, सेवनं, निषेवनं, अनुसेवनं, आचरणं, प्रवृत्तिः *f.*, प्रवर्त्तनं, व्यापारः, व्यवसायः, निष्ठता, अभियोगः, अनुशीलनं, परिशीलनं, अनुसन्धानं.—(Course of occupation, employment) व्यापारः, व्यवसायः, कर्म्म *n.* (न्), उद्योगः, उद्यमः, प्रवृत्तिः *f.*, व्यवहारः, कार्य्यं; 'interesting pursuit,' विनोदः, विनोदजनकव्यापारः.

PURSUIVANT, *s.* राजदूतः, राजदूतपरिचरः, वेत्रधरः, याष्टीकः.

PURSY, *a.* दुःश्वासी -सिनी &c., प्राणकृच्छ्रग्रस्तः -स्ता -स्तं, ह्रस्वस्थूलः &c.

PURULENCE, PURULENCY, *s.* पूयत्वं, सपूयत्वं -ता, पूयपूर्णता, पूययुक्तता.

PURULENT, *s.* सपूयः -या -यं, पूयमयः -यी -यं, पूयरूपः -पा -पं, पूययुक्तः -क्ता -क्तं, पूयपूर्णः -र्णा -र्णं.—(Running with pus) पूयस्रावी -विणी -वि (न्).

To PURVEY, *v. a.* and *n.* खाद्यद्रव्याणि परिकॢप् (c. 10. -कल्पयति -यितुं) or उपकॢप् or सम्भृ (c. 1. -भरति -भर्त्तुं) or युज् (c. 10. योजयति -यितुं) or समायुज्, भोजनपरिकल्पनं कृ, भोजनसम्भारं कृ, आहारयोजनां कृ, आहारनिर्वाहं कृ.

PURVEYANCE, *s.* खाद्यद्रव्यपरिकल्पनं, भोजनपरिकल्पनं, अन्नादिपरिकल्पनं, भोजनसम्भारः, आहारयोजना, आहारनिर्वाहः, परिकल्पनं, निर्वाहः.

PURVEYOR, *s.* भोजनपरिकल्पकः, अन्नादिपरिकल्पकः, भोजनाधिकारी *m.* (न्), भोजनाधिकृतः, आहारयोजकः.

PUS, *s.* पूयं, पूयरक्तं, पूयशोणितं, दूष्यं, मलजं, व्रणजं, प्रसितं, व्रणक्लेदः.

To PUSH, *v. a.* and *n.* (Make a thrust) तड् (c. 10. ताडयति -यितुं), प्रसृ (c. 10. -सारयति -यितुं), प्रसारणं कृ, आहन् (c. 2. -हन्ति -न्तुं), अभिहन्, अभ्याहन्.—(Impel, move by pressure) हस्ताभ्याम् अवलम्ब्य चल् (c. 10. चालयति -यितुं) or सञ्चल् or सृ (c. 10. सारयति -यितुं) or स्थानान्तरीकृ or प्रेर् or प्रणुद् or नुद् or कृष् or समाकृष्.—(Push aside, push out) अपसृ in caus., बहिष्कृ, बहिःकृ.—(Push forward) प्रसृ, प्रचल् in caus., अग्रे चल् or सृ, अग्रे नी.

PUSH, PUSHING, *s.* ताडनं, आहतिः *f.*, आघातः, अभिघातः, अभ्याघातः, प्रहारः, प्रसारणं, अपसारणं, सारणं.—(Impelling) प्रणोदः, प्रेरणं -णा, वेगः.—(Vigorous effort, onset) सुयत्नः, आक्रमः -मणं.

PUSHED, *p. p.* ताडितः -ता -तं, आहतः &c., अभिहतः &c., प्रसारितः -ता -तं, अपसारितः &c., सारितः &c., चालितः &c., प्रेरितः -ता -तं, प्रणोदितः &c.. प्रणुन्नः -न्ना -न्नं, स्थानान्तरीकृतः &c., बहिष्कृतः &c.

PUSHING, *a.* (Enterprising) साहसिकः -की -कं, साहसशीलः -ला -लं, साहसबुद्धिः -द्धिः -द्धि, उद्योगी -गिनी &c., अत्युद्योगी &c., उद्योगशीलः -ला -लं, अत्युद्यमी &c., धृष्टः -ष्टा -ष्टं, प्रगल्भः -ल्भा -ल्भं, प्रतिभानवान् -वती -वत् (त्).

PUSILLANIMITY, *s.* भीरुता, कातरता, धैर्य्यहीनता, शौर्य्यहीनता, वीर्य्यहीनता, निर्वीर्य्यं, कार्पण्यं, कृपणबुद्धित्वं, क्लीवता, भीरुहृदयत्वं, कापुरुषत्वं.

PUSILLANIMOUS, *a.* भीरुहृदयः -या -यं, कृपणबुद्धिः -द्धिः -द्धि, कातरबुद्धिः &c., धैर्य्यहीनः -ना -नं, शौर्य्यहीनः &c., पौरुषहीनः &c.

PUSS, PUSSY, *s.* मार्जारः, विडालः. *See* CAT.

PUSTULE, *s.* स्फोटः -टकः, विस्फोटः, रक्तवटी, रक्तवरटी, वटी, वरटी, व्रणः, तनुव्रणः, गण्डः, गुटिका. *See* PIMPLE.

PUSTULOUS, *a.* स्फोटपूर्णः -र्णा -र्णं, स्फोटमयः -यी -यं, सस्फोटः -टा -टं.

To PUT, *v. a.* (Lay, place, set) धा (c. 3. दधाति, धातुं), स्था in caus. (स्थापयति -यितुं), ऋ in caus. (अर्पयति -यितुं), निविश् (c. 10. -वेशयति -यितुं), सन्निविश्, न्यस् (c. 4. -अस्यति -असितुं), विन्यस्, आरुह् in caus. (-रोपयति -यितुं), दा (c. 3. ददाति, दातुं), धृ (c. 1. धरति, धर्त्तुं), कृ (c. 8. करोति, कर्त्तुं). *See To* LAY, PLACE.—(Apply) आधा, संयुज् (c. 10. -योजयति -यितुं), आयुज्, युज्, ऋ or सम् in caus.—(Incite) प्रवृत् in caus., प्रोत्सह् in caus., प्रेर्.—(Put a question), *see To* PROPOSE.—(Put about, as a ship, &c.) नौमार्गं परिवृत् (c. 10. -वर्त्तयति -यितुं), मार्गपरिवर्त्तनं कृ, गतिपरिवर्त्तनं कृ.—(Put away) अपसृ (c. 10. -सारयति -यितुं), निःसृ, बहिष्कृ, दूरीकृ.—(Put aside, put by) न्यस्, सन्न्यस्, व्युदस्, निधा, रक्ष्, परिरक्ष्.—(Put down, lay down) न्यस्, उपन्यस्, निधा, अवधा, निक्षिप्.—(Put down), *see To* REPRESS, DEGRADE.—(Put forth, extend) प्रसृ in caus.—(Put forth), *see To* SPROUT, BUD.—(Put forth), *see To* EXERT; 'he puts forth his strength,' कृतशक्तिर् भवति.—(Put off), *see To* POSTPONE.—(Put off, divest one's self) वस्त्राणि अवतॄ (c. 10. -तारयति -यितुं), उत्कृष्, उन्मुच्, अवमुच्, विमुच्, उच्छद्, अपनह्.—(Put off), *see To* DISCARD.—(Put off from land) तीराद् अपगम् or अपया or अपसृ.—(Put on clothes, dress) वस्त्रं परिधा or पिधा, वस्, प्रवस्, विवस्, प्रतिवस्, वेष्ट्, परिवेष्ट्, प्रवेष्ट्, आछद्, प्रवृ, संव्ये, परिव्ये, परिधा. वस्त्राणि परिधा or आछद् or आमुच्, प्रसाध्, वस्त्र्, संवस्त्र्, *see To* DRESS, INVEST.—(Put on armour) नह् (c. 4. नह्यति -ते, नद्धुं), सन्नह्, दंशनं सन्नह्, वर्म्म (c. 10. वर्म्मयति -यितुं), संवर्म्म.—(Put on shoes) पादुके अधिरुह् (c. 1. -रोहति -रोढुं) or रुह् or आरुह् in caus.—(Put on, assume) ग्रह्, धृ (c. 10. धारयति -यितुं), स्वीकृ, अङ्गीकृ.—(Put out, extinguish) शम् in caus., उपशम्, प्रशम्, निशम्, निर्वा in caus.; 'having put out the fire,' अग्निं शमयित्वा or निशाम्य.—(Put out, extend) प्रसृ in caus.—(Put out), *see To* CONFUSE, DISCONCERT.—(Put out the eyes) लोचने उत्पट् in caus. or उत्कृष् or उच्छिद्.—(Put to it), *see To* DISTRESS, PERPLEX.—(Put together) सन्धा, समाधा, संयुज्.—(Put up, lodge) उष्, उत्तरणगृहे वस्, रथाद् अवतॄ.—(Put up with) सह् (c. 1. सहते, सोढुं), विषह्.—(Put up), *see To* PACK.—(Put up), *see To* EXPOSE.—(Put upon), *see To* DECEIVE.—(Put in order) विरच्, रच्, विन्यस्, सज्जीकृ.—(Put in mind), *see To* REMIND.—(Put in practice), *see To* EXERCISE, PRACTISE.—(Put in fear), *see To* FRIGHTEN.—(Put in writing), *see To* COMMIT TO WRITING.—(Put in jeopardy) संशयितं -तां कृ, *see To* JEOPARDY.—(Put to death), *see To* KILL.

PUT, *p. p.* स्थापितः -ता -तं, अर्पितः &c., निहितः &c., निवेशितः &c., न्यस्तः -स्ता -स्तं. *See* PLACED.—(Put on, as clothes) परिहितः -ता -तं.—(Put off, discarded) अवतारितः -ता -तं, अपास्तः -स्ता -स्तं, सन्न्यस्तः &c., व्युदस्तः &c., त्यक्तः -क्ता -क्तं.

PUT, *s.* (Clown) वृषलः, ग्राम्यजनः.—(Harlot) वेश्या.

PUTATIVE, *a.* लोकप्रसिद्धः -द्धा -द्धं, जनप्रसिद्धः &c., लोकमतः -ता -तं.

PUTID, *a.* क्षुद्रः -द्रा -द्रं, कुत्सितः -ता -तं, कृपणः -णा -णं, तुच्छः &c.

PUTIDNESS, *s.* क्षुद्रता, कुत्सितत्वं, तुच्छता -त्वं, कृपणता, कार्पण्यं.

PUT-OFF, *s.* (An excuse) अपदेशः, व्यपदेशः, छद्म *n.* (न्), छलं.

PUTREFACTION, *s.* पूतिः *f.*, पूतत्वं -ता, गलितत्वं, गलनं, विगलनं, गलितावस्था, विलयः -यनं, दौर्गन्ध्यं, दौर्गन्धिः *m.*, दुर्गन्धता, पूतिगन्धः.

PUTREFIED, *p. p.* गलितः -ता -तं, विगलितः &c., पूतीभूतः &c., विलीनः -ना -नं.

To PUTREFY, *v. a.* पूतीकृ, गल् in caus. (गालयति, गलयति -यितुं), विगल्, गलितीकृ, विली in caus. (-लापयति -यितुं).

To PUTREFY, *v. n.* गल् (c. 1. गलति -लितुं), विगल्, गलितः -ता -तं भू, पूतीभू, विली (c. 4. -लीयते -लेतुं), प्रविली, दुर्गन्धः -न्धा -न्धं भू, पूतिगन्धिकः -का -कं भू.

PUTRESCENCE, *s.* गलनं, विगलनं, विलयः -यनं, पूतिः *f.*, पूतत्वं.

PUTRESCENT, *a.* गलन् -लन्ती -लत् (त्), विगलन् &c., विलीयमानः -ना -नं.

PUTRID, *a.* पूतः -ता -तं, पूतिगन्धः -न्धा -न्धं, दुर्गन्धः -न्धा -न्धं, दुर्गन्धी -न्धिनी -न्धि (न्), पूतिगन्धिकः -का -कं, उग्रगन्धिः -न्धिः -न्धि, गलितः -ता -तं, विगलितः &c., विलीनः -ना -नं.

PUTRIDNESS, PUTRIDITY, *s.* पूतत्वं -ता, पूतिः *f.*, दुर्गन्धता, दौर्गन्ध्यं, दौर्गन्धिः *m.*, पूतिगन्धिता, गलितत्वं -ता, विगलितत्वं, विलीनता.

PUTTY, *s.* काचबन्धनलेपः, काचबन्धनयोग्यो विलेपः, उदपेषं.

To PUTTY, *v. a.* पूर्व्वोक्तलेपेन काचं बन्ध् (c. 9. बध्नाति, बन्द्धुं).

To PUZZLE, *v. a.* मुह् (c. 10. मोहयति -यितुं), विमुह्, व्यामुह्, भ्रम् (c. 10. भ्रमयति -यितुं), भ्रान्तिं जन्, निरुत्तरीकृ, बुद्धिभ्रान्तिं कृ, शल्यं कृ. *See To* POSE.

PUZZLE, *s.* (Enigma) गूढं, कूटं, प्रवह्लिः *f.* -ह्लिका, प्रहेलिका, अन्तर्लापिका.—(Perplexity) व्यस्तता, मोहः, व्यामोहः, भ्रान्तिः *f.*, भ्रमः, व्याकुलता, व्यग्रता, बुद्धिभ्रान्तिः *f.*, बुद्धिभ्रमः.

PUZZLED, *p. p.* मोहितः -ता -तं, विमोहितः &c., भ्रान्तः -न्ता -न्तं, सम्भ्रान्तः &c., भ्रान्तहृदयः -या -यं, व्यस्तः -स्ता -स्तं, निरुत्तरीकृतः -ता -तं, इतिकर्त्तव्यतामूढः -ढा -ढं.

PUZZLE-HEADED, *a.* भ्रान्तबुद्धिः -द्धिः -द्धि, व्यस्तबुद्धिः &c., जडबुद्धिः &c.

PUZZLING, *part.* or *a.* भ्रमजनकः -का -कं, मोहजनकः &c. *See* PERPLEXING.

PYGMY, *s.* वामनः, खर्वः, खर्वः, वामनमूर्त्तिः *m.*, ह्रस्वमूर्त्तिः, ह्रस्वकायः.

PYGMY, PYGMEAN, *a.* वामनः -ना -नं, वामनतनुः -नुः -नु. *See* DWARFISH.

PYLORUS, *s.* जठरस्य अधःस्थमुखं, जठराधोमुखं, जठराधोद्वारं.

PYRAMID, *s.* सूच्यग्रस्तम्भः, सूच्याकारस्तम्भः, शुण्डाकारस्तम्भः, सूचिः -ची *f.*, शिखा, शङ्कुः *m.*, सूक्ष्माग्रस्तम्भः.

PYRAMIDAL, PYRAMIDICAL, *a.* सूच्यग्रः -ग्रा -ग्रं, सूच्याकारः -रा -रं, सूच्यग्रस्तम्भाकारः &c., शुण्डाकारः &c., सूक्ष्माग्रस्तम्भाकृतिः -तिः -ति, शङ्कुरूपः -पा -पं, शिखावलः -ला -लं, शिखरी -रिणी &c.

PYRE, *s.* चितिः -ती *f.*, चिता, चित्या, श्मशानाग्निः *m.* *See* PILE.

PYRITES, *s.* विटमाक्षिकं, सुवर्णमाक्षिकं, स्वर्णमाक्षिकं, माक्षिकं, आवर्त्तः, सुवर्णमुखी, कामारिः *m.*, मधुधातुः *m.*, आग्नेयप्रस्तरः; 'iron pyrites,' नीलमृत्तिका, तण्डुलीयः -यकः; 'hepatic iron pyrites,' रूप्यमाक्षिकं, कांस्यमाक्षिकं.

PYRITIC, *a.* माक्षिकसम्बन्धी -न्धिनी &c., माक्षिकगुणकः -का -कं.

PYROTECHNY, *s.* अग्निक्रीडाविद्या, आग्नेयक्रीडाविद्या, अग्निशिल्पं.

PYRRHIC, *s.* (Foot in prosody) सुप्रियः, लल.

PYRRHONIST, *s.* नास्तिकः, शास्त्राविश्वासी *m.* (न्), चार्वाकः, धर्म्मनिन्दकः.

Q.

QUACK, *s.* (Cry of a duck or goose) हंसनादः, हंसरावः, हंसचीत्कारः, क्वक्शब्दः.—(Empiric, pretender to medical skill) दुश्चिकित्सकः, मिथ्याचिकित्सकः, मिथ्यावैद्यः, छद्मवैद्यः, वैद्यम्मन्यः, वैद्यमानी *m.* (न्), आयुर्वेदानभिज्ञः.

To QUACK, *v. n.* हंसवद् नद् (c. 1. नदति -दितुं) or रु (c. 2. रौति, रवितुं) or चीत्कृ or कृ, हंसनादं कृ, क्वक् शब्दं कृ.—(Pretend to medical skill) दुश्चिकित्सां कृ, मिथ्याचिकित्सनं कृ, आयुर्वेदविरोधेन चिकित्सां कृ.

QUACKERY, *s.* दुश्चिकित्सा -त्सनं, मिथ्याचिकित्सा -त्सनं, आयुर्वेदविरुद्धा चिकित्सा, आयुर्वेदानभिज्ञता.

QUADRAGESIMA, *s.* चत्वारिंशद्दिवसोपवासः, चत्वारिंशद्दिनोपवासः.

QUADRAGESIMAL, *a.* चत्वारिंशद्दिनोपवाससम्बन्धी -न्धिनी -न्धि (न्).

QUADRANGLE, *s.* चतुरस्रं, चतुष्कोणः, चतुर्भुजः; 'formed by four houses,' चतुःशालं -ला -लकं, चतुश्शाला, प्रकोष्ठः.

QUADRANGULAR, *a.* चतुष्कोणः -णा -णं, चतुरस्रः -स्रा -स्रं, चतुर्भुजः -जा -जं.

QUADRANT, *s.* (Fourth part) पादः, चतुर्थभागः, तुरीयभागः.—(Of a circle) वर्त्तुलपादः, त्रिज्या, पदं.—(The instrument) तुरीययन्त्रं, सूर्य्ययन्त्रं.

QUADRATE, *To* QUADRATE, *see* SQUARE, *To* SQUARE.

QUADRATIC, *a.* चतुष्कोणीयः -या -यं, वर्गीयः -या -यं, चतुरस्रीयः &c.

QUADRATURE, *s.* (Of a circle, &c.) वर्गीकरणं.

QUADRENNIAL, *a.* चतुर्वर्षीयः -या -यं, चातुर्वार्षिकः -की -कं, चातुरब्दिकः &c.

QUADRILATERAL, *a.* चतुर्भुजः -जा -जं, चतुःपार्श्वीयः -या -यं, चतुःपार्श्वः -र्श्वा -र्श्वं, चतुःपार्श्वयुक्तः -क्ता -क्तं, चतुःपार्श्वविशिष्टः -ष्टा -ष्टं.

QUADRILITERAL, *a.* चतुरक्षरः -रा -रं, चतुर्वर्णः -र्णा -र्णं.

QUADRILLE, *s.* चतुर्नृत्यं, सम्मुखस्थानां स्त्रीपुरुषाणां नृत्यं.

QUADRIMESTRAL, *a.* चतुर्मास्यः -स्या -स्यं, चातुर्मासिकः -की -कं.

QUADRIPARTILE, *a.* चतुर्विधः -धा -धं, चतुर्भागः -गा -गं, चतुर्विभागः &c.

QUADRISYLLABLE, *s.* चतुरक्षरं, चतुरक्षरविशिष्टः शब्दः, चतुरक्षरः शब्दः.

QUADRIVIAL, *a.* चतुष्पथीयः -या -यं, चतुर्मार्गीयः -या -यं.

QUADRIVIUM, *s.* (Place where four roads meet) चतुष्पथं, चतुर्मार्गं.

QUADRUPED, *s.* चतुष्पदः -दी, चतुष्पादः, चतुष्पाद् *m. f. n.*, चतुष्पादः पशुः, चतुष्पदपशुः *m.*, चतुष्पदप्राणी *m.* (न्), चतुर्गतिः -तिः -ति.

QUADRUPLE, *a.* चतुर्गुणः -णा -णं, चतुर्विधः -धा -धं, चतुष्टयः -यी -यं.

To QUADRUPLE, QUADRUPLICATE, *v. a.* चतुर्गुणं -णां कृ, चतुर्गुणीकृ, चतुर्विधीकृ.

To QUAFF. *v. a.* बाहुल्येन पा (c. 1. पिबति पातुं) or आपा or निपा.

QUAFFED, *p. p.* पीतः -ता -तं, आपीतः -ता -तं, निपीतः -ता -तं.

QUAFFER, *s.* पाता *m.* (तृ), पायी *m.* (न्), अतिपायी *m.*, बहुपायी.

QUAGGY, *a.* पङ्किलः -ला -लं, पङ्कमयः -यी -यं, बहुपङ्कः -ङ्का -ङ्कं.

QUAGMIRE, *s.* पङ्कः, कुपङ्कः, पङ्किलभूः *f.*, कार्दमभूमिः *f.*, सपङ्कभूमिः *f.*, पङ्ककर्वटः, अनूपभूः *f.*, पङ्कस्थानं.

To QUAIL. *v. n.* कम्प् (c. 1. कम्पते -म्पितुं), प्रकम्प्, विकम्प्, सद् (c. 1. सीदति, सत्तुं), अवसद्, विषद्, क्षि in pass. (क्षीयते), प्रली (c. 4. -लीयते -लेतुं).

QUAIL, *s.* (The bird) वर्त्तिका, वर्त्तकः, वर्त्तकपक्षी *m.* (न्), कणिखेलः, गञ्जिकायः, लावः, लावकः, गरुद्योधी *m.* (न्), भारती, विष्किलिङ्गी.

QUAINT, *a.* (Odd) विलक्षणः -णा -णं, असङ्कृतः -ता -तं, अपरूपः -पा -पं, प्राचीनरीत्यनुरूपः -पा -पं.—(Over exact) अतिसूक्ष्मः -क्ष्मा -क्ष्मं.

QUAINTLY, *adv.* विलक्षणं, वैलक्षण्येन, असङ्कृतं, प्राचीनरीत्यनुरूपेण.

QUAINTNESS, *s.* वैलक्षण्यं, विलक्षणता, असङ्कृतत्वं, अपरूपता, अतिसूक्ष्मता.

To QUAKE, *v. n.* कम्प् (c. 1. कम्पते -म्पितुं), प्रकम्प्, विकम्प्, अभिकम्प्, वेप् (c. 1. वेपते -पितुं), प्रवेप्, त्रस् (c. 4. त्रस्यति -सितुं), वित्रस्, उद्विज् (c. 6. -विजते -जितुं), ह्वल् (c. 1. ह्वलति -लितुं), विह्वल्, प्रह्वल्.

QUAKE, *s.* कम्पः, प्रकम्पः, उत्कम्पः, कम्पनं, वेपनं, प्रवेपणं, वेपथुः *m.*

QUAKER, *s.* कम्पान्वितः -ता, कम्पनः -ना, कम्पमानः -ना, सकम्पः.

QUAKING, *part.* कम्पमानः -ना -नं, वेपमानः -ना -नं, कम्पितः -ता -तं.

QUALIFICATION, *s.* (That which fits a person for any office, &c.) योग्यता, उपयुक्तता, उपयोगिता, क्षमता, कार्य्यक्षमता, गुणविशिष्टता, गुणवैशिष्ट्यं, गुणता.—(Endowment) गुणः, विशेषणं.—(Modification, limitation) मर्य्यादा, नियमनं, परिच्छेदः -दनं, अवच्छेदः -दनं, शमनं, परिमितत्वं, नियतत्वं, परिमाणं, न्यूनत्वं, न्यूनीकरणं, विशेषः; 'without qualification,' अविशेषणः -णा -णं.

QUALIFIED, *p.p.* (Fitted) योग्यः -ग्या -ग्यं, उपयुक्तः -क्ता -क्तं, उपयोगी -गिनी -गि (न्), क्षमः -मा -मं, कार्य्यक्षमः -मा -मं, कर्म्मक्षमः &c., अलङ्कर्म्मीणः -णा -णं, उचितः -ता -तं, पर्य्याप्तः -प्ता -प्तं, गुणवान् -वती -वत् (त्), गुणी &c., गुणोपेतः -ता -तं.—(Modified) नियमितः -ता -तं, नियतः &c., निबद्धः -द्धा -द्धं, समर्य्यादः -दा -दं, सपरिमाणः -णा -णं, परिमितः -ता -तं, परिच्छिन्नः -न्ना -न्नं, शमितः &c.

To QUALIFY, *v. a.* (Make fit) योग्यं -ग्यां कृ, उपयुक्तं -क्तां कृ, क्षमं -मां कृ, कार्य्यक्षमं -मां कृ, उपयोगिनं -गिनीं कृ, पर्य्याप्तं -प्तां कृ, गुणवन्तं -वतीं कृ, योग्यीकृ, क्षमीकृ, उपयुक्तगुणान् दा.—(Modify, limit, diminish) नियम् (c. 1. -यच्छति -यन्तुं), निबन्ध् (c. 9. -बध्नाति -बन्द्धुं), समर्य्यादं -दां कृ, परिमा, परिमितं -तां कृ, सपरिमाणं -णां कृ, परिच्छिद्, शम्, उपशम्, प्रशम्, न्यूनीकृ, ह्रस्, लुप्.

QUALITY, *s.* (Property) गुणः, धर्म्मः; 'good quality,' सद्गुणः, सुगुणः, गुणः; 'possessed of good qualities,' सद्गुणः -णा -णं, गुणी गुणिनी -णि (न्), सद्गुणी &c., सुगुणी &c., गुणवान् -वती -वत् (त्), गुणान्वितः -ता -तं, गुणोपेतः -ता -तं, गुणसागरः -रा -रं, गुणाकरः -रा -रं, गुणयुक्तः -क्ता -क्तं, गुणाश्रयः -या -यं; 'the possession of good qualities,' गुणता, गुणवत्ता; 'destitute of them,' गुणहीनः -ना -नं; 'the loss of them,' गुणभ्रंशः; 'a collection or heap of them,' गुणसंग्रहः, गुणौघः, गुणपूगं; 'variety of quality,' गुणान्तरं; 'bad quality,' दुर्गुणः -णं, अवगुणः, असद्गुणः; 'possessed of bad qualities,' दुर्गुणी &c.; 'essential or inherent quality,' अनुगतधर्म्मः, वस्तुशक्तिः *f.*—(Distinguishing property) धर्म्मः, भावः, स्वभावः, विशेषगुणः, विशेषधर्म्मः, विशेषः, लक्षणं, गुणलक्षणं, स्वभावलक्षणं, रूपं, स्वरूपं, शीलः -लं.—(Nature, disposition) भावः, स्वभावः, प्रकृतिः *f.*, शीलः -लता; 'good quality,' सद्भावः.—(Character, whether good or bad) भावः, सदसद्भावः, गुणागुणं, गुणावगुणं, सत्त्वं, सत्त्वासत्त्वं.—(High rank) श्रेष्ठपदं, पदश्रेष्ठता उत्कृष्टपदं, पदोत्कृष्टता, कुलीनता.—(People of rank) कुलीनवर्गः, श्रेष्ठपदस्थाः *m. pl.*, कुलीनजनाः *m. pl.* कौलीनं.

QUALM, *s.* (Nausea) वमनेच्छा, विवमिषा, उत्क्लेशः.—(Of conscience) मनस्तापः, अन्तःकरणतापः, ईश्वरतापः, ईश्वरसन्तापः, पश्चात्तापः.

QUALMISH, *a.* वमनेच्छुः -च्छुः -च्छु, विवमिषुः &c., वमनोन्मुखः -खा -खं.

QUANDARY, *s.* सन्देहः, संशयः, सम्भ्रमः, व्यस्तता, व्यामोहः.

QUANTITY, *s.* (Magnitude, a mass or collection of indeterminate dimensions) परिमाणं, प्रमाणं, परिमितिः *f.*, मानं, मात्रा, भागः, अंशः; 'a quantity of water equivalent to a piece of gold,' सुवर्णखण्डसमो or सुवर्णखण्डपरिमाणो or सुवर्णखण्डपरिमितो जलांशः.—(Great quantity, abundance) बाहुल्यं, बहुत्वं -ता, प्राचुर्य्यं, प्रचुरता, प्रायः, आधिक्यं, महाभागः or expressed by the adjectives बहु, प्रचुर, अधिक prefixed; 'in great quantities,' बाहुल्येन, बहुशस्, अनेकशस्, प्राचुर्य्येण.—(Great quantity, collection) सञ्चयः, निचयः, प्रचयः, समूहः, वृन्दं, ओघः, संग्रहः, पुञ्जः, राशिः *m.*, पूगः, पुञ्जः -ञ्जं, निवहः, वारः. *See* HEAP.—(Small quantity) अल्पभागः, अल्पांशः, अल्पं -ल्पिका, अल्पमात्रं, मात्रा, स्तोकं, मुष्टिमात्रं, मुष्टिपरिमाणं; 'in small quantities,' अल्पशस्, *see* LITTLE.—(Measure, in prosody) मात्रा.—(In arithmetic or algebra) राशिः *m. f.*; 'known quantity,' व्यक्तराशिः *m. f.*, रूपं; 'unknown quantity,' अव्यक्तराशिः, अव्यक्तः; 'negative,' क्षयः; 'infinite,' अनन्तराशिः; 'figurative,' क्षेत्रराशिः.

QUANTUM, *s.* परिमाणं, निरूपितांशः, निरूपितभागः, उपयुक्तभागः.

QUARANTINE, *s.* चत्वारिंशद्दिनपर्य्यन्तं गमनागमननिषेधः or संसर्गनिषेधः, चत्वारिंशद्दिवसपर्य्यन्तं गमनागमनावरोधः.

QUARREL, *s.* विवादः, कलहः -हं, वाग्युद्धं, वाक्कलहः -हं, वादयुद्धं, विप्रलापः, वाक्कलिः *m.*, विसंवादः, विप्रयोगः, विप्रतिपत्तिः *f.*, द्वन्द्वं, द्वैधं, विरोधोक्तिः *f.*, वाग्विरोधः, मैत्रीभङ्गः, सौहृदभङ्गः, वैरं, वैरिता; 'quarrel in fun,' क्रीडाकलहः.

To QUARREL, *v. n.* कलहं कृ, कलह (nom. कलहायते), विवद् (c. 1. -वदते -दितुं), विसंवद्, विप्रलप् (c. 1. -लपति -पितुं), व्यवक्रुश् (c. 1. -क्रोशति -क्रोष्टुं), वाक्कलहं कृ, वाग्युद्धं कृ, युध् (c. 4. युध्यते, योद्धुं), वैर (nom. वैरायते), द्वन्द्वं कृ.

QUARRELER, *s.* विवादी *m.* (न्), कलहकारी *m.* (न्), कलिकारकः.

QUARRELING, *s.* कलहकरणं, विवादकरणं, व्यवक्रोशनं, कत्थनं.

QUARRELSOME, *a.* कलहकारी -रिणी -रि (न्), कलहकारः -री -रं, कलहप्रियः -या -यं, कलिकारी &c., कलिकारकः -का -कं, कलिप्रियः -या -यं, विवादार्थी -र्थिनी &c., विवादी &c., विवादशीलः -ला -लं, विवादप्रियः -या -यं, युयुत्सुः -त्सुः -त्सु, सद्वन्द्वः -न्द्वा -न्द्वं, शीघ्रक्रोधी &c., आशुक्रोधी &c., क्रोधशीलः &c.

QUARRELSOMENESS, *s.* कलहकारिता, विवादशीलता, क्रोधशीलता, युयुत्सा.

QUARRY, *s.* (For stone) आकरः, खनिः -नी *f.*, खानिः -नी *m. f.*, प्रस्तरखानिः *f.*, पाषाणस्थली, पाषाणस्थानं, पाषाणकन्दरः, प्रस्तरोत्पत्तिस्थानं, पाषाणभूमिः *f.*—(Of a hawk, &c.) श्येनानुसृतः पक्षी, श्येनानुसृतं पश्वादि, आमिषं.

QUARRYMAN, *s.* प्रस्तरखनकः, पाषाणखनकः, पाषाणखनिकः.

QUART, *s.* कुडवः, अर्द्धप्रस्थस्य चतुर्थांशः or पादः.

QUARTAN, *s.* (Ague) चातुर्थकः, चातुर्थिकः, त्र्याहिकः.

QUARTER, *s.* (Fourth part) पादः, चतुर्थांशः, चतुर्थभागः, तुरीयभागः, तुरीयांशः, तुरीयः, चतुर्भागः, पादिकः, पादिनः, अर्द्धार्द्धः, ढः; 'three quarters, or a whole minus a quarter,' पादोनः -ना -नं.—(Region or quarter of the sky) दिक् *f.* (श्), दिशा, दिशः *f.* (श्), आशा, काष्ठा, ककुभ् *f.*, हरित् *f.*, दिग्विभागः, खनिः -नी *m. f.*, विदेशिनी; the four quarters are, East प्राची, पूर्व्वदिक् *f.*, पूर्व्वकाष्ठा, South अवाची, दक्षिणा, दक्षिणाशा, West प्रतीची, पश्चिमाशा, पश्चिमकाष्ठा, North उदीची, उत्तरा, उत्तराशा; 'intermediate quarter or point,' विदिक् *f.* (श्), प्रदिक्, अपदिशं; these are 'South-east,' दक्षिणपूर्व्वा; 'South-west,' नैर्ऋतिः *f.*, दक्षिणपश्चिमा; 'North-west,' वायवी, पश्चादुत्तरा, पश्चादुदीची, उत्तरपश्चिमा; 'North-east,' प्रागुत्तरा, प्रागुदीची, उत्तरपूर्व्वा; 'Regent of a quarter,' दिक्पालः, लोकपालः; 'the eight regents,' अष्टदिक्पालाः *m. pl.*, *see* REGENT; 'quarter of the wind,' वायवी; 'from every quarter,' चतुर्दिग्भ्यः; 'in every quarter,' चतुर्दिक्षु; 'from various quarters,' नानादिग्भ्यः.—(Region, in general) देशः, प्रदेशः, उद्देशः, अपदेशः; 'from various quarters,' नानादेशेभ्यः, नानादिग्देशेभ्यः.—(Quarters, lodgings) वासस्थानं, आवासस्थानं.

वसतिस्थानं, वसतिः f., निवसतिः f., निकेतनं; 'of an army,' सैन्यनिवेशः -शनं, सैन्यनिकेतः -तनं, बलस्थितिः f., सैन्यस्थितिः f., कटकः; 'head-quarters,' सेनापतिनिकेतः -तनं.—(Indulgence shewn in battle) जीवदानं, प्राणदानं, दया, क्षमा, कृपा, धर्म्मः; 'quarter shall be given to him,' तस्य दया or धर्म्मो भविष्यति; 'quarter!' दयस्व, क्षमस्व, क्षम्यतां.—(Quarter of a year) वत्सरपादः, मासत्रयं, त्रिमासं.—(Close quarters) बाहुबाहवि, हस्ताहस्ति; 'to come to close quarters in battle,' बाहुयुद्धं कृ.

To QUARTER, *v. a.* (Divide into four parts) चतुर्भागीकृ, चतुरंशीकृ, चतुर्धा कृ, चतुर्धा खण्ड् or विभिद् or विछिद्, चतुर्भागशः कृ, चतुःखण्डशः कृ.—(Lodge) वस् in caus.

To QUARTER, *v. n.* (Lodge) वस्, निवस्, प्रतिवस्, वासं कृ.

QUARTER-DAY, *s.* पाददिनं, पाददिवसः, वत्सरपाददिवसः, त्रिमासान्तदिनं.

QUARTER-DECK, *s.* नौपृष्ठस्य पश्चिमभागः or उन्नतभागः.

QUARTERED, *p. p.* चतुर्भागीकृतः -ता -तं, चतुर्धा विभिन्नः -न्ना -न्नं, चतुर्धा खण्डितः -ता -तं.—(Lodged) वासितः -ता -तं.

QUARTERLY, *a.* त्रैमासिकः -की -कं, त्रिमासीनः -ना -नं, पादिकः -की -कं.

QUARTERLY, *adv.* त्रिमासान्ते, मासत्रयान्ते, मासत्रयावसाने.

QUARTO, *s.* चतुःपत्रकपुस्तकं, चतुःफलकपुस्तकं, चतुःपत्रकः -कं.

QUARTZ, *s.* काचमणिः m., सितमणिः, स्फटिकः. *See* CRYSTAL.

To QUASH, *v. a.* (Crush, subdue) खण्ड्, मृद्, दम्, प्रदम्, पराजि, वशीकृ.—(Annul) लुप् (c. 6. लुम्पति, लोप्तुं), लोपं कृ, खण्ड्, निवृत् in caus., प्रचारनिवर्त्तनं कृ, प्रचारखण्डनं कृ, व्यवस्थितिभङ्गं कृ, व्यवस्थितिखण्डनं कृ, नियमोच्छेदं कृ.

QUASI, Expressed by कु, कल्प, देशीय, देश्य &c. in comp.; as, 'a quasi-poet,' कुकविः m., कविकल्पः, कविदेशीयः; 'a quasi king,' राजदेशीयः.

QUATERNARY, QUATERNION, *s.* चतुष्टयं, चतुष्कं.

QUATRAIN, *s.* चतुष्पादकविता, चतुष्पदकविता, चतुष्पदश्लोकः.

To QUAVER, *v. n.* (Sing with tremor of the voice) स्वरभङ्गेन or स्वरकम्पेन or कम्पनस्वरेण गै (c. 1. गायति, गातुं), शारीरं कृ.—(Vibrate) कम्प्, स्फुर्.

QUAVER, *s.* (In singing) शारीरः -रं, स्वरकम्पः, स्वरभङ्गः.—(Note in music) गान्धर्वविद्यायां शीघ्रतालसूचकं चिह्नं.

QUAY, *s.* घट्टः, घट्टी, उत्तरणस्थानं, नौकोत्तरणस्थानं, गुल्मः.

QUEAN, *s.* बन्धकी, पुंश्चली, कुलटा, गणिका, भ्रष्टा, वारस्त्री.

QUEEN, *s.* (Wife of a king) राजपत्नी, राजमहिषी, महिषी, राज्ञी, देवी, नृपपत्नी, नृपवल्लभा, भट्टिनी; 'principal queen, one who has been inaugurated and crowned,' पट्टमहिषी, पट्टदेवी, पट्टाभिषिक्तराज्ञी; 'queen mother,' राजजननी.—(Woman who is the sovereign of a kingdom) राज्ञी, राज्यकारिणी महिषी.—(At chess) प्रधानः.

QUEENLY, QUEENLIKE, *a.* राज्ञीसदृशः -शी -शं, राज्ञीयोग्यः -ग्या -ग्यं.

QUEEN'S METAL, *s.* कांस्यं -स्यकं, कंसः -सं, कंशः -शं.

QUEER, *a.* विलक्षणः -णा -णं, असङ्गतः -ता -तं, अपरूपः -पा -पं.

QUEERLY, *adv.* विलक्षणं, वैलक्षण्येन, असङ्गतं, अपरूपं, अद्भुतं.

QUEERNESS, *s.* विलक्षणता, वैलक्षण्यं, असङ्गतत्वं, अपरूपता, अद्भुतता.

To QUELL, *v. a.* (Cause to cease, allay) निवृत् (c. 10. -वर्त्तयति -यितुं), शम् (c. 10. शमयति -यितुं), प्रशम्, उपशम्.—(Subdue, crush) दम्, प्रदम्, पराजि, खण्ड्, मृद्, वशीकृ.

QUELLED, *p. p.* निवर्त्तितः -ता -तं, शमितः -ता -तं, पराजितः &c., वशीकृतः &c.

QUELLER, *s.* पराजेता m. (तृ), पराजयी m. (न्), दमकः, शमकः.

To QUENCH, *v. a.* (Extinguish) निर्वा in caus. (-वापयति -यितुं), शम्, (c. 10. शमयति -यितुं) उपशम्, प्रशम्.—(Allay) शम्, उपशम्, प्रशम्, शान्तिं कृ; 'to quench the thirst,' तृष्णां छिद् (c. 7. छिनत्ति, छेत्तुं), तृष्णाछेदं कृ, तृष्णाशान्तिं कृ, तृष्णां शम्, पिपासाछेदं कृ, पिपासाविच्छेदं कृ, वैतृष्ण्यं कृ.

QUENCHABLE, *a.* शमनीयः -या -यं, शाम्यः -म्या -म्यं, विच्छेदनीयः -या -यं.

QUENCHED, *p.p.* शमितः -ता -तं, निर्वाणः -णा -णं, छिन्नः -न्ना -न्नं, विच्छिन्नः &c.

QUENCHING, *s.* शमनं, शान्तिः f., छेदः; 'of the thirst,' पिपासाविच्छेदः, तृष्णाछेदः.

QUENCHLESS, *s.* अशमनीयः -या -यं, अनिर्वापणीयः &c., अविच्छेदनीयः &c.

QUERIST, *s.* प्रष्टा m. (ष्टृ), पृच्छकः, प्रश्नकृत्. *See* INTERROGATOR.

QUERULOUS, *a.* विलापशीलः -ला -लं, विलपनशीलः &c., विलापी -पिनी -पि (न्), विलापकारी -रिणी &c., परिदेवनशीलः &c., परिदेवनकारी &c., परिदेवी &c., परिदेवकः -का -कं.

QUERULOUSLY, *adv.* विलापेन, सविलापं, सपरिदेवनं, विलापशीलत्वात्.

QUERULOUSNESS, *s.* विलापशीलता -त्वं, विलापकारित्वं, परिदेवनशीलता.

QUERY, *s.* प्रश्नः, आकांक्षा, आशङ्का, संशयः, सन्देहः, अनुयोगः.

QUEST, *s.* अन्वेषणं, अनुसन्धानं, अनुसरणं, जिज्ञासा, शोधनं; 'in quest,' अन्वेषी -षिणी -षि (न्), अर्थी -र्थिनी &c.

QUESTION, *s.* (Interrogatory) प्रश्नः, पृच्छा -च्छनं, प्रच्छनं -ना, अनुयोगः, पर्य्यनुयोगः, अनुयोजनं, सम्प्रश्नः, जिज्ञासा, आकांक्षा, आशङ्का, अर्थः; 'question and answer,' प्रश्नोत्तरं; 'a string of questions,' प्रश्नमाला, प्रश्नावलिः f.—(Inquiry, investigation) अनुसन्धानं, जिज्ञासा, निरूपणं, परीक्षा, पर्य्येषणा, विचारः -रणा, परीष्टिः f., वितर्कः.—(Subject of debate or controversy) वादविषयः, वादानुवादविषयः, वादास्पदं, विचारविषयः, विचारास्पदं, वितर्कविषयः; 'the topic in question,' प्रस्तुतविषयः, प्रस्तावः, प्रसङ्गः, प्रसक्तिः f.—(Doubt, subject of doubt) सन्देहः, संशयः, विकल्पः, वितर्कः, शङ्का, आशङ्का.

To QUESTION, *v. a.* (Interrogate) प्रच्छ् (c. 6. पृच्छति, प्रष्टुं), अनुप्रच्छ्, परिप्रच्छ्, समनुप्रच्छ्, अभिप्रच्छ्, प्रश्नं कृ, पृच्छनं, प्रच्छनं कृ, ज्ञा in des., (जिज्ञासति -ते -सितुं), अनुयुज्, प्रश्नेन परीक्ष्, प्रश्नोत्तरक्रमेण ज्ञा in des.—(Examine) परीक्ष्, अनुसन्धा, ज्ञा in des., निरूप्, विचर्.—(Doubt of dispute) शङ्क् (c. 1. शङ्कते -ङ्कितुं), आशङ्क्, अभिशङ्क्, परिशङ्क्, विशङ्क्, संशङ्क्, संशयस्थं -स्थां कृ, सन्देहस्थं -स्थां कृ, विचर्, वितर्क्.

QUESTIONABLE, *a.* शङ्कनीयः -या -यं, आशङ्कनीयः &c., शङ्कार्हः -र्हा -र्हं, विचार्य्यः -र्य्या -र्य्यं, विचारणीयः -या -यं, वितर्क्यः -र्क्या -र्क्यं, सन्दिग्धः -ग्धा -ग्धं, संशयस्थः -स्था -स्थं, सन्देहस्थः &c., संशययुक्तः -क्ता -क्तं, संशयापन्नः -न्ना -न्नं, वैकल्पिकः -की -कं.

QUESTIONABLENESS, *s.* शङ्कनीयता, आशङ्कनीयता, विचार्य्यता, सन्दिग्धता.

QUESTIONABLY, *adv.* शङ्कनीयं, आशङ्कनीयं, सन्दिग्धं, शङ्कापूर्व्वं, सशङ्कं.

QUESTIONARY, *a.* प्रश्नमयः -यी -यं, प्रश्नात्मकः -का -कं, पृच्छकः -का -कं.

QUESTIONED, *p. p.* (Interrogated) पृष्टः -ष्टा -ष्टं, अभिपृष्टः &c., अनुयुक्तः -क्ता -क्तं.—(Doubted) शङ्कितः -ता -तं, आशङ्कितः &c., संशयितः &c.

QUESTIONER, *s.* प्रष्टा m. (ष्टृ), पृच्छकः, प्रच्छकः, प्रश्नकर्त्ता m. (र्त्तृ), प्राट् m. (च्छ्), अनुयोक्ता m. (क्तृ), अनुयोगकृत् m., जिज्ञासुः m., जिज्ञासाकारी m. (न्), कथङ्कथिकः.

QUESTIONLESS, *adv.* असंशयं, अनाशङ्कनीयं, निःसंशयं, सुनिश्चितं.

QUIBBLE, *s.* वाक्छलं, वक्रोक्तिः f., वक्रवाक्यं, वक्रभणितं, कैतववादः, अर्थापत्तिः f., छलपादः, कपटवादः, श्लेषः, अपदेशः, व्यपदेशः, अपलापः.

To QUIBBLE, *v. n.* वाक्छलं कृ, वक्रोक्तिं कृ, अर्थापत्तिं कृ, वक्रं or वक्रवाक्यं वद् (c. 1. वदति -दितुं), अपदेशं कृ, अपलप्, व्यपदिश्, अपदिश्.

QUIBBLER, *s.* वाक्छलकारी *m.* (न्), अर्थापत्तिकृत् *m.*, वक्रोक्तिवादी *m.* (न्).

QUIBBLING, *s* वाक्छलकरणं, वक्रोक्तिः *f.*, अर्थापत्तिः *f.*, अर्थापत्तिकरणं.

QUICK, *a.* (Swift) शीघ्रः -घ्रा -घ्रं, त्वरितः -ता -तं, द्रुतः -ता -तं, तूर्णः -र्णा -र्णं, सत्वरः -रा -रं, त्वरान्वितः -ता -तं, क्षिप्रः -प्रा -प्रं, अविलम्बः -म्बा -म्बं, अविलम्बितः -ता -तं, अविलम्बी -म्बिनी -म्बि (न्), तुरः -रा -रं, सत्वरितः &c.—(Quick in motion) त्वरितगतिः -तिः -ति, द्रुतगतिः &c., शीघ्रगः -गा -गं, शीघ्रगामी -मिनी -मि (न्), वेगवान् -वती -वत् (त्), महावेगः -गा -गं, अविलम्बगतिः &c.; 'a quick pace,' द्रुतपदं, अविलम्बितक्रमः.—(Quick in action) आशुकारी &c., क्षिप्रकारी &c., शीघ्रकारी &c., शीघ्रकर्म्मा -र्म्मा -र्म्म (न्), अविलम्बितकर्म्मा &c. —(In apprehension) शीघ्रबुद्धिः -द्धिः -द्धि, शीघ्रग्राही &c. *See* SHARP; 'to be quick,' त्वर् (c. 1. त्वरते -रितुं), शीघ्र (nom. शीघ्रायते); 'be quick,' त्वरतां, त्वरस्व, सन्त्वरस्व.—(Living, moving with life) सजीवः -वा -वं, जीवी &c., जीवभूतः -ता -तं, चलितः -ता -तं, चलः -ला -लं, चलमानः -ना -नं, स्पन्दितः -ता -तं, स्पन्दमानः -ना -नं.—(Quick with child) चलितगर्भा, स्पन्दितगर्भा, गर्भवती, *see* PREGNANT.

QUICK, *adv.* शीघ्रं, त्वरितं, सत्वरं, क्षिप्रं, द्रुतं, आशु, शीघ्र in comp. *See* QUICKLY.

QUICK, *s.* (Sensitive part of the flesh, living flesh) मर्म्म *n.* (न्), मर्म्मस्थलं, मर्म्मस्थानं, मर्म्मदेशः; 'to pierce to the quick,' मर्म्म भिद्; 'cutting or piercing to the quick,' मर्म्मभेदः, मर्म्मस्पर्शनं, मर्म्मताडनं; 'that pierces to the quick,' मर्म्मभेदी -दिनी -दि (न्), मर्म्मस्पृक् *m. f. n.* (श्), मर्म्माविद्.

To QUICKEN, *v. a.* (Make alive) सजीवं -वां कृ, सजीवीकृ, जीव् (c. 10. जीवयति -यितुं), संजीव्, जीवं दा, जीवनं दा.—(Accelerate) त्वर् (c. 10. त्वरयति -यितुं), संत्वर्, गतिं वृध् in caus., गतिवर्धनं कृ, शीघ्रीकृ, क्षेप (nom. क्षेपयति -यितुं), द्रुततरं -रां कृ.—(Stimulate, incite) उद्दीप् (c. 10. -दीपयति -यितुं), उत्तिज् (c. 10. -तेजयति -यितुं), वीर्यं दा or वृध्, तेजो वृध्.

To QUICKEN, *v. n.* (Become living) सजीवः -वा -वं भू, सजीवीभू, जीवित्वं प्राप्, चैतन्यं प्राप्.—(As a woman with child) स्पन्द् (c. 1. स्पन्दते -न्दितुं), चल् (c. 1. चलति -लितुं), चलितगर्भा भू, स्पन्दितगर्भा भू.—(Have increased motion) शीघ्रतरं or द्रुततरं गम् or चल्, शीघ्र (nom. शीघ्रायते), त्वर् (c. 1. त्वरते -रितुं).

QUICKENED, *p. p.* (Made alive) सजीवः -वा -वं, सजीवीकृतः -ता -तं, जीवभूतः &c., जीवितः &c.—(Accelerated) त्वरितः -ता -तं, वर्धितगतिः -तिः -ति, वेगितः &c.

QUICKENING, *part.* or *a.* जीवदः -दा -दं, उद्दीपकः -का -कं. *See* LIFE-GIVING.

QUICKENING, *s.* (Of the child in the womb) स्पन्दनं, गर्भचलनं, गर्भस्पन्दनं.

QUICK-LIME, *s.* तप्तचूर्णं, तप्तकर्क्करः -रं, तप्तलेपः, उष्णलेपः.

QUICKLY, *adv.* शीघ्रं, त्वरितं, सत्वरं, क्षिप्रं, द्रुतं, आशु, सहसा, तूर्णं, लघु, अविलम्बितं, अविलम्बं, चपलं, द्रुतपदं, अविलम्बितपदं, अरं, शीघ्र or त्वरित or क्षिप्र in comp.; as, 'going quickly,' शीघ्रगः -गा -गं, शीघ्रगामी &c., त्वरितगतिः; 'spoken quickly,' त्वरितोदितः -ता -तं; 'acting quickly,' शीघ्रकारी &c., क्षिप्रकारी &c., आशुकारी &c.—(Soon, without delay) अचिरेण, अचिरात्, सद्यस्, आशु, सपदि, झटिति, अविलम्बेन.

QUICKNESS, *s.* शीघ्रता -त्वं, सत्वरता -त्वं, द्रुतता -त्वं, क्षिप्रता, शैघ्र्यं, त्वरा, त्वरणं, अविलम्बः, लघुता, वेगिता.

QUICK-SAND, *s.* आर्द्रसिकताः *pl.*, जलार्द्रसिकताः, अनूपसिकताः, द्रवसिकताः.

QUICK-SCENTED, *a.* शीघ्रघ्राणः -णा -णं, तीक्ष्णघ्राणः &c., सूक्ष्मघ्राणः &c.

QUICK-SIGHTED, QUICK-EYED, *a.* शीघ्रदृष्टिः -ष्टिः -ष्टि, तीक्ष्णदृष्टिः &c., सूक्ष्मदृष्टिः &c., सूक्ष्मदर्शी -र्शिनी -र्शि (न्), प्रखरदृष्टिः &c.

QUICK-SIGHTEDNESS, *s.* सूक्ष्मदर्शिता, दृष्टिसूक्ष्मता, दृष्टितीक्ष्णता, सूक्ष्मदृष्टिः *f.*

QUICKSILVER, *s.* पारदः, पारः, पारतः, रसः, रसधातुः *m.*, दिव्यरसः, सिद्धधातुः *m.*, रसराजः, रसनाथः, चपलः, सूतः -तं, रेतस् *n.*, दारदः, खलमूर्त्तिः *f.*, देहदः, पतङ्गं, खेचरः, मृत्युनाशकः, रुद्रजं, शिववीजं, हरवीजं, अशोकं, अमरः, मुकुन्दः, अचिन्त्यजः -जा -जं, योगवाही.

QUICK-WITTED, *a.* शीघ्रबुद्धिः -द्धिः -द्धि, सूक्ष्मबुद्धिः &c., तीक्ष्णबुद्धिः &c.

QUIESCENCE, *s.* शान्तता, शान्तिः *f.*, निश्चलता, अचलता, नैश्चल्यं, चलनाभावः, निश्चलभावः, चेष्टानिवृत्तिः *f.*, चेष्टाभावः, निवृत्तिः *f.*, निर्वृतिः *f.*, विश्रामः, विश्रान्तिः *f.*, स्थिरता, समाधानं; 'of mind,' मनःशान्तिः *f.*, सौमनस्यं.

QUIESCENT, *a.* निश्चलः -ला -लं, अचलः &c., अचरः -रा -रं, निश्चेष्टः -ष्टा -ष्टं, निवृत्तचेष्टः &c., शान्तः -न्ता -न्तं, स्थिरः -रा -रं, समाहितः -ता -तं, सुसमाहितः &c., निर्वृतः -ता -तं, निवृत्तः -त्ता -त्तं, विरतः -ता -तं. —(In grammar) अनुच्चारितः -ता -तं, लुप्तोच्चारः -रा -रं; 'quiescent mark,' विरामः.

QUIET, *a.* (Not moving) निश्चलः -ला -लं, अचलः -ला -लं, अचरः -रा -रं, स्थिरः -रा -रं, सुस्थिरः &c.—(Calm, not agitated, at rest) शान्तः -न्ता -न्तं, प्रशान्तः &c., उपशान्तः &c., निशान्तः &c., शमितः -ता -तं, शमी -मिनी -मि (न्), सुस्थिरः -रा -रं, स्थिरः -रा -रं, स्वस्थः -स्था -स्थं, अक्षुब्धः -ब्धा -ब्धं, अव्याकुलः -ला -लं, निराकुलः &c., समाहितः -ता -तं, विश्रान्तः -न्ता -न्तं, निर्वृतः -ता -तं, निवृत्तः -त्ता -त्तं.—(Free from wind) निर्वातः -ता -तं, निवृत्तवातः &c., निवृत्तवायुः -युः -यु.—(Mild, gentle) सौम्यः -म्या -म्यं, सौम्यवृत्तिः -त्तिः -त्ति, मृदुः -द्वी -दु, मन्दः -न्दा -न्दं, अनुग्रः -ग्रा -ग्रं, असाहसिकः -की -कं, अचण्डः -ण्डा -ण्डं.—(Unmolested) निर्विघ्नः -घ्ना -घ्नं, अविघ्नितः -ता -तं, निरुपद्रवः -वा -वं, निरुपप्लवः &c., निष्कण्टकः -का -कं, अबाधः -धा -धं, अप्रतिबन्धः -न्धा -न्धं, प्रतिबन्धहीनः -ना -नं, स्वस्थः -स्था -स्थं.—(Silent) तूष्णीकः -का -कं, निःशब्दः -ब्दा -ब्दं, निश्शब्दः &c.; 'be quiet!' तूष्णीम्भव, तूष्णीमास्यतां, विरम.

QUIET, *s.* शान्तिः, शमः, शान्तता, प्रशान्तिः *f.*, उपशमः, निर्वृतिः *f.*, निवृत्तिः *f.*, विश्रामः, विश्रान्तिः *f.*, स्वस्थता, स्वास्थ्यं, समाधानं, निरुपद्रवता, उपद्रवाभावः, निर्विघ्नता, निरुपप्लवता, प्रतिबन्धहीनता, प्रतिबन्धाभावः, निष्कण्टकत्वं, कण्टकाभावः, निश्चलता, स्थिरता.

To QUIET, *v. a.* शम् (c. 10. शमयति -यितुं), प्रशम्, उपशम्, शान्त्व् or सान्त्व् (c. 10. सान्त्वयति -यितुं), अभिशान्त्व्, परिशान्त्व्, उपसान्त्व्, निवृत् (c. 10. -वर्त्तयति -यितुं), विरम् (c. 10. -रमयति -यितुं), निर्विघ्नीकृ, निरुपद्रवीकृ, निश्चलीकृ, स्थिरीकृ.

QUIETISM, *s.* शमः, शान्तिः *f.*, निवृत्तिमार्गः, वैराग्यं. According to the Vedánta system there are six stages of this state, or six duties to be performed by him who practices it, viz. श्रद्धा, समाधानं, तितिक्षा, उपरतिः *f.*, दमः, शमः.

QUIETIST, *s.* वेदान्ती *m.* (न्), वेदान्तज्ञः, वेदान्तगः, वेदान्तसेवी *m.* (न्), वेदान्तमार्गी *m.* (न्), वेदान्ताधिकारी *m.*, निवृत्तमार्गी *m.*

QUIETLY, *adv.* शान्तं, शान्त्या, स्थैर्य्येण, निर्वृतिपूर्व्वं, शान्तवत्, अव्याकुलं,

निराकुलं, अक्षुब्धं, अक्षोभेण, अनुग्रं, अचण्डं, मन्दं, स्वस्थं, स्वास्थ्येन, सशमं, निःशब्दं, तूष्णीं, निश्चलं.

QUIETNESS, *s.* शान्तता, प्रशान्तता, शान्तिः *f.*, स्थिरता, निश्चलता, नैश्चल्यं, अक्षुब्धता, अक्षोभः, अव्याकुलत्वं. *See* QUIET, *s.*

QUIETUDE, *s.* शान्तिः *f.*, शमः. *See* QUIETNESS, QUIET, *s.*

QUILL, *s.* (Feather) पक्षः, पर्णः; 'for writing,' कलमः; लेखनी, आलेखनी.—(Of a porcupine) शललो -लं, शलः -लं.—(Of a lute, &c.) रवः, परिवादः, शारिका, कोणः.

QUILT, *s.* तूलिका, तूला -ली, उत्तरप्रच्छदः, उत्तरच्छदः, शयनीयप्रच्छदः, शय्याप्रच्छदपटः, शय्याच्छादनं, तूलादिनिर्म्मितः प्रच्छदः, आस्तरणं, आस्तरः, संस्तरः, स्तरिमा *m.* (न्).

To QUILT, *v. a.* तूलादि निवेशयित्वा निषिव् (c. 4. -षीव्यति -सेवितुं) or परिषिव् or विषिव् or संसिव् or सिव्.

QUINARY, *a.* पञ्चकः -का -कं, पञ्चरूपः -पा -पं, पञ्चाङ्गः -ङ्गी -ङ्गं.

QUINCE, *s.* (The tree) श्रीफलः may be used.—(The fruit) श्रीफलं.

QUINDECAGON, *s.* पञ्चदशकोणः -णं, पञ्चदशभुजः, पञ्चदशास्रं -स्री.

QUINQUAGESIMA, *a.* ख्रीष्टपुनरुत्थानोत्सवात् पूर्व्वं पञ्चाशत्तमदिवसः.

QUINQUENNIAL, *a.* पाञ्चवर्षिकः -की -कं, पञ्चवर्षिकः &c., पञ्चवर्षीयः -या -यं, पाञ्चाब्दिकः -की -कं.

QUINSY, *s.* अधिमांसकः, घटसर्पः, गण्डमाला, कण्ठरोगः.

QUINTESSENCE, *s.* सारः, सारांशः, पञ्चमसारः, उत्तमसारः, परमसारः.

QUINTUPLE, *a.* पञ्चगुणः -णा -णं, पञ्चविधः -धा -धं, पञ्चाङ्गः -ङ्गी -ङ्गं.

QUIP, *s.* (Taunt, sarcasm) क्षेपः, अवक्षेपः, व्यञ्जना -नं.

QUIRE, *s.* (Band of singers) गायकगणः, गायकचक्रं.—(Of paper) पत्रचतुर्विंशकं.

QUIRISTER, *s.* सहगायकः, सहगायनः, गायकगणाध्यक्षः.

QUIRK, *s.* (Fancy) मनोलौल्यं, बुद्धिचापल्यं, लहरी, छन्दस्, अवहृतिः *m.*, दुर्वासना, मृषार्थकं.—(Taunt) क्षेपः, अवक्षेपः.—(Quibble) वाक्छलं, वक्रोक्तिः *f.*

QUIRKISH, *a.* चपलः -ला -लं, लोलः -ला -लं, वाक्छलमयः -यी -यं.

To QUIT, *v. a.* (Give up, abandon) त्यज् (c. 1. त्यजति, त्यक्तुं), परित्यज्, संत्यज्, हा (c. 3. जहाति, हातुं), विहा, अपहा, अपाहा, प्रहा, विसृज्, उत्सृज्, अतिसृज्, व्यपसृज्, अपास्, व्युदस्, उज्झ्, प्रोज्झ्, मुच्, विमुच्, रह्, विरह्, परिहृ, वृज्, परिवृज्, विवृज्.—(Depart from) अपगम् (c. 1. -गच्छति -गन्तुं), विगम्, व्यपगम्, अपया, अपे, व्यपे, अपसृ, प्रस्था, विप्रस्था.—(Clear) शुध्, परिशुध्, मुच्, विमुच्, निस्तॄ in caus.—(Perform one's duty) स्वकार्य्यं or स्वकर्म्म सम्पद् (c. 10. -पादयति -यितुं) or विधा.

QUIT, *a.* मुक्तः -क्ता -क्तं, विमुक्तः &c., विमोचितः -ता -तं, ऋणमुक्तः &c., उत्तीर्णः -र्णा -र्णं, अवतीर्णः -र्णा -र्णं, उपकारमुक्तः &c., शोधितः -ता -तं.

QUITE, *adv.* सर्व्वथा, सर्व्वतस्, सर्व्वशस्, साकल्येन, सकलं, सम्यक्, अशेषतस्, अशेषेण, पर्य्याप्तं, विश्वतस्, अखिलेन, निखिलेन, अन्यूनं, सर्व्वभावेन.—(To a great degree, very) अति or सु prefixed, अत्यन्तं, अतिशयं -येन; 'quite fresh,' अतिनवः -वा -वं, अतिसद्यस्कः -स्का -स्कं, सद्यस्कालीनः -ना -नं.—(Not quite) ईषदूनः -ना -नं, अल्पोनः &c.

QUITS, अन्योन्यं or परस्परम् ऋणमुक्तौ *m. du.*, or उपकारमुक्तौ.

QUITTANCE, *s.* निस्तारः, मुक्तिः *f.*, मोक्षः, निष्कृतिः *f.*, उत्तरणं, शुद्धिः *f.*, शोधनं, अपनयनं; 'from debt or obligation,' ऋणमुक्तिः *f.*, ऋणमोक्षः, ऋणशुद्धिः *f.*, ऋणशोधनं, ऋणापनयनं, ऋणापाकरणं, ऋणापनोदनं, विगणनं; 'of a grudge,' वैरशुद्धिः *f.*

QUITTED, *p. p.* त्यक्तः -क्ता -क्तं, परित्यक्तः &c., रहितः -ता -तं, विरहितः &c., उत्सृष्टः -ष्टा -ष्टं, विसर्जितः &c., उज्झितः &c., प्रोज्झितः &c.

QUIVER, *s.* तूणः -णा -णी, तूणीरः, शरधिः *m.*, इषुधिः *m.*, शराश्रयः, बाणाश्रयः, निषङ्गः, अपासङ्गः, उपासङ्गः, तुलसारिणी, कोलिः *f.*; 'having a quiver,' तूणी -णिनी &c.; 'carrying one,' धृतेषुधिः -धिः -धि, तूणधरः -रा -रं.

To QUIVER, *v. n.* स्फुर् (c. 6. स्फुरति -रितुं), प्रस्फुर्, विस्फुर्, कम्प् (c. 1. कम्पते -म्पितुं), विकम्प्, प्रकम्प्, अभिकम्प्, स्पन्द् (c. 1. स्पन्दते -न्दितुं), परिस्पन्द्, वेप् (c. 1. वेपते -पितुं), प्रवेप्, त्रस् (c. 4. त्रस्यति -सितुं), वित्रस्, ह्वल् (c. 1. ह्वलति -लितुं), विह्वल्, प्रह्वल्; 'his lips quiver,' ओष्ठाधरौ स्फुरतः; 'his lip quivers,' अधरः स्फुरति; 'his arm quivered,' बाहुः पुस्फोर.

QUIVERED, *a.* तूणी -णिनी -णि (न्), धृतेषुधिः -धिः -धि, सतूणः -णा -णं.

QUIVERING, *part.* or *a.* स्फुरन् -रन्ती -रत् (त्), स्फुरितः -ता -तं, प्रस्फुरितः &c., स्पन्दमानः -ना -नं, स्पन्दितः &c., कम्पमानः -ना -नं, प्रकम्पमानः &c., कम्पितः &c., वेपमानः -ना -नं, सकम्पः -म्पा -म्पं, चञ्चलः -ला -लं; 'having a quivering lip,' स्फुरिताधरः -रा -रं, प्रस्फुरिताधरः &c., स्फुरदोष्ठी -ष्ठिनी &c.

QUIVERING, *s.* स्फुरणं, स्फुरितं, विस्फुरणं, प्रस्फुरणं, स्फूर्त्तिः *f.*, स्पन्दनं, कम्पनं, वेपनं; 'of the lip,' अधरस्फुरणं.

QUIZ, *s.* (Odd fellow) अपरूपजनः, विलक्षणजनः.—(One who ridicules others) उपहासकः, अवक्षेपकः, परिहासकृत् *m.*, अवज्ञाकारी *m.*

To QUIZ, *v. a.* अवहस् (c. 1. -हसति -सितुं), अपहस्, अवहासभूमिं कृ, अपहासास्पदं कृ, अवज्ञास्पदं कृ, अवज्ञाभूमिं कृ, अवक्षिप्.

QUOIF, QUOIFFURE, QUOIN, *see* COIF, COIFFURE, &c.

QUOIT, *s.* (Circular ring of iron) चक्रं, लोहचक्रं, लौहचक्रं, चक्रनं; 'game of quoits,' चक्रक्रीडा.

To QUOIT, *v. a.* लोहचक्राणि क्षिप् (c. 6. क्षिपति, क्षेप्तुं), चक्रक्रीडां कृ.

QUONDAM, *a.* पूर्व्वः -र्व्वा -र्व्वं, प्राक्तनः -नी -नं. *See* FORMER.

QUORUM, *s.* कार्य्यनिर्वाहक्षमसंख्या, कार्य्यनिर्वाहोपयुक्तसंख्या, कार्य्यनिर्वाहोचितसंख्या, कार्य्यनिर्वाहावरसंख्या, कार्य्यसाधकावरसंख्या.

QUOTA, *s.* उपयुक्तांशः, उपयुक्तभागः, यथायोग्यांशः, यथोचितांशः.

QUOTATION, *s.* (The act) अवतरणं, अवतारणं, उद्धारः, उद्धरणं, उपन्यासः, उपन्यसनं, of the Vedas श्रुतादानं.—(Passage quoted) उपन्यस्तवाक्यं, उद्धृतवाक्यं, उपन्यस्तवचनं, उद्धृतलेखः, अवतारितवाक्यं, उपनीतवाक्यं, प्रमाणार्थम् अमुकग्रन्थोद्धृतम् अनुवादकवाक्यं.

To QUOTE, *v. a.* अवतॄ (c. 10. -तारयति -यितुं), अवतरणं कृ, उपन्यस् (c. 4. -अस्यति -असितुं), उपन्यासं कृ, उद्धृ (c. 1. -हरति -हर्त्तुं), उद्धारं कृ, प्रमाणार्थम् अमुकग्रन्थाद् अनुवादकवाक्यम् उद्धृ or उपनी (c. 1. -नयति -नेतुं).

QUOTED, *p. p.* अवतीर्णः -र्णा -र्णं, अवतारितः -ता -तं, उद्धृतः -ता -तं, उपन्यस्तः -स्ता -स्तं, प्रमाणार्थम् उपनीतः -ता -तं.

QUOTH, *v. defect.* Expressed by आह, उवाच &c.

QUOTIDIAN *a.* प्रात्यहिकः -की -कं, प्रात्याह्निकः &c., ऐकाहिकः &c., अन्वाहिकः &c., प्रातिदैनिकः &c., आह्निकः &c., अन्येद्युष्कः -ष्का -ष्कं; 'fever,' प्रात्याहिकज्वरः, अन्येद्युष्कः.

QUOTIENT, *s.* लब्धिः *f.*, आप्तं, फलं, क्षेत्रफलं, भागः.

R.

RABBIT, *s.* शशः, शशकः, लम्बकर्णः, लोमकर्णः -र्णकः, मृदुलोमकः; 'its skin,' शशोर्णः, शशलोम *n.* (न्), शशचर्म्म *n.*, शशाजिनं.

RABBLE, *s.* अन्त्यजातीयाः *m. pl.*, प्राकृतजनाः *m. pl.*, अन्त्याः *m. pl.*,

खला: *m. pl.*, हीनवर्णा: *m. pl.*, पृथग्जना: *m. pl.*, अधमजातीया: *m. pl.*, अधमजनसमूह:, नीचजनसमूह:, प्राकृतजनसम्मर्द:.

RABID, *a.* उन्मत्त: -त्ता -त्तं, उन्माद: -दा -दं, उन्मादवान् -वती -वत् (त्), मत्त: -त्ता -त्तं, प्रमद: -दा -दं, वातुल: -ला -लं; 'a rabid dog,' अलर्क:, अलक:.

RABIDLY, *adv.* उन्मत्तवत्, मत्तवत्, सोन्मादं, उन्मादेन, प्रमदवत्.

RABIDNESS, *s.* उन्मत्तता, उन्माद:, सोन्मादता, प्रमदता. *See* MADNESS.

RACE, *s.* (Lineage) वंश:, सन्तति: *f.*, सन्तान:, अन्वय:, कुलं, जाति: *f.*, अन्ववाय:, गोत्रं, वंशपरम्परा, वंशावलि: *f.*, वंशवितति: *f.*, पुत्रपौत्रादिवंशपरम्परा, तनु: *m.*, अभिजन:, प्रवरं, वर्ण:, जननं, अनूकं, सगोत्रं; 'human race,' मनुष्यजाति: *f.*, नृजाति: *f.*—(A running or course) चर्य्या, धावनं, मार्ग:; 'horse-race,' अश्वचर्य्या, अश्वधावनं, अश्वमार्ग:.—(Ginger) गुल्ममूलं.

To RACE, *v. n.* अग्रोपस्थानेच्छया धाव् (c. 1. धावति -वितुं), अग्राभिगमनेच्छया धाव्, परस्परजिगीषया धाव्, जवेन धाव्.

RACE-COURSE, *s.* चर्य्याभूमि: *f.*, चर्य्यास्थानं, धावनभूमि: *f.*, धावनस्थानं.

RACE-HORSE, *s.* जवाश्व:, जवन:, जवी *m.* (न्), जवाधिक:, धावक:.

RACER, *s.* धावक:, धावनकृत्. *See* RACE-HORSE.

RACK, *s.* (For hay) गवादनी, द्रोणी -णि: *f.*—(Instrument of torture) यातनायन्त्रं, यातनयन्त्रं, प्रमाथयन्त्रं.—(Extreme pain) यातना, अतिव्यथा, तीव्रवेदना, तीक्ष्णवेदना.

To RACK, *v. a.* यत् (c. 10. यातयति -यितुं), यातनयन्त्रेण व्यथ् (c. 10. व्यथयति -यितुं) or प्रमथ् (c. 10. -माथयति -यितुं), अत्यन्तं व्यथ् or पीड् (c. 10. पीडयति -यितुं), यातनां कृ.

RACKED, *p. p.* अतिव्यथित: -ता -तं, अतिपीडित: &c., प्रमाथित: &c., प्रमथित: &c.

RACKET, *s.* (Confused noise) कोलाहल:, कलकल:, कलरव:, हलहलाशब्द:, कालकील:, रास:, तुमुलं.—(In tennis) गुलिकाताडनी, गुलिकाप्रक्षेपणी, गुलिकाप्रणोदनी, गुलिकाक्षेपणयष्टि: *m.*, गुलिकाप्रणोदनयन्त्रं.

RACKETY, *a.* कोलाहलकारी -रिणी -रि (न्), तुमुलकारी &c., तुमुली &c.

RACY, *a.* रसिक: -का -कं, रसी -सिनी -सि (न्), रसवान् -वती -वत् (त्), सरस: -सा -सं, सुरस: &c., तीक्ष्णरस: &c., उग्ररस: &c.

RADIANCE, RADIANCY, *s.* प्रभा, दीप्ति: *f.*, तेजस् *n.*, उज्ज्वलता, प्रकाशता, छवि: *f.*, उद्भास:, भाजिष्णुता, घर्म्मरश्मि: *m.* *See* BRIGHTNESS, BRILLIANCY, LUSTRE.

RADIANT, *a.* देदीप्यमान: -ना -नं, प्रकाशमान: &c., द्योतमान: &c., दीप्तिमान् -मती -मत् (त्), प्रदीप्तिमान् &c., प्रभावान् &c., सुप्रभ: -भा -भं, तेजोमय: -यी -यं, कान्तिमान् &c., किरणमय: -यी -यं, मरीचिमाली -लिनी-लि (न्), विशद: -दा -दं. *See* BRIGHT, BRILLIANT, LUSTROUS.

RADIANTLY, *adv.* अतितेजसा, सुप्रभं, उज्ज्वलं, सुप्रकाशं.

To RADIATE, *v. n.* स्फुर् (c. 6. स्फुरति -रितुं), किरण (nom. किरणायते), दीप् in freq. (देदीप्यते), वर्च्चस् (nom. वर्च्चायते), अंशु (nom. अंशूयति), किरणरूपेण स्फुर्, किरणान् पत् (c. 10. पातयति -यितुं).

RADIATION, *s.* किरणस्फुरणं, रश्मिस्फुरणं, अंशुपातनं, किरणपातनं, रश्मिविकिरणं, अंशुविकिरणं, दीप्तिविकिरणं.

RADICAL, *a.* (Original, fundamental) मौलिक: -की -कं, मौल: -ली -लं, मूलिक: -की -कं, मूली -लिनी -लि (न्), वास्तव: -वी -वं.—(Natural) स्वाभाविक: -की -कं, प्राकृतिक: &c., स्वभावज: -जा -जं, सात्त्विक: -की -कं.—(Primitive) मूलिक: &c., *see* the word.

RADICALLY, *adv.* मूलतस्, आमूलं, समूलं, स्वभावतस्, जातितस्.

To RADICATE, *v. a.* मूलतो रुह् in caus. (रोपयति -यितुं) बद्धमूलं -लां कृ.

RADISH, *s.* मूलक: -कं, कन्दमूलं, सेकिमं, पाटीर:, पटीरं, हरिपर्णं, हस्तिपर्णं.

RADIUS, *s.* (Of a circle) त्रिज्या, व्यासार्द्धं, व्यासार्द्धरेखा, कर्कट:.—(Of the equator) भूकर्ण:.—(Of a wheel) अर:.

RAFF, *s.* अधमजातीया: *m. pl.*, हीनवर्णा:, अन्त्यजातीया: &c. *See* RABBLE.

RAFFLE, *s.* गुटिकापात:, महामूल्यद्रव्यप्राप्त्यर्थं गुटिकापातनं.

To RAFFLE, *v. n.* महामूल्यद्रव्यप्राप्त्यर्थं गुटिका: पत् (c. 10. पातयति -यितुं).

RAFT, *s.* उडुप: -पं, तरण: -णी, तरणि: *m.*, प्लव:, प्लवाका, तरण्ड:, तरत् *n.*, तर्णि: *m.*, तारण:, वहित्रं, वारिरथ:, कोल:, भेल: -लक:, होड:.

RAFTER, *s.* गृहस्थूणा, वेश्मस्थूणा, पटलस्थूणा, स्थूणा, पटलकाष्ठं, पटलदारु: *m.*, गृहदारु: *m.*, गृहकाष्ठं, दीर्घस्थूणा, दीर्घकाष्ठं, दीर्घदारु: *m.*

RAG, *s.* (Piece of tattered cloth) वस्त्रखण्ड:, जीर्णवस्त्रखण्ड:, जर्जरवस्त्रखण्ड:, पटखण्ड:, चीरं, चीवरं, कर्पट:, कन्था, लक्तकं, कर:.—(Ragged garment) जीर्णवस्त्रं, जर्ज्जरवस्त्रं; 'dressed in rags,' *see* RAGGED; 'a bundle of rags,' चीरसमूह:, करोत्कर:.

RAGAMUFFIN, *s.* चीरवासा: *m.* (स्), कर्पटी *m.* (न्), खल:, धूर्त:, अधमजातीय:.

RAGE, *s.* (Great anger, fury) क्रोध:, कोप:, प्रकोप:, अतिक्रोध:, अतिकोप:, क्रोधावेश:, कोपावेश:, संरम्भ:, प्रतिरम्भ:, संरब्धता, अमर्ष:, क्रुध् *f.*, उग्रता -त्वं, रौद्रं -द्रता, चण्डता, उच्चण्डता, राग:, अतिराग:, उत्ताप:, सन्ताप:, कोपाकुलता, प्रतिघ:; 'in a rage,' संरब्ध: -ब्धा -ब्धं, संरम्भी -म्भिणी &c., क्रुद्ध: -द्धा -द्धं, क्रोधी -धिनी &c., जातक्रोध: -धा -धं, कोपाकुल: -ला -लं, जातामर्ष: -र्षा -र्षं, क्रोधाविष्ट: -ष्टा -ष्टं.—(Violence, vehemence) संरम्भ:, उग्रता, तीक्ष्णता, अतितीक्ष्णता, तैक्ष्ण्यं, रौद्रता, तीव्रता, तिग्मता.—(Agitation) क्षोभ:, व्याक्षोभ:, वेग:, अतिक्षोभ:.

To RAGE, *v. n.* (Be angry) क्रुध् (c. 4. क्रुध्यति, क्रोद्धुं), संक्रुध्, रुष् (c. 4. रुष्यति, रोषितुं), कुप् (c. 4. कुप्यति, कोपितुं), प्रकुप्, क्रोधाकुल: -ला -लं भू, कोपाकुल: -ला -लं भू, संरब्ध: -ब्धा -ब्धं भू, संरब्धीभू.—(Become violent or intense) उग्रतर: -रा -रं भू, तीक्ष्णतर: -रा -रं भू, रौद्रतर: -रा -रं भू, रौद्रीभू, तिग्मतर: -रा -रं भू, भृश (nom. भृशायते), उच्चण्ड: -ण्डा -ण्डं भू, क्षुभ् (c. 4. क्षुभ्यति, क्षोभितुं).

RAGEFUL, *a.* क्रोधी -धिनी -धि (न्), क्रोधान्वित: -ता -तं, कोपान्वित: &c., कोपाकुल: -ला -लं, कोपी &c., संरम्भी &c., सकोप: -पा -पं.

RAGGED, *a.* जर्ज्जर: -रा -रं, जर्ज्जरीक: -का -कं, जीर्ण: -र्णा -र्णं, छिन्न: -न्ना -न्नं, विच्छिन्न: &c., विषमधार: -रा -रं; 'ragged garment,' जीर्णवस्त्रं, जर्ज्जरवस्त्रं, छिन्नवस्त्रं, भिक्षुसंघाटी *m.* (न्), कर्पट:, चीरं, चीवरं, कन्था; 'dressed in ragged garments,' चीरवासा: -सा: -स: (स्), कर्पटधारी -रिणी -रि (न्), कर्पटिक:, चीवरी &c.

RAGGEDNESS, *s.* जर्ज्जरता, जर्ज्जरीकता, जीर्णता, छिन्नवस्त्रता, छिन्नता.

RAGING, *part.* or *a.* उग्र: -ग्रा -ग्रं, रोषण: -णा -णं, वेगी -गिनी -गि (न्), महावेग: -गा -गं, उदीर्णवेग: &c., संरम्भी &c., संरब्ध: -ब्धा -ब्धं, तीक्ष्ण: -क्ष्णा -क्ष्णं, तीव्र: -व्रा -व्रं, चण्ड: -ण्डा -ण्डं, उच्चण्ड: &c.

RAGMAN, *s.* चीरव्यापारी *m.* (न्), चीरविक्रेता *m.* (तृ), छिन्नवस्त्रव्यापारी.

RAGOUT, *s.* मिष्टान्नं, सव्यञ्जनाहार:, व्यञ्जनं, उपस्कर:.

RÁHU, *s.* (The ascending node, fabled as a demon, the son of Singhiká, with the tail of a dragon. His head was cut off by Vishnu, at the churning of the ocean; but being immortal, by having tasted the amrit, the head and tail retained their separate existence, and were transferred to the stellar sphere. The head, or Ráhu, became the cause of eclipses, by endeavouring at various times to swallow the sun and moon. The tail was called Ketu, or the descending node, *see* PLANET) राहुः, सिंहिकासूनुः *m.*, सैंहिकः, सैंहिकेयः, ग्रहः, ग्रहकल्लोलः, खेटः, विधुन्तुदः, सूर्य्यग्रहः. An eclipse is called राहुग्राहः, राहुग्रासः, राहुसंस्पर्शः.

RAIL, *s.* लोहस्तम्भः, लोहशङ्कुः *m.*, लोहावरणं. *See* RAILING.

To RAIL, *v. a.* (Inclose with rails) लोहस्तम्भेन परिवेष्ट् or परिवृ or आवृ or अवरुध् or संरुध्, लोहस्तम्भावृतं -तां कृ.

To RAIL, *v. n.* (Reproach, revile, abuse) निन्द्, अपवद्, तिरस्कृ, आक्रुश्, अवगुर्, अवक्षिप्, अधिक्षिप्, परिक्षिप्, क्षिप्, शप्, अभिशप्, परिशप्, आक्षर्, गर्ह्, भर्त्स्, कुत्स्, मुखरीकृ, गुप् in des., उपालभ्.

RAILED AT, *p.p.* आक्रुष्टः -ष्टा -ष्टं, उपालब्धः -ब्धा -ब्धं, अधिक्षिप्तः -प्ता -प्तं.

RAILER, *s.* निन्दकः, आक्रोशकः, उपक्रोष्टा *m.* (ष्टृ), कुत्सावादी *m.* (न्), अपवादकः, निर्भर्त्सकः, उपालम्भकारी *m.*, अवक्षेपकः.

RAILING, *s.* (Reviling) निन्दा -न्दनं, अपवादः, परिवादः, परीवादः, तिरस्कारः, उपालम्भः, जुगुप्सा, वाक्पारुष्यं, आक्रोशः-शनं, उपक्रोशः, दुर्वाक्यं, धिक्क्रिया.—(Fence) आवरणं, लोहावरणं, आवारः, कटघ्नं, *see* FENCE.

RAILLERY, *s.* अपहासः, परिहासः, परीहासः, प्रहसनं, हासिका.

RAIL-ROAD, RAIL-WAY, *s.* लोहवर्त्म *n.* (न्), लोहमार्गः अयोवर्त्म *n.* (न्).

RAIMENT, *s.* वस्त्रं, वासस् *n.*, वसनं, वेशः, अम्बरं, आच्छादनं, परिधानं, प्रसाधनं, संव्यानं, सिचयः, प्रच्छादनं, परिच्छदः; 'clothed in white raiment,' शुक्लाम्बरधारी -रिणी -रि (न्), शुक्लवासाः -साः -सः (स्).

To RAIN, *v. n.* वृष् (c. 1. वर्षति -ते -र्षितुं), अभिवृष्, प्रवृष्, अभिप्रवृष्, वर्षणं कृ, वृष्टिं कृ, मेघेभ्यः पत् (c. 1. पतति -तितुं), वृष्टिं सु (c. 1. स्रवति, स्रोतुं), जलं or तोयं सु; 'to rain slightly or softly,' शीक् (c. 1. शीकते -कितुं); 'to rain heavily,' अतिवृष्टिं कृ; 'to cease to rain,' निर्वृष्; 'it rains,' वर्षन्ति मेघाः, वृष्टिर् मेघेभ्यः पतति.

To RAIN, *v. a.* वृष् (c. 1. वर्षति -ते -र्षितुं), अभिवृष्, प्रवृष्, अभिप्रवृष्, सु (c. 1. स्रवति, स्रोतुं or c. 10. स्रावयति -यितुं), पत् (c. 10. पातयति -यितुं), शीक् (c. 1. शीकते -कितुं); 'the clouds rain water,' जलं स्रवन्ति मेघाः; 'the clouds rained blood,' मेघाः शोणितं ववृषुः; 'the sky rained blood,' स्रावयामास शोणितं व्योम, शिशीके शोणितं व्योम.

RAIN, *s.* वृष्टिः *f.*, वर्षः -र्षं, आवृष्टिः *f.*, खजलं, घनाम्बु *n.*, मेघाम्बु *n.*, खवारि *n.*, मेघजलं, गोघृतं, पर्जन्यः, परामृतं; 'soft rain,' शीकरः; 'heavy rain,' अतिवृष्टिः *f.*; 'untimely rain,' अकालवृष्टिः *f.*; 'shower of rain,' धारासम्पातः, धारासारः; 'broken or partial rain,' खण्डवृष्टिः *f.*—(Rains, season of the rains) वर्षाः *m. pl.*, वर्षकालः, वृष्टिकालः, मेघकालः, मेघागमः, प्रावृट् *f.* (ष्), प्रावृट्कालः, प्रावृषा. *See* RAINY.

RAIN-BOW, *s.* इन्द्रधनुस् *n.*, इन्द्रचापः, शक्रधनुस् *n.*, इन्द्रायुधं, देवायुधं, शक्रशरासनं, मेघधनुः *m.*, सुरधनुः *m.*, मणिधनुः *m.*, वायुफलं, धनुष्यं, कौशिकायुधं, परामृतं.

RAINED, *p. p.* वर्षितः -ता -तं, अभिवर्षितः -ता -तं, प्रवर्षितः &c.

RAINNESS, *s.* वर्षुकत्वं, वार्षिकत्वं, बहुवृष्टित्वं, वृष्टिबाहुल्यं.

RAINWATER, *s.* वर्षाम्बु *n.*, वृष्टिजलं, वर्षजलं, वृष्टिवारि *n.*

RAINY, *a.* वर्षुकः -का -कं, वार्षिकः -की -कं, वर्षिकः &c., वृष्टिमान् -मती -मत् (त्), बहुवृष्टिः -ष्टिः -ष्टि, वर्षी -र्षिणी -र्षि (न्), प्रावृषिकः -की -कं. *See* PLUVIAL; 'rainy cloud,' वर्षुकमेघः, वर्षुकाब्दः; 'a rainy day,' दुर्दिनं, वार्दलं; 'rainy night,' वर्षारात्रः; 'rainy season,' वृष्टिकालः, वर्षकालः, वर्षाकालः, मेघागमः, मेघकालः, प्रावृट् *f.* (ष्), प्रावृट्कालः, प्रावृषा, घनकालः, जलदकालः, घनसमयः, जलदागमः, तपात्ययः, चातकानन्दनः.

To RAISE, *v. a.* (Lift, raise up) उत्स्था in caus. (-थापयति -यितुं, rt. स्था), उत्तुल् (c. 10. -तोलयति -यितुं), उन्नम् (c. 10. -नमयति -नामयति -यितुं), उन्नी (c. 1. -नयति -नेतुं), उद्धृ (c. 1. -हरति -हर्त्तुं), उच्छ्रि (c. 1. उच्छ्रयति -यितुं, rt. श्रि), समुच्छ्रि, प्रोच्छ्रि, उत्कृष्.—(Erect, elevate, set up) उत्स्था in caus., स्था in caus., उन्नम्, उच्छ्रि, उत्क्षिप्, समुत्क्षिप्, उद्बृह् (c. 6. -बृहति -बर्हितुं), उद्यम् (c. 1. -यच्छति -यन्तुं), समुद्यम्, अभ्युद्यम्, अधिरुह् in caus. (-रोपयति -यितुं), आरुह्, रुह्, अर्द्धीकृ, उच्चीकृ, उच्चैः कृ.—(Erect, build) निर्मा, विनिर्मा.—(Elevate, exalt) उन्नम्, उच्छ्रि, उद्यम्, उद्धन् (c. 2. -हन्ति -न्तुं), उन्नतिं कृ; 'in rank,' पदवृद्धिं कृ, उत्कृष्टपदे or श्रेष्ठपदे नियुज् or प्रतिपद् (c. 10. -पादयति -यितुं), प्रतिपत्तिं कृ or दा.—(Increase, enhance) वृध् in caus., संवृध्, अधिकीकृ, अधिकं -कां कृ.—(Produce, make) उत्पद् in caus., जन् (c. 10. जनयति -यितुं), संजन्.—(Excite, incite) उत्पद्, जन्, उत्थप्, उत्स्था, उद्युज्, नियुज्, प्रवृत्.—(Levy), *see* *To* LEVY.—(Raise one's voice) उच्चैःस्वरेण भाष् or वद्, उच्चैर् वद्, उच्चवाक्यम् उदीर्.—(Raise a clamor) उत्क्रुश् (c. 1. -क्रोशति -क्रोष्टुं), उच्चैःस्वरेण घुष्, उद्घुष्, उच्चशब्दं कृ, महाशब्दं कृ, उच्चैर्घुष्टं कृ.—(Crops, cattle, &c.) उत्पद् in caus.—(Dust) रजः or रेणुम् उद्धू (c. 5. -धूनोति -धोतुं) or समुद्धू.—(Raise a siege) अवरोधत्यागं कृ.

RAISED, *p. p.* (Lifted, raised up) उत्थापितः -ता -तं, उत्तोलितः &c., उन्नमितः &c., उन्नतः -ता -तं, उच्छ्रितः &c., समुच्छ्रितः &c., उद्यतः -ता -तं, उद्धृतः &c., समुद्धृतः &c., उत्कर्षितः &c., उद्बर्हितः &c., उत्थितः &c., उद्गाहितः &c., उत्क्षिप्तः -प्ता -प्तं, उद्गूर्णः -र्णा -र्णं; 'is raised,' उत्थाप्यते.—(Erected, set up) उत्थापितः &c., स्थापितः &c., रोपितः &c., अधिरोपितः &c., अर्द्धीकृतः &c., उद्धृतः -ता -तं.—(Produced) उत्पादितः -ता -तं, उत्पन्नः -न्ना -न्नं, जनितः &c., जातः &c.—(Raised on high) अर्द्धीकृतः &c., उच्चीकृतः &c., कृतोच्चैस्, उच्चैःकृतः &c.; 'having the hands raised,' उच्छ्रितपाणिः -णिः -णि, उत्थितहस्तः -स्ता -स्तं; 'having the arms raised,' उद्बाहुः -हुः -हु, उद्यतबाहुः &c.; 'having the spear raised,' उद्यतशूलः -ला -लं; 'having the weapon raised,' उद्यतायुधः -धा -धं; 'sitting with the feet raised,' प्रौढपादः -दा -दं; 'dust raised by the hoofs,' रजः खुरोद्धूतं; 'the dust is raised by the wind,' वातेन रज उद्धूयते.

RAISER, *s.* उत्थापकः, उत्तोलकः, उन्नायकः, उन्नेता *m.* (तृ), उद्धारकः.

RAISIN, *s.* (Dried grape) यक्षाम्री, शुष्कद्राक्षा, शुष्कमृद्वीका.

RAISING, *s.* उत्थापनं, उत्थानं, अभ्युत्थानं, उत्थितिः *f.*, उत्तोलनं, उच्छ्रयः, समुच्छ्रयः, उच्छ्रायः, समुच्छ्रायः, उच्छ्रितिः *f.*, उत्कर्षः, उन्नतिः, समुन्नतिः *f.*, उन्नयनं; 'of a weapon to strike,' शस्त्रोत्थापनं, शस्त्रोद्यमः.

RAISING, *part.* उत्थापकः -का -कं, उत्थापयन् -यन्ती -यत् (त्), उत्थाप्य indec.; 'raising a dreadful dust,' रजो घोरम् उद्धून्वन् -न्वती &c. or उद्धून्वानः -ना -नं or उद्धूय or समुद्धूय indec.

RÁJAH, RÁJA, *s.* (King) राजा *m.* (न्) *see* KING.

RÁJPOOT, *s.* (Man of the military tribe) राजपुत्रः, *see* MILITARY, *a.*

RAKE, *s.* (Libertine) व्यसनी *m.* (न्), स्त्रीव्यसनी *m.*, लम्पटः, नागरः, धूर्त्तः, विटः, *see* LIBERTINE.—(The tool) तृणसंग्रहणी, घाससंग्रहणी, दन्तयुक्तः शुष्कतृणादिसंग्रहणयोग्यो दण्डः or यष्टिः.

To RAKE, *v. a.* (Gather or clear with a rake) पूर्व्वोक्तयन्त्रेण संग्रह् (c. 9. -गृह्णाति -ग्रहीतुं) or शुध्.—(Collect) संग्रह्, संचि, समानी.

To RAKE, *v. n.* (Lead a dissolute life) लम्पटवद् आचर् (c. 1.-चरति

-रितुं), लाम्पट्यं कृ, व्यभिचर्, भोगासक्तः -क्ता -क्तं भू, विषयासक्त &c. भू.

RAKISH, *a.* व्यसनी -निनी -नि (न्), व्यसनीयः -या -यं, लाम्पटिकः -की -कं, लम्पटस्वभावः -वा -वं, व्यभिचारी &c., छेकः -का -कं. *See* DISSOLUTE, LIBERTINE.

RAKISHNESS, *s.* व्यसनिता, व्यभिचारः, लम्पटता. *See* LIBERTINISM.

To RALLY, *v.a.* (Restore to order troops thrown into confusion) पिच्छलसैन्यान् or विद्रुतसैन्यान् or भग्नव्यूहसैन्यान् पुनर् व्यूहीकृ or व्यूह् (c. 1. -ऊहते -हितुं) or पुनः समूहीकृ or पुनर् व्यूहक्रमेण रच्, पुनः संग्रह्.—(Jest, banter) अवहस्, अपहस्, अवहासभूमिं कृ, अधिक्षिप्, मुखरीकृ.

To RALLY, *v. n.* (Recover order) पुनर् व्यूहीभू or समूहीभू.—(Recover strength) पुनर् बलं लभ् (c. 1. लभते, लब्धुं), समुत्था (c. 1. -तिष्ठति -थातुं, rt. स्था), प्रत्याश्वस् (c. 2. -श्वसिति -तुं), पुनः स्वस्थः -स्था -स्थं भू.

RAM, *s.* (Male sheep) मेषः, उरभ्रः, मेढ्रः, मेण्ढः, मेढ्रः -ढ्रकः, मेठः, अविः *m.*, एडकः, ऊर्णायुः *m.*, उरणः -णकः, रोमशः, लोमशः, वृष्णिः *m.*, भेडः, हुडुः *m.*, सम्फालः, संस्फालः.—(Battering ram), *see* the word.—(The sign aries) मेषः.

To RAM, *v. a.* बलात् or बलेन निविश् (c. 10. -वेशयति -यितुं) or प्रविश्, अतिबलेन निविश्, अतिबलेन प्रणुद् (c. 6. -णुदति -णोत्तुं), अतिबलेन ताडयित्वा निविश् or अन्तः प्रविश् or सम्बाध् (c. 1. -बाधते -धितुं) or सम्पीड् (c. 10. -पीडयति -यितुं).

RÁMA, *s.* The name common to three incarnations of Vishnu, viz. 1. Paraśu Ráma, or Ráma with the axe, the sixth avatár or incarnation of Vishnu. He was a Brahman, the son of the holy sage Jamadagni, and born at the beginning of the second or Treta age, for the purpose of repressing the tyranny, and punishing the violence of the Kshatriya or military tribe. He appears to typefy the class of Brahmans, and their contest with the Kshatriyas. Some of his names are परशुरामः -मकः, परशुधरः, पर्शुरामः, जमदग्निसुतः, जामदग्न्यः. 2. Rámachandra or the moon-like Ráma, the seventh incarnation of Vishnu. He was born into the world as the son of Daśaratha, king of Oude, and great grandson of Raghu, at the close of the second or Treta age, for the purpose of destroying the demons who infested the earth, and especially Rávana, the Daitya sovereign of Ceylon. His names are रामचन्द्रः, रघुनन्दनः, रघूद्वहः, रघुवरः, रघुनाथः, राघवः, रावणारिः *m.*, रावणजित् *m.*, दशास्यजित् *m.*, मखत्राता *m.* (तृ), रामभद्रः. 3. Balaráma, or the strong Ráma, according to some the eighth incarnation of Vishnu. He was born at the end of the Dwápara, or third age, as the seventh son of Vasudeva and Devakí, and therefore elder brother of Krishna, but was transferred from the womb of Devakí to that of Rohiní the other wife of Vasudeva. Hence one of his names सङ्कर्षणः. He is sometimes regarded as an incarnation of the serpent Ananta or Śesha, and hence called, अनन्तः, शेषः. His other names are बलरामः, बलदेवः, बलभद्रः, बलः, बललः, हलायुधः, हलभृत् *m.*, हली *m.* (न्), सीरपाणिः *m.*, कृष्णाग्रजः, अच्युताग्रजः, प्रियमधुः *m.*, मधुप्रियः, मुष्टिकान्तकः, गुप्तचरः, रेवतीरमणः, रेवतीशः. *See* BALARÁMA.

To RAMBLE, *v. n.* इतस्ततो भ्रम् (c. 4. भ्राम्यति, भ्रमितुं) or परिभ्रम् or विहृ (c. 1. -हरति -हर्त्तुं) or पर्यट् (c. 1. -अटति -टितुं), इतस्ततो भ्रमणं कृ or परिभ्रमणं कृ, विहारं कृ.

RAMBLE, *s.* भ्रमणं, परिभ्रमणं, विहारः, विहरणं, पर्यटनं, इतस्ततो विहारः, इतस्ततोगमनं.

RAMBLER, *s.* विहारी *m.* (न्), परिभ्रमकः, भ्रमणकारी *m.* (न्), भ्रमणकृत् *m.*

RAMBLING, *s.* इतस्ततो विहारः or विहरणं or भ्रमणं. *See* RAMBLE.

RAMIFICATION, *s.* (Small branch) उपशाखा, क्षुद्रशाखा, सूक्ष्मशाखा, मूलखण्डः.—(State of having many branches) बहुशाखत्वं, सूक्ष्मशाखाबाहुल्यं.

RAMIFIED, *p. p.* बहुशाखी -खिनी -खि (न्), शाखी &c., सशाखः -खा -खं, सूक्ष्मशाखामयः -यी -यं, उपशाखामयः &c., बहुशाखाविशिष्टः -ष्टा -ष्टं.

To RAMIFY, *v. a.* बहुशाखीकृ, उपशाखारूपेण पृथक्कृ or विभिद्.

To RAMIFY, *v. n.* शाखा (nom. शाखायते), सूक्ष्मशाखारूपेण विस्तॄ in pass. (-स्तीर्य्यते), उपशाखारूपेण भिन्नीभू or विभिद् in pass. or विच्छिद् in pass.

RAMIFYING, *part.* शाखी -खिनी -खि (न्), शाख्यः -ख्या -ख्यं. *See* RAMIFIED.

RAMMER, *s.* मुद्गरः, दीर्घमुद्गरः, घनः, दीर्घघनः, ताडनी.

RAMMISH, *a.* उग्रगन्धः -न्धा -न्धं, तीक्ष्णगन्धः &c., उग्रगन्धिः -न्धिः -न्धि.

RAMMISHNESS, *s.* उग्रगन्धत्वं, तीक्ष्णगन्धत्वं, उग्रत्वं, दौर्गन्ध्यं *m.*

RAMOUS, *a.* शाखी -खिनी -खि (न्), शाख्यः -ख्या -ख्यं, काण्डीरः -रा -रं.

To RAMP, *v. n.* प्लु (c. 1. प्लवते, प्लोतुं), वल्ग्, नृत्, क्रीड्, विस्फुल्.

RAMP, *s.* प्लवः -वनं, प्लुतं, वल्गितं, कम्पः -म्पा, उत्प्लुतं, उत्फालः.

RAMPANCY, *a.* अतिवृद्धिः *f.*, उत्सेकः, उद्रेकः, मर्य्यादातिक्रमः, अपरिमितता, अतिरिक्तता, अतिक्रमः, उत्क्रमः, आधिक्यं.

RAMPANT, *a.* अतिरिक्तः -क्ता -क्तं, उद्रिक्तः &c., उत्सिक्तः &c., मर्य्यादातीतः -ता -तं, अतिक्रान्तमर्य्यादः -दा -दं, उत्क्रान्तमर्य्यादः &c., अतिमर्य्यादः &c., अपरिमितः &c.

RAMPART, *s.* प्राकारः, वप्रः, चयः, धूलिकेदारः, धूलिकुट्टिमं, प्रगण्डी.

RAMROD, *s.* चूर्णसंहननी, चूर्णसम्पीडनी, चूर्णप्रणोदनी, चूर्णप्रणोदकदण्डः, आग्नेयनाडीसम्बद्धो लोहदण्डः स च नाडीमुखनिविष्टो भूत्वा आग्नेयचूर्णगुलिकादि संहतीकरोति.

RANCID, *a.* उग्रगन्धः -न्धा -न्धं, उग्रगन्धिकः -का -कं, उग्ररसः -सा -सं, तीक्ष्णरसः &c., विरसः &c., कुरसः &c., पर्युषितः -ता -तं.

RANCIDNESS, RANCIDITY, *s.* उग्ररसत्वं, तीक्ष्णरसत्वं, विरसता, वैरस्यं, कुरसता.

RANCOR, *s.* अतिद्वेषः, द्रोहबुद्धित्वं, अतिद्रोहः, दीर्घद्वेषः, अतिमात्सर्य्यं, अतिमात्सरता, विषपूर्णता, दंशः, दंशशीलता, अतिदंशः, जिघांसा. *See* MALIGNITY, MALICE.

RANCOROUS, *a.* अतिद्वेषी -षिणी -षि (न्), दीर्घद्वेषी &c., दंशी &c., अतिदंशी, दंशशीलः -ला -लं, द्रोहबुद्धिः -द्धिः -द्धि, अतिद्रोही -हिणी &c., अतिमत्सरी &c., जिघांसुः -सुः -सु, विषहृदयः -या -यं, विषपूर्णः -र्णा -र्णं. *See* MALIGNANT.

RANCOROUSLY, *adv.* अतिद्वेषेण, सद्रोहं, अतिद्रोहेण, सदंशं, सविषं.

RANDOM, *a.* सन्धानहीनः -ना -नं, सन्धानरहितः -ता -तं, अभिसन्धिहीनः &c., अभिसन्धानहीनः &c., आकस्मिकः -की -कं, आगन्तुकः -का -कं, अनियमितः -ता -तं, अनियतः -ता -तं, अनिरूपितः &c., अयन्त्रितः &c., निर्यन्त्रणः -णा -णं, यादृच्छिकः -की -कं, आपतिकः &c., दैवागतः -ता -तं, दैवोपस्थितः &c., अकस्मादुपस्थितः &c., अकस्मादागतः &c., अकस्मादुत्पन्नः -न्ना -न्नं, अकस्मात्कृतः &c., अशृङ्खलः -ला -लं; 'at random,'

अकस्मात्, सन्धानं विना, अभिसन्धानं विना, अनियतं, अयन्त्रितं, निर्यन्त्रणं, यदृच्छया, अशृङ्खलं; to talk at random,' प्रलप् (c. 1. -लपति -पितुं).

RANDY, *a.* उन्मत्तः -त्ता -त्तं, मत्तः &c., उच्छृङ्खलः -ला -लं.

To RANGE, *v. a.* (Arrange, dispose) विन्यस्, विरच्, विधा, संविधा, प्रतिविधा, व्यूह्, व्यूहीकृ, क्रमेण स्था, पंक्तिक्रमेण विन्यस्.

To RANGE, *v. n.* (Wander) भ्रम् (c. 4. भ्राम्यति, भ्रमितुं), परिभ्रम्, भ्रमणं कृ, चर्, पर्यट्, विचर् (c. 1. -चरति -रितुं), विहृ (c. 1. -हरति -हर्त्तुं), गाह् (c. 1. गाहते -हितुं), व्रज्, प्रव्रज्, पर्यटनं कृ.—(Lie in a particular direction, be situated) वृत् (c. 1. वर्त्तते -र्त्तितुं), स्था (c. 1. तिष्ठति, स्थातुं).

RANGE, *s.* (A row, rank) पंक्तिः *f.*, श्रेणिः -णी *f.*, राजिः -जी *f.*, राजिका, आवलिः -ली, पद्धतिः *f.*, वीथिः -थी, ततिः *f.*, आलिः -ली *f.*, पालिः -ली *f.*, माला, विञ्जोली.—(Class, grade) वर्गः, गणः, वर्णः.—(Reach, compass, extent, room) विषयः, गोचरः -रं, परिमाणं, प्रसरः; 'the range of sight,' चक्षुर्विषयः, नयनविषयः; 'of an arrow,' बाणगोचरः -रं, शरायणं, बाणायणं; 'within range of the ear,' कर्णगोचरः -रा -रं; 'the utmost range,' पारः; 'beyond the range,' अविषयः -या -यं, विषयातिक्रान्तः -न्ता -न्तं, विषयातीतः &c., अगम्यः -म्या -म्यं, अपारणीयः -या -यं.—(Kitchen range) पाकोपकरणपंक्तिः *f.*—(Range of mountains) कुलपर्व्वतः, कुलगिरिः *m.*, कुलशैलः; 'range of mountains supposed to encircle the earth,' चक्रवालः, लोकालोकः. *See* the names of the seven ranges under MOUNTAIN.

RANGED, *p. p.* विन्यस्तः -स्ता -स्तं, व्यवस्थापितः &c., व्यूढः -ढा -ढं.

RANGER, *s.* परिभ्रमकः.—(Keeper of a forest) अरण्यरक्षकः -रक्षी *m.* (न्), अरण्यपालः -लकः, अरण्याध्यक्षः.

RANK, (Line, row) पंक्तिः *f.*, श्रेणिः -णी *f.*, राजिः -जी *f.*, राजिका, आवलिः -ली, पद्धतिः *f.*, ततिः *f.*, आलिः -ली *f.*, पालिः -ली *f.*—(Station in life) पदं, पदविः -वी *f.*, आस्पदं, स्थानं, वृत्तिः *f.*—(High station, high rank or dignity) उच्चपदं, परमपदं, उच्चपदता, उच्चपदविः *f.*, प्रतिपत्तिः *f.*, उत्कृष्टपदं, उत्कर्षः, कुलोत्कर्षः, औत्कर्ष्यं, उत्कृष्टता, अभिजातता, आभिजात्यं, आभिजनं, उन्नतिः *f.*, समुन्नतिः *f.*, कुलीनता, कौलीनं, प्रधानता, मान्यता, सेव्यता, मर्य्यादा, मानं; 'man of high rank,' उच्चपदस्थः, उच्चपदभाक् *m.* (ज्), पदभाक् *m.*, प्रतिपत्तिमान् *m.* (त्), अभिजातः, अभिजनवान् *m.* (त्), कुलीनः. *See* HIGH-BORN.—(Class, order) वर्गः, गणः, वर्णः.—(Ranks of the army, line of soldiers) व्यूहः, सैन्यपंक्तिः *f.*, दण्डः; 'breaking the ranks,' व्यूहभङ्गः, व्यूहभेदः.

RANK, *a.* (Luxuriant in growth) अतिवर्धिष्णुः -ष्णुः -ष्णु, अतिवर्धी -र्धिनी -र्धि (न्), अतिवर्धनः -ना -नं, अतिस्फीतः -ता -तं, अतिपीनः -ना -नं.—(Strong to the smell or taste) उग्रगन्धः -न्धा -न्धं, उग्रगन्धिकः -का -कं, उग्ररसः -सा -सं, उग्रः -ग्रा -ग्रं, तीक्ष्णगन्धः &c., तीक्ष्णरसः &c.

To RANK, *v. a.* (Place in a line) पंक्तिक्रमेण स्था in caus. (स्थापयति -यितुं) or विन्यस् or विरच्.—(Place in a particular class or station) वर्णक्रमेण or वर्गक्रमेण विरच् (c. 10. -रचयति -यितुं) or विन्यस्, यथावर्गं or यथावर्णं स्था in caus., विशेषपदस्थं -स्थां कृ, विशेषगणाभ्यन्तरं -रां कृ, विशेषवर्गाभ्यन्तरं -रां कृ.

To RANK, *v. n.* (Be placed or stand in a line) पंक्तिक्रमेण स्था.—(Be placed in a particular class or station) विशेषपदस्थः -स्था -स्थं भू, विशेषगणाभ्यन्तरः -रा -रं भू, विशेषवर्गाभ्यन्तरः -रा -रं भू, विशेषपदयुक्तः -क्ता -क्तं भू, यथावर्गं स्था.

To RANKLE, *v. n.* (Be inflamed, fester) अन्तस् तप् in pass. (तप्यते), अन्तर् दह् (c. 4. दह्यति -ते, दग्धुं), व्रणवत् पक्वः -क्वा -क्वं भू or पूय् (c. 1. पूयते -यितुं) or सपूयः -या -यं भू.—(Become more violent or virulent) उग्रतरः -रा -रं भू, तीक्ष्णतरः -रा -रं भू, रौद्रतरः -रा -रं भू, तिग्मतरः -रा -रं भू, चण्डतरः -रा -रं भू, भृश (nom. भृशायते).

RANKNESS *s.* (Too great luxuriance) अतिवृद्धिः *f.*, अधिकवृद्धिः *f.*, अतिवर्धनं, अत्यन्तवर्धनं, अतिस्फीतिः *f.*, अतिस्फातिः *f.*, अतिपीनता, उत्सेकः, उद्रेकः.—(Of smell or taste) उग्रता, तीक्ष्णता, उग्रगन्धता, तीक्ष्णगन्धता, उग्ररसत्वं, उग्रस्वादः, उग्रवासः.

To RANSACK, *v. a.* (Plunder, pillage), *see* the words.—(Search by turning things over) अस्तव्यस्तीकृत्य अन्विष् (c. 4. -इष्यति -एषितुं) or अनुसन्धा (c. 3. -दधाति -धातुं), अनुसन्धानार्थं or अन्वेषणार्थम् अस्तव्यस्तीकृ.

RANSACKED, *p. p.* लुण्ठितः -ता -तं, अन्वेषणार्थम् अस्तव्यस्तीकृतः -ता -तं.

RANSOM, *s.* परिक्रयणमूल्यं, परिक्रयमूल्यं, त्राणमूल्यं, तारणमूल्यं, निस्तारमूल्यं, उद्धारमूल्यं, निष्कृतिमूल्यं, त्राणं, उद्धारः, मुक्तिः, मोक्षः; 'he gave his life a ransom for many,' बहूनां त्राणाय or बहूनां मोक्षाय स्वप्राणान् ददौ.

To RANSOM. *v. a.* मूल्यं दत्त्वा परिक्री (c. 9. -क्रीणीते -क्रेतुं), सममूल्यकद्रव्यं दत्त्वा परिक्री or त्रै (c. 1. त्रायते -त्रातुं) or परित्रै, मूल्यं दत्त्वा निस्तॄ (c. 10. -तारयति -यितुं) or तॄ or उद्धृ (c. 1. -हरति -हर्त्तुं) or मुच् (c. 6. मुञ्चति, मोक्तुं) or मोक्ष् (c. 10. मोक्षयति -यितुं).

RANSOMED, *p. p.* परिक्रीतः -ता -तं, त्रातः -ता -तं, निस्तारितः -ता -तं.

RANSOMER, *s.* परिक्रेता *m.* (तृ), त्राता *m.* (तृ), निस्तारकः, परिक्रयकृत्.

To RANT, *v. n.* उच्चैःस्वरेण शब्दालङ्कारमयं फल्गुवाक्यं वद् (c. 1. वदति -दितुं), उच्चैःस्वरेण शब्दमात्रमयं वाक्यं वद्, अतिशब्दनवाक्यं वद्, उच्चैःस्वरेण प्रलप्.

RANT, *s.* शब्दमात्रमयं फल्गुवाक्यं or निरर्थकवाक्यं, शब्दमात्रवाक्यं, अलङ्कारमात्रमयम् अतिशब्दनवाक्यं, प्रलापः.

RANTER, *s.* शब्दमात्रवादी *m.* (न्), शब्दमात्रवक्ता *m.* (क्तृ), महाशब्दकवाक्यवादी *m.*, प्रलापी *m.*

To RAP, *v. a.* (Strike with a quick, sharp blow) लघु or लघुप्रहारेण तड् (c. 10. ताडयति -यितुं), लघु प्रहृ (c. 1. -हरति -हर्त्तुं) or आहन् (c. 2. -हन्ति -न्तुं) or अभिहन्.—(Snatch or hurry away) हृ, अपहृ, अभिहृ, ग्रह्, कृष्, समाकृष्.—(Seize the mind, affect with rapture) मनो or चित्तं हृ or अपहृ, हृदयं हृ or ग्रह्, परमहर्षेण मुह् (c. 10. मोहयति -यितुं).

RAP, *s.* लघुप्रहारः, लघ्वाघातः, आघातः, आहतिः *f.*, ताडनं.

RAPACIOUS, *a.* हरणशीलः -ला -लं, अपहरणशीलः &c., अपहारबुद्धिः -द्धिः -द्धि, अपहारप्रवणः -णा -णं, अपहारकः -का -कं, अपहारी -रिणी -रि (न्), ग्रसनशीलः &c., ग्रसनबुद्धिः &c., ग्रहणशीलः -ला -लं, सर्व्वग्राही &c., सर्व्वहारी &c., सर्व्वग्रासी &c., लुब्धः -ब्धा -ब्धं, अतिलुब्धः &c., अतिलोभी &c., लोभी &c., विप्रलुम्पकः -का -कं, हिंसकः &c., साहसिकः -की -कं.

RAPACIOUSLY, *adv.* हरणशीलत्वात्, अपहारबुद्ध्या, अतिलोभेन.

RAPACIOUSNESS, RAPACITY, *s.* हरणशीलता, अपहारशीलत्वं, अपहारबुद्धिः *f.*, अपहारकत्वं, अपहारिता, ग्रहणशीलता, लुब्धता, अतिलोभः, साहसिकत्वं.

RAPE, *s.* बलात्कारेणाभिगमः, बलात्कारसम्भोगः, स्त्रीहरणं, कन्याहरणं, धर्षणं, स्त्रीधर्षणं, बलात्कारधर्षणं, हठधर्षणं, कन्यादूषणं, हठसम्भोगः, साहसं, राक्षसं.

RAPID, *a.* शीघ्रः -घ्रा -घ्रं, त्वरितः -ता -तं, सत्वरः -रा -रं, त्वरान्वितः -ता -तं, द्रुतः &c., क्षिप्रः -प्रा -प्रं, तूर्णः -र्णा -र्णं, वेगवान् -वती -वत् (त्), महावेगः -गा -गं, शीघ्रगः -गा -गं. *See* QUICK, SWIFT.

RAPIDITY, RAPIDNESS, *s.* शीघ्रता, त्वरा, सत्वरता, द्रुतता, शैघ्र्यं, वेगः, महावेगः, क्षिप्रता, तरस् *n.*, तूर्णता. *See* QUICKNESS, VELOCITY.

RAPIDLY, *adv.* शीघ्रं, त्वरितं, सत्वरं, क्षिप्रं, द्रुतं, अशनैस्, महावेगेन, शीघ्र in comp.; 'going rapidly,' शीघ्रगामी -मिनी &c.

RAPIER, *s.* क्षुद्रखड्गः, क्षुद्रकृपाणः, कृपाणः, निस्त्रिंशः.

RAPINE, *s.* लुण्ठनं, लुण्ठा, लुण्टनं, अपहारः -रणं, युद्धेनापहारः -रणं, हरणं, उपद्रवः, विप्लवः, हठः. *See* PILLAGE, PLUNDER.

To RAPINE, *v. a.* लुण्ठ्, अपहृ, उपद्रु. *See To* PILLAGE, PLUNDER.

RAPPER, *s.* ताडयिता *m.* (तृ), ताडकः, प्रहर्त्ता *m.* (र्त्तृ).

RAPT, *a.* हर्षमोहितः -ता -तं, सम्मोहितः &c., परमहृष्टः -ष्टा -ष्टं, परमानन्दितः -ता -तं, हर्षोन्मत्तः -त्ता -त्तं, आनन्दमत्तः &c., मत्तः &c.

RAPTURE, *s.* परमहर्षः, परमानन्दः, अत्यानन्दः, अत्यमहर्षः, हर्षसम्मोहः, आनन्दमोहः, मोहावस्था, आनन्दावेशः, आह्लादावेशः, हर्षावेशः, परमसुखं, ब्रह्मसुखं, ब्रह्मानन्दः, प्रहर्षः, प्रमदः, उन्मदः, मादः, हर्षोन्मत्तता, हर्षोन्मादः, रोमहर्षः, पुलकितत्वं; 'to feel rapture,' अत्यन्तं हृष् or प्रहृष्.

RAPTURED, *a.* हर्षमोहितः -ता -तं. *See* ENRAPTURED, ECSTASIED.

RAPTUROUS, *a.* मादनः -ना -नं, उन्मादनः &c., मोहनः &c., परमानन्ददः -दा -दं, परमानन्दकरः -रा -रं, परमहर्षदः &c., सपुलकः -का -कं. *See* ECSTATIC.

RAPTUROUSLY, *adv.* सपरमानन्दं, परमहर्षेण, परमाह्लादेन, समादं.

RARE, *a* (Not frequent, scarce) विरलः -ला -लं, विरलागतः -ता -तं, दुर्लभः -भा -भं, दुर्लभ्यः -भ्या -भ्यं, दुष्प्रापः -पा -पं, दुष्प्राप्यः -प्या -प्यं, अलभ्यः -भ्या -भ्यं, अप्राप्यः &c., असाधारणः -णा -णं, असामान्यः -न्या -न्यं, अप्रसिद्धः -द्धा -द्धं, क्वाचित्कः -त्की -त्कं, कादाचित्कः &c., कार्हिचित्कः &c., चिरचेष्टितः -ता -तं.—(Unusually excellent) परमोत्कृष्टः -ष्टा -ष्टं, अनुत्कृष्टः &c., सर्वोत्कृष्टः &c., परमः -मा -मं, उत्तमः &c., अनुत्तमः &c., अद्भुतः -ता -तं, अतुल्यः -ल्या -ल्यं, अपूर्व्वः -र्व्वा -र्व्वं, सौन्दर्य्यविरलः -ला -लं.—(Thin, not dense) सूक्ष्मः -क्ष्मा -क्ष्मं, अघनः -ना -नं.

RAREFACTION, *s.* तापप्रयुक्तसूक्ष्मता -त्वं, तापजनितसूक्ष्मता, सूक्ष्मता, सौक्ष्म्यं. —(The act) सूक्ष्मीकरणं.

RAREFIED, *p. p.* सूक्ष्मः -क्ष्मा -क्ष्मं, सूक्ष्मीभूतः -ता -तं, सूक्ष्मीकृतः &c.

To RAREFY, *v. a.* सूक्ष्मीकृ, सूक्ष्मं -क्ष्मां कृ, सूक्ष्मतां कृ or जन्.

To RAREFY, *v. n.* सूक्ष्मीभू, सूक्ष्मः -क्ष्मा -क्ष्मं भू, सूक्ष्मतरः -रा -रं भू.

RARELY, *adv.* विरलं, वैरल्येन, क्वचित्, कदाचित्, कर्हिचित्, यथाकथाच, कथमपि, दुर् in comp.; as, 'rarely to be met with,' दुर्लभः -भा -भं, दुष्प्रापः -पा -पं.

RARENESS, *s.* (Infrequency, scarceness) विरलता -त्वं, वैरल्यं, दौर्लभ्यं, दुर्लभता, दुर्लभ्यता, अप्रसिद्धता -त्वं, दुष्प्रापत्वं, असामान्यता, असाधारणता, क्वाचित्कता -त्वं.—(Unusual excellence) अनुत्कृष्टता, परमोत्कृष्टता, सर्वोत्कृष्टता, उत्तमता, अतुल्यता, अपूर्व्वता.—(Thinness) सूक्ष्मता, सौक्ष्म्यं.

RARITY, *s.* (Scarceness), *see* the last.—(Rare thing) दुर्लभवस्तु *n.*, दुर्लभद्रव्यं, उत्कृष्टद्रव्यं, कौतुकं, कौतूहलं.

RASCAL, *s.* धूर्त्तः, दुर्जनः, दुरात्मा *m.* (न्), दुर्वृत्तः, कृष्णकर्म्मा *m.* (न्), खलः, अधमवृत्तिः *m.*, दुष्टजनः, पापात्मा *m.*, जघन्यवृत्तिः *m.*, नीचवृत्तिः *m.*, अपकृष्टवृत्तिः, पापिष्ठः, शठः, दुष्कर्म्मा *m.*

RASCALITY, *s.* धूर्त्तता, दुर्जनता -त्वं, दौर्जन्यं, दौरात्म्यं, दुरात्मत्वं, दुर्वृत्तत्वं, खलता, दुष्टता, पापिष्ठता -त्वं, शठता, जघन्यता, अपकृष्टता, अधमवृत्तित्वं, कैतवं, वञ्चनं.

RASCALLY, *a.* दुर्वृत्तः -त्ता -त्तं, पापिष्ठः -ष्ठा -ष्ठं, अधमवृत्तिः -त्तिः -त्ति, जघन्यवृत्तिः &c., शठः -ठा -ठं, कापटिकः -की -कं, दुष्टः -ष्टा -ष्टं.

To RASE, *v. a.* (Graze) घृष् (c. 1. घर्षति -र्षितुं). *See To* RAZE.

RASH, *a.* अविमृश्यकारी -रिणी -रि (न्), असमीक्ष्यकारी &c., अविचार्य्यकारी &c., साहसी &c., साहसिकः -की -कं, आत्ययः -त्या -त्यं, गमकारी &c., प्रमत्तः -त्ता -त्तं, अपरिणामदर्शी &c., अदूरदर्शी &c., असावधानः -ना -नं, अविचारी &c.—(Of measures) अविचार्य्य कृतः -ता -तं, अविमृश्य कृतः &c., अविचारपूर्व्वः -र्व्वा -र्व्वं, असमीक्षापूर्व्वः &c., अनवेक्षापूर्व्वः &c.

RASH, *s.* (Eruption) दद्रुः *m.*, खर्ज्जूः *f.*, ददर्दः, स्फोटोत्पत्तिः *f.*, विस्फोटः, वरटी, रक्तवरटी, रक्तस्फोटोत्पत्तिः *f.*, रक्तस्फोटः.

RASHER, *s.* (Of bacon) वल्लूरखण्डः, वल्लूरछेदः, शूकरमांसखण्डः.

RASHLY, *adv.* अविचार्य्य, असमीक्ष्य, अविमृश्य, सहसा, अनवेक्षया, अविचारेण, अविचारपूर्व्वं, असमीक्षापूर्व्वं, अनवेक्षापूर्व्वं, दर्पात्, दर्पेण.

RASHNESS, *s.* अविमृश्यकारिता -त्वं, असमीक्ष्यकारिता -त्वं, अविचार्य्यकारिता, गमकारित्वं, साहसं, साहसिकत्वं, विषमसाहसं, दुःसाहसं, अविचारः, अविचारिता, अनवेक्षा, असमीक्षा, अविवेकः, असावधानता, अपरिणामदर्शनं, मदः, दर्पः; 'of youth,' यौवनदर्पः.

RASP, *s.* घर्षणी, घर्षणयन्त्रं, निर्घर्षणकः, घर्षकः, आघट्टकः.

To RASP, *v. a.* पूर्व्वोक्तयन्त्रेण घृष् (c. 1. घर्षति -र्षितुं).

RASPBERRY, *s.* कण्टकगुल्मफलं, कण्टकस्तम्बफलं.

RASPED, *p. p.* पूर्व्वोक्तयन्त्रेण घर्षितः -ता -तं, आघर्षितः &c.

RASURE, *s.* (Scraping) घर्षणं, उल्लेखनं, तक्षणं. *See* ERASURE.

RAT, *s.* उन्दुरुः *m.*, उन्दरुः *m.*, उन्दरः, इन्दुरः, इन्दुरुः *m.*, मूषिकः -का, मुषकः -का, मूषी *m.*, (न्), मूषीकः -का, आखुः *m.*, बिलेशयः, वज्रदन्तः, तुदुमः, धान्यारिः *m.*, महिन्धकः, खनकः; 'swarm of rats,' आखूत्थः; 'rat-hole,' मूषिकविवरं, आखुविलं, मूषिकोत्करः.

To RAT, *v. n.* (Desert one's party and go over to the opposite) स्वपक्षं त्यक्त्वा अन्यपक्षम् or विपरीतपक्षम् आश्रि (c. 1. -श्रयति -यितुं).

RATABLE, *a.* शुल्कयोग्यः -ग्या -ग्यं, करयोग्यः &c., शुल्कस्थानं.

RATAN, *s.* वेत्रसः, कीचकः, वेणुः *m.*, वेत्रः -त्रं, वंशः, वानीरः, वञ्जुलः, भेदी *m.* (न्) छिद्रिकः.

RAT-CATCHER, *s.* मूषिकघाती *m.* (न्), मूषिकग्राही *m.*, आखुघातः -तकः.

RATE, *s.* (Price) मूल्यं, अर्घः.—(Degree of price or value) अर्घबलाबलं, मूल्यबलाबलं, मूल्यप्रमाणं, अर्घपरिमाणं, अर्घप्रमाणं; 'market rate,' आपणिकः.—(Proportion, degree) प्रमाणं, परिमाणं, मानं, मितिः *f.*, परिमितिः *f.*; 'at the rate of,' प्रमाणेन -णतस्.—(Degree of velocity) वेगः, गतिः *f.*, गतिप्रमाणं, गतिमानं, गतिमितिः *f.*; 'rate of the velocity of light,' प्रकाशकिरणगतिमितिः *f.*; 'at a quick rate,' द्रुतगत्या, लघुगत्या, द्रुतपदं.—(Settled allowance) निरूपितमूल्यं, नियतमूल्यं, परिमितमूल्यं.—(Tax, assessed sum) शुल्कः -ल्कं, करः, देयं, ग्राह्यं.—(At any rate) तावत्.

To RATE, *v. a.* (Set a value on, fix the value) मूल्यं निरूप् (c. 10. -रूपयति -यितुं), अर्घं निरूप्, अर्घबलाबलं निरूप् or निर्णी, अर्घपरिमाणं निरूप्, मूल्यप्रमाणं निरूप्, द्रव्यादिमूल्यं निरूप् or ख्या in caus., अर्घं संख्या in caus. (-ख्यापयति -यितुं), अर्घसंख्यापनं कृ, मूल्यनिर्णयं कृ, मूल्यनिरूपणं कृ.—(Fix the magnitude or proportion) प्रमाणं or परिमाणं निरूप् or निर्णी, प्रमाणनिरूपणं कृ, प्रमाणनिर्णयं कृ. —(Chide, scold) निन्द् (c. 1. निन्दति -न्दितुं), उपालभ् (c. 1. -लभते -लब्धुं) भर्त्स्.

RATED, *p. p.* निरूपितमूल्यः -ल्या -ल्यं, निर्णीतमूल्यः &c., संख्यातः -ता -तं,

संख्यापितः &c., परिसंख्यातः &c.—(Chid) निन्दितः -ता -तं, उपालब्धः -ब्धा -ब्धं.

RATHER, *adv.* (Preferably) वरं usually followed by न च or न पुनर् as 'rather death than poverty,' वरं मृत्युर् न च दारिद्र्यं. The root शिष् with वि may be used to express the sense of 'rather,' as 'rather death than dishonour,' अपमानात् प्राणत्यागो विशिष्यते or the sense may be expressed by some other construction, as 'I would rather that the sons of Dhritaráshtra should kill me in the battle,' यदि मां धार्त्तराष्ट्रा रणे हन्युस् तन् मे क्षेमतरं भवेत्. *See* PREFERABLE, PREFERABLY.—(Somewhat, a little) ईषत्, किञ्चित्, किमपि; 'rather less,' ईषदूनः -ना -नं, किञ्चिदूनः -ना -नं.

RATI, *s.* (The wife of Kámadeva the god of love) रतिः *f.*, कामपत्नी, कामप्रिया, कामकला, स्मरप्रिया, कामिः *f.*, रागलता, प्रीतिः *f.*, रेवा, मायावती, केलिकिला.

RATIFICATION, *s.* सत्याकृतिः *f.*, सत्याकरणं, सत्यापनं, सत्यङ्कारः, सत्यकरणं, दृढीकरणं, स्थिरीकरणं, संस्तम्भः, निश्चयकरणं, निश्चितकरणं.

RATIFIED, *p. p.* सत्याकृतः -ता -तं, दृढीकृतः -ता -तं, स्थिरीकृतः &c.

RATIFIER, *s.* सत्यापकः, सत्यकारी *m.* (न्), सत्यङ्कारी *m.*, दृढकारी *m.*, स्थिरकारी *m.*, निश्चयकारी *m.*, संस्तम्भकारी *m.*

To RATIFY, *v. a.* सत्याकृ, सत्यं -त्यां कृ, सत्य (nom. in caus. सत्यापयति -यितुं), दृढीकृ, स्थिरीकृ, दृढ (nom. दृढयति -यितुं), निश्चयं कृ, संस्तम्भ् (c. 5. -स्तभ्नोति -स्तम्भितुं, c. 10. -स्तम्भयति -यितुं).

RATING, *s.* (Chiding) निन्दा, भर्त्सनं, निर्भर्त्सनं, उपालम्भः.

RATIO, *s.* प्रमाणं, मानं, परिमाणं, क्रमः. *See* PROPORTION.

To RATIOCINATE, *v. n.* विचारं कृ, विचर् (c. 10. -चारयति -यितुं), वितर्कं कृ.

RATIOCINATION. *s.* विचारः -रणं, वितर्कः -र्कणं, तर्कविद्या, तर्कज्ञानं.

RATION, *s.* आहारभागः, आहारांशः, निरूपिताहारांशः.

RATIONAL, *a.* (Having the faculty of reasoning) ज्ञानशक्तिकः -का -कं, ज्ञानशक्तिसम्पन्नः -न्ना -न्नं, चिच्छक्तिकः &c., सचेतनः -ना -नं, सचेताः -ताः -तः (स्), बुद्धिजीवी -विनी -वि (न्), तर्कशक्तिकः &c., तर्कशक्तिसम्पन्नः -न्ना -न्नं, सज्ञानः -ना -नं, बुद्धिमान् -मती -मत् (त्), तर्कज्ञः -ज्ञा -ज्ञं.—(Agreeable to reason) युक्तः -क्ता -क्तं, उपयुक्तः &c., यथायुक्तः &c., यथायोग्यः -ग्या -ग्यं, यथोचितः -ता -तं, न्याय्यः -य्या -य्यं, युक्तिसिद्धः -द्धा -द्धं, न्यायसिद्धः &c., न्यायानुसारी -रिणी &c., यथार्थः -र्था -र्थं, युक्तिमान् &c., सयुक्तिकः -का -कं, उपपत्तिमान् &c., उपपन्नः -न्ना -न्नं, तर्कविद्यानुसारी &c.

RATIONALE, *s.* (Detailed account of principles) उपपत्तिः *f.*

RATIONALISM. *s.* हेतुवादः, कारणवादः, हेतुदर्शनं, हैतुकत्वं.

RATIONALIST, *s.* हेतुवादी *m.* (न्), कारणवादी *m.*, हेतुदर्शी, हैतुकः.

RATIONALITY, RATIONALNESS, *s.* (Power of reasoning) ज्ञानशक्तिः *f.*, चिच्छक्तिः *f.*, तर्कशक्तिः *f.*—(Reasonableness) युक्तता, युक्तिः *f.*, उपयुक्तता, युक्तिसिद्धता, न्यायसिद्धता.

RATIONALLY, *adv.* युक्तं, यथायुक्तं, न्यायतस्, न्यायानुसारेण, तर्कानुसारेण -तस्, उपपन्नं, यथोचितं, युक्तितस्, यथार्थं, तर्कविद्यानुसारेण.

To RATTLE, *v. n.* क्वण् (c. 1. क्वणति -णितुं), शिञ्ज् (c. 2. शिङ्क्ते, c. 1. शिञ्जते -ञ्जितुं), विशिञ्ज्, ध्वन् (c. 1. ध्वनति -नितुं), स्तन् (c. 1. स्तनति -नितुं), स्वन् (c. 1. स्वनति -नितुं), विरु (c. 2. -रौति -रवितुं), झणझणा (nom. झणझणायते), झम्झम (nom. झम्झमायते), झम्झमं कृ, झम्झा (nom. झम्झायते), क्वणितं कृ, शिञ्जितं कृ, झणझणशब्दं कृ.—(Utter words in a clattering manner) जल्प्, चटचटशब्दं कृ,

चटचट (nom. चटचटायते), चटचट.

To RATTLE, *v. a.* ध्वन् in caus. (ध्वनयति, ध्वानयति -यितुं), क्वण् in caus., स्वन् in caus., स्तन् in caus., शिञ्ज् in caus.

RATTLE, *s.* (Rattling nosse) क्वणितं, क्वणनं, स्तनितं, स्तननं, ध्वनिः *m.*, ध्वनितं, शिञ्जितं, झम्झमं, झम्झा, झनत्कारः, झणझणशब्दः.—(Clattering talk) जल्पनं, जल्पितं, चटचटशब्दः.—(Instrument for making a rattling sound) शिञ्जिनी, क्वणनी, झम्झनी.

RATTLING, *s.* क्वणितं, क्वणनं, झम्झनं; 'of thunder,' रसितं, स्तनितं, गर्जितं, मेघनिर्घोषः. *See* RATTLE.

RATTLING, *part.* क्वणन् -णन्ती -णत् (त्), क्वणितः -ता -तं, झम्झनकारी -रिणी -रि (न्), शिञ्जी -ञ्जिनी -ञ्जि (न्), ध्वनन् &c., स्वनन् &c.

To RAVAGE, *v. a.* उपप्लु (c. 1. -प्लवते -प्लोतुं), उपद्रु (c. 1. -द्रवति -द्रोतुं), बाध् (c. 1. बाधते- धितुं), प्रबाध्, परिबाध्, अवमृद् (c. 1. -मर्दति -र्दितुं), विप्लवं कृ, उपप्लवं कृ, उपद्रवं कृ, अवमर्दं कृ.

RAVAGE, *s.* उपप्लवः, विप्लवः, उपद्रवः, अवमर्दः -र्दनं, उपमर्दः, बाधा -धनं, प्रबाधा, उत्पातः, उच्छेदः, विनाशः.

RAVAGED, *p. p.* उपद्रुतः -ता -तं, विप्लुतः &c., उपप्लुतः &c., अवमर्दितः &c., प्रबाधितः &c., विनाशितः &c., उच्छिन्नः -न्ना -न्नं.

RAVAGER, *s.* उपद्रवी *m.* (न्), विप्लवकारी *m.* (न्), प्रबाधकः, अवमर्दकः.

RÁVANA, *s.* (The Daitya sovereign of Ceylon, fabled as having ten faces. He was killed by Rámachandra) रावणः, लङ्कापतिः *m.*, लङ्केशः, दशाननः, दशास्यः, दशमुखः, दशग्रीवः, दशकण्ठः.

To RAVE, *v. n.* (Be delirious, talk incoherently) चित्तविभ्रमात् or भ्रान्तचित्तत्वात् प्रलापं कृ, चित्तविप्लवात् प्रलप् (c. 1. -लपति -पितुं), चैतन्यनाशाद् जल्प् (c. 1. जल्पति -ल्पितुं) or जल्पनं कृ.—(Wander in mind) भ्रान्तचित्तः -त्ता -त्तं भू, चैतन्यरहितः -ता -तं भू, नष्टचेतनः -ना -नं भू, बुद्धिभ्रष्टः -ष्टा -ष्टं भू, उन्मद् (c. 4. -माद्यति -मदितुं), प्रमद्.

To RAVEL, *v. a.* (Untwist) उद्ग्रन्थ् (c. 9. -ग्रथ्नाति, c. 1. -ग्रन्थति -न्थितुं), समुद्ग्रन्थ्, तन्तोद्ग्रन्थनं कृ, तन्तून्मुन्थनं कृ, विश्लिष् in caus.—(Entangle, entwist) ग्रन्थ्, ग्रन्थिलीकृ, आकुञ्च्, संश्लिष्टीकृ, व्यावृत् in caus.

RAVELED, *p. p.* (Untwisted) उद्ग्रथितः -ता -तं, समुद्ग्रथितः &c., उद्ग्रन्थितः &c., विश्लिष्टः -ष्टा -ष्टं.—(Twisted) ग्रथितः &c., आकुञ्चितः &c., संश्लिष्टः -ष्टा -ष्टं.

RAVELIN, *s.* दुर्गबहिःस्थितः सेतुद्वययुक्तः परिकूटविशेषः.

RAVELINGS, *s. pl.* उद्ग्रथिततन्तवः *m. pl.*, विश्लिष्टतन्तवः, उद्ग्रथिततन्तूनि *n. pl.*

RAVEN, *s.* द्रोणकाकः, काकोलः, काकालः, दग्धकाकः, पर्वतकाकः, अरण्यवायसः, वनाश्रयः, क्रूररावी *m.* (न्), पललप्रियः, महाप्राणः, दरा -री, काकपक्षी *m.* (न्).

To RAVEN, *v. a.* and *n.* अतिगृध्नत्वेन भक्ष् (c. 10. भक्षयति -यितुं), अतिलोभेन आमिषं ग्रस् (c. 1. ग्रसते -सितुं), गृध् (c. 4. गृध्यति, गर्धितुं), घस्मरः -रा -रं भू, हिंसनशीलः -ला -लं भू.

RAVENOUS, *a.* अतिघस्मरः -रा -रं, अतिबुभुक्षुः -क्षुः -क्षु, अतिक्षुधितः -ता -तं, क्षुधापीडितः &c., क्षुधातुरः -रा -रं, आमिषलोभी -भिनी -भि (न्), अतिभक्षकः -का -कं, ग्रसनशीलः -ला -लं, हरणशीलः &c., हिंसनशीलः -ला -लं. *See* HUNGRY.

RAVENOUSLY, *adv.* अतिक्षुधितवत्, अतिघस्मरवत्, अतिबुभुक्षया.

RAVENOUSNESS, *s.* अतिबुभुक्षा, अतिघस्मरत्वं, अतिभक्षकत्वं, अतिक्षुधा.

RAVER, *s.* चित्तविभ्रमात् प्रलापी *m.* (न्), भ्रान्तचित्तत्वात् प्रलापी *m.*

RAVÍ, *s.* (River in the Panjáb) ऐरावती.

RAVINE, *s.* दरा -री, दरीभूः *f.*, कन्दरः -री, द्रोणी, निम्नभूमिः *f.*

RAVING, *s.* चित्तविभ्रमप्रयुक्तः प्रलापः or जल्पः -ल्पनं, चित्तविभ्रमः, चित्तविप्लवः, चैतन्यनाशः, ज्ञानभ्रान्तिः *f.*—(The disease) प्रलापवायुः *m.*, प्रलापवातः.

To ravish, *v. a.* (Have carnal knowledge of by force) बलात्कारेण अभिगम् (c. 1. -गच्छति -गन्तुं) or सम्भोगं कृ, धृष् (c. 10. धर्षयति -यितुं), प्रधृष्, बलात्कारेण कन्यां दुष् (c. 10. दूषयति -यितुं) or हृ (c. 1. हरति, हर्त्तुं) or अपहृ, परामृश् (c. 6. -मृशति -मष्टुं), प्रमथ् in caus. (-माथयति -यितुं), बलात्कारसम्भोगं कृ, हठधर्षणं कृ, हठसम्भोगं कृ, धर्षणं कृ, हठधर्षणं कृ.—(Seize, carry away by force) हृ, अपहृ, व्यपहृ.—(Enrapture) मनो or चित्तं हृ or परमहर्षेण मुह् (c. 10. मोहयति -यितुं).

Ravished, *p. p.* धर्षितः -ता -तं, हठधर्षितः &c., बलात्कारेण दूषितः &c., बलात्कारेणाभिगतः &c., प्रमाथितः &c., हृतः &c., अपहृतः &c.—(Enraptured), *see* the word.

Ravisher, *s.* स्त्रीहर्त्ता *m.* (र्त्तृ), स्त्रीहारी *m.* (न्), कन्याहर्त्ता *m.*, धर्षकः, हठधर्षकः, हठदूषकः, बलात्कारदूषकः, कन्यादूषकः, स्त्रीप्रमाथी *m.*, प्रमाथी *m.*, हर्त्ता *m.*, अभिहर्त्ता *m.*, अपहारी *m.*, रतहिण्डकः.

Ravishing, *s.* स्त्रीहरणं, स्त्रीधर्षणं, बलात्कारेणाभिगमः. *See* Rape.

Ravishing, *part.* or *a.* चित्तहारी -रिणी -रि (न्), चित्तापहारी &c., मनोहरः -रा -रं, चित्तमोहनः -ना -नं, चित्तमोही &c.

Ravishment, *s.* (Of a woman) स्त्रीहरणं, कन्याहरणं, धर्षणं, बलात्कारेणाभिगमनं.—(Of the senses) चित्तहरणं, चित्तापहरणं, मनोहरणं, चित्तमोहः -हनं, *see* Enravishment, Rapture.

Raw, *a.* (Undressed, uncooked) आमः -मा -मं, अपक्वः -क्वा -क्वं, असिद्धः -द्धा -द्धं, असंस्कृतः -ता -तं, अनुपस्कृतः &c.; 'half-dressed, nearly raw,' आपक्वः -क्वा -क्वं, यातयामः -मा -मं.—(Unripe, crude) अपक्वः -क्वा -क्वं, अपरिपक्वः &c., अपरिणतः -ता -तं, कलः -ला -लं.—(Inexperienced) अपक्वः &c., अविपक्वबुद्धिः -द्धिः -द्धि, अपरिपक्वबुद्धिः &c., *see* the word.—(Not covered with skin) चर्म्मरहितः -ता -तं, विगतचर्म्मा -र्म्मा -र्म्म (न्), विचर्म्मा &c., निश्चर्म्मा &c., अचर्म्मा &c., त्वग्रहितः &c.—(Damp and cold) आर्द्रशीतलः -ला -लं, आर्द्रशिशिरः -रा -रं.—(Raw flesh) आममांसं, क्रव्यं; 'smell of it,' विस्रं; 'eater of it,' आममांसादः, क्रव्यादः, *see* Cannibal.—(Raw fruit) आमफलं, शलाटुः -टुः -टु.

Raw-boned, *a.* त्वगस्थिमात्रभूतः -ता -तं, केवलास्थिमयः -यी -यं.

Rawness, *s.* (State of being uncooked or unripe) आमता, अपक्वता, अपक्तिः *f.*, अपाकः, अपरिपाकः, अपरिपक्वता, असिद्धता, असंस्कृतत्वं, अनुपस्कृतत्वं, अपरिणतत्वं, अपरिणतिः *f.*, अपरिणामः, असिद्धिः *f.*, कलता.—(Inexperience) अपाकः, अपरिपाकः, अपक्वता, अपक्वबुद्धित्वं, अविपक्वबुद्धित्वं.—(Dampness and coldness) आर्द्रशीतता, आर्द्रशीतलता.—(Of smell) विस्रता.

Ray, *s.* (Of light) किरणः, रश्मिः *m.*, मरीचिः *m. f.*, करः, अंशुः *m.*, अभीशुः *m.*, अभीषुः *m.*, मयूखः, गभस्तिः *m. f.*, दीधितिः *m.*, अर्कत्विट् *f.* (ष्) पादः, उस्रः, रुचिः *f.*, त्विषिः *m.*, विभा, अर्चिस् *f.*, भानुः *m.*, शिपिः *m.*, धृष्णिः *m.*, पृश्निः *f.*, वीचिः *f.*, घृणिः *m.*, उपधृतिः *f.*, पृश्निः *f.*, स्योनः, स्यूमः; 'ray of the sun,' सूर्य्यरश्मिः *m.*, सूर्य्यकरः; 'of the meridian sun,' खर्कराटः; 'of the moon,' चन्द्रपादः, शशिपादः, शशिकरः, शशिमयूखः, सोमांशुः *m.*; 'pencil or stream of rays,' करजालं, अंशुजालं.

Rayless, *a.* किरणहीनः -ना -नं, रश्मिहीनः &c., निस्तेजाः -जाः -जः (स्).

To raze, *v. a.* (Demolish) उच्छिद् (c. 7. -छिनत्ति -छेत्तुं), उद्धृ, संहृ, नश् or विनश् in caus., ध्वंस् or विध्वंस् in caus., अधःपत् or निपत् in caus., लुप्, विलुप्, उन्मूल्. *See* Erase.

Razed, *p. p.* उच्छिन्नः -न्ना -न्नं, उन्मूलितः -ता -तं, विनाशितः &c.

Razor, *s.* क्षुरः, खुरः, क्षौरी, क्षौरयन्त्रं, क्षौरिकयन्त्रं, वृद्धिपत्रं; 'the edge of a razor,' क्षुरधारा; 'sharp as a razor,' क्षुरधाराभः -भा -भं.

Razor-case, *s.* क्षुरभाण्डं, खुरभाण्डं, क्षुराधारः, क्षुरालिकः.

Razor-strop, *s.* क्षुरतेजनी, खुरतेजनी, क्षुरतेजनचर्म्म *n.* (न्).

Razure, *s.* उच्छेदः -दनं, विनाशः -शनं, व्यामर्षः -र्षणं, लोपः.

Re. This prefix is expressed in Sanskrit by पुनर् or प्रति, by the former when 're' signifies again, as in the verbs, 're-absorb,' 're-appear;' by the latter when it signifies back, as in the verbs, 're-demand,' 'repay.' In cases where the word formed with 're' is not given in this Dictionary, the student must take the simple verb or noun, and use the above prefixes.

To reach, *v. a.* (Arrive at, attain to) प्राप् (c. 5. -आप्नोति -आप्तुं), सम्प्राप्, अवाप्, अनुसम्प्राप्, उपसम्प्राप्, आप्, आगम् (c. 1. -गच्छति -गन्तुं), अभिगम्, अधिगम्, उपगम्, गम्, आया (c. 2. -याति -तुं), अभिया, समाया, उपाया, उपस्था (c. 1. -तिष्ठति -स्थातुं), आसद् (c. 10. -सादयति -यितुं), इ (c. 2. एति -तुं), अभी, ऋ (c. 1. ऋच्छति, अर्त्तुं), आपद्, प्रतिपद्, अभिपद्, अश् (c. 5. अश्नुते, अशितुं), उपाश्, समश्, स्पृश्, आविश्.—(Extend to) व्याप्, *see* the next.—(Reach out, stretch out) प्रसृ in caus., प्रग्रह्, दा.

To reach, *v. n.* (Extend, stretch unto) व्याप् (c. 5. -आप्नोति -आप्तुं), वितन् in pass., (-तन्यते), प्रसृ (c. 1. -सरति -सर्त्तुं), गम् (c. 1. गच्छति, गन्तुं) आगम्, या (c. 2. याति -तुं), आया, विस्तृ in pass., (-स्तीर्य्यते) or expressed by पर्य्यन्त or प्रमाण or परिमाण in comp. as 'a staff that reaches to the forehead,' ललाटपर्य्यन्तो दण्डः or ललाटपर्य्यन्तपरिमाणो दण्डः; 'How far does the wall reach?' किम्पर्य्यन्तः or किम्प्रमाणः or किम्परिमाणः स प्राकारः; 'it reaches from the mountain to the sea,' पर्व्वतादारभ्य समुद्रपर्य्यन्तं विस्तीर्य्यते.—(Be received) प्राप् in pass., (-आप्यते) प्राप्तः -प्ता -प्तं भू.

Reach, *s.* (Extend, compass, range) पर्य्यन्तः -न्तं, प्रमाणं, परिमाणं, विषयः, प्रसरः, गोचरः -रं; 'the utmost reach,' पारः; 'the reach of a man,' पौरुषं, पुरुषविषयः; 'of the eye,' चक्षुर्विषयः; 'of an arrow,' बाणगोचरः -रं; 'beyond the reach,' अविषयः -या -यं, विषयातिक्रान्तः -न्ता -न्तं, विषयातीतः -ता -तं, अगम्यः -म्या -म्यं, अतीतः &c., अतिगः -गा -गं, अपारणीयः -या -यं, अति prefixed; 'beyond the reach of the wise,' धीमताम् अपि अविषयः -या -यं; 'beyond the reach of the understanding,' बुद्ध्यगम्यः -म्या -म्यं, बुद्ध्यग्राह्यः -ह्या -ह्यं, बुद्ध्यतीतः -ता -तं, बोधातीतः &c.; 'beyond the reach of mortals,' अतिमानुषः -षा -षं, अतिमर्त्यः -र्त्या -र्त्यं, जनातिगः -गा -गं; 'within the reach,' विषय in comp., गम्यः -म्या -म्यं, ग्राह्यः &c.; 'within the reach of the understanding,' बुद्धिगम्यः -म्या -म्यं; 'within reach of the hand,' हस्तग्राह्यः &c., हस्तस्पर्शनीयः -या -यं, हस्तप्राप्यः &c.

Reached, *p. p.* (Attained) प्राप्तः -प्ता -प्तं, अनुप्राप्तः &c., आगतः -ता -तं, अधिगतः &c., आसादितः &c., आपन्नः -न्ना -न्नं, प्रपन्नः &c.; 'having reached,' प्राप्य, आसाद्य.—(Stretched forth) प्रसारितः -ता -तं, उच्छ्रितः &c., दत्तः -त्ता -त्तं.

Reaching, *part.* गामी -मिनी -मि (न्), गः गा गं in comp.; as, 'reaching beyond,' अतिगः -गा -गं, अतीतः -ता -तं or expressed by पर्य्यन्त in comp. *See* under *To* reach, *v. n.*

To re-act, *v. n.* प्रतिकृ, प्रतिहन् (c. 2. -हन्ति -न्तुं), प्रत्याहन्, प्रतिकारं

कृ, प्रतिकृतिं कृ, प्रतिक्रियां कृ, प्रतीकारं कृ, प्रतिघातं कृ, प्रत्याघातं कृ.

Re-acting, re-active, *part.* or *a.* प्रतिकारकः -का -कं, प्रतीकारकः &c., प्रतिकारी -रिणी -रि (न्), प्रतिघातकः -का -कं, प्रत्याघातकः &c.

Re-action, *s.* प्रतिक्रिया, प्रतिकृतिः *f.*, प्रतिकारः, प्रतीकारः, प्रतिघातः, प्रत्याघातः, कर्म्मान्तरं; 'action and reaction,' आघातप्रत्याघातौ *m. du.*

To read, *v. a.* (Peruse) पठ् (c. 1. पठति -ठितुं), सम्पठ्, अधी (c. 2. अधीते, अध्येतुं, rt. इ), अधिगम् (c. 1. -गच्छति -गन्तुं), अधिगा used only in the 3d pret. átm. (अध्यगीष्ट), अध्ययनं कृ, पठनं कृ.—(Read out or aloud) वच् in caus. (वाचयति -यितुं), अनुवच्, श्रु in caus. (श्रावयति -यितुं), पठ्, सम्पठ्; 'he reads the letter,' पत्रं वाचयति.—(Read to one's self) स्वाध्यायं कृ.—(Read through) पारम् अधी or अधिगम्, पारायणं कृ, साकल्येन पठनं कृ or अध्ययनं कृ; 'one who reads through,' पारायणिकः, पारायणी *m.* (न्); 'one who has read through the Vedas,' वेदपारगतः; 'easy to be read,' सुपठनीयः -या -यं, सुवाच्यः -च्या -च्यं.

To read, *v. n.* (Be studious, practise reading) अध्ययनं कृ, पठनं कृ, अभ्यस् (c. 4. -अस्यति -सितुं), अभ्यासं कृ, विद्याभ्यासं कृ.

Read, *p.p.* or *a.* अधीतः -ता -तं, पठितः -ता -तं, निपठितः &c., अधिगतः &c., आगमितः &c.; 'one who has read the Vedas,' अधीतवेदः.—(Read out) श्रावितः -ता -तं, वाचितः &c., अनुवाचितः &c.—(Studied) अभ्यस्तः -स्ता -स्तं.—(Well-read) स्वधीतः -ता -तं, स्वधीती -तिनी -ति (न्), कृताध्ययनः -ना -नं, विद्यासम्पन्नः -न्ना -न्नं, अभ्यस्तविद्यः &c.

Readable, *a.* पठनीयः -या -यं, अध्ययनीयः -या -यं, अध्येतव्यः -व्या -व्यं, पाठ्यः -ठ्या -ठ्यं, अधिगम्यः -म्या -म्यं, अधिगमनीयः &c., श्राव्यः &c.

Reader, *s.* अध्येता *m.* (तृ), अध्ययनी *m.* (न्), अध्यायी *m.*, पठिता *m.* (तृ), पाठकः, अध्ययनकारी *m.* (न्), अध्ययनकृत् *m.*, पठनकारी *m.*, अधीयानः; 'one who has read through,' पारायणिकः, पारायणी *m.*; 'public reader,' पाठकः.

Readily, *adv.* (Willingly) कामं, कामतस्, प्रकामं, इच्छातस्, पर्य्याप्तं.—(Quickly, promptly) शीघ्रं, आशु, त्वरितं, अविलम्बेन, झटिति, अचिरेण, अचिरात्.—(Easily) सुखेन, सुखं, अनायासेन, अल्पायासेन, निरायासं, सुकरं, अयत्नेन, अयत्नतस्, अदुःखेन, अकष्टेन, अक्लेशेन, सु or सुख prefixed, *see* Easily.—(Without being asked) अयाचितं.

Readiness, *s.* (Promptness, quickness) प्रत्युत्पन्नता, उद्युक्तता -त्वं, शीघ्रता, अविलम्बः, अविलम्बत्वं; 'of mind or wit,' प्रत्युत्पन्नमतित्वं.—(Willingness) सकामत्वं -ता, कामनत्वं, इच्छुता, इच्छुकत्वं, पर्य्याप्तिः *f.*, पर्य्याप्तता.—(State of preparation) सिद्धता, सिद्धिः *f.*, प्रस्तुतत्वं, उद्यतत्वं.

Reading, *s.* (Act of reading, perusal) अध्ययनं, पठनं, पाठः -ठनं, अधीतिः *f.*, अध्यायः, अध्ययः, प्राध्ययनं, निपाठः, निपठः, पठिः *f.*, निपठितिः *f.*, अधिगमः -मनं; 'reading through,' पारायणं, पारगमनं; 'reading to one's self,' स्वाध्यायः, स्वाध्ययनं; 'ignorant of reading and writing,' अलिपिज्ञः.—(Reading out, causing to be heard) वाचनं, अनुवाचनं, श्रावणं.—(Committing to memory upon reading) पाठः, अभ्यासः.—(Suspension of reading) अनध्यायः; 'day on which it is suspended,' अनध्यायदिवसः.—(Matter read) अध्ययनं, पाठः.—(Variation in reading, in a copy or edition) पाठान्तरं, पाठभेदः, द्विरूपपाठः, द्विरूपः, पाठः; 'false reading,' अपपाठः.

Reading-desk, *s.* अध्ययनमञ्चः, मञ्चः, मञ्चकः अध्ययनफलकः -कं.

Reading-room, *s.* पाठशाला, पठनशाला, अध्ययनशाला.

To re-admit, *v. a.* पुनः प्रविश् (c. 10. -वेशयति -यितुं), पुनर् ग्रह्.

Ready, *a.* (Prepared, said of things) सज्जः -ज्जा -ज्जं, प्रस्तुतः -ता -तं, सुप्रस्तुतः &c., सज्जितः &c., सज्जीभूतः -ता -तं, सज्जीकृतः &c., उपकल्पितः &c., परिकल्पितः &c., कल्पितः &c., उपक्लृप्तः -प्ता -प्तं, सिद्धः -द्धा -द्धं, संस्कृतः &c., आयोजितः &c., आयुक्तः -क्ता -क्तं, उपस्थितः -ता -तं; 'to be ready,' सज्जीभू, सज्ज् in pass. (सज्यते), प्रस्तुतीभू, सिद्धीभू; 'to make ready,' *see To* prepare; 'go and make ready,' गत्वा सज्जीकुरु.—(Prepared, said of persons) उद्यतः -ता -तं, समुद्यतः &c., अभ्युद्यतः &c., उद्युक्तः -क्ता -क्तं, आयुक्तः &c., उन्मुखः -खा -खं, अभिमुखः &c., कल्पः -ल्पा -ल्पं; 'ready to go,' गन्तुम् उद्यतः -ता -तं, गमनोद्यतः &c., गमनोन्मुखः &c.; 'ready to burst forth,' भेदोन्मुखः &c. or expressed by the desiderative, see *on the point of*, under Point, *s.*—(Prompt) प्रत्युत्पन्नः -न्ना -न्नं, प्रगल्भः -ल्भा -ल्भं; 'ready wit,' प्रत्युत्पन्नमतित्वं; 'having it,' प्रत्युत्पन्नमतिः -तिः -ति.—(Quick) शीघ्रः -घ्रा -घ्रं, त्वरितः -ता -तं, द्रुतः &c., क्षिप्रः -प्रा -प्रं, अविलम्बी &c., अविलम्बितः -ता -तं.—(Easy) सुखः -खा -खं, सुकरः -रा -रं, सुगमः -मा -मं, लघुः -घुः -घ्वी -घु, अनायासी &c.—(Opportune) उपयुक्तः -क्ता -क्तं, समयोपयुक्तः &c., अनुकूलः -ला -लं.—(Expert) कुशलः -ला -लं, दक्षः -क्षा -क्षं, निपुणः -णा -णं, पटुः &c.—(At hand, in hand, present) उपस्थितः -ता -तं, निकटः -टा -टं, हस्तगतः -ता -तं, हस्तस्थः -स्था -स्थं, विद्यमानः -ना -नं, वर्त्तमानः &c.; 'ready money,' उपस्थितमुद्रा; 'buying with ready money,' रोकः.—(Willing) सकामः -मा -मं, इच्छुः -च्छुः -च्छु, इच्छुकः -का -कं, पर्य्याप्तः -प्ता -प्तं.

Ready, *adv.* प्रस्तुतं, सुप्रस्तुतं, उद्यतं, समुद्यतं, पर्य्याप्तं.

Ready-made, *a.* प्रस्तुतः -ता -तं, उपस्थितः &c., सिद्धः -द्धा -द्धं.

Ready-witted, *a.* प्रत्युत्पन्नमतिः -तिः -ति, विदग्धः -ग्धा -ग्धं, विदग्धमतिः &c.

Real, *a.* सत्यः -त्या -त्यं, वास्तविकः -की -कं, वास्तवः -वी -वं, तथ्यः -थ्या -थ्यं, यथार्थः -र्था -र्थं, प्रकृतः -ता -तं, सन् -सती -सत् (त्), सात्त्विकः -की -कं, तात्त्विकः -की -कं, अवितथः -था -थं, अकृत्रिमः -मा -मं, अकल्पितः -ता -तं, सत्यकः -का -कं, ऋतः -ता -तं, यथातथ्यः &c., यथातथः &c., विद्यमानः -ना -नं, परमार्थः -र्था -र्थं, पारमार्थिकः -की -कं, गतालीकः -का -कं, निर्मायिकः -की -कं, अकपटः -टा -टं, निष्कपटः &c., निष्कपटी &c., अन्वर्थः &c.—(In law) स्थावरः -रा -रं, जङ्गमेतरः -रा -रं; 'real property,' स्थावरं, स्थावरधनं.

Reality, *s.* सत्यता -त्वं, सत्यं, वास्तविकत्वं, वास्तवत्वं, तथ्यता -त्वं, यथार्थता, याथार्थ्यं, तत्त्वं, तत्त्वार्थः, सत्त्वं, सत्ता, अस्तित्वं, प्रकृतता -त्वं, प्रकृतिभावः, विद्यमानता, अकृत्रिमता, अकल्पितत्वं, याथातथ्यं; 'a reality,' सत्त्वं, तत्त्वं, सत्यं, सत्यविषयः, वस्तु *n.*, अस्ति indec.; 'in reality,' वस्तुतस्, तत्त्वतस्.

Realization, *s.* सिद्धिः *f.*, साधनं, सिद्धीकरणं, सत्यीकरणं, स्वीकरणं, आत्मीयकरणं, आत्मसात्करणं; 'of an object,' अर्थसिद्धिः *f.*, फलसिद्धिः *f.*

To realize, *v. a.* साध् (c. 10. साधयति -यितुं), सिद्धीकृ, सिद्धिं कृ, सिद्धतां कृ or जन्, सत्यीकृ, स्वीकृ, आत्मीयं -यां कृ, आत्मसात्कृ; 'to realize any object,' अर्थसिद्धिं कृ, फलसिद्धिं कृ.

Realized, *p. p.* सिद्धः -द्धा -द्धं, सिद्धीकृतः -ता -तं, सिद्धार्थः -र्था -र्थं.

Really, *adv.* वस्तुतस्, अर्थतस्, तत्त्वतस्, परमार्थतस्, यथार्थं, यथार्थतस्, सत्यं, तथ्यं, यथातथ्यं; 'the star appears higher than it really is,' नक्षत्रं वास्तवस्थानाद् उच्चदेशे दृश्यते.

Realm, *s.* राष्ट्रं, राज्यं, विषयः, लोकः. *See* Kingdom.

REAM, *s.* रीमाख्यो लेखनपत्राणां मुद्राङ्कनपत्राणां वा महाभारः.

To RE-ANIMATE *v. a.* पुनर् आश्वस्, (c. 10. -श्वासयति -यितुं), प्रत्याश्वस्, पुनर् जीव् (c. 10. जीवयति -यितुं) or संजीव्, पुनर्जीवनं दा, पुनर्जीवितं -तां कृ.

REANIMATED, *p. p.* पुनराश्वासितः -ता -तं, आश्वासितः &c., प्रत्याश्वासितः &c., प्रत्याश्वस्तः -स्ता -स्तं, पुनर्जीवितः &c., संजीवितः &c.

REANIMATION, *s.* पुनराश्वासनं, प्रत्याश्वासनं, पुनर्जीवनदानं, संजीवनं.

To REAP, *v. a.* (Cut with a sickle) लू (c. 9. लुनाति, लवितुं), लवित्रेण छिद् (c. 7. छिनत्ति, छेत्तुं) or अवछिद् or कृत् (c. 6. कृन्तति, कर्त्तितुं) or अवकृत् or दो or दा (c. 4. द्यति c. 2. दाति -तुं) or निर्दो or छो (c. 4. छ्यति, छातुं) or अवछो, लवनं कृ.—(Gather) संग्रह् (c. 9. -गृह्णाति -ग्रहीतुं), चि (c. 5. -चिनोति, चेतुं), अवचि, संचि; 'to reap corn,' शस्यसंग्रहं कृ; 'to reap the fruits of any thing,' फलसिद्धिं कृ, फलप्राप्तिं कृ, फलं भुज् or अनुभू or प्राप्, फलभोगी -गिनी &c., भू; 'of an action,' कर्म्मफलं भुज् or प्राप्.

REAPED, *p. p.* लूनः -ना -नं, लवित्रछिन्नः -न्ना -न्नं, कर्त्तितः -ता -तं, छातः &c., अवछातः &c., छितः &c., दातः &c., निर्दातः &c., दितः -ता -तं, संगृहीतः &c., सञ्चितः -ता -तं.

REAPER, *s.* लवकः, लविता *m.* (तृ), शस्यलवकः, छेदकः, छेत्ता *m.* (तृ), शस्यछेदकः, शस्यछिद् *m.*, शस्यछेत्ता *m.* (तृ), निर्दाता *m.*, शस्यसंग्रही *m.* (न्), शस्यसंग्राहकः, शस्यसञ्चयी *m.*, लवनकारी *m.*, कार्त्तकः.

REAPING, *s.* लवनं, लावः, अभिलावः, शस्यलावः, लवः, शस्यछेदः -दनं, छेदनं, शस्यसंग्रहः, शस्यकर्त्तनं, दातिः *f.*, दानं.

REAPING-HOOK, *s.* लवित्रं, लवाणकं, लवाकः, शस्यकर्त्तनी, शस्यछेदनी.

REAR, *s.* (That which is behind) पश्चाद्भागः, पाश्चात्यभागः, पश्चिमभागः, पार्ष्णिः *m.*, पृष्ठं; 'in the rear,' पश्चात्, पृष्ठतस्, पश्चाद्भागे; 'in our rear,' अस्मत्पश्चात्.—(Rear of an army) पार्ष्णिः *m. f.*, व्यूहपार्ष्णिः *m.*, प्रत्यासारः, प्रत्यासरः, प्रतिसरः, सञ्चयः, सञ्जनं; 'a body of forces in the rear,' पार्ष्णित्रं; 'an enemy in the rear,' पार्ष्णिग्राहः; 'bringing up the rear,' प्रतिगृह्य.

To REAR, *v. a.* (Raise to maturity, bring up) पुष् (c. 10. पोषयति -यितुं), परिपुष्, पाल् (c. 10. पालयति -यितुं), प्रतिपाल्, भृ (c. 3. बिभर्त्ति, c. 1. भरति, भर्त्तुं), सम्भृ, संवृध् (c. 10. -वर्धयति -यितुं), वृध्, परिवृध्, विनी (c. 1. -नयति -नेतुं), अनुनी, पोषणं कृ, पालनं कृ, पालनपोषणं कृ.—(Raise, lift) उत्था in caus. (-थापयति -यितुं, rt. स्था), उन्नम् (c. 10. -नमयति -यितुं), उच्छ्रि (c. 1. -श्रयति -यितुं, rt. श्रि), उत्तुल्, उन्नी, उद्यम्, उद्धृ, उद्वह्, उच्चीकृ, ऊर्द्ध्वीकृ.

To REAR, *v. n.* (As a horse) अश्ववत् पुरूवकं कृ.

REARED, *p. p.* (Brought up) पोषितः -ता -तं, पुष्टः -ष्टा -ष्टं, पालितः -ता -तं, प्रतिपालितः &c., भृतः &c., सम्भृतः &c., संवर्धितः -ता -तं, परिवर्धितः &c., वर्धितः &c.—(Raised, elevated) उत्थापितः -ता -तं, उच्छ्रितः &c., अभ्युच्छ्रितः &c., उन्नतः &c.

REAR-GUARD, *s.* पार्ष्णित्रं, व्यूहपार्ष्णित्रं, सैन्यपार्ष्णित्रं.

REARING, *s.* (Educating) पोषणं, पोषः, पालनं, भरणं, संवर्धनं, परिवर्धनं, वर्धनं.—(Elevating) उत्थापनं, उन्नयनं, उन्नमनं, उच्छ्रितिः *f.*—(Of a horse) पुरूवकं.

REAR-WARD, *s.* *See* REAR, REAR-GUARD.

REASON, *s.* (Reasoning faculty, understanding) बुद्धिः *f.*, धीः *f.*, मनस् *n.*, मतिः *f.*, चित्तं, चेतस् *n.*, ज्ञानं, चिच्छक्तिः *f.*, चेतना, चित् *f.*, तर्कशक्तिः *f.*, अनुमानशक्तिः *f.*, आकलनशक्तिः *f.*, मानसं, प्रज्ञा, उपलब्धिः *f.*, शेमुषी, मनीषा, स्वान्तं.—(Right, justice) युक्तता, युक्तिः *f.*, उपपत्तिः *f.*, उपपन्नता, योग्यता, यथायोग्यता, यथार्थता, याथार्थ्यं, न्यायः, न्याय्यता, सामञ्जस्यं, सम्यक्त्वं; 'with reason,' युक्तं, यथायुक्तं, यथायोग्यं, न्यायतस्, सम्यक्.—(Cause, ground) हेतुः *m.*, कारणं, निमित्तं -त्तकं, निदानं, निबन्धनं, प्रयोजनं; 'by reason of,' हेतोः हेतौ, निमित्ते, कृते, अर्थं, कारणात्, or expressed simply by the abl. c.; as, 'by reason of anger,' कोपात्; 'for this reason,' अनेन हेतुना, अतःकारणात्, तस्य हेतोः, तदर्थं; 'for some reason,' केनापि कारणेन; 'for what reason,' केन हेतुना, कस्य हेतोः, किमर्थं; 'without reason,' कारणेन विना, हेतुना विना, अकस्मात्; 'He assigns a reason,' स हेतुम् आह; 'the reason of their barrenness is the absence of seed,' तेषां वन्ध्यत्वे बीजाभावः कारणं; 'the reason of the indistinctness is as follows,' अथ अस्पष्टत्वे हेतुर् उच्यते.

To REASON, *v. n.* (Deduce inferences, exercise the faculty of reason) तर्क् (c. 10. तर्कयति -यितुं) वितर्क्, अनुतर्क्, अनुमा (c. 2. -माति -तुं), ऊह् (c. 1. ऊहते -हितुं), अपोह्, प्रोह्, वितर्कं कृ, वितर्कणं कृ, ऊहं कृ, ऊहापोहं कृ, अर्थापत्तिं कृ, सिद्धासिद्धविचारं कृ.—(Argue, debate) विवद्, विसंवद्, विचर्, वितर्क्, वादानुवादं कृ.

REASONABLE, *a.* (Having the faculty of reason), *see* RATIONAL.—(Conformable to reason, just, right) युक्तः -क्ता -क्तं, उपयुक्तः &c., योग्यः -ग्या -ग्यं, यथायुक्तः &c., यथायोग्यः &c., यथोचितः -ता -तं, युक्तिमान् -मती -मत् (त्), सयुक्तिकः -का -कं, उपपन्नः -न्ना -न्नं, उपपत्तिमान् -मती &c., यथार्थः -र्था -र्थं, न्याय्यः -य्या -य्यं, न्यायानुसारी -रिणी -रि (न्), न्यायानुरूपः -पा -पं, न्यायसिद्धः -द्धा -द्धं, युक्तिसिद्धः &c., यथान्यायः -या -यं, तात्त्विकः -की -कं.—(Moderate) परिमितः -ता -तं, मितः &c., सपरिमाणः -णा -णं, नियतः -ता -तं, समः -मा -मं.—(Acting or thinking rationally), समदर्शी &c., न्यायकारी &c., न्यायवृत्तिः -त्तिः -त्ति, समवृत्तिः &c.

REASONABLENESS, *s.* (Faculty of reason) ज्ञानशक्तिः *f.*, चिच्छक्तिः *f.*, तर्कशक्तिः.—(Conformity to reason), युक्तता, उपयुक्तता, योग्यता, यथायोग्यता, युक्तिः *f.*, उपपत्तिः *f.*, उपपन्नता, यथार्थता, याथार्थ्यं, न्याय्यता -त्वं, न्यायसिद्धता, युक्तिसिद्धता, औचित्यं, सम्भवः, सम्भूतिः *f.*, सम्भावना.—(Moderation) परिमितता, समता, अनतिक्रमः, मर्य्यादानतिक्रमः.

REASONABLY, *adv.* (Conformably with reason) युक्तं, यथायोग्यं, उपपन्नं, न्यायतस्, न्यायानुसारेण, न्यायानुरूपेण, यथान्यायं, यथार्थं, यथोचितं, युक्तितस्.—(Moderately) परिमितं, नियतं, समं.

REASONER, *s.* तर्की *m.* (न्), तार्किकः, वितर्की *m.*, ऊही *m.* (न्), प्रोही *m.*, प्रोहः, विचारकः, तर्ककारी *m.*, वितर्ककारी, नैयायिकः, न्यायविद् *m.*, प्रतिपादकः. *See* LOGICIAN.

REASONING, *s.* तर्कः, वितर्कः -र्कणं, विचारः, ऊहः -हनं, प्रोहः, अभ्यूहः, ऊहापोहः, अपोहः -हनं, व्यूहः, निरूहः, न्यायः, अनुमानं, अध्याहारः, अर्थापत्तिः *f.*, अनुमानोक्तिः *f.*; 'art or science of reasoning,' तर्कविद्या, तर्कशास्त्रं, तर्कज्ञानं, विचारविद्या; 'chain of reasoning,' तर्कप्रबन्धः, अनुमानप्रबन्धः; 'skill in it,' तार्किक्यं.

REASONLESS, *a.* (Destitute of reason) बुद्धिहीनः -ना -नं, निर्बुद्धिः -द्धिः -द्धि, ज्ञानहीनः &c.—(Without a reason) अहेतुकः -का -कं, निर्हेतुकः &c., निष्कारणः -णा -णं.

To RE-ASSUME *v. a.* प्रत्यादा, पुनर् आदा or ग्रह् or प्रतिग्रह्.

RE-ASSURANCE, *s.* पुनराश्वासनं, पुनराशा, प्रत्याशा, आश्वासनं.

To RE-ASSURE, *v. a.* पुनर् आश्वस् (c. 10. -श्वासयति -यितुं), प्रत्याश्वस्.

RE-ASSURED, *p. p.* पुनराश्वासितः -ता -तं, पुनराश्वस्तः -स्ता -स्तं, प्रत्याश्वसितः &c.

RE-ASSURING, *part.* or *a.* पुनराश्वासकः -का -कं, प्रत्याश्वासकः &c., आश्वासकः &c.

REBEL, *s.* राजद्रोही *m.* (न्), राजाभिद्रोही *m.*, राजयुध्वा *m.* (न्), राजप्रतियोधी *m.*, स्वामिद्रोही *m.*, राजशासनत्यागी *m.*, राजप्रतीपः, राजप्रतीपकारी *m.*, राजविपरीतकारी *m.*, राजविरोधी *m.*, राजविरुद्धाचारी *m.*, कलहकारी *m.*, अवशः, प्रतीपः, विपरीतकारी *m.*

To REBEL, *v. n.* राजद्रोहं कृ, राजानम् अभिद्रुह् (c. 4. -द्रुह्यति -द्रोहितुं -द्रोग्धुं) राजाभिद्रोहं कृ, स्वामिद्रोहं कृ, राजशासनत्यागं कृ, राजशासनलंघनं कृ, राजानं प्रतियुध् (c. 4. -युध्यते -योद्धुं), प्रकृतिक्षोभं कृ, प्रकृतिकलहं कृ.

REBELLION, *s.* राजद्रोहः, राजाभिद्रोहः, राजयुद्धं, राजशासनत्यागः, स्वामिद्रोहः, प्रकृतिक्षोभः, प्रकृतिकलहः, राजशासनलंघनं, राजोपद्रवः, उपद्रवः, प्रकोपः, कोपः, खण्डनं.

REBELLIOUS, *a.* राजद्रोही -हिणी -हि (न्), राजाभिद्रोही &c., राजध्रुक् *m.f.n.* (द्रुह्), राजप्रध्रुक्, द्रोही &c., प्रध्रुक् *m.f.n.*, राजप्रतीपः -पा -पं, राजप्रतीपकारी &c., प्रतीपः -पा -पं, राजविपरीतकारी &c., विपरीतकारी &c., उपद्रवी &c., राजोपद्रवी &c., राजशासनलंघी &c., राजशासनत्यागी &c., लंघितशासनः -ना -नं, उल्लंघितशासनः &c., राजावशः -शा -शं. *See* REBEL. *s.*

To REBOUND *v. n.* उत्पत् (c. 1. -पतति -तितुं), परापत्, उत्प्लु (c. 1. -प्लवते -प्लोतुं), प्रतिहन् in pass. (-हन्यते).

REBOUND, *s.* उत्पतनं, परापतनं, प्रतिघातः, प्रतिहतिः *f.*, प्रतिहननं, उत्प्लुतं.

REBUFF, *s.* (Repercussion) प्रतिघातः, प्रतिहतिः *f.*, प्रतिहननं, पराहननं. (Check, defeat) पराभवः, पराजयः, अपजयः.—(Refusal) प्रत्यादेशः, अवधीरणा.

To REBUFF, *v. a.* प्रतिहन् (c. 2. -हन्ति -न्तुं), पराहन्, प्रत्यादिश्, अवधीर्, पराजि.

To REBUILD *v. a.* पुनर् निर्मा or विनिर्मा (c. 2. -माति -तुं), पुनर्निर्माणं कृ.

REBUILT, *p.p.* पुनर्निर्मितः -ता -तं, पुनर्विनिर्मितः &c., पुनर्निचितः &c.

REBUKABLE, *a.* निन्दनीयः -या -यं, निन्द्यः -न्द्या -न्द्यं, निन्दार्हः -र्हा -र्हं.

To REBUKE, *v. a.* निन्द् (c. 1. निन्दति -न्दितुं), प्रतिनिन्द्, विनिन्द्, उपालभ् (c. 1. -लभते -लब्धुं), भर्त्स् (c. 10. भर्त्सयते -यितुं), प्रत्यादिश् (c. 6. -दिशति -देष्टुं), गर्ह् c. 1. गर्हते -र्हितुं), विगर्ह्, गुप् in des., (जुगुप्सते -प्सितुं), आक्रुश् c. 1. -क्रोशति -क्रोष्टुं), क्षिप् (c. 6. क्षिपति क्षेप्तुं), तर्ज् (c. 10. तर्जयति -यितुं).

REBUKE, *s.* निन्दा -न्दनं, परीवादः, परिवादः, भर्त्सनं, भर्त्सनवाक्यं, परिभाषणं, उपालम्भः, प्रत्यादेशः, आक्रोशः, उपक्रोशः, जुगुप्सा, वाग्दण्डः, शब्ददण्डः.

REBUKER, *s.* निन्दकः, परिवादकः, प्रत्यादेशकः, भर्त्सनकारी *m.* (न्).

REBUS, *s.* प्रवह्लिः *f.*, -ह्लिका. *See* RIDDLE.

To REBUT, *v. a.* निरस् (c. 4. -अस्यति -असितुं), उपमर्दं कृ, खण्ड्. *See* REPEL.

To RECALL, *v. a.* (Call back, take back, bring back) पुनर् आदा (c. 3. -ददाति -दातुं) प्रत्यादा, पुनर् आनी (c. 1. -नयति -नेतुं), प्रत्यानी, प्रत्यानयनं कृ, प्रत्यावर्त्तनं कृ, प्रतिनिवर्त्तनं कृ, निवर्त्तनं कृ, निवृत् or प्रतिनिवृत् or प्रत्यावृत् in caus.—(Revoke, annul) निवृत् (c. 10. वर्त्तयति -यितुं), प्रत्यादिश् (c. 6. -दिशति -देष्टुं), खण्ड् (c. 10. खण्डयति -यितुं), निवर्त्तनं कृ, खण्डनं कृ, लोपं कृ.—(Call to mind) स्मृ (c. 1. स्मरति, स्मर्त्तुं), अनुस्मृ, अनुचिन्त्, अनुबुध्.

RECALL, *s.* प्रत्यानयनं, पुनरानयनं, प्रत्यावर्त्तनं, प्रत्यादानं, पुनरादानं.

RECALLED, *p.p.* (Called back, brought back) प्रत्यानीतः -ता -तं, पुनरानीतः &c., प्रत्यावर्त्तितः &c., प्रतिनिवर्त्तितः &c., निवर्त्तितः &c.,—(Revoked, annulled) निवर्त्तितः -ता -तं, खण्डितः &c., प्रत्यादिष्टः -ष्टा -ष्टं, लुप्तः -प्ता -प्तं.—(Called to mind) स्मृतः -ता -तं, उद्बुद्धः -द्धा -द्धं, उद्वाहितः -ता -तं.

To RECANT, *v. a.* पूर्व्वोक्तविपरीतं वद् (c. 1. वदति -दितुं), पूर्व्वोदितविपरीतं वद्, पूर्व्वोक्तखण्डनं कृ, पूर्व्वोक्तलोपं कृ, अनुशयं कृ, विप्रतिपत्तिं कृ.

RECANTATION, *s.* पूर्व्वोक्तविपरीतवादः, पूर्व्वोदितविपरीतवादः, पूर्व्वोक्तखण्डनवादः, पूर्व्वोक्तखण्डनं, पूर्व्वोक्तलोपः, अनुशयः, विप्रतिपत्तिः *f.*

To RECAPITULATE *v. a.* संक्षेपतः पुनः कथ् (c. 10. कथयति -यितुं), वाक्यसारम् अनुवद् (c. 1. -वदति -दितुं) or अनुवच् (c. 2. -वक्ति -क्तुं), संक्षेपेण वाक्यं पुनर् वद्, सारविषयान् पुनर् वद् or अनुवद्, सारप्रकरणानि पुनर्वद् or पुनर्वच्.

RECAPITULATED, *p. p.* संक्षेपतः पुनरुक्तः -क्ता -क्तं or पुनःकथितः -ता -तं.

RECAPITULATION, *s.* संक्षेपतः पुनःकथनं or पुनरुक्तिः *f.* or पुनर्वचनं or अनुवादः, संक्षेपेणानुवादः, पूर्व्वकथितानुवादः, संक्षेपतः पुनर्व्याख्या.

To RECEDE, *v. a.* अपक्रम् (c. 1. -क्रामति -क्रमितुं), व्यपक्रम्, अपसृ (c. 1. -सरति -सर्त्तुं), निवृत् (c. 1. -वर्त्तते -र्त्तितुं), परावृत्, अपावृत्, प्रतिनिवृत्, अवस्था (c. 1. -तिष्ठते -स्थातुं), पलाय् (c. 1. पलायते -यितुं, rt. इ), विपलाय्, अपसृप् (c. 1. -सर्पति -सर्प्तुं), अपगम् (c. 1. -गच्छति -गन्तुं), अपया (c. 2. -याति -तुं), अपे (c. 2. अपैति -तुं, rt. इ).

RECEIPT, *s.* (Act of receiving) आदानं, ग्रहणं, प्रतिग्रहणं, प्राप्तिः *f.*, अवाप्तिः *f.*, प्रापणं, लब्धिः *f.*, उपलब्धिः *f.*—(Income) आयः, आगमः, उदयः, आदायः, उत्पन्नं, प्राप्तिः *f.*, लाभः, लब्धिः *f.*, फलं; 'of money or property,' धनागमः, धनोदयः, अर्थागमः, फलोदयः; 'receipts of trade,' पण्याया; 'receipt and expenditure,' आयव्ययौ *m. du.*—(Note of ackowledgment) मुक्तिपत्रं, विगणनपत्रं, प्रत्ययकारिपत्रं, प्रत्ययकारी लेखः, प्रत्ययकारिणी, स्वीकारपत्रं, स्वीकरणपत्रं, स्वीकारलेखः, सरस्वतीदानं, आदानपत्रं, आगमपत्रं, आगमलेख्यं.—(Recipe, prescription of ingredients) साधनलेखः, योगलेखः, संयोगलेखः, लेखः, लेख्यं.

RECEIVABLE, *a.* आदेयः -या -यं, उपादेयः &c., ग्राह्यः -ह्या -ह्यं, ग्रहणीयः -या -यं, ग्रहीतव्यः -व्या -व्यं, प्रतिग्राह्यः &c., प्रापणीयः -या -यं, प्राप्यः -प्या -प्यं, लभ्यः -भ्या -भ्यं, उपलभ्यः &c., स्वीकरणीयः &c.

To RECEIVE, *v. a.* (Take, get, obtain) आदा (c. 3. -ददाति -दत्ते -दातुं), उपादा, ग्रह् (c. 9. गृह्णाति, गृह्णीते, ग्रहीतुं), प्रतिग्रह्, अभिग्रह्, सम्प्रग्रह्, संग्रह्, आप् (c. 5. आप्नोति, आप्तुं), प्राप्, अवाप्, लभ् (c. 1. लभते, लब्धुं), उपलभ्, प्रतीष् (c. 6. -इच्छति -एषितुं), प्रतिपद् (c. 4. -पद्यते -पत्तुं), आपद्, अभिपद्, समापद्.—(Allow) स्वीकृ, अङ्गीकृ, ग्रह्, अनुग्रह्.—(Admit) प्रविश् in caus., आविश्, ग्रह्.—(Hold, contain) धा, आधा, आदा.—(Entertain a guest) सत्कृ, आतिथ्यं कृ, सत्कारं कृ, सम्भू (c. 10. -भावयति -यितुं), सम्भावनं कृ, आदरं कृ, स्वागतं कृ or वद्.

RECEIVED, *p. p.* or *a.* (Taken, accepted, obtained) आदत्तः -त्ता -त्तं, आत्तः &c., उपादत्तः &c., उपात्तः &c., गृहीतः -ता -तं, प्रतिगृहीतः &c., प्राप्तः -प्ता -प्तं, आप्तः &c., अवाप्तः &c., लब्धः -ब्धा -ब्धं, उपलब्धः &c.; 'received as wages,' भृतिरूपेण लब्धः &c.—(Generally admitted) लोकप्रसिद्धः -द्धा -द्धं, सर्व्वत्र प्रचलः -ला -लं; 'received practice,' लोकव्यवहारः; 'received doctrine,' आम्नायः; 'received expression,' आप्तवचनं, आप्तोक्तिः *f.*

RECEIVER, *s.* ग्राही *m.* (न्), ग्राहकः, ग्रहीता *m.* (तृ), प्रतिग्रहीता *m.*, प्रतिग्राहकः, आदाता *m.* (तृ), आदायी *m.* (न्), उपादाता *m.*, उपादायी *m.*,

प्रतिग्रहकृत् m., आप्ता m. (प्तृ), प्रापकः, लब्धा m. (ब्धृ), उपलब्धा m., प्रतीच्छकः.—(Vessel for receiving) आधारः, द्रवाधारः, आधानं, भाजनं, पात्रं, द्रवाशयः, आशयः.

Recency, s. नवता -त्वं, नूतनत्वं, अभिनवता, प्रत्यग्रता. *See* Newness.

Recent, a. नूतनः -ना -नी -नं, नवः -वा -वं, अभिनवः &c., नवीनः -ना -नं, प्रतिनवः &c., नूत्नः -त्ना -त्नं, प्रत्यग्रः -ग्रा -ग्रं, इदानीन्तनः -नी -नं, अधुनातनः &c., अर्वाचीनः -ना -नं, अप्राचीनः &c., सद्यस्कः -स्का -स्कं, सद्यस्कालीनः -ना -नं, आधुनिकः -की -कं, अचिरः -रा -रं, अव्यवहितदीर्घकालः -ला -लं.

Recently, adv. नूतनकाले, नूतनं, अव्यवहितदीर्घकाले. *See* Lately.

Receptacle, s. आधारः, पात्रं, भाजनं, आशयः, निधानं, निधिः m., आधानं, आश्रयः, अधिश्रयः, अधिकरणं, गर्भः, आस्पदं, विन्यासः, वीजं. The word आशयः is especially used in composition thus, 'the receptacle of the blood,' रक्ताशयः; 'of the food,' अन्नाशयः, आमाशयः; 'of bile,' पित्ताशयः.

Reception, s. (Receiving) आदानं, उपादानं, ग्रहणं, प्रतिग्रहः -हणं, आधानं.—(Admission) स्वीकारः, स्वीकरणं, अङ्गीकारः, अङ्गीकरणं, ग्रहणं.—(Entrance) प्रवेशनं, प्रवेशः.—(Entertainment) सत्कारः, सत्क्रिया, संग्रहः, सम्भावनं -ना; 'of friends,' मित्रसंग्रहः.

Recess, s. (In a wall, &c., secret or retired spot) गर्भः, कोणः, विविक्तस्थानं, गूढस्थानं, निभृतस्थानं, गुप्तस्थानं.—(Place of retirement) परावर्त्तनस्थानं, अपावर्त्तनस्थानं, अपक्रमणस्थानं.—(Remission of business) विरामः, विरतिः f., विश्रामः, निवृत्तिः f., कार्य्यनिवृत्तिः f., कार्य्यत्यागः, विरामकालः, विश्रामकालः.

Recession, s. अपक्रमणं, अपावर्त्तनं, परावर्त्तनं, परावृत्तिः f., अपसरणं.

Recipe, s. *See* under Receipt, Prescription.

Recipient, s. (Person) ग्राही m. (न्), आदाता m. (तृ), ग्राहकः, आश्रयिता m. *See* Receiver.—(Thing) आधारः, आशयः, पात्रं. *See* Receiver.

Reciprocal, a. परस्परः -रा -रं, अन्योन्यः -न्या -न्यं, इतरेतरः -रा -रं, व्यतिकरः -रा -रं, इतरेतराश्रयः -या -यं, मिथस् in comp. The sense of "reciprocal" is often expressed by the prepositions वि, आ, अव, अति, प्रति, प्र in combination. *See* Mutual.—(Alternate, in reciprocal succession) परस्परानुगामी -मिनी -मि (न्), परस्परानुवर्त्ती &c., अन्योन्यानुगामी &c., अन्योन्यानुवर्त्ती &c.

Reciprocally, adv. परस्परं -रं, अन्योन्यं, इतरेतरं, मिथस्, उभयतस्, परस्पर in comp.; 'mutually connected,' व्यतिषक्तः -क्ता -क्तं, मिथःसम्बद्धः -द्धा -द्धं, *see* Mutually.

To reciprocate, v. a. परस्परं परिवृत् (c. 10. -वर्त्तयति यितुं), परस्परपरिवर्त्तनं कृ, अन्योन्यं परिवृत्, व्यतिकरं कृ, व्यतिहृ, व्यतिहारं कृ; 'to reciprocate gifts,' परस्परं दानप्रतिदानं कृ; 'to reciprocate assistance,' प्रत्युपकारं कृ; 'civilities,' प्रतिपूजनं कृ, *see To* interchange.

Reciprocation, s. परिवर्त्तनं, विनिमयः, व्यतिकरः, व्यतिहारः. *See* Interchange.

Reciprocity, reciprocalness, s. परस्परता, अन्योन्यता -त्वं, व्यतिकरः, व्यतिहारः, व्यतीहारः, परस्परयोगः, इतरेतरयोगः, परस्परभावः, व्यतिषङ्गः. *See* Mutuality.

Recital, recitation, s. (Repetition, reading out in a loud voice) पठनं, पाठः, अनुवादः, आवर्णं, वाचनं, अनुवाचनं, उल्लेखः -खनं, उच्चारणं, उद्घोषः -षणं, उद्गारः.—(Narration) कथनं, आख्यानं, उपकथनं, ख्यापनं, वर्णनं.

Recitative, s. (Cadence introductory to a song) तेनः.

To recite, v. a. (Repeat, read out) पठ् (c. 1. पठति -ठितुं), सम्पठ्, अनुवद् (c. 1. -वदति -दितुं), श्रु (c. 10. श्रावयति -यितुं), आश्रु, संश्रु, वच् (c. 10. वाचयति -यितुं), अनुवच्, उच्चर् (c. 10. -चारयति -यितुं), उद्घुष् (c. 10. -घोषयति -यितुं), पठनं कृ.—(Narrate) कथ् (c. 10. कथयति -यितुं), आख्या (c. 2. -ख्याति -तुं), ख्या in caus., वर्ण्, अनुवर्ण्, व्याहृ, उदाहृ, निरूप्, विवरणं कृ, वृत् in caus.

Recited, p.p. (Repeated, read out) पठितः -ता -तं, श्रावितः &c.; 'being recited,' पठ्यमानः -ना -नं.—(Narrated) कथितः -ता -तं, आख्यातः &c., वर्णितः &c.

Reciter, s. पठकः, पठिता m. (तृ), पठनकारी m. (न्), श्रावकः, श्रावयिता m. (तृ), अनुवादकः, उच्चारकः, उच्चारणकारी m., कथकः, उपकथकः, आख्यायकः.

To reck, v. a. and n. अपेक्ष्, अवधा, मन्, प्रतिमन्. *See To* care.

Reckless, a. अनवधानः -ना -नं, असावधानः &c., अनवहितः -ता -तं, प्रमत्तः -त्ता -त्तं, साहसिकः -की -कं, साहसी -सिनी -सि (न्), निरपेक्षः -क्षा -क्षं, निःशङ्कः -ङ्का -ङ्कं.

Recklessly, adv. अनवहितं, साहसेन -सात्, साहसबुद्ध्या, प्रमत्तं.

Recklessness, s. साहसं, साहसशीलता, साहसबुद्धिः f., अनवधानं -नता, असावधानता, प्रमादः, प्रमत्तता.

To reckon, v. a. (Count, number) गण् (c. 10. गणयति -यितुं), विगण्, परिगण्, प्रगण्, संख्या (c. 2. -ख्याति -तुं), परिसंख्या, सम्परिख्या, कल् (c. 10. कलयति -यितुं), गणनां कृ.—(Esteem, account) मन्, सम्मन्, प्रतिमन्, गण्, विगण्,

To reckon, v. n. (Reason with one's self, conclude) वितर्क् (c. 10. -तर्कयति -यितुं), तर्क्, अनुमा, ऊह्, अवगम्.—(Consider, think) मन् (c. 4. मन्यते, मन्तुं), तर्क्, वितर्क्, बुध्.—(Reckon on, count upon) अवलम्ब्, समालम्ब्, संश्रि, समाश्रि, उपाश्रि, विश्वस्.—(Reckon with, settle accounts) विगणनं कृ, सिद्धिं कृ, ऋणसिद्धिं कृ.

Reckoned, p. p. गणितः -ता -तं, विगणितः &c., परिगणितः &c., मतः &c., संख्यातः &c.

Reckoner, s. गणकः, विगणकः, गणयिता m. (तृ), गुणकः, गुणकारः.

Reckoning, s. (The act) गणनं -ना, विगणनं -ना, संख्यानं, परिसंख्यानं, गुणनं.—(Statement of account with another) विगणनपत्रं, विगणनापत्रं, गणनपत्रं, विगणनलेखः, संख्यापत्रं.—(Statement of expense) व्ययपत्रं, व्ययलेखः.—(Esteem, estimation) मानं, सम्मानं, मतिः f.

To reclaim, v. a. (Demand to have restored, take back) मदीयम् एतत् प्रतिदातव्यम् इति ज्ञापयित्वा ग्रह् (c. 9. गृह्णाति, ग्रहीतुं), मदीयम् एतत् प्रत्यर्पणीयम् इत्युक्त्वा ग्रह्, पुनर् लभ्, प्रतिलभ्, पुनर् ग्रह्, पुनः प्राप्, पुनः स्वीकृ.—(Call back from error, vice, &c.) पापात् or दुष्कर्म्मणो निवृत् (c. 10. -वर्त्तयति -यितुं) or विनिवृत् or परावृत् or विरम् (c. 10. -रमयति -यितुं), अधर्म्माद् निवर्त्तयित्वा धर्म्मे प्रवृत् in caus. or प्रयुज् in caus. or नियुज् in caus., पापाद् विप्रतिसृ in caus. (-सारयति -यितुं), विप्रतिसारं जन्.—(Make fit for cultivation) कृषियोग्यं -ग्यां कृ.

Reclaimable, a. (From vice) पापनिवर्त्तयितव्यः -व्या -व्यं, पापनिवर्त्तनीयः -या -यं, दुष्कर्म्मपरावर्त्तनीयः &c., कुकर्म्मनिवर्त्तनीयः, शक्यविप्रतिसारः -रा -रं, उपदेशावश्यः -श्या -श्यं.—(That may be taken again) प्रतिलभ्यः -भ्या -भ्यं, पुनर् लभ्यः &c. or ग्रहणीयः -या -यं.

RECLAIMED, *p. p.* (Taken again) पुनर् गृहीतः -ता -तं, पुनः प्राप्तः -प्ता -प्तं, प्रतिलब्धः -ब्धा -ब्धं, पुनर् लब्धः &c.—(From vice) पापनिवर्त्तितः -ता -तं, निवृत्तपापः -पा -पं, जातविप्रतिसारः -रा -रं.

RECLAMATION, *s.* (Taking again) पुनर्ग्रहणं, पुनर्लब्धिः *f.*, पुनरुपलब्धिः *f.*, प्रतिलब्धिः, पुनःप्राप्तिः *f.*, प्रत्युद्धरणं.—(From vice, &c.) पापनिवर्त्तनं, दुष्कर्म्मनिवर्त्तनं, दुष्कर्म्मपरावर्त्तनं.

To RECLINE, *v. n.* (Lean) अवलम्ब् (c. 1. -लम्बते -म्बितुं), समालम्ब्, संश्रि (c. 1. -श्रयति -ते -यितुं), समाश्रि, उपाश्रि, निली (c. 4. -लीयते -लेतुं), अवलम्बनं कृ.—(Lie) शी (c. 2. शेते, शयितुं), अधिशी, संविश् (c. 6. -विशति -वेष्टुं), उपविश्, निषद् (c. 6. -षीदति -षत्तुं), पत् (c. 1. पतति -तितुं). *See To* LIE, *v. n.*

RECLINING, *part.* (Leaning) अवलम्बी -म्बिनी -म्बि (न्), अवलम्बितः -ता -तं, संश्रितः -ता -तं, समाश्रितः &c., उपाश्रितः &c., निलीनः -ना -नं, निलीयमानः -ना -नं.—(Lying) शयानः -ना -नं, शयः -या -यं, शयितः -ता -तं, संविष्टः -ष्टा -ष्टं, उपविष्टः &c., निषण्णः -ण्णा -ण्णं, निषीदन् -दन्ती -दत् (त्), पतितः -ता -तं; 'on a bed,' शयने संविष्टः &c.

RECLUSE, *s.* विविक्तवासी *m.* (न्), विविक्तसेवी *m.*, एकान्तवासी *m.*, एकान्तसेवी *m.*, विजनवासी *m.*, एकाकी *m.*, अरण्यवासी *m.*, वनवासी *m.*, वनस्थः, वानप्रस्थः.

RECLUSENESS, *s.* विविक्तता, विविक्तवासित्वं, विविक्तसेवा, वानप्रस्थत्वं.

RECOGNITION, *s.* प्रत्यभिज्ञानं, प्रत्यभिज्ञा, अभिज्ञानं, अनुज्ञानं, स्वीकारः, स्वीकरणं, अङ्गीकारः, अङ्गीकरणं, स्मरणं, स्मृतिः *f.*, अनुस्मृतिः *f.*, संवित्तिः *f.*

RECOGNIZANCE, *s.* प्रतिज्ञापत्रं -त्रकं, प्रतिभूः *m.*, प्रातिभाव्यं, दर्शनप्रतिभूः *m.*, दर्शनप्रातिभाव्यं, पारिभाव्यं, लग्नकः, प्रात्ययिकपत्रं -त्रकं, अङ्गीकारपत्रं.

To RECOGNIZE, *v. a.* (Recover the knowledge of, recollect) प्रत्यभिज्ञा (c. 9. -जानाति -नीते -ज्ञातुं), अभिज्ञा, समभिज्ञा, अनुज्ञा, अनुस्मृ (c. 1. -स्मरति -स्मर्त्तुं), प्रतिस्मृ, स्मृ, परिचि (c. 5. -चिनोति -चेतुं), निश्चि, प्रत्यभिज्ञानं कृ.—(Admit, acknowledge) स्वीकृ, अङ्गीकृ, अङ्गीकारं कृ, अनुग्रह्, ग्रह्.

RECOGNIZED, *p. p.* प्रत्यभिज्ञातः -ता -तं, अभिज्ञातः &c., अनुज्ञातः &c., अनुस्मृतः &c., परिचितः &c., अङ्गीकृतः &c., स्वीकृतः &c.—(Generally acknowledged) लोकसिद्धः -द्धा -द्धं, प्रसिद्धः &c.

To RECOIL, *v. n.* परापत् (c. 1. -पतति -तितुं), विवृत् (c. 1. -वर्त्तते -र्त्तितुं), परावृत्, अकस्मात् परावृत्, पश्चात् प्रु or पत् or गम्.

RECOIL, *s.* अकस्माद् विवर्त्तः -र्त्तनं or परावर्त्तः -र्त्तनं, परापतनं.

RECOILING, *part.* अकस्माद् विवर्त्तमानः -ना -नं or परापतन् -तन्ती -तत् (त्).

To RECOLLECT, *v. a.* स्मृ (c. 1. स्मरति, स्मर्त्तुं), अनुस्मृ, प्रतिस्मृ, संस्मृ, अनुसंस्मृ, अभिसंस्मृ, अनुचिन्त् (c. 10. -चिन्तयति -यितुं), समनुचिन्त्, अनुबुध् (c. 4. -बुध्यते -बोद्धुं), अनुध्यै (c. 1. -ध्यायति -ध्यातुं), उपध्यै.—(Recognise) प्रत्यभिज्ञा, अभिज्ञा.—(Try to recollect) स्मृ in des. (सुस्मूर्षते -र्षितुं); 'trying to recollect,' सुस्मूर्षमाणः -णा -णं.—(Recollect one's self) धैर्य्यं कृ, धैर्य्यावलम्बनं कृ.

RECOLLECTED, *p. p.* स्मृतः -ता -तं, अनुस्मृतः &c., अनुचिन्तितः &c., प्रत्यभिज्ञातः &c.

RECOLLECTION, *s.* स्मृतिः *f.*, स्मरणं, संस्मृतिः *f.*, संस्मरणं, अनुस्मृतिः *f.*, स्मरः, स्मर्तृत्वं, स्मरत्वं, अनुचिन्ता, अनुबोधः, आध्यानं, आध्या, ध्यानं, संस्कारः, चिन्ता; 'of a former birth,' जातिस्मरत्वं; 'proximate cause of recollection,' स्मृतिहेतुः *m.*

To RECOMMEND, *v. a.* (Commend to another's kind treatment by favourable representations) गुणवर्णनेन or यशोवर्णनेन अमुकजनम् आदरणीयमिति or अनुग्रहार्हमिति or सत्कारार्हमिति बुध् (c. 10. बोधयति -यितुं) or उद्दिश् (c. 6. -दिशति -देष्टुं), गुणप्रशंसापूर्व्वम् अमुकजनं सत्कारार्हम् इति बोधयित्वा परस्मिन् सम् in caus. (-अर्पयति -यितुं), सद्गुणशालित्वाद् अमुकः सत्करणीय इति or अनुग्रहणीय इति ज्ञापयित्वा परस्मिन् सम्, गुणवर्णनेन परार्पम् अनुग्रहं प्रार्थ्.—(Commend, praise) प्रशंस् (c. 1. -शंसति -सितुं), अभिप्रशंस्, स्लाघ्, कृत्, अनुकृत्, वर्ण्, गुणवर्णनं कृ.—(Advise) उपदिश्, आदिश्.—(Commit) सम् or न्यस् in caus., *see* COMMIT.

RECOMMENDATION, *s.* (Favourable mention) गुणप्रशंसा -सनं, गुणव्याख्या, गुणवर्णनं, गुणवादः, यशोवर्णनं, गुणकीर्त्तनं, गुणवर्णनेन परार्थम् अनुग्रहप्रार्थनं.—(Letter of recommendation) गुणवर्णनपत्रं, गुणव्याख्यापत्रं, गुणप्रशंसापत्रं, वर्णनपत्रं, यशोवर्णनपत्रं, प्रशंसापत्रं, साहित्यपत्रं.—(That which recommends) प्रसादकारणं, अनुग्रहकारणं, अनुरागकारणं, प्रसादहेतुः *m.*, कृपाकारणं, कृपाहेतुः *m.*—(Advice) उपदेशः, आदेशः, प्रेरणा.

RECOMMENDATORY, *a.* गुणप्रशंसकः -का -कं, गुणवर्णकः &c., गुणप्रकाशकः &c.

RECOMMENDED, *p. p.* प्रशंसितः -ता -तं, प्रशस्तः -स्ता -स्तं, स्लाघितः -ता -तं.

To RECOMPENSE, *v. a.* (Reward) परितुष् (c. 10. -तोषयति -यितुं), सन्तुष्, पारितोषिकं दा, सम्भू in caus.—(Make a return or requital) प्रतिफलं दा, निष्कृतिं दा, प्रतिदानं कृ, प्रतिकृतिं or प्रतिक्रियां कृ, शोधनं कृ, शुद्धिं कृ, परिशोधनं कृ, निस्तारं कृ, निष्कृ, प्रतिकृ, प्रत्युपकृ, अपाकृ, शुध् in caus.—(Make amends for a loss) क्षतिनिष्कृतिं कृ, हानिनिष्कृतिं कृ, क्षतिपूरणं कृ, हानिपूरणं कृ.

RECOMPENSE, *s.* (Reward) पारितोषिकं, फलं, प्रतिफलं.—(Return, requital) प्रतिफलं, निष्कृतिः *f.*, प्रतिकृतिः *f.*, प्रतिक्रिया, प्रतीकारः, निस्तारः, निर्यातनं, शुद्धिः *f.*, शोधनं, परिशुद्धिः *f.*, परिशोधनं, उपकारमोक्षः, प्रत्युपकारः, सुकृतं.—(Amends for a loss) क्षतिपूरणं, हानिपूरणं, क्षतिनिष्कृतिः *f.*, हानिनिष्कृतिः *f.*, हानिमूल्यं.

RECOMPENSED, *p. p.* परितोषितः -ता -तं, सन्तोषितः &c., सम्भावितः &c., प्रतिफलितः &c., प्रतिकृतः &c., प्रत्युपकृतः &c., गृहीतफलः -ला -लं.

RECOMPENSING, *part.* पारितोषिकः -की -कं, तुष्टिकरः -रा -रं, निष्कारकः &c.

RECONCILABLE, *a.* सन्धेयः -या -यं, सन्धातव्यः -व्या -व्यं, समाधेयः -या -यं.

To RECONCILE, *v. a.* (Restore to friendship or union) सन्धा (c. 3. -दधाति -धत्ते -धातुं), समाधा, सन्धिं कृ, सन्धानं कृ, समाधानं कृ, समाधिं कृ, अन्योन्यवैरित्वं or अन्योन्यद्वेषं शम् (c. 10. शमयति -यितुं), वैरशान्तिं कृ, वैरशमनं कृ, विवादशान्तिं कृ, पुनःसख्यं कृ, पुनर्मैत्र्यं कृ, पुनःसौहृदं कृ, पुनःप्रीतिं कृ, पुनरैक्यं कृ, एकीकृ, मिल् in caus. (मेलयति -यितुं), सम्मिल्, सह मिल्, मेलनं कृ.—(Bring to acquiescence, content, or submission) सान्त्व् (c. 10. सान्त्वयति -यितुं), साम् (c. 10. सामयति -यितुं), अनुनी (c. 1. -नयति -नेतुं), तुष् (c. 10. तोषयति -यितुं), सन्तुष्, परितुष्, सम्परितुष्, तुष्टिं नी.—(Make consistent) सदृशीकृ, सङ्गतं -तां कृ, सम्मतीकृ, एकवाक्यतां कृ, अनुवादित्वं कृ.

RECONCILED, *p. p.* सन्धितः -ता -तं, समाहितः -ता -तं, कृतसन्धिः -न्धिः -न्धि, शान्तवैरः -रा -रं, शान्तद्वेषः -षा -षं, शान्तविवादः -दा -दं, एकीकृतः -ता -तं; 'to be reconciled,' सन्धा (c. 3. -दधाति -धत्ते -धातुं or pass. -धीयते), सह मिल् (c. 6. मिलति, मेलितुं), पुनर्मैत्र्यं गम् or इ, पुनःसख्यं गम्, एकीभू, तुष्टिं गम् or इ, परितोषं गम्; 'to be reconciled to one's enemy,' शत्रुणा or शत्रुणा सह सन्धा; 'to one's brother,' भ्रात्रा सह मिल्.

RECONCILER, *s.* सन्धाता *m.* (तृ), समाधाता *m.*, सन्धानकर्त्ता *m.* (र्तृ), सन्धिकृत् *m.*

RECONCILIATION, RECONCILEMENT, *s.* (The act) सन्धानं, समाधानं, सन्धानकरणं, सन्धिकरणं, वैरशमनं, मेलनं, सम्मेलनं, एकीकरणं, सान्त्वनं, साम *n.* (न्), शाम *n.*, शामनं.—(The state) सन्धिः *m.*, समाधिः *m.*, वैरशान्तिः *f.*, साम *n.* (न्), पुनःसख्यं, पुनर्मैत्र्यं, पुनर्मैत्री, पुनःप्रीतिः *f.*, पुनःस्नेहः, संवित्तिः *f.*, ऐक्यं, एकता.

RECONDITE, *a.* गूढः -ढा -ढं, निगूढः &c., निगूढार्थः -र्था -र्थं, गहनः -ना -नं, परमगहनः &c., गहनार्थः &c., गुप्तार्थः &c., गुह्यार्थः &c., गम्भीरार्थः &c., दुर्ज्ञेयः -या -यं, दुर्गम्यः -म्या -म्यं, अगम्यः &c., दुर्बोधः -धा -धं, दुरवबोधः &c., गम्भीरः -रा -रं, रहस्यः -स्या -स्यं.

To RECONDUCT, *v. a.* पुनर् नी (c. 1. नयति, नेतुं), प्रतिनी, प्रत्यानी.

To RECONNOITRE, RECONNOITER, *v. a.* कियद्दूरात् or नातिदूराद् अवेक्ष् (c. 1. -ईक्षते -क्षितुं) or निरीक्ष् or वीक्ष् or परीक्ष् or दृश् or अनुदृश् or आलोक् or अवलोक् or आलोच् or अनुसन्धा or निरूप्.

RECONNOITRED, *p. p.* कियद्दूराद् अवेक्षितः -ता -तं or निरूपितः &c.

To RECONQUER, *v. a.* पुनर् जि or पराजि or विजि, पुनर् वशीकृ.

To RECONSIDER, *v. a.* पुनर् विचर् or विगण् or चिन्त्, प्रतिचिन्त्, पुनर् निरूप् or अनुसन्धा or परीक्ष्, पुनर् वितर्क्, पुनर्विचारं कृ.

RECONSIDERED, *p. p.* पुनर्विचारितः -ता -तं, पुनर्निरूपितः &c., प्रतिचिन्तितः &c.

To RECORD, *v. a.* पत्रे or लेख्ये or लेख्यपत्रे आरुह् in caus. (-रोपयति -यितुं) or समारुह् or अभिलिख् (c. 6. -लिखति -लेखितुं) or लिख्, लेख्यपत्रे समृ in caus. (-अर्पयति -यितुं) or ऋ in caus. or निविश् (c. 10. -वेशयति -यितुं) or न्यस्, लेख्यारूढं -ढां कृ, पत्रारूढं -ढां कृ, पट्टारूढं -ढां कृ.

RECORD, *s.* लेख्यं, लेखः, लेख्यप्रसङ्गः, लेख्यपत्रं, लेखप्रमाणं, लेख्यप्रमाणं, लिखितं, लिखनं, पत्रं -त्री -त्रिका, पत्रकं, पटः, पट्टः, आगमः, आम्नायः, साक्ष्यं.

RECORDED, *p. p.* लेख्यारूढः -ढा -ढं, लेख्यारोपितः -ता -तं, लेख्यपत्रारूढः &c., लेख्यसमर्पितः -ता -तं, पट्टारूढः &c., पटारूढः &c., अभिलिखितः -ता -तं, लिखितः &c., पत्रलिखितः &c., आम्नातः &c.

RECORDER, *s.* कायस्थः, लेखकः, लिपिकरः, लिपिकारः, अभिलेखकः, अभिलेखनकृत्.—(Officer) नगरव्यवहारदर्शी *m.* (न्), प्रधानविचारकः.

To RECOUNT, *v. a.* कथ् (c. 10. कथयति -यितुं), आख्या (c. 2. -ख्याति -तुं or caus. ख्यापयति -यितुं), ख्या, श्रु (c. 10. श्रावयति -यितुं), वर्ण् (c. 10. वर्णयति -यितुं), आचक्ष्, निविद् in caus.

RECOUNTED, *p. p.* कथितः -ता -तं, आख्यातः &c., समाख्यातः &c., निवेदितः &c.

RECOURSE, *s.* आश्रयः -यणं, समाश्रयः -यणं, उपाश्रयः -यणं, संश्रयः -यणं, आशयः, अवलम्बनं, उपस्थितिः *f.*, उपगमनं, प्रत्यागमनं; 'to have recourse,' आश्रि (c. 1. -श्रयति -यितुं), समाश्रि, उपाश्रि, समुपाश्रि, संश्रि, अभिश्रि, अवलम्ब् (c. 1. -लम्बते -म्बितुं), उपस्था (c. 1. -तिष्ठति -स्थातुं), आस्था, उपगम्; 'having recourse,' आश्रित्य, आश्रितः -ता -तं, आस्थाय, उपस्थाय.

To RECOVER, *v. a.* (Regain) प्रतिलभ् (c. 1. -लभते -लब्धुं), प्रत्युपलभ्, पुनर् लभ्, पुनर् उपलभ्, अनुप्राप् (c. 5. -आप्नोति -आप्तुं), प्रत्यवाप्, पुनः प्राप्, पुनर् अवाप्, प्रत्यादा (c. 3. -ददाति -दत्ते -दातुं), पुनर् आदा, पुनर् ग्रह् (c. 9. गृह्णाति, ग्रहीतुं), प्रतिग्रह्, प्रतिपद् (c. 4. -पद्यते -पत्तुं), पुनर् आपद्, प्रत्याहृ (c. 1. -हरति -ते -हर्तुं), प्रत्युद्धृ, उद्धृ; 'to recover one's consciousness,' संज्ञां लभ्, चैतन्यं लभ्, स्वप्रकृतिम् आपद् or प्रतिपद्; 'one who has done so,' लब्धसंज्ञः, स्वप्रकृतिमापन्नः; 'to recover recollection,' स्मृतिं लभ्.—(Restore from sickness, &c.) स्वस्थं -स्थां कृ, रोगं शम् in caus., रोगाद् विमुच् or मुच्, रोगं निवृत् in caus., रोगं नश् in caus. or निरस्, समुत्था in caus. प्रतिकृ, समाधा, प्रतिसमाधा, *see To* CURE.

To RECOVER, *v. n.* (Regain health, be restored from sickness) रोगात् समुत्था (c. 1. -तिष्ठति -थातुं, rt. स्था) or उत्था or मुच् in pass. (मुच्यते) or विमुच्, रोगमुक्तः -क्ता -क्तं भू, शान्तरोगः -गा -गं भू, निवृत्तरोगः &c. भू, पुनः स्वस्थः -स्था -स्थं भू, पुनः सुस्थः -स्था -स्थं भू, पुनर् निरामयः -या -यं भू, पुनर् आरोग्यं or स्वास्थ्यं गम् or इ.—(From loss of consciousness or fainting) प्रत्याश्वस् (c. 2. -श्वसिति -तुं), संज्ञां लभ् (c. 1. लभते, लब्धुं), चैतन्यं लभ्, चेतनां प्राप्, स्वप्रकृतिम् आपद् (c. 4. -पद्यते -पत्तुं) or प्रतिपद्, प्रकृतिमापन्नः -न्ना -न्नं भू.—(Regain one's former state, come right) पूर्ववद् भू, यथास्थितः -ता -तं भू, स्वस्थः -स्था -स्थं भू, पूर्वावस्थां or पूर्वस्थितिं or पूर्ववृत्तिम् आपद् or प्रतिपद् or गम्.

RECOVERABLE *a.* प्रतिलभ्यः -भ्या -भ्यं, पुनर्लभ्यः &c., पुनःप्राप्यः -प्या -प्यं.

RECOVERED, *p. p.* (Regained) प्रतिलब्धः -ब्धा -ब्धं, प्रत्युपलब्धः &c., पुनर्लब्धः &c., पुनरुपलब्धः &c., पुनः प्राप्तः -प्ता -प्तं, अनुप्राप्तः &c., पुनर् अवाप्तः &c., प्रत्यवाप्तः &c., पुनर्गृहीतः -ता -तं, प्रत्युद्धृतः &c., प्रत्याहृतः &c., आपन्नः -न्ना -न्नं, प्रतिपन्नः &c., प्रतिकृतः &c.—(From sickness) रोगसमुत्थितः -ता -तं, समुत्थितः &c., रोगोत्थितः &c., रोगमुक्तः -क्ता -क्तं, मुक्तरोगः -गा -गं, निवृत्तरोगः &c., गतरोगः &c., विगतरोगः &c., नष्टरोगः &c., निरस्तरोगः &c., शान्तरोगः &c., स्वस्थः -स्था -स्थं, निरामयः -या -यं; 'from a fever,' गतज्वरः -रा -रं, ज्वरमुक्तः &c.—(From unconsciousness or fainting) लब्धसंज्ञः -ज्ञा -ज्ञं, लब्धचैतन्यः -न्या -न्यं, लब्धचेताः -ताः -तः (स्), स्वप्रकृतिमापन्नः -न्ना -न्नं. —(One who has recovered his recollection) लब्धस्मृतिः -तिः -ति.

RECOVERY, *s.* (Regaining) पुनर्लब्धिः *f.*, पुनर्लाभः, पुनरुपलब्धिः *f.*, प्रत्युपलब्धिः *f.*, प्रतिलब्धिः *f.*, प्रतिलम्भः, पुनःप्राप्तिः *f.*, पुनःप्रापणं, पुनरवाप्तिः *f.*, प्रत्यवाप्तिः *f.*, अनुप्राप्तिः *f.*, अवाप्तिः *f.*, पुनरादानं, पुनर्ग्रहणं, प्रतिग्रहणं, प्रत्युद्धरणं, प्रत्युद्धारः, अवहारः, प्रत्यानयनं, आनयनं, प्रतीकारः. —(From sickness) रोगसमुत्थानं, समुत्थानं, रोगोत्थानं, रोगमुक्तिः *f.*, रोगमुक्तता, रोगनिवृत्तिः *f.*, स्वास्थ्यं, स्वस्थता, आरोग्यं, निरामयता -त्वं, निरामयं, कल्यता -त्वं.

RECREANT, *a.* (Cowardly) कातरः -रा -रं, क्लीवः -वा -वं, भीरुः -रुः रु.—(Apostate) धर्म्मभ्रष्टः -ष्टा -ष्टं, सङ्कुलभ्रष्टः &c., त्यक्तसङ्कुल्यः -ल्या -ल्यं, उल्लंघितधर्म्मः -र्म्मा -र्म्मं.

To RECREATE, *v. a.* (Divert, gratify) विनुद् (c. 10. -नोदयति -यितुं), आनन्द् in caus., रम् in caus., सुख्, सन्तुष्, परितुष्, प्री, तृप्, ह्लाद्, सुखं कृ, प्रीतिं दा.—(Refresh) आश्वस् (c. 10. -श्वासयति -यितुं), प्रत्याश्वस्, समाश्वस्, सुख् (c. 10. सुखयति -यितुं).

RECREATED, *p. p.* विनोदितः -ता -तं, आश्वासितः &c., परितोषितः -ता -तं.

RECREATION, *s.* विनोदः -दनं, विश्रामः, विश्रान्तिः *f.*, विहारः, विहरणं, क्रीडा, मनोविनोदः, मनोरञ्जनं, विलासः, खेला, रमणं, कौतुकं; 'to take recreation,' विहृ (c. 1. -हरति -हर्तुं), मनो विनुद् (c. 10. -नोदयति -यितुं), रम्, क्रीड्, विश्रम्.

RECREATIVE, *a.* विनोदकः -का -कं, मनोरञ्जकः &c. *See* REFRESHING, *a.*

To RECRIMINATE, *s.* प्रत्यभियोगं कृ, प्रत्यपवादं कृ, प्रत्यारोपं कृ, प्रत्यारोपणं कृ; 'to criminate and recriminate,' अभियोगप्रत्यभियोगं कृ, वादानुवादं कृ.

Recrimination, *s.* प्रत्यभियोगः, प्रत्यपवादः, प्रत्यारोपः -पणं; 'crimination and recrimination,' अभियोगप्रत्यभियोगौ *m. du.*, अन्योन्यदोषारोपः -पणं, परस्परदोषारोपः, वादानुवादः.

Recriminatory, recriminative, *a.* प्रत्यारोपकः -का -कं, प्रत्यपवादकः &c., प्रत्यभियोगी -गिनी -गि (न्), प्रत्यारोपकारी &c.

To recruit, *v. a.* (Repair) प्रतिकृ, प्रतिसंकृ, स्वस्थं -स्थां कृ, सुस्थं -स्थां कृ, सुस्थ (nom. सुस्थयति -यितुं), पूर्व्ववत्तं -वर्त्तीं -वत् कृ, समाधा, प्रतिसमाधा.—(Restore exhausted strength) क्षीणबलं वृध् (c. 10. वर्धयति -यितुं), क्षीणसत्त्वं वृध्, तेजो or सत्त्वं वृध्, आप्यस् in caus., आप्यै in caus.—(Supply with new soldiers) नवसैन्ययुक्तं -क्तां कृ.

To recruit, *v. n.* (Recover energy or strength) बलं or सत्त्वं लभ् (c. 1. लभते, लब्धुं), स्वसत्त्वं लभ् or प्राप्, स्वतेजो लभ्, स्ववीर्य्यं प्राप्, स्वप्रकृतिं लभ्, पुनः स्वास्थ्यं गम् or इ, पुनः स्वस्थः -स्था -स्थं भू, पुनः सुस्थः &c. भू.—(Raise new soldiers) नवसैन्यसंग्रहं कृ, नूतनसैन्यसंग्रहं कृ, बलाधिक्यं कृ.

Recruit, *s.* नवसैन्यः, नूतनसैन्यः, नवसैनिकः, नवीनसैन्यः, शस्त्राभ्यासी *m.* (न्), अस्त्रशिक्षाकारी *m.*, नूतनाभ्यासी *m.*, नवाभ्यासी *m.*

Recruited, *p. p.* (In strength) लब्धबलः -ला -लं, लब्धसत्त्वः -त्त्वा -त्त्वं, प्राप्तबलः &c., वर्धितबलः &c., पुनः स्वस्थभूतः -ता -तं, आप्यायितः &c., प्रत्याश्वस्तः -स्ता -स्तं.—(As an army) नवसैन्ययुक्तः -क्ता -क्तं, नूतनसैन्ययुक्तः &c.

Rectangle, *s.* समकोणाकृतिः *f.*, समकोणः, समास्रं, आयतसमकोणः, आयतसमास्रं, आयतसमलम्बः, समचतुष्कोणः, समचतुरस्रं, समकोणमूर्त्तिः *f.*, आयतः.

Rectangular, *a.* समचतुष्कोणः -णा -णं, समचतुरस्रः -स्रा -स्रं, समकोणः -णा -णं, समकोणाकृतिः -तिः -ति, आयतः -ता -तं.

Rectifiable, *a.* शोधनीयः -या -यं, संशोधनीयः &c., शोध्यः -ध्या -ध्यं.

Rectification, *s.* शोधनं, संशोधनं, शुद्धिः *f.*, विशुद्धिः *f.*, प्रतिसमाधानं.

Rectified, *p. p.* शोधितः -ता -तं, विशोधितः &c., प्रतिसमाहितः &c.

To rectify, *v. a.* शुध् (c. 10. शोधयति -यितुं), विशुध्, संशुध्, शुद्धीकृ, समाधा (c. 3. -दधाति -धत्ते -धातुं), प्रतिसमाधा, शोधनं कृ, यथार्थं -र्थां कृ, तथ्यं -थ्यां कृ, समञ्जसं -सां कृ, सम्यक् कृ.

Rectilinear, rectilineal, *a.* सरलरेखः -खा -खं, सरलरेखाविशिष्टः -ष्टा -ष्टं, सरलरेखामयः -यी -यं.

Rectitude, *s.* सारल्यं, सरलता -त्वं, ऋजुता, आर्जवं, मर्य्यादा, अवक्रता, अजिह्मता, शुद्धता, शुचिता, मतिशुद्धता, साधुता, दाक्षिण्यं, सत्यशीलता, विमलता, न्यायिता, अशठता, सच्चरितं, संस्था, स्थितिः *f.*, व्यवस्थितिः *f.*, सम्यग्वृत्तित्वं, अव्यभिचारः, यथोचितं, याथातथ्यं; 'law of retitude,' नीतिः *f.*; 'path of rectitude,' सत्पथः, सन्मार्गः; 'deviation from the path of rectitude,' सत्पथभ्रंशः, सत्पथत्यागः, सन्मार्गभ्रंशः, विमार्गगमनं, उन्मार्गगमनं, उत्पथगमनं, कुपथगमनं, यथोचितभ्रंशः, मर्य्यादात्यागः, मर्य्यादालंघनं.

Rector, *s.* ग्रामपुरोहितः, ग्रामगुरुः *m.*, ग्रामाचार्य्यः, ग्रामधर्म्माध्यक्षः.

Rectory, *s.* ग्रामपुरोहितवसतिः *f.*, ग्रामाचार्य्यगृहं, ग्रामगुरुनिकेतनं.

Rectum, *s.* अधःस्थो मलाशयः, जघन्यस्थो मलाशयः, पश्चिमनाडी.

Recumbence, recumbency, *s.* शयनं, पतनं, कुक्षिशयनं, कुक्षिशय्या.

Recumbent, *a.* शयानः -ना -नं, शयः -या -यं, शायी -यिनी -यि (न्), शयितः -ता -तं, कुक्षिशयः -या -यं, कुक्षिशायी &c., संविष्टः -ष्टा -ष्टं. *See* Reclining, Lying down.

To recur, *v. n.* (Happen again) पुनर् उपस्था (c. 1. -तिष्ठति -स्थातुं), पुनः सम्भू, पुनः संवृत् or वृत्, पुनर् आगम् or उपागम्, पुनः सम्पद्, पुनर् आपत् or निपत्, पुनर् घट्; 'from time to time,' वारं वारं or पुनः पुनर् or अनुवारम् उपस्था.—(To the mind or thought) स्फुर् (c. 6. स्फुरति -रितुं), मनसि स्फुर्, पुनः स्मृ, पुनःस्मृतः -ता -तं भू.

Recurrence, recurrency, *s.* पुनरुपस्थितिः *f.*, पुनरुपस्थानं, पुनरागमनं, पुनर्वर्त्तनं, पुनरुपागमः, पुनःसम्भवः, पुनःसम्भूतिः *f.*, पुनरुत्पत्तिः *f.*, पुनर्घटना.—(To the mind) स्मरणं, स्मृतिः *f.*, पुनःस्मरणं, स्फुरणं.

Recurrent, recurring, *a.* अनुवारमागामी -मिनी -मि (न्), वारं वारम् उपस्थायी &c., पुनःपुनरागामी &c., पुनःपुनर्वर्त्ती &c.

Recusant, recusancy, *s.* *See* Non-conformist, non-conformity.

Red, *a.* रक्तः -क्ता -क्तं, लोहितः -ता -हिनी -तं, रक्तवर्णः -र्णा -र्णं, लोहितवर्णः &c., रोहितः -ता -हिणी -तं, शोणितः -ता -तं, शोणः -णा -णी -णं, सिन्दूरवर्णः &c., कषायः -या -यं, मञ्जिष्ठः -ष्ठी -ष्ठं; 'dark red,' अरुणः -णा -णं, घनारुणः &c.; 'pale red,' श्वेतरक्तः -क्ता -क्तं, पाटलः -ला -लं.

Red, *s.* रक्तः, लोहितः, रोहितः, शोणितः, रक्तवर्णः, अरुणः.

To redden, *v. a.* रक्तीकृ, लोहितीकृ, अरुणीकृ, शोणितीकृ, रक्तवर्णीकृ.

To redden, *v. n.* अरुणीभू, रक्तीभू, लोहित (nom. लोहितायति -ते), लोहितीभू.

Reddened, *p. p.* रक्तीकृतः -ता -तं, अरुणीकृतः &c., अरुणितः &c., लोहितीकृतः -ता -तं, पाटलितः &c., पाटलीकृतः &c., सिन्दूरितः &c.

Reddish, *a.* ईषद्रक्तः -क्ता -क्तं, आरक्तः &c., आलोहितः -ता -तं.

Reddishness, *s.* ईषद्रक्तता, आरक्तता, आलोहितता, ईषल्लोहितता.

To redeem, *v. a.* (Ransom, purchase back) परिक्री (c. 9. -क्रीणीते -क्रेतुं), परिक्रयं कृ, परिक्रयणं कृ, अवहृ, अवहरणं कृ.—(Save, deliver) त्रै (c. 1. त्रायते, त्रातुं), परित्रै, संत्रै, मुच् (c. 6. मुञ्चति, मोक्तुं, c. 10. मोचयति -यितुं), परिमुच्, उद्धृ (c. 1. -हरति -हर्त्तुं), समुद्धृ, मोक्ष् (c. 10. मोक्षयति -यितुं), निस्तॄ (c. 10. -तारयति -यितुं), सन्तॄ, उत्तॄ, तॄ, उद्धारं कृ.—(Compensate, make amends for) निष्कृतिं कृ, हानिनिष्कृतिं कृ, क्षतिनिष्कृतिं कृ, हानिपूरणं कृ.

Redeemable, *a.* परिक्रेयः -या -यं, परिक्रेतव्यः -व्या -व्यं, अवहार्य्यः -र्य्या -र्य्यं.

Redeemed, *p. p.* परिक्रीतः -ता -तं, त्रातः &c., परित्रातः &c., मुक्तः -क्ता -क्तं, परिमुक्तः &c., उद्धृतः -ता -तं, निस्तारितः &c.

Redeemer, *s.* (Ransomer) परिक्रेता *m.* (तृ), परिक्रयकृत्.—(Saviour) त्राता *m.* (तृ), उद्धर्त्ता *m.*, समुद्धर्त्ता *m.*, उद्धारकः, मोक्षकः, परिमोचकः, निस्तारकः, तारकः; 'of the world,' जगत्त्राता *m.*, जगदुद्धारकः.

Re-delivery, *s.* प्रत्यर्पणं, प्रतिसमर्पणं, पुनःसमर्पणं, अवहारः.

Redemption, *s.* (Ransom) परिक्रयः -यणं, अवहरणं.—(Rescue, salvation) त्राणं, परित्राणं, उद्धारः, समुद्धारः, उद्धरणं, मुक्तिः *f.*, मोक्षः -क्षणं, परिमोक्षणं, परिमुक्तिः *f.*, निस्तारः, निस्तरणं, तारणं, निष्कृतिः *f.*

Red-haired, *a.* रक्तकेशः -शा -शं, रक्तकेशी -शिनी -शि (न्).

Red-hot, *a.* अग्निवर्णः -र्णा -र्णं, तापरक्तः -क्ता -क्तं, तप्तः -प्ता -प्तं, उपतप्तः &c., सन्तप्तः &c., अभितप्तः &c., रक्ततप्तः &c., उत्तापरक्तः -क्ता -क्तं.

Red-lead, *s.* सिन्दूरं -रिका, रक्तचूर्णं. *See* Minium.

Red-legged, *a.* रक्तपादः -दा -दं, लोहितपादः &c., रक्तजंघः -घा -घं.

Redness, *s.* रक्तत्वं -ता, रक्तिमा *m.* (न्), लौहित्यं, लोहितत्वं -ता, अरुणिमा *m.* (न्), शोणिमा *m.* (न्), शोणितत्वं -ता.

Redolence, redolency, *s.* सुगन्धः, आमोदः, सुवासः. *See* Fragrance.

Redolent, *a.* सुरभिः -भिः -भि, सुगन्धिकः -का -कं, सुगन्धिः -न्धिः -न्धि, सुवासिकः -की -कं, परिमलयुक्तः -क्ता -क्तं, तिक्तः &c. *See* Fragrant.

To redouble, *v. a.* (Repeat often) पुनःपुनः कृ, मुहुर्मुहुः कृ, असकृत् कृ, अभीक्ष्णं कृ.—(Increase by repeated efforts) अनेकयत्नान्

कृत्वा or पुनःपुनर् यत्नं कृत्वा वृध् (c. 10. वर्धयति -यितुं) or प्रवृध् or अधिकीकृ or अधिकतरीकृ or अधिकतरं -रां कृ; 'to redouble one's efforts,' पुनः पुनर् यत्नं कृ, मुहुर्मुहुर् उद्योगं कृ.

REDOUBLED, *p. p.* पुनःपुनः कृतः -ता -तं, मुहुर्मुहुः कृतः &c., असकृत्कृतः &c., पौनःपुनिकः -की -कं, वर्धितः -ता -तं, प्रवृद्धः -द्धा -द्धं, अधिकीकृतः &c.

REDOUBT, *s.* दुर्गबहिःस्थितं प्राकारप्राचीरादि, दुर्गप्राकारः, प्राचीरं.

REDOUBTABLE, *a.* भीमः -मा -मं, महावीर्य्यः -र्य्या -र्य्यं, महाप्रतापः -पा -पं.

To REDOUND, *v. n.* (Conduce, bring about) नी (c. 1. नयति, नेतुं), आनी, आवह् (c. 1. -वहति -वोढुं), साध् (c. 10. साधयति -यितुं), सम्पद् (c. 10. -पादयति -यितुं), जन् (c. 10. जनयति -यितुं), संजन्.—(Result) अवसो (c. 4. -स्यति -सातुं), पर्य्यवसो, परिणामः -मा -मं भू in comp., सपरिणामः -मा -मं भू.

To REDRESS, *v. a.* प्रतिकृ, समाधा (c. 3. -दधाति -धातुं), प्रतिसमाधा, सन्धा, साध् (c. 10. साधयति -यितुं), उद्धृ (c. 1. -हरति -हर्त्तुं), उपायं कॢप् (c. 10. कल्पयति -यितुं), प्रतिसमाधानं कृ, प्रतीकारं कृ, उद्धारं कृ, दुःखाद् or क्लेशाद् मुच्, क्लेशमुक्तिं कृ.

REDRESS, *s.* प्रतिकारः, प्रतीकारः, प्रतिक्रिया, समाधानं, प्रतिसमाधानं, उपायः, उद्धारः, उद्धरणं, परिच्छेदः, क्लेशमुक्तिः *f.*, दुःखमुक्तिः *f.*

REDRESSED, *p. p.* प्रतिकृतः -ता -तं, समाहितः &c., परिच्छिन्नः -न्ना -न्नं.

To REDUCE, *v. a.* (Bring to a former state) पूर्ववत् कृ, पूर्वावस्थां or पूर्वस्थितिं नी (c. 1. नयति, नेतुं) or आनी or गम् in caus.—(Bring to any state) नी, आनी, गम् in caus. (गमयति -यितुं), कृ in comp.; 'to reduce to proverty,' दारिद्र्यं गम्, दरिद्रीकृ; 'to subjection,' वशीकृ; 'to one's own power,' स्ववशीकृ, आत्मसात्कृ; 'to ashes,' भस्मसात्कृ, भस्मीकृ; 'to a heap of ashes,' भस्मराशीकृ; 'to nothing,' निष्किञ्चनीकृ. Or expressed by आपन्न or सम्पन्न in comp.; as, 'to reduce to poverty,' दारिद्र्यापन्नं -न्नां कृ.—(Diminish, lower) न्यूनीकृ, अल्पीकृ, लघूकृ, ऊनीकृ, न्यून् (c. 10. न्यूनयति -यितुं), ऊन्, ह्रस् (c. 10. ह्रासयति -यितुं), लघ (nom. लघयति -यितुं), कन् (c. 10. कनयति -यितुं), शिथिलीकृ; 'to reduce one's strength,' बलं or वीर्य्यं शिथिलीकृ.—(Make thin) कृशीकृ, क्षीणीकृ, मांसक्षयं कृ, क्षि in caus. (क्षपयति -यितुं), शुष्कीकृ.—(Subdue) वशीकृ, पराजि, विजि, जि, सह्.—(In arithmetic) रूपान्तरं कृ, रूपं दा or कृ.—(Reduce to order), *see To* METHODIZE, ARRANGE.

REDUCED, *p. p.* (Brought to a former state) पूर्ववत्कृतः -ता -तं, पूर्ववन्नीतः &c., पूर्वावस्थाकृतः &c., पूर्वदशाक्रमितः &c., पूर्वस्थितिकृतः &c.—(Brought to any state) गमितः -ता -तं, परिगमितः &c., गतः -ता -तं, कृतः &c. in comp. भूतः &c. in comp.; 'reduced to poverty,' दारिद्र्यगतः -ता -तं, दारिद्र्यकृतः &c., दरिद्रीकृतः &c., दरिद्रीभूतः &c., गतधनः -ना -नं, गतविभवः -वा -वं, प्रचलितविभवः &c., शिथिलवसुः -सुः -सु, *see* POVERTY; 'reduced to misery,' कृच्छ्रगतः -ता -तं, कृच्छ्रक्रमितः &c.; 'reduced to ashes,' भस्मीकृतः &c., भस्मीभूतः &c., भस्मसात्कृतः &c.; 'to powder,' चूर्णीकृतः &c.; 'to nothing,' निष्किञ्चनः -ना -नं.—(Brought into subjection) वशीकृतः -ता -तं, वशीभूतः &c.—(Diminished, lowered) न्यूनीकृतः -ता -तं, न्यूनीभूतः &c., अल्पीकृतः &c., लघूकृतः &c., शिथिलीकृतः &c., शिथिलितः &c.; 'in strength of body,' शिथिलबलः -ला -लं, क्षीणबलः &c., विकलबलः &c., क्षीणः &c., कृशः -शा -शं.

REDUCIBLE, *a.* आनेयः -या -यं, आनेतव्यः -व्या -व्यं, करणीय in comp.; as, 'reducible to a former state,' पूर्ववत्करणीयः &c.; 'to ashes,' भस्मसात्करणीयः &c., भस्मीकरणीयः &c.

REDUCTION, *s.* (Bringing to any state) करणं in comp.; as, 'reduction to ashes,' भस्मीकरणं; 'to powder,' चूर्णीकरणं.—(Diminution, impairment) न्यूनीकरणं, न्यूनता -त्वं, अल्पीकरणं, लघूकरणं, ऊनीकरणं, ह्रासः, वैकल्यं, विकलीकरणं, शिथिलीकरणं, शैथिल्यं.—(Subjugation) वशीकरणं, विजयः, खण्डनं.—(In arithmetic) रूपान्तरं, रूपान्तरकरणं.

REDUNDANCE, REDUNDANCY, *s.* आधिक्यं, अधिकता -त्वं, अतिरेकः, उद्रेकः, आतिरेक्यं, अतिरिक्तता, आतिशय्यं, उत्सेकः, उद्वर्त्तः, गाढता. *See* EXCESS, EXUBERANCE.

REDUNDANT, *a.* अधिकः -का -कं, अतिरिक्तः -क्ता -क्तं, उद्रिक्तः &c., समतिरिक्तः &c., अतिशय in comp., अतिशयितः -ता -तं, अतिशयी -यिनी &c., अतिशायनः -ना -नं, अत्यन्तः -न्ता -न्तं, व्यर्थः -र्था -र्थं, उत्सिक्तः &c., उद्वर्त्तः -र्त्ता -र्त्तं, गाढः -ढा -ढं. *See* EXCESSIVE, EXUBERANT.

REDUNDANTLY, *adv.* अतिरिक्तं, उद्रिक्तं, अतिशयेन, सातिशयं, व्यर्थं.

To REDUPLICATE, *v. a.* (Double) द्विगुणीकृ.—(A syllable or letter) आम्रेड् (c. 10. -म्रेडयति -यितुं), अक्षराम्रेडनं कृ, अक्षराभ्यासं कृ, अक्षरद्वित्वं कृ, द्विरुक्तिं कृ.

REDUPLICATED, *p. p.* आम्रेडितः -ता -तं, अभ्यस्तः -स्ता -स्तं, द्विरुक्तः -क्ता -क्तं.

REDUPLICATION, *s.* आम्रेडनं, आम्रेडितं, द्विरुक्तिः *f.*; 'of a letter,' द्वित्वं; 'the reduplicated syllable,' अभ्यासः; 'word formed by reduplication,' प्रतिशब्दः. Reduplication is denoted by the symbol द्वि.

RED-WOOD, *s.* (Kind of red sandal) पत्राङ्गं, रक्तचन्दनं.

To RE-ECHO, RE-ECHOING, *see To* ECHO, ECHOING.

REED. *s.* नलः, नडः, वेत्रं -त्रः, वेतसः -सी, वेणुः *m.*, वंशः, शरः, धमनः, नालः -ली, नाडिः -डी *f.*, कीचकः, तृणं, तृणध्वजः, तृणकेतुः *m.*, पोटगलः, कुषिरन्ध्रः, छिद्रान्तरः, खसीरकः, त्वक्सारः, शतपर्वा *m.* (न्), मस्करः; 'leaf of a reed,' वेतसपत्रं; 'reed-mat,' नलपट्टिका; 'reed for writing, reed pen,' कलमः, लेखनी, आलेखनी.

REEDY, *a.* (Abounding with reeds) वेत्रकीयः -या -यं, वैत्रकः -की -कं, वेत्रवान् -वती -वत् (त्), वेत्रमयः -यी -यं, वेत्रपूर्णः -र्णा -र्णं, नडकीयः -या -यं, नडसः -सा -सं, नड्वलः -ला -लं, नलमयः -यी -यं, वेतस्वान् -स्वती -स्वत् (त्), वेतसपूर्णः -र्णा -र्णं, शरमयः &c.—(Sounding like a reed) कीचकस्वरः -रा -रं.

REEF, *s.* (Of a sail) वातवसनपुटः, नौकावसनपुटः.—(Of rocks) समुद्रमध्ये शैलसेतुः *m.* or शैलश्रेणी or शैलपंक्तिः *f.*

To REEF, *v. a.* वातवसनानि संहृ (c. 1. -हरति -हर्त्तुं) or संवृ or सम्पुटीकृ.

REEFY, *a.* शैलसेतुपूर्णः -र्णा -र्णं, शैलश्रेणीपूर्णः -र्णा -र्णं.

REEK, *s.* वाष्पः, उष्णवाष्पः, तप्तजलवाष्पः, धूमः -मिका, फेनः, स्वेदः.

To REEK, *v. n.* वाष्प (nom. वाष्पायते), वाष्पम् उद्गृ or उत्क्षिप् or उद्वम् in caus. or मुच्, वाष्पोद्गतिं कृ, वाष्पोद्गारं कृ, धूम (nom. धूमायते).

REEKING, REEKY, *a.* वाष्पायमानः -ना -नं, वाष्पोद्गारी -रिणी &c., वाष्पमयः -यी -यं, वाष्पार्द्रः -र्द्रा -र्द्रं, आर्द्रः &c., धूममयः -यी -यं, धूमायमानः -ना -नं.

REEL, *s.* (For winding thread) आवापनं.—(Lively dance) लघुनृत्यं.—(Movement on one side) विचलनं, चलनं.

To REEL, *v. n.* विचल् (c. 1. -चलति -लितुं), सञ्चल्, चल्, इतस्ततो विचल्, एकपार्श्वे पत् in des. (पिपतिषति -षितुं, पित्सति -त्सितुं).

To RE-ENFORCE, *s.* बलाधिक्यं कृ, सेनाधिक्यं कृ. *See* RE-INFORCE.

To RE-ENTER, *v. a.* पुनः प्रविश् (c. 6. -विशति -वेष्टुं), पुनर् आगम्.

To RE-ESTABLISH, *v. a.* पुनः स्था in caus. (स्थापयति -यितुं) or प्रतिष्ठा, पुनः संस्था.

REFECTION, *s.* अल्पाहारः, लघुभोजनं, अल्पभोजनं, लघ्वाहारः, आहारः, उपहारः, अल्पाभ्यवादनं, श्रमापहारः, श्रमपरिच्छेदः, क्लमपरिच्छेदः, शरीराप्यायनं.

REFECTORY. *s.* उपहारगृहं, उपहारशाला, आहारशाला, भोजनशाला.

To REFER, *v. a.* (Deliver over, consign to another for decision) निष्पादनार्थं परस्मिन् समृ in caus. (-अर्पयति -यितुं) or न्यृ or निक्षिप् or न्यस् or परस्मै प्रतिपद् in caus.—(Leave to the decision of another) परविचारं प्रार्थयित्वा कार्य्यं or अर्थं त्यज् (c. 1. त्यजति, त्यक्तुं) or अपास् (c. 4. -अस्यति -सितुं) or विसृज् (c. 6. -सृजति -स्रष्टुं) or अवसृज् or मुच् or अवमुच् or हा.—(Assign) आरुह् in caus. (-रोपयति-यितुं), समारुह्, अध्यारुह्, अभिसम्बन्ध् (c. 9. -बध्नाति-बन्धुं), सम्बन्ध्.

To REFER, *v. n.* (Have reference) अपेक्ष् (c. 1. -ईक्षते -क्षितुं), अवेक्ष्, प्रतीक्ष्, उद्दिश् (c. 6. -दिशति -देष्टुं), समुद्दिश्, निर्दिश्, अभिसम्बन्ध् in pass. (-बध्यते), सम्बन्ध् in pass.—(Allude) उद्दिश्, समुद्दिश्, सूच् (c. 10. सूचयति -यितुं).

REFERABLE, *a.* आरोपणीयः -या -यं, समारोपणीयः &c., अध्यारोपणीयः &c., समर्पणीयः -या -यं, अर्पणीयः &c., सम्बन्धनीयः -या -यं, अभिसम्बन्धनीयः -या -यं, सम्बन्धीयः -या -यं.

REFEREE, *s.* मध्यस्थः, प्रमाणपुरुषः, स्थेयः, निर्णेता *m.* (तृ), विचारकृत्.

REFERENCE, *s.* (Directing or consigning to another for information, &c.) समर्पणं, अर्पणं, प्रतिपादनं, निवेदनं, आरोपणं, समारोपणं, आरोपः.—(Relation, regard, allusion) अपेक्षा, अवेक्षा, प्रतीक्षा, उद्देशः, समुद्देशः, सम्बन्धः, अभिसम्बन्धः, अन्वयः, समन्वयः, विषयत्वं -ता, विषयः, सम्पर्कः, गोचरत्वं -ता; 'containing a reference,' सापेक्षः -क्षा -क्षं; 'in reference to,' अपेक्षया, अपेक्ष्य, प्रतीक्ष्य, उद्दिश्य, उद्देशेन, समुद्दिश्य, सापेक्षं.

REFERRED, *p. p.* (Consigned or directed to another) परसमर्पितः -ता -तं, परप्रतिपादितः &c., परनिवेदितः &c., अर्पितः &c., प्रस्थापितः &c.—(Assigned) आरोपितः -ता -तं, समारोपितः &c., अध्यारोपितः &c., अभिसम्बद्धः -द्धा -द्धं, निर्दिष्टः -ष्टा -ष्टं, उद्दिष्टः &c.

REFERRIBLE *a.* आरोपणीयः -या -यं. *See* REFERABLE, *a.*

To REFINE, *v. a.* (Purify) शुध् (c. 10. शोधयति -यितुं), संशुध्, विशुध्, शुद्धीकृ, शोधनं कृ, विमलीकृ, निर्मलीकृ, पवित्रीकृ, विमल (nom. विमलयति -यितुं), मलं हृ or अपनी.—(Make elegant or polite, polish) परिष्कृ, संस्कृ, शिष्टीकृ, शिष्टं -ष्टां कृ, सभ्यं -भ्यां कृ, शिष्टतां or सभ्यतां जन् (c. 10. जनयति -यितुं) or दा, सूक्ष्मीकृ.

To REFINE, *v. n.* (Become pure) शुध् (c. 4. शुध्यति -ते, शोद्धुं), संशुध्, विशुध्, शुद्धीभू, विमलीभू.—(Be over nice) अतिसूक्ष्मीभू, अतिसूक्ष्मतां सेव्.

REFINED, *p. p.* (Purified) शोधितः -ता -तं, संशोधितः &c., शुद्धः -द्धा -द्धं, संशुद्धः &c., विशोधितः &c., शुद्धीकृतः &c., विमलीकृतः &c., निर्मलीकृतः &c., हृतमलः -ला -लं, पवित्रीकृतः &c.—(Polished) परिष्कृतः -ता -तं, संस्कृतः &c., शिष्टः -ष्टा -ष्टं, सभ्यः -भ्या -भ्यं, सभ्यतापन्नः -न्ना -न्नं, सभ्यतासम्पन्नः &c.—(Nice, over nice) सूक्ष्मः -क्ष्मा -क्ष्मं, अतिसूक्ष्मः &c.

REFINEMENT *s.* (Act of purifying) शोधनं, संशोधनं, विशोधनं, शुद्धीकरणं, शोधः.—(Purity) शुद्धिः *f.*, संशुद्धिः *f.*, विशुद्धिः *f.*, शोधितत्वं, शुद्धता -त्वं, पवित्रता, *see* PURITY.—(Act of polishing) परिष्कारः, परिष्कृतिः *f.*, परिष्करणं, संस्कारः, संस्कृतिः *f.*, संस्करणं, सभ्यकरणं, शिष्टकरणं.—(State of being polished, elegance) शिष्टता -त्वं,

सभ्यता -त्वं, परिष्कारः, परिष्कृतत्वं, सुजनता, सौजन्यं; 'of manners,' शिष्टाचारत्वं, सभ्याचारत्वं, सभ्याचारसम्पन्नता, शिष्टाचारसम्पन्नता, सभाचातुर्य्यं, सुशीलता, सुनीतिः *f.*, विनयः; 'of mind,' मनःशुद्धिः *f.*, चित्तशुद्धिः *f.*—(Nicety, over nicety) सूक्ष्मता, अतिसूक्ष्मता, सौक्ष्म्यं, अतिसौक्ष्म्यं.

REFINER, *s.* शोधकः, संशोधकः, शोधयिता *m.* (तृ), मलापहारकः.—(Of metals) धातुशोधकः, धातुमलहारी *m.* (न्), धातुकलङ्कहारी *m.*

REFINING, *s.* (Of metals) धातुशोधनं, धातुमलापहारः, धातुकलङ्कहरणं.

To REFIT, *v. a.* प्रतिसंकृ, प्रतिकृ, समाधा, प्रतिसमाधा, जीर्णोद्धारं कृ, जीर्णसमाधानं कृ, पुनः क्लृप् or परिक्लृप्, पुनः सज्जीकृ, पुनः समायुज्. *See To* REPAIR.

To REFLECT, *v. a.* (Throw back, cause to return, as a mirror, &c.) प्रतिक्षिप् (c. 6. -क्षिपति -क्षेप्तुं) प्रतिहन् (c. 2. -हन्ति -न्तुं), पराहन्, परावृत् in caus. (-वर्त्तयति -यितुं), प्रत्यावृत्, परावर्त्तनं कृ, प्रतिक्षेपं कृ, प्रतिबिम्ब (nom. प्रतिबिम्बयति -यितुं), बिम्ब, प्रतिबिम्बितं -तां कृ, प्रतिबिम्बं कृ, प्रतिमूर्त्तिं कृ, प्रतिरूपं कृ; 'a body which reflects all the rays of light,' पदार्थो यस्मात् सर्व्वकिरणाः परावर्त्तन्ते or पराव्रजन्ति, पदार्थो यः सर्व्वकिरणान् परावर्त्तयति; 'a lake which reflects the stars,' ताराप्रतिबिम्बं सरस्, ताराछायं सरस्; 'the mirror reflects the image,' दर्पणो मूर्त्तिबिम्बं प्रतिक्षिपति, दर्पणो मूर्त्तिं प्रतिबिम्बयति, दर्पणो मूर्त्तिप्रतिबिम्बं करोति.

To REFLECT, *v. n.* (In the mind, consider) चिन्त् (c. 10. चिन्तयति -यितुं), संचिन्त्, विचिन्त्, मनसा विचर् (c. 10. -चारयति -यितुं), ध्यै (c. 1. ध्यायति, ध्यातुं), अनुध्यै, संध्यै, अभिध्यै, विमृश् (c. 6. -मृशति -म्रष्टुं), परिमृश्, वितर्क् (c. 10. -तर्कयति -यितुं), अनुतर्क्, तर्क्, भू (c. 10. भावयति -यितुं), विभू, सम्भू, मनसा विगण् (c. 10. -गणयति -यितुं), समाधा (c. 3. -धत्ते -धातुं), निरूप् (c. 10. -रूपयति -यितुं), अवेक्ष् (c. 1. -ईक्षते -क्षितुं), समवेक्ष्, समीक्ष्, प्रसमीक्ष्, मन् (c. 4. मन्यते, मन्तुं), चिन्तां कृ, विचारणां कृ.—(Bring reproach, cast censure upon) तिरस्कारम् आवह्, कलङ्कं or दोषं क्षिप् (c. 6. क्षिपति, क्षेप्तुं), यशोहानिं or कीर्त्तिहानिं or कलङ्कम् आवह्, यशो or कीर्त्तिं न्यूनीकृ.

REFLECTED, *p. p.* (Thrown back, as in a mirror, &c.) प्रतिबिम्बितः -ता -तं, बिम्बितः &c., बिम्बागतः &c., बिम्बगतः &c., प्रतिहतः &c., प्रतिक्षिप्तः -प्ता -प्तं, परावर्त्तितः -ता -तं, पराहतः &c., प्रतिफलितः &c., संक्रान्तः -न्ता -न्तं; 'reflected in water,' जलप्रतिबिम्बितः -ता -तं; 'to be reflected,' परावृत् (c. 1. -वर्त्तते -र्त्तितुं), प्रतिहन् in pass. (-हन्यते); 'the rays of the sun are reflected,' सूर्य्यकिरणाः परावर्त्तन्ते; 'it is seen by reflected light,' परावृत्तकिरणैर् विलोक्यते; 'reflected image,' प्रतिबिम्बं, बिम्बः -म्बं, प्रतिच्छाया, छाया, प्रतिच्छन्दः -न्दकं, प्रतिफलनं; 'reflected light,' प्रतिभा.

REFLECTING, *part.* or *a.* (Throwing back as a mirror, &c.) परावर्त्तनकारी -रिणी -रि (न्), प्रतिबिम्बकारी &c., बिम्बप्रतिक्षेपकः -का -कं, प्रतिक्षेपकः &c., परावर्त्तकः &c.; 'a lake reflecting the stars,' ताराप्रतिबिम्बं सरस्, ताराछायं सरस्.—(Given to meditation) चिन्ताशीलः -ला -लं, ध्यानशीलः &c., विचारशीलः &c., चिन्तयन् -यन्ती -यत् (त्), चिन्तावान् &c. *See* MEDITATIVE.

REFLECTION, *s.* (Act of throwing back) प्रतिक्षेपः -पणं, प्रतिहतिः *f.*, परावर्त्तनं, प्रतिबिम्बकरणं, संक्रान्तिः *f.*; 'reflection of rays of light,' किरणपरावर्त्तनं; 'the angle of reflection,' परावर्त्तनकोणः.—(That which is reflected, image &c. reflected) प्रतिबिम्बं, बिम्बं -म्बः, प्रतिच्छाया, छाया, छायात्मा *m.* (न्), प्रतिभासः, आभासः,

प्रतिमा, प्रतिरूपं, प्रतिमूर्त्तिः *f.*, प्रतिफलं -लनं, प्रतिकृतिः *f.*; 'reflection of the moon,' प्रतिमेन्दुः *m.*—(Consideration, thought) चिन्ता -न्तनं, सुचिन्ता, विचारः, विचारणा -णा, विमर्शः, ध्यानं, आध्यानं, अभिध्यानं, अनुध्यानं, चर्चा, समाधिः *m.*, समाधानं, भावना, सम्भावना, चिन्तितं, चिन्तितिः *f.*, चिन्तिया.—(Reproach, censure) कलङ्कः, कीर्त्तिहानिः *f.*, यशोहानिः *f.*

REFLECTOR, *s.* (Something polished for reflecting) प्रतिबिम्बकः, आदर्शः, दर्शनं, दर्पणः.—(One who considers) विचारकृत् *m.*, विचारकः, चिन्ताकारी *m.* (न्).

REFLEXIBILITY, *s.* परावर्त्तनीयता, परावर्त्तनयोग्यता, प्रतिबिम्बयोग्यता.

REFLEXIBLE, *a.* परावर्त्तनीयः -या -यं, परावर्त्तनक्षमः -मा -मं, परावर्त्तनयोग्यः &c., प्रतिबिम्बयोग्यः &c., प्रतिक्षेपणीयः -या -यं, प्रतिहननीयः -या -यं.

REFLEXIVE, *a.* पूर्व्वापेक्षकः -का -कं, पूर्व्वोद्देशकः &c., पूर्व्वप्रतीक्षकः &c.

REFLUENT, *a.* परावर्त्ती -र्त्तिनी -र्त्ति (न्), पश्चात्प्रवाही &c., विपरिवर्त्ती &c.

REFLUX, REFLUENCE, *s.* पश्चाद्वेला, विपरीतवेला, पश्चात्प्रवाहः, विपरीतप्रवाहः, वेलाया विपरीतगतिः *f.*, वेलापरावर्त्तः -र्त्तनं, वेलापरिवर्त्तनं, वेलाविपरिवर्त्तनं.

To REFORM, *v. a.* (Cause to cease from wickedness, bad conduct, &c.) पापात् or दुष्कर्म्मणो निवृत् (c. 10. -वर्त्तयति -यितुं) or विनिवृत् or परावृत् or परिवृत् or विरम् (c. 10. -रमयति -यितुं), अधर्म्मात् or कुकर्म्मणो निवर्त्तयित्वा धर्म्मे प्रवृत् in caus. or नियुज् in caus., पापाद् विप्रतिसृ in caus. (-सारयति -यितुं), विप्रतिसारं जन्, पापनिवर्त्तनं कृ, पापपरिवर्त्तनं कृ, निवृत्तपापं -पां कृ; 'to reform a bad habit,' दोषनिवर्त्तनं कृ, दोषखण्डनं कृ.—(Amend, correct) शुध् (c. 10. शोधयति -यितुं), विशुध्, समाधा, प्रतिसमाधा, प्रतिकृ प्रतिसंकृ. *See To* RECTIFY.

To REFORM, *v. n.* (Cease from bad conduct and return to good) पापात् or दुष्कर्म्मणो निवृत् (c. 1. -वर्त्तते -र्त्तितुं) or विनिवृत् or परावृत् or विरम् (c. 1. -रमति -रन्तुं), अधर्म्मात् or कुकर्म्मणो निवृत्य धर्म्मप्रवृत्तिं कृ or धर्म्मे प्रवृत्, पापाद् विप्रतिसृ (c. 1. -सरति -सर्त्तुं) विप्रतिसारं कृ, विप्रतीसारं कृ, निवृत्तपापः -पा -पं भू, पापत्यागं कृ, पापपरित्यागं कृ, दोषत्यागं कृ, त्यक्तपापः -पा -पं भू, त्यक्तदोषः -षा -षं भू.

REFORM, REFORMATION, *s.* पापनिवर्त्तनं, दोषनिवर्त्तनं, पापनिवृत्तिः *f.*, दोषनिवृत्तिः *f.*, निवर्त्तनं, निवृत्तिः *f.*, परिवर्त्तनं, परिवृत्तिः *f.*, विनिवर्त्तनं, पापत्यागः, दोषत्यागः, दोषपरित्यागः, दोषखण्डनं, दोषपरिच्छेदः, दोषच्छेदः, दोषप्रतिकारः, दोषप्रतीकारः, दोषशोधनं, दोषसमाधानं, प्रतिसमाधानं, विप्रतिसारः, विप्रतीसारः, शोधनं.—(Of religion) धर्म्मपरिवर्त्तनं, दुष्टधर्म्मपरिवर्त्तनं, धर्म्मपरिवृत्तिः *f.*, दूषितधर्म्मशोधनं, धर्म्मशोधनं.

REFORMED, *p. p.* निवृत्तपापः -पा -पं, निवृत्तदोषः -षा -षं, त्यक्तपापः &c., त्यक्तदोषः &c., गतपापः &c., गतदोषः &c., विगतदोषः &c., हृतदोषः &c., गतमायः -या -यं, विरतपापः &c., विनिवृत्तपापः &c., खण्डितदोषः &c., छिन्नदोषः &c., शोधितः -ता -तं, शुद्धः -द्धा -द्धं, विशोधितः &c., जातविप्रतीसारः -रा -रं, कृतविप्रतीसारः &c.

REFORMER, *s.* निवर्त्तकः, पापनिवर्त्तकः, पापनिवृत्तिकर्त्ता *m.* (र्त्तृ), दोषनिवर्त्तकः, दोषखण्डकः, दोषच्छेदकः, दोषहारी *m.* (न्), शोधनकारी *m.*, शोधकः.—(Of religion) धर्म्मशोधकः, दूषितधर्म्मशोधकः.

To REFRACT, *v. a.* वक्रीकृ, गतिवक्रतां कृ, वक्रगतिं कृ; 'to refract rays of light,' किरणवक्रतां कृ.

REFRACTED, *p. p.* वक्रीभूतः -ता -तं, वक्रीकृतः &c.; 'to be refracted,' वक्रीभू; 'the rays are refracted downwards,' अधो वक्रीभवन्ति किरणाः.

REFRACTION, *s.* किरणवक्रता, किरणवक्रीभावः, किरणवक्रीभवनं, किरणवक्रगतिः *f.*, किरणवक्रीकरणं.

REFRACTORINESS, *s.* प्रतीपता -त्वं, विप्रतीपता, अवश्यता, दुःशास्यता, अविनेयता, दुःसाध्यता, दुर्दान्तता, अविधेयता, दुर्निग्रहता, अनायत्तता.

REFRACTORY, *a.* प्रतीपः -पा -पं, विप्रतीपः &c., प्रतीपकारी -रिणी -रि (न्), विपरीतकारी &c., अवश्यः -श्या -श्यं, दुःशास्यः -स्या -स्यं, दुःशासनः -ना -नं, अविनेयः -या -यं, अविधेयः &c., दुर्निग्रहः -हा -हं, दुःसाध्यः -ध्या -ध्यं, अनिवार्य्यः -र्य्या -र्य्यं, उल्लंघितशासनः -ना -नं. *See* INTRACTABLE, PERVERSE; 'to be refractory,' प्रतीप (nom. प्रतीपायते), प्रतीपीभू.

REFRAGABLE, *a.* खण्डनीयः -या -यं, खण्ड्यः -ण्ड्या -ण्ड्यं, खण्डितव्यः &c.

To REFRAIN, *v. a.* (Restrain) यम्, नियम्, विनियम्, संयम्, निग्रह्, निरुध्, अवरुध्, संवृ, वृ, निवृ, निषिध्, निवृत् in caus.

To REFRAIN, *v. n.* (Forbear, restrain one's self) निवृत् (c. 1. -वर्त्तते -र्त्तितुं) with abl. c., विरम् (c. 1. -रमति -रन्तुं) with abl. c., आत्मानं यम् (c. 1. यच्छति, यन्तुं) or संयम्, परिहृ (c. 1. -हरति -हर्त्तुं) with acc., वृज् (c. 10. वर्जयति -यितुं) with acc., परिवृज्, विवृज्, प्रोज्झ्, त्यज्, हा; 'he should refrain from eating flesh,' निवर्त्तेत मांसभक्षणात् or मांसं वर्जयेत्.

REFRANGIBLE, *a.* वक्रीकरणीयः -या -यं, वक्रीभवनीयः &c., वक्रताक्षमः &c.

To REFRESH, *v. a.* (Invigorate, relieve from fatigue) क्लान्तिं or श्रमं हृ (c. 1. हरति, हर्त्तुं), श्रमापहारं कृ, क्लान्त्यपहारं कृ, क्लान्तिच्छेदं कृ, श्रमच्छेदं कृ, विश्रान्तिं दा, आप्यै (c. 10. -प्याययति -यितुं), समाप्यै, बलं or तेजो or सत्त्वं वृध् (c. 10. वर्धयति -यितुं), सत्त्वं or वीर्य्यं दा.—(Revive, cheer) आश्वस् (c. 10. -श्वासयति -यितुं), प्रत्याश्वस्, पुनर् आश्वस्, पुनर् जीव् (c. 10. जीवयति -यितुं), पुनर्जीवनं दा, सुख् (c. 10. सुखयति -यितुं), आनन्द् in caus., तुष् in caus., ह्लाद् in caus.—(Cool) शीतल (nom. शीतलयति -यितुं), शीतलीकृ, निर्वा in caus. (-वापयति -यितुं), निर्वापणं कृ.—(Make new or fresh) नवीकृ.

REFRESHED, *p. p.* (Relieved from fatigue) हृतक्लान्तिः -न्तिः -न्ति, हृतश्रमः -मा -मं, हृतक्लमः &c., अपहृतक्लान्तिः &c., अपहृतश्रमः &c., गतक्लमः &c., गतश्रमः &c., विगतश्रमः &c., छिन्नक्लान्तिः &c., छिन्नश्रमः &c., विश्रान्तः -न्ता -न्तं, विम्लानः -ना -नं, आप्यायितः -ता -तं.—(Revived, cheered) आश्वासितः &c., समाश्वासितः &c., प्रत्याश्वस्तः -स्ता -स्तं, आनन्दितः -ता -तं, अनुभूतसुखः -खा -खं.—(Cooled) शीतलीकृतः -ता -तं, निर्वापितः &c.—(Made fresh) नवीकृतः -ता -तं.

REFRESHING, *a.* क्लान्तिहरः -रा -रं, क्लान्तिहारकः -का -कं, श्रान्तिहरः &c., श्रमहारी -रिणी -रि (न्), श्रमापहारी &c., श्रमापहः -हा -हं, क्लान्त्यपहः &c., श्रान्त्यपहः &c., क्लान्तिच्छिद् *m. f. n.*, विश्रान्तिदः -दा -दं, श्रमच्छेदकः -का -कं, आप्यायकः -का -कं, आश्वासकः &c., आनन्ददः -दा -दं, बलवर्धकः &c., निर्वापकः &c.

REFRESHMENT, *s.* (Act of refreshing) श्रमापहारः, श्रमापहरणं, क्लान्तिहरणं, क्लान्त्यपहारः, क्लान्त्यपहरणं, क्लान्तिच्छेदः, श्रमच्छेदः, श्रान्तिच्छेदः, आप्यायः -यनं, विश्रान्तिदानं, बलवर्धनं, सत्त्ववर्धनं, सत्त्वदानं, आश्वासनं, विम्लापनं.—(State) विश्रान्तिः *f.*, विश्रामः, विम्लानिः *f.*, विम्लानता.—(Food, slight repast) उपाहारः, लघुभोजनं, लघ्वाहारः, अल्पाहारः, आहारः.

REFRIGERANT, *a.* तापहरः -रा -रं, सन्तापहरः &c., दाहहरः &c., दाहनाशकः -का -कं, शीतलकारी -रिणी -रि (न्), निर्वापकः -का -कं.

REFRIGERANT, *s.* (Medicine) निर्वापणं, दाहहारकं, तापनाशकम् औषधं.

To REFRIGERATE, *v. a.* तापं or दाहं हृ (c. 1. हरति, हर्त्तुं) or नश्

(c. 10. नाशयति -यितुं), शीतलीकृ, शीतल (nom. शीतलयति -यितुं), निर्वा in caus. (-वापयति -यितुं).

REFRIGERATION, *s.* निर्वापनं, निर्वाणं, तापहरणं, दाहहरणं, शीतलीकरणं.

REFUGE, *s.* (Shelter, protection) आश्रयः, समाश्रयः, आश्रयणं, संश्रयः, शरणं, आशयः, अयनं, आयः, गतिः *f.*, अवस्थानं, अरणं.—(That which shelters, cause of protection) आश्रयः, शरणं, संश्रयः, आश्रयभूतः -ता -तं, शरणभूतः -ता -तं, आश्रयस्थानं, शरण्यं, शरण्युः *m.*, पालकः, रक्षकः.—(Resource, expedient) गतिः *f.*, आश्रयः, उपायः, युक्तिः *f.*; 'to take refuge,' आश्रि (c. 1. -श्रयति -यितुं), समाश्रि, संश्रि, उपाश्रि, समुपाश्रि, शरणार्थं गम् (c. 1. गच्छति, गन्तुं) or आगम् or उपे (c. 2. उपैति -तुं, rt. इ), अवलम्ब् (c. 1. -लम्बते -म्बितुं), आश्रयणं कृ; 'having but one refuge,' अनन्यगतिः -तिः -ति, अनन्यगतिकः -का -कं; 'come for refuge,' शरणागतः -ता -तं, शरणार्थम् आगतः &c., शरणापन्नः -न्ना -न्नं, प्रपन्नः &c.; 'seeking refuge,' शरणार्थी -र्थिनी &c., शरणैषी &c.; 'one who affords refuge,' शरणार्पकः.

REFUGEE, *s.* शरणागतः, शरणार्थम् आगतः, शरणार्थी *m.* (न्), शरणैषी *m.* (न्), शरणार्थम् आश्रितः, अवलम्बी *m.* (न्), अवलम्बितः, प्रपन्नः; 'protector of refugees, kind to them,' शरणागतपालकः, शरणागतवत्सलः, प्रपन्नपालः -लकः.

REFULGENCE, *s.* प्रतापः, अतितेजस् *n.*, महातेजस् *n.*, उज्ज्वलता, अतिप्रभा, विभा.

REFULGENT, *a.* प्रतापवान् -वती -वत् (त्), अतिप्रतापी -पिनी -पि (न्), सुप्रभः -भा -भं, उज्ज्वलः -ला -लं, द्योती &c., विभ्राजमानः -ना -नं. *See* SPLENDID, BRIGHT.

To REFUND, *v. a.* प्रतिदा (c. 3. -ददाति -दातुं), पुनर् दा or प्रदा or प्रयम्.

REFUSAL, *s.* (Denial of a thing demanded) प्रत्याख्यानं, प्रत्यादेशः, अपह्नवः, अपह्नुतिः *f.*, अपलापः, निरसनं, निरासः, निराकरणं, निराकृतिः *f.*, अपवादः, निह्नवः, निह्नुतिः *f.*, निषेधः, प्रतिषेधः, व्यपाकृतिः *f.*, प्रणयविहतिः *f.*—(Declining to accept) अग्रहणं, अप्रतिग्रहः, अपरिग्रहः, अस्वीकारः, अस्वीकरणं, अनङ्गीकारः, अनङ्गीकरणं, निरसनं, निराकरणं, अननुज्ञानं.—(Of a lover) अवधीरणं -णा, धीरता -त्वं.—(Right of buying or taking in preference) पूर्व्वक्रयाधिकारः, पूर्व्वग्रहणाधिकारः.

To REFUSE, *v. a.* (Deny a request or demand, decline to do what is asked) प्रत्याख्या (c. 2. -ख्याति -तुं), अन्तःख्या, अतिख्या, प्रत्यादिश् (c. 6. -दिशति -देष्टुं), अपह्नु (c. 2. -ह्नुते -ह्नोतुं), निह्नु, अपलप् (c. 1. -लपति -पितुं), निरस् (c. 4. -अस्यति -असितुं), अपास्, निराकृ, प्रत्याचक्ष् (c. 2. -चष्टे), अपवद् (c. 1. -वदति -दितुं), निषिध् (c. 1. -षेधति -षेद्धुं), प्रतिषिध्, अपव्यय् (c. 1. -व्ययते -यितुं), प्रत्यादेशं कृ, निरासं कृ, न अनुज्ञा, न अनुमन्, न सम्मन्.—(Decline to accept, reject) न ग्रह् (c. 9. गृह्णाति, ग्रहीतुं), न प्रतिग्रह्, अग्रहणं कृ, न स्वीकृ, न अङ्गीकृ, निरस्, अपास्, निराकृ, अवधीर् (c. 10. अवधीरयति -यितुं). The sense of 'refuse' may be expressed simply by the negative particle न; as, 'to refuse to give,' न दा or even by अलं as अलन्दा.

REFUSE, *a.* उच्छिष्टः -ष्टा -ष्टं, अवशिष्टः &c., असारः -रा -रं, निःसारः &c.

REFUSE, *s.* उच्छिष्टं, अवशिष्टं, शेषः, अवशेषः, शेषभागः, उद्वर्त्तः, जुष्टं, समुज्झितं, असारः, असारद्रव्यं, निःसारद्रव्यं, मलं. *See* LEAVINGS.

REFUSED, *p. p.* प्रत्याख्यातः -ता -तं, प्रत्यादिष्टः -ष्टा -ष्टं, अपह्नुतः -ता -तं, निरस्तः -स्ता -स्तं, निराकृतः -ता -तं, अपवादितः &c., निषिद्धः -द्धा -द्धं, अस्वीकृतः &c., अनङ्गीकृतः &c., अननुज्ञातः -ता -तं, अननुमतः &c., असम्मतः &c., अवधीरितः &c.

REFUTABLE, *a.* खण्डनीयः -या -यं, खण्ड्यः -ण्ड्या -ण्ड्यं, खण्डितव्यः -व्या -व्यं, प्रत्याख्येयः -या -यं, निरसनीयः &c., उपमर्दनीयः &c., खण्डनशक्यः -क्या -क्यं.

REFUTATION, *s.* खण्डनं, वाक्यखण्डनं, पक्षाघातः, बाधा -धः, निरासः, वाक्यनिरासः, वाक्यनिरसनं, निराकरणं, वाक्यनिराकरणं, प्रत्याख्यानं, उपमर्दः, अधरीकरणं, आधर्षणं, विक्षेपः, वितण्डा, जल्पः, अनिश्चयः; 'other side of the argument,' उत्तरपक्षः.

To REFUTE, *v. a.* वाक्यं खण्ड् (c. 10. खण्डयति -यितुं) or निरस् (c. 4. -अस्यति -असितुं) or निराकृ, बाध् (c. 1. बाधते -धितुं), प्रत्याख्या (c. 2. -ख्याति -तुं), अधरीकृ, आधृष् (c. 10. -धर्षयति -यितुं), संसूच् (c. 10. -सूचयति -यितुं), विक्षिप् (c. 6. -क्षिपति -क्षेप्तुं), उपमर्दं कृ, वाक्योपमर्दं कृ, अपवद्, वितण्डां कृ.

REFUTED, *p. p.* खण्डितः -ता -तं, निरस्तः -स्ता -स्तं, निराकृतः -ता -तं, बाधितः &c., अधरीकृतः &c., प्रत्याख्यातः &c., आधर्षितः &c., विक्षिप्तः -प्ता -प्तं, उपमर्दितः &c., निर्धूतः &c., वितण्डितः &c., निस्तीर्णः -र्णा -र्णं, विखण्डितः &c.

REFUTER, *s.* उपमर्दकः, वाक्यखण्डकः, बाधकः, निरासकारी *m.* (न्).

To REGAIN, *v. a.* प्रतिलभ् (c. 1. -लभते -लब्धुं), पुनर् लभ्, पुनर् उपलभ्, पुनः प्राप् (c. 5. -आप्नोति -आप्तुं), पुनर् आप्, पुनर् अवाप्, अनुप्राप्, प्रत्यवाप्, प्रत्यादा (c. 3. -ददाति -दत्ते -दातुं), पुनर् आदा, प्रतिपद् (c. 4. -पद्यते -पत्तुं), पुनर् आपद्, प्रत्याहृ, पुनर् ग्रह्. *See To* RECOVER, *v. a.*

REGAINED, *p. p.* प्रतिलब्धः -ब्धा -ब्धं, पुनर्लब्धः &c., पुनरुपलब्धः &c., प्रत्युपलब्धः &c., पुनः प्राप्तः -प्ता -प्तं, पुनराप्तः &c., पुनरवाप्तः &c., प्रतिपन्नः -न्ना -न्नं, आपन्नः &c. *See* RECOVERED.

REGAL, *a.* राजकीयः -या -यं, राजयोग्यः -ग्या -ग्यं, राजार्हः -र्हा -र्हं, नृपोचितः -ता -तं, राजसम्बन्धी -न्धिनी &c., ऐश्वरः -री -रं, ऐशिकः -की -कं, ऐशः -शी -शं. *See* KINGLY, PRINCELY, MAJESTIC.—(Man of the regal class) राजन्यः, विराट् *m.* (ज्), क्षत्रियः, मूर्द्धाभिषिक्तः, बाहुजः,

To REGALE, *v. a.* सन्तुष् (c. 10. -तोषयति -यितुं), तुष्, सन्तृप् (c. 10. -तर्पयति -यितुं), तृप्, संवृध् (c. 10. -वर्धयति -यितुं), सुख् (c. 10. सुखयति -यितुं), आनन्द् in caus.; 'with choice food,' परमान्नैः or भोजनविशेषैः सन्तुष्, उत्तमाहारं भुज् in caus.—(Regale one's self) उत्तमान्नैः सन्तुष् (c. 4. -तुष्यति -तोष्टुं) or आत्मानं सन्तुष् in caus., or सन्तृप् (c. 4. -तृप्यति) or आत्मानं सन्तृप् in caus., उत्तमाहारं कृ, उत्तमभोजनं कृ, उत्सवं कृ, महोत्सवं कृ.

REGALED, *p. p.* सन्तोषितः -ता -तं, सन्तर्पितः &c., संवर्धितः -ता -तं.

REGALIA, *s.* राजलक्षणानि *n. pl.*, राजचिह्नानि *n. pl.*, राजलिङ्गानि *n. pl.*, नृपचिह्नानि *n. pl.*, नृपलिङ्गानि *n. pl.*, नृपलक्षणानि *n. pl.*, राजैश्वर्यचिह्नानि *n. pl.*

REGALITY, *s.* राजत्वं -ता, नृपत्वं, राज्यं. *See* KINGSHIP, ROYALTY.

To REGARD, *v. a.* (Look at, observe) अवेक्ष् (c. 1. -ईक्षते -क्षितुं), अपेक्ष्, प्रतीक्ष्, प्रत्यवेक्ष्, अभिप्रेक्ष्, प्रेक्ष्, निरीक्ष्, वीक्ष्, समीक्ष्, ईक्ष्, दृश् (c. 1. पश्यति, द्रष्टुं), प्रतिदृश्, अनुदृश्, अभिदृश्, आलोक् (c. 10. -लोकयति -यितुं), समालोक्, आलोच्, आलक्ष्, समालक्ष्, लक्ष्.—(Point or be directed towards) उद्दिश् (c. 6. -दिशति -देष्टुं), समुद्दिश्.—(Mind, heed) मन् (c. 4. मन्यते, मन्तुं), अनुमन्, मननं कृ, अपेक्ष्, अवेक्ष्, अवेक्षणं कृ, अपेक्षां कृ, अवधा (c. 3. -धत्ते -धातुं), अवधानं कृ, सावधानः -ना -नं भू, अवहितः -ता -तं भू or अस्.—(Esteem,

REG

respect) मन् (c. 10. मानयति -यितुं), सम्मन्, प्रतिमन्, अभिमन्, पूज्, सेव्, निषेव्, भज्, अवेक्ष्, आदृ, अभिनन्द्, सम्मानं कृ.—(Keep, observe) पाल्, प्रतिपाल्, सेव्, निषेव्, उपसेव्.—(Have relation to) प्रतीक्ष्, अपेक्ष्, उद्दिश्.

Regard, *s.* (Look) दृष्टिः *f.*, लक्ष्यं, *see* Look.—(Attention of the mind towards any thing, respect unto) प्रतीक्षा, अवेक्षा, अपेक्षा, अवेक्षणं, अन्ववेक्षा, निरीक्षा -क्षणं, उद्देशः, आस्था, अनुसन्धानं; 'regard to results,' फलोद्देशः.—(Relation, reference) अपेक्षा, प्रतीक्षा, उद्देशः, समुद्देशः, सम्बन्धः, अन्वयः, समन्वयः, विषयत्वं -ता, विषयः, सम्पर्कः; 'having regard to,' सापेक्षः -क्षा -क्षं; 'in regard to,' अपेक्षया, अपेक्ष्य, प्रतीक्ष्य, उद्दिश्य, उद्देशेन, सापेक्षं, विषये.—(Esteem, respect) मानं, सम्मानं, मान्यता -त्वं, आदरः, पूजा.—(Love, affection) स्नेहः, प्रणयः, प्रश्रयः, प्रेम *n.* (न्), अनुरागः, अनुरक्तिः *f.*, प्रीतिः *f.*

Regarded, *p. p.* प्रतीक्षितः -ता -तं, अवेक्षितः &c., अपेक्षितः &c., मतः &c.

Regardful, *a.* प्रतीक्षकः -का -कं, अवेक्षकः &c., अवेक्षाकारी -रिणी -रि (न्), अपेक्षकः &c.—(Heedful) सावधानः -ना -नं, अवहितः -ता -तं.

Regardfully, *adv.* सावेक्षं, सापेक्षं, अपेक्षया, अवेक्षया, सावधानं.

Regarding, *part.* प्रतीक्षकः -का -कं, अपेक्षकः &c., सापेक्षः -क्षा -क्षं.—(Relating to) सम्बन्धी -न्धिनी &c., विषयकः -का -कं.

Regardless, *a.* निरपेक्षः -क्षा -क्षं, अनपेक्षः &c., अनपेक्षकः -का -कं, अपेक्षाहीनः -ना -नं, उपेक्षकः &c., विरक्तः -क्ता -क्तं, उदासीनः -ना -नं, अनुत्सुकः &c.

Regardlessly, *adv.* निरपेक्षं, अनपेक्षं, अनपेक्षया, अनवेक्षया, उपेक्षया.

Regardlessness, *s.* अनपेक्षा, अनवेक्षा, निरपेक्षता -त्वं, उपेक्षा.

Regatta, *s.* नौकाक्रीडा, नौकाकौतुकं, बहुनौकानां क्रीडायुद्धं.

Regency, *s.* राजप्रतिनिधेर् अधिकारः or पदं, राजप्रतिनिधित्वं.—(Body of persons governing vicariously) राजप्रतिनिधिमण्डलं, राजप्रतिनिधिसमाजः.

Regeneracy, *s.* पुनर्जन्म *n.* (न्), पुनर्जातत्वं, पुनर्जातावस्था.

To regenerate, *v. a.* पुनर् जन् (c. 10. जनयति -यितुं), पुनर्जन्म दा, पुनर्जातं -तां कृ, जन्मान्तरं दा, पुनः सृज् (c. 6. सृजति, स्रष्टुं).

Regenerate, regenerated, *a.* पुनर्जातः -ता -तं, पुनर्भवः -वा -वं, द्विजन्मा -न्मा -न्म (न्), पुनर्जन्मा &c., पुनर्भूः -भूः -भु, द्विजः -जा -जं, पुनः सृष्टः -ष्टा -ष्टं, पुनरुत्पन्नः -न्ना -न्नं.

Regeneration, *s.* पुनर्जन्म *n.* (न्), पुनर्जातिः *f.*, पुनर्भवं, पुनर्जन्मावस्था, द्विजन्मावस्था, पुनर्जातावस्था, जन्मान्तरं, पुनरुत्पत्तिः *f.*, नवसृष्टिः *f.*, नव्यसृष्टिः *f.*

Regent, *s.* (Ruler) अधिपतिः *m.*, शासिता *m.* (तृ), शास्ता *m.*, शासकः.—(Vicarious ruler) राजप्रतिनिधिः *m.*—(Regent of the quarter) दिक्पालः; 'the eight regents of the quarters,' अष्टदिक्पालाः *m. pl.* These are, 'of the East,' इन्द्रः; 'of the S. E.' अग्निः or वह्निः; 'of the S.,' यमः or पितृपतिः *m.*; 'of the S. W.,' नैर्ऋतिः; 'of the W.,' वरुणः; 'of the N. W.,' मरुत्; 'of the N.,' कुवेरः; 'of the N. E.,' ईशः or शिवः. Their elephants are ऐरावतः, पुण्डरीकः &c., *see* under Elephant.

Regent, *a.* शासनकारी -रिणी &c., शासिता -त्री -तृ (तृ), राज्याधिकारी &c.

Regicide, *s.* (Killer of a king) राजघातुकः, राजघाती *m.* (न्), राजघातकः, राजहा *m.* (न्), राजहन्ता *m.* (न्तृ), राजघः, राजघ्नः, राजहिंसकः, नृपहा *m.* &c.—(Killing of a king) राजहत्या, राजवधः, राजघातः, नृपघातः, राजहिंसा.

Regime, *s.* *See* Government, Administration.

Regimen, *s.* (Regulation of diet) पथ्यं, पथ्यापथ्यं, पथ्यापथ्यविचारः, पथ्यापथ्यनियमः; 'violation of it,' अपथ्यं; 'one under it,' पथ्याशी -शिनी -शि (न्).

Regiment, *s.* सैन्यदलं, सैन्यव्यूहः, सैन्यगुल्मः, सैन्यसमूहः, सैन्यगणः.

Regimental, *a.* सैन्यदलसम्बन्धी -न्धिनी -न्धि (न्), सैन्यगुल्मविषयकः -का -कं.

Regimentals, *s.* सैन्यवेषः, सैन्यवेशः, सैन्यदलविशेषको वेशः.

Region, *s.* (Country) देशः, प्रदेशः, विषयः, राष्ट्रं, भूमिः *f.*, चक्रं, मण्डलं, प्रान्तः, धिष्ण्यं, निर्गः; 'the lower regions,' अधोलोकः, अधोभुवनं, अवाची; 'the upper regions,' ऊर्द्ध्वलोकः, ऊर्द्ध्वभुवनं, उदीची; 'centre of a region,' मध्यदेशः.—(Quarter of the sky) दिक् *f.* (श्), दिशा, दिशाः *f.* (स्), दिशी, आशा, काष्ठा, खनिः *m. f.*, *see* Quarter.—(Part of the body) देशः, चक्रं, मण्डलं; 'the region of the heart,' हृदयदेशः; 'of the liver,' यकृद्देशः; 'umbilical region,' नाभिदेशः, स्वाधिष्ठानचक्रं; 'of the head,' मस्तकमण्डलं.

Register, *s.* लेख्यं, लेखः, लेख्यपत्रं, पञ्जिः -ञ्जी *f.*, पञ्जिका, पदभञ्जिका.

To register, *v. a.* लेख्ये or लेख्यपत्रे आरुह् in caus. (-रोपयति -यितुं) or समारुह् or अभिलिख् (c. 6. -लिखति -लेखितुं), or लिख्, लेख्यारूढं -ढां कृ. *See* *To* record.

Registered, *p. p.* लेख्यारूढः -ढा -ढं, लेख्यारोपितः &c., अभिलिखितः &c., लेख्यसमर्पितः &c. *See* Recorded.

Registrar, *s.* लेखकः, अभिलेखकः, कायस्थः, पञ्जिकाकारकः, लिपिकृत्.

Registry, registration, *s.* (The act of registering) अभिलिखनं, अभिलेखनं, लेख्यारोपणं, लेख्यसमर्पणं, नामाभिलेखनं, नामाभिलिखनं.—(The place) अभिलिखनस्थानं, लेख्यस्थानं, लेखस्थानं, लेख्यगृहं.

Regnant, *a.* शासनकारी -रिणी -रि (न्), राज्याधिकारी -रिणी &c., राज्याधिकारयुक्तः -क्ता -क्तं, राज्यधारी &c., प्रबलः -ला -लं.

Regress, regression, *s.* व्यतिक्रमः, विपरीतगतिः *f.*, परावर्त्तः -र्त्तनं.

Regret, *s.* पश्चात्तापः, अनुतापः, अनुशोकः, अनुशोचनं, मनस्तापः, तापः, सन्तापः, उद्वेगः, अनुशयः, शोकः, खेदः, उत्कण्ठा, औत्कण्ठ्यं, उत्सुकता, औत्सुक्यं, दुःखं, मनोदुःखं, मनोव्यथा, उद्भ्रमः, उत्कः.

To regret, *v. a.* अनुतप् in pass. (-तप्यते), पश्चात् तप्, सन्तप्, तप्, अनुशुच् (c. 1. -शोचति -चितुं), शुच्, खिद् (c. 4. खिद्यते, खेत्तुं), उद्विज् (c. 6. -विजते -जितुं), उत्कण्ठ् (c. 1. -कण्ठते -ण्ठितुं), उत्सुक (nom. उत्सुकायते), अनुशी (c. 2. -शेते -शयितुं), उन्मनस् (nom. उन्मनायते), दु (c. 5. दुनोति c. 4. दूयते, दोतुं), विदु, अवदु.

Regretful, *a.* अनुशोचकः -का -कं, अनुतापी -पिनी -पि (न्), पश्चात्तापी &c., उत्कण्ठितः -ता -तं, उत्सुकः -का -कं, उद्विग्नः -ग्ना -ग्नं, उत्कः -त्का -त्कं.

Regretted, *p. p.* अनुशोचितः -ता -तं, शोचितः &c., अवदूनः -ना -नं.

Regular, *a.* (According to rule) यथाविधि: -धिः -धि, वैधिकः -की -कं, वैधः -धी -धं, सविधिः -धिः -धि, विधियुक्तः -क्ता -क्तं, विध्यनुसारी -रिणी -रि (न्), नैयमिकः -की -कं, नियमानुसारी &c., यथामार्गः -र्गा -र्गं, यथाशास्त्रः -स्त्रा -स्त्रं, यथापद्धतिः -तिः -ति, सूत्रानुसारी &c., ससूत्रः -त्रा -त्रं, सौत्रः -त्री -त्रं.—(According to established usage) आचारिकः -की -कं, व्यवहारिकः &c., व्यावहारिकः &c., यथाव्यवहारः -रा -रं, यथारीतिः -तिः -ति, यथामार्गः -र्गा -र्गं, मार्गानुसारी &c., नित्यः -त्या -त्यं, नैत्यिकः -की -कं, स्थावरः -रा -रं.—(Governed by rule, steady in a course, said of persons) नियमनिष्ठः -ष्ठा -ष्ठं, नियमशीलः -ला -लं, नियमपरः -रा -रं, नियमी &c., नियमानुसारी &c., नियमानुयायी &c., विधिनिष्ठः &c., विध्यनुयायी &c., विधिवर्त्ती

&c., नियमवर्त्ती &c., विध्यनुवर्त्ती &c., यथामार्गचारी &c., यथाविधिचारी &c., यथानियमाचारी &c., अव्यभिचारी &c., व्यवस्थितः -ता -तं. —(In due order or course) यथाक्रमः -मा -मं, यथानुक्रमः &c., क्रमिकः -का -कं, क्रमकः &c., सक्रमः -मा -मं, क्रमानुगतः -ता -तं, क्रमानुसारी &c., अनुक्रामः -मा -मं, यथापर्य्यायः -या -यं, पारम्परिकः -की -कं, अनुलोमः -मा -मं, अनुपूर्व्वः -र्व्वा -र्व्वं, आनुलोमिकः -की -कं, अविकलः -ला -लं.—(Periodical) नियतकालिकः -की -कं, नियतः -ता -तं, नित्यः -त्या -त्यं.

Regularity, *s.* (Agreeableness to rule) विध्यनुसारः -रिता, नियमानुसारः -रिता, यथाविधिता, सविधिता, नैयमिकत्वं, सूत्रानुसारः -रिता, नियमः, ससूत्रता.—(Steadiness in a course, observance of rule) नियमनिष्ठा, विधिनिष्ठा, नियमशीलता, नियमपरता, विध्यनुवर्त्तनं, नियमानुयायिता, नियमानुवर्त्तित्वं, अव्यभिचारः, व्यवस्थितिः *f.*—(Method, regular course) क्रमः, अनुक्रमः, यथाक्रमता, सक्रमता, क्रमिकता -त्वं, यथानुक्रमता, पर्य्यायः, व्यवस्था, व्यवस्थितिः *f.*, परिपाटिः -टी *f.*, पारिपाट्यं, परम्परा, पारम्पर्य्यं, आनुपूर्व्यं, आनुपूर्व्वी, आनुलोम्यं.—(Regular arrangement) विन्यासः, विन्यसनं, व्यूहनं, व्यूढिः *f.*, रचनं -ना, विरचना.

Regularly, *adv.* (According to rule) यथाविधि, विधिवत्, विधितस्, विध्यनुसारेण, विध्यनुरूपेण, यथानियमं, नियमानुसारेण, यथामार्गं, मार्गानुसारेण, यथापद्धति, यथासूत्रं, विधिपूर्व्वं -र्व्वकं.—(Methodically, in due order or course) यथाक्रमं, यथानुक्रमं, सक्रमं, क्रमतस्, क्रमशस्, क्रमेण, क्रमात्, यथापर्य्यायं, पर्य्यायेण, अनुपूर्व्वशस्, आनुपूर्व्येण, शनकैः, शनैः शनैः.

To regulate, *v. a.* (Adjust by rule) विधिवत् or यथाविधि व्यवस्था in caus. (-स्थापयति -यितुं) or परिक्लृप् (c. 10. -कल्पयति -यितुं) or संविधा (c. 3. -दधाति -धातुं) or विधा, यथासूत्रं विधा, सूत्र (nom. सूत्रयति -यितुं), परिमाणं निरूप् (c. 10. -रूपयति -यितुं), परिमा, परिमितं -तां कृ.—(Direct, subject to rules and good management) अनुशास् (c. 2. -शास्ति -शासितुं), समनुशास्, शास्, विनियम् (c. 1. -यच्छति -यन्तुं), नियम्, विधा, संविधा, विधृ (c. 10. -धारयति -यितुं), अनुशासनं कृ.—(Dispose, put in good order) विधा, संविधा, परिक्लृप्, व्यवस्था in caus., प्रणी, सम्प्रणी, विन्यस्, विरच्, व्यूह्, व्यवस्थां कृ, नियमं कृ.

Regulated, *p. p.* व्यवस्थितः -ता -तं, व्यवस्थापितः &c., विनियतः -ता -तं, नियतः &c., नियमितः &c., विहितः &c., अनुशासितः &c., शासितः &c., यन्त्रितः -ता -तं, परिमितः &c., प्रमितः &c., सूचितः &c.; 'well regulated,' सुव्यवस्थितः -ता -तं, सुविहितः &c., सुयन्त्रितः &c.; 'ill-regulated,' अव्यवस्थितः -ता -तं, अयन्त्रितः &c.; 'having regulated,' विनियम्य.

Regulation, *s.* (The act of regulating) व्यवस्थापनं, व्यवस्थितिः *f.*, विनियमः, व्यवस्था, अनुशासनं, शासनं, विधानं, संविधानं, परिकल्पनं, विधारणं -णा, यन्त्रणं, प्रणयनं, अनुनयः -यनं.—(Rule) नियमः, विनियमः, विधिः *m.*, विधानं, व्यवस्था, व्यवस्थितिः *f.*, स्थितिः *f.*, सूत्रं, क्रमः, मर्य्यादा.

Regulator, *s.* नियन्ता *m.* (न्तृ), विनियन्ता *m.*, अनुशासकः, शासकः, शास्ता *m.* (स्तृ), अनुशास्ता *m.*, विधाता *m.* (तृ), व्यवस्थापकः, परिकल्पकः.

Rehearsal, *s.* (Repetition of the words of another) पठनं, पाठः, अनुवादः, वाचनं, अनुवाचनं, उल्लेखः -खनं.—(Narration) कथनं, आख्यानं.—(Recital in preparation for the public representation) भाव्यनुकरणं, पूर्व्वाभिनयः -यनं.

To rehearse, *v. a.* (Repeat the words of another) पठ् (c. 1. पठति -ठितुं), सम्पठ्, अनुवद्, पठनं कृ, अनुवादं कृ.—(Narrate) कथ्, आख्या, श्रु in caus.—(Recite, preparatory to a public representation) भाव्यनुकरणं कृ, पूर्व्वाभिनयं कृ.

Rehearsed, *p. p.* पठितः -ता -तं, अनुवादितः &c., पूर्व्वाभिनीतः -ता -तं.

To reign, *v. n.* राज्यं कृ, राजत्वं कृ, राज्यपालनं कृ, राज्यशासनं कृ, राज्याधिकारं कृ, राजव्यवहारं कृ, राजकार्य्यं कृ, आधिपत्यं कृ, सिंहासनारूढः -ढा -ढं भू.

Reign, *s.* राज्यं, राजत्वं -ता, आधिपत्यं.—(Period of rule) राज्यशासनकालः, राज्यकालः, आधिपत्यकालः.—(Prevalence), *see* the word.

Reigning, *part.* or *a.* राज्यकारी -रिणी -रि (न्), राज्यशासनकारी &c., राज्यारूढः -ढा -ढं, सिंहासनारूढः &c., राजपदारूढः &c., राज्याधिकारी &c.

To re-imburse, *v. a.* प्रतिदा, पुनर् दा, क्षतिपूरणं कृ, हानिपूरणं कृ, निष्कृतिं दा, अपाकृ, प्रतिकृ, प्रत्युपकृ, परिशोधनं कृ.

Re-imbursement, *s.* पुनर्दानं, प्रतिदानं, क्षतिपूरणं, हानिपूरणं, परिशोधनं.

Rein, *s.* (Of a horse) रश्मिः *m.*, अभीशुः *m.*, अभीषुः *m.*, प्रग्रहः, प्रग्राहः, वसुः *m.*, वागा, वल्गा, दन्तालिका.—(Reins), *see* the word.

To rein, *v. a.* अश्वं रश्मिभिर् यम् (c. 1. यच्छति, यन्तुं) or संयम् or नियम् or निग्रह् (c. 9. -गृह्णाति -ग्रहीतुं) or प्रग्रह्.

Re-infect, *a.* अकृतार्थः -र्था -र्थं, असिद्धार्थः &c., अकृतार्थीभूतः &c.

To re-inforce, re-inforcement. *See To* recruit.

Reins, *s. pl.* (Lower part of the back) कटिः -टी, कटिदेशः, श्रोणिः -णी *f.*, श्रोणिदेशः, कटिपश्चाद्भागः.—(Kidneys), *see* Kidney.

To re-instate, *v. a.* पुनः स्था in caus. (स्थापयति -यितुं), प्रतिष्ठा, प्रत्यवस्था, पुनर् अवस्था, पुनर् नियुज् (c. 10. -योजयति -यितुं), पुनः स्थापनं कृ.

Re-instated, *p. p.* पुनः स्थापितः -ता -तं, पुनर् अवस्थापितः &c. or नियोजितः &c.

Re-instatement, *s.* पुनःस्थापनं -ना, पुनरवस्थापनं, प्रतिष्ठापनं -ना, प्रत्यवस्थापनं, पुनर्नियोगः, पुनर्नियोजनं.

To re-iterate, *v. a.* (Say again) पुनर् वद्, पुनःपुनर् वद्, मुहुर् वद्, अनुवद्, पुनरुक्तिं कृ, आम्रेड्.—(Do again) पुनः कृ, पुनःपुनः कृ, मुहुः कृ, वारं वारं कृ, मुहुर् मुहुः कृ.

Re-iterated, *p. p.* पुनःपुनः कृतः -ता -तं, वारं वारं कृतः &c., मुहुर् मुहुः कृतः &c., पौनःपुनिकः -की -कं, पुनरुक्तः -क्ता -क्तं, पुनःपुनरुक्तः &c.

Re-iteration, *s.* पुनःपुनःकरणं, मुहुःकरणं, पौनःपुन्यं, पुनरुक्तिः *f.*, पौनरुक्त्यं, पुनर्वचनं, अनुवादः, आम्रेडनं, समभिहारः.

To reject, *v. a.* निरस् (c. 4. -अस्यति -सितुं), अपास्, व्युदस्, प्रत्याख्या (c. 2. -ख्याति -तुं), निराकृ, पराकृ, प्रतिक्षिप् (c. 6. -क्षिपति -क्षेप्तुं), विक्षिप्, त्यज् (c. 1. त्यजति, त्यक्तुं), निर्णुद् (c. 6. -णुदति -णोत्तुं), प्रत्यादिश् (c. 6. -दिशति -देष्टुं), अपाहा (c. 3. -जहाति -हातुं), प्रत्याचक्ष् (c. 2. -चष्टे), निर्धू (c. 5. -धूनोति -धोतुं), अपव्यध् (c. 4. -विध्यति -व्यद्धुं), अपवाध्, वृज् (c. 10. वर्जयति -यितुं), अवधीर् (c. 10. अवधीरयति -यितुं), न स्वीकृ, न ग्रह्, अस्वीकारं कृ, अग्रहणं कृ. *See To* refuse.

Rejected, *p. p.* निरस्तः -स्ता -स्तं, अपास्तः &c., व्युदस्तः &c., प्रत्याख्यातः -ता -तं, निराकृतः -ता -तं, पराकृतः &c., प्रतिक्षिप्तः -प्ता -प्तं, निक्षिप्तः &c., विक्षिप्तः &c., प्रत्यादिष्टः -ष्टा -ष्टं, अपविद्धः -द्धा -द्धं, निर्धूतः -ता -तं, अवधीरितः &c., त्यक्तः -क्ता -क्तं, परित्यक्तः &c., वर्जितः &c., अस्वीकृतः &c.

Rejection, *s.* निरसनं, निरासः, निराकृतिः *f.*, निराकरणं, निकृतिः *f.*, प्रत्याख्यानं, प्रत्यादेशः, प्रतिक्षेपः, त्यागः, परित्यागः, वर्जनं, अपवर्जनं,

विसर्जनं, अस्वीकारः, अनङ्गीकारः, अग्रहणं, अवधीरणं -णा.

To rejoice, *v. n.* आनन्द् (c. 1. -नन्दति -न्दितुं), अभिनन्द्, विनन्द्, नन्द्, हृष् (c. 4. हृष्यति, हर्षितुं), प्रहृष्, संहृष्, सम्प्रहृष्, ह्लाद् (c. 1. ह्लादते -दितुं), आह्लाद्, प्रह्लाद्, उल्लस् (c. 1. -लसति -सितुं), समुल्लस्, प्रोल्लस्, रम् (c. 1. रमते, रन्तुं), अभिरम्, आरम्, संरम्, तुष् (c. 4. तुष्यति, तोष्टुं), परितुष्, सन्तुष्, मुद् (c. 1. मोदते -दितुं), प्रमुद्, प्रतिमुद्, प्री (c. 4. प्रीयते, प्रेतुं), सम्प्री, मद् (c. 4. माद्यति, मदितुं), आनन्दितः -ता -तं भू, हृष्टः -ष्टा -ष्टं भू, हर्षं or आनन्दं गम् or इ.

To rejoice, *v. a.* आनन्द् (c. 10. -नन्दयति -यितुं), अभिनन्द्, नन्द्, हृष्, (c. 10. हर्षयति -यितुं), प्रहृष्, परिहृष्, ह्लाद् (c. 10. ह्लादयति -यितुं), प्रह्लाद्, आह्लाद्, रम् (c. 10. रमयति -यितुं), उल्लस् (c. 10. -लासयति -यितुं), तुष् (c. 10. तोषयति -यितुं), सन्तुष्, तृप् (c. 10. तर्पयति -यितुं), प्रमुद् (c. 10. -मोदयति -यितुं), मुद्, प्री (c. 9. प्रीणाति, c. 10. प्रीणयति -यितुं), आनन्दं or हर्षं जन् (c. 10. जनयति -यितुं), आनन्दितं -तां कृ, आनन्दं दा.

Rejoiced, *p. p.* आनन्दितः -ता -तं, नन्दितः &c., आह्लादितः &c., हर्षितः &c., हृष्टः -ष्टा -ष्टं, प्रहर्षितः -ता -तं, उल्लसितः &c., उल्लासितः &c., तुष्टः -ष्टा -ष्टं, परितुष्टः &c., हर्षयुक्तः -क्ता -क्तं, हर्षाविष्टः -ष्टा -ष्टं; 'in mind,' हृष्टमनाः -नाः -नः (स्), हृष्टमानसः -सा -सं, हृष्टहृदयः -या -यं.

Rejoicing, *part. act.* नन्दकः -का -कं, आनन्दकः &c., नन्दनः -ना -नं, आनन्दनः &c., आनन्ददः -दा -दं, आनन्दकरः -रा -रं, हर्षदः -दा -दं, हर्षकः -का -कं, हर्षप्रदः &c., आह्लादकः &c., मोदकः &c., हर्षणः -णा -णं, उत्सवकरः -रा -रं.—*Neut. part.* हर्षमाणः -णा -णं, रममाणः -णा -णं, मोदमानः -ना -नं, प्रीयमाणः &c., सम्प्रीयमाणः &c.

Rejoicing, *s.* आनन्दः -न्दनं, हर्षः -र्षणं, आह्लादः -दनं, नन्दनं, प्रमोदः -दनं, सन्तोषणं, *see* Joy.—(Public rejoicing) उत्सवः, उत्सवकरणं.

To rejoin, *v. n.* प्रतिवच् (c. 2. -वक्ति -क्तुं), पुनर्वच्, प्रतिवद्, प्रत्युत्तरं कृ.

Rejoinder, *s.* प्रतिवाक्यं, प्रतिवचनं, उत्तरं, प्रत्युत्तरं, उत्तरपक्षः, प्रत्युक्तिः *f.*, प्रत्युक्तं, प्रतर्पं, कक्षा, उत्तरोत्तरं. *See* Reply.

To relapse, *v. n.* पुनः पत् (c. 1. पतति -तितुं), पुनर् आगम् (c. 1. -गच्छति -गन्तुं), पुनर् आवृत् (c. 1. -वर्त्तते -र्त्तितुं), प्रत्यावृत्, पर्यावृत्, आवृत्, पुनर्ग्रस्तः -स्ता -स्तं भू, पुनः पीडितः &c. भू, पुनराविष्टः -ष्टा -ष्टं भू; 'relapse into a former state,' पूर्व्वावस्थां or पूर्व्वदशां गम् or आपद् or इ or प्राप्, पूर्व्ववद् भू; 'relapse into vice,' पुनर् व्यसनी भू, पुनर् व्यभिचारी भू, पुनर् व्यभिचारं कृ, पुनर् व्यभिचर्, पुनर् धर्म्माद् भ्रंश्, पुनर् धर्म्मं त्यज्, पुनः सत्पथाद् भ्रंश् or च्यु or विचल् or उत्क्रम्; 'relapse into a fever,' पुनर् ज्वरग्रस्तः -स्ता -स्तं भू, पुनर्ज्वरी -रिणी &c. भू, पुनर्ज्वरातुरः -रा -रं भू.

Relapse, *s.* पुनःपतनं, आवृत्तिः *f.*, आवर्त्तनं, प्रत्यावृत्तिः *f.*, प्रत्यावर्त्तनं, पर्यावर्त्तः, प्रत्यागमः; 'into a former state,' पूर्व्वावस्थाप्राप्तिः *f.*; 'into vice,' पुनर्व्यभिचारः, पुनर्धर्म्मत्यागः, पुनर्धर्म्माद्भ्रंशः, पुनःसत्पथाद्भ्रंशः; 'into a fever,' पुनर्ज्वरग्रस्तता.

To relate, *v. a.* कथ् (c. 10. कथयति -यितुं), संकथ्, आख्या (c. 2. -ख्याति -तुं), समाख्या, ख्या in caus. (ख्यापयति -यितुं), अभिख्या, शंस् (c. 1. शंसति -सितुं), श्रु in caus., आश्रु, संश्रु, वद्, निविद्, आविद्, आचक्ष्, समाचक्ष्, प्रचक्ष्, वर्ण्, उपवर्ण्, अनुवर्ण्, संवर्ण्, निगद्, उदाहृ, व्याहृ, अभिधा, विवृ, विवरणं कृ, कृत्, अनुकृत्, वृत् in caus., कथनं कृ, *see* *To* narrate, tell; 'to relate over again,' पुनर् आख्या, सम्प्रत्याचक्ष्.

To relate, *v. n.* (Have reference) उद्दिश् (c. 6. -दिशति -देष्टुं), अपेक्ष् (c. 1. -ईक्षते -क्षितुं), विषयकः -का -कं भू, सम्बन्ध् in pass. (-बध्यते), सम्बद्धः -द्धा -द्धं भू, सम्बन्धी &c. भू. *See* *To* refer.

Related, *p. p.* (Narrated) कथितः -ता -तं, आख्यातः -ता -तं, समाख्यातः &c., *see* Told.—(Connected) सम्बद्धः -द्धा -द्धं, सम्बन्धी -न्धिनी -न्धि (न्), ससम्बन्धः -न्धा -न्धं, कृतसम्बन्धः -न्धा -न्धं, अनुबद्धः &c., अनुसम्बद्धः &c., सम्पृक्तः -क्ता -क्तं, सम्पर्क्की -र्क्किणी &c., अनुषङ्गी &c., आनुषङ्गिकः -की -कं, संसक्तः -क्ता -क्तं, सान्वयः -या -यं, अन्वितः -ता -तं, समन्वितः &c.; 'mutually related,' व्यतिषक्तः &c.—(Related by consanguinity, or by blood on the father's side) गोत्रसम्बन्धी -न्धिनी &c., गोत्रसम्बद्धः -द्धा -द्धं, एकगोत्रः -त्रा -त्रं, सगोत्रः &c., गोत्रजः -जा -जं, एकगोत्रजः &c., गोत्री &c., एकशरीरः -रा -रं, एकशरीरसम्बन्धी &c., एकरक्तः -क्ता -क्तं, एकरक्तसम्बन्धी &c., एकशरीरावयवः -वा -वं, एकशरीरान्वयी &c., सकुल्यः -ल्या -ल्यं, सजातीयः -या -यं, स्वजातीयः &c., सवंशीयः &c., स्ववंशीयः &c., आत्मीयसम्बन्धी &c., *see* Kindred, *a.*—(Related by blood on the mother's side or by marriage) योनिसम्बन्धी &c., योनिसम्बद्धः -द्धा -द्धं, शरीरसम्बन्धी &c., आप्तसम्बन्धी &c., यौनः -नी -नं.

Relater, *s.* कथकः, आख्यायकः, ख्यापकः, उपकथकः, काथिकः.

Relating, *part.* (Having reference) विषयकः -का -कं, सम्बन्धी -न्धिनी -न्धि (न्), उद्देशकः -का -कं or expressed by the affix ईय, *see* Reference, Regard, Regarding.

Relation, *s.* (Act of telling) कथनं, आख्यानं, उपकथनं, उपाख्यानं, ख्यापनं, वर्णनं -ना, शंसनं, विवरणं, व्याहरणं, अनुकीर्त्तनं, निरूपणं, श्रावणं, निवेदनं, उद्गारः; 'exact relation of particulars,' वस्तुकथनं, वृत्तान्तकथनं, वस्तुस्थितिकथनं.—(Reference) विषयत्वं, सम्बन्धः, उद्देशः, अन्वयः, अपेक्षा, गोचरत्वं; 'in reference to,' अपेक्षया, उद्दिश्य, *see* Reference, Regard.—(Connexion) सम्बन्धः -न्धित्वं, अभिसम्बन्धः, सम्पर्कः, अन्वयः, समन्वयः, सन्दर्भः, अनुषङ्गः, संसक्तिः *f.*, समासक्तिः *f.*, संसर्गः; 'mutual relation,' अन्योन्यसम्बन्धः, मिथःसम्बन्धः, व्यतिषङ्गः; 'intimate and inseparable relation, as of properties with substances,' समवायः, समवायसम्बन्धः, नित्यसम्बन्धः; 'as of material with produce,' समवायिकारणं.—(Connexion by blood, alliance of kin) एकशरीरता, एकशरीरसम्बन्धः, एकशरीरान्वयः, एकशरीरावयवत्वं, ज्ञातित्वं, ज्ञातिभावः, सम्बन्धित्वं, बन्धुता, बान्धवत्वं, सजातित्वं, सगर्भत्वं, समानोदर्य्यता, सोदर्य्यता, सगोत्रत्वं, एकगोत्रता, समगोत्रता, गोत्रसम्बन्धः, एकरक्तसम्बन्धः, समरक्तसम्बन्धः, सपिण्डता, एकपिण्डता, सापिण्ड्यं.—(Connexion on the mother's side, or by marriage) योनिसम्बन्धः, शरीरसम्बन्धः, आप्तभावः, आप्तता.—(Kinsman) बान्धवः, बन्धुः *m.*, बन्धुजनः, गोत्रबन्धुः *m.*, ज्ञातिः *m.*, स्वज्ञातिः *m.*, गोत्रजनः, गोत्रपुरुषः, गोत्रजः, सम्बन्धी *m.* (न्), सपिण्डः, समानोदकः, कुटुम्बी *m.*, स्वकुटुम्बी, *see* Kinsman; 'relations,' बन्धुवर्गः, बान्धवाः *m. pl.*, ज्ञातिवर्गः, बान्धवगणः, *see* Kindred; 'having relations,' सबान्धवः -वा -वं, कौटुम्बिकः -की -कं. The सपिण्डः is a relation connected by the offering of the funeral cake to the manes of common ancestors; the समानोदकः is connected by the offering of water only.

Relationship, *s.* सम्बन्धः, सम्बन्धित्वं, बन्धुता -त्वं, बान्धवत्वं -ता, ज्ञातित्वं, ज्ञातिभावः, ज्ञातेयं, सजातित्वं. *See* under Relation.

Relative, *a.* (Having relation) सम्बन्धी -न्धिनी -न्धि (न्), सम्बन्धकः -का -कं, सम्बन्धीयः -या -यं, विषयकः -का -कं, अनुषङ्गी &c., आनुषङ्गिकः -की -कं, सम्पर्क्की &c., ससम्बन्धः -न्धा -न्धं, ससम्पर्कः -र्का -र्कं, सान्वयः -या -यं, उद्देशकः -का -कं, परायणः -णा -णं.—(Not absolute) अन्यापेक्षकः -का -कं, अन्यसापेक्षः -क्षा -क्षं, सापेक्षः &c., अन्योद्देशकः &c., अकेवलः -ला -लं.—(Correlative, mutually related) अन्योन्यसम्बन्धी &c., अन्योन्याश्रितः -ता -तं, अन्योन्यान्वितः &c.—(In grammar) तत्पदापेक्षकः -का -कं, तत्पदापेक्षी &c.

RELATIVE, *s.* बन्धुः *m.*, बान्धवः, सम्बन्धी *m.* (न्), ज्ञातिः *m.* *See* KINSMAN.

RELATIVELY, *adv.* अपेक्षया, अन्यापेक्षया, सापेक्षं, उद्देशेन, उद्दिश्य, अन्योद्देशेन, अन्यमुद्दिश्य, अन्यमपेक्ष्य, अन्यसापेक्षं. *See* REGARD.

To RELAX, *v. a.* शिथिलीकृ, शिथिल (nom. शिथिलयति -ते -यितुं), श्लथ् (c. 10. श्लथयति -यितुं), प्रश्लथ्, श्रथ् (c. 1. श्रथति, c. 10. श्रथयति -यितुं), श्रन्थ् (c. 9. श्रथ्नाति, श्रन्थितुं), श्लथीकृ, स्रंस् (c. 10. स्रंसयति -यितुं), विस्रंस्, स्रस्तीकृ, विस्रस्तीकृ, विगल् in caus.—(Remit) मुच् (c. 6. मुञ्चति, मोक्तुं, c. 10. मोचयति -यितुं), विमुच्, अवमुच्, अवसृज् (c. 6. -सृजति -स्रष्टुं), विसृज्.—(Abate, diminish) शम् (c. 10. शमयति -यितुं), उपशम्, लघूकृ, न्यूनीकृ; 'relax one's efforts,' उद्योगशैथिल्यं कृ.—(Relax the mind) विनुद् (c. 10. -नोदयति -यितुं), विनोदनं कृ, मनोविनोदं कृ.—(The bowels) कोष्ठमृदुतां जन्, नाडिमृदुतां जन्, कोष्ठलघुतां जन्, लघुकोष्ठतां कृ, अतिसारं or सारणं जन्, *see* *To* PURGE.—(Untie) उद्ग्रन्थ्, उन्मुच्, वियुज्, विसन्धा, विपाश्, उत्सूत्रीकृ.

To RELAX, *v. n.* शिथिलीभू, शिथिल (nom. शिथिलायते), श्लथ (nom. श्लथायते), श्रथ (nom. श्रथायते), श्रन्थ् (c. 1. श्रन्थते -न्थितुं), श्लथीभू, स्रंस् (c. 1. स्रंसते -सितुं), स्रस्तीभू.—(Abate) शम् (c. 4. शाम्यति, शमितुं), उपशम्, प्रशम्, न्यूनीभू.—(Remit in close attention) उद्योगशैथिल्यं कृ, शिथिलोद्योगः -गा -गं भू.

RELAXATION, *s.* (Act) शिथिलीकरणं, श्रन्थनं, श्रथनं, विस्रंसनं, मोचनं.—(State) शैथिल्यं, शिथिलता, विस्रंसा, विस्रंसः, प्रश्रयः, मुक्तिः *f.*, मुक्तता.—(Abatement, remission) शमः, उपशमः, शान्तिः *f.*, उपशान्तिः *f.*, न्यूनता.—(Amusement, remission of labor) विनोदः -दनं, मनोविनोदः, विश्रामः, विश्रान्तिः *f.*, उद्योगविश्रामः, उद्योगविश्रान्तिः *f.*, उद्योगविच्छेदः, उद्योगशैथिल्यं, अनध्यायः.—(Of bowels) कोष्ठमृदुता, मृदुकोष्ठता, कोष्ठलघुता, लघुकोष्ठता, अतिसारः, सारणं.

RELAXED, *p. p.* शिथिलितः -ता -तं, शिथिलीकृतः &c., शिथिलः -ला -लं, श्लथः -था -थं, प्रश्लथः &c., विश्लथः &c., स्रस्तः -स्ता -स्तं, विस्रस्तः &c., विगलितः -ता -तं, मुक्तः -क्ता -क्तं, मोचितः -ता -तं; 'in the body,' विश्लथाङ्गः -ङ्गा -ङ्गं, स्रस्ताङ्गः &c.; 'in strength,' शिथिलबलः -ला -लं, शिथिलशक्तिः -क्तिः -क्ति; 'in the bowels,' मृदुकोष्ठः -ष्ठा -ष्ठं, लघुकोष्ठः &c.; 'one who has relaxed his hold,' स्रस्तहस्तः -स्ता -स्तं, शिथिलितहस्तः &c.

RELAXING, *part.* or *a.* शैथिल्यकारी -रिणी -रि (न्), शैथिल्यजनकः -का -कं, ग्लानिकारकः &c., ग्लानिकरः &c., बलशैथिल्यकारकः &c., बलशैथिल्यजनकः &c.

RELAY, *s.* मार्गे निरूपितस्थानेषु सज्जीकृतो जवाश्वगणः, जवाश्वस्थानं.

To RELEASE, *v. a.* मुच् (c. 6. मुञ्चति, मोक्तुं, c. 10. मोचयति -यितुं), विमुच्, प्रविमुच्, निर्मुच्, मोक्ष् (c. 10. मोक्षयति -यितुं), विमोक्ष्, उद्धृ (c. 1. -हरति -हर्तुं), त्रै (c. 1. त्रायते, त्रातुं), परित्रै, निस्तॄ (c. 10. -तारयति -यितुं), उत्सृज्, विसृज्, त्यज्. *See* *To* FREE, LIBERATE.

RELEASE, *s.* मुक्तिः *f.*, विमुक्तिः *f.*, मोक्षः -क्षणं, विमोक्षः -क्षणं, मोचनं, विमोचनं, उद्धारः, उद्धरणं, समुद्धरणं, त्राणं, परित्राणं, निस्तारः, निस्तरणं, उत्सरणं, विसर्जनं, त्यागः; 'from confinement,' बन्धनमुक्तिः *f.*

RELEASED, *p. p.* मुक्तः -क्ता -क्तं, विमुक्तः &c., मोचितः -ता -तं, विमोचितः &c., मोक्षितः &c., उद्धृतः &c., *see* LIBERATED; 'from obligation,' ऋणमुक्तः -क्ता -क्तं, उत्तीर्णः -र्णा -र्णं, अपतीर्णः &c.; 'from confinement,' बन्धनमुक्तः &c.

RELEASER, *s.* मोचकः, विमोचकः, उद्धर्त्ता *m.* (र्त्तृ). *See* LIBERATOR.

To RELENT, *v. n.* दयार्द्रः -र्द्रा -र्द्रं भू, दयार्द्रचित्तः -त्ता -त्तं भू, दयार्द्रीभू, मृदूभू, मृदुचित्तः -त्ता -त्तं भू, दयां कृ, करुणां कृ, कृपां कृ, सकरुणः -णा -णं भू, करुण (nom. करुणायते), कृपा (nom. कृपायते), पुनर् दयां कृ, पुनर् अनुग्रहं कृ, कोमलचित्तः -त्ता -त्तं भू, स्निग्धीभू, द्रवीभू, शम् (c. 4. शाम्यति, शमितुं), शान्तिं or सान्त्वं गम्.

RELENTLESS, *a.* निर्दयः -या -यं, निष्करुणः -णा -णं, अकरुणः &c., निष्कृपः -पा -पं, अशाम्यः -म्या -म्यं, अशमनीयः -या -यं, उग्रदण्डः -ण्डा -ण्डं, उग्रः -ग्रा -ग्रं, निष्ठुरः -रा -रं, कठोरः &c., पाषाणहृदयः -या -यं, निर्द्दयहृदयः &c.; 'a relentless foe,' दृढवैरी *m.* (न्).

RELENTLESSLY, *adv.* निर्दयं, निष्करुणं, निष्कृपं, निष्ठुरं, कठोरं, उग्रदण्डेन.

RELEVANCE, RELEVANCY, *s.* प्रासङ्गिकत्वं, प्रसङ्गयोग्यता, प्रसङ्गानुसारः, प्रसङ्गसङ्गतिः *f.*, प्रसङ्गौचित्यं, प्रसङ्गान्वयः, प्रकरणयोग्यता, प्रकरणानुसारः, प्रकरणसङ्गतिः *f.*, प्राकरणिकत्वं, प्रस्तावानुसारः, प्रस्तावान्वयः, प्रस्तावौचित्यं, प्रस्तावानुषङ्गः, प्रस्तुतानुषङ्गः, प्रस्तुतसङ्गतिः *f.*, युक्तिः *f.*, योग्यता, यौक्तिकत्वं, विषयकत्वं.

RELEVANT, *a.* प्रासङ्गिकः -की -कं, प्रसङ्गानुसारी -रिणी -रि (न्), प्रसङ्गसङ्गतः -ता -तं, प्रसङ्गोचितः -ता -तं, प्रसङ्गयोग्यः -ग्या -ग्यं, प्रसङ्गसदृशः -शी -शं, प्रसङ्गान्वयी &c., प्रकरणयोग्यः &c., प्रकरणानुसारी &c., प्रकरणसङ्गतः &c., प्राकरणिकः -की -कं, प्रस्तावोचितः -ता -तं, प्रस्तावानुसारी &c., प्रस्तावानुषङ्गी &c., प्रस्तुतानुषङ्गी &c., प्रस्तावसदृशः -शी -शं, प्रास्ताविकः -की -कं, यौक्तिकः -की -कं, प्रयुक्तः -क्ता -क्तं, युक्तिमान् -मती -मत् (त्), प्रतीक्षकः -का -कं, अपेक्षकः &c., उद्देशकः &c., विषयकः &c.

RELIANCE, *s.* विश्वासः, प्रत्ययः, विश्रम्भः, निष्ठा, आश्रयः, उपाश्रयः, संश्रयः, समाश्रयः, आशयः, शरणं, श्रायः, अवलम्बनं, तन्त्रता.

RELIC, *s.* शेषः -षं, अवशेषः -षं, शिष्टं, अवशिष्टं, अवशिष्टांशः, नष्टशिष्टांशः, परिशेषः, परिशिष्टं, शेषभागः, अवशिष्टभागः, शेषखण्डः.—(Corpse) शवः -वं.

RELICT, *s.* (Widow) विधवा, गतभर्तृका, मृतपतिका.

RELIEF, *s.* (Removal of pain or distress, alleviation) दुःखशमनं, दुःखशान्तिः *f.*, दुःखोद्धरणं, दुःखापहरणं, दुःखापहारः, दुःखमोचनं, दुःखमुक्तिः *f.*, दुःखपरिहारः, दुःखापनयनं, श्रमापनयनं, श्रमापहारः, श्रमपरिहारः, अनिष्टापनयनं, दुःखपरिमार्जनं, उद्धरणं, उद्धारः, शमनं, प्रशमनं.—(Ease or alleviation obtained) सुखं, शान्तिः *f.*, प्रशान्तिः *f.*, शमः, उपशमः, शान्तता, विश्रान्तिः *f.*, विश्रामः, स्वास्थ्यं, स्वस्थता, सुस्थता, सुस्थितिः *f.*, निर्वृतिः *f.*, समाधानं.—(In sculpture), *see* BASS-RELIEF.

RELIEVABLE, *a.* उद्धरणीयः -या -यं, शमनीयः &c., शाम्यः -म्या -म्यं.

To RELIEVE, *v. a.* (Free from pain, remove distress) उद्धृ (c. 1. -हरति -हर्तुं), दुःखम् अपहृ or हृ or अपनी (c. 1. -नयति -नेतुं), दुःखाद् मुच् (c. 6. मुञ्चति, मोक्तुं, c. 10. मोचयति -यितुं), दुःखं शम् (c. 10. शमयति -यितुं), दुःखशमनं कृ, दुःखोद्धरणं कृ, दुःखापहरणं कृ, श्रमम् अपहृ or हृ, श्रमापनयनं कृ, श्रमापहरणं कृ, दुःखमोचनं कृ.—(Alleviate) शम् (c. 10. शमयति -यितुं), प्रशम्, उपशम्, शान्तिं दा or कृ, शमनं कृ, प्रशमनं कृ, विश्रामं दा, विश्रान्तिं दा, लघ (nom. लघयति -यितुं), लघूकृ.—(Help) उपकृ, साहाय्यं कृ, सहायत्वं कृ, उपचर्.—(Relieve guard) सैनिकपरिवर्त्तनं कृ, रक्षकपरिवृत्तिं कृ, जागरणाद् मुच्.—(Set off by contrast) विपरीतगुणप्रकाशेन अधिकशोभां दा.

RELIEVED, *p.p.* (Freed from pain, &c.) मुक्तदुःखः -खा -खं, शान्तदुःखः

&c., शमितदुःखः &c., दुःखमुक्तः -क्ता -क्तं, श्रममुक्तः &c., मुक्तः &c., दुःखोद्धृतः -ता -तं, उद्धृतः &c., उद्धृतदुःखः -खा -खं, उद्धृतश्रमः -मा -मं, परिहृतदुःखः &c., विगतदुःखः &c., गतदुःखः &c., विगतश्रमः &c.; 'relieved of anxiety,' विगतोद्वेगः -गा -गं, गताधिः -धिः -धि; 'of fever,' विगतज्वरः -रा -रं, गतज्वरः &c., ज्वरमुक्तः &c., शान्तज्वरः &c.—(Alleviated) शान्तः -न्ता -न्तं, शमितः -ता -तं, प्रशमितः &c., उपशान्तः &c., प्राप्तविश्रामः -मा -मं, प्राप्तविरामः -मा -मं.—(Helped) उपकृतः -ता -तं.—(Relieved from watching) जागरणमुक्तः -क्ता -क्तं.—(Set off by contrast) विपरीतगुणप्रकाशेन प्राप्तशोभः -भा -भं.

Religion, *s.* धर्म्मः, ईश्वरभक्तिः *f.*, देवभक्तिः *f.*, भक्तिः *f.*, ईश्वरसेवा. *See* Piety.—(System of faith) धर्म्मः, धर्म्ममार्गः, मतं, मार्गः; 'establishment of a religion,' धर्म्मसंस्थापनं; 'extinction of one,' धर्म्मोच्छेदः; 'good religion,' सद्धर्म्मः; 'of the same religion,' सधर्म्मा -र्म्मा -र्म्म (न्), एकधर्म्मा &c., अपृथग्धर्म्मशीलः -ला -लं.

Religious, *a.* (Devoted to the practice of religion) धार्म्मिकः -की -कं, धर्म्मपरः -रा -रं, धर्म्मपरायणः -णा -णं, धर्म्मशीलः -ला -लं, भक्तिमान् -मती -मत् (त्), भजनशीलः &c., पुण्यात्मा -त्मा -त्म (न्), पुण्यशीलः &c., धर्म्माचारी &c., भक्तिनिष्ठः &c., व्रती &c., कर्म्मनिष्ठः &c., क्रियानिष्ठः &c., क्रियावान् &c., कर्म्मिष्ठः &c., नियमनिष्ठः &c., नियमशीलः &c., नियमपरः -रा -रं, *see* Pious.—(Pertaining to religion) धर्म्मसम्बन्धी &c., धर्म्मविषयकः -का -कं, धर्म्मप्रकरणः -णा -णं, धर्म्म in comp., देव in comp.; 'religious rite,' कर्म्म *n.* (न्), क्रिया, दैवकर्म्म *n.*

Religiously, *adv.* धार्म्मिकवत्, ईश्वरभक्त्या. *See* Piously.

Religiousness, *s.* धार्म्मिकत्वं, धर्म्मशीलता, कर्म्मनिष्ठा, नियमनिष्ठा, नियमपरता.

To relinquish, *v. a.* त्यज् (c. 1. त्यजति, त्यक्तुं), परित्यज्, संत्यज्, हा (c. 3. जहाति, हातुं), विहा, अपहा, अपाहा, प्रहा, प्रोज्झ् (c. 6. -उज्झति -ज्झितुं), उज्झ्, विमुच् (c. 6. -मुञ्चति -मोक्तुं), उत्सृज् (c. 6. -सृजति -स्रष्टुं), विसृज्, अपसृज्, व्यपसृज्, अतिसृज्, परिहृ (c. 1. -हरति -हर्त्तुं), प्रत्यादिश् (c. 6. -दिशति -देष्टुं), रह् (c. 10. रहयति -यितुं), विरह्, वृज् (c. 10. वर्जयति -यितुं), पृष्ठतः कृ.

Relinquished, *p. p.* त्यक्तः -क्ता -क्तं, परित्यक्तः &c., उत्सृष्टः -ष्टा -ष्टं, प्रोज्झितः -ता -तं, समुज्झितः &c., उज्झितः &c., प्रोत्सारितः &c.

Relinquishment, *s.* त्यागः, त्यजनं, परित्यागः, उत्सागः, विसर्जनं, विसर्गः, उत्सर्जनं, उत्सर्गः, प्रोज्झनं, वर्जनं, विमोचनं, मोचनं, परिहारः, परिहरणं, प्रत्यादेशः; 'of right or title,' स्वत्वनिवृत्तिः *f.*, सत्त्वानिवृत्तिः *f.*, स्वत्वत्यागः.

Reliquary, *s.* शिष्टभाण्डं, शिष्टपात्रं, शिष्टसम्पुटकः, अवशिष्टभाण्डं.

Relish, *s.* रुचिः *f.*, स्वादः -दनं, आस्वादः -दनं, रसः, *see* Taste.—(Relish for, liking for) अभिरुचिः *f.*, रुचिः *f.*, अभिनन्दनं, अभिलाषः, अनुमोदनं.—(Something eaten with food to increase the pleasure of eating or to provoke thirst) अवदंशः, उपदंशः, खर्जिका, मद्यपासनं.

To relish, *v. a.* (Give a nice taste) रसं दा, सुरसं दा, सुस्वादं दा, स्वादूकृ, सरसं -सां कृ, सरसीकृ, सुरसीकृ, स्वादुरसीकृ.—(Taste) आस्वाद् (c. 1. -स्वादति -दितुं), रसम् आस्वाद्, रस् (c. 10. रसयति -यितुं), प्राश् (c. 9. -अश्नाति -अशितुं), प्राशनं कृ, आस्वादनं कृ, रसास्वादनं कृ.—(Like the taste of) रुच् (c. 10. रोचयति -यितुं), अभिरुच्, अभिनन्द्. *See To* like.

To relish, *v. n.* (Have a nice taste) स्वद् (c. 1. स्वदते, स्वादते -दितुं), सुरसः -सा -सं भू, सरसः -सा -सं भू, सरसीभू, स्वादुरसीभू, रुचिरः -रा -रं भू.

Relished, *p. p.* आस्वादितः -ता -तं, रुचितः &c., अनुमोदितः -ता -तं.

Reluctance, reluctancy, *s.* अकामः, अकामता, निष्कामता, अनिच्छा, अनिच्छुता, विमुखता, अरुचिः *f.*, अनभिरुचिः *f.*, अस्पृहा, असन्तोषः.

Reluctant, *a.* अनिच्छुः -च्छुः -च्छु, अकामः -मा -मं, निष्कामः -मा -मं, अनिच्छुकः -का -कं, विमुखः -खा -खं, विमतः -ता -तं, असन्तोषी -षिणी -षि (न्).

Reluctantly, *adv.* अकामतस्, अकामेन, अनिच्छया, अनिच्छातस्, कृच्छ्रेण, निष्कामं, परिक्लिष्टं.

To rely, *v. n.* अवलम्ब् (c. 1. -लम्बते -म्बितुं), समालम्ब्, आलम्ब्, आश्रि (c. 1. -श्रयति -ते -यितुं), समाश्रि, उपाश्रि, संश्रि, विश्वस् (c. 2. -श्वसिति -तुं), विश्रम्भ् (c. 1. -श्रम्भते -म्भितुं), अवलम्बनं कृ.

Relying, *part.* अवलम्बी -म्बिनी -म्बि (न्), अवलम्बितः -ता -तं, आश्रितः -ता -तं, उपाश्रितः &c., संश्रितः &c., विश्वासी &c., विश्रम्भी &c., संश्रय in comp.

To remain, *v. n.* (Continue) स्था (c. 1. तिष्ठति, स्थातुं), अवस्था, पर्य्यवस्था, वृत् (c. 1. वर्त्तते -र्त्तितुं), आस् (c. 2. आस्ते), *see To* continue. *v. n.*—(Dwell, reside) स्था, अधिष्ठा, वृत्, वस् (c. 1. वसति -स्तुं), निवस्, आवस्, निली.—(Be left) शिष् in pass. (शिष्यते), अवशिष्, समवशिष्, परिशिष्, उच्छिष्, शिष्टः -ष्टा -ष्टं भू, सर्वशिष्टः &c. भू, उच्छिष्टः &c. भू, उद्धृत्; 'by subtracting two from six, four remain,' षड्भ्यो द्वयस्य वर्जनेन चत्वारः शिष्यन्ते; 'that which remains of the whole,' सर्व्वशेषः -षा -षं; 'those who remained alive, or those who remained out of the slain,' हतशेषः -षा -षं, हतशिष्टः -ष्टा -ष्टं.

Remainder, *s.* शेषः -षं, अवशेषः, अवशिष्टं, शिष्टं, उच्छिष्टं, परिशिष्टं, परिशेषः, शिष्टांशः, अवशिष्टांशः, शेषभागः, शेषखण्डः -ण्डं, परभागः, उद्धर्त्तः, उद्धृतं, उच्छेषणं, स्थितं.—(In arithmetic) अन्तरं, अन्तरितं: 'for the remainder of one's life,' यावज्जीवं.

Remaining, *part.* or *a.* शिष्टः -ष्टा -ष्टं, अवशिष्टः &c., अवशेषितः -ता -तं, उच्छिष्टः &c., परिशिष्टः &c., शेषः -षा -षं, उद्धृतः -ता -तं, उद्धर्त्तः -र्त्ती -र्त्तं, अन्तरितः -ता -तं, उद्वरितः -ता -तं.

Remains, *s. pl.* शेषाणि *n. pl.*, शिष्टानि. *See* Remainder, Relic, Corpse.

To remand, *v. a.* पुनः प्रेर् (c. 10. प्रेरयति -यितुं, rt. ईर्) or प्रस्था in caus. (-स्थापयति -यितुं), पुनर् आह्वे (c. 1. -ह्वयति -ह्वातुं), पुनराह्वानं कृ, पुनरर्पणं कृ.

Remark, *s.* (Act of taking notice) अवेक्षा -क्षणं, निरीक्षा, अपेक्षा, निरूपणं, आलोकनं, *see* Observation.—(Notice expressed in words) लिखितं, चर्चा, व्याख्या, अभिधानं, ग्रहणं, कथनं. *See* Note, Notice.

To remark, *v. a.* अवेक्ष्, अपेक्ष्, निरूप्, भण्. *See To* observe, notice.

Remarkable, *a.* (Notable, extraordinary) प्रसिद्धः -द्धा -द्धं, विशिष्टः -ष्टा -ष्टं, विशेष in comp., लोकप्रसिद्धः &c., ख्यातः -ता -तं, लोकख्यातः &c., उत्कृष्टः -ष्टा -ष्टं, स्मरणीयः -या -यं, स्मरणार्हः -र्हा -र्हं, अपूर्व्वः -र्व्वा -र्व्वं, आश्चर्य्यः -र्य्या -र्य्यं, अद्भुतः -ता -तं.—(To be observed) विभाव्यः -व्या -व्यं, *see* Observable, Noticeable.

Remarkably, *adv.* विशिष्टप्रकारेण, उत्कृष्टप्रकारेण, अद्भुतं, स्मरणीयं.

Remarked, *p. p.* अभिहितः -ता -तं, भणितः &c., कथितः &c., निरूपितः &c.

Remarried, *p. p.* पुनरूढः -ढा -ढं, पुनर्विवाहितः -ता -तं, पुनरुद्वाहितः &c.

Remediable, *a.* प्रतिकार्य्यः -र्य्या -र्य्यं, प्रतीकार्य्यः &c., उपायसाध्यः -ध्या -ध्यं, उपायप्रतिकार्य्यः &c., चिकित्स्यः -त्स्या -त्स्यं, चिकित्सनीयः -या -यं,

चिकित्सितुं शक्यः &c., शमनीयः -या -यं, उपायपरिहार्य्यः &c., परिहार्य्यः &c., समाधेयः -या -यं, प्रतिसमाधेयः &c., परिच्छेद्यः -द्या -द्यं, उपाययोग्यः -ग्या -ग्यं, उपचारयोग्यः &c., शक्यप्रतिकारः -रा -रं, शक्यपरिच्छेदः -दा -दं, शक्योपचारः -रा -रं, शक्योपायः -या -यं, विद्यमानप्रतीकारः &c.

REMEDIAL, *a.* प्रतिकारकः -का -कं, प्रतीकारी -रिणी -रि (न्), उपायसाधकः -का -कं, उपायदः -दा -दं, उपायकारी &c., परिहारकः &c., अभिघाती &c., प्रतिघाती &c.

REMEDIED, *p. p.* प्रतिकृतः -ता -तं, परिच्छिन्नः -न्ना -न्नं, परिहृतः -ता -तं, चिकित्सितः -ता -तं, शमितः &c., उपायसाधितः &c., उपायप्रतिकृतः &c., लब्धौषधः -धा -धं.

REMEDILESS, *a.* निरुपायः -या -यं, अनुपायः &c., उपायहीनः -ना -नं, निरुपचारः -रा -रं, उपचारशून्यः -न्या -न्यं, उपायासाध्यः -ध्या -ध्यं, गतिहीनः -ना -नं, अप्रतिकारः -रा -रं, अपरिच्छेदः -दा -दं. *See* IRREMEDIABLE, INCURABLE.

REMEDY, *s.* (Medicine) भेषजं, भैषज्यं, भेषजं, औषधं, अगदः, वैद्योपचारः.—(That which cures or counteracts an evil of any kind) प्रतिकारः, प्रतीकारः, प्रतिक्रिया, प्रतिविधिः *m.*, उपायः, उपचारः, परिच्छेदः, प्रतिसमाधानं, समाधानं, अभिघातः, प्रतिघातः, उपचर्य्या, उपक्रमः, चिकित्सा; 'mild remedy,' सामोपायः, सामोपचारः, सौम्योपचारः; 'violent remedy,' राक्षसोपायः.

To REMEDY, *v. a.* प्रतिकृ, प्रतिसमाधा (c. 3. -दधाति -धातुं), समाधा, उपायेन प्रतिकृ or शम् (c. 10. शमयति -यितुं), कित् in des. (चिकित्सति -त्सितुं), स्वस्थं -स्थां कृ, परिच्छिद् (c. 7. -छिनत्ति -छेत्तुं), उपचारं कृ, उपायप्रयोगं कृ, भिषज (nom. भिषज्यति), औषधीकृ; 'by mild measures,' सामोपायैः प्रतिकृ.

To REMEMBER, *v. a.* स्मृ (c. 1. स्मरति, स्मर्त्तुं), अनुस्मृ, संस्मृ, अनुसंस्मृ, अभिसंस्मृ, अनुचिन्त् (c. 10. -चिन्तयति -यितुं), समनुचिन्त्, अनुबुध् (c. 4. -बुध्यते -बोद्धुं), स्मरणं कृ, हृदये कृ, मनसि कृ.—(Recollect) स्मृ, अभिज्ञा. *See To* RECOLLECT.

REMEMBERED, *p. p.* स्मृतः -ता -तं, संस्मृतः &c., हृदयस्थः -स्था -स्थं, हृद्गतः &c.

REMEMBERER, *s.* स्मर्त्ता *m.* (र्तृ), स्मरणकृत्, स्मृतिमान् *m.* (त्), अनुचिन्तकः.

REMEMBRANCE, *s.* स्मरणं, स्मृतिः *f.*, संस्मृतिः *f.*, संस्मरणं, अनुस्मृतिः *f.*, स्मर्तृत्वं, अविस्मृतिः *f.*, अनुचिन्ता, धारणं -णा, अवधारणं; 'continual remembrance,' सततस्मरणं. *See* RECOLLECTION.—(Memorial, memento) स्मारकवस्तु *n.*, स्मारकविषयः, स्मारणं, स्मरणार्थकवस्तु *n.*, स्मृतिचिह्नं; 'of friendship,' प्रीतिदानं, प्रीतिदायं. *See* MEMORIAL.

REMEMBRANCER, *s.* स्मारकः, स्मारणः -णं, उद्बोधकः, स्मरणकारी *m.* (न्).

To REMIND, *v. a.* स्मृ (c. 10. स्मारयति -यितुं), संस्मृ, अनुस्मृ, बुध् (c. 10. बोधयति -यितुं), उद्बुध्, प्रबुध्, प्रतिबुध्, सूच् (c. 10. सूचयति -यितुं), स्मारणं कृ, स्मृतिं or स्मरणं जन् (c. 10. जनयति -यितुं), सूचनं कृ. The construction of the sentence will require 2 acc.; as, 'the Kandalí with its flowers reminds me of her eyes,' कुसुमैः कन्दली स्मारयति मां लोचने तस्याः; 'the Vimba reminds me of her lower lip,' विम्बं स्मारयति माम् अधरं तस्याः.

REMINDED, *p. p.* स्मारितः -ता -तं, उद्बोधितः -ता -तं, उद्बुद्धः -द्धा -द्धं.

REMINDING, REMINDER, *part.* or *s.* स्मारकः -का -कं, स्मृतिजनकः -का -कं, स्मारणः -णा -णं, उद्बोधकः -का -कं, उपलम्भकः -का -कं.

REMINISCENCE, *s.* स्मृतिः *f.*, स्मरणं. *See* MEMORY, RECOLLECTION.

REMISS, *a.* अनवधानः -ना -नं, अनवहितः -ता -तं, असावधानः &c., उपेक्षकः -का -कं, निरपेक्षः -क्षा -क्षं, मन्दादरः -रा -रं, अव्यवसायी -यिनी -यि (न्), अव्यवसायवान् -वती -वत् (त्), शिथिलः -ला -लं, शिथिलोद्योगः -गा -गं, शिथिलयत्नः -त्ना -त्नं, अलसः -सा -सं, प्रमत्तः -त्ता -त्तं.

REMISSION, *s.* (Relaxation) शैथिल्यं, शिथिलता, मोचनं, मुक्तिः *f.*—(Abatement) शान्तिः *f.*, उपशान्तिः *f.*, शमः, उपशमः.—(Release) मुक्तिः *f.*, विमुक्तिः *f.*, मोक्षः, उद्धारः, निस्तारः, विसर्जनं.—(Pardon) क्षमा, क्षान्तिः *f.*, मोचनं, मुक्तिः *f.*, निष्कृतिः *f.*; 'of sin,' पापमोचनं, पापमुक्तिः *f.*, पापमार्जना.—(Intermission) विरामः, विरतिः *f.*, अवरतिः *f.*, निवृत्तिः *f.*, विच्छेदः, छेदः; 'of study, &c.,' अनवकाशः, अनध्यायः, अध्ययनविरामः, अध्ययननिवृत्तिः *f.*

REMISSLY, *adv.* अनवधानेन, अनवहितं, मन्दादरं, अनपेक्षया, सशैथिल्यं.

REMISSNESS, *s.* अनवधानं -नता, अनवहितत्वं, उपेक्षा, अनपेक्षा, अनवेक्षा, अव्यवसायः, प्रमादः, प्रमत्तता, शैथिल्यं, शिथिलता, यत्नशैथिल्यं, अयत्नः.

To REMIT, *v. a.* (Relax, slacken) शिथिलीकृ, शिथिल (nom. शिथिलयति -यितुं), मुच् (c. 6. मुञ्चति, मोक्तुं, c. 10. मोचयति -यितुं), विमुच्, अवसृज्, विसृज्.—(Abate, diminish) शम् (c. 10. शमयति -यितुं), उपशम्, न्यूनीकृ, लघूकृ.—(Release, relinquish) मुच्, विमुच्, मोक्ष्, विसृज् (c. 6. -सृजति -स्रष्टुं), अवसृज्, त्यज्.—(Pardon) क्षम् (c. 1. क्षमते -ति, क्षन्तुं), संक्षम्, मुच्, विमुच्, पापमोचनं कृ.—(Transmit, as money, &c.) संचर् in caus., धनादि संक्रम् in caus., हुण्डिकापत्रद्वारा or लेख्यपत्रादिद्वारा धनं सम् in caus.

To REMIT, *v. n.* (Become less intense) शिथिलीभू, शम् (c. 4. शाम्यति शमितुं), उपशम्, प्रशम्, न्यूनीभू.

REMITTANCE, *s.* (The act) हुण्डिकापत्रद्वारा or लेख्यपत्रादिद्वारा धनसमर्पणं or धनसंक्रान्तिः *f.*—(The sum) लेख्यपत्रद्वारा समर्पितधनं.

REMITTED, *p. p.* मुक्तः -क्ता -क्तं, मोचितः -ता -तं, अवसृष्टः -ष्टा -ष्टं, शान्तः -न्ता -न्तं, उपशान्तः &c., क्षान्तः &c., त्यक्तः -क्ता -क्तं.

REMITTENT, *a.* विषमः -मा -मं, सततः -ता -तं, अविरतः -ता -तं; 'fever,' विषमज्वरः, सततज्वरः.

REMNANT, *s.* शेषः -षं, शिष्टं, अवशिष्टं, उच्छिष्टं. *See* REMAINDER.

REMONSTRANCE, *s.* आपत्तिः *f.*, आपत्तिवादः, आपत्तिभाषणं, आपत्तिलेखः, प्रत्यादेशकवादः, प्रबोधवाक्यं, औपदेशिकवादः. *See* EXPOSTULATION.

To REMONSTRATE, *v. n.* आपत्तिं कृ, आपत्तिपूर्व्वं वद् (c. 1. वदति -दितुं) or भाष्, आपत्तिवादं कृ, प्रत्यादिश् (c. 6. -दिशति -देष्टुं). *See To* EXPOSTULATE.

REMORSE, *s.* पश्चात्तापः, पश्चात्सन्तापः, अनुतापः, मनस्तापः, अनुशोकः, अनुशोचनं, अन्वाधिः *m.*, अनुशयः.

REMORSEFUL, *a.* पश्चात्तापी -पिनी -पि (न्), अनुतापी &c., अनुतप्तः -प्ता -प्तं.

REMORSELESS, *a.* निर्दयः -या -यं, उग्रदण्डः -ण्डा -ण्डं. *See* RELENTLESS.

REMOTE, *a.* दूरः -रा -रं, दूरस्थः -स्था -स्थं, दूरस्थितः -ता -तं, दूरस्थायी -यिनी -यि (न्), दूरवर्त्ती -र्त्तिनी &c., विदूरः &c., विप्रकृष्टः -ष्टा -ष्टं, असन्निकृष्टः &c., असन्निहितः -ता -तं, दविष्ठः -ष्ठा -ष्ठं, दवीयान् -यसी -यः (स्), अनुपस्थायी &c., अनुपस्थः -स्था -स्थं, गोपस्थः &c., गोपस्थाता -त्री -तृ (तृ), असमीपः -पा -पं, आरातीयः -या -यं, परः -रा -रं.

REMOTELY, *adv.* दूरं, दूरात् -रेण, विदूरं, विप्रकृष्टं, असमीपं.

REMOTENESS, *s.* दूरता -त्वं, विदूरता -त्वं, दूरस्थता, असन्निधानं, असान्निध्यं, विप्रकर्षः, असमीपता, असामीप्यं, असन्निकर्षः.

REMOVABLE, *a.* अपनेयः -या -यं, अपनेतव्यः -व्या -व्यं, अपनयनीयः -या -यं, अपहरणीयः -या -यं, अपहार्य्यः -र्य्या -र्य्यं, हार्य्यः &c., परिहार्य्यः &c., अपादेयः -या -यं, व्यावर्त्यः -र्त्या -र्त्यं, विनेयः -या -यं, अपसार्य्यः &c., स्थानान्तरकरणीयः &c.

REMOVAL, *s.* (Act of removing or causing to change place) अपनयनं, विनयनं, अपसारणं, उत्सारणं, निःसारणं, सारणं, अपहरणं,

हरणं, अपहारः, परिहारः, अपकर्षणं, अपादानं, अपवर्त्तनं, अपनोदः -दनं, अपनुत्तिः *f.*, चालनं, विचालनं, स्थानान्तरीकरणं, स्थलान्तरीकरणं. —(State of being removed, change of place, going away) स्थानभेदः, स्थलभेदः, स्थानान्तरं, स्थलान्तरं, अपगमः, अपायः, विचलनं, अपसरः -रणं, अपयानं, व्यावृत्तिः *f.*, व्यावृतिः *f.*—(Act of displacing or expelling) निरसनं, निरासः, अपासनं, निराकरणं, निराकृतिः *f.*, अपाकृतिः *f.*, अपाकरणं, निष्कासनं, निःकासनं, अपसारणं, अपनोदनं, वहिष्करणं, दूरीकरणं, निकृतिः *f.*; 'from an office,' पदात् or स्थानात् प्रभ्रंशनं or निराकरणं, पदभ्रंशनं.—(Putting an end to) खण्डनं, नाशः -शनं, परिच्छेदः, उच्छेदः, उद्धरणं, अभिघातः, प्रतिघातः, साधनं, सिद्धिः *f.*, प्रतिकारः, प्रतीकारः; 'removal of obstacles,' विघ्ननाशनं, विघ्नसिद्धिः *f.*, विघ्नखण्डनं; 'of ignorance,' अज्ञानखण्डनं; 'of disease,' रोगनाशः, रोगप्रतीकारः; 'of fear,' भयप्रतीकारः.

To REMOVE, *v. a.* (Take away) अपनी (c. 1. -नयति -नेतुं), विनी, व्यपनी, अपसृ (c. 10. -सारयति -यितुं), उत्सृ, निःसृ, सृ, अपहृ (c. 1. -हरति -हर्त्तुं), हृ, अपकृष् (c. 1. -कर्षति -क्रष्टुं), व्यपकृष्, अवकृष्, अपादा (c. 3. -ददाति -दातुं), अपनुद् (c. 6. -नुदति -नोत्तुं), अपानुद्, व्यपनुद्, व्यपानुद्, अपोह् (c. 1. अपोहते -ति -हितुं, rt. ऊह्), व्यपोह्. —(Move, cause to change place) विचल् (c. 10. -चालयति -यितुं), चल्, स्थानान्तरं गम् in caus., स्थानान्तरीकृ, स्थलान्तरीकृ, अन्यत्र कृ. —(Displace, expel) निरस् (c. 4. -अस्यति -सितुं), अपास्, निराकृ, अपाकृ, निष्कस् (c. 10. -कासयति -यितुं), अपसृ in caus., अपनुद्, अपसिध् (c. 1. -सेधति -सेद्धुं), वहिष्कृ, वहिः कृ, दूरीकृ; 'from an office, &c.,' पदात् or स्थानात् प्रभ्रंश् (c. 10. -भ्रंशयति -यितुं) or भ्रंश् or च्यु in caus. (च्यावयति -यितुं) or निराकृ.—(Put an end to) खण्ड् (c. 10. खण्डयति -यितुं), नश् (c. 10. नाशयति -यितुं), उद्धृ (c. 1. उद्धरति, उद्धर्त्तुं, rt. हृ), उच्छिद् (c. 7. -छिनत्ति -छेत्तुं), परिच्छिद्, प्रतिकृ; 'doubt is removed,' अपनीयते or निर्णीयते संशयः.

To REMOVE, *v. n.* (Move or change place) चल् (c. 1. चलति -लितुं), विचल्, स्थानान्तरं गम् (c. 1. गच्छति, गन्तुं), स्थलान्तरं गम् or या.—(Change residence) वासान्तरं गम् or या, गृहान्तरं गम्.—(Go away) अपगम्, अपसृ (c. 1. -सरति -सर्त्तुं), अपया (c. 2. -याति -तुं).

REMOVE, *s.* (Removing or changing place), *see* REMOVAL.—(Going away) अपगमः, अपसरः -रणं, अपयानं.—(Step in a scale) पदं, पदविः -वी *f.*, क्रमः.

REMOVED, *p.p.* (Taken away) अपनीतः -ता -तं, अपसारितः &c., उत्सारितः &c., निःसारितः &c., अपहृतः -ता -तं, हृतः &c., अपकर्षितः &c., अपनोदितः &c., अपोढः -ढा -ढं.—(Moved, changed in place) चालितः -ता -तं, विचालितः &c., स्थानान्तरीकृतः -ता -तं, स्थानान्तरगतः &c., स्थानान्तरकृतः &c., स्थानान्तरक्रमितः &c., स्थानान्तरप्राप्तः -प्ता -प्तं, स्थलान्तरीकृतः &c., व्यावृत्तः -त्ता -त्तं, व्यावृतः &c.—(Displaced, expelled) निरस्तः -स्ता -स्तं, अपास्तः &c., उदस्तः &c., परास्तः &c., निराकृतः -ता -तं, अपाकृतः &c., निष्कासितः &c., वहिष्कृतः &c., दूरीकृतः &c., निर्धूतः -ता -तं, अवधूतः &c., निकृतः &c., विप्रकृतः &c., अवकृष्टः -ष्टा -ष्टं, अवसृष्टः &c., प्रत्यादिष्टः -ष्टा -ष्टं, प्रत्याख्यातः -ता -तं; 'from office,' स्थानभ्रष्टः -ष्टा -ष्टं, स्थानात्प्रभ्रंशितः &c., पदच्यावितः -ता -तं.

REMOVER, *s.* अपनेता *m.* (तृ), अपनायकः, विनायकः, अपहारकः, अपहारी *m.* (न्), हारी *m.*, हारकः, हरः in comp., अभिहरः, अपकर्षी *m.* (न्), अपनोदकः, अपहः in comp., हः in comp., घ्नः in comp., नाशकः, नाशी *m.*, खण्डकः in comp.; 'remover of obstacles,' विघ्नविनायकः, विघ्नहारी *m.*, विघ्नहरः, विघ्ननाशकः, विघ्ननाशनः; 'of fear,' भयापहः; 'of disease,' रोगघ्नः, रोगहः, रोगान्तकः; 'of wind,' मारुतापहः.

To REMUNERATE, *v. a.* *See To* RECOMPENSE, REWARD, COMPENSATE.

REMUNERATED, *p. p.* गृहीतपारितोषिकः -का -कं, गृहीतवेतनः -ना -नं.

REMUNERATION, *s.* पारितोषिकं, वेतनं, फलं, निस्तारः, *see* COMPENSATION.

RENCOUNTER. *s.* *See* ENCOUNTER, CLASH, COLLISION.

To REND, *v. a.* दॄ (c. 9. दृणाति, दरितुं -रीतुं, c. 10. दारयति -यितुं), विदॄ, अवदॄ, भिद् (c. 7. भिनत्ति, भेत्तुं), विभिद्, निर्भिद्, विदल् (c. 10. -दलयति -यितुं), विदलीकृ, दल्, छिद्, व्यवछिद्, विछिद्, खण्ड् (c. 10. खण्डयति -यितुं); 'in two,' द्विधा भिद् or छिद्, द्विखण्डीकृ.

RENDER, *s.* (One who tears) विदारकः, दारकः, विभेदकः.

To RENDER, *v. a.* (Pay back, restore) प्रतिदा, पुनर् दा, प्रत्यृ in caus. (प्रत्यर्पयति -यितुं, rt. ऋ), प्रतिपद् in caus.—(Give, afford) दा, प्रदा, प्रयम् (c. 1. -यच्छति -यन्तुं), प्रतियम्, प्रतिपद् (c. 10. -पादयति -यितुं), ऋ in caus. (अर्पयति -यितुं), उपस्था in caus., उपक्लृप्.—(Cause to be, make, effect) कृ, जन् (c. 10. जनयति -यितुं), साध् (c. 10. साधयति -यितुं), उत्पद् (c. 10. -पादयति -यितुं), युक्तं -क्तां कृ, विशिष्टं -ष्टां कृ, कल् (c. 10. कलयति -यितुं). Or more commonly expressed by the use of the caus. form of any verb; as, 'to render proud,' दृप् in caus. (दर्पयति -यितुं); 'to render fat,' प्यै in caus. (प्याययति -यितुं); 'to render illustrious,' यशस्विनं कृ, कीर्त्तिं दा.—(Translate) भाषान्तरीकृ, अवतॄ.

RENDERED, *p. p.* (Restored) प्रतिदत्तः -त्ता -त्तं, प्रत्यर्पितः -ता -तं, प्रतिपादितः &c.—(Given) दत्तः -त्ता -त्तं, अर्पितः &c.—(Made, caused to be) कृत in comp., जात in comp., जनितः -ता -तं, or expressed by the pass. part. of the caus. form; 'rendered poor,' दरिद्रीकृतः -ता -तं; 'rendered proud,' जातदर्पः -र्पा -र्पं, दर्पितः -ता -तं; 'rendered beautiful,' शोभितः -ता -तं; 'rendered populous,' वासितः -ता -तं; 'rendered unfriendly,' विकारितः -ता -तं.

RENDERING, *s.* (Version) भाषान्तरं, पाठः, पाठान्तरं.

RENDEZ-VOUS, *s.* समागमस्थानं, सङ्गमस्थानं, सङ्केतस्थानं, सङ्केतस्थलं.

To RENDEZ-VOUS, *v. n.* सङ्केतस्थाने समागम् (c. 1. -गच्छति -गन्तुं) or संगम्.

RENDING, *s.* विदारः -रणं, दारणं, विदरः, विभेदनं, भिदा, स्फुटनं.

RENEGADE, RENEGADO, *s.* स्वपक्षत्यागी *m.* (न्), स्वधर्म्मत्यागी *m.*, स्वधर्म्मभ्रष्टः.

To RENEW, *v. a.* (Make new) नवीकृ, नवीनीकृ, नवं -वां कृ, नवीनं -नां कृ, नूतनं -नां -नीं कृ, नूतनीकृ.—(Restore to a former state repair) पूर्व्ववत् कृ, पूर्व्वावस्थां or पूर्व्वदशां गम् (c. 10. गमयति -यितुं) or नी (c. 1. नयति, नेतुं), प्रतिसमाधा, प्रतिकृ, प्रतिसंकृ, उद्धृ (c. 1. उद्धरति, उद्धर्त्तुं, rt. हृ), उद्धरणं कृ, जीर्णोद्धारं कृ.—(Make or do again) पुनः कृ, वारं वारं कृ, मुहुः कृ.—(Begin again) पुनर् आरभ्, पुनरारम्भं कृ.

RENEWABLE, *a.* नवीकरणीयः -या -यं, पुनःकरणीयः &c., उद्धरणीयः &c.

RENEWAL, *s.* (Making new) नवीकरणं, नवीनीकरणं, नूतनीकरणं. (Restoration to a former state, repairing) पूर्व्ववत्करणं, प्रतिसमाधानं, सन्धानं, समाधानं, उद्धरणं, उद्धारः, जीर्णोद्धारः.—(Doing again, beginning again) पुनःकरणं, पुनरारम्भः.

RENEWED, *p. p.* नवीकृतः -ता -तं, नवीनीकृतः &c., पुनःकृतः &c., पूर्व्ववत्कृतः &c.

To RENOUNCE, *v. a.* (Disown, disclaim) प्रत्याख्या (c. 2. -ख्याति -तुं), प्रत्यादिश् (c. 6. -दिशति -देष्टुं), निह्नु (c. 2. -ह्नुते -ह्नोतुं), अपह्नु, निरस्

(c. 4. -अस्यति -सितुं), अपास्, उदस्, व्युदस्, निराकृ, प्रत्याचक्ष्, न स्वीकृ, न ग्रह्, न अङ्गीकृ.—(Relinquish) त्यज् (c. 1. त्यजति, त्यक्तुं), परित्यज्, संत्यज्, हा (c. 3. जहाति, हातुं), विहा, अपहा, अपाहा, उत्सृज् (c. 6. -सृजति -स्रष्टुं), विसृज्, अवसृज्, व्यपसृज्, अपसृज्, प्रोज्झ् (c. 6. -उज्झति -ज्झितुं), उज्झ्, पृष्ठतः कृ; 'to renounce the world,' सन्न्यस्, सन्न्यासं कृ, सर्व्वसङ्गान् परित्यज्.

Renounced, *p. p.* प्रत्याख्यातः -ता -तं, प्रत्यादिष्टः -ष्टा -ष्टं, त्यक्तः -क्ता -क्तं, परित्यक्तः &c., निरस्तः -स्ता -स्तं, अपास्तः &c., सन्न्यस्तः &c.

To renovate, *v. a.* नवीकृ, नवीनीकृ, नूतनीकृ, पूर्व्ववत्कृ. *See To* renew.

Renovated, *p.p.* नवीकृतः -ता -तं, पूर्व्ववत्कृतः &c. *See* Renewed.

Renovation, *s.* नवीकरणं, नवीनीकरणं, नवता, नवीनता, नूतनावस्था, नवताप्राप्तिः *f.*, उद्धारः. *See* Renewal.

Renown, *s.* कीर्त्तिः *f.*, ख्यातिः *f.*, यशस् *n.*, विश्रुतिः *f.*, प्रतिपत्तिः *f.*, प्रख्यातिः *f.*, प्रतिख्यातिः *f.*, आख्या, प्रख्या. *See* Fame.

Renowned, *a.* कीर्त्तिमान् -मती -मत् (त्), यशस्वी -स्विनी -स्वि (न्), ख्यातः -ता -तं, आख्यातः &c., प्रख्यातः &c., प्रसिद्धः -द्धा -द्धं, सुप्रसिद्धः &c., जगत्प्रसिद्धः &c., ख्यातापन्नः -न्ना -न्नं, प्रतिष्ठितः -ता -तं, आख्यासम्पन्नः -न्ना -न्नं, प्रथितः -ता -तं, विश्रुतः &c., महायशाः -शाः -शः (स्), प्राप्तयशाः &c., कीर्त्तियुतः -ता -तं, कीर्त्तियुक्तः -क्ता -क्तं, नामधारी &c., रूढः -ढा -ढं.

Rent, *p.p.* (Torn) विदारितः -ता -तं, विदीर्णः -र्णा -र्णं, दारितः &c., दीर्णः &c., प्रविदारितः &c., दलितः -ता -तं, विदलितः &c., भिन्नः -न्ना -न्नं, विभिन्नः &c., पाटितः -ता -तं, स्फुटः -टा -टं, स्फुटितः -ता -तं.

Rent, *s.* (Tear) छिद्रं, भेदः, भित्तिः *f.*, भङ्गः, विदरः, दरी, दारणं, छेदः.—(Revenue) करः, महाकरः, उत्पन्नं, *see* Produce.—(Sum paid for any thing held of another) करः, मूल्यं; 'raising the rent of land,' परिवाधः.

To rent, *v. a.* (Grant the possession of lands &c., by lease, for a certain sum) पट्टोलिकापूर्व्वं निरूपितमूल्यमपेक्ष्य क्षेत्रगृहादि परप्रयोजनीयं दा, आविहितकालाद् वार्षिकमूल्यमपेक्ष्य क्षेत्रगृहादि परहस्ते समृ in caus.—(Take or hold by lease) पट्टोलिकापूर्व्वं वार्षिकमूल्यं प्रतिज्ञाय क्षेत्रगृहादि परहस्ताद् ग्रह् (c. 9. गृह्णाति, ग्रहीतुं) or परहस्ताद् गृहीत्वा प्रयुज् or परहस्ताद् गृहीत्वा अध्यास् or अधिवस्.

Rental, rent-roll, *s.* करपरिसंख्या, करपरिसंख्यापत्रं.

Renter, *s.* (One who leases) पट्टदायी *m.* (न्), पट्टदः.—(One who takes on lease) पट्टादायी *m.* (न्), पट्टग्राही *m.*, पट्टधारी *m.*, पट्टोलिकाधारी *m.*

Renunciation, *s.* प्रत्याख्यानं, प्रत्यादेशः, त्यागः, परित्यागः, उत्सर्गः, उत्सर्जनं, विसर्गः, विसर्जनं, निरसनं, निरासः, प्रोज्झनं, वर्जनं, परिहारः, अस्वीकारः, अग्रहणं; 'of the world,' सन्न्यासः, सन्न्यासित्वं, सर्व्वसङ्गपरित्यागः.

Repaid, *p. p.* प्रतिदत्तः -त्ता -त्तं, प्रत्यर्पितः -ता -तं, प्रतिकृतः -ता -तं.

To repair, *v. a.* (Restore to a sound state, after decay, &c.) प्रतिसमाधा (c. 3. -दधाति -धत्ते -धातुं), पुनः समाधा, पुनः सन्धा, उद्धृ (c. 1. उद्धरति, उद्धर्त्तुं, rt. हृ), उद्धारं कृ, जीर्णोद्धारं कृ, जीर्णोद्धरणं कृ, प्रतिकृ, प्रतिसंकृ, पुनः स्वस्थं -स्थां कृ or स्वस्थीकृ, पुनः सुस्थं -स्थां कृ or सुस्थ (nom. सुस्थयति -यितुं), साध् (c. 10. साधयति -यितुं), पूर्व्ववत् कृ, सन्धानं कृ, प्रतिसमाधानं कृ.—(Make good a loss) क्षतिं पृ (c. 10. पूरयति -यितुं) or सम्पृ, क्षतिपूरणं कृ, क्षतिनिष्कृतिं कृ, क्षतिं निष्कृ or शुध् (c. 10. शोधयति -यितुं), हानिपूरणं कृ, हानिप्रतिकारं कृ.

To repair, *v. n.* (Have recourse, go to) आश्रि (c. 1. -श्रयति -यितुं), श्रि, आश्रयणं कृ, शरणार्थं गम् (c. 1. गच्छति, गन्तुं) or आगम् or उपगम् or अभिगम् or प्रतिगम् or या (c. 2. याति -तुं) or अभिया or प्रयाया or इ (c. 2. एति -तुं), अभ्युपे.

Repair, *s.* प्रतिसमाधानं, सन्धानं, पुनः सन्धानं, समाधानं, साधनं, उद्धारः, जीर्णोद्धारः, जीर्णोद्धरणं, प्रतिकारः, प्रतीकारः, प्रतिकरणं, स्वस्थकरणं, सुस्थकरणं, पूर्व्ववत्करणं.

Repaired, *p. p.* जीर्णोद्धृतः -ता -तं, पुनः सन्धितः -ता -तं, पुनः साधितः &c., प्रतिसमाहितः &c., पुनः समाहितः &c., पूर्व्ववत्कृतः &c., प्रतिकृतः &c., स्वस्थीकृतः &c., स्वस्थः -स्था -स्थं, सुस्थीकृतः &c., सुस्थितः &c.

Repairer, *s.* जीर्णोद्धारकः, जीर्णोद्धर्त्ता *m.* (र्त्तृ) सन्धाता *m.* (तृ).

Reparable. *a.* सन्धेयः -या -यं, समाधेयः &c., प्रतिसमाधेयः &c., साध्यः -ध्या -ध्यं, साधनीयः -या -यं, प्रतिकार्य्यः -र्य्या -र्य्यं, उद्धार्य्यः &c. उद्धरणीयः -या -यं.

Reparation, *s.* (Repair), *see* above.—(Amends) क्षतिपूरणं, हानिपूरणं, क्षतिनिष्कृतिः *f.*, हानिनिष्कृतिः *f.*, क्षतिशोधनं. *See* Indemnity, Compensation.

Repartee, *s.* रसिकोत्तरं, सरसोत्तरं, सरसप्रत्युक्तिः *f.*, भङ्गिः *f.*

Repast, *s.* आहारः, भोजनं, भक्षणं, भक्षिका, अशनं, प्राशनं, अभ्याहारः; 'light repast,' लघुभोजनं, लघ्वाहारः, अल्पाहारः, उपाहारः, फलाहारः.

To repay, *v. a.* प्रतिदा (c. 3. -ददाति -दत्ते -दातुं), पुनर् दा or प्रदा, पुनर् ऋ in caus. (अर्पयति -यितुं), प्रत्यृ, पुनः प्रतिपद् (c. 10. -पादयति -यितुं) or प्रयम् (c. 1. -यच्छति -यन्तुं), निर्यत् (c. 10. -यातयति -यितुं), निवृत् (c. 10. -वर्त्तयति -यितुं), प्रतिकृ.—(Requite) प्रतिकृ, निर्यत्, प्रतिफल (nom. प्रतिफलयति -यितुं); 'to repay a kindness,' प्रत्युपकारं कृ, प्रत्युपकृ; 'an injury,' प्रत्यपकृ, प्रत्यपकारं कृ.—(Compensate) प्रतिफलं दा, निष्कृतिं दा or कृ, निस्तारं कृ, अपाकृ, निष्कृ, *see To* compensate, recompense.

Repayment, *s.* प्रतिदानं, पुनर्दानं, प्रत्यर्पणं, पुनरर्पणं, प्रतिपादनं, पुनःप्रतिपादनं, निर्यातनं, निवर्त्तनं, प्रतिफलं. *See* Requital, Recompense, Compensation.

To repeal, *v. a.* परावृत् (c. 10. -वर्त्तयति -यितुं), निवृत्, प्रचारपरावर्त्तं कृ, प्रचारनिवर्त्तनं कृ, लुप् (c. 6. लुम्पति, लोप्तुं), लोपं कृ, प्रचारलोपं कृ, खण्ड् (c. 10. खण्डयति -यितुं), प्रचारखण्डनं कृ, अवरुह् in caus. (-रोपयति -यितुं), प्रचारभङ्गं कृ, प्रचारभञ्जनं कृ, उच्छिद्, उच्छेदं कृ, प्रचारोच्छेदं कृ, प्रचाररोधं कृ.

Repeal, *s.* परावर्त्तः -र्त्तनं, निवर्त्तनं, प्रचारपरावर्त्तः, प्रचारनिवर्त्तनं, लोपः, प्रचारलोपः, खण्डनं, अवरोपः -पणं, भङ्गः, प्रचारभङ्गः, अनुशयः, उच्छेदः, निरुद्धरणं.

Repealable, *a.* परावर्त्यः -र्त्या -र्त्यं, निवर्त्यः &c., लोपनीयः -या -यं.

Repealed, *p. p.* परावृत्तः -त्ता -त्तं, परावर्त्तितः -ता -तं, निवर्त्तितः &c., निवृत्तः -त्ता -त्तं, लुप्तः -प्ता -प्तं, खण्डितः -ता -तं, अवरोपितः &c., उच्छिन्नः -न्ना -न्नं.

Repealer, *s.* परावर्त्तकः, लोपकारी *m.* (न्), परावर्त्तवादी *m.* (न्).

To repeat, *v. a.* (Say again) पुनर् वद् (c. 1. वदति -दितुं), अनुवद्, मुहुर् वद्, अनुवच् (c. 2. -वक्ति -क्तुं), पुनर् वच्, पुनरुक्तिं कृ, पुनर्वचनं कृ, मुहुर्वचनं कृ, आम्रेड् (c. 1. -म्रेडति -डितुं), पुनर् भाष्, मुहुर्भाषणं कृ.—(Do or make again) पुनः कृ, पुनः पुनः कृ, मुहुः कृ, पुनर् विधा, पुनर् अनुष्ठा or आवृत् in caus., मुहुर् अनुष्ठा, वारं वारं कृ.—(Rehearse, recite) पठ् (c. 1. पठति -ठितुं), सम्पठ्, अनुवद्, कथ् (c. 10. कथयति -यितुं), आख्या (c. 2. -ख्याति -तुं), समाख्या, श्रु (c. 10. श्रावयति -यितुं), गॄ (c. 9. गृणाति, गरितुं -रीतुं), पठनं कृ.—

(Tell) कथ्, वद्.—(A sound or word) आम्रेडः, आम्रेडनं वा.

REPEATED, *p. p.* (Said again) पुनरुक्तः -क्ता -क्तं, मुहुरुक्तः &c., पुनर्भाषितः -ता -तं; 'said twice,' द्विरुक्तः -क्ता -क्तं.—(Done again or often) पुनः कृतः -ता -तं, पुनरावृत्तः -त्ता -त्तं, पुनरावर्त्तितः -ता -तं, पुनः पुनः कृतः &c., मुहुः कृतः &c., वारं वारं कृत &c., पौनःपुनिकः -की -कं, अभीक्ष्णः -क्ष्णा -क्ष्णं; 'twice,' द्विरावृत्तः &c.—(Recited, told) पठितः -ता -तं, कथितः &c.

REPEATEDLY, *adv.* पुनः, पुनर्, मुहुस्, मुहुर्मुहुस्, वारं वारं, अनुवारं, असकृत्, भूयस्, भूयोभूयस्, बहुवारं, वारेण, शश्वत्, अनेकशस्.

REPEATER, *s.* अनुवादकः, अनुवादी *m.* (न्), कथकः, आख्यायकः.

To REPEL, *v. a.* प्रतिहन् (c. 2. -हन्ति -न्तुं), पराहन्, व्याहन्, प्रतिसृ (c. 10. -सारयति -यितुं), अपास्, प्रतिवृ (c. 10. -वारयति -यितुं), निवृ, वृ, अपानुद् (c. 6. -नुदति -नोत्तुं), व्यपानुद्, अपनुद्, प्रतिक्षिप् (c. 6. -क्षिपति -क्षेप्तुं), समवक्षिप्, प्रतिबाध् (c. 1. -बाधते -धितुं), निरस् (c. 4. -अस्यति -असितुं), अपासृ, परास्, निराकृ, अपाकृ, प्रतिकृ, अपोह् (c. 1. -ऊहते -हितुं), अपावृत् in caus., प्रत्यादिश् (c. 6. -दिशति -देष्टुं), निवृत् in caus. *See To* RESIST.

REPELLED, *p. p.* पराहतः -ता -तं, प्रतिहतः &c., व्याहतः &c., प्रतिसारितः -ता -तं, प्रतिवारितः &c., परास्तः -स्ता -स्तं, निरस्तः &c., निराकृतः &c., अपावृत्तः -त्ता -त्तं, अपनोदितः -ता -तं.

REPELLENT, REPELLING, *a.* or *part.* प्रतिघाती -तिनी -ति (न्), प्रतिवारकः -का -कं, निवारकः &c., प्रतिवारणः -णा -णं, प्रतिसारकः &c., प्रतिकारकः -का -कं; 'a repellent,' प्रतिकारः -रं, प्रतीकारः -रं.

REPELLING, *s.* प्रतिघातः -तनं, प्रतिसारणं, प्रतिवारणं, निवारणं, वारणं, निराकरणं, निरसनं, परासनं, प्रतिकारः, प्रतिकरणं.

To REPENT, *v. n.* (Feel regret or remorse) अनुतप् in pass. (-तप्यते), पश्चात् तप्, प्रत्यनुतप्, पश्चात् सन्तप्, तप्, मनसा तप्, अनुशुच् (c. 1. -शोचति -चितुं), पश्चात् शुच्, खिद् in pass. (खिद्यते), पश्चात् खिद्, अनुशी (c. 2. -शेते -शयितुं), पापस्मृत्या पीड् in pass., अनुतापं कृ, पश्चात्तापं कृ, अनुतप्तः -प्ता -प्तं भू, सन्तप्तः &c. भू, अनुशोकं कृ, अनुशयं कृ.—(Change the mind) मनः परिवृत् (c. 10. -वर्त्तयति -यितुं) or परावृत् or व्यावृत्, अन्यमानसीभू.

REPENTANCE, *s.* पश्चात्तापः, अनुतापः, सन्तापः, पश्चात्सन्तापः, मनस्तापः, अनुशोकः, अनुशोचनं, अनुशयः, दुष्कृतखेदः, पापखेदः, खेदः, पश्चात्खेदः, अन्वाधिः *m.*, पश्चाच्छोकः, विसूरितं, विप्रतीसारः, विप्रतिसारः, निवर्त्तनं, पश्चात्तापबुद्धिः *f.*, अनुतापबुद्धिः *f.*—(Change of mind) मनःपरिवर्त्तनं, मनःपरावर्त्तनं, मनोव्यावर्त्तः.

REPENTANT, *a.* अनुतापी -पिनी -पि (न्), पश्चात्तापी &c., अनुतप्तः -प्ता -प्तं, अनुशोचकः -का -कं, अनुशयी -यिनी &c., पश्चात्तापयुक्तः -क्ता -क्तं, पश्चात्तापान्वितः -ता -तं, जातानुतापः -पा -पं, जातपश्चात्तापः &c., जातानुशोकः -का -कं, जातानुशयः -या -यं, पापस्मृतिपीडितः -ता -तं, दुष्कृतस्मृतिपीडितः &c., जातखेदः -दा -दं, खेदान्वितः &c., अनुतापबुद्धिः -द्धिः -द्धि, पश्चात्तापबुद्धिः &c., शाकुणः -णी -णं.

REPENTED, *p.p.* अनुशोचितः -ता -तं, पश्चात् शोचितः &c., अनुशयितः &c.

REPERCUSSION, *s.* प्रतिघातः, प्रतिहतिः *f.*, प्रतिहननं, प्रतिसारणं, परापतनं.

REPERCUSSIVE, *a.* प्रतिघाती-तिनी-ति (न्), पराघाती &c., प्रतिसारकः-का-कं.

REPERTORY, *s.* कोषः, कोषागारं, भाण्डागारं, सञ्चयागारं, भाण्डगृहं.

REPETITION, *s.* (Saying again) अनुवादः, पुनर्वादः, पुनरुक्तिः *f.*, पौनरुक्त्यं, पुनःकथनं, पुनर्वचनं, पुनरुच्चारणं, मुहुर्वचनं, मुहुर्भाषा, पुनर्भाषा, अनुलापः; 'saying twice,' द्विरुक्तिः *f.*—(Doing again) पुनःकरणं, मुहुःकरणं, पुनर्विधानं, पुनरनुष्ठानं, पुनरावृत्तिः *f.*, पुनरावर्त्तनं, आवृत्तिः *f.*, आवर्त्तनं, पौनःपुन्यं; 'doing twice,' द्विरावृत्तिः *f.*—(Of a word or sound) आम्रेडनं, आम्रेडितं.—(A word repeated) कथितपदं, कथितवाक्यं.—(Of an act) क्रियासमभिहारः, क्रियावृत्तिः *f.*—(Recital, rehearsal) पठनं, पाठः, अनुवादः; 'from memory,' अभ्यसनं, अभ्यासः.

To REPINE, *v. n.* व्यथ् (c. 1. व्यथते -थितुं), शुच् (c. 1. शोचति -चितुं), तप् in pass. (तप्यते), परितप्, सन्तप्, आत्मानं तप् in caus. or व्यथ् in caus., खिद् in pass. (खिद्यते), अवसद् (c. 1. -सीदति -सत्तुं), ग्लै, परिग्लै, म्लै.

REPINING, *s.* आत्मव्यथा, मनस्तापः, मनःसन्तापः, मनोव्यथा, अवसादः.

To REPLACE, *v. a.* (Put again in its place) स्वस्थाने पुनर् ऋ in caus. (अर्पयति -यितुं) or पुनर् धा (c. 3. दधाति, धातुं) or पुनर् आधा or पुनः स्था in caus. (स्थापयति -यितुं) or पुनर् न्यस्, प्रतिसृ (c. 10. -सारयति -यितुं), पुनराधानं कृ, पुनरर्पणं कृ, पुनःस्थापनं कृ.—(Supply the place of) उपकॢप् (c. 10. -कल्पयति -यितुं), उपसृज् (c. 6. -सृजति -स्रष्टुं), उपसर्जनं कृ, प्रतिनिधिं दा.

REPLACED, *p. p.* पुनरर्पितः -ता -तं, पुनःस्थापितः &c., प्रतिसारितः &c.

To REPLENISH, *v. a.* पॄ (c. 10. पूरयति -यितुं), पुनः पॄ, पुनः सम्पॄ.

REPLENISHED, *p. p.* पूरितः -ता -तं, सम्पूर्णः -र्णा -र्णं, समृद्धः -द्धा -द्धं.

REPLETE, *a.* पूर्णः -र्णा -र्णं, सम्पूर्णः -र्णा -र्णं, परिपूर्णः &c., पर्याप्तः -प्ता -प्तं, पूरितः -ता -तं, संकीर्णः -र्णा -र्णं, आकीर्णः &c., आढ्यः -ढ्या -ढ्यं in comp., मयः -यी -यं in comp.; 'replete with knowledge,' विद्यापूर्णः &c., सम्पूर्णविद्यः -द्या -द्यं; 'with guile,' मायामयः &c.

REPLETION, *s.* (State of being completely filled) पूर्णता, परिपूर्णता, सम्पूर्णता, पर्याप्तिः *f.*, पूर्त्तिः *f.*, आपूर्त्तिः *f.*, परिपूर्त्तिः *f.*, आभोगः.—(Fulness of the blood or system from eating, &c.) अतितुष्टिः *f.*, अतिसौहित्यं, रक्तबाहुल्यं, रक्तवृद्धिः *f.*, रक्ताधिक्यं.

REPLICANT, *s.* उत्तरवादी *m.* (न्), प्रतिवादी *m.*, उत्तरपक्षी *m.*

REPLIED, *p. p.* प्रत्युक्तः -क्ता -क्तं, पुनरुक्तः &c. *See* ANSWERED.

To REPLY, *v. a.* प्रतिवच् (c. 2. -वक्ति -क्तुं), प्रतिवद् (c. 1. -वदति -दितुं), पुनर् वद्, अनुवद्, पुनर् वच्, प्रतिब्रू, पुनर् ब्रू, प्रतिभाष्, पुनर् भाष्, प्रतिभण्, पुनर् भण्; 'he replied,' प्रत्युवाच, पुनराह, प्रत्याह, *see To* ANSWER.—(In law) उत्तरं वद्, उत्तरं कृ, प्रतिवद्.

REPLY, *s.* (Answer) प्रतिवचनं, प्रतिवाक्यं, प्रत्युक्तिः *f.*, प्रत्युक्तं, उत्तरं, प्रत्युत्तरं, प्रतिवाक् *f.* (च्), प्रतिवादः, प्रतिवाणी -णिः *f.*—(In disputation) उत्तरं, प्रत्युत्तरं, कक्षा, उद्ग्राहः, कोटिः *f.*, प्रत्यर्थं.

To REPORT, *v. a.* (Give an account, relate) आविद् (c. 10. -वेदयति -यितुं), निविद्, विद्, आख्या, ख्या in caus., ज्ञा in caus., विज्ञा in caus., कथ्, संकथ्, शंस्, घुष् in caus.—(Give an official account) अधिकारपूर्व्वं विज्ञापनं कृ or आवेदनं कृ or विज्ञा in caus.

REPORT, *s.* (Account given, statement) आवेदनं, विज्ञापनं, विज्ञप्तिः *f.*, वादः, कथा; 'written report,' आवेदनपत्रं, विज्ञापनपत्रं, लेखः.—(Rumor, common talk) प्रवादः, जनप्रवादः, जनवादः, जनश्रुतिः *f.*, जनवार्त्ता, जनरवः, जनवदन्ती, लोकप्रवादः, लोकवार्त्ता, वार्त्ता, किंवदन्ती, वदन्ती, वादः, उपश्रुतिः *f.*, रवः, वृत्तान्तः, आख्या, चर्चा, उद्घोषः.—(Reputation) कीर्त्तिः *f.*, ख्यातिः *f.*, यशस् *n.*; 'good report,' सुख्यातिः *f.*; 'evil,' कुख्यातिः *f.*, कुकीर्त्तिः *f.*, अकीर्त्तिः *f.*, कौलीनं.—(Sound, noise) शब्दः, ध्वनिः *m.*, क्वणः -णितं.

REPORTED, *p.p.* (Related) आवेदितः -ता -तं, कथितः &c., विज्ञप्तः -प्ता -प्तं, विज्ञापितः -ता -तं, आख्यातः &c., शंसितः &c.—(Rumored) घोषितः -ता -तं, उद्घोषितः &c., कीर्त्तितः &c.

REP

REPORTER, *s.* वृत्तान्तलेखकः, समाचारलेखकः, वाक्यसारलेखकः.

To REPOSE, *v. n.* (Lie, rest) शी (c. 2. शेते, शयितुं), संविश् (c. 6. -विशति -वेष्टुं), विश्रम् (c. 4. -श्राम्यति -श्रमितुं), शयनं कृ, *see To* LIE.—(Rest on) अवलम्ब्, समालम्ब्, संश्रि, समाश्रि, उपाश्रि, निली, अवलम्बनं कृ.—(Confide in) विश्वस्, विश्रम्भ्.

REPOSE, *s.* विश्रामः, विश्रान्तिः *f.*, विश्रमः, शमः, शान्तिः, विरामः, श्रमच्छेदः, क्लान्तिच्छेदः, श्रमनिवृत्तिः *f.*, निर्वृतिः *f.*, शीः *f.*

REPOSED, *p. p.* विश्रान्तः -न्ता -न्तं, गतश्रमः -मा -मं, गतक्लमः &c., नष्टश्रमः &c., अपहृतश्रमः &c., निवृत्तश्रमः &c., छिन्नक्लान्तिः -न्तिः -न्ति.

To REPOSIT, *v. a.* निधा (c. 3. -दधाति -धातुं), न्यस् (c. 4. -अस्यति -असितुं), न्यासीकृ, रक्षणार्थं न्यस् or निधा, रक्ष् (c. 1. रक्षति -क्षितुं), संरक्ष्, निधिं कृ.

REPOSITED, *p.p.* न्यस्तः -स्ता -स्तं, निहितः -ता -तं, रक्षितः -ता -तं.

REPOSITORY, *s.* निधिः *m.*, निधानं, आधारः, कोषः, आगारं, भाण्डं, भाजनं, पात्रं, कोष्ठः-ष्ठकं, रक्षणस्थानं; 'of corn,' धान्यागारं, धान्यकोष्ठकं.

To REPREHEND, *v. a.* *See To* BLAME, REPROVE, &c.

REPREHENSIBLE, *a.* निन्द्यः -न्द्या -न्द्यं, निन्दनीयः -या -यं, गर्ह्यः -र्ह्या -र्ह्यं, गर्हणीयः -या -यं, विगर्ह्यः &c., परिभाषणीयः &c., दूषणीयः &c., दूष्यः -ष्या -ष्यं, दूषणार्हः -र्हा -र्हं, दोषवान् -वती -वत् (त्), सदोषः -षा -षं, निन्दापात्रं, निन्दाभाजनं, परिभाषणीयः &c.

REPREHENSION, *s.* निन्दा -न्दनं, उपालम्भः. *See* REPROOF, BLAME.

To REPRESENT, *v. a.* (Exhibit) दृश् (c. 10. दर्शयति -यितुं), प्रदृश्, *see To* SHOW.—(Describe) वर्ण् (c. 10. वर्णयति -यितुं), अनुवर्ण्, विवृ, निरूप्; 'in writing or drawing,' लिख् (c. 6. लिखति, लेखितुं), आलिख्, विलिख्.—(Personate) रूप् (c. 10. रूपयति-यितुं), अभिनी, वेशं धृ or भृ.—(State respectfully) निविद् (c. 10. -वेदयति -यितुं), विज्ञा in caus. (-ज्ञापयति -यितुं), निवेदनं कृ, विज्ञापनं कृ.—(Stand in the place of) प्रतिनिधिर् भू or अस्, प्रतिभूर् अस्, प्रतिपुरुषो भू or अस्.

REPRESENTATION, *s.* (Act of exhibition) दर्शनं, प्रदर्शनं, प्रकाशनं; 'on the stage,' अभिनयः -यनं.—(Description) वर्णनं -ना, अनुवर्णनं, उपवर्णनं, निरूपणं.—(Respectful statement) निवेदनं, विज्ञापनं -ना, विज्ञप्तिः *f.*, आवेदनं, उपन्यासः, उपपादनं,—(Delineation, sketch) आलेख्यं, आलेखनं, लेख्यं.—(Image, likeness, picture) प्रतिरूपं, प्रतिकृतिः *f.*, प्रतिमा, प्रतिमानं, प्रतिमूर्त्तिः *f.*, मूर्त्तिः *f.*, प्रतिनिधिः *m.*, प्रतिबिम्बं, प्रतिच्छाया, प्रतिच्छन्दः -न्दकं, चित्रं, चित्रलेखा.

REPRESENTATIVE, *a.* प्रदर्शकः -का -कं, उद्बोधकः -का -कं, प्रतिरूपकः &c.

REPRESENTATIVE, *s.* प्रतिनिधिः *m.*, प्रतिभूः *m.*, प्रतिपुरुषः, उपसर्जनं.

REPRESENTED, *p. p.* (Exhibited) दर्शितः -ता -तं, प्रदर्शितः &c.—(Described) वर्णितः -ता -तं.—(In a picture, &c.) चित्रलिखितः -ता -तं, आलिखितः &c., *see* PAINTED.—(Stated respectfully) निवेदितः -ता -तं, आवेदितः &c., विज्ञापितः &c., विज्ञप्तः -प्ता -प्तं, उपन्यस्तः -स्ता -स्तं, उपपादितः &c.—(Having substitutes) सप्रतिनिधिः -धिः -धि, सप्रतिभूः -भूः -भु.

To REPRESS, *v. a.* निग्रह् (c. 9. -गृह्णाति -ग्रहीतुं), नियम् (c. 1. -यच्छति -यन्तुं), संयम्.

REPRESSED, *p. p.* निगृहीतः -ता -तं, संयतः &c., जातनिग्रहः -हा -हं.

REPRESSION, *s.* निग्रहः -हणं, संयमः -मनं, निगृहीतिः *f.*, यन्त्रणं.

REPRESSIVE, *a.* नियामकः -का -कं, निग्रहकारी -रिणी -रि (न्).

REPRIEVE, *a.* दण्डविलम्बः -म्बनं, दण्डनविलम्बः, आकालान्तराद् दण्डत्यागः or दण्डयापनं, दण्डकालयापनं, दण्डकालान्तरनयनं, परावर्त्तः, दण्डकालपरावर्त्तः, दण्डपरावर्त्तः.

To REPRIEVE, *v. a.* दण्डविलम्बनं कृ, दण्डविलम्बं कृ, आकालान्तराद् दण्डनं त्यज् or या in caus., शिक्षाविलम्बनं कृ, दण्डं or दण्डकालं परावृत् (c. 10. -वर्त्तयति -यितुं), दण्डकालपरावर्त्तं कृ, प्राणदानं कृ, प्राणदण्डविलम्बं कृ.

To REPRIMAND, *v. a.* निन्द् (c. 1. निन्दति -न्दितुं), प्रत्यादिश् (c. 6. -दिशति -देष्टुं), उपालभ् (c. 1. -लभते -लब्धुं), गर्ह्, विगर्ह्, अभिशंस्, क्षिप्, भर्त्स्, शब्दताडनं कृ, मुखदण्डनं कृ, वाग्दण्डं कृ, धिग्दण्डं कृ. *See To* REPROVE.

REPRIMAND, *s.* उपालम्भः, वाग्दण्डः, शब्ददण्डः, शब्दताडनं, धिग्दण्डः, मुखदण्डः -ण्डनं, प्रत्यादेशः, प्रत्यादेशवाक्यं, भर्त्सनवाक्यं, अभिशंसनं, निन्दा.

REPRIMANDED, *p.p.* उपालब्धः -ब्धा -ब्धं, प्रत्यादिष्टः -ष्टा -ष्टं, अभिशस्तः &c.

To REPRINT, *v. a.* पुनर् मुद्र् (nom. मुद्रयति -यितुं), पुनर् मुद्रीकृ.

REPRINTED, *p.p* पुनर्मुद्रितः -ता -तं, पुनर्मुद्रीकृतः &c., पुनर्मुद्राङ्कितः &c.

REPRISAL, *s.* प्रत्यपहारः, प्रत्यपहरणं, प्रत्यपकारः, प्रत्यपकरणं, प्रतिपीडनं, क्षतिपूरणार्थम् अपहरणं or अपहारः, हानिपूरणार्थं प्रत्यपहरणं or प्रतिहरणं.

To REPROACH, *v. a.* निन्द् (c. 1. निन्दति -न्दितुं), विनिन्द्, प्रतिनिन्द्, प्रणिन्द्, तिरस्कृ, परिवद् (c. 1. -वदति -दितुं), परिभाष् (c. 1. -भाषते -षितुं), उपालभ् (c. 1. -लभते -लब्धुं), गर्ह्, विगर्ह्, परिगर्ह्, कुत्स्, अभिकुत्स्, भर्त्स्, अपवद्, आक्रुश्, समाक्रुश्, उपक्रुश्, गुप् in des., तर्ज्, क्षिप्, अधिक्षिप्, दोषम् आरुह् in caus., दोषं क्षिप्, दोषारोपं कृ, दोषीकृ, वाक्पारुष्यं कृ, धिक्कृ, धिक्पारुष्यं कृ. *See To* BLAME, CENSURE.

REPROACH, *s.* निन्दा -न्दनं, तिरस्कारः, तिरस्क्रिया, परिवादः, परीवादः, परिभाषा -षणं, गर्हा -र्हणं, उपालम्भः, उपक्रोशः, आक्रोशः, जुगुप्सा, परुषोक्तिः *f.*, परुषवचनं, वाक्पारुष्यं, धिक्पारुष्यं, धिक्क्रिया, दुर्वाक्यं, दुरुक्तं, कुत्सा, घृणा, ऋतीया, पर्यनुयोगः, अर्हणं, वाच्यता, वचनीयता, ह्रणीया, रीढ्या, क्षिः *m.*, अपकारगीः *f.*

REPROACHABLE, *a.* निन्द्यः -न्द्या -न्द्यं, परिभाषणीयः &c., गर्ह्यः -र्ह्या -र्ह्यं.

REPROACHED, *p. p.* निन्दितः -ता -तं, तिरस्कृतः &c., उपालब्धः -ब्धा -ब्धं, परिभाषितः &c., गर्हितः &c., अभिक्रुष्टः -ष्टा -ष्टं, धिक्कृतः &c.

REPROACHFUL, *a.* (Opprobrious) निन्दकः -का -कं, परिवादकः &c., कुत्सावादी -दिनी -दि (न्), निन्दात्मकः &c., घृणाकरः -रा -रं, निन्दामयः -यी -यं.—(Shameful) गर्ह्यः -र्ह्या -र्ह्यं, लज्जाकरः -रा -री -रं, लज्जाप्रदः -दा -दं.

REPROACHFULLY, *adv.* सनिन्दं, निन्दया, सतिरस्कारं, सासूयं, सपरिवादं.

REPROBATE, *a.* दुष्टः -ष्टा -ष्टं, दुराचारः -रा -रं, दुरात्मा -त्मा -त्म (न्), धर्म्मत्यागः -गा -गं, त्यक्तधर्म्मा -र्म्मा -र्म्म (न्), दुष्टभावः -वा -वं, पापात्मा &c., पापचेताः -ताः -तः (स्), त्यक्तलज्जः -ज्जा -ज्जं, दुःशीलः -ला -लं.

REPROBATE, *s.* दुष्टजनः, कुलनाशः -शनः, वृषलः, हतपरलोकः.

To REPROBATE, *v. a.* गर्ह् (c. 1. गर्हते -र्हितुं), विगर्ह्, गर्हापूर्व्वम् असम्मतिं सूच् (c. 10. सूचयति -यितुं), निन्द् (c. 1. निन्दति -न्दितुं), घृणां कृ, त्यक्तृ.

REPROBATED, *p. p.* गर्हितः -ता -तं, गर्हापूर्व्वं निन्दितः &c., विगर्हितः &c.

REPROBATION, *s.* (Act) गर्हा -र्हणं, विगर्हणं -णा, निन्दा -न्दनं, घृणा.—(State) अतिदुष्टता, त्यक्तत्वं, गर्ह्यता.

To RE-PRODUCE, *v. a.* प्रत्युत्पद् (c. 10.-पादयति-यितुं), पुनर् उत्पद् or जन्.

REPRODUCED, *p. p.* प्रत्युत्पन्नः -न्ना -न्नं, प्रत्युत्पादितः -ता -तं, पुनरुत्पन्नः &c.

REPRODUCTION, *s.* प्रत्युत्पादनं, प्रत्युत्पत्तिः *f.*, पुनरुत्पादनं, पुनरुत्पत्तिः *f.*

REPROOF, *s.* निन्दा -न्दनं, परिभाषणं, परिवादः, परीवादः, उपालम्भः, प्रत्यादेशः, निन्दावाक्यं, भर्त्सनवाक्यं, भर्त्सना, वाग्दण्डः, मुखदण्डः, शब्ददण्डः. *See* CENSURE, CHIDING.

Reprovable, *a.* निन्द्यः -न्द्या -न्द्यं, निन्दनीयः -या -यं, परिभाषणीयः &c.

To reprove, *v. a.* निन्द् (c. 1. निन्दति -न्दितुं), प्रतिनिन्द्, विनिन्द्, प्रणिन्द्, प्रत्यादिश् (c. 6. -दिशति -देष्टुं), उपालभ् (c. 1. -लभते -लब्धुं), परिवद्, अपवद्, परिभाष्, अपभाष्, गर्ह्, विगर्ह्, भर्त्स्, गुप् in des., कुत्स्, अभिकुत्स्, क्षिप्, अधिक्षिप्, तिरस्कृ, वाग्दण्डं कृ, आक्रुश्, उपक्रुश्, धिक्कृ. *See To* censure.

Reproved, *p. p.* निन्दितः -ता -तं, प्रत्यादिष्टः -ष्टा -ष्टं, उपालब्धः -ब्धा -ब्धं.

Reprover, *s.* निन्दकः, प्रत्यादेशकः, परिवादकः, वाग्दण्डकारी *m.* (न्).

Reptile, *s.* उरगः, उरोगामी *m.* (न्), उरोगः, उरोगमः, उरङ्गः, उरङ्गमः, सर्पः, सरीसृपः, सर्पी *m.* (न्), कृमिः *m.*, बिलवासी *m.* (न्), बिलेवासी *m.*, बिलौकाः *m.* (स्), अपदः, अपादः, बहुपादः.

Reptile, *a.* (Creeping) सर्पी -र्पिणी -र्पि (न्), सर्पन् -र्पन्ती -र्पत् (त्), सर्पणः -णा -णं.—(Relating to a reptile) सार्पः -र्पी -र्पं, कृमिलः -ला -लं.

Republic, *s.* लोकप्रभुत्वं, सर्व्वलोकप्रभुत्वं, लोककर्तृकप्रभुत्वं, प्रजाप्रभुत्वं, सर्व्ववर्णप्रभुत्वं, सर्व्ववर्णाधिपत्यं, साधारणप्रभुत्वं, साधारणाधिपत्यं, साधारणजनप्रभुत्वं, लोकसाधारणाधिपत्यं, सर्व्वप्रजाधिपत्यं, लोककर्तृकराज्यं, सामान्यजनकर्तृकराज्यं, लोकपालितं राज्यं, साधारणजनपालितराज्यं, प्रजापालितराज्यं.

Republican, *a.* लोकप्रभुत्वसम्बन्धी -न्धिनी -न्धि (न्), प्रजाप्रभुत्वसम्बन्धी &c., लोकाधिपत्यसम्बन्धी &c., लोकप्रभुत्वविषयकः -का -कं, लोकप्रभुत्वानुसारी &c., लोकप्रभुत्वानुरूपः -पा -पं.

Republican, *s.* लोकप्रभुत्ववादी *m.* (न्), लोकाधिपत्यपक्षपाती *m.*, लोकप्रभुत्वावलम्बी *m.*, प्रजाधिपत्यवादी *m.*, प्रजाधिपत्यानुग्राही *m.*, प्रजानाथः, लोकनाथः.

Republicanism, *s.* लोकप्रभुत्वपक्षपातः, लोकाधिपत्यपक्षपातः, लोकप्रभुत्वावलम्बनं, प्रजाधिपत्यवादः, लोकाधिपत्यानुग्रहः.

To repudiate, *v. a.* प्रत्याख्या (c. 2. -ख्याति -तुं), निराकृ, निरस्, प्रत्यादिश्, त्यज्, परित्यज्, प्रत्याचक्ष्, निर्नुद्, अपध्वंस्. *See To* reject.

Repudiated, *p. p.* प्रत्याख्यातः -ता -तं, निराकृतः &c., प्रत्यादिष्टः -ष्टा -ष्टं.

Repudiation, *s.* प्रत्याख्यानं, निरसनं, निरासः, निराकरणं, निराकृतिः *f.*, त्यागः, परित्यागः, प्रत्यादेशः, *see* Rejection.—(Divorce) विवाहसम्बन्धत्यागः, विवाहसम्बन्धमुक्तिः *f.*, दाम्पत्यमुक्तिः *f.*, भार्य्यानिराकरणं.

Repugnance, repugnancy, *s.* प्रतिकूलता, प्रातिकूल्यं, विरोधः, विरुद्धता, वैपरीत्यं, विमुखता, विमतिः *f.*, अनिच्छा.

Repugnant, *a.* प्रतिकूलः -ला -लं, विरुद्धः -द्धा -द्धं, विपरीतः -ता -तं, विरोधी -धिनी &c., विमुखः -खा -खी -खं. *See* Opposed, Adverse.

Repulse, *s.* प्रतिघातः, प्रतिहतिः *f.*, पराहननं, प्रतिहननं, प्रतिसारणं, निवारणं, वारणं, अपाकृतिः *f.*, विद्रवः, विद्रावणं, पराजयः, अपजयः.

To repulse, *v. a.* पराहन् (c. 2. -हन्ति -न्तुं), प्रतिहन्, प्रतिसृ. *See To* repel.

Repulsed, *p. p.* पराहतः -ता -तं, प्रतिहतः &c., व्याहतः &c., निहतः &c., आहतः &c., प्रहतः &c., प्रतिसारितः &c., प्रतिक्षिप्तः -प्ता -प्तं, विद्रावितः &c., निवारितः &c., अपाकृतः &c., पराजितः &c., प्रत्याख्यातः &c.

Repulsion, *s.* प्रतिसारकत्वं, प्रतिघातकत्वं, प्रतिसारणगुणः, प्रतिसारणशक्तिः *f.*, प्रतिहननशक्तिः *f.*, प्रतिहननं, प्रतिसारणं. *See* Repulse.

Repulsive, *a.* (Repelling) प्रतिघाती -तिनी -ति (न्), प्रतिघातकः -का -कं, प्रतिसारकः -का -कं, निवारकः &c., वारकः &c.—(Forbidding) अप्रीतिजनकः -का -कं, त्रासजनकः &c., त्रासकरः -री -रं, अमङ्गलः -ला -लं, अप्रसन्नमुखः -खी -खं.

Reputable, *a.* (In good esteem) मान्यः -न्या -न्यं, सम्मान्यः &c., माननीयः -या -यं, आदरणीयः &c., प्रशंसनीयः &c., मानार्हः -र्हा -र्हं, सम्मानार्हः &c., श्लिष्टः -ष्टा -ष्टं.—(Conferring reputation, not disgraceful) मानदः -दा -दं, मानप्रदः &c., मानदायी -यिनी &c., यशस्यः -स्या -स्यं, यशस्करः -री -रं, कीर्त्तिकरः -री -रं, ख्यातिकरः &c., सुप्रतिष्ठः -ष्ठा -ष्ठं, श्लाघ्यकरः &c.

Reputably, *adv.* समानं, यथा सुख्यातिर् उत्पद्यते तथाप्रकारेण.

Reputation, *s.* कीर्त्तिः *f.*, ख्यातिः *f.*, विख्यातिः *f.*, प्रतिष्ठा, समाख्या, यशस् *n.*, परिख्यातिः *f.*, प्रतिख्यातिः *f.*, प्रविख्यातिः, प्रकीर्त्तिः *f.*, कीर्त्तना -नं, प्रतिपत्तिः *f.*, प्रथा, सम्प्रथा, मर्य्यादा, समाज्ञा, प्रसिद्धिः *f.*, गौरवं, चारित्रं; 'one who has established a reputation,' लब्धप्रतिष्ठः -ष्ठा -ष्ठं, प्राप्तप्रतिष्ठः &c.; 'good reputation,' सुकीर्त्तिः *f.*, सत्कीर्त्तिः *f.*, सुख्यातिः *f.*; 'bad reputation,' कुकीर्त्तिः *f.*, दुष्कीर्त्तिः *f.*, अकीर्त्तिः, अपकीर्त्तिः *f.*, कुख्यातिः *f.*, अख्यातिः *f.*, अयशस् *n.*, वाच्यता.

To repute, *v. a.* गण् (c. 10. गणयति -यितुं), विगण्, मन् (c. 4. मन्यते, मन्तुं, c. 10. मानयति -यितुं), संख्या, परिसंख्या, कृत् (c. 10. कीर्त्तयति -यितुं).

Repute, *s.* कीर्त्तिः *f.*, ख्यातिः *f.*, प्रसिद्धिः *f.* *See* Reputation.

Reputed, *p. p.* मतः -ता -तं, गणितः &c., विगणितः &c., कीर्त्तितः &c.

Request, *s.* (Entreaty) प्रार्थनं -ना, अर्थना, अभ्यर्थना, अर्थः, याचना, याञ्चा, स्वार्थनिवेदनं, अर्थविज्ञापना, सनिः -नी *m. f.*—(Desire) आकांक्षा, अभिकांक्षा, कांक्षा, इच्छा, स्पृहा, अभ्येषणा.—(State of being desired or held in estimation) अपेक्षा, आकांक्षा, मान्यता -त्वं, माननीयता; 'general request,' लोकमान्यता.

To request, *v. a.* प्रार्थ् (c. 10. -अर्थयते -ति -यितुं), अभ्यर्थ्, सम्प्रार्थ्, अर्थ्, याच् (c. 1. याचति -ते -चितुं), अभियाच्, प्रयाच्, सम्प्रयाच्, संयाच्, अर्थं निविद् (c. 10. -वेदयति -यितुं) or विज्ञा in caus. (-ज्ञापयति -यितुं), वृ (c. 9. वृणीते, वरितुं -रीतुं, c. 10. वारयति -यितुं), कांक्ष्, आकांक्ष्, अभिकांक्ष्.

Requested, *p. p.* प्रार्थितः -ता -तं, अभ्यर्थितः &c., अर्थितः &c., याचितः &c., अर्दितः -ता -तं.

To require, *v. a.* (Ask, demand) प्रार्थ् (c. 10. -अर्थयति -ते -यितुं), याच् (c. 1. याचति -चितुं), अभियाच्.—(Need, call for) आकांक्ष् (c. 1. -कांक्षति -क्षितुं), अभिकांक्ष्, कांक्ष्, अर्ह् (c. 1. अर्हति -र्हितुं), प्रार्थ्; or expressed by भू or अस् in conjunction with the nouns प्रयोजनं, उपयोगः or कार्य्यं. *See To* need. The desid. form may sometimes be used to express the sense of 'require,' thus; 'three quantities being given, it is required to find a fourth,' त्रीन् राशीन् निर्दिश्य चतुर्थो जिज्ञास्यते (desid. pass. of ज्ञा).

Required, *p. p.* आकांक्षितः -ता -तं, अभिकांक्षितः &c., प्रार्थितः &c.

Requisite, *a.* आकांक्षितः -ता -तं, आकांक्षणीयः -या -यं, अभिकांक्षितः &c., प्रयोजनीयः &c., प्रयोजनार्हः -र्हा -र्हं, अवश्यकः -का -कं, आवश्यकः -की -कं, अवश्यप्रापणीयः &c. *See* Needful.

Requisite, *s.* अवश्यकवस्तु *n.*, अवश्यकद्रव्यं, अवश्यकविषयः; 'requisites,' प्रयोजनीयद्रव्यसामग्री, उपकरणसाहित्यं. *See* Necessaries.

Requisition, *s.* आकांक्षा, अभिकांक्षा, कांक्षा, प्रार्थनं -ना, अभ्यर्थनं -ना, अर्थना, याचनं -ना, अपेक्षा -क्षणं; 'is in requisition,' सेव्यतां याति.

Requital, *s.* (Recompense, return) प्रतिफलं, प्रतिदानं, निस्तारः, निष्कृतिः *f.*, प्रत्युपकारः, पारितोषिकं, उपकारमोक्षः, उपकारशुद्धिः *f.*, शुद्धिः *f.*, परिशोधः, परिवर्त्तनं.—(Retaliation) प्रतिकारः, प्रतीकारः, प्रतिकृतिः *f.*, प्रतिक्रिया, प्रत्यपकारः, प्रतिकर्म्म *n.* (न्), प्रतिहिंसा, निर्यातनं.

To requite, *v. a.* (Compensate, repay) प्रतिफलं दा, प्रतिदा, प्रतिफल (nom. प्रतिफलयति -यितुं), निष्कृतिं दा, प्रत्युपकृ, निस्तारं कृ, पारि-

तोषिकं दा.—(Retaliate) प्रतिकृ, विप्रतिकृ, प्रत्यपकृ, प्रतिकारं कृ, प्रतिहिंस् (c. 1. -हिंसति -सितुं, c. 7. -हिनस्ति), निर्यत् (c. 10. -यातयति -यितुं).

Requited, *p.p.* प्रतिफलितः -ता -तं, प्रतिकृतः &c., विप्रतिकृतः &c., निर्यातितः &c.

To resalute, *v. a.* प्रत्यभिनन्द् (c. 1. -नन्दति -न्दितुं), प्रतिनन्द्, प्रत्यभिवद्, प्रत्यर्च्.

To rescind, *v. a.* लुप् (c. 6. लुम्पति, लोप्तुं), लोपं कृ, खण्ड् (c. 10. खण्डयति -यितुं), उच्छिद् (c. 7. -छिनत्ति -छेत्तुं), परिच्छिद्, उच्छिद्, भङ्गं कृ, भञ्ज्. *See To* repeal.

Rescinded, *p.p.* लुप्तः -प्ता -प्तं, खण्डितः &c., उच्छिन्नः -न्ना -न्नं, परिच्छिन्नः &c.

Rescission, *s.* लोपः, खण्डनं, उच्छेदः, परिच्छेदः, भङ्गः, उद्धरणं, निरुद्धरणं, अवरोपः -पणं, अनुशयः, विप्रतिपत्तिः *f.*; 'of sale,' क्रयानुशयः. *See* Repeal.

Rescript, *s.* शासनं, आज्ञापत्रं, शासनपत्रं, राजाज्ञा, निबन्धः.

To rescue, *v. a.* त्रै (c. 1. त्रायते, त्रातुं), परित्रै, संत्रै, उद्धृ (c. 1. -हरति -हर्त्तुं), समुद्धृ, रक्ष् (c. 1. रक्षति -क्षितुं), परिरक्ष्, अभिरक्ष्, संरक्ष्, मुच् (c. 6. मुञ्चति, मोक्तुं, c. 10. मोचयति -यितुं), विमुच्, निर्मुच्, मोक्ष् (c. 10. मोक्षयति -यितुं), विमोक्ष्, निस्तॄ (c. 10. -तारयति -यितुं), तॄ, उद्धरणं कृ, उद्धारं कृ, रक्षणं कृ; 'from confinement,' बन्धनाद् मुच्.

Rescue, *s.* त्राणं, परित्राणं, उद्धरणं, उद्धारः, समुद्धारः, समुद्धरणं, रक्षा -क्षणं, परिरक्षणं, निस्तारः, निस्तरणं, तारणं, मुक्तिः *f.*, मोचनं, विमोचनं, मोक्षः -क्षणं, परिमोक्षणं; 'to the rescue!' त्राहि, त्रायस्व.

Rescued, *p.p.* उद्धृतः -ता -तं, समुद्धृतः &c., त्राणः -णा -णं, त्रातः -ता -तं, रक्षितः -ता -तं, परिरक्षितः &c., मुक्तः -क्ता -क्तं, मोचितः -ता -तं, विमोचितः &c., निस्तारितः &c.; 'from confinement,' मुक्तबन्धनः -ना -नं, बन्धनमुक्तः -क्ता -क्तं.

Rescuer, *s.* त्राता *m.* (तृ), उद्धर्त्ता *m.* (र्त्तृ), रक्षकः, मुक्तिदाता *m.* (तृ), उद्धारकः, मोचकः, निवर्त्तकः. *See* Deliverer.

Research, *s.* अन्वेषणं -णा, पर्येषणं -णा, अनुसन्धानं, परीष्टिः *f.*, संवीक्षणं, गवेषणं -णा, निरूपणं, जिज्ञासा, मीमांसा, मार्गणं, मृगणा, मृगया, मृगः, विचारणा, तत्त्वानुसन्धानं, विचयः, वीचयनं, विचयनं.

Resemblance, *s.* (Likeness) औपम्यं, सादृश्यं, सदृशता, सरूपता, सारूप्यं, समता, साम्यं, समानता, तुल्यता -त्वं, तुला, तौल्यं, सारूप्यं, सरूपता, उपमा, उपमितिः *f.*, उपमानं -नता, अनुकारः, अनुहारः, *see* Likeness.—(Something similar, a representation) उपमा, प्रतिमा -मानं, प्रतिरूपं, प्रतिभासः, प्रतिकृतिः *f.*, प्रतिमूर्त्तिः *f.*, प्रतिच्छाया, प्रतिबिम्बं, प्रतिनिधिः *m.*

To resemble, *v. a.* (Be like) सदृशः -शी -शं भू or अस्, सदृशीभू, अनुकृ (c. 8. -करोति -कर्त्तुं), तुल्यः -ल्या -ल्यं भू, समः -मा -मं भू, समानः -ना -नं भू, उपमः -मा -मं भू, सरूपः -पा -पं भू, अनुरूपः -पा -पं भू; 'the son resembles his father,' पुत्रः पितुर् अनुकरोति or पुत्रः पितृरूपो भवति or पुत्रः पित्रा सदृशाकारो भवति; 'no one resembles him,' अनेन सदृशः कश्चिन् नास्ति or तस्य तुल्यः or तेन तुल्यः or तेन समो न कोऽपि भवति. A nominal verb may sometimes express the sense of 'resemble,' thus; 'he resembles a lion,' सिंहायते; 'it resembles heaven,' स्वर्गीयते.—(Liken) उपमा (c. 2. -माति, c. 3. -मिमीते -मातुं), सदृशीकृ, समीकृ, समान (nom. समानयति -यितुं).

Resembling, *part.* अनुकारी -रिणी -रि (न्), सदृशः -शी -शं, तुल्यः -ल्या -ल्यं, समः -मा -मं, समाकारः -रा -रं, सरूपः -पा -पं, रूपभृत् *m.f.n.*, रूपभृत् *m.f.n.*, सवर्णः -र्णा -र्णं &c. *See* Like.

To resent, *v. n.* अपकारम् अपेक्ष्य कुप् (c. 4. कुप्यति, कोपितुं) or प्रकुप् or क्रुध् (c. 4. क्रुध्यति, क्रोद्धुं) or रुष् (c. 4. रुष्यति, रोषितुं) or रोषं कृ or मन्युं कृ, अपकारमपेक्ष्य प्रत्यपकाराय or प्रतिकाराय मनः कृ, अपकारमपेक्ष्य जातमन्युः -न्युः -न्यु भू or जातक्रोधः -धा -धं भू, अपकारमपेक्ष्य क्रोधात् प्रत्यपकारं कृ in des., हिंसाम् अपेक्ष्य जातक्रोधत्वात् प्रतिहिंसां कृ in des. (चिकीर्षति -र्षितुं) or प्रतिद्रोहाय मनः कृ.

Resentful, *a.* समन्युः -न्युः -न्यु, जातमन्युः &c., प्रतिहिंसाबुद्धिः -द्धिः -द्धि, प्रतिद्रोहबुद्धिः &c., प्रत्यपकारबुद्धिः &c., क्रोधशीलः -ला -लं, कोपशीलः &c., प्रतिहिंसाशीलः &c., दंशी -शिनी -शि (न्), सासूयः -या -यं.

Resentment, *s.* मन्युः *m.*, क्रोधः, कोपः, रोषः, प्रकोपः, प्रतिद्रोहबुद्धिः *f.*, प्रत्यपकारबुद्धिः *f.*, प्रतिहिंसाबुद्धिः *f.*, दंशः, द्वेषः, असूया, ईर्ष्या, मात्सर्यं.

Reservation, *s.* (Keeping back, concealing) गोपनं, गुप्तिः *f.*, उपसंहारः, उपसंहरणं, उपसंहृतिः *f.*, संहरणं, संहृतिः *f.*, प्रत्याहारः, प्रत्याहरणं, संवृतिः *f.*, संवरणं, अपवरणं, अपावरणं, धृतिः *f.*, धरणं, विधृतिः *f.*, विधरणं, विनिग्रहः, निभृते स्थापनं.—(Mental reservation) मनोगुप्तिः *f.*, मनोगोपनं, मनोसंवृतिः *f.*, मनोसंवरणं, निह्नुतिः *f.*, अपह्नुतिः *f.*, निह्नवः, अपह्नवः.—(Custody, keeping in store) रक्षा -क्षणं, परिरक्षणं, संग्रहणं, सञ्चयः -यनं.

To reserve, *v. a.* (Keep back, withhold to a future time) उपसंहृ (c. 1. -हरति -हर्त्तुं), प्रत्याहृ, संहृ, विधृ (c. 1. -धरति -धर्त्तुं, c. 10. -धारयति -यितुं), विनिग्रह् (c. 9. -गृह्णाति -ग्रहीतुं), निग्रह्, आकालान्तरात् or कालान्तरं यावद् उपसंहृ or रक्ष् (c. 1. रक्षति -क्षितुं) or परिरक्ष्.—(Lay up, keep in store to a future time) रक्ष्, परिरक्ष्, आकालान्तरात् or परकालं यावद् रक्ष् or निधा (c. 3. -दधाति -धातुं) or सन्न्यस् (c. 4. -अस्यति -सितुं) or संचि (c. 5. -चिनोति -चेतुं) or संग्रह्.—(Conceal to another time) आकालान्तराद् गुप् (c. 1. गोपायति, c. 10. गोपयति, गोप्तुं) or गोपनं कृ or निभृते स्था in caus. (स्थापयति -यितुं) or संवृ (c. 5. -वृणोति -वरितुं, c. 10. -वारयति -यितुं) or अपवृ or अपावृ or संवरणं कृ; 'in the mind,' मनसा गुप्, मनोगोपनं कृ.—(Suffer to remain to another time) आकालान्तरात् शिष् (c. 10. शेषयति -यितुं) or परिशिष् or अवशिष् or रक्ष्; 'one should reserve one's money for a time of want,' आपदर्थं धनं रक्षेत्.

Reserve, *s.* (Withholding, keeping back), *see* Reservation.—(Something concealed in the mind, withheld from disclosure) मनोगुप्तिः *f.*, मनोगुप्तं, निह्नुतिः *f.*, अपह्नुतिः *f.*—(Restraint) यन्त्रणं, निग्रहः, विनिग्रहः, निगृहीतिः *f.*—(In manner, disinclination to talk) कथाविरक्तिः *f.*, कथाविमुखता, कथावैरक्त्यं, वाग्यतत्वं, वाग्यतिः *f.*, वाग्यन्त्रणं, अल्पभाषणं, कथापराङ्मुखता, संलापपराङ्मुखता, आलापविरक्तिः *f.*, धीरता.—(Stock laid up) सञ्चयः, सञ्चितं, संग्रहः, निचयः.—(Stratagem in reserve, double resource) द्वैधं.—(Of an army) प्रतिग्रहः, परिग्रहः, सन्नहनं, पार्ष्णित्रं, पतद्ग्रहः. *See* Rear-guard.—(Without reserve), *see* Unreservedly.—(In reserve) निभृते, गोपने, गुप्तं. *See* the next.

Reserved, *p.p.* or *a.* (Kept back or concealed to a future time) आकालान्तरात् or परकालं यावद् रक्षितः -ता -तं or उपसंहृतः -ता -तं or विधारितः &c. or विधृतः &c. or गुप्तः -प्ता -प्तं or निभृते स्थापितः -ता -तं or संवृतः &c.—(Left remaining) शिष्टः -ष्टा -ष्टं, अवशेषितः -ता -तं, आकालान्तराद् अवशेषितः &c.—(Restrained in manner, disinclined to talk) वाग्यतः -ता -तं, वाग्यन्त्रितः &c., यन्त्रितकथः -था -थं, यन्त्रितवाक् *m.f.n.* (च्), कथाविरक्तः -क्ता -क्तं,

संवादविरक्तः &c., कथाविमुखः -खा -खी -खं, कथापराङ्मुखः &c., संलापविमुखः &c., आलापविरक्तः &c., अनालापी -पिनी -पि (न्), अल्पभाषी -षिणी &c., अल्पालापी &c., परिमितालापी &c., परिमितकथः &c., गूढभावः -वा -वं, गूढस्वभावः &c., लज्जाशीलः -ला -लं, धीरः -रा -रं.

RESERVEDLY, *adv.* वाग्यतस्, वाग्यतत्वात्, परिमितवाचा, गूढभावेन.

RESERVEDNESS, *s.* वाग्यतत्वं, कथाविरक्तिः *f.*, धीरता. *See* RESERVE.

RESERVOIR, *s.* जलाशयः, तडागः, जलाधारः, उदकाधारः, निपानं, खातं, वापी, अम्भोनिधिः *m.*, जलदानगृहं, सरोवरः, क्रीडासरस् *n.*, वरासनं, तल्लः.

To RESIDE, *v. n.* वस् (c. 1. वसति, वस्तुं), निवस्, अधिवस्, आवस्, समावस्, प्रतिवस्, वासं कृ, वृत्, स्था, आश्रि, निली, अध्यास्. *See* *To* DWELL.—(Reside together or with) संवस्, सहवासं कृ; 'resided,' उषितः -ता -तं.

RESIDENCE, *s.* (Act of dwelling) वासः -सनं, वसनं, वसतिः *f.*, निवसतिः *f.*, निवासः, अधिवासनं -सिता, अधिष्ठानं, अधिष्ठितिः *f.*, अवस्थितिः *f.*, स्थितिः *f.*, संस्थितिः *f.*, प्रतिष्ठा, वर्त्तनं, निलयनं, आश्रयणं, अध्यासः -सनं; 'residence abroad,' प्रवासः.—(Place of dwelling) वसतिः *f.*, वासः, वासस्थानं, निवसतिः *f.*, निवासः, निवासस्थानं, निवासभूयं, गृहं, आवासः, अधिवासः, समावासः, आवसथः, वास्तुः -स्तु *m. n.*, स्थानं, अवस्थानं, प्रतिष्ठा, आयतनं, निकेतनं, आलयः, निलयः, निलायिता, क्षितिः *f.*; 'permanent residence,' स्थिरप्रतिष्ठा, स्थावरप्रतिष्ठा; 'changing of residence,' गृहान्तरगमनं, स्थानान्तरगमनं, स्थलान्तरकरणं. *See* DWELLING.

RESIDENT, *a.* वासी -सिनी -सि (न्), निवासी &c., वासकारी &c., स्थायी &c., स्थः -स्था -स्थं in comp., संस्थः -स्था -स्थं in comp., निलायी &c., कृतवासः -सा -सं, कृतालयः -या -यं, आश्रितः -ता -तं, समाश्रितः &c., समावासितः &c., अवस्थितः &c., अधिष्ठितः &c.; 'resident in Mathurá,' मथुरावासी &c., मथुरानिवासी &c.; 'in the city,' नगरस्थः &c.; 'the people resident there,' तत्रस्था जनाः.

RESIDENT, *s.* वासी *m.* (न्); 'temporary resident,' आगन्तुः -न्तुकः.

RESIDENTIARY, *a.* वासी -सिनी &c., वासकारी &c. *See* RESIDENT, *a.*

RESIDUARY, RESIDUAL, *a.* शेषसम्बन्धी -न्धिनी &c.; 'legatee,' शेषभागी *m.* (न्), शेषाधिकारी *m.*, शेषरिक्थभागी *m.*, शेषरिक्थभाक् *m.* (ज्).

RESIDUE, *s.* शेषः -षं, अवशेषः, अवशिष्टं, परभागः, *see* REMAINDER.

To RESIGN, *v. a.* (Give up) त्यज् (c. 1. त्यजति, त्यक्तुं), परित्यज्, संत्यज्, उत्सृज् (c. 6. -सृजति -स्रष्टुं), विसृज्, अवसृज्, उत्सर्गं कृ, उत्सर्जनं कृ, हा (c. 3. जहाति, हातुं), विहा, प्रहा, प्रोज्झ्, सन्न्यस्, प्रत्यादिश्; 'by writing,' त्यागपत्रेण उत्सृज्; 'to resign a title or claims,' अधिकारत्यागं कृ, स्वत्वत्यागं कृ, स्वत्वनिवृत्तिं कृ.—(Commit) सम् ऋ in caus. (-अर्पयति -यितुं), ऋ in caus., न्यस्, निक्षिप्, न्यासीकृ, प्रतिपद् in caus., परिदा, समर्पणं कृ.—(Submit to) सह् (c. 1. सहते, सोढुं), विषह्, क्षम् (c. 1. क्षमते, क्षन्तुं), तिज् in des.

RESIGNATION, *s.* (Giving up) त्यागः, परित्यागः, उत्सर्गः, उत्सर्जनं, विसर्जनं, सन्न्यसनं, सन्न्यासः; 'written resignation,' त्यागपत्रं, परित्यागपत्रं, त्यागलेखः; 'of claim,' स्वत्वत्यागः, स्वत्वनिवृत्तिः *f.*—(Committing, yielding) समर्पणं, अर्पणं, निक्षेपः, न्यसनं, न्यासीकरणं.—(Submission) क्षमा, क्षान्तिः *f.*, तितिक्षा, सहनं, सहिष्णुता, धीरता, मर्षः, शान्तिः *f.*, सन्तोषवृत्तिः *f.*—(To the will of God) ईश्वरेच्छासन्तोषवृत्तिः *f.*, ईश्वरेच्छानुवृत्तिः *f.*, ईश्वरेच्छानुवर्त्तनं, ईश्वरेच्छानुमतिः *f.*, ईश्वरेच्छानुरोधः, ईश्वरेच्छापरितोषः, भगवदिच्छानुमतिः *f.*, तितिक्षा, ईश्वरसंकल्पानुवृत्तिः *f.*

RESIGNED, *p. p.* or *a.* (Given up) त्यक्तः -क्ता -क्तं, परित्यक्तः &c., उत्सर्जितः -ता -तं, उत्सृष्टः -ष्टा -ष्टं, सन्न्यस्तः -स्ता -स्तं.—(Submissive) क्षान्तः -न्ता -न्तं, क्षमावान् -वती -वत् (त्), सहिष्णुः -ष्णुः -ष्णु, तितिक्षुः &c., शान्तः &c., *see* PATIENT.—(To the will of God) ईश्वरेच्छासन्तोषवृत्तिः -त्तिः -त्ति, ईश्वरेच्छानुवर्त्ती -र्त्तिनी -र्त्ति (न्), ईश्वरेच्छानुरोधी &c., ईश्वरेच्छासन्तुष्टः -ष्टा -ष्टं, ईश्वरेच्छाभिमतः -ता -तं, ईश्वरेच्छानुमतः &c., ईश्वरसङ्कल्पानुवर्त्ती &c., भगवत्सङ्कल्पपरितुष्टः &c., यतचित्तः -त्ता -त्तं, शान्तचेताः -ताः -तः (स्).

RESILIENCE, RESILIENCY, *s.* प्रतिघातः. *See* REBOUND.

RESIN, *s.* सर्ज्जरसः, यक्षधूपः, अरालः, रालः, वृक्षधूपः, वृक्षनिर्य्यासः, शालनिर्य्यासः, सर्ज्जमणिः *m.*, सुरधूपः, धूपनः, सर्ज्जरसः, रसाङ्कः, दधि *n.*, तीक्ष्णतैलं, अग्निवल्लभः, वह्निवल्लभः, महारूपः, बहुरूपः, कलकलः, धूनकः.

RESINOUS, *a.* सर्ज्जरसगुणकः -का -कं, यक्षधूपसगुणः -णा -णं.

To RESIST, *v. a.* or *n.* (Oppose, withstand) प्रतिकृ, विप्रतिकृ, विप्रकृ, विरुध् (c. 7. -रुणद्धि -रोद्धुं), प्रतिरुध्, प्रतिकूल (nom. प्रतिकूलयति -यितुं), प्रतिकूलः -ला -लं भू, पर्य्यवस्था (c. 1. -तिष्ठति -स्थातुं), प्रत्यवस्था, प्रत्याहन् (c. 2. -हन्ति -न्तुं), व्याहन्, निहन्, प्रतीप (nom. प्रतीपायते), प्रतियुध्, प्रतिसमास् (c. 2. -आस्ते -आसितुं), परिपन्थ (nom. परिपन्थयति -यितुं), विपक्षतां कृ, विरोधं कृ, प्रतिरोधं कृ, प्रातिकूल्यं कृ.—(Hinder) निवृ (c. 10. -वारयति -यितुं), बाध् (c. 1. बाधते -धितुं), प्रतिबन्ध् (c. 9. -बध्नाति -बन्द्धुं), रुध्, निरुध्.—(Check) निग्रह् (c. 9. -गृह्णाति -ग्रहीतुं), विनिग्रह्, स्तम्भ् (c. 10. स्तम्भयति -यितुं), प्रतिष्टम्भ्.

RESISTANCE, *s.* प्रतिकारः, प्रतीकारः, विप्रतिकारः, प्रतिक्रिया, विरोधः, प्रतिरोधः, प्रतिकूलता, प्रातिकूल्यं, प्रतियोगः -गिता, पर्य्यवस्थानं, पर्य्यवस्था, पर्य्यवस्थितिः *f.*, प्रत्यवस्थानं, प्रत्यवस्थितिः *f.*, प्रतिच्छेदः, निकारः, प्रतिबन्धः -न्धकता, प्रतिष्टम्भः, निग्रहः -हणं, अवग्रहः, निवारणं, प्रतियत्नः, प्रत्युपायः.—(In mechanics) प्रत्याघातः, प्रतिघातः.

RESISTED, *p. p.* प्रतिकृतः -ता -तं, विप्रतिकृतः &c., विप्रकृतः &c., प्रतिरुद्धः -द्धा -द्धं, रुद्धः &c., पर्य्यवस्थितः &c., प्रत्यवस्थितः &c., प्रतिष्टब्धः -ब्धा -ब्धं, निवारितः -ता -तं, प्रतिहतः &c., व्याहतः &c.

RESISTER, *s.* विरोधी *m.* (न्), प्रतिरोधी *m.*, प्रतियोगी *m.*, पर्य्यवस्थाता *m.* (तृ), प्रत्यवस्थाता *m.*, प्रतिरोधकः, प्रतिघाती *m.*, विरोधकारी *m.*

RESISTLESS, *s.* अप्रतिकार्य्यः -र्य्या -र्य्यं, अनवग्रहः -हा -हं. *See* IRRESISTIBLE.

RESOLUTE, *a.* दृढनिश्चयः -या -यं, स्थिरनिश्चयः &c., दृढसंकल्पः -ल्पा -ल्पं, स्थिरमतिः -तिः -ति, स्थिरचेताः -ताः -तः (स्), सुस्थिरचेताः &c., स्थितधीः -धीः -धि, वज्रसंकल्पः -ल्पा -ल्पं, स्थिरः -रा -रं, सुस्थिरः &c., धीरः -रा -रं, सुधीरः &c., धैर्य्यवान् -वती -वत् (त्), धृतिमान् &c., साङ्कल्पिकः -की -कं, प्रगल्भः -ल्भा -ल्भं, व्यवसायी -यिनी -यि (न्), कृतनिश्चयः &c.

RESOLUTELY, *adv.* दृढनिश्चयपूर्व्वं, सुस्थिरनिश्चयं, सुस्थिरं, स्थिरचेतसा.

RESOLUTENESS, *s.* स्थिरमतित्वं, दृढसंकल्पता, धैर्य्यं. *See* the next.

RESOLUTION, *s.* (Fixed purpose, determination) निश्चयः, विनिश्चयः, सङ्कल्पः, व्यवसायः, अध्यवसायः, निर्णयः, दृढनिश्चयः, दृढसङ्कल्पः, स्थिरनिश्चयः, कल्पः, मतिः *f.*, दृढमतिः *f.*, सम्प्रधारणा.—(Constancy) स्थिरमतित्वं, स्थिरता, सुस्थिरता, स्थैर्य्यं, धीरता, धैर्य्यं, धृतिः *f.*, धृतिमत्त्वं, धारणं -णा, प्रगल्भता, प्रागल्भ्यं, आग्रहः, निर्बन्धः.—(Decision or proposition offered for determination) निश्चयः, निर्णयः, उपन्यासः.—(Separation of parts), *see* DISSOLUTION, SOLUTION.

RESOLVABLE, *s.* विलयनीयः -या -यं, विभाज्यः -ज्या -ज्यं, विभेद्यः -द्या -द्यं.

To RESOLVE, *v. a.* (Dissolve) विली in caus., विद्रु in caus., *see* DISSOLVE, LIQUEFY.—(Separate component parts) पृथक्कृ,

विभज्, वियुज्, विभिद्, विच्छिद्, विश्लिष् in caus., विद्रु in caus., मूलतत्त्वशोधनं कृ, उपोद्घातं कृ.—(Resolve doubts or difficulties) संशयान् छिद् (c. 7. छिनत्ति, छेत्तुं) or उच्छिद्, व्याख्या (c. 2. -ख्याति -तुं), *see To* SOLVE.—(Constitute by resolution) निश्चयपूर्व्वं व्यवस्था in caus. or संस्था or विधा or कॢप्.

To RESOLVE, *v. n.* (Determine in the mind) निश्चयं कृ, विनिश्चयं कृ, निर्णयं कृ, सङ्कल्पं कृ, मनसा निश्चि (c. 5. -चिनोति -चेतुं) or निर्णी (c. 1. -णयति -णेतुं) or संकॢप् (c. 10 -कल्पयति -यितुं), व्यवसो (c. 4. -स्यति -सातुं), अध्यवसो, मतिं कृ, बुद्धिं कृ, मनः कृ with dat. or loc. c.; as, 'he resolves to go,' गमनाय मनः or मतिं करोति, गमनाय निश्चयं करोति; 'he resolves to do that,' तत् कर्त्तुं व्यवस्यति; 'he is resolved to sacrifice his life,' स्वप्राणान् परित्यक्तुं व्यवसितो ऽस्ति.—(Dissolve), *see* DISSOLVE, MELT.

RESOLVED, *p. p.* (Analyzed) पृथक्कृतः -ता -तं, व्याकृतः &c., विभक्तः -क्ता -क्तं.—(Determined) कृतनिश्चयः -या -यं, कृतसङ्कल्पः -ल्पा -ल्पं, निश्चितः -ता -तं, सुनिश्चितः &c., सङ्कल्पितः &c., साङ्कल्पिकः -की -कं, व्यवसितः -ता -तं, प्रयतितः &c., कृतबुद्धिः -द्धिः -द्धि; 'having resolved on going to the forest,' वनगमनाय कृतबुद्धिः or वनं गन्तुं व्यवसितः.

RESOLVENT, *s.* (In medicine) द्रावकः, द्रावणं, शोषघ्नः, शोषद्रुत्.

RESOLVER, *s.* (Of doubts) संशयच्छेत्ता *m.* (त्तृ), संशयोच्छेदी *m.* (न्).

RESONANCE, *s.* अनुनादः, व्यनुनादः, प्रोद्घोषणं, उद्घोषणं, प्रतिध्वनिः *m.*

RESONANT, *a.* अनुनादी -दिनी -दि (न्), अनुनादः -दा -दं, प्रोद्घुष्टः -ष्टा -ष्टं, संघुष्टः &c., परिसंघुष्टः &c., उपघुष्टः &c., निह्रादी &c., मुखरितः -ता -तं.

To RESORT, *v. n.* आश्रि (c. 1. -श्रयति -यितुं), श्रि, आश्रयणं कृ, गम् (c. 1. गच्छति, गन्तुं), उपगम्, प्रतिगम्, अभिगम्, आगम्, उपे (c. 2. उपैति -तुं, rt. इ), अभ्युपे, अभिसृ (c. 1. -सरति -सर्त्तुं), या (c. 2. याति -तुं), प्रतिया, प्रत्याया, अभिया, या, सेव् (c. 1. सेवते -वितुं); 'resorted to,' आश्रितः -ता -तं; 'having resorted to,' आश्रित्य.

RESORT, *s.* (Act of going or betaking one's self) आश्रयणं, श्रयणं, उपगमः -मनं, अभ्युपगमः -मनं, प्रतिगमनं, अभिगमः -मनं, गमनं, अभिसारणं.—(Place of resort) गमनागमनस्थानं, अभिगमनस्थानं, अभिसारणस्थानं, आश्रयणस्थानं, आश्रयः, समाश्रयः, आयतनं, आशयः; 'resort of man,' लोकयात्रा.—(Refuge, means of relief) गतिः *f.*, उपायः.

To RESOUND, *v. a.* अनुनद् (c. 10. -नादयति -यितुं), व्यनुनद्, अभिनद्, आनद्, सन्नद्, नद्, ध्वन् (c. 10. ध्वनयति -यितुं), प्रतिध्वन्, प्रतिध्वनिं कृ.

To RESOUND, *v. n.* ध्वन् (c. 1. ध्वनति -नितुं), प्रतिध्वन्, प्रध्वन्, स्वन् (c. 1. स्वनति -नितुं), प्रतिस्वन्, स्तन् (c. 1. स्तनति -नितुं), प्रोघुष् (c. 1. -घोषति -षितुं), परिसंघुष्, गुञ्ज् (c. 1. गुञ्जति -ञ्जितुं), प्रक्ष्वेड् (c. 1. -क्ष्वेडति -डितुं), रस् (c. 1. रसति -सितुं).

RESOUNDING, *part.* (Sounding with) अनुनादः -दा -दं, निर्घुष्टः -ष्टा -ष्टं, परिसंघुष्टः &c., उपकूजितः -ता -तं, विकूजितः &c.

RESOURCE, *s.* गतिः *f.*, उपायः, अभ्युपायः, युक्तिः *f.*, प्रयुक्तिः *f.*, उपपत्तिः *f.*, तरणोपायः, कॢप्तिः *f.*, कल्पना; 'other resource,' गत्यन्तरं, अन्योपायः, अन्यगतिः *f.*; 'having no other resource,' अनन्यगतिः -तिः -ति, अनन्यगतिकः -का -कं; 'having no resource,' अगतिकः -का -कं, गतिहीनः -ना -नं, निरुपायः -या -यं; 'last resource,' चरमगतिः *f.*, चरमोपायः, अगतिकगतिः *f.*—(Resources) विभवः, वित्तं, सम्भवः, धनं, अर्थः, आगमः, आयः; 'of small resources,' अल्पविभवः -वा -वं; 'of concealed resources,' उपगुप्तवित्तः -त्ता -त्तं.

RESOURCELESS, *a.* अगतिकः -का -कं, गतिहीनः -ना -नं, निरुपायः -या -यं.

To RESPECT, *v. a.* (Regard, relate to) अपेक्ष् (c. 1. अपेक्षते -क्षितुं, rt. ईक्ष्), अवेक्ष्, प्रतीक्ष्, उद्दिश् (c. 6. -दिशति -देष्टुं), विषयकः -का -कं भू, सम्बन्ध् in pass. (-बध्यते), सम्बद्धः -द्धा -द्धं भू, सम्बन्धी -न्धिनी -न्धि भू.—(Esteem, reverence) मन् (c. 10. मानयति -यितुं), प्रतिमन्, सम्मन्, पूज् (c. 10. पूजयति -यितुं), सम्पूज्, अभिपूज्, आदृ (c. 6. -द्रियते -दर्त्तुं), सेव् (c. 1. सेवते -वितुं, c. 10. सेवयति -यितुं), भज् (c. 1. भजति, भक्तुं), अर्ह् (c. 10. अर्हयति -यितुं), अर्च् (c. 1. अर्चति -र्चितुं, c. 10. अर्चयति -यितुं), अभ्यर्च्, समभ्यर्च्, समर्च्, सम्भू (c. 10. -भावयति -यितुं), पुरस्कृ, आदरं कृ, सम्मानं कृ.

RESPECT, *s.* (Relation, reference, regard) अपेक्षा, प्रतीक्षा, उद्देशः, विषयत्वं -ता, सम्बन्धः, अवेक्षा, अन्ववेक्षा, सन्धानं; 'with respect to,' अपेक्षया, अपेक्ष्य, प्रतीक्ष्य, उद्दिश्य, उद्देशेन, प्रति affixed; as, 'with respect to me,' मां प्रति.—(Esteem, reverence) मानं, सम्मानं, आदरः, मान्यत्वं, पूजा, अर्हा -र्हणं -णा, सम्भावना, अर्चा, अर्चनं -ना, अभ्यर्चा -र्चनं, सेवा -वनं, पुरस्कारः, प्रतीतिः *f.*, सत्कारः, अनुनयः, भक्तिः *f.*, सम्भ्रमः, मर्य्यादा; 'much respect,' बहुमानं.—(Respects, act of reverence) प्रणिपातः, प्रणामः, प्रणतिः *f.*, प्रणिपतनं, अभिवादनं, नमस्कारः, नमस्, नमस्या, वन्दनं, अभिवन्दनं; 'to pay one's respects,' प्रणिपत्, प्रणम्, नमस्कृ, अभिवद्, अभिवन्द्, वन्दनं कृ, प्रणामं कृ.—(Regard, view) अवेक्षा, अन्ववेक्षा, प्रतीक्षा, दृष्टिः *f.*; 'respect of persons,' भेददृष्टिः *f.*, पक्षदृष्टिः, पक्षपातः.—(Particular) विषयः, प्रकरणं.

RESPECTABILITY, *s.* मान्यता, सम्मान्यता, आर्य्यता -त्वं, गौरवं, गुरुता -त्वं, मर्य्यादा, प्रतिष्ठा; 'family respectability,' कुलमर्य्यादा.

RESPECTABLE, *a.* आर्य्यः -र्य्या -र्य्यं, मान्यः -न्या -न्यं, माननीयः -या -यं, सम्मान्यः &c., आदरणीयः -या -यं, पूजनीयः -या -यं, पूज्यः -ज्या -ज्यं, पूजनार्हः -र्हा -र्हं, प्रतीक्ष्यः -क्ष्या -क्ष्यं, प्रतीक्षणीयः -या -यं, अर्च्यः -र्च्या -र्च्यं, अर्चनीयः -या -यं, गुरुः -र्व्वी -रु, सगौरवः -वा -वं, गौरवितः -ता -तं, मर्य्यादावान् -वती -वत् (त्), मर्य्यादापालकः -का -कं, कुलमर्य्यादापालकः &c., मानी -निनी -नि (न्), पुरस्करणीयः &c., शिष्टः -ष्टा -ष्टं, सम्भावितः -ता -तं, भद्रकः -का -कं, अकुत्सितः -ता -तं, प्रतिष्ठितः &c., सप्रतिष्ठः -ष्ठा -ष्ठं; 'highly respectable,' परममान्यः &c.; 'a respectable person,' आर्य्यजनः, आर्य्यकः, आर्य्यमिश्रः, सज्जनः, सुजनः; 'respectable woman,' आर्य्यिका, आर्य्यका, कुलपालिका, कुलमर्य्यादापालिका, कुलस्त्री, कुलवधूः *f.*—(Moderate, fair) मध्यमः -मा -मं.

RESPECTABLY, *adv.* आर्य्यं, सगौरवं, समर्य्यादं, आर्य्यवत्, मान्यवत्, शिष्टवत्, आर्य्यजनवत्, आर्य्य in comp.; as, 'respectably dressed,' आर्य्यवेशः -शा -शं.

RESPECTED, *p. p.* सम्मानितः -ता -तं, पूजितः &c., आदृतः &c., कृतादरः -रा -रं, सेवितः -ता -तं, अर्चितः &c., प्रतीक्षितः &c.

RESPECTER, *s.* पूजकः, सम्पूजकः, आदरकृत्, प्रतीक्षकः, अवेक्षकः.

RESPECTFUL, *a.* आदरकारी -रिणी -रि (न्), आदृतः -ता -तं, दत्तादरः -रा -रं, कृतादरः &c., सादरः -रा -रं, आदरपूर्व्वः -र्व्वा -र्व्वं, आदरशीलः -ला -लं, आदरयुक्तः -क्ता -क्तं, मानकारी &c., मर्य्यादाशीलः &c., समर्य्यादः -दा -दं, प्रतीतः -ता -तं, सम्प्रतीतः &c.

RESPECTFULLY. *adv.* सादरं, समानं, आदरपूर्व्वं, आदरपुरःसरं, ससम्मानं, सम्मानपूर्व्वं, समर्य्यादं, अर्चापूर्व्वकं.

RESPECTFULNESS, *s.* आदरशीलता, मर्य्यादाशीलता, सादरत्वं, मर्य्यादा.

RESPECTING, *part.* प्रतीक्षकः -का -कं, अपेक्षकः &c., उद्देशकः &c.,

अपेक्ष्य, प्रतीक्ष्य, उद्दिश्य, प्रति affixed with an acc. c.

RESPECTIVE, *a.* (Relative, not absolute) सापेक्षः -क्षा -क्षं, अपेक्षकः -का -कं, ससम्बन्धः -न्धा -न्धं. *See* RELATIVE.—(Several) इतरेतरः -रा -रं, अन्योन्यः -न्या -न्यं, *see* SEVERAL; 'respective inclination,' इतरेतरकाम्या.—(Own) expressed by doubling the pronouns स्व, स्वकीय, स्वीय, स्वक, निज, आत्म, आत्मीय &c.; thus, 'in their respective stations,' स्वेषु स्वेषु स्थानेषु or simply by doubling the noun; thus, 'they dwell each in their respective houses,' गृहे गृहे प्रत्येकं वसन्ति.

RESPECTIVELY, *adv.* इतरेतरं, अन्योन्यं, प्रत्येकं, प्रति or अनु prefixed, or more usually expressed by doubling a pronoun or noun, *see* the last.

RESPIRATION, *s.* श्वासप्रश्वासं, श्वासोच्छ्वासं, श्वासः, श्वसनं, उच्छ्वसनं, प्राणः.

RESPIRATORY, *a.* श्वासप्रश्वासकारी -रिणी &c., श्वासोच्छ्वाससम्बन्धी &c.

To RESPIRE, *v. n.* श्वासप्रश्वासं कृ, श्वासोच्छ्वासं कृ, श्वस् (c. 2. श्वसिति -तुं), आश्वस्, उच्छ्वस्, प्रश्वस्, प्राण् (c. 2. प्राणिति -तुं, rt. अन्).

RESPITE, *s.* विश्रामः, विश्रान्तिः *f.*, विरामः, विरतिः *f.*, निवृत्तिः *f.*, उपशमः, अपशमः, शमः, शान्तिः *f.*, विच्छेदः, अवरतिः *f.* *See* REPRIEVE.

To RESPITE, *v. a.* विश्रामं दा, विश्रान्तिं दा, विश्रम् in caus. (-श्रामयति -यितुं), विरामं दा, अवकाशं दा. *See To* REPRIEVE.

RESPLENDENCE, RESPLENDENCY, *s.* प्रतापः, तेजस् *n.*, अतितेजस्. *See* SPLENDOR.

RESPLENDENT, *a.* प्रतापी -पिनी -पि (न्), सुप्रभः -भा -भं, देदीप्यमानः -ना -नं, प्रकाशमानः &c., विभ्राजमानः &c., अत्यादित्यः -त्या -त्यं, भानुमान् -मती -मत् (त्). *See* SPLENDID.

To RESPOND, *v. n.* प्रतिवच् (c. 2. -वक्ति -क्तुं), प्रतिवद् (c. 1. -वदति -दितुं), प्रतिब्रू, प्रतिभाष्, प्रतिशंस्. *See To* ANSWER, REPLY, CORRESPOND.

RESPONDENT, *s.* (In law) प्रतिवादी *m.* (न्), उत्तरवादी *m.*, प्रतिपक्षी *m.*, उत्तरपक्षी *m.*, समाधानपक्षी *m.*—(Party or cause of the respondent) उत्तरपक्षः, प्रतिपक्षः, समाधानपक्षः.

RESPONSE, *s.* (Answer) प्रतिवाक्यं, प्रतिवचनं, उत्तरं, *see* REPLY.—(In disputations) प्रतिवादः, उत्तरं, प्रत्युत्तरं, समाधानं.—(Of an oracle) शकुनः -नं, प्रश्नः, प्रसादः, देववाणी, आकाशवाणी.—(In a litany, &c.) उत्तरवाक्यं.

RESPONSIBILITY, *s.* अनुयोगाधीनता, अनुसन्धानाधीनता, विचाराधीनता, आह्वानाधीनता, अभियोज्यता, अनुयोज्यता, अभियोजनीयता, पर्यनुयोगाधीनता, पर्यनुयोज्यता, अनुसन्धानयोग्यता, आह्वानयोग्यता, आह्वेयता, उत्तरदानाधिकारः, उत्तरदानाधीनता, पृच्छाधीनता.

RESPONSIBLE, *a.* (Liable to account or answer) अनुयोगाधीनः -ना -नं, पर्यनुयोगाधीनः &c., अनुसन्धानाधीनः &c., आह्वानाधीनः &c., आह्वेयः -या -यं, विचाराधीनः -ना -नं, अभियोज्यः -ज्या -ज्यं, अनुयोज्यः &c., पर्यनुयोज्यः &c., अनुयोजनीयः -या -यं, अनुयोक्तव्यः -व्या -व्यं, अभियोक्तव्यः &c., पृच्छाधीनः &c., आह्वानयोग्यः &c., अभियोक्त्राह्वानाधीनः &c., उत्तरदानाधिकारी -रिणी -रि (न्), उत्तरदानाधीनः -ना -नं; 'a responsible person,' अनुयोगाधीनजनः, यः प्रत्युत्तरं or प्रतिवाक्यं दातुम् अर्हति or येन प्रत्युत्तरं दातव्यम् ईदृशो जनः.—(Admitting or requiring an answer) प्रतिवाक्यः -क्या -क्यं.

RESPONSION, *s.* प्रतिवचनं, प्रतिवाक्यं, उत्तरकरणं, प्रत्युत्तरकरणं.

RESPONSIVE, *a.* उत्तरकारी -रिणी -रि (न्), उत्तरदायकः -का -कं, उत्तरदायी &c.

REST, *s.* (Cessation of action or motion) विश्रामः, विश्रान्तिः *f.*, विश्रमः, निर्वृतिः *f.*, निवृत्तिः *f.*, विरामः, विरतिः *f.*, अवरतिः *f.*, उपरतिः *f.*, चेष्टानिवृत्तिः *f.*, व्यापारनिवृत्तिः *f.*, श्रमनिवृत्तिः *f.*, निश्चलता, श्रमच्छेदः, निर्व्यापारता, निरुद्यमता, व्यापाराभावः, उद्योगनिवृत्तिः *f.*, स्थिरता, नैश्चल्यं, अचलता, चलनाभावः. *See* QUIESCENCE.—(Tranquillity, ease, quiet) सुखं, शान्तिः *f.*, शमः, उपशमः, शान्तता, प्रशान्तिः *f.*, स्वस्थता, स्वास्थ्यं, सौख्यं, समाधानं.—(Sleep, repose) निद्रा, निद्रावस्था, निद्रादशा, स्वप्नः, शयनं; 'at rest,' शान्तः -न्ता -न्तं, निर्वृतः -ता -तं, विश्रान्तः -न्ता -न्तं, निश्चलः -ला -लं, निर्व्यापारः -रा -रं, निश्चेष्टः -ष्टा -ष्टं, निरुद्यमः -मा -मं, निरुद्योगः -गा -गं.—(Pause in music or poetry) यतिः *f.*, अवसानं.—(That which is left) शिष्टं, अवशिष्टं, उच्छिष्टं, शेषः -षं, अवशेषः, *see* REMAINDER.—(The others) शिष्टजनाः *m.pl.*, अवशिष्टजनाः *m.pl.*, इतरे *m.pl.*, अपरे *m.pl.*, अन्ये *m. pl.* *See* ET-CÆTERA.

To REST, *v. n.* (Cease from action or motion, be still) विश्रम् (c. 4. -श्राम्यति -श्रमितुं), निश्चलीभू, निश्चलः -ला -लं भू, विरम् (c. 1. -रमति -रन्तुं), आरम्, उपरम्, निवृत् (c. 1. -वर्त्तते -र्त्तितुं), निर्वृत्, विनिवृत्, स्थिरीभू.—(Be tranquil, quiet) शम् (c. 4. शाम्यति, शमितुं), उपशम्, प्रशम्, सुखी -खिनी -खि भू, स्वस्थः -स्था -स्थं भू.—(Repose, sleep) शी (c. 2. शेते, शयितुं), स्वप् (c. 2. स्वपिति -तुं), संविश् (c. 6. -विशति -वेष्टुं), निद्रा, शयनं कृ, स्वप्नं कृ, निद्रां कृ.—(Lean on) अवलम्ब् (c. 1. -लम्बते -म्बितुं), समालम्ब्, आलम्ब्, संश्रि (c. 1. -श्रयति -ते -यितुं), समाश्रि, उपाश्रि, अवस्था (c. 1. -तिष्ठति -स्थातुं), निली (c. 4. -लीयते -लेतुं), सन्निली, अवलम्बनं कृ.—(Confide) विश्वस्, विश्रम्भ्.—(Remain) स्था, वृत्.

To REST, *v. a.* (Lay to rest, cause to rest) शी in caus. (शाययति -यितुं), विश्रम् (c. 10. -श्रामयति -यितुं), संविश् (c. 10. -वेशयति -यितुं), शयनं कृ.—(Lay, place on a support) अवलम्ब् in caus. (-लम्बयति -यितुं), न्यस् (c. 4. -अस्यति -सितुं), निधा, आधा, निविश्, स्था in caus., धृ in caus., समृ, आधारं कृ, आश्रयं कृ.

RESTED, *p.p.* (Relieved from fatigue) विश्रान्तः -न्ता -न्तं, गतक्लमः -मा -मं, गतश्रमः -मा -मं, *see* REFRESHED.—(Laid on for support) अवलम्बितः -ता -तं, आश्रितः -ता -तं, निलीनः -ना -नं, निषण्णः -ण्णा -ण्णं, निहितः &c., न्यस्तः -स्ता -स्तं; 'having rested upon,' अवलम्ब्य, उपधाय.

RESTING, *part.* अवलम्बी -म्बिनी -म्बि (न्), अवलम्बितः -ता -तं, आश्रितः &c., संश्रितः &c., सन्निष्ठमानः -ना -नं; 'her face resting on her hand,' हस्तनिहितवदना; 'resting on the head,' मस्तकस्थः -स्था -स्थं; 'a vessel resting on his head,' मस्तकोपस्थितभाण्डः.

RESTING-PLACE, *s.* विश्रामस्थानं, विश्रमस्थानं, शयनस्थानं, उपधानं.

RESTITUTION, *s.* प्रतिदानं, प्रत्यर्पणं, परिदानं, हृतप्रतिदानं, हृतप्रत्यर्पणं, हृतपरिदानं, पुनरर्पणं, प्रत्यानयनं. *See* RESTORATION.

RESTIVE, RESTIFF, *a.* दुर्दम्यः -म्या -म्यं, दुर्विनीतः -ता -तं, दुर्विनेयः -या -यं, दुर्वश्यः -श्या -श्यं, अदम्यः &c., अवश्यः &c., अविनेयः &c., प्रतीपः -पा -पं, विषमः -मा -मं, दुर्निग्रहः -हा -हं, दुर्द्धरः -रा -रं, दुष्टः -ष्टा -ष्टं; 'horse,' शूकलः, शूलकः; 'elephant,' अंकुशदुर्द्धरः.

RESTIVENESS, *s.* दुर्दम्यता, दुर्विनीतता, अवश्यता, प्रतीपता, दुष्टता.

RESTLESS, *a.* (Unquiet) अशान्तः -न्ता -न्तं, शान्तिहीनः -ना -नं, अनिर्वृतः -ता -तं, अशान्तचित्तः -त्ता -त्तं, अस्वस्थः -स्था -स्थं, व्यग्रः -ग्रा -ग्रं, व्यग्रचित्तः &c., परिप्लवः -वा -वं, आकुलः -ला -लं, विह्वलः -ला -लं, असमाहितः -ता -तं.—(Fidgety, always moving) चञ्चलः -ला -लं, चपलः -ला -लं, सदाचलः &c., सततगतिः -तिः -ति, सदा-

गतिः &c., निरास्पदः -दा -दं, अत्यन्तीनः -ना -नं.—(Sleepless) निर्निद्रः -द्रा -द्रं, विनिद्रः &c., अनिद्रः &c., उन्निद्रः &c., निद्राहीनः -ना -नं, स्वप्नहीनः &c.

Restlessly, *adv.* अशान्तं, अशान्त्या, चञ्चलं, सचाञ्चल्यं, अनिर्वृतं.

Restlessness, *s.* अशान्तिः *f.*, शान्तिहीनता, अनिर्वृतिः *f.*, अस्वस्थता, अस्वास्थ्यं, चञ्चलता, चाञ्चल्यं, चपलता, व्यग्रता, व्याकुलता, असमाधानं, असमाहितत्वं.

Restorable, *a.* परावर्त्त्यः -र्त्त्या -र्त्त्यं, प्रतिदेयः -या -यं, प्रत्यर्पणीयः &c.

Restoration, *s.* (Act of giving back) प्रतिदानं, प्रत्यर्पणं, परावर्त्तनं, परावृत्तिः *f.*, परिदानं, हृतप्रतिदानं, हृतपरिदानं, हृतप्रत्यर्पणं.—(Bringing back, or replacing in a former state) प्रत्यानयनं, उद्धरणं, उद्धारः, पूर्व्ववत्करणं, पूर्व्वस्थितिस्थापना, पूर्व्वदशास्थापनं, पूर्व्वदशानयनं, पुनःस्थापनं -ना.—(Repairing) जीर्णोद्धारः, जीर्णोद्धरणं, नष्टोद्धारः, नष्टोद्धरणं.—(Recovery) समुत्थानं, रोगात्समुत्थानं. *See* Recovery.

Restorative, *a.* तेजोदायकः -का -कं, तेजस्करः -रा -रं, सत्त्वदः -दा -दं, अग्निदायकः &c., अग्निदः &c., तेजोवर्धकः &c. *See* Invigorating.

Restorative, *s.* अग्निदायकम् or तेजोदायकम् औषधं, तेजोवर्धनं.

To restore, *v. a.* (Give back) प्रतिदा (c. 3. -ददाति -दत्ते -दातुं), परिदा, प्रत्यृ in caus. (-अर्पयति -यितुं), प्रतिपद् (c. 10. -पादयति -यितुं), पुनः प्रतिपद्, पुनर् ऋ in caus., पुनर् दा, पुनः प्रदा, परावृत् in caus. (-वर्त्तयति -यितुं), प्रयम् (c. 1. -यच्छति -दातुं), पुनः प्रयम्, निर्यत् (c. 10. -यातयति -यितुं), समुपाकृ, प्रत्यर्पणं कृ, प्रतिदानं कृ, परावर्त्तं कृ.—(Replace) पुनः स्था in caus. (स्थापयति -यितुं), प्रतिष्ठा, प्रतिरुह् in caus., प्रतिधा, *see* Replace.—(Bring back to its former state, repair) पूर्व्ववत् कृ, पूर्व्वस्थितिम् आनी or गम् in caus., पूर्व्वदशाम् आनी or प्रत्यानी, उद्धृ (c. 1. उद्धरति, उद्धर्त्तुं, rt. हृ), जीर्णोद्धारं कृ, प्रतिकृ, प्रतिसंस्कृ, साध्, *see To* repair.—(Bring back) प्रत्यानी (c. 1. -नयति -नेतुं), प्रतिनी, पुनर् आनी.—(Restore to life) जीव् in caus., *see To* re-animate.—(To health), *see To* cure, recover.

Restored, *p. p.* (Given back) प्रतिदत्तः -त्ता -त्तं, परिदत्तः &c., प्रत्यर्पितः -ता -तं, पुनरर्पितः &c., प्रतिपादितः &c., प्रत्यापन्नः -न्ना -न्नं, प्रदत्तः -त्ता -त्तं, परावृत्तः -त्ता -त्तं, परावर्त्तितः -ता -तं.—(Replaced) पुनःस्थापितः -ता -तं, प्रतिष्ठापितः &c.—(Repaired) उद्धृतः -ता -तं, जीर्णोद्धृतः &c., प्रतिसंस्कृतः &c.—(Brought back) प्रत्यानीतः -ता -तं, पुनरानीतः &c.—(To life) प्राप्तजीवनः -ना -नं.—(To one's senses) लब्धचेताः -ताः -तः (स्), प्राप्तचैतन्यः -न्या -न्यं. *See* Recovered.

Restorer, *s.* प्रतिदाता *m.* (तृ), उद्धर्त्ता *m.* (र्त्तृ), जीर्णोद्धर्त्ता, जीर्णोद्धारकः.

To restrain, *v. a.* निग्रह् (c. 9. -गृह्णाति -ग्रहीतुं), विनिग्रह्, सन्निग्रह्, नियम् (c. 1. -यच्छति -यन्तुं), विनियम्, संयम्, परियम्, अभ्यायम्, यम्, निरुध् (c. 7. -रुणद्धि -रोद्धुं), अवरुध्, सन्निरुध्, संरुध्, निवृ (c. 10. -वारयति -यितुं), वृ, संहृ (c. 1. -हरति -हर्त्तुं), प्रत्याहृ, उपसंहृ, विधृ (c. 10. -धारयति -यितुं), यन्त्र् (c. 10. यन्त्रयति -यितुं), बाध्, निषिध्, प्रतिषिध्, प्रतिबन्ध्, नियमनं कृ, आकलनं कृ, आकल्.

Restrainable, *a.* निग्रहीतव्यः -व्या -व्यं, निग्रहणीयः -या -यं, नियन्तव्यः &c., नियम्यः -म्या -म्यं, निवारणीयः &c., संहरणीयः &c., प्रत्याहरणीयः &c., आकलनीयः &c.

Restrained, *p. p.* निगृहीतः -ता -तं, नियमितः &c., नियतः &c., संयतः &c., संयमितः &c., यतः &c., यन्त्रितः &c., नियन्त्रितः &c., रुद्धः -द्धा -द्धं, निरुद्धः &c., विधृतः -ता -तं, विधारितः &c., निवारितः &c., प्रत्याहृतः &c., उपसंहृतः &c., बाधितः &c., आकलितः &c., बद्धः -द्धा -द्धं, निबद्धः &c., प्रतिबद्धः &c., धैर्य्यशाली -लिनी &c.; 'in desire,' यतेन्द्रियः -या -यं, बद्धकामः -मा -मं.

Restrainer, *s.* नियन्ता *m.* (न्तृ), यन्ता *m.*, नियामकः, निग्रहीता *m.*, निरोधकः.

Restraint, *s.* निग्रहः -हणं, नियमनं, संयमः -मनं, संयामः, यमः, यतिः *f.*, नियतिः *f.*, यमनं, निगृहीतिः *f.*, यन्त्रणं, नियन्त्रणं, निरोधः, अवरोधः, प्रतिरोधः, उपरोधः, रोधः, सम्प्रतिरोधकः -कं, संग्रहः, प्रग्रहः, वियमः, वियामः, वारणं, निवारणं, आवरणं, प्रतिबन्धः, निबन्धः -न्धनं, बाधः -धा -धनं, आकलनं, दमः -मनं, स्तम्भः, गुप्तिः *f.*, निषेधः, प्रतिषेधः; 'self-restraint,' आत्मसंयमः, आत्मयमः, दान्तिः *f.*, नैयत्यं; 'absence of restraint,' निर्यन्त्रणं.—(Of speech) वाग्यमः -मनं, वाग्यतत्वं.—(In law, limitation) आसेधः; 'of time,' कालासेधः; 'of place,' स्थानासेधः; 'from living away from home,' प्रवासासेधः; 'from employment,' कर्म्मासेधः.

To restrict, *v. a.* निबन्ध् (c. 9. -बध्नाति -बन्द्धुं), परिमा (c. 2. -माति -तुं), परिमितं -तां कृ, सपरिमाणं -णां कृ, नियम् (c. 1. -यच्छति -यन्तुं), संयम्, निग्रह् (c. 9. -गृह्णाति, ग्रहीतुं), निरूप् (c. 10. -रूपयति -यितुं), मर्य्यादां or सीमां निरूप्, समर्य्यादं -दां कृ, ससीमं -मां कृ.

Restricted, *p. p.* निबद्धः -द्धा -द्धं, परिमितः -ता -तं, मितः &c., नियतः &c., नियमितः &c., समर्य्यादः -दा -दं, सावधिकः -का -कं, ससीमः -मा -मं; 'as a word,' मितार्थः, योगरूढः. *See* Limited.

Restriction, *s.* निबन्धः -न्धनं, बन्धः -न्धनं, नियमः -मनं, संयमः, नियतिः *f.*, निग्रहः, मर्य्यादा, सीमा, परिसीमा, अवधिः *m.*, परिमितिः *f.*, परिमितता, परिमाणं, परिच्छेदः, विशेषः -षणं; 'without restriction,' अनिबन्धनः -ना -नं, अविशेषणः -णा -णं.

Restrictive, *a.* निबन्धनः -ना -नं, नियामकः -का -कं, परिमापनः -ना -नं, परिच्छेदकः &c., मर्य्यादानिरूपकः &c., सीमानिरूपकः &c.

To result, *v. n.* (Issue, proceed) उत्पद् (c. 4. -पद्यते -पत्तुं), समुत्पद्, जन् (c. 4. जायते, जनितुं), उपजन्, सिध् (c. 4. सिध्यति, सेद्धुं), प्रभू (c. 1. -भवति -वितुं), उद्भू, अनुभू in pass., प्रवृत् (c. 1. -वर्त्तते -र्त्तितुं), अनुवृत्, निःसृ, उदि.—(End in) अवसो (c. 4. -स्यति -सातुं), पर्य्यवसो, निष्पद् in pass., विगम्, निर्गम्, अपगम्.

Result, *s.* (Consequence, issue) परिणामः, फलं, उत्पत्तिः *f.*, सिद्धिः *f.*, प्रयुक्तिः *f.*, प्रयोगः, उत्पन्नं, उद्भूतं, निष्पन्नं, उत्तरं, फलमुत्तरं, फलोदयः, फलोत्पत्तिः *f.*, निर्गमः, शेषः, अन्तः, उदर्कः, जन्यं, अनुभवः, भव्यं, अनुसारः, अनुवर्त्तनं, अन्वयः, प्रत्ययः, अनुषङ्गः, योगः, कार्य्यं, अर्थः, फलितार्थः, अवसानं, अवसायः, पर्य्यवसानं, गुणः, परिपाकः, *see* Effect; 'unexpected result,' विपाकः; 'happy result,' शुभफलं.—(Result of reasoning, conclusion) सिद्धान्तः, सिद्धिः *f.*, निश्चितार्थः, मथितार्थः, निर्णीतार्थः, उपपत्तिः *f.*, अनुभूतिः *f.*, अनुमितिः *f.*, घटितार्थः.

Resulting, *part.* प्रयुक्तः -क्ता -क्तं, उत्पन्नः -न्ना -न्नं, जातः -ता -तं, जनितः &c., जन्यः -न्या -न्यं, उद्भूतः &c., अनुवृत्तः -त्ता -त्तं, प्रवृत्तः &c., अनुसारी -रिणी &c., अनुयायी &c., फल in comp., प्रभव in comp., उद्भव in comp.; 'pain resulting from sin,' पापप्रयुक्तं दुःखं; 'fever resulting from fasting,' उपवासप्रयुक्तो ज्वरः; 'obedience resulting from fear,' भयप्रयुक्ता भक्तिः; 'resulting from that,' तत्फलः -ला -लं.

Resumable, *a.* प्रत्याहरणीयः -या -यं, प्रत्याहार्य्यः -र्य्या -र्य्यं, अवहार्य्यः &c.

Resumé, *s.* सारः, सारार्थः, सारसंग्रहः, संग्रहः, उपसंहारः.

To resume, *v. a.* (Take back or again) पुनर् आदा (c. 3. -ददाति

-दत्ते -दातुं), प्रत्यादा, पुनर् ग्रह् (c. 9. गृह्णाति, ग्रहीतुं), प्रत्याहृ (c. 1. -हरति -हर्तुं), पुनर् आहृ, पुनर् हृ, अपहृ, अनुप्राप् (c. 5. -आप्नोति -आप्तुं), पुनः प्राप्, प्रत्यवाप्, पुनर् लभ्.—(Take up again after interruption, begin again) प्रकृतम् or प्रस्तुतम् or मूलविषयम् अनुसृ (c. 1. -सरति -सर्तुं), प्रकृतप्रसङ्गं कृ, प्रकृतानुसरणं कृ, पुनर् आरभ् (c. 1. -रभते -रब्धुं), पुनःप्रसङ्गं कृ, पुनर् वद् or ब्रू; 'he resumed,' पुनराह.

RESUMED, *p.p.* प्रत्याहृतः -ता -तं, अपहृतः &c., पुनर्गृहीतः -ता -तं.

RESUMING, *part.* दत्तापहारी -रिणी -रि (न्), प्रत्याहारकः -का -कं.

RESUMPTION, *s.* प्रत्याहरणं, प्रत्याहारः, पुनराहरणं, पुनर्हरणं, अपहारः, अपहरणं, पुनर्ग्रहणं, प्रत्यादानं, पुनरादानं; 'of a grant,' दत्तापहारः, दत्तापहरणं.

RESURRECTION, *s.* मृतोत्थानं, मृतोत्थितिः *f.*, मृतलोकोत्थानं, पुनरुत्थानं, पुनरुत्थितिः *f.*, मृतपुनरुत्थानं, न्यायदिने or विचारदिने मृतलोकानां पुनरुत्थितिः *f.* or श्मशानादुत्थितिः *f.*; 'resurrection day,' मृतोत्थानकालः.

To RESUSCITATE, *v.a.* प्रतिजीव् (c. 10. -जीवयति -यितुं), संजीव्, उज्जीव्, जीव्, पुनः सजीवं -वां कृ, उत्था in caus. *See To* REVIVE.

RESUSCITATED, *p. p.* संजीवितः -ता -तं, प्रतिजीवितः &c., पुनः सजीवीकृतः &c.

RESUSCITATION, *s.* प्रतिजीवनं, सञ्जीवनं, पुनः सजीवीकरणं, पुनरुत्थापनं.

RETAIL, RETAILING, *s.* अल्पविक्रयः, खण्डविक्रयः, क्षुद्रविक्रयः, अल्पपण्यया, अल्पविपणः, अल्पवाणिज्यं, खण्डवाणिज्यं, क्षुद्रवाणिज्यं.

To RETAIL, *v. a.* अल्पशः or खण्डशो विक्री (c. 9. -क्रीणाति -णीते -क्रेतुं), अल्पविक्रयं कृ, खण्डविक्रयं कृ, अल्पपण्यायां कृ, पण् (c. 1. पणते -णितुं), खण्डवाणिज्यं कृ.

RETAILER, *s.* खण्डविक्रयी *m.* (न्), खण्डविक्रयकारी *m.*, अल्पविक्रयकारी *m.*, विपणी *m.* (न्), प्रापणिकः, आपणिकः, खण्डवाणिज्यकृत् *m.*, खण्डवणिक् *m.* (ज्).

To RETAIN, *v. a.* (Keep, hold) धृ (c. 10. धारयति -यितुं, c. 1. धरति, धर्तुं), सन्धृ, धा (c. 3. दधाति, धत्ते, धातुं), रक्ष् (c. 1. रक्षति -क्षितुं), संरक्ष्, अभिरक्ष्, धारणं कृ.—(Keep back) विधृ, निग्रह्, विनिग्रह् सन्निग्रह्, संहृ, उपसंहृ.—(Hire, engage) वेतनेन or मूल्येन ग्रह्, निरूपितवेतनं प्रतिज्ञाय कर्म्मणि नियुज् or स्था in caus.—(Remember), *see* the word.

RETAINED, *p. p.* धृतः -ता -तं, धारितः &c., विधृतः &c., स्थापितः &c.

RETAINER, *s.* (Dependant, adherent) आश्रितः, आश्रयी *m.* (न्), अनुचरः, अनुजीवी *m.* (न्), उपजीवी *m.*, भाक्तिकः, भृत्यः, अवलम्बी *m.*, अनुवर्त्ती *m.*, अनुगामी *m.*, अनुचारी *m.*, अनुयायी *m.*, अनुगः, सपक्षः, सेवकः, पार्श्वकः; 'an old retainer,' चिराश्रितः, चिरसेवकः; 'body of retainers,' परिवारः, भृत्यवर्गः, सेवकवर्गः, अनुयायिवर्गः.

RETAINING, *s.* धारणं, धरणं, धृतिः *f.*, रक्षणं, नियोजनं, स्थापनं.

To RETALIATE, *v. a.* प्रतिकृ, विप्रतिकृ, विप्रकृ, प्रत्यपकृ, वैरप्रतिकारं कृ, प्रत्यपकारं कृ, प्रतिफल (nom. प्रतिफलयति -यितुं), प्रतिफलं दा, प्रतियातं कृ, प्रतिहिंस् (c. 7. -हिनस्ति, c. 1. -हिंसति -सितुं), प्रतिहिंसां कृ, वैरशुद्धिं कृ, वैरोद्धारं कृ, निर्यत् (c. 10. -यातयति -यितुं), वैरनिर्यातनं कृ.

RETALIATED, *p.p.* प्रतिकृतः -ता -तं, विप्रतिकृतः &c., विप्रकृतः &c., प्रत्यपकृतः &c., प्रतिफलितः -ता -तं, निर्यातितः -ता -तं.

RETALIATION, *s.* प्रतिकारः, प्रतीकारः, प्रतिकृतिः *f.*, प्रतिक्रिया, प्रतिकर्म्म *n.* (न्), विप्रतिकारः, विप्रकारः, विप्रकृतिः *f.*, प्रत्यपकारः, वैरप्रतिक्रिया, वैरप्रतिकारः, प्रतिविधिः *m.*, प्रतिफलं, प्रतियातः, प्रतिहिंसा, वैरशुद्धिः *f.*, वैरोद्धारः, निर्यातनं, वैरनिर्यातनं, अपकारः, अपक्रिया, अपकरणं, समाधिः *m.*, लुट्टं.

To RETARD, *v. a.* (Diminish the velocity of motion) वेगरोधं कृ, वेगावरोधं कृ, वेगं or गतिं रुध् (c. 7. रुणद्धि, रोद्धुं) or अवरुध् or विधृ (c. 10. -धारयति -यितुं), वेगविधारणं कृ, वेगविलम्बनं कृ, गतिविलम्बनं कृ, गतिमन्दतां कृ, मन्दगतिं -तिं -ति कृ.—(Cause delay) विलम्ब् (c. 10. -लम्बयति -यितुं), विलम्बं कृ, विलम्बनं कृ, मन्दतां कृ, मन्दं -न्दां कृ.—(Hinder) रुध्, निरुध्, प्रतिरुध्, अवरुध्, संरुध्, बाध्, स्तम्भ्, प्रतिबन्ध्.

RETARDATION, RETARDING, *s.* वेगरोधः, वेगावरोधः, वेगविधारणं, वेगविलम्बनं, गतिविलम्बनं, गतिप्रतिबन्धः, वेगसंकोचः, रोधः, अवरोधः, विलम्बनं.

RETARDED, *p. p.* रुद्धवेगः -गा -गं, अवरुद्धवेगः &c., रुद्धगतिः -तिः -ति, अवरुद्धगतिः &c., विलम्बितः -ता -तं, विलम्बितवेगः -गा -गं, विलम्बितगतिः -तिः -ति, विधारितवेगः &c.; 'gradually retarded motion,' क्षीयमाणो वेगः, क्षीयमाणा गतिः.

RETARDING, *part.* विलम्बी -म्बिनी &c., वेगरोधकः -का -कं, वेगावरोधकः &c.

To RETCH, *v. n.* वमितुं or छर्दयितुं यत्नं कृ or उद्गमं कृ or उद्गम्, वमनोद्यमं कृ.

RETENTION, *s.* धारणं -णा, धृतिः *f.*, धरणं, आग्रहः, ग्रहः, संग्रहः -हणं.—(Faculty of the mind) धारणाशक्तिः *f.*, धारणा, स्मृतिः *f.*, मेधा.

RETENTIVE, *a.* (As memory) धारणावान् -वती -वत् (त्), धारणाशक्तिविशिष्टः -ष्टा -ष्टं, धारणाशक्तियुक्तः -क्ता -क्तं.—(Retaining) धारकः -का -कं, धरः -रा -रं, आग्रही -हिणी &c.; 'of moisture,' क्लेदधारकः -का -कं; 'of life,' दुर्मरः -रा -रं.

RETENTIVENESS, *s.* धारणाशक्तिः *f.*, धारणाक्षमता, धारकत्वं, धृतिः *f.*, दृढता.

RETICULAR, RETICULATED, *a.* जालाकारः -रा -रं, जालाकृतिः -तिः -ति, जालरूपः -पा -पं, व्यत्यस्तरेखाविशिष्टः -ष्टा -ष्टं, जालवद् अन्तरालविशिष्टः &c.

RETICULATION, *s.* जालकर्म्म *n.* (न्), जालाकारकर्म्म *n.*, जालवत्कर्म्म *n.*

RETICULE, *a.* स्त्रीलोकेन हस्तेन भृतं सूच्यादिधारणयोग्यो लघुकोषः.

RETINA, *s.* नेत्रान्तःस्थितचित्रपत्रं, नेत्रान्तःस्थचित्रपत्रं.

RETINUE, *s.* परिवारः, परिवर्हः, वर्हः, परिग्रहः, तन्त्रं, परिकरः, परिजनः, परिजनाः *m. pl.*, परिचराः *m. pl.*, अनुचराः *m. pl.*, परिचरवर्गः, सहचरवर्गः, भृत्यवर्गः, परिच्छदः.

To RETIRE, *v. n.* अपक्रम् (c. 1. -क्रामति -क्रमितुं), व्यपक्रम्, परावृत् (c. 1. -वर्त्तते -र्त्तितुं), प्रतिनिवृत्, निवृत्, पार्श्वे परावृत्, अवस्था (c. 1. -तिष्ठते -स्थातुं), अपसृ (c. 1. -सरति -सर्त्तुं), अपया (c. 2. -याति -तुं), अपगम् (c. 1. -गच्छति -गन्तुं), व्यपगम्, चल् (c. 1. चलति -लितुं), पलाय् (c. 1. पलायते -यितुं, rt. इ), विपलाय्.—(Retire into privacy or private life) विविक्ततां or विविक्तवृत्तिम् आस्था or सेव्, सर्व्वसङ्गान् न्यस् (c. 4. -अस्यति -सितुं) or त्यज्, सङ्गसन्न्यासं कृ, गृहसन्न्यासं कृ, विविक्तदेशे वस्.

RETIRED, *a.* (Sequestered, secluded) विविक्तः -क्ता -क्तं, विजनः -ना -नं, निभृतः -ता -तं, एकान्तः -न्ता -न्तं, निर्जनः &c., निःशलाकः -का -कं.—(Secret) गूढः -ढा -ढं, गुप्तः -प्ता -प्तं, प्रच्छन्नः -न्ना -न्नं; 'a retired spot,' विविक्तस्थानं, निर्जनस्थानं, निर्जनदेशः, रहःस्थानं; 'a place whence water has retired,' परापः -पा -पं, परेपः -पा -पं; 'leading a retired life,' विविक्तसेवी -विनी -वि (न्).

RETIREMENT, *s.* (Act of retiring) परावर्त्तः -र्त्तनं, प्रतिनिवर्त्तनं, निवर्त्तनं, पार्श्वपरिवर्त्तनं, अपक्रमः -मणं, अपसरणं, अपगमः -मनं, पलायनं.—(Act of retiring into privacy or private life) विविक्तसेवनं, विविक्तवृत्तिसेवनं, विविक्तवाससेवनं, विविक्तदेशे वासः, सङ्गसन्न्यासः, गृहसन्न्यासः.—(Private or retired life or state) विविक्तता -त्वं,

विविक्तवृत्तिः *f.*, विविक्तदशा, एकान्तता, एकान्तवृत्तिः *f.*—(Place of retirement) विविक्तस्थानं, निर्जनस्थानं, निभृतस्थानं, निषद्या.

RETIRING, *part.* or *a.* (Withdrawing) परावर्त्ती -र्त्तिनी -र्त्ति (न्), अपक्रामन् -मन्ती -मत् (त्), पार्श्वपरिवर्त्ती &c.—(Not forward or bold) विविक्तसेवी &c., एकान्तसेवी &c., विविक्तप्रियः -या -यं, एकान्तप्रियः &c., अप्रगल्भः -ल्भा -ल्भं, अधृष्टः -ष्टा -ष्टं, मन्दास्यविशिष्टः -ष्टा -ष्टं, मन्दस्वभावः -वा -वं. *See* RESERVED.

To RETORT, *v. a.* प्रतिक्षिप् (c. 6. -क्षिपति -क्षेप्तुं), प्रत्यवक्षिप्, पुनः क्षिप् or अवक्षिप्, प्रतिकृ, प्रत्यारुह् in caus. (-रोपयति -यितुं). *See To* RECRIMINATE.

To RETORT, *v. n.* प्रत्यपवद् (c. 1. -वदति -दितुं), प्रत्यपवादं कृ, प्रत्यवक्षेपं कृ, प्रत्युत्तरं कृ, प्रतिनिन्द् (c. 1. -निन्दति -न्दितुं), पुनर् निन्द्, प्रत्यारोपं कृ.

RETORT, *s.* (Return of an accusation or incivility) प्रत्यपवादः, प्रत्यवक्षेपः, प्रत्यारोपः, प्रत्यभियोगः, प्रत्युत्तरं, प्रतिनिन्दा, विप्रकृतिः *f.*, विप्रकारः, विप्रतिकारः, प्रतिकारः.—(Vessel in chemistry for distillation) वकः, वकयन्त्रं, मूषः -षी -षा -षिका; 'glass retort,' काचवकः, काचवकयन्त्रं.

To RETRACE, *v. a.* (One's steps) निवृत्, प्रतिनिवृत्. *See To* RETURN.

To RETRACT, *v. a.* or *n.* कथितत्यागं कृ, उक्तत्यागं कृ, उक्तास्वीकारं कृ, कथितास्वीकारं कृ, उक्तप्रत्यादेशं कृ, व्यतिक्रमं कृ, अनुशयं कृ, निवृत् (c. 1. -वर्त्तते -र्त्तितुं) with abl.; 'induce to retract,' निवृत् in caus. *See To* RECANT, RECALL.

RETRACTATION, RETRACTION, *s.* कथितत्यागः, उक्तत्यागः, उक्तप्रत्यादेशः, उक्तास्वीकारः, कथितास्वीकारः, निवर्त्तनं, निवृत्तिः *f.*, अनुशयः, व्यतिक्रमः. *See* RECANTATION.

RETRACTED, *p. p.* अनुशयितः -ता -तं, प्रत्यादिष्टः -ष्टा -ष्टं, व्यतिक्रान्तः -न्ता -न्तं.

RETREAT, *s.* (Act of retiring) अपक्रमः -मणं, अपसरणं, अपयानं, परावर्त्तः, परावृत्तिः *f.*, अपावर्त्तनं, अपावृत्तिः *f.*, परिवर्त्तः -र्त्तनं, विप्रयाणं, प्रतिप्रयाणं, अपायः, अपगमः -मनं, उपक्रमः, निवर्त्तनं, प्रतिनिवर्त्तनं, वक्रमः.—(Of an army) पलायनं, विपलायनं, प्रपलायनं, द्रावः, विद्रवः, प्रद्रावः, सन्द्रावः, उद्द्रावः, द्रवः, संयुगे निवर्त्तनं.—(Place of retirement) विविक्तस्थानं, विविक्तदेशः, निर्जनस्थानं, निर्जनदेशः, निभृतस्थानं, रहःस्थानं, परावर्त्तनस्थानं.

To RETREAT, *v. n.* (Retire) अपक्रम् (c. 1. -क्रामति -क्रमितुं), व्यपक्रम्, परावृत्, अपया, अपगम्, *see To* RETIRE.—(As an army) पलाय् (c. 1. पलायते -यितुं, rt. इ), विपलाय्, प्रपलाय्, सम्पलाय्, प्रद्रु (c. 1. -द्रवति -द्रोतुं), विद्रु, विप्रद्रु, अपधाव् (c. 1. -धावति -वितुं), प्रधाव्.—(Withdraw into privacy), *see To* RETIRE.

RETREATED, *p. p.* परावृत्तः -त्ता -त्तं, अपावृत्तः &c., पलायितः -ता -तं.

To RETRENCH, *v. a.* (Cut off, curtail) छिद् (c. 7. छिनत्ति, छेत्तुं), अवछिद्, अवकृत् (c. 6. -कृन्तति -कर्त्तितुं), लू (c. 9. लुनाति, लवितुं), लुप् (c. 6. लुम्पति, लोप्तुं), खण्ड्, छेदनं कृ.—(Lessen expenses, &c.) व्ययं न्यूनीकृ or अल्पीकृ or ह्रस् in caus. or संहृ.

RETRENCHMENT, *s.* छेदः, अवच्छेदः, लोपः, व्ययच्छेदः, व्ययलोपः, न्यूनव्ययः.

RETRIBUTION, *s.* प्रतिफलं, प्रतिक्रिया, प्रतिकृतिः *f.*, प्रतिकारः, निष्कृतिः *f.*

RETRIBUTIVE, RETRIBUTORY, *a.* प्रतिफलप्रदः -दा -दं, प्रतिफलदायकः -का -यिका -कं, प्रतिफलदः &c., परिशोधकः -का -कं, प्रतिकारकः -का -कं, प्रतिकारी -रिणी -रि (न्).

RETRIEVABLE, *a.* उद्धरणीयः -या -यं, पुनरुद्धरणीयः &c., पुनःप्रापणीयः &c.

To RETRIEVE, *v. a.* उद्धृ (c. 1. -हरति -हर्त्तुं), समुद्धृ, पुनर् उद्धृ, पुनः प्राप् (c. 5. -आप्नोति -आप्तुं), पुनर् लभ्, पुनर् आनी, उद्धारं कृ, उद्धरणं कृ. *See To* RECOVER, RESTORE.

RETRIEVED, *p. p.* उद्धृतः -ता -तं, समुद्धृतः &c., पुनः प्राप्तः -प्ता -प्तं.

To RETROCEDE, *v. n.* प्रतिगम् (c. 1. -गच्छति -गन्तुं), विपरीतं गम्, परावृत्.

RETROCESSION, *s.* प्रतिगमनं, पश्चाद्गमनं, विपरीतगमनं, परावर्त्तनं.

RETROGRADATION, *s.* प्रतिक्रमः, व्यतिक्रमः, विपरीतगतिः *f.*, वक्रगतिः *f.*

RETROGRADE, *a.* विपरीतगामी -मिनी -मि (न्), प्रतिगामी &c., व्यतिक्रान्तः -न्ता -न्तं, विपरीतगतिकः -का -कं, परावृत्तः -त्ता -त्तं, प्रतीपः -पा -पं, प्रातीपिकः &c.—(In astronomy) वक्रगतिः -तिः -ति, वक्रः -क्रा -क्रं.

To RETROGRADE, *v. n.* (Go backward) परावृत् (c. 1. -वर्त्तते -र्त्तितुं), विपरीतं गम् (c. 1. गच्छति, गन्तुं), प्रतिगम्, पश्चाद् गम्, प्रतिक्रम् (c. 1. -क्रामति -क्रमितुं), व्यतिक्रम्, व्यतिक्रमं कृ.—(Decline) क्षीणसत्त्वः -त्त्वा -त्त्वं भू, मूलसत्त्वाद् भ्रंश्. *See To* DEGENERATE, DECLINE.

RETROGRESSION, *s.* पश्चाद्गमनं, विपरीतगमनं, प्रतिगमनं, व्यतिक्रमः.

RETROSPECT, *s.* गतावलोकनं, अतीतावलोकनं, गतकालावलोकनं, अतीतकालावलोकनं, भूतावलोकनं, भूतकालावलोकनं, अनुदर्शनं, अनुदृष्टिः *f.*, पश्चाद्दर्शनं, पश्चाद्दृष्टिः *f.*, पश्चादवलोकनं, अन्ववलोकनं.

RETROSPECTIVE, *a.* (Looking back) पश्चाद्दर्शी -र्शिनी -र्शि (न्), पश्चादवलोकी &c., गतावलोकी &c., गतकालावलोकी &c., अनुदर्शी &c.—(Relating to what is past) गतापेक्षकः -का -कं, भूतापेक्षकः &c., अतीतापेक्षकः &c., गतकालापेक्षकः &c., गतकालापेक्षी -क्षिणी &c., गतकालसापेक्षः -क्षा -क्षं, भूतकालसापेक्षः &c.

RETROSPECTIVELY, *adv.* गतापेक्षया, गतकालापेक्षया, गतकालसापेक्षं, भूतापेक्षया.

To RETURN, *v. n.* (Come back, go back) पुनर् आगम् (c. 1. -गच्छति -गन्तुं), प्रत्यागम्, प्रतिगम्, निवृत् (c. 1. -वर्त्तते -र्त्तितुं), प्रत्यावृत्, प्रतिनिवृत्, सन्निवृत्, पर्यावृत्, उपावृत्, व्यावृत्, विनिवृत्, आवृत्, पुनर् आवृत्, प्रतिया (c. 2. -याति -तुं), प्रत्याया, पुनर् आया, प्रत्युपया, प्रत्ये (c. 2. प्रत्येति -तुं, rt. इ), पुनर् इ, प्रतिक्रम् (c. 1. -क्रामति -क्रमितुं), प्रतिपद् (c. 4. -पद्यते -पत्तुं), पुनर् अभिपद्, पुनर् उपस्था (c. 1. -तिष्ठति -स्थातुं), प्रत्युपस्था, पुनर् आव्रज्; 'he returned to the place whence he came,' प्रतिजगाम यथागतं.—(Turn back or round) परावृत्, परिवृत्, पर्यावृत्, परिवर्त्तनं कृ.—(Answer), *see* REJOIN, RETORT.

To RETURN, *v. a.* (Give back) प्रतिदा (c. 3. -ददाति -दातुं), पुनर् दा, परिदा, प्रत्यृ in caus., पुनर् स्मृ, प्रतिपद्, *see To* RESTORE.—(Bring or send back) पुनर् नी or आनी, पुनर् आनी in caus. (-नाययति -यितुं), पुनर् गम् in caus., पुनः प्राप् in caus.—(Give in recompense) प्रतिकृ, प्रतिफलं दा, प्रतिफलाय दा, प्रतिदा; 'to return a benefit,' प्रत्युपकृ; 'an injury,' प्रत्यपकृ, प्रतिहिंस्, प्रतिहिंसां कृ; 'to return evil for good,' परेणोपकारे कृते प्रत्यपकारं कृ or आचर्, उपकारात् प्रति अपकारं कृ, उपकारं प्राप्य अपकारं कृ; 'to return good for evil,' परेणापकारे कृते प्रत्युपकारं कृ or आचर्.—(Render an official account), *see To* REPORT.

RETURN, *s.* (Coming back) पुनरागमनं, प्रत्यागमः -मनं, प्रतिगमनं, प्रत्यावृत्तिः *f.*, प्रत्यावर्त्तनं, निवर्त्तनं, निवृत्तिः *f.*, प्रतिनिवृत्तिः *f.*, सन्निवृत्तिः *f.*, पर्यावृत्तिः *f.*, पर्यावर्त्तः -र्त्तनं, पुनरावृत्तिः *f.*, आवृत्तिः *f.*, परावृत्तिः *f.*, उपयातं.—(Turning back or round) परावर्त्तनं, परावृत्तिः *f.*, परिवृत्तिः *f.*—(Periodical revolution) परिवर्त्तः -र्त्तनं, परिवृत्तिः *f.*, पुनरावर्त्तः, पुनरावृत्तिः *f.*, विवर्त्तः, पर्ययः, पर्यायः; 'of the seasons,' ऋतुपरिवर्त्तः, ऋतुपर्यायः.—(Repayment) प्रतिदानं, परिदानं.—(Requital) प्रतिक्रिया, प्रतिकृतिः *f.*, प्रतिकर्म्म *n.* (न्),

प्रतिकारः, प्रतीकारः, प्रतिफलं, *see* REQUITAL; 'return of a benefit,' प्रत्युपकारः, उपकारमोक्षः; 'of an injury,' प्रत्यपकारः; 'of good for evil,' परेणापकारे कृते तस्य प्रत्युपकाराचरणं.—(Profit, return of trade) उत्पन्नं, फलं, फलोदयः, लाभः, लब्धिः *f.*, प्राप्तिः *f.* —(Official statement), *see* REPORT.—(In return for) प्रति with abl. c., विनिमयेन, हेतोः, हेतौ, *see* FOR.

RETURNED, *p. p.* पुनरागतः -ता -तं, प्रत्यागतः &c., प्रतिगतः &c., आगतः &c., पुनरायातः &c., प्रत्यावृत्तः -त्ता -त्तं, प्रतिनिवृत्तः &c., विनिवृत्तः &c., निवृत्तः &c., पुनरावृत्तः &c., परावृत्तः &c.—(Given back) प्रतिदत्तः -त्ता -त्तं, परिदत्तः &c.—(Requited) प्रतिकृतः -ता -तं, प्रतिफलितः &c.

RE-UNION, *s.* पुनर्योगः, पुनःसंयोगः, पुनःसंसर्गः, पुनर्मेलनं, पुनःसन्धिः *m.*, पुनःसन्धानं, प्रतिसमाधानं, पुनःसमागमः.—(Assembly) सभा.

To RE-UNITE, *v. a.* पुनः संयुज्, पुनः सन्धा, पुनः संसृज्, पुनर् एकीकृ.

RE-UNITED, *p. p.* पुनःसंयुक्तः -क्ता -क्तं, पुनःसंसृष्टः -ष्टा -ष्टं, पुनर्मिलितः -ता -तं.

To REVEAL, *v. a.* प्रकाश् (c. 10. -काशयति -यितुं), विकाश्, विवृ (c. 5. -वृणोति -वृणुते -वरितुं -रीतुं), अपवृ, अपावृ, व्यक्तीकृ, व्यञ्ज् (c. 7. -अनक्ति -अंक्तुं, c. 10. -अञ्जयति -यितुं) प्रकटीकृ, प्रकट (nom. प्रकटयति -यितुं), आविष्कृ, प्रादुष्कृ.—(Tell) सूच्, ज्ञा in caus., ख्या in caus., निविद्.—(A secret) रहस्यभेदं कृ.

REVEALED, *p. p.* प्रकाशितः -ता -तं, विवृतः &c., आविष्कृतः &c., प्रादुष्कृतः &c., व्यक्तीकृतः &c., सूचितः &c., ज्ञापितः &c., प्रकटितः -ता -तं.

REVEALER, *s.* प्रकाशकः, विवरणकृत्, सूचकः, ज्ञापकः, ख्यापकः; 'of a secret,' रहस्यभेदकः, रहस्यप्रकाशकः.

REVEALING, REVEALMENT, *s.* प्रकाशनं, विवरणं, विवृतिः *f.*, व्यक्तीकरणं, प्रकटीकरणं, आविष्करणं, स्पष्टीकरणं; 'of a secret,' रहस्यभेदः,

To REVEL, *v. n.* अतिशयहास्यशब्देन उत्सवं कृ, रात्रिकाले हासिकादिशब्देन उत्सवं कृ or अतिशयतुमुलेन सम्प्रीतिं कृ or केलिं कृ; 'one who revels in his lusts,' कामकामी *m.* (न्).

REVEL, *s.* अतिशयहास्यशब्देन उत्सवः, हासिकादिशब्देन सम्प्रीतिः *f.* or केलिः *m. f.*; 'master of the revels,' केलिसचिवः.

REVELATION, *s.* प्रकाशनं, विवरणं, प्रादुष्करणं, आविष्करणं, स्पष्टीकरणं, प्रकाशितवाक्यं, ईश्वरप्रत्यादेशः. *See* REVEALING.

REVELER, *s.* अतिशयहास्यशब्देन or अतिशयहासिकादिशब्देन उत्सवकारी *m.* (न्), सम्प्रीतिरतः, सम्प्रीतिप्रसक्तः, सम्प्रीतिप्रियः, पानोत्सुकः, पानासक्तः.

REVELRY, *s.* अतिशयहासिकादिशब्देन उत्सवकरणं. *See* REVEL.

To REVENGE, *v. a.* प्रतिकृ, वैरशुद्धिं कृ, वैरप्रतिक्रियां कृ, वैरप्रतिकारं कृ, अपकारशुद्धिं कृ, अपकारं प्राप्य प्रत्यपकृ, हिंसां प्राप्य प्रतिहिंस् (c. 7. -हिनस्ति, c. 1. -हिंसति -सितुं), परेणापकारे कृते प्रत्यपकारं कृ, अपकारात् प्रति अपकारं कृ, परेण द्रोहे कृते प्रतिद्रोहं कृ, वैरोद्धारं कृ, वैरनिर्यातनं कृ, निर्यत् (c. 10. -यातयति -यितुं), अपकारमोक्षं कृ; 'to revenge an insult,' अवलेपप्रतिकारं कृ, अवलेपशुद्धिं कृ.

REVENGE, *s.* वैरशुद्धिः *f.*, वैरप्रतिक्रिया, वैरप्रतिकारः, वैरप्रतिकृतिः *f.*, वैरनिर्यातनं, वैरोद्धारः, अपकारशुद्धिः *f.*, प्रतिकारः, प्रतीकारः, प्रतिक्रिया, प्रतिकृतिः *f.*, प्रतिकर्म्म *n.* (न्), विप्रतिकारः, प्रतिहिंसा, प्रत्यपकारः, प्रतिद्रोहः, निर्यातनं, प्रतिफलं, प्रतिविधिः *m.*—(Feeling or desire of revenge) प्रतिहिंसाबुद्धिः *f.*, प्रतिद्रोहबुद्धिः *f.*, प्रत्यपकारबुद्धिः *f.*, प्रतिक्षेपः, प्रत्यपकारेच्छा, प्रतिद्रोहेच्छा, वैरिता, जिघांसा.

REVENGED, *p. p.* प्रतिकृतः -ता -तं, निर्यातितः &c., वैरशुद्धः -द्धा -द्धं.

REVENGEFUL, *a.* प्रतिहिंसाबुद्धिः -द्धिः -द्धि, प्रतिद्रोहबुद्धिः &c., प्रत्यपकारबुद्धिः &c., प्रतिहिंसाशीलः -ला -लं, प्रतिहिंसेच्छुः -च्छुः -च्छु, प्रतिद्रोहेच्छुः &c., प्रत्यपकारेच्छुः &c., प्रतिकारेच्छुः &c., निर्यातनशीलः &c., दंशी -शिनी -शि (न्), द्विषन्तपः -पा -पं.

REVENGEFULLY, *adv.* प्रतिहिंसाबुद्ध्या, प्रत्यपकारबुद्ध्या, प्रतिद्रोहशीलत्वात्.

REVENGEFULNESS, *s.* प्रतिहिंसाशीलत्वं, प्रतिहिंसाबुद्धिः *f.*, प्रत्यपकारशीलता.

REVENGER, *s.* प्रतिकारकः, प्रतिहिंसकः, वैरशोधकः, प्रत्यपकारकः.

REVENUE, *s.* बलिः *m.*, करः, आयः, राजस्वं, राजधनं, राजकरः -रं, उत्पन्नं, नृपांशः, राजांशः, उपस्वत्वं, भागधेयः, कारः, लाभः, प्राप्तिः *f.*

To REVERBERATE, *v. a.* (Send or beat back) प्रतिक्षिप् (c. 6. -क्षिपति -क्षेप्तुं), प्रतिप्रक्षिप्, प्रतिहन् (c. 2. -हन्ति -न्तुं), प्रतिहननं कृ, प्रतिघातं कृ.

To REVERBERATE, *v. n.* प्रतिध्वन् (c. 1. -ध्वनति -नितुं), प्रतिध्वनिं कृ, प्रतिध्वननं कृ, प्रतिनद् (c. 1. -नदति -दितुं), अनुनद्, व्यनुनद्, प्रतिनादं कृ, प्रतिगर्ज् (c. 1. -गर्जति -र्जितुं), प्रतिगर्जनं कृ; 'cause to reverberate,' अनुनद् in caus., व्यनुनद्, प्रतिनद्. *See To* RESOUND.

REVERBERATING, *part.* प्रतिध्वनन् -नन्ती -नत् (त्), प्रतिगर्जन् &c., प्रतिनादयन् &c.

REVERBERATION, *s.* (Sending or beating back) प्रतिक्षेपः -पणं, प्रतिप्रक्षेपः -पणं, प्रतिघातः, प्रतिहननं.—(Of sound) प्रतिध्वनिः *m.*, प्रतिध्वननं, प्रतिनादः, अनुनादः, व्यनुनादः, प्रतिगर्जनं -ना, प्रतिशब्दः, प्रतिनिनदः.

To REVERE, *v. a.* पूज् (c. 10. पूजयति -यितुं), अभिपूज्, सम्पूज्, मन् (c. 10. मानयति -यितुं), सम्मन्, अर्च् (c. 1. अर्चति -र्चितुं, c. 10. अर्चयति -यितुं), समर्च्, अभ्यर्च्, उपास् (c. 2. -आस्ते -आसितुं), सेव् (c. 1. सेवते -वितुं, c. 10. सेवयति -यितुं), आदृ (c. 6. -द्रियते -दर्त्तुं), भज् (c. 1. भजते, भक्तुं), नमस्कृ, पुरस्कृ, सत्कृ, पूजां कृ, आदरं कृ. *See* OBEISANCE.

REVERED, *p. p.* पूजितः &c., सेवितः &c., अर्चितः &c. *See* HONOURED.

REVERENCE, *s.* पूजा -जनं, मानं, सम्मानं, अर्चनं -ना, अर्चा, अभ्यर्चा -र्चनं, आदरः, सेवा -वनं, अर्हा -र्हणं -णा, भक्तिः *f.*, श्रद्धा, नमस् ind., सत्कारः, सपर्य्या, आराधनं, पुरस्कारः, मान्यत्वं, बहुमानं, सम्भ्रमः, उपासना; 'act of reverence,' नमस्कारः, नमस्या, प्रणामः, प्रणतिः *f.*, नमस्, अभिवादनं, अभिवन्दनं; 'your reverence,' भगवान् *m.* (त्), भवान् *m.*

To REVERENCE, *v. a* पूज्, सम्पूज्, नमस् (nom. नमस्यति). *See To* REVERE.

REVERENCED, *p. p.* पूजितः -ता -तं, आदृतः &c., सम्मानितः &c., उपासितः &c.

REVEREND, *a.* पूज्यः -ज्या -ज्यं, पूजनीयः -या -यं, पूजार्हः -र्हा -र्हं, अर्च्यः -र्च्या -र्च्यं, अर्चनीयः -या -यं, आर्य्यः -र्य्या -र्य्यं, मान्यः -न्या -न्यं, सम्मान्यः &c., माननीयः -या -यं, अर्चार्हः &c., अर्ह्यः -र्ह्या -र्ह्यं, अर्हणीयः &c., आदरणीयः &c., नमस्कार्य्यः -र्य्या -र्य्यं, नमस्यः -स्या -स्यं, उपास्यः &c., उपासनीयः &c.. श्रद्धेयः &c., पूजिलः -ला -लं, भट्टारः -रा -रं.

REVERENTIAL, REVERENT, *a.* सादरः -रा -रं, आदरयुक्तः -क्ता -क्तं, पूजकः -का -कं, सम्पूजकः &c., पूजाकारी -रिणी &c., आदरबुद्धिः -द्धिः -द्धि, आदरकारी &c., भक्तिमान् -मती -मत् (त्), भक्तिसूचकः -का -कं, आदरसूचकः &c.

REVERENTIALLY, *adv.* सादरं, समानं, सनमस्कारं, आदरपूर्वं, शिरसा.

REVERIE, *s.* ध्यानं, चिन्ता, भावना, अनर्थकध्यानं, विशृङ्खलध्यानं, अप्रकृतध्यानं, अनर्थकचिन्ता, अनर्थकवासना, अनर्थकभावना, बुद्धिविलासः.

REVERSAL, *s.* परावर्त्तः -र्त्तनं, परावृत्तिः *f.*, प्रत्यावर्त्तनं, परिवर्त्तनं.

To REVERSE, *v. a.* (Turn upside down) परावृत् (c. 10. -वर्त्तयति -यितुं), परिवृत्, पर्यस्, विपर्यस्, अधोमुखीकृ, *see To* OVERTURN, INVERT.—(Change to the contrary) परिवृत्, विपरीतं -तां कृ, विपर्यस्तं -स्तां कृ, व्यत्यस्तं -स्तां कृ, विपर्यासं कृ, विपर्ययं कृ, वैपरीत्यं कृ, व्यतिक्रमं कृ.

(In law, overthrow a decision) परावृत्, परावर्त्तं कृ, परावृत्तिं कृ.

REVERSE, *s.* (Change, vicissitude) परिवर्त्तनं, परिवृत्तिः *f.*, आवृत्तिः *f.*, पर्य्यायः, अवस्थान्तरं, परिणामः, विकारः.—(The contrary) विपर्य्ययः, विपर्य्यासः, व्यत्ययः, व्यत्यासः, विपर्य्यायः, प्रत्यवायः, विपरीतं, वैपरीत्यं, व्यतिक्रमः, विपक्षः, प्रतिपक्षः.—(Reverse of) expressed by इतर, *see* OPPOSITE, *a.*—(Misfortune) कार्य्यविपत्तिः *f.*, *see* MISFORTUNE.

REVERSE, *a.* विपरीतः -ता -तं, विपर्य्यस्तः -स्ता -स्तं, व्यत्यस्तः &c., व्यतिक्रान्तः -न्ता -न्तं, विरुद्धः -द्धा -द्धं, अपसव्यः -व्या -व्यं, प्रसव्यः &c., सव्यः &c., प्रतीपः -पा -पं, विप्रतीपः &c., प्रतीकः -का -कं, विपक्षः -क्षा -क्षं, प्रतिपक्षः &c., विलोमः -मा -मं, प्रतिलोमः &c., प्रातीपिकः -की -कं, अर्वाचीनः -ना -नं, प्रतिकूलः -ला -लं, वामः -मा -मं; 're-verse order,' व्यतिक्रमः.

REVERSED, *p. p.* विपर्य्यस्तः -स्ता -स्तं, पर्य्यस्तः &c., व्यतिक्रान्तः -न्ता -न्तं, व्यत्यस्तः -स्ता -स्तं, अपवृत्तः -त्ता -त्तं.—(Turned upside down or with the end downwards) अधोमुखीकृतः -ता -तं, अधोमुखः -खा -खं, अधःकृतः -ता -तं, अधरोत्तरः -रा -रं, अधराग्रः -ग्रा -ग्रं.—(As a sentence) परावृत्तः -त्ता -त्तं, परावर्त्तितः -ता -तं.

REVERSELY, *adv.* विपर्य्ययेण, व्यतिक्रमेण, विपरीतं, वैपरीत्येन, आदिपश्चात्.

REVERSIBLE, *a.* परावर्त्त्यः -र्त्त्या -र्त्त्यं, परावर्त्तनीयः -या -यं, परिवर्त्तनीयः &c.

REVERSION, *s.* परावर्त्तः -र्त्तनं, परावृत्तिः *f.*, प्रत्यावर्त्तनं, प्रत्यावृत्तिः *f.*, पर्यावृत्तिः *f.*, पर्यावर्त्तनं, परिवर्त्तनं, आवृत्तिः *f.*—(Succession, right to future possession) उत्तराधिकारः, अन्यभोगोत्तराधिकारः, अन्यभोगोत्तरप्राप्तिः *f.* -प्रापणं.

REVERSIONARY, *a.* अन्यभोगोत्तरप्राप्यः -प्या -प्यं, अन्यभोगोत्तरप्रापणीयः -या -यं, उत्तरप्रापणीयः &c., उत्तरभोग्यः -ग्या -ग्यं, क्रमेण भोग्यः &c.

To REVERT, *v. n.* प्रत्यावृत् (c. 1. -वर्त्तते -र्त्तितुं), परावृत्, पर्यावृत्, प्रतिनिवृत्, परिवृत्, आवृत्, पुनर् आवृत्, प्रत्यागम्, पुनर् आगम्.

REVERTIBLE, *a.* परावर्त्त्यः -र्त्त्या -र्त्त्यं, परिवर्त्तनीयः -या -यं, परिवर्त्त्यः &c.

To REVIEW, *v. a.* (Look back on) पश्चाद् अवलोक् (c. 1. -लोकते -कितुं, c. 10. -लोकयति -यितुं), पश्चाद् दृश् (c. 1. पश्यति, द्रष्टुं), अनुदृश्, गतावलोकनं कृ, गतकालावलोकनं कृ, पश्चादवलोकनं कृ.—(Examine again, revise) पुनः परीक्ष् (c. 1. -ईक्षते -क्षितुं), पुनर् निरूप् (c. 10. -रूपयति -यितुं), पुनर् अनुसन्धा (c. 3. -दधाति -धातुं), पुनर् आलोक् or अवलोक् or समवलोक् or दृश्, पुनर् विचर्, पुनर्विचारं कृ.—(Inspect) निरूप्, परीक्ष्, अनुसन्धा, दृश्.—(A book, &c.) काव्यग्रन्थादेर् गुणदोषौ परीक्ष् or प्रकाश्, गुणदोषविवेचनं कृ, दोषादोषविचारं कृ, ग्रन्थदोषादोषविचारं कृ.

REVIEW, *s.* (Looking back) पश्चाद्दर्शनं, पश्चाद्दृष्टिः *f.*, पश्चादवलोकनं, अनुदर्शनं, अनुदृष्टिः *f.*, गतावलोकनं.—(Examining again) पुनः-परीक्षा, पुनर्निरूपणं, पुनरनुसन्धानं, पुनर्दर्शनं, पुनर्दृष्टिः *f.*, पुनर्विचारः.—(Inspection) निरूपणं, दर्शनं, निरीक्षणं, परीक्षणं.—(Of a book) काव्यग्रन्थादेर् गुणदोषविवेचनं or गुणदोषविचारः, ग्रन्थगुणदोषविवेचनं or गुणदोषप्रकाशनं or दोषादोषप्रकाशनं.

REVIEWER, *s.* ग्रन्थदोषादोषप्रकाशकः, ग्रन्थगुणदोषविवेचकः -विचारकः.

To REVILE, *v. a.* तिरस्कृ, निन्द् (c. 1. निन्दति -न्दितुं), आक्रुश् (c. 1. -क्रोशति -क्रोष्टुं), समाक्रुश्, भर्त्स् (c. 10. भर्त्सयते -ति -यितुं), सम्भर्त्स्, कुत्स्, अभिकुत्स्, तर्ज्, उपालभ्, अपवद्, शप्, अभिशप्, क्षिप्, परिक्षिप्, अधिक्षिप्, अतिब्रू, मुखरीकृ, भष्, गुप् in des., अभिशंस्, *see* *To* REPROACH, ABUSE; 'to revile in return,' प्रत्याक्रुश्.

REVILED, *p. p.* निन्दितः -ता -तं, तिरस्कृतः &c., आक्रुष्टः -ष्टा -ष्टं, उपालब्धः -ब्धा -ब्धं, निर्भर्त्सितः &c., जुगुप्सितः &c., अभिशस्तः -स्ता -स्तं.

REVILER, *s.* निन्दकः, आक्रोशकः, आक्रोष्टा *m.* (ष्टृ), उपक्रोष्टा *m.*, निर्भर्त्सकः.

REVILING, *s.* निन्दा -न्दनं, तिरस्कारः, आक्रोशः -शनं, उपक्रोशः, पारुष्यं, परुषोक्तिः *f.*, परुषवचनं, निर्भर्त्सनं, जुगुप्सा, मौखर्य्यं, अपवादः, अभिवादः, तर्जनं, उपालम्भः, कुत्सा -त्सनं, गालिप्रदानं, क्षेपः, अवक्षेपः, परिभाषणं.

REVISAL, *s.* पुनर्दृष्टिः *f.*, अनुदृष्टिः *f.*, अनुदर्शनं, पुनःशोधः -धनं, पुनःपरीक्षा.

To REVISE, *v. a.* (Review), *see* the word.—(Amend) शुध् (c. 10. शोधयति -यितुं), परिशुध्, संशुध्, विशुध्, पुनः शुध्, शोधनं कृ, पुनःशोधनं कृ.

REVISED, *p. p.* शोधितः -ता -तं, पुनःशोधितः &c., पुनर्निरूपितः &c.

REVISION, *s.* पुनर्दृष्टिः *f.*, अनुदृष्टिः *f.*, पुनःशोधः -धनं, शुद्धिः *f.*, पुनरावृत्तिः *f.*

REVIVAL, *s.* (Return to life) पुनर्जीवनं, प्रतिजीवनं, सञ्जीवनं, उज्जीवनं, पुनःप्राणनं, पुनर्जीवनप्राप्तिः *f.*, पुनश्चैतन्यप्राप्तिः *f.*, *see* RECOVERY.—(Return to a vigorous or healthy state) पुनःस्वास्थ्यप्राप्तिः *f.*, पुनःस्वास्थ्यं, समुत्थानं, समुत्थितिः *f.*, पुनःसंस्थितिः *f.*, पुनरुपस्थितिः *f.*, पुनःप्रवृत्तिः *f.*—(Recovery from misfortune) विपदुद्धारः, आपदुद्धारः, पुनरुद्धारः.

To REVIVE, *v. n.* उज्जीव् (c. 1. -जीवति -वितुं), विजीव्, प्रतिजीव्, संजीव्, पुनर् जीव्, जीवनं or संज्ञां or चैतन्यं पुनः प्राप् or लभ् or आपद् or प्रतिपद्, समुत्था (c. 1. समुत्तिष्ठति -त्थातुं, rt. स्था), उत्था, प्रत्याश्वस् (c. 2. -श्वसिति -तुं), समाश्वस्, प्रत्यापन्नजीवनः -ना -नं भू, प्रत्यागतप्राणः -णा -णं भू, प्रत्यापन्नचेतनः -ना -नं भू. *See* *To* RECOVER.

To REVIVE, *v. a.* जीव् (c. 10. जीवयति -यितुं), प्रतिजीव्, संजीव्, उज्जीव्, पुनर् जीव्, पुनः सजीवं -वां कृ, पुनः सजीवीकृ, पुनर् उत्था in caus. (उत्थापयति -यितुं, rt. स्था) or समुत्था, पुनः संस्था, प्रत्याश्वस् (c. 10. -श्वासयति -यितुं), समाश्वस्, *see* *To* RECOVER, *v. a.*—(Renew) नवीकृ.

REVIVED, *p. p.* प्रतिजीवितः -ता -तं, सञ्जीवितः &c., पुनः सजीवीकृतः &c., प्रत्यापन्नजीवनः -ना -नं, प्रत्यागतप्राणः -णा -णं, प्रत्यापन्नसंज्ञः -ज्ञा -ज्ञं, प्रत्याश्वस्तः -स्ता -स्तं, समाश्वासितः -ता -तं.—(Renewed) नवीकृतः -ता -तं, नवीभूतः &c.

REVOCABLE, *a.* परावर्त्त्यः -र्त्त्या -र्त्त्यं, परावर्त्तनीयः -या -यं, लोप्यः -प्या -प्यं.

REVOCATION, *s.* परावर्त्तः -र्त्तनं, परावृत्तिः *f.*, लोपः, खण्डनं, प्रत्यादेशः, अनुशयः, विप्रतिपत्तिः *f.* *See* RECALL, REPEAL.

To REVOKE, *v. a.* परावर्त्तं कृ, परावृत्, लुप्, खण्ड्, लोपं कृ, अनुशयं कृ, प्रत्यादिश् (c. 6. -दिशति -देष्टुं). *See* *To* RECALL, REPEAL.

To REVOLT, *v. n.* शासनत्यागं कृ, अधिकारत्यागं कृ, राजद्रोहं कृ, राजाभिद्रोहं कृ, स्वस्वामित्यागं कृ, स्वपक्षत्यागं कृ, द्रोहं कृ. *See* *To* REBEL.

REVOLT, *s.* राजद्रोहः, राजाभिद्रोहः, शासनत्यागः, अधिकारत्यागः, स्वस्वामित्यागः, स्वपक्षत्यागः, शासनपरित्यागः, कोपः, प्रकोपः. *See* REBELLION.

REVOLTER, *s.* शासनत्यागी *m.* (न्), राजद्रोही *m.*, स्वस्वामित्यागी *m.* (न्).

REVOLTING, *a.* बीभत्सजनकः -का -कं, घृणोत्पादकः &c., अतिद्वेषजनकः &c., परमद्वेषजनकः &c., अत्यन्तद्वेषजनकः &c., गर्ह्यः -र्ह्या -र्ह्यं, गर्हणीयः &c., कुत्सितः -ता -तं; 'revolting appearance,' बीभत्सदर्शनं.

REVOLUTION, *s.* (Revolving) परिवर्त्तनं, परिवर्त्तः, परिवृत्तिः *f.*, आवर्त्तनं, आवृत्तिः *f.*, आवर्त्तः, विवर्त्तः -र्त्तनं, परिवर्त्तिः *f.*, परावृत्तिः *f.*, भ्रमणं, परिभ्रमणं, भ्रान्तिः, *f.*, घूर्णिः *f.*, घूर्णनं; 'of a wheel,' चक्रावर्त्तः, चक्रगतिः *f.*—(Motion of a body round a fixed point) भ्रमणं, परिभ्रमणं.—(Motion of any thing which brings it back to the same point) परिवृत्तिः *f.*, परिवर्त्तनं, आवर्त्तः, पुनरावर्त्तः, पर्य्ययः, पर्य्यायः, विपर्य्ययः; 'of the seasons,' ऋतुपर्य्यायः; 'of all the seasons,' सर्व्वर्तुपरिवर्त्तः; 'of employment or duty,' कर्म्मविपर्य्ययः; 'of time,' कालचक्रं.—(Continued course) गतिः *f.*,

प्रवृत्तिः *f.*, चक्रगतिः *f.*; 'of a planet,' ग्रहगतिः.—(Change in the government) राज्यपरिवर्त्तनं, राज्यरीतिपरिवर्त्तनं, राज्यव्यवस्था-परिवर्त्तनं, राज्यस्थितिपरिवर्त्तनं.

REVOLUTIONARY, *a.* राज्यपरिवर्त्तनसम्बन्धी -न्धिनी &c., राज्यपरिवर्त्तकः -का -कं.

REVOLUTIONIST, *s.* राज्यपरिवर्त्तकः, राज्यरीतिपरिवर्त्तकः, राज्यस्थिति-परिवर्त्तकः.

To REVOLVE, *v. n.* परिवृत् (c. 1. -वर्त्तते -र्त्तितुं), विवृत्, सम्परिवृत्, विपरिवृत्, व्यावृत्, आवृत्, भ्रम् (c. 4. भ्राम्यति, c. 1. भ्रमति -मितुं), परिभ्रम्, घूर्ण् (c. 1. घूर्णति -ते -र्णितुं), विघूर्ण्, व्याघूर्ण्, परिघूर्ण्, लुठ् (c. 6. लुठति -ठितुं), लुट् (c. 1. लोटति -टितुं); 'the earth revolves on its own axis,' स्वाक्षोपरि भ्रमति पृथिवी; 'pains and pleasures revolve like a wheel,' चक्रवत् परिवर्त्तन्ते दुःखानि च सुखानि च.

To REVOLVE, *v. a.* (Cause to turn round) भ्रम् in caus. (भ्रमयति, भ्रामयति -यितुं), परिवृत् (c. 10. -वर्त्तयति -यितुं), विवृत् आवृत्, घूर्ण् in caus. (घूर्णयति -यितुं), परिघूर्ण्, विघूर्ण्, व्याघूर्ण्, संसृ (c. 10. -सारयति -यितुं), लुठ् (c. 10. लोठयति -यितुं) or लुट्.—(In the mind) मनसा विचर् (c. 10. -चारयति -यितुं) or विगण् or विमृश् or वितर्क् or विवेचनं कृ.

REVOLVED, *p. p.* परिवर्त्तितः -ता -तं, परिवृत्तः -त्ता -त्तं, परावृत्तः &c., विवृत्तः &c., विवर्त्तितः -ता -तं, भ्रान्तः -न्ता -न्तं, घूर्णितः &c.; 'in the mind,' मनसा विचारितः &c.

REVOLVING, *part.* परिवर्त्ती -र्त्तिनी -र्त्ति (न्), परिवर्त्तमानः -ना -नं, विवर्त्तमानः &c., आवर्त्तमानः &c., भ्रमन् -मन्ती -मत् (त्), भ्रमी -मिणी &c., घूर्णायमानः &c.

REVULSION, *s.* विपरीतकर्षणं, पश्चात्कर्षणं, प्रतिकर्षणं, पराकर्षणं.

To REWARD, *v. a.* पारितोषिकं दा, वरं दा, प्रतिफलं दा, फलं दा, दानेन परितुष् (c. 10. -तोषयति -यितुं) or सन्तुष् or सम्भू (c. 10. -भावयति -यितुं), दक्षिणां दा, प्रतिफल (nom. प्रतिफलयति -यितुं). *See To* RECOMPENSE, REQUITE.

REWARD, *s.* पारितोषिकं, प्रतिफलं, फलं, दक्षिणा, वरः, वेतनं, प्रतिदानं, मानं, बहुमानं, *see* RECOMPENSE; 'worthy of a reward,' दक्षिणार्हः -र्हा -र्हं, दक्षिणीयः -या -यं, दक्षिण्यः -ण्या -ण्यं; 'the reward of learning,' विद्याधरः.

REWARDED, *p. p.* गृहीतपारितोषिकः -का -कं, गृहीतदक्षिणः -णा -णं, गृहीतवेतनः -ना -नं, प्रतिफलितः -ता -तं, परितोषितः &c., दानपरितोषितः &c.

REWARDER, *s.* फलदाता *m.* (तृ), प्रतिफलदः, वरदाता *m.*, वरदः.

RHAPSODIC, RHAPSODICAL, *a.* असम्बद्धः -द्धा -द्धं, अबद्धः &c., असङ्गतः -ता -तं, विसङ्गतः &c., अयुक्तिकः -का -कं, अनर्थकः &c., निरन्वयः -या -यं, अनन्वितः -ता -तं.

RHAPSODY, *s.* असम्बद्धकाव्यं, असम्बद्धवाक्यं, असङ्गतवाक्यं, असम्बद्धकविता.

RHETORIC, *s.* अलङ्कारविद्या, अलङ्कारशास्त्रं, शब्दालङ्कारविद्या, काव्यालङ्कारादिविषयका विद्या, शब्दालङ्कारः, वाङ्मयविद्या, साहित्यशास्त्रं, प्रवचनविद्या, प्रवचनशास्त्रं, परार्थानुमानं, वाङ्मयं.

RHETORICAL, *a.* आलङ्कारिकः -की -कं, अलङ्कारविद्यासम्बन्धी -न्धिनी -न्धि (न्), अलङ्कारशास्त्रसम्बन्धी &c., अलङ्कारी &c., अलङ्कारविषयकः -का -कं, अलङ्काररूपः -पा -पं, प्रवचनविद्यासम्बन्धी &c., वाङ्मयः -यी -यं; 'rhetorical expression,' अलङ्कारः.

RHETORICALLY, *adv.* अलङ्कारविद्यानुसारेण, अलङ्कारशास्त्रानुसारेण, अलङ्कारशास्त्रवत्.

RHETORICIAN, *s.* अलङ्कारविद्याज्ञः, अलङ्कारशास्त्रज्ञः, अलङ्कारशास्त्रपण्डितः, अलङ्कारशास्त्राध्यापकः, प्रवचनपटुः *m.* *See* ORATOR.

RHEUM, *s.* श्लेष्मा *m.* (न्), श्लेष्मकः, दूषिः -षी *f.*, दूषिका, दूषीका, क्लेदनः, क्लेदकः, वातुलं, पिञ्जटः, कफः, नेत्रमलं.

RHEUMATIC, *a.* (Pertaining to rheumatism) वातरोगसम्बन्धी -न्धिनी &c., वातुलः -ला -लं, वातीयः -या -यं.—(Affected with it) वातरोगी -गिणी -गि (न्), वातग्रस्तः -स्ता -स्तं, वायुग्रस्तः &c., वातुलः -ला -लं, वातूलः &c., वातकी &c., वाताहतः -ता -तं, वातोपहतः &c., पवनाहतः &c.

RHEUMATISM, *s.* वातरोगः, वायुरोगः, वातामयः, वातव्याधिः *m.*, वातः, वायुः *m.*, रसवातः, अनिलामयः, अनिलरोगः, अनिलः, धनुर्वातः, पटीरं, गृध्रसी; 'acute rheumatism,' वातरक्तं, वातगुल्मः, वातशोणितं; 'chronic, from dyspepsia,' आमवायुः *m.*, आमवातः; 'rheumatism in the joints,' सन्धिवातः, सन्धिवायुः *m.*; 'shooting rheumatism in the bones,' अस्थिशूलः -लं, अस्थितोदः.

RHEUMY, *a.* श्लेष्मलः -ला -लं, श्लेष्मणः -णा -णं, श्लेष्मवान् -वती -वत् (त्), श्लेष्ममयः -यी -यं, श्लेष्मयुक्तः -क्ता -क्तं; 'rheumy eyed,' क्लिन्नाक्षः -क्षा -क्षं. *See* BLEAR-EYED.

RHINOCEROS, *s.* खड्गः, खड्गी *m.* (न्), एकशृङ्गः, गण्डः -ण्डकः, गण्डाङ्गः, एकचरः, वनोत्साहः, तैतिलः; 'its horn,' खड्गः; 'the female,' खड्गधेनुः *f.*

RHOMB, RHOMBUS, *s.* विषमचतुरस्रं, विषमचतुष्कोणः.

RHUBARB, *s.* रेवसं, रेवाचिनी. These are Mahrattí words.

RHYME, *s.* (Correspondence of sounds in poetry) यमकः -कं, अन्त्ययमकः -कं, अन्त्यशब्दयमकः -कं, अन्त्यशब्दसमता, अनुप्रासः, मित्राक्षरं.—(A word to correspond in sound to another) यमकशब्दः, यमकः -कं.—(Poetry) कविता, काव्यं.

To RHYME, *v. n.* (Correspond in sound) यमकः -का -कं भू, यमकशब्दो भू.—(Make rhyme) कवितां कृ, काव्यं कृ, अनुप्रासं कृ.

RHYMELESS, *a.* यमकहीनः -ना -नं, अयमकः -का -कं, अननुप्रासः -सा -सं.

RHYTHM, RHYTHMUS, *s.* तालः, लयः, गाथा, तालबन्धनं, तालबद्धता.

RHYTHMICAL, *a.* तालबद्धः -द्धा -द्धं, लयबद्धः &c., तालसम्बन्धी -न्धिनी &c.

RIB, *s.* (Bone of an animal) पर्शुका, पार्शुका, पर्शुः *m.*, पार्श्वास्थि *n.*, पार्श्वकः, वंक्रिः *m.*; 'the ribs collectively,' पञ्जरं -रः, पिञ्जरं -रः, पार्श्वं.—(Of a boat) पोलिन्दः.—(Of an umbrella, &c.) शलाका, —(A thin slip of wood) शलाका.—(A prominent line) रेखा.

RIBALD, *a.* दुर्मुखः -खा -खं, अशुद्धभाषी -षिणी -षि (न्), अवाच्यभाषी &c., अवाच्यः -च्या -च्यं, अवद्यः &c., गर्ह्यः -ह्या -ह्यं, दुरुक्तः -क्ता -क्तं, कुत्सितः -ता -तं.

RIBALDRY, *s.* दुरुक्तिः *f.*, दुर्वचनं, कुत्सितवाक्यं, अवद्यं, अवाच्यं, व्यङ्गं.

RIBBED, *p. p.* or *a.* सशलाकः -का -कं, शलाकी -किनी &c., रेखाङ्कितः -ता -तं.

RIBBON, RIBAND, *s.* पट्टः, दुकूलपट्टः, दीर्घदुकूलखण्डः, दीर्घपट्टः, बन्धनी.

RICE, *s.* (The grain in the husk) शालिः *m.*, व्रीहिः *m.*, धान्यं, धान्योत्तमं, स्तम्बकरिः *m.*, जीवसाधनं.—(The grain without the husk, or after threshing) तण्डुलः, धान्यास्थि *n.*, धान्यसारः, शालिसारः; 'a grain of rice,' तण्डुलकणः.—(Wild rice) नीवारः; 'a grain of it,' नीवारकणः.—(A white rice growing in deep water) कलमः.—(Red sort, growing in moist soil) षष्टिकः -का; 'fit for growing it,' षष्टिक्यः -क्या -क्यं.—(Large or fragrant sort) महाव्रीहिः *m.*, महाशालिः *m.*—(New rice) नवधान्यं, नवान्नं. One hundred and eighty varietes of rice are enumerated.—(Boiled rice) अन्नं, ओदनः -नं, भक्तं, अन्धस् *n.*, भिस्सा, दीदिविः *m.*; 'scum of it,' मासरः, आचामः, निस्रावः, विस्रावः.—(Scorched) भिस्सटा, भिस्सिटा, भिस्मिटा, भिस्मिष्टा, भिस्मिका, दग्धिका.—(Fried rice) धानाः *f. pl.*, धानाकाः *f. pl.*; 'the meal of it,' धानाचूर्णं.—(Rice flattened by threshing) धान्यचमसः, पृथुकः -कं.—(Oblation of rice) अर्घः, अर्घ्यं, चरुः *m.*—(Heap of rice for presentation) धान्यधेनुः *f.*, धान्याचलः, तण्डुलौघः.—(Rice-water) तण्डुलोदकं, तण्डुलाम्बु *n.*, तण्डुलीयः.—(Rice-gruel) यवागूः *f.*, उष्णिका, आचामा, विलेपी, तरला, धान्याम्लं.—(Rice-field) शालिक्षेत्रं.—(Rice-milk) पायसः -सं.—(Rice-husk) तुषः.—(Ear of rice) कणिशः -शं, धान्यशीर्षकं.—(Granary for rice) कुशूलः, व्रीह्यगारं.—(Having rice, bearing it, made of it) व्रीहिमयः -यी -यं, व्रीहिकः -का -कं, व्रीही -हिणी -हि (न्), व्रैहः -ही -हं, व्रैहेयः -यी -यं, शालेयः -यी -यं, शालिमयः &c.

RICH, *a.* (Wealthy) धनी -निनी -नि (न्), धनवान् -वती -वत् (त्), सधनः -ना -नं, महाधनः -ना -नं, बहुधनः &c., वित्तवान् &c., वसुमान् &c., अर्थवान् &c., अर्थान्वितः -ता -तं, सार्थः -र्था -र्थं, धनसम्पन्नः -न्ना -न्नं, धनिकः -का -कं, धनाढ्यः -ढ्या -ढ्यं, धनसमृद्धः -द्धा -द्धं, धनविपुलः -ला -लं, लक्ष्मीवान् &c., श्रीमान् &c., सश्रीकः -का -कं, कोषवान् &c., सम्पत्तिमान् &c., समृद्धः &c., धनेश्वरः &c., लक्ष्मीशः, इभ्यः -भ्या -भ्यं; 'extremely rich person,' अतिधनी &c., लक्षाधीशः, कोटीश्वरः, कोट्यधीशः, लक्षपतिः *m.*, कुबेरः.—(Abounding in) आढ्यः -ढ्या -ढ्यं, पूर्ण in comp., बहु in comp., बहुल in comp., प्रचुर in comp., सम्पन्न in comp., समृद्ध in comp., पुष्कल in comp., मय in comp., अधिक in comp.; 'rich in good qualities,' गुणाढ्यः &c., गुणसम्पन्नः -न्ना -न्नं.—(Fertile) स्फीतः -ता -तं, पीनः -ना -नं, बहुफलदः -दा -दं.—(Costly, splendid) महार्घः -र्घा -र्घं, महामूल्यः -ल्या -ल्यं, बहुमूल्यः &c., अतिशोभनः -ना -नं, अतिशोभान्वितः -ता -तं, तैजसः -सी -सं, अतितैजसः &c., प्रतापवान् &c.—(As a dish) घृतपूर्णः -र्णा -र्णं, घृतप्लुतः -ता -तं, घृतमयः -यी -यं.

RICHES, *s.* धनं, वित्तं, वसु *n.*, अर्थः, सम्पत्तिः *f.*, द्रव्यं, विभवः, लक्ष्मीः *f.*, श्रीः *f.*, राः *m.* (रै), सम्पद् *f.*—(State of having great riches) धनाढ्यता, धनबाहुल्यं, धनप्राचुर्य्यं, धनसमृद्धिः *f.*, धनवैपुल्यं, धनैश्वर्य्यं, धनसम्पत्तिः *f.*, महाधनत्वं, सधनता; 'desirous of riches,' धनार्थी -र्थिनी -र्थि (न्); 'desire of riches,' धनाशा, धनतृष्णा; 'pride of riches,' धनदर्पः; 'puffed up by riches,' धनगर्वितः -ता -तं.

RICHLY, *adv.* (With riches) सधनं, धनबाहुल्येन, बहुधनेन, महाधनेन.—(Splendidly) महामूल्येन, अतिशोभया, अतिशोभापूर्व्वं.—(Abundantly) बाहुल्येन, अतिबहुलं, प्राचुर्य्येण, वैपुल्येन, विपुलं, अतिविपुलं, समृद्धा.

RICHNESS, *s.* (Opulence) धनाढ्यता, सधनता, धनबाहुल्यं, धनसमृद्धिः *f.*, धनसम्पत्तिः *f.*, धनिकता, सश्रीकता, *see* RICHES.—(Fertility) स्फीतता, पीनता, स्फीतिः *f.*, बहुफलता.—(Costliness, splendor) महार्घता, महामूल्यता, शोभा, अतिशोभा, तेजस् *n.*, प्रतापः.—(Abundance) बाहुल्यं, प्राचुर्य्यं, वैपुल्यं, समृद्धिः *f.*, समृद्धता.—(Of a dish) घृतपूर्णता, मिष्टता.

RICK, *s.* (Stack) चितिः *f.*, चयः, उत्करः, राशिः *m.*, निचयः, निकरः, ओघः; 'of hay,' तृणोत्करः, तृणचितिः *f.*, *see* HAY-RICK.

RICKETS, *s. pl.* बालरोगः, बालव्याधिः *m.*, बालामयः.

RICKETY, *a.* शिथिलसन्धिः -न्धिः -न्धि, अदृढसन्धिः &c., अस्थिरः -रा -रं, अनवस्थितः -ता -तं, विचलः -ला -लं, चलस्वभावः -वा -वं, स्खलितगतिः -तिः -ति.

To RID, *v. a.* (Free from encumbrance, &c.) विघ्नात् or भारात् मुच् (c. 6. मुञ्चति, मोक्तुं) or शुध् (c. 10. शोधयति -यितुं) or विशुध् or उद्धृ (c. 1. -हरति -हर्त्तुं) or मोक्ष् (c. 10. मोक्षयति -यितुं), विघ्नं or भारम् अपनी or विनी or हृ, निर्विघ्नीकृ; 'to rid of thieves,' कण्टकान् उद्धृ, कण्टकोद्धरणं कृ, कण्टकशोधनं कृ, निष्कण्टकीकृ; 'of thorns,' शल्योद्धारं कृ, शल्यानि उद्धृ.

RID, *a.* मुक्तः -क्ता -क्तं, विमुक्तः &c., शोधितः -ता -तं, वर्जितः &c., रहितः &c., विगत in comp., वीत in comp., गत in comp., हीन in comp., हृत in comp., निर् or स prefixed; 'rid of thieves or thorns,' कण्टकमुक्तः -क्ता -क्तं, मुक्तकण्टकः -का -कं, विगतकण्टकः &c., वीतकण्टकः &c., कण्टकहीनः -ना -नं, हृतकण्टकः &c., निष्कण्टकः &c.; 'to be rid of,' मुच् in pass. (मुच्यते), विमुच्; 'to get rid of,' अपास्, निरस्, निराकृ, त्यज्, परित्यज्, अपसृज्, अपहा, *see To* DISCARD; 'to be got rid of,' त्याज्यः -ज्या -ज्यं, अपासनीयः -या -यं, निराकरणीयः &c.

RIDDANCE, *s.* मुक्तिः *f.*, मोचनं, मुक्तता, मोक्षः -क्षणं, उद्धारः, उद्धरणं, शोधनं, शुद्धिः *f.*, निस्तारः, त्राणं, परित्राणं.

RIDDLE, *s.* प्रवह्लिः *f.* -ह्लिका, प्रहेलिका, प्रश्नदूती, कूटप्रश्नः, दृष्टकूटं गूढप्रश्नः, गूढं, गूढवाक्यं, श्लेषः, श्लेषोक्तिः *f.*; different kinds are सर्व्वतोभद्रः, वर्द्धमानः, अन्तर्लापिका, बहिर्लापिका.—(Large sieve) शोधनी, बृहच्चालनी, महाचालनी.

To RIDDLE, *v. a.* (Clean grain) पूर्व्वोक्तयन्त्रेण शुध् (c. 10. शोधयति -यितुं), or शोधनं कृ or उत्पवनं कृ.—(Perforate) व्यध्, छिद्र्, छिद्रपूर्णं -र्णां कृ, सच्छिद्रीकृ.

To RIDE, *v. n.* (Be carried on horseback) अश्वेन वह् in pass. (उह्यते), अश्वेन सञ्चर् (c. 1. -चरति -रितुं) or चर्, अश्वेन गम् (c. 1. गच्छति, गन्तुं) or या (c. 2. याति -तुं), अश्ववाहनेन गम् or या or चल्.—(On an elephant) गजेन वह् in pass. or सञ्चर् or गम् or या or चल्, गजवाहनेन चल् or व्रज्.—(Be borne on a fluid, &c.) वह् in pass., प्लु (c. 1. प्लवते, प्लोतुं).

To RIDE, *v. a.* (Sit on a horse) अश्वम् आरुह् (c. 1. -रोहति -रोढुं) or अधिरुह् or अध्यारुह् or समारुह् or अधिक्रम् (c. 1. -क्रामति -क्रमितुं), अश्वारूढः -ढा -ढं भू, अश्वारोही -हिणी -हि भू, अश्वारोहणं कृ.—(Sit on an elephant) गजारूढः -ढा -ढं भू, गजारोही &c. भू, गजम् आरुह्.—(On the back of a peacock) मयूरपृष्ठारूढः -ढा -ढं भू, मयूरपृष्ठम् आरुह् or आश्रि.—(A chariot) यानारूढः -ढा -ढं भू, यानम् आरुह्, यानारोहणं कृ.

RIDE, *s.* अश्वेन गमनं or चलनं, अश्वेन विहरणं, अश्वारोहणं; 'to take a ride,' अश्वेन विहारं कृ or विहृ, अश्वेन भ्रमणं कृ or परिभ्रमणं कृ.

RIDER, *s.* (On a horse) अश्वारोही *m.* (न्), अश्वारोढा *m.* (ढ्), अश्वारूढः, *see* HORSE-MAN.—(In general) आरोढा *m.*, आरोही *m.*, रोहकः.

RIDGE, *s.* (Of a mountain) कटकः -कं, कूटं, दन्तः, उपत्यकः.—(Of earth, a mound) सेतुः *m.*, पिण्डलः, पिण्डिलः, धरणः, आलिः -ली *f.*, संवरः, जङ्गालः.—(Back, top) पृष्ठं, अग्रं.

RIDGY, *a.* सकटकः -का -कं, कटकाकारः -रा -रं, कटकरूपः -पा -पं.

RIDICULE, *s.* उपहासः, परिहासः, अपहासः, अवहासः, प्रहासः, प्रहसनं, उपहसनं, उपहसितं, उपहसनीयता, विहसितं, हसनं, हास्यं, हासिका, परिभाषणं, अवक्षेपः, अवहेला, अवज्ञा, उत्प्रासनं, उत्स्मयः -यनं.

To RIDICULE, *v. a.* उपहस् (c. 1. -हसति -सितुं), अवहस्, अपहस्, उपहासभूमिं कृ, अवहासभूमिं कृ, अवहासास्पदं कृ, अवहासास्पदीकृ, अपहासास्पदीकृ, हास्यास्पदीकृ, अवहासस्थानं कृ, उत्स्मि (c. 1. -स्मयते -स्मेतुं).

अभिक्षिप्, अवक्षिप्, आक्षिप्. *See To* DERIDE.

RIDICULED, *p. p.* उपहसितः -ता -तं, अवहसितः &c., आक्षिप्तः -प्ता -प्तं.

RIDICULOUS, *a.* उपहास्यः -स्या -स्यं, अवहास्यः &c., परिहास्यः &c., हास्यः &c., हास्यजनकः -का -कं, हासजनकः, हासकरः -री -रं, हास्योत्पादकः &c., हासोत्पादकः &c., उपहासयोग्यः -ग्या -ग्यं, उपहासार्हः -र्हा -र्हं, उपहासविषयः -या -यं, हास्यास्पदः -दा -दं, तथ्यः -थ्या -थ्यं.

RIDICULOUSLY, *adv.* हास्यप्रकारेण, उपहास्यप्रकारेण, उपहास्यं.

RIDICULOUSNESS, *s.* उपहास्यता, अपहास्यता, परिहास्यता, हास्यत्वं.

RIDING, *s.* अश्वारोहणं, हयारोहः, अश्वारोहणविद्या, अश्वविद्या.

RIDING, *part.* आरोही -हिणी -हि (न्), आरूढः -ढा -ढं, आरोह in comp., रोहक in comp., आश्रयी &c.; 'riding on a horse,' अश्वारोही &c.; 'on an elephant,' गजारूढः &c.; 'on the back of a peacock,' मयूरपृष्ठारूढः &c., मयूरपृष्ठाश्रयी &c.

RIDING-SCHOOL, *s.* अश्वारोहणशाला, अश्वशिक्षाशाला, हयशिक्षाशाला.

RIFE, *a.* प्रसिद्धः -द्धा -द्धं, प्रबलः -ला -लं. *See* PREVALENT.

RIFENESS, *s.* प्रसिद्धता, प्रसिद्धिः *f.*, बाहुल्यं. *See* PREVALENCE.

RIFF-RAFF, *s.* खलाः *m. pl.*, पृथग्जनाः, अधमवर्गाः &c. *See* RABBLE.

To RIFLE, *v. a.* हृ (c. 1. हरति, हर्तुं), अपहृ, अभिहृ. *See To* ROB.

RIFLE, *s.* (Kind of gun) सीताकर्षेण घुमिरीकृता गुलिकाप्रक्षेपणी.

RIFT, *s.* छिद्रं, भित्तिः *f.*, भङ्गः. *See* CLEFT, FISSURE.

To RIFT, *v. a.* भिद्, विभिद्, छिद्. *See To* CLEAVE, SPLIT.

To RIG, *v. a.* सज्जीकृ, सज्ज् (c. 1. सज्जति -ज्जितुं), समसज्जं -ज्जां कृ.—(A ship) नावं समुद्रयानार्थं वातवसनादिना सज्जीकृ or समायुज्. *See To* EQUIP.

RIG, RIGGING, *s.* सज्जा, सज्जनं -ना, नौकासज्जा -ज्जनं, वातवसनादिसज्जा, रज्ज्वादिसज्जनं, वसनरज्ज्वादि, वसनं, परिच्छदः.

RIGGED, *p. p.* सज्जीकृतः -ता -तं, सज्जितः &c., वसनरज्ज्वादियुक्तः &c.

RIGHT, *a.* (Just, fit, proper) युक्तः -क्ता -क्तं, उपयुक्तः &c., यथायुक्तः &c., यथायोग्यः -ग्या -ग्यं, सम्यङ् समीची सम्यक्, समञ्जसः -सा -सं, योग्यः &c., न्याय्यः -य्या -य्यं, उचितः -ता -तं, यथोचितः &c., समीचीनः -ना -नं, यथार्थः -र्था -र्थं, याथार्थिकः -की -कं, समुचितः &c., साधुः -धुः -ध्वी -धु, लभ्यः -भ्या -भ्यं, *see* PROPER.—(True, correct) ऋतः -ता -तं, सत्यः -त्या -त्यं, तथ्यः -थ्या -थ्यं, अवितथः -था -थं, यथार्थः &c., शुद्धः -द्धा -द्धं.—(Straight) सरलः -ला -लं, ऋजुः -जुः -जु, अजिह्मः -ह्मा -ह्मं; 'a right line,' सरलरेखा.—(Not left) दक्षिणः -णा -णं, अपसव्यः -व्या -व्यं, अवसव्यः &c., वामेतरः -रा -रं; 'right and left,' सव्यापसव्यः -व्या -व्यं; 'to the right,' प्रदक्षिणः -णा -णं; 'winding to the right,' दक्षिणावर्त्ती -र्त्तिनी -र्त्ति (न्); 'the right side,' *see* RIGHT, *s.*; 'the right hand,' दक्षिणपाणिः *m.*, अग्रपाणिः *m.*, अग्रहस्तः, अग्रकरः; 'being on the right hand,' दक्षिणस्थः -स्था -स्थं; 'right ascension, in astronomy,' विषुवांशः.

RIGHT, *s.* (Justice, propriety) धर्म्मः, न्यायः, नीतिः *f.*, न्याय्यत्वं -ता, न्यायिता, न्यायता, युक्तिः *f.*, युक्तता, योग्यता, उपयुक्तता, उपयोगिता, यथायोग्यता, यथार्थता, याथार्थ्यं, सामञ्जस्यं, सम्यक्त्वं, औचित्यं, उचितत्वं, समञ्जसं; 'right and wrong,' धर्म्माधर्म्मं, युक्तायुक्तं, न्यायान्यायं, हिताहितं.—(Correctness) सत्यता, सत्यं, ऋतं, अवितथं, समञ्जसं, शुद्धता.—(Just claim, title) अधिकारः -रित्वं, स्वत्वं, स्वाम्यं, सत्ता; 'to have a right,' अर्ह् (c. 1. अर्हति -र्हितुं); 'a woman has no right to independence,' स्त्री न स्वातन्त्र्यम् अर्हति.—(The right side, not the left) दक्षिणं, अपसव्यं, अवसव्यं, वामेतरं, दक्षिणदिक् *f.* (श्), दक्षिणपार्श्वः, दक्षिणाङ्गं; 'right and left,' सव्यापसव्यं; 'upon the right side,' दक्षिणस्थः -स्था -स्थं; 'on the right,' दक्षिणपार्श्वे, दक्षिणतस्, दक्षिणेन.—(One's own right) स्वाधिकारः, स्वस्वत्वं, 'to set to rights,' *see To* RIGHT, *v. a.*

RIGHT, *adv.* (Justly) युक्तं, यथायुक्तं, यथायोग्यं, यथोचितं, यथान्यायं, धर्म्मतस्, न्यायतस्, समञ्जसं, सम्यक्, यथार्थं, स्थाने.—(Truly) सत्यं, ऋतं, अञ्जसा, अर्थतस्, यथार्थतस्.—(In a straight line) सरलं, ऋजु, अजिह्मं, अवक्रं.—(To a great degree) सु or अति prefixed.

RIGHT, *interj.* साधु, भद्रं, युक्तं, स्वस्ति, बाढं.

To RIGHT, *v. a.* (Restore to a right position, set to rights) सुस्थ (nom. सुस्थयति -यितुं), सुस्थं -स्थां कृ, स्वस्थ (nom. स्वस्थयति -यितुं), स्वस्थं -स्थां कृ, *see To* RESTORE, *v. a.*—(Do justice to) न्यायं कृ.

To RIGHT, *v. n.* (Become right) सुस्थः -स्था -स्थं भू, स्वस्थः -स्था -स्थं भू.—(Become erect) ऋजुः -जुः -जु भू, ऋजूभू.

RIGHT-ANGLE, *s.* समकोणः, समलम्बः, समलम्बकोणः, समलम्बत्रिभुजः.

RIGHTEOUS, *a.* धार्म्मिकः -की -कं, न्यायाचारः -रा -रं, न्यायाचारी -रिणी &c., न्यायपरः -रा -रं, पुण्यः -ण्या -ण्यं, साधुः -धुः -ध्वी -धु, धर्म्मवर्त्ती &c. *See* JUST.

RIGHTEOUSLY, *adv.* धर्म्मतस्, न्यायतस्, धर्म्मानुसारेण. *See* JUSTLY.

RIGHTEOUSNESS, *s.* धर्म्मः, धर्म्मता, धार्म्मिकता -त्वं, न्यायः, न्याय्यता, न्यायिता, साधुता -त्वं, पुण्यता, शुचिता. *See* JUSTICE.

RIGHTFUL, *a.* (Having a just title) अधिकारी -रिणी -रि (न्), अधिकारवान् -वती -वत् (त्), साधिकारः -रा -रं, स्वत्वाधिकारी &c.—(Agreeable to justice), *see* JUST.

RIGHTFULLY, *adv.* अधिकारेण, अधिकारतस्, साधिकारं. *See* JUSTLY.

RIGHTFULNESS, *s.* अधिकारिता, अधिकारवत्त्वं, साधिकारत्वं, *see* JUSTICE.

RIGHT-HAND, *s.* दक्षिणपाणिः *m.*, दक्षिणहस्तः, दक्षिणकरः, अग्रहस्तः, *see* RIGHT, *a.*

RIGHT-HANDED, *a.* दक्षिणहस्तसेवी -विनी -वि (न्), दक्षिणसाची &c.

RIGHTLY, *adv.* युक्तं, सम्यक्, धर्म्मतस्, धर्म्मेण, न्यायतस्, यथान्यायं, यथायोग्यं, यथाधर्म्मं, यथार्थं, यथोचितं, समञ्जसं, स्थाने, *see* JUSTLY, FITLY.—(Truly) सत्यं, ऋतं, अञ्जसा, यथार्थं -र्थतस्, *see* TRULY.

RIGHTNESS, *s.* यथार्थता, याथार्थ्यं, सत्यता, सामञ्जस्यं, सम्यक्त्वं, शुद्धता.

RIGID, *a.* (Stiff, not pliant) दृढः -ढा -ढं, स्तब्धः -ब्धा -ब्धं, स्तब्धीकृतः -ता -तं, घनः -ना -नं, कठिनः -ना -नं, स्तिमितः -ता -तं, अशिथिलः -ला -लं, अमृदुः -दुः -द्वी -दु.—(Strict, severe) कठोरः -रा -रं, कर्कशः -शा -शं, उग्रः -ग्रा -ग्रं, नियतः -ता -तं, सूक्ष्मः -क्ष्मा -क्ष्मं, सूक्ष्मदर्शी &c.

RIGIDITY, RIGIDNESS, *s.* दृढता, स्तब्धता, घनता, कठिनता, काठिन्यं, दार्ढ्यं, कठोरता, कर्कशता, कार्कश्यं, उग्रता -त्वं, अशिथिलता, अशैथिल्यं; 'of the eye-lids,' वर्त्मावबन्धः.

RIGIDLY, *adv.* दृढं, सुदृढं, स्तब्धं, स्तब्धतया, स्तब्धत्वेन, सकाठिन्यं, सदार्ढ्यं, सकार्कश्यं, कठोरं, कठिनं, अशिथिलं.

RIGMAROLE, *s.* अनर्थककथा, निरर्थककथा, असम्बद्धार्थिका दीर्घकथा.

RIGOR, *s.* (Stiffness) दृढता, कठिनता, कठोरता, काठिन्यं, *see* RIGIDITY.—(Severity) उग्रता, उग्रदण्डता -त्वं, कठोरता, कर्कशता, निष्ठुरता, नैष्ठुर्य्यं.—(Intensity) *see* the word.

RIGOROUS, *a.* (Severe) उग्रदण्डः -ण्डा -ण्डं, उग्रः -ग्रा -ग्रं, उग्रतदण्डः &c., कठोरः -रा -रं, निष्ठुरः -रा -रं, कठिनः -ना -नं, क्रूरः &c., कर्कशः -शा -शं.—(Exact) सूक्ष्मः -क्ष्मा -क्ष्मं. *See* STRICT.

RIGOROUSLY, *adv.* उग्रत्वेन, उग्रं, उग्रदण्डेन, कठोरं, निष्ठुरं, नैष्ठुर्य्येण.

RILL, *s.* अल्पनदी, क्षुद्रनदी, अल्पसरित् *f.*, सूक्ष्मसरित्, क्षुद्रसरित् *f.*

RIM, *s.* प्रान्तः, अन्तः, धार् -रा, प्रान्तभागः, अन्तभागः, उत्सङ्गः, पार्श्वः; 'of a cup,' पात्रप्रान्तः, पात्रकण्ठः, पात्रपार्श्वः.

RIME, *s.* तुषारः, नीहारः, कुज्झटिः *f.* -टिका. *See* HOAR-FROST.

RIMY, *a.* तुषारमयः -यी -यं, नीहारमयः &c., कुज्झटिकामयः &c.

RIND, *s.* त्वक् *f.* (च्), त्वचा, वल्कं -ल्कलं, शल्कं -ल्कलं, चर्म्म *n.* (न्), छल्लिः -ल्ली *f.*, शल्लकं, चोचं -चकं, चोलकं, चीरं, अण्डकोषः; 'having rind,' त्वचीयान् -यसी -यः (स्), त्वचिष्ठः -ष्ठा -ष्ठं.

RING, *s.* (Circle) मण्डलं, परिमण्डलं, चक्रं, चक्रवालं, वलयः -यं, वर्त्तुलः.—(Of metal) लोहचक्रं, लोहवलयः -यं; 'of a chain,' लोहलः.—(Ornament for the finger) अङ्गुलीयकं, अङ्गुरीयकं, अङ्गुरीयः -यं, अङ्गुलीकः -कं, ऊर्म्मिका, करारोटः, वालकः; 'seal-ring,' अङ्गुलिमुद्रा -द्रिका, मुद्रा, वेढिः -ढी *f.*; 'ring for the toes or feet,' नूपुरः, पादाङ्गदं, पादकटकः, मञ्जीरं; 'marriage-ring,' कौतुकं, मङ्गलसूत्रं, *see* MARRIAGE; 'sacred ring of kuśa grass worn during religious ceremonies,' पवित्रं -त्रकं.—(Circle of persons) मण्डलं; 'dancing in a ring,' मण्डलनृत्यं, हल्लीषं -षकं.—(Arena) रङ्गः.—(Ringing sound) क्वणितं, शिञ्जितं, क्वणः, घण्टाशिञ्जितं, घण्टाशब्दः, झनत्कारः, झञ्झा -ञ्झनं.

To RING, *v. a.* (Cause to ring or sound, as a bell) घण्टां वद् (c. 10. वादयति -यितुं) or क्वण् (c. 10. क्वाणयति -यितुं) or नद् (c. 10. नादयति -यितुं), घण्टाम् आहन् (c. 2. -हन्ति -न्तुं), घण्टाक्वणनं कृ, घण्टावादनं कृ.

To RING, *v. n.* (Sound, as a bell) क्वण् (c. 1. क्वणति -णितुं), शिञ्ज् (c. 2. शिंक्ते, c. 1. शिञ्जते -ञ्जितुं), विशिञ्ज्, किङ्किणा (nom. किङ्किणायते), ध्वन् (c. 1. ध्वनति -नितुं), झण्ड् (c. 1. झण्डति -ण्डितुं), झञ्झा (nom. झञ्झायते), क्वणितं कृ, शिञ्जितं कृ, झनत्कारं कृ, घण्टावत् शब्दं कृ.

RINGED, *a.* (Fitted with rings) साङ्गुलीयः -या -यं, सवलयः -या -यं.

RINGER, *s.* घण्टावादकः, घण्टाघाती *m.* (न्), घण्टाताडकः.

RINGING, *s.* घण्टावादनं, क्वणनं, क्वणितं, शिञ्जितं, झञ्झनं, झनत्कारः.

RING-LEADER, *s.* मुख्यः, मुखरः, प्रमुखः, प्रवर्त्तकः, प्रयोजकः, नायकः.

RINGLET, *s.* अलकः, अलकान्तः, कर्कारालः, कुरलः. *See* CURL.

RING-WORM, *s.* कोठः, दद्रुः *m.*, दद्रूः *m.*, गजकर्णी, खर्जूः *f.*

To RINSE, *v. a.* (Wash out the mouth) आचम् (c. 1. -चामति -चमितुं), आचमनं कृ, जलम् or उदकम् उपस्पृश् (c. 6. -स्पृशति -स्प्रष्टुं), उपस्पर्शं कृ, गण्डूषं कृ, शुषिप्रणीं कृ.—(Cleanse by the introduction of water) जलं निक्षिप्य शुध् (c. 10. शोधयति -यितुं) or प्रक्षल् or परिमृज्; 'one who has rinsed his mouth,' आचान्तः.

RINSING, *s.* (The mouth) आचमनं, आचाम्यं, उपस्पर्शः, गण्डूषः, शुषिप्रणीः *f.*; 'water for rinsing the mouth,' आचमनीयं, आचाम्यं.

RIOT, *s.* (Tumult, uproar) तुमुलं, कोलाहलः, डिम्बः, डिम्बाहवः, डमरः, डामरः, विप्लवः, आहवः, कालकीलः, सम्भ्रमः, चमत्कारः.—(Popular disturbance) प्रकृतिक्षोभः, प्रजाक्षोभः, प्रकृतियुद्धं, ग्रामयुद्धं, ग्राममद्गुरिका.—(Noisy festivity) अतिशयशब्देन or अतिशयतुमुलेन उत्सवकरणं, *see* REVEL.—(To run riot) मर्य्यादाम् अतिक्रम् or लङ्घ्.

To RIOT, *v. n.* (Raise an uproar) तुमुलं कृ, कोलाहलं कृ, डिम्बं कृ, विप्लवं कृ.—(Revel) अतिशयशब्देन or अतिशयतुमुलेन उत्सवं कृ.

RIOTER, *s.* तुमुलकारी *m.* (न्), डिम्बकारी *m.*, क्षोभकारी *m.*, क्षोभकृत् *m.*

RIOTOUS, *a.* तुमुलकारी -रिणी -रि (न्), कोलाहलकारी &c., डिम्बकारी &c., महाशब्दकारी &c., क्षोभकारी &c., महाशब्देन or अतिशयतुमुलेन उत्सवकारी &c.

RIOTOUSLY, *adv.* अतिशयतुमुलेन, अतितुमुलेन, कोलाहलेन, महाशब्देन.

To RIP, *v. a.* (Tear) दृ (c. 10. दारयति -यितुं), विदृ, पट् (c. 10. पाटयति -यितुं), विपट्, विभिद्, निकृत्, विनिकृत्, विदारणं कृ; 'ripping open,' विदार्य्य.

RIP, *s.* विदारः -रणं -णा, विदरः, पाटनं, विपाटनं, विभेदः.

RIPE, *a.* (As fruit, &c.) पक्वः -क्वा -क्वं, परिपक्वः &c., पक्त्रिमः -मा -मं, विपक्त्रिमः &c., सुपक्वः -क्वा -क्वं, पाकिमः -मा -मं, पक्वतापन्नः -न्ना -न्नं, पक्वदशापन्नः &c., पक्वदशाप्राप्तः -प्ता -प्तं, परिणतः -ता -तं, पाकोन्मुखः -खा -खं, फलोन्मुखः &c., विनाशोन्मुखः &c., शृतः -ता -तं.—(Brought to perfection, complete) सिद्धः -द्धा -द्धं, सम्पन्नः -न्ना -न्नं, व्युत्पन्नः &c., प्रौढः -ढा -ढं.—(In years, &c.) प्रवृद्धः -द्धा -द्धं, वृद्धः &c., प्रौढः &c.—(Ready) उद्यतः -ता -तं, उन्मुख in comp., *see* READY.

To RIPEN, *v. n.* पक्वः -क्वा -क्वं भू, परिपक्वः -क्वा -क्वं भू, पच् in pass. (पच्यते), परिपच्, पक्वीभू, पक्वतां गम्. *See To* MATURE, *v. n.*

To RIPEN, *v. a.* पच् (c. 1. पचति, पक्तुं, c. 10. पाचयति -यितुं), पक्वं -क्वां कृ, परिपक्वं -क्वां कृ, पक्वीकृ, पाकं कृ or जन्. *See To* MATURE, *v. a.*

RIPENED, *p. p.* पक्वः -क्वा -क्वं, परिपक्वः &c., परिणतः &c., *see* MATURED.

RIPENING, *part.* (Making ripe) पाचकः -का -कं, पाचनः -ना -नं, परिपाकी -किणी &c.—(Becoming ripe) पच्यमानः -ना -नं, परिपच्यमानः &c.

RIPENESS, *s.* पाकः, परिपाकः, पक्वता -त्वं, परिपक्वता, पक्तिः *f.*, विपाकः, पक्वभावः, पक्वदशा, पक्वावस्था, परिणामः, परिणतिः *f.*, परिणतता. *See* MATURITY.

RIPPED, *p. p.* विदारितः -ता -तं, विदीर्णः -र्णा -र्णं, विपाटितः &c.

RIPPLE, *s.* वीचिः -ची *f.*, वीचिका, ऊर्म्मिः -र्म्मी *f.*, ऊर्म्मिका, सूक्ष्मोर्म्मिः, भङ्गिः *f.*

To RIPPLE, *v. n.* चलोर्म्मिः -र्म्मिः -र्म्मि भू, चलवीचिः -चिः -चि भू, ऊर्म्मिमान् -मती -मत् भू, सवीचिः -चिः -चि भू, वीचिभङ्गुरः -रा -रं भू.

To RIPPLE, *v. a.* वीचियुक्तं -क्तां कृ, वीचिमन्तं -मतीं -मत् कृ, चलवीचिं कृ.

RIPPLING, *part.* चलोर्म्मिः -र्म्मिः -र्म्मि, चलवीचिः &c., वीचिमाली -लिनी &c.

To RISE, *v. n.* (Get up) उत्था (c. 1. उत्तिष्ठति -थातुं, rt. स्था), समुत्था; 'he rose from his seat,' आसनाद् उदस्थात् or उदतिष्ठत्; 'from bed,' शयनाद् उत्था, शयनं or शय्यां त्यज्, सुप्तोत्थितः -ता -तं भू.—(Move upward, ascend) ऊर्द्ध्वं गम् (c. 1. गच्छति, गन्तुं), उद्गम्, समुद्गम्, उच्चैर् गम्, उच्चैर् व्रज् (c. 1. व्रजति -जितुं), उदि (c. 1. उदयति c. 2. उदेति -तुं, rt. इ), समुदि, अभ्युदि, उत्पत् (c. 1. -पतति -तितुं), ऊर्द्ध्वम् आक्रम् (c. 1. -क्रमते -मितुं), आक्रम्, उद्वृत् (c. 1. -वर्त्तते -र्त्तितुं), आरुह् (c. 1. -रोहति -रोढुं), उच्चर् (c. 1. -चरति -रितुं), ऊर्द्ध्वगतः -ता -तं भू, उन्नतः -ता -तं भू, आरोहणं कृ; 'the sun rises,' उदयति सूर्य्यः. The mountain behind which the heavenly bodies are supposed by the Hindus to rise is called उदयः, उदयपर्वतः &c., *see* MOUNTAIN.—(Become erect) उन्नम् (c. 1. -नमति -नन्तुं), उन्नतः -ता -तं भू, समुन्नम्, उत्था.—(Appear) दृश् in pass. (-दृश्यते), लक्ष् in pass., उत्पद् in pass., प्रतिभा (c. 2. -भाति -तुं), उद्भा, निर्भा, प्रभू, आविर्भू, प्रादुर्भू, आत्मानं दृश् in caus.—(Originate, issue, take rise) उत्पद् (c. 4. -पद्यते -पत्तुं), समुत्पद्, जन् (c. 4. जायते, जनितुं), प्रजन्, उपजन्, प्रभू, उद्भू, सम्भू, प्रसृ (c. 1. -सरति -सर्त्तुं), निःसृ, विनिःसृ, उद्गम्, निर्गम्, प्रवृत् (c. 1. -वर्त्तते -र्त्तितुं), उदि, उत्पन्नः -न्ना -न्नं भू.—(Increase) वृध् (c. 1. वर्धते -र्धितुं), प्रवृध्, अधिकीभू, अधिकतरीभू, अधिकतरः -रा -रं भू, उत्तरोत्तरं वृध्.—(Be excited) उद्दीप्तः -प्ता -प्तं भू, उद्दीप् (c. 4. -दीप्यते -दीपितुं), उत्पद् in pass.—(From death) श्मशानाद् उत्था or समुत्था; 'all the dead rose,' सर्व्वे मृता उदतिष्ठन्.—(To heaven) स्वर्गारोहणं कृ.—(Be promoted) प्रतिपत्तिं or पदवृद्धिं प्राप्, श्रेष्ठपदे or उत्कृष्टपदे नियुक्तः -क्ता -क्तं भू.—(As the sea) क्षुभ् : -आ -भं भू.

RISE, *s.* (Getting up) उत्थानं, समुत्थानं, उत्थितिः *f.*—(Moving upwards, ascent) ऊर्द्ध्वगमनं, ऊर्द्ध्वगतिः *f.*, उद्गमः -मनं, समुद्गमः -मनं, उन्नतिः *f.*, उदयः -यनं, समुदयः, उद्वर्त्तनं, समुत्क्रमः, उत्पातः, उत्पतनं; 'falls and rises,' पातोत्पाताः *m. pl.*; 'rise of the sun,' सूर्य्योदयः.—(Origin, production) उत्पत्तिः *f.*, उद्भवः, उद्गमः, सम्भवः, प्रभवः, प्रवृत्तिः *f.*, मूलं, आरम्भः, आगमः, उपक्रमः, उपस्थितिः *f.*, उपस्थानं.—(Promotion) पदवृद्धिः *f.*, प्रतिपत्तिः *f.*—(Increase) वृद्धिः *f.*, प्रवृद्धिः *f.*, वर्धनं.—(To give rise to) उत्पद् (c. 10. -पादयति -यितुं), समुत्पद्, जन् (c. 10. जनयति -यितुं).

RISEN, *p. p.* उत्थितः -ता -तं, अभ्युत्थितः &c., समुत्थितः &c., उन्नतः -ता -तं, समुन्नतः &c., प्रत्युन्नतः &c., उदितः &c., समुदितः &c., अभ्युदितः &c., उत्पतितः -ता -तं, समुत्पतितः &c., ऊर्द्ध्वगतः &c., उद्वर्त्तितः &c., उद्भूतः -ता -तं; 'from bed or sleep,' शयनोत्थितः -ता -तं, सुप्तोत्थितः &c., त्यक्तशय्यः -य्या -य्यं, त्यक्ततल्पः -ल्पा -ल्पं.

RISIBILITY, *s.* हसनशीलता, हसनशक्तिः *f.*, हसनेच्छा, हसनसामर्थ्यं.

RISIBLE, *a.* हसनशीलः -ला -लं, हसनशक्तिकः -का -कं, हसनसमर्थः &c.

RISING, *s.* (Getting up) उत्थानं, समुत्थानं, उत्थितिः *f.*, समुत्थितिः *f.*, अभ्युत्थानं; 'from a seat,' आसनादुत्थानं; 'from bed,' शयनादुत्थानं; 'rising to receive a visitor,' प्रत्युत्थानं, प्रत्युद्गमः -मनं, अभ्युत्थानं.—(Ascent, going upwards) उदयः -यनं, उद्गमः, उन्नतिः *f.*, ऊर्द्ध्वगमनं, ऊर्द्ध्वगतिः *f.*, समुदयः, अभ्युदयः, समुद्गमः, उत्पतनं, समुत्पतनं, उत्पातः, उद्वर्त्तनं, आरोहः -हणं; 'of the sun,' सूर्य्योदयः; 'of a planet,' उच्छ्रयः; 'of a sign,' लग्नं, होरा.—(Insurrection) प्रजाक्षोभः, प्रकृतिक्षोभः.—(Tumor), *see* the word.

RISING, *part.* उदयी -यिनी -यि (न्), उदयमानः -ना -नं, उत्पतन् -तन्ती -तत् (त्), उत्पतिता -त्री -तृ (तृ), उत्पतिष्णुः -ष्णुः -ष्णु, उदितः -ता -तं; 'rising sun,' प्रथमोदितसूर्य्यः; 'warmth of it,' प्रथमोदितादित्यतापः.

RISING-GROUND, *s.* उन्नतभूभागः, उन्नतभूमिभागः, उच्चभूभागः, उच्चस्थानं.

RISK, *s.* संशयः, शङ्का, सन्देहः, विकल्पः, भयं, भयहेतुः *m.*, सङ्कटं; 'of life,' जीवितसंशयः, *see* JEOPARDY, PERIL, DANGER.

To RISK, *v. a.* संशयस्थं -स्थां कृ, सन्देहस्थं -स्थां कृ, शङ्कास्थं -स्थां कृ, शङ्कास्पदीकृ, शङ्कास्पदं कृ. *See To* JEOPARD, HAZARD.

RISKED, *p. p.* संशयितः -ता -तं, शङ्कास्पदीकृतः &c., सन्देहास्पदीकृतः &c.

RITE, *s.* (Religious observance) क्रिया, विधिः *m.*, विधानं, कर्म्म *n.* (न्), देवकर्म्म *n.*, दैवकर्म्म *n.*, देवक्रिया, दैवक्रिया, देवकार्य्यं, दैवकार्य्यं, संस्कारः, नियमः, रीतिः *f.*, कल्पः, संविधानं, आचारः, आचरणं, शास्त्रविधानं, शास्त्रविधिः *m.*, शास्त्रकर्म्म *n.*, शास्त्रोक्तकर्म्म *n.*, शास्त्रविधानं, शास्त्रविधिः *m.*, अनुष्ठानं, व्रतं, यमः, नियामः; 'marriage rite,' विवाहविधिः *m.*, *see* MARRIAGE; 'funeral rite,' उत्तरक्रिया, अन्त्यक्रिया, अन्तसत्क्रिया, मृतशरीरसत्कर्म्म *n.* (न्), *see* OBSEQUIES, FUNERAL; 'rite of investiture with the sacrificial thread,' उपनयनं, *see* INVESTITURE; 'rite of oblation to the manes,' पितृकर्म्म *n.*, पितृक्रिया, *see* MANES. The following are the sanskáras, or rites purificatory of the bodies of the three classes in this life, and qualifying them for the next, explained in Manu Bk. 2. 27 *et seq.*: 1. Sacrifice on conception, गर्भाधानं. 2. On the quickening of the fœtus, पुंसवनं. 3. A rite consisting of partition and arrangement of the hair of the mother in the fourth, sixth, or eighth month of gestation, सीमन्तोन्नयनं. 4. Giving the new-born infant honey and clarified butter out of a golden spoon, before separating the navel-string, जातकर्म्म *n.* 5. Naming the child on the tenth or twelfth day after birth, नामकर्म्म *n.* or नामकरणं. 6. Carrying the child out to see the sun in the fourth month after birth, निष्क्रमणं. 7. Feeding the child with boiled rice in the sixth month after birth, or on the cutting of the first tooth, अन्नप्राशनं. 8. Tonsure, or shaving the head all but one lock, in the first or third year after birth, चूडाकर्म्म *n.* or चूडाकरणं or चूडाकार्य्यं. 9. Investiture with a peculiar thread or cord, called the sacrificial thread, worn over the left shoulder and under the right, performed on youths of the three classes at ages varying from eight to sixteen, from eleven to twenty-two, and from twelve to twenty-four, respectively, उपनयनं. 10. Cutting off the hair entirely, performed on Brahmans at sixteen on Kshatriyas at twenty-two, and on Vaiśyas at twenty-four years of age, केशान्तः. 11. Ceremony performed by youths of the first class on returning from the house of their preceptor to that of their natural parents, समावर्त्तनं. 12. Marriage, in the thirty-sixth or eighteenth year, विवाहः.—(Inauspicious rite) अशुभकर्म्म *n.* (न्), अशुभकार्य्यं; 'rites and ceremonies,' आचारविचाराः *m. pl.*; 'performing a rite,' क्रियानुष्ठानं; 'mode of performing a rite,' क्रियाविधिः *m.*, प्रयोगः.

RITUAL, *a.* (Pertaining to rites, consisting of them) वैधिकः -की -कं, वैधः -धी -धं, विधि in comp., विधिरूपः -पा -पं, विधिमयः -यी -यं, विध्युक्तः -क्ता -क्तं, विधिसम्बन्धी -न्धिनी &c., विधिविषयकः -का -कं, क्रियासम्बन्धी &c., क्रियाविषयकः &c., क्रिया in comp., शास्त्रोक्तः -क्ता -क्तं, आचारिकः -की -कं, कल्प्यः -ल्पी -ल्पं.

RITUAL, *s.* क्रियापद्धतिः -ती, संस्कारपद्धतिः *f.*, कर्म्मपद्धतिः *f.*, विधिपद्धतिः *f.*, विधानपद्धतिः *f.*, पद्धतिः -ती, संस्कारशास्त्रं, विधिशास्त्रं, क्रियाविधिः *m.*, विधिः *m.*

RITUALIST, *s.* क्रियाविधिज्ञः, संस्कारशास्त्रज्ञः, क्रियावान् *m.* (त्).

RIVAL, *s.* स्पर्धी *m.* (न्), प्रतिस्पर्धी *m.*, प्रतियोगी *m.* (न्), प्रतिपक्षः, सपत्नः, विजिगीषुः *m.*, जिगीषुः *m.*, *see* RIVAL, *a.*; 'a kingdom without a rival,' असपत्नं राज्यं; 'a rival wife,' सपत्नी.

RIVAL, *a.* स्पर्धी -र्धिनी -र्धि (न्), विस्पर्धी &c., प्रतिस्पर्धी &c., परिस्पर्धी &c., प्रतियोगी &c., विजिगीषुः -षुः -षु, जिगीषुः &c., परस्परविजिगीषुः &c., परस्पराभिभवेच्छुः -च्छुः -च्छु, एकार्थेच्छुः &c., एकार्थाभिलाषी &c., एकार्थी &c., एकार्थदृष्टिः -ष्टिः -ष्टि, एकार्थप्रवृत्तः -त्ता -त्तं, एकार्थोद्युक्तः -क्ता -क्तं, संघर्षी &c., परस्परसंघर्षी &c., जयेच्छुः &c., अभिभवेच्छुः &c.

To RIVAL, *v. a.* स्पर्ध् (c. 1. स्पर्धते -र्धितुं), विस्पर्ध्, प्रतिस्पर्ध्, आस्पर्ध् with instr. c., जि in des. (जिगीषति -षितुं), विजि in des., पराभिभवनाय or परस्पराभिभवनाय यत् (c. 1. यतते -तितुं) or उद्योगं कृ, परजयार्थं यत्, परस्परं संघृष् (c. 1. -घर्षति -र्षितुं), एकार्थम् अभिलष् or आकांक्ष्, एकार्थप्रापणाय यत्; 'he rivals Indra,' शक्रेण or शक्रेण सह स्पर्धते; 'one who rivals the beauty of the moon,' चन्द्रच्छायापरिस्पर्धी.

RIVALING, RIVALLING, *part.* स्पर्धी -र्धिनी &c. *See* RIVAL, *a.*

RIVALRY, *s.* स्पर्धा or स्पर्द्धा, प्रतिस्पर्धा, आस्पर्धा, जिगीषा, विजिगीषा, प्रतियोगिता -त्वं, प्रतिपक्षता -त्वं, सापत्न्यं, सपत्नत्वं, संघर्षः, परस्परसंघर्षः, पराभिभवेच्छा, परस्पराभिभवेच्छा, परस्पराभिभवनाय उद्योगः, परजयेच्छा, परस्परजयेच्छा, एकार्थाभिलाषः, एकार्थाकांक्षा, एकार्थप्रापणाय परस्परोद्योगः, एकार्थदृष्टिः *f.*, एकार्थप्रवृत्तिः *f.*, अहम्पूर्व्विका.

RIVEN, *p. p.* विदीर्णः -र्णा -र्णं, विदारितः -ता -तं, छिन्नः -न्ना -न्नं, विभिन्नः &c.

RIVER, *s.* नदी, सरित् *f.*, सिन्धुः *f.*, आपगा, निम्नगा, स्रोतस् *n.*, कुल्या, स्रोतोवहा, स्रोतोवहा, स्रोतस्वती, स्रोतस्विनी, पयस्विनी, स्रवन्ती, द्रवन्ती, समुद्रगा, जलधिगा, सागरगामिनी, तरङ्गिणी, तटिनी, शैवलिनी, ह्रदिनी, ह्रादिनी, पर्वतजा, रोधोवक्रा, रोधवक्रा, समुद्रदयिता, समुद्रकान्ता, कूलवती, कूलङ्कषा, धुनी, धेना, जम्बालिनी, द्वीपवती, निर्झरिणी, उद्मः, नदः. This last is applied only to a river of which the personification is male, as the Indus सिन्धुः, Brahmaputra ब्रह्मपुत्रः, Sona शोणः, हिरण्यबाहुः; 'bed of a river,' नदीपात्रं, नदीमातृकं; 'bank of a river,' नदीतीरं, नदीकूलं; 'current,' नदीवेगः, नदीरयः, नदीवेला; 'water of a river,' सरिज्जलं; 'source,' सरिन्मुखं; 'mouth,' सिन्धुसङ्गमः, सम्भेदः; 'watered by rivers,' नदीमातृकः -का -कं, जलमातृकः &c.; 'one who knows the course of rivers,' नदीज्ञः; 'bathing in a river,' नदीस्नः -स्ना -स्नं; 'the bend of a river,' नदीवङ्कः; 'relating to a river,' नादेयः -यी -यं.—(River of heaven), स्वर्णदी, सुरनदी, *see* GANGES, MILKY-WAY.

RIVET, *s.* कीलः -लकः, लोहकीलकः, सूक्ष्मकीलकः, शलाका.

To RIVET, *v. a.* (Fasten with a rivet) कील् (c. 10. कीलयति -यितुं), कीलकेन बन्ध् (c. 9. बध्नाति, बन्द्धुं), कीलकबद्धं -द्धां कृ.—(Fix or fasten firmly) दृढं बन्ध्, दृढीकृ; 'to rivet the attention,' चित्ताभिनिवेशं कृ or जन्, अभिनिविष्टचित्तं -त्तां कृ.

RIVETED, *p. p.* कीलकबद्धः -द्धा -द्धं, कीलितः -ता -तं, दृढीकृतः -ता -तं; 'having the attention riveted,' अभिनिविष्टचित्तः -त्ता -त्तं; 'by sound,' नादलुब्धः &c.

RIVULET, *s.* अल्पनदी, क्षुद्रनदी, अल्पसरित् *f.*, क्षुद्रसरित् *f.*, अल्पाम्भस् *n.*, अल्पस्रोतस् *n.*, क्षुद्रस्रोतस् *n.*, कुसरित् *f.*

ROAD, *s.* मार्गः, पथः, पन्थाः *m.* (पथिन्), अध्वा *m.* (न्), वर्त्म *n.* (न्), वर्त्मनिः -नी *f.*, अयनं, वर्त्तनं -नी, वर्त्तनिः *f.*, सरणिः -णी *f.*, सृतिः *f.*, पदविः -वी, पद्धतिः -ती *f.*, पद्या, पद्वा *m.* (न्), पद्वः, उपनिष्क्रमणं, सञ्चरः, एकपदी, एकपाद्, तरः, वीथिः *f.*, शरणिः *f.*, माथः, माठः, माठ्यः, प्रपाथः, पित्सलं, सुक्रमः; 'public road, high road,' राजमार्गः, राजपथः, महापथः, महावर्त्म *n.*; 'a good road,' सुपथः, सुपन्थाः *m.*, अतिपन्थाः *m.*, सत्पथः, सन्मार्गः; 'a bad road,' कुपथः, कुमार्गः, कापथः, विपथः, कदध्वा *m.* (न्), दुरध्वः, व्यध्वः; 'a wrong road,' विमार्गः, उन्मार्गः, विपथः, उत्पथः; 'unbeaten road,' अक्षुण्णमार्गः; 'a common road,' प्रचारः; 'difficult road,' दुर्गः, दुर्गमार्गः, दुर्गसञ्चरः, दुर्गमवर्त्म *n.*, कान्तारः -रं; 'long and lonesome road,' प्रान्तरं, शून्यमार्गः; 'place where four roads meet,' चतुष्पथं, शृङ्गाटं -टकं; 'where three roads meet,' त्रिकं; 'the want of a road,' अपथं, अपन्थाः *m.*; 'road-side,' मार्गपार्श्वः; 'on the road-side,' मार्गपार्श्वे; 'on the road,' पथि, मार्गमध्ये, अध्वनि, अध्वमध्ये.

To ROAM, *v. n.*, भ्रम् (c. 4. भ्राम्यति, भ्रमितुं), परिभ्रम्, अट् (c. 1. अटति -ते -टितुं), पर्यट्, विचर् (c. 1. -चरति -रितुं), संचर्, इतस्ततो भ्रम् or चर् or विहृ (c. 1. -हरति -हर्तुं), गाह् (c. 1. गाहते -हितुं), भ्रमणं कृ, परिभ्रमणं कृ, विहारं कृ; 'as a mendicant,' परिव्रज्, व्रज्.

ROAMING, *s.* भ्रमणं, परिभ्रमणं, इतस्ततो भ्रमणं, नानादिग्भ्रमणं, विहारः, विहरणं, अटनं, पर्यटनं, अटाट्या; 'as of a religious mendicant,' व्रज्या, परिव्रज्या, व्रजनं, व्रजितं.

ROAMING, *part.* भ्राम्यन् -म्यन्ती -म्यत् (त्), भ्रमन् &c., परिभ्रमन्, भ्रमणकारी -रिणी -रि (न्), अटमानः -ना -नं, विहारी &c., परिव्रजन् &c., व्रज्यावान् -वती, वत् (त्).

ROAN, *a.* (Horse) शुक्लबिन्दुचित्रितो नीलवर्णाश्वः or श्यामवर्णाश्वः.

To ROAR, *v. n.* (Make a loud continued sound) गर्ज् (c. 1. गर्जति -र्जितुं), परिगर्ज्, नर्द् (c. 1. नर्दति -र्दितुं), विनर्द्, रु (c. 2. रौति, रवितुं), विरु, संरु, रस्, वाश्, रद्, गज्, हम्भ् (nom. हम्भायते -यितुं), हुङ्कृ, हूङ्कृ, हुङ्कारं कृ, अनुहुङ्कृ, गर्जनं कृ.—(Cry out, bawl) नद् (c. 1. नदति -दितुं), विनद्, प्रणद्, उत्क्रुश् (c. 1. -क्रोशति -क्रोष्टुं), विक्रुश्, प्रक्रुश्, चित्कारं कृ, चीत्कारं कृ, चीत् शब्दं कृ, घुष्, प्रक्ष्विड् (c. 1. क्ष्वेडति -डितुं), नादं कृ; 'from pain,' आर्त्तनादं कृ.

ROAR, ROARING, *s.* (Loud continued sound) गर्जनं -ना, गर्जितं, परिगर्जनं, नर्दनं, नर्दितं, रावः, विरावः, दीर्घध्वनिः *m.*, दीर्घरावः, दीर्घरुतं, दीर्घनिर्घोषः, रासः, हम्भा, हम्भारावः, घनध्वनिः *m.*, गम्भीरशब्दः, गम्भीरध्वनिः *m.*, हुङ्कारः, हुङ्कृतं, हुङ्कृतिः *f.*, फूत्कारः, फुत्कारः, घर्घरितं.—(Crying out) नादः, उत्क्रोशः, चित्कारः, चीत्कारः, घोषः, निर्घोषः, उद्घोषः, उत्क्रुष्टं, विक्रुष्टं, क्ष्वेडितं, प्रक्ष्वेडितं.—(Of a lion) सिंहनादः -दकः, सिंहध्वनिः *m.*, सिंहनर्दः -र्दनं.—(Of the clouds) मेघनिर्घोषः, घनध्वनिः *m.*, मेघनादः, मेघगर्जनं, घनशब्दः, घनस्वनः.—(Of the sea) समुद्रनादः, महार्णवस्वनः.

ROARING, *part.* गर्जन् -र्जन्ती -र्जत् (त्), गर्जनकारी -रिणी -रि (न्), नर्दन् &c., विनर्दन् &c., नर्दी &c., नर्दमानः -ना -नं, नादी &c., रावी -विणी &c.; 'like a lion,' सिंहनर्दी &c., सिंहनादी &c.

To ROAST, *v. a.* भ्रस्ज् (c. 1. भृज्जति -ते, भष्टुं, भर्ष्टुं), भृज् (c. 1. भर्जते -र्जितुं), पच् (c. 1. पचति, पक्तुं); 'on a spit,' शूले आरोप्य or समारोप्य पच्, शूलाकृ, भटित्रीकृ, भटित्रं -त्रां कृ, शूलाकृत्य पच् or संस्कृ or सिद्धीकृ.—(Heat) तप्, दह्.

ROASTED, ROAST, *a.* भृष्टः -ष्टा -ष्टं, भ्रष्टः &c., भर्जितः -ता -तं, पाचितः -ता -तं, परिपाचितः &c., अङ्गारपरिपाचितः &c.; 'on a spit,' शूलाकृतः -ता -तं, शूल्यः -ल्या -ल्यं, भटित्रः -त्रा -त्रं; 'roast meat,' शूलिकं, शूल्यं, शूल्यमांसं, भटित्रं.

ROASTING, *s.* भर्जनं, पाचनं, अङ्गारपरिपाचनं, शूलाकरणं.

To ROB, *v. a.* धनद्रव्यादि हृ (c. 1. हरति, हर्तुं) or अपहृ or अभिहृ, चुर् (c. 10. चोरयति -यितुं), स्तेन् (c. 10. स्तेनयति -यितुं), मुष् (c. 9. मुष्णाति, मोषितुं), परिमुष्, प्रमुष्, लुण्ठ्, लुण्ट्, कल्, लुप्, विलुप्. *See To* STEAL, PLUNDER.

ROBBED, *p. p.* हृतधनः -ना -नं, हृतद्रव्यः -व्या -व्यं, अपहृतद्रव्यः &c., हृतस्वः -स्वा -स्वं, लुण्ठितः -ता -तं, मुषितः -ता -तं, अपहारितः &c.

ROBBER, *s.* चौरः, प्रसह्यचौरः, दस्युः *m.*, धनहारी *m.* (न्) धनहर्त्ता *m.* (र्तृ), अपहारकः, अपहारी *m.* (न्), अभिहर्त्ता *m.*, परस्वापहारी *m.*, धनहरः, स्तेनः, साहसिकः, तस्करः, लुण्टाकः, स्तेयकृत् *m.*, स्तेयकारी *m.*, परास्कन्दी *m.*, रजनीचरः, निशाचरः, मोषकः, परिमोषी *m.*, मायलः, वटाधीकः, प्रतिरोधी *m.* (न्), प्रतिरोधकः.

ROBBERY, *s.* चौर्य्यं, स्तेयं, चौरिका, चौरत्वं, स्तैन्यं, अपहारः, धनापहारः -रणं, अपहरणं, अपहारणं, धनापहरणं, अभिहारः, अभ्याहारः, धनाभिहारः, अभिग्रहणं, हरणं, धनहरणं, परस्वहरणं, परस्वापहरणं, लुण्ठनं, लुण्टनं, मोषणं, मुष्टं, तास्कर्य्यं, साहसं.

ROBE, *s.* वसनं, मानवसनं, वस्त्रं, मानवस्त्रं, मानपरिच्छदः, मानसूचकवस्त्रं,

सभावस्त्रं, सभावसनं, उत्कृष्टवस्त्रं, राजकीयवस्त्रं, राजवस्त्रं, राजवसनं.

To ROBE, *v. a.* or *n.* **वसनं** or **वस्त्रं परिधा, मानवस्त्रं परिधा.** *See To* DRESS.

ROBED, *p. p.* **सुवस्त्रवेष्टितः -ता -तं, मानवस्त्रवेष्टितः** &c., **सवसनः -ना -नं.**

ROBUST, *a.* **दृढाङ्गः -ङ्गा -ङ्गं, दृढशरीरः -रा -रं, मांसलः -ला -लं, वज्रदेहः -हा -हं, दृढदेहः** &c., **व्यूढोरस्कः -स्का -स्कं, पृथुशरीरः -रा -रं, उरस्वान् -स्वती -स्वत् (त्), उरसिलः -ला -लं, बलवान्** &c., **महाबाहुः** &c., *see* LUSTY; 'to be robust,' **उरस्** (nom. **उरस्यति**).

ROBUSTLY, *adv.* **मांसलवत्, बलवत्, महाबलेन, सवीर्य्यं, ससत्त्वं, सबलं.**

ROBUSTNESS, *s.* **दृढाङ्गता, मांसलता -त्वं, शरीरदृढता, वीर्य्यं.** *See* LUSTINESS.

ROCK, *s.* **शिला, स्थूलपाषाणः, स्थूलप्रस्तरः, स्थूलोपलः, बृहदुपलः, बृहत्पाषाणः, बृहदश्मा** *m.* (**न्**), **स्थूलदृषद्** *f.*, **पाषाणः, अश्मा** *m.* (**न्**), **प्रस्तरः, दृषद्** *f.*, **उपलः, ग्रावा** *m.* (**न्**), **शैलः, जलघूपलः, निश्चलाङ्गः, काठः, कूपकः, कूपिका, पारारुकः, परारुकः, पारटीटः**; 'a rock fallen from a height,' **गण्डशैलः**; 'hard as a rock,' **शिलाघनः -ना -नं, शिलादृढः -ढा -ढं, शैलसारः -रा -रं.**

To ROCK, *v. a.* **इतस्ततः प्रचल्** (c. 10. **-चालयति -यितुं**) or **संचल्** or **विचल्** or **चल्, आन्दोलनं कृ, आन्दोल्** (c. 10. **आन्दोलयति -यितुं**).

To ROCK, *v. n.* **इतस्ततो विचल्** (c. 1. **-चलति -लितुं**) or **प्रचल्, दोल्.** *See To* REEL.

ROCKED, *p. p.* **इतस्ततो विचालितः -ता -तं** or **सञ्चालितः** &c., **प्रचलायितः** &c.

ROCKET, *s.* **अग्निवाणः, सधूपः, भुशुण्डी, शतघ्नी, तारा.**

ROCKING, *part.* or *a.* **दोलायमानः -ना -नं, इतस्ततो विचलमानः -ना -नं.**

ROCK-SALT, *s.* **सिन्धुलवणं, सिन्धुजं, सिन्धूद्भवं, सिन्धुमन्थजं, सिन्धूपलं, सिन्धुजन्म** *n.* (**न्**), **सितशिवं.**

ROCKY, *a.* **शैलः -ली -लं, शिलेयः -यी -यं, शिलामयः -यी -यं, शैलमयः** &c., **शिलापूर्णः -र्णा -र्णं, शिलावान् -वती -वत् (त्), अश्मरः -रा -रं, अश्ममयः** &c., **आश्मनः -नी -नं, दार्षदः -दी -दं, औपलः -ली -लं, प्रस्तरमयः** &c., **उपलपूर्णः** &c.

ROD, *s.* **दण्डः, वेत्रं, यष्टिः** *m. f.*, **वेणुः** *m.*, **वेणुदलं, शलाका, शल्यं**; 'metallic rod,' **लोहदण्डः, लोहयष्टिः** *m. f.*—(For punishing) **दण्डः, ताडनी, वेणुः** *m.*, **वेणुदलं.**

RODOMONTADE, *s.* **गर्वितवाक्यं, दाम्भिकवाक्यं, शून्यकथा.** *See* RANT.

ROE, *s.* (Female deer) **हरिणी, मृगी, मृगवधूः** *f.*—(Of fish) **मीनाण्डं.**

ROGUE, *s.* **धूर्त्तः, कितवः, वञ्चकः, प्रवञ्चकः, कूटकः, कूटकारः, शठः, प्रतारकः, तस्करः, कुहकः, कपटिकः, छिद्रवरः, कैरवः, चाटः, शोठः, स्थगः, शङ्करीकः, पिशुनः.**

ROGUERY, ROGUISHNESS, *s.* **धूर्त्तता, कैतवं, कूटता, तस्करता, तस्करविद्या, तास्कर्य्यं, शठता, शाठ्यं, वञ्चनं, कपटः, वञ्चकता, पैशुन्यं, पैशुनं, दण्डाजिनं.**

ROGUISH, *a.* **धूर्त्तः -र्त्ता -र्त्तं, शठः -ठा -ठं, कितवः** &c. *See* KNAVISH.

To ROLL, *v. a.* (Cause to turn or revole) **लुट्** (c. 10. **लोटयति -यितुं**), **प्रलुठ्, आवृत्** (c. 10. **-वर्त्तयति -यितुं**), **व्यावृत्, अनुवृत्, विवृत्, भ्रम्** (c. 10. **भ्रमयति -यितुं**), **संसृ** (c. 10. **-सारयति -यितुं**), **सृ, संचल्** (c. 10. **-चालयति -यितुं**), **घूर्ण्** (c. 10. **घूर्णयति -यितुं**), **परिघूर्ण्**; 'he rolls the wheel along the ground,' **चक्रम् अनुवर्त्तयति भूमौ**; 'to roll back,' **पश्चाद् अनुवृत्, पश्चाद् वृत्, व्यावृत्, पश्चात् संसृ**; 'to roll away,' **अपवृत्, अपसृ, समपसृ.**—(Roll up into a ball) **गुटिकीकृ, गुलिकीकृ, गोलीकृ, पिण्डीकृ, वर्त्तुलीकृ, लुण्डीकृ.**—(Wrap around) **अवगुण्ठ्** (c. 10. **-गुण्ठयति -यितुं**), **परिवेष्ट्.**

To ROLL, *v. n.* (Turn round) **लुट्** (c. 6. **लुठति -ठितुं**), **प्रलुठ्, परि-लुठ्, लुट्** (c. 1. **लोटति -टितुं**), **लुड्, लुल्, आवृत्** (c. 1. **-वर्त्तते -र्त्तितुं**), **विवृत्, व्यावृत्, परिवृत्, विपरिवृत्, उपावृत्, परावृत्, सम्परिवृत्, भ्रम्** (c. 1. **भ्रमति -मितुं**), **परिभ्रम्, घूर्ण्** (c. 1. **घूर्णति -ते -र्णितुं**), **विघूर्ण्, व्याघूर्ण्, परिघूर्ण्, लुठनं कृ**; 'the dog rolled at his master's feet,' **कुक्कुरः स्वामिचरणयोर् लुलोठ**; 'he rolls on the ground,' **भूमौ परावर्त्तते** or **लुठनं करोति.**—(Roll about, toss about) **इतस्ततो विचल्** (c. 1. **-चलति -लितुं**) or **प्रचल्, इतस्ततो लुठ्** or **लुल्, दोल्** (nom. **दोलायते**), **घूर्ण्**; 'one who rolls about in sleep,' **प्रचलायितः, घूर्णितः**; 'one whose eyes roll about,' **प्रचलितनयनः, लोलाक्षिः.**—(Roll on) **अतिवृत्**; 'time rolls on,' **अतिवर्त्तते कालः.**—(A horse that rolls itself on the ground) **उपावृत्तः, लुठितः.**

ROLL, *s.* (Act of rolling) **लुठनं.**—(A mass made round, thing rolled up) **वर्त्तुलः, गोलकः, पिण्डः, गुटिका, दीर्घगोलकः**; 'a roll of cotton,' **तूलनाली.**—(Round loaf) **उण्डेरकः, संयावः.**—(List) **नामावलिः -ली** *f.*, *see* LIST.

ROLLED, *p. p.* **लुठितः -ता -तं, लोठितः** &c., **प्रलोठितः** &c., **आवर्त्तितः -ता -तं, विवर्त्तितः** &c., **अनुवर्त्तितः** &c.; 'rolled back,' **व्यावृत्तः -त्ता -त्तं, व्यावर्त्तितः -ता -तं**; 'rolled up,' **वर्त्तुलीकृतः -ता -तं, पिण्डीकृतः** &c., **लुण्डीकृतः** &c., **संश्यानः -ना -नं.**

ROLLER, *s.* (Instrument) **चक्रं, वर्त्तनयन्त्रं, वर्त्तनी, परिवर्त्तकयन्त्रं, परिवर्त्तनी, वर्त्तुलयन्त्रं.**—(For cakes) **वेल्लनं.**—(Bandage) **पट्टः.**

ROLLING, *s.* **लुठनं, लोठनं, लोटनं, लुण्ठनं, परिलोठनं, प्रलोठनं, लुण्ठा, लुण्टा, लुण्ठी, आवर्त्तनं, उपावर्त्तनं, वेल्लनं, आघूर्णनं.**

ROLLING, *part.* **लुठन् -ठन्ती -ठत् (त्), लुण्ठन्** &c., **लोलमानः -ना -नं, लोलः -ला -लं, लुठितः -ता -तं, प्रचलितः** &c., **प्रचलायितः -ता -तं, इतस्ततो विचलमानः -ना -नं**; 'having a rolling eye,' **लोलनयनः -ना -नं, प्रचलितनयनः** &c.; 'a river rolling gold,' **कनकवाहिनी**; 'rolling and tossing about in sleep,' **प्रचलायितः -ता -तं, घूर्णितः** &c.

ROLLING-PIN, *s.* (For making cakes) **वेल्लनं.**

ROMANCE, *s.* **अद्भुतकथा, कल्पितकथा, कूटार्थकथा, कूटार्थोपाख्यानं, अभूतकथा, असम्भवकथा, मृषार्थककथा, भङ्गपुराणं, माहात्म्यं, अद्भुतरसात्मका कथा.**

To ROMANCE, *v. n.* **अद्भुतकथां क्लृप्** or **रच्** or **लिख्, अद्भुतकथोपाख्यानं कृ.**

ROMANTIC, *a.* (Said of persons) **अद्भुतप्रियः -या -यं, असम्भवप्रियः** &c., **विलक्षणप्रियः** &c., **विचित्रप्रियः** &c., **लोलः -ला -लं, अद्भुतवृत्तिः -त्तिः -त्ति, अशृङ्खलवृत्तिः** &c., **लोलवृत्तिः** &c.—(Said of things) **अद्भुतरसरूपः -पा -पं, अद्भुतरसात्मकः -का -कं, अद्भुतः -ता -तं, विलक्षणः -णा -णं, विचित्रः -त्रा -त्रं, वासनाकल्पितः -ता -तं, आश्चर्य्यकरः -रा -रं, चित्तापहारी -रिणी** &c., **हृदयग्राही** &c., **मनोहरः** &c.—(Improbable) **असम्भवः -वा -वं.**

ROMP, *s.* (Boisterous girl) **प्रगल्भा, प्रचण्डा, चण्डी, अधीरा, निर्लज्जा, विलासिनी, अविनीता, चञ्चला, चपला, क्रीडाशीला, खेलाशीला.**—(Noisy or rude play) **अविनयक्रीडा, अविनयखेला, अविनीतक्रीडा, अशिष्टक्रीडा, शब्दसहितक्रीडा.**

To ROMP, *v. n.* **अविनयेन क्रीड्** (c. 1. **क्रीडति -ते -डितुं**) or **दिव्** (c. 4. **दीव्यति -ते, देवितुं**), **अतिशब्देन क्रीड्, महाशब्देन क्रीड्** or **क्रीडां कृ** or **खेलां कृ.**

ROMPING, *part.* or *a.* **अविनयक्रीडापरः -रा -रं, अविनीतः -ता -तं, अविनयदेवी -विनी** &c.

ROOD, *s.* No exact equivalent in Sanskrit. **दण्डः** is a pole of four cubits. *See* the measures of length under MEASURE.

ROOF, *s.* पटलः -लं -ला, छादनं, आच्छादनं, छादं, चालः, कुटलं, कटनं, छदिस् *f.*; 'the wooden frame of a roof,' वलभिः -भी *m. f.*, गोपानसी; 'the edge,' वलीकः -कं, नीध्रं, नीव्रं.—(Of the mouth) तालु *n.*, तालुका.

To ROOF, *v. a.* पटलेन आच्छद् (c. 10. -छादयति -यितुं) or आवृ (c. 5. -वृणोति -वरितुं -रीतुं), सपटलं -लां कृ, पटल (nom. पटलयति -यितुं).

ROOFED, *p.p.* सपटलः -ला -लं, पटलाच्छादितः -ता -तं, पटलाच्छन्नः -न्ना -न्नं.

ROOFLESS, *a.* पटलहीनः -ना -नं, निष्पटलः -ला -लं, निराश्रयः -या -यं.

ROOK, *s.* काकजातीयः पक्षी, काकः, वायसः. *See* CROW.

ROOKERY, *s.* काकाश्रयः, काकालयः, काकाशयः, काकस्थानं, काकायतनं.

ROOM, *s.* (Space, compass, free course) अवकाशः, प्रसरः, अवसरः, अन्तरं, विषयः, अपसरणं; 'want of room,' अनवकाशः; 'the water flows out to make room for the stone,' पाषाणाय विषयं दत्त्वा जलं बहिर्गच्छति; 'room! make room!' अपसर, अवसर.—(Place for reception or admission of any thing) स्थानं, आस्पदं, पदं, भूमिः *f.*, प्रदेशः; 'room for suspicion,' शङ्कास्पदं; 'room for fear,' भयस्थानं; 'there was no room to hold all,' सर्व्वधारणाय स्थानं नाभवत्.—(Opportunity) अवसरः, अवकाशः.—(Stead, lieu) स्थानं, स्थलं, भूमिः *f.*; 'in the room of,' स्थाने, भूमौ, स्थले.—(Apartment) शाला -लिका, आगारः -रं, कोष्ठः -ष्ठकं, गृहं, कक्षः, कुटी, आवासः, प्रकोष्ठः, स्थलं -ली; 'inner room,' उपरोधकं, अन्तर्गृहं, गर्भगृहं, गर्भागारं, गर्भः; 'top room, upper room,' शिरोगृहं, चन्द्रशालिका, उपरिशाला.

ROOMINESS, *s.* सावकाशत्वं, विस्तीर्णता, विशालता, असम्बाधता, विपुलता.

ROOMY, *a.* सावकाशः -शा -शं, असम्बाधः -धा -धं, विस्तीर्णः -र्णा -र्णं, विपुलः -ला -लं, विशालः -ला -लं, विस्तृतः -ता -तं.

ROOST, *s.* पक्षिणां वासयष्टिः *m.* or निवासयष्टिः *m.* or शयनयष्टिः, पक्षिणां वासदण्डः or वासस्थानं or निलयनस्थानं.

To ROOST, *v.n.* पक्षिवत् तरुशाखायां or दण्डाग्रे स्वप् (c. 2. स्वपिति -तुं) or शी (c. 2. शेते, शयितुं), यष्ट्यग्रे or तरुशाखायां स्वप्नार्थं निली (c. 4. -लीयते -लेतुं) or निवस् or अधिवस् or वस् or निषद् or अवस्था or आश्रि.

ROOSTING, *part.* तरुशाखायां निलीयमानः -ना -नं, तरुशायी -यिनी -यि (न्).

ROOT *s.* (That part of a plant or tree which enters the earth) मूलं, अंघ्रिः *m.*, अंह्रिः *m.*, ब्रध्नः, ब्रध्नः, पादः, चरणः -णं, पदं, वृक्षमूलं, वृक्षांघ्रिः *m.*; 'firm roots,' दृढमूलं, धरणमूलं; 'having firm roots,' दृढमूलः -ला -लं, बद्धमूलः &c.; 'to the roots, by the roots,' आमूलं, समूलं, मूलतस्; 'to pluck up by the roots,' उन्मूल् (c. 10. -मूलयति -यितुं), समूलं or आमूलम् उत्पट्; 'from root to top,' आमूलशिखरं, आमूलचूडं; 'to take root,' मूलं बन्ध्; 'fibrous root,' शिफा, जटा; 'from a radicant branch,' अवरोहः; 'bulbous root,' कन्दः -न्दं; 'root-digger,' मूलोत्पाटजीवी *m.* —(Lower part of any thing) अधोभागः, अधमभागः, ग्राहः; the latter is only applied to parts of the body of animals; as, 'the root of the tail,' पुच्छग्राहः; 'of the hair,' केशग्राहः. —(Original, source, first cause) मूलं, बीजं, योनिः *m. f.*, आदिः *m.*, हेतुः *m.*, मूलहेतुः *m.*, प्रथमहेतुः *m.*, निदानं, कारणं, मूलकारणं, आदिकारणं, आदिहेतुः *m.*, गर्भः; 'having for its root,' मूल or मूलक in comp.; as, 'happiness, having its root in contentment,' सन्तोषमूलकं सुखं; 'strife having its root in avarice,' लोभमूलः कलहः.—(Root of a word, radical word) शब्दयोनिः *f.*, प्रकृतिः *f.*; 'relation of a root to its ramification,' प्रकृतिविकृतिभावः.—(Of a number) मूलं.—(Of a square or cube) पदं, मूलं; 'square root,' वर्गमूलं, वर्गपदं; 'cube-root,' घनमूलं, घनपदं.

To ROOT, *v. a.* (Plant deep in the earth) बद्धमूलं -लां कृ, दृढमूलं -लां कृ, दृढं रुह् in caus. (रोपयति -यितुं), दृढं निखन्, दृढरोपणं कृ.—(Root up) उन्मूल् (c. 10. -मूलयति -यितुं), समुन्मूल्, मूलात् or समूलम् उद्धृ (c. 1. -हरति -हर्त्तुं) or समुद्धृ or उत्पट् (c. 10. -पाटयति -यितुं) or उच्छिद् (c. 7. -छिनत्ति -छेत्तुं) or व्यपरुह् in caus.

To ROOT, *v. n.* मूलं बन्ध् (c. 9. बध्नाति, बन्द्धुं), बद्धमूलः -ला -लं भू.

ROOTED, *p. p.* बद्धमूलः -ला -लं, दृढमूलः &c.; 'rooted up,' उन्मूलितः -ता -तं, उच्छिन्नमूलः -ला -लं, निकृत्तमूलः &c., उद्धृतमूलः &c., उत्पाटितः -ता -तं, उत्खातः &c.

ROPE, *s.* रज्जुः *m. f.*, गुणः, सूत्रं, दामा *f.* (न्), दाम *n.* (न्), दामनी, वराटकः, वराटः, वटाकरः, शुल्वः, पाशः, सन्दानं, शुल्बं, गलः, पवित्रकं, वटः -टी -टं, उद्ग्राहिनी, सुम्बं, पाशिसयी, वटीगुणः; 'of a ship,' नौरज्जुः *m. f.*; 'of a well,' उद्घाटनं, घटीयन्त्रं; 'hanging by a rope,' रज्जुवलसी *m.* (न्).

To ROPE, *v. n.* रज्जुं यन्त्, सूत्रं बन्ध्, सूत्ररूपेण विततीभू.

ROPE-DANCER, *s.* कलायनः, सूत्रायनः, रज्जुयायी *m.* (न्), प्लवकः, केलकः.

ROPE-LADDER, *s.* रज्जुनिर्म्मितसोपानं, सूत्रसोपानं, रज्जुसोपानं.

ROPE-MAKER, *s.* रज्जुकारः -रकः, रज्जुकारी *m.* (न्), रज्जुकृत्, गुणकारः.

ROPINESS, *s.* रज्जुत्वं, गुणत्वं, ससूत्रता, सूत्रपूर्णता, सान्द्रता, श्यानता.

ROPY, *a.* रज्जुगुणकः -का -कं, श्यानः -ना -नं, सूत्रमयः -यी -यं.

ROSARY, *s.* जपमाला, अक्षमाला, अक्षसूत्रं, जपसूत्रं, माला, सूत्रं, स्मरणी; 'fingers used as a rosary,' करमाला.

ROSE, *s.* (The tree) जवापुष्पः, ओड्रपुष्पः, पिण्डपुष्पः, हेमपुष्पः, जवा, जपा, ओड्रः, उड्रः, उद्रः.—(Flower) जपा, जपा, जवापुष्पं, ओड्रपुष्पं, हेमपुष्पं.

ROSE-APPLE, *s.* (The tree) जम्बूः *f.*, जम्बुः *f.*, जम्बुकः, जम्बूकः; 'a large kind,' राजजम्बूः *f.*—(The fruit) जम्बूः *f.*, जम्बुः *f.*, जम्बु *n.*, जाम्बवं, जम्बुफलं.

ROSE-COLORED, ROSEATE, *a.* पाटलः -ला -लं, पाटलवर्णः -र्णा -र्णं, जवावर्णः &c.

ROSE-WATER, *s.* पुष्पद्रवः, जवापुष्पद्रवः, जवापुष्पजलं.

ROSIN, *s.*, *see* RESIN.

ROSY, *a.* (Rose-colored) पाटलः -ला -लं, जवावर्णः -र्णा -र्णं.—(Formed like a rose, full of roses) जवारूपः -पा -पं, जवामयः -यी -यं.

To ROT, *v. n.* गल् (c. 1. गलति -लितुं), विगल्, गलितः -ता -तं भू, विगलितः -ता -तं भू, विली (c. 4. -लीयते -लेतुं), प्रविली, क्षि (c. 4. क्षीयते), दुर्गन्धः -न्धा -न्धं भू.

To ROT, *v. a.* गल् (c. 10. गलयति, गालयति -यितुं), विगल्, गलितीकृ, विगलितीकृ, विली in caus. (-लापयति -यितुं).

ROTATION, *s.* (Circular motion of a wheel, &c.) आवर्त्तः -र्त्तनं, आवृत्तिः *f.*, परिवर्त्तः -र्त्तनं, परिवृत्तिः *f.*, चक्रावर्त्तनं, चक्रावर्त्तः, चक्रगतिः *f.*, भ्रमणं, भ्रान्तिः *f.*, घूर्णनं, घूर्णिः *f.*—(Vicissitude of succession) पर्य्यायः, पर्य्ययः, विपर्य्ययः, आनुपूर्व्यं, आनुपूर्वी, क्रमः, परिवर्त्तनं; 'in rotation,' पर्य्यायेण, पर्य्यायानुसारेण, पर्य्यायानुक्रमेण, चक्रवत्.

ROTATORY, ROTARY, *a.* चक्रवदावर्त्ती -र्त्तिनी -र्त्ति (न्), चक्रावर्त्ती &c., चक्रवत्परिवर्त्ती &c., चाक्रिकः -की -कं, चक्रगतिः -तिः -ति, चक्रगामी -मिनी &c.; 'rotatory motion,' चक्रावर्त्तः, चक्रवदावर्त्तः.

ROTE, *s.* शब्दावर्त्तनं, शब्दावृत्तिः *f.*, शब्दमात्रावर्त्तनं, आवर्त्तनं, अभ्यासः, अभ्यसनं, रूपं; 'to learn by rote,' शब्दावर्त्तनं कृ, अभ्यस् (c. 4.

-अस्यति -सितुं); 'learnt by rote,' मुखस्थः -स्था -स्थं, कण्ठस्थः &c., अभ्यस्तः -स्ता -स्तं.

ROTTEN, *a.* गलितः -ता -तं, विगलितः &c., विलीनः -ना -नं, विशीर्णः -र्णा -र्णं, शीर्णः &c., क्षीणः -णा -णं, पूतः -ता -तं, पूतीभूतः &c., दुर्गन्धः -न्धा -न्धं.—(Unsound) क्षीणसारः -रा -रं, क्षीणसत्त्वः -त्त्वा -त्त्वं, असारः -रा -रं.

ROTTENNESS, *s.* गलितत्वं -ता, विगलितत्वं, क्षीणता, विलीनता, पूतत्वं, असारता.

ROTUND, ROTUNDITY, *s.* *See* ROUND, ROUNDNESS.

ROTUNDA, ROTUNDO, *s.* वर्त्तुलगृहं, वर्त्तुलभवनं, वर्त्तुलशाला.

To ROUGE, *v. a.* सौन्दर्य्यवर्धनार्थं कपोलौ रञ्ज् (c. 10. रञ्जयति -यितुं) or रक्तवर्णीकृ or रक्तेन लिप्.

ROUGH, *a.* (Not smooth or even) विषमः -मा -मं, असमः -मा -मं, असमानः -ना -नं, अश्लक्ष्णः -क्ष्णा -क्ष्णं, रुक्षः -क्षा -क्षं, रूक्षः -क्षा -क्षं.—(Rugged) रुक्षः -क्षा -क्षं, रूक्षः &c., परुषः -षा -षं.—(To the touch) दुःस्पर्शः -र्शा -र्शं, दुःखस्पर्शः -र्शा -र्शं.—(Harsh, not soft) परुषः -षा -षं, रुक्षः -क्षा -क्षं, रूक्षः &c., परुषवृत्तिः -त्तिः -त्ति, कर्कशः -शा -शं, कठिनः -ना -नं, अमृदुः -दुः -दु, अमसृणः -णा -णं, असौम्यः -म्या -म्यं, अस्निग्धः -ग्धा -ग्धं, अकोमलः -ला -लं.—(Severe) निष्ठुरः -रा -रं, कर्कशः -शा -शं, उग्रः -ग्रा -ग्रं, कटुः -टुः -टु, कठोरः -रा -रं. (Coarse, not finished, not polished) असंस्कृतः -ता -तं, अपरिष्कृतः &c., असंस्कारितः &c., अशिष्टः -ष्टा -ष्टं, असभ्यः -भ्या -भ्यं, घनः -ना -नं, स्थूलः -ला -लं; 'rough measurement,' स्थूलमानं; 'to measure in a rough way,' स्थूलाकारेण मा.—(Clumsy) स्थूलः -ला -लं, अनिपुणः -णा -णं, अदक्षः -क्षा -क्षं, अकुशलः -ला -लं, अपटुः -टुः -टु.—(With waves or tempest, as the sea) क्षुब्धः -ब्धा -ब्धं, व्याक्षुब्धः &c., विक्षुब्धः &c., संक्षुब्धः &c., अनिलक्षुब्धः &c., पवनक्षुब्धः &c., वायुक्षुब्धः &c., पवनाहतः -ता -तं, तरङ्गाकुलः -ला -लं, महातरङ्गः -ङ्गा -ङ्गं, बृहत्तरङ्गः &c., तरङ्गितः -ता -तं, वेलाकुलः -ला -लं; 'a rough sea,' क्षुब्धार्णवः, वायुक्षुब्धसमुद्रः, वातं.—(Having a rough or hairy skin) दृढलोमा -मा -म (न्), स्थूललोमा &c., लोमावृतः -ता -तं, लोमशः -शा -शं.

To ROUGH-CAST, *v. a.* स्थूलाकारेण क्लृप् (c. 10. कल्पयति -यितुं), स्थूलरूपेण कृ or निर्मा or विधा, स्थूलाकारं दा, स्थूलरूपं कृ or दा, स्थूलसंस्कारं कृ or दा.

ROUGH-DRAUGHT, *s.* पाण्डुलेख्यं, स्थूलालेख्यं, पाण्डुलेख्यमात्रं, वस्तुमात्रं.

To ROUGH-DRAW, *v. a.* स्थूलरूपेण लिख् (c. 6. लिखति -लेखितुं) or आलिख्, स्थूलालेख्यं कृ, पाण्डुलेख्यं कृ, आलेख्यारम्भं कृ, चित्रारम्भं कृ.

To ROUGH-HEW, *v. a.* स्थूलरूपेण तक्ष् (c. 1. तक्षति -क्षितुं) or छिद्, स्थूलाकारं दा.

ROUGH-HEWN, *p. p.* स्थूलरूपेण कल्पितः -ता -तं, स्थूलाकारेण तष्टः -ष्टा -ष्टं, असंस्कृताकारः -रा -रं, असंस्कृतरूपः -पा -पं, अपरिष्कृताकारः -रा -रं.

ROUGHLY, *adv.* रुक्षं, रूक्षं, सरौक्ष्यं, विषमं, परुषं, सपारुष्यं, पारुष्येण, कर्कशं, सकार्कश्यं, कठोरं, कठिनं, सकाठिन्यं, निष्ठुरं, सनैष्ठुर्य्यं, स्थूलं.

ROUGHNESS, *s.* (Unevenness) विषमता, वैषम्यं, रुक्षता, रूक्षता, रौक्ष्यं, असमता, अश्लक्ष्णता, असमानता.—(Ruggedness) रुक्षता, रूक्षता, परुषता -त्वं, पारुष्यं.—(To the touch) दुःखस्पर्शता, दुःस्पर्शता.—(Harshness) परुषता, पारुष्यं, रुक्षता, कर्कशता, कार्कश्यं, कठिनता, काठिन्यं, अमृदुता, असौम्यता, अकोमलता.—(Severity) निष्ठुरता, नैष्ठुर्य्यं, उग्रता, कटुता, कठोरता.—(Want of finish) असंस्कृतता, अपरिष्कारः, अशिष्टता, स्थूलता.—(Of the sea, &c.) क्षुब्धता, संक्षुब्धता, ऊर्म्मिप्रलोठनं, तरङ्गप्रलोठनं, तरङ्गाकुलत्वं, सवातत्वं, वातं.

ROUGH-RIDER, *s.* अश्वदमकः, अश्वदमी *m.* (न्). *See* HORSE-BREAKER.

ROUGH-SHOD, *a.* सायसपादुकायुक्तः -क्ता -क्तं, सायसखुरत्रयुक्तः -क्ता -क्तं.

ROUND, *a.* (Circular) वर्त्तुलः -ला -लं, वर्त्तुलाकारः -रा -रं, वर्त्तुलाकृतिः -तिः -ति, वर्त्तुलरूपः -पा -पं, चक्राकारः -रा -रं, चक्राकृतिः -तिः -ति, चाक्रिकः -की -कं, चाक्रेयः -यी -यं, वृत्तः -त्ता -त्तं, वृत्ताकारः -रा -रं, मण्डलाकारः -रा -रं, मण्डलाकृतिः -तिः -ति, मण्डलरूपः -पा -पं, मण्डली -लिनी -लि (न्), वलयाकारः &c., वलयाकृतिः &c., कङ्कणाकारः &c., कुण्डलाकारः &c.—(Globular) गोलाकारः -रा -रं, गोलाकृतिः -तिः -ति, वर्त्तुलः -ला -लं, वर्त्तुलाकारः &c., मण्डलाकारः &c., गुडः -डा -डं, घटी -टिनी &c., निस्तलः -ला -लं.—(Cylindrical) दीर्घवर्त्तुलः -ला -लं, लम्बवर्त्तुलः &c., लम्बवर्त्तुलाकारः &c., दीर्घगोलाकारः &c.—(Plump) पीनः -ना -नं, उन्नतः -ता -तं, *see* PLUMP.—(Plain) अवक्रः -क्रा -क्रं, व्यक्तः -क्ता -क्तं.—(As a number) शून्यात्मकः -का -कं; 'a round number,' शून्यात्मकसंख्या.

ROUND, *s.* (Circle) मण्डलं, परिमण्डलं, चक्रं, वर्त्तुलः, गोलः, वलयः, निघः, वटः.—(Revolution) आवृत्तिः *f.*, आवर्त्तनं, परिवर्त्तनं, पर्य्यायः, चक्रं, *see* REVOLUTION.—(Circuitous course) वक्रमार्गः, वक्रगतिः *f.*

ROUND, *adv.* चक्रवत्, मण्डलवत्, वलयवत्, गोलवत्, मण्डलतस्, मण्डलरूपेण, चक्ररूपेण, परि prefixed; 'to turn round,' परिवृत्, *see* *To* REVOLVE; 'to come round, change opinion,' मतिं परिवृत्, अन्यमानसीभू; 'to look round,' सर्व्वमुखः परिवृत्.—(On all sides) समन्ततस्, समन्तात्, आसमन्तात्, सर्व्वतस्, विश्वतस्, परितस्, सर्व्वदिक्षु, चतुर्दिक्षु.—(Circuitously) वक्रमार्गेण, वक्रं.

ROUND, *prep.* परि or अभि prefixed, परितस् or अभितस् affixed; 'the planets move round the sun,' रविं परितो ग्रहा भ्रमन्ति; 'the moon moves round the earth,' पृथिवीम् अभितो भ्रमति चन्द्रः; 'to get round one,' *see* *To* CIRCUMVENT.

To ROUND, *v. a.* (Make round) वर्त्तुलीकृ, मण्डलीकृ, परिमण्डलीकृ, मण्डल (nom. मण्डलयति -यितुं), परिमण्डल, गोलीकृ.—(Go round) परितो गम्, परितो या, परिगम्, अभितो गम्.

ROUNDABOUT, *a.* (Circuitous) वक्रः -क्रा -क्रं, जिह्मः -ह्मा -ह्मं, कुटिलः &c.

ROUNDABOUT, *adv.* (On all sides) समन्ततस्, समन्तात्, परितस्, *see* ROUND, *adv.*

ROUNDED, *p. p.* मण्डलीकृतः -ता -तं, मण्डलितः -ता -तं, परिमण्डलितः &c., वर्त्तुलीकृतः &c., वृत्तः -त्ता -त्तं; 'well-rounded,' सद्वृत्तः &c.

ROUNDLY, *adv.* (Plainly, openly) अवक्रं, व्यक्तं, स्पष्टं, सुस्पष्टं, सुव्यक्तं.—(Peremptorily) सुनियतं, दृढोक्त्या, दार्ढ्येन.

ROUNDNESS, *s.* वर्त्तुलता -त्वं, वर्त्तुलाकारता, मण्डलाकारता, चक्राकारता, गोलाकारता, गोलत्वं, मण्डलत्वं, परिमण्डलता, मण्डलाकृतिः *f.*, वर्त्तुलाकृतिः *f.*—(Plumpness) पीनता, उन्नतिः *f.*, स्थूलता.—(Plainness) अवक्रता, व्यक्तता, स्पष्टता.

ROUND-SHOULDERED, *a.* कुब्जः -ब्जा -ब्जं, उन्नतस्कन्धः -न्धा -न्धं, वक्रपृष्ठः &c.

To ROUSE, *v. a.* (Awake) प्रबुध् (c. 10. -बोधयति -यितुं), प्रतिबुध्, विबुध्, बुध्, जागृ in caus. (जागरयति -यितुं), निद्रां भञ्ज्, शयनाद् उत्था in caus., निद्राभङ्गं कृ, प्रबोधनं कृ, बोधनं कृ.—(Excite, stimulate) उत्तिज् (c. 10. -तेजयति -यितुं), प्रोत्सह् (c. 10. -साहयति -यितुं), उत्सह्, उत्था in caus. (उत्थापयति -यितुं, rt. स्था), समुत्था, उद्युज् (c. 10. -योजयति -यितुं), उद्बुध्, प्रबुध्, उद्दीप्, दीप्, उत्तप्, प्रवृत्, प्ररुच्, चुद्, प्रचुद्, संचुद्, चेष्ट् in caus.

To ROUSE, *v. n.* प्रबुध् (c. 4. -बुध्यते -बोद्धुं), प्रतिबुध्, जागृ (c. 2. जागर्त्ति,

जागरितुं), उत्था (c. 1. -तिष्ठति -ते -थातुं, rt. स्था), शयनाद् उत्था.

Roused, *p. p.* (From sleep) प्रबोधितः -ता -तं, प्रबुद्धः -द्धा -द्धं, जागरितः -ता -तं, भग्ननिद्रः -द्रा -द्रं.—(Excited) उत्तेजितः -ता -तं, प्रोत्साहितः &c., उत्थापितः &c., उद्बोधितः &c., उत्तापितः &c., उत्तप्तः -प्ता -प्तं, संरब्धः -ब्धा -ब्धं.

Rout, *s.* (Mob) अधमलोकसंघः, जनसम्मर्दः. *See* Mob, Rabble.—(Of an army) विद्रावः, विद्रवः, प्रद्रावः, उद्द्रावः, सन्द्रावः, द्रावः, द्रवः, सन्द्रावः, सैन्यभङ्गः, व्यूहभङ्गः, व्यूहभेदः, सैन्यव्यूहभङ्गः, भङ्गः, भेदः, पलायनं, विपलायनं, प्रपलायनं, पलायितं, बलव्यसनं, व्यसनं, डमरं, डामरः -रं; 'total rout,' सुपलायितं.—(Fashionable assembly) शिष्टलोकसभा, सभ्यलोकसमाजः.

To rout, *v. a.* विद्रु (c. 10. -द्रावयति -यितुं), प्रद्रु, सन्द्रु, द्रु, विद्रुतीकृ, सैन्यव्यूहान् भञ्ज् (c. 7. भनक्ति, भंक्तुं) or भिद्, विध्वंस् (c. 10. -ध्वंसयति -यितुं).

Route, *s.* मार्गः, पथः, पदवी, गतिः *f.* *See* Road.

Routed, *p. p.* विद्रुतः -ता -तं, विद्रावितः &c., भयद्रुतः &c., भयविप्लुतः -ता -तं, पलायितः -ता -तं, विपलायितः &c., प्रपलायितः &c., पिच्छलः -ला -लं, उत्पिच्छलः &c. समुत्पिञ्जः -ञ्जा -ञ्जं, समुत्पिञ्जलः &c., भग्नव्यूहः -हा -हं, कान्दिशीकः -का -कं, कन्दिशीकः &c.

Routine, *s.* नित्यकर्म्म *n.* (न्), नित्यकृत्यं, नित्यक्रमः, पर्य्यायः, नित्यपर्य्यायः, नित्यपाठः, परिपाठः; 'daily routine,' दैनिकक्रमः, आह्निकक्रमः, आह्निकं.

To rove, *v. n.* भ्रम् (c. 4. भ्राम्यति, भ्रमितुं), परिभ्रम्, भ्रमणं कृ, परिभ्रमणं कृ, अट् (c. 1. अटति -टितुं), पर्यट्, अटनं कृ, पर्यटनं कृ, गाह् (c. 1. गाहते -हितुं), विचर् (c. 1. -चरति -रितुं), संचर्, विहृ, व्रज्, प्रव्रज्.

Rover, *s.* परिभ्रमकः, भ्रमणकारी *m.* (न्), परिभ्रमणकारी *m.*, पर्यटनकृत् *m.*, विहारी *m.*, यथेष्टचारी *m.*, अवनिचरः.—(Robber) परिपन्थी *m.*, दस्युः *m.*

Roving, *s.* भ्रमणं, परिभ्रमणं, अटनं, पर्यटनं, विहारः, विहरणं.

Row, *s.* (Line, rank) पंक्तिः *f.*, श्रेणिः -णी *f.*, राजिः -जी *f.*, आवलिः -ली *f.*, पद्धतिः -ती *f.*, राजिका, ततिः *f.*, वीथिः -थी *f.*, आलिः -ली *f.*, पालिः -ली *f.*, धारणी, रेखा, सरणिः -णी *f.*, माला, विञ्झोली; 'in a row,' पंक्तिक्रमेण; 'row of teeth,' दन्तपंक्तिः *f.*; 'two rows of teeth,' द्वे दन्तपंक्ती; 'row of trees,' तरुपंक्तिः *f.*, पादपश्रेणी, पादपवीथिः *f.*; 'of curls,' अलकसंहतिः *f.*; 'of swords,' खड्गश्रेणी, खड्गलेखा; 'row of houses,' वीथिः -थी, गृहपंक्तिः *f.*; 'of four houses,' चतुःशालं, सञ्जवनं, संयवनं.—(Riot, disturbance) कोलाहलः, तुमुलं, विप्लवः, डमरः -रा -रं, डामरः, डिम्बः; 'festive turbulence,' चमत्कारः, चर्चरी.

To row, *v. a.* (Impel a boat by means of an oar) नौकां दण्डेन वह् (c. 10. वाहयति -यितुं) or संचल् (c. 10. -चालयति -यितुं) or चल् or सृ in caus.—(Scold) भर्त्स्, तर्ज्, उपालभ्.

To row, *v. n.* पोतवाहनं कृ, नौकावाहनं कृ, नौदण्डसञ्चालनं कृ, क्षेपणिसञ्चालनं कृ, क्षिपणिसञ्चालनं कृ.

Rowel, *s.* (Of a spur) अश्वतोदनचक्रकं, प्रतोदकण्टकः, कण्टकः.

Rower, *s.* पोतवाहः -हकः, नौकावाहः -हकः, नौदण्डसञ्चालकः, नौदण्डचालकः, क्षेपणिसञ्चालकः, क्षेपणिधरः, नियामकः.

Royal, *a.* राजकीयः -या -यं, राजयोग्यः -ग्या -ग्यं, राजार्हः -र्हा -र्हं, राजोचितः -ता -तं, नृपोचितः &c., ऐशिकः -की -कं, ऐश्वरः -री -रं, राज or नृप in comp., *see* Kingly, Princely, Regal, Majestic, &c.; 'royal attendant,' राजपुरुषः, राजसेवकः, राजपरिचरः; 'royal city,' राजधानं -नी, राजनगरी, राजपुरी, संस्थानं; 'royal dignity,' राजतेजस् *n.*, राजप्रतापः; 'royal duty,' राजधर्म्मः, राजधुरा, राजकार्य्यं; 'royal dynasty,' राजावलिः -ली *f.*; 'royal family,' राजकुलं, राजवंशः; 'royal court,' राजसभा, ईश्वरसभा; 'royal edict,' राजाज्ञा, राजशासनं; 'letter,' राजलेखः, राजपत्रं; 'insignia,' राजलक्षणं, राजलक्ष्मा *m.* (न्), राजचिह्नं; 'mansion,' राजमन्दिरं, राजसदनं, राजवसतिः *f.*; 'seat,' राजशय्या; 'road,' राजमार्गः, राजवर्त्म *n.* (न्); 'elephant,' राजहस्ती *m.* (न्), राजेभः, राजवाह्यः; 'revenue,' राजस्वं, राजधनं; 'audience,' राजदर्शनं; 'audience-chamber,' राजदर्शनशाला; 'seal,' राजमुद्रा, राजचिह्नं; 'amusement,' राजविलासः, राजनर्म्म *n.* (न्); 'circle or court,' राजमण्डली -लं; 'polity,' राजनीतिः *f.*, राजनयः; 'royal will,' राजेच्छा, नृपेच्छा; 'favourite,' राजवल्लभः, नृपवल्लभः; 'sacrifice,' राजसूयं; 'of royal race,' राजवंश्यः -श्या -श्यं, नृपात्मजः -जा -जं, राजबीजी -जिनी -जि (न्).

Royalist, *s.* राजानुगतः, राजानुभक्ती *m.* (न्), राजपक्षीयः, राजपक्षपाती.

Royally, *adv.* राजवत्, नृपवत्, राजरूपेण, राजसदृशं, नृपसदृशं.

Royalty, *s.* राजत्वं -ता, राज्यं, नृपत्वं, राजभूयं, राजसायुज्यं, राजाधिकारः, भूपता -त्वं, नरेन्द्रत्वं -ता, ऐश्वर्य्यं, आधिपत्यं, प्रभुत्वं, प्रभैश्वर्य्यं, महीपत्वं; 'requisites of royalty,' प्रकृतयः *f. pl.*; 'ensigns of royalty,' राजलक्षणानि *n. pl.*, छत्रचामरं.

To rub, *v. a.* घृष् (c. 1. घर्षति -र्षितुं), आघृष्, निर्घृष्, मृद् (c. 9. मृद्नाति मर्दितुं), परिमृद्, पिष् (c. 7. पिनष्टि, पेष्टुं), प्रतिपिष्, निष्पिष्, घर्षणं कृ, मर्दनं कृ.—(The body) संवाह् (c. 1. -वाहति, c. 10. -वाहयति -यितुं); 'they both rubbed his feet with their hands,' कराभ्यां तस्य पादौ संववाहतुः; 'I will rub your feet,' तव चरणौ संवाहयामि.—(Rub, so as to clean) मृज् (c. 2. मार्ष्टि -र्ष्टुं), प्रमृज्, परिमृज्, सम्मृज्, अवमृज्, आमृज्, परिष्कृ, प्रक्षल् (c. 10. -क्षालयति -यितुं), स्वच्छीकृ.—(Grind in a mortar, &c.) चूर्ण्, चूर्णीकृ, पिष्, मृद्, क्षुद्, क्षोदीकृ.—(Polish by friction) घर्षणेन तिज् (c. 10. तेजयति -यितुं) or निष्टप् or मृज् or परिष्कृ.—(Rub one against the other) परस्परं घृष्, परस्परघर्षणं कृ; 'to rub the hands together,' करं करेण घृष् or निष्पिष् or प्रतिपिष्, पाणिं पाणौ विनिष्पिष्; 'the teeth together,' दन्तान् दन्तैर् घृष् or निष्पिष्, दन्तघर्षणं कृ.—(Rub in, spread over, smear with, as unguents, &c.) लिप् (c. 6. लिम्पति, लेप्तुं), अनुलिप्, आलिप्, अञ्ज्, अभ्यञ्ज्, मृद्.—(Rub down, as a horse) अनुलोम मृज्.—(Rub off) अपमृज्, अवमृज्.—(Rub out) अपमृज्, व्यामृज्, प्रमृज्, अवमृज्, व्यामृश् (c. 6. -मृशति -म्रष्टुं), अवमृश्, व्यामर्षं कृ, अवमर्षणं कृ, लोपं कृ.—(Rub up) मृज्, परिष्कृ.

To rub, *v. n.* घृष् (c. 1. घर्षति -र्षितुं), संघृष्, संघट्ट् (c. 1. -घट्टते -ट्टितुं), संघर्षणं कृ, संघर्षं कृ, परस्परसंघर्षं कृ.—(Wear away by friction) घर्षणेन क्षि in pass.—(Pass through with difficulty) दुःखेन or कृच्छ्रेण तॄ.

Rub, *s.* घर्षणं, आघर्षः -र्षणं, संघर्षः, मर्दनं, विमर्दनं, परिमर्दनं, मार्जनं.—(Collision, obstruction) संघट्टः -ट्टनं, समाघातः, सम्मर्दः, प्रतिघातः.—(Difficulty) दुःखं, कृच्छ्रं, दुर्गं, कष्टं, शल्यं, वैषम्यं.

Rubbed, *p. p.* घर्षितः -ता -तं, आघर्षितः &c., संघर्षितः &c., अभिघर्षितः &c., मर्दितः -ता -तं, मृदितः &c., परिमृदितः &c., घृष्टः -ष्टा -ष्टं, मृष्टः &c., प्रमृष्टः &c., परिमृष्टः &c., मार्जितः -ता -तं, परिमार्जितः &c., प्रमार्जितः &c., सम्मार्जितः &c., प्रक्षालितः &c., आघट्टितः &c.—(Rubbed out) अपमृष्टः -ष्टा -ष्टं, व्यामृष्टः &c., निर्मृष्टः &c.

Rubber, *s.* (One that rubs) घर्षकः, मर्दकः, मार्जकः, घर्षणकारी *m.*

(न्), मर्द्दनकारी *m.*, निर्घर्षणकः, आघट्टकः.—(Instrument for rubbing) मार्जनी.

Rubbing, *s.* घर्षणं, आघर्षः -र्षणं, संघर्षः -र्षणं, निर्घर्षणं, मर्द्दनं, परिमर्द्दनं, आघट्टनं, विघट्टनं, मार्जनं, परिमार्जनं.

Rubbish, *s.* उच्छिष्टं, अवस्करः, अपस्करः, मलं, तुच्छद्रव्यं, कुत्सितद्रव्यं.

Rubbish-hole, *s.* उच्छिष्टप्रक्षेपणार्थं गर्त्तः, मलाधारः, अवस्कराधारः.

Rubicund, *a.* ईषद्रक्तः -क्ता -क्तं, आरक्तः &c., पाटलवर्णः -र्णा -र्णं.

Rubric, *s.* रक्ताक्षरलिखितसूत्रं, प्रार्थनापद्धतिसूत्रं, प्रार्थनाग्रन्थसूत्रं.

Ruby, *s.* पद्मरागः, माणिक्यं, लोहितकः, शोणरत्नं, शोणितोपलं -लः, पाटलोपलं -लः, अरुणोपलं -लः, अर्कोपलः, भास्करप्रियं, लक्ष्मीपुष्पः, कुरुविन्दः, पद्मरागमणिः *m.*, महामूल्यः.

Ruby, *a.* (Of the color of the ruby) रक्तवर्णः -र्णा र्णं, लोहितवर्णः &c., शोणितवर्णः &c., पाटलवर्णः &c., पद्मरागवर्णः &c.; 'having ruby lips,' बिम्बोष्ठः -ष्ठा -ष्ठं, (*i. e.* like the fruit of the vimba or bimba) विद्रुमोष्ठः &c. (*i. e.* like coral).

Rudder, *s.* कर्णः, नौकर्णः, अरित्रं, केनिपातः -तकः, पोतरक्षः.

Ruddiness, *s.* रक्तता, अरुणिमा *m.* (न्), रक्तिमा *m.* (न्), अरुणता; 'of countenance,' मुखरागः, कपोलरागः, कपोलरक्तता, मुखारुणिमा *m.* (न्),

Ruddy, *a.* रक्तवर्णः -र्णा -र्णं, अरुणः -णा -णं, अरुणवर्णः &c.; 'ruddy-faced,' रक्तमुखः -खा -खं, अरुणमुखः &c., रक्तकपोलः -ला -लं; 'ruddy-goose, or Brahmany duck,' चक्रवाकः, चक्रः, रात्रिविश्लेषगामी *m.*

Rude, *a.* (Uncivilized, untaught) अशिष्टः -ष्टा -ष्टं, अशिक्षितः -ता -तं, असभ्यः -भ्या -भ्यं, अनक्षरः -रा -रं, निरक्षरः &c., अविद्यः -द्या -द्यं, अपरिष्कृतः -ता -तं, अकृतबुद्धिः -द्धिः -द्धि, विद्याहीनः -ना -नं, विद्याशून्यः -न्या -न्यं, विद्याचारहीनः &c., दुराचारः -रा -रं, दुर्जनः -ना -नं, असभ्यवृत्तिः -त्तिः -त्ति, दौर्जन्यवृत्तिः &c., ग्राम्यः -म्या -म्यं.—(Uncivil, impolite, rough in manner) अविनीतः -ता -तं, अविनयः -या -यं, नष्टविनयः &c., प्रणष्टविनयः &c., कुशीलः -ला -लं, वामशीलः &c., दुःशीलः &c., विशीलः &c., दुर्मर्य्यादः -दा -दं, निर्मर्य्यादः &c., अमर्य्यादः &c., धृष्टः -ष्टा -ष्टं, उद्धतः -ता -तं, समुद्धतः &c., असभ्यः &c., अनार्य्यः -र्य्या -र्य्यं.—(Coarsely executed) स्थूलः -ला -लं, असंस्कृतः -ता -तं, रुक्षः -क्षा -क्षं, रूक्षः &c.—(Clumsy) अदक्षः -क्षा -क्षं, अकुशलः -ला -लं, अनिपुणः -णा -णं, स्थूलः &c.

Rudely, *adv.* अशिष्टं, अशिष्टवत्, असभ्यवत्, अविनीतवत्, अविनयेन, धृष्टवत्, सधार्ष्ट्यं, कुशीलवत्, अनार्य्यवत्.—(Roughly) रुक्षं, रूक्षं, सरौक्ष्यं, स्थूलं, असंस्कृतं.

Rudeness, *s.* (Absence of civilization) अशिष्टता -त्वं, असभ्यता, विद्याहीनता, अनक्षरता -त्वं, निरक्षरता -त्वं, विद्याशून्यता, विद्याचारहीनता, अपरिष्कारः.—(Incivility, impoliteness) अविनीतता -त्वं, अविनयः, कुशीलता, दुःशीलता, वामशीलता, अशीलता, अमर्य्यादा, दुर्मर्य्यादता, धृष्टता, धार्ष्ट्यं, असभ्यता, दौर्जन्यं, औद्धत्यं, अननुनयः, विनयाभावः, अनार्य्यता, अदाक्षिण्यं.—(Roughness, clumsiness) रुक्षता, रूक्षता, स्थूलता, अदक्षता.

Rudiment, *s.* (First principle) मूलतत्त्वं, मूलं, आरम्भः, प्रारम्भः, मूलसूत्रं, प्रथमसूत्रं, प्रथमतत्त्वं, तत्त्वं, सूत्रं, आदिः *m.*, उपक्रमः, परिभाषा; 'the rudiments of learning,' विद्यारम्भः, विद्यातत्त्वानि *n. pl.*; 'of grammar,' व्याकरणारम्भः.—(Original or elemental part of any thing) मूलवस्तु *n.*, मूलावयवः, मूलाङ्गं, मूलद्रव्यं, मूलं, बीजं, मात्रं, भूतमात्रं, तन्मात्रं, वस्तु *n.*, धातुः *m.*

Rudimental, rudimentary, *a.* मूलिकः -का -कं, मौलः -ली -लं, मूल in comp., आरम्भकः -का -कं, प्रारम्भकः &c., प्राथमिकः -की -कं, आदि in comp., प्रथमः -मा -मं, मूलतत्त्वरूपः -पा -पं, मूलतत्त्वसम्बन्धी -न्धिनी &c., मूलतत्त्वविषयकः -का -कं.

To rue, *v. a.* पश्चात् शुच् or खिद् or विषद्, पश्चात्तापं कृ. *See To* regret.

Rue, *s.* (Sort of pot-herb) ब्राह्मी, ब्राह्मिका, ब्रह्मी.

Rueful, *a.* शोकान्वितः -ता -तं, सशोकः -का -कं, विषण्णः -ण्णा -ण्णं; 'having a rueful countenance,' विषण्णवदनः -ना -नं, उद्विग्नवदनः &c., म्लानवदनः &c.

Ruefully, *adv.* सशोकं, सखेदं, सोद्वेगं, सविषादं, विषण्णमुखेन.

Ruffian, *s.* दस्युः, साहसिकः, क्रूरकर्म्मा *m.* (न्), कृष्णकर्म्मा *m.*, घोरकर्म्मा *m.*, अघोरकर्म्मा *m.*, वधोद्यतः, आततायी *m.* (न्), प्राणघातकः.

Ruffle, ruff, *s.* (Frill) ऊर्म्मिमदंशुकमयो वस्त्राञ्चलः or वस्त्रानुबन्धः or वस्त्रालङ्कारः, पुटितदुकूलखण्डः, पुटितदुकूलं, ऊर्म्याकारदुकूलं.—(Plait, fold) ऊर्म्मिका, पुटः, चूणः.—(Discomposure) व्याकुलत्वं, अशान्तिः *f.*, अस्थिरता, सम्भ्रमः, अनिर्वृतिः *f.*

To ruffle, *v. a.* (Pucker, plaid, fold) पुटीकृ, सम्पुटीकृ, संकुच्, सङ्कोचं कृ, चूण् (c. 10. चूणयति -यितुं), पुट्.—(Crumple) संकुच्, सम्मृद्, रूक्षीकृ.—(Agitate) क्षुभ् (c. 10. क्षोभयति -यितुं), विक्षुभ्, *see To* agitate.—(Discompose) व्याकुलीकृ, आकुलीकृ, व्याकुल (nom. व्याकुलयति -यितुं), अशान्तिं or सम्भ्रमं or अनिर्वृतिं जन्, चित्तवेगं जन्, कातरीकृ, अस्थिरीकृ.

Ruffled, *p. p.* or *a.* क्षुब्धः -ब्धा -ब्धं, क्षोभितः -ता -तं, आकुलितः &c., व्याकुलितः &c., व्याकुलः -ला -लं, व्याकुलचेताः -ताः -तः (स्), आकुलचित्तः -त्ता -त्तं, व्यग्रः -ग्रा -ग्रं, अस्वस्थः -स्था -स्थं, अनिर्वृतः -ता -तं, अस्थिरः -रा -रं, गतधृतिः -तिः -ति, कातरः -रा -रं, अनवस्थितः &c., व्यस्तः -स्ता -स्तं, सम्भ्रान्तः &c., अशान्तः -न्ता -न्तं, लुलितः -ता -तं, विलुलितः &c.; 'not to be ruffled,' अक्षोभ्यः -भ्या -भ्यं.

Rug, *s.* आस्तरणं, आस्तरः, स्तरिमा *m.* (न्), संस्तरः, स्तरः, तूलिका, तूला -ली, कम्बलः, रल्लकः, ऊर्णायुः *m.*

Rugged, *a.* रुक्षः -क्षा -क्षं, रूक्षः &c., परुषः -षा -षं, विषमः -मा -मं, असमः -मा -मं, कर्कशः -शा -शं. *See* Rough.

Ruggedness, *s.* रुक्षता, रूक्षता, रौक्ष्यं, परुषता, पारुष्यं, विषमता, वैषम्यं, असमता, कर्कशता, कार्कश्यं. *See* Roughness, *s.*

Ruin, *s.* (Destruction) नाशः, विनाशः, प्रणाशः, क्षयः, ध्वंसः, प्रध्वंसः, परिध्वंसः, परिक्षयः, अत्ययः, व्यसनं, घातः, विघातः, लोपः, उच्छेदः.—(Defeat, overthrow) पराजयः, पराभवः, अभिभवः, सादः -दनं, व्यसनं, भङ्गः; 'of an army,' बलव्यसनं.—(Mischief, bane) क्षतिः *f.*, परिक्षतिः *f.*, दूषणं, अनिष्टं, अपायः, अनर्थः, विषं.—(Of fortune, estate, &c.) सम्पत्तिनाशः, सम्पत्तिभङ्गः, लक्ष्मीभङ्गः, ऐश्वर्य्यभङ्गः, ऐश्वर्य्यनाशः, परिक्षीणता, परिक्षयः, अस्तः -स्तं; 'to go to ruin,' क्षि in pass. (क्षीयते), परिक्षि.—(Of a building) उत्सादनं, उत्सन्नता, गृहक्षयः, जीर्णिः *f.*; 'a building in ruins,' उत्सन्नगृहं, जीर्णगृहं, क्षीणगृहं, उत्सन्नवाटिका; 'a ruined temple,' जीर्णमण्डपः -पं, जीर्णदेवायतनं, चिरन्तनदेवतागारः -रं; 'in ruins,' उत्सन्नः -न्ना -न्नं, क्षीणः &c.

To ruin, *v. a.* (Destroy) नश् (c. 10. नाशयति -यितुं), विनश्, प्रणश्, क्षि (c. 5. क्षिणोति, क्षेतुं, c. 10. क्षययति, क्षपयति -यितुं), ध्वंस् (c. 10. ध्वंसयति -यितुं), विध्वंस्, प्रध्वंस्, दुष् (c. 10. दूषयति -यितुं), सद् (c. 10. सादयति -यितुं), हन् (c. 2. हन्ति -न्तुं, c. 10. घातयति -यितुं), उच्छिद् (c. 7. -छिनत्ति -छेत्तुं), लुप् (c. 6. लुम्पति, लोप्तुं, c. 10. -लोपयति -यितुं), विलुप्, क्षतिं कृ.—(Demolish, pull down) उत्सद्, अवसद्,

अधःपत् (c. 10. -पातयति -यितुं), उत्सादनं कृ, उद्धृ, संहृ, ध्वंस्.—(Deprive of fortune, bring to poverty) सम्पत्तिनाशं कृ, सम्पत्तिभङ्गं कृ, परिक्षीणीकृ, परिक्षयं जन् or कृ, नष्टश्रीकं -कां कृ, दारिद्र्यं गम् in caus.—(By magical incantations) उच्चाटनं कृ.

To RUIN, *v. n.* (Fall into ruin) क्षि in pass. (क्षीयते), परिक्षि, *see To* DECAY.

RUINED, *p. p.* (Destroyed) नष्टः -ष्टा -ष्टं, नाशितः -ता -तं, विनाशितः &c., प्रणष्टः &c., ध्वंसितः -ता -तं, ध्वस्तः -स्ता -स्तं, विध्वस्तः &c., दूषितः -ता -तं, सादितः &c., क्षीणः -णा -णं, विशीर्णः -र्णा -र्णं.—(Demolished, decayed as a building, &c.) उत्सादितः -ता -तं, उत्सन्नः -न्ना -न्नं, जीर्णः -र्णा -र्णं, अधःपातितः -ता -तं, उच्छिन्नः -न्ना -न्नं.—(Deprived of fortune) नष्टश्रीकः -का -कं, गतश्रीकः &c., विगतश्रीकः &c., हतश्रीकः &c., क्षीणधनः -ना -नं, क्षीणार्थः -र्था -र्थं, नष्टार्थः &c., गतविभवः -वा -वं, नष्टलक्ष्मीकः -का -कं, नष्टसम्पत्तिः -त्तिः -त्ति, भग्नसम्पत्तिः &c., क्षतवृत्तिः -त्तिः -त्ति, परिक्षीणः -णा -णं, प्रचलितविभवः &c., लुप्तसर्वस्वः -स्वा -स्वं, नष्टैश्वर्य्यः -र्य्या -र्य्यं.

RUINOUS, *a.* (Destructive, baneful) नाशी -शिनी -शि (न्), नाशकः -का -कं, विनाशकः &c., क्षयकरः -री -रं, घातुकः -का -कं, घाती &c., विघातकः &c., आत्ययिकः -की -कं, दूषकः &c., विध्वंसकः &c., सम्पत्तिनाशकः &c., लक्ष्मीनाशकः &c., कल्याणहरः -रा -रं, कल्याणहारकः &c., कल्याणनाशकः &c., लक्ष्मीभञ्जकः &c., अनर्थकरः &c.—(Fallen to ruins) उत्सन्नः -न्ना -न्नं, जीर्णः -र्णा -र्णं.

RUINOUSLY, *adv.* सनाशं, सक्षयं, विनाशेन, सदूषणं, सध्वंसं.

RULE, *s.* (Government, authority) अधिकारः, अधीकारः, आधिपत्यं, प्रभुत्वं, ईशत्वं, स्वामित्वं, स्वाम्यं, ऐश्वर्य्यं, शासनं, शास्तिः *f.*, अनुशासनं, कर्तृत्वं.—(Regulation, law) विधिः *m.*, विधानं, नियमः, सूत्रं, व्यवस्था, स्थितिः *f.*, धर्म्मः, मर्य्यादा, क्रमः.—(Precept) नियमः, निदेशः, निर्देशः, आदेशः, सूत्रं, कल्पः, शासनं, प्रचोदनं, चोदना.—(Principle, rule of science) सूत्रं, तत्त्वं, नियमः, न्यायः, उक्तवाक्यं.—(Rule of action, course of procedure) क्रियाविधिः *m.*, कर्म्मविधिः *m.*, क्रियाप्रसङ्गः, मर्य्यादा, कार्य्याकार्य्यनियमः.—(Rule of jurisprudence) व्यवहारविधिः *m.*, व्यवहारः, व्यवहारमार्गः.—(Of grammar) शब्दशासनं.—(General rule) साधारणविधिः *m.*, साधारणं, सामान्यविधिः *m.*—(Standard measure) प्रमाणं, परिमाणं, मानं.—(According to rule) यथाविधि, विधिवत्, नियमतस्, यथानियमं, विधिपूर्व्वं -र्व्वकं, यथान्यायं.—(Instrument for ruling lines), *see* RULER.—(Rule of three in arithmetic) त्रैराशिकः -कं -का. It is of three kinds, 1. Direct, क्रमत्रैराशिकः -कं. 2. Inverse, विलोमत्रैराशिकः -कं, व्यस्तत्रैराशिकं. 3. Double, पञ्चराशिकं. The first term or supposition is called त्रिराशिकं; the second or rate प्रमाणं; the third or demand, इच्छा; the fourth or answer, इच्छाफलं.

To RULE, *v. a.* (Govern) शास् (c. 2. शास्ति -सितुं), अनुशास्, प्रशास्, समनुशास्, ईश् (c. 2. ईष्टे, ईशितुं), यम् (c. 1. यच्छति, यन्तुं), नियम्, विनियम्, संनियम्, पाल् (c. 10. पालयति -यितुं), परिपाल्, विनी, प्रणी, वशीकृ, विधा, अधिष्ठा, अध्यास्, अधिकृतः -ता -तं भू, गुप्.—(Mark with lines) रेखाभिर् अङ्क् (c. 10. अङ्कयति -यितुं), वक्ष्यमाणशलाकया रेखाङ्कितं -तां कृ, सरलरेखाभिर् अङ्क्, वर्त्तिभिर् अङ्क्.

To RULE, *v. n.* राज्यं कृ, राज्यपालनं कृ, राज्यशासनं कृ, राज्याधिकारं कृ, प्रभुत्वं कृ, स्वाम्यं कृ, अधिकारं कृ, आधिपत्यं कृ, राजकार्य्यं कृ.

RULED, *p. p.* शासितः -ता -तं, अनुशासितः &c., प्रशासितः &c., पालितः -ता -तं, नियमितः &c.; 'ruled over,' अधिष्ठितः -ता -तं.—(With lines) रेखाङ्कितः -ता -तं; 'a ruled line,' रेखा, वर्त्तिः *f.*, अङ्कः, लेखा.

RULER, *s.* (Governor) शासिता *m.* (तृ), प्रशासिता *m.*, शास्ता *m.*, शासकः, अनुशासकः, अधिपतिः *m.*, अधिष्ठाता *m.* (तृ), स्वामी *m.* (न्), अधिपः, अध्यक्षः, अधिकृतः, ईश्वरः, ईशः, प्रभुः *m.*, पालकः, पालयिता *m.* (तृ), नियन्ता *m.*, नियामकः, अधिकारी *m.* (न्), प in comp.; 'under one ruler,' एकस्वामिकः -का -कं; 'under two,' उभयस्वामिकः &c.—(For ruling lines) शलाका, अङ्कनी, लेखनी, रेखणी.

RULING, *part.* or *a.* पालयन् -यन्ती -यत् (त्), शासत् -सती -सत्, शासिता -त्री -तृ, नियामकः -का -कं.—(Predominant) प्रबलः -ला -लं, प्रभविष्णुः -ष्णुः -ष्णु, प्रधानः -ना -नं, प्रभवः -वा -वं; 'ruling deity,' अधिदैवं.

RUM, *s.* (The spirit) गौडी -डिकं, गुडलं, शीधुः -धु *m. n.* आसवः, हीलुकं, मैरेयं.

RUM, *a.* (Odd) विलक्षणः -णा -णं, असकृतः -ता -तं, अपरूपः -पा -पं.

To RUMBLE, *v. n.* गर्ज् (c. 1. गर्जति -र्जितुं), परिगर्ज्, नर्द् (c. 1. नर्दति -र्दितुं), विनर्द्, गम्भीरशब्दं कृ, गम्भीरध्वनिं कृ, गम्भीरघोषं कृ, गम्भीरनादं कृ, दीर्घनिर्घोषं कृ, घनशब्दं कृ.

RUMBLING, *s.* (Low continued sound) गर्जनं -ना, परिगर्जनं, नर्दनं, गम्भीरशब्दः, गम्भीरध्वनिः *m.*, गम्भीरनिर्घोषः, गम्भीरघोषः, दीर्घनिर्घोषः, दीर्घशब्दः, दीर्घध्वनिः *m.*, निर्घोषः, घोषः.—(Of the clouds) मेघनिर्घोषः, घनशब्दः, घनध्वनिः *m.*, मेघनादः, घनस्वनः, मेघगर्जनं, स्तनितं; 'of wheels,' नेमिशब्दः, नेमिनिर्घोषः.

RUMINANT, RUMINATING, *a.* रोमन्थकारी -रिणी -रि (न्), रोमन्थकरः -रा -रं.

To RUMINATE, *v. n.* (Chew the cud) रोमन्थ (nom. रोमन्थायते) रोमन्थं कृ.—(Muse) पुनः पुनश् चिन्त् or ध्यै or मनसा विचर्.

RUMINATION, *s.* (Chewing the cud) रोमन्थः -न्थं, रोमन्थनं.—(Musing) पौनःपुनिकध्यानं, पौनःपुनिकचिन्ता, पुनः पुनो मनसा विचारणं.

To RUMMAGE, *v. a.* अधरोत्तरीकृत्य or अस्तव्यस्तीकृत्य सूक्ष्मम् अन्विष् or निरूप्, सूक्ष्मान्वेषणार्थम् अधरोत्तरीकृ or अस्तव्यस्तीकृ.

RUMMAGE, RUMMAGING, *s.* सूक्ष्मान्वेषणार्थम् अधरोत्तरीकरणं or अस्तव्यस्तीकरणं.

RUMOR, *s.* लोकप्रवादः, जनप्रवादः, जनवादः, लोकवादः, प्रवादः, किंवदन्तिः -न्ती *f.*, जनश्रुतिः *f.*, लोकश्रुतिः *f.*, जनरवः, वार्त्ता, लोकवार्त्ता, जनवार्त्ता. *See* REPORT.

To RUMOR, *v. a.* प्रवद् (c. 1. -वदति -दितुं) श्रु in caus. *See To* REPORT.

RUMORED, *p. p.* लोकप्रवादेन आवितः -ता -तं, लोकप्रवादात् श्रुतः &c., *see* REPORTED.

RUMP, *s.* नितम्बः, स्फिचौ *f. du.* (स्फिच्), श्रोणिः -णी *f.*, श्रोणिफलकं, कटिप्रोथः.

To RUMPLE, *v. a.* संकुच् (c. 1. -कोचति -चितुं), सम्मृद् (c. 9. -मृद्नाति -मर्दितुं), पुट् (c. 10. पुटयति -यितुं), सम्पुट्, पुटीकृ, सम्पुटीकृ, चूर्ण् (c. 10. चूर्णयति -यितुं), रूक्षीकृ, रूक्षीकृ.

RUMPLE, *s.* सङ्कोचः -चनं, पुटः, सम्मर्दः, मर्दः, कुञ्चनं, भङ्गः, चूर्णः.

RUMPLED, *p. p.* सङ्कोचितः -ता -तं, सम्मर्दितः &c., मर्दितः &c., पुटितः &c.

To RUN, *v. n.* (Move quickly) धाव् (c. 1. धावति -ते -वितुं), प्रधाव्, द्रु (c. 1. द्रवति, द्रोतुं), दु (c. 1. दवति, दोतुं), रंह् (c. 1. रंहति -हितुं), शीघ्रं or द्रुतं चल् (c. 1. चलति -लितुं), द्रुतपदेन चल्, द्रुतक्रमेण सृ (c. 1. सरति, सर्त्तुं) or चर् (c. 1. चरति -रितुं), द्रुतम् इ or गम्.—(As a fluid) द्रु, स्रु (c. 1. स्रवति, स्रोतुं), प्रस्रु, स्यन्द् (c. 1. स्यन्दते -न्दितुं), क्षर् (c. 1. क्षरति -रितुं), गल् (c. 1. गलति -लितुं); 'rivers run into the ocean,' नद्यः समुद्रं द्रवन्ति.—(Melt) विली, प्रली,

द्रु, विद्रु, द्रवीभू.—(Pass, proceed) प्रगम्, प्रचल्, प्रचर्, प्रवृत् (c. 1. -वर्त्तते -र्त्तितुं), प्रसृ.—(As time) अतिवृत्, अतिक्रम्, अती, व्यती.—(As a sore) पूयं स्रु (c. 10. स्रावयति -यितुं), पूय् (c. 1. पूयते -यितुं), पूयं मुच् or उत्सृज्.—(Have a course, go in a particular direction) अमुकदिशं or अमुकदिशि गम्; 'the river runs in a different direction,' नदी भिन्नदिशं गच्छति.—(Flee for escape) पलाय् (c. 1. पलायते -यितुं, rt. इ), विपलाय्, द्रु, विद्रु, प्रद्रु, दिशः or ककुभो भज्.—(Extend) प्रसृ, प्रसृप्, आया, आगम्, वितन् in pass., विस्तृ in pass.—(Run about) परिधाव्, इतस्ततो धाव्, विपरिधाव्.—(Run after) अनुधाव्, पश्चाद् धाव्, अनुद्रु, पश्चाद् द्रु, अनुसृ, अनुगम्, अनुया, अनुवृत्, अनुव्रज्.—(Run against) प्रतिधाव्, प्रतिद्रु, अभिधाव्, अभिद्रु, प्रतिमुखं धाव् or द्रु or आगम्.—(Run at) अभिधाव्, प्रतिधाव्, आक्रम्, अभिक्रम्.—(Run away) पलाय् (c. 1. पलायते -यितुं), विपलाय्, प्रपलाय्, सम्पलाय्, विद्रु, प्रद्रु, विप्रद्रु, प्राद्रु, द्रु, अपधाव्, प्रधाव्, अपगम्, व्यपगम्, अपक्रम्, अपसृप्, व्यपसृप्.—(Run in, enter) निविश्, आविश्, प्रविश्, आगम्, अभिगम्, आया, आश्रि.—(Run into, incur) उपगम्, उपागम्, गम्; 'run into danger,' संशयम् उपगम्, भयम् उपगम्.—(Run off), *see To* RUN AWAY.—(Run on, continue on) प्रवृत्, वृत्, पर्य्यवस्था.—(Run on, prate) जल्प्, प्रलप्.—(Run over), *see To* OVERFLOW.—(Run out) विगम्, निवृत्, विनिवृत्, समाप् in pass., क्षि in pass.—(Run round) परिधाव्, परितो धाव्.—(Run to or towards) अभिद्रु, अभिधाव्, आद्रु, आधाव्, उपद्रु, समुपद्रु, समाद्रु, प्रतिद्रु, समुपधाव्, उपधाव्, प्रतिधाव्.—(For refuge) आश्रि, संश्रि, उपाश्रि, आश्रयणं कृ.—(Run hither and thither) इतस्ततो धाव्, विपरिधाव्.—(Run up, rise, swell) वृध् (c. 1. वर्धते -र्धितुं), उत्तरोत्तरं वृध्, प्रसृप्.—(Run, riot) मर्य्यादाम् अतिक्रम् or अतिगम् or लंघ्, मर्य्यादातिक्रमं कृ.

To RUN, *v. a.* (Drive, push, cause to enter) प्रविश् (c. 10. -वेशयति -यितुं), निविश्.—(A horse) अश्वं चल् in caus, or प्रेर् or प्रणुद्.—(Incur) उपगम्, उपागम्, गम्, आसद्, *see* RISK.—(Run down), *see To* CHASE.—(Run down), *see To* DECRY.—(Run over), *see To* RECOUNT.—(Run through), *see To* EXPEND, SQUANDER.

RUN, *s.* (Running) धावनं, द्रवणं, द्रावः.—(Flight) पलायनं, विपलायनं, प्रपलायनं, द्रावः, द्रवः, विद्रवः, प्रद्रावः.—(Course) गतिः *f.*, चर्य्या, चलनं, क्रमः, प्रवृत्तिः *f.*, मार्गः.—(Flow) स्रवः -वणं, स्रावः, प्रवाहः, प्रस्रावः.—(Prevalence) प्रचारः, प्रचलत्वं, प्रचरणं, प्रचलनं, प्रसिद्धिः *f.*—(Extent) परिमाणं, पर्य्यन्तः -न्तं, विषयः, *see* REACH.—(Voyage) जलयात्रा, समुद्रयात्रा, यात्रा; 'in the long run,' अन्ते, दीर्घकालमपेक्ष्य; 'the run of mankind,' सामान्यलोकः, साधारणलोकः.

RUNAGATE, RUNAWAY, *s.* पलायी *m.* (न्), विपलायी *m.*, प्रपलायी *m.*, युद्धत्यागी *m.*, युद्धपराङ्मुखः, युद्धविमुखः.

RUNDLE, *s.* (Of a ladder) सोपानं, सोपानशलाका, आरोहणशलाका.

RUNNER, *s.* धावकः, धावनकृत्.—(Courier) जंघाकारिकः, जांघिकः, जंघालः, जवी *m.* (न्), प्रजवी *m.*, तरस्वी *m.*, जवनः, जवः, वेगी *m.*, अध्वगः, धावकः, वार्त्ताहरः.—(Branch running along the ground) प्ररोहः, पल्लवः, लतिका, भूमिप्ररोहः.

RUNNING, *part.* or *a.* (Moving quickly) धावन् -वन्ती -वत् (त्), द्रवन् &c., धावमानः -ना -नं.—(Flowing) स्रवन् &c., स्रुतः -ता -तं, स्यन्दी -न्दिनी -न्दि (न्); 'running water,' स्रवज्जलं, प्रवहज्जलं.—(Discharging matter) पूयस्रावी -विणी &c., सपूयः -या -यं.—(Running away) पलायमानः -ना -नं.—(In succession, without any intervening time) अव्यवहितकालेन, अव्यवधानेन, यथाक्रमं, पर्य्यायेण, अनुपूर्व्वशस्.

RUNNET, *s.* दधिसात्करणयोग्यो रसः, दधिसात्करणयोग्यं वस्तु.

RUNNING, *s.* (Act of moving quickly) धावनं, द्रवणं, द्रावः, द्रुतगमनं, द्रुतपदेन चलनं.—(Flowing) स्रवः -वणं, स्रावः, प्रस्रावः, परिस्रावः, प्रस्रवणं, प्रवाहः.—(Discharge of matter) पूयस्रावः; 'running of the nose,' नासास्रावः, नासापरिस्रावः.

RUNT, *s.* (Dwarfish animal) ह्रस्वजन्तुः *m.*, ह्रस्वशरीरो जन्तुः, खर्व्वः.

RUPEE, *s.* रौप्यं, रौप्यमुद्रा, रूप्यमुद्रा, मुद्रा, मुद्रिका; 'half-rupee,' भागः, रौप्यभागः.

RUPTURE, RUPTION, *s.* भङ्गः, भेदः, भञ्जनं, भेदनं, छेदः -दनं, ध्वंसः, विध्वंसः, खण्डनं, स्फोटः -टनं.—(Breach of friendship) स्नेहभङ्गः, स्नेहभेदः, मैत्रीभङ्गः, सौहृदभङ्गः.—(Hernia) अन्त्रवृद्धिः *f.*

To RUPTURE, *v. a.* भञ्ज्, भिद्, खण्ड्; 'a blood-vessel,' उरोक्षतं कृ.

RUPTURED, *p. p.* भग्नः -ग्ना -ग्नं; 'having hernia,' अन्त्रवृद्धिरोगी -गिणी &c.

RURAL, *a.* जाङ्गलः -ली -लं, जङ्गलः -ला -लं, वन्यः -न्या -न्यं, जानपदः -दी -दं, ग्राम्यः -म्या -म्यं, ग्रामीयः -या -यं, आनुग्रामिकः -की -कं, अनागरः -री -रं, अनागरिकः -की -कं.

RUSE, *s.* व्यपदेशः, अपदेशः, उपायः. *See* ARTIFICE, STRATAGEM.

RUSH, *s.* (Kind of grass) दूर्व्वा; 'place full of rushes,' दूर्व्वाविकीर्णभूमिः *f.*

RUSH, *s.* (Impetuous advance or onset) वेगः, आवेगः, महावेगेन धावनं or अभिधावनं, सवेगधावनं, अतिवेगेन गमनं, सवेगगमनं, महावेगेन आपतनं or आपातः or प्रपतनं, अतिवेगेन अवस्कन्दनं, संरम्भः, संरम्भेण or रभसेन आक्रमणं; 'emulative onset,' अहम्पूर्व्विका.

To RUSH, *v. n.* (Move forward with impetuosity) महावेगेन धाव् (c. 1. धावति -वितुं) or अभिधाव्, सवेगं धाव्, अतिवेगेन गम् or चल्, महावेगेन या or सृ or प्रया or प्रसृ.—(Rush upon) महावेगेन आक्रम् (c. 1. -क्रामति -क्रमितुं) or अभिक्रम् or आपत् or आसद्, महावेगपूर्व्वम् अभिधाव् or प्रतिधाव्, समहावेगम् अभिद्रु or प्रतिद्रु or आस्कन्द् or अवलुप्.—(Rush into headlong) अवाङ्मुखेन प्रविश्, अतिवेगेन प्रविश्, अतिसाहसेन प्रविश्, अवाक् or अधोमुखेन पत्.—(Rush forth or out) निर्पत्, प्रपत्, अतिवेगेन निर्गम् or वहिर्गम्; 'water rushed from his eyes,' जलं तस्य नेत्राभ्यां प्रापतत्.

RUSHING, *s.*, *see* RUSH.—*Part.* महावेगः -गा -गं, *see* IMPETUOUS.

RUSHLIGHT, *s.* तृणमयदीपिका, तृणमयवर्त्तियुक्तो दीपकः.

RUSHY, *a.* दूर्व्वामयः -यी -यं, दूर्व्वापूर्णः -र्णा -र्णं, तृणमयः &c., तृणपूर्णः &c.

RUSSET, *a.* कपिशः -शा -शं, कपिशवर्णः -र्णा -र्णं, ताम्रवर्णः &c., श्यावः &c.

RUST, *s.* (Of iron) सिंहानं, सिंहाणं, सिंघाणं, शिंघाणं, मलं, अयोमलं, मण्डुरं, किट्टं, किट्टालः, कलङ्कः, रीतिः *f.*, लोष्टं, धूर्त्तं, पात्रटीरः.

To RUST, *v. n.* सिंहानं or कलङ्कं बन्ध् (c. 9. बध्नाति, बन्द्धुं), सकलङ्कः -ङ्का -ङ्कं भू, कलङ्कावृतः -ता -तं भू, समलः -ला -लं भू, मलावृतः -ता -तं भू.

To RUST, *v. a.* सकलङ्कं -ङ्कां कृ, मलावृतं -तां कृ, कलङ्क (nom. कलङ्कयति -यितुं).

RUSTED, *p. p.* कलङ्कितः -ता -तं, मलावृतः -ता -तं, कलङ्कावृतः &c.

RUSTIC, *a.* (Pertaining to the country) ग्राम्यः -म्या -म्यं, जनपदसम्बन्धी &c., *see* RURAL.—(Boorish, homely) ग्राम्यः -म्या -म्यं, ग्रामीयः -या -यं, ग्रामिकः -की -कं, ग्रामीणः -णा -णं, आनुग्रामिकः

&c., ग्रामजः -जा -जं, असभ्यः -भ्या -भ्यं, अशिष्टः -ष्टा -ष्टं, प्राकृतः -ता -तं.

RUSTIC, *s.* ग्राम्यजनः, ग्रामी *m.* (न्), ग्रामवासी *m.*, ग्रामेवासी *m.*, वृषलः.

RUSTICALLY, *adv.* ग्राम्यजनवत्, ग्रामिकवत्, असभ्यवत्, ग्रामीयप्रकारेण.

To RUSTICATE, *v. a.* ग्रामे वस् in caus. (वासयति -यितुं) or विवस् or प्रवस्.

To RUSTICATE, *v. n.* ग्रामे वस् (c. 1. वसति, वस्तुं) or निवस्, ग्रामं सेव्.

RUSTICITY, *s.* ग्राम्यता -त्वं, ग्रामिकत्वं, ग्रामीयता, असभ्यता, अशिष्टता.

RUSTINESS, *s.* सकलङ्कता, समलता -त्वं, मालिन्यं, मलिनता, मलवत्त्वं.

To RUSTLE, *v. n.* शकशक (nom. शकशकायति -ते), शकशकशब्दं कृ, मर्म्मर (nom. मर्म्मरायति -ते), मर्म्मरं कृ, मर्म्मरशब्दं कृ, काहलं कृ, काहलशब्दं कृ.

RUSTLING, *s.* शकशकशब्दः; 'of leaves,' मर्म्मरः, पत्रकाहलः -ला, पिप्पोला, पर्णध्वनितं; 'of clothes,' मर्म्मरः, वस्त्रध्वनितं.

RUSTLING, *part.* शकशकायन् -यन्ती -यत् (त्), मर्म्मरकारी -रिणी -रि (न्).

RUSTY, *a.* कलङ्की -ङ्किनी -ङ्कि (न्), कलङ्कमयः -यी -यं, सकलङ्कः -ङ्का -ङ्कं, कलङ्कितः -ता -तं, कलङ्कावृतः -ता -तं, मलिनः -ना -नं, समलः -ला -लं, मली -लिनी &c., मलावृतः &c.

RUT, *s.* (In animals) मदः, रतेच्छा, मैथुनेच्छा.—(Mark of a wheel) चक्रचिह्नं, नेमिचिह्नं, चक्राङ्कः, चक्रमार्गः.

RUTHLESS, *a.* निर्दयः -या -यं, दयाहीनः -ना -नं. *See* PITILESS.

RUTTISH, *a.* मत्तः -त्ता -त्तं, मदाविष्टः &c., मदोत्कटः &c., *see* LUSTFUL.

RYOT, *s.* कृषकः, कृषिकः, कर्षकः, कृषिजीवी *m.* (न्), भूस्वाम्यधीनः.

S.

SABBATARIAN, *s.* विश्रामदिनपालकः, विश्रामवारप्रतिपालकः, विश्रामदिनसेवकः.

SABBATH, *s.* विश्रामदिवसः, विश्रामदिनं, विरामदिवसः, विश्रामवारः.

SABBATH-BREAKER, *s.* विश्रामवारभेदकः, विश्रामवारलंघी *m.* (न्), विश्रामदिनभेदी *m.*

SABBATICAL, *a.* विश्रामवारसम्बन्धी &c., पुण्यविश्रामसम्बन्धी &c.

SABLE, *a.* श्यामः -मा -मं, कृष्णवर्णः -र्णा -र्णं, कृष्णः &c., कालः &c.

SABLE, *s.* (Animal with long dark fur) लोमशजन्तुः *m.*, श्यामलोमविशिष्टः क्षुद्रजन्तुः.—(Fish) जलतापिकः, जलतापी *m.* (न्), जलतालुः.

SABOT, *s.* (Wooden shoe) काष्ठपादुका, काष्ठमयपादुका.

SABRE, *s.* चक्रखड्गः, खड्गः, चन्द्रहासः, मण्डलाग्रः, निस्त्रिंशः, कृपाणः.

To SABRE, *v. a.* खड्गेन हन् (c. 2. हन्ति -न्तुं, c. 10. घातयति -यितुं).

SABULOUS, *a.* सिकतामयः -यी -यं, शार्करिकः -की -कं. *See* SANDY.

SACCHARINE, *a.* (Pertaining to sugar) शर्करासम्बन्धी -न्धिनी &c., शार्करः -री -रं, शार्करिकः -की -कं, ऐक्षवः -वी -वं.—(Having the qualites of sugar, sweet) शर्करागुणकः -का -कं, शर्कराधर्म्मकः &c., मिष्टः -ष्टा -ष्टं, मधुरः -रा -रं, सुमधुरः &c.

SACERDOTAL, *a.* पौरोहितः -ती -तं, पौरोहितिकः -की -कं, याजकीयः -या -यं, याजकसम्बन्धी &c., *see* PRIESTLY; 'sacerdotal office,' पौरोहित्यं.

SACHEL, *s.* क्षुद्रकोषः, पुस्तककोषः, लेख्यपत्राधारः, पत्रिकाधारः.

SACHÍ, (The wife of Indra; daughter of the saint Puloman, destroyed by Indra, to prevent his curse for the violation of the daughter) शची, शचिः *f.*, इन्द्राणी, शक्राणी, मघोनी, इन्द्रशक्तिः *f.*, पुलोमजा, पौलोमी.

SACK, *s.* (Coarse canvas bag) शाणकोषः, स्थूलकोषः, शाणमयकोषः, स्यूतः, स्योतः, स्यूतिः *f.*, स्यूनः, स्योनः, प्रसेवः, शाणपुटः, धौतकटः, गोणी.—(Pillage of a town, &c.) नगरलुण्ठनं, ग्रामलुण्ठनं, ग्रामघातः.

To SACK, *v. a.* (A town) नगरं लुण्ट् or लुण्ठ्, नगरलुण्ठनं कृ, *see* PILLAGE.

SACK-CLOTH, SACKING, *s.* शाणं, शाणजं, शाणवसनं, शाणपटः, शाणवस्त्रं, शणपटः, स्थूलशाटिः *m.*, स्थूलशाटकः, स्थूलपटः, स्थूलपट्टः, वराशिः *m.*

SACKED, *p. p.* लुण्ठितः -ता -तं, लुण्टितः &c. *See* PLUNDERED, STORMED.

SACRAMENT, *s.* संस्कारः, महायज्ञः. For the twelve sanskáras or sacred symbolical rites, *see* RITE. The following are the five mahá-yajnas, or great sacraments of the Hindús (as explained in Manu III. 70. *et. seq.*), appointed to be performed every day by the Grihastha, or house-keeper, for the sake of expiating the sin incurred by the involuntary destruction of minute living creatures. They refer respectively to what is due to five objects, viz. himself, the gods, his fore-fathers, spirits or ghosts, and men or guests. 1. Study of Scripture, with prayer and meditation, called ब्रह्मयज्ञः or अहुतः. 2. Offering oblations to the gods in fire, called देवयज्ञः or हुतः. 3. Offering libations of water and cakes to the manes of deceased ancestors, called पितृयज्ञः or प्राशितं or श्राद्धं. 4. Casting the residue of oblations on the ground or in water, as an offering to spirits or goblins, called भूतयज्ञः or बलियज्ञः or प्रहुतः or आहुतः or बलिः *m.* 5. Receiving guests, and especially Brahmans, with hospitality, called नृयज्ञः or मनुष्ययज्ञः or ब्राह्म्यहुतं or ब्राह्म्यं or ब्रह्महुतं. The Vishnu-Purána adds two other sacraments, viz. 'propagation of offspring,' प्रजापतियज्ञः, and 'observance of truth,' सत्ययज्ञः, but these are comparatively modern additions. The Christian idea of a sacrament may be expressed by संस्कारः or ख्रीष्टप्रकल्पितसंस्कारः; as, 'the sacrament of baptism,' जलसंस्कारः or जलसेचनसंस्कारः or मज्जनसंस्कारः; 'of the Lord's Supper,' ख्रीष्टभोजनसंस्कारः or ख्रीष्टमृत्युस्मरणार्थकसंस्कारः.

SACRAMENTAL, *a.* संस्कारसम्बन्धी -न्धिनी &c., महायज्ञसम्बन्धी &c., संस्कारविषयकः -का -कं, संस्कारप्रयुक्तः -क्ता -क्तं, संस्काररूपः -पा -पं.

SACRED, *a.* (Holy, pertaining to God or his worship) पुण्यः -ण्या -ण्यं, पवित्रः -त्रा -त्रं, ईश्वरसम्बन्धी -न्धिनी &c., देवसम्बन्धी &c., ईश्वरपूजासम्बन्धी &c., ईश्वरभजनसम्बन्धी &c., अलौकिकः -की -कं, असांसारिकः -की -कं, धर्म्मविषयकः -का -कं, अमार्गिकः -की -कं, प्रपञ्चेतरः -रा -रं.—(Used for religious purposes) पुण्यकर्म्मोपयोगी -गिनी -गि (न्), पवित्रकर्म्मोपयोगी &c., पुण्यकर्म्मार्थकः -का -कं &c., ईश्वरपूजोपयोगी &c., ईश्वरपूजार्थकः -का -कं.—(Consecrated) संस्कृतः -ता -तं, प्रतिष्ठितः &c., सुप्रतिष्ठितः &c., प्रणीतः &c.—(Inviolable, approaching to a superior being) अलंघनीयः -या -यं, अनुल्लंघनीयः &c., अलंघ्यः -घ्या -घ्यं, अभेद्यः -द्या -द्यं, अनतिक्रमणीयः -या -यं, सशपथः -था -थं, शिवस्वतुल्यः -ल्या -ल्यं, शिवस्वसदृशः -शी -शं, निषिद्धः -द्धा -द्धं.—(Venerable) पूज्यः -ज्या -ज्यं, पूजनीयः -या -यं, सुपूजनीयः &c., पूजार्हः -र्हा -र्हं.—(Relating to holy sages) आर्षः -र्षी -र्षं, आर्षेयः -यी -यं, ऋषिसम्बन्धी &c.; 'sacred spot,' पुण्यस्थानं, पुण्यस्थलं, पुण्यक्षेत्रं, पुण्यतीर्थं, क्षेत्रं; 'sacred grove,' पुण्यवनं, तपोवनं 'sacred thing,' पुण्यवस्तु *n.*; 'thing not to be touched,' ब्रह्मस्वं, देवस्वं, शिवस्वं, गोमांसं; 'sacred writing,' पुण्यशास्त्रं, शास्त्रं, वेदः; 'sacred and profane knowledge,' ज्ञानविज्ञानं.

Sacredness, *s.* पुण्यता -त्वं, पवित्रता -त्वं, अलंघनीयता, पूज्यता, सुपूज्यता.

Sacrifice, *s.* (Of an animal or any other thing to God) यज्ञः, यागः, मेधः, क्रतुः *m.*, अध्वरः, मखः, इज्या, इष्टिः *f.*, यज्ञकर्म्म *n.* (न्), याज्ञिक्यं, यजनं, याजनं, बलिः *m.*, बलिकर्म्म *n.* बलिदानं, प्रयागः, प्रोक्षणं, सत्रं, होमः, हवनं, आहवनं, धृतिः *f.*, दीक्षा, चयनं, सप्ततन्तुः *m.*, सवः, इष्टं, नारायणबलिः *m.*; 'a sacrifice at which sixteen officiating priests are required,' ज्योतिष्टोमं; 'a royal sacrifice performed only by an universal monarch,' राजसूयं, क्रतूत्तमः, क्रतुराजः; 'relating to it,' राजसूयिकः -का -कं; 'officiating priest at it,' राजसूययाजी *m.* (न्); 'sacrifice of a horse, which, performed a hundred times, raises the sacrificer to a level with Indra,' अश्वमेधः; 'horse fit for it,' अश्वमेधिकः, अश्वमेधीयः; 'morning sacrifice,' प्रातर्यज्ञः, प्रातर्हुतं; 'any part of a sacrifice,' यज्ञाङ्गः; 'a supplementary sacrifice performed to atone for any defects in the preceding one,' अवभृथः, यज्ञान्तः, दीक्षान्तः; 'bathing after any sacrifice,' अवभृथः, अवभृथस्नानं; 'accomplishment of a sacrifice,' यज्ञसिद्धिः *f.*; 'remnants of one,' यज्ञशेषः, यज्ञशिष्टं; 'animal for sacrifice, especially a horse,' यज्ञपशुः *m.*, क्रतुपशुः *m.*; 'goat for one,' यज्ञछागः; 'reward of one,' क्रतुफलं; 'a Brahman who sells the benefits of a sacrifice he has performed,' क्रतुविक्रयी *m.* (न्), 'vessel for sacrifice,' यज्ञपात्रं; 'fit for sacrifice,' यज्ञियः -या -यं, याज्ञियः -यी -यं, मेध्यः -ध्या -ध्यं; 'human sacrifice,' नरयज्ञः, नरमेधः; 'ceremonies preliminary to a sacrifice,' दीक्षा; 'a sacrifice preceded by them,' दीक्षणीयेष्टिः *f.*; 'officiating at a sacrifice, or causing one to be performed,' याजनं; 'officiating priest at one,' याजकः, *see* Sacrificer; 'place of sacrifice,' यज्ञभूमिः *f.*, यज्ञस्थानं, यज्ञियशाला, यज्ञशाला; 'ground or terrace leveled and squared, and prepared for a sacrifice,' स्थण्डिलं, चत्वरं, वेदिः -दी *f.*, यज्ञवाटः -टिका; 'altar in the middle of it,' स्थण्डिलसितकं, वेदिः -दी *f.*, आयतनं; 'ascetic who sleeps on such ground,' स्थण्डिलशायी *m.*, स्थण्डिलेशयः; 'shed for a sacrifice,' मण्डपः, यज्ञमण्डपः; 'fire for a sacrifice,' होमाग्निः *m.*; 'pit for this fire,' कुण्डं, होमकुण्डं, यज्ञकुण्डं, हवनी, हविर्धानी; 'post for binding the victim,' यूपः -पं; 'the top of it,' यूपाग्रं; 'ring at the top of it,' यूपकटकः; 'ceremony of erecting it,' यूपोच्छ्रयः.—(Thing offered to God) उपहारः, उत्सर्गः, बलिः *m.*, हुतं, होमः, चरुः *m.*, नैवेद्यं, निवेदनं, कव्यं, कुण्डपाय्यः, *see* Oblation.—(Surrender or loss made for gaining some object, or for obliging another) त्यागः, उत्सर्गः, परित्यागः, विनियोगः, व्ययः, समर्पणं, निवेदनं, अवसानं; 'of one's self,' आत्मपरित्यागः, आत्मसमर्पणं, आत्मनिवेदनं; 'of one's person or life,' स्वदेहविनियोगः, स्वदेहपरित्यागः, स्वप्राणपरित्यागः, स्वजीवितव्ययः; 'at the sacrifice of one's own happiness,' आत्मनः सुखपरित्यागेन, आत्मनः सुखावसानेन.

To sacrifice, *v. a.* (Immolate on an altar, destroy or consume any thing as an atonement or offering) यज् (c. 1. यजति -ते, यष्टुं), हु (c. 3. जुहोति, होतुं), अभिहु, आहु, अभ्युहु, उपहारार्थं हन् (c. 2. हन्ति -न्तुं), उत्सर्गार्थं हन् or उपहृ (c. 1. -हरति -हर्त्तुं) or आहृ or उपहारीकृ, क्रतौ हन्, उत्सर्गपूर्ब्बं हन्, बलिं कृ, बलिदानं कृ, अध्वर (nom. अध्वरीयति), यजनं कृ, याजनं कृ, *see To* immolate. The root यज् is often redundantly followed by यज्ञः or क्रतुः or by other subtantives in the accus. or instr. c.; as, 'he sacrificed a sacrifice,' यज्ञं or यज्ञेन इयाज, इष्टिं or इष्ट्या अयजत्, क्रतुं or क्रतुना अयाक्षीत्; 'he sacrificed a horse,' अश्वं or अश्वेन or अश्वमेधेन ईजे; 'having sacrificed cattle,' पशुभिर् इष्ट्वा; 'sacrificing a horse to the gods,' अश्वेन देवान् ईजानः.—(Surrender or suffer to be lost for the sake of gaining something) त्यज् (c. 1. त्यजति, त्यक्तुं), परित्यज्, उत्सृज् (c. 1. -सृजति -स्रष्टुं), उत्सर्गं कृ, हा (c. 3. जहाति, हातुं, c. 10. हापयति -यितुं), विहा, अपहा, नश् (c. 10. नाशयति -यितुं), प्रणश्, विनश्.—(Devote) विनियुज्, समृ in caus., निविद् in caus., उत्सृज्.

Sacrificed, *p. p.* इष्टः -ष्टा -ष्टं, हुतः -ता -तं, उपहृतः &c., उपहारीकृतः &c., प्रोक्षितः &c.; 'to be sacrificed,' याज्यः -ज्या -ज्यं.—(Surrendered) त्यक्तः -क्ता -क्तं, परित्यक्तः &c., उत्सृष्टः -ष्टा -ष्टं.

Sacrificer, *s.* यष्टा *m.* (ष्टृ), याजकः, याजी *m.* (न्), यज्वा *m.* (न्), यज्ञकृत् *m.*, याज्ञिकः, होता *m.* (तृ), यजन्तः, याजिः *m.*, यजिः *m.*, यज्ञकर्त्ता *m.* (र्त्तृ), यज्ञकारी *m.* (न्), यजमानः, ऋत्विक् *m.* (ज्); 'one who frequently sacrifices,' इज्याशीलः, यागशीलः, यायजूकः; 'performer of the Vrihaspati sacrifice,' स्थपतिः *m.*

Sacrificial, *a.* यज्ञियः -या -यं, याज्ञियः -यी -यं, ऐष्टिकः -की -कं, यज्ञीयः -या -यं, यज्ञसम्बन्धी -न्धिनी &c., यज्ञविषयकः -का -कं, हुतः -ता -तं, आहवनीयकः -का -कं, वैतानः -नी -नं, वैतानिकः -की -कं, पौर्ष्णिकः -की -कं, यज्ञ in comp.—(Fit for a sacrifice) मेध्यः -ध्या -ध्यं, यज्ञियः -या -यं, याज्ञियः &c., यज्ञ in comp.; 'sacrificial vessel,' यज्ञपात्रं, यज्ञभाजनं, पूजाभाण्डं, पात्रीयः; 'sacrificial thread or cord worn over the left shoulder and under the right by the three principal classes,' यज्ञोपवीतं, उपवीतं, यज्ञसूत्रं, पवित्रं, सावित्रं, पञ्चवटः, पञ्चावटः, द्विजायनी; 'one invested with it,' यज्ञोपवीती *m.* (न्), उपवीती *m.*; 'the same cord passed over the right shoulder,' प्राचीनावीतं; 'one so wearing it,' प्राचीनावीती *m.*; 'the same suspended over the neck,' निवीतं; 'one so wearing it,' निवीती *m.*; 'sacrificial fire,' होमाग्निः *m.*, समूह्यः, परिचाय्यः, उपचाय्यः; 'grass,' कुशः -शं, पवित्रकं, पवित्रं, दर्भः, कुथः.

Sacrilege, *s.* देवस्वापहरणं, देवस्वापहारः, देवस्वचौर्य्यं, ब्रह्मस्वहरणं, पुण्यवस्तुहरणं, पुण्यवस्तुदूषणं, पुण्यद्रव्यदूषणं, पवित्रवस्तुदूषणं, धर्म्मातिक्रमः, धर्म्मलोपः, धर्म्मलंघनं.

Sacrilegious, *a.* देवस्वापहारी -रिणी -रि (न्), देवस्वापहारकः -का -कं, देवस्वचौर्य्यसम्बन्धी &c., पुण्यवस्तुहारी &c., पुण्यवस्तुदूषकः -का -कं, पवित्रवस्तुदूषकः &c., पुण्यद्रव्यदूषकः &c., धर्म्मलोपकः &c., धर्म्मातिक्रमी &c.

Sacrilegiously, *adv.* देवस्वापहारेण, पुण्यवस्तुदूषणेन, सधर्म्मलोपं.

Sad, *a.* (Affected with sorrow or melancholy) विषण्णः -ण्णा -ण्णं, विषादी -दिनी -दि (न्), अवसन्नः -न्ना -न्नं, उद्विग्नः -ग्ना -ग्नं, उदासीनः -ना -नं, उदासी -सिनी &c., खेदयुक्तः -क्ता -क्तं, खिन्नः -न्ना -न्नं, दुर्मनाः -नाः -नः (स्), विमनाः &c., उद्विग्नमनाः &c., सन्तमनाः &c., सशोकः -का -कं, शोकार्त्तः -र्त्ता -र्त्तं, अवनतः -ता -तं, परिद्यूनः -ना -नं, सोत्कण्ठः -ण्ठा -ण्ठं, *see* Melancholy.—(Of a sad countenance) म्लानमुखः -खा -खं, म्लानवदनः -ना -नं, दीनमुखः -खी -खं, विषण्णमुखः &c.—(Causing sorrow) शोकजनकः -का -कं, शोकदः -दा -दं, शोचनीयः -या -यं, शोकावहः -हा -हं, दुःखावहः &c., दुःखकरः -री -रं, दुःखदः &c., खेदजनकः &c., क्लेशकः &c., क्लेशकरः &c.—

(Bad, worthless) निर्गुणः -णा -णं, दुष्टः -ष्टा -ष्टं; 'to be sad,' विषद्, अवसद्, खिद् in pass., दुर्मनस्, शुच्, व्यथ्, see MELANCHOLY.

To SADDEN, *v. a.* शुच् (c. 10. शोचयति -यितुं), विषण्णीकृ, उद्विग्नीकृ, शोकान्वितं -तां कृ, शोकार्त्तीकृ, सशोकं -कां कृ. *See To* GRIEVE, *v. a.*

SADDLE, *s.* पर्य्याणं, पर्य्ययणं, पल्ययनं, पल्याणं, अश्वसज्जा, सज्जा.

To SADDLE, *v. a.* सपर्य्याणं -णां कृ, पर्य्याणं निविश् (c. 10. -वेशयति -यितुं), or न्यस् or आरुह् in caus., पर्य्याणयुक्तं -क्तां कृ, सज्जीकृ, सज्ज् (c. 10. सज्जयति -यितुं).

SADDLER, SADDLE-MAKER, *s.* पर्य्याणकारी *m.* (न्), अश्वसज्जाकारः -रकः.

SADDUCEE, *s.* पुनरुत्थानाभाववादी *m.* (न्), परलोकाभाववादी *m.*

SADLY, *adv.* सशोकं, सविषादं, सखेदं, सदुःखं, सोद्वेगं, सक्लेशं, शोचनीयं, शोचनीयप्रकारेण, यथा शोकः or क्लेशो जायते तथाप्रकारेण.

SADNESS, *s.* विषादः, विषण्णता, शोकः, सशोकता, उद्वेगः, उद्विग्नता, अवसादः, अवसन्नता, उदासीनता, औदासीन्यं, खेदः, उत्कण्ठा, आधिः *m.*, मनःपीडा, मनोव्यथा, मनोविषादः. *See* MELANCHOLY, SORROW.

SAFE, *a.* (Free from danger) भयमुक्तः -क्ता -क्तं, भयातीतः -ता -तं, आपदतीतः -ता -तं, आपन्मुक्तः &c., विपदतीतः -ता -तं, विपन्मुक्तः &c., विपत्तिमुक्तः &c., अकुतोभयः -या -यं, निर्भयः -या -यं, अभयः -या -यं, क्षेमम्प्राप्तः -प्ता -प्तं, निर्भयत्वप्राप्तः &c., निःशङ्कः -ङ्का -ङ्कं.—(Free from hurt or injury) सुस्थः -स्था -स्थं, सुरक्षितः -ता -तं, सुपालितः &c., अक्षतः -ता -तं, अपरिक्षतः &c., क्षतिहीनः -ना -नं, अजातक्षतिः -तिः -ति, अजातनाशः -शा -शं, अजातापायः -या -यं, अजातापकारः -रा -रं, निर्व्रणः -णा -णं.—(Safe and sound) सुस्थः -स्था -स्थं, सुस्थशरीरः -रा -रं, कल्यः -ल्या -ल्यं, सुशरीरः -रा -रं, अनामयः -या -यं, निरामयः &c., कुशलः -ला -लं.—(Conferring or causing safety) अभयजनकः -का -कं, अभयकारकः &c., निर्भयत्वजनकः &c., निर्भयः -या -यं, क्षेमकरः -रा -रं, क्षेमजनकः &c., क्षेम्यः -म्या -म्यं, भयहीनः -ना -नं, भयरहितः -ता -तं; 'a safe place,' निर्भयस्थानं.

SAFE, *s.* (For stores &c.) काष्ठोलः लकः, कोष्ठः -ष्ठकं, लोहभाण्डं.

SAFE-CONDUCT, *s.* अभयपत्रं, अभयवाक् *f.* (च्), अभयदानं, अभयप्रदानं.

SAFE-GUARD, *s.* रक्षा -क्षणं, गुप्तिः *f.* *See* PROTECTION.—(Passport) अभयपत्रं.

SAFELY, *adv.* क्षेमेण, सक्षेमं, अक्षतं, क्षतेन विना, अभयेन, निर्भयं, कुशलं, स्वस्तिक्षेमं, सुस्थशरीरेण, निरामयेण, निरामयं, अनामयेन.

SAFETY, *s.* (Freedom from danger) भयमुक्तिः *f.*, अभयं, निर्भयं, आपन्मुक्तिः *f.*, विपन्मुक्तिः *f.*, निर्भयत्वं, अभयत्वं, भयाभावः, भयहीनता, भयशून्यता.—(State of freedom from hurt or injury) सुस्थता, शरीरसुस्थता, क्षेमः -मं, क्षेम्यता, अक्षतं, अक्षतता त्वं, सुरक्षितत्वं, अपरिक्षतता, क्षतिहीनता, कल्यता, कुशलता, कौशल्यं, अनामयं, निरामयत्वं -ता; 'in safety,' क्षेमेण, सक्षेमं, अक्षतं, *see* SAFELY; 'place of safety,' निर्भयस्थानं, आश्रयः. *See* SHELTER.

SAFETY-LAMP, *s.* खानिकप्रयुक्ता अभयदीपिका, अभयप्रदीपः.

SAFETY-VALVE, *s.* अतिबाहुल्येनोत्पद्यमानवाष्पनिर्गमयोग्यं सपिधानछिद्रं.

SAFFLOWER, *s.* कुसुम्भं, अग्निशिखं, वह्निशिखं, वह्निदीपकः, कमलोत्तरं, रक्तसङ्कोचं, पीतः, रोहितं, महारजनं; 'dyed orange with safflower,' कौसुम्भः -म्भी -म्भं.

SAFFRON, *s.* कुङ्कुमं, वाह्लीकं, वाह्लिकं, वरवाह्लीकं, अग्निशिखं, वह्निशिखं, वरः -रं, वरः -रं, काश्मीरजः, काश्मीरजन्म *n.* (न्), पीतकं, पीतनं, पीतचन्दनं, पीतकावेरं, कावेरं, रक्तसंज्ञं, रक्तं, शोणितं, लोहितं, लोहितचन्दनं, गौरं, सूर्य्यसंज्ञं, हरिचन्दनं, घुसृणं, जागुडं, सङ्कोचं, पिशुनं, धीरं, कुचन्दनं.

SAFFRON, *a.* (Having the color or qualities of saffron) कौङ्कुमः -मी -मं, कुङ्कुमवर्णः -र्णा -र्णं, कुङ्कुमरागः -गा -गं, कुङ्कुमारुणः -णा -णं; 'dyed with it,' कुङ्कुमाक्तः -क्ता -क्तं; 'marked with it,' कुङ्कुमाङ्कः -ङ्का -ङ्कं.

SAGACIOUS, *a.* अर्थज्ञः -ज्ञा -ज्ञं, विदग्धः -ग्धा -ग्धं, विदग्धबुद्धिः -द्धिः -द्धि, तीक्ष्णबुद्धिः &c., मेधावी -विनी -वि (न्), प्राज्ञः -ज्ञा -ज्ञं, दूरदर्शी &c., दीर्घदृष्टिः -ष्टिः -ष्टि, चतुरः -रा -रं, चातुरः -री -रं, गम्भीरः -रा -रं, नयविद् *m. f. n.* *See* SHARP.

SAGACIOUSLY, *adv.* विदग्धवत्, सवैदग्ध्यं, दीर्घदृष्ट्या. *See* SHARPLY.

SAGACITY, *s.* विदग्धता, वैदग्ध्यं, बुद्धितीक्ष्णता, अर्थविज्ञानं, दीर्घदृष्टिः *f.*

SAGE, *s.* (Wise man) पण्डितः, बुधः, प्राज्ञः, ज्ञानी *m.* (न्), महाप्रज्ञः, प्रज्ञः, प्रज्ञी *m.* (न्), विदग्धः, सौमेधिकः, *see* PHILOSOPHER.—(Holy sage or saint) मुनिः *m.*, ऋषिः *m.*, सिद्धः, सिद्धपुरुषः, परमार्थविद् *m.*, ब्रह्मज्ञः, ब्रह्मज्ञानी *m.* (न्), ज्ञानी *m.*, आत्मज्ञः, आत्मतत्त्वज्ञः, आत्मयाजी *m.* (न्), मौनी *m.*, वाचंयमः, यती *m.* (न्), यतिः *m.*, यमी *m.*, मुमुक्षुः *m.*, परमहंसः, दासः, वादिशः, मन्ता *m.* (तृ), केवली *m.*, अक्षरजूः *m.* (र्), *see* SAINT for an account of the Rishis.

SAGE, *a.* प्राज्ञः -ज्ञा -ज्ञं, पण्डितः -ता -तं, ज्ञानी &c., वादिः &c., *see* WISE.

SAGELY, *adv.* पण्डितवत्, प्राज्ञवत्, सपाण्डित्यं, सज्ञानं, विज्ञजनवत्.

SAGENESS, *s.* पाण्डित्यं, प्राज्ञता, वैदुष्यं, ज्ञानवत्त्वं, प्रज्ञता. *See* WISDOM.

SAGITTARIUS, *s.* (The sign or constellation) धनुः -नु *m. n.* तौक्षिकः.

SAGO, *s.* No equivalent. सागूः or सागुः may be used.

SAID, *p. p.* उक्तः -क्ता -क्तं, प्रोक्तः -क्ता -क्तं, भाषितः -ता -तं, भणितः -ता -तं, गदितः &c., निगदितः &c., उदितः &c., अभिहितः &c., उदाहृतः &c., उदीरितः &c., जल्पितः &c., लपितः &c., आख्यातः &c., व्याख्यातः &c.; 'well said,' साध्वभिहितः -ता -तं; 'having said,' उक्त्वा.

SAIL, *s.* (Of a ship) वातवसनं, वायुवसनं, नौकावसनं, नौवसनं, नौवस्त्रं, वातवस्त्रं, वायुवस्त्रं, नौकापटः, वायुपटः.—(Ship) नौः *f.*, नौका.

To SAIL, *v. n.* (Move in a ship or by water) नौकया वह् in pass. (उह्यते) or गम् (c. 1. गच्छति, गन्तुं) or चल् (c. 1. चलति -लितुं) or संचर् (c. 1. -चरति -रितुं) or या (c. 2. याति -तुं) or प्लु (c. 1. प्लवते, प्लोतुं), समुद्रेण गम् or या, जलपथेन गम्; 'he sailed over the ocean in a ship,' नौकया समुद्रं पुप्लुवे; 'he sails in the Ganges,' गङ्गायाम् प्लवते; 'he sails on the ocean,' समुद्रेण गच्छति.—(Set sail, impel a ship) नौकां or नावं चल् (c. 10. चालयति -यितुं) or सञ्चल् or वह् (c. 10. वाहयति -यितुं), नौचालनं कृ.—(Pass over in a ship) नौकया तॄ (c. 1. तरति -रितुं -रीतुं) or समुद्रपारं गम्.

SAILING, *s.* समुद्रयानं, समुद्रगमनं, नौकाचालनं, नौकावाहनं.

SAILING, *part.* समुद्रयायी -यिनी -यि (न्), उह्यमानः -ना -नं, प्लवमानः &c.

SAILOR, *s.* नाविकः, समुद्रगः, समुद्रयायी *m.* (न्), समुद्रगामी *m.*, निर्यामः -मकः, पोतवाहः -हकः, नौकावाहकः, नौवाहकः, नौचालकः. *See* MARINER.

SAINT, *s.* सिद्धः, सिद्धजनः, सिद्धपुरुषः, पवित्रलोकः, पुण्यलोकः, पवित्रजनः, ऋषिः *m.*, रिषिः *m.*, मुनिः *m.*, साधुः *m.*, यतेन्द्रियः, नियतेन्द्रियः, जितेन्द्रियः, पूतात्मा *m.* (न्), पुण्यात्मा *m.*, परमार्थविद् *m.*, आत्मज्ञः, परपुरुषः, महापुरुषः, मौनी *m.* (न्), मुमुक्षुः *m.*, यती *m.*, महातपाः *m.* (स्), पावकः, सत्यवचाः *m.* (स्), निर्ग्रन्थः; 'patron-saint,' इष्टदेवता; 'a company of saints,' सिद्धसंघः; 'a succession of saints,' सिद्धपरम्परा; 'the seven great saints forming the Great Bear constellation,' सप्तर्षयः *m. pl.* These are sometimes called Prajápatis, and, as created by

Brahmá, Brahmarshis or Brahmádikas. Their names are मरीचिः, अत्रिः, अङ्गिरस्, पुलस्त्यः or पुलस्तिः, पुलहः, क्रतुः, वशिष्ठः. Some authorities add the names of भृगुः, दक्षः, कश्यपः, नारदः and प्रचेतस् to the list of Brahmarshis or Prajápatis. According to the Vishnu Purána there are three kinds of Rishis or saints. 1. Brahmarshis, ब्रह्मर्षयः *m.pl.*, or saints who are the sons of Brahmá, or Brahmans, such as Maríchi, Atri, Vaśishtha, &c., dwelling in the sphere of Brahmá. 2. Devarshis, देवर्षयः *m. pl.*, or saints who are also demigods, as Nárada, Nara, Náráyana, Kardama, &c., dwelling in the region of the gods. 3. Rájarshis, राजर्षयः *m. pl.*, royal saints or holy personages who are also kings or men of the military class, and who have attained to the rank of Rájarshi from the practice of religious austerities. Such were Ikshwáku, Viśvámitra, son of Gádhi, Purúravas, Dushmanta, &c. Their sphere is the heaven of Indra. Four other classes of Rishis are enumerated in the Amara Kosha, viz. 1. Maharshis, महर्षयः *m. pl.*, or great saints, such as Vyása, the arranger of the Vedas, &c. 2. Paramarshis, परमर्षयः *m. pl.*, or most excellent saints, such as the Muni Bhela, the author of some medical works. 3. Kándarshis, काण्डर्षयः *m. pl.*, or saints and sages who teach a particular kánda or section of the Vedas, as Jaimini, founder of the Púrva Mímánsá system, &c. 4. Śrutarshis, श्रुतर्षयः *m. pl.*, or inspired saints, as the author of the medical work called suśruta, &c.

SAINT-ANTHONY'S FIRE, *s.* *See* ERYSIPELAS.

SAINTED, *p.p.* सिद्धलोकारोपितः -ता -तं, अतिपुण्यः -ण्या -ण्यं, अतिपवित्रः &c.

SAINT-LIKE, SAINTLY, *a.* साधुसदृशः -शी -शं, सिद्धसदृशः &c., पुण्यात्मा -त्मा -त्म (न्), पूतात्मा &c., अतिपुण्यः -ण्या -ण्यं, अतिपवित्रः -त्रा -त्रं, अतिधार्म्मिकः -की -कं.

SAINTLINESS, *s.* अतिपुण्यता, अतिपवित्रता, अतिधार्म्मिकत्वं, सिद्धसादृश्यं.

SAINT-VITUS'-DANCE, *s.* अङ्गस्फुरणं, शरीरस्फुरणं, अङ्गस्फुरणरोगः.

SAKE, *s.* कारणं, हेतुः *m.*, निमित्तं, प्रयोजनं; 'for the sake of,' अर्थे or अर्थं in comp., हेतोः, हेतौ, कारणात्, कृते, निमित्ते with the gen. c. or crude form; 'for one's own sake,' आत्मार्थं; 'for my sake,' मदर्थं -र्थे; 'for his sake,' तदर्थं, तस्य हेतोः; 'for the sake of happiness,' सुखार्थं, सुखहेतोः.

SÁL, *s.* (A tree with a wood yielding resin) सालः, शालः, सर्ज्जः -र्ज्जकः, कार्ष्यः, काश्यः, शस्यसंवरः, सस्यसंवरः, अश्वकर्णकः; 'its resinous juice,' सालरसः, शालनिर्यासः, सर्ज्जरसः.

SALACIOUS, *s.* रतार्थी &c., सुरतार्थी &c., मैथुनार्थी &c., *see* LUSTFUL.

SALACIOUSNESS, *s.* रतार्थित्वं, कामुकत्वं, रतेच्छा. *See* LUSTFULNESS.

SALAD, *s.* शुक्तसर्षपादिना सह खादनीयम् अपक्वशाकादि.

SÁLAGRÁM, *s.* (A species of ammonite stone found in the Gandhak river, and worshipped by the Vaishnavas as a type of Vishnu) सालग्रामः, परमेष्ठी *m.* (न्).

SALAMANDER, *s.* आग्नेयगोधा -धिका, आग्नेयसरटः, अग्निवासी *m.* (न्).

SAL-AMMONIAC, *s.* नवसागरः may be used.

SALARIED, *a.* सवेतनः -ना -नं, वैतनिकः -की -कं, कृतवेतनः -ना -नं.

SALARY, *s.* वेतनं, वर्त्तनं, भृतिः *f.*; 'annual,' वार्षिकं, वार्षिकवेतनं; 'monthly,' मासिकं; 'fixed,' निरूपितवेतनं, प्रकल्पितवेतनं; 'having a fixed salary,' प्रकल्पितवेतनः -ना -नं; 'one who has received his salary,' गृहीतवेतनः -ना -नं.

SALE, *s.* विक्रयः -यणं, विक्रीणनं, पणनं, विपणः -णनं; 'exposed for sale,' क्रेयः -या -यं, क्रय्यः -य्या -य्यं, विक्रेयः &c., क्रेतव्यः -व्या -व्यं, पण्यः -ण्या -ण्यं, क्रयार्थं प्रसारितः -ता -तं, पण्यशालायां प्रसारितः &c., क्रयाणकः -का -कं; 'an article for sale,' पण्यं, पण्यद्रव्यं; 'rescission of sale,' विक्रयानुशयः.

SALEABLE, *a.* विक्रेयः -या -यं, विक्रेतव्यः -व्या -व्यं, विक्रयणीयः &c., विक्रययोग्यः -ग्या -ग्यं, पण्यः -ण्या -ण्यं, पणितव्यः -व्या -व्यं, पण्यार्हः -र्हा -र्हं, क्रेयः &c., क्रेतव्यः &c.

SALESMAN, *s.* विक्रयी *m.* (न्), विक्रेता *m.* (तृ), विक्रयिकः, विक्रयकृत् *m.*

SALIENT, *a.* (Springing, darting) प्लवमानः -ना -नं, स्फुरन् -रन्ती &c. —(Lively, witty) सरसः -सा -सं, रसिकः -का -कं, तीक्ष्णः -क्ष्णा -क्ष्णं, सरसः &c.

SALINE, *a.* लावणिकः -की -कं, लावणः -णी -णं, लवणः -णा -णं, लवणमयः -यी -यं, लवणगुणकः -का -कं, क्षारगुणकः &c. *See* SALT, *a.*

SALIVA, *s.* लाला, मुखस्रावः, मुखरसः, मुखासवः, वक्त्रासवः, वदनासवः, आस्यासवः, निष्ठूतं, निष्ठ्यूतं, सृणिका, सृणीका, स्यन्दिनी, द्राविका, लसिका, मुखनिःसारितं जलं.

SALIVARY, SALIVAL, *a.* (Secreting or conveying saliva) लालोत्पादकः -का -कं, लालावाहकः &c. —(Pertaining to it) लालासम्बन्धी -न्धिनी &c.

To SALIVATE, *v. a.* पारददानेन अतिशयलालाम् उत्पद् (c. 10. -पादयति -यितुं) or स्रु (c. 10. स्रावयति -यितुं) or जन् (c. 10. जनयति -यितुं), पारददानेन मुखव्रणत्वं जन् or मुखरोगं कृ, लालावृद्धिं कृ.

SALIVATION, *s.* अतिशयलालोत्पत्तिः *f.*, अतिशयलालास्रावः, पारदप्रयुक्तं मुखव्रणत्वं, पारदप्रयुक्तो मुखरोगः.

SALLOW, *a.* पाण्डुः -ण्डुः -ण्डु, पाण्डुरः -रा -रं, पाण्डुवर्णः -र्णा -र्णं, पीतवर्णः &c., विवर्णः &c.; 'in complexion,' पाण्डुमुखः -खी -खं.

SALLOWNESS, *s.* पाण्डुता, पाण्डुरता, पाण्डुवर्णः, पीतता, वैवर्ण्यं.

SALLY, *s.* (Issue, rushing out) निष्पतनं, अभिनिष्पतनं, निष्पातः, अभिनिष्पातः, निर्गमः, निःसरणं, अपसरणं, वहिर्गमनं, वहिर्धावनं, निष्क्रमणं.—(Spring, leap) स्फुरणं, उत्पतनं, प्लवनं, उत्प्लवनं.—(Of wit or fancy) बुद्धिविलासः, मतिविलासः, मनोविलासः.—(Of levity or extravagance) बुद्धिचापल्यं, चापल्यं, चापलं, चञ्चलता, विलासः, विलसनं.

To SALLY, *v. n.* निष्पत् (c. 1. -पतति -तितुं), अभिनिष्पत्, निर्पत्, वहिर् धाव् (c. 1. धावति -वितुं), वहिर् गम् (c. 1. गच्छति, गन्तुं), निर्गम्.

SALLY-PORT, *s.* अपसारः, अपसरणद्वारं, निःसरणद्वारं, निर्गमद्वारं.

SALMAGUNDI, *s.* व्यञ्जनादिना सह मिश्रितं छिन्नमांसं or खण्डमांसं.

SALMON, *s.* सुललितमांसः प्रसिद्धमत्स्यभेदः.

SALOON, *s.* रङ्गशाला, महाशाला, नृत्यशाला, दर्शनशाला, शाला.

SALT, *s.* लवणं, रुचकं, क्षारः; 'sea salt,' सामुद्रं, लवणं, सागरोत्थं, वशिरं, वसिरं, अक्षीवं, अक्षिवं; 'rock-salt,' सिन्धुलवणं, सैन्धवं, माणिमन्थं, माणिबन्धं, लवणोत्तमं, सितशिवं, शितशिवं, सितसिवं, शीतशिवं, शीतसिवं; 'lump of salt,' सैन्धवघनः; 'culinary salt,' उद्भिदं; 'mineral or metallic salt,' उपरसः, रसः; 'medicinal salt, impregnated with iron and sulphur called Bit Loben, or Bit Noben,' विट्लवणं, विड्लवणं, विटलवणं, कृष्णलवणं, पाक्यं, रोचकं, क्षारः, विडं, विडगन्धं, विटः, कृतकं, पाक्यं; 'Sochal salt,'

सौवर्चलं, अक्षं, रुचकं; 'the same black,' तिलकं; 'Sambhar salt,' रौमकं, रौमं, रौमलवणं, वसुकं, वसूकं; 'native salt,' स्वयकृतम् ऊषरलवणं.

SALT, *a.* लवणः -णा -णं, लावणः -णी -णं, लावणिकः -की -कं, लवणरसयुक्तः -क्ता -क्तं, लवणमयः -यी -यं, लवणगुणकः -का -कं, लवणयुक्तः -क्ता -क्तं, लवणाक्तः -क्ता -क्तं, क्षारयुक्तः &c., क्षारगुणकः &c., क्षारधर्म्मकः &c., क्षारविशिष्टः -ष्टा -ष्टं, लवणविशिष्टः &c., लवण in comp., क्षार in comp.; 'a salt mine,' लवणाकरः; 'salt flavor,' क्षाररसः, लवणरसः; 'salt sea,' लवणसमुद्रः, लवणार्णवः, लवणाम्बुराशिः *m.*; 'salt soil,' ऊषः, क्षारमृत्तिका; 'having such soil,' ऊषरः -रा -रं, ऊषवान् -वती -वत् (त्).

To SALT, *v. a.* लवणीकृ, लवण (nom. लवणयति -यितुं), लवणाक्तं -क्तां कृ, सलवणं -णां कृ, लवणयुक्तं -क्तां कृ, लवणेन सिच्, सक्षारं -रां कृ.

SALT-CELLAR, *s.* लावणिकं, लवणपात्रं, लवणभाजनं, लवणाधारः.

SALTED, *p. p.* लवणितः -ता -तं, लवणाक्तः -क्ता -क्तं, लवणीकृतः -ता -तं, लावणिकः -की -कं, लावणः -णी -णं, उद्लावणिकः &c., क्षारयुक्तः -क्ता -क्तं.

SALTISH, *a.* ईषल्लवणः -णा -णं, ईषल्लावणिकः -की -कं, ईषल्लवणयुक्तः &c.

SALT-MINE, *s.* लवणाकरः, लवणखानिः -नी *m. f.*, लवणखनिः -नी *f.*

SALTNESS, *s.* लवणत्वं -ता, लावण्यं, सलवणत्वं, लवणयुक्तता, लवणरसः, क्षारयुक्तता, क्षारता, क्षाररसः.

SALT-PETRE, SALT-PETER, *s.* यवक्षारः, यवजः, यवाग्रजः, तर्ष्यः, पाक्यः, तीक्ष्णरसः, तीक्ष्णः, यवलासः.

SALT-WATER, *s.* लवणाम्बु *n.* लवणजलं, लवणोदकं, लवणोदं, लवणाम्भस्.

SALUBRIOUS, *a* आरोग्यकरः -री -रं, आरोग्यजनकः -का -कं, आरोग्यवर्धकः &c., रोगघ्नः -घ्नी -घ्नं, रोगहरः -रा -रं, रोगहारी -रिणी -रि (न्), स्वास्थ्यजनकः &c., अनामयकरः &c., पथ्यः -थ्या -थ्यं, पथ्यकरः &c., व्याधिघ्नः -घ्नी -घ्नं, क्षेम्यः -म्या -म्यं, आरोग्यः -ग्या -ग्यं, अगदः -दा -दं, शरीरहितकारी &c., शरीरहितावहः -हा -हं, पौष्टिकः -की -कं, सात्त्विकः &c., पुष्टिकरः &c., पुष्टिदः -दा -दं.

SALUBRITY, *s.* आरोग्यत्वं, आरोग्यजनकता, पथ्यता, क्षेम्यता, हितता.

SALUTARINESS, *s.* हितता -त्वं, हितकारिता -त्वं, उपकारकता, श्रेयस्कारित्वं.

SALUTARY. *a* (Beneficial) हितः -ता -तं, हितकरः -रा -रं, हितकारी -रिणी &c., हितावहः -हा -हं, हितकारकः -का -कं, हितप्रदः -दा -दं, हितवान् -वती -वत् (त्), श्रेयस्करः -री -रं, श्रेयस्कारी &c., श्रेयस्कारकः &c., उपकारी &c., उपकारकः &c., अर्थकरः &c.—(Wholesome), *see* SALUBRIOUS.

SALUTATION, *s.* अभिवन्दनं, अभिवादः -दनं, वन्दनं, अभिनन्दा -न्दनं, कुशलवादः, कुशलप्रश्नः, आशीर्वादः, कौशलं -ली, क्षेमप्रश्नः, नमस्कारः, नमस्क्रिया, प्रणामः, प्रणतिः *f.*, प्रणिपातः, उपसंग्रहः; 'salutation in return,' प्रत्यभिवादः -दनं. *See* OBEISANCE.

SALUTE, *s.* अभिवादनं, वन्दनं. *See* SALUTATION.—(Kiss) चुम्बनं.

To SALUTE, *v. a.* अभिवन्द् (c. 1. -वन्दते -न्दितुं), वन्द्, संवन्द्, अभिवद् (c. 10. -वादयते -ति -यितुं) अभिनन्द् (c. 1. -नन्दति -न्दितुं), आनन्द्, कुशलवादं कृ, कुशलप्रश्नं कृ, कुशलप्रश्नेन अभिवद् or अभिभाष्, आशिषं ब्रू or वद्, प्रणम् (c. 1. -णमति -णन्तुं), शिरसा प्रणम्, शिरसा अभिवद्, आमन्त्र् (c. 10. -मन्त्रयति -ते -यितुं), सम्मन्त्र्, अर्च्, अभ्यर्च्, नमस्कृ, नमस्कारं कृ, सभाज्, उपस्था (c. 1. -तिष्ठते -स्थातुं), सभुध् in caus.; 'to salute in return,' प्रत्यभिवद्, प्रतिनन्द्, प्रत्यर्च्.—(Kiss) चुम्ब्.

SALUTED, *p. p.* अभिवादितः -ता -तं, अभिवन्दितः &c., अभिनन्दितः &c., आनन्दितः &c., कुशलवाक्यैर् अभिवादितः -ता -तं, नमस्कृतः &c., नमसितः &c., नमस्यितः &c., सत्कृतः &c.; 'having saluted,' अभिवाद्य, प्रणम्य.

SALUTER, *s.* अभिवादयिता *m.* (तृ), अभिवादकः, अभिवन्दी *m.* (न्).

SALVABILITY, *s.* तारणशक्यता, तारणयोग्यता, रक्षणयोग्यता, रक्षणीयता, निस्तार्य्यता, निस्तारयोग्यता, मुक्तियोग्यता, उद्धरणीयत्वं.

SALVABLE, *a.* तारणशक्यः -क्या -क्यं, तारणयोग्यः -ग्या -ग्यं, रक्षणयोग्यः &c., रक्षणीयः -या -यं, त्राणयोग्यः &c., त्राणशक्यः &c., निस्तार्य्यः -र्य्या -र्य्यं, निस्तारयोग्यः &c., मुक्तियोग्यः &c., उद्धरणीयः &c., उद्धारयोग्यः &c.

SALVAGE, *s.* नंक्ष्यमाणनौकारक्षकाणां दत्तं पारितोषिकं.

SALVATION, *s.* (Preservation) रक्षणं, रक्षा, संरक्षणं, त्राणं, परित्राणं, तारणं, उद्धारः, उद्धरणं, क्षेमः -मं, *see* PRESERVATION.—(In theology) तारणं, उद्धारः, मुक्तिः *f.*, मोक्षः, उद्धारगतिः *f.*, पापमुक्तिः *f.* -क्तता, पापमोक्षः -क्षणं, ऊर्द्धगतिः *f.*, परमगतिः *f.*, निस्तारः; 'means of salvation,' तारणोपायः, रक्षणोपायः; 'way of salvation through devotion,' भक्तिमार्गः; 'through works,' कर्म्ममार्गः.

SALVE, *s.* लेपः, प्रलेपः, अनुलेपः, उपदेहः, उपनाहः, उपशमनं, शमनं.

To SALVE, *v. a.* लेपेन or अनुलेपेन शम् (c. 10. शमयति -यितुं) or उपशम्.

SALVER, *s.* रूप्यपात्रं, रूप्यमयशरावः, रूप्यमयभाजनं, पात्रं.

SALVO, *s.* निर्गमः, निर्गमोपायः, निस्तारः, निस्तरणद्वारं, उद्धरणं.

SAL-VOLATILE, *s.* अतिशीघ्रवायुपरिणामशीलं द्रवरूपलवणं.

SAME, *a.* समः -मा -मं, समानः -ना -नं, समीयः -या -यं, स in comp., तुल्यः -ल्या -ल्यं, एक in comp., अभिन्नः -न्ना -न्नं, अनन्यः -न्या -न्यत्, अपरः -रा -रं, अविभिन्नः &c., निर्विशेषः -षा -षं, अभेदः -दा -दं, *see* LIKE; 'of the same form,' समरूपः -पा -पी -पं, समानरूपः &c., समाकारः -रा -रं, एकरूपः &c., अभिन्नरूपः &c., अनन्यरूपः &c., तुल्यरूपः &c., सरूपः &c.; 'of the same kind or species,' समजातीयः -या -यं, समानजातीयः &c., सजातीयः &c., एकजातीयः &c.; 'of the same family,' समानगोत्रः -त्रा -त्रं, समानकुलः -ला -लं; 'of the same class,' समवर्णः -र्णा -र्णं, समानवर्णः &c., सवर्णः &c., एकवर्णः &c.; 'of the same age,' समवयस्कः -स्का -स्कं, समवयाः -याः -यः (स्), सवयाः &c., समानजन्मा -न्मा -न्म (न्), एकवयस्कः &c.; 'occurring at the same time,' समानकालीनः -ना -नं, एककालीनः &c.; 'the same time,' समकालः -लं; 'at the same time,' समकाले -लं, एककाले, एकदा, युगपत्, यौगपद्येन, एकधारे; 'of the same size,' सममात्रः -त्री -त्रं, समपरिमाणः -णा -णं; 'the very same,' समसमानः -ना -नं; 'following the same occupation,' समवृत्तिः -त्तिः -त्ति, तुल्यवृत्तिः &c.; 'he is the same as a father to me,' माम् प्रति पितृस्थाने or पितृभूमौ or पितृवत् or पितृनिर्विशेषो भवति; 'in the same manner,' तद्वत्, तथा, तथैव, एवं, एवम्प्रकारेण, तथाप्रकारेण, तथाविधेन, एवंविधेन, तथाविधं, एवंविधं, एवमेव, तथाहि, तद्रूपेण, तत्प्रकारेण.—(That was mentioned before) पूर्व्वोक्तः -क्ता -क्तं.

SAMENESS, *s.* समता -त्वं, समानता -त्वं, साम्यं, सामान्यं, साम्यता, तुल्यता -त्वं, सदृशता, सादृश्यं, अभिन्नता, अनन्यता, अभेदः, अविभेदः, अभिन्नता, समभावः, एकता, ऐक्यं, अभिन्नभावः, एक in comp., स in comp.; 'sameness of form,' समरूपता, समानरूपता, एकरूपता, सरूपता, सारूप्यं; 'of kind or class,' समजातित्वं, सजातित्वं, सवर्णता, सावर्ण्यं.

SAMÍ, *s.* (A thorny tree with a hard wood) शमी, समी, कान्तारिः *m.*, वनारिः *m.*, सक्तुफला -ली, शिवा; 'a variety of it,' शमीरः, शमीरुः *m.*, शमिरः.

SAMPLE, *s.* (Specimen) आदर्शः, निदर्शनं, प्रतिमा, उपमा, प्रमाणं.

SAMPLER, *s.* सूचिकर्म्मप्रतिमा, बालस्त्रीणां सूचिकर्म्मादर्शः.

SANATIVE, SANATORY, *a.* रोगनाशकः -का -कं, रोगशमकः &c., रोगघ्नः -घ्नी -घ्नं, रोगनिवारकः &c., गदघ्नः &c., आरोग्यजनकः &c., आरोग्यकरः &c.

SANAT-KUMÁRA, *s.* (One of the four mind-born sons of Brahmá, created by him before all other beings, and devoid of all human passion. Therefore called ever-young or ever-pure) सनत्कुमारः, वैधात्रः.

SANCTIFICATION, *s.* (The act) पवित्रीकरणं, पुण्यीकरणं, अन्तःशोधनं, अन्तरात्मशोधनं, पुण्यकरणं, शुचीकरणं, पापहरणं, पापनाशनं, कल्मषहरणं, मलहरणं, *see* PURIFICATION.—(State) पवित्रता, पुण्यता, शुचिता, अन्तःशुद्धिः *f.*, अन्तःशौचं.

SANCTIFIED, *p. p.* पवित्रीकृतः -ता -तं, पुण्यीकृतः &c., पवित्रितः &c., शुचीकृतः &c., नष्टपापः -पा -पं, हृतपापः &c., धूतपापः &c., धूतकल्मषः -षा -षं, पापशुद्धः -द्धा -द्धं, अन्तःशुद्धः &c., वीतकल्मषः &c.

To SANCTIFY, *v. a.* पवित्रीकृ, पुण्यीकृ, अन्तःशुद्धीकृ, पवित्र (nom. पवित्रयति -यितुं), अन्तरात्मानं शुध् (c. 10. शोधयति -यितुं), पापमलं हृ (c. 1. हरति, हर्तुं) or नश् (c. 10. नाशयति -यितुं), शुचीकृ, अन्तःशौचं कृ.

SANCTIFYING, *a.* अन्तःशोधकः -का -कं, अन्तःशुद्धिकरः -री -रं, पुण्यकरः &c.

SANCTIMONIOUS, *a.* दाम्भिकः -की -कं, दम्भी -म्भिनी -म्भि (न्), अतिधार्म्मिकः -की -कं, धर्म्माभिमानी &c., कपटधर्म्मी &c., पुण्यवेशधारी &c., पवित्रवेशधारी &c., अतिपुण्यः -ण्या -ण्यं, अतिपवित्रः -त्रा -त्रं, पवित्रम्मन्यः &c., बकवृत्तिः -त्तिः -त्ति.

SANCTIMONIOUSNESS, SANCTIMONY, *s.* दम्भः, दाम्भिकत्वं -ता, अतिपुण्यता, अतिपवित्रत्वं, धर्म्माभिमानं, पुण्यवेशधारणं, पवित्रवेशधारणं, बकध्यानं, बकवृत्तिः *f.*

SANCTION, *s.* प्रमाणं, प्रामाण्यं, आश्रयः, अनुग्रहः, उपग्रहः, संग्रहः, आग्रहः, आधारः, रक्षा, पालनं, उपकारः, सत्यापनं, दृढीकरणं, स्थिरीकरणं.

To SANCTION, *v. a.* सप्रमाणं -णां कृ, सप्रमाणीकृ, प्रमाणं दा, दृढीकृ, स्थिरीकृ, सत्याकृ, सत्य (nom. in caus. सत्यापयति -यितुं), अनुग्रह् (c. 9. -गृह्णाति -ग्रहीतुं), उपग्रह्, अभिरक्ष्, आश्रयो भू.

SANCTIONED, *p. p.* सप्रमाणीकृतः -ता -तं, दृढीकृतः &c., अनुगृहीतः &c.

SANCTITY, *s.* अतिपुण्यता, अतिपवित्रता, अन्तःशुद्धिः *f.*, अन्तःशुद्धता, मनःशुद्धिः *f.*, अन्तरात्मशुद्धिः *f.*, अन्तःशौचं, अन्तःशुचिता, अन्तःपवित्रता, अन्तःपावित्र्यं, पवित्रता, पुण्यता, पावित्र्यं, शुद्धिः *f.*, विशुद्धिः *f.*, परिशुद्धिः *f.*, साधुता -त्वं.

SANCTUARY, *s.* (Inner part of a temple) गर्भागारं, गर्भगृहं, आगारगर्भः, मन्दिरगर्भः, गर्भः.—(Holy place) देवालयः, पवित्रालयः -यं, पुण्यालयः -यं, देवागारः -रं, पुण्यागारः -रं, शुद्धागारः -रं, महालयः, पवित्रस्थानं, पुण्यस्थानं, वीहारः, *see* TEMPLE.—(Place of refuge) आश्रयस्थानं, आश्रयस्थलं, शरणं, निर्भयस्थानं, शरणस्थानं, संश्रयस्थानं, महालयः.

SAND, *s.* बालुका, सिकताः *f. pl.*, महासूक्ष्मा, प्रवाही, कर्पराशः, इष्टगन्धं.

To SAND, *v. a.* बालुकाकीर्णं -र्णां कृ, बालुकावृतं -तां कृ, सबालुकं -कां कृ.

SANDAL, *s.* (Kind of shoe) कोशी, कोषी, चरणदासी.—(The wood, produced chiefly in the Malaya mountains) चन्दनः -नं, श्रीखण्डः -ण्डं, सारगन्धः, गन्धसारः, मलयजः -जं, भद्रश्रीः *f.*, भद्रश्रयं, तिलपर्णं, तैलपर्णी, वर्णकः, भद्राश्रयः, हरिचन्दनः -नं, भोगिवल्लभं, शीतलप्रदः, पटीरं, गोशीर्षं, चन्द्रकान्तः -न्तं, मलयागुरुः -रु *m. n.*; 'white sandal-wood,' तैलपर्णिकं; 'red,' रक्तचन्दनं, रञ्जनं, कुचन्दनं, पत्राङ्गं, तिलपर्णी, कुङ्कुमागुरु *n.*; 'black,' कृष्णचन्दनं, कृष्णागुरु *n.*; 'unctuous preparation of sandal-wood used as a perfume or unguent,' चन्दनं; 'anointing or perfuming the person with it,' चर्चा, चर्चिका, चार्चिक्यं; 'anointed with it,' चर्चितः -ता -तं.

SANDARAC, SANDARACH, *s.* मसीशोषणचूर्णं, मसिशोषकचूर्णं.

SAND-BAG, *s.* बालुकाकोषः, बालुकाकोशः, बालुकाधारः.

SAND-BANK, *s.* सैकतं, सिकतामयं, परेपः, परापः, पादचत्वरः, पुलिनं.

SANDED, *p.p.* बालुकाकीर्णः -र्णा -र्णं, बालुकावृतः -ता -तं, बालुकावान् &c.

SANDERS, *s.* (Red sanders wood) तिलपर्णी, पत्राङ्गं, पत्रङ्गं, पत्त्राङ्गं, रञ्जनं, रक्तचन्दनं, कुचन्दनं.—(Yellow sanders) पीतद्रुः *m.*, कालेयकः -कं, कालीयकः -कं, हरिद्रवः, दार्वी, पचम्पचा, पचम्पचा, दारुहरिद्रा, पर्जनी.

SAND-GLASS, *s.* बालुकायन्त्रं, बालुकानाली.

SANDS, *s. pl.* सिकताः *f. pl.*, सैकतभूमिः *f.*, परेपभूः *f.*, परापभूः *f.*, परेपभूमिः *f.*

SANDY, *a.* सैकतः -ती -तं, सिकतामयः -यी -यं, सिकतावान् -वती -वत् (त्), बालुकामयः &c., सिकतिलः -ला -लं, बहुबालुकः -का -कं, बहुसिकतः -ता -तं, बालुकाप्रचुरः -रा -रं.

SANE, *a.* प्रकृतिस्थः -स्था -स्थं, स्वस्थः &c., सुस्थः &c., अमत्तः -त्ता -त्तं, अनुन्मत्तः &c., अविक्षिप्तः -प्ता -प्तं, अविकृतः -ता -तं, अवातुलः &c.

SANGUIFEROUS, *a.* रक्तवाहकः -का -कं, रक्तवाही -हिनी -हि (न्), असृग्वहः &c.

SANGUIFICATION, *s.* रक्तोत्पादनं, रक्तोत्पत्तिः *f.*, शोणितोत्पत्तिः *f.*, रक्तवर्धनं.

SANGUINARY, *a.* (Bloody, attended with much blood) रक्तमयः -यी -यं, बहुरक्तः -क्ता -क्तं, बहुरक्तपातसहितः -ता -तं.—(Bloody minded) रक्तप्रियः -या -यं, मारात्मकः -का -कं, जिघांसुः -सुः -सु, क्रूरचेताः -ताः -तः (स्), निष्ठुरः -रा -रं.

SANGUINE, *a.* (Of ardent temperament) उष्णप्रकृतिः -तिः -ति, उष्णस्वभावः -वा -वं, चण्डप्रकृतिः &c., सानुरागः -गा -गं, अनुरागी &c., प्रचण्डः -ण्डा -ण्डं, उत्सुकः -का -कं, तीक्ष्णः -क्ष्णा -क्ष्णं.—(Confident, hopeful) अतिविश्वासी -सिनी -सि (न्), अतिविश्वासशीलः -ला -लं, अत्याशावान् -वती -वत् (त्), अत्याशान्वितः -ता -तं, अत्याकांक्षी &c., सुफलापेक्षी &c., सुखापेक्षी &c., सुखप्रतीक्षः -क्षा -क्षं, भाविलाभासंशयी &c., सुप्रत्याशी &c., आशाबद्धः -द्धा -द्धं.

SANGUINENESS, *s.* अतिविश्वासः, अत्याशा, अत्याकांक्षा, सुफलापेक्षा, सुखापेक्षा, सुखप्रतीक्षा, भाविलाभासंशयः, सुप्रत्याशा.

SANIES, *s.* पूयरक्तं, पूयशोणितं, पूयं, मलजं, क्षतजं. *See* PUS.

SANIOUS, *a.* पूयरक्तवान् -वती -वत् (त्), पूयरक्तस्रावी -विणी -वि (न्).

SANITY, *s.* स्वास्थ्यं, स्वस्थता, सुस्थता, सुस्थितिः *f.*, अमत्तता, अनुन्मत्तता.

SÁNKHYA, *s.* (A system of philosophy ascribed to the Muni Kapila. It asserts duality द्वैतं, or the co-existence of two principles in the universe, viz. spirit and matter. Its doctrines being opposed to the oneness of the Vedas led to the formation of another school called the Vedánta or Uttara-Mímánsá system, asserting the opposite idea of unity एकत्वं or अद्वैतं, and shewing that the end or aim of the Vedas was to inculcate the oneness of Spirit or God) सांख्यः, सांख्यदर्शनं; 'with the commentary,' सांख्यकारिका.

SANSKRIT, *s.* (The classical and sacred language of the Hindús, from which are formed all their modern dialects. The word means highly polished and artificially constructed) संस्कृतं, संस्कृतोक्तिः *f.*, संस्कृतभाषा, ब्राह्मणभाषा, देवभाषा, दैवभाषा, आदिभाषा.

SAP, *s.* (Of plants) सारः, रसः, द्रवः, मज्जा, मज्जा *m.* (न्), निर्यासः, निकरः, सत्त्वं, वृक्षसारः, वृक्षरसः.

To sap, *v. a.* (Undermine) अधस् or अधस्तात् खन् (c. 1. खनति -नितुं), अधोभागे गूढखातं कृ, अधो खात्वा पर्यस् (c. 4. -अस्यति -सितुं) or निपत् (c. 10. -पातयति -यितुं) or नश् (c. 10. नाशयति -यितुं).

Sapan-wood, *s.* रक्तचन्दनं, पत्राङ्गं, पत्राङ्गं, रञ्जनं, कुचन्दनं, पत्तङ्गं, पट्टरञ्जनं.

Sapid, *a.* सुरसः -सा -सं, सरसः &c., मिष्टः -ष्टा -ष्टं, स्वादुः -द्वी -दु, स्वादुरसः -सा -सं, सरस्वान् -स्वती -स्वत् (त्), रसवान् &c. *See* Tasteful.

Sapidity, sapidness, *s.* सुरसता, सरसता, सारस्यं, स्वादुता, मिष्टता.

Sapience, *s.* प्राज्ञत्वं, प्रज्ञता, वैदुष्यं. *See* Wisdom.

Sapient, *a.* विद्वान् -दुषी -द्वत् (त्), प्राज्ञः -ज्ञा -ज्ञं. *See* Wise.

Sapless, *a.* असारः -रा -रं, निःसारः &c., निस्सारः &c., सारहीनः -ना -नं, सारवर्जितः -ता -तं, विरसः -सा -सं, निरसः &c., नीरसः &c., रसहीनः -ना -नं, निस्सत्त्वः -त्त्वा -त्त्वं, सत्त्वहीनः &c., म्लानः -ना -नं.

Sapling, *s.* बालवृक्षः, कोमलवृक्षः, रसार्द्रः पेलववृक्षः, बालद्रुः *m.*

Saponaceous *a.* मेदुरः -रा -रं, चिक्कणः -णा -णं, चिक्किणः &c.

Sapor, *s.* रुचिः *f.*, रसः, स्वादः, आस्वादः. *See* Taste.

Sappan-wood, *s.* *See* Sapan-wood.

Sapper, *s.* खनकः, आखनिकः, सुरुङ्गाखनकः, सौरुङ्गिकः. *See* Miner.

Sapphire, *s.* नीलः, नीलकान्तः, नीलाश्मा *m.* (न्), इन्द्रनीलः, तृणग्राही *m.* (न्), शितिरत्नं, शनिः *m.*

Sapphirine, *a.* नीलमयः -यी -यं, नीलगुणकः -का -कं, नीलोपमः &c.

Sappiness, *s.* सरसता, रसवत्त्वं, रसालता, बहुरसत्वं, बहुसारत्वं.

Sappy, *a.* रसवान् -वती -वत् (त्), सरसः -सा -सं, रसी -सिनी -सि (न्), बहुरसः &c., रसाढ्यः -ढ्या -ढ्यं, सारवान् &c., बहुसारवान् &c., बहुसारः -रा -रं, मज्जावान् &c., ससारः -रा -रं, ससत्त्वः -त्त्वा -त्त्वं, सत्त्ववान् &c., आर्द्रः -र्द्रा -र्द्रं.

Saraswatí, *s.* (The wife of the god Brahmá, or, according to some, of Dharma. She is goddess of speech and eloquence, patroness of music and the arts, and inventress of the Sanskrit language and Devanágarí letters) सरस्वती, वाग्देवी, वागीश्वरी, वाणी, वाक् *f.* (च्), ब्राह्मी, ब्रह्मकन्यका, वाङ्मयी, भारती, शारदा, तपिता, वाग्विलासिनी, वाग्वशी, वाग्वज्ञरी. The name Saraswatí, signifying 'flowing,' is applied to a celebrated river as well as to the goddess of speech. The river rises in the mountains N. E. of Dehli.

Sarcasm, *s.* अवक्षेपः, आक्षेपः, क्षेपः, व्यञ्जना -नं, व्यंग्यः -ग्यं, व्यंग्योक्तिः *f.*, वक्रोक्तिः *f.*, तीक्ष्णवाक्यं, तीक्ष्णवचनं, अरुन्तुदवाक् *f.* (च्), अरुन्तुदवाक्यं, वाग्रसिः *f.*, वागिषुः *m. f.*

Sarcastic, sarcastical, *a.* अरुन्तुदः -दा -दं, अवक्षेपकः -का -कं, सावक्षेपः -पा -पं, साक्षेपः &c., सव्यञ्जनः -ना -नं, तीक्ष्णः -क्ष्णा -क्ष्णं, तिग्मः -ग्मा -ग्मं, कटुः -टुः -टु.

Sarcastically, *adv.* सावक्षेपं, साक्षेपं, सव्यञ्जनं, अरुन्तुदवाचा.

Sarcoma, *s.* मांसवृद्धिः *f.*, अर्बुदः, अधिमांसं. *See* Tumor.

Sarcophagous, *a.* मांसभक्षकः -का -कं, मांसभोजी &c. *See* Carnivorous.

Sarcophagus, *s.* प्रस्तरमयः शवाधारः, पाषाणमयी शवपेटिका.

Sardonic, *a.* (Laugh) विकृतहासः, करालस्मितं, पिशाचस्मितं.

Sardonyx, *s.* (Gem) गोमेदकः -कं, शिवधातुः *m.*, वैदूर्यं.

Sarsaparilla, sarsa, *s.* गन्धवल्कलं, उत्कटं.

Sash, *s.* (Ornamental belt) शोभार्थं भृता दुकूलमयमेखला, कटिबन्धनी, कटिसूत्रं, कटिशृङ्खला, परिकरः.—(Of a window) वातायनकाष्ठं, वातायनपरिगतं काष्ठादि.

Sástra, *s.* (Sacred treatise) शास्त्रं, *see* Shástra.

Satan, *s.* (The devil) पिशाचः, *see* Demon. The Arabic word is शैतान्, from which a Sanskrit word शैतानः or सैतानः may perhaps be formed.

Satanical, *a.* शैतानसम्बन्धी -न्धिनी &c., पैशाचिकः &c. *See* Demoniacal.

Satchel, *s.* पुस्तककोषः, लेख्यपत्रकोषः. *See* Sachel.

To sate, *v. a.* अत्यन्तं or अतिशयेन तृप् in caus., *See To* satiate.

Sated, *p. p.* अतितृप्तः -प्ता -प्तं, अतितर्पितः -ता -तं, अतिपूरितः &c.

Satellite, *s.* (In astronomy) उपग्रहः, चन्द्रः.—(Obsequious follower) अनुपक्षी *m.* (न्), नित्यानुपक्षी *m.*, नित्यानुचारी *m.*, पार्श्वपरिवर्त्ती *m.*

To satiate, *v. a.* अत्यन्तं or अतिशयेन तृप् (c. 10. तर्पयति -यितुं) or सन्तृप् or परितृप् or पृ (c. 10. पूरयति -यितुं) or परिपृ or तुष् (c. 10. तोषयति -यितुं) or सन्तुष् or परितुष्, अतितृप्तिं or अतिसौहित्यं जन् (c. 10. जनयति -यितुं) or कृ, अतितुष्टिं जन् or उत्पद् (c. 10. -पादयति -यितुं), सुहितं -तां कृ.

Satiated, *p. p.* अतितृप्तः -प्ता -प्तं, अतितर्पितः -ता -तं, अतिपूरितः &c., परितृप्तः -प्ता -प्तं, सन्तृप्तः &c., समर्पितः &c., तर्पितः &c., सन्तोषितः &c., परितुष्टः -ष्टा -ष्टं, अतिपूर्णः -र्णा -र्णं, परिपूर्णः &c., पूर्णकामः -मा -मं, परिपूर्णकामः &c., शान्तकामः &c., पर्याप्तकामः &c., प्रतिलब्धकामः &c., सुहितः -ता -तं, अतितुष्टः &c., अतितोषितः &c.

Satiety, *s.* अतितृप्तिः *f.*, परितृप्तिः *f.*, तृप्तिः *f.*, अतितर्पणं, तर्पणं, आतृप्तिः *f.*, अतितृप्तता, अतिपूर्त्तिः *f.*, अतिपूर्णता, परिपूर्त्तिः *f.*, अतितुष्टिः *f.*, अतितुष्टता, परितोषः, परितुष्टिः *f.*, सौहित्यं, सुहितता, कामपर्याप्तिः *f.*, कामशान्तिः *f.*, पूर्णकामत्वं, क्षुधाशान्तिः *f.*, वितृष्णता, आघ्राणः.

Satin, *s.* (The silk) अतिशोभनदुकूलं, अतिरुचिरदुकूलं, श्लक्ष्णदुकूलं.

Satire, *s.* (Discourse or poem in which wickedness is satirized) दुराचारोपहासककविता -भाषणं, सावक्षेपकविता, दुर्वृत्तावक्षेपककविता -भाषणं, दोषोपहासकभाषणं, अरुन्तुदकाव्यं, अवगीतं, अरुन्तुदभाषणं, निन्दोपाख्यानं.—(Keen remark or ridicule) अवक्षेपः, उपहासः, व्यञ्जना, अरुन्तुदवाक् *f.* (च्), विदूषणं, वागसिः *f.*, *see* Sarcasm.

Satirical, *a.* दुराचारोपहासकः -का -कं, दोषोपहासकः &c., दुर्वृत्तावक्षेपकः &c., उपहासकः &c., उपहासात्मकः &c., उपहासरूपः -पा -पं, अवक्षेपकः &c., सावक्षेपः -पा -पं, सोपहासः -सा -सं, साक्षेपः &c., सव्यञ्जनः -ना -नं, अवक्षेपार्थकः &c., अवगीतरूपः -पा -पं, अरुन्तुदः &c. *See* Sarcastic.

Satirically, *adv.* सोपहासं, सावक्षेपं, साक्षेपं, अरुन्तुदं, सव्यञ्जनं.

Satirist, *s.* दोषोपहासकः, दुराचारोपहासी *m.* (न्), दोषावक्षेपकः.

To satirize, *v. a.* अरुन्तुदवाक्यैर् उपहस् or अवक्षिप् or अवगै, सव्यञ्जनं or सावक्षेपं or सोपहासं निन्द्, तीक्ष्णवाचा निन्द्.

Satirized, *p. p.* अरुन्तुदवाक्यैर् अवक्षिप्तः -प्ता -प्तं, अवगीतः -ता -तं.

Satisfaction, *s.* (The state) तुष्टिः *f.*, तृप्तिः *f.*, तोषः, सन्तोषः, परितोषः, इच्छातृप्तिः *f.*, कामतृप्तिः *f.*, इच्छापूर्त्तिः *f.*, इच्छाशान्तिः *f.*, कामशान्तिः *f.*, इच्छानिवृत्तिः *f.*, शान्तिः *f.*, तुष्टता, परितुष्टता, तृप्तता, शान्तता, पर्याप्तिः *f.*, इच्छापर्याप्तिः *f.*, पूर्त्तिः *f.*, परिपूर्त्तिः *f.* सौहित्यं, सुहितता, समाधानं.—(The act) तर्पणं, सन्तर्पणं, तोषणं, सन्तोषणं, परितोषणं, पूरणं, पारणं, आप्यायनं, अवनं, इच्छाशमनं, इच्छाशान्तिः *f.*, इच्छानिवृत्तिः *f.*; 'of hunger,' क्षुधाशान्तिः *f.*—(Gratification) प्रीणनं, तर्पणं, अनुवर्त्तनं.—(Relief from doubt) सन्देहनिवृत्तिः *f.*, संशयनिवृत्तिः *f.*, सन्देहभञ्जनं, सन्देहहरणं.—(Compensation) पारितोषिकं,

see COMPENSATION.—(Payment) निस्तारः, शुद्धिः *f.*

SATISFACTORILY, *adv.* यथासुखं, यथा तुष्टिर् जायते तथा, पर्य्याप्तं

SATISFACTORY, *a.* तुष्टिजनकः -का -कं, तुष्टिजननः -नी -नं, तुष्टिकरः -री -रं, तुष्टिदः -दा -दं, सन्तोषदः &c., सन्तोषदायकः -यिका -कं, तृप्तिजनकः -का -कं, तृप्तिदः &c., सन्तोषकः -का -कं, परितोषकः &c., मनोहरः -रा -रं, मनोयोग्यः -ग्या -ग्यं, इच्छापूरकः -का -कं, कामपूरकः &c., पर्य्याप्तः-प्ता-प्तं,सन्देहहारी &c., सन्देहभञ्जकः -का -कं, संशयनिवर्त्तकः &c.

SATISFIABLE, *a.* आतृप्यः -प्या -प्यं, सन्तर्पणीयः -या -यं, सन्तोषणीयः &c.

SATISFIED, *p. p.* (Having desires gratified) तुष्टः -ष्टा -ष्टं, सन्तुष्टः &c., परितुष्टः &c., सन्तोषितः -ता -तं, तृप्तः -प्ता -प्तं, सन्तर्पितः -ता -तं, तर्पितः &c., तृप्तकामः -मा -मं, वितृप्तकामः &c., पूर्णकामः &c., शान्तकामः &c., निवृत्तकामः &c., पर्य्याप्तकामः &c., पर्य्याप्तः -प्ता -प्तं, आप्यायितः -ता -तं, आप्तकामः -मा -मं, सुहितः -ता -तं, चरितार्थः -र्था -र्थं, कृतार्थः &c., कृतकृत्यः -त्या -त्यं, प्रीतः -ता -तं, प्रसादितः &c., अशितः &c.—(Having doubt removed) निवृत्तसन्देहः -हा -हं, निवृत्तसंशयः -या -यं, हृतसन्देहः -हा -हं, गतसन्देहः &c.; 'to be satisfied,' तृप् (c. 4. तृप्यति, तर्पितुं), तुष् (c. 4. तुष्यति, तोष्टुं); 'fire cannot be satisfied with fuel,' अग्निर् न तृप्यति काष्ठानां.

To SATISFY, *v. a.* (Gratify desires to the full) तुष् (c. 10. तोषयति -यितुं), सन्तुष्, परितुष्, तृप् (c. 10. तर्पयति -यितुं), सन्तृप्, परितृप्, पृ (c. 10. पूरयति -यितुं), परिपृ, कामं पृ, इच्छां पृ or शम् (c. 10. शमयति -यितुं) or निवृत् (c. 10. -वर्त्तयति -यितुं), तृप्तिं or सौहित्यं जन् (c. 10. जनयति -यितुं), तुष्टिं जन् or उत्पद् (c. 10. -पादयति -यितुं), आप्यै in caus. (-प्याययति -यितुं), सुख् (c. 10. सुखयति -यितुं), प्री (c. 9. प्रीणाति, c. 10. प्रीणयति -यितुं), हिंव् (c. 1. हिंवति -वितुं), प्रीतिं कृ, सुखं दा.—(Free from doubt) संशयं or सन्देहं हृ (c. 1. हरति, हर्त्तुं), संशयनिवृत्तिं कृ, संशयच्छेदं कृ, संशयखण्डनं कृ.

SATISFYING, *part.* or *a.* तुष्टिदः -दा -दं, तुष्टिजनकः -का -कं, तुष्टिकरः -री -रं, तृप्तिकरः -री -रं, तृप्तिजनकः &c., सन्तर्पकः &c., सन्तोषकः &c., आप्यायनशीलः &c.

SATIVE, *s.* उद्यानजः -जा -जं, उद्यानरोपितः -ता -तं, क्षेत्रजः -जा -जं.

SATLAJ, *s.* (River) शतद्रुः *f.*, शितद्रुः *f.*, शुतुद्रिः *f.*

SATRAP, *s.* छत्रपः, छत्रपतिः *m.*, मण्डलाध्यक्षः, मण्डलाधिपतिः *m.*

To SATURATE, *v. a.* अतिशयेन or अत्यन्तं सिच् (c. 6. सिञ्चति, सेक्तुं) or निषिच् or आसिच्, अतिशयेन or अत्यन्तं क्लिद् (c. 10. क्लेदयति -यितुं) or परिक्लिद्, अत्यन्तं पृ (c. 10. पूरयति -यितुं) or परिपृ.

SATURATED, *p. p.* अतिसिक्तः -क्ता -क्तं, अतिपूरितः -ता -तं, अतिपूर्णः -र्णा -र्णं.

SATURATION, *s.* अतिशयसेकः, अतिसेचनं, अतिक्लेदनं, अतिपूरणं.

SATURDAY, *s.* शनिवारः, शनिवासरः, मन्दवारः, मन्दवासरः, कृतान्तः.

SATURN, *s.* (The planet, variously fabled as the son of Revatí and Balaráma, or of Chháyá and the sun. His influence is considered to be malignant and inauspicious) शनिः *m.*, शौरिः *m.*, सौरः, सौरिः *m.*, रेवतीभवः, छायासुतः, छायातनयः, छायात्मजः, ब्रह्मण्यः, ब्राह्मण्यः, पातङ्गिः *m.*—(The evil-eyed one) क्रूरदृक् *m.* (श्), क्रूरलोचनः.—(The slow-goer) शनैश्चरः, मन्दः, पङ्गुः *m.*—(Lord of the planets) ग्रहनायकः.—(Lord of seven lights or satellites) सप्तांशुपुङ्गवः, सप्तार्चीः *m.* (स्), सप्तार्चिः. Other names are क्रोडः, आरः.

SATURNALIA, *s. pl.* (Spring festival of the Hindús) होलिका, होली, होलाका, दोलयात्रा, दोलोत्सवः.

SATURNIAN, *a.* सत्ययुगसम्बन्धी -न्धिनी &c., सत्ययुगविषयकः -का -कं.

SATURNINE, *a.* मन्दः -न्दा -न्दं, मन्दप्रकृतिः -तिः -ति, जडः -डा -डं, जडस्वभावः -वा -वं, शीतः -ता -तं, शीतप्रकृतिः -तिः -ति.

SATYR, *s.* वनेचरः, वनचारी *m.* (न्), अरण्यचरः, वनदेवता, अरण्यदेवता.

SAUCE, *s.* व्यञ्जनं, उपस्करः, सूपः, तेमनं, मिष्टान्नं, निष्ठानं, प्रहितं, प्रदिग्धः, लालसीकं, उपकरणं, षाड्वः, पिच्छिलः; 'fish-sauce,' पाकमत्स्यः, मीनाम्बीणः.

SAUCE-PAN, *s.* पिठरः, उखा, पिष्टपचनं, पिष्टपाचकं, कन्दुः *m.f.*, कन्दूः *m.f.*, खोलकः, पाकः.

SAUCER, *s.* शालाजिरः -रं, वैदलं, पात्राधारः, शरावः, पुटकः, पात्रं.

SAUCILY, *adv.* अविनयेन, धृष्टवत्, प्रगल्भं, सप्रागल्भ्यं. *See* IMPUDENTLY.

SAUCINESS, *s.* अविनयः, अविनीतता, धृष्टता, प्रगल्भता, प्रागल्भ्यं, चापल्यं, चपलता, वाक्पारुष्यं, परुषवचनं, पारुष्यं, दुरुक्तिः *f.*, दुरुत्तरं, धृष्टता, उत्तरदायकता.

SAUCY, *a.* अविनीतः -ता -तं, अविनयः -या -यं, धृष्टः -ष्टा -ष्टं, प्रगल्भः -ल्भा -ल्भं, चपलः -ला -लं, उत्तरदायकः-यिका -कं, उत्तरदायी -यिनी-यि (न्).

To SAUNTER, *v. n.* अलसवत् or आलस्येन मन्दं मन्दं परिक्रम् (c. 1. -क्रामति -क्रमितुं) or शनैः शनैः परिभ्रम् (c. 4. -भ्राम्यति -भ्रमितुं) or मन्दं मन्दं व्रज्.

SAUNTERING, *s.* अलसपरिक्रमः, आलस्येन परिक्रमणं, मन्दपरिक्रमणं.

SAUSAGE, *s.* छिन्नमांसव्यञ्जनादिगर्भं जन्तुपुरीतत्.

SAVAGE, *a.* (Uncivilized) अशिष्टः -ष्टा -ष्टं, अशिक्षितः -ता -तं, विद्याचारहीनः -ना -नं, दुराचारः -रा -रं, निराचारः &c., अनाचारी -रिणी -रि (न्), विद्याचारशून्यः -न्या -न्यं, शिक्षाहीनः &c., शिक्षारहितः -ता -तं, असभ्यः -भ्या -भ्यं, आचारहीनः &c., आचारशून्यः &c.—(Cruel, ferocious) क्रूरः -रा -रं, क्रूरकर्म्मशाली &c., क्रूराचारः &c., निष्ठुरः -रा -रं, निर्दयः -या -यं, दारुणः -णा -णं, रौद्रः -द्री -द्रं, रौरवः -वी -वं, *see* FEROCIOUS, INHUMAN.—(As a beast) श्वापदः -दी -दं, श्वापदः -दी -दं.—(Wild, pertaining to the forest) आरण्यः -ण्यी -ण्यं, अरण्यजः -जा -जं, जङ्गलः -ला -लं, जाङ्गलः -ली -लं, वनचरसम्बन्धी &c.—(Pertaining to barbarians) म्लेच्छीयः -या -यं, म्लेच्छसम्बन्धी &c., म्लेच्छ in comp.

SAVAGE, *s.* (Uncivilized person) अशिष्टजनः, अशिक्षितजनः, असभ्यजनः, बर्बरः.—(A foreigner or one of a barbarous tribe, not speaking Sanskrit and not subject to Hindú institutions) म्लेच्छः, म्लेच्छजातिः *m.*, किरातः, पुलिन्दः, शबरः, यवनः, भिल्लः, खुधनः.—(Cruel person, brute) राक्षसः, दैत्यः, क्रूरजनः, क्रूरकर्म्मा *m.* (न्), अघोरकर्म्मा *m.*, पुरुषपशुः *m.*

SAVAGELY, *adv.* अशिष्टवत्, किरातवत्, राक्षसवत्, अतिक्रूरं, अतिनिष्ठुरं.

SAVAGENESS, *s.* अशिष्टता, शिक्षाहीनता, विद्याचारहीनता, दुराचारता -त्वं, अनाचारता -त्वं, असभ्यता, शिक्षाभावः, क्रूरता, क्रौर्य्यं, निष्ठुरता, निर्दयता, दारुणता, दारुण्यं, रौद्रता, उग्रता, पारुष्यं.

SAVANT, *s.* गुणग्राहकः, गुणज्ञः, पण्डितः, विद्वान् *m.* (स्), रसज्ञः, मर्म्मज्ञः, ज्ञानी *m.* (न्), अभिज्ञः, विद्यासम्पन्नः.

To SAVE, *v. a.* (Preserve from injury) रक्ष् (c. 1. रक्षति -क्षितुं), अभिरक्ष्, परिरक्ष्, संरक्ष्, प्रतिरक्ष्, त्रै (c. 1. त्रायते -ति -त्रातुं), परित्रै, सन्त्रै, पाल्, गुप्, तॄ in caus., सन्तॄ in caus., अव्, पर्य्याप् in des., रक्षणं कृ, रक्षां कृ, *see To* PRESERVE; 'save me,' त्राहि मां, त्रायस्व मां, मामव, त्राहि त्राहि.—(Deliver) उद्धृ (c. 1. उद्धरति, उद्धर्त्तुं, rt. हृ), समुद्धृ, मुच्, मोक्ष्, निस्तॄ in caus. (-तारयति -यितुं), सन्तॄ, त्रै, परित्रै.—(In theology) त्रै, उद्धृ, तॄ in caus., पापाद् मुच्.—(Not to lose or spend) न क्षि, न व्ययीकृ, अव्ययीकृ, न नश्

in caus. यथा न क्षीयते or यथा न व्ययीक्रियते तथा कृ.—(Lay by) रक्ष्, निधा, संचि (c. 5. -चिनोति -चेतुं), सञ्चयं कृ, संग्रह्, संग्रहं कृ.—(Prevent) निवृ, वृ, रुध्, निवृत् in caus.

SAVE. (Except) वर्ज्जयित्वा, मुक्त्वा, अपहाय, see EXCEPT, EXCEPTED.

SAVED, *p. p.* (Preserved) रक्षितः -ता -तं, त्रातः -ता -तं, त्राणः -णा -णं, तारितः -ता -तं, सन्तारितः &c., अवितः &c.—(Delivered) मुक्तः -क्ता -क्तं, मोचितः -ता -तं, मोक्षितः &c., उद्धृतः &c., निस्तारितः &c.—(In theology) त्रातः -ता -तं, तारितः &c., कृतनिष्कृतिः -तिः -ति; 'not saved,' अकृतनिष्कृतिः &c.—(Not spent, laid by) अव्ययितः -ता -तं, अव्ययीकृतः &c., रक्षितः &c., सञ्चितः &c.—(Prevented) निवारितः -ता -तं.—(Left) शिष्टः -ष्टा -ष्टं, अवशिष्टः &c.; 'those that were saved out of the slain,' हतशेषाः *m. pl.*, हतशिष्टाः *m. pl.*

SAVING, *s.* (The act) रक्षणं, अव्ययः, सम्पादनं, उपार्जनं -ना, अर्जनं, सञ्चयः, लब्धिः.—(Something saved) रक्षितांशः, अव्ययितांशः, रक्षितधनं, अव्ययितधनं, सञ्चितांशः, सञ्चितधनं, उपार्जितांशः.—(Desire of saving life) प्राणपरीप्सा.

SAVING, *part.* or *a.* (Frugal) अव्ययशीलः -ला -लं, अल्पव्ययी -यिनी -यि (न्), स्वल्पव्ययः -या -यं, परिमितव्ययः &c.—(Securing everlasting salvation) त्राणसाधकः -धिका -कं, मुक्तिसाधकः &c., मोक्षसाधकः &c., उद्धारसाधकः &c., परमगतिसाधकः &c., सद्गतिसाधकः &c.—(Excepting) वर्ज्जयित्वा.

SAVIOUR, *s.* त्राता *m.* (तृ), परित्राता *m.*, उद्धारकः, उद्धर्त्ता *m.* (र्तृ), तारकः, तारणकर्त्ता *m.*, निस्तारकः, त्रायकः, मुक्तिदाता *m.*; 'of the world,' जगदुद्धारकः, जगत्त्राता *m.*

SAVOR, SAVOUR, *s.* (Odor) गन्धः वासः; 'sweet savor,' सुगन्धः, सुगन्धिः *m.*, सुवासः, सौरभ्यं; 'ill savor,' दुर्गन्धः, दौर्गन्धिः *m.*, कुत्सितगन्धः.—(Taste) रसः, स्वादः, रुचिः *f.*, लावण्यं, लवणत्वं.

To SAVOR, *v. n.* (Have a smell or flavor) सगन्धीभू, गन्धविशिष्टः -ष्टा -ष्टं भू, सरसीभू, रसयुक्तः -क्ता -क्तं भू.—(Appear a little like) ईषत्सदृशः -शी -शं भू, ईषत्सदृशगुणः -णा -णं भू or प्रतिभा (c. 2. -भाति -तुं).

SAVORINESS, *s.* सुरसता -त्वं, सौरस्यं, सरसता, स्वादुता, मिष्टता -त्वं.

SAVORY, *a.* (Pleasing to the taste) सुरसः -सा -सं, रसिकः -की -कं, सरसः &c., रसी -सिनी -सि (न्), रसवान् -वती -वत् (त्), स्वादुः -द्वी -दु, मिष्टः -ष्टा -ष्टं, रुचिकरः -रा -रं; 'savory food,' मिष्टान्नं,स्वाद्वन्नं.—(To the smell)सुगन्धी-न्धिनी &c., सुरभिः-भिः-भि.

SAW, *s.* (The instrument) करपत्रं, क्रकचः, क्रकरः, पत्रदारकः, शाणः, वातरायणः, तालाङ्कः, कर्त्तनी.

To SAW, *v. a.* करपत्रेण or क्रकचेन पट् (c. 10. पाटयति -यितुं) or छिद् (c. 7. छिनत्ति, छेत्तुं) or भिद् or विभिद् or विदृ (c. 10. -दारयति -यितुं) or विदल् (c. 10. -दलयति -यितुं) or द्विखण्डीकृ, शाणघर्षणेन विदृ; 'he sawed the wood,' करपत्रेण काष्ठम् अपाटयत्.

SAW-DUST, *s.* विदीर्णकाष्ठचूर्णं, काष्ठविदलं, काष्ठघर्षणजक्षोदः.

SAWED, *p. p.* करपत्रविदीर्णः -र्णा -र्णं, करपत्रच्छिन्नः -न्ना -न्नं, क्रकचभिन्नः -न्ना न्नं, करपत्रविदार्य्यमाणः -णा -णं, करपत्रपाटितः -ता -तं, करपत्रविदारितः -ता -तं, करपत्रघर्षितः &c.

SAWING, *s.* करपत्रेण विदारणं or विपाटनं or विच्छेदः, शाणघर्षणं.

SAW-PIT, *s.* काष्ठपाटनगर्त्तः, काष्ठविदारणगर्त्तः, काष्ठदारणयोग्यो गर्त्तः.

SAWYER, *s.* क्राकचिकः, काष्ठपाटनजीवी *m.* (न्), काष्ठविदारकः.

To SAY, *v. a.* (Speak, utter) वद् (c. 1. वदति -दितुं), ब्रू (c. 2. ब्रवीति, वक्तुं 2 pret. आह), वच् (c. 2. वक्ति -क्तुं), भाष् (c. 1. भाषते -षितुं), गद् (c. 1. गदति -दितुं), निगद्, भण् (c. 1. भणति -णितुं), उदाहृ (c. 1. -हरति -हर्त्तुं), व्याहृ, समुदाहृ, उच्चर् (c. 10. -चारयति -यितुं), उदीर् (c. 10. -ईरयति -यितुं), समुदीर्, ईर्, आलप् (c. 1. -लपति -पितुं), जल्प् (c. 1. जल्पति -ल्पितुं), संजल्प्, उपजल्प्, मन्त्र् (c. 10. मन्त्रयति -यितुं), अभिधा, वाक्यं वद्, वाक्यं ब्रू; आह the irregular 2. pret. of ब्रू is used for 'he says' or 'he said.'—(Declare) कथ् (c. 10. कथयति -यितुं), प्रवद्, समावद्, प्रवच्, आख्या.—(Rehearse) अनुवद्, *see To* RECITE.—(That is to say) अर्थतस्, वस्तुतस्.

SAYING, SAY, *s.* उक्तिः *f.*, वाक्यं, उक्तं, वचनं, वाक् *f.* (च्), भाषणं, भाषितं, लपितं, भणितं, वचस् *n.*, अभिधा, अभिधानं, आख्यानं, कथनं, वादः, प्रवादः, प्रवचनं; 'popular saying,' लोकप्रवादः, जनवादः, लोकवाक्यं, लोकोक्तिः *f.*

SAYING, *part.* वदन् -दन्ती -दत् (त्), भाषन् &c., भाषमाणः -णा -णं. The particle इति, meaning 'so, thus,' is often placed at the end of a speech or quotation, either with or without the participle, which implies 'saying,' as इत्युक्त्वा, इत्यभिधाय or simply इति.

SCAB, *s.* कच्छूः *f.*, कच्छुः *f.*, शुष्कव्रणः, सिध्म *n.* (न्), सिध्मं, पामा *f.*, पाम *n.* (न्), कण्डूः *f.*, कण्डुः, खर्जूः *f.*, खसः, पाचिस् *n.*, किलासः, त्वक्पुष्पं-ष्पिका, विचर्चिका.—(Low fellow) अधमाचारः, अधमवृत्तिः *m.*

SCABBARD, *s.* कोषः, कोशः, खड्गकोषः, असिकोषः, खड्गपिधानं, खड्गाधारः, अस्याधारः, टङ्कः, दुग्रहः, परिवारः, प्रत्याकारः.

SCABBINESS, *s.* कच्छुरता, सिध्मलता -त्वं, पामनता, सिध्मवत्त्वं.

SCABBY, *a.* कच्छुरः -रा -रं, सिध्मलः -ला -लं, सिध्मवान् -वती -वत् (त्), पामनः -ना -नं, कच्छूलः -ला -लं, कच्छुरोगी -गिणी &c.

SCAFFOLD, SCAFFOLDING, *s.* मञ्चः, मञ्चकः, इन्द्रकोषः, कर्णवंशः, ताराङ्कणं.—(For spectators) प्रेक्षामञ्चः -ञ्चकः, प्रेक्षागारं, मञ्चः.—(For the execution of a criminal) वधमञ्चः, घातमञ्चः, वध्यघातमञ्चः, वधस्थानं, घातस्थानं.

To SCALD, *v. a.* अतितप्तजलेन दह् (c. 1. दहति, दग्धुं), सुतप्तजलेन दह्, तप्तजलसम्पर्केण दह्, सुतप्तजलसेकेन दह्.

SCALD, *s.* अतितप्तजलकृतं क्षतं, तप्तजलजक्षतं, तप्तजलसम्पर्कजो दाहः.

SCALDED, *p. p.* अतितप्तजलसम्पर्केण दग्धः -ग्धा -ग्धं, तप्तजलदग्धः &c., तप्तः -प्ता -प्तं, सन्तप्तः -प्ता -प्तं.

SCALDING, *part.* अतिदाहकः -का -कं, अतितापकः &c., ज्वलन् -लन्ती -लत् (त्).

SCALE, *s.* (Balance, pair of scales) तुला, तुलायन्त्रं, मापनयन्त्रं, मापनदण्डः, मापनः, धटः, पदार्थमापनार्थं तुलायन्त्रं; 'goldsmith's scales,' स्वर्णी -र्णिका, नाराची -चिका.—(The cup or dish of a balance) धटः, तुलाधटः.—(Sign of the balance), *see* LIBRA.—(Of a fish) शल्कं, शल्कलं, वल्कं, मत्स्यवल्कं, मीनवल्कं, वल्कलं, शकलं.—(Of an animal) कवचः.—(Thin plate or crust) फलकः -कं, शल्कं, शकलं, वल्कं, पत्रं, पटलं.—(Ladder) सोपानं, सोपानपद्धतिः *f.*, निःश्रेणी.—(Regular gradation or series) श्रेणी -णिः *f.*, श्रेधी, क्रमः, अनुक्रमः, पंक्तिः *f.*, आवली, पर्य्यायः; 'on a small scale,' अल्पपरिमाणः -णा -णं.—(In music) ग्रामः, रागः, वर्णः, *see* GAMUT, MODE.

To SCALE, *v. a.* (Climb) आरुह् (c. 1. -रोहति -रोढुं), अधिरुह्, अवस्कन्द् (c. 1. -स्कन्दति -स्कन्तुं), अधिक्रम्.—(The walls of a fortress, &c.) लंघ् (c. 10. लंघयति -यितुं), अभिलंघ्, उल्लंघ्, अवस्कन्द्, लंघनं कृ,

दुर्गलंघनं कृ.—(Strip of scales) वल्क (nom. वल्कयति -यितुं), वल्कं or वल्कलं हृ or निर्हृ or निष्कृष्, निर्वल्कलीकृ.

To SCALE, *v. n.* (Come off in scales) निर्वल्कलीभू, शकलीभू.

SCALED, *p. p.* लंघितः -ता -तं, उल्लंघितः &c., अवस्कन्दितः -ता -तं.

SCALENE, *a.* (Triangle) विषमत्रिभुजः, विषमत्रिकोणं, असमत्रिभुजः.

SCALL, *s.* कच्छूः *f.*, सिध्म *n.* (न्), शुष्कव्रणः. *See* SCAB.

SCALLOP, *v. a.* (Shell-fish) कम्बुः *m.*. कम्बुभेदः.

To SCALLOP, *v. a.* कम्बुरूपेण छेदाङ्कितं -तां कृ, अर्द्धचन्द्राकारछेदाङ्कितं -तां कृ, खण्डमण्डलरूपछेदाङ्कितं -तां कृ, अर्द्धमण्डलरूपचिह्नैर् वस्त्रान्तं परिछिद्.

SCALP, *s.* मस्तकाग्रत्वक् *f.* (च्), मस्तकाग्रचर्म्म *n.* (न्), शिरोग्रत्वक् *f.*, शिरोस्थित्वक् *f.*, शिरोग्रचर्म्म *n.*, शिरोस्थिचर्म्म *n.*, मस्तकास्थिचर्म्म *n.*

To SCALP, *v. a.* मस्तकाग्रत्वचम् अवछिद् (c. 7. -छिनत्ति -छेत्तुं), मस्तकाग्रचर्म्म अपकृत् or उत्कृत् or निष्कृत्, शिरोस्थिचर्म्म निष्कृष् or निर्हृ or हृ.

SCALPED, *p. p.* हृतमस्तकत्वक् *m. f. n.* (च्), हृतमस्तकचर्म्मा -र्म्मा -र्म्म (न्).

SCALY, *a.* सशल्कः -ल्का -ल्कं, सवल्कः &c., वल्कवान् -वती वत् (त्), वल्कमयः -यी -यं, वल्करूपः -पा -पं, वल्की -ल्किनी -ल्कि (न्), वल्कली &c., शल्की &c., शल्कली &c., शकली &c., वल्कावृतः -ता -तं, शल्कावृतः &c.

SCAMP, *s.* अधमाचारः, दुराचारः, दुर्वृत्तः, दुष्टजनः, जाल्मः, धूर्त्तः, खलः.

To SCAMPER, *v. n.* सत्वरं or त्वरितं धाव् (c. 1. धावति -वितुं) or द्रु or चल्.

To SCAN, *v. a.* (Scrutinize) सूक्ष्मं निरीक्ष् or परीक्ष् or वीक्ष्, सूक्ष्मं दृश् or निरूप्, सूक्ष्मं ज्ञा in des.—(Count the feet of verse) छन्दोमात्रां गण् (c. 10. गणयति -यितुं), छन्दोमात्रागणनं कृ.

SCANDAL, *s.* (Reproachful aspersion or calumny) अपवादः, परिवादः, पिशुनवाक्यं, पिशुनवचनं, पिशुनकथा, पैशुन्यं, असूया, अभ्यसूया, असूयककथा, अभ्यसूयककथा, विगर्हकथा, विगानं, वाग्दोषः.—(Gossiping rumor) जनरवः, लोकप्रवादः, लोकरवः, लोकवादः.—(Cause of reproach, disgrace) कलङ्कः, कलङ्ककारणं, अकीर्त्तिकारणं, अपमानकारणं, अपमानहेतुः *m.*, वचनीयता.—(Cause of stumbling, impediment) स्खलनहेतुः *m.*, स्खलितकारणं, बाधा, विघ्नः, व्याघातः.

To SCANDALIZE, *v. a.* बीभत्सं or अरुचिं or असन्तोषं जन् or कृ, वैकृत्यं जन्, गर्हां जन्, कुत्सां जन्, व्यथ् (c. 10. व्यथयति -यितुं), व्यथां जन् or कृ, क्लेशं दा, बाधां कृ, बाध्, विप्रियं कृ, व्यलीकं कृ.

SCANDALIZED, *p. p.* जातबीभत्सः -त्सा -त्सं, जातबाधः -धा -धं, व्यथितः &c.

SCANDALOUS, *a.* (Disgraceful) कलङ्ककरः -री -रं, अकीर्त्तिकरः &c., कुकीर्त्तिकरः &c., कुख्यातिजनकः &c., लज्जाकरः &c., गर्ह्यः -र्ह्या -र्ह्यं, गर्हणीयः -या -यं, गर्हितः -ता -तं, अपयशस्करः &c., अपयशोजनकः &c., यशोनाशकः &c., यशोघ्नः -घ्नी -घ्नं, अपमानजनकः &c.—(Offensive, causing disgust, &c.) बीभत्सजनकः -का -कं, बीभत्सकरः -री -रं, घृणोत्पादकः &c., कुत्सितः -ता -तं.—(Defamatory) अपवादकः -का -कं, असूयकः &c., असूकः &c., अभ्यसूयकः &c.

SCANDALOUSLY, *adv.* गर्हणीयं, गर्ह्यं, कुत्सितं, गर्ह्यप्रकारेण, कुत्सितप्रकारेण, यथा बीभत्सो जायते तथाप्रकारेण.

SCANDALOUSNESS, *s.* गर्ह्यता, गर्हणीयता, बीभत्सजनकता, घृणाजनकता.

SCANNED, *p. p.* सूक्ष्मं निरूपितः -ता -तं or निरीक्षितः &c. or परीक्षितः &c.

SCANSION, *s.* छन्दोमात्रागणनं, श्लोकमात्रागणनं, छन्दोमात्रापरीक्षा.

SCANT, *To* SCANT, *see* SCANTY, *To* STINT, LIMIT.

SCANTILY, *adv.* अविस्तीर्णं, अविस्तारेण, अबाहुल्येन, अविपुलं, अप्रचुरं, अप्राचुर्य्येण, अपर्य्याप्तं, विकलं, अबहु, अल्पमात्रं, स्वल्पं.

SCANTINESS, *s.* अविस्तीर्णता, अविस्तृतिः *f.*, अबाहुल्यं, अविपुलता, अवैपुल्यं, अप्रचुरता, अप्राचुर्य्यं, अबहुत्वं, अल्पता, स्वल्पता, क्षुद्रता, अपृथुता, सम्बाधता, न्यूनता.

SCANTY, *a.* (Narrow) अविस्तीर्णः -र्णा -र्णं, अविस्तृतः -ता -तं, सङ्कटः -टा -टं, सम्बाध in comp., अपृथुः &c., तनुः &c.—(Small, not full) अल्पः -ल्पा -ल्पं, स्वल्पः &c., क्षुद्रः -द्रा -द्रं, अविपुलः -ला -लं, अबहुलः &c., अप्रचुरः -रा -रं, अभूयिष्ठः -ष्ठा -ष्ठं, विकलः -ला -लं, न्यूनः -ना -नं, अपर्य्याप्तः -प्ता -प्तं, लुप्तः -प्ता -प्तं.—(Niggardly) कृपणः -णा -णं.

SCAPULA, *s.* स्कन्धः, भुजशिरस् *n.*, अंशः, अंसः, बाहुमूलं, फलकः.

SCAPULAR, *a.* स्कन्धसम्बन्धी -न्धिनी -न्धि (न्), स्कन्धविषयकः -का -कं.

SCAR, *s.* (Mark of a wound) क्षतचिह्नं, व्रणचिह्नं, व्रणः -णं, शुष्कव्रणं, शुष्कक्षतं, क्षतं, किणः -णं, क्षारी, क्षताङ्कः, व्रणाङ्कः.—(Any mark) चिह्नं, अङ्कः.

To SCAR, *v. a.* क्षतेन or व्रणेन चिह्न् (c. 10. चिह्नयति -यितुं), क्षतचिह्नितं -तां कृ.

SCARAMOUCH, *s.* भण्डः, वैहासिकः. *See* BUFFOON.

SCARCE, *a.* (Rare) विरलः -ला -लं, विरलागतः -ता -तं, दुर्लभः -भा -भं, दुर्लभ्यः -भ्या -भ्यं, दुष्प्रापः -पा -पं, दुष्प्राप्यः -प्या -प्यं, अप्राप्यः &c., असाधारणः -णा -णी -णं, *see* RARE.—(Small in quantity, deficient) अबहुलः -ला -लं, अप्रचुरः -रा -रं, अपुष्कलः -ला -लं, अविपुलः &c., अल्पः -ल्पा -ल्पं, स्वल्पः &c.

SCARCELY, SCARCE, *adv.* कष्टेन, कृच्छ्रेण, सकृच्छ्रं, दुःखेन, सदुःखं, कष्टं, सकष्टं, आयासेन, कठिनं, काठिन्येन, सकाठिन्यं, दुर् or दुःख prefixed; 'scarcely to be found,' दुर्लभ्यः &c., दुःखप्राप्यः &c.

SCARCITY, SCARCENESS, *s.* (Rareness) विरलता -त्वं, वैरल्यं, दुर्लभता, दौर्लभ्यं, दुर्लभ्यता, दुष्प्रापत्वं, दुष्प्राप्यता, अप्रसिद्धता, असाधारणता, असाधारण्यं, क्वाचित्कता.—(Smallness of quantity, deficiency) अबाहुल्यं, अबहुत्वं, अप्राचुर्य्यं, अप्रचुरता, अपुष्कलता, अविपुलता, अल्पता -त्वं, स्वल्पता, न्यूनता.—(Time of scarcity) दुर्भिक्षं, दुष्कालः, अनाकालं, प्रयामः, नीवाकः, महार्घता.

To SCARE, *v. a.* त्रस् (c. 10. त्रासयति -यितुं), संत्रस्, वित्रस्, भी in caus. (भाययति -यितुं, भीषयति -यितुं), उद्विज् (c. 10. -वेजयति -यितुं), त्रासं कृ, भयहेतुदर्शनेन विद्रु (c. 10. -द्रावयति -यितुं), भयप्रदर्शनेन द्रु.

SCARE-CROW, *s.* काकत्रासकमूर्त्तिः *f.*, काकादित्रासकवस्तु *n.*, काकादित्रासनार्थं क्षेत्रस्थापितं भयानकवस्तु or भयङ्करवस्तु *n.*, पक्षित्रासकमूर्त्तिः *f.*, भयहेतुः *m.*, भयप्रदर्शनं.

SCARED, *p. p.* त्रासितः -ता -तं, वित्रस्तः -स्ता -स्तं, त्रस्तः &c., भीतः -ता -तं.

SCARF, *s.* चैलं, अङ्गवस्त्रं, उपवस्त्रं, उत्तरीयं, सिचयः, अधिकाङ्गं.

SCARF-SKIN, *s.* बाह्यत्वक् *f.* (च्), बहिस्त्वक् *f.*, बाह्यचर्म्म *n.* (न्), अवभासिनी.

SCARIFICATION, *s.* त्वक्छेदः -दनं, त्वग्लिखनं, त्वगुल्लिखनं, लिखनं, उल्लिखनं, प्रोल्लेखनं, रक्तमोक्षणार्थं त्वक्छेदनं or चर्म्मछेदनं.

SCARIFICATOR, SCARIFIER, *s.* त्वक्छेदकः, त्वगुल्लेखकः, त्वक्छेदनयन्त्रं.

SCARIFED, *p. p.* लिखितः -ता -तं, उल्लिखितः &c., छिन्नत्वक् *m. f. n.*, उल्लिखितत्वक्.

To SCARIFY, *v. a.* त्वचं or चर्म्म लिख् (c. 6. लिखति, लेखितुं) or उल्लिख् or प्रोल्लिख् or प्रलिख् or विलिख्, त्वचं छिद् (c. 7. छिनत्ति, छेत्तुं) or विछिद्.

SCAR-LESS, *a.* निर्व्रणः -णा -णं, निर्व्रणः &c., व्रणहीनः -ना -नं, अव्रणः &c.

SCARLET, *a.* सुरक्तः -क्ता -क्तं, रक्तः &c., शोणितः &c., सिन्दूरवर्णः &c.

SCARLET-FEVER, SCARLATINA, *s.* उदर्द्दः, उदर्भः.

SCATE, *s.* (Fish) शङ्कुचिः *m.* -चीः *f.*, शाङ्कुचिः -ची, शङ्कुः *m.*, शङ्कोचः, सङ्कोचः.

To SCATH, *v. a.* क्षतं कृ, क्षतिं कृ, क्षण्, अर्द्, हिंस्. *See To* HURT, DAMAGE.

SCATHED, *p. p.* क्षतः -ता -तं, परिक्षतः &c., विक्षतः &c. अर्द्दितः &c.

SCATHLESS, *a.* अक्षतः -ता -तं, अपरिक्षतः &c., क्षतहीनः -ना -नं, अविक्षतः &c., अक्षितः &c., अहिंसितः &c., अजातक्षतः -ता -तं, अजातापकारः -रा -रं.

To SCATTER, *v. a.* कॄ (c. 6. किरति, करितुं -रीतुं), विकॄ, प्रकॄ, आकॄ, अवकॄ, इतस्ततो or बहुधा विकॄ or विक्षिप् (c. 6. -क्षिपति -क्षेप्तुं), बहुधा क्षिप् or व्यस् (c. 4. -अस्यति -सितुं), विनिर्धू (c. 5. -धूनोति -धवितुं), विधू, विद्रु (c. 10. -द्रावयति -यितुं), विभ्रंश. *See To* DISPERSE, DISSIPATE.

To SCATTER, *v. n.* विकॄ in pass. (-कीर्य्यते), कॄ in pass., बहुधा गम् (c. 1. गच्छति, गन्तुं) or विगम्, विक्षिप् in pass. (-क्षिप्यते).

SCATTERED, *a.* विकीर्णः -र्णा -र्णं, आकीर्णः &c., अवकीर्णः &c., प्रकीर्णः &c., कीर्णः &c., विक्षिप्तः -प्ता -प्तं, व्यस्तः -स्ता -स्तं, सुव्यस्तः &c., उदस्तः &c., बहुधा क्षिप्तः &c., बहुधागतः -ता -तं, प्रसृतः &c., प्रसारितः &c., विधूतः -ता -तं, विनिर्धूतः &c., खण्डितः &c., असंहतः -ता -तं; 'having scattered,' विकीर्य्य; 'being scattered,' कीर्य्यमाणः -णा -णं, अवकीर्य्यमाणः &c., विकीर्य्यमाणः &c.

SCATTERING, *s.* किरणं, विकिरणं, अवकिरणं, कीर्णिः *f.*, विकीर्णिः *f.*, विकिरः, विक्षेपः -पणं, विसारणं, बहुधा क्षेपः, बहुधागमनं.

SCATTERING, *part.* विकिरन् -रन्ती -रत् (त्), विकिरणकारी -रिणी -रि (न्).

SCAVENGER, *s.* अवस्करकः, मलापकर्षी *m.*, मलाकर्षी *m.* (न्), खलपूः *m.*, मार्गशोधकः, मार्गसम्मार्जकः.

SCENE, *s.* (Stage) रङ्गः, रङ्गभूमिः *f.*, रङ्गशाला; 'back of the scenes,' नेपथ्यं; 'behind the scenes,' नेपथ्ये.—(Curtain or hanging of a theatre) अपटी.—(Division of an act) प्रवेशः, पात्रप्रवेशः, अङ्कपरिच्छेदः; 'introductory scene,' प्रवेशकः.—(Place represented) भूमिः *f.*, स्थलं -ली, स्थानाकारः, स्थानप्रतिरूपं, भूमिप्रतिरूपं.—(Place where any thing is represented) रङ्गः, भूमिः *f.*—(Painting representing scenery) चित्रगता गृहवृक्षादिरचना, वर्णगता दृक्पातविषयरचना.—(Assemblage of objects seen at one view) दृक्पातविषयः, दृक्पथगोचरविषयाः *m. pl.*, दृष्टिपातविषयः.

SCENERY, *s.* (Appearance of various natural objects as seen together) जलतृणवृक्षादिसंस्था, पर्व्वतवृक्षादिसंस्था, जलपर्व्वतवृक्षादिरचना, दृष्टिपातविषयरचना, दृक्पातविषयसंस्था, दृक्पथगोचरजलपर्व्वतवृक्षादि.—(Of a theatre) रङ्गभूमौ or रङ्गशालायां गृहवृक्षादिरचना, चित्रगता or वर्णगता गृहवृक्षादिरचना.

SCENIC, SCENICAL, *a.* नाटकीयः -या -यं, अभिनयविषयकः -का -कं.

SCENT, *s.* (Odor, smell) गन्धः, वासः; 'sweet scent,' सुगन्धः, सुवासः, आमोदः, मोदः, वासः, परिमलः, धूपः, सौरभ्यं, सुरभिगन्धः, 'a scent spreading far,' समाकर्षी *m.* (न्), निर्हारी *m.*; 'made up scent,' कृत्रिमधूपः -पकः, वृकधूपः, वकधूपः.—(Power of smelling) घ्राणशक्तिः *f.*, घ्राणेन्द्रियं, घ्राणं; 'having a quick scent,' शीघ्रघ्राणः -णा -णं, तीक्ष्णघ्राणः &c., शीघ्रचेतनः -ना -नं.

To SCENT, *v. a.* (Smell) घ्रा, आघ्रा, उपघ्रा, उपाघ्रा.—(Perfume) वास् (c. 10. वासयति -यितुं), सुरभीकृ, भू in caus., धूप्, सुगन्धीकृ, *see To* PERFUME.

SCENTED, *p. p.* (Smelt) घ्रातः -ता -तं, आघ्रातः &c., घ्राणः -णा -णं.(Perfumed) वासितः -ता -तं, सुवासितः &c., अनुवासितः &c., सुरभितः -ता -तं, सुरभीकृतः &c., सुरभिः -भिः -भि, सुरभिगन्धिः -न्धिः -न्धि, सुगन्धी -न्धिनी -न्धि (न्), गन्धी &c., सुगन्धवान् -वती -वत् (त्), गन्धवान् &c., आमोदितः -ता -तं, भावितः &c., परिमलितः &c., *see* PERFUMED.

SCENTLESS, *a.* निर्गन्धः -न्धा -न्धं, अगन्धः &c., गन्धहीनः -ना -नं.

SCEPTIC, *s.* अविश्वासी *m.* (न्), हैतुकः, सन्दिग्धमतिः *m.*, संशयात्मा *m.* (न्), चार्वाकः, अप्रत्ययी *m.*, संशयकारी *m.*, युक्तिबलेन सर्व्वत्र संशयकारी *m.*

SCEPTICAL, *a.* अविश्वासी -सिनी -सि (न्), अप्रत्ययी &c., संशयालुः -लुः -लु, संशयात्मा -त्मा -त्म (न्), सन्दिग्धमतिः -तिः -ति, सन्दिग्धमानसः -सा -सं, संशयानः -ना -नं, संशयापन्नः -न्ना -न्नं, संशयापन्नमानसः -सा -सं. *See* INFIDEL.

SCEPTICISM, *s.* अविश्वासः, संशयः, सन्दिग्धमतित्वं, *see* INFIDELITY.

SCEPTRE, SCEPTER, *s.* राजदण्डः -ण्डं, राजवेत्रं, राजयष्टिः *m.*, शक्तिः *f.*—(Royal authority or office) राजाधिकारः, छत्रसिंहासनं.

SCEPTRED, SCEPTERED, *a.* राजदण्डधारी -रिणी -रि (न्), दण्डी -ण्डिनी &c.

SCHEDULE, *s.* (Paper, document) पत्रं, लेखः, लेख्यं.—(Paper annexed to a larger document) पत्रानुबन्धः, लेख्यानुबन्धः.—(List), *see* LIST, INVENTORY.

SCHEME, *s.* कल्पना, उपायः, सङ्कल्पः, परिकल्पना, परिकल्पितं, व्यवसायः, अनुसन्धानं, अनुसन्धा, युक्तिः *f.*, प्रयुक्तिः *f.*, प्रयोगः, कल्पितं, उपायकल्पना.

To SCHEME, *v. a.* मनसा क्लृप् or परिक्लृप्, उपायं क्लृप्. *See To* PLAN.

SCHEMER, *s.* उपायकल्पकः, परिकल्पकः, कल्पनाकारी *m.* (न्), उपायी *m.*

SCHEMING, *part.* or *a.* युक्तिमान् -मती -मत् (त्), अनुसन्धानी -निनी -नि (न्), अनुसन्धायी &c., उपायी &c., उपायचिन्तकः -का -कं, विदग्धः -ग्धा -ग्धं; 'a scheming woman,' खोटिः *f.*, खोरिः *f.*, विदग्धा स्त्री.

SCHIRRHUS, *s.* *See* SCIRRHUS.

SCHISM, *s.* शाखा, शाखाभेदः, धर्म्मभेदः, मतभेदः, मार्गभेदः, सम्प्रदायः, धर्म्मविभेदः, मतविभेदः, धर्म्मविच्छेदः.

SCHISMATIC, SCHISMATICAL, *a.* धर्म्मभेदकः -का -कं, मतभेदकः &c., मार्गभेदकः &c., शाखाभेदसम्बन्धी -न्धिनी -न्धि (न्), मार्गभेदसम्बन्धी &c., मार्गभेदविषयकः -का -कं.

SCHOLAR, *s.* (Learner, pupil) शिष्यः, विद्यार्थी *m.* (न्), अन्तेवासी *m.*, छात्रः, अन्तेवासिजनः, अध्यायी *m.*, अध्येता *m.* (तृ), विद्याभ्यासी *m.* (न्), शिक्षिताक्षरः, अधीती *m.*, विद्याभ्यासकृत् *m.*, अक्षरचुञ्चुः, पाठार्थी *m.*; 'head scholar,' पट्टशिष्यः; 'scholar of a scholar,' प्रशिष्यः.—(Learned man) पण्डितः, पण्डितजनः, विद्वान् *m.* (स्), विद्वज्जनः, कृतविद्यः, सर्व्वरसः, रसज्ञः, तात्त्विकः, *see* LEARNED.

SCHOLAR-LIKE, SCHOLARLY, *a.* पण्डितयोग्यः -ग्या -ग्यं, छात्रयोग्यः &c.

SCHOLARSHIP, *s.* पाण्डित्यं, पण्डितत्वं, विद्या, वैदुष्यं, *see* LEARNING.

SCHOLASTIC, SCHOLASTICAL, *a.* पाठशालासम्बन्धी -न्धिनी -न्धि (न्), शालासम्बन्धी &c., पण्डितसभासम्बन्धी &c., पाण्डित्यविषयकः -का -कं.

SCHOLIAST, *s.* भाष्यकारः, टीकाकारः, टीकालेखकः, *see* COMMENTATOR.

SCHOLIUM, *s.* टीका, भाष्यं, टीकाग्रन्थः, आदर्शः, *see* COMMENTARY.

SCHOOL, *s.*, (Place of instruction) पाठशाला, विद्यालयः -यं, विद्यावेश्म *n.* (न्), विद्यागृहं, शिक्षालयः -यं, शिक्षागृहं, विद्याभ्यासगृहं, विद्याभ्यासशाला, अध्ययनशाला, अध्ययनगृहं, मठः, आश्रमः, आवसथः, आवसथ्यः, शाला.—(Body of scholars) शिष्यसमूहः, विद्यार्थिसमूहः, छात्रसमूहः, पाठशाला, शाला.—(Sect of philosophers) शाखा, पण्डितशाखा, शिक्षासम्प्रदायः, शालासम्प्रदायः; 'difference of school,' शाखाभेदः; 'of the same school,' एकशाखः -खा -खं; 'of a good school,' शालाशुद्धः -द्धा -द्धं.—(School or system of philosophy) दर्शनः, तीर्थः. There are six schools or systems of philosophy recognised by the Hindús, viz. 1. Púrva Mímánsá, पूर्व्वमीमांसा, founded by Jaimini, for the purpose of illustrating and explaining the karmakánda, or ritual part of the Vedas. It gives the rationale or meaning of the ritual enjoined in those sacred books, as distinct from the theological or spiritual part of them, and acknowledges the principle of एकत्वं, or oneness, which it was the object of the Vedánta system more fully to investigate. 2. Sánkhya, सांख्यः, ascribed to the Muni Kapila. This system is an attempt to account for the existence of the universe without the Deity, by asserting the principle of द्वैतं or duality, or, in other words, the co-existence of Spirit and matter. 3. Vedánta, वेदान्तः, or Uttara Mímánsá, उत्तरमीमांसा, said to have been founded by Vyása, and subsequently fully developed by its most celebrated teacher शङ्करः or शङ्कराचार्य्यः. This system is wholly concerned with the theological and philosophical part of the Vedas, or that part contained in the chapters called Upanishads, and its teaching is intended to oppose the duality of the Sánkhya system by shewing that the end or aim of the Vedas is एकत्वं, or the oneness of Spirit. It denies the co-existence of matter with Spirit, and hence the conclusion arrived at is the non-existence of any thing but God. 4. Nyáya, न्यायः, founded by the inspired sage Gautama, and the most popular of all the systems. It is neither so mystical as the Vedánta, nor so fanciful as the Sánkhya. Its title signifies 'the fitness of things,' and it may be described as an attempt to treat of almost all subjects, according to a philosophical method and logical arrangement. 5. Vaiśeshika, वैशेषिकं, a branch of the Nyáya, founded by the sage कणादः, to supply what was incomplete in the aphorisms of Gautama. 6. Yoga, योगः or Pátanjala, पातञ्जलं, founded by the sage पतञ्जलिः *m.* Its object is to shew that, even in the body, there may be, to a great extent, union with the Supreme Being. These philosophical systems are contained in sacred writings called Shástras. *See* the word.

To SCHOOL, *v. a.* शिक्ष्, अनुशिक्ष्, उपदिश्, शास्. *See To* TEACH, INSTRUCT.

SCHOOL-BOY, *s.* बालशिष्यः, बालछात्रः, बालाध्यायी *m.* (न्), विद्याभ्यासार्थं पाठशालाम् अभिगच्छति यः कुमारः or बालः or बालकः.

SCHOOL-FELLOW, *s.* सहाध्यायी *m.* (न्), सहपाठकः, समाध्यायी *m.*, एकपाठशालाभिगामी *m.*, एकगुरुः *m.*, एकोपाध्यायः.

SCHOOL-HOUSE, *s.* पाठशाला, पाठगृहं, शिक्षागृहं, शिक्षाशाला, शाला.

SCHOOLING, *s.* शिक्षा -क्षणं, अध्यापनं, उपदेशः, पाठः, विद्यादानं.—(Compensation for instruction) शिक्षावेतनं, शिक्षामूल्यं.

SCHOOLMAN, *s.* तार्किकः, नैयायिकः, न्यायविद् *m.*, तर्कशास्त्रज्ञः.

SCHOOLMASTER, *s.* बालाध्यापकः, बालोपदेशी *m.* (न्), बालोपदेशकः, बालशिक्षकः, अर्भकाध्यापकः, उपाध्यायः, शिक्षागुरुः *m.*, शिक्षादाता *m.* (तृ), विद्यादाता *m.*, पाठशालानायकः, पाठशालाध्यक्षः, आचार्य्यः, गुरुः *m.*, उपाध्यायः, अध्यापकः.

SCHOOLMISTRESS, *s.* बालाध्यापिका, बालोपदेशिनी, उपाध्याया, आचार्य्या, शिक्षादात्री, विद्यादात्री, पाठशालाध्यक्षा, पाठशालानायिका.

SCHOOL-ROOM, *s.* पाठशाला, शिक्षाशाला. *See* SCHOOL-HOUSE.

SCHOONER, *s.* कूपकद्वयविशिष्टा नौका, द्विकूपकनौः *f.*, द्विकूपकः.

SCIATICA, *s.* कटिशिरावेदना, कटिस्नायुवेदना, श्रोणिशिरावेदना.

SCIATICAL, *a.* कटिसम्बन्धी -न्धिनी -न्धि (न्), श्रोणिसम्बन्धी &c.

SCIENCE, *s.* विद्या, विज्ञानं, ज्ञानं, शास्त्रं, व्युत्पत्तिः *f.*, *see* KNOWLEDGE; 'study of science,' विद्याभ्यासः; 'a science,' विद्या; 'book of science,' शास्त्रं, *see* SHÁSTRA; 'sacred science,' श्रुतं, ज्ञानं; 'profane,' विज्ञानं, उपविद्या; 'skilled in sacred science,' शास्त्रविद्, आम्नायविद्-विद्-विद्.

SCIENTIFIC, SCIENTIFICAL, *a.* (According to the principles of science) विद्यासूत्रानुसारी -रिणी -रि (न्), विद्यातत्त्वानुसारी &c., विद्याक्रमानुसारी &c., विद्यासूत्रानुयायी &c., शास्त्रानुसारी &c.—(Well versed in science) विद्यावान् -वती -वत् (त्), ज्ञानी &c., विद्वान् -दुषी -द्वत् (त्), ज्ञानवान् &c., कृतविद्यः -द्या -द्यं, कोविदः -दा -दं, ज्ञातसिद्धान्तः, तात्त्विकः.

SCIENTIFICALLY, *adv.* विद्यासूत्रानुसारेण, विद्यातत्त्वानुसारात्, विद्याक्रमेण.

SCIMITAR, *s.* खड्गः, वक्रखड्गः, न्युब्जखड्गः, असिः *m.*, निस्त्रिंशः, वक्रनिस्त्रिंशः, वक्रकृपाणः, चन्द्रहासः, मण्डलाग्रः, असिरिष्टिः *m.*, धाराविषः, विधुपञ्जरः, करपालः, करवालः, कौक्षेयकः.

To SCINTILLATE, *v. n.* स्फुर् (c. 6. स्फुरति -रितुं), अग्निकणान् or अग्निस्फुलिङ्गान् उत्क्षिप् (c. 6. -क्षिपति -क्षेप्तुं), ज्वलनकणान् मुच् or निःसृ in caus.

SCINTILLATION, *s.* स्फुरणं, अग्निकणस्फुरणं, स्फुलिङ्गस्फुरणं, स्फुलिङ्गज्वलनं, अग्निकणज्वलनं, स्फुलिङ्गोत्क्षेपः, कणोत्क्षेपः.

SCIOLISM, *s.* खण्डपाण्डित्यं, खण्डज्ञानं, खण्डितज्ञानं, पाण्डित्याभासः, अर्द्धपाण्डित्यं, किञ्चिज्ज्ञानं, अल्पज्ञानं, धुवकता -त्वं.

SCIOLIST, *s.* खण्डपण्डितः, खण्डज्ञानी *m.* (न्), अल्पविद्यः, अल्पज्ञः, किञ्चिज्ज्ञः, अल्पविद्यावान् *m.* (त्), धुवकः.

SCION, *s.* अङ्कुरः, पल्लवः, नवपल्लवः, किसलयः, प्ररोहः, प्रवालः.

SCIRRHOUS, *a.* ग्रन्थिमान् -मती -मत् (त्), ग्रन्थिलः -ला -लं, घनीभूतः &c.

SCIRRHUS, SCIRRHOSITY, *s.* मांसग्रन्थिः *m.*, मांसकाठिन्यं, मांसघनता.

SCISSIBLE, SCISSILE *a.* छेदनीयः -या -यं, छेद्यः -द्या -द्यं, कर्त्तनीयः -या -यं.

SCISSORS, *s. pl.* कर्त्तरी, कर्त्तनी, कृपाणी, कर्त्री, छेदनी, खण्डधारा, शरारीमुखी.

To SCOFF, *v. n.* अवक्षिप् (c. 6. -क्षिपति -क्षेप्तुं), क्षिप्, अवज्ञा, तिरस्कृ, मुखरीकृ, अवहस्, उपहस्, अपहस्, विहस्, प्रहस्, अवहासभूमिं कृ, उपहासास्पदं कृ, अपहासास्पदं कृ, गर्ह्, अवगर्ह्, अवगुर्, अवमन्, आक्षर्, भर्त्स्, परिभू, निन्द्, तुच्छीकृ, अवज्ञां कृ. *See To* JEER, MOCK.

SCOFF, *s.* अवक्षेपः, क्षेपः, अवहासः, उपहासः, उपहासोक्तिः *f.*, अवज्ञा, अवज्ञावाक्यं, अवमानोक्तिः *f.*, अवमानं, अवहेला, तिरस्कारोक्तिः *f.*, निन्दोक्तिः *f.*

SCOFFER, *s.* उपहासकः, अवहासकः, अवक्षेपकः, क्षेपकः. *See* MOCKER.

SCOFFING, *s.* अवहासः, उपहासः, तिरस्कारः, तिरस्क्रिया, अवक्षेपणं.

SCOFFINGLY, *adv.* सावक्षेपं, सावहासं, सतिरस्कारं, उपहासेन, सावहेलं.

To SCOLD, *v. a.* or *n.* निन्द् (c. 1. निन्दति -न्दितुं), प्रतिनिन्द्, विनिन्द्, उपालभ् (c. 1. -लभते -लब्धुं), भर्त्स् (c. 10. भर्त्सयति -यितुं), प्रत्यादिश् (c. 6. -दिशति -देष्टुं), तर्ज् (c. 10. तर्जयति -यितुं), आक्रुश्, गर्ह्, विगर्ह्, गुप् in des., क्षिप्, अवक्षिप्, अधिक्षिप्, वाग्दण्डं कृ, तिरस्कृ, परिवद्, परिभाष्. *See To* CHIDE, REPROVE.

SCOLD, *s.* (Foul-mouthed scolding woman) दुर्मुखी, वाग्दुष्टा, कर्कशा,

पूतना, कैकेयी, दुर्गा, कृत्या, महामाया, सदावक्रा, वक्रशीला, अधीरा.

SCOLDED, *p. p.* निन्दितः -ता -तं, उपालब्धः -ब्धा -ब्धं, प्रत्यादिष्टः -ष्टा -ष्टं, तर्जितः -ता -तं, समर्जितः &c., तिरस्कृतः &c., अधिक्षिप्तः -प्ता -प्तं.

SCOLDER, *s.* निन्दकः, उपालम्भकारी *m.* (न्), प्रत्यादेशकः, उपक्रोष्टा *m.* (ष्टृ).

SCOLDING, *s.* निन्दा -न्दनं, उपालम्भः, तर्जनं, भर्त्सनं, निर्भर्त्सनं, वाग्दण्डः, वाक्पारुष्यं, परिवादः, परिभाषणं, धिक्कारः, धिक्क्रिया, तिरस्कारः, तिरस्क्रिया.

SCOLLOP, *To* SCOLLOP, *see* SCALLOP, *To* SCALLOP.

SCONCE, *s.* (Holder of the end of a candle) दीपाग्राधारः, वर्त्याधारः, दीपाग्रधारणयोग्या लोहनलिका.—(Mulct) दण्डः, दण्डलेशः.

To SCONCE, *v. a.* दण्ड् (c. 10. दण्डयति -यितुं). *See To* MULCT, FINE.

SCOOP, *s.* (Kind of ladle) दर्वी, दर्विकः, दार्वी, कम्बिः *f.*, कम्बी, खजिका; 'butter-scoop,' कुन्तलिका.—(Instrument for excavating) खनित्रं, उत्खनित्रं, खात्रं.

To SCOOP, *v. a.* (Lade out), *see To* LADLE.—(Make hollow, excavate) खन् (c. 1. खनति -नितुं), उत्खन्, निखन्, प्रोत्खन्, खनित्रेण शून्यीकृ or शुषिरीकृ or पुट् or पुटीकृ.

SCOOPED, *p. p.* उत्खातः -ता -तं, उत्खनितः -ता -तं, शुषिरीकृतः &c.

SCOPE, *s.* (End, aim) अभिप्रायः, अभिप्रेतं, तात्पर्य्यं, आशयः, अर्थः, उद्देशः, आकूतं, अभिसन्धिः *m.*, अभिसन्धानं, तात्पर्य्यार्थः, आकांक्षा, विवक्षितं, *see* MEANING.—(Limit, compass) अन्तः, पर्य्यन्तः -न्तं, परिमाणं, विषयः.—(Room, space) अवकाशः, प्रसरः, अवसरः.

SCORBUTIC, SCORBUTICAL, *a.* नाविकरक्तपित्तसम्बन्धी -न्धिनी -न्धि (न्), नाविकरक्तपित्तरोगी -गिणी &c.; 'scorbutic affection of the gums,' शीतादः; 'diseased with it,' शीतादरोगी &c.

To SCORCH, *v. a.* बाह्यतस् or बहिस् or बहिर्भागे दह् (c. 1. दहति, दग्धुं) or निदह् or परिदह् or तप् (c. 1. तपति, तप्तुं, c. 10. तापयति -यितुं).

To SCORCH, *v. n.* बाह्यतस् or बहिर्भागे दह् in pass. or तप् in pass.

SCORCHED, *p. p.* बाह्यतस् or बहिर्भागे दग्धः -ग्धा -ग्धं or परिदग्धः &c. or तप्तः -प्ता -प्तं or सन्तप्तः &c. or अभितप्तः &c. or उत्तप्तः &c., भर्जितः -ता -तं, भृष्टः -ष्टा -ष्टं.

SCORCHING, *part.* or *a.* दाहकः -का -कं, तापकः &c., उष्णः -ष्णा -ष्णं, अत्युष्णः &c., प्रखरः -रा -रं, चण्डः &c., नैदाघः -घी -घं.

SCORCHING, *s.* बहिर्दाहः, बहिर्दहनं, बहिर्भागे दाहः, बाह्यतस्तापः.

SCORE, *s.* (Twenty) विंशकं, विंशी *m.* (न्), विंशतिः *f.*—(Notch) छेदः, अवच्छेदः, विच्छेदः.—(Line) रेखा, अङ्कः, वर्त्तिः *f.*—(Account, reckoning) गणना, विगणना, विगणनपत्रं, विगणनलेखः, विगणनापत्रं.—(Reason) हेतुः *m.*, कारणं, निमित्तं; 'on the score of,' हेतोः, हेतौ, कारणात्, कृते, निमित्ते or expressed by the abl. c., or by the affix तस्; 'on the score of relationship,' ज्ञातित्वहेतोः, ज्ञातित्वात्, ज्ञातिभावतस्.

To SCORE, *v. a.* (Notch) छिद्, अवछिद्, छेदं कृ.—(Mark with lines) रेखाङ्कितं -तां कृ, रेखाभिर् अङ्क् (c. 10. अङ्कयति -यितुं) or चिह्न्, अङ्कं कृ, अङ्कनं कृ.—(Set down a debt) ऋणं लिख् or अभिलिख्, ऋणाभिलेखनं कृ, ऋणं लेख्ये आरुह् in caus.—(Set down, take an account of) लिख् (c. 6. लिखति, लेखितुं), अभिलिख्, अङ्क्.

SCORED, *p. p.* अङ्कितः -ता -तं, रेखाङ्कितः &c., लिखितः &c., अभिलिखितः &c.

SCORIA, *s.* रीतिः *f.*, रीतिका, किट्टं, किट्टालः, लोहकिट्टं. *See* DROSS.

SCORN, *s.* अवज्ञा, अवज्ञानं, अवमानं, अवमतिः *f.*, अपमानं, अवहेला -लं -लनं, परिभवः, परिभावः, परिभूतिः *f.*, तिरस्कारः, तिरस्क्रिया, अवलेपः, घृणा, उन्मायः, *see* CONTEMPT; 'object of scorn,' तिरस्कारविषयः, तिरस्कारास्पदं, तिरस्कारपात्रं, परिभवास्पदं, परिभवपदं.

To SCORN, *v. a.* अवज्ञा (c. 9. -जानाति -नीते -ज्ञातुं), अवमन् (c. 4. -मन्यते -मन्तुं), तृणाय मन्, अवधीर्, तिरस्कृ, परिभू, गर्ह्, विगर्ह्, तुच्छीकृ, न्यक्कृ, कुत्स्, उपेक्ष्, कदर्थीकृ, बाध् in des., अवधृ, निन्द्, धिक्कृ. *See To* CONTEMN, DESPISE.

SCORNED, *p.p.* अवज्ञातः -ता -तं, अवमतः &c., अवमानितः &c., अवधीरितः &c., विमानितः &c., तिरस्कृतः -ता -तं, गर्हितः -ता -तं, विगर्हितः &c., परिभूतः &c., अतिनिन्दितः &c., निन्दितः &c.

SCORNER, *s.* अवज्ञाता *m.* (तृ), निन्दकः, अवमन्ता *m.* (न्तृ), अवमानकृत्, अवहेलकृत्, अवज्ञाकारी *m.* (न्), तिरस्कारी *m.*, तिरस्कर्त्ता *m.*, (र्तृ), घृणाकरः.

SCORNFUL, *a.* अवज्ञाकारी -रिणी -रि (न्), अवज्ञानी &c., अवमानी &c., सावहेलः -ला -लं, सावज्ञः -ज्ञा -ज्ञं, परिभवी &c., परिभावी &c., परिभावुकः -का -कं, अवमन्ता -न्त्री -न्तृ (न्तृ), सावलेपः -पा -पं, सोन्मायः -या -यं, अवलिप्तः -प्ता -प्तं, दृप्तः -प्ता -प्तं, तिरस्कारी &c., अवहेलात्मकः -का -कं, निन्दात्मकः &c., अवज्ञारूपः -पा -पं, अवमानार्थकः &c.

SCORNFULLY, *adv.* सावज्ञानं, सावहेलं, सावमानं, सपरिभावं, परिभवेण, सावलेपं, सोन्मायं, सतिरस्कारं, दृप्तवत्, निन्दापूर्व्वं, निन्दकवत्.

SCORNFULNESS, *s.* अवज्ञाशीलता, सावहेलत्वं, अवलिप्तता, सोन्मायत्वं.

SCORPIO, *s.* (The sign) वृश्चिकः, कौर्प्यः, अलिः *m.*

SCORPION, *s.* वृश्चिकः, अलिः *m.*, अली *m.* (न्), आलिः *m.*, आरी *m.* (न्), द्रुणः, द्रोणः, द्रूणः, अलिपकः, अघशीर्नः, लूमविषः, वस्कराटिका; 'its tail or sting,' लूमं -मः.

SCOT, *s.* (Portion of money assessed) करः, देयभागः, देयांशः, देयं.

To SCOTCH, *v. a.* छेदं कृ, छेदैर् अङ्क्, त्वक्छेदं कृ, ईषद् व्रश्च् or छिद्.

SCOT-FREE, *a.* अदण्डितः -ता -तं, अक्षतः -ता -तं, निर्व्रणः -णा -णं.

SCOUNDREL, *s.* धूर्त्तः, दुर्जनः, दुरात्मा *m.* (न्), दुर्वृत्तः, खलः, कृष्णकर्म्मा *m.* (न्), अधमवृत्तिः *m.*, दुष्कृतः, अधन्यवृत्तिः *m.*, कल्लितवृत्तः. *See* RASCAL.

To SCOUR, *v. a.* (Scrub, cleanse by friction) मृज् (c. 1. मार्जति -र्जितुं, c. 2. मार्ष्टि -ष्टुं), सम्मृज्, प्रक्षल् (c. 10. -क्षालयति -यितुं), निर्णिज् (c. 3. -णेनेक्ति -णेक्तुं), धाव् (c. 10. धावयति -यितुं), घर्षणेन शुध् (c. 10. शोधयति -यितुं), निर्घर्षणेन शुध् or परिष्कृ.—(Purge), *see* the word.—(Pass swiftly over) शीघ्रं or सत्वरं तॄ or अतितॄ or अतिक्रम्.—(Run swiftly) शीघ्रं धाव्.

SCOURED, *p. p.* मार्जितः -ता -तं, सम्मार्जितः &c., मृष्टः -ष्टा -ष्टं, सम्मृष्टः &c., प्रक्षालितः -ता -तं, निर्णिक्तः -क्ता -क्तं, घर्षणेन धावितः -ता -तं or धौतः -ता -तं or शोधितः &c., निर्धौतः &c., परिष्कृतः &c.

SCOURER, *s.* वस्त्रनिर्णेजकः, वस्त्रसम्मार्जकः, वस्त्रप्रक्षालकः, वस्त्रधावकः, वस्त्रशोधकः, चैलमार्जकः, चैलधावः -वकः, निर्णेजकः, नेजकः.

SCOURGE, *s.* कशा, कषा, प्रतिष्कशः, प्रतिष्कषः, चलिसङ्गः, चर्म्मदण्डः, रज्जुः *m.f.*, चर्म्मरज्जुः *m.f.*, ताडनी, प्रतोदः.

To SCOURGE, *v. a.* कशया तड् (c. 10. ताडयति -यितुं), रज्जुना or रज्ज्वा or चर्म्मरज्ज्वा तड् or प्रहृ (c. 1. -हरति -हर्त्तुं) or आहन् (c. 2. -हन्ति -न्तुं), कशाघातं कृ, कशाताडनं कृ.

SCOURGED, *p. p.* कशाहतः -ता -तं, कशाताडितः &c. रज्जुताडितः -ता -तं

SCOURGING, *s.* कशाघातः, कशाताडनं, रज्ज्वाघातः, कशाप्रहारः; 'worthy of scourging,' कशार्हः -र्हा -र्हं, कश्यः -श्या -श्यं.

SCOURING, *s.* मार्जनं, सम्मार्जनं, मार्ष्टिः *f.*, परिमार्जनं, प्रक्षालनं, निर्णेकः, निर्णेजनं, धावनं, परिष्कारः, वस्त्रमार्जनं, मलापकर्षणं.

SCOUT, *s.* चारः, चरः, गुप्तचरः, गुप्तदूतः, गूढचारः -री *m.* (न्), गुप्तगतिः *m.*

8 U

गूढदूतः, गूढनिरूपकः, शत्रुचेष्टानिरूपकः, प्रणिधिः *m.* *See* Spy.

To scout, *v. n.* (Act as scout) गूढचारवत् शत्रुचेष्टानिरूपणं कृ.

To scout, *v. a.* गर्ह् (c. 1. गर्हते -र्हितुं), सावज्ञं निराकृ or निरस्.

Scowl, *s.* भ्रूभङ्गः, भ्रूकुटिः *f.*, भ्रूक्षेपः, भ्रूसङ्कोचः, कटाक्षः, अप्रसन्नदृष्टिः *f.*, अप्रसादसूचका कुदृष्टिः *f.*, मुखमालिन्यं.

To scowl, *v. n.* भ्रूभङ्गं कृ, भ्रूकुटिं कृ, कटाक्षेण or भ्रूभङ्गेन दृश् (c. 1. पश्यति, द्रष्टुं), भ्रुवौ संकुच् (c. 1. -कोचति -चितुं), भ्रूसंकोचं कृ.

Scowling, *part.* सभ्रूभङ्गमुखः -खी -खं, मलिनमुखः &c. *See* Frowning.

Scowlingly, *adv.* सभ्रूभङ्गं, सकटाक्षं, भ्रूभङ्गेन, सभ्रूक्षेपं, भ्रूसङ्कोचपूर्व्वं.

Scragginess, *s.* कृशता, परिकृशता, कृशाङ्गता, क्षामता, क्षीणता, कार्श्यं.

Scraggy, scragged, *a.* (Lean) कृशः -शा -शं, परिकृशः &c., कृशाङ्गः -ङ्गी -ङ्गं, क्षामः -मा -मं, शिरालः -ला -लं.—(Rough) रूक्षः -क्षा -क्षं, रूक्षः &c., *see* Rugged.

To scramble, *v. n.* (Climb by seizing with the hands) हस्ताभ्यां धृत्वा or हस्ताभ्याम् अवलम्ब्य आरुह् or अभिरुह्.—(Catch with haste, preventive of another) परनिवारणपूर्व्वं or परनिरसनपूर्व्वं सहसा धृ (c. 1. धरति, धर्त्तुं) or हृ (c. 1. हरति, हर्त्तुं) or झटिति ग्रह् (c. 9. गृह्णाति, ग्रहीतुं).

Scramble, scrambling, *s.* (Seizing with haste, &c.) इष्टद्रव्यग्रहणार्थं परनिवारणपूर्व्वं सहसा हरणं or हरणेच्छा.—(Climbing with the hands) हस्ताभ्याम् अवलम्ब्य आरोहणं.

Scrap, *s.* खण्डः -ण्डकः, लवः, अंशः, भागः, विभागः, शकलः -लं; 'of food,' पिण्डः, पिण्डोलिः *f.*, फेलकः, फेला, लवः. *See* Crum.

Scrap-book, *s.* खण्डकाव्यादिरक्षणपुस्तकं, खण्डकवितादिरक्षणग्रन्थः, खण्डकविताग्रन्थः, श्लोकमुद्रादिरक्षणार्थं पुस्तकं.

To scrape, *v. a.* (Rub the surface with something sharp) लिख् (c. 6. लिखति, लेखितुं), उल्लिख्, विलिख्, प्रलिख्, निर्लिख्, प्रोल्लिख्, तक्ष् (c. 1. तक्षति -क्षितुं), त्वक्ष्, खन् (c. 1. खनति -नितुं), खुर् (c. 6. खुरति, खोरितुं), क्षुर् (c. 6. क्षुरति, क्षोरितुं), उल्लेखनं कृ, तक्षणं कृ.—(Rub with a grating noise) घृष् (c. 1. घर्षति -र्षितुं), घर्षणं कृ, *see To* rub.—(Clean by scraping) घर्षणेन मृज् or प्रक्षल् or निर्णिज्.—(Remove by scraping, scrape off) घर्षणेन अपनी or विनी or मृज् or अपमृज् or अवमृज् or परिमृज् or शुध् in caus., निर्घर्षणं कृ.—(Scrape together) संचि (c. 5. -चिनोति -चेतुं), समाचि, एकीकृ, एकत्र कृ.—(Scrape the feet) पादघर्षणं कृ.

To scrape, *v. n.* (Make a harsh noise) परस्परसंघर्षेण कर्कशशब्दं कृ, परस्परघर्षणं कृ.—(Make an awkward bow) कुप्रणामं कृ.—(Scrape acquaintance) मैत्र्यं कृ, अन्यस्य मैत्र्यम् उपगम्, अन्यस्मिन् प्रीतिं कृ.

Scrape, *s.* (Rubbing) घर्षणं, निर्घर्षणं, तक्षणं, क्षुरणं.—(Bow) कुप्रणामः.—(Difficulty) दुर्गं, दुर्गतिः *f.*, दुर्दशा, दुरवस्था, दुःस्थितिः *f.*, दुःखं, कष्टं, आधिः *m.*

Scraped, *p. p.* उल्लिखितः -ता -तं, प्रोल्लिखितः &c., घर्षितः &c., *see* Rubbed.

Scraper, *s.* (Instrument for scraping) उल्लेखनी -निका, निर्लेखनं -नी, लेखनी, घर्षणी, निर्घर्षणी, निर्घर्षणकः, घर्षणयन्त्रं.—(For the feet) पादोल्लेखनी, पादनिर्लेखनी, पादघर्षणी, पादनिर्घर्षणकः.—(For the tongue) जिह्वोल्लेखनी -निका, जिह्वानिर्लेखनं -नी.—(Kind of shovel) अभ्रिः *f.*, अभ्री, काष्ठकुद्दालः.

Scraping, *s.* (The act) उल्लेखनं, प्रोल्लेखनं, निर्लेखनं, लेखनं, घर्षणं, निर्घर्षणं, खुरणं, क्षुरणं, तक्षणं, खननं; 'the tongue,' जिह्वोल्लेखनं, जिह्वानिर्लेखनं.—(That which is scraped off, scrapings) अवस्करः, अपस्करः, अवकरः, मलं, उच्छिष्टं, कल्कं, विदलं.

To scratch, *v. n.* (Tear or lacerate the skin or surface) त्वचम् उल्लिख् (c. 6. -लिखति -लेखितुं) or प्रोल्लिख् or विलिख् or निर्लिख् or प्रलिख् or लिख्, त्वचं दृ (c. 10. दारयति -यितुं) or विदृ or अवदृ, त्वचं छिद् (c. 7. छिनत्ति, छेत्तुं) or भिद् or निर्भिद्, त्वचं कृत् or निकृत् or क्षुर् (c. 6. क्षुरति, क्षोरितुं) or खुर्, त्वक्छेदं कृ.—(With the nail) नखेन त्वचं दृ or विदृ, नखेन त्वचं लिख् or उल्लिख् or प्रलिख्, नखेन अङ्क् (c. 10. अङ्कयति -यितुं), नखेन त्वक्छेदं कृ or त्वग्भेदं कृ.—(Allay itching by scratching) कण्डू (nom. कण्डूयति -ते), कण्डूयनं कृ, कण्डूयां कृ, कण्डूतिं कृ, नखेन त्वचं घृष् (c. 1. घर्षति -र्षितुं) or विघृष्, त्वग्घर्षणं कृ, त्वग्विघर्षणं कृ, गात्रघर्षणं कृ, गात्रविघर्षणं कृ, 'he scratches his head with his nails,' नखैः or अंगुल्यग्रैर् आत्मनः शिरः or आत्मनः शिरोरुहान् कण्डूयति.—(Scratch the ground, excavate with the claws, as birds, &c.) विष्कॄ (c. 6. -किरते -करितुं -रीतुं), अपस्कृ, भूमिम् आलिख्य विक्षिप्.—(Wound slightly) त्वचं क्षण्, ईषत् क्षण् or परिक्षण्, त्वग्व्रणं कृ, त्वक्क्षतं कृ, ईषद्व्रणं कृ.—(Write roughly), *see To* scrawl.—(Scratch out), *see To* erase.

Scratch, *s.* (Laceration of the skin or surface) त्वक्छेदः, त्वग्भेदः, त्वगुल्लेखनं, त्वग्लेखनं, त्वग्विलेखः, त्वग्दारणं, त्वग्विदारणं, त्वग्विभेदः, त्वक्क्षतं, त्वक्क्षतिः *f.*, त्वक्परिक्षतिः *f.*, परिक्षतिः *f.*—(With the nail) नखलेखा, नखविलेखः, नखछेदः, नखव्रणः -णं, नखक्षतं, नखाङ्कः, नखचिह्नं, नखपदं, नखक्षतिः *f.*, नखपरिक्षतिः *f.*, व्याघ्रनखं -खकं, सुमुखं, शशप्लुतकं.—(With a thorn) कण्टकक्षतं, कण्टकव्रणः.—(Slight wound) त्वग्भेदः, त्वक्क्षतं, त्वग्व्रणः, ईषत्क्षतं, ईषत्त्वग्भेदः, ईषत्त्वक्छेदः.—(Rudely drawn figure), *see* Scrawl.

Scratched, *p. p.* (Lacerated on the surface) लिखितः -ता -तं, उल्लिखितः &c., प्रोल्लिखितः &c., विदारितः &c., दारितः &c., छिन्नत्वक् *m. f. n.* (च्), भिन्नत्वक् *m. f. n.*, क्षतत्वक् *m. f. n.*, परिक्षतत्वक्, क्षतः -ता -तं, परिक्षतः &c.—(With the nail) नखलिखितः -ता -तं, नखोल्लिखितः &c., नखदारितः &c., नखविदारितः &c., नखच्छिन्नः -न्ना -न्नं, नखक्षतः -ता -तं, नखपरिक्षतः &c., नखाङ्कितः &c.—(With a thorn) कण्टकक्षतः -ता -तं, कण्टकच्छिन्नः -न्ना -न्नं.—(Rubbed with the nail) घर्षितः -ता -तं, विघर्षितः &c., नखघर्षितः &c., घृष्टः -ष्टा -ष्टं.

Scratcher, *s.* (One who scratches) त्वग्भेदकः, त्वक्छेदकः, त्वगुल्लेखकः, त्वग्लेखकः त्वग्दारकः, त्वग्विदारकः, उल्लेखकः, कण्डूयनकः, कण्डूतिकारी *m.* (न्), कण्डूयाकृत् *m.*—(Bird that scratches for food) विष्किरः, नखविष्किरः, अपस्करकारी *m.*

Scratching, *s.* (The act of lacerating the surface) उल्लेखनं, प्रोल्लेखनं, विदारणं, त्वगुल्लेखनं, त्वग्लेखनं, त्वग्दारणं, त्वग्विदारणं, त्वक्छेदनं, त्वग्भेदनं, *see* Scratch, *s.*—(Scratching to allay itching) कण्डूयनं, कण्डूया, कण्डूतिः *f.*, कण्डूः *f.*

Scratching, *part.* (Lacerating the surface) लिखन् -खन्ती -खत् (त्), उल्लिखन् &c.—(To allay itching) कण्डूयन् -यन्ती -यत् (त्), कण्डूयमानः -ना -नं.

To scrawl, *v. a.* अस्पष्टं or अस्पष्टाक्षरैः or अस्पष्टक्रमेण लिख् (c. 6. लिखति, लेखितुं) or अङ्क् (c. 10. अङ्कयति -यितुं), अनवधानेन or प्रमादेन लिख्, स्थूलाक्षरैः or कदक्षरैः or अव्यक्ताक्षरैर् लिख्, स्थूलवर्णैः or स्थूलक्रमेण लिख् or आलिख्, अतिशीघ्रं लिख्, अतिक्षिप्रं लिख्.

Scrawl, scrawling, *s.* अस्पष्टलेखः, अस्पष्टलिखनं, स्थूललेखः, स्थूल-

लेख्यं, स्थूलालेख्यं, अस्पष्टाक्षरलिखनं, स्थूलाक्षरलिखनं, कदक्षरलिखनं.

SCRAWLED, *p.p.* अस्पष्टाक्षरैः or स्थूलाक्षरैर् लिखितः -ता -तं or अङ्कितः &c.

To SCREAM, *v. n.* विक्रुश् (c. 1. -क्रोशति -क्रोष्टुं), क्रुश्, रु (c. 2. रौति, रवितुं), विरु, नद् (c. 1. नदति -दितुं), रस् (c. 1. रसति -सितुं), वाश् (c. 1. वाशते -शितुं), उच्चैः or उच्चैःस्वरेण क्रुश्, चीत्कारं कृ, चित्कारं कृ, चीत् शब्दं कृ, चीत्कृ, उच्चनादं कृ, महानादं कृ, उच्चस्वरं कृ, नादं कृ; 'with pain,' आर्त्तनादं कृ, आर्त्तस्वरं कृ.

SCREAM, SCREAMING, *s.* विक्रुष्टं, विक्रोशनं, चीत्कारः, चित्कारः, नादः, उच्चनादः, महानादः, रावः, रुतं, क्रुष्टं, उत्क्रोशः, उत्क्रुष्टं, रासः, स्वरः, उच्चस्वरः, कोलाहलः, चटुः -टु *m. n.*; 'of pain,' आर्त्तनादः, आर्त्तस्वरः, आर्त्तरावः.

To SCREECH, SCREECH, SCREACHING, *see To* SCREAM, SCREAMING.

SCREECH-OWL, *s.* मङ्गलरावी कालपेचकः, कर्कशरावी पेचकभेदः.

SCREEN, *s.* (Partition) व्यवधानं, व्यवधा, तिरस्करिणी, तिरोधानं, अन्तर्धानं, अन्तर्धा, जवनिका, यवनिका, पटः -टं, कटः, प्रतिसीरा, छाया. —(Coarse sieve) स्थूलचालनी.

To SCREEN, *v. a.* (Shelter, protect) छद् (c. 10. छादयति -यितुं), प्रच्छद्, आच्छद्, समाच्छद्, संछद्, गुप् (c. 1. गोपायति, गोप्तुं), अभिगुप्, संगुप्, व्यवधा (c. 3. -दधाति -धातुं), तिरोधा, अन्तर्धा, पिधा, अपिधा, वृ (c. 5. वृणोति -वरितुं -रीतुं, c. 10. वारयति -यितुं), संवृ, आवृ, अपवृ, निवृ, व्यवधानेन रक्ष् or संरक्ष्, गोपनं कृ, संगोपनं कृ, गुप्तिं कृ.—(Sift) शुध्, गालनं कृ, निर्गालनं कृ.

SCREENED, *p. p.* (Protected) छादितः -ता -तं, छन्नः -न्ना -न्नं, प्रच्छादितः &c., आच्छादितः &c., गुप्तः -प्ता -प्तं, गोपितः -ता -तं, संगोपितः &c., गोपायितः &c., व्यवहितः &c., आवृतः &c., संवृतः &c., व्यावृतः &c., अन्तरितः -ता -तं, अन्तर्हितः &c., तिरोहितः &c., व्यवधानरक्षितः &c., व्यवधानगुप्तः -प्ता -प्तं.—(Sifted) शोधितः -ता -तं, निर्गालितः &c.

SCREENING, *part.* व्यवधायकः -का -कं, व्यवधायी -यिनी &c., अन्तर्धायकः &c.

SCREW, *s.* (Spiral bolt or cylinder) आवर्त्तनकीलः -लकः, आवर्त्तनकीलः -लकः, परिवर्त्तनकीलः, सावर्त्तनकीलः, विवर्त्तनकीलः, कीलः -लकः, मलसूत्रं; 'male screw,' नरः; 'female,' नारी.—(Stingy person) कृपणः, दृढमुष्टिः *m.*, गाढमुष्टिः *m.*

To SCREW, *v. a.* (Fasten with screws) आवर्त्तनकीलकैः or आवर्त्तनकीलकैर् बन्ध् (c. 9. बध्नाति, बन्द्धुं), कीलकैर् बन्ध्, मलसूत्रेण बन्ध्. —(Twist) आवृत् (c. 10. -वर्त्तयति -यितुं), आवृत्, परिवृत्.—(Press), *see* the word.—(Oppress) पीड्, बाध्, *see* OPPRESS.—(Drive a screw) कीलं आवर्त्य प्रविश् in caus., कीलं परिवर्त्य प्रविश्.

SCREWED, *p. p.* सावर्त्तनकीलबद्धः -द्धा -द्धं, परिवर्त्तनकीलबद्धः &c., बाधितः &c.

To SCRIBBLE, SCRIBBLED, SCRIBBLING, *see To* SCRAWL, SCRAWLED, &c.

SCRIBBLER, *s.* कुलेखकः, कदक्षरलेखकः, कुग्रन्थकारः, अस्पष्टलेखकः.

SCRIBE, *s.* लेखकः, लिपिकरः, लिपिकारः, लिपिजीवी *m.* (न्), कायस्थः, अक्षरजीवकः, अक्षरजीवी *m.* (न्), अक्षरचनः, अक्षरचणः, अक्षरचञ्चुः, अक्षरचुञ्चुः *m.*, मसिपण्यः, मसिजीवी *m.*, वर्णिकः, वार्णिकः, वर्णी *m.* (न्), लिपिकः, लिपिकरः, लिपिक्षुरः, करणः.

SCRIP, *s.* (Small bag) क्षुद्रकोषः, वस्त्रसम्पुटकः.—(Writing, certificate) लेखः, लेख्यं, पत्रिका, पत्रं, प्रमाणपत्रं.

SCRIPTURAL, *a.* शास्त्रीयः -या -यं, शास्त्रानुसारी -रिणी -रि (न्), यथाशास्त्रः -स्त्रा -स्त्रं, शास्त्रसिद्धः -द्धा -द्धं, श्रुतिसिद्धः &c., शास्त्रोक्तः -क्ता -क्तं, शास्त्रप्रोक्तः &c., वेदोक्तः &c., वेदोदितः -ता -तं, वैदिकः -की -कं, श्रुत्युक्तः &c., श्रुतिविहितः -ता -तं, श्रुतिकथितः &c., श्रुत्युदितः &c.,

यथाश्रुतिः -तिः -ति, औपनिषदः -दी -दं, शास्त्रानुयायी &c., धर्म्मग्रन्थानुसारी &c., धर्म्मग्रन्थप्रोक्तः &c.

SCRIPTURALLY, *adv.* शास्त्रतस्, यथाशास्त्रं, शास्त्रानुसारेण, शास्त्रवत्.

SCRIPTURE, *s.* (Writing) लेखः -खनं, लिपिः *f.*, लिखनं, लेखनं, लिखितं, अक्षरविन्यासः, अक्षरसंस्थानं.—(Sacred writing) श्रुतिः *f.*, श्रुतं, शास्त्रं, ब्रह्म *n.* (न्), कल्पः, आगमः, आम्नायः, प्रमाणं.—(The Bible) धर्म्मग्रन्थः, धर्म्मपुस्तकं. The sacred writings of the Hindús may be arranged under seven heads, viz. 1. Vedas, 2. Upanishads, 3. Vedángas, 4. Upavedas, 5. Shástras, 6. Puránas and 7. Upapuránas. The Student is referred to each separate head for a fuller explanation than is here given of the subdivisions comprised under the several titles. 1. The Vedas are four in number, viz. ऋग्वेदः, यजुर्वेदः, सामवेदः, अथर्ववेदः. 2. The Upanishads, are the theological and philosophical chapters of the Vedas, either detached from, or comprehended in, the principal work, and collectively called वेदान्तः. 3. The Vedángas are six sacred sciences subordinate to the Vedas, viz. Pronunciation, शिक्षा, Description of religious ceremonies, कल्पः, Grammar, व्याकरणं, Prosody, छन्दस्, Astromony, ज्योतिषं, Explanation of difficult and obscure phrases, निरुक्तं -क्तिः. 4. The Upavedas, or Minor vedas, are four, viz. Medicine, आयुर्वेदः, Archery and military art, धनुर्वेदः, Music, गान्धर्ववेदः or गन्धर्ववेदः, Mechanics and the use of tools, &c., शिल्पिशास्त्रं or शस्त्रशास्त्रं. 5. Shástra is a title of very general application, but it is properly restricted to six sacred and philosophical treatises, viz. मीमांसाशास्त्रं, सांख्यशास्त्रं, वेदान्तशास्त्रं, न्यायशास्त्रं containing the branch called वैशेषिकं, योगशास्त्रं and धर्म्मशास्त्रं. The last contains the body of Hindú law; the others are the textbooks of the six Hindú schools of philosophy, *see* SCHOOL. 6. The Puránas are eighteen mythological poems, *see* PURÁNA. 7. The Upapuránas, or inferior Puránas, are also eighteen, *see* under PURÁNA.—(One who is conversant with scripture) वेदविद्, वेदज्ञः, शास्त्रविद्, शास्त्रज्ञः, शास्त्रदर्शी *m.* (न्), बहुवेदार्थदर्शी *m.*, शास्त्राभिज्ञः, शास्त्री *m.*, शास्त्राचरणः, शास्त्रसम्पन्नः, ब्रह्मज्ञः, ब्रह्मविद्, ब्रह्मवेदी *m.*, ब्रह्मवेत्ता *m.* (तृ), वैदिकः, श्रुतिधरः, श्रुतिज्ञः, श्रोत्रियः, छान्दसः, स्थूललक्षः; 'conversancy with it,' ब्रह्मज्ञानं, वेदव्युत्पत्तिः *f.*, शास्त्रव्युत्पत्तिः *f.*, शास्त्रज्ञानं, ब्रह्मवेदः, ब्रह्मविद्या; 'study of scripture,' ब्रह्माभ्यासः, ब्रह्माधिगमः -मनं, वेदाधिगमः -मनं, ब्रह्मसत्रं, वेदाध्ययनं, शास्त्राध्ययनं; 'relating to the study of it,' ब्रह्माधिगामिकः -की -कं; 'teaching it,' वेदाध्यापनं, ब्रह्मोपदेशः; 'teacher of it,' आचार्य्यः, उपाध्यायः, वेदाध्यापकः, ब्रह्मोपदेशकः; 'reading it aloud,' ब्रह्मघोषः; 'holiness derived from reading it,' ब्रह्मवर्चसं; 'savour or excellency of it,' ब्रह्मरसः; 'relating to scripture,' श्रौतः -ती -तं, वैदिकः -की -कं, शास्त्रीयः -या -यं; 'authority of it,' श्रुतिप्रामाण्यं, आगमप्रामाण्यं.

SCRIVENER, *s.* नियमपत्रलेखकः, पत्रलेखकः, लेखकः, लिपिकरः.

SCROFULA, *s.* गण्डमाला, कण्ठमाला, अपची, कण्ठगण्डः, गलगण्डः.

SCROFULOUS, *a.* गण्डमाली -लिनी -लि (न्), कण्ठमाली &c., गण्डमालारोगी &c.

SCROLL, *s.* लेख्यपत्रं -त्रकं, दीर्घपत्रं -त्रकं, पटः, दीर्घपटः, पट्टः, धर्म्मपुस्तकं.

SCROTUM, *s.* अण्डकोशः, अण्डकोषः, मुष्कः, मुष्ककोषः, फलकोशः, फलकोषकः, वृषणः, वृषणकोषः, कोषः -षकः, कोशः, सीमा *m.* (न्), सीमा, अण्डं -ण्डकः, तीक्ष्णं -क्ष्णकः; 'enlargement of it,' कोषवृद्धिः *f.*, वृद्धिः *f.*; 'septum of it,' महावीर्ज्यं, विटपः.

To SCRUB, *v. a.* अतिशयेन or अत्यन्तं मृज् (c. 1. मार्जति -र्जितुं, c. 2. मार्ष्टि -ष्टुं), अतिघर्षणेन मृज्, बलवत् or बलेन मृज्, अतिमार्जनं कृ, अत्यन्तं प्रक्षल् (c. 10. -क्षालयति -यितुं) or निर्णिज् (c. 3. -र्णेनेक्ति -र्णेक्तुं) or धाव् or घृष्. *See To* RUB.

SCRUB, *s.* हीनवृत्तिः *m.*, अधमवृत्तिः *m.*, जघन्यवृत्तिः *m.*, नीचकर्म्मकारी *m.* (न्), नीचकर्म्मा *m.* (न्), कुत्सितकर्म्मा *m.*, अपकर्म्मकृत्, अधमकर्म्मा *m.*, पामरः, व्रातीनः.

SCRUBBED, *p. p.* अतिघर्षणपूर्व्वं or अतिघर्षणेन मार्जितः -ता -तं or निर्णिक्तः -क्ता -क्तं, अतिनिर्णिक्तः &c., सुनिर्णिक्तः &c., सुप्रक्षालितः &c., सुमृष्टः &c., सुघर्षितः &c.

SCRUBBY, *a.* क्षुद्रः -द्रा -द्रं, नीचः -चा -चं, तुच्छः -च्छा -च्छं. *See* MEAN.

SCRUPLE, *s.* (Hesitation) शङ्का, आशङ्का, विकल्पः, संशयः. *See* DOUBT.

To SCRUPLE, *v. n.* शङ्क् (c. 1. शङ्कते -ङ्कितुं), आशङ्क्, अभिशङ्क्, विशङ्क्, विकॢप् (c. 1. -कल्पते -ल्पितुं, c. 10. -कल्पयति -यितुं), त्रस् (c. 4. त्रस्यति -सितुं), विलम्ब्. *See To* HESITATE.

SCRUPULOUS, *a.* (Hesitating) शङ्की -ङ्किनी -ङ्कि (न्), आशङ्की &c., शङ्कान्वितः -ता -तं, आशङ्कान्वितः &c., सशङ्कः -ङ्का -ङ्कं, संशयी &c., सन्देही &c., शङ्काशीलः -ला -लं, आशङ्काशीलः &c.—(Exact, nice, precise) सूक्ष्मः -क्ष्मा -क्ष्मं, अतिसूक्ष्मः &c., सूक्ष्मदृष्टिः -ष्टिः -ष्टि, सूक्ष्मदर्शी -र्शिनी &c., सूक्ष्माचारी &c., अतिसूक्ष्माचारी &c., अत्याचारः -री -रं, अत्याचारी &c.

SCRUPULOUSNESS, *s.* शङ्काशीलता, सशङ्कता, सूक्ष्मता, अतिसूक्ष्मता, सूक्ष्मदृष्टिः *f.*

SCRUTINEER, *s.* सूक्ष्मपरीक्षकः, सूक्ष्मनिरूपकः, निरूपकः. *See* SCRUTINIZER.

To SCRUTINIZE, *v. a.* सूक्ष्मं or अतिसूक्ष्मं निरूप् (c. 10. -रूपयति -यितुं) or परीक्ष् (c. 1. -ईक्षते -क्षितुं) or निरीक्ष् or दृश् (c. 1. पश्यति, द्रष्टुं) or अनुसन्धा (c. 3. -दधाति -धातुं) or ज्ञा in des. (जिज्ञासते -सितुं) or अनुयुज् (c. 7. -युनक्ति -युंक्ते -योक्तुं) or मार्ग् (c. 10. मार्गयति -यितुं), परिमार्ग्.

SCRUTINIZED, *p. p.* अतिसूक्ष्मं निरूपितः -ता -तं or परीक्षितः &c. or निरीक्षितः &c.

SCRUTINIZER, *s.* सूक्ष्मनिरूपकः, सूक्ष्मपरीक्षकः, सूक्ष्मदर्शी *m.* (न्), सूक्ष्मानुसन्धायी *m.*, सूक्ष्मानुसन्धानी *m.*, सूक्ष्मजिज्ञासाकृत् *m.*, निरूपकः, परीक्षकः &c.

SCRUTINY, *s.* सूक्ष्मपरीक्षा, सूक्ष्मनिरूपणं, सूक्ष्मानुसन्धानं, सूक्ष्मदर्शनं, सूक्ष्मनिरीक्षा -क्षणं, सूक्ष्मजिज्ञासा, परीक्षा -क्षणं, निरूपणं, अनुसन्धानं, निरीक्षणं, संवीक्षणं, जिज्ञासा, अनुयोगः.

To SCUD, *v. n.* अतिवेगेन गम् (c. 1. गच्छति, गन्तुं) or चल् (c. 1. चलति -लितुं), सहसा चल्; 'before the wind or a tempest,' अतिवेगेन अनुवातं चल्, वात्यावेगेन अतिशीघ्रं चल् or वह् in pass. (उह्यते), अतिवेगेन वात्याप्रेरितः -ता -तं भू.

SCUD, *s.* वातप्रेरितशीकरः, वातप्रेरितमेघः, वातप्रेरितकुज्झटिका.

SCUFFLE, *s.* विप्लवः, तुमुलं, बाहूबाहवि युद्धं, बाहूबाहवि कलहः, हस्ताहस्ति युद्धं, नियुद्धं, सङ्कुलयुद्धं, रणसङ्कुलं, शरीरसम्बन्धः.

To SCUFFLE, *v. n.* बाहूबाहवि युध् (c. 4. युध्यते, योद्धुं) or नियुद्धं कृ.

To SCULK, *v. n.* निभृते स्था (c. 1. तिष्ठति, स्थातुं) or वृत् (c. 1. वर्त्तते -र्त्तितुं), निभृतस्थाने or गूढस्थाने वृत्, गुप्तः -प्ता -प्तं भू or वृत्, अन्तरितः -ता -तं भू, गुप् in pass. (गुप्यते); 'to skulk off,' अपसृप् (c. 1. -सर्पति -सप्तुं), पलाय् (c. 1. पलायते -यितुं, rt. इ), विपलाय्.

SCULKER, *s.* निभृतवर्त्ती *m.* (न्), निभृतस्थायी *m.* (न्), गुप्तवर्त्ती *m.*

SCULKING, *s.* निभृतवर्त्तनं, निभृतस्थाने or गूढस्थाने वर्त्तनं, अपसर्पणं.

SCULL, *s.* (Bone that surrounds the brain) कपालः -लं, कर्परः, शिरोस्थि *n.*, मस्तकः -कं, शीर्षकं, करोटः -टिः -टी *f.*, मुण्डः -ण्डं, भगालः; 'a chaplet or necklace of sculls,' कपालस्रक् *f.* (ज्), कापाली स्रक्, कपालमाला, कापाली माला; 'pertaining to the scull,' कापालः -ली -लं, कापालिकः -की -कं.—(Short oar) क्षुद्रक्षेपणिः, क्षुद्रदण्डः, ह्रस्वदण्डः.

To SCULL, *v. a.* क्षुद्रदण्डेन नौकां चल् (c. 10. चालयति -यितुं).

SCULL-CAP, *s.* शिरोवेष्टः -ष्टनं, शिरस्कं, शिरोवस्त्रं, मस्तकावरणं -णी.

SCULLER, *s.* क्षुद्रदण्डेन नौकाचालकः, क्षुद्रक्षेपणिचालकः. *See* ROWER.

SCULLERY, *s.* पिठरागारं -रः, भाण्डागारं -रः, पात्रागारं, स्थाल्यागारं, कटाहागारं, कुण्डागारं, पिठरं.

SCULLION, *s.* पिठरादिप्रक्षालकः -का, भाण्डादिमार्जकः -का, कटाहादिशोधकः -का, कुण्डकटाहादिपरिष्कारकः -का.

SCULPTOR, *s.* तक्षकः, तष्टा *m.* (ष्टृ), तक्षा *m.* (न्), त्वष्टा *m.*, मूर्त्तिकारः -रकः, प्रतिमाकारः -रकः, मूर्त्तितक्षकः, प्रतिमातक्षकः, उपमाता *m.* (तृ), उपमाकारः.

SCULPTURE, *s.* तक्षणं, तक्षणकर्म्म *n.* (न्), त्वक्षणं, मूर्त्तितक्षणं, प्रतिमातक्षणं, मूर्त्तिकरणं, प्रतिमाकरणं, उपमाकरणं, उपमातक्षणं.

To SCULPTURE, *v. a.* तक्ष् (c. 1. तक्षति -क्षितुं, c. 5. तक्ष्णोति), त्वक्ष् (c. 1. त्वक्षति -क्षितुं), प्रतिमातक्षणं कृ, मूर्त्तितक्षणं कृ, प्रतिमां कृ, मूर्त्तिं कृ.

SCULPTURED, *p. p.* तष्टः -ष्टा -ष्टं, तक्षितः -ता -तं, त्वष्टः -ष्टा -ष्टं.

SCUM, *s.* (Impure matter or froth which rises to the surface of liquors) मण्डः -ण्डं, मूर्द्धरसः, रसाग्रं, फेनः, पराङ्गः, कारुजः, उत्पीडः, उत्तररसः, उपरिस्थरसः; 'of boiled rice,' निस्रावः, विस्रावः, मासरः, आचामः.—(Refuse, dirt) मलं, अवस्करः, अपस्करः, उच्छिष्टं, अवशिष्टं, कल्कं, उत्तर्षः, जुष्टं, असारद्रव्यं.

To SCUM, *v. a.* मण्डम् अपहृ (c. 1. -हरति -हर्त्तुं) or अपनी, निर्मण्डीकृ.

SCURF, *s.* त्वक्स्नेहः, चर्म्मस्नेहः, शिरश्चर्म्मणि पिण्डितस्नेहः, मस्तकत्वक्स्नेहः, शिरोमज्जा, मस्तकमज्जा, मज्जा, शिरोमलं, चर्म्ममलं.

SCURFY, *a.* त्वक्स्नेहवान् -वती -वत् (त्), चर्म्ममलवान् &c., मलावृतः -ता -तं.

SCURRILITY, *s.* मौखर्य्यं, मुखरत्वं, दुर्मुखता, वाग्दुष्टता, वाक्पारुष्यं, पारुष्यं, परुषवचनं, परुषोक्तिः *f.*, दुर्वचनं, दुरुक्तिः *f.*, दुरुक्तं, दुर्भाषणं, अपभाषणं, दुर्वचस् *n.*, खलोक्तिः *f.*, परोद्वेजकभाषणं, अपशब्दः, न्यक्कं.

SCURRILOUS, *a.* (Using abusive language) मुखरः -रा -रं, दुर्मुखः -खी -खं, वाग्दुष्टः -ष्टा -ष्टं, परुषवाक् *m. f. n.* (च्) परुषोक्तिकः -का -कं, परुषभाषी -षिणी -षि (न्), कटुभाषी &c., मुखशफः -फा -फं, मुखशीलः -ला -लं, अबद्धमुखः &c., परोद्वेगकरभाषी &c., क्षेपकः -का -कं.—(Containing low abuse) परुषः -षा -षं, परुषोक्तिमयः -यी -यं, दुरुक्तः -क्ता -क्तं, दुर्वाच्यः -च्या -च्यं.

SCURVILY, *adv.* कुत्सितं, सकार्पण्यं, तुच्छप्रकारेण, अविनयेन, परुषं.

SCURVINESS, *s.* कुत्सितत्वं, तुच्छता, कार्पण्यं, पामरता, जघन्यता, खलता.

SCURVY, *s.* (The disease) शीतादः, नाविकरक्तपित्तः -त्तं.

SCURVY, *a.* कुत्सितः -ता -तं, तुच्छः -च्छा -च्छं, पामरः -रा -रं, *see* MEAN.

SCUTCHEON, *s.* कुलचिह्नपत्रं, कुलमर्य्यादालक्षणपत्रं, कुलीनलक्षणपत्रं.

SCUTTLE, *s.* (Broad basket) विशालपेटकः, पृथुकरण्डः.—(Hole in the side of a ship) नौपार्श्वच्छिद्रं.

To SCUTTLE, *v. a.* नौकापार्श्वे or नौकातले छिद्राणि कृ, नौपार्श्वं सच्छिद्रं कृ.

To SCUTTLE, *v. n.* (Run off affectedly) वैलक्ष्येण अपधाव्.

SCYTHE, *s.* सङ्कोकः, लवित्रं, लवाग्रकं, शस्यछेदनी, शस्यकर्त्तनी.

SEA, *s.* समुद्रः, अर्णवः, सागरः, जलधिः *m.*, उदधिः *m.*, अब्धिः *m.*, जलनिधिः *m.*, महोदधिः *m.*, वारिधिः *m.*, वारिनिधिः, मीनालयः, *see* OCEAN; 'a rough sea,' क्षुब्धार्णवः, क्षुब्धसमुद्रः, वानं; 'a sea of trouble,' दुःखसागरः; 'ablution or bathing in the sea,' समुद्रस्नानं; 'the seven seas,' सप्तसमुद्राः *m. pl.*, *see* under OCEAN.

SEA-BATHING, *s.* समुद्रस्नानं, समुद्रजलस्नानं.

SEA-BEAT, *a.* तरङ्गाहतः -ता -तं, कल्लोलाहतः &c., उत्तरङ्गः -ङ्गा -ङ्गं.

SEA-COAST, *s.* समुद्रतटं, समुद्रतीरं, जलधितीरं, अब्धितीरं, अब्धितटं.

SEA-FARING, *a.* समुद्रयायी -यिनी -यि (न्), समुद्रगामी &c., समुद्रगः -गा -गं, समुद्रमार्गेण or समुद्रपथेन गमनागमनकारी &c., नौकाजीवी &c., सांयात्रिकः -की -कं.

SEA-FIGHT, *s.* समुद्रयुद्धं, अब्धियुद्धं, नौकायुद्धं, नौयुद्धं.

SEA-GIRT, SEA-ENCIRCLED, *a.* समुद्रमेखलः -ला -लं, अर्णवमेखलः &c., अब्धिमेखलः &c., समुद्ररसनः -ना -नं, जलधिरसनः &c., समुद्रवेष्टितः -ता -तं, समुद्रवलयाङ्कितः &c., समुद्रान्तः -न्ता -न्तं, सागरान्तः &c.

SEA-GREEN, *a.* समुद्रवर्णः -र्णा -र्णं, अब्धिवर्णः &c., श्यामहरित् *m. f. n.*

SEA-GULL, *s.* समुद्रकुक्कुटः -टी, समुद्रचरटः, जलकुक्कुटः -टी, विष्किका, गङ्गाचिल्ली, देवट्टी, समुद्रप्लवः.

SEA-MAN, *s.* समुद्रयायी *m.* (न्), समुद्रगः, नाविकः. *See* SAILOR.

SEAMANSHIP, *s.* नाविकविद्या, नौचालनविद्या, नौकानयनविद्या.

SEA-PORT, *s.* नौकाश्रयः, नौकाश्रयः, समुद्रतीरस्थनगरी.

SEA-SALT, *s.* समुद्रलवणं, सामुद्रं, अक्षीवं, अक्षिवं, वसिरं, वशिरं.

SEA-SHORE, *s.* समुद्रतीरं, समुद्रतटं, समुद्रवेला, वेला, समुद्रान्तः -न्तं, सिन्धुतटं, जलधिरोधस् *n.*, वेलामूलं; 'on the sea-shore,' वेलायां, समुद्रतीरे.

SEA-SICK, *a.* समुद्रामयग्रस्तः -स्ता -स्तं, समुद्ररोगपीडितः -ता -तं.

SEA-SICKNESS, *s.* समुद्रामयः, समुद्ररोगः, ऊर्म्मिप्रलोठनजा वमनेच्छा.

SEA-SIDE, *s.* समुद्रतीरं, समुद्रवेला, समुद्रसमीपभूमिः *f.*

SEA-WATER, *s.* समुद्रजलं, समुद्राम्बु *n.*, सागराम्बु *n.*, समुद्रवारि *n.*, समुद्रोदकं.

SEA-WEED, *s.* समुद्रशाकः, समुद्रतृणं, समुद्ररोही शाकविशेषः.

SEA-WORTHY, *a.* समुद्रगमनयोग्यः -ग्या -ग्यं, समुद्रयानयोग्यः &c., समुद्रतरणयोग्यः &c.

SEAL, *s.* (Stamp) मुद्रा.—(Signet) मुद्रा, प्रत्ययकारिणी, दीनारः.—(Finger-ring seal) अङ्गुलिमुद्रा.—(Seal or tie with a seal for fastening a letter) तालिकः.—(Impression of a seal) मुद्रा.—(Sea-calf) समुद्रवत्सः, मकरः.

To SEAL, *v. a.* मुद्र् (nom. मुद्रयति -यितुं), मुद्रीकृ, समुद्रीकृ, मुद्रितं -तां कृ.—(Mark with a seal) मुद्राङ्कितं -तां कृ, मुद्राचिह्नितं -तां कृ, मुद्रया अङ्क् (c. 10. अङ्कयति -यितुं) or चिह्न् (c. 10. चिह्नयति -यितुं), मुद्रालाञ्छितं -तां कृ.—(Fasten with a seal) मुद्रया बन्ध् (c. 9. बध्नाति, बन्द्धुं).

SEALED, *p.p.* मुद्रितः -ता -तं, मुद्रीकृतः &c., समुद्रः -द्रा -द्रं, समुद्रीकृतः &c.—(Marked with a seal) मुद्राङ्कितः -ता -तं, मुद्राचिह्नितः &c., मुद्रालाञ्छितः &c., अङ्कितः &c., चिह्नितः &c.—(Fastened with a seal) मुद्राबद्धः -द्धा -द्धं, तालिकबद्धः &c.; 'sealed papers,' मुद्रिका.

SEALING, *s.* मुद्रीकरणं, समुद्रीकरणं, मुद्राङ्कनं, मुद्राबन्धनं, अङ्कनं.

SEALING-WAX, *s.* लाक्षा, अलक्तः, अलक्तकं, लक्तकं, राक्षा.

SEAM, *s.* (Suture, joining) सन्धिः *m.*, सीवनं, सेवनी.—(Formed by sewing) सूचिसेवनं, सीवनं.—(Of planks) फलकसन्धिः *m.*, काष्ठसन्धिः *m.*—(Cicatrix) शुष्कव्रणः, रूढव्रणं.

SEAMLESS, *a.* सन्धिहीनः -ना -नं, सन्धिरहितः -ता -तं, निःसन्धिः -न्धिः -न्धि.

SEAMSTRESS, *s.* सूचिका, सूचिकर्म्मोपजीविनी, सूचीशिल्पोपजीविनी.

To SEAR, *v. a.* वहिर्भागं दह् (c. 1. दहति, दग्धुं, c. 10. दाहयति -यितुं), वहिर्मांसं दह्, दाहेन or दहनेन वहिर्भागं दृढीकृ or घनीकृ or कठिनीकृ or शुष्कीकृ.

SEAR, *a.* शुष्कः -ष्का -ष्कं, शीर्णः -र्णा -र्णं, विशीर्णः &c., म्लानः -ना -नं.

To SEARCH, *v. a.* अन्विष् (c. 4. -इष्यति, c. 6. -इच्छति -एषितुं -एष्टुं), अन्वेष् (c. 1. -एषते -षितुं), निरूप् (c. 10. -रूपयति -यितुं), अनुसन्धा (c. 3. -दधाति -धातुं), परीक्ष् (c. 1. -ईक्षते -क्षितुं), अवेक्ष्, निरीक्ष्, संवीक्ष्, मार्ग् (c. 1. मार्गति, c. 10. मार्गयति -यितुं), मृग् (c. 10. मृगयते -ति -यितुं), विचि (c. 5. -चिनोति -चेतुं), ज्ञा in des. (जिज्ञासते -सितुं), चर्च् (c. 1. चर्चति -र्चितुं).

SEARCH, SEARCHING, *s.* अन्वेषणं -णा, पर्य्येषणं -णा, अनुसन्धानं, जिज्ञासा, अन्विष्टिः *f.*, परीष्टिः *f.*, निरूपणं, परीक्षा -क्षणं, संवीक्षणं, निरीक्षा -क्षणं, समीक्षणं, अनुसरणं, मार्गः -र्गणं, शोधनं, अनुयोगः, विचयः, चर्चा, उद्देशः, तर्कः; 'for wealth,' अर्थान्वेषणं, अर्थेहा.

SEARCHED, *p.p.* अन्विष्टः -ष्टा -ष्टं, अन्वेषितः -ता -तं, निरूपितः -ता -तं.

SEARCHER, *s.* अन्वेष्टा *m.* (ष्टृ), अन्वेषी *m.* (न्), अन्वेषकः, निरूपकः, निरूपयिता *m.* (तृ), परीक्षकः, निरीक्षकः, अनुसन्धाता, अनुसन्धायी *m.*, जिज्ञासाकृत्; 'of the heart,' अन्तर्यामी *m.*

SEARED, *p.p.* तप्तलोहदग्धः -ग्धा -ग्धं, दाहेन कठिनीकृतः -ता -तं.

SEASON, *s.* (Fit time or opportunity) अवसरः, अवकाशः, कालः, समयः, प्रस्तावः, प्रसङ्गः, कालयोगः, कालसन्धिः *m.*, सन्धिः *m.*, सुयोगः; 'season for action,' कार्य्यकालः, कार्य्यावसरः, कार्य्यसमयः; 'season for ablution,' स्नानावसरः; 'wrong season,' अकालः, अनवसरः; 'out of season,' अकालेन, अनवसरेण; 'born out of season,' अकालजः -जा -जं.—(Any time) कालः, समयः, वेला, *see* TIME.—(Auspicious moment) मुहूर्त्तः -र्त्तं, लग्नः -ग्नं, शुभलग्नः -ग्नं, शुभमुहूर्त्तः -र्त्तं.—(One of the divisions of the year) ऋतुः *m.*, कालः, समयः; 'revolution of the seasons,' ऋतुपर्य्यायः, *see* REVOLUTION; 'the interval or junction between two seasons,' ऋतुसन्धिः *m.*; 'the seasons collectively,' ऋतुगणः, ऋतुवर्गः; 'the six seasons,' षडृतवः *m. pl.* The year is divided into six seasons, according to the Hindús, viz. 1. Spring, वसन्तः, वसन्तसमयः, comprising, according to the reckoning which refers to the Northern parts of India, the two months of चैत्रः and वैशाखः, *i. e.* from the middle of March to the middle of May, *see* SPRING. 2. The hot season or Summer, ग्रीष्मः, ग्रीष्मकालः, निदाघकालः, comprising the two months of ज्येष्ठः and आषाढः, *i.e.* from the middle of May to the middle of July, *see* SUMMER. 3. The rainy season, the rains, वर्षाः *m. pl.*, वर्षाकालः, वृष्टिकालः, comprising the two months श्रावणः and भाद्रः, *i. e.* from the middle of July to the middle of September, *see* under RAIN, RAINY. 4. The autumnal season, शरद्, शरत्कालः, शरदृतुः *m.*, comprising the two months आश्विनः and कार्त्तिकः, *i. e.* from the middle of September to the middle of November, *see* AUTUMN. 5. The cold season, हेमन्तः, comprising the two months मार्गशीर्षः and पौषः, *i. e.* from the middle of November to the middle of January. 6. The dewy season or season of hoar frost, शिशिरः, शिशिरकालः, comprising the two months माघः and फाल्गुनः, *i. e.* from the middle of January to the middle of March. According to more modern authorities the season of Spring begins with the month Phálguna, or the middle of February. This reckoning will place each of the succeeding seasons a month earlier. Sometimes the word आगमः is used in composition for 'the coming on of a season,' or for the season itself, as 'the rainy season,' वर्षागमः, मेघागमः; 'the hot season,' ग्रीष्मागमः, उष्मागमः.

To SEASON, *v. a.* (Render palatable by the mixture of seasoning) वास् (c. 10. वासयति -यितुं), व्यञ्जनादिना संस्कृ or उपस्कृ, व्यञ्जनादि प्रक्षिप्य सुरसीकृ or रुचिरं -रां कृ or स्वादूकृ.—(Mature, prepare) पच्, पक्वं -क्वां कृ, पक्वीकृ, पक्वतां or परिपाकं कृ or गम्, सिद्धं -द्धां कृ, सिद्धीकृ, उपयुक्तं -क्तां कृ, योग्यं -ग्यां कृ; 'to season the body to heat,' शरीरं घर्म्मसहनयोग्यं कृ.

To SEASON, *v. n.* (Become mature) पक्वः -क्वा -क्वं भू, परिपक्वः -क्वा -क्वं भू, योग्यः -ग्या -ग्यं भू, उपयुक्तः -क्ता -क्तं भू. *See To* MATURE, *v. n.*

SEASONABLE, *a.* (Opportune) समयोपयुक्तः -क्ता -क्तं, प्रसङ्गोपयुक्तः &c., कालोपयुक्तः &c., समयोचितः -ता -तं, कालोचितः &c., कालिकः -की -कं, कालीनः -ना -नं, सामयिकः -की -कं, युक्तकालिकः -की -कं, उपयुक्तकालिकः &c., उचितकालिकः &c., कालानुरूपः -पा -पं, समयानुरूपः &c., प्रसङ्गानुरूपः &c., कालानुसारी -रिणी -रि (न्), समयानुसारी &c., कालानुकूलः -ला -लं, समयानुकूलः &c., कालप्राप्तः -प्ता -प्तं, समयप्राप्तः &c., अवसरप्राप्तः &c., प्रसङ्गप्राप्तः &c., प्राप्तकालः -ला -लं, प्राप्तसमयः -या -यं, प्राप्तावसरः -रा -रं, प्राप्तप्रसङ्गः -ङ्गा -ङ्गं, प्रास्ताविकः -की -कं, प्रस्तावसदृशः -शी -शं, कालसदृशः &c., प्रसङ्गसदृशः &c., प्रासङ्गिकः -की -कं, काल्यः -ल्या -ल्यं, काकतालीयः -या -यं.—(Done in season) कालकृतः -ता -तं, समयकृतः &c.; 'seasonable exertion,' कालकृतोद्योगः.—(Produced in season) कालजः -जा -जं, कालोत्पादितः -ता -तं, कालोत्पन्नः -न्ना -न्नं, कालोद्भवः -वा -वं, कालजातः -ता -तं, आर्त्तवः -वी -वं, ऋतुजः -जा -जं, ऋतुजातः -ता -तं, ऋतूद्भवः -वा -वं, ऋतवीयः -या -यं, ऋतव्यः -व्या -व्यं.

SEASONABLENESS, *s.* कालोपयुक्तता, समयोपयुक्तता, कालयोग्यता, प्रसङ्गयोग्यता, कालौचित्यं, समयौचित्यं, प्रसङ्गौचित्यं, कालोचितत्वं, कालानुकूल्यं, कालानुरूप्यं, कालानुरूपता, समयानुरूप्यं, कालसादृश्यं,. प्रस्तावसादृश्यं, प्रसङ्गसादृश्यं, कालप्राप्तता, समयप्राप्तता, कालिकता -त्वं, कालजता, कालोत्पन्नता, सामयिकत्वं.

SEASONABLY, *adv.* काले, कालतस्, यथाकालं, समये, समयतस्, यथासमयं, समया, कालानुसारेण, समयानुसारेण, उपयुक्तकाले, उपयुक्तसमये, कालोपयुक्तं, यथावसरं, यथावकाशं, यथाप्रसङ्गं, कालानुरूपेण, प्रस्तावानुरूपेण, प्रस्तावसदृशं, स्थाने, योगतस्, वेलायां.

SEASONED, *p. p.* or *a.* (Mixed with seasoning, &c.) वासितः -ता -तं, प्रपस्तः -स्ता -स्तं, सुसंस्कृतः -ता -तं, व्यञ्जनयुक्तः -क्ता -क्तं, व्यञ्जनादिसंस्कृतः &c., सव्यञ्जनः -ना -नं.—(Matured) पक्वः -क्वा -क्वं, सिद्धः -द्धा -द्धं.

SEASONING, *s.* (That which is added to give a relish) व्यञ्जनं, उपस्करः, उपकरणं, तेमनं, प्रहितं, निष्ठानं, सन्धितं, वेसवारः, वेशवारः, वेषवारः, सूदः, मिष्टान्नं, मोदकं, अग्निवर्धनः -नं; 'acid seasoning,' चुक्रः -क्रं, वृक्षाम्लं, तिन्तिडीकं.—(Act of maturing) पचनं, पाकः, पक्वीकरणं, उपयुक्तकरणं.

SEAT, *s.* (That on which one sits, chair, &c.) आसनं, पीठः -ठं, विष्टरः, विस्तरः, आसितं, संवेशः, निषद्यकं.—(Thing spread to sit on) आस्तरणं, आस्तरः, विष्टरः, विस्तरः.—(Seat of justice) धर्म्मासनं, न्यायासनं, विचारासनं.—(Mansion, place of abode or inherence) स्थानं, वासस्थानं, निवासस्थानं, वसतिः *f.*, निवसतिः *f.*, आशयः, आयतनं, आस्पदं, अधिष्ठानं, अधिष्ठितिः *f.*, निकेतनं, निवेशनं, वेश्म *n.* (न्), निलयः -यनं, आलयः, आकरः, मठः; 'seat of consciousness,' अहङ्कारास्पदं, अहङ्काराशयः; 'of diseases,' रोगायतनं, रोगाशयः; 'of enjoyment,' भोगायतनं, भोगास्पदं, सुखास्पदं; 'of joy,' हर्षास्पदं, आनन्दास्पदं; 'of pain,' दुःखायतनं, दुःखास्पदं; 'of sorrow,' शोकास्पदं; 'of avarice,' लोभास्पदं; 'of all happiness and prosperity,' सकलसुखसम्पत्तिवसतिः *f.*; 'of the blood,' रक्ताशयः; 'of the bile,' पित्ताशयः; 'of science,' विद्याकरः; 'of one's ancestors,' आद्यस्थानं, आदिपुरुषस्थानं.

To SEAT, *v. a.* (Cause to sit down) उपविश् in caus. (-वेशयति -यितुं), समुपविश्, आसनं ग्रह् in caus. (ग्राहयति -यितुं), दत्तासनं ग्रह् in caus., दत्तासने उपविश् in caus. or स्था in caus., आसनस्थितं -तां कृ.—(Seat one's self) उपविश् (c. 6. -विशति -वेष्टुं), आसनं ग्रह् (c. 9. गृह्णाति, ग्रहीतुं), आसनपरिग्रहं कृ.—(Install) प्रतिष्ठा in caus. (-ष्ठापयति -यितुं), अधिकारं प्रविश् (c. 10. -वेशयति -यितुं), अधिकारारूढं -ढां कृ, पदारूढं -ढां कृ.—(Settle), *see* the word.

SEATED, *p. p.* (On a seat) उपविष्टः -ष्टा -ष्टं, समुपविष्टः &c., आसीनः -ना -नं, समासीनः &c., आसनोपविष्टः -ष्टा -ष्टं, आसनस्थः -स्था -स्थं, आसनस्थितः -ता -तं, आसनारूढः -ढा -ढं, आसनगतः -ता -तं, आसनाश्रितः &c., आसनमाश्रितः &c., निषण्णः -ण्णा -ण्णं, सन्निषण्णः &c., अध्यासीनः -ना -नं, पीठाध्यासीनः &c., पीठोपविष्टः -ष्टा -ष्टं, पीठस्थः -स्था -स्थं, कृतासनपरिग्रहः -हा -हं; 'seated at ease,' सुखासीनः -ना -नं, सुखोपविष्टः -ष्टा -ष्टं; 'Be seated,' आसनं गृह्यतां, क्रियताम् आसनपरिग्रहः.—(Settled, fixed) स्थितः -ता -तं in comp., स्थः स्था स्थं in comp., निष्ठः -ष्ठा -ष्ठं, निष्ठितः -ता -तं, प्रतिष्ठितः &c., गतः -ता -तं in comp., निविष्टः -ष्टा -ष्टं; 'seated in the soul,' आत्मनिष्ठः -ष्ठा -ष्ठं; 'in the heart,' हृदयस्थः -स्था -स्थं, हृत्स्थः &c.; 'in the mind,' मनोनिष्ठः &c., मनोगतः -ता -तं; 'in the body,' शरीरस्थः &c., देहस्थः &c.; 'in the throat,' कण्ठस्थः &c., कण्ठगतः -ता -तं; 'in the bones,' अस्थिस्थः &c., अस्थिगतः -ता -तं; 'deeply seated,' बद्धमूलः -ला -लं, दृढमूलः &c.

To SECEDE, *v. n.* अपया (c. 2. -याति -तुं), व्यपया, अपगम् (c. 1. -गच्छति -गन्तुं), व्यपगम्, अपे (c. 2. अपैति -तुं), व्यपे, अपसृ (c. 1. -सरति -सर्त्तुं), अपक्रम् (c. 1. -क्रामति -क्रमितुं), धर्म्मं त्यज् (c. 1. त्यजति, त्यक्तुं) or उत्सृज्, भिन्नः -न्ना -न्नं भू, भिन्नमतः -ता -तं भू, विभक्तः -क्ता -क्तं भू, मतान्तरं ग्रह्, मतान्तरम् अवलम्ब्.

SECEDER, *s.* भिन्नमतग्राही *m.* (न्), मतान्तरग्राही *m.*, साधारणधर्म्मत्यागी *m.*

SECESSION, *s.* अपगमः, व्यपगमः, अपयानं, अपसरणं, अपक्रमः -मणं, त्यागः, उत्सर्गः, धर्म्मत्यागः, साधारणधर्म्मत्यागः, मतान्तरग्रहणं.

To SECLUDE, *v. a.* (Cause to keep apart from society, &c.) विविच् (c. 7. -विनक्ति -वेक्तुं, c. 10. -वेचयति -यितुं), विविक्तं -क्तां कृ, जनसंसर्गविविक्तं -क्तां कृ, पृथक्स्थितं -तां कृ, सभाविविक्तं -क्तां कृ, सभापृथक्स्थितं -तां कृ, विविक्तं वस् in caus.—(Shut up, hide) निरुध् (c. 7. -रुणद्धि -रोद्धुं), रुध्, गुप्, गोपनं कृ.—(Seclude one's self) विविक्तं वस् (c. 1. वसति, वस्तुं), विविक्तवासं कृ, एकान्तं or एकान्ततो वस्, जनसंसर्गवर्जनं कृ, सङ्गवर्जनं कृ, सङ्गत्यागं कृ, सभावर्जनं कृ, सन्न्यासं कृ, सन्न्यसनं कृ.

SECLUDED, *p. p.* (Separated from society, &c.) विविक्तः -क्ता -क्तं,

जनसंसर्गविविक्तः &c., सभाविविक्तः &c., पृथक्स्थितः -ता -तं, असक्तः -क्ता -क्तं.—(Living in retirement) विविक्तवासी -सिनी -सि (न्), एकान्तवासी &c., एकान्तस्थितः -ता -तं, विविक्तवृत्तिः -त्तिः -त्ति; 'a secluded spot,' विविक्तस्थानं, प्रान्तरं, प्रान्तरशून्यं, *see* RETIRED.

SECLUSION, *s.* विविक्तता -त्वं, विविक्तं, विविक्तदशा, विविक्तावस्था, विविक्तवृत्तिः *f.*, पृथक्स्थितिः *f.*, पृथक्स्थितत्वं, विविक्तस्थितिः *f.*, एकान्तस्थितिः *f.*, एकान्तत्वं, विविक्तवासः, एकान्तवासः. *See* PRIVACY.

SECOND, *a.* द्वितीयः -या -यं, द्वितीयकः -का -कं, द्वितीयीकः -का -कं; 'second in rank,' द्वितीयपदस्थः -स्था -स्थं; 'in quality,' द्वितीयगुणकः -का -कं; 'second in value, inferior,' अनुत्तमः -मा -मं, उत्तरः -रा -रं, अमुख्यः &c., *see* SECONDARY; 'second to none,' अद्वितीयः -या -यं, अनुत्तरः -रा -रं.

SECOND, *s.* (Helper) साहाय्यकारी *m.* (न्), सहकारी *m.*, उपकारी *m.*, सहायः, उत्तरसाधकः, द्वितीयः; 'the state or office of a second,' द्वितीयत्वं -ता.—(Measure of time, a simple breathing) प्राणपादः, असुपादः, विपलं; 'in three seconds,' त्रिष्वसुपादेषु.—(Any minute measure of time) विपलं, विकला, पलं, क्षणः, त्रुटिः *f.*, निमेषः, निमिषः. A vipala is equal to $\frac{1}{60}$th of a pala or minute, a vikalá to $\frac{1}{60}$th of a kalá or minute of a degree. *See* MOMENT, INSTANT, *and the measures of time under* MEASURE.

To SECOND, *v. a.* (Help, back) उपकृ, उपकारं कृ, साहाय्यं कृ, सहायत्वं कृ, उपग्रह् (c. 9. -गृह्णाति, ग्रहीतुं), अनुग्रह्, पक्षपातं कृ, पक्षोद्ग्राहं कृ, पक्षोपग्रहं कृ, पक्षानुग्रहं कृ.

SECONDARILY, *adv.* अप्रधानतस्, अप्राधान्येन, अमुख्यशस्, गौणतस्, आनुषङ्गिकतस्, द्वितीयतस्, द्वितीयक्रमानुसारेण.

SECONDARINESS, *s.* अप्रधानता, अप्राधान्यं, अमुख्यता, गौणता, गौणिकता.

SECONDARY, *a.* (Not primary) अप्रधानः -ना -नं, अमुख्यः -ख्या -ख्यं, अप्रथमः -मा -मं, अप्राग्र्यः -ग्र्या -ग्र्यं, अनुषङ्गी -ङ्गिणी &c., आनुषङ्गिकः -की -कं, गौणः -णी -णं, गौणिकः -की -कं, उपसृष्टः -ष्टा -ष्टं, गुणभूतः -ता -तं; 'secondary rank,' अप्रधानता, अप्रधानपदं; 'any thing secondary,' अप्रधानं, उपसर्जनं.—(Not first rate) मध्यमः -मा -मं, मध्यमीयः -या -यं, मध्यमगुणकः -का -कं, विगुणः -णा -णं. The prepositions उप and अनु often give the sense of 'secondary;' as, 'a secondary planet,' उपग्रहः; 'a secondary passion or flavour,' उपरसः, अनुरसः; 'symptom,' अनुबन्धः.

SECONDED, *p. p.* अनुगृहीतः -ता -तं, उपगृहीतः &c., उपकृतः -ता -तं.

SECONDER, *s.* अनुग्राही *m.* (न्), उपकारी *m.*, पक्षपाती *m.*, पक्षोद्ग्राही *m.*

SECOND-HAND, *a.* (Not new, used by another) अन्योपभुक्तः -क्ता -क्तं, अन्यभुक्तः &c., अन्योपयोजितः -ता -तं, अन्यव्यवहारितः &c., अन्यपूर्व्वः -र्व्वा -र्व्वं, उच्छिष्टः -ष्टा -ष्टं.—(Not original) अन्यकल्पितः -ता -तं, अन्यसिद्धः -द्धा -द्धं, अन्यकृतः -ता -तं, अन्योक्तः -क्ता -क्तं.

SECONDLY, *adv.* द्वितीयतस्, द्वितीयं, द्वितीयपदे, द्वितीयवारे.

SECOND-RATE, *a.* मध्यमः -मा -मं, मध्यमगुणकः &c., *see* SECONDARY.

SECOND-SIGHT, *s.* दिव्यदृष्टिः *f.*, दिव्यचक्षुस् *n.*, अतिमानुषदृष्टिः *f.*

SECOND-SIGHTED, *a.* दिव्यदृष्टिः -ष्टिः -ष्टि, दिव्यचक्षूः -क्षूः -क्षुः (स्).

SECRECY, *s.* (Concealment, state of being hid or unknown) गुप्तता -त्वं, गुह्यता -त्वं, गुप्तिः *f.*, गोपनं, गोप्यता, गोपनीयता, गूढता, प्रच्छन्नता, रहस्यता -त्वं, संवृतिः *f.*, संवृतता -त्वं, अन्याज्ञातता -त्वं, गुप्तभावः.—(Keeping a secret, forbearance of disclosure) रहस्यगुप्तिः *f.*, रहस्यगोपनं, गुह्यगोपनं, गुह्यरक्षणं *f.*; गुप्तिः *f.*, संवृतिः *f.*, संवृत्तिः *f.*, रहस्यपालनं, रहस्याभेदः, रहस्याविक्षेपः, रहस्याकथनं, रहस्याभाषणं, निह्नवः, निह्नुतिः *f.*, अभाषणं, मौनं, अनुद्घाटनं; 'profound secrecy,' सुगुप्तिः *f.*, सुसंवृत्तिः *f.*, घनसंवृत्तिः *f.*, घनसंवृतिः *f.*—(Privacy) विविक्तता -त्वं, विविक्तभावः, एकान्तता, रहस् *n.*, रहोभावः रहोवासः, निभृतत्वं, *see* SECLUSION.

SECRET, *a.* (Concealed, not known to others) गुप्तः -प्ता -प्तं, गूढः -ढा -ढं, गुह्यः -ह्या -ह्यं, रहस्यः -स्या -स्यं, प्रच्छन्नः -न्ना -न्नं, छन्नः &c., उपच्छन्नः &c., संवृतः -ता -तं, निभृतः -ता -तं, निगूढः &c., अन्तर्हितः -ता -तं, अव्यक्तः -क्ता -क्तं, अप्रकाशः -शा -शं, अन्याज्ञातः -ता -तं, अन्याविदितः &c.; 'very secret,' सुगुप्तः -प्ता -प्तं, सुरहस्यः &c., सुरक्षितः &c.; 'secret sin,' गूढपातकं, प्रच्छन्नपातकं; 'secret intelligence,' गूढवार्त्ता, गूढभाषितं; 'secret door,' गूढद्वारं, अन्तर्द्वारं; 'secret purpose,' गूढार्थः, संवृत्तिः *f.*; 'secret emissary,' गूढचारः, गूढपुरुषः, गुप्तगतिः *m.*—(To be kept secret) गोप्यः -प्या -प्यं, गोपनीयः -या -यं, गुह्यः -ह्या -ह्यं, गोह्यः &c., संवरणीयः &c.—(Keeping a secret) गुह्याभेदी -दिनी &c., गुह्याभेदकः -का -कं, गुह्याभाषी &c., गुह्याकथकः &c., रहस्याभेदी, रहस्याकथकः &c., रहस्यानिवेदी &c.—(Sequestered, retired) विविक्तः -क्ता -क्तं, निभृतः -ता -तं, विजनः -ना -नं, छन्दः -न्दा -न्दं, *see* PRIVATE, RETIRED.—(Occult) गूढः -ढा -ढं, निगूढः &c., अस्पष्टः -ष्टा -ष्टं, अव्यक्तः -क्ता -क्तं; 'secret in operation,' निगूढकार्य्यः -र्य्या -र्य्यं, गूढकार्य्यः &c., अव्यक्तकार्य्यः &c.

SECRET, *s.* (Something concealed or to be kept secret) रहस्यं, गुह्यं, गोप्यं, गोपनीयं, गूढभाषितं, गुह्यभाषितं, गुप्तभाषितं, गुह्यार्थः, गोपनीयार्थः, गुह्यविषयः, गोपनीयविषयः, मर्म्म *n.* (न्), अषडक्षीणः, तृतीयागोचरं, निह्नवः; 'secret counsel,' मन्त्रः, गूढमन्त्रः; 'a well kept secret,' सुगुप्तरहस्यं, सुगुप्तमन्त्रः, सुरक्षितमन्त्रः; 'one who can keep a secret,' रहस्यपालकः, रहस्यरक्षकः, रहस्यगोपनचतुरः, गोपनीयार्थरक्षणचतुरः; 'keeping a secret,' रहस्यगोपनं &c., *see* SECRECY; 'divulging a secret,' रहस्यभेदः, रहस्यविक्षेपः, गुह्यभेदः, रहस्यकथनं, रहस्यप्रकाशनं, अन्तर्भेदः; 'to divulge a secret,' रहस्यं भिद् or प्रकाश् or कथ् or विक्षिप्; 'one who knows secrets,' रहस्यविद्, रहस्यज्ञः, मर्म्मविद्, मर्म्मज्ञः, मार्म्मिकः, मर्म्मवेदी *m.* (न्), मन्त्रज्ञः, मन्त्रविद्, अन्तर्वेदी *m.*; 'diving into the secrets of others,' मर्म्मभेदः, मर्म्मान्वेषणं; 'one who does so,' मर्म्मभेदी *m.* (न्), मर्म्मान्वेषी *m.*—(In secret) रहसि, रहस्, मिथस्, *see* PRIVATELY.

SECRETARY, *s.* लेखकः, लिपिकरः, लिपिकारः -रकः, वर्णिकः, कायस्थः; 'chief secretary,' लेखाधिकारी *m.* (न्).—(Minister), *see* the word.

To SECRETE, *v. a.* (Hide) गुप् (c. 1. गोपायति, गोप्तुं, c. 10. गोपयति -यितुं), गुह् (c. 1. गूहति -हितुं), संवृ (c. 5. -वृणोति -वरितुं, c. 10. -वारयति -यितुं), अपवृ, निह्नु, गोपनं कृ, अपहारं कृ.—(As saliva, bile, &c.) उत्पद् (c. 10. -पादयति -यितुं), जन् in caus., उद्रिच्.

SECRETED, *p. p.* गुप्तः -प्ता -प्तं, संवृतः -ता -तं, अपवारितः &c., उत्पादितः &c.

SECRETION, *s.* (Act of producing) उत्पादनं.—(Matter secreted) मलं, धातुः *m.*, उत्पादितमलं, शरीरमलं, शरीरोत्पादितमलं, शरीररसः; 'of the nose,' नासोत्पादितमलं, नासामलं; 'of the throat,' कफादिमलं, श्लेष्मादिमलं, कफः, श्लेष्मा *m.* (न्); 'of the bowels,' मलं, अन्नमलं, उदरमलं, पुरीषं; 'promoting the animal secretions,' धातुभृत्, धातुवर्द्धकः -का -कं.

SECRETLY, *adv.* रहसि, रहस्, रहस्यं, गुप्तं, सुगुप्तं, निभृतं -ते, सुनिभृतं -ते, प्रच्छन्नं -न्ने, उपांशु, गूढं, गुप्त or गूढ in comp.; as, 'going secretly,' गुप्तगतिः -तिः -ति, गूढचारी &c., *see* PRIVATELY.

SECRETNESS, *s.* गुप्तता -त्वं, गूढता, प्रच्छन्नता, रहस्यता, *see* SECRECY.

SECRETORY, *a.* उत्पादकः -का -कं, मलोत्पादकः &c., मलजनकः &c.

SECT, *s.* शाखा, मार्गः, भिन्नमार्गः, पन्थाः *m.* (पथिन्), पथः, सम्प्रदायः, मतं, पक्षः, गणः, तीर्थः; 'difference of sect,' शाखाभेदः, मतभेदः, मार्गभेदः; 'mark of a sect,' तिलकः -कं.

SECTARIAN, *a.* शाखासम्बन्धी -न्धिनी -न्धि (न्), शाखी &c., शाखिकः -की -कं.

SECTARIAN, SECTARY, *s.* शाखी *m.* (न्), शाखानुयायी &c., शाखावलम्बी *m.*, शाखाश्रयी *m.*, शाखाश्रितः, शाखासेवी, शाखामार्गानुयायी *m.*, भिन्नमार्गानुयायी *m.*

SECTARIANISM, *s.* शाखासेवनं, शाखानुगमनं, शाखाश्रयणं, भिन्नमार्गगमनं.

SECTION, *s.* (Division) परिच्छेदः, छेदः, विच्छेदः, भेदः -दनं, विभागः.—(Of a book) अध्यायः, अध्ययः, सर्गः, पर्व *n.* (न्), काण्डः -ण्डं, खण्डः -ण्डं, परिच्छेदः, विच्छेदः, स्कन्धः, प्रकरणं, प्रस्तावः, अङ्कः, वर्गः, शाखा, उल्लासः, उच्छ्वासः, आश्वासः, उद्यतः, लम्बकः; 'story divided into sections,' खण्डकथा.—(In geometry) मार्गः.

SECTOR, *s.* विच्छेदकः.—(Of a circle) कर्कटद्वयान्तर्गतो वृत्तभागः.

SECULAR, *a.* (Pertaining to this present world, or to things not spiritual) लौकिकः -की -कं, ऐहलौकिकः &c., ऐहिकः -की -कं, इहलोकविषयकः -का -कं, इहलोकसम्बन्धी -न्धिनी &c., प्रापञ्चिकः -की -कं, सांसारिकः &c., संसारविषयकः &c., संसारसम्बन्धी &c., संसारी &c., व्यावहारिकः &c., लोकव्यवहारसम्बन्धी &c., विषयसम्बन्धी &c., प्रपञ्ची &c., इहलोकसापेक्षः -क्षा -क्षं, इहलोकापेक्षकः &c., दृष्टार्थः -र्था -र्थं; 'secular learning,' विज्ञानं, अर्थशास्त्रं.—(Not subject to monastic rules) व्यवहारी &c., व्यवहारिकः &c.

SECULARITY, SECULARNESS, *s.* लौकिकता -त्वं, ऐहिकत्वं -ता, ऐहलौकिकत्वं, ऐहिकबुद्धित्वं, ऐहिकविषयासक्तिः, संसारासक्तिः *f.*, लोकासक्तिः *f.*, इहलोकासक्तिः *f.*, प्रपञ्चासक्तिः *f.*

SECUNDINES, *s.* गर्भवेष्टनं, गर्भकोशः, गर्भकोषः, गर्भाशयः, जरायुः *m.*, गर्भावरणं चर्म्म *n.* (न्), गर्भावेष्टनचर्म्म *n.*

SECURE, *a.* (Free from danger) निर्भयः -या -यं, भयातीतः -ता -तं, अतीतभयः -या -यं, वीतभयः &c., गतभयः &c., अकुतोभयः &c., असम्भाव्यभयः &c., असम्भाव्यापकारः -रा -रं, भयसम्भवातीतः &c., अहार्य्यः -र्य्या -र्य्यं, अनाश्यः -श्या -श्यं, निरुपद्रवः -वा -वं, *see* SAFE.—(Free from fear of danger) निर्भयः -या -यं, अभयः &c., भयहीनः -ना -नं, निःशङ्कः -ङ्का -ङ्कं, अशङ्कः &c., विशङ्कः &c., निरातङ्कः &c., निरपेक्षः -क्षा -क्षं; 'rendering secure,' विधायकः -का -कं.

To SECURE, *v. a.* (Guard from danger) निर्भयं -यां कृ, निर्भयीकृ, भयं निवृ (c. 10. -वारयति -यितुं) or निरस् or निवृत् in caus., भयनिवारणं कृ, भयनिवृत्तिं कृ, भयनिरासं कृ, भयनिरसनं कृ, रक्ष् (c. 1. रक्षति -क्षितुं), अभिरक्ष्, सुरक्षितं -तां कृ, रक्षणं कृ.—(Make certain or sure) स्थिरीकृ, दृढीकृ, सत्याकृ, सुनिश्चयं -यां कृ, सुनिश्चितं -तां कृ, अहार्य्यत्वं जन्, अनाश्यत्वं जन्.—(Make fast or firm) दृढं बन्ध् (c. 9. बध्नाति, बन्द्धुं), दृढीकृ, संस्तम्भ्; 'with a bar,' अर्गलेन बन्ध्.

SECURED, *p. p.* (Guarded from danger) रक्षितः -ता -तं, सुरक्षितः &c., निवृत्तभयः -या -यं, निवारितभयः &c.—(Made sure) स्थिरीकृतः -ता -तं, दृढीकृतः &c.—(Made fast) दृढबद्धः -द्धा -द्धं, सुबन्धः -न्धा -न्धं, अर्गलबद्धः &c., संस्तब्धः -ब्धा -ब्धं.

SECURELY, *adv.* निर्भयं, भयं विना, अभयेन, सक्षेमं, *see* SAFELY.

SECURITY, *s.* (Protection) रक्षा, रक्षणं, संरक्षणं, अभिरक्षणं, गुप्तिः *f.*, गोपनं, त्राणं, परित्राणं, भयनिवारणं, भयनिरासः, भयनिरसनं.—(That which protects) रक्षणं, रक्षकः, त्राणं, आश्रयः, शरणं.—(Freedom from fear or danger) अभयं, निर्भयता -त्वं, भयाभावः, भयहीनता, निःशङ्कता, शङ्काभावः, अहार्य्यता -त्वं, अनाश्यता -त्वं, निर्विघ्नता, निरुपद्रवत्वं, निर्वृतिः *f.*, *see* SAFETY.—(Assurance of safety) अभयवाक् *f.* (च्), *see* SAFETY.—(Securing, rendering firm) दृढीकरणं, स्थिरीकरणं, संस्तम्भनं, क्षेमकरणं, विधायकत्वं.—(Certainty) निश्चयः, निःसंशयत्वं, संशयाभावः, सन्देहाभावः.—(Any thing given or deposited as a security) लग्नकः, बन्धकः, प्रातिभाव्यं, पारिभाव्यं, आधिः *m.*, न्यासः, निक्षेपः, *see* PLEDGE; 'for the payment of a debt,' दानप्रातिभाव्यं, ऋणमार्गणः; 'for appearance,' दर्शनप्रातिभाव्यं, दर्शनपारिभाव्यं, दर्शनप्रतिभूः *m.*—(A person who stands security) प्रतिभूः *m.*, प्रतिनिधिः *m.*

SEDAN, *s.* स्कन्धवाह्यपीठः, स्कन्धवहनयोग्यो पीठः, शिबिका.

SEDATE, *a.* धीरः -रा -रं, गम्भीरः -रा -रं, गम्भीरवृत्तिः -त्तिः -त्ति, गभीरवृत्तिः &c., गुरुवृत्तिः &c., गौरववृत्तिः &c., शान्तः -न्ता -न्तं, अन्तर्वेगहीनः -ना -नं, निरुद्विग्नः -ग्ना -ग्नं, निराकुलः -ला -लं, अव्याकुलः &c., अचञ्चलः -ला -लं.

SEDATELY, *adv.* गम्भीरं, सगाम्भीर्य्यं, धीरवत्, सधैर्य्यं, अव्याकुलं, निराकुलं, सगौरवं, गौरवेण, अचञ्चलं.

SEDATENESS, *s.* धीरता, गम्भीरता -त्वं, गाम्भीर्य्यं, गम्भीरवृत्तित्वं, गभीरता, गभीरवृत्तित्वं, धैर्य्यं, गौरवं, शान्तता, निराकुलता, अव्याकुलता, स्थिरता, स्थैर्य्यं, अचञ्चलता, अचाञ्चल्यं.

SEDATIVE, *a.* शान्तिकः -की -कं, शान्तिदः -दा -दं, शान्तिकरः -रा -रं, शान्तिकर्त्ता -र्त्री -र्त्तृ (र्त्तृ), शमकः -का -कं, उपशमकः -का -कं, उपशायी -यिनी -यि (न्).

SEDATIVE, *s.* (Medicine) शमनं, उपशमनं, ग्राही *m.* (न्).

SEDENTARINESS, *s.* अनुद्योगशीलता, अव्यायामशीलता, गतिहीनता, चलनाभावः.

SEDENTARY, *a.* अनुद्योगशीलः -ला -लं, अव्यायामशीलः &c., अव्यायामी -मिनी -मि (न्), निरुद्योगी &c., गतिहीनः -ना -नं, गतिरहितः -ता -तं, चलनरहितः &c.

SEDIMENT, *s.* मलं, किट्टं, उच्छिष्टं, कल्कं, खलं, शेषं, विनीयः, *see* DREGS; 'having sediment,' खली -लिनी -लि (न्), कल्की &c.

SEDITION, *s.* प्रकृतिकलहः, प्रजाकलहः, कलहः, भेदः, प्रकृतिक्षोभः, प्रजाक्षोभः, राजयुद्धं, राजद्रोहः, राज्यभेदः; 'fomenting sedition,' उपजापः; 'one who does so,' उपजापकः; 'to do so,' उपजप् (c. 1. -जपति -पितुं).

SEDITIOUS, *a.* कलहकारी -रिणी -रि (न्), प्रजाक्षोभकरः -री -रं, प्रकृतिक्षोभकरः &c., राज्यभेदकरः &c., भेदकरः &c., राजद्रोही &c., राजविरुद्धकारी &c., उपजापकः -का -कं.

SEDITIOUSLY, *adv.* उपजापेन, सोपजापं, यथा प्रजाकलहो जायते तथा.

To SEDUCE, *v. a.* (Entice from the path of rectitude) प्रलुभ् (c. 10. -लोभयति -यितुं), विलुभ्, परिलुभ्, लुभ्, सत्पथाद् or सन्मार्गाद् भ्रंश् (c. 10. भ्रंशयति -यितुं) or च्यु in caus. (च्यावयति -यितुं) or अपकृष् (c. 1. -कर्षति -क्रष्टुं), मुह् (c. 10. मोहयति -यितुं), विमुह्, प्रलभ् (c. 1. -लभते -लब्धुं), लल् (c. 10. लालयति -यितुं), दुष्कर्म्मणि प्रवृत् in caus., विरूप् (c. 10. -रूपयति -यितुं), सन्मार्गभ्रष्टं -ष्टां कृ, सन्मार्गच्युतं -तां कृ.—(A woman) छलेन कन्यां दुष् (c. 10. दूषयति -यितुं), सतीत्वाद् भ्रंश् in caus., सतीत्वनाशं कृ, छलेन कन्याम् अभिगम्.

SEDUCED, *p.p.* (Enticed) प्रलोभितः -ता -तं, विलोभितः &c., सन्मार्गभ्रंशितः &c., सन्मार्गभ्रष्टः -ष्टा -ष्टं, आकृष्टः -ष्टा -ष्टं, मोहितः -ता -तं, विमोहितः &c., लालितः &c., प्रोत्साहितः -ता -तं, प्रवर्त्तितः &c.—(As a woman) सतीत्वभ्रंशिता, सतीत्वभ्रष्टा, भ्रष्टा, छलेन नष्टसतीत्वा.

SEDUCER, *s.* प्रलोभकः, विलोभकः, आकर्षकः, मोहकः, विमोहकः, विमोही *m.* (न्), लाली *m.*, लालनकारी *m.*, प्रतारकः.—(Of a woman) छलेन कन्यादूषकः or कन्याभिगन्ता *m.* (न्तृ), कापट्येन सतीत्वनाशकः.

SEDUCIBLE, *a.* प्रलोभनीयः -या -यं, आकर्षणीयः &c., प्रतारणीयः &c., विलोभनीयः &c., हार्य्यः -र्य्या -र्य्यं, भेद्यः -द्या -द्यं.

SEDUCTION, *s.* प्रलोभनं, विलोभनं, आकर्षणं, आकृष्टिः *f.*, सन्मार्गभ्रंशनं, सन्मार्गोत्प्रभ्रंशनं, मोहनं, विमोहनं, लालनं, लोभदर्शनं, प्रतारणं, वञ्चनं, प्रलम्भः.—(Of a woman) कन्याछलं, कन्यकाछलं, छलेन कन्यादूषणं or कन्याभिगमनं or स्त्रीसंग्रहणं, कपटपूर्व्वं सतीत्वनाशः.

SEDUCTIVE, *a.* प्रलोभकः -का -कं, विलोभकः &c., आकर्षकः &c., आकर्षी -र्षिणी -र्षि (न्), मोही &c., विमोहनः -ना -नी -नं, लाली &c., भ्रान्तिजनकः &c.

SEDULITY, SEDULOUSNESS, *s.* आसक्तिः *f.*, प्रसक्तिः *f.*, व्यासङ्गः, उद्योगासक्तिः *f.*, व्यवसायः, उद्योगशीलता. *See* DILIGENCE, INDUSTRY.

SEDULOUS, *a.* उद्योगासक्तः -क्ता -क्तं, कर्म्मासक्तः &c., उद्यमासक्तः &c., उद्योगशीलः -ला -लं, व्यासङ्गी -ङ्गिनी &c., आसक्तः &c., तत्परः &c. *See* INDUSTRIOUS.

SEDULOUSLY, *adv.* आसक्तिपूर्व्वं, यत्नतस्, साभिनिवेशं. *See* INDUSTRIOUSLY.

SEE, *s.* धर्म्माध्यक्षाधिकारः, धर्म्माध्यक्षाधीनमण्डलं, धर्म्माध्यक्षाधीनदेशः, धर्म्माध्यक्षाधीनः प्रदेशः, धर्म्माध्यक्षाधिपत्यं.

To SEE, *v. a.* or *n.* (Perceive by the eye) दृश् (c. 1. पश्यति, द्रष्टुं), अभिदृश्, प्रतिदृश्, परिदृश्, अनुदृश्, प्रदृश्, सन्दृश्, विदृश्, ईक्ष् (c. 1. ईक्षते -क्षितुं), समीक्ष्, वीक्ष्, प्रेक्ष्, निरीक्ष्, अभिवीक्ष्, अभिप्रेक्ष्, सम्प्रेक्ष्, अवेक्ष्, प्रत्यवेक्ष्, आलोक् (c. 10. -लोकयति -यितुं, c. 1. -लोकते -कितुं), समालोक्, अवलोक्, विलोक्, लक्ष् (c. 10. लक्षयति -यितुं), आलक्ष्, समालक्ष्, उपलक्ष्, समुपलक्ष्, संलक्ष्, आलोच् (c. 10. -लोचयति -यितुं, c. 1. -लोचते -चितुं), निर्वर्ण् (c. 10. -वर्णयति -यितुं), सभाज् (c. 10. सभाजयति -यितुं), दृष्टिं कृ, दर्शनं कृ, अवलोकनं कृ, विलोकनं कृ.—(Perceive, understand) ज्ञा (c. 9. जानाति -नीते, ज्ञातुं), परिज्ञा, अवगम् (c. 1. -गच्छति -गन्तुं), अवे (c. 2. अवैति -तुं, rt. इ), बुध्, अवबुध्, उपलभ्, निशम्.—(Experience) अनुभू, भुज्, दृश्.—(Beware) सावधानः -ना -नं भू, अवहितः -ता -तं भू, अवधा.—(See into, examine) निरूप् (c. 10. -रूपयति -यितुं), निरीक्ष्, *see To* EXAMINE, INQUIRE.—(See after) पाल्, रक्ष्, अवेक्ष्; 'see! see!' पश्य, पश्यत.

SEED, *s.* (Of plants, &c.) बीजं -जकं, रोहिः *m.*, इरुः *m.*; 'good seed,' सुबीजं, बीजोत्कृष्टं; 'sowing seed,' बीजारोपः -पणं, वपः -पनं, वापः, उप्तिः *f.*; 'to sow seed,' बीजारोपणं कृ, बीजानि आरुह् in caus.; 'full of seed,' बीजपूर्णः -र्णा -र्णं; 'having it,' बीजवान् -वती &c., बीजी -जिनी &c.; 'growing from it,' बीजप्ररोहः -हा -हं, बीजप्ररोही -हिणी &c., बीजरुहः -हा -हं, बीज्यः -ज्या -ज्यं; 'sown with seed,' बीजितः -ता -तं; 'yielding seed,' बीजप्रदः -दा -दं, बीजसूः -सूः -सु; 'from seed,' बीजतस्.—(Of stone fruits) अष्ठिः *f.*, अष्ठीला -ष्ठिका.—(Of animals, seminal fluid) शुक्रं, रेतस् *n.*, धातुः *m.*, तेजस् *n.*, बीजं, वीर्य्यं, इन्द्रियं, धातुराजकः, आनन्दप्रभवः.—(Origin, source) बीजं, योनिः *m.*, मूलं, आदिः *m.* प्रभवः, उद्भवः.—(Offspring) सन्तानं, अपत्यं, प्रजा, कुलं, वंशः, बीजं.

To SEED, *v. n.* (Produce seed) बीजं दा or प्रदा or उत्पद्, बीज (nom. बीजायते).

To SEED, *v. a.* (Sow seed) बीजारोपं कृ, बीज (nom. बीजयति -यितुं).

SEEDED, *p. p.* बीजितः -ता -तं, बीजवान् -वती -वत् (त्), बीजी -जिनी -जि (न्).

SEEDLESS, *a.* निर्बीजः -जा -जं, बीजहीनः -ना -नं, बीजरहितः -ता -तं.

SEEDLING, *s.* बीजप्ररोहः, बीजप्ररोही *m.* (न्), बीजरुहः, बीजरोही *m.*

SEEDSMAN, *s.* बीजविक्रयी *m.* (न्), बीजविक्रेता *m.* (तृ), बीजव्यापारी *m.*

SEED-TIME, *s.* बीजकालः, बीजारोपणकालः, उप्तिकालः, वापकालः.

SEED-VESSEL, *s.* बीजकोशः, बीजकोषः -षी, बीजगुप्तिः *f.*; 'of the lotus,' बीजमातृकः, कर्णिका, कर्णिकारः.

SEEDY, *a.* बीजी -जिनी -जि (न्), बीजिकः -का -कं, बीजवान् -वती -वत् (त्), बीजपूर्णः -र्णा -र्णं, सबीजः -जा -जं, बहुबीजः -जा -जं, बीजमयः -यी -यं.

SEEING, SEEING THAT, *s.* यस्मात्, येन, यत्. *See* SINCE.

SEEING, *part.* पश्यन् -श्यन्ती -श्यत् (त्), ईक्षमाणः -णा -णं, प्रेक्षमाणः &c.

SEEING, *s.* दृष्टिः *f.*, दर्शनं, ईक्षणं, प्रेक्षणं, सन्दर्शनं. *See* SIGHT.

To SEEK, *v. a.* (Look for, search for, inquire for) अन्विष् (c. 4. -इष्यति, c. 6. -इच्छति -एषितुं -एष्टुं), अन्वेष् (c. 1. -एषते -षितुं), मृग् (c. 10. मृगयते -ति -यितुं), मार्ग् (c. 1. मार्गति, c. 10. मार्गयति -यितुं), परिमार्ग्, निरूप् (c. 10. -रूपयति -यितुं), अनुसन्धा (c. 3. -दधाति -धातुं), ज्ञा in des. (जिज्ञासते -सितुं), विचि (c. 5. -चिनोति -चेतुं), गवेष् (c. 10. गवेषयति -यितुं), अनुयुज् (c. 7. -युनक्ति -युङ्क्ते -योक्तुं), इष् (c. 6. इच्छति, एषितुं), आकांक्ष् (c. 1. -कांक्षति -क्षितुं), भज् (c. 1. भजते, भक्तुं), चेष्ट् (c. 1. चेष्टते -ष्टितुं), चर्च् (c. 1. चर्चति -र्चितुं), अन्वेषणं कृ, जिज्ञासां कृ, अनुयोगं कृ, इतस्ततो गत्वा or इतस्ततः परिक्रम्य अन्वेषणं कृ.—(Solicit, beg for) प्रार्थ् (c. 10. -अर्थयते -ति -यितुं), अर्थ्, अभ्यर्थ्, समभ्यर्थ्, याच् (c. 1. याचति -चितुं), अभियाच्, प्रयाच्, सम्प्रयाच्, भिक्ष् (c. 1. भिक्षते -क्षितुं).

To SEEK, *v. n.* (Make search) अन्वेषणं कृ, जिज्ञासां कृ, अनुसन्धानं कृ.

SEEKER, *s.* अन्वेष्टा *m.* (ष्टृ), अन्वेषी *m.* (न्), अन्वेषणकृत् *m.*, जिज्ञासाकृत्, अनुसन्धाता *m.* (तृ), अनुवर्त्ती *m.*, प्रार्थकः, अर्थी *m.*

SEEKING, *s.* अन्वेषणं -णा, जिज्ञासा, मार्गः -र्गणं. *See* SEARCH.

SEEKING, *part.* अन्विष्यन् -ष्यन्ती -ष्यत् (त्), अन्वेषी -षिणी -षि (न्), अन्वेषमाणः -णा -णं, इच्छन् &c.

To SEEM, *v. n.* दृश् in pass. (दृश्यते), लक्ष् in pass. (लक्ष्यते), प्रतिभा (c. 2. -भाति -तुं), सम्प्रभा, निर्भा, आभा, आभास् (c. 1. -भासते -सितुं); 'you seem astonished,' विस्मित इव प्रतिभासि.

SEEMING, *s.* आभासः, आभा, छाया, बाह्यरूपं, आकारः, आकृतिः *f.*

SEEMINGLY, *adv.* आभासेन, आकारेण, प्रत्यक्षतस्, प्रत्यक्षेण, बाह्यतस्.

SEEMLINESS, *s.* (Comeliness) सुदृश्यता, सुरूपता.—(Propriety) योग्यता -त्वं, युक्तता, उपयुक्तता, औचित्यं. *See* FITNESS.

SEEMLY, *a.* युक्तः -क्ता -क्तं, योग्यः -ग्या -ग्यं, उपयुक्तः &c., उचितः -ता -तं, यथोचितः &c., उपपन्नः -न्ना -न्नं, समञ्जसः -सा -सं, सङ्गतः -ता -तं.

SEEN, *p.p.* दृष्टः -ष्टा -ष्टं, ईक्षितः -ता -तं, प्रेक्षितः &c., आलोकितः &c., अवलोकितः &c., आलोचितः &c., लोकितः &c., आलक्षितः -ता -तं, लक्षितः &c.; 'seen and unseen,' दृष्टादृष्टः -ष्टा -ष्टं; 'not seen or heard before,' अदृष्टाश्रुतपूर्व्वः -र्व्वा -र्व्वं; 'is seen,' दृश्यते, लक्ष्यते; 'to be seen, visible,' दृश्यः -श्या -श्यं, दर्शनीयः -या -यं, प्रेक्षणीयः &c., प्रेक्ष्यः &c., वीक्ष्यः &c., लक्ष्यः &c.; 'having seen,' दृष्ट्वा, प्रेक्ष्य, वीक्ष्य.

Seer, *s.* (One who sees) द्रष्टा *m.* (ष्टृ), दर्शी *m.* (न्), चक्षुष्मान् *m.* (त्); 'far-seer,' दूरदर्शी *m.*—(Prophet) भाविदर्शी *m.*, भाविदर्शकः, भविष्यद्दर्शी *m.*, सिद्धः, सिद्धपुरुषः, सौमेधिकः, *see* Sage.

See-saw, *s.* उच्चतागतं, निम्नोच्चतं, उच्चावचं, पातोत्पातं, आन्दोलनं, इतस्ततो विचलनं or चलनं, गतागतं, प्रतिगतागतं.

To **seethe**, *v. a.* क्वथ् (c. 1. क्वथति -थितुं), उखीये or स्थाल्यां पच्.

Seethed, *p. p.* क्वथितः -ता -तं, स्थालीपक्वः -क्वा -क्वं, उखीयपक्वः &c.

Seether, *s.* उखीयं, ऋचीषं, पिष्टपचनं, स्थाली, पिठरः -रं, उखा.

Segment, *s.* छेदः, परिच्छेदः, विच्छेदः, खण्डः.—(Of a circle) वृत्तखण्डः -ण्डं, वर्त्तुलखण्डः, खण्डमण्डलं, धनुष्यं.

Segregarious, *a.* एकचरः -रा -रं, एकचारी -रिणी -रि (न्), विविक्तचारी &c.

To **segregate**, *v. a.* वियुज्, विश्लिष् in caus. *See To* separate, *v. a.*

Segregation, *s.* वियोगः, विश्लेषः, पृथक्करणं. *See* Separation.

Seignior, *s.* स्वामी *m.* (न्), प्रभुः *m.*, पतिः *m.* *See* Lord.

Seizable, *a.* हार्य्यः -र्य्या -र्य्यं, हरणीयः -या -यं, अपहार्य्यः &c., ग्राह्यः -ह्या -ह्यं, ग्रहणीयः &c., धार्य्यः &c., धरणीयः &c.

To **seize**, *v. a.* (Take by force) हृ (c. 1. हरति, हर्त्तुं), अपहृ, बलेन हृ, बलात्कारेण ग्रह् (c. 9. गृह्णाति, ग्रहीतुं) or अभिग्रह् or परिग्रह् or प्रतिग्रह् or धृ (c. 1. धरति, धर्त्तुं) or कल् (c. 10. कालयति -यितुं), प्रकल्, हरणं कृ.—(Grasp, clutch) ग्रह्, संग्रह्, परिग्रह्, उपसंग्रह्, धृ, ग्रस् (c. 1. ग्रसते -सितुं), परामृश् (c. 6. -मृशति -म्रष्टुं), संहृ, आकल् (-कलयति -यितुं), संग्राहं कृ.—(Attack suddenly, take hold of, as a fever, &c.) आक्रम् (c. 1. -क्रामति -क्रमितुं), आविश् (c. 6. -विशति -वेष्टुं), आक्रमणं कृ, ग्रस्, ग्रस्तः -स्ता -स्तं भू.—(Try to seize) ग्रह् in des. (जिघृक्षति -ते -क्षितुं), हृ in des. (जिहीर्षति -र्षितुं).

Seized, *p. p.* (Taken by force) हृतः -ता -तं, अपहृतः &c., बलेन हृतः &c., बलात्कारेण हृतः &c. or प्रहृतः &c. or गृहीतः -ता -तं or धृतः &c. or प्राप्तः -प्ता -प्तं, सम्प्राप्तः &c.—(Grasped, clutched) गृहीतः -ता -तं, संगृहीतः &c., धृतः &c., ग्रस्तः -स्ता -स्तं, आकलितः &c.—(Attacked suddenly) आक्रान्तः -न्ता -न्तं, आविष्टः -ष्टा -ष्टं, ग्रस्तः &c.; 'by fever,' ज्वरग्रस्तः &c.

Seizer, *s.* हर्त्ता *m.* (र्त्तृ), हारी *m.* (न्), हारकः, हरः, धर्त्ता *m.*, ग्राही *m.*, ग्राहकः, ग्रहीता *m.* (तृ), अपहर्त्ता *m.*

Seizure, *s.* (Taking by force) हरणं, अपहरणं, हारः, अपहारः, बलात्कारेण हरणं or ग्रहणं or ग्रहः or अभिग्रहः -हणं or प्रतिग्रहः -हणं or धरणं.—(Laying hold) ग्रहणं, ग्रहः, संग्राहः, संग्रहणं, परिग्रहणं, धरणं, धृतिः *f.*, ग्रसनं, आकलनं.—(Sudden attack, as of a disease) आक्रमणं, आवेशः, अवतारः, अवतरणं, लंघनं; 'first seizure,' पूर्व्वावतारः.

Seldom, *adv.* विरलं, वैरल्येन, क्वचित्, कदाचित्, कर्हिचित्, दुर् in comp.; 'seldom to be found,' दुर्लभः -भा -भं, दुष्प्रापः &c.; 'seldom to be seen,' दुर्दृश्यः -श्या -श्यं, दुर्लक्ष्यः -क्ष्या -क्ष्यं.

To **select**, *v. a.* उद्धृ (c. 1. उद्धरति, उद्धर्त्तुं, rt. हृ), उद्ग्रह् (c. 9. -गृह्णाति -ग्रहीतुं), वृ (c. 5. वृणोति -णुते, c. 10. वरयति -यितुं, c. 1. वरति -रितुं -रीतुं), आवृ, प्रवृ, व्यावृत् (c. 4. व्यावृत्यते), वृत्, परिगण् (c. 10. -गणयति -यितुं), परिगणनं कृ, उद्धरणं कृ, उद्धारं कृ. *See To* choose.

Select, *a.* उत्कृष्टः -ष्टा -ष्टं, उत्तमः -मा -मं, विशिष्टः &c., *see* Choice.

Selected, *p. p.* उद्धृतः -ता -तं, वृतः -ता -तं, वृत्तः -त्ता -त्तं, व्यावृत्तः &c., परिगणितः -ता -तं, गृहीतः &c., उद्गृहीतः &c., मनोनीतः &c.

Selection, *s.* (Act of choosing) उद्धरणं, उद्धारः, उद्ग्रहणं, ग्रहणं, वरणं, वृतिः *f.*, वरः.—(Thing selected) उद्धृतं.—(Number of things selected) संग्रहः, संहिता, सारः; 'selection of parallel passages,' चूर्णिः *m.*

Self, *a.* or *pron.* (As united to a pronoun, &c. reciprocally, or in composition with an adverb or noun) आत्मा *m.* (न्), आत्म in comp.; 'I will kill myself,' आत्मानं हनिष्यामि; 'blame thyself,' आत्मानं निन्द; 'he shows himself,' आत्मानं दर्शयति; 'for one's self,' आत्मार्थं; 'like one's self,' आत्मवत्; 'comparison with one's self,' आत्मौपम्यं.—(As united to a pronoun, &c. emphatically) स्वयं, स्वतस्; 'I myself will decide,' स्वयं निष्पत्तिं करिष्यामि. The pronoun सः is sometimes joined with the personal pronouns emphatically; as, 'I myself,' सो ऽहं.—(As the first member of a compound word) आत्म or स्व or स्वयं or स्वतः prefixed; 'self done,' आत्मकृतः -ता -तं, स्वयङ्कृतः &c.; 'self-given,' स्वयन्दत्तः -त्ता -त्तं, आत्मदत्तः &c.; 'self-sufficient,' स्वस्थः -स्था -स्थं; 'self-actuating,' स्वयंवहः -हा -हं.—(Of one's self, of one's own accord) स्वयं, स्वतस्; 'decayed of itself,' स्वयंशीर्णः -र्णा -र्णं.

Self-abasement, *s.* आत्मापकर्षः, अहङ्कारत्यागः, स्वाभिमानत्यागः.

Self-abhorrence, *s.* आत्मद्वेषः, आत्मगर्हा -र्हणं, आत्मबीभत्सः.

Self-abuse, *s.* आत्मनिन्दा, आत्मगर्हा, आत्माक्रोशः, आत्मकुत्सा.

Self-accomplished, *a.* आत्मसिद्धः -द्धा -द्धं, स्वतःसिद्धः &c., स्वयंसिद्धः &c.

Self-acquired, *a.* आत्मोपार्जितः -ता -तं, स्वोपार्जितः &c., आत्मार्जितः &c.

Self-advantage, *s.* आत्महितं, स्वहितं, आत्मोदयः, आत्मलाभः, स्वलाभः, आत्मसिद्धिः *f.*, आत्मवृद्धिः *f.*, आत्मविवृद्धिः, स्वार्थः.

Self-affairs, *s. pl.* आत्मकार्य्यं, स्वकार्य्यं, आत्मकर्म्म *n.* (न्), स्वकर्म्म *n.*

Self-aggrandizement, *s.* आत्मविवृद्धिः *f.*, आत्मवृद्धिः *f.*, स्ववृद्धिः *f.*, स्वमहत्त्ववृद्धिः *f.*, आत्मपदवृद्धिः *f.*, स्वपदवृद्धिः *f.*, आत्मोदयः.

Self-applause, *s.* आत्मप्रशंसा, आत्मश्लाघा, आत्मस्तुतिः *f.*

Self-beguiled, *a.* आत्मवञ्चितः -ता -तं, आत्ममोहितः &c., स्वमोहितः &c.

Self-born, self-begotten, *a.* आत्मभूतः -ता -तं, स्वजः -जा -जं, आत्मजः &c., आत्मजातः -ता -तं, स्वजातः &c., आत्मजनितः &c., आत्मोत्पन्नः &c., स्वोत्पन्नः &c.

Self-command, *s.* आत्मसंयमः, आत्मयमनं, अन्तर्यमनं, प्रतिसंस्थानं, दान्तिः *f.*, दमः, दमथः. *See* Self-control.

Self-conceit, *s.* अहङ्कारः, अहम्मतिः *f.*, अहम्मानं, आत्माभिमानं, स्वाभिमानं, ममता, अहमहमिका, अभिमानं, अमर्हासः.

Self-conceited, *a.* अहङ्कारी -रिणी -रि (न्), अहम्मानी -निनी &c., आत्माभिमानी &c., स्वाभिमानी &c., साहङ्कारः -रा -रं, साभिमानः -ना -नं, स्वाभिमानः &c., अभिमानी &c., ममतायुक्तः -क्ता -क्तं. *See* Conceited.

Self-confidence, *s.* आत्मनिष्ठा, आत्मविश्वासः, स्वमतनिष्ठा, स्वबुद्धिनिष्ठा.

Self-confident, *a.* आत्मनिष्ठः -ष्ठा -ष्ठं, स्वमतनिष्ठः &c., स्वबुद्धिनिष्ठः &c.

Self-control, *s.* आत्मसंयमः, आत्मनिग्रहः, आत्मनियमः, आत्मयमनं, आत्मवशः, अन्तर्यमः -मनं, अन्तःसंयमः, संयमः.

Self-convicted, *a.* स्वनिर्णीतापराधः -धा -धं, स्वनिश्चितदोषः -षा -षं.

Self-created, *a.* स्वयङ्कृतः -ता -तं, आत्मकृतः &c., स्वजनितः -ता -तं.

Self-deceit, self-deception, *s.* आत्मवञ्चना, आत्मछलं, आत्मप्रतारणा.

Self-deceived, *a.* आत्मवञ्चितः -ता -तं, स्ववञ्चितः &c., स्वप्रतारितः -ता -तं.

Self-deceiving, *a.* आत्मवञ्चकः -का -कं, आत्मप्रतारकः &c., स्वप्रतारकः &c.

Self-dedication, *s.* आत्मनिवेदनं, आत्मसमर्पणं, स्वदेहविनियोगः.

SELF-DEFENCE, *s.* आत्मरक्षणं, आत्मरक्षा, आत्मत्राणं, स्वरक्षणं, स्वत्राणं. आत्मपरित्राणं, परित्राणं; 'in self-defence,' आत्मरक्षार्थं.

SELF-DELUSION, *s.* आत्मवञ्चनं -ना, आत्ममोहः -हनं, आत्मप्रतारणा.

SELF-DENIAL, *s.* आत्मपरित्यागः, आत्मसंयमः, आत्मनिरोधः, संयमः.

SELF-DENYING, *a.* आत्मपरित्यागी -गिनी -गि (न्), आत्मनियामकः -का -कं, आत्मसंयमी &c., आत्मनिरोधी &c., आत्मत्यागी &c.

SELF-DEPENDENCE, *s.* आत्मनिष्ठा, आत्माश्रयः, स्वतन्त्रता, स्वातन्त्र्यं, आत्मतन्त्रता, आत्मसंश्रयः, आत्माधीनता, आत्माधारः.

SELF-DEPENDENT, *a.* आत्मनिष्ठः -ष्ठा -ष्ठं, आत्माश्रयी -यिणी -यि (न्), आत्माश्रयः -या -यं, आत्माश्रितः -ता -तं, आत्मसंश्रितः &c., स्वतन्त्रः -न्त्रा -न्त्रं, आत्मतन्त्रः &c.

SELF-DESTRUCTION, *s.* आत्मनाशः, आत्मघातः, आत्महननं, आत्महत्या, आत्मव्यापादनं, स्वनाशः, स्वघातः.

SELF-DEVISED, *a.* आत्मकल्पितः -ता -तं, आत्मघटितः &c., स्वयोजितः -ता -तं.

SELF-DEVOTION, *s.* आत्मसमर्पणं, आत्मार्पणं, स्वदेहविनियोगः.

SELF-DISPARAGEMENT, *s.* निर्वेदः, निर्विण्णता, आत्मावमानं, आत्मावज्ञा -ज्ञानं.

SELF-EDUCATED, *a.* आत्मशिक्षितः -ता -तं, स्वशिक्षितः &c., आत्माध्यापितः &c.

SELF-ENJOYMENT, *s.* आत्मसुखं, आत्मसौख्यं, आत्मसन्तोषः, स्वतःसुखं.

SELF-ESTEEM, *s.* अहम्मानं, अहम्मतिः *f.*, आत्ममानं, आत्मसम्मानं, अहङ्कारः.

SELF-EVIDENT, *a.* स्वतःप्रमाणः -णा -णं, स्वतःस्पष्टः -ष्टा -ष्टं, स्वतःसिद्धः -द्धा -द्धं, स्वतःप्रकाशः -शा -शं, स्वतःप्रत्यक्षः -क्षा -क्षं, प्रत्यक्षः &c.

SELF-EXAMINATION, *s.* आत्मपरीक्षा -क्षणं, आत्मविचारः -रणं -णा, आत्मपृच्छा -च्छनं, आत्मजिज्ञासा, आत्मविभावनं.

SELF-EXISTENCE, *s.* स्वयम्भवः, स्वयम्भावः, स्वयंवृत्तिः *f.*, स्वत्वं.

SELF-EXISTENT, *a.* स्वयम्भूः -म्भूः -म्भु, आत्मभूः -भूः -भु, आत्महेतुः -तुः -तु, आत्ममूलः -ला -लं, स्वतःसिद्धः -द्धा -द्धं, अकृत्रिमः -मा -मं.

SELF-GAINED, SELF-GOTTEN, *a.* आत्मोपार्जितः -ता -तं, स्वोपार्जितः &c., आत्मार्जितः &c., स्वहस्तार्जितः &c., स्वभुजोपार्जितः &c., स्वसम्पादितः &c.

SELF-GOVERNMENT, *s.* आत्मशासनं, आत्मशास्तिः *f.*, स्वशासनं, आत्मनियमनं.

SELF-IGNORANCE, *s.* आत्माज्ञानं, आत्माबोधः, आत्माज्ञता, स्वाज्ञानं.

SELF-IMMOLATION, *s.* आत्मघातः, आत्महननं, आत्मोत्सर्गः; 'of a widow after her husband,' अनुगमनं, अग्निप्रवेशः.

SELF-INTEREST, *s.* आत्महितं, स्वहितं, स्वार्थः, *see* SELF-ADVANTAGE.

SELF-INTERESTED, *a.* स्वार्थबुद्धिः -द्धिः -द्धि, स्वार्थी -र्थिनी -र्थि (न्), स्वार्थार्थी &c., स्वार्थनिष्ठः -ष्ठा -ष्ठं, स्वार्थपरः -रा -रं. *See* under INTERESTED.

SELF-INVITED, *a.* आत्माहूतः -ता -तं, आत्मनिमन्त्रितः &c., स्वाहूतः &c.

SELF-KNOWING, *a.* आत्मज्ञः -ज्ञा -ज्ञं, आत्मज्ञानी -निनी -नि (न्), आत्मतत्त्वज्ञः &c.

SELF-KNOWLEDGE, *s.* आत्मज्ञानं, आत्मविद्या, आत्मबोधः, आत्मबुद्धिः *f.*, आत्मवेदनं, आत्मदर्शनं, आत्मतत्त्वज्ञानं, आत्मानुभवः.

SELF-LOVE, *s.* आत्मानुरागः, कामात्मता, आत्मकामः, आत्मस्नेहः, ममता, अहम्मानं, अहम्मतिः *f.*, आत्ममानं, आत्मसम्मानं.

SELF-MOVED, *a.* स्ववहितः -ता -तं, आत्मवहितः &c., स्वयंवहः -हा -हं, स्वचोदितः -ता -तं, आत्मचोदितः &c., अनन्यचोदितः &c., स्वैरी -रिणी -रि (न्).

SELF-MURDER, *s.* आत्मघातः, आत्महत्या, आत्मवधः. *See* SUICIDE.

SELF-MURDERER, *s.* आत्मघातकः, आत्मघाती *m.*, आत्महा *m.* *See* SUICIDE.

SELF-OPINIONATED, *a.* स्वमताग्रही &c., स्वमताभिमानी &c. *See* OPINIATED.

SELF-POSSESSED, *a.* आत्मवान् -वती -वत् (त्), धृतात्मा -त्मा -त्म (न्), स्थिरात्मा &c., स्वस्थः -स्था -स्थं, स्वस्थचित्तः -त्ता -त्तं, आत्मस्थः &c., आत्मनिष्ठः -ष्ठा -ष्ठं, सत्त्वशाली -लिनी -लि (न्), अव्यग्रः -ग्रा -ग्रं, अव्यग्रचित्तः -त्ता -त्तं. *See* COLLECTED.

SELF-POSSESSION, *s.* आत्मनिष्ठा, स्वस्थता, स्वनिष्ठा, स्वास्थ्यं, चित्तस्वास्थ्यं, धृतिः *f.*, धृतात्मता, स्थिरात्मता, सत्त्वं, चित्तसत्त्वं, अव्यग्रता. *See* PRESENCE OF MIND.

SELF-PRAISE, *s.* आत्मप्रशंसा, आत्मस्तुतिः *f.*, आत्मश्लाघा.

SELF-PRESERVATION, *s.* आत्मरक्षा -क्षणं, आत्मत्राणं, आत्मपरित्राणं, स्वत्राणं.

SELF-PRESERVING, *a.* आत्मरक्षकः -का -कं, स्वरक्षः -क्षा -क्षं, आत्मरक्षः -क्षा -क्षं.

SELF-PRODUCED, *a.* आत्मोद्भवः -वा -वं, आत्मसम्भवः &c., आत्मभूतः -ता -तं.

SELF-RELIANCE, *s.* आत्मनिष्ठा, आत्माश्रयः, आत्मविश्वासः, स्वमतनिष्ठा.

SELF-RESPECT, *s.* आत्ममानं -निता, आत्मसम्मानं, अहम्मानं.

SELF-RESTRAINED, *a.* आत्मसंयतः -ता -तं, आत्मनियन्त्रितः &c., आत्मनियमितः &c.

SELF-RESTRAINT, *s.* आत्मसंयमः, आत्मनिग्रहः, आत्मयमनं, आत्मनियमनं, आत्मनिरोधः, अन्तर्यमनं, आत्मवशः, यमः, संयमः, यतिः *f.*, नियतिः *f.*, दमः, दान्तिः *f.*

SELF-RIGHTEOUS, *a.* साधुम्मन्यः -न्या -न्यं, धर्म्माभिमानी -मिनी -नि (न्).

SELF-RIGHTEOUSNESS, *s.* साधुम्मन्यता, धर्म्माभिमानं, मिथ्याधर्म्मित्वं.

SELF-SAME, *a.* समसमानः -ना -नं, अनन्यः &c. *See* SAME, IDENTICAL.

SELF-SATISFIED, *a.* आत्मसन्तुष्टः -ष्टा -ष्टं, आत्मतुष्टः &c., स्वसन्तुष्टः &c., स्वलाभपूर्णः -र्णा -र्णं, निजलाभपूर्णः &c., कृतकृत्यः -त्या -त्यं, कृतार्थः -र्था -र्थं.

SELF-SUFFICIENCY, *s.* स्वस्थता, स्वास्थ्यं, आत्मनिष्ठा, स्वाभिमानं, स्वनिष्ठता.

SELF-SUFFICIENT, *a.* स्वस्थः -स्था -स्थं, स्वनिष्ठः -ष्ठा -ष्ठं, स्वाभिमानी -निनी &c.

SELF-TORMENT, *s.* आत्मद्रोहः, आत्मविडम्बना, आत्मसन्तापः, आत्मवैक्लव्यं.

SELF-TORMENTING, SELF-TORMENTOR, *a.* or *s.* आत्मद्रोही -हिणी -हि (न्), आत्मविडम्बनाकारी -रिणी &c., आत्मविडम्बनाकर्त्ता -र्त्री -र्तृ (र्तृ), आत्मसन्तापकः -का -कं.

SELF-WILL, *s.* स्वेच्छा, स्वैरिता, स्वैरता, स्वाच्छन्द्यं, स्वच्छन्दता, स्वातन्त्र्यं.

SELF-WILLED, *a.* स्वैरी -रिणी -रि (न्), स्वैरः -री -रं, स्वच्छन्दः -न्दा -न्दं, स्वेच्छाचारी -रिणी &c., कामचारी &c., कामचारः -री -रं, स्वैरगतिः -तिः -ति, स्वरुचिः -चिः -चि, स्वतन्त्रः -न्त्रा -न्त्रं, यथेष्टचारी &c.

SELFISH, *a.* स्वार्थपरः -रा -रं, स्वार्थदृष्टिः -ष्टिः -ष्टि, स्वार्थबुद्धिः -द्धिः -द्धि, स्वार्थनिष्ठः -ष्ठा -ष्ठं, स्वार्थपरायणः -णा -णं, स्वार्थलिप्सुः -प्सुः -प्सु, स्वार्थी -र्थिनी -र्थि (न्), स्वार्थार्थी &c., स्वहितैषी -षिणी &c., स्वहितपरः -रा -रं, स्वहितपरायणः -णा -णं, स्वहितदृष्टिः -ष्टिः -ष्टि, स्वार्थलोभी &c., स्वलाभपरः -रा -रं, स्वलाभपरायणः -णा -णं, स्वलाभनिष्ठः -ष्ठा -ष्ठं, स्वलाभदृष्टिः &c., अर्थबुद्धिः &c., आत्मबुद्धिः &c., ममतायुक्तः -क्ता -क्तं, मामकः -की -कं, आत्मग्राही -हिणी &c., आत्मम्भरिः -रिः -रि, अहंक्रियावान् -वती -वत् (त्), केवलः -ला -लं.

SELFISHLY, *adv.* स्वार्थबुद्ध्या, स्वार्थलिप्सया, स्वहितैषया, स्वार्थपरत्वात्, स्वहितपरत्वात्, स्वार्थतस्, अर्थतस्.

SELFISHNESS, *s.* स्वार्थदृष्टिः *f.*, स्वार्थपरता, स्वार्थनिष्ठा, स्वार्थलिप्सा, स्वलाभनिष्ठा, स्वार्थबुद्धिः *f.*, स्वहितनिष्ठा, स्वहितपरता, ममता -त्वं, अहंक्रिया.

To SELL, *v. a.* विक्री (c. 9. -क्रीणाति -णीते -क्रेतुं), विक्रयं कृ, विक्रयणं कृ, विक्रीणानं कृ, पण् (c. 1. पणते -णितुं, पणायति, c. 10. पणयति -यितुं).

To SELL, *v. n.* (Be sold) विक्री in pass. (-क्रीयते); 'it sells at a low price,' अल्पमूल्येन विक्रीयते.

SELLER, *s.* विक्रेता *m.* (तृ), विक्रयी *m.* (न्), विक्रयिकः, विक्रयकारी *m.* (न्), विक्रयकर्त्ता *m.* (र्तृ), पणायिता *m.*; 'buyer and seller,' क्रयविक्रयिकः.

SELLING, *s.* विक्रयः, विक्रयणं, विक्रीणनं, पणनं.

SELVAGE, SELVEDGE, *s.* पटप्रान्तः, वस्त्रप्रान्तः, वस्तिः *m.*, तरी, दशा.

SEMBLANCE, *s.* (Likeness) आभासः -सता -सत्वं, सादृश्यं, सदृशता, औपम्यं, उपमा, प्रतिमा, प्रतिमानं, आभा.—(Form, appearance) आकारः, रूपं, मूर्त्तिः *f.*, विग्रहः.

SEMEN, *s.* शुक्रं, रेतस् *n.*, धातुः *m.*, तेजस् *n.*, बीजं, वीर्य्यं, इन्द्रियं, रेतनं, रेतं, धातुराजकः, हीलं, आनन्दप्रभवः.

SEMI. This prefix may usually be expressed by अर्द्ध, *see* HALF.

SEMI-BREVE, *s.* (In music) दीर्घस्वरः.

SEMICIRCLE, *s.* अर्द्धमण्डलं, अर्द्धवृत्तं, वृत्तार्द्धं, मण्डलार्द्धं, अर्द्धचन्द्रः, चन्द्रार्द्धं; 'used as an hieroglyphick,' नादः.

SEMICIRCULAR, *a.* अर्द्धमण्डलाकारः -रा -रं, अर्द्धवृत्ताकारः &c., अर्द्धवृत्ताकृतिः -तिः -ति, अर्द्धचन्द्राकारः -रा -रं, अर्द्धचन्द्राकृतिः -तिः -ति.

SEMI-DIAMETER, *s.* अर्द्धव्यासः, व्यासार्द्धं, अर्द्धविष्कम्भः.

SEMI-LUNAR, *a.* अर्द्धचन्द्राकारः -रा -रं, अर्द्धचन्द्राकृतिः -तिः -ति.

SEMI-METAL, *s.* उपधातुः *m.*, अर्द्धधातुः *m.*

SEMINAL, *a.* बैजिकः -की -कं, बीज्यः -ज्या -ज्यं, बीजसम्बन्धी -न्धिनी -न्धि (न्), बीजविषयकः -का -कं; 'seminal fluid,' रेतस् *n.*, शुक्रं, *see* SEMEN; 'seminal effusion,' रेतःपातः, सेकः.

SEMINARY, *s.* (Ground where seed is sown) बीजारोपस्थलं -ली, बीजारोहस्थलं.—(Place of education) शिक्षास्थानं, शिक्षालयः, विद्याभ्यासस्थानं.

SEMITONE, *s.* (In music) स्वरांशः, मूर्च्छनं -ना.

SEMIVOWEL, *s.* अन्तस्थः, अर्द्धस्वरः, अर्द्धव्यञ्जनं.

SEMPITERNAL, *a.* नित्यः -त्या -त्यं, नित्यस्थायी -यिनी -यि (न्). *See* ETERNAL.

SEMPSTRESS, *s.* सूचिका, सूचीशिल्पोपजीविनी, सूचिकर्म्मोपजीविनी.

SENATE, *s.* वृद्धसभा, राजमन्त्रिसभा, वृद्धसंघः, वृद्धसदस् *n.*, राजामात्यसभा, श्रेष्ठसभा, शिष्टसभा, महासभा, प्रधानसभा, महासमाजः.

SENATE-HOUSE, *s.* महासभास्थानं, प्रधानसभास्थानं, वृद्धसभास्थानं.

SENATOR, *s.* वृद्धसभासद् *m.*, प्रधानसभासद्, महासभाभ्यन्तरः.

SENATORIAL, *a.* वृद्धसभासम्बन्धी -न्धिनी -न्धि (न्), महासभासम्बन्धी &c.

To SEND, *v. a.* प्रेर् (c. 10. प्रेरयति -यितुं, rt. ईर्), प्रेष् (c. 10. प्रेषयति -यितुं, rt. इष्), सम्प्रेष्, अनुप्रेष्, परिप्रेष्, प्रहि (c. 5. -हिणोति -हेतुं), प्राप् in caus. (प्रापयति -यितुं, rt. आप्) संचर् (c. 10. -चारयति -यितुं), नुद् (c. 6. नुदति, नोत्तुं), प्रतिपद् (c. 10. -पादयति -यितुं), प्रयुज् (c. 10. -योजयति -यितुं) all with 2. acc.; as, 'he sent them to the city,' तान् नगरीं प्रेरयामास; 'I will send a letter to the king,' लेखं राज्ञो हस्तं प्रापयिष्यामि; or with acc. and dat., as, 'he sent a weapon to the king,' अस्त्रं राज्ञे प्राहिणोत्.—(Send away, despatch) प्रस्था in caus. (-स्थापयति -यितुं), अपसृ in caus. (-सारयति -यितुं), प्रया in caus. (-यापयति -यितुं), विसृज्, प्रणुद्, अपास्, सम्प्रेष्, *see* DISMISS.—(Send before or in advance) अग्रे प्रस्था in caus. or प्रया in caus., पुरस्कृ.—(Send for, summon, request or cause to be brought) आह्वे (c. 1. -ह्वयति -ह्वातुं), आनी in caus. (-नाययति -यितुं), उपानी in caus., आगम् in caus., आहृ in caus.; 'he sent for them from the village,' तान् ग्रामाद् आनाययामास or आहूतवान्.—(Send forth, emit, produce) विसृज्, निःसृ in caus., उदीर्, समुदीर्, निरस्, उत्क्षिप्, उत्पद् in caus.—(Cause to fall, as a missile, &c.) पत् in caus., क्षिप्, प्रक्षिप्.

SENDER, *s.* प्रेरकः, प्रेरयिता *m.* (तृ), प्रेषकः, सम्प्रेषकः, प्रेषयिता *m.*, प्रेरणकृत्, प्रेरणकर्त्ता *m.*, प्रयोजकः.

SENDING, *s.* प्रेरणं -णा, प्रेषणं, प्रेषः, प्रस्थापनं, प्रयापणं, क्षेपणं.

SENILE, *a.* वृद्धतासम्बन्धी -न्धिनी -न्धि (न्), वार्धक्यसम्बन्धी &c.

SENILITY, *s.* वृद्धता -त्वं, वार्धक्यं, वृद्धावस्था, वृद्धभावः. *See* OLD AGE.

SENIOR, *a.* ज्येष्ठः -ष्ठा -ष्ठं, वयोज्येष्ठः &c., कालज्येष्ठः &c., ज्यायान् -यसी -यः (स्), अग्रजः -जा -जं, वरीयान् &c., वरिष्ठः &c., श्रेष्ठः &c., *see* ELDER; 'senior in office,' अधिकारज्येष्ठः -ष्ठा -ष्ठं.

SENIOR, *s.* (One who is older) ज्येष्ठः, वयोज्येष्ठः, *see* the last.—(Elderly person) गुरुजनः, वृद्धजनः, आर्य्यजनः.

SENIORITY, *s.* ज्येष्ठता -त्वं, ज्यैष्ठ्यं, वयोज्येष्ठता, वयोज्यैष्ठ्यं, कालज्येष्ठता, कालज्यैष्ठ्यं, अधिकवयस्कता; 'in office,' अधिकारज्येष्ठता, अधिकारज्यैष्ठ्यं; 'according to seniority,' अनुज्येष्ठं.

SENNIGHT, *s.* (Week) सप्ताहं, सप्तरात्रं, *see* WEEK.

SENSATION, *s.* (Feeling) वेदनं -ना, संवेदः, चेतना, चैतन्यं, चित् *f.*, इन्द्रियज्ञानं, इन्द्रियबोधः, इन्द्रियग्रहः -हणं.—(State of excited interest) लोकानुरागः, जनानुरागः.

SENSE, *s.* (Organ of perception or sense) इन्द्रियं, ज्ञानेन्द्रियं, ज्ञानसाधनं, इन्द्रियबुद्धिः *f.*, इन्द्रियज्ञानं, करणं, हृषीकं, अक्षं, अध्यात्म *n.* (न्), विषयि *n.* (न्); 'the five senses or organs collectively,' पञ्चेन्द्रियं, इन्द्रियग्रामः, इन्द्रियवर्गः, इन्द्रियगणः, श्रोत्रादि *n.* These are the eye चक्षुस्, the ear श्रोत्रं, the nose घ्राणं, the tongue जिह्वा, the skin त्वक्, and are called ज्ञानेन्द्रियाणि to distinguish them from the five कर्म्मेन्द्रियाणि or organs of action; *see* ORGAN. To these ten an eleventh, the mind मनस्, is sometimes added. 'Subjugation or restraint of the senses,' इन्द्रियजयः, इन्द्रियदमनं, इन्द्रियनिग्रहः, इन्द्रिययमनं, इन्द्रियनियमनं; 'one who has subdued his senses,' जितेन्द्रियः -या -यं, यतेन्द्रियः &c., यती *m.* (न्); 'perceptible by the senses,' इन्द्रियग्राह्यः -ह्या -ह्यं, इन्द्रियगोचरः -रा -रं; 'by two senses,' द्वीन्द्रियग्राह्यः &c.; 'evident to the senses,' प्रत्यक्षः -क्षा -क्षं, प्रत्यक्षसिद्धः -द्धा -द्धं; 'deadness of the senses,' इन्द्रियस्वापः; 'pleasure of sense,' इन्द्रियसुखं, विषयसुखं; 'perversion of the senses,' इन्द्रियविप्रतिपत्तिः *f.*; 'disorder of them,' इन्द्रियवैकल्यं; 'acuteness of them,' इन्द्रियपाटवं; 'wanting a sense,' विकलेन्द्रियः -या -यं, निरिन्द्रियः &c.—(Object of sense) विषयः, इन्द्रियविषयः, इन्द्रियार्थः, अर्थः, गोचरः. These are five, corresponding to the five senses or organs of perception, viz. 'form' रूपं, 'sound' शब्दः, 'odour' गन्धः, 'flavour' रसः, 'touch' स्पर्शः.—(Perception by the senses, sensation) वेदनं -ना, संवेदः -दनं, बोधः -धनं, इन्द्रियज्ञानं, इन्द्रियबोधः -धनं, इन्द्रियग्रहः -हणं, ग्रहणं, चेतना.—(Perception by the mind, &c.) बोधः, वेदनं, ज्ञानं, अनुबोधः, उपलब्धिः *f.*, ग्रहः -हणं, *see* PERCEPTION.—(Understanding) बुद्धिः *f.*, मतिः *f.*, धीः *f.*, मेधा, चित्.—(Consciousness) चैतन्यं, चेतना, वेदनं, ज्ञानं, संज्ञा; 'internal sense,' अन्तश्चैतन्यं, अन्तःसंज्ञा; 'sense of pleasure,' सुखवेदनं, सुखानुभवः, सुखबोधः; 'to recover one's senses,' संज्ञां or चैतन्यं लभ्; 'one who has done so,' लब्धसंज्ञः -ज्ञा -ज्ञं, लब्धचैतन्यः -न्या -न्यं, लब्धचेताः -ताः -तः (स्); 'to lose one's senses, be out of one's senses,' बुद्धिभ्रष्टः -ष्टा -ष्टं भू, नष्टबुद्धिः -द्धिः -द्धि भू, हतबुद्धिः -द्धिः -द्धि भू, नष्टज्ञानः -ना -नं भू, हतज्ञानः -ना -नं भू, नष्टेन्द्रियः -या

-र्थे भू.—(Opinion) मतं, मतिः *f.*, बुद्धिः *f.*—(Meaning) अर्थः, अभिप्रायः, आकांक्षा, आशयः, उद्देशः, विवक्षितं, विवक्षा, विषयः, छन्दस्; 'sense of words,' शब्दानुशासनं, पदार्थः, भावार्थः, शक्तिः *f.*, विग्रहः; 'second sense,' अर्थान्तरं; 'tenor of the sense,' अर्थानुसन्धानं; 'according to the sense,' अर्थतस्; 'apprehension of the literal sense,' शाब्दबोधः.—(Common sense) सामान्यबुद्धिः *f.*, साधारणबुद्धिः *f.*, साधारणधीः *f.*—(Good sense) सद्बुद्धिः *f.*, सुसङ्गतं, सुसङ्गतवाक्यं, सुबुद्धिः *f.*, सुधीः *f.*, *see* INTELLIGENCE.

SENSELESS, *a.* (Wanting the faculty of perception) अचेतनः -ना -नं, चैतन्यहीनः -ना -नं, विषयग्रहणाशक्तः -क्ता -क्तं, विषयग्रहणाक्षमः -मा -मं, इन्द्रियविषयाग्राही -हिणी -हि (न्), इन्द्रियार्थाग्राही &c.—(Without feeling or consciousness) अचेतनः -ना -नं, विचेतनः &c., चैतन्यहीनः -ना -नं, विसंज्ञः -ज्ञा -ज्ञं, निःसंज्ञः &c., संज्ञाहीनः -ना -नं, नष्टचेतनः -ना -नं, गतचेतनः &c., गतचेताः -ताः -तः (स्), नष्टचेताः &c., नष्टचेष्टः -ष्टा -ष्टं, सुप्तः -प्ता -प्तं, सुप्तबुद्धिः -द्धिः -द्धि.—(Foolish, said of persons) निर्बुद्धिः -द्धिः -द्धि, निर्बोधः -धा -धं, अबुद्धिमान् -मती -मत् (त्), मतिहीनः -ना -नं, अबुधः -धा -धं, अविज्ञः -ज्ञा -ज्ञं, मूढः -ढा -ढं, मुग्धः -ग्धा -ग्धं, प्रमुग्धः &c.—(Unreasonable, said of things) अयुक्तः -क्ता -क्तं, अयुक्तिकः -का -कं, असमञ्जसः -सा -सं, अनुपपन्नः -न्ना -न्नं.—(Unmeaning) अनर्थकः -का -कं, निरर्थकः &c., असङ्गतः -ङ्गा -ङ्गं, अबद्धः &c.

SENSELESSLY, *adv.* अज्ञवत्, अविज्ञवत्, मूर्खवत्, अल्पबुद्ध्या, असङ्गतं.

SENSELESSNESS, *s.* निर्बुद्धित्वं, अज्ञता, अविज्ञता, बुद्धिहीनता, अयुक्तता.

SENSIBILITY, *s.* (Capability of receiving impressions) विषयग्रहणशक्तिः *f.*, विषयग्रहणक्षमता, इन्द्रियविषयग्रहणं, इन्द्रियार्थग्रहणं.—(Acuteness of sensation) शीघ्रग्राहकत्वं, सूक्ष्मग्राहकता, शीघ्रचैतन्यं, शीघ्रचेतनत्वं, सूक्ष्मचैतन्यं, चैतन्यसूक्ष्मता, चलेन्द्रियत्वं, सूक्ष्मेन्द्रियत्वं, *see* SENSITIVENESS.—(Sensation, feeling) चेतना, चैतन्यं, वेदनं -ना, संवेदः, बोधः, ज्ञानं, चित् *f.*, चिच्छक्तिः *f.*—(Consciousness) चैतन्यं, संज्ञा, ससंज्ञता.

SENSIBLE, *a.* (Capable of receiving impressions) विषयग्रहणशक्तः -क्ता -क्तं, विषयग्रहणक्षमः -मा -मं, विषयग्राही -हिणी -हि (न्), इन्द्रियार्थग्राही &c.—(Perceptible by the senses) इन्द्रियज्ञेयः -या -यं, इन्द्रियगोचरः -रा -रं, इन्द्रियवेद्यः -द्या -द्यं, इन्द्रियगम्यः -म्या -म्यं, ऐन्द्रियकः -की -कं, प्रत्यक्षः -क्षा -क्षं, *see* PERCEPTIBLE.—(Having perception of, conscious of) ग्राहकः -का -कं, ग्राही -हिणी &c., वेदनक्षमः -मा -मं, ग्रहणक्षमः -मा -मं, ग्रहणशक्तः -क्ता -क्तं, चेतनः -ना -नं, सचेतनः &c., चेतनावान् -वती -वत् (त्), प्रज्ञानन् -नती -नत् (त्), चेतयमानः -ना.-नं.—(Possessing consciousness) सचेतनः -ना -नं, सचैतन्यः -न्या -न्यं, चैतन्यवान् &c., संज्ञावान् &c., ससंज्ञः -ज्ञा -ज्ञं, लब्धसंज्ञः &c., प्राप्तसंज्ञः &c., प्राप्तचैतन्यः &c., लब्धचैतन्यः &c., आपन्नचेतनः -ना -नं, प्रतिपन्नचेतनः &c., प्राप्तबोधः -धा -धं, लब्धबोधः &c., सज्ञानः -ना -नं, लब्धज्ञानः &c.—(Having acute feeling) शीघ्रग्राहकः -का -कं, शीघ्रचेतनः -ना -नं, सहृदयः -या -यं, अभिज्ञ or ज्ञ in comp.; as, 'sensible of kindness,' उपकाराभिज्ञः -ज्ञा -ज्ञं, उपकारज्ञः &c., *see* SENSITIVE.—(Intelligent, having good sense, said of persons) बुद्धिमान् -मती -मत्, मतिमान् &c., धीमान् &c., मनस्वी -स्विनी &c., विचक्षणः -णा -णं, प्राज्ञः -ज्ञा -ज्ञं, प्रज्ञः &c., ज्ञानी &c., ज्ञानशाली &c., सुधीः -धीः -धि, सुमेधाः -धाः -धः (स्), प्रमानन् &c.; 'a sensible man,' सुधीः *m.*, बुद्धिमान्, बुधजनः; 'a sensible woman,' मनस्विनी, प्रज्ञानवती.—(Reasonable, said of things) युक्तः -क्ता -क्तं, सुयुक्तः &c., सयुक्तिकः -का -कं, उपपन्नः -न्ना -न्नं, सङ्गतः -ता -तं, समञ्जसः -सा -सं.

SENSIBLY, *adv.* (Perceptibly) प्रत्यक्षतस्.—(With good sense) सुबुद्ध्या, विचक्षणवत्, प्राज्ञवत्, सुबुद्धिपूर्वं, विज्ञवत्.

SENSITIVE, *a.* (Capable of perceiving, having sense) चेतनः -ना -नं, चेतकः -का -की -कं, सचेतनः -ना -नं, चेतनावान् -वती -वत् (त्), इन्द्रियविशिष्टः -ष्टा -ष्टं, ज्ञानेन्द्रियविशिष्टः &c., इन्द्रिययुक्तः -क्ता -क्तं, विषयग्रहणशक्तः -क्ता -क्तं, विषयग्रहणक्षमः -मा -मं, विषयग्राही -हिणी &c.—(Having quick or acute sensibility) शीघ्रग्राहकः -का -कं, शीघ्रचेतनः -ना -नं, शीघ्रचैतन्यवान् &c., सूक्ष्मचेतनः &c., सूक्ष्मग्राहकः -का -कं, सूक्ष्मचैतन्यवान् &c., चलेन्द्रियः -या -यं, सूक्ष्मेन्द्रियः &c., सेन्द्रियः &c., सहृदयः -या -यं, हृदयवान् -वती -वत् (त्), कोमलहृदयः &c., करुणार्द्रः -र्द्रा -र्द्रं, सत्त्वः -त्त्वा -त्त्वी -त्त्वं.—(Of shame) लज्जावान् &c., लज्जालुः -लुः -लु, *see* MODEST.—(Having taste) रसास्वादी &c.—(Pertaining to the senses) इन्द्रियसम्बन्धी &c., इन्द्रियविषयकः -का -कं.

SENSITIVELY, *adv.* शीघ्रचेतनवत्, सूक्ष्मचैतन्येन, सूक्ष्मेन्द्रियत्वात्, चलेन्द्रियत्वात्.

SENSITIVENESS, *s.* इन्द्रियसूक्ष्मता, सूक्ष्मेन्द्रियत्वं, चैतन्यसूक्ष्मता, सूक्ष्मचैतन्यं, शीघ्रचेतनत्वं, शीघ्रचैतन्यं, शीघ्रग्राहकता, करुणार्द्रता. *See* SENSIBILITY.

SENSITIVE-PLANT, *s.* स्पर्शलज्जा, लज्जालुः *m.*, लज्जाकारिका, लज्जकारिका, महाभीता, गण्डकारी, गण्डकाली, नमस्कारी, समङ्गा, खदिरी, रक्तपर्णी, सुवहा, युक्तरसा, राज्ञा.

SENSORIUM, *s.* चेतनाशयः, चेतनास्पदं, चैतन्यास्पदं, ज्ञानाशयः.

SENSUAL, *a.* (Devoted to the gratification of the senses) विषयासक्तः -क्ता -क्तं, विषयपरः -रा -रं, विषयपरायणः -णा -णं, विषयप्रवणः -णा -णं, विषयी -यिणी -यि (न्), वैषयिकः -की -कं, विषयसेवी -विनी &c., विषयोपसेवी &c., विषयरतः -ता -तं, विषयाधीनः -ना -नं, विषयवशः -शा -शं, विषयाभिमुखः -खा -खं, विषयतत्परः -रा -रं, विषयलुब्धः -ब्धा -ब्धं, विषयसुखसेवी &c., विषयसुखासक्तः &c., विषयोपभोगव्यग्रः -ग्रा -ग्रं, शिश्नोदरपरायणः -णा -णं, वनितोपभोगतत्परः &c., सम्भोगी &c., भोगासक्तः &c., कामासक्तः &c., इन्द्रियसुखासक्तः &c., इन्द्रियसुखसेवी &c., इन्द्रियाधीनः -ना -नं, इन्द्रियवशः -शा -शं, देहम्भरः -री -रं, दुष्टभावः -वा -वं, विप्रदुष्टभावः &c.—(Pertaining to the senses) वैषयिकः -की -कं, विषयसम्बन्धी &c., ऐन्द्रियकः -की -कं.

SENSUALIST, *s.* विषयी *m.* (न्), विषयासक्तः, विषयसेवी *m.*, विषयायी *m.* (न्), भोगासक्तः, इन्द्रियाधीनः, केलिनागरः. *See* the last.

SENSUALITY, SENSUALNESS, *s.* विषयासक्तिः *f.*, विषयासक्तता, विषयसेवा, विषयोपसेवा, विषयसुखासक्तिः *f.*, इन्द्रियसुखासक्तिः *f.*, इन्द्रियाधीनता, विषयाधीनता, विषयवशता, विषयसङ्गः, विषयव्यासङ्गः, विषयपरता, शारीरिकसुखासक्तिः *f.*, शारीरिकसुखसेवा, शारीरिकविषयानुरागः, भोगासक्तिः *f.*, कामासक्तिः *f.*, वनितोपभोगः.

SENT, *p.p.* प्रेरितः -ता -तं, प्रेषितः -ता -तं, सम्प्रेषितः &c., अनुप्रेषितः &c., प्रहितः -ता -तं, ईरितः &c., गमितः &c., नुन्नः -न्ना -न्नं, नुत्तः -त्ता -त्तं.—(Sent away, despatched) प्रस्थापितः -ता -तं, प्रयापितः &c., सम्प्रेषितः &c., दूतः -ता -तं, प्रणुन्नः -न्ना -न्नं.—(Sent for) आहूतः -ता -तं; 'having sent for,' आनाय्य.

SENTENCE, *s.* (Judgment pronounced, judicial decision) निर्णयपादः, निर्णयः, दण्डनिर्णयः, दण्डकथनं, दण्डाज्ञा, दण्डाभिधानं, दण्डनियोगः, दण्डकल्पनं, दण्डनिवेदनं, दण्डस्थापनं, आधर्षणं, विचारः, तीरितं; 'of death,' प्राणदण्डाज्ञा, प्राणदण्डनिर्णयः, वधदण्डाज्ञा.—(Determination, decision) निश्चयः, निश्चितं, निर्णयः, विचारः, संकल्पः, नि-

आप्तिः *f.*, निर्धारणं.—(Opinion) मतं, मतिः *f.*, बुद्धिः *f.*, बोधः, संकल्पः, निवेदनं.—(Paragraph, period) वाक्यं, वचनं, उक्तं, पाद्धिका, पदं, वाक्यखण्डः, वाक्यपरिच्छेदः, वक्तव्यं; 'a complete sentence,' निरूढः; 'construction of sentences,' वाक्यरचना, वाक्ययोजना; 'rule of constructing sentences,' वाक्यपद्धतिः *f.*—(Maxim) सूत्रं.

To SENTENCE, *v. a.* निर्णयं कृ, दण्डनिर्णयं कृ, दण्डाज्ञां कृ, दण्डकथनं कृ, दण्डनिवेदनं कृ, दण्डाभिधानं कृ, अपराधकथनपूर्व्वं दण्डाभिधानं कृ, दण्डं निर्णी (c. 1. -णयति -णेतुं) or प्रणी; 'to death,' वधदण्डाज्ञां कृ.

SENTENCED, *p. p.* निर्णीतः -ता -तं, निर्णीतदण्डः -ण्डा -ण्डं, प्रणीतः -ता -तं, प्रणीतदण्डः &c., निश्चितः -ता -तं, तीरितः &c., आधर्षितः &c.

SENTENTIOUS, *a.* (Abounding with sentences or maxims) सूत्रमयः -यी -यं, सूत्रप्रायः -या -यं, वाक्यमयः -यी -यं.—(Using short sentences) सूत्रभाषी -षिणी -षि (न्), सूत्रप्रायभाषी &c.

SENTENTIOUSLY, *adv.* सूत्रसादृश्येन, सूत्रतस्, सूत्रवत्.

SENTENTIOUSNESS, *s.* सूत्रभाषणं, सूत्रप्रायभाषणं, सूत्रसादृश्यं.

SENTIENT, *a.* चेतनः -ना -नं, सचेतनः -ना -नं, चेतनावान् -वती -वत् (त्), चैतन्यवान् &c., चैतन्ययुक्तः -क्ता -क्तं, चैतन्यविशिष्टः -ष्टा -ष्टं, चेतकः -का -कं, चेतयमानः -ना -नं, चेतयः -या -यं, विषयग्रहणशक्तिकः -का -कं, विषयग्रहणक्षमः -मा -मं, इन्द्रिययुक्तः -क्ता -क्तं, इन्द्रियवान् &c., इन्द्रियविशिष्टः -ष्टा -ष्टं, इन्द्रियज्ञानविशिष्टः &c., सचेष्टः -ष्टा -ष्टं; 'a sentient being,' प्राणी *m.* (न्), चेतनः, प्राणभृत् *m.*, शरीरी *m.*, देही *m.*, *see* LIVING, *part.*

SENTIMENT, *s.* (Thought, opinion, notion) मतं, मतिः *f.*, बुद्धिः *f.*, कल्पना, मनःकल्पना, बोधः, सङ्कल्पः.—(Sense contained in words) अर्थः, अभिप्रायः, *see* SENSE.—(Feeling, passion) भावः, रसः, रागः, भावः, रुचिः *f.*, *see* PASSION. Eight sentiments or rasas are usually emumerated: 1. Love, शृङ्गारः. 2. Mirth, हास्यः -स्यं. 3. Tenderness, करुणा or कारुण्यं. 4. Anger or rage, रौद्रः -द्रं or क्रोधः. 5. Heroism, वीरः -रं. 6. Terror, भयानकः -कं or भयं. 7. Disgust, बीभत्सः -त्सं. 8. Surprise, अद्भुतः -तं or विस्मयः. Sometimes a ninth is added, 'tranquillity,' शान्तः; or even a tenth, 'paternal tenderness,' वात्सल्यं.

SENTIMENTAL, *a.* (Abounding with sentiment or feeling) रसिकः -का -की -कं, रसमयः -यी -यं, सरसः -सा -सं, रसी -सिनी &c., रसवान् -वती &c., रसरूपः -पा -पं, रसात्मकः -का -कं, भाविकः -का -कं, सरागः -गा -गं, रागवान् &c., रागान्वितः -ता -तं, शृङ्गारी -रिणी &c., सरस्वान् &c.—(Affected) रसानुकारी &c., भावानुकारी &c., विलक्षः -क्षा -क्षं, सवैलक्ष्यः -क्ष्या -क्ष्यं.

SENTIMENTALITY, *s.* रसानुकारिता, भावानुकारिता, वैलक्ष्यं, रसिकत्वं.

SENTINEL, SENTRY, *s.* सेनारक्षः -क्षकः, सैनिकः, रक्षकः, रक्षी *m.* (न्), उपरक्षकः, रक्षिता *m.* (तृ), सैन्यः, उपरक्षणं, परिधिस्थः, अनीकस्थः, सन्नद्धः.

SENTRY-BOX, *s.* रक्षकगृहं, सैनिकगृहं, सैनिकाधारः.

SEPARABLE, *a.* भेद्यः -द्या -द्यं, विभेद्यः -द्या -द्यं, वियोजनीयः -या -यं.

To SEPARATE, *v. a.* वियुज् (c. 7. -युनक्ति -युंक्ते -योक्तुं, c. 10. -योजयति -यितुं), विसंयुज्, विप्रयुज्, विभिद् (c. 7. -भिनत्ति -भेत्तुं), भिद्, विश्लिष् (c. 10. -श्लेषयति -यितुं), विच्छिद् (c. 7. -छिनत्ति -छेत्तुं), विगम् in caus. (-गमयति -यितुं), पृथक् कृ, विभज्, विविच्.

To SEPARATE, *v. n.* वियुज् in pass. (-युज्यते), वियुक्तः -क्ता -क्तं भू, विभिद् in pass. (-भिद्यते), भिद्, विभिन्नः -न्ना -न्नं भू, विश्लिष् (c. 4. -श्लिष्यति -श्लेष्टुं), विच्छिद् in pass., विगम् (c. 1. -गच्छति -गन्तुं), विभक्तः -क्ता -क्तं भू.

SEPARATE, *a.* (Distinct, disconnected) विभिन्नः -न्ना -न्नं, भिन्नः &c., व्यतिरिक्तः -क्ता -क्तं, पृथक्स्थितः -ता -तं, पृथक् indec., विविक्तः -क्ता -क्तं, विसंयुक्तः &c., असम्बद्धः -द्धा -द्धं, असंस्पृष्टः -ष्टा -ष्टं, असंलग्नः -ग्ना -ग्नं, व्यस्तः -स्ता -स्तं, अव्यतिकीर्णः -र्णा -र्णं, विगतः -ता -तं, विरलः -ला -लं, प्रविरलः &c., असाधारणः -णा -णी -णं, प्रगतः &c.

SEPARATED, *p. p.* वियुक्तः -क्ता -क्तं, वियोजितः -ता -तं, विसंयुक्तः -क्ता -क्तं, विप्रयुक्तः &c., पृथक्कृतः -ता -तं, विश्लिष्टः -ष्टा -ष्टं, विश्लेषितः -ता -तं, परिच्छिन्नः -न्ना -न्नं, विच्छिन्नः &c., विभिन्नः &c., भिन्नः &c., विगतः -ता -तं, विभक्तः -क्ता -क्तं, विविक्तः &c., द्वैधीकृतः &c., व्यासक्तः &c., असंसक्तः &c., असंलग्नः -ग्ना -ग्नं, विसंलग्नः &c., विसम्बद्धः -द्धा -द्धं, सान्तरालः -ला -लं, व्यावृत्तः &c.; 'from a lover,' विधुरः -रा -रं, विरही -हिणी &c.

SEPARATELY, *adv.* पृथक्, विरलं, विभिन्नं, विभेदेन, विभागशस्.

SEPARATENESS, *s.* पृथक्त्वं, पार्थक्यं, भिन्नता, विभिन्नता, पृथग्भावः.

SEPARATER, *s.* विभेदकः, विच्छेदकः, विभेदकारी *m.* (न्), पृथक्कारी *m.*

SEPARATION, *s.* (The act) वियोगः, विप्रयोगः, वियोजनं, विभेदः -दनं, विश्लेषः -षणं, प्रविश्लेषः, विच्छेदः -दनं, पृथक्करणं, द्वैधीकरणं, परिच्छेदः, भेदः -दनं, अवच्छेदः, विभागः, प्रविभागः, विगमः, विसंयोगः, व्यासङ्गः, असन्धानं, असंयोगः, सङ्गविच्युतिः *f.*—(The state) भिन्नता, विभिन्नता, विभेदः, भेदः, वियोगः, विप्रयोगः, पृथक्त्वं, पार्थक्यं, पृथग्भावः, विश्लेषः, विश्लिष्टता, विभक्तता, विभक्तभावः, विरहः, व्यतिरेकः, व्यावृत्तिः *f.*—(Of the sexes) द्वन्द्वभेदः, द्वन्द्वभिन्नं, स्त्रीपुरुषभेदः.—(Especially of lovers) विरहः, विश्लेषः, प्रविश्लेषः, विप्रयोगः, वियोगः, विप्रलम्भः, विधुरं, विधुरता, विगमः; 'anguish of separation,' विरहज्वरः, विरहानलः; 'a woman who suffers separation from her lover,' विरहिणी, विरहोत्कण्ठिता, उत्कण्ठिता.

SEPOY, *s.* सैन्यः, सैनिकः. *See* SOLDIER.

SEPTANGULAR, *a.* सप्तकोणः -णा -णं, सप्तास्रः -स्रा -स्री -स्रं.

SEPTEMBER, *s.* भाद्रोत्तरार्द्धं, आश्विनपूर्व्वार्द्धं, भाद्रः, भाद्रपदः, प्रोष्ठपदः, नभस्यः, आश्विनः, आश्वयुजः, इषः.

SEPTENARY, *a.* सप्तसंख्यकः -का -कं, सप्तरूपः -पा -पं.

SEPTENARY, *s.* (Aggregate of seven) सप्तकं.

SEPTENNIAL, *a.* सप्तवर्षिकः -की -कं, साप्तवर्षिकः &c., साप्ताब्दिकः &c.

SEPTIC, SEPTICAL, *a.* गलनकारी -रिणी -रि (न्), विगलनकारी &c., विलयनकारी &c., विगलनकृत् *m. f. n.*, विलयनकृत् *m. f. n.*

SEPTILATERAL, *a.* सप्तपार्श्वकः -का -कं, सप्तभुजः -जा -जं, सप्तबाहुः -हुः -हु.

SEPTUAGENARIAN, *s.* सप्ततिकः -का, सप्ततिवयस्कः -स्का -स्कं.

SEPTUM, *s.* (Of the scrotum) महावीर्य्यं, विटपः, *see* SCROTUM.

SEPTUPLE, *a.* सप्तगुणः -णा -णं, सप्तविधः -धा -धं, सप्तकः -का -कं.

SEPULCHRE, SEPULCHER, *s.* समाधिः *m.*, श्मशानं, सन्धिः *m.*, शवस्थानं, शवमन्दिरं, प्रेतमन्दिरं, प्रेतस्थानं, प्रेतवासः, शववासः, मृतशरीरस्थानं, शवगर्त्तः, अवटः, एडुकं.

SEPULCHRAL, *a.* श्मशानसम्बन्धी -न्धिनी -न्धि (न्), श्माशानिकः -की -कं, श्मशान in comp., श्मशानविषयकः -का -कं; 'sepulchral blossom,' पितृवनसुमनस् *n.*

SEPULTURE, *s.* भूमिखननं, निखननं, खननं, भूमौ निखननं, श्मशाने स्थापनं, *see* BURIAL.—(Rites of sepulture) प्रेतकर्म्म *n.* (न्), अन्त्येष्टिः *f.*, मृतसत्कर्म्म *n.*, अन्त्यकर्म्म *n.* *See* FUNERAL.

SEQUEL, *s.* (That which follows, succeeding part) उत्तरभागः, उत्तरं, शेषभागः, उत्तरार्द्धं, शेषः.—(Consequence) परिणामः, अन्तः, शेषः, अन्वयः, *see* RESULT; 'in the sequel,' शेषे, अन्ते, अग्रे.

SEQUENCE, *s.* अन्वयः, समन्वयः, अनुक्रमः, आनुपूर्व्यं. *See* SUCCESSION.

To sequester, sequestrate, *v. a.* (A benefice, &c.) ऋणशोधनं यावत् धर्म्माध्यापकवृत्तिं परहस्ते सम् in caus. (-अर्पयति -यितुं) or निक्षिप् or परप्रयोजनीयां दा, ऋणापाकरणं यावत् धर्म्माध्यापकवृत्तिं पृथक्कृ or वियुज् (c. 10. -योजयति -यितुं).

Sequestered, *p. p.* (As a benefice, &c.) ऋणशोधनं यावत् परहस्तसमर्पितः -ता -तं or पृथक्कृतः &c. or वियोजितः &c.—(Retired) विविक्तः -क्ता -क्तं, *see* Secluded.

Sequestration, *s.* ऋणशोधनं यावत् परहस्तसमर्पणं or पृथक्करणं.

Seraglio, *s.* (Women's apartments) अन्तःपुरं, अवरोधः -धनं, अवरोधगृहं, अवरोधायनं, स्त्रीगृहं, शुद्धान्तः, विलासभवनं, सुविदल्लं. *see* Harem.—(Palace) राजधानी, राजभवनं, उपकारी -रिका.

Sere, *a.* शुष्कः -ष्का -ष्कं, सुशुष्कः &c., शीर्णः -र्णा -र्णं. *See* Sear.

Serenade, *s.* ज्योत्स्नीकाले or सुरात्रिकाले कामिजनकृतं प्रेमसूचकं गीतवादनं or सङ्गीतकं.

To serenade, *v. a.* or *n.* ज्योत्स्नीकाले प्रेमसूचनार्थं गीतवादनं कृ.

Serene, *a.* (Clear, as sky, &c.) प्रसन्नः -न्ना -न्नं, वितिमिरः -रा -रं, अनभ्रः -भ्रा -भ्रं, निरभ्रः &c., व्यभ्रः &c., गततोयदः -दा -दं.—(Bright) प्रसन्नः -न्ना -न्नं, स्वच्छः -च्छा -च्छं, विमलः -ला -लं, निर्म्मलः &c., अमलः &c., विशदः -दा -दं, शुद्धः -द्धा -द्धं.—(Calm, unruffled) शान्तः -न्ता -न्तं, प्रशान्तः &c., प्रसन्नः -न्ना -न्नं, स्थिरः -रा -रं, अक्षुब्धः -ब्धा -ब्धं, निर्वेगः -गा -गं, वेगहीनः -ना -नं, अनुद्विग्नः -ग्ना -ग्नं, निरुद्वेगः -गा -गं, अव्याकुलः -ला -लं, निराकुलः &c.; 'in mind,' प्रसन्नचेताः -ताः -तः (स्), शान्तचेताः &c., शान्तमनस्कः -स्का -स्कं, शान्तचित्तः -त्ता -त्तं, प्रसन्नचित्तः &c., शान्तात्मा -त्मा -त्म (न्), सुमनस्कः &c.

Serenely, *adv.* प्रसन्नं, प्रसादेन, सप्रसादं, शान्तं, शान्त्या, प्रसन्नचेतसा.

Serenity, sereneness, *s.* (Clearness) प्रसन्नता, प्रसादः, प्रसत्तिः *f.*, स्वच्छता, निर्म्मलता, विमलता, निरभ्रता.—(Calmness) शान्तिः *f.*, शान्तता, प्रसादः, प्रसन्नता, स्थिरता, स्थैर्य्यं, अक्षोभः, अक्षुब्धता, वेगहीनता, निराकुलता.—(Of mind) चित्तशान्तिः *f.*, मनःशान्तिः *f.*, चित्तप्रसादः, चित्तप्रसन्नता.

Serf, *s.* कृषिकर्म्मणि नियोजितो दासः, भूमिकर्षकदासः.

Sergeant, *s.* (Non-commissioned officer) अनधिकारवान् सैनिकाध्यक्षः.

Seriatim, *s.* क्रमशस्, अनुपूर्व्वशस्, आनुपूर्व्येण, यथाक्रमं, अनुक्रमशस्.

Series, *s.* (Continued succession or line) श्रेणी *f.*, श्रेणिः *m. f.*, श्रेधी, पंक्तिः *f.*, आवलिः -ली *f.*, माला, शृङ्खला, परम्परा; 'of causes,' कारणश्रेणी, कारणमाला; 'of inflections,' रूपावलिः -ली.—(Arithmetical) श्रेधी, अनुपातः, चयः; 'last term in the series,' अन्त्यपदं, अन्त्यधनं; 'sum of the series,' सर्व्वधनं.—(Regular succession) क्रमः, अनुक्रमः, पर्य्यायः, आनुपूर्व्यं, आनुपूर्व्वी, पारम्पर्य्यं, पाटः, परिपाटिः -टी *f.*

Serious, *a.* (Grave in manner) गम्भीरवृत्तिः -त्तिः -त्ति, गभीरवृत्तिः &c., गम्भीरस्वभावः -वा -वं, गम्भीरशीलः -ला -लं, गम्भीरमनस्कः -स्का -स्कं, गम्भीरः -रा -रं, गुरुवृत्तिः &c., गुरुस्वभावः &c., मन्दवृत्तिः &c., मन्दस्वभावः &c., धीरः -रा -रं, धीरवृत्तिः &c.—(In earnest, not jesting) अपरिहासी -सिनी -सि (न्), अविनोदी &c., विनोदरहितः -ता -तं, परिहासहीनः -ना -नं, वास्तविकः -की -कं, सद्रूपः -पा -पं.—(Important) गुरुः -र्व्वी -रु, गुर्व्वर्थः -र्था -र्थं, अलघुः -घुः -घ्वी -घु.

Seriously, *adv.* (Gravely) सगौरवं, गौरवेण, सगाम्भीर्य्यं, गम्भीरं, सधैर्य्यं, धीरं, धीरवत्, अलघु, अलाघवेन, मन्दं.—(In earnest) अपरिहासेन, अविनोदेन, अलाघवेन.

Seriousness, *s.* (Gravity of manner, &c.) गम्भीरता, गाम्भीर्य्यं, गौरवं, गुरुता, धीरता, स्वभावगाम्भीर्य्यं, स्वभावगुरुता, स्वभावमन्दता, स्वभावमान्द्यं.—(Earnestness) अपरिहासः, अविनोदः, विनोदाभावः, परिहासाभावः, वास्तविकत्वं.—(Importance) गुरुता, गौरवं, अलघुता, अलाघवं, गुर्व्वर्थत्वं.

Sermon, *s.* धर्म्मविषयवाक्यं, धर्म्मविषयभाषणं, धर्म्मोपदेशविषयवाक्यं, धर्म्मोपदेशकवाक्यं, धर्म्मोपदेशः, धर्म्मकथनं, वाक्यं.

Serous, *a.* मेदुरः -रा -रं, मेदस्वी -स्विनी -स्वि (न्), रक्तद्रवसम्बन्धी &c., धर्म्मोदकसम्बन्धी &c., धर्म्मसारसम्बन्धी &c., धर्म्माम्भोमयः -यी -यं.

Serpent, *s.* सर्पः, भुजङ्गः, भुजङ्गमः, भुजगः, उरगः, उरःसरः, उरङ्गः, उरङ्गमः, सरीसृपः, पन्नगः, व्यालः, अहिः *m.*, नागः, कञ्चुकी, आशीविषः, तक्षकः, पृदाकुः *m.*; 'female serpent,' सर्पी, भुजगी, *see* Snake.

Serpentine, *a.* (Pertaining to a serpent) सर्पसम्बन्धी -न्धिनी -न्धि (न्), सार्प्यः -र्प्यी -र्प्यं, सार्पः -र्पी -र्पं, आहेयः -यी -यं, औरगः -गी -गं.—(Winding like a serpent) सर्पगतिः -तिः -ति, सर्पी -र्पिणी &c., विसर्पी &c., वक्रः -क्रा -क्रं, वक्रगतिः &c., वक्रगामी &c., सर्पगतिवत्; 'serpentine motion,' सर्पगतिः *f.*, विसर्पणं.

Serpigo, *s.* *See* Ring-worm.

Serrate, serrated, *a.* अनुक्रकचः -चा -चं, क्रकचधारः -रा -रं, दन्तुरः -रा -रं, छिन्नधारः &c., सच्छेदः -दा -दं, सावच्छेदः -दा -दं, छेदयुक्तः -क्ता -क्तं.

Serried, *a.* संहतः -ता -तं, सुसंहतः &c., संश्लिष्टः &c., सम्बाधः &c.

Serum, *s.* मेदस् *n.*, वसा, वपा, धर्म्माम्भस् *n.*, त्वगम्भस् *n.*, धर्म्मोदकं, त्वगुदकं, धर्म्मसारः, त्वक्सारः, सौम्यः, रक्तद्रवः, रक्ताम्भस् *n.*, असृक्करः, उदकधातुः *m.*

Servant, *s.* सेवकः, प्रेष्यः, चेटकः, चेटः, किङ्करः, दासः, दाशः, भृत्यः, भृतकः, कर्म्मकरः, कर्म्मकारः, कर्म्मकारी *m.* (न्), अनुचरः, परिचरः, परिचारकः, परिजनः, वेतनोपजीवी *m.* (न्), वेतनजीवी *m.*, सेवोपजीवी *m.*, सेवाजीवी *m.*, भृतिभुक् *m.* (ज्), भृतिजीवी *m.*, अनुजीवी *m.*, नियोज्यः, प्रैष्यः, भरणीयः, वैतनिकः, शुश्रूषकः, चेडः, चेडकः, पार्श्विकः, पार्श्वानुचरः, सैरिन्ध्रः, अर्थी *m.*, भुजिष्यः, दासेरः, दासेयः, गोप्यः -प्यकः; 'old servant,' मूलभृत्यः; 'servant who waits at table,' परिवेष्टा *m.* (ष्टृ), परिवेषकः; 'attentive servant who watches a master's countenance,' लालाटिकः; 'servants, a set of servants,' दासवर्गः, भृत्यवर्गः, सेवकवर्गः; 'relation between master and servant,' सेव्यसेवकभावः.

Servant-maid, *s.* प्रेष्या, चेटी, चेटिका, चेडी -डिका, सेवकी, दासी, कर्म्मकरी, किङ्करी, घोटा, परिचारिका, सैरन्ध्री, सैरिन्ध्री, प्रतीहारी.

To serve, *v. a.* (Attend upon, act as servant to) सेव् (c. 1. सेवते -वितुं, c. 10. सेवयति -यितुं), उपसेव्, उपास् (c. 2. -आस्ते -सितुं), पर्य्युपास्, समुपास्, श्रु in des. (शुश्रूषते -षितुं), आश्रि, प्रतिश्रि, उपस्था (c. 1. -तिष्ठति -ते -स्थातुं), उपचर् (c. 1. -चरति -रितुं), पर्य्युपस्था, उपाचर्, परिचर्, सभाज् (c. 10. सभाजयति -यितुं), उपचारं कृ, उपासनां कृ.—(At table) परिविष् (c. 10. -वेषयति -यितुं), परिवेषणं कृ.—(Obey, be subject to, worship) सेव्, श्रु in des., अनुवृत्, अनुविधा in pass., उपजीव् (c. 1. -जीवति -वितुं), आराध्, उपाराध्.—(Help, assist) उपकृ, उपकारं कृ, साहाय्यं कृ, उपचर्, उपग्रह्, अनुग्रह्.—(Promote one's purpose) अर्थं प्रवृत् (c. 10. -वर्त्तयति -यितुं) or प्रयुज् (c. 10. -योजयति -यितुं) or सम्पद् (c. 10. -पादयति -यितुं) or साध् (c. 10. साधयति -यितुं), इष्टं सम्पद् or साध्.—(Be sufficient for) पर्य्याप्तः -प्ता -प्तं भू, उपयुक्तः -क्ता -क्तं भू, उचितः -ता

-तं भू, पर्य्याप्तिं कृ, निर्वाहं कृ, कृप्, उपकृप्.—(Supply) उपस्था in caus. (-स्थापयति -यितुं), उपकृप् (c. 10. -कल्पयति -यितुं), परिकृप्.—(Be in the place of) स्थाने or स्थले or भूमौ वृत् or भू or उपयुक्तः -क्ता -क्तं भू or प्रयुक्तः -क्ता -क्तं भू.—(Use, manage) प्रयुज्, उपयुज्, विधा.—(Treat) आचर्, विधा.—(Serve out, distribute) पृथक् पृथग् विभज् or दा or परिकृप्.—(Serve up, place on the table) परिविश् (c. 10. -वेशयति -यितुं), परिविष् (c. 10. -वेषयति -यितुं), परिवेषणं कृ, परिवेशनं कृ, अन्नानि परिविश् or परिकृप् or कृप् or उपस्था in caus. or उपहृ; 'one who serves up,' परिवेषकः, उपहर्त्ता *m.* (र्तृ).

To SERVE, *v. n.* (Be in servitude) सेवां कृ, दास्यं कृ, दास (nom. दासायति), सेवको भू, दासो भू.—(Perform duties) कर्म्म कृ or विधा, कार्य्यं कृ or अनुष्ठा, नियोगिकर्म्म कृ.—(Be of use, be sufficient for) उपयुक्तः -क्ता -क्तं भू, उचितः -ता -तं or पर्य्याप्तः -प्ता -प्तं भू.—(Accomplish the end) अर्थं सम्पद् in caus. or साध् in caus.

SERVED, *p. p.* (Attended upon, obeyed, worshipped) सेवितः -ता -तं, उपासितः -ता -तं, शुश्रूषितः &c., उपचरितः &c., परिचरितः &c., वरिवसितः &c., आराधितः &c.—(Assisted) उपकृतः -ता -तं.—(Supplied) उपकॢप्तः -प्ता -प्तं.—(Served up, prepared, presented, as food, &c.) परिवेशितः -ता -तं, परिवेषितः &c., कल्पितः &c., परिकल्पितः &c., उपहृतः &c.

SERVICE, *s.* (Attendance upon, waiting upon) सेवा -वनं, उपसेवा, निषेवणं, शुश्रूषा, उपासनं -ना, उपचारः, उपचारकरणं, उपचारकर्म्म *n.* (न्), उपचर्य्या, परिचरणं, परिचर्य्या, वरिवस्या, अनुगमनं, उपस्थानं.—(State of service) दास्यं, दासत्वं, सेवा, सेवकदशा, प्रेष्यत्वं, भृत्यत्वं, कैङ्कर्य्यं; 'he lives in our service,' अस्मत्सेवया जीवति.—(Waiting at table) परिवेषणं, परिवेशनं.—(Obedience or subjection to) आज्ञासेवनं, आज्ञानुवृत्तिः *f.*, आज्ञाकरत्वं, अनुवृत्तिः *f.*, अनुवर्त्तनं, वश्यता, शुश्रूषा -षणं, अनुरोधः, भक्तिः *f.*, भजनं, उपासनं -ना, उपासा, आराधनं -ना; 'the service of princes,' नृपसंश्रयः; 'diligent in service,' शुश्रूषापरः -रा -रं.—(Benefit, advantage) उपकारः, उपकृतं, उपक्रिया, उपकृतिः *f.*, सुकृतं, हितं, अर्थः, उपयोगः.—(Use) उपयोगः -गित्वं, प्रयोगः, प्रयोजनं, व्यवहारः.—(Employment, business) व्यापारः, कार्य्यं, कर्म्म *n.* (न्), व्यवसायः, वृत्तिः *f.*, प्रवृत्तिः *f.*, व्यवहारः, नियोगः; 'out of service,' निर्व्यापारः -रा -रं, निर्वृत्तिः -त्तिः -त्ति; 'military service,' सैन्यकर्म्म *n.* (न्), सैनिकवृत्तिः *f.*—(Worship) पूजा, पूजोपचारः, उपचारः, उपचर्य्या, भक्तिः *f.*; 'public worship,' साधारणपूजा; 'course of rites,' अनुष्ठानं, *see* RITE; 'conductor of a service,' अनुष्ठाता *m.*—(Set of dishes served up at once) यावन्ति भोजनपात्राणि युगपत् परिवेष्यन्ते, भोजनपात्रसमूहः, भोजनपात्रगणः, भोजनपात्रजातं.

SERVICEABLE, *a.* (Useful) उपयोगी -गिनी -गि (न्), उपयुक्तः -क्ता -क्तं, उपकारकः -का -कं, उपकारी &c., उपकारकारी -रिणी &c., सोपकारः -रा -रं, प्रयोगी &c., प्रयोज्यः -ज्या -ज्यं, प्रायोज्यः &c., व्यवहार्य्यः -र्य्या -र्य्यं.—(Fit for duty) कार्य्यक्षमः -मा -मं, कर्म्मक्षमः &c., कर्म्मोपयुक्तः -क्ता -क्तं, चलत्कर्म्मीणः -णा -णं.

SERVICEABLENESS, *s.* उपयोगिता, उपयुक्तता, उपयोगः, सोपकारता -त्वं.

SERVICEABLY, *adv.* उपयुक्तं, उपयोगेन, सोपयोगं, सोपकारं.

SERVILE, *a.* (Pertaining to servants or slaves) दाससम्बन्धी -न्धिनी -न्धि (न्), दास्यसम्बन्धी &c., दासेयः -यी -यं, दासेरः -री -रं, सेवकः -का -कं, सेवासम्बन्धी &c., शौद्रः -द्री -द्रं, अधमभृतकः -का -कं, नैदेशिकः -की -कं, दास्य in comp.; 'servile-work,' दास्यकर्म्म *n.*—(Cringing) अतिसान्त्वकारी &c., अतिचाटुकारी &c., अतिलाली &c., अतिलालनकारी &c., अत्यनुकूलः -ला -लं, अत्यनुरोधी &c.

SERVILELY, *adv.* अतिलालनपूर्व्वं, अत्यनुकूलं, अत्यनुरोधेन.

SERVILITY, SERVILENESS, *s.* (Mean obsequiousness) अतिलालनं, अत्यनुकूलता, अत्यानुकूल्यं, अतिसान्त्वकारः, अतिसान्त्वनं, अतिचाटुकारः, अत्यनुरोधः, छन्दोनुरोधः, छन्दोनुवृत्तिः *f.*—(Slavery), *see* SERVITUDE.

SERVITOR, *s.* सेवकः, *see* SERVANT.

SERVITUDE, *s.* दास्यं, दासत्वं, सेवा, सेवकदशा, सेवकभावः, दासभावः, दास्ययोगः, भृत्यत्वं, प्रेष्यत्वं, परप्रेष्यत्वं, कैङ्कर्य्यं, पराधीनता, अन्याधीनता, परवशता, परवत्ता, श्ववृत्तिः *f.*

SESAME, SESAMUM, *s.* (The plant or seed) तिलः, सारालः, सुबन्धः, दलाढकः, पूतधान्यं, होम्यधान्यं; 'its blossom,' वज्रपुष्पं; 'barren sesamum, bearing no blossom, &c.,' तिलपिञ्जः, तिलपेजः; 'sown with sesamum, as a field, &c.,' तिल्यः -ल्या -ल्यं, तैलीनः -नी -नं; 'oil of sesamum,' तिलतैलं, तिलरसः, तिलस्नेहः, तैलं; 'ground sesamum,' तिलचूर्णं, तिलकल्कं, तिलकदः; 'sediment after the oil is expressed,' तिलकिट्टं; 'burnt offering of sesamum,' तिलहोमं; 'sesamum made up in the shape of a cow,' तिलधेनुः *f.*; 'sesamum seeds with water,' तिलोदकं; 'with milk and rice,' तिलौदनं; 'made of sesamum,' तिलमयः -यी -यं.

ŚESHA, *s.* (King of the serpents), *see* SNAKE.

SESSION, *s.* (Sitting) उपवेशः -शनं.—(Of a court or assembly) सभा.—(Time or term during which an assembly sits or transacts business) सभा, सभाकालः, सभाकार्य्यकालः, कार्य्यनिर्वाहकालः.

To SET, *v. a.* (Place, put, lay) धा (c. 3. दधाति, धातुं), निधा, आधा, स्था in caus. (स्थापयति -यितुं), न्यस् (c. 4. -अस्यति -सितुं), ऋ in caus. (अर्पयति -यितुं), रुह् in caus. (रोपयति -यितुं), आरुह्, निविश् (c. 10. -वेशयति -यितुं), भृ (c. 1. भरति, भर्त्तुं), दा, कृ; 'one's foot,' पादं न्यस् or ऋ in caus., पादार्पणं कृ.—(Fix) स्था in caus., प्रतिष्ठा, अवस्था, रुह् in caus., बन्ध्.—(Establish, settle) स्था in caus., प्रतिष्ठा, व्यवस्था, प्रकृप् (c. 10. -कल्पयति -यितुं), परिकृप्.—(Fit, adjust, adapt) युज् (c. 10. योजयति -यितुं), आयुज्, समायुज्, समाधा, योग्यं -ग्यां कृ.—(Regulate) विधा, संविधा.—(Plant) रुह् in caus., निरुह्, रोपणं कृ, निखन्.—(Fix jewels, &c., in metal) प्रणिधा, निधा, खच्, युज्; 'is set,' प्रणिधीयते.—(Inlay), *see* the word.—(Sharpen, whet) तिज् (c. 10. तेजयति -यितुं), निशो, निशि, क्ष्णु, तीक्ष्णधारीकृ, तीक्ष्णाग्रीकृ.—(Set a limb) त्रुटितास्थि सन्धा or संयुज्.—(Set about), *see To* BEGIN.—(Set against), *see To* OPPOSE.—(Set apart) पृथक्कृ, उद्धृ, विनियुज्.—(Set aside) विनिधा, *see To* REJECT, ANNUL, OMIT.—(Set before) उपस्था in caus., उपहृ, आहृ; 'as food,' भुज् in caus., परिविष् in caus., परिविश् in caus.—(Set by), *see To* ESTEEM, REGARD, VALUE.—(Set down, lay down) न्यस्, उपन्यस्, निधा, भूमौ न्यस् or धा.—(Set down in writing), *see To* REGISTER, COMMIT TO WRITING.—(Set down), *see To* DEGRADE, REBUKE.—(Set fire) अग्निं दा, *see To* KINDLE.—(Set forth) अभिधा, *see To* PUBLISH, SHOW, DISPLAY, DESCRIBE.—(Set forward) पुरस्कृ, *see To*

ADVANCE, PROMOTE.—(Set free) मुक्तिं दा, मुच्, *see To* FREE.—(Set in order), *see To* DISPOSE, ARRANGE.—(Set at nought), *see To* DESPISE, CONTEMN.—(Set off, show to advantage) शोभां दा, अधिकशोभां दा, शुभ् in caus., प्रकाश् in caus., *see To* EMBELLISH, ADORN.—(Set off against) प्रतिगण्, प्रतिगणनां कृ, समानमूल्यकं -कां ज्ञा, तुल्यमूल्यं -ल्यां ज्ञा.—(Set off with fine words) उपक्षिप्, *see To* EULOGIZE, RECOMMEND.—(Set on), *see To* INCITE, INSTIGATE.—(Set the mind or heart on) मनो निविश् or धा or समाधा or प्रणिधा or युज्, मनो बन्ध्; 'he set his heart upon such an object as this,' एवंविधे अभिलाषे मनो बबन्ध.—(Set on foot) प्रवृत् in caus., आरभ्, समारभ्.—(Set over) अधिकृ, प्रकृ, नियुज्, विनियुज्, सन्नियुज्, अध्यक्षं कृ.—(Set to rights) सुस्थं -स्थां कृ, पुनः सुस्थं कृ, सुस्थ (nom. सुस्थयति -यितुं), प्रतिसमाधा, अनुसन्धा, प्रतिसमाधानं कृ, *see To* CORRECT, REPAIR.—(Set to music) स्वरबद्धं -द्धां कृ.—(Set in motion) संचर् in caus., संचल् in caus.—(Set the teeth on edge) दन्तहर्षं कृ or जन्.—(Set a trap) पाशं युज् (c. 10. योजयति -यितुं), जालं विस्तृ.—(Set sail) नावं or नौकां चल् (c. 10. चालयति -यितुं), समुद्रयानार्थं तीराद् अपगम्, नौकायां तीराद् अपया or अपसृ.—(Set up) स्था in caus., प्रतिष्ठा, संस्था, अवस्था, उत्था, *see To* ERECT, ESTABLISH.

To SET, *v. n.* (Go down, as a heavenly body) अस्तम् इ (c. 2. एति -तुं), अस्तं गम् (c. 1. गच्छति, गन्तुं), अस्तम् or अस्ताचलम् अवलम्ब् (c. 1. -लम्बते -म्बितुं), निर्वाणम् इ or गम्, अस्तमयनं कृ, अस्तावलम्बनं कृ, निम्रुच् (c. 1. -म्रोचति -चितुं), अभिनिम्रुच्; 'western mountain behind which the heavenly bodies set,' अस्तः, अस्ताचलः, अस्तगिरिः *m.*, *see* MOUNTAIN.—(Be fixed hard, congeal) घनीभू, दृढीभू, बन्ध् in pass. (बध्यते), संहन् in pass. (-हन्यते), संहतीभू.—(Flow in a fixed direction) एकदिशं or एकदिशि गम् or सु or द्रु.—(Set forward) अग्रे गम्, पुरो गम्, प्रगम्, प्रया.—(Set in) उपस्था (c. 1. -तिष्ठति -स्थातुं), पर्युपस्था, *see To* BEGIN, *v. n.*—(Set off) यात्रां कृ, प्रस्थानं कृ, प्रक्रम्, प्रचल्, चल्, यात्राम् आरभ्.—(Set out) प्रस्था (c. 1. -तिष्ठति -स्थातुं), विप्रस्था, सम्प्रस्था, प्रत्यभिप्रस्था, प्रया (c. 2. -याति -तुं), या, प्रगम् (c. 1. -गच्छति -गन्तुं), चल् (c. 1. चलति -लितुं), व्रज् (c. 1. व्रजति -जितुं), प्रस्थानं कृ, प्रयाणं कृ; 'he set out for Kashmír,' काश्मीरं or काश्मीरं प्रति चलितः or प्रस्थितः.—(Set to) यत्नेन कृ, यत्नतः कृ, मनो निविश् in caus. or युज्.—(Set up, begin business) वृत्तिम् आरभ्, वृत्त्यारम्भं कृ, पण्यायाम् आरभ्.—(Set up for), *see To* PRETEND.—(Set upon), *see To* ASSAULT, ATTACK.

SET, *s.* (Number of things of the same kind) गणः, समूहः, वर्गः, संघः, श्रेणी, पंक्तिः *f.*; 'a set of dishes,' भोजनपात्रसमूहः; 'a set of numbers,' संख्याश्रेणी.—(Number of persons) जनसमूहः, पंक्तिः *f.*, गणः, वर्गः.

SET, *p. p.* (Placed, put) स्थापितः -ता -तं, अर्पितः &c., न्यस्तः -स्ता -स्तं, विन्यस्तः &c., रोपितः -ता -तं, निवेशितः &c., आहितः &c., निहितः &c., *see* PLACED.—(Inlaid, studded) खचितः -ता -तं, अनुविद्धः -द्धा -द्धं, प्रणिहितः -ता -तं, प्रतिबद्धः &c., क्षुरितः -ता -तं, पिनद्धः -द्धा -द्धं, विन्यस्तः -स्ता -स्तं, जडितः &c., पर्युप्तः -प्ता -प्तं, प्रत्युप्तः &c., करम्बितः &c.; 'with gems,' मणिखचितः -ता -तं, रत्नखचितः &c.; 'with pearls,' मौक्तिकखचितः &c.; 'is set,' प्रणिधीयते.—(Gone down, as the sun, a planet, &c.) अस्तः -स्ता -स्तं, अस्तमितः &c., अस्तगतः &c., अस्तङ्गतः &c., निर्वाणः -णा -णं.—(Set apart) पृथक्कृतः -ता -तं, उद्धृतः &c.—(Set aside) निराकृतः -ता -तं, निरस्तः -स्ता -स्तं, प्रत्याख्यातः -ता -तं.—(Intent on) आसक्तः -क्ता -क्तं, निष्ठः -ष्ठा -ष्ठं, निष्ठितः -ता -तं, निविष्टः -ष्टा -ष्टं, अभिनिविष्टः &c., आहितः -ता -तं, आयुक्तः -क्ता -क्तं.—(Set on foot) प्रवर्त्तितः -ता -तं, प्रवृत्तः -त्ता -त्तं, विसारितः -ता -तं, आरब्धः -ब्धा -ब्धं, समारब्धः &c.—(Set forth) अभिहितः -ता -तं, विहितः &c., पुरस्कृतः &c.—(Set in order) विन्यस्तः -स्ता -स्तं, विहितः &c., व्यवस्थापितः &c., विरचितः &c.—(Set off, adorned) शोभितः -ता -तं, प्रकाशितः &c.—(Set to rights) सुस्थीकृतः -ता -तं, प्रतिसमाहितः &c.—(Set to music) स्वरबद्धः -द्धा -द्धं.—(Set in motion) सञ्चारितः -ता -तं, सञ्चालितः &c.—(Set over) अधिकृतः -ता -तं, नियुक्तः -क्ता -क्तं, विनियुक्तः &c., व्यापृतः -ता -तं.—(Set up) स्थापितः -ता -तं, प्रतिष्ठापितः &c., *see* ESTABLISHED.—(Regular, prescribed, uniform) नियमितः -ता -तं, नियतः &c., एकरूपः -पा -पं, समरूपः &c., निश्चितः &c., नित्यः -त्या -त्यं.—(Fixed in opinion) दृढनिश्चयः -या -यं, स्थिरनिश्चयः &c.

SETACEOUS, *a.* शूकयुक्तः -क्ता -क्तं, बहुशूकः -का -कं. *See* BRISTLY.

SET-DOWN, *s.* अभिमानखण्डनं, दर्पखण्डनं, अपकर्षणं, वाग्दण्डः.

SET-OFF, *s.* सममूल्यकवस्तु *n.*, निस्तारः, परिवर्त्तः, तुल्यवस्तु *n.*

SETON, *s.* सूचिद्वारा त्वगन्तर्निवेशितं सूत्रं or चर्म्मान्तर्निवेशितं सूत्रं.

SETOSE, SETOUS, *a.* शूकविशिष्टः -ष्टा -ष्टं, शूकमयः -यी -यं. *See* BRISTLY.

SETTER, *s.* (Dog) वनपक्षिनिर्देशको मृगयाकुक्कुरः, वन्यपक्षिनिर्देशने शिक्षितो मृगयाश्वा *m.*—(Of precious stones, &c.) योजयिता *m.* (तृ).

SETTING, *s.* (Placing) स्थापनं -ना, अर्पणं, रोपणं, आरोपः -पणं, आधानं, निधानं.—(Of the heavenly bodies) अस्तं, अस्तमयनं, अस्तमयः, अस्तगमनं, अस्तक्रमणं, अस्तावलम्बनं, अवरोपणं.

To SETTLE, *v. a.* (Fix, establish) स्था in caus. (स्थापयति -यितुं), प्रतिष्ठा, संस्था, अवस्था, विधा (c. 3. -दधाति -धातुं), प्रतिनिधा, रुह् in caus., आरुह्, निरुह्.—(Establish in life) प्रतिष्ठा in caus., प्रतिष्ठितं -तां कृ, प्रतिष्ठां कृ.—(Determine, decide) निर्णी (c. 1. -णयति -णेतुं), निश्चि (c. 5. -चिनोति -चेतुं), साध् (c. 10. साधयति -यितुं), सिद्धीकृ, निष्पद् (c. 10. -पादयति -यितुं), निष्पत्तिं कृ, निर्णयं कृ, निश्चयं कृ, परिकॢप् (c. 10. -कल्पयति -यितुं), व्यवसो (c. 4. -स्यति -सातुं), व्यवस्था in caus., निर्धृ (c. 10. -धारयति -यितुं), अवधृ, सम्प्रधृ, तीर् (c. 10. तीरयति -यितुं), निर्धारणं कृ, अवधारणं कृ, सम्प्रधारणं कृ, तीरणं कृ.—(Settle an affair) कार्य्यनिर्णयं कृ, कार्य्यनिष्पत्तिं कृ.—(Compose, quiet) स्थिरीकृ, स्वस्थं -स्थां कृ, शम् in caus.—(Settle a difference or dispute) सन्धा, समाधा, सन्धानं कृ, सन्धिं कृ, शम् in caus., प्रशम्.—(Adjust, arrange) विधा, संविधा, सन्धा, समाधा, रच्, विरच्, विन्यस्.—(Settle a debt, &c.) ऋणं शुध् (c. 10. शोधयति -यितुं) or साध्, ऋणसिद्धिं कृ, ऋणशोधनं कृ, *see To* LIQUIDATE.—(Cause to sink to the bottom) अधो गम् in caus. (गमयति -यितुं), अधः पत् in caus. (पातयति -यितुं), अवसद् in caus.—(Colonize) वस् in caus., अधिवस्.

To SETTLE, *v. n.* (Fall to the bottom) अधो गम् (c. 1. गच्छति, गन्तुं), अधः पत् (c. 1. पतति -तितुं), तले or तलं पत्.—(Sink) सद् (c. 1. सीदति, सत्तुं), निषद्, अवसद्.—(Deposit a sediment) मलम् अधःपत् in caus., मलाधःपातनं कृ.—(Become fixed) अवस्था (c. 1. -तिष्ठति -स्थातुं), प्रतिष्ठा in caus. pass. (-ष्ठाप्यते), प्रतिष्ठितः -ता -तं भू, स्थिरीभू.—(Settle in life, marry) प्रतिष्ठितः -ता -तं भू, प्रतिष्ठां

प्राप्, विवाहं कृ.—(Become calm, still) शम् (c. 4. शाम्यति, शमितुं), विश्रम्, प्रसद्.—(Become compact) संहतीभू, घनीभू.

SETTLED, *p. p.* (Fixed, established) स्थापितः -ता -तं, प्रतिष्ठापितः &c., प्रतिष्ठितः &c., संस्थापितः &c., रोपितः &c.—(Settled in life, married) प्रतिष्ठितः -ता -तं.—(Determined, decided) निर्णीतः -ता -तं, निश्चितः &c., सिद्धः -द्धा -द्धं, निष्पन्नः -न्ना -न्नं, नियतः -ता -तं, नियमितः &c., व्यवस्थापितः &c., परिकल्पितः &c., व्यवसितः &c., साधितः &c., तीरितः &c., निर्धारितः &c.—(As a debt) सिद्धः -द्धा -द्धं, शोधितः -ता -तं, *see* LIQUIDATED.—(Adjusted, arranged) विहितः -ता -तं, समाहितः &c.—(Composed) शमितः &c., स्थिरीकृतः &c.

SETTLEMENT, SETTLING, *s.* (Act of fixing) स्थापनं -ना, प्रतिष्ठापनं, व्यवस्थापनं, प्रतिष्ठा, रोपणं.—(Settlement in life) प्रतिष्ठा, प्रतिष्ठितिः *f.*, विवाहः.—(Marriage settlement) शुल्कः -ल्कं, स्त्रीधनं, स्त्रीवृत्तिः *f.*—(Determining, deciding) निर्णयः -यनं, निश्चयः, निष्पत्तिः *f.*, सिद्धिः *f.*, निर्धारणं -णा, अवधारणं, तीरणं; 'of affairs,' कार्य्यनिर्णयः.—(Of a debt) सिद्धिः *f.*, ऋणसिद्धिः *f.*, शुद्धिः *f.*, शोधनं, ऋणशुद्धिः *f.*, ऋणशोधनं, *see* LIQUIDATION.—(Adjustment, as of differences, &c.) समाधानं, सन्धानं, समाधिः *m.*, सन्धिः *m.*, सन्धिकरणं, सन्धानकरणं, वैरशमनं.—(Colonization) देशान्तराधिवासनं.—(Place colonized, colony) अधिवासितदेशः, प्रदेशः, देशशाखा, राज्यशाखा.

SETTLER, *s.* अधिवासी *m.* (न्), प्रदेशाधिवासी *m.*, देशशाखास्थः.

SEVEN, *a.* सप्त *m. f. n. pl.* (न्), सप्तसंख्यकः -का -कं, सप्तकः -का -की -कं; 'aggregate of seven,' सप्तकं.

SEVEN-FOLD, *a.* सप्तगुणः -णा -णं, सप्तविधः -धा -धं, सप्तगुणितः &c.

SEVEN-FOLD, *adv.* सप्तधा, सप्तविधेन, सप्तगुणितं.

SEVENTEEN, *a.* सप्तदश *m. f. n. pl.* (न्), सप्तदशसंख्यकः -का -कं.

SEVENTEENTH, *a.* सप्तदशः -शी -शं.

SEVENTH, *a.* सप्तमः -मी -मं, साप्तमिकः -की -कं.

SEVENTHLY, *adv.* सप्तमतस्, सप्ततस्, सप्तमस्थाने, सप्तमपदे.

SEVENTIETH, *a.* सप्ततः -ती -तं, सप्ततितमः -मी -मं.

SEVENTY, *s.* सप्ततिः *f. sing.*, सप्ततिसंख्यकः -का -कं; 'they reigned seventy years,' सप्ततिम् अब्दान् राज्यं चक्रुः; 'with seventy arrows,' सप्तत्या शरैः; 'seventy-one,' एकसप्ततिः *f. sing.*; 'seventy-two,' द्वासप्ततिः *f.*; 'seventy-three,' त्रयःसप्ततिः; 'seventy-four,' चतुःसप्ततिः *f.*; 'seventy-five,' पञ्चसप्ततिः *f.*; 'seventy-six,' षट्सप्ततिः *f.*; 'seventy-seven,' सप्तसप्ततिः *f.*; 'seventy-eight,' अष्टासप्ततिः *f.*; 'seventy-nine,' नवसप्ततिः *f.* or ऊनाशीतिः *f.* or एकोनाशीतिः *f.*

To SEVER, *v. a.* (Part, disjoin) वियुज्, विश्लिष् in caus., भिद्, विभिद्, छिद्, विच्छिद्, अवच्छिद्, पृथक्कृ, विभज्.

SEVERAL, *a.* (Consisting of a number, many) बहुः -हुः -ह्वी -हु, अनेकः -का -कं, कतिपय in comp., कतिचित् in comp., *see* MANY, NUMEROUS, FEW.—(Separate, distinct) भिन्नः -न्ना -न्नं, व्यक्तः -क्ता -क्तं, व्यस्तः -स्ता -स्तं, पृथगात्मकः -का -कं, पृथग्व्यक्तिकः &c., अव्यापकः &c., असाधारणः -णा -णी -णं, प्रत्येकः -का -कं.—(Peculiar) स्व in comp., आत्म in comp., प्रातिस्विकः -की -कं.—(Respective) स्व repeated, इतरेतरः -रा -रं, *see* RESPECTIVE.

SEVERALLY, *adv.* पृथक्, पृथक् पृथक्, प्रत्येकं, अनुपूर्वशस्, अनुक्रमशस्, यथाक्रमं, अवयवशस्, व्यक्तितस्, व्यक्तिशस्, प्रति or अनु prefixed.

SEVERALTY, *s.* पृथक्त्वं, पार्थक्यं, व्यक्तिता, व्यस्तता, व्यासः, भिन्नता.

SEVERANCE, *s.* वियोगः, विश्लेषः, विप्रयोगः, विभेदः, पृथक्करणं.

SEVERE, *a.* (Said of persons) निष्ठुरः -रा -रं, कठोरः -रा -रं, उग्रः -ग्रा -ग्रं, उग्रदण्डः -ण्डा -ण्डं, उग्रशासनः -ना -नं, तीक्ष्णदण्डः &c., तीव्रदण्डः &c., दण्डनशीलः -ला -लं, दण्डबुद्धिः -द्धिः -द्धि, भैरवशासनः &c., तीव्रशक्तिः -क्तिः -क्ति, प्रखरः -रा -रं, कठिनः -ना -नं, क्रूरः -रा -रं, परुषः -षा -षं, कटुः -टुः -टु, उद्यतदण्डः -ण्डा -ण्डं, उद्यतबाहुः -हुः -हु, *see* RIGOROUS.—(Said of things) तीक्ष्णः -क्ष्णा -क्ष्णं, तीव्रः -व्रा -व्रं, उग्रः -ग्रा -ग्रं, रौद्रः -द्री -द्रं, प्रखरः -रा -रं, दुःसहः -हा -हं, दुःसह्यः -ह्या -ह्यं, कष्टसह्यः &c.—(Intense, excessive) अत्यन्तः -न्ता -न्तं, अतिशय in comp., अतिशायनः -ना -नं, भृशः -शा -शं, अति prefixed; 'severe pain,' तीव्रवेदना; 'penance,' उग्रतपस् *n.*

SEVERED, *p. p.* वियुक्तः -क्ता -क्तं, विप्रयुक्तः &c., विश्लिष्टः -ष्टा -ष्टं, विभिन्नः -न्ना -न्नं, विच्छिन्नः &c., अवच्छिन्नः &c., छिन्नः &c., प्रभिन्नः &c., विगतः -ता -तं.

SEVERELY, *adv.* निष्ठुरं, नैष्ठुर्य्येण, कठोरं, उग्रं, तीक्ष्णं, तीव्रं.

SEVERITY, *s.* (Said of persons) नैष्ठुर्य्यं, निष्ठुरता, कठोरता, उग्रता, उग्रदण्डता, तीक्ष्णदण्डता, कठिनता, काठिन्यं, क्रूरता, परुषता, पारुष्यं, कटुता, दौरात्म्यं, निकृतिः *f.*, तेजस् *n.*, *see* RIGOR.—(Said of things) उग्रता, तीक्ष्णता -त्वं, तीव्रता, रौद्रता, प्रखरता, दुःसहता, दुःसह्यता.—(Excessive punishment) अतिदण्डः-ण्डनं, दण्डनाधिक्यं.

To SEW, *v. a.* सिव् (c. 4. सीव्यति, सेवितुं), निषिव्, परिषिव्, विषिव्, सीवनं कृ, सेवनं कृ, स्यूतिं कृ, वे, प्रवे.

SEWED, SEWN, *p. p.* स्यूतः -ता -तं, निष्यूतः &c., स्युतः &c., ष्यूतः -ता -तं, उतः &c., प्रोतः &c., पुटितः -ता -तं.

SEWER, *s.* कर्दमाटकः, सङ्करः, नाली, प्रणाली, प्रणालः, मलनिर्गमः, मलवाहिनी, मलमार्गः, मलपथः. *See* DRAIN; 'village sewer,' ग्रामसङ्करः.

SEWING, *s.* सीवनं, सेवनं, स्यूतिः *f.*, ष्यूतिः *f.*, स्युतिः *f.*, निष्यूतिः.

SEX, *s.* (Distinction between male and female) स्त्रीपुरुषभेदः, स्त्रीपुरुषव्यक्तिभेदः, स्त्रीपुरुषलिङ्गं, लिङ्गभेदः.—(Gender) लिङ्गं, जातिः *f.*; 'male sex,' पुरुषजातिः *f.*, पुंजातिः *f.*, पुंलिङ्गं, नरजातिः *f.*; 'female sex,' स्त्रीजातिः *f.*, स्त्रीलिङ्गं; 'separation of the sexes,' स्त्रीपुरुषवियोगः, द्वन्द्वभिन्नं.

SEXAGENARIAN, SEXAGENARY, *a.* षष्टिकः -का -कं, षष्टिकवयस्कः -स्का -स्कं.

SEXANGULAR, *a.* षट्कोणः -णा -णं, षडस्रः -स्रा -स्रं, षड्भुजः &c.

SEXENNIAL, *a.* षडब्दिकः -का -कं, षड्वार्षिकः &c., षड्वर्षीणः -णा -णं.

SEXTANT, *s.* (Sixth part of a circle) वृत्तषडंशः, वृत्तषड्भागः.

SEXTON, *s.* शवगर्त्तखनकः, शवकुण्डकारकः, श्मशानाध्यक्षः, मृतपाः.

SEXUAL, *a.* स्त्रीपुरुषधर्म्मसम्बन्धी -न्धिनी -न्धि (न्), स्त्रीपुरुषभेदसम्बन्धी &c., स्त्रीपुरुषभेदविषयकः -का -कं, स्त्रीपुरुषविशेषणः -णा -णं, स्त्रीपुरुषव्यवसम्बन्धी &c., मैथुनसम्बन्धी &c., लिङ्गसम्बन्धी &c.; 'sexual intercourse,' मैथुनं, मिथुनं, रतिः *f.*, सुरतं, अङ्गसङ्गः, व्यवायः, सम्भोगः, सङ्गः, रतिक्रिया, स्त्रीपुरुषसङ्गः, *see* COPULATION.

SHABBILY, *adv.* (Raggedly) लाटवस्त्रेण, कर्पटवस्त्रैः, जर्ज्जरवस्त्रैः, कर्पटिकवत्.—(Meanly) कुत्सितं, कृपणं, सकार्पण्यं, तुच्छं.

SHABBINESS, *s.* (Raggedness) लाटता, जर्ज्जरता, जीर्णता, सूत्रदारिद्र्यं.—(Meanness) कृपणता, कार्पण्यं, कुत्सितत्वं, तुच्छता, अनुदारता.

SHABBY, *a.* (As clothes, &c.) लाटः -टा -टं, जर्ज्जरः -रा -रं, जर्ज्जरीकः -का -कं, जीर्णः -र्णा -र्णं, सूत्रदरिद्रः -द्रा -द्रं, पाश in comp.; as, 'a shabby umbrella,' छत्रपाशः.—(Mean) कृपणः -णा -णं,

कुत्सितः -ता -तं, तुच्छः -च्छा -च्छं, जघन्यः -न्या -न्यं, कदर्यः -र्या -र्यं; अपकृष्टः &c., अनुदारः &c.

To SHACKLE, *v. a.* निगडेन बन्ध्. *See To* FETTER, HAMPER.

SHACKLE, *s.* निगडः, बन्धनं, शृङ्खला, पाशः, संरोधः. *See* FETTER.

SHACKLED, *p. p.* निगडितः -ता -तं, शृङ्खलितः &c., संरुद्धः -द्धा -द्धं.

SHAD, *s.* (Sort of fish) पाठीनः, मद्गुरः, शृङ्गी *f.*, सहस्रदंष्ट्रः.

SHADDOCK, *s.* (Citrus decumana, a fruit) गिरिजा.

SHADE, *s.* (Obscurity caused by interruption of light) छाया, अनातपः, आतपाभावः, अतेजस् *n.*, सूर्य्यप्रकाशाभावः, अप्रकाशः, श्यामा.—(Obscurity) अन्धकारः, तिमिरं, तमस् *n.*, अप्रकाशत्वं.—(Screen) व्यवधा, व्यवधानं, वितानं, तिरस्करिणी, *see* SCREEN; 'for a lamp,' अश्मन्तकं.—(Degree, gradation) अंशः, भागः, क्रमः.—(Minute difference) अत्यल्पान्तरं, स्वल्पान्तरं, अत्यल्पमात्रं, अत्यल्पं.—(Ghost) अपच्छाया, प्रेतः.

To SHADE, *v. a.* (Shelter from light and heat) आतपं निवृ (c. 10. -वारयति -यितुं) or वृ, सूर्य्यतेजो निवृ, उष्णं निवृ, आतपवारणं कृ, उष्णनिवारणं कृ, उष्णप्रतिबन्धं कृ, छायां कृ.—(Overspread, cover) छद् (c. 10. छादयति -यितुं), प्रच्छद्, आच्छद्, अवतन्, वितन्, वितानीकृ.

SHADED, *p. p.* छादितः -ता -तं, प्रच्छादितः &c., वितानीकृतः -ता -तं.

SHADINESS, *s.* छायायुक्तता, सच्छायत्वं, छायाबाहुल्यं, आतपराहित्यं.

SHADOW, *s.* (Shade representing the form of the body which intercepts the light) छाया, प्रतिच्छाया, प्रतिबिम्बं; 'middle or mean shadow,' मध्यच्छाया.—(Reflection, image reflected) प्रतिबिम्बं, प्रतिच्छाया, छायात्मा *m.* (न्), छाया, प्रतिभासः, प्रतिमूर्त्तिः *f.*, प्रतिरूपं, प्रतिमा; 'shadow of the moon,' प्रतिमेन्दुः *m.*; 'relation of a shadow with its substance,' बिम्बप्रतिबिम्बभावः; 'casting a shadow,' छायाकरः -रा -री -रं.—(Obscurity), *see* SHADE.—(Shelter) आश्रयः, शरणं, संश्रयः.—(Faint resemblance) आभासः, पाण्डुरूपं, ईषत्सदृशरूपं.

To SHADOW, *v. a.* (Overspread, &c.), *see To* SHADE.—(Represent faintly) आभासं दृश् in caus., छायाभासं प्रदृश्, ईषत्सदृशरूपं प्रदृश्, छायाप्रदर्शनं कृ, प्रतिच्छायां कृ, बिम्ब (nom. बिम्बयति -यितुं), प्रतिबिम्ब.

SHADOWED, *p. p.* बिम्बितः -ता -तं, प्रतिबिम्बितः &c., बिम्बागतः &c.

SHADOWLESS, *a.* छायाहीनः -ना -नं, अपच्छायः -या -यं, छायारहितः -ता -तं.

SHADOWY, *a.* (Not bright) मन्दच्छायः -या -यं, न्यूनकान्तिः -न्तिः -न्ति, न्यूनतेजस्कः -स्का -स्कं, मन्दतेजस्कः &c., न्यूनप्रभः -भा -भं, *see* DIM.—(Unsubstantial) छायारूपः -पा -पं, छायात्मकः -का -कं, छायाकारः -रा -रं, छायाकृतिः -तिः -ति, अवास्तविकः -की -कं.

SHADY, *a.* (Abounding with shade, having shade) सच्छायः -या -यं, छायामयः -यी -यं, छायाबहुलः -ला -लं, छायायुक्तः -क्ता -क्तं, छायावृतः -ता -तं, छायाच्छादितः &c., छायाच्छन्नः -न्ना -न्नं.—(Sheltered from the heat) आतपरहितः -ता -तं, आतपशून्यः -न्या -न्यं, आतपहीनः -ना -नं, निरातपः -पा -पं.

SHAFT, *s.* (Arrow) शरः, बाणः, काण्डः -ण्डं; 'shaft of an arrow,' शरकाण्डः.—(Pole of a carriage) धूः *f.* (धुर्), धुरा, कूबरः; 'of a plough,' ईषा, ईशा, हलदण्डः, *see* POLE.—(Handle) दण्डः.—(Of a mine) खनिगर्त्तः, खनिकूपः, खनिकुण्डं, कूपः, अवटः.—(Of a column) शङ्कुः *m.*

SHAG, *s.* (Rough hair) विषमलोम *n.* (न्), स्थूललोम *n.*, दृढलोम.—(Kind of bird) मत्स्यवेधनी, मद्गुः *m.*

SHAGGINESS, *s.* विषमलोमत्वं, लोमप्राचुर्य्यं, लोमशत्वं, प्रचुरलोमत्वं.

SHAGGY, *a.* विषमलोमा -मा -म (न्), दृढलोमा &c., स्थूललोमा &c., प्रचुरलोमा &c., अपरिष्कृतलोमा &c., लोमशः -शा -शं, रोमशः &c.

To SHAKE, *v. a.* क्षुभ् (c. 10. क्षोभयति -यितुं), विक्षुभ्, व्याक्षुभ्, संचल् (c. 10. -चालयति -यितुं), विचल्, चल्, कम्प् (c. 10. कम्पयति -यितुं), प्रकम्प्, प्रतिकम्प्, धू (c. 5. धूनोति, धुनोति, c. 9. धुनाति, धवितुं, धोतुं), आधू, ह्वल् (c. 10. ह्वलयति, ह्वालयति -यितुं), आस्खल् (c. 10. -स्खलयति -यितुं), आन्दोलनं कृ; 'he shakes his head,' तिर्य्यङ् मूर्धानं चालयति.—(One's confidence) शङ्कान्वितं -तां कृ, विश्वासन्यूनतां कृ or जन्.—(Shake off) अवधू, निर्धू, विधू, उद्धू, अपास्, निरस्, निराकृ, मुष्.—(Shake hands) परस्परं पाणिं ग्रह्, अन्योन्यं हस्तं or हस्तौ स्पृश् (c. 6. स्पृशति, स्प्रष्टुं); 'they shake hands,' अन्योन्यं हस्तौ स्पृशतः.

To SHAKE, *v. n.* क्षुभ् (c. 4. क्षुभ्यति, क्षोभितुं), प्रक्षुभ्, संक्षुभ्, कम्प् (c. 1. कम्पते -म्पितुं), विकम्प्, प्रकम्प्, अभिकम्प्, संकम्प्, वेप् (c. 1. वेपते -पितुं), प्रवेप्, ह्वल् (c. 1. ह्वलति -लितुं), विह्वल्, प्रह्वल्, स्फुर् (c. 6. स्फुरति -रितुं), चल् (c. 1. चलति -लितुं), विचल्, वेल्ल् (c. 1. वेल्लति -ल्लितुं), एज् (c. 1. एजते -जितुं), दोल (nom. दोलायते), क्ष्माय् (c. 1. क्ष्मायते -यितुं), आन्दोलितः -ता -तं भू.

SHAKE, *s.* क्षोभः, विक्षोभः, संक्षोभः, कम्पः, विकम्पः. *See* SHAKING.

SHAKEN, *p. p.* क्षुब्धः -ब्धा -ब्धं, विक्षुब्धः &c., संक्षुब्धः &c., व्याक्षुब्धः &c., क्षोभितः -ता -तं, क्षुभितः &c., धूतः -ता -तं, आधूतः &c., धूनः -ना -नं, आधुतः &c., विधूनितः -ता -तं, चलितः &c., प्रचलितः &c., कम्पितः &c., आकम्पितः &c., वेल्लितः &c., प्रेङ्खितः &c., आस्फालितः -ता -तं, आन्दोलितः -ता -तं, स्फुरितः &c., क्ष्मायितः &c., लाडितः &c.; 'by the wind,' अनिलधूतः -ता -तं, अनिलक्षुब्धः -ब्धा -ब्धं, अनिलोद्धतः -ता -तं, पवनाहतः &c., वायुना धूयमानः -ना -नं or विधूयमानः &c.—(Shaken off) निर्धूतः -ता -तं, उद्धूतः &c., विधूतः &c., विधुतः &c., निरस्तः -स्ता -स्तं; 'one who has shaken off his sins,' उद्धूतपापः -पा -पं, मुक्तपापः &c., पापमुक्तः -क्ता -क्तं; 'having shaken off,' अपास्य, विधूय.

SHAKING, *s.* क्षोभः -भणं, विक्षोभः, संक्षोभः, कम्पः -म्पनं, विकम्पः, वेपनं, चलनं, विचलनं, आस्फालनं, आन्दोलनं, वेल्लनं, वेल्लितं, धूननं, विधूननं, धूनिः *f.*, विधुननं, विधुतिः *f.*, विधूतिः, विधुवनं, एजनं, स्फुरणं.

SHAKING, *part.* (Moving about, trembling) चलनः -ना -नं, कम्पनः -ना -नं, सकम्पः -म्पा -म्पं, वेपमानः -ना -नं, चलः -ला -लं, चपलः &c., लोलः &c., कम्प्रः -म्प्रा -म्प्रं, तरलः -ला -लं, दोलायमानः -ना -नं, चलाचलः &c., पारिप्लवः -वी -वं, परिप्लवः &c., क्ष्मायिता -त्री -तृ (तृ), एजिता &c.—(Causing to shake) क्षोभकः -का -कं, क्षोभकारी -रिणी &c., धुन्वन् -न्वती -न्वत् (त्), विधुन्वन् &c., धुन्वानः -ना -नं, एजयन् &c., एजकः -का -कं.

SHAKY, *a.* अस्थिरः -रा -रं, स्खलितः -ता -तं, स्खलद्गतिः -तिः -ति.

SHALLOW, *a.* (Not deep, having little water) गाधः -धा -धं, उत्तानः -ना -नं, गाधजलः -ला -लं, उत्तानजलः &c., ईषज्जलः &c., अल्पजलः &c., अगम्भीरः -रा -रं, अगभीरः &c.; 'a shallow stream,' गाधसरित् *f.*, अल्पसरित्, कुसरित्; 'to become shallow,' चुड्ड् (c. 1. चुड्डति -ड्डितुं), चुड्ड्, चुड्, चुड्ड्.—(Not intellectually deep) अल्पबुद्धिः -द्धिः -द्धि, अल्पमतिः -तिः -ति, अल्पविद्यः -द्या -द्यं, अल्पज्ञः -ज्ञा -ज्ञं, किंचिज्ज्ञः &c., अगम्भीरबुद्धिः &c.

SHALLOW, *s.* (A shoal) सैकतं, पुलिनं, गाधभूमिः *f.*, उत्तानभूमिः.

SHALLOWNESS, *s.* गाधता, उत्तानता, अगम्भीरता, अगाम्भीर्य्यं.

SHAM, *s.* छलं, छद्म *n.* (न्), कैतवं, व्याजः, अपदेशः, व्यपदेशः, कपटः -टं, उपधा, लक्षणं, कूटः -टं, मिषं.

SHAM, *a.* छाद्मिकः -की -कं, सव्याजः -जा -जं, छद्म or कूट or कपट or मिथ्या in comp., *see* PRETENDED; 'sham fight,' क्रीडाकलहः.

To SHAM, *v. a.* or *n.* छद्म कृ, कूटं कृ, व्याजं कृ, कपटं कृ. *See To* PRETEND; 'one who shams sleep,' मिथ्याप्रसुप्तः, प्रसुप्तलक्षणः.

SHAMBLES, *s.* शूना, सूना, शौनविक्रयस्थानं, शौनिकस्थानं, सौनस्थानं.

SHAMBLING, *a.* विषमः -मा -मं, विरूपः -पा -पं, स्थूलः -ला -लं.

SHAME, *s.* (Sensation of conscious guilt) लज्जा.—(Sense of shame, modesty) लज्जा, ह्रीः *f.*, व्रीडा, त्रपा, मन्दाक्षं, ह्रियिया, ह्रिणीया, ह्रीका, ह्रीका, *see* MODESTY; 'one who has cast off all shame,' त्यक्तलज्जः, निरस्तलज्जः.—(Reproach, disgrace) अपमानं, अप्रतिष्ठा, कलङ्कः.—(Cause of shame) लज्जाहेतुः *m.*, लज्जाकारणं, लज्जास्पदं.—(To feel shame), *see To* BLUSH, *v. n.*—(To put to shame) लज्ज् in caus., ह्री in caus., तर्ज् (c. 10. तर्जयति -यितुं); 'putting to shame,' तर्जनं, ह्रेपणं, *see To* SHAME.—(Shame for shame!) धिक्, शान्तं.

To SHAME, *v. a.* (Make ashamed) लज्ज् (c. 10. लज्जयति -यितुं), ह्री in caus. (ह्रेपयति -यितुं), तर्ज् (c. 10. तर्जयति -यितुं), लज्जितं -तां कृ, लज्जान्वितं -तां कृ, सलज्जं -ज्जां कृ.—(Disgrace) अपमानं कृ, कलङ्कं कृ, कलङ्क (nom. कलङ्कयति -यितुं), लज्जां कृ.—(Mock at) अवज्ञा, अवमन्, मुखरीकृ, लघूकृ.

SHAMED, *p. p.* ह्रेपितः -ता -तं, तर्जितः &c., लज्जितः -ता -तं.

SHAMEFACED, *a.* लज्जावान् -वती -वत् (त्), लज्जाशीलः -ला -लं, ह्रीमान् &c., त्रपितः -ता -तं, व्रीडितः &c. *See* BASHFUL, MODEST.

SHAMEFUL, *a.* लज्जाकरः -रा -री -रं, अपमानकरः &c., अकीर्त्तिकरः &c., कीर्त्तिनाशकः -का -कं, गर्ह्यः -र्ह्या -र्ह्यं, गर्हणीयः -या -यं.

SHAMELESS, *a.* (Destitude of shame) निर्लज्जः -ज्जा -ज्जं, अलज्जः &c., विलज्जः &c., लज्जाहीनः -ना -नं, निस्त्रपः -पा -पं, त्रपाहीनः -ना -नं, निरपत्रपः -पा -पं, अनपत्रपः &c., त्यक्तलज्जः &c., निरस्तत्रपः &c., त्रपानिरस्तः -स्ता -स्तं, लज्जोज्झितः -ता -तं, वियातः -ता -तं, धृष्टः -ष्टा -ष्टं.—(Indicating want of shame) अलज्जासूचकः -का -कं, वैयात्यसूचकः &c.

SHAMELESSLY, *adv.* लज्जया विना, लज्जां विना, निर्लज्जं, सवैयात्यं.

SHAMELESSNESS, *s.* निर्लज्जता -त्वं, लज्जाहीनता, त्रपाहीनता, वैयात्यं.

SHAMMING, *s.* छद्मकरणं, छलनं -ना, व्याजकरणं. *See* SHAM, *s.*

To SHAMPOO, *v. a.* हस्ताभ्याम् अङ्गानि संवाह् (c. 10. -वाहयति -यितुं, c. 1. -वाहति -हितुं) or मृद् (c. 9. मृद्नाति, मर्दितुं, c. 10. मर्दयति -यितुं) or सम्पीड्, अङ्गसंवाहनं कृ.

SHAMPOOED, *p. p.* हस्ताभ्यां संवाहितः -ता -तं or मर्दितः -ता -तं.

SHAMPOOER, *s.* संवाहकः, अङ्गसंवाहकः, अङ्गमर्दकः.

SHAMPOOING, *s.* संवाहनं, अङ्गसंवाहनं, अङ्गमर्दनं, उत्सादनं, उद्वर्त्तनं.

SHANK, *s.* (Bone of the leg) जङ्घास्थि *n.*, पादास्थि *n.*, अधमास्थि *n.*—(The leg) जङ्घा.—(The long part of any thing) दीर्घांशः, दीर्घभागः; 'having long shanks,' ऊर्द्ध्वजानुः -नुः -नु, ऊर्द्ध्वज्ञुः &c., दीर्घजङ्घः -ङ्घा -ङ्घं.

To SHAPE, *v. a.* रूप् (c. 10. रूपयति -यितुं), सरूपं -पां कृ, क्लृप् (c. 10. कल्पयति -यितुं), आकारं कृ or दा, संस्कारं कृ, संस्कृ, रच्, विरच्, घट्.

SHAPE, *s.* आकारः, आकृतिः *f.*, रूपं, मूर्त्तिः *f.*, संस्कारः, संस्थानं, विग्रहः, विधानं, वपुस् *n.*, संहननं, कायः, शरीरं. *See* FIGURE.

SHAPED, *p. p.* रूपी -पिणी -पि (न्), साकारः -रा -रं, सरूपः -पा -पं, रूपवान् -वती -वत् (त्), आकार or आकृति or रूप in comp.; 'moon-shaped,' चन्द्राकारः -रा -रं, चन्द्राकृतिः -तिः -ति, चन्द्ररूपः -पी -पं; 'well shaped,' सुरूपः -पी -पं, रूपवान् &c., सिंहसंहननः -ना -नं.

SHAPELESS, *a.* अनाकारः -रा -रं, निराकारः -रा -रं, निराकृतिः -तिः -ति, अरूपी -पिणी -पि (न्), अरूपः -पी -पं, नीरूपः -पा -पं, रूपहीनः -ना -नं, आकारहीनः &c., अमूर्त्तिः -र्त्तिः -र्त्ति, विरूपः &c., अरूपवान् &c.

SHAPELESSNESS, *s.* निराकारता, आकारहीनता, अरूपता, अमूर्त्तिः *f.*

SHAPELY, *a.* सुरूपः -पा -पी -पं, रूपवान् -वती &c., आकारशुद्धः -द्धा -द्धं.

SHARD, *s.* मृण्मयभाण्डशकलं, मृण्मयपात्रखण्डः, काचखण्डः.

SHARE, *s.* (Part, portion) भागः, अंशः, विभागः, उद्धारः, वण्टः -ण्टकः, भाज्यं, भाजितं, अंसः; 'equal share,' समभागः; 'share by share,' अंशांशि.—(Of an estate) ऋक्थभागः, ऋक्थांशः, रिक्थभागः, उद्धारः, औद्धारिकं.—(Of a plough) फालः, पोत्रं, फलं, निरीशं, कुशी, कूटकं.

To SHARE, *v. a.* (Distribute, divide) विभज् (c. 1. -भजति -भक्तुं), प्रविभज्, संविभज्, अंश् (c. 10. अंशयति -यितुं), वण्ट् (c. 10. वण्टयति -यितुं), पृथक् पृथग् विभज्, अंशांशि दा or परिक्लृप्, *see To* DISTRIBUTE.—(Partake) अंशं or भागं ग्रह् (c. 9. गृह्णाति, ग्रहीतुं) or हृ (c. 1. हरति, हर्त्तुं) or भुज्, अन्येन सह भुज् (c. 7. भुनक्ति, भुंक्ते, भोक्तुं), अन्येन सह भज्.

To SHARE, *v. n.* सहभागी -गिनी -गि (न्) भू, अंशी &c. भू, भागी &c. भू, अन्येन सह भोगं कृ or सहोपभोगं कृ, अंशं or भागं प्राप् (c. 5. -आप्नोति -आप्तुं) or लभ् (c. 1. लभते, लब्धुं), अंशं ग्रह् or आदा, सहभोगी &c. भू.

SHARE-HOLDER, *s.* अंशधारी *m.* (न्), भागधारी *m.*, विभागधारी *m.*, अंशभागी *m.*, अंशी *m.*, अंशग्राही *m.* (न्).

SHARED, *p. p.* विभक्तः -क्ता -क्तं, संविभक्तः &c., प्रविभक्तः &c., अंशितः -ता -तं, परिकल्पितः &c., अन्येन सह भुक्तः -क्ता -क्तं or सहोपभुक्तः &c.

SHARER, *s.* भागी *m.* (न्), अंशी *m.*, अंशहारी *m.* *See* PARTAKER.

SHARK, *s.* ग्राहः, तन्तुः *m.*, तन्तुणः, तन्तुनागः, नक्रराजः, मकरः, दृढदंशकः, जलकिराटः, समुद्रारुः *m.*, अवहारः, हाङ्गरः.

SHARP, *a.* (Having a keen edge) तीक्ष्णः -क्ष्णा -क्ष्णं, तीक्ष्णधारः -रा -रं, शितधारः &c., धाराधरः -रा -रं, शितः -ता -तं, निशितः &c., तीव्रः -व्रा -व्रं, तिग्मः -ग्मा -ग्मं, खरः -रा -रं, शातः -ता -तं, निशातः &c., प्रखरः -रा -रं, तेजोवान् -वती -वत् (त्), लविः -विः -वि; 'a sharp sword,' तीक्ष्णखड्गः, निशितनिस्त्रिंशः; 'sharp as a razor,' क्षुरधाराभः -भा -भं.—(Having a sharp point) तीक्ष्णाग्रः -ग्रा -ग्रं, शिताग्रः &c., तीक्ष्णशिखः -खा -खं, शातशिखः &c., सूक्ष्माग्रः &c., तीक्ष्णः &c.—(Acute of mind, quick, ready) तीक्ष्णबुद्धिः -द्धिः -द्धि, सूक्ष्मबुद्धिः &c., शीघ्रबुद्धिः &c., तीव्रबुद्धिः &c., विदग्धः -ग्धा -ग्धं, निपुणमतिः -तिः -ति, कुशलबुद्धिः &c., उत्पन्नमतिः &c., कुशाग्रीयमतिः &c., कुशाग्रमतिः &c., कुशाग्रबुद्धिः &c., प्रखरबुद्धिः &c., निपुणः -णा -णं, पटुः -टुः -टु, चतुरः -रा -रं.—(Quick in perception) शीघ्रग्राही -हिणी &c., सूक्ष्मः -क्ष्मा -क्ष्मं, सूक्ष्मग्राही &c., तीक्ष्णः -क्ष्णा -क्ष्णं; 'a sharp sight,' सूक्ष्मदृष्टिः *f.*, तीक्ष्णदृष्टिः *f.*—(Quick in action, smart) तीक्ष्णकर्म्मा -र्म्मा -र्म्म (न्), शीघ्रकर्म्मा &c., आशुकारी &c., शीघ्रकारी &c., क्षिप्रकारी &c.—(Witty) रसिकः -का -कं, विदग्धः -ग्धा -ग्धं.—(Sour, acid) अम्लः -म्ला -म्लं, अम्लरसः -सा -सं, शुक्तः -क्ता -क्तं, शौक्तिकः -की -कं, अरुन्तुदः -दा -दं.—(Pungent) कटुः -टुः -टु, उग्रः -ग्रा -ग्रं, रूक्षकः -का -कं, *see* PUNGENT.—(Severe, cutting)

तीक्ष्णः -क्ष्णा -क्ष्णं, तीव्रः -व्रा -व्रं, उग्रः -ग्रा -ग्रं, कटुः -टुः -टु, प्रखरः -रा -रं, खरः &c., अरुन्तुदः -दा -दं, मर्म्मस्पृक् *m. f. n.* (श्), मर्म्मवेधी &c., मर्म्मभेदी -दिनी &c.; 'sharp language,' वागसिः *f.*, वागिषुः *m.*, कटुवाक्यं, अरुन्तुदवाक् *f.* (च्); 'sharp pain,' तीव्रवेदना, शूलः -लं. —(Piercing) वेधकः -का -कं, वेधी &c.—(As sound) उदात्तः -त्ता -त्तं, कर्कशः -शा -शं.

SHARP, *s.* (Note) उदात्तः, उदात्तस्वरः, उच्चस्वरः.

SHARP-EDGED, *a.* तीक्ष्णधारः -रा -रं, शितधारः &c., निशितधारः &c.

To SHARPEN, *v. a.* तिज् (c. 10. तेजयति -यितुं), निशो (c. 4. -श्यति -शातुं), शो, निशि (c. 5. -शिनोति -शेतुं), क्ष्णु (c. 2. क्ष्णौति, क्ष्णवितुं), प्रक्ष्णु, संक्ष्णु, तीक्ष्णीकृ, तीक्ष्णधारीकृ, शितधारीकृ, तीक्ष्णाग्रीकृ; 'the appetite,' रुच् in caus.—(Sharpen up) उत्तिज्.

SHARPENED, *p. p.* तेजितः -ता -तं, निशितः -ता -तं, शितः &c., शातः &c., निशातः &c., विशितः &c., क्ष्णुतः &c.; 'as the appetite,' रुचितः &c.

SHARPER, *s.* कितवः, वञ्चकः, धूर्त्तः, कूटकः, प्रतारकः, कुहकः.

SHARPLY, *adv.* तीक्ष्णं, तीव्रं, सतैक्ष्ण्यं, तिग्मं, प्रखरं, अरुन्तुदं, निपुणं.

SHARPNESS, *s.* (Keenness of edge) तीक्ष्णता, तैक्ष्ण्यं, धारातीक्ष्णता, तेजस् *n.*, तीव्रता, तिग्मता, तैग्म्यं.—(Of point) तीक्ष्णाग्रता -त्वं, शिताग्रता.—(Of mind) बुद्धितीक्ष्णता, बुद्धितैक्ष्ण्यं, तीक्ष्णबुद्धित्वं, बुद्धिसूक्ष्मता, विदग्धता, वैदग्ध्यं, निपुणता, नैपुण्यं, बुद्धिकौशल्यं, पटुता, पाटवं, चतुरता, चातुर्य्यं, मतिप्रकर्षः.—(Sourness) अम्लता, शुक्तता.—(Pungency) कटुता, प्रखरता, प्राखर्य्यं, उग्रता, तीक्ष्णता.—(Severity) तीक्ष्णता, तैक्ष्ण्यं, तीव्रता, तिग्मता.—(Of sound) कर्कशता, कार्कश्यं, उदात्तत्वं.

SHARP-NOSED, *a.* खरणाः -णाः -णः (स्), खरणसः -सा -सं, तीक्ष्णनासः &c.

SHARP-POINTED, *a.* तीक्ष्णाग्रः -ग्रा -ग्रं, शिताग्रः &c., सूच्यग्रः &c.

SHARP-SET, *a.* तीक्ष्णक्षुधार्त्तः -र्त्ता -र्त्तं, बुभुक्षार्त्तः &c., तीक्ष्णक्षुधार्त्तः &c.

SHARP-SHOOTER, *s.* शीघ्रवेधी *m.*, लक्ष्यवेधी *m.* (न्), लक्ष्यवेधनकुशलः.

SHARP-SIGHTED, *a.* सूक्ष्मदृष्टिः -ष्टिः -ष्टि, सूक्ष्मदर्शी -र्शिनी -र्शि (न्), तीक्ष्णदृष्टिः &c., तीव्रदृष्टिः &c., काकदृष्टिः &c.

SHARP-WITTED, *a.* तीक्ष्णबुद्धिः -द्धिः -द्धि, सूक्ष्मबुद्धिः &c., शीघ्रबुद्धिः &c.

SHÁSTRA, SHÁSTER, *s.* A term applied to scientific or philosophical treatises and books of law. There are properly only six Shástras, comprising the five philosophical systems (*see* SCHOOL), and the code of legal institutes; viz. 1. मीमांसाशास्त्रं or पूर्व्वमीमांसाशास्त्रं, 2. सांख्यशास्त्रं, 3. वेदान्तशास्त्रं, 4. न्यायशास्त्रं, including under it the वैशेषिकशास्त्रं, 5. योगशास्त्रं, 6. धर्म्मशास्त्रं. The last includes the celebrated code of Manu or मानवधर्म्मशास्त्रं. The term Shástra is also applied to less important branches of literature, and when used in the singular number denotes the body of all that has been written on each subject; as, 'Treatises on rhetoric,' अलङ्कारशास्त्रं; 'poetical works,' काव्यशास्त्रं; 'Treatises on the mechanical arts,' शिल्पिशास्त्रं.

To SHATTER, *v. a.* (Break into many pieces) शतखण्डशः कृ or भिद् or भञ्ज्, सहस्रखण्डशः कृ, बहुखण्डशः कृ or भञ्ज्, शतखण्डीकृ, शतचूर्णीकृ, खण्डविखण्डीकृ, बहुशकलीकृ, खण्डं खण्डं कृ, छिन्नभिन्नीकृ, छेदविच्छेदं कृ, खण्ड्, मृद्, निष्पिष्, परिभञ्ज्, प्रभञ्ज्, पिष्, चूर्ण्.

To SHATTER, *v. n.* शतखण्डशो भू or भिद् in pass., शतचूर्णीभू.

SHATTERED, *p. p.* शतखण्डशो भिन्नः -न्ना -न्नं or भग्नः -ग्ना -ग्नं, शतचूर्णीकृतः -ता -तं, सहस्रखण्डशो भग्नः -ग्ना -ग्नं, छिन्नभिन्नः -न्ना -न्नं.

SHATTERING, *s.* परिभङ्गः, शतखण्डीकरणं, शतचूर्णीकरणं, छेदविच्छेदः.

To SHAVE, *v. a.* (With a razor) क्षौरं कृ, क्षुर् (c. 6. क्षुरति, क्षोरितुं), खुर् (c. 6. खुरति, खोरितुं) मुण्ड् (c. 1. मुण्डति -ण्डितुं, c. 10. मुण्डयति -यितुं), मुण्डनं कृ, आवप् (c. 10. -वापयति -यितुं, c. 1. -वपति -वप्तुं), परिवप्, वप्, वपनं कृ, वापं कृ, क्षुरेण or लुरेण छिद् (c. 7. छिनत्ति, छेत्तुं) or लू (c. 9. लुनाति, लवितुं), भद्राकरणं कृ; 'to shave the head,' शिरोमुण्डनं कृ.—(Pare) तक्ष् (c. 1. तक्षति -क्षितुं), तक्षणं कृ, त्वक्ष्, छिद्, अवछिद्, अवकृत्, क्लृप्.

SHAVED, SHAVEN, *p. p.* मुण्डितः -ता -तं, वापितः &c., परिवापितः &c., कृतक्षौरः -रा -रं, कृतवापनः -ना -नं, क्षुरितः -ता -तं, मुण्डः -ण्डा -ण्डं, कुण्डः -ण्डा -ण्डं; 'a number of shaved heads,' मुण्डमण्डली.

SHAVELING, *s.* मुण्डितशिराः *m.* (स्), वापितशिराः *m.*, मुण्डितः, मुण्डः.

SHAVER, *s.* (One who shaves) मुण्डकः, मुण्डी *m.* (न्), क्षुरी *m.*, मुण्डनकृत् *m.*, क्षौरकारी *m.* (न्), वपनकृत्.—(Boy) माणवकः.

SHAVING, *s.* (Act of cutting with a razor) क्षौरं, क्षौरकरणं, मुण्डनं, वपनं, वपः, वापः, परिवापः, वापनं, आवपनं.—(That which is pared off) तष्टं, विदलं, शकलं, खण्डः, छेदः, तनुछेदः, सूक्ष्मछेदः.

SHAWL, *s.* उत्तरीयं, प्रावरणं, प्रावारः, स्कन्धावरणं, स्कन्धवस्त्रं.

SHE, *pron.* सा (तद्), एषा (एतद्), इयं (इदं), असौ (अदस्).

SHEAF, *s.* शस्यस्तम्बः, शस्यस्तवकः, शस्यगुच्छः -च्छकः, शस्यमुष्टिः -ष्टी *f.*, शस्यभारः, स्तम्बः, स्तवकः, ताडः.

To SHEAR, *v. a.* लू (c. 9. लुनाति, लवितुं), कृत् (c. 6. कृन्तति, कर्त्तितुं), छिद् (c. 7. छिनत्ति, छेत्तुं), आवप् (c. 10. -वापयति -यितुं), परिवप्, वप्, मुण्ड् (c. 1. मुण्डति -ण्डितुं, c. 10. मुण्डयति -यितुं), क्लृप्, वपनं कृ, क्षौरं कृ; 'sheep,' मेषलोम छिद् or अवछिद् or लू.

SHEARED, *p. p.* लूनः -ना -नं, छिन्नलोमा -मा -म (न्), कृत्तलोमा &c.

SHEARER, *s.* छेदकः, छिद् in comp., लोमछिद्, लोमछेदकः, लवकः, लोमछेत्ता *m.* (तृ); 'of sheep,' मेषलोमछिद्.

SHEARING, *s.* छेदनं, लूनिः *f.*, लवनं, लवः, लुः *m.*, कर्त्तनं, कल्पनं, कॢप्तिः *f.*, क्षौरं, वपनं, वापः, परिवापः, मुण्डनं; 'of wool,' लोमछेदनं, लोमकर्त्तनं, मेषलोमछेदः.

SHEARS, *s. pl.*, कर्त्तनी, कर्त्तरी, कल्पनी, कृपाणी, खड्गधारा.

SHEAT-FISH, *s.* बोदालः, वदालः, सहस्रदंष्ट्रः, सहस्रदंष्ट्री *m.* (न्).

SHEATH, *s.* (Case, covering) कोषः, कोशः, पिधानं, तिरोधानं, आवेष्टनं, परिवेष्टनं, वेष्टनं, आवरणं, आच्छादनं, पुटः, पेशी.—(Of a sword) खड्गकोषः, खड्गपिधानं, खड्गाधारः, कोषः, दलं, पेशी, *see* SCABBARD.—(In botany) शुङ्गा, दलं.

To SHEATHE, SHEATH, *v. a.* (Put into a case) कोषे निविश् (c. 10. -वेशयति -यितुं), कोषं प्रविश्, कोषस्थं -स्थां कृ.—(Envelop with a covering) आवेष्ट्, परिवेष्ट्, आच्छद्, परिच्छद्, पिधा, आवृ, परिवृ, कोशेन परिवेष्ट्.

SHEATHED, *p. p.* कोषस्थः -स्था -स्थं, कोशस्थः &c., कोषनिवेशितः -ता -तं.

To SHED, *v. a.* (Let fall, cast) पत् (c. 10. पातयति -यितुं), मुच् (c. 6. मुञ्चति, c. 10. मोचयति -यितुं), निर्मुच्, गल् in caus., गलनं कृ, विगलनं कृ; 'the feathers,' पक्षगलनं कृ.—(Let flow, spill) पत् (c. 10. पातयति -यितुं), स्रु (c. 10. स्रावयति -यितुं, c. 1. स्रवति, स्रोतुं), मुच्, प्रमुच्, सृज् (c. 6. सृजति, स्रष्टुं), उत्सृज्, वृत् in caus., आवृत्, स्कन्द् (c. 10. स्कन्दयति -यितुं), क्षर् (c. 1. क्षरति -रितुं); 'to shed tears,' अश्रूणि पत् in caus., वाष्पं सृज्, अश्रूणि नेत्राभ्याम् आवृत् in caus.; 'to shed blood,' रक्तं स्रु in caus. or मुच् or मोक्ष्.

SHED, *p. p.* गलितः -ता -तं, विगलितः &c., पातितः &c., स्रावितः -ता -तं.

SHED, *s.* (Slight building) मण्डपः, मण्डपिका, मण्डपिका, धामः, वितर्द्धिः -र्द्धी *f.*, विहारः; 'for cattle,' गोष्ठं, गोगोष्ठं, गोस्थानकं, गोगृहं, गोशाला.

SHEDDER, *s.* (Of blood) रक्तस्रावकः, रक्तस्रावी *m.* (न्), रक्तमोचकः, रक्तपातकः, रक्तोत्पादकः, शोणितोत्पादकः, असृक्स्रावी *m.*

SHEEP, *s.* मेषः, अविः *m.*, अविकः, उरभः, उरणः, एडकः, भेडः, रोमशः, लोमशः, बहुरोमा *m.* (न्) ऊर्णायुः *m.*, अजः, *see* RAM; 'female,' मेषी -षिका, एडका, भेडी, उरणी, अविला, जालकिनी; 'flock of sheep,' औरभ्रकं, आविकटः.

SHEEP-COT, SHEEP-FOLD, *s.* मेषस्थानं -नकं, मेषशाला, मेषव्रजः, मेषालयः -यं.

SHEEPISH, *a.* अतिलज्जाशीलः -ला -लं, अतिलज्जावान् -वती -वत् (त्), मेषस्वभावः -वा -वं, मेषशीलः -ला -लं, जनभीतः -ता -तं, सभाभीतः &c.

SHEEPISHNESS, *s.* अतिलज्जा, मेषशीलता, जनभीतिः *f.*, सभाभीतिः *f.*

SHEEP-SHEARER, SHEEP-SHEARING. *See* SHEARER, SHEARING.

SHEEP-SKIN, *s.* मेषचर्म्म *n.* (न्), मेषलोम *n.* (न्), मेषाजिनं, अविचर्म्म.

SHEEP-STEALER, *s.* मेषहर्त्ता *m.* (र्तृ), मेषहारी *m.* (न्), मेषापहारकः.

SHEEP-STEALING, *s.* मेषहरणं, मेषापहारः, मेषापहरणं, मेषचौरं.

SHEER, *a.* (Mere, unmixed) मात्र in comp., मात्रकः -का -कं, केवलः -ला -ली -लं, केवली -लिनी -लि (न्), शुद्धः -द्धा -द्धं, *see* MERE.

To SHEER OFF, *v. n.* अपसृ, अपसृप्, अपसृप्, पलाय्, *see To* DECAMP. —(Move off on one side) पार्श्वं or पार्श्वतो गम् or चल्.

SHEET, *s.* (Of a bed, &c.) प्रच्छदपटः, प्रच्छदवस्त्रं, उत्तरप्रच्छदः, उत्तरच्छदः, शय्याच्छादनं, निचोलः.—(Of paper) पत्रं -त्रकं, पत्रिका, फलकः.—(Of metal) पत्रं, फलकः.—(Of water) वारिराशिः *m.*, वारिपत्वरः.—(Winding sheet) शववस्त्रं.

SHEET-ANCHOR, *s.* बृहल्लङ्करः, महालङ्करः, बृहदङ्कुशः. There is no Sanskrit equivalent for the modern anchor: लङ्करः is borrowed from the Persian.

SHEET-IRON, *s.* लोहपत्रं -त्रकं, लोहपत्रिका, लोहफलकः.

SHE-GOAT, *s.* अजा, छागी. *See* GOAT.

SHELF, *s.* (Board or bracket in a wall) नागदन्तः -न्तकः, नागनिर्य्यूहः, निर्य्यूहः, नागः, सालारं, भित्तिबहिःस्थः फलकः, भित्तिबहिःस्थं दीर्घकाष्ठं; 'set of shelves,' कपाटः -टं.—(Sand-bank) सैकतं.

SHELL, *s.* (Hard covering of an animal) कम्बुः -म्बु *m. n.*, कवचः -चं; 'conch-shell,' शङ्खः, शङ्खकः -कं, शम्बूकः, जलजं, शुक्तिः *f.*, शूचिकामुखं, कम्बुः -म्बुकः; 'bivalve-shell,' कम्बुः *m.*, शम्बुः *m.*, शम्बुकः, शम्बूकः, शम्बुकः, जलशुक्तिः *f.*; 'oyster-shell,' शुक्तिः *f.*, शुक्तिपुटं, शुक्तिपेशी; 'small shell,' क्षुद्रशङ्खः, शुक्तिः *f.*, शङ्खनखः; 'used as a coin,' कपर्दः, कपर्दकः, *see* COWRIE; 'worker or dealer in shells,' शङ्खकारः, शङ्खी *m.* (न्), शाङ्खिकः, काम्बविकः; 'contained in a shell,' शुक्त्यन्तर्गतः -ता -तं.—(Of an egg) अण्डकवचः -चं, पेशी -शिः *f.*, अण्डपुटः -टं, अण्डपेशी.—(Of a nut, &c.) कवचः -चं.—(Of a pea, &c.) बीजकोशः, सिम्बा.—(Husk) त्वक् *f.* (च्), तुषः, कञ्चुकः, कोशः, पुटः.—(Envelope) पुटः, कोशः, कोषः, आवेष्टनं, परिवेष्टनं, पेशी -शिः *f.*—(Outer part) बहिर्भागः, बाह्यभागः, बहिर्भागमात्रं.—(Bomb), *see* the word.

To SHELL, *v. a.* निस्त्वचीकृ, निस्त्वच (nom. निस्त्वचयति -यितुं), त्वच (nom. त्वचयति -यितुं), निस्तुषीकृ, निष्पुटीकृ, त्वचं or पुटं हृ or निर्हृ.

SHELL-CUTTER, *s.* शाङ्खिकः, शङ्खी *m.* (न्), शङ्खच्छेदकः, काम्बविकः.

SHELLED, *p. p.* निस्त्वचः -चा -चं, निस्त्वचीकृतः -ता -तं, निस्तुषितः &c.

SHELL-FISH, *s.* कम्बुस्थः, कम्बुवासी *m.* (न्), शङ्खस्थः, शुक्तिस्थः, कोशस्थः, कोशवासी *m.*, कम्बुयुक्तजन्तुः *m.*, कम्बुस्थमत्स्यः.

SHELLY, *a.* शङ्खी -ङ्खिनी -ङ्खि (न्), शाङ्खिकः -की -कं, काम्बवः -वी -वं, कम्बुमयः -यी -यं, शङ्खमयः &c., कम्बुपूर्णः -र्णा -र्णं, शङ्खाढ्यः &c.

SHELTER, *s.* आश्रयः, समाश्रयः, संश्रयः, आश्रयणं, शरणं, आश्रयः, आयः, छत्रं, अवस्थानं, निवासस्थानं, अवकाशः; 'to take shelter,' आश्रि, समाश्रि, शरणार्थं गम्, *see* under SHELTER; 'being in shelter,' आश्रयस्थः -स्था -स्थं; 'having taken shelter,' आश्रित्य.

To SHELTER, *v. a.* (Give shelter) आश्रयं दा, आश्रयः or शरणं भू.—(Protect, cover) रक्ष्, गुप्, पाल्, छद्, प्रच्छद्, गुप्तिं कृ, गोपनं कृ.—(Shelter one's self) आश्रि (c. 1. -श्रयति -यितुं), समाश्रि.

SHELTERED, *p. p.* or *a.* आश्रितः -ता -तं, समाश्रितः &c., संश्रितः &c., साश्रयः -या -यं.—(From the wind) निर्वातः -ता -तं.

SHELTERING, *part.* आश्रयभूतः -ता -तं, आश्रयदाता -त्री -तृ (तृ).

SHELTERLESS, *a.* निराश्रयः -या -यं, अनाश्रयः &c., आश्रयहीनः -ना -नं.

To SHELVE, *v. n.* प्रवणः -णा -णं भू, प्रवणीभू, पातुकः -का -कं भू, क्रमशः प्रवणीभू or अधोगम् or पत्.

SHELVING, *part.* or *a.* प्रवणः -णा -णं, पातुकः -का -कं, क्रमशः प्रवणः -णा -णं or अधोगामी -मिनी &c.; 'shelving ground,' प्रवः, प्रवणभूमिः.

SHEPHERD, *s.* मेषपालः -लकः, पशुपालः -लकः, अविपालः, पशुरक्षी *m.* (न्), मेषरक्षी *m.*, मेषरक्षकः, मेषपोषकः, औरभ्रिकः, उरभ्रपालः; 'his business,' मेषपालनं, पशुपालनं, पाशुपाल्यं; 'shepherd's boy,' पालदारकः.

SHEPHERDESS, *s.* मेषपाली, मेषपालका, पशुपाली, मेषरक्षिणी.

SHERBET, *s.* शर्बतसंज्ञकं रसिकपानीयं, शर्करादिमिश्रितं मद्यजक्षीरादिरसमयं पानीयं.

SHERIFF, *s.* न्यायसभाध्यक्षः, धर्म्मसभाध्यक्षः, निर्णयपादप्रवर्त्तनाधिकारी *m.* (न्), निर्णयप्रवर्त्तकः, राज्यनियमप्रवर्त्तकः.

SHERRY, *s.* स्पेनाख्यदेशजः प्रसिद्धमद्यविशेषः.

SHEW, *To* SHEW, SHEWN, *see* SHOW, *To* SHOW, &c.

SHIELD, *s.* (Buckler) फलकः -कं, फलं, फरं, चर्म्म *n.* (न्), चर्म्मं, आवरणं, चर्म्मावरणं, आवरकः -कं, स्फुरः, सङ्कराटः, खेटिका, ढालं, अङ्कफलं; 'armed with a shield or bearing one,' फलकी *m.* (न्), फलकपाणिः *m.*, चर्म्मी *m.*, ढाली *m.* (न्), फलकभृत् *m.*—(Defence) रक्षणं, गुप्तिः *f.*, त्राणं.

To SHIELD, *v. a.* रक्ष्, त्रै, गुप्, पाल्, छद्. *See To* PROTECT, COVER.

SHIELDED, *p. p.* रक्षितः -ता -तं, छादितः &c., आवृतः &c., अन्तरितः &c.

To SHIFT, *v. n.* (Change) परिवृत् (c. 1. -वर्त्तते -र्त्तितुं), विवृत्, विपरिवृत्, सम्परिवृत्.—(Move, change place) चल् (c. 1. चलति -लितुं), विचल्, स्थानान्तरं गम् (गच्छति, गन्तुं) or चल् or या, स्थलान्तरं गम्.—(Change clothes) वस्त्रान्तरं परिधा, निवस्.—(Shift for a livelihood) दिननिर्वाहं कृ, अगतिकगतिं कृ.

To SHIFT, *v. a.* (Change) परिवृत् (c. 10. -वर्त्तयति -यितुं), विपरिवृत्, विकृ (c. 8. -करोति -कर्त्तुं), विह्वृ; 'he shifts his course,' स्वमार्गं विकरोति.—(Cause to change place) विचल् (c. 10. -चालयति -यितुं), चल्, स्थानान्तरं गम् in caus., स्थानान्तरीकृ, स्थलान्तरीकृ, अन्यत्र कृ.—(Shift off), *see To* PUT OFF.

SHIFT, *s.* (Expedient) उपायः, गतिः *f.*, युक्तिः *f.*, अभ्युपायः.—(Evasion, trick) छद्म *n.* (न्), छलं, अपदेशः, व्यपदेशः.—(Under garment) अन्तरीयं, अधोवस्त्रं, अधोवसनं, अधोंशुकं.

Shilly-shally, *s.* विकल्पः, अस्थिरता, चापल्यं. *See* Irresolution.

Shin, *s.* जङ्घाग्रभागः, जङ्घायाः पूर्व्वास्थि *n.*, अग्रजङ्घा.

To shine, *v. n.* प्रकाश् (c. 1. -काशते -शितुं, c. 4. -काश्यते), काश्, द्युत् (c. 1. द्योतते -तितुं), विद्युत्, राज् (c. 1. राजति -ते -जितुं), अभिराज्, अभिविराज्, दीप् (c. 4. दीप्यते -पितुं), स्फुर् (c. 6. स्फुरति -रितुं), शुभ् (c. 1. शोभते -भितुं), विशुभ्, भास् (c. 1. भासते -सितुं), आभास्, प्रभास्, अवभास्, भा (c. 2. भाति -तुं), प्रभा, आभा, विभा, उद्भा, चकास् (c. 2. चकास्ति -सितुं), रुच् (c. 1. रोचते -चितुं), ज्वल् (c. 1. ज्वलति -लितुं), उज्ज्वल्, वर्चस् (nom. वर्चायते), ओजस् (nom. ओजायते); 'to shine very brightly,' दीप् in freq. (देदीप्यते), ज्वल् in freq. (जाज्वल्यते), शुभ् in freq. (शोशुभ्यते), अतितेजसा प्रकाश्; 'the fixed stars shine by their own light,' नक्षत्राणि स्वप्रकाशानि भवन्ति; 'planets shine by reflected light,' ग्रहाः परावृत्तकिरणैर् प्रकाश्यन्ते.

Shine, *s.* प्रभा, प्रकाशः, द्युतिः *f.*, तेजस् *n.* *See* Sun-shine.

Shingle, *s.* (Gravel, pebble) शर्करा, शिलाखण्डः, वर्त्तुलशिला, वेलाहतशिला, वेलाहतशर्करा.—(Thin plank) फलकः.

Shining, *part.* or *a.* प्रकाशमानः -ना -नं, दीप्तिमान् -मती -मत् (त्), द्युतिमान् &c., द्योती -तिनी -ति (न्), द्योतमानः -ना -नं, विद्योतमानः &c., शोभमानः &c., देदीप्यमानः &c., विराजमानः &c., प्रभावान् &c., कान्तिमान् &c., तेजस्वी &c., भास्वान् &c., भास्वरः -री -रं, भास्करः -रा -रं, प्रकाशन् -शन्ती -शत् (त्), स्फुरन् &c., भासयन् &c., प्रकाशः -शा -शं, प्रकाशी &c., काशी &c., काशिष्णुः -ष्णुः -ष्णु. *See* Bright.

Shiny, *a.* दीप्तिमान् -मती -मत् (त्), तेजोमयः -यी -यं. *See* Bright.

Ship, *s.* वृहन्नौका, वृहन्नौः *f.*, वृहत्तरणी, नौः *f.*, नौका, वृहत्पोतः, पोतः, तरणिः -णी *f.*, अर्णवयानं, जलयानं, अर्णवपोतः, वोहित्थं, मद्गुः *m.*, प्लवः; 'to take ship,' नौकाम् आरुह् (c. 1. -रोहति -रोढुं); 'ship of war,' युद्धनौः *f.*, युद्धनौका.

Ship, an affix denoting abstract state or office is rendered by ता or त्वं; as, 'a judge,' धर्म्माध्यक्षः; 'judgeship,' धर्म्माध्यक्षता -त्वं; 'a son,' पुत्रः; 'sonship,' पुत्रता -त्वं.

To ship, *v. a.* (Put on board ship) नौकाम् आरुह् in caus. (-रोपयति -यितुं) or प्रविश् (c. 10. -वेशयति -यितुं), नौकायां निविश् or सम् in caus.—(Fix in its place) स्वस्थाने धा or रुह् in caus., स्वस्थानीकृ.

Ship-master, *s.* नौकापतिः *m.*, नौस्वामी *m.* (न्), नौकास्वामी *m.*, नौकाधिपतिः.

Shipment, *a.* नौकारोपणं, नौकाप्रवेशनं, नौकासमर्पणं.

Shipping, *s.* नौकासमूहः, नौकादिसमूहः, नौकासमवायः, नाविकं.

Ship-wreck, *s.* नौभङ्गः, नौकाभङ्गः, नौभेदः, नौकानाशः, नौव्यसनं, नौकाव्यसनं, नौकामज्जनं.—(Destruction) नाशः, विनाशः.

To ship-wreck, *v. a.* नौकां भञ्ज् (c. 7. भनक्ति, भंक्तुं) or भिद् (c. 7. भिनत्ति, भेत्तुं) or नश् (c. 10. नाशयति -यितुं) or विनश्, नौभङ्गं कृ, नौभेदं कृ, नौव्यसनं कृ or जन्, उत्कूल् (c. 10. -कूलयति -यितुं), कूलोपरि क्षिप्.

Ship-wrecked, *p. p.* भिन्ननौकः -का -कं, भग्ननौकः &c., उत्कूलितः -ता -तं, कूलोपरि क्षिप्तः -प्ता -प्तं, सैकतोपरि क्षिप्तः &c.

To shirk, *v. a.* or *n.* छलेन कर्त्तव्यतां त्यज् or परिहृ or हा, छलेन पलाय् (c. 1. पलायते -यितुं, rt. इ) or व्यपदिश् (c. 6. -दिशति -देष्टुं), छलं कृ, छद्म कृ, व्यपदेशं कृ, अपदेशं कृ, अपसृप्, व्यपसृप्, अपक्रम्, अपधाव्.

Shirk, shirker, *s.* कर्त्तव्यत्यागी *m.* (न्), कर्त्तव्यतात्यागी *m.*, छद्मकारी *m.*

Shirt, *s.* अन्तरीयं, अधोवस्त्रं, अधोवसनं, अधोंशुकं, अन्तर्वस्त्रं, अन्तर्वसनं, क्षौमवस्त्रं, क्षौमवसनं, क्षौमाम्बरं.

To shiver, *v. a.* शतखण्डशः कृ or भिद्, सूक्ष्मखण्डशो भिद्, शतखण्डीकृ, सहस्रखण्डशो भञ्ज्, शतचूर्णीकृ, चूर्णीकृ, चूर्ण्, निष्पिष्. *See To* shatter, *v. a.*

To shiver, *v. n.* (Fall or be broken into many small pieces) सहस्रखण्डशो भिद् in pass. or पत्, शतखण्डशो भिद् in pass., शतचूर्णीभू.—(Quake or shake with cold, &c.) शीतार्त्तत्वात् कम्प् (c. 1. कम्पते -म्पितुं) or विकम्प् or प्रकम्प्, हिमार्त्तत्वाद् वेप् (c. 1. वेपते -पितुं) or प्रवेप्, सीत्कारं कृ, शीत्कारं कृ.

Shiver, *s.* (Small fragment) सूक्ष्मखण्डः -खण्डकः, भित्तिः *f.*, शकलः -लं, छेदः, दलं, छिन्नं, भिन्नं; 'into shivers,' सहस्रखण्डशः, सूक्ष्मखण्डशः.—(Shaking) कम्पः, सीत्कारः, *see* Shivering, *s.*

Shivered, *p. p.* सहस्रखण्डशो भिन्नः -न्ना -न्नं, सूक्ष्मखण्डशो भिन्नः &c., शतखण्डीकृतः -ता -तं, छिन्नभिन्नः &c., चूर्णितः &c., जर्ज्जरः -रा -रं.

Shivering, *s.* (The act of shattering) सहस्रखण्डशो भेदः -दनं, शतखण्डीकरणं, शतचूर्णीकरणं, चूर्णीकरणं, निष्पेषः -षणं.—(Quaking, trembling with cold, &c.) शीतार्त्तत्वात् or शीताविष्टत्वात् कम्पः or कम्पनं, विकम्पः -म्पनं, शरीरकम्पः, देहकम्पः, अङ्गकम्पः, वेपनं, वेपथुः *m.*, सीत्कारः, शीत्कारः, सीत्कृतं.

Shivering, *part.* (As with cold) कम्पमानः -ना -नं, विकम्पमानः &c., कम्पनः -ना -नं, कम्पान्वितः -ता -तं, वेपमानः -ना -नं, कम्पितः -ता -तं.

Shoal, *s.* (A shallow) सैकतं, पुलिनं, कूलं, गाधभूमिः *f.*, उत्तानभूमिः *f.*—(Crowd) सङ्घः, सङ्घातः, समूहः; 'of fish,' मत्स्यसङ्घातः, मत्स्यसङ्घः, पोताधानं.

Shock, *s.* (Concussion) क्षोभः, विक्षोभः, संक्षोभः, संघट्टः -ट्टनं, आकस्मिकक्षोभः, आघातः, व्याघातः.—(Impression of terror or disgust) त्रासावेशः, बीभत्सावेशः.—(Pile of sheaves) शस्यस्तम्बोत्करः, शस्यस्तम्बकचितिः *f.* -राशिः *m.*

To shock, *v. a.* (Shake by sudden collision) क्षुभ् (c. 10. क्षोभयति -यितुं), विक्षुभ्, संक्षुभ्, अकस्मात् क्षुभ्, संघट्ट् (c. 10. -घट्टयति -यितुं), आकस्मिकक्षोभं कृ.—(Strike with sudden terror or disgust) आकस्मिकत्रासं कृ or जन् (c. 10. जनयति -यितुं), आकस्मिकसाध्वसं कृ or जन्, बीभत्सं कृ or जन्, दारुण्यं कृ or जन् or उत्पद् in caus., भैरवं जन्.—(Pile sheaves) शस्यस्तम्बान् राशीकृ.

Shocked, *p. p.* (Struck with sudden horror) आकस्मिकत्रासोपहतः -ता -तं, साध्वसोपहतः &c., अकस्मात् साध्वसोपहतः &c. or बीभत्सोपहतः &c.

Shocking, *a.* आकस्मिकत्रासदः -दा -दं, आकस्मिकत्रासकरः -रा -रं, साध्वसकारी -रिणी -रि (न्), त्रासजनकः -का -कं, बीभत्सकरः -रा -रं.

Shod, *p. p.* सपादुकः -का -कं, उपपादुकः -की -कं, पादुकायुक्तः -क्ता -क्तं, सपादत्रः -त्रा -त्रं, उपानद्युक्तः -क्ता -क्तं, उपानद्गुप्तः -प्ता -प्तं, उपानद्गूढः &c.

Shoe, *s.* पादुका, पादत्रं, उपानत् *f.* (ह्), पादूः *f.*, पादपा, पादत्राणं, पादरक्षा, चरणत्राणं, प्राणहिता, वध्रं, पादबन्धनं; 'of a horse,' खुरत्रं, खुरत्राणं.

To shoe, *v. a.* पादुकायुक्तं कृ, सपादुकं कृ, उपानद्युक्तं कृ, पादुकाबन्धनं कृ, पादुकां बन्ध् (c. 9. बध्नाति, बन्धुं).

Shoe-black, shoe-cleaner, *s.* पादुकामार्जकः, पादुकासम्मार्जकः, पादुकामार्जः.

Shoeless, *a.* पादुकाहीनः -ना -नं, अपपादत्रः -त्रा -त्रं, निष्पादुकः -का -कं.

Shoe-maker, *s.* पादुकाकारः, पादुकाकृत् *m.*, पादूकृत् *m.*, पादुकृत् *m.*, चर्म्मकारः -रकः, चर्म्मकृत् *m.*, चर्म्मकारी *m.* (न्), चर्म्मारः; 'shoe-maker's knife,' चर्म्मप्रभेदिका, आरा.

SHOE-STRING, *s.* पादुकाबन्धनं-नी, पादुकाबन्धः, पादुकायोक्त्रं, उपानद्बन्धनं, पादुकाबन्धनसूत्रं, पादुकाबन्धनरज्जुः *m. f.*

To SHOOT, *v. a.* (Let fly, discharge) क्षिप् (c. 6. क्षिपति, क्षेप्तुं), प्रक्षिप्, मुच् (c. 6. मुञ्चति, मोक्तुं), प्रमुच्, मोक्ष् (c. 10. मोक्षयति -यितुं), अस् (c. 4. अस्यति -सितुं), प्रास्, सृज् (c. 6. सृजति, स्रष्टुं), पत् (c. 10. पातयति -यितुं), ईर् (c. 10. ईरयति -यितुं), उदीर्, त्यज्; 'to shoot an arrow,' शरं प्रक्षिप्; 'a dart,' अस्त्रं क्षिप्; 'a bullet from a gun,' आग्नेयनाडेर् लोहगुलिकां प्रक्षिप् or निःसृ in caus.—(Strike with any thing, kill) प्रहृ (c. 1. -हरति -हर्त्तुं), आहन् (c. 2. -हन्ति -न्तुं), हन्, अभ्याहन्, व्यध् (c. 4. विध्यति, व्यद्धुं), आव्यध्; 'with an arrow,' शरेण आहन्.—(Emit) उत्सृज्, विसृज्, निरस्, निःसृ in caus.—(Thrust forward) प्रसृ in caus.

To SHOOT, *v. n.* (With an arrow) शरप्रक्षेपं कृ, शरासनं कृ.—(With a gun) गुलिकाप्रक्षेपं कृ.—(Germinate) स्फुट्, उद्भिद् in pass., प्रोद्भिद्, प्ररुह्, विकस्, अङ्कुर (nom. अङ्कुरयति -यितुं), फुल्ल्.—(As pain) मर्म्म व्यध् (c. 4. विध्यति, व्यद्धुं), मर्म्मवेधनं कृ, शूल् (c. 1. शूलति -लितुं), शूलोपहतः -ता -तं भू, तीक्ष्णवेदनाम् अनुभू, तीव्रवेदनोपहतः -ता -तं भू.

SHOOT, *s.* (Sprout) अङ्कुरः, पल्लवः, किसलयः, किशलयः, किसलः -लं, नवपल्लवः, प्ररोहः, प्रबालः, उद्भिज्जः, उद्भिद् *f.*, विसलं, नवविटपः, बालविटपः.

SHOOTER, *s.* क्षेप्ता *m.* (प्तृ), प्रक्षेप्ता *m.*, शरप्रक्षेपकः, गुलिकाप्रक्षेपकः; 'a good or sharp shooter,' शीघ्रवेधी *m.* (न्).

SHOOTING, *part.* (Sprouting) उद्भिज्जः -ज्जा -ज्जं, उद्भिद् *m. f. n.*, प्ररोही &c.

SHOOTING, *s.* (Act of shooting arrows) शरप्रक्षेपः -पणं, शरासनं, बाणासनं, बाणमोक्षणं, शरमोक्षणं.—(Bullets, &c., with a gun) गुलिकाप्रक्षेपः, गुलिकासनं, गोलासनं.—(Sharp pain) शूलः -लं, तोदः -दनं, वेदना, तीक्ष्णवेदना, तीव्रवेदना.

SHOP, *s.* पण्यशाला, विक्रयशाला, विक्रयगृहं, विक्रयस्थानं, पण्यवीथी-थिः *f.*, पण्यवीथिका, वीथिः -थी *f.*, विपणिः -णी *m. f.*, आपणः, आसनी, पणिः *f.*, आवारिः *m.*; 'work-shop,' शिल्पशाला, शिल्पगृहं.

To SHOP, *v. n.* द्रव्यक्रयणार्थं विक्रयशालाम् अभिगम् (c. 1. -गच्छति -गन्तुं).

SHOP-KEEPER, *s.* आपणिकः, विपणी *m.* (न्), पण्याजीवः, पण्यशालाधिकारी *m.* (न्), व्यापारी *m.*, क्रयविक्रयोपजीवी *m.*, क्रयविक्रयिकः, तुलाधारः.

SHOP-LIFTER, *s.* चिल्लाभः, विक्रयशालास्थद्रव्यापहर्त्ता *m.* (र्त्तृ).

SHOP-LIFTING, *s.* विक्रयशालास्थद्रव्यहरणं, पण्यशालास्थद्रव्यापहरणं.

SHOP-MAN, *s.* विक्रयशालायां सेवकः or कर्म्मकरः, आपणिकः.

SHOPPING, *s.* पण्यशालाभिगमनं, विक्रयशालाभिगमनं, पण्यशालासेवनं.

SHORE, *s.* तीरं, कूलं, तटं, प्रतीरं, रोधस्, वेला, कूलभूः *f.*, मर्य्यादा, अधुमान् *m.* (त्), वप्रः, आयोगः, पाठकः; 'of the sea,' समुद्रतीरं, समुद्रतटं, समुद्रान्तः -न्तं; 'brought to shore,' उत्कूलितः -ता -तं.—(Prop) उपस्तम्भः, उपघ्नः.

To SHORE, *v. a.* (Prop) दीर्घकाष्ठेन उपस्तम्भ् or संस्तम्भ्.

SHORN, *p. p.* (Cut off) छिन्नः -न्ना -न्नं, अवच्छिन्नः &c., लूनः -ना -नं.—(Having the hair or wool cut off) छिन्नकेशः -शा -शं, छिन्नलोमा -मा -म (न्), कृत्तकेशः &c., कृत्तलोमा &c., मुण्डितः -ता -तं, कृतमुण्डनः -ना -नं, कृतवापः -पा -पं, परिवापितः -ता -तं, कृतचूडः -डा -डं.—(Deprived) हृतः -ता -तं, अपहृतः &c., हीनः -ना -नं.

SHORT, *a.* (Not long, not having great extension) ह्रस्वः -स्वा -स्वं, अल्पः -ल्पा -ल्पं, क्षुद्रः -द्रा -द्रं, स्वल्पः -ल्पा -ल्पं, अल्पकः -का -कं, अदीर्घः -र्घा -र्घं; 'very short,' ह्रसिष्ठः -ष्ठा -ष्ठं; 'a short plank,' क्षुद्रफलकः, ह्रस्वफलकः; 'a short distance,' कियद्दूरं, ईषद्दूरं, कियत्पर्य्यन्तं.—(Not long in time) अल्पकालिकः -की -कं, अल्पकालीनः -ना -नं, अदीर्घकालिकः &c., अदीर्घकालीनः &c., अल्पकालस्थायी -यिनी -यि (न्), अचिरस्थायी &c.; 'in a short time,' *see* SHORTLY; 'for a short time,' अल्पकालं, अल्पकालमात्रं, अल्पमात्रं, कियत्कालं, ईषत्कालं; 'a short delay,' क्षणक्षेपः.—(Short in size or measure) ह्रस्वपरिमाणः -णा -णं, अल्पपरिमाणः &c., क्षुद्रपरिमाणः &c., अल्पप्रमाणः &c., अल्पप्रमाणकः -का -कं.—(In stature) ह्रस्वः -स्वा -स्वं, ह्रस्वशरीरः -रा -रं, ह्रस्वाङ्गः -ङ्गी -ङ्गं, अल्पशरीरः &c., अल्पतनुः -नुः -नु, वामनतनुः &c., क्षुद्रतनुः &c., अल्पमूर्त्तिः -र्त्तिः -र्त्ति, ह्रस्वमूर्त्तिः -र्त्तिः -र्त्ति, स्तोककायः -या -यं, वामनः -ना -नं, खर्वः -र्वा -र्वं, अतुङ्गः -ङ्गा -ङ्गं, नीचः -चा -चं, नीचकः -का -कं, पृश्निः -श्निः -श्नि, न्यङ् नीची न्यक्.—(Brief) अविस्तीर्णः -र्णा -र्णं, संक्षिप्तः -प्ता -प्तं, परिमितशब्दकः -का -कं, अल्पशब्दकः &c.—(Insufficient) न्यूनः -ना -नं, हीनः -ना -नं, अपर्य्याप्तः -प्ता -प्तं, अनुपयुक्तः &c.—(Deficient in) हीनः -ना -नं, न्यूनः -ना -नं, विकलः -ला -लं, रहितः -ता -तं, ह्रसितः &c.—(Not of adequate extent) न्यूनपरिमाणः -णा -णं, न्यूनः -ना -नं; 'short of one's expectations,' आशान्यूनः -ना -नं; or expressed by ऋते, विना, अन्तरेण, वर्जयित्वा &c.; as, 'I shall be satisfied with nothing short of Ráma's exile,' नान्येन तुष्येयम् ऋते रामविवासनात्, *see* EXCEPT.—(As a vowel, &c.) लघुः -घुः -घ्वी -घु, ह्रस्वः -स्वा -स्वं; 'a short vowel,' ह्रस्वस्वरः, मात्रा.—(Friable) सुचूर्णनीयः -या -यं, आशुचूर्णनीयः &c., चूर्णगुणकः -का -कं, चूर्णनशीलः -ला -लं, भञ्जनशीलः &c., भिदुरः -रा -रं.—(To be short, come short), *see To* FAIL, *v. n.*—(To cut short), *see To* CURTAIL, LESSEN.—(To fall short), *see To* FAIL, *v. n.*—(To stop short) अकस्मात् स्था or अवस्था, मार्गमध्ये स्था, अर्द्धमार्गे स्था or निवृत्.—(In short) संक्षेपतस्, समासतस्, अल्पशब्दतस्, सङ्क्षेपतस्, वस्तुतस्.

SHORT-BREAD, SHORT-CAKE, *s.* सुभेद्यपिष्टकः, सुचूर्णनीयपिष्टकः.

SHORT-COMING, *s.* दोषः, अपराधः, न्यूनता, अतिपातः, अपक्रिया, उपात्ययः, परित्यागः, छिद्रं, वैकल्यं. *See* FAULT.

To SHORTEN, *v. a.* (Make short) ह्रस् (c. 10. ह्रासयति -यितुं), ह्रस्वीकृ, अल्पीकृ, न्यूनीकृ, वामनीकृ.—(Contract) संक्षिप्, संह्र, संकुच्.

To SHORTEN, *v. n.* अल्पीभू, न्यूनीभू, ह्रस् (c. 1. ह्रसते -सितुं), ह्रस्वीभू.

SHORTENED, *p. p.* ह्रसितः -ता -तं, न्यूनीकृतः -ता -तं, न्यूनीभूतः &c., अल्पीकृतः &c., अल्पीभूतः &c., संक्षिप्तः -प्ता -प्तं, संकुचितः -ता -तं.

SHORT-HAND, *s.* संक्षिप्ताक्षरलिखनं, संक्षिप्ताक्षरलिपिः *f.*, संक्षिप्ताक्षरं; 'the art,' संक्षिप्ताक्षरलेखनविद्या.

SHORT-LIVED, *a.* अल्पायुः -युः -यु or अल्पायूः -यूः -युः (स्), ह्रसितायुः &c., अल्पवयाः -याः -यः (स्), अल्पकालिकः -का -कं, अचिरस्थायी -यिनी -यि (न्), अचिरजीवी &c., अदीर्घजीवी &c., क्षणस्थायी &c., क्षणजीवी &c.

SHORTLY, *adv.* (Quickly, in a little time) अचिरेण, अचिरात्, न चिरेण, न चिरात्, शीघ्रं, सद्यस्, झटिति.—(In a few words) अल्पशब्दतस्, संक्षेपतस्, समासतस्, अविस्तरेण, अविस्तरशस्.

SHORTNESS, *s.* ह्रस्वता -त्वं, ह्रसिमा *m.* (न्), अल्पता -त्वं, क्षुद्रता, अदीर्घता.—(Of time) अल्पकालिकत्वं, कालाल्पता.—(Of life) आयुरल्पता -त्वं.—(Of size or stature) ह्रस्वता, ह्रस्वशरीरता, अल्पशरीरता,

वामनता, खर्वता, नीचता, अतुङ्गता.—(Briefness) अविस्तीर्णता, अविस्तारः, अविस्तरः, संक्षेपः, संक्षिप्तता, संक्षिप्तिः f., उपसंक्षेपः, समस्तता, विस्ताराभावः, अल्पविस्तारः.—(Insufficiency, deficiency) न्यूनता -त्वं, हीनता, अपर्य्याप्तिः f., अल्पत्वं, वैकल्यं, परिमितता.

SHORT-SIGHTED, a. अल्पदृष्टिः -ष्टिः -ष्टि, अल्पदृक् m. f. n. (श्), अल्पदृक्, अदूरदृष्टिः &c., अदीर्घदृष्टिः &c., अदूरदर्शी -र्शिनी &c., अदीर्घदर्शी &c.

SHORT-SIGHTEDNESS, s. अदीर्घदृष्टिः f., अदूरदृष्टिः f., अल्पदृष्टिः f.

SHORT-WINDED, a. दुःश्वासी -सिनी -सि (न्), श्वासकृच्छ्रग्रस्तः -स्ता -स्तं.

SHOT, p. p. (Discharged, as an arrow, &c.) क्षिप्तः -प्ता -प्तं, प्रक्षिप्तः &c., अस्तः -स्ता -स्तं, निरस्तः &c., मुक्तः -क्ता -क्तं, धनुर्मुक्तः &c.; 'as a bullet, &c.,' आग्नेययन्त्रमुक्तः &c., यन्त्रमुक्तः &c.; 'is shot forth,' प्रक्षिप्यते, निःसार्य्यते.—(Struck with an arrow) शराहतः -ता -तं, बाणाहतः &c., शरविद्धः -द्धा -द्धं; 'with a bullet,' गुलिकाहतः -ता -तं.

SHOT, s. (Shooting, discharge of any missile) क्षेपः -पणं, प्रक्षेपः असनं, पातः -तनं, प्रहारः; 'of an arrow,' see SHOOTING, s.—(Missile, weapon) अस्त्रं, मुक्तं.—(Bullet) गुलिका, गुटिका, लोहगुलिका, गुलिः -ली f., सीसकगुलिः f., दूरवेधिनी गुलिका, आग्नेयास्त्रं.—(Flight of an arrow) शरायणं, बाणायणं, शरपातः.—(Of a bullet) गुलिकायनं, गुटिकायनं.—(A good shot, a good marksman) शीघ्रवेधी m. (न्), लक्ष्यवेधी, लक्ष्यवेधनकुशलः.

To SHOT, v. a. गुलिकां निविश् in caus., गुलिकागर्भं -र्भां कृ.

SHOTTED, p.p. गुलिकागर्भः -र्भा -र्भं, आग्नेयगुलिगर्भः &c., लोहगुलिगर्भः &c.

SHOULD. When this auxiliary expresses obligation, it is rendered in Sanskrit by the fut. past. part., see OUGHT. When it expresses present or future time conditionally, it may be rendered by the present tense, or not unfrequently by the conditional tense.

SHOULDER, s. स्कन्धः, अंशः, अंसः, भुजशिरस् n., भुजशिखरं, दोःशिखरं, बाहुमूलं; 'having wide shoulders,' पृथुस्कन्धः -न्धा -न्धं, विपुलस्कन्धः &c., विपुलांशः -शा -शं; 'shoulder-joint,' स्कन्धसन्धिः m., विरु n.; 'upon the shoulder,' स्कन्धे, स्कन्धेन, प्रतिस्कन्धं; 'he bears faggots on his shoulder,' इन्धनं स्कन्धेन वहति; 'the dog is borne on the shoulder,' कुक्कुरः स्कन्धेन उह्यते; 'he places the goat on his shoulder,' छागं स्कन्धे करोति; 'resting on the shoulder,' स्कन्धस्थः -स्था -स्थं.

To SHOULDER, v. a. (Take or place on the shoulder, carry on the shoulder) स्कन्धे कृ or स्था in caus., स्कन्धस्थं -स्थां कृ, स्कन्धे आरुह् in caus., स्कन्धेन वह्.—(Push with the shoulder) स्कन्धेन तड् (c. 10. ताडयति -यितुं).

SHOULDER-BLADE, s. फलकः, स्कन्धफलकः, अंशः, अंसः, भुजशिरस् n., स्कन्धः, कासवरं.

To SHOUT, v. n. (Utter a loud cry) उत्क्रुश् (c. 1. -क्रोशति -क्रोष्टुं), उच्चैःस्वरेण क्रुश् or प्रक्रुश् or विक्रुश्, उच्चैः or उच्चैःस्वरेण नद् (c. 1. नदति -दितुं) or प्रणद् or घुष् (c. 10. घोषयति -यितुं) or उद्घुष्, मुक्तकण्ठं क्रुश्, महानादं कृ, महाघोषं कृ, महाध्वनिं कृ, प्रणादं कृ, उत्क्रोशं कृ, कोलाहलं कृ, चित्कारं कृ, चीत्कृ.—(For joy) हर्षनादं कृ, हर्षघोषं कृ, जयघोषं कृ, जयशब्दं कृ, जयकोलाहलं कृ, किलकिल (nom. किलकिलायति), जयजयेतिशब्दं कृ.

SHOUT, s. (Loud cry) उत्क्रोशः, उत्क्रुष्टं, विक्रुष्टं, प्रणादः, महानादः, निनादः, महाघोषः, घोषणं -णा, उद्घोषणं, कोलाहलः, उच्चैर्घुष्टं, उच्चैःस्वरः, चित्कारः, चीत्कारः, महाध्वनिः m., संहूतिः f., बहुभिः कृता संहूतिः.—(Of joy or triumph) जयघोषः, जयकोलाहलः, जयशब्दः, जयध्वनिः m., जयरवः, जयारवः, हर्षनादः, हर्षस्वनः, जयजयेतिशब्दः.

To SHOVE, v. a. प्रसृ (c. 10. -सारयति -यितुं), संचल् in caus. See To PUSH.

SHOVE, s. प्रसारणं, अपसारणं, सञ्चालनं, प्रहारः. See PUSH, s.

SHOVEL, s. अभ्रिः f., कुद्दालः, कुदालः, काष्ठकुद्दालः.

To SHOW, v. a. (Exhibit) दृश् (c. 10. दर्शयति -यितुं), प्रदृश्, अभिदृश्, निदृश्, प्रतिदृश्, सन्दृश्, विदृश्, दर्शनं कृ, प्रदर्शनं कृ; 'to show cause of fear,' भयहेतुप्रदर्शनं कृ.—(Point out, indicate) निर्दिश् (c. 6. -दिशति -देष्टुं), प्रदिश्, आदिश्, विनिर्दिश्, उद्दिश्, आदिश् in caus. (-देशयति -यितुं), सूच् (c. 10. सूचयति -यितुं), संसूच्; 'show the way,' मार्गम् आदेशय.—(Inform, make known) ज्ञा in caus., बुध् in caus., प्रबुध्, निविद् in caus., आख्या, ख्या, कथ्.—(Manifest) प्रकाश् (c. 10. -काशयति -यितुं), व्यञ्ज्, व्यक्तीकृ, आविष्कृ, प्रादुष्कृ, प्रकटीकृ.—(Show a kindness, favor, &c.) उपकृ, उपकारं कृ, अनुग्रहं कृ, अनुग्रह्.—(Show forth), see To MANIFEST.—(Show off) दम्भार्थं दृश् in caus.—(Show one's self) आत्मानं दृश् in caus., दृश् in pass. (दृश्यते); 'he shows himself as if dead,' आत्मानं मृतवद् दर्शयति.—(Show up), see To EXPOSE.

To SHOW, v. n. दृश् in pass. (दृश्यते), लक्ष् in pass. (लक्ष्यते), प्रतिभा (c. 2. -भाति -तुं).

SHOW, s. (Appearance, semblance) आभासः, भासः, आकारः, आभा, दर्शनं.—(Ostentatious parade) दम्भः, आडम्बरः -रं, दम्भार्थं प्रकाशनं, कौतुकं.—(Pretence) छद्म n. (न्), व्यपदेशः.—(Spectacle) प्रेक्षा -क्षणं, कौतुकं, चमत्कारः.

SHOWER, s. (One who shows) दर्शकः, प्रदर्शकः, दर्शनकृत्, दर्शयिता m. (तृ).

SHOWER, s. (Of rain) धारासारः, धारासम्पातः, धारा, आसारः, वर्षः, वृष्टिः f., आवृष्टिः f., प्रक्षरं, तरमः.—(Of arrows) शरवर्षः, शरवृष्टिः f., शरधारा, पत्रपूगः.—(Of tears) अश्रुधारा.

To SHOWER, v. a. or n. वृष् (c. 1. वर्षति -ते -र्षितुं), धारासारेण वृष्; 'to shower down water,' जलवर्षेण or जलवर्षं वृष्, वारिणा अभिवृष्; 'to shower blood,' रक्तं वृष्; 'to shower arrows,' शरान् वृष्. See To RAIN.

SHOWER-BATH, s. धारायन्त्रगृहं, धारायन्त्रमन्दिरं, धारायन्त्रं, शिरोभिषेचनयन्त्रं, शिरोभिषेचनी, शिरोभिषेकः, शिरःस्नानं.

SHOWERY, a. वर्षुकः -का -कं, बहुवृष्टिः -ष्टिः -ष्टि, वृष्टिमान् -मती -मत् (त्), बहुधारः -रा -रं, वर्षिकः -की -कं. See RAINY.

SHOWING, s. दर्शनं, प्रदर्शनं, सन्दर्शनं, निर्देशः, प्रकाशनं, सूचनं.

SHOW-MAN, s. दर्शकः, प्रदर्शकः, दर्शयिता m. (तृ), कौतुकदर्शकः.

SHOWN, p. p. दर्शितः -ता -तं, प्रदर्शितः &c., सन्दर्शितः &c., निर्दिष्टः -ष्टा -ष्टं, प्रदिष्टः &c., सूचितः -ता -तं, ज्ञापितः &c., प्रकाशितः &c.

SHOWY, a. (Make a fine show) अतिशोभनः -ना -नं, स्वकामशोभनः -ना -नं, अतिदर्शनीयः -या -यं, अतिप्रकाशः -शा -शं, आडम्बरी -रिणी -रि (न्); 'showy learning,' सभापाण्डित्यं.

SHRED, s. खण्डः -ण्डकः, पटखण्डः, वस्त्रखण्डः, दीर्घखण्डः -ण्डकः.

To SHRED, v. a. दीर्घखण्डीकृ, दीर्घखण्डशः कृ or छिद् or व्यवछिद्.

SHREW, s. (Scold) कर्कशा, कुशीला, वामशीला, वक्रशीला, दुःशीला, उग्रशीला, कटुशीला.—(Mouse) वेश्मनकुलः, see SHREW-MOUSE.

SHREWD, a. (Cunning, knowing) विदग्धः -ग्धा -ग्धं, विचक्षणः -णा -णं, चतुरः -रा -रं, चातुरः -री -रं, पक्वबुद्धिः -द्धिः -द्धि, परिपक्वबुद्धिः

&c., पक्कः -क्का -क्कं, परिपक्कः &c., सूक्ष्मबुद्धिः &c., कुबुद्धिः &c., दीर्घबुद्धिः -द्धिः -द्धि, निपुणः -णा -णं, कुशलः -ला -लं, नागरः -रा -रं.—(Proceeding from cunning) विदग्ध in comp., वैदग्ध्यप्रयुक्तः -क्ता -क्तं.

SHREWDLY, *adv.* विदग्धवत्, वैदग्ध्येन, सवैदग्ध्यं, विचक्षणवत्.

SHREWDNESS, *s.* वैदग्ध्यं, वैदग्धं, विदग्धता, विचक्षणता, वैचक्षण्यं, चतुरता, चातुर्य्यं, बुद्धिपक्कता, पक्कता, परिपक्कता, परिपाकः, नैपुण्यं, परिवेदना.

SHREWISH, *a.* कर्कशः -शा -शं, कर्कशस्वभावः -वा -वं, कर्कशशीलः -ला -लं, वामशीलः &c., वक्रशीलः &c., कटुशीलः &c., कुप्रकृतिः -तिः -ति.

SHREW-MOUSE, *s.* वेश्मनकुलः, लिङ्गालिका, दीना, चिक्का.

To SHRIEK, *v. n.* उत्क्रुश् (c. 1. -क्रोशति -क्रोष्टुं), कर्कशस्वरेण क्रुश् or रु or क्रन्द् (c. 1. क्रन्दति -न्दितुं), चित्कारं कृ, चीत्कारं कृ. *See To* SCREAM.

SHRIEK, *s.* रावः, कर्कशरावः, चित्कारः, चीत्कारः, उत्क्रोशः, उत्क्रुष्टं, विक्रुष्टं, नादः, क्रन्दनं, क्रन्दितं, कोलाहलं, हलहलाध्वनिः *m.*

SHRIKE, *s.* (Fork tailed butcher-bird) कलिङ्गः, भिङ्गकः, भृङ्गः, भृङ्गकः, धूम्याटः, धूम्राटः.

SHRILL, *a.* कर्कशः -शा -शं, पटुः -टुः -टु, कर्णवेधकः -का -कं, कर्णवेधी -धिनी -धि (न्), कर्णकटुः -टुः -टु, कलोत्तालः -ला -लं, उत्तालः -ला -लं; 'shrill-voiced,' कर्कशस्वरः -रा -रं, उच्चैःस्वरः &c.

SHRILLNESS, *s.* कर्कशता -त्वं, कार्कश्यं, कटुता, कर्णवेधकत्वं.

SHRILLY, *a.* कर्कशं, कर्कशस्वरेण, उच्चैःस्वरेण, पटुस्वरेण.

SHRIMP, *s.* जलवृश्चिकः, इक्षाकः, गङ्गाटेयः, चिङ्गटः, गलाविलः, गलाविलः, गलानिकः.

SHRINE, *s.* आयतनं, देवतायतनं, देवायतनं, पुण्यतीर्थं, तीर्थं, पुण्यद्रव्यायतनं, पुण्यद्रव्याधारः, पवित्रद्रव्याधारः.

To SHRINK, *v. n.* संकुच् in pass. (-कुच्यते), सङ्कोचम् इ (c. 2. एति -तुं), सङ्कोचं या, कुचनम् इ, कुच् in pass. (कुच्यते), आकुच्, संक्षिप् in pass. (-क्षिप्यते), संहृ in pass. (-ह्रियते), सद् (c. 1. सीदति, सत्तुं); 'as in fear, terror, &c.,' विकम्प् (c. 1. -कम्पते -म्पितुं), वित्रस् (c. 4. -त्रस्यति -सितुं), उद्विज्; 'with shame,' लज्ज् (c. 1. लज्जते -ज्जितुं), विलज्ज्.

To SHRINK, *v. a.* (Cause to contract) संकुच् (c. 1. -कोचति -चितुं), कुच् (c. 1. -कुचति -चितुं, c. 10. -कुचयति -यितुं), सङ्कोचं गम् in caus., सङ्कोचं कृ.

SHRINKING, *s.* सङ्कोचः, आकुचनं, कुचनं, संक्षेपः, *see* CONTRACTION.

To SHRIVEL, *v. n.* संकुच् in pass. (-कुच्यते), आकुच् in pass. (-कुच्यते), कुच्, शॄ in pass. (-शीर्य्यते), विशॄ, संश्यानः -ना -नं भू, वलिपूर्णः -र्णा -र्णं भू, वलिरूपः -पा -पं भू.

To SHRIVEL, *v. a.* (Cause to shrink) संकुच् (c. 1. -कोचति -चितुं), शॄ in caus. (शारयति -यितुं), शीर्णीकृ, विशीर्णीकृ, संश्यानीकृ.

SHRIVELED, *p. p.* सङ्कुचितः -ता -तं, कुचितः &c., आकुचितः &c., शीर्णः -र्णा -र्णं, विशीर्णः &c., संश्यानः -ना -नं, विक्लिन्नः -न्ना -न्नं; 'into wrinkles,' वलिनः -ना -नं, वलिभः -भा -भं, वलिमान् -मती -मत् (त्).

SHROFF, *s.* धनव्यापारी *m.* (न्), मुद्राव्यापारी *m.*, कलोपजीवी *m.*

SHROUD, *s.* (For a corpse) शववस्त्रं, शववसनं, शवपरिधानं, प्रेतवस्त्रं, शवाच्छादनं.—(Cover) आच्छादनं.

To SHROUD, *v. a.* छद् (c. 10. छादयति -यितुं), प्रच्छद्. *See To* SHELTER.

SHROUDED, *p.p.* प्रच्छन्नः -न्ना -न्नं, प्रच्छादितः &c., गूढः -ढा -ढं, उपगूढः &c.

SHRUB, *s.* (Woody plant, dwarf tree) गुल्मः, स्तम्बः, क्षुद्रः, क्षुपः, क्षुपः, अप्रकाण्डः, विस्तारः, क्षुद्रवृक्षः, अल्पवृक्षः.—(Drink), *see* PUNCH.

SHRUBBERY, *s.* गुल्मवाटिका, गुल्मवाटी, वृक्षवाटिका, उपवनं.

SHRUBBY, *a.* गुल्मावृतः -ता -तं, तरुगुल्मावृतः &c., गुल्ममयः -यी -यं.

To SHRUG, *v. a.* or *n.* (The shoulders) असन्तोषसूचनार्थं स्कन्धसङ्कोचं कृ or स्कन्धाकुञ्चनं कृ or स्कन्धोत्कर्षणं कृ or स्कन्धचेष्टनं कृ.

SHRUG, *s.* स्कन्धसङ्कोचः, स्कन्धाकुञ्चनं, स्कन्धोत्कर्षणं, स्कन्धचेष्टा.

SHRUNK, *s.* सङ्कुचितः -ता -तं, कुचितः -ता -तं, आकुचितः &c., संवृतः -ता -तं, शीर्णः -र्णा -र्णं, संश्यानः -ना -नं, संहृतः -ता -तं, संक्षिप्तः -प्ता -प्तं, ह्रसितः -ता -तं, सन्नः -न्ना -न्नं, सङ्कीर्णः -र्णा -र्णं.

To SHUDDER, *v. n.* कम्प् (c. 1. कम्पते -म्पितुं), विकम्प्, स्फुर् (c. 6. स्फुरति -रितुं), विस्फुर्, प्रस्फुर्, वेप् (c. 1. वेपते -पितुं), प्रवेप्, ह्लल् (c. 1. ह्ललति -लितुं), सीत्कारं कृ, शीत्कारोपहतः -ता -तं भू, सीत्कारग्रस्तः -स्ता -स्तं भू.

SHUDDER, SHUDDERING, *s.* अङ्गकम्पः, शरीरकम्पः, अङ्गस्फुरणं, शरीरस्फुरणं, विस्फुरणं, अङ्गवेपनं, कम्पः -म्पनं, विकम्पः -म्पनं, सीत्कारः, सीत्कृतं, शीत्कारः.

To SHUFFLE, *v. a.* (Shove one way and the other) इतस्ततः संचल् (c. 10. -चालयति -यितुं) or चल्, इतस्ततः सृ (c. 10. सारयति -यितुं) or विक्षिप्, बहुधा चल्; 'to shuffle the feet,' पादास्फालनं कृ, पादचापल्यं कृ.—(Mix together) सम्मिश्रीकृ, असत्यव्यस्तीकृ, अधरोत्तरीकृ, संकुलीकृ, सङ्करीकृ, विक्षिप्, सम्मिश्; 'cards,' द्यूतपत्रसम्मिश्रणं कृ.

To SHUFFLE, *v. n.* (Practice evasions) छल कृ, छलं कृ, व्यपदेशं कृ, अपदेशं कृ, व्यपदिश् (c. 6. -दिशति -देष्टुं), कपटं कृ, वक्रवृत्तिः -त्तिः -त्ति भू, चपलः -ला -लं भू.

SHUFFLE, SHUFFLING, *s.* (Mixing, pushing together) सम्मिश्रणं, असत्यव्यस्तीकरणं, इतस्ततः सञ्चालनं or सारणं or विक्षेपः; 'of the feet,' पादास्फालनं, पादचापल्यं.—(Evasion) छद्म *n.* (न्), छलं, अपदेशः, व्यपदेशः, वक्रता, चपलता, चापल्यं.

SHUFFLER, *s.* वक्रवृत्तिः *m.*, चपलवृत्तिः *m.*, छद्मवृत्तिः *m.* छली *m.* (न्).

To SHUN, *v. a.* वृज् (c. 10. वर्जयति -यितुं), परिवृज्, विवृज्, परिहृ (c. 1. -हरति -हर्तुं), प्रोज्झ् (c. 6. प्रोज्झति -ज्झितुं, rt. उज्झ्), उज्झ्, हा (c. 3. जहाति, हातुं), त्यज् (c. 1. त्यजति, त्यक्तुं), परित्यज्, वर्जीकृ.

SHUNNED, *p.p.* वर्जितः -ता -तं, विवर्जितः &c., परिहृतः -ता -तं, प्रोज्झितः -ता -तं, वर्जीकृतः -ता -तं, त्यक्तः -क्ता -क्तं, परित्यक्तः &c.

SHÚDRA, *s.* *See* SÚDRA.

To SHUT, *v. a.* (Close, fasten up) पिधा (c. 3. -दधाति -धातुं), अपिधा, रुध् (c. 7. रुणद्धि, रोद्धुं), निरुध्, अवरुध्, संवृ (c. 5. -वृणोति -वरितुं -रीतुं), बन्ध् (c. 9. बध्नाति, बन्धुं), संहृ (c. 1. -हरति -हर्तुं), संहन् (c. 2. -हन्ति -न्तुं); 'shut the door,' द्वारं पिधेहि or रुन्द्धि; 'they shut the doors,' द्वाराणि पिदधुः or रुरुधुः; 'to shut the mouth,' मुखं संवृ or पिधा; 'the hands,' हस्तौ बन्ध् or संहन्; 'a book,' पुस्तकं बन्ध्; 'the lips,' ओष्ठौ संवृ; 'the eyes,' मील्, निमील्, निमिष्, *see To* CLOSE, *v. a.*—(Contract, compress) संवृ, संहृ, संकुच्, संहन्, सम्पीड्.—(Bar) अर्गलेन बन्ध्.—(Obstruct) रुध्, निरुध्, स्तम्भ्, प्रतिबन्ध्.—(Shut in), *see To* CONFINE, INCLOSE.—(Shut out) बहिष्कृ, निवृ, निराकृ, निषिध्, *see To* EXCLUDE, PRECLUDE.—(Shut up) निरुध्, अवरुध्; 'in a prison,' कारायां निरुध्; 'in a box,' सम्पुटीकृ.

SHUT, *p. p.* रुद्धः -द्धा -द्धं, पिहितः -ता -तं, संवृतः -ता -तं, बद्धः -द्धा -द्धं, पिधानवान् -वती -वत् (त्), सपिधानः -ना -नं; 'as a bud,' अविकचः -चा -चं, मुकुलीकृतः -ता -तं; 'as the eye,' निमीलितः -ता -तं, मुकुलितः &c.

SHUTTER, *s.* अवरोधकं, प्रतिबन्धकं, आच्छादनं, कपाटः; 'of a window,' जालकावरोधकं, जालकाच्छादनं, वातायनावरोधकं.

SHUTTLE, *s.* (Of a weaver) त्रसरः, सूत्रवेष्टनं, सूत्रयन्त्रं, तसरः, मक्षिकः, नाडिचीरं.

SHUTTLE-COCK, *s.* लघुगुलिकाविशेषो यो विनोदार्थं दण्डाहतो भूत्वा इतस्ततः प्रक्षिप्यते.

SHY, *a.* सभाभीतः -ता -तं, सभाभीरुः -रुः -रु, जनभीतः -ता -तं, लोकभीतः &c., भाषणविमुखः -खा -खी -खं, अल्पभाषी -षिणी -षि (न्), आलापविरक्तः -क्ता -क्तं, कातरः -रा -रं, आगमनभीरुः -रुः -रु, भीरुः -रुः -रु.

SHYNESS, *s.* सभाभीतिः *f.*, सभाभीरुता, जनभीतिः *f.*, लोकभीतिः *f.*, सभाकम्पः, भाषणविमुखता, आलापवैरक्त्यं, भीरुता, कातरता.

SIBILANT, *s.* (Letter) ऊष्मः. *See* HISSING.

SICK, *a.* (Inclined to vomit) वमनेच्छुः -च्छुः -च्छु, विवमिषुः -षुः -षु, वमनोन्मुखः -खा -खं, वमी -मिनी -मि (न्), उद्गारी -रिणी &c., छर्देनेच्छुः -च्छुः -च्छु.—(Ill) रोगी -गिणी -गि (न्), रोगार्त्तः -र्त्ता -र्त्तं, रोगातुरः -रा -रं, रोगान्वितः -ता -तं, रोगग्रस्तः -स्ता -स्तं, अस्वस्थः -स्था -स्थं, सामयः -या -यं, व्याधितः -ता -तं, व्याधियुक्तः -क्ता -क्तं, अमी &c., विकारी &c., आमयावी &c., उपतापी &c., अभ्यान्तः -न्ता -न्तं, रुग्णः -ग्णा -ग्णं, *see* ILL, *a.*—(Disgusted) जातबीभत्सः -त्सा -त्सं, द्वेषी -षिणी &c., विकृतः -ता -तं, निर्विण्णः -ण्णा -ण्णं; 'sick of the world,' भवरोगी -गिणी &c., भवार्त्तः -र्त्ता -र्त्तं; 'sick-room,' विशिका.—(To be sick, vomit) वम् (c. 1. वमति -मितुं), छर्द् (c. 10. छर्दयति -यितुं).

To SICKEN, *v. a.* (Disgust) बीभत्सं कृ or जन् (c. 10. जनयति -यितुं), वैकृत्यं जन्.—(Make sick) वमनेच्छां जन्, छर्देनेच्छां जन्, रोगार्त्तीकृ, सरोगीकृ.

To SICKEN, *v. n.* (Fall sick) रोगग्रस्तः -स्ता -स्तं भू, रोगार्त्तः -र्त्ता -र्त्तं भू, ज्वर् (c. 1. ज्वरति -रितुं), सरोगीभू, *see* *To* LANGUISH.—(Feel disgust) बीभत्सोपहतः -ता -तं भू, जातबीभत्सः -त्सा -त्सं भू.

SICKENING, *a.* बीभत्सजनकः -का -कं, विरक्तिजनकः &c., *see* DISGUSTING.

SICKISH, *a.* ईषद्वमनेच्छुः -च्छुः -च्छु, ईषद्रोगी -गिणी -गि (न्).

SICKLE, *s.* लवित्रं, दात्रं, लवाणकं, लवाकः, शस्यकर्त्तनी, शस्यछेदनी, कर्त्तरी, लवग्रः, लवहननं -नी, लवघनः, लवुकः.

SICKLINESS, *s.* सरोगता, रोगिता, रोगाधीनता, रोगशीलता, जन्मरोगिता.

SICKLY, *a.* (Unwell), *see* SICK.—(Habitually ill) सदारोगी -गिणी -गि (न्), नित्यरोगी &c., रोगाधीनः -ना -नं, रोगशीलः -ला -लं; 'by birth or nature,' जन्मरोगी &c., जातिरोगी &c., प्रकृतिरोगी &c., स्वभावरोगी &c.; 'having a sickly countenance,' रुग्णवदनः -ना -नं, रुग्णमुखः &c.

SICKNESS, *s.* (Inclination to vomit, nausea) वमनेच्छा, छर्देनेच्छा, विवमिषा, वमनोन्मुखता, वमः -मनं, वमिः *f.*, वान्तिः *f.*, उत्क्लेशः, उत्क्लेदः, उत्क्षेपः, उद्गारः, छर्दनं, छर्दी, छर्दिः, छर्दिः *f.*, छर्दिस् *f.*, प्रच्छर्दिका.—(Disease) रोगः, व्याधिः *m.*, आमयः, रुज् *f.* (क्), अस्वास्थ्यं, अस्वस्थता, विकारः, असमाधानं, रुग्णावस्था, रोगिता, रोगग्रस्तता, रोगव्याप्तिः *f.*, *see* DISEASE, ILLNESS.

SIDE, *s.* (Of a man or any animal) पार्श्वः, पार्श्वभागः, पक्षः -क्षकः, पक्षभागः, कुक्षिः *m.*, कक्षः, पार्श्वाङ्गं, अर्द्धाङ्गं, अङ्कः, क्रोडः; 'pain in the side,' पार्श्वशूलः -लं, कुक्षिशूलः -लं; 'left side,' वामपार्श्वः, वामाङ्गं; 'turning upon the side,' पार्श्वपरिवर्त्तनं, अङ्कपरिवर्त्तनं; 'removed from the side of a parent,' पितुर् अङ्कात् परिभ्रष्टः, पितृपार्श्वात्परिभ्रष्टः -ष्टा -ष्टं; 'at one's side,' पार्श्वे, पार्श्वतस्; 'staying close at the side,' पार्श्वस्थः -स्था -स्थं, पार्श्वगतः -ता -तं, पार्श्वपरिवर्त्ती -र्त्तिनी &c., उपान्तस्थः -स्था -स्थं; 'sleeping at the side of,' पार्श्वशयः -या -यं.—(Edge, border) प्रान्तः, उपान्तः -न्तं, अन्तः, सीमा, धारा; 'of a wood,' वनान्तः -न्तं, वनधारा; 'of a river,' नदीतीरं, नदीकूलं, नदीतटं; 'of a roof,' पटलप्रान्तः; 'of a mountain,' पर्व्वतधारा, पर्व्वतटङ्कः.—(Declivity or slope of a mountain) उत्सङ्गः, नितम्बः, कटकः.—(Part considered in respect to its direction) दिक् *f.* (श्), दिशा, पार्श्वः or more usually expressed by the affixes तस्, त्र &c.; as, 'on all sides,' सर्व्वतस्, समन्ततस्, समन्तात्, विश्वतस्, परितस्, अभितस्, सर्व्वत्र, सर्व्वदिक्षु चतुर्दिक्षु; 'on both sides,' उभयतस्, उभयत्र, उभयपार्श्वयोः; 'on the other side,' अपरतस्, परतस्; 'on the opposite side,' अभिमुखतस्, विपरीतभागे; 'side by side,' पार्श्वापार्श्वि.—(Any part being in opposition to another) पक्षः; 'side of an argument,' पक्षः; 'both sides of an argument,' पक्षद्वयं; 'taking up a side,' पक्षता; 'another side of the argument,' पक्षान्तरं.—(Party faction) पक्षः; 'one's own side,' आत्मपक्षः, स्वपक्षः; 'having a side,' पक्षवान् &c.; 'one of the opposite side,' विपक्षः, प्रतिपक्षः; 'one of the same side,' सपक्षः, स्वपक्षावलम्बी *m.* (न्), स्वपक्षकः; 'to take a side,' पक्षपातं कृ, *see* *To* SIDE; 'one who takes a side,' पक्षपाती *m.* (न्), पक्षोद्ग्राही *m.*—(Any part of a thing) भागः; 'the outer side,' बाह्यभागः; 'black on the two sides,' द्वयोर् भागयोः श्यामः -मा -मं.—(Branch of a family, separate line) पक्षः; 'relations on the father's side,' पितृपक्षा ज्ञातयः; 'on the mother's side,' मातृपक्षा बान्धवाः; 'noble on both sides,' मातृतःपितृतश्चाभिजनवान् -वती &c.—(Side of a geometrical figure) भुजः, बाहुः *m.*, दोस् *m.*

SIDE, *a.* पार्श्विकः -की -कं, पार्श्वः -र्श्वी -र्श्वं, पार्श्वीयः -या -यं, पार्श्वस्थः -स्था -स्थं, पाक्षिकः -की -कं, पाक्षः -क्षी -क्षं, पार्श्व or पक्ष in comp.; 'a side door,' पक्षद्वारं.

To SIDE, *v. n.* (Embrace or adopt a side) पक्षपातं कृ, पक्षोद्ग्राहं कृ, पक्षं ग्रह् or उद्ग्रह् or अनुग्रह्.

SIDE-BOARD, *s.* पक्षफलकः -कं, पार्श्वफलकः, पार्श्वस्थफलकः.

SIDE-LONG, *a.* अनुपार्श्वः -र्श्वा -र्श्वं, पार्श्विकः -का -कं, आनुपार्श्विकः -की -कं, वक्रः -क्रा -क्रं. तिरश्चीनः -ना -नं, तिर्य्यक् -रश्ची -र्य्यक् (च्); 'side-long glance,' तिर्य्यग्दृष्टिः *f.*, अपाङ्गदृष्टिः.

SIDE-LONG, *adv.* अनुपार्श्वं, पार्श्वतस्, तिर्य्यक्, तिरस्, पार्श्वदिशि.

SIDE-LOOK, *s.* कटाक्षः, नेत्रकटाक्षः, अपाङ्गदृष्टिः *f.*, अपाङ्गदर्शनं, दृष्टिविक्षेपः.

SIDER, *s.* पक्षकः, पक्षधरः, पक्षोद्ग्राही *m.* (न्), पक्षपाती *m.*, पक्षी *m.*

SIDEREAL, SIDERAL, *a.* तारासम्बन्धी -न्धिनी -न्धि (न्), नाक्षत्रिकः -की -कं, नाक्षत्रः -त्री -त्रं, नक्षत्रसम्बन्धी &c., ताराविषयकः -का -कं, ग्रहसम्बन्धी &c., तारामयः -यी -यं, नक्षत्रमयः &c., तारापूर्णः -र्णा -र्णं.

SIDE-SADDLE, *s.* पक्षपर्य्याणं, पक्षपर्य्ययणं, स्त्रीपर्य्याणं, स्त्रीपर्य्ययणं.

SIDESMAN, *s.* पक्षकः, पक्षपाती *m.* (न्), पक्षोद्ग्राही *m.*, पक्षी *m.*, पार्श्विकः, पक्षधारी *m.* *See* PARTISAN.

SIDE-TABLE, *s.* पक्षफलकः -कं, पार्श्वफलकः, पार्श्वस्थफलकः.

SIDE-WAYS, SIDE-WISE, *adv.* तिर्य्यक्, तिरस्, तिरश्चीनं, अनुपार्श्वं, पार्श्वतस्; 'moving side ways,' तिर्य्यक् -रश्ची -र्य्यक् (च्), तिर्य्यग्गामी -मिनी &c., तिरश्चीनः -ना -नं.

SIDING, *s.* (Taking a side) पक्षपातः, पक्षोद्ग्राहः, पक्षता.

To SIDLE, *v. n.*, तिर्य्यग् गम् (c. 1. गच्छति, गन्तुं), तिर्य्यक् चल् or या.

SIDLING, *s.* तिर्य्यक्चलनं, तिर्य्यग्यानं, तिर्य्यग्गमनं, तिर्य्यग्गतिः *f.*—(One of a horse's paces) उत्तेजितः.

SIEGE, *s.* अवरोधः -धनं, प्रतिरोधः, रोधः -धनं, चिरारोधः, रुद्धा, नगरवेष्टनं, नगरपरिवेष्टनं, सैन्यवेष्टनं.

SIEVE, *s.* चालनी -नं, धान्यचालनी, शोधनी, धान्यशोधनी, प्रस्फोटनं -नी, तितउः *m.*, तितउ *n.*, निर्गलनयन्त्रं, पाटीरः, शतपोनः.

To SIFT, *v. a.* (Separate by a sieve) शुध् (c. 10. शोधयति -यितुं), तितउना चल् (c. 10. चालयति -यितुं), चालनयन्त्रेण शुध् or शोधनं कृ, निर्गलनं कृ, प्रस्फुट् in caus.—(Investigate minutely) सूक्ष्मपरीक्षां कृ, सूक्ष्मं परीक्ष्, सूक्ष्मजिज्ञासां कृ, मन्थनं कृ, मथनं कृ.

SIFTED, *p. p.* शोधितः -ता -तं, निर्गलितः &c., चालितः &c., मथितः &c.

SIFTING, *s.* शोधनं, धान्यशोधनं, धान्यचालनं, निर्गलनं, प्रस्फोटनं, धान्यप्रस्फोटनं, मथनं.

To SIGH, *v. n.* दीर्घनिश्वासं कृ, दीर्घनिःश्वासं कृ, दीर्घं निश्वस् or निःश्वस् (c. 2. -श्वसिति -तुं), दीर्घम् उच्छ्वस् or विनिश्वस् or विनिःश्वस् or समुच्छ्वस्, स्तन् (c. 1. स्तनति -नितुं), निस्तन्, सीत्कारं कृ.

SIGH, *s.* दीर्घनिश्वासः, दीर्घनिःश्वासः, दीर्घश्वासः, निःश्वासः, निश्वासः, निःश्वसनं, दीर्घनिःश्वसनं, निश्श्वासः, निश्श्वसनं, उच्छ्वासः, दीर्घोच्छ्वासः, उच्छ्वसितं, दीर्घोच्छ्वसितं, दीर्घश्वसितं, दीर्घश्वसनं, समुच्छ्वासः, समुच्छ्वसितं, विनिश्वासः, स्तननं, स्तनितं.

SIGHING, *part.* दीर्घनिश्वासी -सिनी -सि (न्), निःश्वासी &c., उच्छ्वासी &c., दीर्घोच्छ्वासी &c., दीर्घनिश्वस्य indec., निश्वसन् -सन्ती -सत् (त्), विनिश्वसन् &c.

SIGHT, *s.* (Vision, view, act of seeing) दृष्टिः *f.*, दर्शनं, ईक्षणं, वीक्षणं, वीक्षा, प्रेक्षणं, प्रेक्षा, आलोकः, आलोकनं, अवलोकनं, लोकः -कनं, लक्षणं, आलोचनं -ना, निशामनं, निर्वर्णनं, निध्यानं, निभालनं, निभालनं, सूचना; 'being within sight,' दृष्टिगोचरः -रा -रं, दृष्टिविषयः -या -यं, दृग्गोचरः &c., दृश्यः -श्या -श्यं, दृश्यमानः &c., चक्षुर्ग्राह्यः -ह्या -ह्यं, *see* VISIBLE; 'in sight,' दृष्टिगोचरेण; 'in sight of, in presence of,' साक्षात्, समक्षं, प्रत्यक्षेण, पश्यतस्, दृष्टितस्; 'in sight of many persons,' बहुजनसमक्षं; 'out of sight,' अदृश्यः -श्या -श्यं, *see* INVISIBLE; 'out of one's sight,' परोक्षे, अगोचरेण; 'out of my sight,' ममागोचरेण; 'at sight of,' दर्शनात्, दर्शनेन; 'at sight of the token,' अभिज्ञानदर्शनात्; 'first sight of,' प्रथमदर्शनं, अपूर्व्वदर्शनं; 'at the very first sight,' प्रथमदर्शनात् -ने, प्रथमदर्शनक्षणात्, आप्रथमदर्शनात्, सकृद्दर्शनात्; 'at sight, in commerce,' पत्रदर्शनात्.—(Faculty or sense of sight) दृष्टिः *f.*, दृक् *f.* (श्), चक्षुरिन्द्रियं, नेत्रेन्द्रियं, चक्षुस् *n.*, दृक्शक्तिः *f.*, दृष्टिशक्तिः *f.*, दर्शनशक्तिः *f.*, आलोचकं; 'charming or bewitching the sight,' दृष्टिबन्धः -न्धनं.—(Eye) चक्षुस् *n.*, नेत्रं, नयनं, लोचनं, दृष्टिः *f.*—(Spectacle, show, any thing seen) प्रेक्षा, प्रेक्षणं, कौतुकं; 'fond of sight-seeing,' कौतुकासक्तः -क्ता -क्तं.

SIGHTLESS, *a.* दृष्टिहीनः -ना -नं, नेत्रहीनः &c., काणः -णा -णं.

SIGHTLY, *a.* दर्शनीयः -या -यं, सुदर्शनः -ना -नं, सुदृश्यः -श्या -श्यं.

SIGN, *s.* (Token, mark) लक्षणं, चिह्नं, लाञ्छनं, ध्वजः, अभिज्ञानं, प्रज्ञानं, लिङ्गं, लक्ष्मं, व्यञ्जकः -कं, सूचना, सूचकं; 'good sign,' सुचिह्नं, सुलक्षणं; 'bad sign,' कुलक्षणं, अपलक्षणं, अपचिह्नं, दुर्लक्षणं.—(Motion or action indicating something) संज्ञा, सङ्केतः, इङ्गितं, इङ्गः, आकारः; 'with the fingers,' अङ्गुलिसन्देशः; 'with the head,' शिरःसङ्केतः, मस्तकसङ्केतः, मस्तकसन्देशः; 'understanding signs,' इङ्गितज्ञः -ज्ञा -ज्ञं; 'to make signs,' सङ्केतं कृ, इङ्गितं कृ.—(Portent, prodigy) उत्पातः, अद्भुतं, उपसर्गः, दुर्लक्षणं, दुश्चिह्नं.—(Of the zodiac) राशिः *m.*, *see* ZODIAC; 'rising of a sign,' लग्नं.—(Arithmetical sign) अङ्कः.—(Sign manual) हस्ताक्षरं, स्वाक्षरं, स्वहस्ताक्षरं.—(Of an inn, &c.) ध्वजः, सुराध्वजः.

To SIGN, *v. a.* स्वहस्ताक्षरं or हस्ताक्षरं or नामाक्षरं लिख् (c. 6. लिखति, लेखितुं), स्वाक्षरेण or हस्ताक्षरेण अङ्क् (c. 10. अङ्कयति -यितुं).

SIGNAL, *s.* सङ्केतः, संज्ञा, इङ्गितं, ध्वजः, चिह्नं, प्रकाशचिह्नं.

SIGNAL, *a.* प्रसिद्धः -द्धा -द्धं, स्मरणीयः -या -यं, स्मरणार्हः -र्हा -र्हं, विशिष्टः -ष्टा -ष्टं, विशेष in comp., विचित्रः &c. *See* REMARKABLE.

To SIGNALIZE, *v. a.* प्रसिद्धीकृ, विशिष्टीकृ, प्रसिद्धं -द्धां कृ, स्मरणीयं -यां कृ, विश्रुतीकृ, विचित्रीकृ; 'to signalize one's self,' कीर्त्तिं or यशः प्राप् (c. 5. -आप्नोति -आप्तुं), विशिष् in pass. (-शिष्यते), नाम or प्रतिष्ठां लभ् or प्राप्.

SIGNATURE, *s.* हस्ताक्षरं, स्वहस्ताक्षरं, स्वाक्षरं, नामाक्षरं, हस्तलिखनं.

SIGNED, *p. p.* हस्ताक्षराङ्कितः -ता -तं, स्वाक्षराङ्कितः &c., मुद्राङ्कितः &c.; 'a paper signed and sealed,' मुद्रिका, मुद्राङ्कितपत्रं.

SIGNET, *s.* मुद्रा, मुद्रिका, प्रत्ययकारिणी, नामाक्षरं; 'signet-ring,' अङ्गुलिमुद्रा; 'royal-signet,' राजमुद्रा.

SIGNIFICANCE, *s.* (Meaning) अर्थः, अर्थवत्त्वं, अर्थवत्ता, अभिप्रायः, आकूतं, वाचकता.—(Importance) गौरवं, भारः.—(Force) शक्तिः *f.*

SIGNIFICANT, SIGNIFICATIVE, *a.* (Having a meaning) अर्थवान् -वती -वत् (त्), अर्थान्वितः -ता -तं, अर्थयुक्तः -क्ता -क्तं, सार्थः -र्था -र्थं, सार्थकः -का -कं, आर्थिकः -की -कं, साकूतः -ता -तं, पूर्णार्थः -र्था -र्थं.—(Expressive, indicative) उद्बोधकः -का -कं, बोधकः &c., सूचकः -का -कं, वाचकः &c., अर्थसूचकः &c., अर्थबोधकः &c., अभिधायिकः -का -कं, लाक्षणिकः -की -कं, अर्थप्रकाशकः &c., दर्शकः &c., प्रदर्शकः &c., साङ्केतिकः -की -कं, हेतुगर्भः -र्भा -र्भं; 'significant word,' अभिधेयं, अभिव्याहारः.

SIGNIFICANTLY, *adv.* सार्थं, साकूतं, पूर्णार्थं, पूर्णार्थतस्, अर्थवत्.

SIGNIFICATION, *s.* (Meaning) अर्थः, विवक्षा, विवक्षितं, आकांक्षा, अभिप्रायः, आकूतं; 'etymological signification,' अवयवार्थः.—(Force of words) शक्तिः *f.*, शब्दशक्तिः *f.*, शब्दसामर्थ्यं, निरूढः.—(Act of making known) सूचनं -ना, ज्ञापनं.

SIGNIFIED, *p. p.* सूचितः -ता -तं, ज्ञापितः &c., संज्ञासूचितः &c.

To SIGNIFY, *v. a.* (Make known) सूच् (c. 10. सूचयति -यितुं), संसूच्, ज्ञा in caus. (ज्ञापयति, ज्ञपयति -यितुं), विज्ञा, बुध् in caus.—(By signs) सङ्केतादिद्वारेण सूच्.—(Mean, convey meaning, imply) उद्बुध् (c. 10. -बोधयति -यितुं), वच् in des. (विवक्षति -क्षितुं), अर्थं सूच् or उद्दिश् (c. 6. -दिशति -देष्टुं), अर्थवान् -वती -वत् भू, *see* *To* MEAN.—(Have consequence or importance) गुर्व्वर्थः -र्था -र्थं भू, पूर्णार्थः -र्था -र्थं भू, महार्थः &c. भू, बह्वर्थः &c. भू; 'to signify little,' अल्पार्थः -र्था -र्थं भू, लघ्वर्थः -र्था -र्थं भू. Sometimes expressible by the instr. case after किं; as, 'what signify the splendors of a court?' किं सभाप्रतापेन; 'what does this signify?' किम् अनेन.

SIGN-MANUAL, *s.* हस्ताक्षरं, स्वहस्ताक्षरं; 'of a king,' राजहस्ताक्षरं.

SIGN-POST, *s.* ध्वजस्तम्भः, ध्वजोपस्तम्भः, मार्गसूचनस्तम्भः, मार्गस्तम्भः.

SILENCE, *s.* (Forbearance of speech) मौनं, मौनभावः, मौनित्वं,

अभाषणं, अनालापः, तूष्णीम्भावः, तूष्णीम्भूतत्वं, निःशब्दता, वाग्यतता, निस्वनः, भाषणाभावः; 'suppression of speech, dogged silence,' वाक्स्तम्भः, वाग्रोधः, वाग्बन्धनं, मुखबन्धनं, मुखस्तम्भः, मुखरोधः, वाग्यमनं; 'vow of silence,' मौनव्रतं, वाङ्नियमः; 'condition of a fish,' मीनता; 'to keep silence,' वाचं यम् (c. 1. यच्छति, यन्तुं) or नियम्, वाचं रुध् (c. 7. रुणद्धि, रोद्धुं), मुखं रुध्, वाग्रोधं कृ, तूष्णीम् भू, मौनं कृ, मौनीभू; 'Silence!' मौनं कुरु, तूष्णीम्भव.—(Stillness), *see* the word.

To SILENCE, *v. a.* वाग्रोधं कृ, वाग्बन्धनं कृ, वाक्स्तम्भं कृ, मुखरोधं कृ, निरुत्तरीकृ, अनुत्तरीकृ, निरुत्तरं -रां कृ, अधरीकृ.—(Cause to cease) विरम् (c. 10. -रमयति -यितुं), निवृत् (c. 10. -वर्त्तयति -यितुं).

SILENCED, *p. p.* निरुत्तरः -रा -रं, निरुत्तरीकृतः -ता -तं, हतोत्तरः -रा -रं, अनुत्तरः &c., अनुत्तरीकृतः &c., रुद्धमुखः -खा -खं, बद्धमुखः &c.

SILENT, *a.* (Not speaking) मौनी -निनी -नि (न्), तूष्णीकः -का -कं, अभाषी -षिणी &c., अनालापः -पा -पं, अनालापी &c., निःशब्दः -ब्दा -ब्दं, निर्वचनः -ना -नं, तूष्णीम्भूतः -ता -तं, मूकः -का -कं.—(Habitually silent, speaking little) अल्पभाषी &c., अल्पवादी &c., तूष्णींशीलः -ला -लं, वाग्यतः -ता -तं, वाग्यः -ग्या -ग्यं, वाचंयमः -मा -मं, *see* TACITURN.—(Having the mouth stopped, doggedly silent) रुद्धमुखः -खा -खं, मुद्रितमुखः &c., बद्धमुखः &c.—(Having no answer to return) निरुत्तरः -रा -रं, अनुत्तरः -रा -रं.—(Still) निःशब्दः -ब्दा -ब्दं, निश्शब्दः &c., नीरवः -वा -वं.—(To be silent) तूष्णीम् भू, मौनीभू, मौनं कृ, वाचं यम् (c. 1. यच्छति, यन्तुं), वचनं विरम् (c. 1. -रमति -रन्तुं).

SILENTLY, *adv.* तूष्णीं, तूष्णीकां, समौनं, मौनीभूय, वाग्यतस्, जोषं, निःशब्दं.

SILK, *s.* (Fine thread, &c., produced by caterpillars) कीटजं, कृमिजं, कीटसूत्रं, कीटजसूत्रं, कृमिजसूत्रं, कीटतन्तुः *m.*, कीटकोषः, कीटकोशः, कीटकोषजं, कृमिकोषजं, कौशेयं, कौषेयं.—(Wove silk) दुकूलं, दुगूलं, कौशाम्बरं, कौषाम्बरं, कौशेयं, कौषेयं, कौशेयवस्त्रं, कौशिकवस्त्रं, कौशिकं, कीटकोषजं, पट्टः, चीनांशुकं, वार्हरं, तन्तुसन्ततं, क्षौमं; 'bleached silk,' धौतकौशेयं, पत्रोर्णं.

SILK, SILKEN, *a.* कौशः -शी -शं, कौशिकः -की -कं, कौशेयः -यी -यं, कौषेयः &c., कौषिकः &c., कीटकोषजः -जा -जं, कोशजः &c., कोशप्रभवः -वा -वं, कृमिकोशोत्थः -त्था -त्थं, कोषोद्भवः &c., कृमिकोषोद्भवः &c., दौकूलः -ली -लं, दुकूलमयः -यी -यं; 'a silk garment,' कौशाम्बरं.—(Soft) मृदुः -दुः -दु, कोमलः &c.

SILK-COTTON TREE, *s.* शाल्मलिः -ली *m. f.*, शाल्मलितरुः *m.*, शाल्मलः, शाल्मलिनी, स्थिरायुः *m.*, पिच्छिला, पूरणी, मोचा; 'its gum,' पिच्छा, शाल्मलीवेष्टः; 'another sort of silk-cotton tree,' कूटशाल्मलिः *m. f.*, रोचनः.

SILK-WEAVER, *s.* कीटतन्तुवापः, दुकूलकारः, कौशिकपटकारः.

SILK-WORM, *s.* कोषकारः -रकः, कोशकारः -रकः, तन्तुकीटः, तन्तुकृमिः *m.*, कोशवासी *m.* (न्), कोशस्थः, पुण्डरीकः, पट्टकूलं.

SILKY, *a.* कौशेयः -यी -यं, कौशगुणकः -का -कं. *See* SILKEN.

SILL, *s.* (Of a door) शिला -ली, देहली.—(Of a window) वातायनशिला.

SILLILY, *adv.* मूर्खवत्, मूढवत्, अज्ञवत्, अल्पबुद्ध्या, निर्बोधवत्.

SILLINESS, *s.* मूर्खता, अल्पबुद्धित्वं, निर्बुद्धित्वं, अज्ञता, बुद्धिहीनता.

SILLY, *a.* अल्पबुद्धिः -द्धिः -द्धि, अल्पधीः -धीः -धि, अल्पमेधाः -धाः -धः (स्), दुर्बुद्धिः &c., मन्दबुद्धिः &c., मन्दमतिः -तिः -ति, दुर्मतिः &c., निर्बोधः -धा -धं, मूढसत्त्वः -त्त्वा -त्त्वं, दुर्मेधाः &c., मूर्खः -र्खा -र्खं, मूढः -ढा -ढं, मुग्धः -ग्धा -ग्धं, अनीतिज्ञः -ज्ञा -ज्ञं. *See* FOOLISH.

SILVAN, *a.* आरण्यः -ण्यी -ण्यं, आरण्यकः -की -कं, अरण्यजः -जा -जं, वन्यः -न्या -न्यं, वनजः -जा -जं, वानः -नी -नं, वानेयः -यी -यं, वनस्थः -स्था -स्थं, वनेचरः -रा -रं, वन in comp.

SILVER, *s.* (The metal) रूप्यं, रौप्यं, रजतं, श्वेतं -तकं, सितं, धौतं, शुक्लं, शुभ्रं, महाशुभ्रं, खर्जूरं, खर्जुरं, दुर्वर्णं, चन्द्रलौहं, चन्द्रहासं, राजरङ्गं, इन्दुलोहकं, तारं, ब्राह्मपिङ्गा, अकूप्यं.—(Coin made of silver) रूप्यमुद्रा, रौप्यमुद्रा.

SILVER, *a.* (Made of silver) रूप्यमयः -यी -यं, रौप्यः -प्यी -प्यं, रूप्यनिर्म्मितः -ता -तं, राजतः -ती -तं, रजतमयः &c., रजतनिर्म्मितः &c., रजतकृतः -ता -तं.—(White, like silver) रूप्यवर्णः -र्णा -र्णं, श्वेतः -ता -तं, *see* SILVERY.

To SILVER, *v. a.* रजत (nom. रजतयति -यितुं), रजतोपेतं -तां कृ, रजतान्वितं -तां कृ, रूप्यवर्णीकृ, श्वेतवर्णीकृ.

SILVERED, *p. p.* रजतान्वितः -ता -तं, राजतान्वितः &c., धौतः -ता -तं, रसितः -ता -तं, रूप्योपेतः &c., रूप्यवर्णीकृतः &c. *See* PLATED.

SILVER-SMITH, *s.* रूप्यकारः -रकः, रौप्यकारः -रकः, नाडिन्धमः.

SILVERY, *a.* रूप्यवर्णः -र्णा -र्णं, रौप्यवर्णः -र्णा -र्णं, रूप्यसदृशः -शी -शं, रजतोपमः -मा -मं, श्वेतवर्णः &c., शुक्लवर्णः &c.; 'having a silvery beard,' सितश्मश्रुः -श्रुः -श्रु.

SIMILAR, *a.* तुल्यः -ल्या -ल्यं, सदृशः -शी -शं, समः -मा -मं, समानः -ना -नं, साधारणः -णी -णा -णं, अनुगुणः -णा -णं, सगुणः &c., समगुणः &c., तुल्यगुणः &c., सधर्म्मा -र्म्मा -र्म्म (न्), सधर्म्मी -र्म्मिणी &c., अभ्युपगतः &c. *See* LIKE.

SIMILARITY, *s.* तुल्यता, सदृशता -त्वं, सादृश्यं, समता, समानता, साम्यं, औपम्यं; 'of form,' सारूप्यं, सरूपता, समरूपता; 'of character,' स्वभावसमता, प्रतिभावः. *See* LIKENESS.

SIMILARLY, *adv.* तद्वत्, तथैव, तथा, तुल्यप्रकारेण, एवं, सादृश्येन, एवम्प्रकारेण, तथाप्रकारेण, तथाविधेन, एवंविधेन.

SIMILE, *s.* उपमा, दृष्टान्तः, उदाहरणं, निदर्शनं, उत्प्रेक्षा.

SIMILITUDE, *s.* (Resemblance, form) औपम्यं, उपमा, प्रतिमा -मानं, आकारः, रूपं, मूर्त्तिः *f.*—(Likeness), *see* SIMILARITY, SIMILE.

To SIMMER, *v. n.* शनैः शनैः क्षीणशब्देन क्वथ् in pass. (क्वथ्यते) or पच् in pass. (पच्यते) or श्रा in pass. (श्रायते).

SIMMERING, *s.* शनैः शनैः क्वथनं, शनकैः क्वथनं or श्रपणं.

To SIMPER, *v. n.* अनर्थकहास्यं कृ, अनर्थकस्मितं कृ, अनर्थकहासं कृ, अनर्थकनिःशब्दहासं कृ, कुस्मि (c. 1. -स्मयते -स्मेतुं), कुस्मितं कृ.

SIMPER, *s.* अनर्थकस्मितं, अनर्थकहास्यं, अनर्थकनिःशब्दहास्यं.

SIMPLE, *a.* (Not compound) निरवयवः -वा -वं, अमिश्रितः -ता -तं, अमिश्रः -श्रा -श्रं, शुद्धः -द्धा -द्धं, केवलः -ला -लं, केवली -लिनी -लि (न्), अकृत्रिमः -मा -मं, अव्याकृतः -ता -तं, असङ्कीर्णः -र्णा -र्णं, असमस्तः -स्ता -स्तं; 'simple word,' व्यस्तपदं.—(Artless, plain) सरलः -ला -लं, मायाहीनः -ना -नं, अमायिकः -की -कं, अमायः -या -यं, शुद्धमतिः -तिः -ति, निष्कपटः -टा -टं, अकपटः &c., निर्व्याजः -जा -जं, छलहीनः -ना -नं, अवक्रः -क्रा -क्रं, अजिह्मः -ह्मा -ह्मं, ऋजुः -जुः -जु.—(Neat) विनीतः -ता -तं, निर्भूषणः -णा -णं.—(Not abstruse, not complex) एकार्थः -र्था -र्थं, अगूढार्थः &c., स्पष्टार्थः &c., स्पष्टः -ष्टा -ष्टं, सुगम्यः -म्या -म्यं, व्यक्तः -क्ता -क्तं, भिन्नार्थः &c., *see* PLAIN.—(Foolish, childish) अल्पबुद्धिः -द्धिः -द्धि, दुर्मतिः -तिः -ति, बालिशः -शा -शं, *see* SILLY.

SIMPLE, *s.* (Herb) ओषधिः -धी *f.*, औषधं, तृणं.

SIMPLE-MINDED, *a.* शुद्धबुद्धिः -द्धिः -द्धि, सरलबुद्धिः &c., सरलमतिः &c.

SIMPLETON, *s.* अल्पबुद्धिः *m.*, अल्पधीः *m.*, मन्दबुद्धिः &c., मूर्खः, मूढः.

SIMPLICITY, SIMPLENESS, *s.* (State of being uncompounded) निरवयवत्वं, अमिश्रता, अमिश्रितत्वं, शुद्धता, केवलत्वं, अमिश्रभावः.—(Artlessness, plainness) सरलता, सारल्यं, अमाया, मायाहीनता, अमायिकत्वं, अकापट्यं, निष्कापट्यं, अपटाभावः, अव्याजः, छलहीनता, अवक्रता, ऋजुता, अनन्यभावः, आनीत्वं; 'of mind,' मतिसारल्यं, बुद्धिसारल्यं, मतिशुद्धता.—(Freedom from ornament) विनीतत्वं -ता, अभूषितत्वं, भूषणाभावः, भूषणहीनता.—(Freedom from abstruseness) एकार्थता, स्पष्टार्थता, स्पष्टता, सुगम्यता, व्यक्तता, सुज्ञेयता.—(Childishness) बालिश्यं, *see* SILLINESS.

SIMPLIFIED, *p. p.* लघूकृतः -ता -तं, सुगमीकृतः &c., व्यक्तीकृतः -ता -तं.

To SIMPLIFY, *v. a.* लघूकृ, सुगमीकृ, व्यक्तीकृ, स्पष्टीकृ, अर्थगूढतां हृ, एकार्थीकृ; 'to simplify the subject,' प्रस्तुतलाघवार्थं.

SIMPLY, *adv.* (Merely, solely) केवलं, मात्रं -त्रेण -त्रात्, *see* PLAINLY.

To SIMULATE, *v. a.* छद्म कृ, व्याजं कृ, छद्मवेशं धृ. *See To* PRETEND.

SIMULATION, *s.* छद्म *n.* (न्), व्याजः, अपदेशः, व्यपदेशः. *See* PRETENCE.

SIMULTANEOUS, *a.* समकालिकः -की -कं, समकालीनः -ना -नं, समानकालिकः &c., एककालिकः &c., एककालीनः -ना -नं, एकसमयः -या -यं, यौगपदिकः -की -कं.

SIMULTANEOUSLY, *adv.* युगपत्, एकदा, एककाले, समकाले, यौगपद्येन.

SIMULTANEOUSNESS, *s.* समकालिकता, एककालिकता, यौगपद्यं, कालैक्यं, एककालता, समकालता, समानकालत्वं, युगपद्भावः.

SIN, *s.* पापं, कल्मषं, किल्विषं, पातकं, पाप्मा *m.* (न्), अघं, दुरितं, एनस् *n.*, कलुषं, अभद्रं, अशुभं, वृजनं, वृजिनं, दोषः, अपराधः, दुष्कृतं, कल्कं, अंहस् *n.*, अंघस् *n.*, मन्तुः *m.*, कुल्मलं, कलङ्कः, प्रत्यवायः, किल्बं, अमीवं, पङ्कः -ङ्कं, जङ्गपूगं; 'bad action,' दुष्कर्म्म *n.* (न्), कुकर्म्म *n.*, पापकर्म्म *n.*, अपकर्म्म *n.*, अकर्म्म *n.*, दुष्कृतं, दुष्कृतिः *f.*, असत्कर्म्म *n.*, कुकृत्यं; 'heinous sin,' महापातकं, महापापं, अतिपातकं, अनुपातकं; 'the five heinous sins,' पञ्चमहापातकानि *m. pl.*; these are, 1. Killing a Brahman, ब्रह्महत्या, ब्राह्मणवधः. 2. Stealing gold, सुवर्णस्तेयं. 3. Drinking spirituous liquors, सुरापानं. 4. Intercourse with the wife of a Guru, गुरुतल्पगमनं. 5. Associating with any one guilty of these crimes, तत्संसर्गः; 'secret sins,' प्रच्छन्नपातकानि *n. pl.*, गुप्तपातकानि *n. pl.*; 'awful sin,' अघोरपातकं, अघोरपापं, घोरपापं; 'freed from sin,' पापमुक्तः -क्ता -क्तं; 'restraining sin,' पापविनिग्रहः; 'involved in the consequences of sin,' पापगोचरः -रा -रं; 'equal in sin,' पापसम्मितः -ता -तं; 'a personification of the five heinous sins, or a male whose head is Brahmanicide, whose arms are theft, whose heart is wine-drinking, &c.,' पापपुरुषः.

To SIN, *v. n.* पापं कृ, पातकं कृ, पापकर्म्म कृ, अपराधं कृ, दोषं कृ, अपराध् (c. 4. -राध्यति, c. 5. राध्नोति -राद्धुं), दुष् (c. 4. दुष्यति, दोष्टुं), दुष्कृतं कृ, मन्तु (nom. मन्तूयते).

SINCE, *prep.* or *adv.* (After, from the time that) expressed by the abl. c., either alone or followed by प्रभृति or आरभ्य or अवधि or sometimes preceded by आ; as, 'since childhood,' बाल्यात् or बाल्यतः or बाल्यात् प्रभृति or आबाल्यात्, शैशवात्प्रभृति; 'ever since one's birth,' जन्मतः प्रभृति or जन्मत आरभ्य or आजन्मतः; 'ever since I saw him,' प्रथमदर्शनक्षणात् प्रभृति, or यतः प्रभृति स मे दर्शनपथं गतः (followed by ततः प्रभृति); 'since the time of Vena,' वेणकालात्प्रभृति. The crude form may sometimes be used with the above words in this sense; as, 'since birth,' जन्मप्रभृति or जन्मारभ्य or जन्मावधि.—(Ago, in past time) पुरा, पूर्व्वं, गतकाले, अतीतकाले, पूर्व्वकाले, पुरस्तात्.—(Because that, seeing that) यस्मात्, येन, यतस्, यत्, हि, often expressed by the abl. c. of the abstract affix त्वं, or the instr. c. of the affix ता; as, 'since it was founded on observation,' प्रत्यक्षमूलत्वात्, प्रत्यक्षमूलतया.

SINCERE, *a.* (Said of things or persons) सरलः -ला -लं, सात्त्विकः -की -कं, तात्त्विकः &c., सत्यः -त्या -त्यं, दक्षिण्यः -ण्या -ण्यं, निर्व्याजः -जा -जं, निर्व्यलीकः -का -कं, अमायिकः -की -कं, अमायी -यिनी -यि (न्), अमायः -या -यं, मायाहीनः -ना -नं, निष्कपटः -टा -टं, अकपटः -टा -टं, अकृत्रिमः -मा -मं, अकल्पितः -ता -तं, दम्भरहितः -ता -तं, ऋजुः -जुः -जु, अजिह्मः -ह्मा -ह्मं, अवक्रः -क्रा -क्रं, शुद्धः -द्धा -द्धं, पूतः -ता -तं, वास्तविकः -की -कं, वास्तवः -वी -वं, यथार्थः -र्था -र्थं, निष्प्रपञ्चः -ञ्चा -ञ्चं.—(Said of persons only) सत्यवादी -दिनी -दि (न्), सत्यवाक् *m.f.n.* (च्), सत्यशीलः -ला -लं, शुद्धमतिः -तिः -ति, शुद्धभावः -वा -वं, विमलात्मा -त्मा -त्म (न्), अशठधीः -धीः -धि, उदारः -रा -रं, सत्यव्रतः -ता -तं, शुचिः -चिः -चि, निःशठः -ठा -ठं.

SINCERELY, *adv.* सरलं, सारल्येन, दाक्षिण्येन, निर्व्यलीकं, निर्व्याजं, अमायया, सत्यं, मनःपूर्व्वं, हृदयपूर्व्वं.

SINCERITY, SINCERENESS, *s.* सरलता, सारल्यं, दाक्षिण्यं, सत्यता, निर्व्यलीकता, अमाया, अमायिकत्वं, मायाहीनता, अकृत्रिमता, अकल्पितत्वं, निष्कपटत्वं, अकापट्यं, निष्कापट्यं, ऋजुता, आर्जवं, शुद्धता, वास्तविकता, यथार्थता, सत्यवादित्वं, सत्यशीलता, मतिशुद्धता, उदारता, विमलता, शुचिता, अनन्यभावः.

SINCIPUT, *s.* (Front of the head) मस्तकाग्रभागः, शिरोग्रभागः.

SIN-DESTROYING, *a.* पापनाशी -शिनी -शि (न्), पापनाशकः -का -कं, पापघ्नः -घ्नी -घ्नं, अघघ्नः &c., अघमलापहः -हा -हं, अघमर्षणः -णा -णं, पापशमनः &c.

SINE, *s.* (Of an arc in geometry) ज्या, त्रिज्या; 'versed sine,' इषुः *m.f.*, शरः.

SINECURE, *s.* वेतनयुक्तो निष्कर्म्मकाधिकारः or कर्म्मशून्याधिकारः.

SINEW, *s.* स्नायुः *m.f.*, स्नसा, स्नावः, सिरा, शिरा, सन्धिबन्धनं, ग्रन्थिबन्धनं, स्नायुभेदांशः, वहीरुः *m.*, रसालसा.—(Sinews, strength) बलं, शक्तिः *f.*, मुख्यसाधनं.

SINEWY, *a.* स्नायुमयः -यी -यं, शिरालः -ला -लं. *See* NERVOUS.

SINFUL, *a.* (Said of persons) पापी -पिनी -पि (न्), पापकर्म्मा -र्म्मा -र्म्म (न्), कुकर्म्मा &c., दुष्कर्म्मा &c., दुष्कृती &c., पापकारी -रिणी &c., पापकर्त्ता -र्त्री -र्तृ (र्तृ), पापकरः -री -रं, पापकृत् *m.f.n.*, कुकर्म्मकृत्, कुकर्म्मकारी &c., दुष्कृतकर्म्मा &c., पापकर्म्मी -र्म्मिणी &c., अपराधी &c., एनस्वी &c., किल्विषी &c., पातकी &c., कल्मषी &c., कृष्णकर्म्मा &c., पापाशयः -या -यं, पापपरायणः -णा -णं, पापनिरतः -ता -तं, पापात्मकः -का -कं, पापात्मा -त्मा -त्म (न्), पापबुद्धिः -द्धिः -द्धि, पापमतिः -तिः -ति, मन्दकारी &c., दुष्टचारी &c., व्यसनी -निनी &c., अधर्म्मचारी &c., दुरितः -ता -तं, *see* WICKED; 'very sinful,' पापिष्ठः -ष्ठा -ष्ठं, पापीयान् -यसी -यः (स्), अतिपापी &c.—(Containing sin, said of things) पाप in comp., पापी &c., पापवान् -वती -वत् (त्), दुष्टः -ष्टा -ष्टं, धर्म्मविरुद्धः -द्धा -द्धं, अघवान् &c., अघमयः -यी -यं, कलुषः -षा -षं, कल्की &c., कल्कः -ल्का -ल्कं, प्रत्यवायी &c.; 'sinful actions,' पापकर्म्माणि *n. pl.*

SINFULLY, *adv.* पापवत्, सपापं, दुष्टवत्, दुर्जनवत्, सपातकं.

SINFULNESS, *s.* पापं, पापिष्ठता, पापबुद्धिः *f.*, सपापता, पापनिरतिः *f.*, पापपरत्वं, दुष्टता, शठता, शाठ्यं, धर्म्मविरुद्धता, प्रत्यवायः. *See* WICKEDNESS.

To SING, *v. n.* गै (c. 1. गायति, गातुं), अनुगै, अभिगै, प्रगै, निगै, परिगै, उद्गै, गायनं कृ, गानं कृ.—(As birds, &c.) रु (c. 2. रौति, रवितुं), कल् (c. 10. कलयति -यितुं), कलं रु, वाश् (c. 4. वाश्यते -शितुं), वाशितं कृ.—(Make a humming sound) रणरणशब्दं कृ.

To SING, *v. a.* गै (c. 1. गायति, गातुं); 'to sing an air,' कलं गै; 'a song,' गीतं गै; 'a poem,' काव्यं गै.—(Celebrate in song) उपगै, परिगै, अभिप्रगै, गानेन कृत्, *see* CELEBRATE, CELEBRATED.

To SINGE, *v. a.* बाह्यतो दह् (c. 1. दहति, दग्धुं), बहिर्भागे दह्, ईषद् दह्, अग्निना स्पृश्, अग्निस्पृष्टं -ष्टां कृ. *See To* SCORCH.

SINGED, *p. p.* बाह्यतो दग्धः -ग्धा -ग्धं, बहिर्दग्धः &c., अग्निस्पृष्टः -ष्टा -ष्टं.

SINGER, *s.* गायकः, गाता *m.* (तृ), गायनः, गातुः *m.*, गाथिकः, गाथकः, गाथाकारः, गेष्णुः *m.*, गेष्णः, उद्गाता *m.*; 'female singer,' गात्री, गायकी, गायनी, उद्गात्री.

SINGING, *s.* गायनं, गानं, गीतिः *f.*, गीतं, स्वरयुक्तवाक्योच्चारणं.—(Of birds, &c.) रुतं, पक्षिरुतं, रावः, पक्षिरावः, वाशितं, वाशनं, मधुरुतं, कलः, कलकलः, कलरवः, कलनं. *See* MURMUR.

SINGING, *part.* गायन् -यन्ती -यत् (त्), प्रगायन् &c.

SINGING-MASTER, *s.* गानशिक्षकः, गानविद्याशिक्षकः, गीतोपदेशकः.

SINGLE, *a.* (One, consisting of one only) एकः -का -कं, अद्वितीयः -या -यं, केवलः -ला -ली -लं, एककः -का -कं; 'a single inflection,' एकपदः.—(Sole, alone) एकाकी -किनी -कि (न्), केवलः -ला -ली -लं, केवली &c., एकः -का -कं, अद्वितीयः -या -यं, असहायः -या -यं.—(Not double) अद्वैधः -धी -धं, अद्विकः -का -कं, अद्विगुणः -णा -णं, अद्वितीयः -या -यं.—(Distinct, individual) भिन्नः -न्ना -न्नं, व्यक्तः -क्ता -क्तं, अव्यापकः -का -कं, अविभक्तः &c., *see* PARTICULAR.—(Pure, simple) शुद्धः -द्धा -द्धं, *see* SIMPLE.—(Unmarried) अविवाहितः -ता, अनूढः -ढा, निःसङ्गः -ङ्गा.

To SINGLE, *v. a.* उद्धृ (c. 1. -हरति -हर्त्तुं, rt. हृ), उद्धृ, उद्ग्रह्, *see To* SELECT.

SINGLE-BODIED, *a.* एकदेहः -हा -हं, एकशरीरः -रा -रं, एकाङ्गः &c.

SINGLE-COMBAT, *s.* द्वन्द्वयुद्धं, द्वयोर्युद्धं, द्वन्द्वं, नियुद्धं.

SINGLE-EYED, *a.* एकाक्षः -क्षी -क्षं, एकलोचनः -ना -नं, एकचक्षुः -क्षिणी &c.

SINGLE-HANDED, *a.* असहायः -या -यं, स्वबाहुसहायः &c., एकाकी &c.

SINGLE-HEARTED, *a* एकचित्तः -त्ता -त्तं, अनन्यवृत्तिः -त्तिः -त्ति.

SINGLE-HOOFED, *a.* एकशफः -फा -फं, एकखुरः -रा -रं, एकखुरी -रिणी &c.

SINGLE-MINDED, *a.* शुद्धमतिः -तिः -ति. *See* SIMPLE, SIMPLE-MINDED.

SINGLENESS, *s.* (State of being one, or distinct from all others) एकता, ऐक्यं, केवलत्वं, कैवल्यं, अद्वितीयता, अद्वैधता, भिन्नता.—(Simplicity, sincerity) शुद्धता, अनन्यता, अनन्यभावः; 'of heart,' मतिशुद्धता.

SINGLE-STICK, *s.* (Cudgel) यष्टिः *m.*, दण्डः, वेत्रं, द्विदण्डि indec.; 'fighting with single-stick,' द्विदण्डिप्रहरणं, द्विमुषलिप्रहरणं.

SINGLY, *adv.* (Individually, one by one) प्रत्येकं, एकशस्, एकैकशस्, एकतस्, एकैकं, पृथक्, पृथक् पृथक्.—(Alone, without companions) असहायतस्, अद्वितीयतस्, एकतस्.

SINGULAR, *a.* (Single) एकः -का -कं, *see* SINGLE.—(Existing by itself, unexampled) अद्वितीयः -या -यं, अनुपमः -मा -मं, अप्रतिमः -मा -मं, अपूर्व्वः -र्व्वा -र्व्वं, असदृशः -शी -शं, अनन्यसाधारणः -णा -णी -णं, अनन्यसामान्यः -न्या -न्यं, अपूर्व्वप्रतिमः -मा -मं, अपूर्व्वप्रमाणः -णा -णं, एकमात्रः -त्रा -त्रं.—(Not common, odd) असाधारणः -णा -णी -णं, असामान्यः -न्या -न्यं, असङ्कृतः -ता -तं, विलक्षणः -णा -णं, अप्रसिद्धः -द्धा -द्धं, अपरूपः -पा -पं, अद्भुतः -ता -तं, लोकबाह्यः -ह्या -ह्यं, अलौकिकः -की -कं, लोकोत्तरः -रा -रं.—(The singular number) एकवचनं.

SINGULARITY, *s.* असाधारणता, अद्वितीयता, अप्रतिमता, अनुपमता, असदृशता, असादृश्यं, अपूर्व्वता, असामान्यता, अनन्यसाधारणता, विलक्षणता, वैलक्षण्यं, असङ्कृतत्वं, असङ्कृतिः *f.*, अपरूपता, अद्भुतता, एकता.

SINGULARLY, *adv.* अपूर्व्ववत्, अपूर्व्वं, असङ्कृतं, विलक्षणं, सवैलक्षण्यं, असाधारण्येन, असामान्येन, अद्भुतं, विशेषतस्.

SINISTER, *a.* (Not honest, crooked) असरलः -ला -लं, वक्रः -क्रा -क्रं, अनृजुः -जुः -जु, कुटिलः -ला -लं, वामः -मा -मं, वृजिनः -ना -नं.—(Inauspicious) अमङ्गलः -ला -लं, अकल्याणः -णा -णी, अमङ्गलसूचकः -का -कं.—(Left), *see* the word.

SINISTRALLY, *adv.* वामत्वेन, सव्यत्वेन, वामदिशि, वामदिशं प्रति.

SINISTROUS, *a.* वामस्थः -स्था -स्थं, सव्यस्थः &c., वामवर्त्ती -र्त्तिनी &c.

To SINK, *v. n.* सद् (c. 6. सीदति, सत्तुं), अवसद्, विषद्, व्यवसद्, उत्सद्, संसद्, अधोगम् (c. 1. -गच्छति -गन्तुं), अधो या (c. 2. याति -तुं), अधःपत् (c. 1. पतति -तितुं), अवपत्, पत्.—(In water) मज्ज् (c. 6. मज्जति, मंक्तुं), निमज्ज्, जलमग्नः -ग्ना -ग्नं भू.—(In the mud) पङ्के सद् or पत्.—(In difficulties) कृच्छ्रे सद्, आपदि सद्.—(With fear) भयात् सद् or विषद्.—(Decline) अस्तं गम्, क्षि in pass. (क्षीयते), ध्वंस्, *see To* FAIL.

To SINK, *v. a.* (Cause to sink) अवसद् (c. 10. -सादयति -यितुं), व्यवसद्, सद्, मज्ज् (c. 10. मज्जयति -यितुं), अधोगम् in caus. (-गमयति -यितुं).

SINK, *s.* (Drain) मलनिर्गमः, जलसारणी, गुप्तनाली, गुप्तिः *f.*

SINKING, *part.* सीदन् -दन्ती -दत् (त्), अवसीदन् &c., मज्जन् -ज्जन्ती -ज्जती -ज्जत् (त्), निमज्जन् &c., निमग्नः -ग्ना -ग्नं.

SINLESS, *a.* निष्पापः -पा -पं, अपापः -पा -पं, पापहीनः -ना -नं, पापरहितः -ता -तं, अकल्मषः -षा -षं, निष्कल्मषः &c., अनघः -घा -घं, अकिल्बिषः -षा -षं, वीतकल्मषः &c., अनेनाः -नाः -नः (स्), निरागाः &c., अकल्कः -ल्का -ल्कं, निर्दोषः -षा -षं, निरपराधः -धा -धं, निष्कलङ्कः -ङ्का -ङ्कं, अनमीवः -वा -वं.

SINLESSNESS, *s.* निष्पापता, अपापता, पापहीनता, पापाभावः.

SINNER, *s.* पापी *m.* (न्), पापजनः, पापकारी, पापकृत् *m.*, पापात्मा *m.* (न्), पापकर्म्मी *m.* (न्), एनस्वी *m.* (न्), व्यसनी *m.*, अपुण्यकर्त्ता *m.* (र्तृ), अपुण्यकृत् *m.*, अधोनः, *see* SINFUL; 'an atrocious sinner,' महापातकी *m.* (न्), अतिपातकी *m.*, महापापी *m.*, अतिपापी *m.*, पापमूर्त्तिः *m.*, पापनिधिः *m.*, पापस्वरूपः, पापराशिः *m.*, पापपुरुषः.

SIN-OFFERING, *s.* पापशमनं, पापनाशकप्रायश्चित्तं, पापशमकबलिः *m.*

SINUOSITY, *s.* वक्रता, वक्रिमा *m.* (न्), कुटिलता, भिन्नता, कौटिल्यं.

SINUOUS, *a.* वक्रः -क्रा -क्रं, कुटिलः -ला -लं. *See* WINDING, *a.*

SINUS, *s.* (In surgery) नाडिः -डी *f.*, नाडीव्रणः -णः, नालिः -ली, नालीव्रणः -णः, नालीक्षतं, गतिः *f.*, अवटः -टिः *m.*

To SIP, *v. a.* (Drink in small quantities) अल्पाल्पशस् or अल्पाल्पं पा (c. 1. पिबति, पातुं) or आपा, अल्पशो निपा or चम् (c. 1. चमति -मितुं), ईषत्पानं कृ, आचम् (c. 1. -चामति -मितुं), उपस्पृश् (c. 6.

-स्पृशति -स्प्रष्टुं). The last two words are used especially with reference to sipping water before meals and religious ceremonies from the palm of the hand, and ejecting it again.

SIP, SIPPING, s. ईषत्पानं, अल्पशः पानं, अल्पशो निपानं, ईषन्निपानं, आचमनं, उपस्पर्शः, शुचिप्रणी: *f*.. ओष्ठनिपानं, ओष्ठपानं.

SIPHON, s. कुक्कुटनाडीयन्त्रं, नाडीयन्त्रं, नालीयन्त्रं, वक्रनाडी.

SIPPED, *p.p.* अल्पाल्पशः पीतः -ता -तं, अल्पशो निपीतः -ता -तं.

SIR, s. आर्य्यः, महाशयः, महानुभावः, महेच्छः, महाजनः, सुजनः, श्री prefixed; 'O sir,' आर्य्य. As an address of respect, 'Sir' may often be expressed in Sanskrit by भवान् with the 3d pers. of the verb; as, 'enter, Sir,' प्रविशतु भवान्.

SIRE, s. (Word of address to a king) देव voc. c., श्रीमद्देव, महाराज, राजन्, आयुष्मन्.—(Father) जनकः, जननः, जनिता *m.* (तृ).

SIREN, s. मोहिनी, मोहकारिणी, मायिनी, मायाकारिणी, विमोहिनी.

SIRIUS, s. (Dog-star) लुब्धकः.

SIRLOIN, s. (Of beef) गोपार्श्वमांसं, गोपार्श्वः.

SIRNAME, s. उपनाम *n.* (न्), पद्धतिः -ती *f.* *See* SURNAME.

SIRRAH, s. (Reproachful address) अरे, अरेरे, रे, रै, अये.

SIRUP, s. इक्षुरसः, स्वादुरसः, मधुरसः, मधुररसः, मधुरं, लेह्यं.

SIRUPY, *a.* इक्षुरसमयः -यी -यं. स्वादुरसमयः &c., मधुरः -रा -रं.

SISTER, s. स्वसा *f.* (सृ *nom. pl.* स्वसारः), भगिनी, भगिनीका, भग्नी, स्वयोनिः *f.*, जामिः -मी, यामिः -मी; 'elder sister,' अग्रजा; 'younger sister,' अवरजा; 'sister's husband,' भगिनीपतिः *m.*, स्वसृपतिः; 'sister's son,' भागिनेयः, स्वस्रीयः, स्वस्रियः, स्वस्रेयः; 'sister's daughter,' भागिनेया, स्वस्रीया, स्वस्रिया, स्वस्रेयी.—(Woman of the same faith) धर्म्मभगिनी.

SISTER-IN-LAW, s. (Husband's sister) ननान्दा *f.* (न्दृ), ननन्दा *f.* (न्दृ), नन्दा, पतिस्वसा *f.* (सृ), पत्युः स्वसा *f.*—(Wife's sister) श्याली, श्यालकी, श्यालिका, जायाभगिनी, पत्नीस्वसा *f.*—(Brother's wife) भ्रातृजाया, भ्रातृपत्नी, भ्रातृभार्य्या, प्रजावती.

SISTERHOOD, s. (State of a sister) भगिनीत्वं, स्वसृत्वं.—(Community of sisters or women) स्वसृगणः, भगिनीगणः, स्वसृमण्डली, स्वसृसमूहः, स्त्रीगणः.

SISTERLY, *a.* स्वसृयोग्यः -ग्या -ग्यं, भगिनीयोग्यः &c., स्वस्रीयः -या -यं.

To SIT, *v. n.* उपविश् (c. 6. -विशति -वेष्टुं), समुपविश्, उपोपविश्, उपवेशं कृ, उपवेशनं कृ, आस् (c. 2. आस्ते -सितुं), अध्यास्, समास्, सद् (c. 1. सीदति, सत्तुं), निषद् with loc. or acc. c.; as, 'he sits down on a chair,' पीठे or पीठम् उपविशति; 'on a seat offered,' दत्तासनम् उपविशति.—(Sit by the side of) उपास्, अन्वास्.—(Sit idle) उदास्.—(Incubate) नीडे निली (c. 4. -लीयते -लेतुं), नीडनिलायं कृ, अण्डोपरि उपविश्.—(Press on, bear on) उपस्था, समुपस्था, आक्रम्, पीड्.—(As an assembly) कार्य्यनिर्वाहं कृ.

SÍTÁ, s. (The wife of Rámachandra, and daughter of Janaka, the king of Mithilá. She is called 'earth-born,' as having been turned up from the soil by a plough, as Janaka was ploughing a spot to prepare for a sacrifice) सीता, धरणीसुता, भूमिसम्भवा, भूमिजा, भूपुत्री, जनकात्मजा, जनकसुता, जनकतनया.

SITE, s. स्थानं, स्थलं, पदं, आस्पदं, स्थितिः *f.*, भूमिः *f.*, पदविः -वी *f.*, प्रतिष्ठा -ष्ठानं, धानी, विन्यासः, गाधः.—(Of a house) वास्तुः *m.*, वास्तु *n.*, गृहभूमिः *f.*, वेश्मभूः *f.*, गृहपोतकः, गृहपोटः, पोटः, पोतः -तकः, कुट्टिमं, वाटिका; 'ceremony of purification, &c., of a site,' स्थलशुद्धिः *f.*, वास्तुसंशमनं, वास्तुसंशमनीयं.

SITTING, s. (The act) उपवेशः -शनं, आसना -नं, अध्यासः -सनं -ना, आस्या.—(A seat) आसनं.

SITTING, *part.* आसीनः -ना -नं, अध्यासीनः &c., उपविष्टः -ष्टा -ष्टं, निषीदन् -दन्ती -दत् (त्); 'on a seat,' आसनोपविष्टः &c.

SITUATED, SITUATE, *a.* (Placed or standing with regard to any other object) स्थः स्था स्थं, स्थितः -ता -तं, अवस्थितः &c., संस्थः -स्था -स्थं, संस्थितः -ता -तं, दिश्यः -श्या -श्यं; 'situated near,' समीपस्थः &c., समीपस्थितः &c.; 'situated to the south,' दक्षिणस्थः -स्था -स्थं, दक्षिणदिश्यः &c.; 'towards the east,' पूर्व्वस्थः &c., पूर्व्वदिश्यः &c.; 'well situated,' सुस्थितः -ता -तं, सुसंस्थितः &c.; 'pleasantly situated,' सौवास्तवः -वी -वं.—(With regard to men or things) स्थः स्था -स्थं, स्थितः -ता -तं, अवस्थ in comp., अवस्थाप्राप्तः -प्ता -प्तं, अवस्थापन्नः -न्ना -न्नं; 'well situated,' सुस्थः &c., सुस्थितः &c.; 'so situated,' तदवस्थः -स्था -स्थं; 'how situated?' किमवस्थः -स्था -स्थं; 'badly situated,' दुःस्थितः -ता -तं, दुःस्थः &c.

SITUATION, s. (Place, position) स्थानं, स्थितिः *f.*, अवस्थितिः *f.*, अवस्थानं, आस्पदं, पदं, पदविः -वी *f.*—(State, circumstances) अवस्था, दशा, स्थितिः *f.*, संस्थितिः *f.*, भावः, वृत्तिः *f.*, आस्पदं, पदं; 'disgraceful situation,' परिभवास्पदं, परिभवपदं.—(Office, post) पदं, पदविः -वी, अधिकारः, स्थानं, स्थलं, नियोगः, व्यापारः.

SIVA, s. A celebrated Hindú God, the Destroyer of Creation, and therefore the most formidable of the Hindú Triad. He also personifies reproduction, since the Hindú philosophy excludes the idea of total annihilation without subsequent regeneration. Hence he is sometimes confounded with Brahmá, the Creator, or first person of the Triad. He is the particular god of the Tántrikas, or followers of the books called Tantras. His worshippers are termed Śaivas, and although not so numerous as the Vaishnavas, exalt their god to the highest place in the heavens, and combine in him many of the attributes which properly belong to the other deities. According to them Śiva is Time, Justice, Fire, Water, the Sun, the Destroyer and Creator. As presiding over generation, his type is the Linga, or Phallus, the origin probably of the Phallic emblem of Egypt and Greece. As the god of generation and of justice, which latter character he shares with the god Yama, he is represented riding a white bull. His own colour, as well as that of the bull, is generally white, referring probably to the unsullied purity of Justice. His throat is dark blue; his hair of a light reddish colour, and thickly matted together, and gathered above his head like the hair of an ascetic. He is sometimes seen with two hands, sometimes with four, eight, or ten, and with five faces. He has three eyes, one being in the centre of his forehead, pointing up and down. These are said to denote his view of the three divisions of time, past, present, and future. He holds a trident in his hand to denote, as some say, his relationship to water, or according to others, to show that the three great attributes of Creator, Destroyer, and Regenerator are combined in him. His loins are enveloped in a tiger's skin. In his character of Time, he not only presides over its extinction, but also its astronomical regulation. A crescent or half-moon on his forehead indicates the measure of time by the phases of the moon; a serpent forms one of his necklaces to denote the measure of time by years, and a second necklace of human skulls marks the lapse and revolution of ages, and the extinction and succession of the generations of mankind. He is often represented as entirely covered with serpents, which are the emblems of immortality. They are bound in his hair, round his neck, wrists, waist, arms, and legs; they serve as rings for his fingers, and earrings for his ears, and are his constant companions. Śiva has more than a thousand names, which are detailed at length in the sixty-ninth chapter of the Śiva Purána. The following list of the principal of these will give the best idea of his character and attributes. (The Auspicious one) शिवः, शम्भुः *m.*, शङ्करः, सदाशिवः, श्रीमान् *m.* (त्), भद्रः, भगः.—(The great god or lord) महादेवः, ईश्वरः, महेश्वरः, महेशः, ईशः, ईशानः, नाथः, देवः. —(Lord of the universe, as worshipped at Benares) विश्वेश्वरः, विश्वेशः, विश्वनाथः, सर्व्वेश्वरः.—(Lord of the earth) धरणीश्वरः.—(The seizer) हरः, हरकः, हरिः *m.*—(The Destroyer, a personification of Time that destroys all things) कालः, महाकालः, जगद्घाती *m.* (न्), जगद्भक्षकः, कालञ्जरः.—(The Reproducer, the Conqueror of Death and cause of life and being) भवः, मृत्युञ्जयः, मृत्युवञ्चनः, जगद्योनिः *m.*, भूतात्मा *m.* (न्), जः, भरुः *m.*—(Disperser of the tears of mortals) रुद्रः.—(The terrific or tremendous one) भैरवः, घोरः, भीषणः, भीष्मः, भीमः.—(The fierce one) उग्रः, चण्डः.—(Blue-throat, having a dark blue and beautiful throat, so stained by the acrimony of the poison, which he swallowed on its production at the churning of the ocean; *see* OCEAN) नीलकण्ठः, श्यामकण्ठः, नीलग्रीवः, शितिकण्ठः, कालकण्ठः, श्रीकण्ठः, नीललोहितः.—(Tri-ocular, having three eyes) त्रिलोचनः, त्रिनेत्रः, त्रिदृक् *m.* (श्), त्रिनयनः, त्र्यक्षः.—(Having deformed or unnatural eyes) विरूपाक्षः.—(Moon-crested, having a crescent on his brow) चन्द्रमौलिः *m.*, चन्द्रशेखरः, शशिशेखरः, इन्दुभृत्, चन्द्रापीडः, शशीशः, चन्द्रिलः, सोमः.—(Borne on, or accompanied by the Bull which personifies Justice) वृषवाहनः, वृषभवाहनः, वृषध्वजः, वृषभध्वजः, धर्म्मवाहनः, वृषपतिः *m.*, वृषभगतिः *m.*, वृषपर्व्वा *m.* (न्), वृषाङ्कः, वृषाञ्चनः, वृषारूढः.—(Having matted or braided hair) धूर्जटिः *m.*, जटाधरः, जटाधारी *m.* (न्), जटिलः, जटाटङ्कः, जटाटीरः, कपर्दी *m.* (न्), कपर्दः.—(Having sky-coloured hair) व्योमकेशी *m.* (न्), व्योमकेशः.—(Trident-bearer) शूली *m.* (न्), त्रिशूली *m.*, शूलधरः, पिनाकी *m.*—(Lord of animals or cattle) पशुपतिः *m.*, गोपतिः, गोरक्षः, गोपालकः.—(Lord of spirits) भूतेशः, भूतनाथः, भूतः.—(Bearer of the Ganges, this river having on its descent from heaven alighted on his head, and thence descended upon earth, through a chasm in the Himálaya mountains called Gomukha) गङ्गाधरः.—(Clothed with a tiger's skin) कृत्तिवासाः *m.* (स्), कृत्तिवासः.—(Bound or covered with snakes) अहिबन्धः.—(Having a necklace of human skulls) कपालभृत्, कपाली *m.* (न्), अस्थिमाली *m.*, पुरुषास्थिमाली *m.*, अस्थिधन्वा *m.* (न्), भगाली *m.*—(The white one or yellowish white) शुचिः, गौरः, हरिणः.—(Conqueror and Destroyer of the district and king of Tripura) त्रिपुरजित्, त्रिपुरसूदनः, त्रिपुरदहनः, त्रिपुरान्तकः.—(Presiding over the three Vedas, or the three letters of the mystical syllable *om*) त्र्यम्बकः.—(He of whom one form is water) जलमूर्त्तिः *m.*—(The Steadfast) स्थाणुः *m.*—(The Universal) सर्व्वः. —(The Omnipresent) सर्व्वगः.—(The Omniscient) सर्व्वज्ञः.—(The Imperishable) अक्षरः.—(The Five-faced) पञ्चमुखः, पञ्चाननः, पञ्चवक्त्रः, सर्व्वतोमुखः.—(Scorcher of Cupid, *see* KÁMADEVA) स्मरहरः, कामध्वंसी *m.* (न्), अनङ्गासुहृद्, भर्गः.—(Restorer of his body) पराङ्गदः.—(Lord of Kailása, in the Himálayas, the favourite haunt of both Śiva and Kuvera) गिरीशः, गिरिशः, कैलासौकाः *m.* (स्), कैलासनिकेतनः.—(Lord of Benares) काशीनाथः, काशीशः; hence one of the names of Benares is रुद्रावासः, शिवपुरी.—(Having three residences) त्रिधामा *m.*—(Destroyer of Daksha's sacrifice. That sage having on one occasion made a sacrifice, to which he invited all the gods, excepting his son-in-law Śiva and his daughter Durgá, the latter went unbid, and being received coldly, threw herself into the fire, whence emanated a form of Śiva, who decapitated the sage) दक्षाध्वरध्वंसकृत्, दक्षयज्ञविनाशी *m.* (न्), क्रतुध्वंसी *m.*—(He of whom the seed was cast into Fire) वह्निरेताः *m.* (स्), कृशानुरेताः *m.*—(Teacher of the gṛihya, or book of domestic rites) गृह्यगुरुः.—(Possessor of the head of Brahmá, having in a dispute cut off one of the heads of that deity) ब्रह्ममूर्द्धभृत्.—(Enemy of the demon Pura) पुरारिः *m.*, पुरासुहृद्.—(Enemy of the demon Andhaka) अन्धकरिपुः *m.*—(He who cuts to pieces with his axe) खण्डपरशुः *m.*, खण्डपर्शुः *m.*—(Armed with the Khatwánga or Pánśula) खट्वाङ्गी *m.*, खट्वाङ्गभृत् *m.*, पांशुली *m.* —(Armed with a rope) पाशी *m.*—(Lord of devotion or devotees) योगेशः.—(Lord of gold) हेमकेशः.—(Fond of dancing) नाट्यप्रियः.—(The naked one) दिगम्बरः, दिग्वासाः *m.* (स्), नग्नः.—(Covered with sandal powder) पांशुचन्दनः, पांशुलः. —(Mounted on a dog in his terrific form) श्वाश्वः.—(The perverse) वामः, वामदेवः.—(Husband of Párvatí) पार्व्वतीनाथः. —(Of Durgá) दुर्गापतिः, दक्षजापतिः.—(Of Gaurí) गौरीपतिः.—(Of Umá) उमापतिः.—(Of Bhavání) भवानीपतिः.—(Lord of the Pramathas, his attendants) प्रमथाधिपः.—(Lord of Nandi, one of his chief attendants) नन्दीशः, नन्दीश्वरः, नन्दिवर्धनः. —(Lord of Bhṛingi, one of his chamberlains) भृङ्गीशः.—(Loved of Vishnu) हरिप्रियः.—(Having Vishnu as his dart, that deity having served him for a shaft which set the city of Tripura on fire) हरिशरः. Some of his other names, the derivation of which is not very apparent, are the following: नकुलः, अप्यूढः, शिपिविष्टः, शिविपिष्टः, क्षीरकुः, नाक्रः, मृडः, कुम्भकरः, वारः, ङः *m.*—(Under the emblem of the Phallus) लिङ्गं; 'a worshipper of him under that type,' लिङ्गी *m.*—(A form of Śiva, half male and half female) अर्द्धनारीशः, अर्द्धनारीनटेश्वरः.—(Inferior manifestations of him, called Bhairavas) असिताङ्गः, रुरुः *m.*, चण्डः, क्रोधः, उन्मत्तः, कुपतिः, भीषणः, संहरः, नकुलः.—(His wife) पार्व्वती, दुर्गा, गौरी, उमा, सती, भवानी, *see* PĀRVATĪ; as the symbol of created nature his wife is called प्रकृतिः.—(His sons) कार्त्तिकेयः, गणेशः, *see* KĀRTIKEYA, GANESHA.—(His attendants) प्रमथः, शिवकीर्त्तनः.—(Some of the names of his attendants are) नन्दी *m.*, नन्दिः *m.*, भृङ्गी *m.*, नाडीदेहः, नाडीविग्रहः, नाडीजङ्घः, भृङ्गिरिटः, तण्डुः, पशुः.—(His vehicle or bull) वृषः, नन्दी *m.*—(Temple consecrated to his bull) गोपुटिकः.—(His trident) त्रिशूलं, पिनाकः, महितं, पाशुपतास्त्रं.—(His bow) पिनाकः, अजगवं.—(One of his weapons, a staff with transverse pieces, representing the breast-bone and ribs, surmounted by a skull) खट्वाङ्गं, पांशुलः.—(His rope for binding incorrigible offenders) पाशः.—(His musical instrument, a kind of rattle, shaped like an hour-glass, and held in one hand) डमरुः *m.*—(His serpent earrings) नागकुण्डलं.—(His necklace of skulls) अस्थिमाला, मुण्डमाला.—(His matted hair) जटा, जटाजूटः, कपर्द्दः.—(His superhuman power) विभूतिः *f.*, भूतिः *f.*, *see* SUPERHUMAN, *a.*—(Daitya flayed by him) रुरुः.—(Worshipper of Śiva) शैवः, शैव्यः, शिवज्ञः, पाशुपतिकः. Many plants are sacred to Śiva, as the aśoka, vilva, mango, &c.

SIX, *a.* षट् *m. f. n. pl.* (षष्), षट्संख्यकः -का -कं, षट्कः -ट्का -ट्कं; 'six months,' षण्मासाः *m. pl.*, षण्मासं; 'the six seasons,' षडृतवः *m. pl.*; 'of six months standing,' षाण्मासिकः -की -कं, षण्मास्यः -स्या -स्यं; 'six-fingered,' षडङ्गुलिः -लिः -लि; 'six-angled,' षट्कोणः -णा -णं; 'six-limbed,' षडङ्गः -ङ्गा -ङ्गं; 'six-armed,' षड्भुजः -जा -जं; 'six-faced,' षण्मुखः -खा -खं; 'a yoke of six oxen,' षड्गवं; 'having six feet,' षट्पदः -दा -दं; 'in six ways,' षड्धा; 'the aggregate of six,' षट्कं.

SIX-FOLD, *a.* षड्गुणः -णा -णं, षड्विधः -धा -धं, षट्कः -ट्का -ट्कं.

SIXTEEN, *a.* षोडश *m. f. n. pl.* (न्) षोडशकः -का -कं.

SIXTEENTH, *a.* षोडशः -शी -शं; 'a sixteenth part,' षोडशांशः.

SIXTH, *a.* षष्ठः -ष्ठी -ष्ठं, षष्ठकः -का -कं; 'a sixth part,' षड्भागः, षडंशः; 'a sixth meal,' षष्ठान्नं; 'being or having a sixth,' षष्ठी -ष्ठिनी -ष्ठि (न्).

SIXTHLY, *adv.* षष्ठतस्, षष्ठस्थाने, षष्ठपदे.

SIXTIETH, *a.* षष्टितमः -मी -मं, षष्टः -ष्टी -ष्टं.

SIXTY, *a.* षष्टिः *f.*, षष्टिसंख्यकः -का -कं; 'he reigned sixty years,' षष्टिम् अब्दान् राज्यं चकार; 'sixty-one,' एकषष्टिः; 'sixty-two,' द्वाषष्टिः; 'sixty-three,' त्रयःषष्टिः; 'sixty-four,' चतुःषष्टिः; 'sixty-five,' पञ्चषष्टिः; 'sixty-six,' षट्षष्टिः; 'sixty-seven,' सप्तषष्टिः; 'sixty-eight,' अष्टाषष्टिः; 'sixty-nine,' नवषष्टिः, एकोनसप्ततिः, ऊनसप्ततिः; 'aggregate of sixty,' षष्टिकं; 'bought with sixty,' षष्टिकः -का -कं.

SIZE, *s.* (Bulk) परिमाणं, मानं, परिमितिः *f.*, प्रमाणं, मात्रं, आकारः, आकारमानं, आकृतिः *f.*, आकृतिमानं, महत्त्वमानं, महत्त्वपरिमाणं, आकारपरिमाणं, आकृतिपरिमाणं; 'of the same size,' समपरिमाणः -णा -णं, सममात्रः -त्रा -त्रं; 'of the size of an egg,' अण्डपरिमाणः -णा -णं; 'of the size of a grain of mustard,' सर्षपपरिमाणः -णा -णं; 'of unequal size,' विषमपरिमाणः &c., असमपरिमाणः &c.; of all sizes,' उत्तमाधममध्यमाः *m. pl.*; 'having ascertained the size and distance of the moon,' चन्द्रस्य मानं दूरत्वं च ज्ञात्वा.

SKAIN, SKEIN, *s.* पञ्जिका, पिञ्जिका, पञ्जिः -ञ्जी *f.*, पिञ्जिः -ञ्जी *f.*; 'of silk,' कौशिकसूत्रपञ्जी, कौशिकसूत्रग्रन्थिः *m.*

SKATE, *s.* (For moving on the ice) हिमसंहतजलोपरि विसर्पणयोग्या लोहयुक्तपादुका or स्खलनयोग्यपादुका, स्खलनपादुका.—(The fish), *see* SCATE.

To SKATE, *v. n.* पूर्व्वोक्तपादुकाद्वारेण हिमोपरि or हिमसंहतजलोपरि विसृप् (c. 1. -सर्पति -सर्प्तुं) or संसृप् or स्खल् (c. 1. स्खलति -लितुं).

SKATER, *s.* पूर्व्वोक्तपादुकाद्वारा हिमोपरि विसर्पी *m.* (न्) or संसर्पी *m.*

SKATING, *s.* लोहयुक्तपादुकाद्वारेण हिमोपरि विसर्पणं or संसर्पणं or स्खलनं or रिङ्खणं.

SKEIN, *s.* पञ्जिका, पिञ्जिका, पञ्जिः *f.* *See* SKAIN.

SKELETON, *s.* कङ्कालः, अस्थिपञ्जरः, अस्थिपिञ्जरः, पञ्जरः, संघः, शरीरास्थिमात्रं, देहास्थिमात्रं; 'reduced to a mere skeleton,' त्वगस्थिमात्रशेषः -षा -षं.—(Frame, compages) संस्थानं, व्यूहः, आकारः.—(Of any subject) वस्तुमात्रं, वस्तु *n.*

SKEPTIC, SKEPTICAL, SKEPTICISM. *See* SCEPTIC, INFIDEL, &c.

SKETCH, *s.* (Of a figure, &c.) आलेख्यं, पाण्डुलेख्यं, पाण्डुलेख्यमात्रं, लघ्वालेख्यं, बहिर्लेख्यं, ईषदालेख्यं, किञ्चिदालेख्यं, ईषदङ्कनं, किञ्चिदङ्कनं, ईषद्वर्णनं, स्थूलालेख्यं; 'of a painting,' चित्रारम्भः, पाण्डुचित्रं, चित्रं.—(Of a subject) वस्तुमात्रं, ईषद्वर्णनं, किञ्चिद्वर्णनं, वस्तु *n.*

To SKETCH, *v. a.* बाह्यरेखामात्रं लिख् (c. 6. लिखति, लेखितुं) or आलिख् or विलिख्, पाण्डुलेख्यम् अङ्क् (c. 10. अङ्कयति -यितुं) पाण्डुलेख्यं कृ, लघ्वालेख्यं कृ, स्थूलालेख्यं कृ, किञ्चिदालेख्यं कृ, किञ्चिद्वर्णनं कृ, ईषद्वर्णनं कृ, ईषद् वर्ण् (c. 10. वर्णयति -यितुं) or अनुवर्ण् or उपवर्ण् or संवर्ण्, चित्रारम्भं कृ, पाण्डुचित्रं कृ.

SKETCHED, *p. p.* आलिखितः -ता -तं, किञ्चिदालिखितः &c., चित्रारब्धः, चित्रारम्भः -म्भा -म्भं, किञ्चिद्वर्णितः -ता -तं, बहिरङ्कितः &c.

SKEWER, *s.* शलाका, कीलः -लकः, शङ्कुः *m.*, मांसबन्धनशलाका.

To SKEWER, *v. a.* शलाकया बन्ध् (c. 9. बध्नाति, बन्द्धुं), शलाकाबद्धं -द्धां कृ.

SKIFF, *s.* (Light boat) लघुनौका, क्षुद्रनौका, सुवहनौका.

SKILFUL, *a.* कुशलः -ला -लं, निपुणः -णा -णं, प्रवीणः -णा -णं, पटुः -टुः -ट्वी -टु, विचक्षणः -णा -णं, विशारदः -दा -दं, चतुरः -रा -रं, अभिज्ञः -ज्ञा -ज्ञं, विज्ञः &c., विदग्धः -ग्धा -ग्धं, पेशलः -ला -लं, वैज्ञानिकः -की -कं, कृती -तिनी -ति (न्), युक्तिमान् -मती -मत् (त्), निष्णातः -ता -तं, ज्ञ in comp.; 'skilful in arms,' अस्त्रज्ञः -ज्ञा -ज्ञं, शस्त्रकुशलः &c.; 'skilful in expedients,' उपायज्ञः -ज्ञा -ज्ञं.

SKILFULLY, *adv.* कुशलवत्, कौशल्येन, सकौशल्यं, निपुणवत्, सपाटवं, विचक्षणवत्, चतुरवत्, सचातुर्य्यं, विदग्धवत्, सवैदग्ध्यं, युक्त्या, निपुणं.

SKILFULNESS, *s.* कुशलता, कौशल्यं, निपुणता, नैपुण्यं, प्रवीणता, प्रावीण्यं, पटुता, पाटवं, विचक्षणता, वैचक्षण्यं, चतुरता, चातुर्य्यं, युक्तिः *f.*, युक्तिमत्त्वं, विज्ञता, अभिज्ञता, विदग्धता, वैदग्ध्यं, विचित्रता, व्यवसायः, गुणः.

SKILL, *s.* कुशलता, पाटवं, युक्तिः *f.*, पटुता. *See* SKILFULNESS.

SKILLED, *a.* कुशलः -ला -लं, शिक्षितः -ता -तं, ज्ञ in comp., अभिज्ञ in comp., विद् in comp., कृतमुखः &c., *see* SKILFUL; 'skilled in the śāstras,' शास्त्रज्ञः -ज्ञा -ज्ञं, शास्त्राभिज्ञः &c., शास्त्रविद् *m.f.n.*, शास्त्रतत्त्वज्ञः &c., शास्त्रकुशलः -ला -लं; 'in music,' गान्धर्वतत्त्वज्ञः -ज्ञा -ज्ञं.

SKIM, *s.* (Matter that forms on the surface) मण्डः, फेनः, उत्तरं, उत्तरमलं, *see* SCUM.—(Of milk) दुग्धफेनः -नं, दुग्धतालीयं, शार्करः, शार्करः.

To SKIM, *v. a.* (Clear off the thick matter from the surface) मण्डं or फेनम् अपनी (c. 1. -नयति -नेतुं) or हृ (c. 1. हरति, हर्त्तुं) or अपहृ.—(Skim milk) दुग्धफेनम् अपनी or हृ, दुग्धतालीयम् अपनी or अपहृ.

To SKIM, *v. n.* (Glide along the surface, brush) विसृप् (c. 1. -सर्पति -सर्प्तुं -सर्प्तुं), लघुगत्या वहिर्भागं घृष् (c. 1. घर्षति -र्षितुं).

SKIMMED, *p. p.* हृतमण्डः -ण्डा -ण्डं, हृतफेनः -ना -नं; 'milk,' पत्रलं.

SKIN, *s.* त्वक् *f.* (च्), त्वचा, त्वचं, चर्म्म *n.* (न्), असृग्धरा, रक्ताधारः, असृग्धारा, तनुः -नूः *f.*, शरीरचर्म्म *n.*, शरीरावरणं, देहावरणं, देहकोषः, रोमभूमिः *f.*, मांसहासा, शिपिः *f.*, शिफिः *f.*, वेदनी, नटपर्णं, लावण्यलक्ष्यं.—(Hide) चर्म्म *n.* (न्), कृत्तिः *f.*, दृतिः *f.*, अजिनं, लोम *n.* (न्); 'of a tiger,' व्याघ्रचर्म्म *n.*; 'deer's skin,' मृगचर्म्म *n.*, रङ्क्वाजिनं; 'hare or rabbit's skin,' शशचर्म्म *n.*, शशलोम *n.* (न्), शशकाजिनं, शशोर्णं.—(Of a snake) कञ्चुकः, निर्मोकः. (Bark, rind) त्वक् *f.* (च्), वल्कलः -लं, शल्कलं, शकलं, छल्ली.—(Reduced to mere skin and bone) त्वगस्थिमात्रशेषः -षा -षं, त्वगस्थिभूतः -ता -तं.

To SKIN, *v. a.* त्वच (nom. त्वचयति -यितुं), निस्त्वचीकृ, निश्चर्म्म (nom. निश्चर्म्मयति -यितुं), त्वक्परिपुटनं कृ, त्वक्ष्. *See To* PEEL, FLAY.

SKIN-FLINT, *s.* अतिकृपणः, दृढमुष्टिः *m.*, गाढमुष्टिः *m.* *See* MISER.

SKINNED, *p. p.* निस्त्वचीकृतः -ता -तं, निस्त्वचः -चा -चं, हृतत्वक् *m.f.n.* (च्).

SKINNINESS, *s.* शिरालता, त्वगस्थिमात्रभावः, चर्म्ममात्रभावः, जरूथं.

SKINNY, *a.* शिरालः -ला -लं, त्वगस्थिमात्रमयः -यी -यं, चर्म्ममात्रमयः &c., त्वगस्थिमात्रभूतः -ता -तं, त्वङ्मात्रमयः &c., त्वङ्मयः &c. *See* LEAN.

To SKIP, *v. n.* प्लु (c. 1. प्लवते, प्लोतुं), वल्ग्, नृत्. *See To* LEAP.

SKIP, SKIPPING, *s.* प्लुतं, प्लवः -वनं, उत्प्लुतं, प्लुतिः *f.*, प्लुतगमनं, प्लुतगतिः *f.*, मण्डूकप्लुतं -तिः *f.*, मण्डूकगतिः *f.* *See* LEAP.

SKIPPING, *part.* प्लुतगतिः -तिः -ति, प्लुतगामी -मिनी &c., प्लवकारी &c.

SKIRMISH, SKIRMISHING, *s.* डिम्बः, डिम्बाहवः, डमरः, डिम्बयुद्धं, सेनामुखयुद्धं, ईषद्युद्धं, लघुयुद्धं, उपयुद्धं.

To SKIRMISH, *v. n.* डिम्बयुद्धं कृ, डिम्बाहवं कृ, सेनामुखयुद्धं कृ.

SKIRT, *s.* (Of a garment) वस्त्राञ्चलः -लं, वस्त्रान्तः, वसनाग्रः, वस्त्रसीमा, वसनदशा, वस्त्रदशा, पटान्तः, अञ्चलः, दशा, वस्तिः *m.*, तरी, तरिः *f.*—(Edge, border) प्रान्तः, प्रान्तभागः, अन्तभागः, अन्तः -न्तं, उपान्तः -न्तं, पर्य्यन्तभागः, पर्य्यन्तः -न्तं, परिसरः, सीमा, धारः -रा; 'of a wood,' वनान्तः -न्तं, वनधारा, उपवनं; 'of a mountain,' पर्य्यन्तभूः *f.*

To SKIRT, *v. a.* प्रान्त (nom. प्रान्तयति -यितुं), समन्त, प्रत्यन्त, पर्य्यन्तं कृ.

SKIRTING, *part.* प्रत्यन्तः -न्ता -न्तं, पार्य्यन्तिकः -की -कं, प्रान्तकः -का -कं.

SKITTISH, *a.* खेलाशीलः -ला -लं, खेलापरः -रा -रं, लीलाशीलः -ला -लं, चञ्चलः -ला -लं, चपलः &c., तरलः &c., क्रीडाशीलः &c.

SKITTISHNESS, *s.* खेलाशीलता, चञ्चलता, चपलता, चापल्यं, तरलता.

To SKULK, *v. n.* निभृते स्था or वृत्. *See To* SCULK, LURK.

SKULL, *s.* कपालः, भगालः, शिरोस्थि *n.* *See* SCULL.

SKY, *s.* आकाशः, व्योम *n.* (न्), गगणं, अन्तरीक्षं, अन्तरिक्षं, नभस् *n.*, खं, द्यौः *f.* (दिव्), द्यौ *f.* (द्यो), अम्बरं, दिगन्तरं, दिगन्तरालं, अन्तरालं, अभ्रं, वियत् *n.*, मेघवर्त्म *n.* (न्), मेघवेश्म *n.* (न्), तारापथः, मरुत्पथः, मरुद्वर्त्म *n.*, नाकः, घनपदवी, विष्णुपदं, पुष्करं, अनन्तं, सुरवर्त्म *n.*

SKY-COLOURED, *a.* आकाशवर्णः -र्णा -र्णं, व्योमवर्णः &c., नीलवर्णः &c.

SKY-LARK, *s.* व्याघ्राटः, भरद्वाजः. *See* LARK.

SKY-LIGHT, *s.* पटलगवाक्षः, पटलजालिका, पटलकाचः.

SKY-ROCKET, *s.* आकाशवाणः, आग्नेयवाणः. *See* ROCKET.

SKY-TOUCHING, *a.* व्योमस्पृक् *m.f.n.* (श्), अभ्रंलिहः -हा -हं, नभोलिद् *m.f.n.* (ह्), गगणस्पर्शी -र्शिनी -र्शि (न्), गगणस्पर्शितः -ता -तं.

SLAB, *s.* शिला, शिलापट्टः, शिलापटः, शिलाफलकः. फलकः.

To SLABBER, *v. n.* लालां मुखात् स्रु in caus. *See To* DRIVEL.

SLACK, *a.* शिथिलः -ला -लं, श्लथः &c. *See* LOOSE, REMISS.

To SLACKEN, *v. a.* शिथिलीकृ, शिथिल (nom. शिथिलयति -यितुं), मुच्, *see To* LOOSE, *v. a.*; 'to slacken one's speed,' वेगं or रयं शम् in caus.

To SLACKEN, *v. n.* शिथिलीभू, मन्दीभू. *See To* LOOSE, *v. n.*

SLACKENED, *p. p.* शिथिलितः -ता -तं, शिथिलीकृतः &c., शिथिलीभूतः &c., विगलितः &c., मन्दीभूतः &c., शान्तवेगः -गा -गं, शान्तरयः -या -यं.

SLACKLY, *adv.* शिथिलं, शैथिल्येन. *See* LOOSELY, REMISSLY.

SLACKNESS, *s.* शैथिल्यं, शिथिलता, श्लथता, *see* LOOSENESS, REMISSNESS.

SLAIN, *p. p.* हतः -ता -तं, निहतः &c., व्यापादितः -ता -तं, घातितः -ता -तं, मारितः &c., सूदितः &c., निषूदितः -ता -तं. *See* KILLED.

To SLAKE, *v. a.* (Quench) शम् in caus., उपशम्, प्रशम्, छिद्, *see To* QUENCH.—(Mix with water) जलेन सह मिश्र्, जलसंसृष्टं -ष्टां कृ.

To SLAM, *v. a.* (A door) यथा आकस्मिकशब्दो जायते तथा लघ्वाघातेन द्वारं पिधा or बलवदाघातेन द्वारं बद्धं कृ.

SLAM, *s.* आकस्मिकशब्दः, आकस्मिकध्वनिः *m.*, द्वारघातः.

SLANDER, *s.* अपवादः, परिवादः, पैशुन्यं, पिशुनवाक्यं, असूया, अभ्यसूया, गुणनिन्दा, गुणापवादः, कलङ्कः. *See* CALUMNY, DEFAMATION.

To SLANDER, *v. a.* अपवद् (c. 1. -वदति -दितुं), परिवद्, गुणापवादं कृ, पिशुनवाक्यं वद्, कलङ्क (nom. कलङ्कयति -यितुं), असूय (nom. असूयति -यितुं). *See To* DEFAME, CALUMNIATE.

SLANDERED, *p. p.* अपवादितः -ता -तं, अभिशस्तः -स्ता -स्तं, अभिशापितः &c.

SLANDERER, *s.* अपवादी *m.* (न्), परिवादी *m.*, अपवादकः. *See* DEFAMER.

SLANDEROUS, *a.* अपवादकः -का -कं, पिशुनः -ना -नं, अपवादात्मकः -का -कं, कलङ्कमयः -यी -यं, असूयकः &c. *See* DEFAMATORY.

SLANDEROUSLY, *adv.* सापवादं, सपरिवादं, सासूयं, पिशुनवाक्यपूर्व्वं.

SLANG, *s.* (Low language) खलोक्तिः *f.*, अश्लीलं, अश्लीलाक्षेपः.

SLANT, SLANTING, *a.* वक्रः -क्रा -क्रं, कुटिलः -ला -लं, तिर्य्यङ् -रश्ची -र्य्यक् (च्), वृजिनः -ना -नं, अनृजुः -जुः -जु, विषमः -मा -मं, प्रवणः -णा -णं.

To SLANT, *v. a.* आवृज् (c. 10. वर्जयति -यितुं), वक्रीकृ, तिर्य्यक्कृ, प्रवणीकृ.

To SLANT, *v. n.* आनम् (c. 10. -नमति -नन्तुं), प्रवणीभू, वक्रीभू, तिर्य्यग्भू.

SLANTINGLY, *adv.* तिर्य्यक्, तिरस्, वक्रं, प्रवणं, प्रावण्येन, आवर्ज्य.

SLAP, *s.* चपेटिका, चपेटाघातः, चपेटप्रहारः, तलप्रहारः, तलाघातः, कराघातः, आस्फोटः -टनं, आस्फोटनशब्दः, तलं.

To SLAP, *v. a.* चपेटेन आहन् (c. 2. -हन्ति -न्तुं) or प्रहृ, चपेटाघातं कृ, आस्फुट् (c. 10. -स्फोटयति -यितुं), आस्फोटनं कृ.

SLAP, *adv.* आकस्मिकाघातेन, आकस्मिकप्रहारेण, आस्फोटनशब्देन.

SLASH, *s.* दीर्घच्छेदः -दनं, दीर्घवेधः, दीर्घक्षतं -तिः *f.*, छेदविच्छेदः.

To SLASH, *v. a.* दीर्घच्छेदं कृ, दीर्घक्षतं कृ, छेदविच्छेदं कृ, व्यवछिद् (c. 7. -छिनत्ति -छेत्तुं), विनिकृत्, छिन्नभिन्नीकृ, क्षतविक्षतीकृ.

SLASHING, *part.* छेदविच्छेदकारी -रिणी -रि (न्), दीर्घच्छेदकारी &c.

SLATE, *s.* श्लक्ष्णशिला, तनुशिला, लेख्यसंज्ञकः श्लक्ष्णशिलाफलकः.

To SLATE, *v. a.* श्लक्ष्णशिलाफलकैर् आस्तृ or आछद् or आवृ.

SLATTERN, *s.* वेशप्रमत्ता, वेशप्रमादिनी, अविनीतवेशिनी.

SLAUGHTER, *s.* वधः, घातः -तनं, हननं, निहननं, मारणं, व्यापादनं, निषूदनं, सूदनं, संहारः, विशसनं, वैशसं, प्रतिघातनं, क्षणनं, प्रमयः, आलम्भः, विमर्दनं, निबर्हणं, निर्बर्हणं, प्रमापणं, निकारणं, निशारणं, विशरः, विशारणं, प्रवासनं, निकृन्तनं, परासनं, निर्हिंसनं, निर्वासनं, संज्ञपनं, निर्ग्रन्थनं, निर्गन्धनं, अपासनं, निस्तर्हणं, परिवर्जनं, निर्वापणं, उद्वासनं, उद्वासः, प्रमथनं, क्रथनं, मथनं, उज्जासनं, पिञ्जः, उन्मन्थः, निशुम्भः -म्भनं.

To SLAUGHTER, *v. a.* हन् (c. 2. हन्ति -न्तुं), विशस् (c. 1. -शसति -सितुं), *see To* KILL.

SLAUGHTERED, *p. p.* हतः -ता -तं, विशसितः -ता -तं. *See* KILLED.

SLAUGHTER-HOUSE, *s.* घातस्थानं, आघातस्थानं, आघातः -तनं, शूना, सूना, बध्यस्थानं, हिंसास्थानं, पशुमारणस्थानं, पशुवधस्थानं, प्राणिवधस्थानं.

SLAVE, *s.* दासः, दाशः, दासेयः, दासेरः, सेवकः, चेटकः, चेटः, किङ्करः, प्रेष्यः, प्रैष्यः, प्रैषः, भृत्यः, गोप्यः -प्यकः, नियोज्यः, परजितः, भुजिष्यः, परिचारकः, चेडः -डकः, कर्म्मकरः, कर्म्मकारः, *see* SERVANT; 'female slave,' दासी, दासिका, दाशी, चेटी, चेडी, चेटिका, चेडिका; 'domestic slave,' गृहदासः; 'female slave of a slave,' दासदासी; 'multitude of female slaves,' दासीसभं; 'son of a slave,' दासीपुत्रः; 'dealer in slave-girls,' कन्यापालः; 'born of a slave,' दासेयः -यी, दासेरः; 'to be a slave,' दास (nom. दासायति).

To SLAVE, *v. n.* आयस् (c. 4. -यस्यति -सितुं). *See To* DRUDGE, TOIL.

SLAVERY, *s.* दास्यं, दासत्वं, दासभावः, दासावस्था, दासदशा, प्रेष्यत्वं, परप्रेष्यत्वं, भृत्यत्वं. *See* SERVITUDE, DRUDGERY.

SLAVISH, SLAVISHNESS, SLAVISHLY. *See* SERVILE, SERVILITY, &c.

To SLAY, *v. a.* हन् (c. 2. हन्ति -न्तुं), व्यापद् in caus. *See To* KILL.

SLAYER, *s.* हन्ता *m.* (न्तृ), घातकः, घाती *m.* (न्). *See* KILLER.

SLEDGE, *s.* निश्चक्रयानं, निश्चक्रवाहनं, अचक्रयानं, चक्रशून्यवाहनं.

SLEDGE-HAMMER, *s.* घनः, वृहद्घनः, मुद्गरः, वृहन्मुद्गरः.

SLEEK, *a.* सुखस्पर्शः -र्शा -र्शं, श्लक्ष्णः -क्ष्णा -क्ष्णं, स्निग्धः -ग्धा -ग्धं.

SLEEKNESS, *s.* सुखस्पर्शता, श्लक्ष्णता -त्वं, स्निग्धता -त्वं, सपरुषता.

To SLEEP, *v. n.* स्वप् (c. 2. स्वपिति, स्वप्तुं), प्रस्वप्, सम्प्रस्वप्, संस्वप्, अवस्वप्, निद्रा (c. 2. -द्राति -तुं), शी (c. 2. शेते, शयितुं), निद्रां कृ, स्वप्नं कृ, स्वपनं कृ, सुप्तिं कृ, शयनं कृ, निमील् (c. 1. -मीलति -लितुं), संविश् (c. 6. -विशति -वेष्टुं); 'he sleeps comfortably,' सुखेन or सुस्थः स्वपिति; 'to desire to sleep,' स्वप् in des. (सुषुप्सति -प्सितुं), शी in des. (शिशयिषते).

SLEEP, *s.* निद्रा, स्वप्नः, स्वापः, स्वपनं, सुप्तिः *f.*, सुप्तं, शयनं, शयितं, शीः *f.*, शायिका, संवेशः, सर्व्वेन्द्रियाव्यापारः; 'state of sleep,' निद्रावस्था, स्वप्नावस्था; 'a deep or sound sleep,' सुनिद्रा, सुषुप्तिः *f.*, निर्भरनिद्रा, गाढनिद्रा, सुषुप्त्यवस्था, साधिका; 'very deep or dead sleep,' घोरनिद्रा, अघोरनिद्रा; 'fallen into a deep sleep,' सुनिद्रामग्नः -ग्ना -ग्नं; 'in a sound sleep,' सुषुप्तः -प्ता -प्तं, शेश्यितः -ता -तं शेश्यितवान् &c.; 'arousing from sleep,' निद्राभङ्गः; 'aroused from sleep,' भग्ननिद्रः -द्रा -द्रं; 'to go to sleep,' स्वप्, निद्रा, शी, शयनं कृ, निद्रां गम्; 'he went to sleep,' निदद्रौ, सुष्वाप.

SLEEPER, *s.* शायी *m.* (न्), शयनकृत्, निद्राणः, स्वप्नावस्थः.

SLEEPINESS, *s.* निद्रालुता, निद्राशीलता, शयालुता, शिशयिषा, सुषुप्सा, निद्रेच्छा, स्वप्नेच्छा, शयनेच्छा, स्वापः, तन्द्रा, तन्द्रिका.

SLEEPING, *s.* स्वपनं, स्वापः, शयनं, शायिका. *See* SLEEP.

SLEEPING, *part.* शयानः -ना -नं, स्वपन् -पती -पत् (त्), निद्रान् -द्रान्ती -द्रात् (त्), निद्रायमाणः -णा -णं, निद्राणः -णा -णं, शयितः -ता -तं, शयितवान् -वती -वत् (त्), सुप्तः -प्ता -प्तं, स्वप्नक् *m. f. n.* (ज्); 'soundly,' शेश्यितः -ता -तं, शेश्यितवान् &c.

SLEEPING-ROOM, *s.* शयनगृहं, स्वप्नगृहं, निद्राशाला. *See* BEDROOM.

SLEEPLESS, *a.* निर्निद्रः -द्रा -द्रं, विनिद्रः &c., अनिद्रः &c., उन्निद्रः &c., निद्राहीनः -ना -नं, निद्रारहितः -ता -तं, अनागतनिद्रः &c., विगतनिद्रः &c.

SLEEPLESSNESS, *s.* निर्निद्रता, विनिद्रता -त्वं, अनिद्रता -त्वं, उन्निद्रता, निद्राहीनता, निद्राराहित्यं, निद्राभावः.

SLEEPY, *a.* (Habitually sleepy) निद्रालुः -लुः -लु, शयालुः &c., तन्द्रालुः &c., निद्राशीलः -ला -लं, स्वप्नशीलः &c., नैद्रः -द्री -द्रं, निद्राणः -णा -णं.—(Desirous of sleeping) शिशयिषुः -षुः -षु, सुषुप्सुः -प्सुः -प्सु.—(Overcome by sleep) निद्राकुलः -ला -लं, निद्राक्रान्तः -न्ता -न्तं, निद्राग्रस्तः -स्ता -स्तं, निद्रातुरः -रा -रं.

SLEET, *s.* शीकरः, शीकरवर्षः, शीभवः, सीकरः, तुषारवर्षः.

To SLEET, *v. n.* शीक् (c. 1. शीकते -कितुं), शीकर (nom. शीकरायते).

SLEEVE, *s.* पिप्पलः, बाहुवस्त्रं, बाहुवसनं, दोर्वस्त्रं, दोराच्छादनं; 'to laugh in one's sleeve,' अन्तर्हासं कृ, उद्धर्षनं कृ, उच्चघनं कृ.

SLEIGHT, *s.* (Of hand) हस्तलाघवं, लघुहस्तत्वं, हस्तचापल्यं, कुसृतिः *f.*, माया, कुहकः, इन्द्रजालं, *see* JUGGLERY, LEGERDEMAIN.

SLENDER, *a.* (Thin skin) तनुः -नुः -न्वी -नु, प्रतनुः &c., वितनुः &c., क्षीणः -णा -णं, सूक्ष्मः -क्ष्मा -क्ष्मं, क्षामः -मा -मं, कृशः -शा -शं, शीर्णः -र्णा -र्णं, कृशाङ्गः -ङ्गी -ङ्गं, अविपुलः -ला -लं; 'slender in the waist,' क्षीणमध्यः -ध्या -ध्यं, तनुमध्यः &c., तनुमध्यमः -मा -मं, हरिमध्यः &c., सिंहमध्यः &c., सिंहकटिः -टिः -टि, मृगकटिः &c., मृगमध्यः &c., तनुशरीरः -रा -रं, क्षामाङ्गः -ङ्गा -ङ्गं, कृशोदरः -रा -रं; 'a slender-waisted woman,' सुमध्यमा, तनुमध्यमा, मध्यक्षीणा; 'having a slender stem,' शीर्णनालः -ला -लं.—(Small, inconsiderable) अल्पः -ल्पा -ल्पं, क्षुद्रः -द्रा -द्रं, क्षीणः -णा -णं, लघुः -घुः -घु, अबहुः &c., निर्बलः -ला -लं; 'of slender means,' क्षीणार्थः -र्था -र्थं.

SLENDERNESS, *s.* तनुता, क्षीणता, क्षामता, शीर्णता, सूक्ष्मता, कृशता, कार्श्यं, अल्पता; 'of waist,' मध्यक्षीणता.

To SLICE, *v. a.* तक्ष् (c. 1. तक्षति -क्षितुं), छेदं कृ, परिच्छेदं कृ, छिद् (c. 7. छिनत्ति, छेत्तुं), परिच्छिद्, खण्ड्, खण्डीकृ, पृथुच्छेदं कृ.

SLICE, *s.* छेदः, परिच्छेदः, खण्डः, शकलं; 'of bread,' पूपखण्डः.

To SLIDE, *v. n.* (Move along the surface of snow, ice, &c.) हिमोपरि स्खल् (c. 1. स्खलति -लितुं) or रिङ्ख् (c. 1. रिङ्खति -ङ्खितुं) or रिंख् (c. 1. रिंखति -खितुं) or विसृप् (c. 1. -सर्पति -सर्प्तुं) or संसृप्.—(Slip) च्यु (c. 1. च्यवते, च्योतुं), स्खल्.

SLIDE, SLIDING, *s.* स्खलनं, रिङ्खणं, रिङ्खणं, रिङ्खः, च्यवनं.

SLIGHT, *a.* (Thin, slim) तनुः -नुः -न्वी -नु, सुतनुः -नुः -नु, क्षीणः -णा -णं; 'a slight woman,' लघ्वी, *see* SLENDER.—(Trifling, inconsiderable) अल्पः -ल्पा -ल्पं, स्वल्पः &c., लघुः -घुः -घु, स्तोकः -का -कं, क्षुद्रः -द्रा -द्रं, ईषत् prefixed; 'a slight inspection,'

ईषद्दर्शनं; 'a slight blow,' ईषदाघातः, उपघातः; 'a slight obstacle,' अल्पविघ्नः; 'in a slight degree,' ईषत्, किञ्चित्, कियत्, स्तोकं; 'not in the slightest,' न मनागपि, न किञ्चिदपि, न किमपि, न कियदपि, न सूक्ष्ममपि, न स्तोकमपि, न लेशमपि; 'there is not the slightest movement of the tongue or lips,' जिह्वोष्ठं मनागपि न चलति.

SLIGHT, *s.* (Neglect) अनादरः, उपेक्षा, अवमानं, अवज्ञा, अवधीरणं, ईषदवज्ञा, ईषदुपेक्षा, ईषदवमानं, ईषदनादरः, अनपेक्षा, प्रणिपातलंघनं, अमाननं, अवगणनं -ना.

To SLIGHT, *v. a.* उपेक्ष् (c. 1. -ईक्षते -क्षितुं), ईषद् अवज्ञा (c. 9. -जानाति -ज्ञातुं) or अवमन् (c. 4. -मन्यते -मन्तुं) or अवधीर् (c. 10. -धीरयति -यितुं), अवगण् (c. 10. -गणयति -यितुं), अनादरं कृ, ईषदवज्ञां कृ.

SLIGHTED, *p. p.* उपेक्षितः -ता -तं, ईषदवज्ञातः &c., अवगणितः &c., अवधीरितः -ता -तं, ईषदवधीरितः &c., ईषदवमानितः &c.

SLIGHTER, *s.* उपेक्षकः, उपेक्षाकारी *m.* (न्), मन्दादरः, अनादरकृत्.

SLIGHTINGLY, *adv.* उपेक्षया, अनपेक्षया, अनादरेण, ईषदवज्ञापूर्वं.

SLIGHTLY, *adv.* ईषत्, कियत्, स्तोकं, मनाक्, अल्पमात्रं, अबहु, अभृशं; 'slightly warm,' ईषदुष्णः -ष्णा -ष्णं; 'slightly red,' ईषद्रक्तः -क्ता -क्तं.

SLIGHTNESS, *s.* तनुता, सूक्ष्मता, क्षीणता, अल्पता, लघुता, क्षुद्रता.

SLILY, *adv.* छलेन, सव्याजं, सकपटं, सवैदग्ध्यं, छद्मना, अव्यक्तं; 'going slily,' अव्यक्तगतिः -तिः -ति, गूढगतिः &c.

SLIM, *a.* तनुः -नुः -न्वी -नु, क्षीणः -णा -णं, क्षामः &c. *See* SLENDER.

SLIME, *a.* शिलाजतु *n.*, शैलनिर्यासः, सान्द्रपङ्कः, श्यानपङ्कः, चिक्कणपङ्कः.

SLIMINESS, *s.* सान्द्रता, श्यानता, चिक्कणता, पङ्किलता -त्वं.

SLIMNESS, *s.* तनुता -त्वं, तानवं, क्षीणता, क्षामता. *See* SLENDERNESS.

SLIMY, *a.* सान्द्रः -न्द्रा -न्द्रं, श्यानः -ना -नं, चिक्कणः -णा -णं, चिचिक्कणः &c., पङ्किलः -ला -लं, सान्द्रपङ्कमयः -यी -यं, सान्द्रपङ्कगुणकः &c.

SLING, *s.* (Instrument for throwing stones) गोफणा, प्रस्तरक्षेपणी, पाषाणक्षेपणी, प्रस्तरप्रक्षेपणी, प्रक्षेपणी, भिन्दपालः.—(Pole with ropes for carrying burdens) भारयष्टिः *m. f.*, काचः.

To SLING, *v. a.* (Throw with a sling) गोफणया क्षिप् (c. 6. क्षिपति, क्षेप्तुं) or प्रक्षिप्.—(Hang so as to swing) उद्बन्ध्, ऊर्द्धं बन्ध्, आन्दोल (nom. आन्दोलयति -यितुं), काच (nom. काचयति -यितुं).

To SLINK, *v. n.* अपसृप् (c. 1. -सर्पति -सर्प्तुं), व्यपसृप्, पलाय् (c. 1. पलायते -यितुं, rt. इ), विपलाय्, अपधाव् (c. 1. -धावति -वितुं), अपक्रम्, अपया, निष्पत्.

To SLIP, *v. n.* (Slide) स्खल् (c. 1. स्खलति -लितुं), चल्, रिङ्ग्, रिङ्ख्.—(Glide) विसृप्, संसृप्.—(Stumble, fall) च्यु (c. 1. च्यवते, च्योतुं), भ्रंश् (c. 4. भ्रश्यति, c. 1. भ्रंशते -शितुं), स्रंस् (c. 1. स्रंसते -सितुं), विस्रंस्, आस्रंस्, पत् (c. 1. पतति -तितुं), गल्, विगल्.—(Err) विच्यु, विचल्, भ्रंश्.—(Slip away), *see* *To* SLINK.—(Slip off) स्रंस्, विस्रंस्, विगल्.—(Slip down) प्रच्यु, प्रभ्रंश्, लम्ब्, अवपत्, अवगल्.—(Slip in) छलेन or निभृतं प्रविश् (c. 6. -विशति -वेष्टुं).

To SLIP, *v. a.* (Let slip) शिथिल (nom. शिथिलयति -ते -यितुं), शिथिलीकृ, मुच् (c. 6. मुञ्चति, मोक्तुं), स्रंस् (c. 10. स्रंसयति -यितुं), च्यु (c. 10. च्यावयति -यितुं), हा in caus. (हापयति -यितुं), *see* *To* LOOSE, *v. a.*; 'I will not let slip the occasion,' अवकाशं न शिथिलयिष्ये.—(Neglect, omit), *see* the words.—(Slip in) छलेन or निभृतं प्रविश् in caus. or निविश् in caus.

SLIP, *s.* (Sliding) स्खलनं, रिङ्गणं, रिङ्खणं, रिङ्खः, च्यवनं.—(Stumble, fall) स्खलनं, स्खलितं, च्युतिः *f.*, भ्रंशः, प्रभ्रंशः, पातः, पतनं, स्रंसनं,

विस्रंसा.—(Error) दोषः, भ्रमः, प्रमादः, स्खलनं, अपराधः; 'of the hand,' हस्तदोषः; 'of the tongue,' जिह्वादोषः.—(Twig) शाखिका, प्रशाखिका, पल्लवः, काण्डः.—(Long, narrow piece) खण्डः, दीर्घखण्डः -ण्डकः; 'of cloth,' वस्त्रखण्डः.

SLIPPED, *p. p.* च्युतः -ता -तं, स्खलितः &c., भ्रष्टः -ष्टा -ष्टं, प्रभ्रष्टः &c.; 'from its place,' स्थानच्युतः -ता -तं, पदच्युतः &c.—(Slipped off) स्रस्तः -स्ता -स्तं, विगलितः -ता -तं.

SLIPPER, *s.* (Light shoe) लघुपादुका, लघुपादत्रं, लघुपादपा, पादुका, पादपा, उपानत् *f.* (ह्), वध्रं; 'magical slipper,' योगपादुका, सिद्धिः *f.*

SLIPPERINESS, *s.* चिक्कणता -त्वं, स्निग्धता, स्नैग्ध्यं, श्लक्ष्णता, अस्थिरता.

SLIPPERY, *a.* चिक्कणः -णा -णं, चिचिक्कणः &c., स्निग्धः -ग्धा -ग्धं, मेदुरः -रा -रं, स्नेही -हिनी -हि (न्), श्लक्ष्णः -क्ष्णा -क्ष्णं; 'slippery ground,' निपद्या.—(Unstable, uncertain) अस्थिरः -रा -रं, अनवस्थितः -ता -तं, चञ्चलः -ला -लं, चपलः &c., तरलः &c., लोलः &c., विचलः -ला -लं.

SLIPPING, *s.* स्खलनं, च्युतिः *f.*, च्यवनं, रिङ्गणं, रिङ्खणं. *See* SLIP.

To SLIT, *v. a.* दीर्घच्छेदं कृ, दीर्घच्छेदनं कृ, दीर्घच्छिद्रं कृ, दीर्घवेधनं कृ.

SLIT, *p. p.* छिन्नः -न्ना -न्नं, दीर्घच्छेदान्वितः -ता -तं, विद्धः -द्धा -द्धं.

SLIT, *s.* दीर्घच्छेदः -दनं, दीर्घच्छिद्रं, छेदः, छिद्रं, दीर्घभेदः.

To SLOBBER, *v. n.* लालां सु in caus. *See* *To* SLABBER.

SLOP, *s.* (Soiled water, &c.) मलिनजलं, मलिनजलादि *n.*, समलजलं, अमेध्यजलादि, अमेध्यजलं.—(Water, &c., carelessly thrown about) प्रमादाद् इतस्ततः क्षिप्तं or पातितं जलादि.—(Mess) कर्दमः.

To SLOP, *v. a.* प्रमादाद् इतस्ततो जलादि पत् in caus. or क्षिप्.

SLOPE, *s.* प्रावण्यं, प्रवणभूमिः *f.*, निम्नभूमिः, निम्नता, क्रमप्रवणभूमिः *f.*, क्रमनिम्नभूभागः, क्रमशो निम्नो भूभागः, स्थानं क्रमशः प्रवणं, स्थानं क्रमशो ऽधोगम्यं; 'of a mountain,' उत्सङ्गः, कटकः, शैलकटकः.

To SLOPE, *v. a.* आवृज् (c. 10. -वर्जयति -यितुं), प्रवणीकृ, निम्नीकृ.

To SLOPE, *v. n.* क्रमशः प्रवणः -णा -णं भू, क्रमप्रवणः -णा -णं भू, प्रवणीभू, क्रमशो निम्नः -म्ना -म्नं भू, निम्नीभू.

SLOPING, *part.* or *a.* प्रवणः -णा -णं, क्रमशः प्रवणः &c., क्रमप्रवणः &c., क्रमशो निम्नः -म्ना -म्नं, क्रमशः पातुकः -का -कं, क्रमशो ऽधोगामी -मिनी -मि (न्).

SLOPPY, *a.* पङ्किलः -ला -लं, जलपङ्कमयः -यी -यं, अनूपः -पा -पं.

SLOP-SELLER, *s.* तुच्छवस्त्रविक्रेता *m.* (तृ), सिद्धवस्त्रविक्रयी *m.* (न्).

SLOP-SHOP, *s.* तुच्छवस्त्रादिविक्रयस्थानं, प्रस्तुतवस्त्रविक्रयगृहं.

SLOTH, *s.* तन्द्रा, तन्द्रिः -न्द्री *f.*, तन्द्रिका, आलस्यं, तुन्दपरिमार्जनं, मिद्धं, गुडाका, *see* LAZINESS.—(The animal) पर्णमृगः.

SLOTHFUL, *a.* तन्द्रालुः -लुः -लु, अलसः -सा -सं. *See* LAZY.

SLOTHFULNESS, *s.* तन्द्रालुता, आलस्यं, अलसता. *See* LAZINESS.

To SLOUCH, *v. n.* निम्नगत्या चल्, अलसगत्या चल्, ग्रामिकवत् चर्.

SLOUCHING, *a.* निम्नः -म्ना -म्नं, प्रलम्बः -म्बा -म्बं, निम्नगतिः -तिः -ति.

SLOUGH, *s.* (Muddy place) पङ्कः, महापङ्कः, कुपङ्कः, पङ्काढ्यस्थानं.—(Of a snake) कञ्चुकः, निर्मोकः, जहकः, भुजङ्गनिर्मोकः, भुजङ्गत्वक् *f.* (च्), अहित्वक् *f.*, अहिचर्म्म *n.* (न्), तीक्ष्णा, निर्वयनी.—(From a wound) क्षतगलितमांसं.

SLOVENLINESS, *s.* अविनीतवेशत्वं, वेशप्रमत्तता, अविनीतता -त्वं, अपरिष्कारः, अव्यवस्था, प्रमत्तता, प्रमादः.

SLOVENLY, SLOVEN, *a.* वेशप्रमत्तः -त्ता -त्तं, वेशप्रमादी -दिनी -दि (न्), अविनीतवेशी -शिनी &c., अविनीतपरिच्छदः -दा -दं, अपरिष्कृतवेशः

-शा -शं, अपरिष्कृतपरिच्छदः -दा -दं, अविनीतः -ता -तं, अपरिष्कृतः &c., प्रामादिकः -की -कं.

Slow, *a.* (Not swift, moving slowly) मन्दः -न्दा -न्दं, मन्थरः -रा -रं, मन्दगतिः -तिः -ति, मन्दगमनः -ना -नं, मन्दगामी -मिनी -मि (न्), अद्रुतः -ता -तं, अशीघ्रः -घ्रा -घ्रं, विलम्बितः -ता -तं, विलम्बी -म्बिनी &c.; 'slow fire,' मन्दाग्निः *m.*—(Not ready, not prompt) मन्दः -न्दा -न्दं, मन्थरः &c., अक्षिप्रः -प्रा -प्रं, अत्वरितः -ता -तं, मनाक्करः -रा -रं; 'slow in recognising,' प्रत्यभिज्ञानमन्थरः -रा -रं.—(Behind in time) विलम्बितः -ता -तं, कालातीतः -ता -तं, मन्दः &c., *see* Late, *a.*—(Slow in intellect) मन्दबुद्धिः -द्धिः -द्धि, मन्दमतिः -तिः -ति, मन्दः -न्दा -न्दं, स्थूलबुद्धिः &c., *see* Dull.—(Tedious) दीर्घकालीनः -ना -नं, दीर्घसूत्रः -त्रा -त्रं, दीर्घसूत्री &c., *see* Dilatory.—(In music) विलम्बितः -ता -तं; 'slow time,' विलम्बितवृत्तिः *f.*, तत्त्वं.—(Slow fever) जीर्णज्वरः.

Slow-going, *adv.* मन्दगतिः -तिः -ति, मन्दगामी -मिनी -मि (न्), मन्दगमनः -ना -नं, मन्दगतः -ता -तं, शनैश्चरः -रा -रं, शनैर्गामी &c.

Slowly, slow, *adv.* मन्दं, शनैस्, मन्दं मन्दं, शनैः शनैः, मन्द in comp., मान्द्येन, समान्द्यं, मनाक्, मन्थरं, अद्रुतं, अशीघ्रं, अक्षिप्रं, अत्वरितं, विलम्बितं, विलम्बेन.

Slowness, *s.* मान्द्यं, मन्दता -त्वं, मन्थरता, विलम्बः -म्बनं, विलम्बितत्वं, अद्रुतत्वं, अशीघ्रता, अक्षिप्रता, दीर्घसूत्रता; 'of intellect,' बुद्धिमान्द्यं, मन्दबुद्धित्वं, मन्दता. *See* Dullness.

Slug, *s.* (Kind of snail) शम्बूकहीनः कृमिविशेषः.

Sluggard, *s.* अलसः, आलस्यशीलः, तुन्दपरिमार्जः, तुन्दपरिमृजः.

Sluggish, *a.* तन्द्रालुः -लुः -लु, अलसः -सा -सं, आलस्यशीलः -ला -लं, निद्रालुः -लुः -लु, मन्दः -न्दा -न्दं, मन्दगतिः -तिः -ति, मनाक्करः -रा -रं, शयालुः &c.

Sluggishly, *adv.* आलस्येन, अलसवत्, मन्दं, समान्द्यं, सतन्द्रं, तन्द्रया.

Sluggishness, *s.* तन्द्रालुता, तन्द्रा -न्द्री, तन्द्रिका, आलस्यं, अलसता -त्वं, मन्दता, मान्द्यं, जडता, जाड्यं. *See* Laziness, Indolence.

Sluice, *s.* (Flood-gate) जलद्वारं, जलनिर्गमः, जलवर्त्म *n.* (न्), जलबन्धनद्वारं.—(Stream of water) जलप्रवाहः, जलप्रपातः.

To slumber, *v. n.* (Sleep lightly) लघुनिद्रां कृ, अल्पनिद्रां कृ, ईषन्निद्रां कृ.—(Sleep) स्वप् (c. 2. स्वपिति, स्वप्तुं), प्रस्वप्, निद्रा &c., *see To* sleep.

Slumber, *s.* निद्रा, लघुनिद्रा, अल्पनिद्रा, ध्याननिद्रा, स्वप्नः, *see* Sleep.

To slur, *v. a.* (Soil, sully) मलिन (nom. मलिनयति -यितुं), मलिनीकृ, कलङ्क (nom. कलङ्कयति -यितुं), दुष् in caus.—(Do hurriedly) अतिक्षिप्रं कृ, अतिशीघ्रं कृ or अनुष्ठा, सहसा कृ, त्वरितं कृ, अनवधानेन or अनवेक्षया कृ.—(Pass over lightly, overlook) उपेक्ष्, समुपेक्ष्.—(Pronounce imperfectly) लुप्तवर्णपदेन व्याहृ or उदाहृ or उच्चर्.—(Sing in a gliding way) अविलम्बितपदेन or अविच्छिन्नस्वरेण गै or उच्चर्.

Slur, *s.* (Mark, stigma) कलङ्कः, लाञ्छनं, अपकलङ्कः, अकीर्त्तिचिह्नं, अपमानचिह्नं.—(In music) स्वराविच्छेदचिह्नं.

Slurred, *p. p.* (Soiled) कलङ्कितः -ता -तं, मलिनीकृतः -ता -तं, दूषितः &c.—(Done hurriedly) सहसा कृतः -ता -तं, त्वरितकृतः &c.—(Pronounced imperfectly) लुप्तवर्णपदः -दा -दं, लुप्तवर्णः -र्णा -र्णं, ग्रस्तः -स्ता -स्तं, ग्रस्तवर्णः -र्णा -र्णं.—(Pronounced glidingly or rapidly) अविच्छिन्नस्वरेणोच्चारितः -ता -तं, त्वरितोदितः -ता -तं, निरस्तः -स्ता -स्तं.

Slush, *s.* पङ्ककर्दमः, मृदुपङ्कः, सजलपङ्कः, कर्दमः.

Slut, *s.* अविनीतवेशिनी, अपरिष्कृतवेशिनी, अविनीता, बन्धकी.

Sluttish, *a.* अविनीतवेशी -शिनी &c., अविनीतः -ता &c. *See* Slovenly.

Sly, *a.* विदग्धः -ग्धा -ग्धं, कापटिकः -की -कं, छाद्मिकः -की -कं, छद्मकुशलः -ला -लं, दाम्भिकः -की -कं, सव्याजः -जा -जं, मायान्वितः -ता -तं, बहुमायः -या -यं, भूरिमयः -या -यं, धूर्त्तः -र्त्ता -र्त्तं, व्याजिकः -की -कं, चतुरः -रा -रं; 'sly laugh,' अन्तर्हासः, उपहसितं, उपहसनं.

Slyness, *s.* विदग्धता, वैदग्ध्यं, व्याजः, कपटः, कापट्यं, सव्याजत्वं, धूर्त्तता, छलं, छद्म *n.* (न्), छाद्मिकत्वं, चतुरता, मायः, माया.

To smack, *v. a.* (Kiss with a noise) सशब्दं चुम्ब्, आस्फोटनशब्देन चुम्ब्, सशब्दचुम्बनं कृ.—(The lips) ओष्ठास्फोटनं कृ, ओष्ठविष्वाणनं कृ, ओष्ठसंचारानन्तरम् आस्फोटनशब्दं कृ.—(The face), *see To* slap.—(Crack) आस्फोटनं कृ, आस्फोटनशब्दं कृ; 'a whip,' आस्फोटनशब्देन कशाघातं कृ.

To smack, *v. n.* (Have a taste) स्वादनं कृ, *see To* savor, *v. n.*

Smack, *s.* (Loud kiss) सशब्दचुम्बनं, सास्फोटनचुम्बनं.—(Of the lips) ओष्ठास्फोटनं, ओष्ठविष्वाणनं.—(Crack, slap) आस्फोटनं, आस्फोटनशब्दः, आकस्मिकशब्दः, स्फूत्कारः, क्वणितं, ध्वनितं.—(Taste) आस्वादः, रसः, *see* Savor.

Smack, *adv.* आस्फोटनशब्देन, आकस्मिकशब्देन, आकस्मिकाघातेन.

Small, *a.* अल्पः -ल्पा -ल्पं, क्षुद्रः -द्रा -द्रं, *see* Little, *a.*—(In stature) अल्पतनुः -नुः -नु, अल्पशरीरः -रा -रं, *see* Little, *a.*—(Small quantity) अल्पभागः, *see* Little, *s.*—(In a small degree) ईषत्, *see* Little, *adv.*

Smallage, *s.* अजमोदा, अजमोदाजातीयः शाकभेदः.

Smallest, *a.* अल्पिष्ठः -ष्ठा -ष्ठं, कनिष्ठः &c. *See* Least, *a.*

Smallness, *s.* अल्पता -त्वं, क्षुद्रता, तनुता, सूक्ष्मता, स्तोकता, क्षोदिमा *m.* (न्), अणिमा *m.* *See* Littleness.

Small-pox, *s.* शीतला -ली, रक्तघटी, रक्तवरटी, वसन्तः, वसन्तरोगः, मसूरी -रिका, गुली, विस्फोटः, पापरोगः.

Smart, *a.* (Sharp) तीक्ष्णः -क्ष्णा -क्ष्णं, तीव्रः -व्रा -व्रं, पटुः &c., *see* Sharp.—(Quick, brisk) शीघ्रः -घ्रा -घ्रं, लघुः -घुः -घु, द्रुतः -ता -तं, तीक्ष्णकर्म्मा -र्म्मा -र्म्म (न्), आशुकारी -रिणी &c., शीघ्रकारी &c., *see* Quick, Sharp.—(Witty) रसिकः -का -कं, मार्म्मिकः &c.—(Fine, well-dressed, showy) सुवेशी -शिनी -शि (न्), सुवेशः -शा -शं, शोभनः -ना -नं, शोभनवेशी &c., छेकः -का -कं.

Smart, *s.* (Sharp pain) तीव्रवेदना, तीक्ष्णवेदना, वेदना, तीक्ष्णव्यथा, शूलः -लं, तोदः, तीव्रदुःखं.

To smart, *v. n.* व्यथ् (c. 1. व्यथते -थितुं), तीक्ष्णवेदनां or तीक्ष्णव्यथाम् अनुभू, दुःखोष्णः -ष्णा -ष्णं भू, व्यथोष्णः &c. भू, तप् in pass. (तप्यते).

Smartly, *adv.* (Sharply), *see* Sharply.—(Briskly) द्रुतं, क्षिप्रं, शीघ्रं, लाघवेन.—(Finely) सु prefixed; as, 'smartly dressed,' सुवेशी &c.

Smartness, *s.* (Sharpness), *see* Sharpness.—(Quickness) शीघ्रता, द्रुतता, क्षिप्रता, लघुता, लाघवं; 'of hand,' हस्तलाघवं, लघुहस्तत्वं, हस्तचापल्यं.—(Wittiness, cleverness) रसिकत्वं, सरसत्वं, मार्म्मिकता, पटुता, पाटवं.—(Fineness) शोभा, शोभनत्वं, सुवेशिता.

To smash, *v. a.* भञ्ज्, चूर्ण्, *see To* break, dash, shatter.

Smash, smashed. *See* Shattering, Shattered, Broken.

Smatterer, *s.* चुञ्चुकः, किञ्चिज्ज्ञः, खण्डज्ञानी *m.* (न्), खण्डविद्यावान् *m.* (त्).

SMATTERING, *s.* किञ्चित्, अल्पमात्रं, अल्पिका, अल्पभागः; 'of knowledge,' किञ्चिज्ज्ञानं, खण्डज्ञानं, खण्डपाण्डित्यं, खण्डितपाण्डित्यं, खण्डविद्या.

To SMEAR, *v. a.* लिप् (c. 6. लिम्पति, लेप्तुं), आलिप्, उपलिप्, विलिप्, समालिप्, अञ्ज् (c. 7. अनक्ति, अंक्तुं, c. 10. अञ्जयति -यितुं), अभ्यञ्ज्, दिह् (c. 2. देग्धि -ग्धुं), प्रदिह्, लेपनं कृ, लेपं कृ, उपलेपं कृ, विलेपनं कृ.

SMEARED, *p. p.* लिप्तः -प्ता -प्तं, विलिप्तः &c., उपलिप्तः &c., अवलिप्तः &c., अभ्यक्तः -क्ता -क्तं, अक्तः in comp., दिग्धः -ग्धा -ग्धं, निदिग्धः &c.; 'with blood,' रक्ताक्तः -क्ता -क्तं, शोणिताक्तः &c., रक्तावलिप्तः &c.

SMEARING, *s.* लेपः -पनं, विलेपः -पनं, अवलेपः -पनं, उपलेपः -पनं, लिपिः *f.*, अञ्जनं, अभ्यञ्जनं, अभ्यङ्गः, समालम्भः.

SMELL, *s.* (Faculty or sense of smell) घ्राणं, घ्राणेन्द्रियं, घ्राणशक्तिः *f.*, आघ्राणशक्तिः *f.*, गन्धग्रहणशक्तिः *f.*—(Perception of odour) गन्धग्रहणं, घ्राणं, आघ्राणं, अवघ्राणं, घ्रातिः *f.*—(Odour) गन्धः, वासः; 'bad smell,' दुर्गन्धः, *see* under ODOUR; 'good smell,' सुगन्धः, सुवासः, *see* ODOUR, FRAGRANCE.

To SMELL, *v. a.* (Perceive by the nose) घ्रा (c. 1. जिघ्रति, घ्रातुं), आघ्रा, उपघ्रा, उपाघ्रा, अवघ्रा, शिङ्घ् (c. 1. शिङ्घति -ङ्घितुं), उपशिङ्घ्, घ्राणं कृ, आघ्राणं कृ, अवघ्राणं कृ, घ्राणेन्द्रियेण ग्रह् or ज्ञा or बुध् or अनुभू, नासाद्वारेण ग्रह् or गन्धग्रहणं कृ.

To SMELL, *v. n.* (Have an odour) गन्धी -न्धिनी -न्धि भू or अस्, सगन्धः -न्धा -न्धं भू or अस्, गन्धवान् -वती -वद् भू, गन्धविशिष्टः -ष्टा -ष्टं भू, सवासः -सा -सं भू; 'have a bad smell,' दुर्गन्धी &c. भू, *see* *To* STINK, *v. n.*—(Have the same smell) सगन्धः -न्धा -न्धं भू, समगन्धः -न्धा -न्धं भू, तुल्यगन्धः &c. भू; 'to smell of smoke,' धूमसगन्धः -न्धा -न्धं भू.

SMELLED, SMELT, *p. p.* घ्रातः -ता -तं, घ्राणः -णा -णं, आघ्रातः &c., अवघ्रातः &c., उपघ्रातः &c., शिङ्घितः -ता -तं.

SMELL-FEAST, *s.* पराक्षरुचिः *m.*, परपाकरुचिः *m.* *See* PARASITE.

SMELLING, *part.* (Perceiving by the nose) घ्राणकारी -रिणी -रि (न्), आघ्राणकारी &c., गन्धग्राही &c.—(Having a smell) गन्धवान् -वती -वत् (त्), गन्धी &c., गन्धयुक्तः -क्ता -क्तं, सगन्धः -न्धा -न्धं, वासयुक्तः -क्ता -क्तं.

To SMELT, *v. a.* लोहादि विली in caus. or विद्रु in caus. or द्रवीकृ.

SMELTER, *s.* लोहादिविद्रावकः, लोहादिविलयनकृत्, लोहकारः.

SMELTING, *s.* लोहादिविलयनं, लोहादिविद्रावणं, लोहादिकरणं.

To SMILE, *v. n.* स्मि (c. 1. स्मयते, स्मेतुं), उत्स्मि, स्मितं कृ, मन्दस्मितं कृ, मन्दहास्यं कृ, ईषद्धासं कृ, उपहासं कृ, विहस् (c. 1. -हसति -सितुं), उपहस्, विहासं कृ; 'to smile at,' अभिस्मि, अभ्युत्स्मि; 'to cause to smile,' स्मि in caus. (स्माययति -यितुं); 'to smile on, be propitious,' कृपादृष्टिं कृ, प्रसन्नः -न्ना -न्नं भू, प्रसन्नमुखः -खी -खं भू, कृपावलोकनं कृ.

SMILE, *s.* स्मितं, मन्दस्मितं, स्मयः, उत्स्मयः, विहासः, विहसितं, विहसनं, उपहासः, ईषद्धासः, मन्दहास्यं, मन्दहासः, वक्रोष्ठिका, वक्रोष्ठिः *f.*; 'with a smile,' सस्मितं; 'with a bitter smile,' सामर्षहासं.

SMILING, *part.* or *a.* स्मितः -ता -तं, सस्मितः -ता -तं, स्मेरः -रा -रं, विहासी -सिनी -सि (न्), प्रफुल्लः -ल्ला -ल्लं, विहस्य indec.; 'smiling sweetly,' चारुहासी &c., शुचिस्मितः -ता -तं; 'smiling words,' सस्मितानि वचनानि; 'a smiling countenance,' स्मेरमुखं, हास्यमुखं, हास्यवदनं; 'having a smiling countenance,' स्मेरमुखः -खी -खं, सुहसाननः -ना -नं, प्रसन्नमुखः &c., प्रफुल्लवदनः &c.

SMILINGLY, *adv.* सस्मितं, विहस्य, सविहसितं, सहास्यं.

To SMIRK, *v. n.* विलक्षणस्मितं कृ, कुस्मितं कृ, अपहसितं कृ, विलक्षहास्यं कृ.

SMIRK, *s.* विलक्षणस्मितं, विलक्षस्मितं, विलक्षहास्यं, अपहसितं, अपहास्यं, कुस्मितं, जिह्महसितं, जिह्महास्यं.

To SMITE, *v. a.* (Strike) हन् (c. 2. हन्ति -न्तुं), अभिहन्, निहन्, तड् (c. 10. ताडयति -यितुं), व्यध्, प्रतिव्यध्, प्रहृ, तुद्, *see* *To* STRIKE.—(Kill) हन्, मृ in caus., सूद्, शस् &c., *see* *To* KILL.

SMITER, *s.* हन्ता *m.* (न्तृ), ताडयिता *m.* (तृ), प्रहर्त्ता *m.*, घातकः, घाती *m.*

SMITH, *s.* शिल्पी *m.* (न्), अयोघनेन तप्तलोहादिताडकः.—(Blacksmith) लोहकारः, अयस्कारः, ध्माकारः, ध्मकः.

SMITHERY, SMITHY, *s.* लोहकारशाला, अयस्कारशाला, ध्मकशाला.

SMITING, *s.* हननं, ताडनं, मारणं; 'of the breast,' वक्षस्ताडनं.

SMITTEN, *s.* हतः -ता -तं, निहतः &c., समाहतः &c., उपहतः &c.—(With love) कामोपहतः -ता -तं, काममोहितः &c., कामार्त्तः -र्त्ता -र्त्तं.

SMOCK, SMOCK-FROCK, *s.* स्थूलशाटकः -टी, ग्राम्यजनभृतं शिथिलोत्तरीयं.

SMOKE, *s.* धूमः, धूमिका, धूपः -पिका, दहनकेतनं, मरुद्वाहः, करमालः, खतमालः, व्यामः; 'quantity of smoke,' धूम्या; 'volume of it,' धूमावलिः -ली, धूममाला; 'cloud of it,' धूममेघः, धूमौघः, धूमपटलः -लं; 'absence of it,' विधूमः, धूमाभावः.

To SMOKE, *v. n.* (Emit smoke) धूम (nom. धूमायति -ते), धूमम् उत्सृज् (c. 6. -सृजति -स्रष्टुं) or उत्क्षिप् (c. 6. -क्षिपति -क्षेप्तुं) or निःसृ in caus. or निर्गम् in caus., धूप (nom. धूपायति -ते), धूप (nom. धूपायति -ते).—(Inhale tobacco through a pipe) नालद्वारेण ताम्रकुट्टधूमिकां पिबा, धूमनिपानं कृ.—(Cause to emit smoke) धूम in caus. (धूमाययति -यितुं).

To SMOKE, *v. a.* (Apply smoke, affect by smoke) धूमस्पर्शं -स्पर्शं कृ, धूमोपहतं -तां कृ, धूपीकृ, धूप (nom. धूपयति -यितुं), धूमेन शुष् in caus., धूम (nom. धूमयति -यितुं), धूप् (c. 1. धूपायति -यितुं, धूपितुं), अवधूप्, सधूमीकृ.—(A pipe), *see* under *To* SMOKE, *v. n.*

SMOKED, *p. p.* धूपितः -ता -तं, अवधूपितः &c., धूपीकृतः &c., सधूमीकृतः -ता -तं, धूमशोषितः -ता -तं.

SMOKELESS, *a.* निर्धूमः -मा -मं, विधूमः &c., धूमहीनः -ना -नं.

SMOKER, *s.* धूमपायी *m.* (न्), धूमनिपाता *m.* (तृ), ताम्रकुट्टधूमपायी.

SMOKING, *s.* (Act of emitting smoke) धूमोत्क्षेपः -पणं, धूमोत्सर्जनं.—(Inhaling tobacco-smoke) धूमनिपानं, धूमपानं, ताम्रकुट्टधूमपानं.

SMOKING, *part.* धूमायमानः -ना -नं, धूमोत्क्षेपी -पिणी -पि (न्).

SMOKY, *a.* धूम्रः -म्रा -म्रं, धूमलः -ला -लं, सधूमः -मा -मं, धूममयः -यी -यं, धौमीयः -यी -यं, सधूपः -पा -पं; 'smoky coloured,' धूम्रवर्णः -र्णा -र्णं.—(Having the appearance of smoke) धूमाकारः -रा -रं.

SMOOTH, *a.* (Not rough, having an even surface, glossy) श्लक्ष्णः -क्ष्णा -क्ष्णं, स्निग्धः -ग्धा -ग्धं, स्नेही -हिनी -हि (न्), चिक्कणः -णा -णं, मसृणः -णा -णं, समः -मा -मं, पेशलः -ला -लं, अरूक्षः -क्षा -क्षं, अरूक्षः &c., अरूक्षः -क्षा -क्षं, अखरः -रा -रं, अपरुषः -षा -षं, सुखस्पर्शः -र्शा -र्शं.—(Level) समः -मा -मं, समानः -ना -नं.—(Bland, soft) मृदुः -दुः -दु, मेदुरः -रा -रं, स्निग्धः &c.—(Gently flowing, moving equally) विसृत्वरः -रा -रं, विसारी -रिणी &c., धारावाही &c., समानगतिः -तिः -ति.—(Unruffled, calm) अक्षुब्धः -ब्धा -ब्धं, शान्तः -न्ता -न्तं, निर्वेगः -गा -गं, निस्तरङ्गः -ङ्गा -ङ्गं, प्रसन्नः -न्ना -न्नं.

To SMOOTH, *v. a.* श्लक्ष्ण (nom. श्लक्ष्णयति -यितुं), श्लक्ष्णीकृ, स्निग्धीकृ, समीकृ, समानीकृ.—(Free from obstruction) निर्विघ्नीकृ, *see* *To* EASE.

SMOOTHLY, *adv.* सुखेन, अदुःखेन, निर्विघ्नं, अक्लेशेन. *See* EASILY.

SMOOTHNESS, *s.* श्लक्ष्णता, स्निग्धता, सौम्यं, अरूक्षता, अकर्कशता, मृदुता, समता, समानता; 'of speech,' वाक्चापल्यं, मधुरभाषित्वं, *see* FLUENCY; 'of the sea, &c.,' अक्षुब्धता, शान्तता.

SMOOTH-TONGUED, *a.* चपलजिह्वः -ह्वा -ह्वं, चपलवाक् *m.f.n.* (च्).

To SMOTHER, *v. a.* (Suffocate) श्वासरोधं कृ, श्वासनिरोधं कृ, प्राणरोधं कृ, कण्ठनिरोधं कृ, श्वासावरोधं कृ.—(Suppress) निग्रह्, स्तम्भ्, नियम्, नियन्त्, गुह्, छद्, अन्तः कृ.

SMOTHERED, *p. p.* रुद्धश्वासः -सा -सं, रुद्धप्राणः -णा -णं, निरुद्धकण्ठः -ण्ठा -ण्ठं; 'with dust and mud,' पांशुपङ्काच्छन्नः -न्ना -न्नं.

To SMOULDER, *v. n.* अन्तर्दाहं कृ, अन्तर्ज्वलनं कृ, अन्तर्ज्वाली -लिनी -लि भू, अन्तर्दाहवान् -वती -वद् भू, गूढदाहवान् &c. भू.

SMOULDERING, *part.* अन्तर्दाही -हिनी -हि (न्), अन्तर्ज्वाली &c., अन्तर्दाहवान् -वती -वत् (त्), गूढदाहवान् &c.

To SMUGGLE, *v. a.* निषिद्धवस्तूनि देशान्तरात् छलेन आनी or उपनी or आवह्, शुल्कदानम् अकृत्वा वाणिज्यद्रव्याणि देशान्तरात् छलेन आनी.

SMUGGLED, *p. p.* छलेन देशान्तरादानीतः -ता -तं or विदेशादानीतः &c.

SMUGGLER, *s.* निषिद्धद्रव्यानेता *m.* (तृ), शुल्कदानम् अकृत्वा वाणिज्यवस्तूनि विदेशात् छलेन आनयति यो दस्युः, शुल्कदस्युः *m.*

SMUGGLING, *s.* निषिद्धद्रव्यानयनं, शुल्कादानपूर्वं वाणिज्यवस्तूनां देशान्तरात् छलेनानयनं, शुल्कादानापराधः.

SMUT, *s.* मषी, *see* LAMP-BLACK.—(Obscene language) दुर्वचनं, दुर्भाषणं, अपशब्दः, दुरुक्तिः *f.*, कुत्सितवचनं, कुत्सितवाक्यं.

To SMUT, SMUTCH, *v. a.* मलिनीकृ, मलीमसीकृ, मलिन (nom. मलिनयति -यितुं).

SMUTTY, *a.* मलीमसः -सा -सं, मलिनः -ना -नं. *See* OBSCENE.

SNACK, *s.* अंशः, भागः, *see* SHARE.—(Light repast), *see* REPAST.

SNAFFLE, *s.* (Light bridle) लघुवल्गा, लघुवल्गा, लघुखलीनः.

SNAIL, *s.* शम्बूकः, शम्बूकवासी *m.* (न्), कोशस्थः, कोशवासी *m.*, कवचवासी कृमिः, कम्बुवासी *m.*, कम्बुयुक्तः or कवचयुक्तः कृमिः.

SNAIL-SHELL, *s.* कृमिकोशः, कृमिकोषः, कृमिकवचः, कृमिकम्बुः *m.*, जम्बुकम्बुः *m.*, कम्बुः *m.*, शम्बुः *m.*

SNAKE, *s.* सर्पः, अहिः *m.*, भुजङ्गः, भुजङ्गमः, भुजगः, उरगः, उरङ्गः, उरङ्गमः, उरःसरः, व्यालः, नागः, पन्नगः, सरीसृपः, पवनाशनः, बिलेशयः, बिलवासी *m.* (न्), विषधरः, विषाननः, विषास्यः, विषायुधः, आशीविषः, दीर्घजिह्वः, दीर्घरसनः, द्विजिह्वः, द्विरसनः, दीर्घपृष्ठः, दृक्कर्णः, चक्षुःश्रवाः *m.* (स्), लताजिह्वः, लतारसनः, वायुभक्षः, पवनाशनः, श्वसनाशनः, जिह्मगः, भेकभुक् *m.* (ज्), मण्डूकभुक्, चक्री *m.* (न्), कञ्चुकी *m.*, काकोदरः, कञ्चुकालुः *m.*, गूढपात् *m.*, गूढपादः, कुण्डली *m.* (न्), दन्दशूकः, पृदाकुः *m.*, सृदरः, समकोलः, तक्षकः, तृम्पू *m.*, व्याडः, सर्पी *m.* (न्); 'hooded snake,' फणी *m.* (न्), भोगी *m.*, फणवान् *m.* (त्), भोगवान् *m.*, फणावान्, फणभृत् *m.*, फणधरः, फणाधरः, फणाभरः, फणाकरः, दर्वीकरः; 'female snake,' सर्पी, सर्पिणी, भुजगी, भुजङ्गी; 'variegated snake,' मालुधानः, मातुलाहिः *m.*; 'other sorts of snakes,' गोनसः, गोनासः, तिलित्सः, अजगरः, शयुः *m.*, वाहसः, राजिलः, डुण्डुभः, डुण्डुभः, राजाहिः *m.*, नागभिद् *m.*; 'a water-snake,' जलव्यालः, कालकन्दकः, अलगर्दः, अलगर्द्दः; 'the king of the snakes that inhabit the infernal regions, forming the couch and canopy of Vishnu, and upholding the world which rests on one of his thousand heads,' शेषः, अनन्तः, सर्पेश्वरः, फणीश्वरः; 'other kings and chiefs of the snakes,' वासुकिः *m.*, सर्पराजः, तक्षकः, शङ्खः, महापद्मः; 'the expanded hood of a snake,' फणः -णा, भोगः, स्फटा, स्फोटा, दर्विः -र्वी, दर्विः -र्वी; 'his skin,' कञ्चुकः, निर्मोकः, *see* SLOUGH; 'a snake that has cast his skin,' निर्मुक्तः, मुक्तकञ्चुकः; 'his venom,' गरलं, विषं, क्ष्वेडः; 'his fang,' विषदन्तः, आशी, आशिस् *f.*, सर्पदंष्ट्रः.—(Bitten by a snake) अहिदष्टः -ष्टा -ष्टं, अहिविदष्टः &c.

SNAKE-CATCHER, SNAKE-CHARMER, *s.* व्यालग्राही *m.* (न्), सर्पग्राही *m.*, आहितुण्डिकः, अहितुण्डिकः, जाङ्गुलिकः, विषवैद्यः, सर्पमन्त्री *m.* (न्), मन्त्रवादी *m.*, मन्त्री *m.*, जीवकः.

SNAKE-HOLE, *s.* सर्पविवरं, सर्पबिलं, भुजङ्गबिलं, अहिविवरं.

SNAKE-STONE, *s.* (A jewel said to be found in the head or hood of a snake) सर्पमणिः *m.*, नागमणिः *m.*, फणामणिः *m.*, सर्पफणजः.

SNAKY, *a.* आहेयः -यी -यं, सार्पः -र्पी -र्पं, सार्प्यः -र्पी -र्प्यं, औरगः -गी -गं, सर्पसम्बन्धी -न्धिनी -न्धि (न्), सर्पस्वभावः -वा -वं.

To SNAP, *v. a.* (Break at once) एकपदे or युगपत् or अकस्मात् त्रुट् (c. 6. त्रुटति -टितुं, c. 10. त्रोटयते -यितुं) or भञ्ज् or खण्ड् or स्फुट् or रुज् or छिद् or तक्ष्.—(The fingers) अङ्गुलिस्फोटनं कृ, अङ्गुलिभङ्गं कृ, छोटिकां कृ, मुचुटीं कृ, मुकुटीं कृ.—(Bite suddenly) अकस्माद् दंश् or विदंश्.—(Snap up) अकस्माद् ग्रह् or उद्ग्रह् or उद्ग्राहं कृ, *see To* SNATCH.

To SNAP, *v. n.* (Break suddenly) एकपदे or युगपत् or अकस्मात् त्रुट् (c. 4. त्रुट्यति -टितुं) or स्फुट् (c. 6. स्फुटति -टितुं) or भञ्ज् in pass. or भिद् in pass. or छिद् in pass.—(Make an effort to seize with the teeth, as a dog) श्ववद् or कुक्कुरवद् दन्तैर् ग्रह् in des. (जिघृक्षति -क्षितुं) or दंश् in des.—(Utter angry words) भष् (c. 1. भषति -षितुं).

SNAP, SNAPPING, *s.* (Sudden break) अकस्मात् त्रोटनं or स्फोटनं or स्फुटनं, आकस्मिकभङ्गः, अकस्माद् भञ्जनं or भङ्गः, अकस्मात् खण्डनं.—(Of the fingers) अङ्गुलिस्फोटनं, अङ्गुलिभङ्गः, छोटिका, पुच्छटिः *m.*, मुकुटी, मुचुटी.—(Sudden bite, or effort to seize with the teeth) आकस्मिकदंशः -शनं, अकस्माद् दंशः or दन्तैर् जिघृक्षा.

SNAPPED, *p. p.* अकस्मात् त्रुटितः -ता -तं or भग्नः -ग्ना -ग्नं or स्फुटितः -ता -तं or छिन्नः -न्ना -न्नं or भिन्नः &c.

SNAPPISH, *a.* (Eager to bite or seize) दंशनशीलः -ला -लं, दिदंक्षुः -क्षुः -क्षु, जिघृक्षुः -क्षुः -क्षु, जिगरिषुः -षुः -षु.—(Peevish, currish) कर्कशः -शा -शं, कर्कशशीलः &c., कुक्कुरस्वभावः -वा -वं, श्वस्वभावः -वा -वं.

SNARE, *s.* पाशः, पाशबन्धः, जालं, वागुरा, उन्मायः, कूटः, मोहजालं, कूटयन्त्रं; 'snares of the world,' प्रपञ्चपाशः, भवपाशः.

To SNARE, *v. a.* पाशबद्धं -द्धां कृ, जालबद्धं -द्धां कृ, पाशे or उन्माये or वागुरायां पत् (c. 10. पातयति -यितुं), जाले पातयित्वा बन्ध् (c. 9. बध्नाति, बन्द्धुं), पाशीकृ, पाश (nom. पाशयति -यितुं).

SNARED, *p. p.* पाशबद्धः -द्धा -द्धं, जालबद्धः &c., पाशीकृतः -ता -तं, पाशितः -ता -तं, उन्मायपतितः -ता -तं, वागुरापतितः &c., कीटः -टी -टं.

To SNARL, *v. n.* भष् (c. 1. भषति -षितुं), रै (c. 1. रायति, रातुं), तर्ज्, तर्जनं कृ, गर्ज्, गर्जनं कृ, कर्कशवाक्यं वद्, परुषवाक्यं वद्, कटुवाक्यं वद्.

SNARLER, *s.* भषकः, कुक्कुरस्वभावः, भषशीलः, सदाकर्कशः.

To SNATCH, *v. a.* or *n.* अकस्मात् or झटिति ग्रह् (c. 9. गृह्णाति, ग्रहीतुं) or हृ (c. 1. हरति, हर्तुं) or अभिहृ or धृ (c. 1. धरति, धर्तुं) or कृष् (c. 1. कर्षति, क्रष्टुं) or आकल् (c. 10. -कलयति -यितुं) or प्रकल् (c. 10. -कालयति -यितुं); 'to snatch at,' अकस्माद् जिघृक्षया हस्तं प्रसृ (c. 10. -सारयति -यितुं), अकस्माद् ग्रह् in des. (जिघृक्षति -क्षितुं) or हृ in des. (जिहीर्षति -र्षितुं); 'to snatch away,' अकस्माद् अपहृ

or अपहृ or अपकृष् or विलुप्; 'to snatch out,' अकस्माद् उद्धृ or निर्हृ or उत्कृष्.

SNATCH, SNATCHING, *s.* (Hasty seizing) अकस्माद् हरणं or ग्रहणं or धरणं, आकस्मिकहरणं, अकस्मादाकलनं, आकस्मिकाभिगृध्नुता.—(Short interval) अल्पान्तरं, अल्पावकाशः, क्षणावकाशः.—(Short fit of action) क्षणप्रवृत्तिः *f.*

SNATCHED, *p. p.* अकस्माद् गृहीतः -ता -तं or हृतः -ता -तं or धृतः -ता -तं or अभिद्रुतः &c., अकस्मादाकलितः -ता -तं; 'snatched away,' अकस्माद् अपहृतः -ता -तं or विलुप्तः -प्ता -प्तं; 'snatched out,' उद्धृतः &c.

To SNEAK, *v. n.* कुत्सितजनवत् छलेन अपसृप् (c. 1. -सर्पति -सर्प्तुं) or अपक्रम्, कापुरुषवद् निभृतस्थानम् आस्था (c. 1. -तिष्ठति -स्थातुं) or निभृतस्थाने आत्मानं गुह् or गुप्, कुत्सितजनवद् आचर्, कुत्सितवृत्तिः -त्तिः -त्ति भू.—(Behave with meanness and servility) कृपणवत् or कुत्सितप्रकारेण अतिलालनं कृ or अतिसान्त्वनं कृ.

SNEAKING, *part.* or *a.* कुत्सितवृत्तिः -त्तिः -त्ति, कुत्सिताचारः -रा -रं, कुत्सितप्रकारेण अतिलालनकारी-रिणी-रि(न्) or अतिसान्त्वनकारी &c.

To SNEER, *v. n.* विकृतमुखेन or मुखविकारेण अवज्ञां सूच् (c. 10. सूचयति -यितुं), विकृतहासेन अवमानं सूच्, अवज्ञाहासं कृ, अवज्ञासूचनार्थं विकृतस्मितं कृ or विकृतहासं कृ; 'to sneer at,' अवहस्, *see To* DERIDE.

SNEER, *s.* अवज्ञासूचनार्थं विकृतस्मितं or विकृतहासः, अमर्षहासः, अवज्ञासूचकहासः, अवज्ञाहासः, अवज्ञासूचका मुखविकृतिः *f.*, अवहासः. *See* SARCASM.

SNEERINGLY, *adv.* सावज्ञाहासं, सामर्षहासं, सावहासं, अवहासेन.

To SNEEZE, *v. n.* क्षु (c. 2. क्षौति, क्षवितुं), क्षुतं कृ, क्षवं कृ, छिक्कां कृ, छिक्कनं कृ, छिक्क् (nom. छिक्कति -क्कितुं, छिक्कायते); 'to sneeze upon,' अवक्षु.

SNEEZE, SNEEZING, *s.* क्षुतं, क्षवः, क्षवथुः *m.*, क्षुत् *f.*, क्षुता, छिक्का, छिक्कनं, काशः, प्राणानी, हृच्छिः *m.*, घ्राणदुःखदा.

SNEEZED, *p. p.* क्षुतः -ता -तं; 'sneezed upon,' अवक्षुतः -ता -तं.

SNEEZING, *part.* क्षवकृत् *m.f.n.*, क्षवकारी-रिणी &c., क्षुतवान् -वती &c.

To SNIGGER, *v. n.* अन्तर्हासं कृ, उच्चघनं कृ, उद्घर्षनं कृ, गूढहासं कृ.

To SNIFF, *v. a.* नासाद्वारेण श्वस् (c. 2. -श्वसिति -तुं) or निःश्वस् or श्वासं कृ.

To SNIP, *v. a.* कर्त्तन्या सूक्ष्मच्छेदं कृ or अल्पच्छेदं कृ or छिद्.

SNIPE, *s.* दीर्घचञ्चुः, दीर्घमुखः, दीर्घचञ्चुविशिष्टः पक्षिभेदः.

To SNIVEL, *v. n.* नासिकामलं सु in caus. (स्रावयति -यितुं), नासिकास्रावोपहतः -ता -तं भू.—(Whimper) बालकवत् परिदेव्.

SNIVEL, *s.* नासामलं, नासिकामलं, सिंहानं, सिंहाणं, सिङ्घाणं.

SNIVELING, *s.* नासिकास्रावः, नासास्रावः, नासापरिस्रावः.

SNOB, *s.* सभ्यम्मन्यः, कुलीनलोकव्यवहारानुकारी प्राकृतजनः.

SNOOZE, *To* SNOOZE, *see* NAP, *To* NAP.

To SNORE, *v. n.* स्वप्नमध्ये कर्कशशब्दपूर्व्वं नासाद्वारेण श्वासं कृ or नासया श्वासप्रश्वासं कृ, स्वप्नमध्ये कर्कशस्वरेण नासिकां ध्मा (c. 1. धमति, ध्मातुं) or नासया श्वस् (c. 2. श्वसिति -तुं), निद्रामध्ये कर्कशश्वासं कृ or कर्कशस्वरं कृ, उच्छिङ्खनं कृ, क्रपनं कृ.

SNORE, SNORING, *s.* स्वप्नमध्ये कर्कशश्वासः or सशब्दश्वासः or नासया श्वासः, निद्रामध्ये कर्कशस्वरेण श्वासः, निद्रावस्थायाम् उच्छिङ्खनं or क्रपनं, स्वरः.

To SNORT, *v. n.* नासाद्वारेण उग्रश्वासं कृ, नासिकाद्वारेण फूत्कृ or फूत्कारं कृ or फूत्शब्दं कृ, सूत्कारं कृ, सूत्कृ, सूसूशब्दं कृ.

SNORTING, *s.* नासाद्वारेण उग्रश्वासः or उग्रशब्दसहितश्वासः, सूत्कारः.

SNOT, *s.* नासामलं, नासिकामलं, सिंहानं, सिंहाणं. *See* MUCUS.

SNOUT, *s.* पोत्रं, प्रोथः -थं, नस्तः, नस्या, नासा, नासिका, मुखः.

SNOW, *s.* हिमं, तुषारः, हिमानी, नीहारः, तुहिनं, तौषारं, हिमसंहतिः *f.*, हिमिका, खवाष्पः, भस्मतूलं, कारः; 'a fall of snow,' तुषारपातः, तुषारवर्षः; 'a particle of snow,' हिमकणः, तुषारकणः.

To SNOW, *v. n.* तुषारं वृष् (c. 1. वर्षति -र्षितुं), हिमं वृष्, तुषारकणान् वृष्, हिमकणान् वृष्.

SNOW-BALL, *s.* हिमपिण्डः, तुषारपिण्डः, हिममण्डलं.

SNOW-CAPPED, *a.* हिमशेखरः -रा -रं, हिमशिखरः &c., हिमावृतशिखरः.

SNOW-DRIFT, *s.* हिमसंहतिः *f.*, तुषारसंहतिः, हिमराशिः *m.*, हिमौघः.

SNOW-STORM, *s.* तुषारवर्षः, तुषारपातः, हिमपातः, हिमसम्पातः.

SNOWY, *a.* (Abounding with snow, covered with it) हिमवान् -वती -वत् (त्), हिममयः -यी -यं, हिम्यः -म्या -म्यं, हैमः -मी -मं, हिम in comp., तुषारमयः &c., हिमाढ्यः -ढ्या -ढ्यं, तौषारः -री -रं, हिमावृतः -ता -तं; 'snowy mountain,' हिमाद्रिः *m.*, तुषाराद्रिः, तुहिनाद्रिः, हिमपर्व्वतः, शीताद्रिः *m.*—(White, like snow) हिमाभः -भा -भं, हिमवर्णः -र्णा -र्णं.

To SNUB, *v. a.* प्रत्यादिश्, वाग्रोधं कृ, अपकृष्, दर्पभङ्गं कृ, पराभू.

SNUB-NOSED, *a.* नतनासिकः -का -कं, खुरणसः -सा -सं, खुरणाः -णाः -णः (स्), चिपिटः -टा -टं, चिपिटकः -का -कं, चिपुटः -टा -टं, चिकिनः -ना -नं, अवनाटः -टा -टं, अवटीटः &c., अवभ्रटः &c.

SNUFF, *s.* (Burnt or charred wick) दग्धतूला -ली, तप्ततूला -ली, दग्धपिच्छलं.—(Pulverized tobacco) नस्यं, नस्तं, नासिकाचूर्णं, नासाचूर्णं, अवपीडः, क्षुत्करी; 'to take snuff,' नस्यं पा or निपा.

To SNUFF, *v. a.* (Inhale by the nose) नासाद्वारेण निःश्वस्, उच्छिङ्खनं कृ, *see To* SNUFF, SMELL.—(Crop the snuff of a candle) दग्धतूलाम् अवच्छिद् (c. 7. -छिनत्ति -छेत्तुं) or छिद् or लू, प्रदीपतूलीं छिद् or हृ, दीपिकातूलीम् अवच्छिद्.

SNUFF-BOX, *s.* नस्याधारः, नासिकाचूर्णाधारः, नस्यपात्रं, नस्यभाजनं.

SNUFFERS, *s.* तूलाकर्त्तनी, तूलाछेदनी, प्रदीपतूलाकर्त्तनी, कर्त्तनी.

To SNUFFLE, *v. n.* नासाद्वारेण सूत्शब्दं कृ. *See To* SNORT, SNIFF.

SNUFF-TAKER, *s.* नस्यपायी *m.* (न्), नासिकाचूर्णनिपाता *m.* (तृ).

SNUFFY, *a.* नस्यदूषितः -ता -तं, नासिकाचूर्णमलिनः -ना -नं.

SNUG, *a.* (Close, compact, covered up) संहतः -ता -तं, सुसंहतः &c., संवृतः -ता -तं, आवृतः &c., सुप्रच्छन्नः -न्ना -न्नं, प्रच्छन्नः -न्ना -न्नं, गुप्तः -प्ता -प्तं, गूढः -ढा -ढं, उपगूढः &c.—(Comfortable) सुस्थः -स्था -स्थं, सुस्थितः -ता -तं, स्वस्थः -स्था -स्थं, सुखी -खिनी -खि (न्), सुखः -खा -खं, यथासुखः &c.—(Lying close) निकटशायी &c., पार्श्वापार्श्विशायी &c.

To SNUGGLE, *v. n.* निकटे or अङ्के or पार्श्वतः or पार्श्वापार्श्वि शी.

SNUGLY, *adv.* सुखेन, यथासुखं. *See* CLOSELY, COMFORTABLY.

SNUGNESS, *s.* सुसंहतता, सुप्रच्छन्नता, सुस्थता, सुस्थितिः *f.*, सौख्यं.

SO, *adv.* (Thus) एवं, तथा, इति, इत्थं; 'and so forth,' इत्यादि, इत्यादिप्रकारेण; 'be it so,' एवं भवतु, एवमस्तु, तथास्तु, अस्तु; 'is it so?' कच्चित्.—(In this manner, in such a manner) एवं, तथा, एवंविधं -धेन; 'I must so contrive that my master awake,' यथा स्वामी जागर्त्ति तथा मया कर्त्तव्यं.—(In like manner, after the same manner) तद्वत्, एवं, तथा, एवम्प्रकारेण, तथाविधेन, तथाप्रकारेण, एवंविधेन, एवंविधानेन, एतादृशं.—(To such a degree) एतावत्, ईदृक्, एतादृक्, ईदृशं, एतादृशं, तादृक्, एतत्पर्य्यन्तं, तथा,

इत्थं, इयत्, इयत्पर्य्यन्तं ; 'so far,' तावत्, एतावत्, तदन्तं, तत्पर्य्यन्तं ; 'so many, so much,' तावत् indec., तावान् -वती -वत् (त्), तावत्संख्यकः -का -कं, तत्संख्यकः &c. ; 'so great, so large,' एतावान् &c., एतावन्महान् &c., ईदृशः -शी -शं, ईदृङ्महान् &c. ; 'so long,' तावत् ; 'so long a time,' तावत्कालं ; 'there is no body so small but that it may be divided in half,' न तादृगल्पः परिमाणांशो यस्य अर्द्धं कल्पयितुम् अशक्यं ; 'he is not so sagacious as to discriminate,' न तस्य ईदृग् विज्ञानम् अस्ति परिच्छेत्तुं ; 'am I so weak that the goods in my house are to be carried off by the sea?' किम् अहं दुर्बलो मम गृहस्थभाण्डानि समुद्रेण अपहर्त्तव्यानि ; 'let it be ascertained whether he is worthy to receive so large a salary,' ज्ञायतां किम् उपयुक्त एतावद् वर्त्तनं गृह्णाति ; 'so true is it,' यथार्थम् अस्ति.—(Therefore) ततस्, तस्मात्, तेन.—(So so, indifferent) तावन्मात्रं, यावत्तावत्.—(So and so) expressed by अमुक in comp. ; as, 'Mr. So and so,' अमुकनामा m. (न्), अमुकजनः.

To SOAK, *v. a.* चिरेण जलसिक्तं -क्तां कृ, चिरकालं जलेन सिच् (c. 6. सिञ्चति, सेक्तुं), चिरेण जलस्थं -स्थां कृ, चिरकालं जलेन समाप्लु (c. 10. -प्लावयति -यितुं) or जलसमाप्लुतं -तां कृ or आर्द्रीकृ or क्लिद् (c. 10. क्लेदयति -यितुं) or समुक्ष् (c. 1. -उक्षति -क्षितुं) or अभ्युक्ष्.

SOAKED, *p. p.* चिरेण सिक्तः -क्ता -क्तं, चिरसिक्तः &c., चिरक्लेदितः -ता -तं, चिरजलस्थः -स्था -स्थं, चिरजलस्थितः -ता -तं, प्रक्लिन्नः -न्ना -न्नं, आर्द्रः -र्द्रा -र्द्रं, समुक्षितः -ता -तं.

SOAP, *s.* सर्ज्जिः *f.*, सर्ज्जिका, क्षारः, सर्ज्जक्षारः, अञ्जनं, अभ्यञ्जनं, मार्ज्जनतैलं, मार्ज्जनलेपः, मेदस् *n.*, प्रदेहः, स्नेहः.

To SOAP, *v. a.* सर्ज्जिकया अञ्ज् or अभ्यञ्ज् or लिप्, सर्ज्जिकालिप्तं कृ.

SOAP-BERRY-PLANT, *s.* अरिष्टः, रिष्टः, फेनिलः.

SOAPY, *a.* मेदुरः -रा -रं, चिक्कणः -णा -णं, सर्ज्जिकालिप्तः -प्ता -प्तं.

To SOAR, *v. n.* ऊर्द्ध्वं or ऊर्द्ध्वं गम् (c. 1. गच्छति, गन्तुं), ऊर्द्ध्वं डी (c. 4. डीयते, c. 1. डयते -यितुं), उड्डी, प्रोड्डी, उड्डीनं कृ, उड्डयनं कृ, ऊर्द्ध्वं विहायसा गम् or नभसा गम् or वियति विसृप् (c. 1. -सर्पति -सर्प्तुं), ऊर्द्ध्वगमनं कृ, ऊर्द्ध्वारोहणं कृ, नभोगमनं कृ, उत्क्रमणं कृ.

SOARER, *s.* ऊर्द्ध्वगामी *m.* (न्), आकाशगामी *m.*, उड्डीनकारी *m.*, उड्डयनकृत्.

SOARING, *s.* उड्डीनं, उड्डयनं, ऊर्द्ध्वगमनं, ऊर्द्ध्वगतिः *f.*, नभोगमनं, नभोगतिः *f.*, उपरिगमनं, उत्क्रमणं, ऊर्द्ध्वारोहणं.

SOARING, *part.* उड्डीयमानः -ना -नं, आकाशगामी -मिनी -मि (न्).

To SOB, *v. n.* (Make a convulsive sound in crying) गद्गद (nom. गद्गदति), गद्गदं कृ, क्रन्दनमध्ये गद्गदध्वनिं कृ, गद्गदशब्देन क्रन्द् (c. 1. क्रन्दति -न्दितुं) or रुद् (c. 2. रोदिति -तुं) or प्ररुद्, गद्गदशब्देन क्रन्दनं कृ, छनच्छन (nom. छनच्छनायते), छनच्छनशब्दं कृ.

SOB, SOBBING, *s.* गद्गदः, गद्गदध्वनिः *m.*, गद्गदशब्दः, गद्गदशब्दसहितक्रन्दनं, क्रन्दनं, रोदनं, छनच्छनशब्दः, फूत्कारः, फुत्कारः.

SOBER, *a.* (Not drunk) अमत्तः -त्ता -त्तं, निर्मदः -दा -दं, अक्षीवः -वा -वं, अनागतमदः -दा -दं.—(Temperate in drink) पानाप्रसक्तः -क्ता -क्तं, परिमितपानी -निनी -नि (न्), मितपानी &c., यतपानी &c., पानसंयमी &c.—(Not wild or extravagant, serious) धीरः -रा -रं, स्थिरः -रा -रं, नियतः -ता -तं, नियमी &c., विनीतः -ता -तं, नियतवृत्तिः -त्तिः -त्ति, विचारबुद्धिः -द्धिः -द्धि, विचारशीलः -ला -लं, विचारी &c., समत्तः -त्ता -त्तं, स्थिरमतिः -तिः -ति, स्थिरबुद्धिः -द्धिः -द्धि, गम्भीरवृत्तिः &c.

To SOBER, *v. a.* निर्मदीकृ, मदहीनं -नां कृ, नियतीकृ, स्थिरीकृ, धीरीकृ.

SOBERED, *p. p.* निर्मदीकृतः -ता -तं, विगतमदः -दा -दं, क्षीणक्षैव्यः -व्या -व्यं.

SOBERLY, *adv.* धीरवत्, विनीतवत्, सविनयं, नियतवत्, विचारपूर्वं.

SOBER-MINDED, *a.* धीरमनस्कः -स्का -स्कं, गम्भीरमनस्कः &c., स्थिरबुद्धिः &c.

SOBERNESS, SOBRIETY, *s.* (Freedom from intoxication) अमत्तता, अक्षीवता, निर्मदत्वं, मदहीनता, मदाभावः, क्षैव्याभावः.—(Temperance in drink) पानसंयमः, पानाप्रसक्तिः *f.*, पानाप्रसक्तता, परिमितपानं, मितपानं.—(Seriousness) धीरता, गम्भीरता, गाम्भीर्य्यं, स्थिरता, स्थैर्य्यं, विनीतता, विनयः, विचारशीलता, नियतवृत्तिः *f.*, अमत्तता.

SOCIABLE, *a.* जनसङ्गप्रियः -या -यं, सङ्गप्रियः &c., जनसङ्गासक्तः -क्ता -क्तं, संलापप्रियः -या -यं, सम्भाषणप्रियः &c., सङ्गशीलः -ला -लं, संलापशीलः &c., स्नेहबुद्धिः -द्धिः -द्धि, सुशीलः -ला -लं.

SOCIABILITY, SOCIABLENESS, *s.* सङ्गप्रियता, सङ्गप्रीतिः *f.*, सङ्गासक्तिः *f.*, जनसङ्गप्रीतिः *f.*, जनसङ्गप्रियता, संलापप्रियता, संलापासक्तिः *f.*, संलापशीलता, स्नेहबुद्धिः *f.*, सुशीलता.

SOCIABLY, *adv.* सङ्गासक्तत्वात्, जनसङ्गासक्तत्वात्, स्नेहबुद्ध्या, सुशीलवत्.

SOCIAL, *a.* (Pertaining to society) सांसर्गिकः -की -कं, साङ्गतिकः -की -कं, जनसंसर्गसम्बन्धी -न्धिनी -न्धि (न्), साङ्गमिकः &c., सहवाससम्बन्धी &c., सहवासविषयकः -का -कं, सहभावसम्बन्धी &c. ; 'social duty,' जनाचारः.—(Ready to unite in friendly converse) सङ्गप्रियः -या -यं, सङ्गमशीलः -ला -लं, संसर्गशीलः &c., संवासशीलः &c., समागमशीलः &c., अनेकचरः -रा -रं, समूहचरः &c., *see* SOCIABLE.—(Consisting in mutual converse) संसर्गरूपः -पा -पं, सङ्गरूपः &c., प्रतिभाषणवान् -वती -वत् (त्).

SOCIETY, *s.* (Association, consociation) संसर्गः, सङ्गः, सङ्गमः, सङ्गतिः *f.*, समागमः, सहवासः, संवासः, सहभावः, सार्थं, साहचर्य्यं, साहित्यं, सहायता, साहाय्यं, लोकयात्रा, उपपत्तिः *f.*—(Community, body of people) जनसमूहः, लोकसमूहः, लोकसङ्गः, पंक्तिः *f.*, सभा, समाजः, मण्डली ; 'good society,' सभा ; 'fit for it,' सभ्यः -भ्या -भ्यं ; 'not fit for it,' असभ्यः -भ्या -भ्यं, अपांक्तेयः -या -यं, अपांक्त्यः -क्त्या -क्त्यं, अपांक्तः &c.—(Corporate body) श्रेणी -णिः *m. f.*, ग्रामसङ्घः.

SOCK, *s.* पादवस्त्रं, पादरक्षा -क्षणं, पादत्राणं, पादपरिधानं.

SOCKET, *s.* पात्रं, आधारः, आधानं, गर्भः, कूपः, गर्त्तः, भाजनं.

SOD, *s.* तृणावृतभूमिखण्डः, घासावृतभूमिखण्डः, सतृणभूमिखण्डः.

SOD, *a.* सर्ज्जिः *f.*, सर्ज्जिका, सर्ज्जिकाक्षारः, क्षारः, मृत्तिकाक्षारः, कापोतः, सौवर्चलं, रुचकं, वज्रक्षारः -रं, सुखवर्चकः, क्षुद्रिका, काचमलं.

To SODER, *v. a.* *See To* SOLDER.

SODOMITE, *s.* गुदमैथुनकर्त्ता *m.* (र्त्तृ), गुदमैथुनकारी *m.*, पुंमैथुनकृत्.

SODOMY, *s.* गुदमैथुनं, पुंमैथुनं, पायुमैथुनं.

SOEVER. Expressed by prefixing the relative to the interrogative, with the affixes चित्, अपि or चन ; thus, 'whosoever,' यः कश्चित् ; 'whatsoever,' यत् किञ्चित् ; 'wheresoever,' यत्र कुत्रचित् ; 'whensoever,' यदा कदाचित्, or by doubling the relative, thus यो यः, यद् यत्, यत्र यत्र, यदा यदा ; 'any soever,' कश्चित्, काचित्, किञ्चित् ; 'at any time whatsoever,' कदाचित्.

SOFA, *s.* केलिशयनं, केलिशय्या, पर्य्यङ्कः, शय्या, शयनं, शयनीयं.

SOFT, *a.* (Not hard or rough) मृदुः -द्वी -दु, मृदुलः -ला -लं, कोमलः &c., मसृणः -णा -णं, स्निग्धः -ग्धा -ग्धं, मृदुस्पर्शः -र्शा -र्शं, सुखस्पर्शः -र्शा -र्शं, श्लक्ष्णः -क्ष्णा -क्ष्णं, मेदुरः -रा -रं, सुकुमारः &c., बालेयः -या -यं, मरालः -ला -लं, अखरः -रा -रं, अप्रखरः &c., अकर्कशः -शा -शं, अपरुषः -षा -षं, अनुग्रः -ग्रा -ग्रं, अकठिनः -ना -नं, अकठोरः -रा -रं.—(Wanting firmness, flaccid) शिथिलः -ला -लं, अदृढः -ढा

-ढं, अघनः -ना -नं.—(Mild, gentle) सौम्यः -म्या -म्यं, मृदुः &c., मृदुस्वभावः -वा -वं.—(Weak in mind) अल्पबुद्धिः -द्धिः -द्धि, बालिशबुद्धिः &c., सुवचनीयः -या -यं.—(Having a soft voice) मृदुस्वरः -रा -रं, मधुरस्वरः &c.

Soft, *interj.* नीचैस्, नीचकैस्, तूष्णीं, तूष्णीम्भव, शान्तं.

To soften, *v. a.* मृदूकृ, कोमलीकृ, म्रद (nom. म्रदयति -यितुं), शम् in caus., सान्त्व् or शान्त्वं, दम् in caus., स्निग्धीकृ, करुणार्द्रीकृ. *See To* mollify, melt, *v. a.*

To soften, *v. n.* मृदूभू, कोमलीभू, स्निग्धीभू, शम् (c. 4. शाम्यति, शमितुं), प्रशम्, शान्तः -न्ता -न्तं भू, दयार्द्रीभू. *See To* melt, *v. n.*

Softened, *p. p.* मृदूकृतः -ता -तं, शमितः &c., स्निग्धीभूतः -ता -तं.

Softening, *part.* or *a.* शान्तिदः -दा -दं, शान्तिकः -की -कं, शान्तिकरः -री -रं.

Softly, *adv.* शनैस्, शनैः शनैस्, शनकैस्, मन्दं, मृदु, समार्दवं.

Softness, *s.* मृदुता, मार्दवं, म्रदिमा *m.* (न्), कोमलता, स्निग्धता -त्वं, मृदुस्पर्शता -त्वं, सुखस्पर्शता -त्वं, सुकुमारता -त्वं, सौकुमार्य्यं, अखरता, अकर्कशता -त्वं, अकठिनता, अकाठिन्यं, शिथिलता, शैथिल्यं; 'of voice,' स्वरमधुरता -माधुर्य्यं.

To soil, *v. a.* मलिन (nom. मलिनयति -यितुं), मलिनीकृ, कलङ्क (nom. कलङ्कयति -यितुं), दुष् (c. 10 दूषयति -यितुं), लिप्. *See To* stain.

Soil, *s.* (Dirt, stain) मलं, परिमलं, कलुषं, कलङ्कः, कल्कं, ग्लानिः *f.*, परिग्लानं.—(Mould, earth) मृत्तिका, मृद् *f.*, मृदा, भूमिः *f.*, भूः *f.*, स्थलं -ली, पांशुः *m.*, स्थलं; 'good soil,' मृत्स्ना, मृत्सा, मृद्दिनी; 'fertile soil,' उर्व्वरा, अर्व्वरा; 'dry or barren soil,' मरुः *m.*, मरुस्थलं -ली, ईरिणं -णा, इरिणं; 'salt soil,' ऊषः, ऊषरः, उषः, क्षारमृत्तिका; 'having salt soil,' ऊषरः -रा -रं, ऊषवान् -वती -वत् (त्); 'untilled or waste soil,' खिलः, अप्रहतभूमिः *f.*; 'stony,' शर्करा; 'a black soil,' नीलमृत्तिका, कृष्णमृद् *f.*, कृष्णमृत्तिका, कृष्णभूमिः *f.*; 'pale soil,' पाण्डुमृत्तिका; 'native soil,' जन्मभूमिः *f.*, जन्मवसुधा; 'mountain-soil,' गिरिमृद्; 'soil fertile with every crop,' सर्व्वशस्याढ्यभूमिः *f.*

Soiled, *p. p.* मलिनितः -ता -तं, मलिनीकृतः &c., कलङ्कितः &c., परिमलितः &c., दूषितः -ता -तं, लिप्तः -प्ता -प्तं, अवलिप्तः &c., विलिप्तः &c., कलुषितः &c., मलिनः -ना -नं, कल्की -ल्किनी &c.; 'having soiled hands,' लिप्तहस्तः -स्ता -स्तं.

To sojourn, *v. n.* (Dwell for a time) कियत्कालं or अल्पकालपर्य्यन्तं वस् (c. 1. वसति, वस्तुं) or निवस्, प्रवस्, प्रवासं कृ, कियत्कालं स्था or वृत् or आस् or अध्यास्, देशान्तरे or परदेशे वस्, देशान्तरम् अधिवस् or आवस्, *see To* lodge, *v. n.*

Sojourn, sojourning, *s.* प्रवासः -सनं, प्रवसनं, कियत्कालपर्य्यन्तवासः, अल्पकालनिवासः, अदीर्घवासः, देशान्तरवासः, देशान्तराधिवासः, परदेशवासः, देशान्तरसेवनं, परदेशसेवनं, देशान्तरावलम्बनं.

Sojourner, *s.* प्रवासी *m.* (न्), प्रवसन् *m.* (त्), प्रोषितः, देशान्तरवासी *m.* (न्), देशान्तराधिवासी *m.*, परदेशवासी, देशान्तरसेवी *m.*, परदेशसेवी.

To solace, *v. a.* सान्त्व् or शान्त्व्, आश्वस् in caus., विनुद् (c. 10. -नोदयति -यितुं), *see To* comfort, console; 'to solace one's self,' आत्मानं विनुद्.

Solace, *s.* सान्त्वनं -ना, परिसान्त्वनं, आश्वासनं, विनोदः -दनं, आपत्प्रतीकारः, क्लेशापहरणं, शोकापनोदः -दनं, क्लेशशान्तिः *f.*, शोकशान्तिः *f.*, दुःखशान्तिः *f.*, शोकापहरणं.

Solar, solary, *a.* सौरः -री -रं, सवितृयः -या -यं, सवितृलः -ला -लं, सावनः -नी -नं, सूर्य्यसम्बन्धी -न्धिनी -न्धि (न्), सूर्य्यविषयकः -का -कं, सूर्य्य in comp., अर्क in comp.; 'solary dynasty,' सूर्य्यवंशः; 'solar day,' सौरसावनदिनं, सावनदिनं, सौरदिनं; 'solar month,' सौरमासः, सावनमासः; 'solar year,' सौरवर्षः, अर्कवर्षः.

Sold, *p. p.* विक्रीतः -ता -तं, पणितः &c.; 'having sold,' विक्रीय.

To solder, *v. a.* द्रुतधातुमयलेपेन संलग्नीकृ, द्रुतसीसकादिना सन्धा.

Solder, *s.* द्रुतधातुमयलेपः, द्रुतसीसकादिमयलेपः, धातुमयलेपः.

Soldier, *s.* सैन्यः, सैनिकः, आयुधिकः, आयुधीयः, योद्धा *m.* (द्धृ), योधः, शस्त्रजीवी *m.* (न्), शस्त्राजीवः, शस्त्रधरः, शस्त्रभृत् *m.*, शस्त्रधारी *m.* (न्), शस्त्रोपजीवी *m.*, युद्धोपजीवी *m.*, युद्धजीवी *m.*, अस्त्रधरः, अस्त्रधारी *m.*, अस्त्रभृत् *m.*, अस्त्रजीवः, युधानः, चमूचरः, सेनाचरः, तन्त्री *m.*, काण्डस्पृष्टः, काण्डपृष्ठः; 'man of the military class,' क्षत्रियः, क्षत्रः, क्षत्री *m.*, राजन्यः, राजपुत्रः, विराट् *m.* (ज्).

Soldier-like, soldierly, *a.* सैन्ययोग्यः -ग्या -ग्यं, सैन्योपयुक्तः -क्ता -क्तं, सैनिकः -की -कं, आयुधीयः -या -यं, योधसम्बन्धी &c., सैन्यसम्बन्धी &c.

Soldiery, *s.* सैन्यसमूहः, सैनिकवर्गः, योधसमूहः, राजन्यकं, योद्धृत्वं.

Sole, *s.* (Of the foot) तलं, पादतलं; 'from the sole of the foot to the head,' आपादतलमस्तकात्, आपादमस्तकात्.—(Of a shoe) तलः, पादुकातलः, पादुकाधोभागः.

Sole, *a.* एकः -का -कं, एकाकी -किनी -कि (न्), केवलः -ला -लं, केवली &c., कैवल्यः -ल्या -ल्यं, अद्वितीयः -या -यं. *See* Single.

Solecism, *s.* अपशब्दः, अपभ्रंशः, अशुद्धशब्दः, अशुद्धप्रयोगः, म्लेच्छितं, अपप्रयोगः, अप्रयोगः, अवचनीयता.

Solely, *adv.* केवलं, मात्रं -त्रेण -त्रात्, एकान्ततस्, एकतस्.

Solemn, *a.* (Attended with religious rites) विधिपूर्व्वः -र्व्वा -र्व्वं, देवकर्म्मसहितः -ता -तं, संस्कारसहितः &c., पुण्यविधिसहितः &c., पुण्यसंस्कारसहितः &c., धर्म्मसंस्कारपूर्व्वः -र्व्वा -र्व्वं, धर्म्मसंस्कारसहितः -ता -तं, धर्म्मक्रियासहितः &c.—(Serious, grave) गुरुः -र्व्वी -रु, गुर्व्वर्थः -र्था -र्थं, गम्भीरः -रा -रं, गभीरः &c., गम्भीरार्थः &c., धीरः -रा -रं, अलघुः -घुः -घ्वी -घु.—(Attended with a serious promise, consisting of a solemn asseveration) दृढप्रतिज्ञापूर्व्वः -र्व्वा -र्व्वं, दृढप्रतिज्ञारूपः -पा -पं, गुरुप्रतिज्ञापूर्व्वः &c., दृढनिश्चयपूर्व्वः &c., दृढनिश्चयरूपः &c., दृढनिश्चयात्मकः -का -कं; 'a solemn pledge,' दृढप्रतिज्ञा, अलघुप्रतिज्ञा.

Solemnity, solemnness, *s.* (Seriousness, gravity) गुरुता -त्वं, गौरवं, गम्भीरता, गाम्भीर्य्यं, अलघुता, धीरता.—(Religious ceremony) धर्म्मक्रिया, पुण्यक्रिया, देवक्रिया, संस्कारः, उत्सवः. *See* Rite.

To solemnize, *v. a.* (Perform according to ritual forms) यथाविधि or यथाशास्त्रं कृ or अनुष्ठा (c. 1. -तिष्ठति -ष्ठातुं), विधिवत् कृ or अनुष्ठा or निर्वह् (c. 10. -वाहयति -यितुं), विधिपूर्व्वं कृ or अनुष्ठा.—(Make grave or serious) गम्भीरीकृ, धीरत्वं कृ or जन्, गुरुत्वं or गौरवं कृ or जन्; 'the mind,' चित्तधीरत्वं जन्, चित्तगौरवं कृ.

Solemnly, *adv.* (According to ritual form) यथाविधि, यथाशास्त्रं, विधिवत्, विधिपूर्व्वं, पुण्यविधिपूर्व्वं.—(Seriously) सगौरवं, गौरवेण, गम्भीरं, सगाम्भीर्य्यं, अलघु, अलाघवेन.—(With solemn asseveration) दृढप्रतिज्ञापूर्व्वं, दृढनिश्चयपूर्व्वं, गुरुप्रतिज्ञापूर्व्वं; 'solemnly pledged,' अलघुप्रतिज्ञः -ज्ञा -ज्ञं.

To solicit, *v. a.* प्रार्थ् (c. 10. -अर्थयते -ति -यितुं), अभ्यर्थ्, अर्थ्, विनयेन प्रार्थ् or याच्. *See To* implore, entreat, beg.

Solicitation, *s.* प्रार्थनं -ना, अभ्यर्थना, अर्थः, याचना, सनिः -नी *m. f.*, अध्येषणा; 'affectionate solicitation,' प्रणयः, प्रश्रयः, प्रसरः.

Solicited, *p. p.* प्रार्थितः -ता -तं, अभ्यर्थितः &c., विनयेन याचितः -ता -तं

or उपयाचितः -ता -तं or प्रयाचितः &c. *See* IMPLORED.

SOLICITOR, *s.* प्रार्थयिता *m.* (तृ), प्रार्थकः, याचकः, उपयाचकः.—(Attorney) प्रतिनिधिः *m.*, प्रतिपुरुषः.

SOLICITOUS, *a.* (Eagerly anxious about) उत्सुकः -का -कं, व्यग्रः -ग्रा -ग्रं, उत्कः -त्का -त्कं, उत्कलिकः -ता -तं, सोत्कण्ठः -ण्ठा -ण्ठं.—(Careful, anxious) उद्विग्नः -ग्ना -ग्नं, चिन्तायुक्तः -क्ता -क्तं, चिन्ताग्रस्तः -स्ता -स्तं, चिन्ताक्रान्तः -न्ता -न्तं, विधुरः -रा -रं, चिन्तितः -ता -तं, भावितः &c.

SOLICITUDE, *s.* औत्सुक्यं, उत्सुकता -त्वं, व्यग्रता -त्वं, उत्कण्ठा, उद्विग्नता, उद्वेगः, चिन्ता, चित्तवेदना, हृदयवेदना, अनुध्यानं.

SOLID, *a.* (Hard, firm, compact) घनः -ना -नं, दृढः -ढा -ढं, सुदृढः &c., संहतः -ता -तं, सुसंहतः &c., दृढसन्धिः -न्धिः -न्धि, जरठः -ठा -ठं, ग्रावा -वा -व (न्), कक्खटः -टा -टं, *see* HARD.—(Not hollow) सगर्भः -र्भा -र्भं, गर्भपूर्णः -र्णा -र्णं, अशून्यः -न्या -न्यं.—(Not liquid) अद्रवः -वा -वं, द्रवेतरः -रा -रं, अद्रुतः -ता -तं, घनः -ना -नं, अप्रवाही -हिणी -हि (न्); 'solids,' अद्रवद्रव्याणि *n. pl.*, अद्रवपदार्थाः *m. pl.*—(Substantial) वास्तवः -वी -वं, सारवान् -वती -वत् (त्), घनः -ना -नं; 'solid food,' चर्व्यं; 'solid hoofed,' एकशफः -फा -फं.

SOLID, *s.* (In geometry) घनः; 'its contents,' घनफलं.—(Something not liquid) अद्रवद्रव्यं, अद्रवपदार्थः, घनद्रव्यं, घनपदार्थः.

SOLIDITY, SOLIDNESS, *s.* घनता -त्वं, दृढता -त्वं, संहतत्वं, अद्रवता -त्वं, कठिनता, काठिन्यं, अद्रुतता, अप्रवाहिता.

SOLIDUNGULATE, SOLIDUNGULOUS, *a.* एकशफः -फा -फं, एकखुरः -रा -रं.

SOLILOQUY, *s.* आत्मगतभाषणं, आत्मभाषणं, स्वगतभाषणं, स्वगतवाक्यं.

SOLITARILY, *adv.* विविक्तं, एकान्ततस्, निभृते, रहस्, रहसि, उपांशु.

SOLITARINESS, *s.* विविक्तता, एकान्तत्वं, एकाकित्वं. *See* SOLITUDE.

SOLITARY, SOLITAIRE, *s.* विविक्तवासी *m.* (न्), वनवासी *m. See* RECLUSE.

SOLITARY, *a.* (Living alone, going alone) विविक्तवासी -सिनी -सि (न्), एकान्तवासी &c., विविक्तसेवी &c., एकान्तसेवी &c., विविक्तप्रियः -या -यं, विजनस्थः -स्था -स्थं, विजनसेवी &c., निर्जनस्थः &c., विविक्तचरः -रा -रं, एकचरः &c., एकान्तचरः &c., असंसर्गी -र्गिणी -र्गि, असक्तः -क्ता -क्तं, जनसंसर्गरहितः -ता -तं, जनसंसर्गशून्यः -न्या -न्यं.—(Retired, said of places) निर्जनः -ना -नं, विजनः &c., निर्मनुजः -जा -जं, निर्मनुष्यः -ष्या -ष्यं, विविक्तः -क्ता -क्तं, निभृतः -ता -तं, एकान्तः -न्ता -न्तं, निःशलाकः -का -कं, छन्नः -न्ना -न्नं, छन्दः -न्दा -न्दं, *see* LONELY.—(Single) एकः -का -कं, एकाकी -किनी &c., असहायः -या -यं.

SOLITUDE, *s.* (Lonely state) विविक्तता, विविक्तदशा, विविक्तवृत्तिः *f.*, विविक्तवासित्वं, एकान्तता, एकान्तवृत्तिः *f.*, एकाकिता, जनसंसर्गहीनता, संसर्गाभावः, जनसंसर्गाभावः, असहायता.—(Loneliness, said of places) विविक्तता, निर्जनता, विजनता, निर्मनुष्यता, *see* LONELINESS.—(Lonely place, desert) विविक्तस्थानं, विविक्तस्थलं, अरण्यं, वनं, वल्लुरं, वल्लूरं.

SOLO, *s.* एकाकिगानं, एकाकिगीतं, एकवाद्यस्वरः, एकाकिस्वरः.

SOLSTICE, *s.* अयनं, अयनान्तः, अयनकालः, अयनसन्धिः *m.*, अयनसन्धिकालः, क्रान्तिः *f.*, क्रान्तिकालः; 'summer solstice,' उत्तरायणं, उत्तरक्रान्तिः; 'winter,' दक्षिणायनं, दक्षिणक्रान्तिः *f.*, याम्यायनं.

SOLSTITIAL, *a.* अयनान्तसम्बन्धी -न्धिनी -न्धि (न्), अयनसम्बन्धी &c., क्रान्तिसम्बन्धी &c., अयनान्तकालिकः -का -कं; 'solstitial point,' अयनं, अयनसन्धिः *m.*, अयनान्तः.

SOLUBILITY, SOLUBLENESS, *s.* द्राव्यता -त्वं, विद्राव्यता -त्वं, द्रावणीयता, गलनीयता, गाल्यता -त्वं, विलयनीयता, द्रावणशक्यता.

SOLUBLE, *a.* द्राव्यः -व्या -व्यं, द्रावणीयः -या -यं, विद्राव्यः &c., गाल्यः -ल्या -ल्यं, विलयनीयः -या -यं, द्रावणशक्यः -क्या -क्यं, गलनीयः -या -यं, द्रवार्हः -र्हा -र्हं. *See* DISSOLVABLE.

SOLUTION, *s.* (The act) द्रावणं, विद्रावणं, विलयनं, गलनं, विगलनं.—(The state) द्रवत्वं, द्रुतत्वं, विद्रुतता, विलीनता, समाधानं, संयोगः.—(Chemical union) द्रवमूलकसारूप्यसंयोगः, द्रवमूलकसंयोगः, संयोगः, योगः.—(Explanation) लापनं, लापनिका, व्याख्या-ख्यानं, विख्यापनं, शोधनं, परिशोधनं; 'of a difficult verse,' श्लोकलापनं; 'of a riddle,' छित्तिः *f.*—(Of doubt) संशयनिवृत्तिः *f.*

To SOLVE, *v. a.* (Dissolve) द्रवीकृ, विद्रु in caus., विली in caus.—(Explain, resolve) व्याख्या (c. 2. -ख्याति -तुं), ली in caus. (लापयति -यितुं), लापनं कृ, शुध् (c. 10. शोधयति -यितुं), परिशुध्; 'a problem,' साध् (c. 10. साधयति -यितुं), सिद्धीकृ; 'a doubt,' संशयं छिद् (c. 7. छिनत्ति, छेत्तुं) or उच्छिद्, संशयम् अपनी or अपनुद्.

SOLVED, *p.p.* व्याख्यातः -ता -तं, लापितः &c., छिन्नः -न्ना -न्नं; 'as a problem,' सिद्धः -द्धा -द्धं; 'is solved,' सिध्यति.

SOLVENCY, *s.* ऋणशोधनक्षमता, ऋणशोधनशक्तिः *f.*, ऋणाधिकधनवत्त्वं, ऋणाधिकधनिता, ऋणाधिकधनसम्पत्तिः *f.*, ऋणापकरणक्षमता.

SOLVENT, *a.* (Having the power of dissolving) द्रावकः -का -कं, विद्रावकः &c., द्रावकरः -रा -रं, द्रवकरः &c., स्रावकः -का -कं.—(Able to pay) ऋणशोधनक्षमः -मा -मं, ऋणपरिशोधनक्षमः &c., ऋणापकरणक्षमः &c., ऋणाधिकधनः -ना -नं, ऋणाधिकधनसम्पन्नः -न्ना -न्नं.

SOLVENT, *s.* (Menstruum) द्रावकरसः, योगवाही *m.* (न्), द्रावणं.

SOLVER, *s.* व्याख्याता *m.* (तृ), विख्यापकः, छेत्ता *m.*, उच्छेदी *m.* (न्).

SOMBER, SOMBRE, *a.* न्यूनप्रभः -भा -भं, न्यूनतेजाः -जाः -जः (स्), अल्पतेजाः &c., मन्दप्रभः -भा -भं, मलिनप्रभः &c., धूसरः -री -रं, श्यामः -मा -मं.

SOME, *a.* (A certain quantity of a thing, a small quantity) किञ्चित्, कियत्, ईषत्, अल्पभागः, अल्पांशः, अंशः, अल्पिका, अल्पं; 'some water,' किञ्चिज्जलं, कियज्जलं, ईषज्जलं, जलांशः; 'some seed,' कियन्ति बीजानि; 'some bread,' अपूपांशः, कियान् अपूपः, अपूपाल्पभागः, अपूपस्य अल्पांशः; 'some meat,' किञ्चिन्मांसं, मांसाल्पभागः, मांसाल्पिका; 'for some distance,' कियद्दूरं, कियत्पर्य्यन्तं; 'for some time,' कियत्कालं, किञ्चित्कालं, कतिचित्कालं; 'some time afterwards,' कियत्कालात्परं; 'to some extent,' किञ्चित्, ईषत्.—(A certain number, a few, said of things) अल्पः -ल्पा -ल्पं, कतिपयः -या -यं, कतिचित्, अनेकः -का -कं; 'some days,' कतिपयदिनानि *n. pl.*; 'some paces,' कतिचित्पदानि *n. pl.*, कतिपयपदानि; 'some trees,' कतिपयवृक्षाः *m. pl.*, कतिचिद्वृक्षाः *m. pl.*, कतयश्चिद् वृक्षाः; 'in some trees,' कतिचिद्वृक्षेषु, कतिषुचिद् वृक्षेषु.—(A certain number, few, said of persons) कश्चित् *m. sing.*, काचित् *f.*, कश्चन *m. sing.*, काचन *f.*, को ऽपि *m. sing.*, कापि *f.*, कतिपय in comp., कतिचित्, कतयश्चित् *m. pl.*; 'some persons,' केचित्, केपि, कतिचिज्जनाः *m. pl.*, कतिपयजनाः *m. pl.*, केचिज्जनाः, कतिपयलोकाः *m. pl.*; 'of some persons,' केषाञ्चित्, केषामपि.—(Denoting a person or thing not definite) अमुकः -का -कं, or expressed by the affixes चित्, अपि or चन after the interrogative; as, 'some person,' अमुकजनः, कश्चित्, कश्चिज्जनः; 'having some name or other,' अमुकनामा *m.* (न्); 'some place or other,' अमुकस्थानं, किञ्चित्स्थानं; 'some day,' कदाचित्, कदापि; 'by some means or other,' *see* the next.

SOME-HOW, *adv.* कथञ्चित्, कथञ्चन, कथमपि, कथं कथमपि, यथाकथञ्चित्.

SOME-ONE, SOME-BODY, *s.* कश्चित् *m.*, काचित् *f.*, को ऽपि *m.*, कापि *f.*, कश्चन *m.*, काचन *f.*, कश्चिज्जनः, को ऽपि जनः, अमुकः *m.*, अमुका, अमुकजनः, यः कश्चित्, यः कश्चन; 'of some one,' कस्यचित्, कस्यापि; 'by some one,' केनचित्, केनापि; 'to some one,' कस्मैचित्.

SOMER-SAULT, SOMERSET, *s.* ऊर्द्धपादवलितं, ऊर्द्धचरणवलितं.

SOMETHING, *s.* किञ्चित्, किमपि, किञ्चन, यत्किञ्चित्, अल्पं, स्वल्पं.

SOMETIME, *adv.* (Formerly) पुरा, पूर्व्वं, पूर्व्वकाले, पुरस्तात्, प्राक्.—(At some future time) परकाले, अतःपरं, *see* HEREAFTER.

SOMETIMES, *adv.* कदाचित्, कदापि, कदाचन, कर्हिचित्, जातु.

SOMEWHAT, *s.* किञ्चित्, किमपि, किञ्चन, यत्किञ्चित्. *See* LITTLE, *s.*

SOMEWHAT, *adv.* किञ्चित्, ईषत्, कियत्, आ prefixed, कल्प or देश्य or देशीय affixed; 'somewhat less,' किञ्चिन्न्यूनः -ना -नं, ईषदूनः &c.; 'somewhat eloquent,' पटुकल्पः -ल्पा -ल्पं, पटुदेश्यः -श्या -श्यं, पटुदेशीयः -या -यं; 'somewhat blue,' आनीलः -ला -लं; 'somewhat ruddy,' आताम्रः -म्रा -म्रं.

SOMEWHERE, *adv.* क्वचित्, क्वापि, कुत्रचित्, कुत्रापि, कुत्रचन, यत्रकुत्रचित्, यत्रकुत्रापि; 'from somewhere,' कुतश्चित्, कुतश्चन.

SOMNAMBULISM, *s.* निद्राचारः, निद्रापरिक्रमः, निद्राभ्रमणं, स्वप्नचारः.

SOMNAMBULIST, *s.* निद्राचारी *m.* (न्), निद्रापरिक्रमी *m.*, स्वप्नचारी *m.*

SOMNIFEROUS, SOMNIFIC, *a.* निद्राकरः -री -रं, स्वप्नकारी -रिणी -रि (न्), स्वप्नकृत् *m.f.n.*, निद्राजनकः -का -कं, स्वप्नजनकः &c., सुप्तिजनकः &c., सुप्तिकारकः &c., सौप्तिकः -की -कं, नैद्रः -द्री -द्रं.

SOMNILOQUIST, *s.* निद्राभाषी *m.* (न्), निद्रालापी *m.*, स्वप्नभाषी *m.*

SOMNILOQUISM, *s.* निद्राभाषणं, निद्रालापः, स्वप्नभाषणं, स्वप्नप्रलापः.

SOMNOLENCY, SOMNOLENT, *see* SLEEPINESS, SLEEPY.

SON, *s.* पुत्रः, पुत्रकः, सुतः, सूनुः *m.*, तनयः, नन्दनः, आत्मजः, स्वजः, आत्मसम्भवः, अङ्गजः, शरीरजः, तनुजः, तनूजः, तनूजनिः *m.*, प्रसूतः, दारकः, कुमारः, उद्वहः; 'legitimate son,' औरसः, औरस्यः, उरस्यः; 'son of a rival wife,' सापत्नः; 'of an auspicious mother,' सुभगासुतः; 'of an unmarried woman,' कन्यकाजातः, कानीनः; 'by another's wife,' पारस्त्रैणेयः; 'dutiful and affectionate son,' सत्पुत्रः, सुपुत्रः; 'having a son,' पुत्री *m.* -त्रिणी *f.* (न्), पुत्रवान् *m.* -वती (त्), सपुत्रः -त्रा; 'rejoicing on the birth of a son,' पुत्रोत्सवः, पुत्रानन्दः; 'son and daughter,' पुत्रौ *m. du.*

SON-IN-LAW, *s.* जामाता *m.* (तृ), दुहितुःपतिः *m.*, दुहितृभर्त्ता *m.* (र्तृ), पुत्रिकाभर्त्ता *m.*, विट्पतिः *m.*, विवाह्यः.

SONG, *s.* गीतं, गानं, गीतिः *f.*, गायनं, गेयं, गाथा, गा, गं, खेलिः *f.*, काकली; 'song with music,' सङ्गीतं, सङ्गीतिः *f.*; 'holy song,' सद्गीतं; 'sweet song,' मधुरगीतं; 'song of victory,' जयशब्दः.

SONGSTER, *s.* गायकः, गाथकः, गाथिकः, गीतकुशलः, *see* SINGER.—(Bird) गायकपक्षी *m.* (न्).

SONLESS, *a.* निष्पुत्रः -त्रा -त्रं, अपुत्रः &c., पुत्रहीनः -ना -नं, अपुत्रकः -का -कं, अपुत्री -त्रिणी -त्रि (न्), अपुत्रीकः -का -कं, पुत्ररहितः -ता -तं.

SONNET, *s.* गीतकं, गीतिका, लघुगीतकं, लघुकविता, काव्यबन्धः.

SONOROUS, SONORIFIC, *a.* शब्दनः -ना -नं, शब्दकारः -री -रं, शब्दकरः -रा -रं, ध्वनिकरः &c., ध्वनिकारकः -का -कं, शब्दजनकः -का -कं, नादजनकः &c., शाब्दः -ब्दी -ब्दं, मुखरः -रा -रं, महाशब्दः -ब्दा -ब्दं, नादी -दिनी &c., रवणः -णा -णं.

SONOROUSLY, *adv.* महाशब्देन, महानादेन, महाशब्दपूर्व्वं, महाध्वनिपूर्व्वं.

SONOROUSNESS, *s.* शब्दनत्वं, महाशब्दत्वं, शब्दजनकत्वं, मुखरता.

SONSHIP, *s.* पुत्रत्वं, पुत्रभावः, पुत्रावस्था, पुत्रदशा, पुत्रधर्म्मः.

SOON, *adv.* (In a short time) अचिरेण, अचिरात्, आशु, सद्यस्, अनन्तरं, शीघ्रं, झटिति, सपदि, अञ्जसा, द्राक्, न चिरेण, न चिरात्, माचिरं, हठात्, अदूरात्.—(Without delay) अविलम्बेन, अविलम्बितं, अकालक्षेपेण; 'as soon as,' यावत्, followed by 'so soon,' तावत्, or expressed by च, repeated thus, 'as soon as water was asked, so soon a shower fell into his mouth,' यावद् अम्बु याचितं तावद् धारा मुखे तस्य निपतिता or अम्बु च याचितं धारा च मुखे तस्य निपतिता; or expressed by साक्षात्, *see* IMMEDIATELY.—(Readily, willingly) कामं, प्रकामं.

SOONER, *adv.* (Rather) वरं, *see* RATHER; 'sooner or later,' आदिपश्चात्.

SOOT, *s.* कज्जलं, कज्ज्वलं, दीपकज्जलं, दीपकिट्टं, दीपध्वजः, मषी.

SOOTH, *s.* (Truth) सत्यं, सत्यता; 'in sooth,' सत्यं, सत्यमेव.

To SOOTHE, *v. a.* शम् (c. 10. शमयति -यितुं), उपशम्, प्रशम्, सान्त्व् or शान्त्व् (c. 10. सान्त्वयति -यितुं), उपसान्त्व्, अभिशान्त्व्, साम् (c. 10. सामयति -यितुं), लल् (c. 10. लालयति -यितुं), अनुनी (c. 1. -नयति -नेतुं), परिमृश्, परामृश्, प्रसद् (c. 10. -सादयति -यितुं), अभिप्रसद्, विनुद् in caus., आश्वस् in caus., चप् (c. 1. चपति -पितुं).

SOOTHED, *p. p.* शमितः -ता -तं, शान्तः -न्ता -न्तं, उपशान्तः &c., कृतशान्तिः -न्तिः -न्ति, कृतसान्त्वनः -ना -नं, लालितः -ता -तं, अनुनीतः &c., विनोदितः &c.

SOOTHER, *s.* शमकः, उपशमकः, सान्त्वनकृत्, सान्त्वयिता *m.* (तृ), लालकः.

SOOTHING, *s.* शमनं, शमः, प्रशमनं, उपशमः -मनं, सान्त्वनं -ना, शान्तिः *f.*, सान्त्वः, लालनं, विनोदः -दनं, तापहरणं, प्रसादनं, आश्वासनं.

SOOTHING, *part.* or *a.* शमकः -का -कं, उपशमकः &c., शान्तिकः -की -कं, शमी -मिनी -मि (न्), शमकारी -रिणी &c., शान्तिकरः -रा -रं, सान्त्वनकरः -रा -रं, लाली &c., आश्वासनशीलः -ला -लं, तापहरः -रा -रं, तापहारी &c.

SOOTHSAYER, *s.* दैवज्ञः, सांवत्सरिकः, सावित्रकः. *See* DIVINER.

SOOTHSAYING, *s.* शकुनपरीक्षणं, गणना, दैवज्ञानं. *See* DIVINATION.

SOOTY, *a.* कज्जली -लिनी -लि (न्), कज्जलदूषितः -ता -तं, मषीमयः -यी -यं.

SOP, *s.* यूषादिसिक्तः पिष्टकखण्डः, यूषादिसिक्तः पूपखण्डः or अपूपखण्डः, यूषसिक्तपिष्टकः, जलादिसिक्तपूपखण्डः, सिक्तपिष्टकः, आर्द्रपिष्टकः.

To SOP, *v. a.* अपूपखण्डं or पिष्टकखण्डं यूषादिना सिच् or आर्द्रीकृ.

SOPHIST, SOPHISTER, *s.* आभासवादी *m.* (न्), सिद्धान्ताभासवादी *m.*, सत्याभासवादी *m.*, हेत्वाभासवादी *m.*, हैतुकः, तार्किकः, जल्पकः, चार्वाकः, मिथ्याहेतुवादी *m.*

SOPHISTIC, SOPHISTICAL, *a.* आभासात्मकः -का -कं, सत्याभासकः -का -कं, सिद्धान्ताभासकः &c., सत्याभासी -सिनी -सि (न्), सत्यप्रतिभासकः &c., हेत्वाभासरूपः -पा -पं, हैतुकः -की -कं.

SOPHISTRY, SOPHISM, *s.* आभासः, हेत्वाभासः, सिद्धान्ताभासः, सत्याभासः, पक्षाभासः, प्रतिभासः, सिद्धान्तप्रतिभासः, मिथ्याहेतुः *m.*, वाक्छलं, मक्षिका.

To SOPHISTICATE, *v. a.* अशुद्धद्रव्यसंसर्गेण दुष् (c. 10. दूषयति -यितुं), हीनद्रव्यमिश्रणेन दुष्, दुष्टद्रव्यसम्पर्केण भ्रष्टीकृ.

SOPHISTICATED, *a.* हीनसंसर्गदूषितः -ता -तं, अशुद्धसम्पर्कदूषितः &c., दूषितः &c.

SOPORIFIC, SOPORIFEROUS, *a.* निद्राकारकः -का -कं, निद्राकारी -रिणी -रि (न्), निद्राजनकः -का -कं, उपशायी &c., स्वापनः -ना -नं. *See* SOMNIFEROUS.

SOPPED, *p. p.* यूषादिसिक्तः -क्ता -क्तं, यूषादिसिक्तः &c., जलादिसिक्तः &c.

SORCERER, *s.* अभिचारविद् *m.*, अभिचारी *m.* (न्), मायाकारः. *See* MAGICIAN.

SORCERESS, *s.* मायिनी, मायाकारिणी, माया, पूतना, अभिचारिणी.

SORCERY, *s.* अभिचारः, अभिचारविद्या, मायाविद्या, माया, मायाक्रिया, यज्ञक्रिया, कुविद्या, कुसृतिः *f.*, संवदनं, योगः. *See* MAGIC.

SORDID, *a.* (Filthy) मलिनः -ना -नं, मलवान् -वती -वत् (त्), मलीमसः -सा -सं.—(Mean, vile) कुत्सितः -ता -तं, जघन्यः -न्या -न्यं, जघन्यवृत्तिः -त्तिः -त्ति, अधमः -मा -मं, *see* MEAN, *a.*

SORDIDNESS, *s.* मलिनत्वं, कुत्सितत्वं, जघन्यता, पामरता, अपकृष्टता.

SORE, *s.* क्षतं, व्रणः, त्वक्क्षतं, त्वग्व्रणः, अरुस् *n.*, ईर्म्मं, त्वक्कक्षुरः, विपादिका; 'pain of a sore,' व्रणवेदना; 'cleansing or cicatrising of one,' व्रणशोधनं; 'having one,' व्रणी -णिनी &c.; 'causing one,' व्रणकृत्.

SORE, *a.* (Tender to the touch) स्पर्शासहः -हा -हं, स्पर्शासहनः -ना -नं, स्पर्शार्त्तः -र्त्ता -र्त्तं, स्पर्शदुःखितः -ता -तं; 'a sore eye,' चुल्लः, चिल्लः, पिल्लः; 'having sore eyes,' चुल्लः -ल्ली -ल्लं, चिल्लः -ल्ली -ल्लं, पिल्लः -ल्ली -ल्लं, क्लिन्नाक्षः -क्षा -क्षं.—(Painful, easily pained) वेदनायुक्तः -क्ता -क्तं, सवेदनः -ना -नं, सुलभवेदनः -ना -नं, सुलभव्यथः -था -थं.—(In mind) मनोदुःखी -खिनी -खि (न्), सुलभदुःखः -खा -खं, सुलभतापः -पा -पं.—(Grievous) उग्रः -ग्रा -ग्रं, उग्रक्लेशदः -दा -दं, गुरुक्लेशदः &c., क्लेशदः &c., गुरुः -र्वी -रु.

SORE, SORELY, *adv.* अत्यन्तं, अतिशयेन, अतिशय in comp., उग्रं, भृशं, *see* INTENSELY; 'sorely-grieved,' उग्रशोकः -का -कं.

SORENESS, *s.* स्पर्शासहत्वं, स्पर्शासहनत्वं, स्पर्शार्त्तत्वं, सव्रणत्वं, क्षतत्वं.

SORREL, *s.* अम्लवेतसः, चुक्रः, चुक्रिका, दलाम्लं, शुक्ता, शतवेधी *m.*, सहस्रवेधी *m.* (न्), लोलिका.

SORROW, *s.* शोकः, खेदः, दुःखं, मनोदुःखं, शुच् *f.* (च्), क्लेशः, मन्युः *m.*, शोचनं, मनस्तापः, आधिः *m.*, *see* GRIEF; 'freed from all sorrow,' शोकमुक्तः -क्ता -क्तं, आधिव्याधिनिर्मुक्तः &c.

To SORROW, *v. n.* शुच् (c. 1. शोचति -चितुं), शोचनं कृ, खिद् (c. 4. खिद्यते, खेत्तुं), *see To* GRIEVE, *v. n.*; 'to sorrow much,' शुच् in freq. (शोशुच्यते).

SORROWFUL, *a.* शोकार्त्तः -र्त्ता -र्त्तं, शोकान्वितः -ता -तं, शोकी -किनी -कि (न्), शोकोपेतः -ता -तं, सशोकः -का -कं, दुःखी &c., दुःखान्वितः -ता -तं, दुःखार्त्तः &c., दुःखोपेतः -ता -तं, शोचनः -ना -नं, शोचितः -ता -तं, शोकयुक्तः -क्ता -क्तं, उद्विग्नः -ग्ना -ग्नं, उद्विग्नमनाः -नाः -नः (स्), दुर्मनाः &c., विमनाः &c., उद्विग्नचित्तः -त्ता -त्तं, उदासीनः -ना -नं, उदासी &c., विषादी &c., विषण्णः -ण्णा -ण्णं, समन्युः -न्युः -न्यु, प्रमन्युः &c., परिद्यूनः -ना -नं, *see* SAD.—(Causing sorrow) शोकजनकः -का -कं, शोकदः -दा -दं, दुःखावहः &c., *see* MOURNFUL.

SORROWFULLY, *adv.* सशोकं, सखेदं, सदुःखं, सोद्वेगं, शोकेन, शोकपूर्व्वं.

SORROW-STRICKEN, *a.* शोकार्त्तः -र्त्ता -र्त्तं, शोकातुरः -रा -रं, शोकोपहतः -ता -तं.

SORRY, *a.* (Grieved) दुःखी -खिनी -खि (न्), दुःखितः -ता -तं, *see* GRIEVED.—(Sorry for one's own conduct, pained) अनुतापी &c., पश्चात्तापी &c., अनुतप्तः -प्ता -प्तं, अनुशोचकः -का -कं, अनुशयी &c., सानुशयः -या -यं, जातानुशोकः -का -कं, जातानुतापः -पा -पं, जातानुशयः -या -यं, जातखेदः -दा -दं, खेदयुक्तः -क्ता -क्तं, अनुतापयुक्तः &c.; 'to be sorry,' *see To* REPENT.—(Poor, wretched) तुच्छः -च्छा -च्छं, कृपणः -णा -णं, कुत्सितः -ता -तं or expressed by the affixes क, र, क्र, कल्प, पाश, देशीय, or by the prefixes दुर्, कु, कद् &c.; as, 'a sorry horse,' अश्वतरः, अश्वकः; 'a sorry ox,' वृषभतरः; 'a sorry poet,' कविकल्पः, कुकविः; 'sorry fare,' कदन्नं; 'a sorry wench,' पापीयसी.

SORT, *s.* प्रकारः, जातिः *f.*, भेदः, विधः, व्यक्तिः *f.*, *see* KIND, MANNER.

To SORT, *v. a.* जातिक्रमेण or वर्गक्रमेण or यथावर्गं विरच् (c. 10. -रचयति -यितुं), यथावर्गं or वर्गक्रमेण विन्यस् (c. 4. -अस्यति -सितुं) or व्यस्.

To SORT, *v. n.* युज् in pass. (युज्यते), उपपद् in pass. (-पद्यते). *See To* SUIT.

SOT, SOTTISH, *s.* or *a.* पानासक्तः -क्ता -क्तं, मद्यासक्तः &c., पामरः -रा -रं, सदापायी -यिनी -यि (न्), पानजडः -डा -डं, मद्यपानजडः &c., पानमूढः &c.

SOTTISHNESS, *s.* पानासक्तिः *f.*, मद्यासक्तिः *f.*, पानजडता, पानमूढता.

SOUGHT, *p. p.* अन्विष्टः -ष्टा -ष्टं, अन्वेषितः -ता -तं, मार्गितः -ता -तं, मृगितः &c., इष्टः -ष्टा -ष्टं, गवेषितः -ता -तं; 'long sought for,' चिरवेष्टितः -ता -तं; 'is sought,' अन्विष्यते, इष्यते.

SOUL, *s.* (The immortal essence viewed as an emanation from the Deity) आत्मा *m.* (न्), परमात्मा *m.*, अन्तरात्मा *m.*, चिदात्मा *m.*, अन्तर्यामी *m.* (न्), सच्चिदंशः, चित्कला, चिदाभासः; 'of the universe,' ब्रह्म *n.* (न्), परमात्मा *m.*—(The spirit, vital or intellectual principle) आत्मा *m.* (न्), जीवात्मा *m.*, मनस् *n.*, चेतस्, चित् *f.*, चैतन्यं, चेतनः -ना, प्राणः, जीवः, प्राणात्मा *m.*, शरीरी *m.* (न्), देहवान् *m.* (त्), देही *m.*, शारीरं, पुरुषः, क्षेत्रज्ञः, चैतन्यकारणं, जीवनकला, परसंज्ञकः, धियाम्पतिः *m.*, सबीजः, पुद्गलः; 'union of soul and body,' चिच्छरीरसंयोगः; 'seated in the soul,' आत्मनिष्ठः -ष्ठा -ष्ठं; 'oneness of soul,' आत्मैक्यं, ऐकभावः, तादात्म्यं; 'knowledge of soul,' आत्मज्ञानं, आत्मविद्या; 'the whole soul,' सर्व्वात्मा *m.*, सर्व्वभावः; 'with one's whole soul,' सर्व्वभावेन.—(Self) आत्मा *m.* (न्) स्वः.—(Essence, chief part) सारः, सारांशः, सारता, सारभागः, तत्त्वांशः, सत्त्वांशः, सत्त्वं, तत्त्वार्थं.—(Fire, spirit, life) तेजस् *n.*, सत्त्वं, वीर्य्यं.—(Departed soul) प्रेतः, परेतः, प्रेतनरः, नारकः.—(Person), *see* the word.

SOUND, *a.* (Entire, undecayed) अविकलः -ला -लं, अक्षतः -ता -तं, अभिन्नः -न्ना -न्नं, अखण्डः -ण्डा -ण्डं, अन्यूनः -ना -नं.—(Not diseased, hale) निरामयः -या -यं, अनामयः &c., कल्यः -ल्या -ल्यं, नीरोगः -गा -गं, नीरुजः -जा -जं, अरोगी -गिणी -गि (न्), अरुग्णः -ग्णा -ग्णं, सुस्थः -स्था -स्थं, चङ्गः -ङ्गा -ङ्गं.—(Not hurt) अक्षतः -ता -तं, अपरिक्षतः &c., अजातक्षतः &c., क्षतहीनः -ना -नं, निर्व्रणः -णा -णं, व्रणहीनः -ना -नं, अव्रणः &c., अक्षुण्णः -ण्णा -ण्णं.—(In good condition, safe and sound) सुस्थः -स्था -स्थं, सुस्थितः -ता -तं, अनामयः -या -यं, सुरक्षितः -ता -तं.—(Without flaw) निर्दोषः -षा -षं, दोषहीनः -ना -नं, अनघः -घा -घं, निश्छिद्रः -द्रा -द्रं, विशुद्धः -द्धा -द्धं.—(Correct in views) सत्पथवर्त्ती &c., सत्पथानुसारी &c., सत्यमतधारी &c., *see* ORTHODOX.—(Valid, not to be refuted) अखण्डनीयः -या -यं, अखण्ड्यः -ण्ड्या -ण्ड्यं, सुप्रमाणः -णा -णं, सुप्रमाणवान् -वती &c., सप्रमाणः &c., प्रमाणोपेतः -ता -तं, दृढप्रमाणः &c., धर्म्यः -र्म्या -र्म्यं, युक्तिसिद्धः -द्धा -द्धं.—(Fast, deep, heavy) गाढः -ढा -ढं, निर्भरः -रा -रं, अतिशय or सु or अति prefixed; 'a sound sleep,' सुनिद्रा &c., *see* under SLEEP; 'a sound beating,' अतिताडनं, अतिशयताडनं.

SOUND, *s.* (Noise) शब्दः, ध्वनिः *m.*, स्वनः, निस्वनः, निस्वानः, स्वानः, नादः, निनादः, निनदः, वादितं, अनुनादः, निह्रादः, संह्रादः, निर्घोषः

घोषः, निर्घोषः, रवः, रावः, आरावः, विरावः, संरावः, आरवः, स्वरः, ध्वानः, ध्वनः, निध्वानः, स्वनिः *m.*, स्वनितं, क्वणः, रणः, कुणितं, धुः *m.*, *see* NOISE; 'a mere sound,' शब्दमात्रं; 'musical sound,' क्वणः, क्वाणः, क्वणनं, निक्वणः, निक्वाणः, वादः -दनं; 'of a lute,' प्रक्वाणः, प्रक्वणः; 'tinkling sound,' शिञ्जितं; 'rustling sound,' मर्म्मरः; 'confused sound,' कोलाहलः, कलकलः; 'auspicious,' जयध्वनिः *m.*; 'deep or hollow,' गम्भीरशब्दः, गम्भीरनादः; 'prolonged,' दीर्घनादः, दीर्घरावः.

To SOUND, *v. a.* (Cause to make a noise) ध्वन् (c. 10. ध्वनयति -यितुं), स्वन् (c. 10. स्वनयति -यितुं), नद् (c. 10. नादयति -यितुं), विनद्, अनुनद्, स्तन् (c. 10. स्तनयति -यितुं), शब्दनं कृ, ध्वननं कृ; 'a musical instrument,' वद् (c. 10. वादयति -यितुं), संवद्, वादनं कृ; 'they sounded the conchs and drums,' शङ्खान् पटहांश्च समवादयन्.—(Spread by report), *see To* NOISE.—(Try, examine) परीक्ष् (c. 1. -ईक्षते -क्षितुं), ज्ञा in des. (जिज्ञासते -सितुं), निरूप्, *see To* TRY.—(The depth of water) लम्बसूत्रेण जलवेधं or जलं परिमा (c. 2. -माति -तुं, c. 10. -मापयति -यितुं), लम्बेन जलगाम्भीर्यं परिमा, सूत्रेण or रज्जुना जलपरिमापणं कृ or जलवेधपरीक्षां कृ.

To SOUND, *v. n.* ध्वन् (c. 1. ध्वनति -नितुं), स्वन् (c. 1. स्वनति -नितुं), क्वण् (c. 1. क्वणति -णितुं), स्तन् (c. 1. स्तनति -नितुं), नद् (c. 1. नदति -दितुं), प्रणद्, विनद्, शब्द् (c. 10. शब्दयति -यितुं), रस् (c. 1. रसति -सितुं), ह्राद् (c. 1. ह्रादते -दितुं), रु (c. 2. रौति, रवितुं), विरु, रेभ् (c. 1. रेभते -भितुं), शब्दं कृ, नादं कृ, ध्वनिं कृ.

SOUNDED, *p. p.* (Caused to sound) ध्वनितः -ता -तं, स्वनितः &c., शब्दितः &c., क्वणितः &c., नादितः &c., स्वान्तः -न्ता -न्तं, ध्वान्तः &c., स्वरितः -ता -तं, विरेभितः &c.; 'as a musical instrument,' वादितः -ता -तं.—(Tried) परीक्षितः -ता -तं, जिज्ञासितः &c., निरूपितः &c.—(As water) लम्बसूत्रपरिमापितः -ता -तं, लम्बपरिमापितः &c.

SOUNDING, *part.* or *a.* (Making a noise) शब्दनः -ना -नं, शब्दकरः -रा -रं, नादी -दिनी -दि (न्), निर्ह्रादी &c., संह्रादी &c., स्वनवान् -वती -वत् (त्), सनादः -दा -दं, शब्दायमानः -ना -नं, *see* SONOROUS.—(Causing to sound) वादकः -का -कं, वादनकारी &c.

SOUNDING, *s.* (Causing to sound) शब्दनं, ध्वननं, वादनं, संवादनं.—(Of the depth of water) जलपरिमापणं, जलवेधपरिमापणं; 'soundings,' गाधः, गाधस्थलं; 'mean soundings,' समरज्जुः *f.*

SOUNDING-LEAD, *s.* लम्बः, लम्बकः, लम्बसीसकं. *See* PLUMMET.

SOUNDLY, *adv.* गाढं, बाढं, निर्भरं, दृढं, सुखेन, सु or अति or अतिशय prefixed; 'soundly asleep,' सुसुप्तः &c., *see* under SLEEP.

SOUNDNESS, *s.* (Entireness) अक्षतत्वं, अभिन्नता, अखण्डत्वं, अविकलता, अवैकल्यं.—(State of being healthy or without hurt) कल्यत्वं -ता, निरामयत्वं, अनामयत्वं, स्वास्थ्यं, सुस्थता, सुस्थितिः *f.*, अरोगिता, आरोग्यं, रोगाभावः, अक्षतत्वं, क्षताभावः, व्रणाभावः, क्षतहीनता, निर्व्रणत्वं.—(Validity) अखण्डनीयता, सप्रमाणत्वं.—(Correctness in views) सत्यपथानुसरणं, सत्पथः, सत्यधर्म्मः, *see* ORTHODOXY.—(State of being without flaw) निर्दोषत्वं, दोषहीनता, छिद्रहीनता.

SOUP, *s.* यूषं, यूषः -षं, सूपः, मांसयूषं, निष्क्वाथः, पिच्छिलः.

SOUR, *a.* (Acid) अम्लः -म्ला -म्लं, अम्लरसः -सा -सं, शुक्तः -क्ता -क्तं, शौक्तः -क्ती -क्तं, शौक्तिकः -की -कं, शठः -ठा -ठं, अरुन्तुदः -दा -दं.—(In temper) कर्कशः -शा -शं, कर्कशस्वभावः -वा -वं, वक्रस्वभावः &c., असदाचक्रः -क्रा -क्रं, अरुन्तुदः &c.

To SOUR, *v. a.* (Make acid) अम्लीकृ, शुक्तीकृ, शठीकृ, अम्लरसीकृ.—(Make cross) कर्कशीकृ, वक्रीकृ.

To SOUR, *v. n.* अम्लीभू, शुक्तीभू, अम्लरसीभू, कर्कशीभू, अरुन्तुदीभू.

SOURCE, *s.* (Origin, spring) मूलं, योनिः *m. f.*, उद्भवः, सम्भवः, प्रभवः, हेतुः *m.*, बीजं, गर्भः, आदिः *m.*, उद्गमः, उद्गमस्थानं, उत्पत्तिस्थानं; 'of a river,' सरिन्मुखं; 'the source of the Ganges is in the Himálayas,' गङ्गा हिमवत्प्रभवा or हिमवान् गङ्गायाः प्रभवः.

SOURED, *p. p.* अम्लीभूतः -ता -तं, शुक्तीभूतः &c., कर्कशीभूतः -ता -तं.

SOURISH, *a.* ईषदम्लः -म्ला -म्लं, ईषदम्लरसोपेतः -ता -तं, किञ्चिदम्लः &c.

SOURNESS, *s.* अम्लता -त्वं, अम्लभावः, अम्लः, शुक्तता -त्वं, शठता, चुक्रः.—(Of temper) कर्कशत्वं, कार्कश्यं, भाववक्रता, सदावक्रता.

To SOUSE, *v. a.* (Plunge suddenly) अकस्मात् मस्ज् (c. 10. मज्जयति -यितुं) or निमस्ज् or प्लु in caus. or जलेन सिच्, *see To* IMMERSE.

To SOUSE, *v. n.* (As a hawk) वेगेन पतित्वा नखैर् ग्रह्, *see To* POUNCE.

SOUTH, *s.* दक्षिणा, दक्षिणाशा, दक्षिणदिशा, दक्षिणदिक् *f.* (श्), दक्षिणापथः, दक्षिणापथः, अवाची, अपाची, याम्या; 'lying or pointing towards the south,' दक्षिणस्थः -स्था -स्थं, दक्षिणाभिमुखः -खी -खं, दक्षिणामुखः &c., दक्षिणाप्रवणः -णा -णं, दक्षिणाग्रः -ग्रा -ग्रं, दक्षिणादिश्यः -श्या -श्यं, दक्षिणदिक्स्थः &c.; 'lying to the north and south,' दक्षिणोत्तरस्थः &c., दक्षिणोत्तरः -रा -रं. According to the Hindús, Yama is the Regent of the south.

SOUTH, SOUTHERN, SOUTHERLY, *a.* (Lying towards the south), *see* the last.—(Belonging to the south) दक्षिणः -णी -णं, दाक्षिणः -णी -णं, अवाङ् -वाची -वाक् (च्), अवाचीनः -ना -नं, अवाच्यः -च्या -च्यं, दाक्षिणात्यः -त्या -त्यं, दाक्षिणिकः -की -कं, अप्यः -प्या -प्यं, अपाङ् -पाची -पाक् (च्), अपाचीनः &c., अपाच्यः &c., दक्षिणदेशीयः -या -यं; 'the southern mountain,' दक्षिणाचलः; 'in a southerly direction,' दक्षिणदिशि.

SOUTH-EAST, *s.* दक्षिणपूर्व्वा, प्रागवाची, दक्षिणप्राची, प्राग्दक्षिणा, आग्नेयी. Agni is the Regent of the S. E. quarter.

SOUTH-EAST, SOUTH-EASTERN, SOUTH-EASTERLY, *a.* दक्षिणपूर्व्वः -र्व्वा -र्व्वं, प्रागवाङ् -वाची -वाक् (च्), प्रागवाचीनः -ना -नं, दक्षिणपूर्व्वस्थः -स्था -स्थं, आग्नेयः -यी -यं.

SOUTH-WARD, *adv.* दक्षिणतस्, दक्षिणात्, दक्षिणेन, दक्षिणदिशि.

SOUTH-WEST, *s.* नैर्ऋतिः *f.*, निर्ऋतिः *f.*, दक्षिणपश्चिमा, दक्षिणप्रतीची, पश्चादवाची. The demon Nairṛita or Nirṛiti is the Regent of the S. W. quarter.

SOUTH-WEST, SOUTH-WESTERN, SOUTH-WESTERLY, *a.* दक्षिणपश्चिमः -मा -मं, दक्षिणप्रतीचीनः -ना -नं, दक्षिणपाश्चात्यः -त्या -त्यं, नैर्ऋतिस्थः -स्था -स्थं.

SOUTHERN-WOOD, *s.* (Artemisia) दमनः, दमनकः.

SOUVENIR, *s.* स्मरणार्थकदानं, स्मारकदानं. *See* MEMENTO, MEMORIAL.

SOVEREIGN, *s.* राजा *m.* (न्), महाराजः, अधिराजः, अधिपतिः *m.*, अधीश्वरः, परमराजः, सर्व्वाधिकारी *m.* (न्), सर्व्वेश्वरः, अधीशः. *See* KING.

SOVEREIGN, *a.* परमः -मा -मं, मुख्यः -ख्या -ख्यं, श्रेष्ठः -ष्ठा -ष्ठं, सर्व्वश्रेष्ठः &c., प्रमुखः -खा -खं, प्रधान in comp., *see* PARAMOUNT, SUPREME; 'a sovereign remedy,' महौषधं, परमौषधं, सर्व्वरोगौषधं.

SOVEREIGNTY, *s.* राज्यं, राजत्वं, आधिपत्यं, आधिराज्यं, मुख्याधिकारः, श्रेष्ठाधिकारः, प्रधानाधिकारः, सर्व्वाधिकारः, प्रभुत्वं, स्वाम्यं, ईशत्वं, साम्राज्यं, राजभूयं, भूमिपतित्वं, पार्थिवेन्द्रता; 'over the beasts,' मृगेन्द्रता.

SOW, *s.* शूकरी, सूकरी, वराही, कोली, पङ्कक्रीडा.

To sow, *v. a.* or *n.* (As seed) वप् (c. 1. वपति, वप्तुं), आवप्, निवप्, प्रवप्, संवप्, बीजानि क्षेत्रे विकॄ (c. 6. -किरति -करितुं -रीतुं) or प्रकॄ or कॄ or रुह् in caus. (रोपयति -यितुं) or आरुह्, बीजारोपं कृ, बीजारोपणं कृ, बीजविकिरणं कृ, बीजप्रकिरणं कृ, वपनं कृ, वापं कृ; 'as you sow so shall you reap,' यथा वपनं तथा फलसिद्धिः, यथानुष्ठानं तथा सिद्धिः, कर्मानुसारी लाभः.—(To sow discord) भेदं कृ or जन्.

Sower, *s.* वप्ता *m.* (प्तृ), बीजवप्ता, वापी *m.* (न्), प्रवापी *m.*, वापकः, वपनकृत् *m.*, वपनकर्त्ता *m.* (र्त्तृ), उप्तिकर्त्ता *m.*, बीजारोपकः, बीजारोपणकृत्.

Sowing, *s.* वपनं, वापः, उप्तिः *f.*, बीजारोपः -पणं, बीजविकिरणं.

Sowing-time, *s.* वपनकालः, उप्तिकालः, वापकालः, बीजारोपकालः.

Sown, sowed, *p. p.* उप्तः -प्ता -प्तं, वापितः -ता -तं, पर्युप्तः &c., बीजविकीर्णः -र्णा -र्णं, बीजप्रकीर्णः &c., बीजाकीर्णः &c., बीजितः -ता -तं, उप्यमानः -ना -नं, उप्रिमः -मा -मं; 'is sown,' उप्यते, रोप्यते.

Space, *s.* (In the abstract, mere extension or vacuity) आकाशः -शं, शून्यं, शून्यत्वं -ता, रिक्तं, रिक्तता -त्वं, दिगन्तरं, दिगन्तरालं, व्योम *n.* (न्), गगणं, अन्तरीक्षं, वियत् *n.*; 'infinite space,' महाकाशः -शं, अनन्तं; 'finite,' घटाकाशं, मठाकाशं; 'empty space,' शून्यं, रिक्तं.—(Region, quarter, direction) दिक् *f.* (श्), देशः, प्रदेशः, काष्ठा, ककुभ् *f.*, आशा, हरित् *f.*; 'extending through all space,' दिग्व्यापी -पिनी -पि, अभिव्याप्तः -प्ता -प्तं, चतुर्दिग्व्यापी &c.; 'in the first second the stone falls through a space not exceeding 17 feet,' प्रथमे ऽनुपादे नैकादशहस्तमितदेशम् अतिक्रामति प्रस्तरः; 'the space traversed,' अतिक्रान्तप्रदेशः, अन्तरं.—(Included or intervening space, space between) अभ्यन्तरं, अन्तरालं -लकं, अन्तरं, मध्यं, व्यवधानं, व्यवायः, मार्गः.—(Room) अवकाशः, प्रसरः, अवसरः, आकाशः, विषयः; 'want of space,' अनवकाशः.—(Place, spot) स्थानं, स्थलं -ली, भूमिः *f.*; 'open space near a village,' परीहारः, परिहारः, ग्रामान्तं, ग्रामान्तीयं.—(Space of time) अवधिः *m.*, कालान्तरं, कालावधिः *m.*, अन्तरं.

Spacious, *a.* विस्तीर्णः -र्णा -र्णं, विस्तृतः -ता -तं, विपुलः -ला -लं, असम्बाधः -धा -धं, विशालः -ला -लं, सावकाशः -शा -शं, उरुः -रु -रु.

Spaciousness, *s.* विस्तीर्णता, विस्तारः, विस्तृतिः *f.*, विशालता, विपुलता, असम्बाधता -त्वं, सावकाशता -त्वं, उरुता.

Spade, *s.* खनित्रं, खात्रं, आखनिकः, आखनः, आखानं, आखः, अवदारणं, गोदारणं, खनकः, टङ्कः, टङ्कः, विशिखा. *See* Hoe.

Span, *s.* (From tip of the thumb to that of the little finger) वितस्तिः *m.f.*, पाटकः, किष्कुः *m.*—(From tip of the thumb to that of the fore-finger) प्रादेशः, प्रदेशः.—(To tip of the middle finger) तालः, तलः.—(To tip of the ring-finger) गोकर्णः.

To span, *v. a.* हस्ततलेन or तालेन or प्रतलेन परिमा (c. 2. माति -तुं, c. 10. -मापयति -यितुं) or मा, अङ्गुष्ठकनिष्ठाभ्यां परिमा or प्रमा or मा.

Spangle, *s.* धातुतारा, धातुकणः, वपुकणिका, स्फुरद्धातुकणः, तेजःकणः.

To spangle, *v. a.* स्फुरद्धातुकणिकाभिर् or धातुतारिकाभिर् अलङ्कृ.

To spank, *v. a.* चपेटेन आहन्, चपेटाघातं कृ. *See* *To* slap.

To spank, *v. n.* (Move along impetuously) वेगेन चल्, महावेगेन चल्.

Spar, *s.* (Long piece of wood) दीर्घकाष्ठं, दीर्घदारुः *m.*, काष्ठखण्डः, दारुखण्डः.—(Mineral) धातुखण्डः, स्फुरद्धातुः *m.*, स्फुरद्धातुखण्डः.

To spar, *v. n.* क्रीडायुद्धं कृ, परिहासेन or क्रीडार्थम् अन्योन्यप्रहारं कृ or परस्पराघातं कृ, विनोदार्थं मुष्टियुद्धं कृ or मुष्टामुष्टि युध्.

To spare, *v. a.* (Not to spend, apply frugally) न व्ययीकृ, न व्यय् (c. 10. व्यययति -यितुं, rt. इ), न विक्षिप्, न विनियुज्, परिमितव्ययं कृ, परिमितप्रयोगं कृ, अल्पप्रयोगं कृ, अल्पविनियोगं कृ, अबहुप्रयोगं कृ, परिमितं प्रयुज् or विनियुज्, अबाहुल्येन विनियुज्; 'to spare one's money,' न धनक्षेपं कृ; 'one's time,' न कालक्षेपं कृ.—(Part with without inconvenience) अकृच्छ्रेण or अकष्टेन त्यज् (c. 1. त्यजति, त्यक्तुं), अदुःखेन or अक्लेशेन विसृज् (c. 6. -सृजति -स्रष्टुं, c. 10. सर्जयति -यितुं) or उत्सृज् or हा or विहा or प्रहा, सुखेन त्यज्.—(Omit, forbear) त्यज्, परित्यज्, हा, विहा, विसृज्, उत्सृज्, अवसृज्.—(Leave remaining) शिष् (c. 10. शेषयति -यितुं), अवशिष्, अवशिष्टीकृ.—(Not to destroy), *see* *To* save; 'ones life,' जीव् in caus.

Spare, *a.* (That can be dispensed with, superfluous) अधिकः -का -कं, अतिरिक्तः -क्ता -क्तं, अवशिष्टः -ष्टा -ष्टं, शिष्टः &c., उच्छिष्टः &c., उद्वृत्तः -त्ता -त्तं.—(Scanty) अल्पः -ल्पा -ल्पं, परिमितः -ता -तं, अबहुलः -ला -लं, अबहुः -हुः -हु, *see* Scanty.—(Lean) कृशः -शा -शं, *see* Lean, Meagre.

Spared, *p. p.* न व्ययितः -ता -तं, न व्ययीकृतः &c., विसर्जितः &c., विसृष्टः -ष्टा -ष्टं, त्यक्तः -क्ता -क्तं, अवशेषितः &c. *See* Saved.

Spareness, *s.* कृशता, कार्श्यं, कृशाङ्गता, क्षीणता. *See* Leanness.

Sparing, *a.* परिमितव्ययी -यिनी -यि (न्), अल्पव्ययी &c., परिमितः -ता -तं, अल्पः -ल्पा -ल्पं, अबहुलः -ला -लं. *See* Saving.

Sparingly, *adv.* परिमितं, अल्पशस्, स्तोकशस्; 'eating sparingly,' परिमिताहारः -रा -रं, मिताशनः -ना -नं, मितभुक् *m. f. n.* (ज्).

Spark, *s.* (Of fire) अग्निकणः, वह्निकणः, अग्निकणिका, ज्वलनकणः, कणः -णिका, स्फुलिङ्गः -ङ्गा -ङ्गं -ङ्गकः, विस्फुलिङ्गः, उल्का, अग्निलवः.—(Gay fellow) छेकः, *see* Fop.—(Small particle) कणः, कणिका, लेशः, लवः, अणुः *m.*

Sparkle, *s. see* Spark.—(Luminous particle) तेजःकणः, स्फुरत्कणः.

To sparkle, *v. n.* स्फुर् (c. 6. स्फुरति -रितुं), विस्फुर्, स्फुलिङ्गान् उत्क्षिप् (c. 6. -क्षिपति -क्षेप्तुं) or विक्षिप् or विकॄ, तेजःकणान् विकॄ or विक्षिप्, स्फुल् (c. 6. स्फुलति -लितुं), विस्फुल्. *See* *To* glitter.

Sparkling, *part.* or *a.* स्फुरन् -रन्ती -रत् (त्), स्फुरितप्रभः -भा -भं, स्फुलिङ्गविक्षेपी -पिणी -पि (न्), दीप्तिमान् &c. *See* Glittering.

Sparring, *s.* मौष्टा, क्रीडामौष्टा, मुष्टामुष्टि, क्रीडायुद्धं. *See* Boxing.

Sparrow, *s.* चटकः, चटकपक्षी *m.* (न्), कलविङ्कः -ङ्ककः, कलाविकलः, गृहनीडः, वृषायणः, गृहबलिभुक् *m.* (ज्).

Spasm, *s.* अङ्गग्रहः, ग्रहः, ग्रहामयः, आकर्षः, अङ्गाकर्षः, शूलं, अङ्गशूलं, अङ्गसङ्कोचः, सङ्कोचः, आक्षेपकः, अङ्गाक्षेपकः, अपतन्त्रकः, अपतानकः; 'in the side,' पार्श्वशूलं, पार्श्वग्रहः.

Spasmodic, *a.* अङ्गाकर्षकः -का -कं, अङ्गाकर्षी -र्षिणी -र्षि (न्), अङ्गाक्षेपकः &c., अङ्गसङ्कोचकः -का -कं, अङ्गसङ्कोचनः -ना -नं, अङ्गग्राही -हिणी &c.; 'spasmodic contraction,' आकर्षः, अपतानकः, अपतन्त्रकः.

To spatter, *v. a.* पङ्कादिना सिच्, पङ्कम् अवसिच् or अवकॄ. *See* *To* bespatter.

Spatula, spattle, *s.* लेपनयन्त्रं, लेपनी, प्रलेपनी, प्रलेपकः.

Spavin, *s.* अश्वानां सन्धिशोथः or सन्धिगुल्मः or सन्धिवृद्धिः *f.*

Spavined, *a.* सन्धिशोथरोगी -गिणी -गि (न्), सन्धिगुल्मरोगी &c.

Spawl, *s.* निष्ठ्यूतं, मुखनिःसारितं जलं, मुखनिःसारितलाला.

Spawn, *s.* (Of fish) मत्स्याण्डं, मीनाण्डं, जलाण्डकः, मत्स्यडिम्भः, मत्स्यडिम्बादि *n.*—(Of frogs) भेकाण्डं, मण्डूकाण्डं.

To SPAWN, *v. n.* मत्स्याण्डानि प्रसु, मीनाण्डानि प्रसु or उत्पद् (c. 10. -पादयति -यितुं), भेकाण्डानि प्रसु, अण्डोत्पत्तिं कृ, अण्डप्रसवं कृ.

To SPEAK, *v. n.* वद् (c. 1. वदति -दितुं), प्रवद्, समावद्, वच् (c. 2. वक्ति -क्तुं), प्रवच्, ब्रू (c. 2. ब्रवीति, ब्रूते, वक्तुं), भाष् (c. 1. भाषते -षितुं), प्रभाष्, सम्प्रभाष्, गद् (c. 1. गदति -दितुं), निगद्, भण् (c. 1. भणति -णितुं), आलप् (c. 1. -लपति -पितुं), जल्प् (c. 1. जल्पति -ल्पितुं), उपजल्प्, संजल्प्, वाक्यम् ईर् (c. 10. ईरयति -यितुं) or उदीर्, अह् (used only in the 2d pret. आह), शब्द् (c. 10. शब्दयति -यितुं), अभिशब्द्, संशब्द्.—(Speak of) कथ् (c. 10. कथयति -यितुं), संकथ्, अभिधा (c. 3. -दधाति -धातुं), *see To* MENTION.

To SPEAK, *v. a.* (Utter, pronounce) उच्चर् (c. 10. -चारयति -यितुं), उदाहृ (c. 1. -हरति -हर्त्तुं), व्याहृ, उदीर् (c. 10. -ईरयति -यितुं), समुदीर्, प्रवद् (c. 1. -वदति -दितुं), गद् (c. 1. गदति -दितुं).

SPEAKER, SPEAKING, *s.* or *part.* वक्ता *m.* (क्तृ), वक्त्री *f.*, वादी *m.* -दिनी (न्), भाषी *m.* -षिणी (न्), वाचकः, वदः, अभिभाषी *m.*, वदावदः; 'speaking little,' अल्पभाषी -षिणी -षि (न्), मितभाषी &c.; 'speaking much,' बहुभाषी &c.; 'speaking the truth,' सत्यभाषी &c.; 'pleasant speaker,' प्रियवादी &c., प्रियंवदः -दा -दं.

SPEAKING, *s.* भाषणं, वादः, आलापः -पनं, गदः -दनं, निगदः, उक्तिः *f.*, भणितिः *f.*, उदीरणं, वाक्योदीरणं, उदाहरणं, अभिधानं, उच्चारणं, व्याहरणं, व्याहारः, कथनं.

SPEAR, *s.* शूलः -लं, शक्तिः *f.*, शल्यं, प्रासः, कुन्तः -न्ती, शलाका, कीलः, तोमरः; 'head of one,' शूलाग्रं, फलं.

To SPEAR, *v. a.* शूलेन व्यध् (c. 4. विध्यति, व्यद्धुं). *See To* LANCE.

SPEARMAN, *s.* शूली *m.* (न्), शूलधरः, शक्तिधरः, शक्तिग्रहः, शाक्तीकः, शक्तिहेतिकः, प्रासिकः, कौन्तिकः, शलाकी *m.*, शूलपाणिः *m.*

SPECIAL, *a.* (Designating or belonging to a species) जातिवाचकः -का -कं, जातिविषयकः -का -कं, जातिसम्बन्धी &c., जातीयः -या -यं, जाति in comp.; 'special property or characteristic,' जातित्वं, जातिधर्म्मः, जातिलक्षणं.—(Particular, peculiar) विशेष in comp., विशेषकः -का -कं, सविशेषः -षा -षं, असाधारणः -णा -णं, असामान्यः -न्या -न्यं, अव्यापी -पिनी &c., अव्यापकः -का -कं, अव्याप्यः -प्या -प्यं, अवच्छेदकः -का -कं, सोपाधिकः -की -कं, *see* PARTICULAR; 'special rule,' विशेषविधिः *m.*; 'special text,' विशेषवचनं; 'special duty,' विशेषधर्म्मः; 'special occasion,' समयविशेषः; 'provided for by special mention,' प्रतिपदोक्तः -क्ता -क्तं.—(Extraordinary, uncommon) अप्राकृतः -ती -तं, लोकोत्तरः -रा -रं, अप्रसिद्धः &c.—(Designed for this particular purpose) तदुद्देशकः -का -कं, तदुद्दिष्टः -ष्टा -ष्टं, तन्निमित्तकः -का -कं, तद्धेतुकः -का -कं.—(Special plea in law) प्राङ्न्यायः.

SPECIALLY, *adv.* विशेषतस्, विशेषेण, सविशेषं, असाधारणतस्, मुख्यशस्.

SPECIALTY, *s.* विशेषता, वैशेष्यं, विशेषः, असाधारणत्वं, असाधारण्यं, असामान्यं, अव्यापकत्वं, अव्यापित्वं.

SPECIE, *s.* मुद्राङ्कितसुवर्णरूप्यादि *n.*, मुद्रितसुवर्णादि, मुद्रा, *see* COIN.

SPECIES, *s.* जातिः *f.*, प्रकारः, विशेषः, भेदः, प्रभेदः, जातं, जातिमात्रं, लूनकः, परापरं; 'the human species,' मनुष्यजातिः *f.*; 'the dog species,' श्वजातिः *f.*

SPECIFIC, SPECIFICAL, *a.* विशेषजातीयः -या -यं, जातीयः &c., विशेषजातिविषयकः -का -कं, विशेषजातिसम्बन्धी -न्धिनी &c., व्यञ्जकः -का -कं, विशेष in comp., विशेषकः -का -कं, विशेषणः -णा -णं, असाधारणः -णी -णं, असामान्यः -न्या -न्यं, जाति in comp.; 'specific gravity,' जातीयगुरुत्वं; 'specific character,' जातिस्वभावः, जातिधर्म्मः, जातिलक्षणं, जातित्वं, साधारणं, सामान्यलक्षणं, सामान्यं.

SPECIFIC, *s.* (Remedy) विशेषौषधं, सविशेषौषधं, असाधारणौषधं.

SPECIFICALLY, *adv.* जातितस्, जातित्वेन, स्वभावतस्, निसर्गतस्, विशेषतस्.

SPECIFICATION, *s.* विशेषनिर्देशः, विशेषाभिधानं, विशेषकथनं, विशेषोद्देशः -शनं, विशेषोपदेशः, विशेषपरिसंख्या, विशेषवर्णनं -ना, प्रत्यवयववर्णनं -ना, परिसंख्या -ख्यानं, व्यवच्छेदः -दनं, अवच्छेदः -दनं, निर्देशः, उपदेशः, अभिधानं, भेदनं.

SPECIFIED, *p. p.* निर्दिष्टः -ष्टा -ष्टं, उपदिष्टः &c., उद्दिष्टः &c., परिसंख्यातः -ता -तं, उक्तलक्षणः -णा -णं, निर्दिष्टलक्षणः &c., व्यवच्छिन्नः -न्ना -न्नं, अवच्छिन्नः &c., विशेषितः -ता -तं, भेदितः -ता -तं, वाचनिकः -की -कं; 'about to be specified,' वक्ष्यमाणः -णा -णं; 'it will be specified,' वक्ष्यते.

To SPECIFY, *v. a.* विशेषतस् or अवयवशस् or प्रत्यवयवं कथ् (c. 10. कथयति -यितुं) or अभिधा (c. 3. -दधाति -धातुं), एकैकशो निर्दिश् (c. 6. -दिशति -देष्टुं) or उद्दिश् or समुद्दिश्, एकैकशो दृश् (c. 10. दर्शयति -यितुं), विशेषनिर्देशं कृ, विशेषकथनं कृ, विशेषवर्णनं कृ, विशेष (nom. विशेषयति -यितुं), विशिष् (c. 7. -शिनष्टि -शेष्टुं).

SPECIMEN, *s.* आदर्शः, निदर्शनं, प्रतिरूपं, प्रतिमानं, प्रतिमा, उपमा.

SPECIOUS, *a.* सत्याभासी -सिनी -सि (न्), सत्याभासकः -का -कं, प्रमाणाभासी &c., सत्याभासात्मकः -का -कं, आभासी &c., सत्यसदृशः -शी -शं, सत्यसन्निभः -भा -भं, सत्यसङ्काशः -शा -शं, अविचाररमणीयः -या -यं, आपातरमणीयः &c., अविचारसुन्दरः -री -रं, अविचारदर्शनीयः -या -यं, बहिर्दर्शनीयः &c., बाह्यतो दर्शनीयः &c., सुदृश्यः -श्या -श्यं; 'using specious arguments,' आभासवादी *m.* (न्).

SPECIOUSLY, *adv.* सत्याभासेन, सत्याभासपूर्व्वं, सत्यसदृशं, सव्याजं.

SPECIOUSNESS, *s.* सत्याभासः -सत्वं, सत्यसादृश्यं. *See* PLAUSIBILITY.

SPECK, SPECKLE, *s.* (Spot, mark, stain) चिह्नं, बिन्दुः *m.*, विप्रुट् *f.* (ष्), विप्रुद् *f.*, अङ्कः, कलङ्कः, तिलकः -कं; 'of mud,' पङ्कबिन्दुः *m.*, पङ्कचिह्नं; 'speck or flaw in gold, &c.,' स्फारः; 'in the eye,' पुष्पं, तिलपुष्पं.—(Minute particle) कणः, कणिका, लवः, अणुः *m.*, सूक्ष्मबिन्दुः *m.*

To SPECKLE, *v. a.* चित्र् (c. 10. चित्रयति -यितुं), चित्रीकृ, बिन्दुचित्रितं -तां कृ, बिन्दुचिह्नितं -तां कृ, चित्रविचित्रीकृ, शबलीकृ, कर्बुरीकृ.

SPECKLED, *p. p.* or *a.* चित्रितः -ता -तं, बिन्दुचित्रितः &c., बिन्दुचित्रकः -का -कं, चित्रः -त्रा -त्रं, चित्री -त्रिणी -त्रि (न्), चित्राङ्गः -ङ्गी -ङ्गं, चित्रविचित्रः -त्रा -त्रं, बिन्दुचिह्नितः &c., कर्बुरितः &c., शबलीकृतः &c., तिलकी -किनी &c.; 'a speckled snake,' चित्रसर्पः.

SPECTACLE, *s.* (Show, something wonderful exhibited) प्रेक्षा -क्षणं, कौतुकं, चमत्कारः.—(Any thing seen) प्रेक्षा -क्षणं, दृष्टिविषयः.

SPECTACLES, *s. pl.* उपनेत्रे -त्रे *n. du.*, सुलोचने -ने *n. du.*, दिव्यचक्षुषी *n. du.*, दृष्टिसहायौ *m. du.*, दृष्टिसाहाय्यकारकाचौ *m. du.*, दृगुपकारकौ *m. du.*, दृगुपकारककाचौ *m. du.*, काचद्वयनिर्म्मितम् अधिककिरणपक्षकारकं यन्त्रं.

SPECTATOR, *s.* प्रेक्षकः, प्रेक्षणिकः, प्रेक्षणकः, प्रेक्षी *m.* (न्), प्रेक्षिलोकः, द्रष्टा *m.* (ष्टृ), दर्शी *m.* (न्), प्रेक्षमाणः, पारिषदः, पारिषद्यः, परिषद्यः, पार्षदः, सामाजिकः.

SPECTRE, *s.* छाया, माया, भूतं, प्रेतछाया, प्रेतः, वेतालः, *see* GHOST; 'to raise a spectre,' छायाम् उद्भू (c. 10. -भावयति -यितुं).

SPECULAR, *a.* दर्पणगुणकः -का -कं, आदर्शगुणकः &c., आदर्शधर्म्मकः &c.

To SPECULATE, *v. n.* (Meditate) मनसा विचर् (c. 10. -चारयति -यितुं),

वितर्क् (c. 10. -तर्कयति -यितुं), विमृश् (c. 6. -मृशति -म्रष्टुं), मनसा परिक्लृप् (c. 10. -कल्पयति -यितुं), कल्पनां कृ, परिकल्पनां कृ.—(In commerce) व्यापारं कृ, धनव्यापारं कृ.

SPECULATION, *s.* (Meditation) मानसविचारः, मनसा विचारः -रणं, वितर्कः, परिकल्पना, विमर्शः.—(Scheme) कल्पना, उपायः, युक्तिः *f.*; 'good speculation,' सुकल्पना; 'bad,' कुकल्पना.—(In commerce) व्यापारः, धनव्यापारः.

SPECULATIVE, *a.* (Contemplative) ध्यानशीलः -ला -लं, *see* MEDITATIVE.—(Theoretical, not practical) काल्पनिकः -की -कं, मनःकल्पितः -ता -तं, मानसिकः -की -कं, मनसिजः -जा -जं, मनोभवः -वा -वं, अव्यावहारिकः -की -कं, अव्यवहार्य्यः -र्य्या -र्य्यं, व्यवहारायोग्यः -ग्या -ग्यं.

SPECULATOR, *s.* परिकल्पकः, कल्पनाकृत्.—(In commerce) धनव्यापारी *m.* (न्).

SPECULUM, *s.* दर्पणः -णं, आदर्शः, धातुमयदर्पणं, धातुदर्पणं.

SPEECH, *s.* (Faculty of speech, speaking) वाक् *f.* (च्), वाणी, वाचा, गीः *f.* (गिर्), गिरा, उक्तिः *f.*, वाक्शक्तिः *f.*, वदन्तिः *f.*, निगदः, निगादः, व्याहारः, व्याहृतिः *f.*, भाषणं, भाषा, वचनं, प्रवचनं, वादः, लापः, अभिलापः, लपितं, लपनं, वाग्व्यापारः, शब्दव्यापारः, भणितिः *f.*, निदेशः, भारती, सरस्वती, राधना, कासूः *f.*, शब्दजालं.—(Words, that which is spoken) वाक्यं, वचनं, वचस् *n.*, उक्तिः *f.*, उक्तं, भाषणं, भाषा, भाषितं, लपितं.—(Harangue) वाक्यं, सालङ्कारवाक्यं, अलङ्कारवद्वाक्यं.—(Language) भाषा, उक्तिः *f.*; 'cleverness of speech,' वाक्चातुर्य्यं, वाक्कौशल्यं, वाक्पटुता; 'liberty of speech,' वागप्रतिबन्धः, वाङ्मुक्तिः *f.*; 'control of it,' वाङ्निरोधः, वाग्दण्डः, वाङ्नियमः -मनं; 'softness of speech,' वाङ्माधुर्य्यं; 'stopping one's speech,' वाग्बन्धनं; 'elegance of speech,' शब्दलालित्यं; 'covert speech,' व्याजोक्तिः *f.*; 'bad speech,' दुर्वचनं, दुरुक्तिः *f.*, दुर्भाषणं, दुर्वाक्यं; 'mere speech,' वाङ्मात्रं; 'opening of speech,' वाङ्मुखं; 'of measured speech,' मितवाक् *m.f.n.* (च्), मितभाषी -षिणी &c.; 'Part of speech in grammar,' शब्दः; 'goddess of speech,' सरस्वती, भारती, वाग्देवी, *see* SARASWATĪ.

To SPEECHIFY, *v. n.* वाक्यं वद्, सालङ्कारवाक्यं वद्. *See To* HARANGUE.

SPEECHLESS, *a.* वाग्रहितः -ता -तं, वाचाहीनः -ना -नं, स्तम्भितवाक्. *See* MUTE.

SPEED, *s.* वेगः, शीघ्रता, जवः, प्रजवः, जूतिः *f.*, जवनं, सत्वरता, त्वरा, जूर्णिः *f.*, तूर्णिः *m.*, रयः, रभसः, तरसो, तरस् *n.*, रंहतिः *f.*, रंहस् *n.*, आशुगमनं, त्वरितगतिः *f.*, स्यदः. *See* QUICKNESS.

SPEEDILY, *adv.* शीघ्रं, त्वरितं, सत्वरं, झटिति, सद्यस्, सपदि, आशु, क्षिप्रं, सरभसं, अचिरात्, न चिरेण. *See* QUICKLY.

SPEEDY, *a.* त्वरितः -ता -तं, शीघ्रः -घ्रा -घ्रं, द्रुतः -ता -तं, महावेगः -गा -गं, वेगवान् -वती -वत् (त्), त्वरितगतिः -तिः -ति, शीघ्रगतिः &c., प्रजवी -विणी -वि (न्), तूर्णः -र्णा -र्णं, क्षिप्रः -प्रा -प्रं. *See* QUICK, SWIFT.

SPELL, *s.* (Charm) मन्त्रः, अभिचारमन्त्रः, *see* CHARM; 'book of spells,' मन्त्रशास्त्रं; 'reciter of spells,' मन्त्रवादी *m.* (न्), मन्त्री *m.*—(Turn) वारः, पर्य्यायः, वासरः.

SPELL-BOUND, *a.* अभिमन्त्रितः -ता -तं, अनुमन्त्रितः &c., मन्त्रितः &c.

To SPELL, *v. a.* or *n.* अक्षराणि गण् (c. 10. गणयति -यितुं) or संख्या (c. 2. -ख्याति -तुं), अक्षराणि रच् (c. 10. रचयति -यितुं) or विरच् or विन्यस् (c. 4. -अस्यति -सितुं), यथाक्षरं or यथावर्णं शब्दान् संख्या, अक्षरविरचनं कृ, अक्षरविन्यासं कृ, वर्णविन्यासं कृ, अक्षररचनां कृ, वर्णरचनां कृ, वर्णयोजनां कृ, अक्षरयोजनां कृ.

SPELLED, SPELT, *p. p.* गणिताक्षरः -रा -रं; 'in two ways,' द्विरूपः -पा -पं.

SPELLING, *s.* अक्षरगणना, अक्षरविन्यासः, अक्षरविन्यसनं, अक्षररचना, अक्षरविरचनं, वर्णविन्यासः, वर्णरचना, वर्णयोजना, शुद्धाक्षररचना; 'variation in spelling,' पाठान्तरं, पाठः; 'spelling-book,' अक्षरविन्यासशिक्षापुस्तकं.

SPENCER, *s.* कञ्चुकः, कञ्चुलिका, चक्षिका, ह्रस्वकञ्चुकः, *see* JACKET.

To SPEND, *v. a.* (Expend) व्ययीकृ, व्यय् (c. 1. व्ययति, c. 10. व्यययति -यितुं, rt. इ), उपयुज्, विनियुज्, *see To* EXPEND.—(Consume, exhaust) क्षि, क्षीणीकृ, विक्षिप्, नश् in caus., सद् in caus., *see* EXHAUST.—(Time, &c.) कालं गम् (c. 10. गमयति -यितुं) or वृत् (c. 10. वर्त्तयति -यितुं) or नी (c. 1. नयति, नेतुं) or वह् or या in caus., *see To* PASS, *v. a.*

SPENDING, *s.* व्ययः, व्ययीकरणं, विनियोगः, *see* EXPENDITURE.

SPENDTHRIFT, *s.* व्ययशीलः, अर्थनाशी *m.*, अतिव्ययी *m.*, अर्थघ्नः, *see* PRODIGAL.

SPENT, *p. p.* व्ययीकृतः -ता -तं, व्ययीभूतः -ता -तं, व्ययितः &c., अपचितः &c., विनियुक्तः -क्ता -क्तं, *see* EXPENDED, EXHAUSTED; 'well-spent time,' सत्कालक्षेपः.

SPERM, *s.* शुक्रं, बीजं, धातुः *m.*, धातुराजः -जक, वीर्य्यं. *See* SEMEN.

SPERMACETI, *s.* तिमिमेदस् *n.*, तिमिवसा, तिमिस्नेहः, तिमितैलं.

SPERMATIC, *a.* (Consisting of sperm), *see* SEMINAL.—(Conveying it) शुक्रवाही -हिनी -हि (न्), बीजवाही &c.—(Producing it) शुक्रकरः -री -रं.

To SPEW, *v. a.* वम् (c. 1. वमति -मितुं), उद्वम्, छर्द्. *See To* VOMIT.

SPHERE, *s.* (Globe, orb) मण्डलं, गोलः -लं -लकः, पिण्डः -ण्डं, वर्त्तुलं, भुवनं, *see* ORB; 'celestial sphere,' आकाशमण्डलं.—(Circuit of action, department, province) विषयः, प्रकरणं, धर्म्मः, अधिकारः, नियोगः, निबन्धनं, देशः; 'one's own sphere of action,' स्वधर्म्मः, स्वकर्म्म *n.* (न्).

SPHERICAL, *a.* गोलाकारः -रा -रं, वर्त्तुलाकारः &c., वर्त्तुलः -ला -लं, मण्डली -लिनी -लि (न्), मण्डलाकारः -रा -रं. *See* ORBED.

SPHERICALNESS, *s.* वर्त्तुलत्वं, वर्त्तुलाकारत्वं, गोलाकारता, गोलत्वं.

SPHERICS, *s.* गोलाध्यायः, गोलविद्या, गोलशास्त्रं, मण्डलविद्या.

SPHEROID, *s.* (Oblate) चपटगोलः.—(Prolate) अण्डाकारगोलः.

SPHEROIDAL, *a.* गोलकल्पः -ल्पा -ल्पं, गोलप्रायः &c., गोलसदृशः -शी -शं.

SPHERULE, *s.* लघुगोलः, सूक्ष्मगोलः, क्षुद्रगोलः, सूक्ष्मवर्त्तुलं.

SPICE, *s.* व्यञ्जनं, उपस्करः, तेमनं, मिष्टान्नं. *See* SEASONING.

To SPICE, *v. a.* व्यञ्जनादिना वास् (c. 10. वासयति -यितुं). *See To* SEASON.

SPICED, *p. p.* वासितः -ता -तं, उपस्कृतः &c. *See* SEASONED.

SPICY, *a.* मिष्टः -ष्टा -ष्टं, तिक्तः -क्ता -क्तं, सरसः -सा -सं, सुरसः &c., व्यञ्जनमयः -यी -यं, रसिकः -का -कं, मिश्रः -श्रा -श्रं.

SPIDER, *s.* ऊर्णनाभः, ऊर्णनाभिः *m.*, लूता, लूतिका, तन्तुवायः, तन्त्रवायः, मर्कटः -टकः, मर्ककः, अष्टापदः, अष्टपादः, मालकारकः, जालिकः, लालास्रावः, कृशाक्षः, किन्तनुः *m.*, शलकः, कोशकारः, कोषकारः; 'spider's web,' ऊर्णनाभजालः, मर्कटवासः, आशाबन्धः.

SPIKE, *s.* (Large nail) शङ्कुः *m.*, शलाका, शल्यं, कीलः, शूलः -लं, कण्टकः, लोहकीलः, शिली, *see* NAIL.—(Of corn) कणिशः -शं, कणिशं, धान्यशीर्षकं, शस्यमञ्जरी.

To SPIKE, *v. a.* कील् (c. 10. कीलयति -यितुं), शूल् (c. 1. शूलति -लितुं).

Spiked, *a.* (Having spikes) शङ्कुयुक्तः -क्ता -क्तं, शङ्कुमान् -मती -मत् (त्), शैक्यः -क्या -क्यं.—(Fastened with spikes) कीलितः -ता -तं, शङ्कुबद्धः -द्धा -द्धं.

Spikenard, *s.* जटिला, जटामांसी, जटाला, जटा, जटावती, मांसी, मिसी -सिः *f.*, मिशिः *f.*, मिषिः *f.*, मिषी, तपस्विनी, लोमशा, केशिनी, पेशी, पिशिता, शिफा, नलदं.

Spiky, *a.* तीक्ष्णाग्रः -ग्रा -ग्रं, शैक्यः &c. *See* Pointed.

To **spill**, *v. a.* पत् (c. 10. पातयति -यितुं), सु in caus. *See To* shed.

To **spill**, *v. n.* सु (c. 1. स्रवति, स्रोतुं), पत् in caus. pass. (पात्यते).

To **spin**, *v. a.* (Form threads) तर्कुद्वारेण तन्तून् कृ or जन् (c. 10. जनयति -यितुं) or तन्तुवायं कृ or तन्तुवापं कृ or तान्तवं कृ, तर्कुटीद्वारेण सूत्रतान्तवं कृ, तर्कुद्वारेण सूत्राणि तन् (c. 8. तनोति -नितुं) or वितन्, सूत्रतननं कृ, तन्त्राणि कृ, *see To* weave.—(Draw out), *see To* protract, draw out.—(Cause to whirl) भ्रम् in caus. (भ्रमयति -यितुं), परिवृत् in caus., *see To* revolve, *v. a.*

To **spin**, *v. n.* (Practice spinning) तर्कुद्वारेण तन्तुवायं कृ or तन्तुवापं कृ or तान्तवं कृ, सूत्रतान्तवं कृ, तर्कुटं कृ.—(Whirl) भ्रम् (c. 4. भ्राम्यति, c. 1. भ्रमति -मितुं), परिवृत्, *see To* revolve, *v. n.*

Spinach, spinage, *s.* वास्तुकः or वस्तुकः may perhaps be used.

Spinal, *a.* पृष्ठवंशसम्बन्धी -न्धिनी -न्धि (न्), पृष्ठवंशस्थः -स्था -स्थं.

Spindle, *s.* तर्कुः *f.*, तर्कुटी, तर्कुटं, सूत्रतर्कुटी, सम्पाटः, मेरुयन्त्रं, कार्पासनासिका.

Spindle-shanked, *a.* क्षामजंघः -घा -घं, तनुजंघः &c., दीर्घजंघः &c.

Spine, *s.* पृष्ठवंशः, वंशः, कशेरुः -रु *m. n.*, कशेरुका, रीढकः, पृष्ठास्थि *n.*

Spinner, *s.* तन्तुवायः, तन्तुवापः, तन्तुकारी *m.* (न्), तान्तवकारी *m.*

Spinning, *s.* तान्तवं, तन्तुवायः, तन्तुवापः, तन्त्रवायः, सूत्रतान्तवं, सूत्रतननं, तन्तुकरणं, वायः, वापः.

Spinning-wheel, *s.* तान्तवचक्रं, तन्तुवायचक्रं, तन्तुवापचक्रं.

Spinous, spiny, *a.* कण्टकी -किनी &c., सकण्टकः -का -कं. *See* Thorny.

Spinster, *s.* निवरा, अवरा, अनूढा, अविवाहिता, अपरिणीता.

Spiracle, *s.* वायुपथः, वायुमार्गः, उच्छ्वासः, जलोच्छ्वासः, सूक्ष्मरन्ध्रं, वायुरन्ध्रं, वातायनं, स्वेदमार्गः. *See* Pore, *s.*

Spiral, *a.* आवर्त्ती -र्त्तिनी -र्त्ति (न्), परिवर्त्तकः -का -कं, व्यावर्त्ती &c., चाक्रिकः -की -कं, अलकाकारः -रा -रं, चक्राकारः -रा -रं, जलसूचाकारः &c.

Spirally, *adv.* अलकाकारेण, अलकरूपेण, व्यावर्त्तकप्रकारेण.

Spire, *s.* (Winding line) अलकरूपा व्यावर्त्तकरेखा, आवर्त्तः.—(Steeple, pinnacle) शिखरं, शृङ्गं, शङ्कुः *m.*, शिखा; 'of a house or temple,' गृहशिखरं, प्रासादशिखरं, प्रासादशृङ्गं; *see* Pinnacle; 'of flame,' अग्निशिखा.

Spirit, *s.* (Breath) प्राणः, आत्मा *m.* (न्), असुः *m.*—(Soul) आत्मा *m.* (न्), देही *m.* (न्), शरीरी *m.*, क्षेत्रज्ञः, चैत्यः, *see* Soul.—(Temper, disposition of mind) प्रकृतिः *f.*, भावः, स्वभावः, प्रकृतिभावः, बुद्धिः *f.*, चित्तं, मनस् *n.*, वृत्तिः *f.*; 'proudness of spirit,' चित्तसमुन्नतिः *f.*; 'having a noble spirit,' उदारप्रकृतिः -तिः -ति; 'conquest of one's own spirit,' मनोजयः; 'in good spirits,' हृष्टचित्तः -त्ता -त्तं, हृष्टमनाः -नाः -नः (स्), हर्षवृत्तिः -त्तिः -त्ति, स्वस्थः -स्था -स्थं; 'high spirits,' प्रहर्षः, हृष्टचित्तत्वं; 'lowness of spirits,' विषादः, *see* Lowness; 'in low spirits,' विषण्णः -ण्णा -ण्णं, उदासीनः -ना -नं, *see* Low.—(Life, mettle) तेजस् *n.*, वीर्य्यं, सत्त्वं, ओजस् *n.*, प्रभावः, उत्साहः, प्रोत्साहः, धैर्य्यं, रसः.—(Life, essence, essential qualities) सारः, सारांशः, सत्त्वं, सत्त्वांशः, तत्त्वं; 'in spirit and in letter,' अर्थतो ग्रन्थतश्च.—(Spirituous liquor) सुरा, मद्यं, मदिरा, *see* Spirits.—(Ghost, disembodied spirit) प्रेतः, परेतः, नारकः, छाया, अपच्छाया.—(Goblin) वेतालः, भूतं, पिशाचः; 'evil spirit,' अपदेवता.—(The supreme spirit) ब्रह्म *n.* (न्), परमात्मा *m.*, आत्मा, पुरुषः, नरः, तत्त्वं, सदागतिः *m.*, सच्चिदानन्दं, निष्क्रियं; 'knowledge of it,' ब्रह्मतत्त्वं, ब्रह्मज्ञानं. In modern translations of the Bible the Holy Spirit is rendered by पवित्रात्मा or पवित्र आत्मा.

To **spirit**, *v. a.* आश्वस् in caus. *See To* inspirit, animate.

Spirited, *a.* (Fall of life or animation) तेजोवान् -वती -वत् (त्), तेजस्वी -स्विनी -स्वि (न्), वीर्य्यवान् &c., ओजस्वी &c., ससत्त्वः -त्त्वा -त्त्वं, सत्त्वपूर्णः -र्णा -र्णं, उत्साही &c., सोत्साहः -हा -हं, प्रोत्साही &c., मानी &c.—(As style, &c.) रसिकः -का -कं, सरसः -सा -सं; 'spirited style in poetry,' गौडी.—(In composition denoting state of the mind) प्रकृतिः -तिः -ति in comp., स्वभावः -वा -वं in comp., मनस्कः -स्का -स्कं in comp., *see* Low-spirited, High-spirited, &c.

Spiritless, *a.* निस्तेजाः -जाः -जः (स्), तेजोहीनः -ना -नं, निर्वीर्य्यः -र्य्या -र्य्यं, वीर्य्यहीनः -ना -नं, निर्वीरः -रा -रं, निःसत्त्वः -त्त्वा -त्त्वं, सत्त्वहीनः -ना -नं, नीरसः -सा -सं, विरसः &c., अरतिज्ञः -ज्ञा -ज्ञं.

Spirits, *s. pl.* (Spirituous liquor) सुरा -री, मद्यं, मदिरा, मदः, हाला, वारुणी, शीधुः -धु *m. n.*, सीधुः -धु *m. n.*, शुण्डा, आसवः -वं, वरुणात्मजा, हलिप्रिया, परिस्रुत् *f.*, परिस्रुता, कल्यं -ल्या, कश्यं; 'spirit-drinking,' सुरापानं, मद्यपानं; 'spirit-drinker,' सुरापः -पी *f.*

Spiritual, *a.* (Not material) अमूर्त्तिकः -का -कं, अमूर्त्तः -र्त्ता -र्त्तं, अमूर्त्तिमान् -मती -मत् (त्), निराकारः -रा -रं, निरवयवः -वा -वं, आत्मीयः -या -यं, आत्मिकः -की -कं, आत्मसम्बन्धी -न्धिनी &c., आत्मस्वरूपः -पा -पं, चिद्रूपः &c., आध्यात्मिकः -की -कं, अध्यात्मिकः &c., आधिदैविकः &c., *see* Incorporeal.—(Not gross, pertaining to spirit) पारमार्थिकः -की -कं, परमार्थविषयकः -का -कं, परमार्थसम्बन्धी -न्धिनी &c., ज्ञानमार्गसम्बन्धी &c., निवृत्तिमार्गसम्बन्धी &c., मानसिकः -की -कं, अदृष्टार्थः -र्था -र्थं, नारकः -की -कं, नारः -री -रं, पारत्रिकः -की -कं.—(Not lay, relating to sacred things) धर्म्मविषयकः -का -कं, धर्म्मप्रकरणः -णा -णं, धर्म्मप्रकरणसम्बन्धी &c., अव्यवहारिकः -की -कं, असांसारिकः &c.; 'spiritual knowledge,' परमार्थः; 'spiritual father,' ब्रह्मदाता *m.* (तृ), *see* Preceptor.

Spiritualism, *s.* ज्ञानमार्गः, ज्ञानाभ्यासः, ब्रह्मवादः, निवृत्तिमार्गः.

Spiritualist, *s.* ब्रह्मवादी *m.* (न्), ज्ञानमार्गी *m.*, ज्ञानाभ्यासी, निवृत्तिमार्गी.

Spirituality, *s.* (Immateriality), *see* the word.—(Spiritual nature) पारमार्थिकता -त्वं, परमार्थसम्बन्धिता, परमार्थनिष्ठा.

To **spiritualize**, *v. a.* परमार्थनिष्ठं -ष्ठां कृ, परमार्थासक्तं -क्तां कृ.

Spiritually, *adv.* परमार्थतस्, अदृष्टार्थतस्, परमार्थानुसारतस्.

Spiritually-minded, *a.* परमार्थबुद्धिः -द्धिः -द्धि, परमार्थनिष्ठः -ष्ठा -ष्ठं, परमार्थासक्तः -क्ता -क्तं, परमार्थतत्परः -रा -रं, परमार्थपरायणः -णा -णं.

Spirituous, *a.* सौरिकः -की -कं, शीघ्रमादकः -का -कं, मादकगुणविशिष्टः -ष्टा -ष्टं; 'liquor,' सुरा, *see* Spirits, *s. pl.*

Spit, *s.* (For roasting meat, &c.) शूलः -लं; 'roasted on one,' शूलाकृतः &c., *see* Roasted.—(Spittle) निष्ठ्यूतं, *see* Spittle.

To **spit**, *v. a.* (Put upon a spit) शूलाकृ, शूल् (c. 1. शूलति -लितुं),

शूलीकृ, शूले समारुह् in caus. (-रोपयति -यितुं) or आरुह्, शूलारोपणं कृ, शूल्यं -ल्यां कृ.—(Eject from the mouth) मुखात् निःसृ in caus. (-सारयति -यितुं), निष्ठीव्, *see* the next.

To SPIT, *v. n.* ष्ठीव् or ष्ठिव् (c. 1. ष्ठीवति, c. 4. ष्ठीव्यति, ष्ठेवितुं), निष्ठीव्, क्षीव् or क्षिव् or क्षेव् (c. 1. क्षीवति, क्षेवति, c. 4. क्षीव्यति, क्षेवितुं), श्लेष्मनिरसनं कृ, श्लेष्माणं निरस् (c. 4. -अस्यति -सितुं), लालां मुखात् निःसृ in caus. (-सारयति -यितुं), निरसनं कृ, ष्ठीवनं कृ, निष्ठीवनं कृ, थुथुशब्दं कृ; 'to spit upon,' अवनिष्ठीव्, अवनिष्ठीवनं कृ.

SPIT, *p. p.* ष्ठ्यूतः -ता -तं, निष्ठ्यूतः &c., मुखनिःसारितः &c.; 'having spit,' ष्ठीवित्वा.

SPITE, *s.* द्वेषः, असूया, ईर्ष्या, मात्सर्य्यं, दंशः, द्रोहः, द्रोहबुद्धिः *f.*, अपकारेच्छा, दुष्टभावः, कालकूटं, *see* MALICE; 'in spite of,' अनिच्छया, *see* DESPITE.

To SPITE, *v. a.* द्विष् (c. 2. द्वेष्टि, द्विष्टे, द्वेष्टुं), विद्विष्, प्रद्विष्, द्रुह् (c. 4. द्रुह्यति, द्रोहितुं), अभिद्रुह्, ईर्ष्य् (c. 1. ईर्ष्यति -र्ष्यितुं). *See* *To* RESENT.

SPITEFUL, *a.* द्रोहबुद्धिः -द्धिः -द्धि, ईर्ष्यी -र्ष्यिणी -र्ष्यि (न्), दंशी &c., द्रोही &c., ईर्ष्यालुः -लुः -लु, विषहृदयः -या -यं, सासूयः -या -यं, मत्सरी &c., दुष्टभावः -वा -वं. *See* MALICIOUS, RESENTFUL.

SPITEFULLY, *adv.* द्रोहबुद्ध्या, द्रोहपूर्व्वं, सासूयं, सद्वेषं, समात्सर्य्यं.

SPITEFULNESS, *s.* द्रोहबुद्धित्वं, दंशेरता, दंशकत्वं, मात्सर्य्यं. *See* SPITE.

SPITTING, *s.* ष्ठीवनं, निष्ठीवः -वनं, निष्ठेवः -वनं, निष्ठेवा, निष्ठ्यूतिः *f.*, निष्ठूतिः *f.*, निरसनं, निरासनं, उद्गिरणं; 'spitting upon,' अवनिष्ठीवनं.

SPITTING-POT, SPITTOON, *s.* पतद्ग्रहः, प्रतिग्राहः, प्रतिग्रहः, चर्व्वितपात्रं, चर्व्विताधारः, प्रोग्रहः.

SPITTLE, *s.* लाला, निष्ठ्यूतं, ष्ठ्यूतं, ष्ठीवनं, निष्ठीवनं, निष्ठूतं, मुखस्रावः, मुखासवः, आस्यासवः, द्राविका. *See* SALIVA.

To SPLASH, *v. a.* or *n.* जलम् इतस्ततो विक्षिप् (c. 6. -क्षिपति -क्षेप्तुं) or क्षिप् or विकॄ or अवकॄ, जलविक्षेपं कृ, जलम् अवसिच्, करपत्रं कृ. *See* *To* SLOP.

SPLASH, SPLASHING, *s.* जलविक्षेपः, जलक्षेपः, जलावसेकः, जलावकिरणं; 'in sport,' करपत्रं -त्रिका, करपात्रं; 'noise of it,' झर्झरं.

SPLASHED, *p. p.* पङ्कजलादिदूषितः -ता -तं, पङ्कादिलिप्तः -प्ता -प्तं.

SPLEEN, *s.* (The organ or the disease) प्लीहा *m.* (-हन्), प्लिहा *m.* (न्), प्लीहा *f.*, प्लिहा *f.*, उदरग्रन्थिः *m.*, प्लीहागुल्मः, प्लिहः.—(Anger, spite, melancholy), *see* the words.

SPLEENWORT, *s.* (Plant removing the disease) प्लीहघ्नः, प्लीहशत्रुः *m.*, प्लीहारिः *m.*

SPLENDID, *a.* (Very brilliant) तेजोमयः -यी -यं, अतिशोभनः -ना -नं, अतिदीप्तिमान् -मती -मत् (त्), अतिकान्तिमान् &c., अतिप्रभावान् &c., सुप्रभः -भा -भं, तेजिष्ठः -ष्ठा -ष्ठं, तेजीयान् -यसी -यः (स्), अतितेजसः -सी -सं, अतितेजस्वी -स्विनी &c., महातेजाः -जाः -जः (स्), महाप्रभः -भा -भं, उज्ज्वलः -ला -लं, शोभमानः -ना -नं, शुभ्रः -भ्रा -भ्रं, भास्वान् &c., भासन्तः -न्ता -न्तं, भानुमान् &c., भासुरः -रा -रं, *see* BRILLIANT, BRIGHT.—(Magnificent) महाप्रतापः -पा -पं, प्रतापवान् &c., प्रतापी &c., *see* MAGNIFICENT.

SPLENDIDLY, *adv.* सुप्रभं, अतिशोभया, अतितेजसा, महाप्रतापेन, अतिप्रतापेन, महातेजसा; 'splendidly dressed,' उज्ज्वलवेशधारी -रिणी &c.

SPLENDOR, *s.* महातेजस् *n.*, तेजस् *n.*, अतिशोभा, शोभा, अतिदीप्तिः *f.*, प्रतापः, उज्ज्वलता, बृहद्द्युतिः *f.*, ओजस्विता, प्रभा, प्रतिभा, श्रीः *f.*, छविः *f.*, विभूतिः *f.*, द्युतिः *f.*, *see* MAGNIFICENCE.

SPLENETIC, *a.* वक्रभावः -वा -वं, कर्कशशीलः -ला -लं. *See* PEEVISH, FRETFUL.

SPLENIC, *a.* प्लीहसम्बन्धी -न्धिनी -न्धि (न्), प्लीहासम्बन्धी &c.

To SPLICE, *v. a.* ग्रन्थिम् अकृत्वा संयुज् or सम्बन्ध् or सन्धा.

SPLINTER, *s.* काष्ठखण्डः -ण्डकः, शकलः -लं, भित्तं, भित्तिः *f.*, भिन्नं, विदलं; 'as entered into the flesh,' शल्यं, शलाका, शर्करा.

To SPLINTER, *v. a.* or *n.* बहुखण्डशो भिद् or विद्ॄ. *See* *To* SPLIT, SHIVER.

To SPLIT, *v. a.* भिद् (c. 7. भिनत्ति, भेत्तुं), विभिद्, निर्भिद्, विदॄ (c. 10. -दारयति -यितुं, c. 9. -दृणाति -दरितुं -रीतुं), अवदॄ, दॄ, विदल् (c. 10. -दलयति -यितुं), दल्, विदलीकृ, खण्ड् (c. 10. खण्डयति -यितुं), पट् (c. 10. पाटयति -यितुं), विपट्, छिद्, विच्छिद्, द्वाढ्, शकलीकृ, विश्लेषणं कृ; 'into many pieces,' *see* *To* SHIVER, *v. a.*

To SPLIT, *v. n.* विभिद् in pass. (-भिद्यते), भिद् in pass., विदॄ in pass. (-दीर्य्यते), विदल् (c. 1. -दलति -लितुं), दल्, फल् (c. 1. फलति -लितुं), त्रुट् (c. 6. त्रुटति, c. 4. त्रुट्यति -टितुं), विच्छिद् in pass., पट् in caus. pass. (पाट्यते), शकलीभू; 'into many pieces,' *see* *To* SHIVER, *v. n.*

SPLIT, *s.* भेदः, विभेदः, भित्तिः *f.*, विदारणं, भङ्गः, खण्डनं. *See* CRACK.

SPLIT, *p. p.* भिन्नः -न्ना -न्नं, विभिन्नः &c., भेदितः -ता -तं, विदीर्णः -र्णा -र्णं, विदारितः -ता -तं, विदलितः -ता -तं, दलितः &c., विदलः -ला -लं, विदलीकृतः -ता -तं, जर्ज्जरः -रा -रं.

SPLITTING, *s.* भेदः -दनं, विदारणं, पाटनं, विपाटनं, विदलीकरणं.

To SPOIL, *v. a.* (Plunder) लुण्ठ्, लुण्ट्, अपहृ, अभिद्रु, *see* *To* PLUNDER.—(Injure, corrupt) दुष् (c. 10. दूषयति -यितुं), नश् (c. 10. नाशयति -यितुं), दूषणं कृ, नाशं कृ, क्षतिं कृ.—(Indulge too much) अतिशयेन छन्दो ऽनुवृत्, अत्यन्तं लल्, *see* *To* INDULGE.

To SPOIL, *v. n.* दुष् (c. 4. दुष्यति, दोष्टुं), नश् (c. 4. नश्यति, नंष्टुं).

SPOIL, *s.* (That which is taken in war, plunder) लोप्त्रं, लोत्रं, लोतः -तं, युद्धोपार्जितद्रव्यं, युद्धजितद्रव्यं, युद्धजितधनं, युद्धसम्पादितधनं, युद्धसम्पादितद्रव्यं, *see* PLUNDER.—(In cattle) गोग्रहः.

SPOILED, SPOILT, *p. p.* (Plundered) लुण्ठितः -ता -तं.—(Injured) दूषितः -ता -तं, नाशितः &c., नष्टः -ष्टा -ष्टं, विनाशितः &c., लाटः -टा -टं.—(Too much indulged) अतिलालितः -ता -तं, *see* INDULGED.

SPOILER, *s.* (Plunderer) अपहारकः, अपहारकृत्.—(Injurer) दूषकः.

SPOILING, *s.* (Plundering) अपहारः -रणं, लुण्ठनं.—(Injuring) दूषणं.

SPOKE, *s.* (Of a wheel) अरं, आरा, चक्रसक्थि *n.*; 'a row of spokes,' अरावलिः -ली *f.*; 'a long-spoked wheel,' दीर्घसक्थि चक्रं.

SPOKEN, *p. p.* उक्तः -क्ता -क्तं, भाषितः -ता -तं, वदितः &c., भणितः &c., निगदितः &c., अभिहितः &c., कथितः &c., उदाहृतः -ता -तं, समुदाहृतः &c., अभिव्याहृतः &c., समुदीरितः &c., *see* SAID; 'spoken fast,' त्वरितोदितः -ता -तं, निरस्तः -स्ता -स्तं.

SPOKESMAN, *s.* वक्ता *m.* (कृ), प्रतिनिधिवक्ता *m.*, प्रतिनिधिवादी *m.* (न्).

SPOLIATION, *s.* अपहारः, अपहरणं, हरणं, लुण्ठनं, लुण्टनं. *See* PILLAGE.

SPONDEE, *s.* कर्णः, गगः, गुर्व्वक्षरद्वयं.

SPONGE, *s.* जलशोषणी or इस्पञ्जः or स्पञ्जः may perhaps be used.

To SPONGE, *v. a.* इस्पञ्जादिना मृज् (c. 1. मार्जति, c. 2. मार्ष्टि -र्ष्टुं).

SPONGER, *s.* परान्नपुष्टः, परान्नोत्सुकः, आगन्तुकः. *See* PARASITE.

SPONGINESS, *s.* शिथिलावयवत्वं, विरलावयवत्वं; 'of the gums,' परिदरः.

SPONGY, *a.* शिथिलावयवः -वा -वं, विरलावयवः &c., कोमलावयवः &c.

SPONSOR, *s.* प्रतिभूः *m.*, प्रतिनिधिः *m.*, धर्म्मप्रतिभूः *m.*, धर्म्मप्रतिनिधिः.

SPONTANEOUS, *a.* स्वयंकृतः -ता -तं, स्वेच्छापूर्व्वकः -का -कं, स्वेच्छामूलकः

&c., स्वेच्छाहेतुकः &c., यदृच्छामूलकः &c., स्वतःसिद्धः -द्धा -द्धं, स्वयंजातः -ता -तं, स्वच्छन्दः -न्दा -न्दं, स्वैरः -री -रं, कामहेतुकः -का -कं, स्वाभाविकः -की -कं, सात्त्विकः &c., सांसिद्धिकः &c., अयत्नकृतः -ता -तं, अयत्नभूतः -ता -तं, ऐच्छिकः -की -कं.

SPONTANEOUSLY, *adv.* स्वयं, स्वतस्, स्वच्छन्दात्, स्वभावतस्, स्वेच्छापूर्व्वं, इच्छातस्, स्वेच्छातस्, कामं. *See* VOLUNTARILY.

SPONTANEOUSNESS, SPONTANEITY, *s.* स्वेच्छा, यदृच्छा, स्वसन्तोषः.

SPOON, *s.* चमसः -सं, दर्व्वी, दर्व्विः *f.*, दर्व्विकः, दर्वी, दर्विः *f.*, दर्विकः, दार्वी, कम्बिः *f.*, खजः, खजाकः -का, खजिका, पाणिका, स्रुच् *f.* (च्), स्रुवः -वा; 'wooden-spoon,' तर्दूः *m. f.*, दारुहस्तकः.

SPOONFUL, *s.* चमसपूरणं, दर्व्विपूरणं, कम्बिपूरणं, कम्बिपूरकं.

SPORT, *s.* क्रीडा -डनं, खेला, केलिः -ली *m. f.*, लीला, विलासः, विहारः, देवः -वनं, कूर्द्दनं, नर्म्मन् *n.* (न्), कैलं, रासेरसः, द्रवः, *see* PLAY, PASTIME.—(Mockery) उपहासः, *see* MOCKERY.—(Diversion of the field) मृगया, *see* HUNTING.—(In sport) परिहासेन, लीलया.

To SPORT, *v. n.* क्रीड् (c. 1. क्रीडति -ते -डितुं), रम् (c. 1. रमते, रन्तुं), विलस् (c. 1. -लसति -सितुं), दिव्, विह्, कुर्द्द्, कूर्द्द् &c. *See To* PLAY, *v. n.*

SPORTING, *s.* (Hunting, &c.) मृगया, मृगव्यं; 'fond of it,' मृगयाशीलः.

SPORTIVE, *a.* क्रीडाशीलः -ला -लं, विलासी -सिनी &c., विहारी &c., विलासवान् -वती -वत् (त्), उल्लसः -सा -सं, सविलासः &c., सलीलः -ला -लं, सहेलः &c., समुल्लसितः &c., *see* PLAYFUL, FROLICSOME.

SPORTIVELY, SPORTIVENESS, *see* PLAYFULLY, PLAYFULNESS.

SPORTSMAN, *s.* मृगयाकारी *m.* (न्), मृगव्यकारी *m.*, मृगयाशीलः, मृगयाविहारी *m.*, मृगयुः *m.*, आखेटकः, व्याधः.

SPOT, *s.* (Mark) चिह्नं, लक्षणं, अङ्कः -ङ्कं, लाञ्छनं, पदं, *see* MARK.—(Stain) कलङ्कः, *see* STAIN.—(Dot, speck) विन्दुः *m.*, विप्रुट् *f.* (ष्), विप्रुट् *f.*, चिह्नं, अङ्कः, शून्यं; 'on the body,' तिलः -लकः -कं, *see* under MARK; 'in the moon,' शशः.—(Place, site) स्थानं, स्थलं -ली, देशः, प्रदेशः, पदं, आस्पदं, भूमिः *f.*, क्षेत्रं, भवनं; 'in a certain spot,' एकदेशे; 'on the spot,' तत्रैव.

To SPOT, *v. a.* चिह्न् (c. 10. चिह्नयति -यितुं), कलङ्क (nom. कलङ्कयति -यितुं), मलिन (nom. मलिनयति -यितुं), सकलङ्कं -ङ्कां कृ, शबलीकृ. *See To* STREAK.

SPOTLESS, *a.* निष्कलङ्कः -ङ्का -ङ्कं, कलङ्कहीनः -ना -नं, निर्मलः -ला -लं, निष्कल्मषः -षा -षं, अकल्मषः &c., अनघः &c. *See* SINLESS, BLAMELESS.

SPOTTED, *a.* चिह्नितः -ता -तं, विन्दुचिह्नितः &c., चित्रः -त्रा -त्रं, तिलकी &c., *see* SPECKLED.—(Stained) कलङ्की -ङ्किनी &c., कलङ्कितः &c.

SPOUSAL, SPOUSALS, *see* NUPTIAL, MARRIAGE.

SPOUSE, *s.* (Husband) पतिः, भर्त्ता *m.*—(Wife) भार्य्या, स्त्री.

SPOUT, *s.* प्रणाली, नालः -ली, नलः; 'vessel with a spout,' नलविशिष्टं पात्रं.

To SPOUT, *v. a.* प्रणालीद्वारेण अर्द्धम् उत्क्षिप् (c. 6. -क्षिपति -क्षेप्तुं), नलद्वारा अर्द्धम् उत्क्षिप् or बलवद् उत्क्षिप् or उद्गॄ (c. 10. -गारयति -यितुं) or निःसृ in caus. (-सारयति -यितुं) or निरस् (c 4. -अस्यति -सितुं).

To SPOUT, *v. n.* प्रणालीद्वारेण or नलद्वारेण बलवत् स्रु (c. 1. स्रवति -स्रोतुं) or प्रस्रु or निःस्रु or निर्गम्; 'to spout up or over,' उत्सेचनं कृ, उत्सेकं कृ.—(Mouth), *see* the word.

SPOUTED, *p.p.* बलवद् उत्क्षिप्तः -प्ता -प्तं or निःसारितः -ता -तं, उत्सिक्तः &c.

To SPRAIN, *v. a.* अतिशयेन स्नायुतननं कृ or स्नायुवितननं कृ, अतियत्नप्रयुक्तम् अस्थिस्नायुवितानं कृ, अतियत्नपूर्व्वम् अस्थिस्नायून् वितन् (c. 8. -तनोति -नितुं) or सन्धिबन्धनानि वितन्, अतियत्नपूर्व्वं सन्धिस्नायून् वितत्य गमनशक्तिं हृ; 'one's ankle,' अतिशययत्नपूर्व्वं पादसन्धिवितानं कृ.

SPRAIN, *s.* सन्धिवितानः, स्नायुवितानः, सन्धिवितननं, अतियत्नपूर्व्वः स्नायुतानः, अतितानः, अतिवितानः, अतियामः.

SPRAT, *s.* मलमीनः, तलमीनः, नडमीनः, चिलिचिमः, चिलीचिमः, चिलीचिमिः, चिलिचीमः.

To SPRAWL, *v. n.* हस्तपादादि प्रसार्य्य भूमौ शी (c. 2. शेते, शयितुं), बाहू चरणौ च इतस्ततः प्रसार्य्य भूमौ शी, इतस्ततो विक्षिप्ताङ्गो भूमौ शी, इतस्ततः प्रसारिताङ्गो भूमौ शी, इतस्ततो विक्षिप्तहस्तपादाभ्यां भूमौ शी.

SPRAWLING, *part.* इतस्ततः प्रसारिताङ्गो भूमौ शायी -यिनी -यि (न्).

SPRAY, *s.* (Sprig), *see* the word.—(Small particles of rain, &c.) शीकरः, सीकरः, तुषारः; 'abounding with it,' शीकरौघः -घा -घं.

To SPREAD, *v. a.* (As a carpet, mat, &c.) आस्तॄ (c. 9. -स्तृणाति, c. 5. -स्तृणोति -स्तरितुं -रीतुं), विस्तॄ, परिस्तॄ, संस्तॄ, आस्तरणं कृ; 'to spread a carpet,' पादपटास्तरणं कृ; 'a net,' जालं विस्तॄ.—(Scatter) कॄ (c. 6. किरति, करितुं -रीतुं), विकॄ, विकिरणं कृ.—(Extend, expand) विस्तॄ in caus. (-स्तारयति -यितुं), प्रसृ in caus. (-सारयति -यितुं), विसृ, अतिसृ, वितन् (c. 8. -तनोति -नितुं), व्यातन्, प्रतन्, अतितन्, तन्, विततीकृ, प्रसारणं कृ, विसारणं कृ; 'spreading the wings,' पक्षौ प्रसार्य्य.—(Propagate, publish), *see* the words.

To SPREAD, *v. n.* प्रसृ (c. 1. -सरति -सर्त्तुं), विसृ, प्रसृप् (c. 1. -सर्पति -सर्प्तुं), विसृप्, प्रचर् (c. 1. -चरति -रितुं), प्ररुह् (c. 1. -रोहति -रोढुं), विस्तॄ in pass. (-स्तीर्य्यते), वितन् in pass. (-तन्यते), विततीभू, व्याप्, विजृम्भ्, विप्रस्था.—(As disease, contagion, &c.) विसृप्.

SPREAD, *p. p.* आस्तीर्णः -र्णा -र्णं, आस्तृतः -ता -तं, विस्तीर्णः &c., विस्तृतः -ता -तं, विस्तारितः &c., प्रसारितः &c., प्रसृतः &c., विसृतः &c., विकीर्णः -र्णा -र्णं, प्रवृद्धः -द्धा -द्धं, व्याप्तः -प्ता -प्तं, प्ररूढः -ढा -ढं, विततः -ता -तं, प्रविततः &c., सन्ततः &c., आततः &c., अवततः &c., ततः &c.

SPREAD, *s.* आस्तरणं, प्रसारः -रणं, विस्तारः, प्रसरः, व्याप्तिः *f.*, प्रतानः.

SPREADING, *part.* विसर्पी -र्पिणी -र्पि (न्), विसारी -रिणी &c., विसर्पन् -र्पन्ती -र्पत् (त्), प्रसर्पन् &c., प्रसर्पी &c., प्रतानी -निनी &c., प्रसरः -रा -रं, प्रसरन् &c., प्ररोही -हिणी &c., सान्तानिकः -की -कं; 'a spreading creeper,' लता प्रतानिनी.

SPREADING, *s.* विसर्पणं, प्रसर्पणं, प्रसारः -रणं, प्रसरः, विसरः, विसारः -रणं, प्रतानः, प्रततिः *f.*, सन्ततिः *f.*, विततिः *f.*, वितानः, प्रवर्धनं; 'of a carpet, &c.,' आस्तरणं, आस्तरः.

SPRIG, *s.* उपशाखा, शाखिका, प्रशाखिका, पल्लवः, दलं. *See* SHOOT.

SPRIGHTLINESS, *s.* प्रहर्षः, प्रहृष्टता, प्रफुल्लता, उल्लसता. *See* LIVELINESS.

SPRIGHTLY, *a.* उल्लासवृत्तिः -त्तिः -त्ति, प्रफुल्लः -ल्ला -ल्लं. *See* LIVELY.

To SPRING, *v. n.* (Begin to grow) उद्भिद् (c. 7. -भिनत्ति -भेत्तुं), प्रोद्भिद्, प्ररुह् (c. 1. -रोहति -रोढुं), अङ्कुर (nom. अङ्कुरयति -यितुं), स्फुट्, उद्भूत्, *see To* SHOOT, SPROUT.—(Proceed, arise, issue) उत्पद् (c. 4. -पद्यते -पत्तुं), समुत्पद्, जन् (c. 4. जायते, जनितुं), प्रभू, उद्भू, समुद्भू, सम्भू, निःसृ, प्रवृत्, उदि, अभ्युदि, प्ररुह्.—(Leap) प्लु (c. 1. प्लवते, प्लोतुं), वल्ग् (c. 1. वल्गति -ल्गितुं), आवल्ग्, *see To* LEAP; 'to spring up,' उत्प्लु, उत्पत्, प्रोत्पत्; 'down,' अवप्लु; 'over,' लङ्घ्; 'forth,' प्रस्कन्द्; 'upon,' महावेगेन आपत् or आक्रम् or आस्कन्द्, *see To* RUSH UPON.—(Crack) स्फुट्.—(Start) स्फुर् (c. 6. स्फुरति -रितुं), प्रस्फुर्.

To SPRING, *v. a.* (Produce quickly) अकस्माद् उत्पद् (c. 10. -पाद-

यति -यितुं) or जन् (c. 10. जनयति -यितुं) or संजन्.—(Cause to rise) उत्था in caus. (उत्थापयति -यितुं, rt. स्था), समुत्था, उद्भू in caus.—(Cause to explode) ज्वल् in caus., स्फुट् in caus.—(Crack, burst), *see* the words.

Spring, *s.* (Vernal season) वसन्तः, वसन्तकालः, वसन्तसमयः, पुष्पसमयः, पुष्पमासः, सुरभिः *m.*, ऋतुराजः, मधुः *m.*, मधुसमयः, मधुमासः, कामसखः, कामवल्लभः, पिकानन्दः, इष्यः; 'spring-festival,' वसन्तोत्सवः.—(Leap, bound) प्लवः, प्लुतं, वल्गितं, स्कन्दः, उत्प्लुतं, उद्गमः; 'as of a wolf,' अवलुम्पनं.—(Elasticity) स्थितिस्थापकत्वं -ता.—(Fountain) जलकूपः -पी, कूपः, जलाकरः, स्रोतस् *n.*, निर्झरः, झरः -रा -री, देवकुण्डं, उत्सः; 'spring-water,' कूपोदकं.—(Source of a river) सरिन्मुखं.—(Origin, source) योनिः *m. f.*, मूलं, आदिः *m.*, *see* Source, Rise.—(Prime) प्रौढिः *f.*, प्रौढता.—(Spring-tide) उच्चवेला.

Springe, *s.* पाशः, कूटपाशः, जालं, उन्माथः, वागुरा, कूटयन्त्रं.

Springiness, *s.* स्थितिस्थापकत्वं -ता, स्थितिस्थापकगुणः, वेतसगुणकता.

Springing, *s.* (Leaping), *see* the word.—(Of plants) उद्भेदः, उद्भवनं.

Springy, *a.* स्थितिस्थापकविशिष्टः -ष्टा -ष्टं, वेतसगुणकः -का -कं.

To sprinkle, *v. a.* सिच् (c. 6. सिञ्चति, सेक्तुं), अवसिच्, निषिच्, संसिच्, अवकॄ (c. 6. -किरति -करितुं -रीतुं), अभ्यवकॄ, पर्यवकॄ, समवकॄ, प्रकॄ, विकॄ, कॄ, उक्ष् (c. 1. उक्षति -क्षितुं), अभ्युक्ष्, प्रोक्ष्, समुक्ष्, सेकं कृ, सेचनं कृ, अवसेकं कृ, अवसेचनं कृ, प्रोक्षणं कृ.

To sprinkle, *v. n.* शीक् (c. 1. शीकते -कितुं), च्युत्. *See To* drizzle.

Sprinkled, *p. p.* सिक्तः -क्ता -क्तं, अभिषिक्तः &c., कृताभिषेकः -का -कं, प्रोक्षितः -ता -तं, समुक्षितः &c., अभ्युक्षितः &c., कीर्णः -र्णा -र्णं, आकीर्णः &c., विकीर्णः &c.; 'with water,' जलसिक्तः -क्ता -क्तं; 'with blood,' शोणितोक्षितः -ता -तं; 'having sprinkled,' सिक्त्वा, अभ्युक्ष्य.

Sprinkler, *s.* सेक्ता *m.* (क्तृ), सेचकः, प्रोक्षकः, प्रोक्षणकारी *m.* (न्).

Sprinkling, *s.* सेकः, सेचनं, अवसेकः, अवसेचनं, अभिषेकः, अभिषेचनं, प्रोक्षणं, अभ्युक्षणं, अभिप्रोक्षणं, आसारः, सिक्तता.

Sprite, *s.* छाया, अपच्छाया. *See* Spirit, Spectre, Ghost.

To sprout, *v. n.*, अङ्कुर (nom. अङ्कुरयति -यितुं), स्फुट् (c. 6. स्फुटति -टितुं), फुल्ल् (c. 1. फुल्लति -ल्लितुं), उद्भिद् (c. 7. -भिनत्ति -भेत्तुं), प्रोद्भिद्, प्ररुह् (c. 1. -रोहति -रोढुं), विकस् (c. 1. -कसति -सितुं). *See To* shoot, *v. n.*

Sprout, *s.* अङ्कुरः, प्ररोहः, पल्लवः -वं, नवपल्लवः -वं, किसलयः -यं, किशलयः -यं, किसलः -लं, किशलः -लं, नवविटपः, विटपः, अभिनवोद्भिद् *m.*, उद्भिद् *m.*, उद्भिज्जः, जालकं, विसलं, पत्त्रिणी, पत्रयौवनं.

Sprouted, *p. p.* उद्भिन्नः -न्ना -न्नं, अङ्कुरितः -ता -तं, पल्लवितः -ता -तं.

Sprouting, *part.* उद्भिद् *m. f. n.*, उद्भिज्जः -ज्जा -ज्जं, उद्भिदः -दा -दं, प्ररोही -हिणी -हि (न्), अङ्कुरितः -ता -तं, पल्लवी -विनी &c., पल्लवितः &c.

Sprouting, *s.* उद्भेदः, प्रोद्भेदः, प्ररोहः, उद्भवनं, स्फुटनं, स्फुटता.

Spruce, *s.* विनीतः -ता -तं, विनीतपरिच्छदः -दा -दं, परिमृष्टपरिच्छदः &c., विनीतवेशी -शिनी &c., सुवेशी &c. सुपरिच्छदी &c.

Sprucely, *adv.* विनीतं, विनीतपरिच्छदेन, विनीत in comp. *See* Neatly.

Spruceness, *s.* विनीतता, विनीतवेशित्वं, सुपरिच्छदः. *See* Neatness.

Sprung, *p. p.* उत्पन्नः -न्ना -न्नं, उद्भूतः -ता -तं, सम्भूतः &c., जातः &c., ज in comp., सम्भव in comp., उद्भव in comp., भव in comp.; 'sprung from a noble family,' महाकुलजः -जा -जं, सत्कुलजातः -ता -तं, सत्कुलसम्भवः -वा -वं, महाकुलभवः &c., महाकुलप्रसूतः -ता -तं; 'from a royal family,' राजवंशजः -जा -जं, राजवंश्यः -श्या -श्यं.

Spume, Spumous, Spumy. *See* Froth, Frothy.

Spun, *p. p.* तान्तवः -वी -वं, तन्त्री -न्त्रिणी -न्त्रि (न्), ताकेवः -वी -वं.

Spunge, *To* spunge, spungy. *See* Sponge, &c.

Spur, *s.* (For pricking a horse) प्रतोदः, तोदनं, अश्वतोदनं, कण्टकः.—(Of a cock) नखः.—(Incitement), *see* the word.

To spur, *v. a.* प्रतुद् (c. 6. -तुदति -तोत्तुं), प्रतोदेन तुद् or वितुद् or आतुद्, प्रतोदेन व्यध्.—(Incite), *see* the word.

Spurious, *a.* कृत्रिमः -मा -मं, कल्पितः -ता -तं, काल्पनिकः -की -कं, मिथ्या in comp., कपट or कूट in comp. *See* Counterfeit, False.

Spuriousness, *s.* कृत्रिमता -त्वं, कल्पितत्वं, काल्पनिकता, कूटता.

To spurn, *v. a.* (Kick) पादेन तड्, पादाघातं कृ, चरणाघातं कृ.—(Reject with disdain) गर्ह् (c. 1. गर्हते -र्हितुं), कुत्स् (c. 10. कुत्सयति -यितुं), अवज्ञा (c. 9. -जानाति -ज्ञातुं), अवमन् (c. 4. -मन्यते -मन्तुं), तुच्छीकृ, निराकृ, पराकृ, परिभू, कदर्थीकृ, कदर्थ्, लङ्घ्, गुप् in des., तिरस्कृ, धिक्कृ, *see To* scorn.

Spurned, *p. p.* पादाहतः -ता -तं, चरणाहतः &c., गर्हितः &c., निराकृतः &c.

To spurt, *v. a.* नलिकामुखाद् जलं बलेन निःसृ in caus. (-सारयति -यितुं).

To spurt, *v. n.* सूक्ष्मनालीमुखाद् बलेन or अतिवेगेन निःसृ (c. 1. -सरति -सर्तुं).

Spurt, *s.* सूक्ष्मनालीमुखाद् अतिवेगपूर्व्वो जलप्रवाहः or जलप्रपातः.

To sputter, *v. n.* (Speak spittingly) सनिष्ठीवं or सष्ठीवनं वद् (c. 1. वदति -दितुं), सथुत्कारं वद्, सथूत्कारं वद्, थूत्कृ.—(Throw out small particles) थुपुथुशब्दपूर्व्वं or थुत्कारपूर्व्वं सूक्ष्मकणान् क्षिप्.

Sputtered, *p. p.* थूत्कृतः -ता -तं, सनिष्ठीवम् or सथुत्कारम् उक्तः -क्ता -क्तं.

Spy, *s.* प्रणिधिः *m.*, चारः, गूढचारः, गूढचारी *m.* (न्), गूढपुरुषः, गूढगतिः *m.*, गुप्तचरः, गुप्तगतिः *m.*, गुप्तदूतः, गूढदूतः, मन्त्रगूढः, चरः, सूचकः, देशापेक्षः, रहस्याख्यायी *m.* (न्), पिशुनः, यथार्हवर्णः, चारासरितः, कापटिकः, अवसर्पः, अपसर्पः, प्रतिष्कः -ष्कशः -ष्कषः, स्पशः, उदास्थितः, हेरिकः, अनिरुद्धः, वनगुप्तः.

To spy, *v. a.* (Descry) दृश्, ईक्ष्, प्रेक्ष्, समीक्ष्, *see To* espy.—(Explore, inspect) निरीक्ष्, परीक्ष्, अवेक्ष्, वीक्ष्, समीक्ष्, प्रसमीक्ष्, निरूप् (c. 10. -रूपयति -यितुं), अन्विष्, अनुसन्धा, परिदृश्; 'to spy out a country,' देशनिरूपणं कृ, देशावेक्षणं कृ, देशापेक्षां कृ.

Squab, *a.* ह्रस्वस्थूलः -ला -लं, स्थूलः &c., घनः -ना -नं. *See* Dumpy.

To squabble, *v. n.* कलहं कृ, विवद्, व्यवक्रुश्. *See To* quarrel.

Squabble, *s.* कलहः, विवादः, कलिः *m.*, कलकलः, अपवादः, *see* Quarrel.

Squad, *s.* शस्त्राभ्यासकारी नवसैन्यगुल्मः, नवसैन्यदलं.

Squadron, *s.* सैन्यव्यूहः, सैन्यगुल्मः, सैन्यदलं, सैन्यसमूहः, सैन्यगणः.

Squalid, *a.* कुत्सितः -ता -तं, मलिनः -ना -नं, अमेध्यः &c. *See* Foul.

Squalidity, squalidness, *s.* कुत्सितत्वं, अमेध्यता -त्वं, मालिन्यं, समलता.

To squall, *v. n.* विक्रुश् (c. 1. -क्रोशति -क्रोष्टुं), रु, नद्, वाश्, *see To* scream.

Squall, *s.* (Cry) विक्रुष्टं, उत्क्रोशः, नादः, रावः, चीत्कारः, *see* Scream.—(Of wind, &c) झञ्झावातः, झञ्झानिलः, झञ्झा, *see* Gust.

Squally, *a.* झञ्झावातमयः -यी -यं, झञ्झानिलमयः &c. *See* Gusty.

To squander, *v. a.* व्ययीकृ, व्यय् (c. 1. व्ययति, c. 10. व्यययति -यितुं, rt. इ), अपरिमितव्ययं कृ, अतिव्ययं कृ, अतिशयव्ययं कृ. *See To* lavish.

Squandered, *p. p.* व्ययीकृतः -ता -तं, अतिव्ययितः &c. *See* Lavished.

Squanderer, *s.* अतिव्ययी *m.* (न्), अपरिमितव्ययी *m.* *See* Prodigal, *a.*

Squandering, *s.* (The act) अतिव्ययः, अपरिमितव्ययः, अतिमोक्षणं, *see* Prodigality, *s.*—*Pres. part.* व्ययमानः -ना -नं.

SQUARE, *a.* (Having four equal sides and angles) चतुरस्रः -स्रा -स्रं, चतुष्कोणः -णा -णं, समचतुर्भुजः -जा -जं, समचतुष्कोणः &c., समचतुरस्रः &c.—(Just), *see* JUST, *a.*

SQUARE, *s.* (The figure) चतुष्कोणः, समचतुष्कोणः, चतुरस्रं, समचतुरस्रं, चतुर्भुजः, समचतुर्भुजः, चतुष्कं.—(In arithmetic or algebra) वर्गः, द्विघातः, कृतिः *f.*; 'of a fraction,' भिन्नवर्गः; 'of a cube,' घनवर्गः.—(Open place, court, &c., in a town) चत्वरं, अङ्गनं, प्राङ्गणं, निकर्षणं, सन्निवेशः, स्थानं; 'formed by four houses,' चतुःशालं -ला -लकं.

To SQUARE, *v. a.* (In arithmetic, &c.) द्विघातं कृ, द्विगुणनं कृ, समगुणनं कृ, वर्ग (nom. वर्गयति -यितुं), वर्गं कृ.—(Regulate), *see* the word.

To SQUARE, *v. n.* युज् in pass. (युज्यते). *See To* SUIT, FIT, AGREE.

SQUARED, *p. p.* वर्गितः -ता -तं, आयोजितः &c. *See* REGULATED, ADJUSTED.

SQUARENESS, *s.* चतुष्कोणत्वं, चतुरस्रत्वं, चतुर्भुजत्वं, समचतुर्भुजत्वं.

SQUARE-ROOT, *s.* वर्गमूलं, द्विघातमूलं, मूलं, पदं, वर्गपदं.

To SQUASH, *v. a.* मृद् (c. 9. मृद्नाति, मर्द्दितुं), सम्मृद्, सम्पीड् (c. 10. -पीडयति -यितुं).

SQUASH, *s.* सम्मर्दः, अवमर्दः, मर्दनं, सम्पीडनं, चूर्णनं.

SQUASHED, *p. p.* सम्मर्द्दितः -ता -तं, मर्द्दितः &c., सम्पीडितः &c., चूर्णितः &c.

To SQUAT, *v. n.* उत्कुटुकासनं कृ, मन्दिरासनं कृ, अवसक्थिकासनं कृ; 'one who squats,' कृतावसक्थिकः -का -कं.

SQUAT, *s.* or *a.* (The posture) उत्कुटुकासनं.—(Dumpy), *see* the word.

To SQUEAK, SQUEAL, *v. n.* कर्कशस्वरेण रु (c. 2. रौति, रवितुं) or नद् (c. 1. नदति -दितुं) or रस् (c. 1. रसति -सितुं), कर्कशशब्दं कृ.

SQUEAK, SQUEAL, *s.* कर्कशरावः, कर्कशनादः, चित्कारः. *See* SHRIEK.

SQUEAKING, SQUEALING, *part.* कर्कशरावी -विणी -वि (न्), कर्कशनादी &c.

SQUEAMISH, *a.* वमनेच्छुः -च्छुः -च्छु, वमनोन्मुखः -खा -खं, विवमिषुः &c.

SQUEAMISHNESS, *s.* वमनेच्छा, वमनोन्मुखता, वान्त्युन्मुखता, विवमिषा.

To SQUEEZE, *v. a.* सम्पीड् (c. 10. -पीडयति -यितुं), पीड्, सम्मृद् (c. 9. -मृद्नाति -मर्द्दितुं), चूर्ण्, *see To* PRESS, CRUSH; 'with the hand,' मुष्टिसंग्राहेण पीड्.

SQUEEZE, *s.* सम्मर्दः -र्दनं, मर्दनं, सम्पीडनं, पीडनं, निपीडनं.

SQUEEZED, *p. p.* सम्पीडितः -ता -तं, पीडितः &c., निपीडितः &c., सम्मर्द्दितः -ता -तं, मर्द्दितः &c., *see* CRUSHED; 'with the hand,' मुष्टिसंग्राहपीडितः &c.

SQUIB, *s.* आग्नेयचूर्णगर्भा क्षुद्रनाली या वह्निसम्पर्काद् आकस्मिकशब्देन स्फुटति.—(Sarcastic writing) सव्यङ्ग्यलेखः, *see* LAMPOON.

To SQUINT, *v. n.* तिर्य्यग् दृश् (c. 1. पश्यति, द्रष्टुं), वक्रं दृश्, जिह्मं दृश्, तिर्य्यक् प्रेक्ष् (c. 1. -ईक्षते -क्षितुं), तिर्य्यग्दृष्टिः -ष्टिः -ष्टि भू, वक्रदृष्टिः -ष्टिः -ष्टि भू or अस्.

SQUINT, *s.* तिर्य्यग्दृष्टिः *f.* -ष्टित्वं, वक्रदृष्टिः *f.*, तिर्य्यक्प्रेक्षणं, दृष्टिवक्रता.

SQUINT-EYED, *a.* तिर्य्यग्दृष्टिः -ष्टिः -ष्टि, वक्रदृष्टिः &c., वलिरः -रा -रं, केकरः &c., केकराक्षः -क्षी -क्षं, वलिराक्षः &c., केदरः -रा -रं, दूरेरितेक्षणः -णा -णं, कुञ्चिकः -का -कं, टेरकः &c., टगरः -रा -रं, जिह्मदृष्टिः &c.

SQUIRE, *s.* (Attendant on a warrior) साम्नाहनिकः.—(Gentleman) महाशयः, महानुभावः, आर्य्यः, श्री prefixed, *see* SIR, GENTLEMAN.

SQUIRREL, *s.* वृक्षशायिका, वृक्षमर्कटिका, पर्णमृगः, चमरपुच्छः.

To SQUIRT, *v. a.* सूक्ष्मनालीमुखाद् जलं बलेन निःसृ in caus. (-सारयति -यितुं), नलिकामुखाद् जलम् अतिवेगेन निःसृ in caus. or निरस् (c. 4. -अस्यति -सितुं), वस्तिमुखाद् जलादि निःसृ in caus. or बहिःसृ in caus., धारायन्त्रमुखाद् जलादि बलवद् निःसृ in caus.

SQUIRT, *s.* धारायन्त्रं, नलिका, वस्तिः *m. f.*, धारानाली.

To STAB, *v. a.* कट्टारेण व्यध् (c. 4. विध्यति, व्यद्धुं) or छुर् (c. 6. छुरति -रितुं), त्वक्छेदं कृ, त्वग्भेदं कृ, त्वग्वेधनं कृ, त्वग्व्यधनं कृ. *See To* WOUND.

STAB, *s.* त्वग्भेदः, त्वक्छेदः, वेधः, वेधनं, छुरणं, कट्टाराघातः.

STABBED, *p. p.* छुरितः -ता -तं, विद्धः -द्धा -द्धं, वेधितः -ता -तं, कट्टारविद्धः &c., कट्टारभिन्नः -न्ना -न्नं; 'in the belly,' छुरितोदरः -रा -रं.

STABBER, *s.* त्वग्भेदकः, त्वक्छेदकः, त्वग्वेधकः, कट्टारपाणिः *m.*

STABILITY, *s.* स्थैर्य्यं, स्थिरता -त्वं, स्थायित्वं, स्थास्नुता -त्वं, धृतिः *f.*, धैर्य्यं, स्थावरत्वं, दृढता, दार्ढ्यं, द्रढिमा *m.*, स्तब्धता, दिधिः *f.*

STABLE, *a.* स्थिरः -रा -रं, स्थास्नुः -स्नुः -स्नु, स्थावरः -रा -रं, स्थाणुः -णुः -णु, स्तब्धः -ब्धा -ब्धं, धीरः &c. *See* FIRM.

STABLE, STABLING, *s.* (For horses) अश्वशाला, वाजिशाला, मन्दुरा, मन्दिरा, अश्वस्थानं, अश्वगोष्ठं, प्रग्रीवः -वं.—(For elephants) वारी, गजबन्धनी.

STABLE-BOY, *s.* अश्वपालः -लकः, सादी *m.* (न्). *See* GROOM.

STACK, *s.* राशिः *m.*, उत्करः, चयः, चितिः *f.* *See* HAY-STACK, PILE.

To STACK, *v. a.* राशीकृ, आचि (c. 5. -चिनोति -चेतुं), संचि. *See To* HEAP.

STACKED, *p. p.* चितः -ता -तं, राशीकृतः &c., आचितः &c. *See* HEAPED.

STAFF, *s.* (Stick, mace) दण्डः, वेत्रं, यष्टिः *m. f.*, वेत्रयष्टिः, लगुडः; 'of an ascetic or student,' आषाढः, अषाढः, राम्भः.—(Body of officers) नियोगिगणः, नियोगिसमूहः, अधिकारिसमूहः, अधिकारिणां गणः; 'one who belongs to the staff,' नियोगिगणाभ्यन्तरः.

STAFF-BEARER, *s.* दण्डपाणिः *m.*, दण्डधरः, वेत्रधरः. *See* MACE-BEARER.

STAG, *s.* मृगः, हरिणः, एणः, कुरङ्गः -ङ्गमः. *See* DEER.

STAGE, *s.* (For acting) रङ्गः, रङ्गभूमिः *f.*, रङ्गशाला, नेपथ्यं, भूमिका, नाट्यशाला, आनर्त्तः; 'speaking off the stage,' आकाशभाषणं, आकाशभाषितं.—(Theatre, drama), *see* the words.—(Raised platform) मञ्चः, मञ्चकः.—(Place of rest on a journey) मार्गे or अध्वनि विश्रामस्थानं or अश्वपरिवर्त्तनस्थानं, अवस्थानं.—(Single step or degree, station) पदं, अवस्था, स्थानं, आस्पदं, पदविः -वी *f.*, वृत्तिः *f.*, पर्य्यायः; 'last stage,' चरमावस्था; 'first stage,' प्रथमारम्भः, प्रत्युत्क्रमः, प्रथमचरणः; 'four stages of life,' अवस्थाचतुष्टयं.

STAGE-COACH, *s.* अध्वगवाहनं, मार्गगवाहनं, पथिकयानं, साधारणयानं.

STAGE-MANAGER, *s.* सूत्रधारः, स्थापकः, मारिषः. *See* MANAGER.

STAGE-PLAYER, *s.* नटः, नाटकः, रङ्गावतरणजीवी *m.* (न्). *See* PLAYER.

STAGER, *s.* (Old) ज्ञानवृद्धः, व्यवहारवृद्धः, *see* EXPERIENCED.

To STAGGER, *v. n.* विचल् (c. 1. -चलति -लितुं), संचल्, चल्, इतस्ततो विचल्, भ्रम् (c. 4. भ्राम्यति, भ्रमितुं), दोल (nom. दोलायते), आन्दोल. *see To* VACILLATE, OSCILLATE, HESITATE.

To STAGGER, *v. a.* विचल् in caus. (-चालयति -यितुं), सञ्चल्, इतस्ततो विचल्, भ्रम् in caus., आन्दोलनं कृ, विकल्पं जन्, शङ्कां जन्, साशङ्क -ङ्कां कृ.

STAGNANT, *a.* गतिरहितः -ता -तं, गतिहीनः -ना -नं, प्रवाहरहितः &c., प्रवाहहीनः &c., अप्रवाही -हिणी &c., स्थिरः -रा -रं, वेलाहीनः &c., अचलः -ला -लं, निश्चलः &c., निश्चेष्टः -ष्टा -ष्टं. *See* MOTIONLESS.

To STAGNATE, *v. n.* गतिहीनः -ना -नं भू, प्रवाहहीनः -ना -नं भू, स्थिरीभू, अचलः -ला -लं भू, निश्चलीभू, निश्चेष्टः -ष्टा -ष्टं भू.

STAGNATION, STAGNANCY, *s.* गतिहीनता, गत्यभावः, वेलाहीनता, प्रवाहहीनता, प्रवाहाभावः, अप्रवाहः, स्थिरता, अचलता, निश्चलता.

STAID, *a.* स्थिरः -रा -रं, स्थिरबुद्धिः -द्धिः -द्धि, गम्भीरः &c., धीरः &c.

STAIDNESS, *s.* धीरता, स्थिरता, गम्भीरता, गाम्भीर्य्यं, स्थिरबुद्धित्वं.

To STAIN, *v. a.* कलङ्क (nom. कलङ्कयति -यितुं), मलिन (nom. मलिनयति -यितुं), कलुष (nom. कलुषयति -यितुं), लिप् (c. 6. -लिम्पति, लेप्तुं) दुष् (c. 10. दूषयति -यितुं), लाञ्छ् (c. 1. लाञ्छति -ञ्छितुं), सकलङ्कं -ङ्कां कृ, सकलङ्कीकृ, समलीकृ, विवर्णीकृ.—(Dye) रञ्ज् (c. 10. रञ्जयति -यितुं).

STAIN, *s.* कलङ्कः, लाञ्छनं, चिह्नं, कलुषं, दूषणं, मालिन्यं, मलं, परिमलं, वैवर्ण्यं, विवर्णत्वं, वर्णविकारः, वर्णविकृतिः *f.*

STAINED, *p. p.* कलङ्कितः -ता -तं, मलिनितः &c., कलुषितः &c., लिप्तः -प्ता -प्तं, लाञ्छितः -ता -तं, कलङ्की -ङ्किनी -ङ्कि (न्), विकृतवर्णः -र्णा -र्णं, दूषितः -ता -तं; 'with blood,' रक्तविलिप्तः &c., रक्तमलिनः -ना -नं, *see* BLOOD-STAINED; 'with stained hands,' लिप्तहस्तः -स्ता -स्तं.

STAINLESS, *a.* निष्कलङ्कः -ङ्का -ङ्कं, कलङ्कहीनः -ना -नं, निर्मलः -ला -लं.

STAIR, *s.* सोपानं; 'flight of stairs,' सोपानपङ्क्तिः *f.*, *see* the next.

STAIR-CASE, STAIRS, *s.* सोपानपङ्क्तिः *f.*, सोपानश्रेणिः -णी *f.*, सोपानपंक्तिः *f.*, सोपानं, अधिरोहिणी, आरोहणं, निःश्रेणी, निःश्रयणी -यिणी, शालारं, वल्भिः -भी *f.*, पङ्क्तारः.

STAKE, *s.* (Of wood, &c.) शङ्कुः *m.*, कीलः -लकः, शूलः -लं, स्थाणुः *m.*, स्थूणा, शल्यं, शलाका, निमः, ध्रुवः; 'fastened by a stake,' कीलितः -ता -तं, कीलबद्धः -द्धा -द्धं; 'stake for empaling criminals,' शूलः -लं; 'burning at the stake,' तुषानलः, तुषाग्निः *m.*—(Any thing pledged or wagered) पणः, प्रतिपाणं, आक्षिकपणः, आक्षिकं, ग्लौचिः -ची *f.*, ग्रहः, आधिः *m.*, द्रव्यं, विषयः; 'to be at stake,' *see* JEOPARDY.

To STAKE, *v. a.* (Set or fasten with stakes) कील् (c. 10. कीलयति -यितुं), कीलकैर् बन्ध् or परिवेष्ट्.—(Wager, pledge) पण् (c. 1. पणते -णितुं), परिपण्, पणं कृ, पणनं कृ, न्यस् (c. 4. -अस्यति -सितुं), निक्षिप् (c. 6. -क्षिपति -क्षेप्तुं).

STALE, *a.* उषितः -ता -तं, पर्युषितः &c., विरसः -सा -सं, नीरसः &c., असारः -रा -रं, निःसारः &c., रात्र्यन्तरितः -ता -तं; 'stale food,' पर्युषितभोजनं.—(Worn out, trite) जीर्णः -र्णा -र्णं, वृद्धः -द्धा -द्धं, पुराणः -णा -णं, उच्छिष्टः -ष्टा -ष्टं; 'stale device,' उच्छिष्टकल्पना.

To STALE, *v. n.* मिह् (c. 1. मेहति, मेढुं), मूत्र् (c. 10. मूत्रयति -यितुं), मूत्रं कृ, मूत्रोत्सर्गं कृ, मूत्रत्यागं कृ, प्रस्रावं कृ.

STALENESS, *s.* पर्युषितत्वं, उषितत्वं, विरसता, उच्छिष्टता, जीर्णता.

STALK, *s.* (Of a plant) मञ्जरिः -री, नाली -ला -लं -लः, नालिका, नाडी -डिः *f.* -डं, नाडिका, काण्डः, वृन्तं, पल्लवः -वं, स्तम्भः, कडङ्गः, पिञ्जरं, वोण्टः; 'of sugar-cane,' अङ्कारिका.—(Stately walk) हंसगतिः *f.*, गजगतिः *f.*, साटोपगतिः *f.*

To STALK, *v. n.* गजवत् or हंसवत् क्रम् or चर् or गम्, साटोपं क्रम् or गम् or चल्, गजगतिः -तिः -ति भू, हंसगामी &c. भू. *See* STATELY.

STALKED, *a.* (Having a stalk) मञ्जरितः -ता -तं, काण्डवान् -वती &c.

STALL, *s.* (For a horse) अश्वस्थानं, अश्वगोष्ठं.—(For an ox) गोष्ठं, गोस्थानं.—(Shop) वीथिः -थी, आपणः, साधृतं, *see* SHOP, *a.*

STALLION, *s.* बीजाश्वः, सवृषणो ऽश्वः, अच्छिन्नमुष्को ऽश्वः.

STAMEN, *s.* (Of a flower) पुंकेसरः, पौरुषकेसरः, केसरः.

STAMINA, *s. pl.* बलसाधनं, बलहेतुः *m.*, सारसाधनं, साराङ्गं.

To STAMMER, *v. n.* स्खलद्वाक्येन वद् (c. 1. वदति -दितुं), स्खलितं वद्, स्खलितस्वरेण वद्, गद्गद (nom. गद्गदति), गद्गदवाचा वद्, अस्फुटस्वरेण वद्, अव्यक्ताक्षरैर् वद्, अस्पष्टाक्षरैर् वद्, वाग्वैकल्येन वद्, अस्फुटं वद्, अस्पष्टं वद्, म्लेच्छ् (c. 1. म्लेच्छति, c. 10. म्लेच्छयति -यितुं).

STAMMERER, *s.* स्खलद्वाक्यः, स्खलितवाक्यः, स्खलितस्वरः, वाग्विकलः, स्खलन्ती *m.*, अव्यक्तवादी *m.* (न्), अस्पष्टवादी *m.*, अस्फुटवादी *m.*, मदकलवादी *m.*

STAMMERING, *s.* वाक्स्खलनं, अव्यक्तवादः, अस्फुटवादः, अस्पष्टवादः.

To STAMP, *v. a.* (Strike with the bottom of the foot) पादतलेन प्रहृ (c. 1. -हरति -हर्तुं) or आहन् (c. 2. -हन्ति -न्तुं), पादविक्षम्भं कृ, पादाघातं कृ, पादप्रहारं कृ; 'he stamps on the ground,' भूमौ पादप्रहारं करोति.—(Impress, imprint) अङ्क् (c. 10. अङ्कयति -यितुं), चिह्न् (c. 10. चिह्नयति -यितुं), मुद्र (nom. मुद्रयति -यितुं), मुद्रीकृ.—(Form) कॢप्, संकॢप्, रच्, घट्.—(Pound with the feet) पादाघातेन पिष् (c. 7. पिनष्टि, पेष्टुं) or निष्पिष् or मृद् or चूर्ण्, पादसम्मर्दं कृ.

STAMP, *s.* (Instrument for impressing) मुद्रा, मुद्रिका, मुद्राङ्कनयन्त्रं.—(Impression or mark made) मुद्रा, मुद्रिका, अङ्कः, चिह्नं, न्यासः.—(With the foot) पादाघातः, पादप्रहारः, पादन्यासः, पादविक्षम्भः.—(Character, form) रूपं, स्वरूपं, आकारः, आकृतिः *f.*, संस्कारः, संस्थानं, स्वभावः, प्रकृतिः *f.*, व्यूहनं.—(Stamped paper) मुद्रितपत्रं, मुद्राङ्कितपत्रं.

STAMPED, *p. p.* मुद्रितः -ता -तं, मुद्राङ्कितः &c., मुद्रीकृतः &c., अङ्कितः -ता -तं, चिह्नितः &c., समुद्रः -द्रा -द्रं. *See* IMPRESSED.

STAMPING, *s.* अङ्कनं, मुद्राङ्कनं; 'with the feet,' पादविक्षम्भः, *see* STAMP.

To STANCH, *v. a.* प्रवाहरोधं कृ, प्रस्रावरोधं कृ, प्रस्रावं रुध् (c. 7. रुणद्धि, रोद्धुं) or स्तम्भ् (c. 10. स्तम्भयति -यितुं), प्रवाहं रुध्, शुष् (c. 10. शोषयति -यितुं).

To STANCH, *v. n.* रुद्धप्रवाहः -हा -हं भू, रुद्धप्रस्रावः -वा -वं भू, शुष् (c. 4. शुष्यति), रुद्धः -द्धा -द्धं भू, स्तम्भितः -ता -तं भू.

STANCH, *a.* धीरः -रा -रं, दृढः -ढा -ढं, *see* FIRM; 'a stanch friend,' दृढसुहृद्; 'a stanch partisan,' बद्धपक्षपातः, दृढभक्तिः *m.*

STANCHED, *p.p.* रुद्धः -द्धा -द्धं, रुद्धप्रवाहः -हा -हं, स्तम्भितप्रवाहः &c.

STANCHION, *s.* क्षुद्रस्तम्भः, उपस्तम्भः, अवष्टम्भः, स्थाणुः *m.*, स्थूणा.

STANCHNESS, *s.* दृढता, दार्ढ्यं, धीरता, धैर्य्यं, दृढभक्तित्वं, दृढसौहृदं.

To STAND, *v. n.* (Be erect on the feet) दण्ड (nom. दण्डायते), स्था (c. 2. तिष्ठति, स्थातुं), पादाभ्यां स्था.—(Be stationary) स्था, अवस्था, प्रतिष्ठा, सम्प्रतिष्ठा.—(Be placed) स्था, वृत्.—(Remain) स्था, अवस्था, पर्यवस्था, वृत् (c. 1. वर्त्तते -र्त्तितुं), *see* *To* REMAIN.—(Stop, not to proceed) स्था, संस्था, अवस्था, स्तम्भ् (c. 1. स्तम्भते -म्भितुं), निवृत्, विरम् (c. 1. -रमति -रन्तुं), रुद्धगतिः -तिः -ति भू, स्थिरः -रा -रं भू.—(Be in any state) भू (c. 1. भवति -वितुं), वृत्, अस्.—(Stand by or near) उपस्था, आस्था, अनुष्ठा, समीपं स्था.—(Stand by, support), *see* *To* DEFEND, HELP, SIDE WITH.—(Stand for, in the place of) भूमौ or स्थाने वृत्; 'she stands in the place of a friend,' सखीभूमौ वर्त्तते, *see* *To* REPRESENT.—(Stand for, be a candidate for any office) अमुकपदं प्राप् in des. (प्रेप्सति -प्सितुं, rt. आप्) or अभ्याप् in des. (अभीप्सति), पदप्रेप्सुः -प्सुः -प्सु भू, पदाभिलाषी -षिणी &c. भू, पदकामुकः -का -कं भू.—(Stand off) दूरे or दूरतः स्था, दूरतो वृत्.—(Stand out), *see* *To* PROJECT, PERSIST.—(Stand over) अधिष्ठा.—(Stand round) परिष्ठा, पर्युपस्था, परितः स्था, अभितः स्था.—(Stand up) उत्था (c. 1. उत्तिष्ठति -थातुं, rt. स्था), समुत्था.—(Stand against), *see* *To* OPPOSE, RESIST.

To STAND, *v. a.* (Endure) सह् (c. 1. सहते, सोढुं), विषह्, *see To* BEAR.

STAND, *s.* (Station) स्थानं, पदं, अवस्थानं.—(Stop, halt) स्तम्भः, गतिस्तम्भः, गतिरोधः, स्थितिः *f.*, अवस्थितिः *f.*, यतिः *f.*; 'to bring to a stand,' स्तम्भ् (c. 10. स्तम्भयति -यितुं), विष्टम्भ्, गतिरोधं कृ, गतिं रुध्; 'brought to a stand,' स्तम्भितः -ता -तं, स्तब्धः -ब्धा -ब्धं, रुद्धगतिः -तिः -ति, गतिहीनः -ना -नं.—(Platform) मञ्चः, मञ्चकः; 'for spectators,' प्रेक्षागारं.—(Frame, support, receptacle) मञ्चः, तलः, उपस्तम्भः, वृक्षः, आधारः, पात्रं; 'of a lamp or candle,' दीपाधारः, दीपपादपः, दीपवृक्षः, शिखावृक्षः, शिखातरुः *m.*, दीपपात्रं; 'of a water-jar,' कुम्भं.

STANDARD, *s.* (Ensign) ध्वजः, पताका, केतनं, केतुः *m.*, वैजयन्ती -न्तिका, *see* FLAG.—(Rule, measure) प्रमाणं, परिमाणं, मानं, सूत्रं; 'of gold,' वर्णिका.

STANDARD-BEARER, *s.* ध्वजवान् *m.* (त्), पताकी *m.* (न्), ध्वजी *m.*, ध्वजधारी *m.*, पताकाधारी *m.*, पताकावाही *m.*, वैजयन्तिकः.

STANDING, *part.* or *a.* (In a standing posture) दण्डायमानः -ना -नं.—(Being placed, remaining) स्थ in comp., स्थित or अवस्थित in comp., स्थायी -यिनी -यि (न्), स्थाता -त्री -तृ (तृ); 'on the road,' मार्गस्थः -स्था -स्थं; 'at a window,' वातायनस्थः &c., वातायनाश्रितः -ता -तं.—(Standing up or erect) उत्थितः -ता -तं, उत्थः -त्था -त्थं.—(Standing on end, as the hair) उत्तम्भितः -ता -तं, पुलकितः &c., उन्नतः &c., हृष्टः -ष्टा -ष्टं.—(Lasting) चिरस्थायी &c., स्थायी &c., कालिकः -का -कं, *see* LASTING.—(Stagnant), *see* the word.

STANDING, *s.* (Continuance) स्थायित्वं, स्थितिः *f.*, अवस्थितिः *f.*, संस्थितिः *f.*; 'of long standing,' चिरस्थायी &c., *see* LASTING.—(Station) स्थानं, पदं, पदवी, आस्पदं; 'high standing,' उच्चपदं, *see* RANK.

STANZA, *s.* श्लोकः, गाथा, तूर्णिः *m.*, ग्रन्थः, तोटकं; 'foot or line of a stanza,' पदं, पादः, पद्; 'stanza by stanza,' पद्धस्.

STAPLE, *s.* (Mart, emporium) वाणिज्यनगरी, महाजनकर्म्मयोग्या नगरी.—(Loop of iron) लोहपुटकं, लोहवलयः -यं.

STAPLE, *a.* मुख्यः -ख्या -ख्यं, प्रधानः -ना -नं, वाणिज्यप्रधानः &c.

STAR, *s.* तारा, तारका, तारिका, नक्षत्रं, ऋक्षं, उडुः *f.*, उडु *n.*, उडुः, ज्योतिस् *n.*, ज्योतिषी, भासमः, रात्रिजं, भं; 'fixed stars,' नक्षत्राणि *n. pl.*; 'the stars collectively,' नक्षत्रगणः, नक्षत्रमण्डलं, उडुगणः, भगणः; 'falling star,' उल्का, अग्न्युत्पातः; 'falling of a star,' तारापातः, उल्कापातः; 'polar star,' ध्रुवः, *see* POLAR; 'star under which one is born,' जन्मनक्षत्रं, नाडीनक्षत्रं.

STARBOARD, *s.* (Right side of a ship) नावो दक्षिणपार्श्वः.

STARCH, *s.* आहारः, मण्डः -ण्डं, गोधूमादिजमण्डः, स्तब्धीकरणगुणकः श्यानलेपः or सान्द्रलेपः, स्तार्चसंज्ञकं श्यानद्रव्यं.

STARCH, *a.* स्तब्धः -ब्धा -ब्धं, दृढः -ढा -ढं, कठिनः -ना -नं.

To STARCH, *v. a.* पूर्व्वोक्तश्यानद्रव्येण लिप् or स्तब्धीकृ or दृढीकृ.

STARCHED, *p. p.* स्तब्धीकृतः -ता -तं, दृढीकृतः &c., श्यानद्रव्यलिप्तः &c.

To STARE, *v. n.* अनिमेषदृष्ट्या or अनिमिषदृष्ट्या आलोक् (c. 10. -लोकयति -यितुं, c. 1. -लोकते -कितुं), अनिमिषनयनाभ्यां दृश् (c. 1. पश्यति, द्रष्टुं) or निरीक्ष् (c. 1, -ईक्षते -क्षितुं), विवृतनयनाभ्यां or उत्फुल्लनयनाभ्यां दृश्, स्थिरदृष्ट्या or बद्धदृष्ट्या or शून्यदृष्ट्या निरीक्ष् or आलोक्, अनन्यदृष्ट्या निरीक्ष्, उन्मीलितनयनाभ्यां दृश्, फुल्ललोचनाभ्यां दृश्, उन्मील् (c. 1. -मीलति -लितुं).

STARE, *s.* अनिमेषदृष्टिः *f.*, अनिमिषदृष्टिः *f.*, अनिमेषावलोकनं, स्थिरदृष्टिः *f.*, अनन्यदृष्टिः *f.*, शून्यदृष्टिः *f.*, शून्या दृष्टिः, बद्धदृष्टिः *f.*

STARING, *part.* or *a.* अनिमेषदृष्टिः -ष्टिः -ष्टि, अनिमिषदृष्टिः &c., अनिमेषावलोकी -किनी -कि (न्), विवृतनयनः -ना -नं, उत्फुल्लनयनः &c., फुल्लनयनः &c., फुल्ललोचनः -ना -नं, प्रफुल्ललोचनः &c., शून्यदृष्टिः -ष्टिः -ष्टि, उन्मीलितः -ता -तं, उन्मीलिताक्षः -क्षा -क्षं, विवृताक्षः &c., उन्मिषन् -षन्ती -षत् (त्); 'with astonishment,' विस्मयोत्फुल्लनयनः &c.

STARK, *a.* (Mere, entire) केवलः -ला -लं, अत्यन्तः -न्ता -न्तं, साकल्यः &c.

STARK, *adv.* केवलं, अत्यन्तं, अशेषतस्. *See* ENTIRELY, WHOLLY.

STARLESS, *a.* ताराहीनः -ना -नं, नक्षत्रहीनः &c., हतज्योतीः -तीः -तिः (स्).

STARLIGHT, *s.* ताराप्रकाशः, नक्षत्रप्रकाशः, नक्षत्रप्रभा, ज्योत्स्ना.

STARLING, *s.* (Kind of bird) शारिका, सारिका.

STARRY, *a.* (Belonging to the stars) तारासम्बन्धी -न्धिनी -न्धि (न्), नाक्षत्रः -त्री -त्रं, आर्क्षः -र्क्षी -र्क्षं.—(Abounding with stars, consisting of them) तारकी -किणी &c., तारकितः -ता -तं, तारामयः -यी -यं, नक्षत्रमयः &c., नक्षत्राकीर्णः -र्णा -र्णं, ताराकीर्णः &c., नक्षत्रवान् -वती -वत् (त्), नक्षत्रव्याप्तः -प्ता -प्तं, बहुनक्षत्रः -त्रा -त्रं, प्रचुरतारः -रा -रं; 'starry firmament,' नक्षत्रमण्डलं, भचक्रं, खगोलः; 'starry host,' नक्षत्रगणः, भगणः.

To START, *v. n.* (Move suddenly, as if by a twitch) स्फुर् (c. 6. स्फुरति -रितुं), प्रस्फुर्, अकस्मात् कम्प् (c. 1. कम्पते -म्पितुं) or विकम्प् or स्पन्द् (c. 1. स्पन्दते -न्दितुं), आकस्मिकस्फुरणं कृ.—(From fear) साध्वसात् or साध्वसोपहतत्वात् कम्प्, *see To* QUIVER.—(Commence a journey) प्रस्था (c. 1. -तिष्ठते -ष्ठातुं), प्रस्थानं कृ, *see To* SET OUT.—(Start aside) अकस्मात् स्वस्थानाद् विचल् or भ्रंश् or विच्यु.—(Start up) अकस्मात् or सहसा उत्था (c. 1. उत्तिष्ठति -त्थातुं) or समुत्था, अकस्माद् उत्पद् (c. 4. -पद्यते -पत्तुं) or उद्भू.

To START, *v. a.* (Alarm, rouse) त्रस् in caus. (त्रासयति -यितुं), उत्त्रस्, भी in caus., कम्प् in caus., उत्था in caus. (उत्थापयति -यितुं, rt. स्था), समुत्था in caus.—(Put in motion) चल् (c. 10. चालयति -यितुं), संचल्.—(Produce suddenly) अकस्मात् उत्पद् in caus.—(Propose), *see* the word.

START, *s.* (Sudden motion) स्फुरणं, कम्पः, स्पन्दनं, आकस्मिकस्फुरणं; 'from fear,' साध्वसकम्पः, साध्वसोत्कम्पः.—(Sudden spring) आकस्मिकप्लुतं.—(Sudden effort followed by intermission) सविच्छेदयत्नः, आकस्मिकयत्नः.—(First setting out) गमनारम्भः, प्रस्थानारम्भः.

STARTED, *p. p.* (Suddenly frightened) अकस्मात् त्रासितः -ता -तं or भीषितः &c.—(Put in motion) सञ्चालितः &c.—(Set out) प्रस्थितः -ता -तं.

STARTING, *s.* स्फुरणं, *see* START, *s.*—(Of tears) वाष्पोद्गमः.

STARTING, *part.* स्फुरन् -रन्ती -रत् (त्); 'with fear,' साध्वसोत्कम्पी -म्पिनी &c., त्रासविकम्पी &c.—(As the eyes) निर्दारितः -ता -तं.

To STARTLE, *v. a.* आकस्मिकत्रासेन कम्प् in caus. (कम्पयति -यितुं) or विकम्प्, आकस्मिकत्रासं जन् (c. 10. जनयति -यितुं), आकस्मिकसाध्वसं जन्, अकस्मात् त्रस् in caus. or कम्प् in caus.

To STARTLE, *v. n.* आकस्मिकसाध्वसात् कम्प् (c. 1. कम्पते -म्पितुं) or विकम्प्, आकस्मिकत्रासात् स्फुर् (c. 6. स्फुरति -रितुं).

STARTLED, *p. p.* अकस्मात् त्रासितः -ता -तं or भीषितः -ता -तं or कम्पितः &c.; 'in a very startled manner,' चकितचकितं.

STARVATION, *s.* अनाहारः -रत्वं, निराहारत्वं, निरन्नता -त्वं, अनाहाराय-

सादः, क्षुधावसन्नता, अपुष्टता; 'death by starvation,' अनाहारमृत्युः *m.*, अनाहारनाशः.

To STARVE, *v. n.* अनाहारेण मृ (c. 6. म्रियते, मर्त्तुं), निराहारत्वात् or आहाराभावात् मृ or नश् (c. 4. नश्यति -शितुं) or अवसद् (c. 1. -सीदति -सत्तुं), क्षुधावसन्नत्वात् मृ, क्षुधया मृ.

To STARVE, *v. a.* अनाहारेण हन् (c. 2. हन्ति -न्तुं) or मृ (c. 10. मारयति -यितुं), निराहारत्वेन नश् (c. 10. नाशयति -यितुं); 'one's self,' अनाहारेण or आहारविरहेण आत्मानं हन्.

STARVED, *p. p.* अनाहारावसन्नः -न्ना -न्नं, क्षुधावसन्नः &c., अनाहारमृतः -ता -तं, निराहारः -रा -रं, निरन्नः -न्ना -न्नं, क्षुधापीडितः -ता -तं, क्षुधार्दितः &c.

STARVELING, *s.* अनाहारकृशः &c., अपुष्टः &c., विपुष्टः &c., *see* LEAN.

STARVING, *a.* निराहारः -रा -रं, आहाररहितः -ता -तं, अन्नरहितः &c., निरन्नः -न्ना -न्नं, क्षुधार्त्तः -र्त्ता -र्त्तं. *See* STARVED.

STATE, *s.* (Condition) अवस्था, दशा, स्थितिः *f.*, वृत्तिः *f.*, भावः, गतिः *f.*, ता or त्वं affixed, *see* CONDITION; 'former state,' पूर्व्वस्थितिः *f.*; 'good state,' सुस्थितिः *f.*; 'bad state,' दुःस्थितिः *f.*, दुर्दशा; 'natural state,' स्वभावः; 'state of mind,' चित्तवृत्तिः *f.*; 'the two states of life, viz. happiness and misery,' अवस्थाद्वयं; 'the four states, viz. childhood, youth, manhood, and old age,' अवस्थाचतुष्टयं.—(Grandeur, pomp) ऐश्वर्य्यं, प्रतापः, श्रीः *f.*, ऐश्वर्य्यप्रतापः, राज्यप्रतापः, *see* POMP, MAJESTY.—(Ruling power, government) परमाधिकारः, राज्याधिकारः, राज्यं, राज in comp., *see* GOVERNMENT; 'state affairs,' राजकार्य्यं; 'state elephant,' राजहस्ती *m.*, राजेभः; 'state maxim or rule,' राजधर्म्मः; 'state secret,' राजगुह्यं; 'eight offices of state,' अष्टाधिकाराः *m. pl.* —(Whole body of people united under one government) राज्यं, राष्ट्रं, प्रजागणः, प्रजासमूहः.

To STATE, *v. a.* निविद् (c. 10. -वेदयति -यितुं), आविद्, विज्ञा in caus. (-ज्ञापयति -यितुं), व्यक्तं कथ् (c. 10. कथयति -यितुं) or निगद् (c. 1. -गदति -दितुं), उपन्यस् (c. 4. -अस्यति -सितुं), उपपद् (c. 10. -पादयति -यितुं), वृत्तान्तविवरणं कृ, वृत्तान्तविज्ञापनं कृ, वृत्तान्तव्याख्यां कृ.

STATED, *p. p.* (Told, represented) आवेदितः -ता -तं, निवेदितः &c., व्यक्तं कथितः -ता -तं or निगदितः &c., उपन्यस्तः -स्ता -स्तं, उपपादितः -ता -तं.—(Settled, regular) नियतः -ता -तं, नियमितः &c., नित्यः -त्या -त्यं.

STATELINESS, *s.* गौरवं, आटोपः, साटोपत्वं, प्रौढता, प्रौढिः *f.*, उद्धतिः *f.*, ऐश्वर्य्यं, प्रतापः, विभूतिः *f.* *See* MAJESTY.

STATELY, *a.* साटोपः -पा -पं, प्रौढः -ढा -ढं, गौरववृत्तिः -त्तिः -त्ति, आयतिमान् -मती &c., उद्धतः -ता -तं, *see* MAJESTIC, DIGNIFIED; 'in gait,' साटोपगामी -मिनी -मि (न्), गजगतिः -तिः -ति, हंसगामी &c., खेलगामी &c., खेलगतिः -तिः -ति.

STATEMENT, *s.* आवेदनं, निवेदनं, विज्ञापनं, विज्ञप्तिः *f.*, उपन्यासः, उपपादनं, वृत्तान्तविवरणं, वृत्तान्तविज्ञापनं, वृत्तान्तव्याख्या, पक्षः.

STATESMAN, *s.* राज्यनीतिज्ञः, राज्यनीतिकुशलः, राज्यकर्म्मकुशलः, राजधर्म्मवित् *m.*, राजनीतिविशारदः, नीतिज्ञः, नीतिकुशलः, राजकार्य्यधुरन्धरः, राजकार्य्यभारी *m.* (न्), राजमन्त्री *m.*, चारेक्षणः.

STATESMANSHIP, *s.* नीतिः *f.*, राज्यनीतिः *f.*, नीतिविद्या, राज्यनयः.

STATION, *s.* (Place, post) स्थानं, पदं, पदविः -वी *f.*, आस्पदं, स्थलं, अवस्थानं, अवस्थितिः *f.*, स्थितिः *f.*, वृत्तिः *f.*; 'for cattle,' गोस्थानं, गोष्ठं, गोव्रजः; 'for soldiers,' सैन्यस्थानं, गुल्मस्थानं.—(Resting-place) विश्रामस्थानं.—(Office) नियोगः, अधिकारः, पदं, पदवी.—(Rank) पदं, पदविः -वी *f.*, वृत्तिः *f.*, *see* RANK; 'high station,' उच्चपदं, परमपदं; 'to take one's station,' स्वस्थानम् आश्रि.

To STATION, *v. a.* स्था in caus. (स्थापयति -यितुं), प्रतिष्ठा, अवस्था; 'in any post,' पदे or अधिकारे नियुज् (c. 10. -योजयति -यितुं).

STATIONARY, *a.* (Fixed) स्थावरः -रा -रं, स्थाणुः -णुः -णु, स्थायुकः -का -कं, स्थिरः -रा -रं, अचरः &c., अचलः -ला -लं, निश्चलः &c., अविक्रमः -मा -मं, अचलिष्णुः -ष्णुः -ष्णु, अचरिष्णुः &c., गतिहीनः -ना -नं, वर्त्तिष्णुः &c., वर्त्तनः -ना -नं, सन्निविष्टः -ष्टा -ष्टं.—(Not advancing) अवर्धमानः -ना -नं.

STATIONED, *p. p.* स्थापितः -ता -तं, प्रतिष्ठापितः &c., पदनियुक्तः -क्ता -क्तं.

STATIONER, *s.* लेखसाधनविक्रेता *m.* (तृ), लेखसामग्रीविक्रेता *m.*, लिपिसज्जाविक्रयी *m.* (न्), लेखनपत्रविक्रयी *m.*, लेख्यपत्रादिविक्रेता *m.*

STATIONERY, *s.* लेखसाधनादि *n.*, लेखसाधनं, लिपिसज्जा, लेखसामग्री.

STATISTIC, STATISTICAL, *a.* देशस्थितिसम्बन्धी -न्धिनी &c., देशस्थितिविषयकः -का -कं, देशावस्थाविषयकः &c., देशरीतिविषयकः &c.

STATISTICS, *s. pl.* देशस्थितिविद्या, देशस्थितिरीतिप्रकरणं.

STATUARY, *s.* (Image-carving) मूर्त्तिकरणं, मूर्त्तितक्षणं, प्रतिमाकरणं.—(Image-carver) प्रतिमाकारः, उपमाता *m.* (तृ), तक्षकः.

STATUE, *s.* प्रतिमा, मूर्त्तिः *f.*, प्रतिच्छाया, प्रतिच्छन्दकं, *see* IMAGE.

STATURE, *s.* मूर्त्तिः *f.*, शरीरोच्चता, शरीरपरिमाणं; 'short in stature,' ह्रस्वमूर्त्तिः -र्त्तिः -र्त्ति, *see* SHORT; 'tall,' उच्चमूर्त्तिः &c., दीर्घमूर्त्तिः &c.

STATUTE, *s.* व्यवस्था, नियमः, राजव्यवस्था, विधानं. *See* LAW.

STATUTORY, *a.* व्यवस्थाप्रोक्तः -क्ता -क्तं, नियमस्थापितः &c., विधिस्थापितः &c.

STAVE, *s.* (Of wood) काष्ठफलकः.—(Part of a psalm) गीतखण्डः.

To STAVE, *v. a.* (Make a hole) दण्डाघातेन छिद्र् (c. 10. छिद्रयति -यितुं) or छिद्रं कृ.—(Stave off) विलम्ब् (c. 10. -लम्बयति -यितुं), *see To* DELAY, *v. a.*

To STAY, *v. n.* स्था (c. 1. तिष्ठति, स्थातुं), अवस्था, वृत् (c. 1. वर्त्तते -र्त्तितुं), आस् (c. 2. आस्ते), वस् (c. 1. वसति -स्तुं). *See To* REMAIN, RESIDE.

To STAY, *v. a.* (Stop, hinder) रुध् (c. 7. रुणद्धि, रोद्धुं), स्तम्भ् (c. 10. स्तम्भयति -यितुं), स्था in caus. (स्थापयति -यितुं), निवृ (c. 10. -वारयति -यितुं), धृ (c. 10. धारयति -यितुं), सन्धृ, विलम्ब् (c. 10. -लम्बयति -यितुं), *see To* STOP, HINDER.—(Prop), *see To* PROP.

STAY, STAYING, *s.* (Continuance, act of remaining) स्थितिः *f.*, संस्थितिः *f.*, अवस्थितिः *f.*, संस्था, अवस्थानं, वृत्तिः *f.*, वर्त्तनं, वासः, आसना, आस्था, *see* RESIDENCE.—(Stop, hinderance) रोधः, गतिरोधः, स्तम्भः.—(Prop, support) उपस्तम्भः, अवष्टम्भः, आधारः, *see* SUPPORT.

STAYING, *part.* स्थायी -यिनी -यि (न्), अवस्थायी &c., स्थ in comp., संस्थ in comp., स्थितः -ता -तं. *See* RESIDENT, *a.*

STAY-LACE, *s.* अङ्गिकासूत्रं, चोलिकासूत्रं, कूर्पासकसूत्रं.

STAYS, *s. pl.* अङ्गिका, चोलिका, चोलः -ली, कञ्चुलिका, कूर्पासकः -कं.

STEAD, *s.* स्थानं, स्थलं, भूमिः *f.*; 'in my stead,' मत्स्थाने, मत्स्थले.

STEADFAST, *a.* स्थिरः -रा -रं, धीरः -रा -रं, स्थिरमनस्कः -स्का -स्कं, स्थिरबुद्धिः -द्धिः -द्धि, स्थिरवृत्तिः -त्तिः -त्ति, धृतिमान् -मती -मत् (त्), अचपलः -ला -लं, अचञ्चलः &c., अचपलवृत्तिः &c., अचञ्चलवृत्तिः &c., अव्यभिचारी -रिणी -रि (न्), अव्यभिचारवृत्तिः &c., दृढकारी &c., दृढः -ढा -ढं; 'in faith,' दृढभक्तिः. *See* FIRM, CONSTANT, RESOLUTE.

STEADFASTLY, *adv.* स्थिरं, दृढं, धैर्य्येण, स्थैर्य्येण, दार्ढ्येन, धीरं.

STEADFASTNESS, *s.* स्थिरता, स्थैर्य्यं, धीरता, धृतिः *f.*, दृढता, दार्ढ्यं.

STEADILY, *adv.* स्थिरं, स्थैर्य्येण, धीरं, धैर्य्येण, नित्यं, अनवरतं, नियतं.

STEADINESS, *s.* स्थिरता, स्थैर्य्यं, धृतिः *f.*, धैर्य्यं, निश्चलता, अचापल्यं, अचञ्चलता, अचाञ्चल्यं; 'of conduct,' अव्यभिचारः, मर्य्यादा, धारणा, संस्था, *see* FIRMNESS, CONSTANCY.

STEADY, *a.* स्थिरः -रा -रं, धीरः -रा -रं, निश्चलः -ला -लं, अचलः &c., अस्खलितः -ता -तं, धैर्य्यवान् -वती -वत् (त्), धृतिमान् &c., नियमी &c., *see* FIRM, CONSTANT, RESOLUTE; 'steady in conduct,' अव्यभिचारी &c., मर्य्यादावान् &c., समर्य्यादः -दा -दं, सन्मार्गगामी &c., सत्पथगामी &c., सम्यग्वृत्तिः -त्तिः -त्ति, सम्यग्वर्त्तमानः -ना -नं; 'steady-minded,' स्थिरमतिः -तिः -ति, निश्चलमतिः &c.

To STEADY, *v. a.* स्थिरीकृ, निश्चलीकृ, अचलीकृ, स्थिरतां कृ, स्थैर्य्यं कृ.

STEAK, *s.* मांसखण्डः, मांसच्छेदः.—(Of beef) गोमांसखण्डः.

To STEAL, *v. a.* चुर् (c. 10. चोरयति -यितुं), अपहृ (c. 1. -हरति -हर्त्तुं) हृ, मुष् (c. 9. मुष्णाति, मोषितुं), परिमुष्, प्रमुष्, स्तेन् (c. 10. स्तेनयति -यितुं), चौर्य्यं कृ, स्तेयं कृ.

To STEAL, *v. n.* (Practise theft) चौर्य्यं कृ, चौरं कृ, स्तेयं कृ, चौर्य्यकर्म्म कृ, स्तेयकर्म्म कृ.—(Move silently) अव्यक्तं चल्, निःशब्दं चल्, छलेन गम्.

STEALER, *s.* चौरः, स्तेयी *m.* (न्), स्तेनः, स्तेयकृत् *m.*, हारी *m.*, हर्त्ता *m.* (र्त्तृ), अपहर्त्ता *m.*, हारकः, मोषकः, मोषी *m.*; 'of gold,' स्वर्णहारी *m.*; 'of horses,' वाजिहर्त्ता *m.*; 'of hearts,' हृदयचौरः, *see* THIEF.

STEALING, *s.* चौर्य्यं, चौरं -री -रिका, स्तेयं, अपहारः, *see* THEFT.

STEALTH, *s.* (Stealing), *see* above.—(Secret act) छलं, निभृतकर्म्म *n.* (न्), गूढकर्म्म, प्रच्छन्नकर्म्म, निह्नवः; 'by stealth,' छलेन, निभृतं, रहसि, निह्नवेन, *see* CLANDESTINELY, SECRETLY.

STEALTHILY, *adv.* छलेन, निभृतं, निह्नवेन, रहसि, प्रच्छन्ने, रहस्यं.

STEALTHY, *a.* निभृतः -ता -तं, गुप्तः -प्ता -प्तं, गूढः -ढा -ढं, रहस्यः -स्या -स्यं, छलान्वितः -ता -तं, छलेन कृतः -ता -तं, अव्यक्तः -क्ता -क्तं, अस्पष्टः &c.

STEAM, *s.* वाष्पः, उष्णवाष्पः, तप्ततोयवाष्पः, उष्णोदकवाष्पः, स्वेदः.

To STEAM, *v. n.* वाष्प (nom. वाष्पायते), वाष्पम् उत्सृज् or उत्क्षिप् or मुच्, वाष्पम् उद्, वाष्पोत्सर्गं कृ, वाष्पोद्गारं कृ, वाष्पोद्गमं कृ.

To STEAM, *v. a.* (Expose to steam) वाष्पव्याप्तं -प्तां कृ, वाष्पव्याप्यं -प्यां कृ, वाष्पान्तः स्था in caus. (स्थापयति -यितुं), स्विद् (c. 10. स्वेदयति -यितुं).

STEAM-BOAT, STEAM-VESSEL, *s.* वाष्पीयनौः *f.*, वाष्पीयनौका, वाष्पीयतरी, वाष्पसञ्चालितनौका, आग्नेयनौः *f.*, आग्नेयनौका.

STEAMED, *p. p.* स्वेदितः -ता -तं, वाष्पान्तःस्थापितः &c., वाष्पायितः &c.

STEAM-ENGINE, *s.* वाष्पीययन्त्रं, वाष्पसञ्चालितयन्त्रं.

STEAMER, *s.* वाष्पीयनौः *f.*, वाष्पीयनौका. *See* STEAM-BOAT.

STEED, *s.* तुरङ्गः, तुरङ्गमः, तुरगः, वाजी *m.* (न्), अश्वः. *See* HORSE.

STEEL, *s.* सारलोहः -हं, तीक्ष्णायसं, पिण्डायसं, चित्रायसं, शस्त्रकं, शस्त्रं, लोहः, सारः, चीनजं.—(Weapon) शस्त्रं -स्त्रकं.

STEEL, *a.* सारलोहमयः -यी -यं, तीक्ष्णायसः -सी -सं.

To STEEL, *v. a.* (Make hard) कठिनीकृ, दृढीकृ, निर्दयीकृ.

STEEL-YARD, *s.* मापनदण्डः, तौलदण्डः, तुलादण्डः.

STEEP, *a.* दुरारोहः -हा -हं, प्रवणः -णा -णं, पातुकः -का -कं.

STEEP, *s.* पातुकः, पातुकभूमिः *f.*, प्रवणभूमिः *f.*, प्रपातः, अवः.

To STEEP, *v. a.* चिरकालं जले or जलान्तः स्था in caus. (स्थापयति -यितुं) or जलस्थं -स्थां कृ or जलस्थितं -तां कृ, चिरकालं जलेन समाप्लु (c. 10. -प्लावयति -यितुं) or जलसमाप्लुतं -तां कृ, चिरकालं जलेन सिच् (c. 7. सिञ्चति, सेक्तुं) or जलसिक्तं -क्तां कृ or क्ष्मा in caus. (क्ष्मापयति -यितुं), वास् (c. 10. वासयति -यितुं); 'to steep indigo,' नीलपाचनं कृ, नीलसन्धानं कृ, *see* *To* SOAK, MACERATE.

STEEPED, *p. p.* चिरकालं जलान्तःस्थापितः -ता -तं or जलसिक्तः -क्ता -क्तं, वासितः -ता -तं, भावितः &c., *see* SOAKED; 'having her lips steeped in smiles,' स्मितव्यापिताधरा.

STEEPLE, *s.* शिखरं, शृङ्गं, प्रासादशिखरं, प्रासादशृङ्गं. *See* SPIRE.

STEEPNESS, *s.* दुरारोहत्वं -ता, प्रवणता -त्वं, पातुकता -त्वं, प्रावण्यं.

STEER, *s.* नवचलीवर्दः, वत्सतरः, वत्सः, दम्यः, गडिः *m.*

To STEER, *v. a.* or *n.* (A ship) नौकामार्गं निश्चि (c. 5. -चिनोति -चेतुं), नौकाम् or नावम् आनी (c. 1. -नयति -नेतुं) or वह् (c. 10. वाहयति -यितुं), नौकां चल् (c. 10. चालयति -यितुं), नौपथं or नौमार्गं दृश् (c. 10. दर्शयति -यितुं), नौकानयनं कृ, नौकाचालनं कृ.—(Direct one's own course) स्वमार्गं निश्चि or निर्णी.

STEERER, STEERSMAN, *s.* कर्णधारः, कर्णग्राहः, कर्णिकः, कर्णी *m.* (न्), नौकावाहकः, पोतवाहः -हकः, नौकाचालकः.

STELLAR, *a.* तारकी -किणी &c., नाक्षत्रः -त्री -त्रं, आर्क्षः &c. *See* STARRY.

STELLATE, STELLATED, *a.* ताराकारः -रा -रं, नक्षत्राकारः &c., तारोपमः &c.

STEM, *s.* काण्डः -ण्डं, प्रकाण्डः -ण्डं, स्तम्भः, नालः, दण्डः, वोण्टः, वृन्तं; 'having a slender stem,' शीर्णकाण्डः -ण्डा -ण्डं, शीर्णनालः -ला -लं.

To STEM, *v. a.* प्रतिरुध् (c. 7. -रुणद्धि -रोद्धुं), रुध्, प्रतिकूल (nom. प्रतिकूलयति -यितुं), पर्य्यवस्था (c. 1. -तिष्ठति -स्थातुं), प्रत्यवस्था, स्तम्भ् (c. 10. स्तम्भयति -यितुं), प्रतिस्तम्भ्, प्रतिबन्ध्.

STENCH, *s.* दुर्गन्धः, पूतिगन्धः, कुत्सितगन्धः, पूतिः *f.* *See* STINK.

STENOGRAPHY, *s.* संक्षिप्ताक्षरलिपिः *f.*, संक्षिप्ताक्षरलेखनविद्या.

STENTORIAN, *a.* उच्चस्वरः -रा -रं, उच्चस्वरवान् -वती &c., उरुस्वनः -ना -नं.

To STEP, *v. n.* (Tread, place the feet) पदन्यासं कृ, पादन्यासं कृ, पदपातं कृ, पादपातं कृ, पदक्रमं कृ, पदविक्षेपं कृ, पादनिक्षेपं कृ, पदविष्टम्भं कृ, पादविष्टम्भं कृ, चरणपातं कृ.—(Walk a little way, go) क्रम् (c. 1. क्रामति, क्रमितुं), संक्रम्, क्रमे क्रमे चल् (c. 1. चलति -लितुं) or व्रज् or चर् or गम्.

STEP, *s.* (Of the foot) पदं, क्रमः.—(Placing of the foot in moving) पदन्यासः, पादन्यासः, पदक्रमः, पदपातः, पादपातः, पदविष्टम्भः, पदविक्षेपः, पादविक्षेपः, पादनिक्षेपः, पादप्रक्षेपः, चरणपातः, चरणक्रमः; 'wide step or stride,' विक्रमः; 'at every step, step by step,' प्रतिपदं, अनुपदं, पदे पदे, पदात्पदं, पदशस्, क्रमशस्, क्रमे क्रमे; 'a quick step,' द्रुतपदं.—(Space measured by a step) पदं, क्रमः, पदान्तरं.—(Stage, degree) पदं, पर्य्यायः, क्रमः; 'the first step towards an object,' प्रथमारम्भः, प्रत्युत्क्रमः, प्रथमचरणः.—(Proceeding, action) उपायः, उपचारः, कर्म्म *n.* (न्), क्रिया, पदन्यासः, *see* MEASURE.—(Of a ladder, &c.) सोपानं; 'flight of steps,' सोपानश्रेणी, निःश्रेणी, आरोहणं, अधिरोहिणी, *see* STAIR, STAIR-CASE.

STEP-BROTHER, *s.* वैमात्रः, वैमात्रेयः, विमातृजः, अन्योदर्य्यः. *See* HALF-BROTHER.

STEP-DAUGHTER, *s.* (Husband's daughter) भर्त्तृसुता, सपत्नीसुता.—(Wife's daughter) पत्नीसुता.—(Son's wife) सुतस्त्री, पुत्रवधूः *f.*, स्नुषा.

STEP-FATHER, *s.* श्वशुरः, धर्म्मपिता *m.* (तृ). *See* FATHER-IN-LAW.

STEP-MOTHER, *s.* विमाता *f.* (तृ), सपत्नी माता, सापत्नमाता.

STEP-SISTER, *s.* वैमात्री, वैमात्रेयी, अन्योदर्य्या. *See* HALF-SISTER.

STEP-SON, *s.* (Husband's son) भर्तृसुतः, सपत्नीसुतः.—(Wife's son) पत्नीसुतः.—(Daughter's husband) जामाता *m.*, *see* SON-IN-LAW.

STEPPING-STONE, *s.* सोपानप्रस्तरः, सोपानशिला, सोपानं.

STERILE, *a.* वन्ध्यः -न्ध्या -न्ध्यं, निष्फलः -ला -लं, अफलः &c., अनपत्यः -त्या -त्यं, अनपत्यकः -का -कं, अप्रसूतः -ता -तं. *See* BARREN.

STERILITY, *s.* वन्ध्यता -त्वं, निष्फलता, अफलता -त्वं. *See* BARRENNESS.

STERLING, *a.* अकृत्रिमः -मा -मं, सारः -रा -रं.—(Money) सारधनं.

STERN, *a.* (Severe) निष्ठुरः -रा -रं, कठोरः &c., कर्कशः -शा -शं, कठिनः -ना -नं, उग्रः -ग्रा -ग्रं, निर्दयः -या -यं, दयाहीनः -ना -नं; 'in countenance,' निष्ठुरवदनः -ना -नं, उग्रवदनः &c., निष्ठुरमुखः -खी -खं; 'of stern stuff,' अभेद्यसारः -रा -रं.

STERN, *s.* नावः पश्चाद्भागः, नावः पश्चिमभागः or पाश्चात्यभागः.

STERNLY, *adv.* निष्ठुरं, कठोरं, नैष्ठुर्य्येण, सनैष्ठुर्य्यं. *See* SEVERELY.

STERNNESS, *s.* निष्ठुरता, नैष्ठुर्य्यं, कठोरता, कठिनता, काठिन्यं, उग्रता, *see* SEVERITY; 'of countenance,' मुखनैष्ठुर्य्यं, वदननैष्ठुर्य्यं.

STERNUM, *s.* (Breast-bone) उरोस्थि *n.*, वक्षोस्थि *n.*

STERNUTATION, *s.* क्षुतं -ता, क्षुत् *f.*, क्षवः, छिक्का, छिक्कनं. *See* SNEEZING.

STERNUTATIVE, STERNUTATORY, *a.* क्षुत्करः -री -रं, छिक्ककः -का -कं.

STERNUTATORY, *s.* नस्तं, नस्यं, अवपीडः, क्षुत्करी. *See* SNUFF.

To STEW, *v. a.* शनैः शनैः क्वथ् (c. 1. क्वथति -थितुं). *See To* SEETHE, BOIL.

STEW, *s.* (Meat stewed) व्यञ्जनादिना सह क्वथितं मांसादि, क्वथितमांसादि, रसकः.—(Confusion, fright) व्यग्रता व्याकुलत्वं, कातरता, त्रासः, दुर्दशा.—(Brothel), *see* the word.

STEWARD, *s.* कार्य्याधीशः, अर्थाधिकारी *m.* (न्), भाण्डागाराधिपतिः *m.*, कार्य्याधिपतिः, कर्म्मनिर्वाहकः, कर्म्मसम्पादकः.

STEWARDSHIP, *s.* कार्य्याधीशत्वं, अर्थाधिकारः, भाण्डागाराधिकारः.

STEWED, *p. p.* क्वथितः -ता -तं; 'stewed meat,' क्वथितमांसं, रसकः.

STIBIUM, *s.* स्रोतोञ्जनं, सौवीरं. कापोताञ्जनं, यामुनं, लोचकः.

To STICK, *v. a.* (Cause to adhere) अनुलग्नीकृ, संलग्नीकृ, अनुबन्ध् (c. 9. -बध्नाति -बन्धुं), अनुबद्धीकृ, सञ्ज् (c. 10. सञ्जयति -यितुं), आसञ्ज्, अनुषञ्ज्, संसक्तीकृ, आसक्तीकृ.—(Thrust) प्रसृ (c. 10. -सारयति -यितुं), प्रसारणं कृ.—(Stab), *see To* STAB.

To STICK, *v. n.* (Adhere) अनुबन्ध् (c. 9. -बध्नाति -बन्धुं, c. 4. -बध्यते), सञ्ज् in pass. (सज्यते, सज्जते), अनुसञ्ज्, आसञ्ज्, संसञ्ज्, लग् (c. 1. लगति -गितुं), अनुलग्नः -ग्ना -ग्नं भू, अनुलग्नीभू, संलग्नीभू, अनुबद्धीभू, आसक्तीभू, संसक्तीभू.—(Stop, be arrested) स्तम्भ्, रुद्धगतिः -तिः -ति भू, स्तम्भितगतिः -तिः -ति भू.—(Hesitate), *see* the word.—(Stick out), *see To* PROJECT.—(Stick in the mud) पङ्के मस्ज् (c. 6. मज्जति, मंक्तुं).

STICK, *s.* (Long piece of wood) यष्टिः *m. f.*, यष्टिका, दण्डः, काष्ठं, काष्ठखण्डः, वेत्रं, लगुडः, शम्या, *see* STAFF; 'for churning,' मन्थाः *m.* (मथिन्), दधिचारः, मन्थदण्डकः.—(Thrust, stab), *see* the words.

STICKINESS, *s.* श्यानता, सान्द्रता, पिच्छिलता, अनुलग्नशीलता, संलग्नशीलता.

To STICKLE, *v. n.* दुराग्रहेण or अतिनिर्बन्धेन पक्षपातं कृ or पक्षोद्ग्राहं कृ.

STICKLER, *s.* दुराग्रहेण or अतिनिर्बन्धेन पक्षपाती or पक्षोद्ग्राही *m.* (न्).

STICKY, *a.* श्यानः -ना -नं, सान्द्रः -न्द्रा -न्द्रं, पिच्छिलः -ला -लं, पिच्छिलः &c., अनुलग्नशीलः -ला -लं, संलग्नशीलः &c., स्निग्धः -ग्धा -ग्धं.

STIFF, *a.* (Not flexible) स्तब्धः -ब्धा -ब्धं, कठिनः -ना -नं, दृढः -ढा -ढं, घनः -ना -नं, अशिथिलः -ला -लं, *see* RIGID, FORMAL.

To STIFFEN, *v. a.* स्तब्धीकृ, कठिनीकृ, दृढीकृ, घनीकृ, स्तम्भ्.

To STIFFEN, *v. n.* स्तब्धीभू, कठिनीभू, दृढीभू, घनीभू.

STIFFENED, *p. p.* स्तब्धीकृतः -ता -तं, स्तब्धीभूतः &c., घनीभूतः &c.

STIFFLY, *adv.* स्तब्धं, स्तब्धत्वेन, कठिनं, दृढं, अशिथिलं.

STIFF-NECKED, STIFFHEARTED, *a.* स्तब्धमतिः -तिः -ति. *See* STUBBORN.

STIFFNESS, *s.* स्तब्धत्वं -ता, कठिनत्वं, काठिन्यं, दृढत्वं -ता, दार्ढ्यं, घनता -त्वं, अशिथिलता, अशैथिल्यं. *See* RIGIDITY, FORMALITY.

To STIFLE, *v. a.* (Suffocate) श्वासरोधं कृ, श्वासावरोधं कृ, श्वासं रुध् (c. 7. रुणद्धि, रोद्धुं) or अवरुध्, *see To* SMOTHER.—(Suppress) स्तम्भ् (c. 10. स्तम्भयति -यितुं), नियम्, निग्रह्, *see To* SUPPRESS.

STIFLED, *p. p.* (Suffocated) रुद्धश्वासः -सा -सं, अवरुद्धश्वासः &c.—(Suppressed) स्तम्भितः -ता -तं, उपगूढः -ढा -ढं; 'with stifled utterance,' भिन्नस्वरः -रा -रं, रुद्धस्वरः &c., स्तम्भितवाक् *m. f. n.* (च्).

STIFLING, *part.* श्वासावरोधी -धिनी -धि (न्), श्वासरोधी &c.

STIGMA, *s.* कलङ्कः, लाञ्छनं, अपमानचिह्नं, अभिशस्ताङ्कः, अङ्कः.

To STIGMATIZE, *v. a.* अपमानचिह्नेन अङ्क् (c. 10. अङ्कयति -यितुं), कलङ्क (nom. कलङ्कयति -यितुं), कलङ्कं कृ, अभिशस्ताङ्केन चिह्न् (c. 10, चिह्नयति -यितुं).

STILETTO, *s.* क्षुद्रकट्टारः, क्षुद्रछुरिका. *See* DAGGER.

To STILL, *v. a.* (Quiet, calm) शम् (c. 10. शमयति -यितुं), प्रशम्, उपशम्.—(Make silent) निःशब्दीकृ, *see To* SILENCE.—(Stop) निवृत् (c. 10. -वर्त्तयति -यितुं), निवृ (c. 10. -वारयति -यितुं), स्थिरीकृ.

STILL, *s.* (For distillation) अधोयन्त्रं, वकः, वकयन्त्रं, कावचकयन्त्रं.

STILL, *a.* (Silent) निःशब्दः -ब्दा -ब्दं, निश्शब्दः &c., नीरवः -वा -वं, *see* SILENT.—(Motionless) अचलः -ला -लं, निश्चलः &c., स्थिरः -रा -रं, सन्नः -न्ना -न्नं, *see* MOTIONLESS, QUIET.—(Calm) शान्तः -न्ता -न्तं, प्रशान्तः &c., उपशान्तः &c., निर्वातः -ता -तं, *see* QUIET.

STILL, *adv.* (Until now, even now) अद्यापि, अद्ययावत्, अद्यावधि.—(Nevertheless) तथापि.—(Quietly, silently) शान्तं, तूष्णीं, निःशब्दं.

STILL-BORN, *a.* मृतजातः -ता -तं; 'a still-born child,' मूढगर्भः, मृतगर्भः; 'bearing a still-born child,' नष्टप्रसूतिका.

STILLNESS, *s.* (Freedom from noise) निःशब्दता, नीरवता, शब्दाभावः, *see* SILENCE.—(Freedom from motion) निश्चलता, अचलता, स्थिरता.—(Calmness) शान्तिः *f.*, शान्तता, निर्वृतिः *f.*, अक्षोभः, निर्वातत्वं, वाताभावः, *see* QUIETNESS.

STILT, *s.* पादोत्थापनकाष्ठं, पादोत्थापककाष्ठं, पादोच्चयनकाष्ठं.

STIMULANT, *a.* तेजोवर्धकः -का -कं, दीपकः &c., दीपनः -ना -नं, उद्दीपकः &c., उत्तेजकः &c., प्ररोचकः -का -कं, रोचकः &c., रुचकः &c., प्रोत्साहकः &c., प्रवर्त्तकः &c., उद्बोधकः &c., अग्निवर्धकः -का -कं, चेतनावर्धकः &c., चेतनाप्रदः -दा -दं, चेतनोत्तेजकः &c.

STIMULANT, *s.* तेजोवर्धनं, अग्निवर्धनं, प्ररोचनं, दीपनं, उद्दीपनं, रुचकं, रोचकं, चेतनावर्धनं.

To STIMULATE, *v. a.* उद्दीप् (c. 10. -दीपयति -यितुं), दीप्, उत्तिज् (c. 10. -तेजयति -यितुं), प्ररुच् (c. 10. -रोचयति -यितुं), प्रोत्सह् (c. 10. -साहयति -यितुं), प्रवृत् (c. 10. -वर्त्तयति -यितुं), *see To* EXCITE, ROUSE.—(In medicine) तेजोवर्धनं कृ, चेतनावर्धनं कृ, तेजो वृध् (c. 10. वर्धयति -यितुं), वाजीकृ.

STIMULATED, *p. p.* उद्दीपितः -ता -तं, दीपितः &c., प्रदीप्तः -प्ता -प्तं, उत्तेजितः -ता -तं, तेजितः &c., रुचितः -ता -तं, प्ररुचितः, प्रोत्साहितः -ता -तं, प्रवर्त्तितः &c., चोदितः &c. *See* EXCITED, ROUSED.

STIMULATING, *part.* or *a.* उद्दीपकः -का -कं, उद्दीपनः -ना -नं, उत्तेजकः -का -कं, रञ्जकः &c., प्रोत्साहनः -ना -नं, वाजीकरः -रा -रं. *See* STIMULANT, *a.*

STIMULATION, *s.* उद्दीपनं, दीपनं, प्रदीपनं, उत्तेजनं, प्ररोचनं, प्रोत्साहनं, प्रवर्त्तनं, संवर्धनं, वर्धनं, रञ्जनं, वाजीकरणं.

STIMULUS, *s.* प्रोत्साहः -हनं, प्रवर्त्तः -र्त्तनं, उद्दीपनं, उत्तेजनं, रञ्जकः, इन्द्रियबोधनं. *See* STIMULANT, *s.*

To STING, *v. a.* दंश् (c. 1. दशति, दंष्टुं), विदंश्, दंशनं कृ, दंशं कृ.

STING, *s.* (Of animals) शङ्कुः *m.*, दंशः, कण्टकः; 'of a scorpion,' चलं; 'having a sting in the tail,' शङ्कुपुच्छः -च्छा -च्छं.—(Thrust of a sting into the flesh) दंशः -शनं.—(Point, wit) मर्म्म *n.* (न्).

STINGILY, *adv.* सकार्पण्यं, कृपणवत्, कृपणं, स्वल्पव्ययेन. *See* MANLY.

STINGINESS, *s.* कृपणता, कार्पण्यं, व्ययशङ्का. *See* NIGGARDLINESS.

STINGING, *part.* or *a.* दंशकः -का -कं, दंशनः -ना -नं, मर्म्मस्पृक् *m.f.n.* (श्).

STINGY, *a.* कृपणः -णा -णं, दानविमुखः -खा -खं. *See* MISERLY.

To STINK, *v. n.* दुर्गन्धी -न्धिनी -न्धि भू, पूतिगन्धी &c. भू, कुत्सितगन्धी &c. भू, क्नूय् (c. 1. क्नूयते -यितुं). *See To* SMELL, *v. n.*

STINK, *s.* दुर्गन्धः, दौर्गन्धिः *m.*, कुत्सितगन्धः, पूतिगन्धः, पूतिः *f.*, कुणपः.

STINKING, *a.* दुर्गन्धी -न्धिनी -न्धि (न्), दुर्गन्धः -न्धा -न्धं, दौर्गन्धिकः -की -कं, कुत्सितगन्धिकः &c., पूतिगन्धिकः &c., पूतः -ता -तं, कुणपः -पी -पं, असुरभिः -भिः -भि, क्नूयिता -त्री -तृ (तृ).

To STINT, *v. a.* निबन्ध् (c. 9. -बध्नाति -बन्द्धुं), नियम् (c. 1. -यच्छति -यन्तुं), संयम्, संहृ (c. 1. -हरति -हर्त्तुं), निग्रह् (c. 9. -गृह्णाति -ग्रहीतुं), परिमितं -तां कृ, सपरिमाणं -णां कृ, परिच्छेदं कृ.

STINT, *s.* परिमितत्वं, परिमितिः *f.*, परिमाणं, निबन्धः. *See* RESTRICTION.

STINTED, *p.p.* सपरिमाणः -णा -णं, परिमितः &c., नियमितः &c., *see* LIMITED.

STIPEND, *s.* वेतनं, वर्त्तनं, भृतिः *f.*, निरूपितवेतनं. *See* SALARY.

STIPENDIARY, *a.* वैतनिकः -की -कं, सवेतनः -ना -नं, वेतनग्राही -हिणी &c.

STIPTIC, *a.* रक्तस्रावस्तम्भकः -का -कं. *See* STYPTIC, *a.*

To STIPULATE, *v. n.* पण् (c. 1. पणते -णितुं), पणं कृ, पणनं कृ, नियमं कृ, नियमीकृ, प्रतिज्ञा (c. 9. -जानीते -ज्ञातुं), समयं कृ, संविदं कृ, सङ्केतं कृ, संग्रह्.

STIPULATED, *p. p.* नियमितः -ता -तं, नैयमिकः -की -कं, नियतः -ता -तं, पणितः -ता -तं, सामयिकः -की -कं, संविदितः -ता -तं, सङ्केतितः -ता -तं, प्रतिज्ञातः -ता -तं, निरूपितः &c.; 'stipulated interest,' नियमितवृद्धिः *f.*, कारितावृद्धिः *f.*, कारिता.

STIPULATION, *s.* पणः, नियमः, सङ्केतः, समयः, संविद् *f.*, प्रतिज्ञा, उद्देशः.

To STIR, *v. a.* (Move) चल् (c. 10. चालयति -यितुं), संचल्, *see To* MOVE, *v. a.*—(Agitate, move about) धू (c. 5. धूनोति, धोतुं), आधू, मन्थ् (c. 1. मन्थति -न्थितुं, c. 9. मथ्नाति, c. 1. मथति -थितुं), उन्मन्थ्, निर्मन्थ्, प्रमन्थ्, सम्प्रमन्थ्, लुड् (c. 1. लोडति -डितुं, c. 10. लोडयति -यितुं), आलुड्, समालुड्, परिलुड्, विलुड्.—(Stir up) उद्धू, उत्तिज् (c. 10. -तेजयति -यितुं), प्रवृत् in caus., प्रणुद्, चुद्. *See To* INCITE, INSTIGATE.

To STIR, *v. n.* (Be in motion) चल् (c. 1. चलति -लितुं). *See To* MOVE, *v. n.*

STIR, *s.* सम्भ्रमः, विभ्रमः, वैक्लव्यं, तुमुलं, कोलाहलः, कलहः.

STIRRED, *p. p.* (Agitated) धूतः -ता -तं, मथितः -ता -तं, प्रमथितः &c., आलोडितः &c., चालितः -ता -तं, चलितः &c., व्याघट्टितः -ता -तं.—(Stirred up) उद्धूतः -ता -तं, उत्तेजितः &c., चेष्टितः &c., *see* INSTIGATED.

STIRRING, *part.* चलन् -लन्ती -लत् (त्), चेष्टमानः -ना -नं. *See* MOVING, *part.* and *a.*

STIRRUP, *s.* अश्वारोहिणां पादग्रहणी or पादधारणी or पादधरणी, अश्वारूढानां पादधारणार्थं लोहवलयः -यं.

To STITCH, *v. a.* सिव् (c. 4. सीव्यति, सेवितुं), निषिव्, संसिव्. *See To* SEW.

STITCH, *s.* (Pass of the needle) सूच्यङ्कः, सूचिमार्गः, सूचिचारः, सूचिप्रहारः, सीवनं.—(In the side) पार्श्वशूलः -लं.

STITCHED, *p. p.* स्यूतः -ता -तं, प्रोतः -ता -तं. *See* SEWN, SEWED.

STITCHING, *s.* सीवनं, सेवनं, स्यूतिः *f.* *See* SEWING, *s.*

STOCK, *s.* (Of a tree, &c.) काण्डः -ण्डं, प्रकाण्डः -ण्डं, *see* TRUNK.—(Handle, haft) वारङ्गः, दण्डः, त्सरुः *m.*, स्थूलाग्रं.—(Lineage, family) वंशः, कुलं, आदिः.—(Capital, principal) मूलधनं, धनमूलं, मूलद्रव्यं, मूलं, नीविः -वी, परिपणं, परिवर्त्तं.—(Store) सञ्चयः, सञ्चितं, सम्भारः, सामग्र्यं -ग्री, उपकरणसामग्री, उपकरणसम्भारः, संयोगः; 'common stock,' गणद्रव्यं, गणार्थं.—(In cattle, &c.) गोधनं, पशुसम्पत्तिः *f.*, जीवधनं, पादबन्धनं, यादवं.—(Wooden fetters) हडिः *m.*, पादपाशी, कीलः; 'confined in the stocks,' कीलितः -ता -तं, हडिबद्धः -द्धा -द्धं.

To STOCK, *v. a.* सम्भृ (c. 1. -भरति -भर्तुं), सम्भारं कृ, पॄ (c. 10. पूरयति -यितुं), सञ्चि (c. 5. -चिनोति -चेतुं), उपक्लृप्, सञ्चयं कृ. *See To* STORE.

STOCKADE, *s.* वाट्यं, स्तम्भपंक्तिः *f.*, दुर्गावरोधका शङ्कुपंक्तिः.

STOCKED, *p. p.* सम्भृतः -ता -तं, पूरितः -ता -तं, पूर्णः -र्णा -र्णं, सम्पूर्णः &c., उपक्लृप्तः -प्ता -प्तं, सोपकारः -रा -रं, सोपकारद्रव्ययुक्तः -क्ता -क्तं.

STOCKING, *s.* पादवस्त्रं, पादत्राणं, पादत्रं, पादरक्षा -क्षणं.

STOCK-STILL, *a.* काष्ठवत् स्थिरः -रा -रं or निश्चलः -ला -लं.

STOCKS, *s. pl.* हडिः *m.*, पादपाशी. *See* under STOCK.

STOIC, STOICAL, *a.* उदासी -सिनी -सि (न्), उदासीनः -ना -नं, उदासः -सा -सं, इन्द्रियानधीनः -ना -नं, इन्द्रियासङ्गी -ङ्गिनी &c., कामावसायी &c., कामावसायिता -त्री -तृ (तृ), सुखदुःखाद्यनधीनः &c., कामक्रोधाद्यनधीनः &c., जितेन्द्रियः -या -यं, समबुद्धिः -द्धिः -द्धि, समचित्तः -त्ता -त्तं, अममः -मा -मं, निर्ममः &c., शान्तः -न्ता -न्तं, शान्तचित्तः &c.

STOICALLY, *adv.* उदासीनवत्, औदास्येन, इन्द्रियासङ्गेन, समबुद्ध्या.

STOICISM, *s.* उदासः, औदास्यं, उदासीनता, औदासीन्यं, शमः, शान्तिः *f.*, इन्द्रियासङ्गः, इन्द्रियशमः, कामावसायः -यिता, आत्मसंयमः, अममत्वं -ता, निर्ममत्वं -ता, कामक्रोधाद्यनधीनता, सुखदुःखाद्यनधीनता, जितेन्द्रियत्वं, समबुद्धित्वं, समचित्तत्वं.

STOLEN, *p. p.* चौरहृतः -ता -तं, चौरापहृतः &c., हृतः -ता -तं, अपहृतः &c., मूषितः -ता -तं, मुषितः &c., चौरगतः &c., होढः -ढा -ढं; 'stolen goods,' लोप्त्रं, होढं.

STOLID, *a.* जडः -डा -डं, बुद्धिहीनः -ना -नं, मूर्खः &c. *See* STUPID.

STOLIDITY, *s.* जडता, बुद्धिहीनता, मूर्खता. *See* STUPIDITY.

STOMACH, *s.* जठरः -रं, उदरं, अन्तर्जठरं, कोष्ठः -ष्ठं, पक्वाशयः, अन्नाशयः, आमाशयः, पक्वस्थानं, अन्नकोशः, पिचण्डः, पिचिण्डः; 'pit of the stomach,' मणिपूरं; 'clearing of the stomach,' कोष्ठशुद्धिः *f.*; 'stomach-ache,' जठरव्यथा, उदरवेदना.

To STOMACH, *v. a.* सह् (c. 1. सहते, सोढुं), विषह्. *See To* BEAR, BROOK.

STOMACHIC, *a.* (Strengthening the stomach) अग्निवर्धकः -का -कं, अग्निदः -दा -दं, अग्न्युत्तेजकः -का -कं, रुच्यकः &c., रोचकः &c., वह्निकरः -रा -रं, पाचकः -का -कं.—(Pertaining to the stomach) जाठरः -री -रं, जठरसम्बन्धी &c., अन्नकोशसम्बन्धी &c.

STOMACHIC, *s.* अग्निवर्धनं, रुच्यकं, रोचकः, रोचकौषधं, दीपनं.

STONE, *s.* प्रस्तरः, पाषाणः, शिला, अश्मा *m.* (न्), उपलः, ग्रावा *m.* (न्),

दृषद् *f.*, शर्करा, पर्वतफलं ; 'precious stone,' रत्नं, मणिः *m.* ; 'flat stone for grinding condiments, &c.,' शिलापट्टः, शिला ; 'philosopher's stone,' स्पर्शमणिः *m.*, रसेन्द्रः ; 'throwing stones,' प्रस्तरप्रक्षेपः, उपलप्रक्षेपः ; 'bruised by a stone,' अश्मकुट्टः -ट्टा -ट्टं. —(Of fruit) अष्ठिः *f.*, अष्ठीला -लिका.—(In the bladder) मूत्रकृच्छ्रः, मूत्राश्मा *m.* (न्), अश्मरी, अश्मीरः -रं, शर्करा, सिकता.— (Testicle) मुष्कः.

STONE, *a.* (Made of stone) प्रस्तरमयः -यी -यं, पाषाणमयः &c., अश्ममयः &c., आश्मनः -नी -नं, आश्मिकः -की -कं, पाषाण in comp., प्रस्तर in comp. ; 'stone-ware,' अश्ममयभाण्डं.

To STONE, *v. a.* (Kill or pelt with stones) प्रस्तराघातेन हन् (c. 2. हन्ति -न्तुं) or व्यापद् in caus., प्रस्तरप्रक्षेपं कृ, पाषाणप्रक्षेपं कृ.

STONE-BLIND, *a.* घनान्धः -न्धा -न्धं, घनान्धकः -का -कं, दृढान्धः &c.

STONE-CUTTER, STONE-MASON, *s.* पाषाणदारकः, अश्मदारकः, शैलभेदकः, पाषाणभेदकः ; 'his chisel,' टङ्कः, पाषाणदारणः.

STONE-CUTTING, *s.* पाषाणदारणं, अश्मदारणं, शैलभेदनं, शैलच्छेदः.

STONE-HEARTED, *a.* पाषाणहृदयः -या -यं, प्रस्तरहृदयः &c., निर्दयः -या -यं.

STONE-HORSE, *s.* वीजाश्वः, सवृषणो ऽश्वः, अच्छिन्नमुष्को ऽश्वः.

STONE-PIT, *s.* प्रस्तरखानिः *f.*, पाषाणकन्दरः, प्रस्तरोत्पत्तिकूपः.

STONE'S-THROW, *s.* प्रस्तरपातः, पाषाणपातः, प्रस्तरायणं, शिलापातस्थानं.

STONINESS, *s.* प्रस्तरबाहुल्यं, पाषाणपूर्णता, शिलेयता, शार्करीयता.

STONY, *a.* पाषाणमयः -यी -यं, प्रस्तरमयः &c., अश्ममयः &c., शिलामयः &c., आश्मनः -नी -नं, आश्मः -श्मी -श्मं, आश्मिकः -की -कं, अश्मरः -रा -रं, पाषाणी -णिनी -णि (न्), शार्करीयः -यी -यं, शार्करः -री -रं, शार्करिकः -की -कं, शर्करिकः -की -कं, शार्करकः &c., शर्करिलः &c., शर्करावान् -वती -वत् (त्), शिलेयः -यी -यं, औपलः -ली -लं, दार्षदः -दी -दं.

STOOL, *s.* (Seat) पीठं, पादपः, आसनं -नी, संवेशः, विस्तरः, पिण्डिका ; 'for the feet,' पादपीठं, चरणपीठं, पादासनं, पदासनं, पादपः.— (Evacuation) उच्चारः, उच्चरितं, मलोच्चारः, रेकः ; 'to go to stool,' उच्चर्, गू, पुरीषोत्सर्गं कृ.

To STOOP, *v. n.* नम् (c. 1. नमति, नन्तुं), अवनम्, प्रणम्, अभिप्रणम्, विनम्, सन्नम्, नम्रीभू, नतकायः -या -यं भू, अवनतकायः -या -यं भू, प्रह्वीभू, प्रह्वः -ह्वा -ह्वं भू.—(Condescend, submit, yield), *see* the words.

To STOOP, *v. a.* नम् in caus. (नमयति -यितुं), नम्रीकृ, प्रह्वीकृ, अवनतीकृ.

STOOP, STOOPING, *s.* नतिः *f.*, प्रणतिः *f.*, आनतिः *f.*, अवनतिः *f.*, अवनामः, नम्रता, प्रह्वता ; 'of the body,' अङ्गनतिः, अङ्गावनतिः, कायावनतिः *f.*

STOOPING, *part.* or *a.* नताङ्गः -ङ्गा -ङ्गं, अवनताङ्गः &c., अवनतकायः -या -यं, नम्राङ्गः &c., नतः -ता -तं, आनतः &c., अवनतः &c., प्रणतः &c., नम्रः -म्रा -म्रं, नम्रमूर्त्तिः -र्त्तिः -र्त्ति, प्रणतशिराः -राः -रः (स्), अवाग्रः -ग्रा -ग्रं.

To STOP, *v. a.* (Close, obstruct) रुध् (c. 7. रुणद्धि, रोद्धुं), प्रतिरुध्, संरुध्, निरुध्, प्रतिबन्ध् (c. 9. -बध्नाति -बन्द्धुं), स्तम्भ् (c. 10. स्तम्भयति -यितुं, c. 9. स्तभ्नाति, स्तम्भितुं), विष्टम्भ्, पिधा (c. 3. -दधाति -धातुं), सपिधानं -नां कृ, रोधं कृ, अवरोधं कृ ; 'he stops one end of the pipe with his finger,' नाडेर् एकमुखम् अङ्गुल्या रुणद्धि ; 'he stops his ears with his fingers,' अङ्गुलीभिः कर्णौ पिदधाति, अङ्गुलीः कर्णयोर् निदधाति.—(Arrest progress, make to stand) गतिं रुध्, गतिरोधं कृ, गतिस्तम्भं कृ, गतिस्तम्भनं कृ, स्तम्भ्, विष्टम्भ्, अवस्था in caus. (-स्थापयति -यितुं), संस्था, गतिभङ्गं कृ.—(Cause to cease) निवृत् (c. 10. -वर्त्तयति -यितुं), विनिवृत्, विरम् (c. 10. -रमयति -यितुं), उपरम्, शम् in caus.—(Hinder) निवृ (c. 10. -वारयति -यितुं), वृ, रुध्, बाध्.

To STOP, *v. n.* (Stand still) अवस्था (c. 1. -तिष्ठति -स्थातुं), संस्था, स्था, निश्चलः -ला -लं स्था, रुद्धगतिः -तिः -ति स्था or भू, स्तम्भितगतिः -तिः -ति स्था or भू, स्तम्भ् (c. 1. स्तम्भते -म्भितुं), स्थिरः -रा -रं भू.—(Cease, pause, give over) निवृत् (c. 1. -वर्त्तते -र्त्तितुं), विनिवृत्, विरम् (c. 1. -रमति -रन्तुं), उपरम्, *see To* CEASE, END, *v. n.* —(Stay, tarry) स्था, अवस्था.

STOP, STOPPING, *s.* (Hinderance of progress, obstruction) रोधः, अवरोधः, गतिरोधः, गतिस्तम्भः -म्भनं, गमनस्तम्भः, गमनरोधः, गतिभङ्गः, स्तम्भः -म्भनं, विष्टम्भः, अवष्टम्भनं, *see* HINDERANCE.—(Closing, shutting) प्रतिबन्धः, रोधः, पिधानं.—(Cessation of motion) स्तम्भः, अयानं, गतिस्तम्भः, यानस्तम्भः, अवस्थितिः *f.*, स्थितिः *f.*, यानविरतिः *f.*, गतिविरामः, गमननिवृत्तिः *f.*, विश्रामः, यतिः *f.*—(Cessation) निवृत्तिः *f.*, विनिवृत्तिः *f.*, अवसानं, अवसायः, विरतिः *f.*, विरामः, उपरामः, अवरतिः *f.*, आरतिः *f.*, वियमः, वियामः.—(Rest, in music, &c.) यतिः *f.*, अवसानं, विरामः.—(In punctuation) विश्रामचिह्नं, विरामचिह्नं, अवसानचिह्नं.

STOPPAGE, *s.* स्तम्भः, विष्टम्भः, प्रतिष्टम्भः, अवष्टम्भः, रोधः, प्रतिरोधः, प्रतिबन्धः, अनुबन्धः, *see* STOP, *s.* ; 'in any organ,' माहः, आनाहः.

STOPPED, *p. p.* (Hindered from proceeding) रुद्धः -द्धा -द्धं, रुद्धगतिः -तिः -ति, अवरुद्धः &c., अवरुद्धगतिः &c., स्तम्भितः -ता -तं, स्तम्भितगतिः -तिः -ति, स्तब्धगतिः &c., स्तब्धः -ब्धा -ब्धं, नष्टगतिः &c.—(Closed) रुद्धः -द्धा -द्धं, सपिधानः -ना -नं, स्तम्भितः -ता -तं ; *see* SHUT ; 'by the hand,' कररुद्धः -द्धा -द्धं.—(Ceased, caused to cease) निवृत्तः -त्ता -त्तं, निवर्त्तितः &c.

STOPPED, STOPPLE, *s.* पिधानं, प्रतिबन्धकः, प्रतिबन्धनी, रोधकः, अवरोधकः, अवरोधनी, रोधनी, स्तम्भनी.

STORAX, *s.* शिलाकुसुमं, शिलापुष्पं, शिलोद्भवः, शीतलं. *See* BENZOIN.

STORE, *s.* सञ्चयः, सञ्चितं, संग्रहः, सम्भारः, निचयः, प्रचयः, चयः, संहारः, समाहारः, पर्य्याहारः, सामग्र्यं -ग्री, संयोगः, संघातः, समयः, निधिः *m.*, निधानं, कोषः ; 'store of grain,' धान्यसंग्रहः, धान्यसञ्चयः ; 'of virtue,' धर्म्मकोषः, धर्म्मनिधिः *m.* ; 'hidden store,' गूढसञ्चयः.

To STORE, *v. a.* संचि (c. 5. -चिनोति -चेतुं), सञ्चयं कृ, सम्भृ (c. 1. -भरति -भर्त्तुं), सम्भारं कृ, पृ (c. 10. पूरयति -यितुं), संग्रहं कृ, समाहारं कृ, पर्य्याहारं कृ, पूर्णं -र्णां कृ, सम्पूर्णं -र्णां कृ, सम्पन्नं -न्नां कृ, निधिं कृ. *See To* FURNISH, LAY UP.

STORED, *p. p.* सम्भृतः -ता -तं, पूरितः &c., कोषभूतः &c., पूर्णः -र्णा -र्णं, सम्पूर्णः &c., सम्पन्नः -न्ना -न्नं, उपार्जितः &c., वसितः &c., आवसितः &c., अवसितः &c. ; 'stored grain,' कुशूलधान्यं, चर्ढं.

STORE-HOUSE, *s.* कोषागारः, कोषः, कोशागारः, कोष्ठः -ष्ठकं.

STORE-KEEPER, *s* कोषाध्यक्षः, कोषागाराध्यक्षः, कोष्ठपालः -लकः.

STORE-ROOM, STORE-CLOSET, *s.* कण्डोलः -लकः, कुशूलः, *see* STORE-HOUSE.

STORK, *s.* बकः, सारसः, क्रौञ्चः, दीर्घपाद् *m.* *See* CRANE, HERON.

STORM, *s.* (Of wind, &c.) वात्या, अतिवातः, चण्डवातः, प्रचण्डवातः, झञ्झावातः, झञ्झानिलः, जवानिलः, वातरूषः, वात्यावेगः, पवनाघातः, वातुलः, वातूलः, दुर्दिनं.—(Assault on a fort, &c.) दुर्गलङ्घनं, अवस्कन्दः -न्दनं, दुर्गावस्कन्दः.

To STORM, *v. a.* (Assault a fort) दुर्गं लङ्घ् (c. 10. लङ्घयति -यितुं) or

अवस्कन्द् (c. 1. -स्कन्दति -स्कन्तुं) or आस्कन्द् or समास्कन्द् or समवस्कन्द्, दुर्गलङ्घनं कृ, दुर्गावस्कन्दनं कृ.

To STORM, *v. n.* भृश (nom. भृशायते), उच्चण्डः -ण्डा -ण्डं भू, *see To* RAGE.

STORMY, *a.* वातलः -ला -लं, वातवान् -वती -वत् (त्), वातरः -रा -रं, वातिकः -की -कं, वातमयः -यी -यं, अतिवातमयः &c., वृष्टिवातमयः &c., वृष्टिवातविशिष्टः -ष्टा -ष्टं, अतिवातविशिष्टः &c., वातक्षुब्धः -ब्धा -ब्धं, पवनक्षिप्तः -प्ता -प्तं, वाताहतः -ता -तं; 'stormy sea,' क्षुब्धार्णवः.

STORY, *s.* (Narration, tale) कथा, कथानकं, परिकथा, उपकथा, उपाख्यानं, आख्यानं, आख्यायिका, कथाप्रबन्धः, कथानुबन्धः, वार्त्ता, वृत्तान्तः, चरित्रं, इतिहासः; 'an old story,' पुरावृत्तकथा; 'idle story,' लोककथा; 'remaining only in story,' कथाशेषः -षा -षं.—(Fictitious story), *see* FICTION.—(Floor) भूमिः *f.*, कोष्ठः, फलकः, तलः; 'upper story,' उपरिभूमिः *f.*, *see* FLOOR.

STORY-TELLER, *s.* कथकः, कथोपकथकः, कथाख्यायकः, कथाख्यानवित्.

STOUT, *a.* स्थूलः -ला -लं, स्थूलशरीरः -रा -रं, मांसलः -ला -लं, बलवान् -वती -वत् (त्), महाबलः -ला -लं, महाकायः -या -यं, अंशलः -ला -लं, अंसलः &c., वृहच्छरीरः -रा -रं, वृहदङ्गः -ङ्गा -ङ्गं, मेदस्वी -स्विनी -स्वि (न्).

STOUTNESS, *s.* स्थूलता, शरीरस्थूलता, अङ्गस्थूलता, अङ्गवृहत्त्वं, शरीरवृहत्त्वं, मांसलत्वं, अंशलता, मेदस्विता.

STOVE, *s.* चुल्ली, अङ्गारिणी, अङ्गारगुप्तिः *f.*, अग्निकुण्डं, *see* FIREPLACE.

To STOW, *v. a.* कोशे or कोषे निविश् (c. 10. -वेशयति -यितुं) or निधा (c. 3. -दधाति -धातुं) or स्था in caus., कोशीकृ, भाण्डीकृ, वासनीकृ.

To STRADDLE, *v. n.* पादौ पृथक् कृत्वा स्था (c. 1. तिष्ठति, स्थातुं), प्रगतजङ्घः -ङ्घा -ङ्घं स्था, विगतजङ्घः -ङ्घा -ङ्घं स्था.

To STRAGGLE, *v. n.* व्यभिचर् (c. 1. -चरति -रितुं), असंहतं चल् (c. 1. चलति -लितुं), असंहतः -ता -तं व्रज् (c. 1. व्रजति -जितुं) or चर्, मार्गात् or पथात् विचल्, विस्तीर्णः -र्णा -र्णं भू, प्रविततः -ता -तं भू.

STRAGGLER, *s.* असंहतचारी *m.* (न्), असंहतगामी *m.*, व्यभिचारी *m.*

STRAGGLING, *part.* or *a.* असंहतः -ता -तं, विस्तीर्णः -र्णा -र्णं, प्रविततः &c.

STRAIGHT, *a.* सरलः -ला -लं, ऋजुः -जुः -जु, ऋजुकः -का -कं, अवक्रः -क्रा -क्रं, अजिह्मः -ह्मा -ह्मं, अकुटिलः -ला -लं, अभुग्नः -ग्ना -ग्नं, अकुञ्चः -ञ्चा -ञ्चं, समः -मा -मं, समरेखः -खा -खं, समानः -ना -नं, प्रगुणः -णा -णं; 'a straight line,' सरलरेखा; 'moving in a straight line,' सरलयायी -यिनी &c, अजिह्मगः -गा -गं; 'to be straight,' ऋजूभू, ऋज् (c. 1. अर्जते -र्जितुं).

STRAIGHT, STRAIGHTWAY, *adv.* सद्यस्, तत्काले. *See* FORTHWITH, IMMEDIATELY.

To STRAIGHTEN, *v. a.* ऋजूकृ, सरलीकृ, समीकृ, समरेखीकृ, अवक्रीकृ.

STRAIGHTENED, *p.p.* ऋजूकृतः -ता -तं, सरलीकृतः &c., समीकृतः -ता -तं.

STRAIGHT-FORWARD, *a.* सरलः -ला -लं, ऋजुः -जुः -जु, अवक्रः -क्रा -क्रं, अकुटिलः -ला -लं, अजिह्मः -ह्मा -ह्मं, प्रगुणः -णा -णं. *See* HONEST.

STRAIGHT-FORWARDNESS, *s.* ऋजुता, आर्जवं, अवक्रता. *See* HONESTY.

STRAIGHTLY, *adv.* सरलं, ऋजु, अवक्रं, अजिह्मं, सरल or अजिह्म in comp.

STRAIGHTNESS, *s.* ऋजुता, सरलता, सारल्यं, ऋजुता -त्वं, आर्जवं, ऋजिमा *m.* (न्), अवक्रता, अवक्रिमा *m.*, अकुटिलता, अजिह्मता.

To STRAIN, *v. a.* (Stretch) आयतं तन् (c. 8. तनोति -नितुं), अतिशयेन तन् or विततीकृ.—(Injure by stretching), *see To* SPRAIN.—(Force beyond propriety) आयतं or अतिशयेन कृष् (c. 1. कर्षति, क्रष्टुं) or आकृष् or समाकृष्.—(Make great effort), *see To* STRAIN, *v. n.*—(Filter liquids, &c.) शुध् (c. 10. शोधयति -यितुं), उत्पवनं कृ, गालनं कृ, गल् in caus. (गलयति, गालयति -यितुं), सम्मृज्, *see To* FILTER, *v. a.*

To STRAIN, *v. n.* (Make violent efforts) अतिशयेन यत् (c. 1. यतते -तितुं) or प्रयत्, अतियत्नं कृ, आयम्य उद्यम् (c. 1. -यच्छति -यन्तुं) or चेष्ट् or व्यवसो, अतिशक्ति or अतिसामर्थ्यं यत्नं कृ.—(Filter), *see* the word.

STRAIN, *s.* (Over-exertion) अतियत्नः, अतिशययत्नः, अत्युद्यमः.—(Injury by over-exertion), *see* SPRAIN.—(Stretching, tension) कर्षणं, कर्षः, कृष्टिः *f.*, आकर्षः, आकृष्टिः *f.*, संकर्षणं, विकर्षणं, विततिः *f.*, विततनं.—(Tenor) अन्वयः, अर्थान्वयः, क्रमः, प्रसङ्गः.—(Style) वृत्तिः *f.*, वाग्वृत्तिः *f.*, वाग्व्यापारः.—(Song, sound), *see* the words.

STRAINED, *p.p.* (Stretched) विततः -ता -तं, कृष्टः -ष्टा -ष्टं, आकृष्टः &c., आकर्षितः -ता -तं.—(Forced) क्लिष्टः -ष्टा -ष्टं, अतियत्नपूर्वं कृष्टः -ष्टा -ष्टं or आकृष्टः &c., अतियत्नपूर्वः -र्वा -र्वं.—(Filtered) शोधितः -ता -तं, निर्गलितः &c., सम्मृष्टः -ष्टा -ष्टं.

STRAINER, *s.* शोधनी, शोधनयन्त्रं, चालनं -नी, सम्मार्जनयन्त्रं.

STRAIT, *a.* सङ्कटः -टा -टं, सबाध in comp. *See* NARROW, *a.*

STRAIT, *s.* (Narrow passage) समुद्रसङ्कटं, समुद्रधुनी, सामुद्रधुनी, सङ्कटं.—(Difficulty) सङ्कटं, कृच्छ्रं, कष्टं; 'one who is in straits,' अनुपायः -या -यं, उपायहीनः -ना -नं, कृच्छ्रगतः -ता -तं.

To STRAITEN, *v. a.* बाध् (c. 1. बाधते -धितुं), सबाध्, संकुच् (c. 1. -कोचति -चितुं), पीड् (c. 10. पीडयति -यितुं), सङ्कटीकृ.

STRAITENED, *p. p.* संकुचितः -ता -तं, संकोचितः &c., बाधितः &c., सबाधितः -ता -तं; 'for food,' भोजनव्यग्रः -ग्रा -ग्रं.

STRAIT-LACED, *a.* सूक्ष्मदर्शी &c. *See* STRICT, STIFF.

STRAITNESS, *s.* सङ्कटत्वं, सबाधता, सङ्कोचः. सङ्कुचितत्वं.

STRAND, *s.* तटं, तीरं, कूलं, पुलिनं, समुद्रतीरं. *See* SHORE.

To STRAND, *v. a.* उत्कूल् (nom. उत्कूलयति -यितुं), उत्तीर (nom. उत्तीरयति).

STRANDED, *p. p.* उत्कूलितः -ता -तं, उत्तीरितः -ता -तं, उत्तीरं indec.

STRANGE, *a.* (Foreign) विदेशीयः -या -यं, वैदेशिकः -की -कं, *see* FOREIGN.—(Belonging to others, alien) परकीयः -या -यं, पारक्यः -क्या -क्यं, पर in comp., अन्य in comp., भिन्नः -न्ना -न्नं.—(Wonderful) अद्भुतः -ता -तं, चित्रः -त्रा -त्रं, विचित्रः &c., आश्चर्यः -र्या -र्यं, आश्चर्यकरः &c., *see* WONDERFUL.—(Novel) अपूर्वः -र्वा -र्वं, अभूतपूर्वः -र्वा -र्वं, *see* NOVEL.—(Odd, unusual) विलक्षणः -णा -णं, असङ्गतः -ता -तं, अपरूपः -पा -पं, अलौकिकः -की -कं; 'strange story,' असम्भवकथा.—(Unacquainted) अपरिचितः -ता -तं.

STRANGE, *exclam.* आश्चर्यं, चित्रं, चित्रं चित्रं, अद्भुतं.

STRANGELY, *adv.* अद्भुतं, अद्भुतप्रकारेण, आश्चर्यप्रकारेण, विचित्रं.

STRANGENESS, *s.* (Foreignness) विदेशीयता -त्वं.—(Novelty) अपूर्वता.—(Oddness) वैलक्षण्यं.—(Wonderfulness) अद्भुतता -त्वं, आश्चर्यता, विचित्रता, वैचित्र्यं.

STRANGER, *s.* (Foreigner) विदेशी *m.* (न्), विदेशीयः, वैदेशिकः, वैदेश्यः, अन्यदेशोद्भवः, पारक्यः, प्रोषितः -तवान् *m.* (त्), वहिरङ्गः, *see* FOREIGNER.—(One not of the same family, &c., an unknown person) परपुरुषः, परः, पारक्यः, परलोकः, अन्यजनः, अन्यः, अपरिचितः, उदासीनः.—(One unknowing) अनभिज्ञः -ज्ञा -ज्ञं, अनभ्यस्तः -स्ता -स्तं, अपरिचितः -ता -तं, अनाप्तः -प्ता -प्तं, *see* INEXPERIENCED.—(Accidental visitor) आगन्तुकः, आगन्तुः *m.*, अभ्यागतः.

To STRANGLE, *v. a.* गलहस्त (nom. गलहस्तयति -यितुं), गलमर्दं कृ,

श्वासरोधं कृ, श्वासावरोधं कृ. *See To* SUFFOCATE, CHOKE.

STRANGLED, *p. p.* रुद्धश्वासः -सा -सं, अवरुद्धश्वासः &c. *See* CHOKED.

STRANGLING, STRANGULATION, *s.* श्वासरोधः, श्वासावरोधः, गलहस्तः, गलग्रहः, गलपीडनं, कण्ठपीडनं, श्वाससम्पीडनं. *See* SUFFOCATION.

STRANGURY, *s.* मूत्रकृच्छ्रं, मूत्ररोधः, मूत्रावरोधः, मूत्रावष्टम्भः, मूत्रानुबन्धः, अश्मरी.

STRAP, *s.* चर्म्मबन्धः, चर्म्मपट्टः -ट्टा -ट्टी, वरत्रा. *See* STROP.

To STRAP, *v. a.* (Beat with a strap) चर्म्मरज्जुना तड् or आहन्.

STRATAGEM, *s.* उपायः, अपदेशः, व्यपदेशः, उपक्रमः, छलं, छद्म *n.* (न्), कृप्तिः *f.*, कल्पना, छलितं.

STRATEGY, *s.* व्यूहरचनाविद्या, सैन्यरचनाविद्या, *see* GENERALSHIP.

STRATIFIED, *p. p.* फलकरूपः -पा -पं, आस्तृतः -ता -तं, स्तररूपः &c.

STRATUM, *s.* स्तरः, फलकः -कं, आस्तरणं, आस्तरः, पार्थिवांशपुटः, पार्थिवांशस्तरः; 'of rock,' शिलाफलकः -कं.

STRAW, *s.* पलालः -लं -ली, पलः, नालः -लं, शुष्कनालः, नलः, तृणं, धान्यकल्कं, तुच्छधान्यकं, कडङ्करः, कडङ्गरः; 'of wheat,' गोधूमनालः; 'of barley,' यवनालः; 'fit to be fed with straw,' कडङ्करीयः -या -यं, कडङ्कर्य्यः -र्य्या -र्य्यं; 'hardly worth a straw,' तृणप्रायः -या -यं; 'not to care a straw for,' तृणाय मन्.

To STRAY, *v. n.* भ्रम् (c. 4. भ्राम्यति, भ्रमितुं), व्यभिचर् (c. 1. -चरति -रितुं), विचल् (c. 1. -चलति -लितुं), भ्रंश् (c. 4. भ्रश्यति, भ्रंशितुं), प्रभ्रंश्, च्यु (c. 1. च्यवते, च्योतुं), प्रमद् (c. 4. -माद्यति -मदितुं), मार्गाद् भ्रंश्, पथाद् भ्रंश्, *see To* ERR.—(As a sheep, &c., from the flock) यूथात् परिभ्रंश् or भ्रंश्.

STRAY, STRAYED, *a.* प्रभ्रष्टः -ष्टा -ष्टं, परिभ्रष्टः &c., भ्रष्टः &c., च्युतः -ता -तं, प्रच्युतः &c., विचलितः &c., भ्रान्तः -न्ता -न्तं, दिग्भ्रान्तः &c., दिग्भ्रमी -मिणी &c., पथभ्रष्टः &c., मार्गभ्रष्टः &c., मार्गप्रभ्रष्टः &c., वर्त्मभ्रष्टः &c., नष्टः &c., त्यक्तमार्गः -र्गा -र्गं; 'as a sheep, &c.,' यूथभ्रष्टः -ष्टा -ष्टं; 'a stray animal,' स्वयूथात् परिभ्रष्टः पशुः.

STREAK, *s.* रेखा, लेखा, छेदः, राजिः -जी *f.*, पद्धतिः *f.*, अङ्कः, शिरा.

To STREAK, *v. a.* रेखाभिर् अङ्क् (c. 10. अङ्कयति -यितुं), रेखाङ्कितं -तां कृ, रेखाचित्रितं -तां कृ, शबलीकृ, चित्रीकृ, लिख्.

STREAKED, STREAKY, *p. p.* रेखाङ्कितः -ता -तं, रेखाचित्रितः &c., रेखाविचित्रः -त्रा -त्रं, रेखाचिह्नितः -ता -तं, चित्रितः &c., चित्रः -त्रा -त्रं, विचित्रः &c., चित्राङ्गः -ङ्गा -ङ्गं, शबलः -ला -लं.

STREAM, *s.* (Running water) स्रोतस् *n.*, सरित् *f.*, नदी.—(Current, flow) स्रोतस् *n.*, प्रवाहः, उदकप्रवाहः, जलप्रवाहः, ओघः -घं, जलौघः, वेला, रयः, धारा -रः, वेगः, जलवेगः, प्रवृत्तिः *f.*, प्रस्रवः -वणं, प्रस्रावः, संसृतिः *f.*, कूलङ्कषः, जलचलं, *see* CURRENT; 'against the stream,' प्रतिस्रोतस्; 'floating with the stream,' प्रवाहपतितः -ता -तं.—(As of rain) धारा; 'continued stream,' सन्ततधारा.

To STREAM, *v. n.* सन्ततप्रवाहेण स्रु (c. 1. स्रवति, स्रोतुं) or प्रस्रु, निरन्तरप्रवाहेण स्रु or परिस्रु. *See To* FLOW.

STREAMER, *s.* पताका, दीर्घपताका, केतुवसनः, दीर्घकेतुः *m.* *See* FLAG.

STREAMING, *part.* सन्ततस्रावी -विणी -वि (न्), निरन्तरप्रवाही &c.

STREAMLET, *s.* अल्पस्रोतस् *n.*, अल्पसरित् *f.*, कुसरित्. *See* RIVULET.

STREET, *s.* मार्गः, नगरमार्गः, प्रतोली, रथ्या, वीथिः -थी *f.*, विशिखा, संसरणं, उपनिष्करः, उपनिष्क्रमणं.

STREET-WALKER, *s.* हट्टविलासिनी. *See* PROSTITUTE, HARLOT.

STRENGTH, *s.* बलं, शक्तिः *f.*, सामर्थ्यं, समर्थता, प्राबल्यं, प्रबलता, ऊर्जः, पराक्रमः, विक्रमः, तेजस् *n.*, प्रभावः, सत्त्वं, सारता, क्षमता, तरस् *n.*, विभवः, वैभवं, *see* POWER; 'of arm,' भुजबलं; 'of mind,' बुद्धिविभवः, बुद्धिवैभवं, मनःशक्तिः *f.*, धीशक्तिः *f.*; 'with all one's strength,' यथाबलं, यथाशक्ति, *see* under POWER; 'loss of strength,' बलहानिः *f.*, बलक्षयः, सत्त्वहानिः *f.*; 'on the strength of,' *see* under SCORE.

To STRENGTHEN, *v. a.* (Make strong) सबलं -लां कृ, सबलीकृ, बलवन्तं -वतीं -वत् कृ, बलं दा or वृध् (c. 10. वर्धयति -यितुं), बलवृद्धिं कृ, बलवर्धनं कृ, प्रबलीकृ, बलवत्तरं -रां कृ.—(Confirm, establish), *see* the words.

STRENGTHENED, *p. p.* सबलीकृतः -ता -तं, सबलः -ला -लं, वर्धितबलः &c.

STRENGTHENING, *part.* or *a.* बलवर्धी -र्धिनी -र्धि (न्), बलवर्धकः -का -कं, बलवर्धनः -ना -नं, बलवृद्धिकरः -रा -रं, पुष्टिकारकः -का -कं.

STRENUOUS, *a.* उद्योगी -गिनी -गि (न्), महोत्साहः -हा -हं, महोद्यमः -मा -मं, महाप्रयत्नः -त्ना -त्नं, सोत्साहः &c., सोद्योगः &c. *See* ENERGETIC.

STRENUOUSLY, *adv.* सोत्साहं, प्रयत्नतस्, यत्नतस्. *See* ENERGETICALLY.

STRENUOUSNESS, *s.* उत्साहः, उद्योगः, उद्यमः, सोद्योगत्वं. *See* ENERGY.

STRESS, *s.* प्रभावः, भारः, बलं, प्रणिधानं, गौरवं, गुरुत्वं.

To STRETCH, *v. a.* (Extend, draw out) तन् (c. 8. तनोति -नितुं), वितन्, व्यातन्, प्रतन्, प्रवितन्, अतितन्, विततीकृ, आयम् (c. 1. -यच्छति -यन्तुं), विस्तृ (c. 10. -स्तारयति -यितुं), दीर्घीकृ, *see To* DRAW OUT; 'to stretch one's limbs,' स्वाङ्गम् आयम्.—(Stretch out, as the hand, &c.) प्रसृ in caus. (-सारयति -यितुं), प्रग्रह् (c. 9. -गृह्णाति -ग्रहीतुं), प्रसारणं कृ.—(Strain, force), *see* the words

To STRETCH, *v. n.* तन् in pass. (तन्यते), वितन्, व्यातन्, प्रतन्, विततीभू, प्रततीभू, विस्तृ in pass. (-स्तीर्य्यते), प्रसृ (c. 1. -सरति -सर्तुं), आयम् (c. 1. -यच्छते -यन्तुं), विप्रस्था (c. 1. -तिष्ठति -स्थातुं), द्राघ् (c. 1. द्राघते -घितुं).

STRETCH, *s.* (Extension) विततिः *f.*, प्रततिः *f.*, आयतिः *f.*, आयामः, विस्तारः, विस्तृतिः *f.*—(Effort) यत्नः, प्रयत्नः, उद्यमः.—(Reach, extent) पर्य्यन्तः -न्तं, परिमाणं, प्रसरः, विषयः.

STRETCHED, *p. p.* विततः -ता -तं, प्रविततः &c., आततः &c., विततीकृतः &c., व्यायतः &c., विस्तीर्णः -र्णा -र्णं, विस्तृतः -ता -तं, प्रसृतः &c., जृम्भितः &c., विजृम्भितः &c., उज्जृम्भितः &c.; 'stretched forth,' प्रसारितः -ता -तं.

STRETCHING, *part.* वितन्वन् -न्वती -न्वत् (त्), तन्वन् &c., आयच्छमानः -ना -नं; 'one's limbs,' स्वाङ्गम् आयच्छमानः &c.

To STREW, *v. a.* कॄ (c. 6. किरति, करितुं -रीतुं), विकॄ, प्रकॄ, अवकॄ, समवकॄ, आस्तॄ (c. 9. -स्तृणाति, c. 5. -स्तृणोति -स्तरितुं -रीतुं), विस्तॄ, परिस्तॄ, संस्तॄ, आस्तरणं कृ, आच्छद् (c. 10. -च्छादयति -यितुं), *see To* SCATTER, *v. a.*

STREWED, *p. p.* आकीर्णः -र्णा -र्णं, विकीर्णः &c., प्रकीर्णः &c., अवकीर्णः &c., कीर्णः &c., कीर्य्यमाणः -णा -णं, अवकीर्य्यमाणः &c.

STRICKEN, *p. p.* हतः -ता -तं, उपहतः &c., निहतः &c., *see* STRUCK; 'in years,' वयोवृद्धः -द्धा -द्धं, *see* OLD.

STRICT, *a.* (Said of persons) सूक्ष्मदर्शी -र्शिनी -र्शि (न्), सूक्ष्मः -क्ष्मा -क्ष्मं, कठोरः -रा -रं, कठिनः -ना -नं, निष्ठुरः -रा -रं.—(Of things) समञ्जसः -सा -सं, सूक्ष्मः -क्ष्मा -क्ष्मं, नियतः -ता -तं, सम्यङ् -मीची -म्यक् (च्), दृढः -ढा -ढं, स्थिरः -रा -रं; 'in regimen,' पथ्याशी -शिनी &c.

STRICTLY, *adv.* निष्ठुरं, कठोरं, कठिनं, सूक्ष्मं, सौक्ष्म्येण, दृढं.

STRICTNESS, *s.* कठोरता, निष्ठुरता, नैष्ठुर्य्यं, कठिनता, काठिन्यं, सूक्ष्मता,

सौहृत्यं, सामञ्जस्यं, सम्यक्त्वं, दृढता, स्थिरता, उग्रता.

STRICTURE, s. (Of the urethra) मूत्रावरोधः, निरुद्धप्रकाशः.—(Critical remark) गुणदोषप्रकाशनं, गुणदोषव्याख्या, चर्चा.

STRIDE, s. विक्रमः, दीर्घक्रमः, दीर्घविक्रमः, लङ्घनं, विलङ्घनं.

To STRIDE, *v. n.* विक्रम् (c. 1. -क्रमते -मितुं), लङ्घ् (c. 10. लङ्घयति -यितुं).

STRIFE, s. कलहः -हं, कलिः *m.*, द्वन्द्वं, विरोधः, विप्रतिपत्तिः *f.*

STRIFEFUL, *a.* कलहकारी -रिणी -रि (न्), कलिप्रियः &c. *See* CONTENTIOUS.

To STRIKE, *v. a.* (Hit) तड् (c. 10. ताडयति -यितुं), वितड्, हन् (c. 2. हन्ति -न्तुं), अभिहन्, विहन्, आहन्, समाहन्, प्रहृ (c. 1. -हरति -हर्तुं), तुद्, आतुद्, वितुद्, व्यध्, प्रतिव्यध्, आघातं कृ, प्रहारं कृ, हननं कृ, *see To* HIT, SMITE.—(Cause to sound) वद् (c. 10. वादयति -यितुं), नद् in caus., वादनं कृ.—(Lower a sail) वातवसनम् अवपत् in caus. or अवरुह् in caus. or अवतॄ in caus. or अधःकृ.—(Affect with any feeling) उपहन्, उपहतं -तां कृ, *see To* ASTONISH, SURPRISE, &c.—(Strike down) पत् in caus. (पातयति -यितुं) निपत्, अवपत्, शद् in caus. (शातयति -यितुं), संशद्, आघातेन or प्रहारेण भूमौ पत् in caus.—(Strike out), *see To* EFFACE, ERASE, PRINT, CONTRIVE.

To STRIKE, *v. n.* (Make a blow) ताडनं कृ, आघातं कृ, प्रहारं कृ, *see To* KNOCK, *v. n.*—(Submit), *see To* YIELD.—(Strike against) लग् (c. 1. लगति -गितुं), प्रतिघातं कृ, परस्परसमाघातं कृ, संघट्ट्.—(Strike out, as in swimming, &c.) बाहुप्रसारणं कृ, बाहुप्रहारं कृ.—(Combine to quit work) वेतनासन्तुष्टत्वात् कर्म्मत्यागार्थं कुसाहित्यं कृ.

STRIKE, s. वेतनासन्तुष्टत्वात् कर्म्मत्यागार्थं कर्म्मकारिणां कुसाहित्यं.

STRIKER, s. ताडयिता *m.* (तृ), प्रहर्त्ता *m.* (र्तृ), आघाती *m.* (न्), घाती *m.*

STRIKING, *a.* विस्मयोत्पादकः -का -कं, विस्मापकः &c. *See* IMPRESSIVE.

STRING, s. (Slender cord, line or rope) सूत्रं, गुणः, तन्तुः *m.*, तन्त्री, तन्त्रं, रज्जुः *m.f.*, दाम *n.* (न्), दामनी, दामा, रसना, शुल्बं, शुल्वः -ल्वं, डोरकः, वटः -टी -टं, वराटः -टकः, सुम्बं, पवित्रकं; 'hempen string,' शणसूत्रं, शणतन्तुः *m.*; 'string of a musical instrument,' तन्त्री, तारः; 'of a bow,' ज्या, गुणः, धनुर्गुणः, शिञ्जा -ञ्जिनी, मौर्वी.—(Tie) बन्धः, बन्धनं.—(Line, series) आवलिः -ली *f.*, माला, पंक्तिः *f.*, पद्धतिः -ती *f.*, श्रेणी -णिः *f.*, जालं in comp.; 'string of pearls,' मुक्तावली -लिः *f.*, मुक्ताजालं; 'of beads,' अक्षमाला; 'of words or epithets,' शब्दमाला, शब्दजालं, माला; 'of causes,' कारणमाला.

To STRING, *v. a.* (Furnish with strings) तन्तुयुक्तं -क्तां कृ, तन्तुविशिष्टं -ष्टां कृ.—(String a garland, &c., arrange on a string, as beads, &c.) ग्रन्थ् (c. 9. ग्रथ्नाति, c. 1. ग्रन्थति -न्थितुं), ग्रन्थनं कृ, गुम्फ् (c. 1. गुम्फति -म्फितुं), गुफ् (c. 1. गुफति -फितुं), गुम्फनं कृ, गुम्फं कृ, रच् (c. 10. रचयति -यितुं), विरच्, रचनां कृ, दृभ् (c. 6. दृभति, c. 10. दर्भयति, c. 1. दर्भति -र्भितुं), सन्दर्भं कृ, अन्थ्, अन्थनं कृ, सूत्र (nom. सूत्रयति -यितुं), वट (nom. वटयति -यितुं), सूत्रणं कृ.—(String a bow) धनुर्गुणं or धनुर्ज्याम् आरुह् in caus. (-रोपयति -यितुं), धनुर्गुणारोपणं कृ, धनुः सज्यं कृ, मौर्वीं धनुषि आतन् (c. 8. -तनोति -नितुं).

STRINGED, *a.* तन्त्री -न्त्रिणी -न्त्रि (न्), तान्त्रः -न्त्री -न्त्रं, तन्तुयुक्तः -क्ता -क्तं, तन्तुमान् -मती -मत् (त्), तन्तुविशिष्टः -ष्टा -ष्टं, वटी -टिनी &c.; 'many-stringed,' बहुतन्त्रीकः -का -कं; 'one-stringed,' एकतन्त्रीकः -का -कं, एकतारः -रा -रं; 'stringed-instrument,' ततं.

STRINGENT, *a.* दृढबन्धी -न्धिनी -न्धि (न्), दृढबन्धकः -का -कं, दृढः -ढा -ढं.

STRINGLESS, *a.* निर्गुणः -णा -णं, गुणहीनः -ना -नं, तन्तुहीनः -ना -नं.

STRINGY, *a.* (Consisting of strings or fibres) सूत्रमयः -यी -यं, तन्तुमयः &c., सूत्री -त्रिणी &c., *see* FIBROUS.—(Ropy, viscid) श्यानः -ना -नं.

To STRIP, *v. a.* (Deprive of clothes) विवस्त्र (nom. विवस्त्रयति -यितुं), नग्नीकृ, विवस्त्रीकृ, निर्वस्त्रीकृ, वस्त्रहीनं -नां कृ, *see To* DIVEST.—(Deprive of) हृ (c. 1. हरति, हर्तुं), अपहृ, अपनी, *see To* DEPRIVE, FLEECE, PLUNDER; 'to strip a tree of its leaves,' वृक्षस्य पत्राणि हृ or निर्हृ, वृक्षं निष्पत्रीकृ or निष्पत्र (Nom. निष्पत्रयति -यितुं).

STRIP, s. खण्डः -ण्डकः, सूक्ष्मखण्डः, दीर्घखण्डः; 'of cloth,' वस्त्रखण्डः.

STRIPE, s. (Line) रेखा, दीर्घरेखा, *see* LINE.—(Long narrow piece) दीर्घखण्डः -ण्डकः.—(Lash, stroke) कशाघातः, कशाघातचिह्नं.

To STRIPE, *v. a.* (Make lines), *see To* STREAK.—(Lash) कशया तड्.

STRIPED, *p. p.* नानावर्णरेखाङ्कितः -ता -तं, चित्रितः &c. *See* STREAKED.

STRIPLING, s. माणवकः, वटुः *m.*, कुमारः, बालः, किशोरः, *see* LAD.

STRIPPED, *p. p.* (Of clothes) विवस्त्रः -स्त्रा -स्त्रं, विवस्त्रीकृतः -ता -तं, नग्नीकृतः &c., हृतवस्त्रः &c., हृतवेशः -शा -शं, अवधूतवेशः &c.—(Deprived, robbed) हृतः -ता -तं, अपहृतः &c., लुण्ठितः &c.; 'of one's money,' हृतधनः -ना -नं; 'of one's all,' हृतसर्व्वस्वः -स्वा -स्वं.

To STRIVE, *v. n.* (Make efforts) यत् (c. 1. यतते -तितुं), प्रयत्, यत्नं कृ, प्रयत्नं कृ, व्यवसो (c. 4. -स्यति -सातुं), चेष्ट् (c. 1. चेष्टते -ष्टितुं), विचेष्ट्, आत्मानं चेष्ट्, उद्यम् (c. 1. -यच्छति -यन्तुं), व्यायम्, आयस् (c. 4. -यस्यति -सितुं), घट् (c. 1. घटते -टितुं, c. 10. घटयति -यितुं), उद्योगं कृ, उद्यमं कृ, उत्साहं कृ, व्यवसायं कृ, आयासं कृ, प्रयासं कृ, चेष्टां कृ.—(Contend) कलहं कृ, कलह (nom. कलहायते), युध्, विरुध्, *see To* CONTEND, CONTEST.—(Vie with) स्पर्ध्, *see To* EMULATE.

STRIVING, s. उद्योगकरणं, यत्नकरणं, *see* EXERTION, CONTENTION.

STROKE, s. (Blow) आघातः, अभिघातः, घातः, आहतिः *f.*, हतिः *f.*, प्रहारः, ताडनं, पातः -तनं; 'of a stick,' वेत्राघातः; 'of a sword,' खड्गाघातः; 'of a weapon,' शस्त्रपातः; 'of an oar,' नौकादण्डपातः, नौकादण्डनिपातः.—(Sudden attack, as of disease, &c.) आक्रमः, अवतारः, अवतरणं, आवेशः, लङ्घनं.—(Sudden or bold effort) आकस्मिकयत्नः, साहसिकयत्नः, प्रयत्नः.—(Line drawn) रेखा, लेखा, अङ्कः -ङ्कनं; 'of a pen,' कलमलेखा, कलमरेखा.

To STROKE, *v. a.* (With the hand) पाणिना or हस्तेन शनैर् मृज् (c. 2. मार्ष्टि -र्ष्टुं) or प्रमृज् or विमृज्, पाणिना समालभ् (c. 1. -लभते -लब्धुं) or आलभ्, हस्तेन परामृश् (c. 6. -मृशति -म्रष्टुं) or परिमृश् or विमृश्, हस्तेन परिस्पृश् (c. 6. -स्पृशति -स्प्रष्टुं) or संस्पृश् or परिसंस्पृश्, हस्तेन लल् (c. 10. लालयति -यितुं); 'in one direction, with the hair,' अनुलोमं मृज्, अनुलोम (nom. अनुलोमयति -यितुं).

To STROLL, *v. n.* आलस्येन विहृ or परिभ्रम् or परिक्रम्. *See To* RAMBLE.

STROLL, STROLLING, s. आलस्येन परिक्रमणं or विहारः or इतस्ततः परिक्रमः, यथेष्टपरिक्रमः, यथेष्टविहरणं, यथेष्टचारः. *See* RAMBLE, RAMBLING.

STROLLER, s. यथेष्टविहारी *m.* (न्), यथेष्टचारी *m.* *See* RAMBLER.

STRONG, *a.* (Having power) बलवान् -वती -वत् (त्), बली -लिनी -लि (न्), प्रबलः -ला -लं, महाबलः &c., सबलः &c., *see* POWERFUL; 'very strong,' अतिबलवान् &c., बलीयान् -यसी -यः (स्), बलिष्ठः -ष्ठा -ष्ठं.—(Firm) दृढः -ढा -ढं, सुदृढः &c.—(As smell, &c.)

उग्रः -ग्रा -ग्रं; 'a strong smell,' उग्रगन्धः, अतिगन्धः.—(As wind, &c.) चण्डः -ण्डा -ण्डं, प्रचण्डः &c., तीक्ष्णः -क्ष्णा -क्ष्णं, तीव्रः -व्रा -व्रं, अति prefixed; 'a strong wind,' प्रचण्डवातः, अतिवातः.—(As medicine, &c.) प्रतापी -पिनी &c., प्रभावी &c., प्रबलः -ला -लं, तेजस्वी &c., गुणवान् &c., गुणकारी &c.—(Pungent) कटुः -टुः -टु, उग्रः &c.; 'to be strong,' प्रबलीभू, बलवान् &c. भू, मुर्छ् (c. 1. मूर्च्छति -र्च्छितुं), ओजस् (nom. ओजायते); 'an army a thousand strong,' साहस्रः, सहस्री *m.* (न्).

STRONG-BUILT, STRONG-MADE, *a.* दृढसन्धिः -न्धिः -न्धि, दृढाङ्गः -ङ्गा -ङ्गं.

STRONG-HOLD, *s.* दुर्गं, कोटिः *f.*, कोटः, कोट्टारः, शिखरी *m.* (न्).

STRONGLY, *adv.* बलवत्, सबलं, प्रबलं, दृढं, सुदृढं, प्राबल्येन.

STRONG-MINDED, *a.* दृढमतिः -तिः -ति, दृढबुद्धिः &c., स्थिरबुद्धिः &c.

STRONG-SMELLING, *a.* उग्रगन्धः -न्धा -न्धं, उग्रगन्धी -न्धिनी -न्धि (न्).

STROP, *s.* (For razors) क्षुरतेजनी, क्षुरतेजनी, क्षुरतेजनचर्म्म *n.* (न्).

STRUCK, *p.p.* हतः -ता -तं, आहतः &c., समाहतः &c., अभिहतः &c., प्रहतः &c., उपहतः &c., व्याहतः &c., प्रतिहतः &c., ताडितः -ता -तं, आस्फालितः -ता -तं; 'with astonishment,' विस्मयोपहतः -ता -तं. The use of हत in the first member of a compound is very common; as, 'struck with poverty,' हतसम्पद् -दा -दं, *i. e.* 'one whose fortunes are struck or blasted.'

STRUCTURE, *s.* (A building) भवनं, हर्म्म्यं, मन्दिरं, *see* EDIFICE.—(Organization) व्यूहः -हनं, व्यूढिः *f.*, संव्यूहः -हनं, संस्थानं, संस्थितिः *f.*, विधानं, निर्म्माणं, निर्म्मितिः *f.*; 'of the body,' अङ्गव्यूहनं.

To STRUGGLE, *v. n.* (Make great effort) अत्यन्तं यत्, महायत्नं कृ, तीव्रयत्नं कृ, अतियत्नं कृ, अत्यन्तं चेष्ट्, विचेष्ट्, *see To* STRIVE.—(Contend) युध् (c. 4. युध्यते, योद्धुं), *see To* FIGHT.

STRUGGLE, *s.* (Great effort) महायत्नः, अतियत्नः, तीव्रयत्नः, विचेष्टितं.—(Contest) युद्धं, नियुद्धं, कलहः -हं, *see* CONTENTION.

STRUGGLING, *part.* यतमानः -ना -नं, महायत्नकारी -रिणी &c., विचेष्टमानः -ना -नं.

STRUMPET, *s.* वेश्या, गणिका, पुंश्चली. *See* HARLOT, PROSTITUTE.

STRUNG, *p.p.* ग्रन्थितः -ता -तं, ग्रथितः &c., गुम्फितः -ता -तं, गुफितः &c., अन्वितः -ता -तं, रचितः &c., दृब्धः -ब्धा -ब्धं, सन्दितः -ता -तं, सूत्रितः -ता -तं.—(As a bow) सज्यः -ज्या -ज्यं, अधिज्यः &c., आरोपितज्यः &c.; 'bow-string strung tight on a bow,' मौर्वी धनुषि आतता.

To STRUT, *v. n.* साटोपं or सदर्पं or सगौरवं चल् (c. 1. चलति -लितुं).

STRUT, *s.* साटोपगतिः *f.*, सदर्पगतिः *f.*, सगर्व्वगतिः *f.*, प्रौढगतिः *f.*

STRUTTING, *part.* साटोपगामी -मिनी &c., प्रौढगतिः -तिः -ति. *See* STATELY.

STUBBLE, *s.* भूमिस्थो यवगोधूमादिनालः, भूमिस्था शुष्कनाली, भूमिस्थनालः -ली -लं, छिन्नशस्यनालः -ली, लूनशस्यनालः.

STUBBORN, *a.* स्तब्धः -ब्धा -ब्धं, प्रतीपः -पा -पं, दृढः -ढा -ढं, अविनेयः -या -यं, अवश्यः -श्या -श्यं, दुराग्रही &c. *See* OBSTINATE.

STUBBORNNESS, *s.* स्तब्धता, प्रतीपता, धैर्य्यं, अविनेयता. *See* OBSTINACY.

STUCCO, *s.* सुधा, धवलसुधा, शुक्लसुधा, चूर्णलेपः. *See* PLASTER.

STUCCOED, *a.* सुधाधवलितः -ता -तं, सुधालिप्तः -प्ता -प्तं, सुधामयः -यी -यं; 'a stuccoed house,' सुधाभवनं, सुधामयगृहं.

STUCK, *p.p.* लग्नः -ग्ना -ग्नं, परिलग्नः &c., संलग्नः &c., आसक्तः -क्ता -क्तं.

STUD, *s.* (Ornamental knob) गण्डः -ण्डका, गण्डालङ्कारः.—(Of horses) वाडवं, आश्वं, अश्वीयं, अश्वसमूहः, अश्ववृन्दं, अश्वगणः.

STUDDED, *p.p.* खचितः -ता -तं, प्रतिबद्धः -द्धा -द्धं, *see* SET, INLAID.

STUDENT, *s.* शिष्यः, विद्यार्थी *m.* (न्), छात्रः, अन्तेवासी *m.*, अध्येता *m.* (तृ), अधीयानः, अध्यायी *m.*, *see* SCHOLAR; 'in theology,' ब्रह्मचारी *m.* (न्), लिङ्गी *m.*, व्रती *m.*, *see* under ORDER.

STUDENTSHIP, *s.* ब्रह्मचर्य्यं, ब्रह्मचारित्वं, अन्तेवासित्वं.

STUDIED, *p. p.* (Read) शिक्षितः -ता -तं, अधीतः &c., अधिगतः &c., अभ्यासितः &c., अभ्यस्तः -स्ता -स्तं, पठितः -ता -तं, निपठितः &c.—(Premeditated) पूर्व्वकल्पितः -ता -तं, पूर्व्वसङ्कल्पितः &c.

STUDIOUS, *a.* अध्ययनशीलः -ला -लं, विद्याभ्यासशीलः &c., अध्ययनपरः -रा -रं, अध्ययनपरायणः -णा -णं, अध्ययनासक्तः -क्ता -क्तं, विद्यार्थी -र्थिनी -र्थि (न्), विद्येच्छुः -च्छुः -च्छु, अध्ययनेच्छुः &c., विद्याभ्यासी &c., व्यवसायी &c., अध्यवसायी &c., विद्याप्रसितः -ता -तं, विद्यानिविष्टः -ष्टा -ष्टं, विद्याभ्यासक्ती &c., अध्ययनाभिमुखः -खा -खं, जिज्ञासुः -सुः -सु, पाठेच्छुः &c., पठनेच्छुः &c.

STUDIOUSLY, *adv.* अध्ययनासक्तिपूर्व्वं, विद्याभ्यासेन, विद्याभ्यासक्त्या.

STUDIOUSNESS, *s.* अध्ययनशीलता, विद्याभ्यासशीलता, अध्ययनासक्तिः *f.*, विद्यासक्तिः *f.*, विद्येच्छा, विद्याभ्यासक्तिः, अध्ययनपरता, पाठेच्छा.

STUDY, *s.* (Reading, application to books, &c.) अध्ययनं, पाठः, निपाठः, पठनं, अधिगमः -मनं, प्राध्ययनं, अभ्यासः, विद्याभ्यासः, विद्याभ्यसनं, अधीतिः *f.*, निपठितिः *f.*, निपठः, आवर्त्तनं, *see* STUDIOUSNESS; 'study of the Vedas,' वेदाध्ययनं, वेदाभ्यासः, उपग्रहणं, उपाकर्म्म *n.* (न्), उपाकरणं; 'close study,' सततताध्ययनं, सततताभ्यासः, अनुशीलनं, परिशीलनं; 'desultory study,' शाखाचङ्क्रमणं, चङ्क्रमणं; 'a Brahman who has finished his study,' प्राधीतः, अधीतवेदः, अधीती *m.*—(Subject of study, particular study) अध्ययनं, पाठः, अध्ययनविषयः.—(Apartment for study) अध्ययनमठः, अध्ययनागारं, पाठागारं, ज्ञानमठः, ग्रन्थकुटी.—(Meditation, contrivance) ध्यानं, विचारः, चिन्ता, चर्चा, कल्पना.

To STUDY, *v. a.* (Read, turn over in the mind) पठ् (c. 1. पठति -ठितुं), सम्पठ्, अधी (c. 2. अधीते, अध्येतुं, rt. इ), अधिगम् (c. 1. -गच्छति -गन्तुं), अभ्यस् (c. 4. -अस्यति -सितुं), आवृत् (c. 10. -वर्त्तयति -यितुं), अध्ययनं कृ.—(Attend to) सेव् (c. 1. सेवते -वितुं), उपसेव् निषेव्, आसेव्, समासेव्.—(Ponder, consider, premeditate), *see* the words.

To STUDY, *v. n.* (Apply the mind to reading, &c.) विद्याभ्यासं कृ, विद्याभ्यसनं कृ, अध्ययनं कृ, विद्याभ्यासक्तिं कृ, पाठं कृ.—(Endeavour diligently), *see To* STRIVE.

STUFF, *s.* (Matter, material) वस्तु *n.*, द्रव्यं, प्रकृतिः *f.*, विषयः, पदार्थः, परिणामिद्रव्यं.—(Cloth) पटः, वस्त्रं, वसनं, *see* CLOTH.—(Household furniture) गृहोपस्करादि *n.*, गृहभाण्डानि *n. pl.*, गृहद्रव्याणि *n. pl.*—(Rubbish) तुच्छद्रव्यं, *see* RUBBISH, NONSENSE.

To STUFF, *v. a.* (Fill to excess) अत्यन्तं पृ (c. 10. पूरयति -यितुं), अतिशयेन तृप् in caus.—(Crowd together) सम्बाध्, *see To* CROWD, *v. a.*

To STUFF, *v. n.* अतिशयेन or अतितृप्ति पृ in pass. (पूर्य्यते) or आत्मानं पृ (c. 10. पूरयति -यितुं), अतितृप्ति भुज्. *See To* CRAM, *v. n.*

STUFFED, *p. p.* अतिपूरितः -ता -तं, अतिपूर्णः -र्णा -र्णं. *See* CRAMMED.

STUFFING, *s.* (That which fills up) पूरणं, पूरकः -कं, भरणं, भरकः -कं.—(Seasoning) मांसान्तर्गतं व्यञ्जनादि, *see* SEASONING.

To STULTIFY, *v. a.* मूर्खं कृ, मूढीकृ, मूर्खीकृ, निर्बोधीकृ.

To STUMBLE, *v. n.* स्खल् (c. 1. स्खलति -लितुं), प्रस्खल्, स्खलनं कृ, पादस्खलनं कृ, स्खलितं कृ, च्यु (c. 1. च्यवते, च्योतुं), प्रच्यु, पत्, विचल्, संचल्.

To STUMBLE, *v. a.* स्खल् in caus. (स्खलयति -यितुं), स्खलनं जन् in caus.

STUMBLE, STUMBLING, *s.* स्खलनं, स्खलितं, पादस्खलनं, पतनं, चपच्छेदः.

STUMBLING-BLOCK, *s.* व्याघातजनकपाषाणः, स्खलनजनकप्रस्तरः.

STUMP, *s.* (Of a tree) स्थाणुः *m.* -णु *n.*, ध्रुवः, शङ्कुः *m.*, छिन्नवृक्षस्य भूमिस्थः काष्ठाधोभागः.—(Of a limb) छिन्नाङ्गस्य उच्छिष्टभागः.

STUMPY, *a.* ह्रस्वस्थूलः -ला -लं, स्थूलखर्वः -र्वा -र्वं, ह्रस्वः -स्वा -स्वं.

To STUN, *v. a.* (With a blow) आघातेन मूर्च्छितं -तां कृ, आघातमूर्च्छितं -तां कृ, प्रहारेण मूर्च्छां जन् (c. 10. जनयति -यितुं), आघातेन संज्ञां or चैतन्यं हृ (c. 1. हरति, हर्तुं), प्रहाराकुलं -लां कृ, आघातेन जडीकृ or मूढीकृ or आकुलीकृ or मूढसंज्ञं -ज्ञां कृ, स्तम्भीकृ.—(Deafen) बधिरीकृ, श्रवणशक्तिं हृ, श्रवणेन्द्रियं जडीकृ.—(Confound) मुह् (c. 10. मोहयति -यितुं).

STUNG, *p. p.* दंशितः -ता -तं, दष्टः -ष्टा -ष्टं, तोदितः -ता -तं, प्रतोदितः &c., प्रतुन्नः -न्ना -न्नं, व्यथितः -ता -तं, तीक्ष्णव्यथोपहतः &c.

STUNNED, *p. p.* (By a blow) आघातमूर्च्छितः -ता -तं, प्रहारमूर्च्छितः &c., प्रहाराकुलः -ला -लं, प्रहारमोहितः -ता -तं, आघातमूढः -ढा -ढं, प्रमूढसंज्ञः -ज्ञा -ज्ञं, मूढसंज्ञः &c., प्रहारजडः -डा -डं, जडीकृतः -ता -तं, जडधीः -धीः -धि.—(Deafened) बधिरीकृतः -ता -तं, उपहतकर्णः -र्णा -र्णं.

STUNNING, *a.* कर्णोपघाती -तिनी -ति (न्), श्रवणशक्तिहारी -रिणी &c.

To STUNT, *v. a.* वृद्धिरोधं कृ, वृद्धिविरोधं कृ, वृद्धिव्याघातं कृ, वामनीकृ.

STUNTED, *p. p.* or *a.* रुद्धवृद्धिः -द्धिः -द्धि, वामनाकृतिः -तिः -ति.

STUPEFACTION, *s.* मोहः, सम्मोहः, व्यामोहः, जडता. *See* STUPOR.

STUPEFIED, *p. p.* मोहितः -ता -तं, जडीकृतः &c., जडीभूतः &c., मूढसंज्ञः -ज्ञा -ज्ञं, प्रमूढसंज्ञः &c., स्तम्भितः -ता -तं, स्तम्भितेन्द्रियः -या -यं, मोहितेन्द्रियः &c., स्तब्धः -ब्धा -ब्धं, हृतसंज्ञः &c.

To STUPEFY, *v. a.* मुह् (c. 10. मोहयति -यितुं), सम्मुह्, व्यामुह्, जडीकृ, इन्द्रियस्तम्भं कृ, इन्द्रियस्तम्भनं कृ, इन्द्रियाणि स्तम्भ् (c. 9. स्तभ्नाति, स्तम्भितुं, c. 10. स्तम्भयति -यितुं), विष्टम्भ्, संस्तम्भ्, स्तम्भीकृ.

STUPEFYING, *a.* मोहकः -का -कं, मोहजनकः -का -कं, स्तम्भकः -का -कं, इन्द्रियमोहकः &c., इन्द्रियस्तम्भकः &c., मोहकारी -रिणी &c., मोहकारकः &c.

STUPENDOUS, *a.* विस्मयजनकः -का -कं, विस्मयोत्पादकः &c., विस्मयकारकः &c., अद्भुतः -ता -तं, आश्चर्यः &c., आश्चर्यकरः &c. *See* WONDERFUL.

STUPENDOUSNESS, *s.* अद्भुतता -त्वं, आश्चर्यत्वं, विस्मयजनकता.

STUPID, *a.* मूढः -ढा -ढं, मूर्खः -र्खा -र्खं, प्रमूढः &c., मन्दबुद्धिः -द्धिः -द्धि, जडः -डा -डं, जडबुद्धिः &c., जडमतिः -तिः -ति, मूढमतिः &c., मन्दः -न्दा -न्दं, निर्बुद्धिः -द्धिः -द्धि, निर्बोधः -धा -धं, स्थूलः -ला -लं, स्थूलबुद्धिः &c., स्थूलधीः -धीः -धि, दुर्मतिः -तिः -ति, दुर्बुद्धिः &c., दुर्मेधाः -धाः -धः (स्), मतिहीनः -ना -नं, बुद्धिहीनः &c., अबुधः -धा -धं, अबुद्धिमान् -मती -मत् (त्), अबुद्धिः &c., अविज्ञः -ज्ञा -ज्ञं, अज्ञः &c., मन्थरः -रा -रं, मन्दरः -रा -रं, कुशठः -शठा -शठं, कुशठकः -का -कं, कुत्सितः -ता -तं, अज्ञानः -ना -नं, अज्ञानी &c., कुधीः &c., बर्बरः -रा -रं.

STUPIDITY, STUPIDNESS, *s.* मूढता, मूर्खता, स्थूलता, मन्दता, बुद्धिमन्दता, मन्दबुद्धित्वं, जडता, जडिमा *m.* (न्), बुद्धिजडता, मौर्ख्यं, स्थौल्यं, जाड्यं, मान्द्यं, बुद्धिजाड्यं, निर्बुद्धित्वं, बुद्धिहीनत्वं -ता, अविज्ञता, अज्ञता, अज्ञानं, कुशठता.

STUPIDLY, *adv.* मूर्खवत्, मूढवत्, अविज्ञवत्, सजाड्यं, समान्द्यं.

STUPOR, *s.* मोहः, इन्द्रियस्वापः, इन्द्रियसुप्तिः *f.*, इन्द्रियमोहः, इन्द्रियस्तम्भः, स्तम्भः, व्यामोहः, जडता, जाड्यं, जडिमा *m.* (न्).

STURDINESS, *s.* दृढाङ्गता, शरीरदृढता, दृढता. *See* ROBUSTNESS.

STURDY, *a.* दृढाङ्गः -ङ्गा -ङ्गं, दृढदेहः -हा -हं, *see* STOUT, ROBUST.

To STUTTER, *v. n.* स्खलद्वाक्येन वद्, अस्पष्टं वद्. *See To* STAMMER.

STUTTERER, *s.* स्खलद्वाक्यः, स्खलितवाक् *m.* (च्), वाग्विकलः, मदकलवाक्.

STUTTERING, *s.* वाक्स्खलनं, वाग्वैकल्यं, अस्पष्टोच्चारणं, *see* STAMMERING.

STY, *s.* (For pigs) शूकरस्थानं, *see* PIG-STY.—(In the eye) कुम्भिका.

STYLE, *s.* (Manner) वृत्तिः *f.*, रीतिः *f.*, *see* MODE.—(Of speaking or writing) वाग्वृत्तिः *f.*, शब्दवृत्तिः *f.*, शब्दरीतिः *f.*, वाग्व्यापारः, शब्दरचना, वाक्सरणिः -णी *f.*; 'elegance of style in rhetoric,' गुणः; 'figurative style,' व्यञ्जनावृत्तिः *f.*—(Style of living) वृत्तिः *f.*—(Title) संज्ञा, ख्यातिः *f.*, प्रतिष्ठानाम *n.*—(For writing) लेखनी, कीलः, *see* PEN.—(Pointed iron graver) शलाका, तक्षणी, कीलः.—(Of a dial) शङ्कुः *m.*, कीलः.

To STYLE, *v. a.* संज्ञां कृ or दा, अभिधा, कृत्. *See To* NAME, CALL.

STYLED, *p. p.* संज्ञितः -ता -तं, संज्ञ in comp. *See* NAMED, CALLED.

STYLISH, *a.* सभ्यरीत्यनुसारी -रिणी -रि (न्), सभ्यवृत्त्यनुरूपः -पा -पं, सभ्यव्यवहारसिद्धः -द्धा -द्धं, सभ्यलोकमतः -ता -तं, अतिशोभनः -ना -नं.

STYPTIC, *a.* रक्तावरोधकः -का -कं, रक्तस्तम्भकः &c., रक्तस्रावावरोधी -धिनी &c., रक्तस्रावस्तम्भकः &c., रक्तनिरोधकः &c., स्तम्भकः &c., रक्तस्तम्भनः -ना -नं, कषायी -यिणी &c., कषायान्वितः -ता -तं, कषायः -या -यं.

STYPTIC, *s.* रक्तावरोधकं, रक्तस्तम्भनं, स्तम्भनं. *See* the last.

STYRAX, *s.* कपिशः, अश्मपुष्पं, शीतशिवं. *See* BENZOIN.

STYX, *s.* (River of Hell) वैतरणी, परलोकनदी, प्रेतनदी.

SUAVITY, *s.* मधुरता, माधुर्य्यं, वाङ्माधुर्य्यं, मधुरोक्तित्वं, स्वादुता.

SUBACID, *a.* ईषदम्लः -म्ला -म्लं, काम्लः -म्ला -म्लं, किञ्चिदम्लः &c.

To SUBDIVIDE, *v. a.* अंशांशान् कृ, अंशांशीकृ, अवयवीकृ, प्रतिभागीकृ.

SUBDIVISION, *s.* अंशांशः, अवयवः, शाखा, उपशाखा, प्रतिभागः, भागप्रतिभागः, प्रभागः, प्रत्यङ्गं, उपाङ्गं, अङ्गस्कन्धः, उपप्रकरणं, विशेषः; 'having subdivisions,' अवयवी -विनी -वि (न्), शाखी &c.

To SUBDUE, *v. a.* वशीकृ, पराजि (c. 1. -जयति -ते -जेतुं), विजि (atm. only) संजि, जि, दम् (c. 10. दमयति -यितुं), प्रदम्, अभिभू, पराभू, स्ववशीकृ, आत्मवशीकृ, आत्मवशं नी (c. 1. नयति, नेतुं), स्वाधीनीकृ, आत्माधीनीकृ, स्ववशे स्था in caus. (स्थापयति -यितुं), आत्मायत्तं -त्तां कृ, आत्मायत्तीकृ, स्वायत्तीकृ, भञ्जनं कृ, भञ्ज्. *See To* CONQUER, OVERCOME, SOFTEN.

SUBDUED, *p. p.* वशीकृतः -ता -तं, वशीभूतः &c. दमितः -ता -तं, पराजितः &c., जितः &c., अभिभूतः -ता -तं, पराभूतः &c., दान्तः -न्ता -न्तं, स्ववशीकृतः &c., आत्मवशः -शा -शं, वशी -शिनी -शि (न्), वशः &c., वशङ्गतः -ता -तं, स्ववशनीतः &c., हस्तङ्गतः &c., हस्तगतः &c., दर्परहितः &c., निवृत्तः -त्ता -त्तं. *See* OVERCOME, MORTIFIED, SOFTENED, HUMBLED.

SUBDUER, *s.* दमकः, दमी *m.* (न्), दमनकारी *m.* (न्), जेता *m.* (तृ).

SUBDUING, *s.* वशीकरणं, दमनं, दमः, भङ्गः. *See* SUBJUGATION.

SUBJACENT, *a.* अधःस्थः -स्था -स्थं, अधःस्थितः -ता -तं, अधोवर्त्ती &c.

SUBJECT, *a.* (Under the power of) वशः -शा -शं, वशी -शिनी -शि (न्), अधीनः -ना -नं, आयत्तः -त्ता -त्तं, अभ्यधीनः -ना -नं, भक्तः -क्ता -क्तं, तन्त्रः -न्त्रा -न्त्रं, उपजीवी -विनी -वि (न्), विवशः &c., अनुवशः &c., निघ्नः -घ्ना -घ्नं; 'to another,' परवशः -शा -शं, पराधीनः -ना -नं, परायत्तः &c., परतन्त्रः &c., परच्छन्दः -न्दा -न्दं, परवान् &c., परोपजीवी &c., नाथवान् &c.—(Liable to) अधीनः -ना -नं, योग्यः -ग्या -ग्यं, वशः -शा -शं, अर्ह in comp., नित्य in comp., आस्पदं in comp., पात्रं in comp., *see* OBNOXIOUS; 'subject to disease,' रोगाधीनः -ना -नं, नित्यरोगी &c., सदा-

रोगी &c., रोगास्पदं; 'subject to melancholy,' नित्यविषादी &c., सदाविषादी &c.—(To be subject) वशीभू, अधीनीभू, आयत्तीभू, उपजीव् (c. 1. -जीवति -वितुं).

SUBJECT, *s.* (One that owes allegiance) प्रजा, भक्तः, वश्यः, उपजीवी *m.* (न्); 'subjects, collectively,' प्रजालोकः, प्रजा, प्रजाः *f. pl.*; 'beloved by one's subjects,' प्रजानुरक्तः -क्ता -क्तं, अनुरक्तप्रजः -जा -जं; 'the protection of one's subjects,' प्रजापालनं.—(That which is treated of, a topic, head) विषयः, प्रकरणं, प्रसङ्गः, प्रस्तावः, प्रसक्तिः *f.*, अर्थः, वृत्तान्तः, स्थानं, स्थलं, पदं, अधिकरणं, मार्गः; 'subject in hand,' प्रस्तुतं; 'on such a subject,' एवंविषयः -या -यं; 'this chapter is on the subject of the heavenly bodies, &c.,' अयं सर्गो ग्रहादिविषयकः.—(That in which any thing inheres or exists) अधिकरणं, आधारः, आश्रयः, आशयः, आस्पदं, स्थानं, अधिष्ठानं, व्याप्यं; 'of an inference,' व्याप्यं; 'of any operation or act,' आश्रयः, अधिकरणं, पात्रं, स्थानं, अधिष्ठानं, भूमिः *f.*—(Of a verb, in grammar) कर्त्ता *m.*—(Of a predicate) अनुवाद्यं.—(Of a proposition) साध्यं.

To SUBJECT, *v. a.* (Bring under the power of) वशीकृ, अधीनीकृ, आयत्तीकृ.—(Subjugate), *see To* SUBDUE.—(Make liable) अधीनं -नां कृ, अधीनीकृ, वशीकृ, योग्यं -ग्यां कृ, आस्पदं कृ, आस्पदीकृ; 'to subject one to ridicule,' उपहासास्पदं कृ, उपहासास्पदीकृ; 'to subject to diseases,' रोगाधीनीकृ, रोगाधीनं -नां कृ; 'to a legal process,' विवादास्पदीकृ; 'to trial,' अनुभवारूढं -ढां कृ.

SUBJECTED, *p. p.* वशीकृतः -ता -तं, अधीनीकृतः -ता -तं. *See* SUBJECT, *a.*

SUBJECTION, *s.* (The act) वशीकरणं, अधीनीकरणं.—(The state) वशता -त्वं, वशिता -त्वं, वशं, वश्यता -त्वं, भक्तिः *f.*, निघ्नता, आज्ञाधीनता; 'to another,' पराधीनता, परवशता, परवशित्वं, परवशः, परतन्त्रत्वं, पारतन्त्र्यं, पराश्रितत्वं.

SUBJECTIVE, *a.* अधिकरणसम्बन्धी -न्धिनी -न्धि (न्), अधिष्ठानसम्बन्धी &c., अधिष्ठाननिष्ठः -ष्ठा -ष्ठं, अधिकरणनिष्ठः &c.

SUBJECT-MATTER, *s.* विषयः, प्रस्तावः, प्रसङ्गः, प्रकरणं. *See* under SUBJECT, *s.*

To SUBJOIN, *v. a.* अनुबन्ध् (c. 9. -बध्नाति -बन्द्धुं), आयुज्, समायुज्, संयुज्.

To SUBJUGATE, *v. a.* वशीकृ, करदीकृ, पराजि. *See To* SUBDUE, *v. a.*

SUBJUGATED, *p. p.* वशीकृतः -ता -तं, करदीकृतः &c. *See* SUBDUED.

SUBJUGATION, *s.* वशीकरणं, दमनं, दमः, जयः -यनं, विजयः -यनं, पराजयः, अभिभवः, परिग्रहः, निग्रहः -हणं, भञ्जनं, भङ्गः, दण्डः -ण्डं; 'of one's enemies,' शत्रुदमनं; 'of foreign countries,' दिग्विजयः; 'of one's passions,' इन्द्रियदमः -मनं, इन्द्रियजयः, इन्द्रियनिग्रहः.

SUBJUNCTIVE, *s.* (Mode in grammar) संशयार्थः.

SUBLIMATE, *s.* (Of mercury) रसकर्पूरः, रसपुष्पं.

To SUBLIMATE, *v. a.* ऊर्द्ध्वपातनं कृ, ऊर्द्ध्वं पत् in caus. (पातयति -यितुं).

SUBLIMATION, *s.* ऊर्द्ध्वपातनं, ऊर्द्ध्वकरणं, उच्चीकरणं, पुटपाकः.

SUBLIME, *a.* अत्युच्चः -च्चा -च्चं, अत्युच्छ्रितः -ता -तं, अत्युत्कृष्टः -ष्टा -ष्टं, अत्युन्नतः -ता -तं, अत्युद्धतः -ता -तं, अतिप्रौढः -ढा -ढं. *See* LOFTY.

SUBLIMITY, SUBLIMENESS, *s.* अत्युच्चता, अत्युत्कृष्टता, अत्युत्कर्षः, अत्युद्धतिः *f.*, अत्युन्नतिः *f.*, प्रौढता, अत्यूर्द्ध्वता. *See* LOFTINESS.

SUBLUNARY, *a.* ऐहलौकिकः -की -कं, ऐहिकः -की -कं. *See* MUNDANE.

SUBMARINE, *a.* समुद्राधःस्थः -स्था -स्थं, समुद्रतलस्थः &c., समुद्रस्थः &c.; 'submarine fire,' समुद्रवह्निः *m.*, वडवाग्निः *m.*, वाडवाग्निः *m.*, वाडवानलः, वाडवः, और्वः, अब्ध्यग्निः *m.*, सलिलेन्धनः.

To SUBMERGE, *v. a.* निमज्ज् (c. 10. -मज्जयति -यितुं), जलान्तर् मज्ज्, जलान्तः कृ, जलान्तः स्था in caus. *See To* PLUNGE, INUNDATE.

To SUBMERGE, *v. n.* मज्ज् (c. 6. मज्जति -ज्जितुं), निमज्ज्. *See To* PLUNGE, *v. n.*

SUBMERGED, *p. p.* मज्जितः -ता -तं, निमज्जितः &c., निमग्नः -ग्ना -ग्नं, आप्लावितः -ता -तं, *see* PLUNGED, IMMERSED; 'is submerged,' प्लाव्यते.

SUBMERSION, *s.* निमज्जनं, मज्जनं, आप्लावः -वनं. *See* IMMERSION.

SUBMISSION, *s.* (To the power of another) वशता -त्वं, वशित्वं, वशं, वश्यता, अधीनता, पराधीनता, अनुवर्त्तनं, अनुवृत्तिः *f.*, वशवर्त्तनं, वशीभूतता, *see* SUBJECTION, OBEDIENCE.—(Resignation) क्षमा, क्षान्तिः *f.*, *see* RESIGNATION.

SUBMISSIVE, *a.* वशवर्त्ती -र्त्तिनी -र्त्ति (न्), वश्यः -श्या -श्यं, वशगः -गा -गं, वशानुगः &c., वश्यात्मा -त्मा -त्म (न्), विधेयः -या -यं, विनतः -ता -तं, आनतः &c., दीनः -ना -नं, सविनयः -या -यं, क्षामः &c., अनुविधायी &c. *See* OBEDIENT, DOCILE, RESIGNED.

SUBMISSIVELY, *adv.* सानुवर्त्तनं, क्षमापूर्व्वं, क्षान्तिपूर्व्वं, सविनयं.

SUBMISSIVENESS, *s.* वशवर्त्तित्वं, आज्ञानुवर्त्तित्वं, वश्यता, विनतिः *f.*

To SUBMIT, *v. a.* or *n.* (One's self) वशीभू, वशं गम् (c. 1. गच्छति, गन्तुं) or उपगम् or अभ्युपे (अभ्युपैति -तुं, rt. इ), वशतास्वीकारं कृ, *see To* OBEY.—(Submit to, bear with) सह् (c. 1. सहते, सोढुं), विषह्, क्षम् (c. 1. क्षमते, क्षन्तुं), संक्षम्.—(Submit for another's consideration) परविचारं प्रार्थ् (c. 10. प्रार्थयति -ते -यितुं), परविचारं प्रार्थयित्वा विज्ञा in caus., *see To* REFER, DEFER.

SUBMITTED, *p. p.* (Referred) प्रार्थनापूर्व्वं परविचारार्थं समर्पितः -ता -तं.—(Submitted to) सोढः -ढा -ढं; 'to be submitted to,' क्षन्तव्यः -व्या -व्यं.

SUBORDINATE, *a.* गौणः -णी -णं, अमुख्यः -ख्या -ख्यं, अप्राधान्यः -न्या -न्यं, अप्रधान in comp.; 'any thing or person subordinate,' अप्रधानं, उपसर्ज्जनं.

SUBORDINATELY, *adv.* गौणतस्, अप्रधानतस्, अप्राधान्येन, अमुख्यतस्.

SUBORDINATION, *s.* (State of being under control) वशता, वश्यता, *see* SUBJECTION.—(Inferiority) अप्रधानता, अप्राधान्यं, अमुख्यता, गौणता; 'principle of subordination,' गौणमुख्यन्यायः.

To SUBORN, *v. a.* कुकर्म्मसम्पादने छलेन नियुज् (c. 7. -युनक्ति -योक्तुं, c. 10. -योजयति -यितुं) or प्रयुज्, कूटसाक्ष्यकरणे नियुज्.

SUBORNATION, *s.* कुकर्म्मसाधने नियोजनं, कूटसाक्ष्यसाधनं.

SUBORNED, *p. p.* कुकर्म्मसाधने or कूटसाक्ष्यकरणे नियुक्तः -क्ता -क्तं.

To SUBSCRIBE, *v. a.* or *n.* (Sign with one's own hand) हस्ताक्षरं लिख् (c. 6. लिखति, लेखितुं), स्वहस्ताक्षरं लिख् or अङ्क् (c. 10. अङ्कयति -यितुं), नामलिखनं कृ, नामाङ्कनं कृ, स्वनामाङ्कितं -तां कृ, नामाङ्कितं कृ, *see To* SIGN.—(Promise to pay by signing one's name) हस्ताक्षरम् अभिलिख्य or नामाङ्कनं कृत्वा किञ्चिद् दातुं प्रतिज्ञा (c. 9. -जानीते -ज्ञातुं) or स्वांशं दातुं प्रतिज्ञा or धनांशं दातुं प्रतिज्ञा or अंशं दा in des. (दित्सति -त्सितुं).

SUBSCRIBER, *s.* (One who enters his name) नामाभिलेखकः, हस्ताक्षराभिलेखकः.—(Contributor) अंशदाता *m.* (तृ), अंशदायी *m.*, अंशदित्सुः *m.*

SUBSCRIPTION, *s.* (Act of signing) नामाभिलेखनं, स्वनामलिखनं, नामाङ्कनं, हस्ताक्षरलिखनं.—(Signature), *see* the word.—(Contribution) अंशदानं, धनांशदानं, अनेकसाध्यकार्य्यसाहाय्यकधनदानं.—(Sum contributed) अनेकदत्तधनं, अंशदित्सुसमर्पितधनं.

SUBSEQUENCE, *s.* अनुगमनं, अनुयानं, पश्चाद्यानं, अनुयायिता.

SUBSEQUENT, *a.* पश्चात्कालिकः -का -कं, पश्चात्कालीनः -ना -नं, पाश्चात्यः -त्या -त्यं, परः -रा -रं, पराचीनः -ना -नं, उत्तरः -रा -रं, अवरः &c., कालान्तरीयः -या -यं, पश्चात् in comp.; 'subsequent period,' पश्चात्कालः; 'subsequent rite,' अनुकर्म्म *n.*; 'subsequent mention,' वक्ष्यमाणत्वं.

SUBSEQUENTLY, *adv.* पश्चात्, परं, परतस्, परस्तात्, उत्तरं, उत्तरतस्, उत्तरत्र; 'subsequently to the marriage,' विवाहात् परं or परतस्.

To SUBSERVE, *v. a.* उपकृ, साहाय्यं कृ. *See To* PROMOTE, SERVE.

SUBSERVIENCE, SUBSERVIENCY, *s.* उपयोग: -गिता, उपयुक्तता, उपकारः -रिता, अनुवृत्तिः *f.*, अनुवर्त्तनं, सहकारिता, तन्त्रता, पारतन्त्र्यं.

SUBSERVIENT, *a.* उपयोगी -गिनी -गि (न्), उपकारी -रिणी &c., उपकारकः -का -कं, सहकृत्वा -त्वा -त्व (न्), अधीनः -ना -नं, तन्त्रः -न्त्रा -न्त्रं, वशः -शा -शं, निघ्नः &c. *See* SUBJECT, DEPENDANT.

To SUBSIDE, *v. n.* (Sink) सद् (c. 1. सीदति, सत्तुं), अधोगम् (c. 1. -गच्छति -गन्तुं), अधोया, अधः पत्, *see To* SETTLE, *v. n.*—(Become calm, cease) शम् (c. 4. शाम्यति, शमितुं), प्रशम्, उपशम्, प्रसद्, सम्प्रसद्, विरम् (c. 1. -रमति -रन्तुं), निवृत्, विनिवृत्, विगम्, शान्तः -न्ता -न्तं भू, *see To* CEASE, *v. n.*; 'as the wind,' निर्वा (c. 2. -वाति -तुं), निर्वातीभू.

SUBSIDED, *p. p.* शान्तः -न्ता -न्तं, प्रशान्तः &c., विरतः -ता -तं.

SUBSIDENCE, SUBSIDENCY, *s.* (Sinking) अधःपतनं, अधोगतिः *f.*, अधोगमनं.

SUBSIDIARY, *s.* उपकारी -रिणी &c., उपयोगी -गिनी &c., उपकारकः -का -कं, सहकारी &c., साहाय्यकारी &c.; 'something subsidiary,' उपसर्ज्जनं, उपपदं, *see* SUBSERVIENT, SUBORDINATE, *a.*

SUBSIDY, *s.* धनरूपसाहाय्यं, धनरूपोपकारः, धनरूपसाहित्यं.

To SUBSIST, *v. n.* (Be, exist) वृत् (c. 1. वर्त्तते -र्त्तितुं), भू, अस्, विद् in pass.—(Live, be maintained) जीव् (c. 1. -जीवति -वितुं), उपजीव्, उपजीवनं कृ, निर्वाहं कृ, निर्वह् (c. 1. -वहति -वोढुं), जीवनिर्वाहं कृ, प्राणनिर्वाहं कृ, उदरनिर्वाहं कृ, प्राणयात्रां कृ, शरीरयात्रां कृ, उदरपोषणं कृ.—(Continue) स्था.

SUBSISTENCE, *s.* (Existence), *see* the word.—(Means of subsisting, livelihood) उपजीविका, जीविका, उपजीवनं, उपजीव्यं, जीवनं, जीवनोपायः, वृत्त्युपायः, प्राणयात्रा, शरीरयात्रा, जीवोपकरणं, जीवसाधनं, निर्वाहः, प्राणनिर्वाहः, जीवनिर्वाहः, प्राणधारणं, *see* LIVELIHOOD, LIVING, *s.*; 'bare subsistence,' दिननिर्वाहः, ग्रासाच्छादनं.

SUBSISTENT, *a.* सत्त्ववान् -वती -वत् (त्), जीवी -विनी &c., उपजीवी &c.

SUBSTANCE, *s.* (A real being) वस्तु *n.*, पदार्थः, द्रव्यं, सत्त्वं, अर्थः, भावः, *see* THING.—(Material form, matter) मूर्त्तिः *f.*, मूर्त्तवस्तु *n.*, मूर्त्तद्रव्यं, वस्तु *n.*, द्रव्यं.—(Material or essential part) सारः, सारता, सारांशः, गर्भः, सत्त्वं, तत्त्वं, तत्त्वार्थः, मूलं, अर्थः, वस्तु *n.*, वस्तुता; 'in substance,' अर्थतस्, वस्तुतस्.—(Property, possessions) वसु *n.*, धनं, अर्थः, द्रविणं, द्रव्यं, वित्तं, विभवः, वैभवं, रिक्थं; 'one's whole substance,' सर्व्वस्वं.

SUBSTANTIAL, *a.* (Real) वास्तवः -वी -वं, वास्तविकः -की -कं, वस्त्वात्मकः -का -कं, सात्त्विकः -की -कं, *see* REAL.—(Material) मूर्त्तिमान् -मती &c., मूर्त्तः -र्त्ता -र्त्तं, *see* MATERIAL.—(Having substance or solidity) सारवान् -वती -वत् (त्), सारः -रा -रं, घनः -ना -नं, *see* SOLID.—(Possessed of property) वसुमान् &c., वित्तवान् &c., महाधनः -ना -नं, धनी &c., *see* RICH.

SUBSTANTIALLY, *adv.* वस्तुतस्, अर्थतस्, सारतस्, तत्त्वतस्.

SUBSTANTIALNESS, *s.* वास्तवत्वं, वास्तविकत्वं, सत्त्वं, सारता, सत्ता.

To SUBSTANTIATE, *v. a.* भू in caus., साध्, प्रमाणीकृ. *See To* PROVE.

SUBSTANTIATED, *p. p.* भावितः -ता -तं, विभावितः &c. *See* PROVED.

SUBSTANTIATION, *s.* उपपादनं, साधनं, सिद्धिः *f.*, विभावनं, भावनं.

SUBSTANTIVE, *s.* (In grammar) विशेष्यं, सत्त्ववाचकः, द्रव्यवाचकः, सत्त्वं; 'proper substantive,' नामवाचकः, संज्ञावाचकः, संज्ञा.

SUBSTANTIVE, *a.* सात्त्विकः -की -कं, सत्त्ववाचकः -का -कं, वास्तविकः &c.

To SUBSTITUTE, *v. a.* उपक्लृप् (c. 10. -कल्पयति -यितुं), उपसृज् (c. 6. -सृजति -स्रष्टुं, c. 10. -सर्ज्जयति -यितुं) उपसर्ज्जनं कृ, उपकल्पनं कृ, कल्पनं कृ, परस्थाने क्लृप्, परस्थाने कृ, प्रतिनिधिं कृ.

SUBSTITUTE, *s.* प्रतिनिधिः *m.*, उपसर्ज्जनं, अनुकल्पः, प्रतिपुरुषः, प्रतिहस्तकः, प्रतिकृतिः *f.*, प्रतिच्छन्दः, गौणकल्पः, आदेशः.

SUBSTITUTED, *p.p.* उपकल्पितः -ता -तं, उपसर्ज्जितः &c., परस्थाने कल्पितः -ता -तं, प्रतिनिधिभूतः &c., अतिदिष्टः -ष्टा -ष्टं, अध्यस्तः -स्ता -स्तं; 'to be substituted,' कल्पनीयः -या -यं, कल्प्यः -ल्प्या -ल्प्यं.

SUBSTITUTION, *s.* उपकल्पनं, उपसर्ज्जनं, प्रत्याहारः, आदेशः, अतिदेशः.

SUBSTRATUM, *s.* (Layer), *see* STRATUM.—(In metaphysics) अधिकरणं, आधारः, आश्रयः, स्थानं, पात्रं, *see* BASIS.

To SUBTEND, *v. a.* अभिमुखं or प्रतिमुखं or अधो वितन् in pass.

SUBTERFUGE, *s.* छलं, छद्म *n.* (न्), अपदेशः, व्यपदेशः, छिद्रं.

SUBTERRANEAN, SUBTERRANEOUS, *a.* अन्तर्भौमः -मी -मं, भूम्यन्तर्गतः -ता -तं, गूढः -ढा -ढं; 'a subterranean place,' अन्तर्भूमिः *f.*; 'passage,' गूढमार्गः, सुरुङ्गा.

SUBTILE, SUBTLE, *a.* (Fine, thin) सूक्ष्मः -क्ष्मा -क्ष्मं, अतिसूक्ष्मः &c., अतिलघुः -घुः -घु, निरवयवः -वा -वं, अणुकः -का -कं.—(In intellect, piercing) सूक्ष्मबुद्धिः -द्धिः -द्धि, सूक्ष्मदर्शी -र्शिनी &c., कुशाग्रीयमतिः -तिः -ति, कुशाग्रबुद्धिः &c., कुशाग्रीयः -या -यं, मार्म्मिकः -की -कं, मर्म्मिकः &c., मर्म्मवित्, मर्म्मवेदी &c.—(Sly), *see* SLY.

SUBTILELY, *adv.* सूक्ष्मं, सौक्ष्म्येण, सूक्ष्मबुद्ध्या, ससौक्ष्म्यं.

SUBTILITY, SUBTILENESS, SUBTLETY, *s.* सूक्ष्मता, सौक्ष्म्यं, निरवयवत्वं, अणिमा *m.* (न्), अतिलाघवं; 'of intellect,' बुद्धिसूक्ष्मता, कुशाग्रीयता, मतिप्रकर्षः.—(Cunning, slyness), *see* the words.

To SUBTILIZE, *v. a.* सूक्ष्मीकृ, अतिसूक्ष्मीकृ, सूक्ष्मतां कृ or जन्.

To SUBTRACT, *v. a.* उद्धृ (c. 1. -हरति -हर्त्तुं), उद्धरणं कृ.—(In arithmetic) शुध् (c. 10. शोधयति -यितुं), व्यवकल् (c. 10. -कलयति -यितुं), शोधनं कृ, व्यवकलनं कृ, अन्तरं कृ.—(In algebra) च्युतं कृ, अन्तरं कृ.

SUBTRACTED, *p. p.* उद्धृतः -ता -तं.—(In arithmetic, &c.) शोधितः -ता -तं, व्यवकलितः &c.; 'to be subtracted,' शोध्यः -ध्या -ध्यं, शोधनीयः -या -यं.

SUBTRACTION, *s.* उद्धारः, उद्धरणं.—(In arithmetic) शोधनं, शुद्धिः *f.*, व्यवकलनं, व्यवकलितं, अन्तरं, वर्ज्जनं, वियरं, पतनं.

SUBTRAHEND, *s.* (Sum to be subtracted) शोधकः, च्युतं.

SUBURB, SUBURBS, *s.* शाखानगरं, शाखापुरं, उपनगरं, उपपुरं, नगरोपान्तः -न्तं, नगरपरिसरः, नगरप्रान्तः -न्तं, गृहा, अभिष्यन्दिरमणं.

SUBURBAN, *a.* शाखानगरस्थः -स्था -स्थं, उपनगरस्थः &c., शाखापुरस्थः &c., नगरोपान्तस्थः -स्था -स्थं, नगरोपान्तिकः -की -कं.

SUBVERSION, *s.* ध्वंसः, विध्वंसः, परिध्वंसः, भङ्गः. *See* OVERTHROW.

SUBVERSIVE, *a.* ध्वंसकरः -रा -रं, ध्वंसकारी -रिणी &c., परिध्वंसी &c., विनाशकः &c., *see* DESTRUCTIVE; 'of happiness,' सुखान्तकरः &c.

To SUBVERT, *v. a.* ध्वंस् (c. 10. ध्वंसयति -यितुं), परिध्वंस्, विध्वंस्, नश् (c. 10. नाशयति -यितुं), विनश्, पत् in caus., निर्भिद्. *See To* OVERTHROW.

9 o

SUBVERTED, *p.p.* विध्वंसित: -ता -तं, पातित: &c., विनाशित: -ता -तं, निर्भिन्न: -न्ना -न्नं, *see* OVERTHROWN; 'is subverted,' निर्भिद्यते.

SUCCEDANEOUS, *a.* गौण: -णी -णं, गौणभूत: -ता -तं, उपसर्जन: -ना -नं, आनुकल्पिक: -की -कं; 'a succedaneous rule,' अनुकल्प:.

SUCCEDANEUM, *s.* उपसर्जनं, अनुकल्प:, गौणकल्प:. *See* SUBSTITUTE.

To SUCCEED, *v. n.* (Follow, be subsequent to) पश्चाद् आया (c. 2. -याति -तुं), अनुया, अनुक्रम्, पश्चाद् वृत् (c. 1. वर्त्तते -र्त्तितुं), अनुवृत्, परतो वृत्, परस्ताद् वृत्, उत्तरतो वृत्, अवर: -रा -रं वृत् or भू, उत्तर: -रा -रं वृत् or भू.—(Be successful) सिध् (c. 4. सिध्यति, सेद्धुं), संसिध्, सिद्धार्थीभू, कृतार्थीभू, सिद्धिं गम् or इ, सम्पद् (c 4. -पद्यते -पत्तुं), क्रम् (c. 1. क्रमते -मितुं), *see To* PROSPER, *v. n.*

SUCCEEDED, *p.p.* अनुगत: -ता -तं, अनुयात: &c.; 'by fear,' भयोत्तर: -रा -रं.

SUCCEEDING, *part.* or *a.* अनुयायी -यिनी -यि (न्), अनुग: -गा -गं, क्रमानुयायी &c., क्रमानुग: -गा -गं, उत्तर: -रा -रं, अवर: &c. *See* SUBSEQUENT, *a.*

SUCCESS, *s.* सिद्धि: *f.*, अर्थसिद्धि: *f.*, फलसिद्धि: *f.*, साध्यसिद्धि: *f.*, सम्पत्ति: *f.*, सम्पद् *f.*, उदय:, सफलता, सिद्धार्थता -त्वं, कृतार्थता, चरितार्थता, कृतकृत्यता, श्री: *f.*, लक्ष्मी: *f.*—(Result) निर्गम:, निर्गति: *f.*, परिणाम:.

SUCCESSFUL, *a.* (Of persons) कृतार्थ: -र्था -र्थं, सिद्धार्थ: &c., चरितार्थ: &c., प्राप्तार्थ: &c., कृतकृत्य: -त्या -त्यं, अवृथार्थ: -र्था -र्थं, कृतकाम: -मा -मं, प्राप्तकाम: &c., प्राप्ताश: -शा -शं, आशाप्राप्त: -प्ता -प्तं, कृतार्थीभूत: -ता -तं, श्रीमान् &c., *see* PROSPEROUS.—(Of things) सिद्ध: -द्धा -द्धं, सिद्धिमान् -मती -मत् (त्), सफल: -ला -लं, फलवान् &c., फलित: -ता -तं, सुफल: &c.

SUCCESSFULLY, *adv.* सफलं, सिद्धार्थतस्, कृतार्थतस्, अवृथा, सिद्धा.

SUCCESSION, *s.* (Following of things in order) आनुपूर्व्यं, आनुपूर्वी -र्वी, अनुक्रम:, पर्यायः, विपर्यय:, परम्परा, पारम्पर्य्यं, अन्वय:, समन्वय:, सन्तति: *f.*, श्रेणी, वीप्सा, अनुयायित्वं, अनुयानं, अनुवृत्ति: *f.*, अनुवर्त्तनं, अनुषङ्ग:, क्रम:; 'of office,' कर्म्मविपर्यय:; 'in succession,' अनुपूर्व्वशस्, *see* SUCCESSIVELY.—(Line, series) श्रेणी, आवलि: -ली *f.*, माला; 'of kings,' राजावलि: -ली *f.*, *see* SERIES.—(Right of succeeding to another) उत्तराधिकार: -रिता, अधिकारपर्य्याय:, दाय: -यत्वं, दायाधिकार:.

SUCCESSIVE, *a.* अनुपूर्व: -र्वा -र्वं, आनुक्रमिक: -की -कं, यथाक्रम: -मा -मं, यथानुक्रम: &c., पारम्परिक: -की -कं, परम्पर: -रा -रं, क्रमानुसारी -रिणी -रि (न्), क्रमानुयायी &c., क्रमक: -का -कं, क्रमागत: -ता -तं, क्रमायात: &c., परम्परागत: -ता -तं, परम्परायात: &c., सन्तत: -ता -तं.

SUCCESSIVELY, *adv.* अनुपूर्व्वशस्, अनुक्रमशस्, यथापूर्व्वं, यथाक्रमं, परम्परं, पारम्पर्य्येण, पर्य्यायेण, विपर्य्ययेण, क्रमशस्, क्रमतस्, क्रमेण, क्रमात्, क्रमानुसारेण.

SUCCESSOR, *s.* उत्तराधिकारी *m.* (न्), अवराधिकारी *m.*, क्रमानुयायी *m.*

SUCCINCT, *a.* संक्षिप्त: -प्ता -प्तं, अविस्तीर्ण: -र्णा -र्णं. *See* CONCISE.

SUCCINCTLY, SUCCINCTNESS, *see* CONCISELY, CONCISENESS.

SUCCORY, *s.* (Plant, wild endive) कासनी.

SUCCOUR, *To* SUCCOUR, &c. *See* HELP, *To* HELP, &c.

SUCCULENCE, *s.* सरसता, बहुरसत्वं, सद्रवता, सजलता. *See* JUICINESS.

SUCCULENT, *s.* सरस: -सा -सं, बहुरस: &c., सद्रव: -वा -वं, सजल: -ला -लं, रसमय: -यी -यं, जलमय: &c., आर्द्र: -र्द्रा -र्द्रं. *See* JUICY.

To SUCCUMB, *v. n.* वशीभू, वशं गम्, सद् (c. 1. सीदति, सत्तुं), *see To* YIELD.

SUCH, *a.* (Of this kind) ईदृश: -शी -शं, ईदृक् *m.f.n.* (श्), ईदृक्ष: -क्षा -क्षं, अमूदृश: -शी -शं, अमूदृक्ष: &c.; 'such is the law,' ईदृशी मर्य्यादा.—(Of that kind, of such a kind) तादृश: -शी -शं, तादृक् *m.f.n.* (श्), तादृक्ष: -क्षा -क्षं, एतादृश: &c., एतादृक् &c., एतादृक्ष: &c., एवंविध: -धा -धं, तथाविध: -धा -धं, एवम्भूत: -ता -तं, एवं in comp.; 'such as me,' मादृश: &c., मादृक् &c., मादृक्ष: &c., मद्विध: -धा -धं; 'such as thee,' त्वादृश: &c., त्वादृक् &c., भवादृश: &c.; 'what has such power to burn as fire?' किम् अन्यद् अनलात् प्रभवति दग्धुं.—(Such and such an one) अमुक: -का -कं.

To SUCK, *v. a.* (Draw in with the mouth) चूष् (c. 1. चूषति -षितुं), आचूष्, चूषां कृ, चूषणं कृ, चोषं कृ, चोषणं कृ.—(Draw in milk from the breast, as a child) स्तनं पा (c. 1. पिबति, पातुं) or धे (c. 1. धयति, धातुं), समभिसन्धे, स्तनात् क्षीरं पा or निपा स्तनपानं कृ; 'a child that sucks the breast,' स्तनन्धय: -या -यी -यं.—(The finger or hand) अङ्गुलिं धे or अभिसन्धे or पा, मुष्टिं धे, अङ्गुलिपानं कृ; 'a child that sucks its hand,' मुष्टिन्धय:.—(Imbibe, absorb, suck up) निपा, शुष् in caus., उच्छुष्, रसादानं कृ.

SUCK, *s.* (Act of sucking), *see* SUCTION.—(Milk, &c., sucked) स्तन्यं, दुग्धं, चूष्यं; 'one who gives suck,' स्तन्यदात्री, स्तन्यदायिनी.

SUCKED, *p. p.* चूषित: -ता -तं, चोषित: &c., धीत: -ता -तं, पीत: &c., निपीत: &c.; 'that can be sucked,' चूष्य: -ष्या -ष्यं.

SUCKER, *s.* चोषक:, चूषणकारी *m.* (न्), धाता *m.* (तृ). *See* SUCKLING.

SUCKING, *s.* चूषणं, चूषा, चोष: -षणं; 'the breast,' स्तनपानं, स्तन्यपानं, क्षीरपानं; 'the fingers,' अङ्गुलिपानं.

To SUCKLE, *v. a.* स्तनं धे in caus. (धापयति -यितुं) or उपधे in caus. or पा in caus. (पाययति -यितुं), स्तन्यं दा, स्तनपानं दा, स्तन्यदानेन पुष् (c. 10. पोषयति -यितुं).

SUCKLED, *p. p.* स्तन्यपोषित: -ता -तं, स्तनन्धय: &c.; 'by a bitch,' शुनिन्धय: -या -यं.

SUCKLING, *s.* (The act) स्तन्यदानं, स्तन्यदानेन पोषणं.—(Young child) स्तनन्धय: -या -यी -यं, स्तनपायी -यिनी &c., धाता -त्री (तृ), धय: -या.

SUCTION, *s.* आचूषणं, चूषणं, चोष: -षणं, रसादानं. *See* SUCKING, *s.*

SUDDEN, *a.* आकस्मिक: -की -कं, साहसिक: -की -कं, सहसिक: -का -कं, अकाण्ड: -ण्डा -ण्डं, अकस्मादुत्पन्न: -न्ना -न्नं, अकस्माद्भूत: -ता -तं, एकपात: -ता -तं, अलक्षित: -ता -तं, अचिन्तित: &c., अकल्पित: -ता -तं, अकाण्डनिपाती -तिनी -ति (न्), अकस्माज्जात: -ता -तं, अकाण्डजात: &c.; 'sudden death,' अपमृत्यु: *m.*, अपामृत्यु: *m.*, अलक्षितमृत्यु:, अलक्षितान्त:, अवघात:; 'on a sudden,' अकस्मात्.

SUDDENLY, *adv.* अकस्मात्, सद्यस्, सहसा, एकपदे, एकदा, अकाण्डं, हठात्, काकतालीयवत्; 'suddenly born,' अकाण्डजात: -ता -तं, अकस्माज्जात: &c.

SUDDENNESS, *s.* आकस्मिकत्वं -ता, साहसिकत्वं, अकाण्डत्वं, अकल्पितत्वं.

SUDORIFIC, *a.* स्वेदन: -ना -नं, स्वेदकर: -रा -रं, स्वेदोत्पादक: -का -कं, स्वेदजनक: &c., प्रस्वेदित: -ता -तं, प्रस्वेदितवान् -वती &c.

ŚUDRA, *s.* (Man of the fourth or servile class) शूद्र:, अवरवर्ण: जघन्यज:, वृषल:.

SUDS, *s.* सर्ज्जिकासंसृष्टजलं, मार्ज्जनतैलसंसृष्टजलं, सर्ज्जिव्याप्तजलं.

To SUE, *v. a.* (In law) अभियुज् (c. 7. -युनक्ति -योक्तुं), अभियोगं कृ, व्यवहाराभियोगं कृ, व्यवहारं कृ, व्यवह्, वादं कृ, अभिशंस्. *See To* PROSECUTE.

To SUE, *v. a.* प्रार्थ्, याच्, प्रार्थनापूर्व्वम् अन्विष्. *See To* PETITION.

SUET, *s.* मेदस् *n.*, वसा, मांसस्नेह:, वृक्कादिपरिगतं मेदस्.

To SUFFER, *v. a.* (Feel, undergo) अनुभू, उपगम् (c. 1. -गच्छति -गन्तुं), उपागम्, भुज् (c. 7. भुनक्ति, भुंक्ते, भोक्तुं), उपभुज्, प्राप् (c. 5. -आप्नोति -आप्तुं), ज्ञा, विद्, सेव्, क्षम्, दृश्; 'one who suffers pain,' दुःखभागी -गिनी &c.—(Endure, bear) सह् (c. 1. सहते, सोढुं), विषह्, क्षम् (c. 1. क्षमते, क्षन्तुं), संक्षम्, मृष्, तिज् in des., उपास्.—(Permit, allow) अनुज्ञा, अनुमन्, अनुमतिं दा, *see To* PERMIT.

To SUFFER, *v. n.* (Undergo pain) दुःखम् अनुभू, दुःखभागी -गिनी -गि भू, दुःखी &c. भू, तप् in pass. (तप्यते), सन्तप्, व्यथ् (c. 1. व्यथते -थितुं), क्लिश् (c. 4. क्लिश्यते).

SUFFERABLE, *a.* सहनीयः -या -यं, सह्यः -ह्या -ह्यं, सोढव्यः -व्या -व्यं.

SUFFERANCE, *s.* सहनं, क्षमा, सहत्वं, सहता, साहनं. *See* ENDURANCE.

SUFFERED, *p. p.* (Undergone) अनुभूतः -ता -तं, उपागतः -ता -तं, उपगतः &c., भुक्तः -क्ता -क्तं, उपभुक्तः &c.—(Endured) सोढः -ढा -ढं, विसोढः &c.—(Permitted) अनुज्ञातः -ता -तं, अनिषिद्धः -द्धा -द्धं, अप्रतिबद्धः &c.

SUFFERER, *s.* दुःखभागी *m.* -गिनी *f.* (न्), दुःखानुभवी *m.*, दुःखभोगी *m.*, दुःखभोक्ता *m.* (क्तृ), दुःखी *m.*, दुःखितः, दुःखोपेतः.

SUFFERING, *s.* (Bearing of pain) दुःखानुभवः, दुःखभोगः, दुःखोपभोगः, दुःखोपगमः, दुःखोपागमः, दुःखयोगः, दुःखवेदनं.—(Pain endured) दुःखं, व्यथा, क्लेशः, तापः, परितापः, वेदना, पीडा, कृच्छ्रं, आर्त्तिः *f.*

SUFFERING, *a.* दुःखी -खिनी -खि (न्). *See* SUFFERER, AFFLICTED.

To SUFFICE, *v. n.* क्लृप् (c. 1. कल्पते -ल्पितुं, कल्प्तुं), उपक्लृप्, पर्य्याप्तः -प्ता -प्तं भू, उपयुक्तः -क्ता -क्तं भू, यथेष्टः -ष्टा -ष्टं भू, उचितः -ता -तं भू; 'as much food as will suffice for a year,' संवत्सरनिर्वाहपर्य्याप्तम् अन्नं.

To SUFFICE, *v. a.* तृप् (c. 10. तर्पयति -यितुं), तुष्. *See To* SATISFY.

SUFFICIENCY, *s.* पर्य्याप्तिः *f.*, पर्य्याप्तत्वं -ता, उपयुक्तता -त्वं, यथेष्टता -त्वं, सामर्थ्यं, औचित्यं, योग्यता -त्वं, उचितत्वं, निर्वाहः. *See* COMPETENCE.

SUFFICIENT, *a.* पर्य्याप्तः -प्ता -प्तं, उपयुक्तः -क्ता -क्तं, यथेष्टः -ष्टा -ष्टं, उचितः -ता -तं, समर्थः -र्था -र्थं, योग्यः -ग्या -ग्यं; 'food sufficient for a month,' मासवृत्त्युचितम् अन्नं, *see* ENOUGH, *a.*; 'to be sufficient for,' क्लृप् (c. 1. कल्पते -ल्पितुं).

SUFFICIENTLY, *adv.* पर्य्याप्तं, अलं, यथेष्टं, उपयुक्तं. *See* ENOUGH, *adv.*

To SUFFOCATE, *v. a.* श्वासरोधं कृ, श्वासावरोधं कृ, श्वासं रुध् (c. 7. रुणद्धि, रोद्धुं) or अवरुध्, प्राणं रुध् or अवरुध्, कण्ठं रुध्. *See To* CHOKE, STIFLE.

SUFFOCATED, *p.p.* रुद्धश्वासः -सा -सं, रुद्धप्राणः -णा -णं, निरुद्धकण्ठः &c.

SUFFOCATING, *a.* श्वासरोधकः -का -कं, श्वासावरोधकः &c., प्राणरोधकः &c.

SUFFOCATION, *s.* श्वासरोधः -धनं, श्वासावरोधः, श्वासप्रतिरोधः, प्राणरोधः -धनं, प्राणावरोधः, कण्ठरोधः -धनं, श्वासप्रतिबन्धः, उद्बन्धनं.

SUFFRAGE, *s.* सम्मतं, सम्मतिः *f.*, सम्मतिज्ञापनं, स्वीकारः. *See* VOTE.

To SUFFUSE, *v. a.* समाप्लु (c. 10. -प्लावयति -यितुं), व्याप्, आकॄ.

SUFFUSED, *p. p.* समाप्लुतः -ता -तं, व्याप्तः -प्ता -प्तं, परिगतः -ता -तं, *see* OVERSPREAD; 'eyes suffused with tears,' नेत्राणि समाप्लुतानि वारिणा, वाष्पोपप्लुताक्षः -क्षी -क्षं, वाष्पाविलेक्षणः -णा -णं; 'face suffused with blushes,' ह्रीपरिगतमुखं.

SUFFUSION, *s.* व्याप्तिः *f.*, व्यापनं, व्याप्तता, समाप्लावनं, आच्छादनं.

SUGAR, *s.* शर्करा, गुडशर्करा, गुडोद्भवा, सिता, मिष्टं, इक्षुसारः, वालुकात्मिका; 'coarse sugar,' गुडः; 'raw sugar,' मत्स्यण्डी, फाणितं; 'sugar-mill,' इक्षुयन्त्रं, इक्षुचक्रं.

To SUGAR, *v. a.* शर्करान्वितं -तां कृ, शार्करीकृ, सशर्करं -रां कृ, मिष्टीकृ.

SUGAR-CANDY, *s.* खण्डमोदकः, खण्डः, माक्षिकशर्करा, उपला, शुक्लोपला, शर्करा, सिताखण्डः, दृढगात्रिका.

SUGAR-CANE, *s.* इक्षुः *m.*, इक्षुरः, इक्षुकाण्डं, इक्षुदण्डः, मधुयष्टिः *f.*, मधुतृणं, गुडदण्डः, गुडदारु: *m.*, गुडतृणं, रसालः, महाक्षीरः, विपुलरसः, असिपत्रः, पयोधरः, मृत्युपुष्पः; 'varieties of it,' पुण्ड्रः, पौण्ड्रः, कान्तारकः, खण्डं; 'root of it,' मोरटं, शेखवमूलं.

SUGARED, SUGARY, *a.* शर्करान्वितः -ता -तं, शर्करायुक्तः -क्ता -क्तं, सशर्करः -रा -रं, शार्करः -री -रं, शैखवः -वी -वं, मिष्टः -ष्टा -ष्टं.

To SUGGEST, *v. a.* उपन्यस् (c. 4. -अस्यति -सितुं), समुपन्यस्, सूच् (c. 10. सूचयति -यितुं), सूचनं कृ, मन्त्र् (c. 10. मन्त्रयते -ति -यितुं), मन्त्रणं कृ, प्रबुध् (c. 10. -बोधयति -यितुं), उद्दिश् (c. 6. -दिशति -देष्टुं), आदिश्, उपदिश्, चित् (c. 10 चेतयति -यितुं), प्रयुज् (c. 10. -योजयति -यितुं), समुपस्था in caus.

SUGGESTED, *p. p.* उपन्यस्तः -स्ता -स्तं, सूचितः -ता -तं, मन्त्रितः &c.

SUGGESTION, *s.* उपन्यासः, सूचना -नं, प्रबोधः, मन्त्रणं, बुद्धिः *f.*

SUGGESTIVE, *a.* सूचकः -का -कं, प्रबोधकः &c., चेतकः -का -कं.

SUICIDAL, *a.* आत्मघातकः -का -कं, आत्मघाती -तिनी -ति (न्).

SUICIDE, *s.* (Self-murder) आत्मघातः, आत्महत्या, आत्मवधः, आत्महननं, आत्मव्यापादनं, प्राणत्यागः, देहत्यागः, जीवितत्यागः, जीवोत्सर्गः, प्राणपरित्यागः, काम्यमरणं, आत्मद्रोहः, स्वप्राणहिंसा.—(Self-murderer) आत्मघाती *m.* (न्), आत्मघातकः, आत्महा *m.* (न्), आत्मत्यागी *m.*, आत्मधुक् *m.* (-द्रुह्), आत्मद्रोही *m.*, कृतजीवितत्यागः.

SUI-GENERIS, एकप्रकारः -रा -रं, स्वसदृशः -शी -शं, स्वप्रकृतः -क्या -क्यं.

SUIT, *s.* (Set) गणः, समूहः, *see* SET; 'as of clothes, &c.,' युगं, युग्मं, युगलं, युतकं, यमकं, यमलं; 'a suit of clothes,' वस्त्रयुगं, वस्त्रयुग्मं, वासोयुगं, आच्छादः.—(Petition) अर्थः, प्रार्थनं -ना, अभ्यर्थना, प्रणयः.—(In law) अर्थः, वादः, अभ्यः, व्यवहारः.—(Retinue), *see* SUITE.

To SUIT, *v. n.* युज् in pass. (युज्यते), उपपद् in pass. *See To* FIT, *v. n.*

To SUIT, *v. a.* युज् (c. 10. योजयति -यितुं). *See To* FIT, ADAPT, *v. a.*

SUITABLE, *a.* योग्यः -ग्या -ग्यं, युक्तः -क्ता -क्तं, उपयुक्तः &c., यथायोग्यः &c., उपयोगी -गिनी &c., उचितः -ता -तं, सदृशः -शी -शं, प्रयोक्तव्यः -व्या -व्यं, *see* FIT, FITTING, *a.*; 'suitable to the occasion,' प्रस्तावसदृशः &c., *see* OPPORTUNE.

SUITABLENESS, *s.* योग्यता, युक्तता, उपयुक्तता, उपयोगिता -त्वं, उपयोगः, यथायोग्यता, उपपत्तिः *f.*, याथातथ्यं. *See* FITNESS.

SUITABLY, *adv.* युक्तं, योग्यं, यथायोग्यं, यथोचितं, *see* FITLY.—(Agreeably to) अनुसारेण -रतस्, अनुरूपेण.

SUITE, *s.* परिवारः, अनुचरवर्गः, पोष्यवर्गः. *See* RETINUE.

SUITED, *p. p.* उपयुक्तः -क्ता -क्तं, युक्तः &c., पर्य्याप्तः &c. *See* SUITABLE.

SUITOR, *s.* प्रार्थकः, प्रार्थयिता *m.* (तृ), अर्थी *m.* (न्), आवेदकः, *see* PETITIONER, PROSECUTOR.—(Wooer) विवाहार्थी *m.*, पाणिग्रहार्थी *m.*, प्रणयी *m.*

SULKILY, SULLENLY, *adv.* उदासीनं, उदासीनवत्, अन्तःक्रोधेन, अन्तःकोपेन.

SULKINESS, SULLENNESS, *s.* उदासीनता, अन्तःक्रोधित्वं, अन्तःक्रोधिता, अन्तःकोपिता, अन्तःक्रोधः, मलिनमुखत्वं, मुखमालिन्यं, प्रतीपता. *See* MOROSENESS.

SULKY, SULLEN, *a.* उदासीनः -ना -नं, अन्तःक्रोधी -धिनी -धि (न्), अन्तःकोपी &c., उदासवृत्तिः -त्तिः -त्ति, प्रतीपः &c. *See* MOROSE.

SULLIED, *p. p.* दूषितः -ता -तं, मलिनः &c., कलङ्कितः &c., *see* SOILED.

To SULLY, *v. a.* कलङ्क (nom. कलङ्कयति -यितुं), दुष् in caus. *See* *To* SOIL.

SULLY, *s.* कलङ्कः, मालिन्यं, दूषणं, म्लानिः *f.* *See* SOIL, STAIN.

SULPHATE, *s.* (Of copper) ताम्रगर्भं, तुत्थं.—(Of iron) कासीसं, काशीशं, हंसलोमशं, धातुशेखरः, नयनौषधं; 'green sulphate,' *see* under IRON, *s.*

SULPHUR, *s.* गन्धकः, गन्धिकः, गन्धाश्मा *m.* (न्), सौगन्धिकः, सुगन्धिकः, गन्धमोदनं, अतिगन्धः, क्रूरगन्धः, गन्धपाषाणः, स्वर्णारि *m.*, धातुवैरी *m.* (न्), शुल्वारिः *m.*, पामारिः *m.*, पामघ्नः, कीटघ्नः, शुकपुच्छः.

SULPHUREOUS, *a.* गन्धकमयः -यी -यं, गन्धकयुक्तः -क्ता -क्तं, गन्धकगुणकः -का -कं, गन्धकगुणविशिष्टः -ष्टा -ष्टं, गन्धकधर्म्मकः -का -कं.

SULPHURET, *s.* (Of iron) पांशुकासीसं, ताप्यं, धातुमाक्षिकं.—(Of mercury) कज्जली.

SULTRINESS, *s.* निर्वाततत्वं -ता, अत्युष्णता, वातहीनता, वायुहीनता.

SULTRY, *a.* निर्वातः -ता -तं, अत्युष्णः -ष्णा -ष्णं, वातहीनः -ना -नं, वायुहीनः &c., अत्युष्णवाष्पविशिष्टः -ष्टा -ष्टं; 'sultry vapour,' उष्णवाष्पः, मरीचिका, मृगतृष्णा.

SUM, *s.* (Aggregate, total) संख्या, साकल्यं, समुदायः, समाहारः, समवायः, गणनं.—(Substance, amount) सारः, अर्थः, सारांशः, गर्भः, तात्पर्य्यं.—(Compendium), *see* SUMMARY, *s.*—(Sum of money) धनभागः, धनांशः, कियद्धनं, किञ्चिद्धनं; 'small sum of money,' धनलेशः, धनाल्पिका, किञ्चिद्धनं, अल्पधनं; 'large sum,' धनबाहुल्यं, बहुधनं; 'any very large sum,' परार्द्धं.—(In arithmetic, figures set for an arithmetical operation) राशिः *m.f.*, पिण्डः.—(In sum) संक्षेपतस्, *see* SUMMARILY.

To SUM, *v. a.* (Add together) राशीकृ, संख्या, परिसंख्या, परिगण्, संकल् (c. 10. -कलयति -यितुं), सङ्कलनं कृ, समाहृ, समाहरणं कृ, समीकृ.—(Sum up, condense) उक्तोपसंहारं कृ, उक्तसमाहारं कृ, उक्तप्रत्याहारं कृ, उक्तोपसंक्षेपं कृ, उक्तसारं वद्.

SUMMARILY, *adv.* संक्षेपतस्, संक्षेपात् -पेण, समासतस्, *see* CONCISELY; 'to declare summarily,' संक्षेपतो वद्, सम्प्रभष्.

SUMMARY, *a.* सांक्षेपिकः -की -कं, सामासिकः -की -कं. *See* CONCISE, *a.*

SUMMARY, *s.* संक्षेपः, संग्रहः, सारः, संक्षिप्तग्रन्थः, ग्रन्थस्यविषयानुक्रमणिका. *See* COMPENDIUM.

SUMMED, *p. p.* राशिगतः -ता -तं.—(Summed up) उपसंहृतः -ता -तं.

SUMMER, *s.* ग्रीष्मः, ग्रीष्मकालः, ग्रीष्मसमयः, निदाघकालः, निदाघः, उष्णकालः, उष्णसमयः, उष्णः, उष्णकः, उष्मः, उष्मा *m.* (न्), उष्णागमः, उष्मागमः, उष्मोपगमः, तपः, तपाः *m.* (स्).

SUMMER-HOUSE, *s.* विलासमन्दिरं, केलिगृहं; 'with water-works,' जलमन्दिरं, जलयन्त्रगृहं, जलयन्त्रमन्दिरं, जलयन्त्रनिकेतनं, जलहं, धारागृहं, धारायन्त्रगृहं, समुद्रगृहं.

SUMMIT, *s.* अग्रं, शिखा, शिखरं, शेखरं, शृङ्गं, चूडा, कूटः -टं, पृष्ठं, उच्छ्रायः, उच्छ्रयः. *See* TOP.

To SUMMON, *v. a.* आह्वे (c. 1. -ह्वयति -ह्वातुं), आह्वानं कृ, आह्वान (nom. आह्वानयति -यितुं), आकृ in caus. (-कारयति -यितुं), आकारणं कृ.

SUMMONED, *p. p.* आहूतः -ता -तं, कृताह्वानः -ना -नं, आकारितः &c., आवाहितः &c.; 'one who does not appear when summoned,' आहूतप्रपलायी *m.*

SUMMONER, *s.* आह्वाता *m.* (तृ), आह्वायकः, आह्वानकारी *m.* (न्).

SUMMONS, *s.* आह्वानं, आहूतिः *f.*, हूतिः *f.*, आह्वायः, आकारणं, आवाहनं.

SUMMUM-BONUM, *s.* परमार्थः, परार्थः, उत्तमार्थः.

SUMPTER, SUMPTER-HORSE, *s.* स्थूरी *m.* (न्), स्थौरी. *See* PACK-HORSE.

SUMPTUARY, *a.* व्ययविषयकः -का -कं, व्ययसम्बन्धी -न्धिनी -न्धि (न्).

SUMPTUOUS, *a.* महामूल्यः -ल्या -ल्यं, बहुमूल्यः &c. *See* COSTLY.

SUMPTUOUSLY, *adv.* अतिव्ययपूर्व्वं, महाव्ययपूर्व्वं, अतिव्ययेन.

SUMPTUOUSNESS, *s.* महामूल्यता, बहुमूल्यता, महार्घता, अतिव्ययः.

SUN, *s.* सूर्य्यः, रविः *m.*, भानुः *m.*, अर्कः, आदित्यः, भास्करः, सविता *m.* (तृ), अर्य्यमा *m.* (न्), विवस्वान् *m.* (त्), दिवाकरः, सूरः. The sun has innumerable names in Sanskrit, many of which are more properly epithets than names. Some of them are here collected with their meanings.—(As begetter and nourisher of all things, he is called) सविता *m.* (तृ), सावित्रः, पूषा *m.* (न्), विश्वपाः *m.*—(As causing day-light) दिनकरः, दिवसकरः, दिवाकरः, दिनकृत् *m.*, प्रभाकरः, विभाकरः, अहस्करः, भास्करः.—(As lord of the day) अहर्पतिः *m.*, दिनपतिः, द्युपतिः *m.*, दिनप्रणीः *m.*—(As gem of the day) दिनमणिः *m.*, दिवामणिः *m.*—(As gem of the sky) नभोमणिः *m.*, खमणिः *m.*, वियन्मणिः *m.*—(Enemy of darkness) तिमिररिपुः *m.*, ध्वान्तारातिः *m.*, तमोनुदः, तमोपहः.—(Receptacle of light) भाकोषः, तेजःपुञ्जः.—(Circle of light) भानेमिः *m.*—(Meteor of the sky) खखोल्कः.—(The illuminator of the sky) खद्योतनः, प्रद्योतनः, विरोचनः.—(Eye of the sky) नभश्चक्षुः *m.*—(Eye of the world) जगच्चक्षुः *m.* (स्), लोकचक्षुः *m.*—(Beholder of the deeds of the world) कर्म्मसाक्षी *m.* (न्), जगत्साक्षी *m.*—(Lord of the constellations) ग्रहराजः, ग्रहपतिः *m.*, तपताम्पतिः *m.*, त्विषाम्पतिः *m.*—(Having a thousand rays) सहस्रकिरणः, सहस्रांशुः *m.*—(Garlanded with rays) किरणमाली *m.* (न्), अंशुमाली *m.*, मरीचिमाली *m.*—(Possessed of rays) अंशुमान् *m.* (त्), गभस्तिमान् *m.*, अंशुधरः, किरणः, गभस्तिः *m.*—(Lord of the rays) अंशुभर्त्ता *m.*—(Wielding rays) अंशुहस्तः, गभस्तिहस्तः, अंशुपाणिः.—(Having hot rays) चण्डांशुः *m.*, चण्डकिरणः, घर्म्मांशुः *m.*, तिग्मांशुः *m.*, तीक्ष्णांशुः *m.*, खरांशुः *m.*, चण्डरश्मिः *m.*, चण्डमरीचिः *m.*, उष्णरश्मिः *m.*, चण्डदीधितिः *m.*, अशीतमरीचिः *m.*, अशीतकरः.—(Having bright rays) शुभ्ररश्मिः *m.*—(Possessed of light) प्रतिभावान् *m.* (त्), भास्वान् *m.*, विभावान् *m.*, ज्योतिष्मान् *m.*, विभावसुः *m.*—(The inflamer, or warmer) तपनः, तापनः.—(The Ripener) पचतः, पचेलिमः.—(The scorcher) शुष्णः.—(Burner of the forehead) ललाटन्तपः.—(The surprising light) चित्रभानुः *m.*—(Sporting or roaming in the sky) गगणविहारी *m.*, गगणाध्वगः, खगः, खचरः.—(Symbol in the sky) गगणध्वजः.—(Friend of the lotuses) पद्मबन्धुः *m.*, पद्मिनीकान्तः, पद्मिनीवल्लभः.—(Sprung from the lotus) पद्मगर्भः.—(Seated on a lotus) पद्मासनः.—(Holding a lotus in his hand) पद्मपाणिः *m.*, पद्मकरः.—(Drawn by seven horses) सप्ताश्वः.—(Drawn by green horses) हरिदश्वः.—(Ever-moving) सदागतिः *m.*—(Lord of life) जीवितेशः.—(Possessed of jewels) मणिमान् *m.*—(Best of deities) सुरोत्तमः.—(As son of Kaśyapa) काश्यपेयः, काश्यपिः *m.*—(As descended from Mṛitanda) मार्त्तण्डः, मृताण्डः, मृतण्डः.—(As having been shorn of his beams by Visvakarma, the architect of the gods) विकर्त्तनः.—(As identified with the 12 ádityas) द्वादशात्मा *m.* (न्), द्वादशात्मकः. The 12 ádityas are the offspring of Aditi, and are the emblems of the sun in each month of the year. Hence they are identified with the sun itself. Their names are सूर्य्यः, वरुणः, वेदाङ्गः, भानुः *m.*, इन्द्रः, रविः *m.*, गभस्तिः *m.*, यमः, स्वर्णरेताः *m.*, दिवाकरः, मित्रः, विष्णुः *m.* Other names for the sun, of less obvious derivation, are the following: पतङ्गः, पपीः *m.* (स्), हंसः, इनः, हेलिः *m.*, मिहिरः, भगः, तरणिः *m.*, मित्रः, भट्टारकः, ब्रध्नः, अरुणः, विश्वकर्म्मा *m.*, वरुणः, विष्णुः, कृष्णः. The following are the names of some of the sun's wives: छाया, अश्विनी, प्रभा, संज्ञा, विश्वकर्म्मसुता, त्वाष्ट्री, सवर्णा, शनिप्रसूः *f.*, तपती, त्रसरेणुः *m.*, वरी, सौरी, सूर्य्या. His sons are यमः or वैवस्वतः, शनिः *m.*, अश्विनौ *m. du.* or अश्विनीकुमारौ *m. du.*, कर्णः, सावर्णिः *m.*, सुग्रीवः, रेवन्तः, रैवतः; 'his daughter, or the personified Taptí river,' तपती, तपनतनया, अर्कतनया; 'his charioteer,' अरुणः, अनूरुः *m.*, काश्यपिः *m.*, गरुडाग्रजः, सूरसूतः, सूर्य्यसारथिः *m.*; 'three of his attendants,' माठरः, पिङ्गलः, दण्डः; 'a worshipper of the sun,' सौरः; 'the sun's disk,' सूर्य्यमण्डलं, *see* DISK; 'early morning sun,' बालार्कः, बालातपः, बालमित्रः; 'figure of the sun as drawn for worship,' सूर्य्ययन्त्रं; 'half-yearly passage of the sun,' अयनं, *see* SOLSTICE; 'mansion of the sun,' सूर्य्यनक्षत्रं, महानक्षत्रं; 'region of the sun,' सूर्य्यलोकः.—(Sun and moon) सूर्य्याचन्द्रमसौ *m. du.*, चन्द्रार्कौ *m. du.*, दिवाकरनिशाकरौ *m. du.*, पुष्पवन्तौ *m. du.*, पुष्पदन्तौ *m. du.*

SUN-BEAM, *s.* सूर्य्यरश्मिः *m.*, सूर्य्यकिरणः, सूर्य्यमयूखः, सूर्य्यकरः, सूर्य्यांशुः *m.*, तपनांशुः *m.*, तपनकरः, भानुकरः. *See* RAY, *s.*

SUN-BURNT, *a.* सूर्य्यतप्तः -प्ता -प्तं, रविप्रतप्तः &c., सूर्य्यव्याप्तः &c.

SUNDAY, *s.* भानुवारः, रविवारः, अर्कवारः, आदित्यवारः, भट्टारकवारः, रविवासरः, भानुवासरः, अर्कदिनं, अर्कः.

To SUNDER, *v. a.* वियुज्, विप्रयुज्, पृथक्कृ. *See To* PART, SEPARATE.

SUNDERED, *p. p.* (Divided in sunder) पृथक्कृतः -ता -तं, द्वैधीभूतः -ता -तं, द्वैधीकृतः -ता -तं, विश्लिष्टः -ष्टा -ष्टं, विच्छेदितः -ता -तं, विप्रयुक्तः -क्ता -क्तं.

SUN-DIAL, *s.* छायायन्त्रं, छायामण्डलं, प्रतोदः, सूर्य्यघटी.

SUN-DRIED, *p. p.* आतपशुष्कः -ष्का -ष्कं, आतपशोषितः -ता -तं.

SUNDRY, *a.* नाना *indecl.*, विविधः -धा -धं, नानाविधः &c., पृथग्विधः &c., *see* DIVERS; 'sundries,' नानाद्रव्याणि *n. pl.*, नानाविधवस्तूनि *n. pl.*

SUN-FLOWER, *s.* सूर्य्यकमलः, ओहस्तिनी, वेशदानः, भामकः, दिवाकरः, जामाता *m.* (तृ), विधाबायुः *m.*, वनालिका; 'the flower,' सूर्य्यकमलं.

SUNG, *p. p.* गीतः -ता -तं, परिगीतः &c.; 'by bards,' उपगीतः &c.

SUNK, *p. p.* मग्नः -ग्ना -ग्नं, निमग्नः &c., अवसन्नः -न्ना -न्नं, सन्नः &c., अवगाढः -ढा -ढं, निखातः -ता -तं; 'in mud,' पङ्कमग्नः &c.

SUNKEN, *a.* जलतलस्थः -स्था -स्थं, जलोपगूढः -ढा -ढं.

SUNLESS, *a.* असूर्य्यः -र्य्या -र्य्यं, अनादित्यः -त्या -त्यं, सूर्य्यहीनः &c.

SUNNY, *a.* सूर्य्यतप्तः -प्ता -प्तं, रवितप्तः &c., सूर्य्यव्याप्तः &c., सूर्य्यातपव्याप्तः &c., सातपः -पा -पं, सार्कः -र्का -र्कं.

SUN-RISE, *s.* सूर्य्योदयः, सूर्य्योदयकालः, अरुणोदयः, उदयः, उदयकालः, अभ्युत्थानं; 'before sun-rise,' सूर्य्ये अनुदिते.

SUN-SET, *s.* सूर्य्यास्तं -स्तः, सूर्य्यास्तकालः अस्तः -स्तं, दिनान्तः, दिवावसानं, तिमहु *n.*, उत्सूरः; 'at sun-set,' अस्तङ्गते सूर्य्ये.

SUN-SHINE, *s.* सूर्य्यातपः, आतपः, सूर्य्यप्रकाशः, प्रकाशः, सूर्य्यतापः, सूर्य्यकान्तिः *f.*, सूर्य्यतेजस् *n.*, सूर्य्यद्युतिः *f.*, सूर्य्यालोकः, द्योतः, सूर्य्यकिरणः, कला.

To SUP, *v. n.* or *a.* रात्रिभोजनं कृ, नक्तभोजनं कृ.—(Sip), *see To* SIP.

SUPER. A prefix rendered by अति, अधिक, अतिशय &c., in comp.

To SUPER-ABOUND, *v. n.* अतिबहुलीभू, अतिविपुलीभू, अतिप्रचुरीभू.

SUPER-ABUNDANCE, *s.* अतिबाहुल्यं, अतिवैपुल्यं, अतिप्राचुर्य्यं, आधिक्यं, अतिरिक्तता, आतिरेक्यं, उपचयः. *See* EXUBERANCE.

SUPER-ABUNDANT, *a.* अतिबहुलः -ला -लं, अतिविपुलः &c., अतिप्रचुरः &c., अतिरिक्तः -क्ता -क्तं, अतिशायी -यिनी -यि (न्), अधिकः &c. *See* EXUBERANT.

To SUPER-ADD, *v. a.* अधिकं समायुज् or संयुज्, अधिकसंयोगं कृ.

SUPER-ANNUATED, *a.* अतिवयस्कः -स्का -स्कं, वयोधिकः -का -कं, वयोतीतः -ता -तं, वार्धक्याक्षमः -मा -मं, वार्धक्याशक्तः -क्ता -क्तं.

SUPER-ANNUATION, *s.* अतिवयस्कता, वयोतीतता, वार्धक्याक्षमता.

SUPERB, *a.* अतिशोभनः -ना -नं, स्पर्धी &c. *See* MAGNIFICENT.

SUPERCILIOUS, *a.* ऊर्द्ध्वदृष्टिः -ष्टिः -ष्टि, दर्पादुपेक्षकः -का -कं, *see* LOFTY.

SUPERCILIOUSNESS, *s.* दर्पादुपेक्षा, दर्पात् परोपेक्षा. *See* HAUGHTINESS.

SUPEREROGATION, *s.* अत्याचारः, अतिरिक्ताचारः, अत्याचरणं, अतिरिक्ताचरणं, नियमातिरेकः, विध्यतिरेकः, कर्त्तव्याधिक्यं, काम्यत्वं.

SUPEREROGATORY, *a.* नियमातिरिक्तः -क्ता -क्तं, कर्त्तव्यातिरिक्तः &c., विध्यतिरिक्तः &c., अतिरिक्तः -क्ता -क्तं, काम्यः -म्या -म्यं.

SUPEREXCELLENCE, *s.* अत्युत्कृष्टता, अत्युत्तमता, सर्व्वश्रेष्ठता.

SUPEREXCELLENT, *a.* अत्युत्कृष्टः -ष्टा -ष्टं, अत्युत्तमः -मा -मं, सर्व्वोत्कृष्टः -ष्टा -ष्टं, सर्व्वश्रेष्ठः &c., सर्व्वोत्तमः -मा -मं, श्रेष्ठः &c.

SUPERFICIAL, *a.* (Pertaining to, or being on the surface) बाह्यः -ह्या -ह्यं, वाहीकः -का -कं, वहिःस्थः -स्था -स्थं, वहिर्भागस्थः &c., वहिर्लग्नः -ग्ना -ग्नं, पृष्ठस्थः &c., वहिस् or पृष्ठ in comp.; 'superficial view,' बाह्यदृष्टिः *f.*; 'superficial contents,' पृष्ठफलं.—(Shallow, not deep) अनिम्नः -म्ना -म्नं, अल्पः -ल्पा -ल्पं, *see* SLIGHT; 'superficial scholar,' किञ्चिज्ज्ञः, अल्पज्ञः, चुम्बकः, शास्त्रगण्डः, *see* SMATTERER.

SUPERFICIALLY, *adv.* बाह्यतस्, वहिर्भागे, वहिस्. *See* SLIGHTLY.

SUPERFICIES, *s.* तलं, पृष्ठं, विस्तारः, वहिर्भागः, उपरिस्थभागः.

SUPERFINE, *a.* अत्युत्तमः -मा -मं, अत्युत्कृष्टः -ष्टा -ष्टं, अतिसूक्ष्मः &c.

SUPERFLUITY, *s.* अतिरेकः, आतिरेक्यं, अतिरिक्तता, आधिक्यं, आतिशय्यं, प्रयोजनातिरेकः, प्रयोजनातिरिक्तता, वैयर्थ्यं.

SUPERFLUOUS, *a.* अतिरिक्तः -क्ता -क्तं, अधिकः -का -कं, प्रयोजनातिरिक्तः &c., आवश्यकातिरिक्तः &c., अनर्थकः -का -कं, विफलः -ला -लं.

SUPERHUMAN, *a.* अतिमानुषः -षा -षं, अतिमनुष्यः -ष्या -ष्यं, अतिमर्त्यः -र्त्या -र्त्यं, मानुषातिगः -गा -गं, जनातिगः &c., पुरुषातिगः &c., अपौरुषः -षी -षं; 'having superhuman intellect,' अतिमनुष्यबुद्धिः -द्धिः -द्धि; 'superhuman power,' विभूतिः *f.*, भूतिः *f.*, प्रभावः; 'possessed of it,' विभूतिमान् -मती -मत् (त्).

SUPERINCUMBENT, *a.* उपरिस्थः -स्था -स्थं, उपरिवर्त्ती -र्त्तिनी -र्त्ति (न्).

To SUPERINDUCE, *v. a.* अध्यानी (c. 1. -नयति -नेतुं), अनुनी, अध्यारुह् in caus.

To SUPERINTEND, *v. n.* अधिष्ठा (c. 1. -तिष्ठति -ष्ठातुं), अध्यक्षः -क्षा -क्षं भू, अध्यक्षतां कृ, अवेक्ष्, उपदृश्, कार्य्यावेक्षणं कृ. *See To* OVERSEE.

SUPERINTENDENCE, *s.* अध्यक्षता -त्वं, अधिकारः, अधीकारः, अधिष्ठितिः *f.*, अधिष्ठातृत्वं, अधिष्ठानं, अधिकर्म्म *n.* (न्), अधीशता, अवेक्षणं, कार्य्यावेक्षणं, कार्य्यदर्शनं, कार्य्येक्षणं, कार्य्याधीशता.

SUPERINTENDENT, *s.* अध्यक्षः, अधीशः, अधिकारी *m.* *See* OVERSEER.

SUPERIOR, *a.* (Upper) उपरिस्थः -स्था -स्थं, ऊर्द्ध्वस्थः &c., ऊर्द्ध्वः -र्द्ध्वा -र्द्ध्वं.—(In rank or excellence) श्रेयान् -यसी -यः (स्), श्रेष्ठः -ष्ठा -ष्ठं, गरीयान् &c., वरीयान् &c., वरिष्ठः -ष्ठा -ष्ठं, ज्यायान् &c., ज्येष्ठः &c.,

विशिष्टः -ष्टा -ष्टं, प्रमुखः -खा -खं, प्रधानः -ना -नं, मुख्यः -ख्या -ख्यं, उत्कृष्टः &c., प्रकृष्टः &c., अधिकः -का -कं, प्रभविष्णुः -ष्णुः -ष्णु, वरः -रा -रं, गुरुः -र्वी -रु, अकनिष्ठः &c., *see* PRE-EMINENT; 'of superior worth,' गुणोत्कृष्टः &c., गुणाधिकः -का -कं; 'superior to the best,' परात्परः -रा -रं; 'to be superior,' विशिष् in pass. (-शिष्यते), अतिरिच् in pass. (-रिच्यते); 'action is superior to inaction,' अकर्म्मणः कर्म्म विशिष्यते or अकर्म्मणः कर्म्म ज्यायः; 'intellect is superior to action,' कर्म्मणो बुद्धिर् विशिष्यते or कर्म्मणो बुद्धिर् ज्यायसी.—(Beyond the influence of).

SUPERIOR, *s.* श्रेष्ठः, ज्येष्ठः, गुरुः.—(Of a convent) आश्रमगुरुः.

SUPERIORITY, *s.* श्रेष्ठता, श्रैष्ठ्यं, विशिष्टता, वैशिष्ट्यं, वैशेष्यं, प्रधानता, प्राधान्यं, उत्कृष्टता, उत्कर्षः, प्रमुखत्वं, प्रभविष्णुता, प्राग्भावः, आधिक्यं, ऊर्द्ध्वस्थितिः *f.*, प्राबल्यं, ज्येष्ठता, वरिष्ठता, बलीयस्त्वं, परिव्रढिमा *m.* (न्), *see* PRE-EMINENCE.

SUPERLATIVE, *a.* परमः -मा -मं, अत्यन्तः -न्ता -न्तं, आत्यन्तिकः -की -कं, अतिशय or अति prefixed, *see* EXCESSIVE, SUPREME.—(In grammar) अतिशयार्थवाचकः -का -कं, परमावधिवाचकः &c.

SUPERLATIVELY, *adv.* अत्यन्तं, अतिशयेन, अति prefixed. *See* EXCESSIVELY.

SUPERNATURAL, *a.* अलौकिकः -की -कं, अतिमानुषः -षा -षं, मानुषासाध्यः -ध्या -ध्यं, अपौरुषेयः -यी -यं, मानवासाध्यः &c., अद्भुतः &c. *See* SUPERHUMAN.

SUPERNATURALLY, *adv.* अलौकिकं, अतिमानुषं, अलौकिकप्रकारेण.

SUPERNUMERARY, *a.* or *s.* अतिसंख्यः -ख्या -ख्यं, संख्यातिरिक्तः -क्ता -क्तं, नियतसंख्यातिरिक्तः &c., नियमातिरिक्तः &c., अधिकः -का -कं, अतिरिक्तः &c.

SUPERSCRIPTION, *s.* उपरिलेखः, उपरिस्थलेखः, बहिर्लेखः.

To SUPERSEDE, *v. a.* (Render void) लुप् (c. 6. लुम्पति, लोप्तुं), लोपं कृ; 'this system has superseded all the others,' अयं मार्गः सर्व्वेषाम् अपरेषां लोपस्य कारणं बभूव.—(Set aside, displace) निरस् (c. 4. -अस्यति -सितुं), निराकृ, निःसृ in caus., अपसृ.

SUPERSEDED, *p. p.* निरस्तः -स्ता -स्तं, निराकृतः -ता -तं; 'a superseded wife,' अध्यूढा, अधिविन्ना, कृतसापत्निका, कृतसापत्नका, कृतसापत्नी, कृतसापत्नीका, कृतसपत्निका.

SUPERSTITION, *s.* (Over exactness in religion) अतिभक्तिः *f.*, अत्याचारः, अतिरिक्तभक्तिः *f.*, अतिरिक्ताचारः.—(Belief in supernatural agency, &c.) शकुनपिशाचादिविश्वासः, शकुनपिशाचादिभक्तिः *f.*, पिशाचादिनिष्ठा, शकुनादिविश्वासः.—(False religion) अन्यथाधर्म्मः, मिथ्याधर्म्मः, अन्यथाभक्तिः *f.*, अन्यथामार्गः, अशास्त्रीयभक्तिः *f.*, अविधिनिष्ठा, अविधिश्रद्धा, अवैधक्रिया.

SUPERSTITIOUS, *a.* (Over exact in religion) अत्याचारी -रिणी -रि (न्), अतिरिक्ताचारी &c.—(Credulous regarding supernatural agency, &c.) पिशाचादिविश्वासी &c., शकुनपिशाचादिविश्वासी &c., शकुनादिनिष्ठः -ष्ठा -ष्ठं, पिशाचादिनिष्ठः &c.—(Falsely religious) अन्यथाधर्म्मी -र्म्मिणी &c., अन्यथामार्गी &c., अवैधकर्म्मी &c., असत्यधर्म्मी &c., मिथ्याधर्म्मी &c.—(Proceeding from superstition) मिथ्याधर्म्ममूलकः -का -कं, अत्याचारमूलकः &c., पिशाचादिनिष्ठाप्रयुक्तः -क्ता -क्तं.

SUPERSTRUCTURE, *s.* वास्तूपरिस्थभवनं, उपरिव्यूहनं. *See* STRUCTURE.

To SUPERVENE, *v. n.* अकस्माद् उपस्था (c. 1. -तिष्ठति -स्थातुं) or आगम्.

To SUPERVISE, SUPERVISION, *see To* SUPERINTEND, INSPECT, &c.

SUPINE, *a.* (Lying with the face upward) उत्तानशयः -या -यं, उत्तानः -ना -नं, ऊर्द्ध्वमुखः -खा -खी -खं.—(Indolent) अलसः -सा -सं.

SUPINENESS, *s.* अलसता, आलस्यं, तन्द्रा. *See* INDOLENCE.

SUPPER, *s.* नक्तभोजनं, रात्रिभोजनं, सायम्भोजनं, निशिभोजनं.

To SUPPLANT, *v. a.* (Trip up), *see* the word.—(Displace by stratagem) छलेन निरस् (c. 4. -अस्यति -सितुं) or निराकृ or अपसृ (c. 10. -सारयति -यितुं), वञ्च् (c. 10. वञ्चयति -यितुं), *see To* DISPLACE.

SUPPLE, *a.* कोमलः -ला -लं, मृदुः -दुः -द्वी -दु, सुनम्यः -म्या -म्यं, सुखनम्यः &c., नमनशीलः -ला -लं. *See* PLIANT, FLEXIBLE.

SUPPLEMENT, *s.* परिशिष्टं, परिबृंहणः, उत्तरखण्डः, अतिदेशः, अतिनिर्देशः, न्यूनतापूरणं, न्यूनताभरणं.

SUPPLEMENTAL, SUPPLEMENTARY, *a.* अतिनिर्दिष्टः -ष्टा -ष्टं, अतिदिष्टः &c., अतिनिर्देशकः -का -कं, न्यूनतापूरकः -का -कं, न्यूनताभरकः &c.

SUPPLENESS, *s.* कोमलता, मृदुता, सुनम्यता, नमनशीलता.

SUPPLIANT, SUPPLICANT, *a.* or *s.* अर्थी -र्थिनी -र्थि (न्), प्रार्थकः -का -कं, प्रार्थयिता -त्री -तृ (तृ), मार्गणकः &c., अभ्यर्थयमानः -ना -नं, कृताञ्जलिः -लिः -लि, बद्धाञ्जलिः &c., शरणार्थी &c., शरणागतः -ता -तं.

SUPPLIANTLY, *adv.* कृताञ्जलिवत्, बद्धाञ्जलिवत्, अञ्जलिकर्म्मपूर्व्वं.

To SUPPLICATE, *v. a.* अञ्जलिकर्म्मपूर्व्वं प्रार्थ् (c. 10. -अर्थयते -ति -यितुं) or अभ्यर्थ् or सम्प्रार्थ् or अर्थ्, अञ्जलिं कृत्वा याच्. *See To* ENTREAT.

SUPPLICATED, *p. p.* प्रार्थितः -ता -तं, अनुनीतः -ता -तं. *See* ENTREATED.

SUPPLICATION, *s.* प्रार्थनं -ना, अर्थः, याच्ञा, अनुनयः. *See* ENTREATY.

SUPPLIED, *p. p.* सम्पन्नः -न्ना -न्नं, युक्तः -क्ता -क्तं, सम्भृतः -ता -तं; 'as an ellipsis,' अध्याहृतः -ता -तं; 'is plentifully supplied,' आपूर्य्यते.

To SUPPLY *v. a.* उपस्था in caus. (-स्थापयति -यितुं), उपकॢप्, परिकॢप्. सम्भृ, पृ (c. 10. पूरयति -यितुं), सम्पृ, *see To* FURNISH, PROVIDE.—(Serve instead of), *see To* SERVE.—(Supply an ellipsis) अध्याहृ, अभ्यूह्, ऊह्, अभ्यूहं कृ, समासाध्याहारं कृ.

SUPPLY, *s.* सम्भारः, सम्भृतिः *f.*, सामग्री, *see* STOCK, STORE.—(Supplies) निर्वाहः, यात्रिकं, पाथेयं, *see* PROVISIONS.

To SUPPORT, *v. a.* (Uphold, sustain) आलम्ब् (c. 10. -लम्बयति -यितुं, c. 1. -लम्बते -म्बितुं), अवलम्ब्, समवलम्ब्, धृ (c. 10. धारयति -यितुं, c. 1. धरति, धर्त्तुं), संधृ, परिधृ, अभिधृ, संस्तम्भ्, उपस्तम्भ्, अवष्टम्भ्, विष्टम्भ्, संग्रह्, *see To* MAINTAIN; 'how shall I support life?' कथं जीवितं धरिष्ये; 'to support with the hand,' करालम्बनं कृ; 'this point being supported on the finger,' तस्मिन् बिन्दौ अङ्गुल्या अवलम्बिते.—(Support with food, &c.) भृ (c. 1. भरति, c. 3. बिभर्त्ति, भर्त्तुं), सम्भृ, भरणं कृ, भृतिं दा, पुष् (c. 10. पोषयति -यितुं), पोषणं कृ, पुष्टिं कृ, पाल् (c. 10. पालयति -यितुं), आलम्ब्, आलम्बनं कृ, वृध् in caus., संवृध्, भू in caus.; 'to support a family,' कुलभरणं कृ, कुलालम्बनं कृ, तन्त्र् (c. 10. तन्त्रयते -यितुं); 'to support one's self,' निर्वाहं कृ.—(Bear, endure) सह्, विषह्, *see To* ENDURE, SUFFER.—(Help) उपकृ, उपग्रह्, अनुग्रह्.—(Vindicate, make good), *see To* MAINTAIN.—(Support the courage, &c.), *see To* ENCOURAGE, CONSOLE, &c.

SUPPORT, *s.* (Act of supporting) आलम्बनं, अवलम्बनं, धारणं, उपस्तम्भनं, अवष्टम्भनं, संस्तम्भनं, संग्रहः -हणं; 'support of life,' प्राणधारणं, प्राणोपस्तम्भः, प्राणयात्रा, प्राणस्थितिः *f.*—(Supporting with food, &c.) भरणं, पोषणं, पुष्टिः *f.*, पालनं, प्रतिपालनं, भृत्या, पालनपोषणं, सम्भारः, सम्भृतिः *f.*, संवर्धनं.—(Means of subsistence) उपजीवनं, उपजीविका, *see* MAINTENANCE, SUBSISTENCE.—(That which upholds) आधारः, धारणं, आलम्बः -म्बनं, अवलम्बनं, उपस्तम्भः, अवष्टम्भः, उपघ्नः, आश्रयः, उपलम्बः; 'contiguous support,' अभिकाश्रयः.—(Help), *see* HELP.

SUPPORTABLE, *a.* सह्यः -ह्या -ह्यं, सहनीयः -या -यं. *See* TOLERABLE.

SUPPORTED, *p. p.* (Upheld) आलम्बितः -ता -तं, अवलम्बितः &c., उत्तम्भितः -ता -तं, उपस्तम्भितः &c., अवष्टम्भितः &c., उपष्टब्धः -ब्धा -ब्धं, अवष्टब्धः &c., आधृतः -ता -तं, धारितः &c., आधारितः &c., साधारः -रा -रं; 'with the hand,' करालम्बितः &c., दत्तहस्तः -स्ता -स्तं.—(Maintained) भृतः -ता -तं, सम्भृतः &c., पोषितः &c., *see* MAINTAINED.

SUPPORTER, *s.* (Upholder) आलम्बी *m.* (न्), धारकः, धारी *m.* (न्), धरः, उपस्तम्भकः, अवष्टम्भकः, आलम्बकारी *m.*, उपस्तम्भकारी *m.*, उद्वहः.—(Maintainer) भर्त्ता *m.* (र्तृ), पोषकः, *see* MAINTAINER; 'of a family,' कुलालम्बी *m.* -म्बिनी *f.*, कुलोद्वहः, उपाधिः *m.*

SUPPOSABLE, *a.* मन्तव्यः -व्या -व्यं, भावनीयः -या -यं, कल्पनीयः &c.

To SUPPOSE, *v. a.* (Conceive to be, assume) कॢप् (c. 10. कल्पयति -यितुं), मनसा कॢप्, सम्भू (c. 10. -भावयति -यितुं), विभू, भू, उपन्यस्, अप्रमाणपूर्व्वम् उपन्यस्, आहार्य्यारोपं कृ.—(Imagine, infer) मन् (c. 4. मन्यते, मन्तुं), विभू, तर्क्, अवगम्, अनुमा, आशङ्क्, *see* *To* THINK, INFER.—(Required to exist, presuppose) पूर्व्वं or अग्रे कॢप् or भू in caus., अस्तित्वदर्शनं कृ, अस्तित्वप्रदर्शनं कृ.

SUPPOSED, *p. p.* कल्पितः -ता -तं, भावितः &c., मतः &c., अनुमितः &c.; 'for various reasons it is supposed,' अनेकहेतुभिर् अनुमीयते.

SUPPOSITION, SUPPOSAL, *s.* कल्पना, भावना, अनुमानं, अनुमितिः *f.*, तर्कः, वितर्कः, बुद्धिः *f.*, उपन्यासः, पक्षः. *See* HYPOTHESIS.

SUPPOSITITIOUS, *a.* कृत्रिमः -मा -मं, कल्पितः -ता -तं, छलेन सद्वस्तुस्थाने स्थापितः -ता -तं; 'child,' पुत्रप्रतिनिधिः *m.*

To SUPPRESS, *v. a.* (Conceal) उपगुह् (c. 1. -गूहति -हितुं), निगुह्, गुह्.—(Restrain, obstruct) नियम् (c. 1. -यच्छति -यन्तुं), विनियम्, निरुध् (c. 7. -रुणद्धि -रोद्धुं), अवरुध्, संरुध्, रुध्, निग्रह् (c. 9. -गृह्णाति -ग्रहीतुं), स्तम्भ् (c. 9. स्तभ्नाति, c. 10. स्तम्भयति -यितुं), निवृ (c. 10. -वारयति -यितुं), धृ in caus., विधृ, यन्त्र् (c. 10. यन्त्रयति -यितुं), जि (c. 1. जयति, जेतुं), निवृत् (c. 10. -वर्त्तयति -यितुं); 'to suppress one's passions,' इन्द्रियाणि जि or निग्रह् or दम्; 'one who suppresses his passions,' जितेन्द्रियः; 'to suppress anger,' क्रोधं जि or निग्रह्; or expressed by अन्तर् in comp.; as, 'one who suppresses his anger,' अन्तःक्रोधी *m.* (न्), जितक्रोधः; 'his tears,' अन्तर्वाष्पः; 'to suppress disturbances,' कण्टकमर्द्दनं कृ; 'the voice,' वाक्स्तम्भं कृ, वागरोधं कृ; 'the breath,' श्वासावरोधं कृ.

SUPPRESSED, *p. p.* (Concealed) उपगूढः -ढा -ढं, निगूढः &c.—(Restrained, obstructed) स्तम्भितः -ता -तं, रुद्धः -द्धा -द्धं, निगृहीतः -ता -तं, यतः &c., समुपोढः &c., *see* RESTRAINED; or expressed by अन्तर् in comp.; as, 'suppressed anger,' अन्तःक्रोधः; 'suppressed fever,' अन्तर्दाहः.

SUPPRESSION, *s.* (Restraint, stoppage) नियमनं, निगृहीतिः *f.*, निग्रहः -हणं, यन्त्रणं, संयमः -मनं, रोधः, अवरोधः, स्तम्भः -म्भनं, अवष्टम्भः, आयामः, निवारः -रणं; 'of the breath,' श्वासरोधः, श्वासावरोधः; 'of the voice,' वाक्स्तम्भः; 'of the urine,' मूत्रावरोधः, मूत्रावष्टम्भः; 'of the passions,' इन्द्रियजयः, इन्द्रियनिग्रहः, कामावसायः; 'of feeling,' प्रतिसन्धानं.—(Concealment) गोपनं, अपवारणं, संवरणं, अप्रकाशनं, अपलापः.

To SUPPURATE, *v. n.* पूय् (c. 1. पूयते -यितुं), सपूयः -या -यं भू, पक्वः -क्वा -क्वं भू, पक्वीभू, परिपक्वीभू. *See* *To* MATURATE, *v. n.*

SUPPURATION, *s.* पाकः, परिपाकः, पूयत्वं, संस्रावः, *see* MATURATION.

SUPPURATIVE, *a.* पाचकः -का -कं, पाचनः &c. *See* MATURATIVE.

SUPREMACY, *s.* आधिपत्यं, प्रभुत्वं -ता, प्रधानता -त्वं, प्राधान्यं, प्रधानाधिकारः, ईशिता -त्वं, प्रभविष्णुता -त्वं, ऐश्वर्य्यं, मुख्यता -त्वं, मुख्याधिकारः, स्वाम्यं, स्वामित्वं, श्रेष्ठत्वं.

SUPREME, *a.* (Highest in authority) प्रधानः -ना -नं, सर्व्वप्रधानः &c., ऐशिकः -की -कं, ऐश्वरः -री -रं, सर्व्वोपरिस्थः &c., प्रभुः -भ्वी -भु, प्रभविष्णुः -ष्णुः -ष्णु, आधिकारिकः -की -कं, *see* PRE-EMINENT.—(Highest) परमः -मा -मं, पारमिकः -की -कं, परः -रा -रं, *see* CHIEF; 'supreme monarch,' परमराजः; 'supreme authority,' परमाधिकारः, प्रधानाधिकारः, ऐकपत्यं; 'supreme Being,' प्रधानं, परमब्रह्म *n.* (न्), परब्रह्म *n.*, ब्रह्म *n.*, जगदात्मा *m.* (न्), चिद्रूपं, निर्गुणः, अखिलात्मा *m.*

SUPREMELY, *adv.* परमं, परं, अत्यन्तं, अतिशय or अति prefixed.

SURAT, *s.* (Country on the western side of India) सुराष्ट्रः.

SURD, *s.* (In algebra) करणीगतराशिः *m.*, करणीगतसंख्या, करणीगतः.

SURE, *a.* (Fixed, certain) स्थिरः -रा -रं, आवश्यकः -की -कं, अवश्यकः -का -कं, ध्रुवः -वा -वं, निश्चितः -ता -तं, सुनिश्चितः -ता -तं, असन्दिग्धः -ग्धा -ग्धं, निःसंशयः -या -यं, निःसन्देहः -हा -हं, अवश्यम्भावी -विनी &c.—(Having full confidence, certainly knowing) कृतनिश्चयः -या -यं, सनिश्चयः &c., जातनिश्चयः &c., दृढनिश्चयः &c., निश्चितमनस्कः -स्का -स्कं, निश्चितमनाः -नाः -नः (स्), संशयहीनः -ना -नं, सन्देहहीनः &c., निश्चयी &c.—(Secure) निर्भयः -या -यं; 'I am sure,' मम दृढनिश्चयो विद्यते, मम दृढज्ञानं जायते, मम स्थिरज्ञानं जायते, मम दृढप्रत्याशा विद्यते; 'to be sure,' अवश्यं, *see* CERTAINLY.

SURE, SURELY, *adv.* अवश्यं, नूनं, ध्रुवं, निश्चितं. *See* CERTAINLY.

SURETY, *s.* प्रतिभूः *m.*, प्रातिभाव्यं, पारिभाव्यं, प्रतिनिधिः *m.*, लग्नकः, प्रात्ययिकः, बन्धकः, न्यासः. *See* SECURITY.

SURF, *s.* भङ्गिः -ङ्गी *f.*, भङ्गः, लहरिः -री *f.*, कल्लोलः, तरलायितः.

SURFACE, *s.* पृष्ठं, पृष्ठभागः, तलं -लः, बहिर्भागः, उपरिभागः, उपरिस्थभागः, विस्तारः, तलपर्य्यन्तः, दृश्याङ्गं, दर्शनाङ्गं, मुखं; 'of the earth,' भूतलं, भूपृष्ठं, पृथिवीतलं, क्षितितलं, क्षौणितलं, क्षितिपीठं, भूमुखं, कुतलं, धरोपस्थः; 'of a rock,' शिलातलं.

To SURFEIT, *v. a.* अत्यन्तभोजनदानेन वमनेच्छां जन् (c. 10. जनयति -यितुं), अत्यन्तं तृप् in caus., अतिसौहित्यं जन्. *See* *To* GLUT, *v. a.*

To SURFEIT, *v. n.* अतिभोजनेन वमनेच्छुः -च्छुः -च्छु भू.

SURFEIT, *s.* अतितृप्तिः *f.*, अतिसौहित्यं, अतिभोजनप्रयुक्ता वमनेच्छा.

SURFEITED, *p. p.* अतितृप्तः -प्ता -प्तं, अतिभोजनेन वमनेच्छुः -च्छुः -च्छु.

SURGE, *s.* कल्लोलः, उल्लोलः, महोर्म्मिः *m. f.*, ऊर्म्मिः *m. f.*, भङ्गः, भङ्गिः -ङ्गी *f.*, तरङ्गः, अर्गलः. *See* BILLOW.

SURGEON, *s.* शस्त्रवैद्यः, अस्त्रचिकित्सकः, शालाकी *m.* (न्), कायशल्यादिभिषक् *m.* (ज्), शल्यशास्त्रज्ञः; 'veterinary,' अश्ववैद्यः.

SURGERY, *s.* अस्त्रचिकित्सा, कायचिकित्सा, शस्त्रवैद्यकं, शस्त्रवैद्यकर्म्म *n.* (न्), शल्यशास्त्रं, राक्षसं, आसुरी.

SURGICAL, *a.* अस्त्रचिकित्सासम्बन्धी &c., शस्त्रवैद्यकर्म्मसम्बन्धी &c.

SURLINESS, *s.* कर्कशता, कार्कश्यं, वक्रशीलता, *see* MOROSENESS.

SURLY, *a.* कर्कशः -शा -शं, वक्रशीलः -ला -लं. *See* MOROSE.

To SURMISE, *v. a.* शङ्क्, आशङ्क्, तर्क्, सम्भू in caus. *See* *To* SUSPECT.

SURMISE, *s.* वितर्कः, शङ्का, आशङ्का, संशयः. *See* SUSPICION.

To SURMOUNT, *v. a.* अतिक्रम् (c. 1. -क्रामति -क्रमितुं), अधिक्रम्, अभ्यतिक्रम्, अधिरुह् (c. 1. -रोहति -रोढुं), आरुह्, तीर् (c. 10. तीरयति -यितुं), पार् (c. 10. पारयति -यितुं), तॄ. *See To* OVERCOME.

SURMOUNTABLE, *a.* अतिक्रमणीयः -या -यं, अतिक्रम्यः &c., अधिगम्यः &c.

SURMOUNTED, *p. p.* अतिक्रान्तः -न्ता -न्तं, उत्तीर्णः -र्णा -र्णं, तीर्णः &c.

SURNAME, *s.* पद्धतिः -ती *f.*, कुलनाम *n.* (न्), उपनाम *n.*, उपपदं, रूढिः *f.* Examples of surnames in Sanskrit are शर्म्मन् in विष्णुशर्म्मन्, and दासः in कालिदासः.

To SURNAME, *v. a.* उपनाम दा or कृ, पद्धतिं दा, कुलनाम दा.

SURNAMED, *p. p.* उपनामकः -का -कं, उपनामविशिष्टः -ष्टा -ष्टं.

To SURPASS, *v. a.* अतिक्रम् (c. 1. -क्रामति -क्रमितुं), अतिशी (c. 2. -शेते -शयितुं), अतिचर् (c. 1. -चरति -रितुं), अतिरिच् in pass. (-रिच्यते), विशिष् in pass., श्रेष्ठः -ष्ठा -ष्ठं भू. *See To* EXCEED, EXCEL.

SURPASSABLE, *a.* अतिक्रमणीयः -या -यं, अतिक्रम्यः -म्या -म्यं.

SURPASSED, *p. p.* अतिक्रान्तः -न्ता -न्तं, जितः -ता -तं, विजितः &c., उत्क्रान्तः -न्ता -न्तं, प्रक्रान्तः &c., अतीतः &c., अन्तरितः &c. *See* EXCEEDED.

SURPASSING, *part.* or *a.* अत्यन्तः -न्ता -न्तं, अतिक्रामकः &c., *see* EXCEEDING, *a.*; often expressed by अति; as, 'surpassing the wind,' अत्यनिलः.

SURPLUS, *s.* उद्वर्त्तः, उद्वृत्तं, उच्छिष्टं, अधिकभागः, परभागः, समभिहारः.

SURPLUS, *a.* अधिकः -का -कं, उद्वृत्तः -त्ता -त्तं, उद्वर्त्तः -र्त्ता -र्त्तं.

To SURPRISE, *v. a.* (Strike with wonder) विस्मि in caus. (-स्माययति -स्मापयति -ते -यितुं), विस्मयं जन् (c. 10. जनयति -यितुं), विस्मयं कृ, विस्मापनं कृ, आश्चर्य्यत्वं जन्, चमत्कारं जन्, चमत्कृ.—(Come upon unawares) अकस्मात् or अचिन्तितम् आक्रम् or उपक्रम् or उपस्था or आगम् or आसद् or अवस्कन्द्.

SURPRISE, SURPRISAL, *s.* (Wonder) विस्मयः, आश्चर्य्यत्वं, आश्चर्य्यं, चमत्कारः, चमत्कृतिः *f.*, चमत्क्रिया, चित्रं, अद्भुतरसः, चोद्यं -द्यं, चोद्यं.—(Coming upon unawares) अकस्माद् आक्रमणं or अवस्कन्दः -न्दनं.

SURPRISED, *p. p.* (Struck with wonder) विस्मितः -ता -तं, विस्मयान्वितः &c., विस्मयापन्नः -न्ना -न्नं, आगतविस्मयः -या -यं, जातविस्मयः &c., सविस्मयः &c., विस्मयाकुलः -ला -लं, चमत्कृतः -ता -तं, जातचमत्कारः -रा -रं; 'to be suprised,' विस्मितः -ता -तं भू or अस्, विस्मि (c. 1. -स्मयते -स्मेतुं), विस्मयं गम्.—(Come upon unawares) अकस्माद् आक्रान्तः -न्ता -न्तं or अवस्कन्दितः -ता -तं.

SURPRISING, *part.* or *a.* विस्मयजनकः -का -कं, विस्मयकारकः &c., विस्मापकः &c., विस्मापनः -ना -नं, आश्चर्य्यः -र्य्या -र्य्यं, आश्चर्य्यकरः -रा -रं, आश्चर्य्यकारकः -का -कं, चमत्कारी -रिणी -रि (न्), चमत्कारिकः &c., अद्भुतः -ता -तं, चित्रः -त्रा -त्रं, विचित्रः &c.; 'a very surprising thing,' महदाश्चर्य्यं.

To SURRENDER, *v. a.* (Resign, give up) त्यज्, परित्यज्, उत्सृज्, विसृज्, अवसृज्, उत्सर्गं कृ, उत्सर्जनं कृ, हा, विहा, प्रोज्झ्, सन्न्यस्, प्रत्यादिश्, परादा.—(Commit) सम् in caus. (-अर्पयति -यितुं), ऋ in caus., न्यस्, निक्षिप्, प्रतिपद् in caus., प्रदा, परिदा, दा, प्रयम् (c. 1. -यच्छति -यन्तुं).

To SURRENDER, *v. n.* वशं गम् or उपगम् or अभ्युपे, वशीभू.

SURRENDER, *s.* त्यागः, परित्यागः, उत्सर्गः, उत्सर्जनं. *See* SUBMISSION.

SURRENDERED, *p. p.* त्यक्तः -क्ता -क्तं, परित्यक्तः &c., उत्सृष्टः -ष्टा -ष्टं.

SURREPTITIOUS, *a.* (Done by stealth) छलेन कृतः -ता -तं, *see* CLANDESTINE.—(Introduced fraudulently) छलेन निवेशितः, *see* FRAUDULENT.

SURREPTITIOUSLY, *adv.* छलेन, सकपटं. *See* CLANDESTINELY, FRAUDULENTLY.

SURROGATE, *s.* धर्म्माध्यक्षप्रतिनिधिः *m.*, धर्म्माधिपतिप्रतिनिधिः.

To SURROUND, *v. a.* परिवेष्ट् (c. 1. -वेष्टते -ष्टितुं, c. 10. -वेष्टयति -यितुं), संवेष्ट्, उपवेष्ट्, प्रवेष्ट्, परिवृ, आवृ, परिक्षि, उपस्था, परिगम्, परिसृ, परिचर्, परी, अभिपरी, परिधा, संवल्, प्रदक्षिणीकृ. *See To* ENCOMPASS, INCLOSE.

SURROUNDED, *p. p.* परिवेष्टितः -ता -तं, वेष्टितः &c., परिवृतः -ता -तं, आवृतः &c., वृतः &c., परिगतः -ता -तं, परिवीतः -ता -तं, संवीतः &c., परीतः &c., वलयितः &c., परिक्षिप्तः -प्ता -प्तं, पर्य्यवरुद्धः -द्धा -द्धं, अभिजुष्टः -ष्टा -ष्टं. *See* ENCOMPASSED.

SURROUNDING, *s.* (The act) परिवेष्टनं. *See* ENCOMPASSMENT.

SURROUNDING, *part.* परिवेष्टकः -का -कं, परिवेष्टनकारी -रिणी &c., परिगतः -ता -तं, आवरकः -का -कं, परिचरकः &c.—(Neighbouring), *see* the word; 'surrounding place,' परिस्थलं.

SURTOUT, *s.* उत्तरीयं, प्रावारः -रकः, निचोलः -ली, चलिः *m.*

SURVEILLANCE, *s.* अध्यक्षता, निरूपणं, अवेक्षा. *See* INSPECTION.

To SURVEY, *v. a.* आलोक् (c. 10. -लोकयति -यितुं), अवलोक्, समवलोक्, समालोक्, विलोक्, निरीक्ष् (c. 1. -ईक्षते -क्षितुं), अवेक्ष्, समवेक्ष्, परीक्ष्, निरूप् (c. 10. -रूपयति -यितुं), दृश्, अनुदृश्, सन्दृश्, *see To* INSPECT, EXAMINE, SCRUTINIZE.—(Land) भूमापनं कृ, भूमिमापनं कृ, भूमिं परिमा.

SURVEY, *s.* निरीक्षा -क्षणं, अवलोकनं, निरूपणं, *see* INSPECTION.—(Of land) भूमापनं, भूमिमापनं.

SURVEYED, *p. p.* निरीक्षितः -ता -तं, आलोकितः &c. *See* INSPECTED.

SURVEYOR, *s.* (Of land, &c.) भूमापकः, भूमापनकृत्.

To SURVIVE, *v. a.* (Outlive another) अन्योत्तरं or परोत्तरं जीव् (c. 1. जीवति -वितुं), अन्यमरणोत्तरं जीव्, उत्तरं जीव्, उत्तरजीवी -विनी &c. भू, अधिककालं जीव्, *see To* OUTLIVE.

To SURVIVE, *v. n.* धृ (c. 6. ध्रियते), ध्रियमाणः -णा -णं भू, अवस्था.

SURVIVOR, SURVIVING, *s.* or *part.* ध्रियमाणः -णा -णं, उत्तरजीवी -विनी -वि (न्), परोत्तरजीवी &c., अन्योत्तरजीवी &c., परमरणोत्तरजीवी &c., अवस्थितः -ता -तं, अनुगतः &c.—(Left alive on the field of battle) हतशेषः -षा -षं, हतशिष्टः -ष्टा -ष्टं.

SUSCEPTIBILITY, *s.* ग्रहणशीलता, ग्रहणक्षमता, ग्रहणशक्तिः *f.*, ग्राहकत्वं, वेदनक्षमता, वेदनग्राहकत्वं, ग्रहणोपयुक्तता, वेदनशीलता, वेदनपात्रता, ग्रहणपात्रता.

SUSCEPTIBLE, *a.* ग्राहकः -का -कं, ग्राही -हिणी -हि (न्), ग्रहणशीलः -ला -लं, ग्रहणक्षमः -मा -मं, ग्रहणशक्तः -क्ता -क्तं, वेदनक्षमः &c., वेदनग्राहकः -का -कं, गमनीयः -या -यं; 'of pain,' सुलभदुःखः -खा -खं, शीघ्रदुःखी &c.; 'of disease,' सुलभरोगः -गा -गं, शीघ्ररोगी -गिणी &c.; 'of anger,' सुलभकोपः -पा -पं, शीघ्रकोपी &c.; 'of warm passions,' शीघ्रमनोविकारी &c.

To SUSPECT, *v. a.* (Mistrust, doubt) शङ्क् (c. 1. शङ्कते -ङ्कितुं), आशङ्क्, परिशङ्क्, संशङ्क्, न विश्वस् (c. 2. -श्वसिति -तुं), रेक् (c. 1. रेकते -कितुं), आरेक्, संशयं कृ, संशी, संशयारोपं कृ, भी (c. 3. बिभेति, भेतुं); 'to suspect a fault,' दोषं or अपराधं शङ्क्; 'he suspects me of the crime,' मां दोषिणं परिशङ्कते or मां दोषेण परिशङ्कते; 'why do you suspect me?' किं मां शङ्कसे; 'I suspect the truth of what he says,' तथ्यं वचस् तस्य परिशङ्के; 'I suspect the sincerity of your repentance,' दक्षिण्यस्य ते कृतप-

आशापस्य बिभेमि.—(Imagine, conjecture) तर्क्, समतर्क्, मन्, शङ्क्, *see To* SUPPOSE.

SUSPECTED, *p. p.* शङ्कितदोषः -षा -षं, शङ्कितापराधः -धा -धं, शङ्कितः -ता -तं, आशङ्कितः &c., तर्कितः &c., अविश्वस्तः -स्ता -स्तं; 'to be suspected,' शङ्कनीयः -या -यं, शङ्क्यः -ङ्क्या -ङ्क्यं.

To SUSPEND, *v. a.* (Hang up) उद्बन्ध् (c. 9. -बध्नाति -बन्द्धुं), बन्ध्, उद्बन्धनं कृ, प्रलम्ब् in caus., *see To* HANG.—(Make to depend) अवलम्ब् in caus. (-लम्बयति -यितुं), समवलम्ब्, समालम्ब्.—(Debar) निषिध्, निवृ in caus., वृ in caus.—(Cause to stop for a time) कियत्कालपर्य्यन्तं निवृत् (c. 10. -वर्त्तयति -यितुं), *see To* STAY, DELAY, *v. a.*

SUSPENDED, *p. p.* (Hung up, made to hang) उद्बद्धः -द्धा -द्धं, प्रलम्बितः -ता -तं, लम्बितः &c., आलम्बितः &c., आन्दोलितः &c.; 'in a swing or loop,' शिक्यितः -ता -तं, काचितः &c.; 'suspended round the throat,' कण्ठलग्नः -ग्ना -ग्नं.—(Caused to cease for a time) कियत्कालपर्य्यन्तं निवर्त्तितः -ता -तं.

SUSPENSE, *s.* अनिश्चयः, अनिर्णयः, सन्देहः, संशयः, विकल्पः, अनिर्धारणं, भावसन्धिः *m.*, कृताकृतं; 'in suspense,' दोलायमानः -ना -नं, आन्दोलितमनाः -नाः -नः (स्), सन्देहदोलस्थः -स्था -स्थं, संशयस्थः &c.

SUSPENSION, *s.* (Hanging up) उद्बन्धनं.—(Delaying) विलम्बः -म्बनं.—(Suspension of work, cessation) कर्म्मनिवृत्तिः *f.*, कर्म्मविच्छेदः, निवृत्तिः *f.*, कर्म्मान्तरं, अवसानं.—(Interruption or intermission for a time) कियत्कालपर्य्यन्तं विच्छेदः or निवृत्तिः *f.* or रोधः or निरोधः.—(Causing to depend) अवलम्बनं.

SUSPICION, *s.* शङ्का, आशङ्का, संशयः, वितर्कः, तर्कः, विकल्पः, निह्नवः, अविश्वासः, अप्रत्ययः, कुतर्कः; 'on suspicion,' शङ्कया; 'the suspicion arose,' इति शङ्कितं, इति तर्कितं.

SUSPICIOUS, *a.* (Inclined to suspect) शङ्काशीलः -ला -लं, शङ्काबुद्धिः -द्धिः -द्धि, संशयशीलः -ला -लं, संशयबुद्धिः &c., सन्देहशीलः &c., सन्देहबुद्धिः &c., सन्दिग्धचित्तः -त्ता -त्तं, सन्दिग्धमतिः -तिः -ति, संशयालुः -लुः -लु, शङ्की -ङ्किनी &c., अविश्वासी &c., कुतर्कशीलः -ला -लं, कुतर्कस्वभावः -वा -वं, अप्रत्ययी &c., कुहकचकितः -ता -तं.—(Giving rise to suspicion) शङ्कनीयः -या -यं, आशङ्कनीयः &c., शङ्काजनकः -का -कं, शङ्कापदः -दा -दं, शङ्कोत्पादकः &c., संशयजनकः &c., सन्देहजनकः &c., वितर्क्यः -र्क्या -र्क्यं, वितर्कणीयः -या -यं, शङ्कास्पदं, संशयास्पदं.—(Doubtful) सशङ्कः -ङ्का -ङ्कं, साशङ्कः &c., शङ्कितः -ता -तं, आशङ्कितः &c., *see* DOUBTFUL.

To SUSTAIN, *v. a.* धृ (c. 1. धरति, धर्त्तुं, c. 10. धारयति -यितुं), सन्धृ, अभिधृ, आलम्ब्, भृ (c. 1. भरति, c. 3. बिभर्त्ति, भर्त्तुं), सह्. *See To* SUPPORT, BEAR.

SUSTAINED, *p. p.* धृतः -ता -तं, भृतः &c., आलम्बितः &c. *See* SUPPORTED.

SUSTENANCE, *s.* आहारः, अन्नं, जीविका, उपजीविका. *See* SUPPORT.

SUTLEJ, *s.* (The River) शुतद्रुः.

SUTLER, *s.* सेनाचरः, सेनानुचरः, सेनानुचारी *m.* (न्).

SUTTEE, *s.* (Widow who burns herself) सती, अनुमृता.

SUTURE, *s.* सन्धिः *m.*, सेवनी, सीवनं; 'of the skull,' कपालसन्धिः *m.*, कपालसेवनी, तुन्नसेवनी.

To SWADDLE, *v. a.* दीर्घपट्टकैः परिवेष्ट् (c. 1. -वेष्टते -ष्टितुं) or वेष्ट्.

SWADDLING-CLOTHES, *s.* बालपरिवेष्टनं, शिशुपरिवेष्टनं, बालकवेष्टनं.

SWAG-BELLIED, *a.* लम्बोदरः -रा -रं. *See* POT-BELLIED.

To SWAGGER, *v. n.* *See To* BLUSTER, BULLY, BRAG, STRUT.

SWAIN, *s.* ग्राम्यजनः, क्षेत्री *m.* (न्), मेषपालकः. *See* COUNTRYMAN.

To SWALLOW, *v. a.* गॄ (c. 6. गिरति, गरितुं -रीतुं), निगॄ, अवगॄ, ग्रस् (c. 1. ग्रसते -सितुं), गरणं कृ, गिरणं कृ, निगरणं कृ, निगारं कृ, ग्रसनं कृ, ग्रासं कृ, गिलनं कृ.

SWALLOW, *s.* निगरणः, अन्नमार्गः, अन्नवाहिस्रोतस् *n.*

SWALLOWED, *p.p.* निगीर्णः -र्णा -र्णं, गीर्णः &c., गिरितः -ता -तं, निगिरितः &c., गिलितः -ता -तं, ग्रस्तः -स्ता -स्तं, ग्रसितः -ता -तं.

SWALLOWING, *s* (The act) गिरणं, गरणं, निगरणं, निगारः, निगरः, गीर्णिः *f.*, गिरिः *f.*, गरा, गिलनं, गिलिः *f.*, ग्रसनं, ग्रासः.

SWALLOW-WORT, *s.* (Plant) अर्कः, अर्कपत्रः, सूर्य्यः, मन्दारः, गणरूपः, अर्कपुष्पिका, आदित्यपुष्पिका, अर्कपर्णः, वसुकः, आस्फोतः, विकिरणः.

SWAMP, *s.* अनूपभूः *f.*, कच्छभूः *f.*, अनूपभूमिः *f.*, कच्छः. *See* MARSH.

To SWAMP, *v. a.* *See To* SINK, PLUNGE, OVERWHELM.

SWAMPY, *a.* अनूपः -पा -पं, कच्छः -च्छा -च्छं. *See* MARSHY.

SWAN, *s.* राजहंसः, हंसः, मृदुगमना.

SWARD, *s.* सतृणभूमितलं, तृणसभूमितलं, सतृणभूमिपृष्ठं.

SWARM, *s.* गणः, सङ्घः, वृन्दं, यूथं, कुलं, समूहः, मण्डलं, *see* MULTITUDE; 'of bees,' अलिवृन्दं, अलिकुलं, भ्रमरमण्डलं.

To SWARM, *v. n.* (Collect in crowds) समूहीभू, सङ्घशः समे, सङ्घशो गम् or या or इ, वृन्दीभू.—(Be crowded with) सङ्कीर्णः -र्णा -र्णं भू, आकीर्णः &c. भू, *see* the next.

SWARMING WITH, *a.* आकीर्णः -र्णा -र्णं, सङ्कीर्णः &c., व्याप्तः -प्ता -प्तं, गुप्तः -प्ता -प्तं, उपद्रुतः -ता -तं. *See* CROWDED.

SWARTHINESS, *s.* श्यामता -त्वं, श्यावता, कृष्णवर्णता, कृष्णता.

SWARTHY, *a.* श्यामः -मा -मं, श्यावः -वा -वं, कृष्णवर्णः -र्णा -र्णं.

To SWATHE, *v. a.* दीर्घपट्टकैः or दीर्घवस्त्रखण्डैः परिवेष्ट्.

SWATHE, *s.* दीर्घपट्टः -ट्टकः, परिवेष्टनं, दीर्घवस्त्रखण्डः.

SWATHED, *p. p.* परिवेष्टितः -ता -तं, दीर्घपट्टपरिवेष्टितः -ता -तं.

To SWAY, *v. a.* *See To* BIAS, INFLUENCE, RULE, WIELD.

To SWAY, *v. n.* नम्, आनम्, प्रलम्ब्. *See To* LEAN, INCLINE, *v. n.*

SWAY, *s.* *See* INFLUENCE, POWER, AUTHORITY, RULE.

To SWEAR, *v. n.* शप् (c. 1. शपति -ते, c. 4. शप्यति -ते, शप्तुं), अभिशप्, परिशप्, शपथं कृ, दिव्यं कृ, शपथं शप्; 'he swore by the king,' नृपेण or नृपे शपथं शेपे; 'to swear by heaven,' स्वर्गेण शप्; 'he swore to return,' पुनरागमनाय शपथं चकार; 'made to swear,' शापितः -ता -तं.

To SWEAR, *v. a.* (Cause to take an oath) शप् in caus. (शापयति -यितुं), शपथं or दिव्यं कृ in caus.—(Swear an oath) शपथं शप्.

SWEARER, *s.* शपथकृत्, शपथकर्त्ता *m.* (र्तृ), दिव्यकर्त्ता *m.*

SWEARING, *s.* शपथकरणं, दिव्यकरणं, शपनं, शापः, अभिशापः.

SWEAT, *s.* स्वेदः, घर्म्मः, निदाघः, स्यन्दं, प्रस्वेदः. *See* PERSPIRATION.

To SWEAT, *v.n.* स्विद् (c. 4. स्विद्यति -ते, स्वेत्तुं). *See To* PERSPIRE, *v. n.*

SWEATY, SWEATING, *a.* स्वेदितः -ता -तं, सस्वेदः -दा -दं, स्वेदवान् -वती &c., स्वेदाप्लुतः -ता -तं, घर्म्माप्लुतः &c., स्वेदबिन्दुाङ्कितः &c. *See* PERSPIRING.

To SWEEP, *v. a.* मृज् (c. 2. मार्ष्टि -ष्टुं, c. 1. मार्जति -जितुं), सम्मृज्, परिमृज्, प्रमृज्, आमृज्, मार्जनं कृ, सम्मार्जनं कृ, मार्जन्या or मार्जनयन्त्रेण शुध् (c. 10. शोधयति -यितुं); 'to sweep off or away,' अपमृज्, अवमृज्, *see To* CARRY OFF.

To SWEEP, *v. a.* (Pass with force) महावेगेन चल् or सृ or अतिक्रम्.

SWEEP, *s.* प्रसरः, प्रचरः. *See* COMPASS, RANGE, REACH.

SWEEPER, s. सम्मार्जकः, मार्जकः, अवस्करकः, मलाकर्षी m. (न्), खलपूः m., बहुकरः -रा -री, हड्डकः, हडिकः, अवकृष्टः. See SCAVENGER.

SWEEPING, s. मार्जनं -ना, सम्मार्जनं, परिमार्गः, मलापकर्षणं.

SWEEPINGS, s. pl. अवस्करः, अवकरः, सङ्कारः, सङ्करः, अपस्करः, मलं.

SWEET, a. (To the taste) स्वादुः -दुः -द्वी -दु, मधुरः -रा -रं, सुरसः -सा -सं, मधुः -ध्वी -धु, मिष्टः -ष्टा -ष्टं, वसुः -सुः -सु, मधुमान् -मती -मत् (त्), मधुमयः -यी -यं.—(Pleasing), see PLEASING, PLEASANT; 'a sweet song,' मधुरगीतं, कोमलगीतं -तकं.

SWEET, s. मधु n., मधुरं, मिष्टं, स्वाद्वन्नं, आस्वादः.—(Any thing pleasant) सुखं; 'the sweets of royalty,' राज्यसुखं.

To SWEETEN, v. a. स्वादूकृ, मधुरीकृ, मधुसात्कृ, मिष्टीकृ.

To SWEETEN, v. n. मधुरीभू, मिष्टीभू, मधुर (nom. मधुरायते).

SWEETENED, p. p. मिष्टीकृतः -ता -तं, मधुरीकृतः &c., मधुसाद्भूतः &c.

SWEETHEART, s. प्रियः -या, दयितः -ता, नायकः -यिका, कान्तः -न्ता.

SWEETISH, a. ईषन्मधुरः -रा -रं, ईषत्स्वादुः -दुः -द्वी -दु.

SWEETLY, adv. मधुरं, स्वादु, मधुर in comp. See PLEASINGLY.

SWEETMEAT, s. मोदकः -कं, मिष्टं, मिष्टान्नं, स्वाद्वन्नं, मधुमस्तकं, लडुकं, लड्डुकं, मण्डलं, वायनं, गुल्यः, प्रहेणकं.

SWEETNESS, s. मधुरता, माधुर्य्यं, स्वादुता, स्वाद्यं, सुरसता, मिष्टता, स्वादुः m., मधुरसः, कोमलता. See PLEASANTNESS.

SWEET-SMELLING, a. सुगन्धः -न्धा -न्धं, सुरभिः &c. See FRAGRANT.

SWEET-VOICED, SWEET-TONED, SWEET-SPEAKING, a. चारुस्वनः -ना -नं, मञ्जुस्वनः &c., सुस्वरः -रा -रं, मधुरस्वरः &c., मधुरभाषी -षिणी -षि (न्), मिष्टभाषी &c., प्रियवादी &c., प्रियंवदः -दा -दं.

To SWELL, v. n. श्वि (c. 1. श्वयति -यितुं or pass. शूयते), उच्छ्वि, स्फाय् (c. 1. स्फायते -यितुं), आस्फाय्, शूनीभू, स्फीतीभू, उच्छूनीभू, उच्छूनः -ना -नं भू, पुटवद् भू, वृध्, प्रवृध्, उत्सृप्, see To INCREASE, DILATE, HEAVE, v. n.; 'with air,' see To PUFF, v. n.

To SWELL, v. a. श्वि in caus. (श्वाययति -यितुं), उच्छ्वि in caus., स्फाय् in caus. (स्फावयति -यितुं), वृध् (c. 10. वर्धयति -यितुं), see To INCREASE, DILATE, v. a.

SWELLED, p. p. शूनः -ना -नं, उच्छूनः &c., स्फीतः &c. See SWOLLEN.

SWELLING, SWELL, s. (Tumour) शोथः, शोफः, श्वयथुः m., आध्मानं, मांसवृद्धिः f.; 'white swelling,' पूयालसः; 'of the glands of the neck,' गण्डमाला, see TUMOUR.—(Intumescence), see the word.—(Extension, increase, expansion) विस्तारः, वृद्धिः f., जृम्भः &c.—(Of the sea) ऊर्म्मिप्रलोठनं, ऊर्म्मिविभ्रमः, वानं, वारिराशिः m.

SWELLING, part. शूयमानः -ना -नं, उत्सर्पी -र्पिणी &c., प्रलोठितः -ता -तं.

SWEPT, p. p. मार्जितः -ता -तं, सम्मार्जितः -ता -तं, सम्मृष्टः -ष्टा -ष्टं; 'off,' अपमार्जितः -ता -तं; 'away,' अपहृतः -ता -तं.

To SWERVE, v. n. विचल् (c. 1. -चलति -लितुं), चल्, पराङ्मुखः -खा -खं भू, see To DEVIATE; 'he swerves from his duty,' स्वधर्म्माद्विचलति.

SWIFT, a. त्वरितः -ता -तं, शीघ्रः -घ्रा -घ्रं, शीघ्रगामी -मिनी -मि (न्), शीघ्रगतिः -तिः -ति, त्वरितगतिः &c., महावेगः -गा -गं, वेगवान् -वती -वत् (त्), द्रुतः -ता -तं, द्रुतगतिः -तिः -ति, त्वरान्वितः -ता -तं, लघुगामी &c., जववान् &c., जवी &c., तरस्वी &c., तूर्णः -र्णा -र्णं, प्रतूर्णः &c., वेगवाही &c., क्षिप्रगतिः &c., see QUICK, RAPID; 'as the wind,' वायुवेगसमः -मा -मं, वायुगतिः -तिः -ति.

SWIFTLY, adv. शीघ्रं, त्वरितं, सत्वरं. See QUICKLY, RAPIDLY.

SWIFTNESS, s. शीघ्रता, वेगः, जवः, सौष्ठवं. See RAPIDITY.

To SWIG, SWILL, v. a. अतिपानं कृ, अतिशयपानं कृ, बहुशः पा.

To SWIM, v. a. (Pass a river, &c., by moving the arms in water) बाहुभ्यां नदीं तॄ (c. 1. तरति -रितुं -रीतुं) or नदीतरणं कृ.

To SWIM, v. n. (Move along in water by means of the arms) बाहुभ्यां तरणं कृ, बाहुभ्यां जले सृ (c. 1. सरति, सर्तुं) or विसृ; 'as a fish,' मत्स्यवद् जले विसृ; 'unable to swim,' तरणविद्यायाम् अकुशलः, अप्रवेशः.—(Float) प्लु (c. 1. प्लवते, प्लोतुं), see To FLOAT.

SWIMMER, s. तरणकर्त्ता m. (र्त्तृ), तरणकृत्, प्लवनकृत्.

SWIMMING, s. तरणं, प्लवनं, जलविसरणं, बाहुभ्यां तरणं, बाहुतरणं; 'swimming across a river,' बाहुभ्यां नदीतरणं; 'swimming against the stream,' स्रोतःप्रतीपतरणं, स्रोतःप्रतिकूलतरणं.

SWIMMING, part. जलविसारी -रिणी -रि (न्), प्लवमानः -ना -नं.

To SWINDLE, v. a. or n. प्रतॄ, वञ्च्, परिवञ्च्, छलेन हृ or अपहृ.

SWINDLER, s. प्रतारकः, परस्वापहारी m. (न्), चाटः, पार्श्विकः.

SWINE, s. शूकरः, सूकरः, शूकराः m. pl. See HOG.

To SWING, v. a. इतस्ततो विचल् (c. 10. -चालयति -यितुं) or सञ्चल् or चल्, प्रेङ्ख् (c. 10. प्रेङ्खयति -यितुं), आन्दोलनं कृ, आन्दोल (nom. आन्दोलयति -यितुं), प्रेङ्खोल (nom. प्रेङ्खोलयति -यितुं), प्रेङ्खोलनं कृ.

To SWING, v. n. इतस्ततो विचल् (c. 1. -चलति -लितुं) or सञ्चल् or चल्, दोल (nom. दोलायते -यितुं). See To OSCILLATE.

SWING, s. (Oscillation) आन्दोलनं, प्रेङ्खोलनं, प्रेङ्खणं, इतस्ततो विचलनं.—(Seat, line and other apparatus for swinging) दोला -ली -लं, दोलिका, प्रेङ्खा, प्रेङ्खोलनं, हिन्दोलः -लकः, खट्वा, आन्दोलनं, काचः; 'suspended in a swing,' काचितः -ता -तं, शिक्यितः &c.—(Impetus) वेगः.

SWINGING, part. दोलायमानः -ना -नं, दोदुल्यमानः -ना -नं, प्रेङ्खन् -ङ्खन्ती -ङ्खत् (त्), प्रेङ्खितः -ता -तं, प्रेङ्खोलितः &c., विचलमानः -ना -नं, विचलन् &c., प्रचलितः -ता -तं, काचितः -ता -तं, शिक्यितः &c.

SWINISH, a. सौकरः -री -रं, शौकरः &c., सूकरवृत्तिः -त्तिः -त्ति, शूकरसदृशः -शी -शं, शूकरशीलः -ला -लं, शूकरबुद्धिः -द्धिः -द्धि.

SWITCH, s. पिच्छा, शिथिलदण्डः, कोमलदण्डः, मृदुपल्लवः.

SWIVEL, s. परिवर्त्तनवलयः, भ्रमवलयः, परिवर्त्तननाडिः f.

SWOLLEN, p. p. शूनः -ना -नं, उच्छूनः &c., प्रोच्छूनः &c., संशूनः &c., शोथयुक्तः -क्ता -क्तं, शोफयुक्तः &c., स्फीतः -ता -तं, स्फातः &c., प्रवृद्धः -द्धा -द्धं, प्रस्फुरितः -ता -तं. See INCREASED, DILATED.

To SWOON, v. n. मुर्छ् (c. 1. मूर्च्छति -र्च्छितुं). See To FAINT.

SWOON, s. मूर्च्छा, मूर्च्छनं -ना, मोहः. See FAINTING, s.

SWOONED, p. p. मूर्च्छितः -ता -तं, मूर्च्छापन्नः -न्ना -न्नं. See FAINTED.

SWOONING, part. मूर्च्छितः -ता -तं, गतचेतनः &c., see FAINTING, part.

SWOOP, s. आकस्मिकावपातपूर्व्वं नखैर् ग्रहणं, अकस्माद् ग्रहणं, अकस्माद् अवपातः, अकस्माद् आक्रमणं; 'of a hawk,' श्येनावपातः.

SWORD, s. खड्गः, असिः m., कृपाणः, निस्त्रिंशः, शिरिः m., रिष्टिः m., ऋष्टिः m., पारेरकः; 'sword in hand,' खड्गपाणिः m., कृपाणपाणिः m., खड्गहस्तः; 'having a drawn sword in the hand,' आकृष्टकृपाणपाणिः; 'armed with a sword,' see SWORD-MAN; 'edge of a sword,' असिधारा; 'blade of a sword,' असिपत्रं; 'hilt of a sword,' त्सरुः m.; 'sword-exercise,' खड्गमार्गः, त्सरुमार्गः; 'sword-cut,' खड्गप्रहारः, खड्गाघातः; 'sword-bearer,' खड्गधारी m. (न्); 'sword-belt, or sword-knot,' मेखला, त्सरुनिबन्धनं; 'sword-stick,' कूटः -टं, कूटास्त्रं.

SWORD-MAN, s. खड्गी m. (न्), खड्गधरः, खड्गधारी m. (न्), सखड्गः,

असिभृत् *m.*, आसिकः, असिहेतिः *m.*, नैस्त्रिंशिकः.

Sworn, *p.p.* शापितः -ता -तं, कृतशपथः -था -थं, कृतशापः -पा -पं.

Swung, *p.p.* आन्दोलितः -ता -तं, प्रेङ्खितः &c., प्रेङ्खोलितः -ता -तं.

Sycophancy, *s.* अयनुरोधः, छन्दोनुरोधः, छन्दोनुवृत्तिः, *see* Servility.

Sycophant, *s.* अयनुरोधी *m.* (न्), छन्दोनुरोधी *m.* *See* Servile.

Syllabic, *a.* अक्षरसम्बन्धी -न्धिनी -न्धि (न्), आक्षरिकः -की -कं.

Syllable, *s.* अक्षरं; 'monosyllable,' एकाक्षरं, *see* the word.

Syllabub, *s.* दुग्धफेनं, दुग्धतालीयं, क्षीरफेनं, शाकैकः, शाकेरः.

Syllabus, *s.* सारः, सारार्थः, ग्रन्थसारः, सारांशः. *See* Compendium.

Syllogism, *s.* न्यायः, अवयवी *m.* (न्), अवयवघटितवाक्यं, अवयवयुक्तवाक्यं, अवयवोपेतवाक्यं, आनुपूर्व्यं. A syllogism has five members or अवयवाः, according to the Nyáya system, viz. 1. The proposition or assertion to be proved, प्रतिज्ञा; 2. the reason given, हेतुः; 3. the example or illustration, उदाहरणं; 4. the application, उपनयः; 5. the conclusion, निगमनं. Thus, 1. 'The hill is fiery,' पर्व्वतो वह्निमान्. 2. 'Because it smokes,' धूमवत्त्वात्. 3. 'Whatever smokes is fiery, like a culinary hearth,' यो यो धूमवान् स वह्निमान् यथा महानसः. 4. 'This (hill) has smoke which is always accompanied with fire,' वह्निव्याप्यधूमवान् अयं. 5. 'Therefore it is fiery,' तस्माद् वह्निमान्. According to the Mímánsá school, a syllogism has only the last three members.

Syllogistic, *a.* न्यायसम्बन्धी -न्धिनी -न्धि (न्), न्यायविषयकः -का -कं, न्यायरूपः -पा -पं, नैयायिकः -की -कं, अवयवयुक्तवाक्यसम्बन्धी &c.

Sylph, *s.* तन्वङ्गी, लघ्वङ्गी, लघ्वी, तनुमध्या, विद्याधरी.

Sylvan, *a.* वन्यः -न्या -न्यं, वानः -नी -नं, वनजः &c., *see* Silvan.

Symbol, *s.* लक्षणं, चिह्नं, लिङ्गं, संज्ञा. *See* Emblem, Sign.

Symbolical, *a.* लाक्षणिकः -की -कं, साङ्केतिकः -की -कं, सङ्केतात्मकः -का -कं, सङ्केतरूपः -पा -पं, उद्बोधकः -का -कं, प्रदर्शकः &c., प्रतिरूपकः &c.

Symmetrical, *a.* शुद्धरूपः -पा -पं, शुद्धाकारः -रा -रं, शुद्धरेखः -खा -खं, युक्तरूपः -पी -पं, सम्मितरूपः &c., रूपवान् -वती -वत् (त्).

Symmetry, *s.* आकारशुद्धिः *f.*, आकारशुद्धता, अङ्गसंयोगः, अवयवसंयोगः, अङ्गसंहतिः *f.*, अवयवसंहतिः *f.*, आकारसम्मितिः *f.*

Sympathetic, *a.* समदुःखः -खा -खं, समदुःखी -खिनी -खि (न्), सहदुःखी &c., समदुःखसुखः -खा -खं, समवेदनः -ना -नं. *See* Sympathizing.

To sympathize, *v. n.* समदुःखी -खिनी -खि भू, समदुःखसुखोपहतः -ता -तं भू, समदुःखसुखी &c. भू, अन्येन सह दुःखी -खिनी भू, अन्येन सह सुखी -खिनी भू, परदुःखसुखसहभागी -गिनी भू.

Sympathizing, *part.* or *a.* समदुःखसुखः -खा -खं, एकदुःखसुखः &c., समदुःखी -खिनी -खि (न्), सहदुःखी &c., सहसुखी &c., अन्यदुःखसुखभागी &c., परदुःखसुखभागी &c., परदुःखदुःखी &c., परसुखसुखी &c., समदुःखः &c.

Sympathy, *s.* समदुःखत्वं, समदुःखिता, सहदुःखिता -त्वं, समदुःखसुखिता, अन्यदुःखदुःखिता, परदुःखदुःखिता, अन्यदुःखदुःखं, अनुवेदना, कारुण्यं, अनुकम्पा; 'joyful sympathy,' सुखसुखिता, अनुमोदनं.—(Conformity of temperament) आनुगुण्यं, स्वभावसमता, स्वभावानुगुण्यं, समभावः, भावसाम्यं, प्रकृतिसाम्यं, आनुरूप्यं, साधर्म्यं.

Symphonious, *a.* समस्वरः -रा -रं, समानस्वरः &c. *See* Harmonious.

Symphony, *s.* स्वरैक्यं, स्वरसमता, तालसमता, स्वरसाम्यं, स्वरमेलनं, तानमेलनं, तानमानं, *see* Harmony.—(Air) चर्चरी.

Symptom, *s.* लक्षणं, पूर्व्वलक्षणं, चिह्नं, पूर्व्वचिह्नं, सूचना, प्रज्ञानं, कान्तारं, *see* Indication, Sign; 'of disease,' रोगलक्षणं, लक्षणं, विसूचिका; 'secondary symptom,' अनुबन्धः.

Symptomatic, *a.* सूचकः -का -कं, प्रदर्शकः -का -कं, उद्बोधकः &c., बोधकः &c., लाक्षणिकः -की -कं. *See* Indicative.

Synagogue, *s.* यिहुदीयानां भजनभवनं or पूजामन्दिरं.

Synchronism, *s.* समकालिकता, कालैक्यं, यौगपद्यं, एककालिकता.

To synchronize, *v. n.* एककाले सम्भू or सम्पद्, एकसमये सम्भू, समकाले भू, समकालिकः -का -कं भू or अस्. *See* Simultaneous.

Synchronous, *a.* समकालिकः -की -कं. *See* Simultaneous.

To syncopate, *v.a.* मध्याक्षरं लुप् (c. 6. लुम्पति, लोप्तुं), मध्याक्षरलोपं कृ.

Syncope, *s.* (Fainting) मूर्च्छना.—(In grammar) मध्याक्षरलोपः.

Synecdoche, *s.* (Figure in rhetoric) उपलक्षणं.

Synod, *s.* धर्म्माध्यक्षसभा, धर्म्मोपदेशकसभा, धर्म्मसभा.

Synodal, synodical, *a.* सभ्यः -भ्या -भ्यं; 'month,' चन्द्रमासः.

Synonym, *s.* पर्य्यायः, अपरपर्य्यायः, एकार्थपदं, समानार्थशब्दः, समार्थकशब्दः, तुल्यार्थकशब्दः, उपशब्दः.

Synonymous, *a.* समानार्थः -र्था -र्थं, एकार्थः &c., एकार्थकः -का -कं, तुल्यार्थकः &c., सहार्थः -र्था -र्थं.

Synonymy, *s.* समानार्थत्वं, समार्थत्वं, एकार्थत्वं, तुल्यार्थत्वं.

Synopsis, *s.* ग्रन्थसारात्मकपत्रं, सारपत्रकं. *See* Epitome.

Syntactical, *a.* वाक्यविन्याससम्बन्धी &c., वाक्यरचनाविषयकः -का -कं, पदविन्यासविषयकः &c.; 'syntactical agreement,' अन्वयः.

Syntax, *s.* वाक्यविन्यासः, वाक्यरचना, पदविन्यासः, पदरचना, पदयोजना, वाक्ययोजना, पदान्वयः, अन्वययोजना.

Synthesis, *s.* संयोगः, संयोजनं, योगकरणं. *See* Combination.

Synthetical, *a.* संयोगरूपः -पा -पं, संयोगात्मकः &c., संयोगकारी &c.

Syphilis, *s.* उपदंशः, वृषणकच्छूः *f.* *See* Lues venerea.

Syphon, *s.* *See* Siphon.

Syringe, *s.* वस्तिः *m. f.*, नलिका, अन्तःप्रक्षेपणी. *See* Squirt.

To syringe, *v. a.* वस्तिद्वारेण जलादि अन्तःप्रक्षिप्, अन्तः शुध्.

Syrup, *s.* मधुरं, मधु *n.*, इक्षुरसः, इक्षुरसजः, लेह्यं.

System, *s.* (Plan) कल्पना, अनुसन्धानं, *see* Scheme.—(Method) क्रमः, पर्य्यायः, *see* Method.—(Of the body, constitution) शरीरप्रकृतिः *f.*, देहप्रकृतिः *f.*, प्रकृतिः *f.*, भावः, शरीरं.—(Assemblage of parts adjusted into a regular whole) रीतिः *f.*, स्थितिः *f.*, संस्थानं, संस्थितिः *f.*, मार्गः, क्रमः.—(Systems of philosophy). These are six, *see* under School. The three leading systems are the Nyáya, Vedánta, and Sánkhya.

Systematic, systematically, *see* Methodical, &c.

To systematize, systemize, *v. a.* *See To* methodize.

Systole, *s.* (In anatomy) हृत्पिण्डसङ्कोचः.

T.

Tabosheer, *s.* (Manna of the bamboo) वंशक्षीरी, वंशरोचना, वंशलोचना, त्वक्क्षीरा -री, कर्म्मरी.

Tabby, *a.* चित्रः -त्रा -त्रं, शबलः -ला -लं. *See* Brindled.

Tabernacle, *s.* मण्डपः, दूष्यं, पटमण्डपः. *See* Tent.

Tabes, *s.* क्षयः, क्षयरोगः, क्षयथुः *m.*, शरीरशोषणं.

Table, *s.* (For holding dishes, &c.) फलकः -कं, भोजनफलकः -कं, भोजनाधारः, भोजनासनं, मञ्चः -ञ्चकः, भोजनमञ्चः; 'writing table,'

लिखनफलकं, लिपिफलकं, लिपिसन्नाधारः, लेखसाधनाधारः.—(Persons eating at the same table) सहभोजिनां पंक्तिः *f.*; 'unworthy of eating at the same table with the good,' सद्भिः सह एकपंक्तिभोजनानर्हः -र्हा -र्हं.—(Of stone, metal, &c., for writing) पट्टः, प्रस्तरः, पत्रं -त्रिका.—(Tabular view) पत्रकं, सारणी, प्रस्तरः, चक्रं, *see* SYNOPSIS; 'table of numbers, figures, &c.,' अङ्कजालं, सारणी, कोष्ठकं.—(Table of contents) अनुक्रमणिका, सूचीपत्रं, सूची -चिका, पत्रपञ्जी.

TABLE-CLOTH, *s.* फलकाच्छादनं, फलकावरणं, फलकाच्छादनपटः.

TABLE-LAND, *s.* सानुः -नु *m. n.*, अधित्यका, प्रस्थः, समस्थलं, पर्वतभूमिका, भृगुः *m.*, कटकः, स्नुः *m.*, स्नु *n.*

TABLET, *s.* पत्रं, पत्रिका, पत्रकं, पट्टः, फलकः -कं, प्रस्तरः.

To TABOO, *v. a.* उपभोगासेधं कृ, भोगासेधं कृ. *See To* INTERDICT.

TABOR, *s.* मृदङ्गः, पटहः, पणवः, प्रणवः, आंकी. *See* DRUM.

TABULAR, *a.* पत्रस्थः -स्था -स्थं, पत्रकारूढः -ढा -ढं, फलकस्थः &c.

TACIT, *a.* विवक्षितः -ता -तं, अर्थसिद्धः -द्धा -द्धं, ध्वनितः &c., अनिषेधरूपः &c., मानसः -सी -सं; 'tacit consent,' मानसानुज्ञा, मानसं.

TACITLY, *adv.* विवक्षया, अनिषेधेन, मनसा, ध्वनितार्थतस्, तूष्णीं.

TACITURN, *a.* अनालापशीलः -ला -लं, अल्पवादी -दिनी &c., तूष्णींशीलः -ला -लं, कथाविरक्तः -क्ता -क्तं, आलापविमुखः -खा -खं, भाषणविरक्तः &c., परिमितकथः &c., मौनी &c., अनालापः -पा -पं, तूष्णीकः -का -कं. *See* RESERVED.

TACITURNITY, *s.* आलापविरक्तिः *f.*, अनालापशीलता, अनालापः -पिता, मौनित्वं, मौनं, कथाविरक्तिः *f.*, वाग्यामः. *See* RESERVE.

To TACK, *v. a.* (Fasten, attach) अनुबन्ध् (c. 9. -बध्नाति -बन्द्धुं), आबन्ध्, पिनह्, आनह्, *see To* FASTEN, STITCH.

To TACK, *v. n.* नौमार्गं परिवृत् in caus., नौमार्गपरिवर्त्तनं कृ.

TACK, *s.* (Small nail) क्षुद्रकीलः, कीलकः, क्षुद्रशङ्कुः *m.*

TACKING, *s.* नौमार्गपरिवर्त्तनं, नौमार्गपरिवृत्तिः *f.*, नौपथपरिवृत्तिः.

TACKLE, TACKLING, *s.* नौकासज्जा, नौसज्जा, सज्जा. *See* RIGGING.

To TACKLE, *v. a.* *See To* HARNESS, RIG, SEIZE, LAY HOLD.

TACT, *s.* युक्तिः *f.*, कुशलता, कौशल्यं, विज्ञता, अभिज्ञता. *See* SKILL.

TACTICIAN, *s.* व्यूहरचनकुशलः, व्यूहरचनाभिज्ञः, व्यूहपण्डितः.

TACTICS, *s.* व्यूहरचनविद्या, बलविन्यासविद्या, सैन्यविन्यासविद्या, व्यूहरचना, सैन्यरचना, व्यूहनं.

TACTILE, *a.* स्पर्शनीयः -या -यं, स्पृश्यः -श्या -श्यं. *See* TANGIBLE.

TADPOLE, *s.* भेकशावकः, मण्डूकशावकः, बालमण्डूकः.

TAIL, *s.* पुच्छः -च्छं, लाङ्गूलं, लाङ्गुलं, लङ्गूलं, वालः -ला, वालधिः *m.*, वालहस्तः, लूमं, लोमः, पिच्छः, लञ्जः; 'peacock's tail,' बर्हः -र्हं, पिच्छं, कलापः, मयूरपुच्छं, प्रचलाकः; 'to lift up the tail,' उत्पुच्छ (Nom. उत्पुच्छयते).

TAILED, *a.* पुच्छी -च्छिनी -च्छि (न्), पुच्छवान् -वती -वत् (त्), पिच्छवान् &c., पुच्छान्वितः -ता -तं, लाङ्गूली &c., पिच्छिलः -ला -लं.

TAIL-LESS, *a.* अपुच्छः -च्छा -च्छं, पुच्छहीनः -ना -नं, पुच्छरहितः &c.

TAILOR, *s.* सौचिकः, सूचिकः, सौचिः *m.*, तुन्नवायः, वस्त्रभेदी *m.* (न्), वस्त्रभेदकः, सूचिकर्म्मविद् *m.*

To TAINT, *v. a.* दुष् (c. 10. दूषयति -यितुं), लिप् (c. 6. लिम्पति, लेप्तुं), दोषयुक्तं -क्तां कृ, दूषणं कृ. *See To* CORRUPT, INSPECT, STAIN.

TAINT, *s.* दूषणं, दोषः, कलङ्कः, मलं, लेपः -पनं. *See* STAIN.

TAINTED, *p. p.* दूषितः -ता -तं, लिप्तः -प्ता -प्तं, कलङ्कितः -ता -तं, सकलङ्कः -ङ्का -ङ्कं; 'as meat,' पूतिगन्धिकः -का -कं, दुर्गन्धी -न्धिनी &c.

To TAKE, *v. a.* ग्रह् (c. 9. गृह्णाति -ह्णीते, ग्रहीतुं), प्रतिग्रह्, अभिग्रह्, परिग्रह्, सम्प्रग्रह्, उपसम्प्रग्रह्, आदा (c. 3. -ददाति -दत्ते -दातुं), उपादा, लभ् (c. 1. लभते, लब्धुं), उपलभ्, धा (c. 3. धत्ते, धातुं), प्रतीष् (c. 6. -इच्छति -एषितुं), ग्रहणं कृ, आदानं कृ.—(Seize) हृ (c. 1. हरति, हर्त्तुं), धृ (c. 1. धरति, धर्त्तुं), हरणं कृ.—(Captivate), *see* the word.—(Apprehend) ग्रह्, उपलभ्, अवगम्.—(Feel, experience, be affected by) उपहतः -ता -तं भू, अनुभू, उपगम्, उपागम्, विद्.—(Swallow) गृ, निगृ, ग्रस्, खाद्, पा.—(Admit) ग्रह्, स्वीकृ, अङ्गीकृ.—(Gain possession of) आप्, प्राप्, अर्ज्, उपार्ज्, लभ्, आसद्, अधिगम्, *see To* GAIN.—(Take possession of) आक्रम् (c. 1. -क्रामति -क्रमितुं), आविश्, समाविश्.—(Require) आकाङ्क्ष्, *see To* REQUIRE.—(Take away) अपनी (c. 1. -नयति -नेतुं), नी, अपहृ, हृ, *see To* REMOVE, *v. a.*—(Take back) प्रत्यादा; 'lead back,' प्रतिनी.—(Take down), *see To* PULL DOWN, DEPRESS, WRITE.—(Take in), *see To* COMPREHEND, CHEAT.—(Take off) अपनी, अवतॄ or उत्तॄ in caus., उत्कृष्, *see To* STRIP, DIVEST, IMITATE.—(Take up), *see To* LIFT, UNDERTAKE, OCCUPY, ENGROSS, COMPRISE.—(Take upon one's self) स्वीकृ, *see To* UNDERTAKE. Obs. The word 'take' in English has often no equivalent in Sanskrit, but must be rendered by some other form of expression. It may often be expressed by the roots कृ or भू in conjunction with a noun, and is not unfrequently inherent in the verb without being expressed at all, as in the following examples.—(Take aim) बद्धानुशयः -या -यं भू, लक्ष्यीकृ, अनुसन्धा.—(Take an airing) वायुहेतोः परिक्रम् or विहृ.—(Take breath), *see To* PAUSE, REST.—(Take care, take heed), *see To* HEED.—(Take care of) रक्ष्, *see* under CARE.—(Take a course), *see To* RESORT.—(Take effect) प्रभू, सप्रभावः -वा -वं भू, प्रबलीभू, सफलीभू, *see* EFFICACIOUS.—(Take hold), *see To* SEIZE, HOLD.—(Take in hand), *see To* UNDERTAKE.—(Take leave) आमन्त्र्, आमन्त्रणं कृ, *see* FAREWELL.—(Take notice), *see To* OBSERVE, NOTICE.—(Take pains), *see* under PAIN.—(Take part), *see To* SHARE.—(Take place), *see To* HAPPEN.—(Take root), *see To* ROOT, *v. n.*—(Take to task) निर्भर्त्स्, *see To* REPROVE.—(Take the name) नाम ग्रह्.

To TAKE, *v. n.* (Betake one's self) आश्रि, *see* RECOURSE, RESORT.—(Gain reception, succeed) सिध् (c. 4. सिध्यति, सेद्धुं), सम्पद् (c. 4. -पद्यते -पत्तुं), प्रसिद्धिं प्राप्, प्रसिद्धीभू, लोकप्रसिद्धः -द्धा -द्धं भू.—(Have effect) प्रभू.—(Take after) अनुकृ.

TAKEN, *p. p.* गृहीतः -ता -तं, आदत्तः -त्ता -त्तं, आत्तः &c., उपात्तः &c.—(Gained) प्राप्तः -प्ता -प्तं, आप्तः &c., लब्धः -ब्धा -ब्धं.—(Taken away) अपनीतः -ता -तं, अपहृतः -ता -तं, हृतः &c., *see* REMOVED.—(Taken down) अवपातितः -ता -तं, पातितः -ता -तं, *see* LOWERED, HUMBLED.—(Taken off, as clothes, &c.) अवतारितः -ता -तं, *see* STRIPPED.—(Captivated) मोहितः -ता -तं, हृतचित्तः -त्ता -त्तं, वशीकृतः &c.; 'let it be taken,' गृह्यतां; 'proper to be taken,' ग्रहणीयः -या -यं, आदेयः -या -यं; 'having taken,' गृहीत्वा, आदाय; 'having taken his bow and arrow,' गृहीतेषुकार्म्मुकः, आत्तेषुकार्म्मुकः.

TAKER, *s.* ग्राही *m.* -हिणी *f.* (न्), ग्राहकः -हिका, ग्रहीता *m.* -त्री *f.* (तृ), आदायी *m.* -यिनी *f.*, प्रतिग्रहीता *m.*, हर्त्ता *m.*, हारी *m.*

TAKING, *s.* (The act) ग्रहणं, ग्रहः, ग्राहः, प्रतिग्रहणं, प्रतिग्राहः, आदानं, उपादानं, स्वीकरणं, स्वीकारः; 'taking away,' अपनयनं, हरणं, अपहरणं, *see* REMOVAL.

TAKING, *a.* मनोहारी -रिणी &c., हृदयग्राही &c. *See* CAPTIVATING.

TALC, *s.* अभ्रकं, अभ्रं, अमलं, निर्मलं, गिरिजं, गिरिजामलं, मेघजालं, मेघनालं, शुभ्रं, स्वच्छपत्रं, अम्बरं, अन्तरीक्षं, भृङ्गं; 'calx of it,' अभ्रकभस्म *m.* (न्).

TALE, *s.* कथा, उपाख्यानं, आख्यानं, परिकथा, उदन्तः. *See* STORY.

TALE-BEARER, *s.* कर्णेजपः, कर्णजपः, उपजापकः, पिशुनः, भेदजनकः.

TALE-BEARING, *s.* पैशुन्यं, पिशुनता, उपजापः, कर्णेजापः, दोषानुवादः.

TALENT, *s.* (Endowment) गुणः.—(Great abilities) बुद्धिवैभवं, बुद्धिकौशलं, धीशक्तिः *f.*, बुद्धिप्रभावः, दाक्षिण्यं, *see* GENIUS.

TALENTED, *a.* गुणी -णिनी -णि (न्), गुणवान् &c. *See* under GENIUS.

TALISMAN, *s.* कवचः -चं, संवदनं -ना, यन्त्रं. *See* AMULET.

To TALK, *v. n.* भाष् (c. 1. भाषते -षितुं), सम्भाष्, वद् (c. 1. वदति -दितुं), संवद्, आलप्, मन्त्र्, कथोपकथनं कृ. *See To* CONVERSE.

TALK, *s.* कथोपकथनं, संवादः, सम्भाषा -षणं, आलापः, कथा, कथाप्रसङ्गः, *see* CONVERSATION; 'small talk,' लघुभाषणं; 'fine talk,' शब्दपाण्डित्यं; 'mere talk,' वाङ्मात्रं.—(Report) वदन्तिः -न्ती *f.*

TALKATIVE, *a.* वावदूकः -का -कं, कथनः &c. *See* LOQUACIOUS.

TALKATIVENESS, *s.* वावदूकता, वाचालता. *See* LOQUACIOUSNESS.

TALKER, *s.* वक्ता *m.* (कृ), कथकः, भाषी *m.* (न्), आलापी *m.*, वादी *m.*

TALL, *a.* तुङ्गः -ङ्गा -ङ्गं, उत्तुङ्गः &c., प्रांशुः -शुः -शु, उच्चः -च्चा -च्चं, *see* HIGH; 'in stature,' उच्चदेहः -हा -हं, उच्चमूर्त्तिः -र्त्तिः -र्त्ति, दीर्घदेहः -हा -हं, दीर्घमूर्त्तिः &c., दीर्घतनुः -नुः -नु.

TALLNESS, *s.* उच्चता, तुङ्गता, प्रांशुता, उन्नतिः *f.*; 'of stature,' देहदीर्घता, दीर्घदेहत्वं, शरीरदीर्घता, शरीरोच्चता.

TALLOW, *s.* मेषवपा, मेषवसा, गोवपा, गोवसा, गोमेदस् *n.*

TALLOW-CANDLE, *s.* गोवपामयदीपकः, गोवसानिर्म्मितदीपिका.

TALLOW-CHANDLER, *s.* गोवपाविक्रयी *m.* (न्), मेघादिवपाव्यापारी *m.*

TALLY, *To* TALLY. *See* MATCH, *To* MATCH, *v. n.*

TALON, *s.* नखः, नखरः, कररुहः, करजः. *See* CLAW.

TAMARIND, *s.* (The tree) अम्लिका, अम्लीका, आम्लिका, आम्लीका, अम्लफलः, तिन्तिडी, तिन्तिली, तिन्तिडीकः -का -कं, तिन्तिडिका, चिञ्चा, चुक्रा -क्री, गुरुपत्रा, चारित्रा, चरित्रा, गुरुपत्ना, चक्रः.—(The fruit) अम्लफलं.

TAMARISK, TAMARIX, *s.* (Tree) पिचुलः, पिच्छिलः, झावुः *m.*, झावुकः, बहुग्रन्थिः *m.*, यमदूतका.

TAMBOUR, TAMBOURINE, *s.* मृदङ्गः, पटहः. *See* DRUM.

TAME, *a.* (Not wild) गृह्यः -ह्या -ह्यं, गृहकः -का -कं, ग्राम्यः -म्या -म्यं, गृहपुष्टः -ष्टा -ष्टं, छेकः -का -कं, अहिंस्रः -स्रा -स्रं, गृह or ग्राम in comp.; 'a tame pigeon,' गृहकपोतकः; 'tame hog,' ग्राम्यशूकरः, ग्रामशूकरः, विड्वराहः.—(Subdued, trained) दान्तः -न्ता -न्तं, दमितः -ता -तं, वश्यः -श्या -श्यं, अधीनः -ना -नं, शिक्षितः -ता -तं, उपशान्तः &c.—(Flat, spiritless), *see* the words.

To TAME, *v. a.* दम् (c. 10. दमयति -यितुं), प्रदम्, क्रूरतां शम् (c. 10. शमयति -यितुं), क्रूरताशान्तिं कृ, क्रूरतानाशं कृ, क्रूरताभङ्गं कृ, वशीकृ, निग्रह् (c. 9. -गृह्णाति -ग्रहीतुं), अभिग्रह्.

TAMEABLE, *a.* दमनीयः -या -यं, दम्यः -म्या -म्यं, सुदमः -मा -मं.

TAMED, *p. p.* दमितः -ता -तं, दान्तः -न्ता -न्तं, वशीकृतः -ता -तं, वशीभूतः &c., वशङ्गतः &c., शान्तः &c., शान्तक्रौर्य्यः -र्य्या -र्य्यं.

TAMELY, *adv.* कापुरुषवत्, क्लीववत्, कातरवत्, सकातर्य्यं.

TAMENESS, *s.* गृह्यता, वश्यता, वश्यता, अहिंस्रता, वशीभूतता.

TAMER, *s.* दमकः, दमी *m.* (न्), दमनकारी *m.* *See* SUBDUER.

TAMING, *s.* दमनं, दमः, दमथः -थं, दमथुः *m.* *See* SUBJUGATION.

To TAMPER, *v. a.* (Meddle), *see To* MEDDLE.—(Practise secretly) कुकर्म्मसम्पादनार्थं गूढव्यवहारं कृ or गूढव्यापारं कृ or गूढसंसर्गं कृ, छलेन व्यापृ in pass. or व्यवहृ.

To TAN, *v. a.* (Leather) चर्म्मसन्धानं कृ, चर्म्मपाचनं कृ, दृतिसन्धानं कृ.—(Imbrown) ताम्रीकृ, ताम्रवर्णीकृ, श्यामीकृ.

TAN-PIT, *s.* चर्म्मसन्धानभाण्डं, चर्म्मपाचनभाण्डं, चर्म्मपाचनकुण्डं.

TANGENT, *s.* (In geometry) स्पर्शरेखा, सम्पातरेखा.

TANGIBILITY, *s.* स्पर्शनीयता, स्पृश्यता, स्पर्शवेद्यता.

TANGIBLE, *a.* स्पर्शनीयः -या -यं, स्पृश्यः -श्या -श्यं, संस्पृश्यः &c., स्प्रष्टव्यः -व्या -व्यं, स्पर्शयोग्यः &c., स्पर्शार्हः -र्हा -र्हं, स्पर्शवेद्यः &c., सम्पर्कीयः &c.

To TANGLE, TANGLE, &c. *See To* ENTANGLE, ENTANGLEMENT, &c.

TANJORE, *s.* (The country) चोलः, चोलाः *m. pl.*

TANK, *s.* तडागः, जलाधारः, सरोवरः, वेशन्तः. *See* RESERVOIR.

TANNER, *s.* चर्म्मकारः -री *m.* (न्), चर्म्मारः, चर्म्मसन्धानी *m.*

To TANTALIZE, *v. a.* इष्टवस्तु दर्शयित्वा मनोरथान् जनयित्वा खण्ड् (c. 10. खण्डयति -यितुं), आशाः or मनोरथान् जनयित्वा खण्ड्, स्पृहणीयवस्तु दर्शयित्वा न दा or भग्नाशं -शां कृ or वञ्च् (c. 10. वञ्चयति -यितुं).

TANTALIZED, *p. p.* वञ्चितः -ता -तं, खण्डितः &c., भग्नाशः -शा -शं.

TANTALIZING, *a.* आशाजनकः -का -कं, स्पृहाजनकः &c., वञ्चकः &c.

TANTAMOUNT, *a.* समानार्थकः -का -कं, सममूल्यः &c. *See* EQUIVALENT.

TANTRA, *s.* (A religious treatise, generally in the form of a dialogue between Śiva and Durga, teaching peculiar and mystical formulæ for the worship of the deities, or the attainment of superhuman power. These works are very numerous, and their authority in many parts of India seems, in a great measure, to have superseded that of the Vedas) तन्त्रं; 'a follower of the doctrine taught in the Tantras,' तान्त्रिकः.

To TAP, *v. a.* (Strike a gentle blow) लघुप्रहारं कृ, लघ्वाघातं कृ, लघु प्रहृ or आहन्.—(A cask, &c.) सुरादिभाजने छिद्रं कृ, सुरादिस्रावणार्थं भाण्डं छिद्र् (c. 10. छिद्रयति -यितुं).

TAP, *s.* लघुप्रहारः, लघ्वाघातः, ईषदाघातः, ईषत्प्रहारः.

TAPE, *s.* पट्टः, दीर्घपट्टः, बन्धनी, दीर्घबन्धनी, तनुपट्टः.

TAPER, *s.* क्षुद्रदीपः -पकः, क्षुद्रदीपिका, सूक्ष्मदीपिका.

TAPER, *a.* शुण्डाकृतिः -तिः -ति, शुण्डाकारः -रा -रं, शुण्डारूपः &c.

TAPESTRY, *s.* चित्रजवनिका, जवनिका, चित्रयवनिका, चपटी.

TAPE-WORM, *s.* उदरावेष्टः, नाडीकीटः, नाडीजन्तुः *m.*, नीवा.

TAPTI, *s.* (A river in India) तापी.

TAR, *s.* सरलद्रवः, सरलरसः, सर्ज्जरसः, करालः, रालः.

TARDINESS, *s.* मन्दता, मान्द्यं, विलम्बः -म्बनं. *See* SLOWNESS.

TARDY, *a.* मन्दः -न्दा -न्दं. *See* SLOW, DILATORY.

TARE, *s.* काकः, शस्यक्षेत्ररुहः कक्षभेदः, वन्यघासः.

TARGET, *s.* बाणलक्ष्यं, शरलक्ष्यं, लक्ष्यं, लक्षं, शरव्यं, *see* BUTT.

TARIFF, *s.* सूचिः -ची *f.*, सूचिपत्रं, अनुक्रमणिका. *See* LIST.

To TARNISH, *v. a.* कलङ्क (nom. कलङ्कयति -यितुं), दुष् in caus., *see To* SOIL.

To TARNISH, *v. n.* मलिनीभू, सकलङ्कीभू, दुष् (c. 4. दुष्यति, दोष्टुं).

Tarnished, *p. p.* मलिनितः -ता -तं, कलङ्कितः &c., दूषितः -ता -तं.

To tarry, *v. n.* स्था, अवस्था, विलम्ब्, वस्. *See To* stay, delay.

Tart, *a.* अम्लः -म्ला -म्लं, शुक्तः -क्ता -क्तं. *See* Sour, Sharp.

Tart, *s.* (Kind of pie) शष्कुली, पिष्टकं.

Tartar, *s.* (Of the teeth) दन्तमलं, दन्तशर्करा, पुष्पिका, पिप्पिका, रौचनिकं.

Task, *s.* कार्य्यं, कर्त्तव्यं, व्रतं, कर्म्म *n.* (न्), भारः; 'to take to task,' निर्भर्त्स् (c. 10. -भर्त्सयति -यितुं), निन्द्, *see To* reprove.

To task, *v. a.* भारं न्यस् (c. 4. -अस्यति -सितुं), कार्य्ये नियुज्.

Task-master, *s.* कार्य्यशासकः, कार्य्यकारयिता *m.* (तृ), कर्म्मशासकः.

Tassel, *s.* शिथिलसूत्रमयं प्रलम्बकाभरणं, प्रलम्बः -म्बकः -कं.

Tastable, *a.* प्राशनीयः -या -यं, प्राश्यः &c., आस्वादनीयः &c.

To taste, *v. a.* प्राश् (c 9. -अश्नाति -शितुं), आस्वाद् (c. 1. -स्वादति -दितुं), स्वाद्, लिह् (c. 2. लेढि -ढुं), अवलिह्, रसम् आस्वाद्, आस्वादनं कृ, रसास्वादनं कृ, रस् (c. 10. रसयति -यितुं), रसवेदनं कृ, रसबोधं कृ, रसज्ञानं कृ, रसनं कृ.—(Perceive by the taste) स्वादज्ञानं कृ, स्वादबोधनं कृ, स्वादवेदनं कृ.

To taste, *v. n.* (Have a taste or flavor) स्वद् (c. 1. स्वादते, स्वदते), सरसः -सा -सं भू or अस्, स्वादयुक्तः -क्ता -क्तं भू or अस्.

Taste, *s.* (The sensation excited by applying any thing to the tongue or palate) स्वादः, आस्वादः, रसज्ञानं, रसबोधः, रसवेदनं.—(The sense) रसनेन्द्रियं, आस्वादनशक्तिः *f.*, रसनशक्तिः *f.*, रसनं, रुचिः *f.*—(Flavor) रसः, आस्वादः, रुचिः *f.*; 'the six tastes,' षड्रसाः *m. pl.*; these are, 1. sweet, मधुरः; 2. salt, लवणः; 3. pungent, कटुः; 4. bitter, तिक्तः; 5. sour, अम्लः; 6. astringent, कषायः.—(Relish, liking for) रुचिः *f.*, अभिरुचिः *f.*, सन्तोषः; 'that husband was not to her taste,' स पतिः सन्तोषाय तस्या नाभवत्; 'according to taste,' यथारुचि; 'loss of taste,' अरुचिः *f.*, अरोचकं; 'of similar tastes,' समानशीलः -ला -लं.—(Nice perception, faculty of discerning beauty) रसः, रसिकता, रसज्ञता, रसज्ञानं; 'devoid of taste,' अरसिकः -का -कं, अरसज्ञः -ज्ञा -ज्ञं; 'having taste,' रसज्ञः &c., रसिकः &c., सरसः -सा -सं, रसी -सिनी &c.

Tasted, *p. p.* आस्वादितः -ता -तं, स्वादितः &c., प्राशितः &c., ज्ञातरसः -सा -सं, गृहीतरसः &c., रसितः &c., अनुभवरसिकः &c.

Tasteless, *a.* विरसः -सा -सं, नीरसः &c. *See* Insipid.

Taster, *s.* आस्वादी *m.* (न्), रसास्वादी *m.*, प्राशी *m.*, रसी *m.*

Tasting, *s.* आस्वादः -दनं, स्वादनं, प्राशनं, रसनं, लेहनं.

Tastiness, tastefulness, *s.* रसिकता, सरसत्वं, सौरस्यं, रोचकता.

Tasty, tasteful, *a.* रसिकः -का -कं, सरसः -सा -सं, सुरसः &c., रसवान् -वती -वत् (त्), रसी -सिनी -सि (न्), रोचकः -का -कं, रुचिरः -रा -रं, रुच्यः -च्या -च्यं, रुचिकरः -रा -रं, रसितः -ता -तं. *See* Savory.

Tatter, tattered. *See* Rag, Ragged, Ragamuffin.

To tattle, tattle, tattler. *See To* prate, blab, &c.

Taught, *p. p.* शिक्षितः -ता -तं, उपदिष्टः -ष्टा -ष्टं, अध्यापितः -ता -तं, पाठितः -ता -तं, ज्ञापितः &c., विज्ञापितः &c., लब्धविद्यः -द्या -द्यं.

To taunt, *v. a.* उपालभ् (c. 1. -लभते -लब्धुं), अवक्षिप् (c. 6. -क्षिपति -क्षेप्तुं), आक्षिप्, अधिक्षिप्, परिक्षिप्, तर्ज्, *see To* revile.

Taunt, *s.* आक्षेपः, अवक्षेपः, क्षेपः, उपालम्भः. *See* Sarcasm.

Taunted, *p. p.* आक्षिप्तः -प्ता -प्तं, अवक्षिप्तः &c., उपालब्धः -ब्धा -ब्धं.

Taunting, tauntingly. *See* Sarcastic, Sarcastically.

Taurus, *s.* (The sign or constellation) वृषः, वृषभः, तावुरिः *m.*

Tautology, *s.* पुनरुक्तिः *f.*, पुनरुक्तत्वं, अनुवादः. *See* Repetition.

Tavern, *s.* गञ्जा, मदिरागृहं, मद्यविक्रयस्थानं, *see* Public-house.

Tavern-keeper, taverner, *s.* शौण्डिकः, मद्यविक्रयी *m.* *See* Vintner.

Tawdry, *a.* कुशोभनः -ना -नं, मिथ्याशोभायुक्तः &c., मिथ्याशोभनः &c.

Tawniness, *s.* पिङ्गलता, कपिलता, पिशङ्गता, ताम्रवर्णता.

Tawny, *a.* पिङ्गलः -ला -लं, पिङ्गः -ङ्गा -ङ्गं, कपिलः -ला -लं, पिशङ्गः -ङ्गा -ङ्गं, पिशङ्गी -ङ्गिनी -ङ्गि (न्), पिञ्जरः -रा -रं, ताम्रवर्णः -र्णा -र्णं, अरुणः -णा -णं, कपिलः -ला -लं, कद्रुः -द्रूः -द्रु, आरुः -रुः -रु, श्यावः -वी -वं.

Tax, *s.* करः, शुल्कः -ल्कं, राजकरः -रं, कारः, राजस्वं, *see* Impost; 'exempt from it,' अकरः -रा -रं.—(Burthen) भारः.

To tax, *v. a.* करान् दा in caus. (दापयति -यितुं), करं न्यस् (c. 4. -अस्यति -सितुं), सकरीकृ.—(Impose a burthen) भारं न्यस्.—(Charge, accuse), *see* the words.

Taxable, *a.* कराधीनः -ना -नं, शुल्काधीनः -ना -नं, करयोग्यः -ग्या -ग्यं, करदः -दा -दं; 'taxable article,' शुल्कस्थानं.

Taxation, *s.* करादिन्यासः, करादिव्यवस्थापनं, शुल्कादिस्थापना.

Taxed, *p. p.* सकरः -रा -रं, सशुल्कः -ल्का -ल्कं, करदः -दा -दं.

Tax-gatherer, *s.* करग्रहः, करग्राही *m.* (न्), शुल्कग्राही *m.*

Tea, *s.* No Sanskrit equivalent, चहा may be used.

Tea-pot, *s.* चहापात्रं, चहाधारः, चहाभाजनं.

To teach, *v. a.* उपदिश् (c. 6. -दिशति -देष्टुं), शिक्ष् (c. 10. शिक्षयति -यितुं), अनुशिक्ष्, अभिशिक्ष्, अधी in caus. (अध्यापयति -यितुं, rt. इ), पठ् in caus., शास् &c., *see To* instruct. Sometimes the causal expresses the sense of 'teach;' as, 'he teaches to dance,' नर्त्तयति; 'he teaches to read,' पाठयति.

Teachable, *a.* शिक्षणीयः -या -यं, शिक्ष्यः -क्ष्या -क्ष्यं. *See* Docile.

Teachableness, *s.* शिक्षणीयता, शिक्ष्यता, सुशिक्ष्यता.

Teacher, *s.* उपदेशकः, शिक्षकः, अध्यापकः, बोधकः, अवबोधकः, *see* Instructor; 'of children,' बालाध्यापकः, *see* Pedagogue.

Teaching, *s.* उपदेशः, शिक्षा, अध्यापनं. *See* Instruction.

Teak, *s.* (Tree) वर्णः, शाकः, शाकाख्यः, करच्छदः, खरपत्रः, अर्जुनोपमः, हलीनः.

Teal, *s.* (Kind of duck) कलहंसः, कादम्बः.

Team, *s.* (Of horses) रथसंयोजिता अश्वश्रेणी; 'of oxen,' गोश्रेणी.

Tear, *s.* (Of the eye) अश्रु *n.*, अस्रु *n.*, अस्रं, अस्रं, बाष्पः, नेत्राम्बु *n.*, नेत्रजलं, नेत्रोदकं, नेत्रजं, नयनाम्बु *n.*, नयनजलं, नयनवारि *n.*, नयनसलिलं, विलोचनाम्बु *n.*, लोचनाम्बु *n.*, रोदनं; 'tear-drop,' बाष्पबिन्दुः *m.*, अश्रुबिन्दुः *m.*, अस्रबिन्दुः *m.*, अश्रुकला; 'starting of tears,' बाष्पोद्गमः; 'flood of tears,' अश्रुधारा, धाराश्रु *n.*; 'flowing of tears,' अश्रुपातः, अश्रुस्रावः; 'tears of affection,' प्रेमाश्रु; 'of joy,' हर्षाश्रु *n.*; 'to shed tears,' अश्रूणि पत् (c. 10. पातयति -यितुं) or स्रु in caus. (स्रावयति -यितुं) or वृत् in caus., बाष्प (nom. बाष्पायते), अस्र (nom. अस्रायते), प्ररुद्, रुद्, रोदनं कृ; 'he shed tears of joy,' हर्षात् अश्रूण्य् अपातयत्; 'in tears, having the eyes filled with tears,' जाताश्रुः -श्रुः -श्रु, अश्रुलोचनः -ना -नं, अश्रुनयनः &c., अश्रुमुखः -खी -खं, बाष्पोपप्लुताक्षः -क्षी -क्षं, बाष्पाविलेक्षणः &c., पर्य्यश्रुः -श्रुः -श्रु; 'interrupted by tears,' बाष्पाकुलः -ला -लं.—(Rent), *see* Rent.

To TEAR, *v. a.* दॄ (c. 10. दारयति -यितुं, c. 9. दृणाति, दरितुं -रीतुं), विद्, अवद्, दारणं कृ, विदारणं कृ, विभिद्, *see To* REND, LACERATE, PULL.—(Tear down, off, out, up), *see* under *To* PULL.—(The hair) लुञ्च् &c., *see To* PLUCK.

To TEAR, *v. n.* (Rush along) महावेगेन चल्.—(Be torn or rent) भिद् in pass., विभिद् in pass., *see To* CLEAVE, DIVIDE, *v. n.*

TEARFUL, *a.* साश्रुः -श्रुः -श्रु, सास्रुः &c., सास्रः -स्रा -स्रं, सास्रः &c., सबाष्पः -ष्पा -ष्पं, अश्रुपूर्णः -र्णा -र्णं, बाष्पपूर्णः &c., अश्रुमयः -यी -यं.

TEARFULLY, *adv.* सबाष्पं, सास्रं, साश्रं, बाष्पाकुलवाचा, साश्रुपातं.

TEARING, *s.* दारणं, विदारणं, विदारः, विभेदः -दनं, पाटनं.

To TEASE, *v. a.* बाध् (c. 1. बाधते -धितुं). *See To* ANNOY, TORMENT.

TEASED, *p. p.* बाधितः -ता -तं, पीडितः &c., व्यग्रः -ग्रा -ग्रं.

TEAT, *s.* स्तनाग्रं, स्तनः, *see* NIPPLE; 'having two teats,' द्विस्तनी.

TECHNICAL, *a.* लाक्षणिकः -की -कं, पारिभाषिकः &c., साङ्केतिकः -की -कं, परिभाषितः -ता -तं, विशेषविद्यासम्बन्धी -न्धिनी &c.

TECHNICALLY, *adv.* परिभाषानुसारेण, विशेषकलानुसारेण.

TECHNICALITY, *s.* लाक्षणिकत्वं, पारिभाषिकत्वं, साङ्केतिकत्वं.—(A technical term) परिभाषा, लाक्षणिकः.

TEDIOUS, *a.* दीर्घसूत्रः -त्रा -त्रं, अतिदीर्घः -र्घा -र्घं, खेदजनकः -का -कं, श्रमजनकः &c. *See* LONG, PROLIX, IRKSOME.

TEDIOUSLY, *adv.* अतिदीर्घं, दीर्घसूत्रवत्, सुदीर्घं.

TEDIOUSNESS, *s.* दीर्घसूत्रता, अतिदीर्घता. *See* IRKSOMENESS.

To TEEM, *v. n.* पूर्णगर्भः -र्भा -र्भं भू, अतिपूर्णः -र्णा -र्णं भू.—(Bring forth abundantly) बाहुल्येन उत्पद् (c. 10. -पादयति -यितुं) or जन्.

TEEMING, *part.* पूर्णगर्भः -र्भा -र्भं, परिपूर्णः -र्णा -र्णं, सम्पूर्णः &c., पूर्णः &c., आकुल in comp., आढ्य in comp. *See* PROLIFIC.

TEETH, *s. pl.*, दन्ताः *m. pl.*, *see* TOOTH; 'having teeth,' दन्ती -न्तिनी -न्ति (न्), सदन्तः -न्ता -न्तं, जातदन्तः &c.; 'having good teeth,' सुदन् -दती -दत् (त्); 'woman having fine teeth,' शुभदन्ती; having discolored teeth,' श्यावदन्तः &c.; 'row of teeth,' दन्तपंक्तिः *f.*; 'sensitiveness of the teeth,' दन्तहर्षः.

To TEETH, *v. n.* जातदन्तः -न्ता -न्तं भू, उद्भिन्नदन्तः -न्ता -न्तं भू.

TEETHING, *s.* दन्तोद्भेदः, दन्तोद्भवः, दन्तस्फोटः, दन्तोत्पत्तिः *f.*, दन्तजननं; 'time of teething,' दन्तोद्भेदनकालः.

TEGUMENT, *s.* आवेष्टनं, कवचः -चं, पुटः -टी. *See* INTEGUMENT.

TELESCOPE, *s.* दूरदर्शकयन्त्रं, महादूरदर्शकयन्त्रं, दूरदर्शनयन्त्रं, चाक्षुषयन्त्रं, दृष्टिसाधकयन्त्रं.

TELINGANA, *s.* (The country) अन्ध्रः, आन्ध्रः.

To TELL, *v. a.* कथ् (c. 10. कथयति -यितुं). *See To* RELATE, NARRATE.

To TELL, *v. n.* (Take effect) सफलीभू, सफलीभू, सप्रभावः -वा -वं भू, सिध्.—(Hit the mark), *see* under MARK.—(Tell of) सूच्.

TELLER, *s.* कथकः, कथिकः, आख्यायकः. *See* RELATER.

TELLING, *s.* कथनं, उपकथनं, आख्यानं, *see* RELATION, NARRATION.

TELL-TALE, *s.* सूचकः, सूची *m.* *See* TALE-BEARER, INFORMER.

TEMERITY, *s.* साहसं, दुःसाहसं, विषमसाहसं. *See* RASHNESS.

To TEMPER, *v. a.* शम् (c. 10. शमयति -यितुं). *See To* MODERATE.

TEMPER, *s.* (Of mind) शीलः, प्रकृतिः *f.*, भावः, स्वभावः, संवेदनं; 'good temper,' सद्भावः, *see* GOOD-HUMOUR; 'bad temper,' असद्भावः.—(Calmness, moderation) शान्तिः *f.*, शान्तता, समता, संयमः, रोषाभावः.—(Anger) रोषः.

TEMPERAMENT, *s.* प्रकृतिः *f.*, स्वभावः, भावः, देहप्रकृतिः *f.*, देहस्वभावः, शरीरप्रकृतिः *f.*, जन्मप्रकृतिः *f.*; 'bilious,' पित्तप्रकृतिः *f.*

TEMPERANCE, *s.* (Moderation) संयमः, यमः, परिमितता, अप्रसक्तिः *f.*—(In eating) मिताशनं, अल्पाशनं, मिताहारः -रित्वं, मितभोजनं, अल्पाहारः -रित्वं, परिमिताहारः, परिमितभोजनं -जित्वं.—(In drinking) परिमितपानं, मितपानं, अल्पपानं, मात्रापानं.

TEMPERATE, *a.* (Moderate) संयमी -मिनी &c., संयतः -ता -तं, संयतवृत्तिः -त्तिः -त्ति, संयमशीलः -ला -लं, *see* MODERATE.—(In desires) अल्पाकांक्षी -क्षिणी &c., अप्रसक्तः -क्ता -क्तं, जितेन्द्रियः -या -यं.—(In eating) मिताशनः -ना -नं, परिमिताहारः -रा -रं, मिताहारः &c., मिताहारी -रिणी &c., यताहारः &c., अल्पाहारः &c., अल्पाहारी &c., स्वल्पाहारः &c., मितभोजी &c., नियताहारी &c., लघ्वाहारः -रा -रं, लघ्वाहारी &c., अल्पाशी &c., मिताशी &c.—(In drinking) मितपायी &c., परिमितपायी &c., अल्पपायी &c., मितपानी &c., पानाप्रसक्तः -क्ता -क्तं.—(Not excessive) परिमितः -ता -तं, अतीव्रः -व्रा -व्रं.—(Moderately warm) ईषदुष्णः -ष्णा -ष्णं, मन्दोष्णः &c., अचण्डः -ण्डा -ण्डं, अग्रीष्मः -ष्मा -ष्मं.—(Calm, not violent) शान्तः -न्ता -न्तं, अरोषणः -णा -णं, शान्तिप्रयुक्तः -क्ता -क्तं, अचण्डः -ण्डा -ण्डं, धीरः -रा -रं, धैर्य्यशाली &c.

TEMPERATELY, *adv.* अरोषेण, अक्रोधेन, अतीव्रं, अचण्डं, शान्त्या.

TEMPERATURE, *s.* उष्णानुष्णमानं, उष्णानुष्णप्रमाणं, उष्णशीतमानं, उष्णानुष्णता, उष्णमानं, उष्णप्रमाणं, ग्रीष्माग्रीष्मता.

TEMPERED, *p. p.* शमितः -ता -तं, उपशमितः &c., नियमितः -ता -तं.

TEMPEST, TEMPESTUOUS. *See* STORM, STORMY, HURRICANE.

TEMPEST-TOST, TEMPEST-BEATEN, *a.* पवनाहतः -ता -तं, पवनक्षिप्तः -प्ता -प्तं, पवनाघातप्रेरितः &c., वात्यावेगप्रेरितः &c., अनिलसंक्षुब्धः &c.

TEMPLE, *s.* (Building dedicated to a deity) मन्दिरं, प्रासादः, देवमन्दिरं, देवालयं, देवगृहं, देवभवनं, मण्डपः -पं, देवागारः -रं, देववेश्म *n.* (न्), देवतामन्दिरं, भजनालयं, देवतागारः -रं, देवतायतनं, देवावासः, महालयः -यं, सुरस्थानं, सुरमन्दिरं, सुरगृहं, देवकुलं, यज्ञियशाला, वीहारः, चयनं, विच्छन्दकः, विच्छन्दकः, स्वस्तिकः, सर्वतोभद्रः, नन्द्यावर्त्तः, रुचकः; 'temple dedicated to Siva,' शिवालयं, शिवमन्दिरं; 'open temple,' मण्डपः; 'endowments of a temple,' देवस्वं; 'worship at the entrance of a temple,' द्वारपूजा.—(Of the head) कपोलः, कनारः, शङ्खः, शङ्खकः -कं.

TEMPORAL, *a.* ऐहिकः -की -कं, ऐहलौकिकः -की -कं, लौकिकः &c., सांसारिकः &c., दृष्टार्थः -र्था -र्थं. *See* SECULAR.

TEMPORARILY, *adv.* अल्पकालमात्रं, क्षणमात्रं, अचिरेण, अशाश्वतं.

TEMPORARINESS, *s.* अनित्यता, अचिरस्थायिता, क्षणिकता.

TEMPORARY, *a.* अचिरस्थायी -यिनी -यि (न्), अचिरकालिकः -का -कं, अचिरः -रा -रं, अनित्यः -त्या -त्यं, अशाश्वतः -ती -तं, क्षणिकः -का -कं.

To TEMPORIZE, *v. n.* समयानुरोधं कृ, समयानुवर्त्तनं कृ, कालानुरोधं कृ.

TEMPORIZER, *s.* समयानुरोधी *m.* (न्), कालानुरोधी *m.*, कालानुवर्त्ती *m.*

To TEMPT, *v. a.* (Entice to evil) प्रलुभ् (c. 10. -लोभयति -यितुं), परिलुभ्, लुभ्, आकृष् (c. 1. -कर्षति -क्रष्टुं), मुह् (c. 10. मोहयति -यितुं), प्रलोभनं कृ, विमोहनं कृ.—(Try, prove) परीक्ष् (c. 1. -ईक्षते -क्षितुं), परीक्षां कृ.

TEMPTATION, *s.* (Enticement to evil) प्रलोभनं, विलोभनं, आकर्षणं, आकृष्टिः *f.*, मोहः -हनं, विमोहनं.—(Trial) परीक्षा.

TEMPTED, *p. p.* प्रलोभितः -ता -तं, आकृष्टः -ष्टा -ष्टं, मोहितः &c.; 'by avarice,' लोभाकृष्टः &c.—(Tried) परीक्षितः -ता -तं.

TEMPTER, *s.* प्रलोभकः, विलोभकः, मोहकः, परीक्षकः, परीक्षाकृत्.

TEMPTING, *a.* आकर्षकः -का -कं, विमोहनः -ना -नं. *See* ENTICING.

TEN, *a.* दश *m. f. n. pl.* (न्), दशकः -का -कं, दशसंख्यकः -का -कं; 'aggregate of ten,' दशकं; 'ten days,' दशाहं; 'in ten ways,' दशधा.

TENABLE, *a.* रक्षणीयः -या -यं, प्रतिपादनीयः &c., स्थापनीयः &c.

TENACIOUS, *a.* (Holding fast) संलग्नशीलः -ला -लं, *see* RETENTIVE.—(Persistent in a course) अभिनिविष्टः -ष्टा -ष्टं, आग्रही -हिणी &c., दृढः -ढा -ढं, दृढसङ्कल्पः -ल्पा -ल्पं.—(Of opinions) स्वमताग्रही &c.—(Of life) दुर्मरः -रा -रं.

TENACITY, *s.* अभिनिवेशः, आग्रहः, ग्रहः, दृढता, धृतिः *f.*, धारणा.

TENANT, *s.* अधिवासी *m.* (न्), परस्वामिकक्षेत्राधिवासी *m.*, परस्वामिकगृहाधिवासी *m.*, परस्वत्वयुक्तभूम्यधिवासी *m.*

To TENANT, *v. a.* परस्वामिकभूमिम् अधिवस् (c. 1. -वसति -वस्तुं).

TENANTED, *p. p.* अध्युषितः -ता -तं, अधिष्ठितः &c. *See* OCCUPIED.

TENANTRY, *s.* परस्वामिकक्षेत्राधिवासिनां गणः, अधिवासिगणः.

To TEND, *v. a.* पाल्, रक्ष्, *see* under *To* KEEP; 'cattle,' गोपालनं कृ.

To TEND, *v. n.* (Aim at, be directed or incline towards) अभिसन्धा (c. 3. -दधाति -धातुं), उद्दिश् (c. 6. -दिशति -देष्टुं), अभिप्रे (c. 2. अभिप्रेति -तुं, rt. इ), प्रवणः -णा -णं भू; 'act which tends to a main object,' प्रत्युत्क्रमः, प्रत्युत्क्रान्तिः *f.*, प्रयोगार्थः.—(Conduce, contribute), *see* the words.

TENDENCY, *s.* प्रावण्यं, प्रवणता, प्रवृत्तिः *f.*, प्रवाहः, शीलता or आलुता in comp., *see* INCLINATION; 'to descend,' अधोगतिशीलता.

TENDER, *a.* (Soft) कोमलः -ला -लं, मृदुः -द्वी -दु, आर्द्रः -र्द्रा -र्द्रं.—(Sensible of pain) सुलभदुःखः -खा -खं, सुदुःखितः -ता -तं, *see* SORE.—(Delicate) सुकुमारः -रा -रं, कौमारः -री -रं, पेलवः -वा -वं, मृदुः &c.; 'having a tender frame,' प्रकृतिपेलवः -वा -वं, मृद्वङ्गः -ङ्गी -ङ्गं.—(Young) बालः -ला -लं, कौमारः -री -रं.—(Compassionate) दयालुः -लुः -लु, कारुणिकः -की -कं, आर्द्रः -र्द्रा -र्द्रं, दयार्द्रः &c., सहार्दः &c., *see* PITIFUL.

TENDER, *To* TENDER. *See* OFFER, *To* OFFER.

TENDER-HEARTED, *a.* करुणात्मकः -का -कं, कोमलचित्तः -त्ता -त्तं, कोमलान्तःकरणः -णा -णं, कोमलहृदयः -या -यं, सदयहृदयः &c., दयार्द्रभावः -वा -वं, दयार्द्रचित्तः &c., क्लिन्नहृदयः &c., क्लिन्नहृद्, भावार्द्रः &c.

TENDERLY, *adv.* सकरुणं, सकारुण्यं, करुणं, सदयं, सानुकम्पं.

TENDERNESS, *s.* (Softness) कोमलता -त्वं, मृदुता, मार्दवं, सौकुमार्य्यं, कौमारं, आर्द्रता.—(Compassion, kindness) कारुण्यं, करुणा, कृपा, दया, अनुकम्पा, दयालुता, वात्सल्यं, *see* PITY.

TENDINOUS, *a.* शिरालः -ला -लं, शिरामयः -यी -यं, स्नायुमयः &c.

TENDON, *s.* स्नायुः *m.*, वसा, शिरा, सिरा, स्नावः, सन्धिबन्धनं, ग्रन्थिबन्धनं, नाडी, *see* MUSCLE; 'of the neck,' मन्या.

TENDRIL, *s.* (Of a vine or creeper) लतातन्तुः *m.*, तन्तुः *m.*

TENEMENT, *s.* आयतनं, भवनं, *see* DWELLING; 'earthly,' देहः.

TENET, *s.* मतं, सम्मतं, तत्त्वं, स्थितिः *f.* *See* OPINION, DOGMA.

TENFOLD, *a.* दशगुणः -णा -णं, दशविधः -धा -धं, दशधा indec.

TENOR, *s.* (Course, drift) क्रमः, अन्वयः, प्रसङ्गः, प्रवाहः, अभिप्रायः, तात्पर्य्यं, निदर्शनं.—(Voice) मध्यस्वरः.

TENSE, *a.* आततः -ता -तं, ततः &c. *See* STRETCHED, TIGHT.

TENSE, *s.* (In grammar) कालः; 'Present,' वर्त्तमानकालः; 'Preterite,' अतीतकालः; 'Imperfect,' अद्यतनभूतकालः.

TENSION, *s.* आततिः *f.*, आततत्वं, ततिः *f.*, अशैथिल्यं. *See* TIGHTNESS.

TENT, *s.* दूष्यं, दूर्ष्यं, पटमण्डपः, पटगृहं, पटवेश्म *n.* (न्), पटवासः, पटकुटिः *f.*, वस्त्रगृहं, शिविरं, स्कुलं, पोताच्छादनं, गुल्मी, केणिका, कुटरु *n.*, गुणलयनिका; 'tent-maker,' दूष्यनिर्म्माणजीवी *m.*; 'outer tent, or screen surrounding a tent,' जवनिका, यवनिका.

TENTH, *a.* दशमः -मी -मं; 'tenth day of the month,' दशमी.

TENUITY, *s.* तनुता, तानवं, सूक्ष्मता, सौक्ष्म्यं, क्षीणता.

TENUOUS, *a.* तनुः -नुः -न्वी -नु, सूक्ष्मः -क्ष्मा -क्ष्मं. *See* THIN.

TEPID, *a.* ईषदुष्णः -ष्णा -ष्णं, कोष्णः &c., कवोष्णः &c., मन्दोष्णः &c., कुतपः -पा -पं, अनुष्णाशीतः -ता -तं. *See* LUKEWARM.

TEPIDNESS, *s.* कोष्णता, कवोष्णता, मन्दोष्णता. *See* LUKEWARMNESS.

TERGIVERSATION, *s.* अपदेशः, पलायनं, अपक्रमः, पराङ्मुखता, छलं.

TERM, *s.* (Limit, end) अन्तः, पर्य्यन्तः -न्तं, *see* LIMIT.—(Period) अवधिः *m.*, कालावधिः *m.*, *see* PERIOD; 'of days,' अहर्गणः; 'utmost term,' परमावधिः *m.*; 'of life,' आयुर्मर्य्यादा.—(Word, expression, appellation) संज्ञा, पदं, वाक्यं, शब्दः, वचनं, अभिधानं, आख्या, नाम *n.* (न्), पद्धतिः *f.*—(Conditions) सङ्केतः, प्रतिज्ञा, नियमः, नियमवाक्यं.—(State of intercourse) व्यवहारः, वृत्तिः *f.*, परिचयभावः, परिचयः; 'good terms,' प्रीतिः *f.*, मैत्र्यं, संधित्तिः *f.*; 'ill terms,' वितुष्टं, अतुष्टिः *f.*, अप्रीतिः *f.*—(Time of business) व्यवहारकालः, कार्य्यनिर्वाहकालः, *see* SESSION.—(Of a syllogism) अवयवः.—(Of an arithmetical series) पदं; 'first term,' आदिपदं, मुखं; 'last term,' अन्त्यपदं.

To TERM, *v. a.* अभिधा, आख्या. *See* *To* NAME, CALL, STYLE.

TERMAGANT, *s.* कर्कशा, चण्डी, दुष्टा. *See* SCOLD, SHREW.

TERMED, *p. p.* अभिहितः -ता -तं, स्मृतः &c. *See* NAMED, CALLED.

TERMINABLE, *a.* समर्य्यादः -दा -दं, परिच्छेदनीयः &c., *see* LIMITABLE.

TERMINAL, *a.* अन्तस्थः -स्था -स्थं, पार्य्यन्तः -न्ती -न्तं, आन्तः -न्ती -न्तं.

To TERMINATE, *v. a.* or *n.* अवसो. *See* *To* END, CLOSE, LIMIT.

TERMINATION, *s.* अवसानं, अन्तः, अवधिः *m.*, परिणामः, निष्ठा, *see* END, CONCLUSION.—(In grammar) अन्तः, अन्त्यवर्णः.

TERMLESS, *a.* निरवधिः -धिः -धि, अनन्तः -न्ता -न्तं. *See* ENDLESS.

TERRACE, *s.* (Before a house) आलिन्दः, अलिन्दः, प्रघाणः, प्रघणः, गृहतटी, वीथिः -थी *f.*, देहली -लिः *f.*—(On the roof of a house) प्रासादपृष्ठं, अट्टालः -लिका, तमङ्गकः, पृष्ठं.—(Covered terrace in the yard) वितर्द्दिः *f.*, वेदिका.

TERRAQUEOUS, *a.* जलस्थलमयः -यी -यं, जलस्थलात्मकः -का -कं.

TERRESTRIAL, TERRENE, *a.* (Sublunary) लौकिकः -की -कं, ऐहलौकिकः &c., *see* MUNDANE.—(Earthen, earthly) भौमः -मी -मं, भौमिकः -की -कं, *see* EARTHLY, EARTHEN.—(Going or existing on the earth) भूचरः -री -रं, स्थलचरः &c., भूमिजः -जा -जं, स्थलजः &c., भूलोकस्थः -स्था -स्थं; 'terrestrial globe,' भूगोलः -लकं.

TERRIBLE, TERRIFIC, *a.* भयानकः -का -कं, घोरः -रा -रं, दारुणः -णा -णं, भीमः -मा -मं. *See* FRIGHTFUL, FEARFUL, HORRIBLE.

TERRIBLY, TERRIFIED, &c. *See* FRIGHTFULLY, FRIGHTENED, &c.

To TERRIFY, *v. a.* त्रस् in caus., भी in caus., *see* *To* FRIGHTEN.

TERRITORIAL, *a.* राष्ट्रीयः -या -यं, राष्ट्रसम्बन्धी &c., दैशिकः -की -कं.

TERRITORY, *s.* राष्ट्रं, देशः, प्रदेशः, भूमिः *f.*, राज्यं, अधिकारः.

TERROR, *s.* त्रासः, सन्त्रासः, साध्वसं, भयं. *See* FEAR, FRIGHT.

TERSE, *a.* शुद्धः -द्धा -द्धं, संस्कृतः -ता -तं, संक्षिप्तः -प्ता -प्तं.

TERSENESS, *s.* शुद्धता, शुद्धिः *f.*, संक्षिप्तता, संक्षेपः, संस्कृतत्वं.

TERTIAN, *s.* त्र्याहिकज्वरः, त्र्याहिकः, तृतीयकज्वरः, तृतीयकः.

Tesselated, *a.* अष्टापदानुकारेण नानावर्णप्रस्तरखचितः -ता -तं.

Test, *s.* (Trial) परीक्षा, -क्षणं, कषिः *f.*, उपधा, कषः -षणं, आकषः, निकषः, प्रतीतिः *f.*, परीक्षितं; 'this may be put to the test,' एतत्परीक्षा करणीया, एतत्प्रतीतिर् उत्पाद्या.—(Means of trial) परीक्षासाधनं.

To test, *v. a.* परीक्ष् (c. 1. -ईक्षते -क्षितुं), ज्ञा in des. *See To* try.

Testaceous, *a.* शङ्खवासी -सिनी &c., कम्बुविशिष्टः -ष्टा -ष्टं, कम्बुस्थः &c.

Testament, *s.* (Will) मृतपत्रं, मरणपत्रं, मृत्युपत्रं, मृतलेखः; 'Old Testament,' पुरातननियमः; 'New Testament,' नूतननियमः.

Testamentary, *a.* (Pertaining to a will) मृतपत्रसम्बन्धी &c. -विषयकः -का -कं.—(Given by a will) मृतपत्रदत्तः -त्ता -त्तं.

Testator, *s.* मृतलेखकर्त्ता *m.* (र्त्तृ), मरणलेखकर्त्ता *m.*

Testatrix, *s.* मृतलेखकर्त्री, मृत्युलेखकर्त्री, मरणलेखकर्त्री.

Tested, *p. p.* परीक्षितः -ता -तं, कृतपरीक्षः -क्षा -क्षं. *See* Tried.

Testicle, *s.* अण्डं, मुष्कः, वृषणः, कोषः -षकः, कोशः, फलं, मुष्ककः, तोक्षणं; 'testicles,' अण्डद्वयं, मुष्कद्वयं, अण्डयुग्मं, वृषणद्वयं, वृषणौ *m. du.*; 'enlargement of them,' अण्डवृद्धिः *f.*, अण्डशोफः; 'having them,' सवृषणः -णा -णं, अण्डीरः -रा -रं, अण्डीलः &c.

To testify, *v. a.* or *n.*, साक्ष्यं दा or कृ, प्रमाणं दा, प्रमाण (nom. प्रमाणयति -यितुं). *See To* declare, certify, publish.

Testimonial, *s.* प्रमाणपत्रं, प्रमाणलेखः, प्रामाणिकलेखः.

Testimony, *s.* साक्ष्यं, साक्षिता, प्रमाणं, प्रामाण्यं. *See* Evidence.

Testiness, *s.* कर्कशता, कार्कश्यं, वक्रता, कटुता. *See* Peevishness.

Testy, *a.* कर्कशः -शा -शं, कटुः -टुः -टु. *See* Peevish, Fretful.

Tete-a-tete, *s.* रहःसंलापः, रहःसम्भाषा, रहःप्रत्यासत्तिः *f.*

Tether, *s.* बन्धनरज्जुः *m. f.*, बन्धनसूत्रं, चारणरज्जुः *m. f.*

To tether, *v. a.* दीर्घरज्जुना बद्धा चर् (c. 10. चारयति -यितुं).

Tetrad, *s.* (Aggregate of four) चतुष्टयं, चतुष्कं.

Tetragon, *s.* चतुरस्रं, चतुष्कोणः, चतुर्भुजः.

Tetragonal, *a.* चतुष्कोणः -णा -णं, चतुरस्रः -स्रा -स्रं, चतुर्भुजः -जा -जं.

Text, *s.* (Subject of a comment) मूलं, मूलग्रन्थः, पाठग्रन्थः, प्रतीकं, निदर्शनं, अभिहितत्वं, प्रयोगः.—(Verse or passage of Scripture) वचनं, वाक्यं, सूत्रं, ऋक् *f.* (च्), विधिः *m.*, प्रतीकं, श्रुतिः *f.*; 'of the Vedas,' वेदवचनं, वेदवाक्यं.

Textile, *a.* तान्तवः -वी -वं, तन्त्री -न्त्रिणी -न्त्रि (न्).

Textual, *a.* वाचनिकः -की -कं, मौलिकः -की -कं.

Texture, *s.* (Weaving) ऊतिः *f.*, वापः, व्यूतिः.—(Web, that which is woven) तान्तवं, वस्त्रं.—(Quality of the threads) तन्तुगुणः, सूत्रगुणः.

Than, *adv.* or *conj.* Usually expressed in Sanskrit by the abl. c.; as, 'a store of grain is better than all stores,' धान्यसंग्रहः श्रेयान् सर्व्वसंग्रहात्; 'worthier than I,' अस्मत्तो वरीयान्. Or by न च; as, 'silence is better than speaking untruth,' वरं मौनं न च वचनम् अनृतं [*i. e.* better silence and not speaking untruth]. In modern Sanskrit 'than' is often expressed by अपेक्षया, or अपेक्ष्य; as, 'some of the organs of animals are stronger than those of men,' जन्तूनां कानिचिद् इन्द्रियाणि मनुष्यापेक्षया प्रबलानि; 'acid has a stronger attraction for iron than copper,' अम्लरसं ताम्रम् अपेक्ष्य लोहम् अधिकम् आकर्षति; 'placing the cup on some place higher than one's head,' स्वमस्तकम् अपेक्ष्य उच्चतरे स्थाने पात्रं विन्यस्य; 'than him,' तदपेक्षया; 'than me,' मदपेक्षया.

To thank, *v. a.* धन्यं वद् (c. 1. वदति -दितुं), कृतज्ञताकथनं कृ, कृतज्ञताप्रकाशनं कृ, कृतज्ञतादर्शनं कृ, उपकारस्तुतिं कृ, प्राप्तोपकारस्तुतिं कृ, उपकारस्वीकारं कृ, धन्यवादं कृ; 'to give thanks to God,' ईश्वरं धन्यं वद्, ईश्वरगुणान् वद्, ईश्वरस्य धन्यवादं कृ; 'I thank thee,' त्वां धन्यं वदामि.

Thank, thanks, *s. pl.* धन्यवादः, कृतज्ञतादर्शनं, कृतज्ञताकथनं, कृतज्ञताप्रकाशनं, उपकारस्तुतिः *f.*, उपकाराभिवादः, उपकारस्वीकारः; 'many thanks to you for your kindness,' अनुगृहीतो ऽस्मि तवोपकारेण; 'thanks to thee for the breakfast,' कुशलं ते प्रातराशस्य.

Thankful, *a.* कृतज्ञः -ज्ञा -ज्ञं, उपकारज्ञः &c., कृतज्ञतादर्शकः -का -कं, कृतज्ञताकथकः &c., कृतज्ञताप्रकाशकः &c., उपकाराभिवादकः &c., धन्यवादी -दिनी -दि (न्).

Thankfully, *adv.* कृतज्ञतापूर्व्वं, सधन्यवादं, कृतज्ञवत्, उपकारज्ञवत्.

Thankfulness, *s.* कृतज्ञता, उपकारज्ञता, उपकृतज्ञता.

Thankless, *a.* अकृतज्ञः -ज्ञा -ज्ञं, कृतघ्नः &c. *See* Ungrateful.

Thanksgiving, *s.* धन्यवादः, कृतज्ञताकथनं, कृतज्ञतादर्शनं.

That, *pron.* (Demonstrative) सः सा तत् (त्), एषः एषा एतत् (एतत्), असौ *m. f.* (अदस्); 'that man,' स नरः; 'at that time,' तस्मिन् काले, *see* Then.—(Relative) यः या यत् (यत्) or expressed by a compound; as, 'the man that has great wealth,' महाधनो नरः, *see* Who, Which.—(That is to say) अर्थात्, अर्थतस्, वस्तुतस्.—(So that) तथा यथा, *see* the next.

That, *conj.* Expressed by तथा यथा, यथा, यत्, इति or by the accusative case, as in the following examples; 'do you contrive that I may be liberated from my bonds,' यथा मुच्ये बन्धनात् तथा संविधातुम् अर्हसि; 'I did not expect that I should see you again,' न म आसीद् आशंसा यथा पुनरपि त्वां प्रेक्षिष्ये; 'do you not know that I keep watch in the house?' त्वं न जानासि यथा गृहरक्षां करोमि; 'know that it is impossible to stand before him,' अवेहि यद् अशक्यं तस्याग्रे स्थातुं; 'this is a new doctrine, that having killed an enemy remorse should be felt,' अयं नूतनो न्यायो यद् अरातिं हत्वा सन्तापः क्रियते; 'the pupils said that they had done their task,' कृतकृत्या वयम् इति शिष्या ऊचुः; 'having ascertained that it was a monkey who rang the bell,' मर्कटो घण्टां वादयति इति परिज्ञाय; 'his idea was that an increase of wealth ought to be made,' अर्थवृद्धिः करणीया इति मतिर् बभूव; 'reflecting in his mind that I am happy in possessing such a wife,' धन्यो ऽहं यस्य एतादृशी भार्य्या इति मनसि निधाय; 'I will inform the Guru that the hour of sacrifice has arrived,' उपस्थितां होमवेलां गुरवे निवेदयामि; 'they related that a golden shower had fallen from the clouds,' हिरण्मयीं वृष्टिं नभस्तः पतितां शशंसुः; 'thou sayest that my beloved is pining away,' पर्य्युत्सुकां प्रियां मे कथयसि.—(In order that) expressed by अर्थं in comp., or by the dative case; as, 'what must I do in order that I may get money?' धनप्राप्त्यर्थं or धनप्राप्तये किं मया कर्त्तव्यं.

Thatch, *s.* छदिः *f.*, तृणच्छदिः *f.*, छादं, पटलं, तृणपटलं, कटनं, कुटलं, कुटङ्कः, गृहाच्छादनी.

To thatch, *v. a.* शुष्कतृणादिना or तृणपटलेन गृहाच्छादनं कृ.

Thatched, *p. p.* तृणाच्छादितः -ता -तं, शुष्कतृणछादितः -ता -तं.

Thatcher, *s.* गृहाच्छादनकृत् *m.*, तृणपटलकारः, कोटकः.

To THAW, *v. a.* द्रवीकृ, विद्रु in caus., विद्रावणं कृ. *See To* MELT, *v. a.*
To THAW, *v. n.* द्रवीभू, द्रु (c. 1. द्रवति, द्रोतुं), विद्रु. *See To* MELT, *v. n.*
THAW, *s.* हिमद्रवः, हिमद्रावः, हिमगलनं, हिमक्षरणं.
THE. This definite article may be either expressed by the pronoun सः सा तत्, or is more usually omitted altogether; as, 'the man,' स पुरुषः or पुरुषः; 'the woman,' सा स्त्री or स्त्री; 'the lion,' स सिंहः or सिंहः.
THEATRE, *s.* रङ्गः, रङ्गशाला, नाटकशाला, नाट्यशाला, नाटकगृहं, नाटकमन्दिरं, नृत्यशाला, रङ्गभूमिः *f.*, समाजसन्निवेशः, आनर्त्तः.
THEATRICAL, *a.* नाटकीयः -या -यं, नाट्यसम्बन्धी -न्धिनी &c., नाट्यविषयकः -का -कं, नाटकसम्बन्धी &c., नाट्यशालासम्बन्धी &c.
THEE, *pron.* त्वां acc. c.; 'by thee,' त्वया; 'to thee,' तुभ्यं, ते; 'of thee,' तव, ते.
THEFT, *s.* स्तेयं, चौर्य्यं, चौरं, चौरिका, स्तैन्यं, स्तैनं, चुरा, तास्कर्य्यं, तस्करता, मुष्टं, मुष्टिः *f.*, अपहारः, परद्रव्यापहारः, चौर्य्यकर्म्म *n.* (न्). *See* STEALING.
THEIR, *pron.* तेषां *gen. pl. m.*, तासां *f.*, एतेषां *gen. pl. m.*, एतासां *f.*, एषां *gen. pl. m.*, आसां *gen. pl. f.*
THEISM, *s.* आस्तिक्यं, आस्तिकमतं, आस्तिक्यवादः, ईश्वरवादः.
THEIST, *s.* आस्तिकः, आस्तिक्यवादी *m.* (न्), ईश्वरवादी *m.*
THEM, *pron.* तान् or एतान् *acc. pl.*; 'by them,' तैः; 'of them,' तेषां.
THEME, *s.* (Topic) प्रकरणं, विषयः, *see* SUBJECT.—(Short dissertation) अल्पप्रबन्धः, अल्पलेखः, अल्पप्रसङ्गः.
THEMSELVES, *pron.* Expressed by आत्मा *m.* (न्). *See* MYSELF.
THEN, *adv.* (At that time) तदा, तदानीं, तर्हि, एतर्हि, तस्मिन् काले, तत्काले.—(After that) ततः, अथ, तदनन्तरं, तदुपरि; 'now and then,' कदाचित्, कदापि, *see* under NOW.
THENCE, *adv.* (From that place) ततस्, तस्मात् स्थानात्, तस्माद् देशात्.—(For that reason) तस्मात्, *see* THEREFORE.
THENCEFORTH, THENCEFORWARD, *adv.* ततःप्रभृति, तदाप्रभृति, तत्कालादारभ्य, तत आरभ्य, तदारभ्य, तदवधि, तत्कालावधि.
THEOCRACY, *s.* ईश्वरकर्तृकराज्यं, ईश्वरकर्तृकशासनं, ईश्वरप्रभुत्वं.
THEOGONY, *s.* देवोत्पत्तिः *f.*, देवजन्म *n.* (न्), देववंशः -वंशावली.
THEOLOGIAN, *s.* परमार्थवित् *m.*, परमार्थज्ञानी *m.* (न्), ब्रह्मज्ञानी *m.*, ब्रह्मविद्याज्ञः, अध्यात्मज्ञानी *m.*, अध्यात्मदृक् *m.* (श्), श्रोत्रियः, श्रुताध्ययनसम्पन्नः, धर्म्मशास्त्रज्ञः, वेदान्ती *m.*
THEOLOGICAL, *a.* परमार्थविद्याविषयकः -का -कं, परमार्थविद्यासम्बन्धी -न्धिनी &c., अध्यात्मज्ञानविषयकः &c., औपनिषदः -दी -दं.
THEOLOGY, *s.* परमार्थविद्या, परमार्थज्ञानं, श्रुतिविद्या, धर्म्मविद्या, देवज्ञानं, ब्रह्मज्ञानं, ब्रह्मविद्या, तत्त्वज्ञानं, तत्त्वविद्या, अध्यात्मज्ञानं, अध्यात्मविद्या, श्रोत्रियता, परार्थप्रकरणं.
THEOREM, *s.* (Proposition to be proved) प्रमेयं, प्रमेयोपपाद्यं.
THEORETIC, THEORETICAL, *a.* मानसिकः -की -कं, काल्पनिकः &c., अव्यवहारिकः -की -कं, व्यवहारागम्यः -म्या -म्यं, मनोमयः &c. *See* SPECULATIVE.
THEORETICALLY, *adv.* मनःकल्पनानुसारेण, मनःकल्पनया, कल्पनापूर्वं.
THEORY, *s.* (Speculation, scheme) कल्पना, मनःकल्पना, मानसकल्पना, मानससृष्टिः *f.*, तर्कः, कल्पितं, मनःकल्पितं, अर्थापत्तिः *f.*; 'anxious to establish one's own theory,' स्वकल्पनासाधनेच्छुः -च्छुः -च्छु.—(Exposition of principles) बीजनिर्देशः, उपपत्तिः *f.*
THERAPEUTIC, *a.* रोगशमकः -का -कं, रोगप्रतिकारकः &c., *see* CURATIVE.

THERE, *adv.* तत्र, तत्स्थाने, तस्मिन् स्थाने, तस्मिन् देशे; 'here and there,' इतस्ततस्; 'produced there, or relating to that place,' तत्रत्यः -त्या -त्यं, तत्रस्थः -स्था -स्थं; 'the people residing there,' तत्रस्थजनाः *m. f.*, तत्रत्यजनाः.
THEREABOUTS, *adv.* (Near that place) तत्रोपान्ते, तत्स्थानसमीपे-निकटे, तत्रसमीपे, आदिपश्चात्.—(Nearly), *see* NEARLY, *adv.*
THEREAT, *adv.* तेन, तस्मात्, तदुपरि, ततस्, अतस्.
THEREBY, *adv.* तेन, तेनोपायेन, तद्द्वारा, तद्द्वारेण, अनेनोपायेन.
THEREFORE, *adv.* तेन, तस्मात्, अनेन हेतुना, तेन हेतुना, तस्य हेतोः, तेन कारणेन, तत्कारणात्, अतस्, ततस्, अतःकारणात्, अतोहेतोः, तन्निदानात्, तत्, इति, इति हेतोः.
THEREIN, *adv.* तत्र, तस्मिन्, एतस्मिन्, अस्मिन्, अस्मिन् विषये.
THEREOF, *adv.* तस्य, एतस्य, तदीयः -या -यं; 'belonging to that place,' तत्रत्यः -त्या -त्यं, तत्स्थानिकः -की -कं, तत्स्थानीयः -या -यं, तत्रस्थः &c.
THEREUPON, *adv.* ततस्, अतस्, तत्रोपरि, तदनन्तरं, अत्रान्तरे.
THERMOMETER, *s.* उष्णानुष्णमापनयन्त्रं, शीतोष्णमापनयन्त्रं.
THESE, *pron.* एते *m.* एताः *f.* एतानि *n. pl.* (एतत्), इमे *m.*, इमाः *f.*, इमानि *n. pl.* (इदं), अमी *m. pl.* (अदस्); 'these two,' एतौ *m. du.*, एते *f. du.*
THESIS, *s.* (Proposition) पक्षः, पूर्व्वपक्षः, प्रतिज्ञा.
THEY, *pron.* ते *m.*, ताः *f.*, तानि *n. pl.* (तद्), एते &c., इमे &c. (इदं), अमी *m. pl.* (अदस्); 'they two,' तौ *m. du.*, ते *f. du.*
THICK, *a.* घनः -ना -नं, स्थूलः -ला -लं, सान्द्रः -न्द्रा -न्द्रं, निविडः -डा -डं, अविरलः -ला -लं, नीरन्ध्रः -न्ध्रा -न्ध्रं, श्यानः &c., स्त्यानः &c., *see* DENSE.—(As water, &c., turbid) कलुषः -षा -षं, अनच्छः -च्छा -च्छं, आविलः -ला -लं.
THICK, *adv.* (In quick succession) निरन्तरं, अविरतं, *see* FREQUENTLY.—(Closely) निरन्तरं, अविरलं, निविडं.
To THICKEN, *v. a.* घनीकृ, सान्द्रीकृ, स्थूलीकृ, श्यानीकृ, निविडीकृ.
To THICKEN, *v. n.* घनीभू, सान्द्रीभू, स्थूलीभू, श्यानीभू, निविडीभू.
THICKENED, *p. p.* घनीभूतः -ता -तं, घनीकृतः -ता -तं, स्थूलीभूतः &c.,
THICKENING, *s.* घनीकरणं, घनता. *See* INSPISSATION.
THICKET, *s.* गहनं, वृक्षगहनं, तरुगहनं, वनगहनं, अटः -टं, गुहिनं, विपिनं, गह्वरं, सान्द्रं, प्रस्तारः.
THICK-HEADED, *a.* स्थूलबुद्धिः -द्धिः -द्धि, स्थूलधीः &c. *See* STUPID.
THICKLY, *adv.* निरन्तरं, अविरलं, निविडं, अविरतं, सुसंहतं.
THICKNESS, *s.* घनता -त्वं, स्थूलता, स्थौल्यं, सान्द्रता, नैविड्यं, श्यानता, पीवरत्वं, संहतत्वं, *see* DENSITY. 'Thickness,' as a property of matter, is expressed by पिण्डत्वं.
THICK-SET, *a.* संहतः -ता -तं, सुसंहतः &c., निरन्तरः -रा -रं.
THIEF, *s.* स्तेनः, चौरः, स्तेयी *m.* (न्), चोरः, तस्करः, स्तेयकृत् *m.*, मोषकः, आमोषी *m.* (न्), मोष्टा *m.* (ृ), परस्वापहारी *m.*, अदत्तादायी *m.*, परद्रव्यहारकः, चौर्य्यकृत् *m.*, ऐकागारिकः, मलिम्लुचः. *See* ROBBER, STEALER.
THIEF-TAKER, THIEF-CATCHER, *s.* चौरग्राही *m.* (न्), स्तेनग्राही *m.*
To THIEVE, *v. n.* चौर्य्यं कृ, स्तेयं कृ, तास्कर्य्यं कृ, परद्रव्यहरणं कृ.
THIEVISH, *a.* चौर्य्यासक्तः -क्ता -क्तं, स्तेयासक्तः &c., चौर्य्यशीलः -ला -लं, स्तेयकारी -रिणी -रि (न्), अदत्तपरधनापहारप्रसक्तः -क्ता -क्तं.
THIEVISHNESS, *s.* चौर्य्यासक्तिः *f.*, स्तेयासक्तिः *f.*, चौर्य्यशीलता, तस्करता.
THIGH, *s.* ऊरुः *m.*, सक्थि *n.*, जङ्घा, जाङ्घनी, भपत् *m.*; 'fore part of

the thigh,' प्रतिजङ्घा ; 'having long thighs,' दीर्घसक्थः -क्था -क्थं.

THIMBLE, s. अङ्गुल्यग्रत्राणं, अङ्गुलिमुखत्रं, अग्राङ्गुलित्रं -त्राणं, सूचिचालनी, सूचिप्रणोदनी, सूचिचालनयोग्ययन्त्रं.

THIN, a. (Not thick) तनुः -नुः -न्वी -नु, प्रतनुः &c., वितनुः &c., सूक्ष्मः -क्ष्मा -क्ष्मं, अस्थूलः -ला -लं.—(Slender, lean) तनुः -न्वी -नु, क्षीणः -णा -णं, शीर्णः -र्णा -र्णं, कृशः -शा -शं, कृशाङ्गः -ङ्गा -ङ्गं, जैवातृकः -का -कं, पृश्निः -श्निः -श्नि, शातः -ता -तं, अमांसः -सा -सं ; 'having a thin waist,' तनुमध्यमः -मा -मं, अल्पमध्यमः &c., क्षीणमध्यः -ध्या -ध्यं, शातोदरी.—(Rare, subtil, fine) सूक्ष्मः -क्ष्मा -क्ष्मं, श्लक्ष्णः -क्ष्णा -क्ष्णं, दहरः -रा -रं.—(Not close) विरलः -ला -लं ; 'a thin plank,' सूक्ष्मफलकः, सूक्ष्मदारु m.

To THIN, v. a. तनूकृ, सूक्ष्मीकृ, श्लक्ष्णीकृ, श्लक्ष्ण (nom. श्लक्ष्णयति -यितुं), लेखनं कृ, तक्षणं कृ.—(Make less, close, &c.) विरलीकृ.

THINE, a. तव gen. c., ते gen. c., त्वदीयः -या -यं, तवकः -का -कं, तावकः -की -कं, तावकीनः -ना -नं, त्वत्कः -त्का -त्कं, भवदीयः -या -यं, त्वत् in comp.

THING, s. द्रव्यं, वस्तु n., अर्थः, विषयः, पदार्थः, द्रविणं, वसु n., वित्तं, विभवः, see SUBSTANCE ; 'things,' द्रव्याणि n. pl., वस्तूनि n. pl.

To THINK, v. a. or n. (Reflect) चिन्त् (c. 10. चिन्तयति -यितुं), संचिन्त्, विचिन्त्, परिचिन्त्, प्रविचिन्त्, तर्क् (c. 10. तर्कयति -यितुं), वितर्क्, ध्यै (c. 1. ध्यायति, ध्यातुं), अनुध्यै, उपध्यै, अभिध्यै, प्रध्यै, संध्यै, विमृश्, अनुमृश्, परिमृश्, मनसा विचर्, भू in caus., सम्भू in caus., आलोच्, आलोक्, निरूप्, see *To* REFLECT.—(Suppose) मन् (c. 4. मन्यते, मन्तुं), see *To* IMAGINE ; 'to think of,' अनुस्मृ, see *To* RECOLLECT ; 'to think to one's self,' स्वगतं चिन्त् ; 'one who thinks that it is night,' रात्रिम्मन्यः.

THINKER, s. चिन्तकः, चिन्तयिता m. (तृ), चिन्तनकृत्, मन्ता m.

THINLY, adv. विरलं, वैरल्येन, असंहतं, अस्थूलं, तनु, तानवेन.

THINNED, p. p. तनूकृतः -ता -तं, सूक्ष्मीकृतः &c., तष्टः -ष्टा -ष्टं, त्वष्टः &c.

THINNESS, s. तनुता, तानवं, सूक्ष्मता, क्षीणता, शीर्णता, कृशता, कृशाङ्गता, सौक्ष्म्यं, अस्थूलता.—(Rareness) विरलता, वैरल्यं.

THIRD, a. तृतीयः -या -यं, त्रितयः &c., तृतीयी -यिनी -यि (न्).

THIRD, s. (Third part) तृतीयांशः, तृतीयभागः ; 'two thirds,' द्वौ तृतीयांशौ, द्वौ तृतीयभागौ ; 'having a third,' तृतीयी -यिनी &c.

THIRDLY, adv. तृतीयतस्, तृतीयं, तृतीयपदे, तृतीयस्थाने.

THIRST, s. तृष्णा, तृषा, तृट् f. (ष्), पिपासा, तर्षः -र्षणं, अनुतर्षः, तृषितं, पानेच्छा, उदकेच्छा, उदन्या, अपलाषिका, उपलालिका, धीतिः f. ; 'excessive thirst,' अतितृष्णा ; 'of wealth,' धनतृष्णा, धनाशा ; 'eating to excite thirst,' अवदंशः.

To THIRST, v. n. तृष् (c. 4. तृष्यति, तर्षितुं), वितृष्, पा in des. (पिपासति -सितुं), तृषार्त्तः -र्त्ता -र्त्तं भू, तृषार्त्तीभू, उदन (nom. उदन्यति).

THIRSTING, part. तृष्यन् -ष्यन्ती -ष्यत् (त्), पिपासन् -सन्ती -सत् (त्). *See* the next.

THIRSTY, a. तृषार्त्तः -र्त्ता -र्त्तं, पिपासुः -सुः -सु, तर्षितः -ता -तं, तृषितः &c., तृष्णक् m. f. n. (ज्), तृषातुरः -रा -रं, तृष्णातुरः -रा -रं, पानेच्छुः -च्छुः -च्छु, उदकेच्छुः &c., उदकार्थी -र्थिनी -र्थि (न्), पानार्थी &c., पिपासितः -ता -तं, सतृष्णः -ष्णा -ष्णं, सतृट् m. f. n. (ष्), तृट्परीतः -ता -तं, सतृषः -षा -षं, तृषान्वितः -ता -तं, तृषावान् -वती &c., तृषाकुलः -ला -लं, तृषाविष्टः -ष्टा -ष्टं, तृषाक्रान्तः -न्ता -न्तं.

THIRTEEN, a. त्रयोदश m. f. n. pl. (न्), त्रिदश m. f. n. pl. (न्).

THIRTEENTH, a. त्रयोदशः -शी -शं, त्रिदशः -शी -शं.

THIRTIETH, a. त्रिंशः -शी -शं, त्रिंशत्तमः -मी -मं.

THIRTY, a. त्रिंशत् sing. f., त्रिंशकः -का -कं ; 'the aggregate of thirty,' त्रिंशकं ; 'he reigned thirty years,' त्रिंशतम् अब्दान् राज्यं चकार ; 'with thirty arrows,' त्रिंशता शरैः ; 'thirty-one,' एकत्रिंशत् ; 'two,' द्वात्रिंशत् ; 'three,' त्रयस्त्रिंशत् ; 'four,' चतुस्त्रिंशत् ; 'five,' पञ्चत्रिंशत् ; 'six,' षट्त्रिंशत्, see SEVENTY ; 'thirty-fold,' त्रिंशद्गुणः -णा -णं.

THIS, pron. एषः एषा एतत् (एतद्), अयं इयं इदं (इदं), असौ m. f. (अदस्).

THISTLE, s. गोक्षुरः -रकः, गोखुरः, गोक्षुरिः m., क्षुरः.

THITHER, adv. तत्र, तत्स्थानं प्रति, तद्देशं प्रति, तं देशं प्रति.

THONG, s. वरत्रा, चर्म्मरज्जुः m. f., चर्म्मबन्धः, वध्री, वर्द्ध्री, वध्री, वार्द्ध्री, वार्द्ध -र्द्धी, नद्ध्री, वलिसद्मः, चर्म्मनिर्म्मितो रज्जुः, चर्म्मपट्टी.

THORAX, s. उरस् n., वक्षस् n., वक्षःस्थलं, उरःस्थलं, वक्षस्स्थलं, उरस्स्थलं, पार्श्वं.

THORN, s. (Tree) कण्टकवृक्षः.—(Prickle) कण्टकः -कं, द्रुनखः, द्रुमनखः, तरुनखः, पत्रसूचिः m., दलसूचिः m., शल्यं, शिताग्रः, सिताग्रः, राङ्कलः, वल्किलः, वङ्किलः, पनसः, द्रुमरः ; 'extraction of thorns,' कण्टकोद्धरणं, शल्योद्धरणं ; 'eater of thorns,' कण्टकभुक् m.—(Any thing troublesome) कण्टकः, शल्यं.

THORN-APPLE, s. धत्तूरः, धुस्तूरः, धुस्तुरः, धूस्तूरः, कनकः, कितवः, उन्मत्तः, धूर्त्तः, मातुलः, मदनः, मारः, हेमतरुः m., पुरीमोहः, खरदूषणः, काहलापुष्पः, तीक्ष्णकण्टकः ; 'its fruit,' मातुलपुत्रकः.

THORNLESS, a. निष्कण्टकः -का -कं, अकण्टकः &c., कण्टकहीनः -ना -नं.

THORNY, a. कण्टकितः -ता -तं, कण्टकी -किनी -कि (न्), सकण्टकः -का -कं, बहुकण्टकः &c., प्रचुरकण्टकः &c., कण्टकयुक्तः -क्ता -क्तं.

THOROUGH, a. साद्यन्तः -न्ता -न्तं, पर्य्याप्तः -प्ता -प्तं. *See* COMPLETE.

THOROUGH-BRED, a. (Horse) आजानेयः, कुलीनः, *see* under HORSE.

THOROUGHFARE, s. सर्व्वसाधारणमार्गः, सर्व्वसामान्यपथः, सर्व्वगम्यमार्गः, लोकगम्यपथः, अप्रतिरोधपथः; 'a great thoroughfare,' लोकयात्रा, सर्व्वलोकयात्रा, जनाकीर्णमार्गः, जनाकीर्णं.

THOROUGHLY, adv. साद्यन्तं, पर्य्याप्तं, साकल्येन. *See* COMPLETELY.

THOSE, pron. ते m., ताः f., तानि n. pl. (तद्), अमी m. pl. *See* THESE.

THOU, pron. त्वं (युष्मद्) ; 'to thou and thee,' त्वङ्कृ.

THOUGH, conj. यद्यपि, अपि, तथापि, यदि. *See* ALTHOUGH.

THOUGHT, s. (Operation of the mind, act of thinking) चिन्ता -न्तनं, विचारणं -णा, विचारः, ध्यानं, अभिध्यानं, आध्यानं, भावना, चर्चा, मननं, मनोव्यापारः, अन्तःकरणव्यापारः, चित्तव्यापारः, चित्तचेष्टा, मनश्चेष्टा, अन्तःकरणचेष्टा, see REFLECTION, MEDITATION.—(That which is formed in the mind) बुद्धिः f., मतिः f., मतं, मनस् n., बोधः, मनोगतं, कल्पना, मनःकल्पना, मनःकल्पितं, सङ्कल्पः, मनोगुप्तं, मनसिजं, मनोवृत्तिः f., चित्तवृत्तिः f., हृद्गतं, भावना, तर्कः ; 'inmost thoughts,' अन्तर्गतं मनस् ; 'evil thoughts,' कुकल्पना, कुतर्कः, अपध्यानं ; 'speed of thought,' मनोवेगः, मनोजवं ; 'swift as thought,' मनोजवः -वा -वं, मनोयायी -यिनी &c. ; 'beyond thought,' अचिन्त्यः -न्त्या -न्त्यं, अचिन्तनीयः -या -यं ; 'in thought, word, or deed,' मनोवचनकर्म्मभिः inst. pl.

THOUGHT, p. p. चिन्तितः -ता -तं, मतः &c., भावितः &c., कल्पितः &c.

THOUGHTFUL, a. (Contemplative) चिन्तापरः -रा -रं, see MEDITATIVE.—(Considerate, attentive) विचारशीलः -ला -लं, विचारवान् -वती &c., सविचारः -रा -रं, सचिन्तः -न्ता -न्तं, चिन्तावान् &c., चिन्तायुक्तः -क्ता -क्तं.

THOUGHTFULNESS, s. विचारशीलता, सविचारता, सचिन्तता, मानसत्वं.

THOUGHTLESS, *a.* निश्चिन्तः -न्ता -न्तं, विवेकहीनः -ना -नं, विचारहीनः &c., अविचारशीलः -ला -लं, अनूहः -हा -हं. *See* HEEDLESS, NEGLIGENT.

THOUGHTLESSLY, *adv.* अचिन्तया, निश्चिन्तं, अविचारेण, अविवेकेन; 'thoughtlessly done,' अविचारकृतः -ता -तं, अविवेककृतः &c.

THOUGHTLESSNESS, *s.* अविचारः -रता, अविवेकता, अविवेकः, विचारहीनता, विवेकहीनता, प्रमादः. *See* HEEDLESSNESS.

THOUSAND, *a.* सहस्रं *n. sing.*, दशशतं. The word सहस्रं may be used with the nom. pl. or gen. pl.; as, 'a thousand ancestors,' सहस्रं पितरः or सहस्रं पितॄणां; 'ten thousand,' अयुतः -तं; 'one hundred thousand,' लक्षं -क्षा; 'a thousand times,' सहस्रकृत्वस्; 'in a thousand ways,' सहस्रधा; 'thousand eyed,' सहस्रनयनः -ना -नं; 'a regiment of a thousand men,' सहस्री *m.* (न्), साहस्रः; 'the aggregate of a thousand,' साहस्रं; 'thousand-fold,' सहस्रगुणः -णा -णं; 'by thousands,' सहस्रशस्.

THOUSANDTH, *a.* सहस्रतमः -मी -मं, साहस्रः -स्री -स्रं.

THRALLDOM, *s.* दास्यं, वशता, पारतन्त्र्यं, *see* SERVITUDE, SLAVERY.

To THRASH, *v. a.* निस्तुषीकृ, कण्डनं कृ, पू, तड्. *See To* THRESH.

THREAD, *s.* सूत्रं, तन्तुः *m.*, तन्त्रं, गुणः, सूत्रतन्तुः *m.*, सरत् *n.*, सरित् *f.*, कुत्रं, चीनः, सात्रं; 'point of a thread,' पक्ष्म *n.* (न्), सूत्राग्रं; 'thread of a story or subject,' प्रबन्धार्थः, अर्थप्रबन्धः, अन्वयः, अर्थान्वयः, अर्थसन्दर्भः, कथासन्दर्भः, कथाप्रबन्धः, सन्धानं, अनुसन्धानं; 'thread of hope,' आशातन्तुः *m.*; 'sacrificial thread,' *see* under SACRIFICIAL.

To THREAD, *v. a.* सूत्र (Nom. सूत्रयति -यितुं), गुम्फ्, *see To* STRING.

THREADBARE, *a.* जर्जरीकः -का -कं, जर्जरः -रा -रं, सूत्रदरिद्रः &c.

THREADED, *p. p.* सूत्रितः -ता -तं, गुम्फितः &c., ग्रन्थितः &c., ग्रथितः &c.

THREAT, *s.* भर्त्सनं, निर्भर्त्सनं, तर्जनं, दण्डसूचनं. *See* MENACE.

To THREATEN, *v. a.* भर्त्स् (c. 10. भर्त्सयति -ते -यितुं), निर्भर्त्स्, तर्ज्, *see To* MENACE.—(Declare purpose of punishing) दण्डसूचनं कृ, दण्डप्रदर्शनं कृ, दण्डसङ्कल्पप्रदर्शनं कृ.—(Exhibit the appearance of something evil approaching) अनिष्टसूचनं कृ, अनिष्टावेदनं कृ, *see To* PREBODE.

THREATENED, *p. p.* भर्त्सितः -ता -तं, निर्भर्त्सितः &c., तर्जितः -ता -तं.

THREATENING, *part.* भर्त्सनकारी -रिणी &c., अनिष्टावेदी -दिनी &c.

THREE, *a.* त्रयः *m. pl.*, तिस्रः *f. pl.*, त्रीणि *n. pl.* (त्रि); 'the three worlds,' त्रिभुवनं; 'the aggregate of three,' त्रयं, त्रयी, त्रिकं, त्रितयं. The word त्रयं is often used at the end of a compound to express 'three;' as, 'three months,' मासत्रयं; 'three years,' वर्षत्रयं; 'three steps,' पदत्रयं; 'the three properties,' गुणत्रयं; 'he was seen by three rogues,' स धूर्त्तत्रयेण दृष्टः; 'two or three,' द्वित्राः -त्राः -त्राणि (त्र being here put for त्रि); 'two or three or any number,' द्वित्र्यादिसंख्या, द्वित्राद्याः *m. pl.*; 'three or four,' त्रिचतुराः -राः -राणि; 'rule of three,' त्रैराशिकगणितं, *see* under RULE, *s.*

THREE-FOLD, *a.* त्रिगुणः -णा -णं, त्रिविधः -धा -धं, त्रिवृत् *m. f. n.*

THREE-FOURTHS, *s. pl.* त्रयश् चतुर्थांशाः *m. pl.*, त्रिपादाः, त्र्यंशाः.

THRENODY, *s.* यमगाथा, यमगीतं, यमगानं.

To THRESH, *v. a.* (Corn) धान्यादि मृद् (c. 9. मृद्नाति, मर्दितुं) or पू or परिपू or निस्तुषीकृ, धान्यादिमर्दनं कृ, धान्यादिकण्डनं कृ, अवघातं कृ.—(Beat) तड् (c. 10. ताडयति -यितुं), ताडनं कृ.

THRESHED, *p. p.* मर्दितः -ता -तं, मृदितः &c., निस्तुषितः &c., निस्तुषीकृतः &c., पूतः &c., परिपूतः &c., अपहतः &c., बहुलीकृतः &c.

THRESHING, *s.* धान्यादिमर्दनं, धान्यादिकण्डनं, कण्डनं, निस्तुषीकरणं, अवघातः, पावनं, ताडनं.

THRESHING-FLOOR, *s.* धान्यादिमर्दनस्थानं, धान्यादिकण्डनस्थानं, धान्यमर्दनभूमिः *f.*, खलः, शस्यमर्दनस्थानं.

THRESHOLD *s.* देहली, गृहावग्रहणी, गृहतटी, शिला -ली, द्वारपिण्डी, दण्डिका, असुरः, उदुम्बरः.

THRICE, *adv.* त्रिवारं, वारत्रयं, त्रिः, त्रिकृत्वस्, त्रिगुणः -णा -णी -णं, त्रि in comp.; 'thrice ploughed,' त्रिसीत्यः -त्या -त्यं, त्रिहल्यः -ल्या -ल्यं, त्रिगुणाकृतः -ता -तं.

THRIFT, THRIFTINESS, THRIFTY, &c. *See* FRUGALITY, FRUGAL, &c.

THRILL, *s.* स्फुरणं, स्फूर्त्तिः *f.*, स्फुरितं, हर्षः; 'of joy,' रोमहर्षः -र्षणं, रोमोद्धर्षणं, रोमोद्गमः, रोमोद्भेदः, रोमाञ्चः, पुलकः, पुलकोद्गमः.

To THRILL, *v. n.* स्फुर् (c. 6. स्फुरति -रितुं), हृष् (c. 4. हृष्यति, हर्षितुं).

THRILLING, *part.* स्फुरन् -रन्ती -रत् (त्), स्फुरितः -ता -तं; 'with joy,' हृष्टः -ष्टा -ष्टं, हर्षी -र्षिणी -र्षि (न्), पुलकितः -ता -तं, रोमाञ्चितः &c.

To THRIVE, *v. n.* *See To* FLOURISH, PROSPER, *v. n.*

THRIVING, *v. n.* समृद्धः -द्धा -द्धं. *See* PROSPEROUS, FLOURISHING.

THROAT, *s.* कण्ठः, गलः, ग्रीवा, कन्धरः -रा, कुहरं, कृकः, निगरणः, *see* NECK; 'relating to it,' कण्ठ्यः -ण्ठ्या -ण्ठ्यं; 'seated in it,' कण्ठस्थः -स्था -स्थं, कण्ठगतः -ता -तं; 'up to the throat,' आकण्ठात्; 'dryness of it,' कण्ठशोषः.

To THROB, *v. n.* स्फुर् (c. 6. -स्फुरति -रितुं), विस्फुर्, स्यन्द् (c. 1. स्यन्दते -न्दितुं), प्रतिस्यन्द्, परिस्यन्द्, कम्प्, विकम्प्, वेप्. *See To* PALPITATE, BEAT.

THROB, THROBBING, *s.* स्फुरणं -णा, स्फुरितं, स्यन्दनं, स्यन्दितं, विष्यन्दः, स्यन्दः, कम्पः, स्फोरणं, स्फुटः, स्फरणं, स्फारणं, स्फुलनं; 'of the eye,' चक्षुःस्यन्दः.

THROE, *s.* (Of child-birth) प्रसववेदना, गर्भवेदना, वेधना.

THRONE, *s.* सिंहासनं, नृपासनं, राजासनं, उच्चासनं, भद्रासनं, राजशय्या, महाशय्या, मञ्चः, राजासनमञ्चः.

THRONG, *To* THRONG. *See* CROWD, *To* CROWD.

THRONGED, *p. p.* सङ्कीर्णः -र्णा -र्णं, समाकीर्णः &c., बाधितः -ता -तं.

To THROTTLE, *v. a.* गलग्रहं कृ, गलहस्त. *See To* CHOKE, SUFFOCATE.

THROUGH, *prep.* (From one end or side to the other) पारं, आपाराभ्यन्तरात्, पार्श्वान्तरपर्य्यन्तं, पार्श्वान्तरं यावत्, तीरान्तरं.—(Denoting passage) मध्येन, अन्तरेण or expressed by the inflection of the noun; 'he goes through a fissure in the rock,' गिरिरन्ध्रमध्येन गच्छति; 'through the branches,' विटपान्तरेण.—(By means of, through the agency or influence of) expressed by the abl. or instr. case; as, 'through ambition,' लोभात्, लोभेन; 'through anger,' कोपात्, रोषवशतया; 'through him,' तेन, *see* under BY, *prep.*

THROUGH, *adv.* (From the beginning to the end) साद्यन्तं, आद्यन्तं.—(To the end) शेषपर्य्यन्तं, शेषं यावत्, समाप्तिपर्य्यन्तं, अवसानपर्य्यन्तं, आसमाप्तेः, आशेषात्, *see* THROUGHOUT; 'to carry through, get through,' पार् (c. 10. पारयति -यितुं), तीर् (c. 10. तीरयति -यितुं). *see To* FINISH, *v. a.*

THROUGHOUT, *adv.* (From the beginning to the end) साद्यन्तं,

आद्यन्तं, शेषपर्य्यन्तं.—(Of time) expressed by पर्य्यन्तं, यावत् or आ in comp.; thus, 'throughout the month,' मासपर्य्यन्तं; 'throughout the year,' वर्षपर्य्यन्तं; 'throughout the whole year,' आवर्षान्तात् or वर्षान्तं यावत् (*i. e.* to the end of the year); 'throughout life,' यावज्जीवं, जीवनपर्य्यन्तं, आजीवनान्तात्.

To THROW, *v. a.* क्षिप् (c. 6. क्षिपति, क्षेप्तुं), प्रक्षिप्, अस् (c. 4. अस्यति -सितुं), प्रास्, मुच् (c. 6. मुञ्चति, मोक्तुं), प्रमुच्, ईर् (c. 10. ईरयति -यितुं), समीर्, उदीर्, पत् (c. 10. पातयति -यितुं), सृज्, प्रहृ, प्रेष् in caus.—(Throw away) अपास्, व्युदस्, अपव्यध्, त्यज्, अपहा, विहा, नश् in caus., *see To* LOSE, REJECT; 'one's time,' कालं क्षिप्, कालक्षेपं कृ.—(Throw about) विक्षिप्, इतस्ततः क्षिप्.—(Throw behind one's back) पृष्ठतः कृ or क्षिप्.—(Throw down) पत् in caus., अवपत्, अधःपत्, अधः क्षिप्, अधः कृ, भ्रंश् in caus., प्रभ्रंश्, च्यु in caus., प्रच्यु.—(Throw into disorder) व्यूहान् भञ्ज् or भिद्, पिच्छलीकृ.—(Throw off) अवधू, निर्धू, विधू, निरस्, निराकृ, अपव्यध्.—(Throw out) निरस्, निराकृ; 'as hints, &c.,' सूच्, सूचनां कृ.—(Throw up) उत्क्षिप्, उत्क्षेपं कृ, *see To* VOMIT.—(Throw up), *see To* RESIGN.—(Throw one's self down) स्वदेहावपातं कृ; 'from a cliff,' गिरिशिखराद् अवपातं कृ or प्रपतनं कृ.

THROW, *s.* क्षेपः -पणं, प्रक्षेपः, आक्षेपः, असनं, पातः -तनं, क्षिप्तिः *f.*

THROWER, *s.* क्षेपकः, प्रक्षेपकः, क्षेप्ता *m.* (प्तृ), प्रासकः, क्षेपणकृत्.

THROWN, *p. p.* क्षिप्तः -प्ता -प्तं, प्रक्षिप्तः &c., अस्तः -स्ता -स्तं, प्रास्तः &c., ईरितः -ता -तं, पातितः -ता -तं; 'away,' अपास्तः &c., व्युदस्तः &c., अपविद्धः -द्धा -द्धं, अपसारितः -ता -तं, त्यक्तः -क्ता -क्तं, नष्टः -ष्टा -ष्टं; 'a kindness is thrown away on bad men,' सुकृतम् असत्सु नष्टं; 'thrown down,' पातितः -ता -तं, निपातितः &c., अधःपातितः &c., अधःक्षिप्तः -प्ता -प्तं, अधःकृतः -ता -तं, भ्रंशितः -ता -तं; 'thrown into disorder,' भग्नव्यूहः -हा -हं, भिन्नव्यूहः &c., पिच्छलः -ला -लं, समुत्पिञ्जलः &c.; 'thrown off,' निर्धूतः -ता -तं, अवधूतः &c., अपविद्धः &c.; 'as from a horse, &c.,' निरस्तः -स्ता -स्तं.

THRUM, *s.* (Ends of threads) दशाः *f. pl.*, वस्तयः *f. pl.* (वस्ति).

THRUSH, *s.* (Bird) सारिका, शारिका, मदनसारिका, शलाका, शरारिः *f.*, शरालिः *f.*, सरातिः *f.*, आटिः *f.*, आडिः *f.*, आतिः *f.*

To THRUST, *v. a.* तड् (c. 10. ताडयति -यितुं), प्रसृ (c. 10. -सारयति -यितुं), प्रसारणं कृ; 'aside,' अपसृ, *see To* PUSH.

THRUST, *s.* ताडनं, आघातः, अभिघातः, प्रसारणं, प्रहारः, *see* PUSH.

THUMB, *s.* अङ्गुष्ठः, अङ्गुलः, वृद्धाङ्गुलिः *f.*; 'thumb and forefinger,' सन्तोषः.

To THUMB, *v. a.* अङ्गुलीभिर् अङ्क् (c. 10. अङ्कयति -यितुं) or परामृश् or स्पृश्, अङ्गुल्यङ्कितं -तां कृ. *See To* FINGER, *v. a.*

THUMP, *s.* आघातः, प्रहारः, करघातः, मुष्टिपातः. *See* BLOW.

To THUMP, *v. a.* तड् (c. 10. ताडयति -यितुं), प्रहृ, आहन्. *See To* BEAT.

THUNDER, *s.* गर्जनं -ना, गर्जितं, मेघगर्जितं, मेघनादः, मेघशब्दः, मेघनिर्घोषः, स्फूर्जः, स्फूर्जनं, स्फूर्जथुः *m.*, विस्फूर्जथुः *m.*, विस्फूर्जितं, मेघविस्फूर्जितं, स्तनितं, मेघस्तनितं, स्तननं, मेघस्तननं, स्तनयित्नुः *m.*, घनशब्दः, घनस्वनः, घनरवः, मेघध्वनिः *m.*, परिघोषः, गम्भीरनादः, गर्जिः *m.*, गर्जः, रसितः.

To THUNDER, *v. n.* गर्ज् (c. 1. गर्जति -र्जितुं), परिगर्ज्, स्फूर्ज् (c. 1. स्फूर्जति -र्जितुं), विस्फूर्ज्, स्तन् (c. 1. स्तनति -नितुं), गर्जनं कृ, स्फूर्जनं कृ.

THUNDERBOLT, *s.* वज्रः -ज्रं, वज्राघातः, कुलिशः -शं, भिदुरं, भिदिः *m.*, भिदिरं, भिदुः *m.*, अशनिः *m. f.*, वज्राशनिः *m.*, ह्रादकं, मृदाकरः, शतधारं, शतारं, बहुधारः, शतकोटिः *m.*, पद्मोद्यो, अभोत्थं, त्रिदशाङ्कुशं, गिरिज्वरः, गिरिध्वजः, गिरिकण्टकः, इन्द्रप्रहरणं, स्वरुः *m.*, दम्भोलिः *m.*, ह्रादिनी, पविः *m.*, शम्बः, शम्भः, पेशिः *m.*, भसुरिः *m.*, व्याधामः, मेघभूतिः *f.*, दुम्भूः *m.*, दधीच्यस्थि *n.*, वैद्युतो ऽग्निः; 'fall of a thunderbolt,' वज्रपातः; 'like a thunderbolt,' वज्रप्रायः -या -यं.

THUNDER-CLAP, *s.* स्फूर्जथुः *m.*, वज्रनिर्घोषः, वज्रनिष्पेषः, वज्राघातः, वज्रज्वाला, वज्रपातशब्दः, वज्रस्तनितं, वज्रनिस्वनः.

THUNDER-CLOUD, *s.* घनः, वज्रघनः, मेघः, वज्रमेघः, वज्राभ्रं.

THUNDERER, *s.* वज्री *m.* (न्), वज्रपाणिः *m.*, वज्रधरः, कुलिशभृत्.

THUNDERING, *s.* स्फूर्जनं, गर्जनं, मेघगर्जनं. *See* THUNDER.

THUNDERING, *part.* गर्जन् -र्जन्ती -र्जत् (त्), स्फूर्जथुवान् -वती -वत् (त्).

THUNDER-STORM, *s.* वज्रवर्षः, अशनिवर्षः, कुलिशवर्षः.

THUNDERSTRUCK, *a.* वज्राहतः -ता -तं, वज्रहतः &c., वज्रप्रहतः &c., वज्रताडितः -ता -तं, विद्युद्धतः &c. *See* ASTOUNDED.

THURSDAY, *s.* वृहस्पतिवारः, गुरुवारः, गुरुवासरः, लक्ष्मीवारः.

THUS, *adv.* (In this manner) एवं, इत्थं, अनेन प्रकारेण, एवम्प्रकारेण, उक्तेन प्रकारेण, उक्तप्रकारेण, अनया रीत्या, अनयरीत्या, अतएव.—(So) तथा, तथाहि, इति, एतादृशं.—(Thus much) इयान् -यती -यत् (त्), एतावान् &c.

To THWART, *v. a.* व्याहन्, प्रतिहन्, प्रतिरुध्, *see To* FRUSTRATE, HINDER.

THWARTED, *p. p.* संरुद्धचेष्टः -ष्टा -ष्टं, प्रतिबद्धः &c. *See* FRUSTRATED.

THY, *pron.* तव gen. c. (युष्मत्), त्वदीयः -या -यं.

THYSELF, *pron.* स त्वं, आत्मा *m.* (न्). *See* MYSELF.

TIARA, *s.* मुकुटं, किरीटः, मौलिः *m. f.*, अवतंसः, ललाटपट्टं, चूडा.

TIBIA, *s.* जङ्घायाः पूर्वास्थि *n.* or जङ्घास्थि *n.*

TICK, *s.* (Credit), *see* CREDIT.—(Louse) यूकः, लोमकीटः.

To TICK, *v. n.* (As a clock) कालमापकवत् किटकिटशब्दं कृ or पटपटशब्दं कृ, पटपट (nom. पटपटायते -ति).

TICKET, *s.* पत्रकं, पत्रं, सूचकपत्रं, निदर्शनपत्रं, अङ्कपत्रं.

To TICKET, *v. a.* अङ्कपत्रयुक्तं -क्तां कृ, अङ्कपत्रविशिष्टं -ष्टां कृ.

To TICKLE, *v. a.* कण्डू (nom. कण्डूयति), कण्डूयनं कृ, कण्डूयां कृ.

TICKLER, *s.* कण्डूयनकः, कण्डूतिकारी *m.* (न्), कण्डूयाकृत्.

TICKLISH, *a.* कण्डूयनासहनः -ना -नं, कण्डूयासहः -हा -हं, कण्डूयसहः &c.

TID-BIT, *s.* सुग्रासः, विशिष्टग्रासः, आहारविशेषः, भोजनविशेषः.

TIDE, *s.* वेला, स्रोतस् *n.*, प्रवाहः, रयः; 'of the sea,' समुद्रवेला; 'against the tide,' प्रतिस्रोतस्.

TIDINGS, *s.* वार्त्ता, सन्देशः, समाचारः. *See* NEWS, INTELLIGENCE.

TIDY, TIDINESS, TIDILY. *See* NEAT, NEATNESS, NEATLY.

To TIE, *v. a.* बन्ध् (c. 9. बध्नाति, बन्द्धुं), निबन्ध्, पिनह्; 'together,' सम्बन्ध्, योक्त्र (nom. योक्त्रयति -यितुं), संयुज्, संश्लिष् in caus., सन्धा, संलग्नीकृ, संहृ, ग्रन्थ्, गुम्फ्, *see To* FASTEN, KNIT, &c.; 'with a fetter,' पाशीकृ, पाश (nom. पाशयति -यितुं); 'to tie up a young deer,' मृगपोतकं संयोजयितुं; 'to tie up in a bag,' वस्त्रबद्धं -द्धां कृ.

TIE, *s.* (A fastening, knot) बन्धः -न्धनं -नी, ग्रन्थिः *m.*, बन्धनग्रन्थिः *m.*; 'of a yoke,' आबन्धः, योक्त्रं, योत्रं; 'of a letter or parcel,' तालिकः.—(A fetter) पाशः, बन्धनं.—(String) गुणः, दाम -मा, *see* STRING.—(Attachment, tie of affection, &c.) सङ्गः; 'free from ties,' निःसङ्गः -ङ्गा -ङ्गं, सङ्गवर्जितः -ता -तं, असक्तात्मा -त्मा -त्म (न्).

Tied, *p. p.* बद्धः -द्धा -द्धं, निबद्धः &c., सन्निबद्धः &c., नियन्त्रितः -ता -तं, आबद्धः &c., पिनद्धः -द्धा -द्धं, आनद्धः &c., दृब्धः &c., गुणवान् -वती &c.; 'together,' सम्बद्धः -द्धा -द्धं, आबद्धः &c., संयोजितः -ता -तं, संसक्तः -क्ता -क्तं, संलग्नीकृतः -ता -तं, सन्धानितः &c., सन्धितः &c., सन्दितः &c.; 'tied with a fetter,' पाशितः -ता -तं, पाशीकृतः &c.; 'tied up in,' निबद्धः -द्धा -द्धं; 'a quantity of money tied up in a bag,' वस्त्रबद्धो मुद्रासञ्चयः; 'a man with his arms tied behind him,' पश्चाद्बद्धबाहुः पुरुषः.

Tier, *s.* पंक्तिः *f.*, श्रेणिः -णी *f.*, राजिः -जी *f.* *See* Row, Line.

Tiger, *s.* व्याघ्रः, शार्दूलः, द्वीपी *m.* (न्), चित्रकायः, गुहाशयः, मृगारिः *m.*, मृगाद् *m.*, हिंसारुः *m.*, भयानकः; 'state of one,' व्याघ्रता; 'relating to one,' वैयाघ्रः &c.; 'its skin,' व्याघ्रचर्म्म *n.*

Tight, *a.* (Close, firm) दृढः -ढा -ढं, घनः -ना -नं, संहतः -ता -तं, अशिथिलः -ला -लं, गाढः -ढा -ढं, प्रगाढः &c.—(Tied tight) दृढबद्धः -द्धा -द्धं, सन्निबद्धः &c., दृढसन्धिः -न्धिः -न्धि.—(Tight-drawn) आततः -ता -तं, दृढः &c., *see* Stretched.—(Pinching) सम्बाधकः -का -कं, सम्बाधः -धा -धं, सङ्कोचकः &c.

To tighten, *v. a.* दृढीकृ, दृढ (nom. दृढयति -यितुं), दृढतरीकृ.

Tightly, *adv.* दृढं, गाढं, प्रगाढं; 'tied tightly,' दृढबद्धः -द्धा -द्धं.

Tightness, *s.* दृढता, दार्ढ्यं, घनता, संहतत्वं, सम्बाधता -धकता.

Tigress, *s.* व्याघ्री, शार्दूली, द्वीपिनी, चित्रकायी.

Tigrine, tigrish, *a.* वैयाघ्रः -घ्री -घ्रं, व्याघ्रोपमः -मा -मं.

Tile, *s.* पक्वेष्टका, पक्वेष्टिका, पक्वमृत्तिकाफलकः.

To tile, *v. a.* पक्वेष्टकाभिर् आछद्, पक्वेष्टकाच्छादनं कृ.

Till, *s.* (Money-box) मुद्राभाण्डं, मुद्रापात्रं, मुद्राधारः.

Till, *prep.* or *adv.* यावत्, पर्य्यन्तं, अवधि, आ. The last is prefixed, and governs the abl. c.; 'till now,' अद्य यावत्, इदानीं यावत्, अद्यपर्य्यन्तं, एतत्कालपर्य्यन्तं, अद्यावधि, आवर्त्तमानकालात्; 'till then,' तदानीं यावत्, तत्कालं यावत्, तत्कालपर्य्यन्तं; 'till satisfied,' आतृप्तेः; 'till death,' आमृत्योः, आमरणात्; 'till the whole was mixed together,' आसर्व्वमिश्रणात्, सर्व्वमिश्रणपर्य्यन्तं; 'abide ye there till you have to go to another place,' स्थानान्तरगमनपर्य्यन्तं तत्र तिष्ठत; 'he kept him in prison till he should pay the debt,' यावद् ऋणं न परिशोधयति तावत् तं कारायां बद्धवान्.

To till, *v. a.* कृष् (c. 1. कर्षति, क्रष्टुं), कर्षणं कृ, कृषिं कृ, *see* *To* plough.

Tillage, tilling, *s.* कृषिः *f.*, कृषिकर्म्म *n.* (न्), प्रमृतं. *See* Ploughing.

Tilled, *p. p.* कृष्टः -ष्टा -ष्टं, कर्षितः -ता -तं. *See* Ploughed.

Tiller, *s.* कृषकः, कर्षकः, क्षेत्रकर्षकः, कृषीवलः, कृषिजीवी *m.*

Tilt, *s.* (Kind of awning) वितानं -नकं, आच्छादनं, उल्लोचः.—(Tournament) अश्वारोहिणां क्रीडायुद्धं.

To tilt, *v. a.* (Incline) आवृज् (c. 10. -वर्जयति -यितुं).

To tilt, *v. n.* (Lean) नम्, अवनम्.—(Fight) क्रीडायुद्धं कृ.

Tilted, *p. p.* (Inclined) आवर्जितः -ता -तं.—(Covered) सवितानः -ना -नं.

Timber, *s.* दारुः *m.* -रु *n.*, काष्ठं, दलिकः, विसारं; 'of a door,' नासा.

Timbrel, *s.* मृदङ्गः, पटहः, पणवः. *See* Tabor, Drum.

Time, *s.* (In general) कालः, समयः, वेला, दिष्टः, अनेहा: *m.* (स्), हरिमा *m.* (न्), सर्व्वमूषकः, भसन्तः, अमसः, जहकः; 'lapse of time,' कालगतिः *f.*, कालचक्रं, कालावृत्तिः *f.*, कालपर्य्यायः; 'in the course of time,' कालगत्या, काले गच्छति, दिनेषु गच्छत्सु, कालपर्य्यायेण; 'through the influence of time,' कालवशात्; 'measurement of time,' कालमानं, कालमापनं, कालसाधनं; 'spirit of the time,' कालधर्म्मः; 'to waste one's time,' कालं क्षिप्, कालक्षेपं कृ, *see* *To* spend; 'to make good use of one's time,' सत्कालक्षेपं कृ; 'without loss of time,' अकालक्षेपं -पेण; 'one whose time is come,' प्राप्तकालः.—(Space of time) कालः, समयः, अवधिः *m.*, कालमर्य्यादा, *see* Space; 'for a long time,' चिरं, चिरकालं, चिरात्, *see* Long; 'for a short time,' किञ्चित्कालं, कियत्कालं, *see* Short; 'for the time being,' आपाततस्; 'at this time,' इदानीं, अधुना, एतर्हि, *see* Now; 'at that time,' तदानीं, तत्काले, *see* Then; 'at a certain time,' एकदा; 'at any time,' यदा कदाचित्, कदापि; 'at times,' *see* Sometimes; 'at all times,' सर्व्वदा, सदा; 'at the same time,' युगपत्, एकपदे; 'for such a time,' तावत्कालं; 'former time,' पूर्व्वकालः; 'in former time,' *see* Formerly; 'past time,' गतकालः; 'specific time,' निमित्तकालः; 'during all time,' सर्व्वकालं; 'the three times, or present, past, and future,' त्रिकालं.—(Season) कालः, समयः, प्रसङ्गः; 'in time, out of time,' *see* Seasonably, Unseasonably.—(Particular time, occasion) समयः, कालः, समयविशेषः, विशेषकालः, वारः, वासरः; 'according to the time,' समयानुसारेण; 'auspicious time,' सुवेला, शुभवेला; 'hard times,' आपत्कालः; 'dark times,' कलिकालः; 'from time to time,' वारं वारं, काले काले, अनुवेलं.—(A time, with reference to repetition) कृत्वस् or वारं in comp., गुण in comp., आवृत्ति in comp.; as, 'five times,' पञ्चकृत्वस्; 'three times,' त्रिवारं, वारत्रयं; 'a hundred times,' शतकृत्वस्, शतगुणं; 'for a thousand times,' सहस्रकृत्वस्, सहस्रावृत्तिं; 'often times,' बहुवारं; 'how many times?' कतिकृत्वस्; 'the repetition of texts is a hundred times better than sacrifices,' जपो यज्ञाद् दशगुणैर् विशिष्यते; 'the second number is contained in the first as many times as the fourth in the third,' द्वितीया संख्या प्रथमायां यावद्वारं वर्त्तते यावद्वारं चतुर्थी तृतीयायां; 'gold is nineteen times as heavy as water,' सुवर्णगुरुत्वं जलगुरुत्वमपेक्ष्य एकोनविंशतिगुणं.—(In music) तालः, लयः; 'beating time,' तालः, कुलङ्कः; 'quick time,' द्रुतं, ओघः; 'slow time,' विलम्बितं, विलम्बितवृत्तिः *f.*, तत्त्वं; 'mean time,' मध्यं, घनं; 'out of time,' वैतालिकः -की -कं.—(Measures of time), *see* under Measure.—(Time personified) कालः, उग्रदेवता.

To time, *v. a.* (Adapt to the time) कालयोग्यं -ग्यां कृ, कालोपयुक्तं -क्तां कृ, समयोपयुक्तं -क्तां कृ, कालानुरूपं कृ, कालसदृशं -शीं कृ.—(Regulate the time) कालं परिकॢप् or निर्णी.

Timely, *a.* कालिकः -की -कं, कालीनः &c. *See* Seasonable.

Time-piece, *s.* कालमापनयन्त्रं, कालयन्त्रं. *See* Clock.

Time-server, *s.* कालानुवर्त्ती *m.* (न्), कालानुरोधी *m.*, समयानुरोधी *m.*

Time-serving, *s.* कालानुवर्त्तनं, समयानुवर्त्तनं, कालानुरोधः.

Timid, timorous, *a.* भीरुः -रुः -रु, भीरुहृदयः -या -यं, भयशीलः -ला -लं, हरिणहृदयः &c., कातरः -रा -रं, चकितः -ता -तं, दीनचेतनः -ना -नं, दीनः -ना -नं, असाहसिकः -की -कं, अप्रगल्भः -ल्भा -ल्भं, चकितः -ता -तं. *See* Fearful.

Timidity, timorousness, *s.* भीरुता -त्वं, भयशीलता, कातरता, कातर्य्यं, सभयत्वं, चकितं, चकितता, दीनता, विह्वलता, सत्रासत्वं.

Timidly, timorously, *adv.* सभयं, सत्रासं, सचकितं, सकातर्य्यं.

TIN, *s.* त्रपु *n.*, त्रपुस् *n.*, त्रपुलं, वङ्गं, रङ्गं, पिच्चटं, स्वर्णजं, नागं, कुरूप्यं, कस्तीरं, सुरभं, आपुषं, तीरः, आलीनकं, कुटिलं, चार्ब्बटीरं; 'calx of it,' वङ्गभस्म *n.* (न्); 'made of tin,' त्रापुषः -षी -षं, त्रपुमयः -यी -यं.

To TIN, *v. a.* त्रपुपत्त्रावृतं -तां कृ, वङ्गाच्छादितं -तां कृ, त्रपुलीकृ.

TINCTURE, *s.* (Slight admixture) ईषत्प्रक्षेपः, ईषत्संसर्गः, ईषत्सम्पर्कः, ईषत्सम्मिश्रणं.—(Infusion, extract) निर्यासः, निष्कर्षः.

To TINCTURE, *v. a.* ईषत् प्रक्षिप् (c. 6. -क्षिपति -क्षेप्तुं), ईषत्प्रक्षेपं कृ, ईषत् सम्मिश्र् (c. 10. -मिश्रयति -यितुं), ईषत्सम्मिश्रणं कृ, ईषद्रागं -गां कृ.

TINDER, *s.* शीघ्रदाह्यवस्तु *n.*, शीघ्रज्वलनीयवस्तु *n.*, शीघ्रदाह्यं.

TINGE, *s.* रागः, रङ्गः, ईषद्रागः, ईषद्रङ्गः, छाया.

To TINGE, *v. a.* रञ्ज् (c. 10. रञ्जयति -यितुं), अभिरञ्ज्, *see To* TINCTURE.

TINGED, *p. p.* रञ्जितः -ता -तं, अभिरञ्जितः &c., सरागः -गा -गं.

To TINGLE, *v. n.* तीक्ष्णवेदनोपहतत्वात् स्फुर् (c. 6. स्फुरति -रितुं), तोदवेदनोपहतत्वात् स्फुर् or हृष्, सशूलस्फुरणम् अनुभू or सूच्; 'a speech that makes the ears tingle,' श्रवणविदारणं वचः.

TINGLING, *s.* सशूलस्फुरणं, शूलसहितस्फुरणं, तीक्ष्णवेदनासहितस्फुरणं, तोदसहितस्फुरणं, हर्षः; 'of the feet,' पादहर्षः.

TINKER, *s.* जीर्णभाण्डसन्धाता *m.* (तृ), जीर्णपिठरसन्धानजीवी *m.* (न्).

To TINKLE, *v. n.* शिञ्ज्, विशिञ्ज्, क्वण् (c. 1. क्वणति -णितुं), विरु, झणझणा (nom. झणझणायते), खणखणा (nom. खणखणायते). *See To* JINGLE.

TINKLING, *s.* शिञ्जितं, क्वणितं. *See* JINGLE, JINGLING, CLINK.

TIN-MAN, *s.* त्रपुमयभाण्डकारकः, त्रपुमयभाण्डविक्रेता *m.* (तृ).

TINSEL, *s.* मिथ्याशोभनवस्तु *n.*, मिथ्याशोभायुक्तद्रव्यं, कुशोभनवस्तु.

TINSEL, *a.* मिथ्याशोभनः -ना -नं, मिथ्याशोभायुक्तः -क्ता -क्तं.

TINT, *s.* रागः, रङ्गः, छाया, ईषद्रागः, ईषद्रङ्गः, ईषद्वर्णः.

To TINT, TINTED, &c. *See To* TINGE, TINGED.

TINY, *a.* अतिक्षुद्रः -द्रा -द्रं, अत्यल्पः -ल्पा -ल्पं, सूक्ष्मः -क्ष्मा -क्ष्मं.

TIP, *s.* अग्रं, मुखं, अन्तः, अणिः *m.*, शिखरं, अग्रभागः; 'of the finger,' अङ्गुल्यग्रं, अङ्गुल्यग्रभागः, अङ्गुलिमुखं; 'on the tip of the fingers,' अङ्गुलीनाम् अग्रे; 'of the tongue,' जिह्वाग्रं; 'of the foot,' पादाग्रं, प्रपदं; 'of the hand,' हस्ताग्रं, अग्रपाणिः *m.*, हस्ताग्रभागः; 'of hair,' केशान्तः, केशाग्रं; 'of the fingers as sacred to the gods,' दैवं; 'of an elephant's trunk,' पुष्करं, कर्णिका.

To TIP, *v. a.* (Strike ligthly), *see To* TAP.—(Cover the end) अग्राच्छादनं कृ, अग्रपिधानं कृ, अग्रावरणं कृ; 'with iron,' लोहाग्रं -ग्रां कृ. *See* TIPPED.

TIPPED, *p. p.* अग्र in comp., मुख in comp.; 'with iron,' लोहाग्रः -ग्रा -ग्रं, अयोग्रः &c., अयोमुखः -खा -खं.

TIPPET, *s.* ग्रीवाच्छादनं, ग्रीवापरिधानं, कण्ठाच्छादनं, कण्ठवस्त्रं.

To TIPPLE, *v. n.* वारं वारं मद्यपानं कृ, मुहुर्मुहुः सुरापानं कृ, नित्यपानं कृ, सदापानं कृ, नित्यशो मद्यपानं कृ, पानव्यसनं कृ.

TIPPLER, *s.* सुरापः, मद्यपः, नित्यपायी *m.* (न्). *See* DRUNKARD, SOT.

TIPPLING, *s.* सुरापानं, मद्यपानं, अतिशयमद्यपानं, नित्यपानं, पानव्यसनं, मधुवारः, मधुक्रमः, मद्यलं.

TIPSY, *a.* मद्यविह्वलः -ला -लं, मद्यवशः -शा -शं. *See* DRUNK.

TIPTOE, *s.* पादाग्रं, पदाग्रं, पादाङ्गुष्ठाग्रं, पादाङ्गुल्यग्रं, अग्रपादः, प्रपदं; 'on tip toe,' पादाग्रेण, पदाग्रेण, पादाङ्गुल्यग्रैः, प्रपदेन, पादाङ्गुष्ठास्थितावनिः -निः -नि.

TIPTOP, *s.* अग्राग्रं, अग्रतमभागः, अग्रशिखरं, अग्रशिखा.

TIRADE, *s.* भर्त्सनवाक्प्रबन्धः, निन्दावाक्प्रबन्धः, उपालम्भवाक्यं.

TIRE, *s.* (Of a wheel) चक्रनेमिपरिगतो लोहवलयः.

To TIRE, TIRED. *See To* FATIGUE, FATIGUED, *To* BE FATIGUED.

TIRESOME, *a.* श्रमजनकः -का -कं, कष्टकरः -रा -रं. *See* WEARISOME.

TIRHUT, *s.* (The country) मिथिला, तीरभुक्तिः *f.*, निच्छविः *f.*

TIRING-ROOM, *s.* (In a theatre) नेपथ्यं, शाणी.

TISSUE, *s.* (Brocade), *see* BROCADE.—(Connected string) ग्रन्थः -न्थनं, प्रबन्धः, रचना, क्रमः, व्यूहनं, संव्यूहः, विधानं.

TITAN, *s.* दानवः, दैत्यः, दितिजः, राक्षसः. *See* GIANT.

TITHE, *s.* दशमांशः, दशमभागः, दशमांशरूपो करः.

To TITILLATE, TILILLATION. *See To* TICKLE, &c.

TITLE, *s.* (Head) स्थानं, पदं, विषयः, अधिकरणं, मार्गः.—(Inscription in the beginning of a book, &c.) नामपत्रं -त्त्रकं, अभिधानपत्रं, मुखपत्रं, नामलेखः.—(Name, appellation) नाम *n.* (न्), संज्ञा, अभिधा, अभिधानं, उपाधिः *m.*, आख्या, ख्यातिः *f.*, पद्धतिः *f.*, उक्तिः *f.*, लक्षणं; 'title of honour,' ख्यातिः *f.*, कीर्त्तिः *f.*, उपपदं; 'one who by his prowess has acquired the title of hero,' खड्गस्वार्जितवीरख्यातिः *m.*, खड्गस्वार्जितवीरशब्दः.—(Right) अधिकारः -रित्वं, स्वत्वं, स्वाम्यं, आधिपत्यं; 'written title,' आगमः, आगमपत्रं, *see* TITLE-DEED; 'without it,' आगमरहितः -ता -तं.

TITLE-DEED, *s.* आगमः, क्रयकीला, पट्टोलिका, पांशुकूलं.

TITLE-PAGE, *s.* मुखपत्रं, मुख्यपत्रं, नामपत्रं, अभिधापत्रं.

To TITTER, TITTER, TITTERING. *See To* GIGGLE, &c.

TITTLE, *s.* (Jot) लेशः, लवः, अणुः *m.*, *see* JOT, IOTA.

TITTLE-TATTLE, *s.* आलस्यवचनं, प्रलापः, जल्पः. *See* PRATING, *s.*

TITULAR, *a.* नामधारी -रिणी -रि (न्). *See* NOMINAL.

To, *prep.* Many of the meanings of 'to' are expressed by prepositions or affixes, or by the infin. mood, or are inherent in the inflections of the Sanskrit noun; thus, (Motion to or toward any place) expressed by the acc. case alone, or with प्रति &c. added; as, 'he went to the city,' नगरं or नगरं प्रति जगाम, or by the gen. c., with अन्तिकं &c.; as, 'he sent me to you,' मां तवान्तिकं or तव सकाशम् अप्रैषीत्.—(Motion to any state) by the acc. c.; as, 'he attains to fame,' ख्यातिं याति.—(Adaptation) by the dat. c. or crude form; as, 'that husband was not to her taste,' स पतिस् तस्याः सन्तोषाय नाभवत्; 'suited to royalty,' राजयोग्यः -ग्या -ग्यं, राजार्हः &c.; 'that is pleasing to me,' तन् मह्यं रोचते.—(Address, declaration, compellation) by the acc. c. or dat. c.; as, 'he addressed a speech to the king,' राजानं वचनम् अब्रवीत्; 'speak to me,' मां ब्रूहि; 'I will declare this to my pupils,' शिष्येभ्यः प्रवक्ष्यामि तत्; 'he made it known to the king,' तद् राज्ञे विज्ञापयति.—(Giving) by the dat., gen., or loc. c.; 'he gives sweetmeats to his son,' पुत्राय or पुत्रस्य मोदकान् ददाति.—(Up to, as far as, denoting extent, degree, &c.) आ prefixed to the abl. or acc. c., पर्य्यन्त or अन्त in comp.; as, 'to the ocean,' आसमुद्रात् or समुद्रपर्य्यन्तं; 'to the throat,' आकण्ठात्; 'to the knee,' आजानु; 'the numbers from one up to ten thousand,' एकाद्ययुतान्तसंख्याः.—(Possession, appertainment) by the gen. c.; as, 'money belongs to me,' मम धनं भवति.—(Purpose, intention, object) by the dat. c. or infin. mood, or by अर्थं &c. affixed; as, 'they sat down to consult,' मन्त्रणाय or मन्त्रयितुं or मन्त्रणार्थम् उपविष्टाः; 'the barber came to shave his master,' भर्तृक्षौरकरणाय नापित आगच्छत्; 'he came to make peace,' सन्धिं कर्तुम् आगच्छत्; 'give me something to eat,' आहारार्थं किञ्चित् मम देहि.—(As a sign of the infinitive) expressed by the infinitive, or by यथा &c.; as, 'unable to move,' चलितुम् असमर्थः; 'I desire to hear,' श्रोतुम् इच्छामि; 'I did not expect to see you again,' न म आसीद् आशंसा यथा पुनरपि त्वां प्रेक्षिष्ये. There may be other ways of expressing 'to' in Sanskrit, as in the following examples: 'the peacock dances to the songs of the bees,' शिखी नृत्यति मधुकरगीतैः; 'he performed penance to the deity,' देवम् उद्दिश्य तपस् तेपे; 'the town was speedily reduced to ashes,' नगरी सहसा भस्मसाद् अक्रियत; 'compared to that,' तदपेक्ष्य or तदपेक्षया; 'to the east of the village,' प्राग् ग्रामात्; 'he goes to and fro,' गमनागमनं करोति, *see* FRO; 'to one's face,' प्रत्यक्षं -क्षतम्, समक्षं; 'to a man,' अशेषतस्, अशेषेण; 'I have a debt to pay,' मया ऋणं दातव्यं; 'ready to go,' गन्तुम् उद्यतः, गमनोन्मुखः; 'he causes her to enter the house,' तां गृहं प्रवेशयति.

TOAD, *s.* स्थूलमण्डूकः, स्थूलभेकः, वर्षाभूः *m.*

TOADSTOOL, *s.* गोमयच्छत्रं, विड्जं, विड्जच्छत्रं. *See* FUNGUS.

To TOAST, *v. a.* उपाग्नि धृत्वा शुष्कीकृ, अग्निशुष्कं -ष्कां कृ, अग्निना तप् (c. 10. तापयति -यितुं), भृज्, भ्रस्ज्. *See To* FRY, *v. a.*

TOAST, *s.* दग्धापूपः, दग्धपिष्टकः, अग्निशुष्कापूपः, भृष्टापूपः.

TOASTED, *p. p.* भृष्टः -ष्टा -ष्टं, भर्जितः -ता -तं, अग्निशुष्कः -ष्का -ष्कं.

TOBACCO, *s.* ताम्रकुट्टः -ट्टकः, ताम्रकूटः, ताम्रपत्रिका.

TOBACCONIST, *s.* ताम्रकुट्टविक्रयी *m.* (न्), ताम्रकुट्टव्यापारी *m.*

TOCSIN, *s.* आसन्नभयसूचकघण्टा, भयज्ञापकघण्टा.

TO-DAY, *s.* or *adv.* अद्य; 'of to-day,' अद्यतनः -नी -नं.

To TODDLE, *v. n.* बालकवत् स्खलद्गत्या क्रम् or चर्.

TODDY, *s.* (Of the palm) ताली, तालकी, ताडी -डिः *f.*—(Of the cocoa-nut) नारिकेलासवः, नारिकेरासवः.

TOE, *s.* पादाङ्गुली -लिः *f.*, पादाङ्गुरिः *f.*, पदाङ्गुली -लिः *f.*, पादशाखा, अङ्गुरिः *f.*; 'the great toe,' पादाङ्गुष्ठः; 'the little toe,' पादस्य कनिष्ठाङ्गुली; 'toe-nail,' पादनखः, चरणनखः.

TOGETHER, *adv.* (In company) सह in comp., समं, सहितं, एक in comp., एकत्र; 'going together,' सहगामी -मिनी &c.; 'dancing together,' सहनर्त्तनं; 'drinking together,' सहपानं; 'eating together,' सहभोजनं, एकभोजनं, एकत्र भोजनं; 'fighting together,' सहयुध्वा *m.* (न्); 'all together, in a body,' सङ्घशस्, एकसङ्घे -ङ्घतम्, साकल्येन.—(Into union or junction) सम् prefixed; as, 'to bind together,' सम्बन्ध्; 'to meet together,' सङ्गम्, सम्मिल्; 'having the feet together,' सम्पदं; 'two letters placed together,' सन्निहितवर्णौ *m. du.*—(In the same place) एकत्र, एकस्थाने, एकदेशे.—(At the same time) एककाले, समकाले, युगपत्, सह in comp.; 'born at the same time,' एककालजः -जा -जं, समकालजः &c., सहजः &c.—(With one another) परस्परं, अन्योन्यं; 'quarelling together,' परस्परकलहः, अन्योन्यकलहः.—(Together with) सह, समं, सार्द्धं, सहितं, साकं, all with instr. c.; 'together with him,' तेन सह.

To TOIL, *v. n.* आयस्, श्रम्, क्लिश्. *See To* LABOUR, DRUDGE, FAG.

TOIL, *s.* आयासः, क्लेशः, श्रमः, कष्टं. *See* LABOR, DRUDGERY.

TOILET, *s.* (Act or mode of dressing) वस्त्रमाल्यादिविन्यासः, वस्त्रमाल्यादिरचना, अङ्गसंस्कारः, मण्डनं, नेपथ्यं, भूषणं; 'he makes his toilet,' नेपथ्यं धारयति, वस्त्रविन्यासं करोति; 'one who has finished her toilet,' अवसितमण्डना; 'toilet-table,' भूषणाधारः; 'cover,' भूषणाधाराच्छादनं.

TOILSOME, *a.* कष्टसाध्यः -ध्या -ध्यं, श्रमसाध्यः &c. *See* LABORIOUS.

TOKEN, *s.* लक्षणं, चिह्नं, अभिज्ञानं, सङ्केतः, *see* SIGN, MEMENTO.

TOLA, *s.* (Indian weight for gold and silver) तोलः -लं, तोलकः -कं.

TOLD, *p. p.* कथितः -ता -तं, आख्यातः &c., समाख्यातः &c., उक्तः -क्ता -क्तं, भणितः -ता -तं, आवेदितः &c., निवेदितः &c., ज्ञापितः -ता -तं, ज्ञपितः &c., ख्यापितः &c., ज्ञप्तः -प्ता -प्तं, सन्दिष्टः -ष्टा -ष्टं.

TOLERABLE, *a.* (Bearable) सहनीयः -या -यं, सह्यः -ह्या -ह्यं, सोढव्यः -व्या -व्यं.—(Moderately good) विगुणः -णा -णं, मध्यमगुणः -णा -णं, मध्यमः -मा -मं.

TOLERABLY, *adv.* विगुणं, यावत्तावत्, कल्प or देशीय or देश्य in comp.; 'tolerably clever,' पटुकल्पः -ल्पा -ल्पं, पटुदेशीयः &c.

TOLERANCE, *s.* सहनं, सहिष्णुता, क्षमा. *See* TOLERATION.

TOLERANT, *a.* सहनः -ना -नं, सहिष्णुः -ष्णुः -ष्णु, अनिषेधकारी -रिणी -रि (न्), अप्रतिबन्धकारी &c. *See* PATIENT, INDULGENT.

To TOLERATE, *v. a.* सह्, विषह्, क्षम्, मृष्, तिज् in des., उपेक्ष्, अनिषेधं कृ, अप्रतिबन्धं कृ, अनिवारणं कृ. *See To* SUFFER, PERMIT.

TOLERATED, *p. p.* अनिषिद्धः -द्धा -द्धं, अनिवारितः -ता -तं, उपेक्षितः &c.

TOLERATION, *s.* क्षमा, क्षान्तिः *f.*, तितिक्षा, सहिष्णुता, अनिषेधः, अनिवारणं, अप्रतिबन्धः, उपेक्षा, अप्रतिरोधः, अनिरोधः.

TOLL, *s.* शुल्कः -ल्कं, तारिकं, तार्य्यं, घट्टादिदेयं, करः. *See* TAX.

To TOLL, *v. a.* (A bell) शनैः शनैः or वारं वारं घण्टां वद् in caus.

To TOLL, *v. n.* (As a bell) शनैः शनैः or वारं वारं ध्वनितं कृ.

TOLL-BOOTH, TOLL-HOUSE, *s.* शुल्कस्थानं, शुल्कग्रहणस्थानं.

TOLL-GATHERER, *s.* शौल्किकः, शुल्कग्राही *m.* (न्), करग्राही *m.*

TOMATO, *s.* हिङ्गीरः, हिङ्गुली, वङ्गनः. *See* EGG-PLANT.

TOMB, *s.* समाधिः *m.*, श्मशानं, स्तूपः, प्रेतकुण्डं. *See* GRAVE.

TOMB-STONE, *s.* चित्यं, चैत्यं, चिताचूडकं. *See* GRAVE-STONE.

TO-MORROW, *s.* or *adv.* श्वस्, परेद्युस्, परदिनं, *see* MORROW; 'day after,' परश्वस्; 'belonging to to-morrow,' श्वस्तनः -नी -नं, श्वस्त्यः &c.,

TOM-TOM, *s.* मृदङ्गः, पटहः, दुन्दुभिः *m.*, डिण्डिमः. *See* DRUM.

TON, *s.* सभ्याचारः, सभ्यरीतिः *f.*, सभ्यसम्प्रदायः, शिष्टाचारः.

TONE, *s.* (Sound, note) स्वरः, नादः, ध्वनिः *m.*, विरावः, विरिब्धः, *see* SOUND; 'having a good tone,' सुस्वरः -रा -रं.—(Musical sound) स्वरः, क्वणः, क्वाणः, क्वणनं, निक्वणः, निक्वाणः; 'of a lute,' प्रक्वणः, प्रक्वाणः.—(Seventh part of a scale) मूर्च्छनं -ना; 'half tone,' स्वरांशः; 'quarter tone,' श्रुतिः *f.*—(In medicine) सुभावना, सद्भावना, सद्भावः, तेजस् *n.*, अग्निः *m.*

TONGS, *s. pl.* सन्दंशः, सन्दंशकं -का, कङ्कमुखः.

TONGUE, *s.* जिह्वा, रसना, रसज्ञा, रशना, रसिका, रसाला, रसनं, ललना, लोला, जिह्वः, विलासा, मुखचीरी; 'root of the tongue,' जिह्वामूलं; 'tip of it,' जिह्वाग्रं; 'that is on the tip of it,' जिह्वारूढः -ढा -ढं; 'hold your tongue,' वाचं नियच्छ, तूष्णीम्भव; 'tongue-scraper,' *see* SCRAPER; 'one of the seven tongues of fire,' स्फुलिङ्गिनी; 'tongue of a bell,' लोला; of a bolt,'

कण्टकः.—(Speech) भाषा; 'mother-tongue,' जन्मभाषा.

TONGUE-LESS, *a.* अजिह्वः -ह्वा -ह्वं, जिह्वाहीनः -ना -नं, निर्जिह्वः &c.

TONGUE-TIED, *a.* बद्धजिह्वः -ह्वा -ह्वं, संयन्त्रितजिह्वः &c., यतजिह्वः &c.

TONIC, *a.* रुचकः -का -कं, रोचकः &c., तेजस्करः -रा -रं, दीपकः &c., अग्निवर्धकः &c., अग्निदः -दा -दं, पाचकः -का -कं, दीपनः -ना -नं.

TONIC, *s.* रुचकं, रोचकः, अग्निवर्धनः -नं, पाचकं, दीपनं.

TO-NIGHT, *adv.* अद्य रात्रौ, अद्य निशि, अद्य नक्तं.

TONSIL, *s.* कण्ठान्तर्वर्त्ती श्लेष्माधाराशयो मृदुमांसपिण्डः; 'enlargement of them,' अधिमांसकः, शतघ्नी, गण्डमाला.

TONSURE, *s.* (Shaving the head) क्षौरं, क्षौरकर्म्म *n.* (न्), केशवपनं, शिरोवपनं, मुण्डनं, शिरोमुण्डनं, केशच्छेदः.—(As a sacred rite) चूडाकर्म्म *n.*(न्), चूडाकरणं, चूडा, चौडं, चोलं, चौलकर्म्म *n.*, चूडालक्षणं.

TOO, *adv.* (Over much) अति or सु prefixed, अतीव, अत्यन्तं, एकान्ततस्, एकान्त in comp., *see* EXCESSIVELY; 'too great a load,' अतिभारः; 'he approaches too near the fire,' अग्नेर् अतिसमीपम् उपसर्पति; 'too compassionate,' अतिकरुणः -णा -णं, एकान्तकरुणः &c.; 'too early,' अतिप्रगे, अतिकल्यं; 'too late in the evening,' अतिसायं -ये; 'too long,' सुदीर्घः -र्घा -र्घं.—(Also) चैव, च, अपि, तथा.

TOOL, *s.* उपकरणं, यन्त्रं, साधनं, शस्त्रं, *see* INSTRUMENT; 'a mere tool,' निमित्तमात्रं, कारणमात्रं, उपकरणमात्रं.

TOOTH, *s.* दन्तः, दशनः -नं, रदः, रदनः, दंशः, दंष्ट्रा, खादनः, दाढा, द्विजः, द्विजन्मा *m.* (न्), मुखजः, छद्वरः, दन्दशः, जम्भः, हालुः *m.*, मल्लः *m.*, वक्त्रखुरः, रुचकः, मल्लकः, घटः; 'a row of teeth,' दन्तपंक्तिः *f.*, दन्तावली, *see* TEETH; 'two middle fore teeth,' राजदन्तौ *m. du.*; 'double tooth,' मादिः *f.*; 'decay of a tooth,' द्विजक्षयः.—(Of a saw, comb, wheel, &c.) दन्तः.

TOOTH-ACHE, *s.* दन्तवेदना, दन्तव्यथा, दन्तशूलः, दालनं.

TOOTH-BRUSH, *s.* दन्तधावनं, दन्तकाष्ठं, कूर्चकं.

TOOTHED, *a.* दन्ती -न्तिनी -न्ति (न्), रदी &c., दन्तजातः -ता -तं, दन्त or दत् &c. in comp.; as, 'handsome-toothed,' सुदन् -दती -दत् (त्); 'iron-toothed,' अयोदन्तः -न्ता -न्तं, अयोदत् &c.

TOOTHLESS, *a.* अदन्तः -न्ता -न्तं, निर्दन्तः &c., दन्तहीनः -ना -नं, निर्दशनः -ना -नं, गतदन्तः -न्ता -न्तं, गलितदन्तः &c., नीरदः -दा -दं, अदंष्ट्री -ष्ट्रिणी -ष्ट्रि (न्), भग्नदंष्ट्रः -ष्ट्रा -ष्ट्रं, उद्धृतदंष्ट्रः &c., दशनोच्छिष्टः -ष्टा -ष्टं.

TOOTH-PICK, *s.* दन्तशोधनी, शलाका, दन्तनिर्वेष्टकः.

TOOTH-POWDER, *s.* दन्तपवनं, दन्तशाणं, मिशुचूर्णं. *See* DENTIFRICE.

TOP, *s.* (Highest part, upper end) अग्रं, शिखा, शिखरं, अग्रभागः, पृष्ठं, शृङ्गं, चूडा, शिरस् *n.*, उपरिभागः, शीर्षकं, मस्तकं, तुङ्गः, नीचकी *m.* (न्); 'of a tree,' वृक्षाग्रं, वृक्षशिरस् *n.*; 'fallen from the top of a tree,' वृक्षाग्रात् पतितः; 'of a palace or house,' प्रासादपृष्ठं, गृहपृष्ठं; 'of a mountain,' गिरिशृङ्गं, गिरिपृष्ठं, प्राग्भावः.—(Lid) पिधानं.—(Highest or chief place) मुख्यस्थानं.—(Spinning top) भ्रमरं, भ्रमरक्रीडनकं.

TOP, *a.* (in comp.) उपरिस्थः -स्था -स्थं, अग्रस्थः -स्था -स्थं.

TOPAZ, *s.* पीताश्मा *m.* (न्), पीतस्फटिकः, पीतमणिः *m.*, पीतसारः, पीतरक्तं, पीतः, पुष्परागः, पद्मरागः, गुरुरत्नं.

TOPE, *s.* (Mound of earth) स्तूपः.

TOP-HEAVY, *a.* भाराधिकशिरस्कः -स्का -स्कं, ऊर्द्ध्वगुरुः -रुः -रु.

TOPIC, *s.* विषयः, प्रकरणं, प्रसङ्गः, प्रसक्तिः *f.*, वृत्तान्तः, पदं. *See* SUBJECT.

TOPIC, TOPICAL, *a.* प्राकरणिकः -की -कं, विशेषस्थानिकः -की -कं.

TOP-KNOT, *s.* चूडा, शिखा, शिखण्डः -ण्डकः, शिखरः -रं, शेखरः.

TOPMOST, *a.* सर्व्वोपरिस्थः -स्था -स्थं, सर्व्वाग्रस्थः &c., अग्रतमः -मा -मं.

TOPOGRAPHY, *s.* विशेषस्थानवर्णनं, विशेषस्थलविवरणं, स्थानवर्णनं.

To TOPPLE, *v. n.* ऊर्द्ध्वगुरुत्वाद् अग्रतः पत् (c. 1. पतति -तितुं).

TOPSY-TURVY, *a.* or *adv.* अधरोत्तरः -रा -रं, ऊर्द्ध्वाधरः -रा -रं.

TORCH, *s.* उल्का, ज्वलनकाष्ठं, अग्निकाष्ठं, उल्मुकं, अङ्गारं, अलातं, अग्निकुक्कुटः, कण्ठनीलकः.

TORCH-BEARER, *s.* उल्काधारी *m.* (न्), उल्कावाही *m.* -वाहकः.

To TORMENT, *v. a.* अत्यन्तं पीड् (c. 10. पीडयति -यितुं) or तप् (c. 10. तापयति -यितुं) or सन्तप् or परितप्, यत् (c. 10. यातयति -यितुं), अतीव व्यथ् (c. 10. व्यथयति -यितुं), अतिशयेन बाध् (c. 1. बाधते -धितुं) or क्लिश्, अतियातनां कृ or दा, अतिवेदनां कृ or दा, तीव्रवेदनां कृ or दा, अतिव्यथां कृ or दा, परमदुःखं कृ, विडम्ब् (c. 10. -डम्बयति -यितुं). *See To* HARASS, VEX, ANNOY.

TORMENT, *s.* (Extreme pain) यातना, अतियातना, अतिवेदना, अतिव्यथा, अतिदुःखं, अतिपीडा, तीव्रवेदना, तिग्मवेदना, तिग्मयातना, अतिक्लेशः, परमदुःखं, दारुणदुःखं, दारुणयातना, यमयातना, तापः, परितापः, यन्त्रणं -णा, विडम्बनं -ना, क्लेशः, दुःखं.—(That which gives annoyance) कण्टकः.

TORMENTED, *p. p.* अतिपीडितः -ता -तं, अतिव्यथितः &c., अतिबाधितः &c., विडम्बितः -ता -तं, अर्दितः -ता -तं, तप्तः -प्ता -प्तं, दुःखदग्धः -ग्धा -ग्धं.

TORMENTING, TORMENTER, *a.* and *s.* अतिपीडकः -का -कं, अतिपीडाजनकः &c., अतिक्लेशकरः -री -रं, अतिदुःखकरः &c., अरुन्तुदः -दा -दं, प्रमाथी -थिनी &c., आयासकारी &c., परिक्लेष्टा -ष्ट्री -ष्टृ (ष्टृ).

TORN, *p. p.* विदारितः -ता -तं, विदीर्णः -र्णा -र्णं, दारितः -ता -तं, प्रविदारितः &c., दीर्णः -र्णा -र्णं, दलितः -ता -तं, विदलितः &c., पाटितः -ता -तं, भिन्नः -न्ना -न्नं; 'with the nails,' नखभिन्नः -न्ना -न्नं; 'being torn,' विदीर्य्यमाणः -णा -णं; 'having torn,' विदार्य्य; 'is torn,' विदीर्य्यते.

TORNADO, *s.* घूर्णवातः, घूर्णवायुः *m.*, प्रभञ्जनः. *See* TEMPEST.

TORPID, *a.* जडः -डा -डं, विचेतनः -ना -नं, सुप्तः &c., *see* NUMB.

TORPOR, TORPIDITY, *s.* जडता, जाड्यं, जडिमा *m.* (न्), चैतन्यस्तम्भः, चैतन्यनाशः, सुप्तिः *f.*, स्वापः, मान्द्यं, कुण्ठता, तन्द्रा. *See* NUMBNESS.

TORRENT, *s.* निर्झरः -री, झरः, जलप्रवाहः, जलप्रपातः, जलधारा, ओघः, जलौघः, प्रस्रवणं, स्रोतस् *n.*, रयः; 'of rain,' वृष्टिधारा, धारासारः, धारासम्पातः, तरङ्गः; 'a mountain torrent,' गिरिनदी, गिरिसरित्.

TORRID, *a.* उष्णदग्धः -ग्धा -ग्धं, ग्रीष्मदग्धः &c.; 'zone,' उष्णकटिबन्धः.

TORTOISE, *s.* कूर्म्मः, कच्छपः, कमठः, कामठः, गूढाङ्गः, पञ्चाङ्गगुप्तः, पञ्चगुप्तः, कठिनपृष्ठं, चतुर्गतिः *m.*, क्रोडपादः, उद्धटः, स्वरक्षापतत्पेकः; 'female,' कूर्म्मी, कच्छपी, कमठी, दुलिः -ली *f.*, डुलिः *f.*; 'relating to a tortoise,' कौर्म्मः -र्म्मी -र्म्मं, कामठः -ठी -ठं.

TORTOISE-SHELL, *s.* कूर्म्मकवचः -चं, कूर्म्मकपुः -पु *m. n.*, कूर्म्मपृष्ठं, कौर्म्मं.

TORTUOSITY, *s.* वक्रता, वक्रिमा *m.* (न्), कुटिलत्वं, जिह्मता, तिर्य्यक्त्वं.

TORTUOUS, *a.* वक्रः -क्रा -क्रं, कुटिलः -ला -लं, तिर्य्यङ् -रश्ची -र्य्यक् (च्); 'moving tortuously,' तिर्य्यग्गामी -मिनी &c., कुटिलगामी &c., दन्द्रमणः -णा -णं; 'movement,' चङ्क्रमा -मणं, दन्द्रमं -मणं.

To TORTURE, *v. a.* यत् (c. 10. यातयति -यितुं), यातनयात्यन्तं व्यथ् or प्रमथ् (c. 10. -माथयति -यितुं), यातनां कृ, अत्यन्तं पीड् &c. *See To* TORMENT.

TORTURE, *s.* यातना, अतिव्यथा, व्यथा, प्रमाथः, व्याधिः *m.*, अतिव्याधिः *m.*,

तिग्मव्यथा, तिग्मवेदना, सम्पीडः, उद्वेजनं. *See* TORMENT.

TORTURED, *p. p.* व्यथितः -ता -तं, सन्तप्तः -प्ता -प्तं, प्रमथितः -ता -तं.

TORTURER, *s.* यातनाकारी *m.* (न्), यातनकृत् *m.*, व्यथाकरः, प्रमाथी *m.* (न्), उद्वेजनकरः, सन्तापकः, परिक्लेष्टा *m.* (ष्टृ). *See* TORMENTING.

To TOSS, *v. a.* क्षिप् (c. 6. क्षिपति, क्षेप्तुं), विक्षिप्, उत्क्षिप्, समुत्क्षिप्, क्षुभ् (c. 10. क्षोभयति -यितुं), विक्षुभ्, संक्षुभ्, उद्धू (c. 5. -धूनोति -धोतुं), विधू.

To TOSS, *v. n.* विक्षिप् in pass. (-क्षिप्यते), इतस्ततो विक्षिप् or विचल् (c. 1. -चलति -लितुं) or प्रचल्, इतस्ततो लुट् (c. 6. लुठति -ठितुं) or प्रलुट् or लुल्, घूर्ण् (c. 1. घूर्णति -ते -र्णितुं), विघूर्ण्, व्याघूर्ण्, परिघूर्ण्, उद्धू in pass. (-धूयते), विधू, इतस्ततः प्लु (c. 1. प्लवते, प्लोतुं).

TOSS, *s.* क्षेपः -पणं, उत्क्षेपः -पणं, समुत्क्षेपः, क्षोभः, व्याक्षोभः.

TOSSED, *p. p.* क्षिप्तः -प्ता -प्तं, उत्क्षिप्तः &c., क्षुब्धः -ब्धा -ब्धं, संक्षुब्धः &c., उद्धूतः -ता -तं, विधूतः &c., व्यस्तः -स्ता -स्तं, प्रलोठितः -ता -तं, उद्भ्रान्तः -न्ता -न्तं, विक्षिप्तः &c., विकीर्य्यमाणः -णा -णं, काल्यमानः &c.

TOSSING, *s.* क्षेपणं, उत्क्षेपणं, हननं. *See* ROLLING, *s.* and *part.*

TOTAL, *a.* सम्पूर्णः -र्णा -र्णं, पूर्णः &c., समग्रः -ग्रा -ग्रं, आत्यन्तिकः -की -कं, *see* ENTIRE, COMPLETE; 'total rout,' सुपलायितं.

TOTAL, TOTALITY, *s.* साकल्यं, समुदायः, समस्तिः *f.*, समासः, सामग्र्यं, ऐक्यं, पारायणं, कार्त्स्न्यं, समाम्नायः. *See* WHOLE, *s.*

TOTALLY, *adv.* सर्व्वतस्, सर्व्वशस्, सम्यक्, साकल्येन. *See* ENTIRELY.

To TOTTER, *v. n.* स्खल् (c. 1. स्खलति -लितुं), प्रस्खल्, विचल् (c. 1. -चलति -लितुं), संचल्, चल्, विह्वल् (c. 1. -ह्वलति -लितुं), प्रह्वल्, ह्वल्.

TOTTERING, *part.* स्खलितः -ता -तं, विचलन् -लन्ती -लत् (त्), स्खलितगतिः -तिः -ति, विक्लवगतिः &c., स्खलद्गतिः &c., चलविचलः -ला -लं.

To TOUCH, *v. a.* स्पृश् (c. 6. स्पृशति, स्प्रष्टुं), संस्पृश्, परिस्पृश्, हस्तेन परामृश् or आलभ्, स्पर्शं कृ. *See* *To* HANDLE, MOVE.

To TOUCH, *v. n.* (Come in contact) सम्पर्कम् इ or गम्, संसर्गम् इ or गम्, परस्परस्पर्शं कृ; 'as a vessel,' लग् (c. 1. लगति -गितुं).

TOUCH, *s.* (The sense) स्पर्शः, स्पृष्टिः *f.*, स्पर्शेन्द्रियं.—(The perception, the act of touching) स्पर्शः -र्शनं, संस्पर्शः, परिमर्शः, परिमार्गः, स्पर्शबोधः, स्पर्शज्ञानं, त्वग्ज्ञानं.—(Contact) सम्पर्कः, पृक्तिः *f.*, संस्पर्शः, संसर्गः, *see* CONTACT.—(Touch as a test of gold) परीक्षा.

TOUCHED, *p. p.* स्पृष्टः -ष्टा -ष्टं, संस्पृष्टः &c., *see* MOVED; 'my heart is touched with grief,' उत्कण्ठया संस्पृष्टं हृदयं; 'to be touched,' स्प्रष्टव्यः -व्या -व्यं, स्पृश्यः -श्या -श्यं, स्पर्शनीयः -या -यं.

TOUCHING, *a.* हृदयङ्गमः -मा -मं. *See* MOVING, PATHETIC, *a.*

TOUCH-STONE, *s.* निकषः, कषः, निकषपाषाणः, कषपाषाणः, निकषग्रावा *m.* (न्), आकषः, निकसः, कसः, शाणः, शानः, हेमलः.

TOUCHY, *a.* शीघ्रकोपी -पिनी &c. *See* IRRITABLE, PEEVISH.

TOUGH, *a.* दृढः -ढा -ढं, दुःखभेद्यः -द्या -द्यं, दुर्भेद्यः &c., दुःखछेद्यः &c., दुश्छेद्यः &c., दुःखच्छिद्रः -द्रा -द्रं, कठिनः -ना -नं, शिथिलदृढः &c.

TOUGHNESS, *s.* दृढता, दुर्भेद्यता, दुःखछेद्यता, कठिनता, काठिन्यं.

TOUR, *s.* भ्रमणं, परिभ्रमणं, पर्य्यटनं, विहारः, विहरणं.

TOURIST, *s.* परिभ्रमकः, भ्रमणकारी *m.* (न्), भ्रमणकृत्, विहारी *m.*

TOURNAMENT, TOURNEY, *s.* अश्वारोहिणां क्रीडायुद्धं.

TOW, *s.* स्थूलशणं, शणसूत्रं, स्थूलभङ्गा, शणस्थूलं.

To TOW, *v. a.* रज्जुना or रज्ज्वा कृष्, रज्जुना आकृष्य चल् in caus.

TOWARD, TOWARDS, *adv.* (In the direction of) प्रति, अनु, अभिमुखं, उद्दिश्य; 'towards the city,' नगरं प्रति, नगराभिमुखं; 'he set out towards the north,' उत्तरां दिशमुद्दिश्य प्रस्थितः.—(With respect to) उपरि, उद्दिश्य, उद्देशेन, प्रति affixed; 'towards me,' ममोपरि, मामुद्दिश्य, मां प्रति; 'want of courtesy towards you,' तवोपरि अदाक्षिण्यं; 'not behaving properly towards his father,' पितुरुपरि असदृशव्यवहारी.—(Nearly) प्रायस्; 'towards evening,' अभिसायं.

TOWARD, TOWARDLY, &c. *See* APT, FORWARD, SHARP, &c.

TOWEL, *s.* गात्रमार्जनी, अङ्गमार्जनी, गात्रमार्जनवस्त्रं, वरकं.

TOWER, *s.* प्रासादशिखरं -शृङ्गं, मञ्चः *f.*, दुर्गं. *See* TURRET.

TOWERING, *a.* प्रोन्नतः -ता -तं, उन्नतः -ता -तं. *See* ELEVATED.

TOWN, *s.* नगरं -री, पुरी, *see* CITY; 'town and country,' पुरजनपदं.

TOWN-FOLK, TOWNS-MAN, *s.* नगरजनः, नगरनिवासिजनः. *See* CITIZEN.

TOWN-HALL, *s.* नगरकार्य्यनिर्वाहयोग्या महाशाला.

TOY, *s.* क्रीडनकं, क्रीडाद्रव्यं, क्रीडावस्तु *n.*, खेलनी, क्रीडामृगः.

To TOY, *v. n.* *See* *To* PLAY, SPORT, DALLY, TRIFLE.

TOY-SHOP, *s.* क्रीडाद्रव्यविक्रयस्थानं, क्रीडावस्तुविक्रयगृहं.

TRACE, *s.* अभिज्ञानं, चिह्नं, लक्षणं, अङ्कः, पदवी, लक्ष्मं, *see* MARK, FOOTSTEP.—(Of a carriage, &c.) प्रग्रहः, प्रग्राहः, चर्म्मबन्धः.

To TRACE, *v. a.* (Follow by some mark) अनुसृ, मार्गानुसरणं कृ, वर्त्मानुसरणं कृ, मृग्, मार्ग्, *see* *To* TRACK.—(Mark out) वाह्यरेखाम् अङ्क् (c. 10. अङ्कयति -यितुं) or लिख् (c. 6. लिखति, लेखितुं).

TRACHEA, *s.* श्वासमार्गः, श्वासप्रश्वासमार्गः, प्राणमार्गः.

TRACK, *s.* पदवी -विः *f.*, मार्गः, पथः, पन्थाः *m.*, *see* ROAD, TRACE.

To TRACK, *v. a.* पादानुसरणं कृ, पदानुसरणं कृ, मार्गानुसरणं कृ, अनुपदं या (c. 2. याति -तुं) or गम्, अनुसृ, *see* *To* PURSUE.

TRACKLESS, *a.* पादास्पृष्टः -ष्टा -ष्टं, पादाङ्करहितः &c., पदविहीनः &c.

TRACT, *s.* देशः, प्रदेशः, *see* REGION, COUNTRY.—(Short treatise) लेखः, पत्रिका, अल्पप्रबन्धः, स्वल्पप्रबन्धः.

TRACTABILITY, *s.* विधेयता, विनेयता, वश्यता, सविनयता.

TRACTABLE, *a.* विधेयः -या -यं, वश्यः &c., *see* DOCILE, MANAGEABLE.

TRADE, *s.* (Commerce) वाणिज्यं -ज्या, वणिज्यं, वणिक्कर्म्म *n.* (न्), वणिक्क्रिया, अर्थप्रयोगः, क्रयविक्रयः, व्यापारः, नीवरः, कोशातकी *m.* (न्), *see* COMMERCE.—(Occupation of a man of the third class) वैश्यक्रिया, वैश्यवृत्तिः *f.*—(Occupation) व्यापारः, व्यवसायः, व्यवहारः.

To TRADE, *v. n.* वाणिज्यं कृ, क्रयविक्रयं कृ, व्यापारं कृ, उपक्री.

TRADER, *s.* वणिक् *m.* (ज्), वाणिजिकः &c. *See* MERCHANT.

TRADESMAN, *s.* पत्तनवणिक् *m.* (ज्), नगरवणिक्, *see* SHOP-KEEPER.

TRADITION, *s.* लोककथा, इतिहासः, परम्परागतकथा, परम्परागतवाक्यं, पारम्पर्य्यं, परम्परागताचारः, पारम्पर्य्योपदेशः, पारम्परीयकथा, ऐतिह्यं, इतिह ind., सम्प्रदायः, आम्नायः, पुराणं, पूर्व्वं, धोरणिः *f.*, प्रवादः, आख्यायिका, गुरुक्रमः, घोषः.

TRADITIONAL, TRADITIONARY, *a.* परम्परागतः -ता -तं, परम्परायातः &c., परम्परीणः -णा -णं, पारम्परीयः -यी -यं, परम्पराप्राप्तः -प्ता -प्तं, ऐतिहासिकः -की -कं, पौराणिकः -की -कं, पुराणोक्तः -क्ता -क्तं, साम्प्रदायिकः -की -कं, क्रमागतः -ता -तं, क्रमायातः &c., क्रमप्राप्तः &c., घोषप्राप्तः &c., रूढः -ढा -ढं; 'instruction,' पारम्पर्य्योपदेशः; 'practice,' वंशानुचरितं.

TRADITIONALLY, *adv.* पारम्पर्य्येण, परम्पराक्रमेण, सम्प्रदायतस्.

To TRADUCE, TRADUCED. *See* *To* CALUMNIATE, MALIGN, &c.

TRADUCER, *s.* अपवादकः, अभिशंसी *m.* (न्), *see* CALUMNIATOR.

TRAFFIC, *s.* वाणिज्यं, लोकव्यवहारः, लोकयात्रा, *see* COMMERCE.

To TRAFFIC, *v. n.* वाणिज्यं कृ, पण्. *See To* COMMERCE, TRADE.

TRAGEDIAN, *s.* करुणरसाभिनयकुशलः, करुणारसाभिनेता *m.* (तृ).

TRAGEDY, *s.* दुःखपरिणामकनाटकं, करुणारसप्रधाननाटकं.

TRAGIC, TRAGICAL, *a.* (Pertaining to tragedy) दुःखपरिणामनाटकसम्बन्धी &c., करुणारसप्रधानः -ना -नं, करुणारसविषयकः -का -कं.—(Ending tragically) दुःखपरिणामकः -का -कं, दुष्परिणामी -मिनी &c., दुरन्तः -न्ता -न्तं.

To TRAIL, *v. a.* विकृष् (c. 1. -कर्षति -क्रष्टुं), आकृष्, समाकृष्, कृष्.

To TRAIL, *v. n.* विकृष् in pass. (-कृष्यते), आकृष्, कृष्, कृष्टः -ष्टा -ष्टं भू.

TRAIL, *s.* (Track) पदविः -वी *f.*—(Scent left) गन्धः.

To TRAIN, *v. a.* विनी (c. 1. -नयति -नेतुं), शिक्ष् (c. 10. शिक्षयति -यितुं), अनुशिक्ष्, शास्, अनुशास्, अनुशासनं कृ, नियमनं कृ. *See To* DISCIPLINE.

TRAIN, *s.* (End of a robe) वसनान्तः, मानवस्त्रान्तः, वसनभारः.—(Retinue) परिवारः, परिवर्हः, सामग्र्यं, *see* RETINUE.—(Concatenation) श्रेणी, प्रबन्धः, *see* SERIES, SUCCESSION; 'train of fraud,' कपटप्रबन्धः; 'of reasoning,' तर्कप्रबन्धः, अनुमानप्रबन्धः.—(Regular course) क्रमः, अनुक्रमः.—(Of gunpowder) आग्नेयचूर्णश्रेणी.—(Of a peacock) बर्हः, बर्हभारः.

TRAINED, *p. p.* शिक्षितः -ता -तं, विनीतः -ता -तं, अनुनीतः &c., कृताभ्यासः -सा -सं, दमितः -ता -तं, दान्तः -न्ता -न्तं. *See* DISCIPLINED, EDUCATED.

TRAINING, *s.* शिक्षा, *see* EDUCATION; 'of a horse,' अश्वशिक्षा.

TRAIT, *s.* लक्षणं; 'bad trait,' कुलक्षणं, दुर्लक्षणं; 'good,' सुलक्षणं.

TRAITOR, *s.* (One guilty of treason) राजद्रोही *m.* (न्), शत्रुसेवी *m.*, द्विट्सेवी *m.*, राजशत्रुः, देशद्रोही *m.*, भेत्ता *m.* (तृ), भेदकः, उपजापकः.—(One who betrays his trust) विश्वासघाती *m.* (न्), विश्वासघातकः, वञ्चकः, विसंवादी *m.*, मिथ्याप्रतिज्ञः, विश्रब्धघाती *m.*

TRAITOROUS, *a.* राजापथ्यकारी &c., राजद्रोही &c., *see* TREASONABLE.

TRAMMEL, *To* TRAMMEL. *See* SHACKLE, CLOY, *To* CLOY.

To TRAMP, *v. n.* चरणपातं कृ, पदन्यासं कृ, पदविक्षेपं कृ.

To TRAMPLE, *v. a.* पादाभ्यां मृद् (c. 9. मृद्नाति, मर्दितुं) or सम्मृद् or प्रमृद् or उपमृद् or अवमृद्, पादाघातेन मृद् or क्षुद् (c. 7. क्षुणत्ति, क्षोत्तुं), मर्दनं कृ, उपमर्दनं कृ, अवमर्दनं कृ, पादाभ्याम् आक्रम् or समाक्रम्.

TRAMPLED, *p. p.* पादाभ्यां मर्दितः -ता -तं or सम्मर्दितः &c. or उपमर्दितः &c. or अवमर्दितः &c., पादाहतः -ता -तं, पादमर्दितः &c., पादन्यासमर्दितः &c., पादक्षुण्णः -ण्णा -ण्णं, प्रमथितः -ता -तं.

TRAMPLING, *s.* मर्दनं, उपमर्दः -र्दनं, अवमर्दः -र्दनं, सम्मर्दः -र्दनं, पादाहतिः *f.*, पादाघातः, पदपातः, चरणपातः, पादास्फालनं, पादाभ्यासः, चरणास्कन्दनं, प्रमथनं.

TRANCE, *s.* देहातीतवृत्तिः *f.*, मोहावस्था, समाधिः *m.*, तन्मयावस्था, मूर्च्छना, आवेशः, मोहः, लोकान्तरचित्तवृत्तिः *f.*

TRANQUIL, *a.* शान्तः -न्ता -न्तं, प्रशान्तः &c., स्थिरः -रा -रं, स्वस्थः -स्था -स्थं, शान्तात्मा -त्मा -त्म (न्), स्वस्थचित्तः -त्ता -त्तं, अक्षुब्धः -ब्धा -ब्धं. *See* CALM.

To TRANQUILIZE, *v. a.* शम् (c. 10. शमयति -यितुं), *see To* CALM, COMPOSE.

TRANQUILLITY, *s.* शान्तिः *f.*, शमः, शान्तता, निर्वृतिः *f.*, स्थिरता, अक्षुब्धता, अक्षोभः, स्वस्थता, स्वास्थ्यं, निरुपद्रवता. *See* CALMNESS, COMPOSURE.

To TRANSACT, *v. a.* निर्वह् (c. 10. -वाहयति -यितुं), व्यवहृ (c. 1. -हरति -हर्तुं), विधा (c. 3. -दधाति -धातुं), प्रणी, सम्प्रणी, प्रवृत् in caus., आचर्, समाचर्, अनुष्ठा, तीर् (c. 10. तीरयति -यितुं), पार् (c. 10. पारयति -यितुं), पण् (c. 10. पणयति -यितुं), कृ; 'business,' कर्म्मनिर्वाहं कृ.

TRANSACTED, *p. p.* निर्वाहितः -ता -तं, पणायितः -ता -तं, पणितः -ता -तं, आचरितः -ता -तं.

TRANSACTION, *s.* (The act of doing) निर्वाहः -हणं, प्रवर्त्तनं, विधानं, आचरणं, प्रणयनं, अनुष्ठानं; 'of business,' कर्म्मनिर्वाहः.—(Affair) कर्म्म *n.* (न्), कार्य्यं, व्यापारः, व्यवहारः, वृत्तान्तः, पणाया.

To TRANSCEND, *v. a.* *See To* EXCEED, SURPASS, EXCEL.

TRANSCENDENTAL, *a.* अत्युत्तमः -मा -मं. *See* SURPASSING, SUPERIOR.

TRANSCENDENTLY, *adv.* अत्युत्तमं, अत्यन्तं, अधिकं, अभ्यधिकं, परमं.

To TRANSCRIBE, TRANSCRIPT. *See To* COPY, COPY.

TRANSCRIBER, *s.* लिपिकारः, प्रतिलिपिकारकः, आदर्शकारकः.

To TRANSFER, *v. a.* (Make over, cause to pass) संक्रम् in caus. (-क्रामयति -यितुं), उपसंक्रम्, संचर् in caus. (-चारयति -यितुं), समृ in caus. (-अर्पयति -यितुं), अध्यारुह् in caus. (-रोपयति -यितुं), अपवृत् (c. 10. -वर्त्तयति -यितुं); 'to another,' परस्मिन् or परस्मै or परहस्ते समृ in caus. or संक्रम् in caus.—(Convey from one place to another) स्थानान्तरीकृ, स्थलान्तरीकृ.

TRANSFERABLE, *a.* सङ्क्रमणीयः -या -यं, सञ्चारणीयः &c., परसमर्पणीयः &c.

TRANSFERRED, *p. p.* सङ्क्रामितः -ता -तं, सङ्क्रान्तः -न्ता -न्तं, उपसङ्क्रान्तः &c., सञ्चारितः &c., परहस्तसमर्पितः &c., अध्यस्तः -स्ता -स्तं.

TRANSFIGURATION, *s.* रूपान्तरग्रहणं, मूर्त्त्यन्तरग्रहणं, रूपपरिवर्त्तनं.

To TRANSFIGURE, *v. a.* रूपान्तरीकृ, मूर्त्त्यन्तरं कृ, *see To* TRANSFORM.

TRANSFIGURED, *p. p.* रूपान्तरीकृतः -ता -तं. *See* TRANSFORMED.

To TRANSFIX, *v. a.* व्यध् (c. 4. विध्यति, व्यद्धुं), प्रतिव्यध्, भिद् (c. 7. भिनत्ति, भेत्तुं), शूल् (c. 1. शूलति -लितुं), कील् (c. 10. कीलयति -यितुं), निखन् (c. 1. -खनति -नितुं), छुर् (c. 6. छुरति -रितुं). *See To* PIERCE.

TRANSFIXED, *p. p.* विद्धः -द्धा -द्धं, अतिविद्धः &c., कीलितः -ता -तं, छुरितः &c.; 'through the belly,' छुरितोदरः -रा -रं.

To TRANSFORM, *v. a.* रूपं परिवृत् in caus., रूपपरिवर्त्तनं कृ, रूपान्तरीकृ, विडम्ब् (c. 10. -डम्बयति -यितुं). *See To* METAMORPHOSE.

TRANSFORMATION, *s.* रूपान्तरीकरणं, रूपान्तरं, मूर्त्तिपरिवर्त्तनं, विडम्बनं, व्याकृतिः *f.*, परिणामः. *See* METAMORPHOSIS.

TRANSFORMED, *p. p.* व्याकृतः -ता -तं, विडम्बितः &c. *See* METAMORPHOSED.

To TRANSFUSE, *v. a.* एकपात्राभ्यन्तरात् स्रावयित्वा अन्यपात्रे निविश् (c. 10. -वेशयति -यितुं) or निषिच्, पात्रान्तरीकृ. *See To* TRANSFER.

TRANSFUSION, *s.* सङ्क्रामणं, सङ्क्रान्तिः *f.*, सञ्चारणं, पात्रान्तरीकरणं.

To TRANSGRESS, *v. a.* लङ्घ् (c. 10. लङ्घयति -यितुं), उल्लङ्घ्, अतिक्रम् (c. 1. -क्रामति -क्रमितुं), समतिक्रम्, व्यतिक्रम्, अभ्यतिक्रम्, अतिचर् (c. 1. -चरति -रितुं), व्यभिचर्, उल्लङ्घनं कृ, लङ्घनं कृ, अतिक्रमणं कृ, व्यतिक्रमं कृ, अतिवृत्. *See To* SURPASS.

To TRANSGRESS, *v. n.* अपराध्, अपराधं कृ. *See To* OFFEND, *v. n.*

TRANSGRESSED, *p. p.* उल्लङ्घितः -ता -तं, लङ्घितः &c., विलङ्घितः &c., अतिक्रान्तः -न्ता -न्तं, व्यतिक्रान्तः &c., समतिक्रान्तः &c., उत्क्रान्तः &c., अतीतः &c.

TRANSGRESSION, *s.* (The act of transgressing) लङ्घनं, उल्लङ्घनं, विलङ्घनं, अतिक्रमः -मणं, व्यतिक्रमः, समतिक्रमः, उत्क्रमः -मणं, अतिपातः, अत्याचारः, उपात्ययः, अत्ययः, भङ्गः, लोपः -पनं, अमर्य्यादा.—

(Offence) अपराधः, पापं, पातकं, *see* OFFENCE.

TRANSGRESSOR, *s.* (One who goes beyond) अतिक्रामकः, अतिक्रमी *m.* (न्), उल्लङ्घी *m.*, अत्याचारी *m.*—(Sinner) अपराधी *m.*, *see* OFFENDER.

TRANSIENT, *a.* अचिरस्थायी -यिनी &c., अस्थायी &c., क्षणिकः -का -कं, क्षणविध्वंसी &c., भङ्गुरः -रा -रं, क्षणभङ्गुरः &c., चपलः -ला -लं, अनित्यः -त्या -त्यं, अचिरविनश्वरः -रा -रं, नश्वरः &c., अशाश्वतः -ती -तं. *See* MOMENTARY, TEMPORARY.

TRANSIENTNESS, *s.* अचिरस्थायित्वं, अस्थायिता, अनित्यता.

TRANSIT, *s.* सङ्क्रमः -मणं, सङ्क्रान्तिः *f.*, सङ्क्रामः, क्रान्तिः *f.*, अतिक्रमः -मणं, गतिः *f.*; 'of a star,' तारासङ्क्रमः.

TRANSITION, *s.* सङ्क्रमः -मणं, सङ्क्रान्तिः *f.*, विकारः, सञ्चारः, अवस्थान्तरं, स्थित्यन्तरं, अभिलम्भनं, स्थानान्तरं.

TRANSITIVE, *a.* (Verb) सकर्म्मकः, सकर्म्मक्रिया; 'transitive voice,' परस्मैपदं.

TRANSITORY, *a.* अस्थायी &c., जगन् -गती -गत्. *See* TRANSIENT.

To TRANSLATE, *v. a.* (Remove), *see To* REMOVE, TRANSFER; 'to heaven,' सशरीरं स्वर्गम् आरुह् in caus.—(Into another language) भाषान्तरीकृ, अवतॄ (c. 1. -तरति -रितुं -रीतुं), अवतरणं कृ, विवृ, भाषान्तरे निरूप् (c. 10. -रूपयति -यितुं).

TRANSLATED, *p. p.* (Removed), *see* REMOVED; 'to heaven,' सशरीरस्वर्गारोपितः -ता -तं, सशरीरमुक्तः -क्ता -क्तं.—(Into another language) भाषान्तरीकृतः -ता -तं, अवतीर्णः -र्णा -र्णं, विवृतः -ता -तं, भाषान्तरे निरूपितः -ता -तं; 'Prákrit translated into Sanskrit,' प्राकृतः संस्कृते निरूपितः.

TRANSLATION, *s.* (Removal), *see* REMOVAL; 'to heaven,' सशरीरस्वर्गारोपणं, सशरीरमुक्तिः *f.*—(Into another language) भाषान्तरं, भाषान्तरीकरणं, अवतरणं, अवतारः, विवरणं, भाषान्तरे निरूपणं; 'loose translation,' छायानुहरणं.

TRANSLATOR, *s.* भाषान्तरकारी *m.* (न्), अवतरणकृत्, व्याख्याता *m.* (तृ), अर्थव्याख्याता *m.*, अर्थनिरूपकः. *See* INTERPRETER.

To TRANSMIGRATE, *v. n.* देहान्तरं गम् (c. 1. गच्छति, गन्तुं), शरीरान्तरं गम्, जन्मान्तरं or पुनर्जन्म प्राप्, योनिभ्रमणं कृ.

TRANSMIGRATION, *s.* देहान्तरप्राप्तिः *f.*, देहान्तरगतिः *f.* -गमनं, शरीरान्तरप्राप्तिः *f.*, पुनर्जन्म *n.* (न्), जन्मान्तरं, जन्ममरणं, योनिभ्रमणं, पुनरावृत्तिः *f.*, गतिः *f.*; 'exemption from it,' अपुनरावृत्तिः *f.*

TRANSMISSION, TRANSMITTAL, *s.* सञ्चारः -रणं, सङ्क्रामणं, सङ्क्रान्तिः *f.*, सञ्चालनं, प्रेरणं, प्रापणं, अभिवाह्यं.

To TRANSMIT, *v. a.* संचर् in caus. (-चारयति -यितुं), संक्रम् in caus. (-क्रामयति -यितुं), उपसंक्रम्, प्रेर् (c. 10. प्रेरयति -यितुं), प्राप् in caus.

TRANSMITTED, *p. p.* सञ्चारितः -ता -तं, सङ्क्रामितः &c., प्रेरितः &c.

TRANSMUTATION, *s.* परिणामः, परिणामान्तरं, द्रव्यान्तरं.

To TRANSMUTE, *v. a.* द्रव्यान्तरीकृ, परिणामभेदं कृ, आत्यन्तरं कृ.

TRANSPARENCY, *s.* स्वच्छता -त्वं, अच्छता, प्रसन्नता, प्रसत्तिः *f.*, निर्म्मलता, प्रकाशभेद्यता, किरणभेद्यता, प्रकाशारोधकता.

TRANSPARENT, *a.* (Clear) स्वच्छः -च्छा -च्छं, अच्छः &c., प्रसन्नः -न्ना -न्नं, निर्म्मलः -ला -लं, अमलः &c., स्फटिकप्रभः -भा -भं.—(Transmitting light, not opake) प्रकाशभेद्यः -द्या -द्यं, किरणभेद्यः &c., प्रकाशारोधकः -का -कं, प्रकाशाप्रतिबन्धकः &c., दृष्ट्यरोधकः &c., पारदर्शकः &c., मध्यस्थः -स्था -स्थं.

To TRANSPIRE, *v. n.* प्रसिद्धः -द्धा -द्धं भू, प्रसिद्धीभू, प्रकाशः -शा -शं भू, प्रकाशीभू, प्रचलीभू, लोकविदितः -ता -तं भू.

To TRANSPLANT, *v. a.* स्थानान्तरे रुह् in caus. (रोपयति -यितुं) or रोपणं कृ, उन्मूल्य स्थानान्तरे रुह् in caus., उन्मूल् (c. 10. -मूलयति -यितुं).

TRANSPLANTED, *p. p.* स्थानान्तरे रोपितः -ता -तं, उन्मूलितः -ता -तं.

To TRANSPORT, *v. a.* (Convey, carry) तॄ (c. 10. तारयति -यितुं), सन्तॄ, वह्, आवह्, संवह्, स्थानान्तरीकृ, आनी, *see To* CONVEY.—(As a criminal) विवस् (c. 10. -वासयति -यितुं), प्रवस्, निर्वस्, प्रव्रज् (c. 10. -व्राजयति -यितुं), देशान्तरीकृ, सागरपारे दूरीकृ, स्वदेशाद् दूरीकृ.—(Ravish), *see* the word.

TRANSPORT, *s.* (Conveyance) तारणं, सन्तारणं, वाहनं, आनयनं.—(Of passion) क्रोधावेशः, कोपावेशः.—(Rapture), *see* RAPTURE.

TRANSPORTATION, *s.* विवासः -सनं, प्रवासः -सनं, निर्वासनं, विवासकरणं, प्रव्राजनं, सागरपारे दूरीकरणं, सन्तारणं, सन्तारकत्वं.

TRANSPORTED, *p. p.* (Conveyed) सन्तारितः -ता -तं, तारितः &c., आनीतः &c.—(Exiled) विवासितः &c.—(Enraptured), *see* the word.

To TRANSPOSE, *v. a.* स्थानपरिवर्त्तनं कृ, स्थानविनिमयं कृ, स्थानविपर्य्ययं कृ, स्थानं परिवृत् (c. 10. -वर्त्तयति -यितुं), विपर्यस्.

TRANSPOSED, *p. p.* परिवर्त्तितः -ता -तं, विपर्यस्तः &c., व्यत्यस्तः &c.

TRANSPOSITION, *s.* स्थानपरिवर्त्तनं, स्थानविनिमयः, स्थानविपर्य्ययः, व्यत्यासः, व्यत्ययः, विपर्य्ययः, विपर्य्यासः.—(In arithmetic) तुल्यशुद्धिः *f.*

TRANSVERSE, *a.* तिर्य्यङ् -श्ची -र्य्यक् (च्), व्यत्यस्तः -स्ता -स्तं, विपरीतः &c.

TRANSVERSELY, *adv.* तिर्य्यक्, व्यत्यस्तं, कोणाकोणि, विपरीतं.

TRAP, *s.* उन्माथः, कूटयन्त्रं, कूटः, पाशः, वागुरा, जालं, पञ्जराखेटः, ग्राहः, पातिली. *See* SNARE.

TRAPEZIUM, *s.* विषमचतुरस्रं, विषमचतुर्भुजः, विषमचतुष्कोणः.

TRAPPINGS, *s. pl.* परिच्छदः, भूषणं, परिकर्म्म *n.*, *see* FINERY.—(Of a horse or elephant) परिस्तोमः, वर्णः, आदानं, आस्तरः -रणं, प्रवेणिः -णी *f.*, कुथः.

TRASH, *s.* असारद्रव्यं, तुच्छद्रव्यं, कुत्सितद्रव्यं. *See* RUBBISH.

TRAVAIL, *To* TRAVAIL, *See* under LABOR, *To* LABOR, *v. n.*

To TRAVEL, *v. n.* व्रज्, प्रव्रज्, देशभ्रमणं कृ, देशपर्यटनं कृ, देशाटनं कृ, अध्वना गम्, यात्रां कृ, चर्, विचर्. *See To* JOURNEY.

TRAVEL, TRAVELING, *s.* अध्वगमनं, मार्गगमनं, देशभ्रमणं, भ्रमणं, परिभ्रमणं, पर्यटनं, देशपर्यटनं, अटनं, यात्रा, संयात्रा, व्रज्या, अटाट्या, मार्गक्रमणं, प्रवासः; 'to return from travel,' प्रवासाद् आगम्; 'traveling-carriage,' पारियानिकः; 'companion,' सहचरः.

TRAVELLER, *s.* पथिकः, पान्थः, अध्वगः -गामी *m.* (न्), अध्वन्यः, अध्वनीनः, यात्रिकः, पादविकः, सारणिकः, मार्गस्थः, पथिलः, गन्तुः *m.*, गमथः, यायी *m.* (न्), देशिकः, इत्वरः, प्रोथः, देशिकः, अध्वनि वर्त्तमानः, परदेशसेवी *m.*; 'a great traveller,' बहुदेशदर्शी *m.*

To TRAVERSE, *v. a.* तॄ (c. 1. तरति -रितुं -रीतुं), अतितॄ, सन्तॄ, अतिक्रम् (c. 1. -क्रामति -क्रमितुं), परिक्रम्, पारं गम् (c. 1. गच्छति, गन्तुं), or इ.

TRAVERSED, *p. p.* अतिक्रान्तः -न्ता -न्तं, तीर्णः &c., पारगतः &c., पारमितः &c.

TRAVESTY, *s.* हास्यजनकविडम्बनं, हास्यरसप्रधानानुकरणकाव्यं, हास्यजनकानुकरणकविता, आकारगोपनं.

TRAY, *s.* पात्रं, भाजनं, शरावः, द्रोणिः -णी *f.*, आधारः

TREACHEROUS, *a.* विश्वासघाती &c., मिथ्याप्रतिज्ञः -ज्ञा -ज्ञं, विसंवादी &c., असत्यसन्धः -न्धा -न्धं, अविश्वास्यः &c., *see* PERFIDIOUS, FAITHLESS.

TREACHEROUSLY, TREACHEROUSNESS. *See* PERFIDIOUSLY, &c.

TREACHERY, *s.* विश्वासघातः, विश्वासभङ्गः, विसंवादः, प्रतिज्ञाभङ्गः, उपजापः, उपजपः, धूर्त्तता, अभिमरः. *See* PERFIDY.

TREACLE, *s.* इक्षुसारः, इक्षुरसक्वाथः, शर्कराक्षारः. *See* MOLASSES.

To TREAD, *v. n.* चरणपातं कृ, पदपातं कृ, पादपातं कृ, पदन्यासं कृ, पादार्पणं कृ, पदविष्टम्भं कृ, क्रम् (c. 1. क्रामति, क्रमते -मितुं).

To TREAD, *v. a.* आक्रम् (c. 1. -क्रामति -क्रमितुं), समाक्रम्, पादाभ्याम् आक्रम् or पीड्, पदन्यासं कृ, पादन्यासं कृ, पादार्पणं कृ; 'to tread on one's steps,' पदाक्रमणं कृ; 'one who does so,' पदाक्रामः.—(Crush with the feet) पादाभ्यां मृद् or अवमृद्, *see To* TRAMPLE, STAMP, STEP.

TREAD, *s.* पदन्यासः, पादन्यासः, पदपातः, पादपातः, चरणपातः, क्रमः, विक्रमः, पादाघातः, पादाघातः. *See* STEP, PACE.

TREASON, *s.* राजद्रोहः, राजाभिद्रोहः, राजशरीराभिद्रोहः, राजापकारः, राजापथ्यकारित्वं, राजविरोधः.

TREASONABLE, *a.* राजद्रोही -हिणी -हि (न्), राजाभिद्रोही &c., राजापकारी &c., राजद्रोहसम्बन्धी &c., राजविरोधी &c.

TREASURE, *s.* (Store of valuables) निधिः *m.*, निधानं, कोषः.—(Accumulation of money, &c.) धनसञ्चयः, द्रव्यसञ्चयः, वित्तनिचयः, धनराशिः *m.*, धनसमूहः, सञ्चितधनं.—(Money, &c.) धनं, वित्तं, वसु *n.*—(A treasure) निधिः *m.*, कुलाभिः *m.*—(Divine treasure) निधिः *m.*, सेवधिः *m.*, *see* under KUVERA.

To TREASURE, *v. a.* निधिं कृ, निधा, संचि, कोषीकृ. *See To* HOARD.

TREASURED, *p. p.* सञ्चितः -ता -तं, कोषीकृतः &c., कोषभूतः -ता -तं.

TREASURER, *s.* कोषाध्यक्षः, कोशाध्यक्षः, कोशाधीशः, कोशनायकः, धनाधिकारी *m.* (न्), भाण्डागाराध्यक्षः, धनाध्यक्षः, अर्थाधिकारी *m.*, कनकाध्यक्षः, कोष्ठपालः, गञ्जाधिकारी *m.*, गञ्जाधिपः, धनाधिपः, भाण्डागारी *m.*, भौरिकः.

TREASURERSHIP, *s.* कोषाधिकारः, अर्थाधिकारः, गञ्जाधिकारित्वं.

TREASURY, *s.* कोषः, कोशः, धनागारं, भाण्डागारं, धनशाला, धनगृहं, कोष्ठः -ष्ठकं, गञ्जः -ञ्जं, अर्थसंस्थानं, निधिः *m.*

To TREAT, *v. a.* (Act or behave towards) आचर् (c. 1. -चरति -रितुं), समाचर्, व्यवहृ (c. 1. -हरति -हर्तुं), सेव् (c. 1. सेवते -वितुं), विधा (c. 3. -दधाति -धातुं), प्रणी (c. 1. -णयति -णेतुं), विनी; 'one should treat one's son like a friend,' पुत्रं मित्रवद् आचरेत्; 'to treat ill,' अपकृ, कुव्यवहारं कृ; 'to treat with respect,' पूज्, सत्कृ, *see To* HONOUR; 'with hospitality,' सत्कृ, सत्कारं कृ, आतिथ्यं कृ.—(Give food, &c.) उत्तमान्नेन तृप् (c. 10. तर्पयति -यितुं) or सन्तृप्.—(A disease) उपचारं कृ, प्रयोगं कृ, चिकित्सां कृ.

To TREAT, *v. n.* (Treat of any subject) विषयप्रसङ्गं कृ, प्रसक्तिं कृ, प्रस्तावं कृ, प्रस्तुतं -तां कृ, मथ् (c. 1. मथति -थितुं), मथनं कृ, विचर् (c. 10. -चारयति -यितुं), निरूप् (c. 10. -रूपयति -यितुं); 'to treat at length,' प्रपञ्चनं कृ.—(Negotiate) पण्, *see* the word.

TREAT, *s.* उत्तमान्नतर्पणं, परमान्नभोजनं, *see* FEAST, ENTERTAINMENT.

TREATED, *p. p.* आचरितः -ता -तं, व्यवहृतः &c., व्यवहारितः &c., सेवितः &c.; 'ill-treated,' अपकृतः &c., कुव्यवहारितः -ता -तं; 'well-treated,' सत्कृतः -ता -तं, सुव्यवहारितः &c., सेवितः &c., सेव्यमानः -ना -नं.—(Treated of) प्रस्तुतः -ता -तं, विचारितः -ता -तं, मथितः &c., निरूपितः &c.; 'at length,' प्रपञ्चितः -ता -तं.

TREATISE, *s.* निबन्धः, प्रबन्धः, ग्रन्थः, लेखः, शास्त्रं, पुस्तकं.

TREATMENT, *s.* प्रणयनं, प्रणीतिः *f.*, नयः, आचरणं, प्रयोगः, प्रयुक्तिः *f.*, उपायप्रयोगः; 'of disease,' उपचारः, चिकित्सा.

TREATY, *s.* नियमः, समयः, संविद् *f.* *See* COMPACT, LEAGUE.

TREBLE, *a.* त्रिगुणः -णा -णं, त्रिविधः -धा -धं, त्रिगतः -ता -तं.

TREBLE, *s.* (In music) उच्चस्वनः, उच्चस्वरः, तीक्ष्णस्वरः.

To TREBLE, *v. a.* त्रिगुणीकृ, त्रिगुण (nom. त्रिगुणयति -यितुं).

TREBLY, *adv.* त्रिगुणं, त्रिधा, त्रेधा, त्रिविधं, वारत्रयं.

TREE, *s.* वृक्षः, तरुः *m.*, द्रुमः, पादपः, द्रुः *m.*, वनस्पतिः *m.*, वनराजिः *m.*, क्षितिरुहः, महीरुहः, भूरुहः, फलग्राही *m.* (न्), फलदः, पल्लवी *m.* (न्), रोहिः *m.*, अवनिरुट् *m.* (ह्), अवनिरुहः, स्कन्धी *m.* (न्), विटपी *m.*, शाखी *m.*, अंह्रिपः, गच्छः, पत्री *m.*, कुठः, कुटः, अगमः, पलाशी *m.*, शालः, सालः, अनोकहः, धानस्थतः; 'a village tree, held in veneration,' चैत्यः; 'relating to a tree,' वार्क्षः -र्क्षी -र्क्षं.

TREFOIL, *s.* त्रिपर्णी -र्णा -र्णं, त्रिपत्रः -त्रा -त्रं, त्रिदला.

TRELLIS, TRELLIS-WORK, *s.* जालं -लकं, जालिका, गवाक्षजालं.

To TREMBLE, *v. n.* कम्प् (c. 1. कम्पते -म्पितुं), वेप् (c. 1. वेपते -पितुं), स्फुर् (c. 6. स्फुरति -रितुं), चपल (nom. चपलायते). *See To* QUIVER, SHAKE, *v. n.*

TREMBLING, *part.* कम्पमानः -ना -नं, वेपमानः &c., जातकम्पः -म्पा -म्पं, जातवेपथुः -थुः -थु, उज्ज्वलः -ला -लं, उज्ज्वलन् -लन्ती &c. *See* QUIVERING.

TREMBLING, *s.* कम्पः -म्पनं, प्रकम्पः, उत्कम्पः, वेपनं, प्रवेपणं, स्फुरणं, विधुवनं, उज्ज्वलः; 'of voice,' स्वरभङ्गः, *see* QUIVERING, *s.*

TREMENDOUS, *a.* अतिदारुणः -णा -णं, अतिभयानकः, *see* FEARFUL.

TREMOR, *s.* वेपथुः *m.*, कम्पः, वेपनं, स्फुरणं, स्फूर्त्तिः *f.*, चलनं, विधूतिः *f.*, विधुतिः *f.*, विधूननं, गात्रकम्पः. *See* TREMBLING, *s.*

TREMULOUS, *a.* लोलः -ला -लं, चञ्चलः &c., चपलः &c., कम्पनः -ना -नं, कम्प्रः -म्प्रा -म्प्रं, सकम्पः -म्पा -म्पं, कम्पान्वितः -ता -तं, सोत्कम्पः &c., तरलः -ला -लं, तरलितः -ता -तं, लुलितः &c., आलोलः -ला -लं, चटुलः &c., स्फूर्त्तिमान् -मती &c.

TREMULOUSLY, *adv.* सकम्पं, सवेपनं, सस्फुरणं, चञ्चलं, तरलं.

TREMULOUSNESS, *s.* लोलता, चञ्चलता, चपलता, सकम्पता -त्वं.

TRENCH, *s.* परिखा, खातं, कुल्या, उपकुल्या, परिकूटं, खल्लः, *see* DITCH; 'trench at the foot of a tree,' आलवालं, स्थानकं.

To TRENCH, *v. a.* or *n.* *See To* INTRENCH, ENCROACH.

TRENCHER, *s.* काष्ठमयपात्रं, काष्ठमयभाजनं, काष्ठमयभाण्डं.

TREPIDATION, *s.* कम्पः, भयकम्पः, विभ्रमः. *See* TREMBLING, TERROR.

To TRESPASS, *v. a.* (Pass beyond, exceed propriety) अतिक्रम् (c. 1. -क्रामति -क्रमितुं), उत्क्रम्, मर्य्यादातिक्रमं कृ, मर्य्यादालङ्घनं कृ, सीमातिक्रमणं कृ, सीमोल्लङ्घनं कृ, *see To* TRANSGRESS, OFFEND.—(Intrude, encroach) अनधिकारपूर्व्वम् आक्रम् or आक्रमणं कृ, *see To* INTRUDE, &c.

TRESPASS, *s.* अतिक्रमः, उत्क्रमः, आक्रमणं, मर्य्यादातिक्रमः, अनधिकारप्रवेशः, व्यभिचारः, अमर्य्यादा, अपराधः, द्रोहः.

TRESPASSER, *s.* मर्य्यादातिक्रमी *m.* (न्), अनधिकारप्रवेशकः.

TRESS, *s.* अलकः, कबरः -री -रं, केशवेशः, केशगर्भकः. *See* CURL.

TRIAD, *s.* त्रिकं, त्रयं -यी; 'the Hindú triad,' त्रिमूर्त्तिः *f.*

TRIAL, *s.* (Testing, proving) परीक्षा -क्षणं, अनुभवः, *see* TEST; 'under trial,' अनुभूयमानः -ना -नं; 'subjected to trial,' अनुभवारूढः -ढा -ढं.—(Experience) अनुभवः, अनुभूतिः *f.*, प्रतीतिः *f.*—(Attempt) यत्नः, प्रयत्नः, उद्योगः.—(Judicial trial) विचारः, व्यवहारदर्शनं, धर्म्मविवेचनं; 'day of trial,' विचारदिनं, आह्वानदर्शनं.—(Affliction, calamity), *see* the words.

TRIANGLE, *s.* त्रिकोणः -णं, त्रिभुजः, त्र्यस्रं, त्रिशृङ्गः -ङ्गं, त्रिपुटकः, सूचिः *f.*, त्रिकोणाकृतिः *f.*, त्रिकोणमूर्त्तिः *f.*; 'acute angled,' अन्तर्लम्बः; 'equilateral,' समत्रिभुजः; 'isosceles,' द्विसमत्रिभुजः; 'scalene,'

विषमत्रिभुजः; 'base of a triangle,' भुजः; 'segment of the base,' अबाधा; 'verticle arm,' कोटिः f.; 'area,' त्रिकोणक्षेत्रं.

TRIANGULAR, *a.* त्रिकोणाकृतिः -तिः -ति, त्रिकोणाकारः -रा -रं, त्रिभुजाकारः &c., त्र्यस्राकारः &c., त्र्यस्रः -स्रा -स्रं.

TRIBE, *s.* जातिः f., वर्गः, कुलं, वर्णः, गणः, गोत्रं; 'the four tribes or classes,' चतुर्वर्णं; these are, 1. the sacerdotal, *see* BRAHMIN; 2. the military, *see* under MILITARY, *a.*; 3. the agricultural or mercantile, *see* AGRICULTURIST; 4. the servile, *see* SHÚDRA.

TRIBRACH, *s.* (Foot of three short syllables) तगणः.

TRIBULATION, *s.* क्लेशः, दुःखं, सङ्कटं. *See* DISTRESS, TROUBLE.

TRIBUNAL, *s.* (Court of justice) धर्म्मसभा, न्यायसभा, धर्म्मशाला.—(Seat of a judge) धर्म्मासनं, न्यायासनं.

TRIBUTARY, *a.* or *s.* करदः -दा -दं, शुल्कदः -दा -दं, नैगमः -मी -मं; 'made so,' करदीकृतः -ता -तं.—(Paid in tribute) कररूपः &c.

TRIBUTE, *s.* करः, शुल्कः -ल्कं, करभारः, उपहारः. *See* TAX.

TRICE, *s.* निमेषः, पलं, क्षणः, त्रुटिः f.; 'in a trice,' निमेषमात्रेण.

TRICK, *s.* (Artifice to deceive) छलं, छद्म *n.* (न्), व्यपदेशः, माया, कपटः, व्याजः, कैतवप्रयोगः, *see* FRAUD.—(Bad or strange habit) व्यसनं, दुर्गुणं, दुर्लक्षणं, अपलक्षणं, चेष्टा, कुचेष्टा, क्ष्वेलितं; 'monkey trick,' मर्कटचेष्टा, *see* PRANK.

To TRICK, TRICKERY. *See* *To* DECEIVE, DECEPTION, DECEIT.

TRICKED, *p.p.* वञ्चितः -ता -तं, व्यपदिष्टः -ष्टा -ष्टं. *See* DECEIVED.

To TRICKLE, *v. n.* शनैः शनैः स्यन्द् (c. 1. स्यन्दते -न्दितुं) or स्रु (c. 1. स्रवति, स्रोतुं) or क्षर् or री. *See* *To* OOZE, FLOW.

TRICKLING, *part.* शनैः शनैः स्यन्दमानः -ना -नं. *See* OOZING, *part.*

TRICKLING, *s.* स्यन्दनं, निस्यन्दः, क्षरणं, स्रवः, स्रावः. *See* OOZING, *s.*

TRIDENT, *s.* त्रिशूलः -लं, त्रिशिखं, त्रिशीर्षकः -कं, पिनाकः -कं; 'of Śiva,' *see* under ŚIVA; 'bearer of one,' त्रिशूलपाणिः *m.*

TRIDUAN, *a.* त्र्याहिकः -की -कं, त्र्यहान्तरितः -ता -तं.

TRIED, *p. p.* परीक्षितः -ता -तं, अनुभूतः &c.; 'person,' उपधाशुचिः.

TRIENNIAL, *a.* त्रैवार्षिकः -की -कं, त्र्याब्दिकः &c., त्रिवर्षात्मकः &c.

TRIFLE, *s.* स्वल्पविषयः, अल्पविषयः, लघुविषयः, स्तोकल्पवस्तु.

To TRIFLE, *v. n.* बालकवद् आचर्, बालकवृत्तिं सेव् or आस्था, लघुविषयव्यापृतः -ता -तं भू, खेला (nom. खेलायति), कुड् (c. 6. कुडति -डितुं); 'trifle away,' क्षिप्.

TRIFLER, *s.* लघुविषयव्यापृतः -व्यापारी *m.*, कालक्षेपकः.

TRIFLING, *a.* लघुः -घुः -घु, स्वल्पः -ल्पा -ल्पं, अल्पप्रभावः -वा -वं, लघुप्रभावः &c., अगणनीयः -या -यं, क्षुल्लकः -का -कं, तृणप्रायः -या -यं, तनीयान् -यसी -यः (स्). *See* INCONSIDERABLE.

TRIFOLIATE, *a.* त्रिपर्णः -र्णा -र्णं, त्रिपत्रः -त्रा -त्रं, त्रिदलः -ला -लं.

TRIGONOMETRICAL, *a.* त्रिकोणमितिविषयकः -का -कं -सम्बन्धी -न्धिनी &c.

TRIGONOMETRY, *s.* त्रिकोणमितिः *f.*, त्रिकोणमापनविद्या.

TRILATERAL, *a.* त्रिभुजः -जा -जं, त्रिभुजात्मकः -का -कं.

TRILITERAL, *a.* त्र्यक्षरकः -का -कं, त्र्यक्षररूपः &c., त्रिवर्णः &c.

TRILL, *To* TRILL. *See* QUAVER, *To* QUAVER.

TRILLION, *s.* प्रयुतघनः, धुनः; 'hundred trillion,' अक्षौहिणी.

TRIM, *a.* विनीतः -ता -तं, सुरेखः -खा -खं. *See* NEAT.

TRIM, *s.* (Condition) अवस्था, स्थितिः *f.*—(Gear) सज्जा.

To TRIM, *v. a.* विरच् (c. 10. -रचयति -यितुं), क्ॢप् (c. 10. कल्पयति -यितुं), सुस्थं -स्थां कृ, सुस्थीकृ. *See* *To* ARRANGE, DRESS, CLIP.

TRIMMING, *s.* विरचनं -ना; 'of a garment,' परिग्रहः.

TRINITARIAN, *s.* व्यक्तित्रयैकत्ववादी *m.* (न्), व्यक्तित्रयात्मकदेवताश्रयी *m.*, त्रयैकत्ववादी *m.*, त्रयैकत्वमतावलम्बी *m.*

TRINITY, *s.* व्यक्तित्रयैकत्वं, त्रयैकत्वं, व्यक्तित्रयात्मकदेवता.

TRINKET, *s.* कङ्कणः -णं, मण्डनं, *see* ORNAMENT; 'for the hair,' बालपाश्या, पारितथ्या; 'for the forehead,' ललाटिका, पत्रपाश्या.

TRINOMIAL, *a.* (In mathematics) त्रिपदः -दा -दी -दं.

TRIO, *s.* त्रयं -यी, त्रिकं, त्रितयं, त्रिकूटं. *See* TRIAD.

TRI-OCULAR, *a.* त्रिनयनः -नी -नं, त्रिनेत्रः -त्रा -त्रं, त्रिलोचनः -ना -नं.

To TRIP, *v. a.* (Trip up) स्खल् in caus. (स्खलयति -यितुं), परपादम् आहत्य पत् (c. 10. पातयति -यितुं), उद्घातं कृ, *see* *To* SUPPLANT.

To TRIP, *v. n.* स्खल् (c. 1. स्खलति -लितुं), प्रस्खल्, स्खलनं कृ, *see* *To* STUMBLE.—(Walk lightly) लघुगत्या क्रम् or चर् or चल्.

TRIP, *s.* (Stumble) स्खलनं, उद्घातः.—(Excursion) भ्रमणं, ईषद्भ्रमणं.

TRIPARTITE, *a.* त्रिभागः -गा -गं, त्रिखण्डः -ण्डा -ण्डं, त्र्यंशः -शा -शं.

TRIPE, *s.* अन्त्रं, उदरं, पक्वान्त्रं. *See* ENTRAILS.

TRIPETALOUS, *a.* त्रिदलः -ला -लं, त्रिदलविशिष्टः -ष्टा -ष्टं.

TRIPLE, TRIPLED, *a.* त्रिगुणः -णा -णं, त्रिविधः -धा -धं, त्रिरूपः -पा -पं, त्रिगतः -ता -तं, त्रिवृत् *m. f. n.*, त्रिधा ind., त्रेधा ind.

To TRIPLE, TRIPLET. *See* *To* TREBLE, TRIAD, TRIO.

TRIPLICITY, *s.* त्रैविध्यं, त्रिविधत्वं, त्रैगुण्यं, त्रिरूपता.

TRIPOD, TRIPOS, *s.* (Any thing with three feet) त्रिपदं, त्रिपादं.

TRISYLLABIC, *a.* त्र्यक्षरः -रा -रं, त्र्यक्षरी -रिणी &c., त्र्यच्कः -च्का -च्कं.

TRISYLLABLE, *s.* त्र्यक्षरशब्दः, त्र्यक्षरविशिष्टशब्दः.

TRITE, *a.* उच्छिष्टः -ष्टा -ष्टं, लोकोच्छिष्टः &c., जीर्णः -र्णा -र्णं.

TRITENESS, *s.* उच्छिष्टता, लोकोच्छिष्टता, प्रसिद्धता, जीर्णता.

TRITHEISM, *s.* देवत्रयवादः, देवत्रयमतं, त्रिदेववादः.

To TRITURATE, *v. a.* चूर्ण्, पिष्, संघृष्, संघर्षं कृ. *See* *To* GRIND.

TRITURATION, *s.* सङ्घर्षः -र्षणं, विमर्दः -र्दनं, परिमलः, *see* GRINDING.

TRIUMPH, *s.* (Pomp of a victory) जययात्रा, विजययात्रा, जयोत्सवः.—(Victory) विजयः, जयः, जयश्रीः *f.*—(Joy for victory) जयानन्दः, जयहर्षः, जयोल्लासः, जयगर्वः.

To TRIUMPH, *v.n.* (Celebrate victory with pomp) जययात्रां कृ, विजययात्रां कृ, जयोत्सवं कृ.—(Obtain victory) विजि (c. 1. -जयते -जेतुं), जि, विजयी भू.—(Exult) जयजयशब्दं कृ, जयानन्दं कृ.

TRIUMPHAL, *a.* जय or विजय in comp.; 'triumphal arch,' जयतोरणः.

TRIUMPHANT, *a.* विजयी -यिनी -यि (न्), जयी &c., जयवान् -वती -वत् (त्), विजयवान् &c., विजयमानः -ना -नं, जयशाली &c., जययुक्तः -क्ता -क्तं, प्राप्तजयः -या -यं, लब्धजयः &c., जिष्णुः -ष्णुः -ष्णु, जेता -त्री -तृ (तृ), जैत्रः -त्री -त्रं, जयानन्दी &c., जितशत्रुः -त्रुः -त्रु, क्षतारिः -रिः -रि.

TRIUMPHANTLY, *adv.* सविजयं, सजयानन्दं, सजयदर्पं, जयदर्पेण.

TRIUMVIRATE, *s.* पुरुषत्रयप्रभुत्वं, व्यक्तित्रयप्रभुत्वं.

TRIUNE, *a.* त्र्येकः -का -कं, त्रयात्मकैकः -का -कं.

TRIVIAL, *a.* लघुः -घुः -घ्वी -घु, क्षुद्रः -द्रा -द्रं. *See* TRIFLING.

TRIVIALNESS, *s.* लघुता, लाघवं, क्षुद्रता, अतिक्षुद्रता, स्वल्पता.

TROCHEE, *s.* (Foot of two syllables) तालः, गलः, गलपदं.

TRODDEN, *p.p.* पादमर्दितः -ता -तं, पादमृदितः &c., पादाहतः &c., चरणाहतः &c., चरणानमितः -ता -तं, पादस्पृष्टः -ष्टा -ष्टं, पदस्पृष्टः &c.

TROOP, *s.* (Band, collection) गणः, वृन्दं, यूथं, सङ्घः, समूहः, *see* MULTITUDE; 'in troops,' यूथशस्.—(Of cavalry) अश्वारूढसैनिकगुल्मः.—(Troops) सैन्याः *m. pl.*, सैनिकाः *m. pl.*, *see* FORCES.

TROOPER, s. अश्वारूढसैनिकः, अश्वारूढसैन्यः, see HORSEMAN.

TROPE, s. रूपकं, व्यञ्जनं. See METAPHOR, FIGURE.

TROPHY, s. (Triumphal column) जयस्तम्भः, रणस्तम्भः, यूपः -पं.—(Memorial of victory) जयचिह्नं, जयस्मारकं.

TROPIC, s. (The line) अयनसीमा, क्रान्तिसीमा, दक्षिणोत्तरायणसीमा, अयनांशः.—(Tropics) क्रान्तिवलयः, क्रान्तिवृत्तं, अयनवृत्तं, क्रान्तिमण्डलं.

TROPICAL, a. क्रान्तिवलयसम्बन्धी &c., क्रान्तिवृत्तसम्बन्धी &c., क्रान्तिवलयान्तर्गतः -ता -तं.—(Metaphorical), see the word.

TROT, s. धोरितं -तकं, धौरितकं, धोरणं, धारितं -तकं, धौर्य्यं, धारा.

To TROT, v. n. धोर् (c. 1. धोरति -रितुं), धोरणं कृ, धोरितं कृ.

TROTH, s. भक्तिः f., प्रत्ययः, विश्वासः. See FAITH, TRUTH, FIDELITY.

To TROUBLE, v. a. आयस् (c. 10. -यासयति -यितुं), बाध् (c. 1. बाधते -धितुं), उपरुध् (c. 7. -रुणद्धि -रोद्धुं), क्लिश्, तप्, व्याकुलीकृ, अर्द्, व्यथ्, व्यग्रं -ग्रां कृ, कष्टं कृ, क्लेशं कृ or दा, कृच्छ्रं दा, see To HARASS; 'dont trouble yourself,' अलम् आयासेन.

TROUBLE, s. क्लेशः, कष्टं, आयासः, प्रयासः, दुःखं, बाधः -धा, उपरोधः, पीडा, व्यथा, तापः, सन्तापः, आपद् f., आपत्तिः f., विपद्, विपत्तिः f., दुर्दशा, दुःस्थितिः f., कष्टावस्था, व्यसनं, उपद्रवः, सङ्कटं, see CALAMITY, PERPLEXITY; 'a sea of trouble,' विपत्सागरः.—(Pains) यत्नः, see PAINS.—(That which gives annoyance) कण्टकः -कं, शल्यं, दुःखं.

TROUBLED, p. p. बाधितः -ता -तं, क्लेशितः &c., क्लिष्टः -ष्टा -ष्टं, उपरुद्धः -द्धा -द्धं, दुःखितः -ता -तं, सन्तापितः &c., कातरः -रा -रं, व्यग्रः -ग्रा -ग्रं, उद्विग्नः -ग्ना -ग्नं, विह्वलः -ला -लं, आर्त्त in comp.; as, 'troubled with thirst,' तृषार्त्तः -र्त्ता -र्त्तं; 'with hunger,' क्षुधार्त्तः &c.

TROUBLESOME, a. कष्टकरः -रा -रं, कष्टकारकः -का -कं, कष्टावहः -हा -हं, क्लेशकारी -रिणी -रि (न्), क्लेशावहः -हा -हं, दुःखावहः &c., श्रमावहः &c., आयासहेतुकः -का -कं, कष्टः -ष्टा -ष्टं, दुष्टः &c., विषमः -मा -मं, दुर्निवहः -हा -हं, सकण्टकः -का -कं; 'a troublesome fellow,' कण्टकः.

TROUBLOUS, a. सोपद्रवः -वा -वं, सोपप्लवः &c. See CALAMITOUS.

TROUGH, s. द्रोणिः -णी f., द्रूणिः -णी f.; 'for watering cattle,' निपानं, प्रपा, आहावः, पुस्यं.

TROWEL, s. (Of masons) कर्णी, लेपनयन्त्रं.

TROWSERS, s. pl. जङ्घावस्त्रं, कटिवस्त्रं, जङ्घापरिधानं, कञ्चुकः.

TRUANT, a. कर्म्मविमुखः -खा -खं, कर्म्मपराङ्मुखः &c., विलासी -सिनी -सि (न्), अलसः -सा -सं; 'to play truant,' कर्म्मविमुखः -खा -खं भू, विलस् (c. 1. -लसते -सितुं), अलसवद् आचर्.

TRUCE, s. अवहारः, सावधिकसन्धिः m., निरूपितकालपर्य्यन्तं युद्धनिवृत्तिः f.; 'a truce to jesting,' विरमतु परिहासः.

TRUCK, s. क्षुद्रचक्रः शकटः, नीचचक्रं द्रव्यवाहनं, नीचशकटः.

To TRUCKLE, v. n. अत्यनुरोधं कृ, छन्दोनुरोधं कृ, छन्दोनुवृत्तिं कृ.

TRUCULENT, a. क्रूरः -रा -रं, निष्ठुरः &c. See SAVAGE.

To TRUDGE, v. n. पादाभ्यां व्रज् or चर्, आयासेन व्रज्.

TRUE, a. (Not false) सत्यः -त्या -त्यं, तथ्यः -थ्या -थ्यं, यथार्थः -र्था -र्थं, सम्यङ् -मीची -म्यक् (च्), समीचीनः -ना -नं, ऋतः -ता -तं, सत्यवान् -वती &c., उपपन्नः -न्ना -न्नं, सिद्धः -द्धा -द्धं, see GENUINE, REAL, EXACT; 'true and false,' सदसत्; 'it is very true,' युक्तं, युज्यते, उपपन्नं.—(True to obligations, keeping faith) सत्यप्रतिज्ञः -ज्ञा -ज्ञं, सत्यसन्धः -न्धा -न्धं, सत्यशीलः -ला -लं, सत्यव्रतः -ता -तं, see HONEST, FAITHFUL.

TRUENESS, s. सत्यता, तथ्यता, यथार्थता, सम्यक्त्वं. See TRUTH.

TRUISM, s. स्वतःस्पष्टवाक्यं, स्वतःप्रमाणकवचनं, स्वतःसिद्धवाक्यं.

TRULY, adv. सत्यं, यथार्थं -र्थतस्, अर्थतस्, तत्त्वतस्, वस्तुतस्, सम्यक्, परमार्थतस्, अञ्जसा, एवं. See REALLY, CERTAINLY.

TRUMPERY, s. असारद्रव्यं, तुच्छद्रव्यं, उच्छिष्टं. See TRASH.

TRUMPET, s. (Instrument) तूरी, रणतूरी.—(Flower) पाटलिः m. f., पाटला, फलेरुहा, कृष्णवृन्ता, कुवेराक्षी, अमोघा, मोघा, काचस्थाली, काली, स्थाली, तोयपुष्पी, तोयप्रसा, तोयाधिवासिनी.

To TRUMPET, v. a. तूरीवादनपूर्व्वं प्रकाश्. See To PUBLISH.

TRUMPETER, s. तूरीवादकः, रणतूरीवादकः, तूरीध्मः.

TRUNCHEON, s. गदा, यष्टिः m., दण्डः. See CLUB, CUDGEL.

To TRUNDLE, v. a. and n. See To ROLL, v. a. and n.

TRUNK, s. (Of a tree) स्कन्धः, प्रकाण्डः -ण्डं, काण्डः -ण्डं, गण्डिः m.; 'of a lopped tree,' स्थाणुः m. -णु n., ध्रुवः, शङ्कुः m.—(Of the body) शरीरकाण्डः -ण्डं; 'headless trunk,' कबन्धः, अपमूर्द्धकलेवरं.—(Main body) मुख्यभागः.—(Of an elephant) शुण्डा, शुण्डादण्डः, हस्तः, करः, भुजः.—(Chest, box) भाण्डं.

TRUSS, s. (Of hay, &c.) तृणकूर्चः, तृणभारः, तृणगुच्छः.—(Bandage) पट्टः -ट्टकः, कवलिका, आधारः, बन्धनं.

To TRUSS, v. a. सम्बन्ध्, कूर्चीकृ, कील् (c. 10. कीलयति -यितुं).

TRUST, s. (Confidence) विश्वासः, प्रत्ययः, विस्रम्भः, निष्ठा, समाश्वासः, सम्प्रसादः, see CONFIDENCE, RELIANCE; 'breach of trust,' विश्वासभङ्गः, विश्वासघातः, प्रत्ययभङ्गः, प्रणयभङ्गः.—(Charge) न्यासः, निक्षेपः.—(Credit) कालिका, उद्धारः; 'to buy on trust,' उद्धारं कृ.

To TRUST, v. a. (Confide in) विश्वस् (c. 2. -श्वसिति -तुं), समाश्वस्, see To CONFIDE, v. n.—(Commit in confidence) सम् in caus., see To INTRUST.—(Sell on credit) उद्धारं दा.

To TRUST, v. n. (Be confident) प्रत्याशां कृ, दृढप्रत्याशां कृ, निश्चयं कृ, दृढप्रत्ययं कृ, आशां कृ, विश्वासं कृ, निःसन्देहः -हा -हं भू.—(Rely on) विश्वस्, see To RELY, CONFIDE, v. n.

TRUSTED, p. p. विश्वस्तः -स्ता -स्तं, विश्वसितः &c. See CONFIDED.

TRUSTEE, s. न्यासधारी m. (न्), निक्षेपधारी m.

TRUSTING, part. विश्वासी -सिनी &c., विश्वस्तः &c., see CONFIDING; 'trusting to the strength of one's own arm,' स्वबाहुबलमाश्रितः -ता -तं.

TRUSTWORTHINESS, s. विश्वास्यता, विश्वासार्हत्वं, आप्तता, विश्रब्धता.

TRUSTWORTHY, TRUSTY, a. विश्वासार्हः -र्हा -र्हं, विश्वासयोग्यः -ग्या -ग्यं, विश्वास्यः -स्या -स्यं, आप्तः -प्ता -प्तं, विश्वासपात्रं, विश्वासभूमिः f., विश्रब्धः -ब्धा -ब्धं, विस्रम्भार्हः -र्हा -र्हं, श्रद्धार्हः &c., अहार्य्यः -र्य्या -र्य्यं, अभेद्यः &c.

TRUTH, s. सत्यं, तथ्यं, ऋतं, सम्यक्, अवितथं, तत्त्वं, तत्त्वार्थः, यथार्थवचनं, याथार्थ्यं, सत्त्वं, सत्ता, परमार्थः, पूतं.—(Trueness) सत्यता -त्वं, तथ्यता, यथार्थता, याथार्थ्यं, सम्यक्त्वं, वास्तवत्वं, याथातथ्यं; 'one who speaks the truth,' सत्यवादी m., see VERACIOUS; 'speaking the truth,' see VERACITY; 'one who knows the truth,' तत्त्वविद्, सत्यविद्; 'investigation of truth,' मीमांसा; 'true state of the case,' सत्यवृत्तं, सत्यवृत्तान्तः.—(In truth) सत्यमेव, वस्तुतस्, see TRULY.

TRUTHFUL, TRUTHFULNESS. See TRUE, VERACIOUS, VERACITY.

To TRY, v. a. (Test) परीक्ष् (c. 1. -ईक्षते -क्षितुं), परीक्षां कृ, अनुभू, ज्ञा in des., see To TEST, PROVE, EXAMINE, INVESTIGATE.

To TRY, v. n. (Endeavour) यत् (c. 1. यतते -तितुं), प्रयत्, यत्नं कृ,

प्रयत्नं कृ, चेष्, व्यवसो, उद्यम्, घट्, उपक्रम्, उद्यमं कृ, उद्योगं कृ; 'they tried to kill me,' ते मां हन्तुम् उद्यताः or व्यवसिताः; 'he tries to drink the water,' जलं पातुं व्यवस्यति. Sometimes expressed by the desid. form; as, 'he tries to recollect,' सुस्मूर्षते.

TRYING, *part.* or *a.* परीक्षकः -का -कं, परीक्षाकारी -रिणी -रि (न्).

TUB, *s.* द्रोणी -णिः *f.*, द्रूणी -णिः *f.*; 'bathing tub,' स्नानद्रोणी -णिः *f.*

TUBE, *s.* नलिका, नालः -ली -लिः -ला -लं, नाडी -डिः *f.*, प्रणालः -ली -लिका, नलः, सुषिः *f.*, सुषिरं; 'glass tube,' काचनालः.

TUBER, *s.* (Bulbous root) कन्दः -न्दं.

TUBERCLE, *s.* सूक्ष्मव्रणः, सूक्ष्मगुल्मः, ग्रन्थिः *m.* See PIMPLE.

TUBEROUS, *a.* ग्रन्थिलः -ला -लं, कन्दी -न्दिनी &c. See KNOBBY.

TUBULAR, *a.* नलिकाकारः -रा -रं, नालाकृतिः -तिः -ति, नलिकाकृतिः &c.; 'vessel of the body,' नालः -ली, नाडिः -डी *f.*, तन्त्री, धमनी.

To TUCK, TUCK. See *To* FOLD, FOLD, COMPRESS, CRAM.

TUESDAY, *s.* मङ्गलवारः, भौमवारः, कुलवारः, भौमवासरः.

TUFT, *s.* शिखा, शिखरः -रं, चूडा, शेखरः, स्तबकः, पल्लवः, अवतंसः, *see* CLUMP, CLUSTER, BUNCH; 'of mangoes,' आम्रपल्लवः; 'of hair,' चूडा, केशपिण्डः, लोमपिण्डः, लोमगुच्छकः.

TUFTED, *a.* चूडावान् -वती -वत् (त्), चूडालः -ला -लं, शिखी -खिनी -खि (न्), शिखरी -रिणी &c., शेखरितः -ता -तं.

To TUG, *v. a.* कृष् (c. 1. कर्षति, क्रष्टुं), आकृष्, हृ. See *To* PULL.

TUITION, *s.* उपदेशः, शिक्षा, अध्यापनं, शैष्योपाध्यायिका.

To TUMBLE, *v. n.* पत् (c. 1. पतति -तितुं), *see To* FALL, ROLL, *v. n.*

To TUMBLE, *v. a.* See *To* RUMPLE, DISORDER, THROW DOWN.

TUMBLE, *s.* पातः, अवपातः, प्रपातः, पतनं. See FALL.

TUMBLER, *s.* (Mountebank) प्लवकः, कृशाश्वी *m.* (न्), कलायनः, केलकः, *see* DANCER.—(Glass vessel) काचपात्रं, कटखादकः.

TUMID, TUMEFACTION. See SWELLED, SWOLLEN, SWELLING.

TUMLOOK, *s.* (Country) तमालिका, तमोलिप्ती, तामलिप्तं -प्ती.

TUMOUR, *s.* स्फोटः -टकः, विस्फोटः, गुल्मः, शोफः, श्वयथुः *m.*, व्रणः -णं, अर्बुदः -दं, मांसवृद्धिः *f.*, ग्रन्थिः *m.*; 'on the tongue,' अधिजिह्वः; 'on the eye, &c.,' अधिमांसः -सकः; 'fatty tumour,' मेदोर्बुदं, मेदोग्रन्थिः *m.*

TUMULT, *s.* तुमुलं, कोलाहलः, पटहः. See RIOT, UPROAR.

TUMULTUOUS, *a.* अनवस्थितः -ता -तं, अव्यवस्थितः -ता -तं, अव्यवस्थः -स्था -स्थं, क्षुब्धः -ब्धा -ब्धं, तुमुली &c. See DISORDERLY.

TUN, *s.* (Large cask) वृहद्भाण्डं, वृहद्भाजनं.

TUNE, *s.* (Combination of notes) तानः, तालः, कलः, स्वरः, रागिणी, रागभेदः; 'time and tune,' तानमानं.—(Harmony of sound) तालैक्यं, स्वरैक्यं, *see* HARMONY; 'out of tune,' अपस्वरः -रा -रं, कुस्वरः &c., वैतालिकः -की -कं; 'in tune,' सुस्वरः &c., युक्तस्वरः &c., एकस्वरः &c., तुल्यस्वरः &c.

To TUNE, *v. a.* तानीकृ, युक्तस्वरीकृ, स्वरैक्यं कृ.

TUNEFUL, *a.* सुस्वरः -रा -रं. See HARMONIOUS, MELODIOUS.

TUNNEL, *s.* गूढमार्गः, गुप्तमार्गः, विवरमार्गः, अन्तर्भौममार्गः.

To TUNNEL, *v. a.* गूढमार्गं कृ, शुषिरीकृ, उत्खन् (c. 1. -खनति -नितुं).

TURBAN, *s.* उष्णीषः -षं, वेष्टकं, वेष्टनं, शिरोवेष्टनं, पट्टः.

TURBID, *a.* कलुषः -षा -षं, आविलः -ला -लं, अनच्छः -च्छा -च्छं, मलिनः &c., अनिर्मलः &c., *see* MUDDY; 'becomes so,' कलुषायते.

TURBIDNESS, *s.* कलुषता, कालुष्यं, आविलत्वं. See MUDDINESS.

TURBULENCE, *s.* कलहकारित्वं, तुमुलकारित्वं, अव्यवस्थितत्वं, अनवस्थितत्वं, क्षोभः. See DISORDER, DISTURBANCE.

TURBULENT, *a.* कलहकारी -रिणी -रि (न्), तुमुलकारी -रिणी &c., कलहकारः -री -रं, अव्यवस्थितः &c. See TUMULTUOUS.

TURF, *s.* सतृणभूमिः *f.*, सतृणभूमितलं, स्तम्बः. See SWARD.

TURGID, TURGIDITY. See SWELLED, SWOLLEN, SWELLING.

TURKESTÁN, *s.* (The country) तुरुष्कः, तुरुष्कदेशः.

TURMERIC, *s.* हरिद्रा, काञ्चनी, पीता, गौरी, निशाह्वा, निशा, शर्वरी, वरवर्णिनी, वर्णदाता *m.* (तृ), मङ्गलप्रदा, हेमरागिणी, वर्णिनी, जनेष्टा, कृमिघ्नी, लसा.

TURMOIL, *s.* सन्तापः, व्यग्रता, क्लेशः, तुमुलं in caus. See DISQUIET.

To TURN, *v. a.* (Cause to revolve) आवृत् (c. 10. -वर्त्तयति -यितुं), परिवृत्, विवृत्, वृत् &c., *see To* REVOLVE, *v. a.*, ROLL, *v. a.*—(Change) परिवृत् in caus.—(Bend) साचीकृ, *see To* BEND, *v. a.*—(Make acid) अम्लीकृ.—(Form on a lathe) भ्रमेण or चक्रयन्त्रेण निर्मा or घट् or रच्.—(Make giddy) भ्रम्, *see To* INFATUATE.—(In the mind), *see To* REVOLVE.—(Dissuade) निवृत् in caus.—(Turn away the face) मुखं परिवृत् in caus. —(Turn away, turn off) अपास्; 'to turn away an old servant,' मूलभृत्यम् अपास्, *see To* DISMISS, REJECT, AVERT.—(Turn back) परावृत् in caus.—(Turn down), *see To* FOLD. —(Turn off) *see To* DIVERT.—(Turn out) बहिष्कृ, *see To* OUST.—(Turn over) परिवृत् in caus., *see To* OVERTURN.—(Turn the back) पलाय्, पराङ्मुखः -खा -खं भू, विमुखः &c. भू.—(Turn the mind to) मनः कृ, मतिं कृ or प्रकृ.—(Turn to), *see To* RESORT. 'To turn' may often be expressed by कृ in comp.; as, 'to turn a thing black,' द्रव्यं कृष्णीकृ.

To TURN, *v. n.* (Move round) परिवृत् (c. 1. -वर्त्तते -र्त्तितुं), विवृत्, विपरिवृत्, सम्परिवृत्, आवृत्, वृत्, *see To* REVOLVE, *v. n.*, ROLL, *v. n.*—(Change) परिवृत्, *see To* SHIFT, *v. n.*—(Become sour) अम्लीभू, अम्लभावं or अम्लतां गम् or इ.—(Depend on) अवलम्ब्, समालम्ब्.—(Turn against) प्रतिकूलीभू, विरुद्धः -द्धा -द्धं भू.—(Turn away) पराङ्मुखीभू, पराङ्मुखः -खा -खं भू, विमुखीभू, विमुखः -खा -खं भू.—(Turn back) परिवृत्, परावृत्, निवृत्.—(Turn out), *see To* PROVE, *v. n.*—(Turn round) परिवृत्.—(Turn up) प्रादुर्भू, आविर्भू, सम्भू, उत्पद्, उपस्था. 'To turn' may often be expressed by भू in comp.; as, 'to turn black,' कृष्णीभू; 'to turn to ashes,' भस्मसाद्भू.

TURN, TURNING, *s.* (Revolution) परिवर्त्तनं, आवर्त्तः -र्त्तनं, परिवर्त्तः, परिवृत्तिः *f.*—(Bend, winding) वक्रः, वक्रता; 'of a river,' नदीवक्रः.—(Change) परिवर्त्तनं, विकारः, आवृत्तिः *f.*—(Recurring season, alternation) पर्य्यायः, विपर्य्ययः, परिवृत्तिः *f.*, आवृत्तिः *f.*, वारः, वासरः; 'by turns, in turn,' पर्य्यायेण, क्रमेण, विपर्य्ययेण; 'to do by turns, take turns,' पर्य्यायेण कृ, विद्.—(Occasion) कालः, समयः, अवसरः, वारः.—(Form, cast) आकारः, आकृतिः *f.*, शीलः -लता, भावः, स्वभावः; 'of mind,' मनःस्वभावः, चित्तवृत्तिः *f.* —(Walk to and fro) विहारः, ईषद्विहारः, ईषत्परिक्रमः, इतस्ततः परिक्रमः.—(A good turn) उपकारः.—(An ill turn) अपकारः.

TURN-COAT, *s.* See RENEGADE, TIME-SERVER.

TURNED, *p. p.* (Made to go round) परिवर्त्तितः -ता -तं, आवर्त्तितः &c.—(Bent) साचीकृतः -ता -तं.—(Made acid) अम्लीकृतः -ता -तं,

अम्लीभूतः &c.; 'a sweet thing turned acid,' मधुरम् अम्लभावं गतं.—(Turned adrift) विसर्जितः -ता -तं.—(Turned away) अपास्तः -स्ता -स्तं, प्रतिक्षिप्तः -प्ता -प्तं, *see* DISMISSED, REJECTED; 'having the face turned away,' पराङ्मुखः -खी -खं, विमुखः &c., पराचीनः -ना -नं.—(Turned back) परावृत्तः -त्ता -त्तं, परिवृत्तः &c., निवृत्तः &c.—(Turned out) बहिष्कृतः -ता -तं, बहिःकृतः &c., निष्कासितः &c.; 'out of office,' च्युताधिकारः -रा -रं, हृताधिकारः &c.—(Turned loose) मोचितः -ता -तं.—(Having the eyes turned up) उत्तारलोचनः -ना -नं.—(Turned of ninety) दशमीस्थः -स्था -स्थं, दशमीकृतः -ता -तं.

TURNER, *s.* भ्रमाजीवी *m.* (न्), चक्रजीवी *m.*, चक्री *m.*, कुन्दी *m.*

TURNING, *s.* भ्रमद्वारेण काष्ठद्रव्यघटनं or काष्ठद्रव्यरचनं -ना.

TURNIP, *s.* शिखामूलं, गृञ्जनं.

TURPENTINE, *s.* श्रीवासः, श्रीवासस् *n.*, श्रीरसः, वृक्षधूपः, यक्षधूपः, धूपाङ्गः, पायसः, सरलद्रवः, रसाङ्गः, घृताङ्गः, तिलपर्णः, श्रीवेष्टः, श्रीपिष्टः, सर्ज्जरसः, सालवेष्टः, दधि *n.*

TURPITUDE, *s.* दुष्टता, भावदुष्टता. *See* BASENESS, WICKEDNESS.

TURQUOISE, TURKOIS, *s.* वैदूर्य्यं, हरिताश्मा *m.* (न्), पेरोजं.

TURRET, *s.* प्रासादशृङ्गं, प्रासादशिखरं, गृहशिखरं, शिरोगृहं, वडभिः *f.*, वलभी -भिः *m.f.*, तल्पः, लासकः.

TURTLE, *s.* कूर्म्मः, कच्छपः कमठः, कामठः. *See* TORTOISE.

TURTLE-DOVE, *s.* कलरवः कलध्वनिः *m.*, कपोतः. *See* PIGEON.

TUSK, *s.* दंष्ट्रा, रदः, रदनः दाढकः, दाढा, विषाणं, राक्षसी.

TUSKED, *p.p.* दंष्ट्री -ष्ट्रिणी -ष्ट्रि (न्), दन्ती &c., विषाणी &c.

TUTELARY, *a.* रक्षकः -का -कं, पालकः &c., रक्षणकारी -रिणी &c.; 'a tutelary deity,' लोकपालः -लकः, इष्टदेवता, अधिदेवता.

TUTENAG, *s.* (Metal) तुत्थं, तुत्थकं, तुत्थाञ्जनं.

TUTOR, *s.* उपाध्यायः, गुरुः, धीसखः, धीसचिवः, *see* PRECEPTOR.

TUTORSHIP, *s.* उपाध्यायत्वं, अध्यापकता, आचार्य्यत्वं, उपदेशकत्वं.

To TWADDLE, TWADDLING, &c. *See To* PRATE, PRATING, &c.

TWANG, *s.* (Of a bow, &c.) विस्फारः, विष्फारः, स्फारः, ज्याघोषः, ज्याक्वणितं, टङ्कारः, टः.—(Sharp sound) झनत्कारः, क्वणितं.

To TWANG, *v. a.* क्वण् (c. 10. क्वाणयति -यितुं), रण् (c. 10. रणयति -यितुं), 'he twangs his lute,' वीणां रणयति; 'his bow,' धनुर् विस्फारयति.

To TWANG, *v. n.* क्वण् (c. 1. क्वणति -णितुं), झनत्कारं कृ, टङ्कारं कृ.

TWANGED, *p.p.* विस्फारितः -ता -तं, क्वणितः &c., रणितः &c.

To TWEAK, *v. a.* अकस्माद् अङ्गुल्यग्रैर् गृहीत्वा पीड् or सम्पीड्.

TWEEZERS, *s. pl.* सन्दंशः -शकं -शका, कङ्कमुखं.

TWELFTH, *a.* द्वादशः -शी -शं.

TWELVE, *a.* द्वादश *m.f.n. pl.* (न्), द्वादशकः -का -कं.

TWELVEMONTH, *s.* द्वादशमासं, परिवत्सरः, वत्सरः, वर्षः.

TWENTIETH, *a.* विंशः -शी -शं, विंशतितमः -मी -मं.

TWENTY, *a.* विंशतिः *f. sing.*, द्विदशाः *m.pl.*; 'he reigned twenty years,' विंशतिम् अब्दान् राज्यं चकार; 'with twenty arrows,' विंशत्या शरैः; 'twenty-one,' एकविंशतिः *f. sing.*; 'two,' द्वाविंशतिः; 'three,' त्रयोविंशतिः; 'four,' चतुर्विंशतिः; 'five,' पञ्चविंशतिः; 'six,' षड्विंशतिः; 'seven,' सप्तविंशतिः; 'eight,' अष्टाविंशतिः; 'nine,' नवविंशतिः, ऊनविंशत् *f.*, एकोनविंशत्; 'twenty-first,' एकविंशः -शी -शं, एकविंशतितमः -मी -मं; 'aggregate of twenty,' विंशी *m.* (न्).

TWICE, *adv.* द्विः, द्विवारं, वारद्वयं, द्विकृत्वस्, द्विगुणः -णा -णं, द्विकः -का -कं; 'said twice,' द्विरुक्तः -क्ता -क्तं; 'twice-married,' द्विरूढः -ढा -ढं, पुनरूपोढः &c.; 'twice ploughed,' द्विगुणाकृतः -ता -तं; 'twice-born,' द्विजः -जा -जं; 'ten is twice five,' दश पञ्चभ्यो द्विगुणा भवन्ति.

TWIG, *s.* उपशाखा, प्रशाखिका, अग्रशाखा, शाखिका, पल्लवः.

TWILIGHT, *s.* सन्ध्या, सन्ध्याकालः, सन्ध्यासमयः, सन्धिप्रकाशः, विकालः -लकः, सन्ध्यांशः, उत्सूरः, सबलिः *m.*, अध्वान्तं, निशादिः *m.* Twilight is personified as the daughter of Brahmá, and hence called पितृप्रसूः *f.*, पितृसूः *f.*, ब्रह्मभूतिः *f.*; 'the morning twilight,' पूर्व्वसन्ध्या, प्राक्सन्ध्या, सन्ध्या, दिनादिः *m.*; 'the two twilights,' सन्ध्ये *f. du.*

TWIN, *a.* or *s.* यमः -मा -मं, यमकः -का -कं, यमलः -ला -लं, यमजः -जा -जं; 'twins,' यमौ *m. du.*, यमकौ *m. du.*, यमं, यमलं, द्वन्द्वं, युगलं, युगं; 'one of twins,' यमः, यमकः, नारङ्गः; 'we are twin brothers,' भ्रातराव् आवां यमजौ.

To TWINE, *v. a.* or *n.* परिवेष्ट्, आवेष्ट्, वेष्ट्, समावृत्, व्यावृत्.

TWINE, *s.* शणसूत्रं, शाणसूत्रं, शणतन्तुः *m.* *See* THREAD.

TWINGE, *s.* शूलः -लं, तीव्रवेदना, तीक्ष्णवेदना, तोदः.

To TWINGE, *v. n.* शूल् (c. 1. शूलति -लितुं), शूलोपहतः -ता -तं भू.

TWINING, *s.* परिवेष्टनं, आवेष्टनं, वेष्टनं; 'of a creeper,' लतावेष्टनं; 'a twining plant,' लता, लतिका.

TWINKLE, TWINKLING, *s.* (Of the eye) निमेषः -षकः, निमिषः, उन्मेषः, निमीलनं, उन्मीलनं, व्यामीलनं, मीलनं, निमेषोन्मेषौ *m. du.*, निमीलनोन्मीलने *n. du.*, अक्षिपक्ष्मणः सङ्कोचः, अक्षिस्पन्दनं.—(Tremulous, sparkling) स्फुरणं, स्फुरितं.—(In a twinkling) निमेषमात्रेण.

To TWINKLE, *v. n.* (As the eye) निमेषोन्मेषं कृ, निमीलनोन्मीलनं कृ, निमील् (c. 1. -मीलति -लितुं), उन्मील्, निमिष् (c. 6. -मिषति -मेषितुं), उन्मिष्, लोचने निमील् (c. 10. -मीलयति -यितुं) or उन्मील्.—(Sparkle tremulously) स्फुर् (c. 6. स्फुरति -रितुं), स्फुरणं कृ.

To TWIRL, *v. a.* त्वरितं भ्रम् in caus. or परिवृत् in caus.

To TWIRL, *v. n.* द्रुतं परिवृत् or भ्रम् or घूर्ण्. *See To* REVOLVE, *v. n.*

TWIRL, *s.* त्वरितावृत्तिः *f.*, द्रुतपरिवर्त्तनं, द्रुतपरिवृत्तिः *f.*

To TWIST, *v. a.* व्यावृत् (c. 10. -वर्त्तयति -यितुं), आवृत्, समावृत्, आकुञ्च् (c. 1. -कुञ्चति -ञ्चितुं, c. 10. -कुञ्चयति -यितुं).

To TWIST, *v. n.* व्यावृत् (c. 1. -वर्त्तते -र्त्तितुं), आवृत्, आकुञ्च् in pass.

TWIST, *s.* व्यावर्त्तनं, आवर्त्तः -र्त्तका -र्त्तनं, आकुञ्चनं, कुञ्चनं.

To TWIT, *v. a.* निन्द्, उपालभ्, तिरस्कृ, परिवद्. *See To* REPROACH.

To TWITCH, *v. a.* अकस्माद् आकृष् (c. 1. -कर्षति -कष्टुं) or आक्षिप्.

To TWITCH, *v. n.* स्फुर् (c. 6. स्फुरति -रितुं), विस्फुर्, कम्प्, स्पन्द्.

TWITCH, *s.* स्फुरणं, स्फुरितं, विस्फुरणं, प्रस्फुरणं, स्फूर्त्तिः *f.*, स्पन्दनं, कम्पनं, आकस्मिकाकर्षः, आकस्मिकाक्षेपः.

To TWITTER, TWITTER. *See To* CHATTER, CHATTERING.

TWO, *a.* द्वौ *m. f. du.*, द्वे *n. du.* (द्वि), द्वयं affixed, द्वि prefixed; 'two men,' द्वौ पुरुषौ or पुरुषद्वयं or expressed simply by the dual, पुरुषौ; 'of two men,' द्वयोः पुरुषयोः, or simply पुरुषयोः; 'two months,' द्विमासं, मासद्वयं; 'two hundred,' द्वे शते *n. du.*, शतद्वयं, or simply शते; 'two thousand,' द्वे सहस्रे, सहस्रद्वयं, or simply सहस्रे. The crude form द्वि is chiefly used in Bahuvríhi compounds; as, 'two-armed,' द्विभुजः -जा -जं; 'two-footed,' द्विपादः -दा -दं, द्विपदः &c.; 'two-handed,' द्विहस्तः -स्ता -स्तं; 'two-headed,' द्विमूर्द्धः -र्द्धा -र्द्धं; 'two-formed,' द्विरूपः -पा -पं; 'two-edged,' द्विधारः -रा -रं, उभयततीक्ष्णः -क्ष्णा -क्ष्णं; 'consisting of two,' द्विमयः -यी -यं; 'two-year-old,' द्विवार्षिकः -की -कं; 'in two ways,' द्विधा, द्वैधं; 'two or three,' द्वित्राः -त्राः -त्राणि (त्र).

TWO-FOLD, *a.* द्विगुणः -णा -णं, द्विगुणितः -ता -तं, द्विगुणीकृतः &c., द्विकः -का -कं, द्विविधः -धा -धं, द्वैधः -धी -धं, द्विप्रकारः -रा -रं.

TYMPANITES, *s.* अलसकः, गुल्मोदरं, गुल्मः. *See* FLATULENCE.

TYPE, *s.* (Emblem) लक्षणं, व्यञ्जनं, व्यञ्जकः, चिह्नं, *see* SYMBOL, SIGN, MARK; 'of birth,' उत्पत्तिव्यञ्जकः.—(Figure of something to come) प्रतिरूपं -पकं, प्रतिबिम्बं, दर्शकचिह्नं.—(Printing letter) मुद्राक्षरं.—(In medicine) भावना, स्वरूपं.

TYPICAL, *a.* लाक्षणिकः -की -कं, उद्बोधकः -का -कं, बोधकः &c., प्रतिरूपकः &c., प्रतिबिम्बकः &c. *See* PREFIGURATIVE.

To TYPEFY, TYPEFIED. *See To* PREFIGURE, PREFIGURED.

TYPOGRAPHICAL, *s.* मुद्राङ्कनसम्बन्धी &c., मुद्राक्षरसम्बन्धी &c.

TYPOGRAPHY, *s.* मुद्राङ्कनं, मुद्राक्षरप्रयोगः. *See* PRINTING.

TYRANNIC, TYRANNICAL, *a.* प्रजापीडकः -का -कं, प्रजोपद्रवी -विणी &c., प्रजाबाधकः -का -कं, प्रजोपप्लवी &c. *See* OPPRESSIVE.

TYRANNICALLY, *adv.* सनैष्ठुर्य्यं, सक्रौर्य्यं, प्रजापीडकवत्.

TYRANNICIDE, *s.* (The act) प्रजापीडकहत्या.—(The agent) प्रजापीडकहन्ता *m.* (न्तृ).

To TYRANNIZE, *v. n.* कुशासनं कृ, अनीतिशासनं कृ, असम्यक्शासनं कृ, असम्यक्पालनं कृ, प्रजापीडनं कृ, प्रजोपद्रवं कृ, प्रजोपप्लवं कृ, अन्यायशासनं कृ; 'tyrannized over,' उपद्रुतः -ता -तं.

TYRANNY, *s.* (Absolute monarchy) स्वतन्त्रराज्यं, अनिर्बन्धराज्यं.—(Oppressive rule) कुशासनं, प्रजापीडनं, प्रजोपद्रवः, प्रजोपप्लवः, निष्ठुरता, नैष्ठुर्य्यं, परिप्लवः, *see* OPPRESSION, *To* TYRANNIZE.

TYRANT, *s.* प्रजापीडकः, उपद्रवी *m.*, निष्ठुरः, *see* OPPRESSOR.

TYRO, *s.* नवच्छात्रः, छात्रः, नवशिष्यः, नूतनशिष्यः, नूतनाभ्यासी *m.* (न्), विद्यारम्भकः, क्रियाकारः, किञ्चिज्ज्ञः.

U.

UBIQUITOUS, UBIQUITY. *See* OMNIPRESENT, OMNIPRESENCE.

UDDER, *s.* ऊधस् *n.*, उधस् *n.*, ओधस् *n.*, ओधः, ऊधसं, उधसं, आपीनं, वाघः, वामः; 'of a cow,' गोस्तनः; 'of a bitch,' शुनीस्तनः, सुनारः. Obs. ऊधस् becomes ऊधन् in comp.; as, 'a cow with a full udder,' पीनोध्नी, पीवरस्तनी; 'with an udder like a well,' कुण्डोध्नी.

UGLINESS, *s.* कुरूपता, विरूपता, वैरूप्यं, अपरूपता, असौन्दर्य्यं, अलावण्यं, असौम्यता, कुत्सिताकारता, असौष्ठवं.

UGLY, *a.* कुरूपः -पा -पी -पं, अपरूपः &c., विरूपः &c., रूपहीनः -ना -नं, कदाकारः -रा -रं, कुत्सिताकारः &c., कुत्सितः -ता -तं, कुत्सिताकृतिः -तिः -ति, असुन्दरः -रा -री -रं, असौम्यः -म्या -म्यं, दुर्दर्शनः -ना -नं, विकृताकारः &c.; 'an ugly woman,' कुस्त्री.

ULCER, *s.* व्रणः, क्षतं, नाडीव्रणः, सपूयक्षतं, पूतिव्रणः, रक्तविद्रधिः *m.*, उत्सङ्गी *m.* (न्); 'bottom of one,' उत्सङ्गः.

To ULCERATE, *v. n.* सव्रणीभू, सक्षतीभू, व्रणितः -ता -तं भू, व्रणं जन्.

To ULCERATE, *v. a.* व्रणं कृ, सव्रणीकृ, क्षतं कृ, व्रणम् उत्पद् in caus.

ULCERATED, ULCEROUS, *a.* व्रणी -णिनी -णि (न्), व्रणितः -ता -तं, सव्रणः -णा -णं, सक्षतः -ता -तं, जातव्रणः -णा -णं, व्रणमयः -यी -यं.

ULCERATION, *s.* व्रणित्वं -ता, सव्रणभावः, सक्षतभावः, व्रणबन्धनं.

ULTERIOR, *a.* उत्तरः -रा -रं, अपरः &c., पाश्चात्यः -त्या -त्यं.

ULTIMATE, *a.* अन्तिमः -मा -मं, चरमः &c. *See* LAST, FINAL.

ULTIMATELY, *adv.* अन्ततस्, अन्ते, शेषे, शेषतस्. *See* LASTLY.

ULTIMATUM, *s.* अन्त्यप्रतिज्ञा, अन्त्यवाक्यं, निदानवाक्यं.

ULTRA, *s.* अत्यन्तः -न्ता -न्तं, एकान्तः &c. *See* EXCESSIVE.

UMÁ, *s.* (Wife of Śiva) उमा, सती, *see* DURGÁ.

UMBILICAL, *a.* नाभ्यः -भ्या -भ्यं, नाभिसम्बन्धी &c.; 'umbilical cord,' नाभिः *f.*, नालः, नाभिनाडी, नाभिनाला, गर्भनाडी; 'section of it,' नाभिच्छेदनं; 'region,' नाभिमण्डलं.

UMBRAGE, *s.* असन्तोषः, अतुष्टिः *f.*, अप्रीतिः *f.*; 'to take umbrage,' असन्तुष्टः -ष्टा -ष्टं भू, प्रकुप् (c. 4. -कुप्यति).

UMBRELLA, *s.* छत्रं, छत्त्रा, वारिका, आतपत्रं, आतपवारणं, वस्त्रकुट्टिमं, कावारी; 'state-umbrella,' छत्रं; 'bearer of it,' छत्रधारी *m.* (न्).

UMPIRE, *s.* मध्यस्थः, स्थेयः, प्रमाणपुरुषः, शठः.

UN. This prefix is expressed in Sanskrit by अ, अन्, निर्, वि, अप, दुर् &c., prefixed, or by हीन, रहित, शून्य &c., affixed. In cases where the English word formed with 'un' is not given in this Dictionary, the student must take the simple noun and use one of the above prefixes or affixes.

UNABLE, *a.* अशक्तः -क्ता -क्तं, असमर्थः -र्था -र्थं, अक्षमः -मा -मं, अनीशः -शा -शं, अकल्पः -ल्पा -ल्पं, अपारकः -का -कं.

UNACCENTED, *a.* अनुदात्तः -त्ता -त्तं, अस्वरितः -ता -तं.

UNACCEPTABLE, *a.* अप्रतिग्राह्यः -ह्या -ह्यं, अग्राह्यः &c., अग्रहणीयः &c., अनादेयः -या -यं, अस्वीकार्य्यः -र्य्या -र्य्यं, अलीकः -का -कं.

UNACCOMPANIED, *a.* असहायः -या -यं, असहायवान् -वती -वत् (त्), असहायी -यिनी -यि (न्), असङ्गः -ङ्गा -ङ्गं, एकाकी &c.

UNACCOMPLISHED, *a.* असाधितः -ता -तं, असिद्धः -द्धा -द्धं, असंसिद्धः &c., असम्पन्नः -न्ना -न्नं, अनिष्पन्नः &c., अनुपपन्नः &c., असमाप्तः -प्ता -प्तं, अनधिगतः -ता -तं, अकृतः &c., अनागतवान् &c., असम्पूर्णः &c.

UNACCOUNTABLE. *See* INEXPLICABLE, IRRESPONSIBLE.

UNACCUSTOMED, *a.* अनभ्यस्तः -स्ता -स्तं, अनभ्यासी &c., अकृताभ्यासः -सा -सं; 'to ornament,' अननुभूतभूषणः -णा -णं.

UNACKNOWLEDGED, *a.* अननुज्ञातः -ता -तं, अनङ्गीकृतः -ता -तं.

UNACQUAINTED, *a.* अनभिज्ञः -ज्ञा -ज्ञं, अपरिचितः &c., *see* IGNORANT.

UNACTIONABLE, *a.* अव्यवहार्य्यः -र्य्या -र्य्यं, व्यवहाराविषयः -या -यं.

UNADORNED, *a.* अनलङ्कृतः -ता -तं, अभूषितः &c., अलङ्कारहीनः &c.

UNADULTERATED, *a.* अदूषितः -ता -तं, अमिश्रितः &c., असंसृष्टः &c.

UNAFFECTED, *a.* (Not acted upon) अनुपहतः -ता -तं, अप्रतिहतः &c., निर्विकारः -रा -रं, अविकृतः -ता -तं.—(Unfeigned) अकृत्रिमः -मा -मं, *see* SINCERE, SIMPLE.—(Unmoved) अजातद्रवः -वा -वं.

UNAFFECTEDLY, *adv.* अवैलक्ष्येण, अविलक्षत्वेन, सारल्येन, अमायया.

UNAIDED, *a.* अनुपकृतः -ता -तं, असहायः -या -यं, निःसहायः &c.

UNALIENABLE, *a.* अनादेयः -या -यं, स्थावरः &c., *see* INALIENABLE.

UNALLOYED, *a.* अविमिश्रः -श्रा -श्रं, निर्विमिश्रः &c., अनिश्रमिश्रः &c.

UNALTERABLE, *a.* अविकार्य्यः -र्य्या -र्य्यं. *See* IMMUTABLE.

UNALTERED, *a.* अविकारः -रा -रं, निर्विकारः &c., अविकृतः -ता -तं.

UNAMIABLE, *a.* अप्रियः -या -यं, अप्रीतिजनकः -का -कं.

UNANIMITY, *s.* ऐकमत्यं, चित्तैक्यं, मतैक्यं, एकचित्तता.

UNANIMOUS, *a.* एकचित्तः -त्ता -त्तं, एकमतः -ता -तं, सर्व्वसम्मतः &c.

UNANIMOUSLY, *adv.* एकचित्तीभूय, एकमतीभूय, मतैक्येन.

UNANSWERABLE, *a.* अनुत्तरः -रा -रं, दुरुत्तरः &c., असमाधनीयः &c.

UNAPPROACHABLE, *a.* अगम्यः -म्या -म्यं, अनागम्यः &c., अनभिगमनीयः &c., अगमनीयः &c., दुर्गमः -मा -मं, दुरुपस्थानः -ना -नं, अनुपसार्य्यः -र्य्या -र्य्यं, दुर्धर्षः -र्षा -र्षं, अगः -गा -गं. *See* INACCESSIBLE.

UNAPT, *a.* अयुक्तः -क्ता -क्तं, अनाप्तः -प्ता -प्तं, अकुशलः -ला -लं.

UNARMED, *a.* अशस्त्रः -स्त्रा -स्त्रं, विशस्त्रः &c., निःशस्त्रः &c., शस्त्रहीनः -ना -नं, शस्त्ररहितः -ता -तं, अस्त्रहीनः &c., निरायुधः -धा -धं, अनायुधः &c., अनायुद्धः -द्धा -द्धं, असन्नः -न्ना -न्नं, असज्जितः -ता -तं, असन्नद्धः &c., निर्हेतिः -तिः -ति; 'unarmed state,' वैशस्त्रं.

UNASKED, *a.* अपृष्टः -ष्टा -ष्टं, अयाचितः -ता -तं, अप्रचोदितः &c.

UNASPIRATED, *a.* अल्पप्राणः -णा -णं, अल्पप्राणोच्चारितः &c.

UNASSAILABLE, *a.* अनाक्रमणीयः -या -यं, अनाक्रम्यः -म्या -म्यं.

UNASSISTED, *a.* अनुपकृतः -ता -तं, असहायः -या -यं, निःसहायः &c.

UNASSOCIATED, *a.* असहितः -ता -तं, असक्तः -क्ता -क्तं, निःसङ्गः &c.

UNASSUMING, *a.* अप्रगल्भः -ल्भा -ल्भं, अनभिमानी -निनी &c., निर्गर्वः -र्वा -र्वं, अविकत्थनः -ना -नं, अकत्थनः &c., विनीतः -ता -तं, निभृतः &c.

UNATTAINABLE, *a.* अप्राप्यः -प्या -प्यं, अलभ्यः -भ्या -भ्यं, अगम्यः -म्या -म्यं, अनधिगम्यः &c., अनासाद्यः -द्या -द्यं, दुष्प्रापः -पा -पं, कष्टप्राप्यः &c., दुरासदः -दा -दं, असाध्यः -ध्या -ध्यं, दुर्गमः -मा -मं, अगमः &c.

UNATTENDED, *a.* असहायी -यिनी -यि (न्), असहायवान् -वती -वत् (त्), निरनुचरः -रा -रं, अननुचरः &c., अनुचररहितः -ता -तं, अनुचरहीनः -ना -नं, निरनुगः -गा -गं, असहितः -ता -तं, विपालः -ला -लं, निर्व्यपेक्षः &c.

UNATTESTED, *a.* असाक्षिकः -की -कं, साक्ष्यहीनः -ना -नं, अप्रमाणः &c.

UNAUTHENTIC, *a.* अप्रामाणिकः -की -कं, अप्रमाणयुक्तः -क्ता -क्तं.

UNAUTHORITATIVE, *a.* निष्प्रमाणः -णा -णं, अनाप्तः -प्ता -प्तं.

UNAUTHORIZED, *a.* अप्रामाणिकः -की -कं, विधिहीनः -ना -नं.

UNAVAILING, *a.* व्यर्थः -र्था -र्थं, निष्फलः &c. *See* INEFFECTUAL.

UNAVOIDABLE, *a.* अपरिहार्य्यः -र्य्या -र्य्यं, अनतिक्रमणीयः -या -यं, अनिवार्य्यः &c., अशक्यनिवारः -रा -रं; 'decree,' अहार्य्ययोगः.

UNAWARES, *adv.* अकस्मात्, अचिन्तितं, अतर्कितं. *See* SUDDENLY.

UNBAKED, *a.* अपक्वः -क्वा -क्वं, आमः -मा -मं, अकान्दवः &c.

To UNBAR, *v. a.* निरर्गलीकृ, अनर्गलीकृ, अर्गलम् अपनी or हृ.

UNBEARABLE, *a.* असह्यः -ह्या -ह्यं, असहनीयः &c., *see* INTOLERABLE.

UNBEATEN, *a.* अक्षुण्णः -ण्णा -ण्णं; 'path,' अक्षुण्णमार्गः.

UNBECOMING, *a.* अयुक्तः -क्ता -क्तं, अयोग्यः &c. *See* INDECOROUS.

UNBELIEF, *s.* अविश्वासः, अश्रद्धा, अभक्तिः *f.* *See* INFIDELITY.

UNBELIEVER, UNBELIEVING. *See* INFIDEL, *s.* and *a.*

To UNBEND, UNBENDING. *See* *To* RELAX, FIRM, OBSTINATE.

UNBENT, *p. p.* अनतः -ता -तं, उन्नतः &c., अभुग्नः &c., *see* RELAXED.

UNBIASSED, *a.* समदृष्टिः -ष्टिः -ष्टि, सङ्गहीनः &c. *See* IMPARTIAL.

UNBIDDEN, *a.* अनिमन्त्रितः -ता -तं, अप्रचोदितः &c., अनाज्ञप्तः &c.

To UNBIND, *v. a.* उद्ग्रन्थ्, शिथिलीकृ. *See* *To* LOOSE, *v. a.*

UNBLAMABLE, *a.* अनवद्यः -द्या -द्यं, अनिन्दनीयः -या -यं, अनिन्द्यः &c., अवाच्यः -च्या -च्यं, निरपराधः -धा -धं, अनुपस्कृतः &c. *See* INNOCENT.

UNBLEACHED, *a.* निष्प्रवाणः -णा -णं, निष्प्रवाणिः -णिः -णि, अनाहतः &c., तन्त्रकः -का -कं; 'cloth,' निष्प्रवाणं, अनाहतं, तन्त्रकं, नवाम्बरं.

UNBLEMISHED, *a.* निर्दोषः -षा -षं, अकल्मषः -षा -षं, अक्षतः -ता -तं, अपरिक्षतः &c., निष्कलङ्कः -ङ्का -ङ्कं, निर्मलः &c. *See* PURE.

UNBLEST, *a.* निराशीः -शीः -शिः (स्), निराशिषः -षा -षं, अनाशिषः &c.

UNBLOWN, *a.* अफुल्लः -ल्ला -ल्लं, अस्फुटः -टा -टं, मुद्रितः -ता -तं, अविकसितः &c.; 'flower,' कलिका, कलिः -ली, कोरकः -कं.

To UNBOLT, *v. a.* निरर्गलीकृ, अनर्गलीकृ, निरर्गलं -लां कृ.

UNBORN, *a.* अजातः -ता -तं, अजः -जा -जं, अप्राप्तजन्मा &c.

To UNBOSOM, *v. a.* (One's self) मनोगतचिन्तां प्रकाश् in caus.

UNBOUND, *a.* अबद्धः -द्धा -द्धं, उद्बद्धः &c., उद्दामः &c., अबन्धनः &c.

UNBOUNDED, *a.* अनन्तः -न्ता -न्तं, अयन्तः &c. *See* INFINITE.

UNBRIBABLE, *a.* अनदानेन अभेद्यः -द्या -द्यं, अहार्य्यः -र्य्या -र्य्यं.

UNBRIDLED, *a.* उच्छृङ्खलः -ला -लं, विशृङ्खलः &c., अशृस्यः -स्या -स्यं, निर्मर्य्यादः -दा -दं, उद्दामः -मा -मं, अनर्गलः &c. *See* LICENTIOUS.

UNBREECHED, *a.* कटीपटहीनः -ना -नं, अपाकृतकटीपटः -टा -टं.

UNBROKEN, *a.* अभिन्नः -न्ना -न्नं, अभग्नः -ग्ना -ग्नं, अखण्डितः -ता -तं, अक्षतः &c.—(As a horse) अदमितः &c., अशिक्षितः &c.

To UNBURDEN, *v. a.* भाराद् मुच्, मुक्तभारं -रां कृ, भारमुक्तं कृ.

UNBURNT, *a.* अपक्वः -क्वा -क्वं, अदग्धः &c.; 'brick,' आमेष्टका.

To UNBUTTON, *v. a.* शिथिलीकृ, शिथिल (nom. शिथिलयति -यितुं).

UNCAGED, *a.* उत्पिञ्जरः -रा -रं, पञ्जरमुक्तः -क्ता -क्तं.

UNCALLED, *a.* अनाहूतः -ता -तं, अहूतः &c.; 'for,' *see* NEEDLESS.

UNCEASING, *a.* अविरतः -ता -तं, निरन्तरः &c. *See* CONTINUAL.

UNCEREMONIOUS, *a.* मन्दादरः -रा -रं, निरादरः &c., अनादरः &c.

UNCEREMONIOUSLY, *adv.* अनादरेण, आदरेण विना, मन्दादरं.

UNCERTAIN, *a.* सन्दिग्धः -ग्धा -ग्धं, अनिश्चितः &c., अध्रुवः -वा -वं, अस्थिरः -रा -रं, *see* DOUBTFUL.—(Not confident) संशयी -यिनी &c., सांशयिकः -की -कं, अजातनिश्चयः -या -यं, जातसंशयः &c.

UNCERTAINTY, *s.* अनिश्चयः, अनिर्णयः, सन्देहः, संशयः. *See* DOUBT.

UNCHANGEABLE, *a.* निर्विकारः -रा -रं, अव्ययः &c., *see* IMMUTABLE.

UNCHANGED, *a.* अविकृतः -ता -तं, निर्विकारः -रा -रं, अविकारः &c.

UNCHARITABLE, *a.* दोषदृष्टिः -ष्टिः -ष्टि, दोषदर्शी -र्शिनी &c., छिद्रान्वेषी &c., असूयकः -का -कं, अकृपादृष्टिः &c. *See* CENSORIOUS.

UNCHARITABLY, *adv.* अकृपादृष्ट्या, दोषदर्शनशीलत्वात्.

UNCHASTE, *a.* अविनीतः -ता -तं, असाधुवृत्तः -त्ता -त्तं, पांशुलः -ला -लं, असाधुः -ध्वी -धु, व्यभिचारी &c., अवकीर्णी *m.* (न्), *see* INCONTINENT, PROFLIGATE; 'woman,' असती, असाध्वी, बन्धकी, पुंश्चली, अविनीता, अभिसारिका, धृष्टा, धर्षिणी, व्यभिचारिणी, कुलटा, कुलपांसुला, कामगा, इत्वरी, स्वैरिणी, पांशुला, पांसुला.

UNCHECKED, *a.* अयतः -ता -तं, अनियतः &c., अनिवारितः &c., निरवग्रहः -हा -हं, निरर्गलः -ला -लं, विशृङ्खलः &c., अनिराकृतः -ता -तं.

UNCIRCUMCISED, *a.* अपरिकर्त्तितः -ता -तं, अपरिच्छिन्नः -न्ना -न्नं.

UNCIRCUMCISION, *a.* अपरिकर्त्तनं, अपरिच्छेदः, त्वगच्छेदः.

UNCIVIL, *a.* असभ्यः -भ्या -भ्यं, अविनीतः -ता -तं, अविनयः -या -यं, परुषभाषी -षिणी &c., दुर्मर्य्यादः -दा -दं. *See* RUDE, IMPOLITE.

UNCIVILIZED, *a.* अशिष्टः -ष्टा -ष्टं, &c. *See* RUDE, SAVAGE.

UNCLAIMED, *a.* अस्वामिकः -की -कं, अनधिकृतः -ता -तं, अदायिकः &c.

UNCLE, *s.* (Paternal) पितृव्यः, पितृभ्राता *m.* (तृ), ताततुल्यः, तातगुः *m.*—(Maternal) मातुलः, मातृभ्राता *m.* (तृ).

UNCLEAN, *a.* अशुचिः -चिः -चि, अपवित्रः -त्रा -त्रं. *See* IMPURE.

UNCLEANNESS, *s.* अशौचं, अशुचित्वं, अस्पृश्यत्वं. *See* IMPURITY.

To UNCLOSE, *v. a.* विवृ, अपावृ, उद्घट्. *See* *To* OPEN, OPENED.

UNCLOTHED, *a.* विवस्त्रः -स्त्रा -स्त्रं, अप्रावृतः -ता -तं. *See* NAKED.

UNCLOUDED, *a.* निरभ्रः -भ्रा -भ्रं, अनभ्रः &c., व्यभ्रः &c., निर्मेघः &c.

UNCLOVEN, *a.* (As a hoof) एकशफः -फा -फं, एकखुरः -रा -रं.

UNCOMFORTABLE, *a.* अस्वस्थः -स्था -स्थं, असुस्थः &c., असुखी -खिनी &c.

UNCOMFORTABLENESS, *s.* अस्वस्थता, असुस्थता, अस्वास्थ्यं, असुखं.

Uncomfortably, *adv.* असुखेन, असौख्येन, असुखं, अस्वास्थ्येन.

Uncommon, *a.* असामान्यः -न्या -न्यं, असाधारणः -णी -णं, अप्रसिद्धः -द्धा -द्धं, अप्रकृतः &c., विरलः &c. *See* Rare, Strange.

Uncommonly, *adv.* अत्यन्तं, अतिशयेन, अति, सु. *See* Excessively.

Uncompounded, *a.* निरवयवः -वा -वं, असङ्कीर्णः -र्णा -र्णं, अमिश्रितः &c., अपृक्तः -क्ता -क्तं, केवलशुद्धः &c. *See* Simple, *a.*

Unconcealed, *a.* अगुप्तः -प्ता -प्तं, अगूढः -ढा -ढं, असङ्गुप्तः &c.

Unconcern, unconcerned. *See* Indifference, Indifferent.

Unconcernedly, *adv.* निरपेक्षं, अनपेक्ष -क्षया, उदासीनवत्.

Unconditional, *a.* अप्रतिबन्धः -न्धा -न्धं, अप्रतिबद्धः -द्धा -द्धं, अनिबद्धः &c., अनियमितः -ता -तं, असाङ्केतिकः -की -कं, निष्प्रतिज्ञः &c.

Unconfined, *a.* अबद्धः -द्धा -द्धं, असम्बाधः &c., उच्छृङ्खलः -ला -लं.

Uncongenial, *a.* अननुगुणः -णा -णं, अननुकूलः -ला -लं, प्रतिकूलः &c.

Unconnected, *a.* असम्बद्धः -द्धा -द्धं, असम्बन्धः -न्धा -न्धं, निःसम्बन्धः &c., अबद्धः &c., निर्युक्तिकः -की -कं, निरन्वयः -या -यं, अनन्वितः -ता -तं, असङ्गतः &c., अनुपेतः &c., असम्पर्कीयः -या -यं. *See* Incoherent.

Unconquerable, *a.* अजेयः -या -यं, अजय्यः &c., अनाधृष्यः &c.

Unconquered, *p. p.* अजितः -ता -तं, अपराजितः &c., अनभिभूतः &c.

Unconscionable, *a.* *See* Unreasonable.

Unconscious, *a.* अचेतनः -ना -नं, विसंज्ञः &c., *see* Insensible; 'he is unconscious of his own existence,' आत्मानं न विभावयते.

Unconsciousness, *s.* अचैतन्यं &c. *See* Insensibility.

Unconsecrated, *a.* अप्रतिष्ठितः -ता -तं, अप्रणीतः &c., असंस्कृतः &c., अजातसंस्कारः -रा -रं, अनभिमन्त्रितः -ता -तं, अनाहितः &c.

Unconstrained, *a.* अप्रतिबद्धः &c. *See* Free, Voluntary.

Uncontaminated, *a.* अदूषितः -ता -तं, अलिप्तः -प्ता -प्तं, निर्लिप्तः &c.

Uncontrollable, *a.* अदम्यः -म्या -म्यं. *See* Irrestrainable.

Uncontrolled, *a.* निरवग्रहः -हा -हं, निर्यन्त्रणः -णा -णं, निरर्गलः -ला -लं, अनर्गलः &c., अप्रतिबन्धः -न्धा -न्धं. *See* Unrestrained.

Uncourteous, *a.* असभ्यः -भ्या -भ्यं, निर्नमस्कारः &c. *See* Rude.

Uncouth, *a.* अपरूपः -पा -पं, विरूपः &c. *See* Odd, Strange.

To uncover, *v. a.* अपवृ (c. 5. -वृणोति -वरितुं -रीतुं), अपावृ, विवृ, उच्छद् (c. 10. -छादयति -यितुं). *See* *To* strip, divest.

Uncovered, *p. p.* अपवृतः -ता -तं, अनावृतः &c., विवृतः &c., अनाच्छादितः -ता -तं, अनाच्छन्नः -न्ना -न्नं, अछादितः &c. *See* Stripped.

Uncreated, *a.* असृष्टः -ष्टा -ष्टं, अनुत्पन्नः &c. *See* Increate.

Unction, *s.* अभ्यञ्जनं, अञ्जनं, अभ्यङ्गः, प्रदेहः, आलेपनं, विलेपनं, स्निग्धता, स्नैग्ध्यं, स्नेहः.

Unctuous, *a.* स्निग्धः -ग्धा -ग्धं, स्नेही -हिनी -हि (न्), मेदुरः -रा -रं, चिक्कणः &c., सान्द्रः &c., प्रक्लेदितः &c. *See* Oily, Greasy.

Uncultivated, *a.* अप्रहतः -ता -तं, अकृतः &c., खिलः -ला -लं.

Undaunted, *a.* अभीतः -ता -तं, अभिन्नात्मा &c. *See* Fearless.

Undecayed, *a.* अक्षीणः -णा -णं, अशीर्णः &c., अजातक्षयः -या -यं.

Undecaying, *a.* अक्षयः -या -यं, अव्ययः &c., *see* Imperishable.

To undeceive, *v. a.* भ्रमं or भ्रान्तिं नुद् or अपनी, निर्भ्रमीकृ.

Undecided, *a.* अनिश्चितः -ता -तं, अनिर्णीतः &c., अकृतनिश्चयः -या -यं, अकृतसङ्कल्पः &c.—(Irresolute) सन्दिग्धमानसः &c., *see* the word.

Undefiled, *a.* अदूषितः -ता -तं, अलिप्तः -प्ता -प्तं, निर्मलः -ला -लं.

Undefinable, *a.* अलक्ष्यः -क्ष्या -क्ष्यं, अप्रतर्क्यः &c., अनिर्वचनीयः &c.

Undefined, *a.* अलक्षितः &c. *See* Indefinite, Indeterminate.

Undeniable, *a.* अप्रत्याख्येयः -या -यं. *See* Indisputable.

Under, *prep.* (Below, beneath) अधस्, अधस्तात्, तले, उप in comp.; *see* Underneath; 'under the tree,' वृक्षस्याधस्तात्, वृक्षतले; 'under water,' जलस्याधस्; 'under the bed,' खट्वातले, खट्वाधस्; 'under the hand,' हस्ततलगतः -ता -तं.—(In subjection to) अधीनः -ना -नं, *see* Subject.—(Less than) ऊन or न्यून in comp., अर्वाक्, अवरः -रा -रं; 'a child under two years old,' ऊनद्विवर्षो or ऊनद्विवार्षिको बालः, अप्राप्तद्वितीयवर्षो बालः; 'under sixteen years of age,' ऊनषोडशवर्षः -र्षा -र्षं; 'under the time,' अप्राप्तकालः -ला -लं; 'under a fortnight,' अर्वाक् चतुर्दशाद् अह्नः.—(Under pretext of) व्यपदेशेन, *see* Colour.—(In the time of) काले, समये, मध्ये.

Under, *a.* अधःस्थः -स्था -स्थं, अधोभवः -वा -वं, अधस् in comp., अवर् in comp., *see* Inferior; 'under-current,' अधःप्रवाहः.—(Subordinate) उप in comp.; 'under-master,' उपशिक्षकः, उपगुरुः.

Under-age, *a.* अप्राप्तव्यवहारः, अप्राप्तकालः. *See* Minor.

Under-done, *a.* अपक्वः -क्वा -क्वं, आपक्वः &c., आमः -मा -मं.

Undergarment, *s.* अधोवसनं, अधोंशुकं, अन्तरीयं, अन्तर्वासस् *n.*

To undergo, *v. a.* उपगम्, उपागम्, अनुभू. *See* *To* suffer.

Undergone, *p. p.* उपगतः -ता -तं, उपागतः &c., अनुभूतः -ता -तं.

Underground, *adv.* भूम्यधस्, भूम्यधस्तात्, भूतलाधस्तात्.

Underground, *a.* अन्तर्भौमः -मी -मं, भूम्यधःस्थः -स्था -स्थं, भूम्यधोगतः -ता -तं, अन्तर्भूमिस्थः &c. *See* Subterranean.

Underhand, *a.* छलेन कृतः -ता -तं, तिरस् ind. *See* Clandestine.

To underline, *v. a.* अधोरेखाङ्कितं -तां कृ, अधोरेखया अङ्क्.

Underling, *s.* अवरः, अवरपदस्थः, अनुजीवी *m.* (न्).

To undermine, *v. a.* अधस्तात् खन् (c. 1. खनति -नितुं) or उत्खन् or गूढखातं -तां कृ, अधः or अधस्तात् खात्वा नश् in caus. or पर्यस्.

Undermost, *a.* सर्व्वाधःस्थः -स्था -स्थं, सर्व्वाधरस्थः &c., सर्व्वाधरः &c.

Underneath, *adv.* अधस्तात्, अधस्, अधरस्तात्, अधरेण -रात्, अधरतस्, अधोभागे, अधस्तनः -नी -नं, नीचे.

To underrate, *v. a.* लघूकृ, लघु मन्, अल्पमूल्यीकृ, न्यूनमूल्यीकृ.

To understand, *v. a.* अवगम् (c. 1. -गच्छति -गन्तुं), उपलभ् (c. 1. -लभते -लब्धुं), ज्ञा (c. 9. जानाति, ज्ञातुं), विज्ञा, परिज्ञा, बुध् (c. 1. बोधति -धितुं), अवबुध्, समवबुध्, ग्रह् (c. 9. गृह्णाति, ग्रहीतुं), अवे (c. 2. अवैति -तुं), विद्, ऊह्, अवधृ in caus., मन्, विभू in caus., अनुभू, अवगमं कृ, अवधारणं कृ.

Understanding, *s.* (Intellectual faculty) बुद्धिः *f.*, धीः *f.*, मतिः *f.*, मेधा, मेधस् *n.*, ज्ञानं, ज्ञानशक्तिः *f.*, प्रज्ञा, चित् *f.*, चेतना, आकलनशक्तिः *f.*, शेमुषी; 'eye of the understanding,' ज्ञानचक्षुस् *n.*, ज्ञानदृष्टिः *f.*; 'object of understanding,' बुद्धिविषयः; 'of little understanding,' अल्पबुद्धिः -द्धिः -द्धि, अल्पधीः -धीः -धि, अल्पमेधाः -धाः -धः (स्); 'slow of understanding,' मन्दबुद्धिः -द्धिः -द्धि, मन्दमतिः -तिः -ति.—(Terms of intercourse) स्नेहभावः, स्नेहः, संविज्ञिः *f.*

Understood, *p. p.* अवगतः -ता -तं, उपलब्धः -ब्धा -ब्धं, ज्ञातः -ता -तं, विज्ञातः &c., बुद्धः -द्धा -द्धं, बुधितः -ता -तं, मतः &c., आगमितः &c., विदितः &c., आकलितः &c., ज्ञानारूढः -ढा -ढं, बुद्ध्यारूढः &c., अनुभूतः &c., प्रतिपन्नः -न्ना -न्नं.—(Implied) उपलक्षितः -ता -तं, अर्थसम्बद्धः &c.

To undertake, *v. a.* व्यवसो (c. 4. -स्यति -सातुं), अध्यवसो, आरभ् (c. 1. -रभते -रब्धुं), समारभ्, उपक्रम् (c. 1. -क्रमते -मितुं), अनुष्ठा

आस्था, स्वीकृ, अङ्गीकृ, कृ, प्रवृत्.

UNDERTAKEN, *p. p.* आरब्धः -ब्धा -ब्धं, समारब्धः &c., व्यवसितः -ता -तं, अध्यवसायितः &c., स्वीकृतः &c., अङ्गीकृतः &c.

UNDERTAKER, *s.* अनुष्ठाता *m.* (तृ), व्यवसायी *m.* (न्), आरम्भकः, प्रवर्त्तकः, निर्वाहकः.—(Of funerals) अन्त्यकर्म्मनिर्वाहकः.

UNDERTAKING, *s.* कर्म्म *n.* (न्), कार्य्यं, प्रारब्धं, आरब्धं, प्रारब्धिः *f.*, आरम्भः, प्रारम्भः, व्यवसायः, अध्यवसायः, प्रवृत्तिः *f.*; 'bold,' साहसकर्म्म *n.*, *see* ENTERPRISE; 'to accomplish one's undertakings,' प्रारब्धानि सम्पद्.

To UNDERVALUE, *v. a.* लघूकृ, लघु मन्, तुच्छीकृ, लघुमूल्यीकृ.

UNDESERVED, *a.* अयोग्यः -ग्या -ग्यं, अनुपयुक्तः -क्ता -क्तं, अयुक्तः &c., अयथार्हः -र्हा -र्हं, अगुणसम्पादितः -ता -तं, अकर्म्मसम्पादितः &c.

UNDESERVEDLY, *adv.* अयोग्यं, अनुपयुक्तं, अयथार्हं, निरपराधं.

UNDESERVING, *a.* अनर्हः -र्हा -र्हं, निर्गुणः -णा -णं, अगुणः &c., गुणहीनः -ना -नं, अश्लाघ्यः -घ्या -घ्यं, अयोग्यः &c. *See* UNWORTHY.

UNDESIGNED, *a.* अबुद्धिपूर्व्वः -र्व्वा -र्व्वं, अबोधपूर्व्वः &c., अमतिपूर्व्वकः -का -कं, असङ्कल्पपूर्व्वकः &c., अज्ञानपूर्व्वकः &c., असङ्कल्पकृतः -ता -तं, अबुद्धिकृतः &c., असाङ्कल्पिकः -की -कं, असङ्कल्पितः &c., अनुद्दिष्टः -ष्टा -ष्टं, अनभिप्रेतः &c.

UNDESIGNEDLY, *adv.* अबुद्धिपूर्व्वं -र्व्वकं, अबोधपूर्व्वं, अमतिपूर्व्वं, अबुद्धिपुरःसरं, अज्ञानतस्, अबुद्ध्या, अकामतस्, अमत्या, अनिच्छातस्.

UNDESIGNING, *a.* निष्कपटः -टा -टं. *See* SINCERE, ARTLESS.

UNDESIRABLE, *a.* अस्पृहः -हा -हं, अस्पृहणीयः -या -यं, अनिष्टः -ष्टा -ष्टं, अनाकांक्षणीयः &c., अनाकांक्ष्यः &c., अवाञ्छनीयः &c.

UNDESIROUS, *a.* अनिच्छुः -च्छुः -च्छु, अनाकांक्षी &c., अनभिलाषी &c.

UNDEVIATING, *a.* अव्यभिचारी -रिणी -रि (न्), अविच्युतः -ता -तं, अविप्लुतः &c., अस्खलितः &c., अभ्रष्टः -ष्टा -ष्टं, अविपथगामी &c.

UNDIGESTED, *a.* अजीर्णः -र्णा -र्णं, अपक्वः -क्वा -क्वं, अजातपाकः -का -कं, विदग्धः -ग्धा -ग्धं, आमः -मा -मं, कलः -ला -लं; 'undigested food,' आमांशः.—(Not methodized) अव्यवस्थितः -ता -तं, अकृतव्यवस्थः -स्था -स्थं.

UNDIMINISHED, *a.* अक्षीणः -णा -णं, अक्षतः -ता -तं, अविक्षतः &c., अन्यूनीभूतः &c., अन्यूनीकृतः &c., अलुप्तः -प्ता -प्तं, अनपायः -या -यं, अनपायी -यिनी &c., अजातह्रासः -सा -सं; 'of undiminished glory,' अलुप्तमहिमा &c.

UNDISCIPLINED, *a.* अशिष्टः -ष्टा -ष्टं, अशासितः -ता -तं, अशिक्षितः &c.

UNDISGUISED, *a.* निर्व्याजः -जा -जं, निष्कपटः -टा -टं, अकृत्रिमः &c.

UNDISPUTED, *a.* निर्व्विवादः -दा -दं, अविप्रतिपन्नः &c., अव्याहतः &c.

UNDISTURBED, *a.* निरुपद्रवः -वा -वं, उपद्रवहीनः -ना -नं.—(Not perturbed) अक्षुब्धः -ब्धा -ब्धं, अविक्षोभितः &c., अव्यग्रः &c., निराकुलः &c.

UNDIVIDED, *a.* अभिन्नः -न्ना -न्नं, अखण्डः -ण्डा -ण्डं, अखण्डितः -ता -तं, अविभक्तः -क्ता -क्तं, अविभाजितः &c., अनिर्भिन्नः &c.

To UNDO, *v. a.* उद्ग्रन्थ्, शिथिलीकृ, विकृ. *See To* LOOSE, RUIN.

UNDONE, *p. p.* (Not done) अकृतः -ता -तं, अननुष्ठितः &c., अनाचरितः &c., निष्कृतः &c., असाधितः &c., असम्पादितः &c.; 'left undone,' अन्तरितः -ता -तं, *see* OMITTED.—(Ruined) हतः -ता -तं, नष्टः &c., *see* RUINED; 'I am undone,' हतो ऽस्मि.

UNDOUBTED, *a.* असन्दिग्धः -ग्धा -ग्धं, सुनिश्चितः &c. *See* INDUBITABLE.

UNDOUBTEDLY, *adv.* सुनिश्चितं, असंशयं, अवश्यं, असन्दिग्धं, अथ किं.

To UNDRESS, *v. a.* वस्त्रम् अपतॄ (c. 10. -तारयति -यितुं) or उत्सृ or उत्कृष् or अपनह्, विवस्त्रीकृ, विवसनीकृ, नग्नीकृ. *See To* DIVEST, STRIP.

UNDRESSED, *p. p.* or *a.* विवस्त्रः -स्त्रा -स्त्रं, विवसनः -ना -नं, वस्त्रहीनः -ना -नं, उत्तीर्णवस्त्रः &c., मुक्तवस्त्रः &c.—(Not cooked) अपक्वः -क्वा -क्वं, आमः &c., *see* RAW; 'undressed rice, &c.,' आमान्नं.

UNDRINKABLE, *a.* अपेयः -या -यं, अपानयोग्यः &c., दुष्पानः -ना -नं.

UNDUE, *a.* अयोग्यः -ग्या -ग्यं. *See* IMPROPER, INORDINATE.

To UNDULATE, *v. n.* उन्नतानतीभू, उच्चावचीभू, उत्सृप्, विसृप्.

UNDULATION, *s.* ऊर्म्मिमत्ता -त्त्वं, उन्नतानतत्वं, उत्सर्पः -र्पणं.

UNDULATING, UNDULATORY, *a.* ऊर्म्मिमान् -मती -मत् (त्), उन्नतानतः -ता -तं, उन्नतनीचः -चा -चं, उच्चावचः &c., बन्धुरः -रा -रं, भङ्गुरः &c., उत्सर्पी -र्पिणी &c., उत्सर्पितः -ता -तं, विसर्पी &c., तरलायितः -ता -तं, तरङ्गितः &c.

UNDUTIFUL, *a.* अभक्तः -क्ता -क्तं, अवश्यः &c., स्वधर्म्मविमुखः -खा -खं.

UNEASINESS, *s.* असुखं, अनिर्वृतिः *f.*, क्लेशः, कष्टं, व्यथा, बाधा.

UNEASY, *a.* असुखी -खिनी -खि (न्), असुस्थः -स्था -स्थं, अस्वस्थः &c., अनिर्वृतः -ता -तं, सव्यथः -था -थं, उद्विग्नः &c., जाताशङ्कः &c.

UNEATABLE, *a.* अखाद्यः -द्या -द्यं, अनाद्यः &c., अभक्ष्यः &c.

UNEDUCATED, *a.* अशिक्षितः -ता -तं, निरक्षरः &c. *See* ILLITERATE.

UNEMPLOYED, *a.* निर्व्यापारः -रा -रं, निष्कर्म्मा &c. *See* IDLE.

UNENCUMBERED, *a.* सङ्गहीनः -ना -नं, निःसङ्गः -ङ्गा -ङ्गं, निस्सङ्गः &c.

UNENVIOUS, *a.* अनसूयः -या -यं -यकः -का -कं, निःस्पृहः -हा -हं.

UNEQUAL, *a.* असमः -मा -मं, असमानः -ना -नं, विषमः -मा -मं, न्यूनाधिकः -का -कं; 'unequal division,' विषमविभागः, *see* INADEQUATE.

UNEQUALLED, *a.* अनुपमः -मा -मं, अप्रतिमः &c. *See* INCOMPARABLE.

UNEQUALLY, *adv.* असमं, विषमं, असमानं, वैषम्येण, न्यूनाधिकं.

UNEQUIVOCAL, *a.* सुस्पष्टः -ष्टा -ष्टं, वीतसन्देहः &c. *See* CLEAR.

UNERRING, *a.* अमोघः -घा -घं, अभ्रान्तः -न्ता -न्तं, अमोघपातः -ता -तं, अवन्ध्यपातः &c.; 'of unerring sight,' अमोघदृष्टिः -ष्टिः -ष्टि.

UNEVEN, *a.* (Not level) असमः -मा -मं, विषमः &c., एकपार्श्वविषमः &c., अविस्थितः -ता -तं, उन्नतानतः &c., *see* UNDULATING, ODD.

UNEVENLY, UNEVENNESS. *See* UNEQUALLY, INEQUALITY.

UNEXAMPLED, *a.* अपूर्व्वः -र्व्वा -र्व्वं, अपूर्व्वप्रतिमः -मा -मं, अद्वितीयः &c.

UNEXCEPTIONABLE, *a.* अनवद्यः -द्या -द्यं, निरवद्यः &c., अबाध्यः &c.

UNEXPECTED, *a.* आकस्मिकः -की -कं, अनपेक्षितः -ता -तं, अलक्षितः &c., अतर्कितः &c., अचिन्तितः &c., अकाण्डः -ण्डा -ण्डं, अचिन्तकल्पितः &c., काकतालीयः -या -यं.

UNEXPECTEDLY, *adv.* अकस्मात्, अनपेक्षं, अतर्कितं, अचिन्तितं, काकतालीयवत्.

UNFADING, *a.* अम्लानी -निनी &c., अम्लानिः -निः -नि, अक्षयः -या -यं.

UNFAILING, *a.* अक्षयः -या -यं, अक्षयी -यिणी &c. *See* LASTING.

UNFAIR, *a.* विषमः -मा -मं, असमः &c., अन्याय्यः -य्या -य्यं, अनृजुः -जुः -जु, कूट in comp.—(Of persons) असरलः &c., *see* DISHONEST.

UNFAIRLY, *adv.* विषमं, असमं, असम्यक्, अन्यायेन, अनृजु, अनार्य्येण.

UNFAIRNESS, *s.* वैषम्यं, असमता, असम्यक्त्वं. *See* DISHONESTY.

UNFAITHFUL, *a.* अभक्तः -क्ता -क्तं, *see* FAITHLESS, FALSE; 'to engagements,' विसंवादी &c., असत्यसन्धः -न्धा -न्धं; 'wife,' अपतिव्रता.

UNFAITHFULLY, UNFAITHFULNESS. *See* FAITHLESSLY, FAITHLESSNESS.

UNFASHIONABLE, *a.* सभ्यव्यवहारविरुद्धः -द्धा -द्धं, असभ्यः -भ्या -भ्यं.

To UNFASTEN, *v. a.* उद्ग्रन्थ्, शिथिलीकृ. *See To* LOOSE, *v. a.*

UNFATHOMABLE, *a.* अगाधः -धा -धं, अतलस्पर्शः &c., अनवगाह्यः &c.

UNFAVORABLE, *a.* अप्रसन्नः -न्ना -न्नं, अननुकूलः -ला -लं, विरक्तः -क्ता -क्तं, विमुखः -खी -खं, निरनुरोधः -धा -धं, अहितः -ता -तं, विषमः &c.

UNFAVORABLY, *adv.* अप्रसन्नं, अननुकूलं, अहितं, विषमं, अप्रियं.
UNFEELING, *a.* निर्दयः -या -यं, निष्करुणः -णा -णं, कठिनः &c., जडः -डा -डं, निःस्नेहः -हा -हं, अरसिकः &c. *See* PITILESS.
UNFEIGNED, *a.* अकृत्रिमः -मा -मं, निर्व्याजः &c. *See* GENUINE.
UNFETTERED, *a.* अनर्गलः -ला -लं, विपाशः -शा -शं, विशृङ्खलः &c.
UNFINISHED, *a.* असमाप्तः -प्ता -प्तं, अनिष्पन्नः -न्ना -न्नं, असिद्धः -द्धा -द्धं.
UNFIT, *a.* अयुक्तः -क्ता -क्तं, अयोग्यः -ग्या -ग्यं, अनुचितः -ता -तं, *see* IMPROPER; 'for food,' अभक्ष्यः -क्ष्या -क्ष्यं, अभोज्यः &c.
To UNFIT, *v. a.* अयोग्यं -ग्यां कृ. *See To* DISQUALIFY, DISABLE.
UNFITLY, UNFITNESS. *See* IMPROPERLY, IMPROPRIETY.
UNFLEDGED, *a.* अजातपक्षः -क्षा -क्षं, अनागतपक्षः &c., *see* CALLOW.
UNFLINCHING, *a.* अविकम्पितः -ता -तं, अविकम्प्यः &c., सुधीरः -रा -रं.
To UNFOLD, *v. a.* विस्तृ in caus. (-स्तारयति -यितुं). *See To* EXPAND.
UNFOLDED, *a.* विस्तारितः -ता -तं, दलितः &c. *See* EXPANDED.
UNFORESEEN, *a.* अदृष्टः -ष्टा -ष्टं, अप्रदृष्टः &c., अनपेक्षितः -ता -तं.
UNFORGIVING, *a.* दीर्घद्वेषी -षिणी -षि (न्), अक्षमावान् -वती -वत् (त्).
UNFORMED, *a.* अकृतः -ता -तं, असंस्कृतः &c., अनाकारः -रा -रं.
UNFORTUNATE, *a.* दुर्भाग्यः -ग्या -ग्यं, अधन्यः -न्या -न्यं, दुर्दैवः -वा -वं, मन्दभाग्यः -ग्या -ग्यं, हतभाग्यः &c., हतदैवः -वा -वं, दैवोपहतः -ता -तं, अश्रीमान् -मती -मत् (त्), विपन्नः -न्ना -न्नं, आपन्नः &c., विपद्युक्तः -क्ता -क्तं, विपद्ग्रस्तः -स्ता -स्तं, आपद्ग्रस्तः &c., आपदम्प्राप्तः -प्ता -प्तं, अलक्ष्मीकः -का -कं, अलक्ष्मीवान् &c., दुर्भगः -गा -गं, विफलारम्भः -म्भा -म्भं, तपस्वी -स्विनी &c., अनिष्टः -ष्टा -ष्टं, अमङ्गलः -ला -लं, अकल्याणः &c., अकुशलः &c., अभद्रः &c.
UNFORTUNATELY, *adv.* दुर्दैववशात्, दौर्भाग्यवशात्, दौर्भाग्येन.
UNFOUNDED, *a.* अमूलकः -का -कं, निर्मूलः -ला -लं, अवास्तवः -वी -वं, मिथ्या in comp.; 'unfounded accusation,' मिथ्याभिशंसनं.
UNFREQUENT, *a.* विरलः -ला -लं, विरलागतः &c. *See* INFREQUENT.
UNFREQUENTED, *a.* निर्जनः -ना -नं, विजनः &c., अलोकसेवितः &c.
UNFRIENDLINESS, *s.* अमित्रता, अप्रियता, अप्रीतिः *f.*, अननुकूलता.
UNFRIENDLY, *a.* अप्रियः -या -यं, विप्रियः &c., अहितः &c., अहितेच्छुः -च्छुः -च्छु, अस्नेही -हिनी &c., गतसौहृदः -दा -दं, अस्निग्धः &c.
UNFRUITFUL, *a.* अफलः -ला -लं, निष्फलः &c., विफलः &c., अफलदः -दा -दं, फलहीनः -ना -नं, वन्ध्यः -न्ध्या -न्ध्यं.
UNFRUITFULNESS, *s.* अफलत्वं, निष्फलता, वैफल्यं, फलहीनता.
UNFULFILLED, *a.* अपूर्णः -र्णा -र्णं, असम्पूर्णः &c., अपरिपूर्णः &c.
To UNFURL, *v. a.* शिथिलीकृ, मुच्, समुत्क्षिप्. *See To* LOOSE, *v. a.*
UNFURNISHED, *a.* असज्जः -ज्जा -ज्जं, असज्जितः -ता -तं, रिक्तः -क्ता -क्तं.
UNGAINLY, *a.* अदक्षः -क्षा -क्षं, असुन्दरः -री -रं. *See* CLUMSY.
UNGENEROUS, *a.* अनुदारः -रा -रं, अल्पमनस्कः -स्का -स्कं.
UNGENTLEMANLY, UNGENTEEL, *a.* असभ्यः -भ्या -भ्यं, असभ्यवृत्तिः -त्तिः -त्ति, अशिष्टवृत्तिः &c., सभ्यव्यवहारविरुद्धः -द्धा -द्धं.
UNGODLINESS, *s.* अधर्म्मः -र्म्मता, अधार्म्मिकत्वं, ईश्वराभक्तिः *f.*
UNGODLY, *a.* अधर्म्मचारी &c., अनीश्वरः -रा -रं. *See* IRRELIGIOUS.
UNGOVERNABLE, *a.* अशासनीयः -या -यं, अशास्यः &c., दुःशासनः -ना -नं, दुर्निग्रहः -हा -हं, अदम्यः -म्या -म्यं, अवश्यः &c., उच्छृङ्खलः &c., दुर्निवारः -रा -रं, अनिवार्य्यः &c., दुर्निवार्य्यः &c., अनायत्तः &c.
UNGRACIOUS, *a.* अननुग्राही -हिणी &c., निरुपकारी &c., अनुपकारी &c.
UNGRAMMATICAL, *a.* व्याकरणविरुद्धः -द्धा -द्धं, व्याकरणाननुसारी &c., शब्दशास्त्रविरुद्धः &c.; 'expression,' अपशब्दः, अपभ्रंशः.
UNGRATEFUL, *a.* अकृतज्ञः -ज्ञा -ज्ञं, कृतघ्नः -घ्नी -घ्नं, उपकृतघ्नः &c., अकृतवेदी &c., उपकारानभिज्ञः -ज्ञा -ज्ञं, अप्रत्युपकारी &c., विस्मृतोपकारः -रा -रं, अनुपकारी &c. *See* INGRATE.
UNGUARDED, *a.* अरक्षितः -ता -तं, अगुप्तः -प्ता -प्तं, विपालः -ला -लं.
UNGUENT, *s.* विलेपनं, अनुलेपनं, अभ्यञ्जनं, उपदेहः, *see* OINTMENT.
UNHALLOWED, *a.* असंस्कृतः -ता -तं, अपुण्यः -ण्या -ण्यं, अपवित्रः -त्रा -त्रं.
UNHAPPILY, *adv.* असुखेन, दुःखेन, असौख्येन, अस्वास्थ्येन, अतिदुःखितवत्.
UNHAPPINESS, *s.* असुखं, असौख्यं, दुःखं, अकल्याणं, अकुशलं, अशर्म्म *n.*, अनिर्वृतिः *f.*, अक्षेमः, अभद्रं, निरानन्दता, अस्वास्थ्यं. *See* MISERY.
UNHAPPY, *a.* असुखी -खिनी -खि (न्), दुःखी &c., दुःखितः -ता -तं, निरानन्दः -न्दा -न्दं, अहर्षी -र्षी -र्षि, अहर्षितः -ता -तं, अशर्म्मी -र्म्मी -र्म्मि (न्), अनिर्वृतः -ता -तं, अधन्यः -न्या -न्यं, मन्दभाग्यः &c.
UNHARMED, *a.* अक्षतः -ता -तं, अपरिक्षतः &c. *See* UNHURT.
UNHATCHED, *a.* अण्डस्थः -स्था -स्थं, अण्डस्थायी -यिनी -यि (न्).
UNHEALTHY, *a.* असुस्थः -स्था -स्थं, अस्वस्थः &c., सदारोगी -गिणी &c., रोगी -गिणी &c., सरोगः -गा -गं. *See* SICKLY, INSALUBRIOUS.
UNHEARD, *a.* अश्रुतः -ता -तं, अनाकर्णितः &c., अश्रुतपूर्व्वः &c.
UNHEEDED, *a.* अनपेक्षितः -ता -तं, उपेक्षितः &c., अवधीरितः &c.
UNHINGED, *a.* विसन्धितः -ता -तं, विसन्धीकृतः &c., विसन्धीभूतः &c.
UNHOLY, *a.* अपुण्यः -ण्या -ण्यं, अपवित्रः -त्रा -त्रं, अपूतः -ता -तं.
UNHURT, *a.* अक्षतः -ता -तं, अपरिक्षतः &c., अहतः &c., अनाहतः &c., अजातापकारः -रा -रं, अप्राप्तापकारः &c., निर्व्रणः -णा -णं.
UNICORN, *s.* एकशृङ्गः, खड्गः. *See* RHINOCEROS.
UNIFORM, *a.* एकरूपः -पा -पं, समरूपः &c., समानरूपः &c., समानः -ना -नं, समः -मा -मं, सरूपः &c., एकाकारः -रा -रं, समाकारः &c., एकाकृतिः -तिः -ति, समाकृतिः &c., एकप्रकारः -रा -रं, एकभावः -वा -वं, निर्विकारः &c., अविशेषः -षा -षं, कूटस्थः -स्था -स्थं; 'of uniform thickness,' समानस्थौल्यविशिष्टः -ष्टा -ष्टं.
UNIFORM, *s.* सैन्यवेषः, सैन्यवेशः, सैन्यदलविशेषको वेशः.
UNIFORMITY, *s.* एकरूपता, समरूपता, सारूप्यं, समानरूपता, समता, समानता, साम्यं, समभावः, अविशेषः.
UNIFORMLY, *adv.* समरूपेण, समानरूपेण, सदा, सर्व्वदा.
UNILITERAL, *a.* एकवर्णः -र्णा -र्णं, एकाक्षरकः -का -कं.
UNIMPAIRED, *a.* अक्षतः -ता -तं, अविकलः -ला -लं, अलुप्तः -प्ता -प्तं, अन्यूनः -ना -नं, अनूनः &c., अक्षुण्णः -ण्णा -ण्णं, अनपायः -या -यं, अनुज्झितः -ता -तं, अहतः &c., अक्षीणः &c., अशीर्णः &c., अह्रसितः &c.
UNIMPEACHABLE, *a.* अनिन्द्यः -न्द्या -न्द्यं, अदूषणीयः &c., अदूष्यः &c.
UNIMPEDED, *a.* अविघ्नितः -ता -तं, अविघ्नः &c., अविरोधितः -ता -तं, निष्प्रत्यूहः -हा -हं, अनन्तरायः -या -यं, अविहतः -ता -तं, अनुद्घातः -ता -तं, अविघातगतिः -तिः -ति, निर्निरोधः -धा -धं, असरुद्धः -द्धा -द्धं.
UNIMPORTANT, *a.* लघुः -घुः -घ्वी -घु. *See* LIGHT, TRIFLING.
UNINHABITABLE, *a.* अवास्तव्यः -व्या -व्यं, अवसत्यः &c., अवासयोग्यः &c.
UNINHABITED, *a.* निर्जनः -ना -नं, निर्मनुष्यः -ष्या -ष्यं, निर्मानुषः -षा -षं, निष्पुरुषः &c., पुरुषशून्यः -न्या -न्यं, पुरुषवर्जितः -ता -तं, निष्प्रजः -जा -जं, अप्रजः &c., प्रजाहीनः -ना -नं, वसतिहीनः &c.
UNINJURED, *a.* अक्षतः -ता -तं, अहिंसितः &c. *See* UNHURT.
UNINTELLIGIBLE, *a.* अबोध्यः -ध्या -ध्यं, अबोधनीयः &c., *see* OBSCURE.
UNINTENTIONAL, UNINTENTIONALLY. *See* UNDESIGNED, &c.
UNINTERESTING, *a.* अमनोरञ्जकः -का -कं, अहृदयङ्गमः -मा -मं.
UNINTERRUPTED, *a.* अखण्डितः -ता -तं, निरन्तरः -रा -रं, निरन्तरायः &c., अभग्नः -ग्ना -ग्नं, अविच्छिन्नः -न्ना -न्नं, अपरिच्छिन्नः &c., अविरतः &c.
UNINTERRUPTEDLY, *adv.* निरन्तरं, अविच्छिन्नं, अविरतं, अविरलं.

UNINVITED, *a.* अनाहूतः -ता -तं, अहूतः &c., अनिमन्त्रितः &c.

UNION, *s.* संयोगः, योगः, सन्धिः *m.*, सङ्गः, सम्भूतिः *f.*, *see* JUNCTION.

UNIPAROUS, *a.* एकप्रसूः *f.*, एकसूः *f.*, एकोत्पादिका.

UNIQUE, *a.* एकः -का -कं, एकमात्रः &c. *See* SINGULAR.

UNISON, *s.* स्वरैक्यं, नादैक्यं, ऐक्यं, एकता -त्वं. *See* CONCORD.

UNIT, *s.* एकः, एकाङ्कः, अद्वयं.

UNITARIAN, *s.* अद्वैतवादी *m.* (न्), अद्वयवादी *m.* *See* UNITY.

To UNITE, *v. a.* युज्, संयुज्, सन्धा, एकीकृ, *see To* JOIN, *v. a.*

To UNITE, *v. n.* संयुज् in pass., एकीभू, एकचित्तीभू, *see To* JOIN, *v. n.*

UNITED, *p. p.* संयुक्तः -क्ता -क्तं, संयोजितः &c. *See* JOINED.

UNITEDLY, *a.* एकचित्तीभूय, सम्भूय, एकीभूय, योगतस्.

UNITY, *s.* एकता -त्वं, ऐक्यं, अद्वैतं, अद्वयं; 'the doctrine of unity,' अद्वैतमतं, अद्वैतवादः, अभेदः, अभेदमतं, अभेदवादः, ऐक्यं, निर्द्वन्द्वं; 'holding it,' अद्वैतवादः, अद्वैतदृष्टिः *f.*, अभेदबुद्धिः *f.*; 'holder of it,' अद्वैतवादी *m.*, ऐक्यवादी *m.*, अभेदवादी *m.*, निर्द्वन्द्वः, निर्विकल्पः. As opposed to this is the doctrine of duality, or the assertion of two principles, viz. God and matter. It is termed द्वैतं, द्वैतमतं, द्वैतवादः, भेदमतं, &c.

UNIVERSAL, *a.* (Of place) सार्व्वत्रिकः -की -कं, सर्व्वव्यापी -पिनी &c., सर्व्वत्रव्यापी &c., सर्व्वगतः -ता -तं.—(Of persons, &c.) सर्व्वः -र्व्वा -र्व्वं, सार्व्वः -र्व्वी -र्व्वं, सार्व्वलौकिकः -की -कं, सर्व्वसाधारणः -णा -णी -णं, सर्व्वसम्बन्धी &c., *see* GENERAL; 'spirit,' अखिलात्मा *m.*

UNIVERSALITY, *s.* सार्व्वत्रिकत्वं, सर्व्वसाधारण्यं, सर्व्वव्यापिता.

UNIVERSALLY, *adv.* सर्व्वत्र, सर्व्वतस्, विश्वतस्, विष्वक्.

UNIVERSE, *s.* जगत्सर्व्वं, जगत्कृत्स्नं, जगत्समग्रं, जगत् *n.*, सर्व्वजगत् *n.*, जगती, सर्व्वजगती, विश्वं, विश्वजगत्, चराचरं, विश्वचराचरं, संसारः, लोकः, विश्वलोकः, ब्रह्माण्डं, ब्रह्मगोलः, सृष्टिः *f.*, भूतसृष्टिः *f.*, ब्रह्मसृष्टिः *f.*, प्रत्यक्षसृष्टिः *f.*, त्रिभुवनं, त्रैलोक्यं, ब्रह्माण्डकटाहः, विराड्देहः; 'soul of it,' जगदात्मा *m.* (न्), लोकात्मा *m.*, विश्वात्मा *m.*, परमात्मा *m.*, ब्रह्म *n.* (न्), सूक्ष्मं; 'lord of it,' अधिलोकनाथः.

UNIVERSITY, *s.* विद्यालयमण्डलं, विद्यालयगणः, शालामण्डलं, महाविद्यालयः, राजविद्यालयः, अनेकपाठशालासमूहः.

UNJUST, *a.* (Of persons) अधार्म्मिकः -की -कं, अधर्म्मी -र्म्मिणी &c., निर्धर्म्मः -र्म्मा -र्म्मं, अधर्म्मचारी &c., अन्यायाचारी &c., अन्यायशीलः -ला -लं, अन्यायानुवर्त्ती &c., नीतिहीनः -ना -नं, धर्म्मविमुखः -खा -खं.—(Of actions, &c.) अन्याय्यः -य्या -य्यं, अयथार्थः -र्था -र्थं, अयाथार्थिकः -की -कं, न्यायविरुद्धः -द्धा -द्धं, विषमः -मा -मं, असमञ्जसः -सा -सं, मिथ्या or मृषा in comp.; 'unjust accusation,' मिथ्याभिशंसनं.

UNJUSTIFIABLE, *a.* अनिरसनीयदोषः -षा -षं, अयथान्यायः -या -यं.

UNJUSTLY, *adv.* अन्यायतस्, अधर्म्मतस्, अधर्म्मेण, अयुक्तं.

UNKIND, *a.* अप्रियः -या -यं, अस्निग्धः -ग्धा -ग्धं, विप्रियः -या -यं, अप्रीतः -ता -तं, कृपाहीनः -ना -नं, अकृपः -पा -पं, निष्कृपः &c., निर्दयः -या -यं, दयाहीनः &c., अस्नेही &c., स्नेहहीनः &c., अप्रियङ्करः -रा -रं, अननुग्राही &c., अनुपकारशीलः -ला -लं, गतसौहृदः -दा -दं.

UNKINDLY, *adv.* अप्रियं, अप्रीत्या, अस्नेहेन, अकृपया, अस्निग्धं.

UNKINDNESS, *s.* अप्रीतिः *f.*, अप्रीतता, अप्रियता, अस्नेहः, अदया, अकृपा, अहितता.—(Unkind act) अपकारः, अपकृतं, अहितं.

UNKNOWN, *a.* अज्ञातः -ता -तं, अविदितः &c., अननुभूतः &c., अपरिचितः &c., अगोचरः -रा -रं; 'unknown quantity,' अव्यक्तराशिः *m.*

UNLAWFUL, *a.* अधर्म्यः -र्म्या -र्म्यं, विधिविरुद्धः -द्धा -द्धं, स्मृतिविरुद्धः &c., राजनियमविरुद्धः &c., व्यवस्थाविरुद्धः &c., धर्म्मविरुद्धः &c., धर्म्मरोधी -धिनी &c., धर्म्मशास्त्रविरुद्धः &c., शास्त्रविरुद्धः &c., धर्म्मघ्नः -घ्नी -घ्नं, अस्मार्त्तः -र्त्ती -र्त्तं. *See* ILLEGAL.

UNLAWFULLY, *adv.* अधर्म्मेण, अधर्म्मतस्, विधिविरोधेन, स्मृतिविरोधेन, धर्म्मशास्त्रविरुद्धं, व्यवस्थाविरोधेन. *See* ILLEGALLY.

UNLAWFULNESS, *s.* विधिविरुद्धता, स्मृतिविरुद्धता, *see* ILLEGALITY.

UNLEAVENED, *a.* अकिण्वः -ण्वा -ण्वं; 'bread,' अकिण्वपूपः.

UNLEARNED, *a.* अविद्वान् -दुषी -द्वत् (स्), अकृताध्ययनः -ना -नं, अनधीतः &c., अज्ञानी &c., अज्ञः &c., अवेद्यः &c., *see* ILLITERATE.

UNLESS, *conj.* यदि न, चेन् न, न चेत्, अन्यत्र, वर्ज्जयित्वा, *see* EXCEPT, *prep.*; 'unless you do that,' यदि तन् न करोषि or expressed by the indec. part., with अ prefixed, तद् अकृत्वा.

UNLIKE, *a.* असदृशः -शी -शं, असमः -मा -मं, असमानः -ना -नं, अनीदृशः -शी -शं, अतुल्यः -ल्या -ल्यं, भिन्नः -न्ना -न्नं, अन्यः -न्या -न्यत्.

UNLIKELY, *a.* असम्भवः -वा -वं, दुःसम्भाव्यः &c. *See* IMPROBABLE.

UNLIMITED, *a.* निरवधिः -धिः -धि, अनन्तः -न्ता -न्तं, अप्रान्तः &c., अतिवेलः -ला -लं, अपारः -रा -रं, अतिक्रान्तः &c. *See* INFINITE.

To UNLOAD, *v. a.* भारम् उत्तॄ (c. 10. -तारयति -यितुं) or अवतॄ or अवरुह् in caus. (-रोपयति -यितुं), निर्भारीकृ, रिक्तभारीकृ, रिक्तीकृ; 'a ship,' नौकाभारम् उत्तॄ, नौकास्थद्रव्याणि उत्तॄ or अवरुह् in caus.

UNLOADED, *p. p.* उत्तारितभारः -रा -रं, निर्भारः &c., रिक्तः -क्ता -क्तं.

To UNLOCK, *v. a.* उद्घट् (c. 10. -घाटयति -यितुं), विमुद्रीकृ, उन्मुद्रीकृ, विमुद्र् (nom. -मुद्रयति -यितुं), उन्मुद्र्, उद्घट्ट् (c. 10. -घट्टयति -यितुं).

UNLOCKED, *p. p.* उद्घाटितः -ता -तं, उद्घट्टितः &c., उन्मुद्रः -द्रा -द्रं.

UNLOOKED FOR, *a.* अनपेक्षितः -ता -तं, अदृष्टः -ष्टा -ष्टं, अतर्कितः &c.

To UNLOOSE, *v. a.* शिथिलीकृ, उन्मुच्. *See To* LOOSE, LOOSEN, *v. a.*

UNLUCKY, *a.* निर्भाग्यः -ग्या -ग्यं, अमङ्गलः &c. *See* UNFORTUNATE.

To UNMAN, *v. a.* पौरुषभङ्गं कृ, पौरुषं हृ, पौरुषहीनं -नां कृ.

UNMANAGEABLE, *a.* असाध्यः -ध्या -ध्यं, अविधेयः -या -यं, दुरुपचारः -रा -रं, दुरासदः -दा -दं, विषमः -मा -मं, दुर्विनेयः &c.

UNMANLY, *a.* पौरुषहीनः -ना -नं, पुरुषानर्हः -र्हा -र्हं, पुरुषायोग्यः -ग्या -ग्यं, अपुरुषः -षा -षं, अमनुष्यः &c., क्लीबः -बा -बं.

UNMANNERLY, *a.* अशिष्टः -ष्टा -ष्टं, असभ्यवृत्तिः -त्तिः -त्ति, *see* RUDE.

UNMARKED, *a.* निर्लक्षणः -णा -णं, अलक्षितः -ता -तं, अचिह्नितः &c.

UNMARRIED, *a.* अविवाहितः -ता -तं, अनूढः -ढा -ढं, अनुद्वाहितः &c., निरूढः &c., अकृतविवाहः -हा -हं, अजातविवाहः &c., अकृतोद्वाहः &c., अकृतदारसंग्रहः, वटुः; 'woman,' अनूढा, अपरिणीता, अप्रत्ता, अदत्ता, निवरा, अवरा, अपतिः *f.*, अपतिका, अभर्तृका; 'elder brother unmarried,' परिवित्तः, परिवित्तिः *m.*

To UNMASK, *v. a.* छद्मवेशं हृ, कपटवेशं or विडम्बनम् अपनी.

UNMATCHED, *a.* अप्रतिमः -मा -मं, अनुपमः &c. *See* MATCHLESS.

UNMEANING, *a.* अनर्थकः -का -कं, निरर्थकः &c., अपार्थः -र्था -र्थं, असम्बद्धः -द्धा -द्धं, अबद्धः &c., असङ्गतः &c. *See* NONSENSICAL.

UNMENTIONABLE, *a.* अवाच्यः -च्या -च्यं, अकथनीयः &c., अवद्यः &c.

UNMERCIFUL, UNMERCIFULLY. *See* PITILESS, PITILESSLY.

UNMERITED, *a.* अयोग्यः -ग्या -ग्यं, अनर्हः &c. *See* UNDESERVED.

UNMINDFUL, *a.* निरपेक्षः -क्षा -क्षं, अनवहितः &c., नष्टसंस्मृतिः &c.

UNMIXED, *a.* अमिश्रितः -ता -तं, असङ्कीर्णः -र्णा -र्णं, अव्यतिकीर्णः &c.

UNMOLESTED, *a.* निरुपद्रवः -वा -वं, निरुपप्लवः &c., अविघ्नितः -ता -तं.

UNMOVED, *a.* स्थिरः -रा -रं, अविचलितः -ता -तं, अचलितः &c., अलोलः -ला -लं, निर्विकारः -रा -रं, अनाविद्धः -द्धा -द्धं; 'in mind,' स्थिर-

मतिः -तिः -ति, स्थिरात्मा -त्मा -त्म (न्).

UNMUSICAL, *a.* विस्वरः -रा -रं, अपस्वरः &c., स्वरशून्यः &c.

UNNATURAL, *a.* (Contrary to natural feelings) मनुष्यधर्म्मविरुद्धः -द्धा -द्धं, मनुष्यधर्म्मप्रतिकूलः -ला -लं, स्वधर्म्मविरुद्धः &c., स्वजातिविरुद्धः &c.—(Contrary to the course of nature) सृष्टिक्रमविरुद्धः &c., सृष्टिक्रमबाह्यः -ह्या -ह्यं, निसर्गविरुद्धः &c., विलक्षणः -णा -णं, विलोमः -मा -मं, विरूपः -पा -पं.—(Forced) प्रतियत्नपूर्व्वः -र्व्वा -र्व्वं, *see* FORCED; 'unnatural state,' अनिसर्गः.

UNNECESSARILY, *adv.* निष्प्रयोजनं, हेतुना विना, वृथा in comp., *see* NEEDLESSLY; 'produced unnecessarily,' वृथोत्पन्नः -न्ना -न्नं.

UNNECESSARY, *a.* निष्प्रयोजनः -ना -नं, निष्कारणः &c., अहेतुकः &c., वृथा in comp., *see* NEEDLESS; 'unnecessary slaughter,' वृथाघातः.

To UNNERVE, *v. a.* बलं or धैर्य्यं or पौरुषं हृ or अपहृ.

UNNUMBERED, *a.* अगणितः -ता -तं, असंख्यातः &c., *see* INNUMERABLE.

UNOBSERVED, *a.* अलक्षितः -ता -तं, अनभिलक्षितः &c., अनुपलब्धः &c.; 'the body wastes unobserved,' कायः क्षीयमाणो न लक्ष्यते.

UNOBSTRUCTED, *a.* अविरुद्धः -द्धा -द्धं, अनिरुद्धः &c., अबाधितः -ता -तं, अबाधः -धा -धं, अप्रतिबन्धः &c., अरुद्धमार्गः -र्गा -र्गं, अहतमार्गः &c., निर्विघ्नः -घ्ना -घ्नं, निरर्गलः &c. *See* UNIMPEDED.

UNOCCUPIED, *a.* निर्व्यापारः -रा -रं, निष्क्रियः -या -यं.

UNOFFENDING, *a.* अनपराधी -धिनी &c., निरपराधी &c. *See* INOFFENSIVE.

UNOWNED, *a.* अस्वामिकः -का -कं, अस्वकीयः -या -यं, अनधिकृतः &c.

To UNPACK, *v. a.* निष्कोषीकृ, भाण्डस्थद्रव्याण्य् उद्धृ or निर्हृ.

UNPAID, *a.* अशोधितः -ता -तं, असाधितः &c., अविगणितः &c.

UNPALATABLE, *a.* अरुच्यः -च्या -च्यं, अरुचिरः -रा -रं, अरुचिकरः &c.

UNPARALLELED, *a.* अतुल्यः -ल्या -ल्यं, अपूर्व्वः -र्व्वा -र्व्वं, अदृष्टपूर्व्वः &c., अश्रुतपूर्व्वः &c., अनुपमः &c., अनौपम्यः &c. *See* MATCHLESS.

UNPARDONABLE, *a.* अक्षन्तव्यः -व्या -व्यं, अक्षमार्हः &c., अक्षमणीयः &c.

UNPERCEIVED, *a.* अलक्षितः -ता -तं, अव्यक्तः &c. *See* UNOBSERVED.

UNPLEASANT, *a.* अप्रियः -या -यं, विप्रियः &c. *See* DISAGREEABLE.

UNPLOUGHED, *a.* अकृष्टः -ष्टा -ष्टं, अहलः -ला -लं, अहल्यः -ल्या -ल्यं.

UNPOLISHED, *a.* अपरिष्कृतः -ता -तं, असंस्कृतः &c., अनुपस्कृतः &c.

UNPOPULAR, *a.* लोकाप्रियः -या -यं, जनाप्रियः &c., अलौकिकः -की -कं.

UNPOPULARITY, *s.* लोकाप्रियता, जनाप्रियता, लोकाग्राह्यता, अलौकिकत्वं.

UNPRACTISED, *a.* अनभ्यस्तः -स्ता -स्तं; 'in arms,' अकृतास्त्रः -स्त्रा -स्त्रं.

UNPRECEDENTED, *a.* अपूर्व्वः -र्व्वा -र्व्वं, अपूर्व्वप्रतिमः -मा -मं, अदृष्टपूर्व्वः &c., अजातपूर्व्वः &c., अयथापूर्व्वः &c.—(In law) प्रकीर्णकं.

UNPREMEDITATED, *a.* अपूर्व्वचिन्तितः -ता -तं, अपूर्व्वकल्पितः &c., अचिन्तापूर्व्वः -र्व्वा -र्व्वं, प्रत्युत्पन्नः -न्ना -न्नं. *See* EXTEMPORANEOUS.

UNPRETENDING, *a.* अनभिमानी -निनी &c., अविकत्थनः &c. *See* UNASSUMING.

UNPRINCIPLED, *a.* अधर्म्मनिष्ठः -ष्ठा -ष्ठं, दुराचारी -रिणी &c., दुर्वृत्तः -त्ता -त्तं, सदसद्विचारहीनः -ना -नं, सदसदुपेक्षकः -का -कं.

UNPRODUCTIVE, *a.* निष्फलः -ला -लं, अजनकः &c. *See* BARREN.

UNPROFITABLE, *a.* अनर्थकरः -रा -रं, अनर्थकः -का -कं, अलाभकरः &c., अफलदः &c., फलाजनकः &c. *See* USELESS, PROFITLESS.

UNPROFITABLENESS, *s.* व्यर्थता, वैयर्थ्यं, आनर्थक्यं, विफलता, अनुपयोगः.

UNPROFITABLY, *a.* व्यर्थतस्, निष्फलं, विफलं, मुधा.

UNPROMISING, *a.* अनाशाजनकः -का -कं, अनाशाकारी -रिणी &c.

UNPROPITIOUS, *a.* अननुकूलः -ला -लं, अकुशलः &c., अमङ्गलः &c.

UNPROTECTED, *a.* अरक्षितः -ता -तं, अशरणः -णा -णं, निष्पालकः -का -कं.

UNPUNISHED, *a.* अदण्डितः -ता -तं, अदण्ड्यः -ण्ड्या -ण्ड्यं, अशासितः &c.

UNQUESTIONABLE, UNQUESTIONABLY. *See* INDUBITABLE, &c.

UNQUIET, *a.* अशान्तः -न्ता -न्तं, अनिर्वृतः -ता -तं, निरास्पदः &c.

To UNRAVEL, *v. a.* उद्ग्रन्थ्, व्याकृ, परिशुध्, *see To* RAVEL, DISENTANGLE.

UNREAL, *a.* अवास्तवः -वी -वं, असन् -सती -सत् (त्), आभासात्मकः -का -कं, असारः -रा -रं, अतथ्यः -थ्या -थ्यं, असत्यः &c., अविद्यमानः -ना -नं, अतात्त्विकः -की -कं, अप्रकृतः -ता -तं. *See* ILLUSORY.

UNREASONABLE, *a.* अन्याय्यः -य्या -य्यं, अयोग्यः &c., अनुपपन्नः &c.

UNREGENERATE, *a.* अपुनर्जातः -ता -तं, अपरिवृत्तमनस्कः -स्का -स्कं.

UNRELENTING, *a.* अयोहृदयः -या -यं, पाषाणहृदयः &c., अकरुणः &c.

UNREMITTING, *a.* अविरतः -ता -तं, सततसमानः &c. *See* INCESSANT.

UNRESERVED, *a.* निःशेषः -षा -षं, निरवशेषः &c., पूर्णः -र्णा -र्णं.

UNRESERVEDLY, *adv.* अशेषतस्, निरवशेषतस्, अशेषेण, अपावृतं.

UNRESISTING, *a.* अप्रतिकारः -रा -रं, अप्रतिकारकः &c., अनिवारकः &c.

UNRESTRAINED, *a.* अयन्त्रितः -ता -तं, अयतः -ता -तं, निर्यन्त्रणः -णा -णं, अनियतः &c., अनियन्त्रितः &c., उच्छृङ्खलः -ला -लं, विशृङ्खलः &c., निरवग्रहः -हा -हं, अवशः -शा -शं, उद्दामः -मा -मं, अनर्गलः -ला -लं, निरर्गलः &c., निरङ्कुशः -शा -शं, असृणिः -णिः -णि, अशृणिः &c., अपावृतः -ता -तं, अनावृतः &c., स्वतन्त्रः &c.

UNREVEALED, *a.* अप्रकाशितः -ता -तं, अप्रकटः &c., अप्रसिद्धः &c.

UNRIGHTEOUS, *a.* अधार्म्मिकः -की -कं, निर्धर्म्मः -र्म्मा -र्म्मं, अन्याय्यः &c.

UNRIGHTEOUSNESS, *s.* अधर्म्मः -र्म्मता, अधार्म्मिकत्वं, अन्यायः, असाधुता.

UNRIPE, *a.* अपक्वः -क्वा -क्वं, अपरिपक्वः &c., आमः -मा -मं, असिद्धः -द्धा -द्धं, अपरिणतः &c., अपरिपूतः &c., शलाटुः -टुः -टु, कषणः &c.

UNRIPENESS, *s.* अपक्वता, अपरिपक्वता, आमता, असिद्धता.

UNRIVALLED, *a.* अनुपमः -मा -मं, निःसपत्नः &c. *See* PEERLESS.

UNRUFFLED, *a.* अक्षुब्धः -ब्धा -ब्धं, निर्विकारः &c., शान्तः -न्ता -न्तं.

UNRULY, *a.* दुःशासनः -ना -नं, अवशः &c., वामशीलः -ला -लं.

UNSAFE, *a.* सभयः -या -यं, भययुक्तः -क्ता -क्तं, अनिर्भयः &c.

UNSALEABLE, *a.* अविक्रेयः -या -यं, अपण्यः &c., अपणितव्यः &c.

UNSATISFACTORY, *a.* असन्तोषकः -का -कं, अतुष्टिजनकः &c., अनिर्णायकः.

UNSAVORY, *a.* विरसः -सा -सं, अस्वादुः &c. *See* INSIPID.

UNSCATHED, *a.* अक्षतः -ता -तं, अपरिक्षतः &c. *See* UNHURT.

UNSCRIPTURAL, *a.* अशास्त्रीयः -या -यं, शास्त्रविरुद्धः -द्धा -द्धं, अयथाशास्त्रः &c., अशास्त्रः &c., अशास्त्रोक्तः -क्ता -क्तं, अवेदोक्तः &c., निर्वेदः &c.

UNSCRUPULOUS, *a.* अशङ्की &c., निःशङ्कः -ङ्का -ङ्कं, शङ्काहीनः &c.

To UNSEAL, *v. a.* विमुद्र (nom. विमुद्रयति -यितुं), उन्मुद्र, उन्मुद्रीकृ.

UNSEALED, *a.* उन्मुद्रः -द्रा -द्रं, विमुद्रः &c., मुद्रारहितः -ता -तं.

UNSEARCHABLE, *a.* अतर्क्यः -र्क्या -र्क्यं, दुर्ज्ञेयः &c., अलक्ष्यः &c., दुर्लक्ष्यः &c.; 'whose ways are unsearchable,' अनुपलक्ष्यवर्त्मा *m.*

UNSEASONABLE, *a.* आकालिकः -की -कं, अकालजः -जा -जं, अकाल in comp., *see* INOPPORTUNE; 'rising of clouds,' अकालमेघोदयः.

UNSEASONABLENESS, UNSEASONABLY. *See* INOPPORTUNE, &c.

UNSEEMLY, *a.* अयोग्यः -ग्या -ग्यं, अयुक्तः -क्ता -क्तं, अनुपयुक्तः &c.

UNSEEN, *a.* अदृष्टः -ष्टा -ष्टं, अलक्षितः -ता -तं, अलोकितः &c., अनवलोकितः &c., अनालोचितः &c., अगोचरः -रा -रं. *See* INVISIBLE.

UNSELFISH, *a.* अस्वार्थदृष्टिः -ष्टिः -ष्टि, अनात्मनीनः -ना -नं, निर्ममः &c.

UNSERVICEABLE, *a.* अनुपयुक्तः -क्ता -क्तं, निष्प्रयोजनः &c., व्यर्थः &c.

To UNSETTLE, *v. a.* अस्थिरीकृ, अनवस्थितीकृ, अव्यवस्थितं -तां कृ.

UNSETTLED, *a.* अस्थिरः -रा -रं, अनवस्थितः -ता -तं, अव्यवस्थितः &c.

UNSHACKLED, *a.* विशृङ्खलः -ला -लं, उच्छृङ्खलः &c., अशृङ्खलितः &c.

UNSHAKEN, *a.* अक्षुब्धः -ब्धा -ब्धं, निश्चलः -ला -लं, अकम्पितः &c.

To UNSHEATH, *v. a.* विकोष (nom. विकोषयति -यितुं), विकोषीकृ.

UNSHEATHED, *a.* विकोषः -षा -षं, विकोषीकृतः &c., उच्छ्वसितः &c.

UNSHORN, *a.* अकृतक्षौरः -रा -रं, अकृतचूडः &c., अलूनः -ना -नं.

UNSIGHTLY, *a.* कुदृश्यः -श्या -श्यं, दुर्दर्शनः &c., अदर्शनीयः &c.

UNSKILFUL, *a.* अदक्षः -क्षा -क्षं, अकुशलः -ला -लं, अनिपुणः -णा -णं, अप्रवीणः &c., अनभिज्ञः &c., अदक्षिणः &c. *See* AWKWARD.

UNSKILFULNESS, *s.* अकौशल्यं, अदक्षता, अप्रवीणता, अनैपुण्यं.

UNSOCIABLE, *a.* जनसंसर्गविमुखः -खी -खं, जनसङ्गविमुखः &c., संलापविमुखः &c., असंसर्गशीलः &c., अपरिचेयः &c.

UNSOLICITOUS, *a.* निश्चिन्तः -न्ता -न्तं, अप्रयत्नः &c., प्रयत्नशून्यः &c.

UNSOPHISTICATED, *a.* अदूषितः -ता -तं, अकृत्रिमः &c., शुद्धः -द्धा -द्धं.

UNSOUND, *a.* असुस्थः -स्था -स्थं, असारः -रा -रं, क्षीणसारः &c., सदोषः &c., *see* HOLLOW.—(As doctrine) युक्तिविरुद्धः &c.

UNSPEAKABLE, *a.* अकथनीयः -या -यं, शब्दातिगः &c., *see* INEFFABLE.

UNSTABLE, *a.* अस्थिरः -रा -रं, अधीरः &c., अध्रुवः -वा -वं, अनवस्थितः -ता -तं, अधैर्य्यः &c., चञ्चलः &c. *See* INCONSTANT.

UNSTEADINESS, *s.* अस्थिरता, अस्थैर्य्यं, चञ्चलता, चाञ्चल्यं, अनवस्थितिः *f.*, व्यभिचारः, चपलता, चापल्यं, अधीरत्वं.

UNSTEADY, *a.* अस्थिरः -रा -रं, अधीरः &c., अनवस्थितः -ता -तं, चलस्वभावः -वा -वं, विचलः -ला -लं, व्यभिचारी &c. *See* FICKLE.

UNSTRUNG, *p.p.* उद्ग्रन्थितः -ता -तं, उद्ग्रथितः &c., उत्सूत्रः -त्रा -त्रं, शिथिलितः &c.; 'as a bow,' शिथिलज्यः -ज्या -ज्यं.

UNSUBSTANTIAL, *a.* अवास्तवः -वी -वं, असारः &c. *See* UNREAL.

UNSUCCESSFUL, *a.* (Of persons) अकृतार्थः -र्था -र्थं, अप्राप्तार्थः &c.—(Of things) मोघः -घा -घं, विफलारम्भः &c., निष्फलः -ला -लं.

UNSUCCESSFULLY, *adv.* अकृतार्थतस्, निष्फलं, मोघं, असफलं.

UNSUITABLE, *a.* अयोग्यः -ग्या -ग्यं, अयुक्तः -क्ता -क्तं, अनुपयुक्तः &c., अनुचितः -ता -तं, अस्थानः -ना -नं, अयथातथः &c. *See* IMPROPER.

UNSUITABLENESS, UNSUITABLY. *See* IMPROPRIETY, &c.

UNSUITED, *a.* अयुक्तः -क्ता -क्तं, अनुपयुक्तः &c., विहितः -ता -तं.

UNSULLIED, *a.* निष्कलङ्कः -ङ्का -ङ्कं, निर्मलः -ला -लं, अदूषितः &c.

UNSUPPORTED, *a.* अनालम्बः -म्बा -म्बं, अनवलम्बः &c., निराधारः &c.

UNSURMOUNTABLE, *a.* अलंघ्यः -घ्या -घ्यं, अनतिक्रमणीयः &c., दुरतिक्रमः &c.

UNSURPASSED, *a.* अनतिक्रान्तः -न्ता -न्तं, अजितः &c., अनभिभूतः &c.

UNSUSPECTED, *a.* अशङ्कितः -ता -तं, अतर्कितः &c., असन्दिग्धः -ग्धा -ग्धं.

UNSUSPECTING, *a.* अनाशङ्की &c., अशङ्की &c., अशङ्काशीलः -ला -लं.

UNTAINTED, *a.* अगन्धयुक्तः -क्ता -क्तं, पूतिगन्धरहितः &c., अविकृतः &c.

UNTAMABLE, *a.* अदम्यः -म्या -म्यं, दुर्दमः -मा -मं, अशृक्यः &c.

UNTENABLE, *a.* अप्रतिपाद्यः -द्या -द्यं, अप्रतिपादनीयः &c., अस्थापनीयः &c.

UNTHANKFUL, UNTHANKFULNESS. *See* UNGRATEFUL, &c.

UNTIDY, UNTIDINESS. *See* SLOVENLY, SLOVENLINESS.

To UNTIE, *v. a.* उद्ग्रन्थ्, उन्मुच्, प्रमुच्, शिथिलीकृ, उन्नह् (c. 4. -नह्यति -नद्धुं), उत्सूत्रीकृ, उच्छ्वसनं कृ, विसन्धीकृ. *See* *To* LOOSE, *v. a.*

UNTIED, *p. p.* उद्ग्रन्थितः -ता -तं, उद्ग्रथितः &c., उन्नद्धः -द्धा -द्धं, विगलितः &c., उत्सूत्रः &c., उच्छ्वसितः &c., विघट्टितः &c. *See* LOOSED.

UNTIL, *prep.* यावत्, पर्य्यन्तं, आ prefixed to the abl. *See* TILL.

UNTILLED, *a.* अकृष्टः -ष्टा -ष्टं, अप्रहतः &c. *See* UNCULTIVATED.

UNTIMELY, *a.* आकालिकः -की -कं, अकालजः -जा -जं, अकालभवः -वा -वं, *see* INOPPORTUNE; 'death,' अपमृत्युः *m.*, अपघातः.

UNTO, *prep.* पर्य्यन्त or अन्त in comp., आ prefixed, अन्तिकं. *See* TO.

UNTOLD, *a.* अकथितः -ता -तं, अनुक्तः -क्ता -क्तं, अनाख्यातः &c., असन्दिष्टः -ष्टा -ष्टं, अगणितः &c., असंख्यातः &c.

UNTOUCHED, *a.* अस्पृष्टः -ष्टा -ष्टं, अस्पर्शितः &c., अपृक्तः -क्ता -क्तं.

UNTOWARD, *a.* विषमः -मा -मं, प्रत्यवायः -या -यं. *See* PERVERSE.

UNTRACTABLE, *a.* अवश्यः -श्या -श्यं, दुर्विधेयः &c. *See* INTRACTABLE.

UNTRIED, *a.* अपरीक्षितः -ता -तं, अप्रतीतः &c., अकृतपरीक्षः -क्षा -क्षं.

UNTRODDEN, *a.* अपादाहतः -ता -तं, पादास्पृष्टः &c., पादाक्रान्तहीनः &c.

UNTRUE, *a.* असत्यः -त्या -त्यं, अतात्त्विकः -की -कं. *See* FALSE, &c.

UNTRUTH, *s.* असत्यं, अनृतं, वितथं, अलीकं. *See* FALSEHOOD.

To UNTWIST, UNTWINE, *v. a.* उद्ग्रन्थ्, समुद्ग्रन्थ्. *See* *To* UNRAVEL.

UNUSED, *a.* अनभ्यस्तः -स्ता -स्तं, अनासादितः &c. *See* UNACCUSTOMED.

UNUSUAL, *a.* अप्रसिद्धः -द्धा -द्धं, अव्यावहारिकः -की -कं, अपूर्व्वः -र्व्वा -र्व्वं, अजातपूर्व्वः &c., अदृष्टपूर्व्वः &c., लोकरीतिविरुद्धः -द्धा -द्धं, जनरीतिविरुद्धः &c., अनाचारिकः &c., असाम्प्रदायिकः &c., नानुष्ठेयः -या -यं; 'unusual occurrence,' संविधानकं, *see* RARE.

UNUTTERABLE, *a.* वाग्विभवातिवृत्तः -त्ता -त्तं. *See* INEXPRESSIBLE.

UNWARY, *a.* अनवधानः -ना -नं, निरपेक्षः -क्षा -क्षं, प्रमादी -दिनी &c.

UNWAVERING, *a.* अविचलः -ला -लं, निश्चलः &c. *See* FIRM, CONSTANT.

UNWEARIED, *a.* अश्रान्तः -न्ता -न्तं, अविषादः &c. *See* INDEFATIGABLE.

UNWELCOME, *a.* अनिष्टः -ष्टा -ष्टं, अप्रियः -या -यं, दुरागतः &c.

UNWELL, *a.* अस्वस्थः -स्था -स्थं, असुस्थः &c. *See* under ILL, *a.*

UNWHOLESOME, *a.* अपथ्यः -थ्या -थ्यं, कुपथ्यः &c., अपथ्यकारकः -का -कं, असात्म्यः -त्म्या -त्म्यं, रुजाकरः -रा -रं, गरदः -दा -दं, विषमः -मा -मं, विरुद्धः -द्धा -द्धं, *see* INSALUBRIOUS; 'food,' अपथ्यं; 'eater of it,' अपथ्याशी *m.* (न्).

UNWHOLESOMENESS, *s.* अपथ्यता, असात्म्यं. *See* INSALUBRITY.

UNWIELDY, *a.* स्थूलः -ला -लं, अतिस्थूलः &c., अतिभारी -रिणी &c.

UNWILLING, *a.* अनिच्छुः -च्छुः -च्छु, अनिच्छन् -च्छन्ती -च्छत् (त्), निष्कामः -मा -मं, विमुखः -खा -खं, पराङ्मुखः &c. *See* RELUCTANT.

UNWILLINGLY, UNWILLINGNESS. *See* RELUCTANTLY, RELUCTANCE.

To UNWIND, *v. a.* उद्ग्रन्थ्, समुद्ग्रन्थ्. *See* *To* UNRAVEL.

UNWISE, *a.* निर्बुद्धिः -द्धिः -द्धि, अविद्वान् &c. *See* FOOLISH.

UNWORTHILY, *adv.* अयथार्हं -र्हतस्, अयोग्यं, अनुपयुक्तं, अयुक्तं.

UNWORTHINESS, *s.* अनर्हत्वं -ता, अयोग्यता, अनार्य्यता -त्वं, अपात्रता -त्वं, अनुपयुक्तता, निर्गुणत्वं, अगुणता, गुणाभावः, गुणहीनता.

UNWORTHY, *a.* अनर्हः -र्हा -र्हं, अयोग्यः -ग्या -ग्यं, अनुपयुक्तः -क्ता -क्तं, अनार्य्यः -र्य्या -र्य्यं, अनुचितः -ता -तं, निर्गुणः -णा -णं, गुणहीनः -ना -नं, अगुणी &c.; 'an unworthy object,' अपात्रं; 'an unworthy act,' अकार्य्यं; 'unworthy of eating with the good,' साधुभिः सह एकत्र भोजनानर्हः -र्हा -र्हं.

UNWRITTEN, *a.* अलिखितः -ता -तं, मुखकथितः &c. *See* ORAL.

UNWROUGHT, *a.* अकृतः -ता -तं, असंस्कृतः &c.; 'silver,' अकृतरूप्यं.

UNYIELDING, *a.* अनायम्यः -म्या -म्यं, अशिथिलः -ला -लं. *See* FIRM.

To UNYOKE, *v. a.* वियुज् (c. 7. -युनक्ति -योक्तुं, c. 10. -योजयति -यितुं).

UP, *prep.* or *adv.* उत् prefixed, ऊर्द्ध्वं, उच्चैः, उच्चकैः; 'looking up,' उन्मुखः -खा -खं, ऊर्द्ध्वदृष्टिः -ष्टिः -ष्टि; 'to look up,' ऊर्द्ध्वं दृश्; 'to rise up,' उत्था; 'to go up,' उद्गम्; 'to lift up,' उत्तुल्; 'having the feet up,' ऊर्द्ध्वपादः -दा -दं, ऊर्द्ध्वचरणः &c.—(Up and down) उन्नतानतः -ता -तं, निम्नोन्नतः &c., उच्चावचः -चा -चं; 'ups and downs,' पातोत्पाताः *m. pl.*; 'moving up and down,' समुद्वहन् -हन्ती &c., *see* UNDULATING.—(Up to) पर्य्यन्तं, यावत्, आ,

see under To.—(To an equal height with) द्वघ्नः -घ्नी -घ्नं, द्वयसः -सी -सं, मात्रः -त्री -त्रं; 'water up to the knees,' जानुदघ्नं जलं.

Upanishad, *s.* उपनिषद् *f.* *See* under Scripture.

Upapurána, *s.* उपपुराणं. *See* under Purána, Scripture.

Upas-tree, *s.* (Poison tree) विषवृक्षः, विषपादपः.

To upbraid, *v. a.* निन्द्, उपालभ्. *See To* reproach.

Upheld, *p. p.* उत्तम्भितः -ता -तं, आलम्बितः &c., समुद्धृतः &c.

Uphill, *a.* उत्क्रमस्थः -स्था -स्थं, उत्क्रमणीयः &c., आरोहणीयः &c.

To uphold, *v. a.* उत्तम्भ्, आलम्ब्, धृ, सम्भृ. *See To* support.

Upholsterer, *s.* गृहसज्जाविक्रेता *m.* (तृ), गृहोपस्करकर्त्ता *m.*

Upland, *s.* अधित्यका, उच्चभूमिः *f.*, उच्चदेशः, उच्चभूः *f.*

To uplift, *v. a.* उत्था in caus., उत्तम्, उद्यम्. *See To* raise.

Uplifted, *a.* उद्यतः -ता -तं, उच्छ्रितः &c., अभ्युच्छ्रितः &c., ऊर्द्ध or उत् in comp., *see* Raised; 'with uplifted arm,' उद्बाहुः -हुः -हु, ऊर्द्धबाहुः &c.; 'with uplifted sword,' उद्यतासिः, *see* Raised.

Upon, *prep.* or *adv.* उपरि, अधि, नि, उप, प्रति. *See* On.

Upper, *a.* ऊर्द्धः -र्द्धा -र्द्धं, ऊर्द्धस्थः -स्था -स्थं, उपरिस्थः &c., ऊर्द्धस्थितः -ता -तं, उत्तरः -रा -रं, उत्तरीयः -या -यं, उपरितनः -नी -नं, उत्कृष्टः -ष्टा -ष्टं; 'the upper part of the body,' ऊर्द्धकायः; 'upper line,' ऊर्द्धपंक्तिः *f.*; 'upper chamber,' उपरिस्थप्रकोष्ठः, अट्टः, अट्टालः; 'upper garment,' उत्तरीयं, उत्तरासङ्गः, वरूथं, बृहतिका; 'upper half,' पूर्व्वार्द्धं.

Uppermost, *a.* सर्व्वोपरिस्थः -स्था -स्थं, सर्व्वोर्द्धस्थः &c., उत्तमः -मा -मं, सर्व्वोत्तमः &c.; 'with the end uppermost,' ऊर्द्धाग्रः -ग्रा -ग्रं.

Upraised, *a.* उन्नमितः -ता -तं, उन्नतः &c., उद्धृतः &c., उत्क्षिप्तः &c., समुद्धृतः &c., *see* Raised; 'as the eyelid,' उत्पक्ष्मलः -ला -लं.

Upright, *a.* (Erect) उन्नतः -ता -तं, ऋजुः -जुः -जु, ऋजुकः &c., *see* Erect; 'standing upright,' दण्डः, दण्डवत् स्थायी -यिनी &c., दण्डायमानः -ना -नं.—(In character) सरलः -ला -लं, सच्चरितः -ता -तं, शुद्धमतिः &c., सत्यात्मा &c., *see* Just, Honest.

Uprightly, *adv.* (Erectly) दण्डवत्, ऋजु, आर्जवेन, *see* Justly.

Uprightness, *s.* ऋजुता, आर्जवं, दाक्षिण्यं. *See* Integrity.

Uproar, *s.* कोलाहलः, तुमुलं, हाहाकारः, हलहलाशब्दः, डमरः, डामरः, जनरवः, रासः, कलहः, सम्भ्रमः. *See* Riot.

To uproot, *v. a.* उन्मूल्, समुन्मूल्. *See To* root up.

To upset, *v. a.* पर्यस्, परावृत्, परिवृत्. *See To* overturn.

Upset, *s.* पर्यासः, परिवर्त्तनं, *see* Overturn; 'of a boat,' नौमज्जनं.

Upshot, *s.* गतिः *f.* *See* Result, Consequence.

Upside-down, *a.* अधोमुखः -खी -खं, अधरोत्तरः &c., ऊर्द्धाधरः &c.

Upstart, *s.* आगमनुकः, आगन्तुः *m.*, नवश्रीमान् *m.* (त्).

Upward, upwards, *adv.* ऊर्द्धं, उच्चैः, उच्चकैः, उपरि, उपर्य्युपरि; 'with feet upwards,' ऊर्द्धपादः -दा -दं.—(More than) अधिकं, परं; 'upwards of a thousand,' परःसहस्रः -स्रा -स्रं.

Urbanity, *s.* सुजनता, सौजन्यं, सुशीलता. *See* Politeness.

Urchin, *s.* दुष्टबालकः, कुरूपबालकः, अर्भकः, शिशुः *m.*

Urethra, *s.* (In anatomy) मूत्रमार्गः, मूत्रपथः, मूत्रद्वारं.

To urge, *v. a.* प्रेर्, प्रणुद्, चुद्, प्रचुद्, संचुद्, बाध्, प्रबाध्, आक्रम्, उत्क्षिप्, निर्बन्धं कृ. *See To* press, instigate.

Urged, *p. p.* प्रेरितः -ता -तं, चोदितः &c., प्रचोदितः &c., बाधितः &c.

Urgency, *s.* (Importunacy) निर्बन्धः, अतिनिर्बन्धः, आग्रहः.—(Pressure) प्रेरणा, बाधः -धनं, प्रणोदः, भारः.

Urgent, *a.* बाधकः -का -कं, प्रबाधकः &c., निर्बन्धी -न्धिनी &c.

Urgently, *adv.* निर्बन्धेन, अतिनिर्बन्धेन, आग्रहेण, सबाधं.

Urinal, *s.* मूत्रपात्रं, मूत्राधारः, मूत्रभाजनं.

Urinary, *a.* मूत्रलः -ला -लं, मेही -हिनी -हि (न्), मूत्रसम्बन्धी &c., मूत्र in comp.; 'urinary affection,' मूत्रदोषः, मूत्रकृच्छ्रं.

Urine, *s.* मूत्रं, प्रस्रावः, मेहः -हनं, वस्तिमलं, गुह्यनिष्यन्दः; 'milky urine,' मूत्रशुक्रं; 'passing blood in urine,' रक्तप्रमेहः; 'passing mucus,' लालामेहः; 'suppression of urine,' मूत्ररोधः, मूत्रावरोधः, मूत्रस्तम्भः, मूत्राघातः; 'affection of the urine,' मेहः, प्रमेहः, मेहनशूलः -लं. Of these, twenty-one varieties are enumerated, *see* Diabetes, Gonorrhœa, &c.; 'one suffering from this affection,' मेही *m.*, प्रमेही *m.*

To urine, *v. n.* मूत्र् (c. 10. मूत्रयति -यितुं), मिह्. *See To* piss.

Urn, *s.* जलकुम्भः, जलपात्रं, जलभाजनं, कुम्भः.

Uroscopy, *s.* मूत्रपरीक्षा -क्षणं, मेहपरीक्षा -क्षणं.

Ursa major, *s.* सप्तर्षयः *m. pl.* (-र्षि), चित्रशिखण्डिनः *m. pl.*

Usage, *s.* (Treatment) व्यापारः, व्यवहारः.—(Custom, practice) व्यवहारः, आचारः, रीतिः *f.*, धारा, चर्य्या -र्य्या, प्रचारः, मार्गः, अनुसारः -सरणं; 'family usage,' कुलाचारः, वंशसमाचारः.

Use, *s.* (Employment, application of any thing) प्रयोगः, उपयोगः, प्रयोजनं, प्रयुक्तिः *f.*, व्यापारः, व्यवहारः, सेवनं, उपभोगः, भोगः, योगः; 'use of any article,' द्रव्यप्रयोजनं; 'in general use,' रूढः -ढा -ढं, प्रचलः -ला -लं, सर्व्वप्रयुक्तः &c.; 'out of use,' अव्यवहृतः -ता -तं; 'to make use of,' *see To* use.—(Utility) उपयोगः -गित्वं, उपकारः, अर्थः, फलं, प्रयोजनं; 'what's the use of that to me?' को ऽर्थो मे तेन; 'this instrument is of great use in giving warning of a storm,' इदं यन्त्रं झञ्झावातागमज्ञापकम् अत्युपकारकं; 'of what use?' किमर्थं.—(Occasion for) प्रयोजनं, *see* Need.—(Practice) व्यवहारः, अभ्यासः, अभ्यसनं, प्रचारः.—(For pious uses) धर्म्मार्थं.

To use, *v. a.* (Employ, apply to any purpose) प्रयुज् (c. 7. -युनक्ति -युंक्ते -योक्तुं, c. 10. -योजयति -यितुं), उपयुज्, युज्, सेव् (c. 1. सेवते -वितुं), उपसेव्, विधा, उपभुज्, अभ्यस्, व्यवहृ in caus., व्यापृ in caus., धृ in caus., *see To* employ.—(Make use of, enjoy) प्रयुज्, भुज् (c. 7. भुंक्ते, भोक्तुं), उपभुज्.—(Practise) अभ्यस् (c. 4. -अस्यति -सितुं), अनुष्ठा (c. 1. -तिष्ठति -ष्ठातुं), आस्था, समास्था, आश्रि (c. 1. -श्रयति -यितुं), *see To* practise.—(Habituate) अभ्यस्तं -स्तां कृ, अभ्यस्तीकृ, अभ्यासं कृ.—(To be used), *see* Used.

To use, *v. n.* (Be accustomed) अभ्यस्तः -स्ता -स्तं भू. This verb must often be idiomatically rendered by इति with a noun, and the adverb पूर्व्वं; as, 'it used to be so,' इति पूर्व्वं व्यवहारो वर्त्तते or अवर्त्तत.

Used, *p. p.* (Employed, made use of) प्रयुक्तः -क्ता -क्तं, प्रयोजितः -ता -तं, उपयोजितः &c., व्यवहृतः &c., व्यवहारितः &c., सेवितः &c., उपसेवितः &c., भुक्तः -क्ता -क्तं, उपभुक्तः &c., कृतोपभोगः -गा -गं, धृतः -ता -तं, अभ्यस्तः -स्ता -स्तं; 'clothes used by another,' अन्येन प्रयुक्तं or उपभुक्तं or धृतं वस्त्रं; 'to be used,' प्रयुज् in pass. (-युज्यते), विधा in pass. (-धीयते), सेव् in pass. (सेव्यते), सेव्यतां गम् or या.—(Accustomed) अभ्यस्तः -स्ता -स्तं, कृताभ्यासः -सा -सं, शिक्षितः -ता -तं, अनुभूतः &c.; 'to pain,' अनुभूतवेदनः -ना -नं.

USEFUL, *a.* उपकारकः -का -कं, उपकारी -रिणी -रि (न्), सोपकारः -रा -रं, महोपकारः &c., उपयोगी -गिनी &c., प्रयोगी &c., सार्थकः -का -कं, सार्थः -र्था -र्थं, उपकारकरः -रा -रं, उपकारकारी &c., हितकरः &c., हितकारकः &c., हितः -ता -तं, उपयुक्तः -क्ता -क्तं, योग्यः -ग्या -ग्यं, अर्थकरः &c., अर्थदः -दा -दं, अर्थवान् &c. *See* PROFITABLE.

USEFULLY, *adv.* सोपकारं, सार्थं, सहितं, सफलं, अवृथा, अमुधा.

USEFULNESS, *s.* उपयोगः -गिता, उपकारकता -त्वं, सोपकारत्वं, उपकारित्वं, सार्थत्वं, सार्थकत्वं, हितता, उपयुक्तता, सफलता.

USELESS, *a.* निरर्थकः -का -कं, व्यर्थः -र्था -र्थं, अनर्थः &c., अनर्थकः &c., अनुपयोगी -गिनी &c., निष्प्रयोजनः -ना -नं, निरुपयोगः -गा -गं, अप्रयोजकः -का -कं, अनुपयुक्तः -क्ता -क्तं, असार्थकः -का -कं, अपार्थः &c., अदर्थः &c., किमर्थः &c., निष्कारणः -णा -णं, उपयोगहीनः -ना -नं, विफलः -ला -लं, निष्फलः &c., अयोग्यः &c., अनुपपन्नः -न्ना -न्नं, वृथा in comp.; as, 'useless expense,' वृथाव्ययः.

USELESSLY, *adv.* निरर्थकं, व्यर्थतस्, अनुपयोगेन, वृथा, मुधा.

USELESSNESS, *s.* अनुपयोगः -गिता, व्यर्थता, वैयर्थ्यं, निरर्थकत्वं -ता, अनर्थकत्वं, आनर्थक्यं, उपयोगहीनता, उपयोगाभावः.

USER, *s.* प्रयोक्ता *m.* (क्तृ), भोक्ता *m.*, उपभोक्ता *m.*, स्वादकः -का.

USHER, *s.* (Introducer) प्रवेशकः.—(Under-master) उपशिक्षकः.

To USHER, *v. a.* प्रविश् (c. 10. -वेशयति -यितुं). *See To* INTRODUCE.

USUAL, *a.* व्यावहारिकः -की -कं, व्यवहारिकः &c., प्रायिकः -की -कं, प्रसिद्धः -द्धा -द्धं, लोकप्रसिद्धः &c., लौकिकः -की -कं, यथाव्यवहारः -रा -रं, आचारिकः &c., साम्प्रदायिकः &c., यथारीतिः -तिः -ति, यथासम्प्रदायः -या -यं, यौगिकः &c. *See* CUSTOMARY, COMMON.

USUALLY, *adv.* प्रायशस्, प्रायस्, प्रायेण, सामान्यतस्, साधारण्येन, यथारीति, यथाव्यवहारं, बाहुल्येन, बहुशस्.

USUFRUCT, *s.* भोगः, उपभोगः, फलभोगः, फलभुक्तिः *f.*, भुक्तिः.

USURER, *s.* कुसीदिकः, कौसीदिकः, वार्द्धुषिकः, वार्द्धुषी *m.* -षिः *m.*, कलोपजीवी *m.*, वृद्धिजीवी *m.*, जीवकः, द्वैगुणिकः, *see* MONEY-LENDER.

USURIOUS, *a.* सवृद्धिकः -का -कं, वार्द्धुषिकः -की -कं, कौसीदः -दी -दं.

To USURP, *v. a.* (Seize without right) अनधिकारपूर्व्वं ग्रह्, अनधिकारेण हृ or धृ or आक्रम्, बलेन or बलात्कारेण ग्रह्; 'the throne,' अनधिकारपूर्व्वं राज्यापहारं कृ or राज्यं ग्रह् or अवाप्.

USURPATION, *s.* अनधिकारपूर्व्वं ग्रहणं or आक्रमणं, अनधिकारेण or बलात्कारेण अवाप्तिः *f.*; 'of the throne,' राज्यापहारः -हरणं.

USURPER, *s.* राज्यापहारी *m.* (न्), राज्यहर्त्ता *m.* (न्), आक्रन्दः.

USURY, *s.* कुसीदं, कौसीदं, वार्द्धुष्यं, वृद्धिः *f.*, कुसीदपथः, कुसीदजीवनं, अर्थप्रयोगः, वृद्धिजीविका, प्रयोगः, प्रतिषिद्धवृद्ध्युपजीवित्वं.

USUS LOQUENDI, *s.* रूढिः *f.*, वृत्तिः *f.*, रूढवृत्तिः *f.*, वाग्वृत्तिः *f.*

UTENSIL, *s.* भाण्डं, उपकरणं, उपस्करः, पात्रं, भाजनं, यन्त्रं, अमत्रं; 'domestic,' गृहोपकरणं, गृहोपस्करः; 'culinary,' पाकभाण्डं, पाकपात्रं, स्थालं -ली.

UTERINE, *a.* (Pertaining to the womb) गार्भिकः -की -कं, गार्भः -र्भी -र्भं, यौनः -नी -नं, गर्भाशयसम्बन्धी &c.—(Of the same womb) सहोदरः -रा -रं, एकयोनिः -निः -नि, समयोनिसम्भवः -वा -वं, सोदरः -रा -रं, एकोदरः &c., समानोदरः &c., सनाभिः -भिः -भि.

UTERUS, *s.* योनिः *m. f.*, गर्भकोशः, गर्भाशयः. *See* WOMB.

UTILITY, *s.* उपयोगः -गिता, अर्थः. *See* USEFULNESS, USE.

UTMOST, *a.* उत्तमः -मा -मं, परमः &c., परः -रा -रं, *see* EXTREME; 'the utmost limit,' परममर्य्यादा, परमावधिः *m.*, परमसीमा, परावधिः *m.*; 'to the utmost,' परमं, अत्यन्तं; 'to the utmost of one's power,' यावच्छक्यं, यथाशक्ति, यथाबलं; 'to do one's utmost,' यावच्छक्यं यत्.

UTOPIAN, *a. see* CHIMERICAL; 'scheme,' कल्पनासृष्टिः *f.*

UTTER, *a.* सम्पूर्णः -र्णा -र्णं, परिपूर्णः &c. *See* COMPLETE.

To UTTER, *v. a.* उच्चर् (c. 10. -चारयति -यितुं), उदीर् (c. 10. -ईरयति -यितुं), समुदीर्, ईर्, उदाहृ (c. 1. -हरति -हर्त्तुं), व्याहृ, समुदाहृ.

UTTERABLE, *a.* उच्चारणीयः -या -यं, उच्चार्य्यः &c., उदीर्य्यः &c.

UTTERANCE, *s.* उच्चारः -रणं, उदीरणं, उदाहरणं, व्याहरणं, व्याहारः, उल्लेखः -खनं, उद्गारः; 'easy of utterance,' सुखोच्चार्य्यः -र्य्या -र्य्यं, सुखोच्चः -च्चा -च्चं.

UTTERED, *p. p.* उच्चारितः -ता -तं, उदीरितः &c., उदाहृतः &c., समुदाहृतः &c., व्याहृतः &c., निगदितः &c., उदितः &c., निरस्तः -स्ता -स्तं, उक्तः -क्ता -क्तं; 'being uttered,' उदीर्य्यमाणः -णा -णं.

UTTERLY, *adv.* निरवशेषं, अशेषतस्, सर्व्वथा. *See* WHOLLY.

UTTERMOST, *a.* परमः -मा -मं, उत्तमः &c. *See* UTMOST.

UVULA, *s.* प्रतिजिह्वा, उपजिह्वा -ह्विका, अधोजिह्विका, अलिजिह्वा -ह्विका, तालुजिह्वा, घण्टिका, शुण्डिका, गलशुण्डिका, लोला, लम्बिका, शूना, सूना, पुला.

UXORIOUS, *a.* भार्य्यासक्तः, स्त्रीवुद्धिः *m.*, जायासक्तः, स्त्रीविधेयः, दयिताधीनः, स्वदारनिरतः, कामी *m.* (न्), घस्मरः.

UXORIOUSNESS, *s.* भार्य्यासक्तिः *f.*, जायासक्तता, दयिताधीनता.

V.

VACANCY, *s.* शून्यता -त्वं, रिक्तता -त्वं, शून्यं, रिक्तं.—(Of a throne, &c.) अराजकत्वं, अनायकत्वं, अस्वामिकत्वं.

VACANT, *a.* (Empty) शून्यः -न्या -न्यं, रिक्तः -क्ता -क्तं, वितानः -ना -नं, खिलः -ला -लं.—(Unoccupied) अस्वामिकः -का -कं, अनायकः &c.; 'as a throne,' अराजकः -का -कं.—(Empty of thought,' विचारलक्षणशून्यः -न्या -न्यं; 'vacant gaze,' शून्येक्षणं.

To VACATE, *v. a.* उत्सृज् (c. 6. -सृजति -स्रष्टुं), त्यज्, शून्यीकृ.

VACATION, *s.* अवकाशः, अध्ययनविरामः, अध्ययननिवृत्तिः *f.*, अनध्यायः.

To VACCINATE, *v. a.* रक्तवरटीनिवारणार्थं or वसन्तरोगनिवारणार्थं गोस्फोटपूयलवं बाहुमांसे निविश् (c. 10. -वेशयति -यितुं).

VACCINATION, *s.* बाहुमांसे गोस्फोटपूयलवनिवेशनं.

VACCINE, *a.* गव्यः -व्या -व्यं, गोसम्बन्धी &c., गोविषयकः -का -कं.

To VACILLATE, *v. n.* दोल (nom. दोलायते), विचल्. *See To* WAVER.

VACILLATION, *s.* चञ्चलत्वं -ता, चापल्यं, विचलनं, आन्दोलनं.

VACUITY, *s.* शून्यता, रिक्तता, शून्यं, रिक्तं, शुषिरं, खं, *see* HOLE.

VACUUM, *s.* शून्यं, रिक्तं, शून्यता, रिक्तता -त्वं, निर्वातं.

VAGABOND, *a.* or *s.* अध्वगः -गा -गं, पर्य्यटः -टा -टं, अवनिचरः &c., भ्रमी -मिणी -मि (न्), परिभ्रमी &c., भ्रमणकारी &c., देशाटनकारी *m.*

VAGARY, *s.* मनोलौल्यं, बुद्धिविलासः, बुद्धिचापल्यं, उन्मार्गः.

VAGRANCY, *s.* अध्वभ्रमणं, अध्वपर्य्यटनं, मार्गपरिभ्रमणं.

VAGRANT, *s.* मार्गपरिभ्रमी *m.* (न्), अशुद्धवासकः. *See* VAGABOND.

VAGUE, *a.* अनियतः -ता -तं, अविवक्षितः &c. *See* INDETERMINATE.

VAGUENESS, *s.* अनियतत्वं, अनिर्णयः, अविवक्षा, अविवक्षितत्वं.

VAIN, *a.* (Empty, worthless) शून्यः -न्या -न्यं, रिक्तः -क्ता -क्तं, असारः -रा -रं, निःसारः &c., निरर्थकः &c., *see* EMPTY.—(Fruitless, unavailing) निरर्थकः -का -कं, अनर्थकः &c., व्यर्थः -र्था -र्थं, मोघः -घा -घं, निष्फलः -ला -लं, अदर्थः &c., अपार्थः -र्था -र्थं, वृथा in comp.; 'indulging vain hopes,' मोघाशः -शा -शं.—(Conceited) अभिमानी -निनी -नि (न्), आत्माभिमानी &c., मानी &c., अहङ्कारी &c.,

साभिमानः -ना -नं, साहङ्कारः -रा -रं, अहम्मानी &c., गर्व्वितः -ता -तं, *see* CONCEITED; 'of one's appearance,' दर्शनीयमानी &c.—(In vain) वृथा, मुधा, *see* VAINLY; 'laboring in vain,' वृथोद्यमः -मा -मं, भग्नोद्यमः &c.

VAIN-GLORIOUS, *a.* *See* BOASTFUL, BOASTER, PROUD.

VAINLY, *adv.* वृथा, मुधा, मोघं, व्यर्थतस्, व्यर्थं, निष्फलं.

VAIŚYA, *s.* (Man of the third tribe, or of the class of merchants and husbandmen, fabled as sprung from the thigh of Brahmá) वैश्यः, विट् *m.* (श्), ऊरुजः, ऊरव्यः, अर्य्यः, भूमिस्पृक् *m.* (श्).

VALE, *s.* दरी -रा, ईषन्निम्नभूमिः *f.* *See* VALLEY.

VALEDICTION, *s.* आमन्त्रणं, आपृच्छनं, आशीर्वादः, प्रास्थानिकाशीर्वचनं, प्रस्थानकाले स्वस्तिवचनं, प्रास्थानिकस्वस्तिवचनं.

VALEDICTORY, *a.* आमन्त्रयिता -त्री -तृ (तृ), आशीर्वादी -दिनी &c., स्वस्तिवाचनिकः -की -कं, आशीर्वादात्मकः -का -कं, स्वस्तिवचनरूपः &c.

VALERIAN, *s.* (Plant) जननी, मिषिः -षी *f.*, प्रव्रजिता.

VALET, *s.* पार्श्विकः, वस्त्रपरिकल्पकः, पार्श्वानुचरः, सैरिन्ध्रः.

VALETUDINARIAN, *s.* स्वास्थ्यार्थी *m.* (न्), आरोग्यार्थी *m.*, सदारोगी *m.*

VALIANT, *a.* विक्रान्तः -न्ता -न्तं, वीरः -रा -रं, उरुविक्रमः -मा -मं, भटः -टा -टं, ऊर्जितः &c., *see* HEROIC; 'is valiant,' विक्रमते -ति, पराक्रमति.

VALID, *a.* (Sound, just, that can be supported) सप्रमाणः -णा -णं, सुप्रमाणकः -का -कं, सिद्धप्रमाणः &c., सुप्रामाणिकः -की -कं, बलप्रमाणकः -का -कं, प्रबलः -ला -लं, सबलः &c., अखण्डनीयः -या -यं, सिद्धः -द्धा -द्धं, धर्म्यः -र्म्या -र्म्यं, अविशुद्धः -द्धा -द्धं, निष्पन्नः -न्ना -न्नं, बलवान् -वती &c., सप्रभावः -वा -वं, दृढः -ढा -ढं.—(Having legal force) व्यवहारोपयोगी -गिनी &c., व्यवहारसमर्थः -र्था -र्थं, व्यवहारसाधकः -धिका -कं.

VALIDITY, *s.* सप्रमाणता -त्वं, सबलता, प्रबलता, प्राबल्यं, प्रभावः, सप्रभावत्वं, अखण्डनीयता, सिद्धिः *f.*, सिद्धता, निष्पत्तिः *f.*, धर्म्यता.—(In law) व्यवहारोपयोगिता, व्यवहारसामर्थ्यं.

VALLEY, *s.* दरी -रा, कन्दरः -री, दरीभूः *f.*, दरीभूमिः *f.*, उपत्यका, द्रोणी, पर्व्वतद्रोणी, अद्रिद्रोणी, निम्नभूः *f.*, निम्नभूमिः *f.*, प्रान्तरं, शैलोपशल्यं, पर्व्वतद्वयमध्यभूमिः *f.*

VALOUR, *s.* वीर्य्यं, शौर्य्यं, विक्रमः, पराक्रमः. *See* HEROISM.

VALOROUS, *a.* विक्रान्तः -न्ता -न्तं, शूरः -रा -रं. *See* VALIANT.

VALUABLE, *a.* महामूल्यः -ल्या -ल्यं, बहुमूल्यः &c., महार्घः -र्घा -र्घं, अर्घ्यः -र्घ्या -र्घ्यं, अर्घार्हः -र्हा -र्हं, महार्हः &c., बहुमानयितव्यः -व्या -व्यं, महोपकारकः &c., गुणवान् -वती -वत् (त्). *See* PRECIOUS.

VALUATION, *s.* मूल्यनिरूपणं, मूल्यस्थापनं -ना, अर्घस्थापनं -ना, मूल्यप्रमाणस्थापनं, अर्घपरिमाणनिरूपणं, मूल्यनिर्णयः.

VALUE, *s.* (Price) मूल्यं, अर्घः, *see* PRICE.—(Degree of price) मूल्यप्रमाणं, अर्घप्रमाणं, मूल्यपरिमाणं, अर्घमितिः *f.*, मितिः *f.*, *see* RATE.—(High rate or estimation) महामूल्यं, बहुमूल्यं, महार्घः, बहुमानं, बहुमतिः *f.*—(Real worth) सारता.

To VALUE, *v. a.* मूल्यं निरूप् or स्था in caus., *see* *To* RATE.—(Esteem) मन् (c. 10. मानयति -यितुं), *see* *To* ESTEEM; 'highly,' बहु मन्.

VALUED, *p. p.* or *a.* बहुमतः -ता -तं, बहुमानितः &c., सम्मानितः &c.

VALVE, *s.* कपाटः, कपाटयुक्तद्वारं, पिधानं, सपिधानद्वारं.

VAMPIRE, *s.* राक्षसः, पिशाचः. *See* DEMON.

VAN, *s.* (Of an army, &c.) सेनामुखं, अभिनीमुखं, सेनाग्रं, रणमूर्द्धा *m.* (न्), समरमूर्द्धा *m.*, नासीरं, धारः, शिरस् *n.*; 'in the van,' सेनामुखे, अग्रतस्, अग्रे, पुरस्तात्, पुरतस्.

VAN-GUARD, *s.* सेनापुरःसरं, अग्रेसरसैन्याः *m. pl.*, अग्रगसैन्याः.

VANE, *s.* वायवीदिशालक्षणं, वायुलक्षणं, वायुध्वजः.

To VANISH, *v. n.* अन्तर्धा in pass., तिरोभू. *See* *To* DISAPPEAR.

VANISHED, *p. p.* अन्तर्हितः -ता -तं, नष्टः -ष्टा -ष्टं. *See* DISAPPEARED.

VANITY, *s.* (Emptiness, fruitlessness) शून्यता, रिक्तता, निःसारता, व्यर्थता, निरर्थकता, वैयर्थ्यं, मोघता; 'music, dancing, and such-like vanity,' तूर्य्यवादित्रनृत्यादि असत्कार्य्यं.—(Conceit) अहङ्कारः, आत्माभिमानं, अभिमानं, अहम्मानं, अहम्मतिः *f.*, मानं, गर्व्वः, *see* CONCEIT.

To VANQUISH, *v. a.* जि (c. 1. जयति, जेतुं). *See* *To* CONQUER.

VANTAGE, VANTAGE-GROUND. *See* SUPERIORITY.

VAPID, *a.* विरसः -सा -सं, नीरसः &c., निस्सारः &c. *See* FLAT.

VAPOROUS, VAPORY, *a.* बाष्परूपः -पा -पं, बाष्पमयः -यी -यं.

VAPOUR, *s.* बाष्पः, स्वेदः, धूमः -मिका, फेनः -नता, खबाष्पः; 'hot vapour,' उष्णबाष्पः; 'sultry vapour,' मृगतृष्णा, *see* MIRAGE; 'vapour-bath,' उष्मस्वेदः, उष्णस्वेदः.

To VAPOUR, *v. n.* विकत्थ् (c. 1. -कत्थते -त्थितुं). *See* *To* BOAST, BULLY.

VARIABLE, *a.* अस्थिरः -रा -रं, अनवस्थः -स्था -स्थं, चञ्चलः -ला -लं, विषमः -मा -मं, अनित्यः &c., अनवस्थानः &c. *See* INCONSTANT.

VARIABLENESS, *s.* अस्थिरता, वैषम्यं, विषमता, चाञ्चल्यं, वैरूप्यं.

VARIANCE, *s.* भेदः, द्वैधं, विरोधः, वैमनस्यं, *see* DIFFERENCE, *s.*; 'at variance,' परस्परविरुद्धः -द्धा -द्धं, विप्रतिपन्नः -न्ना -न्नं, विमतः &c.

VARIATION, *s.* भेदः, परिवृत्तिः *f.*, विकारः, अन्यथात्वं. *See* CHANGE.

To VARIEGATE, *v. a.* चित्र (c. 10. चित्रयति -यितुं), चित्रीकृ, शबलीकृ, कर्बुर (nom. कर्बुरयति -यितुं), कर्बुरीकृ. *See* *To* DIVERSIFY.

VARIEGATED, *a.* चित्रः -त्रा -त्रं, चित्रविचित्रः &c., चित्रितः -ता -तं, विचित्रः -त्रा -त्रं, कर्बुरः -रा -रं, कर्बुरितः -ता -तं, शबलः -ला -लं, शबलीकृतः -ता -तं, नानावर्णः -र्णा -र्णं, नानारूपः -पा -पं, शारः -री -रं, शारितः -ता -तं, सारङ्गः -ङ्गी -ङ्गं, अनुविद्धः -द्धा -द्धं, कबरः -रा -रं, किर्म्मीरः -रा -रं, कर्म्मीरः &c., कल्माषः -षा -षी -षं, एतः -ता -ती -तं.

VARIETY, *s.* (Diversity) वैचित्र्यं, विचित्रता, भिन्नता &c.—(Difference in kind) भेदः, प्रभेदः, विभेदः.—(In colour, &c.) चित्रता, नानावर्णता, कर्बुरता, शबलता, शारता.

VARIOUS, *a.* विविधः -धा -धं, अनेकः -का -कं, नानाविधः &c., व्याविधः &c., पृथग्विधः &c., नानारूपः -पी -पं, नानाप्रकारः -रा -रं, नानाजातीयः -या -यं, नाना prefixed, नैकः -का -कं, नैकभेदः -दा -दं, उच्चावचः -चा -चं, *see* SUNDRY, MANIFOLD; 'in various ways,' अनेकधा, नानारूपेण, *see* VARIOUSLY; 'various reading,' पाठान्तरं. The prep. वि sometimes expresses the sense of 'various;' as, 'various employment,' विकर्म्म *n.* (न्).

VARIOUSLY, *adv.* अनेकधा, बहुधा, नानारूपेण, नानाप्रकारेण, नानाविधेन, पृथग्विधेन, बहुविधेन, नाना, विविधं.

VARNISH, *s.* कुङ्कुभः -भका, तेजोदायकतैलं, शोभादायकतैलं.

To VARNISH, *v. a.* कुङ्कुभेन स्निग्धीकृ or तेजो दा, बाह्यशोभां दा.

VARUNA, *s.* (God of the waters, the Hindú Neptune, Regent of the West. He is also Lord of punishment, in which capacity he resembles Yama and Śiva) वरुणः, प्रचेताः *m.* (स्), वारुणीवल्लभः.—(As lord of the waters) अपाम्पतिः *m.*, अप्पतिः *m.*, जलपतिः *m.*, केशः, केशगर्भः.—(As lord of aquatic animals

यादसाम्पतिः m., यादःपतिः m., यादसांनाथः.—(As holding the cord, with which he binds incorrigible offenders under the water) पाशी m. (न्), पाशभृत् m., पाशपाणिः m. His consort is called वरुणानी, वरुणी. His son चर्षणिः m., चर्षणः, वारुणिः m. His váhana or vehicle is a fish.

To VARY, *v. a.* अन्यरूपीकृ, भिन्नरूपीकृ, अन्यथा कृ, विपर्यस्, परिवृत् in caus., विद्, भेदं कृ, भिन्नीकृ, *see To* CHANGE.

To VARY, *v. n.* अन्यथा भू, अन्यरूपीभू, भिन्नरूपीभू, भिन्नीभू, भिन्नः -न्ना -न्नं भू, परिवृत् (c. 1. -वर्त्तते -र्त्तितुं), *see To* CHANGE, DIFFER.

VASCULAR, *a.* नाडीसम्बन्धी &c., नाडीमयः -यी -यं, नाडीविशिष्टः &c.

VASE, *s.* पात्रं, भाजनं, कुम्भः, कलशः -शी; 'golden vase,' गड्डुकः -डूकः, गडुकः, भृङ्गारः, कनकालुका, कनकालुः *f.*

VASSAL, VASSALAGE. *See* DEPENDANT, DEPENDANCE.

VAST, *a.* सुमहान् -हती -हत् (त्), अतिमहान् &c., अतिवृहन् -हती &c., अपरिमितः -ता -तं, पुलः -ला -लं. *See* HUGE, IMMENSE.

VASUDEVA, *s.* (Father of Krishna, and son of Śúra, called Ánakadundubhi, because at his birth the gods sounded with joy the drums of heaven, as foreseeing that Vishnu would take a human form in one of his family) वसुदेवः, आनकदुन्दुभिः m., दुन्दुः.

VAT, *s.* महाभाण्डं, वृहद्भाण्डं; 'indigo vat,' नीलभाण्डं.

VAULT, *s.* (Arched roof) खोडकशीर्षं, *see* ARCH; 'vault of heaven,' खगोलः, नभोमण्डलं.—(Cellar) गुप्तिः *f.*—(Leap) वल्गितं.

To VAULT, *v. a.* or *n.* वल्ग्, लङ्घ्, प्लु. *See To* LEAP, JUMP.

To VAUNT, VAUNTER, VAUNTING. *See To* BOAST, BRAG, &c.

VEAL, *s.* गोवत्समांसं, वत्समांसं, वत्सामिषं.

VEDA, *s.* वेदः. This is the name given to the four most ancient sacred books of the Hindús, viz. the Rich or Rig-veda ऋग्वेदः, the Yajus or Yajurveda यजुर्वेदः, the Sáman or सामवेदः, and the Atharvan or Atharva-veda अथर्ववेदः. Of these the Rig-veda is the most celebrated. It consists of metrical hymns or prayers termed súktas or mantras, each stanza of which is called a rich, addressed chiefly to the gods of the elements, Fire, Air, the Sun, &c., and ascribed to different holy authors or Rishis. The Yajurveda consists principally of prayers and invocations applicable to the consecration of the utensils and materials of sacrificial worship. It is divided into two parts, the white and black, the former of which is attributed to the saint Yájnavalkya, and the latter to Tittiri. The Sáma-veda is little else than a recast of the Rig-veda, being made up of many of the same hymns, broken into parts and arranged anew for the purpose of being chanted during various expiatory ceremonies. The Atharva-veda has little in common with the other three in its character or style. Its language indicates a different and later era, and it may therefore be regarded as a supplement to the three others. Hence it is that many passages are found in Sanskrit writings which limit the number of Vedas to three. Each of the Vedas consists of two distinct component parts, viz. the Mantra portion, and the Bráhmana portion. The Mantra portion is a collection or Sanhitá of súktas, or hymns as above described, the composition of which is supposed to have taken place about twelve or thirteen centuries B. C.; the Bráhmana portion is a collection of rules for the repetition of the Mantras at certain particular ceremonies, with directions for the performance of such ceremonies, and illustrative remarks explanatory of their origin. This portion of the Vedas is supposed to have been composed about seven or eight centuries B. C. The Vedas were collected and arranged into books and chapters by the sage Krishnadwaipáyana, surnamed Vyása, who is supposed to have lived in the eleventh century after Christ; *see* under PURÁNA. The Vedas collectively are often called श्रुतिः *f.* or आम्नायः, and a Bráhman conversant with them श्रोत्रियः or श्रुतिज्ञः.—(The three Vedas) वेदत्रयं -यी, त्रयी; 'duty enjoined by them,' त्रयीधर्म्मः.—(The four Vedas) चतुर्वेदं; 'one who is conversant with them,' चतुर्विद्यः, चतुर्वेदः, चातुर्वैद्यः. The Áyur-veda, or code of medicine, is regarded by some as a part of the Atharva-veda, by others as an Upa-veda, *see* under SCRIPTURE.

VEDÁNGA, *s.* वेदाङ्गं, वेदोपकरणं. *See* under SCRIPTURE.

VEDÁNTA, *s.* (System of Philosophy), *see* under SCHOOL, SCRIPTURE. 'Follower of the Vedánta system,' वेदान्ती *m.* (न्).

To VEER, *v. n.* परिवृत् (c. 1. -वर्त्तते -र्त्तितुं), विपरिवृत्, परिवृत्य भिन्नदिशं गम् or इ, अन्यदिशं गम् or इ.

VEGETABLE, *s.* (Plant, any thing germinating) उद्भिद् *m. f. n.*, उद्भिज्जं, उद्भिदं, ओषधिः -धी *f.*, तृणं; 'the vegetable kingdom,' तृणजातिः *f.* -तं.—(Edible plant) शाकः, शदः; 'abounding with vegetables,' शाकिनः -नी -नं.

VEGETABLE, *a.* उद्भिद् *m. f. n.*, उद्भिज्जः -ज्जा -ज्जं, शाकसम्बन्धी &c.

To VEGETATE, *v. n.* उद्भिद् in pass., स्फुट्. *See To* GERMINATE.

VEGETATION, *s.* (Germination), *see* the word.—(Plants in general) तृणजातिः *f.* -तं, तृणादिजातिः *f.*, तरुगुल्मादि *n.*; 'wild vegetation,' जङ्गलं.

VEHEMENCE, *s.* तैक्ष्ण्यं, तीक्ष्णता, चण्डता, प्रचण्डता, तीव्रता, संरम्भः, वेगः, प्राबल्यं, कुतूहलं, कौतूहलं, रभसः, उग्रता.

VEHEMENT, *a.* तीक्ष्णः -क्ष्णा -क्ष्णं, चण्डः -ण्डा -ण्डं, प्रचण्डः &c., उच्चण्डः &c., तीव्रः -व्रा -व्रं, प्रबलः -ला -लं, उग्रः -ग्रा -ग्रं, कुतूहली -लिनी -लि (न्), कौतूहलान्वितः -ता -तं, बलवान् -वती -वत् (त्).

VEHEMENTLY, *adv.* सतैक्ष्ण्यं, उच्चण्डं, प्रचण्डं, तीव्रं, प्रबलं.

VEHICLE, *s.* (Carriage) वाहनं, यानं, वाहः, वाह्यं, रथः, विमानं दण्डारः, पत्त्रं, धारणं, *see* CARRIAGE; 'a mediate one, as a horse dragging a carriage,' वैनीतकः -कं.—(Medium) द्वारं.—(Fluid in which medicine is taken) अनुपानं.

VEIL, *s.* तिरस्करिणी, अवगुण्ठनं, अवगुण्ठिका, चक्षुपटः, पटः, नेत्रवस्त्रं निचोलः -ला -लं, प्रावृतः -ता -तं, निवृतः -ता -तं, निचोलः -ली -लं, पिधानं, आवरकः, आवरणं, तिरोधानं, छादनं -नी, यवनिका, तिरस्क्रिनी, चीरिः *f.*

To VEIL, *v. a.* अवगुण्ठ् (c. 10. -गुण्ठयति -यितुं), गुण्ठ्, छद् (c. 10.

-च्छादयति -यितुं), आच्छद्, समाच्छद्, प्रच्छद्, संछद्, ऊर्णु (c. 2. ऊर्णोति, ऊर्णौति, ऊर्णुते, ऊर्णुवितुं), प्रोर्णु, निव्ये. *See To* COVER.

VEILED, *p. p.* अवगुण्ठितः -ता -तं, अवगुण्ठनवान् -वती -वत् (त्), छादितः -ता -तं, तिरस्कृतः &c., संवृतः &c., व्यवहितः &c., निचोली -लिनी -लि (न्), ऊर्णुतः -ता -तं.

VEIN, *s.* (In anatomy) शिरा, सिरा, नाडिः -डी *f.*, नालिः -ली *f.*, धमनिः -नी, तन्तुकी, हिंस्रा.—(Of a leaf) पत्रशिरा, पत्रनाडिः -डिका, दलस्नसा.—(Temper, mood) वृत्तिः *f.*, चित्तवृत्तिः *f.*, भावः.

VEINED, VEINY, *a.* शिरालः -ला -लं, धमनीलः -ला -लं.

VELOCITY, *s.* वेगः, जवः, तूर्णिः *m.*, तरस् *n.*, रभसः, रंहस् *n.*, क्षेपिमा *m.* (न्), तूर्णता. *See* SPEED, SWIFTNESS.

VENAL, *a.* पण्यः -ण्या -ण्यं, पणितव्यः &c., क्रेयः &c., क्रय्यः &c.

VENALITY, *s.* पण्यता -त्वं, पणितव्यता, क्रेयता -त्वं.

VENDIBLE, *a.* विक्रेयः -या -यं, पण्यः &c. *See* SALEABLE.

VENERABLE, *a.* आर्य्यः -र्य्या -र्य्यं, पूजनीयः -या -यं, पूजार्हः -र्हा -र्हं, भगवान् -वती -वत् (त्), गुरुः -र्वी -रु, आदर्य्यः -र्य्या -र्य्यं, आदृत्यः &c. *See* REVEREND, RESPECTABLE.

To VENERATE, *v. a.* पूज्, अर्च्, मन्, सभाज्. *See To* REVERE.

VENERATION, *s.* पूजा, अर्चा, आदरः. *See* RESPECT, REVERENCE.

VENEREAL, *a.* मैथुनसम्बन्धी &c., रतिसम्बन्धी &c., मैथुनविषयकः -का -कं; 'disease,' उपदंशः.—(Aphrodisiac), *see* the word.

VENERY, *s.* मैथुनं, रतिः *f.*, रतिक्रीडा, रतिसुखं, सम्भोगः, *see* SEXUAL; 'provocative to it,' वाजीकरणं.

VENESECTION, *s.* शिराच्छेदः, शिरावेधः -व्यधः. *See* PHLEBOTOMY.

VENGEANCE, *s.* प्रतीकारः, प्रतिहिंसा, प्रतिक्रिया, प्रतिफलं, वैरशुद्धिः *f.*, *see* REVENGE; 'to take vengeance,' *see To* REVENGE.

VENIAL, *a.* उपेक्षणीयः -या -यं, क्षमार्हः -र्हा -र्हं, लघुः -घ्वी -घु, अल्पः -ल्पा -ल्पं, उप prep.; 'venial offence,' लघुदोषः, अल्पदोषः, स्वल्पदोषः, स्वल्पापराधः, उपदोषः, उपपातकं.

VENISON, *s.* मृगमांसं, हरिणमांसं, हारिणमांसं, हारिणं मांसं, पार्षतं, ऐणं, रौरवं; 'haunch of venison,' मृगजघनं.

VENOM, *a.* विषं, गरलं, गरं, कालकूटं. *See* POISON.

VENOMOUS, *a.* सविषः -षा -षं, विषपूर्णः -र्णा -र्णं, दंशेरः -रा -रं, दन्दशूकः -का -कं, *see* POISONOUS; 'snake,' विषभुजङ्गः.

VENT, *s.* द्वारं, छिद्रं, रन्ध्रं, मुखं, पथः, मार्गः, उच्छ्वासः.

To VENT, *v. a.* उत्सृज् (c. 6. -सृजति -स्रष्टुं), विसृज्, उद्गृ (c. 6. -गिरति -गरितुं -रीतुं), उदीर्, उच्चर् in caus. *See To* EMIT.

To VENTILATE, *v. a.* (Fan) वीज्, उपवीज्, *see To* FAN.—(Cause the air to pass through) वायुव्याप्यं -प्यां कृ, वायुव्याप्तं -प्तां कृ.

VENTILATED, *p.p.* वायुव्याप्तः -प्ता -प्तं, उपवीजितः &c., अनुवीजितः &c.

VENTILATOR, *s.* वायुयन्त्रं, व्यजनं, दुष्टवायूत्क्षेपकयन्त्रं.

VENTRAL, *a.* औदरिकः -की -कं, उदरकः -का -कं, कौक्ष्यः -क्ष्यी -क्ष्यं.

VENTRICLE, *s.* रन्ध्रं, द्वारं, कोष्ठः, कोषः, कोशः, रक्तकोषः.

VENTRILOQUISM, *s.* गारुडवाणी, ऐन्द्रजालिकवाणी, उदरवादः.

VENTRILOQUIST, *s.* उदरवादी *m.* (न्), गारुडवाणीयुक्तः.

VENTURE, *s.* *see* HAZARD, RISK; 'at a venture,' दैवात्.

To VENTURE, *v. n.* or *a.* *See To* DARE, HAZARD, RISK.

VENTURESOME, *a.* साहसिकः -की -कं, साहसबुद्धिः &c. *See* DARING, *a.*

VENUS, *s.* (In mythology) रतिः *f.*, *see* RATI.—(The planet) शुक्रः, उशना: *m.* (स्), भृगुः *m.*, भार्गवः, कविः *m.*, काव्यः, श्वेतः, श्वेतरथः, षोडशांशुः *m.*, मघाभवः, आस्फुजित् *m.*, दैत्यगुरुः *m.* Śukra, the regent of the planet Venus, is fabled as the son of Bhṛigu, and preceptor of the Daityas or demons.

VERACIOUS, *a.* सत्यवादी -दिनी -दि (न्), सत्यवाक् *m. f. n.* (च्), सत्यवक्ता -क्त्री -कृ (क्), सत्यभाषी &c., ऋतवाक् *m. f. n.*, सत्यवचाः -चाः -चः (स्), सत्यवदनशीलः -ला -लं, सत्यशीलः -ला -लं, सत्याभिधायी &c., अवितथवादी &c., पूतवाक् *m. f. n.*, सत्यगीः -गीः -गिः (र्), सत्यसन्धः -न्धा -न्धं.

VERACITY, *s.* सत्यवादित्वं, सत्यवक्तृत्वं, सत्याभिधानं, सत्यभाषणं, सत्यं, सत्यशीलता, सत्यता, सत्यवद्यं, सत्या.

VERANDA, *s.* वरण्डः -ण्डकः, निष्क्राशः, आवरकः. *See* PORTICO.

VERB, *s.* क्रिया, क्रियापदं; 'form of a verb,' क्रियारूपं, धातुरूपं, आख्यातं; 'root of a verb,' धातुः *m.*; 'subject of one,' क्रियाश्रयः; 'table or list of verbs,' धातुपाठः.

VERBAL, *a.* (Expressed in words) वाचिकः -की -कं, वाचनिकः -की -कं, वाचकः -का -कं, शब्दद्वारकः &c.—(Consisting in words, relating to words) शाब्दः -ब्दी -ब्दं, शाब्दिकः -की -कं, शब्दरूपः -पा -पं, शब्दसम्बन्धी &c.—(Literal) पदानुपदिकः -की -कं, समपदः -दा -दं, शब्दरूपः -पा -पं, *see* LITERAL.—(In grammar) क्रियावाचकः -का -कं, धातुसाधितः -ता -तं.

VERBALLY, *adv.* शब्दद्वारा -रेण, शब्दतस्, यथाशब्दं.

VERBATIM, *adv.* शब्दशस्, शब्दतस्, अक्षरशस्, यथाशब्दं.

VERBENA, *s.* (Kind of grass) दर्भः.

VERBOSE, *a.* बहुशब्दकः -का -कं, बहुवाक्यः -क्या -क्यं, अतिशयोक्तिविशिष्टः -ष्टा -ष्टं, अतिविस्तीर्णः &c., *see* PROLIX.

VERBOSITY, VERBIAGE, *s.* शब्दविस्तारः, बहुशब्दत्वं, अतिशयोक्तिः *f.*, शब्दबाहुल्यं, बहुभाषिता, शब्दाधिक्यं.

VERDANT, *a.* हरितः -ता -रिणी -तं, शादहरितः &c., शाड्वलः -ला -लं, अम्लानः &c.; 'to become so,' हरित (nom. हरितायते).

VERDICT, *s.* निर्णयपादः, निर्णयः, दण्डनिर्णयः. *See* SENTENCE.

VERDIGRIS, *s.* कलङ्कः, ताम्रकलङ्कः, ताम्रमलं, ताम्रकिट्टं.

VERDURE, *s.* शादः, नवशादः, हरितशादः, हरितत्वं, अम्लानिः *f.*

VERGE, *s.* (Rod) दण्डः.—(Brink) प्रान्तः, धारा, *see* BRINK.

To VERGE, *v. n.* *See To* TEND, INCLINE, APPROACH.

VERGER, *s.* दण्डी *m.* (न्), दण्डधरः. *See* MACE-BEARER.

VERIFICATION, *s.* सत्याकृतिः *f.*, सत्याकरणं, सत्यकृतिः *f.*, सत्यङ्कारः, सत्यापनं, सत्यङ्करणं, निर्णेतृत्वं, निर्णायनं.

To VERIFY, *v. a.* सत्याकृ, सत्यङ्कृ, सत्यीकृ, सत्य (nom. caus. सत्यापयति -यितुं), निर्णी, निश्चि, निर्णयं कृ.

VERILY, *adv.* सत्यं, अवश्यं, नूनं. *See* TRULY, CERTAINLY.

VERITABLE, VERITY. *See* TRUE, TRUTH.

VERMICULAR, *a.* कृमिसदृशः -शी -शं, कृमिगतिसदृशः -शी -शं.

VERMIFUGE, *a.* कृमिहरः -रा -रं, कृमिघ्नः -घ्नी -घ्नं, कृमिहारी -रिणी &c.

VERMILION, *s.* सिन्दूरं, सिन्दूरिका, हिङ्गुलः, रक्तं, चूर्णपारदः, सुरङ्गं, चित्राङ्गं, रसगर्भः, हंसपादं, हंसांघ्रिः *m.*, कपिशीर्षकं.

VERMIN, *s.* कृमयः *m. pl.*, गर्त्ताश्रिताः *m. pl.*, बिलेवासिनः *m. pl.*, बिलेशयाः *m. pl.*, मूषिकादिक्षुद्रजन्तवः *m. pl.*, गृहोत्पाताः.

VERNACULAR, *a.* जन्मदेशीयः -या -यं, स्वदेशीयः &c., प्राकृतः -ता -तं; 'language,' जन्मभाषा, प्राकृतभाषा.

VERNAL, *a.* वासन्तः -न्ती -न्तं, वासन्तिकः -की -कं, वसन्तजः -जा -जं, वसन्तोद्भवः -वा -वं, वसन्त in comp.

VERSATILE, *a.* चपलबुद्धिः -द्धिः -द्धि, चपलमतिः -तिः -ति, चञ्चलबुद्धिः

&c., अनेकबुद्धिः &c., चपलः -ला -लं, चञ्चलः &c., अन्यमानसः -सी -सं, अन्यमनस्कः -स्का -स्कं, चपलमनस्कः &c.

VERSATILITY, s. बुद्धिचापल्यं, चपलबुद्धित्वं, चपलता.

VERSE, s. (Metrical composition) पद्यं, कविता, काव्यं, छन्दस् n., गा; 'measured by time,' जातिः f.; 'syllabic,' वृत्तं; 'blank,' मुक्तप्रासः; 'prose and verse,' गद्यपद्यं.—(Stanza) श्लोकः, गाथा, रूपं.—(Line of a stanza) पादः, चरणः -णं, पदं; 'verse by verse,' पादशस्.

VERSED, a. अभिज्ञः -ज्ञा -ज्ञं, निपुणः -णा -णं, कुशलः -ला -लं, विशारदः -दा -दं, निष्ठितः -ता -तं, परिनिष्ठितः &c., see SKILLED, CONVERSANT; 'in all subjects,' सर्व्वविषयज्ञः -ज्ञा -ज्ञं.

VERSIFICATION, s. श्लोकरचना, पदरचना, काव्यरचना, पदयोजना, कविताकरणं, काव्यकरणं, श्लोकत्वं.

VERSIFIER, s. श्लोकरचकः, कविताकर्त्ता m. (र्त्तृ), भविनः.

To VERSIFY, v. n. श्लोकरचनां कृ, पदरचनां कृ, कवितां कृ.

VERSION, s. भाषान्तरं, see TRANSLATION.—(Variation in reading) पाठान्तरं, पाठभेदः, पाठः.

VERTEBRA, s. पृष्ठवंशग्रन्थिः m., पृष्ठवंशसन्धिः m., वंशसन्धिः.

VERTEBRAL, a. वंशग्रन्थिसम्बन्धी &c., वंशसन्धिसम्बन्धी &c.

VERTEBRATED, a. पृष्ठास्थिमान् -मती -मत्, पृष्ठवंशविशिष्टः &c.

VERTEX, s. अग्रं, शिखा, शिखरं, शिरस् n., तुङ्गः.

VERTICAL, a. ऊर्द्ध्वाधरः -रा -रं, see PERPENDICULAR.—(In the zenith) समध्यस्थः -स्था -स्थं.—(Vertical circle, in astronomy) दृङ्मण्डलं; 'passing through nonagesimal point,' दृक्क्षेपवृत्तं; 'prime vertical,' सममण्डलं, पूर्व्वापरवृत्तं.

VERTICALLY, adv. ऊर्द्ध्वाधरं, ऊर्द्ध्वाधररूपेण, see PERPENDICULARLY; 'he places the tube vertically in the vessel,' नलम् उपरि-विधाय नालं पात्रे स्थापयति.

VERTIGO, s. भ्रमरं. See GIDDINESS, DIZZINESS.

VERY, a. (Real) सत्यः -त्या -त्यं, वास्तवः -वी -वं; 'in very deed,' सत्यमेव; 'the very one,' अयं विशेषः; 'I, that very person,' सो ऽहम्.—(Mere) शुद्धः -द्धा -द्धं, मात्र in comp.; 'the very birth of a Bráhman,' ब्राह्मणजन्ममात्रं.—(Emphatic) expressed by एव; as, 'from that very moment,' तत्क्षणादेव; 'this very day,' अद्यैव.

VERY, adv. अति or सु or अतिशय prefixed, अतीव, अतिशयेन, अत्यन्तं, भूरि, सुष्ठु, see EXTREMELY, EXCEEDINGLY; 'very angry,' अत्यमर्षी -र्षिणी &c., अतिक्रोधी &c.; 'very many,' सुबहुः -हुः -हु; 'very far,' सुदूरः -रा -रं; 'very glorious,' अमिततेजाः -जाः -जः (स्); 'very deceitful,' अनल्पमायी &c.; 'love is very suspicious,' स्नेहः परम् आशङ्कते; 'very well,' परमं, बाढं; 'very true,' सत्यमेव, परमं.

VESICLE, s. क्षुद्रस्फोटः, त्वक्स्फोटकः, चर्म्मस्फोटः.

VESPERS, s. सायम्पूजा, सायम्भजनं, सन्ध्यापूजा, सन्ध्याभजनं.

VESPERTINE, a. सायङ्कालिकः -की -कं, सायन्तनः &c. See EVENING, a.

VESSEL, s. (Utensil for holding, as a pot, cup, &c.) पात्रं, भाजनं, भाण्डं, अमत्रं, आधारः, धारकः; 'drinking vessel,' पानपात्रं; 'for holding water,' उदकपात्रं, जलपात्रं, घटः, कलशः.—(Vessel of the body, as a vein, &c.) शिरा, नाडिः -डी f., नालिः -ली, धमनी, वाहिनी, see TUBE.—(Boat, ship) नौः f., नौका, पोतः, वहिनी, वहित्रं, तरणी, जलयानं, बोहित्थं.

VEST, s. वस्त्रं, वेशः, वसनं, उत्तरीयं, प्रावारः. See GARMENT.

To VEST, v. a. (Clothe) वेष्ट्, परिधा.—(Invest), see the word.

VESTED IN, p. p. अधीनः -ना -नं, आयत्तः -त्ता -त्तं, वशः -शा -शं.

VESTIBULE, s. देहली -लिः f., निष्काशः. See PORCH.

VESTIGE, s. चिह्नं, लक्षणं, पदवी, पदाङ्कः. See TRACE.

VESTMENT, VESTURE, s. See DRESS, CLOTHES, GARMENT.

VETCH, s. (Kind of plant) द्विदलं, द्विपत्रं.

VETERAN, s. or a. अभ्यासवृद्धः -द्धा -द्धं, व्यवहारवृद्धः &c., ज्ञानवृद्धः &c., see PRACTISED; 'in arms,' शस्त्राभ्यासवृद्धः, युद्धाभ्यासवृद्धः.

VETERINARY, a. पशुचिकित्सासम्बन्धी &c., अश्वचिकित्सासम्बन्धी &c.; 'veterinary art,' पशुचिकित्सा, अश्वादिचिकित्सा; 'surgeon,' अश्ववैद्यः, पशुवैद्यः.

VETO, s. निषेधः, प्रतिषेधः, अननुमोदनं. See PROHIBITION.

To VEX, v. a. बाध् (c. 1. बाधते -धितुं), क्लिश्, प्रकुप् (c. 10. -कोपयति -यितुं), पीड्, तुद्, व्यथ्, तप् in caus., अर्द्. See *To* HARASS.

VEXATION, s. क्लेशः, व्यथा, बाधा, दुःखं, विडम्बना, आयासः, मन्युः m., सन्तापः; 'cause of trouble,' शल्यं, कण्टकः.

VEXATIOUS, a. क्लेशकः -का -कं, दुःखकरः -री -रं. See DISTRESSING.

VEXED, p. p. दुःखितः -ता -तं. See HARASSED, IRRITATED.

VIAND, VIANDS, s. पक्वान्नं, सिद्धान्नं, अन्नं, खाद्यद्रव्याणि n. pl.

VIATICUM, s. पाथेयं, यात्रिकं, शम्बलं, सम्बलं -लः.

To VIBRATE, v. n. दोल (nom. दोलायते), स्पन्द् (c. 1. स्पन्दते -न्दितुं), स्फुर् (c. 6. स्फुरति -रितुं), कम्प्, भ्रम्. See *To* OSCILLATE.

To VIBRATE, v. a. भ्रम् (c. 10. भ्रमयति -यितुं), स्फुर् in caus. (स्फारयति -यितुं), विस्फुर्, विधू. See *To* BRANDISH.

VIBRATING, part. दोलायमानः -ना -नं, स्पन्दमानः &c. See OSCILLATING.

VIBRATION, s. आन्दोलनं, स्पन्दनं, प्रतिस्पन्दनं, स्फुरणं, स्फारणं, विस्फारः -रणं, स्फूर्त्तिः f., कम्पः -म्पनं, भ्रमणं, भ्रमिः f.

VICAR, s. प्रतिनिधिः m. See SUBSTITUTE, DEPUTY.

VICARIOUS, a. प्रतिनिधिरूपः -पा -पं, प्रातिनिधिकः &c., see SUBSTITUTED.

VICARIOUSLY, adv. प्रतिनिधिरूपेण, उपसर्जनरूपेण, प्रतिनिधितस्.

VICE, s. (Moral evil, depravity) दुष्टता, अधर्म्मः, पापं, व्यभिचारः, see WICKEDNESS.—(An habitual fault) व्यसनं, दुर्गुणः, अवगुणः, दुर्लक्षणं, दोषः, दूषणं; 'in a horse,' दुर्गुणं, दुर्लक्षणं; 'in an elephant,' व्यालत्वं.—(Iron press) सन्दंशः -शका.

VICE-GERENCY, s. प्रतिनिधित्वं, प्रातिनिध्यं. See LIEUTENANCY.

VICE-GERENT, s. प्रतिनिधिः m., प्रतिभूः m. See DEPUTY.

VICE-ROY, s. राजप्रतिनिधिः m., राजप्रतिभूः m., भोगपतिः m.

VICE-ROYALTY, s. राजप्रतिनिधित्वं, राजप्रातिनिध्यं.

VICINITY, s. सन्निधानं, सान्निध्यं. See NEIGHBORHOOD.

VICIOUS, a. व्यसनी -निनी -नि (न्), व्यसनीयः -या -यं, दुष्टः -ष्टा -ष्टं, दुर्वृत्तः -त्ता -त्तं, दुश्चरित्रः -त्रा -त्रं, क्षीणपुण्यः -ण्या -ण्यं, see DEPRAVED.—(Having vices or bad tricks) सव्यसनः -ना -नं, व्यसनी &c., दुर्गुणी &c., दुर्लक्षणी &c.

VICIOUSLY, adv. दुष्टवत्, दुर्वृत्तवत्, व्यसनित्वात्, दुष्टभावेन.

VICIOUSNESS, s. दुष्टता, व्यसनिता -त्वं, दुर्वृत्तता, दुर्गुणत्वं.

VICISSITUDE, s. आवृत्तिः f., परिवृत्तिः f., अनुवृत्तिः, अनुक्रमः.

VICTIM, s. बलिः m., यज्ञपशुः m., देवपशुः m., बध्यः, बध्यपशुः m., उपहारः, उपाकृतः, सत्पशुः m.

To VICTIMIZE, v. a. उपहारीकृ. See *To* SACRIFICE, IMMOLATE.

VICTOR, s. जेता m. (तृ), विजेता m., जयी m. (न्), विजयी m., जैत्रः, जित् m.

VICTORIOUS, *a.* जयी -यिनी -यि (न्), विजयी &c., जेता -त्री -तृ (तृ), जैत्रः -त्री -त्रं, जिष्णुः -ष्णुः -ष्णु, जित्वरः -री -रं, जितारिः -रिः -रि, जितशत्रुः -त्रुः -त्रु, जययुक्तः -क्ता -क्तं, जयवान् -वती -वत् (त्), विजयमानः -ना -नं, विजितवान् &c., प्राप्तजयः -या -यं, लब्धजयः &c., रिपुञ्जयः &c., अरिन्दमः -मा -मं, जः जा जं, जित् जित् जित्.—(Conferring victory) जयावहः -हा -हं, जयप्रदः -दा -दं.

VICTORIOUSLY, *adv.* विजयेन, सविजयं, विजयपूर्व्वं, जयपूर्व्वं.

VICTORY, *s.* जयः, विजयः, जयनं, विजयसिद्धिः *f.*, जयश्रीः *f.*; 'proclamation of victory,' जयघोषः; 'record of it,' जयपत्रं; 'march to it,' जयप्रस्थानं; 'glory of it,' जयश्रीः *f.*; 'flag of victory,' जयपताका; 'shout of victory,' जयध्वनिः *m.*, जयशब्दः, जयारवः.

To VICTUAL, *v. a.* खाद्यद्रव्यैः समायुज् (c. 10. -योजयति -यितुं) or युज्, खाद्यद्रव्याणि परिक्लृप् or सम्भृ. *See To* PURVEY.

VICTUALLER, *s.* अन्नादिविक्रेता *m.* (तृ), खाद्यद्रव्यविक्रेता *m.*, शौण्डिकः.

VICTUALLING-HOUSE, *s.* अन्नविक्रयस्थानं, अन्नविक्रयगृहं, शुण्डा.

VICTUALS, *s. pl.* अन्नं, भोजनं, खाद्यद्रव्यं, आहारः. *See* FOOD.

VIDELICET, *s.* अर्थतस्, अर्थात्, वस्तुतस्, यथा, नाम.

To VIE, *v. n.* स्पर्ध् (c. 1. स्पर्धते -र्धितुं), जि in des., *see To* RIVAL.

To VIEW, *v. a.* अवलोक् (c. 10. -लोकयति -यितुं), आलोक्, प्रेक्ष् (c. 1. प्रेक्षते -क्षितुं, rt. ईक्ष्), वीक्ष्, समीक्ष्, निरीक्ष्, निर्वर्ण्. *See To* SURVEY.

VIEW, *s.* (Act of viewing) अवलोकनं, आलोकनं, दर्शनं, सन्दर्शनं, वीक्षणं, दृष्टिः *f.*—(Reach of the eye) दृष्टिपातः, दृक्पातः, दृष्टिः *f.*; 'in view,' दृष्टिगोचरः -रा -रं, दृग्गोचरः &c.—(That which is presented to the view), *see* PROSPECT.—(Intention) उद्देशः, आशयः, बुद्धिः *f.*; 'with the view of,' बुद्ध्या, उद्दिश्य; 'with what view?' किमुद्दिश्य.—(Opinion) मतं, मतिः *f.*, बुद्धिः *f.*, दृष्टिः *f.*; 'of high views,' ऊर्द्ध्वदृष्टिः -ष्टिः -ष्टि; 'of narrow views,' अल्पदृष्टिः &c., मितबुद्धिः &c., कृपणबुद्धिः &c.; 'a point of view,' पक्षः; 'under one point of view,' एकपक्षे.

VIGIL, *s.* जागरणं, रात्रिजागरणं, जागरः, रात्रिजागरः.

VIGILANCE, *s.* (Wakefulness) जागरा, जागर्य्या, जागर्त्तिः *f.*, प्रबोधः.—(Wariness) सावधानता, अवधानं, समीक्ष्यकारित्वं.

VIGILANT, *a.* (Wakeful) जागरी -रिणी -रि (न्), *see* WAKEFUL.—(Wary) सावधानः -ना -नं, स्वहितः &c., अप्रमत्तः &c. *See* CIRCUMSPECT.

VIGOR, *s.* वीर्य्यं, तेजस् *n.*, सत्त्वं, ओजस् *n.*, प्रभावः, बलं, पौरुषं, सारः -रता, ऊर्जितं; 'in full vigor,' प्रौढबलः -ला -लं.

VIGOROUS, *a.* महावीर्य्यः -र्य्या -र्य्यं, वीर्य्यवान् -वती -वत्, तेजोवान् &c., सारवान् &c., प्रौढसत्त्वः -त्त्वा -त्त्वं, महासत्त्वः &c., प्रौढसामर्थ्यः -र्थ्या -र्थ्यं, रागी -गिणी &c., गुणवान् &c. *See* ENERGETIC.

VIGOROUSLY, *adv.* सवीर्य्यं, महायत्नेन, प्रयत्नतस्, वीर्य्यतस्, सारतस्.

VILE, *a.* अधमः -मा -मं, कुत्सितः -ता -तं, खलः -ला -लं, तुच्छः -च्छा -च्छं, जघन्यः &c., दुष्टः &c., निर्गुणः &c., निकृष्टः &c. *See* LOW, MEAN.

VILENESS, *s.* दुष्टता, खलता, जघन्यता, कौत्सित्यं, निर्गुणत्वं, अनार्य्यता.

To VILIFY, *v. a.* *See To* DEFAME,, TRADUCE, REVILE.

VILLA, *s.* नगरोपान्ते खेलिगृहं or विनोदगृहं.

VILLAGE, *s.* ग्रामः, निवसथः, अवसथः, उपवसथः, संवसथः, प्रतिवसथः, सङ्कसथः, पल्लिः -ल्ली *f.*, कटकः, खेटकः, पद्रः, ग्रामस्थः; 'number of villages,' ग्रामता, ग्रामसङ्घः; 'a hundred villages,' ग्रामशतं; 'chief or head-man of a village,' ग्रामाधिपतिः *m.*, ग्रामाध्यक्षः, ग्रामाधिकृतः, ग्रामेशः, ग्रामनायकः, ग्रामणीः *m.*; 'space near a village,' ग्रामान्तं, उपशल्यं.

VILLAGE, *a.* ग्राम्यः -म्या -म्यं, ग्रामीयः -या -यं, ग्रामीणः -णा -णं, ग्रामिकः -की -कं, ग्राम in comp.; 'village divinity,' ग्रामदेवता; 'village officer,' ग्रामाधिकारी *m.*; 'village priest,' ग्रामयाजकः.

VILLAGER, *s.* ग्रामवासी *m.* (न्), ग्रामेवासी *m.*, ग्रामेवासः, ग्रामस्थः, ग्रामिकजनः, ग्रामी *m.*, ग्रामीणः, ग्राम्यजनः, ग्रामचारी *m.*

VILLAIN, VILLAINOUS, VILLAINY. *See* RASCAL, RASCALLY, &c.

To VINDICATE, *v. a.* शुध् (c. 10. शोधयति -यितुं), दोषात् शुध् or परिशुध्, निर्दोषीकृ, प्रतिपद् (c. 10. -पादयति -यितुं), स्था in caus. (स्थापयति -यितुं), प्रतिपादनं कृ, प्रतिपालनं कृ. *See To* JUSTIFY, SUPPORT.

VINDICATION, *s.* शोधनं, परिशोधनं, परिशुद्धिः *f.*, प्रतिपादनं, स्थापनं, प्रतिपालनं, दोषमुक्तिः *f.* *See* JUSTIFICATION, SUPPORT.

VINDICTIVE, VINDICTIVENESS. *See* REVENGEFUL, &c.

VINE, *s.* द्राक्षा, द्राक्षालता, गुच्छफला, द्राक्षावल्ली, द्राक्षाप्रतती.

VINEGAR, *s.* अम्लरसः, शुक्तं, शुक्तरसः, शौक्तिकं, चुक्रं.

VINEYARD, *s.* द्राक्षावाटिका, द्राक्षावाटी, द्राक्षोद्यानं, द्राक्षाक्षेत्रं.

VINOUS, *a.* द्राक्षामद्यगुणकः -का -कं, मौरिकः -की -कं.

VINTAGE, *s.* (Produce of the vine) द्राक्षोत्पन्नफलं, एकसमये द्राक्षोत्पादितफलं.—(Season of gathering it) द्राक्षाफलसंग्रहकालः.

VINTNER, *s.* मद्यविक्रयजीवी *m.* (न्), मद्यविक्रेता *m.* (तृ), द्राक्षारसविक्रेता *m.*, सुराजीवी *m.*, शौण्डिकः, शुण्डारः, ध्वजवान् *m.*

To VIOLATE, *v. a.* लङ्घ् (c. 10. लङ्घयति -यितुं), अतिक्रम्, अतिचर्, लुप्, *see To* TRANSGRESS, INFRINGE.—(Ravish) धृष् (c. 10. -धर्षयति -यितुं).

VIOLATION, *s.* लङ्घनं, लोपः -पनं, अतिक्रमः, व्यतिक्रमः; 'of a vow,' व्रतलोपनं; 'of a law,' *see* INFRINGEMENT.—(Rape), *see* RAPE.

VIOLATOR, *s.* अतिक्रमी *m.*, दस्युः. *See* INFRINGER, RAVISHER.

VIOLENCE, *s.* (Force) बलं, वेगः, प्राबल्यं.—(Unjust force) बलात्कारः, प्रसभं, प्रमाथः, साहसं, हठः, महासाहसं, द्रोहः, सहोबलं; 'personal violence,' दण्डपारुष्यं, पारुष्यं, उपघातः.—(Vehemence, impetuosity), *see* the words.

VIOLENT, *a.* (Forcible, impetuous) प्रबलः -ला -लं, वेगवान् -वती &c., महावेगः -गा -गं.—(Vehement) चण्डः -ण्डा -ण्डं, उच्चण्डः &c., तीक्ष्णः -क्ष्णा -क्ष्णं, तीव्रः -व्रा -व्रं, उग्रः &c., रोषणः -णा -णं, रौद्रः -द्री -द्रं, गाढः -ढा -ढं, सोत्प्रासः -सा -सं; violent wrath,' गुरुकोपः, *see* SEVERE.—(Acting by violence) साहसी -सिनी -सि (न्), साहसिकः -की -कं, साहसकर्म्मा -र्म्मा -र्म्म (न्), प्रमाथी &c., द्रोही &c.—(Violent death) अपमृत्युः *m.*, अपघातः, दुर्मरणं.

VIOLENTLY, *adv.* (Forcibly, impetuously) प्रसह्य, प्रसभं, बलात्कारेण, बलवत्, प्रबलं, महावेगेन, महाजवेन, *see* FORCIBLY.—(Vehemently) तीव्रं, गाढं, उग्रं, अति prefixed, अतिशयेन; 'violently in love,' अत्यनुरागवान् -वती &c.

VIOLIN, *s.* सारङ्गी, शारङ्गी, पिनाकी.

VIPER, *s.* सर्पः, अहिः *m.*, भुजङ्गः, भुजगः, उरगः. *See* SNAKE.

VIRAGO, *s.* पुरुषस्वभावा, पुरुषवृत्तिः *f.*, वृषभी, कर्कशा.

VIRGIN, *s.* कुमारी -रिका, कन्या, तरुणी, अक्षता, गौरी -रिका, अक्षतयोनिः *f.*, अविद्धयोनिः *f.*, अनन्यपूर्व्वा, पुरुषास्पृष्टा, निवरा, *see* MAID; 'defiler of one,' कन्यादूषकः.

VIRGIN, *a.* कौमारः -री -रं, कानीनः &c., *see* MAIDEN, MAIDENLY.

VIRGINITY, *s.* कौमारं, कुमारीत्वं, कन्यात्वं, अक्षतयोनित्वं, अविद्धयोनित्वं, अज्ञातपुरुषता, पुरुषास्पृष्टता. *See* MAIDENHEAD.

VIRGO, *s.* (The Zodiacal sign) कन्या, पाथेयं.

VIRILE, *a.* पौरुषः -षी -षं, पौरुषेयः -यी -यं, पुरुषसम्बन्धी &c.

VIRILITY, *s.* पौरुषं, पुरुषत्वं, पौरुषता, पुंस्त्वं, पुंस्ता, पुंशक्तिः *f.*, जननशक्तिः *f.*, पुरुषशक्तिः *f.*, ओजस् *n.*

VIRTUAL, *a.* वस्तुसदृशः -शी -शं, वस्तुसङ्काशः -शा -शं, वास्तवः -वी -वं, वास्तविकः -की -कं, गुणसिद्धः -द्धा -द्धं, अर्थसदृशः -शी -शं.

VIRTUALLY, *adv.* वस्तुसादृश्येन, वस्तुतस्, अर्थतस्, सारतस्.

VIRTUE, *s.* (Moral goodness) धर्म्मः, पुण्यं, श्रेयस् *n.*, धर्म्माचरणं, धर्म्माचारः, साधुत्वं, साधुवृत्तिः *f.*, साधुवृत्तं, साधुशीलता, सदाचारः, सुकृतं, सुचरितं -त्रं, सच्चरितं, दर्शनं, नीतिः *f.*; 'personified,' वृषः.—(Strength, power) प्रभावः, शक्तिः *f.*, बलं, प्राबल्यं; 'latent virtue,' मर्म्म *n.*—(Good quality, excellence) गुणः, सद्गुणः, सुगुणः, सुलक्षणं; 'virtue and vices,' गुणागुणाः *m. pl.*, गुणदोषाः *m. pl.*

VIRTUOUS, *a.* धार्म्मिकः -की -कं, धर्म्मी -र्म्मिणी -र्म्मि (न्), पुण्यशीलः -ला -लं, साधुशीलः &c., साधुवृत्तः -त्ता -त्तं, साध्वाचारः -रा -रं, साधुः -ध्वी -धु, धर्म्मचारी -रिणी &c., सुकृती &c., कृती &c., सुकृत् *m. f. n.*, पुण्यभाक् *m. f. n.* (ज्), सात्त्विकः -की -कं, सत्त्वशीलः -ला -लं, न्यायाचारः &c., गुणवान् -वती -वत् (त्), गुणी &c., गुणाश्रयः -या -यं, चारुचरित्रः -त्रा -त्रं, अपकल्मषः -षा -षं, *see* GOOD; 'a virtuous wife,' सती, साध्वी, महासती; 'a virtuous person,' सज्जनः; 'a virtuous young girl,' सद्युवती.

VIRTUOUSLY, *adv.* धर्म्मतस्, धर्म्मेण, धर्म्मानुसारेण, पुण्यवत्.

VIRULENCE, *s.* उग्रता, कटुता, तीक्ष्णता, ज्वाला. *See* MALIGNITY.

VIRULENT, *a.* उग्रः -ग्रा -ग्रं, अतितीक्ष्णः &c. *See* MALIGNANT.

VISAGE, *s.* मुखं, आननं, वदनं, आस्यं, वक्त्रं. *See* FACE.

VISCERA, *s. pl.* अन्त्राणि *n. pl.*, उदरं. *See* BOWELS, ENTRAILS.

VISCERAL, *a.* आन्त्रिकः -की -कं, औदरिकः -की -कं.

VISCID, VISCOUS, *a.* सान्द्रः -न्द्रा -न्द्रं, श्यानः -ना -नं, शीनः &c., घनः -ना -नं, अवलेह्यः -ह्या -ह्यं, स्निग्धः &c. *See* GLUTINOUS, STICKY.

VISHṆU, *s.* विष्णुः. The second person of the Hindú triad, and the most celebrated and popular of all the Indian deities. He is the personification of the preserving power, and became incarnate in nine different forms, for the preservation of mankind in various emergencies. Before the creation of the universe, and after its temporary annihilation, he is supposed to sleep on the waters, floating on the serpent Śesha, and is then identified with Náráyana. Brahmá, the creator, is fabled to spring at that time from a lotus which grows from his navel, whilst thus asleep. Vishṇu's wife is called Lakshmí, and the vehicle on which he rides, Garuḍa. *See* LAKSHMÍ, GARUḌA. His ten avatárs or incarnations are: 1. The Matsya, or Fish. In this avatár Vishṇu descended in the form of a fish to save the pious king Satyavrata, who with the seven Ṛishis and their wives had taken refuge in the ark to escape the deluge which then destroyed the earth. 2. The Kúrma, or Tortoise. In this he descended in the form of a tortoise, for the purpose of restoring to man some of the comforts lost during the flood. To this end he stationed himself at the bottom of the ocean, and allowed the point of the great mountain Mandara to be placed upon his back, which served as a hard axis, whereon the gods and demons, with the serpent Vásuki twisted round the mountain for a rope, churned the waters for the recovery of the amṛita or nectar, and fourteen other sacred things, *see* OCEAN. 3. The Varáha, or Boar. In this he descended in the form of a boar to rescue the earth from the power of a demon called 'golden-eyed,' Hiraṇyáksha. This demon had seized on the earth and carried it with him into the depths of the ocean. Vishṇu dived into the abyss, and, after a contest of a thousand years, slew the monster. 4. The Narasinha, or Man-lion. In this monstrous shape of a creature half-man, half-lion, Vishṇu delivered the earth from the tyranny of an insolent demon called Hiraṇyakaśipu. 5. Vámana, or Dwarf. This avatár happened in the second age of the Hindús or Tretá yug, the four preceding are said to have occurred in the first or Satya yug; the object of this avatár was to trick Bali out of the dominion of the three worlds. Assuming the form of a wretched dwarf he appeared before the king, and asked, as a boon, as much land as he could pace in three steps. This was granted; and Vishṇu, immediately expanding himself till he filled the world, deprived Bali at two steps of heaven and earth, but in consideration of some merit, left Pátála still in his dominion. 6. Paraśuráma. 7. Rámachandra; for an account of both these, *see* RÁMA. 8. Kṛishna, or, according to some, Balaráma, *see* KṚISHNA, RÁMA. 9. Buddha. In this avatár Vishṇu descended in the form of a sage, for the purpose of making some reform in the religion of the Brahmins, and especially to reclaim them from their proneness to animal sacrifice. Many of the Hindús will not allow this to have been an incarnation of their favourite god. 10. Kalki, or White Horse. This is yet to come. Vishṇu, mounted on a white horse, with a drawn scimitar, blazing like a comet, will, according to prophecy, end this present age, viz. the fourth or Kali yug, by destroying the world, and then renovating creation by an era of purity. Many of the names of Vishṇu correspond with those of Kṛishna, who is by many identified with Vishṇu, *see* KṚISHNA. Some of his other names are here given.—(Supporter of the universe) विश्वम्भरः.—(Mover on the waters) नारायणः.—(From whose navel comes the lotus from which Brahmá springs) पद्मनाभः, पद्मनाभिः *m.*—(Sleeper on a lotus) पद्मेशयः, नलिनेशयः.—(The best male) पुरुषोत्तमः.—(The four-armed) चतुर्भुजः.—(Holder of the conch-shell) शङ्खी *m.*—(Discus-handed) चक्रपाणिः *m.*—(Holding a bow made of horn) शार्ङ्गी *m.*—(The seizer) हरिः *m.*—(Foe of the demons) दैत्यारिः *m.*—(Having ten incarnations) दशावतारः.—(Taker of three strides, under the 5th or Dwarf avatár) त्रिविक्रमः, त्रिपाद्.—(Destroyer of Bali) बलिध्वंसी *m.*—(Husband of Lakshmí, or attended by her as the goddess of fortune) लक्ष्मीपतिः *m.*,

लक्ष्मीशः, श्रीपतिः m., श्रीधरः, श्रीनिकेतनः, श्रीनिवासः, श्रीकान्तः.—(Possessing the paradise called Vaikuntha) वैकुण्ठः.—(Having Garuḍa as a vehicle) गरुडध्वजः, तार्क्ष्यध्वजः, तार्क्ष्यनायकः.—(Decapitator of Ráhu) राहुमूर्द्धभिद् m., राहुभेदी m., see Ráhu.—(Having spreading ears) विश्वश्रवाः m.—(Destroyer of the demon Kaiṭabha) कैटभजित्.—(Supporting the earth) कुस्तुभः.—(Present to such as have brought under their passions) अधोक्षजः.—(Lotus-eyed) पुण्डरीकाक्षः.—(Self-born) स्वभूः m.—(Whose armies are everywhere) विष्वक्सेनः. Other names are हरित्, जन्मकीलः, मालः, वासुः m., शौरिः m., विधुः m. A worshipper of Vishṇu is called वैष्णवः.

Visibility, s. दृश्यता, दर्शनीयता, प्रत्यक्षता, प्रेक्षणीयता -त्वं.

Visible, a. दृश्यः -श्या -श्यं, दर्शनीयः -या -यं, प्रत्यक्षः -क्षा -क्षं, प्रत्यक्षभूतः -ता -तं, दृग्गोचरः -रा -रं, दृष्टिगोचरः &c., दृष्टिग्राह्यः -ह्या -ह्यं, चक्षुर्ग्राह्यः &c., प्रेक्षणीयः -या -यं, प्रेक्ष्यः &c., वीक्ष्यः &c., लक्ष्यः &c., लोकनीयः -या -यं, दृष्टिविषयः -या -यं, दृग्विषयः &c., दृग्गम्यः &c., दृष्टिगम्यः &c., व्यक्तः -क्ता -क्तं, अभिव्यक्तः &c., प्रादुर्भूतः -ता -तं, आविर्भूतः &c., प्रकाशः -शा -शं, प्रकाशितः -ता -तं, उद्भूतः &c., समक्षः -क्षी -क्षं, चाक्षुषः -षी -षं, चक्षुष्मान् -ष्मती &c.; 'visible object,' वीक्ष्यं -क्ष्यं.

Visibly, adv. प्रत्यक्षतस् -क्षेण, पश्यतस्, समक्षं, साक्षात्.

Vision, s. (Faculty or act of seeing) दृष्टिः f., दर्शनं, आलोचकं, सन्दर्शनं, दृश्यत्वं, चक्षुरिन्द्रियं.—(Supernatural dream) स्वप्नः, स्वप्नदर्शनं, दर्शनं, सन्दर्शनं.—(Spectre) छाया, अपच्छाया, आभासः.

Visionary, a. मानसिकः -की -कं, मनःकल्पितः -ता -तं, अवास्तवः -वी -वं, अवास्तविकः -की -कं. See Fanciful, Imaginary.

Visit, s. अभ्यागमः -मनं, अभिगमः, दर्शनयात्रा, समायः.

To visit, v. a. अभ्यागम् (c. 1. -गच्छति -गन्तुं), अभिगम्, दर्शनार्थम् आगम् or आया or उपया; 'a lover,' अभिसृ (c. 10. -सारयति -यितुं).

Visitation, s. अभ्यागमनं, अभिगमनं, अभिसारणं, परीक्षणं.

Visitor, s. अभ्यागतः, गृहाभ्यागतः, गृहागतः. See Guest.

Vista, s. (Of trees) वृक्षपंक्तिः f., वृक्षश्रेणी. See Avenue.

Visual, a. दृष्टिसम्बन्धी -न्धिनी &c., चाक्षुषः -षी -षं, चक्षुरिन्द्रियसम्बन्धी &c.; 'visual organ,' चक्षुरिन्द्रियं, नेत्रेन्द्रियं.

Viswakarma, s. (Architect or artist of the gods) विश्वकर्म्मा m. (न्), देवत्वष्टा m. (ष्टृ), देववर्द्धकिः m., त्वष्टा m., देवशिल्पी m.

Vital, a. (Pertaining to life) प्राणसम्बन्धी &c., जीवसम्बन्धी &c., आयुष्यः -ष्या -ष्यं, प्राण in comp., जीव in comp.; 'vital action,' प्राणकर्म्म n. (न्); 'vital air,' प्राणवायुः m.; 'vital principle,' जीवात्मा m.—(Necessary to life) जीवसाधकः -का -कं, जीवनसाधकः &c., प्राणरक्षकः &c., जीवनरक्षकः &c.—(Vital part or spot) मर्म्म n. (न्), मर्म्मस्थानं, मर्म्मस्थलं, प्राणस्थानं; 'piercing a vital part,' मर्म्मभेदः.—(Essential), see the word.

Vitality, s. जीवशक्तिः f., जीवनशक्तिः f., प्राणशक्तिः f., जीवः, प्राणः, ओजस् n., चेतना, चैतन्यं, सजीवत्वं, प्राणकर्म्म n.

Vitals, s. pl. मर्म्माणि n. pl., मर्म्मस्थानं, मर्म्मस्थलं.

To vitiate, v. a. दुष् (c. 10. दूषयति -यितुं). See To corrupt.

Vitiation, s. दूषणं, पांसनं, दुष्टता. See Corruption.

Vitreous, a. काचमयः -यी -यं, काचगुणकः -का -कं, काचसगुणः &c.

To vitrefy, v. a. काचसात्कृ, काचवत्कृ, काचपरिणामं कृ.

Vitriol, s. (Blue) तुत्थं -त्थकं, तुत्थाञ्जनं, ताम्रगर्भः, मूषातुत्थं, तूतकं, शिखिग्रीवं, मयूरकं, नीलाञ्जनं, नीलं, वितुन्नकं, हेमतारं.—(Green) कासीसं, काशीशं, मलीमसः -सं, धातुशेखरः, विषदं.

To vituperate, vituperation. See To blame, censure, &c.

Vivacious, a. तेजोवान् -वती -वत् (त्), उल्लासी &c. See Lively.

Vivacity, s. तेजस् n., उल्लसता, उल्लासः. See Liveliness.

Viva-voce, मुखतस्, मुखद्वारा, मुखद्वारेण.

Vivid, a. सुस्पष्टः -ष्टा -ष्टं, स्फुरन् -रन्ती &c., स्फुरद्रूपः -पा -पं.

To vivify, v. a. जीव् (c. 10. जीवयति -यितुं), संजीव्. See To animate.

Viviparous, a. सचेतनप्रसूः f., सचेतनप्रजा.—(Born from the womb) जरायुजः -जा -जं.

Vixen, s. कर्कशा, चण्डी, क्रोधना. See Scold.

Vizier, s. मन्त्री m. (न्), अमात्यः. See Minister.

Vocable, s. शब्दः, वाक्यं, वचनं, वाचकः. See Word.

Vocabulary, s. शब्दकोषः, शब्दसंग्रहः, कोषः. See Lexicon.

Vocal, a. (Having a voice) वाग्युक्तः -क्ता -क्तं, वाणीयुक्तः &c., सवाक् m. f. n. (च्), वाणीविशिष्टः &c.—(Uttered by the voice) वाचिकः -का -कं, वाणीजातः -ता -तं, वाग्जातः &c.

Vocation, s. वृत्तिः f., व्यापारः, व्यवसायः, कर्म्म n. See Business.

Vocative, s. (Case in grammar) सम्बोधनं, सम्बुद्धिः f., आमन्त्रणं, अष्टमी विभक्तिः.

To vociferate, v. n. उच्चैर् घुष् or उत्क्रुश्. See To clamour, cry.

Vociferation, s. घोषणं -णा, उत्क्रोशः. See Exclamation.

Vociferous, a. महाघोषः -षा -षं, उच्चघोषणः &c. See Clamorous.

Vogue, s. प्रचारः, लोकप्रचारः, व्यवहारः, प्रचरः, रीतिः f.

Voice, s. स्वरः, वाणी, गीः f. (गिर्), गिरा, शब्दः, रवः, वाक् f. (च्), कण्ठरवः, वचनं, वचस् n., उक्तिः f., व्याहारः, व्याहृतिः f., भाषितं, लपितं, कण्ठध्वनिः m.; 'having a sweet voice,' मधुरस्वरः -रा -रं; 'having an unpleasant voice,' असौम्यस्वरः -रा -रं, खरस्वरः &c.; 'having the voice of a lion,' सिंहनादः -दा -दं; 'having a cracked voice,' भग्नस्वरः &c.; 'change of voice,' स्वरभेदः, स्वरविकारः.—(In grammar) वाच्यं, पदं; 'active voice,' कर्तृवाच्यं, परस्मैपदं; 'middle,' आत्मनेपदं; 'passive,' कर्मणिवाच्यं, भाववाच्यं.

Void, a. (Empty) शून्यः -न्या -न्यं, रिक्तः -क्ता -क्तं, शून्याकारः -रा -रं, see Empty.—(Null) निरर्थकः -का -कं, see Null.—(Devoid) हीनः -ना -नं, शून्यः &c., see Devoid, Destitute.

Void, s. शून्यं, रिक्तं, शून्यता. See Vacuum.

To void, v. a. उच्चर्, उत्सृज्, उत्सर्गं कृ, हद् (c. 1. हदति -दितुं), गु (c. 6. गुवति -वितुं). See To evacuate, excrement, &c.

Voided, p. p. उच्चरितः -ता -तं, गूनः -ना -नं, हन्नः -न्ना -न्नं.

Volatile, a. (Passing quickly into the aeriform state) अतिशीघ्रवायुपरिणामशीलः -ला -लं, वायुपरिणामशीलः &c., वायुपरिणामी -मिनी &c.—(Fickle) चपलः -ला -लं, चञ्चलः &c.

Volatility, s. चञ्चलता, चाञ्चल्यं, चपलता, चापल्यं, अस्थिरता.

Volcanic, a. ज्वालामुखीसम्बन्धी -न्धिनी &c., अद्रिवह्निसम्बन्धी &c.

Volcano, s. ज्वालामुखी, अद्रिवह्निः m., ज्वलनपर्वतः, आग्नेयपर्वतः.

Volition, s. (Act of will) सङ्कल्पः.—(Will), see Will.

Volley, s. वर्षः, वृष्टिः f., पातः; 'of stones,' शिलावर्षः, अश्मवर्षः.

Volubility, s. वाक्चापल्यं, वाक्चपलता. See Fluency.

Voluble, a. वाक्चपलः -ला -लं, चपलजिह्वः &c., see Fluent, Glib.

Volume, s. (Book) पुस्तकं.—(Of smoke) धूमावलिः -ली, धूमसंहतिः f.—(Of dust) रेणुसंहतिः f., रजोमेघः, धूलीपटलः -लं.

VOLUMINOUS, *a.* विस्तीर्णः -र्णा -र्णं, विस्तारमयः -यी -यं, बहुपुस्तकः -का -कं; 'a voluminous work,' ग्रन्थविस्तरः.

VOLUNTARILY, *adv.* कामतस्, इच्छातस्, बुद्धिपूर्व्वं, इच्छापूर्व्वकं, इच्छापुरःसरं, सङ्कल्पपूर्व्वं, स्वेच्छापूर्व्वकं, कामं, प्रकामं, निकामं, यथेष्टं, यथेप्सितं, स्वात्मसन्तोषेण, इष्टं.

VOLUNTARY, *a.* (Intentional) बुद्धिपूर्व्वः -र्व्वा -र्व्वं, ऐच्छिकः -की -कं, *see* INTENTIONAL.—(Spontaneous) ऐच्छिकः &c., कामिकः -की -कं, आभिकामिकः &c., काम्यः -म्या -म्यं, *see* SPONTANEOUS.

VOLUNTEER, *s.* स्वेच्छापूर्व्वकसैन्यः, स्वेच्छापूर्व्वकयोद्धा *m.* (द्धृ).

To VOLUNTEER, *v. a.* अयाचितं कृ in des. (चिकीर्षति -र्षितुं).

VOLUPTUARY, *s.* विषयी *m.* (न्), व्यसनी *m.*, विषयासक्तः, भोगी *m.*, सम्भोगी *m.*, उग्ररागः, पामरः. *See* SENSUALIST.

VOLUPTUOUS, *a.* विषयी -यिणी &c. *See* SENSUAL, LUXURIOUS.

VOLUTE, *s.* व्यावर्त्तनं, आवर्त्तः -र्त्तनं, व्यावर्त्तकालङ्कारः.

To VOMIT, *v. a.* or *n.* वम् (c. 1. वमति -मितुं), छर्द् (c. 10. छर्दयति -यितुं), वमनं कृ, छर्दनं कृ.—(Vomit up) उत्क्षिप् (c. 6.-क्षिपति -क्षेप्तुं), उद्गॄ (c. 6. -गिरति -गरितुं -रीतुं), उद्वम् (c. 10. -गमयति -यितुं), उत्तॄ (c. 10. -तारयति -यितुं).

VOMIT, *s.* (Matter vomited) वान्तं, वान्तिः *f.*—(Emetic), *see* EMETIC.

VOMITED, *p. p.* वान्तः -न्ता -न्तं, उद्वान्तः &c., उत्क्षिप्तः -प्ता -प्तं, विछर्दितः -ता -तं, उद्गतः &c., उद्गीर्णः -र्णा -र्णं, उद्गीर्णः &c., समुद्गीर्णः &c., उद्धृतः -ता -तं, उद्वान्तः -न्ता -न्तं.

VOMITING, *s.* वमनं, वमः, वमथुः *m.*, वान्तिः *f.*, छर्दनं, प्रच्छर्दिका, उत्क्षेपः -पणं, उद्गारः, उद्वमः, ऊर्द्ध्वशोधनं. *See* SICKNESS.

VOMITIVE, *a.* वान्तिकृत्, वान्तिदः -दा -दं. *See* EMETIC, *a.*

VORACIOUS, *a.* घस्मरः -री -रं. *See* GLUTTONOUS, GREEDY, &c.

VORTEX, *s.* आवर्त्तः -र्त्तिका, भ्रमः. *See* EDDY, WHIRLPOOL.

VOTARY, *s.* भक्तः, भक्तिमान् *m.* (त्), भक्तिलः, सेवकः, उपासकः, आसक्तः, परायणः, आश्रितः; 'of Krishna,' कृष्णाश्रितः, कृष्णाश्रितः.

VOTE, *s.* सम्मतिः *f.*, सम्मतं, सम्मतासम्मतप्रकाशनं, स्वीकारास्वीकारप्रकाशः, सम्मतिख्यापनं. *See* SUFFRAGE.

To VOTE, *v. n.* सम्मतासम्मतं प्रकाश् (c. 10. -काशयति -यितुं) or ख्या in caus. (ख्यापयति -यितुं), सम्मतिप्रकाशनं कृ, सम्मतिं प्रकाश्.

To VOTE, *v. a.* (Elect by vote) सम्मतिपूर्व्वं वृ or नियुज्.—(Give by vote) सम्मतिपूर्व्वं दा or प्रदा or प्रतिपद्.

VOTER, *s.* सम्मतिप्रकाशकः, सम्मतासम्मतप्रकाशकः.

VOTIVE, *a.* व्रतपूर्व्वं समर्पितः -ता -तं, व्रतानुसारेण समर्पितः &c.

To VOUCH, *v. a.* साक्ष्येण प्रमाणीकृ or दृढीकृ, प्रमाणं दा.

VOUCHER, *s.* प्रमाणपत्रं, प्रमाणलेखः, साधनपत्रं, साधनलेखः, निर्णयपत्रं, निर्णेता *m.* (तृ), प्रत्ययकारिणी, आगमः.

To VOUCHSAFE, *v. a.* अनुदा, प्रदा, दातुम् अर्ह् (c. 1. अर्हति -र्हितुं).

To VOUCHSAFE, *v. n.* अर्ह्. *See To* DEIGN, CONDESCEND, *v. n.*

VOW, *s.* व्रतः -तं, सङ्कल्पः, प्रतिज्ञा, नियमः; 'taking a vow on one's self,' व्रतसंग्रहः; 'faithful to one,' संशितव्रतः -ता -तं, यतव्रतः &c.; 'violation of one,' क्षतव्रतः; 'under a vow,' व्रतबद्धः -द्धा -द्धं, सङ्कल्पबद्धः &c., धृतव्रतः -ता -तं.

To VOW, *v. a.* व्रतपूर्व्वं or सङ्कल्पपूर्व्वं प्रतिज्ञा or दातुं प्रतिज्ञा or समृ in caus. (-अर्पयति -यितुं). *See To* PROMISE.

To VOW, *v. n.* (Make a vow) व्रतं कृ, सङ्कल्पं कृ, प्रतिज्ञां कृ, प्रतिज्ञां समारुह् (c. 1. -रोहति -रोढुं), प्रतिज्ञारोहणं कृ.

VOWEL, *s.* मातृका, स्वरः, वर्णः, अच्वर्णः, अमक्षरं; 'short vowel,' ह्रस्वस्वरः, मात्रा; 'ending in one,' अजन्तः -न्ता -न्तं; 'long vowel,' दीर्घस्वरः, दीर्घवर्णः; 'ending in one,' दीर्घवर्णान्तः &c.

VOYAGE, *s.* समुद्रयानं, जलयानं, जलयात्रा, संयात्रा.

To VOYAGE, *v. n.* समुद्रयानं कृ, समुद्रेण or जलेन या or गम्.

VOYAGER, *s.* समुद्रयायी *m.* (न्), जलयात्रिकः, वारिपथोपजीवी.

VRIHASPATI, *s.* (Preceptor of the gods, and regent of the planet Jupiter. He is the son of Angiras) बृहस्पतिः *m.*, गुरुः *m.*, सुराचार्य्यः, सुरप्रियः, सुरेज्यः, गीष्पतिः *m.*, वाचस्पतिः *m.*, धिषणः, जीवः, आङ्गिरसः, चित्रशिखण्डिजः. His son is called भरद्वाजः.

VULCAN, *s.* विश्वकर्म्मा *m.* (न्), देवशिल्पी *m.* *See* VISWAKARMA.

VULGAR, *a.* प्राकृतः -ती -तं, असभ्यः -भ्या -भ्यं, लौकिकः -की -कं, ग्राम्यः -म्या -म्यं, अश्लीलः &c., जघन्यः &c. *See* COMMON, LOW.

VULGARISM, *s.* (In language) अपशब्दः, कुशब्दः.

VULGARITY, *s.* असभ्यता, अशिष्टता, जघन्यता. *See* LOWNESS.

VULNERABLE, *a.* भेद्यः -द्या -द्यं, भेदनीयः &c., वेध्यः &c., वेधनीयः -या -यं; 'vulnerable point,' छिद्रं, मर्म्म *n.* (न्), मर्म्मस्थानं.

VULTURE, *s.* गृध्रः, दाक्षाय्यः, भासः, दूरदर्शी *m.*, दीर्घदर्शी *m.*

VYÁSA, *s.* (The arranger of the Vedas and Puránas, supposed to have lived about the 11th century after Christ. He is called 'island-born,' from having been born on an island in the Ganges) व्यासः, द्वैपायनः, कृष्णद्वैपायनः, कृष्णः.

W.

WAD, WADDING, *s.* आग्नेयचूर्णरोधनवस्तु *n.*, चूर्णरोधनी, चूर्णस्तम्भनं.

To WADDLE, *v. n.* हंसवत् चर् or क्रम्, हंसगतिः -तिः -ति भू.

WADDLE, WADDLING, *s.* हंसगतिः *f.*, हंसवद् गतिः *f.*, विषमगतिः.

To WADE, *v. n.* दुःखेन पादाभ्यां जले चर् or क्रम्, कष्टेन पादाभ्यां गाधजले क्रम्, दुःखेन पादाभ्यां जलपारं गम्.

WAFER, *s.* (Thin cake) तनुपिष्टकः, सूक्ष्मपिष्टकः, शष्कुलकः.—(For letters) वेफर् or वैफर् must be used.

To WAFT, *v. a.* शनैः शनैर् वायौ or वायुना वह् (c. 10. वाहयति -यितुं) or आनी, वायुना प्रेर् or प्रणुद् or उपनुद्.

To WAFT, *v. n.* शनैः शनैर् वायौ or वायुना वह् in pass. (उह्यते).

WAFTED, *p. p.* शनैर् वायुप्रेरितः -ता -तं or उपनुन्नः -न्ना -न्नं.

To WAG, *v. a.* इतस्ततः संचल् (c. 10. -चालयति -यितुं) or चल्.

To WAG, *v. n.* इतस्ततः संचल् (c. 10. -चलति -लितुं) or विचल् or चल्.

WAG, *s.* परिहासवेदी *m.* (न्), रसज्ञः, विदूषकः, धन्वी *m.* (न्).

To WAGE, *v. a.* (War) विग्रह् (c. 9. -गृह्णाति -ग्रहीतुं), विग्रहं कृ.

WAGER, *s.* पणः, आक्षिकपणः, नीविः -वी *f.*, प्रतिज्ञा.

To WAGER, *v. a.* पण् (c. 1. पणते -णितुं), विपण्. *See To* BET.

WAGES, *s.* वेतनं, भृतिः *f.*, भाटिः *f.*, भाटकः, वर्त्तनं. *See* HIRE.

WAGGERY, WAGGISH. *See* DROLLERY, WIT, WITTY.

WAGON, *s.* शकटः -टी -टं, गन्त्री, गन्त्रीरथः, वाहनं, चातुरं.

WAGONER, *s.* शाकटिकः, शकटवाहकः, गन्त्रीवाहकः, चातुरिकः.

WAG-TAIL, *s.* खञ्जनः -निका, खञ्जरीटः, खञ्जखेलः, खञ्जखेटः, कणाटीरः -रकः, कणाटीनः, भरद्वकः, गूढनीडः, हापुत्री, काककदः, काकच्छर्दिः *m.*

To WAIL, *v. n.* परिदेव्, आक्रन्द्, विलप्. *See To* LAMENT, MOAN.

WAILING, *s.* परिदेवनं, आक्रन्दनं. *See* LAMENTATION.

WAIN, *s.* शकटः -टी -टं, अनोगवं. *See* WAGON.

WAINSCOT, *s.* भित्तिबहिःस्थं काष्ठफलकमयं पटलं, भित्तिपटलं.

Waist, *s.* मध्यः -ध्यं, मध्यमः -मं, मध्यस्थलं, अवलग्नः -ग्नं, विलग्नः -ग्नं, उद्यानं, कटिदेशः, कटितटं, कटिः -टी *m. f.*

Waist-coat, *s.* कटिवस्त्रं, मध्यवस्त्रं, मध्यमवस्त्रं, अन्तरीयं.

To **wait**, *v. n.* (Stay) स्था (c. 1. तिष्ठति, स्थातुं), *see To* stay, stop.—(Wait for) प्रतीक्ष् (c. 1. -ईक्षते -क्षितुं), अपेक्ष्, प्रतिपाल् (c. 10. -पालयति -यितुं), *see To* await, expect; 'one's arrival,' आगमनं प्रतीक्ष्; 'wait a moment,' क्षणं तिष्ठ, क्षणम् अपेक्षस्व.—(Wait upon) उपास् (c. 2. -आस्ते -सितुं), उपचर्, परिचर्, सेव्, उपस्था, श्रु in des., *see To* attend; 'at table,' परिविष् (c. 10. -वेषयति -यितुं), परिवेषणं कृ.

Wait, *s.* (To lie in wait) पराक्रमणार्थं निभृते स्था.

Waiter, *s.* परिवेषकः, परिवेष्टा *m.* (ष्टृ), परिचरः, सेवकः.

To **waive**, *v. a.* त्यज्, परित्यज्. *See To* wave.

To **wake**, *v. a.* जागृ in caus., प्रबुध् in caus., *see To* awake.

To **wake**, *v. n.* जागृ (c. 2. जागर्त्ति -गरितुं). *See To* awake, *v. n.*

Wakeful, *a.* जागरणशीलः -ला -लं, जागरूकः -का -कं, जागरः -रा -रं, जागरी -रिणी &c., जागरिता -त्री -तृ (तृ), निद्राविमुखः -खा -खं, अनिद्राशीलः -ला -लं, अनिद्रः -द्रा -द्रं, विनिद्रः &c., उन्निद्रः &c., रात्रिजागरः &c.

Wakefulness, *s.* जागरणशीलता, जागरणं, रात्रिजागरणं, जागर्य्या, जागृतिः *f.*, जागरः, जाग्रदवस्था, जागरूकता, निद्राविमुखता, निद्राभावः, अनिद्रा, अस्वप्नः, अस्वापः, उन्निद्रता, औन्निद्र्यं, विनिद्रत्वं, योगिनिद्रा, प्रबोधः.

Waking, *s.* जागरणं, प्रजागरः, जागरः, प्रबोधः -धनं.

To **walk**, *v. n.* (Go on the feet) पादाभ्यां गम् (c. 1. गच्छति, गन्तुं) or या (c. 2. याति -तुं), पादाभ्यां क्रम् (c. 1. क्रामति, c. 4. क्राम्यति, क्रमितुं), पादाभ्यां चल् or चर्; 'backwards and forwards,' गमनागमनं कृ.—(Walk about, as for pleasure, &c.) परिक्रम्, विहृ (c. 1. -हरति -हर्त्तुं), परिक्रमं कृ.—(Walk off), *see To* decamp.

Walk, walking, *s.* पादगमनं, पादचारः, पादव्रजनं, पादक्रमणं, क्रमणं, पादाभ्यां गमनं; 'walking about,' परिक्रमः; 'for pleasure,' विहारः, विहरणं.—(Place for walking) विहारस्थानं, गमनागमनमार्गः, पदगमार्गः.

Walker, *s.* पादचारी *m.* (न्), पादयायी *m.*, पादगः, पदगः.

Wall, *s.* (Of a house, &c.) भित्तिः *f.*, भित्तिका, कुड्यं, कुड्यकं.—(A surrounding or inclosing wall) प्राकारः, प्राचीरं, परिसरः, सालः.—(Wall of bones, rubbish, &c.) एडुकं, ऐडुकं.

Walled, *a.* प्राकारीयः -या -यं, प्राकारावृतः &c., प्राचीरावृतः &c.

Wallet, *s.* सोपकारद्रव्यकोषः, सोपकारद्रव्याधारः, क्षुद्रकोषः.

To **wallow**, *v. n.* पङ्के लुठ् (c. 6. लुठति -ठितुं) or प्रलुठ् or क्रीड् (c. 1. क्रीडति -डितुं); 'a pig that wallows in mire,' पङ्कक्रीडः.

Walnut, *s.* (Tree) अक्षोटः, आक्षोटः, अक्षोडः, पीलुः *m.*, कन्दरालः -लकः, कर्परालः.

Waltz, *s.* विवर्त्तनृत्यं, विवर्त्तननृत्यं, परिवर्त्तननृत्यं.

Wan, *a.* पाण्डुः -ण्डुः -ण्डु, विवर्णः -र्णा -र्णं, पाण्डुवर्णः &c.

Wand, *s.* दण्डः, वेत्रं, यष्टिः *m. f.*, वेत्रयष्टिः; 'of death,' कालदण्डः.

To **wander**, *v. n.* भ्रम् (c. 4. भ्राम्यति, भ्रमितुं), परिभ्रम्, अट् (c. 1. अटति -ते -टितुं), पर्यट्, विहृ, विचर्, परिक्रम्, प्रव्रज्, परिगम्, भ्रमणं कृ, *see To* rove, ramble; 'to wander from,' *see To* stray.

Wanderer, *s.* भ्रमणकारी *m.* (न्), भ्रमी *m.*, परिभ्रमी *m.*, विहारी *m.*

Wandering, *s.* भ्रमणं, परिभ्रमणं, प्रव्रज्या. *See* Roaming.

To **wane**, *v. n.* क्षि in pass. (क्षीयते), परिक्षि, प्रक्षि, संक्षि, ह्रस्.

Wane, *s.* क्षयः, क्षितिः *f.*, परिक्षयः, अपक्षयः, ह्रासः, तेजःक्षयः, तेजोह्रासः; 'of the moon,' इन्दुक्षयः, कृष्णपक्षः, अपरपक्षः.

Waned, *p. p.* क्षीणः -णा -णं, क्षीणकलः -ला -लं, कलाक्षीणः &c., अपक्षीणः &c., निष्कलः -ला -लं, प्राप्तक्षयः -या -यं, जातक्षयः &c., जातह्रासः -सा -सं; 'a waned moon,' कलाशेषः.

Wanness, *s.* पाण्डुता, विवर्णता, वैवर्ण्यं, कालिमा *m.* (न्).

To **want**, *v. a* or *n.* (Be without) हीनः -ना -नं भू or अस्, *see To* lack; 'he wants wisdom,' बुद्धिहीनः or निर्बुद्धिर् अस्ति.—(Have need of) आकाङ्क्ष् (c. 1. -काङ्क्षति -क्षितुं), अपेक्ष् (c. 1. -ईक्षते -क्षितुं), *see To* need.—(Desire, wish) इष् (c. 6. इच्छति, एषितुं), आकाङ्क्ष्, काङ्क्ष्, *see To* desire.—(Be deficient) न्यूनीभू.—(Be in poverty) दरिद्रा (c. 2. दरिद्राति -द्रितुं).

Want, *s.* (Absence of any thing) अभावः, असम्भवः, अविषयः, विरहः, अप्राप्तिः *f.*, राहित्यं, रहितत्वं, शून्यत्वं, अदर्शनं; 'from want of rain,' वृष्टेरभावात्; 'from want of food,' आहारविरहात्; 'want of money,' धनाभावः.—(Occasion for) प्रयोजनं, *see* Need.—(Deficiency) न्यूनता.—(Indigence) दारिद्र्यं, धनाभावः, द्रव्याभावः.

Wanting, *a.* न्यूनः -ना -नं, अविद्यमानः &c. *See* Deficient.

Wanton, *a.* (Frolicsome) विलासी -सिनी -सि (न्), विलासवान् -वती -वत् (त्), *see* Playful.—(Lascivious) कामुकः -का -कं, कामी &c., लाली &c., *see* Lustful; 'a wanton woman,' पुंश्चली, बन्धकी, लालिनी.—(Self-willed, unrestrained) स्वैरः -री -रं, स्वैरी &c., कामचारी &c., स्वेच्छः -च्छा -च्छं.

To **wanton**, *v. n.* विलस् (c. 1. -लसति -सितुं), क्रीड्. *See To* play.

Wantonly, *adv.* कामुकवत्, विलासेन, स्वेच्छया, यथेच्छं, यथेष्टं.

Wantonness, *s.* कामुकत्वं, लीला, विलासः, लालित्यं, स्वैरिता.

War, *s.* विग्रहः, युद्धं, प्रयुद्धं, सङ्ग्रामः, रणं, संयुगः, सम्परायः -यकं, भीमरः, राटिः *f.*, *see* Battle; 'one skilled in it,' सांयुगीनः.

To **war**, *v. n.* (Make war) विग्रहं कृ, विग्रह् (c. 9. -गृह्णाति -ग्रहीतुं), युद्धं कृ, युध् (c. 4. युध्यते, योद्धुं), संग्राम् (c. 10. -ग्रामयते -यितुं), संग्रामं कृ; 'wishing to make war,' सिसंग्रामयिषुः -षुः -षु; 'war-chariot,' स्यन्दनः; 'war-cry,' सिंहनादः; 'war-horse,' योधहरः, *see* Charger; 'war-dance,' वीरजयन्तिका.

To **warble, warbling**. *See To* quaver, sing, Singing.

To **ward**, *v. a.* (Off) प्रतिवृ (c. 10. -वारयति -यितुं), निवृ, प्रतिहन् (c. 2. -हन्ति -न्तुं), प्रतिकृ, निरुध्, अपसिध्, प्रतिषिध्, अपोह्; 'a blow,' प्रतिघातं कृ, परित्राणं कृ, हस्तवारणं कृ, हस्तधारणं कृ, पर्य्यासिं कृ.

Ward, *s.* (Of a town) पुरार्द्धविस्तरः.—(Custody) रक्षा.—(One under a guardian) नाथाधीनः, बालः, शिशुः *m.*, किशोरः.

Warden, *s.* रक्षकः, नाथः, अध्यक्षः, अधिकारी *m.* (न्), पालः.

Warder, *s.* दौवारिकः, द्वाराध्यक्षः, रक्षकः, दर्शकः, *see* Door-keeper.

Ward-robe, *s.* वस्त्राधारः, वस्त्रभाण्डं.—(Clothes) वस्त्रसमूहः.

Ware, wares, *s.* पण्यं, विट्पण्यं, द्रव्यं. *See* Commodity.

Warehouse, *s.* पण्यशाला, पण्यद्रव्यशाला, विक्रेयद्रव्यशाला.

Warfare, *s.* युद्धं, सङ्ग्रामः, विग्रहः. *See* War, Battle.

Warily, wariness. *See* Cautiously, Caution, &c.

Warlike, *a.* (Pertaining to war) साङ्ग्रामिकः -की -कं, सामरिकः &c., साम्परायिकः &c.—(Disposed for war) रणप्रियः -या -यं, रणकामी -मिनी &c., रणासक्तः -क्ता -क्तं, रणोत्सुकः -का -कं, रणशूरः -रा -रं, रणवीरः &c., युयुत्सुः -त्सुः -त्सु.

Warm, *a.* उष्णः -ष्णा -ष्णं, ईषदुष्णः &c., कदुष्णः -ष्णा -ष्णं, उष्णकः &c., ईषदुष्णकः &c., तप्तः -प्ता -प्तं, ईषत्तप्तः &c., घर्म्म in comp., *see* Hot; 'water,' घर्म्मपयस् *n.*—(Suffering from heat) घर्म्मार्त्तः -र्त्ता -र्त्तं.

To warm, *v. a.* ईषत् तप् (c. 10. तापयति -यितुं) or सन्तप् or प्रतप्, किञ्चित् तप्, ईषदुष्णीकृ; 'the feet,' पादौ प्रतप्; 'to warm one's self at the fire,' अग्नितापं सेव्.

Warmed, *p. p.* ईषत्तप्तः -प्ता -प्तं, किञ्चित्तप्तः &c., ईषदुष्णीकृतः &c.

Warm-hearted, *a.* हृदयी -यिनी &c., हृदयालुः -लुः -लु, स्नेही &c.

Warmly, *adv.* उष्णं, सोष्मं, कदुष्णं, प्रचण्डं, सस्नेहं, स्नेहेन.

Warmth, warmness, *s.* उष्णता, उष्णः, कदुष्णता, उष्मः, कोष्णता, कोष्णं, तापः, ईषत्तापः, उत्तापः, रौद्रः -द्रं. *See* Heat, Hotness.

To warn, *v. a.* (Caution, admonish) प्रत्यादिश् (c. 6. -दिशति -देष्टुं), सन्दिश्, प्रदिश्, उपदिश्, पूर्व्वं प्रबुध् in caus., चित् in caus. (चेतयति -यितुं), *see To* caution, &c.—(Apprise) विज्ञा in caus. (-ज्ञापयति -यितुं), सूच्.

Warned, *p. p.* प्रत्यादिष्टः -ष्टा -ष्टं, प्रबोधितः &c., विज्ञापितः &c.

Warning, *s.* प्रत्यादेशः, प्रबोधः -धनं, पूर्व्वबोधः -धनं, सन्देशः.

To warp, *v. a.* साचीकृ, वक्रीकृ, कुच् (c. 10. कुचयति -यितुं), आकुच्, संकुच् (c. 1. -कोचति -चितुं), आकृष्, संवृ.

To warp, *v. n.* संकुच् or कुच् in pass., तुग्. *See To* shrink, *v. n.*

To warrant, *v. a.* प्रमाणं दा, अधिकारं or अधिकारित्वं दा, सप्रमाणं -णां कृ, सप्रमाणीकृ, प्रमाणीकृ. *See To* sanction, authorise.

Warrant, *s.* (Authority, sanction) अधिकारित्वं, प्रमाणं, अनुज्ञा, आश्रयः.—(Writ) आज्ञापत्रं, शासनपत्रं, अनुज्ञापत्रं, अधिकारपत्रं.

Warranted, *p. p.* सप्रमाणः -णा -णं, साश्रयः -या -यं, साधारः &c.

Warranty, *s.* निर्दोषपत्रं, निश्छिद्रपत्रं, प्रमाणपत्रं.

Warren, *s.* शशकालयः, शशकस्थानं, शशकाश्रयः.

Warrior, *s.* (Soldier) योद्धा *m.* (द्धृ), योधः, युयुधानः, प्रहारी *m.*, *see* Soldier.—(Hero) भटः, सुभटः, वीरः, रथी *m.*, स्यन्दनारोहः, रणपण्डितः, विक्रान्तः, जाल्मी *m.*, भजः, *see* Hero.

Wart, *s.* चर्म्मकीलः -लं, किणः, मांसाङ्कुरः, अधिमांसं.

Wary, *a.* सावधानः -ना -नं, विचक्षणः -णा -णं. *See* Cautious.

To wash, *v. a.* जलेन धाव् (c. 10. धावयति -यितुं) or प्रधाव्, जलेन मृज् (c. 1. मार्जति, c. 2. मार्ष्टि -ष्टुं) or सम्मृज् or प्रक्षल् (c. 10. -क्षालयति -यितुं) or क्षल्, जलेन शुध् (c. 10. शोधयति -यितुं) or निर्णिज् (c. 3. -णेनेक्ति -णेक्तुं) or पू, स्ना in caus. (स्नापयति, स्नपयति -यितुं); 'to wash the face,' मुखमार्जनं कृ, मुखप्रक्षालनं कृ; 'the feet,' पादौ प्रक्षल्; 'the hands,' हस्तौ प्रक्षल्; 'to wash out the mouth,' आचम्, उपस्पृश्, *see To* rinse.

To wash, *v. n.* स्नानं कृ, अभिषेकं कृ, स्ना (c. 2. स्नाति -तुं), जलाभिषेकं कृ.

Wash, *s.* (Act of washing) धावनं, प्रक्षालनं, क्षालनं, मार्जनं, स्नानं, अभिषेकः, *see* Washing.—(Sloppy food for pigs, &c.) अमेध्यजलादिमिश्रितम् उच्छिष्टान्नं or भुक्तोच्छिष्टं or भुक्तसमुज्झितं.—(Materials to smear over) लेपः, विलेपः, प्रलेपः, लेपनं.

Washed, *p. p.* क्षालितः -ता -तं, प्रक्षालितः &c., मार्जितः -ता -तं, जलमार्जितः &c., धावितः -ता -तं, धौतः &c., निर्धौतः &c., निर्णिक्तः -क्ता -क्तं, स्नापितः &c., स्नपितः &c., स्नातः -ता -तं; 'by waves,' ऊर्म्मिरुग्णः -ग्णा -ग्णं.

Washerman, *s.* वस्त्रधावकः, वस्त्ररजकः, रजकः, वस्त्रनिर्णेजकः, निर्णेजकः, वस्त्रनेजकः, वस्त्रमार्जकः, मार्जः, वस्त्रप्रक्षालकः, भस्मकारः, कर्म्मकीलकः.

Washerwoman, *s.* वस्त्रधावकी, वस्त्रनिर्णेजकी, वस्त्ररजकी, रजकी.

Washing, *s.* प्रक्षालनं, क्षालनं, धावनं, मार्जनं, निर्णेकः, निर्णेजनं, अवनेजनं, स्नानं, अभिषेकः, अवसेचनं; 'of clothes,' वस्त्रक्षालनं, वस्त्रप्रक्षालनं, वस्त्रमार्जनं; 'of the feet,' पादप्रक्षालनं, पादयोः क्षालनं, पादधावनं, पादावसेचनं, पादावनेजनं.

Washy, *a.* जलगुणकः -का -कं, अतिद्रवगुणकः &c., अतिद्रवरूपः &c.

Wasp, *s.* वरटा -टी, वरटः, गन्धोली, गन्धाली, भ्रमरकीटः, वरलः, वरोलः, वरेणः, वारला, भृङ्गः, भृङ्गरोलः, विषशूकः, विषशृङ्गी, ब्राह्मणी, तैलाटी, तृणषट्पदः, पेशस्कृत् *m.*, इडाषिका.

Waspish, *a.* कर्कशः -शा -शं, शीघ्रकोपी -पिनी &c., वरटशीलः &c.

To waste, *v. a.* व्ययीकृ, व्यय् (c. 1. व्ययति, c. 10. व्यययति -यितुं, rt. इ), क्षि (c. 1. क्षयति, c. 5. क्षिणोति, c. 10. क्षपयति, क्षययति -यितुं), उपक्षि, क्षयं कृ, क्षीणीकृ, विक्षिप् (c. 6. -क्षिपति -क्षेप्तुं), निःक्षिप्, क्षिप्, नश् (c. 10. नाशयति -यितुं), नाशं कृ; 'to waste time,' कालक्षेपं कृ, कालहरणं कृ, कालक्षयं कृ, कालं क्षिप्.

To waste, *v. n.* क्षि in pass. (क्षीयते), परिक्षि, अपचि in pass. (-चीयते), सद् (c. 1. सीदति, सत्तुं), ह्रस् (c. 1. ह्रसते -सितुं), परिहा in pass. (-हीयते), प्रहा in pass., क्षै (c. 1. क्षायति, क्षातुं), क्षीणीभू, नश् (c. 4. नश्यति).

Waste, wasted, *a.* or *p. p.* (Expended uselessly) अपचितः -ता -तं, व्ययितः &c., व्ययीकृतः &c., व्ययीभूतः &c.—(Diminished) क्षीणः -णा -णं, परिक्षीणः &c., क्षयितः -ता -तं, क्षामः -मा -मं, विशीर्णः &c.; 'wasted with hunger,' क्षुत्क्षामः -मा -मं.—(Refuse) उच्छिष्टः -ष्टा -ष्टं, निःसारः -रा -रं.—(As land) खिलः -ला -लं, जङ्गलः -ला -लं, जाङ्गलः -ली -लं, शून्यः -न्या -न्यं, अप्रहतः -ता -तं.—(To lay waste) उपद्रु, उपप्लवं कृ, बाध्, पीड्, *see To* ravage.

Waste, *s.* क्षयः, परिक्षयः, उपक्षयः, अपक्षयः, क्षिया, क्षितिः *f.*, अपचयः, व्ययः, अपव्ययः, नाशः, क्षेपः, विक्षेपः; 'of time,' कालक्षेपः, कालक्षयः, कालनाशः, कालहरणं, कालयापः -पनं, कालव्ययः; 'of breath,' वाग्व्ययः, वाक्क्षेपः, वाक्क्षयः.—(Desert ground) जङ्गलं, जङ्गलभूमिः *f.*, शून्यं, *see* Desert.

Wasteful, *a.* व्ययशीलः -ला -लं, अपव्ययी -यिनी -यि. *See* Prodigal.

Waste-pipe, *s.* परीवाहः, परिवाहः, उच्छिष्टजलमार्गः.

Wasting, *part.* क्षीयमाणः -णा -णं, अपक्षीयमानः &c., क्षयी -यिणी &c.

Watch, *s.* (Guard) रक्षा, रक्षणं.—(Person watching) रक्षकः, रक्षी *m.* (न्), रक्षिता *m.* (तृ); 'body of watchmen,' रक्षकजनाः *m. pl.*, रक्षकगणः, रक्षिगणः.—(Eighth part of the day, or three hours) प्रहरः, यामः; 'last watch of the night,' अपररात्रः.—(Small time-piece) कालमापनी, कालमापनयन्त्रं.

To watch, *v. n.* (Keep awake) जागृ (c. 2. जागर्त्ति, जागरितुं), जागरणं कृ.—(Keep guard) रक्षां कृ, रक्षार्थं जागृ.—(Watch for) अपेक्ष् (c. 1. -ईक्षते -क्षितुं), प्रतीक्ष्.—(Be vigilant) सावधानः -ना -नं भू or स्था, सचेतनः -ना -नं स्था.

To watch, *v. a.* (Guard) रक्ष् (c. 1. रक्षति -क्षितुं), पाल् (c. 10. पालयति -यितुं), परिपाल्.—(Observe) निरूप्, निरीक्ष्, वीक्ष्, अवेक्ष्.—(Watch over) अधिष्ठा (c. 1. -तिष्ठति -ष्ठातुं).

Watched, *p. p.* रक्षितः -ता -तं, अभिरक्षितः &c., निरूपितः &c.

Watchful, *a.* जागरः -रा -रं, प्रजागरः &c., जागरी -रिणी &c., जागरूकः -का -कं, प्रबुद्धः -द्धा -द्धं, सावधानः -ना -नं, अप्रमादी -दिनी &c., अपेक्षी -क्षिणी &c. *See* Vigilant.

Watch-house, watch-box, *s.* उट्टाटः, पिठरं. *See* Guard-room.

Watching, *s.* जागरणं, जागर्य्या, जागर्त्तिः *f.*, जागरिया, निरूपणं;

'alternate watching and sleeping,' उपशायः, विशायः.

WATCHMAKER, *s.* कालमापमकारः, कालमापनविक्रयी *m.* (न्).

WATCHMAN, *s.* रक्षकः, गृहाभिपाली *m.* (न्), गृहपालकः, आरक्षकः, प्रहरी *m.* (न्), यामिकः; 'who announces the hours,' वैबोधिकः, वैतालिकः.

WATCHWORD, *s.* सम्भाषा -षणं, रणसम्भाषा, संविद् *f.*, रणसंविद्.

WATER, *s.* जलं, वारि *n.*, अम्बु *n.*, अम्भस् *n.*, सलिलं, उदकं, उदं, पयस् *n.*, तोयं, पानीयं, आपः *f. pl.* (अप्), नीरं, वार् *f. n.*, पाथस् *n.*, कीलालं, पुष्करं, अर्णस् *n.*, पेयं, सलं, संवरं, शंवरं, सर्वं -वरं, सर्व -वरः, क्षीरं, पायं, अरं, कमलं, कोमलं, पीथा, अमृतं, जीवनं, जीवनीयं, भुवनं, वनं, कबन्धं, कं, अर्णं, सर्वतोमुखं, मेघपुष्पं, घनरसः, वह्निमारकं, दहनारातिः *m.*, नीचगं, कुलीनसं, कृत्स्नं, कृपीटं, पावनं, शरलकं, तृषाहं; 'warm water,' उष्णोदकं, घर्मोदकं, घर्माम्बु *n.*; 'cold water,' शीतोदकं; 'boiling water,' पक्ववारि *n.*, तप्तजलं, तप्तोदकं, हरणं; 'land and water,' स्थलजलं; 'place where water is distributed,' प्रपा; 'holy water for the feet,' पाद्यं, पादोदकं, चरणोदकं; 'bread and water,' अन्नोदकं; 'growing in water,' जलोद्भवः -वा -वं, जलभूः -भूः -भु; 'living on water,' अम्भक्षः -क्षा -क्षं; 'living in water,' जलचरः -रा -रं, जलचारी -रिणी &c.; 'water-animal,' जलजन्तुः *m.*; 'having much water,' बहूदकः -का -कं; 'having clean water,' अच्छोदः -दा -दं, *see* OCEAN.

To WATER, *v. a.* (Irrigate) सिच्, उक्ष्, *see To* IRRIGATE.—(Supply with water) जलं दा, जलं पा in caus. (पाययति -यितुं), जलदानं कृ.

To WATER, *v. n.* (As the mouth, eyes, &c.) जलं स्रु (c. 10. स्रावयति -यितुं) or पत् in caus.; 'the mouth waters,' लालायते.

WATER-CARRIER, *s.* उदकवाहः, उदवाहः, अम्बुवाहः, दृतिहारः -री *m.* (न्).

WATER-CLOSET, *s.* पायुक्षालनवेश्म *n.* (न्), शौचकूपः.

WATER-COURSE, *s.* जलमार्गः, जलवाहनी, उदकमार्गः. *See* DRAIN.

WATERED, *p. p.* सिक्तः -क्ता -क्तं, जलसिक्तः &c., सलिलसिक्तः &c.; 'well watered,' जलप्रायः -या -यं; 'by rivers,' नदीमातृकः -का -कं; 'by rain,' देवमातृकः &c.

WATERFALL, *s.* निर्झरः, झरः, वारिप्रवाहः, सरः -री, झरा, जलनिर्गमः.

WATER-FOWL, *s.* जलकुक्कुटः, जलविहङ्गमः, गोरङ्कुः *m.*, राजभट्टिका.

WATERING, *s.* सेकः, सेचनं, सिञ्चनं, निषेकः, अवसेकः -सेचनं.

WATERING-PLACE, *s.* जलपानस्थानं, उदकपानस्थानं, प्रपा.

WATERING-POT, *s.* सेकपात्रं, सेचनपात्रं, सेचनघटः, कलसः.

WATER-LILY, *s.* उत्पलं, पद्मः, जलकमलं. *See* LOTUS.

WATER-MAN, *s.* पोतवाहः, नाविकः, पोतवणिक् *m.* (ज्), घटिकः.

WATER-MELON, *s.* तरम्बुजं, पृहल्लोलं.

WATER-MILL, *s.* जलयन्त्रं, जलचक्रं, उदकयन्त्रं.

WATER-POT, *s.* घटः, कलशः, कलसः, जलकलशः, जलाधारकलशः, उदकपात्रं, उदपात्रं, उदकुम्भः, निपः, कुटः, अलुः *f.*, आलुः *f.*; 'of a religious student,' कमण्डलुः -लु *m. n.*, कुण्डी -ण्डिका.

WATERPROOF, *a.* जलाभेद्यः -द्या -द्यं, जलाव्याप्यः &c., उदकाभेद्यः &c.

WATER-SNAKE, *s.* जलव्यालः, जलभुजङ्गः, जलसर्पः.

WATER-SPOUT, *s.* जलचक्रः, उदचक्रः, उदकचक्रः.

WATER-WHEEL, *s.* (For raising water) घटीयन्त्रं, विलोमं.

WATER-WORK, *s.* जलयन्त्रं, उदयन्त्रं, उदकयन्त्रं.

WATERY, *a.* (Pertaining to water) जलसम्बन्धी &c., औदकः -की -कं, आप्यः -प्या -प्यं, जलसः -सा -सं, उदकलः -ला -लं.—(Consisting of it) जलमयः -यी -यं, जलरूपः -पा -पं, अम्मयः &c.—(Abounding with it) जलाढ्यः -ढ्या -ढ्यं, सजलः &c., जलप्रायः -या -यं, अम्बुमान् -मती -मत् (त्), बहूदकः -का -कं, बहुजलः -ला -लं, ससलिलः &c., साम्भाः &c., *see* MARSHY; 'watery wave,' जलोर्म्मिः *m. f.*

WATTLE, *s.* काष्ठशलाकाग्रथितम् अवरोधकं, काष्ठशलाकाग्रथितस्तम्भः.

To WATTLE, *v. a.* काष्ठशलाकाः परस्परं ग्रन्थ्. *See To* INTERWEAVE.

WAVE, *s.* ऊर्म्मिः *m. f.*, ऊर्म्मिका, जलोर्म्मिः *f.*, तरङ्गः, जलतरङ्गः, वीचिः *m. f.*, भङ्गः, भङ्गिः -ङ्गी *f.*, भङ्गिः *f.*, कल्लोलः, उल्लोलः, जललता, पयोराशिः *f.*; 'wave-crowned,' ऊर्म्मिमाली -लिनी -लि (न्), जलोर्म्मिमाली &c.

To WAVE, *v. a.* (Move this way and that way) इतस्ततः संचल् in caus. (-चालयति -यितुं) or चल् or आस्फल् in caus., भ्रम् (c. 10. भ्रमयति -यितुं), इतस्ततो विधू.—(Put aside, give up) त्यज् (c. 1. त्यजति, त्यक्तुं), विसृज् (c. 6. -सृजति -स्रष्टुं), हा, विहा.

To WAVE, *v. n.* इतस्ततश् चल् (c. 1. चलति -लितुं) or विचल्.

WAVELESS, *a.* अवीचिः -चिः -चि, निस्तरङ्गः -ङ्गा -ङ्गं. *See* UNRUFFLED.

To WAVER, *v. n.* दोल (nom. दोलायते), विचल् (c. 1. -चलति -लितुं).

WAVY, *a.* ऊर्म्मिमान् -मती -मत् (त्), भङ्गुरः -रा -रं, बन्धुरः &c., तरङ्गितः -ता -तं, उन्नतानतः &c., चलः -ला -लं. *See* UNDULATING.

WAX, *s.* (Of bees) सिक्थं -क्थकं, मधूच्छिष्टं, मधुजं, शिक्थं, उच्छिष्टमोदनं, द्रावकं, आर्चं.—(For sealing) लाक्षा, अलक्तः.—(Of the ear) कर्णमलं.

To WAX, *v. a.* सिक्थकेन लिप् or अञ्ज्, सिक्थकाक्तं -क्तां कृ.

To WAX, *v. n.* (Increase) वृध्; 'as the moon,' कलावृद्धो भू.

WAXEN, WAXY, *a.* सिक्थकमयः -यी -यं, सैक्थिकः &c., सिक्थसगुणः &c.

WAY, *s.* (Road, path) मार्गः, पथः, पन्थाः *m.* (पथिन्), अध्वा *m.* (न्), वर्त्म *n.* (न्), अयनं, *see* ROAD; 'one who has lost his way,' मार्गभ्रष्टः, वर्त्मवर्जितः, दिग्भ्रान्तः; 'to give way,' मार्गं दा, पन्थानं त्यज्; 'make way! make way!' अपसर, अपसरत, अपसर, अन्तरम् अन्तरं.—(Space, distance) अन्तरं, मार्गं, पर्य्यन्तं, दूरं; 'for a little way,' कियत्पर्य्यन्तं, कियद्दूरं, ईषद्दूरं; 'a great way,' अतिदूरं.—(Direction) दिक् *f.* (श्), मार्गः; 'to point out the way,' दिक्प्रदर्शनं कृ, मार्गं दृश् in caus., मार्गप्रदर्शनं कृ; 'this way, this way!' इत इतः; 'which way?' कुत्र, कां दिशं; 'in both ways,' उभयत्र.—(Manner, method, course) प्रकारः, रीतिः *f.*, विधिः *m.*, विधानं, क्रमः, मार्गः; 'way to act,' क्रियाविधिः *m.*, कृत्यविधिः *m.*, *see* MANNER. Often expressed by the affix धा; as, 'in one way,' एकधा; 'in two ways,' द्विधा; 'in three,' त्रिधा; 'in a hundred,' शतधा; 'in many,' बहुधा, अनेकधा; 'in how many?' कतिधा; 'that may be written in two ways,' द्विधालेख्यः -ख्या -ख्यं. Or by the affixes था, तस्, &c.; as, 'in both ways,' उभयथा, उभयतस्.

WAYFARER, *s.* पथिकः, अध्वगः, मार्गिकः, अध्वन्यः. *See* TRAVELLER.

To WAYLAY, *v. a.* पराक्रमणार्थं मार्गे निभृतं स्था.

WAYWARD, &c. *See* FROWARD, PERVERSE, WILFUL.

WAY-WORN, *a.* अध्वश्रान्तः -न्ता -न्तं, मार्गश्रान्तः &c., यानश्रान्तः &c.

WE, *pron.* वयं *nom. pl.* (अस्मद्); 'we two,' आवां *nom. du.*

WEAK, *a.* दुर्बलः -ला -लं, निर्बलः &c., अबलः &c., अल्पबलः &c., अल्पशक्तिः -क्तिः -क्ति, अकल्पः -ल्पा -ल्पं, निःसत्त्वः -त्त्वा -त्त्वं, निस्तेजाः -जाः -जः (स्), *see* FEEBLE, INFIRM.—(In mind) अल्पबुद्धिः -द्धिः -द्धि, अल्पधीः -धीः -धि, विकलबुद्धिः &c., विकलान्तःकरणः -णा -णं.—

(Weak point or side) छिद्रं, मर्म्मस्थानं.

To WEAKEN, *v. a.* दुर्बलीकृ, बलं हृ (c. 1. हरति, हर्त्तुं), बलक्षयं कृ, शक्तिक्षयं कृ, शक्तिभङ्गं कृ, शक्तिह्रासं कृ. *See To* DEBILITATE.

WEAKENED, *p. p.* क्षीणबलः -ला -लं, हृतबलः &c., दुर्बलीकृतः -ता -तं, हृतौजाः -जाः -जः (स्), क्षीणसत्त्वः -त्त्वा -त्त्वं. *See* ENFEEBLED.

WEAKENING, *a.* बलक्षयकारी -रिणी -रि (न्), सत्त्वक्षयकारी &c.

WEAKNESS, *s.* दुर्बलता, दौर्बल्यं, निर्बलता, अबलं, अशक्तिः *f.*, बलहीनता, बलक्षयः, शक्तिक्षयः, बलक्षीणता, बलहानिः *f.*, शक्तिभङ्गः, *see* DEBILITY.—(Foible) छिद्रं.

WEAL, *s.* क्षेमं, कल्याणं, शुभं, श्रेयस्, भद्रं, कुशलं, *see* WELFARE; 'weal and woe,' शुभाशुभं, भद्राभद्रं.

WEALTH, *s.* धनं, वसु *n.*, वित्तं, विभवः, वैभवं, सम्पत्तिः *f.*, द्रविणं, द्रव्यं, राः *m.* (रै), रिक्थं, स्वापतेयं, हिरण्यं, द्युम्नं, स्वापतेयं, भोग्यं, *see* RICHES; 'in grain,' धान्यधनं, धान्यार्थः; 'in cattle,' गोधनं, चर्म्मधनं.

WEALTHINESS, *s.* महाधनता, सधनत्वं. *See* RICHNESS, OPULENCE.

WEALTHY, *a.* धनी -निनी -नि (न्). *See* RICH, OPULENT.

To WEAN, *v. a.* त्यक्तस्तन्यं -न्यां कृ, स्तन्यवियुक्तं -क्तां कृ, स्तन्यं त्यज् in caus. (त्याजयति -यितुं), स्तन्यत्यागं कृ.—(From the world) सङ्गविमुखं -खां कृ, विषयविमुखं -खां कृ, त्यक्तसङ्गं -ङ्गां कृ, विरक्तं -क्तां कृ.

WEANED, *p. p.* त्यक्तस्तन्यः -न्या -न्यं, त्यक्तस्तनः -ना -नं. *See To* WEAN.

WEANING, WEANEDNESS, *s.* स्तन्यत्यागः; 'from the world,' सङ्गत्यागः, वैराग्यं, विषयासक्तिः, इन्द्रियासक्तिः, विषयविमुखता, प्रत्याहारः.

WEAPON, *s.* शस्त्रं, आयुधं, अस्त्रं, प्रहरणं, हेतिः *f.*, परियातः, वधत्रं, शस्त्रास्त्रं.

To WEAR, *v. a.* (Impair, consume by attrition, &c.) क्षि in caus. (क्षपयति, क्षययति -यितुं), क्षयं कृ, घृष् (c. 1. घर्षति -र्षितुं), घर्षणेन नश्.—(Carry on the body, as clothes, &c.) धृ (c. 10. धारयति -यितुं, c. 1. धरति, धर्त्तुं), भृ (c. 3. बिभर्त्ति, c. 1. भरति, भर्त्तुं), धा (c. 3. धत्ते, धातुं), परिधा, आच्छद् (c. 10. -च्छादयति -यितुं), वस् (c. 2. वस्ते -सितुं); 'he wears clothes,' वासांसि बिभर्त्ति.—(Wear out by use, &c.) जीर्णं -र्णां कृ, जीर्णीकृ, जर्ज्जरीकृ, जर्ज्जरं -रां कृ.—(Wear out, consume by fatigue, &c.) सद् (c. 10. सादयति -यितुं), अवसद्, खिद् (c. 10. खेदयति -यितुं), ग्लै in caus. (ग्लपयति -यितुं), *see To* FATIGUE.

To WEAR, *v. n.* (Waste away) क्षि in pass. (क्षीयते), सद्. *see To* WASTE, *v. n.*—(Wear out by use) जॄ (c. 4. जीर्य्यति), परिजॄ, जीर्णः -र्णा -र्णं भू, जीर्णीभू, जर्ज्जरः -रा -रं भू, जर्ज्जरीभू.—(Wear off), *see To* PASS AWAY.

WEAR, *s.* (Waste through use) क्षयः, परिक्षयः, अपक्षयः, उपभोगः, भोगः.—(Friction) घर्षणं, आघर्षणं.—(Dam in a river) सेतुः *m.*, जलप्रवाहबन्धः.

WEARER, *s.* धारी *m.* (न्), धरः, वसिता *m.* (तृ), भृत् *m.*

WEARIED, *p. p.* श्रान्तः -न्ता -न्तं, क्लान्तः &c. *See* FATIGUED.

WEARINESS, *s.* श्रमः, श्रान्तिः *f.*, क्लान्तिः *f.*, खेदः. *See* FATIGUE.

WEARING, *part.* or *a.* (Carrying) धारी -रिणी -रि (न्), धरः -रा -रं, उद्वहन् -हन्ती &c.—(Consuming) क्षयकारी &c.—(Fit to wear) परिधानोपयोगी -गिनी &c., परिधानयोग्यः -ग्या -ग्यं.

WEARISOME, *a.* श्रमजनकः -का -कं, खेदजनकः &c., आयासजनकः &c., श्रान्तिकरः -री -रं, श्रमकरः &c., श्रमकारकः -का -कं, आयासजनकः &c., जाड्यजनकः &c., जाड्यप्रदः -दा -दं. *See* TEDIOUS.

To WEARY, *v. a.* आयस् (c. 10. -यासयति -यितुं). *See To* FATIGUE.

To WEARY, *v. n.* खिद् (c. 4. खिद्यते), श्रम् (c. 4. श्राम्यति), आयस् (c. 4. -यस्यति).

WEARY, *a.* श्रान्तः -न्ता -न्तं, क्लान्तः &c., खिन्नः -न्ना -न्नं, ग्लानः -ना -नं, म्लानः &c., तन्द्रालुः -लुः -लु, जातखेदः -दा -दं. *See* FATIGUED.

WEASEL, *s.* नकुलः, बभ्रूषः, बभ्रुः *m.*, मूषिवदनः.

WEATHER, *s.* कालः, समयः, दिनं; 'fine weather,' सुदिनं, सुदिनाहः -हं, वसन्ताहः; 'bad weather,' दुर्दिनं, वार्दलं.

To WEATHER, *v. a.* दुःखेन पार् (c. 10. पारयति -यितुं) or तीर् (c. 10. तीरयति -यितुं), कष्टेन तीरं or पारं गम्, दुःखेन तॄ.

WEATHER-BEATEN, *a.* वाताहतः -ता -तं, वातवृष्ट्याहतः ता -तं, अभ्रावकाशिकः -का -कं.

WEATHER-COCK, *s.* प्रासादशृङ्गाग्रे स्थापितं कुक्कुटाकारं वायुलक्षणं.

WEATHER-GLASS. *s* वायुमापकयन्त्रं, वायुगुरुत्वज्ञापकयन्त्रं.

WEATHER-PROOF, *a.* वातवृष्ट्यभेद्यः -द्या -द्यं, वृष्ट्यभेद्यः &c.

WEATHER-WISE, *a.* कालदर्शनकुशलः -ला -लं, कालविद् *m. f. n.*

To WEAVE, *v. a.* वे (c. 1. वयति, वातुं), वप् (c. 1. वपति -प्तुं), ऊय् (c. 1. ऊयते -यितुं), गुम्फ् (c. 6. गुम्फति -म्फितुं), गुफ्, रच् (c. 10. रचयति -यितुं), विरच्.

To WEAVE, *v. n.* (Practise weaving) वायं कृ, तन्तुवायं कृ, वापं कृ, तन्तुवापं कृ, सूत्रवापं कृ, तन्तुव्यूतिं कृ, सूत्रवेष्टनं कृ.

WEAVER, *s.* तन्तुवायः, तन्तुवापः, तन्त्रवायः, तन्त्रवापः, तन्द्रवायः, कुविन्दः, कुपिन्दः, पटकारः, सूचीशिल्पोपजीवी *m.* (न्).

WEAVING, *s.* वायः, वापः, तन्तुवायः, तन्तुवापः, सूत्रवायः, ऊतिः *f.*, व्यूतिः *f.*, व्युतिः *f.*, तानवं, वाणिः *f.*, वेणिः *f.*, सूत्रवेष्टनं, पटनिर्म्माणं, विरचना, प्रसरः; 'Room for weaving,' तन्तुशाला.

WEB, *s.* तन्तुसन्ततं -तिः *f.*, सूत्रसन्ततिः *f.*, तन्त्रं, जालं.—(Of the eye) पटलं.—(Of a spider) ऊर्णनाभजालः, *see* SPIDER.

WEB-FOOTED, *a.* जालपादः -दा -दं, जालपाद्, जालाकारपादः &c.

To WED, *v. a.* विवह्, परिणी, पाणिग्रहणं कृ. *See To* MARRY.

WEDDED, *p. p.* or *a.* विवाहितः -ता -तं, परिणीतः &c., कृतकरग्रहः -हा -हं, *see* MARRIED; 'wedded woman,' ऊढा; 'wedded couple,' दम्पती *m. du.*—(Strongly attached) आसक्तः -क्ता -क्तं, रतः -ता -तं; 'to one's own opinion,' स्वमतरक्षी -क्षिणी &c.

WEDDING, *s.* विवाहोत्सवः, विवाहपर्व्व *n.* (न्), विवाहः, उद्वाहकर्म्म *n.* (न्), विवाहसंस्कारः, विवाहक्रिया; 'wedding dress,' विवाहनेपथ्यं, वैवाहिकनेपथ्यं.

WEDGE, *s.* कीलः, कीलकः, शङ्कुः *m.*

To WEDGE, *v. a.* संहन्, सम्पीड्, सम्बाध्, बाध्, सम्मृद्.

WEDLOCK, *s.* विवाहसम्बन्धः, विवाहितावस्था, दारकर्म्म *n.* (न्).

WEDNESDAY, *s.* बुधवारः, सौम्यवारः -वासरः, कुलाकुलवारः.

WEED, *s.* कक्षः, स्तम्बः, तृणं, कण्टकः -कं; 'instrument for destroying weeds,' स्तम्बघ्नः.—(Widow's weeds) चीरं, चीवरं.

To WEED, *v. a.* कक्षम् उद्धृ (c. 1. -हरति -हर्त्तुं), तृणानि उत्पट् (c. 10. -पाटयति -यितुं) or उच्छिद्, वितृणीकृ.

WEEDING, *s.* कक्षोद्धरणं, कक्षोच्छेदः, तृणोद्धरणं, कण्टकोद्धरणं.

WEEDY, *a.* कक्षपूर्णः -र्णा -र्णं, कक्षबहुलः -ला -लं, तृणपूर्णः &c.

WEEK, *s.* सप्ताहं, वारसप्तकं, दिनसप्तकं; 'week-day,' वारः.

WEEKLY, *a.* साप्ताहिकः -की -कं, सप्ताह्निकः &c., सप्तदैनिकः &c.

WEEKLY, *adv.* सप्ताहे सप्ताहे, प्रतिसप्ताहं.

To WEEP, *v. n.* रुद् (c. 10. रोदिति -तुं), क्रन्द् (c. 1. क्रन्दति -न्दितुं), अश्रूणि पत् in caus., *see To* CRY; 'weep not,' मा रोदीः.

WEEPING, *s.* क्रन्दनं, रोदनं, अश्रुपातः. *See* LAMENTATION.

WEEPING, *part.* रुदन् -दती &c., अश्रुलोचनः -नी -नं, उपप्लुताक्षः &c.

To WEIGH, *v. a.* (In a balance) तुल् (c. 10. तुलयति -यितुं), तूल् (c. 10. तूलयति -यितुं), तोलनं कृ, तुलनां कृ.—(Raise, as an anchor, &c.) उत्तुल्.—(Ponder) विगण् (c. 10. -गणयति -यितुं), मनसा विचर्, *see To* PONDER; 'to weigh alternatives,' विकृप् (c. 10. -कल्पयति -यितुं). 'Weighs upon,' विडम्बयति; 'weighs down,' *see To* OUTWEIGH.

To WEIGH, *v. n.* (Have weight) भारी -रिणी -रि भू or अस्, भारवान् -वती -वद् अस् or भू, भारान्वितः -ता -तम् अस् or भू; 'what does this weigh?' एतत् किम्भारम् अस्ति or एतस्य किं भारपरिमाणं.—(Be important) गुरुः -र्वी -रु भू.

WEIGHED, *p. p.* (In a balance) तुलितः -ता -तं, तुलयाधृतः &c., उन्मितः &c., तुलामितः &c.—(Pondered) सुविचारितः -ता -तं.

WEIGHER, *s.* तोलनकारी *m.* (न्), तुलाधारणविद्, तुलनाकृत्.

WEIGHING, *s.* तोलनं, तुलाधारणं.—(Pondering) विगणनं -ना.

WEIGHT, *s.* (Weight or quantity ascertained by balance) भारः, भारपरिमाणं, उन्मानं, मितिः *f.*, परिमाणं, भारमितिः *f.*, तोलः, तुला, गुरुत्वं -ता, गौरवं, गरिमा *m.* (न्), भरः; 'of deficient weight,' न्यूनतोलः -ला -लं.—(Mass to weigh with) तोलं, उन्मानं. For the different weights, *see* under MEASURE; 'measure by weight,' तुलामानं.—(Ponderous load, burden) भारः, धुरा, धूः *f.* (धुर्), *see* BURDEN.—(Importance, influence) गौरवं, गुरुत्वं -ता, प्रभावः, भारः, प्रमाणं; 'of little weight,' अल्पप्रभावः -वा -वं, अल्पप्रमाणः -णा -णं, लघुप्रभावः &c.

WEIGHTY, *a.* (Having weight) भारी -रिणी -रि (न्), गुरुः -र्वी -रु, *see* HEAVY, PONDEROUS.—(Important, influential) गुरुः &c., सप्रमाणः -णा -णं, *see* IMPORTANT.

WEIR, *s.* जलप्रवाहबन्धकः, जलबन्धकः, जलप्रतिबन्धकः.

WELCOME, *s.* स्वागतं, अभिनन्दनं, आनन्दनं, सभाजनं, सभाजनं, आमन्त्रणं, आप्रच्छनं; 'word of welcome,' स्वागतवचनं, *see* SALUTATION; 'of a guest,' आगतस्वागतं.

WELCOME, *a.* स्वागतः -ता -तं.—(Grateful) सुखदः -दा -दं.

To WELCOME, *v. a.* स्वागतम् इति वद् (c. 1. वदति -दितुं), स्वागतवचनेन पूज् (c. 10. पूजयति -यितुं), स्वस्ति or स्वस्तिवचनं वद्, आमन्त्र् (c. 10. -मन्त्रयति -यितुं), प्रशंस् (c. 1. -शंसति -सितुं); 'a new-comer,' आगतस्वागतं कृ, आगतसत्कारं कृ.

WELCOMED, *p. p.* स्वागतपूजितः -ता -तं, सत्कृतः &c., समुपवेशितः &c.

To WELD, *v. a.* अयोघनाघातेन तप्तलोहं तप्तलोहेन संयुज्.

WELFARE, *s.* कुशलं, कौशलं, कौशल्यं, कुशलता, कल्याणं, क्षेमं, क्षेमकुशलं, मङ्गलं, माङ्गल्यं, सुखं, शुभं, भद्रं, हितं, श्रेयस् *n.*, श्वःश्रेयसं, भूतिः *f.*, सुस्थितिः *f.*, स्थितिः *f.*, अभीष्टं, अभीप्सितं, भविकं, भावुकं, भव्यं, शिवं.

WELL, *a.* (In health) स्वस्थः -स्था -स्थं, सुस्थः &c., निरामयः -या -यं, नीरोगः -गा -गं, *see* HEALTHY.—(Fortunate, happy) कुशलः -ला -लं, क्षेमः -मा -मं, हितः -ता -तं, सुखी -खिनी -खि (न्); 'Is it well?' किं क्षेमम् अस्ति.

WELL, *s.* (For water) कूपः, कूपकः, प्रहिः *m.*, अन्धुः *m.*, जलकूपी, कूपी, निपानं, उदपानं, उदकाधारः, जलाधारः, जलाश्रिका, आपीनः, चूडकः, कोट्टारः; 'wooden frame or upper part of a well,' नेमिः *f.*, त्रिका; 'cover or facing,' वीनाहः; 'reservoir near a well,' आहावः, निपानं, उपकूपजलाशयः; 'well-water,' कूपोदकं, कौपं; 'well-digger,' कूपखनिता *m.* (तृ).—(Of a ship) गुप्तिः *f.*

WELL, *adv.* सु or अति prefixed, सुष्ठु, साधु, सम्यक्, युक्तं, यथायोग्यं, भद्रं, उत्तमरूपेण; 'well off,' सुस्थितः -ता -तं, सुस्थः -स्था -स्थं; 'well said,' स्वभिहितः -ता -तं, सूक्तः -क्ता -क्तं, साध्वभिहितः -ता -तं, साधूक्तः &c., भद्रमुक्तः &c.

WELL, *exclam.* भद्रं, बाढं, साधु, अस्तु, भवतु, तथेति; 'very well,' बाढं, कामं; 'well then,' तद्भद्रं; 'well done!' साधु.

WELL-AFFECTED, *a.* सुरक्तः -क्ता -क्तं, हितबुद्धिः -द्धिः -द्धि, सुशीलः &c.

WELL-BALANCED, *a.* समतोलः -ला -लं, समानतोलः -ला -लं.

WELL-BEHAVED, *a.* विनीतः -ता -तं, साधुवृत्तिः -त्तिः -त्ति, साध्वाचारः -रा -रं, सुचरितः -ता -तं, सदाचारः &c., सुनीतः -ता -तं.

WELL-BEING, *s.* कुशलं, क्षेमं, सुस्थता, सुस्थितिः *f.* *See* WELFARE.

WELL-BORN, *a.* कुलीनः -ना -नं, सत्कुलीनः &c., सुजन्मा -न्मा -न्म (न्), सुजातः -ता -तं, अभिजातः &c., साधुजः &c. *See* NOBLE.

WELL-BRED, *a.* सुविनीतः -ता -तं, सुशिष्टः -ष्टा -ष्टं, सुशीलः -ला -लं.

WELL-DISPOSED, *a.* हितबुद्धिः -द्धिः -द्धि, सुशीलः &c. *See* WELL-WISHER.

WELL-DOER, *s.* सुकर्म्मी *m.* (न्), सुकृती *m.* (न्). *See* VIRTUOUS.

WELL-DONE, *a.* सुकृतः -ता -तं, सुचरितः &c. *Exclam.* साधु.

WELL-DRESSED, *a.* सुवेशः -शा -शं, सुवेषी -षिणी &c., सुवेष्टितः -ता -तं.

WELL-FORMED, *a.* सुरूपः -पी -पं, सुरूपी -पिणी &c., शुभाकारः -रा -रं.

WELL-INFORMED, *a.* बहुज्ञः -ज्ञा -ज्ञं, सुज्ञः &c., बहुश्रुतः -ता -तं.

WELL-KNIT, *a.* सुसंहतः -ता -तं, दृढसन्धिः -न्धिः -न्धि.

WELL-KNOWN, *a.* सुज्ञातः -ता -तं, प्रसिद्धः -द्धा -द्धं. *See* NOTORIOUS.

WELL-MADE, *a.* सुरूपः -पा -पं, सुरूपी -पिणी &c., सुघटितः -ता -तं.

WELL-MEANING, *a.* सदभिप्रायः -या -यं, सदाशयः &c., सुशीलः &c.

WELL-NIGH, *adv.* प्रायस्, प्रायशस्. *See* NEARLY.

WELL-READ, *a.* स्वधीतः -ता -तं, स्वधीती -तिनी -ति (न्), अधीती &c., सर्व्वशास्त्रपारगः -गा -गं, ग्रन्थी -न्थिनी &c., बहुज्ञः &c.

WELL-SPENT, *a.* सुव्ययितः -ता -तं; 'time,' सत्कालक्षेपः.

WELL-WISHER, *s.* हितैषी -षिणी *m.f.*, प्रियैषी -षिणी *m.f.*, हितेप्सुः *m.f.*, हितप्रेप्सुः *m.f.*, श्रेयोर्थी -र्थिनी, हितकामः -मा.

To WELTER, *v. n.* लुठ् (c. 6. लुठति -ठितुं), प्रलुठ्. *See To* WALLOW.

WELTERING, *part.* लुठन् -ठन्ती -ठत् (त्). *See* ROLLING, *part.*

WEN, *s.* मांसवृद्धिः *f.*, मेदोर्बुदं, गलगण्डः. *See* TUMOUR.

WENCH, *s.* योषा, योषिता, तरुणी, कन्या, बन्धकी, गणिका.

To WENCH, WENCHING. *See To* FORNICATE, FORNICATION.

To WEND, *v. n.* गम्, या, इ, सृ, आवृत्, अभिवृत्, *see To* GO; 'hither he wends his way,' इत एवाभिवर्त्तते.

WEST, *s.* (The quarter of the sky) पश्चिमा, पश्चिमदिशा, पश्चिमदिक् *f.* (श्), पश्चिमाशा, प्रतीची, अपरा, चरमा, वारुणी, मध्यः -ध्यं. The god Varuna is fabled as the Regent of the West.

WEST, WESTERLY, WESTERN, *a.* पश्चिमः -मा -मं, प्रत्यङ् -तीची -त्यक् (च्), प्रतीच्यः -च्या -च्यं, प्रतीचीनः -ना -नं, चरमः -मा -मं, अपरः -रा -रं, पाश्चात्यः -त्या -त्यं. 'Madyadesha is west of Prayága,' मध्यदेशः प्रयागात् पश्चिमः; 'as far as the western ocean,' आपश्चिमसमुद्रात्.—(Facing the west) प्रत्यङ्मुखः -खी -खं, पश्चिमाभिमुखः &c.

WESTWARD, *adv.* पश्चात्, प्रत्यक्, पश्चिमदिशि, पश्चिमतस्.

WET, *a.* आर्द्रः -र्द्रा -र्द्रं, जलार्द्रः &c., क्लिन्नः -न्ना -न्नं, सिक्तः -क्ता -क्तं, जलसिक्तः &c., समुक्षितः -ता -तं, अनूपः -पा -पं. *See* MOIST.

WET, *s.* आर्द्रता, क्लेदः -दं, तेमः, स्तेमः, जलं. *See* MOISTURE.

To WET, *v. a.* क्लिद् (c. 10. क्लेदयति -यितुं). *See To* MOISTEN.

Wether, *s.* छिन्नवृषणो मेषः, मुष्कशून्यो मेषः.

Wetness, *s.* आर्द्रता, क्लिन्नता, जलार्द्रता, सिक्तता -त्वं.

Wet-nurse, *s.* धात्रेयी, उपमाता, उपमात्री, पयःप्रसविणी, स्तन्यदानेन पोषयित्री or पालयित्री.

To whack, Whack. *See To* strike, beat, blow.

Whale, *s.* तिमिः *m.*, तिमिङ्गिलः, तिमिङ्गिलगिलः, मीनरः, समुद्राहः *m.*, मकरः, राघवः, बृहन्मीनः.

Wharf, *s.* घट्टः, उपः, तरस्थानं, तरणस्थानं, गुल्मः.

What, *pron. rel.* (That which) यद्.—(What kind, what like, which) यादृशः -शी -शं, यादृक्षः -क्षा -क्षं, यः या यद्.

What, *pron. inter.* कः का किं, कौ *m. du.*, के *f. n. du.*, के *m. pl.*, काः *f. pl.*, कानि *n. pl.*; 'what?' किं, किमु, किमुत, किंस्वित्; 'what kind?' कीदृशः -शी -शं, कीदृक्षः -क्षा -क्षं, कीदृक् *m. f. n.* (श्), किम्भूतः -ता -तं; 'on what account?' किमर्थं; 'what then?' किं तर्हि, किमु; 'what else?' अथ किं; 'what do you wish to say?' किम् असि वक्तुकामः; 'what is he doing?' किंव्यापारः सः; 'what is his name?' किन्नामधेयः सः; 'to what degree?' किम्पर्य्यन्तं; 'what is that to me?' किं मम तेन; 'what though?' यद्यपि.

What, *interj.* कथं, किं, किमुत, उत, उत्, ननु, स्वित्.

Whatever, whatsoever, *pron.* यत्किञ्चित्, यद्यद्, यद्, यावत्; 'whatever wealth is in the world,' यत्किञ्चिद् or यावद् जगत्यस्ति धनम् अस्ति.

Wheat, *s.* गोधूमः, सुमनाः *m.* (स्), सुमनः, धान्यं, प्रवटः, रसालः, अपूपः, गन्धविह्वलः, भूमखः *f.*, गोरक्षमखः *f.*, शितशूकः, म्लेच्छभोजनः, सितशिंशिकः, निस्तुषक्षीरः, बहुदुग्धः.

Wheaten, *a.* गोधूममयः -यी -यं, गोधूमात्मकः -का -कं, गोधूम in comp.

To wheedle, wheedler, wheedling. *See To* coax, flatter, &c.

Wheel, *s.* चक्रं, रथाङ्गं, रथपादः, रथ्यं, मण्डलं, उपधिः *m.*, औपधेयं, नभिः *m.*, दूम्भूः *f.*; 'its circumference,' नेमिः -मी, प्रधिः *m.*, चक्रपरिधिः *m.*; 'potter's wheel,' कुलालचक्रं.

To wheel, *v. a.* परिवृत् (c. 10. -वर्त्तयति -यितुं), विवृत्, आवृत्, व्यावृत्.

To wheel, *v. n.* परिवृत् (c. 1. -वर्त्तते -र्त्तितुं), विवृत्, व्यावृत्, सम्परिवृत्.

Wheelbarrow, *s.* हस्तसञ्चालितम् एकचक्रयुक्तं वाहनं.

Wheeled, *a.* चक्रवान् -वती -वत् (त्), चक्री -क्रिणी -क्रि (न्), चक्रयुक्तः -क्ता -क्तं; 'two-wheeled carriage,' द्विचक्रयुक्तो रथः.

Wheel-wright, *s.* रथकारः, रथकृत्, रथकरः, चक्रकारः.

To wheeze, *v. n.* कासश्वासं कृ, कृच्छ्रेण श्वासं कृ, प्रतिश्रुतं कृ.

Whelp, *s.* शावः -वकः, शिशुः *m.*, वत्सः; 'of a lion,' सिंहशावकः.

When, *adv.* (At the time that) यदा, यर्हि, or expressed by काले, समये, &c. in comp.; as, 'when he was dying,' मरणकाले.—(At what time?) कदा, कर्हि.

Whence, *adv.* (Interrog.) कुतस्, कस्माद् देशात् &c., कस्मात् स्थानात् &c.; 'whence have you come?' कुतः समागतो ऽसि.—(Indef.) यतस्, यस्माद् देशात् &c.; 'to return whence one came,' प्रतिगन्तुं यथागतं.

Whenever, whensoever, *adv.* यदा यदा, यर्हि यर्हि, यदाकदाचित्.

Where, *adv.* (In which place) यत्र.—(In what place?) कुत्र, क्व.

Whereas, *adv.* यस्मात्, येन, यतस्. यत्. *See* Since.

Whereby, *adv.* (By which) येन.—(By what?) केन.

Wherefore, *adv.* (For which reason) यतस्, येन, यत्, यदर्थं, तन्निमित्तं.—(For what reason?) किमर्थं, किम्, केन हेतुना, कस्य हेतोः, किन्निमित्तं, केन निमित्तेन.

Wherein, *adv.* (In which) यस्मिन्, यत्र.—(In what?) कस्मिन्, कुत्र.

Whereof, *adv.* (Of which) यस्य.—(Of what?) कस्य.

Wherever, wheresoever, *adv.* यत्र कुत्रचित्, यत्र कुत्रापि, यत्र यत्र, कुत्रापि, कुत्रचित्, यत्र क्वचित्.

Whereupon, *adv.* यदनन्तरं, यदान्तरे, तदनन्तरं, तदान्तरे.

Wherry, *s.* दण्डसञ्चालिता or क्षेपणिसञ्चालिता लघुनौका.

To whet, *v. a.* निशो, निशि, क्ष्णु, तिज्. *See To* sharpen.

Whether, *adv.* किं, किंवा, वा, उत. The particle वा, either with or without किं, usually expresses the sense of 'whether,' as in the following examples; 'whether you kill me or whether you release me,' मां मारयत वा मुञ्चत वा; 'do you know whether he is virtuous or not?' वेत्सि किं धार्म्मिको न वा; 'whether or not he does that,' तत् करोतु न करोतु वा.—(Whether of twain, which of two) कतरः -रा -रत्.

Whet-stone, *s.* शाणः -णी, शानः, शाणाश्म *n.* (न्), भ्रमः, क्षारकः, वागरः, सानकः.

Whey, *s.* मस्तु *n.*, दधिमण्डः -ण्डं, दुग्धमण्डं, दध्युत्तरं.

Which, *pron.* (Relat.) यः या, यद्, यौ *m. du.*, ये *f. n. du.*, ये *m. pl.*, याः *f. pl.*, यानि *n. pl.*, *see* Who.—(Interrog.) कः का किं, कौ *m. du.*, के *f. n. du.*, के *m. pl.*, काः *f. pl.*, कानि *n. pl.*

Whichever, *pron.* Expressed by doubling the relative, thus यद् यद् &c.

Whiff, *s.* फुत्कृतं, फुत्कारः, फूत्कृतं, फूत् indec. *See* Puff.

While, whilst, *adv.* यावत्, यावत्कालं, यत्कालं, यस्मिन् काले, यत्पर्य्यन्तं, यदा; 'whilst he thought on this the messenger arrived,' यावत् तत् चिन्तयति दूतः समागच्छति. The sense of whilst may sometimes be expressed by मध्ये, *see* During, or by the locative absolute, or some similar form of expression; as, स तदेव चिन्तयति दूतस् समागच्छति.

While, *s.* कालः, समयः; 'a long while,' बहुकालः; 'for a long while,' बहुकालं, चिरकालं, चिरं; 'after a long while,' चिरात्; 'a little while,' अल्पकालः; 'for a little while,' अल्पकालं, किञ्चित्कालं; 'in a little while,' अचिरेण -रात्, क्षणान्तरे, कियता कालेन; 'for a while,' कियत्कालं, आपाततस्; 'a long while ago,' पुरा, पूर्व्वकाले; 'one while,' कदाचित्.—(Worth while) सफलः -ला -लं, फलवान् -वती -वत् (त्), उपयोगी -गिनी &c.

To while, *v. a.* विनोदेन कालं गम् (c. 10. गमयति -यितुं) or नी (c. 1. नयति, नेतुं), विनुद् in caus. (नोदयति -यितुं).

Whim, *s.* मनोलौल्यं, चापलं, चापल्यं. *See* Freak, Caprice.

To whimper, *v. a.* बालकवत् क्रन्द् or रुद् or रु or कूज्.

Whimsical, *a.* चपलः -ला -लं, लोलः &c., *see* Capricious, Freakish.

To whine, *v. n.* कूज् (c. 1. कूजति -जितुं), अनुकूज्. *See To* murmur.

Whine, *s.* कूजनं, कूजितं, विलपनं, कलरुतं, काकुः *f.*, काकूक्तिः *f.*

To whip, *v. a.* कशया or चर्म्मरज्ज्वा or रज्ज्वा तड् (c. 10. ताडयति -यितुं) or दण्ड् or शास् (c. 2. शास्ति -सितुं). *See To* lash.

Whip, *s.* कशा, कषा, चर्म्मयष्टिः *f.*, प्रतिष्कषः, भीमा. *See* Scourge.

Whipped, *p. p.* कशाहतः -ता -तं, दण्डितः &c.; 'whipped horse,' प्रतिकशाश्वः.

Whipping, *s.* कशाघातः, कषाघातः, कशाताडनं, ताडनं; 'worthy of it,' कश्यः -श्या -श्यं, कशार्हः -र्हा -र्हं.

To whirl, *v. a.* भ्रम् (c. 10. भ्रमयति -यितुं). *See To* turn, twirl.

To WHIRL, *v. n.* भ्रम् (c. 4. भ्राम्यति, c. 1, भ्रमति -मितुं), अतिशीघ्रं परिवृत् (c. 1. -वर्त्तते -र्त्तितुं) or घूर्ण्. *See To* REVOLVE, *v. n.*

WHIRLED, *p. p.* भ्रान्तः -न्ता -न्तं, उद्भ्रान्तः &c., शीघ्रं परिवर्त्तितः &c.

WHIRL, WHIRLING, *s.* भ्रमः -मणं, भ्रान्तिः *f.*, भ्रमिः *f.*, विभ्रमः, आवृत्तिः *f.*

WHIRLPOOL, *s.* जलावर्त्तः, जलभ्रमः, जलगुल्मः, आवर्त्तः -र्त्तका, आवर्त्तिनी, भ्रमिः *m.*, भ्रमः, भ्रमरकः, अवघूर्णः. *See* EDDY.

WHIRLWIND, *s.* चक्रवातः, वातावर्त्तः, वातमण्डली, वायुगुल्मः, वात्या, भ्रमिः *m.*, वातभ्रमः, आवर्त्तः, निर्घातः, भ्रान्तिः *f.*, कुनाभिः *m.*, पताका.

To WHISK, *v. a.* अतिक्षिप्रं चल् (c. 10. चालयति -यितुं), अतिलाघवेन चल्; 'he whisks his tail,' परिपुच्छयति.

WHISK, *s.* लघुक्षेपः, आकस्मिकक्षेपः.—(For flies, &c.) चामरं.

WHISKER, *s.* पक्ष्म *n.* (न्), गुम्फः, गण्डलोम *n.* (न्), मुखलोम *n.*

To WHISPER, *v. n.* जप् (c. 1. जपति -पितुं), प्रजप्, नीचस्वरेण or नीचवाचा वद् (c. 1. वदति -दितुं), नीचैर् वद्, उपांशु वद्; 'to whisper into the ear,' कर्णम् उपजप्, कर्णे कथ्, कर्णे जप् or वद्; 'to whisper to one's neighbour,' जनान्तिकं वद्.

WHISPER, WHISPERING, *s.* जपः -पनं, जापः, कर्णेजपनं, कर्णेकथनं, कर्णवादः, उपांशुवादः, उपांशुकथनं, नीचैर्वादः; 'in a whisper,' उपांशु, जनान्तिकं.

WHISPERER, *s.* कर्णेजपः, कर्णजपः, कर्णेकथकः, कर्णोपजापकः.

To WHISTLE, *v. n.* ओष्ठाधरसङ्कोचपूर्व्वं श्वासोत्क्षेपं कृत्वा शीशशब्दं कृ or सीस्शब्दं कृ or कीचकवत् पटुशब्दं कृ, वेणुवत् कर्कशशब्दं कृ, ओष्ठशब्दं कृ.

WHISTLE, *s.* (The sound) शीशशब्दः, सीस्शब्दः, ओष्ठशब्दः, कीचकशब्दः.—(Instrument for whistling) वंशः -शी, ध्वनिनालः.

WHIT, *s.* लेशः, लवः, लवलेशः; 'not a whit,' न मनागपि.

WHITE, *a.* शुक्लः -क्ला -क्लं, श्वेतः -ता -तं, धवलः -ला -लं, सितः -ता -तं, श्येतः -ता -नी -तं, शुभ्रः -भ्रा -भ्रं, शुचिः -चिः -चि, अवदातः -ता -तं, विशदः -दा -दं, गौरः -री -रं, धौतः -ता -तं, पाण्डुरः -रा -रं, अमलः -ला -लं, विमलः &c., रजतः -ता -तं, कर्कः -र्का -र्कं, रुरुः -रुः -रु, अर्जुनः -नी -नं, शितिः -ती -ति, अर्जुनच्छविः -विः -वि, वलक्षः -क्षा -क्षं; 'yellowish white,' हरिणः -णा -णं.

WHITE, *s.* (The colour) शुक्लः, धवलः, श्वेतः, सितः, वलक्षः.—(Of the eye) शुक्लमण्डलं, विड्मरं.

To WHITEN, *v. a.* शुक्ल (nom. शुक्लयति -यितुं), धवल (nom. धवलयति -यितुं), शुक्लीकृ, धवलीकृ, आदीप् (c. 10. -दीपयति -यितुं).

To WHITEN, *v. n.* शुक्लीभू, धवलीभू, श्वेतीभू, विशदीभू.

WHITENED, *p. p.* धवलितः -ता -तं, धवलीकृतः &c., शुक्लीकृतः -ता -तं.

WHITENESS, *s.* शुक्लता -त्वं, शुक्लिमा *m.* (न्), शौक्ल्यं, धवलतं -ता, धावल्यं, शुभ्रता, श्वेतता, सितत्वं, सितिमा *m.* (न्), वैशद्यं.

WHITES, *s.* (Fluor albus) प्रदरः, प्रदरामयः.

WHITEWASH, *s.* सुधा, शुक्ललेपः, धवललेपः, धवलसुधा.

To WHITEWASH, *v. a.* सुधया लिप् (c. 6. लिम्पति, लेप्तुं) or आलिप्, सुधया धवलीकृ or धवल (nom. धवलयति -यितुं).

WHITEWASHED, *p. p.* सुधाधवलितः -ता -तं, सुधालिप्तः &c.; 'house,' सुधाभवनं.

WHITHER, *adv.* (Interrog.) कुत्र, क्व; 'whither shall I go?' क्व गच्छामि.—(Relat.) यत्र.

WHITHERSOEVER, *adv.* यत्र कुत्रचित्, यत्र कुत्रापि.

WHITISH, *a.* ईषच्छुक्लः -क्ला -क्लं, ईषत्पाण्डुः -ण्डुः -ण्डु, धूसरः -रा -रं.

WHITLOW, *s.* नखम्पचः, चिप्पं, कुणिः *m.*, नखशूलः -लं, नखव्रणः.

To WHIZ, *v. n.* शीशशब्दं कृ, सीस्शब्दं कृ, रणरणशब्दं कृ.

WHO, *pron.* (Relat.) यः या यद्, यौ *m. du.*, ये *f. n. du.*, ये *m. pl.*, याः *f. pl.*, यानि *n. pl.* The relative pronoun is not much used in Sanskrit excepting at the beginning of a sentence; as, 'he who desires great riches is not wise,' यो बहुधनम् आकांक्षति स बुद्धिहीनः. In other cases it is more usually expressed by स च or is inherent in a compound word or indecl. part.; thus, 'in that city there dwelt a king who was beloved by his subjects,' तस्मिन् नगरे वसति राजा स च प्रजावल्लभः; 'a saint who has subdued his organs of sense,' जितेन्द्रियो मुनिः; 'by all the birds who had assembled,' सर्व्वैः पक्षिभिर् मिलित्वा.—(Interrog.) कः का किं, कौ *m. du.*, के *f. n. du.*, के *m. pl.*, काः *f. pl.*, कानि *n. pl.*; 'who are you?' कस् त्वं; 'who's there,' को ऽत्र.

WHOEVER, WHOSOEVER, WHOSO, *pron.* यः कश्चित् *m.*, या काचित् *f.*, यत्किञ्चित् *n.*, यः कोपि *m.*, या कापि *f.*, यत्किमपि *m.*, यो यः *m.*, या या *f.*, यद्यद् *n.*

WHOLE, *a.* सर्व्वः -र्व्वा -र्व्वं, सकलः -ला -लं, समग्रः -ग्रा -ग्रं, विश्वः -श्वा -श्वं, कृत्स्नः -त्स्ना -त्स्नं; 'the whole earth,' सर्व्वमही; 'the whole world,' सर्व्वलोकः; 'the whole night,' सर्व्वरात्रः; 'the whole day,' सर्व्वाह्णः; 'the whole business from beginning to end,' साद्यन्तं कर्म्म, आगमनिर्गमौ *m. du.*; 'for the whole month,' मासपर्य्यन्तं; 'whole number,' अभिन्नसंख्या.

WHOLE, *s.* साकल्यं, समुदायः, कार्त्स्न्यं, कार्त्स्नं, सामग्र्यं, आखिल्यं, सार्व्वं, समासः, समस्तः -स्तिः *f.*, व्याप्तिः *f.*

WHOLENESS, *s.* सामग्र्यं, सम्पूर्णता, अभिन्नता. *See* ENTIRENESS.

WHOLESALE, *s.* or *a.* समस्तविक्रयः, महाविक्रयः, अखण्डविक्रयः.

WHOLESOME, *a.* पथ्यः -थ्या -थ्यं, हितः -ता -तं. *See* SALUBRIOUS.

WHOLLY, *adv.* सर्व्वतस्, सर्व्वशस्, सर्व्वथा, साकल्येन, सम्यक्, अशेषतस्, अत्यन्तं, सर्व्वभावेन, सर्व्वतोभावेन. *See* ENTIRELY.

WHOOP, *s.* (The cry) हूप्; 'war-whoop,' सिंहनादः, क्ष्वेडा -डितं.

To WHOOP, *v. n.* हूप्शब्दं कृ, उच्चैःस्वरेण क्रुश्. *See To* SHOUT.

WHORE, *s.* वेश्या, गणिका, पुंश्चली, बन्धकी. *See* HARLOT.

WHOREDOM, WHOREMONGER. *See* FORNICATION, HARLOTRY, &c.

WHORESON, *s.* वेश्यापुत्रः, गणिकापुत्रः, पुंश्चलीजः.

WHOSE, *pron.* (Relat.) यस्य *m.*, यस्याः *f.* The relative 'whose' is not often expressed in Sanskrit, but is frequently inherent in a compound, or rendered by तस्य च &c., *see* WHO; as, 'a wife whose husband is abroad,' प्रोषितभर्तृका स्त्री.—(Interrog.) कस्य *m.*, कस्याः *f.*

WHY, *adv.* किमर्थं, किं, केन हेतुना, किन्निमित्तं, कस्य हेतोः, *see* WHEREFORE; 'why inquire into my story?' किं ते मम वृत्तान्तप्रश्नेन; 'why conceal it?' संवरणे किं कारणं; 'why do you do this?' किमर्थं तत् करोषि.

WICK, *s.* (Of a lamp, &c.) तूला -ली, वर्त्तिः *f.*, वर्त्तिका, तैलिनी, तैलमाली, दशा, दशाकर्षः, पिच्छलं, दीपकूपी, दीपखोरी.

WICKED, *a.* (Said of persons) दुष्टः -ष्टा -ष्टं, पापी -पिनी -पि (न्), दुर्वृत्तः -त्ता -त्तं, दुरात्मा -त्मा -त्म (न्), पापात्मा &c., अपुण्यः -ण्या -ण्यं, शठः -ठा -ठं, पामरः -रा -रं, खलः -ला -लं, नैकृतिकः -की -कं, नैष्कृतिकः &c., अधार्म्मिकः -की -कं, दुष्टमानसः -सा -सं, दुश्चरित्रः -त्रा -त्रं, विकर्म्मिकः &c., *see* SINFUL; 'a wicked man,' दुर्जनः, असज्जनः.—(Of actions) दुष्टः -ष्टा -ष्टं, पाप in comp., *see* SINFUL;

'a wicked act,' पापकर्म्म n. (न्); 'very wicked,' पापिष्ठः -ष्ठा -ष्ठं, दुरिष्टः &c.

WICKEDLY, *adv.* दुष्टं, दुष्टवत्, सपापं, दुर्जनवत्, दुर्वृत्तवत्, खलवत्.

WICKEDNESS, *s.* पापं, दुष्कृतं, दुष्कृतिः *f.*, कुकर्म्म *n.* (न्), दुष्कर्म्म *n.*, कुकृत्यं, कुसृतिः *f.*, निकृतिः *f.*, निकारः, दुष्टता, दौष्ट्यं, दौरात्म्यं, दौर्जन्यं, दुर्जनत्वं, असाधुता, विप्रकारः, कौकृत्यं, असत्कर्म्म *n.*, *see* SINFULNESS; 'great wickedness,' पापिष्ठता, पापीयस्त्वं, दुरिष्टं.

WICKER, *a.* वैदलः -ली -लं, वैणवः -वी -वं, वैणुकेयः -यी -यं, वैत्रकः -की -कं, वंशादिदलनिर्म्मितः -ता -तं; 'wicker-work,' वैदलं.

WICKET, *s.* क्षुद्रद्वारं, उपद्वारं, द्वारकं, खडक्किका.

WIDE, *a.* विशालः -ला -लं, पृथुः -थुः -थु, विस्तीर्णः -र्णा -र्णं, विपुलः -ला -लं, विप्रकृष्टः -ष्टा -ष्टं; 'wide-spread,' बहुविस्तीर्णः -र्णा -र्णं, समततः -ता -तं, बहुप्रतानी &c.; 'wide-awake,' प्रबुद्धः -द्धा -द्धं; 'wide-mouthed,' गुहामुखः -खा -खं; 'wide-open,' उत्फुल्लः -ल्ला -ल्लं.

WIDE, WIDELY, *adv.* विस्तीर्णं, विस्तरेण, विपुलं, प्रचुरं, अत्यन्तं, बहु or अति or सु prefixed, *see* EXTENSIVELY.

To WIDEN, *v. a.* प्रथ् (c. 10. प्रथयति -यितुं), पृथूकृ, विशालीकृ.

WIDENESS, *s.* विशालता, पृथुता, विस्तृतिः *f.* *See* BROADNESS.

WIDOW, *s.* विधवा, रण्डा, विश्वस्ता, विश्वस्या, गतभर्तृका, मृतपतिका, अभर्तृका, निर्नाथा, अनाथा, अवीरा, यतिनी, वृषभी, कात्यायनी, वितनुः *f.*; 'widow before puberty,' बालविधवा, बालरण्डा; 'widow that burns with the body of her husband,' सती; 'the act of doing so,' अग्निप्रवेशः, सहमरणं, सहगमनं, अनुगमनं, अन्वारोहणं; 'stone by which she ascends the pyre,' धर्म्मशिला.

WIDOWED, *a.* हृतभर्तृका, हृतपतिका.—(Stripped) हृतः -ता -तं.

WIDOWER, *s.* मृतभार्य्यः, मृतपत्नीकः, विधुरः, अयोगः.

WIDOWHOOD, *s.* वैधव्यं, वैधव्यदशा, विधवात्वं, निर्नाथता, रण्डावस्था, व्रतभङ्गः.

WIDTH, *s.* विशालता, परिणाहः, व्यासः, परिसरः. *See* BREADTH.

To WIELD, *v. a.* हस्तेन धृ (c. 1. धरति, c. 10. धारयति -यितुं) or धा (c. 3. दधाति, धातुं) or विधा, हस्तेन भृ (c. 1. भरति, c. 3. बिभर्त्ति, भर्तुं), हस्तेन प्रयुज् or उपयुज् or प्रणी.

WIFE, *s.* भार्य्या, स्त्री, पत्नी, जाया, दाराः *m. pl.*, दारा, वधूः *f.*, बधूः *f.*, कलत्रं, गृहिणी, गेहिनी, पाणिगृहीता, सहधर्म्मिणी, सधर्म्मिणी, दयिता, कान्ता, वल्लभा, प्रिया, प्रियतमा, रमणी, नायिका, प्राणेशा, प्राणसमा, प्रेयसी, प्रेष्ठा, वनिता, द्वितीया, महिला, क्षेत्रं, परिग्रहः, गृहं, गृहाः *m. pl.*, भूता, अर्द्धाङ्गं, वामाङ्गं, दम् indec.; 'virtuous and faithful wife,' पतिव्रता, सती, साध्वी, सुव्रता, धर्म्मदाराः *m. pl.*, पतिप्राणा, सुचरित्रा; 'one who has a family,' कुटुम्बिनी, पुरन्ध्रिः -न्ध्री; 'a superseded wife,' अध्यूढा, अधिविन्ना, कृतसापत्निका -त्नीका, कृतसापत्नी, कृतसापत्नका, कृतसपत्निका; 'wife of one husband,' एकभर्तृका; 'rival wife,' सपत्नी; 'one's own wife,' स्वकीया, स्वीया; 'wife of another,' परकीया, परस्त्री, परदाराः *m. pl.*; 'well-born wife,' कुलस्त्री; 'wife of one's bosom,' वक्षःसम्मर्द्दिनी; 'unfaithful wife,' अपतिव्रता, असती; 'taking a wife,' दारपरिग्रहः, दारसंग्रहः, दारक्रिया; 'along with one's wife, or having a wife,' सवधूकः, सपत्नीकः, सभार्य्यः; 'condition of a wife,' भार्य्यात्वं, पत्नीत्वं; 'one whose husband is abroad,' प्रोषितभर्तृका; 'wife's property,' स्त्रीधनं.

WIG, *s.* उपकेशः, कृत्रिमकेशः, केशमयमस्तकाभरणं.

WIGHT, *s.* जनः, माणवकः, नागरः; 'unlucky wight,' तपस्वी *m.* (न्).

WILD, *a.* (Pertaining to or inhabiting a forest or wilderness, not tame) आरण्यः -ण्यी -ण्यं, आरण्यकः -का -कं, वन्यः -न्या -न्यं, अरण्यजः -जा -जं, वनजः &c., आरण्यीयः -या -यं, जाङ्गलः -ला -लं, जाङ्गलः -ली -लं, वनेचरः -रा -रं, वनचारी -रिणी -रि (न्), वन in comp., अरण्य in comp., *see* DESERT, *a.*; 'wild-animal, wild-beast,' अरण्यपशुः *m.*, वनपशुः *m.*, आरण्यपशुः *m.*; 'wild hog,' अरण्यशूकरः, आरण्यशूकरः, वनशूकरः; 'wild goat,' वनच्छागः; 'wild elephant,' वनगजः; 'wild fowl,' वनकुक्कुटः, वृषकुक्कुटः, रज्जुदालकः; 'wild duck,' कामिकः; 'wild stag,' अरण्यमृगः, व्यालमृगः.—(Growing without culture) अरण्य in comp., वन in comp.; 'wild flower,' वनपुष्पं; 'wild fruit,' वनफलं; 'wild rice,' अरण्यधान्यं, तृणधान्यं, नीहारः.—(Irregular, disorderly) विषमः -मा -मं, उच्छृङ्खलः -ला -लं, प्रकीर्णः -र्णा -र्णं, *see* IRREGULAR.—(Absurd) अयुक्तिकः -का -कं, अनर्थकः -का -कं.—(Mad) उन्मत्तः -त्ता -त्तं.—(Savage, desert), *see* the words.

WILDERNESS, WILD, *s.* अरण्यं, वनं, जङ्गलं, शून्यारण्यं, मरुदेशः, मरुस्थलं, मरुः *m.*, जाङ्गलभूमिः *f.*, प्रान्तरं. *See* DESERT, *s.*

WILD-GOOSE-CHASE, *s.* मृगतृष्णा, हेममृगानुगमनं, हेममृगानुधावनं.

WILDLY, *adv.* विषमं, उच्छृङ्खलं, उन्मत्तवत्, सोन्मादं, व्याकुलं.

WILDNESS, *s.* (Uncultivated state) वन्यता, आरण्यता, जङ्गलत्वं.—(Savageness) रौद्रता, दारुणता, अशिष्टता.—(Irregularity) विषमता, उच्छृङ्खलता.—(Madness) उन्मत्तता, विक्षिप्तता.

WILE, *s.* माया, छलं, छद्म *n.* (न्), कपटः -टं, उपायः, व्यपदेशः.

WILFUL, *a.* स्वैरी -रिणी -रि (न्). *See* WILLFUL.

WILL, *s.* (Faculty which is exercised in deciding) इच्छा, सङ्कल्पशक्तिः *f.*, निश्चयशक्तिः *f.*—(Inclination, choice, liking) इच्छा, सङ्कल्पः, वशः -शं, अभिप्रायः, अभिलाषः, आकांक्षा, अभिप्रेतं, अभिमतं, इष्टं, छन्दस् *n.*; 'the will of God,' परमेश्वरेच्छा; 'of one's own will, at will,' इच्छातस्, स्वेच्छातस्, स्वेच्छानुसारेण, यथाकामं, कामतस्; 'ill-will,' दुष्टभावः, दुष्टबुद्धिः *f.*; 'good will,' हितेच्छा, हितकाम्या; 'subject to the will of another,' परवशः -शा -शं; 'following one's own will,' स्वेच्छाचारी -रिणी -रि (न्), *see* WILFUL; 'against the will of,' अनिच्छया, अनिच्छातस्, अनभिप्रेतेन.—(Testament) मृतपत्रं, मृत्युपत्रं, मृतलेखः, मृत्युलेखः.—(Will-with-a wisp), *see* IGNIS FATUUS.

To WILL, *v. a.* (Determine, decide in the mind) सङ्कल्पं कृ, निश्चयं कृ, निश्चि, निर्णी, संकॢप् (c. 10. -कल्पयति -यितुं), मनसा निश्चि or निर्णयं कृ.—(Wish, desire) इष् (c. 6. इच्छति, एषितुं), अभिलष्, आकांक्ष्.—(Command), *see To* COMMAND.—(Dispose of by testament) मृतपत्रेण दा or प्रदा or ऋ in caus.

WILLED, *p. p.* सङ्कल्पितः -ता -तं, साङ्कल्पिकः -की -कं, इष्टः -ष्टा -ष्टं.

WILLFUL, *a.* स्वैरी -रिणी -रि (न्), यथेष्टचारी &c., यथाकामी &c., स्वैरः -री -रं, स्वैरवृत्तः -त्ता -त्तं, स्वैरगतिः -तिः -ति, स्वैरगामी -मिनी &c., यादृच्छिकः -की -कं, छान्दसः -सी -सं. *See* SELF-WILLED.

WILFULLY, *adv.* यथाकामं, यथेष्टं, स्वैरवत्, यदृच्छया, इच्छातस्, कामं.

WILFULNESS, *s.* स्वैरिता, स्वैरता, स्वैरं, स्वेच्छा, स्वेच्छाचारः, यथेष्टचारः, स्वातन्त्र्यं, स्वतन्त्रता, यदृच्छा, प्राकाम्यं. *See* SELF-WILL.

WILLING, *a.* (Not averse, ready) इच्छुः -च्छुः -च्छु, इच्छुकः -का -कं, सकामः -मा -मं, सानुरागः -गा -गं.—(Received of choice, assented to) इष्टः -ष्टा -ष्टं, यथेष्टः &c., अभीष्टः &c., अनुमतः -ता -तं, सम्मतः &c., यथेप्सितः &c.

WILLINGLY, *adv.* कामं, प्रकामं, कामतस्, इच्छातस्, यथेप्सितं, तथेति.

WILLINGNESS, *s.* सकामत्वं, इच्छुता, इच्छुकत्वं, सानुरागता, सम्मतिः *f.*

WILY, *a.* मायी -यिनी -यि (न्), बहुमायः -या -यं. *See* CUNNING.

To WIN, *v. a.* (Gain by conquest) जि (c. 1. जयति, जेतुं), विजि, प्रतिजि.—(Gain, obtain) अर्ज्, प्राप्, लभ्, *see To* OBTAIN.—(Win over) आराध् (c. 10. -राधयति -यितुं), अनुरञ्ज्, प्रसाद्, संग्रह्, *see To* CONCILIATE.

To WINCE, *v. n.* विकम्प् (c. 1. -कम्पते -म्पितुं), विस्फुर् (c. 6. -स्फुरति -रितुं).

WIND, *s.* (Air in motion) वायुः *m.*, अनिलः, वातः, पवनः, मरुत् *m.*, मरुतः, मारुतः, वातिः *f.*, समीरणः, समीरः, समिरः, सदागतिः *m.*, सततगतिः *m.*, आशुगः, पवमानः, प्रभञ्जनः, गन्धवहः, गन्धवाहः, प्रधावनः, धवायकः, जगत्प्राणः, नभस्वलः, श्वसनः, स्पर्शनः, मातरिश्वा *m.* (न्), पृषदश्वः, पृषताश्वः, पृषताम्पतिः *m.*, प्रजीनः, श्वतसः, तान्द्रमः, लघटिः *m.*, विश्वायुः *m.*, यः.—(Air) वायुः *m.*, स्पर्शः; 'against the wind,' प्रतिवातं; 'cold wind,' हिमानिलः; 'swift as the wind,' वायुवेगसमः -मा -मं, वायुगतिः -तिः -ति; 'like the wind,' वायुसमः -मा -मं, वायुभूतः -ता -तं.—(Flatulence) वायुः *m.*, वातः, *see* FLATULENCE; 'to break wind,' पर्द् (c. 1. पर्दते -र्दितुं), शृध् (c. 10. शर्धयति -यितुं).

To WIND, *v. a.* (Blow a horn, &c.) शङ्खं ध्मा.—(Cause to turn or twist) आवृत् (c. 10. -वर्त्तयति -यितुं), परिवृत्, *see To* TWIST, *v. a.* —(Wind up, as a discourse, &c.) उपसंहृ (c. 1. -हरति -हर्तुं), प्रत्याहृ, उपसंहारं कृ, प्रत्याहारं कृ.

To WIND, *v. n.* (Proceed in a winding direction) विसृप् (c. 1. -सर्पति -सर्प्तुं), वक्रं or कुटिलं गम्.—(Turn, twine), *see* the words.

WIND-BOUND, *a.* वातरुद्धः -द्धा -द्धं, वायुप्रतिबद्धः &c., वातबद्धः &c.

WIND-FALL, *s.* आगन्तुकलाभः, आकस्मिकलाभः, अलभ्यलाभः.

WINDING, *s.* वक्रता, वक्रं, वक्रिमा *m.* (न्), पुटः, आवृत्तिः *f.*, व्यावर्त्तनं; 'of a river,' रोधोवक्रता, वक्रं, वङ्कः, पुटभेदः.

WINDING, *part.* विसर्पी -र्पिणी -र्पि (न्), वक्रगामी &c.

WINDING-SHEET, *s.* शववस्त्रं, शववसनं. *See* SHROUD.

WIND-MILL, *s.* वायुसञ्चालितचक्रं, वायुचक्रं, वातचक्रं.

WINDOW, *s.* वातायनं, जालं -लकः -लिका, गवाक्षः -क्षकः, गृहाक्षः, प्रग्रीवः, मुखं, गृहमुखं; 'at the window,' वातायनगतः, वातायनस्थः, वातायनाश्रितः; 'having a window,' जाली -लिनी &c.

WINDY, *a.* वातलः -ला -लं, वातवान् -वती -वत् (त्), वायवः -वी -वं, वायव्यः -व्या -व्यं, वातमयः -यी -यं. *See* STORMY.

WINE, *s.* मद्यं, द्राक्षारसः, द्राक्षामद्यं, द्राक्षासवः, द्राक्षासुरा, मदिरा, मधु *n.*, मध्वासवः, माध्वी -ध्वीकं, माध्वकं, मधुमाध्वीकं, माधवकः, मार्द्वीकं, सुरा -री, हाला, कश्यं, रसितः, महानन्दा, कादम्बरी, पक्वरसः; 'wine personified,' सुरा -री; 'wine-drinker, wine-bibber,' मद्यपः, सुरापः, मद्यपायी *m.*; 'wine-drinking,' मद्यपानं.

WINE-GLASS, *s.* मद्यपात्रं, सुराभाजनं, चषकः, *see* DRINKING-VESSEL.

WINE-MERCHANT, *s.* द्राक्षारसविक्रेता *m.* (तृ), मद्यविक्रयी *m.*

WINE-PRESS, *s.* द्राक्षापेषणयन्त्रं, द्राक्षापेषणी.

WING, *s.* (Of a bird, &c.) पक्षः, पक्ष *n.* (न्), गरुत् *m.*, देहधिः *m.*, पत्रं, पतत्रं, छदः -दनं, तनुरुहः, तनूरुहः, वाजः, बाहुकुत्थः; 'spreading its wings,' पक्षौ प्रसार्य; 'under the wing,' पक्षाधस्; 'root of a wing,' पक्षमूलं, पक्षतिः *f.*—(Of an army) पक्षः, सेनापक्षः, सैन्यपक्षः, पार्श्वस्थदलं, चक्रं.—(Of a house) गृहपक्षः, गृहपार्श्वभागः.

WINGED, *a.* पक्षी -क्षिणी -क्षि (न्), पक्षवान् -वती &c., सपक्षः -क्षा -क्षं, पक्षयुक्तः -क्ता -क्तं, जातपक्षः &c., पत्री &c., पतत्री &c.

WINK, *s.* (Of the eye) निमेषः -षकः, निमिषः, निमीलनं, मीलनं, उन्मीलनं, उन्मीलितं, विकूणनं, कर्करटः, अक्षिपक्ष्मणः सङ्कोचः.—(Sign, or hint made by the eye) नेत्रसङ्केतः, अक्षिसंज्ञा, अक्षिसङ्कोचसंज्ञा, भ्रूसंज्ञितं, अपाङ्गदर्शनं, इङ्गितं.

To WINK, *v. n.* (Close the eyelids quickly) निमिष् (c. 6. -मिषति -मेषितुं), मिष्, निमील् (c. 1. -मीलति -लितुं), मील्, उन्मील्, अक्षिपक्ष्म संकुच् (c. 1. -कोचति -चितुं), क्षप् (c. 10. क्षपयति -यितुं), चूण्, अक्षिसङ्कोचं कृ.—(Make a sign with the eye) अक्षिपक्ष्मसङ्कोचेन सङ्केतं कृ or संज्ञां कृ, नेत्रसङ्केतं कृ.—(Wink at) उपेक्ष्, *see To* CONNIVE.

WINKING, *part.* निमिषन् -षन्ती -षत् (त्), निमीलन् &c., सङ्कटाक्षः -क्षा -क्षं, सङ्कुचिताक्षः &c.—(Winking at) उपेक्षी -क्षिणी &c.

WINNER, *s.* जेता *m.* (तृ), जयी *m.* (न्), विजेता *m.*, विजयी *m.*

WINNING, *a.* अनुरञ्जकः -का -कं, मनोहरः &c., मिष्टयुः -युः -यु.

To WINNOW, *v. a.* शुध् (c. 10. शोधयति -यितुं), निष्पावं कृ, पू, परिपू, प्रस्फुट् (c. 10. -स्फोटयति -यितुं), प्रस्फोटनं कृ. *See To* THRESH.

WINNOWED, *p. p.* पूतः -ता -तं, परिपूतः &c., बहुलीकृतः -ता -तं.

WINNOWER, *s.* पावकः, निष्पावकः, प्रस्फोटनकारी *m.* (न्).

WINNOWING, *s.* निष्पावः, पवनं, पवः, प्रस्फोटनं, बहुलीकरणं, उत्कारः, निकारः; 'winnowing-fan or basket,' सूर्पः -र्पं, शूर्पः -र्पं, प्रस्फोटनं.

WINTER, *s.* हेमन्तः -न्तं, हैमनं, हेमन्तकालः, हिमकालः, शीतकालः, शिशिरः -रं, हिमर्त्तुः *m.*, शीतर्त्तुः, हिमागमः, हैमलं.

To WINTER, *v. n.* हेमन्तकालं गम् (c. 10. गमयति -यितुं) or नी.

WINTERY, *a.* हैमन्तः -न्ती -न्तं, हैमन्तिकः -की -कं, हैमः -मी -मं, हैमनः -नी -नं, हिमकालसम्बन्धी &c.; 'weather,' हिमदुर्दिनं.

To WIPE, *v. a.* मृज् (c. 2. मार्ष्टि -र्ष्टुं, c. 1. मार्जति -र्जितुं), प्रमृज्, आमृज्, परिमृज्, सम्मृज्, प्रक्षल् (c. 10. -क्षालयति -यितुं), मृद्, *see To* RUB; 'the mouth,' मुखं प्रमृज्; 'the eyes,' नेत्रे परिमृज्; 'tears from the eyes,' नेत्राभ्याम् अश्रूणि प्रमृज्.—(Wipe away, wipe off) अपमृज्, अवमृज्, निःक्षिप्; 'dirt or defilement,' मलम् अपमृज्, निर्लेपं कृ.

WIPE, *s.* मार्जः -र्जनं, प्रक्षालनं.—(Blow) प्रहारः, आघातः.

WIPED, *p. p.* मार्जितः -ता -तं, प्रमार्जितः &c.; 'with the hand,' समुद्धस्तः &c.

WIPER, *s.* मार्जनी, मार्जनवस्त्रं, प्रक्षालनी, वरकं.

WIRE, *s.* तारः -रा, लोहतारा, लोहतन्तुः *m.*, लोहसूत्रं, लोहतन्त्री, शलाका, धातुसूत्रं, तन्तुः *m.*, सूत्रं, तन्त्री -न्त्रं.

To WIREDRAW, *v. a.* लोहोद्वर्त्तनं कृ, लोहतारोद्वर्त्तनं कृ.

WIRY, *a.* तन्तुमयः -यी -यं, तन्तुसगुणः -णा -णं, तन्तुप्रायः &c.

WISDOM, *s.* ज्ञानं, विज्ञानं, प्रज्ञा, बुद्धिः *f.*, प्राज्ञता, विज्ञता, मेधा, वैदुष्यं, विद्वत्ता, पाण्डित्यं, मनीषा, मतिः *f.*, विवेकः, हिताहितविवेकः, धीः *f.*; 'god of wisdom,' गणेशः.

WISE, *a.* (Having wisdom) विद्वान् -दुषी -द्वत् (त्), ज्ञानी -निनी -नि (न्), ज्ञानवान् -वती -वत् (त्), प्राज्ञः -ज्ञा -ज्ञं, प्रज्ञः &c., बुद्धिमान् -मती &c., मतिमान् &c., धीमान् &c., प्रज्ञावान् &c., पण्डितः -ता -तं, विज्ञः -ज्ञा -ज्ञं, विवेकी -किनी &c., प्रज्ञी &c., मेधावी -विनी &c., सविवेकः -का -कं, कोविदः -दा -दं, सुधीः -धीः -धि, सुबोधः -धा -धं, कृतधीः &c., धीरः -रा -रं, विशेषज्ञः -ज्ञा -ज्ञं, कृतज्ञः &c., निपुणदृक् *m. f. n.* (श्), प्रेक्षावान् &c., मर्म्मज्ञः &c.; 'a wise man,' विद्वज्जनः, बुधः, *see* LEARNED.—(Dictated by wisdom) ज्ञानप्रयुक्तः -क्ता -क्तं, बुद्धिप्रयुक्तः &c., ज्ञानमूलकः -का -कं, बुद्धिमूलकः &c.

WISE, *s.* *See* MANNER, WAY; 'in no wise,' न कथचन.

WISEACRE, *s.* पण्डितम्मन्यः, ज्ञम्मन्यः, अल्पबुद्धिः *m.*

WISELY, *adv.* विद्वज्जनवत्, प्राज्ञवत्, विज्ञवत्, सज्ञानं, सविवेकं, विवेकपूर्व्वं, सम्यक्, सुष्ठु, युक्तं.

To WISH, *v. n.* इष् (c. 6. इच्छति, एषितुं), अभिलष् (c. 1. -लषति -षितुं), वाञ्छ् (c. 1. वाञ्छति -ञ्छितुं), काङ्क्ष् (c. 1. काङ्क्षति -ङ्क्षितुं), आकाङ्क्ष्, *see To* DESIRE. Often expressed by the desid. form of a root; as, 'to wish to obtain,' आप् in des. (ईप्सति -प्सितुं), लभ् in des. (लिप्सते -प्सितुं); 'to wish to go,' गम् in des. (जिगमिषति -षितुं).

To WISH, *v. a.* (Well to one) इष्टं or मङ्गलम् or कल्याणम् आशंस् (c. 1. -शंसते -सितुं) or आशास् (c. 2. शास्ते -सितुं) or प्रार्थ्.—(Wish one ill) अनिष्टं or अमङ्गलम् आशंस् or प्रार्थ्.

WISH, *s.* इच्छा, अभिलाषः, आकाङ्क्षा, इष्टं, स्पृहा, मनोरथः, ईप्सितं, *see* DESIRE; 'according to one's wish,' यथाभिमतं; 'earnest wish,' कौतूहलं, कुतूहलं, *see* LONGING.

WISHED, *p. p.* इष्टः -ष्टा -ष्टं, अभीष्टः -ष्टा -ष्टं. *See* DESIRED.

WISHING, *part.* or *a.* इच्छुः -च्छुः -च्छु, आकाङ्क्षी &c. *See* DESIROUS.

WISP, *s.* (Of straw) शुष्कतृणकूर्च्चकः, शुष्कनालगुच्छकः.

WISTFULL, WISTFULLY. *See* EARNEST, EAGER, EAGERLY.

WIT, *s.* (Understanding) बुद्धिः *f.*, मतिः *f.*, धीः *f.*; 'one who has lost his wits,' नष्टबुद्धिः -द्धिः -द्धि.—(Quickness of fancy) बुद्धिपाटवं, बुद्धिचातुर्य्यं, बुद्धिविलासः, बुद्धिकौशलं, बुद्धितीक्ष्णता, वैदग्ध्यं, विदग्धता.—(Humour) रसः, रसिकवाक्यं, रसिकोक्तिः *f.*, नर्म्मोक्तिः *f.*, नर्म्म *n.* (न्), मर्म्म *n.*—(A wit, man of wit) रसज्ञः, नर्म्मज्ञः, नर्म्मवेदी *m.* (न्), परिहासवेदी *m.*, नर्म्मभाषी *m.*—(To wit) वस्तुतस्, अर्थतस्.

WITCH, *s.* मायिनी, पूतना, डाकिनी. *See* SORCERESS.

WITCHCRAFT, *s.* माया, अभिचारः, पूतनात्वं. *See* SORCERY.

WITH, *prep.* (Denoting cause, means, instrument) usually expressed by the instrumental case; as, 'with a sword,' खड्गेन; 'with grief,' शोकेन.—(In opposition to, against) instr. c., with or without सह; as, 'to fight with one's enemies,' शत्रुभिः or शत्रुभिः सह युध् or expressed by उपरि or by the dat. or gen. c., in such phrases as, 'he is angry with his son,' पुत्रस्योपरि or पुत्राय or पुत्रस्य क्रुध्यति.—(In company, together with, along with) सह, सार्द्धं, समं, साकं, सहितं, सत्रं -त्रा, अमा all with the instrum. c.; 'along with me,' मया सह; 'along with him,' तेन सह. The preposition सम्, prefixed to roots, gives this sense of 'with;' as, 'to live in company with,' संवस्.—(Associated, attended, connected with) सहितः -ता -तं in comp. or expressed by the instr. c., with or without सह, or by पूर्व्व or पुरःसर in comp.; as, 'associated with enemies,' शत्रुसहितः -ता -तं or शत्रुभिः सहितः &c.—(Denoting manner) expressed by instr. c., or by स in comp. with the accus. n., or by पूर्व्वं or पूर्व्वकं or पुरःसरं affixed; as, 'with anger,' कोपेन, सकोपं, कोपपूर्व्वं, कोपपूर्व्वकं, कोपपुरःसरं; 'with respect,' सादरं; 'with affection,' प्रीतिपूर्व्वं.—(Among) मध्ये. To express a person with any thing in his possession, or a thing in connection with something else, a compound adjective may often be used; thus, 'a man with a stick in his hand,' दण्डहस्तः पुरुषः; 'a man with riches,' सधनः or धनवान् पुरुषः; 'a ship with two masts,' द्विकूपका नौः or कूपकद्वययुक्ता नौः.

WITHAL, *adv.* समं, तथैव, अपिच, अपरञ्च. *See* LIKEWISE.

To WITHDRAW, *v. a.* अपनी (c. 1. -नयति -नेतुं), विनी, व्यपनी, अपकृष् (c. 1. -कर्षति -कर्ष्टुं), अपाकृष्, अपहृ (c. 1. -हरति -हर्त्तुं), व्यपहृ, उपसंहृ, प्रतिसंहृ, संहृ.

To WITHDRAW, *v. n.* अपक्रम् (c. 1. -क्रामति -क्रमितुं), अपसृ (c. 1. -सरति -सर्त्तुं), परावृत्, अवस्था, पलाय्, चल्. *See To* RETIRE.

WITHDRAWAL, *s.* (Taking back) अपनयः -यनं, अपहरणं, उपसंहारः -हरणं.—(Retiring) अपक्रमः, अपायः, *see* RETIREMENT.

WITHDRAWN, *p. p.* अपनीतः -ता -तं, उपसंहृतः &c., परावृत्तः -त्ता -त्तं.

To WITHER, *v. n.* विशॄ in pass. (-शीर्य्यते), म्लै (c. 1. म्लायति, म्लातुं), नश् (c. 4. नश्यति), सद्, क्षि. *See To* FADE, *v. n.*

To WITHER, *v. a.* नश् (c. 10. नाशयति -यितुं). *See To* FADE, *v. a.*

WITHERED, *p. p.* विशीर्णः -र्णा -र्णं, म्लानः -ना -नं, शुष्कः -ष्का -ष्कं, गतरसः -सा -सं, *see* FADED; 'a withered leaf,' जीर्णपर्णं; 'having a withered arm or hand,' विकलपाणिकः -का -कं, कुकरः -रा -रं, कुणिः *m.*, कूणिः, कोणिः.

WITHERS, *s.* (Of an elephant, &c.) स्कन्धदेशः, स्कन्धः, आसनं.

WITHHELD, *p. p.* उपसंहृतः -ता -तं, प्रत्याहृतः &c., अपहृतः &c., विधृतः &c., विधारितः &c., निगृहीतः &c., उच्छिन्नः -न्ना -न्नं.

To WITHHOLD, *v. a.* उपसंहृ (c. 1. -हरति -हर्त्तुं), प्रत्याहृ, संहृ, विधृ (c. 10. -धारयति -यितुं), उच्छिद् (c. 7. -छिनत्ति -छेत्तुं), निग्रह्, विनिग्रह्, नियम्, निरुध्. *See To* RESTRAIN, RETAIN.

WITHIN, *prep.* (In the inner part) अन्तर्, अभ्यन्तरे, अन्तरे; 'within the house,' गृहाभ्यन्तरे; 'being within the house,' गृहान्तर्वर्त्ती -र्त्तिनी &c., गृहान्तर्गतः -ता -तं, गृहान्तःस्थः -स्था -स्थं.—(Not later than) मध्ये, अर्वाक्, *see* UNDER; 'within a year,' संवत्सरमध्ये; 'within ten days,' दशाहमध्ये.—(In the limits or compass of) गोचरः -रा -रं, विषय in comp., गम्य or ग्राह्य &c. in comp.; 'within hearing,' कर्णगोचरः -रा -रं; 'within sight,' दृष्टिगोचरः -रा -रं, दृग्गोचरः &c., दृष्टिगम्यः -म्या -म्यं, दृष्टिविषयः -या -यं; 'within arrow-shot,' बाणगोचरः -रा -रं; 'within reach of the hand,' हस्तग्राह्यः -ह्या -ह्यं, हस्तप्राप्यः &c., हस्तवर्त्ती -र्त्तिनी &c.

WITHIN, *adv.* अन्तर्, अभ्यन्तरे, *see* INWARDLY; 'gone within,' अन्तर्गतः -ता -तं; 'being within,' अन्तर्भवः -वा -वं, अन्तर्वर्त्ती &c.

WITHOUT, *prep.* (Not with) विना with instr. or acc. c., ऋते with abl. or acc. c., अन्तरेण with abl. or acc. or gen., अन्तरा, व्यतिरेकेण in comp., व्यतिरिक्तं, पृथक्, अ prefixed; 'without ornament,' भूषणेन विना or भूषणं विना; 'without feeling,' रसाद् ऋते; 'without punishment,' दण्डव्यतिरेकेण, दण्डमन्तरेण; 'without delay,' अविलम्बेन; 'without beginning or end,' अनाद्यन्तः -न्ता -न्तं; 'without doubt,' असंशयं; 'without reason,' असम्भावनीयं; 'without cause,' प्रयोजनं विना, अकस्मात् or expressed by the loc. abs., असति प्रयोजने.—(Destitute of) हीनः -ना -नं, विहीनः &c., रहितः -ता -तं, विरहितः &c. or expressed by अ, निर्, वि &c. prefixed; 'without money,' धनहीनः -ना -नं, धनरहितः &c., अधनः -ना -नं, निर्धनः &c.; 'how can I go without you?' कथं त्वद्विहीनो यास्यामि.—(Unless, if not, except) यदि न, अन्तरेण with acc., or expressed by the indec. part. with अ or न prefixed; 'without you do that,' यदि न तत् करोषि or तद् अकृत्वा; 'without drinking any water,' पानीयम् अपीत्वा; 'it cannot be seen without a telescope,' दूरदर्शकयन्त्रमन्तरेण न दृश्यते; 'this cannot be ascertained without algebra,' बीजगणितम् अन्तरेण न ज्ञायते तत्.—(On the outside of) बहिस्, बहिर्भागे, अन्तरेण; 'without the fort,' दुर्गबहिस्, दुर्गबहिर्भागे, दुर्गादन्तरेण.

WITHOUT, *adv.* (Not within) बहिस्, अवस्.—(Externally) बाह्यतस्.

To WITHSTAND, *v. a.* पर्यवस्था (c. 1. -तिष्ठति -स्थातुं), प्रतिकूल (nom. प्रतिकूलयति -यितुं), विरुध्. *See To* RESIST, OPPOSE.

WITNESS, *s.* (Testimony) साक्ष्यं, साक्षिता, प्रमाणं; 'false witness,' कूटसाक्ष्यं, मिथ्यासाक्ष्यं, असत्यसाक्ष्यं.—(Person who gives testimony) साक्षी *m.* (न्), प्रमाता *m.* (तृ), साक्ष्यदाता *m.*, साक्ष्यकारी *m.*; 'false witness,' कूटसाक्षी *m.*, कौटसाक्षी *m.*, कूटकार: -रक:; 'having witnesses,' साक्षिमान् -मती -मत् (त्); 'proved by them,' साक्षिभावित: -ता -तं; 'absence of them,' साक्ष्यभाव:; 'examination of a witness,' साक्षिपरीक्षा.—(One who is personally present) प्रत्यक्षदर्शी *m.*, साक्षाद्द्रष्टा *m.*, *see* EYE-WITNESS.

To WITNESS, *v. a.* (See by personal presence) प्रत्यक्षं or प्रत्यक्षतस् or स्वचक्षुषा दृश् (c. 1. पश्यति, द्रष्टुं), साक्षाद् दृश्, प्रत्यक्षदर्शनं कृ.—(Attest) साक्ष्यं दा, साक्ष्येण प्रमाणीकृ, *see To* ATTEST.

To WITNESS, *v. n.* साक्ष्यं दा, साक्ष्यं कृ, साक्षितां दा, साक्षी भू, प्रमाणीकृ, प्रमाणीभू. *See To* TESTIFY.

WITNESSED, *p. p.* (Seen in person) प्रत्यक्षदृष्ट: -ष्टा -ष्टं, साक्षाद्दृष्ट: &c., स्वचक्षुषा दृष्ट: &c.—(Attested) प्रमाणीकृत: -ता -तं, साक्षिक: -की -कं, ससाक्षिक: &c.

WITTICISM, *s.* रसिकवाक्यं, रसिकोक्ति: *f.*, सरसोक्ति: *f.*, सरसवाक्यं, नर्म्मोक्ति: *f.*, नर्म्मभाषणं, विनोदवाक्यं.

WITTILY, *adv.* सरसं, रसिकोक्त्या, बुद्धिविलासेन, नर्म्मोक्त्या.

WITTINGLY, *adv.* ज्ञानतस्, बुद्धिपूर्व्वं, कामतस्. *See* KNOWINGLY.

WITTY, *a.* (Of persons) रसज्ञ: -ज्ञा -ज्ञं, नर्म्मज्ञ: &c., रसवेदी -दिनी -दि (न्), नर्म्मवेदी &c., नर्म्मभाषी -षिणी &c., नर्म्मवक्ता -क्त्री -क्तृ (क्तृ), विदूषक: -का -कं, विदग्ध: -धा -धं.—(Of sayings, &c.) रसिक: -का -कं, सरस: -सा -सं, रसी -सिनी &c., रसवान् -वती -वत् (त्).

WIZARD, *s.* अभिचारविद् *m.*, मायाकार:. *See* MAGICIAN.

WOE, *s.* दु:खं, शोक:, दुर्गति: *f.*, *see* MISERY, SORROW, CALAMITY.—(Exclam.) हा, बत, धिक्.

WOEFUL, WOEFULLY, &c. *See* SORROWFUL, CALAMITOUS, &c.

WOLF, *s.* वृक:, कोक:, अरण्यश्वा *m.* (न्), ईहामृग:, ईहावृक:, छागभोजी *m.* (न्), जनाशन:.

WOMAN, *s.* स्त्री, नारी, अङ्गना, वनिता, योषित् *f.*, योषिता, योषा, जोषित् *f.*, जोषिता, जोषा, नरी, मानवी, महिला, अबला, मनुषी, मानुषी, कामिनी, वामा, विलासिनी, प्रमदा, मानिनी, वधू: *f.*, महेला -लिका, महेला, ललना, ललिता, रमणी, रामा, प्रकृति: *f.*, सीमन्तिनी, प्रतीपदर्शिनी, भरण्या, परिगृह्या; 'a young woman,' तरुणी, कन्या, बाला, युवती, यूनी, नवयौवना; 'assembly of young women,' यौवतं, यौवनं; 'an old woman,' वृद्धा, वृद्धस्त्री, जरती, पलिता, पलिक्नी; 'a woman of good family,' कुलस्त्री, कुलनारी, कुलाङ्गना; 'a beautiful woman,' सुन्दरी, प्रमदा, कान्ता, सुभगा, नितम्बिनी, वामलोचना; 'an excellent woman,' वराङ्गना, वरारोहा, उत्तमा, वरवर्णिनी, मत्तकाशिनी, मत्तकासिनी, स्त्रीरत्नं; 'a passionate woman,' कोपना, भामिनी; 'virtuous woman,' सती, साध्वी, सुचरित्रा, कुलस्त्री, कुलपालिका; 'clever woman,' सरस्वती; 'woman who has borne a child,' प्रसूता -तिका; 'married woman,' सभर्तृका, सनाथा; 'woman-killer,' स्त्रीघातक:; 'woman-hater,' स्त्रीद्वेषी *m.* The Hindus divide women into four classes, corresponding to the four classes of men. These are, 1. पद्मिनी, comprising the most excellent women; 2. चित्रिणी or हरिणी or मृगी, comprising well-educated, accomplished, and beautiful women; 3. शङ्खिनी, comprising women who are tall, neither stout nor thin, with long hair, irascible, and with strong passions; 4. हस्तिनी, comprising women who are short, stout, with curly hair and furious passions.

WOMAN-HOOD, *s.* स्त्रीता, स्त्रीत्वं, नारीत्वं, स्त्रैणं, स्त्रीधर्म्म:.

WOMANISH, WOMANLY, *a.* स्त्रैण: -णी -णं. *See* FEMININE.

WOMANKIND, *s.* स्त्रीजाति: *f.*, स्त्रीप्रकृति: *f.*, स्त्रीजना: *m. pl.*

WOMB, *s.* गर्भाशय:, गर्भस्थानं, योनि: *m. f.*, योनी, गर्भकोश:, जरायु: *m.*, गर्भ:, कोष:, उदरं, जठर: -रं, मातृकुक्षि: *m.*, उल्वं, कलल: -लं, चत्वाल:, धरा.

WON, *p. p.* जित: -ता -तं, निर्जित: &c., उपार्जित: -ता -तं.

WONDER, *s.* (The emotion) विस्मय:, आश्चर्यं -र्यत्वं, चमत्कार:, चित्रं, विचित्रकं.—(A wonder, cause of wonder) आश्चर्यं, अद्भुतं, अद्भुतवस्तु *n.*, कौतुकं, चमत्कार:, चमत्कृति: *f.*, चित्रं, विचित्रता, *see* MARVEL; 'a great wonder,' महदाश्चर्यं; 'wonder of the world,' भुवनाद्भुतं.

To WONDER, *v. n.* विस्मि (c. 1. -स्मयते -स्मेतुं), विस्मयापन्न: -न्ना -न्नं भू, विस्मित: -ता -तं भू, सविस्मय: -या -यं भू, विस्मयान्वित: -ता -तं भू, कुहुकुह (nom. कुहुकुहायते). *See To* MARVEL.

WONDERFUL, WONDROUS, *a.* आश्चर्य: -र्या -र्यं, अद्भुत: -ता -तं, चित्र: -त्रा -त्रं, विचित्रक: &c., चित्री -त्रिणी &c., विस्मापक: &c. *See* MARVELLOUS.

WONDER-STRUCK, *a.* विस्मित: -ता -तं, विस्मयाकुल: -ला -लं.

WONDER-WORKING, *a.* आश्चर्यकर्म्मा -र्म्मा -र्म्म (न्), अद्भुतकर्म्मा &c., चित्रकर्म्मा &c., विचित्रकर्म्मा &c.

WONT, *To* BE WONT. *See* USED, HABITUATED, *To* USE.

WONTED, *a.* आभ्यासिक: -की -कं, व्यावहारिक: &c. *See* CUSTOMARY.

To WOO, *v. a.* विवाहार्थं याच् (c. 1. याचति -चितुं) or प्रार्थ् (c. 10. -अर्थयति -ते -यितुं), विवाहार्थम् आराध् or चित्ताराधनं कृ.

WOOD, *s.* (Forest) वनं, अरण्यं, विपिनं, काननं, *see* FOREST.—(Substance of trees, timber) काष्ठं, दारु: *m.* -रु *n.*

WOOD-APPLE, *s.* (The tree) कपित्थ:.—(The fruit) कपित्थं.

WOOD-COCK, *s.* वनकुक्कुट:, अरण्यकुक्कुट:, वृक्षकुक्कुट:.

WOOD-CUTTER, *s.* वृक्षछिद् *m.*, वनछिद्, छेत्ता *m.* (तृ), स्थाणुछेद:.

WOODED, *a.* वृक्षावृत: -ता -तं, तरुगुल्मावृत: &c., सवृक्ष: -क्षा -क्षं.

WOODEN, *a.* काष्ठमय: -यी -यं, दारुमय: &c., काष्ठी -ष्ठिनी -ष्ठि (न्), काष्ठघटित: -ता -तं, दारुघटित: &c., दारव: -वी -वं, दारुज: -जा -जं, अधिदार्व: -र्वी -र्वं, काष्ठ in comp., दारु in comp.

WOOD-HOUSE, *s.* काष्ठरक्षणस्थानं, इध्मस्थानं, दारुकाष्ठस्थानं.

WOOD-LAND, *s.* वृक्षावृतभूमि: *f.*, तरुगुल्मावृतभूमि: *f.* -भू: *f.*

WOODMAN, *s.* वनचारी *m.*, वनजीवी *m.*, आटविक:. *See* FORESTER.

WOOD-NYMPH, *s.* वनदेवता, वनदेवी, अरण्यदेवता -देवी.

WOOD-PECKER, *s.* दार्वाघाट:, दार्वाघात:, काष्ठकुट्ट:, शतपत्रक:, शतच्छद:, भद्रनामा *m.* (न्), कुठाकु: *m.*, कुठारु: *m.*

WOOD-PIGEON, *s.* हारितः, हारीतः, वनपारावतः, वनकपोतः.

WOOD-SORREL, *s.* चाङ्गेरी, कुचाङ्गेरी, चुक्रिका, दन्तशठा, अम्ली, अम्ललोणिका, अम्ललोलिका, अश्मन्तक, चलस् *n.*

WOODY, *a.* (Abounding with wood) बहुवृक्षावृतः -ता -तं, वृक्षाकीर्णः -र्णा -र्णं, प्रचुरवृक्षः -क्षा -क्षं, वार्क्षः -र्क्षी -र्क्षं.—(Ligneous) काष्ठमयः -यी -यं.—(Silvan) आरण्यकः &c., *see* SILVAN.

WOOER, *s.* विवाहार्थप्रार्थकः, विवाहार्थयाचकः, स्त्र्युपासकः.

WOOF, *s.* (In weaving) वाणिः -णी *f.*

WOOING, *s.* विवाहार्थं प्रार्थनं, विवाहार्थं स्त्र्याराधनं.

WOOL, *s.* ऊर्णा, मेषलोमन् *n.* (न्), अविलोम *n.*, मेषरोम *n.*, मेषाङ्गरुहं, अङ्गरुहं.

WOOLLEN, *a.* और्णः -र्णी -र्णं, और्णिकः -की -कं, ऊर्णामयः -यी -यं, मेषलोममयः -यी -यं, मेषलोमनिर्म्मितः -ता -तं, मेषलोमजः -जा -जं, आविकः -की -कं, राङ्कवः -वी -वं, मृगरोमजः &c.; 'woollen cloth,' और्णवस्त्रं, और्णपटः, अविपटः, आविकः, औरभ्रं, जालिका; 'garment,' और्णवासस् *n.*, वालवासस् *n.*

WOOLLY, *a.* लोमशः -शा -शं, रोमशः &c., रोमवान् -वती -वत् (त्), लोमवान् &c., ऊर्णासदृशः -शी -शं; 'woolly hair,' वर्ब्बरः, वर्ब्बरीकः, वर्वरी.

WORD, *s.* (Single component part of a sentence) शब्दः, पदं, वाचकः, वर्णात्मा *m.* (न्), वाक्यं; 'word for word,' यथाशब्दं; 'force of a word,' शब्दशक्तिः *f.*, निरूढः; 'sense,' शब्दार्थः; 'acceptation,' शब्दानुशासनं; 'low word,' अपशब्दः, अवाक्षरं; 'radical form of a word,' प्रकृतिः *f.*—(Discourse, language) उक्तिः *f.*, वाक्यं, वचनं, वाक् *f.* (च्), वचस् *n.*; 'mere words,' वाङ्मात्रं; 'bad words,' दुरुक्तिः *f.*, दुर्वाक्यं, दुर्वचनं; 'waste of words,' वाग्व्ययः; 'war of words,' वाग्युद्धं; 'a word in season,' प्राप्तकालवचनं; 'a man of few words,' अल्पभाषी *m.* (न्), मितभाषी *m.*, मितवाक् *m.*, वाग्दरिद्रः.—(Promise) वचनं, प्रतिज्ञा; 'to break one's word,' विसंवद्, *see* PROMISE.—(Tidings) समाचारः, संवादः, सन्देशः.—(In a word) समासतस्.

To WORD, *v. a.* शब्दद्वारा व्याख्या (c. 2. -ख्याति -तुं), शब्दतो व्याख्या, शब्दरचनां कृ, शब्दयोजनां कृ, शब्दविन्यासं कृ.

WORDINESS, *s.* शब्दविस्तारः, शब्दबाहुल्यं, बहुशब्दत्वं.

WORDY, *a.* बहुशब्दकः -का -कं, शाब्दिकः -की -कं, शाब्दः -ब्दी -ब्दं, बहुवाङ्मयः -यी -यं, वाग्मी -ग्मिनी -ग्मि (न्).

To WORK, *v. n.* (Labor, make exertion) श्रम् (c. 4. श्राम्यति, श्रमितुं), परिश्रम्, श्रमं कृ, उद्योगं कृ, उद्यमं कृ, उत्साहं कृ, यत्नं कृ, व्यवसायं कृ, कर्म्म कृ, आयस् (c. 4. -यस्यति -सितुं), आयासं कृ, यत्, चेष्ट्, व्यवसो, उद्यम्.—(Operate, act) कृ, चेष्ट्, फलम् उत्पद्, प्रभू, *see To* OPERATE.

To WORK, *v. a.* (Move, cause to move) चल् (c. 10. चालयति -यितुं), संचल्, संचर् (c. 10. -चारयति -यितुं), सृ in caus.—(Form by labour) कृ, घट् (c. 10. घटयति -यितुं), निर्मा, रच्, विधा, कॢप्, *see To* MAKE, MANUFACTURE.—(Produce, bring about) उत्पद् (c. 10. -पादयति -यितुं), सम्पद्, जन् (c. 10. जनयति -यितुं), साध्, कृ.—(Cause to labour) आयस् (c. 10. -यासयति -यितुं), क्लिश् (c. 10. क्लेशयति -यितुं), श्रम् (c. 10. श्रमयति -यितुं), सद् (c. 10. सादयति -यितुं), अवसद्.—(Manage) प्रणी, नी, नियम्, वह् in caus., निर्वह्.—(Embroider), *see* the word.

WORK, *s.* (Employment) कर्म्म *n.* (न्), व्यापारः, कार्य्यं, व्यवसायः, *see* OCCUPATION; 'a laborious work,' श्रमकर्म्म *n.*—(Labour, exertion) श्रमः, आयासः, क्लेशः, उद्योगः, उत्साहः, उद्यमः, यत्नः, कष्टं.—(That which is done or made) कर्म्म *n.* (न्), कार्य्यं, क्रिया, कृतिः *f.*, कृतं.—(Composition, work of an author) ग्रन्थः, क्रिया, कृतिः *f.*—(Religious act) कर्म्म *n.* (न्), क्रिया, अनुष्ठानं; 'good works,' सत्कर्म्म *n.*, सत्क्रिया, सुकर्म्म *n.*, पुण्यकर्म्म *n.*, धर्म्मकार्य्यं, धर्म्मकृत्यं, पुण्यं, साधनं; 'way of salvation by works,' कर्म्ममार्गः; 'one who seeks salvation by works,' कर्म्ममार्गी (न्), धूमपथः, धूमधीः *m.*; 'rich in good works,' पुण्यपुञ्जः; 'reward of them,' पुण्यफलं; 'abandonment of them,' कर्म्मत्यागः.—(Needle-work), *see* EMBROIDERY, NEEDLE-WORK.

WORK-HOUSE, *s.* कर्म्मशाला, कर्म्मगृहं, दरिद्रालयः.

WORK-MAN, *s.* कर्म्मकरः, कर्म्मकारः, कर्म्मारः, कारुः *m.*, शिल्पकारः.

WORKMANSHIP, *s.* घटना, निर्म्माणं, रचना, विरचना, आकृतिः *f.*

WORKSHOP, *s.* शिल्पशाला, शिल्पगृहं, आवेशनं, प्रावेशनं.

WORKING, *s.* (Act of labouring) उद्योगकरणं, उत्साहकरणं, कर्म्मकरणं, आयासकरणं, श्रमकरणं.—(Operation) चेष्टा.

WORK-WOMAN, *s.* कर्म्मकारी -रिणी, कर्म्मकरी, शिल्पकारी.

WORLD, *s.* (Universe) जगत् *n.*, जगती, लोकः, चराचरं, *see* UNIVERSE.—(The earth) लोकः, भुवनं, पृथिवी, भूः *f.*, भवः, भूलोकः, भूगोलः, जगत् *n.*, जीवाधारः, जीवाजीवाधारः, विश्वं, विष्टपं; 'creator of the world,' जगत्स्रष्टा *m.* (ष्टृ); 'destruction of the world,' जगत्क्षयः, जगद्विनाशः; 'destroyer of it,' जगद्घाती *m.*; 'end of the world,' जगदन्तः, कल्पः, भववीतिः *f.*; 'to the end of the world,' आकल्पात्; 'ends of the world,' दिगन्ताः *m. pl.*; 'the three worlds,' त्रिभुवनं, त्रैलोक्यं, लोकत्रयं, भुवनत्रयं, जगत्त्रयं; 'soul of the world,' जगदात्मा *m.*, लोकात्मा *m.*—(Mundane existence) संसारः, संसरणं, संसृतिः *f.*, इहलोकवासः, भूलोकवासः, जगन्निवासः, प्रपञ्चः, कष्टकारकः, संसारमार्गः, संसारचक्रं, संसारावर्त्तः, मोहास्पदं, मायाचक्रं, मायाजालं, विषयजालं, लोकयात्रा, प्रवृत्तिमार्गः; 'this world,' इहलोकः; 'the next world,' परलोकः, लोकान्तरं, प्रेतलोकः; 'the world above,' ऊर्द्धलोकः; 'belonging to this world,' ऐहलौकिकः -की -कं, ऐहिकः &c.; 'belonging to the next world,' पारलौकिकः -की -कं, पारत्रिकः &c., आमुष्मिकः &c.; 'in this world,' इह, इहलोके; 'in the next world,' परत्र, अमुत्र, प्रेत्य; 'renunciation of the world,' सन्न्यसनं, सर्व्वसङ्गपरित्यागः; 'one who renounces it,' सन्न्यासी *m.* (न्); 'deadness to the world,' वैराग्यं, विषयविरक्तिः *f.*; 'sick of the world,' भवरोगी -गिणी &c., भवार्त्तः -र्त्ता -र्त्तं; 'snares of the world,' मोहजालं, मायाजालं, मोहपाशः.—(Mankind) लोकः, लोकाः *m. pl.*, जीवलोकः, जनाः *m. pl.*; 'fear of the world,' लोकलज्जा.—(Customs of men) लोकमार्गः, लोकरीतिः *f.*, लोकप्रचारः, जनरीतिः *f.*, जनप्रचारः; 'one who has seen the world,' बहुदृष्टः.

WORLDLINESS, *s.* लौकिकता, विषयासक्तिः *f.*, प्रपञ्चासक्तिः, देहाभिमानं.

WORLDLING, विषयी *m.* (न्), प्रपञ्चासक्तः. *See* WORLDLY.

WORLDLY, *a.* (Pertaining to this world) लौकिकः -की -कं, सांसारिकः -की -कं, ऐहिकः &c., ऐहलौकिकः &c., प्रापञ्चिकः &c., दृष्टार्थः -र्था -र्थं, संसारी -रिणी -रि (न्), लौक्यः -क्या -क्यं.—(Devoted to it) विषयासक्तः -क्ता -क्तं, विषयाधीनः -ना -नं, प्रपञ्चासक्तः -क्ता -क्तं, इहलोकनिष्ठः -ष्ठा -ष्ठं, इहलोकासक्तः &c., संसारनिष्ठः &c., संसारैकनिष्ठः &c.

WORLDLY-MINDED, *a.* ऐहिकबुद्धिः -द्धिः -द्धि, ऐहिकदृष्टिः -ष्टिः -ष्टि, इहलोकदृष्टिः &c., प्रपञ्चबुद्धिः &c., संसारैकलक्ष्यः -क्ष्या -क्ष्यं.

WORLDLY-WISE, *a.* संसारज्ञानी -निनी -नि (न्), व्यवहारज्ञानी &c.

WORLDLY-WISDOM, *s.* सांसारिकज्ञानं, संसारज्ञानं, व्यवहारज्ञानं.

WORM, *s.* कृमिः *m.*, क्रिमिः *m.*, कीटः -टकः, गण्डूपदः -दी, किचुलुकः, महीलता, शिली, भूलता, रज्जूः *f.*, कोकसः, तण्डुरीणः, कृपणः.—(In the inside of the body) कृमिः *m.*, क्रिमिः *m.*, मीवा, अन्नादः, लेलिहः; 'the disease,' कृमिरोगः; 'affected by it,' कृमी -मिणी -मि (न्); 'destroying worms,' कृमिघ्नः -घ्नी -घ्नं, कृमिहरः -रा -रं; 'having them,' कृमिलः -ला -लं.

WORM-EATEN, *a.* कृमिखादितः -ता -तं, कृमिभक्षितः &c., कृमिनिष्कुषितः &c.

WORMY, *a.* कृमिलः -ला -लं, कृमी -मिणी &c., कृमिमयः -यी -यं.

WORN, *p.p.* धृतः -ता -तं, धारितः &c., भृतः -ता -तं, परिहितः &c.; 'is worn,' धार्य्यते, भ्रियते.—(Worn away) घर्षितः -ता -तं, मृष्टः -ष्टा -ष्टं, उन्मृष्टः &c., आघट्टितः &c.—(Worn out, decayed) जीर्णः -र्णा -र्णं, जर्जरः -रा -रं, जर्जरीकः -का -कं, जरठः -ठा -ठं.—(Worn out, fatigued) श्रान्तः -न्ता -न्तं, *see* FATIGUED.

To WORRY, *v. a.* बाध्, क्लिश्, व्यथ्, आयस्. *See To* TEASE.

WORSE, *a.* दुष्टतरः -रा -रं, कष्टतरः &c., खलतरः &c., अधिकदुष्टः -ष्टा -ष्टं, पापीयान् -यसी -यस् (स्), विशेषदुष्टः &c., गरीयान् &c., अनुत्तमः -मा -मं; 'better and worse,' परापरः -रा -रं.—(More sick) अधिकरोगी -गिणी &c.

WORSE, *adv.* दुष्टतरं, कष्टतरं, खलतरं, अधिकदुष्टं, पापीयस्.

WORSHIP, *s.* पूजा, पूजनं, भजनं, भक्तिः *f.*, अर्चा, अर्चनं -ना, अभ्यर्चा -र्चनं, समभ्यर्चनं, उपासना, उपासा, उपास्तिः *f.*, उपचर्य्या, सेवा, आराधनं -ना, नमस्या, सपर्य्या, अर्हणं -णा, इज्या, नमस्कारः, अपचितिः *f.*; 'of the gods,' देवपूजा, देवभक्तिः *f.*, देवतार्चनं.—(Your worship) भगवान् *m.* (त्), भवान् *m.*

To WORSHIP, *v. a.* पूज् (c. 10. पूजयति -यितुं), अभिपूज्, सम्पूज्, अर्च् (c. 1. अर्चति -र्चितुं, c. 10. अर्चयति -यितुं), अभ्यर्च्, समर्च्, समभ्यर्च्, भज् (c. 1. भजते, भक्तुं), उपास् (c. 2. -आस्ते -सितुं), आराध् (c. 10. -राधयति -यितुं), सेव् (c. 1. सेवते -वितुं, c. 10. सेवयति -यितुं), नमस् (nom. नमस्यति), सभाज् (c. 10. सभाजयति -यितुं), मह्, स्तु in des., अर्ह्; 'by sacrifice,' यज् (c. 1. यजति, यष्टुं, ईजितुं).

WORSHIPFUL, *a.* पूजार्हः -र्हा -र्हं, पूजनीयः -या -यं, अर्चनीयः &c., भट्टारः -रा -रं, भट्टारकः &c., नमस्यः -स्या -स्यं, उपास्यः -स्या -स्यं, अभीज्यः &c., भावमिश्रः -श्रा -श्रं, अर्च्यः &c. *See* HONOURABLE.

WORSHIPPED, *p. p.* पूजितः -ता -तं, अर्चितः &c., समभ्यर्चितः &c., अञ्चितः &c., नमस्यितः &c., नमसितः &c., उपासितः &c. *See* HONOURED.

WORSHIPPER, *s.* पूजकः, अर्चकः, उपासकः, उपासिता *m.* (तृ), सेवकः, सेविता *m.* (तृ), आराधकः, भजकः, पूजाकारी *m.* (न्).

WORST, *a.* दुष्टतमः -मा -मं, कष्टतमः -मा -मं, पापिष्ठः -ष्ठा -ष्ठं, सर्व्वपापिष्ठः &c., खलतमः -मा -मं, गरिष्ठः -ष्ठा -ष्ठं.

WORST, *s.* (Most evil state) दुष्टतमदशा, कष्टतमदशा.

To WORST, *v. a.* अभिभू, पराभू, पराजि (c. 1. -जयति -जेतुं), जि.

WORSTED, *s.* और्णसूत्रं, और्णतन्तुः *m.*, ऊर्णामयसूत्रं.

WORTH, *s.* (Value) अर्घः, मूल्यं, सारता, अर्घः, *see* VALUE; 'of little worth,' अल्पमूल्यः -ल्या -ल्यं, अल्पार्घः -र्घा -र्घं, अपार्घः -र्घा -र्घं.—(Excellence) सारत्वं, गुणः, गुणता, मान्यता.

WORTH, *a.* मूल्य in comp., अर्घ in comp., अर्हः -र्हा -र्हं, उपयुक्तः -क्ता -क्तं, योग्यः -ग्या -ग्यं; 'worth much,' बहुमूल्यः -ल्या -ल्यं; 'worth little,' अल्पमूल्यः &c.; 'how much is this worth?' किम्मूल्यम् एतत्; 'worth while,' क्षमार्हः -र्हा -र्हं, क्षमयोग्यः -ग्या -ग्यं, *see* WHILE.

WORTHILY, *adv.* योग्यं, युक्तं, उपयुक्तं. *See* PROPERLY, RIGHTLY.

WORTHINESS, *s.* योग्यता, उपयुक्तता, युक्तता, अर्हता, पात्रता, सगुणत्वं.

WORTHLESS, *a.* निर्गुणः -णा -णं, गुणहीनः -ना -नं, गुणरहितः -ता -तं, निर्गुणी -णिनी -णि (न्), विगुणः -णा -णं, असारः -रा -रं, निःसारः &c., सारहीनः -ना -नं, तृणप्रायः -या -यं, अधमः -मा -मं, अप्रमूल्यः -ल्या -ल्यं, अप्रशस्तः -स्ता -स्तं; 'of worthless character,' अगुणशीलः -ला -लं; 'a worthless object,' निःसारद्रव्यं, अद्रव्यं, अपात्रं.

WORTHLESSNESS, *s.* निर्गुणत्वं, गुणहीनता, वैगुण्यं, असारता, निःसारता.

WORTHY, *a.* (Deserving) अर्हः -र्हा -र्हं, योग्यः -ग्या -ग्यं, उपयुक्तः -क्ता -क्तं, उचितः -ता -तं, समुचितः &c., सदृशः -शी -शं, अनुरूपः -पा -पं, or expressed by the fut. pass. part.; 'worthy of death,' मरणार्हः -र्हा -र्हं, मरणोचितः -ता -तं, वधार्हः &c., वध्यः -ध्या -ध्यं; 'worthy of honour,' मानार्हः &c., मान्यः -न्या -न्यं; 'of praise,' श्लाघ्यः -घ्या -घ्यं; 'worthy to be called,' ख्यातव्यः -व्या -व्यं; 'possessing a husband worthy of her,' अनुरूपभर्तृभागिनी; 'to be worthy,' अर्ह् (c. 1. अर्हति -र्हितुं), *see To* DESERVE; 'a worthy object or person,' पात्रं, सत्पात्रं, भाजनं, गुणपात्रं, गुणभाजनं.—(Possessing worth or excellence) आर्य्यः -र्य्या -र्य्यं, गुणी -णिनी -णि (न्), गुणवान् -वती -वत् (त्), मान्यः -न्या -न्यं, अधिगुणः -णा -णं, भद्रकः -का -कं.

WORTHY, *s.* (Man of worth) आर्य्यजनः, सज्जनः, मानपात्रं.

WOUND, *s.* (Injury to the flesh) व्रणः -णा -णं, क्षतं, क्षतिः *f.*, परिक्षतं, अरुस् *n.*, ईर्म्मं, वेधः -धनं, प्रहारः, आघातः, उद्घातः, अस्त्राघातः, लूनकः; 'flesh-wound,' त्वग्भेदः, त्वक्छेदः.

To WOUND, *v. a.* क्षण् (c. 8. क्षणोति -णितुं), परिक्षण्, व्रण् (c. 10. -व्रणयति -यितुं), व्रणं कृ, क्षतं कृ, व्यध् (c. 4. विध्यति, व्यद्धुं), परिव्यध्, प्रतिव्यध्, व्रश्च् (c. 6. वृश्चति, व्रश्चितुं), प्रव्रश्च्, भिद्, छिद्, विद्, रिष्, छि, अर्द्, जर्जरीकृ. *See To* HURT.

WOUND, *p.p.* वेष्टितः -ता -तं, परिवेष्टितः &c.; 'wound up,' उपसंहृतः &c.

WOUNDED, *p. p.* क्षतः -ता -तं, परिक्षतः &c., व्रणितः &c., कृतव्रणः -णा -णं, विद्धः -द्धा -द्धं, भिन्नः -न्ना -न्नं, भिन्नदेहः -हा -हं, अस्त्राहतः -ता -तं, रिष्टः -ष्टा -ष्टं, जर्जरितः -ता -तं, जर्जरीकृतः &c., जर्जरः -रा -रं; 'mortally,' भिन्नमर्म्मा -र्म्मा -र्म्म (न्).

WOVE, WOVEN, *p.p.* ऊतः -ता -तं, उतः &c., व्यूतः -ता -तं, व्युतः &c., ओतः -ता -तं, स्यूतः &c., तन्त्री -न्त्रिणी -न्त्रि (न्), तन्तुनिर्म्मितः -ता -तं, तान्तवः -वी -वं, निर्म्मितः -ता -तं; 'wove cloth,' तान्तववस्त्रं, तन्तुसन्ततं; 'wove silk,' दुकूलं, क्षौमं, क्षोमं.

To WRANGLE, WRANGLING. *See To* QUARREL, QUARRELING, DISPUTE.

To WRAP, *v. a.* आवेष्ट् (c. 1. -वेष्टते -ष्टितुं, c. 10. -वेष्टयति -यितुं), परिवेष्ट्, आच्छद् (c. 10. -छादयति -यितुं), परिच्छद्, अवगुण्ठ् (c. 10. -गुण्ठयति -यितुं), कोशस्थं -स्थां कृ, वासनीकृ; 'I wrap myself up,' आत्मानम् अवगुण्ठयामि.

WRAPPED, *p.p.* वेष्टितः -ता -तं, आवेष्टितः &c., अवगुण्ठितः -ता -तं; 'in an envelope,' वासनस्थः -स्था -स्थं, कोशस्थः &c.

WRAPPER, *s.* वेष्टनं, आवेष्टनं, प्रच्छदपटः, प्रावारः, निचोलः, निचोलं, वासनं, पुटः, पिधानं, चलिः *m.*, अंशुकः, निवृतः, वृहतिका.

WRATH, *s.* क्रोधः, कोपः, रोषः, रुट् *f.* (ष्), रुषिः *f.* *See* ANGER.

WRATHFUL, *a.* कोपी -पिनी &c., क्रुद्धः -द्धा -द्धं. *See* ANGRY.

To WREAK, *v. a.* कृ, प्रणी, विधा. *See To* EXECUTE.

WREATH, *s.* माला, माल्यं, स्रक् *f.* (स्रज्), हारः, दाम *n.* (न्), आवलिः -ली, *see* GARLAND; 'of smoke,' धूमावली -लिः *f.*

To wreathe, *v. a.* ग्रन्थ् (c. 9. ग्रथ्नाति, c. 1. ग्रन्थति -न्थितुं, c. 10. ग्रन्थयति -यितुं), गुम्फ् (c. 1. गुम्फति -म्फितुं), गुफ् (c. 1. गुफति -फितुं), गुम्फनं कृ, दृभ् (c. 10. दर्भयति -यितुं), सन्दृभ्, मालया वेष्ट्.

Wreck, *s.* (Shipwreck) नौभङ्गः, नौव्यसनं.—(Wrecked ship) भग्ननौका, भिन्ननौका, भिन्ननौः *f.*, नष्टनौका, नष्टनौः *f.*, उत्कूलितनौः *f.*

To wreck, *v. a.* नौभङ्गं कृ, नौव्यसनं कृ, नौकानाशं कृ, नावं भञ्ज् or भिद् or नश् (c. 10. नाशयति -यितुं), उत्कूल् (c. 10. -कूलयति -यितुं).

Wrecked, *p. p.* भिन्ननौकः -का -कं, भग्ननौकः &c., नष्टनौकः &c., उत्कूलितः &c.

To wrench, *v. a.* साहसिकाकुञ्चनं or तीव्राकुञ्चनं कृत्वा आकृष् (c. 1. -कर्षति -कर्ष्टुं), बलवदाकुञ्चनपूर्व्वम् आकृष्य अपहृ (c. 1. -हरति -हर्त्तुं), बलवद् आकृष्य उद्धृ, पीड् (c. 10. पीडयति -यितुं).

Wrench, *s.* साहसिकाकुञ्चनपूर्व्वम् आकर्षणं or आकर्षः.

To wrest, *v. a.* बलवद् or साहसेन अपहृ. *See To* wrench.

To wrestle, *v. n.* बाहुयुद्धं कृ, बाहुप्रहरणं कृ, मल्लयुद्धं कृ.

Wrestler, *s.* बाहुयोधी *m.* (न्), बाहुप्रहर्त्ता *m.* (र्त्तृ), मल्लः, कल्लः, रङ्गावतारी *m.* (न्); 'king's wrestler,' उसिक्कः, उल्लतः.

Wrestling, *s.* बाहुयुद्धं, मल्लयुद्धं, मल्लक्रीडा, मल्लयात्रा, माल्लवी.

Wretch, *s.* (Bad man) हताशः, काल्मः, पापः, पापीयान् *m.* (स्), पापिष्ठः, दुरात्मा *m.* (न्), नराधमः, खलः, चण्डालः, लट्वः, लड्डुः.—(Poor creature) मन्दभाग्यः, तपस्वी *m.* (न्), हताशः, कृपणः.

Wretched, *a.* अतिदुःखी -खिनी -खि (न्), अतिदुःखान्वितः -ता -तं, अतिदीनः -ना -नं, दीनः &c., अधन्यः -न्या -न्यं. *See* Miserable.

Wretchedness, wretchedly. *See* Misery, Miserably.

To wriggle, *v. n.* देहम् इतस्ततः क्षिप्रं संचल् (c. 10. -चालयति -यितुं).

To wring, *v. a.* (Twist or press violently) बलवद् or साहसेन आकुञ्च् (c. 1. -कुञ्चति -ञ्चितुं, c. 10. कुञ्चयति -यितुं) or पीड् (c. 10. पीडयति -यितुं) or सम्पीड्.—(Wring off) बलवदाकुञ्चनं कृत्वा or बलवद् आकृष्य उद्धृ or निर्हृ or उत्कृष्.—(Wring out water, &c.) बलवत् पीडयित्वा जलं निर्गम् in caus., or निःसृ in caus.

Wrinkle, *s.* वलिः -ली *f.*, चर्म्मरेखा, त्वग्रेखा, रेखा, चर्म्मलेखा, चर्म्मतरङ्गः, तरङ्गः, ऊर्म्मिः *m. f.*, ऊर्म्मिका, त्वगूर्म्मिः *m. f.*, भङ्गः, चर्म्मभङ्गः, त्वक्शैथिल्यं, त्वक्सङ्कोचः, चर्म्मसङ्कोचः; 'on the brow,' ललाटरेखा, ललाटलेखा.

To wrinkle, *v. a.* त्वचं or चर्म्म संकुच् (c. 1. -कोचति -चितुं) or कुच् (c. 1. कुचति -चितुं) or आकुञ्च्. *See To* contract.

Wrinkled, wrinkly, *a.* वलिनः -ना -नं, वलिमान् -मती -मत् (त्), वलिभः -भा -भं, ऊर्म्मिमान् &c., रेखाङ्कितः -ता -तं, सरेखः -खा -खं.

Wrist, *s.* मणिबन्धः -न्धनं, कलापं, प्रकोष्ठः, प्रवेष्टः, चोलकी *m.* (न्), मणिः *m. f.*

Writ, *s.* लेखः, लेख्यं, लेखपत्रं; 'Holy writ,' श्रुतिः *f.*, श्रुतं.

To write, *v. a.* or *n.* (With a pen) लिख् (c. 6. लिखति, लेखितुं), अभिलिख्, लेखनं कृ, लिखनं कृ, लिपिं कृ; 'to write down,' अभिलिख्, लेख्यारूढं -ढां कृ, पत्रारूढं -ढां कृ.—(Compose) ग्रन्थ् (c. 9. ग्रथ्नाति, c. 1. ग्रन्थति -न्थितुं), ग्रन्थनं कृ, रच् (c. 10. रचयति -यितुं), कॢप् (c. 10. कल्पयति -यितुं), निबन्ध्.

Writer, *s.* (One who writes) लेखकः, लिख् in comp. (ख्), लिपिकरः, लेखनकारी *m.* (न्), लिपिकारः.—(Clerk) कायस्थः, *see* Scribe.—(Composer) ग्रन्थकारः, ग्रन्थकर्त्ता *m.* (र्त्तृ), रचकः.

To writhe, *v. a.* or *n.* तीव्रवेदनोपहतत्वाद् अङ्गानि इतस्ततः संचल् (c. 10. -चालयति -यितुं) or आकृष् or अङ्गाकुञ्चनं कृ.

Writhing, *s.* अङ्गाकुञ्चनं, अङ्गाकर्षः, इतस्ततो ऽङ्गसञ्चालनं.

Writing, *s.* (The act) लेखनं, लिखनं, लेखः -खा, अभिलेखनं, लिपिः *f.*, लिपिका, लिबिः -बी *f.*—(Composition) रचना, ग्रन्थनं, ग्रन्थकरणं.—(Written letters or characters) अक्षरविन्यासः, अक्षररचना.—(Any thing written) लिखितं, लेखः, लेख्यं, लेख्यपत्रं, पत्रं -त्रकं; 'committed to writing,' लेख्यारूढः -ढा -ढं, पत्रारूढः &c.; 'writing materials,' लिपिसज्जा, लेखसाधनं, लेखनसामग्री.

Writing-master, *s.* लेखशिक्षकः, लेखनशिक्षकः, लेखोपदेशकः.

Writing-paper, *s.* लेखनपत्रं, लिखनपत्रं, लेख्यपत्रं.

Written, *p. p.* लिखितः -ता -तं, लेखितः &c.; 'document,' लेख्यं.

Wrong, *a.* (Not fit or right) अयुक्तः -क्ता -क्तं, अयोग्यः -ग्या -ग्यं, अनुपयुक्तः -क्ता -क्तं, अनुपपन्नः -न्ना -न्नं, *see* Improper.—(Erroneous) अयथार्थः -र्था -र्थं, अनृतः -ता -तं, वितथः -था -थं, असत्यः &c., असम्यक् -मीची -म्यक् (च्), अशुद्धः -द्धा -द्धं, दोषी -षिणी -षि (न्), सदोषः -षा -षं, अपराधी &c., असन् -सती -सत्, *see* False, Incorrect.—(Unjust, acting improperly) अन्याय्यः -य्या -य्यं, अन्यायी -यिनी &c., न्यायविरुद्धः -द्धा -द्धं, अयथान्यायः -या -यं, *see* Unjust.—(Reverse) विपरीतः -ता -तं; 'wrong road,' उन्मार्गः, विमार्गः.

Wrong, *s.* (Injury, injustice) अपकारः, अपकृतं, अपराधः, अन्यायः.—(Error) भ्रमः, भ्रान्तिः *f.*, दोषः, अपराधः, अयाथार्थ्यं, अयुक्तं, अयाथातथ्यं; 'in the wrong,' भ्रमयुक्तः -क्ता -क्तं, भ्रान्तियुक्तः &c., भ्रमी -मिणी &c., सदोषः -षा -षं, दोषी &c., अपराधी &c.

Wrong, wrongly, *adv.* अयुक्तं, अन्यथा, अयथायुक्तं, अयथायोग्यं, अयथार्थं, अन्यायतस्, अयथान्यायं, वृथा, मिथ्या.

To wrong, *v. a.* अपकृ, अन्यायं कृ, अपराध्. *See To* injure.

Wronged, *p. p.* अपकृतः -ता -तं, प्राप्तापकारः -रा -रं, कृतापकारः &c.

Wrongful, wrongfully. *See* Unjust, Unjustly.

Wrong-headed, wrong-headedness. *See* Perverse, &c.

Wroth, *a.* कोपाविष्टः -ष्टा -ष्टं, रोषाविष्टः &c. *See* Angry.

Wrought, *p. p.* (Done) कृतः -ता -तं, *see* Performed.—(Worked, elaborated) संस्कृतः -ता -तं, संस्कारितः &c., क्लृप्तः -प्ता -प्तं, कल्पितः &c., सिद्धः -द्धा -द्धं; 'wrought iron,' कुशी; 'wrought gold,' कोषः, कृतहेमं.—(Stirred) उत्तेजितः -ता -तं.

Wry, *a.* वक्रः -क्रा -क्रं, विकृतः -ता -तं; 'wry-faced,' विकृताननः &c.

Wry-necked, *a.* वक्रग्रीवः -वा -वं, विकृतग्रीवः &c., वक्रकन्धरः &c.

Wryness, *s.* वक्रता, वक्रिमा *m.* (न्), विकृतिः *f.*, विरूपता, वैरूप्यं.

X.

Xantippe, *s.* कर्कशा, कैकेयी, वक्रशीला, दुर्मुखी, पूतना.

Xenodochy, *s.* अतिथिपूजनं, अतिथिसेवा, अतिथिसत्कारः.

Y.

Yacht, *s.* क्रीडानौका, क्रीडानौः *f.*, केलिनौका, केलिनौः *f.*

Yam, *s.* आलुः -लु *m. n.*, आलुकं, मधुमूलं, मध्वालुकं, सुकन्दः, खगडालुः -लुकं, लक्ष्मणकन्दः.

Yama, *s.* (God of Naraka or Hell, Regent of the South, or lower world, and judge of departed souls, corresponding to the grecian god Pluto, or to the judge of hell, Minos. His abode is in the infernal city of Yamapur, whither the Hindús believe that a departed soul immediately repairs, and receiving a just sentence from Yama, ascends to Swarga, the first heaven, or descends to Naraka, the snaky hell, or assumes on earth the form of some animal, unless its offences have been such as deserve condemnation to a vegetable or even to a mineral prison. As god of justice and lord of punishment, Yama corresponds with Śiva and Varuna, and in this character is represented as bearing a cord or noose. Yama is often identified with Death and Time. He is the son of Súrya or the Sun, and brother of the personified Yamuná or Jumná river) यमः, यमराजः, यमराट् *m.* (ज्), यमनः, शमनः.—(As Death or Time or the Destroyer) कृतान्तः, मृत्युः *m.*, कालः, कालान्तकः, अन्तकः, कालकुण्डः.—(Regent of the South) दक्षिणाशापतिः *m.*—(Lord of the dead) प्रेतपतिः *m.*, प्रेतराजः, परेतराट् *m.* (ज्), परेतराजः.—(Lord of deceased ancestors) पितृपतिः *m.*—(God of the śráddha) श्राद्धदेवः, श्राद्धदेवता.—(God of justice) धर्मराजः, धर्मः.—(The impartial judge) समवर्त्ती *m.*—(God of punishment) दण्डधरः, दण्डी *m.* (न्), दण्डयामः, अधिदण्डनेता *m.* (तृ), दण्डः.—(Bearer of the cord or noose) पाशी *m.* (न्), पाशभृत् *m.*, पाशपाणिः *m.*—(Son of the sun) वैवस्वतः, सूर्य्यपुत्रः, सूर्य्यतनयः, अर्कतनयः, अर्कनन्दनः.—(Brother of Yamuná) यमुनाभ्राता *m.*—(The variegated one) चित्रः. The pain or punishment inflicted by Yama is called यातना. 'One of his attendants,' कालपुरुषः.

Yamuná, *s.* (A river, commonly called Jumná, which rises on the south side of the Himálayas, and after a course of 378 miles, falls into the Ganges at Prayága or Allahabad. The personified river is considered to be the daughter of Súrya or the Sun, and sister of Yama) यमुना, सूर्य्यतनया, सूर्य्यपुत्री, अर्कतनया, यमस्वसा *f.* (सृ), शमनस्वसा *f.*, कालिन्दी.

Yard, *s.* अङ्गनं, प्राङ्गणं, चत्वरं, अजिरं, *see* Court-yard.—(The measure) गजः.—(Of a ship) नौवसनकाष्ठं, नौवसनदण्डः.

Yarn, *s.* (Woollen thread) ऊर्णासूत्रं, और्णसूत्रं, और्णतन्तुः *m.*, ऊर्णामयसूत्रं.—(Long yarn) दीर्घसूत्रं.

To yawn, *v. n.* जृम्भ् (c. 1. जृम्भते -म्भितुं), विजृम्भ्, प्रजृम्भ्, जभ or जम्भ् (c. 1. जभते, जम्भते -म्भितुं), जृम्भणं कृ, जृम्भं कृ, विजृम्भणं कृ, ग्लै (c. 1. ग्लायति, ग्लातुं). *See To* gape.

Yawn, yawning, *s.* जृम्भः -म्भणं, जृम्भा -म्भिका, विजृम्भणं, जृम्भितं, विजृम्भितं, हाफिका, हम्मी *n.* (न्), उपपुष्पिका.

Yawner, *s.* जृम्भकः, जृम्भी *m.* (न्), विजृम्भकः, जृम्भणकारी *m.*

Ye, *pron.* यूयं (*nom. pl.* (युष्मद्).

Yea, *adv.* बाढं, आम, सत्यं, हुम्, तथेति, अपरञ्च; 'yea and nay,' स्वीकारास्वीकारौ *m. du.*, स्वीकृतास्वीकृतं.

Year, *s.* वत्सरः, वर्षः, संवत्सरः, परिवत्सरः, अब्दः, समा, समाः *m.* (स्), संवत् ind., हायनः, वरिषं, कालग्रन्थिः *m.*, ऋतुवृत्तिः *f.*, सर्वर्त्तुपरिवर्त्तः, माससमानः, युगांशकः, शरद् *f.*, शरदा; 'half-year,' वर्षार्द्धं, अब्दार्द्धं, षण्मासं, अयनं; 'last year,' गतवर्षः, परुत् indec.; 'belonging to it,' परुत्नः -त्नी -त्नं; 'the present year,' वर्त्तमानवर्षः, ऐषमस्; 'year before last,' परारि indec.; 'belonging to it,' परारित्नः -त्नी -त्नं; 'next year,' परवर्षः, आगामिवत्सरः, उत्तरवत्सरः; 'events of the year,' वर्षफलं; 'throughout the year, to the end of it,' आवर्षान्तात्; 'for a year,' वर्षपर्य्यन्तं; 'year after year,' वर्षे वर्षे, वत्सरे वत्सरे, प्रतिवत्सरं; 'solar year,' सौरवर्षः; 'sidereal year,' नाक्षत्रवर्षः.

Yearly, *a.* वार्षिकः -की -कं, प्रतिवार्षिकः &c., सांवत्सरिकः -की -कं, सांवत्सरः -री -रं, आब्दिकः -की -कं, प्रतिसांवत्सरिकः &c., वर्षिकः -का -कं, समीनः -ना -नं; 'half-yearly,' षाण्मासिकः -की -कं.

Yearly, *adv.* प्रतिवर्षं, प्रतिवत्सरं, प्रत्यब्दं, अनुवत्सरं, वत्सरे वत्सरे, वर्षे वर्षे, अयने अयने.

To yearn, *v. n.* वत्सल (nom. वत्सलायते), वात्सल्यं सूच् (c. 10. सूचयति -यितुं), वत्सकामा भू, वत्सलीभू, स्निह् (c. 4. स्निह्यति, स्नेहितुं), उत्सुक (nom. उत्सुकायते).

Yearning, *s.* वत्सलता, वात्सल्यं, उत्सुकता, औत्सुक्यं, स्नेहः.

Yeast, *s.* सुरामण्डः, मद्यमण्डः, यवमण्डः, कारोत्तमः, कारोत्तरः, किण्वः -ण्वं, नग्नहूः -हु *m. n.*, अभिषवः, कादम्बरीबीजं, सुराभागः. In some parts of India ताडी or ताड़ी, *i. e.* toddy or the fermented juice of the tád or palm tree is much used as yeast.

To yell, *v. n.* रु (c. 2. रौति, रवितुं), रस्, नद्. *See To* scream.

Yell, *s.* रुतं, रावः, दीर्घरुतं, दीर्घरावः, चित्कारः. *See* Scream.

Yelling, *part.* दीर्घरावः -वी -वं, दीर्घनादी -दिनी -दि (न्).

Yellow, *a.* पीतः -ता -तं, गौरः -री -रं, पीतलः -ला -लं, हरिद्राभः -भा -भं, पीतवर्णः -र्णा -र्णं, गौरवर्णः &c.

Yellow-bird, yellow-hammer, *s.* हरिद्राङ्गः.

Yellowish, *a.* ईषत्पीतः -ता -तं, ईषत्पीतवर्णः -र्णा -र्णं; 'yellowish white,' हरिणः -णा -णं, पाण्डुः -ण्डुः -ण्डु, पाण्डुरः -रा -रं.

Yellowness, *s.* पीतता, गौरता -त्वं, पीतवर्णः, हरिद्रावर्णः.

To yelp, *v. a.* भष्, रै, रु, रस्. *See To* bark, yell.

Yeoman, *s.* गृहस्थः, गृहाधिकारी *m.* (न्), क्षेत्रपतिः *m.*

Yes, *adv.* बाढं, आम्, हूम्, सत्यं, तथेति, परमं, एवं, ओम्, अथकिं, स्वीकृतं.

Yester, *a.* ह्यस्तनः -नी -नं, ह्यस्त्यः -स्त्या -स्त्यं, पर्य्युषितः -ता -तं.

Yesterday, *s.* ह्यस्, पूर्व्वेद्युस्, गतदिवसः, गतदिनं, कल्यं; 'relating to yesterday,' ह्यस्तनः -नी -नं, ह्यस्त्यः -स्त्या -स्त्यं.

Yesternight, *s.* गतरात्रिः *f.*, गता रात्रिः, गता यामिनी.

Yet, *conj.* तथापि, परन्तु, अपि, किन्तु. *See* Nevertheless.

Yet, *adv.* (Over and above) अधिकं, परं.—(Hitherto) अद्य यावत्, अद्यपर्य्यन्तं, अद्यापि, *see* Hitherto, Still.

To yield, *v. a.* (Produce, bear) उत्पद् (c. 10. -पादयति -यितुं), जन् (c. 10. जनयति -यितुं), दा (c. 3. ददाति, दातुं), प्रदा; 'fruit,' फलं दा or प्रदा, फल्.—(Give, grant, concede) अनुदा, प्रदा, दा, वितॄ (c. 1. -तरति -रितुं -रीतुं), अनुज्ञा, प्रोत्सृ in caus., *see To* concede.—(Deliver up, surrender) उत्सृज् (c. 6. -सृजति -स्रष्टुं), विसृज्, अवसृज्, त्यज् (c. 1. त्यजति, त्यक्तुं), हा, विहा.

To yield, *v. n.* वशीभू, वशं गम् or उपगम्. *See To* submit.

Yielding, *a.* (Bearing fruit) फलदः -दा -दं, फलप्रदः &c., फलवान् -वती -वत् (त्), फलन् -लन्ती &c., फलोत्पादकः -का -कं.—(Compliant) अनुकूलः -ला -लं, अनुरोधी -धिनी &c., *see* Compliant.

Yojana, *s.* (A measure of distance, equal to five miles, or, according to some, to nine miles) योजनं.

Yoke, *s.* (For the necks of oxen) युगः -गं, प्रासङ्गः, आबन्धः; 'of a plough,' कुशः; 'pin of the yoke,' युगकीलः -लकः; 'tie of it,' योक्त्रं, योत्रं, आबन्धः.—(Yoke or pair of oxen) गोयुगं, गोमिथुनं.—(Fit for the yoke) युग्यः -ग्या -ग्यं, प्रासङ्ग्यः &c.

To yoke, *v. a.* युज् (c. 7. युनक्ति, c. 10. योजयति -यितुं), नियुज्.

Yoked, *p. p.* युक्तः -क्ता -क्तं, नियुक्तः &c., संसक्तयुगः -गा -गं; 'is yoked,' युज्यते; 'a yoked animal,' युग्यः, प्रासङ्ग्यः, शाकटः;

'having yoked the steeds,' युक्ततुरङ्गः -ङ्गा -ङ्गं.

YOKE-FELLOW, s. सहचरः, सहवर्त्ती m. (न्), सहभावी m.

YOLK, s. (Of an egg) अण्डमध्यं, अण्डमध्यभागः, अण्डहृदयं, अण्डकुसुमं, अण्डमध्यस्थः पीतभागः.

YON, YONDER, a. नातिदूरस्थः -स्था -स्थं, ईषद्दूरस्थः -स्था -स्थं.

YON, YONDER, adv. नातिदूरे -रतस्, ईषद्दूरे -रतस्.

YORE, adv. (Of yore) पुरा, प्राक्काले, प्राक्, पुरस्तात्.

YOU, pron. (For thou, in the sing.) त्वं nom. sing.—(In the plur.) यूयं nom. pl. (युष्मद्); 'of you,' युष्माकं; 'you two,' युवां. The honorific pron. भवान् m. (त्), is often used for 'you,' with the 3d pers. sing. of the verb.

YOUNG, a. बालः -ला -लं, युवा m., युवतिः -ती f., यूनी f., युव n. (न्), तरुणः -णा -णं, अल्पवयाः -याः -यः (स्), अल्पवयस्कः -स्का -स्कं, अभिनववयस्कः &c., बालिशः -शा -शं, कौमारः -री -रं, किशोरः -रा -रं, अभिनवः -वा -वं, प्रतिनवः &c., वयस्थः -स्था -स्थं, वयःस्थः &c.; 'a young man,' कुमारः, युवजनः, बालजनः, तरुणः, रूढवयाः m. (स्); 'young woman,' तरुणी, कुमारी, कन्या, युवती, बाला, नवयौवना; 'a young bird,' see YOUNG, s.

YOUNG, s. (Young one of any animal) शावकः, शिशुः m., पोतः -तकः, अपत्यं, पाकः -का, अर्भकः, डिम्भः, पृथुकः, प्रथुकः, वर्करः -री, कुणकः; 'a young bird,' पक्षिशावकः; 'a young mouse,' मूषिकशावकः; 'a young elephant,' गजशिशुः m.; 'a young deer,' मृगपोतकः.

YOUNGER, a. कनीयान् -यसी -यः (स्), कनिष्ठः -ष्ठा -ष्ठं, यवीयान् &c., यविष्ठः &c., अनुजः -जा -जं, अनुजातः -ता -तं, अनुजन्मा -न्मा -न्म (न्), जघन्यजः -जा -जं, अवरजः &c., अवरवयस्कः -स्का -स्कं, अवरः -रा -रं.

YOUNGSTER, s. कुमारकः, बालजनः, किशोरः, वटुः. See LAD.

YOUR, YOUR'S, pron. तव gen. sing., युष्माकं gen. pl. (युष्मद्), भवतः gen. sing., भवतां gen. pl. (भवत्), त्वदीयः -या -यं, भवदीयः &c., भावत्कः -त्का -त्कं, यौष्माकः -की -कं, यौष्माकीनः -ना -नं.

YOURSELF, pron. (Reciprocally) आत्मा m. (न्); as, 'blame yourself,' आत्मानं निन्द; 'for yourself,' आत्मार्थं.—(Emphatically) स्वयं, स्वतस्; 'you yourself,' स त्वं, see SELF.

YOUTH, s. (Early part of life) यौवनं, यौवनावस्था, यौवनकालः, यौवनदशा, कौमारं, तारुण्यं, तारुण्यदशा, तारुण्यकालः, सौकुमार्य्यं, शैशवं, प्रथमवयस् n., पूर्व्ववयस् n., प्रत्यग्रवयस् n., कैशोरं; 'prime or heyday of youth,' नवयौवनं, यौवनप्रौढिः f.; 'pride of youth,' यौवनदर्पः.—(A young man) तरुणः, कुमारः -रकः, युवजनः, युवा m. (न्), बालजनः, अबालः, किशोरः, वटुः m., वटुकः, वेकटः.—(Young persons) तरुणजनाः m. pl., युवजनाः m. pl., बालजनता.—(State of being young) तारुण्यं, बालत्वं -ता.

YOUTHFUL, a. यौवनवान् -वती -वत् (त्), बालः -ला -लं, यौवनेयकः -की -कं, अल्पवयाः -याः -यः (स्). See YOUNG.

YOUTHFULNESS, s. तारुण्यं, बालता -त्वं, सौकुमार्य्यं, बालिश्यं.

Z.

ZANY, s. भण्डः, वैहासिकः, विदूषकः. See BUFFOON.

ZEAL, s. उत्तापः, चण्डता, उत्कटता, उग्रता, उष्मः, तैक्ष्ण्यं, तीक्ष्णता, व्यग्रता, उद्योगः, अनुद्योगः, प्रौढिः f., औत्सुक्यं, अत्यनुरागः, अत्यनुरक्तिः f., अत्युत्सुकता, उत्सुकता, आस्था. See EARNESTNESS.

ZEALOT, s. अत्यनुरक्तः, अतिव्यग्रः, अत्यासक्तः, अतितीक्ष्णः.

ZEALOUS, a. व्यग्रः -ग्रा -ग्रं, अतिव्यग्रः &c., उत्तप्तः -प्ता -प्तं, चण्डः -ण्डा -ण्डं, उत्कटः &c., तीक्ष्णः -क्ष्णा -क्ष्णं, अत्यनुरक्तः -क्ता -क्तं, अत्यनुरागी -गिणी -गि (न्), अत्युत्सुकः -का -कं, उत्सुकः &c., अत्युद्योगी -गिनी &c., उद्योगी &c., उद्युक्तः -क्ता -क्तं, इष्टार्थोद्युक्तः &c., समुद्यतः -ता -तं, अत्युद्यमी &c., अत्यासक्तः -क्ता -क्तं, उग्रः -ग्रा -ग्रं, तीक्ष्णकर्म्मा -र्म्मा -र्म्म (न्), प्रयत्नवान् -वती -वत् (त्).

ZEALOUSLY, adv. अतिव्यग्रं, अत्युद्योगेन, अत्यनुरागेण.

ZEBRA, s. वनगर्दभः, अरण्यगर्दभः, वनरासभः.

ZEDOARY, s. (A plant) शटिः -टी f., कर्च्चूरकः, कर्चूरकः, वेधमुख्यकः, द्राविडकः, काल्यः -ल्यकः, सुम्पलुकः.

ZENITH, s. खमध्यं, ऊर्द्ध्वस्वस्तिकः -कं, ऊर्द्ध्वदिशा, खस्वस्तिकं, शिरोबिन्दुः m., ऊर्द्ध्वः; 'zenith distance,' नतं, नतांशः, नतभागः; 'pointing to zenith and nadir,' ऊर्द्ध्वाधरः -रा -रं.

ZEPHYR, s. वसन्तवायुः m., मन्दवायुः m., मन्दानिलः, मृदुवातः, सुखस्पर्शवायुः m., सुगन्धवायुः m., चारुवायुः m., मन्दमारुतः, वासन्तः.

ZERO, s. (Cipher, naught) शून्यं, बिन्दुः, वटः.

ZEST, s. रुचिः f., स्वादः, आस्वादः, अभिरुचिः f. See RELISH.

ZIGZAG, a. वक्रः -क्रा -क्रं, कुटिलः -ला -लं, जिह्मः -ह्मा -ह्मं, वक्राकारः -रा -रं, कुटिलगतिः -तिः -ति, घुणाक्षरः -रा -रं; 'zig-zag lightning,' विद्युल्लता, असिलता.

ZINC, s. (Kind of metal) वङ्गं, दस्ता.

ZODIAC, s. राशिचक्रं, ज्योतिश्चक्रं, राशिमण्डलं, भचक्रं, भमण्डलं, भागनं, रिम्फं; 'a sign of the zodiac,' राशिः m., लग्नं, भं; 'the twelve signs collectively,' राशिगणः, भगणः, राशिकुण्डली, मेषवृषादयः m. pl. These are, 1. Aries, मेषः; 2. Taurus, वृषः, वृषभः; 3. Gemini, मिथुनः, द्वन्द्वः, मिथुनं; 4. Cancer, कर्कटः, कर्कः, कर्कटराशिः m.; 5. Leo, सिंहः, आरण्यराशिः m.; 6. Virgo, कन्या; 7. Libra, तुला, तुलाधारः, घटः; 8. Scorpio, वृश्चिकः, कौर्प्यः, अलिः m.; 9. Sagittarius, धनुः -नु m. n., तौक्षिकः; 10. Capricornus, मकरः, मकरराशिः m.; 11. Aquarius, कुम्भः, कुम्भराशिः m.; 12. Pisces, मीनः, मीनराशिः m., मीनलग्नं, झषः. Of the twelve signs there are two divisions, one called उत्तरगोलः, consisting of the six signs, from Aries to Virgo, the other called दक्षिणगोलः, comprising the remaining six signs. 'The rising of a sign,' लग्नं, उदयः; 'setting,' अस्तं; 'rising sign,' उदयलग्नं; 'setting sign,' अस्तलग्नं; 'circuit of the sun through the zodiac,' भागनं, भगणः; 'passage of the sun through a sign,' सूर्य्यसङ्क्रान्तिः f., रविसङ्क्रान्तिः f., सूर्य्यसङ्क्रमणं; 'of a planet,' राशिभोगः; 'passage of the sun or a planet from one sign into another,' सङ्क्रान्तिः f., सङ्क्रमः.

ZODIACAL, a. राशिचक्रसम्बन्धी -न्धिनी &c., भचक्रसम्बन्धी &c.

ZONE, s. (Girdle) मेखला, रसना, कलापः, see GIRDLE.—(Of the earth) भूमेखला, भूवलयः -यं, भूकटिबन्धः; 'torrid zone,' क्रान्तिवलयः, मध्यदेशः.

ZOOGRAPHER, s. प्राणिवर्णनकृत्, पश्वादिविवरणकृत्.

ZOOGRAPHY, s. प्राणिवर्णनं, पश्वादिविवरणं, प्राणिवर्णना.

ZOOLOGICAL, a. प्राणिविद्यासम्बन्धी -न्धिनी &c., प्राणिज्ञानसम्बन्धी &c.

ZOOLOGY, s. प्राणिविद्या, प्राणिविषयका विद्या, प्राणिविषयकं ज्ञानं, जीवजन्तुविद्या, पश्वादिविद्या, पश्वादिशास्त्रं.

ZOOTOMY, s. प्राणिव्यवच्छेदः, प्राणिव्यवच्छेदविद्या, पश्वादिशवव्यवच्छेदः, पश्वादिव्यवच्छेदविद्या, प्राणिशरीरव्यवच्छेदः

APPENDIX.

A.

To abase, *v. a.* अभिमानखण्डनं कृ, लघूकृ, लाघवं कृ.

Abased, *p. p.* खण्डिताभिमानः -ना -नं, त्यक्ताभिमानः &c., नष्टाभिमानः &c., हतगर्वः -र्वा -र्वं, हताहङ्कारः -रा -रं, हृतदम्भः -म्भा -म्भं.

Abasement, *s.* (The act) अभिमानखण्डनं.—(State) मानभङ्गः, अभिमानभङ्गः, मानहानिः *f.*, मानविध्वंसः, नम्रता, लाघवस्वीकारः.

Abatement, *s.* (The act) न्यूनीकरणं.—(State) न्यूनता, क्षयः, ह्रासः, शान्तिः *f.*, *see* Diminution, Mitigation.

Abbey, *s.* योगिगृहं, योग्यालयः. Abbot, *s.* मठाधिपतिः *m.*

Abbreviation, *s.* संक्षेपः, संक्षिप्तता ; 'mark of,' संक्षेपचिह्नं.

To abdicate, *v. a.* (A throne) सिंहासनत्यागं कृ, छत्रचामरत्यागं कृ.

To abhor, *v. a.* अत्यन्तं द्विष्, अत्यन्तद्वेषं कृ, अतिद्वेषं कृ.

Abhorrence, *s.* अतिद्वेषः, अत्यन्तद्वेषः, परमद्वेषः, विकृतं.

Ability, *s.* (Mental) बुद्धिविभवः, बुद्धिवैभवं, बुद्धिपाटवं.

To abjure, *v. a.* शपथपूर्व्वं त्यज्, सशपथं or शपथं कृत्वा त्यज्.

Able. As a termination expressing 'admitting of,' 'susceptible of,' rendered in Sanskrit by the future pass. part.; thus, 'eatable,' खाद्यः -द्या -द्यं, खादनीयः &c., खादितव्यः &c.

To be able, *v. n.* पृ (c. 10. पारयति -यितुं). शक् must take the 5th conj., unless used to give a pass. sense to the infin.

Ablution, *s.* (Of the body) अङ्गस्नानं ; 'of the feet,' पादप्रक्षालनं ; 'of the head,' शिरःस्नानं ; 'of the mouth,' मुखमार्जनं, मुखधावनं, मुखशुद्धिः *f.*, आचमनं ; 'morning a.,' प्रातःस्नानं ; 'by rubbing earth on the body,' मृत्तिकास्नानं ; 'by rubbing cowdung,' गोमयस्नानं ; 'by rubbing ashes,' भस्मस्नानं ; 'servant who assists at a.,' स्नापकः ; 'rules of a.,' शौचविधिः *m.* ; 'one who performs a.,' स्नायी *m.* (न्) ; 'cloth put on after a.,' स्नानवस्त्रं.

Ably, *adv.* ससामर्थ्यं, शक्तितस्, सविभवं, सकौशल्यं, सपाटवं.

To abolish, *v. a.* खण्ड् (c. 10. खण्डयति -यितुं), खण्डनं कृ, निवृत् in caus.

Abolition, *s.* खण्डनं, भङ्गः, अवरोपणं, निवर्त्तनं, निवृत्तिः *f.*

Abomination, *s.* (Object of) अतिद्वेषपात्रं, बीभत्सविषयः.

Aborigines, *s. pl.* प्रथमस्थितलोकाः *m. pl.*, प्राचीनलोकाः *m. pl.*

About. (On the point of) उन्मुख &c., *see* under Point.

Abreast, *adv.* समपार्श्वतस्, पार्श्वपंक्तितस्.

Absence, *s.* अवर्त्तमानता, अविद्यमानता, विप्रकर्षः, परोक्षता.—(Of mind) अनवधानं -नता, अप्रस्तुतलक्षता.

Absent, *a.* (In mind) अनवहितः -ता -तं, अन्यहृदयः -या -यं, भ्रान्तहृदयः &c., अतन्मनस्कः -स्का -स्कं, अप्रस्तुतलक्षः, अन्यासक्तचित्तः -त्ता -त्तं.

Absolute, *a.* (Despotic) स्वाधीनः -ना -नं, स्वायत्तः -त्ता -त्तं, अपराधीनः &c.—(Unconditional) प्रतिबन्धहीनः -ना -नं, निष्प्रतिबन्धः &c.

Absorption, *s.* (Into the Deity) मुक्तिः *f.*, मोक्षः, निर्वाणं.

Abstinence, *s.* अल्पाहारः, अल्पभोजनं, आहारनियमः, संयमः.

To abut, *v. n.* सीमासंयोगं कृ, सीमासन्धिं कृ, स्पृश्, लग्.

Acacia, *s.* (Kind of tree) शमी.

Academical, *a.* विद्यालयसम्बन्धी -न्धिनी &c., मठसम्बन्धी &c.

Accelerated, *p. p.* वर्धितवेगः -गा -गं, वर्धितगतिः -तिः -ति, त्वरितः &c.

Acceleration, *s.* वेगवर्धनं, वेगवृद्धिः *f.*, गतिवर्धनं, गतिवृद्धिः *f.*

To accentuate, *v. a.* स्वरयुक्तं -क्तां कृ, सस्वरोच्चारणं कृ, सस्वरपठनं कृ.

Accentuated, *p. p.* स्वरितः -ता -तं, स्वरयुक्तः -क्ता -क्तं, सस्वरः &c.

Accentuation, *s.* सस्वरोच्चारः -रणं, प्लुतोच्चारणं, स्वरपालनं.

Accidental, *a.* (Non-essential) असहजः -जा -जं, आगन्तुकः -का -कं आहार्य्यः -र्य्या -र्य्यं, अस्वाभाविकः -की -कं.—(Happening by chance) दैवजातः -ता -तं, दैवागतः &c., दैवोपस्थितः &c., दैवघटितः &c., दैवहेतुकः -का -कं, दैवयोगिकः &c., अकारणजातः &c., अकारणागतः &c., अकारणोत्पन्नः -न्ना -न्नं, अकारणभूतः &c., अकारणोद्भवः -वा -वं, अकस्माज्जातः &c., अकस्मादुत्पन्नः -न्ना -न्नं, अकस्माद्भूतः -ता -तं, यदृच्छाभूतः &c., अनिमित्तभूतः &c., आगन्तुकः -का -कं.

Accidentally, *adv.* दैववशात्, अदृष्टवशात्, यदृच्छया.

To accost, *v. a.* सम्बुध् (c. 10. -बोधयति), प्राग्भाषणं कृ, आदिभाषणं कृ.

Accoucheur, *s.* प्रसवकारी वैद्यः, प्रसववैद्यः, सूतिवैद्यः.

Accoutred, *p. p.* सायुधः -धा -धं, सशस्त्रः &c., उपात्तशस्त्रः &c.

To accredit, *v. a.* सत्य (nom. caus. सत्यापयति -यितुं), सत्यापनं कृ.

Accretion, *s.* अन्यसंयोगवर्धनं, अन्यसंयोगवृद्धिः *f.*, समुत्थानं.

Accurate, *a.* सम्यङ् -मीची -म्यक् (च्), शुद्धः -द्धा -द्धं, सूक्ष्मः &c.

Accusation, *s.* दोषारोपः -पणं, अपराधारोपः -पणं.—(False) मिथ्याभियोगः, मिथ्याभिशंसनं.

Aconite, *s.* (A poison) वत्सनाभः, प्राणहारकं.

Acoustic, *a.* श्रवणसम्बन्धी -न्धिनी &c., श्रुतिविषयकः -का -कं.

Acoustics, *s. pl.* ध्वनिविद्या, श्रवणविषयका विद्या.

Acrostic, *s.* आद्याक्षरबन्धः, प्रथमाक्षरबन्धः, पूर्व्वाक्षरबन्धः.

To actuate, *v. a.* प्रवृत् (c. 10. -वर्त्तयति -यितुं), प्रेर् (c. 10. प्रेरयति -यितुं).

Actuated, *p. p.* प्रवर्त्तितः -ता -तं, प्रेरितः &c. *See* Influenced.

Acute-angle, *s.* अनार्लम्बकोणः, न्यूनकोणः, लघुकोणः ; 'acute-angled,' अनार्लम्बः -म्बा -म्बं.

Adagio, *s.* (Slow time in music) विलम्बितं.

Adamantine, *a.* वज्रसदृशः -शी -शं, वज्रप्रायः &c., वज्रः -ज्रा -ज्रं.

Addition, *s.* (In arithmetic) योगः, सङ्कलनं.

To adjourn, *v. a.* आकालान्तरात् त्यज्, कालान्तरपर्य्यन्तं त्यज्.

To adjust, *v. a.* व्यवस्था in caus. Adjustment, *s.* व्यवस्थापनं.

Adrift, *a.* or *adv.* प्रवाहाधीनः -ना -नं, ओघाधीनः -ना -नं.

Adult, *a.* वयःस्थः -स्था -स्थं, वयस्थः &c., प्राप्तयौवनः -ना -नं.

Adulterated, *p. p.* हीनद्रव्यसंसर्गदूषितः -ता -तं, हीनमिश्रणदूषितः &c., हीनसम्पर्कदूषितः ; 'with water,' जलसंसृष्टः -ष्टा -ष्टं.

Adultery, *s.* (In a male) परभार्य्यागमनं, परस्त्रीगमनं.—(In a female) परगमनं, परपुरुषगमनं, अन्यगमनं.

To adumbrate, *v. a.* छायां दृश् in caus., आभासं दृश् in caus.

Adumbration, *s.* छायाप्रदर्शनं, छायाभासः, आभासः, छाया.

COLLECTION, *s.* जातं, कलापः; 'miscellaneous c.,' सर्व्वसङ्ग्रहः.

COLLUSION, *s.* प्रतारणासङ्केतः, कपटमन्त्रः. COLOCYNTH, मृगादनी.

COLONY, *s.* (The people) देशशाखास्थजनाः *m. pl.*—(Country colonized) देशशाखा, राज्यशाखा, देशान्तरस्थराज्यशाखा.

COLUMN, *s.* (Pillar) गोलस्तम्भः.—(Of troops) दण्डः.

COMBUSTIBLE, *a.* शीघ्रदहनीयः -या -यं, शीघ्रज्वलनीयः &c., सहजज्वलनीयः &c., शीघ्रज्वालाग्राही &c., आशुज्वलनीयः &c., सुखज्वलनीयः &c.

COMFORT, *s.* (Ground of c.) सुखहेतुः *m.*, सुखकारणं, सुखास्पदं.

COMMENSALITY, *s.* पंक्तिभोजनं, एकपंक्तिभोजनं, पंक्तिव्यवहारः.

COMMENSURATE, *a.* समपरिमाणः -णा -णं, सममात्रः &c., सममानः -ना -नं.

COMMITTEE, *s.* नियुक्तसभा. COMMITMENT, *s.* कारागृहप्रेषणं.

COMMON, *s.* (Ground) गोप्रचारः, गोचारः, वज्रः, वज्रं.

COMPARATIVE, *a.* अन्यापेक्षः -क्षा -क्षं, सापेक्षः &c., अन्यासापेक्षः &c.

COMPARATIVELY, *adv.* अन्यापेक्ष्य, अन्यद्रव्यमपेक्ष्य, सापेक्षं.

COMPARED, *p. p.* Expressed by अपेक्ष्य; as, 'chalk is heavy when compared with wood,' कर्कटः काष्ठमपेक्ष्य गुरुः भवति.

COMPASS, *s.* परिसरः.—(Point of the c.) दिग्विभागः, दिक् *f.* (श्), दिशा, *see* POINT, QUARTER; 'the eight points,' अष्टदिशाः *f. pl.*; 'collectively,' दिग्चक्रं; 'determining the points of c.,' दिक्साधनं; 'to box the c.,' दिक्कथनं कृ; 'building open to all the points of c.,' सर्व्वतोभद्रं.

To COMPETE, *v. n.* स्पर्ध्. *See To* RIVAL, VIE, COPE.

COMPETENCY, *s.* द्रव्यानुकूल्यं, योगक्षेमपर्य्याप्तधनं, द्रव्यानुकूलता.

To COMPLETE, *v. a.* तीर् (c. 10. तीरयति -यितुं), पार् (c. 10. पारयति -यितुं).

CONCAVE, *a.* मध्यनिम्नः -म्ना -म्नं, गगणाकारः -रा -रं, गगणाकृतिः -तिः -ति, अघःकटाहाकृतिः &c., कटाहाकाशाकृतिः &c.

To CONCEAL, *v. a.* संवृ (c. 5. -वृणोति -वरितुं). CONCEALMENT, *s.* संवरणं.

To CONCEIVE, (In womb) गर्भवती भू, गर्भान्तर् धृ, गर्भधारणं कृ.

CONCLUSION, *s.* (In Logic) निगमनं; 'illogical,' अपसिद्धान्तः.

To CONDEMN, *v. a.* अपराधकथनपूर्व्वं दण्डाभिधानं कृ or दण्डनियोजनं कृ or वध्यं निर्दिश् (c. 6. -दिशति -देष्टुं).

CONDITION, *s.* (Stipulation) सङ्केतः, सन्धिः *m.*, प्रतिबन्धः; 'on one condition I will restore (it),' एकेन सन्धिना प्रत्यर्पयामि.

CONDITIONAL, *a.* साङ्केतिकः -की -कं, सप्रतिबन्धः &c., सापेक्षः &c.

To CONDOLE, *v. n.* समदुःखी भू, सहशोकं कृ. CONDOLENCE, सहशोकः.

CONE, *s.* शङ्कुः *m.*, सूचिखातः, गोपुच्छाकृतिः *f.*

CONFESSOR, *s.* दोषश्रोतृगुरुः *m.*, दोषश्रवणगुरुः *m.*

CONFIDANT, CONFIDANTE, *s.* एकात्मसखा (खि), एकात्ममित्रं, रहस्यमित्रं, रहस्यास्पदं, रहस्यपात्रं, सध्रीची *f.*, सखीजनः.

To CONGRATULATE, *v. a.* अभिनन्द्, अभिवन्द्, अनुमुद्, सहानन्दं कृ, सहानन्दोक्तिं कृ, सहानन्दकथनं कृ, सहानन्दप्रकाशनं कृ, अनुमोदनं कृ.

CONGRATULATED, *p. p.* अभिनन्दितः -ता -तं, अभिवन्दितः &c., अनुमोदितः &c.

CONGRATULATION, *s.* अभिनन्दनं, अभिवन्दनं, सहानन्दोक्तिः -कथनं.

CONGRATULATORY, *a.* सहानन्दसूचकः -का -कं, सहानन्दप्रकाशकः &c.

CONIC SECTION, *s.* शङ्कुच्छित्रं. CONJUGATION, *s.* आख्यानं, रूपाख्यानं.

CONJUNCTION, *s.* (In astron.) योगः, संयोगः; 'auspicious c.,' सुयोगः. This is applied to seven conjunctions, viz. to the occurrence upon Sunday of the nakshatra हस्तः, and thence in order respectively of श्रवणः, अश्विनी, अनुराधा, पुष्यः, रेवती and रोहिणी; 'inauspicious c.,' कुयोगः, पापग्रहः.

CONJUNCTLY, CONJOINTLY, *adv.* सम्भूय, संयोगतस्, यौगपद्येन.

CONSIDERATION, *s.* (Of pros and cons) कार्य्याकार्य्यविचारः, कर्त्तव्याकर्त्तव्यविचारः, सदसद्विचारः; 'minute c.,' सूक्ष्मविचारः, गुरुलघुविचारः; 'in c. of,' अपेक्ष्य.

CONSTRUCTION, *s.* (Of words) पदान्वयः, वाक्यपद्धतिः *f.*, पदयोजना.

To CONSTRUE, *v. a.* अन्वयलापनं कृ, अन्वयलापनिकां कृ, लापनं कृ.

CONTOUR, *s.* रूपरेखा, आकाररेखा, बाह्यरेखा, शरीररेखा.

CONTRIVANCE, *s.* प्रयोगः, प्रयुक्तिः *f.* *To* CONTRIVE, संविधा.

CONVEX, *a.* मध्योन्नतः -ता -तं, अधोमुखदुन्दुभ्याकारः -रा -रं.

CONVICTION, *s.* सापराधीकरणं, अपराधस्थापनं, सदोषीकरणं.

COPPER, *s.* मर्कटास्यं; 'calx of c.,' ताम्रभस्म *n.*; 'sulphate,' ताम्रगर्भः.

COPULATIVE, *a.* (In conjunction) उभयान्वयी -यिनी -यि (न्).

CORRELATIVE, *a.* अन्योन्यान्वयी &c., अन्योन्याश्रितः -ता -तं, परस्पराश्रितः &c.

COURSE, *s.* प्रवृत्तिः *f.*, प्रवाहः; 'of course,' सहजगत्या, सहजरीत्या.

COURT-MARTIAL, *s.* सैनिकन्यायसभा, सैनिकधर्म्मसभा.

COVERED, *p. p.* आकीर्णः -र्णा -र्णं, व्याप्तः -प्ता -प्तं; 'is c.,' आव्रियते.

COVEY, *s.* (Of partridges) तैत्तिरं. COW-POX, *s.* गोस्तनशीतला.

CRANIOLOGY, *s.* कपालसामुद्रिकं, कपालविद्या, कपालशास्त्रं.

CREATION, *s.* उदयः, भूतसृष्टिः *f.*, प्रत्यक्षसृष्टिः *f.*

CREED, *s.* विश्वसनीयविषयसूत्रसङ्ग्रहः, विश्वसनीयविषयमालिका.

CRISIS, *s.* (Of a disease) परिणामदर्शकभेदः, परिणामसूचकभेदः, रूपभेदः, अवस्थान्तरं, स्थित्यन्तरं, भावान्तरं, परिणामज्ञानावसरः.—(Critical juncture) सन्धिः *m.*, प्रसङ्गः.

CRITICAL, *a.* (In judging) सूक्ष्मदर्शी -र्शिनी &c., सूक्ष्मदृष्टिः -ष्टिः -ष्टि.—(Relating to a crisis) परिणामदर्शकभेदसम्बन्धी &c.

To CROSS, (The feet) वेष्टनं कृ. CROSS-LEGGED, *a.* प्रौढपादः -दा -दं.

CURIOSITY, *s.* अपूर्व्वदर्शनोत्सुकता, अश्रुतदर्शनोत्सुकता, अन्वेषणासक्तिः *f.*, गवेषणासक्तिः *f.*—(A rarity) कौतुकं.

CURIOUS, *a.* अपूर्व्वदर्शनोत्सुकः -का -कं, अन्वेषणासक्तः -क्ता -क्तं.

CURSED, *p. p.* आक्रुष्टः -ष्टा -ष्टं, शापग्रस्तः &c., अतिद्वेष्यः &c.

CURVED, *a.* अङ्कुशाकारः -रा -रं. CUT, *s.* (Of the flesh) त्वक्छेदः.

CUTTING, *a.* मर्म्मवेधकः -का -कं, मर्म्मभेदी &c., मर्म्मस्पृक् *m. f. n.* (श्), मर्म्माविद्; 'language,' वाग्विषः *f.*

CYLINDER, *s.* समखातः, लम्बवर्त्तुलं, वर्त्तुलस्तम्भः.

CYLINDRICAL, *a.* लम्बवर्त्तुलाकारः -रा -रं, वर्त्तुलस्तम्भाकारः &c.

D.

DAILY, *a.* दैनन्दिनः -नी -नं; 'daily bread,' नित्यान्नं, नित्यभोजनं.

DARKENED, *p. p.* कलुषीकृतः -ता -तं. DARKNESS, (Great) तामिस्रं.

DEAD, *p. p.* निर्वाणः -णा -णं, प्राणवियुक्तः -क्ता -क्तं, लोकान्तरगतः -ता -तं, लोकान्तरप्राप्तः &c., परलोकगतः &c. If the dead person was a worshipper of Vishnu, he may be called in covert language, वैकुण्ठवासी, if of Śiva, कैलासवासी.

DEATH, *s.* निर्वाणं, निवृत्तिः *f.*, महापथः, महापथगमनं, महाप्रस्थानं, देहयात्रा, देहान्तः, परलोकगमनं, देहावसानं; 'violent d.,' दुर्मरणं; 'snare of d.,' यमपाशः, कालपाशः, मृत्युपाशः; 'exempt from decay and d.,' अजरामरः -रा -रं; 'fear of d.,' जीवितसंशयः.

DECIMAL, *s.* दशांशः, दशमभागः. DECEIVER, व्यपदेष्टृ *m.*

DECOMPOSITION, *s.* पञ्चताप्राप्तिः *f.*, पञ्चत्वापत्तिः *f.*, तत्त्वपृथक्करणं.

To DEFACE, *v. a.* आकारभङ्गं कृ, स्वरूपभङ्गं कृ, रूपभङ्गं कृ.

DEGENERACY, *s.* मूलगुणक्षीणता, मूलसत्त्वहानिः *f.*, मूलधर्म्मभ्रष्टता.

DEGENERATE, *a.* मूलगुणक्षीणः -णा -णं, मूलगुणभ्रष्टः -ष्टा -ष्टं, मूलसत्त्वभ्रष्टः

&c., मूलसत्त्वपतितः &c., क्षीणधर्म्मा -र्म्मा -र्म्म (न्).

DEISM, *s.* केवलेश्वरमतं. DEIST, *s.* केवलेश्वरवादी *m.* (न्).

To DELIBERATE, *v. n.* समर्थ् (c. 10. समर्थयति -यितुं), समर्थनं कृ.

DELIBERATION, *s.* कर्त्तव्याकर्त्तव्यविचारः, कार्य्याकार्य्यविचारः, पूर्व्वापरविचारः, समर्थनं -ना.

DELICACY, *s.* (Food) उत्तमान्नं, परमान्नं. DELICATE, *a.* प्रकृतिपेलवः &c.

DEMOCRACY, *s.* लोकप्रभुत्वं, सामान्यजनकर्तृकराज्यं, लोकाधिपत्यं.

DENOMINATOR, *s.* (Of a fraction) छेदः -दकः.

DESIGN, *s.* मनोगतं, मनोरथः, कल्पना, इङ्गितं, निश्चितं.

DESPOT, *s.* स्वाधीनराजा *m.*, स्वायत्तराजा *m.*, स्वतन्त्रराजा.

DESPOTISM, *s.* स्वतन्त्रता, स्वातन्त्र्यं, अनिर्बन्धशासनं.

DESSERT, *s.* भोजनोत्तरफलाहारः, मुखशुद्धिः *f.*, मुखवासः.

To DESTINE, *v. a.* पूर्व्वनियोगं कृ, पूर्व्वनियोजनं कृ, पूर्व्वकल्पनां कृ.

DESTINATION, *s.* नियोजितविषयः, नियुक्तविषयः, नियुक्तस्थानं.

DESTINED, *p. p.* पूर्व्वनियोजितः -ता -तं, पूर्व्वनियुक्तः &c., दैवकृतः &c.

DESTINY, *s.* दैवयोगः, कर्म्मफलं, कर्म्मयोगः, दैवदशा, भवितव्यं, ब्रह्मलिखितं; 'fulfilment of destiny,' कर्म्मभोगः.

DEVOTEE, *s.* वैरागी *m.* (न्), वैरागिकः. DEVOTION, भक्तियोगः.

DIAGONAL, *s.* कर्णरेखा. DIAGONAL, *a.* कर्णाकृतिः -तिः -ति, कर्णरेखाकृतिः &c., कोणस्थः -स्था -स्थं, कोणगामी &c.

DIAL, *s.* शङ्कुयन्त्रं, कीलयन्त्रं. DIAL-PLATE, *s.* शङ्कुवृत्तं.

DIAMETER, *s.* मध्यरेखा, मध्यसूत्रं, गर्भसूत्रं, वृत्तार्द्धरेखा.

DIARRHŒA, *s.* सङ्ग्रहणी. DIARTHROSIS, *s.* चलसन्धिः *m.*

DIARY, *s.* दिनवृत्तपत्रं, दिनवृत्तलेखः, दिनचरित्रलेखः, आह्निकपत्रं.

DIFFERENTIAL CALCULUS, *s.* वैलक्षण्यगणितं.

DIFFICULT, *a.* दुःखी -खिनी -खि (न्), कष्टसाध्यः -ध्या -ध्यं, श्रमसाध्यः &c., आयाससाध्यः &c., प्रयत्नसाध्यः &c., दुर्गमः -मा -मं, दुष्करः &c., सुदुष्करः &c.

To DIG UP, *v. a.* उत्खन्. DIGGING, *s.* उत्खननं.

DIGRESSION, *s.* अवान्तरकथा, शाखा. DILIGENTLY, अतन्द्रितस्.

DIMPLE, *s.* हनुकूपिका. DIPHTHONG, *s.* सन्ध्यक्षरः.

DIRECTION, *s.* (Line or course in which a body moves) दिक् *f.* (श्); 'in the direction,' दिशि; 'a line is straight which goes in one direction, and curved which goes continually in a different direction,' या रेखा एकां दिशं गच्छेत् सा सरला या च प्रतिपदं भिन्नदिशं गच्छेत् सा वक्रा.

DIRECTORY, *s.* पद्धतिग्रन्थः, पद्धतिः *f.* DIRGE, *s.* शोकगीतं.

DISCHARGE, *s.* (Of matter) पूयस्रावः, पूयं; 'to discharge matter,' पूयं सु in caus., पूय् (c. 1. पूयते -यितुं).

DISCOMPOSED, *a.* गतधृतिः -तिः -ति, गतधैर्य्यः -र्य्या -र्य्यं, गतगाम्भीर्य्यः &c.

DISCOMPOSURE, *s.* अस्वास्थ्यं, असमाधानं, अशान्तिः *f.*, शान्तिभङ्गः.

DISCORD, *s.* वैस्वर्य्यं, विस्वरता, स्वरमेलनाभावः.

To DISENTANGLE, *v. a.* उद्ग्रन्थ्. DISENTANGLED, उद्ग्रथितः -ता -तं.

To DISINHERIT, *v. a.* अंशहीनं -नां कृ, अनंशीकृ, वृत्तिच्छेदनं कृ.

DISPENSATION, *s.* (Divine) ईश्वरकर्तृकसुखदुःखनियोगः.—(License) विधिमोचनं, विधिमुक्तिः *f.*, नियममुक्तिः *f.*

DISPROPORTION, *s.* प्रमाणवैषम्यं, परिमाणवैषम्यं, प्रमाणवैकल्यं.

DISPROPORTIONATE, *a.* विषमपरिमाणकः -का -कं, न्यूनाधिकः -का -कं.

DISPUTED, *p. p.* विप्रतिपन्नः -न्ना -न्नं, विप्रतिपद्यमानः &c., वादास्पदं.

To DISSUADE, *v. a.* निवारणोपदेशं कृ, परावर्त्तनोपदेशं कृ, परावृत् in caus., परावर्त्तनं कृ, निवृत्तिं कृ, निवारणं कृ.

DISTILLATION, *s.* सन्धिका, अन्तर्दहनं, मद्यनिस्सारणं.

To DIVIDE, *v. a.* (In Arith.) भज्, हृ, भाजनं कृ, भजनं कृ.

DIVIDED, भक्तः -क्ता -क्तं, भाजितः -ता -तं; 'the product is divided by the first number,' वधः प्रथमेन ह्रियते.

DIVISIBILITY, *s.* (As a property of matter) सावयवत्वं.

DIVISION, *s.* (In Arith.) भजनं, भाजनं, लब्धं. DIVISOR, वियोजकः.

DIVORCE, *s.* विवाहसम्बन्धमुक्तिः *f.* -मोचनं, दाम्पत्यमुक्तिः *f.*

DOGMA, *s.* मूलतत्त्वं, मूलवाक्यं. DOG-LATIN, *s.* पिशाचभाषा.

DONE, *p. p.* विहितः -ता -तं. DOSE, *s.* औषधपरिमाणं.

DRAMATIS-PERSONÆ, *s.* पात्रं, पात्रवर्गः.

DREAM, *s.* (Bad) दुःस्वप्नः; 'creation of d.,' स्वप्नसृष्टिः *f.*; 'interpretation of d.,' स्वप्नविचारः; 'interpreter,' स्वप्नविचारी *m.*

DRIVING, *s.* सारथ्यं. DRONE, *s.* मधुमक्षिकानरः.

DROPSY, *s.* आध्मानं. DROUGHT, अवृष्टिः *f.*

To DROWN, *v. n.* जलमृत्युं प्राप्. DRUGGIST, *s.* योगविद्.

DULNESS, *s.* जडता, जाड्यं. DURATION, *s.* दीर्घत्वं, दैर्घ्यं.

DUTY, *s.* आवश्यककार्य्यं; 'general d.,' साधारणधर्म्मः; 'peculiar d.,' स्वधर्म्मः, विशेषधर्म्मः; 'minor d.,' उपधर्म्मः, गौणधर्म्मः; 'neglect of one's d.,' स्वधर्म्मत्यागः.

DYSPEPSIA, *s.* अग्निमान्द्यं, मन्दपाकः. DYNAMICS, गतिविद्या.

E.

ECLIPSE, *s.* ग्रासः; 'day of e.,' ग्रहपर्व्व *n.* (न्), राहुपर्व्व *n.*; 'duration of e.,' स्थितिः *f.*; 'total e.,' मीलनं.

EFFECT, (To take) प्रभू. EFFACED, *p. p.* चितीर्णः -र्णा -र्णं.

EFFLUVIUM, *s.* गन्धपरमाणुः *m.* EFFRONTERY, औद्धत्यं.

EITHER, *pron.* (One of two) एकतरः -रा -रं.—(Of many) एकतमः &c.

ELASTIC, *a.* पूर्व्वस्थितिगामी -मिनी &c., पूर्व्वस्थितिप्रापकः -का -कं, स्थितिस्थापकविशिष्टः -ष्टा -ष्टं, वेतसवृत्तिः -त्तिः -त्ति.

ELEMENT, *s.* (As earth, air, &c.) भूतं, महाभूतं; 'the five e., or earth, air, fire, water and ákásha,' पञ्चभूतानि, पञ्चमहाभूतानि, पञ्चता -त्वं, धातुजातं; 'reduction to order of the five e.,' पञ्चीकरणं; 'relation of an e. with its combinations,' प्रकृतिविकृतिभावः; 'the five subtile rudiments of the five e.,' पञ्चतन्मात्राणि.—(Seven elements of the body) सप्तधातवः *m. pl.* (तु). These are, 1. chyle, रसः; 2. blood, रक्तं; 3. flesh, मांसं; 4. fat, मेदस्; 5. marrow, मज्जा; 6. bone, अस्थि; 7. semen, शुक्रं.

ELLIPSE, *s.* अधिककलत्रिकं, कक्षः.

ELLIPSIS, *s.* पदन्यूनता, पदाकांक्षा, पदापेक्षा, वाक्यन्यूनता, वाक्याकांक्षा; 'supplying an e.,' आकांक्षापूरणं; 'word required to supply an e.,' अध्याहार्य्यपदं; 'word brought to supply an e.,' अध्याहृतपदं -वाक्यं.

EMIGRANT, *s.* स्वदेशत्यागी *m.*, देशान्तराधिवासी, अन्यदेशवासी.

ENDOWED, *p. p.* यौतकयुक्तः -क्ता -क्तं, यौतकसम्पन्नः &c., वृत्तियुक्तः &c.

ENTHUSIASM, *s.* आवेशः, अत्युत्साहः, परमोत्साहः, अत्यासक्तिः *f.*

EQUATOR, *s.* (Terrestrial) विषुववृत्तं, विषुवरेखा, विषुवचक्रं, विषुवमण्डलं, विषुवद्वृत्तं, भूमध्यरेखा; 'radius of equator,' भूकरणः.—(Celestial) नाडीवृत्तं.

EQUILIBRIUM, *s.* तुलासाम्यं, तुलासमता, समानगुरुत्वं.

EQUINOCTIAL, (Point) गोलसन्धिः *m.*, विषुवं, क्रान्तिपातः.

ESCAPE, *s.* उद्धारः. ESCAPED, (In battle) हतशेषः -षा -षं.

ESOTERIC, *a.* गुप्तोक्तः -क्ता -क्तं, एकान्तोपदिष्टः &c., रहःकथितः &c.

ESPIONAGE, *s.* चेष्टानिरूपणं, चारद्वारावलोकनं, चारद्वारदर्शनं.
ESPRIT, *s.* अभिमानं; 'de corps,' स्वगणाभिमानं; 'de pays,' देशाभिमानं.
ESSENTIAL, *s.* आवश्यकविषयः, आवश्यकवस्तु *n.*, सारः.
ETIQUETTE, *s.* सभ्याचाररीतिः *f.*, शिष्टाचाररीतिः *f.*, आदरोपचाररीतिः *f.*; 'royal etiquette,' राजोपचारः, राजोपचाररीतिः *f.*
EVERGREEN, *a.* सदाहरितपर्णः -र्णा -र्णं, सदार्द्रपर्णकः -का -कं.
EVIDENCE, *s.* प्रमाणं; 'of sense,' प्रत्यक्षप्रमाणं; 'of inference,' अनुमानप्रमाणं; 'of analogy,' उपमानप्रमाणं; 'of ordeal,' दिव्यप्रमाणं; 'of profession,' भोगप्रमाणं; 'documentary evidence,' लेखप्रमाणं; 'ocular,' दृक्प्रत्ययः.
EXACT, *a.* सम्यङ् -मीची -म्यक् (च्). EXACTION, *s.* बलात्कारः.
EXCLUDED, *p. p.* रुद्धप्रवेशः -शा -शं, अवरुद्धप्रवेशः &c., प्रतिषिद्धप्रवेशः.
EXCLUSIVE, *a.* अनन्यग्राह्यः -ह्या -ह्यं, अन्याग्राह्यः &c., इतराग्राह्यः &c.
EXCRESCENCE, *s.* अङ्कुरः, कीलः; 'on a goat's neck,' मणिः *m.*
EXECUTIVE, *a.* राज्यनियमप्रवर्त्तकः -का -कं, राज्यनियमप्रवर्त्तनाधिकारी, राज्यविधिप्रवर्त्तकः &c.
EXECUTOR, *s.* मृतलेखप्रवर्त्तकः, मृतलेखप्रवर्त्तकः.
To EXPECTORATE, *v. n.* कफोद्गिरणं कृ, श्लेष्मोद्गिरणं कृ.
EXTEMPORARY, *a.* समयकल्पितः -ता -तं, समयोपस्थितः &c., पूर्व्वविचारहीनः -ना -नं, पूर्व्वविचाररहितः -ता -तं, पूर्व्वचिन्ताहीनः &c.
EYE, *s.* अक्षकं; 'of favour,' कृपादृष्टिः *f.*, कृपावलोकनं.

F.

FALLIBLE, *a.* भ्रमपात्रं, सम्भावितभ्रमः -मा -मं, भ्रमार्हः &c.
FAR-GONE, (In love) दूरारूढप्रणयः -या -यं.
To FATHER, *v. a.* पितृत्वारोपं कृ, पितृतारोपणं कृ.
FAULTLESS, *a.* (In form) अनवद्याङ्गः -ङ्गी -ङ्गं.
FEAR, *s.* आतङ्कः. FEATURE, *s.* मुखलक्षणं, मुखचिह्नं.
FETTER, *s.* संरोधः. *To* FETTER, *v. a.* संरुध्.
FEVER, *s.* (Arising from vitiation of the humour bile) पित्तज्वरः.—(Of the humour phlegm) कफज्वरः.—(Of the humour wind) वातज्वरः.—(Of the three humours) त्रिदोषात्मकज्वरः.—(Of the bile and wind) पित्तवातज्वरः.—(Of the bile and phlegm) पित्तकफज्वरः.—(With ague) शीतज्वरः; 'illusions of f.,' ज्वरसृष्टिः *f.*; 'inflammatory f.,' दाहज्वरः; 'slow f.,' जीर्णज्वरः.
FIGURE, *s.* (In geometry) क्षेत्रं.—(In arithmetic) अङ्कः; 'figures,' अङ्कविद्या.—(Emblem) प्रतिरूपं, प्रतिबिम्बं.—(In rhetoric) अलङ्कारः. The following are some of the common figures in rhetoric: 'Simile,' उपमा; 'Breaking the natural order of words in a sentence,' अनन्वयः; 'Identification of the objects of a comparison,' रूपकं; 'Irony,' आक्षेपः; 'Alliteration,' अनुप्रासः; 'Comparison,' उत्प्रेक्षा; 'Hyperbole,' अतिशयोक्तिः *f.*; 'Explanation of any peculiar condition, by coupling cause with effect,' विशेषोक्तिः *f.*; 'Dilating upon an idea, or accumulating expressions to throw light on an idea,' दीपकं; 'Dissimilitude of things compared in some respect to each other,' व्यतिरेकः; 'Describing the past or future as present,' भाविकं; 'Inverse comparison, or comparing new objects with some known object, as the moon, &c.,' प्रतीपं; 'Identity of objects compared to one another,' समं; 'Connexion of different objects by common properties,' सामान्यं; 'Punning on words,' श्लेषः; 'Climax,' सारं; 'Rhetorical use of the word *without*,' विनोक्तिः *f.*; 'Rhetorical use of the word *with* or *along with*,' सहोक्तिः *f.*; 'Change,' परिणामः; 'Recollection,' स्मृतिः *f.*; 'Mistake,' भ्रान्तिः *f.*; 'Doubt,' सन्देहः; 'Applying a simile to other than its obvious application,' अपह्नुतिः *f.* And the following, the meaning of which is doubtful, प्रासः, उल्लेखः, तुल्ययोगिता, चर्वणा.
FINE, *s.* साहसं; 'to be paid to the king,' राजदण्डः.
FINGER, *s.* (Fore) प्रदेशिनी, तर्जनी.—(Middle) मध्यमा.—(Third or ring finger) अनामिका.—(Little) कनिष्ठा.
FIRE, *s.* (Sacred or sacrificial) होमाग्निः *m.*, गृह्याग्निः, हुतं; 'hole or enclosed space for preserving it,' अग्निकुण्डं, कुण्डं, होमकुण्डं, होमशाला; 'maintainer of it,' अग्निहोत्री *m.* (न्), अग्निहोता *m.* (तृ); 'maintenance of it,' अग्निहोत्रं; 'particular wood for kindling it,' अरणिः -णी, गणिकारी -रिका, पलाशः, खदिरः; 'widower's sacred fire,' विधुराग्निः.
FISH, *s.* वल्कवान् *m.* (त्). FISHERMAN, *s.* मत्स्यग्राहकः.
FLAMINGO, *s.* मरालः. FLIGHT, (Of arrow) शरायणं, वातरायणं.
To FLOAT, *v. n.* (As a boat) तॄ.—(In the air) वायौ वह्.
FLOUR, *s.* धान्यचूर्णं. *To* FLOW, द्रु (c. 1. द्रवति, द्रोतुं).
FOCUS, *s.* किरणसमुदयस्थलं, किरणसमुदयबिन्दुः *m.*, किरणसमाहारस्थलं.
FONTENELLE, *s.* (In anatomy) ब्रह्मरन्ध्रं चक्रं.
FOOD, *s.* अभ्यवहारः, अभ्यवहार्य्यं, जेमनं; 'heavy f.,' भ्रष्टान्नं; 'savory f.,' मिष्टान्नं; 'wholesome f.,' सदन्नं; 'loathing of f.,' अन्नद्वेषः; 'non-observant of the distinction of f.,' सर्व्वभक्षः, सर्व्वान्नभोजी &c.
FOOT, *s.* (Hollow of) तलहृदयं; 'fallen at the feet of,' चरणगतः -ता -तं, चरणपतितः &c., पादलग्नः -ग्ना -ग्नं; 'water presented to wash the feet,' पाद्यं.—(Of a verse) पदं, चरणं, पादः.
FORCEPS, *s.* कङ्कमुखं. FORE-LOCK, *s.* भ्रमरकः, भ्रमरालकः.
FORE-SKIN, *s.* शेफाग्रचर्म्म *n.* (न्), लिङ्गाग्रचर्म्म *n.*, अग्रचर्म्म.
FORMAL, *a.* यथामार्गी -र्गी -र्गि, यथाविधिः -धिः -धि, यथापद्धति: &c.
FORMALIST, *s.* कर्म्मनिष्ठः, क्रियानिष्ठः, बाह्यधर्म्मनिष्ठः, बाह्यधर्म्मवृत्तिः *m.*, बाह्योपचारी -रिणी &c.
FORTIFICATION, *s.* (Science) दुर्गप्राकारादिरचनविद्या.
FOSTER-MOTHER, *s.* उपमाता *f.* (तृ), पालकमाता.
FRACTION, *s.* अपूर्णाङ्कः; 'vulgar f.,' शुद्धापूर्णाङ्कः; 'common measure of a f.,' अपवर्त्तः -र्त्तकः; 'reduction of a fraction to a common denominator,' सवर्णनं, अंशसवर्णनं.
FREELY, *adv.* यदृच्छया. FREQUENT, *a.* पौनःपुनिकः -की -कं.
FRICTION, *s.* व्याघट्टनं, सङ्घट्टनं, संहर्षः.
FRIEND, *s.* स्वकदुःखसुखः; 'acquired f.,' कृत्रिममित्रं; 'false f.,' कपटमित्रं, असन्मित्रं, दुर्मित्रं; 'friends and relations,' सुहृत्सम्बन्धिनः *m.pl.*
FROM, *prep.* अप, वि. FRONT, *s.* पुरोभागः.
FRONTISPIECE, *s.* ग्रन्थाग्रवर्त्तिचित्रं, ग्रन्थाग्रस्थचित्रं.
FROST-BITTEN, *a.* हिमदग्धः -ग्धा -ग्धं, हिमग्रस्तः -स्ता -स्तं.
FROZEN, *p. p.* हिमस्तब्धः -ब्धा -ब्धं, हिमस्तम्भितः &c., हिमग्रस्तः &c.
FUNCTION, *s.* (In alg.) कर्म्म *n.* FUR, *s.* सलोमचर्म्म *n.*

G.

GANDHARBA. Their chief is called चित्ररथः.

GANESHA, *s.* (As having a rat for his vehicle, or attended by this animal as an emblem of sagacity) मूषिकाङ्कः, मूषिकाञ्चनः, मूषिकवाहनः.

GANGES, *s.* (As mother of Kártikeya) कुमारसूः. 'The Ganges of heaven,' स्वर्गङ्गा, आकाशगङ्गा; 'of the infernal regions,' भोगवती.

GARLIC, *s.* कन्दः. GENTLEMAN, *s.* सभ्यजनः, सभ्यपुरुषः.

GEOLOGICAL, *s.* भूस्तरविद्यासम्बन्धी -न्धिनी &c. -विषयकः -का -कं.

GEOLOGIST, *s.* भूस्तरविद्याज्ञः, भूस्तरनिरूपकः, क्षितिरचनावित्.

GEOLOGY, *s.* भूस्तरविद्या, भूस्तरनिरूपणविद्या, क्षितिरचनाविद्या, क्षितिरचनाशास्त्रं, भूकथनशास्त्रं.

GEOMETRY, *s.* क्षेत्रमितिः *f.*, क्षेत्रतत्त्वविद्या, भूमितिविद्या.

GOD, *s.* (Of gods) देवाधिदेवः; 'inferior g.,' उपदेवः, उपदेवता; 'local g.,' स्थलदेवता; 'presiding g.,' अधिदेवः, अधिदेवता; 'tutelar g.,' इष्टदेवः, इष्टदेवता; 'recitation of the names of g.,' नामोच्चारणं; 'mother of the g.,' अदितिः *f.*; 'of the Daityas or demons,' दितिः *f.*

GONG, *s.* घटी, घण्टा. GOOD-BY, स्वस्ति. *See* ADIEU.

GRAIN, *s.* (Awned or bearded) शूकधान्यं; 'inferior g.,' उपधान्यं; 'lending g. at interest,' धान्यवर्धनं; 'against the g.,' विलोमः.

GRAMMAR, *s.* (Rules of) शब्दशासनं, शब्दशास्तिः.

To GRATIFY, *v. a.* विनुद् in caus. GRATIFICATION, विनोदः.

GRAVITY, *s.* (Centre of) गुरुत्वकेन्द्रं.

To GROW, *v. n.* समृध्, प्रचुरीभू, अधिकीभू.

GRUEL, *s.* मन्थः. GULF, *s.* (Bay) खातं.

H.

HABITUALLY, *adv.* सदा or शील or नित्य in comp.; 'habitually dejected,' सदाविषादी -दिनी &c., नित्यविषादी &c.; 'silent,' तूष्णीशीलः -ला -लं.

HAIR, *s.* (Falling off of the h.) इन्द्रलुप्तः -प्तं -प्तकः; 'dressed or tufted h.,' केशपाशः; 'parting of the h.,' सीमन्तः; 'ceremony of adjusting the parting during gestation,' सीमन्तोन्नयनं; 'line of h.,' रोमावलिः -ली; 'against the h.,' प्रतिलोमः &c., विलोमः &c.; 'with the h.,' अनुलोमः &c.

HALF, (With numerals); 'Thirteen and a half,' सार्द्धत्रयोदश.

HANDKERCHIEF, *s.* (Pocket) नासामार्जनी.

HARANGUE, *s.* वाक्प्रबन्धः, भाषणं, सालङ्कारभाषणं.

HAVING, *part.* Often expressed by a Bahuvríhi compound; thus, 'speech, having joy for its subject,' वाक्यम् आनन्दविषयकं; 'a man having his father alive,' जीवत्पितृकः पुरुषः.

HEART, *s.* (Purity of) अन्तःशौचं; 'knowledge of the h.,' अन्तर्ज्ञानं; 'singleness of h.,' अनन्यभावः; 'the h. and the life,' अन्तर्वंशौ; in heart and deed, or with all one's heart,' सबाह्याभ्यन्तरं, सर्व्वात्मना.

HEATHEN, *s.* मूर्त्तिपूजकः. HEATHENISM, *s.* मूर्त्तिपूजा.

HEAVEN, *s.* (Seat of the blessed) उत्तमलोकः, दिव्यलोकः, ऊर्द्ध्वलोकः. The heaven of Brahmá is ब्रह्मलोकः, सत्यलोकः, देवलोकः; 'of Vishṇu,' वैकुण्ठं, विष्णुलोकः; 'of Śiva,' कैलासः, शिवलोकः; 'of Indra,' स्वर्गः, स्वर्गलोकः, इन्द्रलोकः, देवलोकः, सुरलोकः, सुरालयः.—(State of final beatitude) मुक्तिः *f.*, मोक्षः, अपवर्गः, कैवल्यं, उद्धारः, सिद्धिः *f.*, ब्रह्मसुखं, ब्रह्मसायुज्यं, निर्वाणं, ब्रह्मप्राप्तिः *f.*, श्रेयस् *n.*, निःश्रेयस्, महोदयः, निर्वृतिः *f.*, अपुनरावृत्तिः *f.*, अपुनर्भवः, परमगतिः *f.*, उत्तमगतिः *f.*, परमपदं, सर्व्वदुःखक्षयः; 'The four states of heavenly bliss,' चतुर्विधामुक्तिः *f.* These are, 1. 'Residence in heaven with the Deity,' सलोकता, सालोक्यं; 2. 'Bearing the likeness of the Deity in heaven,' सरूपता, सारूप्यं; 3. 'Being ever near or in the presence of the Deity,' समीपता, सामीप्यं; 4. 'Absorption into the essence of the Deity,' सायुज्यं.

HEAVENLY-MINDED, *a.* परमार्थबुद्धिः -द्धिः -द्धि, परमार्थासक्तः -क्ता -क्तं.

HEEL, *s.* पृष्णिः *f.* HEIR-APPARENT, *s.* (State of) यौवराज्यं.

HELIOTROPE, *s.* ग्रन्थिमान् *m.* (त्), हस्तिशुण्डी, अस्थिसंहारः.

HELL, *s.* (Region under the earth, or residence of the Nágas, Asuras, Daityas, &c., and not to be confounded with Naraka or the place of punishment) पातालं, अधोभुवनं, नागलोकः. There are seven of these Pátálas or lower regions, सप्तपातालं. These are, 1. अतलं, 2. वितलं, 3. पातालं, 4. रसातलं, 5. महातलं, 6. सुतलं, 7. तलातलं.—(Place of punishment after death) नरकः, निरयः, नारकः. The Naraka, or Tartarus of the Hindús, is divided into numerous different places of torture; such as, 'the place paved with swords,' असिपत्रं; 'the place where the leaves of the trees are swords,' असिपत्रवनं; 'the place of great darkness,' अन्धतामिस्रं; 'a place in which the wicked are baked like pots,' तप्तकुम्भः, कुम्भीपाकः; 'the place of burning sand,' तप्तवालुकः &c., *see* under HELL, p. 340; 'abiding in h.,' नरकवासः; 'descending to h.,' अधःपतनं, अधोगतिः *f.*, नरकपतनं; 'judge of h.,' यमः; 'his messenger,' यमदूतः; 'road to h.,' नरकमार्गः, अधःपथः, धूम्रमार्गः; 'punishment of h.,' यमदण्डः; 'pit of h.,' नरककुण्डं. Eighty-six of these pits are enumerated.

HELLEBORE, *s.* कटुरोहिणी, कटुकी. HEMORRHAGE, रक्तप्रवाहः.

HEMP, *s.* विजया. HERCULEAN, *a.* महाप्रयत्नसाध्यः -ध्या -ध्यं.

HEREDITARY, *a.* पितृप्राप्तः -प्ता -प्तं, पितृक्रमायातः &c., दायलब्धः &c.

HERO, *s.* महारथः, युधिष्ठिरः, भीष्मः; 'drink of hero in battle, to elevate courage,' वीरपानं; 'post of danger wished for by heroes,' वीराशंसनं.

HERPES, *s.* विसर्पः, विसर्पिका, दद्रुः *m.*, पामः -मा (न्).

HILLOCK, *s.* उपपर्व्वतः. HINDER, (Part) पाश्चात्यभागः.

HONEY, *s.* (Of flowers) सुधा. HOOD, (Of snake) दर्वी, स्फटा.

HORIZON, *s.* क्षितिजं, कुजं; 'sensible or visible horizon,' दृष्टिमर्य्यादा, चक्रवालं; 'glow of the horizon,' दिग्दाहः.

HORIZONTAL, *a.* क्षितिजैकसूत्रः -त्रा -त्रं, क्षितिजसमसूत्रः &c.

HORSE-BACK, (Mounted on) अश्वारूढः -ढा, अश्वारोहः &c.

HORSE-RADISH, *s.* शोभाञ्जनः. HOSPITAL, *s.* रोगिशाला.

HOSTILE, *a.* अमित्रः -त्रा -त्रं. HOSTILITY, अमित्रता.

HUMOUR, *s.* The three humours of the body are, 1. 'phlegm,' कफः; 2. 'bile,' पित्तं; 3. 'air or wind,' वायुः *m.*, वातः; 'disorder of any h.,' धातुनाशः; 'vitiation of three h.,' त्रिदोषं, सन्निपातः; 'excess of any of the three h.,' प्रकोपः, उल्वणं; 'disorder resulting from vitiation of the phlegm,' कफविकारः, कफरोगः; 'of the bile,' पित्तविकारः; 'of the wind,' वातविकारः, वायुविकारः.

Hungry, *a.* दग्धोदरः -रा -रं, क्षुधानलविदग्धः -ग्धा -ग्धं.
Hydraulics, *s.* उदकगतिविद्या, जलगतिविद्या -शास्त्रं.
Hydrogen, *s.* जलजनकवायुः *m.*, उदकजनकवायुः *m.* -वाष्पः.
Hydrostatics, *s.* उदकस्थितिविद्या, उदकस्थितिशास्त्रं.
Hyperbola, *s.* अनकलक्षितं; 'opposite,' अत्यूनकलक्षितं.

I.

Impregnated, *p.p.* संसृष्टः -ष्टा -ष्टं, गुणमिश्रितः &c., गुणयुक्तः &c.
Included, *p.p.* अन्तर्भूतः -ता -तं, अन्तःपाती &c., प्रतिष्ठितः -ता -तं.
Incoherent, (Speech) प्रलापः; 'one who talks so,' प्रलापी.
Indra, *s.* (As lord of the Eastern quarter) प्राचीपतिः *m.*, प्राचीनबर्हिः *m.* (स्). His vehicle is the elephant ऐरावतः.
To infect, *v. a.* उपहन्. Infected, *p. p.* उपहतः -ता -तं.
Inferior, *a.* अधोभवः -वा -वं. Infernal, (Region) अवाची.

K. L. M. N. O. P. R.

Kámadeva, *s.* (As having an odd number of arrows) विषमेषुः.
—(As having blossoms for arrows) पञ्चवाणः. His vehicle is a parrot, शुकः. Hence he is called शुकवाहः -हनः.
Kártikeya, *s.* (As god of war) महाशक्तिः *m.*, सिद्धसेनः.
Lay, *a.* व्यवहारिकः -की -कं. Layman, व्यवहारी *m.*
Litigated, (Under litigation) विप्रतिपद्यमानः -ना -नं.
Longer, (For a longer time) अधिककालं.
Manu, *s.* The names of the seven Manus are, 1. स्वायम्भुवः, 2. स्वारोचिषः, 3. उत्तमः, 4. तामसः, 5. रैवतः, 6. चाक्षुषः, 7. वैवस्वतः. The last is the Manu of the present period.
Near, (A well) उपकूपं. Next, *a.* उत्तरः -रा -रं.
Obtuse-angled, *a.* अधिककोणः -णा -णं, विशालकोणः &c.
Passover, *s.* निस्तारोत्सवः. Pasturage, *s.* चरणस्थानं.
Pattern, *s.* दृष्टान्तः. Pavement, *s.* प्रस्तरबन्धनं.
Perplexed, *a.* उपायहीनः -ना -नं. Persecution, *s.* दौरात्म्यं.
To recoil, *v. n.* (As in fear) विकम्प् (c. 1. -कम्पते -म्पितुं).

FINIS.

ERRATA.

AGREEABLE, l. 3. *for* comfortable, *read* conformable.
l. 4. *for* योग्याः, *read* योग्यः.

ALOFT, *for* उर्द्ध्वं, *read* ऊर्द्ध्वं.

ANGRILY, *adv.* *for* कोपेण, *read* कोपेन.

To APPRAISE, l. 2. *for* भूल्यं, *read* मूल्यं.

ARMOUR-BEARER, f broken, *read* सान्नहनिकः.

ATONEMENT, l. 1. *for* प्रायश्चित्तः, *read* प्रायश्चित्तं.

To AUGMENT, *v. n.* l. 3. *transpose* वृंह् in caus., to *v. a.*

To BARTER, *v. a.* l. 3. *for* भाण्डं प्रति, *read* भाण्डात् प्रति.

BASHFUL, l. 2. *for* क्रीडितः, *read* व्रीडितः.

BEFORE, l. 14. *for* पूब्वकाले, *read* पूर्व्वकाले.

BEING, l. 1. *for* सत्त्वः, *read* सत्त्वं.

BEQUEST, *for* उासन्ने, *read* आसन्ने.

To BESTIR, l. 3. *for* व्यवसो c. 1., *read* व्यवसो c. 4.

BICIPITAL, *for* द्विमुर्द्धः, *read* द्विमूर्द्धः.

BIT, l. 5. *for* किञ्ज्ञित्स्थूलतरं, *read* किञ्चित्स्थूलतरं.

BLAZING, l. 1. *for* ज्वालन्, *read* ज्वलन्.

To BLOW, *v. a.* l. 7. *for* नासिकं, *read* नासिकां.

BROTHERLY, *adv.* *for* प्रातृकप्रकारेण, *read* भ्रातृकप्रकारेण.

CARAWAY, l. 1. *for* अजसादा, *read* अजमोदा.

CHASE, *s.* l. 2. *for* भृगयायै, *read* मृगयायै.

To CHECK, *v. a.* l. 3. *for* c. 9., *read* c. 7.

To CHECKER, *v. a.* *for* छित्रयति, *read* चित्रयति.

CIPHER, *s.* l. 1. *for* अङ्कं, *read* अङ्कः.

To CONCLUDE, *v. a.* *for* निवृत्, *read* निर्वृत्.

To CONDEMN, *v. a.* l. 5. *for* c. 1., *read* c. 9.

COOK, *s.* l. 1. *for* सदः, *read* सूदः.

COUPLE, *s.* l. 5. *for* शुङ्खला, *read* शृङ्खला.

COURSE, *s.* l. 15. *for* भोजनपत्राणि, *read* -पात्राणि.

To COURT, *v. a.* l. 6. *for* c. 1., *read* c. 2.

To CRACK, *v. n.* l. 2. *for* विद्, *read* षिद्.

To DASH, *v. a.* l. 5. *for* पह्, *read* प्रह्.

DEBAUCH, l. 3, *for* व्यासनावेशः *read* व्यसनावेशः.

DECISION, l. 1. *for* -यणं, *read* -यनं.

DECREASE, l. 2. *for* न्यनीभावः, *read* न्यूनीभावः.

To DELIGHT, *v. n.* l. 4. *for* तोष्यति, *read* तुष्यति.

To DESIGN, *v. a.* l. 4. *for* abl. case, *read* dat. case.

DETRACTION, l. 3. *for* अभ्यसया, *read* अभ्यसूया.
l. 4. *for* गणापवादः, *read* गुणापवादः.

DEVOTED, l. 4. *for* सक्तिमान्, *read* भक्तिमान्.

DISCREETLY, *adv.* *for* सुविचार्य्यं, *read* सुविचार्य्य.

DOG, *s.* l. 2. *for* मृगदशकः, *read* मृगदंशकः.

To ELUCIDATE, l. 3. *for* दष्टान्तेन, *read* दृष्टान्तेन.

ENTANGLEMENT, *s.* l. 2. *for* सङ्कर्य्यं, *read* साङ्कर्य्यं.

ESSENTIAL, *a.* l. 4. *for* गूर्व्वर्थः, *read* गुर्व्वर्थः.

EUROPEAN, *s.* *for* उरोपीयः, *read* यूरोपीयः.

To EVADE, *v. a.* l. 1. *for* पलायित्वा, *read* पलायमानः.

To EXCEL, l. 3. *for* अन्येति, *read* अत्येति.

EXTENUATION, l. 2. *for* पापापेक्षा, *read* पापोपेक्षा.

EYE, *s.* l. 18. *for* book, *read* hook.

To FABRICATE, *v. a.* *for* -मीयते, *read* -मायते.

To FEAST, *v. n.* *for* मन्तुष्, *read* सन्तुष्.

FIRE, l. 8. *for* अपाम्पितः, *read* अपाम्पित्तः.

GAOL, *s.* *for* बन्धनगुहं, *read* बन्धनगृहं.

IMMATURENESS, l. 4. *for* अपूष्कलता, *read* अपुष्कलता.

INTO, l. 16. *for* जलसास्कृतः, *read* जलसात्कृतः.

KINDLY, l. 2. *for* स्नेहंन, *read* स्नेहेन.

KRISHNA, l. 9. *for* sister, *read* brother.

LOUSY, l. 1. *for* युकालः, *read* यूकालः.

LYING, *part.* l. 4. *for* अधमूर्द्धशयः, *read* अवमूर्द्धशयः.

MEDICINE, l. 5. *for* साम्योपचारः, *read* सौम्योपचारः.

To MOVE, *v. a.* l. 6. *for* सामाकृष्, *read* समाकृष्.

PERCEPTIBLE, l. 5. *for* द्रष्टिग्राह्यः, *read* दृष्टिग्राह्यः.

PIT, l. 2. *for* मुत्रपुटं, *read* मूत्रपुटं.

PORTION, l. 4. *for* क्षुद्रयांसः, *read* क्षुद्रयांशः.

To POSTPONE, l. 3. *for* पिलम्ब्, *read* विलम्ब.

PRACTICE, l. 4. *for* वृतिः, *read* वृत्तिः.

To PROJECT, *v. a.* l. 5. *for* plain, *read* plan.

TURKOIS, *for* वैदुर्य्यं, *read* वैदूर्य्यं.

TRÜBNER & CO.'S PUBLICATIONS

RELATING TO

SANSKRIT AND PÂLI.

Aitareya Brahmanam of the Rig Veda: containing the Earliest Speculations of the Brahmans on the meaning of the Sacrificial Prayers, and on the Origin, Performance and Sense of the Rites of the Vedic Religion. Edited and Translated by Martin Haug. In 2 Vols. Crown 8vo. Vol. I. Contents, Sanskrit Text, with Preface, Introductory Essay, and a Map of the Sacrificial Compound at the Soma Sacrifice, pp. 312. Vol. II. Translation with Notes, pp. 544. £2 2*s.*

Arnold (E.)—The Iliad and Odyssey of India. 8vo. sd., pp. 24. 1*s.*

Arnold (E.)—The Indian Song of Songs. From the Sanskrit of the Gita Govinda of Jayadeva. 8vo. cl., pp. xvi. and 144. 1875. 5*s.*

Âryabhatiya, (The), with the Commentary Bhatadîpikâ of Paramadiçvara, edited by Dr. H. Kern. 4to. pp. xii. and 107. 9*s.*

Atharva Veda Prâtiçâkhya; or Çâunakíyá Caturádhyáyika (The). Text, Translation, and Notes. By William D. Whitney, 8vo. pp. 286, boards. £1 11*s.* 6*d.*

Auctores Sanscriti.—Edited for the Sanskrit Text Society under the supervision of Th. Goldstücker. Vol. I., containing the Jaiminîya-Nyâya-Mâlâ-Vistara. Parts I. to V., pp. 1 to 400, large 4to. sewed. Each part 10*s.*

Ballantyne (J. R.)—First Lessons in Sanskrit Grammar; together with an Introduction to the Hitopadésa. Sec. ed. 8vo. cloth, pp. viii. and 110. 1873. 3*s.* 6*d.*

Benfey (Th.)—A Practical Grammar of the Sanskrit Language, for the use of Early Students. Royal 8vo. cl. pp. viii. and 296. 10*s.* 6*d.*

Bhagavad-Gita (A Commentary on the Text of the); or the Discourse between Krishna and Arjuna of Divine Matters. A Sanskrit Philosophical Poem. By H. Chintamon. 8vo. cloth, pp. 118. 6*s.*

Brhat-Sanhitá; or, Complete System of Natural Astrology of Varâha-Mihira. Translated from Sanskrit into English by Dr. H. Kern. Will be completed in Nine Parts. Parts 1 to 6. Price 2*s.* each part.

Brown (C. P.)—Sanskrit Prosody and Numerical Symbols Explained. Demy 8vo. cloth, pp. 64. 3*s.* 6*d.*

Burnell (A.C., M.R.A.S.)—Catalogue of a Collection of Sanskrit Manuscripts. Part I. Vedic Manuscripts. Fcap. 8vo. pp. 64, sewed. 1870. 2*s.*

Burnell (A. C.)—The Sâmavidhânabrâhmana (being the Third Brâhmana), of the Sâma Veda. Edited, together with the Commentary of Sâyana, an English Translation, Introduction, and Index of Words. Volume I.—Text and Commentary, with Introduction. 8vo. pp. xxxviii. and 104. 12*s.* 6*d.*

Burnell (A. C.)—The Vamçabrâhmana (being the Eighth Brâhmana) of the Sâma Veda. Edited, together with the Commentary of Sâyana, a Preface and Index of Words. 8vo. sd. pp. xliii., 12, and xii., with 2 coloured plates. 10*s.* 6*d.*

Burnell (A. C.)—The Devatâdhyâyabrâhmana (being the Fifth Brahmana) of the Sâma Veda. The Sanskrit Text edited, with the Commentary of Sâyana, an Index of Words, etc. 8vo. pp. 34. 5*s.*

Burnell (A. C.)—On the Aindra School of Sanskrit Grammarians. Their Place in the Sanskrit and Subordinate Literatures. 8vo. pp. 120. 10*s.* 6*d.*

Burnell (A. C.)—Dayadaçaçloki. Ten Slokas in Sanskrit, with English Translation. 8vo. pp. 11. 2*s.*

Burnell (A. C.)—Elements of South-Indian Palæography, from the 4th to the 17th century A.D. 4to. pp. 98. With 30 plates. 1875.—A new Edition in the Press.

Colebrooke.—The Life and Miscellaneous Essays of Henry Thomas Colebrooke. The Biography by his Son, Sir T. E. Colebrooke. The Essays edited by Professor Cowell. 3 vols. 8vo. cl. —Vol. I. The Life. With Portrait and Map. pp. xii. and 492. 14*s.*—Vols. II. and III. The Essays. A New Edition, with Notes by E. B. Cowell, Professor of Sanskrit in the University of Cambridge. pp. xvi.-544, and x.-520. 1873. 28*s.*

Childers (R.C.)—A Pali-English Dictionary, with Sanskrit Equivalents, and with numerous Quotations, Extracts, and References. Imperial 8vo. Double Columns. Part I. pp. 1-276. 24*s.* Part II., pp. 346. Complete in 1 Vol., pp. xxii. and 622 cloth. 1875. £3 3*s.*

Cowell and Eggeling.—Catalogue of Buddhist Sanskrit Manuscripts in the Possession of the Royal Asiatic Society (Hodgson Collection). 8vo. sd., pp. 56. 2*s.* 6*d.*

Cowell (E. B.)—A short Introduction to the Ordinary Prakrit of the Sanskrit Dramas. With a List of Common Irregular Prakrit Words. 8vo. cloth, pp. 40. 1875. 3*s.* 6*d.*

Cunningham (A.)—The Ancient Geography of India. I. The Buddhist Period, including the Campaigns of Alexander, and the Travels of Hwen-Thsang. With 13 Maps. 8vo. cloth, pp. xx. 590. 1870. 28*s.*

Cunningham.—The Bhilsa Topes; or, Buddhist Monuments of Central India: comprising a brief Historical Sketch of the Rise, Progress, and Decline of Buddhism. With 33 Plates, 8vo. cloth, pp. xxxvi. 370. 1854. £2 2*s.*

D'Alwis (James)—A Descriptive Catalogue of Sanskrit, Pali, and Sinhalese Literary Works of Ceylon. In Three Volumes. Vol. I., pp. xxxii. and 244, sewed. 1870. 8*s.* 6*d.* Vols. II. and III. in preparation.

Davids (T. W. Rhys)—Three Inscriptions of Parâkrama Bâhu the Great, from Pulastipura, Ceylon. 8vo. pp. 20. 1*s.* 6*d.*

Davids (T. W. Rhys)—Sigiri, the Lion Rock, near Pulastipura, and the 39th Chapter of the Mahâvamsa. 8vo. pp. 30. 1*s.* 6*d.*

Dathávansa (The); or, the History of the Tooth-Relic of Gotama Buddha. The Pali Text, and its Translation into English, with Notes, by M. Coomâra Swâmy, Mudeliár. Demy 8vo. cloth, pp. 174. 1874. 10*s.* 6*d.*

English Translation only. With Notes. Demy 8vo. cloth, pp. 100. 1874. 6*s.*

Eitel (E. J.)—Buddhism: its Historical, Theoretical, and Popular Aspects. In Three Lectures. Sec. Ed. 8vo. sd., pp. 130. 5*s.*

Gautama.—The Institutes of Gautama. Edited with an Index of Words by Adolf Friederich Stenzler, Ph.D, 8vo. cloth, pp. 80.

Goldstücker (Theodor)—A Dictionary, Sanskrit and English, extended and improved from the Second Edition of the Dictionary of Professor H. H. Wilson, with his sanction and concurrence. Together with a Supplement, Grammatical Appendices, and an Index, serving as a Sanskrit-English Vocabulary. Parts I. to VI. 4to. pp. 400. 1856-1863. 6*s.* each.

Goldstücker (T.)—Panini; His Place in Sanskrit Literature. An Investigation of some Literary and Chronological Questions which may be settled by a study of his Work. By T. Goldstücker. Imperial 8vo. cloth, pp. 268. £2 2*s.*

Griffith (R. T. H.)—Scenes from the Ramayana, Meghaduta, etc. Translated. 2nd ed. Cr. 8vo. pp. xviii., 244, cloth. 6*s.*

Hardy (R. Spence)—Christianity and Buddhism Compared. 8vo. sd. pp. 138. 6*s.*

Indian Antiquary (The.)—A Journal of Oriental Research in Archæology, History, Literature, Languages, Philosophy, Religion, Folklore, etc. Edited by James Burgess, M.R.A.S., F.R.G.S. 4to. Published 12 numbers per annum. Subscription £2 per annum.

Jataka (The), together with its Commentary. Now first published in Pali by V. Fausböll, with a Translation by R. C. Childers. To be completed in five volumes. Text. Vol. I. Part I. Roy. 8vo. sewed, pp. 224. 7*s.* 6*d.*

Kistner (O.)—Buddha and his Doctrines. A Bibliographical Essay. Imp. 8vo., pp. iv. and 32, sewed. 2*s.* 6*d.*

Kusa Jataka.—An Eastern Love Story. A Buddhistic Legendary Poem, with other Stories. By T. Steele. Cr. 8vo. cl. pp. xii. and 260. 1871. 6*s.*

Laghu Kaumudí.—A Sanskrit Grammar. By Varadarája. With an English Version, Commentary and References. By James R. Ballantyne. 8vo. cloth, pp. xxxvi. and 424. £1 11*s.* 6*d.*

Maha-Vira-Charita; or, the Adventures of the Great Hero Rama. An Indian Drama in Seven Acts. Translated into English Prose from the Sanskrit of Bhavabhûti. By John Pickford, M.A. Crown 8vo. cloth. 5*s.*

Maino-i-Khard (The Book of the)—The Pazand and Sanskrit Texts, as arranged by Neriosengh Dhaval. With an English translation, a Glossary of the Pazand texts, containing the Sanskrit, Rosian, and Pahlavi equivalents, etc. By E. W. West. 8vo. sewed, pp. 484. 1871. 16*s.*

Manava-Kalpa-Sutra; being a portion of this ancient Work on Vaidik Rites, together with the Commentary of Kumarila-Swamin. A facsimile of the MS. No. 17 in the Library of H. M. Home Government for India. With a Preface by T. Goldstücker. Oblong folio, cl., pp. 268 of letterpress and 121 leaves of facsimiles. £4 4s.

Megha-Duta (The) (Cloud-Messenger) — By Kālidāsa. Translated from the Sanskrit into English verse, with Notes and Illustrations. By the late H. H. Wilson. The Vocabulary by F. Johnson. New Edition. 4to. cloth, pp. xi. and 180. 10s. 6d.

Muir.—Original Sanskrit Texts, on the Origin and History of the People of India, their Religion and Institutions. Collected, Translated, and Illustrated by John Muir, D.C.L., LL.D., Ph.D.

Vol. I. Mythical and Legendary Accounts of the Origin of Caste, with an Inquiry into its existence in the Vedic Age. Sec. Ed., re-written and greatly enlarged. 8vo. pp. xx. 532, cloth. 1868. 21s.

Vol. II. The Trans-Himalayan Origin of the Hindus, and their Affinity with the Western Branches of the Ayran Race. Sec. Ed. Revised, with Additions. 8vo. cloth, pp. xxxii. and 512. 1871. 21s.

Vol. III. The Vedas; Opinions of their Authors, and of later Indian Writers, on their Origin, Inspiration, and Authority. Sec. Ed., revised and enlarged. 8vo. cloth, pp. xxxii. 312. 1868. 16s.

Vol. IV. Comparison of the Vedic with the later representations of the principal Indian Deities. Sec. Ed., revised. 8vo. cloth, pp. xvi. and 524. 1873. 21s.

Vol. V. Contributions to a Knowledge of the Cosmogony, Mythology, Religious Ideas, Life and Manners of the Indians in the Vedic Age. 8vo. cloth, pp. xvi. 492. 1870. 21s.

Müller (Max)—Lecture on Buddhist Nihilism. (Translated from the German.) Fcap. 8vo. sewed. 1869. 1s.

Naganada; or the Joy of the Snake-World. A Buddhist Drama in Five Acts. Translated into English Prose by Palmer Boyd. With an Introduction by Prof. Cowell. 8vo. cloth, pp. xvi. and 100. 4s. 6d.

Naradiya Dharma Sastram; or, the Institutes of Narada. Translated for the first time from the unpublished Sanskrit original. By Dr. Julius Jolly. With Preface, Notes and Index. 8vo. cloth, pp. xxxv. 144. 10s. 6d.

Pandit's (A) Remarks on Professor Max Müller's Translation of the "Rig-Veda." Sanskrit and English. Fcap. 8vo. sewed. 1870. 6d.

Oriental Congress.—Report of the Proceedings of the Second International Congress of Orientalists held in London, 1874. Royal 8vo. paper, pp. 76. 5s.

Prakrita-Prakasa; or, the Prakrit Grammar of Vararuchi, with the Commentary (Manorama) of Bhamaha. First compl. ed., with Notes, an English Translation, and Index of Prakrit words, to which is prefixed an easy Introduction to Prakrit Grammar. By E. B. Cowell. Sec. issue, with new Preface, and corrections. 8vo. pp. xxxii. and 204. 14s.

Rámáyan of Válmíki. Translated into English verse. By R. T. H. Griffith. 5 vols. 8vo. cloth, pp. 472, 504, 576, 440, and 368. 1870-1875. £4 4s.

Ramayana.—Weber (Dr. Albr.) on the Râmâyana. Translated from the German by the Rev. D. C. Boyd. 8vo. sewed, pp. 130. 5s.

Ram Jasan.—A Sanskrit and English Dictionary. Being an Abridgment of Professor Wilson's Dictionary. With an Appendix explaining the use of Affixes in Sanskrit. Royal 8vo. cloth, pp. ii. and 707. 28s.

Rig-Veda.—The Hymns of the Rig-Veda in the Samhitá and Pada Text, without the Commentary of the Sâyana. Edited by Prof. Max Müller. In 2 vols. 8vo. paper, pp. 1704. £3 3s.

Rig-Veda-Sanhita: The Sacred Hymns of the Brahmans. Translated and explained by F. Max Müller. Vol. I. Hymns to the Maruts, or the Storm-Gods. 8vo. cloth, pp. clii. and 264. 1869. 12s. 6d.

Rig-Veda.—Index Verborum quae continentur in M. Mülleri recensione Rig Vedae, una cum Sarvânukrama, sive indice autorum, deorum, metrorum, etc. (Separate Impression from the Fifth and Sixth Volumes of Rig-Veda-Sanhita, together with the Commentary of Sayanacharya. Edited by Dr. Max Müller.) 4to. pp. 162 and 762. £2 2s.

Rig-Veda Sanhita.—A Collection of Ancient Hindu Hymns, constituting the Fifth to Eighth Ashtakas, or books of the Rig-Veda, the oldest Authority for the Religious and Social Institutions of the Hindus. Translated from the Original Sanskrit by H. H. Wilson, Ed. by E. B. Cowell. Vols. I. to III. 8vo. pp. 400, 376 and 550. £3 3s. Vol. IV. 8vo. pp. 214. 14s. (Vols. V. and VI. in the Press.)

Sabdakalpadruma, the well-known Sanskrit Dictionary of Rajáh Radhakanta Deva. In Bengali characters. 4to. Parts 1 to 17. (In course of publication.) 3s. 6d. each part.

Schlagintweit (E.)—Buddhism in Tibet. Illustrated by Literary Documents and Objects of Religious Worship. With an Account of the Buddhist Systems preceding it in India. Folio Atlas of 20 Plates, and 20 Tables of Native Prints in the Text. Royal 8vo. pp. xxiv. and 404. £2 2s.

Schleicher (A.)—Compendium of the Comparative Grammar of the Indo-European, Sanskrit, Greek, and Latin Languages. Translated from the 3rd German Ed. by H. Bendall. Part I. 8vo. cloth, pp. 184. 7s. 6d.

Surya-Siddhanta (Translation of the)—A Text Book of Hindu Astronomy, with Notes and Appendix, &c. By W. D. Whitney. 8vo. boards, pp. iv. and 354. £1 11s. 6d.

Sutta Nipáta; or, the Dialogues and Discourses of Gotama Buddha. Translated from the Pali, with Introduction and Notes, by Sir M. Coomára Swamy. Cr. 8vo. cloth, pp. xxxvi. and 160. 1874. 6s.

Táittiríya-Prátiçákhya, with its Commentary, the Tri-bháshyaratna: Text, Translation, and Notes. By W. D. Whitney, Prof. of Sanskrit in Yale College, New Haven. 8vo. pp. 469. 1871. 25s.

Trübner's Bibliotheca Sanscrita. A Catalogue of Sanskrit Literature, chiefly printed in Europe. To which is added a Catalogue of Sanskrit Works printed in India; and a Catalogue of Pali Books. Constantly for sale by Trübner & Co. Cr. 8vo. sd., pp. 84. 2s. 6d.

Vachaspatya, a Comprehensive Dictionary in Sanskrit. Compiled by Taranatha Tarkavachaspati. Alphabetically arranged, with a Grammatical Introduction and Copious Citations from the Grammarians and Scholiasts, from the Vedas, etc. Parts I. to VII. 4to. 1873-6. 18s. each Part.

Vishnu-Purána (The); a System of Hindu Mythology and Tradition. Translated from the original Sanskrit, and Illustrated by Notes derived chiefly from other Purânas, by the late H. H. Wilson. Edited by Fitzedward Hall. In 6 vols. 8vo. Vol. I. pp. cxl. and 200; Vol. II. pp. 343; Vol. III. pp. 348; Vol. IV. pp. 346; Vol. V. pp. 392, cloth. 10s. 6d. each. Vol. V., Part 2, containing the Index, and completing the Work, is in the Press.

Wheeler.—The History of India from the Earliest Ages. By J. Talboys Wheeler, Assistant Secretary to the Government of India in the Foreign Department, Secretary to the Indian Record Commission, Author of "The Geography of Herodotus," etc. etc.

Vol. I. The Vedic Period and the Maha Bharata. Demy 8vo. cl., pp. lxxv. and 576. 18s.

Vol. II. The Ramayana and the Brahmanic Period. Demy 8vo. cl., pp. lxxxviii. and 680, with two Maps. 21s.

Vol. III. Hindu, Buddhist, Brahmanical Revival. Demy 8vo. cl., pp. 484 with two maps. 18s.

Vol. IV. Part I. pp. xxxii. and 320. 14s.

Whitney (W. D.)—Oriental and Linguistic Studies. The Veda; the Avesta; the Science of Language. Cr. 8vo. cl., pp. x. and 418. 12s.

Whitney (W. D.)—Oriental and Linguistic Studies. Second Series. Crown 8vo. cloth, pp. 446. 12s.

Williams (Monier)—A Dictionary, English and Sanskrit. Published under the Patronage of the Honourable East India Company. 4to. cloth, pp. xii. 862. 1855. £3 3s.

Wilson.—Works of the late Horace Hayman Wilson.

Vols. I. and II. Essays and Lectures chiefly on the Religion of the Hindus, by the late H. H. Wilson. Ed. by Dr. R. Rost. 2 vols. cloth, pp. xiii. and 399, vi. and 416. 21s.

Vols. III., IV. and V. Essays Analytical, Critical, and Philological, on Subjects connected with Sanskrit Literature. Ed. by Dr. Rost. 3 vols. 8vo. cloth, pp. 408, 406, and 390. Price 36s.

Vols. VI., VII., VIII., IX., and X. Vishnu Purána, a System of Hindu Mythology and Tradition. Translated from original Sanskrit. Ed. by Fitzedward Hall. Vols. I. to V. 8vo. cloth, pp. cxl. and 200, 344, 344, 146. £2 12s. 6d.

Vol. V., Part 2, containing the Index, and completing the Work, is in the Press.

Vols. XI. and XII. Select Specimens of the Hindus. Translated from the Original Sanskrit. 3rd ed. 2 vols. 8vo. cl. pp. lxi. and 384; and iv. and 418. 21s.

Wilson (H. H.)—A Dictionary in Sanskrit and English. Translated, amended, and enlarged from an original compilation prepared by learned Natives for the College of Fort William. The Third Edition edited by Jagunmohana Tarkalankara and Khettramohana Mookerjee. Published by Gyanendrachandra Rayachoudhuri and Brothers. 4to. pp. 1008. Calcutta, 1874. £3 3s.